# The Practitioner's Income Tax Act

19th Edition
2001

The **Income Tax Act** and **Income Tax Application Rules**
fully annotated, as amended to **February 1, 2001**
*Consolidated with*
February 2000 budget proposals; Draft Legislation to February 1, 2001;
Press Releases and other tax proposals
*plus*
The **Income Tax Regulations** and all draft regulations to February 1, 2001;
Canada-US and Canada-UK tax conventions; Tax Tables;
**Interpretation Act**; Topical Index

*Editor*
David M. Sherman, B.A., LL.B., LL.M.
of the Ontario Bar

*Contributing Editors*
Barbara Brougham, M.A.    Carol Klein Beernink, B.A., LL.B.
Scott McVicar, B.A.

© 2001 Thomson Canada Limited

All rights reserved. This copyright applies to indexes and other matter added to this publication. No part of this publication covered by the publisher's copyright may be reproduced, stored in a retrieval system, or transmitted, in any form or by any means, electronic, mechanical, photocopying, recording, or otherwise, without the prior written permission of the publisher.

This publication is designed to provide accurate and authoritative infomation. It is sold with the understanding that the publisher is not engaged in rendering legal, accounting or other professional advice. If legal advice or other expert assistance is required, the services of a competent professional should be sought. The additions are the work of the editors and should in no way be construed as being either official or unofficial policy of any governmental body.

**Canadian Cataloguing in Publication Data**

The National Library of Canada has catalogued this publication as follows:

Main entry under title:

The Practitioner's Income Tax Act

2nd ed. (Mar. 1992)–
Annual.
Editor: David M. Sherman
ISSN 1193 1701
ISBN 0-459-28605-6 (19th ed.)

I. Canada. Income Tax Act.   2. Income tax — Law and legislation — Canada.
I. Sherman, David M. (David Maurice), 1957 –.

KE5753.9.P682        343.7105'2        C92-032121-6 rev.
KF6499.ZA2P73

*[Handwritten notes:]*

B) Redemption of Pref shares
Proceeds            1,200,000
Less: PUC              4,000
D.D.                1,196,000

Proceeds on redemption   1,200,000
Less: DD                 1,196,000
                             4,000
Less: ACB                      NIL
Cap. gain                    4,000

Effects on income
Cap gain on old shares     200,000
D.D.                     1,196,000
Cap. gain on redemp'n        4,000
                         1,400,000
= Accrued gain since V-Day

Estate Planning Question
Date of incorp. – 1968
PUC = 4,000
V-Day = 600,000
Current FMV = 2,000,000

Father will exchange his common shares for 12,000 Pref. retractable shares, voting 890  FMV $100/each + Total PUC = 4,000

A) What are tax consequences to father?

B) What are tax consequences when father ultimately redeems pref. shares for FMV

**CARSWELL**
A THOMSON COMPANY

One Corporate Plaza
2075 Kennedy Road
Scarborough, Ontario
M1T 3V4

Customer Relations:
Toronto: 1-416-609-3800
Elsewhere in Canada: 1-800-387-5164
Fax: 1-416-298-5094
World Wide Web: http://www.carswell.com
E-mail: orders@carswell.com

* But Common shares held by sons have ↑ed by 800,000 but not corresponding ↑ in ACB ∴ Future cap. gain of $800,000

# TABLE OF CONTENTS

| | |
|---|---|
| Introduction | v |
| Important Amending Bills since 1988 Tax Reform | xi |
| Table of Proposed Amendments | xiii |
| Tax Reference Tables | xxi |
| Table of Concordance | lv |
| Overview Table of Sections: Income Tax Act | lxxv |
| Detailed Table of Sections: Income Tax Act | lxxxi |
| Income Tax Act, Annotated | 1 |
| Detailed Table of Sections: Income Tax Application Rules | 1871 |
| Income Tax Application Rules | 1875 |
| Income Tax Regulations | |
|     Detailed Table of Sections | 1921 |
|     Parts I to LXXXV | 1945 |
|     Schedules I to VI, VIII and IX | 2467 |
| Selected Remission Orders | 2507 |
| Tax Conventions (Treaties) | |
|     Income Tax Conventions Interpretation Act | 2537 |
|     Canada–United States (including Technical Explanation) | 2541 |
|     Canada–United Kingdom | 2617 |
|     Current Status of Tax Treaties | 2631 |
| Interpretation Act | 2633 |
| Index | 2647 |

---

Solution

A) 86(2) applies because FMV (2,000,000) > the cost of non-share consideration (nil) and FMV of new shares (1,200,000)
∴ Consider the 800,000 a gift to the sons.

* No deemed dividend on redemption because PUC of new shares = PUC of old shares and no boot is received.

Deemed proceeds of disp'n of old shares:
Lesser of:
(a) cost of non-sh consideration + gift    800,000 *
(b) FMV of old shares                      2,000,000

Capital gain on disposition of old shares on reorg:
  Deemed proceeds        800,000
  ACB of old shares      600,000   (V-Day)
  Cap gain               200,000

Cost of new shares
  ACB of old shares                        600,000
  Less cost of non-sh. cons.  nil
      gift               800,000      800,000
  ACB of new shares                           nil

# SAMPLE ROLLOVER PROBLEM 85(1)

## Facts

|  | FMV | Book (NBV) | V-Day | UCC | Cap. cost |
|---|---|---|---|---|---|
| Bldg | 300,000 | 50,000 | 275,000 | 200,000 | 225,000 |
| Equipment | 100,000 | 25,000 | 200,000 | 150,000 | 250,000 |
| Raw land | 25,000 | 2,500 | | | |
| Land | 187,500 | 12,500 | 62,500 | NIL | 12,500 |
| Inventory | 125,000 | 125,000 | | | |
| Prepaid rent | 5,000 | 5,000 | | | |
| Goodwill | 200,000 | 12,500 | 100,000 | NIL | 25,000 |
| TOTAL ASSETS | 942,500 | 232,500 | | | |

Liabilities $75,000 (Book + FMV)

## Notes
1) Raw land has no structure + is speculative investment
2) $56,250 of net capital losses — median method used

---

### ① 

|  | Tax Value | FMV | Elected Amount | Consideration Debt | Shares | Effect on taxable in. |
|---|---|---|---|---|---|---|
| Inventory | 125,000 | 125,000 | 125,000 | 125,000 | NIL | NIL |
| Land | 62,500 | 187,500 | 137,500* | 137,500 | 50,000 | NIL |
| Bldg | 200,000 | 300,000 | 200,000 | 200,000 | 100,000 | NIL |
| Goodwill | NIL | 200,000 | 1 | NIL | 200,000 | NIL |
|  | 387,500 | 812,500 | 462,501 | 462,500 | 350,000 | |
|  |  |  |  | (75,000) | liabilities assumed | |
|  |  |  |  | 387,500 | New debt | |

* increase by 75,000 (3/4 inclusion rate) to utilize net cap. loss → remember 2001 inclusion rate has ∆ed !!

---

### ② 

a) Elected transfer price                           462,501
   Allocation of ACB to debt consid:
        Debt assumed           75,000
        New debt issued       387,500      462,500
        ACB of shares                            1

b) Proceeds of D (812,500 − 462,500)    350,000
   ACB                                                      1
                                                       ―――――
   Cap. gain                                        349,999

*Handwritten notes at top:*

Required. (1) Under sec 85 what is the maximum debt vs. share capital that can be taken back w/o causing an ↑ in taxable income

(2) a) Determine cost of consideration
b) Tax consequences on a subsequent sale at FMV to an arm's length party

# INTRODUCTION

This is the nineteenth edition of *The Practitioner's Income Tax Act* (PITA), a complement to Carswell's *Stikeman Income Tax Act, Annotated*, now in its 29th edition. (Both PITA and the Stikeman Act were formerly published under the "De Boo" name. Richard De Boo Publishers merged with Carswell in 1991.)

In this edition we have retained the innovations that have made PITA the country's leading Income Tax Act:

- shaded boxes showing all draft legislation and draft regulations in context
- Department of Finance technical notes, in context, accompanying draft legislation and draft regulations
- shaded boxes with press releases and budget materials that announce pending changes, reproduced in context
- "Notes" that explain many of the provisions, guide the reader's understanding, and describe all changes since 1989 as well as all previous versions of the legislation that are still relevant
- reference tables of individual, corporate and payroll tax rates, R&D incentive rates, treaty withholding rates, foreign exchange rates, interest rates, limitation periods and penalties (the Table of Dollar Amounts now appears in the Topical Index under "Dollar limits")
- comprehensive, expert annotations to Related Provisions, Definitions (including terms defined in the *Interpretation Act*), Regulations, Remission Orders, Interpretation Bulletins, Information Circulars, Income Tax Technical News, Advance Tax Rulings, Forms, Application Policies and Registered Plans Division newsletters
- editorial headings for paragraphs in many long subsections, to make the subsection easier to scan (e.g., 53(1), 80(2), 95(2))
- annotations, footnotes and titles to clarify errors and omissions in the legislation
- editorial annotations to all Regulations to show the current reference to provisions in the Act that have been renumbered since the Regulation was enacted
- the full text of numerous Remission Orders relating to the Act
- the full text of the *Interpretation Act*
- a comprehensive, expert Topical Index that includes many terms not explicitly found in the legislation as well as acronyms, and that reflects *all* the latest draft legislation.

**What's New in This Edition?**

This edition, current to February 1, 2001, reflects the following new developments since the 18th edition, which was current to July 15, 2000:

- the proclamation into force of Bill C-23, the *Modernization of Benefits Act*, which changed all references to "spouse" to include a "common-law partner", defined to include a same-sex partner
- the October 18, 2000 Economic Statement (mini-budget)
- the draft legislation of December 21, 2000, implementing both the February 28, 2000 federal budget and the October 18, 2000 Economic Statement
- the draft legislation of August 8, 2000, dealing with authorized foreign banks (Canadian branches of foreign banks)
- the promulgation of various sets of amendments to the regulations and the release of new draft regulations
- the enactment of Bill C-24, the large GST bill, on October 20, 2000 (the bill included a number of amendments to the *Income Tax Act*)
- release by the CCRA of new Interpretation Bulletins, Information Circulars, Forms, Guides, etc.
- various news releases, Backgrounders and notices from the Department of Finance, the CCRA and Agriculture Canada on a wide range of issues, including non-resident trusts and foreign investment entities; tax treaty changes; payroll and capital taxes; automobile dollar limits; taxable employee benefits; workers' compensation awards; the Alternative Minimum Tax; non-resident T2 returns; DRUPA partnerships; flow-through mining expenditures; surtax on deposit-taking institutions; the Canadian Venture Exchange; ceiling amounts for housing benefits; prescribed drought regions, and relief for heating expenses
- new case law developments in numerous areas

*Handwritten note at bottom:*

NOTE → IF tax cost > FMV do not use 85(1)

Introduction

- new annotations for the CCRA's **Registered Charities Newsletters**, which provide administrative interpretation relating to approximately 20 provisions of the Act
- the release by the Department of Finance of over 50 pages of additional **comfort letters**, obtained by the Editor under the Access to Information Act and shown as Proposed Amendments throughout the legislation.

Additional words have been added editorially in square brackets to clarify many of the official headings in both the Act and the Regulations.

In addition, further improvements have been made to the "Notes" annotations, to provide additional explanations of how many of the provisions of the Act operate; to reflect new announcements of CCRA administrative policy; and to refer to significant case law developments and publication of useful articles.

### *Proposed amendments*

Note that proposed amendments, as shown in shaded boxes through the Act, generally are expected to be enacted as proposed. It is only in rare cases that proposed legislation is not enacted, although sometimes minor changes are made. Where there is some doubt that a proposal will be passed, the Notes generally provide useful information in this respect.

### Revised Statutes of Canada, 1985, Fifth Supplement

When Canada's federal statutes were renumbered and consolidated into the *Revised Statutes of Canada, 1985* (RSC 1985), which were proclaimed into force on December 12, 1988, the *Income Tax Act* was not included.

The Statute Revision Commission had originally planned to renumber the Act, but after representations from those who work with it (both in and outside government), the Commission eventually agreed to include the Act in the RSC 1985 without renumbering it. Renumbering would have changed all the provision numbers, so as to do away with references ending in ".1", ".2" and so on and to eliminate gaps left by repealed provisions.

As of March 1, 1994, the Governor in Council (cabinet) proclaimed into force the RSC 1985, Fifth Supplement, which contains the "revised" *Income Tax Act* and *Income Tax Application Rules*.

The RSC 1985 (5th Supp.) is generally effective for taxation years ending after November 1991. For certain purposes, it is effective for payments made, or other events occurring, after November 1991. ITAR section 73 sets out these application dates.

Although there was no general renumbering of the provisions, there were many other changes. Paragraph letters for definitions (e.g., in section 54) were entirely eliminated, so that definitions can be published in both French and English in their alphabetical order. Some formulas in the legislation were changed from "descriptive" to "algebraic" form. The language throughout the Act was made gender-neutral (as has been the Department of Finance's drafting style since 1989). Certain application provisions of previous enacting legislation have been incorporated into the Act (e.g., section 237.2). In theory, all of the changes are non-substantive.

The RSC 1985 (5th Supp.) as proclaimed was current only to November 30, 1991. It therefore did not reflect Bill C-18 (1991 technical bill), Bill C-75 (1992 transportation industry assistance bill), Bill C-80 (1992 Child Benefit bill), Bill C-92 (1992 technical bill) and other minor amendments from December 1991 through February 1994. This was rectified with Bill C-15, the *Income Tax Amendments Revision Act*, which was enacted following proclamation of the Fifth Supplement and received Royal Assent on May 12, 1994 as SC 1994, c. 7.

Pursuant to section 4 of the *Revised Statutes of Canada, 1985 Act*, SC 1987, c. 48, the consolidation of the RSC 1985 is not intended to change the law. Therefore, the changes made to the Act in the 5th Supplement and by the *Income Tax Amendments Revision Act* should be considered non-substantive.

The RSC 1985 (5th Supp.) was first included in the 6th edition of PITA, published in August 1994.

### Beyond the Act

The following appear after the text of the *Income Tax Act*:

- *Income Tax Application Rules:* referred to as the "ITARs". Part I provides transitional rules for the 1971 tax reform changes to the Act. Some of these rules, such as those dealing with dispositions of property held since before 1972, are still relevant. Part II of the ITARs provides transitional rules for the RSC 1985 (5th Supp.), as described above. "Notes" annotations are provided where appropriate. A "Definitions" annotation appears at the end of every section.
- *Income Tax Regulations:* Where the Regulations refer to provisions of the Act that have been renumbered by the RSC 1985 (5th Supp.), the new numbering is shown in square brackets to assist the reader. "Notes"

## Introduction

annotations have been provided where appropriate, recording all changes since 1990. As with the Act, draft regulations and other proposed amendments are reproduced in shaded boxes in context. Detailed "Related Provisions" annotations are provided to Part XI and Schedule II (capital cost allowances), and to Reg. 8300–8520 (pension plans). A "Definitions" annotation appears at the end of every section.

- *Remission Orders:* these provide relief from income tax as approved by the federal Cabinet. The remission orders printed are those that are of general interest; some remission orders that apply only to specific named taxpayers are not included.
- *Income Tax Conventions Interpretation Act:* this Act provides rules for the interpretation of Canada's tax treaties. It is annotated with Notes.
- *Canada-U.S. Tax Treaty:* consolidated with the amendments made by the 1995 and 1997 Protocols. Detailed annotations such as Related Provisions and Notes are provided. The appropriate portions of the three official Technical Explanations to the treaty are reproduced immediately after each Article of the treaty, thus eliminating the need to flip back and forth while reading the treaty.
- *Canada-U.K. Tax Treaty*
- *List of Canada's other tax treaties and current treaty negotiations:* the list has been updated.
- *Topical Index:* we strive to make the Index as helpful as possible, by including many terms that do not appear in the text of the Act but which will be sought by practitioners. (For example, "change of control" and "carryforward" are two terms often used by practitioners but which are lacking from our competitor's *Income Tax Act* index.) We also include references to the Canada-U.S. tax treaty and the *Interpretation Act* where appropriate. As well, the Index includes an innovative "Dollar amounts" entry which many practitioners find indispensable. All proposed amendments in draft legislation are reflected in the Index.

## Technical Explanation of Notes Annotations

It is important that you not be misled in your expectations of what is in the Notes. We therefore set out below a detailed explanation of the methodology used in constructing the Notes annotations.

The primary goal is *relevance to today*. We have generally eliminated information that is of no relevance for current practitioners.

In building the Notes, we have followed these principles:

1. Notes are descriptive and clear, rather than formal.
2. Non-substantive changes are ignored.
3. Changes since 1988 Tax Reform are described.
4. Rules that still depend on the date of previous events are preserved.
5. Rules that affect the cost base of property are preserved.
6. Repealed provisions are summarized.
7. Helpful comments are provided to explain provisions.

### 1. Notes are descriptive and clear, rather than formal

The Notes are descriptions of what has really changed, rather than formal "xxxx was substituted for yyyy" statements. With History annotations, you must study every past amendment, determine whether it is relevant, and determine how the legislation read with application to a given set of transactions. We have tried to save you time by summarizing the changes, where possible, clearly and concisely, without sacrificing completeness and accuracy.

Where a provision was repealed and replaced, but the substance was to add or delete a specific subparagraph or phrase, the change is described in terms of that addition or deletion rather than by reprinting the old version and leaving it to the reader to slog through the text word by word looking for differences. Changes are described in terms of their substantive effect, not their legal form. For example, paragraph 85(1.1)(g) was amended by the 1994 tax amendments bill (Bill C-70), enacted in June 1995. Technically, it was repealed and re-enacted as a different paragraph, with three subparagraphs, (i), (ii) and (iii), which did not previously exist. Examining the words, one finds that paragraphs (i) and (ii) are identical to what previously appeared in the body of the paragraph. Only subparagraph (iii) is new. The description of the change, therefore, is "85(1.1)(g)(iii) added".

Furthermore, when a change was made retroactive to the date of introduction of an earlier amendment, the text of the earlier version is not reproduced in the Notes, since it is now deemed never to have had any application and thus never to have been in force. Where appropriate, we have added explanation of the nature of such amendments.

Introduction

The Notes are not intended to be word-for-word precise in the way that History annotations are. They are intended to provide what you need when dealing with the Act as it stands today and for the past six years. If you are dealing with years long past and need to see the *exact* wording, consult the *Stikeman Income Tax Act*.

## 2. Non-substantive changes are ignored

A formal description of changes in the legislation reflects drafting changes and other non-substantive changes. The Notes do not waste your time with such changes. These include, for example, drafting changes where the third person generic pronoun "he" was replaced with "the taxpayer", or where "shall be deemed" was changed to "is deemed". For the most part, the changes introduced in the RSC 1985 (5th Supp.) revision of the Act are non-substantive and so are ignored. However, where those changes affect the structure of the Act (e.g., definitions that moved from paragraphs to being "above" the paragraph level in a subsection), they are described in the Notes.

## 3. Changes since 1988 Tax Reform are described

The 1988 Tax Reform exercise produced an Act that looked quite different from the previous edition. Wholesale changes were made throughout the Act. 1988 is now many years past, and changes before 1989, or even 1994, are irrelevant to most practitioners in most cases.

You may want to know about changes since 1988 Tax Reform, however. If you are generally familiar with the operation of a provision but have not looked at it for a year or two, a quick outline of what has changed will help you orient yourself and more quickly familiarize yourself with the statute as it reads now.

As well, you may in 2001 be dealing with 1993–2000 tax issues, particularly when it comes to audits of corporate and personal tax returns. It is therefore important to know whether the legislation you are reading has the same application for 1997 or 1998 as it does today. (Whether it had the same application in, say, 1983, however, is generally irrelevant.)

We have therefore included an outline of changes introduced since 1988 Tax Reform. A list of the important amending bills can be found following this Introduction.

Where the changes made were retroactive to 1993 or earlier, we have generally not provided the text of the former version, but have provided instead an outline of the change. Where the changes are recent, enough information is provided about the earlier version to allow you to know exactly how it applied for 1994 to 2000.

We have generally not provided annotations where changes were made by 1988 Tax Reform or earlier legislation (but see 4 below). We assume you no longer care what the rules were in 1987.

## 4. Rules that still depend on the date of previous events are preserved

Simply deleting all History annotations from before 1991 would have been easy. It would also have been irresponsible. The legislation that has amended the Act over the years is rife with "applicable after ...", "applicable with respect to shares issued after ...", "applicable with respect to acquisitions of property after ...", and the like.

The only way to delete the History and yet not mislead practitioners has been to analyze every amending provision to determine whether it is still relevant. Here are some examples of rules we have preserved:

- Section 7: the stock option rules depend both on when the agreement was entered into and on when the shares were issued. We have preserved the rules that apply for shares issued before May 23, 1985 and the rules that apply to stock option agreements that predate April 1, 1977.
- Subsection 12(4): the requirement for annual accrual of investment income applies only to investment contracts "last acquired after 1989". The three-year accrual rules still apply for earlier investments.
- Subsections 20(8), 40(1.1), 44(1.1): amendments were introduced by the 1981 Budget, effective for transactions after November 12, 1981 other than pursuant to the terms of an agreement in writing that predated the budget. Since transactions today can conceivably still take place pursuant to agreements signed in 1981 or earlier, the old rules are mentioned.
- The "old" attribution rules in sections 74 and 75 still apply to attribute income from property transferred before May 23, 1985.
- The rules in section 111 limiting the use of losses on the acquisition of control depend on the date of acquisition. Where losses from an acquisition that predates the current rules might still be usable today (e.g., net capital losses can be carried forward indefinitely, non-capital losses for seven years), the wording of the old rules is reproduced.

In most cases, where changes were made applicable after a given date or as of a given taxation year, the older wording is not preserved. Where changes were made applicable with respect to transactions or events after a

# Introduction

specific date (e.g., acquisition of control, issuance of shares, etc.), the provision has been analyzed to determine whether the earlier rules are still relevant today. If they are, they are reproduced, or enough information is given about the changes (e.g., "paragraph (c) added") so that you can apply the earlier rules.

### 5. Rules that affect the cost base of property are preserved

Even where amendments were effective as of a given date or year, they may still be important today. This will particularly be the case where the provision in question is one that affects the cost, capital cost or adjusted cost base of property. You likely do not need to go back and reconstruct the provision as it applied in 1985 for purposes of the taxpayer's 1985 tax return, but if an event in 1985 affected the adjusted cost base of land that the taxpayer is selling today, you need to know how the provision in question is to be read for that event at that time.

We have therefore taken great care to preserve information about amendments to provisions that affect the cost of property. Extensive annotations thus appear for section 53, sections 85 to 88, and other provisions (e.g., 66.2(5), 107(4)) that change the cost or capital cost of property.

Note that we preserve *only* the changes that are still relevant to today. If you are trying to work out a problem for, say, the 1987 taxation year, do not expect the Notes to be complete! If a transaction took place in 1987 and you want to track its effect on the cost of property today, however, the Notes should have what you need.

### 6. Repealed provisions are summarized

We have violated, in one respect, our rule that changes before 1989 are generally irrelevant unless they have application today. Where a section or subsection was repealed and not replaced, you may wonder what you're missing. Even if the provision was repealed many years ago, we generally provide a brief outline of the subject matter of the provision, when it was repealed, and, if appropriate, where the provision was moved to.

### 7. Helpful comments are provided to explain provisions

Explanatory comments are provided in the Notes to clarify the operation or effect of a provision, to refer to important case law that changes the meaning of the legislation, to refer to useful published articles or to add the Editor's perspective. These continue to be extended with each edition, so that many of the conceptually difficult provisions are explained.

David Sherman
Thornhill, Ontario
February 2001
Fax (905) 889-3246
email: ds@davidsherman.ca
http://www.davidsherman.ca

Topic → Intercompany Dividends ; Sales/Redemption of Shares

Financial records of A which is owned by B

| | |
|---|---|
| R/E after 1971 | 337,500 |
| PUC | 90,000 |
| ACB of B's shares | 127,500 |
| FMV | 1,312,500 |

B → A

**Case 1** – B receives a dividend of 337,500 from A then sells shares to another company for 975,000

a) 337,500 received tax free – no Part I tax (112(1)) and no Part IV as long as A does not receive a dividend refund

b) div. is attributable to post 71 earnings ∴ 55(2) does not apply and gain is as follows:

| | |
|---|---|
| Proceeds | 975,000 |
| ACB | 127,500 |
| cap. gain | 847,500 |

**Case 2** – A pays a dividend to B of 1,185,000 and B sells the shares then valued at 127,000

| | | |
|---|---|---|
| Dividend received | | 1,185,000 |
| Less – div. attributable to post 71 income | 337,500 | |
| div. subject to Part 4 | NIL | 337,500 |
| Deemed proceeds | | 847,500 |
| Add – actual proceeds | | 127,500 |
| | | 975,000 |
| Less: ACB | | 127,500 |
| Cap. gain | | 847,500 |

**Case 3** – X co subscribes for a new class of shares of A for 1,312,500. A then redeems old shares owned by B for their FMV of 1,312,500

Deemed dividend on redemption:

| | |
|---|---|
| Redemption amount paid | 1,312,500 |
| Less: PUC | 90,000 |
| D.D | 1,222,500 |
| Less – part of div. designated as separate (337,500) – part 4 tax (nil) | (337,500) |
| Other part of div. deemed not to be a dividend | 885,000 |

P of D on shares redeemed:

| | |
|---|---|
| Redemption Am't paid | 1,312,500 |
| Less: Desig. D.D. | (337,500) |
| Proceeds of Disp^n | 975,000 |
| ACB | 127,500 |
| | 847,500 |

# IMPORTANT AMENDING BILLS SINCE 1988 TAX REFORM

*(as referred to in "Notes" annotations)*

| Bill or Budget | Bill No. | Citation | Royal Assent |
|---|---|---|---|
| 1988 tax reform | C-139 | S.C. 1988, c. 55 | September 13, 1988 |
| 1988 Tax Court bill | C-146 | S.C. 1988, c. 61 | September 22, 1988 (in force January 1, 1991) |
| 1989 Budget | C-28 | S.C. 1990, c. 39 | October 23, 1990 |
| 1990 pension bill | C-52 | S.C. 1990, c. 35 | June 27, 1990 |
| 1990 garnishment/collection bill | C-51 | S.C. 1990, c. 34 | June 27, 1990 |
| 1990 GST | C-62 | S.C. 1990, c. 45 | December 17, 1990 |
| 1990 Budget/1991 Budget/1991 technical bill (first released July 1990) (original) | C-18 | S.C. 1991, c. 49 | December 17, 1991 |
| 1990 Budget/1991 Budget/1991 technical bill (RSC-redrafted) | C-15 | S.C. 1994, c. 7, Sch. II | May 12, 1994 |
| 1992 transportation assistance bill (original) | C-75 | S.C. 1992, c. 29 | June 23, 1992 |
| 1992 transportation assistance bill (RSC-redrafted) | C-15 | S.C. 1994, c. 7, Sch. VI | May 12, 1994 |
| 1992 child tax benefit bill (original) | C-80 | S.C. 1992, c. 48 | October 15, 1992 |
| 1992 child tax benefit bill (RSC-redrafted) | C-15 | S.C. 1994, c. 7, Sch. VII | May 12, 1994 |
| 1992 Budget/1992 technical bill (original) | C-92 | S.C. 1993, c. 24 | June 10, 1993 |
| 1992 Budget/1992 technical bill (RSC-redrafted) | C-15 | S.C. 1994, c. 7, Sch VIII | May 12, 1994 |
| 1992 Economic Statement/1993 Budget | C-9 | S.C. 1994, c. 8 | May 12, 1994 |
| Department of National Revenue Act amending bill | C-2 | S.C. 1994, c. 13 | May 12, 1994 |
| 1993 technical bill | C-27 | S.C. 1994, c. 21 | June 15, 1994 |
| 1994 tobacco tax reduction bill | C-32 | S.C. 1994, c. 29 | June 23, 1994 |
| 1994 Budget | C-59 | S.C. 1995, c. 3 | March 26, 1995 |
| 1994 tax amendments bill | C-70 | S.C. 1995, c. 21 | June 22, 1995 |

— Part I: debt forgiveness and foreclosure
— Part II: foreign affiliates
— Part III: securities held by financial institutions
— Part IV: eligible funeral arrangements
— Part V: real estate investment trusts
— Part VI: mutual fund reorganizations
— Part VII: objections and appeals
— Part VIII: securities lending arrangements
— Part IX: general (amendments from more than one Part)

| Bill or Budget | Bill No. | Citation | Royal Assent |
|---|---|---|---|
| 1995 cultural property bill | C-93 | S.C. 1995, c. 38 | December 5, 1995 (in force July 12, 1996) |
| Department of Human Resources Development | C-11 | S.C. 1996, c. 11 | May 29, 1996 (in force July 12, 1996) |
| 1995 Budget | C-36 | S.C. 1996, c. 21 | June 20, 1996 |

## Amending Bills

| | | | |
|---|---|---|---|
| Employment insurance bill | C-12 | S.C. 1996, c. 23 | June 20, 1996 |
| GST technical amendments | C-70 | S.C. 1997, c. 10 | March 20, 1997 |
| Bankruptcy and insolvency bill | C-5 | S.C. 1997, c. 12 | April 25, 1997 |
| 1996 Budget | C-92 | S.C. 1997, c. 25 | April 25, 1997 |
| 1997 Budget (first bill) | C-93 | S.C. 1997, c. 26 | April 25, 1997 |
| 1997 Budget (main bill) | C-28 (Div. A) | S.C. 1998, c. 19 | June 18, 1998 |
| 1995-97 technical bill | C-28 (Div. B) | S.C. 1998, c. 19 | June 18, 1998 |
| 1998 Budget (first bill) | C-36 | S.C. 1998, c. 21 | June 18, 1998 |
| Canada Customs & Revenue Agency Act | C-43 | S.C. 1999, c. 17 | April 29, 1999 (in force November 1, 1999) |
| 1999 Budget (first bill) | C-71 | S.C. 1999, c. 26 | June 17, 1999 |
| 1998 Budget (main bill) | C-72 | S.C. 1999, c. 22 | June 17, 1999 |
| Same-sex partners bill | C-23 | S.C. 2000, c. 12 | June 29, 2000 (in force July 31, 2000) |
| 1999 Budget (main bill) | C-25 | S.C. 2000, c. 19 | June 29, 2000 |
| 2000 Budget (first bill) | C-32 | S.C. 2000, c. 14 | June 29, 2000 |
| 2000 GST bill | C-24 | S.C. 2000, c. 30 | October 20, 2000 |

Note: The "RSC-redrafted" bills were re-drafts of the original bills, revised to be consistent with the revisions to the Act made in the R.S.C. 1985 (5th Supp.) version which was proclaimed in force March 1, 1994, but which generally is effective retroactive to December 1, 1991. The redrafted versions of the bills are intended to be identical in meaning to the originals, differing only in that they make the bills conform to the new form of the Act. The consolidated Act as printed in this edition reflects the redrafted amendments.

---

Solution

Cash available for distribution — 2,531,200

Am't distributed as:
- PUC — 140,000
- CSOH – prior to liquidation — 560,000
- – created on liquidation — 235,200 → 795,200

Surplus created on the liquidation:
- Recaptured CCA — 560,000
- Termination costs — (70,000)
- Corp. taxes — (212,800) → 277,200

Undistributed Income on Hand – plug (UIOH) — 1,318,800

Total — 2,531,200

Tax created on distribution
- Corp. taxes – 15% of UIOH — (197,820)
- Personal taxes on v-day surplus — 25% of 277,200 — (69,300)

2,264,080

*Handwritten notes at top:*

Question on components of cash avail. for dist'n + liquid'n value

Facts:
- Cash avail. for dist'n — 2,531,200
- Term'n payroll costs — 70,000
- Corp. taxes — 212,800
- PUC — 140,000
- Pre-V-Day gain on invest. — 235,200
- Recaptured CCA — 560,000

- Company formed prior to V-Day
- 1971 Pre CSOH was 560,000
- Corp. tax on dist'n — 15%
- Personal tax on post V-Day surplus — 25%

# TABLE OF PROPOSED AMENDMENTS

The following table will assist readers in finding, in the shaded boxes throughout the Act and Regulations, the proposed amendments announced at various times, as well as Department of Finance "comfort letters" issued for amendments that have not yet appeared as draft legislation. If you know the subject-matter of announced changes but cannot find them in the legislation, scan the "Subject" column (or consult the Topical Index). If you know the date on which the changes were announced, use the first column, which lists the proposals in chronological order.

Where proposals do not include (and have not been superseded by) draft legislation, the relevant portions of the announcement or press release are reproduced in shaded boxes under the provisions of the Act or Regulations that are expected to be amended.

Except where indicated, all press releases and draft legislation emanate from the federal Department of Finance (Distribution Centre: telephone 613-995-2855, fax 613-996-0518). See the various Special Releases of Carswell's *Canada Tax Service*, *Tax Times* (the "pink sheets") and TaxPartner.

| Bill no. or date of Public Statement | Subject | Reproduced at section no. |
|---|---|---|
| Draft legislation, December 20, 1991 | Interest deductibility | 20(1)(c), (qq) [sic], 20(3.1), (3.2), 20.1 [sic], 20.2 [sic] |
| Press releases, March 2, 1993 and October 1, 1993 | Limit on deductibility of provincial payroll and capital taxes | 18 [end] |
| Draft legislation, August 8, 1994 | Capital gains exemption (legislation enacted in Bill C-59) | Reg. 2800(2) application |
| Draft regulations, September 27, 1994 | Tax shelter and CCA (films and video tape) | Reg. 1100(21)(e), (21.1) |
| Press release, October 14, 1994 | Limit on deductibility of provincial payroll and capital taxes | 18 [end] |
| Federal budget, February 27, 1995 (legislation enacted in 1996) | Certified film productions | (see December 12, 1995 draft regulations) |
| Draft legislation and regulations, June 1, 1995 | Securities held by financial institutions (legislation enacted in 1998; regulations still pending) | Reg. 304(1)(c)(ii), 2402, 2405(3), (5), 2411(4), (5), 6201(5), (5.1), 6209(b), 8102–8105, 9000–9003, 9100–9104, 9200–9204 |
| Letter from Dept. of Finance, September 12, 1995 | Re business fiscal period | 249.1(1) |
| Notice of Ways and Means Motion, December 12, 1995 (most legislation enacted in 1998; regulations still pending) (1995 budget measures) | Interference with remittance | 227(5.2)–(5.4) |
| | Certified film productions | Reg. 1100(1)(m), 1100(2)(a)(iii), 1101(5k.1), 1106, 6701, Sch. II Cl. 10(s), (w), (x), Cl. 12(r) |
| Press release, December 27, 1995 | Limit on deductibility of provincial payroll and capital taxes | 18 [end] |
| Letter from Dept. of Finance to CBA/CICA, June 17, 1996 | Requirement for non-resident to post security | 216(4) |

## Table of Proposed Amendments

| Bill no. or date of Public Statement | Subject | Reproduced at section no. |
|---|---|---|
| Draft regulations, June 20, 1996 | Canadian film or video production tax credit | Reg. 1106(1), (7) |
| | Resource and processing allowances: successoring not available | (see November 30, 2000 draft regulations (miscellaneous)) |
| Letter from Dept. of Finance, September 3, 1996 | Tiered trusts as "designated beneficiaries" | 210 |
| Notice of Ways and Means Motion, October 2, 1996 | Taxpayer emigration | (see Bill C-43 (Sept. 2000)) |
| Press release, November 29, 1996 | Limit on deductibility of provincial payroll and capital taxes | 18 [end] |
| Press release, December 19, 1996 | Segregated fund policies and other annuity contracts | 12.2(1), 204.4(1), 206(1)"foreign property"; Reg. 304(1) |
| Letter from Dept. of Finance, August 6, 1997 | Re application of Large Corporations Tax to joint debt | 181.2(3) |
| Letter from Dept. of Finance, October 8, 1997 | Parent-subsidiary transfers as part of series | 88(1)(c)(v) |
| Press release, October 23, 1997 | Foreign property limit for segregated funds | 12.2(1), 204.4(1), 206(1)"foreign property" |
| Draft legislation and regulations, October 29, 1997 | New film or video production services tax credit | (legislation enacted in 1998); Reg. 9300 |
| Draft legislation and regulations, November 14, 1997 | Impaired loans | (legislation enacted in 1998); Reg. 9103(2) |
| Press release, November 25, 1997 | Limit on deductibility of provincial payroll and capital taxes | 18 [end] |
| Federal budget, February 24, 1998 (most items enacted in 1999) | First Nations taxation | 81(1)(a) |
| Letter from Dept. of Finance, April 29, 1998 | Re registered charity as prescribed investor | Reg. 1106(7)(b) |
| Press release, July 22, 1998 | Prescribed stock exchanges | Reg. 3201 |
| Press release, July 28, 1998 | Abandonment of 1996 proposal re seniors' benefit | 118(3) |
| Letters from Dept. of Finance, September 15, 1998 and November 17, 1997 | Loss deferral rules | 40(3.3)–(3.5) |
| Letter from Dept. of Finance, October 9, 1998 | Re application of Reg. 3200, 3201 for purposes of ITA 38(a.1) | Reg. 3200 |
| Press release, October 27, 1998 | Segregated funds | 12.2(1), 206(1)"foreign property" |
| Draft legislation and regulations, October 27, 1998 (legislation enacted in 1999) | Canadian film or video production tax credit | Reg. 1106(8) |
| | Qualified investments for RESPs | Reg. 221(2), 4900, 4901 |
| | Branch tax (corporate immigration) | Reg. 808(1.1) |
| Letter from Dept. of Finance, December 10, 1998 | Trusts with no prospectus filed to be qualified investments | Reg. 4900(1)(d) |
| Press release, December 18, 1998 | Limit on deductibility of provincial payroll and capital taxes | 18 [end] |
| Press release, December 18, 1998 | Income inclusion on conversion of U.S. IRA | 248(1)"foreign retirement arrangement" |

## Table of Proposed Amendments

| Bill no. or date of Public Statement | Subject | Reproduced at section no. |
|---|---|---|
| | Foreign stock exchange index units | Reg. 4900(1) |
| Draft legislation, December 23, 1998 | Taxpayer migration and trusts | (see Bill C-43 (Sept. 2000)) |
| Letter from Dept. of Finance, December 23, 1998 | Re application of subpara. 55(3)(a)(iii) | 55(3)(a)(iii) |
| Notice of Ways and Means Motion, February 11, 1999 (see the August 8, 2000 draft legislation) | Authorized foreign banks | 18(5), 126(2), 181.3(3), 190.13, 248(1)"authorized foreign bank" |
| Federal budget, February 16, 1999 (most legislation enacted by 1999 Budget bill | First Nations taxation | 81(1)(a) |
| | Non-resident trusts | 94(1) (and see the June 22, 2000 draft legislation) |
| | Foreign-based investment funds | 94.1(1) (and see the June 22, 2000 draft legislation) |
| | RRSP withdrawals under HBP and LLP | Part X.3 |
| Letter from Dept. of Finance, February 19, 1999 | Re anomaly resulting from interaction of sections 55 and 93 | 55(3)(a) |
| Letter from Dept. of Finance, March 17, 1999 | Re transfer of SIN and business numbers to nominee | 241(4) |
| Press release, April 15, 1999 (see Bill C-43 (Sept. 2000)) | Tax rollover for Canadian shareholders of foreign corporations | 44(1), 85.1(5), (6) |
| Press release, May 11, 1999 (see the August 8, 2000 draft legislation) | Conversion of foreign bank subsidiaries into foreign bank branches | 248(1)"authorized foreign bank" |
| Letters from Dept. of Finance, May 12, 1999 and July 2, 1998 | Application of subsec. 84(4.1) | 84(4.1) |
| Department of Foreign Affairs and International Trade news releases, May 26, 1999 and June 4, 1998 (see Bill C-43 (Sept. 2000)) | Amendments re *Foreign Publishers Advertising Services Act* | 19(5)"Canadian newspaper or periodical" |
| Draft legislation, June 3, 1999 (see Bill C-43 (Sept. 2000)) | Donations of ecologically sensitive land | 118.1(12) |
| Letter from Dept. of Finance, June 11, 1999 | Re interaction of ITA 136(2)(c) and Reg. 4900(12) | 136(2)(c) |
| Press release, June 16, 1999 (see Bill C-43 (Sept. 2000)) | Technical change to the $1,000 tax-free amount for emergency service volunteers | 8(1)(a), 81(4) |
| Press release, July 20, 1999 | Technical change for RESPs | 146.1(1)"education savings plan" |
| July 23, 1999 draft legislation | Resource expenditures | (see Bill C-43 (Sept. 2000)); Reg. 1102(1)(a) |
| Technical backgrounder re taxpayer migration and trusts, September 10, 1999 (see Bill C-43 (Sept. 2000)) | Changes to security requirements | 220(4.5)–(4.71) |

## Table of Proposed Amendments

| Bill no. or date of Public Statement | Subject | Reproduced at section no. |
|---|---|---|
| Press release, October 19, 1999 | Residence deduction for the clergy | 8(1)(c) |
| Press release, November 30, 1999 | Update on proposals for the taxation of non-resident trusts and foreign investment funds | 94 |
| November 30, 1999 draft legislation (incorporated in Bill C-43 (Sept. 2000)) | Technical amendments (superseding the June 3, 1999 draft legislation re ecological gifts and implementing news releases of April 15 ($1,000 tax free amount for emergency services) and June 16, 1999 (extension of s. 85.1 to foreign corporations) among others | throughout the Act |
| November 30, 1999 draft regulations | Insurance business policy reserves | Reg. 1400(3), 1401(1)(b), 1404(3)C, 1408(1) definitions |
| | Foreign affiliates | Reg. 5900(2), (3), 5902, 5903, 5905, 5907(1.3), (1.4) |
| | Registered Pension Plans | Reg. 8300(8)(a), 8301(4)(b)(ii.2), 8500(1.1), (7)(d), (8), 8501(6.1), (6.2), 8502(d)(ii), (k) |
| Letter from Dept. of Finance, December 9, 1999 | Tiered trusts as "designated beneficiaries" | 210 |
| December 17, 1999 draft legislation and regulations | Taxpayer migration | (incorporated in Bill C-43 (Sept. 2000)); Reg. 600(c) |
| | Trusts | (incorporated in Bill C-43 (Sept. 2000)) |
| Press release, December 17, 1999 | Limit on deductibility of provincial payroll and capital taxes | 18 [end] |
| Press release, January 25, 2000 | Allowing provinces to impose tax on income | 117(2) |
| Press release, February 7, 2000 | Redemption requirements for LSVCCs | 204.81(1), 211.8(1)(a) |
| Letter from Dept. of Finance, February 15, 2000 | Recaptured CCA on donation of property to charity | 216(1) |
| Letter from Dept. of Finance, February 21, 2000 | Amalgamation of farmers' and fishermen's insurers | 87(1) |
| CCRA press release, February 22, 2000 | Emergency volunteers | 81(4) |
| Federal budget, February 28, 2000 (and see Budget Update of October 18, 2000; December 21, 2000 draft legislation) | Adjustments to the CCA system | Reg. Part XI |
| | Attendant care expenses | 64 |
| | Capital gains deferral | 44.1 |
| | Capital gains inclusion rate | 38(a) |
| | Communication of taxpayer information | 241(3)(c) |
| | Deferred stock option benefits | 7(8)–(16) |
| | Disability tax credit | 118.3(1), (2) |
| | Donation of stock option shares | 110(1)(d.01) |
| | Donations of ecological gifts | 38(a.2), 118.1(10.1)–(10.5) |

## Table of Proposed Amendments

| Bill no. or date of Public Statement | Subject | Reproduced at section no. |
|---|---|---|
| | Electrical generating equipment, and heat or water production and distribution equipment | Reg. Sch. II:Cl. 1 |
| | Extension of foreign property rules to segregated funds | 206(1)"foreign property" |
| | First Nations taxation | 81(1)(a) |
| | Foreign resource expenses | 66(4) (also 66.7(2.1)–(2.3), 79.1(2), (2.1)) |
| | Foreign tax credit | 126(9) |
| | Foreign tax credits: oil and gas production sharing | 126(5) |
| | Government assistance: SR&ED | 37(1)(d.1) |
| | Income not earned in a province | 120(1) |
| | Individual surtax | 180.1(1) |
| | M&P rate for producing steam for sale | 125.1(2) |
| | Medical expense tax credit | 118.2(2)(l.21) |
| | Non-resident-owned investment corporations | 133(8)"non-resident-owned investment corporation" |
| | Offsetting of interest on personal tax overpayment and underpayments | 161.1 |
| | Personal-use property | 46(5) |
| | Rail assets | Reg. Sch. II:Cl. 35 |
| | SR&ED | 127(9)"SR&ED qualified expenditure pool" |
| | Scholarships, fellowships and bursaries | 56(3) |
| | Separate class election for M&P equipment | Reg. 1101(5p) |
| | Simplified film tax incentives | 125.4 |
| | Tax payable by individuals | 117(2) |
| | Tax reduction for corporations | 123.4 |
| | Thin capitalization | 18(4)–(8) |
| | Weak currency debt (kiwi loans) | 20.3 |
| CCRA press release, March 2, 2000 | Internet filing | 150.1 |
| Letter from Dept. of Finance, March 14, 2000 | LSVCC mergers | 204.85(3)(c) |
| Draft regulations, April 18, 2000 | Registered pension plans | (see November 30, 2000 draft regulations) |
| Notice of Ways and Means Motion, June 5, 2000 | throughout the Act | (incorporated in Bill C-43 (Sept. 2000)) |
| Letter from Dept. of Finance, May 15, 2000 | Butterfly reorganization | 55(3.3) |
| Letter from Dept. of Finance, June 6, 2000 | Butterfly reorganization | 248(1)"taxable Canadian property" |
| Bill C-40 (*Courts Administration Act*), First Reading June 15, 2000 | Consequential amendments | heading before 169, and 176(2) |

## Table of Proposed Amendments

| Bill no. or date of Public Statement | Subject | Reproduced at section no. |
|---|---|---|
| Draft legislation, June 22, 2000 | Non-resident trusts | 94 and others |
| | Foreign-based investment funds | 94.1–94.3 and others |
| Letter from Dept. of Finance, July 4, 2000 | Eligible investments for deferred income plans | 204.4(2)(a)(ii)(A) |
| Letter from Dept. of Finance, July 11, 2000 | Penalty re third-party misrepresentations | 163.2(10) |
| Draft legislation, August 8, 2000 | Authorized foreign banks and other incidental changes | 14(14) and :14 (15), 18(1)(v), 20.2, 76.1, 126(1.1), 142.6(1.1)–(2), 142.7, 153(6), 181.3(3), (4), (5), 190.13, 190.14, 212(13.3), 218.2 (new Part XIII.1), 248(1) and others |
| Draft regulations, August 8, 2000 | Authorized foreign banks and other incidental changes | Reg. 404(1), 413(3), 808(1), (2), (5)(j)(ii), (6)(a), (8), 5301(1)(b), (4), (8), (10), 7900, 8201, 9204(2.1), 9204(5)(a), 9204(5.1) |
| Letter from Dept. of Finance, August 16, 2000 | Change in year-end for mutual fund trust | 132.11(1) |
| Press release, September 7, 2000 | New effective date for foreign investment entity and trust tax proposals | 94.3 |
| Bill C-43 (First Reading September 20, 2000) | Amendments re *Foreign Publishers Advertising Services Act* | 19(1), (5), (5.1), (6)–(8), 19.01 |
| | Resource expenditures | 66.1(6)"Canadian exploration expense"(d)(i), (k.1), 66.1(9)(a), 66.2(5)"Canadian development expense"(i.1) |
| | Technical amendments (superseding the November 30, 1999 draft technical legislation, the June 3, 1999 draft legislation re ecological gifts and implementing news releases of April 15 ($1,000 tax free amount for emergency services) and June 16, 1999 (extension of s. 85.1 to foreign corporations) among others) | throughout the Act |
| | Taxpayer migration | 114, 114.1, 115, 128.1, 128.3, 220(4.5)–(4.71), 248(1)"taxable Canadian property" and others |
| | Trusts | 107, 107.4, 108(1), 108(7), 248(1)"disposition", (25.1), (25.2) and others |
| Agriculture and Agri-Food Canada news releases, September 20, 2000 | Prescribed drought regions: Saskatchewan, Alberta | Reg. 7305 |
| Letter from Dept. of Finance, September 28, 2000 | Re "specified property" rule | 88(1)(c.4) |

## Table of Proposed Amendments

| Bill no. or date of Public Statement | Subject | Reproduced at section no. |
|---|---|---|
| Federal Economic Statement and Budget Update, October 18, 2000 (see December 21, 2000 draft legislation) | includes NWMM and tax measures; supplementary information | 14(1), 20(1)(b), 38, 80(13), 85.1, 89(1)"capital dividend account", 110(1)(d), 110.6(2)(a), 117(2), 118(1)B, 118.3(1), 118.6(2), 122.5, 122.61(1), 127(9)"flow-through mining expenditure" |
| Draft regulations, November 30, 2000 (pre-published in the Canada Gazette, Part I, December 9, 2000) (previously released on April 18, 2000) | Registered pension plans | Reg. 8302(3); 8303(2), (6); 8304(2); 8307(4), (6); 8500(8); 8503(2), (2.1), (3); 8504(11); 8510(6); 8514. |
| Draft regulations, November 30, 2000 (pre-published in the Canada Gazette, Part I, December 9, 2000) (Reg. 1202(5)(c) previously released June 20, 1996) | Miscellaneous | Reg. 1202(5)(c), 1216, 3200, 3201, Part LXII, 6210 |
| Press release, December 12, 2000 | Limit on deductibility of provincial payroll and capital taxes | 18 (end) |
| Draft legislation, December 21, 2000 | Re Federal Budget, February 28, 2000 and Budget Update, October 18, 2000 | throughout the Act |
| Press release and Backgrounder, December 21, 2000 | Flow-through share investment tax credit | 127(9)"flow-through mining expenditure" |
|  | Alternative Minimum Tax rate on capital gains | 127.52(1)(d)(i) |
|  | Offset interest | 161.1 |
|  | Surtax on deposit-taking institutions | 190.1(1.2) |
|  | Canadian Venture Exchange | Reg. 3200 |

*Tax planning activities accomplished w/ sec 85(1) rollover:*

1) Spin off assets from one corp. to another. This could be done with redundant assets ∴ alleviating immediate tax consequences ∴ purify corp. for the purpose of 500,000 cap. gains exemption

2) Consolidate business operations within one corporation for loss utilization, tax planning purpose or other business reason

3) For both arm's length acquisitions and divestitures of business in order to minimize or defer taxes payable by vendor

4) Transfer assets of unincorporated business to a Canadian corp.ⁿ to allow the business the opp. to take advantage of small bus. rate and 500K exemption

5) Income splitting / estate planning

# SAMPLE CALCULATION OF NET FAIR MARKET VALUE OF REDUNDANT ASSET

### Facts
FMV = 225,000
ACB = 56,250
Provincial corp rate 15.5%
Assume 75% cap gains inclusion rate

| | | |
|---|---|---|
| Fair market value | 225,000 | |
| ACB | 56,250 | |
| Cap. gain | 168,750 | |
| TCG | 126,563 | |
| | | |
| Federal tax @ 28% | 35,438 | (Effective rate 29.12%) |
| Surtax @ 4% | 1,418 | (Remember surtax on tax!) |
| Refundable taxes @ 6.67% | 8,442 | |
| Provincial taxes @ 15.5% | 19,617 | |
| Total corp. tax | 64,915 | |
| | | |
| Refundable tax | | |
| 26.67% × TCG | 33,754 | |
| | | |
| Net corp. tax | 31,161 | |

Maximum dividend:

| | | |
|---|---|---|
| Proceeds | 225,000 | |
| * Less: Cap. dividend | (42,187) | |
| Corp. tax | (64,915) | |
| Refundable tax | 33,754 | 151,652 |
| | | |
| Grossed up by 25% | | 189,565 |
| Federal tax @ 29% (hypo rate) | | 54,974 |
| Dv. tax credit 13.33% × 189,565 | | (25,269) |
| | | 29,705 |
| Provincial tax @ 53% | | 15,744 |
| Provincial surtax @ 10% | | 1,574 |
| Total personal tax | | 47,023 |

| | | |
|---|---|---|
| Gross redundant asset | | 225,000 |
| Less: Corp. tax | 31,161 | |
| Per. tax | 47,023 | (78,184) |
| Net FMV of redundant asset | | 146,816 |

# TAX REFERENCE TABLES

## INDIVIDUALS
Federal Tax Rates — 2000/2001 . . . . . . . . . . . . . . . . . . . . . . . . . . . . . . . . . . . . . . . . . . . . xxiii
Indexed Federal Personal Tax Credits . . . . . . . . . . . . . . . . . . . . . . . . . . . . . . . . . . . . . . . xxiii
2000 Provincial Tax Rates . . . . . . . . . . . . . . . . . . . . . . . . . . . . . . . . . . . . . . . . . . . . . . . . xxiv
2001 Provincial Tax Rates . . . . . . . . . . . . . . . . . . . . . . . . . . . . . . . . . . . . . . . . . . . . . . . . xxvi
2000 Personal Tax Credits — Combined Federal and Provincial Values . . . . . . . . . . . . . . . . . xxvii
2001 Federal and Provincial Non-refundable Tax Credits . . . . . . . . . . . . . . . . . . . . . . . . . . xxix
2000 and 2001 Québec Personal Tax Credits . . . . . . . . . . . . . . . . . . . . . . . . . . . . . . . . . . xxx
Canada/Québec Pension Plan Contributions . . . . . . . . . . . . . . . . . . . . . . . . . . . . . . . . . . xxxi
Employment Insurance Contributions . . . . . . . . . . . . . . . . . . . . . . . . . . . . . . . . . . . . . . . xxxii
Registered Retirement Savings Plan (RRSP)/Deferred Profit Sharing Plan (DPSP) Contributions . . . xxxii
Automobile Limits — Prescribed Amounts . . . . . . . . . . . . . . . . . . . . . . . . . . . . . . . . . . . xxxii
Employer-Provided Automobiles — Taxable Benefits . . . . . . . . . . . . . . . . . . . . . . . . . . . xxxiv

## CORPORATIONS
Federal Corporate Income Tax Rates for Active Business Income . . . . . . . . . . . . . . . . . . . . xxxv
Provincial Corporate Income Tax Rates for Active Business Income . . . . . . . . . . . . . . . . . . xxxv
Combined Federal and Provincial Corporate Income Tax Rates for Active Business Income . . . . . xxxv
Provincial Manufacturing and Processing (M&P) Tax Incentives . . . . . . . . . . . . . . . . . . . . . xxxvii
Federal Research and Development (R&D) Tax Incentives . . . . . . . . . . . . . . . . . . . . . . . xxxviii
Provincial Research and Development (R&D) Tax Incentives . . . . . . . . . . . . . . . . . . . . . . xxxix

## PROVINCIAL PAYROLL TAXES
Manitoba . . . . . . . . . . . . . . . . . . . . . . . . . . . . . . . . . . . . . . . . . . . . . . . . . . . . . . . . . . . xli
Ontario . . . . . . . . . . . . . . . . . . . . . . . . . . . . . . . . . . . . . . . . . . . . . . . . . . . . . . . . . . . . xli
Québec . . . . . . . . . . . . . . . . . . . . . . . . . . . . . . . . . . . . . . . . . . . . . . . . . . . . . . . . . . . . xli
Newfoundland . . . . . . . . . . . . . . . . . . . . . . . . . . . . . . . . . . . . . . . . . . . . . . . . . . . . . . . xlii

## OTHER
Prescribed Interest Rates . . . . . . . . . . . . . . . . . . . . . . . . . . . . . . . . . . . . . . . . . . . . . . . xliii
Foreign Exchange Rates . . . . . . . . . . . . . . . . . . . . . . . . . . . . . . . . . . . . . . . . . . . . . . . . xliv
Tax Treaty Withholding Rates . . . . . . . . . . . . . . . . . . . . . . . . . . . . . . . . . . . . . . . . . . . . xlv
Limitations and Contingent Dates . . . . . . . . . . . . . . . . . . . . . . . . . . . . . . . . . . . . . . . . . xlix
Penalties and Offences . . . . . . . . . . . . . . . . . . . . . . . . . . . . . . . . . . . . . . . . . . . . . . . . . li
Table of Dollar Amounts (see under "Dollar amounts" in Topical Index)

# REQUIRED:
a) Calculate net proceeds from sale of assets
b) Calculate net proceeds from sale of shares

|  | Proceeds | Income Business | INV (TCG) | CDA | RDTOH |
|---|---|---|---|---|---|
| Opening |  | Nil | Nil | Nil | Nil |
| Cash | 6000 | Nil |  |  |  |
| Inventory | 55500 | 10500 |  |  |  |
| Land | 30000 |  | 11250 | 3750 |  |
| Building | 58500 | 37500 | 4500 | 1500 |  |
| Equipment | 18000 | (9000) |  |  |  |
| Goodwill | 70500 | 52875 | Nil | 17625 |  |
| Liabilities | (30000) |  |  |  |  |
| Taxes | (26297) Ⓐ | 91875 | 15750 |  |  |
| RDTOH | 4200 Ⓑ |  |  | 4200 | 4200 |
|  | 186,423 |  |  | 22875 | 4200 |

Funds avail for dist'n      186423
Less: PUC                   (15000)
Deemed div. on winding up   171,423         Ⓐ 20% × 91875
Less: Cap. dividend         (22875)         (43.5 + 6.67) × 15750
Deemed taxable dividend*    148548
  *sufficient to clear RDTOH              Ⓑ 26.67% × 15,750

TCG on disp'n of shares on w-up:
Actual proceeds from dist'n   186,423
Less: Deemed dividend         171,423
Proceeds                       15,000
Cost                          (15000)
Cap. gain                        NIL

Funds distributed on wind-up                186,423
Deemed taxable div.            148548
Grossed up @ 25%                37137
                               185,685
Cap gain                          NIL
Taxable income                 185,685
Combined Fed/Prov tax 45%       83,558
Less: DTC
 (1.55 × 13⅓% of 185,685)      38,365    (45193)
                           Net cash retained  141,230

Sale of Shares                  Tax @ 45% = 60,750      ∴ Sale of
  Proceeds    195,000                                    assets is
  ACB         (15,000)          Net proceeds             preferred
             180,000            195,000 - 60,750
  TCG        135,000              = 134,250

Case Facts:

|  | FMV | Cost | UCC |
|---|---|---|---|
| Cash | 6000 | 6000 | |
| Inventory | 55500 | 45000 | |
| Land | 30000 | 15000 | |
| Bldg | 58500 | 52500 | 15000 |
| Equip. | 18000 | 37500 | 27000 |
| Goodwill | 70500 | NIL | |
| Liabilities | (30000) | (30000) | |

PUC = 15,000
R/E 111,000

Tax rates
marg. tax rate 45%
prov. tax rate 55%
SB rate 20% on ABI
43.5% on other +
refundable tax of 6.67% on investment income

## TAX REFERENCE TABLES
(These tables were prepared with the assistance of KPMG LLP)

### INDIVIDUALS

#### FEDERAL TAX RATES

**2000**

| Taxable Income | Tax on Lower Limit | Tax Rate on Excess | Rate | Surtax Threshold |
|---|---|---|---|---|
| $0 — 30,004 | $ — | 17% | 5% | $15,500 |
| 30,005 — 60,009 | 5,101 | 25% | | |
| 60,010 and over | 12,602 | 29% | | |

**2001**

| Taxable Income | Tax on Lower Limit | Tax Rate on Excess |
|---|---|---|
| $0 — 30,754 | $ — | 16% |
| 30,755 — 61,509 | 4,921 | 22% |
| 61,510 — 100,000 | 11,687 | 26% |
| 100,001 and over | 21,694 | 29% |

#### Notes:

The 2000 federal budget announced the following changes to the federal tax rates and brackets:
- Effective January 1, 2000 the brackets will be indexed to inflation with the inflation adjustment based on the change in the average inflation rate over the 12-month period ending September 30 of the previous year in comparison to the same period of the year prior to that.
- The tax rate applicable to the middle bracket decreased to 24% (from 26%) effective July 1, 2000. The rate for 2000 is therefore 25%.
- The federal surtax applies to basic federal tax (net of applicable credits) in excess of the threshold amount noted. This threshold increased to $18,500 (from $12,500) effective July 1, 2000. The threshold for 2000 is therefore $15,500.

The October 18, 2000 mini-budget announced further changes to the federal tax rates and brackets for 2001:
- The 17% tax rate applicable to the lowest bracket decreased to 16%.
- The middle bracket tax rate decreased from 24% to 22%.
- The top bracket was divided into two, with a rate of 26% applying to income between $61,510 and $100,000, and the top 29% rate applying to income in excess of $100,000.
- The high-income surtax was eliminated.

#### INDEXED FEDERAL PERSONAL TAX CREDITS

|  | 2000 | 2001[5] |
|---|---|---|
| Basic personal credit: 118(1)B(c) | $ 1,229 | $ 1,186 |
| Maximum married credit or equivalent-to-spouse credit for a related dependant who is under 18, the taxpayer's parent or grandparent, or infirm: 118(1)B(a), (b) | 1,044 | 1,007 |
| — spouse's or dependant's income threshold above which credit is reduced: 118(1)B(a), (b) | 614 | 629 |
| Infirm dependants: | | |
| — under age 18 [Note 1] | 500 | 560 |
| — age 18 or over: 118(1)B(d), (e) [Note 2] | 406 | 560 |
| Age 65 or older: 118(2) [Note 3] | 600 | 579 |

xxiii

# Tax Reference Tables

| | | |
|---|---|---|
| — net income threshold | 26,284 | 26,941 |
| Maximum pension credit: 118(3) | 170 | 160 |
| Disability credit: 118.3 | 730 | 960 |
| Caregiver: 118(1)B(c.1) | 406 | 560 |
| Medical expense credit: 118.2 | | |
| — maximum reduction of allowable medical expenses | 1,637 | 1,678 |
| GST credit: 122.5 | | |
| — for eligible individual, qualified relation (spouse or dependant under 19 for whom equivalent-to-spouse credit claimed) [Note 4] | 205 | 207 |
| — for each qualified dependant | 107 | 109 |
| — net income threshold | 26,284 | 26,941 |
| Tax (clawback) on old age security benefits: 180.2 | | |
| — net income threshold | 53,960 | 55,309 |

**Notes:**

1. The 2000 federal budget introduced a new credit for those supporting children eligible for the disability credit. The amount of the credit is reduced by child and attendant care expenses claimed in respect of the child exceeding $2,000.
2. The income threshold for infirm dependants age 18 or over above which the credit is reduced is $4,845 for 2000 and $4,966 for 2001.
3. The federal age amount, $3,619 for 2001 ($3,531 for 2000), which is used to determine the credit, is reduced by 15% of the excess of a taxpayer's net income over $26,941 for 2001 ($26,284 for 2000). The age credit is reduced to zero when net income exceeds $51,068 for 2001 ($49,284 for 2000).
4. For 2000, the basic credit for each eligible individual is $202 with a one-time supplement of $3 (total $205). The basic credit for each qualified dependant is $106 with a one-time supplement of $1 (total $107).
5. Some credits have gone down for 2001 because they are now 16% of an amount rather than 17%.

## 2000 PROVINCIAL TAX RATES

| | Tax Rates (as a % of Basic Federal Tax) | Bracket 1 | Bracket 2 | Bracket 3 | Rates | Thresholds | Flat Tax |
|---|---|---|---|---|---|---|---|
| British Columbia (a)(d) | | 8.4% $0-30,004 | 12.4% 30,005-60,009 | 14.4% 60,010 and over | 30% 15 | $5,300 8,660 | |
| Alberta (b)(e) | 44.0% | | | | | | .5% of taxable income |
| Saskatchewan (b)(f) | 48.0 | | | | 10 15 | — 4,000 | 1.5% of net income 1.5% of net income |
| Manitoba (a)(g) | | 8.0% $0-29,590 | 12.2% 29,591-59,180 | 13.6% 59,181 and over | | | 2% of net income 2% of net income over $30,000 |
| Ontario (a)(h) | | 6.4% $0-30,004 | 9.6% 30,005-60,009 | 11.2% 60,010 and over | 20 36 | 3,561 4,468 | |
| Québec (i) | | 19.0% $0-26,000 | 22.5% 26,001-52,000 | 25.0% 52,001 and over | | | |
| New Brunswick (a)(j) | | 9.9% $0-29,590 | 15.2% 29,591-59,180 | 17.0% 59,181 and over | 8 | 13,500 | |
| Nova Scotia (a)(k) | | 9.8% $0-29,590 | 14.9% 29,591-59,180 | 16.7% 59,181 and over | 10 | 10,000 | |
| Prince Edward Island (b)(l) | 57.5 | | | | 10 | 5,200 | |
| Newfoundland (b)(m) | 62.0 | | | | 6 10 | 250 7,050 | |
| Yukon Territory (c)(n) | 49.0 | | | | 5 | 6,000 | |
| N.W.T./Nunavut (c) | 45.0 | | | | | | |

## Tax Reference Tables

**Notes:**

(a) British Columbia, Manitoba, Ontario, New Brunswick and Nova Scotia are using the tax-on-income method of calculating their provincial income tax beginning with the 2000 taxation year. This new system applies the provincial tax rate to taxable income, which must be the same for both federal and provincial purposes. Provincial non-refundable credits reduce provincial tax, and the surtax rates are then applied to net provincial tax in excess of the threshold amounts indicated.

(b) Alberta, Saskatchewan, P.E.I. and Newfoundland are switching to the new tax-on-income method in 2001. For 2000, they are retaining the tax-on-tax method of calculating their provincial tax. Their tax rate is applied to basic federal tax (net of applicable credits), and the surtax rates are then applied to provincial tax in excess of the threshold amounts indicated.

(c) The territories are not switching to the tax-on-income system in 2001.

(d) B.C. has retained its 1999 tax-on-tax rate of 49.5% as the basis for calculating its new rates (i.e., 17% × 49.5% = 8.4%). The province is following the federal reductions announced in the 2000 budget — its middle tax rate is based on an effective federal rate of 25% (i.e., 25% × 49.5% = 12.4%) and its brackets will be indexed for inflation.

The province's second-tier surtax rate decreased from 19% to 15% effective January 1, 2000 as announced in the 1999 budget. The first tier surtax rate and the surtax thresholds have not changed.

(e) Alberta eliminated its surtax of 8% on provincial tax in excess of $3,500 effective January 1, 2000.

(f) Saskatchewan reduced its flat tax rate from 2% to 1% effective July 1, 2000. The rate for 2000 is therefore 1.5%.

Saskatchewan's 15% high-rate surtax and 10% "Deficit Surtax" both apply to basic Saskatchewan tax plus the flat tax.

(g) Manitoba announced in its 1999 budget that its tax-on-tax rate would decrease to 47% (from 50%) effective July 1, 1999. This 47% tax-on-tax rate is therefore used to calculate the province's new tax-on-income rates (i.e., 17% × 47% = 8.0%). The province is not passing along the federal reductions announced in the 2000 budget that would otherwise have occurred automatically under the tax-on-tax system. Its middle tax rate is based on the higher effective federal rate of 26% (i.e., 26% × 47% = 12.2%) and its brackets have not been indexed to inflation. The two levels of surtax in the province have not changed.

(h) Ontario announced in its 1999 budget that its tax-on-tax rate would decrease to 38.5% (from 40.5%) effective July 1, 1999. This 38.5% tax-on-tax rate is used to calculate the province's new tax-on-income rates applicable to the two top brackets (i.e., 29% × 38.5% = 11.2%). As indicated in its 2000 budget, the province is using the equivalent of a 37.5% tax-on-tax rate to compute the rate applicable to the lowest bracket (i.e., 17% × 37.5% = 6.4%).

Ontario is following the federal reductions announced in the 2000 budget — its middle tax rate is based on an effective federal rate of 25% (i.e., 25% × 38.5% = 9.6%) and its brackets will be indexed for inflation. However, in order to offset the tax savings generated by the reductions in rates applicable to the lower and middle brackets, Ontario has lowered its surtax thresholds as indicated in the table.

(i) Québec has always had a separate tax system, administered by the province itself. Taxpayers file a separate provincial return and calculate provincial taxes based on Québec taxable income, which need not be the same as federal taxable income. They are also able to use a simplified method of calculating their taxes.

Residents of Québec and taxpayers carrying on business in Québec receive a reduction of their federal taxes equal to 16.5% of basic federal tax. Québec's surtax (called a contribution to the anti-poverty fund) of 0.3% of Québec tax payable was eliminated for taxation years ending after 1999.

(j) As announced in its 2000 budget, New Brunswick's tax-on-tax rate used as the basis for calculating its new rates decreased to 57% (from 60%) effective July 1, 2000. The tax-on-tax rate used as the basis for the new tax-on-income rates is therefore 58.5% for 2000 (i.e., 17% × 58.5% = 9.9%).

The province is not passing along the federal reductions announced in the 2000 budget that would otherwise have occurred automatically under the tax-on-tax system. Its middle tax rate is based on the higher effective rate of 26% (i.e., 26% × 58.5% = 15.2%) and its brackets have not been indexed to inflation. The province's surtax has not changed.

(k) Nova Scotia has retained its 1999 tax-on-tax rate of 57.5% as the basis for calculating its new rates (i.e., 17% × 57.5% = 9.8%). The province is not passing along the federal reductions announced in the 2000 budget that would otherwise have occurred automatically under the tax-on-tax system. Its middle tax rate is based on the higher effective federal rate of 26% (i.e., 26% × 57.5% = 14.9%) and its brackets have not been indexed to inflation. The provinces's surtax has not changed.

# Tax Reference Tables

(l) Prince Edward Island reduced its basic rate from 58.5% to 57.5% effective January 1, 2000.

(m) Effective January 1, 2000, Newfoundland's tax rate was reduced from 69% to 62%. At the same time, the province instituted a two-tier surtax system as indicated in the table. Previously, surtax applied at a rate of 10% on Newfoundland tax in excess of $7,900.

(n) Yukon decreased its basic rate from 50% to 49% effective January 1, 2000. It also plans to further reduce the rate to 46% effective January 1, 2001 and to 44% effective January 1, 2002.

## 2001 PROVINCIAL TAX RATES (subject to further changes in 2001) (a)

| | Tax Rates (as a % of Taxable Income) | Brackets | Surtax Rate | Threshold |
|---|---|---|---|---|
| British Columbia (b) | 8.4% | $0-30,484 | | |
| | 11.9 | 30,485-60,969 | | |
| | 16.7 | 60,970-70,000 | | |
| | 18.7 | 70,001-85,000 | | |
| | 19.7 | 85,001 and over | | |
| Alberta (c) | 10.5 | All income | | |
| Saskatchewan (d) | 11.5 | 0-30,000 | | |
| | 13.5 | 30,001-60,000 | | |
| | 16.0 | 60,001 and over | | |
| Manitoba (e) | 10.9 | 0-30,544 | | |
| | 16.2 | 30,545-61,089 | | |
| | 17.5 | 61,090 and over | | |
| Ontario (f) | 6.20 | 0-30,814 | | |
| | 9.24 | 30,815-61,629 | 20% | 3,560 |
| | 11.16 | 60,630 and over | 36 | 4,491 |
| Québec (g) | 18.0 | 0-26,000 | | |
| | 22.5 | 26,001-52,000 | | |
| | 25.0 | 52,001 and over | | |
| New Brunswick | 9.68 | 0-29,590 | | |
| | 14.82 | 29,591-59,180 | | |
| | 16.52 | 59,181 and over | 8 | 13,500 |
| Nova Scotia | 9.77 | 0-29,590 | | |
| | 14.95 | 29,591-59,180 | | |
| | 16.67 | 59,181 and over | 10 | 10,000 |
| Prince Edward Island | 9.8 | 0-30,754 | | |
| | 13.8 | 30,755-61,509 | | |
| | 16.7 | 61,510 and over | 10 | 5,200 |
| Newfoundland | 10.57 | 0-29,590 | | |
| | 16.16 | 29,591-59,180 | | |
| | 18.02 | 59,181 and over | 9 | 7,032 |

### Notes:

(a) The three territories are not included in the table as they are not switching to the tax-on-income system in 2001. Their tax-on-tax and surtax rates for 2001 are as follows:
  - Northwest Territories — 45%
  - Nunavut — 45%
  - Yukon Territory — 46%
  - Yukon surtax — 5% of Yukon tax in excess of $6,000.

(b) British Columbia is indexing its brackets starting in 2001 using the same formula as that used federally, but based on the B.C. inflation rate, which is 1.6% for 2001. B.C.'s surtaxes have now been incorporated into its tax brackets.

(c) Alberta's new system will apply a flat tax rate to all taxable income. As well, no surtaxes will apply.

(d) Saskatchewan's tax reform proposes a reduction in rates and an increase in brackets as follows, applicable in 2003 when the system is fully implemented:

| | |
|---|---|
| 11.0% | $ 0-35,000 |
| 13.0 | 35,001-100,000 |
| 15.0 | 100,001 and over |

## Tax Reference Tables

(e) Manitoba plans on reducing its middle rate to 15.6% and increasing the threshold for its highest bracket to $65,000 in 2002.

(f) Ontario is indexing its brackets starting in 2001 using the same formula as that used federally, but based on the Ontario inflation rate, which is 2.7% for 2001.

(g) Québec's 2000 budget announced further reductions in the low, middle and high rates to 17%, 22% and 24% respectively for 2002. The province will also index its brackets for inflation commencing January 1, 2003.

## 2000 PERSONAL TAX CREDITS — COMBINED FEDERAL AND PROVINCIAL VALUES

| | Dollar Amount (a) | Federal | B.C. (c) | Alta. | Sask. | Man. |
|---|---|---|---|---|---|---|
| Basic personal | $7,231 | $1,229 | $1,838 | $1,770 | $1,819 | $1,807 |
| Spousal (d) | 6,140 | 1,044 | 1,560 | 1,503 | 1,545 | 1,534 |
| Equivalent-to-spouse (d) (e) | 6,140 | 1,044 | 1,560 | 1,503 | 1,545 | 1,534 |
| Infirm dependants | | | | | | |
| under age 18 (f) | 2,941 | 500 | 747 | 720 | 740 | 735 |
| age 18 and over (g) | 2,386 | 406 | 606 | 584 | 600 | 596 |
| Age 65 and over (h) (l) | 3,531 | 600 | 897 | 864 | 888 | 882 |
| Disability (i) (l) | 4,293 | 730 | 1,091 | 1,051 | 1,080 | 1,073 |
| Caregiver (j) | 2,386 | 406 | 606 | 584 | 600 | 596 |
| Pension (k) (l) | 1,000 | 170 | 254 | 245 | 252 | 250 |
| Canada Pension Plan | | | | | | |
| Employed | 1,330 | 226 | 338 | 326 | 335 | 332 |
| Self-employed | 2,660 | 452 | 676 | 651 | 669 | 665 |
| Employment Insurance | 936 | 159 | 238 | 229 | 235 | 234 |
| Education (l) | | | | | | |
| Per month — full time | 200 | 34 | 51 | 49 | 50 | 50 |
| Per month — part time | 60 | 10 | 15 | 15 | 15 | 15 |
| Tuition fees (m) | | | | | | |
| Interest paid on student loans (n) | | | | | | |
| Medical expenses (o) | | | | | | |

| | Ont. | N.B. | N.S. | P.E.I. | Nfld. | Yukon | N.W.T./Nunavut |
|---|---|---|---|---|---|---|---|
| Basic personal | $1,690 | $1,948 | $1,936 | $1,936 | $1,991 | $1,832 | $1,782 |
| Spousal (d) | 1,435 | 1,654 | 1,644 | 1,644 | 1,691 | 1,555 | 1,514 |
| Equivalent-to-spouse (d) (e) | 1,435 | 1,654 | 1,644 | 1,644 | 1,691 | 1,555 | 1,514 |
| Infirm dependants | | | | | | | |
| under age 18 (f) | 687 | 792 | 787 | 787 | 810 | 745 | 725 |
| age 18 and over (g) | 558 | 643 | 639 | 639 | 657 | 604 | 588 |
| Age 65 and over (h) (l) | 825 | 951 | 945 | 945 | 972 | 894 | 870 |
| Disability (i) (l) | 1,003 | 1,157 | 1,149 | 1,149 | 1,182 | 1,087 | 1,058 |
| Caregiver (j) | 558 | 643 | 639 | 639 | 657 | 604 | 588 |
| Pension (k) (l) | 234 | 269 | 268 | 268 | 275 | 253 | 247 |
| Canada Pension Plan | | | | | | | |
| Employed | 311 | 358 | 356 | 356 | 366 | 337 | 328 |
| Self-employed | 622 | 717 | 712 | 712 | 733 | 674 | 656 |
| Employment Insurance | 219 | 252 | 251 | 251 | 258 | 237 | 231 |
| Education (l) | | | | | | | |
| Per month — full time | 47 | 54 | 54 | 54 | 55 | 51 | 49 |
| Per month — part time | 14 | 16 | 16 | 16 | 17 | 15 | 15 |

**Notes:**

(a) The 2000 federal budget re-introduced full indexation to most credit amounts. The inflation factor used is the same as that applied to the federal tax brackets.

(b) The federal credit values are calculated at a rate of 17%. For those provinces that have not yet switched to the tax-on-income system, the combined federal and provincial credit values reflect basic federal tax and provincial tax only. They do not include federal surtax or any provincial surtaxes on flat taxes. For those provinces that have switched to the new system, the provincial portion of the combined value is calculated based on the province's lowest tax rate. The federal portion of the combined value is unchanged.

(c) B.C. introduced its own personal and spousal credits for 2000 in the amount of $300 each, resulting in an additional credit value of $25 per taxpayer, calculated at the province's lowest rate.

## Tax Reference Tables

(d) The spousal amount of $6,140 is reduced by the excess of the spouse's net income over $614. The credit is therefore reduced to zero where the spouse's net income exceeds $6,754.

(e) The equivalent-to-spouse credit is calculated in the same way as the spousal credit. Eligible dependants are those under age 18 related to the taxpayer, the taxpayer's parents/grandparents, or any other person who is related to the taxpayer and is infirm.

(f) The 2000 federal budget introduced a new credit for those supporting children eligible for the disability credit. The amount of $2941 is reduced by child and attendant care expenses claimed in respect of the child exceeding $2,000. The credit is reduced to zero when these expenses total $4,941.

(g) The infirm dependant amount of $2,386 is reduced by the excess of the dependant's net income over $4,845. The credit is therefore reduced to zero where the dependant's net income exceeds $7,231.

(h) The age amount of $3,531 is reduced by 15% of the excess of the taxpayer's net income over $26,284. The credit is therefore reduced to zero where net income exceeds $49,824.

(i) The disability credit is transferable to a supporting person. The transferable amount of $4,293 is reduced by the excess of the dependant's taxable income over $7,231. The credit is therefore reduced to zero where the dependant's taxable income exceeds $11,524.

(j) The caregiver tax credit is available to providers of in-home care for elderly or infirm relatives. The amount of $2,386 is reduced by the excess of the dependant's net income over $11,661. The credit is therefore reduced to zero where the dependant's net income exceeds $14,047.

(k) The pension credit is calculated based on the lesser of eligible pension income and $1,000. This amount is not indexed for inflation.

(l) These credits are transferable to a spouse. The amounts available for transfer are reduced by the excess of the spouse's net income over $7,231.

(m) The tuition credit is calculated as a percentage of tuition and mandatory ancillary fees paid for the calendar year. The tuition and education credits are both transferable to a spouse, parent or grandparent. The maximum amount transferable for both credits is $5,000 less the excess of the student's net income over $7,231. Any amounts not transferred may be carried forward by the student.

(n) Interest paid on student loans under both federal and provincial programs is eligible for the credit. The credit is not transferable, but it may be carried forward for five years if not claimed in the year earned.

(o) The medical credit is calculated based on qualified medical expenses in excess of the lesser of 3% of net income or $1,637.

A refundable medical expense tax credit is also available equal to the lesser of $507 and 25% of qualifying medical expenses. It is reduced at a rate of 5% of the excess of net family income over $17,664.

## Tax Reference Tables

## 2001 FEDERAL AND PROVINCIAL NON-REFUNDABLE TAX CREDITS (a)

| | Federal (b) Dollar Amount | Federal (b) Value of Credit | B.C. (c) Dollar Amount | B.C. (c) Value of Credit | Alberta Dollar Amount | Alberta Value of Credit | Saskatchewan (d) Dollar Amount | Saskatchewan (d) Value of Credit | Manitoba Dollar Amount | Manitoba Value of Credit |
|---|---|---|---|---|---|---|---|---|---|---|
| Rate applied to credits | | 16.0% | | 8.4% | | 10.0% | | 11.5% | | 10.9% |
| Rate applied to donations in excess of $200 | | 29.0% | | 19.7% | | 12.75% | | 16.0% | | 17.5% |
| Basic personal | $7,412 | $1,186 | $8,000 | $672 | $12,900 | $1,290 | $8,000 | $920 | $7,361 | $802 |
| Spousal/Equivalent to spouse | 6,294 | 1,007 | 6,850 | 575 | 12,900 | 1,290 | 8,000 | 920 | 6,251 | 681 |
| — Net income threshold | 629 | | 685 | | 0 | | 800 | | 625 | |
| Age 65 and over | 3,619 | 579 | 3,587 | 301 | 3,619 | 362 | 3,619 | 416 | 3,595 | 392 |
| — Net income threshold | 26,941 | | 26,705 | | 26,941 | | 26,941 | | 26,757 | |
| Infirm dependents | | | | | | | | | | |
| — Under age 18 | 3,500 | 560 | 2,988 | 251 | | | | | | |
| — Age 18 and over | 3,500 | 560 | 2,424 | 204 | 3,500 | 350 | 2,446 | 281 | 2,429 | 265 |
| Disability | 6,000 | 960 | 4,362 | 366 | 6,000 | 600 | 4,400 | 506 | 4,370 | 476 |
| Caregiver | 3,500 | 560 | 2,424 | 204 | 3,500 | 350 | 2,446 | 281 | 2,429 | 265 |
| — net income threshold | 11,953 | | 11,848 | | 11,953 | | 11,953 | | 11,871 | |
| Pension | 1,000 | 160 | 1,000 | 84 | 1,000 | 100 | 1,000 | 115 | 1,000 | 109 |
| Canada Pension Plan (e) | 1,496 | 239 | 1,496 | 126 | 1,496 | 150 | 1,496 | 172 | 1,496 | 163 |
| Employment Insurance | 877 | 140 | 877 | 74 | 877 | 88 | 877 | 101 | 877 | 96 |
| Education — per month: | | | | | | | | | | |
| — Full time | 400 | 64 | 200 | 17 | 400 | 40 | 200 | 23 | 400 | 44 |
| — Part time | 120 | 19 | 60 | 5 | 120 | 12 | 60 | 7 | 120 | 13 |

| | Ontario (f) Dollar Amount | Ontario (f) Value of Credit | New Brunswick Dollar Amount | New Brunswick Value of Credit | Nova Scotia Dollar Amount | Nova Scotia Value of Credit | P.E.I. Dollar Amount | P.E.I. Value of Credit | Newfoundland Dollar Amount | Newfoundland Value of Credit |
|---|---|---|---|---|---|---|---|---|---|---|
| Rate applied to credits | | 6.2% | | 9.68% | | 9.77% | | 9.8% | | 10.57% |
| Rate applied to donations in excess of $200 | | 11.16% | | 16.52% | | 16.67% | | 16.7% | | 18.02% |
| Basic personal | $7,426 | $460 | $7,231 | $700 | $7,231 | $706 | $7,412 | $726 | $7,410 | $783 |
| Spousal/Equivalent to spouse | 6,306 | 391 | 6,140 | 594 | 6,140 | 600 | 6,294 | 617 | 6,055 | 640 |
| — Net income threshold | 631 | | 614 | | 614 | | 629 | | 606 | |
| Age 65 and over | 3,626 | 225 | 3,531 | 342 | 3,531 | 345 | 3,619 | 355 | 3,482 | 368 |
| — Net income threshold | 26,994 | | 26,284 | | 26,284 | | 26,941 | | 25,921 | |
| Infirm dependents | | | | | | | | | | |
| — Under age 18 | | | | | | | | | | |
| — Age 18 and over | 2,450 | 152 | 2,386 | 231 | 2,386 | 233 | 2,446 | 240 | 2,353 | 249 |
| Disability | 4,409 | 273 | 4,293 | 416 | 4,293 | 419 | 4,400 | 431 | 4,233 | 447 |
| Caregiver | 2,450 | 152 | 2,386 | 231 | 2,386 | 233 | 2,446 | 240 | 2,353 | 249 |
| — net income threshold | 11,976 | | 11,661 | | 11,661 | | 11,953 | | 11,500 | |
| Pension | 1,027 | 64 | 1,000 | 97 | 1,000 | 98 | 1,000 | 98 | 1,000 | 106 |
| Canada Pension Plan (e) | 1,496 | 93 | 1,496 | 145 | 1,496 | 146 | 1,496 | 147 | 1,496 | 158 |
| Employment Insurance | 877 | 54 | 877 | 85 | 877 | 86 | 877 | 86 | 877 | 93 |
| Education — per month: | | | | | | | | | | |
| — Full time | 205 | 13 | 200 | 19 | 200 | 20 | 200 | 20 | 200 | 21 |
| — Part time | 62 | 4 | 60 | 6 | 60 | 6 | 60 | 6 | 60 | 6 |

### Notes:

(a) The three territories have not switched to the tax-on-income system in 2001 and therefore will use the same non-refundable credit amounts as those indicated for federal purposes.

(b) Like the federal tax brackets, the non-refundable credit amounts are adjusted for inflation. The credits are calculated at 16% instead of 17% (see 117(2) and 248(1) "appropriate percentage".)

(c) B.C. uses the B.C. inflation rate for indexing its non-refundable credits, just as it does for its brackets.

(d) Saskatchewan introduced two new credits in 2001 in addition to those listed in the table. A $172 credit per child is available for dependents under the age of 18, and a $57 credit is available for those aged 65 and over. These credits will increase each year until 2003, when the provinces's tax reform measures are fully implemented. The child credit dollar amount is slated to increase to $2,000 per child in 2002, and to $2,500 per child in 2003. The age credit supplement dollar amount is slated to increase to $750 in 2002, and to $1,000 in 2003. Neither of these credits are income-tested.

Tax Reference Tables

(e) Commencing in 2001, self-employed individuals may deduct one-half of their CPP contributions in calculating their net income. The remaining one-half continues to be claimed as a credit.
(f) Ontario uses the Ontario inflation rate for indexing its non-refundable credits, just as it does for its brackets.

## 2000 AND 2001 QUÉBEC PERSONAL TAX CREDITS (a)

|  | Dollar Amount 2000 | Dollar Amount 2001 | Value of credit 2000 22% | Value of credit 2001 21.5% |
|---|---|---|---|---|
| Basic personal | $5,900 | $5,900 | $1,298 | 1,268 |
| Spousal (b) | 5,900 | 5,900 | 1,298 | 1,268 |
| Person living alone or with dependant (c) | 1,050 | 1,050 | 231 | 226 |
| Single parent (d) | 1,300 | 1,300 | 286 | 279 |
| Dependent children (d) |  |  |  |  |
| First | 2,600 | 2,600 | 572 | 559 |
| Second and subsequent | 2,400 | 2,400 | 528 | 516 |
| Other related dependants age 19 or over (e) | 2,400 | 2,400 | 528 | 516 |
| Dependant in full-time attendance at a post-secondary school (per semester) (d)(f) | 1,650 | 1,650 | 363 | 355 |
| Infirm dependants age 19 or over (e) | 5,900 | 5,900 | 1,298 | 1,268 |
| Age 65 or older (c)(i) | 2,200 | 2,200 | 484 | 473 |
| Disability (g)(i) | 2,200 | 2,200 | 484 | 473 |
| Pension (c)(h)(i) | 1,000 | 1,000 | 220 | 215 |
| Québec Pension Plan (j) | 1,330 | 1,496 | 293 | 322 |
| Employment Insurance | 936 | 877 | 206 | 189 |
| Health Services Fund | 1,000 | 1,000 | 220 | 215 |
| Union and professional dues (k) |  |  |  |  |
| Tuition fees (l) |  |  |  |  |
| Interest paid on student loans (m) |  |  |  |  |
| Medical expenses (n) |  |  |  |  |
| Refundable credit for child care expenses (o) |  |  |  |  |
| Refundable credit for adoption expenses (p) |  |  |  |  |
| Refundable housing credit for live-in parents (q) |  |  |  |  |
| Refundable credit for home support of elderly persons living alone (r) |  |  |  |  |
| Refundable credit for the treatment of infertility (s) |  |  |  |  |

**Notes:**
(a) Many of these credits are income-tested. In all cases, net income must be calculated under both the regular filing system and the simplified filing system even if the simplified system is not used.
"Net family income" means the total income of both spouses, as calculated under the simplified system, minus $26,000. "Family income" means the total income of both spouses as calculated under the simplified system
(b) The spousal amount of $5,900 is reduced by the amount of the spouse's net income. There is no equivalent-to-spouse credit in Québec.
(c) The amounts for a person living alone, age 65 and over, and pension income are added together and reduced by 15% of net family income (see note (a)).
(d) The amounts for a single parent, dependent children, and dependent post-secondary students are added together and reduced by the amount of the dependant's net income.
(e) The amounts for other related dependants and infirm dependants are reduced by the amount of the dependant's net income.
(f) The amount for a dependant attending a post-secondary school may only be claimed by a supporting person and is limited to two semesters per year.
(g) The disability credit is transferable to a supporting person. The amount available for transfer is reduced by any income tax payable by the dependant.
(h) The pension credit is calculated based on the lesser of eligible pension income and $1,000.
(i) These credits are transferable to a spouse. The amounts available for transfer are reduced by any income tax payable by the spouse.

Tax Reference Tables

(j) Starting in 2000, self-employed taxpayers may deduct 50% of their QPP or CPP contributions in calculating net income (under either the general or the simplified system). The remaining 50% of the contributions can be claimed as a non-refundable credit.

(k) The credit for union and professional dues is calculated based on the annual fees paid in the year. The portion of professional dues relating to liability insurance is allowed as a deduction and is not included in calculating the credit.

(l) The tuition credit is calculated based on tuition, professional examination, and mandatory ancillary fees paid for the calendar year. The credit is not transferable, but may be carried forward to future years by the student.

(m) Interest paid on student loans but unclaimed in a particular year may be carried forward indefinitely.

(n) The medical credit is calculated based on qualified medical expenses in excess of 3% of family income (see note (a)).

A refundable medical expense tax credit is also available equal to 25% of qualifying medical expenses, net of the 3% reduction. It is reduced at a rate of 5% of the excess of family income over $17,500 (see note (a)).

(o) Child care expenses paid in the year are eligible for a refundable tax credit at a rate that varies from 26% to 75%. The rate of credit falls as net family income rises (see note (a)).

(p) A refundable credit is available equal to 25% of specified adoption expenses, to a maximum credit of $3,750 ($3,000 for adoptions finalized prior to 2000).

(q) The refundable tax credit with respect to housing of a parent is $550 for each live-in parent aged 70 or over at the end of the year.

(r) Beginning in 2000, the refundable credit for home support of persons age 70 and over living alone is equal to 23% of eligible expenses paid to obtain certain home support services. The credit is capped at $2,760. If the expense also qualifies for the Québec medical expense credit, it cannot be claimed for this credit as well.

(s) The costs associated with artificial insemination and *in vitro* fertilization paid during the year by an individual or his/her spouse will give rise to a refundable credit of 25% of all eligible expenses to a maximum annual credit of $3,750 per couple, commencing in 2000.

## CANADA/QUÉBEC PENSION PLAN CONTRIBUTIONS

| Year | Year's Maximum Pensionable Earnings $ | Year's Basic Exemption $ | Maximum Contributory Earnings $ | Employee and Employer Rate % | Maximum Employee / Employer Contribution $ | Self-Employed Annual Maximum Contribution $ |
|---|---|---|---|---|---|---|
| 1990 | 28,900 | 2,800 | 26,100 | 2.2 | 574.20 | 1,148.40 |
| 1991 | 30,500 | 3,000 | 27,500 | 2.3 | 632.50 | 1,265.00 |
| 1992 | 32,200 | 3,200 | 29,000 | 2.4 | 696.00 | 1,392.00 |
| 1993 | 33,400 | 3,300 | 30,100 | 2.5 | 752.50 | 1,505.00 |
| 1994 | 34,400 | 3,400 | 31,000 | 2.6 | 806.00 | 1,612.00 |
| 1995 | 34,900 | 3,400 | 31,500 | 2.7 | 850.50 | 1,701.00 |
| 1996 | 35,400 | 3,500 | 31,900 | 2.8 | 893.20 | 1,786.40 |
| 1997 | 35,800 | 3,500 | 32,300 | 3.0 | 969.00 | 1,938.00 |
| 1998 | 36,900 | 3,500 | 33,400 | 3.2 | 1,068.80 | 2,137.60 |
| 1999 | 37,400 | 3,500 | 33,900 | 3.5 | 1,186.50 | 2,373.00 |
| 2000 | 37,600 | 3,500 | 34,100 | 3.9 | 1,329.90 | 2,659.80 |
| 2001 | 38,300 | 3,500 | 34,800 | 4.3 | 1,496.40 | 2,992.80 |

# Tax Reference Tables

## EMPLOYMENT INSURANCE CONTRIBUTIONS

| | Year | Maximum Yearly Insurable Earnings $ | Employee's Premium Rate % | Employer's Premium Rate % | Maximum Yearly Employee Premium $ | Maximum Yearly Employer Premium $ |
|---|---|---|---|---|---|---|
| | 1990 | 33,280 | 2.25 | 3.15 | 748.80 | 1,048.32 |
| Jan.-June | 1991 | 35,360 | 2.25 | 3.15 | 397.80 | 556.92 |
| July-Dec. | 1991 | 35,360 | 2.80 | 3.92 | 495.04 | 693.06 |
| | 1992 | 36,920 | 3.00 | 4.20 | 1,107.60 | 1,550.64 |
| | 1993 | 38,740 | 3.00 | 4.20 | 1,162.20 | 1,627.08 |
| | 1994 | 40,560 | 3.07 | 4.30 | 1,245.19 | 1,744.08 |
| | 1995 | 42,380 | 3.00 | 4.20 | 1,271.40 | 1,779.96 |
| | 1996 | 39,000 | 2.95 | 4.13 | 1,150.50 | 1,610.70 |
| | 1997 | 39,000 | 2.90 | 4.06 | 1,131.00 | 1,583.40 |
| | 1998 | 39,000 | 2.70 | 3.78 | 1,053.00 | 1,474.20 |
| | 1999 | 39,000 | 2.55 | 3.57 | 994.50 | 1,392.30 |
| | 2000 | 39,000 | 2.40 | 3.36 | 936.00 | 1,310.40 |
| | 2001 | 39,000 | 2.25 | 3.15 | 877.50 | 1,228.50 |

## REGISTERED RETIREMENT SAVINGS PLAN (RRSP) / DEFERRED PROFIT SHARING PLAN (DPSP) CONTRIBUTIONS

| Year | RRSP Deduction Limit (a) | DPSP Employer Deduction Contribution Limit (c) |
|---|---|---|
| 1991 | $11,500 | $6,250 |
| 1992 | 12,500 | 6,750 |
| 1993 | 12,500 | 6,750 |
| 1994 | 13,500 | 7,250 |
| 1995 | 14,500 | 7,750 |
| 1996–2002 | 13,500 | 6,750 |
| 2003 | 13,500 | 7,250 |
| 2004 | 14,500 | 7,750 |
| 2005 | 15,500 | indexed |
| 2006 | indexed (b) | |

**Notes:**

(a) The RRSP deduction limit (defined in 146(1)) is generally the "money purchase limit" (see 147.1(1)) for the immediately preceding calendar year.

(b) After 2005, the deduction limit will be indexed by the growth in the average industrial wage in Canada.

(c) ½ of the "money purchase limit" with annual indexing after 2004 in accordance with the growth in average industrial wages.

## AUTOMOBILE LIMITS — PRESCRIBED AMOUNTS

The income tax rules for automobiles are quite extensive. Below is a brief summary of some of the common rules related to the ownership/use of an automobile.

Deductibility of Automobile Expenses
- Automobile expenses are deductible:
  (i) by an employee
  — if, as an employee, you are required by the terms of employment to use the automobile and are not receiving a (non-taxable) reasonable allowance based on the number of kilometres you drive for employment purposes.
  (ii) by a self-employed individual and/or business
  — if they are reasonable and incurred for the purposes of earning income from a business.
- Limitations on amounts deductible

## Tax Reference Tables

| Date car purchased/leased | 13(7)(g) Maximum Depreciable Cost(1)(6) | 67.3 Monthly Deductible Lease(2)(6) | 67.3 Maximum Prescribed Cost | 67.2 Monthly Deductible Interest(6) | 18(1)(r) Allowances(3) cents/km All prov. | Yukon/NWT |
|---|---|---|---|---|---|---|
| June 18, 1987-Aug. 31, 1989 | $20,000 | $600 | $23,529 | $250 | 27/21 | 31/25 |
| Sept. 1, 1989-Dec. 31, 1990 | 24,000 | 650 | 28,235 | 300 | 31/25 | 35/29 |
| Jan. 1, 1991-Dec. 31, 1995 | 24,000+GST+PST (4) | 650+GST+PST | (a) | 300 | 31/25 | 35/29 |
| Jan. 1, 1996-Dec. 31, 1996 | 24,000+GST+PST (4) | 650+GST+PST | (a) | 300 | 33/27 | 37/31 |
| Jan. 1, 1997-Dec. 31, 1997 | 25,000+GST+PST (5) | 550+GST+PST | (b) | 250 | 35/29 | 39/33 |
| Jan. 1, 1998-Dec. 31, 1999 | 26,000+GST+PST (5) | 650+GST+PST | (c) | 250 | 35/29 | 39/33 |
| Jan. 1, 2000 — Dec. 31, 2000 | 27,000+GST+PST (5) | 700+GST+PST | (d) | 250 | 37/31 | 41/35 |
| Jan. 1, 2001 — Dec. 31, 2001 | 30,000+GST+PST (5) | 800+GST+PST | (e) | 300 | 41/35 | 45/39 |

$$(a)\ \frac{(\$24{,}000 + GST(4) + PST)}{.85} \qquad (b)\ \frac{(\$25{,}000 + GST(5) + PST)}{.85} \qquad (c)\ \frac{(\$26{,}000 + GST(5) + PST)}{.85}$$

$$(d)\ \frac{(\$27{,}000 + GST(5) + PST)}{.85} \qquad (e)\ \frac{(\$30{,}000 + GST(5) + PST)}{.85}$$

### Notes:

(1) An automobile (i.e., defined to be a vehicle designed for highway and street use with a maximum seating capacity for eight passengers) purchased after June 17, 1987 at a cost equal to or in excess of the depreciable limit is allocated as a separate Class 10.1 asset. In the year of disposition, a Class 10.1 vehicle is not subject to recapture and is eligible for one-half of what would otherwise be the normal capital cost allowance deduction. The cost of other automobiles is included in the Class 10 pool. The CCA rate for both classes is 30% declining balance (½ in the year of acquisition).

(2) The maximum deductible monthly lease charge becomes more complicated when the leasee pays a refundable amount to the lessor or is eligible for reimbursements in respect of the lease.

Where the "manufacturer's suggested list price" (MSLP) of the leased auto exceeds the "prescribed cost" shown in the column on the right, the maximum deductible lease charge shall not exceed the lesser of

(i) the maximum monthly deductible lease amount shown in this column; and

(ii) the actual lease charge multiplied by the ratio of

$$(\text{maximum depreciable cost})/(MSLP \times 0.85)$$

(3) The employer who pays a tax-free car allowance to an employee may not deduct the portion of the allowance (if any) in excess of the amounts noted. The high limit relates to the first 5,000 employment-related kilometres driven in the year and the lower limit relates to any excess kilometres driven in the year.

(4) Net of GST input tax credits.

(5) HST replaced the GST and PST in New Brunswick, Nova Scotia, and Newfoundland effective April 1, 1997. In these cases, the amounts should be net of HST input tax credits.

(6) There is a further limitation where there is an element of personal use. Generally, the amount deductible is determined by taking the expense limits as above and applying an allocation formula. The allocation formula is generally based on business or employment kilometres driven over total kilometres driven.

### Types of Expenses and Amounts Deductible

Some of the more common types of expenses, including applicable GST/HST and PST, include the following:

- fuel (gas, propane, oil, etc.)
- insurance
- maintenance and repairs
- licensing or registration
- interest (see Table)
- lease payments (see Table)
- capital cost allowance (see Notes)

## EMPLOYER-PROVIDED AUTOMOBILES — TAXABLE BENEFITS

An employee who uses an employer-provided automobile for personal use is annually subject to two taxable benefits:
(1) a standby charge based upon the car's purchase price or lease costs; and
(2) an operating benefit based upon the car's operating costs.

*Method to Calculate Taxable Benefits*
- Operating Benefit (6(1)(k))
  (1) Beginning in 2001, 16¢ per km of personal use (15¢ for 2000, 14¢ for 1998 and 1999) or 13¢ (12¢ for 2000, 11¢ for 1999) if you are employed principally in selling or leasing automobiles
    Less: amounts reimbursed by the employee within 45 days of the following year.
  (2) where business km>50%;
    — can elect to calculate benefit as ½ of standby charge.
- Standby Charge (6(1)(e), 6(2))
  — 2% of the original cost including all applicable taxes (or 2/3 monthly lease cost) × number of months available to you (for automobile sales people, 1.5% per month of the average cost of the dealer's cars acquired in the year)
  — the benefit is reduced where business use is 90% or more of the kilometres, and personal use is less than 12,000 km in the year
    [2% × number of months available × (personal use km/1000 × number of months available)]
- Allowance Benefit (6(1)(b))
  — An employee may receive an allowance to cover certain costs of operating an automobile for employment use. The allowance is non-taxable if:
    (1) reasonable
    (2) based solely on number of kilometres driven in the performance of your employment duties. (Non-taxable allowance can be in excess of prescribed amounts under certain circumstances), and
    (3) no reimbursement for any automobile related expenses is provided in addition to the employee's tax-free automobile allowance (other than for supplementary business insurance, parking and toll and ferry charges).

Tax Reference Tables

## CORPORATIONS
### FEDERAL INCOME TAX RATES FOR ACTIVE BUSINESS INCOME

|  | Effective January 1, 2001* |  |  |  | Effective January 1, 2000* |  |  |
|---|---|---|---|---|---|---|---|
|  | General Non-manufacturing Income | General Manufacturing Income | Small Business Income up to $200,000 (a) | Small Business Income from $200,000 to $300,000 (b) | General Non-manufacturing Income | General Manufacturing Income | Small Business Income up to $200,000 (a) |
| General corporate rate | 38.00% | 38.00% | 38.00% | 38.00% | 38.00% | 38.00% | 38.00% |
| Less federal abatement | (10.00) | (10.00) | (10.00) | (10.00) | (10.00) | (10.00) | (10.00) |
|  | 28.00 | 28.00 | 28.00 | 28.00 | 28.00 | 28.00 | 28.00 |
| Add surtax @ 4% (c) | 1.12 | 1.12 | 1.12 | 1.12 | 1.12 | 1.12 | 1.12 |
|  | 29.12 | 29.12 | 29.12 | 29.12 | 29.12 | 29.12 | 29.12 |
| Less rate reductions (d) | (1.00) | (7.00) | (16.00) | (7.00) | — | (7.00) | (16.00) |
|  | 28.12 | 22.12 | 13.12 | 22.12 | 29.12 | 22.12 | 13.12 |

*See the following Notes for the actual dates on which these rates and other rate changes are effective.

### PROVINCIAL INCOME TAX RATES FOR ACTIVE BUSINESS INCOME

|  | Effective January 1, 2001* |  |  |  | Effective January 1, 2000* |  |  |
|---|---|---|---|---|---|---|---|
|  | General Non-manufacturing Income | General Manufacturing Income | Small Business Income up to $200,000 (a) | Small Business Income from $200,000 to $300,000 (b) | General Non-manufacturing Income | General Manufacturing Income | Small Business Income up to $200,000 (a) |
| British Columbia (e) | 16.5% | 16.5% | 4.5% | 16.5% | 16.5% | 16.5% | 5.5/4.75% |
| Alberta (f) | 15.5/13.5 | 14.5/13.5 | 6.0/5.0 | 15.5/5.0 | 15.5 | 14.5 | 6.0 |
| Saskatchewan (g) | 17.0 | 10.0 | 8.0 | 17.0 | 17.0 | 10.0 | 8.0 |
| Manitoba (h) | 17.0 | 17.0 | 6.0 | 17.0 | 17.0 | 17.0 | 7.0 |
| Ontario (i) | 14.0 | 12.0 | 6.5 | 14.0 | 15.5/14.5 | 13.5/12.5 | 8.0/7.0 |
| Québec (j) | 9.0 | 9.0 | 9.0 | 9.0 | 8.9 | 8.9 | 8.9 |
| New Brunswick (k) | 17.0 | 17.0 | 4.5 | 17.0 | 17.0 | 17.0 | 4.5 |
| Nova Scotia | 16.0 | 16.0 | 5.0 | 16.0 | 16.0 | 16.0 | 5.0 |
| Prince Edward Island | 16.0 | 7.5 | 7.5 | 16.0 | 16.0 | 7.5 | 7.5 |
| Newfoundland | 14.0 | 5.0 | 5.0 | 14.0 | 14.0 | 5.0 | 5.0 |
| Yukon Territory (l) | 15.0 | 2.5 | 2.5/6.0 | 15.0 | 15.0 | 2.5 | 2.5/6.0 |
| Northwest Territories/Nunavut | 14.0 | 14.0 | 5.0 | 14.0 | 14.0 | 14.0 | 5.0 |

*See the following Notes for the actual dates on which these rates and other rate changes are effective.

### COMBINED FEDERAL AND PROVINCIAL INCOME TAX RATES FOR ACTIVE BUSINESS INCOME

|  | Effective January 1, 2001* |  |  |  | Effective January 1, 2000* |  |  |
|---|---|---|---|---|---|---|---|
|  | General Non-manufacturing Income | General Manufacturing Income | Small Business Income up to $200,000 (a) | Small Business Income from $200,000 to $300,000 (b) | General Non-manufacturing Income | General Manufacturing Income | Small Business Income up to $200,000 (a) |
| British Columbia (e) | 44.6% | 38.6% | 17.6% | 38.6% | 45.6% | 38.6% | 18.6/17.9% |
| Alberta (f) | 43.6/41.6 | 36.6/35.6 | 19.1/18.1 | 37.6/27.1 | 44.6 | 36.6 | 19.1 |
| Saskatchewan (g) | 45.1 | 32.1 | 21.1 | 39.1 | 46.1 | 32.1 | 21.1 |
| Manitoba (h) | 45.1 | 39.1 | 19.1 | 39.1 | 46.1 | 39.1 | 20.1 |
| Ontario (i) | 42.1 | 34.1 | 19.6 | 36.1 | 44.6/43.6 | 35.6/34.6 | 21.1/20.1 |
| Québec (j) | 37.2 | 31.2 | 22.2 | 31.2 | 38.0 | 31.0 | 22.0 |
| New Brunswick (k) | 45.1 | 39.1 | 17.6 | 39.1 | 46.1 | 39.1 | 17.6 |
| Nova Scotia | 44.1 | 38.1 | 18.1 | 38.1 | 45.1 | 38.1 | 18.1 |
| Prince Edward Island | 44.1 | 29.6 | 20.6 | 38.1 | 45.1 | 29.6 | 20.6 |
| Newfoundland | 42.1 | 27.1 | 18.1 | 36.1 | 43.1 | 27.1 | 18.1 |
| Yukon Territory (l) | 43.1 | 24.6 | 15.6/19.1 | 37.1 | 44.1 | 24.6 | 15.6/19.1 |
| Northwest Territories/Nunavut | 42.1 | 36.1 | 18.1 | 36.1 | 43.1 | 36.1 | 18.1 |

*See the following Notes for the actual dates on which these rates and other rate changes are effective.

## Tax Reference Tables

**Notes:**

(a) The first $200,000 of active business income earned by a Canadian-controlled private corporation (CCPC) is eligible for the small business deduction (SBD), equal to 16% of such income. See ITA 125. This $200,000 limit must be shared by associated corporations, and is also reduced on a straight-line basis when the associated group's taxable capital (computed for Large Corporations Tax purposes) employed in Canada in the preceding year exceeds $10 million. The phase-out of the $200,000 limit is as follows:

| Taxable Capital | Business Limit |
|---|---|
| $10 million or less | $200,000 |
| 11 million | 160,000 |
| 12 million | 120,000 |
| 13 million | 80,000 |
| 14 million | 40,000 |
| 15 million or more | 0 |

(b) The 2000 federal budget announced that the rate applicable to income of a CCPC between $200,000 and $300,000 will decrease to 21% effective January 1, 2001 (prorated for taxation years that straddle this date). See ITA 123.4(3). The same limitations that apply to the first $200,000 of income will also apply to this additional $100,000. Income eligible for this lower rate will be reduced if the corporation has manufacturing and processing (M&P) income subject to the M&P credit or income from resource activities.

(c) A 4% corporate surtax is levied on the 28% federal tax before applying any other rate reductions or credits. The federal surtax does not apply to a non-resident-owned investment corporation nor to the capital gains refund received by a mutual fund or investment corporation.

(d) The 2000 federal budget announced that the general corporate rate will be reduced over a five-year period from 28% down to 21%. See ITA 123.4(2). The first 1% reduction is effective January 1, 2001, and must be prorated for taxation years that straddle that date. The October 18, 2000 mini-budget announced the timetable for further reductions — a 2% reduction (to 25%) as of January 1, 2002, a further 2% reduction (to 23%) as of January 1, 2003 and a final 2% reduction (to 21%) as of January 1, 2004. These reductions do not apply to corporations that already receive rate reductions due to the M&P credit or the SBD, and it will not apply to investment income that benefits from refundable tax provisions or income from resource activities.

(e) The 2000 B.C. budget announced a reduction in the small business tax rate from 5.5% to 4.75% effective July 1, 2000. Effective January 1, 2001, the rate is further reduced to 4.5%. For taxation years that straddle these dates, the rate reductions must be prorated accordingly.

(f) Alberta's news release in September 2000 proposed the following changes to its rates, to be implemented as of April 1 each year:

| Year | General and M&P Rate | Small Business Rate | Small Business Limit |
|---|---|---|---|
| 2001 | 13.5% | 5.0% | $300,000 |
| 2002 | 11.5 | 4.0 | 400,000 |
| 2003 | 10.0 | 3.0 | |
| 2004 | 8.0 | | |

(g) Saskatchewan's manufacturing rate includes the maximum 7% reduction available for manufacturing profits allocated to the province. This base amount of 7% is multiplied by the corporation's allocation of income to Saskatchewan to arrive at the net Saskatchewan tax rate reduction. The resulting percentage is then applied to the corporation's Saskatchewan share of Canadian manufacturing and processing profits to determine the amount of the tax reduction.

(h) Manitoba's 1999 budget announced that the province's small business rate will be reduced by 1% each January until the year 2002, when it will be 5%. For taxation years that straddle these dates, the rate reduction must be prorated accordingly.

(i) The 2000 Ontario budget announced a reduction in the general corporate rate and the M&P rate which will be phased in over six years. When fully implemented in 2005, both rates will be 8%. Effective May 2, 2000, the general corporate rate is reduced to 14.5% (from 15.5%) and the M&P rate is reduced to 12.5% (from 13.5%). On January 1, 2001, these rates will be further reduced to 14.0% and 12.0% respectively. For taxation years that straddle these dates, the rates must be prorated accordingly.

In its 2000 budget, the government announced an acceleration of the cuts announced in the 1998 budget by decreasing the small business rate to 7.0% effective May 2, 2000 and applying the 0.5% per year reduction from that point until January 1, 2005, at which time the rate will further decrease to 4.0%. For taxation years that straddle these dates, the rates must be prorated accordingly.

An Ontario surtax is levied on corporations claiming the Ontario SBD in order to gradually reduce the benefit of the deduction where taxable income exceeds $200,000. Currently, the surtax applies to taxable

## Tax Reference Tables

income between $200,000 and $500,000, with the deduction being completely eliminated at taxable income of approximately $500,000.

The 2000 budget announced several changes to these thresholds that will be phased in over five years, as indicated below. The benefit of the lower small business rate will be extended to taxable income up to $400,000, and the range for the application of the surtax will increase to between $400,000 and $1,000,000. The surtax rate will increase each year to coincide with the reduction in the small business rate. The surtax rates indicated below are computed on the basis that the general corporate rate will remain at 14%.

|  | Small business rate | Taxable income limit | Phase-out range | Surtax rate |
|---|---|---|---|---|
| Jan. 1, 2001 | 6.5% | $240,000 | $240,000-$600,000 | 5.0% |
| Jan. 1, 2002 | 6.0 | 280,000 | 280,000-700,000 | 5.333 |
| Jan. 1, 2003 | 5.5 | 320,000 | 320,000-800,000 | 5.667 |
| Jan. 1, 2004 | 5.0 | 360,000 | 360,000-900,000 | 6.000 |
| Jan. 1, 2005 | 4.0 | 400,000 | 400,000-1,000,000 | 6.667 |

(j) Corporations were previously required to make a contribution to the Québec anti-poverty fund equal to 2.8% of their Québec tax payable for the year. This surtax was eliminated effective November 27, 1999, reducing Québec's corporate tax rates to 8.9% (from 9.15%). For taxation years that straddle this date, the rate reduction must be prorated accordingly.

The 2000 budget introduced the establishment of a Youth Fund to support youth job creation. This fund will be financed in part by corporations carrying on business in the province, who will be required to contribute 1.6% of income taxes payable for the year. This contribution is not included in the rates indicated above for 2000 as it is only effective for any taxation year, or part thereof, included in the three-year period beginning March 15, 2000; however, it is included in the rates for 2001 as it is in effect for the whole year.

(k) New Brunswick's 2000 budget announced a decrease in the small business rate to 4.5% (from 6%) effective January 1, 2000. For taxation years that straddle this date, the rate reduction must be prorated accordingly.

(l) Small business corporations carrying on manufacturing and processing in the Yukon are taxed at a rate of 2.5%, the same rate that applies to all other manufacturing and processing corporations. Non-manufacturing CCPCs are subject to the 6% tax rate.

## PROVINCIAL MANUFACTURING AND PROCESSING (M&P) TAX INCENTIVES

| Province | Rate | Description | Notes |
|---|---|---|---|
| British Columbia | 3% | Non-refundable tax credit for purchases of qualifying M&P equipment used in the province. | Qualifying M&P equipment is that which qualifies for federal investment tax credit (ITC) purposes and is purchased after March 31, 2000.<br>The credit is considered to be government assistance and reduces the capital cost of the equipment for federal purposes.<br>Unused credits may be carried forward 10 years and carried back 3 years. |
| Saskatchewan | 6%<br>7% prior to March 26, 1999 | Non-refundable tax credit for purchases of qualifying M&P equipment used in the province. | Qualifying M&P equipment is that which qualifies for federal ITC purposes. Used equipment also qualifies if it has been subject to provincial sales tax when purchased.<br>The credit is considered to be government assistance and reduces the capital cost of the equipment for federal purposes.<br>Unused credits may be carried forward 7 years and carried back 3 years. |
| Manitoba | 10% | Non-refundable tax credit for purchases of qualifying M&P equipment used in the province. | Qualifying M&P equipment is that which qualifies for federal ITC purposes and is purchased prior to July 1, 2003.<br>The credit is considered to be government assistance and reduces the capital cost of the equipment for federal purposes.<br>Unused credits may be carried forward 7 years and carried back 3 years. |
| Québec<br>100% Deduction | 100% of capital cost of equipment | Deduction allowed in computing Québec net income for purchases of qualifying M&P and other equipment used in the province, as well as intangible assets acquired as part of a technology transfer.<br>Two-year deduction allowed in computing paid-up capital for capital tax purposes. | Qualifying M&P equipment is that which would otherwise be included in classes 39 and 43, as well as computer processing equipment and associated systems software which would otherwise be included in classes 10 and 40.<br>There is no half-year rule applicable to this new class, and the available-for-use rules do not apply. Each qualified property is included in a separate class 12.<br>The equipment must be used mainly to earn business income, must not have been used before its acquisition, must be used within a reasonable period after its acquisition, and must be used in Québec for a minimum of 730 days following its acquisition. |
| Québec<br>25% Supplementary Deduction | 25% of capital cost allowance claimed for qualifying equipment | Supplementary deduction allowed in computing Québec net income for purchases of qualifying M&P and other equipment used in the province over and above the 100% deduction outlined above. | Qualifying M&P and other equipment is the same as that which is eligible for the 100% deduction described above, however it must be acquired prior to April 1, 2005. |

## Tax Reference Tables

| Province | Rate | Description | Notes |
|---|---|---|---|
| Québec<br>20% Additional deduction | 20% of capital cost allowance claimed for qualifying equipment | Additional deduction allowed in computing Québec net income for purchases of qualifying M&P and other equipment used in the province over and above the 100% deduction outlined above. | Qualifying M&P and other equipment is the same as that which is eligible for the 100% deduction described above.<br>The additional deduction applies to taxpayers who carry on part of their business outside the province, prorated by their provincial allocation percentage. |
| Nova Scotia | 30%<br>15% effective January 1, 2001 | Non-refundable tax credit for purchases of qualifying M&P equipment used in the province. | Qualifying M&P equipment is that which qualifies for federal ITC purposes and is purchased prior to January 1, 2003.<br>The credit is considered to be government assistance and reduces the capital cost of the equipment for federal purposes.<br>Unused credits may be carried forward 7 years and carried back 3 years. |
| Prince Edward Island | 10% | Non-refundable tax credit for purchases of qualifying M&P equipment used in the province. | Qualifying M&P equipment is that which qualifies for federal ITC purposes.<br>The credit is considered to be government assistance and reduces the capital cost of the equipment for federal purposes.<br>Unused credits may be carried forward 7 years and carried back 3 years. |

## FEDERAL RESEARCH AND DEVELOPMENT (R&D) TAX INCENTIVES

### Federal Investment Tax Credits (ITCs) (a) (ss. 127, 127.1)

| Type of Entity | Nature of Expenditure | ITC Rate on Total Expenditures up to Expenditure Limit (b) | Refund Rate | ITC Rate on Total Expenditures in excess of Expenditure Limit (b) | Refund Rate |
|---|---|---|---|---|---|
| Qualifying CCPCs (c) | Current | 35% | 100% | 20% | 40% |
|  | Capital | 35% | 40% | 20% | 40% |
| Individuals & Unincorporated Businesses | Current & Capital | 20% | 40% | 20% | 40% |
| Other Corporations | Current & Capital | 20% | — | 20% | — |

### Notes:

(a) Federal ITCs earned in a taxation year can either be applied against federal taxes payable in that year, refunded to the claimant (if applicable), carried forward and claimed in the 10 subsequent years or carried back and applied against federal taxes payable in the 3 prior years.

ITC claims must be identified on a prescribed form and filed with the Canada Customs and Revenue Agency within 12 months of the entity's filing due date for its regular income tax return.

ITCs claimed in one year are deducted from the company's R&D expenditure pool in the subsequent year. Provincial ITCs, which are considered to be government assistance, are deducted from the R&D pool in the year claimed.

For taxation years commencing after February 28, 2000, provincial "super-deductions" (i.e., deductions for amounts in excess of actual expenditures) are considered to be government assistance and a portion must be deducted from the R&D pool in the year claimed. For qualifying CCPCs, the value of the assistance will be equal to the applicable provincial small business corporate tax rate multiplied by the amount by which the deduction exceeds the actual expenditure. For all other corporations, the tax rate used to determine the value will be the maximum provincial rate applicable to active business income.

The value thus determined will reduce the balance of R&D expenditures used to calculate ITCs.

(b) The $2 million expenditure limit applies to both current and capital expenditures.

(c) Qualifying CCPCs are those with taxable income (on an associated group basis) for the preceding year of not more than $200,000.

For those associated CCPCs with taxable income of between $200,000 and $400,000, the $2 million expenditure limit is reduced by $10 for every $1 of taxable income over $200,000.

The $2 million expenditure limit is also phased-out for those associated CCPCs with taxable capital (for LCT purposes) of between $10 and $15 million in the prior year. The expenditure limit is reduced by $4 for every $10 by which taxable capital exceeds $10 million.

The ability to claim the 35% ITC rate and related 100% refund is therefore eliminated once taxable income exceeds $400,000 or taxable capital exceeds $15 million.

### *Federal R&D expenditure pool*

Eligible Canadian R&D expenditures, both current and capital, are aggregated in a pool each year and may be deducted in whole or in part. Any amounts not deducted in the current year may be carried forward indefinitely.

## Tax Reference Tables

Foreign current expenditures are also included in the R&D pool, however they must be deducted in the current year.

Government and non-government assistance (which includes provincial ITCs) receivable by the taxpayer reduces the amount of eligible expenditures in the year. For taxation years commencing after February 28, 2000, this will include the value of provincial super-deductions (see note (a) above).

Eligible expenditures for the year are reduced when R&D assets, from which the taxpayer received an ITC in any of the 10 previous years, are converted to commercial use or sold during the year.

Eligible expenditures incurred in a year must be identified on a prescribed form and filed with the Canada Customs and Revenue Agency within 12 months of the entity's filing due date for its regular income tax return.

### Qualifying R&D expenditures

Qualifying Canadian current expenditures include the following:

- salaries or wages of employees directly engaged in R&D (salaries and wages of specified employees are limited to 5 times the year's maximum CPP pensionable earnings and exclude remuneration based on profits or bonuses);
- cost of materials consumed or transformed in R&D;
- lease costs relating to machinery and equipment used in R&D;
- eligible expenditures incurred by contractors performing R&D directly on behalf of the taxpayer;
- eligible expenditures incurred by certain third parties where the taxpayer may exploit the results of the R&D.

### Proxy election for overhead expenses

The proxy election adds 65% of qualifying R&D salaries and wages to the expenditures eligible for federal ITCs (but not to the R&D pool itself). This "notional overhead" amount replaces administration and other overhead costs that are often difficult to support. Overhead costs include the cost of materials transformed in the R&D process, as well as office and other types of supplies. The overhead costs that are replaced by the proxy election are excluded from the R&D expenditure pool. Once the election is made, it is irrevocable for that taxation year.

The salary of a specified employee (one who does not deal at arm's length with the taxpayer) is limited in a number of ways when calculating the amount of salaries and wages eligible for the election. Only 75% of such employees' salaries can be included in eligible salaries, and the maximum per employee is 2.5 times the year's maximum CPP pensionable earnings. Remuneration based on profits and bonuses is also excluded.

## PROVINCIAL RESEARCH AND DEVELOPMENT (R&D) TAX INCENTIVES

| Province | Rate | Description | Definitions |
|---|---|---|---|
| British Columbia | 10% | Refundable and non-refundable tax credit for eligible expenditures incurred in B.C. after August 31, 1999 and before September 1, 2004 by a corporation with a permanent establishment (PE) in the province. | Eligible expenditures are those that qualify for federal ITC purposes. CCPCs are eligible for the refundable credit on expenditures up to their expenditure limit (as it is defined for federal purposes). The credit is not refundable for other corporations and for a CCPC's expenditures in excess of the expenditure limit.<br>The credit is considered to be government assistance and reduces federal expenditures for both the R&D deduction and ITCs. The credit can only be claimed once all discretionary deductions have been claimed.<br>Unused non-refundable credits may be carried forward 10 years and carried back 3 years. All or part of the credit can be renounced each year. |
| Saskatchewan | 15% | Non-refundable tax credit for eligible expenditures incurred in Saskatchewan after March 19, 1998 by a corporation with a PE in the province. | Eligible expenditures are those that qualify for federal ITC purposes. The credit is considered to be government assistance and reduces federal expenditures for both the R&D deduction and ITCs.<br>Unused credits may be carried forward 7 years and carried back 3 years, but not to taxation years ending prior to March 20, 1998. All or part of the credit can be renounced each year. |
| Manitoba | 15% | Non-refundable tax credit for eligible expenditures incurred in Manitoba by a corporation with a PE in the province. | Eligible expenditures are those that qualify for federal ITC purposes. The credit is considered to be government assistance and reduces federal expenditures for both the R&D deduction and ITCs.<br>Unused credits may be carried forward 7 years and carried back 3 years. All or part of the credit can be renounced each year. |

# Tax Reference Tables

| Province | Rate | Description | Definitions |
|---|---|---|---|
| Ontario R&D Super Allowance | CCPCs — 35% and 52.5% Others — 25% and 37.5% | Deduction allowed in computing Ontario net income for eligible expenditures incurred in the province. | Eligible expenditures are those that qualify for federal ITC purposes, and are reduced by federal ITCs and any government assistance received, which includes the OITC and the OBRI (see below). The higher rates are available when eligible expenditures incurred in a year exceed a three-year moving average. Unlike the federal legislation that became effective for taxation years commencing after February 28, 2000, the super-allowance benefit will not be considered as government assistance for Ontario purposes. |
| Ontario Innovation Tax Credit (OITC) | 10% | Refundable tax credit for eligible expenditures incurred in Ontario by a corporation with a PE in the province. | Eligible expenditures are those that qualify for federal ITC purposes. 100% of current expenditures and 40% of capital expenditures qualify for the credit. Effective for taxation years ending after May 4, 1999, the credit is available to all corporations with taxable income of less than $200,000 and taxable paid-up capital (for Ontario capital tax purposes) of less than $25 million in the preceding year. |
| Ontario Business-Research Institute Tax Credit (OBRI) | 20% | Refundable tax credit for eligible expenditures incurred in Ontario as part of an eligible research institute contract. | An eligible research institute contract is an R&D contract between a corporation with a PE in Ontario and an eligible research institute (i.e., certain post-secondary and hospital research institutions, prescribed non-profit research organizations). Eligible expenditures, as defined for federal ITC purposes, are limited to $20 million per year. |
| Québec R&D Wage Tax Credit | Canadian controlled corporations — 40% Others — 20% | Refundable tax credit for R&D wages paid to employees of a PE in Québec. Also available for 50% of amounts paid to an unrelated subcontractor for R&D performed by employees in Québec. | To be eligible for the 40% rate in respect of a maximum of $2 million in qualifying expenditures, the corporation must have less than $25 million in assets on an associated basis. For corporations with assets between $25 and $50 million, the 40% rate is gradually reduced to 20%. The $2 million limit must be shared by associated corporations. The credit may be claimed by a corporation that does not have a PE in Québec. The credit reduces eligible expenditures for federal purposes, but is not taxable in Québec. |
| Québec R&D Super-deduction | Canadian controlled corporations — 460% Others — 230% | Deduction allowed in computing Québec net income in lieu of refundable R&D wage tax credit if election made by the taxpayer. Effective for taxation years beginning after June 30, 1999. | Expenditures eligible for the R&D wage tax credit are also used to compute the super-deduction. The 460% rate applies to those expenditures eligible for the 40% credit (see above). Any unused super-deduction cannot be carried forward. The super-deduction is grossed-up to account for the proportion of business carried on outside Québec. Due to the changes announced in the 2000 federal budget relating to provincial super-deductions the Quebec government has eliminated all provincial R&D super-deductions effective for taxation years beginning after February 29, 2000. |
| Québec Incremental R&D tax credit or super-deduction | Canadian controlled corporations — 15% credit or 190% super-deduction | Refundable tax credit or super-deduction allowed in computing Québec net income for incremental eligible R&D expenditures. Effective for taxation years beginning after June 30, 1999 and ending before July 1, 2004. Eliminated for taxation years beginning after February 29, 2000. | To be eligible, the Canadian-controlled corporation must have less than $25 million in assets on an associated group basis. Eligible R&D expenditures include R&D wages, R&D subcontracts and contract payments to/for R&D entities and projects (see below). The amount of the credit or super-deduction is based on the excess of the current year's eligible R&D expenditures over the average of such expenditures for the previous three years. Rules for the 190% super-deduction election parallel those for the regular super-deduction described above. The incremental super-deduction is also eliminated for taxation years beginning after February 29, 2000. |
| Québec Credit for contract payments to/for R&D entities and projects | 40% | Refundable tax credit for contract and other payments to certain eligible entities. Only 80% of payments to unrelated persons is eligible. | Eligible entities include universities, public research centres, and private research consortiums. Other types of eligible payments include expenditures in respect of pre-competitive research projects, environmental technology innovation projects, and catalyst projects. |
| New Brunswick | 10% | Non-refundable tax credit for eligible expenditures incurred in N.B. by a corporation with a PE in the province. | Eligible expenditures are those that qualify for federal ITC purposes. The credit is considered to be government assistance and reduces federal expenditures for both the R&D deduction and ITCs. Unused credits may be carried forward 7 years and carried back 3 years. The credit can be renounced each year. |
| Nova Scotia | 15% | Refundable tax credit for eligible expenditures incurred in N.S. by a corporation with a PE in the province. | Eligible expenditures are those that qualify for federal ITC purposes. The credit is considered to be government assistance and reduces federal expenditures for both the R&D deduction and ITCs. |
| Newfoundland | 15% | Refundable tax credit for eligible expenditures incurred in Newfoundland by a corporation with a PE in the province. | Eligible expenditures are those that qualify for federal ITC purposes. The credit is considered to be government assistance and reduces federal expenditures for both the R&D deduction and ITCs. |

## Tax Reference Tables

### PROVINCIAL PAYROLL TAXES

*Note:* In addition to the payroll taxes listed below, all provinces require payment of workers' compensation premiums by most employers in respect of most employees. These assessments, which vary by industry and in some cases by employer, are technically not "taxes".

### WHAT CONSTITUTES "PAYROLL"?

Payroll encompasses all payments, benefits and allowances included in computing employment income under the *Income Tax Act*. The federal government had proposed to limit the deductibility of provincial capital and payroll taxes, other than for those provinces who agree to harmonize their provincial sales tax with the federal Goods and Services Tax. However, at the time of writing, the federal government is still negotiating its proposals with the provincial authorities and no legislation has yet been introduced. See press releases reproduced at the end of ITA s. 18.

### MANITOBA HEALTH AND POST-SECONDARY EDUCATION TAX LEVY

| Annual Payroll | Rate of Tax % |
|---|---|
| $ 0 — 1,000,000 | Nil |
| 1,000,001 — 2,000,000 | 4.30 |
| 2,000,001 — and over | 2.15 |

Monthly instalments must be made, and a monthly return filed, by the 15th of the month following the month in which the remuneration is paid. An annual return must be filed on or before March 31 of the following calendar year. Where the corporation has an annual payroll of less than the exemption amount, it must still file an annual declaration of its total payroll. The annual payroll limits apply to associated corporations.

### ONTARIO EMPLOYER HEALTH TAX (EHT)

Employers are exempt from tax on the first $400,000 of Ontario payroll. Payroll in excess of this amount attracts tax at a rate of 1.95%.

Associated corporations must enter into an agreement allocating the exemption amount between them and must file the agreement with their annual returns.

Employers must pay monthly EHT instalments based on the previous month's payroll. However, instalments need not be remitted until the cumulative monthly payroll exceeds the exemption amount for the year.

Effective January 1, 2000, employers with annual payroll of less than $600,000 are not required to pay instalments. They must remit their EHT once a year along with their annual return.

An annual EHT return must be filed by March 15th of the following year. Employers with multiple accounts are permitted to file separate returns for each account.

### QUÉBEC HEALTH SERVICES FUND (HSF)

Employer contributions to the HSF apply at a rate of 4.26%. However, employers with payroll of less than $5 million are eligible for reduced rates as follows:

| | July 1, 1999 Rate | July 1, 2000 Rate |
|---|---|---|
| < $1,000,000 | 3.75% | 2.70% |
| 2,000,000 | 3.88 | 3.09 |
| 3,000,000 | 4.01 | 3.48 |
| 4,000,000 | 4.13 | 3.87 |
| > 5,000,000 | 4.26 | 4.26 |

Corporations that already enjoy an exemption from income and capital tax for their first 5 taxation years (first 3 years for those incorporated prior to March 25, 1997) are also exempted from making HSF contributions on the first $500,000 of wages paid. This exemption amount increases to $700,000 effective July 1, 2000. The exemption must be prorated for taxation years that straddle this date, that are less than 365 days and in which eligibility for the tax holiday ceases.

Instalments of HSF must be made on the 15th of the month following the month in which the remuneration was paid. All employers whose average monthly remittances (income tax, QPP, HSF) exceed $50,000 must remit instalments four times a month.

### QUÉBEC MANPOWER TRAINING TAX

Employers who are subject to the *Act to Foster the Development of Manpower Training* and whose annual payroll exceeds $250,000 are required to participate in the development of worker training by allotting an amount representing at least 1% of their payroll to eligible training expenditures.

## Tax Reference Tables

Employers whose eligible training expenditures are lower than the minimum participation required must make a contribution equal to the difference between the two amounts. This contribution must be remitted by the last day of February following the taxation year.

### NEWFOUNDLAND HEALTH AND POST-SECONDARY EDUCATION TAX

This tax applies at a rate of 2% to annual payroll in excess of $400,000 ($150,000 prior to April 1, 2000). The rate was previously decreased to 1% for employers in renewable resource industries such as fishing, forestry and agriculture, but effective April 1, 2000, the 2% rate now applies to all employers.

Instalments must be made, and a monthly return filed, by the 15th of the month following the month in which the remuneration is paid.

An annual return must be filed by the end of February, along with an annual agreement allocating the exemption among associated companies.

---

**REQUIRED** — Use capitalized cash flow method to cal. FMV

**Facts**
- UCC @ V-Day (30% assets): 1,200,000
- Redundant assets, net of tax: 180,000
- Income before tax: 375,000
- Sus. cap. reinvestment: 45,000
- Depreciation: 75,000
- Rate of return – 12%   Tax rate 50%
- Cap rate 20% or 5 times

**SOLUTION**

| | |
|---|---:|
| Net income before tax | 375,000 |
| Add depreciation | 75,000 |
| Cash flow before tax | 450,000 |
| Less taxes @ 50% | (225,000) |
| | 225,000 |

Sustainably cap. reinvestment

$$\frac{45,000 \times .50 \times .30}{.12 + .30} \times \left(1 - \frac{.12}{2(1+.12)}\right) \quad 29,790 \quad (45000 - 15,210)$$

Cash flow after tax    195,210
Cap rate (multiplier)   × 5
                       976050

Add Tax shield on eval UCC

$$\frac{1,200,000 \times .50 \times .30}{.12 + .30} \quad 428,571$$

Add Redundant asset    180,000

↳ FMV                                    1,584,621

## OTHER
## PRESCRIBED INTEREST RATES (Reg. 4301)
### Federal

The federal prescribed interest rate is adjusted quarterly. The quarterly interest rate is calculated by taking the average equivalent yield of Government of Canada 90-day treasury bill (rounded to the next highest whole percentage) sold by the Department of Finance during the first month of the immediately preceding quarterly period (Reg. 4301).

*Interest Charge Applicable to*

| | Taxable Benefits (a) | Overpaid Taxes (b) | Underpaid Taxes (b) |
|---|---|---|---|
| Jan. 1994 to Mar. 1994 | 5% | 7% | 7% |
| Apr. 1994 to Jun. 1994 | 4% | 6% | 6% |
| Jul. 1994 to Sep. 1994 | 6% | 8% | 8% |
| Oct. 1994 to Dec. 1994 | 7% | 9% | 9% |
| Jan. 1995 to Mar. 1995 | 6% | 8% | 8% |
| Apr. 1995 to Jun. 1995 | 8% | 10% | 10% |
| Jul. 1995 to Sep. 1995 | 9% | 11% | 13% |
| Oct. 1995 to Mar. 1996 | 7% | 9% | 11% |
| Apr. 1996 to Jun. 1996 | 6% | 8% | 10% |
| Jul. 1996 to Dec. 1996 | 5% | 7% | 9% |
| Jan. 1997 to Mar. 1997 | 4% | 6% | 8% |
| Apr. 1997 to Jun. 1997 | 3% | 5% | 7% |
| Jul. 1997 to Mar. 1998 | 4% | 6% | 8% |
| Apr. 1998 to Mar. 2000 | 5% | 7% | 9% |
| Apr. 2000 to Mar. 2001 | 6% | 8% | 10% |

**Notes:**

(a) This prescribed interest rate applies to taxable benefits of employees and shareholders arising on interest-free and low-interest loans, as well as to loans that avoid the attribution rules.

(b) Since July 1995, the formula for determining the rate of interest charged on unpaid taxes includes an increase of two percentage points. This rate applies to all overdue taxes, penalties, interest, insufficient instalment payments and unpaid employee tax deduction, as well as unpaid Canada Pension Plan contributions and Employment Insurance premiums. Thus, the prescribed rate applied to all refunds of tax overpayments is 2% below the rate applied to underpaid taxes.

The 1999 federal budget introduced a mechanism whereby a corporation may request that, for any period of time where interest is calculated both on overpaid and underpaid taxes, the two amounts be offset. Eligible amounts include tax (other than instalments), interest accrued prior to the period of overlapping balances, and penalties. Interest will only be payable on the net balance owing, with the rate of interest depending on whether there is a net overpayment or underpayment. This provision applies for any period after 1999, regardless of the taxation year to which the amounts relate.

For earlier periods, see Notes to Reg. 4301.

### Provincial

The federal prescribed rates are also used by all of the provinces, except for Ontario and Québec, in the calculation of interest on corporate income taxes. The federal interest rates also apply to all provincial personal taxes, except for Québec.

Ontario uses the federal rate for overpaid taxes as the base for determining its rates. The rate used to calculate interest charges on underpaid tax is set at three percentage points higher than the base rate, and the rate used for overpaid tax is set at two percentage points lower than the base rate. The prime rate is used on amounts refunded to taxpayers whose tax issues, under the objections and appeals process, are resolved in the taxpayer's favour.

Québec sets the rate for underpaid taxes based on the average of Canada's prime rate over the preceding three months plus 3%. The interest rate on overpaid taxes is determined quarterly based on the rate applicable to Québec Savings Bonds on the first day of the third month of the preceding quarter.

## Tax Reference Tables

**FOREIGN EXCHANGE RATES**
From *Bank of Canada Review* and calculated using the rates for the last Wednesday of each month.

| Average Yearly | European Euro | French Franc | German Mark | Japanese Yen | Pound Sterling | Swiss Franc | U.S. Dollar |
|---|---|---|---|---|---|---|---|
| 1989 |  | .1858 | .6304 | .00861 | 1.9415 | .7246 | 1.1842 |
| 1990 |  | .2147 | .7234 | .00809 | 2.0808 | .8430 | 1.1668 |
| 1991 |  | .2039 | .6934 | .00852 | 2.0275 | .8027 | 1.1458 |
| 1992 |  | .2288 | .7757 | .00955 | 2.1302 | .8627 | 1.2083 |
| 1993 |  | .2279 | .7804 | .01165 | 1.9372 | .8734 | 1.2898 |
| 1994 |  | .2469 | .8444 | .01339 | 2.0929 | 1.0024 | 1.3659 |
| 1995 | 1.7758 | .2754 | .9591 | .01470 | 2.1671 | 1.1633 | 1.3726 |
| 1996 | 1.7079 | .2667 | .9068 | .01255 | 2.1283 | 1.1051 | 1.3636 |
| 1997 | 1.5652 | .2375 | .7994 | .01145 | 2.2682 | .9548 | 1.3844 |
| 1998 | 1.6668 | .2520 | .8450 | .01139 | 2.4587 | 1.0258 | 1.4831 |
| 1999 | 1.5847 | .2416 | .8102 | .01311 | 2.4038 | .9901 | 1.4858 |
| 2000 | 1.3704 | .2089 | .7007 | .01378 | 2.2499 | .8793 | 1.4852 |

---

FACTS: Income under Div B for Co. — 86% of inc. earned in Cda

| | |
|---|---|
| Div. from foreign investments | 138,000 (before 20,700 in tax w/h) |
| Cdn. interest income | 276,000 |
| Manufacturing profits | 1,196,000 |
| Dividends from taxable Cdn. corps | 414,000 |
| Foreign business profits | 92,000 (before 29,440 in tax w/h) |
| Income under div. B | 2,116,000 |

Qualified prop. purchased — 2,800,000 (Class 43 (ITC))   Donations 55,200   Non Cap loss <fwd → 102,080

M+P Deduction — 54,320   Non bus FTC 20,700   Bus FTC 29,440

Required — Calculate maximum ITC that can be deducted. What is remaining ITC and its impact on future years.

ITC = 10% of 2,800,000 = 289,000

| | | |
|---|---|---|
| Income under Div. B before CCA on elig. property | | 2,116,000 |
| Less CCA (2,800,000 × 30% × ½) | | 420,000 |
| Income under Div B | | 1,696,000 |
| Less: non-cap. losses | 102,080 | |
| charitable | 55,200 | |
| dividends | 414,000 | 571,280 |
| | | 1,124,720 |
| Tax @ 38% | | 427,394 |
| Less abatement (10% × 86% × 1,124,720) | | (96,726) |
| Add surtax (4% × [427,394 − (.10 × 1,124,720)]) | 12,517 | |
| | | 343,265 |
| Less M+P, + FTC's | | <104,460> |
| | | 238,805 |
| less ITC | | 238,805 |
| | | nil |

Remaining tax credit 4,195 can be carried forward 10 years
UCC balance in Class 43 ↓ by 238,805 in following year.

## TAX TREATY WITHHOLDING RATES
### Schedule of Non-Resident Tax Rates for Treaty Countries *

| Country (a) | Interest (b) | Dividends (c) | Royalties (d) | Pensions/Annuities (e) |
|---|---|---|---|---|
| Algeria | 15 | 15 | 0/15 | 15/25 |
| Argentina | 12.5 | 10/15 | 3/5/10/15 | 15/25 |
| Australia | 15 | 15 | 10 | 15/25 |
| Austria | 10 | 5 | 0/10 | 25 |
| Bangladesh | 15 | 15 | 10 | 15/25 |
| Barbados | 15 | 15 | 10 | 15/25 |
| Belgium | 15 | 15 | 10 | 25 |
| Brazil | 15 | 15/25 | 15/25 | 25 |
| Bulgaria ** | 10 | 10/15 | 0/10 | 10/15/25 |
| Cameroon | 15 | 15 | 15 | 25 |
| Chile | 15 | 10/15 | 15 | 15/25 |
| China, People's Republic (f) | 10 | 10/15 | 10 | 25 |
| Croatia | 10 | 5/15 | 10 | 10/15 |
| Cyprus | 15 | 15 | 10 | 15/25 |
| Czech Republic (g) | 10 | 10/15 | 10 | 15/25 |
| Denmark | 10 | 5/10/15 | 0/10 | 25 |
| Dominican Republic | 18 | 18 | 18 | 18/25 |
| Egypt | 15 | 15 | 15 | 25 |
| Estonia | 10 | 5/15 | 10 | 10/15/25 |
| Finland | 10 | 10/15 | 10 | 15/20/25 |
| France | 10 | 5/10/15 | 0/10 | 25 |
| Germany | 15 | 15 | 10 | 15/25 |
| Guyana | 15/25 | 15 | 10 | 25 |
| Hungary | 10 | 5/10/15 | 10 | 10/15/25 |
| Iceland | 10 | 5/15 | 0/10 | 15/25 |
| India | 15 | 15/25 | 10/15/20 | 25 |
| Indonesia | 10 | 10/15 | 10 | 15/25 |
| Ireland | 15 | 0/15 | 0/15 | 0/15 |
| Israel | 15 | 15 | 15 | 15/25 |
| Italy | 15 | 15 | 10 | 15/25 |
| Ivory Coast | 15 | 15 | 10 | 15/25 |
| Jamaica | 15 | 15 | 10 | 15/25 |
| Japan | 10 | 5/15 | 10 | 25 |
| Jordan | 10 | 10/15 | 10 | 25 |
| Kazakhstan | 10 | 5/15 | 10 | 15/25 |
| Kenya | 15 | 15/25 | 15 | 15/25 |
| Korea, Republic of | 15 | 15 | 15 | 25 |

**Notes:**

\* The rates indicated in the table apply to payments from Canada to the applicable treaty country; in some cases, a treaty may provide for a different rate of withholding tax on payments from the other country to Canada. The treaties should be consulted to determine if specific conditions, exemptions or tax sparing provisions apply for each type of payment. Certain treaties provide that if the country, subsequent to the signature of the treaty with Canada, signs a treaty with another member of the Organization for Economic Cooperation and Development, and that country agrees to accept a lower rate of withholding, the lower rate will automatically apply to the treaty with Canada.

\*\* New treaties signed but not ratified. Until ratification, the withholding tax rate is generally 25%.

xlv

## Schedule of Non-Resident Tax Rates for Treaty Countries (continued) *

| Country (a) | Interest (b) | Dividends (c) | Royalties (d) | Pensions/Annuities (e) |
|---|---|---|---|---|
| Kyrgyzstan | 15 | 15 | 0/10 | 15/25 |
| Latvia | 10 | 5/15 | 10 | 10/15/25 |
| Lebanon ** | 10 | 5/15 | 5/10 | 15/25 |
| Lithuania | 10 | 5/15 | 10 | 10/15/25 |
| Luxembourg | 10 | 5/15 | 0/10 | 25 |
| Malaysia | 15 | 15 | 15 | 15/25 |
| Malta | 15 | 15 | 10 | 15/25 |
| Mexico | 15 | 10/15 | 15 | 15/25 |
| Morocco | 15 | 15 | 10 | 25 |
| Netherlands | 10 | 5/10/15 | 0/10 | 15/25 |
| New Zealand | 15 | 15 | 15 | 15/25 |
| Nigeria | 12.5 | 12.5/15 | 12.5 | 25 |
| Norway | 15 | 15 | 10/15 | 0/25 |
| Pakistan | 15 | 15 | 15 | 25 |
| Papua New Guinea | 10 | 15 | 10 | 15/25 |
| Philippines | 15 | 15 | 10 | 25 |
| Poland | 15 | 15 | 10 | 15/25 |
| Portugal ** | 10 | 10/15 | 10 | 15/25 |
| Romania | 15 | 15 | 10/15 | 15/25 |
| Russian Federation | 10 | 10/15 | 0/10 | 25 |
| Singapore | 15 | 15 | 15 | 25 |
| Slovakia (g) | 10 | 10/15 | 10 | 15/25 |
| Slovenia ** | 10 | 5/15 | 10 | 15/25 |
| South Africa | 10 | 5/15 | 6/10 | 25 |
| Spain | 15 | 15 | 10 | 15/25 |
| Sri Lanka | 15 | 15 | 10 | 15/25 |
| Sweden | 10 | 5/10/15 | 0/10 | 25 |
| Switzerland | 10 | 5/10/15 | 0/10 | 15/25 |
| Tanzania | 15 | 20/25 | 20 | 15/25 |
| Thailand | 15 | 15 | 15 | 25 |
| Trinidad & Tobago | 10 | 5/15 | 10 | 15/25 |
| Tunisia | 15 | 15 | 15/20 | 25 |
| Ukraine | 10 | 5/15 | 10 | 25 |
| United Kingdom (h) | 10 | 10/15 | 10 | 10/25 |
| United States (i) | 10 | 5/10/15 | 0/10 | 15/25 |
| Uzbekistan | 10 | 5/15 | 5/10 | 25 |
| Vietnam | 10 | 5/10/15 | 7.5/10 | 15/25 |
| Zambia | 15 | 15 | 15 | 15/25 |
| Zimbabwe | 15 | 10/15 | 10 | 15/25 |

**Notes:**

\* The rates indicated in the table apply to payments from Canada to the applicable treaty country; in some cases, a treaty may provide for a different rate of withholding tax on payments from the other country to Canada. The treaties should be consulted to determine if specific conditions, exemptions or tax sparing provisions apply for each type of payment. Certain treaties provide that if the country, subsequent to the signature of the treaty with Canada, signs a treaty with another memeber of the Organization for Economic Cooperation and Development, and that county agrees to accept a lower rate of withholding, the lower rate will automatically apply to the treaty with Canada.

\*\* New treaties signed but not ratified. Until ratification, the withholding tax rate is generally 25%.

## Tax Reference Tables

(a) Canada is negotiating or renegotiating its tax treaties or protocols with the following countries, as of January 15, 2001:

| | | | |
|---|---|---|---|
| Armenia | Gabon | Moldova | Turkey |
| Australia | Germany | Mongolia | United Arab Emirates |
| Barbados | Greece | Norway | United Kingdom |
| Belgium | Ireland | Romania | United States |
| Colombia | Italy | St. Lucia | Venezuela |
| Czech Republic | Kuwait | Senegal | |
| Ecuador | Mauritius | Singapore | |
| Egypt | Mexico | Slovak Republic | |

(b) Certain interest is exempt from withholding tax either by the *Income Tax Act* (e.g., paragraph 212(1)(b)) or by the treaty.

(c) *Dividends:*

Dividends subject to Canadian withholding tax include taxable dividends (other than capital gains dividends paid by certain entities) and capital dividends.

The withholding tax rate on dividends generally varies depending on the percentage ownership of the total issued capital or percentage ownership of the voting rights owned by the recipient.

Some treaties have specific rules for dividends paid by non-resident-owned investment corporations.

Canada has indicated that in its treaty negotiations it is prepared to reduce the 10% tax rate to 5% over a five-year period on "direct" dividends.

(d) *Royalties:*

Royalties are generally defined as payments for the use of, or right to use, any cultural property and any copyright of scientific work, any patent, trademark, design or model, plan, secret formula or process, and information concerning industrial, commercial, or scientific experience.

Paragraph 212(1)(d) generally exempts from withholding tax cultural royalties for a copyright in respect of the production or reproduction of any literary, dramatic, musical, or artistic work, other than a motion picture film or a videotape or other means for use in connection with television. However, several treaties exempt all cultural royalties from tax.

Canada announced that in its treaty negotiations it is prepared to eliminate the withholding tax on arm's-length payments in respect of rights to use patented information or information concerning scientific experience. It also stated that it is prepared to negotiate, on a bilateral basis, exemptions from withholding taxes for payments for the use of computer software. As such, the more recent treaties generally contain an exemption for such payments.

(e) *Pensions and annuities:*

The terms "pension", "periodic pension payment" and "annuity" are defined, for treaty purposes, in the *Income Tax Conventions Interpretation Act*, to the extent the terms are not fully or partially defined in the treaty or are defined in the treaty by reference to the laws of Canada.

Section 217 provides for an election whereby the non-resident, in certain circumstances, would not be subject to withholding tax at the rate of 25% but would file normal Canadian tax returns and would be subject to Part I tax.

The withholding tax rate varies depending on, among other attributes, if the payment is a lump-sum or periodic payment, or if the payment is a pension or annuity.

Some treaties provide for exemption for certain types of pensions or for an exemption up to a threshold amount. Some pensions are taxable only in the source country.

(f) The treaty does not apply to Hong Kong.

(g) The treaty with the former Czechoslovakia is considered in force with respect to both the Czech Republic and Slovakia.

(h) *United Kingdom (Great Britain and Northern Ireland) (see text of treaty near the end of this book):*

Interest — Interest is defined as income from debt-claims of every kind, whether or not secured by mortgage, and whether or not carrying a right to participate in the debtor's profits, including premiums and prizes attaching to bonds and debentures, as well as income assimilated to income from money lent by the tax law of Canada or the U.K. as the case may be. There are certain exemptions under the treaty. See also Note (b).

Dividends — The 10% withholding tax rate applies if the recipient of the dividend is a company that controls, directly or indirectly, at least 10% of the voting power of the payer. See also Note (c).

Royalties — Cultural royalties, excluding royalties in respect of films or motion pictures, and videotapes or other media for use in television broadcasting, are taxable only in the resident country. See also Note (d).

Pensions/Annuities — Pensions are defined to include any payment under a superannuation, pension or retirement plan, and certain other amounts, but exclude any payments in settlement of all future entitlements or payments under an income-averaging annuity contract (IAAC). Pensions are taxable only in the resident country.

Annuities are defined as periodic payments payable during a person's lifetime or for a specified period of time, under an obligation to make the payments in return for money or money's worth. The definition excludes pensions, any payments in settlement of all future entitlements and IAACs. Annuities are subject to tax in the payer country at a rate of 10%. See also Note (e).

(i) *United States (see text of treaty near the end of this book):*

Interest — Interest is defined as income from debt-claims of every kind, whether or not secured by mortgage, and whether or not carrying a right to participate in the debtor's profits, including premiums and prizes attaching to bonds and debentures, as well as income assimilated to income from money lent by the tax law of Canada or the U.S. as the case may be. There are certain exemptions under the treaty including interest paid in connection with an arm's-length sale on credit of equipment, merchandise or services. See also Note (b).

Dividends — The 5% withholding tax rate applies if the recipient of the interest is a company that is the beneficial owner of at least 10% of the voting stock of the payer. The rate of Canadian branch tax is also limited to 5% on cumulative branch profits exceeding $500,000 Cdn. The first $500,000 Cdn. of cumulative branch profits are exempt from withholding tax. The 10% tax rate applies to dividends from a non-resident-owned investment corporation if the recipient of the interest is a company that is the beneficial owner of at least 10% of the voting stock of the payer. See also Note (c).

Royalties — Royalties are generally defined as payments for the use of, or right to use, any cultural property and any copyright of scientific work, any patent, trademark, design or model, plan, secret formula or process, and information concerning industrial, commercial or scientific experience. The definition also includes gains from the alienation of any intangible property or rights in such property to the extent that such gains are contingent on the productivity, use or subsequent disposition of such property or rights. See also Note (d).

The following royalties are exempt from withholding tax:

- Cultural royalties, excluding royalties in respect of films or motion pictures, and videotapes or other media for use in television broadcasting.
- Payments for the use, or right to use, computer software.
- Payments for the use, or right to use, patents or information concerning industrial, commercial or scientific experience (excluding any such information in relation to a rental or franchise agreement).
- Payments in respect of broadcasting as may be agreed to between the countries.

Pensions/Annuities — Pensions are defined to include any payment under a superannuation, pension or other retirement arrangement, and certain other amounts, but exclude IAACs. Effective in 1998, payments of Old Age Security and Canada/Québec Pension Plan benefits to U.S. residents will be taxable only in the U.S. and will not be subject to Canadian withholding tax. Further, Canadian tax withheld on such benefits in 1996 and 1997 will be refunded (net of regular Canadian income tax) to any U.S. resident whose U.S. tax would be less than the Canadian tax. Conversely, the U.S. will not withhold tax on social security benefits paid to Canadian residents and only 85% of such benefits will be taxable by Canada. Canada will issue refunds for any U.S. tax withheld on benefits in 1996 and 1997. These refunds will be made automatically based on information provided by the U.S.

Annuities are defined as periodic payments payable during a person's lifetime or for a specified period of time, under an obligation to make the payments in return for adequate and full consideration (other than services rendered). The definition excludes non-periodic payments or any annuity the cost of which was tax deductible in the country in which it was acquired. See also Note (e).

## LIMITATIONS AND CONTINGENT DATES

| Subject | Required or Permitted Action | Within (Limitation) | Of (Precipitating Event) | Income Tax Act (Sections) |
|---|---|---|---|---|
| Appeal to Tax Court of Canada | Filing of notice of appeal to Tax Court of Canada | 90 days | Mailing of notice of confirmation or reassessment, or service of notice of objection | 169(1) |
| Assessment for Previous Years (General) | Assessment, reassessment, or additional assessment of tax, interest, penalties under Part I by Minister | 3 years | Mailing of notice of original assessment | 152(3.1), (4)(c) |
| (Mutual fund trusts and non-CCPCs) | | 4 years | | 152(3.1) |
| (Amounts carried back from subsequent years) | | 3 years | Expiration of normal assessment period (see above) | 152(4)(b) |
| Collection | Refraining from commencement of collection proceedings regarding unpaid tax | 90 days | Mailing of notice of assessment or reassessment | 225.1 |
| Death of Taxpayer | Filing of return by legal representatives | 6 months | Death of taxpayer from November through June 15; April 30 or June 15 otherwise | 150(1)(b), (d) |
| Deferred Profit Sharing Plans | Remittance of tax equal to fair market value of security | 10 days | Acquisition of non-qualified investment or use of trust property as security for loan | 198(2) |
| Director's Liability | Action against director for corporation's failure to deduct, withhold or remit tax | 2 years | Ceasing to be a director | 227.1(4) |
| Interest offset | Apply to offset refund interest against arrears interest | 90 days | Mailing of notice of assessment or final court decision | 161.1(3)(c) |
| Keeping books and records | Retention of records for tax purposes | 6 years | End of taxation year | 230(4)(a), (b) |
| | Retention of duplicate charitable donation receipts | 2 years | End of calendar year | 230(4)(a), Reg. 5800(c) |
| | Retention of general corporate records | 2 years | Dissolution of corporation or charity | 230(4)(a), Reg. 5800(a), (b), (d), (e) |
| Objection to Assessment | Filing Notice of Objection | 90 days | Mailing of notice of assessment | 165(1) |
| | | 1 year (alternative for individuals and testamentary trusts) | Balance-due day for original return (see 248(1)) | 165(1) |
| Prosecution of Offences | Laying of information or making complaint | 8 years | Arising of the matter | 244(14) |
| Recovery of Overpayment | Refund by Minister of overpayment upon taxpayer's filing return | 3 years | End of taxation year | 164(1)(a) |

## Tax Reference Tables

| Subject | Required or Permitted Action | Within (Limitation) | Of (Precipitating Event) | Income Tax Act (Sections) |
|---|---|---|---|---|
| *Refunds — Losses or Carry-backs* | Application for refund | | Mailing of notice of original assessment | 164(1)(b) |
| (Mutual fund trusts and non-CCPCs) | | 7 years | | 152(3.1)(a), (4)(b) |
| (Other) | | 6 years | | 152(3.1)(b), (4)(b) |
| *Refunds — Other* | | | | |
| (Mutual fund trusts and non-CCPCs) | | 4 years | | 152(3.1)(a) |
| (Other) | | 3 years | | 152(3.1)(a) |
| (Individuals and testamentary trusts) | | | Anytime, for 1985 or later years, with Revenue Canada's consent | 152(4.2), 164(1.5) |
| *Refunds — Non-resident Withholding Tax Improperly Withheld* | | 2 years | End of calendar year in which amount paid to Receiver General | 227(6) |
| *Sale by Non-residents* | Notice to Minister of name and address of purchaser, description of property and sale price | 10 days | Disposition of taxable Canadian property by non-resident | 116(3) |
| *Withholdings* | Remittance of tax withheld from employees' salaries | 7 days | Employer ceasing to carry on business | Reg. 108(2) |
| | Remittance of tax withheld from payments to non-residents | 15 days | End of month during which tax withheld | 215(1): Information Circular 77-16R3, para. 51 |

## PENALTIES AND OFFENCES
*Penalties*

| ITA Provisions | Violation | Penalty |
|---|---|---|
| 66(14.5) | Late designation of Canadian exploration expense or Canadian development expense | .0025 times amount designated per month or partial month of lateness (maximum $100 per month, maximum $8,000) |
| 85(8), 96(6) | Late filed election on rollover into corporation or on rollover into or out of partnership | .0025 times amount of deferral per month or partial month of lateness (maximum $100 per month, maximum $8,000) |
| 93(6) | Late filed election to treat proceeds of disposition of share of foreign affiliate as a dividend | .0025 times amount elected per month of lateness (maximum $100 per month, maximum $8,000) |
| 96(6) | (See under 85(8) above) | |
| 110.6(29) | Late filed election (or amended election) to trigger capital gains exemption to February 22, 1994 | 1/300 of the taxable capital gain (or increased taxable capital gain) for each month or part month past deadline (generally April 30, 1995) |
| 146(13.1) | RRSP issuer extending a prohibited advantage to annuitant | Amount of the advantage (minimum $100) |
| 162(1) | Failure to file annual return | 5% of year's unpaid tax plus 1% per complete month (up to 12 months) from due date |
| 162(2) | Failure to file annual return after demand (subsequent occurrence within 3 years) | 10% of year's unpaid tax plus 2% per complete month (up to 20 months) from due date |
| 162(3) | Failure of trustee in bankruptcy, etc., to file annual return | $10 for each day of default (maximum $50) |
| 162(4) | Failure to complete or deliver non-resident ownership certificate (Forms NR601, NR602) or ownership certificate (T600) prior to negotiation of foreign bearer coupon or warrant (s. 234(1)) | $50 |
| 162(5) | Failure to provide information on prescribed form | $100 for each failure (unless mitigating circumstances) |
| 162(6) | Failure to provide Social Insurance Number on request | $100 for each failure (unless applied for number within 15 days) |
| 162(7) | Failure to file information return or comply with duty or obligation imposed by Act or Regulation (not specifically provided for) | $25 per day of default (minimum $100, maximum $2,500) |
| 162(7.1) | Failure to file partnership return | $25 per day of default (minimum $100, maximum $2,500) |
| 162(8) | Failure to file partnership information return after demand (subsequent occurrence within 3 years) | Additional penalty of $100 per partner for each month or partial month of default, up to a maximum of 24 months |
| 162(9) | Failure by promoter to apply for tax shelter identification number | 3% of shelters sold prior to issuance of number ($500 minimum) |
| 162(10)(a) | Failure to furnish foreign-based information under 233.1 to 233.4, knowingly or with gross negligence | $500 per month during which return not filed (maximum 24 months) |

## Tax Reference Tables

| ITA Provisions | Violation | Penalty |
|---|---|---|
| 162(10)(b) | Failure to comply with demand to file return under 233 re dealings with non-residents | $1,000 per month during which return not filed (maximum 24 months) |
| 162(10.1) | Additional penalty where number of months under 162(10) exceeds 24 | 5% of the value of property transferred or loaned to foreign trust, or of the cost of foreign property or foreign affiliate |
| 163(1) | Failure to report amount in annual return, where taxpayer had failed to report an amount in returns filed in 3 previous years | 10% of unreported amount (unless penalized under s. 163(2)) |
| 163(2) | False statement or omission in document knowingly or with gross negligence | 50% of tax on understatement of income ($100 minimum) |
| 163(2.2) | False statement or omission in respect of renunciation in respect of resource expenses, knowingly or with gross negligence | 25% of excess renunciation |
| 163(2.21), (2.22) | False statement or omission re flow-through share look-back rule, knowingly or with gross negligence | 25% of excess renunciation |
| 163(2.3) | False statement or omission relating to the allocation of assistance with respect to exercises expenditures under ss. 66(12.691) or (12.701) | 25% of excess renunciation |
| 163(2.4) | False statement or omission re foreign-based information (ss. 233–233.7) | 5% of the value of the property, minimum $24,000 ($2,500 re distribution from non-resident trust) |
| 163.1 | Late or insufficient instalments 190.21 — Part VI, 189(8) — Part V | 50% of interest payable on instalments for year exceeding $1,000 or 25% of interest payable if no instalments had been made during year, whichever is greater |
| 163.2(2), (3) | Third party civil penalty: "planner's penalty" | Minimum $1,000, maximum the person's "gross entitlements" |
| 163.2(4), (5) | Third party civil penalty: "filer's penalty" | Minimum $1,000, maximum the other person's penalty (capped at $100,000 plus "gross entitlements") |
| 180.1(4) | Penalties in respect of Part I.1 tax | Same as under sections 162 to 163.1 |
| 180.2(6) | Penalties in respect of Part I.2 tax | Same as under sections 162 to 163.1 |
| 181.7 | Penalties in respect of Part I.3 tax | Same as under sections 162 to 163.1 |
| 183(3) | Penalties in respect of Part II tax | Same as under sections 162 to 163.1 |
| 183.2(2) | Penalties in respect of Part II.1 tax | Same as under sections 162 to 163.1 |
| 187(3) | Penalties in respect of Part IV tax | Same as under sections 162 to 163.1 |
| 187.6 | Penalties in respect of Part IV.1 tax | Same as under sections 162 to 163.1 |
| 189(8) | Penalties in respect of Part V tax | Same as under sections 162 to 163.1 |
| 190.21 | Penalties in respect of Part VI tax | Same as under sections 162 to 163.1 |
| 191.4(2) | Penalties in respect of Part VI.1 tax | Same as under sections 162 to 163.1 |
| 204.7(3) | Penalties in respect of Part X.2 tax | Same as under sections 162 to 163.1 |
| 204.87 | Penalties in respect of Part X.3 tax | Same as under sections 162 to 163.1 |
| 204.93 | Penalties in respect of Part X.4 tax | Same as under sections 162 to 163.1 |
| 207(3) | Penalties in respect of Part XI tax | Same as under sections 162 to 163.1 |

## Tax Reference Tables

| ITA Provisions | Violation | Penalty |
|---|---|---|
| 207.2(3) | Penalties in respect of Part XI.1 tax | Same as under sections 162 to 163.1 |
| 207.4(2) | Penalties in respect of Part XI.2 tax | Same as under sections 162 to 163.1 |
| 207.7(4) | Penalties in respect of Part XI.3 tax | Same as under sections 162 to 163.1 |
| 208(4) | Penalties in respect of Part XII tax | Same as under sections 162 to 163.1 |
| 209(5) | Penalties in respect of Part XII.1 tax | Same as under sections 162 to 163.1 |
| 210.2(7) | Penalties in respect of Part XII.2 tax | Same as under sections 162 to 163.1 |
| 211.6 | Penalties in respect of Part XII.3 tax | Same as under sections 162 to 163.1 |
| 211.6(5) | Penalties in respect of Part XII.4 tax | Same as under sections 162 to 163.1 |
| 211.91(3) | Penalties in respect of Part XII.6 tax | Same as under sections 162 to 163.1 |
| 219(3) | Penalties in respect of Part XIV tax | Same as under sections 162 to 163.1 |
| 220(3.5) | Late-filed election under ITA 13(4), 14(6), 21, 44(1), 66.7(7)(c), 66.7(7)(d), 66.7(7)(e), 66.7(8)(c), 66.7(8)(d), 66.7(8)(e), 70(6.2), 70(7)(a), 70(9.1), 70(9.2), 70(9.3), 72(2), 73(1), 104(14), Reg. 1103(1), Reg. 1103(2), Reg. 1103(2d) | $100 per complete month of lateness (maximum $8,000) |
| 227(8), (9) | Failure to withhold or deduct tax, or to remit tax, withheld or deducted (first occurrence) | 10% of amount not withheld, deducted or remitted |
|  | Subsequent occurrence after assessment of penalty in the same year | 20% of amount not withheld, deducted or remitted and, after 1992, only if the failure was made knowingly or under circumstances amounting to gross negligence |
| 235 | Failure to file corporate return under Parts I, I.3 or VI | .0025 times total of Part I.3 and Part VI tax per complete month of lateness (maximum 40 months) |
| 247(11) | Penalties re transfer pricing (Part XVI.1) | Same as under sections 162 to 163.1 |

**Notes:**

The burden of proof of a penalty under s. 163 is on the Minister: s. 163(3). Any penalty may be waived by the Minister: s. 220(3.1). A penalty can be imposed under s. 163 before a fine or imprisonment (see "Offences" table below), but once a conviction for an offence has been entered no penalty can apply: ss. 238(3), 239(3). See also Notes to 238(1).

Some penalties are implemented in the form of separate taxes. For example, the penalty for an excessive capital dividend election is enacted as the Part III tax. See Parts II.1 to XII.2 generally (not all of these taxes are penalty taxes).

### Offences

| ITA Provisions | Violations | Penalty |
|---|---|---|
| 238(1) | Failure to file return in required time and manner | On summary conviction, fine from $1,000 to $25,000, and imprisonment for up to 12 months |
|  | Failure of non-resident to notify Minister of particulars of sale of taxable Canadian property |  |
|  | Failure to issue receipts or make deposits with respect to political contributions in accordance with s. 127 |  |
|  | Failure to deduct or withhold tax |  |

## Tax Reference Tables

| ITA Provisions | Violations | Penalty |
|---|---|---|
| | Failure to keep proper books and records of account | |
| | Failure to comply with compliance order of court under s. 238(2) | |
| 239(1), (2) | False or deceptive statements in document. Alteration, falsification or destruction of books or records of account to evade payment of taxes. Wilful evasion or attempt to evade payment of taxes | On summary conviction, fine from 50% to 200% of tax sought to be evaded, and imprisonment for up to 2 years. On indictment, fine from 100% to 200% of tax sought to be evaded, and imprisonment for up to 5 years |
| 239(2.1) | Providing incorrect tax shelter identification number | On summary conviction, fine from 100% to 200% of cost to other person of interest in shelter, and imprisonment for up to 2 years |
| 239(2.2), (2.21) | Unauthorized communication or use of information | On summary conviction, fine of up to $5,000 and imprisonment for up to 1 year |
| 239(2.3) | Unauthorized disclosure of Social Insurance Number | On summary conviction, fine of up to $5,000 and imprisonment for up to 1 year |

**Notes:**

Saving provisions in s. 238(3) and s. 239(3) prevent double penalties from being assessed, but only if the prosecution is instituted before the penalty is assessed.

liv

# TABLE OF CONCORDANCE

The Revised Statutes of Canada, 1985, Fifth Supplement was proclaimed in force as of March 1, 1994. Although there was no general renumbering of the provisions of the *Income Tax Act*, a substantial number of structural changes were made. The table relates the provisions of the former Act to the corresponding provisions of the Fifth Supplement, as amended by 1994, c. 7 (Bill C-15), the *Income Tax Amendments Revision Act*. Note that only those provisions that have underwent structural changes are included in the table.

| Income Tax Act R.S.C. 1952, c. 148 as amended Section | R.S.C. 1985 5th Supplement as amended Section | Income Tax Act R.S.C. 1952, c. 148 as amended Section | R.S.C. 1985 5th Supplement as amended Section |
|---|---|---|---|
| 8 | 8 | (c) | "disposition of property" |
| (1.1) | — | (d) | "proceeds of disposition" |
| 12 | 12 | | |
| (11) | (11) | (i) | (a) |
| (a) | "investment contract" | (ii) | (b) |
| (i) | (a) | (iii) | (c) |
| (ii) | (b) | (iv) | (d) |
| (iii) | (c) | (v) | (e) |
| (iv) | (d) | (vi) | (f) |
| (v) | (e) | (vii) | (g) |
| (vi) | (f) | (viii) | (h) |
| (vii) | (g) | (d.1) | "timber resource property" |
| (viii) | (h) | | |
| (ix) | (i) | (i) | (a) |
| (x) | (j) | (A) | (i) |
| (xi) | (k) | (B) | (ii) |
| (b) | "anniversary day" | (I) | (A) |
| (i) | (a) | (II) | (B) |
| (ii) | (b) | (ii) | (b) |
| (iii) | (c) | (A) | (i) |
| 12.2 | 12.2 | (B) | (ii) |
| (11) | (11) | (e) | "total depreciation" |
| (a) | "exempt policy" | (f) | "undepreciated capital cost" |
| (b) | "anniversary day" | | |
| (i) | (a) | (i) | A |
| (ii) | (b) | (ii) | B |
| — | (12) | (ii.1) | C |
| — | (13) | (ii.2) | D |
| 13 | 13 | (iii) | E |
| (15) | (15) | (iv) | F |
| (b) | (b) | (A) | (a) |
| — | (i) | (B) | (b) |
| — | (ii) | (v) | G |
| (21) | (21) | (vi) | H |
| — | "appropriate minister" | (vii) | I |
| (a) | "conversion" and "conversion cost" | (viii) | J |
| (b) | "depreciable property" | (g) | "vessel" |

lv

## Table of Concordance

| Income Tax Act R.S.C. 1952, c. 148 as amended Section | R.S.C. 1985 5th Supplement as amended Section | Income Tax Act R.S.C. 1952, c. 148 as amended Section | R.S.C. 1985 5th Supplement as amended Section |
|---|---|---|---|
| — | (23.1) | (B) | (e) |
| 14 | 14 | (C) | (f) |
| (5) | (5) | (c) | "small business development bond" |
| (a) | "cumulative eligible capital" | (i) | (a) |
| (i) | A | (ii) | (b) |
| (ii) | B | (d) | "joint election" |
| (iii) | C | (i) | — |
| (iii.1) | D | (ii) | — |
| (A) | (a) | (e) | "property used for specified purposes" |
| (B) | (b) | (i) | (a) |
| (iii.2) | D.1 | (A) | (i) |
| (iv) | E | (B) | (ii) |
| (A) | (a) | (ii) | (b) |
| (B) | (b) | (f) | "specified property" |
| (v) | F | (i) | (a) |
| (A) | P | (ii) | (b) |
| (B) | Q | (iii) | (c) |
| (I) | (a) | (iv) | (d) |
| (II) | (b) | 15.2 | 15.2 |
| (C) | R | (3) | (3) |
| (b) | "eligible capital expenditure" | (a) | "qualifying debt obligation" |
| (i) | (a) | (i) | (a) |
| (ii) | (b) | (ii) | (b) |
| (iii) | (c) | (ii.1) | (c) |
| (A) | (i) | (iii) | (d) |
| (B) | (ii) | (A) | (i) |
| (C) | (iii) | (B) | (ii) |
| (D) | (iv) | (C) | (iii) |
| (iv) | (d) | (b) | "small business bond" |
| (v) | (e) | (c) | "joint election" |
| (vi) | (f) | (i) | (a) |
| (A) | (i) | (ii) | (b) |
| (B) | (ii) | (d) | "eligible issuer" |
| (C) | (iii) | (i) | (a) |
| (D) | (iv) | (ii) | (b) |
| (c) | "adjustment time" | 18 | 18 |
| (i) | (a) | (3) | (3) |
| (ii) | (b) | (a) | "land" |
| (iii) | (c) | (i) | (a) |
| 15.1 | 15.1 | (ii) | (b) |
| (3) | (3) | (iii) | (c) |
| (a) | "eligible small business corporation" | (b) | "interest on debt relating to the acquisition of land" |
| (i) | (a) | (i) | (a) |
| (ii) | (b) | (ii) | (b) |
| (b) | "qualifying debt obligation" | (A) | (i) |
| (i) | (a) | (B) | (ii) |
| (ii) | (b) | (C) | (iii) |
| (ii.1) | (c) | (5) | (5) |
| (iii) | — | (a) | "outstanding debts to |
| (iv) | (d) | | |
| (A) | | | |

lvi

## Table of Concordance

| Income Tax Act R.S.C. 1952, c. 148 as amended Section | R.S.C. 1985 5th Supplement as amended Section | Income Tax Act R.S.C. 1952, c. 148 as amended Section | R.S.C. 1985 5th Supplement as amended Section |
|---|---|---|---|
| | specified non-residents" | — | (16.2) |
| | (a) | — | (16.3) |
| (i) | (i) | (18) | (18) |
| (A) | (A) | (a) | "qualifying inventory" |
| (I) | (B) | | |
| (II) | (ii) | (b) | "specified transaction" |
| (B) | (b) | | |
| (ii) | "specified non-resident shareholder" | (i) | (a) |
| (b) | | (ii) | (b) |
| | "specified shareholder" | (iii) | (c) |
| (c) | (a) | — | (27.1) |
| (i) | (b) | **35** | **35** |
| (ii) | (c) | (2) | (2) |
| (iii) | (d) | (a) | "mining property" |
| (iv) | | (b) | "prospector" |
| **19** | **19** | **37** | **37** |
| (5) | (5) | (7) | (7) |
| (a) | "Canadian issue" | (a) | "approved" |
| (i) | (a) | (b) | "scientific research and experimental development" |
| (A) | (i) | | |
| (B) | (ii) | | |
| (C) | (iii) | (c) | (8)(a) |
| (D) | (iv) | (d) | (b) |
| (ii) | (b) | (e) | (c) |
| (A) | (i) | (f) | (d) |
| (B) | (ii) | **37.1** | **37.1** |
| (C) | (iii) | (5) | (5) |
| (D) | (iv) | (a) | "base period" |
| (E) | (v) | (i) | (a) |
| (F) | (vi) | (ii) | (b) |
| (b) | "Canadian newspaper or periodical" | (b) | "expenditure base" |
| (i) | (a) | (i) | (a) |
| (ii) | (b) | (ii) | (b) |
| (A) | (i) | (A) | (i) |
| (B) | (ii) | (I) | (A) |
| (iii) | (c) | (II) | (B) |
| (iv) | (d) | (B) | (ii) |
| (v) | (e) | (C) | (iii) |
| (A) | (i) | (c) | "qualified expenditure" |
| (B) | (ii) | | |
| (C) | (iii) | (i) | (a) |
| (I) | (A) | (ii) | (b) |
| (II) | (B) | (iii) | (c) |
| (III) | (C) | (d) | "research property" |
| (IV) | (D) | (e) | "scientific research and experimental development" |
| (V) | (E) | | |
| (VI) | (F) | — | 37.2 |
| (d) | "substantially the same" | **40** | 37.3 |
| | | | **40** |
| (e) | "United States" | — | (8) |
| (i) | (a) | **44** | **44** |
| (ii) | (b) | — | (8) |
| **20** | **20** | **47.1** | **47.1** |
| — | (1.1) | — | (26.1) |
| — | (1.2) | **54** | **54** |

lvii

## Table of Concordance

| Income Tax Act R.S.C. 1952, c. 148 as amended Section | R.S.C. 1985 5th Supplement as amended Section | Income Tax Act R.S.C. 1952, c. 148 as amended Section | R.S.C. 1985 5th Supplement as amended Section |
|---|---|---|---|
| (a) | "adjusted cost base" | (D) | (iv) |
| (i) | (a) | (I) | (A) |
| (ii) | (b) | (II) | (B) |
| (iii) | (c) | (iv) | (d) |
| (iv) | (d) | (v) | (e) |
| (b) | "capital property" | (vi) | (f) |
| (i) | (a) | (h) | "proceeds of disposition" |
| (ii) | (b) |  |  |
| (c) | "disposition" | (i) | (a) |
| (i) | (a) | (ii) | (b) |
| (ii) | (b) | (iii) | (c) |
| (A) | (i) | (iv) | (d) |
| (B) | (ii) | (v) | (e) |
| (C) | (iii) | (vi) | (f) |
| (D) | (iv) | (vii) | (g) |
| (iii) | (c) | (viii) | (h) |
| (iv) | (d) | (ix) | (i) |
| (v) | (e) | (x) | (j) |
| (A) | (i) | (xi) | (k) |
| (B) | (ii) | (i) | "superficial loss" |
| (C) | (iii) | (i) | (a) |
| (D) | (iv) | (ii) | (b) |
| (vi) | (f) | (iii) | (c) |
| (vii) | (g) | (iv) | (d) |
| (d) | "eligible capital property" | (v) | (e) |
|  |  | 56 | 56 |
| (e) | "listed personal property" | — | (1.1) |
|  |  | 59 | 59 |
| (i) | (a) | (3.4) | (3.4) |
| (ii) | (b) | (a) | "successor corporation" |
| (iii) | (c) | (b) | "stated percentage" |
| (iv) | (d) | (i) | (a) |
| (v) | (e) | (A) | (i) |
| (f) | "personal-use property" | (B) | (ii) |
| (i) | (a) | (C) | (iii) |
| (A) | (i) | (ii) | (b) |
| (B) | (ii) | (A) | (i) |
| (C) | (iii) | (B) | (ii) |
| (ii) | (b) | (C) | (iii) |
| (iii) | (c) | (c) | "specified predecessor" |
| (g) | "principal residence" | (i) | (a) |
| (i) | (a) | (ii) | (b) |
| (i.1) | (a.1) | — | 60.001 |
| (ii) | (b) | — | 60.02 |
| (A) | (i) | — | 60.11 |
| (B) | (ii) | 61 | 61 |
| (iii) | (c) | (4) | (4) |
| (A) | (i) | (a) | "annual annuity amount" |
| (B) | (ii) |  |  |
| (iii.1) | (c.1) | (b) | "income-averaging annuity contract" |
| (A) | (i) |  |  |
| (B) | (ii) | (i) | (a) |
| (I) | (A) | (A) | (i) |
| (II) | (B) | (I) | (A) |
| (C) | (iii) | (II) | (B) |

lviii

## Table of Concordance

| Income Tax Act R.S.C. 1952, c. 148 as amended Section | R.S.C. 1985 5th Supplement as amended Section | Income Tax Act R.S.C. 1952, c. 148 as amended Section | R.S.C. 1985 5th Supplement as amended Section |
|---|---|---|---|
| (B) | (ii) | (C) | (iii) |
| (ii) | (b) | (v.1) | (f) |
| (iii) | (c) | (vi) | (g) |
| (iv) | (d) | (vii) | (h) |
| (c) | "qualifying payment" | (c) | "Canadian resource property" |
| **63** | **63** | | |
| (3) | (3) | (i) | (a) |
| (a) | "child care expense" | (ii) | (b) |
| (i) | (a) | (A) | (i) |
| (A) | (i) | (B) | (ii) |
| (B) | (ii) | (iii) | (c) |
| (C) | (iii) | (iv) | (d) |
| (D) | (iv) | (v) | (e) |
| (ii) | (b) | (vi) | (f) |
| (A) | (i) | (vii) | (g) |
| (B) | (ii) | (d) | "drilling or exploration expense" |
| (C) | (iii) | | |
| (iii) | (c) | (i) | (a) |
| (A) | (i) | (ii) | (b) |
| (I) | (A) | (iii) | (c) |
| (II) | (B) | (g.2), (g.3) | "expense" |
| (B) | (ii) | (d.1) | "flow-through share" |
| (iv) | (d) | (i) | (a) |
| (b) | "earned income" | (ii) | (b) |
| (i) | (a) | (e) | "foreign exploration and development expenses" |
| (ii) | (b) | | |
| (iii) | (c) | | |
| (iv) | (d) | (i) | (a) |
| (c) | "eligible child" | (ii) | (b) |
| (i) | (a) | (iii) | (c) |
| (ii) | (b) | (iv) | (d) |
| (iii) | (c) | (v) | (e) |
| (iv) | (d) | (f) | "foreign resource property" |
| (d) | "supporting person" | | |
| (i) | (a) | (g) | "joint exploration corporation" |
| (ii) | (b) | | |
| (iii) | (c) | (g.11) | "original owner" |
| **66** | **66** | (i) | (a) |
| (15) | (15) | (ii) | (b) |
| (a) | "agreed portion" | (g.2), (g.3) | "outlay" |
| (i) | (a) | (g.4) | "predecessor owner" |
| (ii) | (b) | (i) | (a) |
| (a.1) | "assistance" | (ii) | (b) |
| (b) | "Canadian exploration and development expenses" | (iii) | (c) |
| | | (h) | "principal-business corporation" |
| (i) | (a) | (i) | (a) |
| (ii) | (b) | (ii) | (b) |
| (iii) | (c) | (iii) | (c) |
| (iv) | (d) | (iv) | (d) |
| (v) | (e) | (A) | (i) |
| (A) | (i) | (B) | (ii) |
| (B) | (ii) | (v) | (e) |
| | | (vi) | (f) |

lix

## Table of Concordance

| Income Tax Act R.S.C. 1952, c. 148 as amended Section | R.S.C. 1985 5th Supplement as amended Section | Income Tax Act R.S.C. 1952, c. 148 as amended Section | R.S.C. 1985 5th Supplement as amended Section |
|---|---|---|---|
| (vii) | (g) | (B) | (ii) |
| (h.01) | "production" | (C) | (iii) |
| (i) | (a) | (b) | "cumulative |
| (ii) | (b) |  | Canadian |
| (iii) | (c) |  | exploration |
| (iv) | (d) |  | expense" |
| (v) | (e) | (i) | A |
| (vi) | (f) | (ii) | B |
| (h.02) | "reserve amount" | (iii) | C |
|  | A | (iv) | D |
| (i) | (a) | (iv.1) | E |
| (ii) | (b) | (iv.2) | E.1 |
| after (ii) | B | (v) | F |
| (h.1) | "selling instrument" | (vi) | G |
| (i) | "shareholder | (vii) | H |
|  | corporation" | (A) | (a) |
| (i) | (a) | (B) | (b) |
| (ii) | (b) | (viii) | I |
| — | (15.1) | (ix) | J |
| **66.1** | **66.1** | (x) | K |
| (6) | (6) | (xi) | L |
| (a) | "Canadian exploration | (xii) | M |
|  | expense" | (c) | "restricted expense" |
| (i) | (a) | (i) | (a) |
| (i.1) | (b) | (ii) | (b) |
| (A) | (i) | (iii) | (c) |
| (B) | (ii) | (iv) | (d) |
| (ii) | (c) | (v) | (e) |
| (A) | (i) | (vi) | (f) |
| (B) | (ii) | (d) | "specified purpose" |
| (C) | (iii) | (i) | (a) |
| (D) | (iv) | (ii) | (b) |
| (ii.1) | (d) | (iii) | (c) |
| (A) | (i) | — | (6.1) |
| (B) | (ii) | **66.2** | **66.2** |
| (C) | (iii) | (5) | (5) |
| (D) | (iv) | (a) | "Canadian development |
| (I) | (A) |  | expense" |
| (II) | (B) | (i) | (a) |
| (ii.2) | (e) | (A) | (i) |
| (iii) | (f) | (B) | (ii) |
| (A) | (i) | (C) | (iii) |
| (B) | (ii) | (D) | (iv) |
| (C) | (iii) | (E) | (v) |
| (D) | (iv) | (i.1) | (b) |
| (E) | (v) | (ii) | (c) |
| (F) | (vi) | (A) | (i) |
| (iii.1) | (g) | (B) | (ii) |
| (A) | (i) | (ii.1) | (d) |
| (B) | (ii) | (A) | (i) |
| (iv) | (h) | (B) | (ii) |
| (v) | (i) | (iii) | (e) |
| (vi) | (j) | (iv) | (f) |
| (vii) | (k) | (v) | (g) |
| (A) | (i) | (vi) | (h) |

lx

## Table of Concordance

| Income Tax Act R.S.C. 1952, c. 148 as amended Section | R.S.C. 1985 5th Supplement as amended Section | Income Tax Act R.S.C. 1952, c. 148 as amended Section | R.S.C. 1985 5th Supplement as amended Section |
|---|---|---|---|
| (vii) | (i) | (v) | F |
| (A) | (i) | (A) | (a) |
| (B) | (ii) | (B) | (b) |
| (C) | (iii) | (I) | (i) |
| (b) | "cumulative Canadian development expense" | (II) | (ii) |
|  |  | (C) | (c) |
|  |  | (vi) | G |
| (i) | A | (vii) | H |
| (ii) | B | (viii) | I |
| (iii) | C | (ix) | J |
| (iii.1) | D | (c) | "disposition" and "proceeds of disposition" |
| (iii.2) | D.1 |  |  |
| (iv) | E | — | (5.1) |
| (v) | F | **66.7** | **66.7** |
| (A) | (a) | (4) | (4) |
| (B) | (b) | (b) | (b) |
| (I) | (i) | (i) | — |
| (II) | (ii) | (A) | (i) |
| (C) | (c) | (I) | (A) |
| (vi) | G | (II) | (B) |
| (vii) | H | (B) | after (B) |
| (vii.1) | I | (5) | (5) |
| (viii) | J | (b) | (b) |
| (ix) | K | (i) | — |
| (A) | (a) | (A) | (i) |
| (B) | (b) | (I) | (A) |
| (x) | L | (II) | (B) |
| (A) | (a) | (B) | after (B) |
| (B) | (b) | — | (18) |
| (xi) | M | **69** | **69** |
| (xii) | N | — | (12.1) |
| (xiii) | O | — | (12.2) |
| — | (5.1) | **70** | **70** |
| **66.4** | **66.4** | (10) | (10) |
| (5) | (5) | (a) | "child" |
| (a) | "Canadian oil and gas property expense" | (i) | (a) |
|  |  | (ii) | (b) |
| (i) | (a) | (iii) | (c) |
| (ii) | (b) | (b) | "share of the capital stock of a family farm corporation" |
| (iii) | (c) |  |  |
| (iv) | (d) |  |  |
| (v) | (e) | (i) | (a) |
| (A) | (i) | (A) | (i) |
| (B) | (ii) | (B) | (ii) |
| (C) | (iii) | (C) | (iii) |
| (b) | "cumulative Canadian oil and gas property expense" | (D) | (iv) |
|  |  | (ii) | (b) |
|  |  | (iii) | (c) |
| (i) | A | (c) | "interest in a family farm partnership" |
| (ii) | B |  |  |
| (iii) | C | (i) | (a) |
| (iii.1) | D | (A) | (i) |
| (iii.2) | D.1 | (B) | (ii) |
| (iv) | E | (C) | (iii) |

lxi

## Table of Concordance

| Income Tax Act R.S.C. 1952, c. 148 as amended Section | R.S.C. 1985 5th Supplement as amended Section | Income Tax Act R.S.C. 1952, c. 148 as amended Section | R.S.C. 1985 5th Supplement as amended Section |
|---|---|---|---|
| (D) | (iv) | (III) | (C) |
| (ii) | (b) | (B) | (ii) |
| (iii) | (c) | (C) | (iii) |
| — | (11) | (D) | (iv) |
| (11) | (12) | (E) | (v) |
| 73 | 73 | (F) | (vi) |
| — | (6) | (G) | (vii) |
| 74.3 | 74.3 | (iv) | (d) |
| — | (2) | (A) | (i) |
| 74.4 | 74.4 | (B) | (ii) |
| (1) | (1) | (v) | (e) |
| — | "designated person" | (b.1) | "designated property" |
| 80.4 | 80.4 | (i) | (a) |
| (7) | (7) | (A) | (i) |
| (a) | "home purchase loan" | (B) | (ii) |
| (i) | (a) | (ii) | (b) |
| (ii) | (b) | (iii) | (c) |
| (iii) | (c) | (iv) | (d) |
| (b) | "prescribed rate" | (c) | "paid-up capital" |
| (i) | (a) | (i) | (a) |
| (ii) | (b) | (ii) | (b) |
| (iii) | (c) | (A) | (i) |
| 82 | 82 | (B) | (ii) |
| — | (1.1) | (C) | (iii) |
| 87 | 87 | (D) | (iv) |
| — | (2.01) | (E) | (v) |
| 88 | 88 | (iii) | (c) |
| — | (1.41) | (f) | "private corporation" |
| 89 | 89 | (i) | (a) |
| (1) | (1) | (ii) | (b) |
| (a) | "Canadian corporation" | (g) | "public corporation" |
| (i) | (a) | (i) | (a) |
| (ii) | (b) | (ii) | (b) |
| (b) | "capital dividend account" | (A) | (i) |
|  | (a) | (B) | (ii) |
| (i) | (i) | (iii) | (c) |
| (A) | (A) | (A) | (i) |
| (I) | (B) | (B) | (ii) |
| (II) | (C) | (i) | "taxable Canadian corporation" |
| (III) | (I) |  |  |
| 1. | (II) | (i) | (a) |
| 2. | (III) | (ii) | (b) |
| 3. | (ii) | (j) | "taxable dividend" |
| (B) | (A) | (i) | (a) |
| (I) | (B) | (ii) | (b) |
| (II) | (C) | — | (1.01) |
| (III) | (I) | 94.1 | 94.1 |
| 1. | (II) | (2) | (2) |
| 2. | (III) | (a) | "designated cost" |
| 3. | (b) | (i) | A |
| (ii) | (c) | (ii) | B |
| (iii) | (i) | (iii) | C |
| (A) | (A) | (iv) | D |
| (I) | (B) | (b) | "non-resident entity" |
| (II) |  | — | (3) |

lxii

## Table of Concordance

| Income Tax Act R.S.C. 1952, c. 148 as amended Section | R.S.C. 1985 5th Supplement as amended Section | Income Tax Act R.S.C. 1952, c. 148 as amended Section | R.S.C. 1985 5th Supplement as amended Section |
|---|---|---|---|
| **95** | **95** | (i) | (a) |
| (1) | (1) | (ii) | (b) |
| (a) | "controlled foreign affiliate" | (c) | "relevant cost base" |
| (i) | (a) | — | (4.1) |
| (ii) | (b) | **102** | **102** |
| (iii) | (c) | (a) | (1) |
| (iv) | (d) | (b) | (2) |
| (v) | (e) | **108** | **108** |
| (a.1) | "excluded property" | (1) | (1) |
| (i) | (a) | (a) | "accumulating income" |
| (ii) | (b) | (i) | (a) |
| (iii) | (c) | (ii) | (b) |
| (iv) | (d) | (A) | (i) |
| (v) | (e) | (B) | (ii) |
| (A) | (i) | (C) | (iii) |
| (B) | (ii) | (iii) | (c) |
| (b) | "foreign accrual property income" | (b) | "beneficiary" |
| (i) | A | (c) | "capital interest" |
| (A) | (a) | (i) | (a) |
| (B) | (b) | (ii) | (b) |
| (C) | (c) | (d) | "cost amount" |
| (D) | (d) | (i) | (a) |
| (ii) | B | (A) | (i) |
| (ii.1) | C | (B) | (ii) |
| (A) | (a) | (C) | (iii) |
| (B) | (b) | (ii) | (b) |
| (iii) | D | A | A |
| (iv) | E | (I) | (i) |
| (v) | F | (II) | (ii) |
| (c) | "foreign accrual tax" | (III) | (iii) |
| (i) | (a) | B | B |
| (A) | (i) | C | C |
| (B) | (ii) | D | D |
| (ii) | (b) | (d.1) | "eligible real property gain" |
| (d) | "foreign affiliate" | (d.11) | "eligible real property loss" |
| (e) | "participating percentage" | (d.12) | "excluded property" |
| (i) | (a) | (d.2) | "eligible taxable capital gains" |
| (ii) | (b) | (i) | (a) |
| (A) | (i) | (ii) | (b) |
| (B) | (ii) | (A) | A |
| (f) | "relevant tax factor" | (B) | B |
| (i) | (a) | (e) | "income interest" |
| (ii) | (b) | (f) | "inter vivos trust" |
| (f.1) | "surplus entitlement percentage" | (f.1) | "non-qualifying real property" |
| (g) | "taxation year" | (i) | (a) |
| (4) | (4) | (ii) | (b) |
| (a) | "direct equity percentage" | (f.2) | "pre-1972 spousal trust" |
| (i) | (a) | (i) | (a) |
| (ii) | (b) | (ii) | (b) |
| (b) | "equity percentage" | | |

lxiii

# Table of Concordance

| Income Tax Act R.S.C. 1952, c. 148 as amended Section | R.S.C. 1985 5th Supplement as amended Section | Income Tax Act R.S.C. 1952, c. 148 as amended Section | R.S.C. 1985 5th Supplement as amended Section |
|---|---|---|---|
| (g) | "preferred beneficiary" | (ii) | (b) |
| (i) | (a) | (iii) | B |
| (ii) | (b) | (b.2) | "pre-1986 capital loss balance" |
| (iii) | (c) | (i) | A |
| (g.1) | "qualified farm property" | (A) | F |
| | | (B) | G |
| (g.2) | "qualified small business corporation share" | (ii) | B |
| | | | H |
| | | (A) | (a) |
| (h) | "settlor" | (B) | (b) |
| (i) | (a) | (C) | I |
| (ii) | (b) | (iii) | C |
| (A) | (i) | (iv) | D |
| (B) | (ii) | (v) | E |
| (i) | "testamentary trust" | (c) | (9) |
| (i) | (a) | (i) | (a) |
| (ii) | (b) | (ii) | (b) |
| (iii) | (c) | (9) | (10) |
| (A) | (i) | (10) | (11) |
| (B) | (ii) | **113** | **113** |
| (j) | "trust" | (3) | (3) |
| pre (i) | pre (f) | (a) | "relevant tax factor" |
| (i) | (f) | (b) | "non-business-income tax" |
| (i.1) | (g) | | |
| after (i.1) | pre (a) | **115** | **115** |
| (ii) | (a) | — | (6) |
| (iii) | (b) | **116** | **116** |
| (iv) | (c) | — | (7) |
| (v) | (d) | **118.1** | **118.1** |
| (vi) | (e) | (1) | (1) |
| | | "total cultural gifts" | "total cultural gifts" |
| **111** | **111** | (d) | (c) |
| — | (7.11) | (e) | (d) |
| (8) | (8) | **120** | **120** |
| (a) | "net capital loss" | (4) | (4) |
| (i) | (a) | (a) | "income earned in the year in a province" |
| (A) | A | | |
| (B) | B | | "tax otherwise payable under this Part" |
| (ii) | (b) | (c) | |
| (A) | (i) | | (a) |
| (B) | (ii) | (i) | (i) |
| (b) | "non-capital loss" | (A) | (ii) |
| (i) | A | (B) | (b) |
| (A) | E | (ii) | |
| (B) | F | **122.3** | **122.3** |
| (ii) | B | (2) | (2) |
| (iii) | C | (a) | "specified employer" |
| (iv) | D | (i) | (a) |
| (v) | D.1 | (ii) | (b) |
| (b.1) | "farm loss" | (iii) | (c) |
| (i) | A | (b) | "tax otherwise payable under this Part for the year" |
| | (a) | | |
| (A) | (i) | | |
| (B) | (ii) | **124** | **124** |

lxiv

# Table of Concordance

| Income Tax Act R.S.C. 1952, c. 148 as amended Section | R.S.C. 1985 5th Supplement as amended Section | Income Tax Act R.S.C. 1952, c. 148 as amended Section | R.S.C. 1985 5th Supplement as amended Section |
|---|---|---|---|
| (4) | (4) | (i) | processing" |
| (a) | "taxable income earned in the year in a province" | (ii) | (a) |
|  | | (iii) | (b) |
| (b) | "province" | (iv) | (c) |
| **125** | **125** | (v) | (d) |
| (7) | (7) | (vi) | (e) |
| (a) | "active business carried on by a corporation" | (vi.1) | (f) |
|  | | (vi.2) | (g) |
| (b) | "Canadian-controlled private corporation" | (vii) | (h) |
|  | | (viii) | (i) |
| (c) | "income of the corporation for the year from an active business" | (ix) | (j) |
|  | | (x) | (k) |
|  | | (A) | (l) |
|  | | (B) | (i) |
| (i) | (a) | **126** | (ii) |
| (ii) | (b) | (7) | **126** |
| (d) | "personal services business" | (a) | (7) |
|  | | (i) | "business-income tax" |
| (i) | (a) | (ii) | (a) |
| (ii) | (b) | (c) | (b) |
| (iii) | (c) | | "non-business-income tax" |
| (iv) | (d) | (i) | (a) |
| (e) | "specified investment business" | (ii) | (b) |
|  | | (iii) | (c) |
| (i) | (a) | (iv) | (d) |
| (ii) | (b) | (v) | (e) |
| (f) | "specified partnership income" | (vi) | (f) |
|  | | (vii) | (g) |
| (i) | A | (viii) | (h) |
| (A) | (a) | (ix) | (i) |
| (I) | G | (d) | "tax for the year otherwise payable under this Part" |
| (II) | H |  | |
| (B) | (b) | (i) | (a) |
| (I) | M | (A) | A |
| (II) | (i) | (B) | B |
| (III) | (ii) | (ii) | (b) |
| (IV) | K | (iii) | (c) |
|  | L | (e) | "unused foreign tax credit" |
| (ii) | B | | |
| (A) | (a) | (i) | A |
| (B) | (b) | (ii) | B |
| (I) | N | (iii) | C |
| (II) | O | **127** | **127** |
| (g) | "specified partnership loss" | (2) | (2) |
|  | A | (a) | "income for the year from logging operations in the province" |
| (i) | B | | |
| (ii) | | | "logging tax" |
| **125.1** | **125.1** | (b) | |
| (3) | (3) | **127.1** | **127.1** |
| (a) | "Canadian manufacturing and processing profits" | — | (2.1) |
|  | | **127.2** | **127.2** |
| (b) | "manufacturing or | (6) | (6) |

lxv

## Table of Concordance

| Income Tax Act R.S.C. 1952, c. 148 as amended Section | R.S.C. 1985 5th Supplement as amended Section | Income Tax Act R.S.C. 1952, c. 148 as amended Section | R.S.C. 1985 5th Supplement as amended Section |
|---|---|---|---|
| (a) | "share-purchase tax credit" | (iv) | (d) |
| (i) | A | (c) | "qualifying taxed capital gains" |
| (ii) | B | (i) | (a) |
| (iii) | C | (ii) | (b) |
| (b) | "unused share-purchase tax credit" | (iii) | (c) |
|  |  | (iv) | (d) |
|  |  | (v) | (e) |
| (i) | A | (d) | "non-qualifying real property" |
| (ii) | B |  |  |
| (iii) | C |  |  |
| 127.3 | 127.3 | 131 | 131 |
| (2) | (2) | (6) | (6) |
| (a) | "scientific research and experimental development tax credit" | (a) | "capital gains redemptions" |
|  |  | (i) |  |
|  |  | (A) | C |
|  |  | (B) | D |
|  | A |  | K |
| (i) | (a) |  | L |
| (ii) | (b) |  | M |
| (iii) | (c) |  | N |
| (iv) | (d) | (ii) | A |
| (v) | (e) | (iii) | B |
| — | B | (b) | "capital gains dividend account" |
| (b) | "unused scientific research and experimental development tax credit" | (i) | (a) |
|  |  | (ii) | (b) |
|  |  | (iii) | (c) |
|  |  | (iv) | (d) |
|  |  | (v) | (e) |
| (i) | A | (vi) | (f) |
| (ii) | B | (vii) | (g) |
| (iii) | C | (c) | "non-qualifying real property capital gains dividend account" |
| 129 | 129 |  |  |
| (4) | (4) |  |  |
| (a) | "Canadian investment income" |  |  |
|  |  | (i) | (a) |
| (i) | — | (ii) | (b) |
| (A) | A | (iii) | (c) |
| (I) | K | (iv) | (d) |
| (II) | L | (c.1) | "non-qualifying real property" |
| (B) | — |  |  |
| (I) | M | (i) | (a) |
| (II) | N | (ii) | (b) |
| (ii) | B | (A) | (i) |
| (iii) | C | (B) | (ii) |
| (b) | "foreign investment income" | (iii) | (c) |
| 130.1 | 130.1 | (A) | (i) |
| (9) | (9) | (B) | (ii) |
| (a) | "liabilities" | (iv) | (d) |
| (b) | "non-qualifying taxed capital gains" | (v) | (e) |
|  |  | (vi) | (f) |
| (i) | (a) | (d) | "refundable capital gains tax on hand" |
| (ii) | (b) |  |  |
| (iii) | (c) | (i) | A |

lxvi

## Table of Concordance

| Income Tax Act R.S.C. 1952, c. 148 as amended Section | R.S.C. 1985 5th Supplement as amended Section | Income Tax Act R.S.C. 1952, c. 148 as amended Section | R.S.C. 1985 5th Supplement as amended Section |
|---|---|---|---|
| (A) | (a) | (D) | (iv) |
| (B) | (b) | (E) | (v) |
| (C) | (c) | (iii) | (c) |
| (ii) | B | (iv) | (d) |
| **132** | **132** | (A) | (i) |
| (4) | (4) | (B) | (ii) |
| (a) | "capital gains redemptions" | (v) | (e) |
|  |  | (vi) | (f) |
| (i) |  | (e) | "taxable dividend" |
| (A) | C | (9) | (9) |
| (B) | D | (a) | "allowable refundable tax on hand" |
|  | K |  |  |
|  | L | (i) | A |
|  | M | (ii) | B |
|  | N | (ii.1) | C |
|  | A | (iii) | D |
| (ii) | B | (A) | M |
| (iii) | "refundable capital gains tax on hand" | (B) | L |
| (b) |  | — | N |
|  | A | (iv) | E |
| (i) | (a) | (v) | F |
| (A) | (b) | (b) | "cumulative taxable income" |
| (B) | (c) |  |  |
| (C) | B | (i) | A |
| (ii) |  | (ii) | B |
| **133** | **133** | — | L |
| (8) | (8) | (A) | M |
| (a) | "allowable refund" | (B) | N |
| pre. (i) | C | (iii) | C |
| (i) | A | — | P |
| (ii) | B | (A) | Q |
| (b) | "Canadian property" | (B) | R |
| (i) | (a) | (iv) | D |
| (ii) | (b) | (v) | E |
| (c) | "capital gains dividend account" | **135** | **135** |
| pre. (i) | A | (4) | (4) |
| (i) | (a) | (a) | "allocation in proportion to patronage" |
| (ii) | (b) |  | (a) |
| (iii) | B | (i) | (i) |
| (iv) | (a) | (A) | (ii) |
| (v) | (c) | (B) | (b) |
|  | M | (ii) | "consumer goods or services" |
|  | N | (b) | "customer" |
| (d) | "non-resident-owned investment corporation" | (c) | "income of the taxpayer attributable to business done with members" |
|  | (a) | (d) |  |
| (i) | (i) |  |  |
| (A) | (ii) |  |  |
| (B) | (iii) |  | "member" |
| (C) | (b) | (e) | "non-member customer" |
| (ii) | (i) | (f) | "payment" |
| (A) | (ii) | (g) |  |
| (B) | (iii) | (i) | (a) |
| (C) |  |  |  |

lxvii

## Table of Concordance

| Income Tax Act R.S.C. 1952, c. 148 as amended Section | R.S.C. 1985 5th Supplement as amended Section | Income Tax Act R.S.C. 1952, c. 148 as amended Section | R.S.C. 1985 5th Supplement as amended Section |
|---|---|---|---|
| (ii) | (b) | (A) | (i) |
| (iii) | (c) | (B) | (ii) |
| **137** | **137** | (C) | (iii) |
| (6) | (6) | (iii) | (c) |
| (a) | "allocation in proportion to borrowing" | (iv) | (d) |
|  | (a) | — | **137.2** |
|  | (b) | **138** | **138** |
| (i) | "bonus interest payment" | (12) | (12) |
| (ii) | (a) | (a) | "accumulated 1968 deficit" |
| (a.1) | (b) |  | (a) |
| (i) | "credit union" | (i) | (b) |
| (ii) | (a) | (ii) | (i) |
| (b) | (i) | (A) | (ii) |
| (i) | (ii) | (B) | (iii) |
| (A) | (iii) | (C) | "amount payable" |
| (B) | (iv) | (b.1) | "Canada security" |
| (C) | (v) | (c) | "cost" |
| (D) | (vi) | (d) | "gross investment revenue" |
| (E) | (vii) | (e) |  |
| (F) | (b) | (i) | A |
| (G) | (i) | (ii) | B |
| (ii) | (ii) | (iii) | C |
| (A) | (iii) | (iv) | D |
| (B) | (c) | (v) | E |
| (C) | "maximum cumulative reserve" | (vi) | F |
| (iii) |  | (e.1) | "interest" |
| (c) | A | (f) | "life insurance policy" |
|  | B | (g) | "life insurance policy in Canada" |
| (i) | "member" |  | "maximum tax actuarial reserve" |
| (ii) |  | (h) |  |
| (d) | **137.1** | (j) | "non-segregated property" |
| **137.1** | (5) |  |  |
| (5) | "deposit insurance corporation" | (k) | "participating life insurance policy" |
| (a) |  | (k.1) | "policy loan" |
|  | (a) | (l) | "property used by it in the year in, or held by it in the year in the course of" |
| (i) | (i) |  |  |
| (A) | (A) |  |  |
| (I) | (B) |  |  |
| (II) | (ii) |  |  |
| (B) | (A) | (l.1) | "qualified related corporation" |
| (I) | (B) |  |  |
| (II) | (b) | (m) | "relevant authority" |
| (ii) | "member institution" | (i) | (a) |
| (b) | (a) | (ii) | (b) |
| (i) | (b) | (n) | "segregated fund" |
| (ii) | "investment property" | (o) | "surplus funds derived from operations" |
| (c) | (a) |  |  |
| (i) | (i) | (i) | A |
| (A) | (ii) | (i.1) | B |
| (B) | (iii) | (ii) | C |
| (C) | (iv) | (iii) | D |
| (D) | (v) | (iv) | E |
| (E) | (b) | (v) | F |
| (ii) |  | (vi) | G |

lxviii

# Table of Concordance

| Income Tax Act R.S.C. 1952, c. 148 as amended Section | R.S.C. 1985 5th Supplement as amended Section | Income Tax Act R.S.C. 1952, c. 148 as amended Section | R.S.C. 1985 5th Supplement as amended Section |
|---|---|---|---|
| (vii) | H | (B) | S |
| | M | (iii) | C |
| | N | (A) | T |
| (p) | (15) | (B) | U |
| (q) | (12) | (v) | "1975-76 excess policy reserves" |
| | "1975 branch accounting election deficiency" | (i) | A |
| (i) | A | (ii) | B |
| (A) | (a) | (w) | "1975-76 excess additional group term reserve" |
| (B) | (b) | | |
| (ii) | B | (i) | A |
| (iii) | C | (ii) | B |
| (iv) | D | — | 142.1 |
| (A) | (a) | 143 | 143 |
| (B) | (b) | (4) | (4) |
| (v) | E | (a) | "adult" |
| | P | (b) | "congregation" |
| (A) | (a) | (c) | "family" |
| (B) | (b) | (i) | (a) |
| after cl. (B) | Q | (ii) | (b) |
| (vi) | F | (d) | "member of a congregation" |
| (vii) | G | | |
| (r) | "1975-76 excess policy dividend deduction" | (i) | (a) |
| | | (ii) | (b) |
| (i) | A | (e) | "religious organization" |
| (A) | P | | |
| (B) | Q | (f) | "total charitable gifts", "total Crown gifts", "total cultural gifts" |
| (ii) | B | | |
| (A) | R | | |
| (B) | S | | |
| (iii) | C | | |
| (A) | T | 145 | 145 |
| (B) | U | (1) | (1) |
| (s) | "1975-76 excess policy dividend reserve" | (a) | "registered supplementary unemployment benefit plan" |
| (i) | A | | |
| (A) | (a) | | |
| (B) | (b) | | |
| (C) | (c) | | |
| (D) | (d) | (b) | "supplementary unemployment benefit plan" |
| (E) | (e) | | |
| (ii) | B | 146 | 146 |
| (t) | "1975-76 excess investment reserve" | (1) | (1) |
| | | (a) | "annuitant" |
| (i) | A | (i) | (a) |
| (ii) | B | (ii) | (b) |
| (u) | "1975-76 excess capital cost allowance" | (b) | "benefit" |
| | | (i) | (a) |
| (i) | A | (ii) | (b) |
| (A) | P | (iii) | (c) |
| (I) | (a) | (iv) | (d) |
| (II) | (b) | (v) | (e) |
| (B) | Q | (vi) | (f) |
| (ii) | B | (c) | "earned income" |
| (A) | R | (i) | (a) |

lxix

## Table of Concordance

| Income Tax Act R.S.C. 1952, c. 148 as amended Section | R.S.C. 1985 5th Supplement as amended Section | Income Tax Act R.S.C. 1952, c. 148 as amended Section | R.S.C. 1985 5th Supplement as amended Section |
|---|---|---|---|
| (A) | (i) | (k) | "spousal plan" |
| (B) | (ii) | (i) | (a) |
| (C) | (iii) | (A) | (i) |
| (ii) | (b) | (B) | (ii) |
| (ii.1) | (b.1) | (ii) | (b) |
| (iii) | (c) | (l) | "unused RRSP deduction room" |
| (A) | (i) | | (a) |
| (B) | (ii) | (i) | (b) |
| (iv) | (d) | (ii) | (i) |
| (A) | (i) | (A) | (ii) |
| (B) | (ii) | (B) | (A) |
| (v) | (e) | (I) | (B) |
| (A) | (i) | (II) | |
| (B) | (ii) | **146.1** | **146.1** |
| (vi) | (f) | (1) | (1) |
| (vii) | (g) | (a) | "beneficiary" |
| (c.1) | "issuer" | (b) | "educational assistance payment" |
| (d) | "maturity" | | |
| (d.1) | "net past service pension adjustment" | (c) | "education savings plan" |
| (e) | "non-qualified investment" | (c.1) | "post-secondary educational institution" |
| (f) | "premium" | | |
| (i) | (a) | (i) | (a) |
| (ii) | (b) | (ii) | (b) |
| (g) | "qualified investment" | (d) | "pre-1972 income" |
| (i) | (a) | (d.1) | "qualifying educational program" |
| (ii) | (b) | | |
| (iii) | (c) | (e) | "refund of payments" |
| (iv) | (d) | (f) | "registered education savings plan" |
| (g.1) | "RRSP deduction limit" | | |
| (g.2) | "RRSP dollar limit" | (g) | "tax-paid-income" |
| (h) | "refund of premiums" | (i) | A |
| (i) | (a) | (ii) | — |
| (ii) | (b) | (A) | B |
| (i) | "registered retirement savings plan" | (B) | C |
| | | (h) | "trust" |
| (i.1) | "retirement income" | (i) | (a) |
| (i) | (a) | (ii) | (b) |
| (A) | (i) | (iii) | (c) |
| (B) | (ii) | (iv) | (d) |
| (ii) | (b) | (v) | (e) |
| (A) | (i) | **146.2** | **146.2** |
| (B) | (ii) | — | (23) |
| (j) | "retirement savings plan" | **146.3** | **146.3** |
| | | (1) | (1) |
| (i) | (a) | (a) | "annuitant" |
| (ii) | (b) | (i) | (a) |
| (A) | (i) | (ii) | (b) |
| (B) | (ii) | (iii) | (c) |
| (C) | (iii) | (b) | "carrier" |
| (I) | (A) | (i) | (a) |
| (II) | (B) | | |

lxx

## Table of Concordance

| Income Tax Act R.S.C. 1952, c. 148 as amended Section | R.S.C. 1985 5th Supplement as amended Section | Income Tax Act R.S.C. 1952, c. 148 as amended Section | R.S.C. 1985 5th Supplement as amended Section |
|---|---|---|---|
| (ii) | (b) | (c.1) | "interest" |
| (iii) | (c) | (e) | "policy loan" |
| (iv) | (d) | (e.1) | "premium" |
| (b.1) | "minimum amount" | (i) | (a) |
| (i) | (a) | (ii) | (b) |
| (ii) | (b) | (iii) | (c) |
| (iii) | (c) | (A) | (i) |
| (c) | "property held" | (B) | (ii) |
| (d) | "qualified investment" | (C) | (iii) |
| (i) | (a) | (D) | (iv) |
| (ii) | (b) | (E) | (v) |
| (iii) | (c) | (F) | (vi) |
| (e) | "registered retirement income fund" | (G) | (vii) |
| | | (e.2) | "proceeds of the disposition" |
| (f) | "retirement income fund" | (i) | (a) |
| (i) | (a) | (A) | A |
| (ii) | (b) | — | B |
| | | (B) | C |
| **148** | **148** | (I) | (i) |
| (9) | (9) | (II) | (ii) |
| (a) | "adjusted cost basis" | (III) | (iii) |
| (i) | A | (ii) | (b) |
| (ii) | B | (A) | (i) |
| (iii) | C | (B) | (ii) |
| (iii.1) | D | (iii) | (c) |
| (iv) | E | (iv) | (d) |
| (v) | F | (A) | (i) |
| (v.1) | G | (B) | (ii) |
| (v.2) | G.1 | (e.3) | "relevant authority" |
| (vi) | H | (f) | "tax anniversary date" |
| (vi.1) | I | (g) | "value" |
| (vii) | J | (i) | (a) |
| (viii) | K | (ii) | (b) |
| — | L | — | (9.1) |
| (ix) | (a) | **149.1** | **149.1** |
| (x) | (b) | (1) | (1) |
| (xi) | (c) | (a) | "charitable foundation" |
| (a.1) | "amount payable" | (b) | "charitable organization" |
| (b) | "cash surrender value" | | |
| (b.1) | "child" | (i) | (a) |
| (c) | "disposition" | (ii) | (b) |
| (i) | (a) | (iii) | (c) |
| (ii) | (b) | (iv) | (d) |
| (iii) | (c) | (c) | "charitable purposes" |
| (iv) | (d) | (d) | "charity" |
| (iv.1) | (e) | (e) | "disbursement quota" |
| (v) | (f) | (i) | A |
| (vi) | (g) | (A) | (a) |
| (vii) | (h) | (B) | (b) |
| (viii) | (i) | (C) | (c) |
| (ix) | (j) | — | B |
| (A) | (i) | (ii) | (a) |
| (B) | (ii) | (iii) | (b) |
| (x) | (k) | (iv) | C |

lxxi

## Table of Concordance

| Income Tax Act R.S.C. 1952, c. 148 as amended Section | R.S.C. 1985 5th Supplement as amended Section | Income Tax Act R.S.C. 1952, c. 148 as amended Section | R.S.C. 1985 5th Supplement as amended Section |
|---|---|---|---|
| (A) | D | (B) | (ii) |
| (B) | E | (a.1) | "excluded share" |
| (C) | F | (i) | (a) |
| (D) | (a) | (ii) | (b) |
| (v) | (b) | (A) | (i) |
| (A) | G | (B) | (ii) |
| (B) | (a) | (a.2) | "non-participating share" |
| (e.1) | (b) | (i) | (a) |
| | "non-qualified investment" | (A) | (i) |
| (i) | (a) | (B) | (ii) |
| (A) | (i) | (ii) | (b) |
| (I) | (A) | (a.3) | "paid-up capital value" |
| (II) | (B) | — | A |
| (III) | (C) | — | B |
| (B) | (ii) | (b) | "initial base" |
| (ii) | (b) | (i) | (a) |
| (iii) | (c) | (ii) | (b) |
| (iv) | (d) | (c) | "initial non-qualified investment" |
| (v) | (e) | | |
| (vi) | (f) | | (a) |
| (f) | "private foundation" | (i) | (b) |
| (g) | "public foundation" | (ii) | "non-qualified investment" |
| (i) | (a) | (d) | |
| (A) | (i) | | "qualified investment" |
| (B) | (ii) | (e) | (a) |
| (ii) | (b) | (i) | (b) |
| (A) | (i) | (ii) | (c) |
| (B) | (ii) | (iii) | (d) |
| (h) | "qualified donee" | (iv) | (e) |
| (j) | "related business" | (vi) | (i) |
| (k) | "specified gift" | (A) | (ii) |
| (l) | "taxation year" | (B) | (A) |
| 152 | 152 | (I) | (B) |
| — | (1.111) | (II) | |
| 172 | 172 | (vii) | (f) |
| — | (6) | (viii) | (g) |
| — | 187.7 | (ix) | (h) |
| 188 | 188 | (x) | (i) |
| (5) | (5) | (f) | "revoked plan" |
| (a) | "net asset amount" | 204.9 | 204.9 |
| — | A | — | (1.1) |
| — | B | 211 | 211 |
| (b) | "net value" | (1) | (1) |
| — | A | "participating life insurance policy etc." | "participating life insurance policy" |
| — | B | | "policy loan" |
| 194 | 194 | | "segregated fund" |
| (3) | (3) | — | 218.1 |
| — | "debt obligation" | 219 | 219 |
| 204 | 204 | (7) | (7) |
| (a) | "equity share" | (a) | "attributed surplus for the year" |
| (i) | (a) | | "Canadian investment |
| (A) | (i) | | |
| (B) | (ii) | | |
| (ii) | (b) | | |
| (A) | (i) | | |

lxxii

Table of Concordance

| Income Tax Act R.S.C. 1952, c. 148 as amended Section | R.S.C. 1985 5th Supplement as amended Section | Income Tax Act R.S.C. 1952, c. 148 as amended Section | R.S.C. 1985 5th Supplement as amended Section |
|---|---|---|---|
| (b) | fund" "accumulated 1968 deficit" | or "insurer" "life insurance corporation" | "insurer" "life insurance corporation" |
| (b.1) | "maximum tax actuarial reserves" | or "life insurer" | "life insurer" |
| (b.2) | "surplus funds derived from operations" | — | "Part VII refund" |
| (c) | "tax deferred account" | — | "Part VIII refund" |
| (i) | A | — | "qualifying share" |
| (ii) | B | — | "refundable Part VII tax on hand" |
| — | 223.1 | — | "refundable Part VIII tax on hand" |
| — | (1) | — | "scientific research and experimental development financing contract" |
| — | (2) | | |
| 230.1 | 230.1 | | |
| — | (7) | — | "scientific research and experimental development tax credit" |
| 232 | 232 | | |
| (1) | (1) | | |
| (a) | "judge" | | |
| (b) | "custodian" | — | "share-purchase tax credit" |
| (c) | "lawyer" | | |
| (d) | "officer" | — | "unused scientific research and experimental development tax credit" |
| (e) | "solicitor-client privilege" | | |
| — | 237.2 | | |
| 248 | 248 | — | "unused share-purchase tax credit" |
| (1) | (1) | | |
| "corporation" | "corporation" | | |
| | "corporation incorporated in Canada" | 251 (4) | 251 (4) |
| | | (a) | "related group" |
| "insurance corporation" | "insurance corporation" | (b) | "unrelated group" |

lxxiii

# OVERVIEW TABLE OF SECTIONS
## Income Tax Act

*(A detailed table of sections follows this overview.)*

1 — Short title

### PART I — INCOME TAX

**DIVISION A — LIABILITY FOR TAX**
2

**DIVISION B — COMPUTATION OF INCOME**
*Basic Rules*
3 and 4

**Subdivision a — Income or Loss from an Office or Employment**
*Basic Rules*
5
*Inclusions*
6 and 7
*Deductions*
8

**Subdivision b — Income or Loss from a Business or Property**
*Basic Rules*
9 to 11
*Inclusions*
12 to 17
*Deductions*
18 to 21
*Ceasing to Carry on Business*
22 to 25
*Special Cases*
26 to 37

**Subdivision c — Taxable Capital Gains and Allowable Capital Losses**
38 to 55

**Subdivision d — Other Sources of Income**
56 to 59.1

**Subdivision e — Deductions in Computing Income**
60 to 66.8

**Subdivision f — Rules Relating to Computation of Income**
67 to 80.5

**Subdivision g — Amounts Not Included in Computing Income**
81

**Subdivision h — Corporations Resident in Canada and Their Shareholders**
82 to 89

lxxv

Overview Table of Sections

**Subdivision i — Shareholders of Corporations Not Resident in Canada**
90 to 95

**Subdivision j — Partnerships and Their Members**
96 to 103

**Subdivision k — Trusts and Their Beneficiaries**
104 to 108

**Division C — COMPUTATION OF TAXABLE INCOME**
110 to 114.2

**Division D — TAXABLE INCOME EARNED IN CANADA BY NON-RESIDENTS**
115 to 116

**Division E — COMPUTATION OF TAX**

**Subdivision a — Rules Applicable to Individuals**
117
*Annual Adjustment of Deductions and Other Amounts*
117.1 to 122.51

**Subdivision a.1 — Child Tax Benefit**
122.6 to 122.64

**Subdivision b — Rules Applicable to Corporations**
123 to 125.3
*Canadian Film or Video Production Tax Credit*
125.4
*Film or Video Production Services Tax Credit*
125.5

**Subdivision c — Rules Applicable to All Taxpayers**
126 to 127.41

**Division E.1 — MINIMUM TAX**
127.5 to 127.55

**Division F — SPECIAL RULES APPLICABLE IN CERTAIN CIRCUMSTANCES**
*Bankruptcies*
128
*Changes in Residence*
128.1 to 128.3
*Private Corporations*
129
*Investment Corporations*
130
*Mortgage Investment Corporations*
130.1
*Mutual Fund Corporations*
131
*Mutual Fund Trusts*
132 to 132.2
*Non-Resident-Owned Investment Corporations*
133 to 134.1
*Patronage Dividends*
135

*Cooperative Corporations*
136
*Credit Unions, Savings and Credit Unions and Deposit Insurance Corporations*
137 to 137.2
*Insurance Corporations*
138 to 141.1
*Financial Institutions*
142.2 to 142.6
*[Proposed] Conversion of Foreign Bank Affiliate to Branch*
142.7
*Communal Organizations*
143 and 143.1
*Cost of Tax Shelter Investments*
143.2

### Division G — DEFERRED AND OTHER SPECIAL INCOME ARRANGEMENTS
*Employees Profit Sharing Plans*
144
*Registered Supplementary Unemployment Benefit Plans*
145
*Registered Retirement Savings Plans*
146
*Home Buyers' Plan*
146.01
*Lifelong Learning Plan*
146.02
*Registered Education Savings Plans*
146.1
*Registered Home Ownership Savings Plans*
146.2
*Registered Retirement Income Funds*
146.3
*Deferred Profit Sharing Plans*
147
*Registered Pension Plans*
147.1 to 147.4
*Life Insurance Policies*
148
*Eligible Funeral Arrangements*
148.1

### Division H — EXEMPTIONS
*Miscellaneous Exemptions*
149
*Charities*
149.1

### Division I — RETURNS, ASSESSMENTS, PAYMENT AND APPEALS
*Returns*
150 and 150.1
*Estimate of Tax*

## Overview Table of Sections

151
*Assessment*
152
*Payment of Tax*
153 to 160.4
*Interest*
161
*Offset of Refund Interest and Arrears Interest*
161.1
*Penalties*
162 to 163.1
*Misrepresentation of a Tax Matter by a Third Party*
163.2
*Refunds*
164
*Objections to Assessments*
165
*General*
166 to 167
*Revocation of Registration of Certain Organizations and Associations*
168

**Division J — APPEALS TO THE TAX COURT OF CANADA AND THE FEDERAL COURT**
169 to 180

**PART I.1 — INDIVIDUAL SURTAX**

180.1

**PART I.2 — TAX ON OLD AGE SECURITY BENEFITS**

180.2

**PART I.3 — TAX ON LARGE CORPORATIONS**

181 to 181.71

**PART II — TOBACCO MANUFACTURERS' SURTAX**

182 and 183

**PART II.1 — TAX ON CORPORATE DISTRIBUTIONS**

183.1 and 183.2

**PART III — ADDITIONAL TAX ON EXCESSIVE ELECTIONS**

184 and 185

**PART IV — TAX ON TAXABLE DIVIDENDS RECEIVED BY PRIVATE CORPORATIONS**

186 to 187

**PART IV.1 — TAXES ON DIVIDENDS ON CERTAIN PREFERRED SHARES RECEIVED BY CORPORATIONS**

187.1 to 187.61

**PART V — TAX IN RESPECT OF REGISTERED CHARITIES**

187.7 to 189

## PART VI — TAX ON CAPITAL OF FINANCIAL INSTITUTIONS

190

*Calculation of Capital Tax*
190.1 to 190.17
*Administrative Provisions*
190.2 to 190.211

## PART VI.1 — TAX ON CORPORATIONS PAYING DIVIDENDS ON TAXABLE PREFERRED SHARES

191 to 191.4

## Part VII — REFUNDABLE TAX ON CORPORATIONS ISSUING QUALIFYING SHARES

192 and 193

## PART VIII — REFUNDABLE TAX ON CORPORATIONS IN RESPECT OF SCIENTIFIC RESEARCH AND EXPERIMENTAL DEVELOPMENT TAX CREDIT

194 and 195

## PART IX — TAX ON DEDUCTION UNDER SECTION 66.5

196

## PART X — TAXES ON DEFERRED PROFIT SHARING PLANS AND REVOKED PLANS

198 to 204

## PART X.1 — TAX IN RESPECT OF OVER-CONTRIBUTIONS TO DEFERRED INCOME PLANS

204.1 to 204.3

## PART X.2 — TAX IN RESPECT OF REGISTERED INVESTMENTS

204.4 to 204.7

## PART X.3 — REGISTERED LABOUR-SPONSORED VENTURE CAPITAL CORPORATIONS

204.8 to 204.87

## PART X.4 — TAX IN RESPECT OF OVERPAYMENTS TO REGISTERED EDUCATION SAVINGS PLANS

204.9 to 204.93

## PART X.5 — PAYMENTS UNDER REGISTERED EDUCATION SAVINGS PLANS

204.94

## PART XI — TAX IN RESPECT OF CERTAIN PROPERTY ACQUIRED BY TRUSTS, ETC., GOVERNED BY DEFERRED INCOME PLANS

205 to 207

## PART XI.1 — TAX IN RESPECT OF CERTAIN PROPERTY HELD BY TRUSTS GOVERNED BY DEFERRED INCOME PLANS

207.1 and 207.2

## PART XI.2 — TAX IN RESPECT OF DISPOSITIONS OF CERTAIN PROPERTY

207.3 to 207.4

## PART XI.3 — TAX IN RESPECT OF RETIREMENT COMPENSATION ARRANGEMENTS

207.5 to 207.7

## Overview Table of Sections

**PART XII — TAX IN RESPECT OF CERTAIN ROYALTIES, TAXES, LEASE RENTALS, ETC., PAID TO A GOVERNMENT BY A TAX EXEMPT PERSON**

208

**PART XII.1 — TAX ON CARVED-OUT INCOME**

209

**PART XII.2 — TAX ON DESIGNATED INCOME OF CERTAIN TRUSTS**

210 to 210.3

**PART XII.3 — TAX ON INVESTMENT INCOME OF LIFE INSURERS**

211 to 211.5

**PART XII.4 — TAX ON QUALIFYING ENVIRONMENTAL TRUSTS**

211.6

**XII.5 — RECOVERY OF LABOUR-SPONSORED FUNDS TAX CREDIT**

211.7 to 211.9

**XII.6 — TAX ON FLOW-THROUGH SHARES**

211.91

**XIII — TAX ON INCOME FROM CANADA OF NON-RESIDENT PERSONS**

212 to 218.1

**XIII.1 — [Proposed] ADDITIONAL TAX ON AUTHORIZED FOREIGN BANKS**

218.2

**XIV — ADDITIONAL TAX ON NON-RESIDENT CORPORATIONS**

219 to 219.3

**XV — ADMINISTRATION AND ENFORCEMENT**

*Administration*
220 to 221.2
*Collection*
222 to 229.1
*General*
230 to 237.2
*Offences and Punishment*
238 to 243
*Procedure and Evidence*
244

**XVI — TAX AVOIDANCE**

245 and 246

**XVI.1 — TRANSFER PRICING**

247

**XVII — INTERPRETATION**

248 to 260

# Detailed Table of Sections

## INCOME TAX ACT

1          Short title

### PART I — INCOME TAX
### DIVISION A — LIABILITY FOR TAX

2
| | |
|---|---|
| 2(1) | Tax payable by persons resident in Canada |
| 2(2) | Taxable income |
| 2(3) | Tax payable by non-resident persons |

### DIVISION B — COMPUTATION OF INCOME
#### Basic Rules

| | |
|---|---|
| 3 | Income for taxation year |
| 4 | |
| 4(1), (2) | Income or loss from a source or from sources in a place |
| 4(3) | Deductions applicable |
| 4(4) | [Repealed] |

#### Subdivision a — Income or Loss from an Office or Employment
#### Basic Rules

| | |
|---|---|
| 5 | |
| 5(1) | Income from office or employment |
| 5(2) | Loss from office or employment |

#### Inclusions

| | |
|---|---|
| 6 | |
| 6(1) | Amounts to be included as income from office or employment |
| 6(1)(a) | value of benefits |
| 6(1)(b) | personal or living expenses |
| 6(1)(c) | director's or other fees |
| 6(1)(d) | allocations, etc., under [employees] profit sharing plan |
| 6(1)(e) | standby charge for automobile |
| 6(1)(e.1) | [Repealed] |
| 6(1)(f) | [private] employment insurance [plan] benefits |
| 6(1)(g) | employee benefit plan benefits |
| 6(1)(h) | employee trust |
| 6(1)(i) | salary deferral arrangement payments |
| 6(1)(j) | reimbursements and awards |
| 6(1)(k), (1)(l) | automobile operating expense benefit |
| 6(1.1) | Parking cost |
| 6(2) | Reasonable standby charge |
| 6(2.1) | Automobile salesman |
| 6(2.2) | [Repealed] |
| 6(3) | Payments by employer to employee |
| 6(4) | Group term life insurance |
| 6(5) | [Repealed] |
| 6(6) | Employment at special work site or remote location |
| 6(7) | Cost of property or service [includes GST, etc.] |
| 6(8) | Idem [GST rebate] |
| 6(9) | Amount in respect of interest on employee debt |
| 6(10) | Contributions to an employee benefit plan |
| 6(11), (12) | Salary deferral arrangement |
| 6(13) | Application |
| 6(14) | Part of plan or arrangement |
| 6(15) | Forgiveness of employee debt |
| 6(15.1) | Forgiven amount |
| 6(16) | Disability-related employment benefits [transportation, parking, attendant] |
| 6(17) | Definitions |

lxxxi

## Detailed Table of Sections

| | |
|---|---|
| 6(18) | Group disability benefits — insolvent insurer |
| 6(19) | Benefit re housing loss |
| 6(20) | Benefit re eligible housing loss |
| 6(21) | Housing loss |
| 6(22) | Eligible housing loss |
| 6(23) | Employer-provided housing subsidies |
| 7 | |
| 7(1) | Agreement to issue securities to employees |
| 7(1) | [Proposed] Agreement to issue securities to employees |
| 7(1.1) | Employee stock options |
| 7(1.11) | Non-arm's length relationship with trusts |
| 7(1.2) | [Repealed under former Act] |
| 7(1.3) | Order of disposition of shares |
| 7(1.3) | [Proposed] Order of disposition of securities |
| 7(1.31) | [Proposed] Disposition of newly-acquired security |
| 7(1.4) | Exchange of options |
| 7(1.5) | Rules where shares exchanged |
| 7(1.5) | [Proposed] Rules where securities exchanged |
| 7(1.6) | [Proposed] Emigrant |
| 7(2) | Securities held by trustee [deemed held by employee] |
| 7(2) | [Proposed] Securities held by trustee [deemed held by employee] |
| 7(3) | Special provision [taxable benefit is under s. 7 only] |
| 7(4) | Application of subsec. (1) |
| 7(5) | Non-application of this section |
| 7(6) | Sale to trustee for employees |
| 7(7) | Definitions |
| 7(7) | [Proposed] Definitions |
| 7(8) | [Proposed] Deferral in respect of non-CCPC employee options |
| 7(9) | [Proposed] Meaning of "qualifying acquisition" |
| 7(10) | [Proposed] Election for purposes of subsection (8) |
| 7(11) | [Proposed] Meaning of "specified value" |
| 7(12) | [Proposed] Identical options — order of exercise |
| 7(13) | [Proposed] Revoked election |
| 7(14) | [Proposed] Deferral deemed valid |
| 7(15) | [Proposed] Withholding |
| 7(16) | [Proposed] Prescribed form for deferral |

### Deductions

| | |
|---|---|
| 8 | |
| 8(1) | Deductions allowed |
| 8(1)(a) | volunteers' [emergency workers'] deduction |
| 8(1)(b) | legal expenses of employee |
| 8(1)(c) | clergyman's residence |
| 8(1)(c) | [Proposed] clergy residence |
| 8(1)(d) | teachers' exchange fund contribution |
| 8(1)(e) | expenses of railway employees |
| 8(1)(f) | sales expenses |
| 8(1)(g) | transport employee's expenses |
| 8(1)(h) | travel expenses |
| 8(1)(h.1) | motor vehicle travel expenses |
| 8(1)(i) | dues and other expenses of performing duties |
| 8(1)(j) | motor vehicle and aircraft costs |
| 8(1)(k), (l) | [Repealed under former Act] |
| 8(1)(l.1) | C.P.P. contributions and U.I.A. [E.I.] premiums |
| 8(1)(m) | employee's registered pension plan contributions |
| 8(1)(m.1) | [Repealed under former Act] |
| 8(1)(m.2) | employee RCA contributions |
| 8(1)(n) | salary reimbursement |
| 8(1)(n.1) | reimbursement of disability payments |
| 8(1)(o), (o.1) | forfeited amounts |
| 8(1)(p) | musical instrument costs |
| 8(1)(q) | artists' employment expenses |

lxxxii

## Detailed Table of Sections

| | |
|---|---|
| 8(1.1) | |
| 8(2) | General limitation |
| 8(3) | [Repealed under former Act] |
| 8(4) | Meals |
| 8(5) | Dues not deductible |
| 8(6)–(8) | [Repealed under former Act] |
| 8(9) | Presumption |
| 8(10) | Certificate of employer |
| 8(10) | [Proposed] Certificate of employer |
| 8(10) | [Proposed] Certificate of employer |
| 8(11) | Goods and services tax |
| 8(12) | Forfeiture of securities by employee |
| 8(13) | Work space in home |

### Subdivision b — Income or Loss from a Business or Property
### Basic Rules

| | |
|---|---|
| 9 | |
| 9(1) | Income |
| 9(2) | Loss |
| 9(3) | Gains and losses not included |
| 10 | |
| 10(1) | Valuation of inventory |
| 10(1.01) | Adventures in the nature of trade |
| 10(1.1) | Certain expenses included in cost |
| 10(2) | Continuation of valuation |
| 10(2.1) | Methods of valuation to be same |
| 10(3) | Incorrect valuation |
| 10(4) | Fair market value |
| 10(5) | [Meaning of] Inventory |
| 10(6) | Artistic endeavour |
| 10(7) | Value in later years |
| 10(8) | Definition of "business that is an individual's artistic endeavour" |
| 10(9) | Transition |
| 10(10) | Acquisition of control |
| 10(11) | Acquisition of control |
| 10(12) | [Proposed] Removing property from [Canadian] inventory [of non-resident] |
| 10(13) | [Proposed] Adding property to [Canadian] inventory [of non-resident] |
| 10(14) | [Proposed] Work in progress |
| 11 | |
| 11(1) | Proprietor of business |
| 11(2) | Reference to "taxation year" |

### Inclusions

| | |
|---|---|
| 12 | |
| 12(1) | Income inclusions |
| 12(1)(a) | services, etc., to be rendered [or goods to be delivered] |
| 12(1)(b) | amounts receivable |
| 12(1)(c) | interest |
| 12(1)(c) | [Proposed] interest |
| 12(1)(d) | reserve for doubtful debts |
| 12(1)(d.1) | reserve for guarantees, etc. |
| 12(1)(e) | reserves for certain goods and services, etc. |
| 12(1)(e.1) | [insurer's] negative reserves |
| 12(1)(f) | insurance proceeds expended |
| 12(1)(g) | payments based on production or use |
| 12(1)(g.1) | proceeds of disposition of right to receive production |
| 12(1)(h) | previous reserve for quadrennial survey |
| 12(1)(i), (i.1) | bad debts recovered |
| 12(1)(i.1) | [Proposed] bad debts recovered |
| 12(1)(j) | dividends from resident corporations |
| 12(1)(k) | dividends from other corporations |
| 12(1)(k) | [Proposed] foreign corporations, trusts and investment entities [dividends, etc.] |

lxxxiii

## Detailed Table of Sections

| | |
|---|---|
| 12(1)(l) | partnership income |
| 12(1)(m) | benefits from trusts |
| 12(1)(n) | employees profit sharing plan |
| 12(1)(n.1) | employee benefit plan |
| 12(1)(n.2) | forfeited salary deferral amounts |
| 12(1)(n.3) | retirement compensation arrangement |
| 12(1)(o) | royalties, etc. |
| 12(1)(o.1) | [Proposed] foreign oil and gas production taxes |
| 12(1)(p) | certain payments to farmers |
| 12(1)(q) | employment tax deduction |
| 12(1)(r) | inventory adjustment [depreciation, etc.] |
| 12(1)(s) | reinsurance commission |
| 12(1)(t) | investment tax credit |
| 12(1)(u) | home insulation or energy conversion grants |
| 12(1)(v) | research and development deductions |
| 12(1)(w) | subsec. 80.4(1) benefit |
| 12(1)(x) | inducement, reimbursement, [refund] etc. |
| 12(1)(x.1) | fuel tax rebates |
| 12(1)(y) | automobile provided to partner |
| 12(1)(z) | amateur athlete trust payments |
| 12(1)(z.1) | qualifying environmental trusts |
| 12(1)(z.2) | dispositions of interests in qualifying environmental trusts |
| 12(1)(z.3) | debt forgiveness |
| 12(1)(z.4) | eligible funeral arrangements |
| 12(1)(z.5) | resource loss |
| 12(1)(z.6) | refunds [of countervailing or anti-dumping duties] |
| 12(2) | Interpretation |
| 12(2.1) | Receipt of inducement, reimbursement, etc. |
| 12(2.2) | Deemed outlay or expense |
| 12(3) | Interest income [accrual to year-end] |
| 12(4) | Interest from investment contract [annual accrual] |
| 12(4.1) | Impaired debt obligations |
| 12(5)–(8) | [Repealed under former Act] |
| 12(9) | Deemed accrual |
| 12(9.1) | Exclusion of proceeds of disposition |
| 12(10) | [Repealed under former Act] |
| 12(10.1) | Income from RHOSP |
| 12(10.2) | NISA receipts |
| 12(10.3) | Amount credited or added not included in income |
| 12(11) | Definitions |
| 12.1 | Cash bonus on Canada Savings Bonds |
| 12.2 | |
| 12.2(1) | Amount to be included [annually from life insurance policy] |
| 12.2(2)–(4.1), (5) | [Repealed under former Act] |
| 12.2(6), (7) | [Repealed under former Act] |
| 12.2(8) | Deemed acquisition of interest in annuity |
| 12.2(9) | [Repealed under former Act] |
| 12.2(10) | Riders |
| 12.2(11) | Definitions |
| 12.2(12) | Application of subsecs. 138(12) and 148(9) |
| 12.2(13) | Application of subsec. 148(10) |
| 12.3 | Transition inclusion re unpaid claims reserve |
| 12.4 | Bad debt inclusion |
| 13 | |
| 13(1) | Recaptured depreciation |
| 13(2) | Idem [luxury automobile] |
| 13(3) | "Taxation year", "year" and "income" of individual |
| 13(4) | Exchanges of property |
| 13(4.1) | Replacement for a former property |
| 13(5) | Reclassification of property |
| 13(5.1) | Rules applicable [leasehold interest] |

## Detailed Table of Sections

| | |
|---|---|
| 13(5.2) | Idem [rent deemed to be CCA] |
| 13(5.3) | Idem [disposition of option] |
| 13(5.4) | Idem |
| 13(5.5) | Lease cancellation payment |
| 13(6) | Misclassified property |
| 13(7) | Rules applicable |
| 13(7)(a) | [change in use] |
| 13(7)(b) | [change in use] |
| 13(7)(c) | [partial use to produce income] |
| 13(7)(d) | [partial change in use] |
| 13(7)(e) | [non-arm's length acquisition] |
| 13(7)(e.1) | [capital gains exemption election] |
| 13(7)(f) | [change in control] |
| 13(7)(g) | [luxury automobile] |
| 13(7)(h) | [luxury automobile — non-arm's length acquisition] |
| 13(7.1) | Deemed capital cost of certain property |
| 13(7.2) | Receipt of public assistance |
| 13(7.3) | Control of corporations by one trustee |
| 13(7.4) | Deemed capital cost |
| 13(7.5) | Deemed capital cost |
| 13(8) | Disposition after ceasing business |
| 13(9) | Meaning of "gaining or producing income" |
| 13(10) | Deemed capital cost |
| 13(11) | Deduction in respect of property used in performance of duties |
| 13(12) | Application of para. 20(1)(cc) [lobbying expenses] |
| 13(13) | Deduction under *Canadian Vessel Construction Assistance Act* |
| 13(14) | Conversion cost |
| 13(15) | Where subsec. (1) and subdivision c do not apply |
| 13(16) | Election concerning vessel |
| 13(17) | Separate prescribed class concerning vessel |
| 13(18) | Reassessments |
| 13(18.1) | Ascertainment of certain property |
| 13(19), (20) | Disposition of deposit [vessel construction] |
| 13(21) | Definitions |
| 13(21.1) | Disposition of building |
| 13(21.2) | Loss on certain transfers [within affiliated group] |
| 13(22) | Deduction for insurer |
| 13(23) | Deduction for life insurer |
| 13(23.1) | Application of subsec. 138(12) |
| 13(24) | Acquisition of control |
| 13(25) | Early change of control |
| 13(26) | Restriction on deduction before available for use |
| 13(27)–(29) | Interpretation — available for use |
| 13(30), (31) | Transfers of property |
| 13(32) | Leased property |
| 13(33) | Consideration given for depreciable property |
| 14 | |
| 14(1) | Inclusion in income from business [eligible capital property] |
| 14 | |
| 14(1) | [Proposed] Eligible capital property — inclusion in income from business |
| 14(1.01) | [Proposed] Election re: capital gain |
| 14(1.1) | Deemed taxable capital gain |
| (1.1) | [Proposed] Deemed taxable capital gain |
| (1.1)(2) | Amount deemed payable |
| (1.1)(3) | Acquisition of eligible capital property |
| (1.1)(3) | [Proposed] Acquisition of eligible capital property |
| (1.1)(4) | References to "taxation year" or "year" |
| (1.1)(5) | Definitions |
| (1.1)(6) | Exchange of property |
| (1.1)(7) | Replacement property for a former property |
| (1.1)(8) | Deemed residence in Canada |

lxxxv

## Detailed Table of Sections

| | |
|---|---|
| (1.1)(9) | Effect of election under subsec. 110.6(19) |
| (1.1)(10) | Deemed eligible capital expenditure |
| (1.1)(11) | Receipt of public assistance |
| (1.1)(12) | Loss on certain transfers [within affiliated group] |
| (1.1)(13) | Deemed identical property |
| (1.1)(14) | [Proposed] [Non-resident] Ceasing to use [eligible capital] property in Canadian business |
| (1.1)(15) | [Proposed] [Non-resident] Beginning to use [eligible capital] property in Canadian business |
| 15 | |
| 15(1) | Benefit conferred on shareholder |
| 15(1.1) | Conferring of benefit |
| 15(1.2) | Forgiveness of shareholder debt |
| 15(1.21) | Forgiven amount |
| 15(1.3) | Cost of property or service |
| 15(1.4) | [Repealed] |
| 15(2) | Shareholder debt |
| 15(2.1) | Persons connected with a shareholder |
| 15(2.2) | When s. 15(2) not to apply — non-resident persons |
| 15(2.3) | When s. 15(2) not to apply — ordinary lending business |
| 15(2.4) | When s. 15(2) not to apply — certain employees |
| 15(2.5) | When s. 15(2) not to apply — certain trusts |
| 15(2.6) | When s. 15(2) not to apply — repayment within one year |
| 15(2.7) | Employee of partnership |
| 15(3) | Interest or dividend on income bond or debenture |
| 15(4) | Idem, where corporation not resident |
| 15(5) | Automobile benefit |
| 15(6) | [Repealed under former Act] |
| 15(7) | Application of subsecs. (1), (2) and (5) |
| 15(8) | [Repealed] |
| 15(9) | Deemed benefit to shareholder by corporation |
| 15.1 | |
| 15.1(1) | Interest on small business development bonds |
| 15.1(2) | Rules for small business development bonds |
| 15.1(3) | Definitions |
| 15.1(4) | Money borrowed |
| 15.1(5) | False declaration |
| 15.1(6) | Disqualification |
| 15.1(7) | Exception |
| 15.2 | |
| 15.2(1) | Interest on small business bond |
| 15.2(2) | Rules for small business bonds |
| 15.2(3) | Definitions |
| 15.2(4) | Status of interest |
| 15.2(5) | False declaration |
| 15.2(6) | Partnerships |
| 15.2(7) | Deemed eligible issuer |
| 16 | |
| 16(1) | Income and capital combined |
| 16(2), (3) | Obligation issued at discount |
| 16(4), (5) | Where subsec. (1) does not apply |
| 16(6) | Indexed debt obligations |
| 16(7) | Impaired indexed debt obligations |
| 16.1 | |
| 16.1(1) | Leasing properties |
| 16.1(2), (3) | Assignments and subleases |
| 16.1(4) | Amalgamations and windings-up |
| 16.1(5) | Replacement property |
| 16.1(6) | Additional property |
| 16.1(7) | Renegotiation of lease |
| 17 | |
| 17(1) | Amount owing by non-resident [deemed interest income] |
| 17(2) | Anti-avoidance rule — indirect loan |

Detailed Table of Sections

17(3) Exception to anti-avoidance rule — indirect loan
17(4) Anti-avoidance rule — loan through partnership
17(5) Anti-avoidance rule — loan through trust
17(6) Anti-avoidance rule — loan to partnership
17(7) Exception
17(8) Exception
17(9) Exception
17(10) Determination of whether related and controlled foreign affiliate status
17(11) Determination of whether related
17(11.1) [Proposed] Determination of whether persons related
17(11.2) [Proposed] Back-to-back loans
17(12) Determination of controlled foreign affiliate status
17(13) Extended definition of controlled foreign affiliate
17(14) Anti-avoidance rule — where rights or shares issued, acquired or disposed of to avoid tax
17(15) Definitions

## Deductions

18
18(1) General limitations
18(1)(a) general limitation
18(1)(b) capital outlay or loss
18(1)(c) limitation re exempt income
18(1)(d) annual value of property
18(1)(e) reserves, etc.
18(1)(e.1) unpaid claims under insurance policies
18(1)(f) payments on discounted bonds
18(1)(g) payments on income bonds
18(1)(h) personal and living expenses
18(1)(i) limitation re employer's contribution under supplementary unemployment benefit plan
18(1)(j) limitation re employer's contribution under deferred profit sharing plan
18(1)(k) limitation re employer's contribution under profit sharing plan
18(1)(l) use of recreational facilities and club dues
18(1)(l.1) *Petroleum and Gas Revenue Tax Act* payments
18(1)(m) royalties, etc.
18(1)(n) political contributions
18(1)(o) employee benefit plan contributions
18(1)(o.1) salary deferral arrangement
18(1)(o.2) retirement compensation arrangement
18(1)(p) limitation re personal services business expenses
18(1)(q) limitation re cancellation of lease
18(1)(r) certain automobile expenses
18(1)(s) loans or lending assets
18(1)(t) payments under [Income Tax] Act
18(1)(u) RSP/RIF fees
18(1)(v) [Proposed] Interest — authorized foreign bank
18(2) Limit on certain interest and property tax
18(2.1) Where taxpayer member of partnership
18(2.2) Base level deduction
18(2.3) Associated corporations
18(2.4) Failure to file agreement
18(2.5) Special rules for base level deduction
18(3) Definitions
18(3.1) Costs relating to construction of building or ownership of land
18(3.2) Included costs
18(3.3) Completion
18(3.4), (3.5) Where subsec. (3.1) does not apply
18(3.6) Undue delay
18(3.7) Commencement of footings
18(4) Limitation re deduction of interest by certain corporations [thin capitalization]
18(5) Definitions
18(5.1) Person deemed not to be specified shareholder
18(6) Loans made on condition

lxxxvii

## Detailed Table of Sections

| | |
|---|---|
| 18(7) | [Repealed under former Act] |
| 18(8) | Where subsec. (4) does not apply |
| 18(9) | Limitation respecting prepaid expenses |
| 18(9.01) | Group term life insurance |
| 18(9.02) | [Proposed] Application of subsec. (9) to insurers |
| 18(9.1) | Penalties, bonuses and rate-reduction payments |
| 18(9.2) | Interest on debt obligations |
| 18(9.3)–(9.8) | Interest on debt obligations |
| 18(10) | Employee benefit plan |
| 18(11) | Limitation [on interest expense] |
| 18(12) | Work space in home |
| 18(13) | When subsec. (15) applies to money lenders |
| 18(14) | When subsec. (15) applies to adventurers in trade |
| 18(15) | Loss on certain properties [transferred within affiliated group] |
| 18(16) | Deemed identical property |
| 18.1 | |
| 18.1(1) | Definitions |
| 18.1(2) | Limitation on the deductibility of matchable expenditure |
| 18.1(3) | Deduction of matchable expenditure |
| 18.1(4) | Amount of deduction |
| 18.1(5) | Special rules |
| 18.1(6) | Proceeds of disposition considered income |
| 18.1(7) | Arm's length disposition |
| 18.1(8) | Non-arm's length disposition |
| 18.1(9) | Special case |
| 18.1(10) | Amount of deduction if non-arm's length disposition |
| 18.1(11) | Partnerships |
| 18.1(12) | Identical property |
| 18.1(13) | Application of section 143.2 |
| 18.1(14) | Debt obligations |
| 18.1(15) | Non-applicability of section 18.1 |
| 18.1(15) | [Proposed] Non-applicability of s. 18.1 |
| 19 | |
| 19(1) | Limitation re advertising expense |
| 19(1) | [Proposed] Limitation re advertising expense — newspapers |
| 19(2) | [Repealed under former Act] |
| 19(3) | Where subsec. (1) does not apply |
| 19(4) | [Repealed under former Act] |
| 19(5) | Definitions |
| 19(5.1) | [Proposed] Interpretation ["Canadian citizen"] |
| 19(6) | Trust property |
| 19(6) | [Proposed] Trust property |
| 19(7) | Grace period |
| 19(7) | [Proposed] Grace period |
| 19(8) | Non-Canadian newspaper or periodical |
| 19(8) | [Proposed] Non-Canadian newspaper |
| 19.01 | |
| 19.01(1) | [Proposed] Definitions |
| 19.01(2) | [Proposed] Limitation re advertising expenses — periodicals |
| 19.01(3) | [Proposed] 100% deduction |
| 19.01(4) | [Proposed] 50% deduction |
| 19.01(5) | [Proposed] Application |
| 19.01(6) | [Proposed] Editions of issues |
| 19.1 | |
| 19.1(1) | Limitation re advertising expense on broadcasting undertaking |
| 19.1(2) | Exception |
| 19.1(3) | [Repealed under former Act] |
| 19.1(4) | Definitions |
| 20 | |
| 20(1) | Deductions permitted in computing income from business or property |
| 20(1)(a) | capital cost of property |

lxxxviii

## Detailed Table of Sections

| | |
|---|---|
| 20(1)(b) | cumulative eligible capital amount |
| 20(1)(b) | [Proposed] cumulative eligible capital amount |
| 20(1)(c) | interest |
| 20(1)(d) | compound interest |
| 20(1)(e) | expenses re financing |
| 20(1)(e) | [Proposed] expenses re financing |
| 20(1)(e.1) | annual fees, etc. [re borrowings] |
| 20(1)(e.2) | premiums on life insurance used as collateral |
| 20(1)(f) | discount on certain obligations |
| 20(1)(g) | share transfer and other fees |
| 20(1)(h), (i) | [Repealed under former Act] |
| 20(1)(j) | repayment of loan by shareholder |
| 20(1)(k) | [Repealed under former Act] |
| 20(1)(l) | doubtful or impaired debts |
| 20(1)(l.1) | reserve for guarantees, etc. |
| 20(1)(m) | reserve in respect of certain [future] goods and services |
| 20(1)(m.1) | manufacturer's warranty reserve |
| 20(1)(m.2) | repayment of amount previously included in income |
| 20(1)(n) | reserve for unpaid amounts |
| 20(1)(o) | reserve for quadrennial survey |
| 20(1)(p) | bad debts |
| 20(1)(q) | employer's contributions to registered pension plan |
| 20(1)(r) | employer's contributions under retirement compensation arrangement |
| 20(1)(s), (t) | [Repealed under former Act] |
| 20(1)(u) | patronage dividends |
| 20(1)(v) | mining taxes |
| 20(1)(v.1) | resource allowance |
| 20(1)(w) | employer's contributions under profit sharing plan |
| 20(1)(x) | employer's contributions under registered supplementary unemployment benefit plan |
| 20(1)(y) | employer's contributions under deferred profit sharing plan |
| 20(1)(z), (z.1) | cancellation of lease |
| 20(1)(aa) | landscaping of grounds |
| 20(1)(bb) | fees paid to investment counsel |
| 20(1)(cc) | expenses of representation [lobbying] |
| 20(1)(dd) | investigation of site |
| 20(1)(ee) | utilities service connection |
| 20(1)(ff) | payments by farmers |
| 20(1)(gg) | [Repealed] |
| 20(1)(hh) | repayments of inducements, etc. |
| 20(1)(hh.1) | repayment of obligation |
| 20(1)(ii) | inventory adjustment |
| 20(1)(jj) | reinsurance commission |
| 20(1)(kk) | exploration and development grants |
| 20(1)(ll) | repayment of interest |
| 20(1)(mm) | cost of substances injected in reservoir |
| 20(1)(nn) | Part XII.6 tax |
| 20(1)(oo), (pp) | salary deferral arrangement |
| 20(1)(qq) | disability-related modifications to buildings |
| 20(1)(qq) [sic] | [Proposed] interest on share purchase |
| 20(1)(rr) | disability-related equipment |
| 20(1)(ss) | qualifying environmental trusts |
| 20(1)(tt) | acquisition of interests in qualifying environmental trusts |
| 20(1)(uu) | debt forgiveness |
| 20(1)(vv) | countervailing or anti-dumping duty |
| 20(1)(ww) | split income |
| 20(1.1) | Application of subsec. 13(21) |
| 20(1.2) | Application of subsec. 12.2(11) |
| 20(2) | Borrowed money |
| 20(2.1) | Limitation of expression "interest" |
| 20(2.2) | Limitation of expression "life insurance policy" |
| 20(2.3) | Sectoral reserve |

## Detailed Table of Sections

| | |
|---|---|
| 20(2.4) | Specified percentage |
| 20(3) | Borrowed money |
| 20(3.1) | [Proposed] Borrowed money |
| 20(3.2) | [Proposed] Idem |
| 20(4)–(4.2) | Bad debts from dispositions of depreciable property |
| 20(4.2) | [Proposed] Bad debts re: eligible capital property |
| 20(4.3) | [Proposed] Deemed allowable capital loss |
| 20(5), (5.1) | Sale of agreement for sale or mortgage included in proceeds of disposition |
| 20(6) | Special reserves |
| 20(7) | Where para. (1)(m) does not apply |
| 20(8) | No deduction in respect of property in certain circumstances |
| 20(9) | Application of para. (1)(cc) |
| 20(10) | Convention expenses |
| 20(11) | Foreign taxes on income from property exceeding 15% |
| 20(12) | Foreign non-business income tax |
| 20(12.1) | Foreign tax where no economic profit |
| 20(13) | Dividend on share from foreign affiliate of taxpayer |
| 20(14) | Accrued bond interest |
| 20(14.1) | Interest on debt obligation |
| 20(15) | Regulations |
| 20(16), (16.1) | Terminal loss |
| 20(16.2) | Reference to "taxation year" and "year" of individual |
| 20(16.3) | Disposition after ceasing business |
| 20(17) | Reduction of inventory allowance deduction |
| 20(18) | Definitions |
| 20(19) | Annuity contract |
| 20(20) | Life insurance policy [disposed of] |
| 20(21) | Debt obligation |
| 20(22) | Deduction for [insurer's] negative reserves |
| 20(23) | [Repealed under former Act] |
| 20(24) | Amounts paid for undertaking future obligations |
| 20(25) | Manner of election |
| 20(26) | Transition deduction re unpaid claims reserve |
| 20(27) | Loans, etc., acquired in ordinary course of business |
| 20(27.1) | Application of subsecs. 13(21) and 138(12) |
| 20(28), (29) | Deduction [for building] before available for use |
| 20(30) | Specified reserve adjustment |
| 20.01 | |
| 20.01(1) | PHSP [private health services plan] premiums |
| 20.01(2) | Limit |
| 20.01(3) | Equivalent coverage |
| 20.1 | |
| 20.1(1) | Borrowed money used to earn income from property |
| 20.1(2) | Borrowed money used to earn income from business |
| 20.1(3) | Deemed dispositions |
| 20.1(4) | Amount payable for property |
| 20.1(5) | Interest in partnership |
| 20.1(6) | Refinancings |
| 20.2 | |
| 20.2(1) | [Proposed] Interest — authorized foreign bank — interpretation |
| 20.2(2) | [Proposed] Formula elements |
| 20.2(3) | [Proposed] Interest deduction |
| 20.2(4) | [Proposed] Branch amounts |
| 20.2(5) | [Proposed] Notional interest |
| 20.3 | |
| 20.3(1) | [Proposed] Weak currency debt [Kiwi loans] — interpretation |
| 20.3(2) | [Proposed] Interest and gain |
| 20.3(3) | [Proposed] Hedges |
| 20.3(4) | [Proposed] Repayment of principal |
| 20.1 | |
| 20.1(1) | [Proposed] Money borrowed for distribution |

## Detailed Table of Sections

| | |
|---|---|
| 20.1(2) | [Proposed] Equity |
| 20.1(3) | [Proposed] Alternative determination |
| 20.1(4) | [Proposed] Limits on allocation |
| 20.1(5) | [Proposed] Invalid designations |
| 20.1(6) | [Proposed] Designation |
| 20.1(7) | [Proposed] Definition: equity |
| 20.1(8) | [Proposed] Definitions |
| 20.1(9) | [Proposed] Expenditure pool amount |
| 20.2 | |
| 20.2(1) | [Proposed] Money borrowed for distribution |
| 20.2(2) | [Proposed] Definition: adjusted equity |
| 20.2(3) | [Proposed] Carrying value of property |
| 21 | |
| 21(1) | Cost of borrowed money |
| 21(2) | Borrowed money used for exploration or development |
| 21(2) | [Proposed] Borrowed money used for exploration or development |
| 21(3) | Borrowing for depreciable property |
| 21(4) | Borrowing for exploration, etc. |
| 21(5) | Reassessments |

### Ceasing to Carry on Business

| | |
|---|---|
| 22 | |
| 22(1) | Sale of accounts receivable |
| 22(2) | Statement by vendor and purchaser |
| 23 | |
| 23(1) | Sale of inventory |
| 23(2) | [Repealed under former Act] |
| 23(3) | Reference to property in inventory |
| 24 | |
| 24(1) | Ceasing to carry on business |
| 24(2) | Business carried on by spouse [or common-law partner] or controlled corporation |
| 24(3) | Where partnership has ceased to exist |
| 24.1 | [Repealed] |
| 25 | |
| 25(1) | Fiscal period of business disposed of by individual |
| 25(2) | Election |
| 25(3) | Dispositions in the extended fiscal period |

### Special Cases

| | |
|---|---|
| 26 | |
| 26(1) | Banks — inclusions in income |
| 26(2) | Banks — deductions from income |
| 26(3) | Write-offs and recoveries |
| 26(4) | Definition of "Minister's rules" |
| 27 | |
| 27(1) | Application of Part I to Crown corporation |
| 27(2) | Presumption |
| 27(2) | [Proposed] Presumption |
| 27(3) | Transfers of land for disposition |
| 28 | |
| 28(1) | Farming or fishing business [cash method] |
| 28(1.1) | Acquisition of inventory |
| 28(1.2) | Valuation of inventory |
| 28(1.3) | Short fiscal period |
| 28(2) | Where joint farming or fishing business |
| 28(3) | Concurrence of Minister |
| 28(4), (4.1) | Non-resident |
| 28(5) | Accounts receivable |
| 29 | |
| 29(1) | Disposition of animal of basic herd class |
| 29(2) | Reduction in basic herd |
| 29(3) | Interpretation |

xci

## Detailed Table of Sections

| | |
|---|---|
| 30 | Improving land for farming |
| 31 | |
| 31(1) | Loss from farming where chief source of income not farming |
| 31(1.1) | Restricted farm loss |
| 31(2) | Determination by Minister |
| 32 | |
| 32(1) | Insurance agents and brokers [unearned commissions] |
| 32(2) | Reserve to be included |
| 32(3) | Additional reserve |
| 32.1 | |
| 32.1(1) | Employee benefit plan deductions |
| 32.1(2) | Allocation |
| 32.1(3) | Income of employee benefit plan |
| 33 | [Repealed under former Act] |
| 33.1 | |
| 33.1(1) | International banking centres — definitions |
| 33.1(2) | Interpretation |
| 33.1(3) | Designation and exemption |
| 33.1(4) | Income or loss from an international banking centre business |
| 33.1(5) | Restriction |
| 33.1(6) | Election |
| 33.1(7) | Election restriction |
| 33.1(8) | Limitation |
| 33.1(9) | Exception |
| 33.1(10) | No deduction permitted |
| 33.1(11) | Application |
| 33.1(12) | Return |
| 34 | Professional business |
| 34.1 | |
| 34.1(1) | Additional business income [off-calendar fiscal period] |
| 34.1(2) | Additional income election |
| 34.1(3) | Deduction |
| 34.1(4) | Deemed December 31, 1995 income |
| 34.1(5) | Deemed December 31, 1995 income |
| 34.1(6) | Deemed December 31, 1995 income |
| 34.1(7) | Maximum December 31, 1995 income |
| 34.1(8) | No additional income inclusion |
| 34.1(9) | Death of partner or proprietor |
| 34.2 | [1995 stub period reserve] |
| 34.2(1) | Definitions |
| 34.2(2) | Computation of December 31, 1995 income |
| 34.2(3) | Business defined |
| 34.2(4) | Reserve |
| 34.2(5) | Reserve included in income |
| 34.2(6) | No reserve |
| 34.2(7) | Anti-avoidance rule |
| 34.2(8) | Death of partner or proprietor |
| 35 | |
| 35(1) | Prospectors and grubstakers |
| 35(2) | Definitions |
| 36 | Railway companies |
| 37 | |
| 37(1) | Scientific research and experimental development |
| 37(1.1) | Business of related corporations |
| 37(1.2) | Deemed time of capital expenditure |
| 37(2) | Research outside Canada |
| 37(3) | Minister may obtain advice |
| 37(4) | Where no deduction allowed under section |
| 37(5) | Where no deduction allowed under sections 110.1 and 118.1 |
| 37(6) | Expenditures of a capital nature |
| 37(6.1) | Amount referred to in para. (1)(h) |

## Detailed Table of Sections

| | |
|---|---|
| 37(7) | Definitions |
| 37(8) | Interpretation |
| 37(9) | Salary or wages |
| 37(9.1) | Limitation re specified employees |
| 37(9.2) | Associated corporations |
| 37(9.3) | Agreement among associated corporations |
| 37(9.4) | Filing |
| 37(9.5) | Deemed corporation |
| 37(10) | Time for election |
| 37(11) | Filing requirement |
| 37(12) | Misclassified expenditures |
| 37(13) | Non-arm's length contract — linked work |
| 37.1, 37.2, 37.3 | [Repealed] |

**Subdivision c — Taxable Capital Gains and Allowable Capital Losses**

| | |
|---|---|
| 38 | Taxable capital gain and allowable capital loss |
| 39 | |
| 39(1) | Meaning of capital gain and capital loss [and business investment loss] |
| 39(2) | Capital gains and losses in respect of foreign currencies |
| 39(3) | Gain in respect of purchase of bonds, etc., by issuer |
| 39(4) | Election concerning disposition of Canadian securities |
| 39(4.1) | Members of partnerships |
| 39(5) | Exception |
| 39(6) | Definition of "Canadian security" |
| 39(7) | Unused share-purchase tax credit |
| 39(8) | Unused scientific research and experimental development tax credit |
| 39(9) | Deduction from business investment loss |
| 39(10) | Idem, of a trust |
| 39(11) | Recovery of bad debt |
| 39(11) | [Proposed] Recovery of bad debt |
| 39(12) | Guarantees |
| 39(13) | Repayment of assistance |
| 39.1 | |
| 39.1(1) | Definitions |
| 39.1(2) | Reduction of capital gain |
| 39.1(3) | Reduction of taxable capital gain |
| 39.1(4) | Reduction in share of partnership's taxable capital gains |
| 39.1(5) | Reduction in share of partnership's income from a business |
| 39.1(6) | Reduction of capital gains |
| 39.1(7) | Nil exempt capital gains balance |
| 40 | |
| 40(1) | General rules |
| 40(1.01) | [Reserve on] Gift of non-qualifying security |
| 40(1.1) | [Farm or small business] Property disposed of to a child |
| 40(2) | Limitations |
| 40(2)(a) | [reserve — limitations] |
| 40(2)(b) | [principal residence] |
| 40(2)(c) | [land used in farming business] |
| 40(2)(d) | [disposition of bond] |
| 40(2)(e) | [Repealed] |
| 40(2)(e.1) | [disposition of debt of related person] |
| 40(2)(e.2) | [settlement of commercial obligation] |
| 40(2)(f) | [right to a prize] |
| 40(2)(g) | [various losses deemed nil] |
| 40(2)(h) | [shares of controlled corporation] |
| 40(2)(i) | [shares of certain corporations] |
| 40(2)(j) | [Repealed under former Act] |
| 40(3) | Deemed gain where amounts to be deducted from ACB exceed cost plus amounts to be added to ACB |
| 40(3.1) | Deemed gain for certain partners |
| 40(3.11) | Amount of gain |
| 40(3.12) | Deemed loss for certain partners |

xciii

## Detailed Table of Sections

| | |
|---|---|
| 40(3.13) | Artificial transactions |
| 40(3.131) | Specified member of a partnership |
| 40(3.14) | Limited partner |
| 40(3.15) | Excluded interest |
| 40(3.16) | Amounts considered not to be substantial |
| 40(3.17) | Whether carrying on business before February 22, 1994 |
| 40(3.18) | Deemed partner |
| 40(3.19) | Non-application of subsec. (3) |
| 40(3.2) | Non-application of subsec. (3.1) |
| 40(3.3) | When subsection (3.4) applies |
| 40(3.4) | Loss on certain properties |
| 40(3.5) | Deemed identical property |
| 40(3.6) | Loss on shares |
| 40(3.7) | [Proposed] Losses of non-resident |
| 40(4) | Disposal of principal residence to spouse or trust for spouse [or common-law partner] |
| 40(5) | [Repealed] |
| 40(6) | Special rule concerning principal residence |
| 40(7) | Property in satisfaction of interest in trust |
| 40(7.1) | Effect of election under subsec. 110.6(19) |
| 40(8) | Application of subsec. 70(10) |
| 40(9) | Additions to taxable Canadian property |
| 40(9) | [Proposed] Additions to taxable Canadian property |
| 41 | |
| 41(1) | Taxable net gain from disposition of listed personal property |
| 41(2) | Determination of net gain |
| 41(3) | Definition of "listed-personal-property loss" |
| 42 | Dispositions subject to warranty |
| 43 | Part dispositions |
| 43 | |
| 43(1) | [Proposed] General rule for part dispositions |
| 43(2) | [Proposed] Ecological gifts |
| 43(3) | [Proposed] Payments out of trust income, etc. |
| 43.1 | |
| 43.1(1), (2) | Life estates in real property |
| 44 | |
| 44(1) | Exchanges of property |
| 44(1) | [Proposed] Exchanges of property |
| 44(1.1) | Farm property disposed of to child |
| 44(2) | Time of disposition and of receipt of proceeds |
| 44(3) | Where subsec. 70(3) does not apply |
| 44(4) | Deemed election |
| 44(5) | Replacement property |
| 44(6) | Deemed proceeds of disposition |
| 44(7) | Where subpara. (1)(e)(iii) does not apply |
| 44(8) | Application of subsec. 70(10) |
| 44.1 | |
| 44.1(1) | [Proposed] [Small business share rollover] Definitions |
| 44.1(2) | [Proposed] Capital gain deferral |
| 44.1(3) | [Proposed] Special rule — re: eligible pooling arrangements |
| 44.1(4) | [Proposed] Special rule — re: acquisitions on death |
| 44.1(5) | [Proposed] Special rule — re: breakdown of relationships |
| 44.1(6) | [Proposed] Special rule — re: eligible small business corporation share exchanges |
| 44.1(7) | [Proposed] Special rule — re: active business corporation share exchanges |
| 44.1(8) | [Proposed] Special rule — re: carrying on an active business |
| 44.1(9) | [Proposed] Special rule — re: qualifying disposition |
| 44.1(10) | [Proposed] Special rule — re: exceptions |
| 44.1(11) | [Proposed] Determination rule |
| 44.1(12) | [Proposed] Anti-avoidance rule |
| 45 | |
| 45(1) | Property with more than one use [change in use] |
| 45(2) | Election where change of use |

xciv

## Detailed Table of Sections

| | |
|---|---|
| 45(3) | Election concerning principal residence |
| 45(4) | Where election cannot be made |
| 46 | |
| 46(1) | Personal-use property |
| 46(1) | [Proposed] Personal-use property |
| 46(1)(a) | |
| 46(1)(b) | |
| 46(2) | Where part only of property disposed of |
| 46(2) | [Proposed] Where part only of property disposed of |
| 46(3) | Properties ordinarily disposed of as a set |
| 46(4) | Decrease in value of personal-use property of corporation, etc. |
| 46(5) | [Proposed] Excluded property |
| 47 | |
| 47(1) | Identical properties [averaging rule] |
| 47(2) | Where identical properties are bonds, etc. |
| 47(3) | [Repealed under former Act] |
| 47(3) | [Proposed] Securities acquired by employee |
| 47(4) | [Repealed under former Act] |
| 47.1 | Indexed Security Investment Plans |
| 47.1(1)–(26) | [Repealed under former Act] |
| 47.1(26.1) | Application of section 47.1 of R.S.C., 1952, c. 148 |
| 47.1(27) | |
| 47.1(28) | Transition for 1986 |
| 48 | [Repealed] |
| 48.1 | |
| 48.1(1) | Gain when small business corporation becomes public[ly listed] |
| 48.1(2) | Time for election |
| 48.1(3) | Late filed election |
| 48.1(4) | Penalty for late filed election |
| 48.1(5) | Unpaid balance of penalty |
| 49 | |
| 49(1) | Granting of options |
| 49(2), (2.1) | Where option expires |
| 49(3) | Where option to acquire exercised |
| 49(3.01) | Option to acquire specified property exercised |
| 49(3.1) | Where option to dispose exercised |
| 49(3.2) | Option granted before February 23, 1994 |
| 49(4) | Reassessment where option exercised in subsequent year |
| 49(5) | [Extension or renewal of option] |
| 49.1 | No disposition where obligation satisfied |
| 50 | |
| 50(1), (1.1) | Debts established to be bad debts and shares of bankrupt corporation |
| 50(2) | Where debt a personal-use property |
| 50(3) | Disposal of RHOSP properties |
| 51 | |
| 51(1), (2) | Convertible property |
| 51(3) | Computation of paid-up capital |
| 51(4) | Application |
| 51.1 | Conversion of debt obligation |
| 52 | |
| 52(1) | Cost of certain property value of which included in income |
| 52 | |
| 52(1) | [Proposed] Cost of certain property the value of which included in income |
| 52(1.1) | [Repealed] |
| 52(1.1) | Idem, where owner non-resident |
| 52(2) | Cost of property received as dividend in kind |
| 52(3) | Cost of stock dividend |
| 52(4) | Cost of property acquired as prize |
| 52(5) | [Repealed under former Act] |
| 52(6) | Cost of right to receive from trust |
| 52(7) | Cost of shares of subsidiary |

## Detailed Table of Sections

| | |
|---|---|
| 52(8) | Cost of shares of immigrant corporation |
| 53 | |
| 53(1) | Adjustments to cost base [additions to ACB] |
| 53(1)(a) | [negative ACB] |
| 53(1)(b) | [share, where 84(1) applied] |
| 53(1)(b.1) | [share of immigrant corporation] |
| 53(1)(c) | [share, where contribution of capital made] |
| 53(1)(d) | [share of foreign affiliate] |
| 53(1)(d.01) | [share of demutualized insurer] |
| 53(1)(d.1) | [capital interest in trust] |
| 53(1)(d.1) | |
| 53(1)(d.2) | [unit in mutual fund trust] |
| 53(1)(d.3) | [share] |
| 53(1)(e) | [partnership interest] |
| 53(1)(f) | [substituted property] |
| 53(1)(f.1) | [property disposed of at loss by other corporation] |
| 53(1)(f.11) | [property disposed of at loss by other person] |
| 53(1)(f.12) | [commercial obligation owing to taxpayer] |
| 53(1)(f.2) | [share, after transfer of other shares to corporation] |
| 53(1)(g) | [bond, mortgage, etc.] |
| 53(1)(g.1) | [indexed debt obligation] |
| 53(1)(h) | [land] |
| 53(1)(i) | [land used in farming] |
| 53(1)(j) | [share or fund unit taxed as stock option benefit] |
| 53(1)(j) | [Proposed] share or fund unit taxed as stock option benefit |
| 53(1)(k) | [expropriation asset] |
| 53(1)(l) | [interest in related segregated fund trust] |
| 53(1)(m) | [offshore investment fund property] |
| 53(1)(m) | [Proposed] [offshore investment fund property] |
| 53(1)(m.1) | [Proposed] [interest in foreign investment entity] |
| 53(1)(n) | [surveying and valuation costs] |
| 53(1)(o) | [real property — remainder interest] |
| 53(1)(p) | [flow-through entity after 2004] |
| 53(1)(q) | [history preservation rules — debt forgiveness] |
| 53(1)(r) | [flow-through entity before 2005] |
| 53(1.1) | Deemed contribution of capital |
| 53(2) | Amounts to be deducted [from ACB] |
| 53(2)(a) | [share] |
| 53(2)(b) | [share of non-resident corporation] |
| 53(2)(b.1) | [capital interest in non-resident trust] |
| 53(2)(b.2) | [property of corporation after change in control] |
| 53(2)(c) | [partnership interest] |
| 53(2)(d) | [part of property retained] |
| 53(2)(e) | [share] |
| 53(2)(f) | [consideration from joint exploration corporation] |
| 53(2)(f.1) | [share of joint exploration corporation] |
| 53(2)(f.2) | [resource expenses renounced by joint exploration corporation] |
| 53(2)(g) | [debt forgiveness] |
| 53(2)(g.1) | [history preservation rules — debt forgiveness] |
| 53(2)(h) | [capital interest in trust] |
| 53(2)(h) | [Proposed] [capital interest in trust] |
| 53(2)(i) | [capital interest in non-resident trust] |
| 53(2)(i) | [Proposed] [capital interest in non-resident trust] |
| 53(2)(j) | [unit of non-resident unit trust] |
| 53(2)(j) | [Proposed] [unit of non-resident unit trust] |
| 53(2)(k) | [assistance received or receivable] |
| 53(2)(l) | [debt obligation] |
| 53(2)(l.1) | [indexed debt obligation] |
| 53(2)(m) | [amounts deducted from income] |
| 53(2)(n) | [expropriation asset] |
| 53(2)(o) | [right to receive partnership property] |

## Detailed Table of Sections

| | |
|---|---|
| 53(2)(p) | [debt owing by corporation] |
| 53(2)(q) | [interest in related segregated fund trust] |
| 53(2)(r) | [Repealed under former Act] |
| 53(2)(s) | [government assistance — amount elected under 53(2.1)] |
| 53(2)(t) | [right to acquire shares or fund units] |
| 53(2)(u) | [non-qualifying real property] |
| 53(2)(v) | [excessive capital gains election] |
| 53(2)(w) | [Proposed] [interest in foreign investment entity] |
| 53(2.1) | Election |
| 53(3) | Application of paras. (2)(i) and (j) |
| 53(4) | Recomputation of adjusted cost base on transfers and deemed dispositions |
| 53(4) | [Proposed] Recomputation of adjusted cost base on transfers and deemed dispositions |
| 53(4)(a) | |
| 53(4)(b) | |
| 53(5) | Recomputation of adjusted cost base on other transfers |
| 53(6) | Recomputation of adjusted cost base on amalgamation |
| 54 | Definitions |
| 54.1 | |
| 54.1(1) | Exception to principal residence rules |
| 54.1(2) | Definition of "property" |
| 54.2 | Certain shares deemed to be capital property |
| 55 | |
| 55(1) | Definitions |
| 55(2) | Deemed proceeds or capital gain |
| 55(3) | Application |
| 55(3.01) | Interpretation for para. (3)(a) |
| 55(3.02) | [Proposed] Distribution by a specified corporation |
| 55(3.1) | Where para. (3)(b) not applicable |
| 55(3.2) | Interpretation of para. (3.1)(b) |
| 55(3.3) | Interpretation of "specified shareholder" changed |
| 55(4) | Avoidance of subsec. (2) |
| 55(5) | Applicable rules |

### Subdivision d — Other Sources of Income

| | |
|---|---|
| 56 | |
| 56(1) | Amounts to be included in income for year |
| 56(1)(a) | pension benefits, unemployment insurance benefits, etc. |
| 56(1)(a.1) | benefits under CPP/QPP |
| 56(1)(b) | support |
| 56(1)(c), (c.1) | [Repealed] |
| 56(1)(c.2) | reimbursement of support payments |
| 56(1)(d) | annuity payments |
| 56(1)(d.1) | [Repealed under former Act] |
| 56(1)(d.2) | idem [annuity payments] |
| 56(1)(e), (f) | disposition of income-averaging annuity contract |
| 56(1)(g) | supplementary unemployment benefit plan |
| 56(1)(h) | registered retirement savings plan, etc. [RRSP or RRIF] |
| 56(1)(h.1) | Home Buyers' Plan |
| 56(1)(h.2) | Lifelong Learning Plan |
| 56(1)(i) | deferred profit sharing plan |
| 56(1)(j) | life insurance policy proceeds |
| 56(1)(k) | [Repealed under former Act] |
| 56(1)(l), (1.1) | legal expenses [awarded or reimbursed] |
| 56(1)(m) | [Repealed] |
| 56(1)(n) | scholarships, bursaries, etc. |
| 56(1)(o) | research grants |
| 56(1)(p) | refund of scholarships, bursaries and research grants |
| 56(1)(q) | education savings plan payments |
| 56(1)(r) | financial assistance |
| 56(1)(s) | grants under prescribed programs |
| 56(1)(t) | registered retirement income fund |
| 56(1)(u) | social assistance [welfare] payments |

xcvii

## Detailed Table of Sections

| | |
|---|---|
| 56(1)(v) | workers' compensation |
| 56(1)(w) | salary deferral arrangement |
| 56(1)(x)–(z) | retirement compensation arrangement |
| 56(1)(aa) | [benefit from registered national arts service organization] |
| 56(1.1) | Application of subsec. 12.2(11) |
| 56(2) | Indirect payments |
| 56(3) | [Repealed under former Act] |
| 56(3) | [Proposed] Exemption for scholarships, fellowships, bursaries and prizes |
| 56(4) | Transfer of rights to income |
| 56(4.1) | Interest free or low interest loans |
| 56(4.2) | Exception |
| 56(4.3) | Repayment of existing indebtedness |
| 56(5) | Exception for split income |
| 56(6), (7) | [Repealed] |
| 56(8) | CPP/QPP benefits for previous years |
| 56(9) | Meaning of "income for the year" |
| 56(10) | Severability of retirement compensation arrangement |
| 56(11) | Disposition of property by RCA trust |
| 56(12) | [Repealed] |
| 56.1 | |
| 56.1(1) | Support |
| 56.1(2) | Agreement |
| 56.1(3) | Prior payments |
| 56.1(4) | Definitions |
| 56.2 | Reserve claimed for debt forgiveness |
| 56.3 | Reserve claimed for debt forgiveness |
| 57 | |
| 57(1) | Certain superannuation or pension benefits |
| 57(2) | Exception |
| 57(3) | Limitation |
| 57(4) | Certain payments from pension plan |
| 57(5) | Payments to widow, etc., of contributor |
| 58 | |
| 58(1) | Government annuities and like annuities |
| 58(2) | Annuities before 1940 |
| 58(3) | Limitation |
| 58(4) | Capital element |
| 58(5) | Spouses [or common-law partners] |
| 58(6) | Pension benefits |
| 58(7) | Enlargement of annuity |
| 59 | |
| 59(1) | Consideration for foreign resource property |
| 59 | |
| 59(1) | [Proposed] Consideration for foreign resource property |
| 59 | |
| 59(1.1) | [Proposed] Partnerships [look-through rule] |
| 59(2) | Deduction under former section 64 in preceding year |
| 59(3), (3.1) | [Repealed under former Act] |
| 59(3.2) | Recovery of exploration and development expenses |
| 59(3.3) | Amounts to be included in income |
| 59(3.4) | Definitions |
| 59(3.5) | Variation of stated percentage |
| 59(4) | [Repealed under former Act] |
| 59(5) | Definitions of "disposition" and "proceeds of disposition" |
| 59(5) | [Proposed] Definition of "proceeds of disposition" |
| 59(6) | Definitions in regulations under section 65 |
| 59.1 | Involuntary disposition of resource property |

### Subdivision e — Deductions in Computing Income

| | |
|---|---|
| 60 | Other deductions |
| 60(a) | capital element of annuity payments |
| 60(b) | support |

xcviii

## Detailed Table of Sections

| | |
|---|---|
| 60(c), (c.1) | [Repealed] |
| 60(c.2) | repayment of support payments |
| 60(d) | interest on death duties |
| 60(e)–(h) | [Repealed under former Act] |
| 60(e) | [Proposed] CPP/QPP contributions on self-employed earnings |
| 60(e) | [Proposed] CPP/QPP contributions on self-employed earnings |
| 60(i) | premium or payment under RRSP or RRIF |
| 60(j) | transfer of superannuation benefits [to RRSP] |
| 60(j.01) | [No longer relevant] |
| 60(j.02) | payment to registered pension plan |
| 60(j.03) | repayments of pre-1990 pension benefits |
| 60(j.04) | repayments of post-1989 pension benefits |
| 60(j.1) | transfer of retiring allowances [to RRSP] |
| 60(j.2) | transfer to spousal RRSP [before 1995] |
| 60(k) | [Repealed under former Act] |
| 60(l) | transfer of refund of premium under RRSP [on death] |
| 60(m) | estate tax applicable to certain property |
| 60(m.1) | succession duties applicable to certain property |
| 60(n) | repayment of pension or benefits |
| 60(o) | legal [or other] expenses [of objection or appeal] |
| 60(o.1) | legal expenses |
| 60(p) | [Repealed] |
| 60(q) | refund of income payments |
| 60(r) | amounts included under subsec. 146.2(6) [RHOSP] |
| 60(s) | repayment of policy loan |
| 60(t) | RCA distributions |
| 60(u) | RCA dispositions |
| 60(v) | contribution to a provincial pension plan |
| 60(v.1) | UI and EI benefit repayment |
| 60(w) | tax under Part I.2 |
| 60(x) | CESG repayment |
| 60.001 | Application of subpara. 60(c.1)(i) |
| 60.01 | Eligible amount |
| 60.02 | Application of subpara. 60(v)(iii) |
| 60.1 | |
| 60.1(1) | Support |
| 60.1(2) | Agreement |
| 60.1(3) | Prior payments |
| 60.1(4) | Definitions |
| 60.11 | Application of subpara. 60.1(1)(a)(ii) |
| 60.2 | |
| 60.2(1) | Refund of undeducted past service AVCs |
| 60.2(2) | Definition of "balance of the annuitized voluntary contributions" |
| 61 | |
| 61(1), (2) | Payment made as consideration for income-averaging annuity |
| 61(3) | [Repealed under former Act] |
| 61(4) | Definitions |
| 61.1 | |
| 61.1(1) | Where income-averaging annuity contract ceases to be such |
| 61.1(2) | Where annuitant dies and payments continued |
| 61.2 | Reserve for debt forgiveness for resident individuals |
| 61.3 | |
| 61.3(1) | Deduction for insolvency with respect to resident corporations |
| 61.3(2) | Reserve for insolvency with respect to non-resident corporations |
| 61.3(3) | Anti-avoidance |
| 61.4 | Reserve for debt forgiveness for corporations and others |
| 62 | |
| 62(1) | Moving expenses |
| 62(2) | Moving expenses of students |
| 62(3) | Definition of "moving expenses" |

xcix

## Detailed Table of Sections

| | |
|---|---|
| 63 | |
| 63(1) | Child care expenses |
| 63(2) | Income exceeding income of supporting person |
| 63(2.1) | Taxpayer and supporting person with equal incomes |
| 63(2.2) | Expenses while at school |
| 63(2.3) | Amount deductible |
| 63(3) | Definitions |
| 63(4) | Commuter's child care expense |
| 63.1 | [See 64.1] |
| 64 | Attendant care expenses |
| 64.1 | Individuals absent from Canada |
| 65 | |
| 65(1) | Allowance for oil or gas well, mine or timber limit |
| 65(2) | Regulations |
| 65(3) | Lessee's share of allowance |
| 66 | |
| 66(1) | Exploration and development expenses of principal-business corporations |
| 66(2) | Expenses of special product corporations |
| 66(3) | Expenses of other taxpayers |
| 66(4) | Foreign exploration and development expenses |
| 66(4.1) | [Proposed] Country-by-country FEDE allocations |
| 66(4.2) | [Proposed] Method of allocation |
| 66(4.3) | [Proposed] FEDE deductions where change of individual's residence |
| 66(5) | Dealers |
| 66(5) | [Proposed] Dealers |
| 66(6)–(9) | [Repealed under former Act] |
| 66(10) | [Repealed effective 2007] |
| 66(10.1) | [Repealed effective 2007] |
| 66(10.2) | [Repealed effective 2007] |
| 66(10.3), (10.4) | [Repealed effective 2007] |
| 66(11) | Acquisition of control |
| 66(11.1), (11.2) | [Repealed under former Act] |
| 66(11.3) | Control |
| 66(11.4) | Change of control |
| 66(11.5) | Early change of control |
| 66(12) | Computation of exploration and development expenses |
| 66(12.1) | Limitations of Canadian exploration and development expenses |
| 66(12.2), (12.3) | Unitized oil or gas field in Canada |
| 66(12.4) | Limitation of foreign exploration and development expenses |
| 66(12.4) | [Proposed] Limitation of FEDE |
| 66(12.41) | [Proposed] Limitations of foreign resource expenses |
| 66(12.42) | [Proposed] Partnerships |
| 66(12.5) | Unitized oil or gas field in Canada |
| 66(12.6) | Canadian exploration expenses to flow-through shareholder |
| 66(12.601) | Flow-through share rules for first $1 million of Canadian development expenses |
| 66(12.6011) | Taxable capital amount |
| 66(12.6012) | Taxable capital employed in Canada |
| 66(12.6013), (12.602) | Amalgamations and mergers |
| 66(12.61) | Effect of renunciation |
| 66(12.62) | Canadian development expenses to flow-through shareholder |
| 66(12.63) | Effect of renunciation |
| 66(12.64) | [Repealed] |
| 66(12.65) | [Repealed] |
| 66(12.66) | Expenses in the first 60 days of year [or throughout next calendar year] |
| 66(12.67) | Restrictions on renunciation |
| 66(12.671) | Prohibited relationship |
| 66(12.68) | Filing selling instruments |
| 66(12.69) | Filing re partners |
| 66(12.6901) | Consequences of failure to file |
| 66(12.691) | Filing re assistance |
| 66(12.7) | Filing re renunciation |

## Detailed Table of Sections

| | |
|---|---|
| 66(12.7001) | Consequences of failure to file |
| 66(12.701) | Filing re assistance |
| 66(12.702) | Consequences of failure to file |
| 66(12.71) | Restriction on renunciation |
| 66(12.72) | [Repealed] |
| 66(12.73) | Reductions in renunciations |
| 66(12.74) | Late filed forms |
| 66(12.741) | Late renunciation |
| 66(12.75) | Penalty |
| 66(13) | Limitation |
| 66(13.1) | Short taxation years |
| 66(13.1) | [Proposed] Short taxation year |
| 66(14) | Amounts deemed deductible under this subdivision |
| 66(14.1) | Designation respecting Canadian exploration expense |
| 66(14.2) | Designation respecting cumulative Canadian development expense |
| 66(14.3) | Definition of "adjusted cumulative Canadian development expense" |
| 66(14.4) | Special cases |
| 66(14.5) | Penalty for late designation |
| 66(14.6) | Deduction of carved-out income |
| 66(15) | Definitions |
| 66(15.1) | Application of subsecs. 66.1(6), 66.2(5), 66.4(5) and 66.5(2) |
| 66(15.1) | [Proposed] Other definitions |
| 66(16) | Partnerships |
| 66(17) | Non-arm's length partnerships |
| 66(18) | Members of partnerships |
| 66(18) | [Proposed] Members of partnerships |
| 66(19) | Renunciation by corporate partner, etc. |
| 66(20) | Specified amount |
| 66.1 | [Canadian exploration expenses] |
| 66.1(1) | Amount to be included in income |
| 66.1(2) | Deduction for certain principal-business corporations |
| 66.1(3) | Expenses of other taxpayer |
| 66.1(4), (5) | [Repealed under former Act] |
| 66.1(6) | Definitions |
| 66.1(6.1) | Application of subsecs. 66(15), 66.2(5) and 66.4(5) |
| 66.1(7) | Share of partner |
| 66.1(8) | [Repealed] |
| 66.1(9) | Canadian development expenses for preceding years |
| 66.1(10) | Certificate ceasing to be valid |
| 66.1(11) | [Repealed under former Act] |
| 66.2 | [Canadian development expenses] |
| 66.2(1) | Amount to be included in income |
| 66.2(2) | Deduction for cumulative Canadian development expenses |
| 66.2(3), (4) | [Repealed under former Act] |
| 66.2(5) | Definitions |
| 66.2(5.1) | Application of subsecs. 66(15), 66.1(6) and 66.4(5) |
| 66.2(6) | Presumption |
| 66.2(7) | Exception |
| 66.2(8) | Presumption |
| 66.21 | |
| 66.21(1) | [Proposed] Definitions |
| 66.21(2) | [Proposed] Application of subsection 66(15) |
| 66.21(3) | [Proposed] Amount to be included in income |
| 66.21(4) | [Proposed] Deduction for cumulative foreign resource expense |
| 66.21(5) | [Proposed] Individual changing residence |
| 66.3 | |
| 66.3(1) | Exploration and development shares |
| 66.3(2) | Deductions from paid-up capital |
| 66.3(3) | Cost of flow-through shares |
| 66.3(4) | Paid-up capital |
| 66.4 | [Canadian oil and gas property expenses] |

## Detailed Table of Sections

| | |
|---|---|
| 66.4(1) | Recovery of costs |
| 66.4(2) | Deduction for cumulative Canadian oil and gas property expense |
| 66.4(3), (4) | [Repealed under former Act] |
| 66.4(5) | Definitions |
| 66.4(5.1) | Application of subsecs. 66(15) and 66.1(6) |
| 66.4(6) | Share of partner |
| 66.4(7) | Exception |
| 66.5 | |
| 66.5(1) | Deduction from income |
| 66.5(2) | Definition of "cumulative offset account" |
| 66.5(3) | Change of control |
| 66.6 | Acquisition from tax-exempt [person] |
| 66.7 | |
| 66.7(1) | Successor of Canadian exploration and development expenses |
| 66.7(2) | Successor of foreign exploration and development expenses |
| 66.7(2.1) | [Proposed] Country-by-country successor FEDE allocations |
| 66.7(2.2) | [Proposed] Method of allocation |
| 66.7(2.3) | [Proposed] Successor of foreign resource expenses |
| 66.7(3) | Successor of Canadian exploration expense |
| 66.7(4) | Successor of Canadian development expense |
| 66.7(5) | Successor of Canadian oil and gas property expense |
| 66.7(6) | Where subsec. 29(25) of ITAR and subsecs. (1) to (5) do not apply |
| 66.7(7) | Application of subsec. 29(25) of ITAR and subsecs. (1), (3), (4) and (5) |
| 66.7(8) | Application of subsec. (2) |
| 66.7(8) | [Proposed] Application of ss. (2) and (2.3) |
| 66.7(9) | Canadian development expense becoming Canadian exploration expense |
| 66.7(10) | Change of control |
| 66.7(11) | Idem |
| 66.7(12) | Reduction of Canadian resource expenses |
| 66.7(12.1) | Specified amount |
| 66.7(13) | Reduction of foreign resource expenses |
| 66.7(13.1) | [Proposed] Reduction of foreign resource expenses |
| 66.7(13.2) | [Proposed] Specified amount — foreign resource expenses |
| 66.7(14) | Disposal of Canadian resource properties |
| 66.7(15) | Disposal of foreign resource properties |
| 66.7(15.1) | [Proposed] Disposal of foreign resource properties — ss. (2.3) |
| 66.7(16) | Non-successor acquisitions |
| 66.7(17) | Restriction on deductions |
| 66.7(18) | Application of subsec. 66(15) |
| 66.7(18) | [Proposed] Application of interpretation provisions |
| 66.8 | |
| 66.8(1) | Resource expenses of limited partner |
| 66.8(2) | Expenses in following fiscal period |
| 66.8(3) | Interpretation |

**Subdivision f — Rules Relating to Computation of Income**

| | |
|---|---|
| 67 | General limitation re expenses |
| 67.1 | |
| 67.1(1) | Expenses for food, etc. |
| 67.1(2) | Exceptions |
| 67.1(3) | Fees for convention, etc. |
| 67.1(4) | Interpretation |
| 67.2 | Interest on money borrowed for passenger vehicle |
| 67.3 | Limitation re cost of leasing passenger vehicle |
| 67.4 | More than one owner or lessor |
| 67.5 | |
| 67.5(1) | Non-deductibility of illegal payments |
| 67.5(2) | Reassessments |
| 68 | Allocation of amounts in consideration for disposition of property |
| 69 | |
| 69(1) | Inadequate considerations |
| 69(1.1) | Idem, where subsec. 70(3) applies |

## Detailed Table of Sections

| | |
|---|---|
| 69(1.2) | Idem |
| 69(2) | [Repealed] |
| 69(3) | [Repealed] |
| 69(4)–(7) | Shareholder appropriations |
| 69(7.1) | [Repealed under former Act] |
| 69(8) | Fair market value of resource output disposed of to Crown |
| 69(9) | Fair market value of resource output acquired from Crown |
| 69(10) | Certain persons deemed to be same person |
| 69(11) | Deemed proceeds of disposition |
| 69(12) | Reassessments |
| 69(12.1), (12.2) | [Repealed] |
| 69(13) | Amalgamation or merger |
| 69(14) | New taxpayer |
| 70 | |
| 70(1) | Death of a taxpayer |
| 70(2) | Amounts receivable |
| 70(3) | Rights or things transferred to beneficiaries |
| 70(3.1) | Exception |
| 70(3.1) | [Proposed] Exception |
| 70(4) | Revocation of election |
| 70(5) | Capital property of a deceased taxpayer |
| 70(5.1) | Eligible capital property of deceased |
| 70(5.2) | Resource properties and land inventories of a deceased taxpayer |
| 70(5.3) | Fair market value |
| 70(5.3) | [Proposed] Fair market value |
| 70(5.4) | NISA on death |
| 70(6) | Where transfer or distribution to spouse [or common-law partner] or spouse trust |
| 70(6.1) | Transfer or distribution of NISA to spouse [or common-law partner] or trust |
| 70(6.2) | Election |
| 70(7) | Special rules applicable in respect of trust for benefit of spouse [or common-law partner] |
| 70(8) | Meaning of certain expressions in subsec. (7) |
| 70(9) | Transfer of farm property to child |
| 70(9.1) | Transfer of farm property from spouse's [or common-law partner's] trust to settlor's children |
| 70(9.1) | [Proposed] Transfer of farm property from trust to settlor's children |
| 70(9.2) | Transfer of family farm corporations and partnerships |
| 70(9.3) | Transfer of family farm corporation or partnership from spouse's [or common-law partner's] trust to children of settlor |
| 70(9.3) | [Proposed] Transfer of family farm corporation or partnership from trust to children of settlor |
| 70(9.4), (9.5) | [Repealed under former Act] |
| 70(9.6) | Transfer to parent |
| 70(9.7) | [Repealed under former Act] |
| 70(9.8) | Leased farm property |
| 70(10) | Definitions |
| 70(11) | Application of subsec. 138(12) |
| 70(12) | Value of NISA |
| 70(13) | Capital cost of certain depreciable property |
| 70(14) | Order of disposal of depreciable property |
| 71 | [Repealed under former Act] |
| 72 | |
| 72(1) | Reserves, etc., for year of death |
| 72(2) | Election by legal representative and transferee re reserves |
| 73 | |
| 73(1) | *Inter vivos* transfer of property of spouse, etc., or trust |
| 73 | |
| 73(1) | [Proposed] *Inter vivos* transfers by individuals |
| 73(1.01) | [Proposed] Qualifying transfers |
| 73(1.02) | [Proposed] Exception for transfers |
| 73(1.1) | Interpretation |
| 73(1.1) | [Proposed] Interpretation |
| 73(1.2) | [Repealed under former Act] |
| 73(2) | Capital cost and amount deemed allowed to spouse, etc., or trust |

ciii

## Detailed Table of Sections

| | |
|---|---|
| 73(3) | *Inter vivos* transfer of farm property to child |
| 73(4) | *Inter vivos* transfer of family farm corporations and partnerships |
| 73(5) | Disposition of a NISA |
| 73(6) | Application of subsec. 70(10) |
| 74 | [Repealed under former Act] |
| 74.1 | |
| 74.1(1) | Transfers and loans to spouse [or common-law partner] |
| 74.1(2) | Transfers and loans to minors |
| 74.1(3) | Repayment of existing indebtedness |
| 74.2 | |
| 74.2(1) | Gain or loss deemed that of lender or transferor |
| 74.2(2) | Deemed gain or loss |
| 74.2(3) | [Proposed] Election for subsection (1) to apply |
| 74.2(4) | [Proposed] Application of subsection (3) |
| 74.3 | |
| 74.3(1) | Transfers or loans to a trust |
| 74.3(2) | Definition of "designated person" |
| 74.4 | |
| 74.4(1) | Definitions |
| 74.4(2) | Transfers and loans to corporations |
| 74.4(3) | Outstanding amount |
| 74.4(4) | Benefit not granted to a designated person |
| 74.5 | |
| 74.5(1) | Transfers for fair market consideration |
| 74.5(2) | Loans for value |
| 74.5(3), (4) | Spouses [or common-law partners] living apart |
| 74.5(5) | Definition of "designated person" |
| 74.5(6) | Back to back loans and transfers |
| 74.5(7) | Guarantees |
| 74.5(8) | Definition of "specified person" |
| 74.5(9) | Transfers or loans to a trust |
| 74.5(10) | [Repealed] |
| 74.5(11) | Artificial transactions |
| 74.5(12) | Where sections 74.1 to 74.3 do not apply |
| 74.5(13) | Exception from attribution rules [kiddie tax] |
| 75 | |
| 75(1) | [Repealed under former Act] |
| 75(2) | Trusts |
| 75(3) | Exceptions |
| 75.1 | |
| 75.1(1) | Gain or loss deemed that of transferor |
| 75.1(2) | Definition of "child" |
| 76 | |
| 76(1), (2) | Security in satisfaction of income debt |
| 76(3) | Section enacted for greater certainty |
| 76(4) | Debt deemed not to be income debt |
| 76(5) | Definitions of certain expressions |
| 76.1 | [Proposed] |
| 76.1(1) | [Proposed] Non-resident moving debt from Canadian business |
| 76.1(2) | [Proposed] Non-resident assuming debt |
| 77 | [Repealed] |
| 78 | |
| 78(1), (2) | Unpaid amounts |
| 78(3) | Late filing |
| 78(4) | Unpaid remuneration and other amounts |
| 78(5) | Where subsec. (1) does not apply |
| 79 | |
| 79(1) | Definitions |
| 79(2) | Surrender of property |
| 79(3) | Proceeds of disposition for debtor |
| 79(4) | Subsequent payment by debtor |

## Detailed Table of Sections

| | |
|---|---|
| 79(5) | Subsequent application with respect to employee or shareholder debt |
| 79(6) | Surrender of property not payment or repayment by debtor |
| 79(7) | Foreign exchange |
| 79.1 | |
| 79.1(1) | Definitions |
| 79.1(2) | Seizure of property |
| 79.1(2) | [Proposed] Seizure of property |
| 79.1(2.1) | [Proposed] Exception |
| 79.1(3) | Creditor's capital gains reserves |
| 79.1(4) | Creditor's inventory reserves |
| 79.1(5) | Adjustment where disposition and reacquisition of capital property in same year |
| 79.1(6) | Cost of seized properties for creditor |
| 79.1(7) | Treatment of debt |
| 79.1(8) | Claims for debts |
| 80 | |
| 80(1) | Definitions |
| 80(2) | Application of debt forgiveness rules |
| 80(2)(a) | [when obligation settled] |
| 80(2)(b) | [interest deemed to be obligation] |
| 80(2)(c) | [ordering of rules] |
| 80(2)(d) | [applicable fraction] |
| 80(2)(d) | [Proposed] [applicable fraction] |
| 80(2)(e) | [where applicable fraction reduces loss] |
| 80(2)(f) | [cumulative eligible capital] |
| 80(2)(g) | [amount paid in satisfaction of debt] |
| 80(2)(g.1) | [amount paid in satisfaction of debt] |
| 80(2)(h) | [debt replaced with debt] |
| 80(2)(i) | [multiple debts settled] |
| 80(2)(j) | ["related" and "controlled"] |
| 80(2)(k) | [foreign currency obligation] |
| 80(2)(l) | [debt replaced with debt to third party] |
| 80(2)(m) | [amount reducible only to zero] |
| 80(2)(n) | [where debt owed by partnership] |
| 80(2)(o) | [where joint liability for debt] |
| 80(2)(p), (q) | [death of debtor] |
| 80(3) | Reductions of non-capital losses |
| 80(4) | Reductions of capital losses |
| 80(5) | Reductions with respect to depreciable property |
| 80(6) | Restriction with respect to depreciable property |
| 80(7) | Reductions of cumulative eligible capital |
| 80(8) | Reductions of resource expenditures |
| 80(9) | Reductions of adjusted cost bases of capital properties |
| 80(10) | Reduction of adjusted cost bases of certain shares and debts |
| 80(11) | Reduction of adjusted cost bases of certain shares, debts and partnership interests |
| 80(12) | Capital gain where current year capital loss |
| 80(13) | Income inclusion |
| 80(14) | Residual balance |
| 80(14.1) | Gross tax attributes |
| 80(15) | Members of partnerships |
| 80(16) | Designations by Minister |
| 80(17) | [Repealed] |
| 80(18) | Partnership designations |
| 80.01 | |
| 80.01(1) | Definitions |
| 80.01(2) | Application |
| 80.01(3) | Deemed settlement on amalgamation |
| 80.01(4), (5) | Deemed settlement on winding-up |
| 80.01(6) | Specified obligation in relation to debt parking |
| 80.01(7) | Parked obligation |
| 80.01(8) | Deemed settlement after debt parking |
| 80.01(9) | Statute-barred debt |

cv

## Detailed Table of Sections

| | |
|---|---|
| 80.01(10) | Subsequent payments in satisfaction of debt |
| 80.01(11) | Foreign currency gains and losses |
| 80.02 | |
| 80.02(1) | Definitions |
| 80.02(2) | General rules for distress preferred shares |
| 80.02(3) | Substitution of distress preferred share for debt |
| 80.02(4) | Substitution of commercial debt obligation for distress preferred share |
| 80.02(5) | Substitution of distress preferred share for other distress preferred share |
| 80.02(6) | Substitution of non-commercial obligation for distress preferred share |
| 80.02(7) | Deemed settlement on expiry of term |
| 80.03 | |
| 80.03(1) | [Definitions] |
| 80.03(2) | Deferred recognition of debtor's gain on settlement of debt |
| 80.03(3) | Surrender of capital property |
| 80.03(4)–(6) | [Repealed] |
| 80.03(7) | Alternative treatment |
| 80.03(8) | Lifetime capital gains exemption |
| 80.04 | |
| 80.04(1) | Definitions |
| 80.04(2) | Eligible transferee |
| 80.04(3) | Application |
| 80.04(4) | Agreement respecting transfer of forgiven amount |
| 80.04(5) | Consideration for agreement |
| 80.04(5.1) | No benefit conferred |
| 80.04(6) | Manner of filing agreement |
| 80.04(7) | Filing by partnership |
| 80.04(8) | Related corporations |
| 80.04(9) | Assessment of taxpayers in respect of agreement |
| 80.04(10) | Liability of debtor |
| 80.04(11) | Joint liability |
| 80.04(12) | Assessments in respect of liability |
| 80.04(13) | Application of Division I |
| 80.04(14) | Partnership members |
| 80.1 | |
| 80.1(1) | Expropriation assets acquired as compensation for or as consideration for sale of foreign property taken by or sold to foreign issuer |
| 80.1(2) | Election re interest received or to be received on expropriation assets acquired by taxpayer |
| 80.1(3) | Where interest amount and capital amount received at same time |
| 80.1(4) | Assets acquired from foreign affiliate of taxpayer as dividend in kind or as benefit to shareholder |
| 80.1(5) | Assets acquired from foreign affiliate of taxpayer as consideration for settlement, etc., of debt |
| 80.1(6) | Assets acquired from foreign affiliate of taxpayer on winding-up, etc. |
| 80.1(7) | Definition of "adjusted principal amount" |
| 80.1(8) | Currency in which adjusted principal amount to be computed or expressed |
| 80.1(9) | Election in respect of two or more expropriation assets acquired by taxpayer |
| 80.2 | Reimbursement by taxpayer [resource royalties] |
| 80.3 | [Income deferrals — livestock] |
| 80.3(1) | Definitions |
| 80.3(2) | Income deferral from the destruction of livestock |
| 80.3(3) | Inclusion of deferred amount |
| 80.3(4) | Income deferral for sales in prescribed drought region |
| 80.3(5) | Inclusion of deferred amount |
| 80.3(6) | Where subsecs. (2) and (4) do not apply |
| 80.4 | |
| 80.4(1) | Loans [to employees] |
| 80.4(1.1), (2) | Interpretation |
| 80.4(3) | Where subsecs. (1) and (2) do not apply |
| 80.4(4) | Interest on loans for home purchase or relocation |
| 80.4(5) | [No longer relevant] |
| 80.4(6) | Deemed new home purchase loans |
| 80.4(7) | Definitions |
| 80.4(8) | Persons connected with a shareholder |

cvi

# Detailed Table of Sections

80.5          Deemed interest

## Subdivision g — Amounts Not Included in Computing Income

81
| | |
|---|---|
| 81(1) | Amounts not included in income |
| 81(1)(a) | statutory exemptions |
| 81(1)(b) | War Savings Certificate |
| 81(1)(c) | ship or aircraft of non-residents |
| 81(1)(d) | service pension, allowance or compensation |
| 81(1)(e) | war pensions |
| 81(1)(f) | Halifax disaster pensions, grants or allowances |
| 81(1)(g) | compensation by Federal Republic of Germany |
| 81(1)(g.1) | income from personal injury award property |
| 81(1)(g.2) | income from income exempt under para. (g.1) |
| 81(1)(g.3) | hepatitis C trust |
| 81(1)(h) | social assistance |
| 81(1)(i) | RCMP pension or compensation |
| 81(1)(j) | [Repealed under former Act] |
| 81(1)(k) | employees profit sharing plan |
| 81(1)(l) | prospecting |
| 81(1)(m) | interest on certain obligations |
| 81(1)(n) | Governor General |
| 81(1)(o), (p) | [Repealed] |
| 81(1)(q) | provincial indemnities |
| 81(1)(r) | foreign retirement arrangements |
| 81(1)(s) | [Repealed under former Act] |
| 81(1.1) | [Repealed under former Act] |
| 81(2) | M.L.A.'s expense allowance |
| 81(3) | Municipal officers' expense allowance |
| 81(3.1) | Travel expenses |
| 81(3.1) | [Proposed] Travel expenses |
| 81(4) | [Repealed under former Act] |
| 81(4) | [Proposed] Payments for volunteer [emergency] services |
| 81(5) | Election |

## Subdivision h — Corporations Resident in Canada and Their Shareholders

82
| | |
|---|---|
| 82(1) | Taxable dividends received |
| 82(1.1) | Limitations as to subpara. (1)(a)(i) |
| 82(2) | Certain dividends [deemed] received by taxpayer |
| 82(3) | Dividends received by spouse [or common-law partner] |

83
| | |
|---|---|
| 83(1) | Qualifying dividends |
| 83(2), (2.1) | Capital dividend |
| 83(2.2)–(2.4) | Where subsec. (2.1) does not apply |
| 83(3) | Late filed elections |
| 83(3.1) | Request for election |
| 83(4) | Penalty for late filed election |
| 83(5) | Unpaid balance of penalty |
| 83(6) | Definition of "qualifying dividend" |
| 83(7) | Amalgamation where there are tax-deferred preferred shares |

84
| | |
|---|---|
| 84(1) | Deemed dividend |
| 84(2) | Distribution on winding-up, etc. |
| 84(3) | Redemption, etc. |
| 84(4) | Reduction of paid-up capital |
| 84(4.1) | Deemed dividend on reduction of paid-up capital |
| 84(4.2) | Deemed dividend on term preferred share |
| 84(4.3) | Deemed dividend on guaranteed share |
| 84(5) | Amount distributed or paid where a share |
| 84(6) | Where subsec. (2) or (3) does not apply |
| 84(7) | When dividend payable |
| 84(8) | Where subsec. (3) does not apply |

cvii

## Detailed Table of Sections

| | |
|---|---|
| 84(9) | Shares disposed of on redemptions, etc. |
| 84(10) | Reduction of contributed surplus |
| 84(11) | Computation of contributed surplus |
| 84.1 | |
| 84.1(1), (2) | Non-arm's length sale of shares |
| 84.1(2) | Idem |
| 84.1(2.01), (2.1) | Rules for para. 84.1(2)(a.1) |
| 84.1(2.2) | Rules for para. 84.1(2)(b) |
| 84.1(3) | Addition to paid-up capital |
| 84.2 | |
| 84.2(1) | Computation of paid-up capital in respect of particular class of shares |
| 84.2(2), (3) | Debt deficiency |
| 85 | |
| 85(1) | Transfer of property to corporation by shareholders [rollover] |
| 85(1.1) | Definition of "eligible property" |
| 85(1.11) | [Proposed] Exception |
| 85(1.2) | Application of subsec. (1) |
| 85(1.3) | Meaning of "wholly owned corporation" |
| 85(1.4) | Definitions |
| 85(2) | Transfer of property to corporation from partnership |
| 85(2.1) | Computing paid-up capital |
| 85(3) | Where partnership wound up |
| 85(4) | [Repealed] |
| 85(5) | Rules on transfers of depreciable property |
| 85(5.1) | [Repealed] |
| 85(6) | Time for election |
| 85(7) | Late filed election |
| 85(7.1) | Special cases |
| 85(8) | Penalty for late filed election |
| 85(9) | Unpaid balance of penalty |
| 85.1 | |
| 85.1(1) | Share for share exchange |
| 85.1(2) | Where subsec. (1) does not apply |
| 85.1(2.1) | Computation of paid-up capital |
| 85.1(3) | Disposition of shares of foreign affiliate |
| 85.1(4) | Exception |
| 85.1(5) | [Proposed] Foreign share for foreign share exchange |
| 85.1(6) | [Proposed] Where subsec. (5) does not apply |
| 86 | |
| 86(1), (2) | Exchange of shares by a shareholder in course of reorganization of capital |
| 86(2.1) | Computation of paid-up capital |
| 86(3) | Application |
| 86(4) | Computation of adjusted cost base |
| 86.1 | [Proposed] Foreign spin-offs |
| 86.1(1) | [Proposed] Eligible distribution not included in income |
| 86.1(2) | [Proposed] Eligible distribution |
| 86.1(3) | [Proposed] Cost adjustments |
| 86.1(4) | [Proposed] Inventory |
| 86.1(5) | [Proposed] Reassessments |
| 87 | |
| 87(1) | Amalgamations |
| 87(1.1) | Shares deemed to have been received by virtue of merger |
| 87(1.2) | New corporation continuation of a predecessor |
| 87(1.2) | [Proposed] New corporation continuation of a predecessor |
| 87(1.3) | [Repealed under former Act] |
| 87(1.4) | Definition of "subsidiary wholly-owned corporation" |
| 87(1.5) | Definitions |
| 87(2) | Rules applicable |
| 87(2)(a) | taxation year |
| 87(2)(b) | inventory |
| 87(2)(c) | method adopted for computing income |

cviii

## Detailed Table of Sections

87(2)(d)     depreciable property
87(2)(d.1)     depreciable property acquired from predecessor corporation
87(2)(e)     capital property
87(2)(e.1)     partnership interest
87(2)(e.2)     security or debt obligation
87(2)(e.3)     financial institutions — specified debt obligation
87(2)(e.4), (e.5)     financial institutions — mark-to-market property
87(2)(f)     eligible capital property
87(2)(f.1)     [Repealed]
87(2)(g)     reserves
87(2)(g.1)     continuation
87(2)(g.2)     financial institution rules
87(2)(g.3)     superficial losses
87(2)(g.4)     superficial losses — capital property
87(2)(h), (h.1)     debts
87(2)(i), (j)     special reserve
87(2)(j.1)     inventory adjustment
87(2)(j.2)     prepaid expenses and matchable expenditures
87(2)(j.3)     employee benefit plans, etc. [SDAs, RCAs]
87(2)(j.4)     accrual rules
87(2)(j.5)     cancellation of lease
87(2)(j.6)     continuing corporation
87(2)(j.7)     certain transfers and loans [attribution rules]
87(2)(j.8)     international banking centre business
87(2)(j.9)     Part VI and Part I.3 tax [pre-1992]
87(2)(j.91)     Part I.3 and Part VI tax
87(2)(j.92)     subsec. 125(5.1) [small business deduction]
87(2)(j.93)     mining reclamation trusts [and qualifying environmental trusts]
87(2)(j.94)     film or video productions
87(2)(j.95)     [Proposed] non-resident trusts and foreign investment entities
87(2)(k)     certain payments to employees
87(2)(l), (l.1)     scientific research and experimental development
87(2)(l.2)     definition of "predecessor corporation"
87(2)(l.21)     [debt forgiveness rules]
87(2)(l.3)     replacement property
87(2)(m)     reserves
87(2)(m.1)     [charitable] gift of non-qualifying security
87(2)(n)     outlays made pursuant to warranty
87(2)(o)     expiration of options previously granted
87(2)(p)     consideration for resource property disposition
87(2)(q)     registered [pension] plans [and DPSPs]
87(2)(r)–(s.1)     [Repealed under former Act]
87(2)(t)     pre-1972 capital surplus on hand
87(2)(u)     shares of foreign affiliate
87(2)(v)     gifts [charitable donations]
87(2)(w)     [Repealed under former Act]
87(2)(x)     taxable dividends
87(2)(y)     contributed surplus
87(2)(y.1)     [Repealed]
87(2)(z)     foreign tax carryover
87(2)(z.1)     capital dividend account
87(2)(z.2)     application of Part III
87(2)(aa)     refundable dividend tax on hand
87(2)(bb)     mutual fund and investment corporations
87(2)(bb.1)     flow-through entities
87(2)(cc)     non-resident-owned investment corporation
87(2)(dd)–(hh)     [Repealed under former Act]
87(2)(ii)     public corporation
87(2)(jj)     interest on certain obligations
87(2)(kk)     disposition of shares of controlled corporation
87(2)(ll), (mm)     para. 20(1)(n) and subpara. 40(1)(a)(iii) amounts

## Detailed Table of Sections

| | |
|---|---|
| 87(2)(nn) | refundable Part VII tax on hand |
| 87(2)(oo) | investment tax credit |
| 87(2)(oo.1) | refundable investment tax credit and balance-due day |
| 87(2)(pp) | cumulative offset account computation |
| 87(2)(qq) | continuation of corporation [investment tax credit] |
| 87(2)(rr) | tax on taxable preferred shares |
| 87(2)(ss) | transferred liability for Part VI.1 tax |
| 87(2)(tt) | livestock — inclusion of deferred amount |
| 87(2)(uu) | fuel tax rebates |
| 87(2.01) | Application of subsec. 37.1(5) |
| 87(2.1) | Non-capital losses, etc., of predecessor corporations |
| 87(2.11) | Vertical amalgamations |
| 87(2.2) | Amalgamation of insurers |
| 87(3) | Computation of paid-up capital |
| 87(3.1) | Election for non-application of subsec. (3) |
| 87(4) | Shares of predecessor corporation |
| 87(4.1), (4.2) | Exchanged shares |
| 87(4.3) | Exchanged rights |
| 87(4.4) | Flow-through shares |
| 87(5) | Options to acquire shares of predecessor corporation |
| 87(5.1) | Adjusted cost base of option |
| 87(6) | Obligations of predecessor corporation |
| 87(6.1) | Adjusted cost base |
| 87(7) | [Obligations of predecessor corporation] |
| 87(8) | Foreign merger |
| 87(8) | [Proposed] Foreign merger |
| 87(8.1) | Definition of "foreign merger" |
| 87(8.1) | [Proposed] Definition of "foreign merger" |
| 87(9) | Rules applicable in respect of certain mergers [triangular amalgamation] |
| 87(10) | Share deemed listed |
| 87(11) | Vertical amalgamations |
| 88 | |
| 88(1) | Winding-up [of subsidiary] |
| 88(1)(a), (a.1) | [property of subsidiary] |
| 88(1)(a.2) | [partnership interest] |
| 88(1)(a.3) | [specified debt obligation] |
| 88(1)(b) | [shares of subsidiary] |
| 88(1)(c) | [cost to parent] |
| 88(1)(c.1) | [eligible capital property] |
| 88(1)(c.2) | ["specified person" and "specified shareholder"] |
| 88(1)(c.3) | [substituted property] |
| 88(1)(c.4) | ["specified property"] |
| 88(1)(c.5) | ["specified subsidiary corporation"] |
| 88(1)(c.6) | [control acquired by way of articles of arrangement] |
| 88(1)(c.7) | [depreciable property] |
| 88(1)(c.8) | [Proposed] ["specified class"] |
| 88(1)(d) | [increase in cost amounts (bump)] |
| 88(1)(d.1) | [rules not applicable] |
| 88(1)(d.2) | [when control acquired] |
| 88(1)(d.3) | [control acquired due to death] |
| 88(1)(e) | [Repealed under former Act] |
| 88(1)(e.1) | [reserves] |
| 88(1)(e.2) | [rules applicable] |
| 88(1)(e.3) | [investment tax credit] |
| 88(1)(e.4) | [employment tax credit] |
| 88(1)(e.5) | [Repealed] |
| 88(1)(e.6) | [charitable donations] |
| 88(1)(e.61) | [donation of non-qualifying securities] |
| 88(1)(e.7) | [foreign tax credit] |
| 88(1)(e.8) | [investment tax credit — expenditure limit] |
| 88(1)(e.9) | [instalments and refundable ITCs] |

## Detailed Table of Sections

| | |
|---|---|
| 88(1)(f) | [depreciable property] |
| 88(1)(g) | [insurance corporation] |
| 88(1)(h) | [financial institution — mark-to-market property] |
| 88(1)(i) | [financial institution — mark-to-market property] |
| 88(1.1) | Non-capital losses, etc., of subsidiary |
| 88(1.2) | Net capital losses of subsidiary |
| 88(1.3) | Computation of income and tax of parent |
| 88(1.4) | Qualified expenditure of subsidiary |
| 88(1.41) | Application of subsec. 37.1(5) |
| 88(1.5) | Parent continuation of subsidiary |
| 88(1.5), (1.6) | [Proposed] Parent continuation of subsidiary |
| 88(1.7) | Interpretation |
| 88(2) | Winding-up of [other] Canadian corporation |
| 88(2.1) | Definition of "pre-1972 capital surplus on hand" |
| 88(2.2) | Determination of pre-1972 capital surplus on hand |
| 88(2.3) | Actual cost of certain depreciable property |
| 88(3) | Dissolution of foreign affiliate |
| 88(4) | Amalgamation deemed not to be acquisition of control |
| 88(4) | [Proposed] Amalgamation deemed not to be acquisition of control |
| 88.1 | [Repealed] |
| 89 | |
| 89(1) | Definitions |
| 89(1.01) | Application of subsec. 138(12) |
| 89(1.1) | Capital dividend account where control acquired |
| 89(1.2) | Capital dividend account of tax-exempt corporation |
| 89(2) | Where corporation is beneficiary |
| 89(3) | Simultaneous dividends |
| 89(4)–(6) | [Repealed under former Act] |
| 89.1 | [Repealed under former Act] |

### Subdivision i — Shareholders of Corporations Not Resident in Canada

| | |
|---|---|
| 90 | Dividends received from non-resident corporation |
| 91(1) | Amounts to be included in respect of share of foreign affiliate |
| 91 | |
| 91(1) | [Proposed] Amounts to be included in respect of share of foreign affiliate |
| 91(2) | Reserve where foreign exchange restriction |
| 91(3) | Reserve for preceding year to be included |
| 91(4) | Amounts deductible in respect of foreign taxes |
| 91(5), (6) | Amounts deductible in respect of dividends received |
| 91(7) | [Proposed] Shares acquired from a partnership |
| 92 | |
| 92(1) | Adjusted cost base of share of foreign affiliate |
| 92(2), (3) | Deduction in computing adjusted cost base |
| 92(4) | [Proposed] Disposition of a partnership interest |
| 92(5) | [Proposed] Deemed gain from the disposition of a share |
| 92(6) | [Proposed] Formula |
| 93 | |
| 93(1), (1.1) | Election re disposition of share in foreign affiliate |
| 93(1.2) | [Proposed] Disposition of a share of a foreign affiliate held by a partnership |
| 93(1.3) | [Proposed] Deemed election |
| 93(2) | Loss limitation on disposition of share |
| 93(2) | [Proposed] Loss limitation on disposition of share |
| 93(2.1) | [Proposed] Loss limitation — disposition of share by partnership |
| 93(2.2), (2.3) | [Proposed] Loss limitation — disposition of partnership interest |
| 93(3) | Exempt dividends |
| 93(3) | [Proposed] Exempt dividends |
| 93(4) | Loss on disposition of shares of foreign affiliate |
| 93(5) | Late filed elections |
| 93(5.1) | Special cases |
| 93(6) | Penalty for late filed election |
| 93(7) | Unpaid balance of penalty |

## Detailed Table of Sections

| | |
|---|---|
| 93.1 | |
| 93.1(1) | [Proposed] Shares held by a partnership |
| 93.1(2) | [Proposed] Where dividends received by a partnership |
| 94 | |
| 94(1) | Application of certain provisions to trusts not resident in Canada |
| 94(2) | Rights and obligations |
| 94(3) | Deduction in computing taxable income |
| 94(4) | Deduction from foreign accrual property income |
| 94(5) | Adjusted cost base of capital interest in trust |
| 94(6) | Where financial assistance given |
| 94(7) | [Repealed] |
| 94 | [Proposed] Treatment of Trusts with Canadian Contributors |
| 94(1) | [Proposed] Definitions |
| 94(2) | [Proposed] Rules of application |
| 94(3) | [Proposed] Liabilities of non-resident trust and others |
| 94(4) | [Proposed] Excluded provisions |
| 94(5) | [Proposed] Ceasing to reside in Canada |
| 94(6) | [Proposed] Becoming or ceasing to be an exempt foreign trust |
| 94(7) | [Proposed] Limit to amount recoverable |
| 94(8) | [Proposed] Recovery limit |
| 94(9) | [Proposed] Determination of fair market value-special case |
| 94.1 | |
| 94.1(1) | Offshore investment fund property |
| 94.1(2) | Definitions |
| 94.1(3) | Interpretation |
| 94.1 | [Proposed] Foreign Investment Entities — Accrual Treatment |
| 94.1(1) | [Proposed] Definitions |
| 94.1(2) | [Proposed] Conditions for application of tax regime for foreign investment entities |
| 94.1(3) | [Proposed] Income inclusion and deduction |
| 94.1(4) | [Proposed] Exceptions |
| 94.1(5) | [Proposed] Income allocation |
| 94.1(6) | [Proposed] Fresh start year |
| 94.1(7) | [Proposed] Loss allocation |
| 94.1(8) | [Proposed] Specified tax allocation |
| 94.1(9) | [Proposed] Adjusted cost base |
| 94.1(10) | [Proposed] Property deemed owned by an entity |
| 94.1(11) | [Proposed] Significant interest in an entity |
| 94.1(12) | [Proposed] Entity treated as controlled foreign affiliate |
| 94.1(13) | [Proposed] Exception for qualifying dispositions and issues |
| 94.1(14) | [Proposed] Qualifying disposition |
| 94.1(15) | [Proposed] Qualifying issue |
| 94.1(16) | [Proposed] Demand for information |
| 94.1(17) | [Proposed] Effect of insufficient information |
| 94.2 | [Proposed] Foreign Investment Entities — Mark-to-market |
| 94.2(1) | [Proposed] Definitions |
| 94.2(2) | [Proposed] Rules of application |
| 94.2(3) | [Proposed] Where mark-to-market method applies |
| 94.2(4) | [Proposed] Mark-to-market |
| 94.2(5) | [Proposed] Non-resident periods excluded |
| 94.2(6) | [Proposed] Foreign partnership — member becoming resident |
| 94.2(7) | [Proposed] Foreign partnership — members ceasing to be resident |
| 94.2(8) | [Proposed] Application of subsecs. (6) and (7) |
| 94.2(9) | [Proposed] Tracked interests |
| 94.2(10) | [Proposed] Treatment of foreign insurance policies |
| 94.2(11) | [Proposed] Change of status of entity |
| 94.2(12) | [Proposed] Cost of participating interest |
| 94.2(13) | [Proposed] Deferral amount where same interest reacquired |
| 94.2(14) | [Proposed] Fresh start re change of status of entity |
| 94.2(15) | [Proposed] Fresh start after emigration of taxpayer |
| 94.2(16) | [Proposed] Fresh start re change of status of tax-exempt entity |
| 94.2(17) | [Proposed] Superficial dispositions |

## Detailed Table of Sections

| | |
|---|---|
| 94.3 | |
| 94.3(1) | [Proposed] Definitions and rules of application |
| 94.3(2) | [Proposed] Prevention of double taxation |
| 95 | |
| 95(1) | Definitions for this subdivision |
| 95(1) | [Proposed] Definitions re foreign affiliates |
| 95(2) | Determination of certain components of foreign accrual property income |
| 95(2)(a) | [income related to active business] |
| 95(2)(a.1) | [income from sale of property] |
| 95(2)(a.2) | [income from insurance] |
| 95(2)(a.3) | [income from Canadian debt and lease obligations] |
| 95(2)(a.3) | [Proposed] [income from Canadian debt and lease obligations] |
| 95(2)(a.4) | [income from partnership debt and lease obligations] |
| 95(2)(b) | [services deemed not active business] |
| 95(2)(c) | [rollover of FA shares to another FA] |
| 95(2)(d), (d.1) | [foreign merger] |
| 95(2)(e), (e.1) | [windup of foreign affiliate] |
| 95(2)(f) | [capital gains and losses of foreign affiliate] |
| 95(2)(g) | [debt settlement — currency fluctuation] |
| 95(2)(g) | [Proposed] [currency fluctuation] |
| 95(2)(g.1) | [debt forgiveness rules] |
| 95(2)(g.2) | [Proposed] [foreign spin-off election] |
| 95(2)(g.2) | [Proposed] [application of foreign investment entity rules] |
| 95(2)(h) | [share transactions — currency fluctuation] |
| 95(2)(i) | [settlement of debt relating to excluded property] |
| 95(2)(j) | [ACB of partnership interest] |
| 95(2)(k) | [change in business — fresh start rule] |
| 95(2)(l) | [trading or dealing in debt] |
| 95(2)(m) | ["qualifying interest"] |
| 95(2.1) | Rule for definition "investment business" |
| 95(2.2) | Rule for para. (2)(a) |
| 95(2.2) | [Proposed] Rule for subsec. (2) |
| 95(2.3) | Application of para. (2)(a.1) |
| 95(2.4) | Application of para. (2)(a.3) |
| 95(2.5) | Definitions for para. (2)(a.3) |
| 95(3) | Definition of "services" |
| 95(4) | Definitions |
| 95(4.1) | Application of subsec. 87(8.1) |
| 95(5) | Income bonds or debentures issued by foreign affiliates |
| 95(6) | Where rights or shares issued, acquired or disposed of to avoid tax |
| 95(6)(a) | |
| 95(6)(a) | |
| 95(6)(b) | |
| 95(6)(b) | |
| 95(7) | Stock dividends from foreign affiliates |

### Subdivision j — Partnerships and Their Members

| | |
|---|---|
| 96 | |
| 96(1) | General rules |
| 96(1.1) | Allocation of share of income to retiring partner |
| 96(1.2) | Disposal of right to share in income, etc |
| 96(1.3) | Deductions |
| 96(1.4) | Right deemed not to be capital property |
| 96(1.5) | Disposition by virtue of death of taxpayer |
| 96(1.6) | Members of partnership deemed to be carrying on business in Canada |
| 96(1.7) | Gains and losses |
| 96(1.7) | [Proposed] Gains and losses |
| 96(1.8) | Loan of property |
| 96(1.9) | [Proposed] Application of sections 94.1 and 94.2 |
| 96(2) | Construction |
| 96(2.1) | Limited partnership losses [at-risk rule] |
| 96(2.2), (2.3) | At-risk amount |

cxiii

## Detailed Table of Sections

| | |
|---|---|
| 96(2.4) | Limited partner |
| 96(2.5) | Exempt interest |
| 96(2.6), (2.7) | Artificial transactions |
| 96(3) | Agreement or election of partnership members |
| 96(3) | [Proposed] Agreement or election of partnership members |
| 96(4) | Election |
| 96(5) | Late filing |
| 96(5.1) | Special cases |
| 96(6) | Penalty for late-filed election |
| 96(7) | Unpaid balance of penalty |
| 96(8), (9) | Foreign partnerships |
| 96(9) | [Proposed] Application of foreign partnership rule |
| 97 | |
| 97(1) | Contribution of property to partnership |
| 97(2) | Rules where election by partners |
| 97(3), (3.1) | [Repealed] |
| 97(4) | Where capital cost to partner exceeds proceeds of disposition |
| 98 | |
| 98(1) | Disposition of partnership property |
| 98(2) | Deemed proceeds |
| 98(3) | Rules applicable where partnership ceases to exist [rollout] |
| 98(4) | Where subsec. (3) does not apply |
| 98(5) | Where partnership business carried on as sole proprietorship |
| 98(6) | Continuation of predecessor partnership by new partnership |
| 98.1 | |
| 98.1(1) | Residual interest in partnership |
| 98.1(2) | Continuation of original partnership |
| 98.2 | Transfer of interest on death |
| 99 | |
| 99(1) | Fiscal period of terminated partnership |
| 99(2) | Fiscal period of terminated partnership for individual member |
| 99(3), (4) | Validity of election |
| 100 | |
| 100(1) | Disposition of an interest in a partnership |
| 100(2), (2.1) | Gain from disposition of interest in partnership |
| 100(3) | Transfer of interest on death |
| 100(4) | Loss re interest in partnership |
| 101 | Disposition of farmland by partnership |
| 102 | |
| 102(1) | Definition of "Canadian partnership" |
| 102(2) | Member of a partnership |
| 103 | |
| 103(1) | Agreement to share income, etc., so as to reduce or postpone tax otherwise payable |
| 103(1.1) | Agreement to share income, etc., in unreasonable proportions |
| 103(2) | Definition of "losses" |

### Subdivision k — Trusts and Their Beneficiaries

| | |
|---|---|
| 104 | |
| 104(1) | Reference to trust or estate |
| 104(1) | [Proposed] Reference to trust or estate |
| 104(1.1) | [Proposed] Restricted meaning of "beneficiary" |
| 104(1.1) | [Proposed] Restricted meaning of beneficiary |
| 104(2) | Taxed as individual |
| 104(3) | [Repealed under former Act] |
| 104(4) | Deemed disposition by trust |
| 104(4) | [Proposed] Deemed disposition by trust |
| 104(4.1) | [Proposed] Mark-to-market property |
| 104(5) | Idem [depreciable property] |
| 104(5) | [Proposed] Depreciable property [deemed disposition] |
| 104(5.1) | Idem [NISA Fund No. 2] |
| 104(5.2) | Rules for trusts [resource property] |
| 104(5.2) | [Proposed] Resource property |

cxiv

## Detailed Table of Sections

| | |
|---|---|
| 104(5.3) | Election |
| 104(5.31) | Revocation of election |
| 104(5.4) | Exempt beneficiary |
| 104(5.5) | Beneficiary |
| 104(5.6), (5.7) | Designated contributor |
| 104(5.8) | Trust transfers |
| 104(5.8) | [Proposed] Trust transfers |
| 104(6) | Deduction in computing income of trust |
| 104(6) | [Proposed] Deduction in computing income of trust |
| 104(7) | Non-resident beneficiary |
| 104(7.01) | [Proposed] Trusts deemed to be resident in Canada |
| 104(7.1) | Capital interest greater than income interest |
| 104(7.2) | Avoidance of subsec. (7.1) |
| 104(8), (9) | [Repealed under former Act] |
| 104(10) | Where property owned for non-residents |
| 104(11) | Dividend received from non-resident-owned investment corporation |
| 104(12) | Deduction of amounts included in preferred beneficiaries' incomes |
| 104(13) | Income of beneficiary |
| 104(13) | [Proposed] Income of beneficiary |
| 104(13.1), (13.2) | Amounts deemed not paid |
| 104(14) | Election by trust and preferred beneficiary |
| 104(14.01) | Late, amended or revoked election |
| 104(14.02) | Late, amended or revoked election |
| 104(14.1) | NISA election |
| 104(15) | Allocable amount for preferred beneficiary |
| 104(16)–(17.2) | [Repealed under former Act] |
| 104(18) | Trust for minor |
| 104(19) | Taxable dividends |
| 104(20) | Designation in respect of non-taxable dividends |
| 104(21) | Taxable capital gains |
| 104(21.01)–(21.03) | Late, amended or revoked designation |
| 104(21.1), (21.2) | Beneficiary's taxable capital gain |
| 104(21.2) | [Proposed] Beneficiaries' taxable capital gain |
| 104(21.3) | Net taxable capital gains of trust determined |
| 104(21.4) | [Proposed] Deemed gains |
| 104(22) | Designation of foreign source income by trust |
| 104(22.1) | Foreign tax deemed paid by beneficiary |
| 104(22.2) | Recalculation of trust's foreign source income |
| 104(22.3) | Recalculation of trust's foreign tax |
| 104(22.4) | Definitions |
| 104(23) | Testamentary trusts |
| 104(24) | Amount payable |
| 104(24) | [Proposed] Amount payable |
| 104(25), (25.1), (26) | [Repealed under former Act] |
| 104(27) | Pension benefits |
| 104(27.1) | DPSP benefits |
| 104(28) | [Death benefit deemed received by beneficiary] |
| 104(29) | Amounts deemed payable to beneficiaries [resource income] |
| 104(30), (31) | Tax under Part XII.2 |
| 105 | |
| 105(1) | Benefits under trust |
| 105(2) | Upkeep, etc. |
| 106 | |
| 106(1) | Income interest in trust |
| 106(1.1) | Cost of income interest in a trust |
| 106(1.1) | [Proposed] Cost of income interest in a trust |
| 106(2) | Disposition by taxpayer of income interest |
| 106(3) | Proceeds of disposition of income interest |
| 107 | |
| 107(1) | Disposition by taxpayer of capital interest |
| 107(1.1) | Cost of capital interest in a trust |

cxv

## Detailed Table of Sections

| | |
|---|---|
| 107(1.1) | [Proposed] Cost of capital interest in a trust |
| 107(2) | Capital interest distribution by personal or prescribed trust |
| 107(2) | [Proposed] Distribution by personal trust |
| 107(2.001) | [Proposed] No rollover on election by a trust |
| 107(2.002) | [Proposed] No rollover on election by a beneficiary |
| 107(2.01) | Distribution of principal residence |
| 107(2.01) | [Proposed] Distribution of principal residence |
| 107(2.1) | Other distributions |
| 107(2.1) | [Proposed] Other distributions |
| 107(2.11) | [Proposed] Gains not distributed to beneficiaries |
| 107(2.2) | Flow-through entity |
| 107(3) | Cost of property other than non-depreciable capital property |
| 107(4) | Where trust in favour of spouse [or common-law partner] |
| 107(4) | [Proposed] Trusts in favour of spouse, common-law partner or self |
| 107(4.1) | Where subsec. 75(2) applicable to trust |
| 107(5) | Distribution to non-resident |
| 107(5) | [Proposed] Distribution to non-resident |
| 107(5.1) | [Proposed] Instalment interest |
| 107(6) | Loss reduction |
| 107.1 | Distribution by employee trust or employee benefit plan |
| 107.1 | [Proposed] Distribution by employee trust, employee benefit plan or similar trust |
| 107.2 | Distribution by a retirement compensation arrangement |
| 107.3 | |
| 107.3(1) | Treatment of beneficiaries under qualifying environmental trusts |
| 107.3(2) | Transfers to beneficiaries |
| 107.3(3) | Ceasing to be a qualifying environmental trust |
| 107.3(4) | Application |
| 107.4 | |
| 107.4(1) | [Proposed] Qualifying disposition |
| 107.4(2) | [Proposed] Application of paragraph (1)(a) |
| 107.4(3) | [Proposed] Tax consequences of qualifying dispositions |
| 107.4(4) | [Proposed] Fair market value of vested interest in trust |
| 108 | |
| 108(1) | Definitions |
| 108(2) | Where trust is a unit trust |
| 108(3) | Income of a trust in certain provisions |
| 108(3) | [Proposed] Income of a trust in certain provisions |
| 108(4) | Trust not disqualified |
| 108(4) | [Proposed] Trust not disqualified |
| 108(5) | Interpretation |
| 108(6) | Variation of trusts |
| 108(6) | [Proposed] Variation of trusts |
| 108(7) | [Proposed] Interests acquired for consideration |

### DIVISION C — COMPUTATION OF TAXABLE INCOME

| | |
|---|---|
| 109 | [Repealed under former Act] |
| 110 | |
| 110(1) | Deductions permitted |
| 110(1)(a)–(c) | [Repealed under former Act] |
| 110(1)(d) | employee options |
| 110(1)(d.01), (d.1) | [Proposed] charitable donation of employee option securities |
| 110(1)(d.2) | prospector's and grubstaker's shares |
| 110(1)(d.3) | employer's shares [where election made re DPSP] |
| 110(1)(e)–(e.2) | [Repealed under former Act] |
| 110(1)(f) | deductions for payments |
| 110(1)(g)–(i) | [Repealed under former Act] |
| 110(1)(j) | home relocation loan |
| 110(1)(k) | Part VI.1 tax |
| 110(1.1)–(1.3) | [Repealed under former Act] |
| 110(1.4) | Replacement of home relocation loan |
| 110(1.5) | Value of share under stock option |
| 110(1.5) | [Proposed] Determination of amounts relating to employee security options |

cxvi

## Detailed Table of Sections

| | |
|---|---|
| 110(1.6) | [Proposed] Meaning of "specified event" |
| 110(1.7) | [Proposed] Definitions in subsection 7(7) |
| 110(2) | Charitable gifts |
| 110(2.1)–(9) | [Repealed under former Act] |
| 110(2.1) | [Proposed] Charitable donation — proceeds of disposition of employee option securities |
| 110.1 | |
| 110.1(1) | Deduction for gifts |
| 110.1(1)(a) | charitable gifts |
| 110.1(1)(b) | gifts to Her Majesty |
| 110.1(1)(c) | gifts to institutions |
| 110.1(1)(d) | ecological gifts |
| 110.1(1)(d) | [Proposed] ecological gifts |
| 110.1(1.1) | Limitation on deductibility |
| 110.1(2) | Proof of gift |
| 110.1(2) | [Proposed] Proof of gift |
| 110.1(3) | Gifts of capital property |
| 110.1(4) | Gifts made by partnership |
| 110.1(5) | Ecological gifts |
| 110.1(5) | [Proposed] Ecological gifts |
| 110.1(6) | Non-qualifying securities |
| 110.1(7) | Corporation ceasing to exist |
| 110.2 | Definitions [lump-sum averaging] |
| 110.2(1) | |
| 110.2(2) | Deduction for lump-sum payments |
| 110.3 | [Repealed under former Act] |
| 110.4 | [Repealed] |
| 110.5 | Additions for foreign tax deductions |
| 110.6 | |
| 110.6(1), (1.1) | [Capital gains exemption — ] Definitions |
| 110.6(2) | Capital gains deduction — qualified farm property |
| 110.6(2.1) | Capital gains deduction — qualified small business corporation shares |
| 110.6(3) | [Repealed] |
| 110.6(4) | Maximum capital gains deduction |
| 110.6(4) | [Proposed] Maximum capital gains deduction |
| 110.6(5) | Deemed resident in Canada |
| 110.6(6) | Failure to report capital gain |
| 110.6(7), (8) | Deduction not permitted |
| 110.6(9) | Average annual rate of return |
| 110.6(10) | [Repealed under former Act] |
| 110.6(11) | Where deduction not permitted |
| 110.6(12) | Spousal trust deduction |
| 110.6(12) | [Proposed] Trust deduction |
| 110.6(13) | Determination under para. 3(b) |
| 110.6(14) | Related persons, etc. [miscellaneous rules re shares] |
| 110.6(15) | Value of assets of corporations |
| 110.6(16) | Personal trust |
| 110.6(17) | Order of deduction |
| 110.6(18) | [Repealed] |
| 110.6(19) | Election for property owned on February 22, 1994 |
| 110.6(20) | Application of subsec. (19) |
| 110.6(21) | Effect of election on non-qualifying real property |
| 110.6(22) | Adjusted cost base |
| 110.6(23) | Disposition of partnership interest |
| 110.6(24) | Time for election |
| 110.6(25) | Revocation of election |
| 110.6(26) | Late election |
| 110.6(27) | Amended election |
| 110.6(28) | Election that cannot be revoked or amended |
| 110.6(29) | Amount of penalty |
| 110.6(30) | Unpaid balance of penalty |

## Detailed Table of Sections

| | |
|---|---|
| 110.7 | |
| 110.7(1) | Residing in prescribed zone [northern Canada deduction] |
| 110.7(2) | Specified percentage |
| 110.7(3) | Restriction |
| 110.7(4), (5) | Board and lodging allowances, etc. |
| 111 | |
| 111(1) | Losses deductible |
| 111(1.1) | Net capital losses |
| 111(2) | Year of death |
| 111(3) | Limitation on deductibility |
| 111(4) | Acquisition of control [capital losses] |
| 111(5) | Idem [business or property losses] |
| 111(5.1) | Computation of undepreciated capital cost |
| 111(5.2) | Computation of cumulative eligible capital |
| 111(5.3) | Doubtful debts and bad debts |
| 111(5.4) | Non-capital loss |
| 111(5.5) | Restriction |
| 111(6), (7) | Limitation |
| 111(7.1) | Effect of election by insurer under subsec. 138(9) in respect of 1975 taxation year |
| 111(7.11) | Application of subsec. 138(12) |
| 111(7.2) | Non-capital loss of life insurer |
| 111(8) | Definitions |
| 111(9) | Exception |
| 111(10) | Fuel tax rebate loss abatement |
| 111(11) | Fuel tax rebate — partnerships |
| 111.1 | Order of applying provisions |
| 112 | |
| 112(1) | Deduction of taxable dividends received by corporation resident in Canada |
| 112(2) | Dividends received from non-resident corporation |
| 112(2.1), (2.2) | Where no deduction permitted |
| 112(2.2) | [Proposed] Guaranteed shares |
| 112(2.21) | [Proposed] Exceptions |
| 112(2.22), (2.3) | [Proposed] Interpretation |
| 112(2.4) | Where no deduction permitted |
| 112(2.5) | Application of subsec. (2.4) |
| 112(2.6) | Definitions |
| 112(2.7) | Change in agreement or condition |
| 112(2.8) | Loss sustained by investor |
| 112(2.9) | Related corporations |
| 112(3) | Loss on share that is capital property |
| 112(3.01) | Loss on share that is capital property — excluded dividends |
| 112(3.1) | Loss on share held by partnership |
| 112(3.11), (3.12) | Loss on share held by partnership — excluded dividends |
| 112(3.2) | Loss on share held by trust |
| 112(3.3) | Loss on share held by trust — special cases |
| 112(3.31), (3.32) | Loss on share held by trust — excluded dividends |
| 112(4) | Loss on share that is not capital property |
| 112(4.01) | Loss on share that is not capital property — excluded dividends |
| 112(4.1) | Fair market value of shares held as inventory |
| 112(4.11) | Fair market value of shares held as inventory — excluded dividends |
| 112(4.2) | Loss on share held by trust |
| 112(4.21), (4.22) | Loss on share held by trust — excluded dividends |
| 112(4.3) | [Repealed] |
| 112(5) | Disposition of share by financial institution |
| 112(5.1) | Share held for less than one year |
| 112(5.2) | Adjustment re dividends |
| 112(5.21) | Subsection (5.2) — excluded dividends |
| 112(5.3) | Adjustment not applicable |
| 112(5.4) | Deemed dispositions |
| 112(5.5) | Stop-loss rules not applicable |
| 112(5.6) | Stop-loss rules restricted |

Detailed Table of Sections

112(6)      Meaning of certain expressions
112(6)(a)    ["dividend", "taxable dividend"]
112(6)(b)    ["control"]
112(6)(c)    ["financial institution", "mark-to-market property"]
112(7)      Rules where shares exchanged
113
113(1)      Deduction in respect of dividend received from foreign affiliate
113(2)      Additional deduction
113(3)      Definitions
113(4)      Portion of dividend deemed paid out of exempt surplus
114          Individual resident in Canada for only part of year
114          [Proposed] Individual resident in Canada for only part of year
114.1       Application of subsec. 115(2)
114.2       Deductions in separate returns

### DIVISION D — TAXABLE INCOME EARNED IN CANADA BY NON-RESIDENTS

115
115(1)      Non-resident's taxable income [earned] in Canada [and taxable Canadian property]
115(2)      Idem [persons deemed employed in Canada]
115(3)      Property deemed to include interests and options
115(4)      Non-resident's income from Canadian resource property
115(4.1)    [Proposed] Foreign resource pool expenses
115(5)      Interpretation of "partnership"
115(6)      Application of subsec. 138(12)
115.1
115.1(1)    Competent authority agreements
115.1(2)    Transfer of rights and obligations
115.2       Non-Residents with Canadian Investment Service Providers
115.2(1)    Definitions
115.2(2)    Not carrying on business in Canada
115.2(3)    Interpretation
115.2(4)    Transfer pricing
116
116(1)      Disposition by non-resident person of certain property
116(1)      [Proposed] Disposition by non-resident person of certain property
116(2)      Certificate in respect of proposed disposition
116(3)      Notice to Minister
116(4)      Certificate in respect of property disposed of
116(5), (5.1)   Liability of purchaser
116(5.1)    [Proposed] Gifts, etc.
116(5.2)    Certificates for dispositions
116(5.2)    [Proposed] Certificates for dispositions
116(5.3)    Liability of purchaser in certain cases
116(5.4)    Presumption
116(6)      Definition of "excluded property"
116(7)      Application of subsec. 138(12)

### DIVISION E — COMPUTATION OF TAX
### Subdivision a — Rules Applicable to Individuals

117
117(1)      Tax payable under this Part
117(2)      1988 and subsequent taxation years rates
117(2)      [Proposed] Rate for 2000
117(2)      [Proposed] Rates for years after 2000
117(3)      [Proposed] Minimum thresholds for 2004
117(3)–(5.2)   [Repealed under former Act]
117(6), (7)   [Repealed]
117.1
117.1(1)    Annual adjustment [indexing]
117.1(1.1)   Adjustment of certain amounts
117.1(2)    [Repealed]
117.1(3)    Rounding

## Detailed Table of Sections

| | |
|---|---|
| 117.1(4) | Consumer Price Index |
| 117.1(5)–(8) | [Repealed under former Act] |
| 118 | |
| 118(1) | Personal credits |
| 118(1)(a) | married status |
| 118(1)(b) | wholly dependent person ["equivalent to spouse" credit] |
| 118(1)(b.1) | [Repealed] |
| 118(1)(c) | single status |
| 118(1)(c.1) | in-home care of relative [caregiver credit] |
| 118(1)(d) | dependants |
| 118(1)(e) | additional amount [re dependant] |
| 118(2) | Age credit |
| 118(3) | Pension credit |
| 118(3.1) | [Proposed] Minimum amounts for 2004 |
| 118(4) | Limitations re subsec. (1) |
| 118(5) | Support |
| 118(6) | Definition of "dependant" |
| 118(7) | Definitions |
| 118(8) | Interpretation |
| 118.1 | |
| 118.1(1) | Definitions |
| 118.1(2) | Proof of gift |
| 118.1(2) | [Proposed] Proof of gift |
| 118.1(2.1) | Ordering |
| 118.1(3) | Deduction by individuals for gifts |
| 118.1(4) | Gift in year of death |
| 118.1(4) | [Proposed] Gift in year of death |
| 118.1(5) | Gift by will |
| 118.1(5.1) | [Proposed] Direct designation — insurance proceeds |
| 118.1(5.2) | [Proposed] Rules applicable re: subsection (5.1) |
| 118.1(5.3) | [Proposed] Direct designation — RRSPs and RRIFs |
| 118.1(6) | Gift of capital property |
| 118.1(7) | Gifts of art |
| 118.1(7) | [Proposed] Gifts of art [by artist] |
| 118.1(7.1) | Gifts of cultural property |
| 118.1(7.1) | [Proposed] Gifts of cultural property |
| 118.1(8) | Gifts made by partnership |
| 118.1(9) | Commuter's charitable donations |
| 118.1(10) | Determination of fair market value |
| 118.1(10.1) | Determination of fair market value [cultural property] |
| 118.1(10.1) | [Proposed] Determination of fair market value [cultural or ecological property] |
| 118.1(10.2) | [Proposed] Request for determination by the Minister of the Environment |
| 118.1(10.3) | [Proposed] Duty of Minister of the Environment |
| 118.1(10.4) | [Proposed] Ecological gifts — redetermination |
| 118.1(10.5) | [Proposed] Certificate of fair market value |
| 118.1(11) | Assessments |
| 118.1(11) | [Proposed] Assessments |
| 118.1(12) | Ecological gifts [fair market value] |
| 118.1(12) | [Proposed] Ecological gifts [fair market value] |
| 118.1(13) | Non-qualifying securities |
| 118.1(14) | Exchanged security |
| 118.1(15) | Death of donor |
| 118.1(16) | Loanbacks |
| 118.1(17) | Ordering rule |
| 118.1(18) | Non-qualifying security defined |
| 118.1(19) | Excepted gift |
| 118.1(20) | Financial institution defined |
| 118.2 | |
| 118.2(1) | Medical expense credit |
| 118.2(2) | Medical expenses |
| 118.2(2)(a) | [medical and dental services] |

## Detailed Table of Sections

| | |
|---|---|
| 118.2(2)(b) | [attendant or nursing home care] |
| 118.2(2)(b.1) | [attendant] |
| 118.2(2)(b.2) | [group home care] |
| 118.2(2)(c) | [full-time attendant at home] |
| 118.2(2)(d) | [nursing home care] |
| 118.2(2)(e) | [school, institution, etc.] |
| 118.2(2)(f) | [ambulance fees] |
| 118.2(2)(g) | [transportation] |
| 118.2(2)(h) | [travel expenses] |
| 118.2(2)(i) | [devices] |
| 118.2(2)(i.1) | [devices for incontinence] |
| 118.2(2)(j) | [eyeglasses] |
| 118.2(2)(k) | [various] |
| 118.2(2)(l) | [guide dogs, etc.] |
| 118.2(2)(l.1) | [transplant costs] |
| 118.2(2)(l.2) | [alterations to home] |
| 118.2(2)(l.21) | [Proposed] [home construction costs] |
| 118.2(2)(l.3) | [lip reading and sign language training] |
| 118.2(2)(l.4) | [sign language services] |
| 118.2(2)(l.5) | [moving expenses] |
| 118.2(2)(l.6) | [driveway alterations] |
| 118.2(2)(l.7) | [van for wheelchair] |
| 118.2(2)(l.8) | [caregiver training] |
| 118.2(2)(l.9) | [therapy] |
| 118.2(2)(l.91) | [tutoring services] |
| 118.2(2)(m) | [prescribed devices] |
| 118.2(2)(n) | [drugs] |
| 118.2(2)(o) | [lab tests] |
| 118.2(2)(p) | [dentures] |
| 118.2(2)(q) | [health plan premiums] |
| 118.2(3) | Deemed medical expense |
| 118.2(4) | Deemed payment of medical expenses |
| 118.3 | |
| 118.3(1) | Credit for mental or physical impairment |
| 118.3(2) | Dependant having impairment |
| 118.3(3) | Partial dependency |
| 118.3(4) | Department of Human Resources Development |
| 118.3(4) | [Proposed] Additional information |
| 118.4 | |
| 118.4(1) | Nature of impairment |
| 118.4(2) | Reference to medical practitioners, etc. |
| 118.4(2) | [Proposed] Reference to medical practitioners, etc. |
| 118.5 | |
| 118.5(1) | Tuition credit |
| 118.5(1)(a) | [institution in Canada] |
| 118.5(1)(b) | [university outside Canada] |
| 118.5(1)(c) | [cross-border commuter] |
| 118.5(2) | Application to deemed residents |
| 118.5(3) | Inclusion of ancillary fees and charges |
| 118.6 | |
| 118.6(1) | [Education credit — ] Definitions |
| 118.6(1) | [Proposed] Definitions |
| 118.6(2) | Education credit |
| 118.6(3) | Disabled students |
| 118.61 | |
| 118.61(1) | Unused tuition and education tax credits |
| 118.61(2) | Deduction of carryforward |
| 118.62 | Credit for interest on student loan |
| 118.7 | Credit for UI [EI] premium and CPP contribution |
| 118.8 | Transfer of unused credits to spouse [or common-law partner] |
| 118.81 | Tuition and education tax credits transferred |

## Detailed Table of Sections

| | |
|---|---|
| 118.9 | Transfer to parent or grandparent |
| 118.91 | Part-year residents |
| 118.92 | Ordering of credits |
| 118.93 | Credits in separate returns |
| 118.94 | Tax payable by non-resident |
| 118.95 | Credits in year of bankruptcy |
| 119 | [Obsolete] |
| 119 | [Proposed] Former resident — credit for tax paid |
| 120 | |
| 120(1) | Income not earned in a province |
| 120(1) | [Proposed] Income not earned in a province |
| 120(2), (2.1) | Amount deemed paid in prescribed manner [Quebec abatement] |
| 120(2.2) | Amount deemed paid [First Nations tax] |
| 120(3) | Definition of "the individual's income for the year" |
| 120(3) | [Proposed] Definition of "individual's income for the year" |
| 120(3.1) | [Repealed under former Act] |
| 120(4) | Definitions |
| 120.1 | [Repealed] |
| 120.2 | |
| 120.2(1) | Minimum tax carry-over |
| 120.2(2) | [Repealed under former Act] |
| 120.2(3) | Additional tax determined |
| 120.2(4) | Where subsec. (1) does not apply |
| 120.2(4) | [Proposed] Where subsection (1) does not apply |
| 120.3 | CPP/QPP disability [or other] benefits for previous years |
| 120.31 | Lump-sum payments |
| 120.31(1) | Definitions |
| 120.31(2) | Addition to tax payable |
| 120.31(3) | Notional tax payable |
| 120.4 | Tax on split income [Kiddie tax] |
| 120.4(1) | Definitions |
| 120.4(2) | Tax on split income |
| 120.4(3) | Tax payable by a specified individual |
| 121 | Deduction for taxable dividends |
| 122 | |
| 122(1) | Tax payable by *inter vivos* trust |
| 122(1.1) | Deductions [personal credits] not permitted [to trust] |
| 122(2) | Where subsec. (1) does not apply |
| 122(3) | [Repealed under former Act] |
| 122.1 | [Repealed under former Act] |
| 122.2 | |
| 122.3 | |
| 122.3(1) | Deduction from tax payable where employment out of Canada [Overseas employment tax credit] |
| 122.3(1.1) | Excluded income |
| 122.3(2) | Definitions |
| 122.4 | [Repealed under former Act] |
| 122.5 | |
| 122.5(1) | [GST credit] Definitions |
| 122.5(2) | Persons not eligible individuals, qualified relations or qualified dependants |
| 122.5(3) | Deemed payment on account |
| 122.5(3.1) | Adjustment of certain amounts [annual indexing] |
| 122.5(4) | Months specified |
| 122.5(5) | Exceptions |
| 122.5(6) | Qualified relation of deceased eligible individual |
| 122.5(7) | Effect of bankruptcy |
| 122.51 | |
| 122.51(1) | [Refundable medical expense supplement — ] Definitions |
| 122.51(2) | Deemed payment on account of tax |

### Subdivision a.1 — Canada Child Tax Benefit

| | |
|---|---|
| 122.6 | Definitions |

cxxii

## Detailed Table of Sections

122.61
122.61(1) Deemed overpayment [Child Tax Benefit]
122.61(2) Exceptions
122.61(3) Non-residents and part-year residents
122.61(3.1) Effect of bankruptcy
122.61(4) Amount not to be charged, etc.
122.61(5) Annual adjustment [indexing]
122.61(5.1) [Repealed]
122.61(6) Adjustment to certain amounts
122.61(6.1) Exception
122.61(7) Rounding
122.62
122.62(1) Eligible individuals
122.62(2) Extension for notices
122.62(3) Exception
122.62(4) Person ceasing to be an eligible individual
122.62(5) Death of cohabiting spouse [or common-law partner]
122.62(6) Separation from cohabiting spouse [or common-law partner]
122.62(7) Person becoming a cohabiting spouse [or common-law partner]
122.62(8), (9) [Repealed]
122.63
122.63(1)–(3) Agreement
122.64
122.64(1) Confidentiality of information
122.64(2) Communication of information
122.64(3) Taxpayer's address
122.64(4) Offence
122.64(5) [Repealed]

### Subdivision b — Rules Applicable to Corporations

123
123(1) Rate for corporations
123(2) [Repealed under former Act]
123.1, 123.2 Corporation surtax
123.3 Refundable tax on CCPC's investment income
123.4, 123.5 [Repealed under former Act]
123.4 [Proposed] Corporation Tax Reductions
123.4(1) [Proposed] Definitions
123.4(2) [Proposed] General deduction from tax
123.4(3) [Proposed] CCPC deduction
124
124(1) Deduction from corporation tax
124(2)–(2.2) [Repealed under former Act]
124(3) Crown agents
124(4) Definitions
124.1, 124.2 [Repealed under former Act]
125
125(1) Small business deduction
125(1.1) [Repealed under former Act]
125(2) Interpretation of "business limit"
125(3) Associated corporations
125(4) Failure to file agreement
125(5) Special rules for business limit
125(5.1) Business limit reduction
125(6) Corporate partnerships
125(6.1) Corporation deemed member of partnership
125(6.2) Specified partnership income deemed nil
125(6.3) Partnership deemed to be controlled
125(7) Definitions
125(8)–(15) [Repealed under former Act]
125.1
125.1(1) Manufacturing and processing profits deductions [M&P credit]

Detailed Table of Sections

125.1(2)     Generating electrical energy for sale
125.1(2)     [Proposed] Electrical energy and steam
125.1(3)     Definitions
125.1(4)     Determination of gross revenue
125.1(5)     Interpretation
125.2
125.2(1), (2)     Deduction of [pre-1992] Part VI tax
125.2(3)     Definition of "unused Part VI tax credit"
125.3
125.3(1), (1.1)     Deduction of [pre-1992] Part I.3 tax
125.3(2)     Special rules
125.3(3)     Acquisition of control
125.3(4)     Definitions

### Canadian Film or Video Production Tax Credit

125.4
125.4(1)     Definitions
125.4(2)     Rules governing labour expenditure of a corporation
125.4(3)     Tax credit
125.4(4)     Exception
125.4(5)     When assistance received
125.4(6)     Revocation of a certificate

### Film or Video Production Services Tax Credit

125.5
125.5(1)     Definitions
125.5(2)     Rules governing Canadian labour expenditure of a corporation
125.5(3)     Tax credit
125.5(4)     Canadian film or video production
125.5(5)     When assistance received
125.5(6)     Revocation of certificate

### Subdivision c — Rules Applicable to All Taxpayers

126
126(1)     Foreign tax deduction [foreign tax credit]
126(1.1), (2)     [Proposed] Authorized foreign bank
126(2.1)     Amount determined for purposes of para. (2)(b)
126(2.2)     Non-residents' foreign tax deduction
126(2.2)     [Proposed] Non-resident's foreign tax deduction
126(2.21)     [Proposed] Former resident — deduction
126(2.22)     [Proposed] Former resident — trust beneficiary
126(2.23)     [Proposed] Where foreign credit available
126(2.3)     Rules relating to unused foreign tax credit
126(3)     Employees of international organizations
126(4)     Portion of foreign tax not included
126(4)     [Proposed] Portion of foreign tax not included
126(4.1)     No economic profit
126(4.1)     [Proposed] No economic profit
126(4.2)     Short-term securities acquisitions
126(4.3)     Exceptions
126(4.4)     Dispositions ignored
126(5)     Foreign tax
126(5)     [Proposed] Foreign oil and gas levies
126(5.1)     Deductions for specified capital gains
126(6)     Construction of subsecs. (1) and (2)
126(6)     [Proposed] Rules of construction
126(7)     Definitions
126(8)     Deemed separate source
126(9)     [Proposed] Computation of qualifying incomes and losses
126.1
126.1(1)     [1993 UI premium tax credit] Definitions
126.1(2), (3)     Associated employers
126.1(4)     Business carried on by another employer

# Detailed Table of Sections

| | |
|---|---|
| 126.1(5) | Definition of "specified employer" |
| 126.1(6), (7) | UI premium tax credit |
| 126.1(8) | Definition of "UI premium tax credit" |
| 126.1(9) | Allocation by associated employers |
| 126.1(10) | Allocation by the Minister |
| 126.1(11) | UI premium tax credit — associated employers |
| 126.1(12), (13) | Prepayment of UI premium tax credit |
| 126.1(14), (15) | Excess prepayment |
| 127 | |
| 127(1) | Logging tax deduction [credit] |
| 127(2) | Definitions |
| 127(3) | Contributions to registered parties and candidates [political contribution credit] |
| 127(3.1) | Issue of receipts |
| 127(3.2) | Deposit of amounts contributed |
| 127(4) | Definitions |
| 127(4.1) | Definition of ["money contribution"] "amount contributed" |
| 127(4.2) | Allocation of amount contributed among partners |
| 127(5) | Investment tax credit |
| 127(6) | Investment tax credit of cooperative corporation |
| 127(7) | Investment tax credit of testamentary trust [or communal organization] |
| 127(8) | Investment tax credit of partnership |
| 127(8.1) | Investment tax credit of limited partner |
| 127(8.2) | Expenditure base |
| 127(8.3), (8.4) | Investment tax credit not allocated to limited partners |
| 127(8.5), (9) | Definitions |
| 127(9.1) | Control acquired before the end of the year |
| 127(9.1)(a) | |
| 127(9.2) | Control acquired after the end of the year |
| 127(10) | Ascertainment of certain property |
| 127(10.1) | Additions to investment tax credit |
| 127(10.2) | Expenditure limit determined |
| 127(10.3) | Associated corporations |
| 127(10.4) | Failure to file agreement |
| 127(10.5) | [Repealed under former Act] |
| 127(10.6) | Expenditure limit determination in certain cases |
| 127(10.7) | Further additions to investment tax credit [repaid assistance] |
| 127(10.8) | Further additions to investment tax credit [expired assistance] |
| 127(11) | Interpretation |
| 127(11.1) | Investment tax credit |
| 127(11.2) | Time of expenditure and acquisition |
| 127(11.3) | Decertification of approved project property |
| 127(11.4) | [Repealed] |
| 127(11.5) | Adjustments to qualified expenditures |
| 127(11.6) | Non-arm's length costs |
| 127(11.7) | Definitions |
| 127(11.8) | Interpretation for non-arm's length costs |
| 127(12)–(12.3) | Interpretation |
| 127(13) | Agreement to transfer qualified expenditures |
| 127(14) | Identification of amounts transferred |
| 127(15) | Invalid agreements |
| 127(16) | Non-arm's length parties |
| 127(17) | Assessment |
| 127(18), (19) | Reduction of qualified expenditures |
| 127(20) | Agreement to allocate |
| 127(21) | Failure to allocate |
| 127(22) | Invalid agreements |
| 127(23) | Partnership's taxation year |
| 127(24) | Exclusion from qualified expenditure |
| 127(25) | Deemed contract payment |
| 127(26) | Unpaid amounts |
| 127(27) | Recapture of investment tax credit |

cxxv

## Detailed Table of Sections

| | |
|---|---|
| 127(28) | Recapture of investment tax credit of partnership |
| 127(29) | Recapture of investment tax credit of allocating taxpayer |
| 127(30) | Addition to tax |
| 127(31) | Tiered partnership |
| 127(32) | Meaning of cost |
| 127(33) | Certain non-arm's length transfers |
| 127(34), (35) | Recapture of investment tax credit |
| 127.1 | |
| 127.1(1) | Refundable investment tax credit |
| 127.1(2) | Definitions |
| 127.1(2.01) | Addition to refundable investment tax credit |
| 127.1(2.1) | Application of subsec. 127(9) |
| 127.1(3) | Deemed deduction |
| 127.2 | |
| 127.2(1) | [Pre-1987] Share-purchase tax credit |
| 127.2(2) | Persons exempt from tax |
| 127.2(3) | Trust |
| 127.2(3.1) | Exclusion of certain trusts |
| 127.2(4) | Partnership |
| 127.2(5) | Cooperative corporation |
| 127.2(6) | Definitions |
| 127.2(7) | Definition of "tax otherwise payable" |
| 127.2(8) | Deemed cost of acquisition |
| 127.2(9) | Partnership |
| 127.2(10) | Election re first holder |
| 127.2(11) | Calculation of consideration |
| 127.3 | |
| 127.3(1) | [Pre-1986] Scientific research and experimental development tax credit |
| 127.3(2) | Definitions |
| 127.3(3) | Trust |
| 127.3(3.1) | Exclusion of certain trusts |
| 127.3(4) | Partnership |
| 127.3(5) | Cooperative corporation |
| 127.3(6) | Deduction from cost |
| 127.3(7) | Partnership |
| 127.3(8) | Definition of "tax otherwise payable" |
| 127.3(9) | Election re first holder |
| 127.3(10) | Calculation of consideration |
| 127.4 | |
| 127.4(1) | [Labour-sponsored funds tax credit] Definitions |
| 127.4(1.1) | Amalgamations or mergers |
| 127.4(2) | Deduction of labour-sponsored funds tax credit |
| 127.4(3), (4) | [Repealed] |
| 127.4(5) | Labour-sponsored funds tax credit limit |
| 127.4(5.1) | Deemed original acquisition |
| 127.4(6) | Labour-sponsored funds tax credit |
| 127.41 | |
| 127.41(1) | Part XII.4 tax credit [qualifying environmental trust beneficiary] |
| 127.41(2) | Reduction of Part I tax |
| 127.41(3) | Deemed payment of Part I tax |

### Division E.1 — Minimum Tax

| | |
|---|---|
| 127.5 | Obligation to pay minimum tax |
| 127.51 | Minimum amount determined |
| 127.52 | |
| 127.52(1) | Adjusted taxable income determined |
| 127.52(2) | Partnerships |
| 127.52(2.1) | Specified member of a partnership |
| 127.52(3) | Definitions |
| 127.53 | |
| 127.53(1) | Basic exemption |
| 127.53(2) | Multiple trusts |

## Detailed Table of Sections

127.53(3) Failure to file agreement
127.531 Basic minimum tax credit determined
127.54
127.54(1) Definitions
127.54(2) Foreign tax credit
127.55 Application of section 127.5

### DIVISION F — SPECIAL RULES APPLICABLE IN CERTAIN CIRCUMSTANCES

#### Bankruptcies

128
128(1) Where corporation bankrupt
128(2) Where individual bankrupt
128(3) [Repealed]

#### Changes in Residence

128.1
128.1(1) Immigration
128.1(1)(a) year-end, fiscal period
128.1(1)(b) deemed disposition
128.1(1)(c) deemed acquisition
128.1(1)(c.1) deemed dividend to immigrating corporation
128.1(1)(c.2) deemed dividend to shareholder of immigrating corporation
128.1(1)(d) foreign affiliate
128.1(2) Paid-up capital adjustment
128.1(3) Paid-up capital adjustment
128.1(4) Emigration
128.1(4)(a) year-end, fiscal period
128.1(4)(a.1) [Proposed] fiscal period
128.1(4)(b) deemed disposition
128.1(4)(b) [Proposed] deemed disposition
128.1(4)(c) reacquisition
128.1(4)(d) individual
128.1(4)(d) [Proposed] individual — elective disposition
128.1(4)(d.1) [Proposed] employee CCPC stock option shares
128.1(4)(e) deemed [taxable Canadian] property
128.1(4)(f) losses on election
128.1(5) [Proposed] Instalment interest
128.1(6) [Proposed] Returning former resident
128.1(7) [Proposed] Returning trust beneficiary
128.1(8) [Proposed] Post-emigration loss
128.1(9) [Proposed] Information reporting
128.1(10) [Proposed] Definitions
128.2
128.2(1), (2) Cross-border mergers
128.2(3) Windings-up excluded
128.3 [Proposed] Former resident — replaced shares

#### Private Corporations

129
129(1) Dividend refund to private corporation
129(1.1) Dividends paid to bankrupt controlling corporation
129(1.2) Dividends deemed not to be taxable dividends
129(2) Application to other liability
129(2.1) Interest on dividend refund
129(2.2) Excess interest on dividend refund
129(3) Definition of "refundable dividend tax on hand"
129(3.1)–(3.5) [Repealed]
129(3.1) [Proposed] Application
129(4) Definitions
129(4.1), (4.2), (4.3), (5) [Repealed]
129(6) Investment income from associated corporation deemed to be active business income
129(7) Meaning of "taxable dividend"
129(8) Application of section 125

Detailed Table of Sections

## Investment Corporations

130
130(1)     Deduction from tax
130(2)     Application of subsecs. 131(1) to (3.2) and (6)
130(3)     Meaning of expressions "investment corporation" and "taxed capital gains"
130(4)     Wholly owned subsidiaries

## Mortgage Investment Corporations

130.1
130.1(1)     Deduction from tax
130.1(2)     Dividend equated to bond interest
130.1(3)     Application of subsec. (2)
130.1(4)     Election re capital gains dividend
130.1(4.1)     Application of subsecs. 131(1.1) to (1.4)
130.1(4.2)     [Proposed] Reporting
130.1(4.3)     [Proposed] Allocation [for 2000]
130.1(5)     Public corporation
130.1(6)     Meaning of "mortgage investment corporation"
130.1(7)     How shareholders counted
130.1(8)     First taxation year
130.1(9)     Definitions

## Mutual Fund Corporations

131
131(1)     Election re capital gains dividend
131(1.1)     Deemed date of election
131(1.2)     Request to make election
131(1.3)     Penalty
131(1.4)     Assessment and payment of penalty
131(1.5)     [Proposed] Reporting
131(1.6)     [Proposed] Allocation [for 2000]
131(2)     Capital gains refund to mutual fund corporation
131(3)     Application to other liability
131(3.1)     Interest on capital gains refund
131(3.2)     Excess interest on capital gains refund
131(4)     Application of section 84
131(5)     Dividend refund to mutual fund corporation
131(6)     Definitions
131(7)     Definition of "taxed capital gains"
131(8), (8.1)     Meaning of "mutual fund corporation"
131(9)     Reduction of refundable capital gains tax on hand
131(10)     Restricted financial institution
131(11)     Rules respecting prescribed labour-sponsored venture capital corporations

## Mutual Fund Trusts

132
132(1)     Capital gains refund to mutual fund trust
132(2)     Application to other liability
132(2.1)     Interest on capital gains refund
132(2.2)     Excess interest on capital gains refund
132(3)     Application of subsec. 104(20)
132(4)     Definitions
132(5)     Definition of "taxed capital gains"
132(6)     Meaning of "mutual fund trust"
132(6.1)     Election to be mutual fund
132(6.2), (7)     [Proposed] Retention of status as mutual fund trust
132.1
132.1(1)     Amounts designated by mutual fund trust
132.1(2)     Adjusted cost base of unit where designation made
132.1(3)     Limitation on current year deduction
132.1(4)     Carryover of excess
132.1(5)     Where designation has no effect

## Detailed Table of Sections

132.11
132.11(1)   Taxation year of mutual fund trust
132.11(2)   Electing trust's share of partnership income and losses
132.11(3)   Electing trust's income from other trusts
132.11(4)   Amounts paid or payable to beneficiaries
132.11(4)   [Proposed] Amounts paid or payable to beneficiaries
132.11(5)   Special rules where change in status of beneficiary
132.11(6)   Additional income of electing trust
132.11(7)   Deduction
132.11(8)   Anti-avoidance
132.2
132.2(1)    Mutual funds — qualifying exchange [rollover]
132.2(2)    Definitions

### Non-Resident-Owned Investment Corporations

133
133(1)      Computation of income
133(2)      Non-resident-owned investment corporations
133(3)      Special tax rate
133(4)      No deduction for foreign taxes
133(5)      [Repealed under former Act]
133(6)      Allowable refund to non-resident-owned investment corporations
133(7)      Application to other liability
133(7.01)   Interest on allowable refund
133(7.02)   Excess interest on allowable refund
133(7.1)    Election re capital gains dividend
133(7.2)    Simultaneous dividends
133(7.3)    Application of subsecs. 131(1.1) to (1.4)
133(8)      Definitions
133(9)      Definitions
134         Non-resident-owned corporation not a Canadian corporation, etc.
134.1       [Proposed]
134.1(1)    [Proposed] NRO — transition
134.1(2)    [Proposed] Application

### Patronage Dividends

135
135(1)      Deduction in computing income
135(2)      Limitation where non-member customer
135(2.1)    Deduction carried over
135(3)      Amount to be deducted or withheld from payment to customer
135(4)      Definitions
135(5)      Holding out prospect of allocations
135(6)      Amount of payment to customer
135(7)      Payment to customer to be included in income
135(8)      Patronage dividends

### Cooperative Corporations

136
136(1)      Cooperative not private corporation
136(2)      Definition of "cooperative corporation"

### Credit Unions, Savings and Credit Unions, and Deposit Insurance Corporations

137
137(1)      [Repealed under former Act]
137(2)      Payments pursuant to allocations in proportion to borrowing
137(3)      Additional deduction
137(4)      Amount deemed deductible under section 125
137(4.1)    Payments in respect of shares
137(4.2)    Deemed interest not a dividend
137(4.3)    Determination of preferred-rate amount of a corporation
137(5)      Member's income
137(5.1), (5.2)  Allocations of taxable dividends and capital gains
137(6)      Definitions

cxxix

## Detailed Table of Sections

| | |
|---|---|
| 137(7) | Credit union not private corporation |
| 137.1 | |
| 137.1(1) | Amounts included in income of deposit insurance corporation |
| 137.1(2) | Amounts not included in income |
| 137.1(3) | Amounts deductible in computing income of deposit insurance corporation |
| 137.1(4) | Limitation on deduction |
| 137.1(5) | Definitions |
| 137.1(5.1) | Deeming provision |
| 137.1(6) | Deemed not to be a private corporation |
| 137.1(7) | Deposit insurance corporation deemed not a credit union |
| 137.1(8) | Deemed compliance |
| 137.1(9) | Special tax rate |
| 137.1(10) | Amounts paid by a deposit insurance corporation |
| 137.1(10.1) | Principal amount of an obligation to pay interest |
| 137.1(11) | Deduction by member institutions |
| 137.1(12) | Repayment excluded |
| 137.2 | Computation of income for 1975 and subsequent years |

### Insurance Corporations

| | |
|---|---|
| 138 | |
| 138(1) | Insurance corporations |
| 138(2) | Insurer's income or loss |
| 138(3) | Deductions allowed in computing income [of life insurer] |
| 138(3.1) | Excess policy dividend deduction deemed deductible |
| 138(4) | Amounts included in computing income |
| 138(4.01)–(4.4) | Life insurance policy |
| 138(4.5) | Application |
| 138(4.6) | Completion |
| 138(5) | Deductions not allowed |
| 138(5.1) | No deduction |
| 138(5.2) | [Repealed] |
| 138(6) | Deduction for dividends from taxable corporations |
| 138(7) | [Repealed] |
| 138(8) | No deduction for foreign tax |
| 138(9) | Computation of income |
| 138(9.1) | [Repealed under former Act] |
| 138(10) | Application of financial institution rules |
| 138(11) | [Repealed] |
| 138(11.1) | Identical properties |
| 138(11.2) | Computation of capital gain on pre-1969 depreciable property |
| 138(11.3) | Deemed disposition |
| 138(11.31) | Exclusion from deemed disposition |
| 138(11.4) | Deduction of loss |
| 138(11.41) | [Repealed] |
| 138(11.5) | Transfer of insurance business by non-resident insurer |
| 138(11.6) | Time of election |
| 138(11.7) | Computation of paid-up capital |
| 138(11.8) | Rules on transfers of depreciable property |
| 138(11.9) | Computation of contributed surplus |
| 138(11.91) | Computation of income of non-resident insurer |
| 138(11.92) | Computation of income where insurance business is transferred |
| 138(11.93) | Property acquired on default in payment |
| 138(11.94) | Transfer of insurance business by resident insurer |
| 138(12) | Definitions |
| 138(13) | Variation in "tax basis" and "amortized cost" |
| 138(14) | Meaning of certain expressions |
| 138(15) | Definition not to apply |
| 138(16) | [Repealed under former Act] |
| 138.1 | |
| 138.1(1) | Rules relating to segregated funds |
| 138.1(2) | Rules relating to property in segregated funds at end of 1977 taxation year |
| 138.1(3) | Capital gains and capital losses of related segregated fund trusts |

Detailed Table of Sections

| | |
|---|---|
| 138.1(4) | Election and allocation |
| 138.1(5) | Adjusted cost base of property in related segregated fund trust |
| 138.1(6) | Definition of "acquisition fee" |
| 138.1(7) | Where subsecs. (1) to (6) do not apply |
| 139 | Conversion of insurance corporations into mutual corporations |

## Demutualization of Insurance Corporations

| | |
|---|---|
| 139.1 | |
| 139.1(1) | Definitions |
| 139.1(2) | Rules of general application |
| 139.1(3) | Special cases |
| 139.1(4) | Consequences of demutualization |
| 139.1(5) | Fair market value of ownership rights |
| 139.1(6) | Paid-up capital — insurance corporation |
| 139.1(7) | Paid-up capital — holding corporation |
| 139.1(8) | Policy dividends |
| 139.1(9) | Payment and receipt of premium |
| 139.1(10) | Cost of taxable conversion benefit |
| 139.1(11) | No shareholder benefit |
| 139.1(12) | Exclusion of benefit from RRSP and other rules |
| 139.1(13) | RRSP registration rules, etc. |
| 139.1(14) | Retirement benefit |
| 139.1(15) | Employee-paid insurance |
| 139.1(16) | Flow-through of conversion benefits to employees and others |
| 139.1(17) | Flow-through of share benefits to employees and others |
| 139.1(18) | Acquisition of control |
| 139.2 | Mutual holding corporations |
| 140 | |
| 140(1) | [Insurance corporation] Deductions in computing income |
| 140(2) | Inclusion in computing income |
| 141 | |
| 141(1) | Definitions |
| 141(2) | Life insurance corporation deemed to be public corporation |
| 141(3) | Holding corporation deemed to be public corporation |
| 141(4) | Specified period |
| 141(5) | Exclusion from taxable Canadian property |
| 141(5) | [Proposed] Exclusion from taxable Canadian property |
| 141.1 | [Insurance corporation] deemed not to be a private corporation |
| 142, 142.1 | [Repealed] |

## Financial Institutions
### Interpretation

| | |
|---|---|
| 142.2 | |
| 142.2(1) | Definitions |
| 142.2(1) | [Proposed] Definitions |
| 142.2(2) | Significant interest |
| 142.2(3) | Rules re significant interest |
| 142.2(4) | Extension of meaning of "related" |
| 142.2(5) | Significant interest — transition |

### Income from Specified Debt Obligations

| | |
|---|---|
| 142.3 | |
| 142.3(1) | Amounts to be included and deducted |
| 142.3(2) | Failure to report accrued amounts |
| 142.3(3) | Exception for certain obligations |
| 142.3(4) | Impaired specified debt obligations |

### Disposition of Specified Debt Obligations

| | |
|---|---|
| 142.4 | |
| 142.4(1) | Definitions |
| 142.4(2) | Scope of section |
| 142.4(3) | Rules applicable to disposition |
| 142.4(4) | Inclusions and deductions re disposition |

Detailed Table of Sections

142.4(5) Gain or loss not amortized
142.4(6) Gain or loss from disposition of obligation
142.4(7) Current amount
142.4(8) Residual portion of gain or loss
142.4(9) Disposition of part of obligation
142.4(10) Penalties and bonuses
142.4(11) Payments received on or after disposition

## Mark-to-Market Properties

142.5
142.5(1) Income treatment for profits and losses
142.5(2) Mark-to-market requirement
142.5(3) Mark-to-market debt obligation
142.5(4) Transition — deduction re non-capital amounts
142.5(5) Transition — inclusion re non-capital amounts
142.5(6) Transition — deduction re net capital gains
142.5(7) Transition — inclusion re net capital gains
142.5(8) First deemed disposition of debt obligation
142.5(9) Transition — property acquired on rollover

## Additional Rules

142.6
142.6(1) Becoming or ceasing to be a financial institution
142.6(1.1) [Proposed] Ceasing to use property in Canadian business
142.6(1.2) [Proposed] Beginning to use property in a Canadian business
142.6(1.3) [Proposed] Specified debt obligation marked to market
142.6(2) Deemed disposition not applicable
142.6(2) [Proposed] Deemed disposition not applicable
142.6(3) Property not inventory
142.6(4) Property that ceases to be inventory
142.6(5) Debt obligations acquired in rollover transactions
142.6(6) Definition of "rollover transaction"
142.6(7) Superficial loss rule not applicable
142.6(8) Accrued capital gains and losses election
142.6(9) Accrued capital gains election limit
142.6(10) Accrued capital losses election limit

## [Proposed] Conversion of Foreign Bank Affiliate to Branch

142.7
142.7(1) [Proposed] Definitions
142.7(2) [Proposed] Amalgamation and merger
142.7(3) [Proposed] Branch-establishment rollover

## Communal Organizations

143
143(1) Communal organizations
143(2) Election in respect of income
143(3) Refusal to accept election
143(3.1) Election in respect of gifts
143(4) Definitions
143(5) Specification of family members
143.1
143.1(1) Amateur athletes' reserve funds
143.1(2) Amounts included in beneficiary's income
143.1(3) Termination of amateur athlete trust
143.1(4) Death of beneficiary

## Cost of Tax Shelter Investments

143.2
143.2(1) Definitions
143.2(2) At-risk adjustment
143.2(3) Amount or benefit not included
143.2(4), (5) Amount or benefit
143.2(6) Amount of expenditure

cxxxii

## Detailed Table of Sections

| | |
|---|---|
| 143.2(7) | Repayment of indebtedness |
| 143.2(8) | Limited-recourse amount |
| 143.2(9), (10) | Timing |
| 143.2(11) | Short-term debt |
| 143.2(12) | Series of loans or repayments |
| 143.2(13), (14) | Information located outside Canada |
| 143.2(15) | Assessments |

### DIVISION G — DEFERRED AND OTHER SPECIAL INCOME ARRANGEMENTS

#### Employees Profit Sharing Plans

| | |
|---|---|
| 144 | |
| 144(1) | Definitions |
| 144(2) | No tax while trust governed by a plan |
| 144(3) | Allocation contingent or absolute taxable |
| 144(4)–(4.2) | Allocated capital gains and losses |
| 144(5) | Employer's contribution to trust deductible |
| 144(6) | Beneficiary's receipts deductible |
| 144(7) | Beneficiary's receipts that are not deductible |
| 144(7.1) | Where property other than money received by beneficiary |
| 144(8) | Allocation of credit for dividends |
| 144(8.1) | Foreign tax deduction [foreign tax credit] |
| 144(8.2) | [Repealed] |
| 144(9) | Deduction for forfeited amounts |
| 144(10) | Payments out of profits |
| 144(11) | Taxation year of trust |

#### Registered Supplementary Unemployment Benefit Plans

| | |
|---|---|
| 145 | |
| 145(1) | Definitions |
| 145(2) | No tax while trust governed by plan |
| 145(3) | Amounts received taxable |
| 145(4) | Amounts received on amendment or winding-up of plan |
| 145(5) | Payments by employer deductible |

#### Registered Retirement Savings Plans

| | |
|---|---|
| 146 | |
| 146(1) | Definitions |
| 146(1.1) | [Repealed] |
| 146(2) | Acceptance of plan for registration [ — conditions] |
| 146(3) | Idem |
| 146(4) | No tax while trust governed by plan |
| 146(5) | Amount of RRSP premiums deductible |
| 146(5.1) | Amount of spousal RRSP premiums deductible |
| 146(5.2) | [Repealed under former Act] |
| 146(5.21) | Anti-avoidance |
| 146(5.3)–(5.5) | [Repealed under former Act] |
| 146(6) | Disposition of non-qualified investment |
| 146(6.1) | Recontribution of certain withdrawals |
| 146(7) | Recovery of property used as security |
| 146(8) | Benefits taxable |
| 146(8.01) | Subsequent re-calculation |
| 146(8.1) | Deemed receipt of refund of premiums |
| 146(8.2) | Amount deductible |
| 146(8.21) | Premium deemed not paid |
| 146(8.3) | Spousal RRSP payments [attribution rule] |
| 146(8.4) | [Repealed under former Act] |
| 146(8.5) | Ordering |
| 146(8.6) | Spouse's [or common-law partner's] income |
| 146(8.7) | Where subsec. (8.3) does not apply |
| 146(8.8), (8.9) | Effect of death where person other than spouse [or common-law partner] becomes entitled |
| 146(8.91) | Amounts deemed receivable by spouse [or common-law partner] |
| 146(9) | Where disposition of property by trust |
| 146(10) | Where acquisition of non-qualified investment by trust |

cxxxiii

# Detailed Table of Sections

| | |
|---|---|
| 146(10.1) | Where tax payable [income from non-qualified investment] |
| 146(11) | Life insurance policies |
| 146(11.1) | Exception |
| 146(12), (13) | Change in plan after registration |
| 146(13.1) | RRSP advantages |
| 146(13.2) | Maturity after age 69 |
| 146(13.3) | Notice |
| 146(14) | Premiums paid in taxation year |
| 146(15) | Plan not registered at end of year entered into |
| 146(16) | Transfer of funds |
| 146(17)–(19) | [Repealed under former Act] |
| 146(20) | Credited or added amount deemed not received |
| 146(21) | Prescribed provincial pension plans |
| 146(22) | Deemed payment of RRSP premiums and provincial pension plan contributions [extension of contribution deadline] |

## Home Buyers' Plan

| | |
|---|---|
| 146.01 | |
| 146.01(1) | Definitions |
| 146.01(2) | Special rules |
| 146.01(3) | Repayment of eligible amount |
| 146.01(4) | Portion of eligible amount not repaid |
| 146.01(5) | Where individual becomes a non-resident |
| 146.01(6) | Death of individual |
| 146.01(7) | Exception |
| 146.01(8) | Filing of prescribed form |
| 146.01(9)–(13) | [Repealed] |

## Lifelong Learning Plan

| | |
|---|---|
| 146.02 | |
| 146.02(1) | Definitions |
| 146.02(2) | Rule of application |
| 146.02(3) | Repayment of eligible amount |
| 146.02(4) | If portion of eligible amount not repaid |
| 146.02(5) | Ceasing residence in Canada |
| 146.02(6) | Death of individual |
| 146.02(7) | Exception |

## Registered Education Savings Plans

| | |
|---|---|
| 146.1 | |
| 146.1(1) | Definitions |
| 146.1(2) | Conditions for registration |
| 146.1(2.1) | RESP is revocable |
| 146.1(2.2) | Waiver of conditions for accumulated income payments |
| 146.1(3) | Deemed registration |
| 146.1(4) | Registration of plans without prospectus |
| 146.1(4.1) | Obligation to file amendment |
| 146.1(5) | Trust not taxable |
| 146.1(6) | Subscriber not taxable |
| 146.1(6.1) | Transfers between plans |
| 146.1(7) | Educational assistance payments |
| 146.1(7.1) | Other income inclusions |
| 146.1(7.2) | Excluded amount |
| 146.1(8)–(10) | [Repealed] |
| 146.1(11) | Trust deemed to be *inter vivos* trust |
| 146.1(12) | Deemed date of registration |
| 146.1(12.1) | Notice of intent to revoke registration |
| 146.1(12.2) | Notice of revocation |
| 146.1(13) | Revocation of registration |
| 146.1(13.1) | RESP information |
| 146.1(14) | [Repealed] |
| 146.1(15) | Regulations |

cxxxiv

Detailed Table of Sections

## Registered Home Ownership Savings Plans
146.2     [Repealed under former Act or irrelevant]

## Registered Retirement Income Funds
146.3
146.3(1)     Definitions
146.3(1.1)     [Repealed]
146.3(2)     Acceptance of fund for registration
146.3(3)     No tax while trust governed by fund
146.3(3.1)     Exception
146.3(4)     Disposition or acquisition of property by trust
146.3(5)     Benefits taxable
146.3(5.1)     Amount included in income
146.3(5.2)     [Repealed under former Act]
146.3(5.3)     Ordering
146.3(5.4)     Spouse's income
146.3(5.5)     Where subsec. (5.1) does not apply
146.3(6)     Where last annuitant dies
146.3(6.1)     Designated benefit deemed received
146.3(6.11)     Transfer of designated benefit
146.3(6.2)     Amount deductible
146.3(7)     Acquisition of non-qualified investment by trust
146.3(8)     Disposition of non-qualified investment
146.3(9)     Tax payable where non-qualified investment acquired
146.3(10)     Recovery of property used as security
146.3(11)–(13)     Change in fund after registration
146.3(14)     Transfers
146.3(15)     Credited or added amount deemed not received

## Deferred Profit Sharing Plans
147
147(1)     Definitions
147(1.1)     Participating employer
147(2)     Acceptance of plan for registration
147(2.1)     Terms limiting contributions
147(2.2)     Reallocation of forfeitures
147(3)     Acceptance of employees profit sharing plan for registration
147(4)     Capital gains determined
147(5)     Registration date
147(5.1)     Contribution limits
147(5.11)     Compensation
147(6)     Deferred plan not employees profit sharing plan
147(7)     No tax while trust governed by plan
147(8)     Amount of employer's contribution deductible
147(9)     Limitation on deduction
147(9.1)     No deduction
147(10)     Amounts received taxable
147(10.1), (10.2)     Single payment on retirement, etc.
147(10.3)     Amount contributed to or forfeited under a plan
147(10.4)     Income on disposal of shares
147(10.5)     Order of disposal of shares
147(10.6)     Commencement of annuity after age 69
147(11), (12)     Portion of receipts deductible
147(13)     Appropriation of trust property by employer
147(14), (14.1)     Revocation of registration
147(15)     Rules applicable to revoked plan
147(16)     Payments out of profits
147(17)     Interpretation of "other beneficiary"
147(18)     Inadequate consideration on purchase from or sale to trust
147(19)     Transfer to RPP, RRSP or DPSP
147(20)     Taxation of amount transferred
147(21)     Restriction re transfers

Detailed Table of Sections

147(22) Excess transfer

## Registered Pension Plans

147.1
147.1(1) Definitions
147.1(2) Registration of plan
147.1(3) Deemed registration
147.1(4) Acceptance of amendments
147.1(5) Additional conditions
147.1(6) Administrator
147.1(7) Obligations of administrator
147.1(8) Pension adjustment limits
147.1(9) Idem — multi-employer plans
147.1(10) Past service benefits
147.1(11) Revocation of registration — notice of intention
147.1(12) Notice of revocation
147.1(13) Revocation of registration
147.1(14) Anti-avoidance — multi-employer-plans
147.1(15) Plan as registered
147.1(16) Separate liability for obligations
147.1(17) Superintendent of Financial Institutions
147.1(18) Regulations
147.2
147.2(1) Pension contributions deductible — employer contributions
147.2(2) Employer contributions — defined benefit provisions
147.2(3) Filing of actuarial report
147.2(4) Amount of employee's pension contributions deductible
147.2(4)(a) service after 1989
147.2(4)(a) [Proposed] service after 1989
147.2(4)(b) service before 1990 while not a contributor
147.2(4)(c) service before 1990 while a contributor
147.2(5) Teachers
147.2(6) Deductible contributions when taxpayer dies
147.3
147.3(1) Transfer — money purchase to money purchase, RRSP or RRIF
147.3(2) Transfer — money purchase to defined benefit
147.3(3) Transfer — defined benefit to defined benefit
147.3(4) Transfer — defined benefit to money purchase, RRSP or RRIF
147.3(4.1) Transfer of surplus — defined benefit to money purchase
147.3(5) Transfer to RPP, RRSP or RRIF for spouse [or common-law partner] on marriage [or partnership] breakdown
147.3(6) Transfer — pre-1991 contributions
147.3(7) Transfer — lump sum benefits on death
147.3(7.1) [Proposed] Transfer where money purchase plan replaces money purchase plan
147.3(8) Transfer where money purchase plan replaces defined benefit plan
147.3(9), (10) Taxation of amount transferred
147.3(11) Division of transferred amount
147.3(12) Restriction re transfers
147.3(13) Excess transfer
147.3(13.1) Withdrawal of excessive transfers to RRSPs and RRIFs
147.3(14) Deemed transfer
147.3(14.1) Transfer of property between provisions
147.3(15) [Repealed]
147.4
147.4(1) RPP annuity contract
147.4(2) Amended contract
147.4(3) New contract
147.4(4) RPP annuity contract beginning after age 69

Detailed Table of Sections

## Life Insurance Policies

148
148(1) Amounts included in computing policyholder's income
148(1.1) Amount included in computing taxpayer's income
148(2) Deemed proceeds of disposition
148(3) Special rules for certain policies
148(4) Income from disposition
148(4.1), (5) [Repealed under former Act]
148(6) Proceeds receivable as annuity
148(7), (8) Disposition at non-arm's length and similar cases
148(8.1) *Inter vivos* transfer to spouse [or common-law partner]
148(8.2) Transfer to spouse [or common-law partner] at death
148(9) Definitions
148(9.1) Application of subsec. 12.2(11)
148(10) Life annuity contracts

## Eligible Funeral Arrangements

148.1
148.1(1) Definitions
148.1(2) Exemption for eligible funeral arrangements
148.1(3) Income inclusion on return of funds

### DIVISION H — EXEMPTIONS
## Miscellaneous Exemptions

149
149(1) Miscellaneous exemptions
149(1)(a) employees of a country other than Canada
149(1)(b) members of the family and servants of employees of a country other than Canada
149(1)(c) municipal authorities
149(1)(d) corporations owned by the Crown
149(1)(d) [Proposed] corporations owned by the Crown
149(1)(d.1) corporations 90% owned by the Crown
149(1)(d.1) [Proposed] corporations 90% owned by the Crown
149(1)(d.2) wholly-owned corporations
149(1)(d.2) [Proposed] wholly-owned corporations
149(1)(d.3) 90% owned corporations
149(1)(d.4) combined [Crown] ownership
149(1)(d.4) [Proposed] combined [Crown] ownership
149(1)(d.5) municipal corporations
149(1)(d.6) [subsidiaries of municipal corporations]
149(1)(d.6) [Proposed] subsidiaries of municipal corporations
149(1)(e) certain organizations
149(1)(f) registered charities
149(1)(g), (h) [Repealed under former Act]
149(1)(h.1) Association of Universities and Colleges of Canada
149(1)(i) certain housing corporations
149(1)(j) non-profit corporations for scientific research and experimental development
149(1)(k) labour organizations
149(1)(l) non-profit organizations
149(1)(m) mutual insurance corporations
149(1)(n) housing companies
149(1)(o) pension trusts
149(1)(o.1), (o.2) pension corporations
149(1)(o.3) prescribed small business investment corporations
149(1)(o.4) master trusts
149(1)(p) trusts under profit sharing plan
149(1)(q) trusts under a registered supplementary unemployment benefit plan
149(1)(q.1) RCA trusts
149(1)(r) trusts under registered retirement savings plan
149(1)(s) trusts under deferred profit sharing plan
149(1)(s.1) trust governed by eligible funeral arrangement
149(1)(s.2) cemetery care trust

cxxxvii

## Detailed Table of Sections

| | |
|---|---|
| 149(1)(t) | farmers' and fishermen's insurer |
| 149(1)(u) | registered education savings plans |
| 149(1)(v) | amateur athlete trust |
| 149(1)(w) | trusts to provide compensation |
| 149(1)(x) | registered retirement income funds |
| 149(1)(y) | trusts to provide vacation pay |
| 149(1)(z) | qualifying environmental trust |
| 149(1.1) | Exception |
| 149(1.1) | [Proposed] Exception |
| 149(1.11) | [Proposed] Election |
| 149(1.2) | Income test [for municipal corporation] |
| 149(1.2) | [Proposed] Income test [for municipal corporation] |
| 149(1.3) | Capital ownership [by municipality] |
| 149(2) | Determination of income |
| 149(3), (4) | Application of subsec. (1) |
| 149(4.1), (4.2) | Income exempt under 149(1)(t) |
| 149(4.3) | Computation of taxable income of insurer |
| 149(5) | Exception re investment income of certain clubs |
| 149(6) | Apportionment rule |
| 149(7) | [Prescribed form for R&D corporation — ] Time for filing |
| 149(7.1) | Penalty for failure to file on time |
| 149(8) | Interpretation of para. (1)(j) |
| 149(9) | Rules for determining gross revenue |
| 149(10) | Exempt corporations [becoming or ceasing to be exempt] |
| 149(11) | [Repealed] |
| 149(12) | Information returns |

### Charities

| | |
|---|---|
| 149.1 | |
| 149.1(1) | Definitions |
| 149.1(1.1) | Exclusions |
| 149.1(1.2) | Authority of Minister |
| 149.1(2) | Revocation of registration of charitable organization |
| 149.1(3) | Revocation of registration of public foundation |
| 149.1(4) | Revocation of registration of private foundation |
| 149.1(4.1) | Revocation of registration of registered charity |
| 149.1(5) | Reduction |
| 149.1(6) | Devoting resources to charitable activity |
| 149.1(6.1) | Charitable purposes |
| 149.1(6.2) | Charitable activities |
| 149.1(6.3) | Designation as public foundation, etc. |
| 149.1(6.4) | National arts service organizations |
| 149.1(6.5) | Revocation of designation |
| 149.1(7) | Designation of associated charities |
| 149.1(8), (9) | Accumulation of property |
| 149.1(10) | Deemed charitable activity |
| 149.1(11) | [Repealed under former Act] |
| 149.1(12) | Rules |
| 149.1(13) | Designation of private foundation as public |
| 149.1(14) | Information returns |
| 149.1(15) | Information may be communicated |
| 149.1(16)–(19) | [Repealed under former Act] |
| 149.1(20) | Rule regarding disbursement excess |
| 149.1(21) | Definition of "disbursement excess" |

### DIVISION I — RETURNS, ASSESSMENTS, PAYMENT AND APPEALS
### Returns

| | |
|---|---|
| 150 | |
| 150(1) | Filing returns of income — general rule |
| 150(1)(a) | corporations |
| 150(1)(b) | deceased individuals |
| 150(1)(c) | trusts or estates |

Detailed Table of Sections

| | |
|---|---|
| 150(1)(d) | individuals |
| 150(1)(e) | designated persons |
| 150(1.1) | Exception |
| 150(2) | Demands for returns |
| 150(3) | Trustees, etc. |
| 150(4) | Death of partner or proprietor |
| 150.1 | |
| 150.1(1) | Definition of "electronic filing" |
| 150.1(2) | Filing of return by electronic transmission |
| 150.1(3) | Deemed date of filing |
| 150.1(4) | Declaration |
| 150.1(5) | Application to other Parts |
| 150.1(5) | [Proposed] Application to other Parts |

## Estimate of Tax

| | |
|---|---|
| 151 | Estimate of tax |

## Assessment

| | |
|---|---|
| 152 | |
| 152(1) | Assessment |
| 152(1.1) | Determination of losses |
| 152(1.11) | Determination pursuant to subsec. 245(2) |
| 152(1.111) | Application of subsec. 245(1) |
| 152(1.12) | When determination not to be made |
| 152(1.2) | Provisions applicable |
| 152(1.3) | Determination binding |
| 152(1.4) | Determination in respect of a partnership |
| 152(1.5) | Notice of determination |
| 152(1.6) | Absence of notification |
| 152(1.7) | Binding effect of determination |
| 152(1.8) | Time to assess |
| 152(2) | Notice of assessment |
| 152(3) | Liability not dependent on assessment |
| 152(3.1) | Definition of "normal reassessment period" |
| 152(3.2) | Determination of deemed overpayment [Child Tax Benefit] |
| 152(3.3) | Notice of determination [Child Tax Benefit] |
| 152(3.4) | Determination of UI premium tax credit |
| 152(3.5) | Notice of determination [UI premium tax credit] |
| 152(4) | Assessment and reassessment [limitation period] |
| 152(4.01) | Assessment to which para. 152(4)(a) or (b) applies |
| 152(4.1) | Where waiver revoked |
| 152(4.2) | [Reassessment with taxpayer's consent] |
| 152(4.3) | Consequential assessment |
| 152(4.4) | Definition of "balance" |
| 152(5) | Limitation on assessments |
| 152(6) | Reassessment where certain deductions claimed [carrybacks] |
| 152(6.1) | [Proposed] Reassessment where amount included in income under subsec. 91(1) is reduced |
| 152(7) | Assessment not dependent on return or information |
| 152(8) | Assessment deemed valid and binding |
| 152(9) | Alternative basis for assessment |
| 152(10) | [Proposed] Where tax deemed not to be assessed |

## Payment of Tax

| | |
|---|---|
| 153 | |
| 153(1) | Withholding |
| 153(1.1) | Undue hardship |
| 153(1.2) | Election to increase withholding |
| 153(1.3), (1.4) | [Repealed] |
| 153(2) | [Repealed] |
| 153(3) | Deemed effect of deduction |
| 153(4) | Unclaimed dividends, interest and proceeds |
| 153(5) | Deemed effect of remittance |
| 153(6) | [Proposed] Meaning of "designated financial institution" |

cxxxix

## Detailed Table of Sections

| | |
|---|---|
| 154 | |
| 154(1) | Agreements providing for tax transfer payments |
| 154(2) | Tax transfer payment |
| 154(3) | Payment deemed received by individual |
| 154(4) | Payment deemed received by Receiver General |
| 154(5) | Amount not to include refund |
| 155 | |
| 155(1) | [Instalments — ] Farmers and fishermen |
| 155(2) | Definition of "instalment base" |
| 156 | |
| 156(1) | [Instalments — ] Other individuals |
| 156(2) | Payment by mutual fund trusts |
| 156(3) | Definition of "instalment base" |
| 156.1 | |
| 156.1(1) | [Instalments exemption — ] Definitions |
| 156.1(1.1) | Values of A and B in "net tax owing" |
| 156.1(1.2) | Value of D in "net tax owing" |
| 156.1(1.3) | Value of F in "net tax owing" |
| 156.1(2), 156.1(3) | No instalment required |
| 156.1(4) | Payment of remainder |
| 157 | |
| 157(1) | Payment by corporations |
| 157(2) | Special case [co-op or credit union] |
| 157(2.1) | Idem [$1,000 threshold] |
| 157(2.1) | [Proposed] $1,000 threshold |
| 157(3) | Private, mutual fund and non-resident-owned investment corporations |
| 157(4) | Definitions |
| 158 | Payment of remainder |
| 159 | |
| 159(1) | Person acting for another |
| 159(2) | Certificate before distribution |
| 159(3) | Personal liability |
| 159(3.1) | Appropriation of property |
| 159(4), (4.1) | Election on emigration |
| 159(5) | Election where certain provisions applicable [on death] |
| 159(5.1) | Idem [pre-1972 professional business] |
| 159(6) | Idem |
| 159(6.1) | Election where subsec. 104(4) applicable |
| 159(6.1) | [Proposed] Election where subsec. 104(4) applicable |
| 159(7) | Form and manner of election and interest |
| 160 | |
| 160(1) | Tax liability re property transferred not at arm's length |
| 160(1.1) | Joint liability where subsec. 69(11) applies |
| 160(1.2) | Joint liability — tax on split income |
| 160(2) | Assessment |
| 160(3) | Discharge of liability |
| 160(3.1) | Fair market value of undivided interest |
| 160(4) | Special rules re transfer of property to spouse [or common-law partner] |
| 160.1 | |
| 160.1(1) | Where excess refunded |
| 160.1(1.1) | Liability for refunds by reason of section 122.5 [GST credit] |
| 160.1(2) | [Repealed] |
| 160.1(2.1) | Liability for refunds by reason of section 122.61 [Child Tax Benefit] |
| 160.1(2.2) | Liability for excess refunds under section 126.1 to partners [UI premium tax credit] |
| 160.1(3) | Assessment |
| 160.1(4) | Where amount applied to liability |
| 160.2 | |
| 160.2(1) | Joint and several liability in respect of amounts received out of or under RRSP |
| 160.2(2) | Joint and several liability in respect of amounts received out of or under RRIF |
| 160.2(3) | Minister may assess recipient |
| 160.2(4) | Rules applicable |

## Detailed Table of Sections

160.3
160.3(1) Liability in respect of amounts received out of or under RCA trust
160.3(2) Minister may assess recipient
160.3(3) Rules applicable
160.4
160.4(1) Liability in respect of transfers by insolvent corporations
160.4(2) Indirect transfers
160.4(3) Minister may assess recipient
160.4(4) Rules applicable

### Interest

161
161(1) General [interest on late balances]
161(2) Interest on instalments
161(2.1) Exception
161(2.2) Contra interest [offset interest]
161(3) [Repealed]
161(4) Limitation — farmers and fishermen
161(4.01) Limitation — other individuals
161(4.1) Limitation — corporations
161(5) Participation certificates
161(6) Income of resident from a foreign country in blocked currency
161(6.1) Foreign tax credit adjustment
161(6.2) Flow-through share renunciations
161(7) Effect of carryback of loss, etc.
161(8) Certain amounts deemed to be paid as instalments
161(9) Definitions of "instalment base", etc.
161(10) When amount deemed paid
161(11) Interest on penalties
161(12) [Repealed]

### Offset of Refund Interest and Arrears Interest

161.1
161.1(1) Definitions
161.1(2) Concurrent refund interest and arrears interest
161.1(3) Contents of application
161.1(4) Reallocation
161.1(5) Repayment of refund
161.1(6) Consequential reallocations
161.1(7) Assessments

### Penalties

162
162(1) Failure to file return of income
162(2) Repeated failure to file
162(2.1) Failure to file — non-resident corporation
162(3) Failure to file by trustee
162(4) Ownership certificate
162(5) Failure to provide information on form
162(6) Failure to provide identification number
162(7) Failure to comply
162(7.1) Failure to make partnership information return
162(8) Repeated failure to file
162(8.1) Rules where partnership liable to a penalty
162(9) [Repealed]
162(10) Failure to furnish foreign-based information
162(10.1) Additional penalty
162(10.11) [Proposed] Application to trust contributions
162(10.2) Shares or debt owned by controlled foreign affiliate
162(10.3) Application to partnerships
162(10.3) [Proposed] Application to partnerships
162(10.4) Application to non-resident trusts
162(11) Effect of subsequent events

cxli

Detailed Table of Sections

163
163(1) Repeated failures [to report income]
163(2) False statements or omissions
163(2.1) Interpretation
163(2.2) False statement or omission
163(2.21) False statement or omissions with respect to look-back rule
163(2.22), (2.3) Penalty
163(2.4) False statement or omission [re foreign asset reporting]
163(2.41) [Proposed] Application to trust contributions
163(2.5) Shares or debt owned by controlled foreign affiliate
163(2.6) Application to partnerships
163(2.6) [Proposed] Application to partnerships
163(2.7) Application to partnerships
163(2.8) Application to members of partnerships
163(2.9) Where partnership liable to penalty
163(2.91) Application to non-resident trusts
163(3) Burden of proof in respect of penalties
163(4) Effect of carryback of losses etc.
163.1 Penalty for late or deficient instalments

## Misrepresentation of a Tax Matter by a Third Party

163.2
163.2(1) Definitions
163.2(2) Penalty for misrepresentations in tax planning arrangements
163.2(3) Amount of penalty
163.2(4) Penalty for participating in a misrepresentation
163.2(5) Amount of penalty
163.2(6) Reliance in good faith
163.2(7) Non-application of subsec. (6)
163.2(8) False statements in respect of a particular arrangement
163.2(9) Clerical services
163.2(10) Valuations
163.2(11) Exception
163.2(12) Special rules
163.2(13) Assessment void
163.2(14) Maximum penalty
163.2(15) Employees

## Refunds

164
164(1) Refunds
164(1.1) Repayment on objections and appeals
164(1.2) Collection in jeopardy
164(1.3) Notice of application
164(1.31) Application of subsecs. 225.2(4), (10), (12) and (13)
164(1.4) Provincial refund
164(1.5) [Late refund of overpayment]
164(1.6) Refund of UI premium tax credit
164(1.7) Limitation of repayment on objections and appeals
164(1.8) Request to pay refund to province
164(2) Application to other debts
164(2.1) Application respecting refunds under s. 122.5 [GST credit]
164(2.2) Application respecting refunds re section 122.61 [Child Tax Benefit]
164(2.3) [Child Tax Benefit] Form deemed to be a return of income
164(3)–(3.2) Interest on refunds and repayments
164(4) Interest on interest repaid
164(4.1) Duty of Minister
164(5), (5.1) Effect of carryback of loss, etc.
164(5.1) [Proposed] Interest — disputed amounts
164(6) Where disposition of property by legal representative of deceased taxpayer
164(6.1) Realization of deceased employees' options
164(7) Definition of "overpayment"

Detailed Table of Sections

164.1 [Repealed]

## Objections to Assessments

165
165(1) Objections to assessment
165(1.1) Limitation of right to object to assessments or determinations
165(1.11) Objections by large corporations
165(1.12) Late compliance
165(1.13) Limitation on objections by large corporations
165(1.14) Application of subsec. (1.13)
165(1.15) Partnership
165(1.2) Determination of fair market value [Limitation on objections]
165(2) Service
165(2.1) Application
165(2.1) [Proposed] Application
165(3) Duties of Minister
165(3.1), (3.2), (4) [Repealed]
165(5) Validity of reassessment
165(6) Validity of notice of objection
165(7) Notice of objection not required

## General

166 Irregularities
166.1
166.1(1) Extension of time [to object] by Minister
166.1(2) Contents of application
166.1(3), (4) How application made
166.1(5) Duties of Minister
166.1(6) Date of objection or request if application granted
166.1(7) When order to be made
166.2
166.2(1) Extension of time [to object] by Tax Court
166.2(2) How application made
166.2(3) Copy to Commissioner
166.2(4) Powers of Court
166.2(5) When application to be granted
167
167(1) Extension of time to appeal
167(2) Contents of application
167(3) How application made
167(4) Copy to Deputy Attorney General
167(5) When order to be made

## Revocation of Registration of Certain Organizations and Associations

168
168(1) Notice of intention to revoke registration
168(2) Revocation of registration

### DIVISION J — APPEALS TO THE TAX COURT OF CANADA AND THE FEDERAL COURT

169
169(1) Appeal
169(1.1) [Proposed] Ecological gifts
169(2) Limitation of right to appeal from assessments or determinations
169(2.1) Limitation on appeals by large corporations
169(2.2) Waived issues
169(3) Disposition of appeal on consent
169(4) Provisions applicable
170
170(1) [Informal Procedure appeals — ] Notice to Commissioner
170(2) Notice, etc., to be forwarded to Tax Court of Canada
171
171(1) Disposal of appeal
171(1.1) [Proposed] Ecological gifts
171(2), (3) [Repealed under former Act]

cxliii

## Detailed Table of Sections

| | |
|---|---|
| 171(4) | [Repealed] |
| 172 | |
| 172(1), (2) | [Repealed under former Act] |
| 172(3) | Appeal from refusal to register, revocation of registration, etc. |
| 172(4) | Deemed refusal to register |
| 172(5) | Idem |
| 172(6) | Application of subsec. 149.1(1) |
| 173 | |
| 173(1) | References to Tax Court of Canada |
| 173(2) | Time during consideration not to count |
| 174 | |
| 174(1) | Reference of common questions to Tax Court of Canada |
| 174(2) | Application to Court |
| 174(3) | Where Tax Court of Canada may determine question |
| 174(4) | Determination final and conclusive |
| 174(4.1) | Appeal |
| 174(5) | Time during consideration of question not counted |
| 175 | Institution of appeals |
| 176 | |
| 176(1) | Notice, etc., to be forwarded to Tax Court of Canada |
| 176(2) | Documents to be transferred to Federal Court |
| 176(2) | [Proposed] Documents to be transferred to Federal Court of Appeal |
| 177, 178 | [Repealed under former Act] |
| 179 | Hearings *in camera* |
| 179.1 | No reasonable grounds for appeal |
| 180 | |
| 180(1) | Appeals to Federal Court of Appeal |
| 180(2) | No jurisdiction in Tax Court of Canada or Federal Court–Trial Division |
| 180(3) | Summary disposition of appeal |

### PART I.1 — INDIVIDUAL SURTAX

| | |
|---|---|
| 180.1 | |
| 180.1(1) | Individual surtax |
| 180.1 | |
| 180.1(1) | [Proposed] Individual surtax |
| 180.1(1.1) | Foreign tax deduction |
| 180.1(1.2), (1.3) | Deduction from tax [investment tax credit] |
| 180.1(1.4) | [Proposed] Former resident — credit for tax paid |
| 180.1(2) | Meaning of tax payable under Part I |
| 180.1(2) | [Proposed] Meaning of tax payable under Part I |
| 180.1(3) | Return |
| 180.1(4) | Provisions applicable to Part |

### PART I.2 — TAX ON OLD AGE SECURITY BENEFITS

| | |
|---|---|
| 180.2 | |
| 180.2(1) | Definitions |
| 180.2(2) | Tax payable |
| 180.2(3) | Withholding |
| 180.2(4) | Determination of amount to be withheld |
| 180.2(5) | Return |
| 180.2(6) | Provisions applicable to this Part |

### PART I.3 — TAX ON LARGE CORPORATIONS

| | |
|---|---|
| 181 | |
| 181(1) | Definitions |
| 181(2) | Prescribed expressions |
| 181(3) | Determining values and amounts |
| 181(4) | Limitations respecting inclusions and deductions |
| 181.1 | |
| 181.1(1) | Tax payable |
| 181.1(2) | Short taxation years |
| 181.1(3) | Where tax not payable |

Detailed Table of Sections

| | |
|---|---|
| 181.1(4), (5) | Deduction |
| 181.1(6) | Definitions |
| 181.1(7) | Acquisition of control |
| 181.2 | |
| 181.2(1) | Taxable capital employed in Canada |
| 181.2(2) | Taxable capital |
| 181.2(3) | Capital |
| 181.2(4) | Investment allowance |
| 181.2(5) | Value of interest in partnership |
| 181.2(6) | Loan |
| 181.3 | |
| 181.3(1) | Taxable capital employed in Canada of financial institution |
| 181.3(2) | Taxable capital of financial institution |
| 181.3(3) | Capital of financial institution |
| 181.3(4) | Investment allowance of financial institution |
| 181.3(4) | [Proposed] Investment allowance of financial institution |
| 181.3(5) | [Proposed] Interpretation |
| 181.4 | Taxable capital employed in Canada of non-resident |
| 181.5 | |
| 181.5(1) | Capital deduction |
| 181.5(2)–(6) | Related corporations |
| 181.5(7) | Related corporations that are not associated |
| 181.6 | Return |
| 181.7 | Provisions applicable to Part |
| 181.71 | Provisions applicable — Crown corporations |

### PART II — TOBACCO MANUFACTURERS' SURTAX

| | |
|---|---|
| 182 | |
| 182(1) | Surtax |
| 182(2) | Definitions |
| 183 | |
| 183(1) | Return |
| 183(2) | Payment |
| 183(3) | Provisions applicable |

### PART II.1 — TAX ON CORPORATE DISTRIBUTIONS

| | |
|---|---|
| 183.1 | |
| 183.1(1) | Application of Part |
| 183.1(2) | Tax payable |
| 183.1(3) | Stock dividend |
| 183.1(4) | Purchase of shares |
| 183.1(5) | Indirect payment |
| 183.1(6) | Where subsec. (2) does not apply |
| 183.1(7) | Where subsec. 110.6(8) does not apply |
| 183.2 | |
| 183.2(1) | Return |
| 183.2(2) | Provisions applicable to Part |

### PART III — ADDITIONAL TAX ON EXCESSIVE ELECTIONS

| | |
|---|---|
| 184 | |
| 184(1) | [Repealed under former Act] |
| 184(2) | Tax on excessive elections |
| 184(2.1) | Reduction of excess |
| 184(3) | Election to treat excess as separate dividend |
| 184(3.1), (3.2) | Election to treat dividend as loan |
| 184(4) | Concurrence with election |
| 184(5) | Penalty |
| 185 | |
| 185(1) | Assessment of tax |
| 185(2) | Payment of tax and interest |
| 185(3) | Provisions applicable to Part |
| 185(4) | Joint and several liability from excessive elections |

cxlv

Detailed Table of Sections

185(5)      Assessment
185(6)      Rules applicable

### PART IV — TAX ON TAXABLE DIVIDENDS RECEIVED BY PRIVATE CORPORATIONS

186
186(1)      Tax on assessable dividends
186(1.1)      Reduction where Part IV.1 tax payable
186(2)      When corporation controlled
186(3)      Definitions
186(4)      Corporations connected with particular corporation
186(5)      Deemed private corporation
186(6)      Partnerships
186.1      Exempt corporations
186.2      Exempt dividends
187
187(1)      Information return
187(2)      Interest
187(3)      Provisions applicable to Part

### PART IV.1 — TAXES ON DIVIDENDS ON CERTAIN PREFERRED SHARES RECEIVED BY CORPORATIONS

187.1      Definition of "excepted dividend"
187.2      Tax on dividends on taxable preferred shares
187.3
187.3(1)      Tax on dividends on taxable RFI shares
187.3(2)      Time of acquisition of share
187.4      Partnerships
187.5      Information return
187.6      Provisions applicable to Part
187.61      Provisions applicable — Crown corporations

### PART V — TAX IN RESPECT OF REGISTERED CHARITIES

187.7      Application of subsec. 149.1(1)
188
188(1), (2)      Revocation tax
188(3), (4)      Transfer of property tax
188(5)      Definitions
189
189(1)      Tax regarding non-qualified investment
189(2)      Computation of interest on debt
189(3)      Share deemed to be debt
189(4)      Computation of interest with respect to a share
189(5)      Share substitution
189(6)      Taxpayer to file return and pay tax
189(7)      Interest
189(8)      Provisions applicable to Part

### PART VI — TAX ON CAPITAL OF FINANCIAL INSTITUTIONS

190
190(1)      Definitions
190(1.1)      Prescribed meanings
190(2)      Application of subsecs. 181(3) and (4)

## Calculation of Capital Tax

190.1
190.1(1)      Tax payable
190.1(1.1)      Additional tax payable by life insurance corporations
190.1(1.2)      Additional tax payable by deposit-taking institutions
190.1(2)      Short taxation years
190.1(3), (4)      Deduction
190.1(5)      Definitions
190.1(6)      Acquisition of control
190.11      Taxable capital employed in Canada
190.12      Taxable capital
190.13      Capital

Detailed Table of Sections

| | |
|---|---|
| 190.14 | Investment in related institutions |
| 190.14 | |
| 190.14(1) | [Proposed] Investment in related institutions |
| 190.14(2) | [Proposed] Interpretation |
| 190.15 | |
| 190.15(1) | Capital deduction |
| 190.15(2–(6) | Related financial institution |
| 190.16 | |
| 190.16(1) | Capital allowance |
| 190.16(2) — 190.16(4) | Related life insurance corporation |
| 190.16(5) | Provisions applicable to Part |
| 190.17 | |
| 190.17(1) | Enhanced capital deduction |
| 190.17(2) | Related financial institution |
| 190.17(3) | Minister's powers |
| 190.17(4) | Least amount allocated |
| 190.17(5) | Provisions applicable to Part |

## Administrative Provisions

| | |
|---|---|
| 190.2 | Return |
| 190.21 | Provisions applicable to Part |
| 190.211 | Provisions applicable — Crown corporations |

### PART VI.1 — TAX ON CORPORATIONS PAYING DIVIDENDS ON TAXABLE PREFERRED SHARES

| | |
|---|---|
| 191 | |
| 191(1) | Definitions |
| 191(2), (3) | Substantial interest |
| 191(4) | Deemed dividends |
| 191(5) | Where subsec. (4) does not apply |
| 191.1 | |
| 191.1(1) | Tax on taxable dividends |
| 191.1(2) | Dividend allowance |
| 191.1(3) | Associated corporations |
| 191.1(4) | Total dividend allowance |
| 191.1(5) | Failure to file agreement |
| 191.1(6) | Dividend allowance in short years |
| 191.2 | |
| 191.2(1) | Election |
| 191.2(2) | Time of election |
| 191.2(3) | Assessment |
| 191.3 | |
| 191.3(1) | Agreement respecting liability for tax |
| 191.3(1.1) | Consideration for agreement |
| 191.3(2) | Manner of filing agreement |
| 191.3(3) | Assessment |
| 191.3(4) | Related corporations |
| 191.3(5) | Assessment of transferor corporation |
| 191.3(6) | Payment by transferor corporation |
| 191.4 | |
| 191.4(1) | Information return |
| 191.4(2) | Provisions applicable to Part |
| 191.4(3) | Provisions applicable — Crown corporations |

### PART VII — REFUNDABLE TAX ON CORPORATIONS ISSUING QUALIFYING SHARES

| | |
|---|---|
| 192 | |
| 192(1) | Corporation to pay tax |
| 192(2) | Definition of "Part VII refund" |
| 192(3) | Definition of "refundable Part VII tax on hand" |
| 192(4) | Corporation may designate amount |
| 192(4.1) | Computing paid-up capital after designation |
| 192(5) | Presumption |
| 192(6) | Definition of "qualifying share" |
| 192(7) | Effect of obligation to acquire shares |

cxlvii

Detailed Table of Sections

| | |
|---|---|
| 192(8) | Late designation |
| 192(9) | Penalty for late designation |
| 192(10) | Deemed deduction |
| 192(11) | Restriction |
| 193 | |
| 193(1) | Corporation to file return |
| 193(2) | Corporation to make payment on account of tax |
| 193(3), (4) | Interest |
| 193(5) | Evasion of tax |
| 193(6) | Undue deferral |
| 193(7) | Avoidance of tax |
| 193(7.1) | Tax on excess |
| 193(8) | Provisions applicable to Part |

### PART VIII — REFUNDABLE TAX ON CORPORATIONS IN RESPECT OF SCIENTIFIC RESEARCH AND EXPERIMENTAL DEVELOPMENT TAX CREDIT

| | |
|---|---|
| 194 | |
| 194(1) | Corporation to pay tax |
| 194(2) | Definition of "Part VIII refund" |
| 194(3) | Definitions |
| 194(4) | Corporation may designate amount |
| 194(4.1) | Computing paid-up capital after designation |
| 194(4.2) | Where amount may not be designated |
| 194(5) | Presumption |
| 194(6) | Definition of "scientific research and experimental development financing contract" |
| 194(7) | Late designation |
| 194(8) | Penalty for late designation |
| 194(9) | Restriction |
| 195 | |
| 195(1) | Corporation to file return |
| 195(2) | Corporation to make payment on account of tax |
| 195(3), (4) | Interest |
| 195(5) | Evasion of tax |
| 195(6) | Undue deferral |
| 195(7) | Avoidance of tax |
| 195(7.1) | Tax on excess |
| 195(8) | Provisions applicable to Part |

### PART IX — TAX ON DEDUCTION UNDER SECTION 66.5

| | |
|---|---|
| 196 | |
| 196(1) | Tax in respect of cumulative offset account |
| 196(2) | Return |
| 196(3) | Instalments |
| 196(4) | Provisions applicable to Part |

### PART X — TAXES ON DEFERRED PROFIT SHARING PLANS AND REVOKED PLANS

| | |
|---|---|
| 198 | |
| 198(1) | Tax on non-qualified investments and use of assets as security |
| 198(2) | Payment of tax |
| 198(3) | Trustee liable for tax |
| 198(4) | Refund of tax on disposition of non-qualified investment |
| 198(5) | Refund of tax on recovery of property given as security |
| 198(6)–(8) | Special rules relating to life insurance policies |
| 199 | |
| 199(1) | Tax on initial non-qualified investments not disposed of |
| 199(2) | Refund |
| 200 | Distribution deemed disposition |
| 201 | Tax where inadequate consideration on purchase or sale |
| 202 | |
| 202(1) | Returns and payment of estimated tax |
| 202(2) | Consideration of application for refund |
| 202(3) | Provisions applicable to Part |

## Detailed Table of Sections

| | |
|---|---|
| 202(4) | Provisions applicable to refunds |
| 202(5) | Interest |
| 202(6) | Deemed payment of tax |
| 203 | Application to other taxes |
| 204 | Definitions |

### PART X.1 — TAX IN RESPECT OF OVER-CONTRIBUTIONS TO DEFERRED INCOME PLANS

| | |
|---|---|
| 204.1 | |
| 204.1(1) | Tax payable by individuals [before 1991] |
| 204.1(2) | Amount deemed repaid |
| 204.1(2.1) | Tax payable by individuals — contributions after 1990 |
| 204.1(3) | Tax payable by deferred profit sharing plan |
| 204.1(4) | Waiver of tax |
| 204.2 | |
| 204.2(1) | Definition of "excess amount for a year in respect of registered retirement savings plans" [before 1991] |
| 204.2(1.1) | Cumulative excess amount in respect of RRSPs |
| 204.2(1.2) | Undeducted RRSP premiums |
| 204.2(1.3) | Group RRSP amount |
| 204.2(1.31) | Qualifying group RRSP premium |
| 204.2(1.32) | Qualifying arrangement |
| 204.2(1.4) | Deemed receipt where RRSP or RRIF amended |
| 204.2(1.5) | Transitional amount |
| 204.2(2) | Where terminated plan deemed to continue to exist |
| 204.2(3) | When retirement savings plan deemed to be a registered plan |
| 204.2(4) | Definition of "excess amount" for a DPSP |
| 204.3 | |
| 204.3(1) | Return and payment of tax |
| 204.3(2) | Provisions applicable to Part |

### PART X.2 — TAX IN RESPECT OF REGISTERED INVESTMENTS

| | |
|---|---|
| 204.4 | |
| 204.4(1) | Definition of "registered investment" |
| 204.4(2) | Acceptance of applicant for registration |
| 204.4(3) | Revocation of registration |
| 204.4(4) | Suspension of revocation |
| 204.4(5) | Cancellation of revocation |
| 204.4(6) | Successor trust |
| 204.4(7) | Deemed registration of registered investment |
| 204.5 | Publication of list in *Canada Gazette* |
| 204.6 | |
| 204.6(1)–(3) | Tax payable |
| 204.7 | |
| 204.7(1) | Return and payment of tax |
| 204.7(2) | Liability of trustee |
| 204.7(3) | Provisions applicable to Part |

### PART X.3 — LABOUR-SPONSORED VENTURE CAPITAL CORPORATIONS

| | |
|---|---|
| 204.8 | |
| 204.8(1) | Definitions |
| 204.8(2) | When venture capital business discontinued |
| 204.8(3) | Date of issue of Class A shares |
| 204.81 | |
| 204.81(1) | Conditions for registration |
| 204.81(2) | Registration number |
| 204.81(3) | Successive registrations |
| 204.81(4) | Determination of cost |
| 204.81(5) | Registration date |
| 204.81(6) | Revocation of registration |
| 204.81(7), (8) | Notice of intent to revoke registration |
| 204.81(8.1) | Voluntary de-registration |
| 204.81(8.2) | Application of subsection 248(7) |

Detailed Table of Sections

| | |
|---|---|
| 204.81(9) | Right of appeal |
| 204.82 | |
| 204.82(1) | Recovery of credit |
| 204.82(2) | Liability for tax |
| 204.82(2.1) | Determination of investment shortfall |
| 204.82(2.2) | Investment shortfall |
| 204.82(3) | Recovery of credit |
| 204.82(4) | Penalty |
| 204.82(5) | Provincially registered LSVCCs |
| 204.82(6) | Further matching of amounts payable to a province |
| 204.83 | |
| 204.83(1) | Refunds for federally registered LSVCCs |
| 204.83(2) | Refunds of amounts payable to provinces |
| 204.84 | Penalty |
| 204.841 | Penalty tax where venture capital business discontinued |
| 204.85 | |
| 204.85(1) | Dissolution of federally registered LSVCCs |
| 204.85(2) | Dissolution of other LSVCCs |
| 204.85(3) | Amalgamations and mergers |
| 204.86 | |
| 204.86(1) | Return and payment of tax for federally-registered LSVCCs |
| 204.86(2) | Return and payment of tax for other LSVCCs |
| 204.87 | Provisions applicable to Part |

**PART X.4 — TAX IN RESPECT OF OVERPAYMENTS TO REGISTERED EDUCATION SAVINGS PLANS**

| | |
|---|---|
| 204.9 | |
| 204.9(1) | Definitions |
| 204.9(1.1) | Application of subsec. 146.1(1) |
| 204.9(2) | Agreements before February 21, 1990 |
| 204.9(3) | Refunds from unregistered plans |
| 204.9(4) | New beneficiary |
| 204.9(5) | Transfers between plans |
| 204.91 | |
| 204.91(1) | Tax payable by subscribers |
| 204.91(2) | Waiver of tax |
| 204.91(3) | Marriage [or common-law partnership] breakdown |
| 204.91(4) | Deceased subscribers |
| 204.92 | Return and payment of tax |
| 204.93 | Provisions applicable to Part |

**PART X.5 — PAYMENTS UNDER REGISTERED EDUCATION SAVINGS PLANS**

| | |
|---|---|
| 204.94 | |
| 204.94(1) | Definitions |
| 204.94(2) | Charging provision |
| 204.94(3) | Return and payment of tax |
| 204.94(4) | Administrative rules |

**PART XI — TAX IN RESPECT OF CERTAIN PROPERTY ACQUIRED BY TRUSTS, ETC., GOVERNED BY DEFERRED INCOME PLANS**

| | |
|---|---|
| 205 | Application of Part |
| 206 | |
| 206(1) | Definitions |
| 206(1.1) | Exception where substantial Canadian presence |
| 206(1.2) | Partnerships |
| 206(1.3) | Interpretation |
| 206(1.4) | Rights in respect of foreign property |
| 206(1.5) | Identical property |
| 206(2) | Tax payable |
| 206(2.01) | [Tax payable by] Registered investments |
| 206(2.1) | Exemption |
| 206(3) | [Repealed] |
| 206(3.1) | Reorganizations, etc. |

cl

Detailed Table of Sections

| | |
|---|---|
| 206(3.1) | [Proposed] Acquisition of qualifying security |
| 206(3.2) | [Proposed] Qualifying security |
| 206(4) | Non-arm's length transactions |
| 206(4) | [Proposed] Non-arm's length transactions |
| 206.1 | Tax in respect of acquisition of shares |
| 207 | |
| 207(1) | Return and payment of tax |
| 207(2) | Liability of trustee |
| 207(3) | Provisions applicable to Part |

### PART XI.1 — TAX IN RESPECT OF CERTAIN PROPERTY HELD BY TRUSTS GOVERNED BY DEFERRED INCOME PLANS

| | |
|---|---|
| 207.1 | |
| 207.1(1) | Tax payable by trust under registered retirement savings plan [holding non-qualified investment] |
| 207.1(2) | Tax payable by trust under deferred profit sharing plan [holding non-qualified investment] |
| 207.1(3) | Tax payable by trust under registered education savings plan [holding non-qualified investment] |
| 207.1(4) | Tax payable by trust under registered retirement income fund [holding non-qualified investment] |
| 207.1(5) | [Repealed] |
| 207.2 | |
| 207.2(1) | Return and payment of tax |
| 207.2(2) | Liability of trustee |
| 207.2(3) | Provisions applicable to Part |

### PART XI.2 — TAX IN RESPECT OF DISPOSITIONS OF CERTAIN PROPERTIES

| | |
|---|---|
| 207.3 | Tax payable by institution or public authority |
| 207.31 | Tax payable by recipient of an ecological gift |
| 207.31 | [Proposed] Tax payable by recipient of an ecological gift |
| 207.4 | |
| 207.4(1) | Return and payment of tax |
| 207.4(2) | Provisions applicable to Part |

### PART XI.3 — TAX IN RESPECT OF RETIREMENT COMPENSATION ARRANGEMENTS

| | |
|---|---|
| 207.5 | |
| 207.5(1) | Definitions |
| 207.5(2) | Election |
| 207.6 | |
| 207.6(1) | Creation of trust |
| 207.6(2) | Life insurance policies |
| 207.6(3) | Incorporated employee |
| 207.6(4) | Deemed contribution |
| 207.6(5) | Resident's arrangement |
| 207.6(5.1) | Resident's contribution |
| 207.6(6) | Prescribed plan or arrangement |
| 207.6(7) | Transfers |
| 207.7 | |
| 207.7(1) | Tax payable |
| 207.7(2) | Refund |
| 207.7(3) | Payment of tax |
| 207.7(4) | Provisions applicable to Part |

### PART XII — TAX IN RESPECT OF CERTAIN ROYALTIES, TAXES, LEASE RENTALS, ETC., PAID TO A GOVERNMENT BY A TAX EXEMPT PERSON

| | |
|---|---|
| 208 | |
| 208(1) | Tax payable by exempt person |
| 208(1.1) | Definition of "specified stage" |
| 208(2) | Return and payment of tax |
| 208(3) | Liability of trustee |
| 208(4) | Provisions applicable to Part |

### PART XII.1 — TAX ON CARVED-OUT INCOME

| | |
|---|---|
| 209 | |
| 209(1) | Definitions |
| 209(2) | Tax |

cli

# Detailed Table of Sections

| | |
|---|---|
| 209(3) | Return |
| 209(4) | Payment of tax |
| 209(5) | Provisions applicable to Part |
| 209(6) | Partnerships |

## PART XII.2 — TAX ON DESIGNATED INCOME OF CERTAIN TRUSTS

| | |
|---|---|
| 210 | Designated beneficiary |
| 210.1 | Application of Part |
| 210.2 | |
| 210.2(1) | Tax on income of trust |
| 210.2(1.1) | Amateur athlete trusts |
| 210.2(2) | Designated income |
| 210.2(3) | Tax deemed paid by beneficiary |
| 210.2(4) | Designations in respect of partnerships |
| 210.2(5) | Returns |
| 210.2(6) | Liability of trustee |
| 210.2(7) | Provisions applicable to Part |
| 210.3 | |
| 210.3(1) | Where no designated beneficiaries |
| 210.3(2) | Where beneficiary deemed not designated |

## PART XII.3 — TAX ON INVESTMENT INCOME OF LIFE INSURERS

| | |
|---|---|
| 211 | |
| 211(1) | Definitions |
| 211(2) | Riders and changes in terms |
| 211.1 | |
| 211.1(1) | Tax payable |
| 211.1(2) | Taxable Canadian life investment income |
| 211.1(3) | Canadian life investment income |
| 211.1(4) | Short taxation year |
| 211.2 | Return |
| 211.3 | |
| 211.3(1) | Instalments |
| 211.3(2) | Annualized tax payable |
| 211.4 | Payment of remainder of tax |
| 211.5 | |
| 211.5(1) | Provisions applicable to Part |
| 211.5(2) | Interest on instalments |

## PART XII.4 — TAX ON QUALIFYING ENVIRONMENTAL TRUSTS

| | |
|---|---|
| 211.6 | |
| 211.6(1) | Charging provision |
| 211.6(2) | Computation of income |
| 211.6(3) | Return |
| 211.6(4) | Payment of tax |
| 211.6(5) | Provisions applicable to Part |

## PART XII.5 — RECOVERY OF LABOUR-SPONSORED FUNDS TAX CREDIT

| | |
|---|---|
| 211.7 | |
| 211.7(1) | Definitions |
| 211.7(2) | Amalgamations and mergers |
| 211.8 | |
| 211.8(1) | Disposition of approved share |
| 211.8(1.1) | Rules of application |
| 211.8(2) | Withholding and remittance of tax |
| 211.8(3) | Liability for tax |
| 211.9 | Refund |

## PART XII.6 — TAX ON FLOW-THROUGH SHARES

| | |
|---|---|
| 211.91 | |
| 211.91(1) | Tax imposed |
| 211.91(2) | Return and payment of tax |
| 211.91(3) | Provisions applicable to Part |

Detailed Table of Sections

**PART XIII — TAX ON INCOME FROM CANADA OF NON-RESIDENT PERSONS**

212
212(1)　　　Tax
212(1)(a)　　management fee
212(1)(b)　　interest
212(1)(c)　　estate or trust income
212(1)(d)　　rents, royalties, etc.
212(1)(e)　　timber royalties
212(1)(f)　　[Repealed]
212(1)(g)　　patronage dividend
212(1)(h)　　pension benefits
212(1)(i)　　[Repealed under former Act]
212(1)(j)　　benefits
212(1)(j.1)　retiring allowances
212(1)(k)　　supplementary unemployment benefit plan payments
212(1)(l)　　registered retirement savings plan payments
212(1)(m)　　deferred profit sharing plan payments
212(1)(n)　　income-averaging annuity contract payments
212(1)(o)　　other annuity payments
212(1)(p)　　payments from RHOSP
212(1)(q)　　registered retirement income fund payments
212(1)(r)　　registered education savings plan
212(1)(s)　　home insulation or energy conversion grants
212(1)(t)　　NISA Fund No. 2 payments
212(1)(u)　　amateur athlete trust payments
212(1)(v)　　payments under an eligible funeral arrangement
212(2)　　　Tax on dividends
212(3)　　　Replacement obligations
212(4)　　　Interpretation of "management or administration fee or charge"
212(5)　　　Motion picture films
212(6)　　　Interest on provincial bonds from wholly-owned subsidiaries
212(7)　　　Where subsec. (6) does not apply
212(8)　　　Bonds issued after December 20, 1960 in exchange for earlier bonds
212(9)　　　Exemptions
212(10)　　　Trust beneficiaries residing outside of Canada
212(11)　　　Payment to beneficiary as income of trust
212(11.1), (11.2)　[Repealed under former Act]
212(12)　　　Deemed payments to spouse, etc.
212(13)　　　Rent and other payments
212(13.1)　　Application of Part XIII tax where payer or payee is a partnership
212(13.2)　　Application of Part XIII tax where non-resident operates in Canada
212(13.3)　　[Proposed] Application of Part XIII to authorized foreign bank
212(14)　　　Certificate of exemption
212(15)　　　Certain obligations
212(16)　　　Payments for temporary use of rolling stock
212(17)　　　Exception
212(18)　　　Return by financial institutions and registered securities dealers
212(19)　　　Tax on registered securities dealers
212.1
212.1(1)–(3)　Non-arm's length sales of shares by non-residents
212.1(4)　　Where section does not apply
212.2
212.2(1)　　Application
212.2(2)　　Deemed dividend
213
213(1), (2)　Tax non-payable by non-resident person
213(3)　　　Corporation deemed to be foreign business corporation
214
214(1)　　　No deductions
214(2)　　　Income and capital combined
214(3)　　　Deemed payments

cliii

## Detailed Table of Sections

| | |
|---|---|
| 214(3.1) | Time of deemed payment |
| 214(4) | Securities |
| 214(5) | Interpretation |
| 214(6) | Deemed interest |
| 214(7), (7.1) | Sale of obligation |
| 214(8) | Meaning of "excluded obligation" |
| 214(9) | Deemed resident |
| 214(10) | Reduction of tax |
| 214(11) | Application of para. 212(1)(b) |
| 214(12) | Where subsec. (2) does not apply |
| 214(13) | Regulations respecting residents |
| 214(14) | Assignment of obligation |
| 214(15) | Standby charges and guarantee fees |
| 215 | |
| 215(1) | Deduction and payment of tax |
| 215(1.1)–(3) | Exception — corporate immigration |
| 215(4) | Regulations creating exceptions |
| 215(5) | Regulations reducing deduction or withholding |
| 215(5) | [Proposed] Regulations reducing deduction or withholding |
| 215(6) | Liability for tax |
| 216 | |
| 216(1)–(3) | Alternatives re rents and timber royalties |
| 216(4) | Optional method of payment |
| 216(5) | Disposition by non-resident of interest in real property, timber resource property or timber limit |
| 216(6) | Saving provision |
| 216(7) | Election |
| 216(8) | Restriction on deduction |
| 217 | |
| 217(1) | Alternative re Canadian benefits |
| 217(2) | Part I return |
| 217(3) | Taxable income earned in Canada |
| 217(4) | Tax credits — limitation |
| 217(5) | Tax credits allowed |
| 217(6) | Special credit |
| 218 | |
| 218(1), (2) | Loan to wholly-owned subsidiary |
| 218(3) | Election |
| 218(4) | Application of election |
| 218.1 | Application of s. 138.1 |

### PART XIII.1 — [PROPOSED] ADDITIONAL TAX ON AUTHORIZED FOREIGN BANKS

| | |
|---|---|
| 218.2 | |
| 218.2(1) | [Proposed] Branch interest tax |
| 218.2(2) | [Proposed] Taxable interest expense |
| 218.2(3) | [Proposed] Where tax not payable |
| 218.2(4) | [Proposed] Rate limitation |
| 218.2(5) | [Proposed] Provisions applicable to Part |

### PART XIV — ADDITIONAL TAX ON NON-RESIDENT CORPORATIONS

| | |
|---|---|
| 219 | |
| 219(1) | Additional tax [branch tax] |
| 219(1.1) | Excluded gains |
| 219(1.1) | [Proposed] Excluded gains |
| 219(2) | Exempt corporations |
| 219(3) | Provisions applicable to Part |
| 219(4) | Non-resident insurers |
| 219(5) | [Repealed under former Act] |
| 219(5.1) | Additional tax on insurer |
| 219(5.2) | Election by non-resident insurer |
| 219(5.3) | Deemed payment of dividend |
| 219(6) | [Repealed under former Act] |
| 219(7) | Definitions |

Detailed Table of Sections

219(8)     Meaning of "qualified related corporation"
219.1     Corporate emigration
219.2     Limitation on rate of branch tax
219.3     Effect of tax treaty

### PART XV — ADMINISTRATION AND ENFORCEMENT
## Administration

220
220(1)     Minister's duty
220(2)     Officers, clerks and employees
220(2.01)     Delegation
220(2.1)     Waiver of filing of documents
220(3)     Extensions for returns
220(3.1)     Waiver of penalty or interest
220(3.2)     Late, amended or revoked elections
220(3.21)     Designations and allocations
220(3.3)     Date of late election, amended election or revocation
220(3.4)     Assessments
220(3.5)     Penalty for late filed, amended or revoked elections
220(3.6), (3.7)     Unpaid balance of penalty
220(4), (4.1)     Security
220(4.2)     Surrender of excess security
220(4.3)     Security furnished by a member institution of a deposit insurance corporation
220(4.4)     Additional security
220(4.5)     [Proposed] Security for departure tax
220(4.51)     [Proposed] Deemed security
220(4.52)     [Proposed] Limit
220(4.53)     [Proposed] Inadequate security
220(4.54)     [Proposed] Extension of time
220(4.6)     [Proposed] Security for tax on distributions of taxable Canadian property to non-resident beneficiaries
220(4.61)     [Proposed] Limit
220(4.62)     [Proposed] Inadequate security
220(4.63)     [Proposed] Extension of time
220(4.7)     [Proposed] Undue hardship
220(4.71)     [Proposed] Limit
220(5)     Administration of oaths
220(6)     Assignment by corporation
220(7)     Effect of assignment
221
221(1)     Regulations
221(2)     Effect
221(3)     Regulations binding Crown
221(4)     Incorporation by reference
221.1     Application of interest
221.2     Re-appropriation of amounts

## Collection

222     Debts to Her Majesty
222.1     Court costs
223
223(1)     Definition of "amount payable"
223(2)     Certificates
223(3)     Registration in court
223(4)     Costs
223(5)     Charge on property
223(6)     Creation of charge
223(7)     Proceedings in respect of memorial
223(8)     Presentation of documents
223(9)     Sale, etc.
223(10)     Completion of notices, etc.
223(11)     Application for an order

## Detailed Table of Sections

| | |
|---|---|
| 223(11.1) | Deemed security |
| 223(12) | Details in certificates and memorials |
| 223.1 | |
| 223.1(1) | Application of subsecs. 223(1) to (8) and (12) |
| 223.1(2) | Application of subsecs. 223(9) to (11) |
| 224 | |
| 224(1)–(1.2) | Garnishment |
| 224(1.3) | Definitions |
| 224(1.4) | Garnishment |
| 224(2), (3) | Minister's receipt discharges original liability |
| 224(4) | Failure to comply with subsec. (1), (1.2) or (3) requirement |
| 224(4.1) | Failure to comply with subsec. (1.1) requirement |
| 224(5), (6) | Service of garnishee |
| 224.1 | Recovery by deduction or set-off |
| 224.2 | Acquisition of debtor's property |
| 224.3 | |
| 224.3(1) | Payment of moneys seized from tax debtor |
| 224.3(2) | Receipt of Minister |
| 225 | |
| 225(1) | Seizure of chattels |
| 225(2) | Sale of seized property |
| 225(3) | Notice of sale |
| 225(4) | Surplus returned to owner |
| 225(5) | Exemptions from seizure |
| 225.1 | |
| 225.1(1)–(5) | Collection restrictions |
| 225.1(6) | Where subsecs. (1) to (4) do not apply |
| 225.1(7) | Idem — large corporations |
| 225.1(8) | Definition of "large corporation" |
| 225.2 | |
| 225.2(1) | Definition of "judge" |
| 225.2(2) | Authorization to proceed forthwith |
| 225.2(3) | Notice of assessment not sent |
| 225.2(4) | Affidavits |
| 225.2(5) | Service of authorization and of notice of assessment |
| 225.2(6) | How service effected |
| 225.2(7) | Application to judge for direction |
| 225.2(8) | Review of authorization |
| 225.2(9) | Limitation period for review application |
| 225.2(10) | Hearing *in camera* |
| 225.2(11) | Disposition of application |
| 225.2(12) | Directions |
| 225.2(13) | No appeal from review order |
| 226 | |
| 226(1), (2) | Taxpayer leaving Canada |
| 227 | |
| 227(1) | Withholding taxes |
| 227(2) | Return filed with person withholding |
| 227(3) | Failure to file return |
| 227(4) | Trust for moneys deducted |
| 227(4.1) | Extension of trust |
| 227(4.2) | Meaning of security interest |
| 227(4.3) | [Proposed] Application to Crown |
| 227(5) | Payments by trustees, etc. |
| 227(5.1) | Definition of "specified person" |
| 227(5.2) | "Person" includes partnership |
| 227(5.2) | [Proposed] Interference with remittance |
| 227(5.3) | [Proposed] Exception where all cheques stopped |
| 227(5.4) | [Proposed] Other exceptions |
| 227(6) | Excess withheld, returned or applied |
| 227(6.1) | Repayment of non-resident shareholder loan |

### Detailed Table of Sections

| | |
|---|---|
| 227(7) | Application for assessment |
| 227(7.1) | Application for determination |
| 227(8) | Penalty |
| 227(8.1) | Joint and several liability |
| 227(8.2) | Retirement compensation arrangement deductions |
| 227(8.3) | Interest on amounts not deducted or withheld |
| 227(8.4) | Liability to pay amount not deducted or withheld |
| 227(8.5) | [Repealed] |
| 227(9) | Penalty |
| 227(9.1) | Penalty |
| 227(9.2) | Interest on amounts deducted or withheld but not remitted |
| 227(9.3) | Interest on certain tax not paid |
| 227(9.4) | Liability to pay amount not remitted |
| 227(9.5) | Payment from same establishment |
| 227(10) | Assessment |
| 227(10.01), 227(10.1) | Part XII.5 [assessment] |
| 227(10.2) | Joint and several liability re contributions to RCA |
| 227(10.3)–(10.9) | [Repealed] |
| 227(11) | Withholding tax |
| 227(12) | Agreement not to deduct void |
| 227(13) | Minister's receipt discharges debtor |
| 227(14) | Application of other Parts |
| 227(15) | Partnership included in "person" |
| 227(16) | Municipal or provincial corporation excepted |
| 227(16) | [Proposed] Municipal or provincial corporation excepted |
| 227.1 | |
| 227.1(1) | Liability of directors for failure to deduct |
| 227.1(2), (3) | Limitations on liability |
| 227.1(4) | Limitation period |
| 227.1(5) | Amount recoverable |
| 227.1(6) | Preference |
| 227.1(7) | Contribution |
| 228 | Applying payments under collection agreements |
| 229 | Receipt of taxes by banks |
| 229.1 | |
| 229.1(1) | [Repealed] |
| 229.1(2) | [Coming into force] |

### General

| | |
|---|---|
| 230 | |
| 230(1) | Records and books |
| 230(1.1), (2) | [Repealed under former Act] |
| 230(2.1) | Idem, lawyers |
| 230(3) | Minister's requirement to keep records, etc. |
| 230(4) | Limitation period for keeping records, etc. |
| 230(4.1) | Electronic records |
| 230(4.2) | Exemptions |
| 230(5) | Exception |
| 230(6) | Exception where objection or appeal |
| 230(7) | Exception where demand by Minister |
| 230(8) | Permission for earlier disposal |
| 230.1 | |
| 230.1(1) | Records and books re political contributions |
| 230.1(2) | Return of information |
| 230.1(3) | Application of subsecs. 230(3) to (8) |
| 230.1(4), (5) | [Repealed] |
| 230.1(6) | Definitions |
| 230.1(7) | Definition of "amount contributed" |
| 231 | Definitions |
| 231 | [Proposed] Definitions |
| 231.1 | |
| 231.1(1) | [Audits,] inspections |

clvii

## Detailed Table of Sections

| | |
|---|---|
| 231.1(2) | Prior authorization |
| 231.1(3) | Application |
| 231.2 | |
| 231.2(1) | Requirement to provide documents or information |
| 231.2(2) | Unnamed persons |
| 231.2(3) | Judicial authorization |
| 231.2(4) | Service of authorization |
| 231.2(5) | Review of authorization |
| 231.2(6) | Powers on review |
| 231.2(7) | [Repealed under former Act] |
| 231.3 | |
| 231.3(1) | Search warrant |
| 231.3(2) | Evidence in support of application |
| 231.3(3) | Evidence |
| 231.3(4) | Contents of warrant |
| 231.3(5) | Seizure of document |
| 231.3(6) | Retention of things seized |
| 231.3(7) | Return of things seized |
| 231.3(8) | Access and copies |
| 231.4 | |
| 231.4(1) | Inquiry |
| 231.4(2) | Appointment of hearing officer |
| 231.4(3) | Powers of hearing officer |
| 231.4(4) | When powers to be exercised |
| 231.4(5) | Rights of witness at inquiry |
| 231.4(6) | Rights of person whose affairs are investigated |
| 231.5 | |
| 231.5(1) | Copies |
| 231.5(2) | Compliance |
| 231.5(2) | [Proposed] Compliance |
| 231.6 | |
| 231.6(1) | Definition of "foreign-based information or document" |
| 231.6(2) | Requirement to provide foreign-based information |
| 231.6(3) | Notice |
| 231.6(4) | Review of foreign information requirement |
| 231.6(5),(6) | Powers on review |
| 231.6(7) | Time during consideration not to count |
| 231.6(8) | Consequence of failure |
| 231.7 | |
| 231.7(1) | [Proposed] Compliance order |
| 231.7(2) | [Proposed] Contempt of court |
| 231.7(3) | [Proposed] Appeal |
| 232 | |
| 232(1) | [Solicitor-client privilege] Definitions |
| 232(2) | Solicitor-client privilege defence |
| 232(3) | Seizure of certain documents where privilege claimed |
| 232(3.1) | Examination of certain documents where privilege claimed |
| 232(4) | Application to judge |
| 232(5) | Disposition of application |
| 232(6) | Order to deliver or make available |
| 232(7) | Delivery by custodian |
| 232(8) | Continuation by another judge |
| 232(9) | Costs |
| 232(10) | Directions |
| 232(11), (12) | Prohibition |
| 232(13) | Authority to make copies |
| 232(14) | Waiver of claim of privilege |
| 232(15) | Compliance |
| 233 | |
| 233(1) | Information return |
| 233(2) | Partnerships |

## Detailed Table of Sections

| | |
|---|---|
| 233(3) | Application to members of partnerships |
| 233.1 | |
| 233.1(1) | Definitions |
| 233.1(2) | Reporting person's information return |
| 233.1(3) | Reporting partnership's information return |
| 233.1(4) | *De minimis* exception |
| 233.1(5) | Deemed member of partnership |
| 233.2 | |
| 233.2(1) | Definitions |
| 233.2(2) | Non-arm's length indicators |
| 233.2(2) | [Proposed] Rule of application |
| 233.2(3) | Partnerships |
| 233.2(4) | Filing information on specified foreign trusts |
| 233.2(4) | [Proposed] Filing information on foreign trusts |
| 233.2(4.1) | [Proposed] Similar arrangements |
| 233.2(5) | Joint filing |
| 233.3 | |
| 233.3(1) | Definitions |
| 233.3(2) | Application to members of partnerships |
| 233.3(3) | Returns respecting foreign property |
| 233.4 | |
| 233.4(1) | Reporting entity |
| 233.4(2) | Rules of application |
| 233.4(2) | [Proposed] Rules of application |
| 233.4(3) | Application to members of partnerships |
| 233.4(4) | Returns respecting foreign affiliates |
| 233.5 | Due diligence exception |
| 233.6 | |
| 233.6(1) | Returns respecting distributions from non-resident trusts |
| 233.6(2) | Excluded trust defined |
| 233.7 | Exception for first-year residents |
| 234 | |
| 234(1)–(3) | Ownership certificates |
| 234(4)–(6) | [Repealed under former Act] |
| 234.1 | [Repealed under former Act] |
| 235 | Penalty for failing to file corporate returns [large corporations] |
| 236 | Execution of documents by corporations |
| 237 | |
| 237(1) | Social Insurance Number |
| 237(1.1) | Production of number |
| 237(2) | Number required in information returns |
| 237(3) | Authority to communicate number |
| 237(4) | Authority to communicate number [for demutualization] |
| 237.1 | |
| 237.1(1) | Definitions |
| 237.1(2) | Application |
| 237.1(3) | Identification |
| 237.1(4) | Sales prohibited |
| 237.1(5) | Providing tax shelter number |
| 237.1(6), (6.1) | Deductions and claims disallowed |
| 237.1(6.2) | Assessments |
| 237.1(7) | Information return |
| 237.1(7.1) | Time for filing return |
| 237.1(7.2) | Time for filing — special case |
| 237.1(7.3) | Copies to be provided |
| 237.1(7.4) | Penalty |
| 237.1(8) | Application of sections 231 to 231.3 |
| 237.2 | Application of section 237.1 |

### Offences and Punishment

| | |
|---|---|
| 238 | |
| 238(1) | Offences and punishment |

| | |
|---|---|
| 238(2) | Compliance orders |
| 238(3) | Saving |
| 239 | |
| 239(1) | Other offences and punishment |
| 239(1.1) | Offences re refunds and credits |
| 239(2) | Prosecution on indictment |
| 239(2.1) | Providing incorrect tax shelter identification number |
| 239(2.2), (2.21) | Offence with respect to confidential information |
| 239(2.22) | Definitions |
| 239(2.3) | Offence with respect to an identification number |
| 239(3) | Penalty on conviction |
| 239(4) | Stay of appeal |
| 240 | |
| 240(1) | Definition of "taxable obligation" and "non-taxable obligation" |
| 240(2) | Interest coupon to be identified in prescribed manner — offence and punishment |
| 241 | |
| 241(1) | Provision of information |
| 241(2) | Idem, in legal proceedings |
| 241(3) | Communication where proceedings have been commenced |
| 241(3.1) | Circumstances involving danger |
| 241(3.2) | Registered charities |
| 241(3.2) | [Proposed] Registered charities |
| 241(4) | Where taxpayer information may be disclosed |
| 241(4.1) | Measures to prevent unauthorized use or disclosure |
| 241(5) | Disclosure to taxpayer or on consent |
| 241(6) | Appeal from order or direction |
| 241(7) | Disposition of appeal |
| 241(8) | Stay of order or direction |
| 241(9) | [Repealed under former Act] |
| 241(10) | Definitions |
| 241(11) | PGRT Act references |
| 242 | Officers, etc., of corporations |
| 243 | Power to decrease punishment |

**Procedure and Evidence**

| | |
|---|---|
| 244 | |
| 244(1) | Information or complaint |
| 244(2) | Two or more offences |
| 244(3) | Venue |
| 244(4) | Limitation period |
| 244(5) | Proof of service by mail |
| 244(6) | Proof of personal service |
| 244(7) | Proof of failure to comply |
| 244(8) | Proof of time of compliance |
| 244(9) | Proof of documents |
| 244(10) | Proof of no appeal |
| 244(11) | Presumption |
| 244(12) | Judicial notice |
| 244(13) | Proof of documents |
| 244(13.1) | [Repealed] |
| 244(14) | Mailing date |
| 244(15) | Date when assessment made |
| 244(16) | Forms prescribed or authorized |
| 244(17) | Proof of return in prosecution for offence |
| 244(18) | Idem, in proceedings under Division J of Part I |
| 244(19) | Proof of statement of non-receipt |
| 244(20) | Members of partnerships |
| 244(21) | Proof of return filed |
| 244(22) | Filing of information returns |

**PART XVI — TAX AVOIDANCE**

| | |
|---|---|
| 245 | [General Anti-Avoidance Rule — GAAR] |

Detailed Table of Sections

| | |
|---|---|
| 245(1) | Definitions |
| 245(2) | General anti-avoidance provision [GAAR] |
| 245(3) | Avoidance transaction |
| 245(4) | Where subsec. (2) does not apply |
| 245(5) | Determination of tax consequences |
| 245(6) | Request for adjustments |
| 245(7) | Exception |
| 245(8) | Duties of Minister |
| 246 | |
| 246(1) | Benefit conferred on a person |
| 246(2) | Arm's length |

### PART XVI.1 — TRANSFER PRICING

| | |
|---|---|
| 247 | |
| 247(1) | Definitions |
| 247(2) | Transfer pricing adjustment |
| 247(3) | Penalty |
| 247(4) | Contemporaneous documentation |
| 247(5) | Partner's gross revenue |
| 247(6) | Deemed member of partnership |
| 247(7) | Exclusion for loans to certain controlled foreign affiliates |
| 247(8) | Provisions not applicable |
| 247(9) | Anti-avoidance |
| 247(10) | No adjustment unless appropriate |
| 247(11) | Provisions applicable to Part |

### PART XVII — INTERPRETATION

| | |
|---|---|
| 248 | |
| 248(1) | Definitions |
| 248(2) | Tax payable |
| 248(3) | Rules applicable in relation to the Province of Quebec [deemed trusts] |
| 248(4) | Interest in real property |
| 248(5) | Substituted property |
| 248(6) | "Class" of shares issued in series |
| 248(7) | Receipt of things mailed |
| 248(8) | Occurrences as a consequence of death |
| 248(9) | Definitions |
| 248(9.1) | How trust created |
| 248(9.2) | Vested indefeasibly |
| 248(10) | Series of transactions |
| 248(11) | Compound interest |
| 248(12) | Identical properties |
| 248(13) | Interests in trusts and partnerships |
| 248(14) | Related corporations |
| 248(15) | Goods and services tax — change of use |
| 248(16) | Goods and services tax — input tax credit and rebate |
| 248(17) | Application of subsec. (16) to passenger vehicles and aircraft |
| 248(18) | Goods and services tax — repayment of input tax credit |
| 248(19) | When property available for use |
| 248(20) | Partition of property |
| 248(21) | Subdivision of property |
| 248(22) | Matrimonial regimes |
| 248(23) | Dissolution of a matrimonial regime |
| 248(23.1) | Transfers after death |
| 248(24) | Accounting methods |
| 248(25) | Beneficially interested |
| 248(25.1) | [Proposed] Trust-to-trust transfers |
| 248(25.2) | [Proposed] Trusts to ensure obligations fulfilled |
| 248(25.3) | [Proposed] Cost of trust interest |
| 248(25.4) | [Proposed] Where acquisition by another of right to enforce |
| 248(26) | Debt obligations |
| 248(27) | Parts of debt obligations |

clxi

## Detailed Table of Sections

| | |
|---|---|
| 248(28) | Limitation respecting inclusions, deductions and tax credits |
| 249 | |
| 249(1) | Definition of "taxation year" |
| 249(2) | References to certain taxation years and fiscal periods |
| 249(3) | Deemed year end where fiscal period exceeds 365 days |
| 249(4) | Year end on change of control |
| 249.1 | |
| 249.1(1) | Definition of "fiscal period" |
| 249.1(2) | Not a member of a partnership |
| 249.1(3) | Subsequent fiscal periods |
| 249.1(4) | Alternative method |
| 249.1(5) | Alternative method not applicable to tax shelter investments |
| 249.1(6) | Revocation of election |
| 249.1(7) | Change of fiscal period |
| 250 | |
| 250(1) | Person deemed resident |
| 250(2) | Idem |
| 250(3) | Ordinarily resident |
| 250(4) | Corporation deemed resident |
| 250(5) | Deemed non-resident |
| 250(5) | [Proposed] Deemed non-resident |
| 250(5.1) | Continued corporation |
| 250(6) | Residence of international shipping corporation |
| 250(6.1) | [Proposed] Residence of *inter vivos* trusts |
| 250(7) | Residence of a qualifying environmental trust |
| 250.1 | [Proposed] Non-resident person's taxation year and income |
| 251 | |
| 251(1) | Arm's length |
| 251(2) | Definition of "related persons" |
| 251(3) | Corporations related through a third corporation |
| 251(3.1) | Relation where amalgamation or merger |
| 251(3.2) | Amalgamation of related corporations |
| 251(4) | Definitions concerning groups |
| 251(5) | Control by related groups, options, etc. |
| 251(6) | Blood relationship, etc. |
| 251.1 | |
| 251.1(1) | Definition of "affiliated persons" |
| 251.1(2) | Affiliation where amalgamation or merger |
| 251.1(3) | Definitions |
| 251.1(4) | Interpretation |
| 252 | |
| 252(1) | Extended meaning of "child" |
| 252(2) | Relationships |
| 252(3) | Extended meaning of "spouse" and "former spouse" |
| 252(4) | [Repealed.] |
| 252.1 | Union [as] employer |
| 253 | Extended meaning of "carrying on business" [in Canada] |
| 253.1 | [Proposed] Investments in limited partnerships [deemed not carrying on business] |
| 254 | Contract under pension plan |
| 255 | "Canada" |
| 256 | |
| 256(1) | Associated corporations |
| 256(1.1) | Definition of "specified class" |
| 256(1.2) | Control, etc. |
| 256(1.3) | Parent deemed to own shares |
| 256(1.4) | Options and rights |
| 256(1.5) | Person related to himself, herself or itself |
| 256(1.6) | Exception |
| 256(2) | Corporations associated through a third corporation |
| 256(2.1) | Anti-avoidance |
| 256(3)–(5) | Saving provision |

clxii

# Detailed Table of Sections

| | |
|---|---|
| 256(5.1), (6) | Control in fact |
| 256(6.1) | [Proposed] Simultaneous control |
| 256(6.2) | [Proposed] Application to control in fact |
| 256(7) | Acquiring control |
| 256(8) | Deemed exercise of right |
| 256(8.1) | Corporations without share capital |
| 256(9) | Date of acquisition of control |
| 257 | Negative amounts |
| 258 | |
| 258(1) | [Repealed under former Act] |
| 258(2) | Deemed dividend on term preferred share |
| 258(3) | Deemed interest on preferred shares |
| 258(4) | Exception |
| 258(5) | Deemed interest on certain shares |
| 259 | |
| 259(1) | Proportional holdings in trust property |
| 259(2) | Proportional holdings in corporate property |
| 259(3) | Election |
| 259(4) | Requirement to provide information |
| 259(5) | Definitions |
| 260 | |
| 260(1) | Definitions |
| 260(2) | Non-disposition |
| 260(3), (4) | Disposition of right |
| 260(5) | Deemed dividend |
| 260(6) | Non-deductibility |
| 260(6.1) | Deductible amount |
| 260(7) | Dividend refund |
| 260(8) | Non-resident withholding tax |
| 260(9) | Restricted financial institution |

*Assume 2/3 incl. ---

ROLLOVER PROBLEM
DEPRECIABLE ASSET

Facts – FMV = 150,000   Cap cost
UCC = 40,500   45,000

Elected T. Price = 120,000
to offset cap. loss of 56,250

Consideration
note – 120,000
com. shares
(w/ stated value)   30,000

Required – show tax consequences of this transaction

The 85(1) election will result in the following:

Recapture (40,500 – 45000)                       4,500
TCG (120,000 – 45000) × 2/3*                    50,000
                                                 54,500

Less: 95 net cap loss adjusted to 2000 rate              Inc. taxable
      56,250 × 2/3 × 4/3                         50,000   income ↓
                                                          4,500

ACB of consideration
 – note    120,000
   shares    nil

PUC of common shares
Legal stated cap of sh. issued                    30,000
Less PUC reduction:
 (a) ↑ in LSC               30,000 (1)
 (b) elected amount  120,000
     boot            120,000
     excess, if any       0      NIL (2)
                          (1) – (2)     30,000
PUC for tax purposes                     nil

Cap. cost of transferred property to corp for CCA and recapture purposes is equal to aggregate of:
(a) cap. cost to transferor    45,000
(b) TCG 2/3 (120 – 45)         50,000
                               95,000
↳ Basis for future write-offs

Cap cost for future cap gains = elected amount
= 120,000

**REQUIRED:** a) Calculate federal Part I tax + provincial tax
b) Calculate RDTOH as at Dec 31/00

Net income for the tax purposes ......... 279,375
Less: Net cap. losses (limited to TCG's) 56,250
      Non cap. losses                     56,250
      Taxable dividends                   28,125   140,625
      Taxable income                               138,750

Part I Tax on taxable income
    Tax + surtax 29.12%                            40,404

    Add refundable tax 6.67% of lesser of
    (a) Agg. Inv. Income
        (56,250 + 67,500 + 28,125
        − 56,250 − 28,125)           67,500

    (b) Taxable inc. less inc. elig.
        for SBD
        138,750 − 127,500            11,250 *
                                                    750
                                                   41,154
    less: SBD * (16% × 127,500)                   (20,400)
                Part I tax payable                 20,754
        Provincial tax  12% × 138,750              16,650
                                                   37,404

Part IV Tax on Taxable Div. Received
    Taxable dividends subject to Part IV tax 28,125 × 1/3   9,375

RDTOH:
    Refundable portion of Part I        3,000
    Part IV tax                         9,375
                                       12,375 → RDTOH

* 16% of least of
    Income from active business   127,500 *
    Taxable income                138,750
    Business limit                200,000

**CASE FACTS:** 12% Prov. tax rate   Refund. Part I — $3000

Taxable portfolio dividends     28125  (received Oct 100)
Cdn. source interest income     67500
ABI                             127500
TCG                             56,250
                    DNB Inc.    279375

**Loss c/fwds:**
Net  103,125
Non   56,250

DN of 168,750 paid

# INCOME TAX ACT

### An Act Respecting Income Taxes

REVISED STATUTES OF CANADA 1985, c. 1 (5TH SUPPLEMENT), AS AMENDED BY 1994, cc. 7, 8, 13, 21, 28, 29, 38, 41; 1995, cc. 1, 3, 11, 17, 18, 21, 38, 46; 1996, cc. 6, 11, 21, 23; 1997, cc. 10, 12, 25, 26; 1998, cc. 19, 21, 34; 1999, c. 10, 17, 22, 26, 31; 2000, cc. 9, 12, 14, 19, 30.

**1. Short title** — This Act may be cited as the *Income Tax Act*.

## PART I — INCOME TAX

### DIVISION A — LIABILITY FOR TAX

**2. (1) Tax payable by persons resident in Canada** — An income tax shall be paid, as required by this Act, on the taxable income for each taxation year of every person resident in Canada at any time in the year.

**Related Provisions**: 2(2) — Calculation of taxable income; 94(3)(a) [proposed] — Application to trust deemed resident in Canada; 96 — Partnerships and their members; 104 — Trusts and estates; 114 — Residence for part of year; 126 — Foreign tax credit; 127.5 — Alternative minimum tax; 149 — Exempt persons; 250 — Extended meaning of resident.

**Notes**: Tax on Canadian residents applies to income from all sources worldwide, subject to the foreign tax credit (see 126) and Canada's tax treaties with other countries. See 2(2). Tax on non-residents is limited to Canadian-source income; see 2(3) and s. 212. For the meaning of "resident in Canada", see Notes to 250(1).

**Interpretation Bulletins**: IT-106R2: Crown corporation employees abroad; IT-193 SR: Taxable income of individuals resident in Canada during part of a year (Special Release); IT-221R2: Determination of an individual's residence status; IT-447: Residence of a trust or estate.

**(2) Taxable income** — The taxable income of a taxpayer for a taxation year is the taxpayer's income for the year plus the additions and minus the deductions permitted by Division C.

**Related Provisions**: 3 — Income for taxation year; 15.1(2)(c) — Issuer of small business development bond; 33.1 — Calculation of income for international banking centre; 110.5 — Additions for foreign tax deductions; 248(1) — "Taxable income" may not be less than nil.

**Notes**: Division C is sections 109 to 114.2.

**(3) Tax payable by non-resident persons** — Where a person who is not taxable under subsection (1) for a taxation year

(a) was employed in Canada,

(b) carried on a business in Canada, or

(c) disposed of a taxable Canadian property,

at any time in the year or a previous year, an income tax shall be paid, as required by this Act, on the person's taxable income earned in Canada for the year determined in accordance with Division D.

**Related Provisions [subsec. 2(3)]**: 94(3)(a) [proposed] — Application to trust deemed resident in Canada; 96(1.6) — Members of partnership deemed carrying on business in Canada; 114 — Residence for part of year; 115(2)(d) — Non-resident deemed employed in Canada; 120(1) — Federal surtax on non-resident's income not earned in a province; 150(1)(a), 150(1.1)(b) — Requirements for non-residents to file tax returns; 212–219 — Tax on non-residents; 217(3)(a) — Non-resident who makes election is deemed employed in Canada; 250.1(a) — Taxation year of non-resident person; 253 — Extended meaning of carrying on business in Canada; Canada-U.S. Tax Convention, Art. VII — Business profits of U.S. resident.

**Notes**: Division D is sections 115 to 116.

A person who was resident in Canada in any previous year can in some cases be deemed employed in Canada in respect of remuneration paid by a Canadian resident. See 115(2)(c) and (d).

Passive income, such as interest, dividends, rent and royalties, is not subject to tax under 2(3). It is taxed under Part XIII (withholding tax) instead, and the non-resident is generally not required or permitted to file a return. See s. 212, 216 and 217.

For discussion of 2(3)(b), see Constantine Kyres, "Carrying on Business in Canada", 45(5) *Canadian Tax Journal* 1629–71 (1995).

**Interpretation Bulletins [subsec. 2(3)]**: IT-113R4: Benefits to employees — stock options; IT-168R3: Athletes and players employed by football, hockey and similar clubs; IT-171R2: Non-resident individuals — computation of taxable income earned in Canada and non-refundable tax credits; IT-176R2: Taxable Canadian property — Interests in and options on real property and shares; IT-193 SR: Taxable income of individuals resident in Canada during part of a year (Special Release); IT-221R2: Determination of an individual's residence status; IT-262R2: Losses of non-residents and part-year residents; IT-298: Canada-U.S. Tax Convention — number of days "present" in Canada; IT-379R: Employees profit sharing plans — allocations to beneficiaries; IT-393R2: Election re tax on rents and timber royalties — non-residents; IT-420R3: Non-residents — income earned in Canada; IT-421R2: Benefits to individuals, corporations and shareholders from loans or debt; IT-434R: Rental of real property by individual.

**Definitions [s. 2]**: "business", "employed" — 248(1); "employed in Canada" — 115(2)(d); "non-resident", "person", "property" — 248(1); "resident in Canada" — 250; "taxable Canadian property" — 248(1); "taxable income" — 2(2), 248(1); "taxable income earned in Canada" — 115(1), 248(1); "taxation year" — 249, 250.1(a); "taxpayer" — 248(1).

**Forms [s. 2]**: NR73: Determination of residency status (leaving Canada); NR74: Determination of residency status (entering Canada); T4058: Non-residents and temporary residents of Canada [guide].

## DIVISION B — COMPUTATION OF INCOME

### Basic Rules

**3. Income for taxation year** — The income of a taxpayer for a taxation year for the purposes of this Part is the taxpayer's income for the year determined by the following rules:

(a) determine the total of all amounts each of which is the taxpayer's income for the year (other than a taxable capital gain from the disposition of a property) from a source inside or outside Canada, including, without restricting the generality of the foregoing, the taxpayer's income for the year from each office, employment, business and property,

(b) determine the amount, if any, by which

  (i) the total of

    (A) all of the taxpayer's taxable capital gains for the year from dispositions of property other than listed personal property, and

    (B) the taxpayer's taxable net gain for the year from dispositions of listed personal property,

  exceeds

  (ii) the amount, if any, by which the taxpayer's allowable capital losses for the year from dispositions of property other than listed personal property exceed the taxpayer's allowable business investment losses for the year,

(c) determine the amount, if any, by which the total determined under paragraph (a) plus the amount determined under paragraph (b) exceeds the total of the deductions permitted by subdivision e in computing the taxpayer's income for the year (except to the extent that those deductions, if any, have been taken into account in determining the total referred to in paragraph (a)), and

(d) determine the amount, if any, by which the amount determined under paragraph (c) exceeds the total of all amounts each of which is the taxpayer's loss for the year from an office, employment, business or property or the taxpayer's allowable business investment loss for the year,

and for the purposes of this Part,

(e) where an amount is determined under paragraph (d) for the year in respect of the taxpayer, the taxpayer's income for the year is the amount so determined, and

(f) in any other case, the taxpayer shall be deemed to have income for the year in an amount equal to zero.

**Related Provisions**: 94(3)(a) [proposed] — Application to trust deemed resident in Canada; 115(1)(b), (b.1), (c) — Application of s. 3 to a non-resident.

**Notes**: The term "income" as defined by s. 3 is called "net income" on the CCRA's income tax return forms.

Although 3(a) is worded very broadly, the courts have applied it restrictively, so that income from unenumerated sources is generally not taxable. See *Fries*, [1990] 2 C.T.C. 439 (SCC) (strike pay); *Layton*, [1995] 2 C.T.C. 2408 (TCC) (grant under Shipbuilders' Workers Adjustment Program); *Bellingham*, [1996] 1 C.T.C. 187 (FCA) (amount received following expropriation); *Schwartz*, [1996] 1 C.T.C. 303 (SCC) (damages for breach of employment contract before it began); *Fortino*, [1997] 2 C.T.C. 2184 (TCC), aff'd [2000] 1 C.T.C. 349 (FCA) (non-competition agreement); *Frank Beban Logging Ltd.*, [1998] C.T.C. 2493 (TCC) (voluntary compensation by government for stopping logging operations); and *Fournier*, [1999] 4 C.T.C. 2247 (TCC) (compensation for harassment of employee). In all these cases the amount in question was found not to be income from a taxable "source".

3(b) requires taxable capital gains (³/₄ of current-year capital gains) and allowable capital losses (³/₄ of current-year capital losses) to be netted against each other, with listed personal property losses factored into 3(b)(i)(B) (personal-use property losses are not otherwise deductible). Allowable business investment losses are claimed under 3(d) rather than under 3(b). Losses (including capital losses) of prior and later years are allowed under s. 111 and claimed under 2(2) as optional deductions in computing *taxable* income rather than under s. 3.

3(f) added by 1991 technical bill, effective 1990, to ensure that a taxpayer with no income is treated as having income of $0 (in response to two Tax Court cases that declined to consider a spouse with no income as having the "lower" income of two spouses for purposes of 63(2)). See *McLaren*, [1990] 2 C.T.C. 429 (FCTD).

**Definitions [s. 3]**: "allowable business investment loss", "allowable capital loss" — 38(b), 248(1); "amount", "business" — 248(1); "Canada" — 255; "employment" — 248(1); "foreign resource property" — 66(15), 248(1); "listed personal property" — 54, 248(1); "office", "property" — 248(1); "taxable capital gain" — 38(a), 248(1); "taxable net gain" — 41(1), 248(1); "taxation year" — 11(2), 249; "taxpayer" — 248(1).

**I.T. Application Rules**: 20(3)(c), 20(5)(c).

**Interpretation Bulletins**: IT-98R2: Investment corporations; IT-134R: Capital gains and losses on dispositions of business property by an individual; IT-138R: Computation and flow-through of partnership income; IT-169: Price adjustment clauses; IT-193 SR: Taxable income of individuals resident in Canada during part of a year (Special Release); IT-206R: Separate businesses; IT-232R3: Losses — their deductibility in the loss year or other years; IT-256R: Gains from theft, defalcation or embezzlement; IT-262R2: Losses of non-residents and part-year residents; IT-270R2: Foreign tax credit; IT-334R2: Miscellaneous receipts; IT-365R2: Damages, settlements and similar receipts; IT-377R: Director's, executor's or juror's fees; IT-381R3: Trusts — capital gains and losses and the flow-through of taxable capital gains to beneficiaries; IT-393R2: Election re tax on rents and timber royalties — non-residents; IT-395R: Foreign tax credit — foreign-source capital gains and losses; IT-420R3: Non-residents — income earned in Canada; IT-434R: Rental of real property by individual; IT-484R2: Business investment losses; IT-490: Barter transactions; IT-495R2: Child care expenses.

**Advance Tax Rulings**: ATR-40: Taxability of receipts under a structured settlement; ATR-50: Structured settlement; ATR-68: Structured settlement.

**Forms**: T776: Statement of real estate rentals.

**4. (1) Income or loss from a source or from sources in a place** — For the purposes of this Act,

(a) a taxpayer's income or loss for a taxation year from an office, employment, business, property or other source, or from sources in a particular place, is the taxpayer's income or loss, as the case may be, computed in accordance with this Act on the assumption that the taxpayer had during the taxation year no income or loss except from that source or no income or loss except from those sources, as the case may be, and was allowed no deductions in computing the taxpayer's income for the taxation year except such deductions as may reasonably be regarded as wholly applicable to that source or to those sources, as the case may be, and except such part of any other deductions as may reasonably be regarded as applicable thereto; and

(b) where the business carried on by a taxpayer or the duties of the office or employment performed by the taxpayer was carried on or were performed, as the case may be, partly in one place and partly in another place, the taxpayer's income or loss for the taxation year from the business carried on, or the duties performed, by the taxpayer in a particular place is the taxpayer's income or loss, as the case may be, computed in accordance with this Act on the assumption that the taxpayer had during the taxation year no income or loss except from the part of the business that was carried on in that particular place or no income or loss except from the part of those duties that were performed in that particular place, as the case may be, and was allowed no deductions in computing the taxpayer's income for the taxation year except such deductions as may reasonably be regarded as wholly applicable to that part of the business or to those duties, as the case may be, and except such part of any other deductions as may reasonably be regarded as applicable thereto.

**Related Provisions**: 96(1)(f) — Source of income preserved when flows through partnership; 108(5) — Source of income lost when flows through trust.

**Interpretation Bulletins**: IT-362R: Patronage dividends.

**(2) Idem** — Subject to subsection (3), in applying subsection (1) for the purposes of this Part, no deductions permitted by sections 60 to 64 apply either wholly or in part to a particular source or to sources in a particular place.

**Notes**: Reference to "63" in 4(2) changed to "64" by 1993 technical bill, effective for 1989 and later taxation years (i.e., since the introduction of s. 64).

**(3) Deductions applicable** — In applying subsection (1) for the purposes of subsections 104(22) and (22.1) and sections 115 and 126,

(a) subject to paragraph (b), all deductions permitted in computing a taxpayer's income for a taxation year for the purposes of this Part, except any deduction permitted by any of paragraphs 60(b) to (o), (p), (r) and (v) to (w), shall apply either wholly or in part to a particular source or to sources in a particular place; and

(b) any deduction permitted by subsection 104(6) or (12) shall not apply either wholly or in part to a source in a country other than Canada.

**Notes**: 4(3) amended by 1993 technical bill, this version effective for taxation years that begin in 1993 or later. For earlier years ending after November 12, 1981, read:

(3) The following rules apply for the purposes of this Act:

(a) in applying paragraph (1)(b) for the purposes of sections 115 and 126, subject to paragraph (b), all deductions permitted in computing a taxpayer's income for a taxation year for the purposes of this Part shall apply either wholly or in part to a particular source or to sources in a particular place; and

(b) in applying subsection (1) for the purposes of subsections 104(22) and (22.1) and sections 115 and 126,

(i) any deduction permitted by any of paragraphs 60(b) to (o), (p), (r) and (v) to (w) shall not apply either wholly or in part to a particular source or to sources in a particular place, and

(ii) any deduction permitted by subsection 104(6) or (12) shall not apply either wholly or in part to a source in a country other than Canada.

**(4) [Repealed]**

**Notes**: 4(4) repealed by 1995 Budget, effective for taxation years that end after July 19, 1995. See new 248(28), which is broader and has replaced it. For earlier taxation years since 1990, read:

(4) **Limitation respecting inclusions and deductions** — Unless a contrary intention is evident, no provision of this Part shall be read or construed to require the inclusion or to permit the deduction, either directly or indirectly, in computing a taxpayer's income for a taxation year or the taxpayer's income or loss for a taxation year from a particular source or from sources in a particular place, of any amount to the extent that that amount has been directly or indirectly included or deducted, as the case may be, in computing such income or loss for the year or any preceding taxation year under, in accordance with or because of any other provision of this Part.

4(4) amended by 1991 technical bill, effective 1990, to prevent double-counting across two different years as well as in one year.

**Interpretation Bulletins**: IT-421R2: Benefits to individuals, corporations and shareholders from loans or debt.

**Definitions [s. 4]**: "amount", "business" — 248(1); "Canada" — 255; "employment", "office", "property" — 248(1); "taxation year" — 11(2), 249; "taxpayer" — 248(1).

**Interpretation Bulletins [s. 4]**: IT-256R: Gains from theft, defalcation or embezzlement; IT-270R2: Foreign tax credit; IT-377R: Director's, executor's or juror's fees; IT-420R3: Non-residents — income earned in Canada.

## Subdivision a — Income or Loss from an Office or Employment

### Basic Rules

**5. (1) Income from office or employment** — Subject to this Part, a taxpayer's income for a taxation year from an office or employment is the salary, wages and other remuneration, including gratuities, received by the taxpayer in the year.

**Related Provisions**: 4(1) — Income or loss from a source or from sources in a place; 6 — Amounts included as income from office or employment; 8(1)(n) — Reimbursement of salary for periods when not employed; 87(2)(k) — Amalgamations — Amount received by employee from new corporation; 110.2(1)"qualifying amount" — Retroactive spreading of certain lump-sum payments over prior years; 115(1)(a)(i) — Non-resident's taxable income earned in Canada; 149(1)(a), (b) — Exempt individuals; 153(1)(a) — Withholding; Canada-U.S. tax treaty, Art. XV, XVI — Taxation of dependent personal services.

**Notes**: Section 26 of the *Employment Insurance Act* (S.C. 1996, c. 23), as amended by 1997 Budget (first bill), states:

> 26. For the purposes of this Part, Part IV, the *Income Tax Act* and the *Canada Pension Plan*, benefits paid to a claimant while employed under employment benefits, or under similar benefits that are the subject of an agreement under section 63, are not earnings from employment.

EI benefits are taxed under 56(1)(a)(iv).

In *Duguay*, 2000 CarswellNat 1190 (TCC), hospital employees who were union officers were paid by the union as reimbursement for days they took off work to participate in union activities. These indemnity payments were held taxable under 5(1).

**Interpretation Bulletins**: IT-68R2: Exemption: professors and teachers from other countries; IT-75R3: Scholarships, fellowships, bursaries, prizes, and research grants; IT-113R4: Benefits to employees — stock options; IT-167R6: Registered pension plans — employee's contributions; IT-196R2: Payments by employer to employee; IT-202R2: Employees' or workers' compensation; IT-213R: Prizes from lottery schemes and giveaway contests; IT-257R: Canada Council grants; IT-266: Taxation of members of provincial legislative assemblies; IT-292: Taxation of elected municipal officers; IT-316: Awards for employees' suggestions and inventions; IT-334R2: Miscellaneous receipts; IT-365R2: Damages, settlements and similar receipts; IT-389R: Vacation-with-pay plans established under collective agreements; IT-470R: Employees' fringe benefits; IT-515R2: Education tax credit.

**Advance Tax Rulings**: ATR-21: Pension benefit from an unregistered pension plan; ATR-45: Share appreciation rights plan; ATR-64: Phantom stock award plan.

**(2) Loss from office or employment** — A taxpayer's loss for a taxation year from an office or employment is the amount of the taxpayer's loss, if any, for the taxation year from that source computed by applying, with such modifications as the circumstances require, the provisions of this Act respecting the computation of income from that source.

**Related Provisions**: 4(1) — Income or loss from a source or from sources in a place; 8(13) — Loss from home office disallowed; 111(1)(a), 111(8)"non-capital loss" — Carryover of loss from employment to prior or later years.

**Definitions [s. 5]**: "amount", "employment", "office", "salary or wages" — 248(1); "taxation year" — 249; "taxpayer" — 248(1).

## Inclusions

**6. (1) Amounts to be included as income from office or employment** — There shall be included in computing the income of a taxpayer for a taxation year as income from an office or employment such of the following amounts as are applicable:

(a) **value of benefits** — the value of board, lodging and other benefits of any kind whatever received or enjoyed by the taxpayer in the year in respect of, in the course of, or by virtue of an office or employment, except any benefit

(i) derived from the contributions of the taxpayer's employer to or under a registered pension plan, group sickness or accident insurance plan, private health services plan, supplementary unemployment benefit plan, deferred profit sharing plan or group term life insurance policy,

(ii) under a retirement compensation arrangement, an employee benefit plan or an employee trust,

(iii) that was a benefit in respect of the use of an automobile,

(iv) derived from counselling services in respect of

(A) the mental or physical health of the taxpayer or an individual related to the taxpayer, other than a benefit attributable to an outlay or expense to which paragraph 18(1)(l) applies, or

(B) the re-employment or retirement of the taxpayer, or

(v) under a salary deferral arrangement, except to the extent that the benefit is included under this paragraph because of subsection (11);

**Related Provisions**: 6(1)(e) — Standby charge for automobile; 6(1)(e.1) — Additional 7% for GST; 6(1)(f) — Insurance benefits received by employer; 6(1)(g) — Employment benefit plan; 6(1)(i) — Salary deferral arrangement payments; 6(1)(k), (l) — Automobile operating expense benefits; 6(1.1) — Parking costs are taxable benefits; 6(4) — Group term life insurance — taxable benefit; 6(6) — Employment at special work site or remote location; 6(7) — Cost of property or service includes taxes; 6(11)–(14) — Salary deferral arrangement; 6(15), (15.1) — Forgiveness of employee debt; 6(16) — Disability-related employment benefits; 6(18)(a) — No benefit from top-up disability payments where insurer insolvent; 6(19)–(22) — Benefit from reimbursement for loss in value of housing; 6(23) — Benefit from housing subsidy; 7(3) — No benefit from stock option agreement except as provided under s. 7; 15(5) — Automobile benefit to shareholder; 18(1)(r) — Limitation on employer deductibility — automobile expenses; 20.01 — Deduction to self-employed person for private health services plan premiums; 56(1)(a) — Amounts included in income; 56(1)(w) — Salary deferral arrangement; 56(1)(x)–(z) — Retirement compensation arrangement; 81(3.1) — No tax on allowance or reimbursement for part-time employee's travel expenses; 153(1)(a) — Withholding of tax by employer; 248(1) — "retiring allowance" excludes counselling services.

**Notes**: The exclusion at the end of 6(1)(a)(i) for group term life insurance paid by an employer no longer applies. See 6(4).

For discussion of how to determine the value of benefits, see Christopher Chen and Randall Timm, "Valuation of Non-Cash Wages", 10(5) *Taxation of Executive Compensation & Retirement* (Federated Press) 73–88 (1999). See also *Wisla*, [2000] 1 C.T.C. 2823 (TCC), where the value of a gold ring given by an employer for long service was its scrap value because the ring was stamped with the employer's logo.

In addition to the exclusions in 6(1)(a)(i) to (v), Interpretation Bulletin IT-470R lists other benefits considered non-taxable under CCRA administrative policy. These include: free or subsidized school services for the employee's children; reimbursement of certain moving expenses on relocation; payment of club dues that benefit the employer's business; discounts offered to all employees (but normally not below the employer's cost); annual gift or wedding gift up to $100 not deducted by the employer; subsidized meals where the employee pays a reasonable amount to cover the cost of the food; uniforms or special clothing needed for the job; transportation to the job provided by the employer; use of the employer's recreational facilities; and transportation passes for bus, rail and airline employees (except where travelling on a space-confirmed basis). Employer-provided child care is also considered not to be a taxable benefit (VIEWS doc RCT 5-8359). An allowance for moving expenses up to $650 may be non-taxable; see Notes to 6(1)(b). The value of a Christmas or other party may be taxed if it exceeds $100 per employee; see Income Tax Technical News No. 15. See also 6(6) and 6(16) for other legislated exceptions.

Revenue Canada stated in a technical interpretation dated September 10, 1999 (VIEWS doc 9921735) that providing free coffee and tea to employees is a taxable benefit!

Reimbursements of losses from the January 1998 ice storm are effectively made non-taxable by remission order. See the *Ice Storm Employee Benefits Remission Order* (reproduced after the Regulations).

Frequent-flyer points earned on employer-paid travel are a taxable benefit when used, valued at the lowest equivalent ticket sold for the flight on which the points are used: *Giffen and Mommersteeg*, [1995] 2 C.T.C. 2767 (TCC).

Special street clothes for a plainclothes policeman were held not to be a taxable benefit in *Huffman*, [1990] 2 C.T.C. 132 (FCA).

For the valuation of housing benefits paid to employees in remote areas, see Notes to 6(6).

For more detail on taxable vs. non-taxable benefits, see CCRA Guide T4130, *Employers' Guide to Payroll Deductions*, on *TaxPartner* or the CCRA web site.

The benefit from automobile operating costs, which was formerly taxable under 6(1)(a), is now taxable under 6(1)(k) and (l).

6(1)(a) will not catch payments from an employer's disability insurer that escape the scope of 6(1)(f) by not being periodic, since 6(1)(a) is a more general provision: *Whitehouse*, [2000] 1 C.T.C. 2714 (TCC).

6(1)(a)(iii) amended by 1993 technical bill, effective 1993. For 1982 to 1992, read:

> (iii) that was a benefit in relation to the use of an automobile, except to the extent that the benefit related to the operation of the automobile,

6(1)(a)(iv), exclusion of certain counselling services, added by 1989 Budget, effective 1988.

6(1)(a)(v) added by 1991 technical bill, effective 1986.

**Regulations**: 200(2)(g), 200(3) (information returns).

**Remission Orders**: *Ice Storm Employee Benefits Remission Order*, P.C. 1998-2047.

**Interpretation Bulletins**: IT-54: Wage loss replacement plans — changes in plans established before June 19, 1971; IT-63R5: Benefits, including standby charge for an automobile, from the personal use of a motor vehicle supplied by an employer — after 1992; IT-75R3: Scholarships, fellowships, bursaries, prizes, and research grants; IT-85R2: Health and welfare trusts; Benefits to employees — stock options; IT-160R3: Personal use of aircraft; IT-167R6: Registered pension plans — employee's contributions; IT-168R3: Athletes and players employed by football, hockey and similar clubs; IT-196R2: Payments by employer to employee; IT-227R: Group term life insurance premiums; IT-334R2: Miscellaneous receipts; IT-339R2: Meaning of "private health services plan"; IT-357R2: Expenses of training; IT-365R2: Damages, settlements and similar receipts; IT-389R: Vacation-with-pay plans established under collective agreements; IT-421R2: Benefits to individuals, corporations and shareholders from loans or debt; IT-428: Wage loss replacement plans; IT-432R2: Benefits conferred on shareholders; IT-470R: Employees' fringe benefits; IT-502: Employee benefit plans and employee trusts; IT-529: Flexible employee benefit programs.

**I.T. Technical News**: No. 6 (payment of mortgage interest subsidy by employer); No. 13 (employer-paid educational costs); No. 12 (1998 deduction limits and benefit rates for automobiles); No. 15 (Christmas parties and employer-paid special events; employer payment of professional membership fees).

**Advance Tax Rulings**: ATR-8: Self-insured health and welfare trust fund; ATR-21: Pension benefit from an unregistered pension plan; ATR-23: Private health services plan; ATR-45: Share appreciation rights plan.

**Forms**: T4130: Employer's guide to payroll deductions — taxable benefits [guide].

(b) **personal or living expenses** — all amounts received by the taxpayer in the year as an allowance for personal or living expenses or as an allowance for any other purpose, except

(i) travel, personal or living expense allowances

(A) expressly fixed in an Act of Parliament, or

(B) paid under the authority of the Treasury Board to a person who was appointed or whose services were engaged pursuant to the *Inquiries Act*, in respect of the discharge of the person's duties relating to the appointment or engagement,

(ii) travel and separation allowances received under service regulations as a member of the Canadian Forces,

(iii) representation or other special allowances received in respect of a period of absence from Canada as a person described in paragraph 250(1)(b), (c), (d) or (d.1),

(iv) representation or other special allowances received by a person who is an agent-general of a province in respect of a period while the person was in Ottawa as the agent-general of the province,

(v) reasonable allowances for travel expenses received by an employee from the employee's employer in respect of a period when the employee was employed in connection with the selling of property or negotiating of contracts for the employee's employer,

(vi) reasonable allowances received by a minister or clergyman in charge of or ministering to a diocese, parish or congregation for expenses for transportation incident to the discharge of the duties of that office or employment,

(vii) reasonable allowances for travel expenses (other than allowances for the use of a motor vehicle) received by an employee (other than an employee employed in connection with the selling of property or the negotiating of contracts for the employer) from the employer for travelling away from

    (A) the municipality where the employer's establishment at which the employee ordinarily worked or to which the employee ordinarily reported was located, and

    (B) the metropolitan area, if there is one, where that establishment was located,

in the performance of the duties of the employee's office or employment,

(vii.1) reasonable allowances for the use of a motor vehicle received by an employee (other than an employee employed in connection with the selling of property or the negotiating of contracts for the employer) from the employer for travelling in the performance of the duties of the office or employment,

(viii) [Repealed]

(ix) allowances (not in excess of reasonable amounts) received by an employee from the employee's employer in respect of any child of the employee living away from the employee's domestic establishment in the place where the employee is required by reason of the employee's employment to live and in full-time attendance at a school in which the language primarily used for instruction is the official language of Canada primarily used by the employee if

    (A) a school suitable for that child primarily using that language of instruction is not available in the place where the employee is so required to live, and

    (B) the school the child attends primarily uses that language for instruction and is not farther from that place than the community nearest to that place in which there is such a school having suitable boarding facilities;

and, for the purposes of subparagraphs (v), (vi) and (vii.1), an allowance received in a taxation year by a taxpayer for the use of a motor vehicle in connection with or in the course of the taxpayer's office or employment shall be deemed not to be a reasonable allowance

(x) where the measurement of the use of the vehicle for the purpose of the allowance is not based solely on the number of kilometres for which the vehicle is used in connection with or in the course of the office or employment, or

(xi) where the taxpayer both receives an allowance in respect of that use and is reimbursed in whole or in part for expenses in respect of that use (except where the reimbursement is in respect of supplementary business insurance or toll or ferry charges and the amount of the allowance was determined without reference to those reimbursed expenses);

**Related Provisions**: 6(6) — Employment at special work site or remote location; 6(16) — Disability-related employment benefits; 8(1) — Deductions allowed; 8(1)(a) — Deduction from income of volunteer firefighter or emergency worker; 8(1)(c) — Clergyman's residence; 8(1)(f) — Salesman's expenses; 8(1)(g) — Transport employee's expenses; 8(1)(h) — Travelling expenses; 8(1)(h.1) — Motor vehicle travelling expenses; 8(11) — GST rebate deemed not a reimbursement; 18(1)(r) — Limitation on employer deductibility — automobile expenses; 81(3.1) — No tax on allowance or reimbursement for part-time employee's travel expenses; 153(1)(a) — Withholding of tax by employer.

**Notes**: The term "personal or living expenses" is given an extended definition in 248(1).

6(1)(b)(i)(A) has the effect of excluding MPs' allowances from tax, since they are fixed in s. 63 of the *Parliament of Canada Act*. The parallel exclusions for allowances of members of provincial legislatures and municipal officers are in 81(2) and 81(3).

A non-accountable allowance for incidental employee moving expenses of up to $650 is non-taxable if the employee certifies having spent at least that much: *Employers' Guide to Payroll Deductions — Taxable Benefits*, Chapter 2.

The per-kilometre amounts in Reg. 7306 are generally accepted as being "reasonable" amounts for purposes of 6(1)(b).

The CCRA announced on Nov. 3, 2000 a change to the policy for the taxable benefit on a combined flat-rate and reasonable per-kilometre allowance (*Employers' Guide — Taxable Benefits*): Previously, only the flat-rate portion was taxable, and the reasonable per-km portion was excluded from income. Starting Jan. 1, 2001, the total combined allowance is considered taxable and must be included in the employee's income; the employee can claim allowable expenses.

6(1)(b)(vii) and (vii.1) amended by 1991 technical bill, effective 1990. For earlier years, read "allowances (not in excess of reasonable amounts)" in place of "reasonable allowances". The effect of the amendment is that the entire allowance is taxed if it is unreasonable. In such a case, a deduction may be available under 8(1)(f) or (h), however.

6(1)(b)(viii) repealed by 1998 Budget, effective for 1998 and later taxation years. The $500 exemption for volunteer firemen's allowances has been replaced by an expanded $1,000 deduction for volunteer emergency workers under 8(1)(a) (but which is to be replaced by an exemption in 81(4)). Before 1998, read:

    (viii) such part of the total of allowances received by a person who is a volunteer fireman from a government, municipality or other public authority for expenses incurred by the person in respect of, in the course of, or by virtue of the discharge of the person's duties as a volunteer fireman, as does not exceed $500, or

6(1)(b)(xi) amended by 1991 technical bill, effective 1988, to deem an allowance not to be reasonable rather than to deem it to be in excess of a reasonable amount, and to add the exceptions for supplementary business insurance, parking, toll and ferry charges. A taxpayer may elect to have the amendment not apply for 1988 and 1989.

6(1)(b)(xi) further amended by 1993 technical bill, effective 1993, to delete the word "parking" (before "toll and ferry charges"). Parking is now dealt with under 6(1.1).

**Remission Orders**: *Ice Storm Employee Benefits Remission Order*, P.C. 1998-2047.

**Interpretation Bulletins**: IT-168R3: Athletes and players employed by football, hockey and similar clubs; IT-470R: Employees' fringe benefits; IT-516R2: Tuition tax credit; IT-518R: Food, beverages and entertainment expenses; IT-522R: Vehicle, travel and sales expenses of employees.

**Forms**: T4130: Employer's guide to payroll deductions — taxable benefits [guide].

(c) **director's or other fees** — director's or other fees received by the taxpayer in the year in respect of, in the course of, or by virtue of an office or employment;

**Related Provisions**: 153(1)(a) — Withholding of tax by employer.

**Interpretation Bulletins**: IT-168R3: Athletes and players employed by football, hockey and similar clubs; IT-377R: Director's, executor's or juror's fees; IT-470R: Employees' fringe benefits; IT-518R: Food, beverages and entertainment expenses.

(d) **allocations, etc., under [employees] profit sharing plan** — amounts allocated to the taxpayer in the year by a trustee under an employees profit sharing plan as provided by section 144 except subsection 144(4), and amounts required by subsection 144(7) to be included in computing the taxpayer's income for the year;

**Related Provisions**: 8(1)(o.1) — Deduction for forfeited amounts; 12(1)(n) — Income inclusion — amount received from EPSP; 128.1(10)"excluded right or interest"(a)(v) — No deemed disposition of rights on emigration; 144(9) — Deductions for forfeited amounts; 153(1)(a) — Withholding of tax at source.

**Interpretation Bulletins**: IT-379R: Employees profit sharing plans — allocations to beneficiaries.

(e) **standby charge for automobile** — where the taxpayer's employer or a person related to the employer made an automobile available to the taxpayer, or to a person related to the taxpayer, in the year, the amount, if any, by which

(i) an amount that is a reasonable standby charge for the automobile for the total number of days in the year during which it was made so available

exceeds

(ii) the total of all amounts, each of which is an amount (other than an expense related to the operation of the automobile) paid in the year to the employer or the person related to the employer by the taxpayer or the person related to the taxpayer for the use of the automobile;

**Related Provisions**: 6(1)(a)(iii) — Automobile benefits excluded from general inclusion of benefits; 6(1)(e.1) — 7% added to benefit before 1996 to reflect GST; 6(1)(k), (l) — Operating expense benefit; 6(2) — Calculation of reasonable standby charge; 6(2.1) — Reduced standby charge for automobile salesman; 6(7) — Cost of automobile includes GST effective 1996; 8(1)(f)(vii) — Salesman's expenses; 12(1)(y) — Partnerships — auto provided to partner or employee of partner; 15(5) — Automobile benefit to shareholder; 153(1)(a) — Withholding of tax by employer.

**Notes**: See Notes to 6(2).

**Regulations**: 200(2)(g), 200(3) (information returns).

**Interpretation Bulletins**: IT-63R5: Benefits, including standby charge for an automobile, from the personal use of a motor vehicle supplied by an employer — after 1992; IT-168R3: Athletes and players employed by football, hockey and similar clubs.

**I.T. Technical News**: No. 12 (1998 deduction limits and benefit rates for automobiles).

(e.1) [Repealed]

**Notes**: Before 1996, 6(1)(e.1) required inclusion of a benefit of 7% to account for GST. The actual GST paid by the employer on the goods or services was not included in the benefit, per former 6(7). This rule has now been reversed, and the GST is specifically included in the benefit: see 6(7).

6(1)(e.1) repealed by 1997 GST/HST bill, effective for 1996 and later taxation years. For 1992 to 1995, read:

(e.1) **goods and services tax** — the total of all amounts each of which is 7% of the amount, if any, by which

(i) an amount (in this paragraph referred to as the "benefit amount") that would be required under paragraph (a) or (e) to be included in computing the taxpayer's income for the year in respect of a supply, other than a zero-rated supply or an exempt supply, (within the meanings assigned by Part IX of the *Excise Tax Act*) of property or a service if no amount were paid to the employer or to a person related to the employer in respect of the amount that would be so required to be included

exceeds

(ii) the amount, if any, included in the benefit amount that can reasonably be attributed to tax imposed under an Act of the legislature of a province that is a prescribed tax for the purposes of section 154 of the *Excise Tax Act*;

6(1)(e.1) added by 1990 GST, effective 1991, and amended by 1992 technical bill, effective 1992.

Prescribed taxes under s. 154 of the *Excise Tax Act* are, generally, provincial retail sales taxes, land transfer taxes, special sales taxes that do not exceed 12%, amusement taxes, hotel taxes, etc. See the *Taxes, Duties and Fees (GST) Regulations*, reproduced in the *Practitioner's Goods and Services Tax, Annotated* and the *Canada GST Service*. Such taxes are not included in the base price for purposes of calculating GST.

(f) **[private] employment insurance [plan] benefits** — the total of all amounts received by the taxpayer in the year that were payable to the taxpayer on a periodic basis in respect of the loss of all or any part of the taxpayer's income from an office or employment, pursuant to

(i) a sickness or accident insurance plan,

(ii) a disability insurance plan, or

(iii) an income maintenance insurance plan

to or under which the taxpayer's employer has made a contribution, not exceeding the amount, if any, by which

(iv) the total of all such amounts received by the taxpayer pursuant to the plan before the end of the year and

(A) where there was a preceding taxation year ending after 1971 in which any such amount was, by virtue of this paragraph, included in computing the taxpayer's income, after the last such year, and

(B) in any other case, after 1971,

exceeds

(v) the total of the contributions made by the taxpayer under the plan before the end of the year and

(A) where there was a preceding taxation year described in clause (iv)(A), after the last such year, and

**S. 6(1)(f)(v)(B)**        Income Tax Act, Part I, Division B

(B) in any other case, after 1967;

**Related Provisions**: 6(18) — No taxable benefit on top-up disability payments where insurer insolvent; 8(1)(n.1)(iii) — Deduction for certain amounts reimbursed to employer; 56(1)(a)(iv) — Income inclusion for benefit under *Employment Insurance Act*; 110.2(1)"qualifying amount" — Retroactive spreading of lump-sum payment over prior years; 139.1(13) — Effect of demutualization of insurance corporation on group insurance policy; 153(1)(a) — Withholding of tax at source.

**Notes**: Under 6(1)(f), employment insurance plan benefits such as disability insurance (not to be confused with federal EI benefits — see 56(1)(a)(iv)) are exempt if the employee paid *all* the premiums, and taxable if the employer paid *any* premiums (with a reduction for any premiums paid by the employee). Note that premiums deducted at payroll are paid by the *employee*.

Where 6(1)(f) does not apply because the payments are not periodic (on a litigation settlement), 6(1)(a) does not apply since it is a more general provision, and the payment is non-taxable: *Whitehouse*, [2000] 1 C.T.C. 2714 (TCC).

**Regulations**: 200(2)(f) (information return).

**I.T. Application Rules**: 19 (where plan established before June 19, 1971).

**Interpretation Bulletins**: IT-54: Wage loss replacement plans; IT-85R2: Health and welfare trusts for employees; IT-99R5: Legal and accounting fees; IT-428: Wage loss replacement plans; IT-529: Flexible employee benefit programs.

**Advance Tax Rulings**: ATR-8: Self-insured health and welfare trust fund.

**I.T. Technical News**: No. 12 (1998 deduction limits and benefit rates for automobiles).

**Forms**: T4E: Statement of employment insurance benefits; T4130: Employer's guide to payroll deductions — taxable benefits [guide].

(g) **employee benefit plan benefits** — the total of all amounts each of which is an amount received by the taxpayer in the year out of or under an employee benefit plan or from the disposition of any interest in any such plan, other than the portion thereof that is

(i) a death benefit or an amount that would, but for the deduction provided in the definition of that term in subsection 248(1), be a death benefit,

(ii) a return of amounts contributed to the plan by the taxpayer or a deceased employee of whom the taxpayer is an heir or legal representative, or

(iii) a superannuation or pension benefit attributable to services rendered by a person in a period throughout which the person was not resident in Canada;

**Related Provisions**: 6(10) — Contributions; 6(14) — Salary deferral arrangement — part of benefit plan; 12(1)(n) — Employees profit sharing plan; 12(1)(n.1) — Employee benefit plan; 18(1)(o) — Employee benefit plan contributions; 32.1 — Employee benefit plan deductions; 56(1)(a) — Benefits — pension and employee; 104(13)(b) — Trusts — income payable to beneficiary; 107.1 — Distribution by employee benefit plan; 128.1(10)"excluded right or interest"(a)(vi), (b) — No deemed disposition of rights on emigration; 153(1)(a) — Withholding of tax by employer; 212(17) — No non-resident withholding tax.

**Notes**: 6(1)(g)(iii) amended by 1990 pension bill, to change "during which" to "throughout which", effective 1988.

**Interpretation Bulletins**: IT-499R: Superannuation or pension benefits; IT-502: Employee benefit plans and employee trusts; IT-529: Flexible employee benefit programs.

**I.T. Technical News**: No. 11 (reporting of amounts paid out of an employee benefit plan).

**Advance Tax Rulings**: ATR-17: Employee benefit plan — purchase of company shares; ATR-39: Self-funded leave of absence.

(h) **employee trust** — amounts allocated to the taxpayer for the year by a trustee under an employee trust;

**Related Provisions**: 6(1)(a) — Value of benefits; 12(1)(n) — Employees profit sharing plan; 12(1)(n.1) — Employee benefit plan; 32.1 — Employee benefit plan deductions; 104(6) — Deductions in computing income of trust; 104(13) — Income payable to beneficiary; 107.1 — Distribution by employee trust; 128.1(10)"excluded right or interest"(e)(i) — No deemed disposition of rights on emigration; 153(1)(a) — Withholding of tax by employer; 212(17) — No non-resident withholding tax.

**Regulations**: 200(2)(g) (information return).

**Interpretation Bulletins**: IT-502: Employee benefit plans and employee trusts; IT-529: Flexible employee benefit programs.

(i) **salary deferral arrangement payments** — the amount, if any, by which the total of all amounts received by any person as benefits (other than amounts received by or from a trust governed by a salary deferral arrangement) in the year out of or under a salary deferral arrangement in respect of the taxpayer exceeds the amount, if any, by which

(i) the total of all deferred amounts under the arrangement that were included under paragraph (a) as benefits in computing the taxpayer's income for preceding taxation years

exceeds

(ii) the total of

(A) all deferred amounts received by any person in preceding taxation years out of or under the arrangement, and

(B) all deferred amounts under the arrangement that were deducted under paragraph 8(1)(o) in computing the taxpayer's income for the year or preceding taxation years;

**Related Provisions**: 6(11) — Salary deferral arrangement; 20(1)(oo), (pp) — Salary deferral arrangement — deductions; 56(1)(w) — Benefits — salary deferral arrangement; 128.1(10)"excluded right or interest"(a)(vii), (b) — No deemed disposition of rights on emigration; 153(1)(a) — Withholding of tax by employer.

**Interpretation Bulletins**: IT-529: Flexible employee benefit programs.

(j) **reimbursements and awards** — amounts received by the taxpayer in the year as an award or reimbursement in respect of an amount that would, if the taxpayer were entitled to no reimbursements or awards, be deductible under subsection 8(1) in computing the income of the taxpayer, except to the extent that the amounts so received

(i) are otherwise included in computing the income of the taxpayer for the year, or

(ii) are taken into account in computing the amount that is claimed under subsection 8(1) by the taxpayer for the year or a preceding taxation year;

**Related Provisions**: 153(1)(a) — Withholding of tax by employer.

**Notes**: 6(1)(j) added by 1989 Budget, effective for amounts received after 1989.

**Interpretation Bulletins**: IT-99R5: Legal and accounting fees.

(k) **automobile operating expense benefit** — where

(i) an amount is determined under subparagraph (e)(i) in respect of an automobile in computing the taxpayer's income for the year,

(ii) amounts related to the operation (otherwise than in connection with or in the course of the taxpayer's office or employment) of the automobile for the period or periods in the year during which the automobile was made available to the taxpayer or a person related to the taxpayer are paid or payable by the taxpayer's employer or a person related to the taxpayer's employer (each of whom is in this paragraph referred to as the "payor"), and

(iii) the total of the amounts so paid or payable is not paid in the year or within 45 days after the end of the year to the payor by the taxpayer or by the person related to the taxpayer,

the amount in respect of the operation of the automobile determined by the formula

$$A - B$$

where

A is

(iv) where the automobile is used primarily in the performance of the duties of the taxpayer's office or employment during the period or periods referred to in subparagraph (ii) and the taxpayer notifies the employer in writing before the end of the year of the taxpayer's intention to have this subparagraph apply, 1/2 of the amount determined under subparagraph (e)(i) in respect of the automobile in computing the taxpayer's income for the year, and

(v) in any other case, the amount equal to the product obtained when the amount prescribed for the year is multiplied by the total number of kilometres that the automobile is driven (otherwise than in connection with or in the course of the taxpayer's office or employment) during the period or periods referred to in subparagraph (ii), and

B is the total of all amounts in respect of the operation of the automobile in the year paid in the year or within 45 days after the end of the year to the payor by the taxpayer or by the person related to the taxpayer; and

**Related Provisions**: 6(1)(a)(iii) — Automobile benefits excluded from general inclusion of benefits; 6(1.1) — Parking is not an operating cost; 6(2.2) — Optional calculation of operating benefits; 12(1)(y) — Automobile benefit to partner or employee of partner; 15(5) — Automobile benefit to shareholder; 153(1)(a) — Withholding of tax by employer; 257 — Formula cannot calculate to less than zero.

**Notes**: 6(1)(k) added by 1993 technical bill, effective 1993. Where *any* operating costs in respect of an employer-owned automobile are paid by the employer, 6(1)(k) deems the taxable benefit to be a flat number of cents per personal-use kilometre as follows:

| Taxation year | Regular employee | Auto salesperson |
|---|---|---|
| 1993 | 12¢ | 12¢ |
| 1994-95 | 12¢ | 9¢ |
| 1996 | 13¢ | 10¢ |
| 1997-99 | 14¢ | 11¢ |
| 2000 | 15¢ | 12¢ |
| 2001 | 16¢ | 13¢ |

(See Reg. 7305.1.) Driving between home and the employer's place of business is considered personal use for this purpose. The benefit inclusion can be avoided if the employee repays all the benefits by February 14 of the new year (6(1)(k)(iii)). If, for example, the employer paid only the insurance, or only a single repair bill, repayment by the employee can avoid an income inclusion potentially far greater than the value of the benefits paid.

The amount per personal-use kilometre (16¢ for 2001) includes 5% (0.8¢ for 2001) of GST deemed collected by the employer, which must be remitted to the CCRA as GST collected under subpara. 173(1)(d)(vi)(A) of the *Excise Tax Act*. See the *Automobile Operating Expense Benefit (GST/HST) Regulations*, reproduced in *The Practitioner's GST Annotated* and the *Canada GST Service*. (In the Harmonized Sales Tax provinces, the percentage is 11% rather than 5%.)

Certain employees can opt by December 31 of the year to have their benefit calculated as one-half the standby charge. See 6(1)(k)(iv).

**Regulations**: 7305.1 (amount prescribed for 6(1)(k)(v)).

**Interpretation Bulletins**: IT-63R5: Benefits, including standby charge for an automobile, from the personal use of a motor vehicle supplied by an employer — after 1992.

**I.T. Technical News**: No. 10 (1997 deduction limits and benefit rates for automobiles); No. 12 (1998 deduction limits and benefit rates for automobiles).

(l) **idem** — the value of a benefit in respect of the operation of an automobile (other than a benefit to which paragraph (k) applies or would apply but for subparagraph (k)(iii)) received or enjoyed by the taxpayer in the year in respect of, in the course of or because of, the taxpayer's office or employment.

**Related Provisions**: 6(1)(a)(iii) — Automobile benefits excluded from general inclusion of benefits; 15(5) — Automobile benefit to shareholder; 153(1)(a) — Withholding of tax by employer.

**Notes:** 6(1)(l) added by 1993 technical bill, effective 1993.

**Interpretation Bulletins:** IT-63R5: Benefits, including standby charge for an automobile, from the personal use of a motor vehicle supplied by an employer — after 1992.

**I.T. Technical News:** No. 12 (1998 deduction limits and benefit rates for automobiles).

**(1.1) Parking cost** — For the purposes of this section, an amount or a benefit in respect of the use of a motor vehicle by a taxpayer does not include any amount or benefit related to the parking of the vehicle.

**Related Provisions**: 6(1)(a)(iii), 6(1)(e), (k) — Benefit in respect of the use of an automobile; 6(16)(a) — Parking costs are non-taxable benefit for disabled employee; 15(5) — Automobile benefit to shareholder.

**Notes:** 6(1.1) added by 1993 technical bill, effective 1993. Since parking is deemed not to be a benefit in respect of the use of a motor vehicle, it is not included in the "standby fee" benefit (6(1)(e), 6(2)), nor in the "operating costs" benefit (6(1)(k)). Instead, it is covered by 6(1)(a), and the benefit is determined based on its "value" (fair market value) — even where the actual benefit to the taxpayer is much less than the market value (see *Richmond*, [1998] 3 C.T.C. 2552 (TCC)).

**Interpretation Bulletins:** IT-63R5: Benefits, including standby charge for an automobile, from the personal use of a motor vehicle supplied by an employer — after 1992.

**I.T. Technical News:** No. 12 (1998 deduction limits and benefit rates for automobiles).

**(2) Reasonable standby charge** — For the purposes of paragraph (1)(e), a reasonable standby charge for an automobile for the total number of days (in this subsection referred to as the "total available days") in a taxation year during which the automobile is made available to a taxpayer or to a person related to the taxpayer by the employer of the taxpayer or by a person related to the employer (both of whom are in this subsection referred to as the "employer") shall be deemed to be the amount determined by the formula

$$\frac{A}{B} \times [2\% \times (C \times D) + \frac{2}{3} \times (E - F)]$$

where

A is the lesser of

    (a) the total number of kilometres that the automobile is driven (otherwise than in connection with or in the course of the taxpayer's office or employment) during the total available days, and

    (b) the value determined for B for the year under this subsection in respect of the standby charge for the automobile during the total available days,

except that the amount determined under paragraph (a) shall be deemed to be equal to the amount determined under paragraph (b) unless

    (c) the taxpayer is required by the employer to use the automobile in connection with or in the course of the office or employment, and

    (d) all or substantially all of the distance travelled by the automobile in the total available days is in connection with or in the course of the office or employment;

B is the product obtained when 1,000 is multiplied by the quotient obtained by dividing the total available days by 30 and, if the quotient so obtained is not a whole number and exceeds one, by rounding it to the nearest whole number or, where that quotient is equidistant from two consecutive whole numbers, by rounding it to the lower of those two numbers;

C is the cost of the automobile to the employer where the employer owns the vehicle at any time in the year;

D is the number obtained by dividing such of the total available days as are days when the employer owns the automobile by 30 and, if the quotient so obtained is not a whole number and exceeds one, by rounding it to the nearest whole number or, where that quotient is equidistant from two consecutive whole numbers, by rounding it to the lower of those two numbers;

E is the total of all amounts that may reasonably be regarded as having been payable by the employer to a lessor for the purpose of leasing the automobile during such of the total available days as are days when the automobile is leased to the employer; and

F is the part of the amount determined for E that may reasonably be regarded as having been payable to the lessor in respect of all or part of the cost to the lessor of insuring against

    (a) loss of, or damage to, the automobile, or

    (b) liability resulting from the use or operation of the automobile.

**Related Provisions**: 6(2.1) — Reduced benefit for automobile salesperson; 12(1)(y) — Automobile benefit to partner or employee of partner; 15(5) — Rule applies to calculate automobile benefit to shareholder; 85(1)(e.4) — Transfer of passenger vehicle to corporation by shareholder.

**Notes:** In simple terms, the standby charge (taxable income inclusion) for making a car available to an employee is 24% per year of the *original* cost of the vehicle to the employer, or ⅔ of the leasing cost if it is leased.

The CCRA takes the position that "all or substantially all", used in 6(2)A(d), means 90% or more.

An unlicensed and uninsured vehicle is not considered "available" for purposes of the standby charge: *Hewitt*, [1996] 1 C.T.C. 2675 (TCC). However, a vehicle is "available" even if it is not used: *Cheung*, [1998] 3 C.T.C. 2729 (TCC).

**Interpretation Bulletins:** IT-63R5: Benefits, including standby charge for an automobile, from the personal use of a motor vehicle supplied by an employer — after 1992.

**I.T. Technical News:** No. 12 (1998 deduction limits and benefit rates for automobiles).

**Forms:** T4130: Employer's guide to payroll deductions — taxable benefits [guide].

**(2.1) Automobile salesman** — Where in a taxation year

(a) a taxpayer was employed principally in selling or leasing automobiles,

(b) an automobile owned by the taxpayer's employer was made available by the employer to the taxpayer or to a person related to the taxpayer, and

(c) the employer has acquired one or more automobiles,

the amount that would otherwise be determined under subsection (2) as a reasonable standby charge shall, at the option of the employer, be computed as if

(d) the reference in the formula in subsection (2) to "2%" were read as a reference to "1½%", and

(e) the cost to the employer of the automobile were the greater of

  (i) the quotient obtained by dividing

    (A) the cost to the employer of all new automobiles acquired by the employer in the year for sale or lease in the course of the employer's business

  by

    (B) the number of automobiles described in clause (A), and

  (ii) the quotient obtained by dividing

    (A) the cost to the employer of all automobiles acquired by the employer in the year for sale or lease in the course of the employer's business

  by

    (B) the number of automobiles described in clause (A).

**Notes**: As well as a reduced standby charge, automobile salespersons are also eligible for a reduced calculation of the benefit for operating costs. See Notes to 6(1)(k).

**Interpretation Bulletins**: IT-63R5: Benefits, including standby charge for an automobile, from the personal use of a motor vehicle supplied by an employer — after 1992.

**I.T. Technical News**: No. 12 (1998 deduction limits and benefit rates for automobiles).

**(2.2)** [Repealed]

**Notes**: 6(2.2) repealed by 1993 technical bill, effective 1993. For 1988 to 1992, it provided an alternate calculation of the operating expense benefit. This rule is now in 6(1)(k)(iv).

**(3) Payments by employer to employee** — An amount received by one person from another

(a) during a period while the payee was an officer of, or in the employment of, the payer, or

(b) on account, in lieu of payment or in satisfaction of an obligation arising out of an agreement made by the payer with the payee immediately prior to, during or immediately after a period that the payee was an officer of, or in the employment of, the payer,

shall be deemed, for the purposes of section 5, to be remuneration for the payee's services rendered as an officer or during the period of employment, unless it is established that, irrespective of when the agreement, if any, under which the amount was received was made or the form or legal effect thereof, it cannot reasonably be regarded as having been received

(c) as consideration or partial consideration for accepting the office or entering into the contract of employment,

(d) as remuneration or partial remuneration for services as an officer or under the contract of employment, or

(e) in consideration or partial consideration for a covenant with reference to what the officer or employee is, or is not, to do before or after the termination of the employment.

**Related Provisions**: 87(2)(k) — Amalgamation — Amount received by employee from new corporation; 153(1)(a) — Withholding of tax by employer.

**Interpretation Bulletins**: IT-75R3: Scholarships, fellowships, bursaries, prizes, and research grants; IT-168R3: Athletes and players employed by football, hockey and similar clubs; IT-196R2: Payments by employer to employee; IT-247: Employer's contributions to pensioners' premiums under provincial medical and hospital services plans; IT-334R2: Miscellaneous receipts; IT-337R3: Retiring allowances; IT-365R2: Damages, settlements and similar receipts; IT-470R: Employees' fringe benefits; IT-515R2: Education tax credit; IT-529: Flexible employee benefit programs.

**(4) Group term life insurance** — Where at any time in a taxation year a taxpayer's life is insured under a group term life insurance policy, there shall be included in computing the taxpayer's income for the year from an office or employment the amount, if any, prescribed for the year in respect of the insurance.

**Related Provisions**: 18(9)(a)(iii), 18(9.01) — Limitation on deduction for premiums paid; 139.1(15) — Effect of demutualization of insurance corporation; 139.1(16), (17) — Flow-through of demutualization benefits by employer to employee; 153(1)(a) — Withholding of tax by employer.

**Notes**: 6(4) amended by 1994 Budget, effective for insurance provided in respect of periods that are after June 1994. Group term life insurance is now a fully taxable benefit, where previously the first $25,000 of coverage was exempt. For insurance provided in respect of periods from January 1 to June 30, 1994, there was a special transitional version of 6(4). From 1974–1993, the pre-1994 version applied.

**Regulations**: 2700–2704 (prescribed amount).

**Interpretation Bulletins**: IT-85R2: Health and welfare trusts for employees; IT-227R: Group term life insurance premiums; IT-529: Flexible employee benefit programs.

**(5)** [Repealed]

**Notes**: 6(5) repealed by 1994 Budget, effective 1995. It provided an interpretation of "policy year" for the 1972–94 versions of 6(4).

**(6) Employment at special work site or remote location** — Notwithstanding subsection (1), in computing the income of a taxpayer for a taxation year from an office or employment, there shall not be included any amount received or enjoyed by the taxpayer in respect of, in the course or by virtue of the office or employment that is the value of, or an allowance (not in excess of a reasonable amount) in respect of expenses the taxpayer has incurred for,

(a) the taxpayer's board and lodging for a period at

(i) a special work site, being a location at which the duties performed by the taxpayer were of a temporary nature, if the taxpayer maintained at another location a self-contained domestic establishment as the taxpayer's principal place of residence

(A) that was, throughout the period, available for the taxpayer's occupancy and not rented by the taxpayer to any other person, and

(B) to which, by reason of distance, the taxpayer could not reasonably be expected to have returned daily from the special work site, or

(ii) a location at which, by virtue of its remoteness from any established community, the taxpayer could not reasonably be expected to establish and maintain a self-contained domestic establishment,

if the period during which the taxpayer was required by the taxpayer's duties to be away from the taxpayer's principal place of residence, or to be at the special work site or location, was not less than 36 hours; or

(b) transportation between

(i) the principal place of residence and the special work site referred to in subparagraph (a)(i), or

(ii) the location referred to in subparagraph (a)(ii) and a location in Canada or a location in the country in which the taxpayer is employed,

in respect of a period described in paragraph (a) during which the taxpayer received board and lodging, or a reasonable allowance in respect of board and lodging, from the taxpayer's employer.

**Related Provisions**: 110.7 — Deduction for residents of northern Canada.

**Notes**: Note that a special work site under 6(6)(a)(i) need not be remote in the sense of isolated. For someone based in Calgary, for example, Toronto can be a "special work site".

The CCRA has published the following for rent and utilities paid to employees living in a prescribed zone without developed rental markets (RC4054, *Ceiling Amounts for Housing Benefits Paid in Prescribed Zones*):

- Common shelter
  2001 — $134 per month
  2000 — $130 per month

- *Apartment or duplex*
  2001 — $360 per month, rent only
  — $174 per month, utilities only
  — $534 per month, rent and utilities

  2000 — $350 per month, rent only
  — $169 per month, utilities only
  — $519 per month, rent and utilities

- *House or trailer*
  2001 — $601 per month, rent only
  — $266 per month, utilities only
  — $867 per month, rent and utilities

  2000 — $585 per month, rent only
  — $259 per month, utilities only
  — $844 per month, rent and utilities

See also T4130, *Employer's Guide — Taxable Benefits*, chapter 3.1.

**Interpretation Bulletins**: IT-91R4: Employment at special work sites or remote work locations; IT-168R3: Athletes and players employed by football, hockey and similar clubs; IT-254R2: Fishermen — employees and seafarers — value of rations and quarters; IT-470R: Employees' fringe benefits; IT-518R: Food, beverages and entertainment expenses; IT-522R: Vehicle, travel and sales expenses of employees.

**Forms**: TD4: Declaration of exemption — Employment at special work site.

**(7) Cost of property or service [includes GST, etc.]** — To the extent that the cost to a person of purchasing a property or service or an amount payable by a person for the purpose of leasing property is taken into account in determining an amount required under this section to be included in computing a taxpayer's income for a taxation year, that cost or amount payable, as the case may be, shall include any tax that was payable by the person in respect of the property or service or that would have been so payable if the person were not exempt from the payment of that tax because of the nature of the person or the use to which the property or service is to be put.

**Related Provisions**: 6(1)(e.1) — Benefit of 7% added before 1996 in place of including GST.

**Notes**: 6(7) amended by 1997 GST/HST bill, effective for 1996 and later taxation years. For 1991 to 1995, read:

(7) Goods and services tax — To the extent that an amount required to be included in computing the income of a taxpayer for a taxation year under paragraph (1)(a) or (e) is determined by reference to the cost to a person of any property or service, that cost shall, for the purposes of those paragraphs, be determined without reference to any goods and services tax payable by that person in respect of the property or service.

The change requires that GST payable by the employer be included in the calculation of a taxable benefit, rather than calculated and included as a separate benefit, as it was under 6(1)(e.1) before 1996. The reference to the "nature of the person" means that GST not paid by provincial governments and status Indians is still included in the value of the taxable benefit. Thus, the employee who is the consumer cannot benefit from the employer's special status.

6(7) added by 1990 GST, effective 1991.

**Interpretation Bulletins**: IT-63R5: Benefits, including standby charge for an automobile, from the personal use of a motor vehicle supplied by an employer — after 1992.

**I.T. Technical News**: No. 12 (1998 deduction limits and benefit rates for automobiles).

**(8) Idem [GST rebate]** — Where

(a) an amount in respect of an expense is deducted under section 8 in computing the income of a taxpayer for a taxation year from an office or employment, or

(b) an amount is included in the capital cost to a taxpayer of a property described in subparagraph 8(1)(j)(ii) or (p)(ii),

and a particular amount is paid to the taxpayer in a particular taxation year as a rebate under the *Excise Tax Act* in respect of any goods and services tax included in the amount of the expense, or the capital cost of the property, as the case may be, the particular amount

(c) to the extent that it relates to an expense referred to in paragraph (a), shall be included in computing the taxpayer's income from an office or employment for the particular year, and

(d) to the extent that it relates to the capital cost of property referred to in paragraph (b), shall be deemed, for the purposes of subsection 13(7.1), to have been received by the taxpayer in the particular year as assistance from a government for the acquisition of the property.

**Related Provisions**: 8(11) — GST rebate deemed not to be reimbursement.

**Notes**: 6(8) added by 1990 GST, effective 1991.

**(9) Amount in respect of interest on employee debt** — Where an amount in respect of a loan or debt is deemed by subsection 80.4(1) to be a benefit received in a taxation year by an individual, the amount of the benefit shall be included in computing the income of the individual for the year as income from an office or employment.

**Related Provisions**: 6(23) — Taxable benefit from employer-provided housing subsidy; 15(9) — Deemed benefit to shareholder.

**Regulations**: 200(2)(g) (information return).

**Remission Orders**: *Ice Storm Employee Benefits Remission Order*, P.C. 1998-2047.

**Interpretation Bulletins**: IT-171R2: Non-resident individuals — computation of taxable income earned in Canada and non-refundable tax credits; IT-421R2: Benefits to individuals, corporations and shareholders from loans or debt.

**I.T. Technical News**: No. 6 (payment of mortgage interest subsidy by employer).

**(10) Contributions to an employee benefit plan** — For the purposes of subparagraph (1)(g)(ii),

(a) an amount included in the income of an individual in respect of an employee benefit plan for a taxation year preceding the year in which it was paid out of the plan shall be deemed to be an amount contributed to the plan by the individual; and

(b) where an amount is received in a taxation year by an individual from an employee benefit plan that was in a preceding year an employee trust, such portion of the amount so received by the individual as does not exceed the amount, if any, by which the lesser of

(i) the amount, if any, by which

(A) the total of all amounts allocated to the individual or a deceased person of whom the individual is an heir or legal representative by the trustee of the plan at a time when it was an employee trust

exceeds

(B) the total of all amounts previously paid out of the plan to or for the benefit of the individual or the deceased person at a time when the plan was an employee trust, and

(ii) the portion of the amount, if any, by which the cost amount to the plan of its property immediately before it ceased to be an employee trust exceeds its liabilities at that time that

(A) the amount determined under subparagraph (i) in respect of the individual

is of

(B) the total of amounts determined under subparagraph (i) in respect of all individuals who were beneficiaries under the plan immediately before it ceased to be an employee trust

exceeds

(iii) the total of all amounts previously received out of the plan by the individual or a deceased person of whom the individual is an heir or legal representative at a time when the plan was an employee benefit plan to the extent that the amounts were deemed by this paragraph to be a return of amounts contributed to the plan

shall be deemed to be the return of an amount contributed to the plan by the individual.

**Interpretation Bulletins**: IT-498: The deductibility of interest on money borrowed to reloan to employees or shareholders; IT-502: Employee benefit plans and employee trusts.

**(11) Salary deferral arrangement** — Where at the end of a taxation year any person has a right under a salary deferral arrangement in respect of a taxpayer to receive a deferred amount, an amount equal to the deferred amount shall be deemed, for the purposes only of paragraph (1)(a), to have been received by the taxpayer as a benefit in the year, to the extent that the amount was not otherwise included in computing the taxpayer's income for the year or any preceding taxation year.

**Related Provisions**: 6(1)(a)(v) — Taxable benefit income inclusion; 6(1)(i) — SDA payment taxed; 6(12)–(14) — SDA — Rules; 8(1)(o) — Forfeited amounts; 20(1)(oo), (pp) — SDA — deduction to employer; 56(1)(w) — Benefit from SDA — included in income.

**Advance Tax Rulings**: ATR-39: Self-funded leave of absence; ATR-45: Share appreciation rights plan; ATR-64: Phantom stock award plan.

**(12) Idem** — Where at the end of a taxation year any person has a right under a salary deferral arrangement (other than a trust governed by a salary deferral arrangement) in respect of a taxpayer to receive a deferred amount, an amount equal to any interest or other additional amount that accrued to, or for the benefit of, that person to the end of the year in respect of the deferred amount shall be deemed at the end of the year, for the purposes only of subsection (11), to be a deferred amount that the person has a right to receive under the arrangement.

**(13) Application** — Subsection (11) does not apply in respect of a deferred amount under a salary deferral arrangement in respect of a taxpayer that was established primarily for the benefit of one or more non-resident employees in respect of services to be rendered in a country other than Canada, to the extent that the deferred amount

(a) was in respect of services rendered by an employee who

(i) was not resident in Canada at the time the services were rendered, or

(ii) was resident in Canada for a period (in this subsection referred to as an "excluded period") of not more than 36 of the 72 months preceding the time the services were rendered and was an employee to whom the arrangement applied before the employee became resident in Canada; and

(b) cannot reasonably be regarded as being in respect of services rendered or to be rendered during a period (other than an excluded period) when the employee was resident in Canada.

**Related Provisions:** 18(1)(o.1) — Salary deferral arrangement — no deduction of outlays for non-residents.

**(14) Part of plan or arrangement** — Where deferred amounts under a salary deferral arrangement in respect of a taxpayer (in this subsection referred to as "that arrangement") are required to be included as benefits under paragraph (1)(a) in computing the taxpayer's income and that arrangement is part of a plan or arrangement (in this subsection referred to as the "plan" under which amounts or benefits not related to the deferred amounts are payable or provided, for the purposes of this Act, other than this subsection,

(a) that arrangement shall be deemed to be a separate arrangement independent of other parts of the plan of which it is a part; and

(b) where any person has a right to a deferred amount under that arrangement, an amount received by the person as a benefit at any time out of or under the plan shall be deemed to have been received out of or under that arrangement except to the extent that it exceeds the amount, if any, by which

(i) the total of all deferred amounts under that arrangement that were included under paragraph (1)(a) as benefits in computing the taxpayer's income for taxation years ending before that time

exceeds

(ii) the total of

(A) all deferred amounts received by any person before that time out of or under the plan that were deemed by this paragraph to have been received out of or under that arrangement, and

(B) all deferred amounts under that arrangement that were deducted under paragraph 8(1)(o) in computing the taxpayer's income for the year or preceding taxation years.

**Related Provisions:** 6(1)(g) — Employee benefit plan benefits; 56(10) — Severability of retirement compensation arrangement.

**(15) Forgiveness of employee debt** — For the purpose of paragraph (1)(a),

(a) a benefit shall be deemed to have been enjoyed by a taxpayer at any time an obligation issued by any debtor (including the taxpayer) is settled or extinguished; and

(b) the value of that benefit shall be deemed to be the forgiven amount at that time in respect of the obligation.

**Related Provisions:** 6(15.1) — Meaning of "forgiven amount"; 15(1.2) — Forgiveness of shareholder loans; 79(3)F(b)(i) — Where property surrendered to creditor; 80(1)"forgiven amount"B(b) — Debt forgiveness rules do not apply to amount of benefit; 80.01 — Deemed settlement of debts.

**Notes:** 6(15) amended by 1994 tax amendments bill (Part I), essentially to refer to the "forgiven amount" as now defined in 6(15.1). For taxation years that end before February 22, 1994 (for obligations settled or extinguished after February 17, 1987), read:

(15) Forgiven employee loans — For the purposes of paragraph (1)(a), the value of the benefit received or enjoyed by a taxpayer, in circumstances where a loan or other obligation to pay an amount is settled or extinguished at any time without any payment by the taxpayer or by payment by the taxpayer of an amount that is less than the amount of the obligation outstanding at that time, shall be deemed to be the amount, if any, by which the amount of the obligation outstanding at that time exceeds the amount so paid, if any.

**Interpretation Bulletins:** IT-421R2: Benefits to individuals, corporations and shareholders from loans or debt.

**(15.1) Forgiven amount** — For the purpose of subsection (15), the "forgiven amount" at any time in respect of an obligation issued by a debtor has the meaning that would be assigned by subsection 80(1) if

(a) the obligation were a commercial obligation (within the meaning assigned by subsection 80(1)) issued by the debtor;

(b) no amount included in computing income because of the obligation being settled or extinguished at that time were taken into account;

(c) the definition "forgiven amount" in subsection 80(1) were read without reference to paragraphs (f) and (h) of the description of B in that definition; and

(d) section 80 were read without reference to paragraphs (2)(b) and (q) of that section.

**Related Provisions**: 80.01(1)"forgiven amount" — Application of definition for purposes of s. 80.01; 248(26) — Liability deemed to be obligation issued by debtor; 248(27) — Partial settlement of debt obligation.

**Notes**: 6(15.1) added by 1994 tax amendments bill (Part I), effective for taxation years that end after February 21, 1994.

**(16) Disability-related employment benefits [transportation, parking, attendant]** — Notwithstanding subsection (1), in computing an individual's income for a taxation year from an office or employment, there shall not be included any amount received or enjoyed by the individual in respect of, in the course of or because of the individual's office or employment that is the value of a benefit relating to, or an allowance (not in excess of a reasonable amount) in respect of expenses incurred by the individual for,

(a) the transportation of the individual between the individual's ordinary place of residence and the individual's work location (including parking near that location) if the individual is blind or is a person in respect of whom an amount is deductible, or would but for paragraph 118.3(1)(c) be deductible, because of the individual's mobility impairment, under section 118.3 in computing a taxpayer's tax payable under this Part for the year; or

(b) an attendant to assist the individual in the performance of the individual's duties if the individual is a person in respect of whom an amount is deductible, or would but for paragraph 118.3(1)(c) be deductible, under section 118.3 in computing a taxpayer's tax payable under this Part for the year.

**Related Provisions**: 6(1.1) — Parking normally a taxable benefit; 64 — Attendant care expenses; 118.4(1) — Nature of impairment.

**Notes**: 6(16) added by 1991 Budget, effective 1991.

**Interpretation Bulletins**: IT-519R2: Medical expense and disability tax credits and attendant care expense deduction.

**(17) Definitions** — The definitions in this subsection apply in this subsection and subsection (18).

**"disability policy"** means a group disability insurance policy that provides for periodic payments to individuals in respect of the loss of remuneration from an office or employment.

**Notes**: See Notes at end of 6(17).

**"employer"** of an individual includes a former employer of the individual.

**Notes**: See Notes at end of 6(17).

**"top-up disability payment"** in respect of an individual means a payment made by an employer of the individual as a consequence of the insolvency of an insurer that was obligated to make payments to the individual under a disability policy where

(a) the payment is made to an insurer so that periodic payments made to the individual under the policy will not be reduced because of the insolvency, or will be reduced by a lesser amount, or

(b) the following conditions are satisfied:

(i) the payment is made to the individual to replace, in whole or in part, periodic payments that would have been made under the policy to the individual but for the insolvency, and

(ii) the payment is made under an arrangement by which the individual is required to reimburse the payment to the extent that the individual subsequently receives an amount from an insurer in respect of the portion of the periodic payments that the payment was intended to replace.

For the purposes of paragraphs (a) and (b), an insurance policy that replaces a disability policy is deemed to be the same policy as, and a continuation of, the disability policy that was replaced.

**Related Provisions**: 8(1)(n) — Reimbursement under (b)(ii) not deductible as salary reimbursement; 8(1)(n.1) — Limited deduction for reimbursements under (b)(ii).

**Notes [6(17)]**: 6(17) added by 1995-97 technical bill, effective for payments made after August 10, 1994. See Notes to 6(18).

**(18) Group disability benefits — insolvent insurer** — Where an employer of an individual makes a top-up disability payment in respect of the individual,

(a) the payment is, for the purpose of paragraph (1)(a), deemed not to be a benefit received or enjoyed by the individual;

(b) the payment is, for the purpose of paragraph (1)(f), deemed not to be a contribution made by the employer to or under the disability insurance plan of which the disability policy in respect of which the payment is made is or was a part; and

(c) if the payment is made to the individual, it is, for the purpose of paragraph (1)(f), deemed to be an amount payable to the individual pursuant to the plan.

**Related Provisions**: 6(17) — Definitions; 8(1)(n.1) — Reimbursement to employer.

**Notes**: 6(18) added by 1995-97 technical bill, effective for payments made after August 10, 1994 (the day before the Superintendent of Financial Institutions took control of Confederation Life). It is worded in terms of a generic insolvent insurer, but was specifically designed to deal with employer-sponsored disability plans insured by Confederation Life. (Department of Finance news release, October 4, 1994.)

**(19) Benefit re housing loss** — For the purpose of paragraph (1)(a), an amount paid at any time in respect of a housing loss (other than an eligible housing loss) to or on behalf of a taxpayer or a person who does not deal at arm's length with the taxpayer in respect of, in the course of or because of, an office or employment is deemed to be a benefit received by the taxpayer at that time because of the office or employment.

**Related Provisions**: 6(20) — Eligible housing loss only partly taxed; 6(21) — Meaning of "housing loss"; 6(23) — Employer-provided housing subsidy is taxable.

**Notes**: 6(19)–(22) provide that a benefit to cover a "housing loss" (see 6(21)) is fully taxable, unless it is an "eligible housing loss" (see 6(22) and 248(1)"eligible relocation" — generally a loss on a work-triggered move of 40 km or more), in which case the first $15,000 is exempt and the balance is only half-taxed.

6(19) added by 1998 Budget, effective

(a) for the 2001 and later taxation years in respect of an eligible relocation in connection with which the individual begins employment at a new work location before October 1998; and

(b) in any other case, after February 23, 1998.

(The start-work date was moved from June 30 to Sept. 30, 1998 as announced in a Dept. of Finance news release April 14, 1998.)

**Interpretation Bulletins**: IT-470R: Employees' fringe benefits.

**(20) Benefit re eligible housing loss** — For the purpose of paragraph (1)(a), an amount paid at any time in a taxation year in respect of an eligible housing loss to or on behalf of a taxpayer or a person who does not deal at arm's length with the taxpayer in respect of, in the course of or because of, an office or employment is deemed to be a benefit received by the taxpayer at that time because of the office or employment to the extent of the amount, if any, by which

(a) one half of the amount, if any, by which the total of all amounts each of which is so paid in the year or in a preceding taxation year exceeds $15,000

exceeds

(b) the total of all amounts each of which is an amount included in computing the taxpayer's income because of this subsection for a preceding taxation year in respect of the loss.

**Notes**: 6(20) added by 1998 Budget, effective on the same basis as 6(19). See Notes to 6(19).

**Interpretation Bulletins**: IT-470R: Employees' fringe benefits.

**(21) Housing loss** — In this section, "housing loss" at any time in respect of a residence of a taxpayer means the amount, if any, by which the greater of

(a) the adjusted cost base of the residence at that time to the taxpayer or to another person who does not deal at arm's length with the taxpayer, and

(b) the highest fair market value of the residence within the six-month period that ends at that time

exceeds

(c) if the residence is disposed of by the taxpayer or the other person before the end of the first taxation year that begins after that time, the lesser of

(i) the proceeds of disposition of the residence, and

(ii) the fair market value of the residence at that time, and

(d) in any other case, the fair market value of the residence at that time.

**Related Provisions**: 6(22) — Meaning of "eligible housing loss".

**Notes**: 6(21) added by 1998 Budget, effective on the same basis as 6(19).

**Interpretation Bulletins**: IT-470R: Employees' fringe benefits.

**(22) Eligible housing loss** — In this section, "eligible housing loss" in respect of a residence designated by a taxpayer means a housing loss in respect of an eligible relocation of the taxpayer or a person who does not deal at arm's length with the taxpayer and, for these purposes, no more than one residence may be so designated in respect of an eligible relocation.

**Related Provisions**: 248(1) — Definition of "eligible relocation".

**Notes**: 6(22) added by 1998 Budget, effective on the same basis as 6(19).

**Interpretation Bulletins**: IT-470R: Employees' fringe benefits.

**(23) Employer-provided housing subsidies** — For greater certainty, an amount paid or the value of assistance provided by any person in respect of, in the course of or because of, an individual's office or employment in respect of the cost of, the financing of, the use of or the right to use, a residence is, for the purposes of this section, a benefit received by the individual because of the office or employment.

**Related Provisions**: 80.4(1), (1.1) — Taxable benefit on loan to employee.

**Notes**: 6(23) added by 1998 Budget, effective on the same basis as 6(19). It overrides some of the case law ruling that certain amounts paid to compensate for higher mortgage costs on relocation were not taxable (see *Krull and Hoefele*, [1996] 1 C.T.C. 131 (FCA)).

**Definitions [s. 6]**: "adjusted cost base" — 54, 248(1); "amount" — 248(1); "arm's length" — 251(1); "automobile" — 248(1); "benefit" — 6(18)(a); "benefit amount" — 6(1)(e.1)(i); "business" — 248(1); "Canada" — 255; "contribution" — 6(1)(b); "cost" — 6(7); "cost amount", "death benefit", "deferred amount" — 248(1); "deferred payment" — 8(1)(n.1)(i); "deferred profit sharing plan" — 147(1), 248(1); "disability policy" — 6(17); "dividend" — 248(1); "eligible housing loss" — 6(22); "eligible relocation" — 248(1); "employed", "employee", "employee benefit plan", "employee trust" — 248(1); "employees profit sharing plan" — 144(1), 248(1); "employer" — 6(2), (17), 248(1); "employment" — 248(1); "forgiven amount" — 6(15.1); "goods and services tax", "group term life insurance policy" — 248(1); "housing loss" — 6(21); "individual", "insurance policy", "life insurance policy", "Minister", "motor vehicle", "non-resident" — 248(1); "obligation" — 248(26); "office" — 248(1); "payor" — 6(1)(k)(ii); "person", "personal or living expenses" — 248(1); "policy year" — 6(5); "prescribed", "private health services plan" — 248(1); "proceeds of disposition" — 54 [technically does not apply to 6(21)(c)(i)]; "profit sharing plan" — 147(1), 248(1); "property" — 248(1); "province" — *Interpretation Act* 35(1); "registered pension plan", "regulation" — 248(1); "related" — 251(2); "resident in Canada" — 250; "retirement compensation arrangement", "salary deferral arrangement", "self-contained domestic establishment", "superannuation or pension benefit" — 248(1); "supplementary unemployment benefit plan" — 145(1), 248(1); "taxation year" — 249; "taxpayer" — 248(1); "top-up disability payment" — 6(17); "Treasury Board" — 248(1); "writing" — *Interpretation Act* 35(1).

**7. (1) Agreement to issue securities to employees** — Subject to subsection (1.1), where a particular qualifying person has agreed to sell or issue securities of the particular qualifying person, or of a qualifying person with which it does not deal at arm's length, to an employee of the particular qualifying person or of a qualifying person with which it does not deal at arm's length,

### Proposed Amendment — 7(1) opening words

**7. (1) Agreement to issue securities to employees** — Subject to subsections (1.1) and (8), where a particular qualifying person has agreed to sell or issue securities of the particular qualifying person (or of a qualifying person with which it does not deal at arm's length) to an employee of the particular qualifying person (or of a qualifying person with which the particular qualifying person does not deal at arm's length),

**Application**: The December 21, 2000 draft legislation, subsec. 1(1), will amend the opening words of subsec. 7(1) to read as above, applicable to 2000 et seq.

**Technical Notes**: Under subsection 7(1), an employee who acquires a security under an employee option agreement is deemed to have received, in the year the security is acquired, a benefit from employment equal to the excess of the fair market value of the security over the amount paid by the employee to acquire the security. Subsection 7(1) is subject to subsection 7(1.1). Subsection 7(1.1) provides that, where the security is acquired under an option granted to an arm's length employee by a Canadian-controlled private corporation (CCPC), subsection 7(1) is to be read so as to deem the employment benefit to have been received in the year the employee disposes of the security, rather than in the year the employee acquires the security.

Subsection 7(1) is amended so that it is also subject to new subsection 7(8). Subsection 7(8) provides that, where an employee acquires a security after February 27, 2000 under an option granted by a corporation (other than a CCPC) or by a mutual fund trust, subsection 7(1) is to be read so as to deem the employment benefit to have been received in the year the employee disposes of the security. In order for subsection 7(8) to apply, the acquisition must be a qualifying acquisition as described in new subsection 7(9), and the employee must elect to defer recognition of the benefit in accordance with new subsection 7(10). (See the commentary on those subsections for further details.)

It should be noted that amended subsection 7(1.3) provides rules for determining the order of the disposition of identical properties. In effect, securities for which a deferral is provided under subsection 7(1.1) or (8) are considered to be disposed of only after identical securities for which no deferral is provided and, then, in the order in which the employee acquired them. New subsection 47(3) provides that securities that are acquired after February 27, 2000, and for which a deferral is provided under subsection 7(1.1) or (8), are deemed, for the purpose of the cost-averaging rule in subsection 47(1), not to be identical to any other securities owned by the taxpayer. Consequently, each of the deferral securities will have its own unique adjusted cost base (ACB). Finally, it should be noted that, under amended paragraph 53(1)(j), the ACB of a security that is acquired after February 27, 2000, and for which a deferral is provided under subsection 7(1.1) or (8), is determined as though the employment benefit were recognized, for tax purposes, at the time the security is acquired. (See the commentary on those provisions for further details.)

(a) if the employee has acquired securities under the agreement, a benefit equal to the amount, if any, by which

(i) the value of the securities at the time the employee acquired them

exceeds the total of

(ii) the amount paid or to be paid to the particular qualifying person by the employee for the securities, and

(iii) the amount, if any, paid by the employee to acquire the right to acquire the securities

is deemed to have been received, in the taxation year in which the employee acquired the securities, by the employee because of the employee's employment;

(b) if the employee has transferred or otherwise disposed of rights under the agreement in respect of some or all of the securities to a person with whom the employee was dealing at arm's length, a benefit equal to the amount, if any, by which

(i) the value of the consideration for the disposition

exceeds

(ii) the amount, if any, paid by the employee to acquire those rights

shall be deemed to have been received, in the taxation year in which the employee made the disposition, by the employee because of the employee's employment;

(c) if rights of the employee under the agreement have, by one or more transactions between persons not dealing at arm's length, become vested in a person who has acquired securities under the agreement, a benefit equal to the amount, if any, by which

(i) the value of the securities at the time the person acquired them

exceeds the total of

(ii) the amount paid or to be paid to the particular qualifying person by the person for the securities, and

(iii) the amount, if any, paid by the employee to acquire the right to acquire the securities,

is deemed to have been received, in the taxation year in which the person acquired the securities, by the employee because of the employee's employment, unless at the time the person acquired the securities the employee was deceased, in which case such a benefit is deemed to have been received by the person in that year as income from the duties of an employment performed by the person in that year in the country in which the employee primarily performed the duties of the employee's employment;

(d) if rights of the employee under the agreement have, by one or more transactions between persons not dealing at arm's length, become vested in a particular person who has transferred or otherwise disposed of rights under the agreement to another person with whom the particular person was dealing at arm's length, a benefit equal to the amount, if any, by which

(i) the value of the consideration for the disposition

exceeds

(ii) the amount, if any, paid by the employee to acquire those rights

shall be deemed to have been received, in the taxation year in which the particular person made the disposition, by the employee because of the employee's employment, unless at the time the other person acquired the rights the employee was deceased, in which case such a benefit shall be deemed to have been received by the particular person in that year as income from the duties of an employment performed by the particular person in that year in the country in which the employee primarily performed the duties of the employee's employment; and

(e) if the employee has died and immediately before death owned a right to acquire securities under the agreement, a benefit equal to the amount, if any, by which

(i) the value of the right immediately after the death

exceeds

(ii) the amount, if any, paid by the employee to acquire the right

shall be deemed to have been received, in the taxation year in which the employee died, by the employee because of the employee's employment, and paragraphs (b), (c) and (d) do not apply.

**Related Provisions**: 7(1.1) — Stock option granted by CCPC; 7(1.4) — Exchange of options; 7(1.5) — Rules where shares exchanged; 7(2) — Shares held by trustee; 7(8) — Deferral re non-CCPC options; 8(12) — Return of employee shares by trustee; 53(1)(j) — Addition to ACB of share; 104(1), (2) — Employee of trustee deemed to be employee of mutual fund trust; 110(1)(d) — Deduction of ½ of the taxable benefit; 110.6(19)(a)(i)(A)B — Election to trigger capital gains exemption — no income inclusion; 128.1(1)(b)(v) [to be repealed], 128.1(10)"excluded right or interest"(c) [draft] — Stock options excluded from deemed disposition on immigration; 128.1(4)(b)(vi) [to be repealed], 128.1(10)"excluded right or interest"(c) [draft] — Stock options excluded from deemed disposition on emigration; 153(1)(a) — Withholding of tax by employer; 164(6.1) — Exercise or disposition of employee stock option by legal representative of deceased employee.

**Notes**: Simplified, a stock option is taxed as follows: No benefit is recognized when the option is granted (7(3)). A benefit is recognized when the option is exercised (7(1)(a)), unless the employer is a Canadian-controlled private corporation dealing at arm's length from the employee, in which case the benefit is only recognized when the shares are disposed of (7(1.1)). (For other corporations, deferral may be available under new 7(8)–(16).) In either case an offsetting deduction of ½ of the benefit may be available under 110(1)(d) or (d.1). The benefit is normally added to the cost base of the shares under 53(1)(j). The same rules apply to units of mutual fund trusts, which are effectively treated the same as shares of public corporations.

Note that the identical-property averaging rule in 47(1) may apply where there are multiple blocks of shares due to exercising stock options at different times. See Marsha Reid, "Stock Options and the Application of the Identical Properties Rule", 12(1) *Taxation of Executive Compensation and Retirement* (Federated Press) 307-310 (July/Aug. 2000). But see also proposed 7(1.3).

7(1) amended by 1998 Budget, effective for 1998 and later taxation years. The substantive changes were to change "corporation" to "qualifying person" (defined in 7(7) to include a mutual fund trust), and "shares" to "securities" (defined in 7(7) to include units of an MFT). Before 1998, read "shares" instead of "securities" in 7(1)(e), and read the opening words and 7(1)(a)–(c) as:

7. (1) **Agreement to issue shares to employees** — Subject to subsection (1.1), where a corporation has agreed to sell or issue shares of the capital stock of the corporation or of a corporation with which it does not deal at arm's length to an employee of the corporation or of a corporation with which it does not deal at arm's length,

(a) if the employee has acquired shares under the agreement, a benefit equal to the amount, if any, by which

(i) the value of the shares at the time the employee acquired them

exceeds

(ii) the total of the amount paid or to be paid to the corporation by the employee for the shares and any amount paid by the employee to acquire the right to acquire the shares

shall be deemed to have been received, in the taxation year in which the employee acquired the shares, by the employee because of the employee's employment;

(b) if the employee has transferred or otherwise disposed of rights under the agreement in respect of some or all of the shares to a person with whom the employee was dealing at arm's length, a benefit equal to the amount, if any, by which

(i) the value of the consideration for the disposition

exceeds

(ii) the amount, if any, paid by the employee to acquire those rights

shall be deemed to have been received, in the taxation year in which the employee made the disposition, by the employee because of the employee's employment;

(c) if rights of the employee under the agreement have, by one or more transactions between persons not dealing at arm's length, become vested in a person who has acquired shares under the agreement, a benefit equal to the amount, if any, by which

(i) the value of the shares at the time that person acquired them

exceeds

(ii) the total of the amount paid or to be paid to the corporation by that person for the shares and any amount paid by the employee to acquire the right to acquire the shares

shall be deemed to have been received, in the taxation year in which the person acquired the shares, by the employee because of the employee's employment, unless at the time the person acquired the shares the employee was deceased, in which case such a benefit shall be deemed to have been received by the person in that year as income from the duties of an employment performed by the person in that year in the country in which the employee primarily performed the duties of the employee's employment;

7(1)(a)–(d) amended by 1991 technical bill, effective 1988, to add subparagraph (ii) in each case and to deal with non-arm's length transferees where the employee is deceased. 7(1)(e) added by 1991 technical bill, effective for deaths after July 13, 1990.

Opening words of 7(1), "Subject to subsection (1.1)", added by 1977 Budget, effective for agreements entered into after March 1977.

**Interpretation Bulletins**: IT-96R6: Options granted by corporations to acquire shares, bonds, or debentures and by trusts to acquire trust units; IT-113R4: Benefits to employees — stock options; IT-171R2: Non-resident individuals — computation of taxable income earned in Canada and non-refundable tax credits.

**Information Circulars**: 89-3: Policy statement on business equity valuations.

**I.T. Technical News**: No. 1 (convertible preferred shares); No. 7 (stock options plans — receipt of cash in lieu of shares); No. 19 (Securities option plan — disposal of securities option rights for shares; Disposition of identical properties acquired under a section 7 securities option; Change in position in respect of GAAR — section 7).

**Advance Tax Rulings**: ATR-15: Employee stock option plan; ATR-64: Phantom stock award plan.

**(1.1) Employee stock options** — Where after March 31, 1977 a Canadian-controlled private corporation (in this subsection referred to as "the corporation") has agreed to sell or issue a share of the capital stock of the corporation or of a Canadian-controlled private corporation with which it does not deal at arm's length to an employee of the corporation or of a Canadian-controlled private corporation with which it does not deal at arm's length and at the time immediately after the agreement was made the employee was dealing at arm's length with

(a) the corporation,

(b) the Canadian-controlled private corporation, the share of the capital stock of which has been agreed to be sold by the corporation, and

(c) the Canadian-controlled private corporation that is the employer of the employee,

in applying paragraph (1)(a) in respect of the employee's acquisition of the share, the reference in that paragraph to "the taxation year in which the employee acquired the securities" shall be read as a reference to "the taxation year in which the employee disposed of or exchanged the securities".

**Related Provisions**: 7(1.3) — Order of disposition of securities; 7(1.4) — Exchange of options; 7(1.5) — Exchange of shares; 7(1.6) — Emigration does not trigger benefit from deemed disposition; 7(1.8) — Parallel rule for non-CCPCs where qualifying acquisition; 47(3)(a) — No averaging of cost on disposition of securities; 128.1(1)(4)(d.1) — Emigration of taxpayer — calculation of gain; 110(1)(d), (d.1) — Deduction of ¼ of the taxable benefit.

**Notes**: 7(1.1) closing words amended by 1998 Budget, effective for 1998 and later taxation years, to change "shares" to "securities" (twice).

7(1.1) added by 1977 Budget, effective for agreements entered into after March 1977.

Closing words (after para. (c)) amended by 1985 Budget, effective for shares acquired after May 22, 1985. For shares acquired earlier, read:

> paragraph (1)(a) does not apply in respect of the employee's acquisition of the share unless the employee disposes of the share, otherwise than as a consequence of his death, within two years from the date he acquired it.

That rule is now reflected in 110(1)(d.1).

See also Notes to 7(1).

**Interpretation Bulletins**: IT-96R6: Options granted by corporations to acquire shares, bonds, or debentures and by trusts to acquire trust units; IT-113R4: Benefits to employees — stock options; IT-171R2: Non-resident individuals — computation of taxable income earned in Canada and non-refundable tax credits.

**I.T. Technical News**: No. 19 (Change in position in respect of GAAR — section 7).

**Advance Tax Rulings**: ATR-15: Employee stock option plan.

**(1.11) Non-arm's length relationship with trusts** — For the purposes of this section, a mutual fund trust is deemed not to deal at arm's length with a corporation only if the trust controls the corporation.

**Notes**: 7(1.11) added by 1998 Budget, effective for 1998 and later taxation years.

**(1.2)** [Repealed under former Act]

**Notes**: 7(1.2) added by 1977 Budget, effective for agreements entered into after March 1977. Repealed by 1985 Budget, effective for shares acquired after May 22, 1985, as this rule is now reflected in 7(1.1) and 110(1)(d.1). For cases where it is in force, read:

> (1.2) **Idem** — Where a taxpayer has acquired a share in circumstances such that, if he had not disposed of it within two years from the date he acquired it, paragraph (1)(a) would not have applied to the acquisition by reason of subsection (1.1), the reference in paragraph (1)(a) to "the taxation year in which he acquired the shares" shall be read as "the taxation year in which he disposed of the shares".

**(1.3) Order of disposition of shares** — For the purpose of subsection (1.1), a taxpayer shall be deemed to dispose of shares that are identical properties in the order in which the taxpayer acquired them.

### Proposed Amendment — 7(1.3)

**(1.3) Order of disposition of securities** — For the purposes of this subsection, subsections (1.1) and (8), subdivision c, subparagraph 110(1)(d.1)(ii) and subsection 147(10.4), and subject to subsection (1.31) and paragraph (14)(c), a taxpayer is deemed to dispose of securities that are identical properties in the order in which the taxpayer acquired them and, for this purpose,

(a) where a taxpayer acquires a particular security (other than under circumstances to which subsection (1.1) or (8) or 147(10.1) applies) at a time when the taxpayer also acquires or holds one or more other securities that are identical to the particular security and are, or were, acquired under circumstances to which any or subsections (1.1) or (8) or 147(10.1) applied, the taxpayer is deemed to have acquired the

## S. 7(1.3)(a)

particular security at the time immediately preceding the earliest of the times at which the taxpayer acquired those other securities; and

(b) where a taxpayer acquires, at the same time, two or more identical securities under circumstances to which either subsection (1.1) or (8) applied, the taxpayer is deemed to have acquired the securities in the order in which the agreements under which the taxpayer acquired the rights to acquire the securities were made.

**Application**: The December 21, 2000 draft legislation, subsec. 1(2), will amend subsec. 7(1.3) to read as above, applicable to securities acquired, but not disposed of, before February 28, 2000 and to securities acquired after February 27, 2000.

**Technical Notes**: Subsection 7(1.3) provides, for the purposes of subsection 7(1.1), a rule for determining the order in which a taxpayer disposes of shares that are identical properties. The rule is relevant in that subsection 7(1.1) defers recognition, for tax purposes, of the employment benefit arising from an employee's acquisition of a share under an option granted by a Canadian-controlled private corporation (CCPC) until the employee disposes of the share. The rule deems the employee to dispose of identical shares in the order in which the employee acquired them — that is, on a first-in-first-out basis.

Subsection 7(1.3) is amended in a number of ways. First, it is amended so that it also applies for the purpose of new subsection 7(8) and for the purposes of existing subdivision c, subparagraph 110(1)(d)(ii) and subsection 147(10.4).

- Subsection 7(8) is similar to existing subsection 7(1.1) in that it defers recognition, for tax purposes, of the employment benefit arising from a taxpayer's acquisition of certain employee option securities until the securities are disposed of. Subsection 7(8) applies to publicly-listed shares, and mutual fund trust units, acquired after February 27, 2000. Extending the application of subsection 7(1.3) to subsection 7(8) ensures that it is possible to determine when a particular security for which a deferral has been provided under subsection 7(8) has been disposed of and, consequently, when the employment benefit that is associated with the taxpayer's acquisition of the security is to be recognized for tax purposes.

- Subdivision c sets out rules for determining taxable capital gains and allowable capital losses when a taxpayer disposes of capital property. Extending the application of subsection 7(1.3) to subdivision c ensures that, when a taxpayer disposes of a security that is identical to other securities owned by the taxpayer, the security that the taxpayer is considered to have disposed of for purposes of the employee security option rules in section 7 is also the security that the taxpayer is considered to have disposed of for purposes of the capital gains rules.

- Paragraph 110(1)(d.1) allows a taxpayer to deduct a portion of the employment benefit that the taxpayer is deemed, by subsection 7(1), to have received when disposing of a share acquired under an employee option granted by a CCPC. Subparagraph 110(1)(d.1)(ii) requires that, in order to qualify for the deduction, the taxpayer must not dispose of the share within two years of acquiring it. Extending the application of subsection 7(1.3) to subparagraph 110(1)(d.1)(ii) en-

sures that, in those cases where the taxpayer holds identical shares, a determination can be made as to when a particular security that was acquired under a CCPC option is disposed of and, consequently, whether or not the taxpayer has satisfied the two-year hold requirement.

- Subsection 147(10.4) provides that, where a taxpayer disposes of shares which the taxpayer received as part of a lump sum payment on withdrawing from a deferred profit sharing plan (DPSP) and in respect of which the taxpayer filed an election under subsection 147(10.1), the taxpayer is to include in income, in the year of disposition, an amount equal to the excess of the fair market value of the shares when they were withdrawn over the cost amount of the shares to the DPSP. The application of subsection 7(1.3) to subsection 147(10.4) is consequential on the repeal of subsection 147(10.5), which contains an ordering rule for subsection 147(10.4) that is identical to the rule in existing subsection 7(1.3).

Second, subsection 7(1.3) is amended to provide two rules for determining, for the purpose of that subsection, the order in which identical securities are considered to have been acquired.

- Paragraph 7(1.3)(a) provides that, where a taxpayer who holds securities that were acquired under circumstances to which any of subsections 7(1.1) or (8) or subsection 147(10.1) applied (referred to in these notes as "deferral securities") acquires identical securities that are not deferral securities, the new securities are deemed to have been acquired immediately before the earliest acquisition of the deferral securities. The effect of this deeming rule, in conjunction with the ordering rule for dispositions, is that a taxpayer holding both deferral and non-deferral securities is considered to dispose of the non-deferral securities first.

- Paragraph 7(1.3)(b) provides that, when a taxpayer acquires a number of identical deferral securities at one time, the securities are deemed to have been acquired in the order in which the options under which the securities are acquired were granted. The effect of this deeming rule, in conjunction with the ordering rule for dispositions, is that a taxpayer who acquires identical securities under different options at the same time is considered to dispose of those securities in the order in which the relevant options were granted.

Third, subsection 7(1.3) is amended so that it is subject to new subsection 7(1.31) and paragraph 7(14)(c).

- New subsection 7(1.31) contains a special rule allowing a taxpayer who disposes of a security that is identical to other securities owned by the taxpayer to designate the most recently acquired security as the security being disposed of, provided certain conditions are met.

- New subsection 7(14) allows the Minister of National Revenue to treat an invalid deferral of an employment benefit arising from a taxpayer's acquisition of an employee option security as a valid deferral under new subsection 7(8) by sending a written notice to this effect to the taxpayer. If the taxpayer has not disposed of the security before the time the notice is sent, paragraph 7(14)(c) deems the taxpayer to have disposed of it at that time for the purposes of section 7. This ensures that the employment benefit is recognized and taxed at that time. Paragraph 7(14)(c) also deems the taxpayer to have reacquired the security immediately after that time, but not under an employee option agreement. Thus, from that point on, the security is treated, for the purposes of the ordering rule in subsection 7(1.3), as a non-deferral security.

It should be noted that new subsection 47(3) provides that securities that are acquired after February 27, 2000, and for which a deferral is provided under subsection 7(1.1) or (8) or 147(10.1), are deemed, for the purpose of the cost-averaging rule in subsection 47(1), not to be identical to any other securities owned by the taxpayer. Consequently, the adjusted cost base (ACB) of each such security, and thus the capital gain or loss on the disposition of the security, is determined without regard to the ACB of any other securities owned by the taxpayer. (See the commentary on new subsection 47(3), and the examples provided as part of that commentary, for further details.)

Amended subsection 7(1.3) applies to securities acquired after February 27, 2000. It also applies to securities acquired, but not disposed of, before February 28, 2000.

**Related Provisions**: 7(1.31) — Disposition of newly-acquired security; 47(3) — No cost averaging for securities for which deferral provided; 248(12) — Identical properties.

**Notes**: 7(1.3) added by 1977 Budget, effective for agreements entered into after March 1977.

**I.T. Technical News**: No. 19 (Change in position in respect of GAAR — section 7).

## Proposed Addition — 7(1.31)

**(1.31) Disposition of newly-acquired security** — Where a taxpayer acquires, at a particular time, a particular security under an agreement referred to in subsection (1) and, on a day that is no later than 30 days after the day that includes the particular time, the taxpayer disposes of a security that is identical to the particular security, the particular security is deemed to be the security that is so disposed of if

(a) no other securities that are identical to the particular security are acquired, or disposed of, by the taxpayer after the particular time and before the disposition;

(b) the taxpayer identifies the particular security as the security so disposed of in the taxpayer's return of income under this Part for the year in which the disposition occurs; and

(c) the taxpayer has not so identified the particular security, in accordance with this subsection, in connection with the disposition of any other security.

**Application**: The December 21, 2000 draft legislation, subsec. 1(2), will add subsec. 7(1.31), applicable to securities acquired, but not disposed of, before February 28, 2000 and to securities acquired after February 27, 2000.

**Technical Notes**: New subsection 7(1.31) contains a special provision which applies when a taxpayer disposes of a security that is identical to other securities owned by the taxpayer. The provision deems a particular security, as designated by the taxpayer, to be the security that is the subject of the disposition. In order for this subsection to apply, certain conditions must be met.

First, the particular security must have been acquired under an employee option agreement, as described in subsection 7(1).

Second, the disposition must occur no later than 30 days after the taxpayer acquires the particular security.

Third, there must be no other acquisitions or dispositions of identical securities in the intervening period; that is, after the acquisition of the particular security and before the disposition in respect of which the designation is being made. It should be noted, however, that this does not preclude the taxpayer from acquiring other identical securities at the same time as the particular security is acquired, or from disposing of other identical securities at the same time as the disposition in respect of which the designation is being made.

Fourth, the taxpayer must make the designation in the return of income that is filed for the year in which the disposition occurs. It is expected that the Minister of National Revenue will accept, as the form of designation, the calculation of the capital gain or loss in respect of the disposition on the basis that it is the particular security that is the subject of the disposition.

Finally, the taxpayer must not have designated the particular security in connection with the disposition of any other security.

*Example*

*On May 1, 2000, Joseph acquires 750 shares of his corporate employer on the open market. On May 1, 2001, he acquires another 750 shares on the open market. On May 1, 2002, he acquires an additional 1,000 shares under employee stock options. Immediately thereafter, he sells 1,500 shares. In his return of income for 2002, he designates the 1,000 stock option shares as constituting part of the shares that were sold. Pursuant to subsections 7(1.3) and (1.31), the 1,500 shares being sold by Joseph are deemed to be comprised of the 1,000 stock option shares and 500 of the 750 shares that Joseph acquired on the open market on May 1, 2000.*

It should be noted that the provisions of subsection 7(1.31) accommodate the practice of specific identification that is currently permitted by the Canada Customs and Revenue Agency (CCRA). (See CCRA's Income Tax Technical News No. 19, dated June 16, 2000, for further details.) The significance of subsection 7(1.31) for the purpose of new paragraph 110(1)(d.01) should also be noted. That paragraph allows a taxpayer to deduct a portion of the employment benefit that the taxpayer is deemed by subsection 7(1) to have received in respect of the taxpayer's acquisition of a qualifying employee option security, if the taxpayer disposes of the security by donating it to a qualifying charity within 30 days after its acquisition.

It should also be noted that new subsection 47(3) provides that securities to which subsection 7(1.31) apply are deemed, for the purpose of the cost-averaging rule in subsection 47(1), not to be identical to any other securities owned by the taxpayer. Consequently, the adjusted cost base (ACB) of each such security, and thus the capital gain or loss on the disposition of the security, is determined without regard to the ACB of any other securities owned by the taxpayer. (See the commentary on new subsection 47(3), and the examples provided as part of that commentary, for further details.)

**S. 7(1.31)**      Income Tax Act, Part I, Division B

**Related Provisions**: 47(3)(b) — No averaging of cost on disposition of securities; 248(12) — Identical properties.

**(1.4) Exchange of options** — Where

(a) a taxpayer disposes of rights under an agreement referred to in subsection (1) or (1.1) to acquire securities of a particular qualifying person that made the agreement or of a qualifying person with which it does not deal at arm's length (which rights and securities are referred to in this subsection and paragraph 110(1)(d) as the "exchanged option" and the "old securities", respectively),

> **Proposed Amendment — 7(1.4)(a)**
>
> (a) a taxpayer disposes of rights under an agreement referred to in subsection (1) or (1.1) to acquire securities of a particular qualifying person that made the agreement or of a qualifying person with which it does not deal at arm's length (which rights and securities are referred to in this subsection as the "exchanged option" and the "old securities", respectively),
>
> **Application**: Bill C-43 (First Reading September 20, 2000), subsec. 1(1), will amend para. 7(1.4)(a) to read as above, applicable to 1998 et seq.
>
> **Technical Notes**: Subsection 7(1.4) contains special provisions that apply when an individual disposes of rights to acquire securities under an employee security option agreement in exchange for other such rights. Paragraph 7(1.4)(a) uses the terms "exchanged option" and "old securities" to refer to the rights that have been disposed of and the securities that could have been acquired thereunder. Paragraph 7(1.4)(a) extends this terminology to paragraph 110(1)(d), which provides a special deduction in respect of certain security option benefits.
>
> Paragraph 7(1.4)(a) is amended to remove the reference to "paragraph 110(1)(d)". This amendment is strictly consequential to changes to paragraph 110(1)(d), which no longer uses these terms.

(b) the taxpayer receives no consideration for the disposition of the exchanged option other than rights under an agreement with a person (in this subsection referred to as the "designated person") that is

    (i) the particular person,

    (ii) a qualifying person with which the particular person does not deal at arm's length immediately after the disposition,

    (iii) a corporation formed on the amalgamation or merger of the particular person and one or more other corporations,

    (iv) a mutual fund trust to which the particular person has transferred property in circumstances to which subsection 132.2(1) applied, or

    (v) a qualifying person with which the corporation referred to in subparagraph (iii) does not deal at arm's length immediately after the disposition

to acquire securities of the designated person or a qualifying person with which the designated person does not deal at arm's length (which rights and securities are referred to in this subsection as the "new option" and the "new securities", respectively), and

(c) the amount, if any, by which

    (i) the total value of the new securities immediately after the disposition

exceeds

    (ii) the total amount payable by the taxpayer to acquire the new securities under the new option

does not exceed the amount, if any, by which

    (iii) the total value of the old securities immediately before the disposition

exceeds

    (iv) the amount payable by the taxpayer to acquire the old securities under the exchanged option,

for the purposes of this section,

(d) the taxpayer is deemed not to have disposed of the exchanged option and not to have acquired the new option,

> **Proposed Amendment — 7(1.4)(d)**
>
> (d) the taxpayer is deemed (other than for the purpose of subparagraph (9)(d)(ii)) not to have disposed of the exchanged option and not to have acquired the new option,
>
> **Application**: The December 21, 2000 draft legislation, subsec. 1(3), will amend para. 7(1.4)(d) to read as above, applicable to 2000 et seq.
>
> **Technical Notes**: Under subsection 7(1), an employee who disposes of an employee security option will generally be treated, for income tax purposes, as having received a benefit from employment at the time of the disposition. Subsection 7(1.4) provides an exception to this treatment in connection with qualifying dispositions under which an employee's option is exchanged for a new option. Subsection 7(1.4) accomplishes this by deeming the exchange not to have occurred for the purposes of section 7.
>
> Subsection 7(1.4) is amended so that this deeming rule does not apply for the purpose of new subparagraph 7(9)(d)(ii). New subsection 7(9) sets out some of the conditions that must be met to be eligible, under new subsection 7(8), to defer taxation of the employment benefit associated with the acquisition of a security under an employee option agreement. The specific condition set out in subparagraph 7(9)(d)(ii) applies if the employee had received the option in exchange for other options. The amendment to subsection 7(1.4) is consequential on the introduction of subparagraph 7(9)(d)(ii) and ensures that the condition in that subparagraph can be applied.

(e) the new option is deemed to be the same option as, and a continuation of, the exchanged option, and

(f) if the designated person is not the particular person, the designated person is deemed to be the same person as, and a continuation of, the particular person.

**Notes**: 7(1.4) amended by 1998 Budget, effective for 1998 and later taxation years. The substantive changes were to extend the rules from shares of corporations to cover units of a mutual fund trust (see Notes to 7(1)). For earlier years since 1988, read:

(1.4) For the purposes of this section and paragraph 110(1)(d), where

(a) a taxpayer disposes of rights under an agreement referred to in subsection (1) or (1.1) to acquire shares of the capital stock of a particular corporation that made the agreement or of a corporation with which the particular corporation does not deal at arm's length (which rights and shares are referred to in this subsection and paragraph 110(1)(d) as the "exchanged option" and the "old shares", respectively),

(b) the taxpayer receives no consideration for the disposition of the exchanged option other than rights under an agreement with

(i) the particular corporation,

(ii) a corporation with which the particular corporation does not deal at arm's length immediately after the disposition,

(iii) a corporation formed on the amalgamation or merger of the particular corporation and one or more other corporations, or

(iv) a corporation with which the corporation referred to in subparagraph (iii) does not deal at arm's length immediately after the disposition

to acquire shares of its capital stock or of the capital stock of a corporation with which it does not deal at arm's length (which rights and shares are referred to in this subsection and paragraph 110(1)(d) as the "new option" and the "new shares", respectively), and

(c) the amount, if any, by which

(i) the total value of the new shares immediately after the disposition

exceeds

(ii) the total amount payable by the taxpayer to acquire the new shares under the new option

does not exceed the amount, if any, by which

(iii) the total value of the old shares immediately before the disposition

exceeds

(iv) the amount payable by the taxpayer to acquire the old shares under the exchanged option,

the following rules apply:

(d) the taxpayer shall be deemed not to have disposed of the exchanged option and not to have acquired the new option,

(e) the new option shall be deemed to be the same option as, and a continuation of, the exchanged option, and

(f) the corporation referred to in subparagraph (b)(ii), (iii) or (iv), as the case may be, shall be deemed to be the same corporation as, and a continuation of, the particular corporation.

7(1.4) amended by 1991 technical bill, effective 1988, to expand its application from amalgamations and mergers to other reorganizations, and to restrict its application to cases where the taxpayer derives no economic gain on the exchange. A taxpayer could elect by notifying Revenue Canada in writing to have the old rule apply to dispositions from January 1, 1989 to July 13, 1990.

7(1.4) added by 1985 technical bill (and amended with retroactive effect in 1987), effective for rights acquired on an amalgamation or merger occurring after 1984.

**Interpretation Bulletins**: IT-96R6: Options granted by corporations to acquire shares, bonds, or debentures and by trusts to acquire trust units; IT-113R4: Benefits to employees — stock options.

**(1.5) Rules where shares exchanged** — For the purposes of this section and paragraph 110(1)(d.1), where

(a) a taxpayer disposes of or exchanges shares of a Canadian corporation that were acquired by the taxpayer under an agreement referred to in subsection (1.1) (in this subsection referred to as the "exchanged shares"),

(b) the taxpayer receives no consideration for the disposition or exchange of the exchanged shares other than shares (in this subsection referred to as the "new shares") of

(i) the corporation,

(ii) a corporation with which the corporation does not deal at arm's length immediately after the disposition or exchange,

(iii) a corporation formed on the amalgamation or merger of the corporation and one or more other corporations, or

(iv) a corporation with which the corporation referred to in subparagraph (iii) does not deal at arm's length immediately after the disposition or exchange, and

(c) the total value of the new shares immediately after the disposition or exchange does not exceed the total value of the old shares immediately before the disposition or exchange,

the following rules apply:

(d) the taxpayer shall be deemed not to have disposed of or exchanged the exchanged shares and not to have acquired the new shares,

(e) the new shares shall be deemed to be the same shares as, and a continuation of, the exchanged shares,

(f) the corporation that issued the new shares shall be deemed to be the same corporation as, and a continuation of, the corporation that issued the exchanged shares, and

(g) where the exchanged shares were issued under an agreement, the new shares shall be deemed to have been issued under that agreement.

**Proposed Amendment — 7(1.5)**

**(1.5) Rules where securities exchanged** — For the purposes of this section and paragraphs 110(1)(d) to (d.1), where

(a) a taxpayer disposes of or exchanges securities of a particular qualifying person that were acquired by the taxpayer under circumstances to which either subsection (1.1) or (8) applied (in this subsection referred to as the "exchanged securities"),

(b) the taxpayer receives no consideration for the disposition or exchange of the exchanged securities other than securities (in this subsection referred to as the "new securities") of

(i) the particular qualifying person,

(ii) a qualifying person with which the particular qualifying person does not deal at arm's length immediately after the disposition or exchange,

(iii) a corporation formed on the amalgamation or merger of the particular qualifying person and one or more other corporations,

(iv) a mutual fund trust to which the particular qualifying person has transferred property in circumstances to which subsection 132.2(1) applied, or

(v) a qualifying person with which the corporation referred to in subparagraph (iii) does not deal at arm's length immediately after the disposition or exchange, and

(c) the total value of the new securities immediately after the disposition or exchange does not exceed the total value of the old securities immediately before the disposition or exchange,

the following rules apply:

(d) the taxpayer is deemed not to have disposed of or exchanged the exchanged securities and not to have acquired the new securities,

(e) the new securities are deemed to be the same securities as, and a continuation of, the exchanged securities, except for the purpose of determining if the new securities are identical to any other securities,

(f) the qualifying person that issued the new securities is deemed to be the same person as, and a continuation of, the qualifying person that issued the exchanged securities, and

(g) where the exchanged securities were issued under an agreement, the new securities are deemed to have been issued under that agreement.

**Application**: The December 21, 2000 draft legislation, subsec. 1(4), will amend subsec. 7(1.5) to read as above, applicable to dispositions and exchanges of securities by a taxpayer that occur after February 27, 2000.

**Technical Notes**: Subsection 7(1.5) contains a special rule that applies for the purposes of the rules in subsection 7(1.1) and paragraph 110(1)(d.1). Subsection 7(1.1) provides that, if an arm's length employee acquires a share under an option granted by a Canadian-controlled private corporation (CCPC), recognition of the employment benefit for tax purposes is deferred until the employee disposes of the share. When the employee disposes of the share and is taxed on the employment benefit, paragraph 110(1)(d.1) allows the employee to deduct a portion of the benefit if the share has been held for at least two years.

Under subsection 7(1.5), a qualifying exchange of shares acquired under an option granted by a CCPC for other shares is deemed not to be a disposition for the purposes of subsection 7(1.1) and paragraph 110(1)(d.1), and the new shares are deemed to be a continuation of the old shares. Consequently, taxation of the employment benefit associated with the old shares is deferred until the employee disposes of the new shares, and the two-year hold requirement for the deduction is based on the combined amount of time that the old and new shares are held. To qualify, the exchange must be for shares of a corporation within the corporate group (including corporations formed on an amalgamation or merger), the employee must receive no consideration for the disposition of the old shares other than the new shares, and the value of the new shares must be no greater than the value of the old shares.

Subsection 7(1.5) is amended so that it also applies to exchanges of employee option securities acquired under circumstances to which new subsection 7(8) applies. Subsection 7(8), which applies to publicly-listed shares and mutual fund trust units acquired under employee option agreements after February 27, 2000, defers recognition of the employment benefit associated with the acquisition of the security until the security is disposed of, provided certain conditions are met. (See the commentary on subsection 7(8) for further details.) The extension of subsection 7(1.5) to these securities ensures that the deferral provided by subsection 7(8) does not cease if the security is exchanged for another qualifying security.

Subsection 7(1.5) is also amended so that it applies for purposes of new paragraph 110(1)(d.01), which allows a special deduction in computing income when an employee donates an employee option security acquired after February 27, 2000 to a qualifying charity. The extension of subsection 7(1.5) to these circumstances ensures that the special deduction is not lost if the employee exchanges the option security for another qualifying security, in accordance with subsection 7(1.5), and donates the new security to charity.

Finally, subsection 7(1.5) is amended so that the rule in paragraph 7(1.5)(e) which deems the new securities to be the same securities as, and a continuation of, the old securities does not apply so as to deem the new securities to be identical to securities to which they would not otherwise be identical. This ensures that the rules in subsections 7(1.3) and (1.31), which deem identical securities to be disposed of in a particular order, do not apply to identify a particular security as the security that is disposed unless the security is, in fact, identical to the security that is the subject of the disposition.

It should be noted that where a taxpayer acquires an employee option security after February 27, 2000, and the security is acquired under circumstances to which subsection 7(1.1) or (8) applied, the employment benefit that will be recognized only at the time of the disposition of the security is, nevertheless, added to the adjusted cost base of the security at the time the security is acquired pursuant to amended paragraph 53(1)(j). Thus, if the security is exchanged for another security under circumstances to which subsection 7(1.5) applies but for which there is no rollover for capital gains purposes, the benefit is taken into account in determining the capital gain or loss on the disposition of the old security.

**Related Provisions**: 47(3)(a) — No averaging of cost on disposition of securities; 110(1)(d) — Employee stock options.

**Notes**: 7(1.5) amended by 1993 technical bill, effective for 1992 and later taxation years, to have the opening words apply to "this section" rather than "subsection (1.1)". The effect is to have 7(1.5) apply recursively to multiple share exchanges.

Amended by 1991 technical bill, effective 1988, to expand its application from 85.1(1) exchanges and 87(4) amalgamations to other reorganizations, and to restrict its application to cases where the taxpayer derives no economic gain on the exchange. A taxpayer may elect, by notifying Revenue Canada in writing, to have the old rule apply to dispositions from January 1, 1989 to July 13, 1990.

Amended by 1985 Budget, effective for shares acquired after May 22, 1985: added reference to 110(1)(d.1) in opening words, and "or exchanged" in para. (a).

7(1.5) added by 1985 technical bill, effective for shares acquired on an amalgamation, merger or share for share exchange occurring after 1984.

**Interpretation Bulletins**: IT-96R6: Options granted by corporations to acquire shares, bonds, or debentures and by trusts to acquire trust units; IT-113R4: Benefits to employees — stock options.

### Proposed Addition — 7(1.6)

**(1.6) Emigrant** — For the purposes of this section and paragraph 110(1)(d.1), a taxpayer is deemed not to have disposed of a share solely because of subsection 128.1(4).

**Related Provisions**: 128.1(4)(d.1) — Calculation of gain from deemed disposition on emigration.

**Application**: Bill C-43 (First Reading September 20, 2000) (taxpayer migration), subsec. 1(2), will add subsec. 7(1.6), applicable after 1992.

**Technical Notes**: Subsection 7(1.1) provides that the employment benefit in respect of shares of a Canadian-controlled private corporation issued under an employee stock option plan is, under certain conditions, to be included in the employee's income only in the taxation year in which the employee disposes of or exchanges the shares.

New subsection 7(1.6) applies where an individual who holds shares emigrates from Canada and is treated as having disposed of the shares under subsection 128.1(4) of the Act. In those circumstances, subsection 7(1.6) deems the shares, for the purposes of section 7 and paragraph 110(1)(d.1) of the Act, not to have been disposed of because of the emigration. As a result, emigration from Canada will not by itself trigger an income inclusion under section 7. However, because the share will still be treated as having been disposed of for the purposes of the Act, the emigrant individual will realize any gain that has accrued on the share since it was acquired. See the commentary on new paragraph 128.1(4)(d.1) for additional information.

**Notes**: Under 128.1(4), emigration from Canada triggers a disposition of most capital property, triggering tax on accrued capital gains. The rule does not apply, however, for purposes of triggering income under 7(1.1).

**(2) Securities held by trustee [deemed held by employee]** — If a security is held by a trustee in trust or otherwise, whether absolutely, conditionally or contingently, for an employee, the employee is deemed, for the purposes of this section and paragraphs 110(1)(d) and (d.1),

### Proposed Amendment — 7(2) opening words

**(2) Securities held by trustee [deemed held by employee]** — If a security is held by a trustee in trust or otherwise, whether absolutely, conditionally or contingently, for an employee, the employee is deemed, for the purposes of this section and paragraphs 110(1)(d) to (d.1),

**Application**: The December 21, 2000 draft legislation, subsec. 1(5), will amend the opening words of subsec. 7(2) to read as above, applicable to 2000 et seq.

**Technical Notes**: Subsection 7(2) provides that, where a trust holds securities for an employee, acquisitions and dispositions of the securities by the trust are treated as acquisitions and dispositions by the employee for the purposes of section 7 and paragraphs 110(1)(d) and (d.1).

Subsection 7(2) is amended so that it also applies for the purpose of new paragraph 110(1)(d.01). Paragraph 110(1)(d.01) allows an employee to deduct a portion of the amount of the benefit that the employee is deemed by subsection 7(1) to have received in respect of the acquisition of certain employee option securities where the securities (or, under certain circumstances, proceeds from the disposition of such securities) are donated to a qualifying charity.

(a) to have acquired the security at the time the trust began to so hold it; and

(b) to have exchanged or disposed of the security at the time the trust exchanged it or disposed of it to any person other than the employee.

**Related Provisions**: 8(12) — Forfeiture of securities by employee; 104(21.2) — Capital gains exemption flowed through trust; 110.6(16) — Personal trust.

**Notes**: 7(2) amended by 1998 Budget, effective for 1998 and later taxation years, to change "share" to "security" throughout.

7(2)(b) added by 1985 Budget, effective for shares acquired after May 22, 1985.

**Interpretation Bulletins**: IT-113R4: Benefits to employees — stock options.

**(3) Special provision [taxable benefit is under s. 7 only]** — If a particular qualifying person has agreed to sell or issue securities of the particular person, or of a qualifying person with which it does not deal at arm's length, to an employee of the particular person or of a qualifying person with which it does not deal at arm's length,

(a) except as provided by this section, the employee is deemed to have neither received nor enjoyed any benefit under or because of the agreement; and

(b) the income for a taxation year of any person is deemed to be not less than its income for the year would have been if a benefit had not been conferred on the employee by the sale or issue of the securities.

**Notes**: 7(3) amended by 1998 Budget, effective for 1995 and later taxation years, except that, in respect of benefits conferred before

March 1998, read "person" in 7(3)(b) as "corporation". For taxation years from 1972 to 1994, read:

(3) Where a corporation has agreed to sell or issue shares of the capital stock of the corporation or of a corporation with which it does not deal at arm's length to an employee of the corporation or of a corporation with which it does not deal at arm's length

(a) no benefit shall be deemed to have been received or enjoyed by the employee under or by virtue of the agreement for the purpose of this Part except as provided by this section; and

(b) the income for a taxation year of the corporation or of a corporation with which it does not deal at arm's length shall be deemed to be not less than its income for the year would have been if a benefit had not been conferred on the employee by the sale or issue of the shares to the employee or to a person in whom the employee's rights under the agreement have become vested.

7(3)(a) is a relieving rule that ensures no benefit is taxable under other rules, such as s. 6. The effect of 7(3)(b) is that an employer (or non-arm's length person) cannot reduce its income by claiming a deduction in connection with the sale or issue of its shares to the employee (or a person who has acquired the employee's rights) — even though employee costs are normally deductible to an employer.

The 1998 amendment to 7(3) was made effective 1995, but has no effect on agreements entered into before March 1998 unless the employee makes the election referred to in Notes to 7(7) "qualifying person".

**Interpretation Bulletins**: IT-96R6: Options granted by corporations to acquire shares, bonds, or debentures and by trusts to acquire trust units; IT-113R4: Benefits to employees — stock options.

**I.T. Technical News**: No. 7 (stock options plans — receipt of cash in lieu of shares).

**Advance Tax Rulings**: ATR-64: Phantom stock award plan.

**(4) Application of subsec. (1)** — For greater certainty it is hereby declared that, where a person to whom any provision of subsection (1) would otherwise apply has ceased to be an employee before all things have happened that would make that provision applicable, subsection (1) shall continue to apply as though the person were still an employee and as though the employment were still in existence.

**Interpretation Bulletins**: IT-113R4: Benefits to employees — stock options.

**(5) Non-application of this section** — This section does not apply if the benefit conferred by the agreement was not received in respect of, in the course of, or by virtue of, the employment.

**(6) Sale to trustee for employees** — If a particular qualifying person has entered into an arrangement under which securities of the particular person, or of a qualifying person with which it does not deal at arm's length, are sold or issued by either person to a trustee to be held by the trustee in trust for sale to an employee of the particular person or of a qualifying person with which it does not deal at arm's length,

(a) for the purposes of this section (other than subsection (2)) and paragraphs 110(1)(d) and (d.1),

> **Proposed Amendment — 7(6)(a) opening words**
>
> (a) for the purposes of this section (other than subsection (2)) and paragraphs 110(1)(d) to (d.1),
>
> **Application**: The December 21, 2000 draft legislation, subsec. 1(6), will amend the opening words of para. 7(6)(a) to read as above, applicable to 2000 et seq.
>
> **Technical Notes**: Subsection 7(6) provides a rule which applies where an employer (or a non-arm's length person) has entered into an arrangement under which its securities (or securities of a non-arm's length person) are sold or issued to a trustee for sale to an employee. It provides that, for the purposes of section 7 and paragraphs 110(1)(d) and (d.1), the employee's rights under the arrangement are treated as having arisen under an employee security option agreement.
>
> Paragraph 7(6)(a) is amended so that this rule also applies for the purpose of new paragraph 110(1)(d.01). Paragraph 110(1)(d.01) allows an employee to deduct a portion of the amount of the benefit that the employee is deemed by subsection 7(1) to have received in respect of the acquisition of certain employee option securities where the securities (or, under certain circumstances, proceeds from the disposition of such securities) are donated to a qualifying charity.

(i) any particular rights of the employee under the arrangement in respect of those securities are deemed to be rights under a particular agreement with the particular person under which the particular person has agreed to sell or issue securities to the employee,

(ii) any securities acquired under the arrangement by the employee or by a person in whom the particular rights have become vested are deemed to be securities acquired under the particular agreement, and

(iii) any amounts paid or agreed to be paid to the trustee for any securities acquired under the arrangement by the employee or by a person in whom the particular rights have become vested are deemed to be amounts paid or agreed to be paid to the particular person for securities acquired under the particular agreement; and

(b) subsection (2) does not apply in respect of securities held by the trustee under the arrangement.

**Notes**: 7(6) amended by 1998 Budget, effective 1998 and later taxation years. The substantive changes were to extend the rules from shares of corporations to cover units of a mutual fund trust (see Notes to 7(1)), but it was also restructured to improve readability. For earlier years, read:

(6) Where a corporation has entered into an arrangement under which shares of the capital stock of the corporation or of a corporation with which it does not deal at arm's length are sold or issued by either corporation to a trustee to be held by the trustee in trust for sale to an employee of the corporation or of a corporation with which it does not deal at arm's length,

(a) for the purposes of this section (except subsection (2)) and paragraphs 110(1)(d) and (d.1), any rights of the employee under the arrangement in respect of those shares, any shares acquired thereunder by the employee or by a person in whom those rights have become vested, and any amounts paid or agreed to be paid to the trustee for any shares acquired thereunder by the employee or any such person, shall be deemed to be, respectively, rights under, shares acquired under, and amounts paid or agreed to be paid to the corporation for shares acquired under, an agreement with the corporation under which the corporation has agreed to sell or issue shares to the employee; and

(b) subsection (2) does not apply in respect of shares held by the trustee under the arrangement.

7(6) amended by 1991 technical bill, effective 1988, to apply for the purposes of 110(1)(d) and (d.1).

**Advance Tax Rulings**: ATR-15: Employee stock option plan.

**(7) Definitions** — The definitions in this subsection apply in this section and in paragraph 110(1)(d).

### Proposed Amendment — 7(7) opening words

**(7) Definitions** — The definitions in this subsection apply in this section and in subsection 47(3), paragraphs 53(1)(j) and 110(1)(d) and (d.01) and subsections 110(1.5), (1.6) and (2.1).

**Application**: The December 21, 2000 draft legislation, subsec. 1(7), will amend the opening words of subsec. 7(7) to read as above, applicable after 1997, except that

(a) it does not apply to a right under an agreement to which the subsec. as enacted by S.C. 1999, c. 22, s. 3(7), does not (except for the purpose of applying para. 7(3)(b)) apply; and

(b) before 2000, the opening words of the subsec., as amended, shall be read as:

"(7) The definitions in this subsection apply in this section and in paragraph 110(1)(d) and subsections 110(1.5) and (1.6)."

**Technical Notes**: Subsection 7(7) defines the expressions "qualifying person" and "security" for the purposes of section 7 and paragraph 110(1)(d). "Qualifying person" is defined as a corporation or a mutual fund trust. "Security" is defined as a share issued by a corporation or a unit of a mutual fund trust.

Subsection 7(7) is amended so that the definitions also apply for the purposes of new subsection 47(3), amended paragraph 53(1)(j), new paragraph 110(1)(d.01), amended subsection 110(1.5) and new subsections 110(1.6) and (2.1).

- New subsection 47(3) exempts from the cost-averaging rule in subsection 47(1) certain securities acquired either under an employee option agreement or on withdrawal from a deferred profit sharing plan.

- Amended paragraph 53(1)(j) adds, to the adjusted cost base of an employee option security, the employment benefit that subsection 7(1) deems the employee to have received in connection with the acquisition of the security.

- New paragraph 110(1)(d.01) and subsection 110(2.1) allow an employee to deduct a portion of the employment benefit that the employee is deemed, by subsection 7(1), to have received in connection with the acquisition of a qualifying employee option security if, within 30 days of the acquisition, the employee do-

nates the security (or proceeds from the disposition of the security) to a qualifying charity.

- Amended subsection 110(1.5) and new subsection 110(1.6) contain interpretative rules that apply for purposes of determining if the conditions for the deduction in paragraph 110(1)(d) are satisfied. Paragraph 110(1)(d) allows an employee to deduct a portion of the employment benefit that the employee is deemed, by subsection 7(1), to have received in connection with the exercise or disposition of rights under a security option agreement.

The extension of subsection 7(7) to these provisions is consequential on either the introduction of the relevant provision, or an amendment to the relevant provision. For subsections 110(1.5) and (1.6), the extension of subsection 7(7) applies after 1997. In all other cases, it applies after 1999.

**"qualifying person"** means a corporation or a mutual fund trust.

**Notes**: Definition "qualifying person" added by 1998 Budget, effective 1995 but, except for the purpose of applying 7(3)(b), does not apply to a right under an agreement made before March 1998 to sell or issue trust units to an individual unless

(a) the right was outstanding at the end of February 1998 and was not disposed of before March 1998 in circumstances to which 7(1)(b) applies; and

(b) the individual so elects in writing filed with Revenue Canada by the later of

(i) the filing-due date for the individual's taxation year that includes the earlier of

(A) the time of the individual's death, and

(B) the time that the right was first disposed of after February 1998, and

(ii) December 31, 1999.

**"security"** of a qualifying person means

(a) if the person is a corporation, a share of the capital stock of the corporation; and

(b) if the person is a mutual fund trust, a unit of the trust.

**Notes**: Definition "security" added by 1998 Budget, effective on the same basis as the addition of 7(7)"qualifying person".

### Proposed Addition — 7(8)–(16)

**Technical Notes**: New subsections 7(8) to (16) contain special rules allowing for the deferral of taxation on the employment benefit realized when an employee acquires securities (i.e., shares of the capital stock of a corporation or units of a mutual fund trust) under an option granted by the employer or a person not dealing at arm's length with the employer, provided certain conditions are met. The deferral will cease when the employee disposes of the security, dies or ceases to be resident in Canada.

The following are the main features of the deferral measure.

- The deferral is available only in respect of securities acquired after February 27, 2000 by Canadian residents.

- If the employee option security is a share, the deferral is available only if the share is of a class of shares listed on a Canadian or foreign prescribed stock exchange.

- The deferral does not apply to options granted by Canadian-controlled private corporations (CCPCs), since a deferral is already available on such options under subsection 7(1.1).

- The deferral is available only if the employee is entitled to a deduction under paragraph 110(1)(d). Generally speaking, an employee is entitled to a deduction under that paragraph when the following conditions are satisfied:
  - the amount paid by the employee to acquire the security was not less than the fair market value of the security when the option was granted;
  - the employee was dealing at arm's length, immediately after the option was granted, with the employer, the entity that granted the option and the entity whose securities could be acquired under the option; and
  - if the security is a share, it is an ordinary common share.
- If the employee option security is a share, the deferral is not available if the employee was, immediately after the option was granted, a specified shareholder of the employer, the corporation that granted the option or the corporation whose shares could be acquired under the option.
- The deferral is subject to an annual limit of $100,000. The limit is based on the year in which the options vest (i.e., first become exercisable), and on the fair market value of the underlying securities when the options were granted. Thus, for options vesting in a given year, an employee will be able to defer taxation on the acquisition of securities having a total fair market value (determined at the time the options were granted) not exceeding $100,000.
- The deferral is not automatic: it requires that the employee file an election with an entity that is involved in the option agreement (i.e., the employer, the entity that granted the option or the entity whose securities were acquired under the option). The elective nature of the deferral allows an employee who has options in excess of the $100,000 limit vesting in a particular year to choose those options for which the deferral will be claimed.
- The deferred amount is to be reported as a special item on the employee's T4 slip in the year in which the security is acquired. The employee is required to include the deferred amount in computing income from employment when completing the tax return for the year in which the deferral ceases.

There are a number of other provisions in the Act that relate to securities for which a deferral is provided under new subsection 7(8). First, deferral securities are subject to the rules in amended subsection 7(1.3), which determine the order in which identical securities are disposed of by a taxpayer. Second, deferral securities are subject to the security-for-security exchange rules in amended subsection 7(1.5), which provide for a continued deferral of the employment benefit associated with the old security, if certain conditions are met. Third, deferral securities are subject to new subsection 47(3), which has the effect of excluding such securities from the cost-averaging rule in subsection 47(1). Finally, pursuant to amended paragraph 53(1)(j), the employment benefit associated with a deferral security is added to the adjusted cost base of the security when the security is acquired, even though the benefit is not taxed until the employee disposes of the security. (See the commentary on those provisions, and in particular the examples provided as part of the commentary on subsection 47(3), for further details.)

**Notice of Ways and Means Motion, federal budget, February 28, 2000**: *Deferred Stock Option Benefits*

(10) That the provisions of the Act which deem an individual who acquires a security under an option granted to the individual as an employee of a corporation (other than a Canadian-controlled private corporation), or as an employee of a mutual fund trust, to have received an employment benefit under subsection 7(1) of the Act that is required to be included in income be amended to provide

(a) that the income inclusion determined in connection with an individual's acquisition of a particular security after February 27, 2000 be deferred from the year in which the security is acquired to the earlier of the year in which the security is disposed of and the year in which the individual dies or becomes non-resident,

(b) that, in the case of an option granted to an employee to acquire a share of the capital stock of a corporation, the deferral not be available if, at the time the option was granted, the employee was a specified shareholder of the employer, of the corporation granting the option or of the corporation whose shares could be acquired under the option,

(c) that the deferral not be available in respect of a particular security acquired by an individual unless

(i) the individual would, if there were no deferral, be entitled in the year the security was acquired to deduct an amount under paragraph 110(1)(d) of the Act in respect of the employment benefit, and

(ii) where the security is a share of the capital stock of a corporation, it is of a class of shares that is listed on a stock exchange referred to in section 3200 or 3201 of the *Income Tax Regulations*,

(d) that the deferral of the income inclusion determined in connection with an individual's acquisition of a particular security under an option that had been granted to the individual by a particular entity, and that had vested in the individual in a particular year, be available only if the specified value of the particular security does not exceed $100,000 less the total of all amounts each of which is the specified value of a related security and, for this purpose,

(i) the specified value of a security acquired under an option is the fair market value of the security at the time the option was granted,

(ii) a security is a related security if

(A) it was acquired by the individual under an option that had been granted to the individual by the particular entity (or by an entity that was not dealing at arm's length with the particular entity) and that had vested in the individual in the particular year, and

(B) the income inclusion determined in connection with its acquisition is deferred because of this measure, and

(iii) the provisions of subsection 7(1.4) of the Act, dealing with exchanged options, apply, and

(e) that the deferral of the income inclusion be available only if arrangements have been established, in accordance with the budget documents tabled by the Minister of Finance in the House of Commons on February 28,

2000, to ensure accurate and timely reporting of the employment benefit.

**Federal budget, supplementary information, February 28, 2000**: *Employee Stock Options*

Many corporations use stock options to encourage their employees to take an ownership stake in the corporation, most notably in the fast-growing high-technology industries. These options provide employees with the right to acquire shares in their employer for a predetermined price — the exercise price.

The current tax treatment of employee stock options is as follows:

- A taxable employment benefit equal to the difference between the fair market value of the share at the time the option is exercised and the amount paid by the employee to acquire the share is generally included in income in the year the option is exercised.
- In the case of Canadian-controlled private corporations (CCPCs), the taxable employment benefit is generally not included in income until the year of disposition of the share acquired under the option.
- Where certain conditions are met, a deduction in respect of the employee stock option benefit is provided that essentially results in the benefit being taxed at the same rate as capital gains.

To assist corporations in attracting and retaining high-calibre workers and make our tax treatment of employee stock options more competitive with the United States, the budget proposes to allow employees to defer the income inclusion from exercising employee stock options for publicly listed shares until the disposition of the shares, subject to an annual $100,000 limit (see below). Employees disposing of such shares will be eligible to claim the stock option deduction in the year the benefit is included in income. The new rules will also apply to employee options to acquire units of a mutual fund trust. The proposed rules are generally similar to those for Incentive Stock Options in the United States.

Employee stock options granted by CCPCs are not affected by the proposed measure.

*Eligible Employees*

Eligible employees are those who at the time the option is granted:

- deal at arm's-length with the employer and any related corporation; and
- are not specified shareholders (specified shareholders are generally those who own 10 per cent or more of a company's shares).

*Eligible Options*

An eligible option is one under which:

- the share to be acquired is an ordinary common share;
- the share is of a class of shares traded on a prescribed Canadian or foreign stock exchange; and
- the total of all amounts payable to acquire the share, including the exercise price and any amount payable to acquire the option, is not less than the fair market value of the share at the time the option is granted.

The proposal applies to eligible options exercised after February 27, 2000, irrespective of when the option was granted or became vested.

*$100,000 Limit*

There will be a $100,000 annual limit on the amount of options that an employee can be granted which will be eligible for deferral. The same limit applies in the United States. This limit will apply:

- to the value of the stock options that vest (first become exercisable) in the employee each year (the "value of a stock option" is the fair market value of the underlying share at the time the option is granted); and
- across all stock option plans of the employer corporation and related corporations.

*Example*

Gerry is an employee of a company that has an employee stock option plan. On January 1, 2001, Gerry's employer grants options to acquire 16,000 shares. Options to acquire 4,000 shares vest immediately, and the remaining options vest in equal parts on January 1 of each of 2002, 2003 and 2004. The fair market value of the shares on January 1, 2001 is $10.

Because, at the time the options were granted, the fair market value of the shares underlying the options that vest in each of the years 2001-2004 does not exceed $100,000, Gerry will be able to defer the income inclusion from exercising all the options.

Had the options all vested in the same year, only 10,000 of the underlying shares would have qualified for the deferral.

There are no restrictions on how many of the options Gerry can exercise in any given year.

*Reporting Arrangements*

Deferral of taxation of the employment benefit arising from the exercise of an employee option will depend on the employer having an arrangement in place to ensure that:

- the employer, or an agent of the employer, can monitor compliance with the $100,000 limit; and
- the related employment benefit and the stock option deduction can be reported on an information slip in the year the share is disposed of.

Consultations will be held in the coming months with stakeholders and other interested parties on the design of appropriate reporting arrangements. It is intended that specific proposals based on these consultations will be made public in sufficient time for employers to have reporting arrangements in place by the end of this year.

*Deferral Period*

The income inclusion for a share acquired under an employee stock option will be deferred until the time the employee disposes of the share or, if earlier, the time the employee dies or becomes a non-resident.

The measure applies to options exercised after February 27, 2000.

**Department of Finance news release, May 9, 2000**: *Finance Minister Clarifies Certain Income Tax Measures in the 2000 Budget*

Finance Minister Paul Martin today announced several clarifications to measures announced in the 2000 budget. These clarifications will ensure the smooth conduct of business transactions while consultations take place.

. . . . .

*Employee Stock Options*

The 2000 budget included a measure allowing employees to defer the income inclusion from exercising employee stock options for publicly listed shares until the disposition of the shares, subject to a $100,000 annual vesting limit. Minister Martin today confirmed that the reporting requirements for the stock option proposal will not require employers to track dispositions of shares acquired under a stock option plan. The reporting forms will concentrate on the benefit at the time of exercise and on compliance with the $100,000 annual limit.

.....

For further information: Employee Stock Options, Catherine Cloutier, (613) 996-0598.

**Department of Finance news release Backgrounder, December 21, 2000**: *Deferral of Taxation on Employee Stock Options*

The February 2000 budget included a measure allowing employees who acquire publicly listed shares under employee stock options after February 27, 2000, to defer taxation of the associated stock option benefit until the disposition of the shares, subject to a $100,000 annual vesting limit.

On May 9, 2000, Finance Minister Paul Martin announced a clarification of how deferred benefits would be reported by employers for tax purposes. Specifically, employers would be required to report deferred stock option benefits on employees' T4 slips for the year in which the stock option shares are acquired. The onus would then be on the employee to include the deferred benefits in income from employment on the tax return for the year in which the employee disposes of the shares.

The proposed legislation released today contains a number of additional changes, as well as some refinements, to the deferral measure that have not been previously announced. The most significant are as follows:

- Where the employer, the corporation granting the option and the corporation whose shares are acquired by a taxpayer under an employee stock option are not the same corporation, each is jointly liable for reporting the deferred stock option benefit to the Minister of National Revenue on the taxpayer's T4 slip for the year in which the taxpayer acquires the share. However, when one corporation fulfills the obligation to report, all are considered to have fulfilled the obligation. This allows the parties involved in the stock option plan to determine who is best able to report the deferred benefit. (For further details, see proposed subsection 200(5) of the *Income Tax Regulations* and the related commentary in Appendix A to the explanatory notes.)

- An employee who wishes to defer taxation of a stock option benefit must file a deferral election with one of the parties who will be responsible for reporting the deferred stock option benefit to the Minister of National Revenue (see above). For shares acquired in 2000, the election must be filed on or before February 15, 2001. Thereafter, the deadline will be January 15 of the year following the year in which the share is acquired. (See proposed subsection 7(10) of the *Income Tax Act* and the related explanatory notes for further details.)

- The proposed legislation requires that the deferral election be in prescribed form and manner. The Minister of National Revenue has indicated that, for shares acquired in 2000, the election must be in the form of a letter from the employee containing the following information:

    (1) a request to have the deferral provisions apply;

    (2) the amount of the stock option benefits, related to qualifying shares acquired after February 27, 2000, that are being deferred;

    (3) confirmation that the employee was resident in Canada when the shares were acquired; and

    (4) confirmation that the $100,000 annual vesting limit has not been exceeded.

- Employees who wish to revoke an election to defer may do so by filing a written notification to this effect with the person with whom the election was filed. The deadline for filing such a notice in respect of shares acquired in 2000 is 60 days after the day on which the legislation that enacts these measures receives Royal Assent. Thereafter, the deadline is January 15 of the year following the year in which the share is acquired. (See proposed subsection 7(13) and the related explanatory notes for further details.)

- Given that employers were expected to determine compliance with the $100,000 annual vesting limit, the budget proposed that the limit would apply only to stock option plans of the particular employer and related corporations. Thus, if options from unrelated corporations were to vest in an individual in the same year, there would be a separate $100,000 limit for each such group. However, given that employees are better able than their employers to determine the extent to which they have already utilized the limit, the proposed legislation does not impose on the employer an obligation to determine compliance with the limit. Rather, compliance with the limit is a condition that the employee must determine is satisfied in filing an election to defer. Accordingly, employees will be expected to track their usage of the limit. Given that the onus for compliance has been removed from the employer, the limit has been designed so that there is only one $100,000 limit for the employee for each vesting year, rather than a separate limit per corporate group. (See proposed paragraph 7(10)(c) and the related explanatory notes for further details.)

- The proposed legislation contains provisions for determining the order in which identical shares are considered to be disposed of for the purposes of the stock option rules. In general terms, an employee will be considered to dispose of stock option shares for which a deferral has been provided only after having disposed of all other identical shares, and then to dispose of deferral shares on a first-in first-out basis. (See proposed amendments to subsection 7(1.3) and the related explanatory notes for further details.)

- The proposed legislation contains a requirement for employees with deferred stock option benefits to file, on an annual basis, a prescribed form containing prescribed information concerning the acquisition and disposition of stock option shares. The Minister of National Revenue has indicated that the form to be used for this purpose is Form T1212, Statement of Deferred Stock Option Benefits. The employee is required to file the form with the return of income for the year, beginning with the 2000 return. (See proposed subsection 7(16) and the related explanatory notes for further details.)

- The proposed legislation ensures that the deferral on a stock option share does not cease if the share is exchanged for another share in a qualifying exchange.

(See proposed amendments to subsection 7(1.5) and the related explanatory notes for further details.)

- Under the proposed legislation, deferral shares are excluded from the cost-averaging rule for determining the adjusted cost base of identical properties for purposes of the capital gains rules. (See proposed subsection 47(3) and the related explanatory notes for further details.)

- The proposed legislation adds the amount of a deferred stock option benefit to the adjusted cost base of the stock option share when the share is acquired, even though the amount is not taxed until the employee disposes of the share. (See proposed amendments to paragraph 53(1)(j) and the related explanatory notes for further details.)

- The proposed legislation contains an amendment to the *Canada Pension Plan* (CPP). The proposed amendment ensures that deferred stock option benefits are taken into account, for contribution purposes, in the year in which the shares are acquired rather than in the year in which the shares are disposed of. This ensures that employers — who have no reporting obligations under the *Income Tax Act* in respect of such amounts beyond the year of acquisition — are able to comply with their remittance obligations under the CPP.

The Canada Customs and Revenue Agency is currently preparing amendments to the Insurable Earnings and Collection of Premiums Regulations to ensure that non-cash remuneration is not taken into account in determining the base upon which employment insurance premiums are calculated.

**(8) Deferral in respect of non-CCPC employee options** — Where a particular qualifying person (other than a Canadian-controlled private corporation) has agreed to sell or issue securities of the particular qualifying person (or of a qualifying person with which it does not deal at arm's length) to a taxpayer who is an employee of the particular qualifying person (or of a qualifying person with which the particular qualifying person does not deal at arm's length), in applying paragraph (1)(a) in respect of the taxpayer's acquisition of a security under the agreement, the reference in that paragraph to "the taxation year in which the employee acquired the securities" shall be read as a reference to "the taxation year in which the employee disposed of or exchanged the securities" if

(a) the acquisition is a qualifying acquisition; and

(b) the taxpayer elects, in accordance with subsection (10), to have this subsection apply in respect of the acquisition.

**Technical Notes**: When an employee acquires a security under an option granted by an employer or a person not dealing at arm's length with the employer, paragraph 7(1)(a) deems the employee to have received a taxable employment benefit equal to the fair market value of the security at the time it is acquired less the amount paid by the employee to acquire the security. In most cases, the benefit is recognized in the year in which the security is acquired. However, in the case of shares acquired under options granted to arm's length employees by Canadian-controlled private corporations (CCPCs), recognition of the benefit is deferred, by virtue of subsection 7(1.1), from the year in which the employee acquires the share to the year in which the employee disposes of the share.

New subsection 7(8) extends, with some modifications and limitations, the deferral currently available for CCPC options to options granted by corporations that are not CCPCs and to options granted by mutual fund trusts. In order to be eligible for the deferral, the acquisition must be a qualifying acquisition as defined in new subsection 7(9), and the employee must file an election to defer in accordance with new subsection 7(10). (See the commentary on those subsections for further details.)

*Example*

In 2001, Jean exercises an option to acquire a share of the capital stock of his employer. The exercise price is $10, which was the fair market value of the share when the option was granted. At the time of acquisition, the share is worth $100. The acquisition is a qualifying acquisition, as described in subsection 7(9), and Jean files an election under subsection 7(10) to defer recognition of the employment benefit in respect of the acquisition. Jean sells the share in 2003, when the share is worth $300. He owns no other shares of the employer.

On Jean's T4 slip for 2001, the employer reports the deferred employment benefit of $90 (= $100 − $10). In filing his tax return for 2003, Jean reports the $90 benefit as employment income as well as the capital gain of $200 (= $300 − ($10 + $90)) realized on the sale of the share.

When recognition of an employment benefit is deferred under subsection 7(8), it is deferred until the employee disposes of the security. It should be noted that, if the employee does not sell the security before death, there will be a deemed disposition under section 70 at the time of death. Likewise, if the employee ceases to be resident in Canada before selling the security, there will be a deemed disposition under section 128.1 at the time of emigration. The exemption of certain employee option securities from the deemed disposition rules on emigration (as provided for under subsection 7(1.6) as proposed in Bill C-43, tabled in the House of Commons on September 20, 2000) will not apply to securities for which a deferral is provided under subsection 7(8). Consequently, employment benefits that are deferred under subsection 7(8) will be taxed no later than the year in which the employee dies or ceases to be resident in Canada.

**Related Provisions**: 7(1.3) — Order of disposition of securities; 7(9) — Meaning of "qualifying acquisition"; 7(14) — Deferral deemed valid at CCRA's discretion; 7(15) — No source withholding required when deferred benefit included; 7(16) — Prescribed form required while security held; 47(3)(a) — No averaging of cost on disposition of securities.

**Regulations**: 200(5) (information return).

**(9) Meaning of "qualifying acquisition"** — For the purpose of subsection (8), a taxpayer's acquisition of a security under an agreement made by a particular qualifying person is a qualifying acquisition if

(a) the acquisition occurs after February 27, 2000;

(b) the taxpayer would, if this Act were read without reference to subsection (8), be entitled to deduct an amount under paragraph 110(1)(d) in respect of the acquisition in computing income for the taxation year in which the security is acquired;

(c) if the particular qualifying person is a corporation, the taxpayer was not, at the time immediately after the agreement was made, a specified shareholder of any of the following:

(i) the particular qualifying person,

(ii) any qualifying person that, at that time, was an employer of the taxpayer and was not dealing at arm's length with the particular qualifying person, and

(iii) the qualifying person of which the taxpayer had, under the agreement, a right to acquire a security; and

(d) if the security is a share,

(i) it is of a class of shares that, at the time the acquisition occurs, is listed on a prescribed stock exchange, and

(ii) where rights under the agreement were acquired by the taxpayer as a result of one or more dispositions to which subsection (1.4) applied, none of the rights that were the subject of any of the dispositions included a right to acquire a share of a class of shares that, at the time the rights were disposed of, was not listed on any prescribed stock exchange.

**Technical Notes**: New subsection 7(9) sets out the requirements that must be met for the acquisition of a security under an employee option agreement to be considered to be a qualifying acquisition for the purposes of subsection 7(8). If the acquisition is a qualifying acquisition, subsection 7(8) provides for the recognition (and, thus, the taxation) of the associated employment benefit to be deferred, at the election of the employee, from the year the employee acquires the security to the year the employee disposes of the security.

In order for an employee's acquisition of a security under an option agreement to be a qualifying acquisition, the following conditions must be satisfied.

*Timing of Acquisition*

Paragraph 7(9)(a) requires that the acquisition occur after February 27, 2000. There are no constraints as to when the option was granted, or when it vested (i.e., first became exercisable). Thus, for example, an acquisition of a security in 2001 will not fail to be a qualifying acquisition because the option under which the acquisition occurs was granted in 1998 and vested in 1999.

*Entitlement to Deduction under Paragraph 110(1)(d)*

Paragraph 7(9)(b) requires that the employee be entitled to a deduction under paragraph 110(1)(d) in respect of the security. This means that the following conditions must also be satisfied.

- The amount paid by the employee to acquire the security (including any amount paid to acquire the right to acquire the security) must be not less than the fair market value of the security when the option was granted, unless the employee acquired the option as a result of one or more exchanges of options to which subsection 7(1.4) applied. Where there have been such exchanges, there are a number of conditions relating to the exercise price that must be satisfied. (See the commentary on amended paragraph 110(1)(d) for further details.)

- At the time immediately after the option was granted, the employee must have been dealing at arm's length with the employer, the entity granting the option and the entity whose securities could be acquired under the option. If there were any exchanges of options to which subsection 7(1.4) applied, this requirement applies to the original option.

- If the security is a share, it must be a prescribed share as described in section 6204 of the *Income Tax Regulations*. In general terms, a prescribed share is an ordinary common share.

*Non-Specified Shareholder*

Paragraph 7(9)(c) requires that, at the time immediately after the option was granted, the employee not be a specified shareholder of the employer, the entity granting the option or the entity whose securities could be acquired under the option. (In general terms, a person is a "specified shareholder" of a corporation, as defined in subsection 248(1), if the person owns, directly or indirectly, at least 10% of the issued shares of any class of the capital stock of the corporation or a related corporation.) If there were any exchanges of options to which subsection 7(1.4) applied, this condition applies to the original option since each new option is deemed to be the same as, and a continuation of, the original option.

*Publicly-Listed Share*

Paragraph 7(9)(d) requires that, if the security is a share, it be of a class of shares listed on a Canadian or foreign stock exchange described in section 3200 or 3201 of the Regulations. Furthermore, if there were any exchanges of options to which subsection 7(1.4) applied, none of the shares that could have been acquired under any of the options being disposed of were, at the time of the exchange, of a class of shares that was not listed on such a stock exchange. Thus, an employee's acquisition of a publicly-listed share under an option acquired as a result of one or more exchanges of options to which subsection 7(1.4) applied will not qualify for deferral if any of the previously-exchanged options allowed the employee to acquire shares that, at the time of the exchange, were unlisted.

This requirement ensures that the $100,000 annual vesting limit in new paragraph 7(10)(c) cannot be circumvented by establishing a class of shares exclusively for employee options which would have little or no fair market value at the time the options are granted but which would have the potential for growth, in absolute dollars, that is similar to other shares of the corporation.

**(10) Election for purposes of subsection (8)** — For the purpose of subsection (8), a taxpayer's election to have that subsection apply in respect of the taxpayer's acquisition of a particular security under an agreement referred to in subsection (1) is in accordance with this subsection if

(a) the election is filed, in prescribed form and manner at a particular time that is before January 16 of the year following the year in which the acquisition occurs, with a person who would be required to file an information return in respect of the acquisition if subsection (8) were read without reference to paragraph (8)(b);

(b) the taxpayer is resident in Canada at the time the acquisition occurs; and

(c) the specified value of the particular security does not exceed the amount by which

(i) $100,000

exceeds

(ii) the total of all amounts each of which is the specified value of another security acquired by the taxpayer at or before the particular time under an agreement referred to in subsection (1), where

(A) the taxpayer's right to acquire that other security first became exercisable in the year that the taxpayer's right to acquire the particular security first became exercisable, and

(B) at or before the particular time, the taxpayer has elected in accordance with this subsection to have subsection (8) apply in respect of the acquisition of that other security.

**Technical Notes**: New subsection 7(8) provides for the recognition (and, thus, the taxation) of the employment benefit in connection with a qualifying acquisition of an employee option security to be deferred until disposition of the security, if the employee makes an election to defer in accordance with new subsection 7(10). It should be noted that subsection 7(13) allows an employee to revoke an election made in accordance with subsection 7(10). The effect of such a revocation is that the election is deemed never to have been made. (See the commentary on subsection 7(13) for further details.)

In order for an election to defer recognition of the employment benefit associated with the acquisition of an employee option security to be in accordance with subsection 7(10), the following conditions must be satisfied.

*Timing, Form and Manner of Election*

Paragraph 7(10)(a) requires that the employee file the election on or before January 15th of the year following the year in which the security is acquired. However, if the security is acquired in 2000, the filing deadline is extended to February 15, 2001.

Paragraph 7(10)(a) requires that the election be filed with a person who will be required to report the deferred employment benefit to the Minister of National Revenue. Under proposed subsection 200(5) of the Regulations, each of the following will be jointly liable for so reporting the deferred employment benefit: the employer, the entity that granted the option and the entity whose security is acquired under the option. (See [under proposed Reg. 200(5)] for further details.)

Finally, paragraph 7(10)(a) requires that the employee file the election in such prescribed form and manner as is determined by the Minister of National Revenue.

*Residency Status of Employee*

Paragraph 7(10)(b) requires that, when the employee acquires the security in respect of which the election is made, the employee be resident in Canada.

*$100,000 Annual Vesting Limit*

Paragraph 7(10)(c) requires that the election be in respect of a particular security which has a specified value that, when added to the total specified value of certain other employee option securities, does not exceed $100,000. The other securities that are relevant for this purpose are those in respect of which the employee has filed (at or before the time that the election in respect of the particular security is filed) an election in accordance with subsection 7(10) and that were acquired under options that vested (i.e., first became exercisable) in the same year as the option under which the particular security is acquired.

It should be noted that where options are exchanged for other options under subsection 7(1.4), the new options are deemed to be the same as, and a continuation of, the original options. Therefore, to the extent that all or a portion of the rights under the old options had vested before the exchange, a corresponding portion of the new rights would be considered to have vested at the same time as the old options.

The specified value of a security acquired under an employee option agreement is determined in accordance with new subsection 7(11). In many instances, the specified value will be the fair market value of the security at the time the option was granted. However, if there have been exchanges under subsection 7(1.4) or the security has been subject to splits or consolidations, the specified value will be the initial fair market value adjusted to take into account such events. (See the commentary on new subsection 7(11) for further details.)

The following examples illustrate the application of the $100,000 annual vesting limit. In each example, it is assumed that all other conditions for the deferral are met.

*Example 1*

*In January 2001, Suzanne's corporate employer grants her options to acquire 16,000 company shares. The exercise price is $10 a share, which is the fair market value of the shares at the time the options are granted. Half of the options vest in 2001, the other half in 2002. Suzanne exercises all of the options in 2004, at which time the shares have a fair market value of $100 each. Suzanne wishes to take maximum advantage of the deferral available under subsection 7(8).*

*The 8,000 shares that Suzanne acquired under the options that vested in 2001 have a total specified value of $80,000 (= 8,000 × $10). The 8,000 shares that Suzanne acquired under the options that vested in 2002 also have a total value of $80,000. Since the total specified value for each vesting year does not exceed $100,000, Suzanne elects to defer on all of the options.*

*On Suzanne's T4 slip for 2004, the employer reports the deferred employment benefit of $1,440,000 (= 16,000 × ($100 − $10)) as a special memo item. This amount will be taxable only when Suzanne disposes of the shares.*

*Example 2*

*The facts are the same as in example 1, except that all of the options vest in 2001.*

Since the shares that Suzanne acquired under options that vested in 2001 have a total specified value of $160,000, which is in excess of the $100,000 vesting limit for 2001, Suzanne cannot elect to defer on all of the options. She elects to defer on 10,000 options, which have a total specified value of $100,000.

On Suzanne's T4 slip for 2004, the employer reports the deferred employment benefit of $900,000 (= 10,000 × ($100 − $10)) as a special memo item which is taxable only in the year of disposition, and the remaining employment benefit of $540,000 (= 6,000 × ($100 − $10)) as employment income which is taxable in 2004.

*Example 3*

On January 1, 2001, Mario's corporate employer grants him options to acquire 10,000 company shares. The exercise price is $10 a share, which is the fair market value of the shares at the time the options are granted. The options vest on January 1, 2003. On July 1, 2002, his employer grants him options on another 10,000 shares. The exercise price is $5 a share, which is the fair market value of the shares at that time. These options vest on July 1, 2003. Mario exercises all of the $10 options on January 1, 2003, when the shares have a fair market value of $100. He exercises all of the $5 options on July 1, 2003, when the shares have a fair market value of $150.

The specified value of the options that vested in January 2003 is $100,000 (= 10,000 × $10). The specified value of the options that vested in July 2003 is $50,000 (= 10,000 × $5). Since the total specified value of options vesting in 2003 exceeds $100,000, Mario cannot defer on all of the options. He wishes to defer on those options which will maximize the amount of employment benefit that is deferred.

The employment benefit on the options exercised in January is $90 (= $100 − $10) per share and $145 (= $150 − $5) per share on the options exercised in July. Accordingly, Mario elects to defer on all of the options exercised in July (which have a specified value of $50,000 and a deferred employment benefit of $1,450,000 (= 10,000 × $145)). He also elects to defer on half of the options exercised in January (which also have a specified value of $50,000 but a deferred employment benefit of $450,000 (= 5,000 × $90)). The employment benefit of $450,000 on the remaining options exercised in January is taxable in 2003.

On Mario's T4 slip for 2003, the employer reports the total deferred employment benefit of $1,900,000 (= $1,450,000 + $450,000) as a special memo item which is taxable only in the year of disposition, and the remaining employment benefit of $450,000 as employment income which is taxable in 2003.

**Related Provisions**: 7(11) — Meaning of "specified value"; 7(12) — Order of exercise of identical options; 7(13) — Revocation of election.

**Forms**: T1212: Statement of deferred stock option benefits.

**(11) Meaning of "specified value"** — For the purpose of paragraph (10)(c), the specified value of a particular security acquired by a taxpayer under an agreement referred to in subsection (1) is the amount determined by the formula

$$A/B$$

where

A is the fair market value, determined at the time the agreement was made, of a security which was the subject of the agreement at the time the agreement was made; and

B is

(a) except where paragraph (b) applies, 1, and

(b) where the number or type of securities that are the subject of the agreement has been modified in any way after the time the agreement was made, the number of securities (including any fraction of a security) which it is reasonable to consider the taxpayer would, at the time the particular security was acquired, have a right to acquire under the agreement in lieu of one of the securities that were the subject of the agreement at the time the agreement was made.

**Technical Notes**: New subsection 7(11) defines the term "specified value" of a security acquired under an employee option agreement for purposes of the $100,000 annual vesting limit in new paragraph 7(10)(c). The $100,000 limit is relevant in determining whether or not the employee can elect to defer taxation on the employment benefit arising from the acquisition of the security.

In many instances, the specified value is the fair market value of the security at the time the option was granted. However, if there have been exchanges under subsection 7(1.4) or the security has been subject to splits or consolidations, the specified value is the initial fair market value adjusted to take into account such events.

More specifically, the specified value of a security acquired under an employee security option is defined as the amount determined by the formula A/B.

Amount A in the formula is the fair market value of a security that could be acquired under the option at the time the option was granted. Where there have been one or more exchanges under subsection 7(1.4), the original option is the option that is relevant in determining amount A since that subsection deems each new option to be the same as, and a continuation of, the original option.

Where there have been no exchanges of options and no other modifications to the number or type of securities that can be acquired under the option, amount B in the formula is "1". In any other case, amount B is the number of securities that it is reasonable to consider that the employee could acquire, after taking all such exchanges and modifications into account, in lieu of one security under the original option at the time it was granted. The most common modifications that would be relevant for this purpose (other than exchanges under subsection 7(1.4)) are structural changes, such as splits and consolidations, in the securities that are the subject of the option.

The following examples illustrate the determination of the specified value of a security acquired under an employee security option where there have been modifications to the original option.

*Example 1*

*Richard is granted an option to acquire a share for $20, which is the fair market value of the share at the time the option is granted. There is a 4-for-1 share* split, with an automatic adjustment to Richard's option allowing him to acquire 4 shares at an exercise price of $5 each. Immediately after the split, Richard exercises his option and acquires all 4 shares.

Amount A in the "specified value" formula is $20, which is the fair market value, at the time the option was granted, of the particular security that could be acquired under the option at that time. Amount B in the formula is 4, since Richard was able to acquire 4 shares in lieu of the 1 share that could be acquired under the option at the time the option was granted. Therefore, the specified value of each share acquired under the option is $5 (= $20/4).

*Example 2*

Anne's employer, Company X, grants her options to acquire 10 shares. The exercise price is $10 a share, which is the fair market value of a Company X share at the time of grant. Company X is acquired by Company Y at a time when Company X shares are worth $100 each and Company Y shares are worth $200 each. Anne's options are exchanged for options to acquire 5 Company Y shares at an exercise price of $20 a share. Anne exercises the options immediately after the exchange.

Amount A in the "specified value" formula is $10, which is the fair market value, at the time the original option was granted, of a Company X share. Amount B in the formula is 0.5, since Anne was able to acquire only 1/2 of a Company Y share in lieu of 1 Company X share. Therefore, the specified value of each Company Y share is $20 (= $10/0.5).

*Example 3*

The facts are the same as in Example 2 except that, before Anne exercises the options, there is 4-for-1 split of Company Y shares. There is an automatic adjustment to Anne's options, allowing her to acquire 20 Company Y shares for $5 each. Anne exercises the options immediately after the split.

Amount A is $10, which is the fair market value, at the time the original option was granted, of a Company X share. Amount B is 2, since Anne was able to acquire 2 Company Y shares in lieu of 1 Company X share. Therefore, the specified value of each Company Y share is $5 (= $10/2).

**(12) Identical options — order of exercise** — Unless the context otherwise requires, a taxpayer is deemed to exercise identical rights to acquire securities under agreements referred to in subsection (1)

(a) where the taxpayer has designated an order, in the order so designated; and

(b) in any other case, in the order in which those rights first became exercisable and, in the case of identical rights that first became exercisable at the same time, in the order in which the agreements under which those rights were acquired were made.

**Technical Notes**: New subsection 7(12) provides a special rule for determining the order in which identical options are considered to be exercised. This is relevant primarily for purposes of applying the $100,000 annual vesting limit in paragraph 7(10)(c) to a particular security acquired under an employee option agreement.

In applying the $100,000 limit, it is necessary to determine the vesting year for the option being exercised (i.e., the year in which the option to acquire the security first became exercisable). It is also necessary to determine the vesting year of any other employee option securities for which the employee has elected a deferral under subsection 7(8). If there are identical options that have vested in different years, absent new subsection 7(12) it may not be possible to determine, when an option is exercised, which particular option is being exercised and, thus, what the vesting year is for the particular option.

Where this is the case, subsection 7(12) allows the employee to designate those options which are considered to have been exercised. If the employee does not so designate, identical options are considered to have been exercised in the order in which they first became exercisable, and identical options that first became exercisable at the same time, but were granted at different times, are considered to have been exercised in the order in which they were granted.

*Example*

On July 1, 2001, Kevin's corporate employer grants him options on 20,000 company shares. The exercise price is $10 a share, which is the fair market value of the shares at that time. Half of the options vest immediately; the other half vest on July 1, 2002.

On July 1, 2002, Kevin's employer grants him options on another 20,000 company shares. The exercise price is $10 a share, which is the fair market value of the shares at that time. Again, half the options vest immediately; the other half on July 1, 2003.

On July 1, 2005, Kevin acquires 30,000 shares under his options.

Unless Kevin designates which particular options are considered to have been exercised, he is considered to have exercised the 10,000 options that vested on July 1, 2001 and the 20,000 options that vested on July 1, 2002 (10,000 of which were granted in 2001 and 10,000 of which were granted in 2002). Since the total specified value on the options that vested in 2001 is $100,000, Kevin can elect to defer, under subsection 7(8), the full employment benefit on those options. However, since the total specified value on the options that vested in 2002 is $200,000, he can elect to defer on only half of those options.

To maximize the deferral available to him, Kevin designates the options exercised as being the 10,000 options that vested on July 1, 2001 and July 1, 2003, and 10,000 of the 20,000 options that vested on July 1, 2002. This keeps him within the $100,000 limit for each vesting year and, thus, allows him to defer the employment benefit on all of the 30,000 options exercised. No deferral will be available, however, when he subsequently exercises the remaining 10,000 options that vested on July 1, 2002.

It should be noted that the designation permitted under subsection 7(12) may be used in respect of options exercised before February 28, 2000, where the designation will allow for a deferral which might not otherwise be allowed on options exercised after February 27, 2000.

*Example*

In 1996, Hélène is granted options that have a total specified value of $400,000. Half of the options vest in 1997; the other half in 1998. In 1999, Hélène exercises half of the options and, in July 2000, she exercises the remaining options. To maximize the deferral under subsection 7(8), Hélène chooses to designate half of the options vested in each of 1997 and 1998 as the options which she exercised in 1999. This allows her to designate the remaining options as the options which she exercised in July 2000 and, since the total specified value for options exercised and deferred from each of the vesting years does not exceed $100,000, she is able to elect to defer the employment benefit on all of the options exercised in 2000.

**Related Provisions**: 248(12) — Identical properties.

**(13) Revoked election** — For the purposes of this section (other than this subsection), an election filed by a taxpayer to have subsection (8) apply to the taxpayer's acquisition of a security is deemed never to have been filed if, before January 16 of the year following the year in which the acquisition occurs, the taxpayer files with the person with whom the election was filed a written revocation of the election.

**Technical Notes**: New subsection 7(13) allows for the revocation of an election made in accordance with subsection 7(10) to defer recognition of a security option benefit under subsection 7(8).

Where an election is revoked in accordance with subsection 7(13), the election is deemed never to have been made. As a result, the employment benefit associated with the acquisition of the security is taxed in the year of acquisition, rather than in the year of disposition. Furthermore, the "specified value" of the security (as defined in subsection 7(11)) ceases to be relevant for the purpose of applying the $100,000 annual vesting limit in paragraph 7(10)(c) to other employee option securities in respect of which the employee wishes to defer taxation under subsection 7(8).

In order for subsection 7(13) to apply, the employee must file a written revocation of the election with the person with whom the election was filed. Generally, the revocation request must be filed on or before January 15th of the year following the year in which the security was acquired. However, if the security was acquired in 2000, the filing deadline is extended to 60 days after the day on which the legislation providing for the revocation receives royal assent.

In being able to revoke an election, an employee has the ability to re-instate all or part of the $100,000 vesting limit for a particular year. This will be significant when the total specified value of securities that can be acquired under options vesting in that year exceeds $100,000.

*Example*

On April 30, 2001, Francine's corporate employer grants her options to acquire 10,000 shares of the company. The exercise price is $10 a share, which is the fair market value of the shares at that time. The options vest immediately and expire on April 30, 2005. On September 30, 2001, Francine's employer grants her options to acquire another 5,000 company shares. The exercise price is $15 a share, which is the fair market value of the shares at that time. The options vest immediately and expire on September 30, 2005.

Francine exercises all of the $10 options on April 30, 2005, when the fair market value is $100 a share. She files an election at that time to defer, under subsection 7(8), recognition of the employment benefit of $900,000 (= 10,000 × ($100 − $10)). Since the total specified value of the shares in respect of which the election is made is $100,000 (= 10,000 × $10), the election fully utilizes the deferral limit for the 2001 vesting year.

Francine exercises the remaining options on September 30, 2005, when the fair market value is $295 a share. She wishes to defer recognition of as much of the employment benefit of $1,400,000 (= 5,000 × ($295 − $15)) as possible. However, because of the previous election on the $10 options, she has no deferral room available. Since she needs $75,000 (= 5,000 × $15) of deferral room, she immediately files with the employer a written request to revoke the election previously made on 7,500 of the $10 options. This provides her with sufficient room to make an election to defer the employment benefit on all of the $15 options.

On Francine's T4 slip for 2005, the benefit of $675,000 associated with the 7,500 options on which the election was revoked is reported as employment income which is taxable in 2005. The remaining benefit of $1,625,000 (= 1/4 ($900,000) + $1,400,000) is reported as a deferred amount, which is to be taxed in the year in which Francine disposes of the shares.

**(14) Deferral deemed valid** — For the purposes of this section and paragraph 110(1)(d), where a taxpayer files an election to have subsection (8) apply in respect of the taxpayer's acquisition of a particular security and subsection (8) would not apply to the acquisition if this section were read without reference to this subsection, the following rules apply if the Minister so notifies the taxpayer in writing:

(a) the acquisition is deemed, for the purpose of subsection (8), to be a qualifying acquisition;

(b) the taxpayer is deemed to have elected, in accordance with subsection (10), to have subsection (8) apply in respect of the acquisition; and

(c) if, at the time the Minister sends the notice, the taxpayer has not disposed of the security, the taxpayer is deemed (other than for the purpose of subsection (1.5)) to have disposed of the security at that time and to have acquired the security immediately after that time other than under an agreement referred to in subsection (1).

**Technical Notes**: New subsection 7(14) contains rules to allow the Minister of National Revenue to treat an invalid deferral of an employment benefit realized on the acquisition of an employee option security as a valid deferral under subsection 7(8).

Specifically, subsection 7(14) deals with situations in which an employee files an election to have an employment benefit deferred under subsection 7(8) but the conditions for the deferral are not satisfied. This could be because either the acquisition of the security in question was not a qualifying acquisition as defined in subsection 7(9) or the election was not made in accordance with subsection 7(10).

When this occurs, subsection 7(14) allows the Minister, upon so notifying the employee in writing, to treat the acquisition as having been a qualifying acquisition and to treat the election as having been made in accordance with subsection 7(10). If the employee still holds the security at the time the notice is sent, the employee is deemed to have disposed of the security at that time and to have reacquired the security immediately thereafter, but not under an employee option agreement. (The provision deeming a disposition and reacquisition of the security does not apply for purposes of the security-for-security exchange rules in subsection 7(1.5).)

In applying the provisions of subsection 7(14), the Minister can ensure that an employment benefit that was incorrectly treated as a deferred amount under subsection 7(8), and thus was not taxed in the year of acquisition, is taxable in the year in which the Minister sends the necessary notice or, if earlier, in the year in which the security is disposed of. It also ensures that the specified value of the security in question is applied against the employee's $100,000 vesting limit for the year in which the right to acquire the security first became exercisable.

It is expected that the Minister would apply the provisions of subsection 7(14) when the year in which the security was acquired is statute-barred.

**(15) Withholding** — Where, because of subsection (8), a taxpayer is deemed by paragraph (1)(a) to have received a benefit from employment in a taxation year, the benefit is deemed to be nil for the purpose of subsection 153(1).

**Technical Notes**: New subsection 7(15) contains a special provision which has the effect of exempting employers from withholding and reporting obligations on employment benefits that employees are deemed, by paragraph 7(1)(a), to have received on the disposition of securities in respect of which a deferral was provided under subsection 7(8).

Under subsection 153(1), an employer is required to withhold tax from an employee's remuneration and to remit that tax to the Receiver General on behalf of the employee and, under subsection 200(1) of the Regulations, the employer is required to report the remuneration to the Minister of National Revenue in an annual information return. Remuneration, for this purpose, would normally include any amount that the employee is deemed by paragraph 7(1)(a) to have received as a benefit from employment in connection with the acquisition of a security under an employee option agreement.

However, where the employment benefit is in respect of a security acquired under circumstances to which subsection 7(8) applied, subsection 7(15) deems the employment benefit to be nil for the purposes of subsection 153(1). Consequently, the employer has no obligation to withhold or remit tax, or to file an information return, in respect of the employment benefit recognized on the disposition of the security. The employee is, nevertheless, required to include the full amount of the benefit in computing employment income for the year in which the disposition occurs.

It should be noted that, under proposed subsection 200(5) of the Regulations, the employer will be required, in the year in which the employee acquires the security, to report the amount of the deferred employment benefit as a special item on the employee's T4 slip. It should also be noted that, since the acquisition itself is not a taxable event, it also does not give rise to any obligation on the part of the employer to withhold or remit tax on the amount of the deferred employment benefit. (See further details on the reporting requirements under proposed [Reg.] 200(5).)

**(16) Prescribed form for deferral** — Where, at any time in a taxation year, a taxpayer holds a security that was acquired under circumstances to which subsection (8) applied, the taxpayer shall file with the Minister, with the taxpayer's return of income for the year, a prescribed form containing prescribed information relating to the taxpayer's acquisition and disposition of securities under agreements referred to in subsection (1).

**Technical Notes**: Under new subsection 7(16), an employee who acquires securities under an employee option agreement, and elects to defer recognition of the related employment benefits under new subsection 7(8), is required to file a prescribed form, containing prescribed information, with the annual tax return for each year in which such securities are held.

Using this form, the employee will have to provide information on transactions relating to such securities, including acquisitions of new deferral securities and dispositions of existing deferral securities. This form will assist employees in complying with their obligations to include deferred employment benefits in computing employment income for the year in which there is a disposition of the related securities.

**Forms**: T1212: Statement of deferred stock option benefits.

**Application**: The December 21, 2000 draft legislation, subsec. 1(8), will add subsecs. 7(8) to (16), applicable to 2000 *et seq.* except that,

(a) in applying para. 7(10)(a) to securities acquired in 2000, the reference to "January 16" shall be read as a reference to "February 16"; and

(b) a written request under subsec. 7(13) to revoke an election in respect of a security acquired in 2000 is deemed to have been filed in a timely manner if it is filed on or before the day that is 60 days after the day on which the amending legislation receives Royal Assent.

**Definitions [s. 7]**: "amount" — 248(1); "arm's length" — 7(1.11), 251(1); "Canadian-controlled private corporation" — 125(7), 248(1); "Canadian corporation" — 89(1), 248(1); "class of shares" — 248(6); "corporation" — 248(1), *Interpretation Act* 35(1); "designated person" — 7(1.4)(b); "disposed", "disposition" — 7(1.6), 248(1); "employee", "employer", "employment" — 248(1); "exchanged option" — 7(1.4)(a); "exchanged securities", "exchanged shares" — 7(1.5)(a); "identical" — 248(12); "Minister" — 248(1); "mutual fund trust" — 132(6)–(7), 132.2(1)(q), 248(1); "new option" — 7(1.4)(b); "new securities", "new shares" — 7(1.4)(b); "old securities", "old shares" — 7(1.4)(a); "person", "prescribed" — 248(1); "prescribed stock exchange" — Reg. 3200, 3201; "property" — 248(1); "qualifying acquisition" — 7(9); "qualifying person" — 7(7); "resident in Canada" — 250; "securities", "security" — 7(7); "share", "specified shareholder" — 248(1); "specified value" — 7(11); "taxation year" — 249; "taxpayer" — 248(1); "trust" — 104(1), 248(1), (3); "written" — *Interpretation Act* 35(1)"writing".

S. 8(1)  Income Tax Act, Part I, Division B

## Deductions

**8. (1) Deductions allowed** — In computing a taxpayer's income for a taxation year from an office or employment, there may be deducted such of the following amounts as are wholly applicable to that source or such part of the following amounts as may reasonably be regarded as applicable thereto:

(a) **volunteers' [emergency workers'] deduction** — in respect of each employer of the taxpayer that is a government, municipality or public authority, the lesser of $1,000 and the total of all amounts received in the year by the taxpayer from the employer that are

(i) included in the taxpayer's income for the year from an office or employment, and

(ii) from the performance, as a volunteer, of the taxpayer's duties as

(A) an ambulance technician,

(B) a firefighter, or

(C) a person who assists in the search or rescue of individuals or in other emergency situations,

except that no amount may be so deducted in respect of an employer if the taxpayer is employed in the year, otherwise than as a volunteer, by the employer in connection with the performance of any of the duties referred to in subparagraph (ii) or of similar duties;

### Proposed Repeal — 8(1)(a)

**Application**: Bill C-43 (First Reading September 20, 2000), subsec. 2(1), will repeal para. 8(1)(a), applicable to 1998 et seq.

**Technical Notes**: Paragraph 8(1)(a) provides for a deduction of up to $1,000 in respect of amounts received by an individual (and included in the individual's income) from a government, municipality or public authority for the performance, as a volunteer, of the taxpayer's duties as an ambulance technician, a firefighter or a person who assists in the search or rescue of individuals or in other emergency situations. This deduction is replaced by an equivalent exemption under subsection 81(4). For information on this exemption, see the commentary on new subsection 81(4).

**Department of Finance news release, June 16, 1999**: *Technical Change to the $1,000 Tax-Free Amount for Emergency Service Volunteers*

In recognition of the important role of volunteers in providing emergency services to rural communities, the 1998 budget increased from $500 to $1,000 the annual amount that volunteer firefighters can receive on a tax-free basis from a public authority. This treatment was also extended to volunteer ambulance technicians and other emergency service volunteers.

Prior to the 1998 change, municipalities were not required to report the first $500 paid in allowances to their volunteer firefighters since this amount was excluded from income for income tax purposes. [See former 6(1)(b)(viii) — ed.] The 1998 budget required that all compensation paid by a public authority to a volunteer emergency service provider be included in income with the individual being able to claim an offsetting deduction of up to $1,000.

Some municipalities and other public authorities have made representations that the previous income exclusion approach was easier for them to administer since they did not need to issue reporting slips to volunteers earning no more than the tax-free amount. To simplify administration for public authorities, amendments to the *Income Tax Act* will be proposed at the earliest opportunity to replace the current deduction of up to $1,000 for compensation received by volunteer emergency service providers with a corresponding exclusion from employment income for income tax purposes [see 81(4) — ed.]. This change will have no income tax implications for volunteer emergency service providers.

For further information: Lise Potvin, Personal Income Tax Division, (613) 992-6729; Karl Littler, Senior Advisor, Tax Policy, Office of the Minister of Finance, (613) 996-7861; Jean-Michel Catta, Public Affairs and Operations Division, (613) 996-8080.

**Related Provisions**: 8(10) — Employer's certificate required; 81(4) — Exemption for volunteer emergency worker's income.

**Notes**: 8(1)(a) added by 1998 Budget, effective for 1998 and later taxation years. It replaces the former $500 exemption for volunteer firemen under 6(1)(b)(viii), but will be moved to 81(4) as per the Proposed Amendment above.

The allowance for volunteer firemen was set at $300 in 1961 and increased to $500 in 1980 and $1,000 in 1998.

Former 8(1)(a) repealed by 1988 tax reform, effective 1988. This was a general employment expense deduction of up to $500, available to all employees without any requirement that expenses actually have been incurred. 8(2) prohibits any deduction for employment expenses unless specifically allowed. 8(1)(b) to (q) allow specific expenses.

**Forms**: T2200: Declaration of conditions of employment.

(b) **legal expenses of employee** — amounts paid by the taxpayer in the year as or on account of legal expenses incurred by the taxpayer to collect or establish a right to salary or wages owed to the taxpayer by the employer or former employer of the taxpayer;

**Related Provisions**: 6(1)(j) — Reimbursements and awards; 6(8) — GST rebate included in income; 60(o.1)(i)(B) — Legal expenses re retiring allowance.

**Notes**: Since "salary or wages" is defined in 248(1) to include all income taxed under s. 5, 6 or 7, the deduction in 8(1)(b) applies to legal expenses to recover any amount taxed under those sections (e.g., a stock option benefit under s. 7, or a disability insurance benefit taxed under 6(1)(f)).

See also Notes to 60(o).

8(1)(b) amended by 1989 Budget, effective for amounts paid after 1989, to add a deduction for legal expenses to "establish a right to" salary or wages.

**Interpretation Bulletins**: IT-99R5: Legal and accounting fees.

**Forms**: T777: Statement of employment expenses; T4044: Employment expenses [guide].

(c) **clergyman's residence** — where the taxpayer is a member of the clergy or of a religious order or a regular minister of a religious denomination, and is in charge of or ministering to a diocese, parish or congregation, or engaged exclusively in full-time administrative service by appointment of a religious order or religious denomination, an amount equal to

(i) the value of the residence or other living accommodation occupied by the taxpayer in the course of or by virtue of the taxpayer's office or employment as such a member or minister so in charge of or ministering to a diocese, parish or congregation, or so engaged in such administrative service, to the extent that that value is included in computing the taxpayer's income for the year by virtue of section 6, or

(ii) rent paid by the taxpayer for a residence or other living accommodation rented and occupied by the taxpayer, or the fair rental value of a residence or other living accommodation owned and occupied by the taxpayer, during the year but not, in either case, exceeding the taxpayer's remuneration from the taxpayer's office or employment as described in subparagraph (i);

### Proposed Amendment — 8(1)(c)

(c) **clergy residence** — where, in the year, the taxpayer

(i) is a member of the clergy or of a religious order or a regular minister of a religious denomination, and

(ii) is

(A) in charge of a diocese, parish or congregation,

(B) ministering to a diocese, parish or congregation, or

(C) engaged exclusively in full-time administrative service by appointment of a religious order or religious denomination,

the amount, not exceeding the taxpayer's remuneration for the year from the office or employment, equal to

(iii) the total of all amounts included in computing the taxpayer's income for the year under section 6 in respect of the residence or other living accommodation occupied by the taxpayer in the course of, or because of, the taxpayer's office or employment as such a member or minister so in charge of or ministering to a diocese, parish or congregation, or so engaged in such administrative service, or

(iv) rent paid by the taxpayer for the taxpayer's principal place of residence (or other principal living accommodation) ordinarily occupied during the year by the taxpayer, or the fair rental value of such a residence (or other living accommodation) owned by the

taxpayer or the taxpayer's spouse or common-law partner, not exceeding the lesser of

(A) the greater of

(I) $1,000 multiplied by the number of months (to a maximum of ten) in the year, during which the taxpayer is a person described in subparagraphs (i) and (ii), and

(II) one-third of the taxpayer's remuneration for the year from the office or employment, and

(B) the amount, if any, by which

(I) the fair rental value of the residence or living accommodation

exceeds

(II) the total of all amounts each of which is an amount deducted, in connection with the same accommodation or residence, in computing an individual's income for the year from an office or employment or from a business (other than an amount deducted under this paragraph by the taxpayer), to the extent that the amount can reasonably be considered to relate to the period, or a portion of the period, in respect of which an amount is claimed by the taxpayer under this paragraph;

**Application**: The December 21, 2000 draft legislation, subsec. 2(1), will amend para. 8(1)(c) to read as above, applicable to 2001 et seq.

**Technical Notes**: Paragraph 8(1)(c) allows certain members of the clergy or of religious orders, as well as certain regular ministers of religious denominations, to deduct an amount in respect of their living accommodation. To be eligible for the deduction, the individuals have to be in charge of, or ministering to, a diocese, parish or congregation, or engaged exclusively in full-time administrative service by a religious order or a religious denomination. The amount of the deduction depends upon whether the living accommodation they occupy is (a) supplied to them by virtue of their employment, (b) rented by them or (c) owned by them.

Where the living accommodation is supplied by virtue of the employment, the amount of the deduction is equal to the value of the benefit derived from the supply of the living accommodation, to the extent that the value is already included in income. Where the living accommodation is rented by the clergy person, the amount of the deduction is equal to the amount of rent paid. Where the living accommodation is owned by the clergy person, the deduction is equal to the fair rental value of the living accommodation. In the latter two cases, the amount of the deduction for a particular year cannot exceed the amount of the remuneration for the year.

This amendment to paragraph 8(1)(c) deals with living accommodations rented or owned by individuals who are otherwise eligible to the deduction under that paragraph.

**S. 8(1)(c)**      Income Tax Act, Part I, Division B

In these cases, it limits the amount of the deduction to the least of three amounts:

- the individual's remuneration for the year from the office or employment,
- the greater of
  - 1/3 of the individual's total remuneration from the employment for the year, and
  - $1,000 per month (to a maximum of ten months) in the year during which an individual meets the conditions set out in subparagraphs 8(1)(c)(i) and (ii), and
- the fair rental value of the residence (reduced by the total of all other amounts deducted in computing an individual's income from a business or from an office or employment in connection with the same accommodation). This is relevant where, for example, two spouses who are members of the clergy occupy the same accommodation.

**Department of Finance news release Backgrounder, December 21, 2000**: *Clergy Residence Deduction*

Under existing paragraph 8(1)(c) of the *Income Tax Act*, certain members of the clergy or of religious organizations are allowed to claim a deduction in respect of their residence. Where the employer provides the clergy residence, the deduction for the residence offsets the corresponding taxable housing benefit, and where the clergy person provides their own residence, the deduction is equal to the rent paid for the residence or the fair rental value of the residence, and cannot exceed the amount of the clergy person's remuneration for the year.

In order to ensure that the level of the tax assistance is appropriate, in a news release dated October 19, 1999, the Minister of Finance proposed a legislative change for the calculation of the deduction in circumstances where the clergy person provides his or her own residence. It was proposed that in such circumstances the deduction be limited to the lesser of the following two amounts:

- the housing allowance paid or earmarked by the clergy person's employer; and
- the greater of $10,000 and 50% of the clergy person's ordinary remuneration (exclusive of any benefit related to the provision of housing).

At that time, the Minister sought the views of religious organizations on the changes under consideration. Further to comments received, the parameters of the proposal have been revised. First, the requirement for earmarking has been dropped. Instead, it is proposed to amend subsection 8(10) in order to require that the employees claiming the clergy residence deduction file with their income tax returns a prescribed form signed by their employers to the effect that the employees meet the requirements concerning their status and function as clergy.

Second, the revised proposal would generally limit the amount of the deduction to the least of the following three amounts:

- the clergy person's total remuneration from the office or employment;
- 1/3 of that total remuneration or $10,000, whichever is greater; and
- the fair rental value of the residence (reduced by other amounts deducted in connection with the same residence).

It is proposed that these amendments apply to the 2001 and subsequent taxation years.

**Department of Finance news release, October 19, 1999**: *Legislative Changes Proposed to Residence Deduction for the Clergy*

Finance Minister Paul Martin today announced his intention to propose legislative changes to the tax deduction allowed to a clergy person under the *Income Tax Act* in respect of the person's residence.

The Minister said that the changes are necessary in order to ensure that the tax deduction continues to be appropriate in circumstances where the clergy person provides his or her own residence. Mr. Martin stated that consultations with the religious sector on the parameters of the proposal will begin this fall. Under the existing clergy residence deduction, certain members of the clergy or of religious organizations are allowed to claim a deduction in respect of their residence. The deduction recognizes, among other things, that the personal residence of a clergy person often serves as an office or meeting place for members of a congregation or parish.

In instances where the employer provides the clergy residence, the deduction for the residence offsets the corresponding housing taxable benefit, and the clergy person pays income tax only on the salary component of his or her employment income. No legislative change is proposed in these circumstances.

A legislative change is proposed, however, where the clergy persons provide their own residence. In these circumstances, the existing clergy residence deduction could, in some cases, offset all of the clergy person's remuneration. In this instance, the amount of the deduction is equal to the rent paid for the residence or, if it is owned by the clergy person, the fair rental value of the residence. This deduction has been available regardless of whether the residence is used by the taxpayer in the performance of religious duties. This level of tax assistance is not appropriate.

Consequently, in circumstances where the clergy person provides his or her residence, it is proposed that the clergy residence deduction be limited for years after 2000 to the lesser of:

(a) the amount of the housing allowance included in the clergy person's income, and

(b) the greater of $10,000 and 50 per cent of the clergy person's ordinary remuneration (i.e., excluding the housing allowance) from that employment.

Under the proposed change, a deduction in respect of a clergy residence will only be available to the extent that a housing allowance is included in the clergy person's income. Employers who currently do not pay such an allowance will be allowed to earmark a reasonable portion of the clergy person's remuneration in respect of a housing allowance.

The Minister of Finance indicated that he is confident that the consultations will ensure that the appropriate level of tax assistance is provided for the clergy residence in circumstances where the clergy person provides the residence. He also noted that affected parties will be given sufficient time to renegotiate, if necessary, working arrangements to comply with any income tax change that may be implemented as a result of these consultations.

The Minister requested that members of the religious sector who wish to have their views considered should submit their comments on the proposal before the end of the year to: Tax Legislation Division, Department of Finance, L'Esplanade Laurier, 17th Floor, East Tower, 140 O'Connor Street, Ottawa, Ontario, K1A 0G5.

For further information: Lucie Vermette, Tax Legislation Division, (613) 992-5636; Nathalie Gauthier, Press Secretary, (613) 996-7861; Jean-Michel Catta, Public Affairs and Operations Division, (613) 996-8080

**Related Provisions**: 8(10) — Employer's certificate required; 146(1)"earned income"(a)(i) — Earned income for RRSP purposes includes value of residence.

**Notes**: Revenue Canada issued the following news release on May 21, 1999 (perhaps superseded by the draft legislation above):

*Revenue Canada to Clarify Tax Treatment of Residence Deduction for the Clergy*

Revenue Canada today announced that it will not appeal recent Tax Court of Canada decisions in cases concerning the deduction for the annual rental value of clergy residences.

The Court rendered decisions in 49 cases on April 22, 1999. These cases were mutually selected as test cases with the understanding that guidance was being sought from the Court. The Court has provided criteria that will assist the Department in ensuring that those who are entitled to the deduction receive it.

In order to reflect the Court's decisions, Revenue Canada will work with representatives of the religious sector to develop a new interpretation bulletin on this subject, to inform clients of the new guidelines and how they will be applied.

New Interpretation Bulletin IT-141R, released May 4, 2000, contains the latest policy in this area, as well as a summary of the 1999 TCC decisions under 8(1)(c).

**Interpretation Bulletins**: IT-99R5: Legal and accounting fees; IT-141R: Clergy Residence Deduction.

(d) **teachers' exchange fund contribution** — a single amount, in respect of all employments of the taxpayer as a teacher, not exceeding $250 paid by the taxpayer in the year to a fund established by the Canadian Education Association for the benefit of teachers from Commonwealth countries present in Canada under a teachers' exchange arrangement;

**Notes**: "Commonwealth" is defined in the *Interpretation Act* (reproduced at the end of this book) as the association of countries listed in the Schedule to that Act.

(e) **expenses of railway employees** — amounts disbursed by the taxpayer in the year for meals and lodging while employed by a railway company

(i) away from the taxpayer's ordinary place of residence as a relieving telegrapher or station agent or on maintenance and repair work, or

(ii) away from the municipality and the metropolitan area, if there is one, where the taxpayer's home terminal was located, and at a location from which, by reason of distance from the place where the taxpayer maintained a self-contained domestic establishment in which the taxpayer resided and actually supported a spouse or common-law partner or a person dependent upon the taxpayer for support and connected with the taxpayer by blood relationship, marriage or common-law partnership or adoption, the taxpayer could not reasonably be expected to return daily to that place,

to the extent that the taxpayer has not been reimbursed and is not entitled to be reimbursed in respect thereof;

**Related Provisions**: 6(6) — Employment — remote and special work sites; 6(8) — GST rebate included in income; 8(1)(h) — Travelling expenses; 8(11) — GST; 67.1 — Expenses for food, etc..

**Notes**: 8(1)(e) amended by 2000 same-sex partners bill to add reference to "common-law partner" and "common-law partnership", effective for the 2001 and later taxation years, or earlier by election (see Notes to 248(1)"common-law partner").

**Interpretation Bulletins**: IT-518R: Food, beverages and entertainment expenses.

**Information Circulars**: 73-21R7: Away from home expenses.

**Forms**: TL2: Claim for meals and lodging expenses.

(f) **sales expenses** — where the taxpayer was employed in the year in connection with the selling of property or negotiating of contracts for the taxpayer's employer, and

(i) under the contract of employment was required to pay the taxpayer's own expenses,

(ii) was ordinarily required to carry on the duties of the employment away from the employer's place of business,

(iii) was remunerated in whole or part by commissions or other similar amounts fixed by reference to the volume of the sales made or the contracts negotiated, and

(iv) was not in receipt of an allowance for travel expenses in respect of the taxation year that was, by virtue of subparagraph 6(1)(b)(v), not included in computing the taxpayer's income,

amounts expended by the taxpayer in the year for the purpose of earning the income from the employment (not exceeding the commissions or other similar amounts referred to in subparagraph (iii) and received by the taxpayer in the year) to the extent that such amounts were not

(v) outlays, losses or replacements of capital or payments on account of capital, except as described in paragraph (j),

(vi) outlays or expenses that would, by virtue of paragraph 18(1)(l), not be deductible in computing the taxpayer's income for the year if the employment were a business carried on by the taxpayer, or

(vii) amounts the payment of which reduced the amount that would otherwise be included in computing the taxpayer's income for the year because of paragraph 6(1)(e);

**Related Provisions**: 6(1)(b)(v) — Allowance for travelling expenses; 6(8) — GST rebate included in income; 8(1)(h) — Travelling expenses; 8(1)(h.1) — Motor vehicle travelling expenses; 8(1)(j) — Auto and aircraft costs; 8(4) — Limitation — meals; 8(9) — Limitation — aircraft expenses; 8(10) — Employer's certificate; 8(13) — Work space in home; 18(1)(h) — Personal or living expenses; 18(1)(l) — Use of recreational facilities and club dues;

## S. 8(1)(f) — Income Tax Act, Part I, Division B

18(1)(r) — Limitation on employer deductibility; 67.1 — 50% limitation on expenses for meals and entertainment; 67.3 — Limitation re cost of leasing passenger vehicle; Reg. 102(2)(d)(i) — Effect of deduction on source withholdings.

**Notes**: See Notes to 8(13) re meaning of "required".

8(1)(f)(vii) added by 1991 technical bill, effective 1990, so that where an amount paid by the employee reduces the standby charge under 6(1)(e), that amount cannot be deducted under 8(1)(f).

**Interpretation Bulletins**: IT-352R2: Employee's expenses, including work space in home expenses; IT-421R2: Benefits to individuals, corporations and shareholders from loans or debt; IT-518R: Food, beverages and entertainment expenses; IT-522R: Vehicle, travel and sales expenses of employees.

**I.T. Technical News**: No. 12 (1998 deduction limits and benefit rates for automobiles).

**Forms**: T777: Statement of employment expenses; T2200: Declaration of conditions of employment; TD1X: Statement of remuneration and expenses (For use by commission remunerated employees); T4044: Employment expenses [guide].

(g) **transport employee's expenses** — where the taxpayer was an employee of a person whose principal business was passenger, goods, or passenger and goods transport and the duties of the employment required the taxpayer, regularly,

　(i) to travel, away from the municipality where the employer's establishment to which the taxpayer reported for work was located and away from the metropolitan area, if there is one, where it was located, on vehicles used by the employer to transport the goods or passengers, and

　(ii) while so away from that municipality and metropolitan area, to make disbursements for meals and lodging,

amounts so disbursed by the taxpayer in the year to the extent that the taxpayer has not been reimbursed and is not entitled to be reimbursed in respect thereof;

**Related Provisions**: 6(1)(b)(vii) — Allowance for travelling expenses; 6(8) — GST rebate included in income; 8(1)(h) — Travelling expenses; 8(11) — GST rebate deemed not to be reimbursement; 67.1 — Expenses for food, etc.

**Interpretation Bulletins**: IT-254R2: Fishermen — employees and seafarers — value of rations and quarters; IT-518R: Food, beverages and entertainment expenses.

**Information Circulars**: 73-21R7: Away from home expenses.

**Forms**: TL2: Claim for meals and lodging expenses.

(h) **travel expenses** — where the taxpayer, in the year,

　(i) was ordinarily required to carry on the duties of the office or employment away from the employer's place of business or in different places, and

　(ii) was required under the contract of employment to pay the travel expenses incurred by the taxpayer in the performance of the duties of the office or employment,

amounts expended by the taxpayer in the year (other than motor vehicle expenses) for travelling in the course of the office or employment, except where the taxpayer

　(iii) received an allowance for travel expenses that was, because of subparagraph 6(1)(b)(v), (vi) or (vii), not included in computing the taxpayer's income for the year, or

　(iv) claims a deduction for the year under paragraph (e), (f) or (g);

**Related Provisions**: 6(8) — GST rebate included in income; 8(1)(h.1) — Motor vehicle travel expenses; 8(1)(j) — Auto and aircraft costs; 8(4) — Limitation — meals; 8(9) — Limitation — aircraft expenses; 8(10) — Employer's certificate; 67.1 — 50% limitation on expenses for meals; 81(3.1) — No tax on allowance or reimbursement for part-time employee's travel expenses; Reg. 102(2)(d)(i) — Effect of deduction on source withholdings.

**Notes**: 8(1)(h) amended by 1991 technical bill, effective 1988, to exclude motor vehicle expenses, now dealt with under 8(1)(h.1).

**Interpretation Bulletins**: IT-266: Taxation of members of provincial legislative assemblies; IT-421R2: Benefits to individuals, corporations and shareholders from loans or debt; IT-522R: Food, beverages and entertainment expenses; IT-522R: Vehicle, travel and sales expenses of employees.

**Information Circulars**: 73-21R7: Away from home expenses; 74-6R2: Power saw expenses.

**I.T. Technical News**: No. 12 (1998 deduction limits and benefit rates for automobiles).

**Forms**: T777: Statement of employment expenses; T2200: Declaration of conditions of employment; TD1X: Statement of remuneration and expenses; T4044: Employment expenses [guide].

(h.1) **motor vehicle travel expenses** — where the taxpayer, in the year,

　(i) was ordinarily required to carry on the duties of the office or employment away from the employer's place of business or in different places, and

　(ii) was required under the contract of employment to pay motor vehicle expenses incurred in the performance of the duties of the office or employment,

amounts expended by the taxpayer in the year in respect of motor vehicle expenses incurred for travelling in the course of the office or employment, except where the taxpayer

　(iii) received an allowance for motor vehicle expenses that was, because of paragraph 6(1)(b), not included in computing the taxpayer's income for the year, or

　(iv) claims a deduction for the year under paragraph (f);

**Related Provisions**: 6(8) — GST rebate included in income; 8(1)(j) — Motor vehicle and aircraft costs; 8(10) — Certificate of employer; 18(1)(r) — Limitation on employer deductibility; 67.3 — Limitation re cost of leasing passenger vehicle; 81(3.1) — No tax on allowance or reimbursement for part-time employee's travel expenses; Reg. 102(2)(d)(i) — Effect of deduction on source withholdings.

**Notes**: 8(1)(h.1) added by 1991 technical bill, effective 1988. Motor vehicle expenses were previously dealt with together with other travelling expenses under 8(1)(h).

**Interpretation Bulletins**: IT-421R2: Benefits to individuals, corporations and shareholders from loans or debt; IT-522R: Vehicle, travel and sales expenses of employees.

**I.T. Technical News**: No. 12 (1998 deduction limits and benefit rates for automobiles).

**Forms**: TD1X: Statement of remuneration and expenses; T777: Statement of employment expenses; T2200: Declaration of conditions of employment; T4044: Employment expenses [guide].

(i) **dues and other expenses of performing duties** — amounts paid by the taxpayer in the year as

(i) annual professional membership dues the payment of which was necessary to maintain a professional status recognized by statute,

(ii) office rent, or salary to an assistant or substitute, the payment of which by the officer or employee was required by the contract of employment,

(iii) the cost of supplies that were consumed directly in the performance of the duties of the office or employment and that the officer or employee was required by the contract of employment to supply and pay for,

(iv) annual dues to maintain membership in a trade union as defined

(A) by section 3 of the *Canada Labour Code*, or

(B) in any provincial statute providing for the investigation, conciliation or settlement of industrial disputes,

or to maintain membership in an association of public servants the primary object of which is to promote the improvement of the members' conditions of employment or work,

(v) annual dues that were, pursuant to the provisions of a collective agreement, retained by the taxpayer's employer from the taxpayer's remuneration and paid to a trade union or association designated in subparagraph (iv) of which the taxpayer was not a member,

(vi) dues to a parity or advisory committee or similar body, the payment of which was required under the laws of a province in respect of the employment for the year, and

(vii) dues to a professions board, the payment of which was required under the laws of a province,

to the extent that the taxpayer has not been reimbursed, and is not entitled to be reimbursed in respect thereof;

**Related Provisions**: 6(8) — GST rebate included in income; 8(1)(l.1) — Employer's portion of UI/EI premiums and CPP contributions deductible; 8(5) — Certain dues not deductible; 8(10) — Employer's certificate; 8(11) — GST rebate deemed not to be reimbursement; 8(13) — Limitation on home office expenses; Reg. 102(2)(d)(i) — Effect of deduction on source withholdings.

**Notes**: This amount is claimed on Line 212 of the T1 General income tax return; the T1 Guide notes that only amounts "relating to employment" should be claimed. A person carrying on business in a professional practice should instead deduct professional membership dues against income from that business or practice.

Even though 8(1)(i) allows a deduction for union dues, strike pay received is not taxable: *Fries*, [1990] 2 C.T.C. 439 (SCC). See Notes to s. 3. Also, an amount paid as additional dues to fund a strike is deductible as "annual" dues even where it is a one-time assessment: *Lucas*, [1987] 2 C.T.C. 23 (FCTD).

See Notes to 8(13) re meaning of "required".

8(1)(i)(vii) added by 1995-97 technical bill, effective 1996. It allows deduction of dues that an employee is required to pay to a professions board such as *L'Office de professions du Québec*.

**Regulations**: 100(3)(b) (deduction of dues by employer reduces source withholding).

**Interpretation Bulletins**: IT-103R: Dues paid to a union or to a parity or advisory committee; IT-158R2: Employees' professional membership dues; IT-352R2: Employees' expenses, including work space in home expenses.

**Information Circulars**: 74-6R2: Power saw expenses.

**Forms**: T1 General — Line 212; T777: Statement of employment expenses; T2200: Declaration of conditions of employment; TD1X: Statement of remuneration and expenses; T4044: Employment expenses [guide].

(j) **motor vehicle and aircraft costs** — where a deduction may be made under paragraph (f), (h) or (h.1) in computing the taxpayer's income from an office or employment for a taxation year,

(i) any interest paid by the taxpayer in the year on borrowed money used for the purpose of acquiring, or on an amount payable for the acquisition of, property that is

(A) a motor vehicle that is used, or

(B) an aircraft that is required for use

in the performance of the duties of the taxpayer's office or employment, and

(ii) such part, if any, of the capital cost to the taxpayer of

(A) a motor vehicle that is used, or

(B) an aircraft that is required for use

in the performance of the duties of the office or employment as is allowed by regulation;

**Related Provisions**: 6(8) — GST rebate included in income or reduces capital cost of vehicle or aircraft; 8(1)(f) — Salesman's expenses; 8(1)(q) — Artists' employment expenses; 8(9) — Limitation — aircraft expenses; 13(7) — Capital cost allowance — rules applicable; 13(7.1) — Deemed capital cost of certain property; 13(11) — Deductions under 8(1)(j)(ii) deemed claimed as CCA; 67.2 — Interest on money borrowed for passenger vehicle; 67.3 — Limitation re cost of leasing passenger vehicle; 80(9)(c) — Reduction of capital cost on debt forgiveness ignored for purposes of para. 8(1)(j); 80.4 — Loans; Reg. 102(2)(d)(i) — Effect of deduction on source withholdings.

**Notes**: 8(1)(j) amended by 1991 technical bill, retroactive to 1988, to change "automobile" to "motor vehicle" so as to apply to vans and pick-ups (see 248(1)); to add reference to (h.1); and to apply to interest on the balance of a debt incurred when buying the vehicle or aircraft.

**Regulations**: 1100(1)(a)(x), (x.1) (CCA rate is 30%).

**Interpretation Bulletins**: IT-421R2: Benefits to individuals, corporations and shareholders from loans or debt; IT-478R2: CCA — recapture and terminal loss; IT-504R2: Visual artists and writers;

**S. 8(1)(j)**      Income Tax Act, Part I, Division B

IT-522R: Vehicle, travel and sales expenses of employees; IT-525R: Performing artists.

**I.T. Technical News**: No. 12 (1998 deduction limits and benefit rates for automobiles).

**Forms**: T777: Statement of employment expenses; TD1X: Statement of remuneration and expenses; T4044: Employment expenses [guide].

(k), (l) [Repealed under former Act]

**Notes**: 8(1)(k) and (l) repealed by 1988 tax reform. These were deductions for unemployment insurance premiums and Canada Pension Plan contributions. A credit is now provided in 118.7 instead.

(l.1) **C.P.P. contributions and U.I.A. [E.I.] premiums** — any amount payable by the taxpayer in the year

  (i) as an employer's premium under the *Employment Insurance Act*, or

  (ii) as an employer's contribution under the *Canada Pension Plan* or under a provincial pension plan as defined in section 3 of the *Canada Pension Plan*,

in respect of salary, wages or other remuneration, including gratuities, paid to an individual employed by the taxpayer as an assistant or substitute to perform the duties of the taxpayer's office or employment if an amount is deductible by the taxpayer for the year under subparagraph (i)(ii) in respect of that individual;

**Related Provisions**: 8(1)(i) — Expenses of performing duties; 60(e) — Deduction for ½ of self-employed person's CPP contributions; 118.7 — Credit for taxpayer's own CPP contributions; 126.1 — Employer's UI premium tax credit for 1993.

**Notes**: EI premiums and CPP contributions paid by an employer carrying on business are deductible under 9(1) as ordinary business expenses, pursuant to generally accepted accounting principles. 8(1)(l.1) applies only to an employer whose deduction for employee expenses arises as a deduction from employment income under 8(1)(i)(ii). Premiums and contributions paid by the employee generate a credit under s. 118.7 (for self-employed persons there is also a deduction under 60(e)).

*Unemployment Insurance Act* changed to *Employment Insurance Act* by EI bill (S.C. 1996, c. 23), effective June 30, 1996.

**Interpretation Bulletins**: IT-352R2: Employee's expenses, including work space in home expenses.

(m) **employee's registered pension plan contributions** — the amount in respect of contributions to registered pension plans that, by reason of subsection 147.2(4), is deductible in computing the taxpayer's income for the year;

**Related Provisions**: 20(1)(q) — Employer's contribution to registered pension plan; 60(j) — Transfer of superannuation benefits; 60(j.01) — Transfer of surplus; 60(j.02) — Payment to registered pension plan; 60(j.03) — Repayments of pre-1990 pension benefits; 60(j.04) — Repayments of post-1989 pension benefits; 60.2(1) — Refund of undeducted past service AVCs; 127.52(1)(a) — Limitation on deduction for minimum tax purposes; 146(1)"earned income"(a)(i), 146(1)"earned income"(c)(i) — Earned income for RRSP counted before deduction under 8(1)(m); 146(5) — Amount of RRSP premium deductible; 146(16) — RRSP — deduction on transfer of funds; 149 — Exemptions.

**Notes**: 8(1)(m) amended by 1990 pension bill, effective 1991. Before 1991, it provided specific rules for deductible employee RRSP contributions, with a cap of $3,500. See now 147.2(4).

**Regulations**: 100(3)(a) (deduction of RPP contributions from payroll reduces source withholding).

**Interpretation Bulletins**: IT-167R6: Registered pension plans — employee's contributions.

**Information Circulars**: 72-13R8: Employee's pension plans.

**Advance Tax Rulings**: ATR-2: Contribution to pension plan for past service.

(m.1) [Repealed under former Act]

**Notes**: 8(1)(m.1) repealed by 1990 pension bill, effective 1991. It provided a deduction for mandatory employee RPP contributions in excess of $3,500 per year (former 8(1)(m) allowed the first $3,500). See 147.2(4) for contributions now deductible.

(m.2) **employee RCA contributions** — an amount contributed by the taxpayer in the year to a pension plan in respect of services rendered by the taxpayer where the plan is a prescribed plan established by an enactment of Canada or a province or where

  (i) the plan is a retirement compensation arrangement,

  (ii) the amount was paid to a custodian (within the meaning assigned by the definition "retirement compensation arrangement" in subsection 248(1)) of the arrangement who is resident in Canada, and

  (iii) either

    (A) the taxpayer was required, by the terms of the taxpayer's office or employment, to contribute the amount, and the total of the amounts contributed to the plan in the year by the taxpayer does not exceed the total of the amounts contributed to the plan in the year by any other person in respect of the taxpayer, or

    (B) the plan is a pension plan the registration of which under this Act was revoked (other than a plan the registration of which was revoked as of the effective date of its registration) and the amount was contributed in accordance with the terms of the plan as last registered;

    (C) [Repealed]

**Related Provisions**: 18(11)(e) — No deduction for interest on money borrowed to make deductible contribution; 60(t)(ii) — Amount included under para. 56(1)(x) or (z) or subsec. 70(2); 60(u)(ii) — Deduction where amount included under para. 56(1)(y); 146(1)"earned income"(a)(i), 146(1)"earned income"(c)(i) — Earned income for RRSP counted before deduction for 8(1)(m.2); 207.6(6) — Rules re prescribed plan or arrangement.

**Notes**: See Notes to 248(1)"retirement compensation arrangement".

8(1)(m.2)(iii)(C) added by 1992 technical bill, effective 1992, but repealed retroactive to its introduction by 1993 technical bill. It referred to "a prescribed plan or arrangement", words which were incorporated into the opening words of 8(1)(m.2) by 1993 technical bill. For 1990 and 1991, ignore everything in the opening words after the first "where".

8(1)(m.2) added by 1990 pension bill, effective 1989 and later taxation years.

**Regulations**: 100(3)(b.1) (payroll deduction of employee contribution reduces source withholding); 6802, 6802.1(1) (prescribed plans).

**Forms**: T4041: Retirement compensation arrangements guide.

(n) **salary reimbursement** — an amount paid by or on behalf of the taxpayer in the year pursuant to an arrangement (other than an arrangement described in subparagraph (b)(ii) of the definition "top-up disability payment" in subsection 6(17)) under which the taxpayer is required to reimburse any amount paid to the taxpayer for a period throughout which the taxpayer did not perform the duties of the office or employment, to the extent that

(i) the amount so paid to the taxpayer for the period was included in computing the taxpayer's income from an office or employment, and

(ii) the total of amounts so reimbursed does not exceed the total of amounts received by the taxpayer for the period throughout which the taxpayer did not perform the duties of the office or employment;

**Related Provisions**: 8(1)(n.1) — Reimbursement of top-up disability payments.

**Notes**: Opening words of 8(1)(n) amended by 1995-97 technical bill, effective for arrangements entered into after August 10, 1994, to add the parenthetical exclusion of arrangements under 6(17). A deduction for such repayments is provided under 8(1)(n.1).

(n.1) **reimbursement of disability payments** — where,

(i) as a consequence of the receipt of a payment (in this paragraph referred to as the "deferred payment") from an insurer, a payment (in this paragraph referred to as the "reimbursement payment") is made by or on behalf of an individual to an employer or former employer of the individual pursuant to an arrangement described in subparagraph (b)(ii) of the definition "top-up disability payment" in subsection 6(17), and

(ii) the reimbursement payment is made

(A) in the year, other than within the first 60 days of the year if the deferred payment was received in the immediately preceding taxation year, or

(B) within 60 days after the end of the year, if the deferred payment was received in the year,

an amount equal to the lesser of

(iii) the amount included under paragraph 6(1)(f) in respect of the deferred payment in computing the individual's income for any taxation year, and

(iv) the amount of the reimbursement payment;

**Notes**: 8(1)(n.1) added by 1995-97 technical bill, effective for reimbursement payments made after August 10, 1994. It provides a deduction to an individual who reimburses a top-up disability payment (see 6(17) and (18)). The deduction is limited to the amount included under 6(1)(f) on the payment by the insurer. For a plan funded solely by employee contributions, there is no 6(1)(f) inclusion, so there is no deduction for the reimbursement. If employer contributions were made to the plan, the reimbursement will be deductible, but reduced for the individual's contributions which reduced the 6(1)(f) inclusion.

(o) **forfeited amounts** — where at the end of the year the rights of any person to receive benefits under a salary deferral arrangement in respect of the taxpayer have been extinguished or no person has any further right to receive any amount under the arrangement, the amount, if any, by which the total of all deferred amounts under the arrangement included in computing the taxpayer's income for the year and preceding taxation years as benefits under paragraph 6(1)(a) exceeds the total of

(i) all such deferred amounts received by any person in that year or preceding taxation years out of or under the arrangement,

(ii) all such deferred amounts receivable by any person in subsequent taxation years out of or under the arrangement, and

(iii) all amounts deducted under this paragraph in computing the taxpayer's income for preceding taxation years in respect of deferred amounts under the arrangement;

**Related Provisions**: 12(1)(n.2) — Inclusions — forfeited salary deferral amounts.

(o.1) **Idem** — an amount that is deductible in computing the taxpayer's income for the year because of subsection 144(9);

**Related Provisions**: 6(1)(d) — Income inclusion from allocations under employees profit sharing plan.

**Notes**: 8(1)(o.1) added by 1993 technical bill, effective 1992.

**Interpretation Bulletins**: IT-379R: Employees profit sharing plans — allocations to beneficiaries.

(p) **musical instrument costs** — where the taxpayer was employed in the year as a musician and as a term of the employment was required to provide a musical instrument for a period in the year, an amount (not exceeding the taxpayer's income for the year from the employment, computed without reference to this paragraph) equal to the total of

(i) amounts expended by the taxpayer before the end of the year for the maintenance, rental and insurance of the instrument for that period, except to the extent that the amounts are otherwise deducted in computing the taxpayer's income for any taxation year, and

(ii) such part, if any, of the capital cost to the taxpayer of the instrument as is allowed by regulation; and

**Related Provisions**: 6(8) — GST rebate included in income or reduces capital cost of instrument; 8(1)(q) — Artists' employment expenses deduction; 13(7), (7.1) — Capital cost allowance — rules applicable; 13(11) — Deduction under 8(1)(p)(ii) deemed claimed

**S. 8(1)(p)**  Income Tax Act, Part I, Division B

as CCA; 80(9)(c) — Reduction of capital cost on debt forgiveness ignored for purposes of 8(1)(p).

**Regulations**: IT-379R: Employees profit sharing plans — allocations to beneficiaries; 1100(1)(a)(viii); Sch. II:Cl. 8(i) (CCA rate is 20%).

**Interpretation Bulletins [para. 8(1)(p)]**: IT-257R: Canada Council grants; IT-478R2: CCA — recapture and terminal loss; IT-525R: Performing artists.

(q) **artists' employment expenses** — where the taxpayer's income for the year from the office or employment includes income from an artistic activity

(i) that was the creation by the taxpayer of, but did not include the reproduction of, paintings, prints, etchings, drawings, sculptures or similar works of art,

(ii) that was the composition by the taxpayer of a dramatic, musical or literary work,

(iii) that was the performance by the taxpayer of a dramatic or musical work as an actor, dancer, singer or musician, or

(iv) in respect of which the taxpayer was a member of a professional artists' association that is certified by the Minister of Communications,

amounts paid by the taxpayer before the end of the year in respect of expenses incurred for the purpose of earning the income from those activities to the extent that they were not deductible in computing the taxpayer's income for a preceding taxation year, but not exceeding a single amount in respect of all such offices and employments of the taxpayer equal to the amount, if any, by which

(v) the lesser of $1,000 and 20% of the total of all amounts each of which is the taxpayer's income from an office or employment for the year, before deducting any amount under this section, that was income from an artistic activity described in any of subparagraphs (i) to (iv),

exceeds

(vi) the total of all amounts deducted by the taxpayer for the year under paragraph (j) or (p) in respect of costs or expenses incurred for the purpose of earning the income from such an activity for the year.

**Notes**: The *Department of Canadian Heritage Act* (S.C. 1995, c. 11), in force July 12, 1996, provides:

46. **Other references** — Every reference made to the Minister of Communications, the Minister of Multiculturalism and Citizenship and the Secretary of State of Canada in relation to any matter to which the powers, duties and functions of the Minister of Canadian Heritage extend by virtue of this Act, in any other Act of Parliament or in any order, regulation or other instrument made under any Act of Parliament shall, unless the context otherwise requires, be read as a reference to the Minister of Canadian Heritage.

8(1)(q) added by 1991 technical bill, effective for amounts paid after 1990. Note that the activity must both fall into one of (i) through (iv) *and* be "artistic".

**Interpretation Bulletins**: IT-257R: Canada Council grants; IT-504R2: Visual artists and writers; IT-525R: Performing artists.

**Forms [para. 8(1)(q)]**: T777: Statement of employment expenses; T4044: Employment expenses [guide].

**(1.1)** [Not included in R.S.C. 1985]

**Notes**: 8(1.1) added by 1990 pension bill. Because it applied to the 1986 taxation year only, it was not included in the R.S.C. 1985 (5th Supp.) consolidation.

**(2) General limitation** — Except as permitted by this section, no deductions shall be made in computing a taxpayer's income for a taxation year from an office or employment.

**Notes**: This rule is the converse of that for self-employed individuals, who can deduct any expenses to earn business income that are not specifically prohibited, when calculating income under generally accepted commercial principles for purposes of 9(1).

**Interpretation Bulletins**: IT-352R2: Employee's expenses, including work space in home expenses; IT-377R: Director's, executor's or juror's fees; IT-478R2: CCA — recapture and terminal loss.

**(3)** [Repealed under former Act]

**Notes**: 8(3) repealed by 1988 tax reform, effective 1988. This provision restricted the availability of the employment expense deduction under 8(1)(a) (repealed at the same time).

**(4) Meals** — An amount expended in respect of a meal consumed by a taxpayer who is an officer or employee shall not be included in computing the amount of a deduction under paragraph (1)(f) or (h) unless the meal was consumed during a period while the taxpayer was required by the taxpayer's duties to be away, for a period of not less than twelve hours, from the municipality where the employer's establishment to which the taxpayer ordinarily reported for work was located and away from the metropolitan area, if there is one, where it was located.

**Related Provisions**: 67.1 — 50% limitation on expenses for meals.

**Interpretation Bulletins**: IT-522R: Vehicle, travel and sales expenses of employees.

**Information Circulars**: 73-21R7: Away from home expenses.

**Forms**: T777: Statement of employment expenses; TD1X: Statement of remuneration and expenses (for use by commission remunerated employees); T4044: Employment expenses [guide].

**(5) Dues not deductible** — Notwithstanding subparagraphs (1)(i)(i), (iv), (vi) and (vii), dues are not deductible under those subparagraphs in computing a taxpayer's income from an office or employment to the extent that they are, in effect, levied

(a) for or under a superannuation fund or plan;

(b) for or under a fund or plan for annuities, insurance (other than professional or malpractice liability insurance that is necessary to maintain a professional status recognized by statute) or similar benefits; or

(c) for any other purpose not directly related to the ordinary operating expenses of the committee or similar body, association, board or trade union, as the case may be.

**Related Provisions**: 8(1)(i)(i), (iv) — Professional and union dues deductible.

**Notes**: Opening words of 8(5) and 8(5)(c) amended by 1995-97 technical bill, effective 1996, to add reference to 8(1)(i)(vii) in the opening words and the word "board" in 8(5)(c).

**Interpretation Bulletins**: IT-103R: Dues paid to a union or to a parity or advisory committee; IT-158R2: Employees' professional membership dues.

**(6)–(8)** [Repealed under former Act]

**Notes**: 8(6), (7) and (8) repealed by 1990 pension bill, effective 1991. 8(6) defined "contribution limit" for the pre-1991 8(1)(m). 8(7) was a special rule for RPP contributions by teachers. 8(8) allowed a deduction for mandatory employee contributions to an RPP for arrears.

**(9) Presumption** — Notwithstanding any other provision of this Act, the total of all amounts that would otherwise be deductible by a taxpayer pursuant to paragraph (1)(f), (h) or (j) for travelling in the course of the taxpayer's employment in an aircraft that is owned or rented by the taxpayer, may not exceed an amount that is reasonable in the circumstances having regard to the relative cost and availability of other modes of transportation.

**Related Provisions**: 67 — General requirement that expenses be reasonable.

**Interpretation Bulletins**: IT-522R: Vehicle, travel and sales expenses of employees.

**(10) Certificate of employer** — An amount otherwise deductible for a taxation year under paragraph (1)(a), (f), (h) or (h.1) or subparagraph (1)(i)(ii) or (iii) by a taxpayer shall not be deducted unless a prescribed form signed by the taxpayer's employer certifying that the conditions set out in that paragraph or subparagraph, as the case may be, were met in the year in respect of the taxpayer is filed with the taxpayer's return of income for the year.

### Proposed Amendment — 8(10)

**(10) Certificate of employer** — An amount otherwise deductible for a taxation year under paragraph (1)(f), (h) or (h.1) or subparagraph (1)(i)(ii) or (iii) by a taxpayer shall not be deducted unless a prescribed form signed by the taxpayer's employer certifying that the conditions set out in that paragraph or subparagraph, as the case may be, were met in the year in respect of the taxpayer is filed with the taxpayer's return of income for the year.

**Application**: Bill C-43 (First Reading September 20, 2000), subsec. 2(2), will amend subsec. 8(10) to read as above, applicable to 1998 et seq.

**Technical Notes**: Subsection 8(10) provides that expenses will not be deductible by an employee under certain provisions unless the employee files with the return of income a prescribed form signed by the employer to the effect that the employee met the requirements of the relevant provisions for the deductibility of such expenses. The amendment to subsection 8(10) deletes a reference to paragraph 8(1)(a) and is strictly consequential on the repeal of that paragraph. The deduction available under that paragraph has been replaced with an equivalent exemption under subsection 81(4). For information on this exemption, see the commentary on new subsection 81(4).

### Proposed Amendment — 8(10)

**(10) Certificate of employer** — An amount otherwise deductible for a taxation year under paragraph (1)(c), (f), (h) or (h.1) or subparagraph (1)(i)(ii) or (iii) by a taxpayer shall not be deducted unless a prescribed form, signed by the taxpayer's employer certifying that the conditions set out in the applicable provision were met in the year in respect of the taxpayer, is filed with the taxpayer's return of income for the year.

**Application**: The December 21, 2000 draft legislation, subsec. 2(2), will amend subsec. 8(10) to read as above, applicable to 2001 et seq.

**Technical Notes**: Subsection 8(10) provides that a deduction will not be allowed to an employee under certain provisions unless the employee files with the return of income a prescribed form signed by the employer to the effect that the employee met the requirements of the relevant provisions. The amendment to subsection 8(10) adds a reference to paragraph 8(1)(c) with respect to the requirements set out in subparagraphs 8(1)(c)(i) and (ii).

**Related Provisions**: 67 — General requirement that expenses be reasonable; 81(4)(b) — Certification re exemption for volunteer emergency worker.

**Notes**: 8(10) amended by 1998 Budget, effective for 1998 and later taxation years, to add reference to 8(1)(a).

8(10) amended by 1991 technical bill, effective 1988, to add reference to 8(1)(h.1).

**Interpretation Bulletins**: IT-352R2: Employees' expenses, including work space in home expenses; IT-522R: Vehicle, travel and sales expenses of employees.

**Information Circulars**: 73-21R7: Away from home expenses; 74-6R2: Power saw expenses.

**Forms**: T2200: Declaration of conditions of employment; T4044: Employment expenses [guide].

**(11) Goods and services tax** — For the purposes of this section and section 6, the amount of any rebate paid or payable to a taxpayer under the *Excise Tax Act* in respect of the goods and services tax shall be deemed not to be an amount that is reimbursed to the taxpayer or to which the taxpayer is entitled.

**Related Provisions**: 6(8) — GST rebate included in income.

**Notes**: 8(11) added by 1990 GST, effective 1991.

**(12) Forfeiture of securities by employee** — If, in a taxation year,

    (a) an employee is deemed by subsection 7(2) to have disposed of a security (as defined in subsection 7(7)) held by a trust,

    (b) the trust disposed of the security to the person that issued the security,

    (c) the disposition occurred as a result of the employee not meeting the conditions necessary for title to the security to vest in the employee, and

    (d) the amount paid by the person to acquire the security from the trust or to redeem or cancel the security did not exceed the amount paid to the person for the security,

the following rules apply:

(e) there may be deducted in computing the employee's income for the year from employment the amount, if any, by which

(i) the amount of the benefit deemed by subsection 7(1) to have been received by the employee in the year or a preceding taxation year in respect of the security

exceeds

(ii) any amount deducted under paragraph 110(1)(d) or (d.1) in computing the employee's taxable income for the year or a preceding taxation year in respect of that benefit, and

(f) notwithstanding any other provision of this Act, the employee's gain or loss from the disposition of the security is deemed to be nil and section 84 does not apply to deem a dividend to have been received in respect of the disposition.

**Notes**: 8(12) amended by 1998 Budget, retroactive to its introduction, to change "share" to "security" and "corporation" to "person". See Notes to 7(1).

8(12) added by 1991 technical bill, effective for 1988 and later taxation years.

**Interpretation Bulletins**: IT-113R4: Benefits to employees — stock options.

**(13) Work space in home** — Notwithstanding paragraphs (1)(f) and (i),

(a) no amount is deductible in computing an individual's income for a taxation year from an office or employment in respect of any part (in this subsection referred to as the "work space") of a self-contained domestic establishment in which the individual resides, except to the extent that the work space is either

(i) the place where the individual principally performs the duties of the office or employment, or

(ii) used exclusively during the period in respect of which the amount relates for the purpose of earning income from the office or employment and used on a regular and continuous basis for meeting customers or other persons in the ordinary course of performing the duties of the office or employment;

(b) where the conditions set out in subparagraph (a)(i) or (ii) are met, the amount in respect of the work space that is deductible in computing the individual's income for the year from the office or employment shall not exceed the individual's income for the year from the office or employment, computed without reference to any deduction in respect of the work space; and

(c) any amount in respect of a work space that was, solely because of paragraph (b), not deducti-

ble in computing the individual's income for the immediately preceding taxation year from the office or employment shall be deemed to be an amount in respect of a work space that is otherwise deductible in computing the individual's income for the year from that office or employment and that, subject to paragraph (b), may be deducted in computing the individual's income for the year from the office or employment.

**Related Provisions**: 18(12) — Parallel rule for self-employed individual.

**Notes**: CCRA Views doc. 2000-0022015 states:

In your letter, you stated that the office in your home meets local zoning regulations. There is no statutory requirement that the work space be zoned or assessed for commercial or business use in order for an individual to be entitled, if that individual otherwise qualifies, to deduct an amount in respect of a work space in the home.

...

Confusion has arisen over the reference to the word "required" in the Act and form T2200 and the fact that a work at home arrangement may be voluntarily entered into by an employee. Although a work at home arrangement may be voluntarily entered into, in our view, once an employee and the employer have entered into a formal work at home arrangement, the employee is "required" to provide a work space in his or her home and pay for some additional costs associated with providing this work space. In our view, an employee under an informal work at home arrangement would not be entitled to deduct office in the home expenses.

8(13) added by 1991 technical bill, effective 1991, to limit employees' home office expenses in the same way that 1988 tax reform did for the self-employed (see 18(12)).

**Interpretation Bulletins**: IT-352R2: Employee's expenses, including work space in home expenses.

**Forms**: T777: Statement of employment expenses; T4044: Employment expenses [guide].

**Definitions [s. 8]**: "additional voluntary contribution", "amount", "annuity", "automobile", "borrowed money", "business" — 248(1); "Canada" — 255; "capital cost" — 13(7)–(7.4), 128.1(1)(c), 128.1(4)(c); "common-law partner", "common-law partnership" — 248(1); "Commonwealth" — *Interpretation Act* 35(1); "connected" — 251(6); "deferred amount", "employed", "employee", "employer", "employment", "goods and services tax", "individual", "Minister" — 248(1); "month" — *Interpretation Act* 35(1); "motor vehicle", "office", "person", "prescribed", "property" — 248(1); "province" — *Interpretation Act* 35(1); "registered pension plan", "regulation" — 248(1); "reimbursement payment" — 8(1)(n.1)(i); "resident" — 250; "retirement compensation arrangement", "salary deferral arrangement", "salary or wages" — 248(1); "security" — 7(7); "self-contained domestic establishment", "share" — 248(1); "taxable income" — 2(2), 248(1); "taxation year" — 249; "taxpayer" — 248(1); "trust" — 104(1), 248(1), (3).

**Interpretation Bulletins [s. 8]**: IT-168R3: Athletes and players employed by football, hockey and similar clubs.

## Subdivision b — Income or Loss from a Business or Property

### Basic Rules

**9. (1) Income** — Subject to this Part, a taxpayer's income for a taxation year from a business or prop-

Subdivision b — Income or Loss from a Business or Property                                   S. 10(1)

erty is the taxpayer's profit from that business or property for the year.

**Related Provisions**: 9(3) — Capital gains and losses not included; 18 — Limitations on various deductions; 18.1 — Limitation on deduction for matchable expenditure; 19, 19.01, 19.1 — Limitations on deductions for advertising expenses; 23 — Sale of inventory after ceasing to carry on business; 80(13) — Income inclusion on forgiveness of debt; 95(1) — Extended definition of "income from property" for FAPI purposes; 112(4)–(5.6) — Restrictions on losses on shares held as inventory; 115(1)(a)(ii) — Non-resident's taxable income earned in Canada; 142.5(1) — Mark-to-market rules for securities held by financial institutions; 143.2(6) — Reduction in expenditure allowed for tax shelter investment; 247 — Calculation of profit on transactions with non-residents; 248(24) — Equity and consolidation methods of accounting not to be used; Canada-U.S. tax treaty, Art. VII — Business profits of U.S. resident; Art. XIV — Independent personal services; Art. XVI — Artistes and athletes; Art. XVII — Withholding re personal services.

**Notes**: "Profit" is normally to be calculated in accordance with "well accepted principles of business (or accounting) practice" or "well accepted principles of commercial trading": *Symes*, [1994] 1 C.T.C. 40 at 52 (SCC); *Canderel Ltd.*, [1998] 2 C.T.C. 35 (SCC). These are usually but not always the same as generally accepted accounting principles (GAAP), set out in the Canadian Institute of Chartered Accountants' *CICA Handbook*. However, in many cases the Act provides specifically for different treatment (in 9(3) and ss. 10–37). Under *Canderel*, the determination of profit is a question of law, not to be delegated to accountants.

Penalties and fines are normally deductible if they are incurred in the course of doing business: *65302 British Columbia Ltd. (formerly Veekans Poultry)*, [2000] 1 C.T.C. 57 (SCC).

For discussion of whether a person is earning business income under 9(1) (as an independent contractor) or employment income, see Notes to 248(1)"employee".

For discussion of when there may be no business because there is no reasonable expectation of profit, see Notes to 18(1)(h).

**Interpretation Bulletins**: IT-75R3: Scholarships, fellowships, bursaries, prizes, and research; IT-92R2: Income of contractors; IT-95R: Foreign exchange gains and losses; IT-104R2: Deductibility of fines or penalties; IT-129R: Lawyers' trust accounts and disbursements; IT-200: Surface rentals and farming operations; IT-213R: Prizes from lottery schemes and giveaway contests; IT-223: Overhead expense insurance vs. income insurance; IT-233R: Lease-option agreements; sale-leaseback agreements; IT-257R: Canada Council, grants; IT-261R: Prepayment of rents; IT-314: Income of dealers in oil and gas leases; IT-359R2: Premiums and other amounts re leases; IT-373R: Farm woodlots and tree farms; IT-425: Miscellaneous farm income; IT-434R: Rental of real property by individual; IT-454: Business transactions prior to incorporation; IT-459: Adventure or concern in the nature of trade; IT-493: Agency cooperative corporations. See also list at end of s. 9 and annotation to 18(1)(a).

**Information Circulars**: 77-11: Sales tax reassessments — deductibility in computing income.

**I.T. Technical News**: No. 1 (sales commission expenses of mutual-fund limited partnerships); No. 5 (lease agreements); No. 8 (proceeds of sale of a condominium — first closing date or second closing date; treatment of United States unitary state taxes); No. 12 ("millennium bug" expenditures); No. 16 (*Canderel, Toronto College Park* and *Ikea* cases; *Continental Bank* case).

**Advance Tax Rulings**: ATR-4: Exchange of interest rates; ATR-15: Employee stock option plan; ATR-20: Redemption premium on debentures; ATR-23: Private health services plan; ATR-45: Share appreciation rights plan; ATR-50: Structured settlement; ATR-62: Mutual fund distribution limited partnership — amortization of selling commissions.

**Forms**: T776: Statement of real estate rentals; T2032: Statement of professional activities; T2042: Statement of farming income and expenses; T2121: Fishing income and expense statement; T2124: Statement of business activities; T4002: Business and professional income [guide]; T4036: Rental income [guide].

**(2) Loss** — Subject to section 31, a taxpayer's loss for a taxation year from a business or property is the amount of the taxpayer's loss, if any, for the taxation year from that source computed by applying the provisions of this Act respecting computation of income from that source with such modifications as the circumstances require.

**Related Provisions**: 18 — Limitations on various deductions; 18.1 — Limitation on deduction for matchable expenditure; 96(8)(b), (c) — Business loss of partnership that previously had only non-resident partners; 103(2) — Meaning of "losses" in subsec. 103(1); 111(1)(a) — Carryover of loss to prior or later year; 111(8) — "non-capital loss"; 112(4)–(4.3) — Loss on share held as inventory.

**Notes**: For discussion of when business losses may be denied because there is no reasonable expectation of profit, see Notes to 18(1)(h).

**Interpretation Bulletins**: IT-328R3: Losses on shares on which dividends have been received. See also list at end of s. 9.

**I.T. Technical News**: No. 16 (*Tonn, Mastri, Mohammad* and *Kaye* cases).

**Advance Tax Rulings**: See under 9(1).

**(3) Gains and losses not included** — In this Act, "income from a property" does not include any capital gain from the disposition of that property and "loss from a property" does not include any capital loss from the disposition of that property.

**Notes**: Capital gains and losses are excluded from the calculation of income under s. 9 because they are dealt with separately under 3(b) and sections 38 through 55.

**Definitions [s. 9]**: "amount", "business" — 248(1); "capital gain" — 39(1)(a), 248(1); "capital loss" — 39(1)(b), 248(1); "property" — 248(1); "taxation year" — 11(2), 249; "taxpayer" — 248(1).

**Interpretation Bulletins [s. 9]**: IT-99R5: Legal and accounting fees; IT-102R2: Conversion of property, other than real property, from or to inventory; IT-189R2: Corporations used by practising members of professions; IT-216: Corporation holding property as agent for shareholder; IT-218R: Profit, capital gains and losses from the sale of real estate, including farmland and inherited land and conversion of real estate from capital property to inventory and vice versa; IT-273R2: Government assistance — general comments; IT-293R: Debtor's gain on settlement of debt; IT-297R2: Gifts in kind to charity and others; IT-346R: Commodity futures and certain commodities; IT-403R: Options on real estate; IT-404R: Payments to lottery ticket vendors; IT-417R2: Prepaid expenses and deferred charges; IT-423: Sale of sand, gravel or topsoil; IT-446R: Legacies; IT-461: Forfeited deposits; IT-479R: Transactions in securities; IT-490: Barter transactions; IT-504R2: Visual artists and writers.

**10. (1) Valuation of inventory** — For the purpose of computing a taxpayer's income for a taxation year from a business that is not an adventure or concern in the nature of trade, property described in an inventory shall be valued at the end of the year at the cost at which the taxpayer acquired the property or its fair market value at the end of the year, whichever is lower, or in a prescribed manner.

**Related Provisions**: 10(1.01) — Adventure in the nature of trade — no writedown until sale; 10(1.1) — Certain expenses included in cost; 10(2) — Valuation of inventory property;

**S. 10(1)**      Income Tax Act, Part I, Division B

12(1)(r) — Income inclusion — inventory adjustment; 28(1.1), (1.2) — Inventory of farming or fishing business; 86.1(4) — Value of shares in inventory after foreign spin-off; 87(2)(b) — Amalgamations — inventory; 96(8)(b) — Cost of inventory of partnership that previously had only non-resident partners; 112(4.1) — Fair market value of share held as inventory; 142.5(1) — Mark-to-market rules for securities held by financial institutions.

**Notes**: The costs of inventory are normally required to be included in the cost of inventory under 10(1) and deducted only when the inventory is sold, rather than when they are incurred.

The Supreme Court of Canada ruled in *Friesen*, [1995] 2 C.T.C. 369, that 10(1) could be used to claim a deduction by writing down inventory, including land inventory, even if the taxpayer owned only one asset in inventory. However, this was reversed by 10(1.01), for cases where the property is held as an adventure in the nature of trade.

10(1) amended by 1995-97 technical bill, effective on the same basis as the addition of 10(1.01). The substance of the amendments was to exclude an adventure in the nature of trade (now covered under 10(1.01)) and to clarify that the reference to cost is to the original cost of the property. Before the amendment, since 1972, read:

(1) For the purpose of computing income from a business, inventory shall be valued at its cost to the taxpayer or its fair market value, whichever is lower, or in such other manner as may be permitted by regulation.

**Regulations**: 1102(1)(b) (no capital cost allowance for property described in inventory); 1801 (inventory generally may be valued at fair market value); 1802 (valuation of animals).

**Interpretation Bulletins**: IT-51R2: Supplies on hand at end of a fiscal period; IT-102R2: Conversion of property, other than real property, from or to inventory; IT-142R3: Settlement of debts on the winding-up of a corporation; IT-153R3: Land developers — subdivision and development costs and carrying charges on land; IT-165R: Returnable containers; IT-328R3: Losses on shares on which dividends have been received; IT-459: Adventure or concern in the nature of trade; IT-504R2: Visual artists and writers. See also list at end of s. 10.

**(1.01) Adventures in the nature of trade** — For the purpose of computing a taxpayer's income from a business that is an adventure or concern in the nature of trade, property described in an inventory shall be valued at the cost at which the taxpayer acquired the property.

**Related Provisions**: 10(9) — Grandfathering of writedown taken before 10(1.01) applies; 10(10) — Writedown required before change in control of corporation; 18(14)–(16) — Superficial loss rule for property held as adventure in the nature of trade.

**Notes**: 10(1.01) added by 1995-97 technical bill, effective

(a) for taxation years that end after December 20, 1995;

(b) in respect of a business that is an adventure or concern in the nature of trade, for taxation years that end before December 21, 1995, except where

(i) the taxpayer's filing-due date for the year is after December 20, 1995, or

(ii) the taxpayer has valued the inventory of the business for that year at less than the cost at which the taxpayer acquired the property, which valuation was reflected in a return of income, notice of objection or notice of appeal filed or served under the Act before December 21, 1995; and

(c) in respect of a business that is an adventure or concern in the nature of trade, for fiscal periods of a partnership that end before December 21, 1995, except where

(i) the filing-due dates of all of the partners for their taxation years that include the end of the fiscal period are after December 20, 1995, or

(ii) the partnership has valued the inventory of the business for that fiscal period at less than the cost at which the partnership acquired the property, which valuation was reflected in a return of income, notice of objection or notice of appeal filed or served under the Act before December 21, 1995 by any partner.

10(1.01) implements the press release announcement of December 20, 1995, which effectively overturns the Supreme Court of Canada decision in *Friesen*, [1995] 2 C.T.C. 369. Under 10(1.01), inventory that has dropped in value cannot be written down (which would generate a loss for tax purposes) if the property is held as an adventure in the nature of trade. Thus, for example, if a taxpayer owns a single piece of land that was purchased for resale purposes, and it drops in value, it cannot be written down until it is sold.

The distinction between "business" and "adventure in the nature of trade" was not previously important in income tax law, despite the extensive case law on "income" vs. "capital property". It is relevant for GST purposes, however. For the CCRA's discussion, see GST Policy Statement P-059, "Business vs. Adventure or Concern in the Nature of Trade Relating to Sales of Real Property" (March 3, 1993), in David M. Sherman, *GST Memoranda, Bulletins & Policies* (Carswell, annual). See also Interpretation Bulletin IT-459, "Adventure or Concern in the Nature of Trade".

In *Stremler*, [2000] 2 C.T.C. 2172 (TCC), the Tax Court held that 10(1.01) does not restrict the annual deduction of carrying costs; it applies only to writedown of the inventory itself. Carrying costs were deductible under general accounting principles per *Canderel*, [1998] 2 C.T.C. 35 (SCC).

**Interpretation Bulletins**: IT-459: Adventure or concern in the nature of trade.

**(1.1) Certain expenses included in cost** — For the purposes of subsections (1), (1.01) and (10), where land is described in an inventory of a business of a taxpayer, the cost at which the taxpayer acquired the land shall include each amount that is

(a) described in paragraph 18(2)(a) or (b) in respect of the land and for which no deduction is permitted to the taxpayer, or to another person or partnership that is

(i) a person or partnership with whom the taxpayer does not deal at arm's length,

(ii) if the taxpayer is a corporation, a person or partnership that is a specified shareholder of the taxpayer, or

(iii) if the taxpayer is a partnership, a person or partnership whose share of any income or loss of the taxpayer is 10% or more; and

(b) not included in or added to the cost to that other person or partnership of any property otherwise than because of paragraph 53(1)(d.3) or subparagraph 53(1)(e)(xi).

**Notes**: 10(1.1) amended by 1995-97 technical bill, effective on the same basis as the addition of 10(1.01), effectively to extend its application to 10(1.01) and 10(10). From 1988 until the amendment took effect (generally December 21, 1995), read:

(1.1) For the purpose of subsection (1), the cost to a particular taxpayer of land that is described in the inventory of a business carried on by the taxpayer shall include each amount described in paragraph 18(2)(a) or (b) in respect of that land for which no deduction is permitted to the taxpayer or to another person in respect of whom the taxpayer was a person, corporation or partnership described in subparagraph (b)(i), (ii) or (iii) of the definition "interest on debt relating to the acquisition of land" in subsection 18(3), where that amount was not included in or added to the cost to that other person of any property otherwise than because of paragraph 53(1)(d.3) or subparagraph 53(1)(e)(xi).

10(1.1) previously amended by 1991 technical bill, retroactive to 1988.

**Interpretation Bulletins**: IT-153R3: Land developers — subdivision and development costs and carrying charges on land. See also list at end of s. 10.

**(2) Continuation of valuation** — Notwithstanding subsection (1), for the purpose of computing income for a taxation year from a business, the inventory at the commencement of the year shall be valued at the same amount as the amount at which it was valued at the end of the preceding taxation year for the purpose of computing income for that preceding year.

**Related Provisions**: 10(2.1) — Methods of valuation to be the same from year to year.

**Interpretation Bulletins**: See list at end of s. 10.

**(2.1) Methods of valuation to be same** — Where property described in an inventory of a taxpayer's business that is not an adventure or concern in the nature of trade is valued at the end of a taxation year in accordance with a method permitted under this section, that method shall, subject to subsection (6), be used in the valuation of property described in the inventory at the end of the following taxation year for the purpose of computing the taxpayer's income from the business unless the taxpayer, with the concurrence of the Minister and on any terms and conditions that are specified by the Minister, adopts another method permitted under this section.

**Notes**: 10(2.1) amended by 1995-97 technical bill, effective on the same basis as the addition of 10(1.01). The substance of the amendment was to exclude the rule from applying to property held as an adventure in the nature of trade. From 1990 until the amendment took effect (generally December 21, 1995), read:

(2.1) Where property described in the inventory of a business of a taxpayer at the end of a taxation year is valued in accordance with a method provided for under this section, that method shall, subject to subsection (6), be used in the valuation of property described in the inventory of that business at the end of the following taxation year for the purpose of computing the taxpayer's income from that business unless the taxpayer, with the concurrence of the Minister and on such terms and conditions as are specified by the Minister, adopts another method provided for under this section.

**Interpretation Bulletins**: IT-459: Adventure or concern in the nature of trade.

**(3) Incorrect valuation** — Where the inventory of a business at the commencement of a taxation year has, according to the method adopted by the taxpayer for computing income from the business for that year, not been valued as required by subsection (1), the inventory at the commencement of that year shall, if the Minister so directs, be deemed to have been valued as required by that subsection.

**Interpretation Bulletins**: See list at end of s. 10.

**(4) Fair market value** — For the purpose of subsection (1), the fair market value of property (other than property that is obsolete, damaged or defective or that is held for sale or lease or for the purpose of being processed, fabricated, manufactured, incorporated into, attached to, or otherwise converted into property for sale or lease) that is

(a) work in progress at the end of a taxation year of a business that is a profession means the amount that can reasonably be expected to become receivable in respect thereof after the end of the year; and

(b) advertising or packaging material, parts, supplies or other property (other than work in progress of a business that is a profession) that is included in inventory means the replacement cost of the property.

**Related Provisions**: 10(5) — Property deemed to be inventory; 34 — Election to exclude work in progress from professional income.

**Interpretation Bulletins**: IT-51R2: Supplies on hand at end of fiscal period. See also list at end of s. 10.

**(5) [Meaning of] Inventory** — Without restricting the generality of this section,

(a) property (other than capital property) of a taxpayer that is advertising or packaging material, parts or supplies or work in progress of a business that is a profession is, for greater certainty, inventory of the taxpayer;

(b) anything used primarily for the purpose of advertising or packaging property that is included in the inventory of a taxpayer shall be deemed not to be property held for sale or lease or for any of the purposes referred to in subsection (4); and

(c) property of a taxpayer, the cost of which to the taxpayer was deductible by virtue of paragraph 20(1)(mm), is, for greater certainty, inventory of the taxpayer having a cost to the taxpayer, except for the purposes of that paragraph, of nil.

**Related Provisions**: 10(4) — Fair market value of work in progress, advertising or packaging materials, parts and supplies; 34 — Election to exclude work in progress from professional income.

**I.T. Application Rules**: 23(3), (4).

**Interpretation Bulletins**: IT-51R2: Supplies on hand at end of fiscal period; IT-457R: Election by professionals to exclude work in progress from income. See also list at end of s. 10.

**(6) Artistic endeavour** — Notwithstanding subsection (1), for the purpose of computing the income of an individual other than a trust for a taxation year from a business that is the individual's artistic endeavour, the value of the inventory of the business for that year shall, if the individual so elects in the individual's return of income under this Part for the year, be deemed to be nil.

**Related Provisions**: 10(7) — Effect of election; 10(8) — Artistic endeavour.

**Notes**: The effect of an artist electing under 10(6) to value inventory at nil is to allow the costs associated with creating the inventory to be deducted in the year they are incurred, rather than waiting for the inventory to be sold. This recognizes the difficulty in valuing works of art and the long period of time it can take for art to be sold.

**Interpretation Bulletins**: IT-212R3: Income of deceased persons — rights or things; IT-504R2: Visual artists and writers. See also list at end of s. 10.

**(7) Value in later years** — Where an individual has made an election pursuant to subsection (6) for a taxation year, the value of the inventory of a business that is the individual's artistic endeavour shall, for each subsequent taxation year, be deemed to be nil unless the individual, with the concurrence of the Minister and on such terms and conditions as are specified by the Minister, revokes the election.

**Interpretation Bulletins**: IT-504R2: Visual artists and writers. See also list at end of s. 10.

**(8) Definition of "business that is an individual's artistic endeavour"** — For the purpose of this section, "business that is an individual's artistic endeavour" means the business of creating paintings, prints, etchings, drawings, sculptures or similar works of art, where such works of art are created by the individual, but does not include a business of reproducing works of art.

**Interpretation Bulletins [subsec. 10(8)]**: IT-504R2: Visual artists and writers. See also list at end of s. 10.

**(9) Transition** — Where, at the end of a taxpayer's last taxation year at the end of which property described in an inventory of a business that is an adventure or concern in the nature of trade was valued under subsection (1), the property was valued at an amount that is less than the cost at which the taxpayer acquired the property, after that time the cost to the taxpayer at which the property was acquired is, subject to subsection (10), deemed to be that amount.

**Notes**: 10(9) added by 1995-97 technical bill, effective on the same basis as the addition of 10(1.01). It provides grandfathering for an inventory writedown that was taken before 10(1.01) applied. The amount to which the writedown was taken is deemed to be the new cost for purposes of 10(1.01).

**Interpretation Bulletins**: IT-459: Adventure or concern in the nature of trade.

**(10) Acquisition of control** — Notwithstanding subsection (1.01), property described in an inventory of a corporation's business that is an adventure or concern in the nature of trade at the end of the corporation's taxation year that ends immediately before the time at which control of the corporation is acquired by a person or group of persons shall be valued at the cost at which the corporation acquired the property, or its fair market value at the end of the year, whichever is lower, and, after that time, the cost at which the corporation acquired the property is, subject to a subsequent application of this subsection, deemed to be that lower amount.

**Related Provisions**: 139.1(18) — Holding corporation deemed not to acquire control of insurer on demutualization; 249(4) — Year-end triggered on change of control; 256(6)–(9) — Whether control acquired.

**Notes**: 10(10) added by 1995-97 technical bill, effective on the same basis as the addition of 10(1.01). It requires an inventory writedown before a change in control of a corporation. This prevents loss trading in corporations that have an unrealized loss in property held as an adventure in the nature of trade. The reference to the year that ends immediately before the change in control is to the year-end triggered under 249(4).

**Interpretation Bulletins**: IT-459: Adventure or concern in the nature of trade.

**(11) Acquisition of control** — For the purposes of subsections 88(1.1) and 111(5), a corporation's business that is at any time an adventure or concern in the nature of trade is deemed to be a business carried on at that time by the corporation.

**Notes**: 10(11) added by 1995-97 technical bill, effective on the same basis as the addition of 10(1.01).

**Interpretation Bulletins**: IT-459: Adventure or concern in the nature of trade.

### Proposed Addition — 10(12)–(14)

**(12) Removing property from [Canadian] inventory [of non-resident]** — If at any time a non-resident taxpayer ceases to use, in connection with a business or part of a business carried on by the taxpayer in Canada immediately before that time, a property that was immediately before that time described in the inventory of the business or the part of the business, as the case may be, (other than a property that was disposed of by the taxpayer at that time), the taxpayer is deemed

(a) to have disposed of the property immediately before that time for proceeds of disposition equal to its fair market value at that time; and

(b) to have received those proceeds immediately before that time in the course of carrying on the business or the part of the business, as the case may be.

**Technical Notes**: Section 10 sets out rules for the valuation of inventory for the purpose of computing a taxpayer's income or loss from a business. These amendments ensure the appropriate measurement of a non-resident's income or loss from a business carried on in Canada.

New subsection 10(12) applies to a non-resident taxpayer who ceases to use a property, described in the inventory of a business or part of a business that is carried on by the taxpayer in Canada, otherwise than by a disposition of the property. For example, subsection 10(12) applies if a non-resident taxpayer removes a property from the inventory of a business or part of a business carried on in Canada and adds that property to the inventory of a business or part of a business carried on by the taxpayer in another country. The time at which the taxpayer ceases to use the property in connection with a business or part of a business in Canada is referred to in this note as the "particular time".

Where new subsection 10(12) applies, the taxpayer is treated as having disposed of the property immediately before the particular time, for proceeds equal to the property's fair market value at that time. The taxpayer is treated as having received the proceeds in the course of carrying on the business in which the property was formerly used, in the taxation year that includes the particular time.

**Related Provisions**: 10(14) — Inventory includes work in progress of a professional; 14(14) — Parallel rule for eligible capital property; 142.6(1.1) — Parallel rule for non-resident financial institution.

**Notes**: This replaces a more specific rule for farming inventory that appeared in 28(4.1).

**(13) Adding property to [Canadian] inventory [of non-resident]** — If at any time a property becomes included in the inventory of a business or part of a business that a non-resident taxpayer carries on in Canada after that time (other than a property that was, otherwise than because of this subsection, acquired by the taxpayer at that time), the taxpayer is deemed to have acquired the property at that time at a cost equal to its fair market value at that time.

**Technical Notes**: New subsection 10(13) applies to a non-resident taxpayer who adds a property (otherwise than by acquiring the property) to the inventory of a business or part of a business that is carried on in Canada by the taxpayer. For example, new subsection 10(13) applies if a taxpayer removes a property from the inventory of a business or part of a business carried on in another country and adds that property to the inventory of a business or part of a business carried on in Canada by the taxpayer. The time at which the taxpayer adds the property to the inventory of the business or part of a business in Canada is referred to in this note as the "particular time".

Where new subsection 10(13) applies, the taxpayer is deemed to have acquired the property at the particular time at a cost equal to the property's fair market value at that time.

**Related Provisions**: 10(14) — Inventory includes work in progress of a professional.

**(14) Work in progress** — For the purposes of subsections (12) and (13), property that is included in the inventory of a business includes property that would be so included if paragraph 34(a) did not apply.

**Technical Notes**: Section 34 provides an exception to full accrual accounting in calculating the income of a business that is a professional practice by allowing the income to be determined without taking into account any professional work in progress at a year end.

New subsection 10(14) provides, for the purposes of new subsections 10(12) and 10(13), that a property included in the inventory of a business includes professional work in progress that would be so included if paragraph 34(a) (the basic rule described above) did not apply. Any work in progress that would ordinarily be described in an inventory will thus be subject to the deemed disposition under subsection 10(12) or the deemed acquisition under subsection 10(13).

**Related Provisions**: 14(15) — Parallel rule for eligible capital property; 142.6(1.2) — Parallel rule for non-resident financial institution.

**Notes**: 34(a) refers to the work in progress that a professional (lawyer, physician, etc.) has elected to exclude from inventory.

**Application**: Bill C-43 (First Reading September 20, 2000) (taxpayer migration), s. 3, will add subsecs. 10(12) to (14), applicable after December 23, 1998.

**Definitions [s. 10]**: "adventure or concern in the nature of trade" — see Notes to 10(1.01); "amount" — 248(1); "artistic endeavour" — 10(8); "business" — 248(1); "Canada" — 255, *Interpretation Act* 35(1); "capital property" — 54, 248(1); "control" — 256(6)–(9); "corporation" — 248(1), *Interpretation Act* 35(1); "cost" — 10(9); "fair market value" — 10(4); "filing-due date" — 248(1); "fiscal period" — 249.1; "individual" — 248(1); "inventory" — 10(5), 248(1); "Minister", "non-resident" — 248(1); "partnership" — see Notes to 96(1); "person", "prescribed", "property", "regulation" — 248(1); "taxation year" — 11(2), 249; "taxpayer" — 248(1); "trust" — 104(1), 248(1), (3).

**Interpretation Bulletins [s. 10]**: IT-98R2: Investment corporations; IT-189R2: Corporations used by practising members of professions; IT-283R2: CCA — video tapes, videotape cassettes, films, computer software and master recording tapes; IT-345R: Special reserve — loans secured by mortgages; IT-452: Utility service connections; IT-473R: Inventory valuation.

**11. (1) Proprietor of business** — Subject to sections 34.1 and 34.2, where an individual is a proprietor of a business, the individual's income from the business for a taxation year is deemed to be the individual's income from the business for the fiscal periods of the business that end in the year.

**(2) Reference to "taxation year"** — Where an individual's income for a taxation year includes income from a business the fiscal period of which does not coincide with the calendar year, unless the context otherwise requires, a reference in this subdivision or section 80.3 to a "taxation year" or "year" shall, in respect of the business, be read as a reference to a fiscal period of the business ending in the year.

**Related Provisions [s. 11]**: 14(4) — Eligible capital property rules — references to "taxation year" or "year"; 20(16.2) — Terminal loss rules — reference to "taxation year" and "year"; 34.1 — Additional income adjustment where fiscal year is not calendar year; 34.2 — Reserve for 1995 stub-period income; 96(1)(f) — Income inclusion from partnership in taxation year in which partnership's year ends; 25(1) — Fiscal period for individual proprietor of business disposed of; 249(2)(b) — Where end of fiscal period coincides with end of taxation year.

**Notes [s. 11]**: 11(1) amended to be made subject to 34.1 and 34.2 by 1995 Budget, effective 1995.

In 11(2), "subdivision" changed to "Division" by 1989 Budget, effective 1988, but then changed back to "subdivision or section 80.3" by 1993 technical bill, retroactive to 1988. The intent had been to have 11(2) apply to 80.3, but the earlier change unintentionally made it apply to the capital gains rules (ss. 38–55) as well.

**Definitions [s. 11]**: "business" — 248(1), 249.1; "calendar year" — *Interpretation Act* 37(1)(a); "fiscal period" — 248(1), 249.1; "individual" — 248(1); "taxation year" — 249.

**Regulations [s. 11]**: 1104(1) (taxation year of individual for capital cost allowance purposes).

**Interpretation Bulletins [s. 11]**: IT-151R5: Scientific research and experimental development expenditures; IT-184R: Deferred cash purchase tickets issued by Canadian Wheat Board.

## Inclusions

**12. (1) Income inclusions** — There shall be included in computing the income of a taxpayer for a taxation year as income from a business or property such of the following amounts as are applicable:

(a) **services, etc., to be rendered [or goods to be delivered]** — any amount received by the taxpayer in the year in the course of a business

(i) that is on account of services not rendered or goods not delivered before the end of the year or that, for any other reason, may be regarded as not having been earned in the year or a previous year, or

(ii) under an arrangement or understanding that it is repayable in whole or in part on the return or resale to the taxpayer of articles in or by means of which goods were delivered to a customer;

**Related Provisions**: 12(1)(x) — Inducements, reimbursements, etc. included in income; 12(2) — Rule is for greater certainty only; 20(1)(m) — Deductions — reserve for goods and services; 20(1)(m.1) — Deductions — manufacturer's warranty reserve; 20(1)(m.2) — Deductions — repayment of amount previously included in income; 20(24) — Amounts paid for undertaking future obligations; 68 — Allocation of amounts paid for combination of services and property.

**Notes**: Although 12(1)(a)(i) requires an income inclusion, an offsetting deduction is normally allowed by 20(1)(m).

**Interpretation Bulletins**: IT-154R: Special reserves; IT-165R: Returnable containers; IT-321R: Insurance agents and brokers — unearned commissions; IT-457R: Election by professionals to exclude work in progress from income; IT-531: Eligible funeral arrangements.

**I.T. Technical News**: No. 18 (*Oerlikon Aérospatiale* case).

**Forms**: T2124: Statement of business activities.

(b) **amounts receivable** — any amount receivable by the taxpayer in respect of property sold or services rendered in the course of a business in the year, notwithstanding that the amount or any part thereof is not due until a subsequent year, unless the method adopted by the taxpayer for computing income from the business and accepted for the purpose of this Part does not require the taxpayer to include any amount receivable in computing the taxpayer's income for a taxation year unless it has been received in the year, and for the purposes of this paragraph, an amount shall be deemed to have become receivable in respect of services rendered in the course of a business on the day that is the earlier of

(i) the day on which the account in respect of the services was rendered, and

(ii) the day on which the account in respect of those services would have been rendered had there been no undue delay in rendering the account in respect of the services;

**Related Provisions**: 12(2) — Rule is for greater certainty only; 34 — Professional business; 68 — Allocation of amounts in consideration for disposition of property; 78 — Unpaid amounts; 138(11.5)(k) — Transfer of business by non-resident insurer.

**Notes**: For one interpretation of "undue delay", a phrase used in 12(1)(b)(ii), see *DHM Energy Consultants Ltd. v. Canada*, [1995] G.S.T.C. 3 (TCC).

**Interpretation Bulletins**: IT-129R: Lawyers' trust accounts and disbursements; IT-170R: Sale of property — when included in income computation.

(c) **interest** — subject to subsections (3) and (5) [should be (4.1) — ed.], any amount received or receivable by the taxpayer in the year (depending on the method regularly followed by the taxpayer in computing the taxpayer's income) as, on account of, in lieu of payment of or in satisfaction of, interest to the extent that the interest was not included in computing the taxpayer's income for a preceding taxation year;

**Proposed Amendment — 12(1)(c)**

(c) **interest** — subject to subsections (3) and (4.1), any amount received or receivable by the taxpayer in the year (depending on the method regularly followed by the taxpayer in computing the taxpayer's income) as, on account of, in lieu of payment of or in satisfaction of, interest to the extent that the interest was not included in computing the taxpayer's income for a preceding taxation year;

**Application**: Bill C-43 (First Reading September 20, 2000), s. 4, will amend para. 12(1)(c) to read as above, applicable to taxation years that end after September 1997.

**Technical Notes**: Paragraph 12(1)(c) requires that any interest received or receivable by a taxpayer in a taxation year be included in computing the taxpayer's income for the year. The existing reference in paragraph 12(1)(c) to subsection 12(5) is corrected to refer instead to subsection 12(4.1).

**Related Provisions**: 12(3) — Accrued interest taxable to corporation, partnership and certain trusts; 12(4) — Annual accrual of interest even if unpaid; 12(4.1) — Impaired debt obligations; 12(9.1) — Exception for certain interests in prescribed debt obligations; 12.1 — Cash bonus on Canada Savings Bonds; 16 — Income and capital combined; 16(3) — Bonds purchased at a discount; 16(6) — Indexed debt obligations — amount deemed received as interest; 17 — Interest deemed received on loan to non-resident; 18(9.1) — Penalties, bonuses and rate reduction payments; 20(1)(c) — Deduction for interest paid; 20(14) — Accrued bond interest; 20(14.1) — Interest on debt obligation; 81(1)(m) — Interest on certain obligations exempt; 137(4.1) — Interest deemed received on certain reductions of capital by credit union; 142.5(3)(a), (b) — Mark-to-market debt obligation; 218 — Loan to wholly-owned subsidiary; 258(3) — Certain dividends on preferred shares deemed to be interest; 258(5) — Deemed interest on certain shares; Canada-U.S. tax treaty, Art. XI — Taxation of interest.

**Notes**: Where a government bond is purchased at a discount, the difference to maturity may be deemed to be interest; see 16(3). Where a bond is sold with accrued interest, payment received in respect of the interest is taxable; see 20(14).

12(1)(c) amended by 1995-97 technical bill to add "subject to subsections (3) and (5)" and to change "the taxpayer's profit" to "the taxpayer's income", effective on the same basis as the addition of 12(4.1).

**Regulations**: 201(1)(b) (information return).

Subdivision b — Income or Loss from a Business or Property  S. 12(1)(i.1)(ii)

**Interpretation Bulletins**: IT-265R3: Payments of income and capital combined; IT-396R: Interest income.
**Advance Tax Rulings**: ATR-61: Interest accrual rules.
**Forms**: T5 Segment; T5 Summary: Return of investment income; T5 Supplementary: Statement of investment income.

(d) **reserve for doubtful debts** — any amount deducted under paragraph 20(1)(l) as a reserve in computing the taxpayer's income for the immediately preceding taxation year;

**Related Provisions**: 87(2.2) — Amalgamation of insurance corporations; 88(1)(g) — Winding-up of subsidiary insurance corporations; 138(11.5)(k) — Transfer of business by non-resident insurer; 138(11.91)(d) — Computation of income for non-resident insurer; 142.3(1)(c) — Amount deductible in respect of specified debt obligation; Reg. 2405(3)"gross Canadian life investment income"(d) — Inclusion in life insurer's income.
**Interpretation Bulletins**: IT-442R: Bad debts and reserve for doubtful debts.

(d.1) **reserve for guarantees, etc.** — any amount deducted under paragraph 20(1)(l.1) as a reserve in computing the taxpayer's income for the immediately preceding taxation year;

(e) **reserves for certain goods and services, etc.** — any amount

(i) deducted under paragraph 20(1)(m) (including any amount substituted by virtue of subsection 20(6) for any amount deducted under that paragraph), paragraph 20(1)(m.1) or subsection 20(7), or

(ii) deducted under paragraph 20(1)(n),

in computing the taxpayer's income from a business for the immediately preceding year;

**Related Provisions**: 66.2(2)(b)(ii)(B), 66.4(2)(a)(ii)(B) — Deductions for resource expenses; 87(2.2) — Amalgamation of insurance corporations; 88(1)(g) — Winding-up of subsidiary insurance corporations; 138(11.91)(d) — Computation of income of non-resident insurer.
**Interpretation Bulletins**: IT-73R5: The small business deduction; IT-154R: Special reserves.

(e.1) **[insurer's] negative reserves** — where the taxpayer is an insurer, the amount prescribed in respect of the insurer for the year;

**Related Provisions**: 20(22) — Deduction in following year; 87(2.2) — Amalgamation of insurance corporations; 88(1)(g)(i) — Windup of subsidiary insurance corporation; 138(11.5)(j.1) — Transfer of business by non-resident insurer; 138(11.91)(d.1)(ii) — Computation of income for non-resident insurer.
**Notes**: 12(1)(e.1) added by 1996 Budget, effective for 1996 and later taxation years. It requires income inclusion for an insurer's "negative reserves", which must be included in income but are allowed an offsetting deduction the next year under 20(22). Negative policy reserves generally arise where the present value of future premiums exceeds the present value of future estimated benefits and expenses in respect of the insurer's policies. See Reg. 1400(2).
An earlier 12(1)(e.1), proposed in the July 12, 1994 draft legislation on debt forgiveness, was not enacted. See now 56.3.
**Regulations**: 1400(2) (amount prescribed).

(f) **insurance proceeds expended** — such part of any amount payable to the taxpayer as compensation for damage to, or under a policy of insurance in respect of damage to, property that is depreciable property of the taxpayer as has been expended by the taxpayer

(i) within the year, and

(ii) within a reasonable time after the damage, on repairing the damage;

**Related Provisions**: 13(21)"proceeds of disposition"(c) — Depreciable property — proceeds of disposition.

(g) **payments based on production or use** — any amount received by the taxpayer in the year that was dependent on the use of or production from property whether or not that amount was an instalment of the sale price of the property, except that an instalment of the sale price of agricultural land is not included by virtue of this paragraph;

**Interpretation Bulletins**: IT-423: Sale of sand, gravel or topsoil; IT-426: Shares sold subject to an earnout agreement; IT-462: Payment based on production or use.

(g.1) **proceeds of disposition of right to receive production** — any proceeds of disposition to which subsection 18.1(6) applies;

**Notes**: 12(1)(g.1) added by 1995-97 technical bill, effective for dispositions after November 17, 1996.

(h) **previous reserve for quadrennial survey** — any amount deducted as a reserve under paragraph 20(1)(o) in computing the taxpayer's income for the immediately preceding year;

(i) **bad debts recovered** — any amount, other than an amount referred to in paragraph (i.1), received in the year on account of a debt or a loan or lending asset in respect of which a deduction for bad debts or uncollectable loans or lending assets had been made in computing the taxpayer's income for a preceding taxation year;

**Related Provisions**: 12.4 — Bad debt inclusion; 20(1)(p) — Bad debts; 22(1) — Sale of accounts receivable; 26(3) — Banks — write-offs and recoveries; 87(2.2) — Amalgamation of insurance corporations; 88(1)(g) — Winding-up of subsidiary insurance corporations; 111(5.3) — Doubtful debts and bad debts; 138(11.5)(k) — Transfer of business by non-resident insurer; 142.3(1)(c), (g) — Amount deductible in respect of specified debt obligation; 142.5(8)(d)(iv) — First deemed disposition of mark-to-market debt obligation.
**Interpretation Bulletins**: IT-109R2: Unpaid amounts; IT-220R2: CCA — proceeds of disposition of depreciable property; IT-302R3: Losses of a corporation — the effect that acquisitions of control, amalgamations, and windings-up have on their deductibility — after January 15, 1987; IT-442R: Bad debts and reserve for doubtful debts.

(i.1) **idem** — where an amount is received in the year on account of a debt in respect of which a deduction for bad debts under subsection 20(4.2) was made in computing the taxpayer's income for a preceding taxation year, that proportion of ³⁄₄ of the amount that

(i) the amount that was deducted under subsection 20(4.2) in respect of that debt

is of

(ii) the total of the amount that was so deducted under subsection 20(4.2) and the

## S. 12(1)(i.1)(ii) — Income Tax Act, Part I, Division B

amount that was deemed to be an allowable capital loss under subsection 20(4.2) in respect of the debt;

### Proposed Amendment — 12(1)(i.1)

(i.1) **bad debts recovered** — where an amount is received in the year on account of a debt in respect of which a deduction for bad debts was made under subsection 20(4.2) in computing the taxpayer's income for a preceding taxation year, the amount determined by the formula

$$A \times B/C$$

where

A is ½ of the amount so received;

B is the amount that was deducted under subsection 20(4.2) in respect of the debt; and

C is the total of the amount that was so deducted under subsection 20(4.2) and the amount that was deemed by that subsection or subsection 20(4.3) to be an allowable capital loss in respect of the debt.

**Application**: The December 21, 2000 draft legislation, subsec. 3(1), will amend para. 12(1)(i.1) to read as above, applicable in respect of taxation years that end after February 27, 2000 except that, for taxation years that ended after February 27, 2000 and before October 18, 2000, the reference to the fraction "1/2" in the description of A in the para. shall be read as a reference to the fraction "2/3".

**Technical Notes**: Paragraph 12(1)(i.1) requires an inclusion in income in respect of amounts recovered on account of bad debts, where subsection 20(4.2) applied to permit a deduction, or an allowable capital loss in respect of the debt.

Paragraph 12(1)(i.1) is amended, consequential on the amendments to subsections 14(1) and 20(4.2) that reflect the reduced inclusion rate for capital gains [see 38(a) — ed.], by replacing the fraction "3/4" with the fraction "1/2". It is also amended to reflect the restructuring of subsection 20(4.2) into subsection 20(4.2) (deduction) and 20(4.3) (deemed allowable capital loss). In addition, it is restructured as a formula to improve readability. The amount required to be included in income is 1/2 of the amount recovered multiplied by the ratio of the amount that was deducted under subsection 20(4.2) in respect of the debt to the total of the amount deducted under subsection 20(4.2) in respect of the debt and the amount deemed by subsection 20(4.3) (previously part of subsection 20(4.2)) to be an allowable capital loss in respect of the debt. Subsection 39(11) deems the portion of the recovered amount that relates to the allowable capital loss to be a taxable capital gain. That is, the amount by which 1/2 of the recovered debt exceeds the amount required to be included in income under paragraph 12(1)(i.1) is deemed to be a taxable capital gain.

For further details, see the commentary on the amendments to subsections 14(1) to (5), 20(4.2) and 39(11).

These amendments apply in respect of taxation years that end after February 27, 2000 except that, for taxation years that end after February 27, 2000 and before October 18, 2000, the fraction to be used in calculating the amount required to be included in income is 2/3 rather than 1/2.

**Related Provisions**: 39(11) — Bad debt recovery; 89(1)"capital dividend account"(c) — Capital dividend account.

**Interpretation Bulletins**: IT-442R: Bad debts and reserve for doubtful debts.

(j) **dividends from resident corporations** — any amount required by subdivision h to be included in computing the taxpayer's income for the year in respect of a dividend paid by a corporation resident in Canada on a share of its capital stock;

**Related Provisions**: 82(1) — Taxable dividends received; 84, 84.1(1)(b) — Deemed dividends; 139.1(4)(f), (g) — Deemed dividend on demutualization of insurance corporation; 139.2 — Deemed dividend on distribution by mutual holding corporation.

**Notes**: Subdivision h is sections 82 to 89. See Notes to 82(1).

**Interpretation Bulletins**: IT-67R3: Taxable dividends from corporations resident in Canada; IT-269R3: Part IV tax on taxable dividends received by a private corporation or a subject corporation.

**Advance Tax Rulings**: ATR-15: Employee stock option plan.

(k) **dividends from other corporations** — any amount required by subdivision i to be included in computing the taxpayer's income for the year in respect of a dividend paid by a corporation not resident in Canada on a share of its capital stock or in respect of a share owned by the taxpayer of the capital stock of a foreign affiliate of the taxpayer;

### Proposed Amendment — 12(1)(k)

(k) **foreign corporations, trusts and investment entities [dividends, etc.]** — any amount required by subdivision i to be included in computing the taxpayer's income for the year;

**Application**: The June 22, 2000 draft legislation, s. 1, will amend para. 12(1)(k) to read as above, applicable to taxation years that begin after 2000.

**Technical Notes**: Section 12 provides for the inclusion of various amounts in computing a taxpayer's income for a taxation year from business or property. Paragraph 12(1)(k) refers to certain amounts required by existing sections 90 to 95 to be so added.

Paragraph 12(1)(k) is amended so that it refers to all amounts required to be added in computing income under amended sections 90 to 95, including new sections 94 to 94.2.

**Related Provisions**: 90 — Dividends received from non-resident corporation; 258(3) — Certain dividends on preferred shares deemed to be interest; 258(5) — Deemed interest on certain shares.

**Notes**: Subdivision i is sections 90 to 95.

**Interpretation Bulletins**: IT-269R3: Part IV tax on taxable dividends received by a private corporation or a subject corporation.

(l) **partnership income** — any amount that is, by virtue of subdivision j, income of the taxpayer for the year from a business or property;

**Related Provisions**: 96(1)(c)(ii) — Partner taxed on share of partnership's income from business or property.

**Notes**: Subdivision j is sections 96 to 103.

**Interpretation Bulletins**: IT-278R2: Death of a partner or of a retired partner.

**Forms**: T2032: Statement of professional activities.

(m) **benefits from trusts** — any amount required by subdivision k or subsection 132.1(1) to be included in computing the taxpayer's income for the year, except

(i) any amount deemed by that subdivision to be a taxable capital gain of the taxpayer, and

(ii) any amount paid or payable to the taxpayer out of or under an RCA trust (within the meaning assigned by subsection 207.5(1));

**Related Provisions**: 12(1)(n.3) — Retirement compensation arrangement — refund of contributions; 56(1)(x), (z) — Retirement compensation arrangement; 104(13), (14) — Income from trusts; 208 — Tax payable by exempt person.

**Notes**: Subdivision k is sections 104 to 108.

Reference to 132.1(1) added to 12(1)(m) by 1993 technical bill, effective 1988. 132.1(1) provides that a mutual fund trust may designate a specified amount for its taxation year in respect of a trust unit, which generally results in a deduction of that amount in computing the trust's income and a corresponding income inclusion for the taxpayer owning the unit during the year.

(n) **employees profit sharing plan** — any amount received by the taxpayer in the year out of or under

(i) an employees profit sharing plan, or

(ii) an employee trust

established for the benefit of employees of the taxpayer or of a person with whom the taxpayer does not deal at arm's length;

**Related Provisions**: 6(1)(a) — Inclusions — value of benefits; 6(1)(d) — Inclusions — allocations etc. under profit sharing plan; 6(1)(g) — Inclusions — employee benefit plan benefits; 20(1)(w) — Deduction to employer; 32.1 — Employee benefit plan deductions; 107.1 — Distribution by employee trust or employee benefit plan; 144(1) — "Employees profit sharing plan" defined; 144(6), (7) — Beneficiary's receipts.

**Interpretation Bulletins**: IT-502: Employee benefit plans and employee trusts.

(n.1) **employee benefit plan** — the amount, if any, by which the total of amounts received by the taxpayer in the year out of or under an employee benefit plan to which the taxpayer has contributed as an employer (other than amounts included in the income of the taxpayer by virtue of paragraph (m)) exceeds the amount, if any, by which the total of all amounts

(i) so contributed by the taxpayer to the plan, or

(ii) included in computing the taxpayer's income for any preceding taxation year by virtue of this paragraph

exceeds the total of all amounts

(iii) deducted by the taxpayer in respect of the taxpayer's contributions to the plan in computing the taxpayer's income for the year or any preceding taxation year, or

(iv) received by the taxpayer out of or under the plan in any preceding taxation year (other than an amount included in the taxpayer's income by virtue of paragraph (m));

**Related Provisions**: 6(1)(a) — Inclusions — value of benefits; 6(1)(g) — Employee benefit plan benefits; 6(10) — Contributions to an employee benefit plan; 18(1)(o) — No deduction for employee benefit plan contributions; 32.1 — Employee benefit plan deductions; 87(2)(j.3) — Amalgamation — continuation of corporation; 107.1 — Distribution by employee trust or employee benefit plan.

**Interpretation Bulletins**: IT-502: Employee benefit plans and employee trusts.

(n.2) **forfeited salary deferral amounts** — where deferred amounts under a salary deferral arrangement in respect of another person have been deducted under paragraph 20(1)(oo) in computing the taxpayer's income for preceding taxation years, any amount in respect of the deferred amounts that was deductible under paragraph 8(1)(o) in computing the income of the person for a taxation year ending in the year;

**Related Provisions**: 6(1)(a) — Inclusions — value of benefits; 6(1)(i) — Salary deferral arrangement payments; 6(11) — Salary deferral arrangement; 87(2)(j.3) — Amalgamations — continuing corporation.

(n.3) **retirement compensation arrangement** — the total of all amounts received by the taxpayer in the year in the course of a business out of or under a retirement compensation arrangement to which the taxpayer, another person who carried on a business that was acquired by the taxpayer, or any person with whom the taxpayer or that other person does not deal at arm's length, has contributed an amount that was deductible under paragraph 20(1)(r) in computing the contributor's income for a taxation year;

**Related Provisions**: 56(1)(x)–(z) — Employee's income inclusion — amounts received from RCA; 87(2)(j.3) — Amalgamation — continuing corporation; 207.5–207.7 — Tax in respect of retirement compensation arrangements.

**Forms**: T4A-RCA Supp: Statement of amounts paid from an RCA.

(o) **royalties, etc.** — any amount (other than an amount referred to in paragraph 18(1)(m), paid or payable by the taxpayer, or a prescribed amount) that, because of an obligation imposed by statute or a contractual obligation substituted for an obligation imposed by statute, became receivable in the year by

(i) Her Majesty in right of Canada or a province,

(ii) an agent of Her Majesty in right of Canada or a province, or

(iii) a corporation, commission or association that is controlled by Her Majesty in right of Canada or a province or by an agent of Her Majesty in right of Canada or a province

as a royalty, tax (other than a tax or portion of a tax that can reasonably be considered to be a municipal or school tax), lease rental or bonus or as an amount, however described, that can reasonably be regarded as being in lieu of any such

## S. 12(1)(o) — Income Tax Act, Part I, Division B

amount, or in respect of the late receipt or non-receipt of any such amount, and that can reasonably be regarded as being in relation to

(iv) the acquisition, development or ownership of a Canadian resource property of the taxpayer in respect of which the obligation imposed by statute or the contractual obligation, as the case may be, applied, or

(v) the production in Canada

(A) of petroleum, natural gas or related hydrocarbons from a natural accumulation of petroleum or natural gas (other than a mineral resource) located in Canada or from an oil or gas well located in Canada,

(B) of sulphur from a natural accumulation of petroleum or natural gas located in Canada, from an oil or gas well located in Canada or from a mineral resource located in Canada,

(C) to any stage that is not beyond the prime metal stage or its equivalent, of metal, minerals (other than iron or petroleum or related hydrocarbons) or coal from a mineral resource located in Canada,

(D) to any stage that is not beyond the pellet stage or its equivalent, of iron from a mineral resource located in Canada, or

(E) to any stage that is not beyond the crude oil stage or its equivalent, of petroleum or related hydrocarbons from tar sands from a mineral resource located in Canada,

in respect of which the taxpayer had an interest to which the obligation imposed by statute or the contractual obligation, as the case may be, applied;

**Related Provisions**: 18(1)(m) — Deductions — limitations — royalties; 65 — Allowance for oil or gas well, mine or timber limit; 66 — Exploration and development expenses of principal-business corporations; 69(6), (7) — Unreasonable consideration; 80.2 — Reimbursement by taxpayers; 104(29) — Amounts deemed to be payable to beneficiaries; 208 — Tax on certain royalties payable by tax-exempt person; 219(1)(k) — Reduction in branch tax; *Interpretation Act* 8(2.1), (2.2) — Application to exclusive economic zone and continental shelf.

**Notes**: Everything after 12(1)(o)(iii) amended by 1996 Budget, effective for taxation years that begin after 1996. The amendment provides that amounts receivable by the Crown (including interest and penalties) in respect of the late receipt or non-receipt of royalties or similar amounts are included in income. The amendment also causes 12(1)(o) to apply to sulphur royalties; see 248(1)"Canadian field processing". For earlier taxation years since 1989, read:

as a royalty, tax (other than a tax or portion thereof that may reasonably be considered to be a municipal or school tax), lease rental or bonus or as an amount, however described, that may reasonably be regarded as being in lieu of any such amount, and that may reasonably be regarded as being in relation to

(iv) the acquisition, development or ownership of a Canadian resource property, or

(v) the production in Canada

(A) of petroleum, natural gas or related hydrocarbons from a natural accumulation of petroleum or natural gas (other than a mineral resource) or from an oil or gas well,

(B) to any stage that is not beyond the prime metal stage or its equivalent, of metal, minerals (other than iron or petroleum or related hydrocarbons) or coal from a mineral resource,

(C) to any stage that is not beyond the pellet stage or its equivalent, of iron from a mineral resource, or

(D) to any stage that is not beyond the crude oil stage or its equivalent, of petroleum or related hydrocarbons from tar sands from a mineral resource,

situated on property in Canada in which the taxpayer had an interest with respect to which the obligation imposed by statute or the contractual obligation, as the case may be, applied;

Reference to coal in 12(1)(o)(v)(B) [now 12(1)(o)(v)(C)] added by 1991 technical bill, effective for amounts receivable after July 13, 1990.

**Regulations**: 1211 (prescribed amount).

**Remission Orders**: *Syncrude Remission Order*, P.C. 1976-1026 (remission of tax on royalties etc. relating to the Syncrude Project).

**Interpretation Bulletins**: IT-438R2: Crown charges — resource properties in Canada.

**Information Circulars**: 86-3: Alberta Royalty Tax Credit — Individuals.

### Proposed Addition — 12(1)(o.1)

(o.1) **foreign oil and gas production taxes** — the total of all amounts, each of which is the taxpayer's production tax amount for a foreign oil and gas business of the taxpayer for the year, within the meaning assigned by subsection 126(7);

**Application**: The December 21, 2000 draft legislation, subsec. 3(2), will add para. 12(1)(o.1), applicable to taxation years of a taxpayer that begin after the earlier of

(a) December 31, 1999; and

(b) where, for the purposes of subsec. 72(9), a date is designated in writing by the taxpayer and the designation is filed with the Minister of National Revenue on or before the taxpayer's filing-due date for the taxpayer's taxation year that includes the day on which the amending legislation receives Royal Assent, the later of

(i) the date so designated, and

(ii) December 31, 1994.

**Technical Notes**: Subsection 12(1) requires a taxpayer to include certain amounts, as income from a business or property, in computing the taxpayer's income for a taxation year. New paragraph 12(1)(o.1) ensures that any "production tax amount" of the taxpayer for a "foreign oil and gas business" is included in computing the taxpayer's income. Both of these terms are newly defined in subsection 126(7), and are explained more fully in the notes to that provision.

New paragraph 12(1)(o.1) applies to taxation years that begin after 1999. However, in the event that a taxpayer elects to have the new foreign tax credit provisions in section 126 apply to taxation years that begin after a date (no earlier than December 31, 1994) designated by the taxpayer, new paragraph 12(1)(o.1) applies on the same basis.

(p) **certain payments to farmers** — any amount received by the taxpayer in the year as a stabilization payment, or as a refund of a levy, under the *Western Grain Stabilization Act* or as a payment, or a refund of a premium, in respect of the gross revenue insurance program established under the *Farm Income Protection Act*;

**Related Provisions**: 20(1)(ff) — Deductions — payments by farmers.

**Notes**: 12(1)(p) amended by 1992 technical bill, effective 1991, to add the second half of the para. (reference to payment or refund under *Farm Income Protection Act*).

**Regulations**: 234–236 (information slips for farm support payments).

**Remission Orders**: *Farmers' Income Taxes Remission Order*, P.C. 1993-1647 (remission of tax on certain income under 12(1)(p) for 1992, where taxpayer repays insurance payments in later year).

(q) **employment tax deduction** — any amount deducted under subsection 127(13) or (14) of the *Income Tax Act*, chapter 148 of the Revised Statutes of Canada, 1952, by the taxpayer for the year;

**Notes**: The employment tax credit under former 127(13)–(16) was repealed effective 1989, so this paragraph is inoperative.

**I.T. Application Rules**: 69 (meaning of "*Income Tax Act*, chapter 148 of the Revised Statutes of Canada, 1952").

(r) **inventory adjustment [depreciation, etc.]** — the total of all amounts each of which, in respect of a property described in the taxpayer's inventory at the end of the year and valued at its cost amount to the taxpayer for the purposes of computing the taxpayer's income for the year, is an allowance in respect of depreciation, obsolescence or depletion included in that cost amount;

**Related Provisions**: 10(1) — Inventory valuation; 20(1)(ii) — Deductions — inventory adjustment; 87(2)(j.1) — Amalgamations — inventory adjustment.

(s) **reinsurance commission** — the total of all amounts each of which is the maximum amount that an insurer may claim in the year in respect of a reserve for a reinsurance commission for a policy as allowed by regulations made under paragraph 20(7)(c) in respect of a risk the reinsurance of which is assumed by the taxpayer;

**Related Provisions**: 20(1)(jj) — Reinsurance commission — deduction; 87(2.2) — Amalgamation of insurance corporations; 88(1)(g) — winding-up of subsidiary insurance corporations; 138(11.5)(k) — Transfer of business by non-resident insurer.

(t) **investment tax credit** — the amount deducted under subsection 127(5) or (6) in respect of a property acquired or an expenditure made in a preceding taxation year in computing the taxpayer's tax payable for a preceding taxation year to the extent that it was not included in computing the taxpayer's income for a preceding taxation year under this paragraph or is not included in an amount determined under paragraph 13(7.1)(e) or 37(1)(e), subparagraph 53(2)(c)(vi) or (h)(ii) or for I in the definition "undepreciated capital cost" in subsection 13(21) or L in the definition "cumulative Canadian exploration expense" in subsection 66.1(6);

**Related Provisions**: 12(1)(x) — Other government assistance; 70(1) — Death of a taxpayer; 87(2)(j.6) — Amalgamations — continuing corporation; 88(2)(c) — Winding-up of a Canadian corporation.

**Notes**: Investment tax credits claimed may be allocated to reduce the cost of depreciable property (s. 13) or capital property (s. 53) or may be allocated against R&D expenses (s. 37) or Canadian exploration expenses (s. 66.1). If not used in any of these ways, the ITC claimed is taxable under 12(1)(t) on the principle that it is a benefit received from the federal government. For other kinds of assistance, see 12(1)(x).

**Interpretation Bulletins**: IT-210R2: Income of deceased persons — periodic payments and investment tax credit; IT-273R2: Government assistance — general comments.

**Information Circulars**: 78-4R3: Investment tax credit rates.

(u) **home insulation or energy conversion grants** — the amount of any grant received by the taxpayer in the year under a prescribed program of the Government of Canada relating to home insulation or energy conversion in respect of a property used by the taxpayer principally for the purpose of gaining or producing income from a business or property;

**Related Provisions**: 13(7.1) — Deemed capital cost of certain property; 53(2)(k) — Adjustments to cost base; 56(1)(s) — Amounts to be included in income for year — grants under prescribed programs.

**Regulations**: 224 (information return); 5500, 5501 (prescribed program).

(v) **research and development deductions** — the amount, if any, by which the total of amounts determined at the end of the year in respect of the taxpayer under paragraphs 37(1)(d) to (h) exceeds the total of amounts determined at the end of the year in respect of the taxpayer under paragraphs 37(1)(a) to (c.1);

**Related Provisions**: 37(1)(c.1) — Deduction allowed in subsequent year.

**Interpretation Bulletins**: IT-151R5: Scientific research and experimental development expenditures.

(w) **subsec. 80.4(1) benefit** — where the taxpayer is a corporation that carried on a personal services business at any time in the year or a preceding taxation year, the amount deemed by subsection 80.4(1) to be a benefit received by it in the year from carrying on a personal services business;

**Interpretation Bulletins**: IT-421R2: Benefits to individuals, corporations and shareholders from loans or debt.

(x) **inducement, reimbursement, [refund] etc.** — any particular amount (other than a prescribed amount) received by the taxpayer in the year, in the course of earning income from a business or property, from

    (i) a person or partnership (in this paragraph referred to as the "payer") who pays the particular amount

        (A) in the course of earning income from a business or property,

**S. 12(1)(x)(i)(B)**      Income Tax Act, Part I, Division B

(B) in order to achieve a benefit or advantage for the payer or for persons with whom the payer does not deal at arm's length, or

(C) in circumstances where it is reasonable to conclude that the payer would not have paid the amount but for the receipt by the payer of amounts from a payer, government, municipality or public authority described in this subparagraph or in subparagraph (ii), or

(ii) a government, municipality or other public authority,

where the particular amount can reasonably be considered to have been received

(iii) as an inducement, whether as a grant, subsidy, forgivable loan, deduction from tax, allowance or any other form of inducement, or

(iv) as a refund, reimbursement, contribution or allowance or as assistance, whether as a grant, subsidy, forgivable loan, deduction from tax, allowance or any other form of assistance, in respect of

(A) an amount included in, or deducted as, the cost of property, or

(B) an outlay or expense,

to the extent that the particular amount

(v) was not otherwise included in computing the taxpayer's income, or deducted in computing, for the purposes of this Act, any balance of undeducted outlays, expenses or other amounts, for the year or a preceding taxation year,

(vi) except as provided by subsection 127(11.1), (11.5) or (11.6), does not reduce, for the purpose of an assessment made or that may be made under this Act, the cost or capital cost of the property or the amount of the outlay or expense, as the case may be,

(vii) does not reduce, under subsection (2.2) or 13(7.4) or paragraph 53(2)(s), the cost or capital cost of the property or the amount of the outlay or expense, as the case may be, and

(viii) may not reasonably be considered to be a payment made in respect of the acquisition by the payer or the public authority of an interest in the taxpayer or the taxpayer's business or property;

**Proposed Amendment — 12(1)(x) — Provincial SR&ED super-deductions**
**Notice of Ways and Means Motion, federal budget, February 28, 2000**: See under 37(1)(d.1).

**Related Provisions**: 12(1)(t) — Investment tax credits; 12(2.1) — Receipt of inducement, reimbursement, etc.; 12(2.2) — Election to exclude amount from income; 13(7.4) — Deemed capital cost of certain property; 20(1)(hh) — Repayments of inducements, etc.; 37(1)(d.1) — Reduction of R&D pool for provincial super R&D allowance; 53(2)(k) — Reduction in ACB — assistance; 53(2.1) — Election; 80(1)"excluded obligation"(a)(i) — Debt forgiveness rules do not apply where amount included under 12(1)(x); 80.2 — Reimbursement by taxpayer; 87(2)(j.6) — Amalgamations — continuing corporation; 125.4(5) — Canadian film/video credit deemed to be assistance; 125.5(5) — Film/video production services credit deemed to be assistance; 126.1(12) — Prepayment of UI premium tax credit; 127(9) — Meaning of "non-government assistance" for ITC purposes; 127(18) — Reduction of qualified expenditures for ITC to reflect assistance; 248(16)–(18) — Goods and services tax — input tax credit and rebate.

**Notes**: 12(1)(x) applies to a wide range of government assistance including GST input tax credits and rebates (see 248(16)), the Canadian film/video production credit (see 125.4(5)) and the film/video production services credit (see 125.5(5)). Such amounts are first applied against the cost of depreciable property (13), eligible capital expenditures (14(10)), or the adjusted cost base of capital property (53(2)) in many cases. Any amount not so allocated is taxable under 12(1)(x). For investment tax credits, see 12(1)(t).

In *Bois Aisé De Roberval Inc.*, [1999] 4 C.T.C. 2161, the Tax Court ruled that refunds under the *Softwood Lumber Products Export Charge Act* for export charges paid in error were "refunds" under 12(1)(x)(iv).

12(1)(x)(i)(C) added (and previous subpara. split into (A) and (B)) by 1998 Budget, effective for amounts received after February 23, 1998 other than amounts received before 1999 pursuant to an agreement in writing made by that date.

Amended by 1995-97 technical bill, retroactive to amounts received after 1990, to add the word "refund" in 12(1)(x)(iv), and make minor non-substantive drafting changes throughout. The addition of "refund" reverses the effect of *Canada Safeway*, [1998] 1 C.T.C. 120 (FCA), where a refund of federal sales tax was ruled non-taxable.

The reference in 12(1)(x)(vi) to 127(11.5) and (11.6) applies only to taxation years that begin after 1995 (1995 Budget bill; restated in 1995-97 technical bill).

12(1)(x) amended by 1990 GST, effective for amounts received after January 1990 (subparas. (iv), (vi) and (vii)) and May 22, 1985 (subpara. (v)). In subparas. (iv) and (vi), "expense" was changed to "outlay or expense". Subparas. (v) and (vii) formerly read:

(v) was not otherwise included in computing the taxpayer's income for the year or a preceding taxation year,

. . . . .

(vii) does not reduce, pursuant to subsection 13(7.4) or paragraph 53(2)(s), the cost or capital cost of the property, as the case may be, or

12(1)(x) originally added by 1985 Budget, effective for amounts received after May 22, 1985 other than amounts received after that date pursuant to the terms of an agreement in writing entered into before 4:30 p.m. EDST May 23, 1985 or to the terms of a prospectus, preliminary prospectus or registration statement filed before May 24, 1985 with a public authority in Canada pursuant to and in accordance with the securities legislation of Canada or of any province and, where required by law, accepted for filing by such authority.

Subsec. 4(4) of the *Western Grain Transition Payments Act* (1995, c. 17, Sch. II), as amended by 1995-97 technical bill (s. 303), provides, effective for payments made after June 22, 1995:

4. (4) **Tax treatment** — For the purposes of the *Income Tax Act*,

. . . . .

(b) a transition payment received in respect of farmland that was, immediately before its disposition by the applicant, capital property of the applicant shall, where the farmland is disposed of before the payment is received, be considered to be an amount required by subsection 53(2) of that Act to be deducted in computing the adjusted cost base of the farmland to the applicant immediately before the disposition;

(c) a transition payment to which neither paragraph (a) nor (b) applies, received by the applicant, shall be considered to be assistance received in the course of earning income from a business or property in respect of the cost of the property or in respect of an outlay or an expense; and

(d) where, pursuant to an equitable arrangement referred to in paragraph 6(c), a portion of a transition payment received by an applicant is paid to a person or partnership that is leasing farmland from the applicant, that portion paid to the person or partnership is required to be included in computing the income of the person or partnership from a business for the taxation year of the person or partnership in which it is received and the amount so paid is deemed not to be a transition payment received by the applicant for the purposes of paragraphs (a) to (c).

See also Notes at end of 53(2) re payments in respect of farmland that is capital property.

**Regulations**: 234–236 (information slips for farm support payments); 7300 (prescribed amount).

**Interpretation Bulletins**: IT-151R5: Scientific research and experimental development expenditures; IT-232R3: Losses — their deductibility in the loss year or in other years; IT-273R2: Government assistance — general comments.

**I.T. Technical News**: No. 5 (western grain transition payments); No. 7 (lease inducement payments — renewal term); No. 16 (*Canderel*, *Toronto College Park* and *Ikea* cases).

(x.1) **fuel tax rebates** — the total of all amounts each of which is

(i) a fuel tax rebate received in the year by the taxpayer under subsection 68.4(3) [of] the *Excise Tax Act*, or

(ii) the amount determined by the formula

$$10(A - B) - C$$

where

A is the total of all fuel tax rebates under subsections 68.4(2) and (3.1) of that Act received in the year by the taxpayer,

B is the total of all amounts, in respect of fuel tax rebates under section 68.4 of that Act received in the year by the taxpayer, repaid by the taxpayer under subsection 68.4(7) of that Act, and

C is the total of all amounts, in respect of fuel tax rebates under section 68.4 of that Act received in the year, deducted under subsection 111(10) in computing the taxpayer's non-capital losses for other taxation years;

**Related Provisions**: 87(2)(uu) — Fuel tax rebates; 88(1)(e.2) — Winding-up; 111(10) — Fuel tax rebate — loss abatement; 111(11) — Fuel tax rebate — partnerships; 161(7)(a)(viii) — Effect of carry-back of loss, etc.; 164(5)(a) — Effect of carry-back of loss, etc.; 164(5.1)(a) — Effect of carry-back of loss, etc.; 257 — Formula cannot calculate to less than zero.

**Notes**: 12(1)(x.1) originally added by 1992 transportation industry assistance bill, effective 1992. The bill added s. 68.4 to the *Excise Tax Act*, providing a fuel tax rebate for small truckers of up to $500, and also implemented the Loss Offset program, under which businesses could claim a fuel tax rebate under the *Excise Tax Act* of 3¢ per litre of fuel purchased. In exchange the business must bring into income 10 times the amount of rebate received. The second program was thus only of interest to businesses with substantial losses that would not otherwise be used up in the near future. Both programs applied only to fuel purchased in 1991 or 1992.

12(1)(x.1)(ii) amended by 1997 Budget (first bill), effective for 1997 and later taxation years. The 1997 version of the rebate is part of a package announced in fall 1996 to rescue Canadian Airlines International Ltd. from bankruptcy. However, the rebate is available to any airline corporation that has losses and wishes to use it.

For excise taxes paid from 1996 to 2000, airline companies carrying on business in Canada can obtain a rebate of up to $20 million per year of federal excise taxes paid on aviation fuel, in exchange for giving up the right to claim income tax losses. They must give up $10 of accumulated tax losses for each $1 of excise tax rebate. They can, at their discretion, repay the excise tax rebates received and fully reinstate the losses previously exchanged. Airline companies that reinstate their losses in future years are not required to pay an associated interest charge on their repayment of the rebate for the period up to January 1, 2000. After that date, interest will be charged at the prescribed rate.

ETA s. 68.4, which provides the rebate, is reproduced in *The Practitioner's Goods and Services Tax, Annotated* and the *Canada GST Service*.

The 1997 amendment to 12(1)(x.1)(ii) simply added references to 68.4(3.1) and reworded the subparagraph as a formula. For 1992–96, read:

(ii) the amount, if any, by which

(A) 10 times the amount, if any, by which

(I) the total of all fuel tax rebates under subsection 68.4(2) of that Act received in the year by the taxpayer

exceeds

(II) the total of all amounts, in respect of fuel tax rebates under subsection 68.4(2) of that Act received in the year by the taxpayer, repaid by the taxpayer under subsection 68.4(7) of that Act

exceeds

(B) the total of all amounts, in respect of fuel tax rebates under subsection 68.4(2) of that Act received in the year, deducted under subsection 111(10) in computing the taxpayer's non-capital loss for a year;

(y) **automobile provided to partner** — where the taxpayer is an individual who is a member of a partnership or an employee of a member of a partnership and the partnership makes an automobile available in the year to the taxpayer or to a person related to the taxpayer, the amounts that would be included by reason of paragraph 6(1)(e) in the income of the taxpayer for the year if the taxpayer were employed by the partnership;

**Notes**: The benefit in respect of automobile operating costs, under 6(1)(k) or (l), does not appear to apply to partners. Only the benefits under 6(1)(e) are included under this paragraph.

12(1)(y) amended by 1990 GST, effective for taxation years and fiscal periods ending after 1990, to add a reference to 6(1)(e.1), and amended by 1997 GST/HST bill, effective for 1996 and later taxation years, to delete the reference. For 1991-95, read, after "6(1)(e)", the words:

or by reason of paragraph 6(1)(e.1) if that paragraph were read without reference to paragraph 6(1)(a)

GST is now included in the taxable benefit calculation under 6(7) rather than specifically included in income under 6(1)(e.1).

**Interpretation Bulletins**: IT-63R5: Benefits, including standby charge for an automobile, from the personal use of a motor vehicle supplied by an employer — after 1992.

(z) **amateur athlete trust payments** — any amount in respect of an amateur athlete trust required by section 143.1 to be included in computing the taxpayer's income for the year;

**Related Provisions**: 143.1(2) — Amounts included in beneficiary's income.

**Notes**: 12(1)(z) added by 1992 technical bill, effective 1988.

**Forms**: T1061: Canadian amateur athlete trust group information return.

(z.1) **qualifying environmental trusts** — the total of all amounts received by the taxpayer in the year as a beneficiary under a qualifying environmental trust, whether or not the amounts are included because of subsection 107.3(1) in computing the taxpayer's income for any taxation year;

**Related Provisions**: 20(1)(ss) — Deduction for contribution to qualifying environmental trust; 87(2)(j.93) — Amalgamations — continuing corporation; 107.3(2) — Where property of qualifying environmental trust transferred to beneficiary; 107.3(3) — Income where trust ceases to be qualifying environmental trust; 107.3(4) — No income inclusion under 104(13) for amounts payable by trust.

**Notes**: 12(1)(z.1) added by 1994 Budget, effective for taxation years that end after February 22, 1994; and amended by 1997 Budget, effective for taxation years that end after February 18, 1997, to change "mining reclamation trusts" to "qualifying environmental trusts" (the same change was made throughout the Act).

Part XII of the Regulations is to be amended so that amounts included under 12(1)(z.1) will not be included for purposes of the resource allowance.

(z.2) **dispositions of interests in qualifying environmental trusts** — the total of all amounts each of which is the consideration received by the taxpayer in the year for the disposition to another person or partnership of all or part of the taxpayer's interest as a beneficiary under a qualifying environmental trust, other than consideration that is the assumption of a reclamation obligation in respect of the trust;

**Related Provisions**: 20(1)(tt) — Deduction for acquisition of interest in qualifying environmental trust; 39(1)(a)(v) — No capital gain on disposition of interest; 87(2)(j.93) — Amalgamations — continuing corporation; 107.3(1)(b) — Where beneficiary not resident in Canada.

**Notes**: 12(1)(z.2) added by 1994 Budget, effective for taxation years that end after February 22, 1994; and amended by 1997 Budget, effective for taxation years that end after February 18, 1997, to change "mining reclamation trust" to "qualifying environmental trust" (the same change was made throughout the Act).

Part XII of the Regulations is to be amended so that amounts included under 12(1)(z.2) will not be included for purposes of the resource allowance.

(z.3) **debt forgiveness** — any amount required because of subsection 80(13) or (17) to be included in computing the taxpayer's income for the year;

**Notes**: 12(1)(z.3) added by 1994 tax amendments bill (Part IX), effective for taxation years that end after February 21, 1994.

(z.4) **eligible funeral arrangements** — any amount required because of subsection 148.1(3) to be included in computing the taxpayer's income for the year;

**Notes**: 12(1)(z.4) added by 1994 tax amendments bill (Part IX), effective 1993.

**Interpretation Bulletins**: IT-531: Eligible funeral arrangements.

(z.5) **resource loss** — 25% of the taxpayer's prescribed resource loss for the year; and

**Related Provisions**: 20(1)(v.1) — Deduction for resource allowance; 53(1)(e)(i)(B), 53(2)(c)(i)(B) — Para. 12(1)(z.5) ignored for partnership ACB adjustment; 96(1)(d) — Para. 12(1)(z.5) ignored for allocating income at partnership level to partners.

**Notes**: 12(1)(z.5) added by 1996 Budget, effective for taxation years that begin after 1996.

**Regulations**: 1210.1 (prescribed resource loss).

(z.6) **refunds [of countervailing or anti-dumping duties]** — any amount received by the taxpayer in the year in respect of a refund of an amount that was deducted under paragraph 20(1)(vv) in computing income for any taxation year.

**Related Provisions**: 13(21)"undepreciated capital cost"K — Deduction of refund from u.c.c. of depreciable property.

**Notes**: 12(1)(z.6) added by 1998 Budget, effective for amounts received after February 23, 1998.

**(2) Interpretation** — Paragraphs (1)(a) and (b) are enacted for greater certainty and shall not be construed as implying that any amount not referred to in those paragraphs is not to be included in computing income from a business for a taxation year whether it is received or receivable in the year or not.

**(2.1) Receipt of inducement, reimbursement, etc.** — For the purposes of paragraph (1)(x), where at a particular time a taxpayer who is a beneficiary of a trust or a member of a partnership has received an amount as an inducement, whether as a grant, subsidy, forgivable loan, deduction from tax, allowance or any other form of inducement, in respect of the activities of the trust or partnership, or as a reimbursement, contribution, allowance or as assistance, whether as a grant, subsidy, forgivable loan, deduction from tax, allowance or any other form of assistance, in respect of the cost of property or in respect of an expense of the trust or partnership, the amount shall be deemed to have been received at that time by the trust or partnership, as the case may be, as such an inducement, reimbursement, contribution, allowance or assistance.

**Notes**: 12(2.1) added by 1985 Budget, effective with respect to amounts received after May 22, 1985 other than amounts received after that date pursuant to the terms of an agreement in writing entered into before May 23, 1985 or to the terms of a prospectus, preliminary prospectus or registration statement filed before May 24, 1985 with a public authority in Canada in accordance with the securities legislation of Canada or of any province and, where required by law, accepted for filing by such authority.

**Interpretation Bulletins**: IT-273R2: Government assistance — general comments.

## (2.2) Deemed outlay or expense — Where

(a) in a taxation year a taxpayer receives an amount that would, but for this subsection, be included under paragraph (1)(x) in computing the taxpayer's income for the year in respect of an outlay or expense (other than an outlay or expense in respect of the cost of property of the taxpayer) made or incurred by the taxpayer before the end of the following taxation year, and

(b) the taxpayer elects under this subsection on or before the day on or before which the taxpayer's return of income under this Part for the year is required to be filed, or would be required to be filed if tax under this Part were payable by the taxpayer for the year or, where the outlay or expense is made or incurred in the following taxation year, for that following year,

the amount of the outlay or expense shall be deemed for the purpose of computing the taxpayer's income, other than for the purposes of this subsection and paragraphs (1)(x) and 20(1)(hh), to have always been the amount, if any, by which

(c) the amount of the outlay or expense

exceeds

(d) the lesser of the amount elected by the taxpayer under this subsection and the amount so received by the taxpayer,

and, notwithstanding subsections 152(4) to (5), such assessment or reassessment of the taxpayer's tax, interest and penalties under this Act for any taxation year shall be made as is necessary to give effect to the election.

**Related Provisions**: 20(1)(hh) — Repayments of inducements, etc.; 80.2 — Reimbursement by taxpayer; 87(2)(j.6) — Amalgamations — Continuing corporation.

**Notes**: 12(2.2) added by 1990 GST and amended retroactively by 1992 technical bill, effective for amounts received after January 1990. The amendment allows an election in respect of an outlay incurred at any time before (instead of up to 3 years before) the related receipt.

**Interpretation Bulletins**: IT-273R2: Government assistance — general comments.

## (3) Interest income [accrual to year-end] —

Subject to subsection (4.1), in computing the income for a taxation year of a corporation, partnership, unit trust or any trust of which a corporation or a partnership is a beneficiary, there shall be included any interest on a debt obligation (other than interest in respect of an income bond, an income debenture, a small business bond, a small business development bond, a net income stabilization account or an indexed debt obligation) that accrues to it to the end of the year, or becomes receivable or is received by it before the end of the year, to the extent that the interest was not included in computing its income for a preceding taxation year.

**Related Provisions**: 12(4) — Annual accrual for individuals and trusts; 12(4.1) — Impaired debt obligations; 12(9) — Deemed accrual; 12.2(8) — Deemed acquisition of interest in annuity; 16(1) — Blended payments; 20(1)(l) — Reserve for doubtful debts; 20(14.1) — Interest on debt obligation; 20(19) — Annuity contract; 87(2)(j.4) — Amalgamations — continuing corporation; 138(11.5)(k) — Transfer of business by non-resident insurer; 138(12)"gross investment revenue"E(b) — Inclusion in gross investment revenue of insurer; 142.3(1)(c) — No income accrual from specified debt obligation; 142.4(1)"tax basis"(b) — Disposition of specified debt obligation by financial institution; 142.5(3)(a) — Mark-to-market debt obligation; 148(9)"adjusted cost basis"D — Inclusion in "adjusted cost basis".

**Notes**: 12(3) amended by 1992 technical bill to add reference to a net income stabilization account, effective 1991.

Amended by 1993 technical bill to add reference to an indexed debt obligation, effective for debt obligation issued after October 16, 1991. (See 16(6).)

Amended by 1995-97 technical bill, effective on the same basis as the addition to 12(4.1), to change "Notwithstanding paragraph (1)(c)" to "Subject to subsection (4.1)".

See also Notes to 12(4).

**Regulations**: 303 (amount deductible under subsec. 20(19)).

**Interpretation Bulletins**: IT-87R2: Policyholders' income from life insurance policies; IT-142R3: Settlement of debts on the winding-up of a corporation; IT-265R3: Payments of income and capital combined; IT-345R: Special reserve — loans secured by mortgages; IT-396R: Interest income; IT-466: Trust companies.

## (4) Interest from investment contract [annual accrual] — Subject to subsection (4.1), where in a taxation year a taxpayer (other than a taxpayer to whom subsection (3) applies) holds an interest in an investment contract on any anniversary day of the contract, there shall be included in computing the taxpayer's income for the year the interest that accrued to the taxpayer to the end of that day with respect to the investment contract, to the extent that the interest was not otherwise included in computing the taxpayer's income for the year or any preceding taxation year.

**Related Provisions**: 12(4.1) — Impaired debt obligations; 12(9) — Deemed accrual; 12(11) — Investment contract; 20(14.1) — Interest on debt obligation.

**Notes**: 12(4) amended by 1995-97 technical bill, effective on the same basis as the addition to 12(4.1), to add "Subject to subsection (4.1)".

12(4) amended and 12(5)–(8) repealed by 1989 Budget, effective (per 1991 technical bill) for investment contracts last acquired after 1989. For those last acquired before 1990, read:

> (4) **Idem** — Where in a taxation year a taxpayer (other than a corporation, partnership, unit trust or any trust of which a corporation or partnership is a beneficiary) holds an interest in an investment contract on any third anniversary of the contract and in the year or any preceding taxation year he has not made an election under subsection (8) with respect to his interest, there shall be included in computing his income for the year the interest that accrued to him to that time with respect to the investment contract to the extent that the interest was not otherwise included in computing his income for the taxation year or any preceding taxation year, and to the extent that the interest accrued to him after December 31, 1981.
>
> (5) **Exception** — Subsection (3) does not apply to a corporation, partnership or trust (other than a corporation described in any of paragraphs 39(5)(b) to (d), a life insurance corporation or any other corporation, other than a mutual fund corpo-

ration or a mortgage investment corporation, whose principal business is the making of loans or that borrows money from the public in the course of carrying on a business the principal purpose of which is the making of loans)

    (a) for taxation years ending before December 31, 1984, or

    (b) with respect to interest accrued before the beginning of its first taxation year commencing after November 12, 1981,

with respect to an interest in a debt obligation last acquired by it before October 29, 1980 unless the obligation was issued by a person with whom the corporation or trust or any member of the partnership was not dealing at arm's length.

(6) **Application** — Subsection (3) does not apply in computing the income for a taxation year of a taxpayer (other than a corporation described in any of paragraphs 39(5)(b) to (d), a life insurance corporation or any other corporation, other than a mutual fund corporation or a mortgage investment corporation, whose principal business is the making of loans or that borrows money from the public in the course of carrying on a business the principal purpose of which is the making of loans) if the interest of the taxpayer was last acquired before October 29, 1980, and

    (a) the taxpayer could not, after October 28, 1980 and before the end of the taxation year, require the repayment, acquisition, cancellation or conversion of the interest (other than by reason of a failure or default under the terms or conditions thereof),

    (b) the maturity date of the debt obligation has not been extended after October 28, 1980 and before the end of the taxation year, and the terms or conditions relating to payments with respect to interest have not been changed during that period, and

    (c) the debt obligation was issued by a person with whom the taxpayer or, where the taxpayer is a partnership, each member thereof, was dealing at arm's length.

(7) [Applied to 1978 taxation year only]

(8) **Accrued interest may be included in income** — Where a taxpayer (other than a taxpayer to whom subsection (3) applies) who holds an interest in a debt obligation elects in his return of income under this Part for a taxation year, he shall, in computing his income for the year and each subsequent taxation year during which he holds an interest in the debt obligation, include the interest accrued to him on the debt obligation to the end of the year to the extent that it was not otherwise included in computing his income for the year or any preceding taxation year.

The change to subsecs. (4)–(8) was from mandatory reporting of accruing interest every three years to reporting of accruing interest every year. For investments acquired in 1990 or later, accrued interest must be reported by individuals every year on the anniversary date. For corporations, partnerships and certain trusts, accrued income must be reported under 12(3) at year-end, meaning that the income for the year *in which the investment was acquired* must include the income accrued from acquisition date to year-end.

**Regulations**: 201(4) (information return).

**Interpretation Bulletins**: IT-265R3: Payments of income and capital combined; IT-415R2: Deregistration of RRSPs.

**Advance Tax Rulings**: ATR-61: Interest accrual rules.

(4.1) **Impaired debt obligations** — Paragraph (1)(c) and subsections (3) and (4) do not apply to a taxpayer in respect of a debt obligation for the part of a taxation year throughout which the obligation is impaired where an amount in respect of the obligation is deductible because of subparagraph 20(1)(l)(ii) in computing the taxpayer's income for the year.

**Notes**: 12(4.1) added by 1995-97 technical bill, effective

    (a) for taxation years that end after September 1997; and

    (b) for taxation years that end after 1995 and before October 1997, if the taxpayer files an election for amended 20(1)(l) to apply to such years (see Notes to 20(1)(l)).

(5)–(8) [Repealed under former Act]

**Notes**: See under 12(4).

(9) **Deemed accrual** — For the purposes of subsections (3), (4) and (11) and 20(14) and (21), where a taxpayer acquires an interest in a prescribed debt obligation, an amount determined in prescribed manner shall be deemed to accrue to the taxpayer as interest on the obligation in each taxation year during which the taxpayer holds the interest in the obligation.

**Related Provisions**: 16(3) — Obligation issued at discount; 18.1(14) — Right to receive production deemed to be debt obligation; 87(2)(j.4) — Amalgamations — accrual rules; 142.3(1)(c) — No income accrual from specified debt obligation.

**Notes**: 12(9) amended by 1989 Budget, effective (per 1991 technical bill) for investment contracts last acquired after 1989, to delete reference to repealed subsec. (8).

**Regulations**: 7000 (prescribed debt obligation, prescribed manner).

**Interpretation Bulletins**: IT-396R: Interest income; IT-410R: Debt obligations — accrued interest on transfer.

**Advance Tax Rulings**: ATR-61: Interest accrual rules.

(9.1) **Exclusion of proceeds of disposition** — Where a taxpayer disposes of an interest in a debt obligation that is a debt obligation in respect of which the proportion of the payments of principal to which the taxpayer is entitled is not equal to the proportion of the payments of interest to which the taxpayer is entitled, such portion of the proceeds of disposition received by the taxpayer as can reasonably be considered to represent a recovery of the cost to the taxpayer of the interest in the debt obligation shall, notwithstanding any other provision of this Act, not be included in computing the income of the taxpayer, and for the purpose of this subsection, a debt obligation includes, for greater certainty, all of the issuer's obligations to pay principal and interest under that obligation.

**Notes**: 12(9.1) applies to dispositions of stripped bonds. Amended by 1992 technical bill so that it continues to apply to all stripped bonds, including those that are indexed debt obligations. The amendment applies to "dispositions of debt obligations occurring after October 16, 1991", and so technically might be said not to apply to a disposition of an *interest* in a debt obligation. For dispositions before that date, read:

    (9.1) **Exception for certain interests in prescribed debt obligation** — Where a taxpayer disposes of an interest in a debt obligation that, by virtue of paragraph 7000(1)(b) of the *Income Tax Regulations*, is a prescribed debt obligation for the purposes of subsection (9), such portion of the proceeds of the disposition received by him as may reasonably be considered to represent a recovery of the cost to him of the debt obligation shall, notwithstanding any other provision of this Act, not be included in computing his income under this Part.

**Interpretation Bulletins**: IT-396R: Interest income.

**(10) [Repealed under former Act]**

**Notes**: 12(10) repealed by 1989 Budget, effective (per 1991 technical bill) for investment contracts last acquired after 1989. Where it still applies, read:

> (10) Application — Subsection (4) shall not apply in computing the income of a taxpayer for a taxation year if the interest of the taxpayer in the investment contract was last acquired by him before November 13, 1981 and
>
>> (a) the taxpayer could not, after November 12, 1981 and before the end of the taxation year, require the repayment, acquisition, cancellation or conversion of his interest (other than by reason of a failure or default under the terms or conditions thereof), and
>>
>> (b) the maturity date of the contract has not been extended after November 12, 1981 and before the end of the taxation year, and the terms or conditions relating to payments in respect of his interest have not been changed during that period.

**(10.1) Income from RHOSP** — Notwithstanding any other provision of this Act, where an individual was at the end of 1985 a beneficiary under a registered home ownership savings plan (within the meanings assigned by paragraphs 146.2(1)(a) and (h) of the *Income Tax Act*, chapter 148 of the Revised Statutes of Canada, 1952, as they read in their application to the 1985 taxation year), that portion of the income that can reasonably be considered to have accrued under the plan before 1986 (other than the portion thereof that can reasonably be considered to be attributable to amounts contributed after May 22, 1985 to or under the plan) shall not be included in computing the income of the individual or of any other person.

**I.T. Application Rules**: 69 (meaning of "*Income Tax Act*, chapter 148 of the Revised Statutes of Canada, 1952").

**Interpretation Bulletins**: IT-396R: Interest income.

**(10.2) NISA receipts** — There shall be included in computing a taxpayer's income for a taxation year from a property the total of all amounts each of which is the amount determined by the formula

$$A - B$$

where

A   is an amount paid at a particular time in the year out of the taxpayer's NISA Fund No. 2; and

B   is the amount, if any, by which

> (a) the total of all amounts each of which is deemed by subsection 104(5.1) or (14.1) to have been paid out of the taxpayer's NISA Fund No. 2 before the particular time, or is deemed by subsection 70(5.4) or 73(5) to have been paid out of another person's NISA Fund No. 2 on being transferred to the taxpayer's NISA Fund No. 2 before the particular time,

exceeds

> (b) the total of all amounts each of which is the amount by which an amount otherwise determined under this subsection in respect of a payment out of the taxpayer's NISA Fund No. 2 before the particular time was reduced because of this description.

**Related Provisions**: 104(6)(b)(ii.1), (iii) — Limitation on deduction by trust for amount payable to beneficiaries; 104(14.1) — NISA election; 108(1) — "accumulating income"; 125(7)"income of the corporation for the year from an active business"(b) — "Income of the corporation for the year from an active business"; 129(4)"aggregate investment income"(b)(ii) — Exclusion from calculation of refundable dividend tax on hand; 212(1)(t) — NISA Fund No. 2 payments to non-residents; 214(3)(l) — Non-resident withholding tax; 248(9.1) — Whether trust created by taxpayer's will.

**Notes**: 12(10.2) added by 1992 technical bill, effective 1991.

**Regulations**: 201(1)(e) (information return).

**Interpretation Bulletins**: IT-212R3: Income of deceased persons — rights or things; IT-243R4: Dividend refund to private corporations; IT-305R4: Testamentary spouse trusts.

**(10.3) Amount credited or added not included in income** — Notwithstanding any other provision of this Act, an amount credited or added to a taxpayer's NISA Fund No. 2 shall not be included in computing the taxpayer's income solely because of that crediting or adding.

**Notes**: 12(10.3) added by 1992 technical bill, effective 1991.

**Forms**: T1163: Statement A — NISA account information and statement of farming activities for individuals; T1164: Statement B — NISA account information and statement of farming activities for additional farming operations; T1165: Statement C — statement of farming activities for Ontario self directed risk management (SDRM); T1175 Sched. 1: NISA/Farming — calculation of CCA and business-use-of-home expenses.

**(11) Definitions** — In this section,

**"anniversary day"** of an investment contract means

> (a) the day that is one year after the day immediately preceding the date of issue of the contract,
>
> (b) the day that occurs at every successive one year interval from the day determined under paragraph (a), and
>
> (c) the day on which the contract was disposed of;

**Notes**: 12(11)"anniversary day" was 12(11)(b) before re-enactment in R.S.C. 1985 (5th Supp.), effective for taxation years beginning after November 1991. See Table of Concordance.

12(11)(b) (now 12(11)"anniversary day") amended by 1989 Budget, effective (per 1991 technical bill) for investment contracts last acquired after 1989. Where it still applies, read:

> (b) "third anniversary" — "third anniversary" of an investment contract means
>
>> (i) the end of the day that is three years after the end of the calendar year of issue of the contract,
>>
>> (ii) the end of the day that occurs at every successive three year interval from the time determined under subparagraph (i), and
>>
>> (iii) the day on which the contract was disposed of,
>
> and for the purpose of this paragraph, where before 1989 a taxpayer has not disposed of an interest in an investment contract last acquired by him before 1982, the contract shall be deemed to have been issued on December 31, 1988.

**"investment contract"**, in relation to a taxpayer, means any debt obligation other than

(a) a salary deferral arrangement or a plan or arrangement that, but for any of paragraphs (a), (b) and (d) to (l) of the definition "salary deferral arrangement" in subsection 248(1), would be a salary deferral arrangement,

(b) a retirement compensation arrangement or a plan or arrangement that, but for any of paragraphs (a), (b), (d) and (f) to (n) of the definition "retirement compensation arrangement" in subsection 248(1), would be a retirement compensation arrangement,

(c) an employee benefit plan or a plan or arrangement that, but for any of paragraphs (a) to (e) of the definition "employee benefit plan" in subsection 248(1), would be an employee benefit plan,

(d) a foreign retirement arrangement,

(e) an income bond,

(f) an income debenture,

(g) a small business development bond,

(h) a small business bond,

(i) an obligation in respect of which the taxpayer has (otherwise than because of subsection (4)) at periodic intervals of not more than one year, included, in computing the taxpayer's income throughout the period in which the taxpayer held an interest in the obligation, the income accrued thereon for such intervals,

(j) an obligation in respect of a net income stabilization account,

(k) an indexed debt obligation, and

(l) a prescribed contract.

**Related Provisions**: 12(9) — Deemed accrual.

**Notes**: Definition "investment contract" amended by 1991 technical bill, 1992 technical bill and 1993 technical bill. Paras. (a) and (b) are effective 1986; para. (d) is effective 1990; para. (j) is effective 1991; para (k) is effective for debt obligations issued after October 16, 1991 (see 16(6)); para. (l) was formerly numbered (k); and for debt obligations acquired before 1990, read "3 years" in place of "one year" in para. (i).

12(11)"investment contract" was 12(11)(a) before re-enactment in R.S.C. 1985 (5th Supp.), effective for taxation years beginning after November 1991. See Table of Concordance.

**Regulations**: 7000(6) (prescribed contract).

**Interpretation Bulletins [subsec. 12(11)]**: IT-396R: Interest income; IT-415R2: Deregistration of RRSPs.

**Definitions [s. 12]**: "allowable capital loss" — 38(b), 248(1); "amateur athlete trust" — 143.1(1)(a), 248(1); "amount" — 248(1); "anniversary day" — 12(11); "arm's length" — 251(1); "assessment" — 248(1); "assistance" — 79(4), 125.4(5), 248(16), 248(18); "automobile", "bankrupt", "business" — 248(1); "Canada" — 255; "Canadian resource property" — 66(15), 248(1), "controlled" — 256(6), (6.1); "corporation" — 248(1), *Interpretation Act* 35(1); "credit union" — 137(6), 248(1); "deferred amount", "dividend", "employee", "employee benefit plan", "employee trust" — 248(1); "employees profit sharing plan" — 144(1), 248(1); "employer" — 248(1); "foreign affiliate" — 95(1), 248(1); "foreign oil and gas business" — 126(7); "foreign retirement arrangement" — 248(1); "income from property" — 9(1), 9(3); "income bond", "income debenture", "indexed debt obligation", "individual", "insurance corporation", "insurer" — 248(1); "investment contract" — 12(11); "investment corporation" — 130(3), 248(1); "lending asset", "life insurance corporation" — 248(1); "life insurance policy" — 138(12), 248(1); "mineral resource", "mineral" — 248(1); "mortgage investment corporation" — 130.1(6), 248(1); "mutual fund corporation" — 131(8), 248(1); "net income stabilization account", "NISA Fund No. 2" — 248(1); "partnership" — see Notes to 96(1); "payer" — 12(1)(x)(i); "person" — 248(1); "personal services business" — 125(7), 248(1); "prescribed" — 248(1); "prescribed debt obligation" — Reg. 7000; "prescribed resource loss" — Reg. 1210.1; "production tax amount" — 126(7); "property" — 248(1); "province" — *Interpretation Act* 35(1); "qualifying environmental trust — 248(1); "related" — 251(2); "resident in Canada" — 250; "retirement compensation arrangement", "salary deferral arrangement", "share" — 248(1); "small business bond" — 15.2, 248(1); "small business development bond" — 15.1, 248(1); "tar sands" — 248(1); "tax payable" — 248(2); "taxable capital gain" — 38(a), 248(1); "taxation year" — 249; "taxpayer" — 248(1); "trust" — 104(1), 248(1), (3); "unit trust" — 108(2), 248(1).

## 12.1 Cash bonus on Canada Savings Bonds
— Notwithstanding any other provision of this Act, where in a taxation year a taxpayer receives an amount from the Government of Canada in respect of a Canada Savings Bond as a cash bonus that the Government of Canada has undertaken to pay (other than any amount of interest, bonus or principal agreed to be paid at the time of the issue of the bond under the terms of the bond), the taxpayer shall, in computing the taxpayer's income for the year, include as interest in respect of the Canada Savings Bond $1/2$ of the cash bonus so received.

**Related Provisions**: 12(1)(c) — Interest.

**Notes**: The half-taxation of cash bonuses on CSBs was originally intended (in 1974) to give such bonuses treatment similar to capital gains. With the increase in capital gains inclusion rate ($2/3$ for 1988 and 1989, $3/4$ for 1990–Feb. 28, 2000), the treatment of cash bonuses differed from that of capital gains, but it is now the same again.

**Definitions [s. 12.1]**: "amount" — 248(1); "taxation year" — 249; "taxpayer" — 248(1).

**Regulations**: 220 (information return).

**Forms**: T600C: Statement of cash bonus payment — Canada Savings Bonds.

## 12.2 (1) Amount to be included [annually from life insurance policy]
— Where in a taxation year a taxpayer holds an interest, last acquired after 1989, in a life insurance policy that is not

(a) an exempt policy,

(b) a prescribed annuity contract, and

(c) a contract under which the policyholder has, under the terms and conditions of a life insurance policy that was not an annuity contract and that was last acquired before December 2, 1982, received the proceeds therefrom in the form of an annuity contract,

on any anniversary day of the policy, there shall be included in computing the taxpayer's income for the taxation year the amount, if any, by which the accumulating fund on that day in respect of the interest in the policy, as determined in prescribed manner, exceeds the adjusted cost basis to the taxpayer of the interest in the policy on that day.

## Proposed Amendment — RRSP & RRIF annuity contracts

**Department of Finance news release, October 27, 1998**: *Segregated Funds*

Proposed new rules for segregated funds were announced on October 23, 1997. These rules, which are not included in the draft legislation, are intended to put interests in segregated funds offered by life insurers on an equal footing with units in mutual funds for the purposes of the 20% foreign property limit. The October 23, 1997 press release indicated that these rules would begin to apply from January 1999. However, consultation with the insurance industry has indicated the considerable extent of the systems changes that will be required for the insurance industry to monitor these limits, and the need to consider substantial technical amendments to the rules governing the taxation of segregated funds. Given the technical and administrative issues associated with this proposal, the Minister announced that the foreign property rules for segregated funds would apply only as of January 2001.

**Department of Finance news release, October 23, 1997**: *Minister Provides Details of Foreign Property Limit for Segregated Funds*

Finance Minister Paul Martin today announced details of the proposed changes to the *Income Tax Act* that will extend the 20 per cent foreign property investment limit to segregated fund policies held under registered retirement savings plans, registered retirement income funds and other deferred-income vehicles.

A segregated fund policy is an arrangement created by an insurance company, under which investors' returns are based on the return earned by the insurer on a specified group of properties. It is a life insurance product that, from the perspective of an investor, is similar to a mutual fund.

Under the existing law, units in a mutual fund are generally treated as foreign property at any time in a year if more than 20 per cent of the mutual fund's assets in the preceding year consisted of foreign property. On December 19, 1996, Minister Martin announced that beginning in 1998 similar rules would apply to segregated funds subject to transitional measures that would be discussed with the insurance industry.

Further to these consultations, it is proposed that the foreign property limit be phased-in over 4 years for segregated funds created before 1997 and that certain segregated funds no longer issued be exempt from the proposed rules. Where the 20 per cent foreign property limit is exceeded, the special penalty tax in the *Income Tax Act* will apply beginning January 1999 to interests in a segregated fund that are foreign property. The characterization of an interest in a segregated fund as foreign property is generally based on the amount of foreign property held by the fund in the previous year. Consequently, beginning in 1998, insurance companies will need to monitor the level of foreign property in segregated funds that they offer.

The attached appendix describes the proposed new rules in greater detail. Draft legislation to implement these proposals will be released next year.

For further information: Andrew Nicholls, Tax Legislation Division, (613) 995-3586.

## APPENDIX
### Application of Foreign Property Limit to Segregated Funds

1. Introduction

The new foreign property rules for segregated funds will apply in three situations.

First, they will apply where an interest in a segregated fund is held by a tax-exempt taxpayer described in paragraphs 205(a) to (f) of the *Income Tax Act*, such as a registered pension plan (RPP), a trust governed by a registered retirement savings plan (RRSP) or a trust governed by a registered retirement income fund (RRIF). Such taxpayers are subject to tax under Part XI of the Act if they invest too heavily in "foreign property". Under the proposed changes, an interest in a segregated fund will, in some circumstances, become a "foreign property" and the holding of such an interest can result in Part XI tax becoming payable.

A similar penalty tax may apply where an interest in a segregated fund policy is held directly as an RRSP or RRIF (i.e., outside of an RRSP or RRIF trust), or where such an interest is issued under an RPP that is not an RPP trust or corporation. The tax will generally be collected by the insurer that issued the segregated fund policy on behalf of the policyholder that is liable to pay it.

Third, the new rules can result in Part XI tax for an insurer where the Minister accepts a segregated fund administered by the insurer as a "registered investment" under proposed amendments to Part X.2 of the Act.

The application of the proposed rules to these three situations is described below.

2. Tax payable under Part XI of the *Income Tax Act* by trusts governed by RRSPs, RRIFs and RPPs

*General*

A trust governed by an RRSP, RRIF or RPP is generally liable to pay a penalty tax under subsection 206(2) of the Act in respect of a month where the cost amount to the trust of the "foreign property" (as defined in subsection 206(1)) held by the trust exceeds 20 per cent of the cost amount to the trust of all property held by it.

Under paragraph (i) of the definition "foreign property", an interest in a trust is a foreign property, except where the trust is a "registered investment" or where the interest in the trust is prescribed not to be a foreign property under the *Income Tax Regulations*. Under the proposed amendments, after 1998, an interest in a segregated fund will be a treated as an interest in a trust for the purpose of Part XI. As a consequence, a trust governed by an RRSP, RRIF or RPP that holds a segregated fund policy in any month that ends after 1998 may be liable to pay the penalty tax under Part XI.

*When is an Interest in a Segregated Fund Prescribed Not to be a Foreign Property?*

The proposed amendments include a number of transitional provisions described below. However, section 5000 of the Regulations will prescribe an interest in a segregated fund held at a particular time not to be a foreign property in two cases:

- where the particular time is after 1999 and, throughout the last year that ended before the particular time (or at the end of the year that includes the particular time, if the fund was created in the year that includes the particular time), the total cost amount of all the foreign prop-

erty held by the segregated fund does not exceed 20 per cent of the cost amount of all the property held by it; or
- where each policyholder holding an interest in the segregated fund at the particular time held an interest in the fund at the end of 1996 or acquired the interest from another policyholder who held an interest in the fund before 1997.

Transitional rules are proposed for 1999, 2000 and 2001 to give insurers an opportunity to shift the properties held by the segregated funds that they administer from foreign properties to non-foreign properties. To this end, an interest in a segregated fund will be prescribed not to be a foreign property in 1999 where:
- the segregated fund was created before 1997 and, at any time in the first 90 days of 1998, the fair market value (FMV) of all the foreign property held by the fund does not exceed 80 per cent of the FMV of all the property held by the fund;
- the segregated fund was created in 1997 or 1998 and, at any time in the first 90 days of its 1998 taxation year, the FMV of all the foreign property held by the fund does not exceed 20 per cent of the FMV of all of the property held by the fund; or
- the segregated fund was created in 1999 and, at the end of 1999, the cost amount of all of the foreign property held by the fund does not exceed 20 per cent of the cost amount of all of the property held by the fund.

In 2000, an interest in a segregated fund will be prescribed not to be a foreign property if the segregated fund was created before 1997 and, throughout 1999, the cost amount of all the foreign property held by the segregated fund does not exceed 60 per cent of the cost amount of all the property held by the fund.

In 2001, an interest in a segregated fund will be prescribed not to be a foreign property if the segregated fund was created before 1997 and, throughout 2000, the cost amount of all the foreign property held by the segregated fund does not exceed 40 per cent of the cost amount of all the property held by the segregated fund.

*"Cost Amount" for the Purposes of Part XI of the Act*

Under the proposed amendments, where an interest in a segregated fund is, after 1998, treated as "foreign property", the "cost amount" of the interest will be determined on a lagged basis.

Specifically, the "cost amount" of an interest in a segregated fund to an RRSP trust, RRIF trust or RPP will be its adjusted cost base (ACB), except that the ACB adjustments that would otherwise be required in a particular calendar year will not be made until after March of the following calendar year. An interest in a segregated fund will have a known constant ACB throughout each year as ACB adjustments in respect of the year will not be made until the following year, making it possible for taxpayers subject to the foreign property penalty tax to comply with the foreign property limit on an on-going basis.

3. New Foreign Property Limits with respect to Segregated Fund Policies Issued or Effected as RRSPs or RRIFs and Policies Issued under RPPs

*Segregated Fund Policies Issued or Effected as RRSPs or RRIFs*

The new rules will also apply where, after 1998, an individual holds an interest in a segregated fund directly as an RRSP or RRIF (i.e., outside a RRSP or RRIF trust). In general, the policyholder's liability for penalty tax will be determined on a policy-by-policy basis. Where the penalty tax is owing, the insurer that issued the segregated fund will be required to collect the penalty tax on behalf of the policyholder.

A policyholder will be liable to pay the penalty tax in respect of a segregated fund policy for any month where the total cost amount (determined on a lagged basis as described above) at the end of the month of all the interests in segregated funds under the policy that are foreign properties exceeds 20 per cent of the total of
- the cash surrender value of the policy at the end of the month (not including any amount in respect of an interest in a segregated fund), and
- the total cost amount (determined on a lagged basis) at the end of the month of all the interests in segregated funds under the policy.

For this purpose, whether an interest in a segregated fund is a foreign property is determined using the definition of "foreign property" described above.

Where an insurer has issued interests in more than one segregated fund policy, the insurer will be able to treat those policies as one policy for purposes of calculating how much penalty tax is payable. The election will allow policies that derive their value largely from foreign property to be offset by policies that derive their value largely from non-foreign property.

*Segregated Fund Policies Issued under RPPs*

The administrator of an RPP (other than an RPP trust or corporation) may also be liable to pay foreign property tax where the RPP is funded or partially funded by an interest in a segregated fund policy.

The administrator's liability will be determined on an insurer-by-insurer basis. As a consequence, all the segregated fund policies used to fund the RPP that were issued by a particular insurer will be grouped together for this purpose. The administrator will be liable to pay tax in a given month in respect of the policies issued by a particular insurer where the total cost amount (determined on a lagged basis as described above) at the end of the month of all the interests in segregated funds that arise under the policies and that are foreign properties exceeds 20 per cent of the total of
- the cash surrender values, at the end of the month, of all the policies (not including any amount in respect of an interest in a segregated fund), and
- the total cost amount (determined on a lagged basis) at the end of the month of all the interests in segregated funds that arise under the policies.

For this purpose, whether an interest in a segregated fund is a foreign property will be determined using the definition of "foreign property" described above.

Where an RPP is funded with segregated fund policies issued by more than one insurer, the administrator of the RPP will be able to elect to treat all such insurers as one insurer for purposes of determining its penalty tax liability. Where the policies issued by one insurer have a high foreign property content, the election will make it possible for an administrator to offset that high foreign property content with the non-foreign property content of policies issued by other insurers.

The responsibility for collecting and remitting an administrator's penalty tax falls on the insurer, unless the administrator makes the election to treat all insurers as one. Where this election is made, the responsibility for collecting and remitting the penalty tax falls on the administrator.

4. Registered Investments

Under the proposed rules, Revenue Canada will be able to accept a segregated fund as a registered investment under subsection 204.4(1) of the *Income Tax Act*. If a segregated fund is accepted, an interest in the fund will not be a foreign property for the purposes of the Act. However, the insurer administering the segregated fund will be subject to tax under Part XI of the Act if the foreign property held by the segregated fund ever exceeds the 20 per cent foreign property limit.

The proposed amendments include a transitional provision. If a segregated fund that was created before 1997 is accepted by Revenue Canada as a registered investment under subsection 204.4(1) of the Act, the foreign property limit under Part XI in respect of the fund will be 60 per cent in 1999 and 40 per cent in 2000.

### Department of Finance news release, December 19, 1996: *Minister Announces Proposals Affecting Segregated Fund Policies and Other Annuity Contracts*

Finance Minister Paul Martin today announced a number of proposed measures affecting the tax treatment of annuity contracts, including segregated fund policies, offered by insurers.

A segregated fund policy is an arrangement made by a person with an insurer, under which the person's returns are based on the returns earned by the insurer on a specified group of properties. It is a life insurance product that, from the perspective of an investor, is similar to a mutual fund.

The most important measures announced today relate to the 20% foreign property limit set out in Part XI of the *Income Tax Act* for taxpayers such as trusts governed by registered retirement savings plans. Under the existing law, units in a mutual fund are generally treated as foreign property where more than 20% of the mutual fund's assets are foreign property. In order to bridge a gap in the existing law and to provide for a more level playing field, the same characterization will now apply to segregated fund policies

The proposed changes are described in more detail in the attached appendix. It is intended that the new rules applying the foreign property limits will be effective after 1997. This will provide a full opportunity to discuss with representatives of the insurance industry the nature of any transitional measures that might be considered to be appropriate. Once consultations are completed, the Minister intends to table the necessary legislation to implement these proposals in the House of Commons.

For further information: Andrew Nicholls, Tax Legislation Division (613) 995-3586.

### Appendix — Proposed Changes for Segregated Funds and Other Annuities: *Background*

There are a number of different types of RRSPs and RRIFs currently available to Canadians. One type is the RRSP or RRIF trust, which is a trust established to hold "qualified investments" for the benefit of the RRSP or RRIF annuitant. Another type is the RRSP or RRIF deposit, which is a contract under which a financial institution agrees to repay a principal amount deposited plus stipulated interest.

A deferred annuity contract issued by an insurer can also be an RRSP or RRIF. Under a deferred annuity contract, the annuitant is entitled to, or is ultimately entitled to elect to receive, a stream of annuity payments at a later date. Quite often a deferred annuity contract provides for amounts, determined with reference to fixed rates of interest, to accumulate prior to maturity in much the way that funds can accumulate through GICs. Variable or segregated fund annuity contracts can also be issued, under which the amount of a future stream of annuity payments will depend largely on the value of a specified group of properties acquired by the insurer with the premiums contributed. An individual's interest in a segregated fund annuity contract is analogous to an investment in a mutual fund.

The foreign property rules in Part XI of the Income Tax Act limit the extent to which a number of specified taxpayers (including RRSP and RRIF trusts) can invest outside Canada. There is a 20% foreign property limit in this context. However, for these purposes, under the existing rules a segregated fund policy is technically not considered to be foreign property regardless of the nature of the segregated fund's assets. In addition, the existing foreign property rules do not apply to segregated fund policies issued as RRSPs and RRIFs.

In addition, there are two technical anomalies under the existing income tax rules that apply to RRIFs and annuities which are addressed by the proposed amendments described below.

First, RRIF trusts cannot acquire an annuity as a "qualified investment" and the law is not entirely clear on the circumstances in which RRSP trusts can acquire annuities.

Second, annuities that are issued as RRIFs may technically not be exempt from the accrual rules under section 12.2 of the Act. These rules require income accruing under annuity contracts to be reported annually. The application of these rules to RRIFs is particularly anomalous because annuities issued as RRSPs are exempt from these rules.

*Proposed Amendments*

*(a) Qualified Investments*

An annuity contract (including a segregated fund policy) that is issued by a person licensed or otherwise authorized under the laws of Canada or a province to carry on in Canada an annuities business will be allowed to be a qualified investment for an RRSP or RRIF trust. For such an annuity contract to be a qualified investment under an RRSP or RRIF trust under the new rules,

  the contract must be acquired by the trust after 1997,

  the trust must be the only person (other than the insurer who issued the contract) entitled to future rights or benefits under the contract, and

  the timing and amount of the trust's entitlements cannot be affected by the personal circumstances of any individual, other than the length of the life of the individual who was the RRSP or RRIF annuitant immediately after the contract was acquired.

This amendment will be implemented by way of an amendment to Part XLIX of the *Income Tax Regulations*. No change to paragraph (c) of the definition "qualified investment" in subsection 146(1) of the Act is contemplated. However, it is contemplated that subsection 146(11) of the Act will be amended to provide that it does not apply to annuity contracts issued after 1997.

*(b) Accrual Rules*

An annuity contract issued as a RRIF will not be subject to the accrual rules under section 12.2 of the Act.

This amendment will be implemented by way of an amendment to subsection 304(1) of the Regulations. It is contemplated that it will apply to taxation years that begin after 1986, given that the original amendments to the Act that gave rise to the need for this amendment applied after 1986.

*(c) Foreign Property*

An interest in an annuity contract will be "foreign property" for the purposes of the Act if the annuity contract is a segregated fund policy and more than 20% of the segregated fund's assets are "foreign property". As a consequence, if an RRSP or RRIF trust or any other taxpayer described in paragraphs 204(1)(a) to (f) of the Act acquires such a foreign property, it will be included in the 20% foreign property limit set out in Part XI of the Act.

If an insurer issues interests in one or more registered annuity policies directly to an RRSP or RRIF annuitant or to a registered pension plan (RPP), the insurer will be likewise liable to pay a monthly foreign property penalty tax in respect of each RRSP annuitant, RRIF annuitant and RPP equal to the amount, if positive, determined by the formula:

$$1\% \times (A - (20\% \times B))$$

where

A is the total of all premiums and other amounts paid on account of the acquisition by the RRSP annuitant, RRIF annuitant or RPP, as the case may be, of such of those interests outstanding at the end of the month as constitute foreign property, and

B is the total of all premiums and other amounts paid on account of the acquisition by the RRSP annuitant, RRIF annuitant or RPP, as the case may be, of such of those interests as are outstanding at the end of the month.

Issuers of segregated fund policies will be allowed to elect to have their segregated funds registered under Part X.2 of the Act. The result of this election would be to exclude interests in registered segregated funds from the "foreign property" definition. However, as a consequence of the election in respect of a segregated fund, the issuer of the segregated fund would be required to pay any penalty tax under Part XI of the Act in respect of foreign property holdings of the segregated fund.

**Related Provisions**: 12.2(5) — Amounts to be included; 12.2(8)–(11) — Rules and definitions; 20(1)(c)(iv) — Interest deductibility; 20(20) — Disposal of life insurance policy or annuity contract; 56(1)(d.1) — Annuity payments included in income; 87(2)(j.4) — Amalgamation — accrual rules; 94.2(10)(a)(ii) — No application to foreign insurance policy of foreign investment entity; 148(9)"adjusted cost basis"G, 148(9)"adjusted cost basis"L(b) — Adjusted cost basis; 148(10) — Life annuity contracts.

**Notes**: Amended by 1991 technical bill, effective for life insurance policies last acquired after 1989. The present 12.2(1) was formerly 12.2(3); the rules for corporate and individual policyholders have now been combined into one rule. For earlier policies, read:

12.2 (1) **Amount to be included** — In computing the income for a taxation year of a corporation, partnership, unit trust or any trust of which a corporation or partnership is a beneficiary that holds

(a) an interest, last acquired after December 1, 1982, in a life insurance policy or

(b) an interest, last acquired after December 19, 1980 and before December 2, 1982, in an annuity contract under which annuity payments did not commence before December 2, 1982,

that is not

(c) an interest in an exempt policy, or

(d) an interest, last acquired before December 2, 1982, in a contract under which the policyholder has, under the terms and conditions of a life insurance policy that was not an annuity contract, received the proceeds therefrom in the form of an annuity contract,

there shall be included the amount by which the accumulating fund at the end of the calendar year ending in the taxation year, as determined in prescribed manner, in respect of the interest exceeds the adjusted cost basis of the interest to the corporation, partnership, unit trust or trust at the end of that calendar year.

See under 12.2(2)–(4.1).

**Regulations [subsec. 12.2(1)]**: 201(5) (information return); 304 (prescribed annuity contract); 307 (accumulating fund).

**Interpretation Bulletins [subsec. 12.2(1)]**: IT-87R2: Policyholders' income from life insurance policies; IT-355R2: Interest on loans to buy life insurance policies and annuity contracts, and interest on policy loans; IT-365R2: Damages, settlements and similar receipts; IT-415R2: Deregistration of RRSPs.

**Advance Tax Rulings**: ATR-50: Structured settlement; ATR-68: Structured settlement.

**(2)–(4.1) [Repealed under former Act]**

**Notes**: 12.2(2), (3), (4) and (4.1) repealed and replaced by 12.2(3) by 1989 Budget. 12.2(3) then merged into 12.2(1) by 1991 technical bill, effective for life insurance policies last acquired after 1989. For earlier policies, read:

(2) **Interest not disposed of before 1985** — Where, before 1985, a corporation, partnership, unit trust or any trust of which a corporation or partnership is a beneficiary has not disposed of an interest in an annuity contract that was last acquired by it before December 20, 1980,

(a) subsection (1) shall be read without reference to the words "after December 19, 1980 and", and

(b) all that portion of subsection (1) following paragraph (d) thereof shall be read as follows:

"there shall be included the amount by which the accumulating fund at the end of the calendar year ending in the taxation year, as determined in prescribed manner, in respect of the interest exceeds the aggregate of the adjusted cost basis of the interest to the corporation, partnership, unit trust or trust at the end of the calendar year ending in the taxation year and the amount, if any, at the end of that calendar year of unallocated income accrued in respect of the interest before 1982, as determined in prescribed manner.",

for taxation years ending after December 30, 1984, with respect to that interest.

(3) **Third anniversary amounts to be included** — Where in a taxation year a taxpayer (other than a corporation, partnership, unit trust or any trust of which a corporation or partnership is a beneficiary) holds an interest in

(a) a life insurance policy last acquired after December 1, 1982, or

(b) an annuity contract last acquired before December 2, 1982 under which annuity payments did not commence before December 2, 1982,

other than

(c) an exempt policy,

(d) a prescribed annuity contract, or

Subdivision b — Income or Loss from a Business or Property      S. 12.2(8)

(e) a contract under which the policyholder has, under the terms and conditions of a life insurance policy that was not an annuity contract and that was last acquired before December 2, 1982, received the proceeds therefrom in the form of an annuity contract

on a third anniversary of the policy or contract and in the taxation year or any preceding taxation year he has not made an election under subsection (4) in respect of his interest, there shall be included in computing his income for the taxation year the amount by which the accumulating fund on that third anniversary, as determined in prescribed manner, in respect of his interest exceeds the aggregate of the adjusted cost basis of the interest to the taxpayer on that third anniversary and the amount, if any, on that third anniversary of unallocated income accrued in respect of the interest before 1982, as determined in prescribed manner.

(4) **Election** — Where in a taxation year a taxpayer (other than a corporation, partnership, unit trust or any trust of which a corporation or partnership is a beneficiary) who holds an interest in

(a) a life insurance policy (other than an annuity contract) last acquired after December 1, 1982, or

(b) an annuity contract (other than a prescribed annuity contract)

has, in the year or a preceding taxation year, elected in respect of that interest by notifying the issuer thereof in writing, he shall, in computing his income for the year, include the amount by which the accumulating fund at the end of the year, as determined in prescribed manner, in respect of that interest exceeds the aggregate of

(c) the adjusted cost basis to him of the interest at the end of the year, and

(d) the amount, if any, at that time of unallocated income accrued in respect of the interest before 1982, as determined in prescribed manner.

(4.1) **Revocation of election** — Where not later than 120 days after the end of a taxation year a taxpayer revokes an election made under subsection (4) in respect of his interest in a life insurance policy or an annuity contract by notifying the issuer thereof in writing, the following rules apply for that year and each subsequent taxation year:

(a) he shall be deemed for the purposes of subsection (3) not to have made an election under subsection (4) in respect of his interest; and

(b) he is not entitled to make an election under subsection (4) in respect of his interest.

(5) **Idem** — Where in a taxation year subsection (1) applies with respect to a taxpayer's interest in an annuity contract (or would apply if the contract had an anniversary day in the year at a time when the taxpayer held the interest), there shall be included in computing the taxpayer's income for the year the amount, if any, by which

(a) the total of all amounts each of which is an amount determined at the end of the year, in respect of the interest, for any of H to L in the definition "adjusted cost basis" in subsection 148(9)

exceeds

(b) the total of all amounts each of which is an amount determined at the end of the year, in respect of the interest, for any of A to G in the definition referred to in paragraph (a).

**Notes**: 12.2(5) amended by 1989 Budget and by 1991 technical bill, effective for life insurance policies last acquired after 1989. For earlier policies, read:

(5) **Amounts to be included** — Where in a taxation year subsection (1), (3) or (4) applies with respect to a taxpayer's interest in an annuity contract, or would apply if the contract had a third anniversary in the year, and at the end of the year

(a) the aggregate of all amounts each of which is an amount determined under any of subparagraphs 148(9)(a)(vi) to (xi) in respect of his interest

exceeds

(b) the aggregate of all amounts each of which is an amount determined under any of subparagraphs 148(9)(a)(i) to (v.1) in respect of his interest,

there shall be included in computing the income of the taxpayer for the year the amount by which the aggregate determined under paragraph (a) exceeds the aggregate determined under paragraph (b).

(6) **Application** — Subsection (1) does not apply in computing the income of a taxpayer for a taxation year if his interest in the annuity contract was last acquired before December 20, 1980, and

(a) he could not, in the period after December 19, 1980 and before the end of the taxation year, require the repayment, acquisition, cancellation or conversion of his interest (other than by reason of a failure or default under the terms or conditions thereof) and the maturity date of the contract has not been extended and the terms or conditions relating to payments in respect of his interest have not been changed in that period; or

(b) the cash surrender value of his interest has not, in the period referred to in paragraph (a), exceeded the aggregate of premiums paid in respect of the interest.

(7) **Idem** — Subsection (3) does not apply in computing the income of a taxpayer for a taxation year if his interest in the annuity contract was last acquired before December 2, 1982 and

(a) he could not, in the period after December 1, 1982 and before the end of the taxation year, require the repayment, acquisition, cancellation or conversion of his interest (other than by reason of a failure or default under the terms or conditions thereof) and the maturity date of the contract has not been extended and the terms or conditions relating to payments in respect of his interest have not been changed in that period; or

(b) the cash surrender value of his interest has not, in the period referred to in paragraph (a), exceeded the aggregate of premiums paid in respect of the interest.

**Regulations**: 201(5) (information return).

**Interpretation Bulletins**: IT-355R2: Interest on loans to buy life insurance policies and annuity contracts, and interest on policy loans.

**(6), (7)** [Repealed under former Act]
**Notes**: See under 12.2(5).

(8) **Deemed acquisition of interest in annuity** — For the purposes of this section, the first premium that was not fixed before 1990 and that was paid after 1989 by or on behalf of a taxpayer under an annuity contract, other than a contract described in paragraph (1)(d) of this section, or paragraph 12.2(3)(e) of the *Income Tax Act*, chapter 148 of the Revised Statutes of Canada, 1952, or to which subsection (1) of this section or subsection 12.2(4) of the *Income Tax Act*, chapter 148 of the Revised Stat-

utes of Canada, 1952, applies (as those paragraphs and subsections, the numbers of which are those in force immediately before December 17, 1991, read in their application to life insurance policies last acquired before 1990) or to which subsection 12(3) applies, last acquired by the taxpayer before 1990 (in this subsection referred to as the "original contract") shall be deemed to have been paid to acquire, at the time the premium was paid, an interest in a separate annuity contract issued at that time, to the extent that the amount of the premium was not fixed before 1990, and each subsequent premium paid under the original contract shall be deemed to have been paid under that separate contract to the extent that the amount of that subsequent premium was not fixed before 1990.

**Notes**: 12.2(8) amended by 1989 Budget and 1991 technical bill, effective for premiums paid after 1989, and re-enacted in the R.S.C. 1985 (5th Supp.) consolidation. The references to R.S.C. 1952, c. 148 are to the Act before the R.S.C. 1985 (5th Supp.) came into force; the reference to December 17, 1991 is the date of Royal Assent to the 1991 technical bill. For premiums paid before 1990, read:

> (8) **Presumption** — For the purposes of this section, the first premium that was not fixed before December 2, 1982 and that was paid on or after that date by or on behalf of a taxpayer under an annuity contract (other than a contract described in paragraph (1)(d) or (3)(e) or a contract to which subsection (1), (3) or (4) or 12(3) applies or would apply in a year if the contract had a third anniversary in the year) last acquired by the taxpayer before that date (in this subsection referred to as the "original contract") shall be deemed to have been paid to acquire, at the time the premium was paid, an interest in a separate annuity contract issued at that time, to the extent that the amount of the premium was not fixed before December 2, 1982, and each subsequent premium paid under the original contract shall be deemed to have been paid under such separate contract to the extent that the amount of the premium was not fixed before December 2, 1982.

**I.T. Application Rules**: 69 (meaning of "*Income Tax Act*, chapter 148 of the Revised Statutes of Canada, 1952").

**Interpretation Bulletins**: IT-355R2: Interest on loans to buy life insurance policies and annuity contracts, and interest on policy loans.

### (9) [Repealed under former Act]

**Notes**: 12.2(9) repealed by 1989 Budget, effective (per 1991 technical bill) for life insurance policies last acquired after 1989. Where it still applies, read:

> (9) **Rules where premium paid** — Where, at any time after December 1, 1982, a prescribed premium (other than a premium referred to in subsection (8)) has been paid by or on behalf of a taxpayer in respect of an interest in a life insurance policy last acquired on or before that date, and
>
> (a) the policy is not an exempt policy, or
>
> (b) there has been a prescribed increase in any benefit on death under the policy,
>
> this Act applies after that time with respect to his interest in the policy as if
>
> (c) subsections (1), (3) and (4) and 148(4), paragraph 148(2)(b) and clause 148(9)(e.2)(iv)(A) were read without reference to the words "last acquired after December 1, 1982",
>
> (d) subsection (1) were read without reference to paragraph (d) thereof;
>
> (e) subsection (3) were read without reference to paragraph (e) thereof;
>
> (f) subsection 148(6) were not applicable;
>
> (g) subparagraph 148(9)(a)(ix) were read as follows:
>
> > "(ix) in the case of an interest in a life insurance policy (other than an annuity contract), the aggregate of all amounts each of which is the net cost of pure insurance in respect of the interest, as determined in prescribed manner, immediately before the end of the calendar year ending in a taxation year commencing after the later of
> >
> > (A) May 31, 1985, and
> >
> > (B) the end of the year before the year in which subsection 12.2(9) first applied in respect of the interest, and
> >
> > before that time,";
>
> (h) subparagraph 148(9)(c)(ix) were read without reference to clause (A) thereof; and
>
> (i) all that portion of subparagraph 148(9) (e.1)(iii) preceding clause (A) thereof were read as follows:
>
> > (iii) that portion of any amount paid, after the later of May 31, 1985 and the time at which subsection 12.2(9) first applied in respect of the interest, under the policy with respect to
>
> and, for the purposes of this subsection, paragraph 148(10)(d) shall be read without reference to the expression "(other than a conversion into an annuity contract)".

**Regulations**: 309 (prescribed premium, prescribed increase).

### (10) Riders 
— For the purposes of this Act, a rider added at any time after 1989 to a life insurance policy last acquired before 1990 that provides additional life insurance is deemed to be a separate life insurance policy issued at that time unless

(a) the policy is an exempt policy last acquired after December 1, 1982 or an annuity contract; or

(b) the only additional life insurance provided by the rider is an accidental death benefit.

**Related Provisions**: 87(2)(j.4) — Amalgamation — accrual rules; 94.2(10)(a)(ii) — No application to foreign insurance policy of foreign investment entity; Reg. 1408(5) — Similar rule for policy reserves.

**Notes**: 12.2(10) amended by 1989 Budget, and paras. (a), (b) added by 1995-97 technical bill, both amendments effective for riders added after 1989. For riders added after December 1, 1982 and before 1990, read "acquired before December 2, 1982" in place of "before 1990".

### (11) Definitions 
— In this section and paragraph 56(1)(d.1) of the *Income Tax Act*, chapter 148 of the Revised Statutes of Canada, 1952,

**Related Provisions**: 20(1.2) — Definitions in 12.2(11) apply to 20(1)(c).

**I.T. Application Rules**: 69 (meaning of "*Income Tax Act*, chapter 148 of the Revised Statutes of Canada, 1952").

**"anniversary day"** of a life insurance policy means

(a) the day that is one year after the day immediately preceding the day on which the policy was issued, and

(b) each day that occurs at each successive one-year interval after the day determined under paragraph (a);

Subdivision b — Income or Loss from a Business or Property    S. 13(1)

**Notes**: 12.2(11)"anniversary day" was 12.2(11)(b) before the R.S.C. 1985 (5th Supp.) consolidation, effective for taxation years ending after November 1991. See Table of Concordance.

12.2(11)(b) (now 12.2(11)"anniversary day") amended by 1989 Budget and 1991 technical bill, effective for life insurance policies last acquired after 1989. For earlier policies, read:

(b) "third anniversary" — "third anniversary" of a life insurance policy means

(i) the end of the day that is three years after the end of the calendar year of issue of the policy, and

(ii) the end of the day that occurs at every successive three year interval from the time determined under subparagraph (i)

and for the purposes of this paragraph, where before 1985 a taxpayer has not disposed of an interest in an annuity contract last acquired by him before December 2, 1982, the contract shall be deemed to have been issued on December 31, 1984.

**"exempt policy"** has the meaning prescribed by regulation.

**Related Provisions**: 148(9)"adjusted cost basis".

**Notes**: 12.2(11)"exempt policy" was 12.2(11)(a) before the R.S.C. 1985 (5th Supp.) consolidation, effective for taxation years ending after November 1991.

**Regulations**: 306 (meaning of "exempt policy").

**(12) Application of subsecs. 138(12) and 148(9)** — The definitions in subsections 138(12) and 148(9) apply to this section.

**Notes**: 12.2(12) added in the R.S.C. 1985 (5th Supp.) consolidation, effective for taxation years beginning after November 1991. This rule was formerly contained in the opening words to 138(12) and 148(9).

**(13) Application of subsec. 148(10)** — Subsection 148(10) applies to this section.

**Notes**: 12.2(13) added in the R.S.C. 1985 (5th Supp.) consolidation, effective for taxation years beginning after November 1991. This rule was formerly contained in the opening words to 148(10).

**Definitions [s. 12.2]**: "acquired" — 12.2(13), 148(10)(c), (e); "adjusted cost basis" — 148(9), 248(1); "amount" — 12.2(12), 148(9), 248(1); "anniversary day" — 12.2(11); "annuity" — 248(1); "cash surrender value" — 12.2(12), 148(9); "corporation" — 248(1), *Interpretation Act* 35(1); "exempt policy" — 12.2(11); "insurer" — 12.2(13), 148(10)(a); "life insurance policy" — 138(12), 248(1); "life insurer" — 12.2(13), 148(10)(a), 248(1); "person" — 248(1); "person whose life was insured" — 12.2(13), 148(10)(b); "premium" — 12.2(12), 148(9); "prescribed" — 248(1); "prescribed annuity contract" — Reg. 304; "regulation" — 248(1); "taxation year" — 249; "taxpayer" — 248(1); "trust" — 104(1), 248(1), (3); "unit trust" — 108(2), 248(1).

**Interpretation Bulletins [s. 12.2]**: IT-355R2: Interest on loans to buy life insurance policies and annuity contracts, and interest on policy loans; IT-363R2: Deferred profit sharing plans — deductibility of employer contributions and taxation of amounts received by a beneficiary; IT-415R2: Deregistration of RRSPs.

**12.3 Transition inclusion re unpaid claims reserve** — Where an amount has been deducted under subsection 20(26) in computing the income of an insurer for its taxation year that includes February 23, 1994, there shall be included in computing the insurer's income for that taxation year and each subsequent taxation year that begins before 2004, the prescribed portion for the year of the amount so deducted.

**Related Provisions**: 87(2)(g.1) — Amalgamation — continuing corporation; 138(11.5)(k) — Transfer of business by non-resident insurer.

**Notes**: 12.3 amended by 1994 Budget, effective for taxation years that end after February 22, 1994. For earlier years, read:

12.3 Net reserve inclusion — Where a taxpayer has deducted an amount under subsection 20(26) in computing the taxpayer's income for the taxpayer's first taxation year that commences after June 17, 1987 and ends after 1987, there shall be included in computing the taxpayer's income for each of the taxation years ending after 1988 and commencing before 1993, the prescribed amount of the taxpayer's net reserve inclusion for that year.

**Definitions [s. 12.3]**: "amount", "insurer", "prescribed" — 248(1); "taxation year" — 11(2), 249; "taxpayer" — 248(1).

**Regulations**: 8100(1) (prescribed amount of net reserve inclusion for former 12.3); 8101(2) (draft) (prescribed amount).

**12.4 Bad debt inclusion** — Where, in a taxation year, a taxpayer disposes of a property that was a property described in an inventory of the taxpayer and in the year or a preceding taxation year an amount has been deducted under paragraph 20(1)(p) in computing the taxpayer's income in respect of the property, there shall be included in computing the taxpayer's income for the year from the business in which the property was used or held, the amount, if any, by which

(a) the total of all amounts deducted under paragraph 20(1)(p) by the taxpayer in respect of the property in computing the taxpayer's income for the year or a preceding taxation year

exceeds

(b) the total of all amounts included under paragraph 12(1)(i) by the taxpayer in respect of the property in computing the taxpayer's income for the year or a preceding taxation year.

**Related Provisions**: 26(3) — Banks — write-offs and recoveries; 87(2)(g.1) — Amalgamations; 138(11.5)(k) — Transfer of business by non-resident insurer; 142.5(8)(d)(ii) — First deemed disposition of mark-to-market debt obligation.

**Definitions [s. 12.4]**: "amount", "business", "inventory", "property" — 248(1); "taxation year" — 11(2), 249; "taxpayer" — 248(1).

**Interpretation Bulletins**: IT-442R: Bad debts and reserves for doubtful debts.

**13. (1) Recaptured depreciation** — Where, at the end of a taxation year, the total of the amounts determined for E to J in the definition "undepreciated capital cost" in subsection (21) in respect of a taxpayer's depreciable property of a particular prescribed class exceeds the total of the amounts determined for A to D in that definition in respect thereof, the excess shall be included in computing the taxpayer's income for the year.

**Proposed Amendment — Recapture on donation of depreciable property to charity**

**Letter from Department of Finance, February 15, 2000**: See under 216.

**Related Provisions**: 13(3) — Interpretation where taxpayer is an individual; 13(5.2) — Where taxpayer paid rent for property before acquiring it; 13(5.3) — Rules applicable; 13(8) — Property disposed of after ceasing business; 13(13) — Deductions; 13(15) — Vessel disposed of before 1974; 20(16) — Terminal loss where A to D exceed E to J and no property left in class; 28(1)(d) — Inclusion in farming or fishing income when using cash method; 104(5)(b), (c) — Trusts — 21-year deemed disposition rule; 110.6(1) — "investment income"; 115(1)(a)(iii.2) — Non-resident's taxable income earned in Canada; 216(6) — Non-residents. See additional Related provisions and Definitions at end of s. 13.

**Notes**: When depreciable property is sold, the proceeds of disposition, up to the original cost, are deducted from the u.c.c. of the class (see 13(21)"undepreciated capital cost"F). (Any excess over the original cost is a capital gain under 39(1).) If as a result the u.c.c. goes negative, 13(1) requires the balance to be included in income. This is "recapture" of CCA that was claimed; conceptually, too much CCA was claimed, since the property was sold for more than the u.c.c. The pooling of many properties into one class can distort the timing of the recapture, however. If the last asset in the class has been disposed of and the u.c.c. is still positive, a terminal loss can be claimed under 20(16).

**I.T. Application Rules**: 20(2) (income from farming or fishing — property acquired before 1972).

**Interpretation Bulletins**: IT-121R3: Election to capitalize cost of borrowed money; IT-267R2: CCA — vessels; IT-288R2: Gifts of capital properties to a charity and others; IT-418: Partial dispositions of property; IT-478R2: CCA — recapture and terminal loss; IT-481: Timber resource property and timber limits.

**I.T. Technical News**: No. 12 (1998 deduction limits and benefit rates for automobiles); No. 16 (*Continental Bank* case).

**(2) Idem [luxury automobile]** — Notwithstanding subsection (1), where an excess amount is determined under that subsection at the end of a taxation year in respect of a passenger vehicle having a cost to a taxpayer in excess of $20,000 or such other amount as may be prescribed, that excess amount shall not be included in computing the taxpayer's income for the year but shall be deemed, for the purposes of B in the definition "undepreciated capital cost" in subsection (21), to be an amount included in the taxpayer's income for the year by reason of this section.

**Related Provisions**: 13(3) — Interpretation where taxpayer is an individual; 13(7)(g) — Limitation on capital cost of automobile; 13(8) — Disposition after ceasing business; 20(16.1) — Terminal loss — vehicles; 67.2 — Interest on money borrowed for passenger vehicle; Reg. 1100(2.5) — 50% CCA in year of disposition. See additional Related Provisions and Definitions at end of s. 13.

**Notes**: See Notes to 13(7)(g) re prescribed amount for each year.

**Regulations**: 7307(1) (prescribed amount).

**Interpretation Bulletins**: IT-478R2: CCA — recapture and terminal loss; IT-521R: Motor vehicle expenses claimed by self-employed individuals; IT-522R: Vehicle, travel and sales expenses of employees.

**I.T. Technical News**: No. 10 (1997 deduction limits and benefit rates for automobiles).

**(3) "Taxation year", "year" and "income" of individual** — Where a taxpayer is an individual whose income for a taxation year includes income from a business the fiscal period of which does not coincide with the calendar year and depreciable property acquired for the purpose of gaining or producing income from the business has been disposed of,

(a) for greater certainty, each reference in subsections (1) and (2) to a "taxation year" and "year" shall be read as a reference to a "fiscal period"; and

(b) a reference in subsection (1) to "the income" shall be read as a reference to "the income from the business".

**Related Provisions**: 13(8) — Property disposed of after ceasing business; 20(16.2) — Same rule applies for purposes of subsecs. 20(16) and (16.1). See additional Related Provisions and Definitions at end of s. 13.

**Notes**: Before re-enactment in R.S.C. 1985 (5th Supp.), 13(3)(a) applied explicitly for purposes of 20(16) and (16.1) as well. See now 20(16.2).

Since 1995, most individuals use a calendar year as their fiscal period. See Notes at end of 249.1.

**Interpretation Bulletins**: IT-172R: CCA — taxation year of individuals; IT-478R2: CCA — recapture and terminal loss.

**(4) Exchanges of property** — Where an amount in respect of the disposition in a taxation year (in this subsection referred to as the "initial year") of depreciable property (in this section referred to as the "former property") of a prescribed class of a taxpayer would, but for this subsection, be the amount determined for F or G in the definition "undepreciated capital cost" in subsection (21) in respect of the disposition of the former property that is either

(a) property the proceeds of disposition of which were proceeds referred to in paragraph (b), (c) or (d) of the definition "proceeds of disposition" in subsection (21), or

(b) a property that was, immediately before the disposition, a former business property of the taxpayer,

and the taxpayer so elects under this subsection in the taxpayer's return of income for the taxation year in which the taxpayer acquires a depreciable property of a prescribed class of the taxpayer that is a replacement property for the taxpayer's former property,

(c) the amount otherwise determined for F or G in the definition "undepreciated capital cost" in subsection (21) in respect of the disposition of the former property shall be reduced by the lesser of

(i) the amount, if any, by which the amount otherwise determined for F or G in that definition exceeds the undepreciated capital cost to the taxpayer of property of the prescribed class to which the former property belonged at the time immediately before the time that the former property was disposed of, and

(ii) the amount that has been used by the taxpayer to acquire

(A) where the former property is referred to in paragraph (a), before the end of the second taxation year following the initial year, or

(B) in any other case, before the end of the first taxation year following the initial year,

a replacement property of a prescribed class that has not been disposed of by the taxpayer before the time at which the taxpayer disposed of the former property, and

(d) the amount of the reduction determined under paragraph (c) shall be deemed to be proceeds of disposition of a depreciable property of the taxpayer that had a capital cost equal to that amount and that was property of the same class as the replacement property, from a disposition made on the later of

(i) the time the replacement property was acquired by the taxpayer, and

(ii) the time the former property was disposed of by the taxpayer.

**Related Provisions**: 13(4.1) — Replacement property for a former property; 13(18) — Reassessments; 14(6) — Parallel rule for eligible capital property; 44(1) — Parallel rule for capital gains purposes; 44(4) — Deemed election; 44(6) — Deemed proceeds of disposition; 87(2)(l.3) — Amalgamations — replacement property; 96(3) — Election by members of partnership; 220(3.2), Reg. 600(b) — Late filing of election or revocation. See also Related Provisions and Definitions at end of s. 13.

**Notes**: 13(4) allows a "rollover" of undepreciated capital cost for CCA purposes where replacement property is acquired, to prevent recapture under 13(1). For the parallel rule with respect to the adjusted cost base of the property (preventing a capital gain from being recognized), see 44(1); for the parallel rule with respect to eligible capital property, see 14(6). See Notes to 44(1).

Text between paras. (b) and (c) amended by 1995-97 technical bill, effective for dispositions of former properties after the 1993 taxation year. The amendments were consequential on amendments to 13(4.1). For earlier dispositions since April 1977, read:

and the taxpayer so elects under this subsection in the taxpayer's return of income under this Part for the year in which the taxpayer acquires, as a replacement for the former property, a property (in this subsection referred to as a "replacement property"),

**Remission Orders**: *Telesat Canada Remission Order*, P.C. 1999-1335.

**Interpretation Bulletins**: IT-259R3: Exchanges of property; IT-267R2: CCA — vessels; IT-271R: Expropriations — time and proceeds of disposition.

**Information Circulars**: 92-1: Guidelines for accepting late, amended or revoked elections.

## (4.1) Replacement for a former property —

For the purposes of subsection (4), a particular depreciable property of a prescribed class of a taxpayer is a replacement for a former property of the taxpayer if

(a) it is reasonable to conclude that the property was acquired by the taxpayer to replace the former property;

(a.1) it was acquired by the taxpayer and used by the taxpayer or a person related to the taxpayer for a use that is the same as or similar to the use to which the taxpayer or a person related to the taxpayer put the former property;

(b) where the former property was used by the taxpayer or a person related to the taxpayer for the purpose of gaining or producing income from a business, the particular depreciable property was acquired for the purpose of gaining or producing income from that or a similar business or for use by a person related to the taxpayer for such a purpose;

(c) where the former property was a taxable Canadian property of the taxpayer, the particular depreciable property is a taxable Canadian property of the taxpayer; and

(d) where the former property was a taxable Canadian property (other than treaty-protected property) of the taxpayer, the particular depreciable property is a taxable Canadian property (other than treaty-protected property) of the taxpayer.

**Related Provisions**: See Related Provisions and Definitions at end of s. 13.

**Notes**: 13(4.1)(c) amended and (d) added by 1998 Budget, effective for any disposition that occurs in a taxation year that ends after 1997. For earlier dispositions, read:

(c) where the former property was taxable Canadian property (or would have been taxable Canadian property if the taxpayer were non-resident throughout the year in which the former property was disposed of and the former property were used in a business carried on by the taxpayer), the particular depreciable property was taxable Canadian property (or would have been taxable Canadian property if the taxpayer were non-resident throughout the year in which the particular property was acquired and the particular property were used in a business carried on by the taxpayer).

13(4.1)(a) replaced by new (a) and (a.1) by 1995-97 technical bill, effective for dispositions of former properties after the 1993 taxation year except that, where a taxpayer elects in respect of a former property that was disposed of before June 18, 1998 by notifying Revenue Canada in writing on or before the filing-due date for the taxpayer's first taxation year that ends after June 18, 1998, 13(4.1)(a.1) shall, for the purpose of determining whether a property is a replacement property of the former property, be read as follows:

(a.1) it was acquired by the taxpayer for a use that is the same as or similar to the use to which the taxpayer or a person related to the taxpayer put the former property;

Before the amendment (i.e., generally up to the 1993 taxation year), read:

(a) it was acquired by the taxpayer for the same or a similar use as the use to which the taxpayer or a person related to the taxpayer put the former property;

New 13(4.1)(a) is new with the 1995-97 technical bill; the former para. (a) is now (a.1), but was expanded to allow use by a related person (e.g., where a taxpayer rents the acquired property to a subsidiary corporation which uses it in the same or similar business).

13(4.1) amended by 1991 technical bill, to add relief in paras. (a) [now (a.1)] and (b) for replacement property used by a person related to the taxpayer (effective for dispositions of former properties after July 13, 1990); and to have the rule in para. (c) apply whether or not the taxpayer is non-resident (effective for dispositions of former properties after April 2, 1990, other than where pursuant to a written agreement or expropriation notice given before April 3, 1990).

**Interpretation Bulletins**: IT-259R3: Exchanges of property.

**(5) Reclassification of property** — Where one or more depreciable properties of a taxpayer that were included in a prescribed class (in this subsection referred to as the "old class") become included at any time (in this subsection referred to as the "transfer time") in another prescribed class (in this subsection referred to as the "new class"), for the purpose of determining at any subsequent time the undepreciated capital cost to the taxpayer of depreciable property of the old class and the new class

(a) the value of A in the definition "undepreciated capital cost" in subsection (21) shall be determined as if each of those depreciable properties were

(i) properties of the new class acquired before the subsequent time, and

(ii) never included in the old class; and

(b) there shall be deducted in computing the total depreciation allowed to the taxpayer for property of the old class before the subsequent time, and added in computing the total depreciation allowed to the taxpayer for property of the new class before the subsequent time, the greater of

(i) the amount determined by the formula

$$A - B$$

where

A is the total of all amounts each of which is the capital cost to the taxpayer of each of those depreciable properties, and

B is the undepreciated capital cost to the taxpayer of depreciable property of the old class at the transfer time, and

(ii) the total of all amounts each of which is an amount that would have been deducted under paragraph 20(1)(a) in respect of a depreciable property that is one of those properties in computing the taxpayer's income for a taxation year that ended before the transfer time and at the end of which the property was included in the old class if

(A) the property had been the only property included in a separate prescribed class, and

(B) the rate allowed by the regulations made for the purpose of paragraph 20(1)(a) in respect of that separate class had been the effective rate that was used by the taxpayer to calculate a deduction under that paragraph in respect of the old class for the year.

**Related Provisions**: 87(2)(d)(ii)(C) — Amalgamations — depreciable property; 257 — Formula cannot calculate to less than zero. See additional Related Provisions and Definitions at end of s. 13.

**Notes**: 13(5) amended by 1996 Budget, effective for properties of a prescribed class that, after 1996, become included in property of another prescribed class. The amendment clarifies that 13(5) applies as a result of a change to the Act or Regulations; accommodates the simultaneous change in status of more than one property of a prescribed class; and causes 13(5) to apply immediately after a change in status, to deal with a change in status at the very beginning of a taxpayer's taxation year. Before 1997, read:

(5) Transferred property — Where depreciable property of a taxpayer that was included in a prescribed class (in this subsection referred to as the "former class") has been transferred to another prescribed class (in this subsection referred to as the "other class"), for purposes of determining the undepreciated capital cost to the taxpayer of depreciable property of the former class and of the other class at any time after the transfer

(a) the transferred property shall be deemed to be depreciable property of the other class acquired before that time and not depreciable property of the former class acquired before that time; and

(b) an amount equal to the greater of

(i) the amount, if any, by which the capital cost to the taxpayer of the transferred property exceeds the undepreciated capital cost to the taxpayer of depreciable property of the former class immediately before the transfer, and

(ii) the total of all amounts that would have been deducted by the taxpayer in respect of the transferred property under paragraph 20(1)(a) in computing the taxpayer's income for taxation years ending before the transfer had that property been the only property included in a separate prescribed class and had the rate allowed by the regulations made under paragraph 20(1)(a) in respect of that separate class been the effective rate that was used by the taxpayer to calculate a deduction under that paragraph in respect of the former class for taxation years at the end of which the transferred property was included in the former class

shall be included in computing the total depreciation allowed to the taxpayer for property of the other class before that time and not included in computing the total depreciation allowed to the taxpayer for property of the former class before that time.

**Interpretation Bulletins**: IT-190R2: CCA — transferred and misclassified property.

**Information Circulars**: 84-1: Revision of capital cost allowance claims and other permissive deductions.

**(5.1) Rules applicable [leasehold interest]** — Where at any time in a taxation year a taxpayer acquires a particular property in respect of which, immediately before that time, the taxpayer had a leasehold interest that was included in a prescribed class, for the purposes of this section, section 20 and any regulations made under paragraph 20(1)(a), the following rules apply:

(a) the leasehold interest shall be deemed to have been disposed of by the taxpayer at that time for proceeds of disposition equal to the amount, if any, by which

(i) the capital cost immediately before that time of the leasehold interest

exceeds

(ii) the total of all amounts claimed by the taxpayer in respect of the leasehold interest and deductible under paragraph 20(1)(a) in computing the taxpayer's income in previous taxation years;

(b) the particular property shall be deemed to be depreciable property of a prescribed class of the taxpayer acquired by the taxpayer at that time and there shall be added to the capital cost to the taxpayer of the property an amount equal to the capital cost referred to in subparagraph (a)(i); and

(c) the total referred to in subparagraph (a)(ii) shall be added to the total depreciation allowed to the taxpayer before that time in respect of the class to which the particular property belongs.

**Related Provisions**: See Related Provisions and Definitions at end of s. 13.

**Interpretation Bulletins**: IT-464R: CCA — leasehold interests.

**(5.2) Idem [rent deemed to be CCA]** — Where, at any time, a taxpayer has acquired a capital property that is depreciable property or real property in respect of which, before that time, the taxpayer or any person with whom the taxpayer was not dealing at arm's length was entitled to a deduction in computing income in respect of any amount paid or payable for the use of, or the right to use, the depreciable property or real property and the cost or the capital cost (determined without reference to this subsection) at that time of the property to the taxpayer is less than the fair market value thereof at that time determined without reference to any option with respect to that property, for the purposes of this section, section 20 and any regulations made under paragraph 20(1)(a), the following rules apply:

(a) the property shall be deemed to have been acquired by the taxpayer at that time at a cost equal to the lesser of

(i) the fair market value of the property at that time determined without reference to any option with respect to that property, and

(ii) the total of the cost or the capital cost (determined without reference to this subsection) of the property to the taxpayer and all amounts (other than amounts paid or payable to a person with whom the taxpayer was not dealing at arm's length) each of which is an outlay or expense made or incurred by the taxpayer or by a person with whom the taxpayer was not dealing at arm's length at any time for the use of, or the right to use, the property,

and for the purposes of this paragraph and subsection (5.3), where a particular corporation has been incorporated or otherwise formed after the time any other corporation with which the particular corporation would not have been dealing at arm's length had the particular corporation been in existence before that time, the particular corporation shall be deemed to have been in existence from the time of the formation of the other corporation and to have been not dealing at arm's length with the other corporation;

(b) the amount by which the cost to the taxpayer of the property determined under paragraph (a) exceeds the cost or the capital cost thereof (determined without reference to this subsection) shall be added to the total depreciation allowed to the taxpayer before that time in respect of the prescribed class to which the property belongs; and

(c) where the property would, but for this paragraph, not be depreciable property of the taxpayer, it shall be deemed to be depreciable property of a separate prescribed class of the taxpayer.

**Related Provisions**: See Related Provisions and Definitions at end of s. 13.

**Notes**: 13(5.2) applies where a taxpayer has paid rent for property such as a building and later acquires it. In essence, if the property is later sold for a profit, the rent is "recaptured" by treating the rent paid as CCA claimed, which is recaptured under 13(1).

**Regulations**: 1101(5g); Sch. II:Cl. 36 (property under 13(5.2)(c) deemed to be a separate class).

**Interpretation Bulletins**: IT-233R: Lease-option agreements; sale leaseback agreements.

**Forms**: T776: Statement of real estate rentals.

**(5.3) Idem [disposition of option]** — Where, at any time in a taxation year, a taxpayer has disposed of a capital property that is an option with respect to depreciable property or real property in respect of which the taxpayer or any person with whom the taxpayer was not dealing at arm's length was entitled to a deduction in computing income in respect of any amount paid for the use of, or the right to use, the depreciable property or real property, for the purposes of this section, the amount, if any, by which the proceeds of disposition to the taxpayer of the option exceed the taxpayer's cost in respect thereof shall be deemed to be an excess referred to in subsection (1) in respect of the taxpayer for the year.

**Related Provisions**: 49 — Options. See also Related Provisions and Definitions at end of s. 13.

**Interpretation Bulletins**: IT-233R: Lease-option agreements; sale leaseback agreements.

**Forms**: T776: Statement of real estate rentals.

**(5.4) Idem** — Where, before the time of disposition of a capital property that was depreciable property of a taxpayer, the taxpayer, or any person with whom the taxpayer was not dealing at arm's length, was entitled to a deduction in computing income in respect of any outlay or expense made or incurred for the use of, or the right to use, during a period of time, that capital property (other than an outlay or expense made or incurred by the taxpayer or a person with whom the taxpayer was not dealing at arm's length before the acquisition of the property), except where the taxpayer disposed of the property to a person with whom the taxpayer was not dealing at arm's length and that person was subject to the provisions of subsection (5.2) with respect to the acquisition by that person of the property, the following rules apply:

(a) an amount equal to the lesser of

(i) the total of all amounts (other than amounts paid or payable to the taxpayer or a person with whom the taxpayer was not dealing at arm's length) each of which was a deductible outlay or expense made or incurred before the time of disposition by the taxpayer, or by a person with whom the taxpayer was not dealing at arm's length, for the use of, or the right to use, during the period of time, the property, and

(ii) the amount, if any, by which the fair market value of the property at the earlier of

(A) the expiration of the last period of time in respect of which the deductible outlay or expense referred to in subparagraph (i) was made or incurred, and

(B) the time of the disposition

exceeds the capital cost to the taxpayer of the property immediately before that time

shall, immediately before the time of the disposition, be added to the capital cost of the property to the person who owned the property at that time; and

(b) the amount added to the capital cost to the taxpayer of the property pursuant to paragraph (a) shall be added immediately before the time of the disposition to the total depreciation allowed to the taxpayer before that time in respect of the prescribed class to which the property belongs.

**Related Provisions**: 13(5.5) — Lease cancellation payment deemed not to be made for the use of property. See additional Related Provisions and Definitions at end of s. 13.

**(5.5) Lease cancellation payment** — For the purposes of subsection (5.4), an amount deductible by a taxpayer under paragraph 20(1)(z) or (z.1) in respect of a cancellation of a lease of property shall, for greater certainty, be deemed not to be an outlay or expense that was made or incurred by the taxpayer for the use of, or the right to use, the property.

**Related Provisions**: See Related Provisions and Definitions at end of s. 13.

**(6) Misclassified property** — Where, in calculating the amount of a deduction allowed to a taxpayer under subsection 20(16) or regulations made for the purposes of paragraph 20(1)(a) in respect of depreciable property of the taxpayer of a prescribed class (in this subsection referred to as the "particular class"), there has been added to the capital cost to the taxpayer of depreciable property of the particular class the capital cost of depreciable property (in this subsection referred to as "added property") of another prescribed class, for the purposes of this section, section 20 and any regulations made for the purposes of paragraph 20(1)(a), the added property shall, if the Minister so directs with respect to any taxation year for which, under subsection 152(4), the Minister may make any reassessment or additional assessment or assess tax, interest or penalties under this Part, be deemed to have been property of the particular class and not of the other class at all times before the beginning of the year, and, except to the extent that the added property or any part thereof has been disposed of by the taxpayer before the beginning of the year, to have been transferred from the particular class to the other class at the beginning of the year.

**Related Provisions**: See Related Provisions and Definitions at end of s. 13.

**Notes**: 13(6) amended by 1991 technical bill to correct the reference to 152(4), retroactive to April 20, 1983.

**Interpretation Bulletins**: IT-190R2: CCA — transferred and misclassified property.

**Information Circulars**: 84-1: Revision of capital cost allowance claims and other permissive deductions.

**(7) Rules applicable** — Subject to subsection 70(13), for the purposes of paragraphs 8(1)(j) and (p), this section, section 20 and any regulations made for the purpose of paragraph 20(1)(a),

**Notes**: Opening words of 13(7) amended to add "Subject to subsection 70(13)" by 1993 technical bill, effective 1993.

(a) **[change in use]** — where a taxpayer, having acquired property for the purpose of gaining or producing income, has begun at a later time to use it for some other purpose, the taxpayer shall be deemed to have disposed of it at that later time for proceeds of disposition equal to its fair market value at that time and to have reacquired it immediately thereafter at a cost equal to that fair market value;

**Related Provisions**: 13(9) — Gaining or producing income; 45 — Change in use rules — capital property. See additional Related Provisions at end of s. 13.

**Notes**: 13(7)(a) amended by 1991 technical bill, effective for changes in use after May 22, 1985, except that in applying it to changes in use occurring before May 1988, read:

(a) where a taxpayer, having acquired property for the purpose of gaining or producing income therefrom or for the purpose of gaining or producing income from a business, has begun at a later time to use it for some other purpose, the taxpayer shall be deemed to have disposed of it at that later time for proceeds of disposition equal to its fair market value at that time and to have reacquired it immediately thereafter at a cost equal to that fair market value;

**Interpretation Bulletins**: IT-525R: Performing artists.

(b) **[change in use]** — where a taxpayer, having acquired property for some other purpose, has begun at a later time to use it for the purpose of gaining or producing income, the taxpayer shall be deemed to have acquired it at that later time at a capital cost to the taxpayer equal to the lesser of

(i) the fair market value of the property at that later time, and

(ii) the total of

(A) the cost to the taxpayer of the property at that later time determined without reference to this paragraph, paragraph (a) and subparagraph (d)(ii), and

(B) ¾ of the amount, if any, by which

(I) the fair market value of the property at that later time

exceeds the total of

(II) the cost to the taxpayer of the property as determined under clause (A), and

(III) $4/3$ of the amount deducted by the taxpayer under section 110.6 in respect of the amount, if any, by which the fair market value of the property at that later time exceeds the cost to the taxpayer of the property as determined under clause (A);

### Proposed Amendment — 13(7)(b)(ii)(B)

**Application**: The December 21, 2000 draft legislation, subsec. 4(1), will amend cl. 13(7)(b)(ii)(B) by replacing the reference to the fraction "3/4" with a reference to the fraction "1/2" and by replacing the reference to the expression "4/3 of" with a reference to the word "twice", applicable to changes in use of property that occur in taxation years that end after February 27, 2000 except that, for changes in use of property that occur in a taxpayer's taxation year that includes either February 28, 2000 or October 17, 2000, the references to the fraction "1/2" shall be read as a reference to the fraction in para. 38(a), as amended [by the December 21, 2000 draft legislation], that applies to the taxpayer for the year and the reference to the word "twice" shall be read as a reference to the expression "the fraction that is the reciprocal of the fraction in para. 38(a), as amended [by the December 21, 2000 draft legislation], that applies to the taxpayer for the year, multiplied by".

**Technical Notes**: Paragraph 13(7)(b) determines the capital cost to a taxpayer of depreciable property originally acquired for a purpose other than gaining or producing income, where the taxpayer subsequently begins to use the property for the purpose of gaining or producing income. Paragraph 13(7)(d) determines the capital cost of depreciable property where the use made of the property for the purposes of gaining or producing income changes relative to other uses made of the property. Subparagraph 13(7)(d)(i) applies where the income-producing use has increased relative to the other uses made of the property.

The amendments to clauses 13(7)(b)(i)(B) and 13(7)(d)(i)(B) replace the references to the fraction "3/4" with references to the fraction "1/2" and references to the expression "4/3 of" with references to the word "twice". The changes are consequential on the decrease of the inclusion rate for capital gains from 3/4 to 1/2 [see 38(a) — ed.].

These amendments generally apply to changes in use of property that occur in taxation years that end after February 27, 2000. For changes in use of property that occur in a taxpayer's taxation year that includes either February 28, 2000 or October 17, 2000, the references to the fraction "1/2" are to be read as references to the fraction in amended paragraph 38(a) that applies to the taxpayer for the year, and the references to the word "twice" are to be read as references to the expression "the fraction that is the reciprocal of the fraction in paragraph 38(a), that applies to the taxpayer for the year, multiplied by". These modifications are required in order to reflect the capital gains/losses rate for the year.

**Related Provisions**: 13(7)(e) — Rules applicable; 13(9) — Gaining or producing income; 45 — Change in use rules — capital property; 70(12) — Capital cost of depreciable property on death; 248(1) — "cost amount"(a). See additional Related Provisions and Definitions at end of s. 13.

**Notes**: 13(7)(b) amended by 1991 technical bill, effective May 23, 1985, except that in applying 13(7)(b)(ii)(B),

(i) to changes in use of property by a person or partnership in taxation years and fiscal periods ending before 1988, the references therein to "3/4" and "4/3 of" shall be read as references to "1/2" and "2 times", respectively,

(ii) to changes in use of property by an individual or a partnership in taxation years and fiscal periods ending after 1987 and before 1990, the references therein to "3/4" and "4/3" shall be read as references to "2/3" and "3/2", respectively,

(iii) to changes in use of property by a corporation in taxation years ending after 1987 and beginning before 1990 throughout which the corporation was a Canadian-controlled private corporation, the reference therein to "3/4" shall, in respect of the corporation for the year, be read as a reference to the fraction determined as the total of

(A) the proportion of 1/2 that the number of days in the year that are before 1988 is of the number of days in the year,

(B) the proportion of 2/3 that the number of days in the year that are after 1987 and before 1990 is of the number of days in the year, and

(C) the proportion of 3/4 that the number of days in the year that are after 1989 is of the number of days in the year, and

(iv) to changes in use of property by a corporation in taxation years ending after 1987 and beginning before 1990 where throughout the year the corporation was not a Canadian-controlled private corporation, the reference therein to "3/4" shall, in respect of the corporation for the year, be read as a reference to the fraction determined as the total of

(A) the proportion of 1/2 that the number of days in the year that are before July 1988 is of the number of days in the year,

(B) the proportion of 2/3 that the number of days in the year that are after June 1988 and before 1990 is of the number of days in the year, and

(C) the proportion of 3/4 that the number of days in the year that are after 1989 is of the number of days in the year.

This transitional rule tracks the change in capital gains inclusion rates from 1/2 before 1988 to 2/3 in 1988 and 1989 and 3/4 effective 1990. For property acquired before May 23, 1985 or before 1986 pursuant to an agreement entered into in writing before May 23, 1985, delete subparas. (i) and (ii) and the preceding words "a capital cost to the taxpayer equal to the lesser of", and read "its fair market value to the taxpayer at that time".

**Interpretation Bulletins**: IT-148R3: Recreational properties and club dues; IT-160R3: Personal use of aircraft; IT-209R: Inter-vivos gifts of capital property to individuals directly or through trusts; IT-525R: Performing artists.

**I.T. Technical News**: No. 18 (*Cudd Pressure* case).

(c) **[partial use to produce income]** — where property has, since it was acquired by a taxpayer, been regularly used in part for the purpose of gaining or producing income and in part for some other purpose, the taxpayer shall be deemed to have acquired, for the purpose of gaining or producing income, the proportion of the property that the use regularly made of the property for gaining or producing income is of the whole use regularly made of the property at a capital cost to the taxpayer equal to the same proportion of the capital cost to the taxpayer of the whole property and, if the property has, in such a case, been disposed of, the proceeds of disposition of the proportion of the property deemed to

**S. 13(7)(c)**  Income Tax Act, Part I, Division B

have been acquired for gaining or producing income shall be deemed to be the same proportion of the proceeds of disposition of the whole property;

**Related Provisions**: 13(9) — Gaining or producing income. See additional Related Provisions and Definitions at end of s. 13.

**Notes**: 13(7)(c) amended by 1991 technical bill, retroactive to May 1988, to delete, after the first two words, the words "(other than a motor vehicle in respect of which section 67.3 applies)".

**Interpretation Bulletins**: IT-148R3: Recreational properties and club dues; IT-160R3: Personal use of aircraft; IT-217R: Depreciable property owned on December 31, 1971; IT-525R: Performing artists.

(d) **[partial change in use]** — where, at any time after a taxpayer has acquired property, there has been a change in the relation between the use regularly made by the taxpayer of the property for gaining or producing income and the use regularly made of the property for other purposes,

(i) if the use regularly made by the taxpayer of the property for the purpose of gaining or producing income has increased, the taxpayer shall be deemed to have acquired at that time depreciable property of that class at a capital cost equal to the total of

(A) the proportion of the lesser of

(I) its fair market value at that time, and

(II) its cost to the taxpayer at that time determined without reference to this subparagraph, subparagraph (ii) and paragraph (a)

that the amount of the increase in the use regularly made by the taxpayer of the property for that purpose is of the whole of the use regularly made of the property, and

(B) ¾ of the amount, if any, by which

(I) the amount deemed under subparagraph 45(1)(c)(ii) to be the taxpayer's proceeds of disposition of the property in respect of the change

exceeds the total of

(II) that proportion of the cost to the taxpayer of the property as determined under subclause (A)(II) that the amount of the increase in the use regularly made by the taxpayer of the property for that purpose is of the whole of the use regularly made of the property, and

(III) ⁴/₃ of the amount deducted by the taxpayer under section 110.6 in respect of the amount, if any, by which the amount determined under subclause (I) exceeds the amount determined under subclause (II), and

**Proposed Amendment — 13(7)(d)(i)(B)**

**Application**: The December 21, 2000 draft legislation, subsec. 4(2), will amend cl. 13(7)(d)(i)(B) by replacing the reference to the fraction "3/4" with a reference to the fraction "1/2" and by replacing the reference to the expression "4/3 of" with a reference to the word "twice", applicable to changes in use of property that occur in taxation years that end after February 27, 2000 except that, for changes in use of property that occur in a taxpayer's taxation year that includes either February 28, 2000 or October 17, 2000, the references to the fraction "1/2" shall be read as a reference to the fraction in para. 38(a), as amended [by the December 21, 2000 draft legislation], that applies to the taxpayer for the year and the reference to the word "twice" shall be read as a reference to the expression "the fraction that is the reciprocal of the fraction in para. 38(a), as amended [by the December 21, 2000 draft legislation], that applies to the taxpayer for the year, multiplied by".

**Technical Notes**: See under 13(7)(b)(ii)(B).

(ii) if the use regularly made of the property for the purpose of gaining or producing income has decreased, the taxpayer shall be deemed to have disposed at that time of depreciable property of that class and the proceeds of disposition shall be deemed to be an amount equal to the proportion of the fair market value of the property as of that time that the amount of the decrease in the use regularly made by the taxpayer of the property for that purpose is of the whole use regularly made of the property;

**Related Provisions**: 13(4) — Exchange of property; 13(7)(e) — Rules applicable; 13(9) — Gaining or producing income; 44(1) — Exchanges of property; 45(1)(c) — Partial change in use of capital property; 45(2) — Election where change in use; 70(12) — Capital cost of depreciable property on death; 248(1) "cost amount" (a) — Application of 13(7) to determination of cost amount; 256(6) — Controlled corporation. See additional Related Provisions and Definitions at end of s. 13.

**Notes**: 13(7)(d)(i)(B)(II) and (III) amended by 1991 technical bill, effective for changes in use after May 22, 1985, except that in applying 13(7)(d)(i)(B)(III)

(a) to changes in use of property by a person or partnership in taxation years and fiscal periods ending before 1988, the reference therein to "⁴/₃ of" shall be read as a reference to "2 times", and

(b) to changes in use of property by an individual or a partnership in taxation years and fiscal periods ending after 1987 and before 1990, the reference therein to "⁴/₃" shall be read as a reference to "³/₂".

This change tracks the change in capital gains inclusion rates from ½ before 1988 to ⅔ in 1989 and 1990 and ¾ effective 1990.

**Interpretation Bulletins**: IT-160R3: Personal use of aircraft; IT-209R: Inter-vivos gifts of capital property to individuals directly or through trusts.

(e) **[non-arm's length acquisition]** — notwithstanding any other provision of this Act except subsection 70(13), where at a particular time a person or partnership (in this paragraph referred to as the "taxpayer") has, directly or indirectly, in any manner whatever, acquired (otherwise than as a consequence of the death of the transferor) a depreciable property (other than a timber resource property) of a prescribed class from a person or partnership with whom the taxpayer did not deal at arm's length (in this paragraph referred to as the "transferor") and, immediately

Subdivision b — Income or Loss from a Business or Property     S. 13(7)(e)

before the transfer, the property was a capital property of the transferor,

(i) where the transferor was an individual resident in Canada or a partnership any member of which was either an individual resident in Canada or another partnership and the cost of the property to the taxpayer at the particular time determined without reference to this paragraph exceeds the cost, or where the property was depreciable property, the capital cost of the property to the transferor immediately before the transferor disposed of it, the capital cost of the property to the taxpayer at the particular time shall be deemed to be the amount that is equal to the total of

(A) the cost or capital cost, as the case may be, of the property to the transferor immediately before the particular time, and

(B) 3/4 of the amount, if any, by which

(I) the transferor's proceeds of disposition of the property

exceed the total of

(II) the cost or capital cost, as the case may be, to the transferor immediately before the particular time,

(III) 4/3 of the amount deducted by any person under section 110.6 in respect of the amount, if any, by which the amount determined under subclause (I) exceeds the amount determined under subclause (II), and

(IV) the amount, if any, required by subsection 110.6(21) to be deducted in computing the capital cost to the taxpayer of the property at that time

and, for the purposes of paragraph (b) and subparagraph (d)(i), the cost of the property to the taxpayer shall be deemed to be the same amount,

(ii) where the transferor was neither an individual resident in Canada nor a partnership any member of which was either an individual resident in Canada or another partnership and the cost of the property to the taxpayer at the particular time determined without reference to this paragraph exceeds the cost, or where the property was depreciable property, the capital cost of the property to the transferor immediately before the transferor disposed of it, the capital cost of the property to the taxpayer at that time shall be deemed to be the amount that is equal to the total of

(A) the cost or capital cost, as the case may be, of the property to the transferor immediately before the particular time, and

(B) 3/4 of the amount, if any, by which the transferor's proceeds of disposition of the property exceed the cost or capital cost, as the case may be, to the transferor immediately before the particular time

and, for the purposes of paragraph (b) and subparagraph (d)(i), the cost of the property to the taxpayer shall be deemed to be the same amount, and

(iii) where the cost or capital cost, as the case may be, of the property to the transferor immediately before the transferor disposed of it exceeds the capital cost of the property to the taxpayer at that time determined without reference to this paragraph, the capital cost of the property to the taxpayer at that time shall be deemed to be the amount that was the cost or capital cost, as the case may be, of the property to the transferor immediately before the transferor disposed of it and the excess shall be deemed to have been allowed to the taxpayer in respect of the property under regulations made under paragraph 20(1)(a) in computing the taxpayer's income for taxation years ending before the acquisition of the property by the taxpayer;

### Proposed Amendment — 13(7)(e)

**Application**: The December 21, 2000 draft legislation, subsec. 4(3), will amend para. 13(7)(e) by replacing the references to the fraction "3/4" with references to the fraction "1/2" and by replacing the reference to the expression "4/3 of" with a reference to the word "twice", applicable to acquisitions of property that occur in taxation years that end after February 27, 2000 except that, for acquisitions of property in a taxation year that includes either February 28, 2000 or October 17, 2000 of a person or partnership from whom the property was acquired, the references to the fraction "1/2" shall be read as references to the fraction in para. 38(a), as amended [by the December 21, 2000 draft legislation], that applies to the person or partnership from whom the taxpayer acquired the property for the year in which the person or partnership disposed of the property, and the references to the word "twice" shall be read as references to the expression "the fraction that is the reciprocal of the fraction in para. 38(a), as amended [by the December 21, 2000 draft legislation], that applies to the person or partnership from whom the taxpayer acquired the property for the year in which the person or partnership disposed of the property, multiplied by".

**Technical Notes**: Paragraph 13(7)(e) contains special rules which apply to determine the capital cost of depreciable property where the property is acquired on a direct or indirect transfer between persons who do not deal at arm's length.

The amendments to paragraph 13(7)(e) replace the references to the fraction "3/4" with references to the fraction "1/2" and the references to the expression "4/3 of" with references to the word "twice". The changes are consequential to the decrease of the inclusion rate for capital gains from 3/4 to 1/2 [see 38(a) — ed.].

The amendments generally apply to acquisitions of property that occur in taxation years that end after February 27, 2000. For acquisitions of property that occur in a taxation year that includes either February 28, 2000 or October 17, 2000 of a person or partnership from whom the property was acquired, the references in paragraph 13(7)(e) to the fraction "1/2" are to be read as references to the fraction in amended paragraph 38(a) that applies to the person or partnership from whom the taxpayer acquired the property for

## S. 13(7)(e) — Income Tax Act, Part I, Division B

the year in which such person or partnership disposed of the property. The references to the word "twice" are to be read as references to the expression "the fraction that is the reciprocal of the fraction in paragraph 38(a) that applies to the taxpayer for the year, multiplied by". These modifications are required in order to reflect the capital gains/losses rate for the year.

**Related Provisions**: 13(7)(e.1) — Where election made to trigger capital gains exemption; 13(7.3) — Control of corporations by one trustee; 13(21.2) — Transfer of property where u.c.c. exceeds fair market value; 70(12) — Capital cost of depreciable property on death; 85(5) — Similar rule on section 85 rollover; 97(4) — Transfer of depreciable property to partnership; 248(8) — Occurrences as a consequence of death; 256(6) — Controlled corporation. See additional Related Provisions and Definitions at end of s. 13.

**Notes**: 13(7)(e)(i)(B)(IV) added by 1994 Budget, effective 1994. It prevents a gain triggered by the election to use the capital gains exemption (for 1994) from increasing the capital cost for CCA purposes.

13(7)(e) amended by 1988 tax reform, effective for property acquired after May 22, 1985, other than acquisitions occurring before 1986 pursuant to an agreement in writing entered into before May 23, 1985. Opening words amended by 1991 technical bill, effective for property acquired after May 22, 1985, to add parenthetical exclusions for death of transferor and for timber resource property; and amended by 1993 technical bill, effective 1993, to add "except subsection 70(13)" and "immediately before the transfer".

In applying 13(7)(e)(i)(B) and (ii)(B)

(a) to acquisitions of property from a person or partnership in taxation years and fiscal periods ending before 1988, the references therein to "³/₄" and "⁴/₃ of" shall be read as references to "¹/₂" and "2 times", respectively;

(b) to acquisitions of property from an individual or a partnership in taxation years and fiscal periods ending after 1987 and before 1990, the references therein to "³/₄" and "⁴/₃" shall be read as references to "²/₃" and "³/₂", respectively;

(c) to acquisitions of property from a corporation in taxation years ending after 1987 and commencing before 1990 throughout which the corporation was a Canadian-controlled private corporation, the references therein to "³/₄" shall be read as references to the fraction determined as the aggregate of

(i) that proportion of ¹/₂ that the number of days in the year that are before 1988 is of the number of days in the year,

(ii) that proportion of ²/₃ that the number of days in the year that are after 1987 and before 1990 is of the number of days in the year, and

(iii) that proportion of ³/₄ that the number of days in the year that are after 1989 is of the number of days in the year; and

(d) to acquisitions of property by a corporation in taxation years ending after 1987 and commencing before 1990 where at any time in the year the corporation was not a Canadian-controlled private corporation, the references therein to "³/₄" shall be read as references to the fraction determined as the aggregate of

(i) that proportion of ¹/₂ that the number of days in the year that are before July 1988 is of the number of days in the year,

(ii) that proportion of ²/₃ that the number of days in the year that are after June 1988 and before 1990 is of the number of days in the year, and

(iii) that proportion of ³/₄ that the number of days in the year that are after 1989 is of the number of days in the year.

This change tracks the change in capital gains inclusion rates from ¹/₂ before 1988 to ²/₃ in 1988 and 1989 and ³/₄ effective 1990.

**Regulations**: 1102(14) — Class of property preserved on non-arm's length acquisition.

**Interpretation Bulletins**: IT-209R: Inter-vivos gifts of capital property to individuals directly or through trusts; IT-217R: Depreciable property owned on December 31, 1971.

(e.1) **[capital gains exemption election]** — where a taxpayer is deemed by paragraph 110.6(19)(a) to have disposed of and reacquired a property that immediately before the disposition was a depreciable property, the taxpayer shall be deemed to have acquired the property from himself, herself or itself and, in so having acquired the property, not to have been dealing with himself, herself or itself at arm's length;

**Related Provisions**: 69(1) — Effect of acquiring property not at arm's length.

**Notes**: 13(7)(e.1) added by 1994 Budget, effective 1994. It ensures that 13(7)(e)(i) will apply when a taxpayer makes the election to use the capital gains exemption (for 1994).

**Regulations**: 1102(14) — Class of property preserved on deemed reacquisition.

(f) **[change in control]** — where a corporation is deemed under paragraph 111(4)(e) to have disposed of and reacquired depreciable property (other than a timber resource property), the capital cost to the corporation of the property at the time of the reacquisition is deemed to be the amount that is equal to the total of

(i) the capital cost to the corporation of the property at the time of the disposition, and

(ii) ³/₄ of the amount, if any, by which the corporation's proceeds of disposition of the property exceed the capital cost to the corporation of the property at the time of the disposition;

### Proposed Amendment — 13(7)(f)(ii)

**Application**: The December 21, 2000 draft legislation, subsec. 4(4), will amend subpara. 13(7)(f)(ii) by replacing the reference to the fraction "3/4" with a reference to the fraction "1/2", applicable to acquisitions of property that occur in taxation years that end after February 27, 2000 except that, for acquisitions of property that occur in a taxpayer's taxation year that includes either February 28, 2000 or October 17, 2000, the reference to the fraction "1/2" shall be read as a reference to the fraction in para. 38(a), as amended [by the December 21, 2000 draft legislation], that applies to the taxpayer for the year.

**Technical Notes**: Paragraph 13(7)(f) applies to determine the capital cost of a property where a corporation is treated as having disposed of and reacquired depreciable property either under paragraph 111(4)(e) (on an acquisition of control of the corporation) or paragraph 149(10)(b) (where the corporation becomes or ceases to be exempt from tax under Part I on its taxable income).

The amendment to subparagraph 13(7)(f)(ii) replaces the fraction "3/4" with the fraction "1/2". The change is consequential to the decrease of the inclusion rate for capital gains from 3/4 to 1/2 [see 38(a) — ed.].

The amendment applies to acquisitions of property that occur in taxation years of a taxpayer that end after February 27, 2000 except that, for acquisitions of property that occur in a taxation year of a taxpayer that includes either February 28, 2000 or October 17, 2000, the reference in subparagraph 13(7)(f)(ii) to the fraction "1/2" is to be read as a reference to the fraction in amended paragraph 38(a) that applies to the taxpayer for the year. These modifications are

Subdivision b — Income or Loss from a Business or Property  S. 13(7.1)(d)

required in order to reflect the capital gains/losses rate for the year.

**Related Provisions**: See Related Provisions and Definitions at end of s. 13.

**Notes**: 13(7)(f) amended by 1995-97 technical bill, effective April 27, 1995, to delete "or 149(10)(b)" (after "111(4)(e)"). Thus, it no longer applies when a corporation ceases to be exempt from Part I tax.

Exclusion of timber resource property in opening words added by 1991 technical bill, effective for property acquired after May 22, 1985.

13(7)(f) added by 1987 Budget (and amended by subsequent press release and by 1988 tax reform), effective where control of a corporation is acquired by a person or group of persons after January 15, 1987 and where, after June 5, 1987, a corporation becomes or ceases to be exempt from tax under Part I on its taxable income. For taxation years that begin before 1990, the fraction "3/4" is prorated based on the capital gains inclusion rate.

**Interpretation Bulletins**: IT-302R3: Losses of a corporation — the effect that acquisitions of control, amalgamations, and windings-up have on their deductibility — after January 15, 1987.

(g) **[luxury automobile]** — where the cost to a taxpayer of a passenger vehicle exceeds $20,000 or such other amount as may be prescribed, the capital cost to the taxpayer of the vehicle shall be deemed to be $20,000 or that other prescribed amount, as the case may be; and

**Related Provisions**: 13(2) — No recapture on luxury automobile; 13(7)(h) — Where vehicle acquired not at arm's length; 20(16.1) — No terminal loss on luxury automobile; 67.2 — Limitation on interest expense; 67.3 — Limitation on leasing cost; 85(1)(e.4) — Transfer of property to corporation by shareholders; Reg. 1100(2.5) — 50% CCA in year of disposition.

**Notes**: 13(7)(g) limits the capital cost of an automobile to a fixed dollar amount for CCA purposes, on the theory that any additional amount is paid for "luxury" features not necessary for business purposes. The dollar limit is:

| Acquisition date | Limit on cost |
| --- | --- |
| June 18/87–Aug 31/89 | $20,000 |
| Sept 1/89–Dec 31/90 | $24,000 |
| 1991–1996 | $24,000 + GST & PST |
| 1997 | $25,000 + GST/HST & PST |
| 1998–1999 | $26,000 + GST/HST & PST |
| 2000 | $27,000 + GST/HST & PST |
| 2001 | $30,000 + GST/HST & PST |

(See Reg. 7307(1).) For parallel limitations on leasing costs and interest paid, see 67.2 and 67.3. Under s. 201 of the *Excise Tax Act* a similiar limitation applies for GST input tax credits.

Each automobile (see 248(1)"automobile") that is over the threshold is deemed to be in a separate Class 10.1 by Reg. 1101(1af), so that CCA is calculated separately for it rather than being pooled with other Class 10 vehicles.

**Regulations**: 1101(1af) (separate class); 7307(1) (prescribed amount); Sch. II:Cl. 10.1 (class for CCA).

**Interpretation Bulletins**: IT-521R: Motor vehicle expenses claimed by self-employed individuals.

**I.T. Technical News**: No. 10 (1997 deduction limits and benefit rates for automobiles); No. 12 (1998 deduction limits and benefit rates for automobiles).

(h) **[luxury automobile — non-arm's length acquisition]** — notwithstanding paragraph (g), where a passenger vehicle is acquired by a taxpayer at any time from a person with whom the taxpayer does not deal at arm's length, the capital cost at that time to the taxpayer of the vehicle shall be deemed to be the least of

(i) the fair market value of the vehicle at that time,

(ii) the amount that immediately before that time was the cost amount to that person of the vehicle, and

(iii) $20,000 or such other amount as is prescribed.

**Related Provisions**: 20(16.1) — Terminal loss; 67.4 — More than one owner. See additional Related provisions and Definitions at end of s. 13.

**Notes**: Opening words "notwithstanding paragraph (g)" added by 1991 technical bill, retroactive to first enactment of 13(7)(h) in 1988. See Notes to 13(7)(g) re prescribed amount.

**Regulations**: 7307(1) (prescribed amount).

**Interpretation Bulletins [para. 13(7)(h)]**: IT-521R: Motor vehicle expenses claimed by self-employed individuals.

**I.T. Technical News**: No. 10 (1997 deduction limits and benefit rates for automobiles).

**Interpretation Bulletins [subsec. 13(7)]**: IT-102R2: Conversion of property, other than real property, from or to inventory; IT-120R5: Principal residence; IT-218R: Profit, capital gains and losses from the sale of real estate, including farmland and inherited land and conversion of real estate from capital property to inventory and vice versa; IT-478R2: CCA — recapture and terminal loss; IT-522R: Vehicle, travel and sales expenses of employees.

**(7.1) Deemed capital cost of certain property** — For the purposes of this Act, where section 80 applied to reduce the capital cost to a taxpayer of a depreciable property or a taxpayer deducted an amount under subsection 127(5) or (6) in respect of a depreciable property or received or is entitled to receive assistance from a government, municipality or other public authority in respect of, or for the acquisition of, depreciable property, whether as a grant, subsidy, forgivable loan, deduction from tax, investment allowance or as any other form of assistance other than

(a) an amount described in paragraph 37(1)(d),

(b) an amount deducted as an allowance under section 65, or

(b.1) an amount included in income by virtue of paragraph 12(1)(u) or 56(1)(s),

the capital cost of the property to the taxpayer at any particular time shall be deemed to be the amount, if any, by which the total of

(c) the capital cost of the property to the taxpayer, determined without reference to this subsection, subsection (7.4) and section 80, and

(d) such part, if any, of the assistance as has been repaid by the taxpayer, pursuant to an obligation to repay all or any part of that assistance, in respect of that property before the disposition thereof by the taxpayer and before the particular time

exceeds the total of

(e) where the property was acquired in a taxation year ending before the particular time, all amounts deducted under subsection 127(5) or (6) by the taxpayer for a taxation year ending before the particular time,

(f) the amount of assistance the taxpayer has received or is entitled, before the particular time, to receive, and

(g) all amounts by which the capital cost of the property to the taxpayer is required because of section 80 to be reduced at or before that time,

in respect of that property before the disposition thereof by the taxpayer.

**Related Provisions**: 6(8)(d) — GST rebate deemed to be assistance; 12(1)(t) — Investment tax credit; 13(7.2) — Receipt of public assistance; 13(7.4) — Deemed capital cost of certain property; 65 — Allowances; 80(1)"excluded obligation"(a)(iii) — Debt forgiveness rules do not apply where amount has reduced capital cost of property; 80(5) — Reduction in capital cost on settlement of debt; 80(9) — Additional reduction in capital cost for limited purposes; 87(2)(j.6) — Amalgamations — continuing corporation; 127(11.5) — Ignore 13(7.1) for purposes of ITC qualified expenditures; 127(12) — Investment tax credit; 143.2(6) — Reduction in cost of tax shelter investment; 248(16) — GST — input tax credit and rebate; 248(18) — GST — repayment of input tax credit. See additional Related Provisions and Definitions at end of s. 13.

**Notes**: Where a GST input tax credit or other government assistance cannot be applied to reduce the capital cost of depreciable property (under this subsection) or the adjusted cost base of capital property (under 53(2)(k)), it is generally included in income under 12(1)(t) or (x).

Opening words of 13(7.1) amended by 1994 tax amendments bill (Part I) to add "where section 80 applied to reduce the capital cost to a taxpayer of depreciable property", effective for taxation years that end after February 21, 1994.

Reference to s. 80 in 13(7.1)(c) added, and 13(7.1)(g) added, by 1994 tax amendments bill (Part I), effective for taxation years that end after February 21, 1994.

**Interpretation Bulletins**: IT-273R2: Government assistance — General comments; IT-478R2: CCA — recapture and terminal loss.

**(7.2) Receipt of public assistance** — For the purposes of subsection (7.1), where at any time a taxpayer who is a beneficiary of a trust or a member of a partnership has received or is entitled to receive assistance from a government, municipality or other public authority whether as a grant, subsidy, forgivable loan, deduction from tax, investment allowance or as any other form of assistance, the amount of the assistance that may reasonably be considered to be in respect of, or for the acquisition of, depreciable property of the trust or partnership shall be deemed to have been received at that time by the trust or partnership, as the case may be, as assistance from the government, municipality or other public authority for the acquisition of depreciable property.

**Related Provisions**: 53(2)(c)(ix) — Reduction of ACB of partnership interest; 53(2)(h)(v) — Reduction of ACB of capital interest in trust. See also Related Provisions and Definitions at end of s. 13.

**(7.3) Control of corporations by one trustee** — For the purposes of paragraph (7)(e), where at a particular time one corporation would, but for this subsection, be related to another corporation by reason of both corporations being controlled by the same trustee or executor and it is established that

(a) the trustee or executor did not acquire control of the corporations as a result of one or more trusts or estates created by the same individual or by two or more individuals not dealing with each other at arm's length, and

(b) the trust or estate under which the trustee or executor acquired control of each of the corporations arose only on the death of the individual creating the trust or estate,

the two corporations shall be deemed not to be related to each other at that particular time.

**Related Provisions**: 256(6)–(9) — Whether control acquired. Also see Related Provisions and Definitions at end of s. 13.

**Notes**: 13(7.3) added by 1985 Budget, effective for property acquired after May 22, 1985, other than property acquired before 1986 pursuant to an agreement entered into in writing before May 23, 1985.

**(7.4) Deemed capital cost** — Notwithstanding subsection (7.1), where a taxpayer has in a taxation year received an amount that would, but for this subsection, be included in the taxpayer's income under paragraph 12(1)(x) in respect of the cost of a depreciable property acquired by the taxpayer in the year, in the three taxation years immediately preceding the year or in the taxation year immediately following the year and the taxpayer elects under this subsection on or before the day on or before which the taxpayer is required to file the taxpayer's return of income under this Part for the year, or, where the property is acquired in the taxation year immediately following the year, for that following year, the capital cost of the property to the taxpayer shall be deemed to be the amount by which the total of

(a) the capital cost of the property to the taxpayer otherwise determined, applying the provisions of subsection (7.1), where necessary, and

(b) such part, if any, of the amount received by the taxpayer as has been repaid by the taxpayer pursuant to a legal obligation to repay all or any part of that amount, in respect of that property and before the disposition thereof by the taxpayer, and as may reasonably be considered to be in respect of the amount elected under this subsection in respect of the property

exceeds the amount elected by the taxpayer under this subsection, but in no case shall the amount elected under this subsection exceed the least of

(c) the amount so received by the taxpayer,

(d) the capital cost of the property to the taxpayer otherwise determined, and

(e) where the taxpayer has disposed of the property before the year, nil.

**Related Provisions**: 87(2)(j.6) — Amalgamations — continuing corporation; 125.4(5) — Canadian film/video credit is deemed to be assistance; 125.5(5) — Film/video production services credit is deemed to be assistance; 127(11.5) — Ignore 13(7.4) for purposes of ITC qualified expenditures; 220(3.2), Reg. 600(b) — Late filing of election or revocation. See also Related Provisions and Definitions at end of s. 13.

**Interpretation Bulletins**: IT-273R2: Government assistance — general comments; IT-478R2: CCA — recapture and terminal loss.

**Information Circulars**: 92-1: Guidelines for accepting late, amended or revoked elections.

**(7.5) Deemed capital cost** — For the purposes of this Act,

(a) where a taxpayer, to acquire a property prescribed in respect of the taxpayer, is required under the terms of a contract made after March 6, 1996 to make a payment to Her Majesty in right of Canada or a province or to a Canadian municipality in respect of costs incurred or to be incurred by the recipient of the payment

(i) the taxpayer is deemed to have acquired the property at a capital cost equal to the portion of that payment made by the taxpayer that can reasonably be regarded as being in respect of those costs, and

(ii) the time of acquisition of the property by the taxpayer is deemed to be the later of the time the payment is made and the time at which those costs are incurred;

(b) where

(i) at any time after March 6, 1996 a taxpayer incurs a cost on account of capital for the building of, for the right to use or in respect of, a prescribed property, and

(ii) the amount of the cost would, if this paragraph did not apply, not be included in the capital cost to the taxpayer of depreciable property of a prescribed class,

the taxpayer is deemed to have acquired the property at that time at a capital cost equal to the amount of the cost;

(c) where a taxpayer acquires an intangible property as a consequence of making a payment to which paragraph (a) applies or incurring a cost to which paragraph (b) applies,

(i) the property referred to in paragraph (a) or (b) is deemed to include the intangible property, and

(ii) the portion of the capital cost referred to in paragraph (a) or (b) that applies to the intangible property is deemed to be the amount determined by the formula

$$A \times \frac{B}{C}$$

where

A is the lesser of the amount of the payment made or cost incurred and the amount determined for C,

B is the fair market value of the intangible property at the time the payment was made or the cost was incurred, and

C is the fair market value at the time the payment was made or the cost was incurred of all intangible properties acquired as a consequence of making the payment or incurring the cost; and

(d) any property deemed by paragraph (a) or (b) to have been acquired at any time by a taxpayer as a consequence of making a payment or incurring a cost

(i) is deemed to have been acquired for the purpose for which the payment was made or the cost was incurred, and

(ii) is deemed to be owned by the taxpayer at any subsequent time that the taxpayer benefits from the property.

**Related Provisions**: 66.1(6)"Canadian exploration expense"(l), 66.2(5)"Canadian development expense"(j) — Where property is depreciable property, its cost will not be CEE or CDE. See also Related Provisions and Definitions at end of s. 13..

**Notes**: 13(7.5) added by 1996 Budget, effective for taxation years that end after March 6, 1996. It allows certain payments and costs to be treated as the capital cost of depreciable property. Its purpose is to prevent costs associated with the building of roads and similar projects from being considered as eligible capital expenditures while, at the same time, ensuring that classification of such costs as CEE, CDE and FEDE is restricted to the building of temporary access roads. The CCA claimed in respect of such costs can result in a reduction of the resource allowance under Reg. 1210.

**Regulations**: 1102(14.2) (prescribed property for 13(7.5)(a)); 1102(14.3) (prescribed property for 13(7.5)(b)).

**(8) Disposition after ceasing business** — Notwithstanding subsections (3) and 11(2), where a taxpayer, after ceasing to carry on a business, has disposed of depreciable property of the taxpayer of a prescribed class that was acquired by the taxpayer for the purpose of gaining or producing income from the business and that was not subsequently used by the taxpayer for some other purpose, in applying subsection (1) or (2), each reference therein to a "taxation year" and "year" shall not be read as a reference to a "fiscal period".

**Related Provisions**: 13(1) — Recaptured depreciation; 20(16.3) — Same rule for purposes of subsecs. 20(16) and (16.1); 25(3) — Disposition in extended fiscal period. See additional Related Provisions and Definitions at end of s. 13.

**Notes**: Before re-enactment in R.S.C. 1985 (5th Supp.), 13(8) applied for purposes of 20(16) and (16.1) as well. See now 20(16.3).

**Interpretation Bulletins**: IT-172R: CCA — taxation year of individuals; IT-478R2: CCA — recapture and terminal loss.

**(9) Meaning of "gaining or producing income"** — In applying paragraphs (7)(a) to (d) in respect of a non-resident taxpayer, a reference to "gaining or producing income" in relation to a business shall be read as a reference to gaining or producing income from a business wholly carried on in Canada or such part of a business as is wholly carried on in Canada.

**Related Provisions**: See Related Provisions and Definitions at end of s. 13.

**Interpretation Bulletins**: IT-478R2: CCA — recapture and terminal loss.

**I.T. Technical News**: No. 18 (*Cudd Pressure* case).

**(10) Deemed capital cost** — For the purposes of this Act, where a taxpayer has, after December 3, 1970 and before April 1, 1972, acquired prescribed property

(a) for use in a prescribed manufacturing or processing business carried on by the taxpayer, and

(b) that was not used for any purpose whatever before it was acquired by the taxpayer,

the taxpayer shall be deemed to have acquired that property at a capital cost to the taxpayer equal to 115% of the amount that, but for this subsection and section 21, would have been the capital cost to the taxpayer of that property.

**Related Provisions**: See Related Provisions and Definitions at end of s. 13.

**Regulations**: 1102(15) (prescribed property, prescribed manufacturing or processing business).

**(11) Deduction in respect of property used in performance of duties** — Any amount deducted under subparagraph 8(1)(j)(ii) or (p)(ii) of this Act or subsection 11(11) of *The Income Tax Act*, chapter 52 of the Statutes of Canada, 1948, shall be deemed, for the purposes of this section to have been deducted under regulations made under paragraph 20(1)(a).

**Related Provisions**: See Related Provisions and Definitions at end of s. 13.

**Interpretation Bulletins**: IT-522R: Vehicle, travel and sales expenses of employees.

**(12) Application of para. 20(1)(cc) [lobbying expenses]** — Where, in computing the income of a taxpayer for a taxation year, an amount has been deducted under paragraph 20(1)(cc) or the taxpayer has elected under subsection 20(9) to make a deduction in respect of an amount that would otherwise have been deductible under that paragraph, the amount shall, if it was a payment on account of the capital cost of depreciable property, be deemed to have been allowed to the taxpayer in respect of the property under regulations made under paragraph 20(1)(a) in computing the income of the taxpayer

(a) for the year, or

(b) for the year in which the property was acquired,

whichever is the later.

**Related Provisions**: See Related Provisions and Definitions at end of s. 13.

**Interpretation Bulletins**: IT-99R5: Legal and accounting fees.

**(13) Deduction under Canadian Vessel Construction Assistance Act** — Where a deduction has been made under the *Canadian Vessel Construction Assistance Act* for any taxation year, subsection (1) is applicable in respect of the prescribed class created by that Act or any other prescribed class to which the vessel may have been transferred.

**Related Provisions**: See Related Provisions and Definitions at end of s. 13.

**(14) Conversion cost** — For the purposes of this section, section 20 and any regulations made under paragraph 20(1)(a), a vessel in respect of which any conversion cost is incurred after March 23, 1967 shall, to the extent of the conversion cost, be deemed to be included in a separate prescribed class.

**Related Provisions**: 13(17) — Transfer of separate class to same class as vessel. See also Related Provisions and Definitions at end of s. 13.

**Regulations**: 1100(1)(v), 1101(2a).

**Interpretation Bulletins**: IT-267R2: CCA — vessels.

**(15) Where subsec. (1) and subdivision c do not apply** — Where a vessel owned by a taxpayer on January 1, 1966 or constructed pursuant to a construction contract entered into by the taxpayer prior to 1966 and not completed by that date was disposed of by the taxpayer before 1974,

(a) subsection (1) and subdivision c do not apply to the proceeds of disposition

(i) if an amount at least equal to the proceeds of disposition was used by the taxpayer, before May, 1974 and during the taxation year of the taxpayer in which the vessel was disposed of or within 4 months from the end of that taxation year, under conditions satisfactory to the appropriate minister, either for replacement or to incur any conversion cost with respect to a vessel owned by the taxpayer, or

(ii) if the appropriate minister certified that the taxpayer had, on satisfactory terms, deposited

(A) on or before the day on which the taxpayer was required to file a return of the taxpayer's income for the taxation year in which the vessel was disposed of, or

(B) on or before such day subsequent to the day referred to in clause (A) as the appropriate minister specified in respect of the taxpayer,

an amount at least equal to the tax that would, but for this subsection, have been payable by the taxpayer under this Part in respect of the proceeds of disposition, or satisfactory security therefor, as a guarantee that the proceeds of disposition would be used before 1975 for replacement; and

(b) if within the time specified for the filing of a return of the taxpayer's income for the taxation year in which the vessel was disposed of

(i) the taxpayer elected to have the vessel constituted a prescribed class, or

(ii) where any conversion cost in respect of the vessel was included in a separate prescribed class, the taxpayer elected to have the vessel transferred to that class, the vessel shall be deemed to have been so transferred immediately before the disposition thereof, but this paragraph does not apply unless the proceeds of disposition of the vessel exceed the amount that would be the undepreciated capital cost of property of the class to which it would be so transferred.

**Related Provisions**: 13(16) — Election; 13(17) — Prescribed class; 13(18) — Reassessment; 13(19), (20) — Disposition of deposit; 13(21) "appropriate minister"; 96(3) — Election by members of partnership; 150(1) — When return of income due. See additional Related Provisions and Definitions at end of s. 13.

**Notes**: 13(15)(a) redrafted in the R.S.C. 1985 (5th Supp.) consolidation, effective for taxation years ending after November 1991. The previous version referred to "the Minister of Industry, Science and Technology" rather than "the appropriate minister". Also, para. (b) was restructured to split off subparas. (i) and (ii).

13(15) amended effective February 23, 1990 to change "Minister of Regional Industrial Expansion" in para. (a) to "Minister of Industry, Science and Technology".

**(16) Election concerning vessel** — Where a vessel owned by a taxpayer is disposed of by the taxpayer, the taxpayer may, if subsection (15) does not apply to the proceeds of disposition or if the taxpayer did not make an election under paragraph (15)(b) in respect of the vessel, within the time specified for the filing of a return of the taxpayer's income for the taxation year in which the vessel is disposed of, elect to have the proceeds that would be included in computing the taxpayer's income for the year under this Part treated as proceeds of disposition of property of another prescribed class that includes a vessel owned by the taxpayer.

**Related Provisions**: 96(3) — Election by members of partnership. See additional Related Provisions and Definitions at end of s. 13.

**Interpretation Bulletins**: IT-267R2: CCA — vessels.

**(17) Separate prescribed class concerning vessel** — Where a separate prescribed class has been constituted either under this Act or the *Canadian Vessel Construction Assistance Act* by reason of the conversion of a vessel owned by a taxpayer and the vessel is disposed of by the taxpayer, if no election in respect of the vessel was made under paragraph (15)(b), the separate prescribed class constituted by reason of the conversion shall be deemed to have been transferred to the class in which the vessel was included immediately before the disposition thereof.

**Related Provisions**: See Related Provisions and Definitions at end of s. 13.

**Interpretation Bulletins**: IT-267R2: CCA — vessels.

**(18) Reassessments** — Notwithstanding any other provision of this Act, where a taxpayer has

(a) used an amount as described in paragraph (4)(c), or

(b) made an election under paragraph (15)(b) in respect of a vessel and the proceeds of disposition of the vessel were used before 1975 for replacement under conditions satisfactory to the appropriate minister,

such reassessments of tax, interest or penalties shall be made as are necessary to give effect to subsections (4) and (15).

**Notes**: 13(18) redrafted in the R.S.C. 1985 (5th Supp.) consolidation, effective for taxation years ending after November 1991. The previous version referred to "the Minister of Industry, Science and Technology" rather than "the appropriate minister" (now defined in 13(21)).

13(18)(b) amended effective February 23, 1990 to change "Minister of Regional Industrial Expansion" to "Minister of Industry, Science and Technology".

**(18.1) Ascertainment of certain property** — For the purpose of determining whether property meets the criteria set out in the Regulations in respect of prescribed energy conservation property, the Technical Guide to Class 43.1, as amended from time to time and published by the Department of Natural Resources, shall apply conclusively with respect to engineering and scientific matters.

**Related Provisions**: 241(4)(d)(vi.1) — Disclosure of information to Department of Natural Resources. See also Related Provisions and Definitions at end of s. 13.

**Notes**: 13(18.1) added by 1994 Budget, effective for property acquired after February 21, 1994.

**Regulations**: Reg. 8200.1 (prescribed energy conservation property).

**(19) Disposition of deposit [vessel construction]** — All or any part of a deposit made under subparagraph (15)(a)(ii) or under the *Canadian Vessel Construction Assistance Act* may be paid out to or on behalf of any person who, under conditions satisfactory to the appropriate minister and as a replacement for the vessel disposed of, acquires a vessel before 1975

(a) that was constructed in Canada and is registered in Canada or is registered under conditions satisfactory to the appropriate minister in any country or territory to which the British Commonwealth Merchant Shipping Agreement, signed at London on December 10, 1931, applies, and

(b) in respect of the capital cost of which no allowance has been made to any other taxpayer under this Act or the *Canadian Vessel Construction Assistance Act*,

or incurs any conversion cost with respect to a vessel owned by that person that is registered in Canada or is registered under conditions satisfactory to the appropriate minister in any country or territory to which the agreement referred to in paragraph (a) applies, but the ratio of the amount paid out to the amount of the deposit shall not exceed the ratio of the capital cost to that person of the vessel or the conversion cost to that person of the vessel, as the case may be, to the proceeds of disposition of the vessel disposed of, and any deposit or part of a deposit not so paid out before July 1, 1975 or not paid out pursuant to subsection (20) shall be paid to the

**S. 13(19)**      Income Tax Act, Part I, Division B

Receiver General and form part of the Consolidated Revenue Fund.

**Related Provisions**: 13(21)"appropriate minister". See additional Related Provisions and Definitions at end of s. 13.

**Notes**: 13(19) redrafted in the R.S.C. 1985 (5th Supp.) consolidation, effective for taxation years ending after November 1991. The previous version referred to "the Minister of Industry, Science and Technology" rather than "the appropriate minister".

13(19) amended effective February 23, 1990 to change "Minister of Regional Industrial Expansion" to "Minister of Industry, Science and Technology".

**(20) Idem** — Notwithstanding any other provision of this section, where a taxpayer made a deposit under subparagraph (15)(a)(ii) and the proceeds of disposition in respect of which the deposit was made were not used by any person before 1975 under conditions satisfactory to the appropriate minister as a replacement for the vessel disposed of,

(a) to acquire a vessel described in paragraphs (19)(a) and (b), or

(b) to incur any conversion cost with respect to a vessel owned by that person that is registered in Canada or is registered under conditions satisfactory to the appropriate minister in any country or territory to which the agreement referred to in paragraph (19)(a) applies,

the appropriate minister may refund to the taxpayer the deposit, or the part thereof not paid out to the taxpayer under subsection (19), as the case may be, in which case there shall be added, in computing the income of the taxpayer for the taxation year of the taxpayer in which the vessel was disposed of, that proportion of the amount that would have been included in computing the income for the year under this Part had the deposit not been made under subparagraph (15)(a)(ii) that the portion of the proceeds of disposition not so used before 1975 as such a replacement is of the proceeds of disposition, and, notwithstanding any other provision of this Act, such reassessments of tax, interest or penalties shall be made as are necessary to give effect to this subsection.

**Related Provisions**: 13(21)"appropriate minister". See additional Related Provisions and Definitions at end of s. 13.

**Notes**: 13(20) redrafted in the R.S.C. 1985 (5th Supp.) consolidation, effective for taxation years ending after November 1991. The previous version referred to "the Minister of Industry, Science and Technology" rather than "the appropriate minister".

13(20) amended effective February 23, 1990 to change "Minister of Regional Industrial Expansion" to "Minister of Industry, Science and Technology".

**(21) Definitions** — In this section,

**Related Provisions**: 20(1.1) — Definitions in 13(21) apply to regulations made under 20(1)(a); 20(27.1) — Definitions in 13(21) apply to s. 20.

**"appropriate minister"** means the Canadian Maritime Commission, the Minister of Industry, Trade and Commerce, the Minister of Regional Industrial Expansion, the Minister of Industry, Science and Technology or the Minister of Industry or any other minister or body that was or is legally authorized to perform the act referred to in the provision in which this expression occurs at the time the act was or is performed;

**Notes**: 13(21)"appropriate minister" was added in R.S.C. 1985 (5th Supp.) consolidation, effective for taxation years ending after November 1991, because of the changed references in 13(15), (18), (19), (20) and (21)"conversion cost" (see Notes to those provisions). Reference to "Minister of Industry" added by *Department of Industry Act* (1995, c. 1), effective March 29, 1995.

**"conversion"**, in respect of a vessel, means a conversion or major alteration in Canada by a taxpayer;

**Related Provisions**: See Related Provisions and Definitions at end of s. 13.

**Notes**: "Conversion" amended by 1991 technical bill, effective for property acquired after July 13, 1990, to remove requirement for approval by the Minister of Industry, Science and Technology (the "appropriate Minister"). Accelerated CCA for vessels and conversion costs is now verified by Revenue Canada as part of the normal audit process.

13(21)"conversion" was 13(21)(a) before R.S.C. 1985 (5th Supp.) consolidation, effective for taxation years ending after November 1991.

**Interpretation Bulletins**: IT-267R2: CCA — vessels; IT-273R2: Government assistance — general comments.

**"conversion cost"**, in respect of a vessel, means the cost of a conversion;

**Notes**: "Conversion cost" was included in the definition of "conversion" in 13(21)(a) before R.S.C. 1985 (5th Supp.) consolidation, effective for taxation years ending after November 1991.

**Interpretation Bulletins**: IT-267R2: CCA — vessels.

**"depreciable property"** of a taxpayer as of any time in a taxation year means property acquired by the taxpayer in respect of which the taxpayer has been allowed, or would, if the taxpayer owned the property at the end of the year and this Act were read without reference to subsection (26), be entitled to, a deduction under paragraph 20(1)(a) in computing income for that year or a preceding taxation year;

**Related Provisions**: 13(1) — Recapture; 13(5.2)(c) — Certain real property deemed to be depreciable property; 20(1)(a) — Capital cost allowance; 54 — "Capital property"; 88(1)(c.7) — Extended meaning for certain windup rules; 107.4(3)(d) — Rollover of depreciable property to trust; 248(1)"depreciable property" — Definition applies to entire Act. See additional Related Provisions and Definitions at end of s. 13.

**Notes**: The reference to "the end of the year" should not mean that one must determine whether CCA was *actually* available at the end of the year. If depreciable property is converted to inventory during the year, it should remain depreciable property until the day on which it is so converted. See, however, *Sako Auto Leasing v. MNR*, [1993] G.S.T.C. 17 (CITT).

"Depreciable property" amended by 1991 technical bill, effective for property acquired after 1989, to clarify that property not yet "available for use" under 13(26) is still considered depreciable property.

13(21)"depreciable property" was 13(21)(b) before R.S.C. 1985 (5th Supp.) consolidation, effective for taxation years ending after November 1991.

**Regulations**: Part XI (capital cost allowance allowed on depreciable property).

**I.T. Application Rules**: 18, 20 (property acquired before 1972).

**Interpretation Bulletins**: IT-102R2: Conversion of property, other than real property, from or to inventory; IT-128R: CCA — depreciable property; IT-220R2: CCA — proceeds of disposition of depreciable property.

**Forms**: T2085: Capital dispositions supplementary schedule — depreciable property.

**"disposition of property"** includes any transaction or event entitling a taxpayer to proceeds of disposition of property;

### Proposed Repeal — 13(21) "disposition of property"

**Application**: Bill C-43 (First Reading September 20, 2000), subsec. 5(1), will repeal the definition "disposition of property" in subsec. 13(21), applicable to transactions and events that occur after December 23, 1998.

**Technical Notes**: Subsection 13(21) defines the expression "disposition of property" for the purposes of the depreciation recapture rules in section 13.

The definition is repealed, strictly as a consequence of the introduction of the new definition "disposition" in subsection 248(1).

**Related Provisions**: 54"disposition" — Disposition for capital gains purposes. See also Related Provisions and Definitions at end of s. 13.

**Notes**: 13(21)"disposition of property" was para. 13(21)(c) before R.S.C. 1985 (5th Supp.) consolidation, effective for taxation years ending after November 1991.

**Advance Tax Rulings**: ATR-1: Transfer of legal title in land to bare trustee corporation — mortgagee's requirements sole reason for transfer.

**"proceeds of disposition"** of property includes

(a) the sale price of property that has been sold,

(b) compensation for property unlawfully taken,

(c) compensation for property destroyed and any amount payable under a policy of insurance in respect of loss or destruction of property,

(d) compensation for property taken under statutory authority or the sale price of property sold to a person by whom notice of an intention to take it under statutory authority was given,

(e) compensation for property injuriously affected, whether lawfully or unlawfully or under statutory authority or otherwise,

(f) compensation for property damaged and any amount payable under a policy of insurance in respect of damage to property, except to the extent that the compensation or amount, as the case may be, has within a reasonable time after the damage been expended on repairing the damage,

(g) an amount by which the liability of a taxpayer to a mortgagee is reduced as a result of the sale of mortgaged property under a provision of the mortgage, plus any amount received by the taxpayer out of the proceeds of the sale, and

(h) any amount included because of section 79 in computing a taxpayer's proceeds of disposition of the property;

**Related Provisions**: 12(1)(f) — Insurance proceeds received for amount expended; 13(4) — Exchanges of property; 13(21) — Undepreciated capital cost; 13(21.1) — Disposition of a building; 44 — Exchanges of property; 54"proceeds of disposition" — Parallel definition for capital property; 79(3) — Deemed proceeds of disposition when property surrendered to creditor; 248(1) — "Cost amount"(a). See also Related Provisions and Definitions at end of s. 13.

**Notes**: 13(21)"proceeds of disposition" was para. 13(21)(d) before R.S.C. 1985 (5th Supp.) consolidation, effective for taxation years ending after November 1991. See Table of Concordance.

Reference to 79(c) in para. (h) changed to "section 79" by 1994 tax amendments bill (Part I), effective for taxation years that end after February 21, 1994.

**Interpretation Bulletins**: IT-170R: Sale of property — when included in income computation; IT-259R3: Exchanges of property; IT-271R: Expropriations; IT-460: Dispositions — absence of consideration; IT-505: Mortgage foreclosures and conditional sales repossessions.

**"timber resource property"** of a taxpayer means

(a) a right or licence to cut or remove timber from a limit or area in Canada (in this definition referred to as an "original right") if

(i) that original right was acquired by the taxpayer (other than in the manner referred to in paragraph (b)) after May 6, 1974, and

(ii) at the time of the acquisition of the original right

(A) the taxpayer may reasonably be regarded as having acquired, directly or indirectly, the right to extend or renew that original right or to acquire another such right or licence in substitution therefor, or

(B) in the ordinary course of events, the taxpayer may reasonably expect to be able to extend or renew that original right or to acquire another such right or licence in substitution therefor, or

(b) any right or licence owned by the taxpayer to cut or remove timber from a limit or area in Canada if that right or licence may reasonably be regarded

(i) as an extension or renewal of or as one of a series of extensions or renewals of an original right of the taxpayer, or

(ii) as having been acquired in substitution for or as one of a series of substitutions for an original right of the taxpayer or any renewal or extension thereof;

**Related Provisions**: 128.1(4)(b)(i) — timber resource property excluded from deemed disposition on emigration; 248(1)"timber resource property" — Definition applies to entire Act; 248(10) — Series of transactions.

**Notes**: In *ITT Industries of Canada Ltd.*, [2000] 3 C.T.C. 400 (FCA), a replacement 25-year BC tree farm licence, issued when the previous *Forest Act* was repealed, was held to be a timber resource property.

13(21)"timber resource property" was para. 13(21)(d.1) before R.S.C. 1985 (5th Supp.) consolidation, effective for taxation years ending after November 1991. See Table of Concordance.

**Interpretation Bulletins**: IT-393R2: Election re tax on rents and timber royalties — non-residents; IT-418: CCA — partial dispositions of property; IT-481: Timber resource property and timber limits.

**"total depreciation"** allowed to a taxpayer before any time for property of a prescribed class means the total of all amounts each of which is an amount deducted by the taxpayer under paragraph 20(1)(a) in respect of property of that class or an amount deducted under subsection 20(16), or that would have been so deducted but for subsection 20(16.1), in computing the taxpayer's income for taxation years ending before that time;

**Related Provisions**: See Related Provisions and Definitions at end of s. 13.

**Notes**: 13(21)"total depreciation" was para. 13(21)(e) before R.S.C. 1985 (5th Supp.) consolidation, effective for taxation years ending after November 1991.

**Regulations**: Part XI.

**Interpretation Bulletins**: IT-478R2: CCA — recapture and terminal loss.

**"undepreciated capital cost"** to a taxpayer of depreciable property of a prescribed class as of any time means the amount determined by the formula

$$(A + B + C + D + D.1) - (E + E.1 + F + G + H + I + J + K)$$

where

A is the total of all amounts each of which is the capital cost to the taxpayer of a depreciable property of the class acquired before that time,

B is the total of all amounts included in the taxpayer's income under this section for a taxation year ending before that time, to the extent that those amounts relate to depreciable property of the class,

C is the total of all amounts each of which is such part of any assistance as has been repaid by the taxpayer, pursuant to an obligation to repay all or any part of that assistance, in respect of a depreciable property of the class subsequent to the disposition thereof by the taxpayer that would have been included in an amount determined under paragraph (7.1)(d) had the repayment been made before the disposition,

D is the total of all amounts each of which is an amount repaid in respect of a property of the class subsequent to the disposition thereof by the taxpayer that would have been an amount described in paragraph (7.4)(b) had the repayment been made before the disposition,

D.1 is the total of all amounts each of which is an amount paid by the taxpayer before that time as or on account of an existing or proposed countervailing or anti-dumping duty in respect of depreciable property of the class,

E is the total depreciation allowed to the taxpayer for property of the class before that time,

E.1 is the total of all amounts each of which is an amount by which the undepreciated capital cost to the taxpayer of depreciable property of that class is required (otherwise than because of a reduction in the capital cost to the taxpayer of depreciable property) to be reduced at or before that time because of subsection 80(5),

F is the total of all amounts each of which is an amount in respect of a disposition before that time of property (other than a timber resource property) of the taxpayer of the class, and is the lesser of

  (a) the proceeds of disposition of the property minus any outlays and expenses to the extent that they were made or incurred by the taxpayer for the purpose of making the disposition, and

  (b) the capital cost to the taxpayer of the property,

G is the total of all amounts each of which is the proceeds of disposition before that time of a timber resource property of the taxpayer of the class minus any outlays and expenses to the extent that they were made or incurred by the taxpayer for the purpose of making the disposition,

H is, where the property of the class was acquired by the taxpayer for the purpose of gaining or producing income from a mine and the taxpayer so elects in prescribed manner and within a prescribed time in respect of that property, the amount equal to that portion of the income derived from the operation of the mine that is, by virtue of the provisions of the *Income Tax Application Rules* relating to income from the operation of new mines, not included in computing income of the taxpayer or any other person,

I is the total of all amounts deducted under subsection 127(5) or (6), in respect of a depreciable property of the class of the taxpayer, in computing the taxpayers' tax payable for a taxation year ending before that time and subsequent to the disposition of that property by the taxpayer,

J is the total of all amounts of assistance that the taxpayer received or was entitled to receive before that time, in respect of or for the acquisition of a depreciable property of the class of the taxpayer subsequent to the disposition of that property by the taxpayer, that would have been included in an amount determined under paragraph (7.1)(f) had the assistance been received before the disposition, and

K is the total of all amounts each of which is an amount received by the taxpayer before that time in respect of a refund of an amount added to the undepreciated capital cost of depreciable property of the class because of the description of D.1;

**Related Provisions**: 12(1)(f) — Damage to depreciable property — insurance proceeds; 12(1)(t) — Investment tax credit; 13(1) — Recapture where E to J exceed A to D; 13(2) — Recap-

Subdivision b — Income or Loss from a Business or Property    S. 13(21.1)

tured depreciation for vehicle; 13(4) — Exchanges of property; 13(5) — Transferred property; 13(5.2) — Where rent paid on property before its acquisition; 13(7) — Rule affecting capital cost; 13(21) — "timber resource property"; 13(22), (23) — Deductions deemed allowed to insurer for 1977 and 1978; 13(24) — Acquisition of control — limitation re calculation of UCC; 13(26) — Restriction on deduction before available for use; 13(33) — Consideration given for depreciable capital; 20(16) — Terminal loss; 70(12) — Capital cost of depreciable property on death; 87(2)(j.6) — Amalgamations — continuing corporation; 138(11.31)(b) — Change-in-use rule for insurance properties does not apply for purposes of UCC definition; 248(1)"undepreciated capital cost" — Definition applies to entire Act; 257 — Formula cannot calculate to less than zero. See additional Related Provisions and Definitions at end of s. 13.

**Notes**: Put simply and ignoring the special-case exceptions, undepreciated capital cost (UCC) is: (A) the original cost of each property in the class, plus (B) prior years' recapture under 13(1), minus (E) CCA claimed till now, minus (F) the proceeds of disposition of property sold, up to a limit of the original cost. (Excess proceeds over the original cost are treated as a capital gain under 39(1), rather than dealt with under s. 13.) See Notes to 13(1).

D.1 added by 1998 Budget, effective for amounts that become payable after February 23, 1998. See 20(1)(vv).

E.1 added by 1994 tax amendments bill (Part I), effective for taxation years that end after February 21, 1994. It provides a reduction in UCC to the extent required by 80(5). It does not apply, however, to the extent the reduction results from the reduction under 80(5) or (9) of the capital cost of depreciable property. Those reductions are dealt with under 13(7.1)(g).

K added by 1998 Budget, effective for amounts received after February 23, 1998. See 12(1)(z.6).

13(21)"undepreciated capital cost" was 13(21)(f) before R.S.C. 1985 (5th Supp.) consolidation, effective for taxation years ending after November 1991. The previous version, identical in meaning, read:

(f) "undepreciated capital cost" — "undepreciated capital cost" to a taxpayer of depreciable property of a prescribed class as of any time means the amount by which the aggregate of

(i) the capital cost to the taxpayer of each depreciable property of that class acquired before that time,

(ii) all amounts included in the taxpayer's income by virtue of this section for a taxation year ending prior to that time, to the extent that those amounts relate to depreciable property of that class,

(ii.1) all amounts each of which is such part of any assistance as has been repaid by the taxpayer, pursuant to an obligation to repay all or any part of that assistance, in respect of a depreciable property of that class subsequent to the disposition thereof by him that would have been included in an amount determined under paragraph 13(7.1)(d) had the repayment been made before the disposition, and

(ii.2) all amounts each of which is an amount repaid in respect of a property of the class subsequent to the disposition thereof by him that would have been an amount described in paragraph (7.4)(b) had the repayment been made before the disposition,

exceeds the aggregate of

(iii) the total depreciation allowed to the taxpayer for property of that class before that time,

(iv) for each disposition before that time of property (other than a timber resource property) of the taxpayer of that class, the lesser of

(A) the proceeds of disposition of the property minus any outlays and expenses to the extent that they were made or incurred by him for the purpose of making the disposition, and

(B) the capital cost to him of the property,

(v) for each disposition before that time of a timber resource property of the taxpayer of that class, the proceeds of disposition of the property minus any outlays and expenses to the extent that they were made or incurred by him for the purpose of making the disposition,

(vi) where the property of that class was acquired by the taxpayer for the purpose of gaining or producing income from a mine and the taxpayer so elects in prescribed manner and within a prescribed time in respect of that property, an amount equal to that portion of the income derived from the operation of the mine that is, by virtue of the provisions of the *Income Tax Application Rules, 1971* relating to income from the operation of new mines, not included in computing income of the taxpayer or any other person,

(vii) all amounts each of which is an amount deducted under subsection 127(5) or (6), in respect of a depreciable property of that class of the taxpayer, in computing the taxpayer's tax payable for a taxation year ending before that time and subsequent to the disposition of such property by him, and

(viii) all amounts each of which is the amount of any assistance the taxpayer received or was entitled to receive before that time, in respect of or for the acquisition of a depreciable property of that class of the taxpayer subsequent to the disposition of such property by him, that would have been included in an amount determined under paragraph 13(7.1)(f) had the assistance been received before the disposition; and

**Regulations**: Part XI (amounts of depreciation allowed, for E).

**I.T. Application Rules**: 18 (property acquired before 1972).

**Interpretation Bulletins**: IT-172R: CCA — taxation year for individuals; IT-327: CCA — Elections under Regulation 1103; IT-418: CCA — partial dispositions of property; IT-478R2: CCA — recapture and terminal loss; IT-481: Timber resource property and timber limits.

**Information Circulars**: 87-5: Capital cost of property where trade-in is involved.

**"vessel"** means a vessel as defined in the *Canada Shipping Act*.

**Notes**: 13(21)"vessel" was 13(21)(g) before R.S.C. 1985 (5th Supp.) consolidation, effective for taxation years ending after November 1991.

**Interpretation Bulletins**: IT-267R2: CCA — vessels.

**Advance Tax Rulings**: ATR-52: Accelerated rate of CCA for vessels.

**Related Provisions [subsec. 13(21)]**: 20(1.1) — Definitions in 13(21) apply to regulations made under 20(1)(a); 20(27.1) — Definitions in 13(21) apply to s. 20.

**(21.1) Disposition of building** — Notwithstanding subsection (7) and the definition "proceeds of disposition" in section 54, where at any particular time in a taxation year a taxpayer disposes of a building of a prescribed class and the proceeds of disposition of the building determined without reference to this subsection and subsection (21.2) are less than the lesser of the cost amount and the capital cost to the taxpayer of the building immediately before the disposition, for the purposes of paragraph (a) of the description of F in the definition "undepreciated capital cost" in subsection (21) and subdivision c,

(a) where in the year the taxpayer or a person with whom the taxpayer does not deal at arm's length disposes of land subjacent to, or immediately contiguous to and necessary for the use of, the building, the proceeds of disposition of the building are deemed to be the lesser of

(i) the amount, if any, by which

(A) the total of the fair market value of the building at the particular time and the fair market value of the land immediately before its disposition

exceeds

(B) the lesser of the fair market value of the land immediately before its disposition and the amount, if any, by which the cost amount to the vendor of the land (determined without reference to this subsection) exceeds the total of the capital gains (determined without reference to subparagraphs 40(1)(a)(ii) and (iii)) in respect of dispositions of the land within 3 years before the particular time by the taxpayer or by a person with whom the taxpayer was not dealing at arm's length to the taxpayer or to another person with whom the taxpayer was not dealing at arm's length, and

(ii) the greater of

(A) the fair market value of the building at the particular time, and

(B) the lesser of the cost amount and the capital cost to the taxpayer of the building immediately before its disposition,

and, notwithstanding any other provision of this Act, the proceeds of disposition of the land are deemed to be the amount, if any, by which

(iii) the total of the proceeds of disposition of the building and of the land determined without reference to this subsection and subsection (21.2)

exceeds

(iv) the proceeds of disposition of the building as determined under this paragraph,

and the cost to the purchaser of the land shall be determined without reference to this subsection; and

(b) where paragraph (a) does not apply with respect to the disposition and, at any time before the disposition, the taxpayer or a person with whom the taxpayer did not deal at arm's length owned the land subjacent to, or immediately contiguous to and necessary for the use of, the build-

ing, the proceeds of disposition of the building are deemed to be an amount equal to the total of

(i) the proceeds of disposition of the building determined without reference to this subsection and subsection (21.2), and

(ii) 1/4 of the amount by which the greater of

(A) the cost amount to the taxpayer of the building, and

(B) the fair market value of the building immediately before its disposition exceeds the proceeds of disposition referred to in subparagraph (i).

**Proposed Amendment — 13(21.1)(b)(ii)**

**Application**: The December 21, 2000 draft legislation, subsec. 4(5), will amend subpara. 13(21.1)(b)(ii) by replacing the reference to the fraction "1/4" with a reference to the fraction "1/2", applicable to taxation years that end after February 27, 2000 except that, for a taxpayer's taxation year that includes either February 28, 2000 or October 17, 2000, the reference to the fraction "1/2" shall be read as a reference to the fraction determined when the fraction in para. 38(a), as amended [by the December 21, 2000 draft legislation], that applies to the taxpayer for the year is subtracted from 1.

**Technical Notes**: Subsection 13(21.1) sets out rules that in certain cases adjust a taxpayer's proceeds of disposition in respect of land and buildings disposed of by the taxpayer.

The amendment to paragraph 13(21.1)(b) replaces the reference to the fraction "1/4" with a reference to the fraction "1/2", as a consequence of the decrease of the inclusion rate for capital gains and losses from 3/4 to 1/2 [see 38(a) — ed.].

The amendment applies to dispositions of property that occur in taxation years of a taxpayer that end after February 27, 2000 except that, for dispositions of property that occur in a taxation year of a taxpayer that includes either February 28, 2000 or October 17, 2000, the references in paragraph 13(21)(b) to the fraction "1/2" is to be read as a reference to the fraction determined by subtracting the fraction in amended paragraph 38(a) that applies to the taxpayer for the year from 1. These modifications are required in order to reflect the capital gains/losses rate for the year.

**Related Provisions**: 70(5)(c), (d) — Capital property of a deceased taxpayer.

**Notes**: 13(21.1) provides special rules where a building is disposed of for less than its "cost amount" (see 248(1)). Where land and building are sold together, any (terminal) loss on the building is reduced to the extent of any (capital) gain on the sale of the land. This is achieved by increasing the proceeds of disposition of the building by the lesser of the loss on the building and the gain on the sale of the land. The capital gain on the land is then reduced by a corresponding amount.

13(21.1) amended by 1995-97 technical bill, effective for dispositions after April 26, 1995 (but subject to the grandfathering rule reproduced after s. 260), to add "and subsection (21.2)" in the opening words and in 13(21.1)(a)(iii). (Other changes made at the same time were non-substantive, e.g. changing "shall be deemed" to "is deemed".)

The amendment provides that 13(21.1) applies before (21.2), but does not stop 13(21.2) from applying. If, after 13(21.1) applies to a disposition, there still remains a terminal loss, and the disposition is one to which 13(21.2) applies, 13(21.2) may defer the recognition of the remaining loss.

**Interpretation Bulletins [subsec. 13(21.1)]:** IT-220R2: CCA — proceeds of disposition of depreciable property; IT-349R3: Intergenerational transfers of farm property on death.

**(21.2) Loss on certain transfers [within affiliated group]** — Where

(a) a corporation, trust or partnership (in this subsection referred to as the "transferor") disposes at a particular time (otherwise than in a disposition described in any of paragraphs (c) to (g) of the definition "superficial loss" in section 54) of a depreciable property of a particular prescribed class of the transferor,

> **Proposed Amendment — 13(21.2)(a)**
>
> (a) a person or partnership (in this subsection referred to as the "transferor") disposes at a particular time (otherwise than in a disposition described in any of paragraphs (c) to (g) of the definition "superficial loss" in section 54) of a depreciable property of a particular prescribed class of the transferor,
>
> **Application**: Bill C-43 (First Reading September 20, 2000), subsec. 5(2), will amend para. 13(21.2)(a) to read as above, applicable after November 1999 except that, if an individual (other than a trust) so elects in writing and files with the Minister of National Revenue on or before the individual's filing-due date for the taxation year in which the amending legislation is assented to, this amendment does not apply in respect of the disposition of a property by the individual before July 2000
>
> (a) to a person who was obliged on November 30, 1999 to acquire the property pursuant to the terms of an agreement in writing made on or before that day; or
>
> (b) in a transaction, or as part of a series of transactions, the arrangements for which, evidenced in writing, were substantially advanced before December 1999, other than a transaction or series of transactions a main purpose of which can reasonably be considered to have been to enable an unrelated person to obtain the benefit of
>
> > (i) any deduction in computing income, taxable income, taxable income earned in Canada or tax payable under the *Income Tax Act*, or
> >
> > (ii) any balance of undeducted outlays, expenses or other amounts.
>
> **Technical Notes**: Subsection 13(21.2) defers, in certain circumstances, the realization of a loss that would otherwise arise from the transfer of a depreciable property. The subsection applies where the transferor or a person affiliated with the transferor holds the transferred property, or has a right to acquire it, 30 days after the transfer. Until any one of certain events occurs, the transferor is treated as holding a notional depreciable property the capital cost of which is, in effect, the amount of the deferred loss.
>
> Subsection 13(21.2) currently applies only where the transferor is a corporation, partnership or trust. The subsection is amended to apply to transfers by any person or partnership. The practical effect of the change is to make the rule apply to natural persons.
>
> The subsection is also amended to clarify subparagraph 13(21.2)(e)(ii), by replacing references to the "taxpayer" with references to the "transferor." This clarification does not effect any substantive change to the provision.
>
> Amended subsection 13(21.2) applies after November 30, 1999. An optional exception is provided where an individual disposes of a property before July 1, 2000, in a transaction that meets either of two tests. The first test is that the disposition be to a person who was obliged on November 30, 1999 to acquire the property under an agreement in writing. The second test is that the disposition be a transaction (or part of a series) the arrangements for which (evidenced in writing) were substantially advanced by November 30, 1999. Ineligible under the second test is any transaction or series of transactions a main purpose of which was to enable an unrelated person to obtain the benefit of a deduction or balance under the Act.
>
> Where either of these tests is met, the transferor may elect not to have the first amendment described above apply to the disposition. Such an election must be made in writing and filed with the Minister of National Revenue on or before the transferor's filing-due date for the year in which these amendments receive Royal Assent.

(b) the lesser of

(i) the capital cost to the transferor of the transferred property, and

(ii) the proportion of the undepreciated capital cost to the transferor of all property of the particular class immediately before that time that

(A) the fair market value of the transferred property at that time

is of

(B) the fair market value of all property of the particular class immediately before that time

exceeds the amount that would otherwise be the transferor's proceeds of disposition of the transferred property at the particular time, and

(c) on the 30th day after the particular time, a person or partnership (in this subsection referred to as the "subsequent owner") who is the transferor or a person affiliated with the transferor owns or has a right to acquire the transferred property (other than a right, as security only, derived from a mortgage, agreement for sale or similar obligation),

the following rules apply:

(d) sections 85 and 97 do not apply to the disposition,

(e) for the purposes of applying this section and section 20 and any regulations made for the purpose of paragraph 20(1)(a) to the transferor for taxation years that end after the particular time,

(i) the transferor is deemed to have disposed of the transferred property for proceeds equal to the lesser of the amounts determined under subparagraphs (b)(i) and (ii) with respect to the transferred property,

(ii) where 2 or more properties of a prescribed class of the transferor are disposed of at the same time, subparagraph (i) applies as if each property so disposed of had been separately disposed of in the order designated by the taxpayer or, if the taxpayer does not designate an order, in the order designated by the Minister,

> **Proposed Amendment —
> 13(21.2)(e)(ii)**
>
> (ii) where two or more properties of a prescribed class of the transferor are disposed of at the same time, subparagraph (i) applies as if each property so disposed of had been separately disposed of in the order designated by the transferor or, if the transferor does not designate an order, in the order designated by the Minister,
>
> **Application**: Bill C-43 (First Reading September 20, 2000), subsec. 5(3), will amend subpara. 13(21.2)(e)(ii) to read as above, applicable after November 1999.
>
> **Technical Notes**: See under 13(21.2)(a).

(iii) the transferor is deemed to own a property that was acquired before the beginning of the taxation year that includes the particular time at a capital cost equal to the amount of the excess described in paragraph (b), and that is property of the particular class, until the time that is immediately before the first time, after the particular time,

(A) at which a 30-day period begins throughout which neither the transferor nor a person affiliated with the transferor owns or has a right to acquire the transferred property (other than a right, as security only, derived from a mortgage, agreement for sale or similar obligation),

(B) at which the transferred property is not used by the transferor or a person affiliated with the transferor for the purpose of earning income and is used for another purpose,

(C) at which the transferred property would, if it were owned by the transferor, be deemed by section 128.1 or subsection 149(10) to have been disposed of by the transferor,

(D) that is immediately before control of the transferor is acquired by a person or group of persons, where the transferor is a corporation, or

(E) at which the winding-up of the transferor begins (other than a winding-up to which subsection 88(1) applies), where the transferor is a corporation, and

(iv) the property described in subparagraph (iii) is considered to have become available for use by the transferor at the time at which the transferred property is considered to have become available for use by the subsequent owner,

(f) for the purposes of subparagraphs (e)(iii) and (iv), where a partnership otherwise ceases to exist at any time after the particular time, the partnership is deemed not to have ceased to exist, and each person who was a member of the partnership immediately before the partnership would, but for this paragraph, have ceased to exist is deemed to remain a member of the partnership, until the time that is immediately after the first time described in clauses (e)(iii)(A) to (E), and

(g) for the purposes of applying this section and section 20 and any regulations made for the purpose of paragraph 20(1)(a) to the subsequent owner,

(i) the subsequent owner's capital cost of the transferred property is deemed to be the amount that was the transferor's capital cost of the transferred property, and

(ii) the amount by which the transferor's capital cost of the transferred property exceeds its fair market value at the particular time is deemed to have been deducted under paragraph 20(1)(a) by the subsequent owner in respect of property of that class in computing income for taxation years that ended before the particular time.

**Related Provisions**: 14(12) — Parallel rule for eligible capital property; 18(13)–(16) — Parallel rule for share or debt owned by financial institution; 40(3.3), (3.4) — Parallel rule with respect to capital losses; 69(5)(d) — No application on winding-up; 87(2)(g.3) — Amalgamations — continuing corporation; 88(1)(d.1) — No application to property acquired on windup of subsidiary; 139.1(18) — Holding corporation deemed not to acquire control of insurer on demutualization; 251.1 — Affiliated persons; 256(6)–(9) — Whether control acquired.

**Notes**: 13(21.2) prevents the transfer of property with a "pregnant loss" from being used as a method of transferring a high capital cost where property has declined in value. Before this rule, 85(5.1) could be used to prevent 20(16) from giving the transferor a terminal loss, thus transferring the high cost base to the transferee, and effectively allowing the sale of tax losses in certain circumstances (subject to GAAR in s. 245): see *Husky Oil Ltd.*, [1999] 4 C.T.C. 2691 (TCC), and *OSFC Holdings Ltd.*, [1999] 3 C.T.C. 2649 (TCC). For the parallel rule with respect to capital losses, see 40(3.3) and (3.4). For eligible capital property, see 14(12); for certain inventory, see 18(13)–(16).

13(21.2) added by 1995-97 technical bill, effective (subject to the grandfathering rule reproduced after s. 260) for dispositions of property after April 26, 1995 except that, where

(a) a property is disposed of after April 26, 1995 and before June 20, 1996, and

(b) the transferor elects in writing, filed with Revenue Canada by September 30, 1998

read the opening words of 13(21.2)(e)(iii) as:

(iii) the transferor is deemed to own a property that was acquired before the beginning of the taxation year that includes the particular time at a capital cost equal to the amount of the excess described in paragraph (b), and that is of a separate prescribed class that is the same class as the particular class, until the time that is immediately before the first time, after the particular time,

**(22) Deduction for insurer** — For the purposes of E in the definition "undepreciated capital cost" in subsection (21), an insurer shall be deemed to have been allowed a deduction for depreciation for property of a prescribed class under paragraph 20(1)(a) in

Subdivision b — Income or Loss from a Business or Property  S. 13(24)(a)

computing income for taxation years before its 1977 taxation year equal to the total of

(a) the amount determined, immediately after the end of its 1976 taxation year, for E in that definition, with respect to property of the particular prescribed class of the insurer (determined without reference to this subsection),

(b) the lesser of

(i) the amount of its 1975-76 excess capital cost allowance with respect to property of the particular prescribed class of the insurer, and

(ii) that proportion of the amount, if any, by which its 1975 branch accounting election deficiency exceeds the amount determined under subparagraph 138(4.1)(d)(ii) that

(A) the amount of its 1975-76 excess capital cost allowance with respect to property of the particular prescribed class of the insurer

is of

(B) the total of all its 1975-76 excess capital cost allowances with respect to properties of a prescribed class of the insurer, and

(c) the lesser of

(i) the amount, if any, by which

(A) the undepreciated capital cost of property of the particular prescribed class of the insurer immediately after the end of its 1976 taxation year (determined without reference to this subsection),

exceeds

(B) the amount determined under paragraph (b) in respect of property of the particular prescribed class of the insurer, and

(ii) that proportion of the amount, if any, by which its 1975 branch accounting election deficiency exceeds the total of

(A) the amount determined under subparagraph 138(4.1)(d)(ii),

(B) the total of all amounts determined under paragraph (b) with respect to property of a prescribed class of the insurer,

(C) the total described in subclause 138(4.1)(a)(ii)(B)(IV),

(D) the amount determined under subparagraph 138(4.1)(b)(ii), and

(E) the amount determined under subparagraph 138(4.1)(a)(ii)

that

(F) the undepreciated capital cost of property of the particular prescribed class of the insurer immediately after the end of its 1976 taxation year (determined without reference to this subsection),

is of

(G) the total of all amounts each of which is the undepreciated capital cost of property of a prescribed class of the insurer immediately after the end of its 1976 taxation year (determined without reference to this subsection).

**Related Provisions**: See Related Provisions and Definitions at end of s. 13.

**(23) Deduction for life insurer** — For the purposes of E in the definition "undepreciated capital cost" in subsection (21), a life insurer shall be deemed to have been allowed a deduction for depreciation for property of a prescribed class under paragraph 20(1)(a) in computing income for taxation years before its 1978 taxation year equal to the total of

(a) the amount determined immediately after the end of its 1977 taxation year for E in that definition, with respect to property of the particular prescribed class of the insurer (determined without reference to this subsection), and

(b) the amount, if any, by which

(i) the total of all maximum amounts the insurer was entitled to claim with respect to property of the particular prescribed class of the insurer in taxation years ending before 1978 and after 1968

exceeds

(ii) the amount determined under paragraph (a).

**Related Provisions**: See Related Provisions and Definitions at end of s. 13.

**(23.1) Application of subsec. 138(12)** — The definitions in subsection 138(12) apply to this section.

**Notes**: 13(23.1) added in the R.S.C. 1985 (5th Supp.) consolidation. This rule was formerly in the opening words of subsec. 138(12).

**(24) Acquisition of control** — Where control of a corporation has been acquired at any time by a person or group of persons and, within the 12-month period that ended immediately before that time, the corporation or a partnership of which it was a majority interest partner acquired depreciable property (other than property that was owned by the corporation or partnership or by a person that would, if section 251.1 were read without reference to the definition "controlled" in subsection 251.1(2), be affiliated with the corporation throughout the period that began immediately before the 12-month period began and ended at the time the property was acquired by the corporation or partnership) that was not used, or acquired for use, by the corporation or partnership in a business that was carried on by it immediately before the 12-month period began,

(a) for the purposes of the description of A in the definition "undepreciated capital cost" in subsection (21) and of sections 127 and 127.1, the property is, subject to paragraph (b), deemed not to have been acquired by the corporation or partnership before that time and to have been acquired by it immediately after that time; and

(b) where the property was disposed of by it before that time and was not reacquired by it before that time, for the purpose of the description of A in that definition, the property is deemed to have been acquired by the corporation or partnership immediately before the property was disposed of.

**Related Provisions**: 13(25) — Change of control within 12 months of incorporation; 87(2)(j.6) — Amalgamations — continuing corporation; 139.1(18) — Holding corporation deemed not to acquire control of insurer on demutualization; 256(6)–(9) — Whether control acquired. See additional Related Provisions at end of s. 13.

**Notes**: 13(24) amended by 1995-97 technical bill, effective for acquisitions of control after April 26, 1995. The substantive change was to use the definition of "affiliated" in 251.1 instead of a related-persons test. For earlier acquisitions generally since January 16, 1987, read:

(24) Where at any time control of a corporation has been acquired by a person or group of persons and, within the twelve month period ending immediately before that time, the corporation, or a partnership of which it was a majority interest partner (within the meaning assigned by subsection 97(3.1)), acquired depreciable property (other than property that was owned by the corporation or partnership or by a person or persons related to the corporation throughout the period commencing immediately before the twelve month period and ending at the time the property was acquired by the corporation or partnership) that was not used, or acquired for use, by the corporation or partnership in a business that was carried on by it immediately before that twelve month period, for the purposes of A in the definition "undepreciated capital cost" in subsection (21) and of sections 127 and 127.1, the property shall be deemed not to have been acquired by the corporation or partnership before that time and shall be deemed to have been acquired by it immediately after that time, except that, where the property was disposed of by it before that time and not reacquired by it before that time, for the purposes of A in that definition, the property shall be deemed to have been acquired by the corporation or partnership immediately before the property was disposed of.

**Interpretation Bulletins**: IT-302R3: Losses of a corporation — the effect that acquisitions of control, amalgamations, and windings-up have on their deductibility — after January 15, 1987.

**I.T. Technical News**: No. 7 (control by a group — 50/50 arrangement).

**(25) Early change of control** — For the purpose of subsection (24), where a corporation referred to in that subsection was incorporated or otherwise formed in the 12-month period referred to in that subsection, the corporation is deemed to have been, throughout the period that began immediately before the 12-month period and ended immediately after it was incorporated or otherwise formed,

(a) in existence; and

(b) affiliated with every person with whom it was affiliated (otherwise than because of a right referred to in paragraph 251(5)(b)) throughout the period that began when it was incorporated or

otherwise formed and ended immediately before its control is acquired.

**Notes**: 13(25)(b) amended by 1995-97 technical bill, effective for acquisitions of control after April 26, 1995, as a result of the amendment to 13(24). For earlier acquisitions generally since January 16, 1987, read:

(b) related to the person or persons to whom it was related (otherwise than by reason of a right referred to in paragraph 251(5)(b)) throughout the period commencing when it was incorporated or otherwise formed and ending immediately before the control of the corporation was acquired.

**(26) Restriction on deduction before available for use** — In applying the definition "undepreciated capital cost" in subsection (21) for the purpose of paragraph 20(1)(a) and any regulations made for the purpose of that paragraph, in computing a taxpayer's income for a taxation year from a business or property, no amount shall be included in calculating the undepreciated capital cost to the taxpayer of depreciable property of a prescribed class in respect of the capital cost to the taxpayer of a property of that class (other than property that is a certified production, as defined by regulations made for the purpose of paragraph 20(1)(a)) before the time the property is considered to have become available for use by the taxpayer.

**Related Provisions**: 13(27), (28) — Interpretation — available for use; 13(30) — Transfers of property; 13(32) — Leased property; 20(28) — Deduction against rental income from building; 37(1.2) — No R&D deduction for capital expenditure until property available for use; 127(11.2) — No investment tax credit until property available for use; 248(19) — When property available for use. See additional Related Provisions at end of s. 13.

**Notes**: 13(26) provides, in essence, that no CCA can be claimed for the year an asset is acquired, or the next year, if the property is not "available for use" as defined in 13(27) and (28). However, the "two-year rolling start" rule in 13(27)(b) and 13(28)(c) effectively puts a time limit on this limitation. Note that the "half-year rule" in Reg. 1100(2)(a)(i) applies only to property "acquired in the year", so where 13(26) has applied to delay a CCA claim, the full (not half) claim will be available once 13(26) ceases to apply. Reg. 1100(2)(a)(vii) confirms this interpretation.

13(26)–(29) added by 1991 technical bill, applicable with respect to property acquired by a taxpayer after 1989 other than property acquired

(a) from a person with whom the taxpayer was not dealing at arm's length (otherwise than by reason of a right referred to in para. 251(5)(b)) at the time the property was acquired, or

(b) in the course of a reorganization in respect of which, if a dividend were received by a corporation in the course of the reorganization, subsec. 55(2) would not be applicable to the dividend by reason of the application of para. 55(3)(b),

where the property was depreciable property of the person from whom it was acquired and was owned by that person before 1990.

**Regulations**: 1100(2)(a)(i) (CCA in year property becomes available for use); 1104(2) (definition of "certified production").

**Advance Tax Rulings**: ATR-44: Utilization of deductions and credits within a related corporate group.

**(27) Interpretation — available for use** — For the purposes of subsection (26) and subject to subsection (29), property (other than a building or part thereof) acquired by a taxpayer shall be considered

Subdivision b — Income or Loss from a Business or Property — S. 13(27)

to have become available for use by the taxpayer at the earliest of

(a) the time the property is first used by the taxpayer for the purpose of earning income,

(b) the time that is immediately after the beginning of the first taxation year of the taxpayer that begins more than 357 days after the end of the taxation year of the taxpayer in which the property was acquired by the taxpayer,

(c) the time that is immediately before the disposition of the property by the taxpayer,

(d) the time the property

(i) is delivered to the taxpayer, or to a person or partnership (in this paragraph referred to as the "other person") that will use the property for the benefit of the taxpayer, or, where the property is not of a type that is deliverable, is made available to the taxpayer or the other person, and

(ii) is capable, either alone or in combination with other property in the possession at that time of the taxpayer or the other person, of being used by or for the benefit of the taxpayer or the other person to produce a commercially saleable product or to perform a commercially saleable service, including an intermediate product or service that is used or consumed, or to be used or consumed, by or for the benefit of the taxpayer or the other person in producing or performing any such product or service,

(e) in the case of property acquired by the taxpayer for the prevention, reduction or elimination of air or water pollution created by operations carried on by the taxpayer or that would be created by such operations if the property had not been acquired, the time at which the property is installed and capable of performing the function for which it was acquired,

(f) in the case of property acquired by

(i) a corporation a class of shares of the capital stock of which is listed on a prescribed stock exchange,

(ii) a corporation that is a public corporation because of an election made under subparagraph (b)(i) of the definition "public corporation" in subsection 89(1) or a designation made by the Minister in a notice to the corporation under subparagraph (b)(ii) of that definition, or

(iii) a subsidiary wholly-owned corporation of a corporation described in subparagraph (i) or (ii),

the end of the taxation year for which depreciation in respect of the property is first deducted in computing the earnings of the corporation in accordance with generally accepted accounting principles and for the purpose of the financial statements of the corporation for the year presented to its shareholders,

(g) in the case of property acquired by the taxpayer in the course of carrying on a business of farming or fishing, the time at which the property has been delivered to the taxpayer and is capable of performing the function for which it was acquired,

(h) in the case of property of a taxpayer that is a motor vehicle, trailer, trolley bus, aircraft or vessel for which one or more permits, certificates or licences evidencing that the property may be operated by the taxpayer in accordance with any laws regulating the use of such property are required to be obtained, the time all those permits, certificates or licences have been obtained,

(i) in the case of property that is a spare part intended to replace a part of another property of the taxpayer if required due to a breakdown of that other property, the time the other property became available for use by the taxpayer,

(j) in the case of a concrete gravity base structure and topside modules intended to be used at an oil production facility in a commercial discovery area (within the meaning assigned by section 2 of the *Canada Petroleum Resources Act*) on which the drilling of the first well that indicated the discovery began before March 5, 1982, in an offshore region prescribed for the purposes of subsection 127(9), the time the gravity base structure deballasts and lifts the assembled topside modules, and

(k) where the property is (within the meaning assigned by subsection (4.1)) a replacement for a former property described in paragraph (4)(a) that was acquired before 1990 or that became available for use at or before the time the replacement property is acquired, the time the replacement property is acquired,

and, for the purposes of paragraph (f), where depreciation is calculated by reference to a portion of the cost of the property, only that portion of the property shall be considered to have become available for use at the end of the taxation year referred to in that paragraph.

**Related Provisions**: 13(21.2)(e)(iv) — When property considered available for use following transfer to affiliated person; 13(30), (31) — Transfers of property; 20(28) — Deduction before available for use; 87(2)(j.6) — Continuing corporation; 248(19) — When property available for use. See additional Related Provisions at end of s. 13.

**Notes**: 13(27)(d) amended by 1995-97 technical bill, effective for property acquired after 1989 (i.e., retroactive to its introduction). The former version, now deemed never to have applied, read:

(d) the time the property is delivered or made available to the taxpayer and is capable, either alone or in combination with other property in the taxpayer's possession at that time, of producing a commercially saleable product or performing a commercially saleable service, including an intermediate product or service that is used or consumed, or is to be used or consumed, by the taxpayer in producing or providing any such product or service.

See under 13(26) regarding application of 13(26)-(29).

**Regulations**: 1100(2)(a)(vii) (CCA in year property becomes available for use under 13(27)(b)); 3200, 3201 (prescribed stock exchanges for 13(27)(f)(i)).

**(28) Idem** — For the purposes of subsection (26) and subject to subsection (29), property that is a building or part thereof of a taxpayer shall be considered to have become available for use by the taxpayer at the earliest of

(a) the time all or substantially all of the building is first used by the taxpayer for the purpose for which it was acquired,

(b) the time the construction of the building is complete,

(c) the time that is immediately after the beginning of the taxpayer's first taxation year that begins more than 357 days after the end of the taxpayer's taxation year in which the property was acquired by the taxpayer,

(d) the time that is immediately before the disposition of the property by the taxpayer, and

(e) where the property is (within the meaning assigned by subsection (4.1)) a replacement for a former property described in paragraph (4)(a) that was acquired before 1990 or that became available for use at or before the time the replacement property is acquired, the time the replacement property is acquired,

and, for the purpose of this subsection, a renovation, alteration or addition to a particular building shall be considered to be a building separate from the particular building.

**Related Provisions**: 13(21.2)(e)(iv) — When property considered available for use following transfer to affiliated person; 13(30), (31) — Transfers of property; 87(2)(j.6) — Continuing corporation.

**Notes**: See under 13(26) regarding application.

The CCRA takes the position that "all or substantially all", used in 13(28)(a), means 90% or more.

**Regulations**: 1100(2)(a)(vii) (CCA in year property becomes available for use under 13(28)(c)).

**(29) Idem** — For the purposes of subsection (26), where a taxpayer acquires property (other than a building that is used or is to be used by the taxpayer principally for the purpose of gaining or producing gross revenue that is rent) in the taxpayer's first taxation year (in this subsection referred to as the "particular year") that begins more than 357 days after the end of the taxpayer's taxation year in which the taxpayer first acquired property after 1989, that is part of a project of the taxpayer, or in a taxation year subsequent to the particular year, and at the end of any taxation year (in this subsection referred to as the "inclusion year") of the taxpayer

(a) the property can reasonably be considered to be part of the project, and

(b) the property has not otherwise become available for use,

if the taxpayer so elects in prescribed form filed with the taxpayer's return of income under this Part for the particular year, that particular portion of the property the capital cost of which does not exceed the amount, if any, by which

(c) the total of all amounts each of which is the capital cost to the taxpayer of a depreciable property (other than a building that is used or is to be used by the taxpayer principally for the purpose of gaining or producing gross revenue that is rent) that is part of the project, that was acquired by the taxpayer after 1989 and before the end of the taxpayer's last taxation year that ends more than 357 days before the beginning of the inclusion year and that has not become available for use at or before the end of the inclusion year (except where the property has first become available for use before the end of the inclusion year because of this subsection or paragraph (27)(b) or (28)(c))

exceeds

(d) the total of all amounts each of which is the capital cost to the taxpayer of a depreciable property, other than the particular portion of the property, that is part of the project to the extent that the property is considered, because of this subsection, to have become available for use before the end of the inclusion year

shall be considered to have become available for use immediately before the end of the inclusion year.

**Notes**: See under 13(26) regarding application.

**Regulations**: 4609 (prescribed offshore region).

**Forms**: T1031: Subsection 13(29) election re certain depreciable properties, acquired for use in a long term project.

**(30) Transfers of property** — Notwithstanding subsections (27) to (29), for the purpose of subsection (26), property of a taxpayer shall be deemed to have become available for use by the taxpayer at the earlier of the time the property was acquired by the taxpayer and, if applicable, a prescribed time, where

(a) the property was acquired

(i) from a person with whom the taxpayer was not dealing at arm's length (otherwise than because of a right referred to in paragraph 251(5)(b)) at the time the property was acquired by the taxpayer, or

(ii) in the course of a reorganization in respect of which, if a dividend were received by a corporation in the course of the reorganization, subsection 55(2) would not apply to the dividend because of paragraph 55(3)(b); and

(b) before the property was acquired by the taxpayer, it became available for use (determined without reference to paragraphs (27)(c) and (28)(d)) by the person from whom it was acquired.

**Notes**: 13(30) added by 1991 technical bill and amended retroactively by 1992 technical bill, effective for property acquired after 1989. The amendment adds reference to a prescribed time.

**Regulations**: 1100(2.2)(j).

**(31) Idem** — For the purposes of paragraphs (27)(b) and (28)(c) and subsection (29), where a property of a taxpayer was acquired from a person (in this subsection referred to as "the transferor")

(a) with whom the taxpayer was, at the time the taxpayer acquired the property, not dealing at arm's length (otherwise than because of a right referred to in paragraph 251(5)(b)), or

(b) in the course of a reorganization in respect of which, if a dividend were received by a corporation in the course of the reorganization, subsection 55(2) would not apply to the dividend because of the application of paragraph 55(3)(b),

the taxpayer shall be deemed to have acquired the property at the time it was acquired by the transferor.

**Notes**: 13(31) added by 1991 technical bill, applicable to property acquired after 1989.

**(32) Leased property** — Where a taxpayer has leased property that is depreciable property of a person with whom the taxpayer does not deal at arm's length, the amount, if any, by which

(a) the total of all amounts paid or payable by the taxpayer for the use of, or the right to use, the property in a particular taxation year and before the time the property would have been considered to have become available for use by the taxpayer if the taxpayer had acquired the property, and that, but for this subsection, would be deductible in computing the taxpayer's income for any taxation year

exceeds

(b) the total of all amounts received or receivable by the taxpayer for the use of, or the right to use, the property in the particular taxation year and before that time and that are included in the income of the taxpayer for any taxation year

shall be deemed to be a cost to the taxpayer of a property included in Class 13 in Schedule II to the *Income Tax Regulations* and not to be an amount paid or payable for the use of, or the right to use, the property.

**Notes**: 13(32) added by 1991 technical bill, applicable to depreciable property of a person referred to in the subsection that was acquired by that person after 1989.

**(33) Consideration given for depreciable property** — For greater certainty, where a person acquires a depreciable property for consideration that can reasonably be considered to include a transfer of property, the portion of the cost to the person of the depreciable property attributable to the transfer shall not exceed the fair market value of the transferred property.

**Related Provisions**: 68 — Allocation of amounts in consideration for disposition of property; 69(1) — Inadequate considerations.

**Notes**: 13(33) added by 1993 technical bill, effective for property acquired after November 1992. It ensures that on a trade-in (e.g., of a vehicle), no more than the value of the trade-in can be allocated to the transfer of the trade-in for the person who acquires it.

**Related Provisions [s. 13]**: 36 — Railway companies; 37(6) — Scientific research capital expenditures; 45(2) — Election where change in use; 68 — Allocation of amounts in consideration for disposition of property; 70(5) — Depreciable and other capital property of deceased taxpayer; 70(9.1) — Transfer of farm property from spouse's trust to children of settlor; 70(12) — Capital cost of depreciable property on death; 73(2) — Capital cost and amount deemed allowed to spouse, etc. or trust; 73(3)(e) — *Inter vivos* transfer of farm property by farmer to child; 80(9)(c) — Reduction of capital cost on debt forgiveness ignored for purposes of s. 13; 85(5) — Rules on transfers of depreciable property; 87(2)(d) — Amalgamations — depreciable property; 87(2)(l.3) — Amalgamations — replacement property; 88(1)(f) — Winding-up; 97(4) — Where capital cost to partner exceeds proceeds of disposition; 98(3)(e) — Rules where partnership ceases to exist; 98(5)(e) — Rules where partnership business carried on as sole proprietorship; 104(5)(c) — Trust — deemed disposition of property; 104(16) — Trusts — capital cost allowance deduction; 107(2) — Distribution by trust in satisfaction of capital interest; 107.2 — Distribution by retirement compensation arrangement; 132.1(1)(d) — Deemed capital cost of property following mutual fund reorganization; 138(11.8) — Rules on transfer of depreciable property; 138(11.91)(f) — Computation of income of non-resident insurer.

**Definitions [s. 13]**: "acquired" — 256(7)–(9); "affiliated" — 13(25), 251.1; "amount" — 248(1); "amount payable" — 13(23.1), 138(12); "appropriate minister" — 13(21); "arm's length" — 13(7)(e.1), 251; "assessment" — 248(1); "assistance" — 79(4), 125.4(5), 248(16), 248(18); "available for use" — 13(21.2)(e)(iv), 13(27)–(31), 248(19); "business" — 248(1); "calendar year" — *Interpretation Act* 37(1)(a); "Canada" — 255; "capital cost" — 13(7)–(7.4), (10), 13(21.2)(g)(i), 70(12), 128.1(1)(c), 128.1(4)(c), 132.1(1)(d); "capital gain" — 39(1), 248(1); "capital property" — 54, 248(1); "class of shares" — 248(6); "control" — 256(6)–(9); "conversion", "conversion cost" — 13(21); "consequence of the death" — 248(8); "corporation" — 248(1), *Interpretation Act* 35(1); "cost amount" — 248(1); "cost to an insurer of acquiring a mortgage or hypothec" — 13(23.1), 138(12); "depreciable property" — 13(21), 248(1); "disposition" — 13(21) [to be repealed], 248(1) [draft]; "estate" — 104(1), 248(1); "farming" — 248(1); "fiscal period" — 249.1; "fishing", "former business property" — 248(1); "former property" — 13(4); "gaining or producing income" — 13(9); "gross revenue" — 248(1); "income" — 13(3)(b); "individual", "life insurer", "majority interest partner", "Minister", "motor vehicle" — 248(1); "1975 branch accounting election deficiency", "1975-76 excess capital cost allowance" — 13(23.1), 138(12); "non-resident", "passenger vehicle", "person", "prescribed" — 248(1); "prescribed stock exchange" — Reg. 3200, 3201; "property" — 248(1); "province" — *Interpretation Act* 35(1); "public corporation" — 89(1), 248(1); "regulation" — 248(1); "related" — 13(25), 251(2); "replacement property" — 13(4), (4.1); "resident in Canada" — 250; "share", "shareholder", "subsidiary wholly-owned corporation" — 248(1); "tax payable" — 248(2); "taxable Canadian property" — 248(1); "taxation year" — 11(2), 13(3)(a), 13(8), 249; "taxpayer" — 104(1), 248(1); "timber resource property" — 13(21), 248(1); "transferor" — 13(7)(e), 13(21.2)(a), 13(31); "treaty-protected property" — 248(1); "trust" — 104(1), 248(1), (3); "undepreciated capital cost" — 13(21), 248(1); "year" — 11(2), 13(3)(a), 13(8).

**Regulations [s. 13]**: 1105 (prescribed classes of depreciable property).

**I.T. Application Rules [s. 13]**: 20(1), (1.1), (3).

**Interpretation Bulletins [s. 13]**: IT-151R5: Scientific research and experimental development expenditures; IT-297R2: Gifts in kind to charity and others; IT-325R2: Property transfers after separation, divorce and annulment.

**Forms [s. 13]**: T2 SCH 8: Capital cost allowance.

**14. (1) Inclusion in income from business [eligible capital property]** — Where, at the end of a taxation year, the total of all amounts each of which is an amount determined, in respect of a business of a taxpayer, for E in the definition "cumulative eligible capital" in subsection (5) (in this section referred to as an "eligible capital amount") or for F in that definition exceeds the total of all amounts determined for A to D in that definition in respect of the business (which excess is in this subsection referred to as "the excess"),

(a) in the case of a taxpayer (other than

  (i) a corporation,

  (ii) a partnership all the members of which were

    (A) corporations,

    (B) partnerships all the members of which were corporations, or

    (C) partnerships described in this subparagraph, or

  (iii) a partnership that was not a Canadian partnership throughout the year)

who was resident in Canada throughout the year,

  (iv) the amount, if any, that is the lesser of

    (A) the excess, and

    (B) the amount determined for F in the definition "cumulative eligible capital" in subsection (5) at the end of the year in respect of the business

shall be included in computing the taxpayer's income from that business for the year, and

  (v) there shall be included in computing the taxpayer's income from the business for the year the amount determined by the formula

$$A - B - C - D$$

where

A is the excess,

B is the amount determined for F in the definition "cumulative eligible capital" in subsection (5) at the end of the year in respect of the business,

C is ½ of the amount determined for Q in the definition "cumulative eligible capital" in subsection (5) at the end of the year in respect of the business, and

D is such amount as the taxpayer claims, not exceeding the taxpayer's exempt gains balance in respect of the business for the year

(b) in any other case, the amount, if any, by which the excess exceeds ½ of the amount determined for Q in the definition "cumulative eligible capital" in subsection (5) in respect of the business shall be included in computing the taxpayer's income from that business for that year.

### Proposed Amendment — 14(1)

**14. (1) Eligible capital property — inclusion in income from business** — Where, at the end of a taxation year, the total of all amounts each of which is an amount determined, in respect of a business of a taxpayer, for E in the definition "cumulative eligible capital" in subsection (5) (in this section referred to as an "eligible capital amount") or for F in that definition exceeds the total of all amounts determined for A to D in that definition in respect of the business (which excess is in this subsection referred to as "the excess"), there shall be included in computing the taxpayer's income from the business for the year the total of

(a) the amount, if any, that is the lesser of

  (i) the excess, and

  (ii) the amount determined for F in the definition "cumulative eligible capital" in subsection (5) at the end of the year in respect of the business, and

(b) the amount, if any, determined by the formula

$$2/3 \times (A - B - C - D)$$

where

A is the excess,

B is the amount determined for F in the definition "cumulative eligible capital" in subsection (5) at the end of the year in respect of the business,

C is ½ of the amount determined for Q in the definition "cumulative eligible capital" in subsection (5) at the end of the year in respect of the business, and

D is the amount claimed by the taxpayer, not exceeding the taxpayer's exempt gains balance for the year in respect of the business.

**Application**: The December 21, 2000 draft legislation, subsec. 5(1), will amend subsec. 14(1) to read as above, applicable in respect of taxation years that end after February 27, 2000 except that, for taxation years that ended after February 27, 2000 and before October 18, 2000, the reference to the fraction "2/3" in the formula in para. 14(1)(b) shall be read as a reference to the fraction "8/9".

**Technical Notes**: Section 14 provides rules concerning the tax treatment of expenditures and receipts of a taxpayer in respect of "eligible capital properties" and operates on a pooling basis. Annual deductions, which are calculated as a percentage of this pool, may be claimed under paragraph 20(1)(b). (These deductions are referred to in these notes as "depreciation"). Eligible capital property includes goodwill, customer lists, farm quotas and licenses of indeterminate duration.

The cost of eligible capital property is recognized, for income tax purposes, in a pool system similar to the capital cost allowance (CCA) system. Unlike CCA, however, only 3/4 of the cost is added to the pool, and only 3/4 of the proceeds of disposition of eligible capital properties is credited against the pool. Any negative balance at the end of a taxation year must be included in calculating income for the year and may be comprised of a portion analogous to recaptured CCA deductions and a portion analogous to a taxable capital gain, calculated at a 3/4 inclusion rate.

With the reduction in the capital gains inclusion rate to 2/3 announced in the February 2000 budget and to 1/2 announced in the October 2000 Economic Statement and Budget Update [see 38(a) — ed.], only 8/9 or 2/3 of gains in respect of eligible capital property (subject to recapture of depreciation claimed) need be included in computing income. The existing 3/4 inclusion rate is, however, maintained for the purpose of calculating pool balances. The 8/9ths and 2/3rds factors effectively convert the 3/4 inclusion rate for gains to a 2/3 inclusion rate for taxation years that end after February 27, 2000 and before October 18, 2000 and to a 1/2 inclusion rate for taxation years that end after October 17, 2000.

Subsection 14(1) requires certain amounts to be included in a taxpayer's income where, at the end of a taxation year, the amounts required to be deducted from a taxpayer's cumulative eligible capital pool (CEC pool) exceed the amounts required to be added to the CEC pool. Currently the amount required to be included in income is generally equal to the absolute value of any negative CEC pool balance (subject to adjustments related to the 1988 conversion of the pool from a 1/2 to a 3/4 inclusion rate, and to any exempt gains balance that the taxpayer retains in respect of an election regarding gains accrued to February 22, 1994 that can benefit from the capital gains exemption that existed until that time).

The current wording of subsection 14(1) generally provides one rule for individuals (existing paragraph 14(1)(a)) and a second rule for corporations. The amount that individuals must include in income is divided into a recapture of depreciation previously claimed, described in subparagraph 14(1)(a)(iv), and any remaining negative CEC pool balance (subject to the adjustments described above) in excess of the subparagraph 14(1)(a)(iv) amount. This remaining amount is described in subparagraph 14(1)(a)(v), and can be considered as being analogous to a capital gain in respect of eligible capital property. Consistent with the change to the capital gains inclusion rate for all taxpayers, subsection 14(1) is amended to replace the two rules in paragraphs 14(1)(a) and (b) with one rule of general application.

Amended subsection 14(1) applies the previous rule for individuals to all taxpayers. The change reflects the new 1/2 inclusion rate for capital gains by reducing the second amount required to be included in income (generally the absolute value of the negative CEC pool balance, less any depreciation claimed that is required to be included in income under former subparagraph 14(1)(a)(iv) (now paragraph 14(1)(a)). The reduction is accomplished by multiplying the existing formula that describes the second amount by 2/3. The second amount has an inherent recognition of the 3/4 rate because it reflects additions to and subtractions from the CEC pool calculated at 3/4. Since 2/3 of 3/4 equals 1/2, the amendment provides and appropriate recognition of the reduction in the capital gains inclusion rate.

*Example*

Sophie has a cumulative eligible capital pool balance of $750,000 in 1999. This pool balance reflects $100,000 of depreciation claimed since Sophie began carrying on business in 1989. In January 2000, Sophie disposes of eligible capital property to Acme Corporation for proceeds of disposition of $2 million. Sophie claims no depreciation in 2000. Sophie has an exempt gains balance of $50,000, which she claims to reduce her paragraph 14(1)(b) income inclusion for 2000. Applying the amendments described above to section 14, the 2000 taxation year (December 31 year-end) results are as follows:

opening balance: $750,000
less 3/4 × $2 million proceeds of disposition
credit balance: (750,000)
recapture of depreciation claimed (amended paragraph 14(1)(a)): $100,000 income inclusion
residual income inclusion (amended paragraph 14(1)(b)): 2/3 × (A − B − C − D)
A is $750,000
B is $100,000 of depreciation
C (1/2 of depreciation claimed before adjustment time) is nil, and
D is $50,000.
2/3 × (750,000 − 100,000 − 50,000) = $400,000 income inclusion.

These amendments apply to taxation years that end after February 27, 2000 except that, for taxation years that end after February 27, 2000 and before October 18, 2000, the reference to 2/3 in the formula is to be read as a reference to 8/9.

**Notice of Ways and Means Motion, Economic Statement, October 18, 2000**: (12) That the amount required by subsection 14(1) of the Act to be included in computing a taxpayer's income from business (other than in respect of recaptured deductions)

(a) reflect a 2/3 inclusion rate for taxation years that end after February 27, 2000 and before October 18, 2000, and

(b) reflect a 1/2 inclusion rate for taxation years that end after October 17, 2000,

and that the rules for calculating a corporation's capital dividend account be modified to take into account these changes to the inclusion rate.

**Supplementary Information, Economic Statement, October 18, 2000**: *Capital Gains*

[For the full text re the changes to the capital gains inclusion rate, see under s. 38 — ed.]

*Eligible Capital Property*

Eligible capital property refers to items such as goodwill and other intangibles. The treatment of eligible capital property is somewhat analogous to the treatment of depreciable property in that deductions are subject to recapture and, where proceeds of disposition exceed the original cost, the gains are treated similarly to capital gains. Accordingly, the one-half inclusion rate for capital gains will apply to gains on dispositions of eligible capital property for taxation years that end after October 17, 2000.

**Department of Finance news release, May 9, 2000**: *Finance Minister Clarifies Certain Income Tax Measures in the 2000 Budget*

Finance Minister Paul Martin today announced several clarifications to measures announced in the 2000 budget.

These clarifications will ensure the smooth conduct of business transactions while consultations take place.

## Capital Gains Inclusion Rate for Eligible Capital Property

Minister Martin today clarified the tax treatment of the disposition of "eligible capital property" after February 28, 2000. Eligible capital property refers to items such as goodwill and other intangibles. Under the Income Tax Act, the treatment of eligible capital property is somewhat analogous to the treatment of depreciable property in that deductions are subject to recapture and, where proceeds on disposition exceed the original cost, the gains are treated similarly to capital gains. Accordingly, the two-thirds inclusion rate for capital gains will apply to gains on dispositions of eligible capital property.

In addition, the existing pooling system, whereby three-quarters of the cost of such property is depreciated at 7 per cent declining balance, will be maintained. This approach is the most generous for taxpayers and will ease both compliance and administration.

Submissions on these issues may be made to the Tax Policy Branch of the Department of Finance.

For further information: Government Assistance for SR&ED, Eligible Capital Property, Alexandra MacLean, (613) 995-2980.

**Related Provisions**: 14(1.01) — Election to recognize capital gain in place of reducing CEC pool; 14(1.1) — Expenditure relating to qualified farm property; 14(3) — Non-arm's length acquisition of eligible capital property; 14(8) — Deemed residence in Canada; 14(9) — Effect of excessive election for capital gains exemption; 20(1)(b) — Cumulative eligible capital amount; 20(4.2) — Bad debt from disposition of eligible capital property; 24(1) — Ceasing to carry on business; 24(2)(d) — Business carried on by spouse or controlled corporation; 28(1)(d) — Inclusion in farming or fishing income when using cash method; 39(9), (10) — Deduction from business investment loss; 39.1(5) — Partnership income inclusion — exempt capital gains balance; 53(1)(e)(i)(A), (A.2), 53(2)(c)(i)(A), (A.2) — Adjustments to ACB of partnership interest; 70(5.1) — Eligible capital property of deceased; 70(9.8) — Farm property used by corporation or partnership; 73(3) — *Inter vivos* transfer of farm property by farmer to child; 85(1)(d.1) — Rollover of property to corporation; 87(2)(f) — Amalgamation — continuing corporation; 88(1)(c.1) — Windup — Amount to be included under para. 14(1)(b); 98(3)(b) — Rules applicable where partnership ceases to exist; 98(5)(h) — Where partnership business carried on as sole proprietorship; 107(2)(f) — Capital interest distribution by personal or prescribed trust; 107.4(3)(e) — Rollover of eligible capital property to trust; 110.6(17) — Capital gains exemption — ordering rule; 146(1)"earned income"(h) — Amount under 14(1)(a)(v) excluded from earned income for RRSP purposes; 248(1)"eligible capital amount" — Definition applies to entire Act; 257 — Formula cannot calculate to less than zero.

**Notes**: See Notes to 20(1)(b) for an explanation of 14(1).

Closing words of 14(1)(a)(v) repealed by 1995-97 technical bill, effective for fiscal periods that end after February 22, 1994, otherwise than solely because of an election under 25(1). (This rule was replaced by new 14(1.1).) For earlier periods, read:

and, for the purposes of section 110.6 and of paragraph 3(b) as it applies for the purposes of that section, the total of all amounts each of which is the portion of the amount so included that can reasonably be attributed to proceeds of a disposition in the year of a qualified farm property (within the meaning assigned by subsection 110.6(1)) in excess of the taxpayer's cost of the property shall be deemed to be a taxable capital gain of the taxpayer from the disposition in the year of qualified farm property.

14(1)(a)(v) amended by 1994 Budget, effective for fiscal periods that end after February 22, 1994 (otherwise than because of an election under 25(1)). The change results from the elimination of the capital gains exemption, and requires a negative balance in excess of the recapturable amount to be included in income for the year from the business. For earlier fiscal periods, the excess was deemed to be a taxable capital gain eligible for the capital gains exemption, as follows:

(v) the amount, if any, by which the excess exceeds the total of

(A) the amount determined under subparagraph (iv), and

(B) ½ of the amount determined for Q in the definition "cumulative eligible capital" in subsection (5) in respect of the business

shall be deemed to be a taxable capital gain of the taxpayer from a disposition of capital property by the taxpayer in the year and, for the purposes of section 110.6, that property shall be deemed to have been disposed of by the taxpayer in the year;

14(1)(a)(v)(B) and "exceeds ... the business" in 14(1)(b) added by 1991 technical bill, retroactive to 1988, to exclude from the taxable capital gain, or from income, ½ of the deductions claimed under 20(1)(b) before the taxpayer's adjustment time.

The draft legislation of July 12, 1994 (debt forgiveness) proposed amendments to the opening words of 14(1) and to 14(1)(a)(iv)(B) to refer to "F and G" instead of "F". However, those amendments were not included in the December 20, 1994 revision of the draft legislation. See now 14(5)"cumulative eligible capital"F:P.1.

**I.T. Application Rules**: 21(1).

**Interpretation Bulletins**: IT-73R5: The small business deduction; IT-365R2: Damages, settlements and similar receipts; IT-386R: Eligible capital amounts. See also list at end of s. 14.

**Advance Tax Rulings**: ATR-6: Vendor reacquires business assets following default by purchaser.

## Proposed Addition — 14(1.01)

**(1.01) Election re: capital gain** — Where, at any time in a taxation year, a taxpayer disposes of an eligible capital property (other than goodwill) in respect of a business, the cost of the property to the taxpayer can be determined, the proceeds of the disposition (in this subsection referred to as the "actual proceeds") exceed that cost, the taxpayer's exempt gains balance in respect of the business for the year is nil and the taxpayer so elects under this subsection in the taxpayer's return of income for the year,

(a) for the purposes of subsection (5), the proceeds of disposition of the property are deemed to be equal to that cost;

(b) the taxpayer is deemed to have disposed at that time, of a capital property that had at that time an adjusted cost base to the taxpayer equal to that cost, for proceeds of disposition equal to the actual proceeds; and

(c) where the eligible capital property is at that time a qualified farm property (within the meaning assigned by subsection 110.6(1)) of the taxpayer, the capital property deemed by paragraph (b) to have been disposed of by the taxpayer is deemed to have been at that time a qualified farm property of the taxpayer.

**Application**: The December 21, 2000 draft legislation, subsec. 5(1), will add subsec. (1.01), applicable in respect of taxation years that end after February 27, 2000.

**Technical Notes**: The capital gains inclusion rate change [see 38(a) — ed.] is reflected in amendments to subsection 14(1) as described above. These amendments, however, only apply where a taxpayer has a negative CEC pool balance. The result of this is that additions to the CEC pool are still made at the 3/4 rate and dispositions of eligible capital property still reduce pool balances on a 3/4 basis as well.

There may be circumstances in which a taxpayer would prefer to recognize the entire economic capital gain on eligible capital property on a 1/2 or 2/3 basis, for example, if a taxpayer has outstanding capital losses to be used but wants to conserve the CEC pool balance. New subsection 14(1.01) permits a taxpayer to elect to, in effect, remove a particular asset from the CEC pool and recognize a capital gain on the particular asset in the year as if it were ordinary non-depreciable capital property.

This election is only available to recognize gains, not losses, and is not available for goodwill or for other types of property for which the original cost cannot be determined. Further, it cannot be used to recognize a capital gain that can be sheltered by the taxpayer's exempt gains balance.

**(1.1) Deemed taxable capital gain** — For the purposes of section 110.6 and of paragraph 3(b) as it applies for the purposes of that section, an amount included under subparagraph (1)(a)(v) in computing a taxpayer's income for a particular taxation year from a business is deemed to be a taxable capital gain of the taxpayer for the year from the disposition in the year of qualified farm property to the extent of the lesser of

(a) the amount included under subparagraph (1)(a)(v) in computing the taxpayer's income for the particular year from the business, and

(b) the amount determined by the formula

$$A - B$$

where

A is 3/4 of the amount determined in respect of the taxpayer for the particular year equal to the amount, if any, by which

(i) the total of all amounts each of which is the taxpayer's proceeds from a disposition in the particular year or a preceding taxation year that began after 1987 of an eligible capital property in respect of the business that, at the time of disposition, was a qualified farm property (as defined in subsection 110.6(1)) of the taxpayer

exceeds

(ii) the total of all amounts each of which is

(A) an eligible capital expenditure of the taxpayer in respect of the business that was made or incurred in respect of a qualified farm property disposed of by the taxpayer in the particular year or a preceding taxation year that began after 1987, or

(B) an outlay or expense of the taxpayer that was not deductible in computing the taxpayer's income and was made or incurred for the purpose of making a disposition referred to in subparagraph (i), and

B is the total of all amounts each of which is

(i) that portion of an amount deemed by subparagraph (1)(a)(v) (as it applied in respect of the business to fiscal periods that began after 1987 and ended before February 23, 1994) to be a taxable capital gain of the taxpayer that can reasonably be attributed to a disposition of a qualified farm property of the taxpayer, or

(ii) an amount deemed by this section to be a taxable capital gain of the taxpayer for a taxation year preceding the particular year from the disposition of qualified farm property of the taxpayer.

**Proposed Amendment — 14(1.1)**

**(1.1) Deemed taxable capital gain** — For the purposes of section 110.6 and paragraph 3(b) as it applies for the purposes of that section, an amount included under paragraph (1)(b) in computing a taxpayer's income for a particular taxation year from a business is deemed to be a taxable capital gain of the taxpayer for the year from the disposition in the year of qualified farm property to the extent of the lesser of

(a) the amount included under paragraph (1)(b) in computing the taxpayer's income for the particular year from the business, and

(b) the amount determined by the formula

$$A - B$$

where

A is the amount by which the total of

(i) 3/4 of the total of all amounts each of which is the taxpayer's proceeds from a disposition in a preceding taxation year that began after 1987 and ended before February 28, 2000 of eligible capital property in respect of the business that, at the time of the disposition, was a qualified farm property (within the meaning assigned by subsection 110.6(1)) of the taxpayer,

(ii) 2/3 of the total of all amounts each of which is the taxpayer's proceeds from a disposition in the particular year or a preceding taxation year that ended after February 27, 2000 and before October 18, 2000 of eligible capital property in respect of the business that, at the time of the disposition, was a qualified farm property (within the meaning assigned by subsection 110.6(1)) of the taxpayer, and

(iii) ½ of the total of all amounts each of which is the taxpayer's proceeds from a disposition in the particular year or a preceding taxation year that ended after October 17, 2000 of eligible capital property in respect of the business that, at the time of the disposition, was a qualified farm property (within the meaning assigned by subsection 110.6(1)) of the taxpayer

exceeds the total of

(iv) ¾ of the total of all amounts each of which is

(A) an eligible capital expenditure of the taxpayer in respect of the business that was made or incurred in respect of a qualified farm property disposed of by the taxpayer in a preceding taxation year that began after 1987 and ended before February 28, 2000, or

(B) an outlay or expense of the taxpayer that was not deductible in computing the taxpayer's income and that was made or incurred for the purpose of making a disposition referred to in clause (A),

(v) ⅔ of the total of all amounts each of which is

(A) an eligible capital expenditure of the taxpayer in respect of the business that was made or incurred in respect of a qualified farm property disposed of by the taxpayer in the particular year or a preceding taxation year that ended after February 27, 2000 and before October 18, 2000, or

(B) an outlay or expense of the taxpayer that was not deductible in computing the taxpayer's income and that was made or incurred for the purpose of making a disposition referred to in clause (A), and

(vi) ½ of the total of all amounts each of which is

(A) an eligible capital expenditure of the taxpayer in respect of the business that was made or incurred in respect of a qualified farm property disposed of by the taxpayer in the particular year or a preceding taxation year that ended after October 17, 2000, or

(B) an outlay or expense of the taxpayer that was not deductible in computing the taxpayer's income and that was made or incurred for the purpose of making a disposition referred to in clause (A), and

**Application**: The December 21, 2000 draft legislation, subsec. 5(2), will amend the portion of subsec. 14(1.1) before the description of B in para. (b) to read as above, applicable in respect of taxation years that end after February 27, 2000.

**Technical Notes**: Subsection 14(1.1) deems certain amounts included in an individual's income in respect of eligible capital property attributable to qualified farm property to be a taxable capital gain of the individual for the purpose of the capital gains exemption in section 110.6. The amount deemed to be a taxable capital gain is limited to the lesser of two amounts. The first amount is the amount included in the taxpayer's income under subparagraph 14(1)(a)(v) (now paragraph 14(1)(b)). The second amount is the taxable amount of the taxpayer's cumulative net gains from dispositions in the year or in a preceding taxation year commencing after 1987 of qualified farm property that is eligible capital property in respect of the business, minus the amount of such taxable net gains that have already been deemed to be taxable capital gains (either under subsection 14(1.1), or under paragraph 14(1)(a) as it read in respect of fiscal periods that ended before February 23, 1994).

Subsection 14(1.1) is amended consequential on the amendments to subsection 14(1), to change references to subparagraph 14(1)(a)(v) to references to new paragraph 14(1)(b).

Subsection 14(1.1) is also amended to adjust the second amount described above to reflect the reduced inclusion rate for capital gains. In order to properly reflect the taxable portion of gains for different taxation years that begin after 1987, it is necessary to amend variable A in paragraph 14(1.1)(b) to limit the application of the 3/4 inclusion rate for proceeds of dispositions and associated acquisition and selling costs, to dispositions that occurred in taxation years that ended before February 28, 2000, and introduce the 2/3 inclusion rate in respect of dispositions that occur in taxation years that end after February 27, 2000 and before October 18, 2000 and the 1/2 inclusion rate in respect of dispositions that occur in taxation years that end after October 17, 2000. Variable A now includes the taxable portion of net gains at the appropriate inclusion rates.

**Notice of Ways and Means Motion, federal budget, February 28, 2000**: (9) That for the 2000 and subsequent taxation years, . . .

(e) the rules for determining the capital gains deduction under section 110.6 of the Act and any other rules of determination under the Act take into account, where appropriate, the change in determination of a taxpayer's taxable capital gain and allowable capital loss from a disposition of a property.

**Related Provisions**: 110.6(2) — Capital gains exemption for qualified farm property; 257 — Formula cannot calculate to less than zero.

**Notes**: 14(1.1) added by 1995-97 technical bill, effective for fiscal periods that end after February 22, 1994, otherwise than solely because of an election under 25(1). For earlier periods, see the closing words of 14(1)(a)(v).

**(2) Amount deemed payable** — Where any amount is, by any provision of this Act, deemed to be a taxpayer's proceeds of disposition of any property disposed of by the taxpayer at any time, for the purposes of this section, that amount shall be deemed to have become payable to the taxpayer at that time.

**Interpretation Bulletins**: See list at end of s. 14.

**(3) Acquisition of eligible capital property** — Notwithstanding any other provision of this Act, where at any time a person or partnership (in this subsection referred to as the "taxpayer") has, directly or indirectly, in any manner whatever, acquired an eligible capital property in respect of a business from a person or partnership with whom the taxpayer did not deal at arm's length (in this subsection referred to as the "transferor") and the property was an eligible capital property of the transferor (other than property acquired by the taxpayer as a consequence of the death of the transferor), the eligible capital expenditure of the taxpayer in respect of the business shall, in respect of that acquisition, be deemed to be equal to $4/3$ of the amount, if any, by which

(a) the amount determined for E in the definition "cumulative eligible capital" in subsection (5) in respect of the disposition of the property by the transferor

exceeds

(b) the total of all amounts that can reasonably be considered to have been claimed as deductions under section 110.6 by any person with whom the taxpayer was not dealing at arm's length in respect of the disposition of the property by the transferor, or any other disposition of the property before that time,

except that, where the taxpayer disposes of the property after that time, the amount of the eligible capital expenditure deemed by this subsection to be made by the taxpayer in respect of the property shall be determined at any time after the disposition as if the amount determined under paragraph (b) in respect thereof were the lesser of

(c) the amount otherwise so determined, and

(d) the amount, if any, by which

(i) the amount determined under paragraph (a) in respect of the disposition of the property by the transferor

exceeds

(ii) the amount determined for E in the definition "cumulative eligible capital" in subsection (5) in respect of the disposition of the property by the taxpayer.

### Proposed Amendment — 14(3)

**(3) Acquisition of eligible capital property** — Notwithstanding any other provision of this Act, where at any particular time a person or partnership (in this subsection referred to as the "taxpayer") has, directly or indirectly, in any manner whatever, acquired an eligible capital property in respect of a business from a person or partnership with which the taxpayer did not deal at arm's length (in this subsection referred to as the "transferor") and the property was an eligible capital property of the transferor (other than property acquired by the taxpayer as a consequence of the death of the transferor), the eligible capital expenditure of the taxpayer in respect of the business is, in respect of that acquisition, deemed to be equal to $4/3$ of the amount, if any, by which

(a) the amount determined for E in the definition "cumulative eligible capital" in subsection (5) in respect of the disposition of the property by the transferor

exceeds the total of

(b) the total of all amounts that can reasonably be considered to have been claimed as deductions under section 110.6 for taxation years that ended before February 28, 2000 by any person with whom the taxpayer was not dealing at arm's length in respect of the disposition of the property by the transferor, or any other disposition of the property before the particular time,

(b.1) $9/8$ of the total of all amounts that can reasonably be considered to have been claimed as deductions under section 110.6 for taxation years that ended after February 27, 2000 and before October 18, 2000 by any person with whom the taxpayer was not dealing at arm's length in respect of the disposition of the property by the transferor, or any other disposition of the property before the particular time, and

(b.2) $1/2$ of the total of all amounts that can reasonably be considered to have been claimed as deductions under section 110.6 for taxation years that end after October 17, 2000 by any person with whom the taxpayer was not dealing at arm's length in respect of the disposition of the property by the transferor, or any other disposition of the property before that particular time,

except that, where the taxpayer disposes of the property after that particular time, the amount of the eligible capital expenditure deemed by this subsection to be made by the taxpayer in respect of the property shall be determined at any time after the disposition as if the total of the amounts determined under paragraphs (b), (b.1) and (b.2) in respect of the disposition were the lesser of

**Application**: The December 21, 2000 draft legislation, subsec. 5(3), will amend the portion of subsec. 14(3) before para. (c) to read as above, applicable in respect of taxation years that end after February 27, 2000.

**Technical Notes**: Subsection 14(3) provides rules regarding non-arm's length transfers of eligible capital property. In those circumstances, where the vendor has claimed a capital gains exemption under section 110.6 in respect of the disposition, the eligible capital expenditure of the purchaser is reduced in order to prevent the purchaser from depreciating amounts that were exempt from capital gains tax in the hands of the non-arm's length vendor.

Subsection 14(3) is amended, consequential on the amendments to subsection 14(1) that reflect the reduced inclusion rate for capital gains. Because subsection 14(3) reduces the purchaser's eligible capital expenditure, and because eligible capital expenditures are still added to the purchaser's cumulative eligible capital pool at a rate of 3/4, the appropriate fraction in subsection 14(3) remains 4/3 of the proceeds of disposition of the vendor. However, the amount available as a deduction in respect of capital gains under section 110.6 for taxation years that end after February 27, 2000 and before October 18, 2000 must be grossed up by 9/8, and by 3/2 for taxation years that end after October 17, 2000, to correct for the reduced inclusion rate [see 38(a) — ed.] and properly reflect the portion of the proceeds of disposition that has been sheltered from taxation. For further details, see the commentary on the amendments to subsection 14(1).

**Related Provisions**: 110.6(19)(b)(ii) — Where election made to trigger capital gains exemption; 248(8) — Occurrences as a consequence of death.

**Notes**: 14(3) amended by 1991 technical bill, retroactive to 1988, to add the exception after 14(3)(b) through to the end of the subsection, and to add the exclusion, in the opening words, for property acquired as a consequence of the transferor's death.

**Interpretation Bulletins**: See list at end of s. 14.

### (4) References to "taxation year" or "year" —
Where a taxpayer is an individual and the taxpayer's income for a taxation year includes income from a business the fiscal period of which does not coincide with the calendar year, for greater certainty a reference in this section to a "taxation year" or "year" shall be read as a reference to a "fiscal period" or "period".

**Related Provisions**: 11(2) — References to "taxation year" or "year" of an individual.

**Notes**: Since 1995, most individuals use a calendar year as their fiscal period. See Notes at end of 249.1.

### (5) Definitions — In this section,

**"adjustment time"** of a taxpayer in respect of a business is

(a) in the case of a corporation formed as a result of an amalgamation occurring after June 30, 1988, the time immediately before the amalgamation,

(b) in the case of any other corporation, the time immediately after the commencement of its first taxation year commencing after June 30, 1988, and

(c) for any other taxpayer, the time immediately after the commencement of the taxpayer's first fiscal period commencing after 1987 in respect of the business.

**Related Provisions**: 248(1)"adjustment time" — Definition applies to entire Act.

**Notes**: 14(5)"adjustment time" was 14(5)(c) before R.S.C. 1985 (5th Supp.) consolidation, effective for taxation years ending after November 1991. See Table of Concordance.

**"cumulative eligible capital"** of a taxpayer at any time in respect of a business of the taxpayer means the amount determined by the formula

$$(A + B + C + D + D.1) - (E + F)$$

where

A is $3/4$ of the total of all eligible capital expenditures in respect of the business made or incurred by the taxpayer before that time and after the taxpayer's adjustment time,

B is the total of

(a) all amounts each of which is the amount that would have been included under subparagraph (1)(a)(v) in computing the taxpayer's income from the business for a taxation year that ended before that time and after February 22, 1994 if the amount determined for D in that subparagraph for the year were nil,

(b) all amounts included under paragraph (1)(b) in computing the taxpayer's income from the business for taxation years that ended before that time and after the taxpayer's adjustment time, and

(c) all taxable capital gains included, because of the application of subparagraph (1)(a)(v) to the taxpayer in respect of the business, in computing the taxpayer's income for taxation years that began before February 23, 1994.

### Proposed Amendment — 14(5)"cumulative eligible capital"B

B is the total of

(a) $3/2$ of all amounts included under paragraph (1)(b) in computing the taxpayer's income from the business for taxation years that ended before that time and after October 17, 2000,

(b) $9/8$ of all amounts included under paragraph (1)(b) in computing the taxpayer's income from the business for taxation years that ended

(i) before that time, and

(ii) after February 27, 2000 and before October 18, 2000,

(c) all amounts included under paragraph (1)(b) in computing the taxpayer's income from the business for taxation years that ended

(i) before the earlier of that time and February 28, 2000, and

(ii) after the taxpayer's adjustment time,

(d) all amounts each of which is the amount that would have been included under subparagraph (1)(a)(v) in computing the taxpayer's income from the business, if the amount de-

## Subdivision b — Income or Loss from a Business or Property     S. 14(5) cum

> termined for D in that subparagraph for the year were nil, for taxation years that ended
>
>     (i) before the earlier of that time and February 28, 2000, and
>
>     (ii) after February 22, 1994, and
>
> (e) all taxable capital gains included, because of the application of subparagraph (1)(a)(v) to the taxpayer in respect of the business, in computing the taxpayer's income for taxation years that began before February 23, 1994,
>
> **Application**: The December 21, 2000 draft legislation, subsec. 5(4), will amend the description of B in the definition "cumulative eligible capital" in subsec. 14(5) to read as above, applicable in respect of taxation years that end after February 27, 2000.
>
> **Technical Notes**: The definition "cumulative eligible capital" provides the calculation of a taxpayer's eligible capital property pool for the purpose of determining the taxpayer's allowable depreciation in respect of eligible capital property for the year.
>
> Two amendments are proposed to the calculation of cumulative eligible capital:
>
> 1. Variable B in the cumulative eligible capital formula is an add-back for amounts previously included in income under subsection 14(1). Variable B is amended to gross up (by 3/2 and 9/8) the amount to be included in respect of income inclusions under paragraph 14(1)(b). This reflects the continued calculation of the cumulative eligible capital pool on a 3/4 basis, and converts the 1/2-based amount now included under paragraph 14(1)(b) (or the 2/3-based amount for taxation years that end after February 27, 2000 and before October 18, 2000) to a 3/4-based amount. Other amendments to variable B are consequential on the amendments to, and renumbering of, subsection 14(1), which are described in further detail above.
>
> 2. Variable R, which is a component of variable F, is amended to update the reference to subparagraph 14(1)(a)(iv) by adding a reference to amended paragraph 14(1)(a), consequential on the renumbering of subsection 14(1), which is described in further detail above.

C  is 1/2 of the amount, if any, of the taxpayer's cumulative eligible capital in respect of the business at the taxpayer's adjustment time,

D  is the amount, if any, by which

    (a) the total of all amounts deducted under paragraph 20(1)(b) in computing the taxpayer's income from the business for taxation years ending before the taxpayer's adjustment time

exceeds

    (b) the total of all amounts included under subsection (1) in computing the taxpayer's income from the business for taxation years ending before the taxpayer's adjustment time,

D.1  is, where the amount determined by B exceeds zero, 1/2 of the amount determined for Q in respect of the business,

E  is the total of all amounts each of which is 3/4 of the amount, if any, by which

    (a) an amount which, as a result of a disposition occurring after the taxpayer's adjustment time and before that time, the taxpayer has or may become entitled to receive, in respect of the business carried on or formerly carried on by the taxpayer where the consideration given by the taxpayer therefor was such that, if any payment had been made by the taxpayer after 1971 for that consideration, the payment would have been an eligible capital expenditure of the taxpayer in respect of the business

exceeds

    (b) all outlays and expenses to the extent that they were not otherwise deductible in computing the taxpayer's income and were made or incurred by the taxpayer for the purpose of giving that consideration, and

F  is the amount determined by the formula

$$(P + P.1 + Q) - R$$

where

P  is the total of all amounts deducted under paragraph 20(1)(b) in computing the taxpayer's income from the business for taxation years ending before that time and after the taxpayer's adjustment time,

P.1  is the total of all amounts each of which is an amount by which the cumulative eligible capital of the taxpayer in respect of the business is required to be reduced at or before that time because of subsection 80(7),

Q  is the amount, if any, by which

    (a) the total of all amounts deducted under paragraph 20(1)(b) in computing the taxpayer's income from the business for taxation years ending before the taxpayer's adjustment time

exceeds

    (b) the total of all amounts included under subsection (1) in computing the taxpayer's income for taxation years ending before the taxpayer's adjustment time, and

R  is the total of all amounts included under subparagraph (1)(a)(iv) in computing the taxpayer's income from the business for taxation years ending before that time and after the taxpayer's adjustment time;

### Proposed Amendment — 14(5)"cumulative eligible capital"R

R  is the total of all amounts included, in computing the taxpayer's income from the business for taxation years that ended before that time and after the taxpayer's adjustment time, under subparagraph (1)(a)(iv) in respect of taxation years that ended before February 28, 2000 and under

**paragraph (1)(a) in respect of taxation years that end after February 27, 2000;**

**Application**: The December 21, 2000 draft legislation, subsec. 5(5), will amend the description of R in the definition "cumulative eligible capital" in subsec. 14(5) to read as above, applicable in respect of taxation years that end after February 27, 2000.

**Technical Notes**: See under 14(5)"cumulative eligible capital"B.

**Related Provisions**: 14(1) — Inclusion in income from business; 14(1.01) — Election to recognize capital gain in place of reducing CEC pool; 14(3) — Non-arm's length acquisition of eligible capital property; 14(12) — Acquisition of eligible capital property by affiliated person on cessation of business; 20(1)(b) — Annual deduction of 7% of cumulative eligible capital; 20(4.2) — Bad debts; 20(4.3) — Deemed allowable capital loss on bad on disposition of eligible capital property; 24(1) — Ceasing to carry on business; 24(2)(d) — Business carried on by spouse or controlled corporation; 70(5.1) — Eligible capital property of deceased; 87(2)(f) — Amalgamations — cumulative eligible capital; 89(1) — Capital dividend account; 98(3)(b) — Rules where partnership ceases to exist; 98(5)(h) — Where partnership business carried on as sole proprietorship; 248(1)"cumulative eligible capital" — Definition applies to entire Act; 257 — Formula amounts cannot calculate to less than zero.

**Notes**: Description of B amended by 1994 Budget, effective for fiscal periods that end after February 22, 1994 (otherwise than because of an election under 25(1)). The change results from the elimination of the capital gains exemption; see 14(1)(a)(v). B previously read:

B   is the total of all amounts deemed by subparagraph (1)(a)(v) to have been a taxable capital gain of the taxpayer from a disposition of capital property and all amounts included by reason of paragraph (1)(b) in computing the taxpayer's income from the business for taxation years ending before that time and after the taxpayer's adjustment time,

P.1 added by 1994 tax amendments bill (Part I), effective for taxation years that end after February 21, 1994. The draft legislation of July 12, 1994 (debt forgiveness) had proposed to add element G to the main formula; it was changed to P.1 in the second formula instead.

14(5)"cumulative eligible capital" was 14(5)(a) before R.S.C. 1985 (5th Supp.) consolidation effective for taxation years ending after November 1991. The previous version, identical in meaning, read:

(a) "cumulative eligible capital" of a taxpayer at any time in respect of a business of the taxpayer means the amount, if any, by which the aggregate of

(i) ¾ of the aggregate of all eligible capital expenditures in respect of the business made or incurred by the taxpayer before that time and after his adjustment time,

(ii) the aggregate of all amounts deemed by subparagraph (1)(a)(v) to have been a taxable capital gain of the taxpayer from a disposition of capital property and all amounts included by reason of paragraph (1)(b) in computing the taxpayer's income from the business for taxation years ending before that time and after the taxpayer's adjustment time,

(iii) ½ of the amount, if any, of the taxpayer's cumulative eligible capital in respect of the business at his adjustment time,

(iii.1) the amount, if any, by which

(A) the aggregate of all amounts deducted under paragraph 20(1)(b) in computing the taxpayer's income from the business for taxation years ending before his adjustment time

exceeds

(B) the aggregate of all amounts included under subsection (1) in computing the taxpayer's income from the business for taxation years ending before his adjustment time

exceeds the total of

(iv) the aggregate of all amounts each of which is ¾ of the amount, if any, by which

(A) an amount which, as a result of a disposition occurring after the taxpayer's adjustment time and before that time, he has or may become entitled to receive, in respect of the business carried on or formerly carried on by him where the consideration given by him therefor was such that, if any payment had been made by him after 1971 for that consideration, the payment would have been an eligible capital expenditure of the taxpayer in respect of the business

exceeds

(B) all outlays and expenses to the extent that they were not otherwise deductible in computing the taxpayer's income and were made or incurred by him for the purpose of giving that consideration, and

(v) the amount, if any, by which the total of

(A) the aggregate of all amounts deducted under paragraph 20(1)(b) in computing the taxpayer's income from the business for taxation years ending before that time and after his adjustment time, and

(B) the amount, if any, by which

(I) the aggregate of all amounts deducted under paragraph 20(1)(b) in computing the taxpayer's income from the business for taxation years ending before his adjustment time

exceeds

(II) the aggregate of all amounts included under subsection (1) in computing the taxpayer's income for taxation years ending before his adjustment time,

exceeds

(C) the aggregate of all amounts included under subparagraph (1)(a)(iv) in computing the taxpayer's income from the business for taxation years ending before that time and after his adjustment time;

D.1 (originally subpara. (iii.2)) added by 1991 technical bill, retroactive to 1988.

See Notes to 20(1)(b).

**Interpretation Bulletins**: IT-99R5: Legal and accounting fees; IT-143R2: Meaning of eligible capital expenditures; IT-365R2: Damages, settlements and similar receipts; IT-386R: Eligible capital amounts; IT-471R: Merger of partnerships. See also list at end of s. 14.

**Forms**: T2 SCH 10: Cumulative eligible capital deduction.

**"eligible capital expenditure"** of a taxpayer in respect of a business means the portion of any outlay or expense made or incurred by the taxpayer, as a result of a transaction occurring after 1971, on account of capital for the purpose of gaining or producing income from the business, other than any such outlay or expense

(a) in respect of which any amount is or would be, but for any provision of this Act limiting the quantum of any deduction, deductible (otherwise than under paragraph 20(1)(b)) in computing the taxpayer's income from the business, or in respect of which any amount is, by virtue of any provision of this Act other than paragraph 18(1)(b), not deductible in computing that income,

(b) made or incurred for the purpose of gaining or producing income that is exempt income, or

(c) that is the cost of, or any part of the cost of,

(i) tangible property of the taxpayer,

(ii) intangible property that is depreciable property of the taxpayer,

(iii) property in respect of which any deduction (otherwise than under paragraph 20(1)(b)) is permitted in computing the taxpayer's income from the business or would be so permitted if the taxpayer's income from the business were sufficient for the purpose, or

(iv) an interest in, or right to acquire, any property described in any of subparagraphs (i) to (iii),

but, for greater certainty and without restricting the generality of the foregoing, does not include any portion of

(d) any amount paid or payable to any creditor of the taxpayer as, on account or in lieu of payment of any debt or as or on account of the redemption, cancellation or purchase of any bond or debenture,

(e) where the taxpayer is a corporation, any amount paid or payable to a person as a shareholder of the corporation, or

(f) any amount that is the cost of, or any part of the cost of,

(i) an interest in a trust,

(ii) an interest in a partnership,

(iii) a share, bond, debenture, mortgage, note, bill or other similar property, or

(iv) an interest in, or right to acquire, any property described in any of subparagraphs (i) to (iii);

**Related Provisions**: 14(3) — Non-arm's length acquisition of eligible capital property; 87(2)(f) — Amalgamations — cumulative eligible capital; 98(3)(b) — Rules applicable where partnership ceases to exist; 107(2)(f) — Capital interest distribution by personal or prescribed trust; 139.1(4)(b) — Amount payable by insurer on demutualization deemed not to be eligible capital expenditure; 248(1)"eligible capital expenditure" — Definition applies to entire Act.

**Notes**: 14(5)"eligible capital expenditure" was 14(5)(b) before R.S.C. 1985 (5th Supp.) consolidation, effective for taxation years ending after November 1991. See Table of Concordance.

See Notes to 20(1)(b).

For interpretation of "bond, debenture, mortgage, note, bill or other similar property" in (f)(iii), see *Federated Cooperatives Ltd.*, [2000] 2 C.T.C. 2382 (TCC).

**Interpretation Bulletins**: IT-99R5: Legal and accounting fees; IT-104R2: Deductibility of fines or penalties; IT-143R2: Meaning of "eligible capital expenditure"; IT-187: Customer lists and ledger accounts; IT-341R3: Expenses of issuing shares or borrowing money; IT-364: Commencement of business operations. IT-386R: Eligible capital amounts. See also list at end of s. 14.

**"exempt gains balance"** of an individual in respect of a business of the individual for a taxation year means the amount determined by the formula

$$A - B$$

where

A is the lesser of

(a) the amount by which

(i) the amount that would have been the individual's taxable capital gain determined under paragraph 110.6(19)(b) in respect of the business if

(A) the amount designated in an election under subsection 110.6(19) in respect of the business were equal to the fair market value at the end of February 22, 1994 of all the eligible capital property owned by the elector at that time in respect of the business, and

(B) this Act were read without reference to subsection 110.6(20)

exceeds

(ii) the amount determined by the formula

$$0.75(C - 1.1D)$$

where

C is the amount designated in the election that was made under subsection 110.6(19) in respect of the business, and

D is the fair market value at the end of February 22, 1994 of the property referred to in clause (i)(A), and

(b) the individual's taxable capital gain determined under paragraph 110.6(19)(b) in respect of the business, and

B is the total of all amounts each of which is the amount determined for D in subparagraph (1)(a)(v) in respect of the business for a preceding taxation year.

**Related Provisions**: 14(9) — Effect of excessive election; 257 — Formulas cannot calculate to less than zero.

**Notes**: Definition "exempt gains balance" added by 1994 Budget, effective for fiscal periods that end after February 22, 1994 (otherwise than because of an election under 25(1)). It deals with the election to use the capital gains exemption for 1994-95 under 110.6(19). It determines the amount by which the income inclusion under 14(1)(a)(v) can be reduced. In general, the exempt gains balance is the unclaimed portion of the taxable capital gain that was included in income as a result of the election under 110.6(19). Thus, the gain is not taxed again on a later disposition of the eligible capital property.

**(6) Exchange of property** — Where in a taxation year (in this subsection referred to as the "initial year") a taxpayer disposes of an eligible capital property (in this section referred to as the taxpayer's "former property") and the taxpayer so elects under this subsection in the taxpayer's return of income for the year in which the taxpayer acquires an eligible capital property that is a replacement property for the taxpayer's former property, such amount, not exceeding the amount that would otherwise be included in the amount determined for E in the definition "cumulative eligible capital" in subsection (5) (if the description of E in that definition were read without reference to "3/4 of") in respect of a business, as has been used by the taxpayer before the end of the first taxation year after the initial year to acquire the replacement property

(a) shall, subject to paragraph (b), not be included in the amount determined for E in that definition for the purpose of determining the cumulative eligible capital of the taxpayer in respect of the business; and

(b) shall, to the extent of ³/₄ thereof, be included in the amount determined for E in that definition for the purpose of determining the cumulative eligible capital of the taxpayer in respect of the business at a time that is the later of

(i) the time the replacement property was acquired by the taxpayer, and

(ii) the time the former property was disposed of by the taxpayer.

**Related Provisions**: 14(7) — Meaning of a "replacement property"; 96(3) — Election by members of partnership; 220(3.2), Reg. 600(b) — Late filing of election or revocation.

**Notes**: See Notes to 13(4) and 44(1).

Opening words of 14(6) amended by 1995-97 technical bill, effective for dispositions of former properties after the 1993 taxation year. (The condition requiring a taxpayer to acquire a property as a replacement for the former property was moved to 14(7).) For earlier dispositions, read:

(6) Where in a taxation year (in this subsection referred to as the "initial year") a taxpayer has disposed of an eligible capital property (in this section referred to as the taxpayer's "former property"), if the taxpayer so elects under this subsection in the taxpayer's return of income under this Part for the year in which the taxpayer acquires, as a replacement property for the taxpayer's former property, an eligible capital property (in this section referred to as a "replacement property"), such amount not exceeding the amount that would otherwise be included in the amount determined for E in the definition "cumulative eligible capital" in subsection (5) (if the description of E in that definition were read without reference to "³/₄ of") in respect of a business as has been used by the taxpayer before the end of the first taxation year following the initial year to acquire the replacement property

**Interpretation Bulletins**: IT-259R3: Exchanges of property. See also list at end of s. 14.

**Information Circulars**: 92-1: Guidelines for accepting late, amended or revoked elections.

### (7) Replacement property for a former property
— For the purposes of subsection (6), a particular eligible capital property of a taxpayer is a replacement property for a former property of the taxpayer if

(a) it is reasonable to conclude that the property was acquired by the taxpayer to replace the former property;

(a.1) it was acquired by the taxpayer for a use that is the same as or similar to the use to which the taxpayer put the former property;

(b) it was acquired for the purpose of gaining or producing income from the same or a similar business as that in which the former property was used; and

(c) where the former property was used by the taxpayer in a business carried on in Canada, the particular property was acquired for use by the taxpayer in a business carried on by the taxpayer in Canada.

**Notes**: 14(7)(a) replaced by new (a) and (a.1) by 1995-97 technical bill, effective for dispositions of former properties after the 1993 taxation year. (See Notes to 14(6).) For earlier dispositions, read:

(a) it was acquired by the taxpayer for the same or a similar use as the use to which the taxpayer put the former property;

14(7)(c) amended by 1991 technical bill, effective for dispositions of former properties after April 2, 1990 (except where pursuant to a written agreement or expropriation notice before April 3, 1990), to apply whether or not the taxpayer is non-resident.

**Interpretation Bulletins**: IT-259R3: Exchanges of property. See also list at end of s. 14.

### (8) Deemed residence in Canada
— Where an individual was resident in Canada at any time in a particular taxation year and throughout

(a) the preceding taxation year, or

(b) the following taxation year,

for the purpose of paragraph (1)(a), the individual shall be deemed to have been resident in Canada throughout the particular year.

**Related Provisions**: 110.6(5) — Parallel rule for capital gains exemption.

**Notes**: 14(8) added by 1993 technical bill, effective for 1988 and later taxation years. It is a relieving provision for individuals who either cease to be (14(8)(a)), or begin to be (14(8)(b)), resident in Canada during the taxation year, allowing them the benefit of 14(1)(a) rather than 14(1)(b) for the year.

### (9) Effect of election under subsec. 110.6(19)
— Where an individual elects under subsection 110.6(19) in respect of a business, the individual shall be deemed to have received proceeds of a disposition on February 23, 1994 of eligible capital property in respect of the business equal to the amount determined by the formula

$$(A - B)\frac{4}{3}$$

where

A is the amount determined in respect of the business under subparagraph (a)(ii) of the description of A in the definition "exempt gains balance" in subsection (5), and

B is the amount determined in respect of the business under subparagraph (a)(i) of the description of A in the definition "exempt gains balance" in subsection (5).

**Related Provisions**: 257 — Formula cannot calculate to less than zero.

**Notes**: 14(9) added by 1994 Budget, effective for fiscal periods that end after February 22, 1994 (otherwise than because of an election under 25(1)). It applies where the amount designated in an election to use the capital gains exemption in respect of a business exceeds $^{11}/_{10}$ of the fair market value of the eligible capital property. In general, where the excess is greater than $^{4}/_{3}$ of the maximum exempt gains balance that could have been obtained, the balance of the excess is deemed by 14(9) to be proceeds of disposition of eligible capital property.

See also Notes to 14(10).

### (10) Deemed eligible capital expenditure —
For the purposes of this Act, where a taxpayer received or is entitled to receive assistance from a government, municipality or other public authority in respect of, or for the acquisition of, property the cost of which is an eligible capital expenditure of the taxpayer in respect of a business, whether as a grant, subsidy, forgivable loan, deduction from tax, investment allowance or as any other form of assistance, that eligible capital expenditure shall at any time be deemed to be the amount, if any, by which the total of

(a) that eligible capital expenditure, determined without reference to this subsection, and

(b) such part, if any, of the assistance as the taxpayer repaid before

(i) the taxpayer ceased to carry on the business, and

(ii) that time

under a legal obligation to pay all or any part of the assistance

exceeds

(c) the amount of the assistance the taxpayer received or is entitled to receive before the earlier of that time and the time the taxpayer ceases to carry on the business.

**Related Provisions**: 14(5) — Definition of "exempt gains balance"; 14(11) — Assistance deemed received by trust or partnership; 20(1)(hh.1) — Deduction for repayment after ceasing to carry on business.

**Notes**: 14(10) added by 1994 tax amendments bill (Part I), effective for assistance that a taxpayer receives or becomes entitled to receive after February 21, 1994 and repayments of such assistance. See Notes to 12(1)(x). (This was originally 14(9) in the draft legislation of July 12, 1994, but a new 14(9) was enacted before this one.)

**Interpretation Bulletins**: IT-273R2: Government assistance — general comments. See also list at end of s. 14.

### (11) Receipt of public assistance —
For the purpose of subsection (10), where at any time a taxpayer who is a beneficiary under a trust or a member of a partnership received or is entitled to receive assistance from a government, municipality or other public authority, whether as a grant, subsidy, forgivable loan, deduction from tax, investment allowance or as any other form of assistance, the amount of the assistance that can reasonably be considered to be in respect of, or for the acquisition of, property the cost of which was an eligible capital expenditure of the trust or partnership shall be deemed to have been received at that time by the trust or partnership, as the case may be, as assistance from the government, municipality or other public authority for the acquisition of such property.

**Notes**: 14(11) added by 1994 tax amendments bill (Part I), effective on the same basis as 14(10). (This was originally 14(10) in the draft legislation of July 12, 1994.)

**Interpretation Bulletins**: IT-273R2: Government assistance — general comments. See also list at end of s. 14.

### (12) Loss on certain transfers [within affiliated group] — Where

(a) a corporation, trust or partnership (in this subsection referred to as the "transferor") disposes at any time in a taxation year of a particular eligible capital property in respect of a business of the transferor in respect of which it would, but for this subsection, be permitted a deduction under paragraph 24(1)(a) as a consequence of the disposition, and

(b) during the period that begins 30 days before and ends 30 days after the disposition, the transferor or a person affiliated with the transferor acquires a property (in this subsection referred to as the "substituted property") that is, or is identical to, the particular property and, at the end of that period, a person or partnership that is either the transferor or a person or partnership affiliated with the transferor owns the substituted property,

the transferor is deemed, for the purposes of this section and sections 20 and 24, to continue to own eligible capital property in respect of the business, and not to have ceased to carry on the business, until the time that is immediately before the first time, after the disposition,

(c) at which a 30-day period begins throughout which neither the transferor nor a person affiliated with the transferor owns

(i) the substituted property, or

(ii) a property that is identical to the substituted property and that was acquired after the day that is 31 days before the period begins,

(d) at which the substituted property is not eligible capital property in respect of a business carried on by the transferor or a person affiliated with the transferor,

(e) at which the substituted property would, if it were owned by the transferor, be deemed by section 128.1 or subsection 149(10) to have been disposed of by the transferor,

(f) that is immediately before control of the transferor is acquired by a person or group of persons, where the transferor is a corporation, or

(g) at which the winding-up of the transferor begins (other than a winding-up to which subsection 88(1) applies), where the transferor is a corporation.

**Related Provisions**: 13(21.2) — Parallel rule for depreciable capital property; 14(13) — Deemed identical property;

18(13)–(16) — Parallel rule for share or debt owned by financial institution; 40(3.3), (3.4) — Parallel rule re capital losses; 69(5)(d) — No application on winding-up; 87(2)(g.3) — Amalgamations — continuing corporation; 88(1)(d.1) — No application to property acquired on windup of subsidiary; 139.1(18) — Holding corporation deemed not to acquire control of insurer on demutualization; 248(12) — Whether properties are identical; 251.1 — Affiliated persons; 256(6)–(9) — Whether control acquired.

**Notes**: See Notes to 13(21.2).

14(12) added by 1995-97 technical bill, effective (subject to the grandfathering rule reproduced after s. 260) for dispositions of property after April 26, 1995.

**(13) Deemed identical property** — For the purpose of subsection (12),

(a) a right to acquire a property (other than a right, as security only, derived from a mortgage, agreement for sale or similar obligation) is deemed to be a property that is identical to the property; and

(b) where a partnership otherwise ceases to exist at any time after the disposition, the partnership is deemed not to have ceased to exist and each person who, immediately before the partnership would, but for this paragraph, have ceased to exist, was a member of the partnership is deemed to remain a member of the partnership, until the time that is immediately after the first time described in paragraphs (12)(c) to (g).

**Notes**: 14(13) added by 1995-97 technical bill, effective (subject to the grandfathering rule reproduced after s. 260) for dispositions of property after April 26, 1995.

### Proposed Addition — 14(14), (15)

**(14) [Non-resident] Ceasing to use [eligible capital] property in Canadian business** — If at a particular time a non-resident taxpayer ceases to use, in connection with a business or part of a business carried on by the taxpayer in Canada immediately before the particular time, a property that was immediately before the particular time eligible capital property of the taxpayer (other than a property that was disposed of by the taxpayer at the particular time), the taxpayer is deemed to have disposed of the property immediately before the particular time for proceeds of disposition equal to the amount determined by the formula

$$A - B$$

where

A is the fair market value of the property immediately before the particular time, and

B is

(a) where at a previous time before the particular time the taxpayer ceased to use the property in connection with a business or part of a business carried on by the taxpayer outside Canada and began to use it in connection with a business or part of a business carried on by the taxpayer in Canada, the amount, if any, by which the fair market value of the property at the previous time exceeded its cost to the taxpayer at the previous time, and

(b) in any other case, nil.

**Related Provisions**: 10(12) — Parallel rule for inventory; 142.6(1.1) — Parallel rule for non-resident financial institution; 257 — Formula cannot calculate to less than zero.

**Technical Notes**: Section 14 of the *Income Tax Act* provides rules concerning the tax treatment of expenditures and receipts of a taxpayer in respect of eligible capital properties. The rules operate on a pooling basis, and annual deductions, calculated as a percentage of this pool, may be claimed under paragraph 20(1)(b). This section is amended by adding new subsections 14 (14) and (15) of the Act. These rules complement existing or proposed provisions in subsections 10(12) and (13) and 13(9), paragraph 45(1)(d) and new section 76.1 of the Act.

Under new subsection 14(14) of the Act, a non-resident taxpayer that at any particular time ceases to use eligible capital property in a business in Canada — otherwise than by actually disposing of the property — will be treated as having disposed of the property immediately before the particular time. The provision applies, for example, if a taxpayer removes eligible capital property from a business carried on in Canada and begins to use it in a business carried on outside Canada. The taxpayer is deemed to receive proceeds of disposition equal to the property's fair market value immediately before the particular time. If the property was previously used in a business outside Canada, the deemed proceeds are reduced by any excess of the property's fair market value when it began to be used in Canada over its cost at that time. New subsection (15) will have set the cost of the property at the lesser of its cost and fair market value at that time. Therefore, the adjustment to the deemed proceeds on removal of the property from Canada ensures that only the change in value of the property during the time it was used in the Canadian business is taken into account at the time of removal.

New subsection 14(14) applies after June 27, 1999 in respect of an authorized foreign bank, and after August 8, 2000 in any other case.

**(15) [Non-resident] Beginning to use [eligible capital] property in Canadian business** — If at a particular time a non-resident taxpayer ceases to use, in connection with a business or part of a business carried on by the taxpayer outside Canada immediately before the particular time, and begins to use, in connection with a business or part of a business carried on by the taxpayer in Canada, a property that is an eligible capital property of the taxpayer, the taxpayer is deemed to have disposed of the property immediately before the particular time and to have reacquired the property at the particular time for consideration equal to the lesser of the cost to the taxpayer of the property immediately before the particular time and its fair market value immediately before the particular time.

**Technical Notes**: New subsection 14 (15) of the Act treats a non-resident taxpayer that ceases to use eligible capital property in a business outside Canada, and begins using that property in a business in Canada as having dis-

Subdivision b — Income or Loss from a Business or Property     S. 15(1)

posed of the property and reacquired it for an amount equal to the lesser of the cost of the property and its fair market value at the time immediately before it begins to be used in the Canadian business.

New subsection 14(15) applies after June 27, 1999 in respect of an authorized foreign bank, and after August 8, 2000 in any other case.

**Application**: The August 8, 2000 draft legislation, s. 1, will add subsecs. 14(14) and (15), applicable after June 27, 1999 in respect of an authorized foreign bank, and after August 8, 2000 in any other case.

**Related Provisions**: 10(14) — Parallel rule for inventory; 142.6(1.2) — Parallel rule for non-resident financial institution.

**Definitions [s. 14]**: "acquired" — 256(7)–(9); "adjusted cost base" — 54, 248(1); "adjustment time" — 14(5), 248(1); "affiliated" — 251.1; "amount" — 248(1); "arm's length" — 251(1); "assistance" — 79(4), 125.4(5), 248(16), (18); "business" — 248(1); "calendar year" — Interpretation Act 37(1)(a); "Canada" — 255; "Canadian partnership" — 102, 248(1); "capital property" — 54, 248(1); "consequence of the death" — 248(8); "control" — 256(7)–(9); "corporation" — 248(1), Interpretation Act 35(1); "cumulative eligible capital" — 14(5), 248(1); "depreciable property" — 13(21), 248(1); "disposition" — 248(1); "eligible capital amount" — 14(1), 248(1); "eligible capital expenditure" — 14(5), 248(1); "eligible capital property" — 54, 248(1); "exempt gains balance" — 14(5); "exempt income" — 248(1); "fiscal period" — 249.1; "identical" — 14(13), 248(12); "individual", "non-resident" — 248(1); "partnership" — see Notes to 96(1); "property" — 248(1); "replacement property" — 14(6), (7); "resident in Canada" — 14(8), 250; "shareholder" — 248(1); "taxable capital gain" — 38(a), 248(1); "taxation year" — 11(2), 14(4), 249; "taxpayer" — 248(1); "transferor" — 14(3), 14(12)(a); "trust" — 104(1), 248(1), (3); "year" — 11(2), 14(4).

**I.T. Application Rules [s. 14]**: 21(1) (business carried on since before 1972).

**Interpretation Bulletins [s. 14]**: IT-66R6: Capital dividends; IT-123R4: Disposition of eligible capital property; IT-123R6: Transactions involving eligible capital property; IT-143R2: Meaning of eligible capital expenditure; IT-187: Customer lists and ledger accounts; IT-206R: Separate businesses; IT-313R2: Eligible capital property — rules where a taxpayer has ceased carrying on a business or has died; IT-330R: Dispositions of capital property subject to warranty, covenant, etc.; IT-341R3: Expenses of issuing shares or borrowing money; IT-364: Commencement of business operations; IT-467R: Damages, settlements and similar payments; IT-488R2: Winding-up of 90%-owned taxable Canadian corporations.

## 15. (1) Benefit conferred on shareholder —
Where at any time in a taxation year a benefit is conferred on a shareholder, or on a person in contemplation of the person becoming a shareholder, by a corporation otherwise than by

(a) the reduction of the paid-up capital, the redemption, cancellation or acquisition by the corporation of shares of its capital stock or on the winding-up, discontinuance or reorganization of its business, or otherwise by way of a transaction to which section 88 applies,

(b) the payment of a dividend or a stock dividend,

(c) conferring, on all owners of common shares of the capital stock of the corporation at that time, a right in respect of each common share, that is identical to every other right conferred at that time in respect of each other such share, to acquire additional shares of the capital stock of the corporation, and, for the purpose of this paragraph,

(i) where

(A) the voting rights attached to a particular class of common shares of the capital stock of a corporation differ from the voting rights attached to another class of common shares of the capital stock of the corporation, and

(B) there are no other differences between the terms and conditions of the classes of shares that could cause the fair market value of a share of the particular class to differ materially from the fair market value of a share of the other class,

the shares of the particular class shall be deemed to be property that is identical to the shares of the other class, and

(ii) rights are not considered identical if the cost of acquiring the rights differs, or

(d) an action described in paragraph 84(1)(c.1), (c.2) or (c.3),

the amount or value thereof shall, except to the extent that it is deemed by section 84 to be a dividend, be included in computing the income of the shareholder for the year.

**Related Provisions**: 15(1.1) — Where stock dividend paid; 15(1.2), (1.21) — Forgiveness of shareholder debt; 15(1.3), (1.4) — GST on shareholder benefit; 15(5) — Calculation of benefit where automobile available to shareholder; 15(7) — Application; 15(9) — Deemed benefit; 69(4), (5) — Property deemed disposed of by corporation at fair market value; 80.04(5.1) — No benefit conferred where debtor transfers property to eligible transferee under 80.04; 80.1(4) — Assets acquired from foreign affiliate of taxpayer as dividend in kind or as benefit to shareholder; 80.4(2) — Loans; 84(2) — Distribution on winding-up, etc.; 120.4(1)"split income"(a)(i) — Shareholder benefits received by children subject to income splitting tax; 139(a) — Life insurance corporations; 139.1(11) — No application to conversion benefit on demutualization of insurance corporation; 184(3.1) — Election to treat dividend as loan; 214(3)(a) — Deemed dividend for purposes of non-resident withholding tax.

**Notes**: 15(1) applies to appropriations of corporate property (including money) by a shareholder. If a corporation mistakenly pays too much to a shareholder when repaying a loan made by the shareholder, 15(1) should not apply because there is no "benefit" conferred. The corporation has the right to recover the overpayment from the shareholder, and 15(2) and 20(1)(j) would apply instead. See also Notes to 15(2).

The value of a shareholder benefit under 15(1) may have to be calculated by reference to a return on the amount the corporation paid (e.g., to construct a home that is used by the shareholder), rather than by the fair market value (i.e., the market rent on such a home). See *Youngman*, [1990] 2 C.T.C. 10 (FCA), and *Fingold*, [1997] 3 C.T.C. 441 (FCA).

Where a payment for a shareholder's personal benefit was mistakenly posted as a corporate expense rather than as a debit to the shareholder's loan account, 15(1) did not apply: *Chopp*, [1998] 1 C.T.C. 407 (FCA).

15(1)(b) amended by 1991 technical bill, effective July 1988, to add "or a stock dividend", due to a change in the definition of "dividend" in 248(1).

**S. 15(1)**      Income Tax Act, Part I, Division B

15(1)(c) amended by 1992 technical bill and by 1993 technical bill (which retroactively added 15(1)(c)(ii)), effective for benefits conferred after December 19, 1991.

**Interpretation Bulletins**: IT-63R5: Benefits, including standby charge for an automobile, from the personal use of a motor vehicle supplied by an employer — after 1992; IT-96R6: Options to acquire shares, bonds or debentures and by trusts to acquire trust units; IT-116R3: Rights to buy additional shares; IT-119R4: Debts of shareholders and certain persons connected with shareholders; IT-143R2: Meaning of "eligible capital expenditure"; IT-160R3: Personal use of aircraft; IT-169: Price adjustment clauses; IT-256R: Gains from theft, defalcation or embezzlement; IT-291R2: Transfer of property to a corporation under subsection 85(1); IT-357R2: Expenses of training; IT-421R2: Benefits to individuals, corporations and shareholders from loans or debt; IT-432R2: Benefits conferred on shareholders; IT-498: The deductibility of interest on money borrowed to reloan to employees or shareholders; IT-529: Flexible employee benefit programs.

**Information Circulars**: 76-19R3: Transfer of property to a corporation under section 85; 87-2R: International transfer pricing.

**Advance Tax Rulings**: ATR-9: Transfer of personal residence from corporation to its controlling shareholder; ATR-14: Non-arm's length interest charges; ATR-15: Employee stock option plan; ATR-22R: Estate freeze using share exchange; ATR-27: Exchange and acquisition of interests in capital; ATR-29: Amalgamation of social clubs; ATR-35: Partitioning of assets to get specific ownership — "butterfly"; ATR-36: Estate freeze.

**(1.1) Conferring of benefit** — Notwithstanding subsection (1), where in a taxation year a corporation has paid a stock dividend to a person and it may reasonably be considered that one of the purposes of that payment was to significantly alter the value of the interest of any specified shareholder of the corporation, the fair market value of the stock dividend shall, except to the extent that it is otherwise included in computing that person's income under paragraph 82(1)(a), be included in computing the income of that person for the year.

**Related Provisions**: 52(3) — Cost of stock dividend.

**Interpretation Bulletins**: IT-88R2: Stock dividends; IT-432R2: Benefits conferred on shareholders.

**(1.2) Forgiveness of shareholder debt** — For the purpose of subsection (1), the value of the benefit where an obligation issued by a debtor is settled or extinguished at any time shall be deemed to be the forgiven amount at that time in respect of the obligation.

**Related Provisions**: 6(15) — Forgiveness of employee loans; 15(1.21) — Meaning of "forgiven amount"; 79(3)F(b)(i) — Where property surrendered to creditor; 80(1)"forgiven amount"B(b) — Debt forgiveness rules do not apply to amount of benefit; 80.01 — Deemed settlement of debts.

**Notes**: 15(1.2) amended by 1994 tax amendments bill (Part I), essentially to refer to the "forgiven amount" as now defined in 15(1.21). For taxation years that end before February 22, 1994 (for obligations settled or extinguished after February 17, 1987), read:

> (1.2) Forgiveness of shareholder loans — For the purposes of subsection (1), the value of the benefit or advantage conferred on a shareholder, in circumstances where a loan or other obligation to pay an amount is settled or extinguished at any time without any payment by that shareholder or by payment by the shareholder of an amount that is less than the amount of the obligation outstanding at that time, shall be deemed to be the amount, if any, by which the obligation outstanding at that time exceeds the total of the amount, if any,

of the benefit in respect of the obligation that was included in the shareholder's income at the time the obligation arose and the amount so paid, if any.

**Interpretation Bulletins**: IT-119R4: Debts of shareholders and certain persons connected with shareholders; IT-421R2: Benefits to individuals, corporations and shareholders from loans or debt; IT-432R2: Benefits conferred on shareholders.

**(1.21) Forgiven amount** — For the purpose of subsection (1.2), the "forgiven amount" at any time in respect of an obligation issued by a debtor has the meaning that would be assigned by subsection 80(1) if

(a) the obligation were a commercial obligation (within the meaning assigned by subsection 80(1)) issued by the debtor;

(b) no amount included in computing income (otherwise than because of paragraph 6(1)(a)) because of the obligation being settled or extinguished were taken into account;

(c) the definition "forgiven amount" in subsection 80(1) were read without reference to paragraphs (f) and (h) of the description B in that definition; and

(d) section 80 were read without reference to paragraphs (2)(b) and (q) of that section.

**Related Provisions**: 80.01(1)"forgiven amount" — Application of definition for purposes of s. 80.01; 248(26) — Liability deemed to be obligation issued by debtor; 248(27) — Partial settlement of debt obligation.

**Notes**: 15(1.21) added by 1994 tax amendments bill (Part I), effective for taxation years that end after February 21, 1994.

**(1.3) Cost of property or service** — To the extent that the cost to a person of purchasing a property or service or an amount payable by a person for the purpose of leasing property is taken into account in determining an amount required under this section to be included in computing a taxpayer's income for a taxation year, that cost or amount payable, as the case may be, shall include any tax that was payable by the person in respect of the property or service or that would have been so payable of the person were not exempt from the payment of that tax because of the nature of the person or the use to which the property or service is to be put.

**Related Provisions**: 15(1.4) — Inclusion in income to reflect GST.

**Notes**: Before 1996, 15(1.4) required inclusion of a benefit of 7% to account for GST. The actual GST paid on the goods or services was not included in the calculation of the benefit due to former 15(1.3). This rule has now been reversed, and the GST is specifically included in the benefit.

15(1.3) amended by 1997 GST/HST bill, effective for 1996 and later taxation years. For 1991 to 1995, read:

> (1.3) **Goods and services tax** — To the extent that an amount or value of a benefit required under subsection (1) to be included in computing the income of a taxpayer for a taxation year is determined by reference to the cost to a corporation of any property or service, that cost shall, for the purposes of that subsection, be determined without reference to any goods and services tax payable by that corporation in respect of the property or service.

15(1.3) added by 1990 GST, effective for benefits conferred after 1990.

**Interpretation Bulletins**: IT-63R5: Benefits, including standby charge for an automobile, from the personal use of a motor vehicle supplied by an employer — after 1992; IT-432R2: Benefits conferred on shareholders.

**(1.4)** [Repealed]

**Related Provisions**: 15(1.3) — GST excluded from amount of benefit under 15(1).

**Notes**: 15(1.4) repealed by 1997 GST/HST bill, effective for 1996 and later taxation years. For 1992 to 1995, read:

(1.4) **Idem** — Where the amount or value of a benefit (in this subsection referred to as the "benefit amount") (other than a benefit referred to in subsection (5)) would be required under subsection (1) to be included in computing a taxpayer's income for a taxation year in respect of a supply, other than a zero-rated supply or an exempt supply (within the meanings assigned by Part IX of the *Excise Tax Act*), of property or a service if no amount were paid to the corporation or to a person related to the corporation in respect of the amount that would be so required to be included, there shall be included in computing the taxpayer's income for the year the total of all amounts each of which is an amount determined by the formula

$$0.07 (A - B)$$

where

- A is the amount that would be so required under subsection (1) to be included in computing the taxpayer's income for the year; and
- B is the amount, if any, included in the benefit amount that can reasonably be attributed to tax imposed under an Act of the legislature of a province that is a prescribed tax for the purposes of section 154 of the *Excise Tax Act*.

See Notes to 15(1.3) and 6(1)(e.1).

15(1.4) added by 1990 GST, effective for benefits conferred after 1990; amended by 1992 technical bill, effective 1992; and amended by 1993 technical bill, effective 1993. For 1992, ignore the parenthesized words "other than a benefit referred to in subsection (5)". For 1991, it read differently.

**Interpretation Bulletins**: IT-63R5: Benefits, including standby charge for an automobile, from the personal use of a motor vehicle supplied by an employer — after 1992; IT-432R2: Benefits conferred on shareholders.

**(2) Shareholder debt** — Where a person (other than a corporation resident in Canada) or a partnership (other than a partnership each member of which is a corporation resident in Canada) is

(a) a shareholder of a particular corporation,

(b) connected with a shareholder of a particular corporation, or

(c) a member of a partnership, or a beneficiary of a trust, that is a shareholder of a particular corporation

and the person or partnership has in a taxation year received a loan from or has become indebted to the particular corporation, any other corporation related to the particular corporation or a partnership of which the particular corporation or a corporation related to the particular corporation is a member, the amount of the loan or indebtedness is included in computing the income for the year of the person or partnership.

**Related Provisions [subsec. 15(2)]**: 15(2.1) — Persons connected with shareholder; 15(2.2)–(2.6) — Exceptions to 15(2); 15(7) — Application of subsec. 15(2); 20(1)(j) — Repayment of loan by shareholder; 80(1)"excluded obligation"(a)(i) — Debt forgiveness rules do not apply where amount included in debtor's income; 80.4(2), (3) — Deemed interest; 120.4(1)"split income"(a)(i) — Shareholder benefits received by children subject to income splitting tax; 139(a) — Life insurance corporations; 214(3) — Non-residents' Canadian income; 227(6.1) — Repayment of non-resident shareholder loan.

**Notes**: In *Attis*, [1992] 1 C.T.C. 2244, and *Hill (N.T.)*, [1993] 1 C.T.C. 2021 (also known as *Uphill Holdings*), the Tax Court ruled that where a shareholder took advances during the year but cleared out the shareholder loan account through dividends and bonuses after year-end, 15(2) does not apply. The CCRA accepts this result: see IT-119R4, para. 29.

15(2) can be used for a form of advance income averaging by shareholders or family members with low income in early years and high income in later years (e.g., students), by taking a loan from a corporation when the individual wants to recognize income, and paying it back in a subsequent year for a deduction under 20(1)(j). See Notes to 146(10) for another method.

15(2) amended by 1995-97 technical bill, effective for loans made and indebtedness arising in 1990 and later taxation years. The exceptions in former 15(2)(a) and (b) were expanded and moved to new 15(2.2)-(2.7). For earlier loans or indebtedness, read:

(2) Where a person (other than a corporation resident in Canada) or a partnership (other than a partnership each member of which is a corporation resident in Canada) is a shareholder of a particular corporation, is connected with a shareholder of a particular corporation or is a member of a partnership, or a beneficiary of a trust, that is a shareholder of a particular corporation and the person or partnership has in a taxation year received a loan from or has become indebted to the particular corporation, to any other corporation related thereto or to a partnership of which the particular corporation or a corporation related thereto is a member, the amount of the loan or indebtedness shall be included in computing the income for the year of the person or partnership, unless

(a) the loan was made or the indebtedness arose

(i) in the ordinary course of the lender's or creditor's business and, in the case of a loan, the lending of money was part of its ordinary business,

(ii) in respect of an individual who is an employee of the lender or creditor or the spouse of an employee of the lender or creditor to enable or assist the individual to acquire a dwelling or a share of the capital stock of a cooperative housing corporation acquired for the sole purpose of acquiring the right to inhabit a dwelling owned by the corporation, where the dwelling is for the individual's habitation,

(iii) where the lender or creditor is a corporation, in respect of an employee of the corporation, or of another corporation that is related to the corporation, to enable or assist the employee to acquire from the corporation, or a corporation related thereto, previously unissued fully paid shares of the capital stock of the corporation or the related corporation, as the case may be, to be held by the employee for the employee's own benefit, or

(iv) in respect of an employee of the lender or creditor to enable or assist the employee to acquire an automobile to be used by the employee in the performance of the duties of the employee's office or employment, and *bona fide* arrangements were made, at the time the loan was made or the indebtedness arose, for repayment thereof within a reasonable time; or

(b) the loan or indebtedness was repaid within one year from the end of the taxation year of the lender or creditor in which it was made or incurred and it is established, by subsequent events or otherwise, that the repayment was not made as part of a series of loans or other transactions and repayments.

A loan to an employee who is also a shareholder was caught by the former 15(2), even if the loan was made to the employee *qua* employee. This is no longer the case due to 15(2.4)(e).

15(2)(a)(ii) amended by 1991 technical bill, effective 1985, to extend to a share of a co-operative housing corporation.

15(2)(a)(iii) amended by 1991 technical bill, effective for loans made and indebtedness incurred after 1981, to extend to a loan made by a corporation related to the employer corporation.

15(2) amended by 1981 Budget, effective for loans made and indebtedness incurred after 1981, to extend to indebtedness as well as loans. Indebtedness incurred before 1982 is not covered by 15(2).

15(2) amended by 1977 Budget, effective for loans made after March 1977, to extend subpara. (a)(iii) to shares of a related corporation and to modernize the language.

**Interpretation Bulletins**: IT-119R4: Debts of shareholders and certain persons connected with shareholders; IT-421R2: Benefits to individuals, corporations and shareholders from loans or debt; IT-503: Exploration and development shares.

**I.T. Technical News**: No. 3 (paragraphs 15(2)(b) and 20(1)(j)).

**(2.1) Persons connected with a shareholder** — For the purposes of subsection (2), a person is connected with a shareholder of a particular corporation if that person does not deal at arm's length with the shareholder and if that person is a person other than

(a) a foreign affiliate of the particular corporation; or

(b) a foreign affiliate of a person resident in Canada with which the particular corporation does not deal at arm's length.

**Interpretation Bulletins**: IT-119R4: Debts of shareholders and certain persons connected with shareholders.

**(2.2) When s. 15(2) not to apply — non-resident persons** — Subsection (2) does not apply to indebtedness between non-resident persons.

**Related Provisions**: 95(2)(a)(ii) — Whether FAPI on income from loans between non-resident corporations.

**Notes**: 15(2.2) added by 1995-97 technical bill, effective for loans made and indebtedness arising in 1990 or later taxation years. This rule was formerly in 15(8).

**(2.3) When s. 15(2) not to apply — ordinary lending business** — Subsection (2) does not apply to a debt that arose in the ordinary course of the creditor's business or a loan made in the ordinary course of the lender's ordinary business of lending money where, at the time the indebtedness arose or the loan was made, *bona fide* arrangements were made for repayment of the debt or loan within a reasonable time.

**Related Provisions**: 80.4(2), (3) — Deemed interest.

**Notes**: Where 15(2.3) applies, a deemed benefit from interest on the loan will still be included in income unless a market rate of interest is paid. See 80.4(2) and (3).

15(2.3) added by 1995-97 technical bill, effective for loans made and indebtedness arising in 1990 or later taxation years. This rule was formerly in 15(2)(a)(i).

**Interpretation Bulletins**: IT-119R4: Debts of shareholders and certain persons connected with shareholders.

**(2.4) When s. 15(2) not to apply — certain employees** — Subsection (2) does not apply to a loan made or a debt that arose

(a) in respect of an individual who is an employee of the lender or creditor but not a specified employee of the lender or creditor,

(b) in respect of an individual who is an employee of the lender or creditor or who is the spouse or common-law partner of an employee of the lender or creditor to enable or assist the individual to acquire a dwelling or a share of the capital stock of a cooperative housing corporation acquired for the sole purpose of acquiring the right to inhabit a dwelling owned by the corporation, where the dwelling is for the individual's habitation,

(c) where the lender or creditor is a particular corporation, in respect of an employee of the particular corporation or of another corporation that is related to the particular corporation, to enable or assist the employee to acquire from the particular corporation, or from another corporation related to the particular corporation, previously unissued fully paid shares of the capital stock of the particular corporation or the related corporation, as the case may be, to be held by the employee for the employee's own benefit, or

(d) in respect of an employee of the lender or creditor to enable or assist the employee to acquire a motor vehicle to be used by the employee in the performance of the duties of the employee's office or employment,

where

(e) it is reasonable to conclude that the employee or the employee's spouse or common-law partner received the loan, or became indebted, because of the employee's employment and not because of any person's share-holdings, and

(f) at the time the loan was made or the debt was incurred, *bona fide* arrangements were made for repayment of the loan or debt within a reasonable time.

**Related Provisions**: 15(2.7) — Deemed specified employee of a partnership; 80.4(2), (3) — Deemed interest.

**Notes**: Where 15(2.4) applies, a deemed benefit from interest on the loan will still be included in income unless a market rate of interest is paid. See 80.4(2) and (3).

*Bona fide* repayment arrangements for 15(2.4) do not necessarily have to be in writing, contractually binding or with firm repayment dates: *Davidson*, [1999] 3 C.T.C. 2159 (TCC).

15(2.4) amended by 2000 same-sex partners bill to add reference to "common-law partner", effective for the 2001 and later taxation years, or earlier by election (see Notes to 248(1)"common-law partner").

15(2.4) added by 1995-97 technical bill, effective for loans made and indebtedness arising in 1990 or later taxation years, except that 15(2.4)(e) does not apply to loans made and indebtedness arising before April 26, 1995.

15(2.4)(b), (c) and (d) were formerly in 15(2)(a)(ii), (iii) and (iv). 15(2.4)(a) and (e) effectively reverse *Silden*, [1993] 2 C.T.C. 123 (FCA), which had held that a loan to an employee who is also a shareholder was caught by 15(2) even if the loan was made to the employee *qua* employee.

**Interpretation Bulletins**: IT-119R4: Debts of shareholders and certain persons connected with shareholders.

**(2.5) When s. 15(2) not to apply — certain trusts** — Subsection (2) does not apply to a loan made or a debt that arose in respect of a trust where

(a) the lender or creditor is a private corporation;

(b) the corporation is the settlor and sole beneficiary of the trust;

(c) the sole purpose of the trust is to facilitate the purchase and sale of the shares of the corporation, or of another corporation related to the corporation, for an amount equal to their fair market value at the time of the purchase or sale, as the case may be, from or to the employees of the corporation or of the related corporation (other than employees who are specified employees of the corporation or of another corporation related to the corporation), as the case may be; and

(d) at the time the loan was made or the debt incurred, *bona fide* arrangements were made for repayment of the loan or debt within a reasonable time.

**Related Provisions**: 15(2.7) — Deemed specified employee of a partnership; 80.4(2), (3) — Deemed interest.

**Notes**: 15(2.5) added by 1995-97 technical bill, effective for loans made and indebtedness arising in 1990 or later taxation years, except that for loans made and indebtedness arising before June 20, 1996, ignore the parenthesized words in 15(2.5)(c).

**Interpretation Bulletins**: IT-119R4: Debts of shareholders and certain persons connected with shareholders.

**(2.6) When s. 15(2) not to apply — repayment within one year** — Subsection (2) does not apply to a loan or an indebtedness repaid within one year after the end of the taxation year of the lender or creditor in which the loan was made or the indebtedness arose, where it is established, by subsequent events or otherwise, that the repayment was not part of a series of loans or other transactions and repayments.

**Related Provisions**: 80.4(2), (3) — Deemed interest.

**Notes**: Where 15(2.6) applies, a deemed benefit from interest on the loan may still be included in income unless a market rate of interest is paid. See 80.4(2) and (3).

15(2.6) added by 1995-97 technical bill, effective for loans made and indebtedness arising in 1990 or later taxation years. This rule was formerly in 15(2)(b).

**Interpretation Bulletins**: IT-119R4: Debts of shareholders and certain persons connected with shareholders.

**(2.7) Employee of partnership** — For the purpose of this section, an individual who is an employee of a partnership is deemed to be a specified employee of the partnership where the individual is a specified shareholder of one or more corporations that, in total, are entitled, directly or indirectly, to a share of any income or loss of the partnership, which share is not less than 10% of the income or loss.

**Related Provisions**: 248(1) — Definition of "specified employee".

**Notes**: 15(2.7) added by 1995-97 technical bill, effective for loans made and indebtedness arising in 1990 or later taxation years.

**Interpretation Bulletins**: IT-119R4: Debts of shareholders and certain persons connected with shareholders.

**(3) Interest or dividend on income bond or debenture** — An amount paid as interest or a dividend by a corporation resident in Canada to a taxpayer in respect of an income bond or income debenture shall be deemed to have been paid by the corporation and received by the taxpayer as a dividend on a share of the capital stock of the corporation, unless the corporation is entitled to deduct the amount so paid in computing its income.

**Related Provisions**: 15(4) — Where paid by corporation not resident in Canada; 15.1(1), 15.2(1) — Parallel treatment for small business development bonds and small business bonds; 18(1)(g) — Payment on income bonds; 112(2.1) — Where no deductions permitted; 214(3) — Non-residents' Canadian income; 258(2) — Deemed dividend on preferred share.

**Interpretation Bulletins**: IT-52R4: Income bonds and income debentures; IT-243R4: Dividend refund to private corporations; IT-269R3: Part IV tax on taxable dividends received by a private corporation or a subject corporation; IT-527: Distress preferred shares.

**(4) Idem, where corporation not resident** — An amount paid as interest or a dividend by a corporation not resident in Canada to a taxpayer in respect of an income bond or income debenture shall be deemed to have been received by the taxpayer as a dividend on a share of the capital stock of the corporation unless the amount so paid was, under the laws of the country in which the corporation was resident, deductible in computing the amount for the year on which the corporation was liable to pay income or profits tax imposed by the government of that country.

**Related Provisions**: 15(3) — Where paid by corporation resident in Canada; 18(1)(g) — Payment on income bonds; 214(3) — Non-residents' Canadian income; 258 — Deemed dividend on preferred share.

**Interpretation Bulletins**: IT-52R4: Income bonds and income debentures.

**(5) Automobile benefit** — For the purposes of subsection (1), the value of the benefit to be included in computing a shareholder's income for a taxation year with respect to an automobile made available to the shareholder, or a person related to the shareholder, by a corporation shall (except where an amount is determined under subparagraph 6(1)(e)(i) in respect of the automobile in computing the shareholder's income for the year) be computed on the assumption that subsections 6(1), (1.1), (2) and (7) apply, with such modifications as the circumstances require, and as though the references therein to "the employer of the taxpayer", "the taxpayer's employer" and "the employer" were read as "the corporation".

**Related Provisions**: 15(1.4) — No additional GST inclusion under 15(1.4) since already covered by 6(1)(e.1) and 15(5); 15(7) — Application; 214(3)(a) — Non-residents' Canadian income.

**Notes**: See Notes to 6(2).

15(5) amended by 1993 technical bill, effective 1993, to add reference to 6(1.1); and by 1997 GST bill, effective for 1996 and later taxation years, to add reference to 6(7).

**Regulations**: 200(2)(h), 200(4) (information returns).

**Interpretation Bulletins**: IT-63R5: Benefits, including standby charge for an automobile, from the personal use of a motor vehicle supplied by an employer — after 1992.

**(6)** [Repealed under former Act]

**Notes**: 15(6) repealed in 1982. This rule is now included in 15(5).

**(7) Application of subsecs. (1), (2) and (5)** — For greater certainty, subsections (1), (2) and (5) are applicable in computing, for the purposes of this Part, the income of a shareholder or of a person or partnership whether or not the corporation, or the lender or creditor, as the case may be, was resident or carried on business in Canada.

**Interpretation Bulletins**: IT-63R5: Benefits, including standby charge for an automobile, from the personal use of a motor vehicle supplied by an employer — after 1992; IT-119R4: Debts of shareholders and certain persons connected with shareholders; IT-432R2: Benefits conferred on shareholders.

**(8)** [Repealed]

**Notes**: 15(8) repealed by 1995-97 technical bill, effective for loans made and indebtedness arising in 1990 or later taxation years. This rule has been moved to 15(2.2). For earlier loans or indebtedness, read:

(8) Where subsec. (2) does not apply — Subsection (2) does not apply in respect of indebtedness between non-resident persons.

**(9) Deemed benefit to shareholder by corporation** — Where an amount in respect of a loan or debt is deemed by section 80.4 to be a benefit received by a person or partnership in a taxation year, the amount is deemed for the purpose of subsection (1) to be a benefit conferred in the year on a shareholder, unless subsection 6(9) or paragraph 12(1)(w) applies to the amount.

**Notes**: 15(9) amended by 1995-97 technical bill, effective for taxation years that end after November 1991. The amendment corrected an error in the statute revision of R.S.C. 1985, where the words "of the loan or debt" were erroneously substituted for "thereof". The amendment ensures that only the portion of the amount in respect of the loan or debt that is deemed to be a benefit under 80.4 is also deemed to be a benefit for 15(1).

**Regulations**: 200(2)(i) (information return).

**Interpretation Bulletins**: IT-119R4: Debts of shareholders and certain persons connected with shareholders; IT-421R2: Benefits to individuals, corporations and shareholders from loans or debt.

**Definitions [s. 15]**: "Act" — *Interpretation Act* 35(1); "amount", "business" — 248(1); "Canada" — 255; "common share", "common-law partner" — 248(1); "connected" — 15(2.1); "corporation" — 248(1), *Interpretation Act* 35(1); "dividend", "employee" — 248(1); "forgiven amount" — 15(1.21); "goods and services tax", "income bond", "income debenture", "individual" — 248(1); "legislature" — *Interpretation Act* 35(1); "motor vehicle" — 248(1); "obligation" — 248(26); "paid-up capital" — 89(1), 248(1); "person", "property" — 248(1); "province" — *Interpretation Act* 35(1); "resident in Canada" — 250; "series of transactions" — 248(20); "share", "shareholder" — 248(1); "specified employee" — 15(2.7), 248(1); "specified shareholder" — 248(1); "stock dividend" — 248(1); "taxation year" — 249; "taxpayer" — 248(1).

**15.1 (1) Interest on small business development bonds** — Any amount received by a taxpayer as or on account of interest on a small business development bond shall, except for the purposes of Part IV, be deemed to have been received as a taxable dividend.

**Related Provisions**: 15(3) — Parallel rule for income bonds; 15.2(1) — Parallel rule for small business bonds.

**(2) Rules for small business development bonds** — Where a corporation (in this section referred to as the "issuer") has issued an obligation that is at any time a small business development bond, notwithstanding any other provision of this Act,

(a) in computing the issuer's income for a taxation year, no deduction shall be made in respect of any amount paid or payable (depending on the method regularly followed in computing the issuer's income) as or on account of interest on the obligation in respect of a period that includes that time;

(b) except for the purpose of subsection 129(1), to the extent that any amount paid by the issuer as or on account of interest on the obligation is not allowed as a deduction because of paragraph (a), it shall, when paid, be deemed to have been paid as a taxable dividend; and

(c) except for the purposes of paragraph 125(1)(b), the issuer's taxable income for any taxation year that includes a period throughout which the obligation was a small business development bond but

(i) the issuer was not an eligible small business corporation, or

(ii) all or substantially all of the proceeds from the issue of the obligation cannot reasonably be regarded as having been used by the issuer or a corporation with which it was not dealing at arm's length in the financing of an active business carried on in Canada immediately before the obligation was issued

shall be deemed to be an amount equal to the total of

(iii) the amount paid or payable (depending on the method regularly followed in computing the issuer's income) as or on account of interest on the obligation in respect of that period, and

Subdivision b — Income or Loss from a Business or Property    S. 15.1(5)

(iv) the issuer's taxable income otherwise determined for the year.

**Notes**: The CCRA takes the position that "all or substantially all", used in 15.1(2)(c)(ii), means 90% or more.

**(3) Definitions** — In this section,

**"eligible small business corporation"** at any time means a taxable Canadian corporation that at that time is

(a) a small business corporation, or

(b) a cooperative corporation (within the meaning assigned by subsection 136(2)) all or substantially all of the assets of which are used in an active business carried on by it in Canada;

**Notes**: The CCRA takes the position that "all or substantially all" means 90% or more.

**"joint election"** means an election that is made in prescribed form, containing prescribed information, jointly by the issuer of an obligation and the person who is the holder of the obligation at the time of the election, that is filed with the Minister by the holder, and in which the holder and the issuer elect that this section apply to the obligation;

**Forms**: T2216: Joint election for a small business development bond.

**"majority interest partner"** — [Repealed]

**Notes**: Definition "majority interest partner" repealed by 1995-97 technical bill, effective April 27, 1995. The term is now defined in 248(1). The repealed definition merely referred to the one in 97(3.1).

**"qualifying debt obligation"** of a corporation at a particular time means an obligation that is a bond, debenture, bill, note, mortgage or similar obligation issued after February 25, 1992 and before 1995,

(a) the principal amount of which is not less than $10,000 or more than $500,000,

(b) that is issued for a term of not more than 5 years and, except in the event of a failure or default under the terms or conditions of the obligation, not less than one year, and

(c) that was issued not more than 5 years before the particular time,

if the obligation is issued by the corporation

(d) as part of a proposal to, or an arrangement with, its creditors that has been approved by a court under the *Bankruptcy and Insolvency Act*,

(e) at a time when all or substantially all of its assets are under the control of a receiver, receiver-manager, sequestrator or trustee in bankruptcy, or

(f) at a time when, because of financial difficulty, the corporation is in default, or could reasonably be expected to default, on a debt held by a person with whom the corporation was dealing at arm's length and the obligation is issued, in whole or in part, directly or indirectly in exchange or substitution for that debt;

**Notes**: Deadline for issuing obligation extended from end of 1992 to end of 1994 by 1992 Economic Statement, effective for obligations issued after 1992. See also Notes at end of 15.1.

The CCRA takes the position that "all or substantially all", used in paragraph (e), means 90% or more.

**"small business development bond"** at any time means

(a) an obligation that is at that time a qualifying debt obligation issued after 1981 and before 1988 by a Canadian-controlled private corporation in respect of which a joint election was made within 90 days after the later of its issue date and March 30, 1983,

(b) an obligation that is at that time a qualifying debt obligation issued after February 25, 1992 by a Canadian-controlled private corporation in respect of which a joint election was made within 90 days after its issue date, or

(c) an obligation that is at that time a qualifying debt obligation issued by a Canadian-controlled private corporation if

(i) it is reasonable to consider that the corporation and the holder of the obligation intended that this section apply to the obligation, having regard to such factors as may be relevant, including the rate of interest stipulated under the terms of the obligation and the manner in which the corporation and the holder have treated the obligation for the purposes of this Act, and

(ii) the holder files with the Minister a joint election in respect of the obligation within 90 days after the date of notification by the Minister that a joint election in respect of the obligation has not been filed.

**Related Provisions**: 248(1)"small business development bond" — Definition applies to entire Act.

**Notes**: 1992 Economic Statement bill provides that for the purpose of this definition, an election made from Jan. 1, 1993 to August 10, 1994 in respect of an obligation issued in 1993 or 1994 is deemed made on time. (For obligations issued in 1992, the deadline was Sept. 8, 1993.)

**Forms**: T2216: Joint election for a small business development bond.

**(4) Money borrowed** — Notwithstanding any other provision of this Act, an amount paid or payable by a taxpayer pursuant to a legal obligation to pay interest on borrowed money used for the purpose of acquiring a small business development bond shall be deemed to be an amount paid or payable, as the case may be, on borrowed money used for the purpose of earning income from a business or property.

**(5) False declaration** — Where the Minister establishes that an issuer has knowingly or under circumstances amounting to gross negligence made a false declaration in a joint election in respect of an obligation, the reference in subparagraph (2)(c)(iii) to "the amount paid or payable" shall in respect of the obligation be read as a reference to "3 times the amount paid or payable".

**(6) Disqualification** — Where at a particular time an issuer makes a joint election in respect of an obligation and

  (a) the issuer or any other corporation associated at the time the obligation was issued with the issuer,

  (b) an individual who controls or is a member of a related group that controls the issuer, or

  (c) a partnership any member of which, who is a majority interest partner of the partnership, controls, or is a member of a related group that controls, the issuer

had at or before the particular time made a joint election in respect of any small business development bond or small business bond, as the case may be, for the purposes of this section, the issuer shall be deemed not to be an eligible small business corporation in respect of the obligation.

**(7) Exception** — Subsection (6) does not apply in respect of an obligation issued at any time where the issue price of the obligation does not exceed the amount, if any, by which

  (a) $500,000

exceeds

  (b) the total of all amounts each of which is the principal amount outstanding immediately after that time in respect of

   (i) another obligation that is a small business development bond issued by

     (A) the issuer, or

     (B) a corporation associated with the issuer, or

   (ii) a small business bond issued by

     (A) an individual who controls, or is a member of a related group that controls, the issuer, or

     (B) a partnership any member of which, who is a majority interest partner of the partnership, controls, or is a member of a related group that controls, the issuer.

**Related Provisions [s. 15.1]:** 136 — Cooperative not private corporation — exception; 143(1)(k) — Communal organization (e.g. Hutterite colony) may issue small business development bond.

**Notes:** 15.1 rewritten by 1992 Budget/technical bill, effective for obligations issued after February 25, 1992.

Former 15.1 provided substantially the same rules, for small business development bonds (SBDBs) issued from December 12, 1979 through December 31, 1987. As SBDBs have a term of no more than 5 years, the last SBDBs issued under the old system expired in 1992.

**Definitions [s. 15.1]:** "active business", "amount" — 248(1); "arm's length" — 251(1); "associated" — 256; "borrowed money", "business" — 248(1); "Canada" — 255; "Canadian-controlled private corporation" — 125(7), 248(1); "corporation" — 248(1), *Interpretation Act* 35(1); "eligible small business corporation" — 15.1(3); "individual" — 248(1); "issuer" — 15.1(2); "joint election" — 15.1(3); "majority interest partner", "Minister", "person", "prescribed", "principal amount", "property" — 248(1); "qualifying debt obligation" — 15.1(3); "related group" — 251(4); "small business bond" — 15.2(3), 248(1); "small business corporation" — 248(1); "small business development bond" — 15.1(3), 248(1); "taxable Canadian corporation", "taxable dividend" — 89(1), 248(1); "taxable income" — 2(2), 248(1); "taxation year" — 249; "taxpayer" — 248(1).

**Interpretation Bulletins [s. 15.1]:** IT-269R3: Part IV tax on taxable dividends received by a private corporation or a subject corporation; IT-507R: Small business development bonds and small business bonds.

## 15.2 (1) Interest on small business bond —
Any amount received by a taxpayer as or on account of interest on a small business bond shall, except for the purposes of Part IV, be deemed to have been received as a taxable dividend from a taxable Canadian corporation.

**Related Provisions:** 15(3) — Parallel rule for income bonds; 15.1(1) — Parallel rule for small business development bonds.

**(2) Rules for small business bonds** — Where an individual or a partnership (in this section referred to as the "issuer") has issued an obligation that is at any time a small business bond, notwithstanding any other provision of this Act,

  (a) in computing the issuer's income for a taxation year, no deduction shall be made in respect of any amount paid or payable (depending on the method regularly followed in computing the issuer's income) as or on account of interest on the bond in respect of a period that includes that time; and

  (b) for any taxation year that includes a period throughout which the obligation was a small business bond but

   (i) the issuer was not an eligible issuer, or

   (ii) all or substantially all of the proceeds from the issue of the obligation were not used by the issuer in the financing of an active business carried on by the issuer in Canada immediately before the time of the issue of the obligation,

there shall be added to the tax otherwise payable under this Part by the issuer for that taxation year an amount equal to 29% of the amount of interest paid or payable (depending on the method regularly followed in computing the issuer's income) in respect of the bond for that period.

**Notes:** The CCRA takes the position that "all or substantially all", used in 15.2(2)(b)(ii), means 90% or more.

**(3) Definitions** — In this section,

**"eligible issuer"** at any time means

  (a) an individual (other than a trust) who is resident in Canada and who

   (i) has not made a joint election before that time in respect of a small business bond,

   (ii) is not a majority interest partner of a partnership that has made a joint election before that time in respect of a small business bond, and

(iii) neither controls nor is a member of a related group that controls

(A) a corporation that has made a joint election before that time in respect of a small business development bond, or

(B) a corporation that is associated with a corporation referred to in clause (A), or

(b) a partnership

(i) each member of which is an individual (other than a trust) who is resident in Canada,

(ii) each majority interest partner, if any, of which is an eligible issuer, and

(iii) that has not made a joint election before that time in respect of a small business bond;

**"joint election"** means an election that is made in prescribed form, containing prescribed information, jointly by the issuer of an obligation and the person who is the holder of the obligation at the time of the election, that is filed with the Minister by the holder and in which the holder and the issuer elect that the provisions of this section apply with respect to that obligation;

**Related Provisions**: 96(3) — Election by partners.

**Forms**: T2218: Joint election for a small business bond.

**"majority interest partner"** — [Repealed]

**Notes**: Definition "majority interest partner" repealed by 1995-97 technical bill, effective April 27, 1995. The term is now defined in 248(1). The repealed definition merely referred to the one in 97(3.1).

**"qualifying debt obligation"** of an issuer at a particular time means an obligation that is a bill, note, mortgage or similar obligation issued after February 25, 1992 and before 1995,

(a) the principal amount of which is not less than $10,000 or more than $500,000,

(b) that is issued for a term of not more than 5 years and, except in the event of a failure or default under the terms or conditions of the obligation, not less than one year, and

(c) that was issued not more than 5 years before the particular time,

if the obligation is issued

(d) as part of a proposal to, or an arrangement with, the issuer's creditors that has been approved by a court under the *Bankruptcy and Insolvency Act*,

(e) at a time when all or substantially all of the issuer's assets are under the control of a receiver, receiver-manager, sequestrator or trustee in bankruptcy, or

(f) at a time when, because of financial difficulty, the issuer is in default, or could reasonably be expected to default, on a debt incurred in the course of the issuer's business and held by a person with whom the issuer was dealing at arm's length or, where the issuer is a partnership, by a person with whom each member of the partnership was dealing at arm's length, and it is issued, in whole or in part, directly or indirectly in exchange or substitution for that debt,

and the funds from the issue of the obligation are used in Canada in a business of the issuer carried on immediately before the time of issue;

**Notes**: Deadline for issuing obligation extended from end of 1992 to end of 1994 by 1992 Economic Statement bill, effective for obligations issued after 1992. See also Notes at end of 15.2.

The CCRA takes the position that "all or substantially all", used in paragraph (e), means 90% or more.

**"small business bond"** at any time means

(a) an obligation that is at that time a qualifying debt obligation, issued by an individual or a partnership, in respect of which a joint election was made within 90 days after its issue date, or

(b) an obligation that is at that time a qualifying debt obligation issued by an individual or a partnership if

(i) it is reasonable to consider that the issuer and the holder of the obligation intended that this section apply to the obligation, having regard to such factors as may be relevant, including the rate of interest stipulated under the terms of the obligation and the manner in which the issuer and the holder have treated the obligation for the purposes of this Act, and

(ii) the holder files with the Minister a joint election in respect of the obligation within 90 days after the date of notification by the Minister that a joint election in respect of the obligation has not been filed under paragraph (a).

**Related Provisions**: 96(3) — Election by partners; 248(1)"small business bond" — Definition applies to entire Act.

**Notes**: 1992 Economic Statement legislation provides that for the purpose of this definition, an election made from Jan. 1, 1993 to Aug. 10, 1994 in respect of an obligation issued in 1993 or 1994 is deemed made on time. (For obligations issued in 1992, the deadline was Sept. 8, 1993.)

**Forms**: T2218: Joint election for a small business bond.

**(4) Status of interest** — Notwithstanding any other provision of this Act, an amount paid or payable by a taxpayer pursuant to a legal obligation to pay interest on borrowed money used for the purpose of acquiring a small business bond shall be deemed to be an amount paid or payable, as the case may be, on borrowed money used for the purpose of earning income from a business or property.

**(5) False declaration** — Where the Minister establishes that an issuer has knowingly or under circumstances amounting to gross negligence made a false declaration in a joint election in respect of an obligation, the reference in paragraph (2)(b) to "29%" shall, in respect of the obligation, be read as a reference to "87%".

**(6) Partnerships** — For the purpose of paragraph (2)(b), in the case of an issuer that is a partnership, the expression "tax otherwise payable under this Part by the issuer" shall be read as a reference to the "tax otherwise payable under this Part by each member of the partnership" and each member shall add to that member's tax otherwise payable under this Part for the taxation year that includes the period described in paragraph (2)(b) the amount that can reasonably be regarded as that member's share of the amount determined under that paragraph with respect to the partnership.

**(7) Deemed eligible issuer** — Where, but for subparagraphs (a)(i), (ii) and (iii) and (b)(ii) of the definition "eligible issuer" in subsection (3), an individual or a partnership would be an "eligible issuer", the individual or partnership shall be deemed to be an eligible issuer in respect of a small business bond at any time where the issue price of the bond does not exceed the amount, if any, by which

(a) $500,000

exceeds

(b) where the issuer is an individual, the total of all amounts each of which is the principal amount outstanding immediately after that time in respect of

    (i) another obligation that is a small business bond issued by

        (A) the individual, or

        (B) a partnership of which the individual is a majority interest partner, or

    (ii) a small business development bond issued by

        (A) a corporation that is controlled by the individual or by a related group of which the individual is a member, or

        (B) a corporation that is associated with a corporation referred to in clause (A), or

(c) where the issuer is a partnership, the total of all amounts each of which is the principal amount outstanding immediately after that time in respect of

    (i) another obligation that is a small business bond issued by

        (A) the partnership,

        (B) an individual who is a majority interest partner of the partnership, or

        (C) a partnership of which the individual referred to in clause (B) is a majority interest partner, or

    (ii) a small business development bond issued by

        (A) a corporation that is controlled by the individual referred to in clause (i)(B) or by a related group of which the individual is a member, or

        (B) a corporation that is associated with a corporation referred to in clause (A).

**Notes**: 15.2 rewritten by 1992 Budget/technical bill, effective for obligations issued after February 25, 1992.

Former 15.2 provided substantially the same rules, for small business bonds (SBBs) issued from December 12, 1979 through December 31, 1987. As SBBs have a term of no more than 5 years, the last SBBs issued under the old system expired in 1992. The treatment of such bonds to the purchaser (15.2(1)) and the issuer (15.2(2)) was essentially the same as under the current legislation, except that the rate of tax on the issuer under 15.2(2) was 34% (the pre-1988 top personal tax rate) rather than 29% (the current top personal federal tax rate).

**Definitions [s. 15.2]**: "active business", "amount" — 248(1); "arm's length" — 251(1); "associated" — 256; "borrowed money", "business" — 248(1); "Canada" — 255; "control" — 256(6), (6.1); "corporation" — 248(1), *Interpretation Act* 35(1); "eligible issuer" — 15.2(3); "individual" — 248(1); "issuer" — 15.2(2); "joint election" — 15.2(3); "majority interest partner", "Minister", "person", "prescribed", "principal amount", "property" — 248(1); "qualifying debt obligation" — 15.2(3); "related group" — 251(4); "resident in Canada" — 250; "small business bond" — 15.2(3), 248(1); "small business development bond" — 15.1(3), 248(1); "tax otherwise payable under this Part" — 15.2(6); "taxable Canadian corporation", "taxable dividend" — 89(1), 248(1); "taxation year" — 249; "taxpayer" — 248(1); "trust" — 104(1), 248(1), (3).

**Interpretation Bulletins [s. 15.2]**: IT-269R3: Part IV tax on taxable dividends received by a private corporation or a subject corporation; IT-507R: Small business development bonds and small business bonds.

**16. (1) Income and capital combined** — Where, under a contract or other arrangement, an amount can reasonably be regarded as being in part interest or other amount of an income nature and in part an amount of a capital nature, the following rules apply:

(a) the part of the amount that can reasonably be regarded as interest shall, irrespective of when the contract or arrangement was made or the form or legal effect thereof, be deemed to be interest on a debt obligation held by the person to whom the amount is paid or payable; and

(b) the part of the amount that can reasonably be regarded as an amount of an income nature, other than interest, shall, irrespective of when the contract or arrangement was made or the form or legal effect thereof, be included in the income of the taxpayer to whom the amount is paid or payable for the taxation year in which the amount was received or became due to the extent it has not otherwise been included in the taxpayer's income.

**Related Provisions**: 12(1)(c) — Interest income; 12(1)(g) — Amount fully taxable where based on production or use; 12(3) — Accrual of interest income; 16(4), (5) — Application of subsec. (1); 138(12) — "Gross investment revenue" of an insurer; 214(2) — Tax on non-residents.

**Notes**: Despite 16(1), the interest component of structured settlement payments to injury victims is non-taxable if certain conditions are met. See Interpretation Bulletin IT-365R2, para. 5.

**Regulations**: 201(1)(d) (information return).

**Interpretation Bulletins**: IT-233R: Lease-option agreements; sale-leaseback agreements; IT-265R3: Payments of income and capital combined; IT-365R2: Damages, settlements and similar receipts; IT-396R: Interest income.

**Forms**: T5 Segment; T5 Summ: Return of investment income; T5 Supp: Statement of investment income.

**(2) Obligation issued at discount** — Where, in the case of a bond, debenture, bill, note, mortgage or similar obligation issued after December 20, 1960 and before June 19, 1971 by a person exempt from tax under section 149, a non-resident person not carrying on business in Canada, or a government, municipality or municipal or other public body performing a function of government,

(a) the obligation was issued for an amount that is less than the principal amount of the obligation,

(b) the interest stipulated to be payable on the obligation, expressed in terms of an annual rate on

(i) the principal amount thereof, if no amount is payable on account of the principal amount before the maturity of the obligation, or

(ii) the amount outstanding from time to time as or on account of the principal amount thereof, in any other case,

is less than 5%, and

(c) the yield from the obligation, expressed in terms of an annual rate on the amount for which the obligation was issued (which annual rate shall, if the terms of the obligation or any agreement relating thereto conferred on the holder thereof a right to demand payment of the principal amount of the obligation or the amount outstanding as or on account of the principal amount, as the case may be, before the maturity of the obligation, be calculated on the basis of the yield that produces the highest annual rate obtainable either on the maturity of the obligation or conditional on the exercise of any such right) exceeds the annual rate determined under paragraph (b) by more than $1/3$ thereof,

the amount by which the principal amount of the obligation exceeds the amount for which the obligation was issued shall be included in computing the income of the first owner of the obligation who is a resident of Canada and is not a person exempt from tax under section 149 or a government, for the taxation year of the owner of the obligation in which he, she or it became the owner thereof.

**Related Provisions**: 16(5) — Application of subsec. 16(1); 53(1)(g) — Addition to adjusted cost base; 142.4(1)"tax basis"(b) — Disposition of specified debt obligation by financial institution.

**Interpretation Bulletins**: IT-265R3: Payments of income and capital combined.

**(3) Idem** — Where, in the case of a bond, debenture, bill, note, mortgage or similar obligation (other than an obligation that is a prescribed debt obligation for the purpose of subsection 12(9)) issued after June 18, 1971 by a person exempt, because of section 149, from Part I tax on part or all of the person's income, a non-resident person not carrying on business in Canada or a government, municipality or municipal or other public body performing a function of government,

(a) the obligation was issued for an amount that is less than the principal amount of the obligation, and

(b) the yield from the obligation, expressed in terms of an annual rate on the amount for which the obligation was issued (which annual rate shall, if the terms of the obligation or any agreement relating thereto conferred on the holder thereof a right to demand payment of the principal amount of the obligation or the amount outstanding as or on account of the principal amount, as the case may be, before the maturity of the obligation, be calculated on the basis of the yield that produces the highest annual rate obtainable either on the maturity of the obligation or conditional on the exercise of any such right) exceeds $4/3$ of the interest stipulated to be payable on the obligation, expressed in terms of an annual rate on

(i) the principal amount of the obligation, if no amount is payable on account of the principal amount before the maturity of the obligation, or

(ii) the amount outstanding from time to time as or on account of the principal amount thereof, in any other case,

the amount by which the principal amount of the obligation exceeds the amount for which the obligation was issued shall be included in computing the income of the first owner of the obligation

(c) who is resident in Canada,

(d) who is not a government nor a person exempt, because of section 149, from tax under this Part on all or part of the person's taxable income, and

(e) of whom the obligation is a capital property,

for the taxation year in which the owner acquired the obligation.

**Related Provisions**: 16(5) — Application of subsec. 16(1); 20(14) — Treatment of accrued bond interest; 53(1)(g) — Addition to adjusted cost base; 142.4(1)"tax basis"(b) — Disposition of specified debt obligation by financial institution.

**Notes**: 16(3) amended by 1993 technical bill, effective for 1990 and later taxation years, essentially to add 16(3)(e). For earlier years, the closing words after para. (b) read:

the amount by which the principal amount of the obligation exceeds the amount for which the obligation was issued shall be included in computing the income of the first owner of the obligation who is a resident of Canada and is not a person exempt from tax under section 149 or a government, for the taxation year of the owner of the obligation in which he, she or it became the owner thereof.

Opening words of 16(3) amended by 1992 technical bill, effective 1991, to exclude a prescribed debt obligation.

**Regulations**: 7000(1) (prescribed debt obligation).

**Interpretation Bulletins**: IT-265R3: Payments of income and capital combined.

**(4) Where subsec. (1) does not apply** — Subsection (1) does not apply to any amount received by a taxpayer in a taxation year

(a) as an annuity payment; or

(b) in satisfaction of the taxpayer's rights under an annuity contract.

**(5) Idem** — Subsection (1) does not apply in any case where subsection (2) or (3) applies.

**(6) Indexed debt obligations** — Subject to subsection (7) and for the purposes of this Act, where at any time in a taxpayer's taxation year

(a) an interest in an indexed debt obligation is held by the taxpayer,

(i) an amount determined in prescribed manner shall be deemed to be received and receivable by the taxpayer in the year as interest in respect of the obligation, and

(ii) an amount determined in prescribed manner shall be deemed to be paid and payable in respect of the year by the taxpayer as interest under a legal obligation of the taxpayer to pay interest on borrowed money used for the purpose of earning income from a business or property;

(b) an indexed debt obligation is an obligation of the taxpayer,

(i) an amount determined in prescribed manner shall be deemed to be payable in respect of the year by the taxpayer as interest in respect of the obligation, and

(ii) an amount determined in prescribed manner shall be deemed to be received and receivable by the taxpayer in the year as interest in respect of the obligation; and

(c) the taxpayer pays or credits an amount in respect of an amount determined under subparagraph (b)(i) in respect of an indexed debt obligation, the payment or crediting shall be deemed to be a payment or crediting of interest on the obligation.

**Related Provisions**: 20(1)(c) — Interest deduction; 53(1)(g.1) — Addition to adjusted cost base; 53(2)(l.1) — Deduction from adjusted cost base; 138(12)"gross investment revenue"G(a) — Gross investment revenue of insurer; 142.3(2) — Indexed debt obligation not subject to rules re income from specified debt obligations; 142.4(1)"tax basis"(e), (n) — Disposition of specified debt obligation by financial institution; 214(7) — Sale of obligation by non-resident.

**Notes**: 16(6) added by 1992 technical bill, effective for debt obligations issued after October 16, 1991. (It had originally been proposed as 248(25).) Where interest on a security is tied to inflation, the interest paid and the interest received (by the issuer and the purchaser respectively) are determined for tax purposes by Reg. 7001.

Opening words of 16(6) amended by 1995-97 technical bill, effective on the same basis as the addition of 16(7), to add the words "Subject to subsection (7) and".

**Regulations**: 7001 (amounts determined in prescribed manner).

**(7) Impaired indexed debt obligations** — Paragraph (6)(a) does not apply to a taxpayer in respect of an indexed debt obligation for the part of a taxation year throughout which the obligation is impaired where an amount in respect of the obligation is deductible because of subparagraph 20(1)(l)(ii) in computing the taxpayer's income for the year.

**Notes**: 16(7) added by 1995-97 technical bill, effective

(a) for taxation years that end after September 1997; and

(b) for taxation years that end after 1995 and before October 1997, if the taxpayer files an election for amended 20(1)(l) to apply to such years (see Notes to 20(1)(l)).

Under 16(7), interest is not included under 16(6) for the portion of the year in which the indexed debt obligation is impaired. This is consistent with the new accounting rules which provide that recognition of interest income in accordance with the terms of the original debt obligation ceases on the impairment of the obligation.

**Definitions [s. 16]**: "amount", "annuity", "borrowed money", "business" — 248(1); "Canada" — 255; "capital property" — 54, 248(1); "indexed debt obligation", "non-resident", "prescribed" — 248(1); "prescribed debt obligation" — Reg. 7000(1); "principal amount", "property" — 248(1); "received" — 248(7); "regulation" — 248(1); "taxation year" — 249; "taxpayer" — 248(1).

**Interpretation Bulletins [s. 16]**: IT-265R3: Payments of income and capital combined.

**16.1 (1) Leasing properties** — Where a taxpayer (in this section referred to as the "lessee") leases tangible property (other than prescribed property) that would, if the lessee acquired the property, be depreciable property of the lessee, from a person resident in Canada other than a person whose taxable income is exempt from tax under this Part, or from a non-resident person who holds the lease in the course of carrying on a business through a permanent establishment in Canada, as defined by regulation, any income from which is subject to tax under this Part, who owns the property and with whom the lessee was dealing at arm's length (in this section referred to as the "lessor") for a term of more than one year, if the lessee and the lessor jointly elect in prescribed form filed with their returns of income for their respective taxation years that include the particular time when the lease began, the following rules apply for the purpose of computing the income of the lessee for the taxation year that includes the particular time and for all subsequent taxation years:

(a) in respect of amounts paid or payable for the use of, or for the right to use, the property, the lease shall be deemed not to be a lease;

(b) the lessee shall be deemed to have acquired the property from the lessor at the particular time at a cost equal to its fair market value at that time;

(c) the lessee shall be deemed to have borrowed money from the lessor at the particular time, for the purpose of acquiring the property, in a principal amount equal to the fair market value of the property at that time;

(d) interest shall be deemed to accrue on the principal amount of the borrowed money outstanding from time to time, compounded semi-annually, not in advance, at the prescribed rate in effect

(i) at the earlier of

(A) the time, if any, before the particular time, at which the lessee last entered into an agreement to lease the property, and

(B) the particular time, or

(ii) where the lease provides that the amount payable by the lessee for the use of, or the right to use, the property varies according to prevailing interest rates in effect from time to time, and the lessee so elects, in respect of all of the property that is subject to the lease, in the lessee's return of income under this Part for the taxation year of the lessee in which the lease began, at the beginning of the period for which the interest is being calculated;

(e) all amounts paid or payable by or on behalf of the lessee for the use of, or the right to use, the property in the year shall be deemed to be blended payments, paid or payable by the lessee, of principal and interest on the borrowed money outstanding from time to time, calculated in accordance with paragraph (d), applied firstly on account of interest on principal, secondly on account of interest on unpaid interest and thirdly on account of unpaid principal, if any, and the amount, if any, by which any such payment exceeds the total of those amounts shall be deemed to be paid or payable on account of interest, and any amount deemed by reason of this paragraph to be a payment of interest shall be deemed to have been an amount paid or payable, as the case may be, pursuant to a legal obligation to pay interest in respect of the year on the borrowed money;

(f) at the time of the expiration or cancellation of the lease, the assignment of the lease or the sublease of the property by the lessee, the lessee shall (except where subsection (4) applies) be deemed to have disposed of the property at that time for proceeds of disposition equal to the amount, if any, by which

(i) the total of

(A) the amount referred to in paragraph (c), and

(B) all amounts received or receivable by the lessee in respect of the cancellation or assignment of the lease or the sublease of the property

exceeds

(ii) the total of

(A) all amounts deemed under paragraph (e) to have been paid or payable, as the case may be, by the lessee on account of the principal amount of the borrowed money, and

(B) all amounts paid or payable by or on behalf of the lessee in respect of the cancellation or assignment of the lease or the sublease of the property;

(g) for the purposes of subsections 13(5.2) and (5.3), each amount paid or payable by or on behalf of the lessee that would, but for this subsection, have been an amount paid or payable for the use of, or the right to use, the property shall be deemed to have been deducted in computing the lessee's income as an amount paid or payable by the lessee for the use of, or the right to use, the property after the particular time;

(h) any amount paid or payable by or on behalf of the lessee in respect of the granting or assignment of the lease or the sublease of the property that would, but for this paragraph, be the capital cost to the lessee of a leasehold interest in the property shall be deemed to be an amount paid or payable, as the case may be, by the lessee for the use of, or the right to use, the property for the remaining term of the lease; and

(i) where the lessee elects under this subsection in respect of a property and, at any time after the lease was entered into, the owner of the property is a non-resident person who does not hold the lease in the course of carrying on a business through a permanent establishment in Canada, as defined by regulation, any income from which is subject to tax under this Part, for the purposes of this subsection the lease shall be deemed to have been cancelled at that time.

**Related Provisions**: 16.1(5) — Replacement property; 16.1(6) — Additional property; 16.1(7) — Renegotiation of lease; Reg. 1100(1.1)–(1.13) — CCA restrictions on leasing property.

**Notes**: The election under 16.1(1) allows taxpayers to reduce the negative effects of the "leasing property" CCA restrictions in Reg. 1100(1.1)–(1.3).

16.1(1) opening words amended by 1998 Budget bill (based on Dept. of Finance news release, Aug. 18/98) to add "other than a person whose taxable income is exempt from tax under this Part", effective for leases entered into by a taxpayer or partnership after 3:30 pm EDST, August 18, 1998, other than such leases entered into after that time pursuant to an agreement in writing

(a) made before that time under which the taxpayer or partnership was required to enter into the lease and

(b) in respect of which there is no agreement or other arrangement under which the obligation of the taxpayer or partnership to enter into the lease can be changed, reduced or waived if there is a change to the Act or if there is an adverse assessment under the Act,

and for the purpose of the amendment, a lease in respect of which a material change has been agreed to by the parties to the lease, effective at any particular time that is after 3:30 pm EDST, August 18, 1998, is deemed to have been entered into at that particular time.

16.1(1) amended by 1991 technical bill, retroactive to the introduction of the section (see Notes at end of 16.1), except that, in the opening words of the subsection

(a) with respect to leases and subleases entered into after 10 p.m. EDST, April 26, 1989 and before June 12, 1989,

(i) ignore the words "resident in Canada (or from a non-resident person who holds the lease in the course of carrying on a business through a permanent establishment in Canada, as defined by regulation, any income from which is subject to tax under this Part)"; and

(ii) ignore the words "and with whom the lessee was dealing at arm's length", and

(b) with respect to leases and subleases entered into after June 11, 1989 and before July 13, 1990,

(i) ignore the words "any income from which is subject to tax under this Part";

(ii) ignore the words "the earlier of" in 16.1(1)(d)(i); and

(iii) ignore 16.1(1)(d)(i)(A).

In 16.1(1)(i), for leases and subleases entered into before July 13, 1990, ignore the words "any income from which is subject to tax under this Part".

See also Notes at end of 16.1.

**Regulations**: 1100(2)(a)(vi) — Half-year CCA rule inapplicable to property deemed acquired by 16.1(1)(b); 4302 (prescribed rate of interest for 16.1(1)(d)); 8200 (prescribed property); 8201 (permanent establishment).

**Forms**: T2145: Election in respect of the leasing of property.

**(2) Assignments and subleases** — Subject to subsections (3) and (4), where at any particular time a lessee who has made an election under subsection (1) in respect of a leased property assigns the lease or subleases the property to another person (in this section referred to as the "assignee"),

(a) subsection (1) shall not apply in computing the income of the lessee in respect of the lease for any period after the particular time; and

(b) if the lessee and the assignee jointly elect in prescribed form filed with their returns of income under this Part for their respective taxation years that include the particular time, subsection (1) shall apply to the assignee as if

(i) the assignee leased the property at the particular time from the owner of the property for a term of more than one year, and

(ii) the assignee and the owner of the property jointly elected under subsection (1) in respect of the property with their returns of income under this Part for their respective taxation years that include the particular time.

**Notes**: 16.1(2) amended by 1991 technical bill, retroactive to the introduction of the section (see Notes at end of 16.1).

**Forms**: T2146: Election in respect of assigned leases or subleased property.

**(3) Idem** — Subject to subsection (4), where at any particular time a lessee who has made an election under subsection (1) in respect of a leased property assigns the lease or subleases the property to another person with whom the lessee is not dealing at arm's length, the other person shall, for the purposes of subsection (1) and for the purposes of computing that person's income in respect of the lease for any period after the particular time, be deemed to be the same person as, and a continuation of, the lessee, except that, notwithstanding paragraph (1)(b), that other person shall be deemed to have acquired the property from the lessee at the time that it was acquired by the lessee at a cost equal to the amount that would be the lessee's proceeds of disposition of the property determined under paragraph (1)(f) if that amount were determined without reference to clauses (1)(f)(i)(B) and (ii)(B).

**(4) Amalgamations and windings-up** — Notwithstanding subsection (2), where at any time a particular corporation that has made an election under subsection (1) in respect of a lease assigns the lease

(a) by reason of an amalgamation (within the meaning assigned by subsection 87(1)), or

(b) in the course of the winding-up of a Canadian corporation in respect of which subsection 88(1) applies,

to another corporation with which it does not deal at arm's length, the other corporation shall, for the purposes of subsection (1) and for the purposes of computing its income in respect of the lease after that time, be deemed to be the same person as, and a continuation of, the particular corporation.

**(5) Replacement property** — For the purposes of subsection (1), where at any time a property (in this subsection referred to as a "replacement property") is provided by a lessor to a lessee as a replacement for a similar property of the lessor (in this subsection referred to as the "original property") that was leased by the lessor to the lessee, and the amount payable by the lessee for the use of, or the right to use, the replacement property is the same as the amount that was so payable in respect of the original property, the replacement property shall be deemed to be the same property as the original property.

**Notes**: 16.1(5) added by 1991 technical bill, retroactive to the introduction of the section (see Notes at end of 16.1).

**(6) Additional property** — For the purposes of subsection (1), where at any particular time

(a) an addition or alteration (in this subsection referred to as "additional property") is made by a lessor to a property (in this subsection referred to as the "original property") of the lessor that is the subject of a lease,

(b) the lessor and the lessee of the original property have jointly elected under subsection (1) in respect of the original property, and

(c) as a consequence of the addition or alteration, the total amount payable by the lessee for the use of, or the right to use, the original property and the additional property exceeds the amount so payable in respect of the original property,

the following rules apply:

(d) the lessee shall be deemed to have leased the additional property from the lessor at the particular time,

(e) the term of the lease of the additional property shall be deemed to be greater than one year,

(f) the lessor and the lessee shall be deemed to have jointly elected under subsection (1) in respect of the additional property,

(g) the prescribed rate in effect at the particular time in respect of the additional property shall be deemed to be equal to the prescribed rate in effect in respect of the original property at the particular time,

(h) the additional property shall be deemed not to be prescribed property, and

(i) the excess referred to in paragraph (c) shall be deemed to be an amount payable by the lessee for the use of, or the right to use, the additional property.

**Notes**: 16.1(6) added by 1991 technical bill, retroactive to the introduction of the section (see Notes at end of 16.1).

**Regulations**: 4301(c) (prescribed rate for 16.1(6)(g)); 4302 (prescribed rate for 16.1(6)(d).

**(7) Renegotiation of lease** — For the purposes of subsection (1), where at any time

(a) a lease (in this subsection referred to as the "original lease") of property is renegotiated in the course of a *bona fide* renegotiation, and

(b) as a result of the renegotiation, the amount payable by the lessee of the property for the use of, or the right to use, the property is altered in respect of a period after that time (otherwise than because of an addition or alteration to which subsection (6) applies),

the original lease shall be deemed to have expired and the renegotiated lease shall be deemed to be a new lease of the property entered into at that time.

**Related Provisions**: 16(1) — Income and capital combined; 20(1)(c) — Deductions permitted — interest.

**Notes**: 16.1 added by 1989 Budget, effective for leases and subleases entered into after 10 p.m. EDST, April 26, 1989, other than

(a) leases entered into pursuant to an agreement in writing entered into at or before 10 p.m. EDST, April 26, 1989 under which the lessee has the right to require the lease of the property, and

(b) subleases of properties that are subject to leases described in paragraph (a) or to leases entered into at or before 10 p.m. EDST, April 26, 1989.

16.1(5)–(7) added by 1991 technical bill, retroactive to the introduction of the section.

**Definitions [s. 16.1]**: "amount" — 248(1); "arm's length" — 251(1); "borrowed money", "business" — 248(1); "Canada" — 255; "depreciable property" — 13(21), 248(1); "lessee", "lessor" — 16.1(1); "non-resident" — 248(1); "permanent establishment" — Reg. 8201; "person", "prescribed" — 248(1); "prescribed rate" — Reg. 4301, 4302; "principal amount", "property" — 248(1); "resident in Canada" — 250; "taxable income" — 248(1); "taxation year" — 11(2), 249; "taxpayer" — 248(1).

**Regulations [s. 16.1]**: 4302 (prescribed interest rate); 8200 (prescribed property).

**17. (1) Amount owing by non-resident [deemed interest income]** — Where, at any time in a taxation year of a corporation resident in Canada, a non-resident person owes an amount to the corporation, that amount has been or remains outstanding for more than a year and the total determined under paragraph (b) for the year is less than the amount of interest that would be included in computing the corporation's income for the year in respect of the amount owing if that interest were computed at a reasonable rate for the period in the year during which the amount was owing, the corporation shall include an amount in computing its income for the year equal to the amount, if any, by which

(a) the amount of interest that would be included in computing the corporation's income for the year in respect of the amount owing if that interest were computed at the prescribed rate for the period in the year during which the amount was owing

exceeds

(b) the total of all amounts each of which is

(i) an amount included in computing the corporation's income for the year as, on account of, in lieu of or in satisfaction of, interest in respect of the amount owing,

(ii) an amount received or receivable by the corporation from a trust that is included in computing the corporation's income for the year or a subsequent year and that can reasonably be attributed to interest on the amount owing for the period in the year during which the amount was owing, or

(iii) an amount that is included in computing the corporation's income for the year or a subsequent year under subsection 91(1) and that can reasonably be attributed to interest on the amount owing for the period in the year during which the amount was owing.

**Related Provisions**: 17(2)–(6) — Anti-avoidance rules; 17(7)–(9) — Exceptions; 17(10)–(15) — Interpretation.

**Notes**: 17(1) amended by 1998 Budget, effective for taxation years that begin after February 23, 1998. However (per amendment made by the Commons Finance Committee before Third Reading), in its application to a taxation year that includes March 10, 1999, the amount determined under amended 17(1) is deemed to be the total of

(i) the amount that would have been determined under 17(1) if the taxation year had ended at the end of March 10, 1999 and 17(7) were read without everything from "except that..."; and

(ii) the amount that would have been determined under 17(1) if the taxation year had begun immediately after the end of March 10, 1999.

For earlier years, read:

**17. (1) Loan to non-resident** — Where a corporation resident in Canada has lent money to a non-resident person and the loan remained outstanding for one year or longer without interest on the loan computed at a reasonable rate having been included in computing the lender's income, the corporation shall be deemed to have received, on the last day of each taxation year during which the loan was outstanding, interest on the loan at the prescribed rate computed for the period in the taxation year during which it was outstanding.

For a detailed discussion of the new rules, see Penny Woolford-Marshall, "Amendments to Section 17", *International Tax Planning*, 47(3) *Canadian Tax Journal* 640-662 (1999); and Richard Tremblay, "Amendments to Section 17 Anti-Avoidance Rules", VIII(3) *International Tax Planning* (Federated Press) 573-578 (1999).

**Regulations**: 4301(c) (prescribed rate of interest for 17(1)(a)).

**(2) Anti-avoidance rule — indirect loan** — For the purpose of this section and subject to subsection (3), where

(a) a non-resident person owes an amount at any time to a particular person or partnership (other than a corporation resident in Canada), and

(b) it is reasonable to conclude that the particular person or partnership entered into the transaction under which the amount became owing or the particular person or partnership permitted the amount owing to remain outstanding because

(i) a corporation resident in Canada made a loan or transfer of property, or

(ii) the particular person or partnership anticipated that a corporation resident in Canada would make a loan or transfer of property,

either directly or indirectly, in any manner whatever, to or for the benefit of any person or partnership (other than an exempt loan or transfer),

the non-resident person is deemed at that time to owe to the corporation an amount equal to the amount owing to the particular person or partnership.

**Related Provisions**: 17(3) — Exception; 17(15)"exempt loan or transfer" — Definition.

**Notes**: 17(2) amended by 1998 Budget, effective for taxation years that begin after 1999. For earlier years, read:

(2) Exception — Subsection (1) does not apply if a tax has been paid on the amount of the loan under Part XIII.

**(3) Exception to anti-avoidance rule — indirect loan** — Subsection (2) does not apply to an amount owing at any time by a non-resident person to a particular person or partnership where

(a) at that time, the non-resident person and the particular person or each member of the particular partnership, as the case may be, are controlled foreign affiliates of the corporation resident in Canada; or

(b) at that time,

(i) the non-resident person and the particular person are not related or the non-resident person and each member of the particular partnership are not related, as the case may be,

(ii) the terms or conditions made or imposed in respect of the amount owing, determined without reference to any loan or transfer of property by a corporation resident in Canada described in paragraph (2)(b) in respect of the amount owing, are such that persons dealing at arm's length would have been willing to enter into them at the time that they were entered into, and

(iii) if there were an amount of interest payable on the amount owing at that time that would be required to be included in computing the income of a foreign affiliate of the corporation resident in Canada for a taxation year, that amount of interest would not be required to be included in computing the foreign accrual property income of the affiliate for that year.

**Related Provisions**: 17(10), (12), (13), (15) — Definition of "controlled foreign affiliate"; 17(11), (11.1) — Meaning of "related"; 17(11.2) — Back-to-back loans — look-through rule.

**Notes**: 17(3) amended by 1998 Budget, effective for taxation years that begin after 1999. For earlier years, read:

(3) Further exception — Subsection (1) does not apply if the loan was made to a subsidiary controlled corporation and it is established that the money that was lent was used in the subsidiary corporation's business for the purpose of gaining or producing income.

**(4) Anti-avoidance rule — loan through partnership** — For the purpose of this section, where a non-resident person owes an amount at any time to a partnership and subsection (2) does not deem the non-resident person to owe an amount equal to that amount to a corporation resident in Canada, the non-resident person is deemed at that time to owe to each member of the partnership, on the same terms as those that apply in respect of the amount owing to the partnership, that proportion of the amount owing to the partnership at that time that

(a) the fair market value of the member's interest in the partnership at that time

is of

(b) the fair market value of all interests in the partnership at that time.

**Notes**: 17(4) added by 1998 Budget, effective for taxation years that begin after February 23, 1998.

**(5) Anti-avoidance rule — loan through trust** — For the purpose of this section, where a non-resident person owes an amount at any time to a trust and subsection (2) does not deem the non-resident person to owe an amount equal to that amount to a corporation resident in Canada,

(a) where the trust is a non-discretionary trust at that time, the non-resident person is deemed at that time to owe to each beneficiary of the trust, on the same terms as those that apply in respect of the amount owing to the trust, that proportion of the amount owing to the trust that

(i) the fair market value of the beneficiary's interest in the trust at that time

is of

(ii) the fair market value of all the beneficial interests in the trust at that time; and

(b) in any other case, the non-resident person is deemed at that time to owe to each settlor in respect of the trust, on the same terms as those that apply in respect of the amount owing to the trust, an amount equal to the amount owing to the trust.

**Notes**: 17(5) added by 1998 Budget, effective for taxation years that begin after February 23, 1998.

**(6) Anti-avoidance rule — loan to partnership** — For the purpose of this section, where a particular partnership owes an amount at any time to any person or any other partnership (in this subsection referred to as the "lender"), each member of the particular partnership is deemed to owe at that time to the lender, on the same terms as those that apply in respect of the amount owing by the particular partnership to the lender, that proportion of the amount owing to the lender that

(a) the fair market value of the member's interest in the particular partnership at that time

is of

(b) the fair market value of all interests in the particular partnership at that time.

**Notes**: 17(6) added by 1998 Budget, effective for taxation years that begin after February 23, 1998.

**(7) Exception** — Subsection (1) does not apply in respect of an amount owing to a corporation resident in Canada by a non-resident person if a tax has been paid under Part XIII on the amount owing, except that, for the purpose of this subsection, tax under Part XIII is deemed not to have been paid on that portion of the amount owing in respect of which an amount was repaid or applied under subsection 227(6.1).

**Notes**: 17(7) added by 1998 Budget, effective for taxation years that begin after February 23, 1998. However (per amendment made by the Commons Finance Committee before Third Reading), in its application to such a taxation year that ends before March 10, 1999, ignore everything from "except that...".

**(8) Exception** — Subsection (1) does not apply to a corporation resident in Canada for a taxation year of the corporation in respect of an amount owing to the corporation by a non-resident person if the non-resident person is a controlled foreign affiliate of the corporation throughout the period in the year during which the amount is owing and it is established that the amount owing

(a) arose as a loan or advance of money to the affiliate that the affiliate has used, throughout the period that began when the loan or advance was made and that ended at the earlier of the end of the year and the time at which the amount was repaid,

(i) for the purpose of earning

(A) income from an active business, as defined in subsection 95(1), of the affiliate, or

(B) income that was included in computing the income from an active business of the affiliate under subsection 95(2), or

(ii) for the purpose of making a loan or advance to another controlled foreign affiliate of the corporation where, if interest became payable on the loan or advance at any time in the period and the affiliate was required to include the interest in computing its income for a taxation year, that interest would not be required to be included in computing the affiliate's foreign accrual property income for that year; or

(b) arose in the course of an active business, as defined in subsection 95(1), carried on by the affiliate throughout the period that began when the amount owing arose and that ended at the earlier of the end of the year and the time at which the amount was repaid.

**Related Provisions**: 17(10), (12), (13), (15) — Definition of "controlled foreign affiliate"; 212(1)(b) — Part XIII (withholding) tax on interest payments to non-resident; 247(7) — Loan described in 17(3) not subject to transfer pricing rules.

**Notes**: 17(8) added by 1998 Budget, effective for taxation years that begin after February 23, 1998.

**(9) Exception** — Subsection (1) does not apply to a corporation resident in Canada for a taxation year of the corporation in respect of an amount owing to the corporation by a non-resident person if

(a) the corporation is not related to the non-resident person throughout the period in the year during which the amount owing is outstanding;

(b) the amount owing arose in respect of goods sold or services provided to the non-resident person by the corporation in the ordinary course of the business carried on by the corporation; and

(c) the terms and conditions in respect of the amount owing are such that persons dealing at arm's length would have been willing to enter into them at the time that they were entered into.

**Related Provisions**: 17(10), (12), (15) — Definition of "controlled foreign affiliate"; 17(11), (11.1) — Meaning of "related".

**Notes**: 17(9) added by 1998 Budget, effective for taxation years that begin after February 23, 1998.

**(10) Determination of whether related and controlled foreign affiliate status** — For the purpose of this section, in determining whether persons are related to each other and whether a non-resident corporation is a controlled foreign affiliate of a corporation resident in Canada at any time,

(a) each member of a partnership is deemed to own that proportion of the number of shares of a class of the capital stock of a corporation owned by the partnership at that time that

(i) the fair market value of the member's interest in the partnership at that time

is of

(ii) the fair market value of all interests in the partnership at that time; and

(b) each beneficiary of a non-discretionary trust is deemed to own that proportion of the number of shares of a class of the capital stock of a corporation owned by the trust at that time that

    (i) the fair market value of the beneficiary's interest in the trust at that time

is of

    (ii) the fair market value of all the beneficial interests in the trust at that time.

**Related Provisions**: 17(12), (13) — Determination of controlled foreign affiliate status.

**Notes**: 17(10) added by 1998 Budget, effective for taxation years that begin after February 23, 1998.

**(11) Determination of whether related** — For the purpose of this section, in determining whether persons are related to each other at any time, each settlor in respect of a trust, other than a non-discretionary trust, is deemed to own the shares of a class of the capital stock of a corporation owned by the trust at that time.

**Related Provisions**: 17(11.1) — Limitation on meaning of "related".

**Notes**: 17(11) added by 1998 Budget, effective for taxation years that begin after February 23, 1998.

### Proposed Addition — 17(11.1)

**(11.1) Determination of whether persons related** — For the purpose of this section, in determining whether persons are related to each other at any time, any rights referred to in subparagraph 251(5)(b)(i) that exist at that time are deemed not to exist at that time to the extent that the exercise of those rights is prohibited at that time under a law, of the country under the law of which the corporation was formed or last continued and is governed, that restricts the foreign ownership or control of the corporation.

**(11.2) Back-to-back loans** — For the purposes of paragraph (3)(b), where a non-resident person, or a partnership each member of which is non-resident, (in this subsection referred to as the "intermediate lender") makes a loan to a non-resident person, or a partnership each member of which is non-resident, (in this subsection referred to as the "intended borrower") because the intermediate lender received a loan from another non-resident person, or a partnership each member of which is non-resident, (in this subsection referred to as the "initial lender"), the loan that was made by the intermediate lender to the intended borrower is deemed to have been made by the initial lender (and not by the intermediate lender) to the intended borrower (to the extent of the lesser of the amount of the loan made by the initial lender to the intermediate lender and the amount of the loan made by the intermediate lender to the intended borrower) under the same terms and conditions and at the same time as it was made by the intermediate lender.

**Application**: Bill C-43 (First Reading September 20, 2000), subsec. 6(1), will add subsecs. 17(11.1) and (11.2), applicable to taxation years that begin after February 23, 1998.

**Technical Notes**: Section 17 generally applies where a corporation resident in Canada has lent money to a non-resident and that loan remained outstanding for one year or longer without the corporation including interest on the loan, computed at a reasonable rate, in computing its income. Where subsection 17(1) applies, it treats the corporation as having received interest on the loan, computed at a prescribed rate, at the end of each taxation year during which the loan was outstanding.

Subsection 17(9) provides an exception to section 17 where the corporation resident in Canada and the non-resident are unrelated and various other conditions are met. Similarly, paragraph 17(3)(b) provides an exception in the case of an indirect loan to which section 17 would otherwise apply if the parties to the indirect loan are unrelated and various other conditions are met. In determining whether a person is related to a corporation, subparagraph 251(5)(b)(i) provides that a taxpayer that has a right to, or to acquire, some shares of the corporation is deemed to own those shares.

New subsection 17(11.1) provides that, in determining whether two persons are related to each other for the purpose of section 17, certain rights referred to in paragraph 251(5)(b) of the Act, such as rights to acquire shares of the capital stock of a corporation, are to be ignored to the extent that, under the laws of the country in which the corporation was formed or last continued or exists that govern foreign ownership or control of the corporation, the holder of the rights is prohibited from exercising the rights.

New subsection 17(11.2) provides a rule for back-to-back loans that is to apply for the purpose of paragraph 17(3)(b) of the Act. Where an initial lender makes a loan to an intermediate lender and that intermediate lender loans funds to the intended borrower because of that loan by the initial lender, the loan by the intermediate lender to the intended borrower is deemed to have been made by the initial lender and not by the intermediate lender to the extent of the loan made by the initial lender and under the terms and conditions established by the intermediate lender and the intended borrower.

These amendments to subsections 17(11.1) and (11.2) apply to taxation years that begin after February 23, 1998.

**(12) Determination of controlled foreign affiliate status** — For the purpose of this section, in determining whether a non-resident person is a controlled foreign affiliate of a corporation resident in Canada at any time, each settlor in respect of a trust, other than a non-discretionary trust, is deemed to own that proportion of the number of shares of a class of the capital stock of a corporation owned by the trust at that time that one is of the number of settlors in respect of the trust at that time.

**Notes**: 17(12) added by 1998 Budget, effective for taxation years that begin after February 23, 1998.

**(13) Extended definition of controlled foreign affiliate** — For the purpose of this section, where, at any time, two corporations resident in Canada are related (otherwise than because of a right referred to in paragraph 251(5)(b)), any corporation that is a controlled foreign affiliate of one of the corporations at that time is deemed to be a controlled foreign affiliate of the other corporation at that time.

**(14) Anti-avoidance rule — where rights or shares issued, acquired or disposed of to avoid tax** — For the purpose of this section,

(a) where any person or partnership has a right under a contract, in equity or otherwise, either immediately or in the future and either absolutely or contingently, to, or to acquire, shares of the capital stock of a corporation and it can reasonably be considered that the principal purpose for the existence of the right is to avoid or reduce the amount of income that subsection (1) would otherwise require any corporation to include in computing its income for any taxation year, those shares are deemed to be owned by that person or partnership; and

(b) where any person or partnership acquires or disposes of shares of the capital stock of a corporation, either directly or indirectly, and it can reasonably be considered that the principal purpose for the acquisition or disposition of the shares is to avoid or reduce the amount of income that subsection (1) would otherwise require any corporation to include in computing its income for any taxation year, those shares are deemed not to have been acquired or disposed of, as the case may be, and where the shares were unissued by the corporation immediately before the acquisition, those shares are deemed not to have been issued.

**Related Provisions**: 95(6) — Similar rule re foreign accrual property income.

**Notes**: 17(14) added by 1998 Budget, effective for taxation years that begin after February 23, 1998.

**(15) Definitions** — The definitions in this subsection apply in this section.

**"controlled foreign affiliate"** has the meaning that would be assigned by the definition "controlled foreign affiliate" in subsection 95(1) if paragraphs (d) and (e) of that definition read as follows:

"(d) one or more persons resident in Canada with whom the taxpayer does not deal at arm's length, or

(e) the taxpayer and one or more persons resident in Canada with whom the taxpayer does not deal at arm's length".

**Proposed Amendment —
17(15) "controlled foreign affiliate"**

**"controlled foreign affiliate"** has the meaning that would be assigned by the definition "controlled foreign affiliate" in subsection 95(1) if this Act were read without reference to subsection 94.1(12) and if paragraphs (d) and (e) of that definition read as follows:

"(d) one or more persons resident in Canada with whom the taxpayer does not deal at arm's length, or

(e) the taxpayer and one or more persons resident in Canada with whom the taxpayer does not deal at arm's length."

**Application**: The June 22, 2000 draft legislation, s. 2, will amend the definition "controlled foreign affiliate" in subsec. 17(15) to read as above, applicable after 2000.

**Technical Notes**: Subsection 17(15) defines expressions that apply for the purposes of section 17, which provides rules under which imputed interest, in connection with debt owing to a taxpayer from a non-resident person, is included in computing the taxpayer's income. The expression "controlled foreign affiliate" is defined to have the same meaning as it does under subsection 95(1) of the Act, except that for the purpose of section 17 a non-resident corporation must be controlled by Canadian residents in order to be treated as a controlled foreign affiliate of a taxpayer resident in Canada.

The definition "controlled foreign affiliate" in subsection 17(15) is amended so that new subsection 94.1(12) does not apply for the purposes of section 17. Under that new subsection, an election is available so that a foreign affiliate of a taxpayer is treated as a controlled foreign affiliate of the taxpayer.

This amendment applies after 2000.

**Related Provisions**: 17(9) — Rules for determining CFA status; 17(10), (12), (13) — Extended meaning of controlled foreign affiliate.

**Notes**: Definition "controlled foreign affiliate" added by 1998 Budget, effective for taxation years that begin after February 23, 1998.

**"exempt loan or transfer"** means a loan or transfer of property made by a corporation to a person or a partnership where

(a) at the time of the loan or transfer, the corporation was not related to the person or to any member of the partnership, as the case may be;

(b) the loan or transfer of property was not part of a series of transactions or events at the end of which the corporation was related to the person or to any member of the partnership, as the case may be; and

(c) the terms and conditions of the loan or transfer (determined without reference to any other loan or transfer of property to either a person related to the corporation or a partnership any member of which was related to the corporation) are such that persons dealing at arm's length would have been willing to enter into them at the time that they were entered into.

### Proposed Amendment — 17(15) "exempt loan or transfer"

**"exempt loan or transfer"** means

(a) a loan or transfer of property made by a corporation to a person or partnership where

(i) at the time of the loan or transfer, the corporation was not related to the person or to any member of the partnership, as the case may be,

(ii) the loan or transfer of property was not part of a series of transactions or events at the end of which the corporation was related to the person or to any member of the partnership, as the case may be, and

(iii) the terms and conditions of the loan or transfer (determined without reference to any other loan or transfer of property to either a person related to the corporation or to a partnership any member of which was related to the corporation) are such that persons dealing at arm's length would have been willing to enter into them at the time that they were entered into;

(b) a dividend paid by a corporation resident in Canada on shares of a class of its capital stock; and

(c) a payment made by a corporation resident in Canada on a reduction of the paid-up capital in respect of shares of a class of its capital stock (not exceeding the total amount of the reduction).

**Application**: Bill C-43 (First Reading September 20, 2000), subsec. 6(2), will amend the definition "exempt loan or transfer" in subsec. 17(15) to read as above, applicable to taxation years that begin after February 23, 1998.

**Technical Notes**: Subsection 17(15) contains definitions that apply for the purposes of section 17, including the definition "exempt loan or transfer" which is relevant for the purpose of subsection 17(2). Subsection 17(2) does not apply to an exempt loan or transfer of property.

The definition "exempt loan or transfer" is amended to include a transfer of property by a corporation resident in Canada by way of the payment of a dividend to a shareholder or the reduction of the paid-up capital of shares of the corporation.

This amendment applies to taxation years that begin after February 23, 1998.

### Letter from Department of Finance, March 20, 2000:

Dear [xxx]

I am responding to your letter of February 29, 2000, in which you are requesting confirmation that we are prepared to recommend to the Minister of Finance that section 17 of the *Income Tax Act* ("the Act") be amended.

The amendment that you are seeking would ensure that a payment of a dividend or a return of capital by a Canadian corporation to its foreign parent would not be considered a loan or transfer of property for the purposes of subsection 17(2) of the Act. In particular, you suggested that the definition of "exempt loan or transfer" in subsection 17(15) of the Act could be amended to achieve this result.

It was not intended that a loan or transfer of property for the purposes of subsection 17(2) of the Act include dividends or returns of capital paid by a Canadian corporation to its foreign parent. Therefore, we are prepared to recommend to the Minister of Finance that the definition of "exempt loan or transfer" in subsection 17(15) of the Act be amended. That definition would be amended to include dividend payments by a Canadian corporation that are subject to tax under Part XIII and return of capital payments by a Canadian corporation that reduce the paid-up capital of the shares of the corporation. It will be recommended that the amendment apply to taxation years that begin after 1999.

I trust that this letter addresses your concerns. Thank you for bringing this matter to our attention.

Yours sincerely,

Len Farber
General Director, Tax Legislation Division, Tax Policy Branch

**Notes**: Definition "exempt loan or transfer" added by 1998 Budget, effective for taxation years that begin after February 23, 1998.

**"non-discretionary trust"**, at any time, means a trust in which all interests were vested indefeasibly at the beginning of the trust's taxation year that includes that time.

**Related Provisions**: 248(1) "non-discretionary trust" — Definition applies to entire Act; 248(9.2) — Meaning of "vested indefeasibly".

**Notes**: Definition "non-discretionary trust" added by 1998 Budget, effective for taxation years that begin after February 23, 1998.

**"settlor"** in respect of a trust at any time means any person or partnership that has made a loan or transfer of property, either directly or indirectly, in any manner whatever, to or for the benefit of the trust at or before that time, other than, where the person or partnership deals at arm's length with the trust at that time,

(a) a loan made by the person or partnership to the trust at a reasonable rate of interest; or

(b) a transfer made by the person or partnership to the trust for fair market value consideration.

**Notes**: Definition "settlor" added by 1998 Budget, effective for taxation years that begin after February 23, 1998.

This definition is much broader than the definition of "settlor" in 108(1), which applies for the rules on the taxation of trusts.

**Definitions**: "active business", "amount" — 248(1); "arm's length" — 251(1); "business" — 248(1); "Canada" — 255; "class" — 248(6); "controlled foreign affiliate" — 17(10), (12), (13), (15); "corporation" — 248(1), *Interpretation Act* 35(1); "disposition", "dividend" — 248(1); "exempt loan or transfer" — 17(15); "foreign accrual property income" — 95(1), (2), 248(1); "foreign affiliate" — 95(1), 248(1); "non-discretionary trust" — 17(15), 248(1); "non-resident" — 248(1); "paid-up capital" — 89(1), 248(1); "partnership" — see Notes to 96(1); "person", "prescribed" — 248(1); "prescribed rate" — Reg. 4301; "property" — 248(1); "related" — 17(10), (11), (11.1), 251(2)–(6); "resident", "resident in Canada" — 250; "settlor" — 17(15); "share" — 248(1); "taxation year" — 249; "taxpayer" — 248(1); "trust" — 104(1), 248(1), (3); "vested indefeasibly" — 248(9.2).

## Deductions

### 18. (1) General limitations — In computing the income of a taxpayer from a business or property no deduction shall be made in respect of

(a) **general limitation** — an outlay or expense except to the extent that it was made or incurred by the taxpayer for the purpose of gaining or producing income from the business or property;

**Related Provisions**: 7(3)(b) — No deduction to employer for cost of issuing stock options to employees; 18(1)(c) — Limitation re exempt income; 18(9) — Limitation re prepaid expenses; 19, 19.01, 19.1 — Limitations on deductions for advertising expenses; 20(1) — Deductions permitted; 20(16) — Terminal loss; 20.01 — Deduction allowed for private health services plan premiums; 21(1) — Cost of borrowed money; 67 — Unreasonable expenses not allowed; 67.1 — 50% limit on expenses for food and entertainment; Reg. 1102(1)(c) — No CCA unless property acquired for purpose of gaining or producing income.

**Notes**: For discussion of denial of losses on the grounds of no "reasonable expectation of profit", see Notes to 18(1)(h).

**Interpretation Bulletins**: IT-80: Interest on money borrowed to redeem shares, or to pay dividends; IT-99R5: Legal and accounting fees; IT-104R2: Deductibility of fines or penalties; IT-153R3: Land developers — subdivision and development costs and carrying charges on land; IT-185R: Losses from theft, defalcation or embezzlement; IT-211R: Membership dues — associations and societies; IT-223: Overhead expense insurance vs. income insurance; IT-233R: Lease-option agreements; sale-leaseback agreements; IT-261R: Prepayment of rents; IT-265R3: Payments of income and capital combined; IT-316: Awards for employees' suggestions and inventions; IT-339R2: Meaning of "private health services plan"; IT-341R3: Expenses of issuing or selling shares, units in a trust, interests in a partnership or syndicate, and expenses of borrowing money; IT-348R: Costs incurred in conversion to metric measurement; IT-364: Commencement of business operations; IT-373R: Farm woodlots and tree farms; IT-389R: Vacation-with-pay plans established under collective agreements; IT-461: Forfeited deposits; IT-467R: Damages, settlements and similar payments; IT-475: Expenditures on research and for business expansion; IT-487: General limitation on deduction of outlays or expenses; IT-521R: Motor vehicle expenses claimed by self-employed individuals; IT-525R: Performing artists.

**Information Circulars**: 77-11: Sales tax reassessments.

**I.T. Technical News**: No. 12 (meals and beverages at golf clubs); No. 16 (*Tonn, Mastri, Mohammad* and *Kaye* cases; *Scott* case).

**Advance Tax Rulings**: ATR-4: Exchange of interest rates; ATR-20: Redemption premium on debentures; ATR-21: Pension benefit from an unregistered pension plan; ATR-23: Private health services plan; ATR-45: Share appreciation rights plan; ATR-50: Structured settlement.

**Forms**: T2032: Statement of professional activities; T2124: Statement of business activities.

(b) **capital outlay or loss** — an outlay, loss or replacement of capital, a payment on account of capital or an allowance in respect of depreciation, obsolescence or depletion except as expressly permitted by this Part;

**Related Provisions**: 14(5) "eligible capital expenditure" — Definition includes amounts deductible under 20(1)(b); 20(1) — Deductions permitted; 20(10) — Convention expenses; 20(16) — Terminal loss; 24(1) — Ceasing to carry on business; 26(2) — Banks; 30 — Clearing land, levelling land and laying tile drainage; 37(1)(b) — Deductible R&D expenditures on capital.

**Notes**: Capital expenses are not deductible; instead, they are included in the cost of the property for capital gains calculation purposes (39(1)(a)), and, for depreciable property, for capital cost allowance (20(1)(a)).

The distinction between capital and current expenses is not always obvious; for a detailed discussion in the context of buildings, see John Durnford, "The Deductibility of Building Repair and Renovation Costs", 45(3) *Canadian Tax Journal* 395-416 (1997). See also *Canderel Ltd.*, [1998] 2 C.T.C. 35 (SCC); *Toronto College Park Ltd.*, [1998] 2 C.T.C. 78 (SCC); *Johns-Manville Canada Inc.*, [1985] 2 C.T.C. 111 (FCA); and *Central Amusement Ltd.*, [1992] 1 C.T.C. 218 (FCTD).

See also Notes to 54 "capital property".

**Interpretation Bulletins**: IT-104R2: Deductibility of fines or penalties; IT-143R2: Meaning of "eligible capital expenditure"; IT-187: Purchase of customer lists and ledger accounts; IT-233R: Lease-option agreements; sale-leaseback agreements; IT-261R: Prepayment of rents; IT-285R2: Capital cost allowance — general comments; IT-341R3: Expenses of issuing or selling shares, units in a trust, interests in a partnership or syndicate, and expenses of borrowing money; IT-357R2: Expenses of training; IT-364: Commencement of business operations; IT-467R: Damages, settlements and similar payments; IT-475: Expenditures on research and for business expansion.

**I.T. Technical News**: No. 5 (lease agreements).

**Advance Tax Rulings**: ATR-20: Redemption premium on debentures; ATR-50: Structured settlement; ATR-59: Financing exploration and development through limited partnerships.

(c) **limitation re exempt income** — an outlay or expense to the extent that it may reasonably be regarded as having been made or incurred for the purpose of gaining or producing exempt income or in connection with property the income from which would be exempt;

**Related Provisions**: 81(1) — Exempt income; 248(1) "exempt income" — Definition excludes dividends and support amounts.

**Interpretation Bulletins**: IT-341R3: Expenses of issuing or selling shares, units in a trust, interests in a partnership or syndicate, and expenses of borrowing money; IT-467R: Damages, settlements and similar payments.

(d) **annual value of property** — the annual value of property except rent for property leased by the taxpayer for use in the taxpayer's business;

**Related Provisions**: 20(1)(a) — Deduction for capital cost allowance.

(e) **reserves, etc.** — an amount as, or on account of, a reserve, a contingent liability or amount or a sinking fund except as expressly permitted by this Part;

**Related Provisions**: 20(1)(l), (l.1), (m), (m.1), (n), (o) — Reserves specifically allowed; 20(7)(c) — Policy reserves for insurance corporations; 20(26) — Deduction for unpaid claims reserve adjustment; 40(1)(a)(iii) — Capital gains reserve; 61.2–61.4 — Reserves re forgiven debt included in income; 138(3)(a)(ii) — Reserves in respect of life insurance claims; 248(1) — "Insurance policy" includes life insurance policy.

**Notes**: In *Canadian Pacific Ltd. v. Ontario (Min. of Revenue)*, [2000] 2 C.T.C. 331 (Ont. CA), a deferred liability account set up to provide for workers' compensation liabilities was held to be deductible and not "contingent" under 18(1)(e) (in its application under the Ontario *Corporations Tax Act*).

**Interpretation Bulletins**: IT-109R2: Unpaid amounts; IT-215R: Reserves, contingent accounts and sinking funds; IT-321R: Insurance agents and brokers — unearned commissions; IT-442R: Bad debts and reserves for doubtful debts; IT-467R: Damages, settlements and similar payments; IT-518R: Food, beverages and entertainment expenses.

**Advance Tax Rulings**: ATR-50: Structured settlement.

(e.1) **unpaid claims under insurance policies** — an amount in respect of claims that were received by an insurer before the end of the year under insurance policies and that are unpaid at the end of the year, except as expressly permitted by this Part;

**Related Provisions**: 20(7)(c) — Policy reserves for insurance corporations; 20(26) — Deduction for unpaid claims reserve adjustment; 138(3)(a)(ii) — Reserves in respect of life insurance claims.

(f) **payments on discounted bonds** — an amount paid or payable as or on account of the principal amount of any obligation described in paragraph 20(1)(f) except as expressly permitted by that paragraph;

**Interpretation Bulletins**: IT-341R3: Expenses of issuing or selling shares, units in a trust, interests in a partnership or syndicate, and expenses of borrowing money; IT-518R: Food, beverages and entertainment expenses.

(g) **payments on income bonds** — an amount paid by a corporation as interest or otherwise to holders of its income bonds or income debentures unless the bonds or debentures have been issued or the income provisions thereof have been adopted since 1930

(i) to afford relief to the debtor from financial difficulties, and

(ii) in place of or as an amendment to bonds or debentures that at the end of 1930 provided unconditionally for a fixed rate of interest;

**Related Provisions**: 15(3), (4) — Interest or dividend on income bond or debenture; 15.1(2)(a), 15.2(2)(a) — Parallel rules for small business development bonds and small business bonds.

**Interpretation Bulletins**: IT-52R4: Income bonds and debentures; IT-518R: Food, beverages and entertainment expenses.

(h) **personal and living expenses** — personal or living expenses of the taxpayer, other than travel expenses incurred by the taxpayer while away from home in the course of carrying on the taxpayer's business;

**Related Provisions**: 20(1) — Deductions permitted; 20(16) — Terminal loss; 20.01 — Deduction allowed for private health services plan premiums; 56(1)(o)(i) — No deduction for personal or living expenses against research grant income; 67 — Unreasonable expenses not allowed; 67.1 — 50% limit on expenses for food and entertainment; 248(1)"personal or living expenses" — Reasonable expectation of profit required.

**Notes**: The definition of "personal or living expenses" in 248(1) effectively allows 18(1)(h) to be used to deny deductions for expenses of a business where there is no "reasonable expectation of profit" (REOP). See *Moldowan*, [1977] C.T.C. 310 (SCC). The Federal Court of Appeal ruled in *Tonn*, [1996] 1 C.T.C. 205 that where there is no personal element or tax sheltering sought, the loss was deductible. However, in *Mastri*, [1997] 3 C.T.C. 234, the Court came to more or less the opposite conclusion. Note also that unreasonable expenses can be disallowed under s. 67; but see *Mohammad*, [1997] 3 C.T.C. 321 (FCA). In *Kuhlmann*, [1999] 1 C.T.C. 38 (FCA), the Court noted that for an expectation of profit to be unreasonable, it had to be "irrational, absurd and ridiculous". In *Walls and Buvyer*, [2000] 1 C.T.C. 324 (FCA), the Court ruled that the REOP concept does not apply unless there is a personal element to the activity. The Supreme Court of Canada has granted leave to appeal both this case and *Stewart*, [2000] 2 C.T.C. 244 (FCA), also dealing with REOP (Sept. 14/00, files 27724 and 27860).

For a detailed discussion see Brian Nichols, "Chants and Ritual Incantations: Rethinking the Reasonable Expectation of Profit Test", 1996 Canadian Tax Foundation annual conference report, 28:1–28:48.

The CCRA acknowledges that "if there is no personal or non-business motivation behind the losses, the reasonable expectation of profit test will be applied less rigorously" (Income Tax Technical News No. 16).

The Supreme Court of Canada ruled in *Symes*, [1994] 1 C.T.C. 40, that child-care expenses were not deductible as business expenses even though they were required to enable the taxpayer to earn business income. However, in *Scott*, [1998] 4 C.T.C. 103 (FCA), a foot courier was allowed extra food needed as "fuel" for his body.

**Interpretation Bulletins**: IT-143R2: Meaning of "eligible capital expenditure"; IT-223: Overhead expense insurance vs. income insurance; IT-322R: Farm losses; IT-334R2: Miscellaneous receipts; IT-341R3: Expenses of issuing or selling shares, units in a trust, interests in a partnership or syndicate, and expenses of borrowing money; IT-357R2: Expenses of training; IT-373R: Farm woodlots and tree farms; IT-518R: Food, beverages and entertainment expenses; IT-521R: Motor vehicle expenses claimed by self-employed individuals.

**I.T. Technical News**: No. 16 (*Tonn*, *Mastri*, *Mohammad* and *Kaye* cases; *Scott* case).

**Forms**: T2032: Statement of professional activities; T2124: Statement of business activities.

(i) **limitation re employer's contribution under supplementary unemployment benefit plan** — an amount paid by an employer to a trustee under a supplementary unemployment benefit plan except as permitted by section 145;

**Related Provisions**: 20(1)(x), 145(5) — Employer's contribution to supplementary unemployment benefit plan deductible.

(j) **limitation re employer's contribution under deferred profit sharing plan** — an amount paid by an employer to a trustee under a deferred profit sharing plan except as expressly permitted by section 147;

**Related Provisions**: 147(8) — Employer's DPSP contribution deductible.

(k) **limitation re employer's contribution under profit sharing plan** — an amount paid by an employer to a trustee under a profit sharing plan that is not

(i) an employees profit sharing plan,

(ii) a deferred profit sharing plan, or

(iii) a registered pension plan;

**Interpretation Bulletins**: IT-502: Employee benefit plans and employee trusts.

(l) **use of recreational facilities and club dues** — an outlay or expense made or incurred by the taxpayer after 1971,

(i) for the use or maintenance of property that is a yacht, a camp, a lodge or a golf course or facility, unless the taxpayer made or incurred the outlay or expense in the ordinary course of the taxpayer's business of providing the property for hire or reward, or

Subdivision b — Income or Loss from a Business or Property    S. 18(1)(o)

(ii) as membership fees or dues (whether initiation fees or otherwise) in any club the main purpose of which is to provide dining, recreational or sporting facilities for its members;

**Related Provisions**: 8(1)(f)(vi) — Salesman's expenses.

**Interpretation Bulletins**: IT-148R3: Recreational properties and club dues; IT-211R: Membership dues — Associations and societies; IT-470R: Employees' fringe benefits.

**I.T. Technical News**: No. 12 (meals and beverages at golf clubs).

(l.1) *Petroleum and Gas Revenue Tax Act payments* — any amount paid or that became payable in the year to Her Majesty in right of Canada by virtue of an obligation imposed under the *Petroleum and Gas Revenue Tax Act*;

**Related Provisions**: 53(1)(e)(i)(A.1), 53(2)(c)(i)(A.1) — Adjustments to cost base of partnership interest; 104(29) — Flow-through from trust to beneficiaries; 208 — Tax on certain royalties payable by tax-exempt person; 219(1)(k) — Reduction in branch tax.

(m) **royalties, etc.** — any amount (other than a prescribed amount) paid or payable by virtue of an obligation imposed by statute or a contractual obligation substituted for an obligation imposed by statute to

(i) Her Majesty in right of Canada or a province,

(ii) an agent of Her Majesty in right of Canada or a province, or

(iii) a corporation, commission or association that is controlled by Her Majesty in right of Canada or a province or by an agent of Her Majesty in right of Canada or a province

as a royalty, tax (other than a tax or portion of a tax that can reasonably be considered to be a municipal or school tax), lease rental or bonus or as an amount, however described, that can reasonably be regarded as being in lieu of any such amount, or in respect of the late payment or non-payment of any such amount, and that can reasonably be regarded as being in relation to

(iv) the acquisition, development or ownership of a Canadian resource property, or

(v) the production in Canada

(A) of petroleum, natural gas or related hydrocarbons from a natural accumulation of petroleum or natural gas (other than a mineral resource) located in Canada or from an oil or gas well located in Canada,

(B) of sulphur from a natural accumulation of petroleum or natural gas located in Canada, from an oil or gas well located in Canada or from a mineral resource located in Canada,

(C) to any stage that is not beyond the prime metal stage or its equivalent, of metal, minerals (other than iron or petroleum or related hydrocarbons) or coal from a mineral resource located in Canada,

(D) to any stage that is not beyond the pellet stage or its equivalent, of iron from a mineral resource located in Canada, or

(E) to any stage that is not beyond the crude oil stage or its equivalent, of petroleum or related hydrocarbons from tar sands from a mineral resource located in Canada;

**Related Provisions**: 12(1)(o) — Royalties, etc., to be included in income; 66.2(5)"Canadian development expense"(e); 66.4(5)"Canadian oil and gas property expense"(a); 80.2 — Reimbursement by taxpayer; 104(29) — Flow-through from trust to beneficiaries; 208 — Tax on certain royalties payable by tax-exempt person; 219(1)(k) — Reduction in branch tax; *Interpretation Act* 8(2.1), (2.2) — Application to exclusive economic zone and continental shelf.

**Notes**: Everything after 18(1)(m)(iii) amended by 1996 Budget, effective for taxation years that begin after 1996. See Notes to the parallel amendments in 12(1)(o). For earlier taxation years since 1989, read:

as a royalty, tax (other than a tax or portion of a tax that may reasonably be considered to be a municipal or school tax), lease rental or bonus or as an amount, however described, that may reasonably be regarded as being in lieu of any such amount, and that may reasonably be regarded as being in relation to

(iv) the acquisition, development or ownership of a Canadian resource property, or

(v) the production in Canada of

(A) petroleum, natural gas or related hydrocarbons from a natural accumulation of petroleum or natural gas in Canada, other than a mineral resource, or from an oil or gas well in Canada,

(B) metal, minerals (other than iron or petroleum or related hydrocarbons) or coal from a mineral resource in Canada to any stage that is not beyond the prime metal stage or its equivalent,

(C) iron from a mineral resource in Canada to any stage that is not beyond the pellet stage or its equivalent, or

(D) petroleum or related hydrocarbons from tar sands from a mineral resource in Canada to any stage that is not beyond the crude oil stage or its equivalent;

Reference to coal in 18(1)(m)(v)(B) [now 18(1)(m)(v)(C)] added by 1991 technical bill, effective for amounts payable after July 13, 1990.

**Regulations**: 1211 (prescribed amounts).

**Remission Orders**: *Syncrude Remission Order*, P.C. 1976-1026 (remission of tax on royalties etc. relating to the Syncrude Project).

**Interpretation Bulletins**: IT-438R2: Crown charges — resource properties in Canada.

**Information Circulars**: 86-3: Alberta Royalty Tax Credit — Individuals.

(n) **political contributions** — a political contribution;

**Related Provisions**: 127(3) — Tax credit for contributions to registered parties and candidates.

(o) **employee benefit plan contributions** — an amount paid or payable as a contribution to an employee benefit plan;

**Related Provisions**: 6(1)(a)(ii), 6(1)(g) — Employee benefit plan benefits taxable to employee; 12(1)(n.1) — Income inclusion — amounts received by employer from employee benefit plan;

18(10) — Exceptions where para. 18(1)(o) does not apply; 32.1 — Employee benefit plan deductions; 107.1 — Distribution by employee benefit plan.

**Interpretation Bulletins**: IT-502: Employee benefit plans and employee trusts.

**(o.1) salary deferral arrangement** — except as expressly permitted by paragraphs 20(1)(oo) and (pp), an outlay or expense made or incurred under a salary deferral arrangement in respect of another person, other than such an arrangement established primarily for the benefit of one or more non-resident employees in respect of services to be rendered outside Canada;

**Related Provisions**: 6(1)(a)(v) — Value of benefits; 6(1)(i), 56(1)(w) — Salary deferral arrangements — amounts included in income.

**Notes**: 18(1)(o.1) amended by 1991 technical bill, retroactive to 1986, to add reference to 20(1)(pp) and to change "in a country other than Canada" to "outside Canada".

**(o.2) retirement compensation arrangement** — except as expressly permitted by paragraph 20(1)(r), contributions made under a retirement compensation arrangement;

**(p) limitation re personal services business expenses** — an outlay or expense to the extent that it was made or incurred by a corporation in a taxation year for the purpose of gaining or producing income from a personal services business, other than

(i) the salary, wages or other remuneration paid in the year to an incorporated employee of the corporation,

(ii) the cost to the corporation of any benefit or allowance provided to an incorporated employee in the year,

(iii) any amount expended by the corporation in connection with the selling of property or the negotiating of contracts by the corporation if the amount would have been deductible in computing the income of an incorporated employee for a taxation year from an office or employment if the amount had been expended by the incorporated employee under a contract of employment that required the employee to pay the amount, and

(iv) any amount paid by the corporation in the year as or on account of legal expenses incurred by it in collecting amounts owing to it on account of services rendered

that would, if the income of the corporation were from a business other than a personal services business, be deductible in computing its income;

**Related Provisions**: 122.3(1.1) — Restrictions on overseas employment tax credit for incorporated employee; 207.6(3) — Retirement compensation arrangement for incorporated employee; 248(1) — extended definition of "salary or wages".

**Notes**: As well as having its deductions limited by 18(1)(p), a corporation carrying on a personal services business (as defined in 125(7) — effectively an incorporated employee) must pay tax at the full corporate rate (i.e., is ineligible for the small business deduction). See 125(1)(a)(i) and 125(7)"active business".

An incorporated employee also cannot claim the overseas employment tax credit. See 122.3(1.1).

**Interpretation Bulletins**: IT-73R5: The small business deduction; IT-168R3: Athletes and players employed by football, hockey and similar clubs; IT-189R2: Corporations used by practising members of professions.

**(q) limitation re cancellation of lease** — an amount paid or payable by the taxpayer for the cancellation of a lease of property of the taxpayer leased by the taxpayer to another person, except to the extent permitted by paragraph 20(1)(z) or (z.1);

**Interpretation Bulletins**: IT-359R2: Premiums on leases.

**(r) certain automobile expenses** — an amount paid or payable by the taxpayer as an allowance for the use by an individual of an automobile to the extent that the amount exceeds an amount determined in accordance with prescribed rules, except where the amount so paid or payable is required to be included in computing the individual's income;

**Regulations**: 7306 (prescribed rules).

**I.T. Technical News**: No. 10 (1997 deduction limits and benefit rates for automobiles).

**(s) loans or lending assets** — any loss, depreciation or reduction in a taxation year in the value or amortized cost of a loan or lending asset of a taxpayer made or acquired by the taxpayer in the ordinary course of the taxpayer's business of insurance or the lending of money and not disposed of by the taxpayer in the year, except as expressly permitted by this Part;

**Notes**: 18(1)(s) amended by 1991 technical bill, retroactive to 1988, primarily to extend to loans "made" as well as "acquired".

**(t) payments under [Income Tax] Act** — any amount paid or payable under this Act (other than tax paid or payable under Part XII.2 or Part XII.6); and

**Related Provisions**: 60(o) — Expenses of objection or appeal; 20(1)(v) — Deduction for mining taxes; 20(1)(ll) — Deduction for interest repaid; 20(1)(nn) — Deduction for Part XII.6 tax; 20(1)(vv) — Deduction for countervailing and anti-dumping duties; 104(30) — Deduction for Part XII.2 tax paid by trust; 161.1 — Offsetting of non-deductible interest against taxable interest of other years.

**Notes**: 18(1)(t) added by 1989 Budget, effective 1989. It prohibits a deduction from income for any interest, penalties or fines paid under the *Income Tax Act*, as well as for the federal tax itself. Provincial income tax is also non-deductible. Such tax is considered as not paid for the purpose of gaining or producing income, and thus is restricted by 18(1)(a); see *First Pioneer Petroleums Ltd.*, [1974] C.T.C. 108 (FCTD). Note that legal and similar expenses relating to an income tax audit, objection or appeal are deductible under 60(o).

Effective for interest accruing in 2001 and later, 161.1 will allow interest of different years to offset each other, so that (non-deductible) interest payable can be cancelled by (otherwise-taxable) interest on refunds. (This applies to corporations, and is expected to be extended to individuals shortly.)

GST interest and penalties under the *Excise Tax Act*, and penalties under any other statute other than the ITA, are normally deductible if incurred in the course of business: *65302 British Columbia Ltd. (formerly Vekans Poultry)*, [2000] 1 C.T.C. 57 (SCC).

18(1)(t) amended by 1996 Budget, effective for 1997 and later taxation years, to add exclusions for Parts XII.2 and XII.6.

**Interpretation Bulletins**: IT-104R2: Deductibility of fines or penalties.

**Information Circulars**: 77-11: Sales tax reassessments — deductibility in computing income.

(u) **RSP/RIF fees** — any amount paid or payable by the taxpayer for services in respect of a retirement savings plan or retirement income fund under which the taxpayer is the annuitant.

**Related Provisions**: 18(11)(b) — No deduction for interest paid on money borrowed to make RRSP contribution.

**Notes**: 18(1)(u) added by 1996 Budget, effective for amounts paid or payable after March 5, 1996. It prevents RRSP and RRIF administration fees and investment counselling fees from being deductible.

After much back-and-forth, the CCRA now agrees that both management fees and investment counsel fees for an RRSP or RRIF can be paid either from the plan (without conferring a taxable benefit on the annuitant) or by the annuitant (without being considered a contribution to the plan). See private letter of February 20, 1998, reproduced in *The Canadian Taxpayer* Vol. XX No. 6 (March 17, 1998), pp. 46-47 (VIEWS doc. # 9727875).

### Proposed Addition — 18(1)(v)

(v) **Interest — authorized foreign bank** — where the taxpayer is an authorized foreign bank, an amount in respect of interest that would otherwise be deductible in computing the taxpayer's income from a business carried on in Canada, except as provided in section 20.2.

**Application**: The August 8, 2000 draft legislation, subsec. 2(1), will add para. 18(1)(v), applicable after June 27, 1999.

**Technical Notes**: Subsection 18(1) of the Act contains a list of general deductions that are prohibited when determining a taxpayer's income. This list is expanded by adding new paragraph 18(1)(v) of the Act, which denies a deduction to an authorized foreign bank (newly defined in subsection 248(1) of the Act) for any amount in respect of interest that would otherwise be deductible in computing the bank's income from a business carried on in Canada, except as provided in new section 20.2 of the Act. New paragraph 18(1)(v) applies after June 27, 1999.

**Interpretation Bulletins [subsec. 18(1)]**: IT-357R2: Expenses of training.

(2) **Limit on certain interest and property tax** — Notwithstanding paragraph 20(1)(c), in computing the taxpayer's income for a particular taxation year from a business or property, no amount shall be deductible in respect of any expense incurred by the taxpayer in the year as, on account or in lieu of payment of, or in satisfaction of,

(a) interest on debt relating to the acquisition of land, or

(b) property taxes (not including income or profits taxes or taxes computed by reference to the transfer of property) paid or payable by the taxpayer in respect of land to a province or to a Canadian municipality,

unless, having regard to all the circumstances (including the cost to the taxpayer of the land in relation to the taxpayer's gross revenue, if any, from the land for the particular year or any preceding taxation year), the land can reasonably be considered to have been, in the year,

(c) used in the course of a business carried on in the particular year by the taxpayer, other than a business in the ordinary course of which land is held primarily for the purpose of resale or development, or

(d) held primarily for the purpose of gaining or producing income of the taxpayer from the land for the particular year,

except to the extent of the total of

(e) the amount, if any, by which the taxpayer's gross revenue, if any, from the land for the particular year exceeds the total of all amounts deducted in computing the taxpayer's income from the land for the year, and

(f) in the case of a corporation whose principal business is the leasing, rental or sale, or the development for lease, rental or sale, or any combination thereof, of real property owned by it, to or for a person with whom the corporation is dealing at arm's length, the corporation's base level deduction for the particular year.

**Related Provisions**: 10(1.1) — Cost of land inventory; 18(2.1) — Limitations; 18(2.2)–(2.5) — Base level deduction; 18(3) — Definitions; 53(1)(d.3) — Addition to adjusted cost base of share; 53(1)(e)(xi) — Addition to adjusted cost base of partnership interest; 53(1)(h) — Addition to adjusted cost base of land; 80(2)(b) — Application of debt forgiveness rules; 212(1)(b)(iii)(E) — Non-resident withholding tax — interest; 241(4)(b) — Communication of information; 248(1) "business".

**Notes**: 18(2) amended by 1988 tax reform, effective 1988, subject to a five-year transitional rule for 1988–1992. In respect of expenses incurred in respect of land that may reasonably be considered to be held, but not used, in the course of a business carried on in the year by the taxpayer or land used in the course of a business in the ordinary course of which land is held primarily for the purpose of resale or development, for taxation years ending before 1993 (effective date amended by 1993 technical bill), read the portion of subsection 18(2) following paragraph (d) as follows:

except to the extent of the aggregate of

(e) the amount, if any, from the land for the particular year exceeds the aggregate of all amounts deducted in computing his income from the land for the year,

(f) in the case of a corporation whose principal business is the leasing, rental or sale, or the development for lease, rental or sale, or any combination thereof, of real property owned by it, to or for a person with whom the corporation is dealing at arm's length, the corporation's base level deduction for the particular year, and

(g) the specified percentage of the amount by which the aggregate of all such expenses incurred in the particular year exceeds the aggregate of the amounts determined under paragraphs (e) and (f) for the year, and, for the purposes of paragraph (g), "specified percentage" means the aggregate of

(h) that proportion of 100% that the number of days in the particular year that are before 1988 is of the number of days in the year,

(i) that proportion of 80% that the number of days in the particular year that are after 1987 and before 1989 is of the number of days in the year,

(j) that proportion of 60% that the number of days in the particular year that are after 1988 and before 1990 is of the number of days in the year,

(k) that proportion of 40% that the number of days in the particular year that are after 1989 and before 1991 is of the number of days in the year, and

(l) that proportion of 20% that the number of days in the particular year that are after 1990 and before 1992 is of the number of days in the year.

**Interpretation Bulletins**: IT-142R3: Settlement of debts on the winding-up of a corporation; IT-153R3: Land developers — subdivision and development costs and carrying charges on land; IT-355R2: Interest on loans to buy life insurance policies and annuity contracts, and interest on policy loans; IT-360R2: Interest payable in a foreign currency.

**(2.1) Where taxpayer member of partnership** — Where a taxpayer who is a member of a partnership was obligated to pay any amount as, on account or in lieu of payment of, or in satisfaction of, interest (in this subsection referred to as an "interest amount") on money that was borrowed by the taxpayer before April 1, 1977 and that was used to acquire land owned by the partnership before that day or on an obligation entered into by the taxpayer before April 1, 1977 to pay for land owned by the partnership before that day, and, in a taxation year of the taxpayer, either,

(a) the partnership has disposed of all or any portion of the land, or

(b) the taxpayer has disposed of all or any portion of the taxpayer's interest in the partnership

to a person other than a person with whom the taxpayer does not deal at arm's length, in computing the taxpayer's income for the year or any subsequent year, there may be deducted such portion of the taxpayer's interest amount

(c) that was, by virtue of subsection (2), not deductible in computing the income of the taxpayer for any previous taxation year,

(d) that was not deductible in computing the income of any other taxpayer for any taxation year,

(e) that was not included in computing the adjusted cost base to the taxpayer of any property, and

(f) that was not deductible under this subsection in computing the income of the taxpayer for any previous taxation year

as is reasonable having regard to the portion of the land or interest in the partnership, as the case may be, so disposed of.

**(2.2) Base level deduction** — For the purposes of this section, a corporation's base level deduction for a taxation year is the amount that would be the amount of interest, computed at the prescribed rate, for the year in respect of a loan of $1,000,000 outstanding throughout the year, unless the corporation is associated in the year with one or more other corporations in which case, except as otherwise provided in this section, its base level deduction for the year is nil.

**Related Provisions**: 18(2.3), (2.4) — Associated corporations; 18(2.5) — Special rules for base level deduction.

**Regulations**: 4301(c) (prescribed rate of interest).

**Interpretation Bulletins**: IT-153R3: Land developers — subdivision and development costs and carrying charges on land.

**(2.3) Associated corporations** — Notwithstanding subsection (2.2), if all of the corporations that are associated with each other in a taxation year have filed with the Minister in prescribed form an agreement whereby, for the purposes of this section, they allocate an amount to one or more of them for the taxation year and the amount so allocated or the total of the amounts so allocated, as the case may be, does not exceed $1,000,000, the base level deduction for the year for each of the corporations is the base level deduction that would be computed under subsection (2.2) in respect of the corporation if the reference in that subsection to $1,000,000 were read as a reference to the amount so allocated to it.

**Related Provisions**: 18(2.4) — Failure to file agreement.

**Interpretation Bulletins**: IT-153R3: Land developers — subdivision and development costs and carrying charges on land.

**Forms**: T2005: Agreement among associated corporations to allocate an amount to calculate their base level deduction.

**(2.4) Failure to file agreement** — If any of the corporations that are associated with each other in a taxation year has failed to file with the Minister an agreement as contemplated by subsection (2.3) within 30 days after notice in writing by the Minister has been forwarded to any of them that such an agreement is required for the purpose of any assessment of tax under this Part, the Minister shall, for the purpose of this section, allocate an amount to one or more of them for the taxation year, which amount or the total of which amounts, as the case may be, shall equal $1,000,000 and in any such case, the amount so allocated to any corporation shall be deemed to be an amount allocated to the corporation pursuant to subsection (2.3).

**Interpretation Bulletins**: IT-153R3: Land developers — subdivision and development costs and carrying charges on land.

**(2.5) Special rules for base level deduction** — Notwithstanding any other provision of this section,

(a) where a corporation, in this paragraph referred to as the "first corporation", has more than one taxation year ending in the same calendar year and is associated in two or more of those taxation years with another corporation that has a taxation year ending in that calendar year, the base level

Subdivision b — Income or Loss from a Business or Property    S. 18(3.1)(b)

deduction of the first corporation for each taxation year in which it is associated with the other corporation ending in that calendar year is, subject to the application of paragraph (b), an amount equal to its base level deduction for the first such taxation year determined without reference to paragraph (b); and

(b) where a corporation has a taxation year that is less than 51 weeks, its base level deduction for the year is that proportion of its base level deduction for the year determined without reference to this paragraph that the number of days in the year is of 365.

**Related Provisions**: 18(2.2) — Base level deduction.

**Interpretation Bulletins**: IT-153R3: Land developers — subdivision and development costs and carrying charges on land.

**Forms**: T2005: Agreement among associated corporations to allocate an amount to calculate their base level deduction.

**(3) Definitions** — In subsection (2),

**"interest on debt relating to the acquisition of land"** includes

(a) interest paid or payable in a year in respect of borrowed money that cannot be identified with particular land but that may nonetheless reasonably be considered (having regard to all the circumstances) as interest on borrowed money used in respect of or for the acquisition of land, and

(b) interest paid or payable in the year by a taxpayer in respect of borrowed money that may reasonably be considered (having regard to all the circumstances) to have been used to assist, directly or indirectly,

(i) another person with whom the taxpayer does not deal at arm's length,

(ii) a corporation of which the taxpayer is a specified shareholder, or

(iii) a partnership of which the taxpayer's share of any income or loss is 10% or more,

to acquire land to be used or held by that person, corporation or partnership otherwise than as described in paragraph (2)(c) or (d), except where the assistance is in the form of a loan to that person, corporation or partnership and a reasonable rate of interest on the loan is charged by the taxpayer;

**Related Provisions**: 53(1)(h) — Addition to adjusted cost base of land.

**Notes**: 18(3)"interest on debt ..." was 18(3)(b) before R.S.C. 1985 (5th Supp.) consolidation, effective for taxation years ending after November 1991. See Table of Concordance.

**Interpretation Bulletins**: IT-153R3: Land developers — subdivision and development costs, etc.

**"land"** does not, except to the extent that it is used for the provision of parking facilities for a fee or charge, include

(a) any property that is a building or other structure affixed to land,

(b) the land subjacent to any property described in paragraph (a), or

(c) such land immediately contiguous to the land described in paragraph (b) that is a parking area, driveway, yard, garden or similar land as is necessary for the use of any property described in paragraph (a).

**Interpretation Bulletins**: IT-153R3: Land developers — subdivision and development costs, etc.

**Notes**: 18(3)"land" was 18(3)(a) before R.S.C. 1985 (5th Supp.) consolidation, effective for taxation years ending after November 1991. See Table of Concordance.

**(3.1) Costs relating to construction of building or ownership of land** — Notwithstanding any other provision of this Act, in computing a taxpayer's income for a taxation year,

(a) no deduction shall be made in respect of any outlay or expense made or incurred by the taxpayer (other than an amount deductible under paragraph 20(1)(a), (aa) or (qq) or subsection 20(29)) that can reasonably be regarded as a cost attributable to the period of the construction, renovation or alteration of a building by or on behalf of the taxpayer, a person with whom the taxpayer does not deal at arm's length, a corporation of which the taxpayer is a specified shareholder or a partnership of which the taxpayer's share of any income or loss is 10% or more and relating to the construction, renovation or alteration, or a cost attributable to that period and relating to the ownership during that period of land

(i) that is subjacent to the building, or

(ii) that

(A) is immediately contiguous to the land subjacent to the building,

(B) is used, or is intended to be used, for a parking area, driveway, yard, garden or any other similar use, and

(C) is necessary for the use or intended use of the building; and

(b) the amount of such outlay or expense shall be included in computing the cost or capital cost, as the case may be, of the building to the taxpayer, to the person with whom the taxpayer does not deal at arm's length, to the corporation of which the taxpayer is a specified shareholder or to the partnership of which the taxpayer's share of any income or loss is 10% or more, as the case may be.

**Proposed Amendment — 18(3.1)(b)**

(b) the amount of such an outlay or expense shall, to the extent that it would otherwise be deductible in computing the taxpayer's income for the year, be included in computing the cost or capital cost, as the case may be, of the building to the taxpayer, to the person with whom the taxpayer does not deal at arm's length, to the corporation of which the taxpayer is a speci-

**S. 18(3.1)(b)**     Income Tax Act, Part I, Division B

fied shareholder or to the partnership of which the taxpayer's share of any income or loss is 10% or more, as the case may be.

**Application**: The December 21, 2000 draft legislation, subsec. 6(1), will amend para. 18(3.1)(b) to read as above, applicable to outlays and expenses made or incurred after December 21, 2000.

**Technical Notes**: Subsection 18(3.1) denies the immediate deduction of certain costs, generally referred to as construction period soft costs, relating to the construction, renovation or alteration of a building. These costs are required to be added to the cost or capital cost of the building to which they relate.

This amendment to paragraph 18(3.1)(b), which is consequential on the enactment of new section 20.3 dealing with weak currency debt, ensures that the amount of an outlay or expense relating to construction period soft costs is only included in the cost or capital cost of the relevant building to the extent that the amount would otherwise be deductible in computing the taxpayer's income.

**Related Provisions**: 18(3.2)–(3.7) — Interpretation and application of subsec. 18(3.1); 20(29) — Deduction against rental income from building; 53(1)(d.2) — Addition to adjusted cost base of share; 53(1)(e)(xi) — Addition to adjusted cost base of partnership interest; 80(2)(b) — Application of debt forgiveness rules; 241(4) — Communication of information.

**Notes**: 18(3.1)(a) amended by 1988 tax reform and by 1991 technical bill and 1993 technical bill, retroactive to 1988. In respect of buildings acquired before 1990, read "or section 37 or 37.1" after the words "subsection 20(29)".

**Interpretation Bulletins**: IT-121R3: Election to capitalize cost of borrowed money; IT-142R3: Settlement of debts on the winding-up of a corporation; IT-355R2: Interest on loans to buy life insurance policies and annuity contracts, and interest on policy loans.

**(3.2) Included costs** — For the purposes of subsection (3.1), costs relating to the construction, renovation or alteration of a building or to the ownership of land include

   (a) interest paid or payable by a taxpayer in respect of borrowed money that cannot be identified with a particular building or particular land, but that can reasonably be considered (having regard to all the circumstances) as interest on borrowed money used by the taxpayer in respect of the construction, renovation or alteration of a building or the ownership of land; and

   (b) interest paid or payable by a taxpayer in respect of borrowed money that may reasonably be considered (having regard to all the circumstances) to have been used to assist, directly or indirectly,

      (i) another person with whom the taxpayer does not deal at arm's length,

      (ii) a corporation of which the taxpayer is a specified shareholder, or

      (iii) a partnership of which the taxpayer's share of any income or loss is 10% or more,

to construct, renovate or alter a building or to purchase land, except where the assistance is in the form of a loan to that other person, corporation or partnership and a reasonable rate of interest on the loan is charged by the taxpayer.

**(3.3) Completion** — For the purposes of subsection (3.1), the construction, renovation or alteration of a building is completed at the earlier of the day on which the construction, renovation or alteration is actually completed and the day on which all or substantially all of the building is used for the purpose for which it was constructed, renovated or altered.

**Notes**: The CCRA takes the position that "all or substantially all" means 90% or more.

**(3.4) Where subsec. (3.1) does not apply** — Subsection (3.1) does not apply to prohibit a deduction in a taxation year of the specified percentage of any outlay or expense described in that subsection made or incurred before 1992 by

   (a) a corporation whose principal business is throughout the year the leasing, rental or sale, or the development for lease, rental or sale, or any combination thereof, of real property owned by it to or for a person with whom the corporation is dealing at arm's length, or

   (b) a partnership

      (i) each member of which is a corporation described in paragraph (a), and

      (ii) the principal business of which is throughout the year the leasing, rental or sale, or the development for lease, rental or sale, or any combination thereof, of real property held by it, to or for a person with whom each member of the partnership is dealing at arm's length,

and for the purposes of this subsection, "specified percentage" means, in respect of an outlay or expense made or incurred in 1988, 80%, in 1989, 60%, in 1990, 40%, and in 1991, 20%.

**(3.5) Idem** — Subsection (3.1) does not apply in respect of an outlay or expense in respect of a building or the land described in subparagraph (3.1)(a)(i) or (ii) in respect of the building,

   (a) where the construction, renovation or alteration of the building was in progress on November 12, 1981,

   (b) where the installation of the footings or other base support of the building commenced after November 12, 1981 and before 1982,

   (c) if, in the case of a new building being constructed in Canada or an existing building being renovated or altered in Canada, arrangements, evidenced in writing, for the construction, renovation or alteration were substantially advanced before November 13, 1981 and the installation of footings or other base support for the new building or the renovation or alteration of the existing building, as the case may be, commenced before June 1, 1982, or

   (d) if, in the case of a new building being constructed in Canada, the taxpayer was obligated to construct the building under the terms of an agreement in writing entered into before November 13, 1981 and arrangements, evidenced in writing, respecting the construction of the building were substantially advanced before June 1, 1982 and the installation of footings or other base support for the building commenced before 1983,

and the construction, renovation or alteration, as the case may be, of the building proceeds after 1982 without undue delay (having regard to acts of God, labour disputes, fire, accidents or unusual delay by common carriers or suppliers of materials or equipment).

**Related Provisions**: 18(3.7) — Commencement of installation of footings.

**Notes**: 18(3.5) amended by 1991 technical bill, retroactive to 1985, to correct references to provisions of 18(3.1)(a).

**(3.6) Undue delay** — For the purposes of subsection (3.5), where more than one building is being constructed under any of the circumstances described in that subsection on one site or on immediately contiguous sites, no undue delay shall be regarded as occurring in the construction of any such building if construction of at least one such building proceeds after 1982 without undue delay and continuous construction of all other such buildings proceeds after 1983 without undue delay.

**(3.7) Commencement of footings** — For the purposes of this section, the installation of footings or other base support for a building shall be deemed to commence on the first placement of concrete, pilings or other material that is to provide permanent support for the building.

**(4) Limitation re deduction of interest by certain corporations [thin capitalization]** — Notwithstanding any other provision of this Act, in computing the income for a taxation year of a corporation resident in Canada from a business or property, no deduction shall be made in respect of that proportion of any amount otherwise deductible in computing its income for the year in respect of interest paid or payable by it on outstanding debts to specified non-residents that

(a) the amount, if any, by which

(i) the greatest aggregate amount that the corporation's outstanding debts to specified non-residents were at any time in the year,

exceeds

(ii) 3 times the total of

(A) the retained earnings of the corporation at the commencement of the year, except to the extent that those earnings include retained earnings of any other corporation,

(B) the corporation's contributed surplus at the commencement of the year, to the extent that it was contributed by a specified non-resident shareholder of the corporation, and

(C) the greater of the corporation's paid-up capital at the commencement of the year and the corporation's paid-up capital at the end of the year, excluding the paid-up capital in respect of shares of any class of the capital stock of the corporation owned by a person other than a specified non-resident shareholder of the corporation,

**Proposed Amendment — 18(4)(a)**

(a) the amount, if any, by which

(i) the average of all amounts each of which is, in respect of a calendar month that ends in the year, the greatest total amount at any time in the month of the corporation's outstanding debts to specified non-residents,

exceeds

(ii) two times the total of

(A) the retained earnings of the corporation at the beginning of the year, except to the extent that those earnings include retained earnings of any other corporation,

(B) the average of all amounts each of which is the corporation's contributed surplus at the beginning of a calendar month that ends in the year, to the extent that it was contributed by a specified non-resident shareholder of the corporation, and

(C) the average of all amounts each of which is the corporation's paid-up capital at the beginning of a calendar month that ends in the year, excluding the paid-up capital in respect of shares of any class of the capital stock of the corporation owned by a person other than a specified non-resident shareholder of the corporation,

**Application**: The December 21, 2000 draft legislation, subsec. 6(2), will amend para. 18(4)(a) to read as above, applicable to taxation years that begin after 2000.

**Technical Notes**: Subsection 18(4) provides thin capitalization rules for corporations resident in Canada, which limit their deduction for interest on debt owing to certain specified non-residents. The interest is disallowed where the corporation's debt-equity ratio in relation to the specified non-residents exceeds 3 to 1.

Pursuant to changes announced in the 2000 Budget, subsection 18(4) is amended in three ways. First, the debt-equity ratio is changed from the present 3:1 to 2:1, effective for taxation years that begin after 2000.

Second, the method of calculating debt for the debt-equity ratio is modified, effective for taxation years that begin after 2000. Under amended paragraph 18(4)(a), debt is calculated based on a monthly average. This average is calculated by first noting, for each calendar month that ends in a given taxation year, the greatest total amount of the corporation's debt outstanding to specified non-residents at any time in that month. The sum of these amounts is then divided by the number of calendar months that end in the taxation year to arrive at the monthly average debt.

Third, the method of calculating equity for the debt-equity ratio is also modified, effective for taxation years that begin after 2000. While the corporation's retained earnings continue to be calculated at the beginning of the year under amended paragraph 18(4)(a), monthly averages are provided for calculating the corporation's contributed surplus and paid-up capital. The monthly contributed surplus is calculated by first noting, for each calendar month that ends in a given taxation year, the amount of the corporation's contributed surplus at the beginning of that month, to the extent that it was contributed by a specified non-resident shareholder of the corporation. The sum of these amounts is then divided by the number of calendar months that end in the taxation year to arrive at the monthly average contributed surplus. A similar calculation is provided for determining the corporation's paid-up capital for the purpose of the debt-equity ratio.

**Notice of Ways and Means Motion, federal budget, February 28, 2000**: *Thin Capitalization*

(26) That, for taxation years that begin after 2000, the provisions of the Act relating to thinly capitalized corporations be modified

    (a) to reduce, from 3:1 to 2:1, the ratio of debt to equity for the purposes of the limit on interest deductibility in subsection 18(4) of the Act,

    (b) to apply an average ratio of debt to equity for the taxation year in determining the limit on interest deductibility applicable to a corporation under subsection 18(4) of the Act, based on calculations of

        (i) the corporation's retained earnings at the beginning of the year,

        (ii) the corporation's contributed surplus and paid-up capital at the beginning of each month of the year to the extent they are attributable to specified non-residents, and

        (iii) the greatest total amount of debt owing by the corporation to specified non-residents at any time in each month of the year,

    (c) [deferred pending consultation; see below — ed.] to expand the anti-avoidance rule in subsection 18(6) of the Act to deem indebtedness of a corporation to a third party that is guaranteed or secured by a specified non-resident to be debt owing by the corporation to the specified non-resident, and

    (d) to repeal subsection 18(8) of the Act, which provides an exemption for developers and manufacturers of aircraft and aircraft components.

**Federal budget, supplementary information, February 28, 2000**: *Strengthening Thin Capitalization Rules*

The *Income Tax Act* contains rules that restrict the interest deduction that a corporation resident in Canada can claim in respect of debt owing to a specified non-resident — generally, a shareholder whose stake in the corporation represents 25 per cent or more of the votes or value in the corporation or a person who is not at arm's-length with such a shareholder. Under these so-called "thin capitalization" rules, the Canadian corporation may deduct interest on debt to specified non-residents to the extent that such debt does not exceed three times the amount of equity contributed by such non-residents. In the event that such debt exceeds the 3:1 ratio, the interest deduction attributable to the excess is denied for Canadian tax purposes.

A number of factors support modifications to the thin capitalization rules, which were introduced in 1972. First, the permitted 3:1 debt-equity ratio is high compared to actual industry ratios in the Canadian economy, suggesting that the 3:1 ratio permits inappropriately high debt levels. On the other hand, the current rules apply to reduce the amount of interest deductible if debt to specified non-residents at any point in the year exceeds the permitted ratio relative to equity. Therefore, temporarily high debt levels can have a disproportionate impact.

The scope of debts covered by the rules is also very narrow. An anti-avoidance rule in the current law deals with so-called back-to-back arrangements. Where a specified non-resident makes a loan to a third party on condition that the third party make a loan to the Canadian corporation, the lesser amount of the two loans is deemed to be a loan to the corporation from the specified non-resident. This rule does not extend, however, to an arrangement where a Canadian corporation borrows funds from a third party with the aid of a guarantee from a specified non-resident. Such a borrowing is often economically equivalent to a direct loan from the non-resident since the guarantee supports the lender's credit risk associated with the borrowing. This type of arrangement can result in the erosion of the tax base to the same extent as a direct loan from the specified non-resident.

In addition, as a result of a special exemption introduced in the early 1970s, the thin capitalization rules currently do not apply to a corporation whose principal business in Canada is the developing or manufacturing of aircraft or aircraft components. It is not apparent that this exemption is warranted under present conditions.

Finally, other changes to the thin capitalization rules need to be considered. The rules currently apply only to corporations and not to other business arrangements such as partnerships, trusts and branches. Taxpayers may therefore be able to use these structures in order to circumvent the rules. There is also concern that use of financing techniques that do not rely on traditional debt — such as leases from a non-resident parent — may weaken the effectiveness of the rules in protecting the Canadian tax base.

In response to these concerns, the budget proposes that the thin capitalization rules in subsections 18(4) to 18(8) of the *Income Tax Act* be amended in the following manner:

- *The threshold debt-equity ratio in subsection 18(4) will be lowered from 3:1 to 2:1.* The new ratio provides a better measurement of excessive reliance on related-party debt financing in the context of actual Canadian industry debt-equity ratios.

- *The debt-equity ratio will be calculated on an averaged basis.* Specifically, average debt for a fiscal year will be calculated as the average of monthly amounts, each of which is the highest amount of debt to specified non-residents outstanding at any time in the month. Of the three components of equity, retained earnings will continue to be measured at the beginning of the year. The amount of paid-up capital and contributed surplus attributed to specified non-residents will be an average of amounts calculated at the beginning of each month during the taxation year. This manner of applying the limitation will give less weight than the current rules to debt levels that are temporarily high.

- *The conditional loan rule in subsection 18(6) of the Act will be broadened.* The rule will encompass loans to a Canadian corporation from a third party that are guaranteed or secured by a specified non-resident.
- *The exemption for developers and manufacturers of aircraft and aircraft components in subsection 18(8) of the Act will be repealed.*

These four changes will come into effect for taxation years that begin after 2000.

Finally, consultations will be initiated on the extension of the thin capitalization rules to other arrangements and business structures, namely:

- Partnerships that have non-resident members, trusts that have non-resident beneficiaries, and Canadian branches of non-resident companies carrying on business in Canada. Because these arrangements do not involve the issuance of share capital, it is not possible to assess on the basis of the current rules whether or not the entity is "thinly capitalized." Therefore, the rules would have to be adapted in order to measure excessive indebtedness for such vehicles.
- Debt substitutes, such as certain types of leases.

The Government invites public comments with respect to both the proposed changes outlined above and the extension of the thin capitalization rules to other arrangements and business structures.

**Department of Finance news release, May 9, 2000**: *Finance Minister Clarifies Certain Income Tax Measures in the 2000 Budget*

Finance Minister Paul Martin today announced several clarifications to measures announced in the 2000 budget. These clarifications will ensure the smooth conduct of business transactions while consultations take place.

*Thin Capitalization Rules*

The thin capitalization rules in the *Income Tax Act* prevent foreign-owned corporations resident in Canada from using an excessive amount of debt when they capitalize their Canadian operations.

Minister Martin today announced the deferral of the budget measure that broadened the kind of debt covered by the thin capitalization rules to include loans to a Canadian corporation from a third party that are guaranteed or secured by a specified non-resident. In certain circumstances, including guaranteed debt in the scope of the thin capitalization rules has raised concerns. Deferring this element of the thin capitalization provision will enable officials to consult broadly with a view to reaching a consensus on how best to define those guarantees that are equivalent to related party debt. Any resulting proposals will be brought forward on a fully prospective basis.

As indicated in the 2000 budget, interested parties will also be consulted on matters related to other business arrangements such as partnerships, trusts, branches and the use of leases.

. . . . .

For further information: Thin Capitalization Rules, Sanjeev Sivarulrasa, (613) 992-5864.

**Notes**: For discussion of the budget proposals see Elinore Richardson, "Canada Amends its Thin Cap Rules", VIII(1) *Corporate Finance* (Federated Press) 698-704 (2000); and K.A. Siobhan Monaghan, "Proposed Amendments to the Thin Capitalization Rules", VI(2) *Corporate Structures and Groups* (Federated Press) 308-311 (2000). The "deferral" announced on May 9, 2000 is thought by many to mean that the proposal has been shelved indefinitely.

is of

(b) the amount determined under subparagraph (a)(i) in respect of the corporation for the year.

**Related Provisions**: 18(5) — Meaning of certain expressions; 18(5.1) — Person deemed not to be specified shareholder; 18(6) — Loan made on conditions; 18(8) — Exception for manufacturer of aircraft or components; Canada-U.S. tax treaty, Art. XXV:8 — Thin capitalization rules grandfathered from treaty non-discrimination provision.

**Notes**: 18(4) to (8) provide the "thin capitalization" rules. In general, they limit the debt:equity ratio for Canadian subsidiaries of non-residents to 3:1 (to change to 2:1), by limiting the deductibility (under 20(1)(c)) of interest paid to non-resident shareholders. In effect, this forces a non-resident setting up a Canadian subsidiary to provide a certain level of its financing through equity rather than using only debt.

In *Wildenburg Holdings Ltd.*, [1999] 2 C.T.C. 161 (Ont Gen Div); aff'd [2000] 3 C.T.C. 148 (Ont CA), it was held that these rules applied for Ontario corporate tax purposes to holdings through a partnership. However, the CCRA generally does not apply them to a partnership for federal purposes, if there is a *bona fide* partnership and the partners are liable for the partnership debts: 1992 Canadian Tax Foundation annual conference round table, p. 54:8, Q. 12, confirmed by Revenue at the 1998 conference (p. 52:14) and in Income Tax Technical News No. 16.

For deemed interest on non-interest-bearing loans to non-residents, see s. 17.

**Interpretation Bulletins**: IT-59R3: Interest on debts owing to specified non-residents (thin capitalization); IT-121R3: Election to capitalize cost of borrowed money.

**Information Circulars**: 87-2R: International transfer pricing.

**Advance Tax Rulings**: ATR-43: Utilization of a non-resident-owned investment corporation as a holding corporation.

**I.T. Technical News**: No. 15 (back-to-back loans in relation to subsections 18(4) and 18(6)); No. 16 (*Wildenburg Holdings* case).

**(5) Definitions** — Notwithstanding any other provision of this Act (other than subsection (5.1)), in this subsection and subsections (4) to (6),

**Notes**: See under "specified shareholder" below.

**"outstanding debts to specified non-residents"** of a corporation at any particular time in a taxation year means

(a) the total of all amounts each of which is an amount outstanding at that time as or on account of a debt or other obligation to pay an amount

(i) that was payable by the corporation to a person who was, at any time in the year,

(A) a specified non-resident shareholder of the corporation, or

(B) a non-resident person, or a non-resident-owned investment corporation, who was not dealing at arm's length with a specified shareholder of the corporation, and

(ii) on which any amount in respect of interest paid or payable by the corporation is or would be, but for subsection (4), deductible in computing the corporation's income for the year,

but does not include

(b) an amount outstanding at the particular time as or on account of a debt or other obligation to pay an amount to a non-resident insurance corporation to the extent that the amount was, for the non-resident insurance corporation's taxation year that included the particular time, designated insurance property in respect of an insurance business carried on in Canada through a permanent establishment as defined by regulation;

### Proposed Amendment — 18(5) "outstanding debts to specified non-residents"(b)

(b) an amount outstanding at the particular time as or on account of a debt or other obligation to pay an amount to

(i) a non-resident insurance corporation to the extent that the obligation was, for the non-resident insurance corporation's taxation year that included the particular time, designated insurance property in respect of an insurance business carried on in Canada through a permanent establishment as defined by regulation, or

(ii) an authorized foreign bank, if the bank uses or holds the obligation at the particular time in its Canadian banking business;

**Application**: The August 8, 2000 draft legislation, subsec. 2(2), will amend para. (b) of the definition "outstanding debts to specified non-residents" in subsec. 18(5) to read as above, applicable after June 27, 1999.

**Technical Notes**: Subsection 18(5) defines certain expressions for the purpose of the "thin capitalization" rules in subsections 18(4) to (8). In certain circumstances, the thin capitalization rules limit a corporation's deduction of interest expense. The rules' application depends on the amount of the corporation's "outstanding debts to specified non-residents" — a term defined in subsection 18(5).

Paragraph (b) of this definition currently provides an exclusion for certain obligations owing to non-resident insurers. The paragraph is amended to provide as well an exclusion for an obligation owing to an authorized foreign bank, if the bank uses or holds the obligation in its Canadian banking business (defined in a new definition in subsection 248(1) of the Act).

This amendment applies after June 27, 1999.

**Notice of Ways and Means Motion (authorized foreign banks), February 11, 1999**: (10) That, for the purposes of the thin capitalization rules in subsections 18(4) to 18(8) of the Act, an amount outstanding to an authorized foreign bank as or on account of a debt or other obligation be excluded from the definition "outstanding debts to specified non-residents" in subsection 18(5) of the Act if the interest payable to the bank in respect of that amount is included in computing its income from a business carried on in Canada.

**Department of Finance news release, February 11, 1999**: *Thin Capitalization Rules*

A corporation may not deduct interest payments made to "specified non-resident shareholders" — generally, those having a 25% or greater ownership interest in the corporation — to the extent that its relevant debt funding exceeds three times its equity funding. The thin capitalization rules ensure that a corporation's earnings are not paid out to significant non-resident shareholders in the form of tax-deductible interest rather than after-tax dividends.

It is proposed that debt owing to a foreign bank from a Canadian resident corporation in which the foreign bank is a specified non-resident shareholder be excluded from these rules, if the interest payments in respect of that debt are included in the foreign bank's income that is subject to tax under Part I of the *Income Tax Act*. Since there is no risk that this debt funding would lead to the corporation's earnings leaving Canada without being taxed, it need not be taken into account for the purposes of the thin capitalization rules.

**Notes**: Para. (b) amended by 1996 Budget, effective for 1997 and later taxation years (changed from 1996 at Second Reading of the Budget bill). The changes reflect the new definition of "designated insurance property" in 138(12), and clarify that "permanent establishment" has the meaning assigned by the Regulations. For earlier taxation years, read:

> (b) any amount outstanding at the particular time as or on account of a debt or other obligation to pay an amount to a non-resident insurance corporation where the amount outstanding at the particular time was, in the non-resident insurance corporation's taxation year that included the particular time, included, for the purposes of section 138, as property used by it in the year in, or held by it in the year in the course of, carrying on an insurance business through a permanent establishment (within the meaning assigned for the purpose of subsection 112(2)) in Canada,

18(5)"outstanding debts ..." was 18(5)(a) before R.S.C. 1985 (5th Supp.) consolidation, effective for taxation years ending after November 1991. See Table of Concordance.

See also Notes to "specified shareholder" below.

**Regulations**: 8201 (permanent extablishment).

**Advance Tax Rulings**: ATR-43: Utilization of a non-resident-owned investment corporation as a holding corporation.

**"specified non-resident shareholder"** of a corporation at any time means a specified shareholder of the corporation who was at that time a non-resident person or a non-resident-owned investment corporation;

**Notes**: 18(5)"specified non-resident shareholder" was 18(5)(b) before R.S.C. 1985 (5th Supp.) consolidation, effective for taxation years ending after November 1991.

**"specified shareholder"** of a corporation at any time means a person who at that time, either alone or together with persons with whom that person is not dealing at arm's length, owns

(a) shares of the capital stock of the corporation that give the holders thereof 25% or more of the votes that could be cast at an annual meeting of the shareholders of the corporation, or

(b) shares of the capital stock of the corporation having a fair market value of 25% or more of the fair market value of all of the issued and outstanding shares of the capital stock of the corporation,

and, for the purpose of determining whether a particular person is a specified shareholder of a corporation at any time, where the particular person or a person with whom the particular person is not dealing at arm's length has at that time a right under a contract, in equity or otherwise, either immediately or in the future and either absolutely or contingently

(c) to, or to acquire, shares in a corporation or to control the voting rights of shares in a corporation, or

(d) to cause a corporation to redeem, acquire or cancel any of its shares (other than shares held by the particular person or a person with whom the particular person is not dealing at arm's length),

the particular person or the person with whom the particular person is not dealing at arm's length, as the case may be, shall be deemed at that time to own the shares referred to in paragraph (c) and the corporation referred to in paragraph (d) shall be deemed at that time to have redeemed, acquired or cancelled the shares referred to in paragraph (d), unless the right is not exercisable at that time because the exercise thereof is contingent on the death, bankruptcy or permanent disability of an individual.

**Related Provisions**: 18(5.1) — Person deemed not to be specified shareholder.

**Notes**: 18(5) amended by 1992 technical bill. Reference in opening words to subsec. (5.1), and new definition of "specified shareholder", are effective for 1993 and later taxation years, but a corporation could elect for them to apply to its 1989 to 1992 taxation years as well by filing an election with Revenue Canada by December 10, 1993. New para. (b) of "outstanding debts ..." is effective for 1991 and later taxation years, but a corporation could elect for it to apply to its 1985 to 1990 taxation years by filing an election with Revenue Canada by December 10, 1993.

18(5)"specified shareholder" was 18(5)(c) before R.S.C. 1985 (5th Supp.) consolidation, effective for taxation years ending after November 1991. See Table of Concordance.

**Interpretation Bulletins**: IT-59R3: Interest on debts owing to specified non-residents (thin capitalization).

**(5.1) Person deemed not to be specified shareholder** — For the purposes of subsections (4) to (6), where

(a) a particular person would, but for this subsection, be a specified shareholder of a corporation at any time,

(b) there was in effect at that time an agreement or arrangement under which, on the satisfaction of a condition or the occur[r]ence of an event that it is reasonable to expect will be satisfied or will occur, the particular person will cease to be a specified shareholder, and

(c) the purpose for which the particular person became a specified shareholder was the safeguarding of rights or interests of the particular person or a person with whom the particular person is not dealing at arm's length in respect of any indebtedness owing at any time to the particular person or a person with whom the particular person is not dealing at arm's length,

the particular person shall be deemed not to be a specified shareholder of the corporation at that time.

**Notes**: 18(5.1) added by 1992 technical bill, effective for 1993 and later taxation years, but a corporation could elect for it to apply to its 1989 to 1992 taxation years as well by filing an election with Revenue Canada by December 10, 1993.

**(6) Loans made on condition** — Where any loan (in this subsection referred to as the "first loan") has been made

(a) by a specified non-resident shareholder of a corporation, or

(b) by a non-resident person, or a non-resident-owned investment corporation, who was not dealing at arm's length with a specified shareholder of a corporation,

to another person on condition that a loan (in this subsection referred to as the "second loan") be made by any person to a particular corporation resident in Canada, for the purposes of subsections (4) and (5), the lesser of

(c) the amount of the first loan, and

(d) the amount of the second loan

shall be deemed to be a debt incurred by the particular corporation to the person who made the first loan.

**Related Provisions**: 18(5.1) — Person deemed not to be specified shareholder.

**Notes**: This rule catches "back-to-back" loans. However, it may be possible to avoid it with conditional loans. See Steven Kohn, "Application of Subsection 18(6) to Back-to-Back Loans", VI(4) *Corporate Finance* (Federated Press), 558-560 (1998).

**Interpretation Bulletins**: IT-59R3: Interest on debts owing to specified non-residents (thin capitalization).

**I.T. Technical News**: No. 15 (back-to-back loans in relation to subsections 18(4) and 18(6)).

**(7) [Repealed under former Act]**

**Notes**: 18(7), repealed by 1985 technical bill, limited the application of s. 21 where the thin capitalization rules apply. It was repealed because it was superfluous.

**(8) Where subsec. (4) does not apply** — Subsection (4) does not apply in computing the income for a taxation year of a corporation whose principal business in Canada throughout the year was the developing or manufacturing of aircraft or aircraft components.

**Proposed Repeal — 18(8)**

**Application**: The December 21, 2000 draft legislation, subsec. 6(3), will repeal subsec. 18(8), applicable to taxation years that begin after 2000.

**Technical Notes**: Subsection 18(8) exempts from the application of the thin capitalization rules contained in subsection 18(4) corporations whose principal business in Canada throughout the year is the development or manufacturing of aircraft or aircraft components. Pursuant to changes announced in the 2000 Budget, this exemption is repealed, effective for taxation years that begin after 2000.

**S. 18(8)**     Income Tax Act, Part I, Division B

**Interpretation Bulletins**: IT-59R3: Interest on debts owing to specified non-residents (thin capitalization).

**(9) Limitation respecting prepaid expenses** — Notwithstanding any other provision of this Act,

(a) in computing a taxpayer's income for a taxation year from a business or property (other than income from a business computed in accordance with the method authorized by subsection 28(1)), no deduction shall be made in respect of an outlay or expense to the extent that it can reasonably be regarded as having been made or incurred

(i) as consideration for services to be rendered after the end of the year,

(ii) as, on account or in lieu of payment of, or in satisfaction of, interest, taxes (other than taxes imposed on insurance premiums), rent or royalty in respect of a period after the end of the year, or

---
**Proposed Amendment — 18(9)(a)(ii)**

(ii) as, on account of, in lieu of payment of or in satisfaction of, interest, taxes (other than taxes imposed on an insurer in respect of insurance premiums of a non-cancellable or guaranteed renewable accident and sickness insurance policy, or a life insurance policy other than a group term life insurance policy that provides coverage for a period of 12 months or less), rent or royalties in respect of a period that is after the end of the year, or

**Application**: Bill C-43 (First Reading September 20, 2000), subsec. 7(1), will amend subpara. 18(9)(a)(ii) to read as above, applicable to taxation years that begin after 1999 except that, where a taxpayer so elects in writing and files the election with the Minister of National Revenue on or before the taxpayer's filing-due date for the taxpayer's taxation year in which the amending legislation receives Royal Assent, the amendment applies to taxation years that end after 1997.

**Technical Notes**: Subsection 18(9) defers the deduction of certain prepaid expenses to the taxation year to which the expenses relate. Paragraph 18(9)(a) lists the prepaid amounts to which the subsection applies. Currently, these amounts include, amongst other amounts, taxes (other than taxes imposed on insurance premiums).

Subparagraph 18(9)(a)(ii) is amended to provide that only premium taxes imposed on an insurer in respect of a non-cancellable or guaranteed renewable accident and sickness insurance policy or a life insurance policy that is not a group term life insurance policy that provides coverage for a period not exceeding 12 months are excepted from subparagraph 18(9)(a)(ii) and continue to be deductible on a current basis. The amendment to subparagraph 18(9)(a)(ii) is consequential on the addition of subsection 18(9.02) of the Act which requires the deferral of policy acquisition costs (which include premium taxes) generally in respect of non-life insurance policies.

This amendment applies to taxation years that begin after 1999 and, where a taxpayer so elects in writing with respect to both it and new subsection 18(9.02), to the taxpayer's taxation years that end after 1997. The election is to be filed with the Minister of National Revenue on or before the taxpayer's filing-due date for the taxation year in which this amendment receives Royal Assent.

---

(iii) as consideration for insurance in respect of a period after the end of the year, other than

(A) where the taxpayer is an insurer, consideration for reinsurance, and

(B) consideration for insurance on the life of an individual under a group term life insurance policy where all or part of the consideration is for insurance that is (or would be if the individual survived) in respect of a period that ends more than 13 months after the consideration is paid;

(b) such portion of each outlay or expense (other than an outlay or expense of a corporation, partnership or trust as, on account of, in lieu of payment of or in satisfaction of, interest) made or incurred as would, but for paragraph (a), be deductible in computing a taxpayer's income for a taxation year shall be deductible in computing the taxpayer's income for the subsequent year to which it can reasonably be considered to relate;

(c) for the purposes of section 37.1, such portion of each qualified expenditure (within the meaning assigned by subsection 37.1(5)) as was made by a taxpayer in a taxation year and as would, but for paragraph (a), have been deductible in computing the taxpayer's income for the year shall be deemed

(i) not to be a qualified expenditure made by the taxpayer in the year, and

(ii) to be a qualified expenditure made by the taxpayer in the subsequent year to which the expenditure can reasonably be considered to relate;

(d) for the purpose of paragraph (a), an outlay or expense of a taxpayer is deemed not to include any payment referred to in subparagraph 37(1)(a)(ii) or (iii) that

(i) is made by the taxpayer to a person or partnership with which the taxpayer deals at arm's length, and

(ii) is not an expenditure described in subparagraph 37(1)(a)(i); and

(e) for the purposes of section 37 and the definition "qualified expenditure" in subsection 127(9), the portion of an expenditure that is made or incurred by a taxpayer in a taxation year and that would, but for paragraph (a), have been deductible under section 37 in computing the taxpayer's income for the year, is deemed

(i) not to be made or incurred by the taxpayer in the year, and

(ii) to be made or incurred by the taxpayer in the subsequent taxation year to which the expenditure can reasonably be considered to relate.

**Related Provisions**: 6(1)(a)(i), 6(4) — Group term life insurance premiums — taxable benefit; 18(9.01) — Group term life insurance — deductibility of premiums; 18(9.02) — Application to insurers; 20(1)(m.1) — Manufacturer's warranty reserve; 20(1)(m.2) — Repayment of amount previously included in income; 87(2)(j.2) — Amalgamations — prepaid expenses.

**Notes**: 18(9)(a)(iii)(B) added by 1994 Budget, effective for premiums paid after February 1994 for insurance. For premiums paid earlier, read:

> (iii) as consideration for insurance in respect of a period after the end of the year (other than an amount paid in respect of reinsurance by an insurer);

Parenthetical exclusion beginning "other than" in 18(9)(b) added by 1992 technical bill, effective for amounts paid as, on account of, in lieu of payment of or in satisfaction of, interest in respect of a period or part thereof that is after 1991. Prepaid interest is now dealt with in 18(9.2) to (9.8).

18(9)(d) amended by 1995 Budget, effective for payments made after 1995. Formerly read: "for the purpose of paragraph (a), an outlay or expense shall be deemed not to include any payment referred to in clause 37(1)(a)(ii)(E)". The new 18(9)(d) provides an exception to the prohibition of the deduction of prepaid expenses by 18(9)(a), for certain third-party payments.

18(9)(e) added by 1995 Budget, effective for expenditures made or incurred at any time.

**Interpretation Bulletins**: IT-109R2: Unpaid amounts; IT-151R5: Scientific research and experimental development expenditures; IT-211R: Membership dues — associations and societies; IT-233R: Lease-option agreements; sale-leaseback agreements; IT-341R3: Expenses of issuing or selling shares, units in a trust, interests in a partnership or syndicate, and expenses of borrowing money; IT-417R2: Prepaid expenses and deferred charges.

**(9.01) Group term life insurance** — Where

(a) a taxpayer pays a premium after February 1994 and before 1997 under a group term life insurance policy for insurance on the life of an individual,

(b) the insurance is for the remainder of the individual's lifetime, and

(c) no further premiums will be payable for the insurance,

no amount may be deducted in computing the taxpayer's income for a taxation year from a business or property in respect of the premium except that there may be so deducted,

(d) where the year is the taxation year in which the premium was paid or a subsequent taxation year and the individual is alive at the end of the year, the lesser of

(i) the amount determined by the formula

$$A - B$$

and

(ii) ⅓ of the amount determined by the formula

$$A \times \frac{C}{365}$$

where

A is the amount that would, if this Act were read without reference to this subsection, be deductible in respect of the premium in computing the taxpayer's income,

B is the total amount deductible in respect of the premium in computing the taxpayer's income for preceding taxation years, and

C is the number of days in the year, and

(e) where the individual died in the year, the amount determined under subparagraph (d)(i).

**Related Provisions**: 6(4) — Taxable benefit from premiums paid by employer; 87(2)(j.2) — Amalgamations — prepaid expenses; 257 — Formula cannot calculate to less than zero.

**Notes**: 18(9.01) added by 1994 Budget, effective for premiums paid after February 1994 for insurance. It ensures that deductions for premiums for paid-up insurance match, reasonably closely, the inclusions required by Reg. 2703 for purposes of 6(4).

### Proposed Addition — 18(9.02)

**(9.02) Application of subsec. (9) to insurers** — For the purpose of subsection (9), an outlay or expense made or incurred by an insurer on account of the acquisition of an insurance policy (other than a non-cancellable or guaranteed renewable accident and sickness insurance policy or a life insurance policy other than a group term life insurance policy that provides coverage for a period of 12 months or less) is deemed to be an expense incurred as consideration for services rendered consistently throughout the period of coverage of the policy.

**Application**: Bill C-43 (First Reading September 20, 2000), subsec. 7(2), will add subsec. 18(9.02), applicable to taxation years that begin after 1999 except that, where a taxpayer so elects in writing and files the election with the Minister of National Revenue on or before the taxpayer's filing-due date for the taxpayer's taxation year in which the amending legislation receives Royal Assent, subsec. 18(9.02) applies to taxation years that end after 1997.

**Technical Notes**: Currently, policy acquisition costs are deductible for tax purposes on a current basis. New subsection 18(9.02) deems an outlay or expense made by an insurer on account of the acquisition of an insurance policy (other than a non-cancellable or guaranteed renewable accident and sickness policy or a life policy that is not a group term life policy that provides coverage for a period not exceeding 12 months) to be an expense incurred for services rendered consistently throughout the period of coverage of the policy. Where such acquisition costs relate to an insurance policy that covers a period extending beyond the end of the insurer's taxation year, subsection 18(9) of the Act will apply to prorate the deductibility of the costs over the period of coverage of the policy. Generally accepted accounting principles (GAAP) identify policy acquisition costs to include premium taxes, commissions, and other costs directly related to the acquisition of premiums written.

**(9.1) Penalties, bonuses and rate-reduction payments** — Subject to subsection 142.4(10), where at any time a payment, other than a payment that

(a) can reasonably be considered to have been made in respect of the extension of the term of a debt obligation or in respect of the substitution or

**S. 18(9.1)(a)**      Income Tax Act, Part I, Division B

conversion of a debt obligation to another debt obligation or share, or

(b) is contingent or dependent on the use of or production from property or is computed by reference to revenue, profit, cash flow, commodity price or any other similar criterion or by reference to dividends paid or payable to shareholders of any class of shares of the capital stock of a corporation,

is made to a person or partnership by a taxpayer in the course of carrying on a business or earning income from property in respect of borrowed money or on an amount payable for property acquired by the taxpayer (in this subsection referred to as a "debt obligation")

(c) as consideration for a reduction in the rate of interest payable by the taxpayer on the debt obligation, or

(d) as a penalty or bonus payable by the taxpayer because of the repayment by the taxpayer of all or part of the principal amount of the debt obligation before its maturity,

the payment shall, to the extent that it can reasonably be considered to relate to, and does not exceed the value at that time of, an amount that, but for the reduction described in paragraph (c) or the repayment described in paragraph (d), would have been paid or payable by the taxpayer as interest on the debt obligation for a taxation year of the taxpayer ending after that time, be deemed,

(e) for the purposes of this Act, to have been paid by the taxpayer and received by the person or partnership at that time as interest on the debt obligation, and

(f) for the purpose of computing the taxpayer's income in respect of the business or property for the year, to have been paid or payable by the taxpayer in that year as interest pursuant to a legal obligation to pay interest,

    (i) in the case of a reduction described in paragraph (c), on the debt obligation, and

    (ii) in the case of a repayment described in paragraph (d),

        (A) where the repayment was in respect of all or part of the principal amount of the debt obligation that was borrowed money, except to the extent that the borrowed money was used by the taxpayer to acquire property, on borrowed money used in the year for the purpose for which the borrowed money that was repaid was used, and

        (B) where the repayment was in respect of all or part of the principal amount of the debt obligation that was either borrowed money used to acquire property or an amount payable for property acquired by the taxpayer, on the debt obligation to the extent that the property or property substituted therefor is used by the taxpayer in the year for the purpose of gaining or producing income therefrom or for the purpose of gaining or producing income from a business.

**Related Provisions**: 18(9.2) — Prepaid interest on debt obligations; 20(1)(e) — Expenses re financing; 87(2)(j.6) — Amalgamations — continuing corporation; 248(5) — Substituted property.

**Notes**: 18(9.1) applies where a penalty or bonus is paid in respect of the repayment of all or part of a debt obligation before its maturity. It provides, in certain circumstances, that the penalty or bonus is deemed to have been paid and received as interest, to the extent it does not exceed the future interest that would, but for the repayment, have been payable on the obligation. 18(9.1) also applies with respect to certain interest rate reduction payments.

The words "Subject to subsection 142.4(10)" added to opening words of 18(9.1) by 1995-97 technical bill, effective for taxation years that end after February 22, 1994.

18(9.1) added by 1991 technical bill, effective 1985. However, for payments before July 13, 1990, ignore 18(9.1)(e).

**Interpretation Bulletins**: IT-104R2: Deductibility of fines or penalties; IT-341R3: Expenses of issuing or selling shares, units in a trust, interests in a partnership or syndicate, and expenses of borrowing money.

**(9.2) Interest on debt obligations** — For the purposes of this Part, the amount of interest payable on borrowed money or on an amount payable for property (in this subsection and subsections (9.3) to (9.8) referred to as the "debt obligation") by a corporation, partnership or trust (in this subsection and subsections (9.3) to (9.7) referred to as the "borrower") in respect of a taxation year shall, notwithstanding subparagraph (9.1)(f)(i), be deemed to be an amount equal to the lesser of

(a) the amount of interest, not in excess of a reasonable amount, that would be payable on the debt obligation by the borrower in respect of the year if no amount had been paid before the end of the year in satisfaction of the obligation to pay interest on the debt obligation in respect of the year and if the amount outstanding at each particular time in the year that is after 1991 on account of the principal amount of the debt obligation were the amount, if any, by which

    (i) the amount outstanding at the particular time on account of the principal amount of the debt obligation

exceeds the total of

    (ii) all amounts each of which is an amount paid before the particular time in satisfaction, in whole or in part, of the obligation to pay interest on the debt obligation in respect of a period or part thereof that is after 1991, after the beginning of the year, and after the time the amount was so paid (other than a period or part thereof that is in the year where no such amount was paid before the particular time in respect of a period, or part of a period, that is after the end of the year), and

(iii) the amount, if any, by which

(A) the total of all amounts of interest payable on the debt obligation (determined without reference to this subsection) by the borrower in respect of taxation years ending after 1991 and before the year (to the extent that the interest does not exceed a reasonable amount)

exceeds

(B) the total of all amounts of interest deemed by this subsection to have been payable on the debt obligation by the borrower in respect of taxation years ending before the year, and

(b) the amount, if any, by which

(i) the total of all amounts of interest payable on the debt obligation (determined without reference to this subsection) by the borrower in respect of the year or taxation years ending after 1991 and before the year (to the extent that the interest does not exceed a reasonable amount)

exceeds

(ii) the total of all amounts of interest deemed by this subsection to have been payable on the debt obligation by the borrower in respect of taxation years ending before the year.

**Related Provisions**: 18(9.3)–(9.8) — Prepaid interest on debt obligations.

**Notes**: 18(9.2) added by 1992 technical bill, effective for 1992 and later taxation years. The rules in 18(9.2) to (9.8) limit the deductibility of prepaid interest.

**Interpretation Bulletins**: IT-417R2: Prepaid expenses and deferred charges.

**(9.3) Interest on debt obligations** — Where at any time in a taxation year of a borrower a debt obligation of the borrower is settled or extinguished or the holder of the obligation acquires or reacquires property of the borrower in circumstances in which section 79 applies in respect of the debt obligation and the total of

(a) all amounts each of which is an amount paid at or before that time in satisfaction, in whole or in part, of the obligation to pay interest on the debt obligation in respect of a period or part of a period that is after that time, and

(b) all amounts of interest payable on the debt obligation (determined without reference to subsection (9.2)) by the borrower in respect of taxation years ending after 1991 and before that time, or in respect of periods, or parts of periods, that are in such years and before that time (to the extent that the interest does not exceed a reasonable amount),

exceeds the total of

(c) all amounts of interest deemed by subsection (9.2) to have been payable on the debt obligation by the borrower in respect of taxation years ending before that time, and

(d) the amount of interest that would be deemed by subsection (9.2) to have been payable on the debt obligation by the borrower in respect of the year if the year had ended immediately before that time,

(which excess is in this subsection referred to as the "excess amount"), the following rules apply:

(e) for the purpose of applying section 79 in respect of the borrower, the principal amount at that time of the debt obligation shall be deemed to be equal to the amount, if any, by which

(i) the principal amount at that time of the debt obligation

exceeds

(ii) the excess amount, and

(f) the excess amount shall be deducted at that time in computing the forgiven amount in respect of the obligation (within the meaning assigned by subsection 80(1)).

**Related Provisions**: 80(1)"forgiven amount"B(c) — Deduction from forgiven amount as per 18(9.3)(f).

**Notes**: 18(9.3) added by 1992 technical bill, effective for 1992 and later taxation years.

Opening words of 18(9.3) amended by 1994 tax amendments bill (Part I) to add "or the holder of the obligation acquires or reacquires property of the borrower in circumstances in which section 79 applies in respect of the debt obligation", retroactive to the introduction of 18(9.3) (1992 and later taxation years).

The words "at or" in 18(9.3)(a) added by 1994 tax amendments bill (Part I), effective for taxation years that end after February 21, 1994, except that they do not apply to any obligation settled or extinguished

(a) before February 22, 1994;

(b) after February 21, 1994

(i) under the terms of an agreement in writing entered into by that date, or

(ii) under the terms of any amendment to such an agreement, where that amendment was entered into in writing before July 12, 1994 and the amount of the settlement or extinguishment was not substantially greater than the settlement or extinguishment provided under the terms of the agreement;

(c) before 1996 pursuant to a restructuring of debt in connection with a proceeding commenced in a court in Canada before February 22, 1994;

(d) before 1996 in connection with a proposal (or notice of intention to make a proposal) that was filed under the *Bankruptcy and Insolvency Act*, or similar legislation of a country other than Canada, before February 22, 1994; or

(e) before 1996 in connection with a written offer that was made by, or communicated to, the holder of the obligation before February 22, 1994.

(These are the same application rules that apply for 80–80.04.)

18(9.3)(e) amended by 1994 tax amendments bill (Part I), retroactive to the introduction of 18(9.3) (1992 and later taxation years).

18(9.3)(f) amended by 1994 tax amendments bill (Part I), effective on the same conditions as the amendment to 18(9.3)(a). Where the new version does not apply, read:

> (f) for the purpose of applying section 80 in respect of the borrower, where the debt obligation was settled or extinguished in circumstances to which that section applies, the debt obligation shall be deemed to have been settled or extinguished by the payment of an amount equal to the total of
>
>> (i) the amount, if any, of the payment made to settle or extinguish the debt obligation (determined without reference to this subsection), and
>>
>> (ii) the excess amount.

**Interpretation Bulletins**: IT-417R2: Prepaid expenses and deferred charges.

**(9.4) Idem** — Where an amount is paid at any time by a person or partnership in respect of a debt obligation of a borrower

(a) as, on account of, in lieu of payment of or in satisfaction of, interest on the debt obligation in respect of a period or part thereof that is after 1991 and after that time, or

(b) as consideration for a reduction in the rate of interest payable on the debt obligation (excluding, for greater certainty, a payment described in paragraph (9.1)(a) or (b)) in respect of a period or part thereof that is after 1991 and after that time,

that amount shall be deemed, for the purposes of subsection (9.5) and, subject to that subsection, for the purposes of clause (9.2)(a)(iii)(A), subparagraph (9.2)(b)(i), paragraph (9.3)(b) and subsection (9.6), to be an amount of interest payable on the debt obligation by the borrower in respect of that period or part thereof and shall be deemed, for the purposes of subparagraph (9.2)(a)(ii) and paragraph (9.3)(a), to be an amount paid at that time in satisfaction of the obligation to pay interest on the debt obligation in respect of that period or part thereof.

**Notes**: 18(9.4) added by 1992 technical bill, effective for 1992 and later taxation years.

**Interpretation Bulletins**: IT-417R2: Prepaid expenses and deferred charges.

**(9.5) Idem** — Where the amount of interest payable on a debt obligation (determined without reference to subsection (9.2)) by a borrower in respect of a particular period or part thereof that is after 1991 can reasonably be regarded as an amount payable as consideration for

(a) a reduction in the amount of interest that would otherwise be payable on the debt obligation in respect of a subsequent period, or

(b) a reduction in the amount that was or may be paid before the beginning of a subsequent period in satisfaction of the obligation to pay interest on the debt obligation in respect of that subsequent period

(determined without reference to the existence of, or the amount of any interest paid or payable on, any other debt obligation), that amount shall, for the purposes of clause (9.2)(a)(iii)(A), subparagraph (9.2)(b)(i), paragraph (9.3)(b) and subsection (9.6), be deemed to be an amount of interest payable on the debt obligation by the borrower in respect of the subsequent period and not to be an amount of interest payable on the debt obligation by the borrower in respect of the particular period and shall, when paid, be deemed for the purposes of subparagraph (9.2)(a)(ii) and paragraph (9.3)(a) to be an amount paid in satisfaction of the obligation to pay interest on the debt obligation in respect of the subsequent period.

**Related Provisions**: 18(9.4) — Prepaid interest on debt obligations.

**Notes**: 18(9.5) added by 1992 technical bill, effective for 1992 and later taxation years.

**Interpretation Bulletins**: IT-417R2: Prepaid expenses and deferred charges.

**(9.6) Idem** — Where the liability in respect of a debt obligation of a person or partnership is assumed by a borrower at any time,

(a) the amount of interest payable on the debt obligation (determined without reference to subsection (9.2)) by any person or partnership in respect of a period shall, to the extent that that period is included in a taxation year of the borrower ending after 1991, be deemed, for the purposes of clause (9.2)(a)(iii)(A), subparagraph (9.2)(b)(i) and paragraph (9.3)(b), to be an amount of interest payable on the debt obligation by the borrower in respect of that year, and

(b) the application of subsections (9.2) and (9.3) to the borrower in respect of the debt obligation after that time shall be determined on the assumption that subsection (9.2) applied to the borrower in respect of the debt obligation before that time,

and, for the purposes of this subsection, where the borrower came into existence at a particular time that is after the beginning of the particular period beginning at the beginning of the first period in respect of which interest was payable on the debt obligation by any person or partnership and ending at the particular time, the borrower shall be deemed

(c) to have been in existence throughout the particular period, and

(d) to have had, throughout the particular period, taxation years ending on the day of the year on which its first taxation year ended.

**Notes**: 18(9.6) added by 1992 technical bill, effective for 1992 and later taxation years.

**Interpretation Bulletins**: IT-417R2: Prepaid expenses and deferred charges.

**(9.7) Idem** — Where the amount paid by a borrower at any particular time, in satisfaction of the obligation to pay a particular amount of interest on a debt obligation in respect of a subsequent period or part thereof, exceeds the particular amount of that interest, discounted

(a) for the particular period beginning at the particular time and ending at the end of the subsequent period or part thereof, and

(b) at the rate or rates of interest applying under the debt obligation during the particular period (or, where the rate of interest of any part of the particular period is not fixed at the particular time, at the prescribed rate of interest in effect at the particular time),

that excess shall

(c) for the purposes of applying subsections (9.2) to (9.6) and (9.8), be deemed to be neither an amount of interest payable on the debt obligation nor an amount paid in satisfaction of the obligation to pay interest on the debt obligation, and

(d) be deemed to be a payment described in paragraph (9.1)(d) in respect of the debt obligation.

**Notes**: 18(9.7) added by 1992 technical bill, effective for 1992 and later taxation years.

**Regulations**: 4301(c) (prescribed rate of interest).

**Interpretation Bulletins**: IT-417R2: Prepaid expenses and deferred charges.

**(9.8) Idem** — Nothing in any of subsections (9.2) to (9.7) shall be construed as providing that

(a) the total of all amounts each of which is the amount of interest payable on a debt obligation by an individual (other than a trust), or deemed by subsection (9.2) to be payable on the debt obligation by a corporation, partnership or trust, in respect of a taxation year ending after 1991 and before any particular time,

may exceed

(b) the total of all amounts each of which is the amount of interest payable on the debt obligation (determined without reference to subsection (9.2)) by a person or partnership in respect of a taxation year ending after 1991 and before that particular time.

**Notes**: 18(9.8) added by 1992 technical bill, effective for 1992 and later taxation years.

**Interpretation Bulletins**: IT-417R2: Prepaid expenses and deferred charges.

**(10) Employee benefit plan** — Paragraph (1)(o) does not apply in respect of a contribution to an employee benefit plan

(a) to the extent that the contribution

(i) is made in respect of services performed by an employee who is not resident in Canada and is regularly employed in a country other than Canada, and

(ii) cannot reasonably be regarded as having been made in respect of services performed or to be performed during a period when the employee is resident in Canada;

(b) the custodian of which is non-resident, to the extent that the contribution

(i) is in respect of an employee who is non-resident at the time the contribution is made, and

(ii) cannot reasonably be regarded as having been made in respect of services performed or to be performed during a period when the employee is resident in Canada; or

(c) the custodian of which is non-resident, to the extent that the contribution can reasonably be regarded as having been made in respect of services performed by an employee in a particular calendar month where

(i) the employee was resident in Canada throughout no more than 60 of the 72 calendar months ending with the particular month, and

(ii) the employee became a member of the plan before the end of the month following the month in which the employee became resident in Canada,

and, for the purpose of this paragraph, where benefits provided to an employee under a particular employee benefit plan are replaced by benefits provided under another employee benefit plan, the other plan shall be deemed, in respect of the employee, to be the same plan as the particular plan.

**Notes**: 18(10) amended by 1993 technical bill, effective for contributions made after 1992. For earlier contributions, ignore 18(10)(c) and read 18(10)(b) as:

(b) the custodian of which is not resident in Canada, to the extent that the contribution

(i) is in respect of an employee who was

(A) not resident in Canada at the time the contribution was made, or

(B) resident in Canada for a period (in this paragraph referred to as an "excluded period") of not more than 36 of the 72 months preceding the date on which the contribution is made and was a beneficiary under the plan before becoming resident in Canada, and

(ii) cannot reasonably be regarded as having been made in respect of services performed or to be performed during a period (other than an excluded period) when the employee is resident in Canada.

The extension of the exemption from 36 to 60 months after becoming a Canadian resident is consistent with the RCA rules; see 207.6(5.1)(b)(ii). The closing words of 18(10)(c) also allow for a replacement plan to be given the same exemption from the deduction prohibition in 18(1)(o).

**Interpretation Bulletins**: IT-502: Employee benefit plans and employee trusts.

**(11) Limitation [on interest expense]** — Notwithstanding any other provision of this Act, in computing the income of a taxpayer for a taxation year, no amount is deductible under paragraph 20(1)(c), (d), (e), (e.1) or (f) in respect of borrowed money (or other property acquired by the taxpayer) in respect of any period after which the money (or other property) is used by the taxpayer for the purpose of

(a) making a payment after November 12, 1981 as consideration for an income-averaging annuity contract, unless the contract was acquired pursuant to an agreement in writing entered into before November 13, 1981;

(b) paying a premium (within the meaning assigned by subsection 146(1) read without reference to the portion of the definition "premium" in that subsection following paragraph (b) of that definition) under a registered retirement savings plan after November 12, 1981;

(c) making a contribution to a registered pension plan or a deferred profit sharing plan after November 12, 1981, other than

(i) a contribution described in subparagraph 8(1)(m)(ii) or (iii) (as they read in their application to the 1990 taxation year) that was required to be made pursuant to an obligation entered into before November 13, 1981, or

(ii) a contribution deductible under paragraph 20(1)(q) or (y) in computing the taxpayer's income;

(d) making a payment as consideration for an annuity the payment for which was deductible in computing the taxpayer's income by virtue of paragraph 60(l);

(e) making a contribution to a retirement compensation arrangement where the contribution was deductible under paragraph 8(1)(m.2) in computing the taxpayer's income;

(f) making a contribution to a net income stabilization account;

(g) making a contribution to any account under a provincial pension plan prescribed for the purpose of paragraph 60(v); or

(h) making a contribution into a registered education savings plan,

and, for the purposes of this subsection, to the extent that an indebtedness is incurred by a taxpayer in respect of a property and at any time that property or a property substituted therefor is used for any of the purposes referred to in this subsection, the indebtedness shall be deemed to be incurred at that time for that purpose.

**Related Provisions**: 18(1)(u) — Investment counselling and administration fees for RRSP or RRIF are non-deductible; 110.6(1)"investment expense"(a); 248(5) — Substituted property.

**Notes**: 18(11) amended by 1990 pension bill. In subpara. (c)(i), the words "as they read in their application to the 1990 taxation year" added, effective 1991. In subpara. (c)(ii), a reference to para. 20(1)(s) deleted, effective 1992. Para. (e) added, effective 1989.

18(11) amended by 1991 technical bill, effective 1990, to add references to 20(1)(e.1) and (f) and delete reference to 20(1)(k) in opening words, and to add the closing words.

18(11) amended by 1992 technical bill. Parenthetical definition of "premium" in para. (b) added, effective 1992; para. (f) added, effective 1991; closing words amended to apply only "to the extent that" indebtedness is used for one of the listed purposes rather than "where" it is so used.

18(11)(g) added by 1993 technical bill, effective for 1993 and later taxation years. It refers to the Saskatchewan Pension Plan.

18(11)(h) added by 1997 Budget, effective for 1998 and later taxation years.

**Interpretation Bulletins**: IT-124R6: Contributions to registered retirement savings plans; IT-167R6: Registered pension plans — employee's contributions; IT-307R3: Spousal registered retirement savings plans; IT-355R2: Interest on loans to buy life insurance policies and annuity contracts, and interest on policy loans.

**(12) Work space in home** — Notwithstanding any other provision of this Act, in computing an individual's income from a business for a taxation year,

(a) no amount shall be deducted in respect of an otherwise deductible amount for any part (in this subsection referred to as the "work space") of a self-contained domestic establishment in which the individual resides, except to the extent that the work space is either

(i) the individual's principal place of business, or

(ii) used exclusively for the purpose of earning income from business and used on a regular and continuous basis for meeting clients, customers or patients of the individual in respect of the business;

(b) where the conditions set out in subparagraph (a)(i) or (ii) are met, the amount for the work space that is deductible in computing the individual's income for the year from the business shall not exceed the individual's income for the year from the business, computed without reference to the amount and sections 34.1 and 34.2; and

(c) any amount not deductible by reason only of paragraph (b) in computing the individual's income from the business for the immediately preceding taxation year shall be deemed to be an amount otherwise deductible that, subject to paragraphs (a) and (b), may be deducted for the year for the work space in respect of the business.

**Related Provisions**: 8(13) — Parallel rule for employee.

**Notes**: Home office expenses typically include such things as mortgage interest (or rent), property taxes, utilities, insurance and maintenance for the home, all prorated to a figure (often 10-15%) representing the proportion of the office to the home as a whole. The CCRA acknowledges that, where an office is the individual's principal place of business and is not used for personal purposes, the fact the individual works at client locations most of the time does not prevent the home office expenses from being calculated based on the office's square footage as a percentage of the home (VIEWS doc 2000-008905).

A parallel limitation applies to GST input tax credits for home office expenses. See para. 170(1)(a.1) of the *Excise Tax Act*, reproduced in David M. Sherman, *The Practitioner's GST Annotated*.

18(12)(c) provides an indefinite carryforward of allowable home office expenses against any eventual income from the business. Each year, the amount that was not deductible for the previous year because of 18(12)(b) is deductible in the year, but to the extent the business does not generate sufficient income, is again restricted by

18(12)(b). For employees, the same carryforward is provided by 8(13)(c).

18(12)(b) amended to add reference to 34.1 and 34.2 by 1995 Budget, effective 1995. Those sections deal with the change to calendar year-end taxation for individuals and most partnerships.

**Interpretation Bulletins**: IT-504R2: Visual artists and writers; IT-514: Work space in home expenses.

**(13) When subsec. (15) applies to money lenders** — Subsection (15) applies, subject to subsection 142.6(7), when

(a) a taxpayer (in this subsection and subsection (15) referred to as the "transferor") disposes of a particular property;

(b) the disposition is not described in any of paragraphs (c) to (g) of the definition "superficial loss" in section 54;

(c) the transferor is not an insurer;

(d) the ordinary business of the transferor includes the lending of money and the particular property was used or held in the ordinary course of that business;

(e) the particular property is a share, or a loan, bond, debenture, mortgage, note, agreement for sale or any other indebtedness;

(f) the particular property was, immediately before the disposition, not a capital property of the transferor;

(g) during the period that begins 30 days before and ends 30 days after the disposition, the transferor or a person affiliated with the transferor acquires a property (in this subsection and subsection (15) referred to as the "substituted property") that is, or is identical to, the particular property; and

(h) at the end of the period, the transferor or a person affiliated with the transferor owns the substituted property.

**Related Provisions**: 18(14) — Alternate application of subsec. 18(15); 40(2)(g)(i), 54"superficial loss" — Parallel rule for capital property; 248(12) — Identical properties.

**Notes**: In simple terms, 18(13)-(16) deny a loss to persons in the business of lending money (18(13)) or holding property as an adventure in the nature of trade (18(14)), where the property sold or identical property is reacquired within the period from 30 days before to 30 days after the sale, either by the same person or an "affiliated" person (see 251.1). For the parallel superficial loss rule for capital property, see 40(2)(g)(i) and 54"superficial loss". The pregnant loss is suspended in the seller's hands (18(15)), as is done by 40(3.4) for pregnant capital losses and 13(21.2) for terminal losses (see Notes to those provisions).

18(13) replaced by 1995-97 technical bill, effective (subject to the grandfathering rule reproduced after s. 260) for dispositions of property after April 26, 1995, other than a disposition before July 1995 to which 142.6(7)

(a) does not apply; and

(b) would apply if the disposition had occurred after June 1995.

It formerly read:

(13) **Superficial loss** — Subject to subsection 142.6(7) and notwithstanding any other provision of this Act, where a taxpayer (other than an insurer)

(a) who was a resident of Canada at any time in a taxation year and whose ordinary business during that year included the lending of money, or

(b) who at any time in the year carried on a business of lending money in Canada

has sustained a loss on a disposition of property used or held in that business that is a share, or a loan, bond, debenture, mortgage, note, agreement of sale or any other indebtedness, other than a property that is a capital property of the taxpayer, no amount shall be deducted in computing the income of the taxpayer from that business for the year in respect of the loss where

(c) during the period commencing 30 days before and ending 30 days after the disposition, the taxpayer or a person or partnership that does not deal at arm's length with the taxpayer acquired or agreed to acquire the same or identical property (in this subsection referred to as the "substituted property"), and

(d) at the end of the period described in paragraph (c), the taxpayer, person or partnership, as the case may be, owned or had a right to acquire the substituted property,

and any such loss shall be added in computing the cost to the taxpayer, person or partnership, as the case may be, of the substituted property.

Opening words of former 18(13) amended by 1994 tax amendments bill (Part III), effective for dispositions occurring after October 30, 1994, to change "138(5.2)" to "142.6(7)" and to add the words "(other than an insurer)".

**(14) When subsec. (15) applies to adventurers in trade** — Subsection (15) applies where

(a) a person (in this subsection and subsection (15) referred to as the "transferor") disposes of a particular property;

(b) the particular property is described in an inventory of a business that is an adventure or concern in the nature of trade;

(c) the disposition is not a disposition that is deemed to have occurred by section 70, subsection 104(4), section 128.1, paragraph 132.2(1)(f) or subsection 138(11.3) or 149(10);

(d) during the period that begins 30 days before and ends 30 days after the disposition, the transferor or a person affiliated with the transferor acquires property (in this subsection and subsection (15) referred to as the "substituted property") that is, or is identical to, the particular property; and

(e) at the end of the period, the transferor or a person affiliated with the transferor owns the substituted property.

**Related Provisions**: 10(1.01) — No writedown of inventory held as adventure in the nature of trade; 18(13) — Alternate application of subsec. 18(15); 40(2)(g)(i), 54"superficial loss" — Parallel rule for capital property; 248(12) — Identical properties.

**Notes**: See Notes to 18(13). 18(14) added by 1995-97 technical bill, effective for dispositions of property after June 20, 1996, other than a disposition before 1997 to a person or partnership that was obliged on June 20, 1996 to acquire the property pursuant to the terms of an agreement in writing made by that day and, for the purpose of this rule, a person or partnership shall be considered not to be obliged to acquire property where the person or partnership can be excused from performing the obligation if there is a change to the Act or if there is an adverse assessment under the Act.

**(15) Loss on certain properties [transferred within affiliated group]** — If this subsection applies because of subsection (13) or (14) to a disposition of a particular property,

(a) the transferor's loss, if any, from the disposition is deemed to be nil, and

(b) the amount of the transferor's loss, if any, from the disposition (determined without reference to this subsection) is deemed to be a loss of the transferor from a disposition of the particular property at the first time, after the disposition,

(i) at which a 30-day period begins throughout which neither the transferor nor a person affiliated with the transferor owns

(A) the substituted property, or

(B) a property that is identical to the substituted property and that was acquired after the day that is 31 days before the period begins,

(ii) at which the substituted property would, if it were owned by the transferor, be deemed by section 128.1 or subsection 149(10) to have been disposed of by the transferor,

(iii) that is immediately before control of the transferor is acquired by a person or group of persons, where the transferor is a corporation, or

(iv) at which the winding-up of the transferor begins (other than a winding-up to which subsection 88(1) applies), where the transferor is a corporation,

and for the purpose of paragraph (b), where a partnership otherwise ceases to exist at any time after the disposition, the partnership is deemed not to have ceased to exist, and each person who was a member of the partnership immediately before the partnership would, but for this subsection, have ceased to exist is deemed to remain a member of the partnership, until the time that is immediately after the first time described in subparagraphs (b)(i) to (iv).

**Related Provisions**: 13(21.2) — Parallel rule for depreciable capital property; 14(12) — Parallel rule for eligible capital property; 18(16) — Deemed identical property; 40(3.3), (3.4) — Parallel rule for capital losses; 69(5)(d) — No application on winding-up; 87(2)(g.3) — Amalgamations — continuing corporation; 139.1(18) — Holding corporation deemed not to acquire control of insurer on demutualization; 248(12) — Whether properties are identical; 251.1 — Affiliated persons; 256(6)–(9) — Whether control acquired.

**Notes**: See Notes to 18(13). 18(15) added by 1995-97 technical bill, effective for dispositions of property after April 26, 1995.

**(16) Deemed identical property** — For the purposes of subsections (13), (14) and (15), a right to acquire a property (other than a right, as security only, derived from a mortgage, agreement for sale or similar obligation) is deemed to be a property that is identical to the property.

**Notes**: See Notes to 18(13). 18(16) added by 1995-97 technical bill, effective for dispositions of property after April 26, 1995.

### Proposed Amendment — Section 18 — Limitation on deductibility of provincial payroll and capital taxes

**Department of Finance press release, March 2, 1993**: Finance Minister Don Mazankowski today announced that the government would take action, on an interim basis, to effectively deny the deductibility of any increases in provincial payroll and capital taxes. This measure would take effect if provincial payroll and capital tax revenues were increased by way of a rate increase, base change, or the introduction of a new tax.

The 1991 federal Budget proposed a mechanism to limit the impact on federal revenue of the provinces' increasing reliance on such taxes. Discussions with the provinces and affected taxpayers have been held since that time to consider possible modifications of the federal proposal to limit deductibility. Those discussions are continuing, and it is anticipated that a comprehensive solution will be ready for implementation in 1994. Today's measure is intended to apply until that final proposal is brought forward.

Mr. Mazankowski said, "I remain concerned that any provincial actions to increase existing payroll and capital taxes or the introduction of new taxes would further erode federal revenues and put additional pressure on the fiscal framework."

If a province institutes or increases payroll or capital taxes in 1993, an income tax amendment would be sought to ensure that corporations and certain trusts operating in that province are allowed to deduct only a certain percentage of such taxes in computing their income for federal tax purposes. To compute its deductible amount, a taxpayer would simply multiply its total amount of those taxes paid to the province by a percentage prescribed under the *Income Tax Act*. That percentage, which would be determined after consultation with the province on expected revenues, would ensure that the total amount of payroll and capital taxes deducted by all businesses in the province remained the same. It would not, in contrast, ensure that the level of each taxpayer's deductible taxes remained the same. The restriction on deductibility would apply on a prorated basis from the date the provincial tax increase took effect.

The Minister noted that this measure would not restrict the tax policy options of any province. A province may continue to levy these taxes as it sees fit. "However, provinces that increase these taxes will no longer be able to pass part of the cost on to the federal government and taxpayers in other provinces," added Mr. Mazankowski.

The Minister stressed that this is an interim measure and that federal and provincial officials are continuing to work on a longer-term solution.

For further information: Jack Jung, (613) 992-7162; Lawrence Purdy, (613) 996-0602.

**Department of Finance press release, October 1, 1993**: *Extension of Interim Measure to Limit the Deductibility of Provincial Payroll and Capital Taxes*

Finance Minister Gilles Loiselle today announced that proposed limits to the deductibility for federal tax purposes of provincial payroll and capital taxes will be delayed for another year, to allow time for additional consultations with provincial and business representatives. An interim measure announced earlier this year to limit the impact of any increases in these taxes will continue to apply until the revised proposal is in effect. The Minister indicated that federal and provincial officials will continue their discussions on a longer term solution.

The 1991 federal budget proposed to limit the impact of deductible provincial payroll and capital taxes on federal revenue without adding to the overall tax burden. Implementation of the proposal was to begin on January 1, 1992, but was postponed for two years, pending revisions. Today's announcement delays the implementation of the revised proposal until January 1, 1995.

Under the interim measure announced in March 1993, the government would deny the deductibility of any increases in provincial payroll and capital taxes, whether by way of rate increases, base changes, or the introduction of new taxes. "The problems associated with deductible provincial payroll and capital taxes still need to be addressed," Mr. Loiselle said. "Until the revised proposal is in effect, the interim measure protects the federal tax base from any further erosion resulting from provincial actions to increase these taxes."

For further information: Denis Boucher, (613) 996-7861; Jack Jung, (613) 992-7162.

**Department of Finance press release, October 14, 1994**: *Extension of Interim Measure to Limit the Deductibility of Provincial Payroll and Capital Taxes*

Finance Minister Paul Martin today announced that proposed limits to the deductibility for federal tax purposes of provincial payroll and capital taxes will be delayed for another year, and that the interim measure limiting the deductibility of these taxes will continue to apply for 1995.

The Minister indicated that since the deductibility of these taxes was one of the many issues discussed with his provincial and territorial counterparts last June in Vancouver, it would be inappropriate to implement a new policy while these discussions are in progress.

The interim measure has been in place since March 1993 and protects the federal tax base from further erosion resulting from provincial actions to increase payroll and capital taxes. Under this measure, all existing provincial payroll and capital taxes are deductible, but any increases in these taxes, whether by way of rate increases, base changes, or introduction of new taxes, are not deductible.

The Minister noted that the delay in implementation will have no impact on the fiscal situation of the government.

For further information: Jack Jung, Business Income Tax Division, (613) 992-7162.

**Department of Finance press release, December 27, 1995**: *Extension of Interim Measure to Limit the Deductibility of Provincial Payroll and Capital Taxes*

Finance Minister Paul Martin today announced that the interim measure that limits the deductibility of increases in provincial payroll and capital taxes will be extended for another year in view of the current discussions with many provinces on a harmonized sales tax system. Under the interim measure, existing payroll and capital taxes are deductible but any increases in these taxes, whether by way of rate increases, base changes, or new taxes, are not deductible for federal income tax purposes.

Mr. Martin said that the interim measure, which has been in place since March 1993, will continue to apply throughout 1996. However, he noted that provinces which harmonize their sales tax with the federal sales tax will be provided with additional flexibility in other tax fields such as payroll and capital taxes. Because of Quebec's actions to align its sales tax with the GST, the interim measure will not be triggered by the increases in Quebec payroll and capital taxes, which were announced in the province's 1995-96 budget.

The Minister expressed the hope that all provinces would join a harmonized sales tax system. "A harmonized sales tax would be in the best interests of businesses, consumers and both levels of government in Canada," he added.

For further information: Jack Jung, Business Income Tax Division, (613) 992-7162.

**Department of Finance press release, November 29, 1996**: *Interim Measure Extended on Deductibility of Provincial Payroll and Capital Taxes*

Finance Minister Paul Martin today announced that the interim measure limiting the deductibility of increases in provincial payroll and capital taxes will continue to apply throughout 1997.

Under the interim measure, existing provincial payroll and capital taxes would remain deductible for federal income tax purposes, but any increases in these taxes, whether by way of rate increases, base changes, or introduction of new taxes, would not be deductible. [However, Quebec, New Brunswick, Nova Scotia and Newfoundland are not subject to this rule, since they have harmonized their sales taxes with the GST. See the December 27/95 news release above — ed.]

For further information: Céo Gaudet, Business Income Tax Division, (613) 992-4273

**Department of Finance press release, November 25, 1997**: *Extension Of Interim Measure On Deductibility Of Provincial Payroll And Capital Taxes*

Finance Minister Paul Martin today announced that the interim measure that limits the deductibility of increases in provincial payroll and capital taxes will continue to apply in 1998.

Under the interim measure, any existing provincial payroll and capital taxes will remain deductible for federal income tax purposes, but any increases in these taxes by way of rate increases, base changes, or introduction of new taxes would not be deductible.

For further information: Jack Jung, Business Income Tax Division, (613) 992-5011.

**Department of Finance press release, December 18, 1998**: *Government Extends Interim Measure on Deductibility of Provincial Payroll and Capital Taxes*

Finance Minister Paul Martin today announced that the interim measure that limits the deductibility of increases in provincial payroll and capital taxes will continue to apply in 1999.

Under the interim measure, any existing provincial payroll and capital taxes will remain deductible for federal income tax purposes, but any increases in these taxes by way of provincial actions to increase the rate, change the definition of the base, or introduce new taxes would not be deductible.

For further information: Jack Jung, Business Income Tax Division, (613) 992-5011; Jean-Michel Catta, Public Affairs and Operations Division, (613) 992-1574.

**Department of Finance press release, December 17, 1999**: *Extension of Interim Measure on Deductibility of Provincial Payroll and Capital Taxes*

Finance Minister Paul Martin today announced that the interim measure that limits the deductibility of increases in provincial payroll and capital taxes will continue to apply in the year 2000.

Under the interim measure, any existing provincial payroll and capital taxes will remain deductible for federal income tax purposes, but any increases in these taxes by way of provincial actions to increase the rate, change the definition of the base, or introduce new taxes would not be deductible.

For further information: Jack Jung, Business Income Tax Division, (613) 992-5011; Jean-Michel Catta, Public Affairs and Operations Division, (613) 996-8080; Karl Littler, Senior Adviser, Tax Policy, Office of the Minister of Finance, (613) 996-7861.

**Department of Finance press release, December 12, 2000**: *Extension of Interim Measure on Deductibility of Provincial Payroll and Capital Taxes*

Finance Minister Paul Martin today announced that the interim measure that limits the deductibility of increases in provincial payroll and capital taxes will continue to apply in 2001.

Under the interim measure, any existing provincial payroll and capital taxes will remain deductible for federal income tax purposes, but any increases in these taxes by way of provincial actions to increase the rate, change the definition of the base or introduce new taxes would not be deductible.

For further information: Jack Jung, Business Income Tax Division, (613) 992-5011; Karl Littler, Senior Advisor, Tax Policy, Office of the Minister of Finance, (613) 996-7861; Jean-Michel Catta, Public Affairs and Operations, Division, (613) 996-8080.

**Definitions [s. 18]**: "acquired" — 256(7)–(9); "affiliated" — 251.1; "amortized cost", "amount", "annuity" — 248(1); "arm's length" — 251(1); "associated" — 256; "automobile", "authorized foreign bank", "borrowed money", "business" — 248(1); "calendar year" — *Interpretation Act* 37(1)(a); "Canada" — 255; "Canadian banking business" — 248(1); "Canadian resource property" — 66(15), 248(1); "capital property" — 54, 248(1); "class of shares" — 248(6); "control" — 256(6)–(9); "controlled" — 256(6), (6.1); "corporation" — 248(1), *Interpretation Act* 35(1); "debt obligation" — 18(9.1), (9.2); "deferred profit sharing plan" — 147(1), 248(1); "depreciable property" — 13(21), 248(1); "designated insurance property" — 138(12), 248(1); "dividend", "employee", "employee benefit plan" — 248(1); "employees profit sharing plan" — 144(1), 248(1); "employer", "exempt income", "gross revenue", "group term life insurance policy" — 248(1); "identical" — 18(16), 248(12); "income-averaging annuity contract", "income bond", "income debenture" — 248(1); "incorporated employee" — 125(7)"personal services business"(a); "individual", "insurance corporation", "insurance policy", "insurer" — 248(1); "interest on debt relating to the acquisition of land" — 18(3); "inventory" — 248(1); "land" — 18(3); "lending asset", "life insurance corporation" — 248(1); "life insurance policy" — 138(12), 248(1); "mineral resource", "mineral", "Minister" — 248(1); "month" — *Interpretation Act* 35(1); "net income stabilization account", "non-resident" — 248(1); "non-resident-owned investment corporation" — 133(8), 248(1); "outstanding debts to specified non-residents" — 18(5); "paid-up capital" — 89(1), 248(1); "partnership" — see Notes to 96(1); "permanent establishment" — Reg. 8201; "person", "personal or living expenses", "personal services business", "prescribed" — 248(1); "prescribed rate" — Reg. 4301; "principal amount" — 248(1); "profit sharing plan" — 147(1); "property" — 248(1); "province" — *Interpretation Act* 35(1); "received" — 248(7); "registered education savings plan" — 146.1(1), 248(1); "registered pension plan" — 248(1); "registered retirement savings plan" — 146(1), 248(1); "regulation" — 248(1); "resident in Canada" — 250; "retirement compensation arrangement", "retirement income fund", "retirement savings plan", "salary" — 248(1)"salary or wages"; "salary deferral arrangement", "self-contained domestic establishment", "share", "shareholder" — 248(1); "specified non-resident shareholder" — 18(5); "specified shareholder" — 18(5), 18(5.1), 248(1); "substituted property" — 18(13)(g), 248(5); "supplementary unemployment benefit fund" — 145(1), 248(1); "tar sands" — 248(1); "taxation year" — 11(2), 249; "taxpayer" — 248(1); "transferor" — 18(13)(a), 18(14)(a); "trust" — 104(1), 248(1), (3); "writing" — *Interpretation Act* 35(1).

**Interpretation Bulletins [s. 18]**: IT-105: Administrative costs of pension plans.

**18.1 (1) Definitions** — The definitions in this subsection apply in this section.

**"matchable expenditure"** of a taxpayer means the amount of an expenditure that is made by the taxpayer to

(a) acquire a right to receive production,

(b) fulfil a covenant or obligation arising in circumstances in which it is reasonable to conclude that a relationship exists between the covenant or obligation and a right to receive production, or

(c) preserve or protect a right to receive production,

but does not include an amount for which a deduction is provided under section 20 in computing the taxpayer's income.

**Notes**: See Notes at end of 18.1.

**"right to receive production"** means a right under which a taxpayer is entitled, either immediately or in the future and either absolutely or contingently, to receive an amount all or a portion of which is computed by reference to use of property, production, revenue, profit, cash flow, commodity price, cost or value of property or any other similar criterion or by reference to dividends paid or payable to shareholders of any class of shares where the amount is in respect of another taxpayer's activity, property or business but such a right does not include an income interest in a trust, a Canadian resource property or a foreign resource property.

**Related Provisions**: 88(1)(a)(i) — Treatment of right to receive production on windup of corporation; 248(1)"cost amount"(e)(iv) — Definition of cost amount does not apply to right to receive production.

**Notes**: See Notes at end of 18.1.

**I.T. Technical News**: No. 10 (net profits interests and proposed section 18.1).

**"tax benefit"** means a reduction, avoidance or deferral of tax or other amount payable under this Act or an increase in a refund of tax or other amount under this Act.

**Notes**: See Notes at end of 18.1.

**"tax shelter"** means a property that would be a tax shelter (as defined in subsection 237.1(1)) if

(a) the cost of a right to receive production were the total of all amounts each of which is a matchable expenditure to which the right relates; and

(b) subsections (2) to (13) did not apply for the purpose of computing an amount, or in the case of a partnership a loss, represented to be deductible.

**Notes**: See Notes at end of 18.1.

**"taxpayer"** includes a partnership.

**Notes**: See Notes at end of 18.1.

**(2) Limitation on the deductibility of matchable expenditure** — In computing a taxpayer's income from a business or property for a taxation year, no amount of a matchable expenditure may be deducted except as provided by subsection (3).

**Related Provisions**: 18.1(15) — Non-applicability of limitation; 87(2)(j.2) — Amalgamation — continuing corporation; 88(1)(a)(i) — Treatment of right to receive production on windup of corporation.

**Notes**: See Notes at end of 18.1.

**I.T. Technical News**: No. 10 (net profits interests and proposed section 18.1).

**(3) Deduction of matchable expenditure** — If a taxpayer's matchable expenditure would, but for subsection (2) and this subsection, be deductible in computing the taxpayer's income, there may be deducted in respect of the matchable expenditure in computing the taxpayer's income for a taxation year the amount that is determined under subsection (4) for the year in respect of the expenditure.

**Related Provisions**: 18.1(6) — Income inclusion; 18.1(10) — Amount of deduction if non-arm's length disposition; 18.1(14) — Where right to receive production is reasonably certain.

**Notes**: See Notes at end of 18.1.

**(4) Amount of deduction** — For the purpose of subsection (3), the amount determined under this subsection for a taxation year in respect of a taxpayer's matchable expenditure is the amount, if any, that is the least of

(a) the total of

(i) the lesser of

(A) 1/5 of the matchable expenditure, and

(B) the amount determined by the formula

$$(A/B) \times C$$

where

A is the number of months that are in the year and after the day on which the right to receive production to which the matchable expenditure relates is acquired,

B is the lesser of 240 and the number of months that are in the period that begins on the day on which the right to receive production to which the matchable expenditure relates is acquired and that ends on the day the right is to terminate, and

C is the amount of the matchable expenditure, and

(ii) the amount, if any, by which the amount determined under this paragraph for the preceding taxation year in respect of the matchable expenditure exceeds the amount of the matchable expenditure deductible in computing the taxpayer's income for that preceding year,

(b) the total of

(i) all amounts each of which is included in computing the taxpayer's income for the year (other than any portion of such amount that is the subject of a reserve claimed by the taxpayer for the year under this Act) in respect of the right to receive production to which the matchable expenditure relates, and

(ii) the amount by which the amount determined under this paragraph for the preceding taxation year in respect of the matchable expenditure exceeds the amount of the matchable expenditure deductible in computing the taxpayer's income for that preceding year, and

(c) the amount, if any, by which

(i) the total of all amounts each of which is an amount of the matchable expenditure that would, but for this section, have been deductible in computing the taxpayer's income for the year or a preceding taxation year

exceeds

(ii) the total of all amounts each of which is an amount of the matchable expenditure deductible under subsection (3) in computing the taxpayer's income for a preceding taxation year.

**Related Provisions**: 18.1(5) — Rules for determining amount.

**Notes**: See Notes at end of 18.1. 18.1(4) limits the deduction for a matchable expenditure to the least of three amounts. Generally, the first amount is the expenditure prorated over the term of the right to receive production to which the expenditure relates, except that in no event is the term used to be less than 5 years. Added to this amount, however, are amounts that would have been deductible in preceding years under this computation but for the second constraint. The second constraint is the amount of income included in computing income in respect of the right for the year. Added to this amount, however, is income for previous years against which amounts could not be deducted because of the first constraint. The third constraint is the amount that would otherwise have been deductible in computing income up to and including the current taxation year in respect of the taxpayer's right to receive production minus the amounts deductible under 18.1(3) in computing income for preceding taxation years.

**(5) Special rules** — For the purpose of this section,

(a) where a taxpayer's matchable expenditure is made before the day on which the related right to receive production is acquired by the taxpayer, the expenditure is deemed to have been made on that day;

(b) where a taxpayer has one or more rights to renew a particular right to receive production to which a matchable expenditure relates for one or more additional terms, after the term that includes the time at which the particular right was acquired, the particular right is deemed to terminate on the latest day on which the latest possible such term could terminate if all rights to renew the particular right were exercised;

(c) where a taxpayer has 2 or more rights to receive production that can reasonably be considered to be related to each other, the rights are deemed to be one right; and

(d) where the term of a taxpayer's right to receive production is for an indeterminate period, the right is deemed to terminate 240 months after it is acquired.

**Notes**: See Notes at end of 18.1.

**(6) Proceeds of disposition considered income** — Where in a taxation year a taxpayer disposes of all or part of a right to receive production to which a matchable expenditure relates, the proceeds of the disposition shall be included in computing the taxpayer's income for the year.

**Related Provisions**: 12(1)(g.1) — Inclusion in income of proceeds of disposition; 87(2)(j.2) — Amalgamation — continuing corporation.

**Notes**: See Notes at end of 18.1.

**(7) Arm's length disposition** — Subject to subsections (8) to (10), where in a taxation year a taxpayer disposes (otherwise than in a disposition to which subsection 87(1) or 88(1) applies) of all of the taxpayer's right to receive production to which a matchable expenditure (other than an expenditure no portion of which would, if this section were read without reference to this subsection, be deductible under subsection (3) in computing the taxpayer's income) relates, or the taxpayer's right expires, the amount deductible in respect of the expenditure under subsection (3) in computing the taxpayer's income for the year is deemed to be the amount, if any, determined under paragraph (4)(c) for the year in respect of the expenditure.

**Related Provisions**: 87(2)(j.2) — Amalgamation — continuing corporation; 88(1)(a)(i) — Treatment of right to receive production on windup of corporation; 251.1 — Affiliated persons.

**Notes**: See Notes at end of 18.1. 18.1(7) provides that, upon disposition or expiry, a taxpayer may claim a terminal deduction in respect of a right to receive production to which a matchable expenditure relates. However, this terminal deduction is not available where 18.1(8) or (9) applies.

**(8) Non-arm's length disposition** — Subsection (10) applies where

(a) a taxpayer's particular right to receive production to which a matchable expenditure (other than an expenditure no portion of which would, if this section were read without reference to subsections (7) and (10), be deductible under subsection (3) in computing the taxpayer's income) relates has expired or the taxpayer has disposed of all of the right (otherwise than in a disposition to which subsection 87(1) or 88(1) applies);

(b) during the period that begins 30 days before and ends 30 days after the disposition or expiry, the taxpayer or a person affiliated, or who does not deal at arm's length, with the taxpayer acquires a right to receive production (in this subsection and subsection (10) referred to as the "substituted property") that is, or is identical to, the particular right; and

(c) at the end of the period, the taxpayer or a person affiliated, or who does not deal at arm's length, with the taxpayer owns the substituted property.

**Notes**: See Notes at end of 18.1. This provision was not included in the draft legislation of November 18, 1996.

**(9) Special case** — Subsection (10) applies where

(a) a taxpayer's particular right to receive production to which a matchable expenditure (other than an expenditure no portion of which would, if this section were read without reference to subsections (7) and (10), be deductible under subsection (3) in computing the taxpayer's income) relates has expired or the taxpayer has disposed of all of the right (otherwise than in a disposition to which subsection 87(1) or 88(1) applies); and

(b) during the period that begins at the time of the disposition or expiry and ends 30 days after that time, a taxpayer that had an interest, directly or indirectly, in the right has another interest, directly or indirectly, in another right to receive production, which other interest is a tax shelter or a tax shelter investment (as defined by section 143.2).

**Related Provisions**: 18.1(12) — Identical properties.

**Notes**: See Notes at end of 18.1. This provision was not included in the draft legislation of November 18, 1996.

**(10) Amount of deduction if non-arm's length disposition** — Where this subsection applies because of subsection (8) or (9) to a disposition or expiry in a taxation year or a preceding taxation year of a taxpayer's right to receive production to which a matchable expenditure relates,

(a) the amount deductible under subsection (3) in respect of the expenditure in computing the taxpayer's income for a taxation year that ends at or after the disposition or expiry of the right is the least of the amounts determined under subsection (4) for the year in respect of the expenditure; and

(b) the least of the amounts determined under subsection (4) in respect of the expenditure for a taxation year is deemed to be the amount, if any, determined under paragraph (4)(c) in respect of the expenditure for the year where the year includes the time that is immediately before the first time, after the disposition or expiry,

(i) at which the right would, if it were owned by the taxpayer, be deemed by section 128.1 or subsection 149(10) to have been disposed of by the taxpayer,

(ii) that is immediately before control of the taxpayer is acquired by a person or group of persons, if the taxpayer is a corporation,

(iii) at which winding-up of the taxpayer begins (other than a winding-up to which subsection 88(1) applies), if the taxpayer is a corporation,

(iv) if subsection (8) applies, at which a 30-day period begins throughout which neither the taxpayer nor a person affiliated, or who does not deal at arm's length, with the taxpayer owns

(A) the substituted property, or

(B) a property that is identical to the substituted property and that was acquired after the day that is 31 days before the period began, or

(v) if subsection (9) applies, at which a 30-day period begins throughout which no taxpayer who had an interest, directly or indirectly, in the right has an interest, directly or indirectly, in another right to receive production if one or more of those direct or indirect interests in the other right is a tax shelter or tax shelter investment (as defined by section 143.2).

**Related Provisions**: 18.1(11) — Partnerships; 18.1(12) — Identical properties; 139.1(18) — Holding corporation deemed not to acquire control of insurer on demutualization; 256(6)–(9) — Whether and when control acquired.

**Notes**: See Notes at end of 18.1. This provision was not included in the draft legislation of November 18, 1996.

**(11) Partnerships** — For the purpose of paragraph (10)(b), where a partnership otherwise ceases to exist at any time after a disposition or expiry referred to in subsection (10), the partnership is deemed not to have ceased to exist, and each taxpayer who was a member of the partnership immediately before the partnership would, but for this subsection, have ceased to exist is deemed to remain a member of the partnership until the time that is immediately after the first of the times described in subparagraphs (10)(b)(i) to (v).

**Notes**: See Notes at end of 18.1. This provision was not included in the draft legislation of November 18, 1996.

**(12) Identical property** — For the purposes of subsections (8) and (10), a right to acquire a particular right to receive production (other than a right, as security only, derived from a mortgage, agreement of sale or similar obligation) is deemed to be a right to receive production that is identical to the particular right.

**Related Provisions**: 248(12) — Extended definition of identical properties.

**Notes**: See Notes at end of 18.1. This provision was not included in the draft legislation of November 18, 1996.

**(13) Application of section 143.2** — For the purpose of applying section 143.2 to an amount that would, if this section were read without reference to this subsection, be a matchable expenditure any portion of the cost of which is deductible under subsection (3), the expenditure is deemed to be a tax shelter investment and that section shall be read without reference to subparagraph 143.2(6)(b)(ii).

**Notes**: See Notes at end of 18.1. This provision was 18.1(8) in the draft legislation of November 18, 1996.

**(14) Debt obligations** — Where the rate of return on a taxpayer's right to receive production to which a matchable expenditure (other than an expenditure no portion of which would, if this section were read without reference to this subsection, be deductible under subsection (3) in computing the taxpayer's income) relates is reasonably certain at the time the taxpayer acquires the right,

(a) the right is, for the purposes of subsection 12(9) and Part LXX of the *Income Tax Regulations*, deemed to be a debt obligation in respect of which no interest is stipulated to be payable in respect of its principal amount and the obligation is deemed to be satisfied at the time the right terminates for an amount equal to the total of the return on the obligation and the amount that would otherwise be the matchable expenditure that is related to the right; and

(b) notwithstanding subsection (3), no amount may be deducted in computing the taxpayer's income in respect of any matchable expenditure that relates to the right.

**Notes**: See Notes at end of 18.1. This provision was 18.1(9) in the draft legislation of November 18, 1996.

**(15) Non-applicability of section 18.1** — Subject to subsections (1) and (14), this section does not apply to a taxpayer's matchable expenditure in respect of a right to receive production if no portion of the expenditure can reasonably be considered to have been paid to another taxpayer, or to a person with whom the other taxpayer does not deal at arm's length, to acquire the right from the other taxpayer and

(a) the taxpayer's expenditure cannot reasonably be considered to relate to a tax shelter or tax shelter investment (as defined by section 143.2) and none of the main purposes for making the expenditure is that the taxpayer, or a person with whom the taxpayer does not deal at arm's length, obtain a tax benefit; or

(b) before the end of the taxation year in which the expenditure is made, the total of all amounts each of which is included in computing the taxpayer's income for the year (other than any portion of such an amount that is the subject of a reserve claimed by the taxpayer for the year under this Act) in respect of the right to receive production to which the matchable expenditure relates exceeds 80% of the expenditure.

### Proposed Amendment — 18.1(15)

**(15) Non-applicability of s. 18.1** — Subject to subsections (1) and (14), this section does not apply to a taxpayer's matchable expenditure in respect of a right to receive production if

(a) no portion of the expenditure can reasonably be considered to have been paid to another taxpayer, or to a person with whom the other taxpayer does not deal at arm's length, to acquire the right from the other taxpayer and

(i) the taxpayer's expenditure cannot reasonably be considered to relate to a tax shelter or tax shelter investment (as defined in section 143.2) and none of the main purposes for making the expenditure is that the taxpayer, or a person with whom the taxpayer does not deal at arm's length, obtain a tax benefit, or

(ii) before the end of the taxation year in which the expenditure is made, the total of all amounts each of which is included in computing the taxpayer's income for the year (other than any portion of such an amount that is the subject of a reserve claimed by the taxpayer for the year under this Act) in respect of the right to receive production to which the matchable expenditure relates exceeds 80% of the expenditure; or

(b) the expenditure is in respect of commissions or other expenses related to the issuance of an insurance policy for which all or a portion of a risk has been ceded to the taxpayer (in this paragraph referred to as the "reinsurer") and both the reinsurer and the person to whom the expenditure is made or is to be made are insurers subject to the supervision of

(i) the Superintendent of Financial Institutions, in the case of an insurer that is required by law to report to the Superintendent of Financial Institutions, or

(ii) in any other case, the Superintendent of Insurance or other similar officer or authority of the province under whose laws the insurer is incorporated.

**Application**: Bill C-43 (First Reading September 20, 2000), s. 8, will amend subsec. 18.1(15) to read as above, applicable to expenditures made after November 17, 1996.

**Technical Notes**: Section 18.1 restricts the deductibility of an otherwise deductible "matchable expenditure" incurred in respect of a "right to receive production" by prorating the deductibility of the amount of the expenditure over the economic life of the right.

Subsection 18.1(15) describes those matchable expenditures incurred in respect of a right to receive production that are not subject to the matchable expenditure rules in section 18.1.

Concern has been expressed that the matchable expenditure rules may apply to a reinsurer's share of sales commissions or expenses incurred in respect of the issuance of an insurance policy for which all or a portion of a risk has been ceded to the reinsurer. However, the tax deferral advantage associated with expenditures of a reinsurer are already taken into account in the calculation of the policy reserves of the reinsurer.

Subsection 18.1(15) is, therefore, amended to exclude from the matchable expenditure rules expenditures of a reinsurer in respect of commissions or other expenses related to issuance of an insurance policy for which all or a portion of a risk is ceded to the reinsurer. This exception applies only where the reinsurer and the person to whom the reinsurer made the expenditures are both insurers subject to the supervision of the Superintendent of Financial Institutions (in the case where the reinsurer is required by law to report to the Superintendent of Financial Institutions) or, in any other case, the Superintendent of Insurance or similar officer or authority of the province under whose laws the insurer was incorporated.

This amendment applies to expenditures made after November 17, 1996, the original coming-into-force date for section 18.1.

**Related Provisions [subsec. 18.1(15)]**: 12(1)(s), 20(1)(jj) — Reinsurance commissions.

**Notes [s. 18.1]**: 18.1 restricts the deductibility of an otherwise deductible matchable expenditure incurred in respect of a right to receive production by prorating the deductibility of the amount of the expenditure over the economic life of the right. (See Notes to 18.1(4).) It does not create an entitlement to deduct an amount in respect of an expenditure, unless the expenditure is otherwise deductible under existing jurisprudence. The "Backgrounder" accompanying Finance news release 96-082 (November 18, 1996) provides general details about the tax policy concerns that led to 18.1, and news releases of December 19, 1996 and July 30, 1997 announced the transitional relief below. Generally, these concern the use of royalty-type arrangements to effect tax-assisted financing by structuring the arrangements as tax shelters or as debt substitutes.

The original transactions which started this kind of planning were for mutual fund limited partnership commissions, which were financed through these shelters. Originally they were allowed a 100% writeoff, which was eventually restricted by Revenue Canada's administrative position to 1/3 deduction each year. In the months leading up to the November 1996 announcement, the concept had been extended to other areas.

18.1 added by 1995-97 technical bill, effective for every expenditure made by a taxpayer or a partnership after November 17, 1996 other than, in respect of a particular right to receive production, such an expenditure made

(a) before 1997 under an agreement in writing made by the taxpayer or the partnership before 1997 to acquire the particular right

(i) in return for paying selling commissions incurred before 1997 in connection with the distribution of shares of a mutual fund corporation or units of mutual fund trust, or

(ii) to render production services before 1997 for a film or video production,

and, for the purpose of applying this paragraph, the expenditure is deemed to have been made no earlier than the time and only to the extent it is considered for the purposes of the Act to have been made and, if subparagraph (ii) applies, only to the extent the services were rendered at or before that time,

(b) before August 1997 if

(i) the expenditure was made under an agreement in writing made by the taxpayer or the partnership before August 1997 to acquire the particular right in return for paying selling commissions incurred after 1996 and before August 1997 in connection with the distribution of shares of a mutual fund corporation or units of a mutual fund trust that is managed by an administrator of mutual funds,

(ii) the particular right to receive production is identified in an advance income tax ruling request delivered to Revenue Canada before November 18, 1996,

(iii) the total of all such expenditures made by any taxpayer or partnership in respect of all of the rights identified in the advance income tax ruling request does not exceed $30,000,000, and

(iv) all tax shelter investments (as defined in section 143.2 of the Act) that can reasonably be considered to relate to the expenditure were acquired before August 1997,

and, for the purpose of applying this paragraph, an expenditure is deemed to have been made no earlier than the time and only to the extent it is considered for the purposes of the Act to have been made,

(c) before August 1997 if

(i) the expenditure is made under an agreement in writing made by the taxpayer or the partnership before August 1997 to acquire the particular right in return for paying selling commissions incurred after 1996 and before August 1997 in connection with the distribution of shares of a mutual fund corporation or units of a mutual fund trust that is managed by an administrator of mutual funds, other than by an administrator of a mutual fund that is or is related to an administrator to which paragraph (b) refers in respect of commissions incurred in connection with the distribution of the shares or units described in paragraph (b),

(ii) the total of all such expenditures made by any taxpayer or partnership to acquire particular rights in return for paying selling commissions in connection with the distribution of shares of the mutual fund corporation or units of the mutual fund trust that is managed by the administrator of mutual funds or any other person that is related to the administrator does not exceed $10,000,000, and

(iii) all tax shelter investments (as defined in section 143.2 of the Act) that can reasonably be considered to relate to the expenditure were acquired before August 1997,

and, for the purpose of applying this paragraph, an expenditure is deemed to have been made no earlier than the time and only to the extent it is considered for the purposes of the Act to have been made,

(d) before November 1997 under an agreement in writing made by the taxpayer or the partnership before November 1997 to acquire the particular right and to render production services before November 1997 for a film or video production if

(i) at least 75% of the expenditures made in respect of the film or video production by the taxpayer or partnership pertain to services performed in Canada by residents of Canada, and

(ii) all tax shelter investments (as defined in section 143.2 of the Act) that can reasonably be considered to relate to the expenditure were acquired before November 1997,

and, for the purpose of applying this paragraph, the expenditure is deemed to have been made no earlier than the time and only to the extent it is considered for the purposes of the Act to have been made and only to the extent the services are rendered at or before that time,

(e) before 1998, under an agreement in writing made by the taxpayer or the partnership before November 18, 1996 to acquire the particular right and, for the purpose of this paragraph, if the expenditure relates to service obligations to be fulfilled by the taxpayer or partnership, the expenditure is deemed to have been made no earlier than the time and only to the extent it is considered for the purposes of the Act to have been made and only to the extent the services are rendered at or before that time,

(f) before 1998, pursuant to the terms of a document that is a prospectus, preliminary prospectus or registration statement if

(i) the document was filed before November 18, 1996 with a public authority in Canada in accordance with the securities legislation of Canada or of any province and, where required by law, accepted for filing by the public authority,

(ii) the particular right is identified in the document, and

(iii) all the funds raised pursuant to the document were raised before 1997 and all tax shelter investments (as defined in section 143.2 of the Act), that can reasonably be considered to relate to the expenditure, were acquired before August 1997,

and, for the purpose of applying this paragraph, if an expenditure relates to service obligations to be fulfilled by the taxpayer or partnership, the expenditure is deemed to have been made no earlier than the time and only to the extent it is considered for the purposes of the Act to have been made and only to the extent the services are rendered at or before that time, or

(g) before 1998, pursuant to the terms of an offering memorandum distributed as part of an offering of securities if

(i) the memorandum contained a complete or substantially complete description of the securities contemplated in the offering as well as the terms and conditions of the offering,

(ii) the memorandum was distributed before November 18, 1996,

(iii) solicitations in respect of the sale of the securities contemplated by the memorandum were made before November 18, 1996,

(iv) the sale of the securities was substantially in accordance with the memorandum,

(v) the particular right is identified in the document, and

(vi) all the funds raised pursuant to the memorandum were raised before 1997 and all tax shelter investments (as defined in section 143.2 of the Act) that can reasonably be considered to relate to the expenditure were acquired before August 1997,

and, for the purpose of applying this paragraph, if an expenditure relates to service obligations to be fulfilled by the taxpayer or partnership, the expenditure is deemed to have been made no earlier than the time and only to the extent it is considered for the purposes of the Act to have been made and only to the extent the services are rendered at or before that time,

except that paragraphs (e), (f) and (g) apply to an expenditure only if

(h) there is no agreement or other arrangement under which the obligations of the taxpayer or the partnership with respect to the expenditure can be changed, reduced or waived if there is a change to the Act or if there is an adverse assessment under the Act,

(i) where the expenditure is associated with one or more tax shelters sold or offered for sale at a time and in circumstances in which section 237.1 of the Act requires an identification number to have been obtained, the identification number was obtained before that time, and

(j) in the case of an expenditure, including an expenditure to which paragraph (e) applies, made pursuant to a document described in paragraph (f) or (g), a portion of the securities authorized to be sold in 1996 pursuant to the document were after 1995 and before November 18, 1996 sold to, or subscribed for by, a person who was not at the time of sale or subscription

(i) a promoter, or an agent of a promoter, of the securities,

(ii) a grantor of the right to receive production to which the expenditure relates,

(iii) a broker or dealer in securities, or

(iv) a person who did not deal at arm's length with a person referred to in subparagraph (i) or (ii).

**Definitions [s. 18.1]**: "affiliated" — 251.1; "amount" — 248(1); "arm's length" — 251(1); "business" — 248(1); "Canadian resource property" — 66(15), 248(1); "class of shares" — 248(6); "control" — 256(6)–(9); "dividend" — 248(1); "foreign resource property" — 66(15), 248(1); "identical" — 18.1(12); "insurer" — 248(1); "matchable expenditure" — 18.1(1); "partnership" — see Notes to 96(1); "officer", "person" — 248(1); "principal amount", "property" — 248(1); "province" — *Interpretation Act* 35(1); "related" — 251(2)–(6); "right to receive production" — 18.1(1); "share", "shareholder" — 248(1); "substituted property" — 18.1(8)(b); "tax benefit", "tax shelter" — 18.1(1); "taxation year" — 249; "taxpayer" — 18.1(1), 248(1); "trust" — 104(1), 248(1), (3).

**19. (1) Limitation re advertising expense** — In computing income, no deduction shall be made in respect of an otherwise deductible outlay or expense of a taxpayer for advertising space in an issue of a newspaper or periodical for an advertisement directed primarily to a market in Canada unless

(a) the issue is a Canadian issue of a Canadian newspaper or periodical dated after 1975; or

(b) the issue is an issue of a newspaper or periodical dated after December 31, 1988 that would be a Canadian issue of a Canadian newspaper or periodical except that

---

**Proposed Amendment — 19(1)**

**19. (1) Limitation re advertising expense — newspapers** — In computing income, no deduction shall be made in respect of an otherwise deductible outlay or expense of a taxpayer for advertising space in an issue of a newspaper for an advertisement directed primarily to a market in Canada unless

(a) the issue is a Canadian issue of a Canadian newspaper; or

(b) the issue is an issue of a newspaper that would be a Canadian issue of a Canadian newspaper except that

**Application**: Bill C-43 (First Reading September 20, 2000), subsec. 9(1), will amend the portion of subsec. 19(1) before subpara. (b)(i) to read as above, applicable in respect of advertisements placed in an issue dated after May 2000.

**Technical Notes**: See under 19.01.

**Department of Foreign Affairs and International Trade, news releases, May 26, 1999 and June 4, 1999**: See under 19.01.

---

(i) its type has been wholly set in the United States or has been partly set in the United States with the remainder having been set in Canada, or

(ii) it has been wholly printed in the United States or has been partly printed in the United States with the remainder having been printed in Canada.

**Related Provisions**: 19.01 — Limitation for magazines and other periodicals.

**Notes**: 19(1) disallows a deduction for advertising in a foreign periodical aimed at the Canadian market. This is a political/cultural rule designed to force Canadian advertisers to patronize Canadian publications. The term "periodical" is interpreted to require publication at least twice a year: VIEWS doc 9830565 (Sept. 16/99). This will now be legislated; see 19.01(1).

19(1) amended due to Canada-U.S. Free Trade Agreement, effective 1989, to permit a deduction for advertising in newspapers and periodicals printed or typeset in the U.S., provided they meet all the other conditions of the definitions of "Canadian issue" and "Canadian newspaper or periodical".

**(2)** [Repealed under former Act]

**(3) Where subsec. (1) does not apply** — Subsection (1) does not apply with respect to an advertisement in a special issue or edition of a newspaper that is edited in whole or in part and printed and published outside Canada if that special issue or edition is devoted to features or news related primarily to Canada and the publishers thereof publish such an issue or edition not more frequently than twice a year.

**(4)** [Repealed under former Act]

**(5) Definitions** — In this section,

"**Canadian issue**" means,

(a) in relation to a newspaper, an issue, including a special issue,

(i) the type of which, other than the type for advertisements or features, is set in Canada,

(ii) the whole of which, exclusive of any comics supplement, is printed in Canada,

(iii) that is edited in Canada by individuals resident in Canada, and

(iv) that is published in Canada, and

(b) in relation to a periodical, an issue, including a special issue,

(i) the type of which, other than the type for advertisements, is set in Canada,

(ii) that is printed in Canada,

(iii) that is edited in Canada by individuals resident in Canada, and

(iv) that is published in Canada,

but does not include an issue of a periodical

(v) that is produced or published under a licence granted by a person who produces or publishes issues of a periodical that are printed, edited or published outside Canada, or

(vi) the contents of which, excluding advertisements, are substantially the same as the contents of an issue of a periodical, or the contents of one or more issues of one or more periodicals, that was or were printed, edited or published outside Canada;

### Proposed Amendment — "Canadian issue"

**"Canadian issue"** of a newspaper means an issue, including a special issue,

(a) the type of which, other than the type for advertisements or features, is set in Canada,

(b) all of which, exclusive of any comics supplement, is printed in Canada,

(c) that is edited in Canada by individuals resident in Canada, and

(d) that is published in Canada;

**Application:** Bill C-43 (First Reading September 20, 2000), subsec. 9(3), will amend the definition "Canadian issue" in subsec. 19(5) to read as above, applicable in respect of advertisements placed in an issue dated after May 2000.

**Technical Notes:** See under 19.01.

**Notes:** 19(5)"Canadian issue" was 19(5)(a) before R.S.C. 1985 (5th Supp.) consolidation, effective for taxation years ending after November 1991. See Table of Concordance.

**"Canadian newspaper or periodical"** means a newspaper or periodical the exclusive right to produce and publish issues of which is held by one or more of the following:

### Proposed Amendment — "Canadian newspaper"

**"Canadian newspaper"** means a newspaper the exclusive right to produce and publish issues of which is held by one or more of the following:

**Application:** Bill C-43 (First Reading September 20, 2000), subsec. 9(4), will amend the opening words of the definition "Canadian newspaper or periodical" in subsec. 19(5) to read as above, applicable in respect of advertisements placed in an issue dated after May 2000.

**Technical Notes:** See under 19.01.

(a) a Canadian citizen,

(b) a partnership

(i) in which interests representing in value at least ¾ of the total value of the partnership property are beneficially owned by, and

(ii) at least ¾ of each income or loss of which from any source is included in the determination of the income of,

corporations described in paragraph (e) or Canadian citizens or any combination thereof,

(c) an association or society of which at least ¾ of the members are Canadian citizens,

(d) Her Majesty in right of Canada or a province, or a municipality in Canada, or

(e) a corporation

(i) that is incorporated under the laws of Canada or a province,

(ii) of which the chairperson or other presiding officer and at least ¾ of the directors or other similar officers are Canadian citizens, and

(iii) that, if it is a corporation having share capital, is

(A) a public corporation a class or classes of shares of the capital stock of which are listed on a prescribed stock exchange in Canada, other than a corporation controlled by citizens or subjects of a country other than Canada, or

(B) a corporation of which at least ¾ of the shares having full voting rights under all circumstances, and shares having a fair market value in total of at least ¾ of the fair market value of all of the issued shares of the corporation, are beneficially owned by Canadian citizens or by public corporations a class or classes of shares of the capital stock of which are listed on a prescribed stock exchange in Canada, other than a public corporation controlled by citizens or subjects of a country other than Canada,

and, for the purposes of clause (B), where shares of a class of the capital stock of a corporation are owned, or deemed by this definition to be owned, at any time by another corporation (in this definition referred to as the "holding corporation"), other than a public corporation a class or classes of shares of the capital stock of which are listed on a prescribed stock exchange in Canada, each shareholder of the holding corporation shall be deemed to own at that time that proportion of the number of such shares of that class that

(C) the fair market value of the shares of the capital stock of the holding corporation owned at that time by the shareholder

is of

(D) the fair market value of all the issued shares of the capital stock of the holding corporation outstanding at that time,

and, where at any time shares of a class of the capital stock of a corporation are owned, or are deemed by this definition to be owned, by a partnership, each member of the partnership shall be deemed to own at that time the least proportion of the number of such shares of that class that

(E) the member's share of the income or loss of the partnership from any source for its fiscal period that includes that time

is of

(F) the income or loss of the partnership from that source for its fiscal period that includes that time,

and for this purpose, where the income and loss of a partnership from any source for a fiscal period are nil, the partnership shall be deemed to have had income from that source for that period in the amount of $1,000,000;

**Related Provisions**: 19(5.1) — Extended meaning of "Canadian citizen"; 19(6) — Trust property; 19(8) — Anti-avoidance — certain newspapers and periodicals deemed not to be Canadian.

**Notes**: "Canadian newspaper or periodical" (b) and (e)(iii) amended by 1991 technical bill, effective for rights referred to in the definition that are acquired after July 13, 1990 (and rights acquired after 1988 where the acquiror of the right so elects by notifying Revenue Canada in writing by December 10, 1993 (deadline extended by 1992 technical bill, s. 159); and for this purpose, where an individual who is a citizen or subject of a country other than Canada or a corporation controlled by such an individual or individuals has at any time after July 13, 1990 acquired, in an arm's length transaction,

(a) more than ¼ of the shares of a particular corporation that have full voting rights under all circumstances, or

(b) shares of a particular corporation having a fair market value in total of more than ¼ of the fair market value of all of the issued shares of the particular corporation,

the particular corporation and any corporation controlled by the particular corporation shall be deemed to have acquired at that time any right referred to in the definition that is owned by the particular corporation or controlled corporation at that time. For earlier acquisitions of rights, read para. (b) as:

(b) a partnership of which at least ¾ of the members are Canadian citizens and in which interests representing in value at least ¾ of the total value of the partnership property are beneficially owned by Canadian citizens,

and read subpara. (e)(iii) as follows:

(iii) of which, if it is a corporation having share capital, at least ¾ of the shares having full voting rights under all circumstances, and shares representing in total at least ¾ of the paid-up capital, are beneficially owned by Canadian citizens or by corporations other than corporations controlled by citizens or subjects of a country other than Canada;

19(5)"Canadian newspaper or periodical" was 19(5)(b) before R.S.C. 1985 (5th Supp.) consolidation, effective for taxation years ending after November 1991. See Table of Concordance.

**Regulations**: 3200 (prescribed stock exchange for "Canadian newspaper or periodical"(e)(iii)).

**"issue of a non-Canadian newspaper or periodical [para. 19(5)(c)]"** — [Repealed under former Act]

**Notes**: 19(5)(c) repealed effective 1989, due to Canada-U.S. Free Trade Agreement. It defined "issue of a non-Canadian newspaper or periodical", a term no longer used in 19(1).

**"substantially the same"** means more than 20% the same;

---

**Proposed Repeal — "substantially the same"**

**Application**: Bill C-43 (First Reading September 20, 2000), subsec. 9(2), will repeal the definition "substantially the same" in subsec. 19(5), applicable in respect of advertisements placed in an issue dated after May 2000.

**Technical Notes**: See under 19.01.

**Notes**: 19(5)"substantially the same" was 19(5)(d) before R.S.C. 1985 (5th Supp.) consolidation, effective for taxation years ending after November 1991.

**"United States"** means

(a) the United States of America, but does not include Puerto Rico, the Virgin Islands, Guam or any other United States possession or territory, and

(b) any areas beyond the territorial sea of the United States within which, in accordance with international law and its domestic laws, the United States may exercise rights with respect to the seabed and subsoil and the natural resources of those areas.

**Notes**: 19(5)"United States" was 19(5)(e) before R.S.C. 1985 (5th Supp.) consolidation, effective for taxation years ending after November 1991. See Table of Concordance.

---

**Proposed Addition — 19(5.1)**

**(5.1) Interpretation ["Canadian citizen"]** — In this section, each of the following is deemed to be a Canadian citizen:

(a) a trust or corporation described in paragraph 149(1)(o) or (o.1) formed in connection with a pension plan that exists for the benefit of individuals a majority of whom are Canadian citizens;

(b) a trust described in paragraph 149(1)(r) or (x), the annuitant in respect of which is a Canadian citizen;

(c) a mutual fund trust, within the meaning assigned by subsection 132(6), other than a mutual fund trust the majority of the units of which are held by citizens or subjects of a country other than Canada;

(d) a trust, each beneficiary of which is a person, partnership, association or society described in any of paragraphs (a) to (e) of the definition "Canadian newspaper" in subsection (5); and

(e) a person, association or society described in paragraph (c) or (d) of the definition "Canadian newspaper" in subsection (5).

**Notes**: Paras. (a) and (b) refer to pension plans, RRSPs and RRIFs.

**Application**: Bill C-43 (First Reading September 20, 2000), subsec. 9(5), will add subsec. 19(5.1), applicable in respect of advertisements placed in an issue dated after June 1996 except that, in applying the subsec. to advertisements placed in an issue dated after June 1996 and before June 2000, the references in that subsec. to "Canadian newspaper" shall be read as references to "Canadian newspaper or periodical".

**Technical Notes**: In addition, new subsection 19(5.1) provides an extended meaning of "Canadian citizen", in order to ensure that Canadian pension funds and certain other entities that may own Canadian newspapers are considered to be Canadian citizens for the purpose of the ownership requirements of section 19. This amendment applies from July 1996. For periodicals, the amendment applies from July 1996 to May 2000, after which nationality of ownership ceases to be relevant in the context of periodicals.

**Department of Foreign Affairs and International Trade, news releases, May 26, 1999 and June 4, 1999**: See under 19.01.

**(6) Trust property** — Where the right that is held by any person, partnership, association or society described in the definition "Canadian newspaper or periodical" in subsection (5) to produce and publish issues of a newspaper or periodical is held as property of a trust or estate, the newspaper or periodical is not a Canadian newspaper or periodical within the meaning of this section unless each beneficiary under the trust or estate is a person, partnership, association or society so described.

### Proposed Amendment — 19(6)

**(6) Trust property** — Where the right that is held by any person, partnership, association or society described in the definition "Canadian newspaper" in subsection (5) to produce and publish issues of a newspaper is held as property of a trust or estate, the newspaper is not a Canadian newspaper unless each beneficiary under the trust or estate is a person, partnership, association or society described in that definition.

**Application**: Bill C-43 (First Reading September 20, 2000), subsec. 9(6), will amend subsec. 19(6) to read as above, applicable in respect of advertisements placed in an issue dated after May 2000.

**Technical Notes**: See under 19.01.

**(7) Grace period** — Notwithstanding any other provision of this section, where a newspaper or periodical that was at any time after June 30, 1965 a Canadian newspaper or periodical within the meaning of this section subsequently ceases to be such a Canadian newspaper or periodical, the newspaper or periodical shall be deemed to continue to be a Canadian newspaper or periodical within the meaning of this section until the expiration of the 12th month following the month in which it so ceased to be a Canadian newspaper or periodical.

### Proposed Amendment — 19(7)

**(7) Grace period** — A Canadian newspaper that would, but for this subsection, cease to be a Canadian newspaper, is deemed to continue to be a Canadian newspaper until the end of the 12th month that follows the month in which it would, but for this subsection, have ceased to be a Canadian newspaper.

**Application**: Bill C-43 (First Reading September 20, 2000), subsec. 9(6), will amend subsec. 19(7) to read as above, applicable in respect of advertisements placed in an issue dated after May 2000.

**Technical Notes**: [See under 19.01.]

**Department of Foreign Affairs and International Trade, news releases, May 26, 1999 and June 4, 1999**: [See under 19.01.]

**(8) Non-Canadian newspaper or periodical** — Where at any time one or more persons or partnerships that are not described in any of paragraphs (a) to (e) of the definition "Canadian newspaper or periodical" in subsection (5) have any direct or indirect influence that, if exercised, would result in control in fact of a person or partnership that holds a right to produce or publish issues of a newspaper or periodical, the newspaper or periodical is deemed not to be a Canadian newspaper or periodical at that time.

### Proposed Amendment — 19(8)

**(8) Non-Canadian newspaper** — Where at any time one or more persons or partnerships that are not described in any of paragraphs (a) to (e) of the definition "Canadian newspaper" in subsection (5) have any direct or indirect influence that, if exercised, would result in control in fact of a person or partnership that holds a right to produce or publish issues of a newspaper, the newspaper is deemed not to be a Canadian newspaper at that time.

**Application**: Bill C-43 (First Reading September 20, 2000), subsec. 9(6), will amend subsec. 19(8) to read as above, applicable in respect of advertisements placed in an issue dated after May 2000.

**Technical Notes**: See under 19.01.

**Related Provisions**: 256(5.1) — General test for "control in fact".

**Notes**: 19(8) added by 1995 split-run periodicals bill (S.C. 1995, c. 46), effective December 16, 1995 (the day after Royal Assent). However, it does not apply to a newspaper or periodical where the influence that would result in control in fact of a person or partnership that holds the right to produce or publish the newspaper or periodical arose as a consequence of a transaction or series of transactions that was completed before April 1993. (This grandfathering corresponds to the grandfathering of the split-run amendments in Part V.1 of the *Excise Tax Act*, which imposed a tax on the Canadian edition of *Sports Illustrated* but not on the pre-existing split-run editions of *Time* and *Reader's Digest*. Split-run editions are those with Canadian advertising but non-Canadian editorial content. See ss. 35–41.3 of the *Excise Tax Act* (reproduced in *The Practitioner's GST Annotated*). This tax has been eliminated as a result of a World Trade Organization ruling; see Proposed Amendments above.

**Definitions [s. 19]**: "beneficially owned" — 248(3); "Canada" — 255, *Interpretation Act* 35(1); "Canadian citizen" — 19(5.1); "Canadian issue" — 19(5); "Canadian newspaper" — 19(5), (7); "Canadian newspaper or periodical" — 19(5), (8); "class of shares" — 248(6); "corporation" — 248(1), *Interpretation Act* 35(1); "estate" — 104(1), 248(1); "individual" — 248(1); "month" — *Interpretation Act* 35(1); "mutual fund trust" — 132(6)–(7), 248(1); "paid-up capital" — 89(1), 248(1); "partnership" — see Notes to 96(1); "person" — 248(1); "prescribed stock exchange in Canada" — Reg. 3200; "property" — 248(1); "province" — *Interpretation Act* 35(1); "public corporation" — 89(1), 248(1); "resident in Canada" — 250; "share", "shareholder" — 248(1); "substantially" — 19(5); "taxpayer" — 248(1); "trust" — 104(1), 248(1), (3); "United States" — 19(5).

### Proposed Addition — 19.01

**19.01 (1) Definitions** — The definitions in this subsection apply in this section.

**"advertisement directed at the Canadian market"** has the same meaning as the expression "directed at the Canadian market" in section 2 of the *Foreign Publishers Advertising Services Act* and includes a reference to that expression made by or under that Act.

Notes: Section 2 of the *Foreign Publishers Advertising Services Act*, S.C. 1999, c. 23, provides:

> "directed at the Canadian market", in relation to advertising services, means that the target market related to those advertising services consists primarily of consumers in Canada.

**"original editorial content"** in respect of an issue of a periodical means non-advertising content

(a) the author of which is a Canadian and, for this purpose, "author" includes a writer, a journalist, an illustrator and a photographer; or

(b) that is created for the Canadian market and has not been published in any other edition of that issue of the periodical published outside Canada.

**"periodical"** has the meaning assigned by section 2 of the *Foreign Publishers Advertising Services Act*.

Related Provisions: 19.01(6) — Meaning of "edition".

Notes: Section 2 of the *Foreign Publishers Advertising Services Act*, S.C. 1999, c. 23, provides:

> "periodical" means a printed publication that appears in consecutively numbered or dated issues, published under a common title, usually at regular intervals, not more than once every week, excluding special issues, and at least twice every year. It does not include a catalogue, a directory, a newsletter or a newspaper.

**(2) Limitation re advertising expenses — periodicals** — Subject to subsections (3) and (4), in computing income, no deduction shall be made by a taxpayer in respect of an otherwise deductible outlay or expense for advertising space in an issue of a periodical for an advertisement directed at the Canadian market.

**(3) 100% deduction** — A taxpayer may deduct in computing income an outlay or expense of the taxpayer for advertising space in an issue of a periodical for an advertisement directed at the Canadian market if

(a) the original editorial content in the issue is 80% or more of the total non-advertising content in the issue; and

(b) the outlay or expense would, but for subsection (2), be deductible in computing the taxpayer's income.

Related Provisions: 19.01(5) — Calculation of percentage.

**(4) 50% deduction** — A taxpayer may deduct in computing income 50% of an outlay or expense of the taxpayer for advertising space in an issue of a periodical for an advertisement directed at the Canadian market if

(a) the original editorial content in the issue is less than 80% of the total non-advertising content in the issue; and

(b) the outlay or expense would, but for subsection (2), be deductible in computing the taxpayer's income.

Related Provisions: 19.01(5) — Calculation of percentage.

**(5) Application** — For the purposes of subsections (3) and (4),

(a) the percentage that original editorial content is of total non-advertising content is the percentage that the total space occupied by original editorial content in the issue is of the total space occupied by non-advertising content in the issue; and

(b) the Minister may obtain the advice of the Department of Canadian Heritage for the purpose of

(i) determining the result obtained under paragraph (a), and

(ii) interpreting any expression defined in this section that is defined in the *Foreign Publishers Advertising Services Act*.

**(6) Editions of issues** — For the purposes of this section,

(a) where an issue of a periodical is published in several versions, each version is an edition of that issue; and

(b) where an issue of a periodical is published in only one version, that version is an edition of that issue.

Application: Bill C-43 (First Reading September 20, 2000), s. 10, will add s. 19.01, applicable in respect of advertisements placed in an issue dated after May 2000.

Technical Notes: Section 19 precludes the deduction of advertising expenses to the extent that the expenses are incurred for advertisements directed at the Canadian market and placed in a newspaper or periodical that does not meet certain Canadian ownership criteria.

Pursuant to the Canada-U.S. Agreement of June 3, 1999 regarding periodicals, section 19 is amended to exclude advertisements in periodicals from the application of section 19. Instead, new section 19.01 permits full deductibility of expenses for advertisements published in issues of periodicals that contain at least 80% original editorial content, and 50% deductibility for advertising expenses in other periodicals, regardless of the ownership of the periodical.

These amendments apply to advertisements in issues of periodicals published after May 2000.

Definitions [s. 19.01]: "advertisement directed at the Canadian market" — 19.01(5); "Canada" — 255, *Interpretation Act* 35(1); "edition" — 19.01(6); "Minister" — 248(1); "original editorial content", "periodical" — 19.01(1); "taxpayer" — 248(1).

Subdivision b — Income or Loss from a Business or Property    S. 19.1(2)(b)

**Department of Foreign Affairs and International Trade, news release, May 26, 1999**: *Ottawa and Washington Agree on Access to the Canadian Advertising Services Market*

Canadian Heritage Minister Sheila Copps and International Trade Minister Sergio Marchi announced today that an agreement-in-principle has been reached between the Government of Canada and the Government of the United States with regard to the access of foreign periodicals to the Canadian advertising services market.

. . . . .

Under the terms of the agreement, Bill C-55, the *Foreign Publishers Advertising Services Act*, will be enacted, with amendments. The prohibition on foreign publishers selling advertising services aimed primarily at the Canadian market will be amended to allow two limited forms of access:

- a *de minimis* exemption which will allow foreign publishers to publish up to 12% of ads aimed at the Canadian market immediately, up to 15% in eighteen months and 18% thirty-six months after the date of enactment of the *Foreign Publishers Services Act*.

- an exemption which will enable foreign publishers to have access to a greater percentage of the Canadian advertising services market, providing they create majority Canadian content and establish a new periodicals business in Canada. Acquisitions of Canadian publishers will not be permitted.

In addition, the rules governing tax deductibility available to advertisers will be changed to provide full deductibility in any periodical, regardless of the nationality of ownership, that produces at least 80% original or Canadian content. Canadian advertisers will receive half the deduction for ads placed in foreign magazines under the de minimis exemption, as well as ads placed in magazines created by foreign investors that include less than 80% original or Canadian content.

. . . . .

For further information, media representatives may contact: Jacques Lefebvre, Senior Communications Advisor, Office of the Minister of Canadian Heritage, (819) 997-7788; Anne-Sophie Lawless, Media Relations, Department of Canadian Heritage, (819) 997-9314; Leslie Swartman, Office of the Minister for International Trade, (613) 992-7332.

This document is also available on the Web site of the Department of Canadian Heritage (http://www.pch.gc.ca) under News Releases.

*Backgrounder 1: Canada-U.S. Agreement on Magazines*

Bill C-55 will proceed quickly to enactment, with amendments.

The prohibition on foreign publishers selling advertising services aimed primarily at the Canadian market will be amended to allow two controlled forms of access to the Canadian advertising services market:

- an exemption that will allow foreign publishers to invest in Canada, create new businesses and produce a majority of Canadian content if they want to have greater access to advertising revenues.

- a *de minimis* exemption of up to 18% of the advertising in any foreign periodical. This exemption will be phased in over three years from the date of enactment of C-55 (12% immediately, 15% after eighteen months, 18% after thirty-six months).

. . . . .

*Tax Deductibility*

Tax deductibility is currently only available for ads placed in periodicals with a minimum of 75% Canadian ownership [see 19(5)"Canadian newspaper or periodical"(b) — ed.] and that contain at least 80% original content [see 19(5)"Canadian issue"(b)(vi) and 19(5)"substantially the same" — ed.]. This will now be changed to provide full deductibility, regardless of the nationality of ownership, in any periodical that contains at least 80% original or Canadian content. Canadian advertisers will receive half the deduction for ads placed in foreign magazines under the de minimis exemption, as well as for ads placed in magazines created by foreign investors that include less than 80% original or Canadian content.

**Department of Foreign Affairs and International Trade, news release, June 4, 1999**: *Canada and United States Sign Agreement on Periodicals*

The governments of Canada and the United States have signed the formal Agreement ending a long-standing dispute regarding access of foreign periodicals to the Canadian advertising services market.

According to the terms of the Agreement, which comes into effect at the time of signing, the United States has agreed not to take any action under the World Trade Organization Agreements, the North American Free Trade Agreement, or section 301 of the Trade Act of 1974, as amended, in response to Bill C-55.

For its part, Canada has agreed to make certain changes to Bill C-55, the *Foreign Publishers Advertising Services Act*, to its foreign investment policy and to the *Income Tax Act*. All of these changes were explained in the May 26 announcement of the agreement-in-principle.

. . . . .

For further information, media representatives may contact: Jacques Lefebvre, Senior Communications Advisor, Office of the Minister of Canadian Heritage, (819) 997-7788; Leslie Swartman, Office of the Minister for International Trade, (613) 992-7332.

**19.1 (1) Limitation re advertising expense on broadcasting undertaking** — Subject to subsection (2), in computing income, no deduction shall be made in respect of an otherwise deductible outlay or expense of a taxpayer made or incurred after September 21, 1976 for an advertisement directed primarily to a market in Canada and broadcast by a foreign broadcasting undertaking.

**(2) Exception** — In computing income, a deduction may be made in respect of an outlay or expense made or incurred before September 22, 1977 for an advertisement directed primarily to a market in Canada and broadcast by a foreign broadcasting undertaking pursuant to

(a) a written agreement entered into on or before January 23, 1975; or

(b) a written agreement entered into after January 23, 1975 and before September 22, 1976 if the agreement is for a term of one year or less and by its express terms is not capable of being extended or renewed.

**(3)** [Repealed under former Act]

**(4) Definitions** — In this section,

**"foreign broadcasting undertaking"** means a network operation or a broadcasting transmitting undertaking located outside Canada or on a ship or aircraft not registered in Canada;

**"network"** includes any operation involving two or more broadcasting undertakings whereby control over all or any part of the programs or program schedules of any of the broadcasting undertakings involved in the operation is delegated to a network operator.

**Definitions [s. 19.1]**: "broadcasting" — *Interpretation Act* 35(1); "Canada" — 255; "foreign broadcasting undertaking", "network" — 19.1(4); "taxpayer" — 248(1).

**20. (1) Deductions permitted in computing income from business or property** — Notwithstanding paragraphs 18(1)(a), (b) and (h), in computing a taxpayer's income for a taxation year from a business or property, there may be deducted such of the following amounts as are wholly applicable to that source or such part of the following amounts as may reasonably be regarded as applicable thereto:

(a) **capital cost of property** — such part of the capital cost to the taxpayer of property, or such amount in respect of the capital cost to the taxpayer of property, if any, as is allowed by regulation;

**Related Provisions**: 13(5) — Transferred property; 13(5.2) — Rules applicable; 13(6) — Misclassified property; 13(7) — Change in use of depreciable property; 13(11) — Automobile deduction; 13(12) — Lobbying expenses; 13(14) — Conversion cost of vessel; 13(21.2) — Transfer of property where u.c.c. exceeds fair market value; 13(26)–(32) — Restriction on deduction before available for use; 18(3.1)(a) — Costs relating to construction of building or ownership of land; 18(12) — Work space in home; 20(1.1) — Definitions in 13(21) apply to regulations; 20(16) — Terminal loss; 21 — Cost of borrowed money; 28(1)(g) — Deduction from farming or fishing income when using cash method; 34.2(2)(c) — Maximum CCA deemed claimed for purposes of 1995 stub period income; 36 — Railway companies; 37(6) — Scientific research capital expenditures; 67.3 — Limitation re cost of leasing passenger vehicle; 68 — Allocation of cost between property and services; 80(9)(c) — Reduction of capital cost on debt forgiveness ignored for CCA regulations; 85(5) — Rules on transfers of depreciable property; 87(2)(d.1) — Amalgamations — depreciable property acquired from predecessor corporation; 107.2(e) — Distribution of depreciable property by retirement compensation arrangement; 107.4(3)(d) — Rollover of depreciable property to trust; 125.4(4) — No Canadian film/video production credit to corporation if investor can claim CCA; 127.52(1)(b), (c) — Minimum tax — add-back of some CCA; 164(6) — Refund — disposition of property by legal representative of deceased taxpayer; 216(5) — Disposition by non-resident of interest in real property etc. See additional Related provisions and Definitions at end of s. 20.

**Notes**: Capital cost allowance (CCA) is claimed in place of accounting depreciation or amortization. The taxpayer can choose to claim less than the maximum allowable, and thus keep a higher undepreciated capital cost for future years.

When determining CCA on the acquisition of a new asset, note in particular the "available for use" restrictions in 13(26)–(32), and the "half-year rule" in Reg. 1100(2). CCA is allowed by class (pool) rather than by individual asset; the rates are set out in Reg. 1100 and the classes of property are in Schedule II to the Regulations (reproduced at the end of the Regulations). Some assets, however, are each deemed to be a separate class; see Reg. 1101. See also Notes to 13(21)"undepreciated capital cost".

**Regulations**: Part XI (CCA rules); Part XVII (farming and fishing property owned since before 1972); Reg. Sch. II–Sch. VI (classes of property).

**I.T. Application Rules**: 18(2), 20, 26.1(2).

**Interpretation Bulletins**: IT-79R3: CCA — Buildings or other structures; IT-121R3: Election to capitalize cost of borrowed money; IT-128R: CCA — Depreciable property; IT-147R3: CCA — Accelerated write-off of manufacturing and processing machinery and equipment; IT-172R: CCA — Taxation year of individuals; IT-187: Customer lists and ledger accounts; IT-195R4: Rental property — CCA restrictions; IT-267R2: CCA — Vessels; IT-283R2: CCA — video tapes, video tape cassettes, films, computer software and master recording media; IT-285R2: CCA — General comments; IT-304R2: Condominiums; IT-306R2: CCA — Contractor's movable equipment; IT-317R: CCA — Radio and television equipment; IT-324: Emphyteutic lease; IT-325R2: Property transfers after separation, divorce and annulment; IT-327: CCA — Elections under regulation 1103; IT-336R: CCA — Pollution control property; IT-371: Rental property — meaning of "principal business"; IT-422: Definition of tools; IT-464R: CCA — Leasehold interests; IT-465R: Non-resident beneficiaries of trusts; IT-469R: CCA — Earth-moving equipment; IT-472: CCA — Class 8 property; IT-476: CCA — Gas and oil exploration and production equipment; IT-477: CCA — Patents, franchises, concessions and licences; IT-481: Timber resource property and timber limits; IT-482: CCA — Pipelines; IT-485: Cost of clearing or levelling land; IT-492: CCA — Industrial mineral mines; IT-501: CCA — Logging assets.

**Information Circulars**: 84-1: Revision of capital cost allowance claims and other permissive deductions; 87-5: Capital cost of property where trade-in is involved.

**I.T. Technical News**: No. 1 (sales commission expenses of mutual-fund limited partnerships); No. 3 (loss utilization within a corporate group); No. 12 ("millennium bug" expenditures).

**Advance Tax Rulings**: ATR-1: Transfer of legal title in land to bare trustee corporation — mortgagee's requirements sole reason for transfer.

**Forms**: T1-CP Summ: Return in respect of certified productions; T1-CP Supp: Statement of certified productions; T2 SCH 8: Capital cost allowance; T776: Statement of real estate rentals; T777: Statement of employment expenses; T2132: Capital cost allowance schedule (depreciation); T4044: Employment expenses [guide]; T5014: Partnership capital cost allowance schedule.

(b) **cumulative eligible capital amount** — such amount as the taxpayer may claim in respect of a business, not exceeding 7% of the taxpayer's cumulative eligible capital in respect of the business at the end of the year;

> **Proposed Amendment — 20(1)(b)**
>
> (b) **cumulative eligible capital amount** — such amount as the taxpayer claims in respect of a business, not exceeding 7% of the taxpayer's cumulative eligible capital in respect of the business at the end of the year except that, where the year is less than 12 months, the amount allowed as a deduction under this paragraph shall not exceed that proportion of the

Subdivision b — Income or Loss from a Business or Property    S. 20(1)(c)

maximum amount otherwise allowable that the number of days in the taxation year is of 365;

**Application**: The December 21, 2000 draft legislation, subsec. 7(1), will amend para. 20(1)(b) to read as above, applicable to taxation years that begin after December 21, 2000.

**Technical Notes**: Paragraph 20(1)(b) provides a deduction in calculating a taxpayer's income from a business of up to 7% of the taxpayer's cumulative eligible capital pool. Consequential on the examination of the eligible capital property provisions undertaken after the 2000 budget, paragraph 20(1)(b) is amended to introduce a short taxation year rule for eligible capital property.

**Supplementary Information, Economic Statement, October 18, 2000**: *Capital Gains*

[For the full text re the changes to the capital gains inclusion rate, see under s. 38 — ed.]

The existing pooling system, whereby three-quarters of the cost of [eligible capital] property is depreciated at 7% declining balance, will be maintained. This approach is the most generous for taxpayers and will ease both compliance and administration.

**Related Provisions**: 14(1) — Inclusion in income from business; 14(5) — Definitions — "cumulative eligible capital", "eligible capital expenditure"; 24 — Ceasing to carry on business; 28(1)(g) — Deduction from farming or fishing income when using cash method; 34.2(2)(c) — Maximum amount deemed claimed for purposes of 1995 stub period income; 70(5.1) — Eligible capital property of deceased; 70(9.8) — Leased farm property; 87(2)(f) — Amalgamations — cumulative eligible capital; 107(2)(f) — Capital interest distribution by personal or prescribed trust; 111(5.2) — Computation of cumulative eligible capital. See additional Related Provisions and Definitions at end of s. 20.

**Notes**: *Eligible capital property* is goodwill and other purchased intangibles without a fixed lifespan. See Interpretation Bulletin IT-143R2 for details, and see 14(5)"eligible capital expenditure" for the substantive definition. (Patents and other intangibles with a fixed life generally fall under the CCA system and are grouped in Class 14 or 44.) An amount expended on eligible capital property is an *eligible capital expenditure*. ¾ of all eligible capital expenditures constitute the taxpayer's *cumulative eligible capital*. Under 20(1)(b), 7% of the declining balance of cumulative eligible capital can be claimed as a deduction each year. On a sale of eligible capital property, there may be an income inclusion (recapture) under 14(1). On ceasing to carry on business, the taxpayer may deduct the entire remaining balance of cumulative eligible capital under s. 24.

**Interpretation Bulletins**: IT-99R5: Legal and accounting fees; IT-123R4: Disposition of and transactions involving eligible capital property; IT-123R6: Transactions involving eligible capital property; IT-143R2: Meaning of "eligible capital expenditure"; IT-302R3: Losses of a corporation — the effect that acquisitions of control, amalgamations, and windings-up have on their deductibility — after January 15, 1987; IT-313R2: Eligible capital property — rules where a taxpayer has ceased carrying on a business or has died; IT-341R3: Expenses of issuing or selling shares, units in a trust, interests in a partnership or syndicate, and expenses of borrowing money.

**Forms**: T5017: Calculation of deduction for cumulative eligible capital of a partnership.

(c) **interest** — an amount paid in the year or payable in respect of the year (depending upon the method regularly followed by the taxpayer in computing the taxpayer's income), pursuant to a legal obligation to pay interest on

(i) borrowed money used for the purpose of earning income from a business or property (other than borrowed money used to acquire property the income from which would be exempt or to acquire a life insurance policy),

(ii) an amount payable for property acquired for the purpose of gaining or producing income from the property or for the purpose of gaining or producing income from a business (other than property the income from which would be exempt or property that is an interest in a life insurance policy),

(iii) an amount paid to the taxpayer under

(A) an appropriation Act and on terms and conditions approved by the Treasury Board for the purpose of advancing or sustaining the technological capability of Canadian manufacturing or other industry, or

(B) the *Northern Mineral Exploration Assistance Regulations* made under an appropriation Act that provides for payments in respect of the Northern Mineral Grants Program, or

(iv) borrowed money used to acquire an interest in an annuity contract in respect of which section 12.2 applies (or would apply if the contract had an anniversary day in the year at a time when the taxpayer held the interest) except that, where annuity payments have begun under the contract in a preceding taxation year, the amount of interest paid or payable in the year shall not be deducted to the extent that it exceeds the amount included under section 12.2 in computing the taxpayer's income for the year in respect of the taxpayer's interest in the contract,

**Proposed Addition [on hold] — 20(1)(c)(v), (vi)**

(v) borrowed money used to make a loan described in subsection 80.4(1), or

(vi) borrowed money used to make a loan described in subsection 80.4(2), to the extent of the amount included in respect of the loan in computing the taxpayer's income for the year,

**Application**: The December 20, 1991 draft legislation (interest deductibility), subsec. 1(1), will add subparas. 20(1)(c)(v) and (vi), applicable to 1972 et seq. (These amendments are still subject to further revision and are not expected to be enacted soon. See Notes to 20(3.1).)

**Technical Notes**: Paragraph 20(1)(c) is the principal provision dealing with interest deductibility. In addition to a generic description of indebtedness on which interest may be deductible in computing a taxpayer's income, this paragraph identifies certain other obligations in respect of which similar treatment is provided.

This amendment adds two new subparagraphs to paragraph 20(1)(c), dealing with interest on borrowed money used to make employer and shareholder loans described in section 80.4. Subparagraph 20(1)(c)(v) confirms, subject to the overriding condition in paragraph 20(1)(c) and section 67 that the expense be reasonable in the circum-

169

## S. 20(1)(c) — Income Tax Act, Part I, Division B

stances, the deductibility of interest on borrowed money used by a taxpayer to make a loan to an employee or prospective employee.

Subparagraph 20(1)(c)(vi) governs the treatment of borrowed money used by or on behalf of a corporation to make a loan to or for the benefit of one of its shareholders. This provision permits any interest arising on the borrowed money for a particular taxation year to be deducted to the extent of the amount included in the borrower's income for the year from the shareholder loan.

or a reasonable amount in respect thereof, whichever is the lesser;

**Related Provisions**: 9(3) — Capital gains not included in income from property; 15.1(2)(a), 15.1(4) — Small business development bonds; 16(1) — Income and capital combined; 16(6) — Indexed debt obligations — amount deemed paid as interest; 17 — Loan to non-resident; 18(1)(e) — No deduction for contingent reserve; 18(1)(g) — Interest on income bonds; 18(1)(t) — No deduction for interest paid on late payments of income tax; 18(1)(v) — No deduction to authorized foreign bank except under 20.2; 18(2) — Limitation — interest and property taxes on land; 18(4)–(8) — Thin capitalization — limitation on interest deductibility; 18(9)–(9.2) — Prepaid interest; 18(11) — No deduction for interest on money borrowed to make RRSP or certain other contributions; 20(1)(e) — Expense of borrowing money; 20(1)(f) — Amounts paid in satisfaction of the "principal amount"; 20(1)(qq) (draft) — Interest on share purchase; 20(1.2) — Definitions in 12.2(11) apply; 20(2) — Borrowed money; 20(2.1) — Limitation; 20(2.2) — Life insurance policy; 20(3), (3.1) — Borrowed money; 20(14) — Accrued bond interest; 20.1(1) — Borrowed money where property is disposed of; 20.1, 20.2 (draft) — Money borrowed for distribution; 20.3 — Weak currency debt — limitation on interest deduction; 21(1)–(4) — Capitalizing interest; 60(d) — Annual interest accruing in respect of estate tax or succession duties; 67.2 — Interest on money borrowed for passenger vehicle; 80.5 — Deemed interest — employee deduction re funds borrowed to purchase auto or aircraft; 110.6(1) — "investment expense"; 118.62 — Credit for interest paid on student loans; 127.52(1)(b), (c), (c.2), (e.1) — Limitation on deduction for minimum tax purposes; 133(1) — No interest deduction to NRO; 137(4.1) — Interest deemed paid on certain reductions of capital by credit union; 138(5)(b) — Insurers — limitation; 212(1)(b) — Non-resident withholding tax on interest; 218 — Loan to wholly-owned subsidiary. See additional Related Provisions and Definitions at end of s. 20.

**Notes**: 20(1)(c) amended by 1989 Budget and 1991 technical bill, effective for contracts last acquired after 1989. For other cases, in subpara. (iv), in place of the parenthesized words, add "or would apply if the contract had a third anniversary in the year".

The treatment of interest deductibility is in a state of flux, as the Department of Finance is still studying proposals it made in 1991 in response to the *Bronfman Trust* case ([1987] 1 C.T.C. 117 (SCC)). See draft 20(1)(c)(v), (vi), 20.1 and 20.2, as well as the version of 20.1 enacted by 1993 technical bill. See also the articles by Brian Arnold and others in the *Canadian Tax Journal*, 39(6) 1473–1496 (1991); 40(2) 267–303 (1992); 40(3) 533–553 (1992); 43(5) 1216–1244 (1995); 44(2) 227–347 (1996); discussing interest deductibility.

Where a bond is purchased with accrued interest, payment made in respect of the interest may be deductible; see 20(14).

Interest in respect of certain investments is non-deductible for purposes of the Alternative Minimum Tax. See 127.52(1)(b), (c), (c.2) and (e.1).

It has generally been accepted that interest paid on a loan used to acquire common shares is always deductible, since such shares can pay unlimited dividends. However, see *Ludmer*, [1999] 3 C.T.C. 601 (FCA), where the deduction was denied. The Supreme Court of Canada has granted leave to appeal in Ludmer (April 20, 2000).

The Courts have held that interest is only deductible under 20(1)(c), and not under normal principles of s. 9, on the basis that interest is paid on account of capital: *Bowater Cdn. Ltd.*, [1987] 2 C.T.C. 47 (FCA); *Shell Canada Ltd.*, [1999] 4 C.T.C. 313 at 325 (SCC).

The Supreme Court of Canada has granted (April 20, 2000) leave to appeal in *Singleton*, [1999] 3 C.T.C. 446 (FCA), where money was "cycled" to make it deductible: a lawyer withdrew cash from his firm partnership to pay for his home purchase, then borrowed funds to reinvest in the partnership the same day. The FCA ruled that the interest was deductible.

For a useful commentary on the principles of whether and when interest should be deductible, see William Innes, "A Critique of the Decision of the Federal Court of Appeal in *The Queen v. Shell Canada Limited*", *Tax Litigation* (Federated Press), Vol. VI, No. 1 (1997), pp. 350–358. The *Shell* case, which dealt with "Kiwi" loans taken out at a high interest rate in a depreciating (New Zealand) currency and hedged back to US dollars, was reversed by the Supreme Court of Canada and decided in the taxpayer's favour: [1999] 4 C.T.C. 313; this will be overruled for the future by proposed 20.3. See also *Sherway Centre Ltd.*, [1998] 2 C.T.C. 343 (FCA), where participating interest payments on a bond were held to be interest.

Note that no deduction is available under 20(1)(c) unless there was a legal obligation to pay the interest. Otherwise, 18(1)(e) prevents a deduction. See *Barbican Properties Inc.*, [1997] 1 C.T.C. 2383 (FCA).

The Courts may disallow interest deductibility when the purpose of the loan was to shift losses around within a corporate group: *Mark Resources*, [1993] 2 C.T.C. 2259 (TCC); *Canwest Broadcasting*, [1995] 2 C.T.C. 2780 (TCC); *C.R.B. Logging Co.*, [1999] 2 C.T.C. 2279 (TCC).

18(11) also prohibits deduction of interest on loans taken for certain purposes (e.g., RRSP contributions).

For a recent thorough review, see John Owen, "Subparagraph 20(1)(c)(i): What Is Its Purpose?" 48(2) *Canadian Tax Journal* 231-273 (2000).

**Regulations**: 201(1)(b) (information return).

**Interpretation Bulletins**: IT-80: Interest on money borrowed to redeem shares or pay dividends; IT-104R2: Deductibility of fines or penalties; IT-121R3: Election to capitalize cost of borrowed money; IT-153R3: Land developers — subdivision and development costs and carrying charges on land; IT-265R3: Payments of income and capital combined; IT-315: Interest expense incurred for the purpose of winding-up or amalgamation; IT-341R3: Expenses of issuing or selling shares, units in a trust, interests in a partnership or syndicate, and expenses of borrowing money; IT-355R2: Interest on loans to buy life insurance policies and annuity contracts, and interest on policy loans; IT-362R: Patronage dividends; IT-421R2: Benefits to individuals, corporations and shareholders from loans or debt; IT-445: Deduction of interest on borrowed funds which are loaned at less than a reasonable rate; IT-488R2: Winding-up of 90%-owned taxable Canadian corporations; IT-498: Deductibility of interest on money borrowed to reloan to employees or shareholders.

**Information Circulars**: 88-2, paras. 19, 20: General anti-avoidance rule — section 245 of the *Income Tax Act*; 88-2, Supplement, para. 5: General anti-avoidance rule.

**I.T. Technical News**: No. 3 (loss utilization within a corporate group; use of a partner's assets by a partnership; interest-bearing note issued in consideration for the redemption or repurchase of shares); No. 16 (*Sherway Centre* case; *Shell Canada* and *Canadian Pacific* cases; *Parthenon Investments* case); No. 18 (*C.R.B. Logging*, *Ludco Enterprises*, *Byram* and *Singleton* cases).

**Advance Tax Rulings**: ATR-4: Exchange of interest rates; ATR-14: Non-arm's length interest charges; ATR-16: Inter-company dividends and interest expense; ATR-41: Convertible preferred shares; ATR-43: Utilization of a non-resident-owned investment corporation as a holding corporation; ATR-44: Utilization of deductions and credits within a related corporate group; ATR-59: Financing exploration and development through limited partnerships.

Subdivision b — Income or Loss from a Business or Property  S. 20(1)(e)(iii)

**Forms**: T2210: Verification of policy loan interest by the insurer.

(d) **compound interest** — an amount paid in the year pursuant to a legal obligation to pay interest on an amount that would be deductible under paragraph (c) if it were paid in the year or payable in respect of the year;

**Related Provisions**: 18(11) — Limitation; 20(2.1) — Limitation; 20(2.2) — Life insurance policy; 21(1)–(4) — Cost of borrowed money; 67.2 — Interest on money borrowed for passenger vehicle; 67.3 — Limitation re motor vehicle expenses; 127.52(1)(b), (c), (c.2), (e.1) — Limitation on deduction for minimum tax purposes; 138(5)(b) — Insurers — limitation; 248(1) — "Borrowed money". See additional Related Provisions and Definitions at end of s. 20.

**Notes**: The deduction under 20(1)(d) is only for amounts *paid*, while 20(1)(c) allows amount *paid or payable*. This can lead to a technical mismatch of deductions.

**Interpretation Bulletins**: IT-121R3: Election to capitalize cost of borrowed money; IT-355R2: Interest on loans to buy life insurance policies and annuity contracts, and interest on policy loans; IT-362R: Patronage dividends.

**Advance Tax Rulings**: ATR-4; Exchange of interest rates.

**Forms**: T2210: Verification of policy loan interest by the insurer.

(e) **expenses re financing** — such part of an amount that is not otherwise deductible in computing the income of the taxpayer and that is an expense incurred in the year or a preceding taxation year

### Proposed Amendment — 20(1)(e) opening words

(e) **expenses re financing** — such part of an amount (other than an excluded amount) that is not otherwise deductible in computing the income of the taxpayer and that is an expense incurred in the year or a preceding taxation year

**Application**: Bill C-43 (First Reading September 20, 2000), subsec. 11(1), will amend the opening words of para. 20(1)(e) to read as above, applicable with respect to expenses incurred by a taxpayer after November 1999, other than expenses incurred pursuant to a written agreement made by the taxpayer before December 1999.

**Technical Notes**: Section 20 of the Act provides rules relating to the deductibility of certain outlays, expenses and other amounts in computing a taxpayer's income for a taxation year from a business or property.

Paragraph 20(1)(e) of the Act provides for the deduction over a five-year period of expenses incurred in the course of issuing securities, borrowing money, and certain other financing transactions. Amounts paid in respect of the principal of a debt obligation and interest on the obligation are expressly excluded from the application of this paragraph. Paragraph 20(1)(e) is amended to clarify that it does not allow a deduction for profit participation and similar payments — that is, payments dependent on the use of or production from property, or computed by reference to revenue, profits, cash flow, commodity prices or any other similar criterion or by reference to dividend payments. [See proposed 20(1)(e)(iv.1) — ed.] Where such payments are compensation for the use of borrowed money or for the right to pay a debt over time, they would be excluded by the existing paragraph 20(1)(e) — either because they are interest or because they fall within the broad definition of "principal amount" in subsection 248(1) of the Act. The amendment ensures that in no circumstances can participation and similar payments be deducted under paragraph 20(1)(e).

(i) in the course of an issuance or sale of units of the taxpayer where the taxpayer is a unit trust, of interests in a partnership or syndicate by the partnership or syndicate, as the case may be, or of shares of the capital stock of the taxpayer,

(ii) in the course of a borrowing of money used by the taxpayer for the purpose of earning income from a business or property (other than money used by the taxpayer for the purpose of acquiring property the income from which would be exempt),

(ii.1) in the course of incurring indebtedness that is an amount payable for property acquired for the purpose of gaining or producing income therefrom or for the purpose of gaining or producing income from a business (other than property the income from which would be exempt or property that is an interest in a life insurance policy), or

(ii.2) in the course of a rescheduling or restructuring of a debt obligation of the taxpayer or an assumption of a debt obligation by the taxpayer, where the debt obligation is

(A) in respect of a borrowing described in subparagraph (ii), or

(B) in respect of an amount payable described in subparagraph (ii.1),

and, in the case of a rescheduling or restructuring, the rescheduling or restructuring, as the case may be, provides for the modification of the terms or conditions of the debt obligation or the conversion or substitution of the debt obligation to or with a share or another debt obligation,

(including a commission, fee or other amount paid or payable for or on account of services rendered by a person as a salesperson, agent or dealer in securities in the course of the issuance, sale or borrowing, but not including any amount that is paid or payable as or on account of the principal amount of the indebtedness or as or on account of interest) that is the lesser of

### Proposed Amendment — 20(1)(e)

(including a commission, fee, or other amount paid or payable for or on account of services rendered by a person as a salesperson, agent or dealer in securities in the course of the issuance, sale or borrowing) that is the lesser of

**Application**: Bill C-43 (First Reading September 20, 2000), subsec. 11(2), will amend the portion of para. 20(1)(e) between subparas. (ii.2) and (iii) to read as above, applicable on the same basis as the amendment to the opening words.

**Technical Notes**: See under 20(1)(e) opening words.

(iii) that proportion of 20% of the expense that the number of days in the year is of 365 and

## S. 20(1)(e)(iv) — Income Tax Act, Part I, Division B

(iv) the amount, if any, by which the expense exceeds the total of all amounts deductible by the taxpayer in respect of the expense in computing the taxpayer's income for a preceding taxation year,

and, for the purposes of this paragraph,

### Proposed Addition — 20(1)(e)(iv.1)

(iv.1) "excluded amount" means

(A) an amount paid or payable as or on account of the principal amount of a debt obligation or interest in respect of a debt obligation,

(B) an amount that is contingent or dependent on the use of, or production from, property, or

(C) an amount that is computed by reference to revenue, profit, cash flow, commodity price or any other similar criterion or by reference to dividends paid or payable to shareholders of any class of shares of the capital stock of a corporation,

**Application**: Bill C-43 (First Reading September 20, 2000), subsec. 11(3), will add subpara. 20(1)(e)(iv.1), applicable on the same basis as the amendment to the opening words.

**Technical Notes**: See under 20(1)(e) opening words.

(v) where in a taxation year all debt obligations in respect of a borrowing described in subparagraph (ii) or in respect of indebtedness described in subparagraph (ii.1) are settled or extinguished (otherwise than in a transaction made as part of a series of borrowings or other transactions and repayments), by the taxpayer for consideration that does not include any unit, interest, share or debt obligation of the taxpayer or any person with whom the taxpayer does not deal at arm's length or any partnership or trust of which the taxpayer or any person with whom the taxpayer does not deal at arm's length is a member or beneficiary, this paragraph shall be read without reference to the words "the lesser of" and to subparagraph (iii), and

(vi) where a partnership has ceased to exist at any particular time in a fiscal period of the partnership,

(A) no amount may be deducted by the partnership under this paragraph in computing its income for the period, and

(B) there may be deducted for a taxation year ending at or after that time by any person or partnership that was a member of the partnership immediately before that time, that proportion of the amount that would, but for this subparagraph, have been deductible under this paragraph by the partnership in the fiscal period ending in the year had it continued to exist and had the partnership interest not been redeemed, acquired or cancelled, that the fair market value of the member's interest in the partnership immediately before that time is of the fair market value of all the interests in the partnership immediately before that time;

**Related Provisions**: 18(11) — Limitation; 20(1)(e.1) — Deduction for annual fees, etc.; 20(1)(e.2) — Premiums on life insurance used as collateral; 20(3) — Use of borrowed money; 21(1)–(4) — Cost of borrowed money; 53(2)(c)(x) — Deduction from adjusted cost base of partnership interest; 87(2)(j.6) — Amalgamations — continuing corporation; 110.6(1) — "investment expense"; 127.52(1)(b), (c), (c.2), (e.1) — Limitation on deduction for minimum tax purposes; 248(1) — "Borrowed money"; 248(10) — Series of transactions. See additional Related Provisions and Definitions at end of s. 20.

**Notes**: In *Sherway Centre Ltd.*, [1998] 2 C.T.C. 343 (FCA), participatory interest payments to finance a shopping centre were held deductible under 20(1)(e). The proposed amendment above will overrule this decision.

20(1)(e) amended by 1993 technical bill, effective for expenses incurred after 1987, to add subparas. (ii.1) and (ii.2); to add exclusion of an amount under 18(9.1)(c) or (d) (between subparas. (ii.2) and (iii)); and to add the words "in respect of a borrowing described in subparagraph (ii) or indebtedness described in subparagraph (ii.1)" to subpara. (v).

20(1)(e) between (ii.2) and (iii) amended by 1995-97 technical bill, retroactive to expenses incurred after 1987, to delete an unnecessary exclusion for payments described in 18(9.1)(c) or (d) (unnecessary because 20(1)(e) provides a deduction only for amounts not otherwise deductible under the Act).

**Interpretation Bulletins**: IT-99R5: Legal and accounting fees; IT-121R3: Election to capitalize cost of borrowed money; IT-143R2: Meaning of "eligible capital expenditure"; IT-341R3: Expenses of issuing or selling shares, units in a trust, interests in a partnership or syndicate, and expenses of borrowing money.

**I.T. Technical News**: No. 16 (*Sherway Centre* case).

**Advance Tax Rulings**: ATR-49: Long-term foreign debt; ATR-59: Financing exploration and development through limited partnerships.

(e.1) **annual fees, etc. [re borrowings]** — an amount payable by the taxpayer (other than a payment that is contingent or dependent on the use of, or production from, property or is computed by reference to revenue, profit, cash flow, commodity price or any other similar criterion or by reference to dividends paid or payable to shareholders of any class of shares of the capital stock of a corporation) as a standby charge, guarantee fee, registrar fee, transfer agent fee, filing fee, service fee or any similar fee, that can reasonably be considered to relate solely to the year and that is incurred by the taxpayer

(i) for the purpose of borrowing money to be used by the taxpayer for the purpose of earning income from a business or property (other than borrowed money used by the taxpayer for the purpose of acquiring property the income from which would be exempt income),

(ii) in the course of incurring indebtedness that is an amount payable for property acquired for the purpose of gaining or producing income therefrom or for the purpose of gaining or producing income from a business (other than property the income from which would be exempt or property that is an interest in a life insurance policy), or

(iii) for the purpose of rescheduling or restructuring a debt obligation of the taxpayer or an assumption of a debt obligation by the taxpayer, where the debt obligation is

(A) in respect of a borrowing described in subparagraph (i), or

(B) in respect of an amount payable described in subparagraph (ii),

and, in the case of a rescheduling or restructuring, the rescheduling or restructuring, as the case may be, provides for the modification of the terms or conditions of the debt obligation or the conversion or substitution of the debt obligation to or with a share or another debt obligation.

**Related Provisions**: 18(11) — Limitation; 20(3) — Use of borrowed money; 21 — Cost of borrowed money; 87(2)(j.6) — Amalgamations — continuing corporation; 110.6(1) — "investment expense"; 127.52(1)(b), (c), (c.2), (e.1) — Limitation on deduction for minimum tax purposes; 248(1) — "Borrowed money". See additional Related Provisions and Definitions at end of s. 20.

**Notes**: 20(1)(e.1) amended by 1993 technical bill, effective for expenses incurred after 1987, essentially to add subparas. (ii) and (iii) and the closing words. For earlier expenses, read:

(e.1) an amount payable by the taxpayer (other than a payment that is contingent or dependent upon the use or production from property or is computed by reference to revenue, profit, cash flow, commodity price or any other similar criterion or by reference to dividends paid or payable to shareholders of any class of shares of the capital stock of a corporation) as a standby charge, guarantee fee, registrar fee, transfer agent fee, filing fee, service fee or any similar fee, that may reasonably be considered to relate solely to the year and that relates to money borrowed by the taxpayer and used by the taxpayer for the purpose of earning income from a business or property (other than money used by the taxpayer for the purpose of acquiring property the income from which would be exempt);

**Interpretation Bulletins**: IT-121R3: Election to capitalize cost of borrowed money; IT-341R3: Expenses of issuing or selling shares, units in a trust, interests in a partnership or syndicate, and expenses of borrowing money.

**Advance Tax Rulings**: ATR-49: Long-term foreign debt.

(e.2) **premiums on life insurance used as collateral** — such portion of the lesser of

(i) the premiums payable by the taxpayer under a life insurance policy (other than an annuity contract) in respect of the year, where

(A) an interest in the policy is assigned to a restricted financial institution in the course of a borrowing from the institution,

(B) the interest payable in respect of the borrowing is or would, but for subsections 18(2) and (3.1) and sections 21 and 28, be deductible in computing the taxpayer's income for the year, and

(C) the assignment referred to in clause (A) is required by the institution as collateral for the borrowing

and

(ii) the net cost of pure insurance in respect of the year, as determined in accordance with the regulations, in respect of the interest in the policy referred to in clause (i)(A),

as can reasonably be considered to relate to the amount owing from time to time during the year by the taxpayer to the institution under the borrowing;

**Related Provisions**: 127.52(1)(b), (c), (c.2), (e.1) — Limitation on deduction for minimum tax purposes.

**Notes**: 20(1)(e.2) added by 1991 technical bill, effective for premiums payable after 1989.

**Regulations**: 308 (net cost of pure insurance).

**Interpretation Bulletins**: IT-309R2: Premiums on life insurance used as collateral; IT-341R3: Expenses of issuing or selling shares, units in a trust, interests in a partnership or syndicate, and expenses of borrowing money.

(f) **discount on certain obligations** — an amount paid in the year in satisfaction of the principal amount of any bond, debenture, bill, note, mortgage or similar obligation issued by the taxpayer after June 18, 1971 on which interest was stipulated to be payable, to the extent that the amount so paid does not exceed,

(i) in any case where the obligation was issued for an amount not less than 97% of its principal amount, and the yield from the obligation, expressed in terms of an annual rate on the amount for which the obligation was issued (which annual rate shall, if the terms of the obligation or any agreement relating thereto conferred on its holder a right to demand payment of the principal amount of the obligation or the amount outstanding as or on account of its principal amount, as the case may be, before the maturity of the obligation, be calculated on the basis of the yield that produces the highest annual rate obtainable either on the maturity of the obligation or conditional on the exercise of any such right) does not exceed $4/3$ of the interest stipulated to be payable on the obligation, expressed in terms of an annual rate on

(A) the principal amount of the obligation, if no amount is payable on account of the principal amount before the maturity of the obligation, or

(B) the amount outstanding from time to time as or on account of the principal amount of the obligation, in any other case,

the amount by which the lesser of the principal amount of the obligation and all amounts paid in the year or in any preceding year in satisfaction of its principal amount exceeds the amount for which the obligation was issued, and

(ii) in any other case, ¾ of the lesser of the amount so paid and the amount by which the lesser of the principal amount of the obligation and all amounts paid in the year or in any preceding taxation year in satisfaction of its principal amount exceeds the amount for which the obligation was issued;

**Proposed Amendment — 20(1)(f)(ii)**

**Application**: The December 21, 2000 draft legislation, subsec. 7(2), will amend subpara. 20(1)(f)(ii) by replacing the reference to the fraction "3/4" with a reference to the fraction "1/2", applicable in respect of amounts that become payable after February 27, 2000 except that, for amounts that became payable after February 27, 2000 and before October 18, 2000, the reference to the fraction "1/2" shall be read as a reference to the fraction "2/3".

**Technical Notes**: Paragraph 20(1)(f) sets out rules concerning the deductibility of amounts paid by a taxpayer where the amounts paid are in respect of the principal amount of an obligation that was issued for less than its principal amount.

The amendment to subparagraph 20(1)(f)(ii) replaces the reference the fraction "3/4" with a reference to the fraction "1/2", as a consequence of the change of the inclusion rate for capital gains from 3/4 to 1/2 [see 38(a) — ed.]. The amendment applies in respect of amounts paid after February 27, 2000 except that, for amounts paid after February 27, 2000 and before October 18, 2000 the reference to the fraction "1/2" is to be read as a reference to the fraction "2/3". These modifications are required in order to reflect the capital gains/losses rate for the year.

**Related Provisions**: 18(1)(f) — Payments on discounted bonds; 18(11) — Limitation; 110.6(1) — "Investment expense"; 127.52(1)(b), (c), (c.2), (e.1) — Limitation on deduction for minimum tax purposes. See additional Related Provisions and Definitions at end of s. 20.

**Notes**: The term "bond, debenture, bill, note, mortgage or similar obligation" may not include bankers' acceptances. See *Federated Cooperatives Ltd.*, [2000] 2 C.T.C. 2382 (TCC).

**Interpretation Bulletins**: IT-341R3: Expenses of issuing or selling shares, units in a trust, interests in a partnership or syndicate, and expenses of borrowing money.

(g) **share transfer and other fees** — where the taxpayer is a corporation,

(i) an amount payable in the year as a fee for services rendered by a person as a registrar of or agent for the transfer of shares of the capital stock of the taxpayer or as an agent for the remittance to shareholders of the taxpayer of dividends declared by it,

(ii) an amount payable in the year as a fee to a stock exchange for the listing of shares of the capital stock of the taxpayer, and

(iii) an expense incurred in the year in the course of printing and issuing a financial report to shareholders of the taxpayer or to any other person entitled by law to receive the report;

**Related Provisions**: See Related Provisions and Definitions at end of s. 20.

(h), (i) [Repealed under former Act]

**Notes**: 20(1)(h) and (i), repealed in 1984, allowed deductions for certification fees and discounts on bankers' acceptance fees. These are now included in the definition of "borrowed money" in 248(1), and thus deductible over five years under 20(1)(e).

(j) **repayment of loan by shareholder** — such part of any loan or indebtedness repaid by the taxpayer in the year as was by virtue of subsection 15(2) included in computing the taxpayer's income for a preceding taxation year (except to the extent that the amount of the loan or indebtedness was deductible from the taxpayer's income for the purpose of computing the taxpayer's taxable income for that preceding taxation year), if it is established by subsequent events or otherwise that the repayment was not made as part of a series of loans or other transactions and repayments;

**Related Provisions**: 20(3) — Use of borrowed money; 110.6(1) — "investment expense"; 227(6.1) — Repayment of loan by shareholder when shareholder is non-resident; 248(10) — Series of transactions. See additional Related provisions and Definitions at end of s. 20.

**Notes**: 20(1)(j) can be used for a form of income averaging. See Notes to 15(2).

**Interpretation Bulletins**: IT-119R4: Debts of shareholders and certain persons connected with shareholders.

**I.T. Technical News**: No. 3 (paragraphs 15(2)(b) and 20(1)(j)).

(k) [Repealed under former Act]

**Notes**: 20(1)(k), repealed by 1988 tax reform, allowed a deduction for the interest portion of a blended payment combining interest and principal. Such amounts are now deductible under the general rule in 20(1)(c) for interest deductibility, since 16(1) deems the interest portion of such a payment to be interest on a debt obligation.

(l) **doubtful or impaired debts** — a reserve determined as the total of

(i) a reasonable amount in respect of doubtful debts (other than a debt to which subparagraph (ii) applies) that have been included in computing the taxpayer's income for the year or a preceding taxation year, and

(ii) where the taxpayer is a financial institution (as defined in subsection 142.2(1)) in the year or a taxpayer whose ordinary business includes the lending of money, an amount in respect of properties (other than mark-to-market properties, as defined in that subsection) that are

(A) impaired loans or lending assets that are specified debt obligations (as defined in that subsection) of the taxpayer, or

(B) impaired loans or lending assets that were made or acquired by the taxpayer in the ordinary course of the taxpayer's business of insurance or the lending of money

equal to the total of

(C) the percentage (not exceeding 100%) that the taxpayer claims of the prescribed

Subdivision b — Income or Loss from a Business or Property    S. 20(1)(l)

reserve amount for the taxpayer for the year, and

(D) in respect of loans, lending assets or specified debt obligations that are impaired and for which an amount is not deductible for the year because of clause (C) (each of which in this clause is referred to as a "loan"), the taxpayer's specified percentage for the year of the lesser of

(I) the total of all amounts each of which is a reasonable amount as a reserve (other than any portion of which is in respect of a sectoral reserve) for a loan in respect of the amortized cost of the loan to the taxpayer at the end of the year, and

(II) the amount determined by the formula

$$0.9M - N$$

where

M is the amount that is the taxpayer's reserve or allowance for impairment (other than any portion of the amount that is in respect of a sectoral reserve) for all loans that is determined for the year in accordance with generally accepted accounting principles, and

N is the total of all amounts each of which is the specified reserve adjustment for a loan (other than an income bond, an income debenture, a small business bond or small business development bond) for the year or a preceding taxation year;

**Related Provisions**: 12(1)(d) — Income inclusion in following year; 12(4.1) — Regular interest income rules do not apply where 20(1)(l)(ii) applies; 16(7) — Indexed debt obligation rules do not apply where 20(1)(l)(ii) applies; 18(1)(s) — Limitation on deduction by insurer or money lender; 20(1)(p) — Bad debt deduction; 20(2.3) — Sectoral reserve; 20(2.4) — Specified percentage; 20(27) — Non-arm's length acquisition of loan or lending asset; 20(30) — Specified reserve adjustment; 22(1) — Sale of accounts receivable; 34.2(2)(c) — Maximum reserve deemed claimed for purposes of 1995 stub period income; 79.1(8) — Creditor cannot deduct amount for bad or impaired debt where property seized; 87(2)(g) — Amalgamations — reserves; 87(2)(h) — Amalgamations — debts; 87(2.2) — Amalgamation of insurance corporations; 88(1)(g) — Winding-up of subsidiary insurance corporations; 111(5.3) — Doubtful debts and bad debts; 138(5)(a) — Deductions not allowed; 138(11.31)(b) — Change in use rule for insurance properties does not apply for purposes of 20(1)(l); 142.3(1)(c) — Amount deductible in respect of specified debt obligation; 142.3(4) — Specified debt obligation rules do not apply where 20(1)(l)(ii) applies; 149(10)(a.1) — Exempt corporations; 257 — Formula cannot calculate to less than zero; Reg. 2405(3)"gross Canadian life investment income"(d), (i) — Inclusion in life insurer's income for following year. See additional Related Provisions and Definitions at end of s. 20.

**Notes**: 20(1)(l) amended by 1995-97 technical bill, effective

(a) for taxation years that end after September 1997; and

(b) for taxation years that end after 1995 and before October 1997 where the taxpayer elects in writing to have the amendment apply to the year and files the election with Revenue Canada by September 30, 1998.

The amendments reflect the 1995 accounting changes announced by the Canadian Institute of Chartered Accountants, and adopted by the Superintendent of Financial Institutions, in dealing with the recognition and measurement of impaired loans. (Department of Finance news release, November 14, 1997.)

For earlier taxation years that end after February 22, 1994 (taking into account amendments made by 1995-97 technical bill), read:

(l) **reserve for doubtful debts** — a reserve determined as the total of

(i) a reasonable amount in respect of doubtful debts that have been included in computing the income of the taxpayer for that year or a preceding year, and

(ii) where the taxpayer is a financial institution (as defined in subsection 142.2(1)) in the year or a taxpayer whose ordinary business includes the lending of money, an amount in respect of properties (other than mark-to-market properties, as defined in that subsection) that are doubtful loans or lending assets that were made or acquired by the taxpayer in the ordinary course of the taxpayer's business of insurance or the lending of money or that were specified debt obligations (as defined in that subsection) of the taxpayer, equal to the total of

(A) the prescribed reserve amount for the taxpayer for the year, and

(B) in respect of doubtful loans or lending assets for which an amount was not deducted for the year by reason of clause (A) (in this clause referred to as the "loans"), the lesser of

(I) a reasonable amount as a reserve for the loans in respect of the amortized cost of the loans to the taxpayer at the end of the year, and

(II) the product obtained when the total of

1. that part of the reserve for the loans reported in the financial statements of the taxpayer for the year that is in respect of the amortized cost to the taxpayer at the end of the year of the loans, and

2. the total of all amounts included under subsection 12(3) or paragraph 142.3(1)(a) in computing the taxpayer's income for the year or a preceding taxation year to the extent that those amounts reduced the part of the reserve referred to in sub-subclause 1

is multiplied by one minus the prescribed recovery rate,

or such lesser amount as the taxpayer may claim where the lesser amount is the total of a percentage of the amount determined under clause (A) and the same percentage of the amount determined under clause (B);

For prior taxation years generally since 1988, ignore the reference to 142.3(1)(a) in 20(1)(l)(ii)(B)(II)2, and read the opening words of 20(1)(l)(ii) as:

(ii) an amount in respect of doubtful loans or lending assets of a taxpayer who was an insurer or whose ordinary business included the lending of money, made or acquired by the taxpayer in the ordinary course of the taxpayer's business of insurance or the lending of money, equal to the total of

**Regulations**: 8000(a) (prescribed reserve amount).

**I.T. Application Rules**: 23(5)"investment interest".

**Interpretation Bulletins**: IT-109R2: Unpaid amounts; IT-188R: Sale of accounts receivable; IT-291R2: Transfer of property to a corporation under subsection 85(1); IT-302R3: Losses of a corporation — the effect that acquisitions of control, amalgamations, and windings-up have on their deductibility — after January 15, 1987; IT-345R: Special reserve — loans secured by mortgages; IT-442R: Bad debts and reserve for doubtful debts; IT-505: Mortgage foreclosures and conditional sales repossessions.

**Advance Tax Rulings**: ATR-6: Vendor reacquires business assets following default by purchaser.

(l.1) **reserve for guarantees, etc.** — a reserve in respect of credit risks under guarantees, indemnities, letters of credit or other credit facilities, bankers' acceptances, interest rate or currency swaps, foreign exchange or other future or option contracts, interest rate protection agreements, risk participations and other similar instruments or commitments issued, made or assumed by a taxpayer who was an insurer or whose ordinary business included the lending of money in favour of persons with whom the taxpayer deals at arm's length in the ordinary course of the taxpayer's business of insurance or the lending of money, equal to the lesser of

(i) a reasonable amount as a reserve for credit risk losses of the taxpayer expected to arise after the end of the year under or in respect of such instruments or commitments, and

(ii) 90% of the reserve for credit risk losses of the taxpayer expected to arise after the end of the year under or in respect of those instruments or commitments determined for the year in accordance with generally accepted accounting principles,

or such lesser amount as the taxpayer may claim;

**Related Provisions**: 12(1)(d.1) — Income inclusion in following year; 20(27) — Non-arm's length acquisition of loan or lending assets; 34.2(2)(c) — Maximum reserve deemed claimed for purposes of 1995 stub period income; 87(2)(g) — Amalgamations — reserves; 87(2)(h) — Amalgamation — debts; 87(2.2) — Amalgamation of insurance corporations; 88(1)(g) — Winding-up of subsidiary insurance corporations; 149(10)(a.1) — Exempt corporations. See additional Related Provisions and Definitions at end of s. 20.

**Notes**: 20(1)(l.1)(ii) amended by 1995-97 technical bill, effective on the same basis as the amendments to 20(1)(l) (see Notes to 20(1)(l)). For earlier taxation years, read:

(ii) the product obtained when the reserve for credit risk losses of the taxpayer expected to arise after the end of the year under or in respect of such instruments or commitments reported in the financial statements of the taxpayer for the year is multiplied by one minus the prescribed recovery rate,

Reg. 8001, which provided the prescribed recovery rate for the former 20(1)(l.1)(ii), will be repealed.

**Regulations**: 8001 [repealed] (prescribed recovery rate).

(m) **reserve in respect of certain [future] goods and services** — subject to subsection (6), where amounts described in paragraph 12(1)(a) have been included in computing the taxpayer's income from a business for the year or a previous year, a reasonable amount as a reserve in respect of

(i) goods that it is reasonably anticipated will have to be delivered after the end of the year,

(ii) services that it is reasonably anticipated will have to be rendered after the end of the year,

(iii) periods for which rent or other amounts for the possession or use of land or chattels have been paid in advance, or

(iv) repayments under arrangements or understandings of the class described in subparagraph 12(1)(a)(ii) that it is reasonably anticipated will have to be made after the end of the year on the return or resale to the taxpayer of articles other than bottles;

**Related Provisions**: 12(1)(e)(i) — Income inclusion in following year; 20(6) — Special reserves; 20(7) — Where 20(1)(m) does not apply; 20(24) — Amounts paid for undertaking future obligations; 32(1) — Insurance agents and brokers; 34 — Professional business; 34.2(2)(c) — Maximum reserve deemed claimed for purposes of 1995 stub period income; 87(2)(g) — Amalgamations — reserves; 149(10)(a.1) — Exempt corporations. See additional Related Provisions and Definitions at end of s. 20.

**Interpretation Bulletins**: IT-92R2: Income of contractors; IT-154R: Special reserves; IT-165R: Returnable containers; IT-215R: Reserves, contingent accounts; IT-261R: Prepayment of rents; IT-321R: Insurance agents and brokers — unearned commissions; IT-531: Eligible funeral arrangements.

**I.T. Technical News**: No. 18 (*Oerlikon Aérospatiale* case).

(m.1) **manufacturer's warranty reserve** — where an amount described in paragraph 12(1)(a) has been included in computing the taxpayer's income from a business for the year or a preceding taxation year, a reasonable amount as a reserve in respect of goods or services that it is reasonably anticipated will have to be delivered or rendered after the end of the year pursuant to an agreement for an extended warranty

(i) entered into by the taxpayer with a person with whom the taxpayer was dealing at arm's length, and

(ii) under which the only obligation of the taxpayer is to provide such goods or services with respect to property manufactured by the taxpayer or by a corporation related to the taxpayer,

not exceeding that portion of the amount paid or payable by the taxpayer to an insurer that carries on an insurance business in Canada to insure the taxpayer's liability under the agreement in respect of an outlay or expense made or incurred after December 11, 1979 and in respect of the period after the end of the year;

**Related Provisions**: 12(1)(e)(i) — Income inclusion in following year; 20(24) — Amounts paid for undertaking future obligations; 34.2(2)(c) — Maximum reserve deemed claimed for purposes of 1995 stub period income; 87(2)(g), (j) — Amalgamations — reserves; 149(10)(a.1) — Exempt corporations. See additional Related Provisions and Definitions at end of s. 20.

**Interpretation Bulletins**: IT-154R: Special reserves.

(m.2) **repayment of amount previously included in income** — a repayment in the year by the taxpayer of an amount required by paragraph 12(1)(a) to be included in computing the taxpayer's income from a business for the year or a preceding taxation year;

**Related Provisions**: 87(2)(j) — Amalgamations. See additional Related provisions and Definitions at end of s. 20.

**Interpretation Bulletins**: IT-154R: Special reserves.

(n) **reserve for unpaid amounts** — where an amount included in computing the taxpayer's income from the business for the year or for a preceding taxation year in respect of property sold in the course of the business is payable to the taxpayer after the end of the year and, except where the property is real property, all or part of the amount was, at the time of the sale, not due until at least 2 years after that time, a reasonable amount as a reserve in respect of such part of the amount as can reasonably be regarded as a portion of the profit from the sale;

**Related Provisions**: 12(1)(e)(ii) — Income inclusion in following year; 20(8) — No deduction in certain circumstances; 34.2(2)(c) — Maximum reserve deemed claimed for purposes of 1995 stub period income; 66.2(2) — Deduction for cumulative Canadian development expenses; 66.4(2) — Deduction for cumulative Canadian oil and gas property expenses; 72(1)(a) — Reserves, etc., for year of death; 79.1(4), (6)(c) — Deemed amount where property repossessed by creditor; 87(2)(g), (i), (ll) — Amalgamations — reserves; 88(1)(d)(i)(C) — Winding-up; 149(10)(a.1) — Exempt corporations. See additional Related Provisions and Definitions at end of s. 20.

**Notes**: The reserve under 20(1)(n) is limited to 3 years: see 20(8).

No reserve can be claimed under 20(1)(n) for recaptured depreciation under 13(1), since such amount is not "profit from the sale": *Odyssey Industries Inc.*, [1996] 2 C.T.C. 2401 (TCC).

20(1)(n) amended by 1994 tax amendments bill (Part I), effective for taxation years that end after February 21, 1994. The purpose of the amendment is to avoid penalizing creditors who exercise "acceleration" clauses under an agreement where the creditor sold property and received, as part of the consideration, a note payable by the purchaser of the property. The acceleration clause would typically be exercised only if the purchaser defaulted on its obligations to a creditor.

Proposed 20(1)(n.1) in the July 12, 1994 draft legislation on debt forgiveness was not enacted. See now 61.4.

**Interpretation Bulletins**: IT-109R2: Unpaid amounts; IT-123R6: Transactions involving eligible capital property; IT-152R3: Special reserves — sale of land; IT-154R: Special reserves; IT-345R: Special reserves — loans secured by mortgages; IT-442R: Bad debts and reserves for doubtful debts; IT-505: Mortgage foreclosures and conditional sales repossessions.

**Information Circulars**: 88-2, para. 24: General anti-avoidance rule — section 245 of the *Income Tax Act*.

**Forms**: T2069: Election in respect of amounts not deductible as reserves for the year of death.

(o) **reserve for quadrennial survey** — such amount as may be prescribed as a reserve for expenses to be incurred by the taxpayer by reason of quadrennial or other special surveys required under the *Canada Shipping Act*, or the regulations under that Act, or under the rules of any society or association for the classification and registry of shipping approved by the Minister of Transport for the purposes of the *Canada Shipping Act*;

**Related Provisions**: 12(1)(h) — Inclusion into income — previous reserve for quadrennial survey; 87(2)(g) — Amalgamations — reserves; 149(10)(a.1) — Exempt corporations. See additional Related Provisions and Definitions at end of s. 20.

**Regulations**: 3600 (prescribed amount).

(p) **bad debts** — the total of

(i) all debts owing to the taxpayer that are established by the taxpayer to have become bad debts in the year and that have been included in computing the taxpayer's income for the year or a preceding taxation year, and

(ii) all amounts each of which is that part of the amortized cost to the taxpayer at the end of the year of a loan or lending asset (other than a mark-to-market property, as defined in subsection 142.2(1)) that is established in the year by the taxpayer to have become uncollectible and that,

(A) where the taxpayer is an insurer or a taxpayer whose ordinary business includes the lending of money, was made or acquired in the ordinary course of the taxpayer's business of insurance or the lending of money, or

(B) where the taxpayer is a financial institution (as defined in subsection 142.2(1)) in the year, is a specified debt obligation (as defined in that subsection) of the taxpayer;

**Related Provisions**: 12(1)(i) — Income inclusion — bad debts recovered; 12.4 — Bad debt inclusion; 20(1)(l) — Reserve for doubtful debts; 20(27) — Non-arm's length acquisition of loan or lending assets; 22(1) — Sale of accounts receivable; 50(1)(a) — Deemed disposition where debt becomes bad debt; 79.1(7)(d) — Deduction by creditor for bad debt where property seized; 79.1(8) — No deduction for principal amount of bad debt where property seized by creditor; 87(2)(g), (h) — Amalgamations; 87(2.2) — Amalgamation of insurance corporations; 88(1)(g) — Winding-up of subsidiary insurance corporations; 111(5.3) — Doubtful debts and bad debts; 142.3(1)(c) — Amount deductible in respect of specified debt obligation; 142.4(1)"tax basis"(p) — Disposition of specified debt obligation by financial institution; 142.5(8)(d)(i) — First deemed disposition of mark-to-market debt obligation. See additional Related Provisions and Definitions at end of s. 20.

**Notes**: 20(1)(p)(ii) amended by 1995-97 technical bill, effective for taxation years that end after February 22, 1994. For earlier years generally since 1998, read:

(ii) all amounts each of which is that part of the amortized cost to the taxpayer at the end of the year of a loan or lending asset made or acquired in the ordinary course of business by a taxpayer who was an insurer or whose ordinary business included the lending of money established by the taxpayer to have become uncollectable in the year;

**Interpretation Bulletins**: IT-109R2: Unpaid amounts; IT-123R4: Disposition of and transactions involving eligible capital property; IT-123R6: Transactions involving eligible capital property; IT-159R3: Capital debts established to be bad debts; IT-188R: Sale of accounts receivable; IT-291R2: Transfer of property to a corporation under subsection 85(1); IT-302R3: Losses of a corporation — the effect that acquisitions of control, amalgamations, and windings-up have on their deductibility — after January 15, 1987; IT-345R: Special reserve — loans secured by mortgages; IT-442R: Bad debts and reserve for doubtful debts; IT-488R2: Winding-up of

90%-owned taxable Canadian corporations; IT-505: Mortgage foreclosures and conditional sales repossessions.

**Advance Tax Rulings**: ATR-6: Vendor reacquires business assets following default by purchaser.

**(q) employer's contributions to registered pension plan** — such amount in respect of employer contributions to registered pension plans as is permitted by subsection 147.2(1);

**Related Provisions**: 6(1)(a)(i) — Employer's contribution to RPP not a taxable benefit; 18(1)(c) — Limitation re exempt income; 146(5) — Amount of premium deductible. See additional Related Provisions and Definitions at end of s. 20.

**Notes**: 20(1)(q) amended by 1990 pension bill, effective 1991. For employer contributions before 1991, it provided a deduction for employer contributions to an employee's RPP, capped at $3,500, and linked with 20(1)(s) and 20(22). The relevant rules are now in 147.1.

**Interpretation Bulletins**: IT-105: Administrative costs of pension plans.

**Information Circulars**: 72-13R8: Employee's pension plans.

**(r) employer's contributions under retirement compensation arrangement** — amounts paid by the taxpayer in the year as contributions under a retirement compensation arrangement in respect of services rendered by an employee or former employee of the taxpayer, other than where it is established, by subsequent events or otherwise, that the amounts were paid as part of a series of payments and refunds of contributions under the arrangement;

**Related Provisions**: 12(1)(n.3) — Retirement compensation arrangement; 18(1)(o.2) — Retirement compensation arrangement; 87(2)(j.3) — Amalgamations — continuing corporation; 153(1)(p) — Withholding; 227(8.2) — RCA — failure to withhold; 248(10) — Series of transactions. See additional Related Provisions and Definitions at end of s. 20.

**Forms**: T737-RCA: Statement of contributions paid to a custodian of a retirement compensation arrangement.

**(s), (t) [Repealed under former Act]**

**Notes**: 20(1)(s) repealed by 1990 pension bill, effective 1991. Deductible employer contributions to registered pension plans are now determined under 147.2. See Notes to 20(1)(q).

20(1)(t), repealed by 1988 tax reform, allowed a deduction for expenditures on scientific research and experimental development, as permitted by 37 and 37.1. The deduction under 37 is still explicitly available under that section, which is part of the same subdivision as this section.

**(u) patronage dividends** — such amounts in respect of payments made by the taxpayer pursuant to allocations in proportion to patronage as are permitted by section 135;

**Related Provisions**: See Related Provisions and Definitions at end of s. 20.

**(v) mining taxes** — such amount as is allowed by regulation in respect of taxes on income for the year from mining operations;

**Related Provisions**: See Related Provisions and Definitions at end of s. 20.

**Notes**: Other deductions for provincial income taxes are generally not allowed. See Notes to 18(1)(t).

**Regulations**: 3900 (amount allowed).

**(v.1) resource allowance** — such amount as is allowed to the taxpayer for the year by regulation in respect of natural accumulations of petroleum or natural gas in Canada, oil or gas wells in Canada or mineral resources in Canada;

**Related Provisions**: 12(1)(z.5) — Inclusion in income of prescribed resource loss; 20(15) — What can be allowed by regulation; 65 — Depletion allowance; 96(1)(d) — Partnerships — no deduction for resource expenditures; 104(29) — Flow-through from trust to beneficiaries; 219(1)(c) — Branch tax on non-resident corporations. See additional Related Provisions and Definitions at end of s. 20.

**Regulations**: 1210 (amount allowed).

**Forms**: T82: Saskatchewan Royalty Tax Estate Calculation (Individuals).

**(w) employer's contributions under profit sharing plan** — an amount paid by the taxpayer to a trustee in trust for employees of the taxpayer or of a corporation with whom the taxpayer does not deal at arm's length, under an employees profit sharing plan as permitted by section 144;

**Related Provisions**: 12(1)(n) — Receipts from employees profit sharing plan — inclusion in income of employer; 144(5) — Employer's contribution to trust deductible. See additional Related Provisions and Definitions at end of s. 20.

**(x) employer's contributions under registered supplementary unemployment benefit plan** — an amount paid by the taxpayer to a trustee under a registered supplementary unemployment benefit plan as permitted by section 145;

**Related Provisions**: 6(1)(a)(i) — Employer's contribution not a taxable benefit to employee; 18(1)(i) — No deduction except as permitted by s. 145; 145(5) — Payments by employer deductible. See additional Related Provisions and Definitions at end of s. 20.

**(y) employer's contributions under deferred profit sharing plan** — an amount paid by the taxpayer to a trustee under a deferred profit sharing plan as permitted by subsection 147(8);

**Related Provisions**: 18(1)(c) — Limitation re exempt income. See additional Related Provisions and Definitions at end of s. 20.

**(z) cancellation of lease** — the proportion of an amount not otherwise deductible that was paid or that became payable by the taxpayer before the end of the year to a person for the cancellation of a lease of property of the taxpayer leased by the taxpayer to that person that

(i) the number of days that remained in the term of the lease (including all renewal periods of the lease), not exceeding 40 years, immediately before its cancellation and that were in the year

is of

(ii) the number of days that remained in the term of the lease (including all renewal periods of the lease), not exceeding 40 years, immediately before its cancellation,

Subdivision b — Income or Loss from a Business or Property    S. 20(1)(cc)

in any case where the property was owned at the end of the year by the taxpayer or by a person with whom the taxpayer was not dealing at arm's length and no part of the amount was deductible by the taxpayer under paragraph (z.1) in computing the taxpayer's income for a preceding taxation year;

**Related Provisions**: 13(5.5) — Lease cancellation payment not included as rental payment under 13(5.4) for CCA purposes; 18(1)(q) — Limitation re cancellation of lease; 20(1)(z.1) — Cancellation payment where property not owned at end of year; 87(2)(j.5) — Amalgamations — cancellation of lease. See additional Related Provisions and Definitions at end of s. 20.

**Interpretation Bulletins**: IT-359R2: Premiums and other amounts re leases; IT-467R: Damages, settlements, and similar payments.

(z.1) **idem** — an amount not otherwise deductible that was paid or that became payable by the taxpayer before the end of the year to a person for the cancellation of a lease of property of the taxpayer leased by the taxpayer to that person, in any case where

(i) the property was not owned at the end of the year by the taxpayer or by a person with whom the taxpayer was not dealing at arm's length, and

(ii) no part of the amount was deductible by the taxpayer under this paragraph in computing the taxpayer's income for any preceding taxation year,

to the extent of the amount thereof (or in the case of capital property, ¾ of the amount thereof) that was not deductible by the taxpayer under paragraph (z) in computing the taxpayer's income for any preceding taxation year;

### Proposed Amendment — 20(1)(z.1)

**Application**: The December 21, 2000 draft legislation, subsec. 7(3), will amend para. 20(1)(z.1) by replacing the reference to the fraction "3/4" with a reference to the fraction "1/2", applicable in respect of amounts that become payable after February 27, 2000 except that, for amounts that became payable after February 27, 2000 and before October 18, 2000, the reference to the fraction "1/2" shall be read as a reference to the fraction "2/3".

**Technical Notes**: Paragraph 20(1)(z.1) permits a taxpayer to deduct an amount in respect of amounts paid by the taxpayer to a lessee for the cancellation of a lease of a property where the property was not owned at the end of the year by the taxpayer or a non-arm's length person.

The amendment to paragraph 20(1)(z.1) replaces the reference to the fraction "3/4" with a reference to the fraction "1/2", as a consequence of the change of the inclusion rate for capital gains from 3/4 to 1/2.

The amendment applies in respect of amounts paid after February 27, 2000 except that for amounts paid after February 27, 2000 and before October 18, 2000 the reference to the fraction "1/2" is to be read as a reference to the fraction "2/3". These modifications are required in order to reflect the capital gains/losses rate for the year.

**Related Provisions**: 13(5.5) — Lease cancellation payment; 18(1)(q) — Limitation re cancellation of lease; 20(1)(z) — Alternative deduction for cancellation payment; 87(2)(j.5) — Amalgama-

tions — cancellation of lease. See additional Related Provisions and Definitions at end of s. 20.

**Interpretation Bulletins**: IT-359R2: Premiums and other amounts re leases; IT-467R: Damages, settlements, and similar payments.

(aa) **landscaping of grounds** — an amount paid by the taxpayer in the year for the landscaping of grounds around a building or other structure of the taxpayer that is used by the taxpayer primarily for the purpose of gaining or producing income therefrom or from a business;

**Related Provisions**: 18(3.1)(a) — Costs relating to construction of building or ownership of land. See Related Provisions and Definitions at end of s. 20.

**Interpretation Bulletins**: IT-296: Landscaping of grounds; IT-304R2: Condominiums; IT-485: Cost of clearing or levelling land.

(bb) **fees paid to investment counsel** — an amount other than a commission paid by the taxpayer in the year to a person

(i) for advice as to the advisability of purchasing or selling a specific share or security of the taxpayer, or

(ii) for services in respect of the administration or management of shares or securities of the taxpayer,

if that person's principal business

(iii) is advising others as to the advisability of purchasing or selling specific shares or securities, or

(iv) includes the provision of services in respect of the administration or management of shares or securities;

**Related Provisions**: 18(1)(u) — Investment counsel fees for RRSP or RRIF are non-deductible; 87(2.2) — Amalgamation of insurance corporations; 88(1)(g) — Winding-up of subsidiary insurance corporations; 110.6(1) — "investment expense". See additional Related Provisions and Definitions at end of s. 20.

**Notes**: In *Walmsley Estate*, [1999] 2 C.T.C. 2956 (TCC), fees paid by an estate to a lay trustee were held not deductible under 20(1)(bb) on the basis that there was insufficient evidence as to what portion of the fees related to earning income.

**Interpretation Bulletins**: IT-124R6: Contributions to registered retirement savings plans; IT-238R2: Fees paid to investment counsel.

(cc) **expenses of representation [lobbying]** — an amount paid by the taxpayer in the year as or on account of expenses incurred by the taxpayer in making any representation relating to a business carried on by the taxpayer,

(i) to the government of a country, province or state or to a municipal or public body performing a function of government in Canada, or

(ii) to an agency of a government or of a municipal or public body referred to in subparagraph (i) that had authority to make rules, regulations or by-laws relating to the business carried on by the taxpayer,

including any representation for the purpose of obtaining a licence, permit, franchise or trade mark relating to the business carried on by the taxpayer;

**Related Provisions**: 13(12) — Application to depreciable property; 20(9) — Amortizing claim over 10 years. See additional Related Provisions and Definitions at end of s. 20.

**Notes**: A person to whom an amount is paid that is deductible under 20(1)(cc) may be required to register under the *Lobbyists Registration Act*. Contact the Lobbyist Registration Branch at 613-957-2760 for information.

**Interpretation Bulletins**: IT-99R5: Legal and accounting fees.

(dd) **investigation of site** — an amount paid by the taxpayer in the year for investigating the suitability of a site for a building or other structure planned by the taxpayer for use in connection with a business carried on by the taxpayer;

**Related Provisions**: 53(1)(a) — Valuation or surveying costs — addition to adjusted cost base. See additional Related Provisions and Definitions at end of s. 20.

**Interpretation Bulletins**: IT-350R: Investigation of site.

(ee) **utilities service connection** — an amount paid by the taxpayer in the year to a person (other than a person with whom the taxpayer was not dealing at arm's length) for the purpose of making a service connection to the taxpayer's place of business for the supply, by means of wires, pipes or conduits, of electricity, gas, telephone service, water or sewers supplied by that person, to the extent that the amount so paid was not paid

(i) to acquire property of the taxpayer, or

(ii) as consideration for the goods or services for the supply of which the service connection was undertaken or made;

**Related Provisions**: See Related Provisions and Definitions at end of s. 20.

**Interpretation Bulletins**: IT-452: Utility service connections.

(ff) **payments by farmers** — an amount paid by the taxpayer in the year as a levy under the *Western Grain Stabilization Act*, as a premium in respect of the gross revenue insurance program established under the *Farm Income Protection Act* or as an administration fee in respect of a net income stabilization account;

**Related Provisions**: 12(1)(p) — Certain payments made to farmers — income inclusion. See additional Related Provisions and Definitions at end of s. 20.

**Notes**: 20(1)(ff) amended by 1992 technical bill, effective 1991, to add everything after "*Stabilization Act*".

**Forms**: T1163: Statement A — NISA account information and statement of farming activities for individuals; T1164: Statement B — NISA account information and statement of farming activities for additional farming operations; T1165: Statement C — statement of farming activities for Ontario self directed risk management (SDRM); T1175 Sched. 1: NISA/Farming — calculation of CCA and business-use-of-home expenses.

(gg) [Repealed]

**Notes**: 20(1)(gg) added by 1991 Budget, but repealed by 1992 technical bill and moved to 20(1)(qq), retroactive to its introduction (renovations and alterations made after 1990). See Notes to 20(1)(qq).

Former 20(1)(gg), repealed by 1986 Budget, provided a 3% inventory allowance.

(hh) **repayments of inducements, etc.** — an amount repaid by the taxpayer in the year pursuant to a legal obligation to repay all or part of a particular amount

(i) included under paragraph 12(1)(x) in computing the taxpayer's income for the year or a preceding taxation year, or

(ii) that is, because of subparagraph 12(1)(x)(vi) or subsection 12(2.2), not included under paragraph 12(1)(x) in computing the taxpayer's income for the year or a preceding taxation year, where the particular amount relates to an outlay or expense (other than an outlay or expense that is in respect of the cost of property of the taxpayer or that is or would be, if amounts deductible by the taxpayer were not limited because of paragraph 66(4)(b), subsection 66.1(2) or subparagraph 66.2(2)(a)(ii) or 66.4(2)(a)(ii), deductible under section 66, 66.1, 66.2 or 66.4) that would, but for the receipt of the particular amount, have been deductible in computing the taxpayer's income for the year or a preceding taxation year;

**Proposed Amendment — 20(1)(hh)(ii)**

(ii) that is, by reason of subparagraph 12(1)(x)(vi) or subsection 12(2.2), not included under paragraph 12(1)(x) in computing the taxpayer's income for the year or a preceding taxation year, where the particular amount relates to an outlay or expense (other than an outlay or expense that is in respect of the cost of property of the taxpayer or that is or would be, if amounts deductible by the taxpayer were not limited by reason of paragraph 66(4)(b), subsection 66.1(2), subparagraph 66.2(2)(a)(ii), the words "30% of" in clause 66.21(4)(a)(ii)(B), clause 66.21(4)(a)(ii)(C) or (D) or subparagraph 66.4(2)(a)(ii), deductible under section 66, 66.1, 66.2, 66.21 or 66.4) that would, if the particular amount had not been received, have been deductible in computing the taxpayer's income for the year or a preceding taxation year;

**Application**: The December 21, 2000 draft legislation, subsec. 7(4), will amend subpara. 20(1)(hh)(ii) to read as above, applicable to taxation years that begin after 2000.

**Technical Notes**: Subparagraph 20(1)(hh)(i) provides a deduction for the repayment by a taxpayer of certain amounts that were included in the taxpayer's income under paragraph 12(1)(x) as an inducement or assistance. Subparagraph 20(1)(hh)(ii) provides a deduction for the repayment of certain inducements or assistance not included in the taxpayer's income under paragraph 12(1)(x) but that would have been so included but for the application of subparagraph 12(1)(x)(v.1) or subsection 12(2.2)

Subdivision b — Income or Loss from a Business or Property        S. 20(1)(mm)

which allow the netting of the amounts against other costs. Subparagraph 20(1)(hh)(ii) does not apply if the outlays or expenses related to the inducements or assistance were deductible in computing income under any of sections 66, 66.1, 66.2 or 66.4 (or would have been so deductible if certain limits on deductions under those sections were not taken into account).

Subparagraph 20(1)(hh)(ii) is amended so that repayments in respect of outlays or expenses deductible under new section 66.21 are likewise not deductible as a consequence of the application of that subparagraph. This amendment is consequential on the introduction of new rules for the deduction of foreign resource expenses in section 66.21.

**Related Provisions**: 60(s) — Repayment of policy loan; 79(4)(d) — Subsequent payment by debtor following surrender of property deemed to be repayment of assistance; 87(2)(j.6) — Amalgamations — continuing corporation; 148(9)"adjusted cost basis"E — "adjusted cost basis". See additional Related Provisions and Definitions at end of s. 20.

**Notes**: 20(1)(hh)(ii) added by 1990 GST, effective for amounts repaid after January 1990, and amended by 1992 Economic Statement, effective for taxation years ending after December 2, 1992, to change reference to 66.1(2)(a)(ii) to 66.1(2). The change was made because the income-based limit for a principal-business corporation is now in 66.2(1)(b).

**Interpretation Bulletins**: IT-273R2: Government assistance — general comments.

(hh.1) **repayment of obligation** — ¾ of any amount (other than an amount to which paragraph 14(10)(b) applies in respect of the taxpayer) repaid by the taxpayer in the year under a legal obligation to repay all or part of an amount to which paragraph 14(10)(c) applies in respect of the taxpayer;

**Related Provisions**: 79(4)(b) — Subsequent payment by debtor following surrender of property deemed to be repayment of assistance.

**Notes**: 20(1)(hh.1) added by 1994 tax amendments bill (Part I), effective for amounts repaid after February 21, 1994. It allows a deduction for repayment of assistance received in respect of eligible capital property related to a business carried on by the taxpayer. The deduction (3/4 of the amount repaid) applies only where the taxpayer ceases to carry on the business before the repayment. Repayments of assistance before that time are added under 14(9)(b) in computing eligible capital expenditure.

**Interpretation Bulletins**: IT-273R2: Government assistance — general comments.

(ii) **inventory adjustment** — the amount required by paragraph 12(1)(r) to be included in computing the taxpayer's income for the immediately preceding year;

**Related Provisions**: 87(2)(j.1) — Amalgamations — inventory adjustment. See additional Related Provisions and Definitions at end of s. 20.

(jj) **reinsurance commission** — the amount required by paragraph 12(1)(s) to be included in computing the taxpayer's income for the immediately preceding taxation year;

**Related Provisions**: 18.1(15)(b) — Reinsurance commission excluded from matchable expenditure rules; 20(7)(c) — Deduction for policy reserves; 87(2.2) — Amalgamations of insurance corporations; 88(1)(g) — Winding-up of subsidiary insurance corporations. See additional Related Provisions and Definitions at end of s. 20.

(kk) **exploration and development grants** — the amount of any assistance or benefit received by the taxpayer in the year as a deduction from or reimbursement of an expense that is a tax (other than the goods and services tax) or royalty to the extent that

(i) the tax or royalty is, by reason of the receipt of the amount by the taxpayer, not deductible in computing the taxpayer's income for a taxation year, and

(ii) the deduction or reimbursement was included by the taxpayer in the amount determined for J in the definition "cumulative Canadian exploration expense" in subsection 66.1(6), for M in the definition "cumulative Canadian development expense" in subsection 66.2(5) or for I in the definition "cumulative Canadian oil and gas property expense" in subsection 66.4(5);

**Related Provisions**: See Related Provisions and Definitions at end of s. 20.

**Notes**: In 20(1)(kk), the words "other than the goods and services tax" added by 1990 GST, effective 1991. Subpara. (i) reworded, effective for amounts received after January 1990, as "is, by reason of the receipt ... not deductible" instead of "would, if the amount had not been received by him, have been deductible".

(ll) **repayment of interest** — such part of any amount payable by the taxpayer because of a provision of this Act, or of an Act of a province that imposes a tax similar to the tax imposed under this Act, as was paid in the year and as can reasonably be considered to be a repayment of interest that was included in computing the taxpayer's income for the year or a preceding taxation year;

**Related Provisions**: 129(2.2), 131(3.2), 132(2.2), 133(7.02), 164(3.1) — Provisions requiring repayment of interest. See also Related Provisions and Definitions at end of s. 20.

**Notes**: 20(1)(ll) amended by 1993 technical bill, effective for taxation years that begin in 1992 or later, to apply in respect of any provision requiring repayment of interest rather than just 164(3.1), as a result of the addition of 129(2.2), 131(3.2), 132(2.2) and 133(7.02) by 1992 technical bill. For earlier years, read:

(ll) **amount deemed to be tax payable** — such part of any amount payable by the taxpayer by virtue of

(i) paragraph 164(3.1)(a) or (4)(a) or any similar provision of any Act of a province that imposes a tax similar to the tax imposed under this Act, or

(ii) paragraph 18(4)(a) of the *Petroleum and Gas Revenue Tax Act*

as was paid in the year and as may reasonably be considered to be repayment of interest that was included in computing the taxpayer's income for the year or a preceding taxation year;

(mm) **cost of substances injected in reservoir** — the portion claimed by the taxpayer of an amount that is an outlay or expense made or incurred by the taxpayer before the end of the year that is a cost to the taxpayer of any substance injected before that time into a natural reservoir to assist in the recovery of petroleum, natural gas or related hydrocarbons to the extent that that portion was not

(i) otherwise deducted in computing the taxpayer's income for the year, or

(ii) deducted in computing the taxpayer's income for any preceding taxation year,

except that where the year is less than 51 weeks, the amount that may be claimed under this paragraph by the taxpayer for the year shall not exceed the greater of

(iii) that proportion of the maximum amount that may otherwise be claimed under this paragraph by the taxpayer for the year that the number of days in the year is of 365, and

(iv) the amount of such outlay or expense that was made or incurred by the taxpayer in the year and not otherwise deducted in computing the taxpayer's income for the year;

**Related Provisions**: 10(5)(c) — Property deemed to be inventory with cost of nil; 66(13.1) — Short taxation years; 87(2)(j.2) — Amalgamation — continuing corporation. See also Related Provisions and Definitions at end of s. 20.

**Notes**: 20(1)(mm) amended by 1996 Budget, effective for 1996 and later taxation years, to delete former subparas. (iii) and (iv) and to make minor wording changes. For taxation years beginning after July 13, 1990 and ending before 1997, read:

(mm) such portion, as may be claimed by the taxpayer, of an amount that is an outlay or expense made or incurred by the taxpayer before the end of the year that is a cost to the taxpayer of any substance injected before that time into a natural reservoir to assist in the recovery of petroleum, natural gas or related hydrocarbons to the extent that that portion was not

(i) otherwise deducted by the taxpayer in computing the taxpayer's income for the year,

(ii) deducted by the taxpayer in computing the taxpayer's income for any preceding taxation year,

(iii) an outlay or expense described in the definition "Canadian exploration expense" in subsection 66.1(6) or the definition "Canadian development expense" in subsection 66.2(5), or

(iv) a Canadian oil and gas property expense,

except that where the year is less than 51 weeks, the amount that may be claimed under this paragraph by the taxpayer for the year shall not exceed the greater of

(v) that proportion of the maximum amount that may otherwise be claimed under this paragraph by the taxpayer for the year that the number of days in the year is of 365, and

(vi) the amount of such outlay or expense not referred to in any of subparagraphs (i) to (iv) that was made or incurred by the taxpayer in the year;

20(1)(mm) amended by 1991 technical bill, effective for taxation years beginning after July 13, 1990, to add everything after 20(1)(mm)(iv).

(nn) **Part XII.6 tax** — the tax, if any, under Part XII.6 paid in the year or payable in respect of the year by the taxpayer (depending on the method regularly followed by the taxpayer in computing the taxpayer's income);

**Related Provisions**: 18(1)(t) — Part XII.6 tax not non-deductible. See also Related Provisions at end of s. 20.

**Notes**: 20(1)(nn) added by 1996 Budget, effective for 1997 and later taxation years. See 211.91.

Former 20(1)(nn), repealed by 1988 tax reform, provided a deduction for Part VI tax paid. Part VI tax is now reduced by the corporate surtax instead; see 190.1(3) and Notes to 125.2(1).

(oo) **salary deferral arrangement** — any deferred amount under a salary deferral arrangement in respect of another person to the extent that it was

(i) included under paragraph 6(1)(a) as a benefit in computing the income of the other person for the taxation year of the other person that ends in the taxpayer's taxation year, and

(ii) in respect of services rendered to the taxpayer;

**Related Provisions**: 6(1)(i) — Salary deferral arrangement payments; 6(11) — Salary deferral arrangement; 12(1)(n.2) — Forfeited salary deferral amounts; 18(1)(o.1) — Deductions — General limitations — Salary deferral arrangement; 87(2)(j.3) — Amalgamation — continuation of corporation. See additional Related Provisions and Definitions at end of s. 20.

(pp) **idem** — any amount under a salary deferral arrangement in respect of another person (other than an arrangement established primarily for the benefit of one or more non-resident employees in respect of services to be rendered outside Canada) to the extent that it was

(i) included under paragraph 6(1)(i) in computing the income of the other person for the taxation year of the other person that ends in the taxpayer's taxation year, and

(ii) in respect of services rendered to the taxpayer;

**Related Provisions**: 18(1)(o.1) — Salary deferral arrangement; 87(2)(j.3) — Amalgamations — continuation of corporation.

**Notes**: 20(1)(pp) added by 1991 technical bill, effective 1986.

(qq) **disability-related modifications to buildings** — an amount paid by the taxpayer in the year for prescribed renovations or alterations to a building used by the taxpayer primarily for the purpose of gaining or producing income from the building or from a business that are made to enable individuals who have a mobility impairment to gain access to the building or to be mobile within it;

**Related Provisions**: 18(3.1)(a) — Costs relating to construction of building or ownership of land; 20(1)(rr) — Disability-related equipment.

**Notes**: 20(1)(qq) enacted by 1992 Budget/technical bill, this version effective for renovations and alterations made after February 25, 1992. For renovations and alterations made from January 1, 1991 to February 25, 1992, read "prescribed renovations or alterations to a building of the taxpayer" (i.e., the taxpayer must own the building). 20(1)(qq) was originally 20(1)(gg) as added by 1991 Budget but was moved to (qq) retroactively.

**Regulations**: 8800 (prescribed renovations and alterations).

## Proposed Addition [on hold] — 20(1)(qq) [sic]

**(qq)** [sic] **interest on share purchase** — the lesser of

(i) the total of all amounts included in computing the taxpayer's income for the year from a share that was not acquired for the purpose of earning income therefrom or from a business, and

(ii) the total of all amounts of interest paid in, or payable in respect of, the year or the immediately preceding taxation year (depending on the method regularly followed in computing the taxpayer's income) on borrowed money used to acquire the share, to the extent that the amount was not deductible in computing the taxpayer's income for the immediately preceding year.

**Application**: The December 20, 1991 draft legislation (interest deductibility), subsec. 1(2), will add para. 20(1)(qq), applicable to 1972 et seq. [Obviously, it will have to be renumbered.]

**Technical Notes**: Proposed paragraph 20(1)(qq) applies in circumstances where shares of a corporation are acquired, using borrowed funds, for a purpose other than to earn income. This paragraph would typically apply in the context of shares bearing a fixed dividend rate that is lower than the interest rate charged on the funds borrowed to acquire those shares. It would not generally apply for borrowings to acquire common shares.

Paragraph 20(1)(qq) provides an interest deduction on the borrowed funds up to the amount included in the borrower's income from the preferred shares that were acquired with those funds. In other words, a deduction in respect of interest arising on the borrowed funds for a particular taxation year is permitted to the extent of the amount of all dividends received on the shares in that year (or, in the case of an individual shareholder, to the extent of the actual dividends and the dividend "gross-up" required under paragraph 82(1)(b)).

Where the interest expense associated with such a borrowing for a particular year exceeds the income from the relevant shares in that year, paragraph 20(1)(qq) provides that the excess may be added to the interest arising on the borrowing for the following year and deducted to the extent of the income from those shares in that later year.

**Related Provisions**: 20(1)(c) — Deduction — interest; 20(3.1) — Borrowed money.

**Notes**: The proposals relating to interest deductibility are still subject to change, and revisions are expected to be released in the future. They are not expected to be enacted any time soon.

As reproduced above, draft 20(1)(qq)(ii) proposes to allow a one-year carryforward of interest expense on borrowed money used to purchase shares that are not acquired for the purpose of earning income. The Department of Finance has indicated that this rule will be amended to clarify that the carryforward expense is deducted in a first-in, first-out basis, so old interest expense can be deducted first, thereby preserving as much of the current year's interest as possible for carryforward into the following year. The Department has also indicated that the Technical Notes will be amended to clarify that 20(1)(qq) is not intended to restrict the existing availability of a deduction under 20(1)(c), such as where common shares are acquired. See the comments by Brian Ernewein of the Department of Finance in Couzin, Ernewein and Lawlor, "Interest Expense: December 20, 1991 Draft Amendments", *Proceedings of the 1992 Corporate Management Tax Conference* (Toronto: Canadian Tax Foundation), pp. 2:1–2:42.

If this provision is enacted, it will have to be renumbered, due to the intervening enactment of 20(1)(qq) to (ww).

**(rr)** **disability-related equipment** — an amount paid by the taxpayer in the year for any prescribed disability-specific device or equipment;

**Related Provisions**: 20(1)(qq) — Disability-related modifications to buildings. See also Related Provisions and Definitions at end of s. 20.

**Notes**: 20(1)(rr) added by 1992 Budget/technical bill and amended by 1993 technical bill, both effective for amounts paid after February 25, 1992. The later amendment uses "disability-specific" in place of "acquired primarily to assist individuals who have a sight or hearing impairment". Thus, devices can be prescribed for persons who have other kinds of impairments such as mobility impairments; see Reg. 8801(c).

Some of the devices that qualify under 20(1)(rr) are eligible for the medical expense credit under 118.2 if purchased by an individual. See Reg. 5700.

**Regulations**: 8801 (prescribed devices and equipment).

**(ss)** **qualifying environmental trusts** — a contribution made in the year by the taxpayer to a qualifying environmental trust under which the taxpayer is a beneficiary;

**Related Provisions**: 12(1)(z.1) — Inclusion in income of amount received from qualifying environmental trust; 87(2)(j.93) — Amalgamations — continuing corporation.

**Notes**: 20(1)(ss) amended by 1997 Budget to change "mining reclamation trust" to "qualifying environmental trust" (the same change was made throughout the Act), effective for taxation years that end after February 18, 1997 and, for the purpose of amended 20(1)(ss), each contribution made from January 1996 through February 18, 1997 by a taxpayer to a trust (other than a mining reclamation trust as formerly defined in 248(1)) is deemed to have been made on February 19, 1997.

20(1)(ss) added by 1994 Budget, effective for taxation years that end after February 22, 1994; but contributions made to a trust before February 23, 1994 are deemed to have been made on that date for purposes of 20(1)(ss).

Part XII of the Regulations is to be amended so that amounts deductible under 20(1)(ss) will not be deducted for purposes of the resource allowance.

Another version of 20(1)(ss), proposed in the July 12, 1994 debt forgiveness draft legislation, now appears as 20(1)(uu) below.

**(tt)** **acquisition of interests in qualifying environmental trusts** — the consideration paid by the taxpayer in the year for the acquisition from another person or partnership of all or part of the taxpayer's interest as a beneficiary under a qualifying environmental trust, other than consideration that is the assumption of a reclamation obligation in respect of the trust;

**Related Provisions**: 12(1)(z.2) — Inclusion in income on disposition of interest in qualifying environmental trust; 87(2)(j.93) — Amalgamations — continuing corporation.

**Notes**: 20(1)(tt) added by 1994 Budget, effective for taxation years that end after February 22, 1994, and amended by 1997 Budget, effective for taxation years that end after February 18, 1997, to change "mining reclamation trust" to "qualifying environmental trust" (the same change was made throughout the Act).

Part XII of the Regulations is to be amended so that amounts deductible under 20(1)(tt) will not be deducted for purposes of the resource allowance.

(uu) **debt forgiveness** — any amount deducted in computing the taxpayer's income for the year because of paragraph 80(15)(a) or subsection 80.01(10);

**Related Provisions**: 28(1)(g) — Deduction from farming or fishing income when using cash method.

**Notes**: 20(1)(uu) added by 1994 tax amendments bill (Part I), effective for taxation years that end after February 21, 1994.

This para. was first proposed as 20(1)(ss), before enactment of 20(1)(ss) and (tt) by 1994 Budget.

(vv) **countervailing or anti-dumping duty** — an amount paid in the year by the taxpayer as or on account of an existing or proposed countervailing or anti-dumping duty in respect of property (other than depreciable property); and

**Related Provisions**: 12(1)(z.6) — Refund of duties included in income; 13(21)"undepreciated capital cost"D.1, K — Inclusion of duties in u.c.c. of depreciable property.

**Notes**: For a detailed discussion of countervailing and anti-dumping duties, see P.M. Saroli & G. Tereposky, "Changes to Canada's Anti-Dumping and Countervailing Duty Laws for the New Millennium", 79(3) *Canadian Bar Review* 352-368 (2000).

20(1)(vv) added by 1998 Budget, effective for amounts that become payable after February 23, 1998. For the parallel reduction in u.c.c. for depreciable property, see 13(21)"undepreciated capital cost"K.

(ww) **split income** — where the taxpayer is a specified individual in relation to the year, the individual's split income for the year.

**Related Provisions**: 120(3)(c) — No deduction in determining income not earned in a province and income subject to Quebec abatement; 120.4 — Income splitting tax (kiddie tax) payable by child.

**Notes**: 20(1)(ww) added by 1999 Budget, effective for 2000 and later taxation years. It allows a deduction for amounts of "split income" that are taxed at a high rate under the "kiddie tax" (see 120.4). This ensures that amounts taxed under 120.4 are not also taxed at regular rates.

**(1.1) Application of subsec. 13(21)** — The definitions in subsection 13(21) apply to any regulations made under paragraph (1)(a).

**Notes**: 20(1.1) added in the R.S.C. 1985 (5th Supp.) consolidation, effective for taxation years ending after November 1991. This rule was formerly in the opening words of 13(21).

**(1.2) Application of subsec. 12.2(11)** — The definitions in subsection 12.2(11) apply to paragraph (1)(c).

**Notes**: 20(1.2) added in the R.S.C. 1985 (5th Supp.) consolidation, effective for taxation years ending after November 1991. This rule was formerly in the opening words of 12.2(11).

**(2) Borrowed money** — For the purposes of paragraph (1)(c), where a person has borrowed money in consideration of a promise by the person to pay a larger amount and to pay interest on the larger amount,

(a) the larger amount shall be deemed to be the amount borrowed; and

(b) where the amount actually borrowed has been used in whole or in part for the purpose of earning income from a business or property, the proportion of the larger amount that the amount actually so used is of the amount actually borrowed shall be deemed to be the amount so used.

**Related Provisions**: See Related Provisions and Definitions at end of s. 20.

**Regulations**: 304 (prescribed annuity contract) [technically does not apply to this subsection].

**(2.1) Limitation of expression "interest"** — For the purposes of paragraphs (1)(c) and (d), "interest" does not include an amount that is paid after the taxpayer's 1977 taxation year or payable in respect of a period after the taxpayer's 1977 taxation year, depending on the method regularly followed by the taxpayer in computing the taxpayer's income, in respect of interest on a policy loan made by an insurer except to the extent that the amount of that interest is verified by the insurer in prescribed form and within the prescribed time to be

(a) interest paid in the year on that loan; and

(b) interest (other than interest that would, but for paragraph (2.2)(b), be interest on money borrowed before 1978 to acquire a life insurance policy or on an amount payable for property acquired before 1978 that is an interest in a life insurance policy) that is not added to the adjusted cost basis (within the meaning given that expression in subsection 148(9)) to the taxpayer of the taxpayer's interest in the policy.

**Related Provisions**: See Related Provisions and Definitions at end of s. 20.

**Regulations**: 4001 (prescribed time).

**Interpretation Bulletins**: IT-355R2: Interest on loans to buy life insurance policies and annuity contracts, and interest on policy loans.

**Forms**: T2210: Verification of policy loan interest by the insurer.

**(2.2) Limitation of expression "life insurance policy"** — For the purposes of paragraphs (1)(c) and (d), a "life insurance policy" does not include a policy

(a) that is or is issued pursuant to a registered pension plan, a registered retirement savings plan, an income-averaging annuity contract or a deferred profit sharing plan;

(b) that was an annuity contract issued before 1978 that provided for annuity payments to commence not later than the day on which the policyholder attains 75 years of age; or

(c) that is an annuity contract all of the insurer's reserves for which vary in amount depending on the fair market value of a specified group of properties.

**Related Provisions**: 138(12)"life insurance policy". See additional Related Provisions and Definitions at end of s. 20.

**Notes**: 20(2.2)(c) added by 1991 technical bill, effective 1987.

**Interpretation Bulletins**: IT-355R2: Interest on loans to buy life insurance policies and annuity contracts, and interest on policy loans.

**(2.3) Sectoral reserve** — For the purpose of clause (1)(l)(ii)(D), a sectoral reserve is a reserve or an allowance for impairment for a loan that is determined on a sector-by-sector basis (including a geographic sector, an industrial sector or a sector of any other nature) and not on a property-by-property basis.

**Notes**: 20(2.3) added by 1995-97 technical bill, effective on the same basis as the amendment to 20(1)(l).

**(2.4) Specified percentage** — For the purpose of clause (1)(l)(ii)(D), a taxpayer's specified percentage for a taxation year is

(a) where the taxpayer has a prescribed reserve amount for the year, the percentage that is the percentage of the prescribed reserve amount of the taxpayer for the year claimed by the taxpayer under clause (1)(l)(ii)(C) for the year, and

(b) in any other case, 100%.

**Notes**: 20(2.4) added by 1995-97 technical bill, effective on the same basis as the amendment to 20(1)(l).

**Regulations**: 8000(a) (prescribed reserve amount).

**(3) Borrowed money** — For greater certainty, it is hereby declared that where a taxpayer has used borrowed money

(a) to repay money previously borrowed, or

(b) to pay an amount payable for property described in subparagraph (1)(c)(ii) previously acquired,

subject to subsection 20.1(6), the borrowed money shall, for the purposes of paragraphs (1)(c), (e) and (e.1), subsections 20.1(1) and (2), section 21 and subparagraph 95(2)(a)(ii) and for the purpose of paragraph 20(1)(k) of the *Income Tax Act*, Chapter 148 of the Revised Statutes of Canada, 1952, be deemed to have been used for the purpose for which the money previously borrowed was used or was deemed by this subsection to have been used, or to acquire the property in respect of which the amount was payable, as the case may be.

**Related Provisions**: See Related Provisions and Definitions at end of s. 20.

**Notes**: Reference to 95(2)(a)(ii) added to closing words of 20(3) by 1994 tax amendments bill (Part II), effective for expenses incurred in taxation years that begin after 1994 except that, where there has been a change in the taxation year of a foreign affiliate of a taxpayer from February 23 through December 31, 1994, the amendment applies to expenses incurred in taxation years of the foreign affiliate that end after 1994, unless

(a) the foreign affiliate had requested that change in the taxation year in writing before February 22, 1994 from the income tax authority of the country in which it was resident and subject to income tax; or

(b) the first taxation year of the foreign affiliate that began after 1994 began at a time in 1995 that is earlier than the time that that taxation year would have begun if there had not been that change in the taxation year of the foreign affiliate.

20(3) amended by 1993 technical bill. For expenses incurred before 1994, ignore the references to 20.1(6), 20.1(1) and 20.1(2). For expenses incurred before 1988, ignore the references to 20(1)(e) and (e.1).

**I.T. Application Rules**: 69 (meaning of "*Income Tax Act*, chapter 148 of the Revised Statutes of Canada, 1952").

**I.T. Technical News**: No. 3 (use of a partner's assets by a partnership).

### Proposed Addition [on hold] — 20(3.1), (3.2)

**(3.1) Borrowed money** — For the purposes of this Part, where

(a) a shareholder of a particular taxable Canadian corporation uses borrowed money at any time

(i) to make a loan to the particular corporation or another taxable Canadian corporation controlled at that time by the shareholder, the particular corporation or a group of persons of which the shareholder or the particular corporation is a member,

(ii) to make a payment under a guarantee given by the shareholder in respect of

(A) a loan made to, or

(B) an amount payable for property acquired by,

the particular corporation or another taxable Canadian corporation controlled at that time by the shareholder, the particular corporation or a group of persons of which the shareholder or the particular corporation is a member, or

(iii) to acquire from the particular corporation a share of its capital stock where, immediately after that time, the shareholder controls the particular corporation,

(b) the particular corporation or the other corporation, as the case may be, uses the proceeds of the loan, the property or property substituted therefor or the proceeds of the sale of the share for the purpose of earning income (other than exempt income) from a source in Canada, and

(c) the particular corporation or the other corporation, as the case may be, was unable without the shareholder's guarantee to borrow the same amount of money from any person with whom it deals at arm's length on terms comparable to the terms on which the borrowed money was borrowed by the shareholder,

the borrowed money shall be deemed to be used for the purpose of earning income from property for the period commencing at that time and ending at the first particular time at which this subsection would not be applicable in respect of the borrowed money if the borrowed money were used at the particular time to make the loan, to make the payment under the guarantee or to acquire the share, as

## S. 20(3.1)

the case may be, and if this subsection were read without reference to paragraph (c).

**Application**: The December 20, 1991 draft legislation (interest deductibility), subsec. 1(3), proposes to add subsec. 20(3.1), applicable to 1972 *et seq.* except that in its application to any such year with respect to borrowed money used before the Date of Introduction [not yet determined, but will be in the future] for a purpose described in subsec. (3.1), that subsec. shall be read as follows:

(3.1) For the purposes of this Part, where

(a) a shareholder of a particular taxable Canadian corporation uses borrowed money at any time

  (i) to make a loan to the particular corporation or a subsidiary controlled corporation of that corporation,

  (ii) to make a payment under a guarantee given by the shareholder in respect of

   (A) a loan made to, or

   (B) an amount payable for property acquired by,

  the particular corporation or a subsidiary controlled corporation of that corporation, or

  (iii) to acquire from the particular corporation or a subsidiary controlled corporation of that corporation a share of its capital stock where, immediately after that time, the shareholder owns the majority of the issued and outstanding shares of each class of the capital stock of the particular corporation,

(b) the particular corporation or the subsidiary controlled corporation, as the case may be, uses the proceeds of the loan, the property or property substituted therefor or the proceeds of the sale of the share for the purpose of earning income (other than exempt income) from a source in Canada, and

(c) the particular corporation or the subsidiary controlled corporation, as the case may be, was unable without the shareholder's guarantee to borrow the same amount of money from any person with whom it deals at arm's length on terms comparable to the terms on which the borrowed money was borrowed by the shareholder,

the borrowed money shall be deemed to be used for the purpose of earning income from property for the period commencing at that time and ending at the first particular time at which this subsection would not be applicable in respect of the borrowed money if the borrowed money were used at the particular time to make the loan, or payment, as the case may be, and if this subsection were read without reference to paragraph (c).

**Technical Notes**: Proposed subsections 20(3.1) and (3.2) establish rules relating to the income tax treatment of borrowed money used by a taxpayer to support, either directly by way of a loan or indirectly through the assumption of liabilities, a corporation or partnership in which the taxpayer has an interest. These rules would be relied upon only where the direct use of the borrowed funds would not give rise to a reasonable expectation of profit, for instance, where they were used by a taxpayer to make an interest-free loan to his or her private corporation, or were used to acquire preferred shares with little or no dividend entitlement.

Subsection 20(3.1) applies in respect of borrowed money used by a taxpayer for one of three purposes:

- to make a loan to a taxable Canadian corporation of which the taxpayer is a shareholder, or to another taxable Canadian corporation that is controlled — either alone or together with others — by the taxpayer (the "shareholder") or the first corporation;
- to honour a guarantee given by the shareholder on a liability of such a corporation; or
- to acquire shares of a corporation that the shareholder controls.

Such borrowings will be treated as having been made for the purpose of earning income from property (enabling the interest arising thereon to qualify for deduction in computing the shareholder's income), provided that two conditions are met. First, the corporation will be required to use the proceeds generated from the shareholder's loan, the property acquired with the shareholder's guarantee, or the proceeds arising from the shareholder's additional share subscription (as the case may be) for the purpose of earning Canadian-source, non-exempt income. Secondly, the corporation's financial situation must be such that it could not, on its own, have borrowed the money on terms comparable to those obtained by the shareholder.

Where the borrowed money has been used for a qualifying purpose and the other conditions described above have been satisfied, the treatment of the borrowing as being to earn property income will apply until such time as the shareholder ceases to hold a qualifying interest in the corporation, or the corporation ceases to use the funds or property in question for the purpose described above.

Subsection 20(3.1), as described above, would apply only with respect to future borrowings. Two relatively narrow modifications to this explanation are required to describe the rules applying in respect of current borrowings (which rules, in turn, attempt to reflect the administrative practice governing such borrowings). First, such borrowings — other than borrowings used to acquire shares — would be eligible under this subsection only where they were used to make a loan to, or otherwise assume a liability of, a taxable Canadian corporation of which the taxpayer is a shareholder or that is a subsidiary controlled corporation of such a corporation. (The term "subsidiary controlled corporation" is defined in subsection 248(1).) Second, borrowings used to acquire shares would be eligible under subsection 20(3.1) only where the shareholder owns the majority of shares of each class that are issued and outstanding at the relevant time (as opposed to the requirement for future borrowings that the shareholder simply control the corporation).

Finally, it may be noted that neither version of proposed subsection 20(3.1) provides an express exception for artificial transactions. The fact that this exception is not reproduced in this provision (or proposed subsection 20(3.2)) is not meant to indicate that it no longer applies; rather, it is intended to reflect the existence, in section 245, of a general anti-avoidance rule that eliminates the need for such specific prohibitions.

**Related Provisions**: 248(5) — Substituted property.

**Notes**: These proposals are still subject to change, and revisions are expected to be released in the future. They are not expected to be enacted any time soon. 20(3.1) is intended primarily to accommodate the owner/manager situation; that is, where a shareholder is effectively required to borrow money in order to fund the operations of his or her company. It is intended to deal with situations to which 20(1)(c) would not otherwise apply, rather than to restrict the scope of 20(1)(c) in any way. See the comments by Brian Ernewein of the Department of Finance in Couzin,

Ernewein and Lawlor, "Interest Expense: December 20, 1991 Draft Amendments", *Proceedings of the 1992 Corporate Management Tax Conference* (Canadian Tax Foundation), pp. 2:1–2:42.

**(3.2) Idem** — For the purposes of this Part, where

(a) a member of a Canadian partnership uses borrowed money at any time

(i) to make a loan to the partnership, or

(ii) to make a payment in respect of a loan made to, or an amount payable for property acquired by, the partnership,

(b) the partnership uses the proceeds of the loan or the property or property substituted therefor for the purpose of earning income (other than exempt income) from a source in Canada, and

(c) the partnership was unable without the provision of additional security by the member to borrow the same amount of money from any person with whom all of its members deal at arm's length on terms comparable to the terms on which the money was borrowed by the member,

the borrowed money shall be deemed to be used for the purpose of earning income from the partnership for the period commencing at that time and ending at the first particular time at which this subsection would not be applicable in respect of the borrowed money if the borrowed money were used at the particular time to make the loan or payment, as the case may be, and if this subsection were read without reference to paragraph (c).

**Application**: The December 20, 1991 draft legislation (interest deductibility), subsec. 1(3), will add subsec. 20(3.2), applicable to 1972 *et seq.*

**Technical Notes**: Proposed subsection 20(3.2) operates in a manner similar to subsection 20(3.1), but has application with respect to borrowed money used by a taxpayer to make loans or honour certain liabilities of a partnership of which the taxpayer is a member. Borrowed money used for such a purpose will be treated as having been used to earn income from the partnership (enabling the interest arising thereon to qualify for deduction in computing the partner's income), provided two conditions are met. First, the partnership will be required to use the proceeds of the loan from the partner, the proceeds of the loan from a third party that the partner has repaid in whole or in part, or the property in respect of which the partner has satisfied an outstanding liability (as the case may be) for the purpose of earning Canadian-source, non-exempt income. Secondly, the partnership must not have been in a position to borrow, without further security from the partner, the same amount on terms comparable to those obtained by the partner in borrowing the money in question.

The treatment of such borrowings will be maintained throughout the period in which the borrower remains a member of the partnership and the funds or property in question are used for the purpose described above.

**Related Provisions**: 248(5) — Substituted property.

**Notes**: See Notes to draft 20(3.1) above.

**(4) Bad debts from dispositions of depreciable property** — Where an amount that is owing to a taxpayer as or on account of the proceeds of disposition of depreciable property (other than a timber resource property or a passenger vehicle having a cost to the taxpayer in excess of $20,000 or such other amount as may be prescribed) of the taxpayer of a prescribed class is established by the taxpayer to have become a bad debt in a taxation year, there may be deducted in computing the taxpayer's income for the year the lesser of

(a) the amount so owing to the taxpayer, and

(b) the amount, if any, by which the capital cost to the taxpayer of that property exceeds the total of the amounts, if any, realized by the taxpayer on account of the proceeds of disposition.

**Related Provisions**: 20(1)(a) — Capital cost of property; 50(1)(a) — Deemed disposition where debt becomes bad debt; 79.1(7)(d) — Deduction by creditor for bad debt where property seized; 79.1(8) — No deduction for principal amount of bad debt where property seized by creditor. See additional Related Provisions and Definitions at end of s. 20.

**Notes**: Exclusion for expensive passenger vehicle added by 1991 technical bill, effective for amounts established as bad debts after July 13, 1990. (There is no depreciation recapture or terminal loss on such property; see 13(2) and 20(16.1).)

See Notes to 13(7)(g) re prescribed amount for each year.

**Regulations**: 7307(1) (prescribed amount).

**Interpretation Bulletins**: IT-159R3: Capital debts established to be bad debts; IT-220R2: CCA — proceeds of disposition of depreciable property; IT-442R: Bad debts and reserve for doubtful debts.

**I.T. Technical News**: No. 10 (1997 deduction limits and benefit rates for automobiles).

**(4.1) Idem** — Where an amount that is owing to a taxpayer as or on account of the proceeds of disposition of a timber resource property of the taxpayer is established by the taxpayer to have become a bad debt in a taxation year, the amount so owing to the taxpayer may be deducted in computing the taxpayer's income for the year.

**Related Provisions**: 50(1)(a) — Deemed disposition where debt becomes bad debt; 79.1(7)(d) — Deduction by creditor for bad debt where property seized; 79.1(8) — No deduction for principal amount of bad debt where property seized by creditor. See Related Provisions and Definitions at end of s. 20.

**Interpretation Bulletins**: IT-442R: Bad debts and reserve for doubtful debts.

**(4.2) Idem** — Where, in respect of a disposition of eligible capital property by a taxpayer, an amount that comes within the terms of paragraph (a) of the description of E in the definition "cumulative eligible capital" in subsection 14(5) was included in the calculation of the taxpayer's cumulative eligible capital and is established by the taxpayer to have become a bad debt in a taxation year, there shall be de-

**S. 20(4.2)** — Income Tax Act, Part I, Division B

ducted in computing the income of the taxpayer for the year

  (a) the amount, if any, by which

    (i) ¾ of the total of

      (A) the total of all amounts each of which is such an amount that was so established by the taxpayer to be a bad debt in the year, and

      (B) the total of all amounts each of which is such an amount that was so established by the taxpayer to be a bad debt in a preceding taxation year,

exceeds the total of

    (ii) the total of all amounts each of which is

      (A) the taxable capital gain of the taxpayer determined under subsection 14(1) for the year or a preceding taxation year and in respect of which a deduction can reasonably be considered to have been claimed under section 110.6, or

      (B) an amount determined in respect of the taxpayer for D in subparagraph 14(1)(a)(v) for the year or a preceding taxation year, and

    (iii) the total of all amounts deducted by the taxpayer under this subsection in preceding taxation years

and the amount, if any, by which

  (b) ¾ of the amount determined under clause (a)(i)(A) for the year

exceeds

  (c) the amount determined under paragraph (a) for the year

shall be deemed to be an allowable capital loss of the taxpayer from a disposition of capital property by the taxpayer in the year.

---

**Proposed Amendment — 20(4.2), (4.3)**

**(4.2) Bad debts re: eligible capital property** — Where, in respect of one or more dispositions of eligible capital property by a taxpayer, an amount that is described in paragraph (a) of the description of E in the definition "cumulative eligible capital" in subsection 14(5) in respect of the taxpayer is established by the taxpayer to have become a bad debt in a taxation year, there shall be deducted in computing the taxpayer's income for the year the amount determined by the formula

$$(A + B) - (C + D + E + F + G + H)$$

where

A is the lesser of

  (a) ½ of the total of all amounts each of which is such an amount that was so established to have become a bad debt in the year or a preceding taxation year, and

  (b) the amount that is

    (i) where the year ended after February 27, 2000, the amount, if any, that would be the total of all amounts determined by the formula in paragraph 14(1)(b) (if that formula were read without reference to the description of D) for the year, or for a preceding taxation year that ended after February 27, 2000, and

    (ii) where the year ended before February 28, 2000, nil;

B is the amount, if any, by which

  (a) ¾ of the total of all amounts each of which is such an amount that was so established to be a bad debt in the year or a preceding taxation year

exceeds the total of

  (b) ½ of the amount by which

    (i) the value of A

  exceeds

    (ii) the amount included in the value of A because of subparagraph (b)(i) of the description of A in respect of taxation years that ended after February 27, 2000 and before October 18, 2000, and

  (c) ⁹⁄₈ of the amount included in the value of A because of subparagraph (b)(i) of the description of A in respect of taxation years that ended after February 27, 2000 and before October 18, 2000;

C is the total of all amounts each of which is an amount determined under subsection 14(1) or (1.1) for the year, or a preceding taxation year, that ends after October 17, 2000 and in respect of which a deduction can reasonably be considered to have been claimed under section 110.6 by the taxpayer;

D is the total of all amounts each of which is an amount determined under subsection 14(1) or (1.1) for the year, or a preceding taxation year, that ended after February 27, 2000 and before October 18, 2000 and in respect of which a deduction can reasonably be considered to have been claimed under section 110.6 by the taxpayer;

E is the total of all amounts each of which is an amount determined under subsection 14(1) or (1.1) for a preceding taxation year that ended before February 28, 2000 and in respect of which a deduction can reasonably be considered to have been claimed under section 110.6 by the taxpayer;

F is the total of

  (a) ²⁄₃ of the total of all amounts each of which is the value determined in respect of the taxpayer for D in the formula in paragraph 14(1)(b) for the year, or a preceding taxation year, that ends after October 17, 2000, and

(b) 8/9 of the total of all amounts each of which is the value determined in respect of the taxpayer for D in the formula in paragraph 14(1)(b) for the year, or a preceding taxation year, that ended after February 27, 2000 and before October 18, 2000;

G is the total of all amounts each of which is the value determined in respect of the taxpayer for D in the formula in subparagraph 14(1)(a)(v) (as that subparagraph applied for taxation years that ended before February 28, 2000) for a preceding taxation year; and

H is the total of all amounts deducted by the taxpayer under this subsection for preceding taxation years.

**(4.3) Deemed allowable capital loss** — Where, in respect of one or more dispositions of eligible capital property by a taxpayer, an amount that is described in paragraph (a) of the description of E in the definition "cumulative eligible capital" in subsection 14(5) in respect of the taxpayer is established by the taxpayer to have become a bad debt in a taxation year, the taxpayer is deemed to have an allowable capital loss from a disposition of capital property in the year equal to the lesser of

(a) the total of the value determined for A and 2/3 of the value determined for B in the formula in subsection (4.2) in respect of the taxpayer for the year; and

(b) the total of all amounts each of which is

(i) the value determined for C or paragraph (a) of the description of F in the formula in subsection (4.2) in respect of the taxpayer for the year,

(ii) 3/4 of the value determined for D or paragraph (b) of the description of F in the formula in subsection (4.2) in respect of the taxpayer for the year, or

(iii) 2/3 of the value determined for E or G in the formula in subsection (4.2) in respect of the taxpayer for the year.

**Application**: The December 21, 2000 draft legislation, subsec. 7(5), will amend subsec. 20(4.2) to read as above, and add subsec. (4.3), applicable in respect of taxation years that end after February 27, 2000 except that, for taxation years that ended after February 27, 2000 and before October 18, 2000,

(a) the reference to the fraction "1/2" in para. (a) of the description of A in subsec. 20(4.2) shall be read as a reference to the fraction "2/3";

(b) the reference to the fraction "3/2" in the description of B in subsec. 20(4.2) shall be read as a reference to the fraction "9/8";

(c) the reference to the fraction "2/3" in para. 20(4.3)(a) and subpara. 20(4.3)(b)(iii) shall be read as a reference to the fraction "8/9"; and

(d) subpara. 20(4.3)(b)(ii) shall be read without reference to the expression "3/4 of".

**Technical Notes**: Subsection 20(4.2) provides a deduction in computing income of a taxpayer for a bad debt on account of proceeds of disposition of eligible capital property. The deduction is reduced to the extent that the taxpayer has sheltered an income inclusion in respect of eligible capital property using the capital gains exemption in section 110.6, or the taxpayer's exempt gains balance (as defined by subsection 14(5)) in respect of the former $100,000 lifetime capital gains exemption. The amount of the reduction is deemed to be an allowable capital loss. The exempt gains balance is available only to individuals. (In these notes, deductions claimed under paragraph 20(1)(b) are referred to as "depreciation".)

Subsection 20(4.2) is amended consequential on the amendments to subsection 14(1) that reflect the reduced inclusion rate for capital gains [see 38(a) — ed.]. For further detail regarding the amendments to subsection 14(1), see the commentary to that provision. Because the eligible capital property system now incorporates three fractions, one for calculating cumulative eligible capital pool balance (3/4) and two others for calculating income inclusions under subsection 14(1), (2/3 and 1/2, subject to a recapture of depreciation claimed), the amendments to subsection 20(4.2) recognize three different proportions of bad debts as deductible, depending on how the recognition of the proceeds of disposition originally affected the taxpayer. The amount deductible under subsection 20(4.2) in respect of bad debts is determined by the formula (A + B) – (C + D + E + F + G + H). The formula operates as a pool that takes into account bad debts in the year and in preceding years.

Variable A applies for taxation years that end after February 27, 2000. It is equal to the lesser of 1/2 of total bad debts and, generally, the taxpayer's income inclusion under amended paragraph 14(1)(b), which reflects the taxable portion of the taxpayer's gain in respect of eligible capital property. The taxpayer's income inclusion under paragraph 14(1)(b) reflects the 2/3 or the 1/2 inclusion rate for capital gains. Variable B is the amount by which 3/4 of the bad debt exceeds 9/8 or 3/2 of variable A. This ensures that only the appropriate fraction of the bad debt is recognized. Multiplying A by 9/8 or 3/2 converts it from a 2/3- or 1/2-based amount to a 3/4-based amount.

Variables C through H reduce the amount of the taxpayer's deduction to reflect otherwise taxable amounts that have been sheltered by deductions in respect of capital gains. Variables F and G relate to the taxpayer's claim in respect of his or her exempt gains balance, related to the $100,000 lifetime capital gains exemption, as defined in subsection 14(5). Variables F and G are only relevant for individuals. Variables C, D and E describe amounts that have been sheltered by the deduction under section 110.6 in respect of capital gains on qualified farm property. Variable H reduces the deduction by amounts deducted under the provision for prior years, to appropriately adjust the pool, which reflects all bad debts owing to the taxpayer in respect of eligible capital property.

Variables C to G are used to calculate the taxpayer's allowable capital loss under new subsection 20(4.3) as described below.

*Example*

*(The first part of this example is also set out in the commentary to the amendments to subsection 14(1).)*

*Sophie has a cumulative eligible capital pool balance of $750,000 in 1999. This pool balance reflects*

*$100,000 of depreciation claimed since Sophie began carrying on business in 1989. In January 2000, Sophie disposes of eligible capital property to Acme Corporation for proceeds of disposition of $2 million. Sophie claims no depreciation in 2000. Sophie has an exempt gains balance of $50,000, which she claims to reduce her paragraph 14(1)(b) income inclusion for 2000. Applying the proposed amendments to section 14 described above, the 2000 taxation year results are as follows:*

*opening balance: $750,000*

*less ¾ × $2 million proceeds of disposition*

*credit balance: ($750,000)*

*recapture of depreciation claimed (amended paragraph 14(1)(a)): $100,000 income inclusion*

*residual income inclusion (amended paragraph 14(1)(b)): ⅔ × (A – B – C – D)*

*A is $750,000*

*B is $100,000 of depreciation*

*C (½ of depreciation claimed before adjustment time) is nil, and*

*D is $50,000 (exempt gains balance that Sophie is claiming).*

*⅔ × ($750,000 – $100,000 – $50,000) = $400,000 income inclusion.*

*In 2001, the $2 million owed to Sophie becomes a bad debt when Acme Corporation goes bankrupt.*

*Sophie applies amended subsections 20(4.2) and (4.3) to calculate her deduction and allowable capital loss in respect of the bad debt.*

*Deduction ((A + B) – (C + D + E + F + G + H)).*

*A is the lesser of*

*(a) ½ of the bad debt, plus ½ of bad debts from prior years – $1,000,000, and*

*(b) the paragraph 14(1)(b) amount, read without reference to variable D in the 14(1)(b) formula: ⅔ × ($750,000 – $100,000) = $433,333*

*the lesser of (a) and (b) is $433,333*

*B is the amount by which ¾ of the bad debt, plus ¾ of the bad debts from prior years — $1.5 million — exceeds ³⁄₂ of the amount determined for A: ³⁄₂ × $433,333 = $650,000*

*B is $1.5 million – $650,000 = $850,000*

*(A + B) is $433,333 + $850,000 = $1,283,333*

*C is nil, because Sophie has not claimed a deduction under section 110.6 in respect of capital gains related to an income inclusion under subsection 14(1) or (1.1)*

*F(a) is ⅔ of the exempt gains balance that Sophie claimed. ⅔ of $50,000 is $33,333.*

*D, E, F(b) and G are generally the same as C and F(a), except that they apply in respect of taxation years that ended before February 28, 2000 or taxation years that ended after February 27, 2000 and before October 18, 2000. Sophie has not claimed a deduction in respect of capital gains, or claimed anything in respect of her exempt gains balance, for taxation years that ended before February 28, 2000 nor for taxation years that ended after February 27, 2000 and before October 18, 2000.*

*H is nil because Sophie has not claimed an amount under subsection (4.2) for bad debts in prior years.*

*The calculation set out in subsection 20(4.2) therefore allows Sophie a deduction of $1,283,333 – $33,333 = $1,250,000. This deduction corresponds to Sophie's $400,000 income inclusion under paragraph 14(1)(b), plus her recaptured depreciation of $100,000, plus the elimination of her $750,000 pool balance; these three amounts total $1,250,000.*

*Sophie used her exempt gains balance of $50,000 in the 2000 taxation year sale of eligible capital property to shelter a portion of the gain. The $33,333 determined by variable F(a) reduces Sophie's deduction as described above in recognition of this sheltering. The amount of the reduction is $33,333, rather than $50,000, because the new formula for the calculation of Sophie's 2000 taxation year (December 31 year-end) income inclusion under paragraph 14(1)(b) introduces the factor ⅔ to the calculation. (In other words, $33,333 will shelter the same amount of gain under a ½ inclusion rate system as $50,000 did under a ¾ inclusion rate system. In both cases $66,667 can be sheltered.) The amount of the reduction in variable F(a) is deemed by subsection 20(4.3) to be an allowable capital loss, as described below.*

The additional rule set out in existing paragraphs 20(4.2)(b), (c) and the "postamble" (which provides that the reduction of the deduction to recognize untaxed capital gains is deemed to be an allowable capital loss) are being moved to new subsection 20(4.3).

New subsection 20(4.3) provides that where a taxpayer's deduction under subsection 20(4.2) is reduced to recognize the taxpayer's use of a capital gains deduction to offset an income inclusion under subsection 14, the taxpayer is deemed to have an allowable capital loss. The allowable capital loss, in effect, restores the capital gains deduction that was used up in sheltering a gain on what turned out to be a bad debt. The allowable capital loss is equal to the lesser of two amounts. The first amount is ½ of the total bad debts. The second amount is the capital gains exemption amounts or exempt gains balance used up in respect of dispositions of eligible capital property under the ½ inclusion rate system, plus ¾ of capital gains exemption or exempt gains balance used up in respect of dispositions of eligible capital property under the ⅔ inclusion rate system plus ⅔ of capital gains exemption or exempt gains balance used up in respect of dispositions of eligible capital property under the ¾ inclusion rate system. The use of the fraction ¾ converts the ⅔-based exemption claims to a ½ basis for the purpose of calculating an allowable capital loss that will be used to offset capital gains that are included at ½. The fraction ⅔ converts the ¾-based exemption claims to the same rate basis.

These amendments apply in respect of taxation years that end after February 27, 2000 except that, for taxation years that end after February 27, 2000 and before October 18, 2000, the fractions used will be adjusted to reflect a ⅔ inclusion rate. In particular, the references to ½, ³⁄₂ and ⅔ are to be read as references to ⅔, ⁹⁄₈ and ⁸⁄₉, respectively, and subparagraph 20(4.3)(b)(ii) is to be read without the expression "¾ of".

**Related Provisions**: 12(1)(i.1) — Bad debts recovered; 20(4.3) — Deemed allowable capital loss on bad on disposition of eligible capital property; 39(11) — Bad debt recovery; 50(1)(a) — Deemed disposition where debt becomes bad debt; 79.1(7)(d) —

Subdivision b — Income or Loss from a Business or Property     S. 20(7)

Deduction by creditor for bad debt where property seized; 79.1(8) — No deduction for principal amount of bad debt where property seized by creditor; 89(1)"capital dividend account"(c) — Capital dividend account; 257 — Formula cannot calculate to less than zero. See additional Related Provisions and Definitions at end of s. 20.

**Notes**: 20(4.2)(a)(ii) amended by 1994 Budget, effective for taxation years that end after February 22, 1994, as a result of the election in 110.6(19) to use the $100,000 capital gains exemption for 1994. The deduction under 20(4.2) is denied to the extent the debt relates to proceeds of disposition that either resulted in a taxable capital gain that was sheltered by the exemption or, because of the "exempt gains balance" (see 14(5)), did not result in an income inclusion under 14(1).

**Interpretation Bulletins**: IT-123R6: Transactions involving eligible capital property.

**(5) Sale of agreement for sale or mortgage included in proceeds of disposition** — Where depreciable property, other than a timber resource property, of a taxpayer has, in a taxation year, been disposed of to a person with whom the taxpayer was dealing at arm's length, and the proceeds of disposition include an agreement for sale of or mortgage on land that the taxpayer has, in a subsequent taxation year, sold to a person with whom the taxpayer was dealing at arm's length, there may be deducted in computing the income of the taxpayer for the subsequent year an amount equal to the lesser of

(a) the amount, if any, by which the principal amount of the agreement for sale or mortgage outstanding at the time of the sale exceeds the consideration paid by the purchaser to the taxpayer for the agreement for sale or mortgage, and

(b) the amount determined under paragraph (a) less the amount, if any, by which the proceeds of disposition of the depreciable property exceed the capital cost to the taxpayer of that property.

**Related Provisions**: See Related Provisions and Definitions at end of s. 20.

**Interpretation Bulletins**: IT-323: Sale of mortgage included in proceeds of disposition of depreciable property.

**(5.1) Idem** — Where a timber resource property of a taxpayer has, in a taxation year, been disposed of to a person with whom the taxpayer was dealing at arm's length, and the proceeds of disposition include an agreement for sale of or mortgage on land that the taxpayer has, in a subsequent taxation year, sold to a person with whom the taxpayer was dealing at arm's length, there may be deducted in computing the income of the taxpayer for the subsequent year the amount, if any, by which the principal amount of the agreement for sale or mortgage outstanding at the time of the sale exceeds the consideration paid by the purchaser to the taxpayer for the agreement for sale or mortgage.

**Related Provisions**: See Related Provisions and Definitions at end of s. 20.

**(6) Special reserves** — Where an amount is deductible in computing income for a taxation year under paragraph (1)(m) as a reserve in respect of

(a) articles of food or drink that it is reasonably anticipated will have to be delivered after the end of the year, or

(b) transportation that it is reasonably anticipated will have to be provided after the end of the year,

there shall be substituted for the amount determined under that paragraph an amount not exceeding the total of amounts included in computing the taxpayer's income from the business for the year that were received or receivable (depending on the method regularly followed by the taxpayer in computing the taxpayer's profit) in the year in respect of

(c) articles of food or drink not delivered before the end of the year, or

(d) transportation not provided before the end of the year,

as the case may be.

**Related Provisions**: 12(1)(e) — Reserves in respect of certain goods and services, etc., rendered. See additional Related Provisions and Definitions at end of s. 20.

**Interpretation Bulletins**: IT-154R: Special reserves.

**(7) Where para. (1)(m) does not apply** — Paragraph (1)(m) does not apply to allow a deduction

(a) as a reserve in respect of guarantees, indemnities or warranties;

(b) in computing the income of a taxpayer for a taxation year from a business in any case where the taxpayer's income for the year from that business is computed in accordance with the method authorized by subsection 28(1); or

(c) as a reserve in respect of insurance, except that in computing an insurer's income for a taxation year from an insurance business, other than a life insurance business, carried on by it, there may be deducted as a policy reserve any amount that the insurer claims not exceeding the amount prescribed in respect of the insurer for the year.

**Related Provisions**: 12(1)(e) — Income inclusion in following year; 12(1)(s) — Reinsurance commission; 18(1)(e.1) — Unpaid claims under insurance policies; 20(26) — Deduction for unpaid claims reserve adjustment; 87(2.2) — Amalgamation of insurance corporations; 88(1)(g) — Winding-up of subsidiary insurance corporations; 138(3)(a)(i) — Policy reserves for life insurance business; 139.1(8)(b) — No deduction for policy dividend paid on demutualization; Reg. 8100(a) — Unpaid claims reserve adjustment. See additional Related Provisions and Definitions at end of s. 20.

**Notes**: 20(7)(c) amended by 1996 Budget, effective for 1996 and later taxation years, to correspond to changes to Reg. 1400. For earlier taxation years, read:

(c) as a reserve in respect of insurance, except that an insurance corporation may, in computing its income for a taxation year from an insurance business, other than a life insurance business, carried on by it, deduct as policy reserves such amounts as are prescribed for the purposes of this paragraph.

**Regulations**: 1400(1) (amount prescribed for 20(7)(c)); for structured settlement reserves, see Reg. 1400(3)E; for earthquake reserves, see Reg. 1400(3)L.

**Interpretation Bulletins**: IT-154R: Special reserves.

**(8) No deduction in respect of property in certain circumstances** — Paragraph (1)(n) does not apply to allow a deduction in computing the income of a taxpayer for a taxation year from a business in respect of a property sold in the course of the business if

(a) the taxpayer, at the end of the year or at any time in the immediately following taxation year,

(i) was exempt from tax under any provision of this Part, or

(ii) was not resident in Canada and did not carry on the business in Canada; or

(b) the sale occurred more than 36 months before the end of the year.

**Related Provisions**: 149 — Exemptions. See additional Related Provisions and Definitions at end of s. 20.

**Notes**: 20(8)(b) added by 1981 Budget, effective for property sold after November 12, 1981 otherwise than pursuant to the terms in existence on that date of an offer or agreement in writing made or entered into on or before that date.

**Interpretation Bulletins**: IT-152R3: Special reserves — sale of land; IT-154R: Special reserves.

**(9) Application of para. (1)(cc)** — In lieu of making any deduction of an amount permitted by paragraph (1)(cc) in computing a taxpayer's income for a taxation year from a business, the taxpayer may, if the taxpayer so elects in prescribed manner, make a deduction of $1/10$ of that amount in computing the taxpayer's income for that taxation year and a like deduction in computing the taxpayer's income for each of the 9 immediately following taxation years.

**Related Provisions**: 13(12) — Application of 20(1)(cc); 96(3) — Election by members of partnership. See additional Related Provisions and Definitions at end of s. 20.

**Regulations**: 4100 (prescribed manner).

**Interpretation Bulletins**: IT-99R5: Legal and accounting fees.

**(10) Convention expenses** — Notwithstanding paragraph 18(1)(b), there may be deducted in computing a taxpayer's income for a taxation year from a business an amount paid by the taxpayer in the year as or on account of expenses incurred by the taxpayer in attending, in connection with the business, not more than two conventions held during the year by a business or professional organization at a location that may reasonably be regarded as consistent with the territorial scope of that organization.

**Related Provisions**: 67.1(3) — Meals and entertainment included in fee for convention; Canada-U.S. tax treaty, Art. XXV:9 — Fees for convention held in U.S. deductible if would be deductible in Canada. See additional Related Provisions and Definitions at end of s. 20.

**Notes**: 20(10) is a *permissive* provision, not restrictive. If convention expenses can be justified as incurred for the purpose of earning income and not being on account of capital (see 18(1)(a) and (b)), they should be deductible even if they do not meet the restrictions in 20(10). See, however, *Griffith*, [1956] C.T.C. 47 (Exch. Ct.).

**Interpretation Bulletins**: IT-131R2: Convention expenses; IT-357R2: Expenses of training.

**(11) Foreign taxes on income from property exceeding 15%** — In computing the income of an individual from a property other than real property for a taxation year after 1975 that is income from a source outside Canada, there may be deducted the amount, if any, by which,

(a) such part of any income or profits tax paid by the taxpayer to the government of a country other than Canada for the year as may reasonably be regarded as having been paid in respect of an amount that has been included in computing the taxpayer's income for the year from the property,

exceeds

(b) 15% of the amount referred to in paragraph (a).

**Related Provisions**: 20(12) — Deduction for foreign tax as alternative to credit; 104(22)–(22.4) — Foreign tax credit for beneficiaries of trust; 126(1) — Foreign tax credit; 126(7)"non-business-income tax"(b) — Limitation on foreign tax credit; 144(8.1) — Employees profit sharing plan — Foreign tax deduction; Canada-U.S. tax treaty, Art. XXIX:5 — United States S corporations. See additional Related Provisions and Definitions at end of s. 20.

**Notes**: The effect of 126(7)"non-business-income tax"(b) is that for individuals, a foreign tax credit on non-business income can only be claimed up to 15% of the income. The excess is allowed as a deduction under 20(11). See also 20(12).

**Interpretation Bulletins**: IT-201R2: Foreign tax credit — trusts and beneficiaries; IT-506: Foreign income taxes as a deduction from income.

**(12) Foreign non-business income tax** — In computing a taxpayer's income for a taxation year from a business or property, there may be deducted such amount as the taxpayer claims not exceeding the non-business income tax paid by the taxpayer for the year to the government of a country other than Canada (within the meaning assigned by subsection 126(7) read without reference to paragraphs (c) and (e) of the definition "non-business-income tax" in that subsection) in respect of that income, other than any such tax, or part thereof, that can reasonably be regarded as having been paid by a corporation in respect of income from a share of the capital stock of a foreign affiliate of the corporation.

**Related Provisions**: 20(11) — Deduction to limit foreign tax credit of individual; 104(22)–(22.4) — Foreign tax credit for beneficiaries of trust; 126(1) — Foreign tax credit; 126(1.1) — Application to authorized foreign bank; 126(7)"non-business-income tax"(c) — Limitation on foreign tax credit. See additional Related Provisions and Definitions at end of s. 20.

**Notes**: In most cases it will be more advantageous to claim a foreign tax credit under 126 than this deduction. However, sometimes no FTC can be claimed, e.g. because foreign withholding tax applies to income that is not counted as foreign source income under the ITA.

20(12) amended by 1992 technical bill, effective 1992, to add "from a business or property" and "in respect of that income", thus limiting the deduction to foreign taxes paid in respect of income from a business or property and clarifying that the amount claimed is to be deducted in computing income from the source to which the foreign tax relates.

**Interpretation Bulletins**: IT-201R2: Foreign tax credit — trusts and beneficiaries; IT-506: Foreign income taxes as a deduction from income.

**(12.1) Foreign tax where no economic profit** — In computing a taxpayer's income for a taxation year from a business, there may be deducted the amount that the taxpayer claims not exceeding the lesser of

(a) the amount of foreign tax (within the meaning assigned by subsection 126(4.1)) that

(i) is in respect of a property used in the business for a period of ownership by the taxpayer or in respect of a related transaction (as defined in subsection 126(7)),

(ii) is paid by the taxpayer for the year,

(iii) is, because of subsection 126(4.1), not included in computing the taxpayer's business-income tax or non-business-income tax, and

(iv) where the taxpayer is a corporation, is not an amount that can reasonably be regarded as having been paid in respect of income from a share of the capital stock of a foreign affiliate of the taxpayer, and

(b) the portion of the taxpayer's income for the year from the business that is attributable to the property for the period or to a related transaction (as defined in subsection 126(7)).

**Related Provisions**: 20(13) — Deduction for foreign tax on dividend from foreign affiliate; 126(1.1) — Application to authorized foreign bank.

**Notes**: 20(12.1) added by 1998 Budget, effective for 1998 and later taxation years. It provides a business deduction for certain foreign taxes that are not eligible for foreign tax credit due to 126(4.1). Note that if a related transaction involves acquisition of another property in respect of which 126(4.1) could apply independently, foreign tax in respect of that property may not be deducted a second time if it has already been deducted as tax in respect of a related transaction relative to the first property: see 248(28). There is no carryforward of foreign tax amounts not deductible in the year.

**(13) Dividend on share from foreign affiliate of taxpayer** — In computing the income for a taxation year of a taxpayer resident in Canada, there may be deducted such amount in respect of a dividend received by the taxpayer in the year on a share owned by the taxpayer of the capital stock of a foreign affiliate of the taxpayer as is provided by subdivision i.

**Related Provisions**: 20(12.1) — Deduction for foreign tax where no economic profit; 91(5) — Amount deductible in respect of dividends received from foreign affiliate; 93.1(2) — Dividends received from foreign affiliate by partnership; 113(1) — Deduction re dividend received from foreign affiliate. See additional Related Provisions and Definitions at end of s. 20.

**Notes**: Subdivision i is sections 90 to 95.

**(14) Accrued bond interest** — Where, by virtue of an assignment or other transfer of a debt obligation, other than an income bond, an income debenture, a small business development bond or a small business bond, the transferee has become entitled to an amount of interest that accrued on the debt obligation for a period commencing before the time of transfer and ending at that time that is not payable until after that time, that amount

(a) shall be included as interest in computing the transferor's income for the transferor's taxation year in which the transfer occurred, except to the extent that it was otherwise included in computing the transferor's income for the year or a preceding taxation year; and

(b) may be deducted in computing the transferee's income for a taxation year to the extent that the amount was included as interest in computing the transferee's income for the year.

**Related Provisions**: 12(9) — Deemed accrual; 16(3) — Purchase of bond at a discount; 53(2)(l) — Adjusted cost base — amounts to be deducted; 138(12)"gross investment revenue"E(b) — Inclusion in gross investment revenue of insurer; 142.4(1)"tax basis"(m) — Disposition of specified debt obligation by financial institution; 142.4(3)(b) — Disposition of specified debt obligation by financial institution; 142.5(3)(a) — Mark-to-market debt obligation; 214(6) — Deemed interest; 214(9) — Deemed resident. See additional Related provisions and Definitions at end of s. 20.

**Notes**: Paras. (a) and (b) are to be read independently of each other: *Antosko*, [1994] 1 C.T.C. 25 (SCC).

**Regulations**: 211 (information return by financial institution).

**Interpretation Bulletins**: IT-320R2: RRSPs — qualified investments; IT-396R: Interest income; IT-410R: Debt obligations — accrued interest on transfer.

**(14.1) Interest on debt obligation** — Where a person who has issued a debt obligation, other than an income bond, an income debenture, a small business development bond or a small business bond, is obligated to pay an amount that is stipulated to be interest on that debt obligation in respect of a period before its issue (in this subsection referred to as the "unearned interest amount") and it is reasonable to consider that the person to whom the debt obligation was issued paid to the issuer consideration for the debt obligation that included an amount in respect of the unearned interest amount,

(a) for the purposes of subsection (14) and section 12, the issue of the debt obligation shall be deemed to be an assignment of the debt obligation from the issuer, as transferor, to the person to whom the obligation was issued, as transferee, and an amount equal to the unearned interest amount shall be deemed to be interest that accrued on the obligation for a period commencing before the issue and ending at the time of issue; and

(b) notwithstanding paragraph (a) or any other provision of this Act, no amount that can reasonably be considered to be an amount in respect of the unearned interest amount shall be deducted or included in computing the income of the issuer.

**Related Provisions**: See Related Provisions and Definitions at end of s. 20.

**(15) Regulations** — For greater certainty it is hereby declared that, in the case of a regulation made under paragraph (1)(v.1) allowing to a taxpayer an amount in respect of natural accumulations of petroleum or natural gas in Canada, oil or gas wells in Canada or mineral resources in Canada,

(a) there may be allowed to the taxpayer by that regulation an amount in respect of any or all such accumulations, wells or resources; and

(b) notwithstanding any other provision contained in this Act, the Governor in Council may prescribe the formula by which the amount that may be allowed to the taxpayer by that regulation shall be determined.

**Related Provisions**: See Related Provisions and Definitions at end of s. 20.

**Regulations**: 1210 (amount allowed under 20(1)(v.1)).

**(16) Terminal loss** — Notwithstanding paragraphs 18(1)(a), (b) and (h), where at the end of a taxation year,

(a) the total of all amounts used to determine A to D in the definition "undepreciated capital cost" in subsection 13(21) in respect of a taxpayer's depreciable property of a particular class exceeds the total of all amounts used to determine E to J in that definition in respect of that property, and

(b) the taxpayer no longer owns any property of that class,

in computing the taxpayer's income for the year

(c) there shall be deducted the amount of the excess determined under paragraph (a), and

(d) no amount shall be deducted for the year under paragraph (1)(a) in respect of property of that class.

**Related Provisions**: 13(1) — Recapture where E to J exceed A to D; 13(6) — Misclassified property; 13(21.1) — Limitation on disposition of a building; 13(21.2) — Limitation where affiliated person acquires the property; 20(16.1) — No terminal loss for luxury automobile; 20(16.2) — Meaning of "taxation year" and "year"; 20(16.3) — Property disposed of after ceasing business; 28(1)(g) — Deduction from farming or fishing income when using cash method; 164(6)(b) — Disposition of property by legal representative of deceased taxpayer. See additional Related Provisions and Definitions at end of s. 20.

**Notes**: A terminal loss is available as a deduction if all the depreciable property in a class is disposed of and there is still some unused (undepreciated capital cost) "left over". See also Notes to 13(1) and 20(1)(a).

The provision of "separate classes" for many kinds of assets under Reg. 1101 permits a terminal loss to be claimed on the sale of such property for less than its undepreciated capital cost even if the taxpayer owns other similar property.

20(16) amended by 1991 technical bill, effective for taxation years beginning after July 13, 1990. For earlier years since 1985, add the following to the end of the subsection:

and the amount of the excess determined under paragraph (a) shall be deemed to have been deducted under paragraph (1)(a) in computing the taxpayer's income for the year from a business or property.

**Interpretation Bulletins**: IT-172R: CCA — taxation year of individuals; IT-195R4: Rental property — CCA restrictions; IT-288R2: Gifts of capital properties to a charity and others; IT-464R: CCA — leasehold interests; IT-465R: Non-resident beneficiaries of trusts;

IT-478R2: CCA — recapture and terminal loss; IT-522R: Vehicle, travel and sales expenses of employees.

**(16.1) Idem** — Subsection (16) does not apply in respect of a passenger vehicle of a taxpayer that has a cost to the taxpayer in excess of $20,000 or such other amount as is prescribed.

**Related Provisions**: 13(2) — No recapture on luxury automobile; 13(7)(g) — Maximum capital cost of passenger vehicle; 13(8) — Disposition after ceasing business; 20(16.2) — Meaning of "taxation year" and "year"; Reg. 1100(2.5) — 50% CCA in year of disposition. See additional Related Provisions and Definitions at end of s. 20.

**Notes**: 20(16.1) amended by 1992 technical bill, retroactive to its introduction (taxation years and fiscal periods that begin after June 17, 1987 and end after 1987). Although it disallows a terminal loss in respect of a luxury automobile, ½ of the otherwise allowable CCA is allowed in the year of disposition, by Reg. 1100(2.5); see Notes thereto.

See Notes to 13(7)(g) re changes in prescribed amount.

**Regulations**: 7307(1) (prescribed amount).

**Interpretation Bulletins**: IT-478R2: CCA — recapture and terminal loss; IT-521R: Motor vehicle expenses claimed by self-employed individuals; IT-522R: Vehicle, travel and sales expenses of employees.

**I.T. Technical News**: No. 10 (1997 deduction limits and benefit rates for automobiles).

**(16.2) Reference to "taxation year" and "year" of individual** — Where a taxpayer is an individual and the taxpayer's income for a taxation year includes income from a business the fiscal period of which does not coincide with the calendar year, if depreciable property acquired for the purpose of gaining or producing income from the business has been disposed of, each reference in subsections (16) and (16.1) to a "taxation year" and "year" shall, for greater certainty, be read as a reference to a "fiscal period".

**Related Provisions**: 11(2) — References to "taxation year" and "year"; 20(16.3) — Exception — disposition after ceasing business; 249 — Taxation year; 249.1 — Fiscal period.

**Notes**: 20(16.2) added in the R.S.C. 1985 (5th Supp.) consolidation, effective for taxation years ending after November 1991. This rule was formerly in 13(3)(a).

**Interpretation Bulletins**: IT-478R2: CCA — recapture and terminal loss.

**(16.3) Disposition after ceasing business** — Where a taxpayer, after ceasing to carry on a business, has disposed of depreciable property of the taxpayer of a prescribed class that was acquired by the taxpayer for the purpose of gaining or producing income from the business and that was not subsequently used by the taxpayer for some other purpose, in applying subsection (16) or (16.1), each reference in that subsection to a "taxation year" and "year" shall, notwithstanding anything in subsection (16.2), not be read as a reference to a "fiscal period".

**Notes**: 20(16.3) added in the R.S.C. 1985 (5th Supp.) consolidation, effective for taxation years ending after November 1991. This rule was formerly in 13(8).

**Interpretation Bulletins**: IT-478R2: CCA — recapture and terminal loss.

**(17) Reduction of inventory allowance deduction** — [No longer relevant]
**Notes**: 20(17) and (18) should be repealed. They relate to a version of 20(1)(gg), the inventory allowance deduction, that was repealed in 1986.

**(18) Definitions** — [No longer relevant]
**Notes**: See Notes to 20(17).

**(19) Annuity contract** — Where a taxpayer has in a particular taxation year received a payment under an annuity contract in respect of which an amount was by virtue of subsection 12(3) included in computing the taxpayer's income for a taxation year commencing before 1983, there may be deducted in computing the taxpayer's income for the particular year such amount, if any, as is allowed by regulation.
**Related Provisions**: 20(20) — Disposal of annuity where payments have not commenced; 148(9)"adjusted cost basis"I — Amount deducted reduces adjusted cost basis. See additional Related Provisions and Definitions at end of s. 20.
**Regulations**: 303 (amounts that may be deducted).

**(20) Life insurance policy [disposed of]** — Where in a taxation year a taxpayer disposes of an interest in a life insurance policy that is not an annuity contract (otherwise than as a consequence of a death) or of an interest in an annuity contract (other than a prescribed annuity contract), there may be deducted in computing the taxpayer's income for the year an amount equal to the lesser of

(a) the total of all amounts in respect of the interest in the policy that were included under section 12.2 of this Act or paragraph 56(1)(d.1) of the *Income Tax Act*, chapter 148 of the Revised Statutes of Canada, 1952, in computing the taxpayer's income for the year or a preceding taxation year, and

(b) the amount, if any, by which the adjusted cost basis (within the meaning assigned by section 148) to the taxpayer of that interest immediately before the disposition exceeds the proceeds of the disposition (within the meaning assigned by section 148) of the interest that the policyholder, a beneficiary or an assignee became entitled to receive.

**Related Provisions**: 148(2) — Deemed proceeds of disposition; 248(8) — Occurrences as a consequence of death. See additional Related Provisions and Definitions at end of s. 20.
**Notes**: 20(20) amended by 1991 technical bill, effective for dispositions after 1989, to extend to accrued but unreceived income in respect of an annuity (other than a prescribed annuity) under which annuity payments have begun at the time of disposition.
**Regulations**: 304 (prescribed annuity contract — technically does not apply to this subsection).
**I.T. Application Rules**: 69 (meaning of "*Income Tax Act*, chapter 148 of the Revised Statutes of Canada, 1952").
**Interpretation Bulletins**: IT-87R2: Policyholders' income from life insurance policies.

**(21) Debt obligation** — Where a taxpayer has in a particular taxation year disposed of a property that is an interest in a debt obligation for consideration equal to its fair market value at the time of disposition, there may be deducted in computing the taxpayer's income for the particular year the amount, if any, by which

(a) the total of all amounts each of which is an amount that was included in computing the taxpayer's income for the particular year or a preceding taxation year as interest in respect of that property

exceeds the total of all amounts each of which is

(b) the portion of an amount that was received or became receivable by the taxpayer in the particular year or a preceding taxation year that can reasonably be considered to be in respect of an amount described in paragraph (a) and that was not repaid by the taxpayer to the issuer of the debt obligation because of an adjustment in respect of interest received before the time of disposition by the taxpayer, or

(c) an amount in respect of that property that was deductible by the taxpayer by virtue of paragraph (14)(b) in computing the taxpayer's income for the particular year or a preceding taxation year.

**Related Provisions**: 12(9) — Deemed accrual; 142.5(3)(a) — Mark-to-market debt obligation; 142.5(8)(c) — First deemed disposition of mark-to-market debt obligation. See additional Related Provisions and Definitions at end of s. 20.
**Notes**: 20(21)(b) amended by 1991 technical bill, retroactive to 1986, to add the concluding portion, beginning "and that was not repaid". 20(21)(b) amended by 1992 technical bill, effective for dispositions after December 20, 1991; for earlier dispositions, read "at or before that time" in place of "in the particular year or a preceding taxation year".
**Interpretation Bulletins**: IT-396R: Interest income.

**(22) Deduction for [insurer's] negative reserves** — In computing an insurer's income for a taxation year, there may be deducted the amount included under paragraph 12(1)(e.1) in computing the insurer's income for the preceding taxation year.
**Related Provisions**: 87(2.2) — Amalgamation of insurance corporations; 88(1)(g)(i) — Windup of subsidiary insurance corporation; 138(11.91)(d.1) — Computation of income for non-resident insurer. See additional Related Provisions and Definitions at end of s. 20.
**Notes**: 20(22) added by 1996 Budget, effective for 1996 and later taxation years. See Notes to 12(1)(e.1). For former 20(22), see Notes to 20(23).
**Regulations**: 1400(2) (negative reserves).

**(23) [Repealed under former Act]**
**Notes**: 20(22) and (23) repealed by 1990 pension bill, effective 1991. For contributions made to registered pension plans before 1991, they provided a limitation on deductibility to a member of a related group of employers. See also Notes to 20(1)(q) and (s).

**(24) Amounts paid for undertaking future obligations** — Where an amount is included under paragraph 12(1)(a) in computing a taxpayer's income for a taxation year in respect of an undertaking to which that paragraph applies and the taxpayer paid a reasonable amount in a particular taxation year to another person as consideration for the assumption by that other person of the taxpayer's obligations in respect of the undertaking, if the taxpayer and the other person jointly so elect,

(a) the payment may be deducted in computing the taxpayer's income for the particular year and no amount is deductible under paragraph (1)(m) or (m.1) in computing the taxpayer's income for that or any subsequent taxation year in respect of the undertaking; and

(b) where the amount was received by the other person in the course of business, it shall be deemed to be an amount described in paragraph 12(1)(a).

**Related Provisions**: 20(25) — Manner of election; 87(2)(j) — Amalgamations — special reserve. See additional Related Provisions and Definitions at end of s. 20.

**Notes**: 20(24) reworded and amended by 1992 technical bill, effective for 1991 and later taxation years, so that it applies to all cases where 12(1)(a) applies (not just undelivered goods and services) and to refer to 20(1)(m.1).

**Interpretation Bulletins**: IT-154R: Special reserves; IT-321R: Insurance agents and brokers — unearned commissions.

**(25) Manner of election** — An election under subsection (24) shall be made by notifying the Minister in writing on or before the earlier of the days on or before which either the payer or the recipient is required to file a return of income pursuant to section 150 for the taxation year in which the payment to which the election relates was made.

**Related Provisions**: See Related Provisions and Definitions at end of s. 20.

**Interpretation Bulletins**: IT-154R: Special reserves.

**(26) Transition deduction re unpaid claims reserve** — An insurer may deduct, in computing its income for its taxation year that includes February 23, 1994, such amount as the insurer claims not exceeding the amount prescribed to be the insurer's unpaid claims reserve adjustment.

**Related Provisions**: 12.3 — Net reserve inclusion; 20(7)(c) — Deduction for policy reserves; 87(2)(g.1) — Amalgamation; Reg. 1400 — Deduction for policy reserves. See additional Related Provisions and Definitions at end of s. 20.

**Notes**: 20(26) amended by 1994 Budget, effective for taxation years that include February 23, 1994. For earlier years, read:

(26) Deduction re net reserve adjustment — In computing the income from a business of a taxpayer who is an insurer or whose business includes the lending of money for the taxpayer's first taxation year that commences after June 17, 1987 and ends after 1987, there may be deducted an amount equal to the taxpayer's prescribed amount of net reserve adjustment or such lesser amount as the taxpayer may claim.

**Regulations**: 8100 (unpaid claims reserve adjustment).

**(27) Loans, etc., acquired in ordinary course of business** — For the purposes of computing a deduction under paragraph (1)(l), (1.1) or (p) from the income for a taxation year of a taxpayer who was an insurer or whose ordinary business included the lending of money, a loan or lending asset or an instrument or commitment described in paragraph (1)(1.1) acquired from a person with whom the taxpayer did not deal at arm's length for an amount equal to its fair market value shall be deemed to have been acquired by the taxpayer in the ordinary course of the taxpayer's business of insurance or the lending of money where

(a) the person from whom the loan or lending asset or instrument or commitment was acquired carried on the business of insurance or the lending of money; and

(b) the loan or lending asset was made or acquired or the instrument or commitment was issued, made or assumed by the person in the ordinary course of the person's business of insurance or the lending of money.

**Related Provisions**: See Related Provisions and Definitions at end of s. 20.

**Interpretation Bulletins**: IT-442R: Bad debts and reserves for doubtful debts.

**(27.1) Application of subsecs. 13(21) and 138(12)** — The definitions in subsections 13(21) and 138(12) apply to this section.

**Notes**: 20(27.1) added in the R.S.C. 1985 (5th Supp.) consolidation, effective for taxation years ending after November 1991. This rule was formerly contained in the opening words of 13(21) and 138(12).

**(28) Deduction [for building] before available for use** — In computing a taxpayer's income from a business or property for a taxation year ending before the time a building or a part thereof acquired after 1989 by the taxpayer becomes available for use by the taxpayer, there may be deducted an amount not exceeding the amount by which the lesser of

(a) the amount that would be deductible under paragraph (1)(a) for the year in respect of the building if subsection 13(26) did not apply, and

(b) the taxpayer's income for the year from renting the building, computed without reference to this subsection and before deducting any amount in respect of the building under paragraph (1)(a)

exceeds

(c) the amount deductible under paragraph (1)(a) for the year in respect of the building, computed without reference to this subsection,

and any amount so deducted shall be deemed to be an amount deducted by the taxpayer under paragraph (1)(a) in computing the taxpayer's income for the year.

**Related Provisions**: 20(29) — Deduction before available for use. See additional Related Provisions and Definitions at end of s. 20.

**Notes**: 20(28) added by 1991 technical bill, effective for taxation years ending after 1989.

**(29) Idem** — Where, because of subsection 18(3.1), a deduction would, but for this subsection, not be allowed to a taxpayer in respect of an outlay or expense in respect of a building, or part thereof, and the outlay or expense would, but for that subsection and without reference to this subsection, be deducti-

Subdivision b — Income or Loss from a Business or Property     S. 20.01(1)(a)(i)

ble in computing the taxpayer's income for a taxation year, there may be deducted in respect of such outlays and expenses in computing the taxpayer's income for the year an amount equal to the lesser of

(a) the total of all such outlays or expenses, and

(b) the taxpayer's income for the year from renting the building or the part thereof computed without reference to subsection (28) and this subsection.

**Related Provisions**: 18(3.1)(a) — Costs relating to construction of building or ownership of land. See additional Related Provisions and Definitions at end of s. 20.

**Notes**: 20(29) added by 1991 technical bill, effective for outlays and expenses after 1989.

**(30) Specified reserve adjustment** — For the purpose of the description of N in subclause (1)(l)(ii)(D)(II), the specified reserve adjustment for a loan of a taxpayer for a taxation year is the amount determined by the formula

$$0.1(A \times B \times C/365)$$

where

A  is the carrying amount of the impaired loan that is used or would be used in determining the interest income on the loan for the year in accordance with generally accepted accounting principles;

B  is the effective interest rate on the loan for the year determined in accordance with generally accepted accounting principles; and

C  is the number of days in the year on which the loan is impaired.

**Related Provisions**: See Related Provisions and Definitions at end of s. 20.

**Notes**: 20(30) added by 1995-97 technical bill, effective on the same basis as the amendment to 20(1)(l).

**Related Provisions [s. 20]**: 18 — Limitations on deductions; 67 — Expenses must be reasonable; 67.1 — Limitation on expenses for meals and entertainment; 67.2 — Interest on money borrowed for passenger vehicle; 67.3 — Limitation re motor vehicle expenses; 70(13) — Capital cost of depreciable property on death; 78 — Unpaid amounts; 80(9)(c) — Reduction of capital cost on debt forgiveness ignored for purposes of s. 20; 104(5) — Deemed disposition by a trust; 107.2 — Distribution by a retirement compensation arrangement; 132.2(1)(d) — Deemed capital cost of depreciable property following mutual fund reorganization; 138(11.5)(k) — Transfer of business by non-resident insurer; 138(11.8) — Rules on transfer of depreciable property; 138(11.91)(f) — Computation of income of non-resident insurer; 209 — "carved-out income"(a).

**Definitions [s. 20]**: "adjusted cost base" — 54, 248(1); "allowable capital loss" — 38(b), 248(1); "amortized cost", "amount" — 248(1); "amount payable" — (in respect of a policy loan) 20(27.1), 138(12); "anniversary day" — 12.2(11), 20(1.2); "annuity" — 248(1); "arm's length" — 251(1); "assistance" — 79(4), 125.4(5), 248(16), (18); "authorized foreign bank" — 248(1); "available for use" — 13(27)–(31), 248(19); "borrowed money" — 20(2), 248(1); "business" — 248(1); "business-income tax" — 126(7); "calendar year" — Interpretation Act 37(1)(a); "Canada" — 255; "Canadian oil and gas property expense" — 66.4(5), 248(1); "Canadian partnership" — 102(1), 248(1); "capital cost" — 13(7)–(7.4), 70(12), 128.1(1)(c), 128.1(4)(c), 132.2(1)(d); "capital property" — 54, 248(1); "class of shares" — 248(6); "consequence of the death" — 248(8); "controlled" — 256(6), (6.1); "corporation" — 248(1), Interpretation Act 35(1); "cumulative eligible capital" — 14(5), 248(1); "deferred amount" — 248(1); "deferred profit sharing plan" — 147(1), 248(1); "depreciable property" — 13(21), 248(1); "disposition" — 13(21), 20(27.1), 248(1); "dividend" — 248(1); "eligible capital property" — 54, 248(1); "employee" — 248(1); "employees profit sharing plan" — 144(1), 248(1); "employer" — 248(1); "excluded amount" — 20(1)(e)(iv.1); "exempt income" — 248(1); "fiscal period" — 249(2), 249.1; "foreign affiliate" — 95(1), 248(1); "foreign tax" — 126(4.1); "goods and services tax" — 248(1); "income" — from business or property 9(1), (3); "income-averaging annuity contract", "income bond", "income debenture", "individual", "insurance corporation", "insurer" — 248(1); "interest in real property" — 248(4); "interest" — in respect of a policy loan 20(27.1), 138(12); "interest paid" — 20(2.1); "inventory", "lending asset", "life insurance business" — 248(1); "life insurance policy" — 20(2.2), 138(12), 248(1); "mineral resource", "mining reclamation trust", "Minister", "motor vehicle" — 248(1); "net cost of pure insurance" — 148(9)"adjusted cost basis"L(a), Reg. 308; "net income stabilization account" — 248(1); "non-business-income tax" — 126(7); "non-resident", "oil or gas well" — 248(1); "partnership" — see Notes to 96(1); "passenger vehicle", "person" — 248(1); "policy loan" — 138(12); "prescribed" — 248(1); "prescribed annuity contract" — Reg. 304; "principal amount" — 248(1); "proceeds of disposition" — 13(21), 20(27.1); "property" — 248(1); "province" — Interpretation Act 35(1); "qualifying environmental trust", "registered pension plan" — 248(1); "registered retirement savings plan" — 146(1), 248(1); "registered supplementary unemployment benefit plan" — 145(1), 248(1); "regulation" — 248(1); "resident" — 250; "restricted financial institution", "retirement compensation arrangement", "salary deferral arrangement" — 248(1); "sectoral reserve" — 20(2.3); "share", "shareholder" — 248(1); "small business bond" — 15.2(3), 248(1); "small business development bond" — 15.1(3), 248(1); "specified individual" — 120.4(1), 248(1); "specified percentage" — 20(2.4); "specified reserve adjustment" — 20(30); "split income" — 120.4(1), 248(1); "subsidiary controlled corporation"; "superannuation or pension benefit" — 248(1); "taxable Canadian corporation" — 89(1), 248(1); "taxable income" — 2(2), 248(1); "taxation year" — 11(2), 20(16.2), (16.3), 249; "taxpayer" — 248(1); "testamentary trust" — 108(1), 248(1); "timber resource property" — 13(21), 248(1); "Treasury Board" — 248(1); "trust" — 104(1), 248(1, (3); "unit trust" — 108(2), 248(1); "writing" — Interpretation Act 35(1); "year" — 11(2), 20(16.2), (16.3).

**I.T. Application Rules [s. 20]**: 20(3)(b), 20(5)(b).

**20.01 (1) PHSP [private health services plan] premiums** — Notwithstanding paragraphs 18(1)(a) and (h) and subject to subsection (2), there may be deducted in computing an individual's income for a taxation year from a business carried on by the individual and in which the individual is actively engaged on a regular and continuous basis, directly or as a member of a partnership, an amount payable by the individual or partnership in respect of the year as a premium, contribution or other consideration under a private health services plan in respect of the individual, the individual's spouse or common-law partner or any person who is a member of the individual's household if

(a) in the year or in the preceding taxation year

(i) the total of all amounts each of which is the individual's income from such a business for a fiscal period that ends in the year exceeds 50% of the individual's income for the year, or

(ii) the individual's income for the year does not exceed the total of $10,000 and the total referred to in subparagraph (i) in respect of the individual for the year,

on the assumption that the individual's income from each business is computed without reference to this subsection and the individual's income is computed without reference to this subsection and subdivision e; and

(b) the amount is payable under a contract between the individual or partnership and

(i) a person licensed or otherwise authorized under the laws of Canada or a province to carry on in Canada an insurance business or the business of offering to the public its services as trustee,

(ii) a person or partnership engaged in the business of offering to the public its services as an administrator of private health services plans, or

(iii) a person the taxable income of which is exempt under section 149 and that is a business or professional organization of which the individual is a member or a trade union of which the individual or a majority of the individual's employees are members.

**Related Provisions**: 53(2)(c)(xii) — Reduction in ACB of partnership interest; 118.2(2)(q) — Medical expense credit for premiums.

**Notes**: See Notes at end of 20.01.

**(2) Limit** — For the purpose of calculating the amount deductible under subsection (1) in computing an individual's income for a taxation year from a particular business,

(a) no amount may be deducted to the extent that

(i) it is deducted under this section in computing another individual's income for any taxation year, or

(ii) it is included in calculating a deduction under section 118.2 in computing an individual's tax payable under this Part for any taxation year;

(b) where an amount payable under a private health services plan relates to a period in the year throughout which

(i) each of one or more persons

(A) is employed on a full-time basis (other than on a temporary or seasonal basis) in the particular business or in another business carried on by

(I) the individual (otherwise than as a member of a partnership),

(II) a partnership of which the individual is a majority interest partner, or

(III) a corporation affiliated with the individual, and

(B) has accumulated not less than three months of service in that employment since the person last became so employed, and

(ii) the total number of persons employed in a business described in clause (i)(A), with whom the individual deals at arm's length and to whom coverage is extended under the plan, is not less than 50% of the total number of persons each of whom is a person

(A) who carries on the particular business or is employed in a business described in clause (i)(A), and

(B) to whom coverage is extended under the plan,

the amount so deductible in relation to the period shall not exceed the individual's cost of equivalent coverage under the plan in respect of each employed person who deals at arm's length with the individual and who is described in subparagraph (i) in relation to the period;

(c) subject to paragraph (d), where an amount payable under a private health services plan relates to a particular period in the year, other than a period described in paragraph (b), the amount so deductible in relation to the particular period shall not exceed the amount determined by the formula

$$(A/365) \times (B + C)$$

where

A is the number of days in the year that are included in the particular period,

B is the product obtained when $1,500 is multiplied by the number of persons each of whom is covered under the plan, and

(i) is the individual or the individual's spouse or common-law partner, or

(ii) is a member of the individual's household and has attained the age of 18 years before the beginning of the particular period, and

C is the product obtained when $750 is multiplied by the number of members of the individual's household who, but for the fact that they have not attained the age of 18 years before the particular period began, would be included in computing the product under the description of B; and

(d) where an amount payable under a private health services plan relates to a particular period in the year (other than a period described in paragraph (b)) and one or more persons with whom the individual deals at arm's length are described in subparagraph (b)(i) in relation to the particular period, the amount so deductible in relation to the particular period shall not exceed the lesser of the amount determined under the formula set out in paragraph (c) and the individual's cost of equivalent coverage in respect of any such person in relation to the particular period.

**Related Provisions**: 20.01(3) — Cost of equivalent coverage; 118.2(2)(q) — Medical expense credit for premiums.

**Notes**: See Notes at end of 20.01.

**(3) Equivalent coverage** — For the purpose of subsection (2), an amount payable in respect of an individual under a private health services plan in relation to a period does not exceed the individual's cost of equivalent coverage under the plan in respect of another person in relation to the period to the extent that, in relation to the period, the amount does not exceed the product obtained when

(a) the amount that would be the individual's cost of coverage under the plan if the benefits and coverage in respect of the individual, the individual's spouse or common-law partner and the members of the individual's household were identical to the benefits and coverage made available in respect of the other person, the other person's spouse or common-law partner and the members of the other person's household

is multiplied by

(b) the percentage of the cost of coverage under the plan in respect of the other person that is payable by the individual or a partnership of which the individual is a member.

**Notes**: 20.01 amended by 2000 same-sex partners bill to add reference to "common-law partner", effective for the 2001 and later taxation years, or earlier by election (see Notes to 248(1)"common-law partner").

20.01 added by 1998 Budget, effective for amounts that become payable after 1997. In simple terms, it allows a deduction for PHSP premiums (e.g. for an extended health plan, drug plan or dental plan — see 248(1)"private health services plan") for self-employed individuals, to parallel the non-inclusion of such premiums as a taxable benefit to employees under 6(1)(a)(i). 20.01(2)(b) and (d) effectively ensure that the deduction is only available if equivalent coverage is offered to arm's length employees. Where 20.01(2)(b) does not apply, 20.01(2)(c) limits the deduction to $1,500 per family member and $750 per child. Where amounts are not deductible under this section, they should be claimed for medical expense credit under 118.2(2)(q) instead.

**Definitions [s. 20.01]**: "affiliated" — 251.1; "amount" — 248(1); "arm's length" — 251(1); "business" — 248(1); "Canada" — 255, *Interpretation Act* 35(1); "common-law partner" — 248(1); "corporation" — 248(1), *Interpretation Act* 35(1); "cost of equivalent coverage" — 20.01(3); "employed", "employee", "employment" — 248(1); "fiscal period" — 249.1; "individual", "majority interest partner" — 248(1); "month" — *Interpretation Act* 35(1); "partnership" — see Notes to 96(1); "person", "private health services plan" — 248(1); "province" — *Interpretation Act* 35(1); "taxable income" — 248(1); "taxation year" — 249.

**20.1 (1) Borrowed money used to earn income from property** — Where

(a) at any time after 1993 borrowed money ceases to be used by a taxpayer for the purpose of earning income from a capital property (other than real property or depreciable property), and

(b) the amount of the borrowed money that was so used by the taxpayer immediately before that time exceeds the total of

(i) where the taxpayer disposed of the property at that time for an amount of consideration that is not less than the fair market value of the property at that time, the amount of the borrowed money used to acquire the consideration,

(ii) where the taxpayer disposed of the property at that time and subparagraph (i) does not apply, the amount of the borrowed money that, if the taxpayer had received as consideration an amount of money equal to the amount by which the fair market value of the property at that time exceeds the amount included in the total by reason of subparagraph (iii), would be considered to be used to acquire the consideration,

(iii) where the taxpayer disposed of the property at that time for consideration that includes a reduction in the amount of the borrowed money, the amount of the reduction, and

(iv) where the taxpayer did not dispose of the property at that time, the amount of the borrowed money that, if the taxpayer had disposed of the property at that time and received as consideration an amount of money equal to the fair market value of the property at that time, would be considered to be used to acquire the consideration,

an amount of the borrowed money equal to the excess shall, to the extent that the amount is outstanding after that time, be deemed to be used by the taxpayer for the purpose of earning income from the property.

**(2) Borrowed money used to earn income from business** — Where at any particular time after 1993 a taxpayer ceases to carry on a business and, as a consequence, borrowed money ceases to be used by the taxpayer for the purpose of earning income from the business, the following rules apply:

(a) where, at any time (in this paragraph referred to as the "time of disposition") at or after the particular time, the taxpayer disposes of property that was last used by the taxpayer in the business, an amount of the borrowed money equal to the lesser of

(i) the fair market value of the property at the time of disposition, and

(ii) the amount of the borrowed money outstanding at the time of disposition that is not deemed by this paragraph to have been used before the time of disposition to acquire any other property shall be deemed to have been used by the taxpayer immediately before the time of disposition to acquire the property;

(b) subject to paragraph (a), the borrowed money shall, after the particular time, be deemed not to have been used to acquire property that was used by the taxpayer in the business;

(c) the portion of the borrowed money outstanding at any time after the particular time that is not deemed by paragraph (a) to have been used before that subsequent time to acquire property shall be deemed to be used by the taxpayer at that subsequent time for the purpose of earning income from the business; and

(d) the business shall be deemed to have fiscal periods after the particular time that coincide with the taxation years of the taxpayer, except that the first such fiscal period shall be deemed to begin at the end of the business's last fiscal period that began before the particular time.

**Related Provisions [subsec. 20.1(2)]**: 20.1(3) — Deemed dispositions — rules.

**(3) Deemed dispositions** — For the purpose of paragraph (2)(a),

(a) where a property was used by a taxpayer in a business that the taxpayer has ceased to carry on, the taxpayer shall be deemed to dispose of the property at the time at which the taxpayer begins to use the property in another business or for any other purpose;

(b) where a taxpayer, who has at any time ceased to carry on a business, regularly used a property in part in the business and in part for some other purpose,

(i) the taxpayer shall be deemed to have disposed of the property at that time, and

(ii) the fair market value of the property at that time shall be deemed to equal the proportion of the fair market value of the property at that time that the use regularly made of the property in the business was of the whole use regularly made of the property; and

(c) where the taxpayer is a trust, subsections 104(4) to (5.2) do not apply.

**(4) Amount payable for property** — Where an amount is payable by a taxpayer for property, the amount shall be deemed, for the purposes of this section and, where subsection (2) applies with respect to the amount, for the purposes of this Act, to be payable in respect of borrowed money used by the taxpayer to acquire the property.

**(5) Interest in partnership** — For the purposes of this section, where borrowed money that has been used to acquire an interest in a partnership is, as a consequence, considered to be used at any time for the purpose of earning income from a business or property of the partnership, the borrowed money shall be deemed to be used at that time for the purpose of earning income from property that is the interest in the partnership and not to be used for the purpose of earning income from the business or property of the partnership.

**(6) Refinancings** — Where at any time a taxpayer uses borrowed money to repay money previously borrowed that was deemed by paragraph (2)(c) immediately before that time to be used for the purpose of earning income from a business,

(a) paragraphs (2)(a) to (c) apply with respect to the borrowed money; and

(b) subsection 20(3) does not apply with respect to the borrowed money.

**Related Provisions [s. 20.1]**: 20(3) — Use of borrowed money; 87(2)(j.6) — Amalgamations — continuing corporation.

**Notes**: 20.1 added by 1993 technical bill, effective January 1, 1994. It ensures that where borrowed money ceases to be used for income-earning purposes because of a loss of the source of income, part or all of the interest paid on such borrowed money may continue to be deductible in certain circumstances. It is unrelated to the 20.1 and 20.2 proposed earlier, on December 20, 1991 (see below).

For a thorough overview of 20.1, see Ryan Chang & Jane Briant, "Interest Deductibility: New Loss of Source of Income Rules", 43(1) *Canadian Tax Journal* 154–176 (1995).

**Definitions [s. 20.1]**: "amount", "borrowed money", "business" — 248(1); "capital property" — 54, 248(1); "depreciable property" — 13(21), 248(1); "fiscal period" — 249.1; "property", "taxpayer" — 248(1); "time of disposition" — 20.1(2)(a).

### Proposed Addition — 20.2 [Authorized foreign bank interest]

**Technical Notes**: New section 20.2 contains rules that allow an authorized foreign bank operating in Canada to deduct, in computing its income from its Canadian banking business for a taxation year, amounts on account of interest expense. Given new paragraph 18(1)(v) of the Act (see separate note), this new section is comprehensive and exclusive: in computing its Canadian business income, an authorized foreign bank may only deduct amounts on account of interest that are authorized under section 20.2.

Under new section 20.2, each taxation year of an authorized foreign bank is divided into "calculation periods," which may be designated by the bank in its tax return for the year, subject to certain conditions described below, or, in the absence of such a designation, by the Minister of National Revenue. The amount that the bank may deduct on account of interest for a given year is the total of the deductible amounts determined for all the calculation periods in the year. Those deductible amounts may include one or more of the following:

- Interest expense actually incurred by the bank in the period, in relation to actual liabilities of the Canadian banking business to other persons or partnerships;

- Interest expense notionally incurred by the Canadian banking business in the period, in relation to documented "branch advances" from the bank itself to the business; and

- A residual amount, representing interest for the period calculated at the Bank of Canada bank rate on an amount not exceeding the amount by which 95% of the value of the Canadian banking business's assets exceeds the total of its actual liabilities and its branch advances.

These three categories of branch interest expense reflect the fact that an authorized foreign bank's Canadian operations may be funded through some combination of three sources of funds. First, the bank may, in the course of its Canadian operations, borrow directly from other persons or partnerships, recording the resulting obligation as a liability of the Canadian business itself. Second, the bank — typically, the bank's head office or other central source of internal financing — may advance funds to the Canadian business, with the lending unit recording the advance in more or less the same way it would an arm's length loan (and applying comparable terms — see below) and the branch recording it as a notional liability. Third, the bank may use its own, undifferentiated funds to operate the branch, without formally recording an advance to the branch.

Regardless what combination of these three sources is used for a given calculation period, section 20.2 limits the amount that the authorized foreign bank may deduct on account of its Canadian business's interest expense. On the principle that an authorized foreign bank's capital structure will include at least 5% of equity, interest is not deductible to the extent it reflects debt in excess of 95% of the value of the assets of the Canadian banking business at the end of the period.

Reference should also be had to the relationship between interest expense deductions under new section 20.2 and the "branch tax" under Part XIV of the Act, described in connection with the amendments to that Part.

New section 20.2 applies after June 27, 1999, except that a special transitional rule (described in the detailed notes to subsection 20.2(1), below) applies to branch advances made before the day that is 14 days after August 8, 2000.

## 20.2 (1) Interest — authorized foreign bank — interpretation — The following definitions apply in this section.

**"branch advance"** of an authorized foreign bank at a particular time means an amount allocated or provided by, or on behalf of, the bank to, or for the benefit of, its Canadian banking business under terms that were documented, before the amount was so allocated or provided, to the same extent as, and in a form similar to the form in which, the bank would ordinarily document a loan by it to a person with whom it deals at arm's length.

**Technical Notes**: New subsection 20.2 (1) of the Act sets out definitions for the purposes of new section 20.2.

A branch advance of an authorized foreign bank at a particular time means an amount allocated or provided by or on behalf of the bank to or for the benefit of the bank's Canadian banking business under terms that are documented, before the amount is allocated or provided, in a manner similar to the bank's documentation of loans to arms-length parties. It is contemplated that the documentation would relate to terms of the advance itself such as currency, amounts, further advances, time when repayment is required, computation of interest, payment of interest, prepayment rights, extensions and other amendments to terms, use of the funds, and whether or not the loan is considered to be secured. However, separate documentation setting out the terms of such security would not be required.

To accommodate authorized foreign banks that may already have begun to finance their Canadian operations, the requirement for prior documentation is modified in the case of branch advances made before the day that is 14 days after August 8, 2000: such advances need only be documented on or before December 31, 2000.

**"branch financial statements"** of an authorized foreign bank for a taxation year means the unconsolidated statements of assets and liabilities and of income and expenses for the year, in respect of its Canadian banking business,

(a) that form part of the bank's annual report for the year filed with the Superintendent of Financial Institutions as required under section 601 of the *Bank Act*, and accepted by the Superintendent; and

(b) if no filing is so required for the taxation year, that are prepared in a manner consistent with the statements in the annual report or reports so filed and accepted for the period or periods in which the taxation year falls.

**Technical Notes**: The branch financial statements of an authorized foreign bank for a taxation year are the unconsolidated statements of assets and liabilities, and income and expenses, for that year in respect of its Canadian banking business that are required, under the *Bank Act*, to be prepared and filed with the bank's annual report to the Superintendent of Financial Institutions. If no such statements are required to be prepared for the taxation year, the term refers to statements that are prepared in a manner consistent with those that are required to be prepared for the annual report so filed.

**"calculation period"** of an authorized foreign bank for a taxation year means any one of a series of regular periods into which the year is divided in a designation by the bank in its return of income for the year or, in the absence of such a designation, by the Minister,

(a) none of which is longer than 31 days;

(b) the first of which commences at the beginning of the year and the last of which ends at the end of the year; and

(c) that are, unless the Minister otherwise agrees in writing, consistent with the calculation periods designated for the bank's preceding taxation year.

**Technical Notes**: A calculation period of an authorized foreign bank for a taxation year means any of a series of regular periods into which the year is divided in a designation by the bank or in a designation by the Minister, such that:

- the periods in the year are regular (as, for example, monthly, weekly or daily);

- no period is longer than 31 days;

- the year's first period starts at the beginning of the year, and its last one ends at the end of the year; and

- except as authorized in writing by the Minister, the year's periods are consistent with the periods designated for the preceding taxation year.

**(2) Formula elements** — The following descriptions apply for the purposes of the formulae in subsection (3), for any calculation period in a taxation year of an authorized foreign bank.

A is the amount of the bank's assets at the end of the period.

BA is the amount of the bank's branch advances at the end of the period.

IBA is the total of all amounts each of which is a reasonable amount on account of notional interest for the period, in respect of a branch advance, that would be deductible in computing the bank's income for the year if it were interest payable by, and the advance were indebtedness of, the bank to another person and if this Act were read without reference to paragraph 18(1)(v) and this section.

IL is the total of all amounts each of which is an amount on account of interest for the period in respect of a liability of the bank to another person or partnership, that would be deductible in computing the bank's income for the year if this Act were read without reference to paragraph 18(1)(v) and this section.

L is the amount of the bank's liabilities to other persons and partnerships at the end of the period.

**Technical Notes**: New subsection 20.2(2) of the Act sets out five elements that are used in the formulas contained in new subsection (3) (described below). These elements, which are set out in terms of a given calculation period during the taxation year of an authorized foreign bank, are importantly qualified by new subsection (4) (described below).

The elements are identified with letters that reflect their meaning.

A is the amount of the bank's assets used in the Canadian banking business at the end of the relevant calculation period.

BA is the amount of the bank's branch advances at the end of the period.

IBA is that total of all reasonable amounts on account of notional interest for the period, with respect to branch advances, that would (but for new paragraph 18(1)(v) and section 20.2 itself) be deductible if the branch advances were actual indebtedness of the bank to another person and if paragraph 18(1)(v) were ignored. New subsection 20.2(5) of the Act (described below) provides additional guidance as to what is a reasonable amount on account of notional interest.

IL is the total of all amounts on account of interest for the period in respect of a liability of the bank in respect of the Canadian business to another person or partnership that would, but for new paragraph 18(1)(v) and section 20.2 itself, be deductible.

L is the amount of the bank's liabilities in respect of the Canadian business to other persons and partnerships at the end of the period.

**Related Provisions [subsec. 20.2(2)]**: 20.2(4) — Branch amounts; 20.2(5) — Notional interest for IBA.

**(3) Interest deduction** — In computing the income of an authorized foreign bank from its Canadian banking business for a taxation year, there may be deducted on account of interest for each calculation period of the bank for the year,

(a) where the total amount at the end of the period of its liabilities to other persons and partnerships and branch advances is 95% or more of the amount of its assets at that time, an amount not exceeding

(i) if the amount of liabilities to other persons and partnerships at that time does not exceed 95% of the amount of its assets at that time, the amount determined by the formula

$$IL + IBA \times (0.95 \times A - L) / BA$$

and

(ii) if the amount of those liabilities at that time exceeds 95% of the amount of its assets at that time, the amount determined by the formula

$$IL \times (0.95 \times A) / L$$

and

(b) in any other case, the total of

(i) the amount determined by the formula

$$IL + IBA$$

and

(ii) the product of

(A) the amount claimed by the bank, in its return of income for the year, not exceeding the amount determined by the formula

$$(0.95 \times A) - (L + BA)$$

and

(B) the average, based on daily observations, of the Bank of Canada bank rate for the period.

**Technical Notes**: The core of new section 20.2 of the Act is new subsection 20.2(3). This subsection contains formulas that are used to calculate the amount deductible, in computing the Canadian business income of an authorized foreign bank, on account of interest expense for each calculation period of the bank in a taxation year. The bank's maximum deduction on account of interest for the year will be the total of the amounts determined under these formulas for each of the calculation periods in the year.

An ordering principle underlies subsection 20.2(3). Interest expense is deductible first in respect of actual liabilities of the Canadian banking business to other persons or partnerships, to the extent those liabilities do not exceed

95% of the business's assets. Next, to the extent those liabilities are equal to less than 95% of the business's assets, interest may be deducted in respect of branch advances. Finally, if liabilities and branch advances together are less than 95% of assets, the bank may choose to deduct interest, computed by reference to the Bank of Canada bank rate, in respect of a residual "top-up" amount not exceeding the amount by which the 95% figure exceeds the total of liabilities and branch advances.

More specifically, subsection 20.2(3) applies one of three different formulas to the interest-deductibility calculation for a given calculation period. First, if the bank's liabilities to others (element L) at the end of the calculation period by themselves exceed 95% of its assets (A), the formula set out in new subparagraph 20.2(3)(a)(ii) applies for the period. That formula generally allows the bank to deduct that proportion of its actual interest expense in respect of liabilities to others (IL) that 95% of its assets (A) is of its liabilities (L).

Second, if the bank's liabilities to others (L) and its branch advances (BA) at the end of the calculation period total 95% or more of the amount of its assets (A) at that time, but its liabilities alone (i.e. without its branch advances) do not exceed that 95% figure, the formula set out in new subparagraph 20.2(3)(a)(i) applies for the period. In broad terms, that formula allows the bank to deduct its actual interest expense in respect of liabilities to others (IL), together with that proportion of its notional interest expense in respect of branch advances (IBA), that the excess of 95% of its assets is of its liabilities.

Third, if liabilities to others (L) and branch advances (BA) at the end of the calculation period total less than 95% of assets (A), the bank may deduct the total of its actual interest expense in respect of liabilities (IL), its notional interest in respect of its branch advances (IBA), and interest at a specified rate on a residual top-up amount described in new subparagraph 20.2(3)(b)(ii) of the Act. That top-up amount is any amount the bank chooses to claim, not exceeding the amount by which 95% of assets (A) exceeds the total of liabilities (L) and branch advances (BA). The interest rate applicable to this elective top-up is the average, based on daily observations, of the Bank of Canada bank rate for the calculation period.

**Related Provisions [subsec. 20.2(3)]**: 18(1)(v) — No other interest deduction allowed; 20.2(2) — Formula element descriptions; 20.2(4) — Branch amounts; 218.2(2) — Part XIII.1 tax on taxable interest expense; 257 — Formulas cannot calculate to less than zero.

**(4) Branch amounts** — Only amounts that are in respect of an authorized foreign bank's Canadian banking business, and that are recorded in the books of account of the business in a manner consistent with the manner in which they are required to be treated for the purposes of the branch financial statements, shall be used to determine

　(a) the amounts in subsection (2); and

　(b) the amounts in subsection (3) of an authorized foreign bank's assets, liabilities to other persons and partnerships, and branch advances.

**Technical Notes**: New subsection 20.2(4) applies in determining the amounts in the descriptions of the formula elements in subsection (2) — which are used in the formulas in subsection (3) — and the amounts of an authorized foreign bank's assets, liabilities and branch advances for the purpose of subsection (3). Subsection (4) provides that these amounts must be in respect of the bank's Canadian banking business only, and must be recorded in the business's books of account in a manner consistent with the manner in which they are required to be treated for the purposes of the branch financial statements. Effectively, no deduction is permitted in respect of interest or liability amounts that are not recorded in the bank's books of account.

**(5) Notional interest** — For the purposes of the description of IBA in subsection (2), a reasonable amount on account of notional interest for a calculation period in respect of a branch advance is the amount that would be payable on account of interest for the period by a notional borrower, having regard to the time to repayment, the currency in which repayment is required and all other terms, as adjusted by paragraph (c), of the advance, if

　(a) the borrower were a person that dealt at arm's length with the bank, that carried on the bank's Canadian banking business and that had the same credit-worthiness and borrowing capacity as the bank;

　(b) the advance were a loan by the bank to the borrower; and

　(c) any of the terms of the advance (excluding the rate of interest, but including the structure of the interest calculation, such as whether the rate is fixed or floating and the choice of any reference rate referred to) that are not terms that would be made between the bank as lender and the borrower, having regard to all the circumstances, including the nature of the Canadian banking business, the use of the advanced funds in the business and normal risk management practices for banks, were instead terms that would be agreed to by the bank and the borrower.

**Technical Notes**: New subsection 20.2(5) of the Act provides clarification as to what constitutes, in applying the formula element "IBA" set out in subsection 20.2(2), a reasonable amount on account of notional interest in respect of a branch advance. A reasonable amount is described in subsection (5) as the amount that would be payable by a notional borrower, having regard to the time to repayment, the currency and all other terms, if:

- the notional borrower were a person dealing at arm's length with the bank, and carried on the bank's Canadian banking business and had the same credit-worthiness and borrowing capacity as the bank;
- the branch advance were a loan by the bank to the notional borrower; and
- the terms of the advance — excluding the interest rate itself, but including such terms as the method of calculating the interest rate where it is a structured rate that relies on external references, the currency of the loan, the time to repayment, provisions for early repayment and amendment — were terms that would be agreed to by the bank and the notional borrower, having regard to all the circumstances (including but not limited to the nature of the Canadian banking busi-

ness, the use of the advanced funds, the presence or absence of a hedge and normal banking practice).

In essence, a reasonable amount of interest is the amount that would be payable in the circumstances in a transaction between arm's length parties if the other terms of the advance themselves were those that would be agreed to in the circumstances by such parties.

**Application**: The August 8, 2000 draft legislation, s. 3, will add s. 20.2, applicable after June 27, 1999 except that in its application to amounts allocated or provided before August 22, 2000, the definition "branch advance" shall be read as follows:

> "branch advance" of an authorized foreign bank at a particular time means an amount allocated or provided by, or on behalf of, the bank to, or for the benefit of, its Canadian banking business under terms that were documented, on or before December 31, 2000, to the same extent as, and in a form similar to the form in which, the bank would ordinarily document a loan by it to a person with whom it deals at arm's length.

**Notice of Ways and Means Motion (authorized foreign banks), February 11, 1999**: (2) That the amount of interest that may be deducted by an authorized foreign bank in computing its income for a taxation year from its business carried on in Canada be the total of

(a) the total of all amounts payable by the bank as interest, or a reasonable amount of interest, whichever is the lesser, for the year in respect of indebtedness incurred in connection with, and on which the interest is borne by, the bank's business carried on in Canada, to the extent that the total amount of all such indebtedness outstanding at any time in the year does not exceed 95% of the total value of the assets used at that time in connection with the bank's business carried on in Canada, and

(b) the amount equal to the product of

(i) an interest rate to be prescribed by regulation, and

(ii) the amount, if any, by which 95% of the total value of the assets used in the year in connection with the bank's business carried on in Canada exceeds the total amount of all indebtedness described in subparagraph (a).

**Department of Finance news release, February 11, 1999**: *Determining Branch Interest Expense*

It is proposed that a Canadian branch of a foreign bank be permitted to deduct, in computing its income subject to tax in Canada, interest both in respect of money borrowed directly from third parties ("direct debt"), and on account of money borrowed indirectly through its home office ("allocated debt"). Deductibility is allowed only to the extent that the amount of the foreign bank's indebtedness incurred in respect of its Canadian business does not exceed 95% of the value of assets used in connection with its Canadian business.

The amount of interest that may be deducted in respect of direct debt will be based on the actual expenses incurred by the Canadian branch. For administrative simplicity, interest on allocated debt will be deemed to be the excess of the 95% indebtedness limit over the amount of debt directly incurred by the branch, multiplied by a prescribed interest rate. It is not anticipated that a fixed rate or benchmark will be prescribed for this purpose; rather, the prescription will describe relevant criteria such as market rates and the use of funds.

**Department of Finance news release, May 11, 1999**: See under 248(1)"authorized foreign bank".

## Proposed Addition — 20.3 [Weak currency loans]

**Technical Notes**: New section 20.3 limits the deductibility of interest expenses and adjusts foreign exchange gains and losses in respect of weak currency debts and associated hedging transactions.

Where a currency is weak, in that it is expected to decline in value relative to a reference currency, the interest rate on a loan in the weak currency will generally be higher than on a loan on similar terms in the reference currency. The higher rate reflects the market's expectation that the amount of the loan expressed in the weak currency will be worth less in terms of the reference currency when the loan is repaid. Lenders generally demand a higher interest rate to compensate for this expected depreciation. If, as expected, the weak currency depreciates, the borrower will realize a foreign exchange gain when the principal of the loan is repaid in the depreciated foreign currency. In economic terms, this gain compensates for the higher interest payments made during the term of the loan. Hedging transactions may be used to fix the reference currency cost of the interest and principal payments that are required to be made in the weak currency.

To ensure certainty, new section 20.3 sets out specific rules concerning the taxation of weak currency debts to the debtor.

**Notice of Ways and Means Motion, federal budget, February 28, 2000**: *Weak Currency Debt*

(28) That a "weak currency debt" be defined as indebtedness incurred by a taxpayer at a particular time after February 27, 2000, in respect of a borrowing of money or an acquisition of property, in a currency (the "weak currency") other than Canadian currency, where

(a) at any time (the "exchange date") the taxpayer uses the borrowed money or the acquired property, directly or indirectly, to acquire funds, or settle an obligation, in another currency (the "final currency")

(i) which funds are used for the purpose of earning income from a business or property and are not used to acquire funds in a different currency, or

(ii) which obligation was incurred for the purpose of earning income from a business or property and was not incurred to acquire funds in a different currency,

(b) the amount of the indebtedness (together with any other indebtedness that can reasonably be regarded as having been incurred as part of a series of weak currency debt transactions that includes the incurring of the indebtedness) exceeds $500,000, and

(c) the rate at which interest is payable in the weak currency in respect of the indebtedness exceeds by more than 2 percentage points (200 basis points) the rate at which interest would have been payable in the final currency if at the particular time the taxpayer had incurred an equivalent amount of indebtedness in the final currency on the same terms, with such modifications as the difference in currency requires.

(29) That the following rules apply in respect of a weak currency debt of a taxpayer (other than a corporation described in one or more of paragraphs (a), (b), (c) and (e) of

the definition "specified financial institution" in subsection 248(1) of the Act):

(a) no deduction on account of interest that accrues on the indebtedness after the later of June 30, 2000 and the exchange date shall exceed the amount (expressed in Canadian currency) of interest in the final currency that would have accrued after that day if, at the time of incurring the indebtedness, the taxpayer had instead incurred an equivalent amount of indebtedness in the final currency on the same terms, with such modifications as the difference in currency requires;

(b) the taxpayer's foreign exchange gain or loss

(i) on the settlement or extinguishment of the indebtedness, and

(ii) on the settlement of any hedge in respect of the indebtedness

shall be on income account [see 39(2) — ed.]; and

(c) in computing the taxpayer's foreign exchange gain or loss on the settlement or extinguishment of the indebtedness, the amount of any interest on the indebtedness that was not deductible because of this paragraph shall be treated as an additional amount paid by the taxpayer to settle or extinguish the indebtedness.

(30) That in applying the rules described in paragraph (29),

(a) a hedge in respect of the indebtedness be defined as any agreement entered into by the taxpayer

(i) that can reasonably be regarded as having been entered into by the taxpayer primarily to reduce the risk to the taxpayer, with respect to payments of principal or interest on the indebtedness, of currency fluctuations, and

(ii) that is identified by the taxpayer as a hedge in respect of the indebtedness in a written notice filed with the Minister on or before the later of July 31, 2000 and the 30th day after the taxpayer agrees to the hedge;

(b) where there is a hedge in respect of any portion of interest in the weak currency paid or payable on the indebtedness, the amount (expressed in Canadian currency) paid or payable in the weak currency for a period on account of interest be deemed to be that amount minus the amount of any foreign exchange gain, or plus the amount of any foreign exchange loss, on the hedge in respect of the interest paid or payable for the period; and

(c) if the amount (expressed in the weak currency) of the indebtedness is decreased before maturity by a repayment of principal, the amount (expressed in the weak currency) repaid be deemed *ab initio* to have been a separate indebtedness and the amount (expressed in the weak currency) of the original indebtedness be reduced accordingly.

**Federal budget, supplementary information, February 28, 2000**: *Weak Currency Borrowings*

"Weak currency borrowings" are transactions that take advantage of the fact that, where a currency is expected to decline in value relative to some reference currency, the interest rate on a loan in the "weak" currency will be higher than on a loan on similar terms in the reference currency. The higher rate reflects the market's expectation that the borrowed amount will be worth less in terms of the reference currency when the loan is repaid. Lenders demand a higher interest rate to compensate for this expected depreciation.

A taxpayer pursuing tax advantages may borrow in a weak currency, even though that currency is not required in its business. The proceeds of the weak currency loan are converted into a currency that is needed for business purposes, but the interest obligation remains in the weak currency at the higher rate. The higher interest payments form the basis for a claimed interest deduction that is higher than would be available if the taxpayer had borrowed directly in the final currency. If, as expected, the currency of the borrowing depreciates, the taxpayer will realize a foreign exchange gain on maturity when the principal of the loan is repaid in the depreciated foreign currency. While this gain compensates for the higher interest payments, the taxpayer may treat it as a capital gain, which would be taxed at a preferential rate. The full deduction of additional interest, coupled with capital gains treatment of the offsetting appreciation, produces an inappropriate result which has been challenged by the Canada Customs and Revenue Agency.

The Supreme Court of Canada has recently ruled [*Shell Canada Ltd. v. The Queen*, [1999] 4 C.T.C. 313 — ed.] that specific rules in the *Income Tax Act* do not deny the tax benefits sought by proponents of these weak currency structures. However, the disputed transaction preceded the introduction of the Act's General Anti-Avoidance Rule (GAAR). The Government's position that the GAAR applies to weak currency borrowings is currently being adjudicated by the courts. [The government lost the first round: *Canadian Pacific Ltd.*, [2001] 1 C.T.C. 2190 (TCC) — ed.]

While the Government is pursuing its challenge of these transactions under the current law, prudent risk management supports the introduction, for greater certainty, of specific legislative rules defining particular weak currency arrangements and setting out their appropriate tax treatment. Essentially, a weak currency borrowing will be treated for tax purposes as equivalent to a direct borrowing in the currency that is used by the taxpayer to earn income.

The proposed rules will apply when a taxpayer incurs foreign currency indebtedness that meets the following conditions:

- the proceeds from the indebtedness are not used directly in the currency of the debt, but rather are converted into another currency and used in that form by the taxpayer;
- the interest rate on the debt is more than two percentage points above the rate on an equivalent borrowing in the currency used to earn income; and
- the principal amount of the debt exceeds $500,000.

Where these conditions are met, the following rules will apply:

- deductible interest on the indebtedness will be limited to the interest that would have been payable if the taxpayer had incurred an equivalent debt directly in the currency of use;
- the total of interest expenses disallowed over the term of the indebtedness will be subtracted from the foreign exchange gain or loss realized when the debt is repaid; and
- any foreign exchange gain or loss realized on repayment of the debt, and the gain or loss on any associated hedge, will be on income account.

The measure will not apply to corporations whose principal business is the lending of money.

# Part I
Income Tax Act, Part I, Division B

It is proposed that this measure apply as of July 1, 2000, in respect of indebtedness incurred after February 27, 2000. This will allow interested parties an opportunity to comment on the proposal.

*Example*

- Assume that Canco would have to pay interest at 8% on a 2-year Canadian dollar (C$) loan, while it would pay 13% on a 2-year Country F dollar (F$) loan.
- As Canco needs C$1m for use in its business, it borrows F$2m in 2001 and immediately converts the borrowed money into C$1m.
- Canco makes the following payments under the loan:

| Payment | F$ value | Exchange rate | C$ value |
|---|---|---|---|
| (all amounts in 000s) | | | |
| Interest — 2002 | F$260 | 0.4779 | C$124 |
| Interest — 2003 | F$260 | 0.4567 | C$119 |
| Principal — 2003 | F$2,000 | 0.4567 | C$913 |

- Canco realizes a foreign exchange gain when it repays the debt in depreciated F$:

| | |
|---|---|
| Value of principal on borrowing: | C$1,000 |
| Value of principal on repayment: | C$913 |
| Foreign exchange gain: | C$87 |

*Proposed Tax Treatment*

- Since Canco could have borrowed the C$ equivalent of F$2m (C$1m) on the same terms for 8%, Canco's annual interest deduction is limited to 8% of C$1m, i.e., $80,000:

| Year | Interest paid | Deductible | Not deductible in year |
|---|---|---|---|
| (all amounts in 000s) | | | |
| 2002 | C$124 | C$80 | C$44 |
| 2003 | C$119 | C$80 | C$39 |
| Total | C$243 | C$160 | C$83 |

- The amount of the non-deductible interest is aggregated over the term of the loan and deducted in computing the foreign exchange gain realized on repayment of the loan. The resulting gain is treated on income account:

| | |
|---|---|
| Foreign exchange gain: | C$87 |
| Undeducted interest: | C$83 |
| Adjusted foreign exchange gain (loss): | C$4 |

- The application of the rule does not fully eliminate the exchange gain. This is because the rule takes the simplifying approach of allowing an interest deduction over the term of the loan at a fixed percentage (8 per cent) of the original C$ value of the principal. A more accurate — but more complex — approach would treat the non-deductible interest paid each year as a prepayment of principal. Such an approach would only allow an interest deduction in subsequent years for the fixed percentage of the reduced principal — effectively disallowing more interest over the term of the loan than under the proposed rule.

## 20.3 (1) Weak currency debt [Kiwi loans] — interpretation
— The definitions in this subsection apply in this section.

**"exchange date"** in respect of a weak currency debt of a taxpayer means, if the debt is incurred or assumed by the taxpayer

(a) in respect of borrowed money that is denominated in the final currency, the debt that is incurred or assumed by the taxpayer; and

(b) in respect of borrowed money that is not denominated in the final currency, or in respect of the acquisition of property, the day on which the taxpayer uses the borrowed money or the acquired property, directly or indirectly, to acquire funds that are, or to settle an obligation that is, denominated in the final currency.

**Technical Notes**: Under paragraph 20.3(2)(a), the limitation on deductibility of interest in respect of a weak currency debt (also defined in subsection 20.3(1)) applies as of the "exchange date" in respect of the debt. This expression is defined in two ways reflecting two different circumstances. If the weak currency debt is incurred or assumed by the taxpayer in respect of borrowed money denominated in the final currency (defined within the definition "weak currency debt"), the exchange date is the day the debt was assumed or incurred. On the other hand, if the debt is incurred or assumed in respect of borrowed money that is not denominated in the final currency, or in respect of the acquisition of property, the exchange date is the day on which the taxpayer uses the borrowed money or the acquired property, directly or indirectly, to acquire funds or settle an obligation denominated in the final currency. Thus, where the taxpayer holds the borrowed funds or acquired property for a period of time before using them to acquire funds, or settle an obligation, in a different currency, the interest limitation rule does not apply until that initial conversion takes place. The use of the phrase "directly or indirectly" is intended to cause the exchange date to be the date of the first such conversion in currency, even if the initial conversion is an intermediate step to a subsequent conversion into the final currency.

**"hedge"** in respect of a weak currency debt owing by a taxpayer means any agreement made by the taxpayer

(a) that can reasonably be regarded as having been made by the taxpayer primarily to reduce the taxpayer's risk, with respect to payments of principal or interest in respect of the debt, of fluctuations in the value of the weak currency; and

(b) that is identified by the taxpayer as a hedge in respect of the debt in a designation in prescribed form filed with the Minister on or before the 30th day after the day the taxpayer enters into the agreement.

**Technical Notes**: The expression "hedge" is defined in respect of a weak currency debt as any agreement that can reasonably be regarded as having been entered into by the taxpayer primarily to reduce the risk of fluctuations in the value of the weak currency, relative to the final currency of use or some other currency of reference such as Canadian currency, in respect of interest or principal payments on the debt.

It is contemplated that hedges could be in a variety of legal forms such as forward and futures contracts, options, swaps and long positions in assets denominated in foreign currency. A hedge need not eliminate all risk associated with currency exposure in a weak currency debt; a contract that serves to reduce risks only partially is included.

In order to be treated as a hedge for the purposes of section 20.3, an agreement must also be identified by the taxpayer as a hedge in respect of the particular weak currency debt in a designation filed with the Minister of National Revenue within 30 days of the taxpayer entering into the hedge agreement. This requirement for up-front identification of the hedge is designed to eliminate any incentive to report or not report the existence of a hedge based on hindsight regarding its performance.

While this definition generally applies to taxation years that end after February 27, 2000, for hedge agreements entered into prior to July 2000, a hedge designation is considered timely if it is filed on or before the later of July 31, 2000 and the 30th day after the day the taxpayer agrees to the hedge.

**"weak currency debt"** of a taxpayer means a debt in a foreign currency (in this section referred to as the "weak currency"), incurred or assumed by the taxpayer at a particular time after February 27, 2000, in respect of a borrowing of money or an acquisition of property,

(a) where

(i) the borrowed money is denominated in a currency (in this section referred to as the "final currency") other than the weak currency, is used for the purpose of earning income from a business or property and is not used to acquire funds in a currency other than the final currency,

(ii) the borrowed money or the acquired property is used, directly or indirectly, to acquire funds that are denominated in a currency (in this section referred to as the "final currency") other than the weak currency, that are used for the purpose of earning income from a business or property and that are not used to acquire funds in a currency other than the final currency, or

(iii) the borrowed money or the acquired property is used, directly or indirectly, to settle an obligation that is denominated in a currency (in this section referred to as the "final currency") other than the weak currency, that is incurred or assumed for the purpose of earning income from a business or property and that is not incurred or assumed to acquire funds in a currency other than the final currency;

(b) where the amount of the debt (together with any other debt that would, but for this paragraph, be a weak currency debt, and that can reasonably be regarded as having been incurred or assumed by the taxpayer as part of a series of transactions that includes the incurring or assumption of the debt) exceeds $500,000; and

(c) where the rate at which interest is payable in the weak currency in respect of the debt exceeds by more than two percentage points the rate at which interest would have been payable in the final currency if at the particular time the taxpayer had instead incurred or assumed an equivalent amount of debt in the final currency on the same terms (other than the rate of interest), with such modifications as the difference in currency requires.

**Technical Notes**: A "weak currency debt" is defined as a debt denominated in a foreign currency — the weak currency — that is incurred or assumed by the taxpayer after February 27, 2000 in respect of either a borrowing of money or an acquisition of property and that meets a number of other conditions set out in the three paragraphs of the definition.

Paragraph (a) of the definition sets out several alternative conditions, of which one must be met, linking the weak currency to another currency — referred to as the "final currency" — used directly for earning income. The final currency is defined with respect to whichever of these conditions is met. Each subparagraph requires that in order to constitute the final currency, the associated funds must be used, or the associated obligation be incurred or assumed, for the purpose of earning income and not to acquire funds in a different currency. This ensures that if the transaction involves conversion into an intermediate currency or currencies before conversion to the currency employed in the direct income-earning use, only the last currency, directly used for earning income, is considered the "final currency".

The three alternatives are as follows:

(i) The borrowed money advanced by the lender is in the final currency but the taxpayer is obliged to repay the debt in the weak currency.

(ii) The taxpayer uses the borrowed money or acquired property, directly or indirectly, to acquire funds in the final currency. This condition encompasses cases where the weak currency is exchanged into one or more other currencies as an intermediate step prior to being exchanged into the final currency. An example involving property would be the purchase of a commodity on credit where the debt for the unpaid purchase price is denominated in the weak currency and the commodity is subsequently sold for proceeds denominated in the final currency, or sold for proceeds that are used to purchase funds in the final currency.

(iii) The taxpayer uses the borrowed money or acquired property, directly or indirectly, to settle an obligation in the final currency.

Paragraph (b) of the definition specifies that, to be considered a weak currency debt, a debt must be of an amount exceeding $500,000. In determining whether this threshold is met, the debt is combined with any other weak currency debts (that is, debts that would be weak currency debts but for the $500,000 threshold) that were incurred or assumed by the taxpayer as part of a series of transactions. This ensures, for example, that the rules cannot be avoided by structuring a weak currency borrowing as a series of smaller borrowings each of which is exempt because it is below the size threshold.

Paragraph (c) of the definition provides that a debt is only considered a weak currency debt if the interest rate in the weak currency is more than two percentage points (200 basis points) higher than the interest rate that would have obtained in the final currency if the taxpayer had incurred an equivalent amount of debt in the final currency on the same terms, other than the rate of interest. For this purpose, terms other than the interest rate may be varied, but only to the extent required to accommodate the currency difference — e.g. where comparable debt markets in the two currencies have different conventions as to interest payment dates.

**(2) Interest and gain** — Notwithstanding any other provision of this Act, the following rules apply in respect of a weak currency debt of a taxpayer (other than a corporation described in one or more of paragraphs (a), (b), (c) and (e) of the definition "specified financial institution" in subsection 248(1)):

(a) no deduction on account of interest that accrues on the debt after the day that is the later of June 30, 2000 and the exchange date shall exceed the amount of interest that would, if at the time of incurring or assuming the debt the taxpayer had instead incurred or assumed an equivalent amount of debt, the principal and interest in respect of which were denominated in the final currency, on the same terms (other than the rate of interest and with such other modifications as the difference in currency requires), have accrued on the equivalent debt after that day;

(b) the amount, if any, of the taxpayer's gain or loss (in this section referred to as a "foreign exchange gain or loss") for a taxation year

(i) on the settlement or extinguishment of the debt, or

(ii) on the performance or settlement of any hedge in respect of the debt

that arises because of the fluctuation in the value of any currency shall be included or deducted, as the case may be, in computing the taxpayer's income for the year from the business or the property to which the debt relates; and

(c) the amount of any interest on the debt that was, because of this subsection, not deductible is deemed, for the purpose of computing the taxpayer's foreign exchange gain or loss on the settlement or extinguishment of the debt, to be an amount paid by the taxpayer to settle or extinguish the debt.

**Technical Notes**: New subsection 20.3(2) sets out several substantive rules that apply to a taxpayer that is a debtor in respect of a weak currency debt. These rules do not apply to a corporation that is a bank, trust company, credit union or a corporation whose principal business is lending money at arm's length.

Paragraph 20.3(2)(a) limits the amount that may be deducted on account of interest expense in respect of a weak currency debt to the amount that would have been deductible under the Act if the taxpayer had instead incurred or assumed an equivalent amount of debt in the final currency (defined within the definition "weak currency debt" in subsection 20.3(1)) on the same terms (other than the rate of interest). Under the Act, the deductible interest on such a final currency borrowing could not exceed a reasonable amount, generally determined based on market interest rates in the final currency on debts negotiated at the same time and on the same terms as the weak currency debt. Thus, if a taxpayer borrows in a weak currency and converts the proceeds into another currency — the final currency — for use to earn income, the interest deduction for any particular period is limited to the amount that would have been deductible for that period if the taxpayer had instead borrowed directly, and paid interest, in the final currency.

The limitation in paragraph 20.3(2)(a) applies with respect to interest that accrues on a weak currency debt after the later of June 30, 2000 and the exchange date (defined in subsection 20.3(1)) in respect of the debt.

Paragraph 20.3(2)(b) provides that any foreign exchange gain or loss on the settlement or extinguishment of the weak currency debt, or on the performance or settlement of any hedge (defined in subsection 20.3(1)) in respect of the debt, is on income account. Regardless of whether the debt itself is considered to be on capital or income account, it is considered appropriate to treat the foreign currency gains or losses on income account, since foreign exchange gains and losses anticipated by the market will typically be reflected in interest rates and the Act allows deductibility of interest expense. For symmetry, a hedge in respect of the exchange rate movements that produce such gains and losses is also treated as being on income account.

Paragraph 20.3(2)(c) provides that, for the purpose of computing the taxpayer's foreign exchange gain or loss on the settlement or extinguishment of a weak currency debt, any interest expense for which a deduction is denied by new subsection 20.3 is deemed to be an amount paid by the taxpayer to settle or extinguish the debt. This rule ensures that the amount of denied interest reduces the amount of any foreign exchange gain on settlement and increases the amount of any foreign exchange loss on settlement. In economic terms, the higher interest cost of the weak currency debt is generally expected to be offset by a foreign exchange gain on maturity. Since deductibility of the excess interest cost is denied under paragraph 20.3(2)(a), it is considered appropriate to reduce the amount of the foreign exchange gain (or increases the amount of the foreign exchange loss) for tax purposes in recognition that the expected gain or loss can be viewed as compensation for the excess interest expense.

**(3) Hedges** — In applying subsection (2) in circumstances where a taxpayer has entered into a hedge in respect of a weak currency debt, the amount paid or payable in the weak currency for a taxation year on account of interest on the debt, or paid in the weak currency in the year on account of the debt's principal, shall be decreased by the amount of any foreign exchange gain, or increased by the amount of any foreign exchange loss, on the hedge in respect of the amount so paid or payable.

**Technical Notes**: New subsection 20.3(3) indicates how the rules in subsection 20.3(2) are to be applied when a taxpayer has entered into a hedge (defined in subsection 20.3(1)) in respect of a weak currency debt. In applying those rules, the amount (which under the Act is measured in Canadian dollars) paid or payable in the weak currency on account of interest or principal on the debt is decreased by the amount of any foreign exchange gain, or increased by the amount of any foreign exchange loss, on the hedge in respect of the amount so paid or payable. This ensures that in applying the rules in subsection 20.3(2), the hedge is integrated with the weak currency debt.

Thus, with respect to interest expenses, it is the taxpayer's net interest cost incorporating hedge gains or losses that is taken into account rather than the interest cost based solely on the current Canadian dollar value of the interest amounts paid or payable. Likewise, with respect to principal payments, it is the net amount repaid incorporating hedge gains or losses that is taken into account rather than solely the current Canadian dollar value of the principal amount paid.

**(4) Repayment of principal** — If the amount (expressed in the weak currency) outstanding on account of principal in respect of a particular weak currency debt is reduced before maturity (whether by repayment or otherwise), the amount (expressed in the weak currency) of the reduction is deemed, except for the purposes of determining the rate of interest that would have been charged on an equivalent loan in the final currency and applying paragraph (b) of the definition "weak currency debt" in subsection (1), to have been a separate debt from the time the debt was incurred or assumed by the taxpayer.

**Technical Notes**: New subsection 20.3(4) deals with repayments and other reductions in principal owing under a weak currency debt. If the principal amount outstanding (expressed in the weak currency) is reduced before maturity, the amount of the reduction is deemed to have been a separate debt from the time the debt was incurred or assumed by the taxpayer. This ensures that the rules in section 20.3 will operate on each portion of the debt. Thus, for example, paragraph 20.3(2)(a) will limit the amount of interest deductible in respect of a particular portion of the debt based on a comparison with the interest that would have been deductible if an amount equivalent to the particular portion had been borrowed in the final currency. The operation of the rule in respect of the particular portion will not be affected by the repayment of another portion of the principal.

The separate debt rule does not apply for the purpose of determining the rate of interest that would have been charged in the final currency. This ensures that the comparable final currency interest rate is the one that would apply to a borrowing of the entire original amount of the principal, not the rate that would apply to a separate borrowing of a portion of that amount, which might be a higher rate due to a loss of economies of scale. Similarly, the $500,000 threshold in paragraph (b) of the definition "weak currency debt" in subsection 20.3(1) is applied to the entire principal amount and not to any portion of it segregated by the deeming rule.

**Application**: The December 21, 2000 draft legislation, s. 8, will add section 20.3, applicable to taxation years that end after February 27, 2000.

By subsec. 8(3) of the amending legislation, a designation described in para. (b) of the definition "hedge" in subsec. 20.3(1) is deemed to have been filed in a timely manner if it is filed on or before the later of July 31, 2000 and the 30th day after the day the taxpayer agrees to the hedge.

**Definitions [s. 20.3]**: "amount", "borrowed money", "business" — 248(1); "corporation" — 248(1), *Interpretation Act* 35(1); "exchange date" — 20.3(1); "final currency" — 20.3(1)"weak currency"(a)(i)-(iii); "foreign currency" — 248(1); "hedge" — 20.3(1); "Minister", "prescribed", "property", "specific financial institution" — 248(1); "taxation year" — 249; "taxpayer" — 248(1); "weak currency" — 20.3(1)"weak currency debt"; "weak currency debt" — 20.3(1).

## Proposed Addition [on hold] — 20.1 [*sic*], 20.2 [*sic*] [December 1991 version]

**20.1 (1) Money borrowed for distribution** — For the purpose of computing the income of a corporation or partnership (in this section referred to as the "distributor") for a particular taxation year, such part of the total of all amounts each of which is an amount outstanding at a particular time in that year on account of borrowed money

(a) used in a taxation year (in this subsection referred to as the "distribution year") that is the particular year or a taxation year preceding the particular year to make a distribution, and

(b) in respect of which a written designation has not been made under this section

as does not exceed the total of

(c) the lesser of

(i) the amount that would be the distributor's equity under subsection (2) at the beginning of the particular year, and

(ii) the amount that would be the distributor's equity under subsection (2) at the end of the particular year

if each amount owing in respect of borrowed money used by the distributor in or after the distribution year to make a distribution were nil, and

(d) the amount, if any, by which

(i) the total of all amounts each of which is the distributor's non-capital loss for the distribution year, for a taxation year ending after the distribution year and before the particular year or for the particular year

exceeds

(ii) the total of all amounts each of which is the distributor's income for the distribution year, for a taxation year ending after the distribution year and before the particular year or for the particular year shall be deemed to be borrowed money used at the particular time for the purpose of earning income from the business or businesses carried on by the distributor at that time (or, where the distributor is not carrying on business at that time, from the properties of the distributor at that time).

**Application**: See end of s. 20.1.

**Technical Notes**: The overall effect of new sections 20.1 and 20.2 is to treat money borrowed by a corporation or partnership, and used to make a distribution of retained earnings or capital, as having been used for the purpose of earning income from a business or property. Since interest on borrowed money used to earn business or property income may be deducted under paragraph 20(1)(c), new sections 20.1 and 20.2 may permit the deduction of interest on borrowings used to make distributions, subject to certain constraints.

Section 20.1 will govern the treatment of borrowed money used to make distributions after the date on which this legislation is issued in final form, while section 20.2 will apply with respect to borrowings associated with distributions made before that time. For the purposes of the following commentary, however, borrowings and distributions to which section 20.1 will apply are referred to as "future" borrowings and distributions, while those to which section 20.2 will apply are referred to as "current" borrowings and distributions.

The amount of borrowed money eligible for this treatment is determined by reference to the "equity" of the distributor (the corporation or partnership) or, in the case of current distributions, by reference to its "adjusted equity". A distributor's equity is generally the tax cost of its assets, less its debts, while its adjusted equity is generally based on the carrying value of its property, determined under generally accepted accounting principles, less its liabilities.

Section 20.1, which applies to borrowed money used for future distributions, includes two mechanisms for determining whether interest on a particular borrowed amount will be deductible in a particular year. In the usual case, all outstanding amounts of borrowed money used to make distributions in a given year will be totalled, and the total will be compared to the distributor's equity at the beginning and end of the particular year. If the total amount outstanding on account of borrowed money used for distributions is less than or equal to the lesser of the distributor's opening and its year-end equity, the full amount of those borrowings will be treated as having been used to earn business or property income. If, on the other hand, those borrowings exceed the distributor's equity and non-capital losses incurred by the distributor since the year in which the distribution was made, the excess borrowings will continue to be treated as having been used to make distributions. This mechanism is referred to in these notes as the "basic method".

The second mechanism provided by section 20.1 is available to any distributor as an alternative to the system described above. Under this option, borrowed money used to make a future distribution is treated as having been used to acquire one or more of the distributor's properties. The distributor may select which properties to designate in this way, and the subsequent use of those properties will govern the tax treatment of interest on the borrowed money used to make the distribution, in the same manner as if it had actually been used to acquire the properties. This second option is referred to in these notes as the "allocation method".

A distributor may choose to apply the basic method to some future distributions, and the allocation method to others. The allocation method is, however, elective, and may only be chosen within a fixed period after the distributor's tax for the year of the distribution is assessed.

Where borrowed money is used to make a current distribution, section 20.2 provides that a modified version of the basic method — based on the accounting rather than the tax values of the distributor's property — will apply. No allocation method is available for current distributions.

Subsection 20.1(1) provides a short-form approach to the establishment of tax recognition of interest on borrowings used to make future distributions. Under this approach, referred to in these notes as the "basic method", interest deductibility is based on the distributor's equity, measuring equity by reference to holdings of income-producing properties. This basic method may be contrasted to the allocation method, under which borrowed money used for distributions is treated as having been used to acquire particular properties, with the tax treatment of interest on the borrowing following from the use to which that property is put.

The basic method found in subsection 20.1(1) and the allocation method (set out in subsection 20.1(3)) will often produce identical, or at least similar, results. However, there will be situations in which a distributor may prefer one method to the other. For example:

- where the borrowing is a short-term one, and either system will provide interest deductibility over that term, the simplicity of the basic method may make it preferable;
- where a longer-term borrowing has been made, and a distributor with sufficient equity to ensure deductibility has no intention of altering the composition or use of its property, the basic method may again be appropriate; and
- where a distributor prefers to capitalize its interest expense on the borrowed money — under section 21 with respect to depreciable property or under subsection 18(3) for land — the allocation method may prove beneficial.

Certain special expressions are used in describing the basic method provided by subsection 20.1(1) for determining the treatment of interest on borrowed money used to make future distributions. The year in which the borrowed money in question was used for a distribution of retained earnings or capital is called the "distribution year," while the year in respect of which a taxpayer wishes to deduct an interest expense on the borrowed money is called the "particular year."

Subsection 20.1(1) treats borrowings used to make a distribution in the distribution year and outstanding at a particular time in the particular year as having been used at that time for the purpose of earning income from the business or businesses carried on by the distributor at that time. Where the distributor is not carrying on business at that time, the borrowings will be treated as having been used in respect of properties held by the distributor at that time.

The amount of the borrowings used to make distributions in a distribution year which will be treated in this manner

Subdivision b — Income or Loss from a Business or Property    S. 20.1(4)(a)(iii)

is limited to the lesser of the distributor's equity at the beginning of the particular year and its equity at the end of that year (ignoring any liabilities in respect of distributions made in or after the distribution year). Since this test measures equity from year to year, events which alter the distributor's equity may affect the amount of interest which may be deducted. In particular, operating losses occurring after a distribution would reduce equity to the extent they were reflected in a decrease in the tax cost of the distributor's assets. To prevent this result, any excess of non-capital losses for the years between the distribution year and the particular year, inclusive, over income for those years is included in computing the amount of borrowed money eligible for the treatment provided under subsection 20.1(1).

**Related Provisions**: 20.1(2) — Meaning of "equity"; 20.1(3) — Alternative allocation; 20.2 — Earlier money borrowed for distribution.

**(2) Equity** — For the purpose of subsection (1), a distributor's equity at any time in a taxation year is the amount that would be the distributor's equity at that time under subsection (7) if

(a) the cost amount to the distributor of each property

(i) that was not acquired for the purpose of earning income therefrom or from a business,

(ii) that is an interest in a life insurance policy,

(iii) that is property the income from which would be exempt,

(iv) that is land, other than land that can reasonably be considered to have been, in the year, used or held, as the case may be, as described in paragraph 18(2)(c) or (d), or

(v) in respect of which any interest payable for the year would, by reason of subsection 18(3.1), not be deductible in computing the distributor's income for the year

were nil, and

(b) each amount owing in respect of borrowed money used by the distributor to acquire a property described in paragraph (a), or in respect of an amount payable by the distributor to acquire such a property, were nil.

**Technical Notes**: Subsection 20.1(2) makes certain adjustments to a distributor's equity, for the purpose of applying subsection 20.1(1). The general effect of these adjustments is to limit the amount of borrowed money in respect of which a distributor may deduct interest to what might be described as the distributor's income-earning equity. Since the starting-point for any determination of a distributor's equity is the definition in subsection 20.1(7), subsections 20.1(2) and (7) should be read together.

Paragraph 20.1(2)(a) requires that the amount of the distributor's equity be determined under subsection 20.1(7) as though the cost amount of certain types of property were nil. Properties so excluded from the computation of the distributor's equity are: any property not acquired for the purpose of earning income therefrom or from a business; any interest in a life insurance policy; any property

the income from which would be exempt; any land, other than land used in a business (except a real estate business) or held primarily for the purpose of producing income therefrom; and property in respect of which interest payable would, because of subsection 18(3.1), not be deductible.

In addition, paragraph 20.1(2)(b) requires that amounts owing in respect of borrowed money used to acquire property described in paragraph 20.1(2)(a) be ignored in computing a distributor's equity for the purpose of subsection 20.1(1).

**(3) Alternative determination** — For the purposes of this Part, where a distributor has used borrowed money at any time to make a distribution, that portion of the borrowed money that has, in a written designation made under this section, been allocated to a property or qualified expenditure of the distributor shall be deemed to have been used at that time to acquire the property or to make the qualified expenditure.

**Technical Notes**: Subsection 20.1(3) permits the use of a specific allocation method for the treatment of borrowings used to make distributions — that is, borrowed money used, after the date on which these amendments are issued in final form, by a corporation to pay a dividend, to redeem, acquire or cancel a share of its capital stock or to reduce its capital, or by a partnership to make a distribution of profits or capital or otherwise to reduce the interest of any person in the partnership. This optional alternative to the basic method treats such borrowed money as having been used to acquire one or more of the distributor's properties.

To use the allocation method, the distributor must make a written designation, allocating the borrowed money to one or more properties or "qualified expenditures" (defined in subsection 20.1(8) as, in essence, expenditures included in a resource pool or research and development pool of the distributor). In order to be valid, that written designation must accord with the requirements in subsections 20.1(5) and (6).

**Related Provisions**: 20.1(4) — Limits on allocation; 20.1(5) — Invalid designations; 20.1(6) — Form and filing of designation; 20.1(7) — Meaning of "equity".

**(4) Limits on allocation** — The amount allocated for the purpose of subsection (3) to a property or qualified expenditure in respect of borrowed money used at any time by a distributor to make a distribution shall be deemed to be

(a) in the case of a property, the lesser of the amount allocated by the distributor to the property and the amount, if any, by which

(i) in the case of a property that is included in an expenditure pool, the cost to the distributor of the property, and

(ii) in the case of any other property, the cost amount (or, where the property is an eligible capital property, $4/3$ of the cost amount) of the property to the distributor at that time

exceeds

(iii) the total of all amounts each of which is an amount owing immediately before that

211

time in respect of borrowed money used to acquire the property or in respect of an amount payable for the property, and

(b) in the case of a qualified expenditure, the lesser of the amount allocated by the distributor to the expenditure and the amount, if any, by which

(i) the amount of the expenditure

exceeds

(ii) the total of all amounts each of which is an amount owing immediately before that time in respect of borrowed money used to make the expenditure or in respect of an amount payable on account of the expenditure.

**Technical Notes**: Subsection 20.1(4) limits the amount of borrowed money that may be allocated to a given property or qualified expenditure for the purposes of the allocation method. In general, no more may be allocated to an asset than its net tax cost — that is, the amount, if any, by which its tax cost at the time of the distribution exceeds any amounts owing in respect of the asset.

Paragraph 20.1(4)(a) sets out the limits on allocations to properties. The amount allocated to a property (other than an eligible capital property or a property included in an expenditure pool) may not exceed the amount, if any, by which the cost amount of the property to the distributor at the time of distribution exceeds any amounts owing immediately before the distribution in respect of borrowed money used to acquire the asset or in respect of an amount payable for the asset. In the case of an eligible capital property, the limit is based upon ⁴/₃ of the property's cost amount, while for property included in an expenditure pool the limit is based upon the cost to the distributor of the property.

Paragraph 20.1(4)(b) sets out the limit on any allocation to a qualified expenditure. The amount so allocated may not exceed the amount, if any, by which the amount of the expenditure exceeds any amounts owing immediately before the time of distribution in respect of borrowed money used to make the expenditure or in respect of an amount payable on account of the expenditure.

**(5) Invalid designations** — For the purpose of this section, a designation made in respect of borrowed money used at any time by a distributor to make a distribution shall be deemed not to have been made where

(a) the total of all amounts each of which is the amount of that borrowed money allocated under the designation to a property or qualified expenditure exceeds the distributor's equity immediately before that time,

(b) the total of all amounts each of which is the amount of that borrowed money allocated under the designation to a property, or qualified expenditure, included in a particular expenditure pool exceeds the amount, if any, by which

(i) the amount of the particular expenditure pool at that time

exceeds

(ii) the aggregate of all amounts each of which is an amount owing immediately before that time in respect of borrowed money used by the distributor to acquire a property, or to make a qualified expenditure, in respect of which an amount is included in the particular expenditure pool, or in respect of an amount payable on account of such an expenditure or for such a property, or

(c) the designation is revoked in accordance with subsection (6) or another designation made in accordance with subsection (6) is filed in respect of that borrowed money after the time at which the designation was filed.

**Technical Notes**: Subsection 20.1(5) limits the total amount of borrowed money that may be allocated in any designation under subsection 20.1(3), as well as the amount that may be allocated to a particular expenditure pool. A designation which fails to comply with either limitation is deemed not to have been made. In addition, subsection 20.1(5) provides for the repudiation of a designation.

Paragraph 20.1(5)(a) sets out a global limit on allocations under a given designation. The total of all amounts of borrowed money so allocated may not exceed the distributor's equity, determined under new subsection 20.1(7), immediately before the time of distribution.

Paragraph 20.1(5)(b) similarly limits allocations made to particular expenditure pools. The total of all amounts of borrowed money allocated under a given designation to qualified expenditures or properties included in a particular pool may not exceed the amount of the pool, at the time of distribution, less all amounts owing immediately before that time in respect of borrowed money used to make expenditures or acquire property included in the pool, or in respect of amounts payable on account of expenditures or for properties.

Paragraph 20.1(5)(c) provides that a designation may be repudiated, either by explicit revocation or by the subsequent filing of another designation. Any revocation or subsequent filing must be in accordance with the requirements of subsection 20.1(6).

**(6) Designation** — A designation made in respect of borrowed money used at any time by a distributor to make a distribution, or a revocation of such a designation,

(a) shall, in the case of a corporation, be made by the corporation in its return of income under this Part for the taxation year that includes that time or in a prescribed form filed with the Minister within the period ending 90 days after the day on which a notice of assessment of tax payable under this Part for the year or notification that no tax is payable under this Part for the year is mailed to the corporation, and

(b) shall, in the case of a partnership, be made by a taxpayer that has authority to act for the partnership in a prescribed form filed with the Minister within the period ending 120 days after the end of the partnership's fiscal period that

Subdivision b — Income or Loss from a Business or Property    S. 20.1(7)

includes that time (or within such longer period as is permitted in writing by the Minister).

**Technical Notes**: The procedural requirements for designations under the allocation method are set out in subsection 20.1(6). A corporation wishing to apply the allocation method must make its designation either in its return of income under Part I for the taxation year that includes the time of distribution, or in a prescribed form filed within 90 days of the day on which an assessment of its Part I tax for the year (or notification that no such tax is payable) is mailed. In the case of a partnership, the designation must be made by a taxpayer with authority to act for the partnership, and must be made in a prescribed form filed within 120 days of the end of the partnership's fiscal period that includes the time of distribution (or within such longer period as the Minister of National Revenue may allow).

The same requirements apply to the revocation of designations contemplated by paragraph 20.1(5)(c).

**(7) Definition: equity** — For the purposes of this section (other than subsection (1)), a distributor's equity at any time is the amount, if any, by which the total of all amounts each of which is

(a) the amount of money owned by the distributor at that time,

(b) the cost amount to the distributor at that time of a property, other than

   (i) a Canadian resource property,

   (ii) a foreign resource property,

   (iii) an eligible capital property,

   (iv) a property in respect of which an amount is included in the amount determined under subparagraph 37(1)(b)(i) in respect of the distributor,

   (v) a share of the capital stock of a corporation of which the distributor is a specified shareholder, or

   (vi) an interest in a partnership where

   (A) the total of the distributor's share and the share of each person with whom the distributor does not deal at arm's length of the income of the partnership from any source for the fiscal period of the partnership that includes that time is, or may be, 10% or more of that income, or

   (B) the total of the distributor's share and the share of each person with whom the distributor does not deal at arm's length of the total amount that would be paid to all members of the partnership (otherwise than as a distribution of income referred to in clause (A)) if the partnership were wound up at that time is 10% or more of that amount,

(c) an amount equal to $4/3$ of the cumulative eligible capital of the distributor at that time in respect of a business of the distributor, or

(d) the amount of an expenditure pool of the distributor at that time

exceeds the total of all amounts each of which is

(e) an amount owing by the distributor at that time, other than an amount that is required to be paid after that time for the lease or rental of property,

(f) the amount of a reserve deducted, otherwise than under paragraph 20(1)(m.1), in computing the distributor's income for its last taxation year ending before that time,

(g) an amount deducted under subparagraph 40(1)(a)(iii) or 44(1)(e)(iii) in computing the distributor's gain for its last taxation year ending before that time from the disposition of a property,

(h) where the distributor has, in the period commencing 24 months before that time and ending at that time, entered into an agreement for the issue of a flow-through share (within the meaning assigned by paragraph 66(15)(d.1)) of the distributor, the amount, if any, by which the consideration for the share exceeds the aggregate of all amounts renounced in respect of the share under subsection 66(12.6), (12.62) or (12.64) before that time, or

(i) where the distributor is a member of a partnership at that time, the amount, if any, by which

   (i) the total of all amounts required by subsection 53(2) to be deducted in computing the adjusted cost base to the distributor of its interest in the partnership at that time

exceeds the total of

   (ii) the cost to the distributor of that interest determined for the purpose of computing the adjusted cost base to the distributor of that interest at that time, and

   (iii) the total of all amounts required by subsection 53(1) to be added to the cost to the distributor of that interest in computing its adjusted cost base to the distributor at that time.

**Technical Notes**: Subsection 20.1(7) contains the general definition of a distributor's "equity" for the purposes of section 20.1.

A distributor's equity at any time is, in broad terms, the tax cost of the distributor's assets at that time less its liabilities. Most properties are included in the equity calculation at their cost amount: exceptions include eligible capital property, Canadian and foreign resource properties, and properties dealt with under section 37 in respect of research and development. Eligible capital property is included under paragraph 20.1(7)(c), which adds to the distributor's equity an amount equal to $4/3$ of its cumulative eligible capital in respect of a business. Research and development properties form part of the expenditure pools (defined in subsection 20.1(8)), the amount of which is included by paragraph 20.1(7)(d) in equity of

213

both corporations and partnerships. Similarly, resource properties are included in the expenditure pools of corporations.

Shares of corporations of which the distributor is a specified shareholder are not included in equity. This exclusion reflects the fact that the value of a share in a corporation represents part of the value of the corporation's assets. Including the value of the share in the shareholder's equity while also including the value of those assets in the equity of the corporation would count the same value twice, and would artificially expand the overall interest deductibility available to both parties. The same considerations apply to significant (10% or more of income or capital) partnership interests, which are also excluded from equity.

The amounts deducted in computing a distributor's equity at any time are: all amounts owing by the distributor, other than amounts payable after that time as rent for property; reserves other than 20(1)(m.1) manufacturers' warranty reserves; capital gains reserves under subparagraph 40(1)(a)(iii) or 44(1)(e)(iii); unrenounced amounts in respect of flow-through shares; and the distributor's "negative" adjusted cost base in respect of any partnership of which it is a member.

**Notes**: The proposals in 20.1 and 20.2 are still subject to change, and revisions are expected to be released in the future. They are not expected to be enacted any time soon. With the enactment of new sections 20.1–20.3 in the meantime, sections 20.1 and 20.2 as included in the December 20, 1991 draft legislation would presumably be renumbered 20.4 and 20.5 if and when reintroduced.

Brian Ernewein of the Dept. of Finance stated at the 1998 Canadian Tax Foundation annual conference that some of these rules may not be needed in light of *Sherway Centre Ltd.*, [1998] 2 C.T.C. 343 (FCA). Other parts, such as borrowing for distribution, will likely be maintained. Revised draft legislation was expected during 1999. However, nothing has been released.

As reproduced above, draft 20.1(7)(b)(v) proposes to exclude from "equity" any shares of corporations of which the distributor is a "specified shareholder" (10% or more ownership, together with non-arm's length persons, of *any* class of shares). Concerns have been raised that, although double-counting is a legitimate worry, this limitation is unfair in some circumstances. The Department of Finance is receptive to alternative approaches on this issue, and is considering amending the proposals. Finance is also considering rules to carry these provisions through amalgamations and windups, and other changes. See the comments by Brian Ernewein of the Department of Finance in Couzin, Ernewein and Lawlor, "Interest Expense: December 20, 1991 Draft Amendments", *Proceedings of the 1992 Corporate Management Tax Conference* (Toronto: Canadian Tax Foundation), pp. 2:1–2:42.

**(8) Definitions** — For the purposes of this section,

(a) "cumulative Canadian exploration expense", "cumulative Canadian development expense" and "cumulative Canadian oil and gas property expense" have the meanings assigned by paragraphs 66.1(6)(b), 66.2(5)(b) and 66.4(5)(b) [now subsections 66.1(6), 66.2(5) and 66.4(5) — ed.] respectively;

**Technical Notes**: Paragraph 20.1(8)(a) provides that the terms "cumulative Canadian exploration expense", "cumulative Canadian development expense" and "cumulative Canadian oil and gas property expense" are to have the same meaning under section 20.1 as they do for the purposes of the resource rules in sections 66, 66.2 and 66.4. These terms are relevant for the definition of "expenditure pool" in paragraph 20.1(8)(c), and in determining the amount of such pools under subsection 20.1(9).

(b) a "distribution" means

(i) in the case of a corporation, the payment of an amount by the corporation as a dividend, on a redemption, acquisition or cancellation of a share of any class of its capital stock, or on a reduction of the capital in respect of any class of its capital stock, and

(ii) in the case of a partnership, the payment of an amount by the partnership as a distribution of profits or capital or as any other reduction in a person's interest in the partnership;

**Technical Notes**: The term "distribution" is relevant in establishing the range of uses of borrowed money to which section 20.1 applies. Those uses are, in the case of a corporation, the payment of a dividend, the redemption, acquisition or cancellation of a share of its capital stock and the reduction of its capital by any other means. In the case of a partnership, section 20.1 applies to the use of borrowed money to distribute profits or capital or otherwise to reduce the interest of any person in the partnership.

(c) an "expenditure pool" of a distributor means properties and expenditures in respect of which amounts are

(i) included in computing the amount that may be deducted under subsection 37(1) in computing the distributor's income for a taxation year, or

(ii) where the distributor is a corporation, included in computing the amount of the corporation's

(A) total Canadian exploration and development expenses,

(B) cumulative Canadian exploration expense,

(C) cumulative Canadian development expense,

(D) cumulative Canadian oil and gas property expense, or

(E) total foreign exploration and development expenses; and

(d) a "qualified expenditure" of a distributor means an expenditure, other than an expenditure made to acquire a property, that is included in an expenditure pool of the distributor.

**Technical Notes**: Paragraphs 20.1(8)(c) and (d) define the terms "expenditure pool" and "qualified expenditure" for the purposes of section 20.1. The purpose of these definitions is to allow the inclusion in a distributor's equity of the amount of its undeducted resource and research and development expenses.

Paragraph 20.1(8)(c) defines an expenditure pool as properties and expenditures that are included in computing the amount deductible under subsection 37(1) or are included in computing any of the various total (or cumulative) resource expenses. Paragraph 20.1(8)(d) defines a qualified expenditure as an expenditure, other than one made to acquire a property, that is included in an expenditure pool.

**Related Provisions**: 20.1(9) — Expenditure pool amount.

**(9) Expenditure pool amount** — For the purposes of this section, the amount of an expenditure pool of a distributor at any time is

(a) in the case of properties and expenditures in respect of which amounts are included in computing the amount that may be deducted under subsection 37(1) in computing the distributor's income for a taxation year, the amount, if any, by which

(i) the total of the amounts determined under paragraphs 37(1)(a) to (c.1)

would exceed

(ii) the total of the amounts determined under paragraphs 37(1)(d) to (h)

at that time if the distributor's taxation year or fiscal period, as the case may be, that includes that time had ended at that time, or

(b) where the distributor is a corporation,

(i) the total Canadian exploration and development expenses incurred by the corporation before that time except to the extent that such expenses were deducted in computing the income of any taxpayer for a taxation year ending before that time,

(ii) the corporation's cumulative Canadian exploration expense at that time,

(iii) the corporation's cumulative Canadian development expense at that time,

(iv) the corporation's cumulative Canadian oil and gas property expense at that time, or

(v) the total foreign exploration and development expenses incurred by the corporation before that time except to the extent that such expenses were deducted in computing the income of any taxpayer for a taxation year ending before that time.

**Technical Notes**: Subsection 20.1(9) describes the computation of the amount of an expenditure pool at any time. In the case of research and development expenses, the amount of the pool at any time is the amount, if any, by which the amounts determined under paragraphs 37(1)(a) to (c.1) would exceed the amounts determined under paragraphs 37(1)(d) to (h) if the distributor's taxation year or fiscal period had ended at that time. Similarly, in the case of the various resource expenses, the amount of each pool is the amount of undeducted expense at that time. For Canadian exploration expenses, Canadian development expenses and Canadian oil and gas property expenses, that result is achieved by reference to the corporation's cumulative expenses at the relevant time — a figure which takes into account deductions prior to that time. For Canadian and foreign exploration and development expenses, a specific exclusion of amounts deducted in computing income for taxation years before that time is necessary.

**Application**: The December 20, 1991 draft legislation (interest deductibility), s. 2, will add s. 20.1. No specific application date is given in the draft legislation; the Technical Notes (see the second paragraph under 20.1(1) above) state that it will apply to "borrowed money used to make distributions after the date on which this legislation is issued in final form".

**Notes**: 20.1 is expected to be both renumbered and amended. See Notes to 20.1(7) above.

**Definitions [s. 20.1 (December 1991 version)]**: "amount" — 20.1(9), 248(1); "arm's length" — 251(1); "assessment" — 248(1); "borrowed money", "business" — 248(1); "Canadian exploration and development expenses" — 66(15), 248(1); "Canadian resource property" — 66(15), 248(1); "corporation" — 248(1), *Interpretation Act* 35(1); "cost amount" — 248(1); "cumulative Canadian development expense" — 20.1(8)(a), 66.2(5); "cumulative Canadian exploration expense" — 20.1(8)(a), 66.1(6); "cumulative Canadian oil and gas property expense" — 20.1(8)(a), 66.4(5); "cumulative eligible capital" — 14(5), 248(1); "disposition" — 54; "distribution" — 20.1(8)(b); "distribution year", "distributor" — 20.1(1); "dividend" — 248(1); "eligible capital property" — 54, 248(1); "equity" — 20.1(2), (7); "exempt income" — 248(1); "expenditure pool" — 20.1(8)(c), 20.1(9); "fiscal period" — 249(2), 249.1; "foreign exploration and development expenses" — 66(15), 248(1); "foreign resource property" — 66(15), 248(1); "life insurance policy" — 138(12), 248(1); "Minister" — 248(1); "non-capital loss" — 111(8), 248(1); "person", "prescribed", "property" — 248(1); "qualified expenditure" — 20.1(8)(d); "share" — 248(1); "taxation year" — 249; "writing" — *Interpretation Act* 35(1).

**20.2 (1) Money borrowed for distribution** — For the purpose of computing the income of a corporation or partnership (in this section referred to as the "distributor") for a particular taxation year, such part of the amount outstanding at a particular time in that year on account of borrowed money used at any time (in this subsection referred to as the "time of distribution")

(a) in the case of a corporation, to pay a dividend, to redeem, acquire or cancel a share of any class of its capital stock or otherwise to reduce the capital in respect of any class of its capital stock, and

(b) in the case of a partnership, to make a distribution of profits or capital or otherwise to reduce the interest of any person in the partnership,

as does not exceed the distributor's adjusted equity immediately before the time of distribution shall be deemed to be borrowed money used for the purpose of earning income from the business or businesses carried on by the distributor at the particular time or, where the distributor is not carrying on business at that time, from the properties of the distributor at that time.

**Application**: See end of s. 20.2.

**Technical Notes**: Section 20.2 sets out a modified form of the basic method of determining the deemed use of money borrowed by a corporation or partnership and used to make a distribution of retained earnings or capital. This modified method applies with respect to current distributions — those made before the date on which this legislation is issued in final form. The central difference between this modified method and the basic method described in the notes to section 20.1 is the use in this method of the accounting value, rather than the tax value, of the distributor's property as the basis for measuring equity.

Subsection 20.2(1) treats borrowed money used to make current distributions of retained earnings or capital — that is, used for that purpose before the date on which this legislation is issued in final form — and outstanding at a particular time as having been used at that time for the purpose of earning income from the business or businesses carried on by the distributor at that time. Where the distributor is not carrying on business at that time, the borrowings will be treated as having been used in respect of properties held by the distributor at that time. The amount of the borrowings which will be treated in this manner is limited to the distributor's "adjusted equity" immediately before the time of distribution.

**Related Provisions**: 20.1 (December 1991 version) — Later money borrowed for distribution.

**Notes**: The proposals in 20.1 and 20.2 are still subject to change, and revisions are expected to be released in the future. They are not expected to be enacted any time soon. The Department of Finance has stated (in the paper referred to below, at p. 2:23):

> The purpose of section 20.2 is to provide legislative authority for Revenue Canada's practice in this regard. Accordingly, we have not intentionally undertaken any significant "policy" changes with this provision.

Brian Ernewein of the Dept. of Finance stated at the 1998 Canadian Tax Foundation annual conference that revised draft legislation could be expected during 1999. However, nothing had been released by January 15, 2000.

As currently proposed, draft 20.2(1)(a) will treat borrowed funds for redeeming shares the same way as borrowed funds for paying dividends. Under Revenue Canada's administrative assessing practice as set out in Interpretation Bulletin IT-80, however, the test for borrowed funds used to redeem shares (i.e., to return capital to shareholders) is less restrictive than that for paying dividends. Interest on the former is deductible to the extent the capital was used by the corporation for income-earning purposes. The Department of Finance has indicated that it will amend 20.2 to make it consistent with Revenue Canada's administrative practice. Any discrepancies should be brought to the attention of the Department. See the comments by Brian Ernewein of the Department of Finance in Couzin, Ernewein and Lawlor, "Interest Expense: December 20, 1991 Draft Amendments", *Proceedings of the 1992 Corporate Management Tax Conference* (Toronto: Canadian Tax Foundation), pp. 2:1–2:42.

With the enactment of new 20.1 by the 1993 technical bill, these proposed 20.1 and 20.2 will be renumbered 20.2 and 20.3 if and when reintroduced.

**I.T. Technical News**: No. 3 (use of a partner's assets by a partnership).

**(2) Definition: adjusted equity** — For the purposes of this section, the adjusted equity of a distributor at any time is the amount, if any, by which

(a) the carrying value at that time to the distributor of its property

exceeds the total of

(b) the total amount, determined in accordance with generally accepted accounting principles, of all liabilities of the distributor at that time other than liabilities in respect of borrowed money used to acquire properties described in paragraph (3)(d) or in respect of an amount payable to acquire such properties, and

(c) the total amount of any profits or gains, determined in accordance with generally accepted accounting principles, of the distributor from the disposition of property before that time to persons with whom the distributor does not deal at arm's length (to the extent that such profits or gains may reasonably be considered to be included in the amount determined under paragraph (a)).

**Technical Notes**: Subsection 20.2(2) defines "adjusted equity" for the purposes of section 20.2. The basis for computing a distributor's adjusted equity at any time is the carrying value of its property at that time, defined in subsection 20.2(3) as carrying value determined under generally accepted accounting principles (GAAP), subject to certain adjustments. Adjusted equity is the amount, if any, by which that carrying value exceeds the total of the distributor's total GAAP liabilities at that time and any profits or gains from non-arm's length dispositions (to the extent that such profits or gains are reflected in the carrying value of the distributor's property).

In computing a distributor's total liabilities, no account is taken of borrowed money used to acquire a property not acquired for the purpose of earning income, any interest in a life insurance policy or any property the income from which would be exempt. Nor is any account taken of an amount payable to acquire such a property.

**(3) Carrying value of property** — For the purpose of subsection (2), the carrying value at any time to a distributor of its property shall be determined in accordance with generally accepted accounting principles except that

(a) neither the equity nor the consolidation method of accounting shall be used;

(b) no amount may be added to or deducted from the original cost of a property to the distributor (other than amounts in respect of depreciation, depletion or the cost of improvements) in computing its carrying value to the distributor;

(c) subject to paragraph (d), the carrying value at that time to the distributor of any property received by it from a person with whom it was not dealing at arm's length shall be deemed to be the lesser of that value otherwise determined and the cost amount of the property to the distributor at that time; and

(d) the carrying value to the distributor of each property

(i) that was not acquired for the purpose of earning income therefrom or from a business,

(ii) that is an interest in a life insurance policy, or

(iii) the income from which would be exempt,

shall be deemed to be nil.

**Technical Notes**: Subsection 20.2(3) defines "carrying value" for the purposes of subsection (2). The starting-point of the definition is carrying value determined in accordance with generally accepted accounting principles (GAAP), except that the equity and consolidation methods of accounting must not be used. From that basis, the following adjustments are made. First, the only amounts that may be added to or deducted from the original cost of a property are those in respect of depreciation, depletion or the cost of improvements. Secondly, the carrying value of any property received from a non-arm's length person is deemed to be the lesser of the carrying value otherwise determined and the property's cost amount. Finally, the carrying value of any property not acquired for the purpose of earning income, any interest in a life insurance policy or any property the income from which would be exempt, is deemed to be nil.

**Application**: The December 20, 1991 draft legislation (interest deductibility), s. 2, will add s. 20.2. No specific application date is given in the draft legislation; the Technical Notes (see the second paragraph under 20.1(1) above) state that it will apply to distributions "made before the date on which this legislation is issued in final form".

**Notes**: 20.2 is expected to be both renumbered and amended. See under 20.2(1) above.

**Definitions [s. 20.2 (December 1991 version)]**: "adjusted equity" — 20.2(2); "amount" — 248(1); "arm's length" — 251(1); "borrowed money", "business" — 248(1); "carrying value" — 20.2(3); "corporation" — 248(1), *Interpretation Act* 35(1); "cost amount" — 248(1); "disposition" — 54; "distributor" — 20.2(1); "dividend", "exempt income" — 248(1); "life insurance policy" — 138(12), 248(1); "person", "property" — 248(1); "taxation year" — 249; "time of distribution" — 20.2(1).

**21. (1) Cost of borrowed money** — Where in a taxation year a taxpayer has acquired depreciable property, if the taxpayer elects under this subsection in the taxpayer's return of income under this Part for the year,

(a) in computing the taxpayer's income for the year and for such of the 3 immediately preceding taxation years as the taxpayer had, paragraphs 20(1)(c), (d), (e) and (e.1) do not apply to the amount or to the part of the amount specified in the taxpayer's election that, but for an election under this subsection in respect thereof, would be deductible in computing the taxpayer's income (other than exempt income) for any such year in respect of borrowed money used to acquire the depreciable property or the amount payable for the depreciable property; and

(b) the amount or the part of the amount, as the case may be, described in paragraph (a) shall be added to the capital cost to the taxpayer of the depreciable property so acquired by the taxpayer.

**Related Provisions**: 13(10) — Deemed capital cost of certain property; 13(21) — Definitions; 20(3) — Life insurance policy; 21(5) — Reassessments; 80(2)(b) — Application of debt forgiveness rules; 96(3) — Election by members of partnership; 127(11.5)(b)(i) — Ignore s. 21 for purposes of ITC qualified expenditures; 220(3.2), Reg. 600(a) — Late filing of election or revocation.

**Notes**: 21(1) provides an election to capitalize interest and similar expenses and fold them into the cost of depreciable property.

21(1) amended by 1991 technical bill, effective 1988, to add reference to 20(1)(e.1).

**Interpretation Bulletins**: See list at end of s. 21.

**Information Circulars**: 92-1: Guidelines for accepting late, amended or revoked elections.

**Advance Tax Rulings**: ATR-1: Transfer of legal title in land to bare trustee corporation — mortgagee's requirements sole reason for transfer.

**(2) Borrowed money used for exploration or development** — Where in a taxation year a taxpayer has used borrowed money for the purpose of exploration, development or the acquisition of property and the expenses incurred by the taxpayer in respect thereof are Canadian exploration and development expenses, foreign exploration and development expenses, Canadian exploration expenses, Canadian development expenses or Canadian oil and gas property expenses, as the case may be, if the taxpayer elects under this subsection in the taxpayer's return of income under this Part for the year,

(a) in computing the taxpayer's income for the year and for such of the 3 immediately preceding taxation years as the taxpayer had, paragraphs 20(1)(c), (d), (e) and (e.1) do not apply to the amount or to the part of the amount specified in the taxpayer's election that, but for an election under this subsection in respect thereof, would be deductible in computing the taxpayer's income (other than exempt income) for any such year in respect of the borrowed money used for the exploration, development or acquisition of property, as the case may be; and

(b) the amount or the part of the amount, as the case may be, described in paragraph (a) shall be deemed to be Canadian exploration and development expenses, foreign exploration and development expenses, Canadian exploration expenses, Canadian development expenses or Canadian oil and gas property expenses, as the case may be, incurred by the taxpayer in the year.

**Proposed Amendment — 21(2)**

**(2) Borrowed money used for exploration or development** — Where in a taxation year a taxpayer has used borrowed money for the purpose of exploration, development or the acquisition of property and the expenses incurred by the taxpayer in respect of those activities are Canadian exploration and development expenses, Canadian exploration expenses, Canadian development expenses, Canadian oil and gas property expenses, foreign resource expenses in respect of a country, or foreign exploration and development expenses, as the case may be, if the taxpayer so elects under this subsection in the taxpayer's return of income for the year,

(a) in computing the taxpayer's income for the year and for such of the three immediately preceding taxation years as the taxpayer had, paragraphs 20(1)(c), (d), (e) and (e.1) do not apply to the amount or to the part of the amount specified in the taxpayer's election that, but for that election, would be deductible in computing the taxpayer's income (other than exempt income or income that is exempt from tax under this Part) for any such year in respect of the borrowed money used for the exploration, development or acquisition of property, as the case may be; and

(b) the amount or the part of the amount, as the case may be, described in paragraph (a) is deemed to be Canadian exploration and development expenses, Canadian exploration expenses, Canadian development expenses, Canadian oil and gas property expenses, foreign resource expenses in respect of a country, or foreign exploration and development expenses, as the case may be, incurred by the taxpayer in the year.

**Application**: The December 21, 2000 draft legislation, subsec. 9(1), will amend subsec. 21(2) to read as above, applicable to taxation years that begin after 2000.

**Technical Notes**: Subsections 21(2) and (4) apply where a taxpayer has used borrowed money for the purpose of incurring specified resource expenses. Where the taxpayer so elects, financing costs in respect of the borrowed money are not deductible under any of paragraphs 20(1)(c) to (e.1) in computing the taxpayer's income. Instead, except where the deduction under one of those paragraphs relates to exempt income (as defined in subsection 248(1)), those costs are added to the category of resource expenses that the borrowed money was used to incur. The election under subsection 21(2) is made in connection with financing costs incurred in the taxation year during which the related resource expenses were incurred. Elections under subsection 21(4) are made in connection with financing costs incurred after that year, and can only be made for a taxation year if treatment under section 21 has been chosen for all preceding taxation years with regard to the borrowed money to which the financing costs related.

Subsections 21(2) and (4) are amended so that the exception referred to above for exempt income extends to all income that is exempt from tax under Part I. This amendment is made for consistency with proposed paragraph (l) of the definition "investment tax credit" in subsection 127(9) and ensures that subsections 21(2) and (4) cannot be used by entities exempt from tax under subsection 149(1).

Subsections 21(2) and (4) are also amended so that the resource expenses specified under those subsections include foreign resource expenses (as defined in the definition "foreign resource expense" in new section 66.21), determined on a country-by-country basis. This amendment is consequential on the introduction of new rules in section 66.21 for the deduction of foreign resource expenses.

**Related Provisions**: 13(10) — Deemed capital cost of property; 13(21) — Definitions; 21(5) — Reassessments; 66(18) — Expenses incurred by partnerships; 80(2)(b) — Application of debt forgiveness rules; 96(3) — Election by members of partnership; 220(3.2), Reg. 600(a) — Late filing of election or revocation.

**Notes**: 21(2) amended by 1991 technical bill, effective 1988, to add reference to 20(1)(e.1).

**Interpretation Bulletins**: See list at end of s. 21.

**Information Circulars**: 92-1: Guidelines for accepting late, amended or revoked elections.

**(3) Borrowing for depreciable property** — In computing the income of a taxpayer for a particular taxation year, where the taxpayer

(a) in any preceding taxation year

(i) made an election under subsection (1) in respect of borrowed money used to acquire depreciable property or an amount payable for depreciable property acquired by the taxpayer, or

(ii) was, by virtue of subsection 18(3.1), required to include an amount in respect of the construction of a depreciable property in computing the capital cost to the taxpayer of the depreciable property, and

(b) in each taxation year, if any, after that preceding taxation year and before the particular year, made an election under this subsection covering the total amount that, but for an election under this subsection in respect thereof, would have been deductible in computing the taxpayer's income (other than exempt income) for each such year in respect of the borrowed money used to acquire the depreciable property or the amount payable for the depreciable property acquired by the taxpayer,

if an election under this subsection is made in the taxpayer's return of income under this Part for the particular year, paragraphs 20(1)(c), (d), (e) and (e.1) do not apply to the amount or to the part of the amount specified in the election that, but for an election under this subsection in respect thereof, would be deductible in computing the taxpayer's income (other than exempt income) for the particular year in respect of the borrowed money used to acquire the depreciable property or the amount payable for the depreciable property acquired by the taxpayer, and the amount or part of the amount, as the case may be, shall be added to the capital cost to the taxpayer of the depreciable property.

**Related Provisions**: 96(3) — Election by members of partnership; 127(11.5)(b)(i) — Ignore s. 21 for purposes of ITC qualified expenditures; 220(3.2), Reg. 600(a) — Late filing of election or revocation.

**Notes**: 21(3) amended by 1991 technical bill, effective 1988, to add reference to 20(1)(e.1).

**Interpretation Bulletins**: See list at end of s. 21.

**(4) Borrowing for exploration, etc.** — In computing the income of a taxpayer for a particular taxation year, where the taxpayer

(a) in any preceding taxation year made an election under subsection (2) in respect of borrowed money used for the purpose of exploration, development or acquisition of property, and

(b) in each taxation year, if any, after that preceding taxation year and before the particular year, made an election under this subsection covering the total amount that, but for an election under this subsection in respect thereof, would have been deductible in computing the taxpayer's income (other than exempt income) for each such year in respect of the borrowed money used for the exploration, development or acquisition of property, as the case may be,

> **Proposed Amendment — 21(4)(b)–(e)**
>
> (b) in each taxation year, if any, after that preceding taxation year and before the particular year, made an election under this subsection covering the total amount that, but for that election, would have been deductible in computing the taxpayer's income (other than exempt income or income that is exempt from tax under this Part) for each such year in respect of the borrowed money used for the exploration, development or acquisition of property, as the case may be, and
>
> (c) so elects in the taxpayer's return of income for the particular year,
>
> the following rules apply:
>
> (d) paragraphs 20(1)(c), (d), (e) and (e.1) do not apply to the amount or to the part of the amount specified in the election that, but for the election, would be deductible in computing the taxpayer's income (other than exempt income or income that is exempt from tax under this Part) for the particular year in respect of the borrowed money used for the exploration, development or acquisition of property, and
>
> (e) the amount or part of the amount, as the case may be, is deemed to be Canadian exploration and development expenses, Canadian exploration expenses, Canadian development expenses, Canadian oil and gas property expenses, foreign resource expenses in respect of a country, or foreign exploration and development expenses, as the case may be, incurred by the taxpayer in the particular year.

**Application**: The December 21, 2000 draft legislation, subsec. 9(2), will amend para. 21(4)(b) to read as above and add paras. (c), (d) and (e), applicable to taxation years that begin after 2000.

**Technical Notes**: See under 21(2).

if an election under this subsection is made in the taxpayer's return of income under this Part for the particular year, paragraphs 20(1)(c), (d), (e) and (e.1) do not apply to the amount or to the part of the amount specified in the election that, but for an election under this subsection in respect thereof, would be deductible in computing the taxpayer's income (other than exempt income) for the particular year in respect of the borrowed money used for the exploration, development or acquisition of property, and the amount or part of the amount, as the case may be, shall be deemed to be Canadian exploration and development expenses, foreign exploration and development expenses, Canadian exploration expenses, Canadian development expenses or Canadian oil and gas property expenses, as the case may be, incurred by the taxpayer in the particular year.

**Related Provisions**: 96(3) — Election by members of partnership; 220(3.2), Reg. 600(a) — Late filing of election or revocation.

**Notes**: 21(4) amended by 1991 technical bill, effective 1988, to add reference to 20(1)(e.1).

**Interpretation Bulletins**: See list at end of s. 21.

**(5) Reassessments** — Notwithstanding any other provision of this Act, where a taxpayer has made an election in accordance with the provisions of subsection (1) or (2), such reassessments of tax, interest or penalties shall be made as are necessary to give effect thereto.

**Definitions [s. 21]**: "amount", "borrowed money" — 248(1); "Canadian exploration expense" — 66.1(6), 248(1); "Canadian exploration and development expenses" — 66(15), 248(1); "Canadian development expense" — 66.2(5), 248(1); "Canadian oil and gas property expense" — 66.4(5), 248(1); "depreciable property" — 13(21), 248(1); "exempt income" — 248(1); "foreign exploration and development expenses" — 66(15), 248(1); "prescribed", "property", "regulation" — 248(1); "taxation year" — 11(2), 249; "taxpayer" — 248(1).

**Interpretation Bulletins [s. 21]**: IT-109R2: Unpaid amounts; IT-121R3: Election to capitalize cost of borrowed money; IT-142R3: Settlement of debts on the winding-up of a corporation; IT-341R3: Expenses of issuing or selling shares, units in a trust, interests in a partnership or syndicate, and expenses of borrowing money; IT-360R2: Interest payable in a foreign currency.

## Ceasing to Carry on Business

**22. (1) Sale of accounts receivable** — Where a person who has been carrying on a business has, in a taxation year, sold all or substantially all the property used in carrying on the business, including the debts that have been or will be included in computing the person's income for that year or a previous year and that are still outstanding, and including the debts arising from loans made in the ordinary course of the person's business if part of the person's ordinary business was the lending of money and that are still outstanding, to a purchaser who proposes to continue the business which the vendor has been carrying on, if the vendor and the purchaser have executed jointly an election in prescribed form to have this section apply, the following rules are applicable:

(a) there may be deducted in computing the vendor's income for the taxation year an amount equal to the difference between the face value of the debts so sold (other than debts in respect of which the vendor has made deductions under paragraph 20(1)(p)), and the consideration paid by the purchaser to the vendor for the debts so sold;

(b) an amount equal to the difference described in paragraph (a) shall be included in computing the purchaser's income for the taxation year;

(c) the debts so sold shall be deemed, for the purposes of paragraphs 20(1)(l) and (p), to have been included in computing the purchaser's income for the taxation year or a previous year but no deduction may be made by the purchaser under paragraph 20(1)(p) in respect of a debt in respect of which the vendor has previously made a deduction; and

(d) each amount deducted by the vendor in computing income for a previous year under paragraph 20(1)(p) in respect of any of the debts so sold shall be deemed, for the purpose of paragraph 12(1)(i), to have been so deducted by the purchaser.

**Related Provisions**: 13(8) — Disposition of depreciable property after ceasing to carry on business; 96(3) — Election by members of partnership.

**Notes**: The CCRA takes the position that "all or substantially all", used in the opening words of 22(1), means 90% or more.

**Interpretation Bulletins**: IT-188R: Sale of accounts receivable; IT-291R2: Transfer of property to a corporation under subsection 85(1); IT-433R: Farming or fishing — use of cash method; IT-442R: Bad debts and reserve for doubtful debts; IT-471R: Merger of partnership; IT-488R2: Winding-up of 90%-owned taxable Canadian corporations.

**Forms**: T2022: Election in respect of the sale of debts receivable.

**(2) Statement by vendor and purchaser** — An election executed for the purposes of subsection (1) shall contain a statement by the vendor and the purchaser jointly as to the consideration paid for the debts sold by the vendor to the purchaser and that statement shall, subject to subsection 69(1), as against the Minister, be binding upon the vendor and the purchaser in so far as it may be relevant in respect of any matter arising under this Act.

**Definitions [s. 22]**: "amount", "business", "Minister", "person", "prescribed", "property" — 248(1); "taxation year" — 11(2), 249.

**23. (1) Sale of inventory** — Where, on or after disposing of or ceasing to carry on a business or a part of a business, a taxpayer has sold all or any part of the property that was included in the inventory of the business, the property so sold shall, for the purposes of this Part, be deemed to have been sold by the taxpayer in the course of carrying on the business.

**Related Provisions**: 12.4 — Bad debt inclusion on sale of inventory.

**Interpretation Bulletins**: IT-287R2: Sale of inventory; IT-457R: Election by professionals to exclude work in progress from income.

**(2)** [Repealed under former Act]

**Notes**: 23(2) repealed effective May 7, 1974.

**(3) Reference to property in inventory** — A reference in this section to property that was included in the inventory of a business shall be deemed to include a reference to property that would have been so included if the income from the business had not been computed in accordance with the method authorized by subsection 28(1) or paragraph 34(a).

**Definitions [s. 23]**: "business", "inventory", "Minister", "person", "property", "taxpayer" — 248(1).

**24. (1) Ceasing to carry on business** — Notwithstanding paragraph 18(1)(b), where at any time after a taxpayer ceases to carry on a business the taxpayer no longer owns any property that was eligible capital property in respect of the business and that has value, in computing the taxpayer's income for taxation years ending after that time,

(a) there shall be deducted, for the first such taxation year, the amount of the taxpayer's cumulative eligible capital in respect of the business at that time;

(b) no amount may be deducted under paragraph 20(1)(b) in respect of the business;

(c) for the purposes of determining the value of P in the definition "cumulative eligible capital" in subsection 14(5), the amount deducted by the taxpayer under paragraph (a) shall be deemed to be an amount deducted under paragraph 20(1)(b) in computing the taxpayer's income from the business for the taxation year that included that time; and

(d) for the purposes of subsection 14(1), section 14 shall be read without reference to subsection 14(4).

**Related Provisions**: 10(12) — Where non-resident ceases to use inventory in business; 13(8) — Disposition of depreciable property after ceasing to carry on business; 14(12) — Limitation where affiliated person acquires the property; 20(1)(hh.1) — Deduction for repayment of assistance relating to eligible capital expenditure after ceasing to carry on business; 24(2) — Business carried on by spouse or controlled corporation; 25 — Fiscal period for individual proprietor of business disposed of; 28(1)(g) — Deduction from farming or fishing income when using cash method; 70(5.1) — Eligible capital property of deceased taxpayer; 107(2)(f) — Capital interest distribution by personal or prescribed trust; Reg. 8103(6) — Mark-to-market — transition inclusion on ceasing to carry on business; Reg. 9204(5) — Residual portion of specified debt obligation on ceasing to carry on business.

**Notes**: 24(1) amended by 1991 technical bill, effective July 14, 1990, to apply only where the taxpayer has disposed of *all* eligible capital property that has value.

**Interpretation Bulletins**: IT-123R6: Transactions involving eligible capital property; IT-291R2: Transfer of property to a corporation under subsection 85(1); IT-313R2: Eligible capital property — rules where a taxpayer has ceased carrying on a business or has died; IT-488R2: Winding-up of 90%-owned taxable Canadian corporations.

**(2) Business carried on by spouse [or common-law partner] or controlled corporation** — Notwithstanding subsection (1), where at any time an individual ceases to carry on a business and thereafter the individual's spouse or common-law partner, or a corporation controlled directly or indirectly in any manner whatever by the individual, carries on the business and acquires all of the property that was eligible capital property in respect of the business owned by the individual before that time and that had value at that time,

(a) in computing the individual's income for the individual's first taxation year ending after that time, subsection (1) shall be read without reference to paragraph (1)(a) and the reference in paragraph (1)(c) to "the amount deducted by the taxpayer under paragraph (a)" shall be read as a reference to "an amount equal to the taxpayer's cumulative eligible capital in respect of the business immediately before that time";

(b) in computing the cumulative eligible capital of the spouse or common-law partner or the corporation, as the case may be, in respect of the business, the spouse or common-law partner or corporation shall be deemed to have acquired an eligible capital property and to have made an eligible capital expenditure at that time at a cost equal to $4/3$ of the total of

(i) the cumulative eligible capital of the taxpayer in respect of the business immediately before that time, and

(ii) the amount, if any, determined for F in the definition "cumulative eligible capital" in subsection 14(5) in respect of the business of the individual at that time;

(c) for the purposes of determining the cumulative eligible capital in respect of the business of the spouse or common-law partner or corporation after that time, an amount equal to the amount determined under subparagraph (b)(ii) shall be added to the amount otherwise determined in respect thereof for P in the definition "cumulative eligible capital" in subsection 14(5); and

(d) for the purposes of determining after that time

(i) the amount deemed by subparagraph 14(1)(a)(v) to be the spouse's or common-law partner's taxable capital gain, and

(ii) the amount to be included under subparagraph 14(1)(a)(v) or paragraph 14(1)(b) in computing the income of the spouse or common-law partner or corporation

in respect of any subsequent disposition of property of the business, there shall be added to the amount otherwise determined for Q in the second formula in the definition "cumulative eligible capital" in subsection 14(5) the amount, if any, determined for Q in that formula in respect of the business of the individual immediately before the individual ceased to carry on the business.

**Proposed Amendment — 24(2)(d)**

(d) for the purpose of determining after that time the amount required to be included under paragraph 14(1)(b) in computing the income of the spouse, the common-law partner or the corporation in respect of any subsequent disposition of property of the business, there shall be added to the amount otherwise determined for Q in the definition "cumulative eligible capital" in subsection 14(5) the amount, if any, determined for Q in that definition in respect of the business of the individual immediately before the individual ceased to carry on business.

**Application**: The December 21, 2000 draft legislation, s. 10, will amend para. 24(2)(d) to read as above, applicable in respect of taxation years that end after February 27, 2000.

**Technical Notes**: Subsection 24(2) provides a rollover of the cumulative eligible capital of a business of an individual who ceases to carry on the business in circumstances where the eligible capital property of the business is acquired by the individual's spouse or common-law partner or by a corporation controlled by the individual that thereafter carries on the business.

Paragraph 24(2)(d) deals with the calculation of income inclusions under subsection 14(1) for the spouse, common-law partner or corporation. Paragraph 24(2)(d) is amended consequential on the renumbering of subsection 14(1), which is described in further detail above.

**Related Provisions**: 14(12) — Certain property deemed not acquired by affiliated person; 25 — Fiscal period for individual proprietor of business disposed of; 256(5.1), (6.2) — Controlled directly or indirectly.

**Notes**: 24(2) amended by 2000 same-sex partners bill to add reference to "common-law partner", effective for the 2001 and later taxation years, or earlier by election (see Notes to 248(1)"common-law partner").

24(2) amended by 1991 technical bill and 1992 technical bill, both effective July 14, 1990, to apply only where *all* the taxpayer's eligible capital property that has value is transferred to the spouse or corporation, and to prevent an overstatement of the deemed taxable capital gain or amount to be included in income on the subsequent disposition of eligible capital property by the spouse or corporation.

Reference to 14(1)(a)(v) added to 24(2)(d)(ii) by 1994 Budget, effective for fiscal periods that end after February 22, 1994.

**(3) Where partnership has ceased to exist** — Notwithstanding subsection (1), where at any time a partnership ceases to exist in circumstances to which neither subsection 98(3) nor subsection 98(5) applies, there may be deducted, in computing the income for the first taxation year beginning after that time of a taxpayer who was a member of the partnership immediately before that time, an amount determined by the formula

$$A \times \frac{B}{C}$$

where

A is the amount that would, had the partnership continued to exist, have been deductible under subsection (1) in computing its income;

B is the fair market value of the taxpayer's interest in the partnership immediately before that time; and

C is the fair market value of all interests in the partnership immediately before that time.

**Notes**: 24(3) added by 1992 technical bill, effective July 14, 1990.

**Definitions [s. 24]**: "amount", "business", "common-law partner" — 248(1); "controlled directly or indirectly" — 256(5.1),

(6.2); "corporation" — 248(1), *Interpretation Act* 35(1); "cumulative eligible capital" — 14(5), 248(1); "eligible capital property" — 54, 248(1); "individual", "property" — 248(1); "taxation year" — 11(2), 249; "taxpayer" — 248(1).

## 24.1 [Repealed]

**Notes**: 24.1 repealed by 1995 Budget, effective for (judicial) appointments made after 1995. The section is no longer needed because lawyers no longer can defer income through choice of a year-end (see 249.1 and 34.1). Before, when a lawyer became a judge (who earns salary taxed under 5(1) on a current-year basis), there was a problem with deferred income all being taxed at once. For now, there is still a problem with the 10-year reserve under 34.2 being all included in income when the lawyer stops practising law. For appointments made from 1984 through 1995, read:

> 24.1 Judges — Where in a taxation year a taxpayer has been appointed a judge by the Governor General or the Governor in Council or by the lieutenant governor in council of a province and the taxpayer elects in the taxpayer's return of income under this Part for the year to have this section apply to the computation of the taxpayer's income,
>
> (a) the taxpayer's income from a professional practice for a fiscal period ending in that taxation year and commencing in the preceding taxation year shall be deemed to be that proportion of such income that the number of months in the taxation year during which the taxpayer was not a judge is of the number of months in the fiscal period; and
>
> (b) the amount by which the taxpayer's income for that taxation year from the taxpayer's professional practice, computed without reference to this section, exceeds the amount that is deemed by paragraph (a) to be the taxpayer's income for the fiscal period shall be deemed to be income of the taxpayer in the immediately following taxation year.

**Definitions [s. 24.1]**: "fiscal period" — 249(2)(b), 249.1; "Governor General", "Governor in Council", "lieutenant governor in council", "province" — *Interpretation Act* 35(1); "taxation year" — 11(2), 249; "taxpayer" — 248(1).

## 25. (1) Fiscal period of business disposed of by individual 
— Where an individual was the proprietor of a business and disposed of it during a fiscal period of the business, the fiscal period may, if the individual so elects and subsection 249.1(4) does not apply in respect of the business, be deemed to have ended at the time it would have ended if the individual had not disposed of the business during the fiscal period.

**Related Provisions**: 13(8) — Disposition of depreciable property after ceasing to carry on business; 14(1) — Inclusion of eligible capital amount in income from business; 99(2) — Parallel rule where partnership ceases to exist.

**Notes**: The words "and subsection 249.1(4) does not apply in respect of the business" added to 25(1) by 1995 Budget, effective for fiscal periods that begin after 1994. Thus, no election may be made by an individual to extend a fiscal period of a terminated proprietorship if the "alternative-fiscal-period rule" in 249.1(4) applies to the proprietorship's fiscal period.

**Interpretation Bulletins**: IT-172R: Capital cost allowance — taxation year of individuals; IT-179R: Change of fiscal period; IT-313R2: Eligible capital property — rules where a taxpayer has ceased carrying on a business or has died.

**Information Circulars**: 76-19R3: Transfer of property to a corporation under section 85.

**(2) Election** — An election under subsection (1) is not valid unless the individual, at the time when the fiscal period of the business would, if the election were valid, be deemed to have ended, is resident in Canada.

**(3) Dispositions in the extended fiscal period** — Where subsection (1) applies in respect of a fiscal period of a business of an individual, for the purpose of computing the individual's income for the fiscal period,

(a) section 13 shall be read without reference to subsection 13(8); and

(b) section 24 shall be read without reference to paragraph 24(1)(d).

**Interpretation Bulletins**: IT-313R2: Eligible capital property — rules where a taxpayer has ceased carrying on a business or has died; IT-478R2: CCA — recapture and terminal loss.

**Definitions [s. 25]**: "business" — 248(1); "Canada" — 255; "fiscal period" — 249.1; "individual" — 248(1); "resident in Canada" — 250; "taxpayer" — 248(1).

## Special Cases

**26. (1) Banks — inclusions in income** — There shall be included in computing the income of a bank for its first taxation year that commences after June 17, 1987 and ends after 1987 the total of

(a) the total of the specific provisions of the bank, as determined, or as would be determined if such a determination were required, under the Minister's rules, as at the end of its immediately preceding taxation year,

(b) the total of the general provisions of the bank, as determined, or as would be determined if such a determination were required, under the Minister's rules, as at the end of its immediately preceding taxation year,

(c) the amount, if any, by which

(i) the amount of the special provision for losses on trans-border claims of the bank, as determined, or as would be determined if such a determination were required, under the Minister's rules, that was deductible by the bank under subsection (2) in computing its income for its immediately preceding taxation year

exceeds

(ii) that part of the amount determined under subparagraph (i) that was a realized loss of the bank for that immediately preceding taxation year, and

(d) the amount, if any, of the tax allowable appropriations account of the bank, as determined, or as would be determined if such a determination were required, under the Minister's rules, at the end of its immediately preceding taxation year.

**Related Provisions**: 20(1)(l) — Reserve for doubtful accounts; 20(1)(l.1) — Reserve for guarantees; 33.1 — International banking centres; 87(2)(g.1) — Amalgamation — continuing corporation; 142.2–142.6 — Additional rules for financial institutions.

**(2) Banks — deductions from income** — In computing the income for a taxation year of a bank, there may be deducted an amount not exceeding the total of

(a) that part of the total of the amounts of the five-year average loan loss experiences of the bank, as determined, or as would be determined if such a determination were required, under the Minister's rules, for all taxation years before its first taxation year that commences after June 17, 1987 and ends after 1987 that is specified by the bank for the year and was not deducted by the bank in computing its income for any preceding taxation year,

(b) that part of the total of the amounts transferred by the bank to its tax allowable appropriations account, as permitted under the Minister's rules, for all taxation years before its first taxation year that commences after June 17, 1987 and ends after 1987 that is specified by the bank for the year and was not deducted by the bank in computing its income for any preceding taxation year,

(c) that part of the amount, if any, by which

(i) the amount of the special provision for losses on trans-border claims, as determined, or as would be determined if such a determination were required, under the Minister's rules, that was deductible by the bank under this subsection in computing its income for its last taxation year before its first taxation year that commences after June 17, 1987 and ends after 1987

exceeds

(ii) that part of the amount determined under subparagraph (i) that was a realized loss of the bank for that last taxation year

that is specified by the bank for the year and was not deducted by the bank in computing its income for any preceding taxation year,

(d) where the tax allowable appropriations account of the bank at the end of its last taxation year before its first taxation year that commences after June 17, 1987 and ends after 1987, as determined, or as would be determined if such a determination were required, under the Minister's rules, is a negative amount, that part of such amount expressed as a positive number that is specified by the bank for the year and was not deducted by the bank in computing its income for any preceding taxation year, and

(e) that part of the total of the amounts calculated in respect of the bank for the purposes of the Minister's rules, or that would be calculated for the purposes of those rules if such a calculation were required, under Procedure 8 of the Procedures for the Determination of the Provision for Loan Losses as set out in Appendix 1 of those rules, for all taxation years before its first taxation year that commences after June 17, 1987 and ends after 1987 that is specified by the bank for the year and was not deducted by the bank in computing its income for any preceding taxation year.

**Related Provisions**: 87(2)(g.1) — Amalgamation — continuing corporation.

**(3) Write-offs and recoveries** — In computing the income of a bank, the following rules apply:

(a) any amount that was recorded by the bank as a realized loss or a write-off of an asset that was included by the bank in the calculation of an amount deductible under the Minister's rules, or would have been included in the calculation of such an amount if such a calculation had been required, for any taxation year before its first taxation year that commences after June 17, 1987 and ends after 1987, shall, for the purposes of paragraph 12(1)(i) and section 12.4, be deemed to have been deducted by the bank under paragraph 20(1)(p) in computing its income for the year for which it was so recorded; and

(b) any amount that was recorded by the bank as a recovery of a realized loss or a write-off of an asset that was included by the bank in the calculation of an amount deductible under the Minister's rules, or would have been included in the calculation of such an amount if such a calculation had been required, for any taxation year before its first taxation year that commences after June 17, 1987 and ends after 1987 shall, for the purposes of section 12.4, be deemed to have been included by the bank under paragraph 12(1)(i) in computing its income for the year for which it was so recorded.

**(4) Definition of "Minister's rules"** — For the purposes of this section, "Minister's rules" means the *Rules for the Determination of the Appropriations for Contingencies of a Bank* issued under the authority of the Minister of Finance pursuant to section 308 of the *Bank Act* for the purposes of subsections (1) and (2) of this section.

**Definitions [s. 26]**: "amount" — 248(1); "bank" — 248(1), *Interpretation Act* 35(1); "Minister" — 26(4), 248(1); "taxation year" — 249.

**27. (1) Application of Part I to Crown corporation** — This Part applies to a federal Crown corporation as if

(a) any income or loss from a business carried on by the corporation as agent of Her Majesty, or from a property of Her Majesty administered by the corporation, were an income or loss of the corporation from the business or the property, as the case may be; and

(b) any property, obligation or debt of any kind whatever held, administered, entered into or incurred by the corporation as agent of Her Majesty were a property, obligation or debt, as the case may be, of the corporation.

**Related Provisions**: 124(3) — No tax abatement for income earned in a province; 181(1) — Meaning of "long-term debt"; 181.71, 190.211 — Capital taxes apply to federal Crown corporations; 187.61, 191.4(3) — Part IV.1 and VI.1 taxes on preferred share dividends apply to federal Crown corporations.

**Notes**: See Notes to 27(2).

27(1) amended by 1995-97 technical bill, effective generally April 27, 1995, except:

(a) for 181.71, for taxation years that end after June 1989;

(b) for 187.61 and 191.4(3), after 1987; and

(c) for 190.211, after May 23, 1985.

Before the amendment, since September 1984, read:

(1) **Application of Part to Crown corporations** — This Part applies to a prescribed federal Crown corporation as if any income or loss from

(a) a business carried on by the corporation as agent of Her Majesty, and

(b) a property of Her Majesty administered by the corporation,

were an income or loss, as the case may be, of the corporation therefrom.

**Interpretation Bulletins**: IT-347R2: Crown corporations.

(2) **Presumption** — Notwithstanding any other provision of this Act, a prescribed federal Crown corporation and any corporation controlled by such a corporation shall be deemed not to be a private corporation and paragraph 149(1)(d) does not apply thereto.

### Proposed Amendment — 27(2)

(2) **Presumption** — Notwithstanding any other provision of this Act, a prescribed federal Crown corporation and any corporation controlled by such a corporation are each deemed not to be a private corporation and paragraphs 149(1)(d) to (d.4) do not apply to those corporations.

**Application**: Bill C-43 (First Reading September 20, 2000), s. 12, will amend subsec. 27(2) to read as above, applicable to taxation years and fiscal periods that begin after 1998.

**Technical Notes**: Section 27 provides special rules for the application of Part I to federal Crown corporations. It allows the Governor in Council to impose income tax on such corporations by prescribing them under the *Income Tax Regulations*. Subsection 27(2) provides that the tax exemption provided under paragraph 149(1)(d) does not apply to a corporation controlled by a prescribed federal Crown corporation. The amendment to subsection 27(2), which adds a reference to the tax exemptions provided under paragraphs 149(1)(d.1) to (d.4), is strictly consequential on the amendment to paragraph 149(1)(d) and the addition of paragraphs 149(1)(d.1) to (d.4) that were made applicable to taxation years and fiscal periods that begin after 1998.

**Related Provisions**: 181.71, 190.211 — Capital taxes apply to prescribed federal Crown corporations; 187.61, 191.4(3) — Part IV.1 and VI.1 taxes on preferred share dividends apply to prescribed federal Crown corporations; 256(6), (6.1) — Meaning of "control".

**Notes**: 27(2) forces Crown corporations that operate in the commercial sector to pay income tax, so that they do not have a competitive advantage over private-sector corporations. The list of such corporations is in Reg. 7100.

Where assets of a Crown corporation are privatized, bonds of the corporation may qualify as qualified investments for RRSPs and other deferred income plans. See Reg. 4900(1)(q).

**Regulations**: 7100 (prescribed federal Crown corporation).

**Interpretation Bulletins**: IT-347R2: Crown corporations.

(3) **Transfers of land for disposition** — Where land of Her Majesty has been transferred to a prescribed federal Crown corporation for purposes of disposition, the acquisition of the property by the corporation and any disposition thereof shall be deemed not to have been in the course of the business carried on by the corporation.

**Interpretation Bulletins**: IT-347R2: Crown corporations.

**Definitions [s. 27]**: "business" — 248(1); "controlled" — 256(6), (6.1); "corporation" — 248(1), *Interpretation Act* 35(1); "Her Majesty" — *Interpretation Act* 35(1); "private corporation" — 89(1), 248(1); "property" — 248(1).

**28. (1) Farming or fishing business [cash method]** — For the purpose of computing the income of a taxpayer for a taxation year from a farming or fishing business, the income from the business for that year may, if the taxpayer so elects, be computed in accordance with a method (in this section referred to as the "cash method") whereby the income therefrom for that year shall be deemed to be an amount equal to the total of

(a) all amounts that

(i) were received in the year, or are deemed by this Act to have been received in the year, in the course of carrying on the business, and

(ii) were in payment of or on account of an amount that would, if the income from the business were not computed in accordance with the cash method, be included in computing income therefrom for that or any other year, and

(b) with respect to a farming business, such amount, if any, as is specified by the taxpayer in respect of the business in the taxpayer's return of income under this Part for the year, not exceeding the amount, if any, by which

(i) the fair market value at the end of the year of inventory owned by the taxpayer in connection with the business at that time

exceeds

(ii) the amount determined under paragraph (c) for the year,

(c) with respect to a farming business, the amount, if any, that is the lesser of

(i) the taxpayer's loss from the business for the year computed without reference to this paragraph and to paragraph (b), and

(ii) the value of inventory purchased by the taxpayer that was owned by the taxpayer in connection with the business at the end of the year, and

(d) the total of all amounts each of which is an amount included in computing the taxpayer's income for the year from the business because of subsection 13(1), 14(1), 80(13) or 80.3(3) or (5),

minus the total of

(e) all amounts, other than amounts described in section 30, that

(i) were paid in the year, or are deemed by this Act to have been paid in the year, in the course of carrying on the business,

(ii) in the case of amounts paid, or deemed by this Act to have been paid, for inventory, were in payment of or on account of an amount that would be deductible in computing the income from the business for the year or any other taxation year if that income were not computed in accordance with the cash method, and

(iii) in any other case, were in payment of or on account of an amount that would be deductible in computing the income from the business for a preceding taxation year, the year or the following taxation year if that income were not computed in accordance with the cash method,

(e.1) all amounts, other than amounts described in section 30, that

(i) would be deductible in computing the income from the business for the year if that income were not computed in accordance with the cash method,

(ii) are not deductible in computing the income from the business for any other taxation year, and

(iii) were paid in a preceding taxation year in the course of carrying on the business,

(f) the total of all amounts each of which is the amount, if any, included under paragraph (b) or (c) in computing the taxpayer's income from the business for the immediately preceding taxation year, and

(g) the total of all amounts each of which is an amount deducted for the year under paragraph 20(1)(a), (b) or (uu), subsection 20(16) or 24(1), section 30 or subsection 80.3(2) or (4) in respect of the business,

except that paragraphs (b) and (c) do not apply in computing the income of the taxpayer for the taxation year in which the taxpayer dies.

**Related Provisions**: 20(7)(b) — No reserve available under 20(1)(m) when using cash method; 23(3) — Reference to property included in inventory; 28(2) — Limitation where business carried on jointly with other persons; 28(4) — Non-resident; 29–31 — Additional special rules for farmers; 34.2(2)(a) — Para. 28(1)(b) ignored for purposes of 1995 stub period income; 76(1) — Security in satisfaction of income debt; 79(3)F(b)(v)(B)(II) — Proceeds of disposition to debtor on surrender of property — unpaid interest included under 28(1)(e); 80(1)"excluded obligation"(b) — Obligation not subject to debt forgiveness rules; 80.3 — Income deferral from destruction of livestock or drought-induced sales of breeding animals; 85(1)(c.2) — Transfer of property to corporation by shareholders; 87(2)(b) — Amalgamations — inventory; 88(1.6) — Winding-up; 248(1)"cash method" — Definition applies to entire Act.

**Notes**: Reference in 28(1)(d) to 80(13) and (17), and in 28(1)(g) to 20(1)(uu), added by 1994 tax amendments bill (Part I), effective for taxation years that end after February 21, 1994; reference in 28(1)(d) to 80(17) then removed retroactive to its introduction by 1995-97 technical bill.

28(1)(e)(ii) amended and (e)(iii) added by 1995-97 technical bill, effective for amounts paid after April 26, 1995, other than amounts paid pursuant to an agreement in writing made by the payer on or before April 26, 1995. For earlier amounts since 1989, read:

(ii) were in payment of or on account of an amount that would, if the income from the business were not computed in accordance with the cash method, be deductible in computing income therefrom for that or any other taxation year,

28(1)(e.1) added by 1995-97 technical bill, effective for amounts paid after April 26, 1995, other than amounts paid pursuant to an agreement in writing made by the payer on or before April 26, 1995.

28(1) amended by 1988 tax reform and 1991 technical bill, with a phase-in of the new rules for 1989 through 1994. For a fiscal period beginning after 1988 and before 1995 in respect of a farming business that was carried on by the taxpayer before 1989, 28(1)(c)

(a) shall, where the taxpayer so elects for the taxation year in the return of his income under Part I for the year, be read as follows:

"(c) the lesser of

(i) the taxpayer's loss from the business for the year computed without reference to this paragraph and to paragraph (b), and

(ii) the aggregate of

(A) the value at the end of the year of inventory purchased by him in taxation years commencing after 1988 that was owned by him in connection with the business at the end of the year, and

(B) the amount determined by the formula

$$\frac{A}{7} \times B$$

where

A is the number of taxation years of the business (not exceeding 6) commencing after 1988, and

B is the value (determined in accordance with subsection (1.2)) at the end of the year of inventory purchased by him that was owned by him in connection with the business at that time and at the beginning of the first taxation year of the business commencing after 1988 (in this paragraph referred to as the "particular year") which value, in the case of inventory that is a specified animal, shall be determined in accordance with subsection (1.2) as if the animal were acquired in the particular year for a cash cost equal to,

(I) in the case of an animal acquired in the taxation year immediately preceding the particular year, its cash cost otherwise determined,

(II) in the case of an animal acquired in one of the two taxation years immediately preceding the year referred to in subclause (I), ½ of its cash cost otherwise determined, and

(III) in any other case, ¼ of its cash cost otherwise determined,

and for this purpose, where a taxpayer acquired a specified animal from a person with whom he was not dealing at arm's length, he shall be deemed to have acquired the animal at the time that it was acquired by that person, and"

and

(b) shall, in any other case, be read as follows:

"(c) the amount, if any, by which the lesser of

(i) the taxpayer's loss from the business for the year computed without reference to this paragraph and to paragraph (b), and

(ii) the value (determined in accordance with subsection (1.2)) at the end of the year of inventory purchased by him that was owned by him in connection with the business at that time, which value, in the case of inventory that is a specified animal acquired in any taxation year of the business commencing before 1989, shall be determined in accordance with subsection (1.2) as if the animal were acquired in the first taxation year of the business commencing after 1988 (in this paragraph referred to as the "particular year") for a cash cost equal to,

(A) in the case of an animal acquired in the taxation year immediately preceding the particular year, its cash cost otherwise determined,

(B) in the case of an animal acquired in one of the two taxation years immediately preceding the year referred to in clause (A), ½ of its cash cost otherwise determined, and

(C) in any other case, ¼ of its cash cost otherwise determined,

exceeds

(iii) for taxation years commencing in 1989, $15,000,

(iv) for taxation years commencing in 1990, $12,500,

(v) for taxation years commencing in 1991, $10,000,

(vi) for taxation years commencing in 1992, $7,500,

(vii) for taxation years commencing in 1993, $5,000, and

(viii) for taxation years commencing in 1994, $2,500,

and where

(ix) such taxation year is less than 51 weeks, the amount referred to in subparagraph (iii), (iv), (v), (vi), (vii) or (viii), as the case may be, shall be read as that proportion of the amount determined thereunder that the number of days in the year is of 365, and

(x) a taxpayer acquired a specified animal from a person with whom he was not dealing at arm's length, he shall, for the purpose of subparagraph (ii), be deemed to have acquired the animal at the time that it was acquired by that person, and"

References in 28(1)(d) and (g) to ss. 30 and 80.3 added by 1989 Budget, effective for fiscal periods beginning in 1989.

Closing words of 28(1), rendering paras. (b) and (c) inoperative where the taxpayer has died, added by 1991 technical bill, effective for fiscal periods beginning in 1989.

**Regulations:** 1700–1704 (capital cost allowance rates for pre-1972 property of farming or fishing business).

**Interpretation Bulletins:** IT-154R: Special reserves; IT-184R: Deferred cash purchase tickets issued by Canadian Wheat Board; IT-291R2: Transfer of property to a corporation under subsection 85(1); IT-373R: Farm woodlots and tree farms; IT-427R: Livestock of farmers; IT-526: Farming — cash method inventory adjustments.

**Forms:** RC4060: Farming income and NISA [guide]; T1163: Statement A — NISA account information and statement of farming activities for individuals; T1164: Statement B — NISA account information and statement of farming activities for additional farming operations; T1165: Statement C — statement of farming activities for Ontario self directed risk management (SDRM); T1175 Sched. 1: NISA/Farming — calculation of CCA and business-use-of-home expenses; T2034: Election to establish inventory unit prices for animals; T2042: Statement of farming income and expenses; T2121: Statement of fishing activities; T4003: Farming income [guide]; T4004: Fishing income [guide]; TD3F: Fishermen's election for tax deductions at source.

**(1.1) Acquisition of inventory** — Where at any time, and in circumstances where paragraph 69(1)(a) or (c) applies, a taxpayer acquires inventory that is owned by the taxpayer in connection with a farming business the income from which is computed in accordance with the cash method, for the purposes of this section an amount equal to the cost to the taxpayer of the inventory shall be deemed

(a) to have been paid by the taxpayer at that time and in the course of carrying on that business, and

(b) to be the only amount so paid for the inventory by the taxpayer,

and the taxpayer shall be deemed to have purchased the inventory at the time it was so acquired.

**Notes:** 28(1.1) added by 1991 technical bill, effective for taxation years and fiscal periods ending after 1990. Former 28(1.1), repealed by 1991 technical bill effective for taxation years beginning after 1988, defined "inventory" for purposes of 28(1). The definition of "inventory" in 248(1) has been amended to cover that rule.

**Interpretation Bulletins:** IT-427R: Livestock of farmers.

**Forms:** T2034: Election to establish inventory unit prices for animals.

**(1.2) Valuation of inventory** — For the purpose of paragraph (1)(c) and notwithstanding section 10, inventory of a taxpayer shall be valued at any time at the lesser of the total amount paid by the taxpayer at or before that time to acquire it (in this section referred to as its "cash cost") and its fair market value, except that an animal (in this section referred to as a "specified animal") that is a horse or, where the taxpayer has so elected in respect thereof for the taxation year that includes that time or for any preceding taxation year, is a bovine animal registered under the *Animal Pedigree Act*, shall be valued

(a) at any time in the taxation year in which it is acquired, at such amount as is designated by the taxpayer not exceeding its cash cost to the taxpayer and not less than 70% of its cash cost to the taxpayer; and

(b) at any time in a subsequent taxation year, at such amount as is designated by the taxpayer not exceeding its cash cost to the taxpayer and not less than 70% of the total of

(i) its value determined under this subsection at the end of the preceding taxation year, and

(ii) the total amount paid on account of the purchase price of the animal during the year.

**Related Provisions**: 85(1)(c.2) — Transfer of property to corporation by shareholders; 88(1.6) — Winding-up.

**Notes**: 28(1.2) added by 1988 tax reform, and amended by 1991 technical bill, effective for fiscal periods commencing after 1988.

**Regulations**: 1801, 1802 (valuation of inventory).

**Forms**: T2034: Election to establish inventory unit prices for animals.

**(1.3) Short fiscal period** — For each taxation year that is less than 51 weeks, the reference in subsection (1.2) to "70" shall be read as a reference to the number determined by the formula

$$100 - \left(30 \times \frac{A}{365}\right)$$

where

A is the number of days in the taxation year.

**Notes**: 28(1.3) is presumably intended to apply to *both* references to "70%" in 28(1.2).

**(2) Where joint farming or fishing business** — Subsection (1) does not apply for the purpose of computing the income of a taxpayer for a taxation year from a farming or fishing business carried on by the taxpayer jointly with one or more other persons, unless each of the other persons by whom the business is jointly carried on has elected to have his or her income from the business for that year computed in accordance with the cash method.

**Interpretation Bulletins**: IT-373R: Farm woodlots and tree farms.

**(3) Concurrence of Minister** — Where a taxpayer has filed a return of income under this Part for a taxation year wherein the taxpayer's income for that year from a farming or fishing business has been computed in accordance with the cash method, income from the business for each subsequent taxation year shall, subject to the other provisions of this Part, be computed in accordance with that method unless the taxpayer, with the concurrence of the Minister and on such terms and conditions as are specified by the Minister, adopts some other method.

**Interpretation Bulletins**: IT-373R: Farm woodlots and tree farms.

**(4) Non-resident** — Notwithstanding subsections (1) and (5), where at the end of a taxation year a taxpayer who carried on a business the income from which was computed in accordance with the cash method is non-resident and does not carry on that business in Canada, an amount equal to the total of all amounts each of which is the fair market value of an amount outstanding during the year as or on account of a debt owing to the taxpayer that arose in the course of carrying on the business and that would have been included in computing the taxpayer's income for the year if the amount had been received by the taxpayer in the year, shall (to the extent that the amount was not otherwise included in computing the taxpayer's income for the year or a preceding taxation year) be included in computing the taxpayer's income from the business

(a) for the year, if section 114 is not applicable; or

(b) if section 114 is applicable, for the period or periods referred to in paragraph 114(a) in respect of the year.

**Proposed Amendment — 28(4)(a), (b)**

(a) for the year, if the taxpayer was non-resident throughout the year; and

(b) for the part of the year throughout which the taxpayer was resident in Canada, if the taxpayer was resident in Canada at any time in the year.

**Application**: Bill C-43 (First Reading September 20, 2000), subsec. 13(1), will amend paras. 28(4)(a) and (b) to read as above, applicable to 1998 *et seq.*

**Technical Notes**: Section 28 provides rules concerning the computation of income for taxpayers who, for income tax purposes, use the cash-basis method of accounting in respect of farming or fishing businesses. Subsection 28(4) applies, under certain conditions, to require the inclusion of the value of a non-resident taxpayer's accounts receivable in calculating the taxpayer's income for the year. Subsection 28(4.1) applies, under certain circumstances, to treat a non-resident taxpayer as having disposed of inventory owned by the taxpayer for proceeds of disposition equal to its fair market value.

Subsection 28(4) is amended, for the 1998 and subsequent taxation years, as a consequence of changes to section 114 of the Act. The amendment makes no substantive change, but keeps the reference in step with the changes to section 114. For more information about the changes to section 114, see the commentary on that section.

**Related Provisions**: 28(4.1) — Non-resident; 28(5) — Accounts receivable; 128.1(4)(b) — Deemed disposition of property where taxpayer ceases to be resident in Canada; 253 — Extended meaning of "carrying on business in Canada".

**Notes**: 28(4) amended by 1991 technical bill, effective for taxpayers who cease to reside in Canada or cease to carry on business in Canada after July 13, 1990.

**Interpretation Bulletins**: IT-193 SR: Taxable income of individuals resident in Canada during part of a year (Special Release); IT-427R: Livestock of farmers.

**(4.1) Idem** — Notwithstanding subsection (1), where at any time in a taxation year

(a) a taxpayer who carried on a business the income from which is computed in accordance with the cash method is non-resident, and

(b) a property that was inventory owned by the taxpayer in connection with the business is not used in connection with a business carried on in Canada by the taxpayer (other than inventory sold in the course of carrying on the business), the taxpayer shall (except where this subsection applied in respect of the property at an earlier time) be deemed to have disposed of the property at that time in the course of carrying on the business for proceeds of disposition equal to its fair market value at that time and an amount equal to those proceeds shall be included in computing the taxpayer's income from the business

    (c) for the year, if section 114 does not apply, or

    (d) if section 114 applies, for the period or periods in the year referred to in paragraph 114(a).

**Proposed Repeal — 28(4.1)**

**Application**: Bill C-43 (First Reading September 20, 2000), subsec. 13(2), will repeal subsec. 28(4.1), applicable after December 23, 1998.

**Technical Notes**: With the addition of new subsection 10(12) and the amendment of section 128.1 (changes in residence), subsection 28(4.1) has become redundant, and is repealed with application after December 23, 1998.

**Related Provisions**: 10(12) — Non-resident ceasing to use inventory; 28(4) — Non-resident; 253 — Extended meaning of "carrying on business in Canada".

**Notes**: 28(4.1) added by 1991 technical bill, effective for taxpayers who cease to reside in Canada after July 13, 1990 and for property that ceases after July 13, 1990 to be used in connection with a business carried on in Canada.

**Interpretation Bulletins**: IT-427R: Livestock of farmers.

**(5) Accounts receivable** — There shall be included in computing the income of a taxpayer for a taxation year such part of an amount received by the taxpayer in the year, on or after disposing of or ceasing to carry on a business or a part of a business, for, on account or in lieu of payment of, or in satisfaction of debts owing to the taxpayer that arose in the course of carrying on the business as would have been included in computing the income of the taxpayer for the year had the amount so received been received by the taxpayer in the course of carrying on the business.

**Definitions [s. 28]**: "amount", "business" — 248(1), 253; "Canada" — 255; "cash method" — 28(1), 248(1); "farming", "inventory", "Minister", "non-resident", "person", "property" — 248(1); "specified animal" — 28(1.2); "taxation year" — 11(2), 249; "taxpayer" — 248(1).

**Interpretation Bulletins [s. 28]**: IT-156R: Feedlot operators; IT-188R: Sale of accounts receivable; IT-433R: Farming or fishing — use of cash method; IT-505: Mortgage foreclosures and conditional sales repossessions; IT-526: Farming — cash method inventory adjustments.

**29. (1) Disposition of animal of basic herd class** — Where a taxpayer has a basic herd of a class of animals and disposes of an animal of that class in the course of carrying on a farming business in a taxation year, if the taxpayer so elects in the taxpayer's return of income under this Part for the year the following rules apply:

    (a) there shall be deducted in computing the taxpayer's basic herd of that class at the end of the year such number as is designated by the taxpayer in the taxpayer's election, not exceeding the least of

        (i) the number of animals of that class so disposed of by the taxpayer in that year,

        (ii) $^1/_{10}$ of the taxpayer's basic herd of that class on December 31, 1971, and

        (iii) the taxpayer's basic herd of that class of animal at the end of the immediately preceding taxation year; and

    (b) there shall be deducted in computing the taxpayer's income from the farming business for the taxation year the product obtained when

        (i) the number determined under paragraph (a) in respect of the taxpayer's basic herd of that class for the year

is multiplied by

        (ii) the quotient obtained when the fair market value on December 31, 1971 of the taxpayer's animals of that class on that day is divided by the number of the taxpayer's animals of that class on that day.

**Related Provisions**: 28(1)(b) — Optional inclusion of inventory in income; 96(3) — Election by members of partnership.

**Forms**: T2034: Election to establish inventory unit prices for animals.

**(2) Reduction in basic herd** — Where a taxpayer carries on a farming business in a taxation year and the taxpayer's basic herd of any class at the end of the immediately preceding year, minus the deduction, if any, required by paragraph (1)(a) to be made in computing the taxpayer's basic herd of that class at the end of the year, exceeds the number of animals of that class owned by the taxpayer at the end of the year,

    (a) there shall be deducted in computing the taxpayer's basic herd of that class at the end of the year the number of animals comprising the excess, and

    (b) there shall be deducted in computing the taxpayer's income from the farming business for the taxation year the product obtained when

        (i) the number of animals comprising the excess

is multiplied by

        (ii) the quotient obtained when the fair market value on December 31, 1971 of the taxpayer's animals of that class on that day is divided by the number of the taxpayer's animals of that class on that day.

**(3) Interpretation** — For the purposes of this section,

    (a) a taxpayer's "basic herd" of any class of animals at a particular time means such number of the animals of that class that the taxpayer had on hand at the end of [the taxpayer's] 1971 taxation year as were, for the purpose of assessing the taxpayer's tax under this Part for that year, accepted by the Minister, as a consequence of an application made by the taxpayer, to be capital properties and not to be stock-in-trade, minus the numbers, if any, required by virtue of this section to be deducted in computing the taxpayer's basic herd of that class at the end of taxation years of the taxpayer ending before the particular time;

(b) "class of animals" means animals of a particular species, namely, cattle, horses, sheep or swine, that are

(i) purebred animals of that species for which a certificate of registration has been issued by a person recognized by breeders in Canada of purebred animals of that species to be the registrar of the breed to which such animals belong, or issued by the Canadian National Livestock Records Corporation, or

(ii) animals of that species other than purebred animals described in subparagraph (i),

each of which descriptions in subparagraphs (i) and (ii) shall be deemed to be of separate classes, except that where the number of the taxpayer's animals described in subparagraph (i) or (ii), as the case may be, of a particular species is not greater than 10% of the total number of the taxpayer's animals of that species that would otherwise be of two separate classes by virtue of this paragraph, the taxpayer's animals described in subparagraphs (i) and (ii) of that species shall be deemed to be of a single class; and

(c) in determining the number of animals of any class on hand at any time, an animal shall not be included if it was acquired for a feeder operation, and an animal shall be included only if its actual age is not less than,

(i) in the case of cattle, 2 years,

(ii) in the case of horses, 3 years, and,

(iii) in the case of sheep or swine, one year,

except that 2 animals of a class under the age specified in subparagraph (i), (ii) or (iii), as the case may be, shall be counted as one animal of the age so specified.

**Definitions [s. 29]**: "basic herd" — 29(3); "business" — 248(1); "capital property" — 54, 248(1); "farming", "Minister", "person" — 248(1); "taxation year" — 11(2), 249; "taxpayer" — 248(1).

**Interpretation Bulletins [s. 29]**: IT-427R: Livestock of farmers.

## 30. Improving land for farming
— Notwithstanding paragraphs 18(1)(a) and (b), there may be deducted in computing a taxpayer's income for a taxation year from a farming business any amount paid by the taxpayer before the end of the year for clearing land, levelling land or installing a land drainage system for the purposes of the business, to the extent that such amount has not been deducted in a preceding taxation year.

**Related Provisions**: 28(1)(g) — Deduction from farming or fishing income when using cash method.

**Definitions [s. 30]**: "amount", "business", "farming" — 248(1); "taxation year" — 11(2), 249; "taxpayer" — 248(1).

**Interpretation Bulletins [s. 30]**: IT-485: Cost of clearing or levelling land.

## 31. (1) Loss from farming where chief source of income not farming
— Where a taxpayer's chief source of income for a taxation year is neither farming nor a combination of farming and some other source of income, for the purposes of sections 3 and 111 the taxpayer's loss, if any, for the year from all farming businesses carried on by the taxpayer shall be deemed to be the total of

(a) the lesser of

(i) the amount by which the total of the taxpayer's losses for the year, determined without reference to this section and before making any deduction under section 37 or 37.1, from all farming businesses carried on by the taxpayer exceeds the total of the taxpayer's incomes for the year, so determined from all such businesses, and

(ii) $2,500 plus the lesser of

(A) ½ of the amount by which the amount determined under subparagraph (i) exceeds $2,500, and

(B) $6,250, and

(b) the amount, if any, by which

(i) the amount that would be determined under subparagraph (a)(i) if it were read as though the words "and before making any deduction under section 37 or 37.1" were deleted,

exceeds

(ii) the amount determined under subparagraph (a)(i).

**Related Provisions**: 9(2) — Loss from business or property; 31(1.1) — Restricted farm loss; 53(1)(i) — Addition to adjusted cost base for non-deductible losses; 53(2)(c)(i)(B) — Adjusted cost base of interest in partnership; 87(2.1)(a) — Amalgamation — Restricted farm loss carried forward; 96(1) — Restricted farm loss of partner; 101 — Disposition of land used in farming business of partnership; 111(1)(c) — Carryover of restricted farm losses; 111(9) — Restricted farm loss where taxpayer not resident in Canada; 127.52(1)(i)(ii)(B) — Calculation of previous year's restricted farm loss for minimum tax purposes; 128.1(4)(f) — Restricted farm loss limitation on becoming non-resident.

**Notes**: There are three categories of farming losses. No deduction is allowed if the farming is not a business with a reasonable expectation of profit (see 18(1)(h) and 248(1)"personal and living expenses"). Where the farming is a business but is not a chief source of income (see Notes to 31(2) below), 31(1) restricts the loss to $2,500 plus ½ of the next $12,500, to a maximum of $8,750. This is a "restricted farm loss" (see 31(1.1)). Unused restricted farm losses can be carried forward 10 years and back 3 years, but only against farming income; see 111(1)(c). Where 31(1) does not apply, losses are fully deductible against other income, and can also be carried forward for 10 years; see 111(1)(d) and 111(8)"farm loss". See also Notes to 31(2).

31(1) amended by 1994 tax amendments bill (Part I), to delete the closing words (now dealt with by 31(1.1). For taxation years that end before February 22, 1994, read the following at the end:

and for the purposes of this Act the amount, if any, by which the amount determined under subparagraph (a)(i) exceeds the amount determined under subparagraph (a)(ii) is the taxpayer's "restricted farm loss" for the year.

**Interpretation Bulletins**: IT-302R3: Losses of a corporation — the effect that acquisitions of control, amalgamations, and windings-up have on their deductibility — after January 15, 1987.

**(1.1) Restricted farm loss** — For the purposes of this Act, a taxpayer's "restricted farm loss" for a taxation year is the amount, if any, by which

(a) the amount determined under subparagraph (1)(a)(i) in respect of the taxpayer for the year

exceeds

(b) the total of the amount determined under subparagraph (1)(a)(ii) in respect of the taxpayer for the year and all amounts each of which is an amount by which the taxpayer's restricted farm loss for the year is required to be reduced because of section 80.

**Related Provisions**: 80(3)(c) — Reduction in restricted farm loss on debt forgiveness; 248(1)"restricted farm loss" — Definition applies to entire Act. See also Related Provisions to 31(1).

**Notes**: 31(1.1) added by 1994 tax amendments bill (Part I), effective for taxation years that end after February 21, 1994. See Notes to 31(1).

**(2) Determination by Minister** — For the purpose of this section, the Minister may determine that a taxpayer's chief source of income for a taxation year is neither farming nor a combination of farming and some other source of income.

**Notes**: Since the Minister has discretion in making a determination under 31(2), that determination can only be successfully appealed if the taxpayer can show that the Minister (i.e., the CCRA) has not observed correct legal principles in the exercise of the discretion. See, for example, *E. W. Bickle Ltd.*, [1979] C.T.C. 228 and [1981] C.T.C. 25 (FCA); and *Barron*, [1997] 2 C.T.C. 198 (FCA). The legal principles to be applied in determining restricted farm losses were set out by the Supreme Court of Canada in *Moldowan*, [1977] C.T.C. 310.

**Definitions [s. 31]**: "amount", "business", "farming", "Minister" — 248(1); "taxation year" — 11(2), 249; "taxpayer" — 248(1).

**Interpretation Bulletins [s. 31]**: IT-156R: Feedlot operators; IT-232R3: Losses — their deductibility in the loss year or in other years; IT-262R2 — Losses of non-residents and part-year residents; IT-322R: Farm losses; IT-373R: Farm woodlots and tree farms.

**32. (1) Insurance agents and brokers [unearned commissions]** — In computing a taxpayer's income for a taxation year from the taxpayer's business as an insurance agent or broker, no amount may be deducted under paragraph 20(1)(m) for the year in respect of unearned commissions from the business, but in computing the taxpayer's income for the year from the business there may be deducted, as a reserve in respect of such commissions, an amount equal to the lesser of

(a) the total of all amounts each of which is that proportion of an amount that has been included in computing the taxpayer's income for the year or a preceding taxation year as a commission in respect of an insurance contract (other than a life insurance contract) that

(i) the number of days in the period provided for in the insurance contract that are after the end of the taxation year

is of

(ii) the number of days in that period, and

(b) the total of all amounts each of which is the amount that would, but for this subsection, be deductible under paragraph 20(1)(m) for the year in respect of a commission referred to in paragraph (a).

**Related Provisions**: 72(1)(b) — Reserves, etc. for year of death; 87(2)(j.6) — Amalgamation — continuing corporation.

**Notes**: 32(1) amended by 1991 technical bill, effective for taxation years ending after 1990.

**Forms**: T2069: Election in respect of amounts not deductible as reserves for the year of death.

**(2) Reserve to be included** — There shall be included as income of a taxpayer for a taxation year from a business as an insurance agent or broker, the amount deducted under subsection (1) in computing the taxpayer's income therefrom for the immediately preceding year.

**(3) Additional reserve** — In computing a taxpayer's income for a taxation year ending after 1990 from a business carried on by the taxpayer throughout the year as an insurance agent or broker, there may be deducted as an additional reserve an amount not exceeding

(a) where the year ends in 1991, 90%,

(b) where the year ends in 1992, 80%,

(c) where the year ends in 1993, 70%,

(d) where the year ends in 1994, 60%,

(e) where the year ends in 1995, 50%,

(f) where the year ends in 1996, 40%,

(g) where the year ends in 1997, 30%,

(h) where the year ends in 1998, 20%,

(i) where the year ends in 1999, 10%, and

(j) where the year ends after 1999, 0%

of the amount, if any, by which

(k) the reserve that was deducted by the taxpayer under subsection (1) for the taxpayer's last taxation year ending before 1991

exceeds

(l) the amount deductible by the taxpayer under subsection (1) for the taxpayer's first taxation year ending after 1990,

and any amount so deducted by the taxpayer for a taxation year shall be deemed for the purposes of subsection (2) to have been deducted for that year pursuant to subsection (1).

Subdivision b — Income or Loss from a Business or Property    S. 33.1(1) eli

**Related Provisions**: 87(2)(j.6) — Rules applicable — continuing corporation.

**Definitions [s. 32]**: "amount", "business" — 248(1); "taxation year" — 11(2), 249; "taxpayer" — 248(1).

**Interpretation Bulletins [s. 32]**: IT-321R: Insurance agents and brokers — unearned commissions.

## 32.1 (1) Employee benefit plan deductions —
Where a taxpayer has made contributions to an employee benefit plan in respect of the taxpayer's employees or former employees, the taxpayer may deduct in computing the taxpayer's income for a taxation year

(a) such portion of an amount allocated to the taxpayer for the year under subsection (2) by the custodian of the plan as does not exceed the amount, if any, by which

(i) the total of all amounts each of which is a contribution by the taxpayer to the plan for the year or a preceding year

exceeds the total of all amounts each of which is

(ii) an amount in respect of the plan deducted by the taxpayer in computing the taxpayer's income for a preceding year, or

(iii) an amount received by the taxpayer in the year or a preceding year that was a return of amounts contributed by the taxpayer to the plan; and

(b) where at the end of the year all of the obligations of the plan to the taxpayer's employees and former employees have been satisfied and no property of the plan will thereafter be paid to or otherwise be available for the benefit of the taxpayer, the amount, if any, by which

(i) the total of all amounts each of which is a contribution by the taxpayer to the plan for the year or a preceding year

exceeds the total of all amounts each of which is

(ii) an amount in respect of the plan deducted by the taxpayer in computing the taxpayer's income for a preceding year, or, by virtue of paragraph (a), for the year, or

(iii) an amount received by the taxpayer in the year or a preceding year that was a return of amounts contributed by the taxpayer to the plan.

**Related Provisions**: 6(1)(a)(ii), 6(1)(g) — Employee benefit plan benefits taxable; 12(1)(n) — Employer's income inclusion — amounts received from employees profit sharing plan; 12(1)(n.1) — Employee benefit plan; 18(1)(o) — Employee benefit plan contributions; 87(2)(j.3) — Amalgamation — continuation of corporation; 107.1 — Distribution by employee trust or employee benefit plan; 207.6(4) — Deemed contribution.

**Advance Tax Rulings**: ATR-17: Employee benefit plan — purchase of company shares.

**(2) Allocation** — Every custodian of an employee benefit plan shall each year allocate to persons who have made contributions to the plan in respect of their employees or former employees the amount, if any, by which the total of

(a) all payments made in the year out of or under the plan to or for the benefit of their employees or former employees (other than the portion thereof that, by virtue of subparagraph 6(1)(g)(ii), is not required to be included in computing the income of a taxpayer), and

(b) all payments made in the year out of or under the plan to the heirs or the legal representatives of their employees or former employees

exceeds the income of the plan for the year.

**Related Provisions**: 32.1(3) — Income of employee benefit plan.

**(3) Income of employee benefit plan** — For the purposes of subsection (2), the income of an employee benefit plan for a year

(a) in the case of a plan that is a trust, is the amount that would be its income for the year if section 104 were read without reference to subsections 104(4) to (24); and

(b) in any other case, is the total of all amounts each of which is the amount, if any, by which a payment under the plan by the custodian thereof in the year exceeds

(i) in the case of an annuity, that part of the payment determined in prescribed manner to have been a return of capital, and

(ii) in any other case, that part of the payment that could, but for paragraph 6(1)(g), reasonably be regarded as being a payment of a capital nature.

**Regulations**: 300 (prescribed manner).

**Definitions [s. 32.1]**: "amount", "annuity", "employee benefit plan", "person", "prescribed", "property" — 248(1); "taxation year" — 11(2), 249.

**Interpretation Bulletins [s. 32.1]**: IT-502: Employee benefit plans and employee trusts.

## 33. [Repealed under former Act]

**Notes**: 33 repealed by 1988 tax reform. This was a special reserve that could be deducted by taxpayers whose business includes the lending of money on security. The normal reserve for doubtful debts can still be claimed under 20(1)(l) by such taxpayers.

A proposed s. 33 was introduced in draft legislation of July 19, 1995, providing a business income reserve for the 1995 stub period for taxpayers who change from off-calendar to calendar year-end. This was moved to 34.2, enacted by the 1995 Budget bill.

## 33.1 (1) International banking centres — definitions — In this section,

**"eligible deposit"**, at any particular time, means a debt owing at the particular time by a taxpayer that is a prescribed financial institution as or on account of an amount deposited with the taxpayer by

(a) a non-resident person with whom the taxpayer is dealing at arm's length at the particular time, where

(i) at the particular time, the deposit is recorded in the books of account of an international banking centre business of the taxpayer,

(ii) at the particular time, the taxpayer is not obligated, either immediately or in the future and either absolutely or contingently, to repay any portion of the debt to a person other than a non-resident person, and

(iii) before the deposit was recorded in the books of account of the international banking centre business, the taxpayer made reasonable inquiries and had no reasonable cause to believe that any portion of the amount was deposited on behalf of, for the benefit of or as a condition of any transaction with, a person (other than a non-resident person with whom the taxpayer was dealing at arm's length), or

(b) another prescribed financial institution with whom the taxpayer is dealing at arm's length at the particular time, where

(i) at or before the time at which the deposit was made, the prescribed financial institution provided written notice to the taxpayer that the deposit was being made from deposits recorded in the books of account of an international banking centre business of that prescribed financial institution, and

(ii) a reasonable rate of interest is paid or payable by the taxpayer in respect of the deposit;

**Related Provisions**: 212(1)(b)(xi) — Non-resident withholding tax — exemption.

**Notes**: Subpara. (a)(iii) of "eligible deposit" amended by 1991 technical bill, effective for deposits first recorded in the books of account of an IBC business after July 13, 1990, to add the words "with whom the taxpayer was dealing at arm's length".

**Regulations**: 7900 (prescribed financial institution).

**"eligible loan"**, at any particular time, means

(a) a loan or deposit (in this paragraph referred to as a "loan") made by a taxpayer that is a prescribed financial institution to a non-resident person (in this paragraph referred to as the "borrower") with whom the taxpayer is dealing at arm's length at the particular time, where

(i) at the particular time, neither a person other than a non-resident person nor a person with whom the taxpayer is not dealing at arm's length is obligated to the taxpayer, either immediately or in the future and either absolutely or contingently, to pay to the taxpayer any amount in respect of the loan,

(ii) the loan was recorded in the books of account of an international banking centre business of the taxpayer throughout the period commencing with the later of

(A) the time at which the loan was made, and

(B) the earliest of

(I) the time at which the loan was first recorded in the books of account of a branch or office of the taxpayer located in Canada,

(II) the end of the first taxation year in respect of which the taxpayer has made any designation under subsection (3), and

(III) the end of 1992

and ending at the particular time,

(iii) in the case of a loan made before the end of the first taxation year in respect of which the taxpayer has made any designation under subsection (3) (other than a loan recorded in the books of account of an international banking centre business of the taxpayer at the time at which the loan was made) or a loan made to a foreign bank, the taxpayer made reasonable inquiries before the loan was recorded in the books of account of the international banking centre business and had no reasonable cause to believe that the borrower had used or would use any proceeds of the loan, directly or indirectly, for the purpose of

(A) earning income in Canada, or

(B) making a loan to a person other than a non-resident person, and

(iv) in the case of any other loan, the taxpayer, before the loan was recorded in the books of account of the international banking centre business,

(A) obtained a statement signed by or on behalf of the borrower that the borrower would not use any proceeds of the loan, directly or indirectly, for a purpose described in subparagraph (iii), and

(B) had no reasonable cause to believe that the borrower would use any proceeds of the loan, directly or indirectly, for a purpose described in subparagraph (iii),

(b) a loan acquired by a taxpayer that is a prescribed financial institution from a foreign bank with which the taxpayer is not dealing at arm's length at the time the loan was acquired, where the conditions described in subparagraphs (a)(i) to (iii) are met at the particular time, or

(c) a deposit made by a taxpayer that is a prescribed financial institution with another prescribed financial institution with whom the taxpayer is dealing at arm's length at the particular time where, at or before the time at which the deposit was made, the taxpayer provided written notice to the prescribed financial institution that the deposit was being made from deposits recorded in the books of account of an international banking centre business of the taxpayer;

**Regulations**: 7900 (prescribed financial institution).

**"foreign bank"** has the meaning that would be assigned by the definition "foreign bank" in subsection 2(1) of the *Bank Act* if that definition were read without reference to paragraph (g) thereof;

> #### Proposed Amendment — 33.1(1)"foreign bank"
>
> **"foreign bank"** has the meaning assigned by the definition "foreign bank" in section 2 of the *Bank Act* (read without reference to paragraph (g)), except that an authorized foreign bank is not considered to be a foreign bank in respect of its Canadian banking business;
>
> **Application**: The August 8, 2000 draft legislation, s. 4, will amend the definition "foreign bank" in subsec. 33.1(1) to read as above, applicable after June 27, 1999.
>
> **Technical Notes**: Section 33.1 provides special rules for "international banking centres" (IBCs). Subsection 33.1(1) defines certain terms used in the section.
>
> The definition "foreign bank" in subsection 33.1(1) is amended to provide that an authorized foreign bank is not considered to be a foreign bank with respect to its Canadian banking business.

**Notes**: The definition "foreign bank" in s. 2 of the *Bank Act* reads:

> "foreign bank", subject to section 12, means an entity incorporated or formed by or under the laws of a country other than Canada that
>
> (a) is a bank according to the laws of any foreign country where it carries on business,
>
> (b) carries on a business in any foreign country that, if carried on in Canada, would be, wholly or to a significant extent, the business of banking,
>
> (c) engages, directly or indirectly, in the business of providing financial services and employs, to identify or describe its business, a name that includes the word "bank", "banque", "banking" or "bancaire", either alone or in combination with other words, or any word or words in any language other than English or French corresponding generally thereto,
>
> (d) engages in the business of lending money and accepting deposit liabilities transferable by cheque or other instrument,
>
> (e) engages, directly or indirectly, in the business of providing financial services and is affiliated with another foreign bank,
>
> (f) controls another foreign bank, or
>
> (g) is a foreign institution, other than a foreign bank within the meaning of any of paragraphs (a) to (f), that controls a bank named in Schedule II,
>
> but does not include a subsidiary of a bank named in Schedule I;

**"non-resident person"** at any time, with respect to a taxpayer, includes a person that the taxpayer, based on reasonable inquiries, believes at that time to be a person not resident in Canada.

**(2) Interpretation** — For the purposes of this section,

(a) a partnership shall be deemed to be a person;

(b) where a member of a partnership and a person do not deal with each other at arm's length, the partnership and the person shall be deemed not to deal with each other at arm's length;

(c) a partnership is a non-resident person only where all of its members are non-resident persons; and

(d) a deposit made by or to a non-resident person or a loan made to a non-resident person does not include a deposit made by or to, or a loan made to, as the case may be, a fixed place of business in Canada of the non-resident person.

**(3) Designation and exemption** — Where a taxpayer that was, throughout a taxation year, a prescribed financial institution has designated in respect of the year, by filing a prescribed form with the Minister on or before the day that is 90 days after the commencement of the year, a branch or office of the taxpayer in the metropolitan area of Montreal in the Province of Quebec or in the metropolitan area of Vancouver in the Province of British Columbia as a branch or office in which an international banking centre business of the taxpayer is to be carried on and has not revoked that designation by filing a prescribed form with the Minister on or before that day, in computing the income of the taxpayer for the year no amount shall be added or deducted in respect of the taxpayer's income or loss, as the case may be, for the year from the international banking centre business.

**Related Provisions**: 33.1(5) — Restriction; 33.1(6) — Election; 33.1(7) — Election restriction; 33.1(9) — Exception where less than 90% of revenue from eligible loans; 33.1(12) — Return; 87(2)(j.8) — Amalgamations — continuing corporation.

**Regulations**: 7900 (prescribed financial institution).

**Forms**: T781: Designation as an international banking centre; T781-C: Revocation of designation as an international banking centre.

**(4) Income or loss from an international banking centre business** — Subject to subsection (5), the amount of a taxpayer's income or loss, as the case may be, for a taxation year from an international banking centre business shall be determined on the assumption that

(a) the international banking centre business was a separate business carried on by the taxpayer the only income or loss of which was derived from eligible loans for the period in the year during which they were recorded in the books of account of the business; and

(b) the only amount payable for the year by the taxpayer in respect of interest on money borrowed for the purpose of earning income from the business was equal to the total of

(i) the total of all amounts each of which is the interest payable by the taxpayer in respect of an eligible deposit for the period in the year during which it was recorded in the books of account of the business, and

(ii) the amount equal to that proportion of

(A) the total of all amounts each of which is the amount determined in respect of a day in the year equal to the amount, if any, by which

(I) 96% of the total of all amounts each of which is the amount outstanding on account of the principal amount of an eligible loan recorded in the books of account of the business at the end of the day

exceeds

(II) the total of all amounts each of which is the amount outstanding on account of the principal amount of an eligible deposit recorded in the books of account of the business at the end of the day

that

(B) the total determined under subparagraph (i)

is of

(C) the total of all amounts each of which is the amount outstanding on account of the principal amount of an eligible deposit recorded in the books of account of the business at the end of a day in the year.

**Related Provisions**: 33.1(6) — Election; 33.1(10) — No deduction permitted; 33.1(11) — Rules clarifying application of provision; 87(2)(j.8) — Amalgamations — continuing corporation.

**(5) Restriction** — A taxpayer's income for a taxation year from an international banking centre business shall not exceed that proportion of such income determined in accordance with subsection (4) that

(a) the total of all amounts each of which is an amount determined in respect of a day in the year equal to the lesser of

(i) 96% of the total of all amounts each of which is the amount outstanding on account of the principal amount of an eligible loan recorded in the books of account of the business at the end of the day, and

(ii) the total of all amounts each of which is the amount outstanding on account of the principal amount of an eligible deposit recorded in the books of account of the business at the end of the day

is of

(b) 96% of the total of all amounts each of which is the amount outstanding on account of the principal amount of an eligible loan recorded in the books of account of the business at the end of a day in the year.

**Related Provisions**: 33.1(6) — Election.

**(6) Election** — For the purposes of subsections (4) and (5), where a taxpayer so elects in the taxpayer's return of income for a taxation year or in a prescribed form filed with the Minister within 90 days after the day of mailing of a notice of assessment for the year or a notification that no tax is payable for the year, an eligible deposit recorded in the books of account of an international banking centre business of the taxpayer at the end of a day in the year shall be deemed not to have been recorded at any time in the day in the books of account of that business and shall be deemed to have been recorded throughout that day in the books of account of another international banking centre business of the taxpayer designated by the taxpayer in the election.

**Related Provisions**: 33.1(7) — Election restriction.

**Forms**: T781-B: Election re deemed transfers of eligible deposits between international banking centres.

**(7) Election restriction** — A taxpayer may elect, as provided in subsection (6), only in respect of eligible deposits recorded in the books of account of an international banking centre business at the end of a day to the extent that the total of those deposits exceeds 96% of the total of all amounts outstanding on account of the principal amounts of eligible loans recorded in the books of account of the business at the end of the day.

**Notes**: 33.1(7) amended by 1991 technical bill, retroactive to taxation years commencing after December 17, 1987, to add the words "96% of".

**(8) Limitation** — In computing the income of a taxpayer for a taxation year, an amount paid or payable by the taxpayer on a deposit for the period in the year during which it was an eligible deposit shall, notwithstanding any other provision of this Act, be deductible only in computing the income or loss of the taxpayer from an international banking centre business.

**(9) Exception** — Where less than 90% of the revenue of a taxpayer for a taxation year from loans or deposits for the period in the year during which they were recorded in the books of account of an international banking centre business was derived from eligible loans in respect of which employees of the taxpayer actively participated in the solicitation, negotiation, analysis or management thereof while employed at a branch or office designated under subsection (3) as a branch or office in which an international banking centre business of the taxpayer is to be carried on, the amount, if any, of the taxpayer's income for the year from the international banking centre business shall, notwithstanding subsection (3), be included in computing the taxpayer's income for the year.

**(10) No deduction permitted** — Notwithstanding any other provision of this Act, in computing the income of a taxpayer no deduction shall be made in respect of any amount paid or payable in respect of indebtedness of the taxpayer to any person where, under an arrangement of which the taxpayer was aware or ought to have been aware at the time the indebtedness was incurred by the taxpayer, any portion of the indebtedness may reasonably be regarded as having been provided directly or indirectly from proceeds of a loan recorded in the books of account of an international banking centre business of a prescribed financial institution and any person has, in respect of that loan, signed a statement described in subparagraph (a)(iv) of the definition "eligible loan" in subsection (1).

**Regulations**: 7900 (prescribed financial institution).

**(11) Application** — For greater certainty,

(a) where at any time a loan or deposit of a taxpayer ceases to be an eligible loan otherwise than by virtue of its disposition to another person, the taxpayer shall be deemed to have disposed of the loan or deposit in the course of carrying on an international banking centre business and to have received proceeds of disposition therefor equal to the fair market value of the loan or deposit at that time and to have reacquired the loan or deposit immediately after that time at a cost equal to its fair market value at that time;

(b) a taxpayer's loss for a taxation year from an international banking centre business shall not be included in determining the taxpayer's non-capital loss for the year; and

(c) the amount, if any, by which

(i) the amount that would be a taxpayer's income for a taxation year from an international banking centre business if this section were read without reference to subsection (5)

exceeds

(ii) the taxpayer's income for the year from the international banking centre business

shall be added in computing the income of the taxpayer for the year.

**Related Provisions**: 54"superficial loss"(c) — Superficial loss rule does not apply.

**(12) Return** — Every taxpayer that has, in respect of a taxation year, designated a branch or office under subsection (3) as a branch or office in which an international banking centre business of the taxpayer is to be carried on shall, within six months after the end of the year, file with the Minister a return in prescribed form containing prescribed information.

**Forms**: T781-A: International banking centre information return.

**Definitions [s. 33.1]**: "amount" — 248(1); "arm's length" — 251(1); "assessment", "authorized foreign bank", "borrowed money", "business", "Canadian banking business" — 248(1); "carrying on business" — 253; "eligible deposit", "eligible loan" — 33.1(1); "employed" — 248(1); "foreign bank" — 33.1(1); "Minister" — 248(1); "non-capital loss" — 111(8), 248(1); "non-resident" — 33.1(1), 248(1); "office", "person", "prescribed", "principal amount" — 248(1); "partnership" — see Notes to 96(1); "person" — 33.1(2), 248(1); "resident in Canada" — 250; "taxation year" — 249; "taxpayer" — 248(1).

**34. Professional business** — In computing the income of a taxpayer for a taxation year from a business that is the professional practice of an accountant, dentist, lawyer, medical doctor, veterinarian or chiropractor, the following rules apply:

(a) where the taxpayer so elects in the taxpayer's return of income under this Part for the year, there shall not be included any amount in respect of work in progress at the end of the year; and

(b) where the taxpayer has made an election under this section, paragraph (a) shall apply in computing the taxpayer's income from the business for all subsequent taxation years unless the taxpayer, with the concurrence of the Minister and on such terms and conditions as are specified by the Minister, revokes the election to have that paragraph apply.

**Related Provisions**: 10(4)(a) — Valuation of work in progress; 10(5)(a) — Work in progress deemed to be inventory; 23(3) — Reference to property included in inventory; 34.2(2)(b) — Election deemed to have been made for purposes of 1995 stub period income; 70(2) — Rights or things included in income on death; 96(3) — Election by members of partnership.

**Notes**: On the professional's death, work in progress excluded under s. 34 is considered by the CCRA to be taxable as a "right or thing". See IT-212R3 and Notes to 70(2).

**Definitions [s. 34]**: "amount", "business" — 248(1); "lawyer" — 232(1), 248(1); "Minister", "property" — 248(1); "taxation year" — 11(2), 249; "taxpayer" — 248(1).

**I.T. Application Rules [s. 34]**: 23(3)–(5) (where business carried on since before 1972).

**Interpretation Bulletins [s. 34]**: IT-188R: Sale of accounts receivable; IT-189R2: Corporations used by practising members of professions; IT-212R3: Income of deceased persons — rights or things; IT-278R2: Death of a partner or of a retired partner; IT-457R: Election by professionals to exclude work in progress from income; IT-471R: Merger of partnerships.

**Forms [s. 34]**: T2032: Statement of professional activities.

**34.1 (1) Additional business income [off-calendar fiscal period]** — Where

(a) an individual (other than a testamentary trust) carries on a business in a taxation year,

(b) a fiscal period of the business begins in the year and ends after the end of the year (in this subsection referred to as the "particular period"), and

(c) the individual has elected under subsection 249.1(4) in respect of the business and the election has not been revoked,

there shall be included in computing the individual's income for the year from the business, the amount determined by the formula

**S. 34.1(1)**      Income Tax Act, Part I, Division B

$$(A - B) \times \frac{C}{D}$$

where

A  is the total of the individual's income from the business for the fiscal periods of the business that end in the year,

B  is the lesser of

   (i) the total of all amounts each of which is an amount included in the value of A in respect of the business and that is deemed to be a taxable capital gain for the purpose of section 110.6, and

   (ii) the total of all amounts deducted under section 110.6 in computing the individual's taxable income for the year,

C  is the number of days on which the individual carries on the business that are both in the year and in the particular period, and

D  is the number of days on which the individual carries on the business that are in fiscal periods of the business that end in the year.

**Related Provisions**: 11(1) — Determination of income from fiscal period of proprietor; 34.1(3) — Offsetting deduction in following year; 34.1(4) — Effect on 1995 stub period; 34.1(7) — Maximum December 31, 1995 income; 34.1(8) — No additional inclusion on death, bankruptcy or cease of business; 96(1.1), (1.6) — Allocation of share of income to retiring partner; 257 — Formula cannot calculate to less than zero.

**Notes**: 34.1(1) provides the calculation of additional business income to be included each year for individuals retaining an off-calendar year-end. See Notes at end of 34.1. The amount included is deducted in the next year under 34.1(3).

**Forms**: RC4015: Reconciliation of business income for tax purposes [guide]; T1139: Reconciliation of business income for tax purposes.

**(2) Additional income election** — Where

   (a) an individual (other than a testamentary trust) begins carrying on a business in a taxation year and not earlier than the beginning of the first fiscal period of the business that begins in the year and ends after the end of the year (in this subsection referred to as the "particular period"), and

   (b) the individual has elected under subsection 249.1(4) in respect of the business and the election has not been revoked,

there shall be included in computing the individual's income for the year from the business the lesser of

   (c) the amount designated in the individual's return of income for the year, and

   (d) the amount determined by the formula

$$(A - B) \times \frac{C}{D}$$

where

A  is the individual's income from the business for the particular period,

B  is the lesser of

   (i) the total of all amounts each of which is an amount included in the value of A in respect of the business and that is deemed to be a taxable capital gain for the purpose of section 110.6, and

   (ii) the total of all amounts deducted under section 110.6 in computing the individual's taxable income for the taxation year that includes the end of the particular period,

C  is the number of days on which the individual carries on the business that are both in the year and in the particular period, and

D  is the number of days on which the individual carries on the business that are in the particular period.

**Related Provisions**: 34.1(5) — Offsetting deduction in following year; 34.1(6) — Deemed December 31, 1995 income; 34.1(8) — No additional inclusion on death, bankruptcy or cease of business; 96(1.1), (1.6) — Allocation of share of income to retiring partner; 257 — Formula cannot calculate to less than zero.

**Notes**: See Notes at end of 34.1.

**Forms**: RC4015: Reconciliation of business income for tax purposes [guide]; T1139: Reconciliation of business income for tax purposes.

**(3) Deduction** — There shall be deducted in computing an individual's income for a taxation year from a business the amount, if any, included under subsection (1) or (2) in computing the individual's income for the preceding taxation year from the business.

**Notes**: See Notes at end of 34.1.

**(4) Deemed December 31, 1995 income** — For the purpose of section 34.2, where

   (a) at the end of 1994 an individual carried on a particular business no fiscal period of which ended at that time, and

   (b) an amount is included under subsection (1) in computing the individual's income for the 1995 taxation year in respect of

     (i) the particular business, or

     (ii) another business that would, if subsection 34.2(3) applied for the purpose of this subparagraph, be included in the particular business,

subject to subsection (7), the December 31, 1995 income of the individual in respect of the particular business or the other business, as the case may be, is deemed to be the amount that would have been so included if the descriptions of A and B in subsection (1) were read as follows:

"A is the total of the individual's income from the business for the fiscal periods of the business that end in the year (determined as if paragraphs 34.2(2)(a) to (d) applied in computing that income),

B is the lesser of

(i) the total of all amounts each of which is an amount included in the value of A in respect of the business and that is deemed to be a taxable capital gain for the purpose of section 110.6, and

(ii) the total of the maximum amounts deductible under section 110.6 in computing the individual's taxable income for the year,".

**Notes**: See Notes at end of 34.1.

**(5) Deemed December 31, 1995 income** — For the purpose of section 34.2, where

(a) at the end of 1994 an individual carried on a particular business no fiscal period of which ended at that time, and

(b) an amount is included under subsection (2) in computing the individual's income for the 1995 taxation year in respect of another business that would, if subsection 34.2(3) applied for the purpose of this paragraph, be included in the particular business,

the December 31, 1995 income of the individual in respect of the other business is deemed to be the amount that would have been so included if the descriptions of A and B in paragraph (2)(d) were read as follows:

"A is the individual's income from the business for the particular period (determined as if paragraphs 34.2(2)(a) to (d) applied in computing that income),

B is the lesser of

(i) the total of all amounts each of which is an amount included in the value of A in respect of the business and that is deemed to be a taxable capital gain for the purpose of section 110.6, and

(ii) the total of the maximum amounts deductible under section 110.6 in computing the individual's taxable income for the taxation year that includes the end of the particular period,".

**Notes**: See Notes at end of 34.1.

**(6) Deemed December 31, 1995 income** — For the purpose of section 34.2, where

(a) at the end of 1995 an individual carries on a business as a member of a partnership no fiscal period of which ended at the end of 1994,

(b) the business was carried on by a professional corporation as a member of the partnership at the end of 1994,

(c) the professional corporation transferred its interest in the partnership to the individual before the end of 1995,

(d) the individual is a practising member of the professional body under the authority of which the professional corporation practised the profession,

(e) the individual was a specified shareholder of the professional corporation immediately before the transfer,

(f) the professional corporation does not have a share of the income or loss of the partnership for the first fiscal period of the partnership that ends after the end of 1995, and

(g) an amount is included under subsection (2) in computing the individual's income for the 1995 taxation year in respect of the business,

the December 31, 1995 income of the individual in respect of the business is deemed to be the amount that would have been so included if the descriptions of A and B in paragraph (2)(d) were read as follows:

"A is the individual's income from the business for the particular period (determined as if paragraphs 34.2(2)(a) to (d) applied in computing that income),

B is the lesser of

(i) the total of all amounts each of which is an amount included in the value of A in respect of the business and that is deemed to be a taxable capital gain for the purpose of section 110.6, and

(ii) the total of the maximum amounts deductible under section 110.6 in computing the individual's taxable income for the taxation year that includes the end of the particular period,"

and, for the purpose of computing the values of C and D in paragraph (2)(d), the individual is deemed to carry on the business on the days on which the corporation carried on the business.

**Notes**: See Notes at end of 34.1.

**(7) Maximum December 31, 1995 income** — Where an amount was included under subsection (1) in computing an individual's income for the 1995 taxation year from a business and

(a) the individual's December 31, 1995 income otherwise determined under subsection (4) in respect of the business for the purpose of section 34.2

exceeds

(b) the amount that would be described under paragraph (a) if the descriptions of A, B and D in subsection (1) were read as follows:

"A is the individual's income from the business for the particular period (determined as if paragraphs 34.2(2)(a) to (d) applied in computing that income),

B is the lesser of

(i) the total of all amounts each of which is an amount included in the value of A in respect of the business

**S. 34.1(7)(b)**  Income Tax Act, Part I, Division B

and that is deemed to be a taxable capital gain for the purpose of section 110.6, and

(ii) the total of the maximum amounts deductible under section 110.6 in computing the individual's taxable income for the taxation year that includes the end of the particular period,

D  is the number of days on which the individual carries on the business that are in the particular period."

for the purpose of applying subsection 34.2(4) to the 1996 and subsequent taxation years, the December 31, 1995 income of the individual in respect of the business is deemed to be the amount determined under paragraph (b).

**Notes**: See Notes at end of 34.1.

**(8) No additional income inclusion** — Subsections (1) and (2) do not apply in computing an individual's income for a taxation year from a business where

(a) the individual dies or otherwise ceases to carry on the business in the year; or

(b) the individual becomes a bankrupt in the calendar year in which the taxation year ends.

**Related Provisions**: 34.1(9) — Income inclusion on death where election made or separate return filed.

**Notes**: See Notes at end of 34.1.

**(9) Death of partner or proprietor** — Where

(a) an individual carries on a business in a taxation year,

(b) the individual dies in the year and after the end of a fiscal period of the business that ends in the year,

(c) another fiscal period of the business ends because of the individual's death (in this subsection referred to as the "short period"), and

(d) the individual's legal representative

(i) elects that this subsection apply in computing the individual's income for the year, or

(ii) files a separate return of income under subsection 150(4) in respect of the individual's business,

notwithstanding subsection (8), there shall be included in computing the individual's income for the year from the business, the amount determined by the formula

$$(A - B) \times C/D$$

where

A  is the total of the individual's income from the business for fiscal periods (other than the short period) of the business that end in the year,

B  is the lesser of

(i) the total of all amounts, each of which is an amount included in the value of A in respect of the business that is deemed to be a taxable capital gain for the purpose of section 110.6, and

(ii) the total of all amounts deducted under section 110.6 in computing the individual's taxable income for the year,

C  is the number of days in the short period, and

D  is the total number of days in fiscal periods of the business (other than the short period) that end in the year.

**Related Provisions**: 257 — Formula cannot calculate to less than zero; 150(4)(c)C — Additional amount deductible on deceased's separate return.

**Notes**: 34.1(9) added by 1995-97 technical bill, effective for 1996 and later taxation years, but 34.1(9)(d)(ii) does not apply to the 1996 and 1997 taxation years.

**Notes [s. 34.1]**: 34.1 added by 1995 Budget, effective 1995. It provides rules for computing the "additional business income" of individuals who carry on an unincorporated business for which an election to have an off-calendar fiscal period is filed under 249.1(4). An off-calendar year can be retained for business purposes (e.g., for a seasonal business that runs through the winter), but tax must be prepaid through a recognition of income under 34.1 to approximate the income earned to December 31.

**Definitions [s. 34.1]**: "amount", "business" — 248(1); "calendar year" — *Interpretation Act* 37(1)(a); "December 31, 1995 income" — 34.1(4)–(7), 34.2(1); "fiscal period" — 249.1; "individual", "legal representative" — 248(1); "particular period" — 34.1(1)(b), 34.1(2)(a); "partnership" — see Notes to 96(1); "professional corporation" — 248(1); "short period" — 34.1(9)(c); "specified shareholder" — 248(1); "taxable capital gain" — 38, 248(1); "taxation year" — 249; "testamentary trust" — 108(1), 248(1).

**34.2 [1995 stub period reserve] — (1) Definitions** — The definitions in this subsection apply in this section.

**"December 31, 1995 income"** in respect of a business carried on by a taxpayer means the amount determined by the formula

$$(A - B - C + D) \times E$$

where

A  is the total of all amounts each of which is the taxpayer's income from the business for a qualifying fiscal period,

B  is the total of all amounts each of which is the taxpayer's loss from the business for a qualifying fiscal period,

C  is the lesser of

(a) the total of all amounts each of which is an amount included in computing the taxpayer's income or loss from the business for a qualifying fiscal period and that is deemed to be a taxable capital gain for the purpose of section 110.6, and

(b) the total of the maximum amounts deductible under section 110.6 in computing the tax-

Subdivision b — Income or Loss from a Business or Property    S. 34.2(1) spe

payer's taxable income for the taxation year in which the qualifying fiscal periods end,

D is

(a) where the taxpayer is a professional corporation, the total salary or wages deductible in computing the value of A or B in respect of the business that is payable by the corporation to an individual

(i) who is a practising member of the professional body under the authority of which the corporation practised the profession, and

(ii) who is a specified shareholder of the corporation, and

(b) in any other case, nil, and

E is

(a) where the taxpayer is a professional corporation a taxation year of which ended at the end of 1995 because of the application of paragraph 249.1(1)(b), the amount determined by the formula

$$\frac{F - G}{F}$$

where

F is the number of days in all qualifying fiscal periods of the business, and

G is the number of days in the year, and

(b) in any other case, 1.

**Related Provisions**: 34.1(7) — Maximum December 31, 1995 income where additional amount included under 34.1(1); 34.2(2) — Maximum reserves and allowances deemed claimed for qualifying fiscal period; 96(1.1), (1.6) — Allocation of share of income to retiring partner; 257 — Formulas cannot calculate to less than zero.

**Notes**: This is sometimes referred to as "stub period" income. See Notes at end of 34.2.

**"qualifying fiscal period"** of a business of a taxpayer means

(a) where at the end of 1994 the taxpayer carried on the business and no fiscal period of the business ended at that time, a fiscal period of the business that

(i) begins after the beginning of the taxpayer's taxation year that includes the end of 1995, and

(ii) ends

(A) at the end of 1995 because of the application of paragraph 249.1(1)(b) or because of the application of section 25 and paragraph 249.1(1)(b), or

(B) immediately before the end of 1995 because of the application of subsection 99(2) and paragraph 249.1(1)(b),

(b) a fiscal period of the business that ends at the end of 1995 because of the application of paragraph 249.1(1)(b) where

(i) the taxpayer is an individual who carries on the business as a member of a partnership at the end of 1995,

(ii) the individual acquired the individual's interest in the partnership in 1995 from a professional corporation,

(iii) the professional corporation carried on the business at the end of 1994 as a member of the partnership and does not have a share of the income or loss of the partnership for the fiscal period,

(iv) the individual is a practising member of the professional body under the authority of which the professional corporation practised the profession, and

(v) the individual was a specified shareholder of the professional corporation immediately before acquiring the interest, and

(c) where

(i) the taxpayer is a professional corporation that has a taxation year that ends at the end of 1995 because of the application of paragraph 249.1(1)(b), and

(ii) at the end of 1994 the business was carried on by the professional corporation as a member of a partnership, or by an individual

(A) who transferred an interest in the partnership to the professional corporation before the end of 1995,

(B) who is a practising member of the professional body under the authority of which the professional corporation practises the profession,

(C) who was a specified shareholder of the professional corporation immediately after the transfer, and

(D) who does not have a share of the income or loss of the partnership for the first fiscal period of the partnership that ends in 1995,

a fiscal period of the business that ends in that taxation year.

**Notes**: See Notes at end of 34.2.

**"specified percentage"** of a taxpayer for a particular taxation year in respect of a business means

(a) where the first taxation year in which a qualifying fiscal period of the business ends is 1995, or subsection 34.1(4), (5) or (6) applies in respect of the business, and the particular year ends in

(i) 1995, 95%,

(ii) 1996, 85%,

(iii) 1997, 75%,

(iv) 1998, 65%,

(v) 1999, 55%,

(vi) 2000, 45%,

(vii) 2001, 35%,

(viii) 2002, 25%,

(ix) 2003, 15%, and

(x) any other year, 0%, and

(b) where the first taxation year in which a qualifying fiscal period of a business of the taxpayer ends is 1996 and the particular year ends in

(i) 1996, 95%,

(ii) 1997, 85%,

(iii) 1998, 75%,

(iv) 1999, 65%,

(v) 2000, 55%,

(vi) 2001, 45%,

(vii) 2002, 35%,

(viii) 2003, 25%,

(ix) 2004, 15%, and

(x) any other year, 0%.

**Notes**: The normal case is (a); the stub period income normally runs from the former year-end to December 31, 1995. Para. (b) applies only to a corporation or testamentary trust that is a member of a partnership that is subject to the new year-end rules, where the corporation or trust retains a non-calendar year-end. In such a case there can be "stub period" income that is counted in the corporation's or trust's 1996 taxation year.

See also Notes at end of 34.2.

**(2) Computation of December 31, 1995 income** — For the purpose of the definition "December 31, 1995 income" in subsection (1), a taxpayer's income or loss from a business for a qualifying fiscal period shall be computed as if

(a) this Act were read without reference to paragraph 28(1)(b);

(b) the taxpayer had made the election referred to in paragraph 34(a) in respect of the business for the period;

(c) the maximum amount deductible in respect of any reserve, allowance or other amount were deducted; and

(d) the taxpayer had not received any taxable dividend.

**Notes**: "Allowance" in 34.2(2)(c) includes capital cost allowance (CCA). See also Notes at end of 34.2.

**(3) Business defined** — For the purposes of the definition "qualifying fiscal period" in subsection (1) and subparagraphs (6)(b)(i) and (c)(i), a reference to a particular business of a taxpayer includes another business substituted therefor, or for which the particular business was substituted, by the taxpayer where

(a) all or substantially all of the gross revenue of the particular business is derived from the sale, leasing, rental or development of properties or the rendering of services; and

(b) all or substantially all of the gross revenue of the other business is derived from the sale, leasing, rental or development, as the case may be, of similar properties or the rendering of similar services.

**Related Provisions**: 34.2(7) — Anti-avoidance rule re carrying on business.

**Notes**: The CCRA's position is that "all or substantially all" means 90% or more. Note that the extended definition of "gross revenue" in 248(1) will apply for this purpose.

Note that "derived" may be interpreted broadly: see *Kemp*, [1947] C.T.C. 343 (Exch. Ct.); *Hollinger North Shore Exploration Co. Ltd.*, [1963] C.T.C. 51 (SCC); *Bessemer Trust Co.*, [1972] C.T.C. 479 (FCTD).

See also Notes at end of 34.2.

**(4) Reserve** — Subject to subsection (6), where a taxpayer carries on a business in a particular taxation year, there may be deducted in computing the taxpayer's income for the year from the business, as a reserve in respect of December 31, 1995 income, such amount as the taxpayer claims not exceeding the least of

(a) the specified percentage for the particular year of the taxpayer's December 31, 1995 income in respect of the business;

(b) where an amount was deductible under this subsection in computing the taxpayer's income for a preceding taxation year from the business, the amount included under subsection (5) in computing the taxpayer's income for the particular year from the business; and

(c) the taxpayer's income for the particular year computed before deducting any amount under this subsection in respect of the business or under any of paragraph 60(w), sections 61.2 to 61.4 and subsection 80(17).

**Related Provisions**: 18(12)(b) — Reserve ignored for purposes of home office limitations; 34.1(7) — Maximum December 31, 1995 income where additional amount included under 34.1(1); 34.2(3) — Similar business carried on; 34.2(5) — Reserve included in income the following year; 34.2(6) — No reserve on death, bankruptcy or cease of business; 34.2(8) — Reserve deduction in year of death; 53(2)(c)(i.4) — Reduction in ACB of passive partner's partnership interest; 87(2)(j) — Amalgamations — continuing corporation; 96(1)(d) — Reserve ignored in determining income of partnership; 96(1.1), (1.6) — Allocation of share of income to retiring partner; 125(7)"specified partnership income"A(a)H — Reserve deducted from specified partnership income for CCPC that is member of partnership.

**Notes**: The reserve as originally proposed (in 33(4)) by the draft legislation of July 19, 1995 was reduced by "other 1995 deductions", which were a partner's expenses or deductions claimed directly (outside the partnership). In response to objections from many professionals, the Department of Finance deleted this requirement in the revised draft legislation of December 12, 1995 (now enacted as above), thus allowing a larger reserve than had been anticipated for many partners.

See also Notes at end of 34.2.

**Forms**: RC4015: Reconciliation of business income for tax purposes [guide]; T1139: Reconciliation of business income for tax purposes; T4002: Business and professional income [guide].

**(5) Reserve included in income** — There shall be included in computing a taxpayer's income for a taxation year from a business the amount deducted under subsection (4) in computing the taxpayer's income therefrom for the preceding taxation year.

**Related Provisions**: 87(2)(j) — Amalgamations — continuing corporation; 125(7)"specified partnership income"A(a)G — Reserve included in specified partnership income for CCPC that is member of partnership.

**Notes**: See Notes at end of 34.2.

**Forms**: T1139: Reconciliation of business income for tax purposes.

**(6) No reserve** — No deduction shall be made under subsection (4) in computing a taxpayer's income for a taxation year from a business where

(a) at the end of the year or at any time in the following taxation year,

(i) the taxpayer's income from the business is exempt from tax under this Part, or

(ii) the taxpayer is non-resident and does not carry on the business through a permanent establishment (as defined by regulation) in Canada;

(b) the taxpayer is a corporation and the year ends immediately before another taxation year

(i) at the beginning of which the business is not carried on principally by the corporation nor by members of a partnership of which the corporation is a member,

(ii) in which the corporation becomes a bankrupt, or

(iii) in which the corporation is dissolved or wound up (other than in circumstances to which subsection 88(1) applies); or

(c) the taxpayer is an individual, and

(i) at the beginning of the year, the business is not carried on principally by the individual nor by members of a partnership of which the individual is a member,

(ii) the individual dies or becomes a bankrupt in the calendar year in which the taxation year ends, or

(iii) the individual is a trust that ceases to exist in the year.

**Related Provisions**: 34.2(7) — Anti-avoidance rule re carrying on business; 34.2(8) — Optional deduction in year of death; 96(1.1) — Retired partner deemed to continue as member of partnership; 96(1.6) — Members of partnership deemed to be carrying on business in Canada (except where 34.2(7) applies).

**Notes**: The reference to permanent establishment (PE) in 34.2(6)(a)(ii) is used because a non-resident with no PE in Canada can usually claim exemption from Canadian income tax on business income via tax treaty. Canada's tax treaties generally allow Canada to tax non-residents only on business income earned in Canada through a PE in Canada. See, for example, Canada-U.S. Tax Convention, Article VII.

See also Notes at end of 34.2.

Despite the wording of 34.2(6)(a)(ii), Revenue Canada administratively allows the reserve to be claimed for the year preceding emigration. See technical interpretation 973297 (June 3, 1998) on Revenue Canada VIEWS.

**Regulations**: 8201 (permanent establishment).

**(7) Anti-avoidance rule** — Where it is reasonable to conclude that one of the main reasons a person carries on a business or is a member of a partnership is to avoid the application of subparagraph (6)(b)(i) or (c)(i), the person is deemed not to carry on the business, and not to be a member of the partnership, for the purposes of those subparagraphs.

**Notes**: See Notes at end of 34.2.

**(8) Death of partner or proprietor** — Where

(a) an individual carries on a business in a taxation year,

(b) the individual dies in the year,

(c) an amount is included under subsection (5) in computing the individual's income for the year from the business, and

(d) the individual's legal representative

(i) elects that this subsection apply in computing the individual's income for the year, or

(ii) files a separate return of income under subsection 150(4) in respect of the individual's business,

there shall be deducted in computing the individual's income for the year from the business the lesser of

(e) the greatest amount that would have been deductible under subsection (4) in computing the individual's income for the year from the business if the individual had not died, and

(f) any amount that the representative claims.

**Related Provisions**: 150(4)(c)B — Additional amount taxable on deceased's separate return.

**Notes**: 34.2(8) added by 1995-97 technical bill, effective for 1996 and later taxation years. The advantage of a separate return is that personal credits can be claimed separately against the tax owing on the remaining stub-period income; and the tax on that income will apply at graduated rates as though the deceased had no other income.

**Notes [s. 34.2]**: 34.2 added by 1995 Budget, effective 1995. It provides a 10-year reserve for individuals (and certain partnerships and professional corporations) that switched from an off-calendar year to a December 31 year-end as of 1995, as required by 249.1. (An election out of this rule is available under 249.1(4), but then an additional annual income inclusion is required under 34.1.) Because most affected taxpayers would otherwise be required to report more than 12 months of business income for 1995, 34.2 provides a 10-year transitional reserve (i.e., allows the extra income to be recognized gradually over a 10-year period).

The reserve is deducted under 34.2(4) as the "specified percentage", defined in 34.2(1). In essence, up to 95% of the "stub period" income (income from the first 1995 year-end through December 31, 1995) can be deducted for 1995; 85% for 1996, and so on. This forces at least 5% of the stub-period income to be taxed in 1995, 15% by 1996, 25% by 1997, and so on through 85% by 2003 and 100% by 2004. The reserve deducted under 34.2(4) is brought back into income the next year under 34.2(5), and a new reserve can be claimed under 34.2(4). Claiming less reserve than required (i.e., recognizing more income than required) reduces dollar-for-dollar the income that must be recognized in the following year. The calculation for each year is made on Form T1139, in which the CCRA manages to make this relatively simple concept virtually unintelligible.

Note that the reserve is restricted in various ways. For example: the same or similar business must still be carried on (34.2(3)); no reserve can be claimed after death, bankruptcy, windup of corporation, becoming exempt or becoming non-resident with no permanent establishment in Canada (34.2(6), but see 34.2(8)); and stub-period income must be minimized by claiming all possible reserves and CCA (34.2(2)).

**Definitions [s. 34.2]**: "amount", "bankrupt" — 248(1); "business" — 34.2(3), (7), 248(1); "calendar year" — *Interpretation Act* 37(1)(a); "corporation" — 248(1), *Interpretation Act* 35(1); "December 31, 1995 income" — 34.1(4)–(7), 34.2(1); "fiscal period" — 249.1; "gross revenue" — 248(1); "income or loss from a business" — 34.2(2); "individual", "legal representative", "non-resident" — 248(1); "partnership" — see Notes to 96(1); "permanent establishment" — Reg. 8201; "person", "professional corporation" — 248(1); "qualifying fiscal period", "specific percentage" — 34.2(1); "taxation year" — 249; "taxpayer" — 248(1); "trust" — 104(1), 248(1), (3).

## 35. (1) Prospectors and grubstakers — Where a share of the capital stock of a corporation

(a) is received in a taxation year by an individual as consideration for the disposition by the individual to the corporation of a mining property or interest therein acquired by the individual as a result of the individual's efforts as a prospector, either alone or with others, or

(b) is received in a taxation year

(i) by a person who has, either under an arrangement with a prospector made before the prospecting, exploration or development work or as an employer of a prospector, advanced money for, or paid part or all of, the expenses of prospecting or exploring for minerals or of developing a property for minerals, and

(ii) as consideration for the disposition by the person referred to in subparagraph (i) to the corporation of a mining property or interest therein acquired under the arrangement under which that person made the advance or paid the expenses, or if the prospector was the person's employee, acquired by the person through the employee's efforts,

the following rules apply:

(c) notwithstanding any other provision of this Act, no amount in respect of the receipt of the share shall be included

(i) in computing the income for the year of the individual or person, as the case may be, except as provided in paragraph (d), or

(ii) in computing at any time the amount to be determined for F in the definition "cumulative Canadian development expense" in subsection 66.2(5) in respect of the individual or person, as the case may be,

(d) in the case of an individual or partnership (other than a partnership each member of which is a taxable Canadian corporation), an amount in respect of the receipt of the share equal to the lesser of its fair market value at the time of acquisition and its fair market value at the time of disposition or exchange of the share shall be included in computing the income of the individual or partnership, as the case may be, for the year in which the share is disposed of or exchanged,

(e) notwithstanding subdivision c, in computing the cost to the individual, person or partnership, as the case may be, of the share, no amount shall be included in respect of the disposition of the mining property or the interest therein, as the case may be,

(f) notwithstanding sections 66 and 66.2, in computing the cost to the corporation of the mining property or the interest therein, as the case may be, no amount shall be included in respect of the share, and

(g) for the purpose of paragraph (d), an individual or partnership shall be deemed to have disposed of or exchanged shares that are identical properties in the order in which they were acquired.

**Related Provisions**: 35(2) — "prospector"; 81(1)(l) — Income exemption; 110(1)(d.2) — Deduction in computing taxable income; 110.6(19)(a)(i)(A)B — Election to trigger capital gains exemption — no income inclusion; 248(12) — Identical properties.

**Notes**: 35(1) amended by 1985 Budget, effective for shares received after May 22, 1985, to add para. (d) and make minor revisions to the wording of 35(1) to accommodate the new paragraph.

**Interpretation Bulletins**: IT-171R2: Non-resident individuals — computation of taxable income earned in Canada and non-refundable tax credits.

**(2) Definitions** — In this section,

**"mining property"** means a right to prospect, explore or mine for minerals or a property the principal value of which depends on its mineral content;

> **Proposed Amendment — 35(2) "mining property"**
>
> **"mining property"** means
>
> (a) a right, licence or privilege to prospect, explore, drill or mine for minerals in a mineral resource in Canada, or
>
> (b) real property in Canada (other than depreciable property) the principal value of which depends on its mineral resource content;
>
> **Application**: The December 21, 2000 draft legislation, s. 11, will amend the definition "mining property" in subsec. 35(2) to read as above, applicable to shares received after December 21, 2000.

**Technical Notes**: Section 35 applies where:

- a share of the capital stock of a corporation is received by a taxpayer, and
- as detailed in paragraphs 35(1)(a) and (b), the consideration is "mining property" (as defined in subsection 35(2)) that is linked with prospecting or exploring.

Where section 35 applies, paragraph 35(1)(c) provides that the receipt of the share does not result in any immediate income inclusion. Other rules in subsection 35(1) govern the tax consequences resulting from the disposition of the share and the acquisition of the mining property.

The definition "mining property" in subsection 35(2) is amended so that it extends only to minerals in a mineral resource in Canada. "Mineral resource" is defined in subsection 248(1). This amendment is consequential on the introduction of new section 66.21, which deals with foreign resource expenses.

**Related Provisions**: 66.21 — Foreign mining properties.

**Notes**: 35(2)"mining property" was 35(2)(a) before consolidation in R.S.C. 1985 (5th Supp.), effective for taxation years ending after November 1991.

**"prospector"** means an individual who prospects or explores for minerals or develops a property for minerals on behalf of the individual, on behalf of the individual and others or as an employee.

**Notes**: 35(2)"prospector" was 35(2)(b) before consolidation in R.S.C. 1985 (5th Supp.), effective for taxation years ending after November 1991.

**Definitions [s. 35]**: "amount" — 248(1); "Canada" — 255, *Interpretation Act* 35(1); "corporation" — 248(1), *Interpretation Act* 35(1); "depreciable property" — 13(21), 248(1); "employee", "employer" — 248(1); "identical" — 248(12); "individual", "mineral", "mineral resource" — 248(1); "mining property" — 35(2); "person", "property" — 248(1); "prospector" — 35(2); "share" — 248(1); "taxable Canadian corporation" — 89(1), 248(1); "taxation year" — 11(2), 249.

**36. Railway companies** — Where any amount in respect of an expenditure incurred by a taxpayer on or in respect of the repair, replacement, alteration or renovation of depreciable property of the taxpayer of a prescribed class is, under a uniform classification and system of accounts and returns prescribed by the National Transportation Agency pursuant to the *Railway Act*, required to be entered in the books of the taxpayer otherwise than as an expense,

(a) no deduction may be made in respect of that expenditure in computing the income of the taxpayer for a taxation year; and

(b) for the purposes of section 13 and regulations made under paragraph 20(1)(a), the taxpayer shall be deemed to have acquired, at the time the expenditure was incurred, depreciable property of a class prescribed by regulation at a capital cost equal to that amount.

**Related Provisions**: Canada-U.S. tax treaty, Art. VIII:4–Art. VIII:6 — Income from railway business.

**Definitions [s. 36]**: "amount" — 248(1); "depreciable property" — 13(21), 248(1); "prescribed", "regulation" — 248(1); "taxation year" — 249; "taxpayer" — 248(1).

**Regulations**: Sch. II:Cl. 1, Sch. II:Cl. 4, Sch. II:Cl. 6, Sch. II:Cl. 35.

**37. (1) Scientific research and experimental development** — Where a taxpayer carried on a business in Canada in a taxation year, there may be deducted in computing the taxpayer's income from the business for the year such amount as the taxpayer claims not exceeding the amount, if any, by which the total of

(a) the total of all amounts each of which is an expenditure of a current nature made by the taxpayer in the year or in a preceding taxation year ending after 1973

(i) on scientific research and experimental development carried on in Canada, directly undertaken by or on behalf of the taxpayer, and related to a business of the taxpayer,

(i.1) by payments to a corporation resident in Canada to be used for scientific research and experimental development carried on in Canada that is related to a business of the taxpayer, but only where the taxpayer is entitled to exploit the results of that scientific research and experimental development,

(ii) by payments to

(A) an approved association that undertakes scientific research and experimental development,

(B) an approved university, college, research institute or other similar institution,

(C) a corporation resident in Canada and exempt from tax under paragraph 149(1)(j), or

(D) [Repealed]

(E) an approved organization that makes payments to an association, institution or corporation described in any of clauses (A) to (C)

to be used for scientific research and experimental development carried on in Canada that is related to a business of the taxpayer, but only where the taxpayer is entitled to exploit the results of that scientific research and experimental development, or

(iii) where the taxpayer is a corporation, by payments to a corporation resident in Canada and exempt from tax because of paragraph 149(1)(j), for scientific research and experimental development that is basic research or applied research carried on in Canada

(A) the primary purpose of which is the use of results therefrom by the taxpayer in conjunction with other scientific research and experimental development activities undertaken or to be undertaken by or on behalf of the taxpayer that relate to a business of the taxpayer, and

(B) that has the technological potential for application to other businesses of a type unrelated to that carried on by the taxpayer,

(b) the lesser of

(i) the total of all amounts each of which is an expenditure of a capital nature made by the

## S. 37(1)(b)(i) — Income Tax Act, Part I, Division B

taxpayer (in respect of property acquired that would be depreciable property of the taxpayer if this section were not applicable in respect of the property, other than land or a leasehold interest in land) in the year or in a preceding taxation year ending after 1958 on scientific research and experimental development carried on in Canada, directly undertaken by or on behalf of the taxpayer, and related to a business of the taxpayer, and

(ii) the undepreciated capital cost to the taxpayer of the property so acquired as of the end of the taxation year (before making any deduction under this paragraph in computing the income of the taxpayer for the taxation year),

(c) the total of all amounts each of which is an expenditure made by the taxpayer in the year or in a preceding taxation year ending after 1973 by way of repayment of amounts described in paragraph (d),

(c.1) all amounts included by virtue of paragraph 12(1)(v), in computing the taxpayer's income for any previous taxation year,

(c.2) all amounts added because of subsection 127(27), (29) or (34) to the taxpayer's tax otherwise payable under this Part for any preceding taxation year, and

(c.3) in the case of a partnership, all amounts each of which is an excess referred to in subsection 127(30) in respect of the partnership for any preceding fiscal period,

exceeds the total of

(d) the total of all amounts each of which is the amount of any government assistance or non-government assistance (within the meanings assigned to those expressions by subsection 127(9)) in respect of an expenditure described in paragraph (a) or (b) that, at the taxpayer's filing-due date for the year, the taxpayer has received, is entitled to receive or can reasonably be expected to receive,

### Proposed Addition — 37(1)(d.1)

(d.1) the total of all amounts each of which is the super-allowance benefit amount (within the meaning assigned by subsection 127(9)) for the year or for a preceding taxation year in respect of the taxpayer in respect of a province,

**Application**: The December 21, 2000 draft legislation, s. 12, will add para. 37(1)(d.1), applicable to taxation years that begin after February 2000 except that, if a taxpayer's first taxation year that begins after February 2000 ends before 2001, the para. applies to the taxpayer's taxation years that begin after 2000.

**Technical Notes**: Under subsection 37(1), certain expenditures incurred by taxpayer for SR&ED carried on in Canada are accumulated in a SR&ED pool. All or a portion of the undeducted balance of the pool at the end of a taxation year may be deducted in that year. Any remaining balance of the pool at the end of a taxation year may be carried forward to be deducted in a subsequent taxation year.

New paragraph 37(1)(d.1) provides for the reduction of a corporation's SR&ED pool for a taxation year by its super-allowance benefit amount [provincial R&D super-allowance — ed.] (a new expression defined in subsection 127(9)) for the year and preceding taxation years.

**Notice of Ways and Means Motion, federal budget, February 28, 2000**: *Government Assistance — SR&ED*

(31) That for taxation years that end after [to be changed to "that begin after"; see below — ed.] February 2000, where, for the purpose of computing income or taxable income relevant in calculating an income tax payable to a province for a taxation year, a corporation becomes entitled to deduct an amount in computing income or taxable income in respect of an expenditure on scientific research and experimental development and that amount exceeds the amount of the expenditure, the specified percentage of the excess be considered for the purposes of the Act to be government assistance received in the year in respect of scientific research and experimental development, and, for this purpose, the specified percentage is

(a) where the corporation's expenditure limit for the year, as determined by subsection 127(10.2) of the Act, is nil, the maximum provincial tax rate applicable to active business income earned in the province by a corporation for the year, and

(b) in any other case, the provincial tax rate applicable to small business income earned in the province by a corporation for the year.

**Federal budget, supplementary information, February 28, 2000**: *Government Assistance for Scientific Research and Experimental Development*

Various levels of government provide both tax and non-tax assistance to taxpayers in order to achieve a variety of policy objectives. Tax assistance includes investment tax credits (ITCs) and super-deductions (i.e., deductions over 100% of cost). Non-tax assistance includes grants and conditionally repayable contributions. The combined level of assistance can be overly generous with a resultant misallocation of resources.

One of the ways that this misallocation is avoided is to base the cost of the expenditure for federal ITC purposes on the cost of the eligible investment net of any other government assistance or reimbursement that the taxpayer has received or is entitled to receive. This ensures that the ITC is based on the taxpayer's actual costs.

However, not all types of government assistance are treated equally for income tax purposes. Deductions in excess of 100%, commonly known as "super-deductions," are provided in certain provinces. These super-deductions are not considered to be government assistance and thus do not affect the expenditure base for federal ITC purposes, even though they are similar in many respects to provincial ITCs.

To address this issue, the budget proposes to treat provincial deductions for scientific research and experimental development (SR&ED) that exceed the actual amount of the expenditure as government assistance for taxation years ending after February 2000. If a corporation is eligible for SR&ED ITCs at the enhanced rate of 35% (i.e., it is a small Canadian-controlled private corporation), the value of the assistance will be determined at the relevant provincial small business corporate income tax rate that is applicable in that province multiplied by the amount by which the deduction for provincial income tax purposes exceeds the actual amount of the expenditure. For all other corporations, the value of the assistance will be determined as the maximum provincial corporate income tax rate applicable to active business income multiplied by the amount by which the deduction for provincial income tax purposes exceeds the actual amount of the expenditure.

This change will result in SR&ED deductions and credits having comparable value, reduce stacking of benefits and make the tax system fairer.

**Department of Finance news release, May 9, 2000**: *Finance Minister Clarifies Certain Income Tax Measures in the 2000 Budget*

Finance Minister Paul Martin today announced several clarifications to measures announced in the 2000 budget. These clarifications will ensure the smooth conduct of business transactions while consultations take place.

. . . . .

*Government Assistance for Scientific Research and Experimental Development*

Minister Martin announced today that the measure regarding the treatment of provincial deductions for scientific research and experimental development (SR&ED) expenditures will apply to taxation years commencing after February 2000. As originally announced in the budget, this measure would have applied for taxation years ending after February 2000. Under this measure, provincial deductions for SR&ED expenditures that exceed the actual amount of the expenditure will be taken into account in determining government assistance for the purposes of the federal investment tax credit base. Postponing the implementation date addresses concerns about the impact of the timing of this change on corporate budgeting strategies for the year 2000.

. . . . .

For further information: Government Assistance for SR&ED, Alexandra MacLean, (613) 995-2980.

(e) that part of the total of all amounts each of which is an amount deducted under subsection 127(5) in computing the tax payable under this Part by the taxpayer for a preceding taxation year where the amount can reasonably be attributed to

(i) a prescribed proxy amount for a preceding taxation year,

(ii) an expenditure of a current nature incurred in a preceding taxation year that was a qualified expenditure incurred in that preceding year in respect of scientific research and experimental development for the purposes of section 127, or

(iii) an amount included because of paragraph 127(13)(e) in the taxpayer's SR&ED qualified expenditure pool at the end of a preceding taxation year within the meaning assigned by subsection 127(9),

(f) the total of all amounts each of which is an amount deducted under this subsection in computing the taxpayer's income for a preceding taxation year, except amounts described in subsection (6),

(f.1) the total of all amounts each of which is the lesser of

(i) the amount deducted under section 61.3 in computing the taxpayer's income for a preceding taxation year, and

(ii) the amount, if any, by which the amount that was deductible under this subsection in computing the taxpayer's income for that preceding year exceeds the amount claimed under this subsection in computing the taxpayer's income for that preceding year,

(g) the total of all amounts each of which is an amount equal to twice the amount claimed under subparagraph 194(2)(a)(ii) by the taxpayer for the year or any preceding taxation year, and

(h) where the taxpayer is a corporation control of which has been acquired by a person or group of persons before the end of the year, the amount determined for the year under subsection (6.1) with respect to the corporation.

**Related Provisions**: 12(1)(t) — Investment tax credit included in income; 12(1)(v) — Income inclusion where calculation under 37(1) would be negative; 18(9)(d), (e) — Certain prepaid expenses deemed incurred in later taxation year; 37(1.1) — Business of related corporations; 37(1.2) — Deemed time of capital expenditure; 37(4) — No deduction for acquisition of rights: 37(6) — Expenditures of a capital nature; 37(6.1) — Change of control of corporation; 37(7), (8) — Interpretation; 37(11) — Prescribed form required; 53(2)(k) — Deduction from adjusted cost base — government assistance; 87(2)(l) — Amalgamations — SR&ED; 96(1)(e.1) — Partnerships — carryforward of expenses not allowed; 125.4(2)(c) — No film production credit where R&D deduction allowed; 127(9) — "contract payment", "qualified expenditure"; 127(10.1), (10.8) — Additions to investment tax credits; 127(11.2) — Investment tax credit; 139.1(18) — Holding corporation deemed not to acquire control of insurer on demutualization; 149(1)(j) — Non-profit corporation for SR&ED — exemption; 248(1)"scientific research and experimental development" — Definition applicable for purposes of entire Act; 248(16) — GST — input tax credit and rebate; 248(18) — GST — repayment of input tax credit; 256(6)–(9) — Whether control acquired; Reg. 1102(1)(d) — No CCA for capital property deducted under 37(1)(b). See additional Related Provisions and Definitions at end of s. 37.

**Notes**: 37(1) entitles the taxpayer to a full deduction for R&D expenditures, even where they would otherwise be on account of capital and thus prohibited by 18(1)(b). As well, such expenditures are "qualified expenditures" as defined in 127(9) and entitle the taxpayer to investment tax credits of 20–35% (see 127(9)"investment tax credit"(a.1) and 127(10.1)). For the meaning of "scientific research and experimental development", see 37(8) and 248(1).

For discussion of the abandoned restrictions on SR&ED claims for computer software development by banks and other financial institutions, see Notes to 248(1)"scientific research and experimental development".

For discussion of the SR&ED program, see *R&D: Credits Today, Innovation Tomorrow*, proceedings of the Canadian Tax Foundation's 1999 Corporate Management Tax Conference.

Opening words of 37(1) amended by 1995 Budget, effective for taxation years that begin after 1995, to remove the following words after "in a taxation year":

and files with the Minister by the day on or before which the taxpayer's return of income under this Part for the taxpayer's

**S. 37(1)**        Income Tax Act, Part I, Division B

following taxation year is required to be filed, or would be required to be filed if tax under this Part were payable by the taxpayer for that following year, a prescribed form containing prescribed information

The filing requirement and deadline have been moved to 37(11).

Opening words of 37(1) amended by 1994 Budget, effective after February 21, 1994 for expenditures incurred at any time; however, for expenditures incurred in a taxation year that ended before February 22, 1994, the taxpayer may file the prescribed form by June 24, 1995. Before the amendment, read "files ... prescribed form" as "files with the taxpayer's return of income under this Part for the year a prescribed form".

37(1)(a)(i.1) added by 1995 Budget, effective for payments made after 1995. (The rule for third-party payments to a corporation formerly appeared in 37(1)(a)(ii)(D).)

37(1)(a)(ii)(D) repealed by 1995 Budget, effective for payments made after 1995. For expenditures from December 16, 1987 through payments made to the end of 1994, read: "(D) a corporation resident in Canada". The new rule for corporations is in 37(1)(a)(i.1).

Closing words of 37(1)(a)(ii) amended non-substantively by 1995 Budget, effective for payments made after 1995, to add the words "that is", and to change "and provided that" to "but only where".

37(1)(a)(iii) added by 1991 technical bill, effective for payments made after December 15, 1987.

37(1)(c.2) and (c.3) added by 1998 Budget, effective for 1998 and later taxation years.

37(1)(d) amended by 1995 Budget, effective for taxation years that begin after 1995, to change "at the time of filing of the return of income for the year" to "at the taxpayer's filing-due date for the year". (See 248(1)"filing-due date".)

37(1)(e)(iii) added by 1995 Budget, effective for taxation years that begin after 1995.

37(1)(e) amended to add reference to prescribed proxy amount of preceding taxation year (now 37(1)(e)(i)) by 1992 Economic Statement, effective for taxation years ending after December 2, 1992.

37(1)(f.1) added by 1994 tax amendments bill (Part I), effective for taxation years that end after February 21, 1994.

**Regulations**: 2900(4) (prescribed proxy amount for 37(1)(e)).

**Interpretation Bulletins**: IT-121R3: Election to capitalize cost of borrowed money; IT-151R5: Scientific research and experimental development expenditures.

**Information Circulars**: 86-4R3: Scientific research and experimental development; 86-4R3 Supplement 1: Automotive industry application paper; 86-4R3 Supplement 2: Aerospace industry application paper; 94-1: Plastics industry application paper; 94-2: Machinery and equipment industry application paper; 97-1: Administrative guidelines for software development.

**Application Policies**: SR&ED 94-02: Expenditures of sole-purpose SR&ED performers — para. 37(8)(a) of the Act and 2902(a) of the Regulations; SR&ED 95-05: SR&ED capital expenditures — retroactive deductions under subsec. 37(1); SR&ED 96-04: Payments to third parties for SR&ED; SR&ED 96-05: Penalties under subsection 163(2); SR&ED 96-07: Prototypes, custom products, commercial assets, pilot plants and experimental production; SR&ED 96-10: Third party payments — approval process.

**Forms**: T2 SCH 301: Newfoundland scientific research and experimental development tax credit; T2 SCH 340: Nova Scotia research and development tax credit; T2 SCH 360: New Brunswick research and development tax credit; T2 SCH 380: Manitoba research and development tax credit; T2 SCH 403: Saskatchewan research and development tax credit; T661: Claim for scientific research and experimental development expenditures carried on in Canada; T666: British Columbia scientific research and experimental development tax credit; T1129: Newfoundland research and development tax credit (individuals); T4088: Claiming scientific research and experimental development expenditures — guide to form T661.

**(1.1) Business of related corporations** — Notwithstanding paragraph (8)(c), for the purposes of subsection (1), where a taxpayer is a corporation, scientific research and experimental development, related to a business carried on by another corporation to which the taxpayer is related (otherwise than by reason of a right referred to in paragraph 251(5)(b)) and in which that other corporation is actively engaged, at the time at which an expenditure or payment in respect of the scientific research and experimental development is made by the taxpayer, shall be considered to be related to a business of the taxpayer at that time.

**Related Provisions**: See Related Provisions and Definitions at end of s. 37.

**Interpretation Bulletins**: IT-151R5: Scientific research and experimental development expenditures.

**(1.2) Deemed time of capital expenditure** — For the purposes of paragraph (1)(b), an expenditure made by a taxpayer in respect of property shall be deemed not to have been made before the property is considered to have become available for use by the taxpayer.

**Related Provisions**: 13(26) — No CCA until property available for use; 127(11.2) — No investment tax credit until property available for use; 248(19) — When property available for use.

**Notes**: 37(1.2) added by 1991 technical bill, effective for expenditures made by a taxpayer after 1989 other than expenditures in respect of property acquired

    (a) from a person with whom the taxpayer was not dealing at arm's length (otherwise than by reason of a right referred to in 251(5)(b)) at the time the property was acquired, or

    (b) in the course of a reorganization in respect of which, if a dividend were received by a corporation in the course of the reorganization, 55(2) would not be applicable to the dividend by reason of the application of 55(3)(b),

where the property was depreciable property of the person from whom it was acquired (or would, but for s. 37, be depreciable property of the person from whom it was acquired) and was owned by that person before 1990.

**(2) Research outside Canada** — In computing the income of a taxpayer for a taxation year from a business of the taxpayer, there may be deducted expenditures of a current nature made by the taxpayer in the year

    (a) on scientific research and experimental development carried on outside Canada, directly undertaken by or on behalf of the taxpayer, and related to the business; or

    (b) by payments to an approved association, university, college, research institute or other similar institution to be used for scientific research and experimental development carried on outside Canada related to the business provided that the taxpayer is entitled to exploit the results of that scientific research and experimental development.

**Related Provisions**: See Related Provisions and Definitions at end of s. 37.

**Notes**: 37(1) and 37(2) both allow a full deduction for current expenses. Under 37(1), capital expenses are also fully deductible. As well, amounts under 37(1) are eligible for investment tax credits under 127(9)"qualified expenditures", while those under 37(2) are not.

**Interpretation Bulletins**: IT-151R5: Scientific research and experimental development expenditures.

**(3) Minister may obtain advice** — The Minister may obtain the advice of the Department of Industry, the National Research Council of Canada, the Defence Research Board or any other agency or department of the Government of Canada carrying on activities in the field of scientific research as to whether any particular activity constitutes scientific research and experimental development.

**Related Provisions**: 241(4)(a) — Disclosure of taxpayer information in order to obtain advice. See also Related Provisions and Definitions at end of s. 37.

**Notes**: 37(3) amended effective February 23, 1990 to change "Department of Regional Industrial Expansion" to "Department of Industry, Science and Technology". Amended effective March 29, 1995 (1995, c. 1), to "Department of Industry".

**Interpretation Bulletins**: IT-151R5: Scientific research and experimental development expenditures.

**(4) Where no deduction allowed under section** — No deduction may be made under this section in respect of an expenditure made to acquire rights in, or arising out of, scientific research and experimental development.

**Related Provisions**: See Related Provisions and Definitions at end of s. 37.

**Interpretation Bulletins**: IT-151R5: Scientific research and experimental development expenditures.

**(5) Where no deduction allowed under sections 110.1 and 118.1** — Where, in respect of an expenditure on scientific research and experimental development made by a taxpayer in a taxation year, an amount is otherwise deductible under this section and under section 110.1 or 118.1, no deduction may be made in respect of the expenditure under section 110.1 or 118.1 in computing the taxable income of, or the tax payable by, the taxpayer for any taxation year.

**Related Provisions**: See Related Provisions and Definitions at end of s. 37.

**Interpretation Bulletins**: IT-151R5: Scientific research and experimental development expenditures.

**(6) Expenditures of a capital nature** — An amount claimed under subsection (1) that may reasonably be considered to be in respect of a property described in paragraph (1)(b) shall, for the purpose of section 13, be deemed to be an amount allowed to the taxpayer in respect of the property under regulations made under paragraph 20(1)(a), and for that purpose the property shall be deemed to be of a separate prescribed class.

**Related Provisions**: 87(2)(d)(ii)(D) — Amalgamations — depreciable property. See additional Related Provisions and Definitions at end of s. 37.

**Notes**: As a result of 37(6), the recapture provisions of the CCA system (see 13(1)) will apply if the property is later sold. See Notes preceding Reg. 1101 re the effect of separate classes.

**Interpretation Bulletins**: IT-151R5: Scientific research and experimental development expenditures.

**(6.1) Amount referred to in para. (1)(h)** — Where a taxpayer is a corporation control of which was last acquired by a person or group of persons at any time (in this subsection referred to as "that time") before the end of a taxation year of the corporation, the amount determined for the purposes of paragraph (1)(h) for the year with respect to the corporation in respect of a business is the amount, if any, by which

(a) the amount, if any, by which

(i) the total of all amounts each of which is

(A) an expenditure described in paragraph (1)(a) or (c) that was made by the corporation before that time,

(B) the lesser of the amounts determined in respect of the corporation under subparagraphs (1)(b)(i) and (ii) immediately before that time, or

(C) an amount determined in respect of the corporation under paragraph (1)(c.1) for its taxation year ending immediately before that time

exceeds the total of all amounts each of which is

(ii) the total of all amounts determined in respect of the corporation under paragraphs (1)(d) to (g) for its taxation year ending immediately before that time, or

(iii) the amount deducted by virtue of subsection (1) in computing the corporation's income for its taxation year ending immediately before that time

exceeds

(b) the total of

(i) where the business to which the amounts described in clause (a)(i)(A), (B) or (C) may reasonably be considered to have been related was carried on by the corporation for profit or with a reasonable expectation of profit throughout the year, the total of

(A) the corporation's income for the year from the business before making any deduction under subsection (1), and

(B) where properties were sold, leased, rented or developed, or services were rendered, in the course of carrying on the business before that time, the corporation's income for the year, before making any deduction under subsection (1), from any other business substantially all the income of which was derived from the sale, leasing, rental or development, as the case may be, of similar properties or the rendering of similar services, and

(ii) the total of all amounts each of which is an amount determined in respect of a preceding taxation year of the corporation that ended after that time equal to the lesser of

(A) the amount determined under subparagraph (i) with respect to the corporation in respect of the business for that preceding year, and

(B) the amount in respect of the business deducted by virtue of subsection (1) in computing the corporation's income for that preceding year.

**Related Provisions**: 139.1(18) — Holding corporation deemed not to acquire control of insurer on demutualization; 256(6)–(9) — Whether control acquired. See also Related Provisions and Definitions at end of s. 37.

**Notes**: The CCRA takes the position that "substantially all", used in 37(6.1)(b)(i)(B), means 90% or more.

**Interpretation Bulletins**: IT-151R5: Scientific research and experimental development expenditures.

**I.T. Technical News**: No. 7 (control by a group — 50/50 arrangement).

**(7) Definitions** — In this section,

**"approved"** means approved by the Minister after the Minister has, if the Minister considers it necessary, obtained the advice of the Department of Industry or the National Research Council of Canada;

**Notes**: For 37(1)(a)(ii)(B), all Canadian universities and affiliated colleges are approved. For 37(1)(a)(ii)(E), the Natural Sciences and Engineering Research Council, the Medical Research Council and the Social Sciences and Humanities Research Council are generally approved. See Interpretation Bulletin IT-151R5, para. 33.

37(7)"approved" was 37(7)(a) before consolidation in R.S.C. 1985 (5th Supp.), effective for taxation years ending after November 1991.

Amended effective February 23, 1990 to change "Department of Regional Industrial Expansion" to "Department of Industry, Science and Technology"; and effective March 29, 1995 (1995, c. 1) to "Department of Industry".

**Application Policies**: SR&ED 96-10: Third party payments — approval process.

**Interpretation Bulletins**: IT-151R5: Scientific research and experimental development expenditures.

**"scientific research and experimental development"** — [Repealed]

**Notes**: Definition "scientific research and experimental development" repealed by 1995 Budget, effective for work performed after February 27, 1995 except that, for the purposes of 149(1)(j) and (8)(b), the definition still applies to work performed pursuant to an agreement in writing entered into before February 28, 1995. The definition read:

"scientific research and experimental development" has the meaning given to that expression by regulation.

It has been replaced by a definition in 248(1) that applies for all purposes of the Act. See also 37(8).

37(7)"scientific research and experimental development" was 37(7)(b) before consolidation in R.S.C. 1985 (5th Supp.), effective for taxation years ending after November 1991. For former 37(7)(c)–(f), see 37(8)(a)–(d).

**Regulations**: 2900 (meaning of "scientific research and experimental development").

**Information Circulars**: See under 248(1)"scientific research and experimental development".

**(8) Interpretation** — In this section,

(a) references to expenditures on or in respect of scientific research and experimental development

(i) where the references occur in subsection (2), include only

(A) expenditures each of which was an expenditure incurred for and all or substantially all of which was attributable to the prosecution of scientific research and experimental development, and

(B) expenditures of a current nature that were directly attributable, as determined by regulation, to the prosecution of scientific research and experimental development, and

(ii) where the references occur other than in subsection (2), include only

(A) expenditures incurred by a taxpayer in a taxation year (other than a taxation year for which the taxpayer has elected under clause (B)), each of which is

(I) an expenditure of a current nature all or substantially all of which was attributable to the prosecution, or to the provision of premises, facilities or equipment for the prosecution, of scientific research and experimental development in Canada,

(II) an expenditure of a current nature directly attributable, as determined by regulation, to the prosecution, or to the provision of premises, facilities or equipment for the prosecution, of scientific research and experimental development in Canada, or

(III) an expenditure of a capital nature that at the time it was incurred was for the provision of premises, facilities or equipment, where at that time it was intended

1. that it would be used during all or substantially all of its operating time in its expected useful life for, or

2. that all or substantially all of its value would be consumed in,

the prosecution of scientific research and experimental development in Canada, and

(B) where a taxpayer has elected in prescribed form and in accordance with subsection (10) for a taxation year, expenditures incurred by the taxpayer in the year each of which is

(I) an expenditure of a current nature for, and all or substantially all of which was attributable to, the lease of premises, facilities or equipment for the

Subdivision b — Income or Loss from a Business or Property    S. 37(8)

prosecution of scientific research and experimental development in Canada, other than an expenditure in respect of general purpose office equipment or furniture,

(II) an expenditure in respect of the prosecution of scientific research and experimental development in Canada directly undertaken on behalf of the taxpayer,

(III) an expenditure described in subclause (A)(III), other than an expenditure in respect of general purpose office equipment or furniture,

(IV) that portion of an expenditure made in respect of an expense incurred in the year for salary or wages of an employee who is directly engaged in scientific research and experimental development in Canada that can reasonably be considered to relate to such work having regard to the time spent by the employee thereon, and, for this purpose, where that portion is all or substantially all of the expenditure, that portion shall be deemed to be the amount of the expenditure,

(V) the cost of materials consumed in the prosecution of scientific research and experimental development in Canada, or

(VI) $\frac{1}{2}$ of any other expenditure of a current nature in respect of the lease of premises, facilities or equipment used primarily for the prosecution of scientific research and experimental development in Canada, other than an expenditure in respect of general purpose office equipment or furniture;

(b) for greater certainty, references to scientific research and experimental development related to a business include any scientific research and experimental development that may lead to or facilitate an extension of that business;

(c) except in the case of a taxpayer who derives all or substantially all of the taxpayer's revenue from the prosecution of scientific research and experimental development (including the sale of rights arising out of scientific research and experimental development carried on by the taxpayer), the prosecution of scientific research and experimental development shall not be considered to be a business of the taxpayer to which scientific research and experimental development is related; and

(d) notwithstanding paragraph (a), references to expenditures on or in respect of scientific research and experimental development shall not include

(i) any capital expenditure made in respect of the acquisition of a building, other than a prescribed special-purpose building, including a leasehold interest therein,

(ii) any outlay or expense made or incurred for the use of, or the right to use, a building other than a prescribed special-purpose building, and

(iii) payments made by a taxpayer to

(A) a corporation resident in Canada and exempt from tax under paragraph 149(1)(j), an approved research institute or an approved association, with which the taxpayer does not deal at arm's length,

(B) a corporation other than a corporation referred to in clause (A), or

(C) an approved university, college or organization

to be used for scientific research and experimental development

(D) in the case of such a payment to a person described in clause (A) or (B), to the extent that the amount of the payment may reasonably be considered to have been made to enable the recipient to acquire a building or a leasehold interest in a building or to pay an amount in respect of the rental expense in respect of a building, and

(E) in the case of a payment to a person described in clause (C), to the extent that the amount of the payment may reasonably be considered to have been made to enable the recipient to acquire a building, or a leasehold interest in a building, in which the taxpayer has, or may reasonably be expected to acquire, an interest.

**Related Provisions**: 37(1.1) — Business of related corporations; 37(9) — Salary or wages; 37(9.1)–(9.5) — Limitation on payments to specified employees; 37(10) — Time for election; 96(3) — Election by members of partnership; 149(1)(j)(ii)(A) — Non-profit SR&ED corporation's expenditures; 248(1)"scientific research and experimental development" — Definition of SR&ED. See additional Related provisions and Definitions at end of s. 37.

**Notes**: 37(8)(a)(ii) (former 37(7)(c)(ii)) amended by 1992 Economic Statement, effective for taxation years ending after December 2, 1992. For earlier years, read:

(ii) where the references occur other than in subsection (2), include only

(A) expenditures each of which was an expenditure incurred for and all or substantially all of which was attributable to the prosecution, or to the provision of premises, facilities or equipment for the prosecution, of scientific research and experimental development in Canada, and

(B) expenditures of a current nature that were directly attributable, as determined by regulation, to the prosecution, or to the provision of premises, facilities or equipment for the prosecution, of scientific research and experimental development in Canada;

37(8)(d)(ii) (former 37(7)(f)(ii)) amended by 1992 Economic Statement, effective for taxation years ending after December 2, 1992, except that (per 1996 Budget bill, s. 74) it does not apply to taxation years beginning before March 6, 1996 with respect to rental expenses incurred pursuant to a written lease agreement renewed, extended or entered into before June 18, 1987 by the taxpayer or a person with whom the taxpayer did not deal at arm's length at the time the lease was renewed, extended or entered into. For earlier years, read:

(ii) any rental expense incurred in respect of a building other than a prescribed special-purpose building, and

However, see Proposed Amendment below.

37(8)(a) to (d) were 37(7)(c) to (f) before consolidation in R.S.C. 1985 (5th Supp.), effective for taxation years ending after November 1991.

The CCRA takes the position that "all or substantially all" means 90% or more.

**Regulations**: 2900(2)–(4) (meaning of "expenditures directly attributable"); 2903 (prescribed special-purpose building).

**Interpretation Bulletins**: IT-151R5: Scientific research and experimental development expenditures.

**Information Circulars**: 86-4R3: Scientific research and experimental development; 86-4R3 Supplement 1: Automotive industry application paper; 86-4R3 Supplement 2: Aerospace industry application paper; 94-1: Plastics industry application paper; 94-2: Machinery and equipment industry application paper; 97-1: Administrative guidelines for software development.

**Application Policies**: SR&ED 94-02: Expenditures of sole-purpose SR&ED performers — ITA 37(8)(a) and Reg. 2902(a); SR&ED 95-04R: Conflict of interest with regard to outside consultants; SR&ED 96-06: Directly undertaking, supervising or supporting v. "directly engaged" SR&ED salary and wages; SR&ED 2000-01: Cost of materials.

**(9) Salary or wages** — For the purposes of clauses (8)(a)(ii)(A) and (B), an expenditure of a taxpayer does not include remuneration based on profits or a bonus, where the remuneration or bonus, as the case may be, is in respect of a specified employee of the taxpayer.

**Notes**: 37(9) (originally proposed as 37(8) before reconsolidation of the Act in R.S.C. 1985 (5th Supp.)) added by 1992 Economic Statement, effective for taxation years ending after December 2, 1992.

**(9.1) Limitation re specified employees** — For the purposes of clauses (8)(a)(ii)(A) and (B), expenditures incurred by a taxpayer in a taxation year do not include expenses incurred in the year in respect of salary or wages of a specified employee of the taxpayer to the extent that those expenses exceed the amount determined by the formula

$$A \times \frac{B}{365}$$

where

A is 5 times the Year's Maximum Pensionable Earnings (as determined under section 18 of the *Canada Pension Plan*) for the calendar year in which the taxation year ends; and

B is the number of days in the taxation year on which the employee is a specified employee of the taxpayer.

**Related Provisions**: 38(9.2)–(9.5) — Allocation of salary of specified employee of associated corporations.

**Notes**: 37(9.1) added by 1996 Budget, effective for taxation years that begin after March 5, 1996. It limits the amount of claim for SR&ED expense for salary of a "specified employee" (see 248(1)) to 5 times the Year's Maximum Pensionable Earnings (YMPE). This maximum amount is prorated for short taxation years.

The YMPE for 2001 is $38,300. For other years, see the table of CPP rates in the introductory pages.

**(9.2) Associated corporations** — Where

(a) in a taxation year of a corporation that ends in a calendar year, the corporation employs an individual who is a specified employee of the corporation,

(b) the corporation is associated with another corporation (in this subsection and subsection (9.3) referred to as the "associated corporation") in a taxation year of the associated corporation that ends in the calendar year, and

(c) the individual is a specified employee of the associated corporation in the taxation year of the associated corporation that ends in the calendar year,

for the purposes of clauses (8)(a)(ii)(A) and (B), the expenditures incurred by the corporation in its taxation year or years that end in the calendar year and by each associated corporation in its taxation year or years that end in the calendar year do not include expenses incurred in those taxation years in respect of salary or wages of the specified employee unless the corporation and all of the associated corporations have filed with the Minister an agreement referred to in subsection (9.3) in respect of those years.

**Related Provisions**: 37(9.5) — Certain individuals and partnerships deemed to be associated corporations.

**Notes**: 37(9.2) added by 1996 Budget, effective for taxation years that begin after March 5, 1996.

**(9.3) Agreement among associated corporations** — Where all of the members of a group of associated corporations of which an individual is a specified employee file, in respect of their taxation years that end in a particular calendar year, an agreement with the Minister in which they allocate an amount in respect of the individual to one or more of them for those years and the amount so allocated or the total of the amounts so allocated, as the case may be, does not exceed the amount determined by the formula

$$A \times \frac{B}{365}$$

where

A is 5 times the Year's Maximum Pensionable Earnings (as determined under section 18 of the *Canada Pension Plan*) for the particular calendar year, and

B is the lesser of 365 and the number of days in those taxation years on which the individual was a specified employee of one or more of the corporations,

the maximum amount that may be claimed in respect of salary or wages of the individual for the purposes of clauses (8)(a)(ii)(A) and (B) by each of the corporations for each of those years is the amount so allocated to it for each of those years.

**Related Provisions**: 37(9.5) — Certain individuals and partnerships deemed to be associated corporations.

**Notes**: 37(9.3) added by 1996 Budget, effective for taxation years that begin after March 5, 1996.

For the Year's Maximum Pensionable Earnings for formula element A, see Notes to 37(9.1).

**(9.4) Filing** — An agreement referred to in subsection (9.3) is deemed not to have been filed by a taxpayer unless

(a) it is in prescribed form; and

(b) where the taxpayer is a corporation, it is accompanied by

(i) where its directors are legally entitled to administer its affairs, a certified copy of their resolution authorizing the agreement to be made, and

(ii) where its directors are not legally entitled to administer its affairs, a certified copy of the document by which the person legally entitled to administer its affairs authorized the agreement to be made.

**Notes**: 37(9.4) added by 1996 Budget, effective for taxation years that begin after March 5, 1996.

**(9.5) Deemed corporation** — For the purposes of subsections (9.2) and (9.3) and this subsection, each

(a) individual related to a particular corporation,

(b) partnership of which a majority interest partner is

(i) an individual related to a particular corporation, or

(ii) a corporation associated with a particular corporation, and

(c) limited partnership of which a member whose liability as a member is not limited is

(i) an individual related to a particular corporation, or

(ii) a corporation associated with a particular corporation,

is deemed to be a corporation associated with the particular corporation.

**Notes**: 37(9.5) added by 1996 Budget, effective for taxation years that begin after March 5, 1996.

**(10) Time for election** — Any election made under clause (8)(a)(ii)(B) for a taxation year by a taxpayer shall be filed by the taxpayer on the day on which the taxpayer first files a prescribed form referred to in subsection (11) for the year.

**Notes**: 37(10) amended identically by 1995 Budget and 1995-97 technical bill, but with different effective application. For taxation years that end after December 2, 1992, until February 21, 1994, read "... shall be filed with the taxpayer's return of income under this Part for the year". Effective February 22, 1994 for expenditures incurred at any time, for taxation years that began before 1996, read "subsection (11)" as "subsection (1)".

37(10) (originally proposed as 37(9) before reconsolidation of the Act in R.S.C. 1985 (5th Supp.)) added by 1992 Economic Statement, effective for taxation years ending after December 2, 1992.

**(11) Filing requirement** — Subject to subsection (12), no amount in respect of an expenditure that would be incurred by a taxpayer in a taxation year that begins after 1995 if this Act were read without reference to subsection 78(4) may be deducted under subsection (1) unless the taxpayer files with the Minister a prescribed form containing prescribed information in respect of the expenditure on or before the day that is 12 months after the taxpayer's filing-due date for the year.

**Related Provisions**: 127(9)"investment tax credit"(m) — Filing deadline applies to all investment tax credits.

**Notes**: 37(11) added by 1995 Budget, effective for taxation years that begin after 1995. The filing requirement was formerly in the opening words of 37(1). For an earlier version of 37(11) dealing with reclassified expenditures, see under 37(12).

**Forms**: T661: Claim for scientific research and experimental development carried on in Canada; T4088: Claiming scientific research and experimental development expenditures — guide to form T661.

**(12) Misclassified expenditures** — If a taxpayer has not filed a prescribed form in respect of an expenditure in accordance with subsection (11), for the purposes of this Act, the expenditure is deemed not to be an expenditure on or in respect of scientific research and experimental development.

**Notes**: 37(12) deems an expenditure in respect of which the taxpayer has not met the filing requirement in 37(11) not to be an SR&ED expenditure. This will cause it to be classified in accordance with ordinary rules, without reference to the SR&ED provisions. For example, an expenditure on equipment, which would have been an SR&ED capital expenditure if the prescribed form had been filed on time, will generally be treated as depreciable property, while an expenditure that would have been an SR&ED current expenditure will generally be deductible as a current expense under 9(1).

37(12) amended by 1997 Budget, effective for 1997 and later taxation years. For taxation years that began and ended in 1996, read:

(12) Reclassified expenditures — A taxpayer is not required to file the prescribed form referred to in subsection (11) in respect of an expenditure that would be incurred in a taxation year by the taxpayer if this Act were read without reference to subsection 78(4) where the expenditure is reclassified by the Minister on an assessment of the taxpayer's tax payable under this Part for the year, or on a determination that no tax under this Part is payable by the taxpayer for the year, as an expenditure in respect of scientific research and experimental development.

37(12) added to replace 37(11) by 1995 Budget, effective for taxation years that begin after 1995. For earlier taxation years, 37(11) was added by 1994 Budget, effective after February 21, 1994 for expenditures incurred at any time. It read:

(11) For the purpose of subsection (1), a taxpayer is not required to file the prescribed form referred to in that subsection in respect of an expenditure incurred in a taxation year by the taxpayer where the expenditure is reclassified by the

Minister on an assessment of the taxpayer's tax payable under this Part for the year, or on a determination that no tax under this Part is payable by the taxpayer for the year, as an expenditure in respect of scientific research and experimental development.

**(13) Non-arm's length contract — linked work** — For the purposes of this section and sections 127 and 127.1, where

(a) work is performed by a taxpayer for a person or partnership at a time when the person or partnership does not deal at arm's length with the taxpayer, and

(b) the work would be scientific research and experimental development if it were performed by the person or partnership,

the work is deemed to be scientific research and experimental development.

**Notes**: 37(13) added by 1995 Budget, effective for taxation years that begin after 1995. 37(13)(b) amended by 1995-97 technical bill, effective for taxation years that begin after 1995, to delete the words "described in paragraph 2900(1)(d) of the *Income Tax Regulations*" after "development". The change was non-substantive; the definition of SR&ED has been moved from the regulations to 248(1).

**Related Provisions [s. 37]**: 87(2)(l) — Amalgamations — continuing corporation; 127(12.1) — Investment tax credit; 256(8) — Deemed acquisition of shares.

**Definitions [s. 37]**: "acquired" — 256(7)–(9); "amount" — 248(1); "approved" — 37(7); "arm's length" — 251(1); "associated" — 13(9.5), 256; "available for use" — 13(27)–(32), 248(19); "business" — 248(1); "calendar year" — *Interpretation Act* 37(1)(a); "Canada" — 255; "carrying on business" — 253; "control" — 256(6)–(9); "corporation" — 248(1), *Interpretation Act* 35(1); "depreciable property" — 13(21), 248(1); "expenditure" — 37(8)(a), (d), 37(9); "filing-due date" — 150(1), 248(1); "individual" — 248(1); "majority interest partner", "Minister", "person", "prescribed", "property" — 248(1); "received" — 248(7); "regulation" — 248(1); "related to a business" — 37(8)(b); "resident in Canada" — 250(1); "scientific research and experimental development" — 37(8), (13), 248(1), Reg. 2900; "specified employee" — 248(1); "super-allowance benefit amount" — 127(9); "tax payable" — 248(2); "taxable income" — 2(2), 248(1); "taxation year" — 11(2), 249; "taxpayer" — 248(1).

## 37.1, 37.2, 37.3 [Repealed]

**Notes**: 37.1–37.3 repealed by 1995-97 technical bill, effective for 1995 and later taxation years. It provided an additional R&D allowance which was eliminated in 1983 (subject to some grandfathering under 37.2 and 37.3 through 1988), and replaced with an enhanced investment tax credit in s. 127.

37.2 added in R.S.C. 1985 (5th Supp.) consolidation. It previously existed as a rule of application in the 1978 legislation that enacted 37.1. It was overridden by 37.3 anyway.

37.3 added in R.S.C. 1985 (5th Supp.) consolidation. It previously existed as a rule of application in the 1984 amending legislation (1984, c. 1, s. 11).

**Interpretation Bulletins [s. 37.1]**: IT-121R3: Election to capitalize cost of borrowed money; IT-151R5: Scientific research and experimental development expenditures.

## Subdivision c — Taxable Capital Gains and Allowable Capital Losses

**38. Taxable capital gain and allowable capital loss** — For the purposes of this Act,

(a) subject to paragraph (a.1), a taxpayer's taxable capital gain for a taxation year from the disposition of any property is $3/4$ of the taxpayer's capital gain for the year from the disposition of the property;

### Proposed Amendment — 38(a)

(a) subject to paragraphs (a.1) and (a.2), a taxpayer's taxable capital gain for a taxation year from the disposition of any property is $1/2$ of the taxpayer's capital gain for the year from the disposition of the property;

**Application**: The December 21, 2000 draft legislation, subsec. 13(1), will amend para. 38(a) to read as above, applicable to 2000 *et seq.* except that

(a) for a taxation year of a taxpayer that ended before February 28, 2000, the references to the fraction "1/2" in paras. 38(a), (b) and (c) shall be read as references to the fraction "3/4",

(b) for a taxation year of a taxpayer that includes February 28, 2000 but does not include October 18, 2000, the references to the fraction "1/2" in paras. 38(a), (b) and (c) shall be read as references to the fraction that applies to the taxpayer for that year, and for this purpose,

(i) where the amount of the taxpayer's net capital gains from dispositions of property in the period that began at the beginning of the year and ended at the end of February 27, 2000 (in this paragraph referred to as the "first period") exceeds the amount of the taxpayer's net capital losses from dispositions of property in the period that begins at the beginning of February 28, 2000 and ends at the end of the year (in this paragraph referred to as the "second period"), the fraction that applies to the taxpayer for the year is 3/4,

(ii) where the amount of the taxpayer's net capital losses from dispositions of property in the first period exceeds the amount of the taxpayer's net capital gains from dispositions of property in the second period, the fraction that applies to the taxpayer for the year is 3/4,

(iii) where the amount of the taxpayer's net capital gains from dispositions of property in the first period is less than the amount of the taxpayer's net capital losses from dispositions of property in the second period, the fraction that applies to the taxpayer for the year is 2/3,

(iv) where the amount of the taxpayer's net capital losses from dispositions of property in the first period is less than the amount of the taxpayer's net capital gains from dispositions of property in the second period, the fraction that applies to the taxpayer for the year is 2/3,

(v) where the taxpayer has only net capital gains, or only net capital losses, from dispositions of property in each of the first and second periods, the fraction that applies to the taxpayer for the year is the fraction determined by the formula

$$(3/4 \ A + 2/3 \ B) / (A + B)$$

where

A is the net capital gains or the net capital losses, as the case may be, of the taxpayer from dispositions of property in the first period, and

B is the net capital gains or the net capital losses, as the case may be, of the taxpayer from dispositions of property in the second period, and

(vi) where the net capital gains and net capital losses of the taxpayer for the year is nil, the fraction that applies to the taxpayer for the year is 2/3,

(c) for a taxation year of a taxpayer that began after February 27, 2000 and includes October 18, 2000, the references to the fraction "1/2" in paras. 38(a), (b) and (c) shall be read as references to the fraction that applies to the taxpayer for that year, and for this purpose,

(i) where the amount of the taxpayer's net capital gains from dispositions of property in the period that began at the beginning of the year and ended at the end of October 17, 2000 (in this paragraph referred to as the "first period") exceeds the amount of the taxpayer's net capital losses from dispositions of property in the period that begins at the beginning of October 18, 2000 and ends at the end of the year (in this paragraph referred to as the "second period"), the fraction that applies to the taxpayer for the year is 2/3,

(ii) where the amount of the taxpayer's net capital losses from dispositions of property in the first period exceeds the amount of the taxpayer's net capital gains from dispositions of property in the second period, the fraction that applies to the taxpayer for the year is 2/3,

(iii) where the amount of the taxpayer's net capital gains from dispositions of property in the first period is less than the amount of the taxpayer's net capital losses from dispositions of property in the second period, the fraction that applies to the taxpayer for the year is 1/2,

(iv) where the amount of the taxpayer's net capital losses from dispositions of property in the first period is less than the amount of the taxpayer's net capital gains from dispositions of property in the second period, the fraction that applies to the taxpayer for the year is 1/2,

(v) where the taxpayer has only net capital gains, or only net capital losses, from dispositions of property in each of the first and second periods, the fraction that applies to the taxpayer for the year is the fraction determined by the formula

$$(2/3\ A + 1/2\ B) / (A + B)$$

where

A is the net capital gains or the net capital losses, as the case may be, of the taxpayer from dispositions of property in the first period, and

B is the net capital gains or the net capital losses, as the case may be, of the taxpayer from dispositions of property in the second period, and

(vi) where the net capital gains and net capital losses of the taxpayer for the year is nil, the fraction that applies to the taxpayer for the year is 1/2,

(d) for a taxation year of a taxpayer that includes February 27, 2000 and October 18, 2000, the references to the fraction "1/2" in paras. 38(a), (b) and (c) shall be read as references to the fraction that applies to the taxpayer for that year, and for this purpose,

(i) where

(A) the amount by which the amount of the taxpayer's net capital gains from dispositions of property in the period that began at the beginning of the year and ended at the end of February 27, 2000 (in this paragraph referred to as the "first period") exceeds the amount of the taxpayer's net capital losses from dispositions of property in the period that began at the beginning of February 28, 2000 and ended at the end of October 17, 2000 (in this paragraph referred to as the "second period")

exceeds

(B) the amount of the taxpayer's net capital losses from dispositions of property in the period that begins at the beginning of October 18, 2000 and ends at the end of the year (in this paragraph referred to as the "third period"),

the fraction that applies to the taxpayer for the year is 3/4,

(ii) where

(A) the amount by which the amount of the taxpayer's net capital losses from dispositions of property in the first period exceeds the amount of the taxpayer's net capital gains from dispositions of property in the second period

exceeds

(B) the amount of the taxpayer's net capital gains from dispositions of property in the third period

the fraction that applies to the taxpayer for the year is 3/4,

(iii) where

(A) the amount by which the amount of the taxpayer's net capital gains from dispositions of property in the second period exceeds the amount of the taxpayer's net capital losses from dispositions of property in the first period

exceeds

(B) the amount of the taxpayer's net capital losses from dispositions of property in the third period

the fraction that applies to the taxpayer for the year is 2/3,

(iv) where

(A) the amount by which the amount of the taxpayer's net capital losses from dispositions of property in the second period exceeds the amount of the taxpayer's net capital gains from dispositions of property in the first period

exceeds

(B) the amount of the taxpayer's net capital gains from dispositions of property in the third period

the fraction that applies to the taxpayer for the year is 2/3,

(iv) where the taxpayer has net capital gains in each of the first and second periods and the aggregate of the amount of those net capital gains in those periods exceeds the amount of the taxpayer's net capital losses in the third period, the fraction that applies to the taxpayer for the year is the fraction that is determined by the formula

$$(3/4\ A + 2/3\ B) / (A + B)$$

where

A is the net capital gains of the taxpayer from dispositions of property in the first period, and

B is the net capital gains of the taxpayer from dispositions of property in the second period,

(vi) where the taxpayer has net capital losses in each of the first and second periods and the aggregate of the amount of those net capital losses in those periods exceeds the amount of the taxpayer's net capital gains in the third period, the fraction that applies to the taxpayer for the year is the fraction that is determined by the formula

$$(3/4\ A + 2/3\ B) / (A + B)$$

where

A is the net capital losses of the taxpayer from dispositions of property in the first period, and

B is the net capital losses of the taxpayer from dispositions of property in the second period,

(vii) where the taxpayer has only net capital gains, or only net capital losses, from dispositions of property in each of the first, second and third periods, the fraction that applies to the taxpayer for the year is the fraction that is determined by the formula

$$(3/4\ A + 2/3\ B + 1/2\ C) / (A + B + C)$$

where

A is the taxpayer's net capital gains or net capital losses, as the case may be, from dispositions of property in the first period,

B is the taxpayer's net capital gains or net capital losses, as the case may be, from dispositions of property in the second period, and

C is the taxpayer's net capital gains or net capital losses, as the case may be, from dispositions of property in the third period,

(viii) where the amount of the taxpayer's net capital gains from dispositions of property in the first period exceeds the amount of the taxpayer's net capital losses from dispositions of property in the second period and the taxpayer has net capital gains from dispositions of property in the third period, the fraction that applies to the taxpayer for the year is the fraction that is determined by the formula

$$(3/4\ A + 1/2\ B) / (A + B)$$

where

A is the amount by which the taxpayer's net capital gains from dispositions of property in the first period exceeds the amount of the taxpayer's net capital losses from dispositions of property in the second period, and

B is the taxpayer's net capital gains from dispositions of property in the third period,

(ix) where the amount of the taxpayer's net capital losses from dispositions of property in the first period exceeds the amount of the taxpayer's net capital gains from dispositions of property in the second period and the taxpayer has net capital losses from dispositions of property in the third period, the fraction that applies to the taxpayer for the year is the fraction that is determined by the formula

$$(3/4\ A + 1/2\ B) / (A + B)$$

where

A is the amount by which the taxpayer's net capital losses from dispositions of property in the first period exceeds the amount of the taxpayer's net capital gains from dispositions of property in the second period, and

B is the taxpayer's net capital losses from dispositions of property in the third period,

(x) where the amount of the taxpayer's net capital gains from dispositions of property in the second period exceeds the amount of the taxpayer's net capital losses from dispositions of property in the first period and the taxpayer has net capital gains from dispositions of property in the third period, the fraction that applies to the taxpayer for the year is the fraction that is determined by the formula

$$(2/3\ A + 1/2\ B) / (A + B)$$

where

A is the amount by which the taxpayer's net capital gains from dispositions of property in the second period exceeds the amount of the taxpayer's net capital losses from dispositions of property in the first period, and

B is the taxpayer's net capital gains from dispositions of property in the third period,

(xi) where the amount of the taxpayer's net capital losses from dispositions of property in the second period exceeds the amount of the taxpayer's net capital gains from dispositions of property in the first period and the taxpayer has net capital losses from dispositions of property in the third period, the fraction that applies to the taxpayer for the year is the fraction that is determined by the formula

$$(2/3\ A + 1/2\ B) / (A + B)$$

where

A is the amount by which the taxpayer's net capital losses from dispositions of property in the second period exceeds the amount of the taxpayer's net capital gains from dispositions of property in the first period, and

B is the taxpayer's net capital losses from dispositions of property in the third period, and

(xii) in any other case, the fraction that applies to the taxpayer for the year is 1/2, and

in determining the fraction that applies to the taxpayer under paragraphs (a) to (d) for the year, the following rules apply:

(e) the net capital gains of a taxpayer from dispositions of property in a period is the amount, if any, by which the taxpayer's capital gains from dispositions of property in the period exceeds the taxpayer's capital losses from dispositions of property in the period,

(f) the net capital losses of a taxpayer from dispositions of property in a period is the amount, if any, by which the taxpayer's capital losses from dispositions of property in the period exceeds the taxpayer's capital gains from dispositions of property in the period,

(g) the net amount included as a capital gain of the taxpayer for a taxation year from a disposition to which para. 38(a.2) applies or from a disposition to which para. 38(a.1) applies, is deemed to be equal to one half of the capital gain,

(h) the net amount included as a capital gain of the taxpayer for a taxation year from a disposition of property before the year because of subparas. 40(1)(a)(ii) and (iii) is deemed to be a capital gain of the taxpayer from a disposition of property on the first day of the year,

(i) each capital loss that is a business investment loss shall be determined without reference to subsecs. 39(9) and (10),

(j) where an amount is included in computing the income of the taxpayer for the year because of subsec. 80(13) in respect of a commercial obligation that is settled, the amount that would be determined under that subsection in respect of the obligation, if the value of E in the formula in that subsection were 1, is deemed to be a capital gain of the taxpayer from a disposition of property on the day on which the settlement occurs,

(k) the taxpayer's capital gains and losses from dispositions of property (other than taxable Canadian property) while the taxpayer is a non-resident are deemed to be nil;

(l) where an election is made by a taxpayer under para. 104(21.4)(d), subsec. 130.1(4.3), or subsec. 131(1.6), all as amended [by the December 21, 2000 draft legislation], for a year, the portion of the taxpayer's net gains for the year that are to be treated as being in respect of capital gains realized on dispositions of property that occurred in a particular period in the year is that proportion of those net gains that the number of days in the particular period is of the number of days in the year;

(m) where the election made under para. 104(21.4)(d), as amended [by the December 21, 2000 draft legislation], for the year was made by a personal trust, the portion of the taxpayer's net gains for the year that are to be treated as being in respect of capital gains realized on dispositions of property that occurred in a particular period in the year is that proportion of those net gains that the number of days in the particular period is of the number of days that are in all periods in the year in which a net gain was realized;

(n) where in the course of administering the estate of a deceased taxpayer, a capital loss from a disposition of property by the legal representative of a deceased taxpayer is deemed under para. 164(6)(c) to be a capital loss of the deceased taxpayer from the disposition of property by the taxpayer in the taxpayer's last taxation year and not to be a capital loss of the estate, the capital loss is deemed to be from the disposition of a property by the taxpayer immediately before the taxpayer's death;

(o) each capital gain referred to in para. 104(21.4)(a), as amended [by the December 21, 2000 draft legislation], in respect of a beneficiary, shall be determined as if that para. were read without reference to subpara. 104(21.4)(a)(ii);

(p) where no capital gains or losses are realized in the period, the amount of net capital gains or losses for that period is deemed to be nil;

(q) where a net amount is included as a capital gain of a taxpayer for a taxation year because of the granting of an option under subsec. 49(1), the net amount is deemed to be a capital gain of the taxpayer from a disposition of property on the day on which the option was granted;

(r) where a net amount is included as a capital gain of a corporation for its taxation year under subsec. 49(2) because of the expiration of an option that was granted by the corporation, the net amount is deemed to be a capital gain of the corporation from a disposition of property on the day on which the option expired;

(s) where a net amount is included as a capital gain of a trust for its taxation year under subsec. 49(2.1) because of the expiration of an option that was granted by the trust, the net amount is deemed to be a capital gain of the trust from a disposition of property on the day on which the option expired; and

(t) where a net amount is included as a capital gain of a taxpayer for a taxation year because of subsec. 49(3), (3.01) or (3.1), the net amount is deemed to be a capital gain of the taxpayer from a disposition of property on the day on which the option was exercised.

**Technical Notes**: Section 38 defines a taxpayer's taxable capital gain, allowable capital loss and business investment loss from the disposition of property as 3/4 of the taxpayer's capital gain, capital loss or business investment loss from the disposition. The section is amended as a consequence of the changes to the inclusion rates for capital gains and losses from 3/4 to 1/2.

Paragraph 38(a) is also amended to add a reference to new paragraph 38(a.2), which provides that the inclusion rate in respect of qualifying gifts of ecologically sensitive land is 1/4.

These amendments apply to the 2000 and subsequent taxation years with the following exceptions.

In order to determine the inclusion rate for a taxation year of a taxpayer that ends before February 28, 2000, the references to the fraction "1/2" in paragraphs 38(a), (b) and (c) are to be read as references to the fraction "3/4". These modifications are required in order to reflect the capital gains/losses rate for the year.

For a taxation year of a taxpayer that includes February 28, 2000 but does not include October 18, 2000, the references to the fraction "1/2" in paragraphs 38(a), (b) and (c) are to be read as references to the fraction that applies to the taxpayer for that year, determined as follows:

- where the amount of the taxpayer's net capital gains from dispositions of property in the period that begins at the beginning of the year and ends at the end of February 27, 2000 (the first period) exceeds the amount of the taxpayer's net capital losses from dispositions of property in the period that begins at the beginning of February 28, 2000 and ends at the end of the year (the second period), the fraction that applies to the taxpayer for the year is 3/4;

- where the amount of the taxpayer's net capital losses from dispositions of property in the first period exceeds the amount of the taxpayer's net capital gains from dispositions of property in the second period, the fraction that applies to the taxpayer for the year is 3/4;

- where the amount of the taxpayer's net capital gains from dispositions of property in the first period is less than the amount of the taxpayer's net capital losses from dispositions of property in the second period, the fraction that applies to the taxpayer for the year is 2/3;

- where the amount of the taxpayer's net capital losses from dispositions of property in the first period is less than the amount of the taxpayer's net capital gains from dispositions of property in the second period, the fraction that applies to the taxpayer for the year is 2/3;

- where the taxpayer has only net capital gains or only net capital losses from dispositions of property in each of both the first and second periods, the fraction that applies to the taxpayer for the year is the fraction determined by the formula

$$\frac{3/4\ A + 2/3\ B}{(A+B)}$$

where

A is the net capital gains or the net capital losses, as the case may be, of the taxpayer from dispositions of property in the first period, and

B is the net capital gains or the net capital losses, as the case may be, of the taxpayer from dispositions of property in the second period; and

- where the net capital gains and net capital losses of the taxpayer for the year are nil, the fraction that applies to the taxpayer for the year is 2/3.

For a taxation year of a taxpayer that begins after February 27, 2000 and includes October 18, 2000, in order to determine the inclusion rate for the year the references to the fraction "1/2" in paragraphs 38(a), (b) and (c) are to be read as references to the fraction that applies to the taxpayer for that year, determined as follows:

- where the amount of the taxpayer's net capital gains from dispositions of property in the period that begins at the beginning of the year and ends at the end of October 17, 2000 (the first period) exceeds the amount of the taxpayer's net capital losses from dispositions of property in the period that begins at the beginning of October 18, 2000 and ends at the end of the year (the second period), the fraction that applies to the taxpayer for the year is 2/3;
- where the amount of the taxpayer's net capital losses from dispositions of property in the first period exceeds the amount of the taxpayer's net capital gains from dispositions of property in the second period, the fraction that applies to the taxpayer for the year is 2/3;
- where the amount of the taxpayer's net capital gains from dispositions of property in the first period is less than the amount of the taxpayer's net capital losses from dispositions of property in the second period, the fraction that applies to the taxpayer for the year is 1/2;
- where the amount of the taxpayer's net capital losses from dispositions of property in the first period is less than the amount of the taxpayer's net capital gains from dispositions of property in the second period, the fraction that applies to the taxpayer for the year is 1/2;
- where the taxpayer has only net capital gains or only net capital losses from dispositions of property in each of both the first and second periods, the fraction that applies to the taxpayer for the year is the fraction determined by the formula

$$\frac{(2/3\ A + 1/2\ B)}{(A+B)}$$

where

A is the net capital gains or the net capital losses, as the case may be, of the taxpayer from dispositions of property in the first period, and

B is the net capital gains or the net capital losses, as the case may be, of the taxpayer from dispositions of property in the second period and;

- where the net capital gains and net capital losses of the taxpayer for the year are nil, the fraction that applies to the taxpayer for the year is 1/2,

For a taxation year of a taxpayer that includes February 27, 2000 and October 18, 2000, in order to determine the inclusion rate for the year the references to the fraction "1/2" in paragraphs 38(a), (b) and (c) are to be read as references to the fraction that applies to the taxpayer for that year, determined as follows:

- where
  — the amount by which the taxpayer's net capital gains from dispositions of property in the period that begins at the beginning of the year and ends at the end of February 27, 2000 (the first period) exceeds the amount of the taxpayer's net capital losses from dispositions of property in the period that begins at the beginning of February 28, 2000 and ends at the end of October 17, 2000 (the second period)

exceeds

  — the amount of the taxpayer's net capital losses from dispositions of property in the period that begins at the beginning of October 18, 2000 and ends at the end of the year (the third period),

the fraction that applies to the taxpayer for the year is 3/4;

- where
  — the amount by which the taxpayer's net capital losses from dispositions of property in the first period exceeds the amount of the taxpayer's net capital gains from dispositions of property in the second period

exceeds

  — the amount of the taxpayer's net capital gains from dispositions of property in the third period

the fraction that applies to the taxpayer for the year is 3/4;

- where
  — the amount by which the taxpayer's net capital gains from dispositions of property in the second period exceeds the amount of the taxpayer's net capital losses from dispositions of property in the first period

exceeds

  — the amount of the taxpayer's net capital losses from dispositions of property in the third period

the fraction that applies to the taxpayer for the year is 2/3;

- where
  — the amount by which the taxpayer's net capital losses from dispositions of property in the second period exceeds the amount of the taxpayer's net capital gains from dispositions of property in the first period

exceeds

  — the amount of the taxpayer's net capital gains from dispositions of property in the third period

the fraction that applies to the taxpayer for the year is 2/3;

- where the taxpayer has net capital gains in the first and second periods and the aggregate of the amount of those net capital gains exceeds the amount of the taxpayer's net capital losses in the third period, the fraction that applies to the taxpayer for the year is the fraction determined by the formula

$$\frac{(3/4\ A + 2/3\ B)}{(A+B)}$$

where

A is the net capital gains of the taxpayer from dispositions of property in the first period, and

B is the net capital gains of the taxpayer from dispositions of property in the second period;

- where the taxpayer has net capital losses in the first and second periods and the aggregate of the amount of those net capital losses exceeds the amount of the taxpayer's net capital gains in the third period, the fraction that applies to the taxpayer for the year is the fraction determined by the formula

$$\frac{(3/4\ A + 2/3\ B)}{(A+B)}$$

where

> A is the net capital losses of the taxpayer from dispositions of property in the first period, and
>
> B is the net capital losses of the taxpayer from dispositions of property in the second period;

- where the taxpayer has only net gains, or only net capital losses, from dispositions of property in each the first, the second and the third periods, the fraction that applies to the taxpayer for the year is the fraction determined by the formula

$$\frac{(3/4\ A + 2/3\ B + 1/2 C)}{(A+B+C)}$$

where

> A is the net capital gains or the net capital losses, as the case may be, of the taxpayer from dispositions of property in the first period,
>
> B is the net capital gains or the net capital losses as the case may be, of the taxpayer from dispositions of property in the second period, and
>
> C is the net capital gains or the net capital losses as the case may be, of the taxpayer from dispositions of property in the third period;

- where the amount of the taxpayer's net capital gains from dispositions of property in the first period exceeds the amount of the taxpayer's net capital losses from dispositions of property in the second period and the taxpayer has net capital gains from dispositions of property in the third period, the fraction that applies to the taxpayer for the year is the fraction determined by the formula

$$\frac{(3/4\ A + 1/2\ B)}{(A+B)}$$

where

> A is the amount by which the taxpayer's net capital gains from dispositions of property in the first period exceeds the amount of the taxpayer's net capital losses from dispositions of property in the second period, and
>
> B is the taxpayer's net capital gains from dispositions of property in the third period;

- where the amount of the taxpayer's net capital losses from dispositions of property in the first period exceeds the amount of the taxpayer's net capital gains from dispositions of property in the second period and the taxpayer has net capital losses from dispositions of property in the third period, the fraction that applies to the taxpayer for the year is the fraction determined by the formula

$$\frac{(3/4\ A + 1/2\ B)}{(A+B)}$$

where

> A is the amount by which the taxpayer's net capital losses from dispositions of property in the first period exceeds the amount of the taxpayer's net capital gains from dispositions of property in the second period, and
>
> B is the taxpayer's net capital losses from dispositions of property in the third period;

- where the amount of the taxpayer's net capital gains from dispositions of property in the second period exceeds the amount of the taxpayer's net capital losses from dispositions of property in the first period and the taxpayer has net capital gains from dispositions of property in the third period, the fraction that applies to the taxpayer for the year is the fraction determined by the formula

$$\frac{(2/3\ A + 1/2\ B)}{(A+B)}$$

where

> A is the amount by which the taxpayer's net capital gains from dispositions of property in the second period exceeds the amount of the taxpayer's net capital losses from dispositions of property in the first period, and
>
> B is the taxpayer's net capital gains from dispositions of property in the third period;

- where the amount of the taxpayer's net capital losses from dispositions of property in the second period exceeds the amount of the taxpayer's net capital gains from dispositions of property in the first period and the taxpayer has net capital losses from dispositions of property in the third period, the fraction that applies to the taxpayer for the year is the fraction determined by the formula

$$\frac{(2/3\ A + 1/2\ B)}{(A+B)}$$

where

> A is the amount by which the taxpayer's net capital losses from dispositions of property in the second period exceeds the amount of the taxpayer's net capital gains from dispositions of property in the first period, and
>
> B is the taxpayer's net capital losses from dispositions of property in the third period; and

- in any other case, the fraction that applies to the taxpayer for the year is 1/2.

For the purpose of determining the inclusion rate that applies to the taxpayer for the year, the following assumptions are to be made:

- The net capital gains of a taxpayer from dispositions of property in a period is the amount by which the taxpayer's capital gains from dispositions of property in the period exceeds the taxpayer's capital losses from dispositions of property in the period.
- The net capital losses of a taxpayer from dispositions of property in a period is the amount by which the taxpayer's capital losses from dispositions of property in the period exceeds the taxpayer's capital gains from dispositions of property in the period.
- The net amount included as a capital gain of the taxpayer for a taxation year from a disposition of ecological property or from a disposition to which paragraph 38(a.1) applies is one half of the capital gain.
- The net amount included in a capital gain of the taxpayer for a taxation year because of subparagraphs 40(1)(a)(ii) and (iii) is a capital gain of the taxpayer from a disposition of property on the first day of the year.

- Each capital loss that is a business investment loss is determined without reference to subsection 39(9) and 39(10).
- Where an amount is included in computing the income of the taxpayer for the year because of subsection 80(13) in respect of a commercial obligation that is settled, the amount that would be determined under that subsection in respect of the obligation, if the value of E in the formula in that subsection were 1, is a capital gain of the taxpayer from a disposition of property on the day on which the settlement occurred.
- The taxpayer's capital gains and losses from dispositions of property (other than taxable Canadian property) that occur at a time when the taxpayer is a non-resident, are nil.
- Where an election is made by a taxpayer under amended paragraph 104(21.4)(d) or subsections 130.1(4.3) or 131(1.6) for the year, the portion of the net gains of the taxpayer for the year that are to be treated as being in respect of capital gains realized on dispositions of property that occurred in a particular period in the year is that proportion of the net gains that the number of days in that period is of the number of days that are in the year.
- Where the election made under amended paragraph 104(21.4)(d) for the year was made by a personal trust, the portion of the taxpayer's net gains for the year that are to be treated as being in respect of capital gains realized on dispositions of property that occurred in a particular period in the year is that proportion of those net gains that the number of days in the particular period is of the number of days that are in all periods in the year in which a net gains was realized.
- Where, in the course of administering the estate of a deceased taxpayer, a capital loss from disposition of property by the legal representative of a deceased taxpayer is deemed under paragraph 164(6)(c) to be a capital loss of the deceased taxpayer from the disposition of property by the taxpayer in the taxpayer's last taxation year and not to be capital losses of the estate, the capital loss is from the disposition of property by the taxpayer immediately before the taxpayer's death.
- Each capital gain referred to in amended paragraph 104(21.4)(a) in respect of a beneficiary, is to be determined as if that paragraph were read without reference to subparagraph (ii) thereof.
- Where no capital gains or losses are realized in a period, the amount of net capital gains or losses for that period is nil.
- Where a net amount is included as a capital gain of the taxpayer for a taxation year because of the granting of an option under subsection 49(1), the net amount is a capital gain of the taxpayer from a disposition of property on the day on which the option was granted.
- Where a net amount is included as a capital gain of a corporation for its taxation year under subsection 49(2) because of the expiration of an option that was granted by the corporation, the net amount is a capital gain of the corporation from a disposition of property on the day on which the option expired.
- Where a net amount is included as a capital gain of a trust for its taxation year under subsection 49(2.1) because of the expiration of an option that was granted by the trust, the net amount is a capital gain of the trust from a disposition of property on the day on which the option expired.
- Where a net amount is included in respect of an option as a capital gain of a taxpayer for a taxation year because of subsection 49(3), 49(3.01) or 49(3.1), the net amount is a capital gain of the taxpayer from a disposition of property on the day on which the option was exercised.
- Where an amount is included in the income of the taxpayer for the year because of property sold subject to an earn-out agreement, the taxpayer has a capital gain from a disposition of property on the day on which a payment was received under the agreement.

**Notice of Ways and Means Motion, Economic Statement, October 18, 2000**: *Capital Gains Inclusion Rate*

(11) That, for the 2000 and subsequent taxation years,

(a) subject to subparagraph (b), a taxpayer's taxable capital gains, allowable capital losses and allowable business investment losses reflect an inclusion rate for the year for capital gains and losses that is based on

(i) a 3/4 inclusion rate for net capital gains or losses from dispositions of property before February 28, 2000,

(ii) a 2/3 inclusion rate for net capital gains or losses from dispositions of property after February 27, 2000 and before October 18, 2000, and

(iii) a 1/2 inclusion rate for net capital gains or losses from dispositions of property after October 17, 2000,

(b) a taxpayer's taxable capital gain in respect of dispositions to which paragraph 38(a.1) of the Act applies reflect an inclusion rate

(i) of 3/8 for dispositions that occur before February 28, 2000,

(ii) of 1/3 for dispositions that occur after February 27, 2000 and before October 18, 2000, and

(iii) of 1/4 for dispositions that occur after October 17, 2000 and before 2002, and

(c) in determining a taxpayer's inclusion rate for the year

(i) the taxpayer's net capital gains from dispositions of property in a period be the amount, if any, by which the taxpayer's capital gains exceed the taxpayer's capital losses from dispositions of property in the period,

(ii) the taxpayer's net capital losses from dispositions of property in a period be the amount, if any, by which the taxpayer's capital losses exceed the taxpayer's capital gains from dispositions of property in the period,

(iii) the taxpayer's capital gain for a taxation year from a disposition of property before the year be treated as being from a disposition of property on the first day of the year,

(iv) the amount of a business investment loss be determined without reference to subsection 39(9) of the Act,

(v) the amount that would be included in computing the taxpayer's income for the year because of subsection 80(13) of the Act, if the value of E in the formula in that subsection were 1, in respect of a commercial obligation that is settled at any time be treated as a capital gain of the taxpayer from a disposition of property at that time,

(vi) the taxpayer's capital gain or loss from the disposition of property (other than taxable Canadian property) while the taxpayer is non-resident be treated as being nil, and

(vii) the taxpayer's capital gain in respect of a disposition to which paragraph 38(a.1) of the Act applies or in respect of a disposition of ecological property to which the halved inclusion rate applies be treated as being 1/2 the capital gain, and

(d) the halved inclusion rate for certain ecological gifts, the rules for determining the capital gains deduction under section 110.6 of the Act and any other rules of determination under the Act be modified to take into account the inclusion rate for the year.

### Economic Statement, supplementary information, October 18, 2000: *Capital Gains*

In the 2000 budget, the Government reduced the inclusion rate for capital gains from three-quarters to two-thirds, effective February 28, 2000. The Government is now proposing to go further and to reduce the inclusion rate for capital gains to one-half, effective October 18, 2000.

While the calculations for 2000 involve three periods to reflect the different inclusion rates for each period, the calculations are mechanical.

*Capital Gains Tax Rates in Canada and the U.S.*

The changes announced today will reduce the maximum federal tax rate on capital gains for individuals in Canada to 14.5 per cent. This is well below the general U.S. federal tax rate of 20 per cent on gains on assets held for more than one year. The top federal-provincial tax rate on capital gains for individuals in Canada will be reduced from an average of about 31 per cent to about 23 per cent, lower than the typical combined federal-state top tax rate on capital gains in the U.S. of 25 per cent. Moreover, the rates for Canada apply to all capital gains, regardless of the type of asset or the length of time the asset is held, contrary to what is the case in the U.S. (Table A2.15).

Table A2.15 — Top Marginal Tax Rates on Capital Gains for Individuals in Canada and the U.S. (as of January 1, 2001)

|  | Capital gains tax rate Federal only | | Capital gains tax rate Federal plus provincial/state[1] | |
|---|---|---|---|---|
|  | Canada | U.S. | Canada | U.S. |
|  | (per cent) | | | |
| Assets held 1 year or less | 14.5 | 39.6[2] | 23.2 | 44.6[2] |
| Assets held for more than 1 year | 14.5 | 20.0 | 23.2 | 25.0 |
| Assets held for more than 5 years | 14.5 | 18.0[3] | 23.2 | 23.0[3] |
| Small business shares | 0/14.5[4] | 14.0[5] | 0/23.2[4] | 19.0[5] |

Notes:

1. Typical provincial/state rates. Under a 50% inclusion rate, provincial tax rates on capital gains would range from 5.3% to 12.5%. State tax rates range from 0 to 12.0%.
2. Gains on property held for one year or less are taxed as ordinary income.
3. Applies to assets acquired after December 31, 2000 — will only be available for assets disposed of after 2005.
4. Eligible for $500,000 lifetime capital gains exemption and potentially the small business rollover.
5. Available on a maximum of the greater of $10 million or 10 times the cost base of the shares. Shares must be held for more than five years. Small business shares are also potentially eligible for a rollover.

*Applying the Different Inclusion Rates for 2000*

### Computing Taxable Capital Gains/Allowable Capital Losses in Taxation Year 2000 — For Individuals (and Other Taxpayers With Calendar Taxation Years)

Three different capital gains inclusion rates will apply for 2000.

- For the period January 1–February 27, the inclusion rate will be three-quarters.
- For the period February 28–October 17, the inclusion rate will be two-thirds.
- For the period October 18–December 31, the inclusion rate will be one-half.

Accordingly, individuals (and other taxpayers with calendar taxation years) will be required to report separately capital gains and losses realized in each of the three periods.

The approach for determining an individual's taxable capital gain or allowable capital loss and an individual's capital gains inclusion rate for the 2000 taxation year will be based upon the general approach described in the budget documents tabled February 28, 2000. The addition of a third inclusion rate for the year means that an individual's taxable capital gain or allowable capital loss and an individual's inclusion rate will, where the individual has gains or losses in each of the three periods, be calculated in three steps.

If there are no gains or losses in at least one period, the individual's taxable capital gain or allowable capital loss and the inclusion rate for the year can be determined using the same approach set out in the budget documents tabled February 28, 2000. The individual will only need to make the appropriate adjustments to reflect, where necessary, the one-half inclusion rate that applies for the period October 18–December 31.

This situation is illustrated in Example 1.

**S. 38(a)**      Income Tax Act, Part I, Division B

*Example 1*

Eric sells shares in ABC Corporation on January 30, 2000, for a gain of $400. He sells more ABC shares on November 30, 2000, for a gain of $1,500. Finally, he sells shares in XYZ Inc. on December 1, 2000, for a loss of $300.

Because he has no gains or losses in the period February 28–October 17, Eric calculates his taxable capital gain using the approach outlined in the budget documents tabled February 28, 2000.

*Step 1, based on the February 2000 budget documents*

Eric determines separately his net gains for the periods January 1–February 27 and October 18–December 31. For the first period, his net gain is $400; for the last period, his net gain is $1,500 less $300, or $1,200.

Eric uses the formula outlined in the 2000 budget documents, making sure that he adjusts the formula to account for the one-half inclusion rate for the period October 18–December 31.

Taxable Capital Gain =

$$\frac{3}{4} \times \$400 + \frac{1}{2} \times \$1,200 = \$900.$$

*Step 2, based on the February 2000 budget documents*

To determine his inclusion rate for the year, Eric follows the approach outlined in the budget documents tabled February 28, 2000, and divides his taxable capital gain of $900 by his net gain for the year of $1,600 (i.e., $400 plus $1,200):

Inclusion Rate =

$$\$900 \div \$1,600 = 56.25\%.$$

*Gains or Losses in Each of the Three Periods*

**Step 1 — Calculation of Net Gain/Loss for Each Period**

For each of the three periods, the individual will have to compute the net capital gain or loss.

**Step 2 — Calculation of Interim Gain/Loss and Interim Inclusion Rate for the Period January 1–October 17**

The next step requires the individual to compare the net gain or net loss for the period January 1–February 27 with the net gain or net loss for the period February 28–October 17. This will produce an "interim" net gain or net loss and "interim" capital gains inclusion rate for the period January 1–October 17.

Where there is a net gain in one of the two periods and a net loss in the other, the interim net gain or net loss for the period January 1–October 17 will be computed by netting the two. The interim inclusion rate for the period January 1–October 17 will be the inclusion rate for the period to which the larger of the net gain or net loss relates. This is illustrated in Examples 2 and 3.

Where there are net gains in both periods, or net losses in both periods, the individual's interim net gain or net loss for the period January 1–October 17 will be the sum of the net gains or the net losses. The individual's interim inclusion rate for the period January 1–October 17 will be determined using the following formula:

$$(\frac{3}{4} \times A + \frac{2}{3} \times B)/(A + B)$$

where

A    Net gain/loss in the period January 1–February 27, 2000; and

B    Net gain/loss in the period February 28–October 17, 2000.

The use of this formula is demonstrated in Example 4.

**Step 3 — Calculation of Taxable Capital Gain/Allowable Capital Loss and Inclusion Rate for the 2000 Taxation Year**

The third step involves using the interim results from Step 2 and the individual's net gain or net loss for the period October 18–December 31 to determine the individual's inclusion rate for the 2000 taxation year. This inclusion rate will then be used to determine the individual's taxable capital gain or allowable capital loss for the year.

Where there is an interim net gain for the period January 1–October 17 and a net loss for the period October 18–December 31, or an interim net loss for the period January 1–October 17 and a net gain for the period October 18–December 31, the net gain or net loss for the 2000 taxation year will be computed by netting the two. The inclusion rate for the year will be the inclusion rate for the period (either the interim period January 1–October 17 or the period October 18–December 31) to which the larger of the net gain or net loss relates. The individual's taxable capital gain or allowable capital loss for the year will be determined by applying this inclusion rate to the net gain or net loss for the year. This is illustrated in Examples 2 and 4.

Where there is an interim net gain from Step 2 and a net gain in the period October 18–December 31, or an interim net loss from Step 2 and a net loss in the period October 18–December 31, the individual's inclusion rate for the 2000 taxation year will be determined using the following formula:

$$(C \times D + \frac{1}{2} \times E)/(D + E)$$

where

C    Interim inclusion rate for the period January 1–October 17, 2000;

D    Interim net gain/loss for the period January 1–October 17, 2000; and

E    Net gain/loss in the period October 18–December 31, 2000.

The individual's taxable capital gain or allowable capital loss for the year will be determined by applying this inclusion rate to the individual's net gain or net loss for the year. Example 3 illustrates the use of this formula.

*Example 2*

Isadora sells shares in XYZ Inc. on February 1, 2000, for a loss of $400. She sells shares in ABC Corporation on May 15, 2000, for a gain of $1,200. Finally, she sells more shares of XYZ Inc. on December 1, 2000, for a loss of $500.

*Step 1*

Isadora determines separately her net gains and losses for the periods January 1–February 27, February 28–October 17, and October 18–December 31. For the first period, she has a net loss of $400; for the second period, she has a net gain of

260

$1,200; for the third period, she has a net loss of $500.

*Step 2*

Isadora determines her interim net gain and interim inclusion rate for the period January 1–October 17. Her interim net gain is $800 (the $1,200 net gain less the $400 net loss). Because the net gain from the second period is larger than the net loss from the first period, Isadora's interim inclusion rate is two-thirds.

*Step 3*

Isadora compares the interim results from Step 2 with the net loss for the period October 18–December 31. Her net gain for the year is $300 (the interim net gain of $800 minus the net loss of $500). Because the net gain for the interim period is greater than the net loss for the later period, her inclusion rate for the year is the two-thirds inclusion rate associated with the interim period. Isadora applies this inclusion rate to her net gain for the year to determine her taxable capital gain.

Taxable Capital Gain =

$$\frac{2}{3} \times \$300 = \$200.$$

*Example 3*

Doug sells shares in ABC Corporation on February 1, 2000, for a gain of $600. He later sells shares in XYZ Inc. on May 15, 2000, for a loss of $500. Finally, he sells more shares of ABC Corporation on December 1, 2000, for a gain of $400.

*Step 1*

Doug determines separately his net gains and losses for the periods January 1–February 27, February 28–October 17, and October 18–December 31. For the first period, he has a net gain of $600; for the second period, he has a net loss of $500; for the third period, he has a net gain of $400.

*Step 2*

Doug calculates his interim net gain and interim inclusion rate for the period January 1–October 17. His interim net gain is $100 (the $600 gain less the $500 loss). Because the net gain from the first period is larger than the net loss from the second period, Doug's interim inclusion rate is three quarters.

*Step 3*

Doug now uses the interim net gain of $100 and the interim inclusion rate of 3/4 for the period January 1–October 17, along with the net gain of $400 for the period October 18–December 31 to determine his inclusion rate for the year. Doug uses the Step 3 formula.

$$C = \frac{3}{4}, D = \$100, E = \$400.$$

Inclusion Rate =

$$(\frac{3}{4} \times \$100 + \frac{1}{2} \times \$400)/(\$100 + \$400) = 55\%.$$

To determine his taxable capital gain for the year, Doug applies this inclusion rate to his net gain for the year of $500 (i.e., the $100 interim net gain plus the $400 net gain for the period October 18–December 31).

Taxable Capital Gain =

$$55\% \times \$500 = \$275.$$

*Example 4*

Cecil sells shares in ABC Corporation on February 1, 2000, for a gain of $1,000. On September 10, he sells more shares of ABC Corporation for a gain of $1,500. Finally, he sells shares of XYZ Inc. on December 1, 2000, for a loss of $1,100.

*Step 1*

Cecil determines separately his net gains and losses for the periods January 1–February 27, February 28–October 17, and October 18–December 31. For the first period, he has a net gain of $1,000; for the second period, he has a net gain of $1,500; for the third period, he has a net loss of $1,100.

*Step 2*

Cecil calculates his interim net gain and interim inclusion rate for the period January 1–October 17. His interim net gain is $2,500 ($1,000 plus $1,500). His interim inclusion rate is calculated using the Step 2 formula:

A = $1,000, B = $1,500.

Interim Inclusion Rate =

$$(\frac{3}{4} \times \$1,000 + \frac{2}{3} \times \$1,500)/(\$1,000 + \$1,500) = 70\%.$$

*Step 3*

Because the interim net gain for the period January 1–October 17 is larger than the net loss for the period October 18–December 31, Cecil's interim inclusion rate of 70 per cent is his inclusion rate for the year. To determine his taxable capital gain for 2000, Cecil applies this inclusion rate to his net gain of $1,400 (the $2,500 interim net gain minus the $1,100 net loss).

Taxable Capital Gain =

$$70\% \times \$1,400 = \$980.$$

### Taxpayers With Non-Calendar Taxation Years

For taxpayers whose taxation years do not coincide with the calendar year (such as some corporations), the one-half inclusion rate will apply to capital gains realized after October 17, 2000. Similar to individuals, corporations will be required to report separately capital gains and losses realized before February 28, from February 28 to October 17, and after October 17, 2000.

### Loss Carryovers

The treatment of net capital losses carried over from other years will be the same as described in the budget documents tabled February 28, 2000.

### Eligible Capital Property

Eligible capital property refers to items such as goodwill and other intangibles. The treatment of eligible capital property is somewhat analogous to the treatment of depreciable property in that deductions are subject to recapture and, where proceeds of disposition exceed the original cost, the gains are treated similarly to capital gains.

Accordingly, the one-half inclusion rate for capital gains will apply to gains on dispositions of eligible capital property for taxation years that end after October 17, 2000.

The existing pooling system, whereby three-quarters of the cost of such property is depreciated at 7 per cent declining balance, will be maintained. This approach is the most generous for taxpayers and will ease both compliance and administration.

### Mutual Funds and Segregated Funds

As an alternative to specific identification, mutual fund corporations, mutual fund trusts and segregated fund trusts will be permitted to treat their capital gains and capital losses for the year as being earned on an equal daily basis throughout the year for the purposes of determining net capital gains or losses attributable to a particular period in the year. If this option is used by a fund, capital gains allocated to the unitholders must be apportioned to the periods in the year on a consistent basis (other than gains allocated by a segregated fund on a redemption of an interest in the segregated fund in the year).

### Capital Gains Arising From Certain Charitable Donations

The capital gains inclusion rate is reduced by one-half for capital gains arising from certain donations of appreciated publicly traded securities and ecologically sensitive property to a charity. For 2000, the inclusion rate for such capital gains will be based on one-half of the capital gains inclusion rate for the period in which the donation occurred. For 2001 (and future years, where applicable), the inclusion rate will be one-half of the capital gains inclusion rate for that year.

### Notice of Ways and Means Motion, federal budget, February 28, 2000: *Capital Gains Inclusion Rate*

(9) That for the 2000 and subsequent taxation years,

(a) subject to subparagraphs (b) and (c), a taxpayer's taxable capital gain, allowable capital loss and allowable business investment loss reflect a 3/4 inclusion rate in respect of gains and losses from dispositions of property before February 28, 2000 and a 2/3 inclusion rate in respect of other gains and losses for the year,

(b) a taxpayer's taxable capital gain in respect of dispositions to which paragraph 38(a.1) of the Act applies reflect a 3/8 inclusion rate for dispositions that occur before February 28, 2000 and a 1/3 inclusion rate for dispositions that occur after February 27, 2000 and before 2002,

(c) the amount included in a taxpayer's taxable capital gain, in a taxation year that begins after February 27, 2000, in respect of a capital gains reserve reflect a 2/3 inclusion rate,

(d) the deductions permitted in paragraphs 110(1)(d) to (d.3) of the Act in respect of amounts that are included in income for the year (other than amounts that would be included in income for the year if the year had ended on February 27, 2000) be determined as 1/3 of the amounts so included in income rather than as 1/4 of such amounts, and

(e) the rules for determining the capital gains deduction under section 110.6 of the Act and any other rules of determination under the Act take into account, where appropriate, the change in determination of a taxpayer's taxable capital gain and allowable capital loss from a disposition of a property.

### Letter from Department of Finance, September 29, 2000:

Dear [xxx]

This is in reply to your letter dated August 14, 2000 concerning the effective date for the changes to the capital gains inclusion rate announced in the 2000 Budget and also to the representations made by your association at a meeting held on June 7, 2000 with Department of Finance officials.

Your request to make the effective date for the change in the inclusion rate for capital gains either January 1, 2000 or December 16, 1999 was brought to the attention of senior officials within the Department. After further discussion and consideration it was decided that the effective date for the change announced in the 2000 Budget would be maintained. The change is proposed to apply in respect of capital gains from dispositions of property after February 27, 2000 for tax equity reasons.

The concerns that your association expressed concerning the difficulty of factually determining the dates that capital gains and losses are realised by a mutual fund trust or corporation were fully discussed. With these difficulties in mind, we recommended that the mutual fund industry be given two options in calculating its inclusion rate for the taxation year that includes February 27, 2000. The Minister supported these recommendations and the options will be part of the 2000 budget legislation.

One option would be to permit a calculation of an inclusion rate based on factual determinations of gains and losses from dispositions of property in the pre and post budget periods in the year. The second option would be to permit a determination based on the assumption that a mutual fund's net capital gains for the year were earned evenly throughout the year. The number of days in the pre and post budget periods when divided by the number of days in the year would determine the portion of the gains for the year allocable to the pre and post budget periods. These gain amounts for the periods would then be used to determine the fund's effective capital gains inclusion rate for the year.

The effective capital gains inclusion rate for the year will be determined using one of the above options. Once calculated, it will affect the determination of the percentage used to determine a capital gains refund for the year of the fund.

Gross gains allocated to unit holders for the year would be allocated to pre and post budget periods in proportions determined on a basis consistent with the basis adopted by the mutual fund to allocate its gains to such periods. The mutual fund would be required to report to the unit holder the portion of the gains allocable to the pre and post budget periods on the income tax information slips issued to them for the year.

We trust that the foregoing solution to the issues raised by your association will meet with general support.

Yours sincerely,

Len Farber
General Director, Tax Legislation Division, Tax Policy Branch

(a.1) a taxpayer's taxable capital gain for a taxation year from the disposition after February 18, 1997 and before 2002 of any property is 3/8 of the taxpayer's capital gain for the year from the disposition of the property where

(i) the disposition is the making of a gift to a qualified donee (as defined in subsection 149.1(1)), other than a private foundation, of a share, debt obligation or right listed on a prescribed stock exchange, a share of the capital stock of a mutual fund corporation, a unit of a mutual fund trust, an interest in a related segregated fund trust (within the meaning assigned by paragraph 138.1(1)(a)) or a prescribed debt obligation, or

(ii) the disposition is deemed by section 70 to have occurred and the taxpayer is deemed by subsection 118.1(5) to have made a gift described in subparagraph (i) of the property;

### Proposed Amendment — 38(a.1)

**Application**: The December 21, 2000 draft legislation, subsec. 13(2), will amend para. 38(a.1) by replacing the reference to the fraction "3/8" with a reference to the fraction "1/4", applicable to 2000 et seq. except that,

(a) for a taxation year of a taxpayer that includes February 28, 2000 or October 17, 2000, the reference to the fraction "1/4" shall be read as a reference to 1/2 of the fraction in para. 38(a), as amended [by the December 21, 2000 draft legislation], that applies to the taxpayer for the year; and

(b) for a taxation year that ended before February 28, 2000, the reference to the fraction "1/4" shall be read as a reference to the fraction "3/8".

**Technical Notes**: Paragraph 38(a.1) provides a special inclusion rate for capital gains arising as a result of a gift of certain securities to qualified donees. This inclusion rate is one half of the normal inclusion rate.

The amendment to paragraph 38(a.1) replaces the reference to the fraction "3/8" (one-half of 3/4) with a reference to the fraction "1/4" (one-half of 1/2).

The amendment applies to the 2000 and subsequent taxation years except that,

(a) for a taxation year of a taxpayer that includes February 28, 2000 or October 17, 2000, the reference to the fraction "1/4" in paragraph 38(a.1) is to be read as a reference to 1/2 of the fraction in amended paragraph 38(a) that applies to the taxpayer for the year and,

(b) for a taxation year that ends before February 28, 2000 the reference to the fraction "1/4" in paragraph 38(a.1) is to be read as a reference to the fraction "3/8".

### Proposed Addition — 38(a.2)

(a.2) a taxpayer's taxable capital gain for a taxation year from the disposition of a property is 1/4 of the taxpayer's capital gain for the year from the disposition of the property where

(i) the disposition is the making of a gift to a qualified donee (other than a private foundation) of a property described, in respect of the taxpayer, in paragraph 110.1(1)(d) or in the definition "total ecological gifts" in subsection 118.1(1), or

(ii) the disposition is deemed by section 70 to have occurred and the taxpayer is deemed by subsection 118.1(5) to have made a gift described in subparagraph (i) of the property;

**Application**: The December 21, 2000 draft legislation, subsec. 13(3), will add para. 38(a.2), applicable to gifts made by a taxpayer after February 27, 2000 except that,

(a) if the taxpayer's taxation year began after February 28, 2000 and ended before October 17, 2000, the reference to the fraction "1/4" shall be read as a reference to the fraction "1/3"; and

(b) if the taxpayer's taxation year includes either February 28, 2000 or October 17, 2000, the reference to the fraction "1/4" shall be read as a reference to 1/2 of the fraction in para. 38(a), as amended [by the December 21, 2000 draft legislation], that applies to the taxpayer for the year.

**Technical Notes**: The portion of a taxpayer's capital gain that is required to be included in computing income is his or her "taxable capital gain". New paragraph 38(a.2) provides that if a capital gain results from the making of an ecological gift to a qualified donee, only 1/4 of the gain will be a taxable capital gain and hence included in income. The definitions of "ecological gifts" and "total ecological gifts" in paragraph 110.1(1)(d) and subsection 118.1(1) respectively are also amended to provide that the fair market value of such gifts must be certified by the Minister of the Environment. For further detail, see the commentary on section 118.1.

This amendment applies to gifts made after February 27, 2000, except that if the taxpayer's taxation year begins after February 28, 2000 and ends before October 17, 2000, the reference to the fraction "1/4" is to be read as a reference to "1/3", and if the taxpayer's taxation year includes either February 28, 2000 or October 17, 2000, the capital gains inclusion rate will be one half of the rate otherwise calculated for the year under amended paragraph 38(a).

**Notice of Ways and Means Motion, federal budget, February 28, 2000**: *Donations of Ecological Gifts*

(22) That the provisions of the Act relating to ecological gifts be modified to (a) halve the income inclusion rate for capital gains from such gifts (other than gifts made to a private foundation) made after February 27, 2000, [...]

[For the remainder of this proposal, and the accompanying Budget Supplementary Information, see under 118.1(1)"total ecological gifts" — ed.]

(b) a taxpayer's allowable capital loss for a taxation year from the disposition of any property is 3/4 of the taxpayer's capital loss for the year from the disposition of that property; and

### Proposed Amendment — 38(b)

**Application**: The December 21, 2000 draft legislation, subsec. 13(4), will amend para. 38(b) by replacing the reference to the fraction "3/4" with a reference to the fraction "1/2", applicable on the same basis as the amendment to para. 38(a).

**Technical Notes**: See under 38(a).

(c) a taxpayer's allowable business investment loss for a taxation year from the disposition of any property is 3/4 of the taxpayer's business investment loss for the year from the disposition of that property.

### Proposed Amendment — 38(c)

**Application:** The December 21, 2000 draft legislation, subsec. 13(4), will amend para. 38(c) by replacing the reference to the fraction "3/4" with a reference to the fraction "1/2", applicable on the same basis as the amendment to para. 38(a).

**Technical Notes:** See under 38(a).

**Related Provisions [s. 38]:** 11(2) — Fiscal (business) year of individual does not apply to subdivision c; 20(4.3) — Deemed allowable capital loss on bad debt on disposition of eligible capital property; 39 — Capital gains and losses; 83(2), 89(1)"capital dividend account"(a)(i) — Untaxed fraction of gain can be distributed free of tax by corporation as capital dividend; 96(1.7) — Partnership gains and losses; 100(1) — Disposition of interest in a partnership; 104(21) — Flow-through of gain from trust to beneficiary; 110(1)(d.01) — Deduction on donating employee stock-option shares to charity; 110.6 — Capital gains exemption; 111(8)"net capital loss" — Carryover of unused allowable capital loss; 127.52(1)(d)(i) — 30% of gain added to income for minimum tax purposes; 133(1)(d) — Non-resident-owned investment corporation fully taxed on gains; 142.5(6) — Transitional allowable capital loss re mark-to-market property; 142.5(9)(e) — Deemed taxable capital gain where mark-to-market property acquired by financial institution on rollover; 149.1(6.4) — Rule re gifts of public securities applies to gifts to registered national arts service organizations; 248(1)"allowable business investment loss", 248(1)"allowable capital loss", 248(1)"taxable capital gain" — Definitions in s. 38 apply to entire Act; Canada-U.S. tax treaty, Art. XIII — Gains.

**Notes:** Taxable capital gains and allowable capital losses of the current year must be netted against each other. Excess allowable capital losses can generally be carried back three years or forward indefinitely as "net capital losses", and optionally used against taxable capital gains in those other years. See 111 and Notes to s. 3. Allowable business investment losses can be used against any income (see 3(d)) or carried back 3 years or forward 7 years as non-capital losses (see 111(1)(a) and 111(8)"non-capital loss"E). Certain taxable capital gains of individuals are eligible for an offsetting deduction under 110.6 (the capital gains exemption).

38(a.1) added, and (a) amended to add "subject to paragraph (a.1)", by 1997 Budget, effective February 19, 1997. Capital gains on publicly-traded shares, mutual funds or government bonds donated to a charity are taxed at only half the normal rate (i.e., now 1/4 inclusion instead of 1/2 inclusion). This rule may be re-announced in the 2001 Budget if it has been found successful, since it otherwise expires at the end of 2001.

A side effect of 38(a.1) is an increase from 1/2 to 3/4 of the fraction of the gain that goes into a donating corporation's capital dividend account and can be distributed to shareholders tax-free. See Notes to 89(1)"capital dividend account".

When determining the value of a transfer under 38(a.1), the transfer appears to take place when the donor has done everything required to effect the transfer, even if the broker does not respond immediately and the stock price changes before the charity receives the stocks. See Arthur Drache, "The Timing of a Gift", 8(11) *Canadian Not-For-Profit News* (Carswell) p. 84 (Nov. 2000). The case referred to by Drache is *D'Esterre v. M.N.R.* (1956), 15 Tax A.B.C. 356 (TAB).

**Definitions [s. 38]:** "business investment loss" — 39(1)(c), 248(1); "capital gain" — 39(1)(a), 248(1); "capital loss" — 39(1)(b), 248(1); "disposition" — 54 [to be repealed], 248(1); "mineral resource" — 248(1); "mutual fund corporation" — 131(8), 248(1); "mutual fund trust" — 132(6)–(7), 132.2(1)(q), 248(1); "prescribed" — 248(1); "prescribed debt obligation" — Reg. 6210; "prescribed stock exchange" — Reg. 3200, 3201; "private foundation" — 149.1(1), 248(1); "property" — 248(1); "qualified donee" — 149.1(1), 248(1); "share" — 248(1); "taxation year" — 249; "taxpayer" — 248(1); "total ecological gifts" — 118.1(1).

**Regulations:** 3200, 3201 (prescribed stock exchanges for 38(a.1)); 6210 (prescribed debt obligations for 38(a.1).

**Interpretation Bulletins [s. 38]:** IT-484R2: Business investment losses.

**Forms [s. 38]:** T1170: Capital gains on gifts of certain capital property; T4037: Capital gains [guide].

## 39. (1) Meaning of capital gain and capital loss [and business investment loss] — For the purposes of this Act,

(a) a taxpayer's **capital gain** for a taxation year from the disposition of any property is the taxpayer's gain for the year determined under this subdivision (to the extent of the amount thereof that would not, if section 3 were read without reference to the expression "other than a taxable capital gain from the disposition of a property" in paragraph 3(a) and without reference to paragraph 3(b), be included in computing the taxpayer's income for the year or any other taxation year) from the disposition of any property of the taxpayer other than

(i) eligible capital property,

(i.1) an object that the Canadian Cultural Property Export Review Board has determined meets the criteria set out in paragraphs 29(3)(b) and (c) of the *Cultural Property Export and Import Act* and that has been disposed of,

(A) in the case of a gift to which subsection 118.1(5) applies, within the period ending 36 months after the death of the taxpayer or, where written application therefor has been made to the Minister by the taxpayer's legal representative within that period, within such longer period as the Minister considers reasonable in the circumstances, and

(B) in any other case, at any time,

to an institution or a public authority in Canada that was, at the time of the disposition, designated under subsection 32(2) of that Act either generally or for a specified purpose related to that object,

(ii) a Canadian resource property,

(ii.1) a foreign resource property,

(ii.2) a property to the disposition of which subsection 142.4(4) or (5) or 142.5(1) applies,

### Proposed Addition — 39(1)(a)(ii.3)

(ii.3) a property in respect of which subsection 94.2(3) applies to the taxpayer immediately before the time of the disposition,

**Application:** The June 22, 2000 draft legislation, s. 3, will add subpara. 39(1)(a)(ii.3), applicable to dispositions that occur after 2000.

Subdivision c — Taxable Capital Gains  S. 39(1)(c)(vii)

> **Technical Notes:** Paragraph 39(1)(a) contains a description of a taxpayer's capital gain for a taxation year from the disposition of property. This paragraph provides that gains from dispositions of specified properties are to be excluded in determining a capital gain. Under subparagraph 39(1)(a)(ii.2), the specified properties include specified debt obligations, where subsection 142.4(4) or (5) applies to the disposition, and mark-to-market properties where subsection 142.5(1) applies to the disposition. Under subparagraph 39(1)(b)(ii), the same exclusion generally applies with regard to a taxpayer's capital loss.
>
> New subparagraph 39(1)(a)(ii.3) provides a similar exclusion for property in respect of which new subsection 94.2(3) applies to a taxpayer immediately before the time of the disposition. Subsection 94.2(3) sets out the conditions for the application of the mark-to-market taxation regime under subsection 94.2(4) for participating interests in foreign investment entities. Because of paragraph 94.2(5)(b), this exclusion does not apply where the taxpayer is not resident in Canada immediately before the time of the disposition.

 (iii) an insurance policy, including a life insurance policy, except for that part of a life insurance policy in respect of which a policyholder is deemed by paragraph 138.1(1)(e) to have an interest in a related segregated fund trust,

 (iv) a timber resource property, or

 (v) an interest of a beneficiary under a qualifying environmental trust;

(b) a taxpayer's **capital loss** for a taxation year from the disposition of any property is the taxpayer's loss for the year determined under this subdivision (to the extent of the amount thereof that would not, if section 3 were read in the manner described in paragraph (a) of this subsection and without reference to the expression "or the taxpayer's allowable business investment loss for the year" in paragraph 3(d), be deductible in computing the taxpayer's income for the year or any other taxation year) from the disposition of any property of the taxpayer other than

 (i) depreciable property, or

 (ii) property described in any of subparagraphs (a)(i), (ii) to (iii) and (v); and

(c) a taxpayer's **business investment loss** for a taxation year from the disposition of any property is the amount, if any, by which the taxpayer's capital loss for the year from a disposition after 1977

 (i) to which subsection 50(1) applies, or

 (ii) to a person with whom the taxpayer was dealing at arm's length

of any property that is

 (iii) a share of the capital stock of a small business corporation, or

 (iv) a debt owing to the taxpayer by a Canadian-controlled private corporation (other than, where the taxpayer is a corporation, a debt owing to it by a corporation with which it does not deal at arm's length) that is

  (A) a small business corporation,

  (B) a bankrupt (within the meaning assigned by subsection 128(3)) that was a small business corporation at the time it last became a bankrupt, or

  (C) a corporation referred to in section 6 of the *Winding-up and Restructuring Act* that was insolvent (within the meaning of that Act) and was a small business corporation at the time a winding-up order under that Act was made in respect of the corporation,

exceeds the total of

 (v) in the case of a share referred to in subparagraph (iii), the amount, if any, of the increase after 1977 by virtue of the application of subsection 85(4) in the adjusted cost base to the taxpayer of the share or of any share (in this subparagraph referred to as a "replaced share") for which the share or a replaced share was substituted or exchanged,

 (vi) in the case of a share referred to in subparagraph (iii) that was issued before 1972 or a share (in this subparagraph and subparagraph (vii) referred to as a "substituted share") that was substituted or exchanged for such a share or for a substituted share, the total of all amounts each of which is an amount received after 1971 and before or on the disposition of the share or an amount receivable at the time of such a disposition by

  (A) the taxpayer,

  (B) where the taxpayer is an individual, the taxpayer's spouse or common-law partner, or

  (C) a trust of which the taxpayer or the taxpayer's spouse or common-law partner was a beneficiary

as a taxable dividend on the share or on any other share in respect of which it is a substituted share, except that this subparagraph shall not apply in respect of a share or substituted share that was acquired after 1971 from a person with whom the taxpayer was dealing at arm's length,

 (vii) in the case of a share to which subparagraph (vi) applies and where the taxpayer is a trust referred to in paragraph 104(4)(a), the total of all amounts each of which is an amount received after 1971 or receivable at the time of the disposition by the settlor (within the meaning assigned by subsection 108(1)) or by the settlor's spouse or common-law partner as a taxable dividend on the share or on any other share in respect of which it is a substituted share, and

(viii) the amount determined in respect of the taxpayer under subsection (9) or (10), as the case may be.

**Related Provisions [subsec. 39(1)]**: 12(1)(z.1) — Disposition of interest in qualifying environmental trust; 39(2) — Capital gains and losses in respect of foreign currencies; 39(3) — Gain — purchase of bonds by issuer; 39(12) — Amount paid under guarantee deemed to be business investment loss; 40 — Calculation of gain or loss; 44.1(2) — Capital gain on disposition of small business investment that is replaced by another; 55(2) — Deemed capital gain on certain dividends; 80.03(2), (4) — Deemed capital gain on disposition of property following debt forgiveness; 100(4) — Reduction in capital loss on disposition of partnership interest; 104(4.1) — Mark-to-market property can be capital property for trust's 21-year deemed disposition; 110.6 — Capital gains exemption; 118.1(7.1) — Gifts of cultural property; 136 — Cooperative can be private corporation for 39(1)(c); 139.1(4)(a) — Capital gain and loss on ownership rights resulting from demutualization of insurer deemed nil; 144(4) — Deemed capital gain from employees profit sharing plan; 248(1)"capital gain", "capital loss" — Definitions in 39(1) apply to entire Act; Canada-U.S. tax treaty, Art. XIII — Gains.

**Notes**: In general, a capital gain is a gain on the sale of "capital property" as defined in 54. See Notes to that definition for the distinction between a capital gain and an income gain. See also Notes to 38 re application of taxable capital gains, allowable capital losses and allowable business investment losses.

39(1)(b)(i) denies a capital loss on depreciable property because a terminal loss is available under 20(16) instead, once all of the property in the class has been disposed of.

When reading 39(1)(c)(iv)(C), see Notes to 50(1) for s. 6 of the *Winding-up and Restructuring Act*.

39(1)(a)(i.1) amended by 1991 technical bill, effective December 12, 1988, to update the cross-references to the *Cultural Property Import and Export Act* and to extend the time for disposition from 15 months to 36 months or longer.

39(1)(a)(ii.2) added by 1994 tax amendments bill (Part III), effective for dispositions of property occurring after February 22, 1994.

39(1)(a)(v) added by 1994 Budget, effective for taxation years that end after February 22, 1994; and amended by 1997 Budget, effective for taxation years that end after February 18, 1997, to change "mining reclamation trust" to "qualifying environmental trust".

Reference in 39(1)(b)(ii) to 39(1)(a)(ii.1) and (v) added by 1994 Budget, effective for taxation years that end after February 22, 1994. Reference to 39(1)(a)(ii.2) added by 1994 tax amendments bill (Part III), effective for property disposed of after February 22, 1994.

39(1)(c)(iv)(B) and (C) added by 1991 technical bill, retroactive to 1987.

39(1)(c)(vi), (vii) amended by 2000 same-sex partners bill to add reference to "common-law partner", effective for the 2001 and later taxation years, or earlier by election (see Notes to 248(1)"common-law partner").

**Interpretation Bulletins**: IT-123R5: Transactions involving eligible capital property; IT-125R4: Dispositions of resource properties; IT-159R3: Capital debts established to be bad debts; IT-220R2: Capital cost allowance — proceeds of disposition of depreciable property; IT-359R2: Premiums and other amounts re leases; IT-346R: Commodity futures and certain commodities; IT-407R4: Dispositions of cultural property to designated Canadian institutions; IT-426: Shares sold subject to an earnout agreement; IT-444R: Corporations — involuntary dissolutions; IT-481: Timber resource property and timber limits; IT-484R2: Business investment losses. See also list at end of s. 39.

**I.T. Technical News**: No. 16 (*Continental Bank* case).

**Advance Tax Rulings**: ATR-15: Employee stock option plan; ATR-28: Redemption of capital stock of family farm corporation.

**Forms**: T1 Sched. 3: Capital gains (or losses); T2 SCH 6: Summary of dispositions of capital property; T3 Sched. 1: Dispositions of capital property; T1161: List of properties by an emigrant of Canada.

**(2) Capital gains and losses in respect of foreign currencies** — Notwithstanding subsection (1), where, by virtue of any fluctuation after 1971 in the value of the currency or currencies of one or more countries other than Canada relative to Canadian currency, a taxpayer has made a gain or sustained a loss in a taxation year, the following rules apply:

(a) the amount, if any, by which

(i) the total of all such gains made by the taxpayer in the year (to the extent of the amounts thereof that would not, if section 3 were read in the manner described in paragraph (1)(a) of this section, be included in computing the taxpayer's income for the year or any other taxation year)

exceeds

(ii) the total of all such losses sustained by the taxpayer in the year (to the extent of the amounts thereof that would not, if section 3 were read in the manner described in paragraph (1)(a) of this section, be deductible in computing the taxpayer's income for the year or any other taxation year), and

(iii) if the taxpayer is an individual, $200,

shall be deemed to be a capital gain of the taxpayer for the year from the disposition of currency of a country other than Canada, the amount of which capital gain is the amount determined under this paragraph; and

(b) the amount, if any, by which

(i) the total determined under subparagraph (a)(ii),

exceeds

(ii) the total determined under subparagraph (a)(i), and

(iii) if the taxpayer is an individual, $200,

shall be deemed to be a capital loss of the taxpayer for the year from the disposition of currency of a country other than Canada, the amount of which capital loss is the amount determined under this paragraph.

**Related Provisions**: 20.3(2)(b) — Foreign exchange gain on weak currency loan (Kiwi loan) deemed to be income; 80.01(11) — Fluctuation in foreign currency ignored for purposes of debt parking and statute-barred debt rules; 95(2)(g), (h) — Gain or loss of foreign affiliate on fluctuation of foreign currency; 142.3(1)(a), (b) — Foreign currency gain or loss by financial institution on specified debt obligation; 142.4(1)"tax basis"(f), (o) — Disposition of specified debt obligation by financial institution; 144(4) — Deemed capital loss from employees profit sharing plan; 248(1)"amortized cost"(c.1), (f.1) — Effect on amortized cost of loan or lending asset.

**Notes**: 39(2)(a)(iii) and (b)(iii) provide a threshold of $200 per year below which all foreign currency gains and losses of an individual are ignored. This amount has not been increased for inflation since its introduction in 1972.

**Interpretation Bulletins**: IT-95R: Foreign exchange gains and losses. See also list at end of s. 39.

**I.T. Technical News**: No. 15 (tax consequences of the adoption of the "euro" currency).

**(3) Gain in respect of purchase of bonds, etc., by issuer** — Where a taxpayer has issued any bond, debenture or similar obligation and has at any subsequent time in a taxation year and after 1971 purchased the obligation in the open market, in the manner in which any such obligation would normally be purchased in the open market by any member of the public,

(a) the amount, if any, by which the amount for which the obligation was issued by the taxpayer exceeds the purchase price paid or agreed to be paid by the taxpayer for the obligation shall be deemed to be a capital gain of the taxpayer for the taxation year from the disposition of a capital property, and

(b) the amount, if any, by which the purchase price paid or agreed to be paid by the taxpayer for the obligation exceeds the greater of the principal amount of the obligation and the amount for which it was issued by the taxpayer shall be deemed to be a capital loss of the taxpayer for the taxation year from the disposition of a capital property,

to the extent that the amount determined under paragraph (a) or (b) would not, if section 3 were read in the manner described in paragraph (1)(a) and this Act were read without reference to subsections 80(12) and (13), be included or be deductible, as the case may be, in computing the taxpayer's income for the year or any other taxation year.

**Related Provisions**: 80(1)"forgiven amount"B(d) — Debt forgiveness rules do not apply where subsec. 39(3) applies; 248(27) — Purchase of partial obligation treated as purchase of obligation.

**Notes**: Reference to 80(12) and (13) added to closing words of 39(3) by 1994 tax amendments bill (Part I), effective for taxation years that end after February 21, 1994.

**I.T. Application Rules**: 26(1.1) (when obligation was outstanding on January 1, 1972).

**Interpretation Bulletins**: See list at end of s. 39.

**(4) Election concerning disposition of Canadian securities** — Except as provided in subsection (5), where a Canadian security has been disposed of by a taxpayer in a taxation year and the taxpayer so elects in prescribed form in the taxpayer's return of income under this Part for that year,

(a) every Canadian security owned by the taxpayer in that year or any subsequent taxation year shall be deemed to have been a capital property owned by the taxpayer in those years; and

(b) every disposition by the taxpayer of any such Canadian security shall be deemed to be a disposition by the taxpayer of a capital property.

**Related Provisions**: 39(4.1) — Look through partnerships for purposes of 39(4); 39(5) — Taxpayers to whom subsec. (4) inapplicable; 39(6) — Definition of "Canadian security"; 54.2 — Certain shares deemed to be capital property.

**Notes**: The election on form T123 allows permanent treatment of gains (losses) Canadian securities as capital gains (losses), rather than fully includable in (deductible from) business income. Once made, it is effective for all time. Note that there are many exclusions from "Canadian security" in 39(6), due to Reg. 6200.

For a similar administrative rule for commodity trading and commodity futures, see Interpretation Bulletin IT-346R, para. 7.

The words "in prescribed form" added effective for taxation years ending after March 30, 1983. An election made before then need not have been in prescribed form.

**Interpretation Bulletins**: IT-346R: Commodity futures and certain commodities; IT-479R: Transactions in securities. See also list at end of s. 39.

**Forms**: T123: Election on disposition of Canadian securities.

**(4.1) Members of partnerships** — For the purpose of determining the income of a taxpayer who is a member of a partnership, subsections (4) and (5) apply as if

(a) every Canadian security owned by the partnership were owned by the taxpayer; and

(b) every Canadian security disposed of by the partnership in a fiscal period of the partnership were disposed of by the taxpayer at the end of that fiscal period.

**Notes**: 39(4.1) added by 1991 technical bill, effective for dispositions after July 13, 1990.

**(5) Exception** — An election under subsection (4) does not apply to a disposition of a Canadian security by a taxpayer (other than a mutual fund corporation or a mutual fund trust) who at the time of the disposition is

(a) a trader or dealer in securities,

(b) a financial institution (as defined in subsection 142.2(1)),

(c)–(e) [Repealed]

(f) a corporation whose principal business is the lending of money or the purchasing of debt obligations or a combination thereof, or

(g) a non-resident,

or any combination thereof.

**Related Provisions**: 39(4.1) — Members of partnerships; 96(3) — Election by members of partnership.

**Notes**: The term "trader or dealer in securities" covers much more than a *licensed* trader or dealer, and depends on how actively the taxpayer trades. See *Vancouver Art Metal Works Ltd.*, [1993] 1 C.T.C. 346 (FCA); *Arcorp Investments Ltd.*, 2000 CarswellNat 2657 (FCTD, Nov. 10, 2000); and Revenue Canada Round Table, Canadian Tax Foundation 1993 annual conference report, p. 58:31, Q. 52. The term is defined in Reg. 230(1), but only for purposes of requiring information returns.

Opening words of 39(5) amended to add the exclusions for a mutual fund corporation or trust by 1997 Budget, retroactive to 1991 and later taxation years. If

(a) an election under 39(4) is made by a mutual fund corporation or mutual fund trust in prescribed form on or before its filing-due date for its taxation year that includes June 18, 1998, and

(b) the election is in respect of a particular taxation year that ends after 1990 and that is not after the corporation's or trust's taxation year that includes June 18, 1998,

then the election is deemed to have been made in the corporation's or trust's return for the particular year (i.e., made on time).

(See also proposed amendment to Reg. 5100(1)"eligible corporation" with respect to mutual fund corporations.)

39(5)(b)–(e) changed to 39(5)(b) by 1994 tax amendments bill (Part III), effective for dispositions of property occurring after February 22, 1994, other than the disposition of property in a taxation year that begins before November 1994 where the property is mark-to-market property (as defined in 142.2(1)) for the year. Formerly read:

(b) a bank,

(c) a corporation licensed or otherwise authorized under the laws of Canada or a province to carry on in Canada the business of offering to the public its services as trustee,

(d) a credit union,

(e) an insurance corporation,

The change was generally non-substantive; it takes advantage of there being a new definition of "financial institution" to refer to.

**Interpretation Bulletins**: IT-479R: Transactions in securities. See also list at end of s. 39.

### (6) Definition of "Canadian security" — For the purposes of this section, "Canadian security" means a security (other than a prescribed security) that is a share of the capital stock of a corporation resident in Canada, a unit of a mutual fund trust or a bond, debenture, bill, note, mortgage or similar obligation issued by a person resident in Canada.

**Notes**: Prescribed securities, under Reg. 6200, include shares whose value is primarily attributable to real property or resource property; non-arm's length debt; shares or debt acquired not at arm's length or in a section 85 rollover (but see 54.2); exploration and development shares; and shares or debt substituted for any of the above. The 39(4) election does not apply to such securities.

The term "bond, debenture, bill, note, mortgage or similar obligation" may not include bankers' acceptances. See *Federated Cooperatives Ltd.*, [2000] 2 C.T.C. 2382 (TCC).

**Regulations**: 6200 (prescribed security).

**Interpretation Bulletins**: IT-346R: Commodity futures and certain commodities; IT-479R: Transactions in securities. See also list at end of s. 39.

### (7) Unused share-purchase tax credit — The amount of any unused share-purchase tax credit of a taxpayer for a particular taxation year, to the extent that it was not deducted from the taxpayer's tax otherwise payable under this Part for the immediately preceding taxation year, shall be deemed to be a capital loss of the taxpayer from a disposition of property for the year immediately following the particular taxation year.

**Related Provisions**: 127.2(6) — Share-purchase tax credit.

**Notes**: Since the share-purchase tax credit is no longer available, this provision is now obsolete. See Notes to 127.2(1).

**Interpretation Bulletins**: IT-479R: Transactions in securities. See also list at end of s. 39.

### (8) Unused scientific research and experimental development tax credit — The amount of any unused scientific research and experimental development tax credit of a taxpayer for a particular taxation year, to the extent that it was not deducted from the taxpayer's tax otherwise payable under this Part for the immediately preceding taxation year, shall be deemed to be a capital loss of the taxpayer from a disposition of property for the year immediately following the particular taxation year, except that where the taxpayer is an individual the capital loss shall be deemed to be 147% of that amount.

**Related Provisions**: 127.3(2) — Scientific research and experimental development tax credit.

**Notes**: Since the SRTC is no longer available, this provision is now obsolete. See Notes to 127.3(1).

**Interpretation Bulletins**: IT-479R: Transactions in securities. See also list at end of s. 39.

### (9) Deduction from business investment loss — In computing the business investment loss of a taxpayer who is an individual (other than a trust) for a taxation year from the disposition of a particular property, there shall be deducted an amount equal to the lesser of

(a) the amount that would be the taxpayer's business investment loss for the year from the disposition of that particular property if paragraph (1)(c) were read without reference to subparagraph (1)(c)(viii), and

(b) the amount, if any, by which the total of

(i) the total of all amounts each of which is twice the amount deducted by the taxpayer under section 110.6 in computing the taxpayer's taxable income for a preceding taxation year ending before 1988,

(i.1) the total of all amounts each of which is $3/2$ of the amount deducted by the taxpayer under section 110.6 in computing the taxpayer's taxable income for a preceding taxation year ending after 1987 and before 1990, and

(i.2) the total of all amounts each of which is $4/3$ of the amount deducted by the taxpayer under section 110.6 in computing the taxpayer's taxable income for a preceding taxation year ending after 1989

---

**Proposed Amendment — 39(9)(b)(i)–(i.2)**

(i) the total of all amounts each of which is twice the amount deducted by the taxpayer under section 110.6 in computing the taxpayer's taxable income for a preceding taxation year that

(A) ended before 1988, or

(B) begins after October 17, 2000,

(i.1) the total of all amounts each of which is

(A) $3/2$ of the amount deducted under section 110.6 in computing the taxpayer's taxable income for a preceding taxation year that

(I) ended after 1987 and before 1990, or

(II) began after February 27, 2000 and ended before October 18, 2000, or

(B) the amount determined by multiplying the reciprocal of the fraction in paragraph 38(a) that applies to the taxpayer for each of the taxpayer's taxation years that includes either February 28, 2000 or October 18, 2000 by the amount deducted under section 110.6 in computing the taxpayer's taxable income for that year, and

(i.2) the total of all amounts each of which is $4/3$ of the amount deducted under section 110.6 in computing the taxpayer's taxable income for a preceding taxation year that ended after 1989 and before February 28, 2000

**Application**: The December 21, 2000 draft legislation, subsec. 14(1), will amend subparas. 39(9)(b)(i) to (i.2) to read as above, applicable to taxation years that end after February 27, 2000.

**Technical Notes**: Pursuant to subsection 39(9), in computing a business investment loss a taxpayer is required to deduct, from the amount of the business investment loss otherwise determined, the lesser of the amount of the business investment loss and the taxpayer's net capital gains for which a deduction was claimed under section 110.6, to the extent that such gains have not been used to reduce other business investment losses.

In calculating the net capital gains for which a deduction was claimed under section 110.6, such deductions are grossed-up by the reciprocal of the applicable inclusion rate.

Consequential on the change of the inclusion rate for capital gains from 3/4 to 1/2 [see 38(a) — ed.], subparagraphs 39(9)(b)(i) to (i.2) are amended to provide for a reduction in a business investment loss of

- twice the amounts deducted by the taxpayer under section 110.6 for taxation years that ended prior to 1988 or begin after October 17, 2000,
- 3/2 of such amounts deducted for 1988, 1989 and taxation years that begin after February 27, 2000 and end before October 18, 2000,
- 4/3 of such amounts deducted for taxation years that ended after 1989 and before February 28, 2000, and
- an amount equal to the product obtained when the reciprocal of the taxpayer's inclusion rate (the fraction in amended paragraph 38(a) that applies to the taxpayer) for each of the taxpayer's taxation years that include February 28, 2000, or October 18, 2000 is multiplied by amounts deducted under section 110.6 for that taxation year.

exceeds

(ii) the total of all amounts each of which is an amount deducted by the taxpayer under paragraph (1)(c) by virtue of subparagraph (1)(c)(viii) in computing the taxpayer's business investment loss

(A) from the disposition of property in taxation years preceding the year, or

(B) from the disposition of property other than the particular property in the year,

except that, where a particular amount was included under subparagraph 14(1)(a)(v) in the taxpayer's income for a taxation year that ended after 1987 and before 1990, the reference in subparagraph (i.1) to "3/2" shall, in respect of that portion of any amount deducted under section 110.6 in respect of the particular amount, be read as "4/3".

**Related Provisions**: 39(10) — Deduction from business investment loss of trust.

**Notes**: 39(9) prevents "double-dipping" by claiming the capital gains exemption to absorb capital gains while also claiming an allowable business investment loss (i.e., an allowable capital loss on shares or debt of certain Canadian-controlled private corporations) against other income. The idea is that capital gains and losses are supposed to be netted against each other first.

A parallel rule prevents the capital gains exemption from being claimed to the extent ABILs have been claimed in the past. See 110.6(1)"annual gains limit"B(b) and 110.6(1)"cumulative gains limit"(b).

The wording of 39(9)(b) reflects the fact that capital gains were 1/2 taxed from 1972 to 1988, 2/3 taxed in 1988 and 1989, and 3/4 taxed since 1990 (until February 27, 2000). Closing words of 39(9)(b) (after subpara. (ii)) added by 1993 technical bill, effective for 1988 and later taxation years, to be consistent with this principle.

**Interpretation Bulletins**: IT-484R2: Business investment losses. See also list at end of s. 39.

**(10) Idem, of a trust** — In computing the business investment loss of a trust for a taxation year from the disposition of a particular property, there shall be deducted an amount equal to the lesser of

(a) the amount that would be the trust's business investment loss for the year from the disposition of that particular property if paragraph (1)(c) were read without reference to subparagraph (1)(c)(viii), and

(b) the amount, if any, by which the total of

(i) the total of all amounts each of which is twice the amount designated by the trust under subsection 104(21.2) in respect of a beneficiary in its return of income for a preceding taxation year ending before 1988,

(i.1) the total of all amounts each of which is 3/2 of the amount designated by the trust under subsection 104(21.2) in respect of a beneficiary in its return of income for a preceding taxation year ending after 1987 and before 1990, and

(i.2) the total of all amounts each of which is 4/3 of the amount designated by the trust under subsection 104(21.2) in respect of a beneficiary in its return of income for a preceding taxation year ending after 1989

**S. 39(10)(b)(i)**      Income Tax Act, Part I, Division B

### Proposed Amendment — 39(10)(b)(i)–(i.2)

(i) the total of all amounts each of which is twice the amount designated by the trust under subsection 104(21.2) in respect of a beneficiary in its return of income for a preceding taxation year that

    (A) ended before 1988, or

    (B) begins after October 17, 2000,

(i.1) the total of all amounts each of which is

    (A) 3/2 of the amount designated by the trust under subsection 104(21.2) in respect of a beneficiary in its return of income for a preceding taxation year that

        (I) ended after 1987 and before 1990, or

        (II) began after February 27, 2000 and ended before October 18, 2000, or

    (B) the amount determined by multiplying the reciprocal of the fraction in paragraph 38(a) that applies to the trust for each of the trust's taxation years that includes either February 28, 2000 or October 18, 2000 by the amount designated by the trust under subsection 104(21.2) in respect of a beneficiary in its return of income for that year, and

(i.2) the total of all amounts each of which is 4/3 of the amount designated by the trust under subsection 104(21.2) in respect of a beneficiary in its return of income for a preceding taxation year that ended after 1989 and before February 28, 2000

**Application**: The December 21, 2000 draft legislation, subsec. 14(2), will amend subparas. 39(10)(b)(i) to (i.2) to read as above, applicable to taxation years that end after February 27, 2000.

**Technical Notes**: Pursuant to subsection 39(10), in computing a business investment loss of a trust, the trust is required to deduct from the amount of the business investment loss otherwise determined, the lesser of

- the amount of the business investment loss, and
- the amount by which the trust's capital gains exceeds capital losses (net gains) — to the extent that the net taxable capital gains derived from those net gains were the subject of a designation under subsection 104(21.2) in respect of a beneficiary and those net gains have not been used to reduce other business investment losses.

In calculating the net gains required to reduce the business investment loss, amounts designated in respect of beneficiaries under subsection 104(21.2) are grossed-up by the reciprocal of the applicable inclusion rate (the fraction that applies to the trust in amended paragraph 38(a)) of the trust.

Consequential on the change of the inclusion rate for capital gains from 3/4 to 1/2 [see 38(a) — ed.], subparagraphs 39(10)(b)(i) to (i.2) are amended to provide for a reduction in a business investment loss of a trust of

- twice the amounts designated by the trust under subsection 104(21.2) for taxation years that ended prior to 1988 and begin after October 17, 2000,
- 3/2 of such amounts designated for 1988, 1989 and taxation years that begin after February 27, 2000 and end before October 18, 2000,
- 4/3 of such amounts designated for taxation years that ended after 1989 and before February 28, 2000, and
- an amount equal to the product obtained when the reciprocal of the trust inclusion rate (for each of the trust's taxation years that include February 28, 2000 or October 18, 2000) is multiplied by the amounts designated by the trust under subsection 104(21.2) in respect of a beneficiary for that taxation year.

exceeds

    (ii) the total of all amounts each of which is an amount deducted by the trust under paragraph (1)(c) by virtue of subparagraph (1)(c)(viii) in computing its business investment loss

        (A) from the disposition of property in taxation years preceding the year, or

        (B) from the disposition of property other than the particular property in the year,

except that, where a particular amount was included under subparagraph 14(1)(a)(v) in the trust's income for a taxation year that ended after 1987 and before 1990, the reference in subparagraph (i.1) to "3/2" shall, in respect of that portion of any amount deducted under section 110.6 in respect of the particular amount, be read as "4/3".

**Notes**: Closing words of 39(10)(b) (after subpara. (ii)) added by 1993 technical bill, effective for 1988 and later taxation years. See Notes to 39(9).

**Interpretation Bulletins**: IT-484R2: Business investment losses. See also list at end of s. 39.

**(11) Recovery of bad debt** — Where an amount is received in a taxation year on account of a debt (in this subsection referred to as the "recovered amount") in respect of which a deduction for bad debts had been made under subsection 20(4.2) in computing the taxpayer's income for a preceding taxation year, the amount, if any, by which 3/4 of the recovered amount exceeds the amount determined under paragraph 12(1)(i.1) in respect of the recovered amount shall be deemed to be a taxable capital gain of the taxpayer from a disposition of capital property by the taxpayer in the year.

### Proposed Amendment — 39(11)

**(11) Recovery of bad debt** — Where an amount is received in a taxation year on account of a debt (in this subsection referred to as the "recovered amount") in respect of which a deduction for bad debts had been made under subsection 20(4.2) in computing a taxpayer's income for a preceding taxation year, the amount, if any, by which 1/2 of the recovered amount exceeds the amount determined under paragraph 12(1)(i.1) in respect of the recovered amount is deemed to be a taxable capital gain of the taxpayer from a disposition of capital property in the year.

**Application**: The December 21, 2000 draft legislation, subsec. 14(3), will amend subsec. 39(11) to read as above, applicable to taxation years that end after February 27, 2000 except that, for taxation years that ended after February 27, 2000 and before October 18, 2000, the reference to the fraction "1/2" shall be read as a reference to the fraction "2/3".

**Technical Notes**: Subsection 39(11) deems a portion of a recovered bad debt in respect of eligible capital property to be a taxable capital gain. The portion that is deemed to be a taxable capital gain is the amount that relates to the portion of the bad debt that was previously deemed by subsection 20(4.2) (now by subsection 20(4.3)) to be an allowable capital loss. For further detail, see the commentary to subsections 20(4.2) and (4.3).

Subsection 39(11) is amended consequential on the change to the inclusion rate for capital gains [see 38(a) — ed.], by replacing the fraction "3/4" with the fraction "1/2".

This amendment applies in respect of taxation years that end after February 27, 2000 except that, for taxation years that end after February 27, 2000 and before October 18, 2000, the fraction to be used in calculating the deemed taxable capital gain is 2/3 rather than 1/2.

**Notes**: 39(11) amended by 1994 Budget, effective 1995, consequential on the elimination of the capital gains exemption in 110.6. For 1994, add the following to the end of the 1995 version:

and, for the purposes of section 110.6, that property shall be deemed to have been disposed of by the taxpayer on the day on which the taxpayer received the recovered amount.

From June 18, 1987 through the end of 1993, read as for 1994 but read the closing words as "... deemed to have been disposed of by the taxpayer in the year." The change for 1994 ensures that the gain can be exempt for 1994 (see 110.6(3)) if the recovered amount was received before February 23, 1994.

**(12) Guarantees** — For the purpose of paragraph (1)(c), where

(a) an amount was paid by a taxpayer in respect of a debt of a corporation under an arrangement under which the taxpayer guaranteed the debt,

(b) the amount was paid to a person with whom the taxpayer was dealing at arm's length, and

(c) the corporation was a small business corporation

(i) at the time the debt was incurred, and

(ii) at any time in the 12 months before the time an amount first became payable by the taxpayer under the arrangement in respect of a debt of the corporation,

that part of the amount that is owing to the taxpayer by the corporation shall be deemed to be a debt owing to the taxpayer by a small business corporation.

**Related Provisions**: 80(2)(l) — Application of debt forgiveness rules on payment by guarantor.

**Notes**: 39(12) added by 1991 technical bill, effective for amounts paid after 1985.

**Interpretation Bulletins**: IT-484R2: Business investment losses. See also list at end of s. 39.

**(13) Repayment of assistance** — The total of all amounts paid by a taxpayer in a taxation year each of which is

(a) such part of any assistance described in subparagraph 53(2)(k)(i) in respect of, or for the acquisition of, a capital property (other than depreciable property) by the taxpayer that was repaid by the taxpayer in the year where the repayment is made after the disposition of the property by the taxpayer and under an obligation to repay all or any part of that assistance, or

(b) an amount repaid by the taxpayer in the year in respect of a capital property (other than depreciable property) acquired by the taxpayer that is repaid after the disposition thereof by the taxpayer and that would have been an amount described in subparagraph 53(2)(s)(ii) had the repayment been made before the disposition of the property,

shall be deemed to be a capital loss of the taxpayer for the year from the disposition of property by the taxpayer in the year and, for the purpose of section 110.6, that property shall be deemed to have been disposed of by the taxpayer in the year.

**Related Provisions**: 79(4)(a) — Subsequent payment by debtor following surrender of property deemed to be repayment of assistance.

**Notes**: 39(13) added by 1992 technical bill, effective 1991. Assistance repaid while capital property is owned reduces the adjusted cost base of the property (and see 40(3)). If the assistance is repaid after the property has been disposed of, 39(13) allows a capital loss.

**Definitions [s. 39]**: "adjusted cost base" — 54, 248(1); "amount" — 248(1); "arm's length" — 251(1); "bank" — 248(1), Interpretation Act 35(1); "Canada" — 255; "Canadian-controlled private corporation" — 248(1); "Canadian resource property" — 66(15), 248(1); "Canadian security" — 39(6); "capital gain" — 39(1)(a), 248(1); "capital loss" — 39(1)(b), 248(1); "capital property" — 54, 248(1); "common-law partner" — 248(1); "corporation" — 248(1), Interpretation Act 35(1); "credit union" — 137(6), 248(1); "depreciable property" — 13(21), 248(1); "disposition" — 54 [to be repealed], 248(1); "eligible capital property" — 54, 248(1); "fiscal period" — 249(2)(b), 249.1; "foreign resource property" — 66(15), 248(1); "individual", "insurance corporation" — 248(1); "life insurance policy" — 138(12), 248(1); "Minister" — 248(1); "mutual fund corporation" — 131(8), 248(1); "mutual fund trust" — 132(6)–(7), 132.2(1)(q), 248(1); "prescribed" — 248(1); "principal amount" — 248(1), 26(1.1); "property", "qualifying environmental trust" — 248(1); "received" — 248(7); "resident in Canada" — 250; "share", "small business corporation" — 248(1); "taxable capital gain" — 38(a), 248(1); "taxable income" — 2(2), 248(1); "taxation year" — 249; "taxpayer" — 248(1); "timber resource property" — 13(21), 248(1); "trust" — 104(1), 248(1), (3); "unused scientific research and experimental development tax credit" — 127.3(2), 248(1); "unused share-purchase tax credit" — 127.2(6), 248(1).

**Interpretation Bulletins [s. 39]**: IT-297R2: Gifts in kind to charity and others; IT-316: Awards for employees' suggestions and inventions; IT-395R: Foreign tax credit — capital gains and capital losses on foreign property; IT-442R: Bad debts and reserves for doubtful debts; Foreign tax credit — foreign-source capital gains and losses; IT-479R: Transactions in securities.

**39.1 (1) Definitions** — In this section,

**"exempt capital gains balance"** of an individual for a taxation year that ends before 2005 in respect of a flow-through entity means the amount determined by the formula

$$A - B - C - F$$

where

A is

(a) if the entity is a trust referred to in any of paragraphs (f) to (j) of the definition "flow-through entity" in this subsection, the amount determined under paragraph 110.6(19)(c) in respect of the individual's interest or interests therein, and

(b) in any other case, the lesser of

(i) 4/3 of the total of the taxable capital gains that resulted from elections made under subsection 110.6(19) in respect of the individual's interests in or shares of the capital stock of the entity, and

(ii) the amount that would be determined under subparagraph (i) if

(A) the amount designated in the election in respect of each interest or share were equal to the amount determined by the formula

$$D - E$$

where

D is the fair market value of the interest or share at the end of February 22, 1994, and

E is the amount, if any, by which the amount designated in the election that was made in respect of the interest or share exceeds 11/10 of its fair market value at the end of February 22, 1994, and

(B) this Act were read without reference to subsection 110.6(20),

B is the total of all amounts each of which is the amount by which the individual's capital gain for a preceding taxation year, determined without reference to subsection (2), from the disposition of an interest in or a share of the capital stock of the entity was reduced under that subsection, and

C is

(a) if the entity is a trust described in any of paragraphs (d) and (h) to (j) of the definition "flow-through entity" in this subsection, 4/3 of the total of all amounts each of which is the amount by which the individual's taxable capital gain otherwise determined for a preceding taxation year that resulted from a designation made under subsection 104(21) by the trust was reduced under subsection (3),

(b) if the entity is a partnership, 4/3 of the total of all amounts each of which is

(i) the amount by which the individual's share otherwise determined of the partnership's taxable capital gains for its fiscal period that ended in a preceding taxation year was reduced under subsection (4), or

(ii) the amount by which the individual's share otherwise determined of the partnership's income from a business for its fiscal period that ended in a preceding taxation year was reduced under subsection (5), and

> **Proposed Amendment —
> 39.1(1)"exempt capital gains balance"C(a), (b)**
>
> (a) if the entity is a trust described in any of paragraphs (d) and (h) to (j) of the definition "flow-through entity" in this subsection, the total of
>
> (i) 3/2 of the total of all amounts each of which is the amount by which the individual's taxable capital gain (determined without reference to this section), for a preceding taxation year that began after February 27, 2000 and ended before October 18, 2000 that resulted from a designation made under subsection 104(21) by the trust, was reduced under subsection (3),
>
> (ii) 4/3 of the total of all amounts each of which is the amount by which the individual's taxable capital gain (determined without reference to this section), for a preceding taxation year that ended before February 28, 2000 that resulted from a designation made under subsection 104(21) by the trust, was reduced under subsection (3),
>
> (iii) the amount claimed by the individual under subparagraph 104(21.4)(a)(ii) for a preceding taxation year, and
>
> (iv) twice the total of all amounts each of which is the amount by which the individual's taxable capital gain (determined without reference to this section) for a preceding taxation year that began after October 17, 2000 that resulted from a designation made under subsection 104(21) by the trust, was reduced under subsection (3),
>
> (b) if the entity is a partnership, the total of
>
> (i) 3/2 of the total of
>
> (A) the total of all amounts each of which is the amount by which the individual's share of the partnership's taxable capital gains (determined without reference to this section), for its fiscal periods that began after Feb-

ruary 27, 2000 and ended before October 18, 2000, was reduced under subsection (4), and

(B) the total of all amounts each of which is the amount by which the individual's share of the partnership's income from a business (determined without reference to this section), for its fiscal periods that began after February 27, 2000 and ended before October 18, 2000, was reduced under subsection (5),

(ii) 4/3 of the total of

(A) the total of all amounts each of which is the amount by which the individual's share of the partnership's taxable capital gains (determined without reference to this section), for its fiscal periods that ended before February 28, 2000 and in a preceding taxation year was reduced under subsection (4), and

(B) the total of all amounts each of which is the amount by which the individual's share of the partnership's income from a business (determined without reference to this section), for its fiscal periods that ended before February 28, 2000 and in a preceding taxation year, was reduced under subsection (5),

(iii) the product obtained when the reciprocal of the fraction in paragraph 38(a) that applies to the partnership for its fiscal period that includes either February 28, 2000 or October 17, 2000 is multiplied by the total of

(A) the total of all amounts each of which is the amount by which the individual's share of the partnership's taxable capital gains (determined without reference to this section), for its fiscal period that includes either February 28, 2000 or October 17, 2000 and ended in a preceding taxation year, was reduced under subsection (4), and

(B) the total of all amounts each of which is the amount by which the individual's share of the partnership's income from a business (determined without reference to this section), for its fiscal period that includes either February 28, 2000 or October 17, 2000 and ended in a preceding taxation year was reduced under subsection (5), and

(iv) twice the total of

(A) the total of all amounts each of which is the amount by which the individual's share of the partnership's taxable capital gains (determined without reference to this section), for its fiscal periods that began after October 17, 2000 and ended in a preceding taxation year, was reduced under subsection (4), and

(B) the total of all amounts each of which is the amount by which the individual's share of the partnership's income from a business (determined without reference to this section), for its fiscal periods that began after October 17, 2000 and ended in a preceding taxation year, was reduced under subsection (5), and

**Application**: The December 21, 2000 draft legislation, subsec. 15(1), will amend paras. (a) and (b) of the description of C in the definition "exempt capital gains balance" in subsec. 39.1(1) to read as above, applicable to taxation years that end after February 27, 2000.

**Technical Notes**: The exempt capital gains balance of an individual for a taxation year in respect of a flow-through entity represents the unclaimed balance of the capital gains that were included in computing the individual's income as a result of an election made under subsection 110.6(19) to crystallize accrued capital gains in respect of the individual's interest in or shares of the capital stock of the entity.

Where an election is made under subsection 110.6(19), the amount of the gain realized as a result of the election does not affect the adjusted cost base of the property but is instead credited to the exempt capital gains balance account of the taxpayer in respect of the taxpayer's interest in or share of the flow-through entity.

The description of C of the formula in the definition "exempt capital gains balance" in subsection 39.1(1) represents the total of amounts deducted in previous taxation years in respect of capital gains flowed out to the taxpayer from the flow-through entity which had been sheltered under any of subsections 39.1(3) through (5).

The amendments to the description of C in the definition are strictly consequential on the change in the capital gains inclusion rate from 3/4 to 1/2 [see 38(a) — ed.].

Amended paragraph (a) of the description of C in the definition "exempt capital gains balance" requires a reduction of a taxpayer's exempt capital gains balance in respect of a trust by

- 3/2 of the amount by which taxable capital gains from a designation under subsection 104(21) in respect of the taxpayer were reduced under subsection 39.1(3) for taxation years that began after February 27, 2000 and ended before October 18, 2000,

- 4/3 of the amounts by which taxable capital gains from a designation under subsection 104(21) in respect of the taxpayer were reduced under subsection 39.1(3) for taxation years that ended before February 27, 2000,

S. 39.1(1) exe  Income Tax Act, Part I, Division B

- the amount claimed by the individual for a preceding taxation year under amended subparagraph 104(21.4)(a)(ii), and
- twice the total of all amounts each of which is the amount by which the individual's taxable capital gain (determined without reference to section 39), for a preceding taxation year that began after October 17, 2000 that resulted from a designation made under subsection 104(21) by the trust was reduced by reason of subsection 39.1(3) in the taxation year.

Amended paragraph (b) of the description of C in the definition "exempt capital gains balance" requires a reduction in a taxpayer's exempt capital gains balance in respect of a partnership by

- 3/2 of the amount by which the taxpayer's share of taxable capital gains and income of the partnership were reduced under subsections 39.1(4) and (5) for taxation years that began after February 27, 2000 and ended before October 18, 2000,
- 4/3 of the amount by which the taxpayer's share of taxable capital gains and income of the partnership were reduced under subsections 39.1(4) and (5) for taxation years that ended before February 28, 2000, and
- the product obtained when the reciprocal of the fraction in amended paragraph 38(a) that applies to the partnership for the fiscal period of the partnership that includes either February 28, 2000 or October 17, 2000 is multiplied by the total of all amounts by which the taxpayer's share of taxable capital gains and income from the partnership were reduced under subsections 39.1(4) and (5) in the taxation year.

(c) in any other case, the total of all amounts each of which is the amount by which the total of the individual's capital gains otherwise determined under subsection 130.1(4) or 131(1), subsections 138.1(3) and (4) or subsection 144(4), as the case may be, for a preceding taxation year in respect of the entity was reduced under subsection (6), and

F is

(a) if the entity is a trust described in any of paragraphs (g) to (j) of the definition "flow-through entity" in this subsection, the total of all amounts each of which is an amount included before the year in the cost to the individual of a property under subsection 107(2.2) or paragraph 144(7.1)(c) because of the individual's exempt capital gains balance in respect of the entity, and

(b) in any other case, nil;

**Related Provisions**: 39.1(7) — Balance deemed nil after ceasing to be shareholder or beneficiary; 53(1)(p) — Addition to ACB after balance expires at end of 2004; 53(1)(r) — Increase in ACB immediately before disposing of all interests or shares of a flow-through entity; 54"adjusted cost base"(c) — ACB adjustment to flow-through entity preserved through disposition and reacquisition; 87(2)(bb.1) — Amalgamation — flow-through entity considered to be same corporation; 107(2.2) — Cost bump on distribution of property from trust that is a flow-through entity; 132.2(1)(j)(ii) — Effect of mutual fund reorganization; 144(1) — Employees profit sharing plan — unused portion of a beneficiary's exempt capital gains balance; 144(7.1) — Employees profit sharing plan — where

property received by beneficiary; 257 — Formulas cannot calculate to less than zero.

**Notes**: See Notes at end of 39.1. The exempt capital gains balance is the unclaimed balance of the capital gains on flow-through entities that were included in income by making an election under 110.6(19) to recognize accrued gains to February 22, 1994 (when the $100,000 capital gain exemption was eliminated. Under 39.1(2)–(6), the balance can be used against later capital gains until 2004, after which it is added to ACB under 53(1)(p). See also Notes to 39.1(7) for cases where the taxpayer disposes of all of the units of the flow-through entity.

Formula element F added by 1995-97 technical bill, retroactive to 1994. Where the flow-through entity is a trust listed in 39.1(1)"flow-through entity"(g) to (j) and it distributed property in a previous year to the individual in satisfaction of all or a portion of the individual's interests in the trust, F will reduce the exempt capital gains balance by the total of all amounts included in the individual's cost of the property because of elections under 107(2.2) or 144(7.1)(c) (see those provisions).

**"flow-through entity" means**

(a) an investment corporation,

(b) a mortgage investment corporation,

(c) a mutual fund corporation,

(d) a mutual fund trust,

(e) a partnership,

(f) a related segregated fund trust for the purpose of section 138.1,

(g) a trust governed by an employees profit sharing plan,

(h) a trust maintained primarily for the benefit of employees of a corporation or 2 or more corporations that do not deal at arm's length with each other, where one of the main purposes of the trust is to hold interests in shares of the capital stock of the corporation or corporations, as the case may be, or any corporation not dealing at arm's length therewith,

(i) a trust established exclusively for the benefit of one or more persons each of whom was, at the time the trust was created, either a person from whom the trust received property or a creditor of that person, where one of the main purposes of the trust is to secure the payments required to be made by or on behalf of that person to such creditor, and

(j) a trust all or substantially all of the properties of which consist of shares of the capital stock of a corporation, where the trust was established pursuant to an agreement between 2 or more shareholders of the corporation and one of the main purposes of the trust is to provide for the exercise of voting rights in respect of those shares pursuant to that agreement.

**Related Provisions**: 54"adjusted cost base"(c) — ACB adjustment preserved through disposition and reacquisition; 87(2)(bb.1) — Amalgamation — flow-through entity considered to be same corporation; 107(2.2) — Cost bump on distribution of property from trust that is a flow-through entity. See also Definitions at end of 39.1.

**Notes**: See Notes at end of 39.1. Essentially, flow-through entities are entities on which a taxpayer can have both a capital gain on the sale of the interest in the entity, and capital gains flowed out by the entity as a conduit from its own dispositions.

**(2) Reduction of capital gain** — Where at any time after February 22, 1994 an individual disposes of an interest in or a share of the capital stock of a flow-through entity, the individual's capital gain, if any, otherwise determined for a taxation year from the disposition shall be reduced by such amount as the individual claims, not exceeding the amount determined by the formula

$$A - B - C$$

where

A is the exempt capital gains balance of the individual for the year in respect of the entity,

B is

(a) if the entity made a designation under subsection 104(21) in respect of the individual for the year, $4/3$ of the amount, if any, claimed under subsection (3) by the individual for the year in respect of the entity,

(b) if the entity is a partnership, $4/3$ of the total of

(i) the amount, if any, claimed under subsection (4) by the individual for the year in respect of the entity, and

(ii) the amount, if any, claimed under subsection (5) by the individual for the year in respect of the entity, and

### Proposed Amendment — 39.1(2)B(a), (b)

**Application**: The December 21, 2000 draft legislation, subsec. 15(2), will amend paras. (a) and (b) of the description of B in subsec. 39.1(2) by replacing the reference to the expression "4/3 of" with a reference to the word "twice", applicable to taxation years that end after February 27, 2000 except that, where the taxation year of an entity that ends in the taxpayer's taxation year includes either February 28, 2000 or October 17, 2000, the reference to the word "twice" shall be read as a reference to the expression "the fraction that is the reciprocal of the fraction in para. 38(a), as amended [by the December 21, 2000 draft legislation], that applies to the entity for its taxation year that ends in the taxpayer's taxation year, multiplied by".

**Technical Notes**: Subsection 39.1(2) allows an individual with an exempt capital gains balance in respect of a flow through entity to claim a reduction in the capital gain otherwise determined for a taxation year from a subsequent disposition of an interest in or share of the capital stock of the flow-through entity. The reduction is limited to the individual's exempt capital gains balance for the year in respect of the entity.

Paragraphs (a) and (b) of the description of B in subsection 39.1(2) are amended to replace the reference to the expression "4/3 of" with a reference to the word "twice". The amendment is consequential on the reduction in the capital gains inclusion rate from 3/4 to 1/2 [see 38(a) — ed.].

The amendment applies to taxation years that end after February 27, 2000 except that, where the taxation year of an entity that ends in the taxation year of the taxpayer includes either February 28, 2000 or October 17, 2000, the references to the word "twice" in paragraphs (a) and (b) of

the description of B in subsection 39.1(2) are to be read as references to the expression "the fraction that is the reciprocal of the fraction in paragraph 38(a) that applies to the entity for its taxation year that ends in the taxpayer's taxation year, multiplied by". These modifications are required in order to reflect the capital gains/losses rate for the year.

(c) in any other case, the amount, if any, claimed under subsection (6) by the individual for the year in respect of the entity, and

C is the total of all reductions under this subsection in the individual's capital gains otherwise determined for the year from the disposition of other interests in or shares of the capital stock of the entity.

**Related Provisions**: 39.1(6) — Reduction of capital gains on ongoing basis; 110.6(19)–(30) — Election to trigger capital gains exemption; 132.2(1)(j)(ii) — Effect of mutual fund reorganization; 257 — Formula cannot calculate to less than zero.

**Notes**: See Notes at end of 39.1. 39.1(2) allows the elected capital gains exemption under 110.6(19) to be used when the taxpayer's interest in a flow-through entity is sold. For gains flowed out to a taxpayer while the taxpayer still owns the interest, see 39.1(3)–(6).

**(3) Reduction of taxable capital gain** — The taxable capital gain otherwise determined under subsection 104(21) of an individual for a taxation year as a result of a designation made under that subsection by a flow-through entity shall be reduced by such amount as the individual claims, not exceeding $3/4$ of the individual's exempt capital gains balance for the year in respect of the entity.

### Proposed Amendment — 39.1(3)

**Application**: The December 21, 2000 draft legislation, subsec. 15(3), will amend subsec. 39.1(3) by replacing the reference to the fraction "3/4" with a reference to the fraction "1/2", applicable to taxation years that end after February 27, 2000 except that, where the taxation year of an entity that ends in the taxpayer's taxation year includes either February 28, 2000 or October 17, 2000, the reference to the fraction "1/2" shall be read as a reference to the fraction in para. 38(a), as amended [by the December 21, 2000 draft legislation], that applies to the entity for its taxation year that ends in the taxpayer's taxation year.

**Technical Notes**: Subsection 104(21) provides a flow-through mechanism for taxable capital gains of trusts. Where a trust makes a designation under that subsection in respect of a beneficiary, the designated amount is treated as a taxable capital gain of the beneficiary.

Subsection 39.1(3) allows an individual to claim a reduction in the amount of the taxpayer's taxable capital gain otherwise determined for a taxation year as a result of a designation under subsection 104(21) by a flow-through entity. The reduction is limited to 3/4 of the individual's exempt capital gains balance for the year in respect of the entity.

Subsection 39.1(3) is amended to replace the reference to the fraction "3/4" with a reference to the fraction "1/2". The amendment is consequential on the reduction of the inclusion rate for capital gains from 3/4 to 1/2 [see 38(a) — ed.].

The amendment applies to taxation years that end after February 27, 2000 except that, where the taxation year of an entity that ends in the taxation year of the taxpayer includes either February 28, 2000 or October 17, 2000, the

## S. 39.1(3) — Income Tax Act, Part I, Division B

reference in the subsection 39.1(3) to that fraction is to be read as a reference to the fraction in amended paragraph 38(a) that applies to the entity for its taxation year that ends in the taxpayer's taxation year. These modifications are required in order to reflect the capital gains/losses rate for the year.

**Related Provisions**: 104(21.4) — No amount claimable on certain deemed gains of trust.

**Notes**: See Notes at end of 39.1. 39.1(3) allows the elected capital gains exemption under 110.6(19) to be used on capital gains allocated by a trust under 104(21).

**(4) Reduction in share of partnership's taxable capital gains** — An individual's share otherwise determined for a taxation year of a taxable capital gain of a partnership from the disposition of a property (other than property acquired by the partnership after February 22, 1994 in a transfer to which subsection 97(2) applied) for its fiscal period that ends after February 22, 1994 and in the year shall be reduced by such amount as the individual claims, not exceeding the amount determined by the formula

$$A - B$$

where

A is ¾ of the individual's exempt capital gains balance for the year in respect of the partnership, and

B is the total of amounts claimed by the individual under this subsection in respect of other taxable capital gains of the partnership for that fiscal period.

### Proposed Amendment — 39.1(4)

**Application**: The December 21, 2000 draft legislation, subsec. 15(4), will amend the description of A in subsec. 39.1(4) by replacing the reference to the fraction "3/4" with a reference to the fraction "1/2", applicable to taxation years that end after February 27, 2000 except that, where the taxation year of an entity that ends in the taxpayer's taxation year includes either February 28, 2000 or October 17, 2000, the reference to the fraction "1/2" shall be read as reference to the fraction in para. 38(a), as amended [by the December 21, 2000 draft legislation], that applies to the entity for its taxation year that ends in the taxpayer's taxation year.

**Technical Notes**: A member of a partnership is taxed on his or her share of the income of the partnership for its fiscal period that ends in the member's taxation year. For this purpose, taxable capital gains at the partnership level are treated as taxable capital gains of its members to the extent of their respective shares thereof. Subsection 39.1(4) allows an individual to claim a reduction in the individual's share of a partnership's taxable capital gains for a fiscal period that ends in the individual's taxation year. The reduction is limited to 3/4 of the individual's exempt capital gains balance for the year in respect of the partnership.

As a consequence of the reduction of the inclusion rate for capital gains from 3/4 to 1/2 [see 38(a) — ed.], the fraction "3/4" in the description of A in subsection 39.1(4) is replaced by the fraction "1/2".

The amendment applies to taxation years that end after February 27, 2000 except that, where the taxation year of an entity that ends in the taxation year of taxpayer includes either February 28, 2000 or October 17, 2000, the reference

to the fraction "1/2" is to be read as reference to the fraction in amended paragraph 38(a) that applies to the entity for its taxation year that ends in the taxpayer's taxation year. These modifications are required in order to reflect the capital gains/losses rate for the year.

**Related Provisions**: 39.1(1)"exempt capital gains balance"C(b)(i), 39.1(2)B(b)(i) — Reduction in balance to reflect application of subsec. (4); 257 — Formula cannot calculate to less than zero.

**Notes**: See Notes at end of 39.1. 39.1(4) allows the elected capital gains exemption under 110.6(19) to be used on capital gains allocated to the taxpayer by a partnership under 96(1).

**(5) Reduction in share of partnership's income from a business** — An individual's share otherwise determined for a taxation year of the income of a partnership from a business for the partnership's fiscal period that ends in the year and the individual's share of the partnership's taxable capital gain, if any, arising under subparagraph 14(1)(a)(v) shall be reduced by such amount as the individual claims, not exceeding the lesser of

(a) the amount, if any, by which ¾ of the individual's exempt capital gains balance for the year in respect of the partnership exceeds the total of

(i) the amount, if any, claimed under subsection (4) by the individual for the year in respect of the partnership, and

(ii) all amounts, if any, claimed under this subsection by the individual for the year in respect of other businesses of the partnership, and

### Proposed Amendment — 39.1(5)(a)

**Application**: The December 21, 2000 draft legislation, subsec. 15(5), will amend para. 39.1(5)(a) by replacing the reference to the fraction "3/4" with a reference to the fraction "1/2", applicable to taxation years that end after February 27, 2000 except that, where the taxation year of an entity that ends in the taxpayer's taxation year includes either February 28, 2000 or October 17, 2000, the reference to the fraction "1/2" shall be read as a reference to the fraction in para. 38(a), as amended [by the December 21, 2000 draft legislation], that applies to the entity for its taxation year that ends in the taxpayer's taxation year.

**Technical Notes**: Subsection 39.1(5) allows an individual who is a member of a partnership to shelter, with his or her exempt capital gains balance in respect of the partnership, that part of his or her share of the partnership's income from a business that is attributable to an amount included under subparagraph 14(1)(a)(v) in computing the partnership's income from the business.

Paragraph 39.1(5)(a) is amended to replace the fraction "3/4" with the fraction "1/2". The amendment is consequential to the reduction of the inclusion rate for capital gains from 3/4 to 1/2 [see 38(a) — ed.].

The amendment applies to taxation years that end after February 27, 2000 except that, where the taxation year of an entity that ends in a taxpayer's taxation year includes either February 28, 2000 or October 17, 2000, the reference to the fraction "1/2" in paragraph 39.1(5)(a) is to be read as reference to the fraction in amended paragraph 38(a) that applies to the entity for its taxation year that ends in the taxpayer's taxation year. These modifications are re-

Subdivision c — Taxable Capital Gains    S. 40(1)(a)(iii)(D)

quired in order to reflect the capital gains/losses rate for the year.

(b) the amount determined by the formula

$$A \times \frac{B}{C}$$

where

A is the amount included under subparagraph 14(1)(a)(v) in computing the income of the partnership from the business for the fiscal period,

B is the amount that would otherwise be the individual's share of the partnership's income from the business for the fiscal period, and

C is the partnership's income from the business for the fiscal period.

**Related Provisions**: 39.1(1)"exempt capital gains balance"C(b)(ii), 39.1(2)B(b)(ii) — Reduction in balance to reflect application of subsec. (4).

**Notes**: See Notes at end of 39.1.

**(6) Reduction of capital gains** — The total capital gains otherwise determined under subsection 130.1(4) or 131(1), subsections 138.1(3) and (4) or subsection 144(4), as the case may be, of an individual for a taxation year as a result of one or more elections, allocations or designations made after February 22, 1994 by a flow-through entity shall be reduced by such amount as the individual claims, not exceeding the individual's exempt capital gains balance for the year in respect of the entity.

**Related Provisions**: 39.1(1)"exempt capital gains balance"C(c), 39.1(2)B(c) — Reduction in balance to reflect application of subsec. (4).

**Notes**: See Notes at end of 39.1. 39.1(6) allows the elected capital gains exemption under 110.6(19) to be used on various capital gains flowed out to the taxpayer by a mortgage investment corporation (130.1(4)), a mutual fund trust (131(1)), a related segregated fund trust (138.1(3), (4)) or an employees profit sharing plan (144(4)). For a mutual fund trust (or any other trust) where the allocation to the beneficiary is done under 104(21), see 39.1(3).

**(7) Nil exempt capital gains balance** — Notwithstanding subsection (1), where at any time an individual ceases to be a member or shareholder of, or a beneficiary under, a flow-through entity, the exempt capital gains balance of the individual in respect of the entity for each taxation year that begins after that time is deemed to be nil.

**Related Provisions**: 53(1)(r) — Increase in ACB on disposition before 2005.

**Notes**: See Notes at end of 39.1 and to 39.1(1)"exempt capital gains balance". Once the last unit of a particular flow-through entity is sold, the exempt capital gains balance goes to nil. A taxpayer with a leftover balance who is selling all the units of (say) a mutual fund may therefore wish to keep 1 unit, so that if the taxpayer later repurchases units of the same fund, the exempt capital gains balance will be available. Alternatively, 53(1)(r) can operate to increase the ACB of the final shares or units disposed of.

**Notes [s. 39.1]**: 39.1 added by 1994 Budget, effective 1994. It provides for the 1994 elected capital gains exemption under 110.6(19) to be used with respect to "flow-through entities", as defined in 39.1(1), until 2004.

**Definitions [s. 39.1]**: "amount" — 248(1); "capital gain" — 39(1)(a), 248(1); "disposition" — 54 [to be repealed], 248(1); "employees profit sharing plan" — 144(1), 248(1); "exempt capital gains balance" — 39.1(1), (7); "fiscal period" — 249(2)(b), 249.1; "flow-through entity" — 39.1(1); "individual" — 248(1); "investment corporation" — 130(3)(a), 248(1); "mortgage investment corporation" — 130.1(6), 248(1); "mutual fund corporation" — 131(8), (8.1), 248(1); "mutual fund trust" — 132(6)–(7), 132.2(1)(q), 248(1); "partnership" — see Notes to 96(1); "person" — 248(1); "related segregated fund trust" — 138.1(1)(a); "share" — (of corporation) 248(1); "share" — (of partnership's gains) 39.1(4); "shareholder" — 248(1); "taxable capital gain" — 38(a), 248(1); "taxation year" — 11(2), 249; "trust" — 104(1), 248(1).

**40. (1) General rules** — Except as otherwise expressly provided in this Part

(a) a taxpayer's gain for a taxation year from the disposition of any property is the amount, if any, by which

(i) if the property was disposed of in the year, the amount, if any, by which the taxpayer's proceeds of disposition exceed the total of the adjusted cost base to the taxpayer of the property immediately before the disposition and any outlays and expenses to the extent that they were made or incurred by the taxpayer for the purpose of making the disposition, or

(ii) if the property was disposed of before the year, the amount, if any, claimed by the taxpayer under subparagraph (iii) in computing the taxpayer's gain for the immediately preceding year from the disposition of the property,

exceeds

(iii) subject to subsection (1.1), such amount as the taxpayer may claim

(A) in the case of an individual (other than a trust) in prescribed form filed with the taxpayer's return of income under this Part for the year, and

(B) in any other case, in the taxpayer's return of income under this Part for the year,

as a deduction, not exceeding the lesser of

(C) a reasonable amount as a reserve in respect of such of the proceeds of disposition of the property that are payable to the taxpayer after the end of the year as can reasonably be regarded as a portion of the amount determined under subparagraph (i) in respect of the property, and

(D) an amount equal to the product obtained when $1/5$ of the amount determined under subparagraph (i) in respect of the property is multiplied by the amount, if any, by which 4 exceeds the number of preceding taxation years of the taxpayer ending after the disposition of the property; and

**S. 40(1)(b)**      Income Tax Act, Part I, Division B

(b) a taxpayer's loss for a taxation year from the disposition of any property is,

(i) if the property was disposed of in the year, the amount, if any, by which the total of the adjusted cost base to the taxpayer of the property immediately before the disposition and any outlays and expenses to the extent that they were made or incurred by the taxpayer for the purpose of making the disposition, exceeds the taxpayer's proceeds of disposition of the property, and

(ii) in any other case, nil.

**Related Provisions**: 7(1.3) — Order of disposition of securities acquired under stock option agreement; 40(1.1) — Reserve where farm property transferred to child; 40(2) — Limitations; 40(3.3), (3.4) — Limitation on loss where property acquired by affiliated person; 44(1) — Exchanges of property; 53(1)(n) — Survey and valuation costs for disposition included in adjusted cost base; 69(11) — Deemed proceeds of disposition; 72(1)(c) — No reserve for year of death; 79.1(3), (6)(c) — Capital gains reserve where property repossessed by creditor; 84.1(2.1) — Non-arm's length sale of shares; 87(2)(e) — Amalgamations — capital property; 87(2)(m) — Amalgamations — proceeds not due until after end of year; 87(2)(ll) — Amalgamations — continuation of predecessor corporations; 88(1)(d)(i)(C) — Winding-up; 100(2) — Gain from disposition of interest in partnership; 104(6) — Reduction in loss where property disposed of owned by a trust; 112(3) — Loss on share that is capital property.

**Notes**: The basic calculation of a capital gain is in 40(1)(a)(i). "Proceeds of disposition" (s. 54) and "adjusted cost base" (ss. 53, 54) both have detailed defined meanings.

A reserve under 40(1)(a)(iii) must both be "reasonable" (clause (iii)(C), and see Interpretation Bulletin IT-236R4 for Revenue Canada's formula) and be within the "1/5 cumulative per year" rule in clause (iii)(D).

40(1)(a)(iii)(C) amended by 1994 tax amendments bill (Part I), effective for taxation years that end after February 21, 1994, to change "not due to the taxpayer until after" to "payable to the taxpayer after", and to change "may reasonably" to "can reasonably". The purpose of the first amendment was to avoid penalizing creditors who exercise "acceleration" clauses pursuant to an agreement under which the creditor sold property and received, as part of the consideration, a note payable by the purchaser of the property. The acceleration clause would typically be exercised only if the purchaser defaulted on its obligations to a creditor.

The draft legislation of July 12, 1994 had proposed a formula for 40(1)(a)(iii)(C) that was the same as the calculation that Revenue Canada has always used on an administrative basis for calculating a "reasonable" reserve (see Interpretation Bulletin IT-236R4, para. 4). That calculation was not included in the 1994 tax amendments bill, however, so the determination of a "reasonable" reserve is still open to interpretation.

40(1)(a)(iii) amended by 1981 Budget, effective with respect to dispositions occurring after November 12, 1981 otherwise than pursuant to the terms in existence on November 12, 1981 of an offer or agreement in writing made or entered into on or before that date or otherwise than by virtue of an event referred to in 54(h)(ii), (iii) or (iv) [now "proceeds of disposition"(b), (c) or (d)] that occurred on or before that date. For dispositions that are not covered by the amended version, delete clause (D) (the requirement to recognize 1/5 of the reserve annually over five years) and the words "in prescribed form" in clause (A).

**I.T. Application Rules**: 26(3), 26(11).

**Interpretation Bulletins**: IT-66R6: Capital dividends; IT-95R: Foreign exchange gains and losses; IT-99R5: Legal and accounting fees; IT-104R2: Deductibility of fines or penalties; IT-220R2: Capital cost allowance — proceeds of disposition of depreciable property; IT-236R4: Reserves — disposition of capital property; IT-259R3: Exchanges of property; IT-268R4: *Inter vivos* transfer of farm property to child; IT-328R3: Losses on shares on which dividends have been received; IT-426: Shares sold subject to an earnout agreement; IT-461: Forfeited deposits; IT-505: Mortgage foreclosures and conditional sales repossessions.

**Information Circulars**: 88-2, paras. 24, 27: General anti-avoidance rule — section 245 of the *Income Tax Act*.

**Forms**: T3 Sched. 2: Reserves on dispositions of capital property; T2017: Summary of reserves on dispositions of capital property; T2069: Election in respect of amounts not deductible as reserves for the year of death; T5008 Supp: Statement of securities transactions; T4091: Return of securities transactions [guide].

### (1.01) [Reserve on] Gift of non-qualifying security

— A taxpayer's gain for a particular taxation year from a disposition of a non-qualifying security of the taxpayer (as defined in subsection 118.1(18)) that is the making of a gift (other than an excepted gift, within the meaning assigned by subsection 118.1(19)) to a qualified donee (as defined in subsection 149.1(1)) is the amount, if any, by which

(a) where the disposition occurred in the particular year, the amount, if any, by which the taxpayer's proceeds of disposition exceed the total of the adjusted cost base to the taxpayer of the security immediately before the disposition and any outlays and expenses to the extent they were made or incurred by the taxpayer for the purpose of making the disposition, and

(b) where the disposition occurred in the 60-month period that ends at the beginning of the particular year, the amount, if any, deducted under paragraph (c) in computing the taxpayer's gain for the preceding taxation year from the disposition of the security

exceeds

(c) the amount that the taxpayer claims in prescribed form filed with the taxpayer's return of income for the particular year, where the taxpayer is not deemed by subsection 118.1(13) to have made a gift of property before the end of the particular year as a consequence of a disposition of the security by the donee or as a consequence of the security ceasing to be a non-qualifying security of the taxpayer before the end of the particular year.

**Related Provisions**: 72(1)(c) — No reserve for year of death; 87(2)(m.1) — Amalgamation — continuing corporation; 110.1(6), 118.1(13) — Donation of non-qualifying security disallowed.

**Notes**: 40(1.01) added by 1997 Budget, effective for 1997 and later taxation years. When a taxpayer makes a charitable gift of a non-qualifying security, 110.1(6) and 118.1(13) provide that the gift is ignored for purposes of the charitable donations deduction or credit. However, if the donee disposes of the security within 5 years the donor will be treated as having made a gift at that later time. 40(1.01) allows the donor to claim a reserve for the gain realized on making the gift so that the income inclusion can be shifted to a later year — normally the year in which the donor ultimately receives a deduction or credit under 110.1 or 118.1. The reserve cannot be claimed once the donor receives tax recognition for the gift or if the donor becomes non-resident or tax-exempt. If the security is not disposed of within the 5-year period by the donee, the donor will not be required to bring the reserve back into income in the year following expiration of the period.

(For the regular reserve where proceeds of disposition are not received in the year, see 40(1)(a)(iii).)

**(1.1) [Farm or small business] Property disposed of to a child** — Where the property referred to in subparagraph (1)(a)(iii) is property that the taxpayer disposed of to the taxpayer's child, who was resident in Canada immediately before the disposition, and was

(a) any land in Canada or depreciable property in Canada of a prescribed class that was, immediately before the disposition, used by the taxpayer, the taxpayer's spouse or common-law partner, or any of the taxpayer's children in the business of farming,

(b) immediately before the disposition, a share of the capital stock of a family farm corporation of the taxpayer or an interest in a family farm partnership of the taxpayer, or

(c) immediately before the disposition, a share of the capital stock of a small business corporation of the taxpayer,

in computing the amount of any claim in respect of that property under subparagraph (1)(a)(iii), that subparagraph shall be read as if the references therein to "$1/5$" and "4" were references to "$1/10$" and "9" respectively.

**Related Provisions**: 40(8), 70(10) — Extended meaning of "child".

**Notes**: 40(1.1)(a) amended by 2000 same-sex partners bill to add reference to "common-law partner", effective for the 2001 and later taxation years, or earlier by election (see Notes to 248(1)"common-law partner").

40(1.1) added by 1981 Budget, effective with respect to dispositions occurring after November 12, 1981 otherwise than pursuant to the terms in existence on November 12, 1981 of an offer or agreement in writing made or entered into on or before that date or otherwise than by virtue of an event referred to in 54(h)(ii), (iii) or (iv) [now "proceeds of disposition"(b), (c) or (d)] that occurred on or before that date.

**Interpretation Bulletins**: IT-236R4: Reserves — disposition of capital property; IT-268R4: *Inter vivos* transfer of farm property to child; IT-328R3: Losses on shares on which dividends have been received.

**(2) Limitations** — Notwithstanding subsection (1),

(a) **[reserve — limitations]** — subparagraph (1)(a)(iii) does not apply to permit a taxpayer to claim any amount under that subparagraph in computing a gain for a taxation year if

(i) the taxpayer, at the end of the year or at any time in the immediately following year, was not resident in Canada or was exempt from tax under any provision of this Part, or

(ii) the purchaser of the property sold is a corporation that, immediately after the sale,

(A) was controlled, directly or indirectly, in any manner whatever, by the taxpayer,

(B) was controlled, directly or indirectly, in any manner whatever, by a person or group of persons by whom the taxpayer was controlled, directly or indirectly, in any manner whatever, or

(C) controlled the taxpayer, directly or indirectly, in any manner whatever, where the taxpayer is a corporation;

**Related Provisions**: 256(5.1), (6.2) — Controlled directly or indirectly — control in fact.

**Interpretation Bulletins**: IT-236R4: Reserves — disposition of capital property.

(b) **[principal residence]** — where the taxpayer is an individual, the taxpayer's gain for a taxation year from the disposition of a property that was the taxpayer's principal residence at any time after the date (in this section referred to as the "acquisition date") that is the later of December 31, 1971 and the day on which the taxpayer last acquired or reacquired it, as the case may be, is the amount determined by the formula

$$A - \frac{A \times B}{C} - D$$

where

A is the amount that would, if this Act were read without reference to this paragraph and subsections 110.6(19) and (21), be the taxpayer's gain therefrom for the year,

B is one plus the number of taxation years that end after the acquisition date for which the property was the taxpayer's principal residence and during which the taxpayer was resident in Canada,

C is the number of taxation years that end after the acquisition date during which the taxpayer owned the property whether jointly with another person or otherwise, and

D is

(i) where the acquisition date is before February 23, 1994 and the taxpayer or a spouse or common-law partner of the taxpayer elected under subsection 110.6(19) in respect of the property or an interest therein that was owned, immediately before the disposition, by the taxpayer, $4/3$ of the lesser of

(A) the total of all amounts each of which is the taxable capital gain of the taxpayer or of a spouse or common-law partner of the taxpayer that would have resulted from an election by the taxpayer or spouse or common-law partner under subsection 110.6(19) in respect of the property or interest if

(I) this Act were read without reference to subsection 110.6(20), and

(II) the amount designated in the election were equal to the amount, if any, by which the fair market value of the property or interest at the end of February 22, 1994 exceeds the amount determined by the formula

$$E - 1.1F$$

where

E is the amount designated in the election that was made in respect of the property or interest, and

F is the fair market value of the property or interest at the end of February 22, 1994, and

(B) the total of all amounts each of which is the taxable capital gain of the taxpayer or of a spouse or common-law partner of the taxpayer that would have resulted from an election that was made under subsection 110.6(19) in respect of the property or interest if the property were the principal residence of neither the taxpayer nor the spouse or common-law partner for each particular taxation year unless the property was designated, in a return of income for the taxation year that includes February 22, 1994 or for a preceding taxation year, to be the principal residence of either of them for the particular taxation year, and

(ii) in any other case, zero;

**Related Provisions**: 40(4) — Disposal of principal residence to spouse or trust for spouse; 40(5) — Where principal residence is property of trust for spouse; 40(6) — Special rule re principal residence; 40(7.1) — Capital gains exemption election ignored for purposes of determining when property last acquired; 45(3) — Election re principal residence; 257 — Formula amounts cannot calculate to less than zero.

**Notes**: 40(2)(b) allows a complete exemption for a "principal residence" (as defined in s. 54; this does not have to be the main place where the taxpayer lives). As long as the taxpayer has only one principal residence at a time, the "one-plus" rule in 40(2)(b)B ensures that the calendar year in which two residences are owned does not disentitle the taxpayer to a full exemption.

40(2)(b)D amended by 2000 same-sex partners bill to add reference to "common-law partner", effective for the 2001 and later taxation years, or earlier by election (see Notes to 248(1) "common-law partner").

40(2)(b) amended (and made much more complicated) by 1994 Budget, effective for dispositions after February 22, 1994, as a result of the elimination of the capital gains exemption and the election under 110.6(19). For earlier dispositions since April 1977, read:

(b) where the taxpayer is an individual, the taxpayer's gain for a taxation year from the disposition of a property that was the taxpayer's principal residence at any time after the date, (in this section referred to as the "acquisition date") that is the later of December 31, 1971 and the day on which the taxpayer last acquired or reacquired it, as the case may be, is the taxpayer's gain therefrom for the year otherwise determined minus that proportion thereof that

(i) one plus the number of taxation years ending after the acquisition date for which the property was the tax-

payer's principal residence and during which the taxpayer was resident in Canada,

is of

(ii) the number of taxation years ending after the acquisition date during which the taxpayer owned the property whether jointly with another person or otherwise;

**I.T. Application Rules**: 26.1(1) (change of use of property before 1972).

**Interpretation Bulletins**: IT-120R5: Principal residence; IT-268R3: *Inter vivos* transfer of farm property to child; IT-366R: Principal residence: transfer to spouse or spouse trust.

**Forms**: T2091: Designation of a property as a principal residence by an individual; T2091(IND)WS: Principal residence worksheet.

(c) **[land used in farming business]** — where the taxpayer is an individual, the taxpayer's gain for a taxation year from the disposition of land used in a farming business carried on by the taxpayer that includes property that was at any time the taxpayer's principal residence is

(i) the taxpayer's gain for the year, otherwise determined, from the disposition of the portion of the land that does not include the property that was the taxpayer's principal residence, plus the taxpayer's gain for the year, if any, determined under paragraph (b) from the disposition of the property that was the taxpayer's principal residence, or

(ii) if the taxpayer so elects in prescribed manner in respect of the land, the taxpayer's gain for the year from the disposition of the land including the property that was the taxpayer's principal residence, determined without regard to paragraph (b) or subparagraph (i) of this paragraph, less the total of

(A) $1,000, and

(B) $1,000 for each taxation year ending after the acquisition date for which the property was the taxpayer's principal residence and during which the taxpayer was resident in Canada;

**Related Provisions**: 40(4) — Disposal of principal residence to spouse or trust for spouse.

**Notes**: 40(2)(c) offers an alternative principal-residence exemption for farmers. Instead of having the gain on the principal residence exempt and the gain on the farmland taxable, the farmer may elect to have a gain of $1,000 per year exempted on the entire property. (This figure has not increased since 1972.)

**Regulations**: 2300 (prescribed manner).

**Interpretation Bulletins**: IT-120R5: Principal residence; IT-268R3: *Inter vivos* transfer of farm property to child; IT-366R: Principal residence: transfer to spouse or spouse trust.

(d) **[disposition of bond]** — where the taxpayer is a corporation, its loss for a taxation year from the disposition of a bond or debenture is its loss therefrom for the year otherwise determined, less the total of such amounts received by it as, on account or in lieu of payment of, or in satisfaction of interest thereon as were, by virtue of paragraph 81(1)(m), not included in computing its income;

Subdivision c — Taxable Capital Gains          S. 40(2)(g)(iii)

(e) **[disposition to controller or controlled corporation]** — [Repealed]

**Related Provisions**: 53(1)(f.1) — Addition to adjusted cost base; 69(5)(a)(ii) — No application where property appropriated by shareholder on winding-up; 98(5) — Where partnership business carried on as sole proprietorship; 256(5.1) — Controlled directly or indirectly — control in fact.

**Notes**: 40(2)(e) repealed by 1995-97 technical bill, effective (subject to the grandfathering rule reproduced after s. 260) for dispositions of property after April 26, 1995. It has been replaced by 40(3.4). Where it applied, since 1989, read:

> (e) where the taxpayer is a corporation, its loss otherwise determined from the disposition of any property disposed of by it to
> 
> > (i) a person by whom it was controlled, directly or indirectly in any manner whatever, or
> > 
> > (ii) a corporation that was controlled, directly or indirectly in any manner whatever, by a person described in subparagraph (i),
> 
> is nil;

**Advance Tax Rulings**: ATR-57: Transfer of property for estate planning purposes.

(e.1) **[disposition of debt of related person]** — a taxpayer's loss, if any, from the disposition at any time to a particular person or partnership of an obligation that was, immediately after that time, payable by another person or partnership to the particular person or partnership is nil where the taxpayer, the particular person or partnership and the other person or partnership are related to each other at that time or would be related to each other at that time if paragraph 80(2)(j) applied for the purpose of this paragraph;

**Related Provisions**: 40(2)(e.2), 40(2)(g)(ii) — Further limitations on loss on disposition of debt; 53(1)(f.1), (f.11) — Addition to adjusted cost base; 54"superficial loss"(e) — Superficial loss rule does not apply; 80.01(8) — Deemed settlement after debt parking.

**Notes**: 40(2)(e.1) added by 1994 tax amendments bill (Part I), effective for dispositions that occur after July 12, 1994, other than pursuant to agreements in writing entered into by that date. Where a loss is denied by 40(2)(e.1), the transferee is generally entitled to increase its ACB under 53(1)(f.1) or (f.11). The purpose of 40(2)(e.1) is to provide balanced treatment for debtors and creditors under the debt parking rule in 80.01(8) and the stop-loss rules in 40(2), 85(4) and 97(3).

**I.T. Application Rules**: 26(5)(c)(ii)(A) (where property owned since June 18, 1971).

(e.2) **[settlement of commercial obligation]** — a taxpayer's loss on the settlement or extinguishment of a particular commercial obligation (in this paragraph having the meaning assigned by subsection 80(1)) issued by a person or partnership and payable to the taxpayer shall, where any part of the consideration given by the person or partnership for the settlement or extinguishment of the particular obligation consists of one or more other commercial obligations issued by the person or partnership to the taxpayer, be deemed to be the amount determined by the formula

$$A \times \frac{(B-C)}{B}$$

where

A is the amount, if any, that would be the taxpayer's loss from the disposition of the particular obligation if this Act were read without reference to this paragraph,

B is the total fair market value of all the consideration given by the person or partnership for the settlement or extinguishment of the particular obligation, and

C is the total fair market value of the other obligations;

**Related Provisions**: 40(2)(e.2), 40(2)(g)(ii) — Further limitations on loss on disposition of debt; 53(1)(f.12) — Addition to adjusted cost base; 80(2)(h) — Application of debt forgiveness rules; 257 — Formula cannot calculate to less than zero.

**Notes**: 40(2)(e.2) added by 1994 tax amendments bill (Part I), effective for dispositions that occur after December 20, 1994, other than pursuant to agreements in writing entered into by that date.

**I.T. Application Rules**: 26(5)(c)(ii)(A) (where property owned since June 18, 1971).

(f) **[right to a prize]** — a taxpayer's gain or loss from the disposition of

> (i) a chance to win a prize or bet, or
> 
> (ii) a right to receive an amount as a prize or as winnings on a bet,

in connection with a lottery scheme or a pool system of betting referred to in section 205 of the *Criminal Code* is nil;

**Notes**: The present wording of para. 40(2)(f) reverts to an earlier version. It appears that in the R.S.C. 1985 consolidation which came into force in 1994, amendments made in 1985 were overlooked. Those amendments deleted "or bet" from subpara. (i), "or as winnings on a bet" from subpara. (ii), and "or a pool system of betting referred to in section 188.1 [now 205] of the *Criminal Code*". The section of the *Criminal Code* referred to has been repealed.

The receipt of a lottery prize is not taxed, not because any provision of the Act says so, but because it is not considered to be income from a "source" for purposes of ss. 3 and 4(1). (See Interpretation Bulletin IT-213R, para. 1, and Notes to s. 3.) A prize is deemed acquired at its fair market value, however; see 52(4).

**Interpretation Bulletins**: IT-213R: Prizes from lottery schemes, pool system betting and giveaway contests; IT-404R: Payments to lottery ticket vendors.

(g) **[various losses deemed nil]** — a taxpayer's loss, if any, from the disposition of a property, to the extent that it is

> (i) a superficial loss,
> 
> (ii) a loss from the disposition of a debt or other right to receive an amount, unless the debt or right, as the case may be, was acquired by the taxpayer for the purpose of gaining or producing income from a business or property (other than exempt income) or as consideration for the disposition of capital property to a person with whom the taxpayer was dealing at arm's length,
> 
> (iii) a loss from the disposition of any personal-use property of the taxpayer (other than listed personal property or a debt referred to in subsection 50(2)), or

281

**S. 40(2)(g)(iv)**      Income Tax Act, Part I, Division B

(iv) a loss from the disposition of property to

(A) a trust governed by a plan or fund referred to in any of subparagraphs (e)(ii) to (iv) of the definition "disposition" in section 54 under which the taxpayer is a beneficiary or immediately after the disposition becomes a beneficiary, or

> **Proposed Amendment — 40(2)(g)(iv)(A)**
>
> (A) a trust governed by a deferred profit sharing plan, an employees profit sharing plan or a registered retirement income fund under which the taxpayer is a beneficiary or immediately after the disposition becomes a beneficiary, or
>
> **Application**: Bill C-43 (First Reading September 20, 2000), subsec. 14(1), will amend cl. 40(2)(g)(iv)(A) to read as above, applicable to 1998 *et seq.*
>
> **Technical Notes**: Paragraph 40(2)(g) of the Act denies the recognition of losses arising from certain dispositions, including dispositions by a taxpayer to a trust governed by a deferred profit sharing plan, employees profit sharing plan or registered retirement income fund, under which the taxpayer is a beneficiary.
>
> Clause 40(2)(g)(iv)(A) is amended to replace a cross-reference to such trusts with a description of them. This amendment is strictly consequential on the replacement of the definition "disposition" in section 54 with a new definition of the same expression in subsection 248(1).

(B) a trust governed by a registered retirement savings plan under which the taxpayer or the taxpayer's spouse or common-law partner is an annuitant or becomes, within 60 days after the end of the taxation year, an annuitant,

is nil;

**Related Provisions**: 3(b)(ii) — Limitation on use of listed personal property losses; 13(21.2) — Superficial loss rule for depreciable property; 18(13)–(16) — Superficial loss in moneylending business or adventure in nature of trade; 40(2)(e.1) — Limitation on loss where commercial obligation disposed of in exchange for another commercial obligation; 40(3.3), (3.4) — Limitation on loss where property acquired by affiliated person; 41 — Listed personal property losses can offset listed personal property gains; 53(1)(f) — Addition to adjusted cost base — superficial loss; 80(1) — "Unrecognized loss"; 112(3)–(4.22) — Reduction in capital loss on shares where dividends previously paid.

**Notes**: For superficial losses, see the definition of that term in s. 54. Personal-use property losses are disallowed except for listed personal property (LPP) losses, which can be offset against LPP gains. See Notes to 41(1).

In *Byram*, [1999] 2 C.T.C. 149 (FCA), the Court allowed a capital loss on interest-free loans that were issued by a shareholder to a corporation to allow it to earn income and thus pay dividends. The test in 40(2)(g)(ii) is not like that in 20(1)(c), which requires, for interest deductibility, that the borrowed money have been used *directly* for purposes of producing income.

40(2)(g)(iv)(B) amended by 2000 same-sex partners bill to add reference to "common-law partner", effective for the 2001 and later taxation years, or earlier by election (see Notes to 248(1)"common-law partner").

**I.T. Application Rules**: 26(6).

**Interpretation Bulletins**: IT-120R5: Principal residence; IT-124R6: Contributions to registered retirement savings plans; IT-159R3: Capital debts established to be bad debts; IT-160R3: Personal use of aircraft; IT-218R: Profit, capital gains and losses from the sale of real estate; IT-239R2: Deductibility of capital losses from guaranteeing loans and loaning funds in non-arm's length circumstances; IT-325R2: Property transfers after separation, divorce and annulment.

**I.T. Technical News**: No. 18 (*Byram* case).

(h) **[shares of controlled corporation]** — where the taxpayer is a corporation, its loss otherwise determined from the disposition at any time in a taxation year of shares of the capital stock of a corporation (in this paragraph referred to as the "controlled corporation") that was controlled, directly or indirectly in any manner whatever, by it at any time in the year, is its loss therefrom otherwise determined less the amount, if any, by which

(i) all amounts added under paragraph 53(1)(f.1) to the cost to a corporation, other than the controlled corporation, of property disposed of to that corporation by the controlled corporation that were added to the cost of the property during the period while the controlled corporation was controlled by the taxpayer and that can reasonably be attributed to losses on the property that accrued during the period while the controlled corporation was controlled by the taxpayer,

exceeds

(ii) all amounts by which losses have been reduced by virtue of this paragraph in respect of dispositions before that time of shares of the capital stock of the controlled corporation; and

**Related Provisions**: 40(3.3), (3.4) — Limitation on loss where property acquired by affiliated person; 87(2)(kk) — Amalgamations — Continuation of predecessor corporations; 112(3)–(4.22) — Reduction in capital loss on shares where dividends previously paid; 256(5.1), (6.2) — Controlled directly or indirectly — control in fact.

**Notes**: 40(2)(h)(i) amended by 1995-97 technical bill, effective (subject to the grandfathering rule reproduced after s. 260) for dispositions of property after April 26, 1995. (The amendment clarifies that a corporation's loss from the disposition of a controlled corporation's shares is subject to adjustment to take account of previous dispositions of property by the controlled corporation to any other corporation, including the shareholder corporation.) Previously read, since 1989:

(i) all amounts added under paragraph 53(1)(f.1) to the cost to another corporation of property disposed of to that corporation by the controlled corporation that were added to the cost of that property during the period that the controlled corporation was controlled by the taxpayer and that may reasonably be considered to be attributable to losses on the property that accrued during the period that the controlled corporation was controlled by the taxpayer,

(i) **[shares of certain corporations]** — where at a particular time a taxpayer has disposed of a share of the capital stock of a corporation that was at any time a prescribed venture capital corporation or a prescribed labour-sponsored venture capital corporation or a share of the capital stock of a taxable Canadian corporation that was held in a prescribed stock savings plan or of a property substituted for such a share, the taxpayer's loss from the disposition thereof shall be deemed to be the amount, if any, by which

(i) the loss otherwise determined

exceeds

(ii) the amount, if any, by which

(A) the amount of prescribed assistance that the taxpayer (or a person with whom the taxpayer was not dealing at arm's length) received or is entitled to receive in respect of the share

exceeds

(B) the total of all amounts determined under subparagraph (i) in respect of any disposition of the share or of the property substituted for the share before the particular time by the taxpayer or by a person with whom the taxpayer was not dealing at arm's length.

**Related Provisions**: 53(2)(k) — Reduction in adjusted cost base — government assistance; 112(3)–(4.22) — Reduction in capital loss on shares where dividends previously paid; 248(5) — Substituted property.

**Notes**: 40(2)(i)(ii) amended by 1993 technical bill, effective for 1991 and later taxation years, to add the words "or is entitled to receive". Thus, prescribed assistance receivable (as well as received) in respect of a share will reduce the capital loss on disposition of the share. A parallel amendment to 53(2)(k)(i)(C) provides that such assistance does not reduce the ACB of the share.

**Regulations**: 6700, 6700.1 (prescribed venture capital corporation); 6701 (prescribed labour-sponsored venture capital corporation); 6702 (prescribed assistance); 6705 (prescribed stock savings plan).

**Interpretation Bulletins**: IT-273R2: Government assistance — general comments.

(j) [Repealed under former Act]

**Notes**: 40(2)(j), repealed by 1985 Budget, dealt with losses on transfers to an indexed security investment plan, a concept no longer used.

**(3) Deemed gain where amounts to be deducted from ACB exceed cost plus amounts to be added to ACB** — Where

(a) the total of all amounts required by subsection 53(2) (except paragraph 53(2)(c)) to be deducted in computing the adjusted cost base to a taxpayer of any property at any time in a taxation year

exceeds

(b) the total of

(i) the cost to the taxpayer of the property determined for the purpose of computing the adjusted cost base to the taxpayer of that property at that time, and

(ii) all amounts required by subsection 53(1) to be added to the cost to the taxpayer of the property in computing the adjusted cost base to the taxpayer of that property at that time,

the following rules apply:

(c) subject to paragraph 93(1)(b), the amount of the excess shall be deemed to be a gain of the taxpayer for the year from a disposition at that time of the property,

(d) for the purposes of section 93, the definition "foreign accrual property income" in subsection 95(1) and section 110.6, the property shall be deemed to have been disposed of by the taxpayer in the year, and

(e) for the purposes of section 93, the amount of the excess shall be deemed to be proceeds of disposition of the property to the taxpayer.

**Related Provisions**: 40(3.1)–(3.2) — Deemed capital gain or loss for passive partners; 53(1)(a) — Deemed gain added to adjusted cost base of property; 93(1) — Election re disposition of share in foreign affiliate; 98(1)(c) — Where partnership ceases to exist; 98.1(1)(c) — Residual interest in partnership.

**Notes**: 40(3) provides that a "negative" ACB under 53(2) triggers an immediate capital gain. The ACB is then reset to zero by 53(1)(a). 40(3) does not apply to a partnership interest (53(2)(c)) for an active partner, which is allowed to remain negative unless the partnership ceases to exist (98(1)(c)) or the partner withdraws from the partnership (98.1(1)(c)). However, for limited partners and other passive partners, see 40(3.1)–(3.2) below.

40(3) amended by 1991 technical bill, effective 1987, to add the references to sections 93 and 95 in paras. (c) and (d) and to add para. (e). The change ensures that an election under 93(1) may be made by a corporation resident in Canada to treat a portion of the gain arising in respect of the shares of a foreign affiliate as a dividend.

**Interpretation Bulletins**: IT-242R: Retired partners; IT-278R2: Death of a partner or of a retired partner.

**(3.1) Deemed gain for certain partners** — Where, at the end of a fiscal period of a partnership, a member of the partnership is a limited partner of the partnership, or is a member of the partnership who was a specified member of the partnership at all times since becoming a member, except where the member's partnership interest was held by the member on February 22, 1994 and is an excluded interest at the end of the fiscal period,

(a) the amount determined under subsection (3.11) is deemed to be a gain from the disposition, at the end of the fiscal period, of the member's interest in the partnership; and

(b) for the purpose of section 110.6, the interest is deemed to have been disposed of by the member at that time.

**Related Provisions**: 40(3.12) — Election for deemed capital loss where ACB is later positive; 40(3.131) — Specified member of partnership — anti-avoidance rule; 40(3.14) — Limited partner; 40(3.15) — Excluded interest; 40(3.18) — Grandfathered partners; 40(3.19) — Subsec. 40(3.1) takes precedence over 40(3); 40(3.2) — Paras. 98(1)(c) and 98.1(1)(c) take precedence; 53(1)(e)(vi) — Addition to adjusted cost base; 53(2)(c)(i.3), (i.4) — Reduction in adjusted cost base.

**Notes**: A negative ACB normally causes an immediate capital gain, but not for partnership interests; see Notes to 40(3). For limited partners and other passive partners (see 248(1) "specified member"), 40(3.1) deems there to be a capital gain, subject to the rules in 40(3.11)–(3.19) and (3.2).

## S. 40(3.1) — Income Tax Act, Part I, Division B

40(3.1) added by 1994 Budget and amended retroactively by 1995-97 technical bill (to clarify an ambiguity), effective February 22, 1994; but it does not apply to a member of a partnership before the end of the partnership's 5th fiscal period ending after 1994 if the following 5 conditions are met:

(a) the member acquires the partnership interest before 1995; and

(b) all or substantially all of the property (other than money) of the partnership is a film production or an interest in one or more partnerships all or substantially all of the property of which is a film production; and

(c) the principal photography of the production (or, in the case of a television series, an episode of the series) begins before 1995;

(d) the funds used to produce the film production are raised before 1995 and the principal photography of the production is completed, and the funds are expended, before 1995 (or, in the case of a film production prescribed for the purpose of 96(2.2)(d)(ii), the principal photography of the production is completed, and the funds are expended, before March 2, 1995); and

(e) one of the following conditions is met:

(i) the producer of the production has, before February 22, 1994, entered into a written agreement for the pre-production, distribution, broadcasting, financing or acquisition of the production or the acquisition of the screenplay for the production (or has entered into a written contract before February 22, 1994 with a screenwriter to write the screenplay for the production), or

(ii) the producer of the production receives before 1995 a commitment for funding or government assistance (or an advance ruling or active status letter in respect of eligibility for such funding or other government assistance) for the production from a federal or provincial government agency the mandate of which is related to the provision of assistance to film productions in Canada, or

(iii) the production is a continuation of a television series an episode of which satisfies the requirements of paragraph (e).

The version in force before the 1995-97 technical bill, now deemed never to have been in force, read:

(3.1) Where, at the end of a fiscal period of a partnership, a member of the partnership is a limited partner of the partnership or is a member of the partnership who was a specified member of the partnership at all times since becoming a member (except where the member's partnership interest was held by the member on February 22, 1994 and is an excluded interest at the end of the fiscal period), the amount determined under subsection (3.11) shall be deemed to be a gain from the disposition, at the end of the fiscal period, of the member's interest in the partnership and, for the purpose of section 110.6, the interest shall be deemed to have been disposed of by the member at that time.

Former 40(3.1), repealed by 1985 Budget, dealt with losses on the transfer of securities to an indexed security investment plan, a concept no longer used.

**I.T. Technical News**: No. 5 (adjusted cost base of partnership interest).

### (3.11) Amount of gain
— For the purpose of subsection (3.1), the amount determined at any time under this subsection in respect of a member's interest in a partnership is the amount determined by the formula

$$A - B$$

where

A is the total of all amounts required by subsection 53(2) to be deducted in computing the adjusted cost base to the member of the interest in the partnership at that time, and

B is the total of

(a) the cost to the member of the interest determined for the purpose of computing the adjusted cost base to the member of the interest at that time, and

(b) all amounts required by subsection 53(1) to be added to the cost to the member of the interest in computing the adjusted cost base to the member of the interest at that time.

**Related Provisions**: 257 — Formula cannot calculate to less than zero.

**Notes**: 40(3.11) added by 1994 Budget, effective February 22, 1994. This was 40(3.2) in the draft legislation of September 27, 1994. In simple terms, any negative adjusted cost base of a limited or passive partner is deemed to be a capital gain.

### (3.12) Deemed loss for certain partners
— Where a corporation, an individual (other than a trust) or a testamentary trust (each of which is referred to in this subsection as the "taxpayer") is a member of a partnership at the end of a fiscal period of the partnership, the taxpayer shall be deemed to have a loss from the disposition at that time of the member's interest in the partnership equal to the amount that the taxpayer elects in the taxpayer's return of income under this Part for the taxation year that includes that time, not exceeding the lesser of

(a) the amount, if any, by which

(i) the total of all amounts each of which was an amount deemed by subsection (3.1) to be a gain of the taxpayer from a disposition of the interest before that time

exceeds

(ii) the total of all amounts each of which was an amount deemed by this subsection to be a loss of the taxpayer from a disposition of the interest before that time, and

(b) the adjusted cost base to the taxpayer of the interest at that time.

**Related Provisions**: 53(2)(c)(i.2) — Reduction in adjusted cost base.

**Notes**: 40(3.12) added by 1994 Budget, effective February 22, 1994. This was 40(3.3) in the draft legislation of September 27, 1994.

### (3.13) Artificial transactions
— For the purpose of applying section 53 at any time to a member of a partnership who would be a member described in subsection (3.1) of the partnership if the fiscal period of the partnership that includes that time ended at that time, where at any time after February 21, 1994

the member of the partnership makes a contribution of capital to the partnership and

(a) the partnership or a person or partnership with whom the partnership does not deal at arm's length

(i) makes a loan to the member or to a person with whom the member does not deal at arm's length, or

(ii) pays an amount as, on account of, in lieu of payment of or in satisfaction of, a distribution of the member's share of the partnership profits or partnership capital, or

(b) the member or a person with whom the member does not deal at arm's length becomes indebted to the partnership or a person or partnership with whom the partnership does not deal at arm's length,

and it is established, by subsequent events or otherwise, that the loan, payment or indebtedness, as the case may be, was made or arose as part of a series of contributions and such loans, payments or other transactions, the contribution of capital shall be deemed not to have been made.

**Related Provisions**: 251 — Arm's length.

**Notes**: 40(3.13) added by 1994 Budget, effective February 22, 1994. It is an anti-avoidance rule designed to prevent artificial increases in the ACB of a partnership interest that would avoid 40(3.1). It is in part a legislative codification of the principle in *Stursberg*, [1993] 2 C.T.C. 76 (FCA), as it applied to a particular set of facts. This provision was 40(3.4) in the draft legislation of September 27, 1994.

**(3.131) Specified member of a partnership** — Where it can reasonably be considered that one of the main reasons that a member of a partnership was not a specified member of the partnership at all times since becoming a member of the partnership is to avoid the application of subsection (3.1) to the member's interest in the partnership, the member is deemed for the purpose of that subsection to have been a specified member of the partnership at all times since becoming a member of the partnership.

**Related Provisions**: 127.52(2.1) — Parallel rule for minimum tax purposes.

**Notes**: 40(3.131) added by 1995-97 technical bill, effective April 27, 1995. This anti-avoidance rule was originally proposed as 248(28) in the draft legislation of April 26, 1995. A parallel rule appears in 127.52(2.1).

**(3.14) Limited partner** — For the purpose of subsection (3.1), a member of a partnership at a particular time is a limited partner of the partnership at that time if, at that time or within 3 years after that time,

(a) by operation of any law governing the partnership arrangement, the liability of the member as a member of the partnership is limited;

**Proposed Amendment — 40(3.14)(a)**

(a) by operation of any law governing the partnership arrangement, the liability of the member as a member of the partnership is limited (except by operation of a provision of a statute of Canada or a province that limits the member's liability only for debts, obligations and liabilities of the partnership, or any member of the partnership, arising from negligent acts or omissions or misconduct that another member of the partnership or an employee, agent or representative of the partnership commits in the course of the partnership business while the partnership is a limited liability partnership);

**Application**: Bill C-43 (First Reading September 20, 2000), subsec. 14(2), will amend para. 40(3.14)(a) to read as above, applicable after 1997.

**Technical Notes**: Section 40 provides special rules for determining a taxpayer's capital gain or capital loss for a taxation year.

Subsection 40(3.14) provides an extended definition of "limited partner" for the purpose of determining whether a member's interest in a partnership is subject to the negative adjusted cost base rule in subsection 40(3.1).

Paragraph 40(3.14)(a) provides that a member of a partnership is a "limited partner" if, by operation of any law governing the partnership arrangement, the liability of the member as a member of the partnership is limited (e.g., a limited partner of a limited partnership). Concern has been expressed that paragraph 40(3.14)(a) applies to a partner of a "limited liability partnership" in addition to a limited partner of a limited partnership. A limited liability partnership is a new type of partnership the form of which has only recently been permitted under some provincial statutes [e.g., lawyers and chartered accountants in Ontario — ed.].

Unlike a limited partner of a limited partnership, a member of limited liability partnership can be liable for the general debts and obligations of a limited liability partnership. However, a member of a limited liability partnership is not liable for the debts, obligations and liabilities of the partnership, or any member of the partnership, arising from negligent acts or omissions that another member of the partnership or an employee, agent or representative of the partnership commits in the course of the partnership business while the partnership is a limited liability partnership.

Paragraph 40(3.14)(a) is amended to exclude from its application cases where a member's liability is limited by operation of a statutory provision of Canada or a province that limits the member's liability only for the debts, obligations and liabilities of a limited liability partnership, or any member of the partnership, arising from negligent acts or omissions that another member of the partnership or an employee, agent or representative of the partnership commits in the course of the partnership business and while the partnership is a limited liability partnership.

**Letter from Department of Finance re Limited Liability Partnerships**: [See under 96(2.4)(a) — ed.]

(b) the member or a person not dealing at arm's length with the member is entitled, either immediately or in the future and either absolutely or contingently, to receive an amount or to obtain a benefit that would be described in paragraph 96(2.2)(d) if that paragraph were read without reference to subparagraphs (ii) and (vi);

(c) one of the reasons for the existence of the member who owns the interest

(i) can reasonably be considered to be to limit the liability of any person with respect to that interest, and

(ii) cannot reasonably be considered to be to permit any person who has an interest in the member to carry on the person's business (other than an investment business) in the most effective manner; or

(d) there is an agreement or other arrangement for the disposition of an interest in the partnership and one of the main reasons for the agreement or arrangement can reasonably be considered to be to attempt to avoid the application of this subsection to the member.

**Related Provisions**: 96(2.4) — Definition of limited partner for purposes of at-risk amount.

**Notes**: 40(3.14) added by 1994 Budget, effective February 22, 1994. This was 40(3.5) in the draft legislation of September 27, 1994.

40(3.14)(b) amended by 1995-97 technical bill, effective for fiscal periods that end after November 1994. Previously read:

> (b) the member or a person with whom the member does not deal at arm's length is entitled to receive an amount or obtain a benefit that would be described in paragraph 96(2.2)(d) if it were read without reference to subparagraphs 96(2.2)(d)(ii) and (vi);

**(3.15) Excluded interest** — For the purpose of subsection (3.1), an excluded interest in a partnership at any time means an interest in a partnership that actively carries on a business that was carried on by it throughout the period beginning February 22, 1994 and ending at that time, or that earns income from a property that was owned by it throughout that period, unless in that period there was a substantial contribution of capital to the partnership or a substantial increase in the indebtedness of the partnership.

**Related Provisions**: 40(3.16) — Amounts considered not to be substantial; 40(3.17) — Whether carrying on business before February 22, 1994; 53(2)(c)(i.4)(E) — Effect of excluded interest on ACB of partnership with 1995 stub period income.

**Notes**: 40(3.15) added by 1994 Budget, effective February 22, 1994. This was 40(3.6) in the draft legislation of September 27, 1994.

**(3.16) Amounts considered not to be substantial** — For the purpose of subsection (3.15), an amount will be considered not to be substantial where

(a) the amount

(i) was raised pursuant to the terms of a written agreement entered into by a partnership before February 22, 1994 to issue an interest in the partnership and was expended on expenditures contemplated by the agreement before 1995 (or before March 2, 1995 in the case of amounts expended to acquire a film production prescribed for the purpose of subparagraph 96(2.2)(d)(ii) the principal photography of which or, in the case of such a production that is a television series, one episode of the series, commences before 1995 and the production is completed before March 2, 1995, or an interest in one or more partnerships all or substantially all of the property of which is such a film production),

(ii) was raised pursuant to the terms of a written agreement (other than an agreement referred to in subparagraph (i)) entered into by a partnership before February 22, 1994 and was expended on expenditures contemplated by the agreement before 1995 (or before March 2, 1995 in the case of amounts expended to acquire a film production prescribed for the purpose of subparagraph 96(2.2)(d)(ii) the principal photography of which or, in the case of such a production that is a television series, one episode of the series, commences before 1995 and the production is completed before March 2, 1995, or an interest in one or more partnerships all or substantially all of the property of which is such a film production),

(iii) was used by the partnership before 1995 (or before March 2, 1995 in the case of amounts expended to acquire a film production prescribed for the purpose of subparagraph 96(2.2)(d)(ii) the principal photography of which or, in the case of such a production that is a television series, one episode of the series, commences before 1995 and the production is completed before March 2, 1995, or an interest in one or more partnerships all or substantially all of the property of which is such a film production) to make an expenditure required to be made pursuant to the terms of a written agreement entered into by the partnership before February 22, 1994, or

(iv) was used to repay a loan, debt or contribution of capital that had been received or incurred in respect of any such expenditure;

(b) the amount was raised before 1995 pursuant to the terms of a prospectus, preliminary prospectus, offering memorandum or registration statement filed before February 22, 1994 with a public authority in Canada pursuant to and in accordance with the securities legislation of Canada or of a province and, where required by law, accepted for filing by the public authority, and expended before 1995 (or before March 2, 1995 in the case of amounts expended to acquire a film production prescribed for the purpose of subparagraph 96(2.2)(d)(ii), or an interest in one or more partnerships all or substantially all of the property of which is such a film production) on expenditures contemplated by the document that was filed before February 22, 1994;

(c) the amount was raised before 1995 pursuant to the terms of an offering memorandum distributed as part of an offering of securities where

   (i) the memorandum contained a complete or substantially complete description of the securities contemplated in the offering as well as the terms and conditions of the offering,

   (ii) the memorandum was distributed before February 22, 1994,

   (iii) solicitations in respect of the sale of the securities contemplated by the memorandum were made before February 22, 1994,

   (iv) the sale of the securities was substantially in accordance with the memorandum, and

   (v) the funds are expended in accordance with the memorandum before 1995 (except that the funds may be expended before March 2, 1995 in the case of a partnership all or substantially all of the property of which is a film production prescribed for the purpose of subparagraph 96(2.2)(d)(ii) the principal photography of which or, in the case of such a production that is a television series, one episode of the series, commences before 1995 and the production is completed before March 2, 1995, or an interest in one or more partnerships all or substantially all of the property of which is such a film production); or

(d) the amount was used for an activity that was carried on by the partnership on February 22, 1994 but not for a significant expansion of the activity nor for the acquisition or production of a film production.

**Related Provisions**: 40(3.17) — Partnership deemed to have carried on business before February 22, 1994; 40(3.18)(d) — Grandfathering of certain partnership interests.

**Notes**: 40(3.16) added by 1994 Budget, effective February 22, 1994. This was 40(3.7) in the draft legislation of September 27, 1994.

The CCRA takes the position that "all or substantially all" means 90% or more.

**(3.17) Whether carrying on business before February 22, 1994** — For the purpose of subsection (3.15), a partnership in respect of which paragraph (3.16)(a), (b) or (c) applies shall be considered to have actively carried on the business, or earned income from the property, contemplated in the document referred to in that paragraph throughout the period beginning February 22, 1994 and ending on the earlier of the closing date, if any, stipulated in the document and January 1, 1995.

**Notes**: 40(3.17) added by 1994 Budget, effective February 22, 1994. This was 40(3.8) in the draft legislation of September 27, 1994.

The CCRA takes the position that "all or substantially all" means 90% or more.

**(3.18) Deemed partner** — For the purpose of subsection (3.1), a member of a partnership who acquired an interest in the partnership after February 22, 1994 shall be deemed to have held the interest on February 22, 1994 where the member acquired the interest

(a) in circumstances in which

   (i) paragraph 70(6)(d.1) applied,

   (ii) where the member is an individual, the member's spouse or common-law partner held the partnership interest on February 22, 1994,

   (iii) where the member is a trust, the taxpayer by whose will the trust was created held the partnership interest on February 22, 1994, and

   (iv) the partnership interest was, immediately before the death of the spouse or common-law partner or the taxpayer, as the case may be, an excluded interest;

(b) in circumstances in which

   (i) paragraph 70(9.2)(c) applied,

   (ii) the member's parent held the partnership interest on February 22, 1994, and

   (iii) the partnership interest was, immediately before the parent's death, an excluded interest;

(c) in circumstances in which

   (i) paragraph 70(9.3)(e) applied,

   (ii) the trust referred to in subsection 70(9.3) or the taxpayer by whose will the trust was created held the partnership interest on February 22, 1994, and

   (iii) the partnership interest was, immediately before the death of the spouse or common-law partner referred to in subsection 70(9.3), an excluded interest; or

(d) before 1995 pursuant to a document referred to in subparagraph (3.16)(a)(i) or paragraph (3.16)(b) or (c).

**Related Provisions**: 252(2)(a) — Extended meaning of "parent".

**Notes**: 40(3.18) amended by 2000 same-sex partners bill to add reference to "common-law partner", effective for the 2001 and later taxation years, or earlier by election (see Notes to 248(1)"common-law partner").

40(3.18) added by 1994 Budget, effective February 22, 1994. This was 40(3.9) in the draft legislation of September 27, 1994.

**(3.19) Non-application of subsec. (3)** — Subsection (3) does not apply in any case where subsection (3.1) applies.

**Notes**: 40(3.19) added by 1994 Budget, effective February 22, 1994. This was 40(3.91) in the draft legislation of September 27, 1994.

**(3.2) Non-application of subsec. (3.1)** — Subsection (3.1) does not apply in any case where paragraph 98(1)(c) or 98.1(1)(c) applies.

**Notes**: 40(3.2) added by 1994 Budget, effective February 22, 1994. This was 40(3.92) in the draft legislation of September 27, 1994.

**(3.3) When subsection (3.4) applies** — Subsection (3.4) applies when

(a) a corporation, trust or partnership (in this subsection and subsection (3.4) referred to as the "transferor") disposes of a particular capital property (other than depreciable property of a prescribed class) otherwise than in a disposition described in any of paragraphs (c) to (g) of the definition "superficial loss" in section 54;

(b) during the period that begins 30 days before and ends 30 days after the disposition, the transferor or a person affiliated with the transferor acquires a property (in this subsection and subsection (3.4) referred to as the "substituted property") that is, or is identical to, the particular property; and

(c) at the end of the period, the transferor or a person affiliated with the transferor owns the substituted property.

**Related Provisions**: 93(2)–(2.3) — Loss on disposition of share of foreign affiliate; 251.1 — Affiliated persons.

**Notes**: 40(3.3) added by 1995-97 technical bill, effective (subject to the grandfathering rule reproduced after s. 260) for dispositions of property after April 26, 1995. See Notes to 40(3.4).

**I.T. Application Rules**: 26(5)(c)(ii)(A) (where property owned since June 18, 1971).

**(3.4) Loss on certain properties** — If this subsection applies because of subsection (3.3) to a disposition of a particular property,

(a) the transferor's loss, if any, from the disposition is deemed to be nil, and

(b) the amount of the transferor's loss, if any, from the disposition (determined without reference to paragraph (2)(g) and this subsection) is deemed to be a loss of the transferor from a disposition of the particular property at the time that is immediately before the first time, after the disposition,

(i) at which a 30-day period begins throughout which neither the transferor nor a person affiliated with the transferor owns

(A) the substituted property, or

(B) a property that is identical to the substituted property and that was acquired after the day that is 31 days before the period begins,

(ii) at which the property would, if it were owned by the transferor, be deemed by section 128.1 or subsection 149(10) to have been disposed of by the transferor,

(iii) that is immediately before control of the transferor is acquired by a person or group of persons, where the transferor is a corporation,

(iv) at which the transferor or a person affiliated with the transferor is deemed by section 50 to have disposed of the property, where the substituted property is a debt or a share of the capital stock of a corporation, or

(v) at which the winding-up of the transferor begins (other than a winding-up to which subsection 88(1) applies), where the transferor is a corporation,

and, for the purpose of paragraph (b), where a partnership otherwise ceases to exist at any time after the disposition, the partnership is deemed not to have ceased to exist, and each person who was a member of the partnership immediately before the partnership would, but for this subsection, have ceased to exist is deemed to remain a member of the partnership, until the time that is immediately after the first time described in subparagraphs (b)(i) to (v).

**Related Provisions**: 13(21.2) — Parallel rule for depreciable capital property; 14(12) — Parallel rule for eligible capital property; 18(13)–(15) — Parallel rule for share or debt owned by financial institution; 40(3.5) — Deemed identical property; 40(3.6) — Where share in corporation disposed of to the corporation; 69(5)(d) — No application on winding-up; 87(2)(g.3) — Amalgamations — continuing corporation; 93(2)–(2.3), (4) — Loss on disposition of share of foreign affiliate; 112(3)–(4.22) — Reduction in capital loss on shares where dividends previously paid; 139.1(18) — Holding corporation deemed not to acquire control of insurer on demutualization; 248(12) — Whether properties are identical; 256(6)–(9) — Whether control acquired.

**Notes**: 40(3.4) prevents the transfer of property with a "pregnant loss" from being used as a method of transferring a high cost base where property has declined in value. The loss is kept suspended in the transferor's hands, and can be claimed once the property is no longer in the affiliated group. For the parallel rule with respect to depreciable property, see 13(21.2). For eligible capital property, see 14(12); for certain inventory, see 18(13)–(16). See Notes to 13(21.2) re the application of GAAR to this situation.

40(3.4) added by 1995-97 technical bill, effective (subject to the grandfathering rule reproduced after s. 260) for dispositions of property after April 26, 1995.

**(3.5) Deemed identical property** — For the purposes of subsections (3.3) and (3.4),

(a) a right to acquire a property (other than a right, as security only, derived from a mortgage, agreement for sale or similar obligation) is deemed to be a property that is identical to the property;

(b) a share of the capital stock of a corporation that is acquired in exchange for another share in a transaction to which section 51, 85.1, 86 or 87 applies is deemed to be a property that is identical to the other share;

**Proposed Amendment — 40(3.5)(b)**
**Letter from Department of Finance, June 6, 2000**: See under 248(1) "taxable Canadian property".

(c) where subsections (3.3) and (3.4) apply to the disposition by a transferor of a share of the capital stock of a corporation, and after the disposition the corporation is merged with one or more other corporations, otherwise than in a transaction in respect of which paragraph (b) applies to the share, or is wound up in a winding-up to which subsection 88(1) applies, the corporation formed on the merger or the parent (within the meaning assigned by subsection 88(1)), as the case may be, is deemed to own the share while it is affiliated with the transferor; and

(d) where subsections (3.3) and (3.4) apply to the disposition by a transferor of a share of the capital stock of a corporation, and after the disposition the share is redeemed, acquired or cancelled by the corporation, otherwise than in a transaction in respect of which paragraph (b) or (c) applies to the share, the transferor is deemed to own the share while the corporation is affiliated with the transferor.

### Possible Future Amendment — 40(3.3)–(3.5)

**Department of Finance letter, November 17, 1997:**

Mr. Steve Suarez
Bennett Jones Verchere
Toronto, Ontario
Re: Proposed Subsections 40(3.3) to (3.5) — Loss deferral rules

Dear Mr. Suarez:

I am writing further to your recent discussion of proposed *Income Tax Act* subsections 40(3.3) and following, with Lawrence Purdy of this Division.

You have described a situation in which you consider that these provisions may operate inappropriately, and have asked for our comments. As I understand that you have a client for whom this is an immediate concern, we have given this some priority.

Proposed subsections 40(3.3) to (3.5) set out rules that would apply where, in general terms, a corporation, partnership or trust would otherwise realize a loss on disposition of a non-depreciable capital property to an affiliated person. The rules would defer the recognition of that loss until the earliest of several possible subsequent events, the most typical of which is that the property (or an identical property) is no longer held by a person who is affiliated with the initial transferor. Once the property had left the affiliated population, the initial transferor could recognize that deferred loss.

The proposals include a few provisions directed at special circumstances. One of these is proposed paragraph 40(3.5)(b), which is meant to cover cases where shares are exchanged for one another. Paragraph 40(3.5)(b) would treat a share that was acquired in exchange for another share, in a transaction to which section 51, 85.1, 86 or 87 applies, as being identical to the other share. This ensures, for example, that a loss that is deferred on the transfer of a share to an affiliate will not be recognized if the share is merely replaced with another share under one of those provisions. Even though it may be argued that the former share is no longer held by an affiliated person (since that share no longer exists), paragraph 40(3.5)(b) causes the new share in effect to take its place for this purpose.

Your concern, as I understand it, is that paragraph 40(3.5)(b) may apply not only where the section 85.1 exchange takes place after the initial transfer of a share to an affiliated person, but also where the section 85.1 exchange is itself that initial transfer. In other words, paragraph 40(3.5)(b) might apply to any exchange to which section 85.1 applies. If this is the case, then the clear intention of section 85.1 to permit a loss to be realized on such an exchange, at least in some circumstances, would be contradicted — the shares taken back would be deemed to be identical to the shares given up, and the loss would be deferred under subsection 40(3.4).

I agree that this would not be an appropriate result, at least where the vendor and the purchaser (as they are described in subsection 85.1(1)(a)) are not affiliated. That is, I agree that it ought in policy terms to be possible for a vendor to realize a loss on an exchange of shares of an acquired corporation for shares of a purchaser that is not affiliated with the vendor immediately after the exchange.

We will consider further how this policy view can best be accommodated in the proposed legislation. Given the tight time-line we are on, it may not be possible to recommend a clarifying change before the legislation is introduced. In that case, we will recommend that the change be included in a future set of technical amendments. While I cannot, as you know, offer any assurance that either the Minister or Parliament itself will agree with the recommendations we intend to make in this regard, I hope this summary of our views is helpful.

Yours sincerely
Len Farber
Department of Finance, Director General, Tax Legislation Division

**Letter from Department of Finance, September 15, 1998:**

Dear [xxx]

I am writing further to a recent exchange of messages between [xxx] and Lawrence Purdy of this Division, regarding *Income Tax Act* subsections 40(3.3) and following. I understand that you and [xxx] are working together on a particular transaction to which these provisions may be relevant, and that [xxx] has asked that you and he be given the same information.

Subsections 40(3.3) to (3.5) set out rules that apply where, in general terms, a corporation, partnership or trust would otherwise realize a loss on a disposition of a non-depreciable capital property to an affiliated person. The rules defer the recognition of that loss until the earliest of several possible subsequent events, the most typical of which is that the property (or an identical property) is no longer held by a person who is affiliated with the initial transferor. Once the property has left the affiliated population, the initial transferor can recognize that deferred loss.

The provisions include a few rules directed at special circumstances. One of those is paragraph 40(3.5)(b), which is meant to cover cases where shares are exchanged for one another. Paragraph 40(3.5)(b) treats a share that was acquired in exchange for another share, in a transaction to which section 51, 85.1, 86 or 87 applies, as being identical to the other share. This ensures, for example, that a loss that is deferred on the transfer of a share to an affiliate will not be recognized if the share is merely replaced with another share under one of those provisions. Even though it may be argued that the former share is no longer held by an affiliated person (since that share no longer exists), paragraph 40(3.5)(b) causes the new share in effect to take its place for this purpose.

Your concern, which has also been raised with us by others in the past, is that paragraph 40(3.5)(b) may apply not only where the section 85.1 exchange takes place after the initial transfer of a share to an affiliated person, but also where the section 85.1 exchange is itself that initial transfer. In other words, paragraph 40(3.5)(b) might apply to any exchange

**S. 40(3.5)**            Income Tax Act, Part I, Division B

to which section 85.1 applies. If this is the case, then the clear intention of section 85.1 to permit a loss to be realized on such an exchange, at least in some circumstances, would be contradicted — the shares taken back would be deemed to be identical to the shares given up, and the loss would be deferred under subsection 40(3.4).

I agree that this would not be an appropriate result, at least where the vendor and the purchaser (as they are described in subsection 85.1(1) are not affiliated. That is, I agree that it ought in policy terms to be possible for a vendor to realize a loss on an exchange of shares of an acquired corporation for shares of a purchaser that is not affiliated with the vendor immediately after the exchange.

We will recommend that a clarifying change to the relevant rules be included in a future package of amendments. Since the change would be a strictly technical correction to the rules as they were enacted, I expect to recommend that the change apply as of the date the rules themselves took effect — that is, to dispositions of property that occur after April 26, 1995.

As you know, I cannot offer any assurance that either the Minister or Parliament itself will agree with the recommendations we intend to make in this regard. Nonetheless, I hope this summary of our views is helpful.

    Yours sincerely,

    Brian Ernewein
    Director, Tax Legislation Division

**Related Provisions**: 87(2)(g.2) — Amalgamations — continuing corporation.

**Notes**: 40(3.5) added by 1995-97 technical bill, effective (subject to the grandfathering rule reproduced after s. 260) for dispositions of property after April 26, 1995.

**(3.6) Loss on shares** — Where at any time a taxpayer disposes, to a corporation that is affiliated with the taxpayer immediately after the disposition, of a share of a class of the capital stock of the corporation (other than a share that is a distress preferred share as defined in subsection 80(1)),

    (a) the taxpayer's loss, if any, from the disposition is deemed to be nil; and

    (b) in computing the adjusted cost base to the taxpayer after that time of a share of a class of the capital stock of the corporation owned by the taxpayer immediately after the disposition, there shall be added the proportion of the amount of the taxpayer's loss from the disposition (determined without reference to paragraph (2)(g) and this subsection) that

        (i) the fair market value, immediately after the disposition, of the share

    is of

        (ii) the fair market value, immediately after the disposition, of all shares of the capital stock of the corporation owned by the taxpayer.

**Related Provisions**: 53(1)(f.2) — Addition to adjusted cost base; 84(3) — Deemed dividend of excess of proceeds over paid-up capital; 251.1 — Affiliated persons.

**Notes**: 40(3.6) effectively replaces former 85(4)(b). See also Notes to 40(3.4).

40(3.6) added by 1995-97 technical bill, effective (subject to the grandfathering rule reproduced after s. 260) for dispositions of property after April 26, 1995.

### Proposed Addition — 40(3.7)

**(3.7) Losses of non-resident** — If an individual disposes of a property at any time after having ceased to be resident in Canada, for the purposes of applying subsections 100(4), 107(1) and 112(3) to (3.32) and (7) in computing the individual's loss from the disposition,

    (a) the individual is deemed to be a corporation in respect of dividends received by the individual, or deemed under Part XIII to have been paid to the individual, at a particular time that is after the time at which the individual last acquired the property and at which the individual was non-resident; and

    (b) an amount on account of

        (i) each taxable dividend received by the individual at a particular time described in paragraph (a), and

        (ii) each amount deemed under Part XIII to have been paid to the individual at a particular time described in paragraph (a), as a dividend from a corporation resident in Canada, to the extent that the amount can reasonably be considered to relate to the property,

is deemed to be a taxable dividend that was received by the individual and that was deductible under section 112 in computing the individual's taxable income or taxable income earned in Canada for the taxation year that includes that particular time.

**Related Provisions**: 119 — Credit to former resident where stop-loss rule applies; 128.1(6)(b), 128.1(7)(e) — Returning former resident of Canada.

**Application**: Bill C-43 (First Reading September 20, 2000) subsec. 14(3), will add subsec. 40(3.7), applicable to dispositions after December 23, 1998 by individuals who cease to be resident in Canada after October 1, 1996.

**Technical Notes**: Section 40 provides rules for determining a taxpayer's gain or loss from the disposition of a property.

New subsection 40(3.7) is a "stop-loss" rule that may reduce the loss of an individual from the disposition of a property if the individual disposes of the property at any time after having ceased to be resident in Canada. In general terms, this stop-loss rule applies where an individual has received dividends in respect of a property (whether a share, an interest in a partnership or an interest in a trust) during the period of non-residence that begins after the individual last acquired the property.

The Act already includes, in section 112 and related provisions, a comprehensive stop-loss system for corporations. Instead of duplicating that system, new subsection 40(3.7) adapts it to apply to losses otherwise realized by individuals on dispositions of property after they ceased to be resident in Canada, regardless of whether they are resident in Canada at the time of such dispositions.

> For the purposes of applying subsections 100(4), 107(1) and 112(3) to (3.32) and (7), new subsection 40(3.7) deems an individual to be a corporation in respect of dividends received in respect of a property after the last time the individual acquired the property and while the individual was non-resident, and deems any taxable dividends received by the individual during that period to have been deductible under section 112 when received. The effect of this is that some or all dividends received while non-resident may reduce the individual's loss on a share, partnership interest or trust interest.

**(4) Disposal of principal residence to spouse or trust for spouse [or common-law partner]** — Where a taxpayer has, after 1971, disposed of property to an individual in circumstances to which subsection 70(6) or 73(1) applied, for the purposes of computing the individual's gain from the disposition of the property under paragraph (2)(b) or (c), as the case may be,

(a) the individual shall be deemed to have owned the property throughout the period during which the taxpayer owned it;

(b) the property shall be deemed to have been the individual's principal residence

(i) in any case where subsection 70(6) is applicable, for any taxation year for which it would, if the taxpayer had designated it in prescribed manner to have been the taxpayer's principal residence for that year, have been the taxpayer's principal residence, and

(ii) in any case where subsection 73(1) is applicable, for any taxation year for which it was the taxpayer's principal residence; and

(c) where the individual is a trust, the trust shall be deemed to have been resident in Canada during each taxation year during which the taxpayer was resident in Canada.

**Related Provisions**: 40(7.1) — Effect of election to trigger capital gains exemption.

**Notes**: After a spousal rollover, 40(4) allows the combined holding period of both spouses to be counted for purposes of the principal-residence exemption.

**Regulations**: 2301 (prescribed manner of designation).

**Interpretation Bulletins**: IT-120R5: Principal residence; IT-366R: Principal residence — transfer to spouse or spouse trust.

**(5) [Repealed]**

**Notes**: 40(5) repealed by 1992 technical bill, effective for dispositions after 1990. See now amended 54"principal residence" with respect to the principal residence of a spousal trust.

**(6) Special rule concerning principal residence** — Where a property was owned by a taxpayer, whether jointly with another person or otherwise, at the end of 1981 and continuously thereafter until disposed of by the taxpayer, the amount of the gain determined under paragraph (2)(b) in respect of the disposition shall not exceed the amount, if any, by which the total of

(a) the taxpayer's gain calculated in accordance with paragraph (2)(b) on the assumption that the taxpayer had disposed of the property on December 31, 1981 for proceeds of disposition equal to its fair market value on that date, and

(b) the taxpayer's gain calculated in accordance with paragraph (2)(b) on the assumption that that paragraph applies and that

(i) the taxpayer acquired the property on January 1, 1982 at a cost equal to its proceeds of disposition as determined under paragraph (a), and

(ii) the description of B in paragraph (2)(b) is read without reference to "one plus"

exceeds

(c) the amount, if any, by which the fair market value of the property on December 31, 1981 exceeds the proceeds of disposition of the property determined without reference to this subsection.

**Related Provisions**: 40(7.1) — Effect of election to trigger capital gains exemption.

**Notes**: Reference in 40(6)(b)(ii) to 40(2)(b)(i) changed to 40(2)(b)B by 1994 Budget, effective for dispositions after February 22, 1994, as a result of amendment to 40(2)(b).

**Interpretation Bulletins**: IT-120R5: Principal residence; IT-366R: Principal residence — transfer to spouse or spouse trust.

**(7) Property in satisfaction of interest in trust** — Where property has been acquired by a taxpayer in satisfaction of all or any part of the taxpayer's capital interest in a trust, in circumstances to which subsection 107(2) applies and subsection 107(4) does not apply, for the purposes of paragraph (2)(b) and the definition "principal residence" in section 54, the taxpayer shall be deemed to have owned the property continuously since the trust last acquired it.

**Related Provisions**: 40(7.1) — Effect of election to trigger capital gains exemption; 107(2.01) — Principal residence distribution by spouse trust.

**Interpretation Bulletins**: IT-120R5: Principal residence; IT-437R: Ownership of property (principal residence).

**(7.1) Effect of election under subsec. 110.6(19)** — Where an election was made under subsection 110.6(19) in respect of a property of a taxpayer that was the taxpayer's principal residence for the 1994 taxation year or that, in the taxpayer's return of income for the taxation year in which the taxpayer disposes of the property or grants an option to acquire the property, is designated as the taxpayer's principal residence, in determining, for the purposes of paragraph (2)(b) and subsections (4) to (7), the day on which the property was last acquired or reacquired by the taxpayer and the period throughout which the property was owned by the taxpayer this Act shall be read without reference to subsection 110.6(19).

**Notes**: 40(7.1) added by 1994 Budget, effective for dispositions after February 22, 1994. It provides that the capital gains exemption election in 110.6(19) is to be ignored in determining when a principal residence was "last acquired". As a result, the increase in ACB of the property resulting from the election will be ignored in computing the capital gain from the disposition; and the taxation years

## S. 40(7.1)

that ended before February 23, 1994 and during which the taxpayer owned the property will still be relevant in computing the principal residence portion of the gain under 40(2)(b)B.

**Interpretation Bulletins**: IT-120R5: Principal residence.

### (8) Application of subsec. 70(10) —
The definitions in subsection 70(10) apply to this section.

**Notes**: 40(8) added in R.S.C. 1985 (5th Supp.) consolidation, effective for taxation years ending after November 1991. This rule was formerly contained in the opening words of 70(10).

### (9) Additions to taxable Canadian property —
Where a non-resident person disposes of a taxable Canadian property that the person last acquired before April 27, 1995 and that would not be a taxable Canadian property immediately before the disposition if section 115 were read as it applied to dispositions that occurred on April 26, 1995, the person's gain or loss from the disposition is deemed to be the amount determined by the formula

> **Proposed Amendment — 40(9) opening words**
>
> **(9) Additions to taxable Canadian property** — If a non-resident person disposes of a taxable Canadian property
>
> (a) that the person last acquired before April 27, 1995,
>
> (b) that would not be a taxable Canadian property immediately before the disposition if section 115 were read as it applied to dispositions that occurred on April 26, 1995, and
>
> (c) that would be a taxable Canadian property immediately before the disposition if section 115 were read as it applied to dispositions that occurred on January 1, 1996,
>
> the person's gain or loss from the disposition is deemed to be the amount determined by the formula
>
> **Application**: Bill C-43 (First Reading September 20, 2000), subsec. 14(4), will amend the portion of subsec. 40(9) before the formula to read as above, applicable to dispositions that occur after April 26, 1995.
>
> **Technical Notes**: As a result of changes to the definition of "taxable Canadian property," certain properties acquired before April 27, 1995 became taxable Canadian properties on that date. Subsection 40(9) was enacted to provide rules for computing a non-resident person's gain or loss from the disposition of such a property, prorating the amount of gain or loss determined without reference to the subsection according to the number of months the person held the property before May 1995.
>
> Effective October 2, 1996 the definition of "taxable Canadian property" is again amended so that certain properties acquired before that date will have become taxable Canadian properties on that date. Subsection 40(9) is amended to clarify that the formula it sets out applies only to gains or losses realized on the disposition of properties that became taxable Canadian properties on April 27, 1995.

$$A \times B/C$$

where

A is the amount of the gain or loss determined without reference to this subsection;

B is the number of calendar months in the period that begins with May 1995 and ends with the calendar month that includes the time of the disposition; and

C is the number of calendar months in the period that begins with the calendar month in which the person last acquired the property and ends with the calendar month that includes the time of the disposition.

**Notes**: As a result of changes to the definition "taxable Canadian property" in 115(1)(b), certain property acquired before April 26, 1995 will have become taxable Canadian property on that date. 40(9) prorates the gain or loss based on the number of months the taxpayer held the property before May 1995.

40(9) added by 1995-97 technical bill, effective (subject to the grandfathering rule reproduced after s. 260) for dispositions of property after April 26, 1995.

**Definitions [s. 40]**: "acquired" — 256(7)–(9); "acquisition date" — 40(2)(b), 40(7.1); "adjusted cost base" — 54, 248(1); "affiliated" — 251.1; "amount" — 248(1); "arm's length" — 251(1); "business" — 248(1); "Canada" — 255; "capital gain", "capital loss" — 39(1), 248(1); "capital property" — 54, 248(1); "child" — 40(8), 70(10), 252(1); "class of shares" — 248(6); "common-law partner" — 248(1); "control" — 256(6)–(9); "controlled directly or indirectly" — 256(5.1), (6.2); "corporation" — 248(1), *Interpretation Act* 35(1); "deferred profit sharing plan" — 147(1), 248(1); "disposition" — 54 [to be repealed], 248(1); "dividend", "employee" — 248(1); "employees profit sharing plan" — 144(1), 248(1); "excepted gift" — 118.1(19); "excluded interest" — 40(3.15); "exempt income", "farming" — 248(1); "fiscal period" — 249(2)(b), 249.1; "identical" — 40(3.5), 248(12); "individual" — 248(1); "interest in a family farm partnership" — 40(8), 70(10); "last acquired" — 40(7.1); "limited partner" — 40(3.14); "listed personal property" — 54, 248(1); "non-resident" — 248(1); "parent" — 252(2)(a); "partnership" — see Notes to 96(1); "person" — 248(1); "personal-use property" — 54, 248(1); "prescribed" — 248(1); "prescribed labour-sponsored venture capital corporation" — Reg. 6701; "prescribed venture capital corporation" — Reg. 6700, 6700.1, 6700.2; "principal residence", "proceeds of disposition" — 54; "property" — 248(1); "province" — *Interpretation Act* 35(1); "registered retirement income fund" — 146.3(1), 248(1); "registered retirement savings plan" — 146(1), 248(1); "resident in Canada" — 250; "share" — 248(1); "share of the capital stock of a family farm corporation" — 40(8), 70(10); "small business corporation", "specified member" — 40(3.131), 248(1); "substantial" — 40(3.16); "substituted property" — 248(5); "superficial loss" — 54; "taxable Canadian corporation" — 89(1), 248(1); "taxable Canadian property" — 248(1); "taxable dividend" — 89(1), 248(1); "taxable income", "taxable income earned in Canada" — 248(1); "taxation year" — 249; "taxpayer" — 40(3.12), 248(1); "testamentary trust" — 108(1), 248(1); "trust" — 104(1), 248(1), (3); "written" — *Interpretation Act* 35(1) [writing].

**Interpretation Bulletins [s. 40]**: IT-332R: Personal-use property.

### 41. (1) Taxable net gain from disposition of listed personal property —
For the purposes of this Part, a taxpayer's taxable net gain for a taxation year from dispositions of listed personal property is ¾ of the amount determined under subsection (2) to be the taxpayer's net gain for the year from dispositions of such property.

Subdivision c — Taxable Capital Gains    S. 42

> **Proposed Amendment — 41(1)**
>
> **Application**: The December 21, 2000 draft legislation, s. 16, will amend subsec. 41(1) by replacing the reference to the fraction "3/4" with a reference to the fraction "1/2", applicable to taxation years that end after February 27, 2000 except that, for taxation years that include either February 28, 2000 or October 17, 2000, the reference to the fraction "1/2" shall be read as reference to the fraction in para. 38(a), as amended [by the December 21, 2000 draft legislation], that applies to the taxpayer for the year.
>
> **Technical Notes**: Subsection 41(1) defines a taxpayer's taxable net gain for a taxation year from dispositions of listed personal property as 3/4 of the taxpayer's net gain determined under subsection 41(2) from dispositions of such property.
>
> Subsection 41(1) is amended to replace the reference to the fraction "3/4" with a reference to the fraction "1/2". The amendment is consequential on the reduction of the inclusion rate for capital gains from 3/4 to 1/2 [see 38(a) — ed.].
>
> The amendment applies to taxation years that end after February 27, 2000 except that, for a taxpayer's taxation year that includes either February 28, 2000 or October 17, 2000, the reference to the fraction "1/2" in subsection 41(1) is to be read as reference to the fraction in amended paragraph 38(a) that applies to the taxpayer for the year. These modifications are required in order to reflect the capital gains/losses rate for the year.

**Related Provisions**: 127.52(1)(d)(i) — Untaxed ¼ of gain added to income for minimum tax purposes; 248(1) "taxable net gain" — Definition applies to entire Act.

**Notes**: Listed personal property losses can be used under 41(2) to offset listed personal property gains. Like other losses from personal-use property, they cannot be used against ordinary capital gains: see 3(b)(ii) and 40(2)(g)(iii).

**Interpretation Bulletins**: See list at end of s. 41.

**(2) Determination of net gain** — A taxpayer's net gain for a taxation year from dispositions of listed personal property is an amount determined as follows:

(a) determine the amount, if any, by which the total of the taxpayer's gains for the year from the disposition of listed personal property, other than property described in subparagraph 39(1)(a)(i.1), exceeds the total of the taxpayer's losses for the year from dispositions of listed personal property, and

(b) deduct from the amount determined under paragraph (a) such portion as the taxpayer may claim of the taxpayer's listed-personal-property losses for the 7 taxation years immediately preceding and the 3 taxation years immediately following the taxation year, except that for the purposes of this paragraph

(i) an amount in respect of a listed-personal-property loss is deductible for a taxation year only to the extent that it exceeds the total of amounts deducted under this paragraph in respect of that loss for preceding taxation years,

(ii) no amount is deductible in respect of the listed-personal-property loss of any year until the deductible listed-personal-property losses for previous years have been deducted, and

(iii) no amount is deductible in respect of listed-personal-property losses from the amount determined under paragraph (a) for a taxation year except to the extent of the amount so determined for the year,

and the remainder determined under paragraph (b) is the taxpayer's net gain for the year from dispositions of listed personal property.

**Related Provisions**: 46(1) — Personal-use property.

**Interpretation Bulletins**: IT-407R4: Dispositions of cultural property to designated Canadian institutions. See also list at end of s. 41.

**Forms**: T1A: Request for loss carry-back; T3A: Request for loss carry-back by a trust.

**(3) Definition of "listed-personal-property loss"** — In this section, "listed-personal-property loss" of a taxpayer for a taxation year means the amount, if any, by which the total of the taxpayer's losses for the year from dispositions of listed personal property exceeds the total of the taxpayer's gains for the year from dispositions of listed personal property, other than property described in subparagraph 39(1)(a)(i.1).

**Related Provisions**: 152(6) — Reassessment; 164(5), (5.1) — Effect of carryback of loss.

**Interpretation Bulletins [subsec. 41(3)]**: IT-159R3: Capital debts established to be bad debts. See also list at end of s. 41.

**Definitions [s. 41]**: "amount" — 248(1); "disposition" — 54 [to be repealed], 248(1); "listed personal property" — 54, 248(1); "listed-personal-property loss" — 41(3); "property" — 248(1); "taxable net gain" — 41(1), 248(1); "taxation year" — 249; "taxpayer" — 248(1).

**Interpretation Bulletins [s. 41]**: IT-332R: Personal-use property.

**42. Dispositions subject to warranty** — In computing a taxpayer's proceeds of disposition of any property for the purposes of this subdivision, there shall be included all amounts received or receivable by the taxpayer as consideration for warranties, covenants or other conditional or contingent obligations given or incurred by the taxpayer in respect of the disposition, and in computing the taxpayer's income for the taxation year in which the property was disposed of and for each subsequent taxation year, any outlay or expense made or incurred by the taxpayer in any such year pursuant to or by reason of any such obligation shall be deemed to be a loss of the taxpayer for that year from a disposition of a capital property and for the purposes of section 110.6, that capital property shall be deemed to have been disposed of by the taxpayer in that year.

**Related Provisions**: 87(2)(n) — Amalgamations — outlays made pursuant to warranty.

**Definitions [s. 42]**: "amount" — 248(1); "capital property" — 54, 248(1); "disposition" — 54 [to be repealed], 248(1); "property" — 248(1); "taxation year" — 249; "taxpayer" — 248(1).

**Interpretation Bulletins [s. 42]**: IT-330R: Disposition of capital property subject to warranty, covenant, etc.

**43. Part dispositions** — For the purpose of computing a taxpayer's gain or loss for a taxation year from the disposition of a part of a property, the adjusted cost base to the taxpayer, immediately before the disposition, of that part is such portion of the adjusted cost base to the taxpayer at that time of the whole property as may reasonably be regarded as attributable to that part.

### Proposed Amendment — 43

**43. (1) General rule for part dispositions** — For the purpose of computing a taxpayer's gain or loss for a taxation year from the disposition of part of a property, the adjusted cost base to the taxpayer, immediately before the disposition, of that part is the portion of the adjusted cost base to the taxpayer at that time of the whole property that can reasonably be regarded as attributable to that part.

**Technical Notes**: Section 43 is a rule governing the disposition of a part of a property. For the purpose of computing a taxpayer's gain or loss from the disposition of a part of a property, a portion of the adjusted cost base (ACB) of the whole property must be allocated to the part on a reasonable basis.

Existing section 43 is renumbered as subsection 43(1) strictly as a consequence of the introduction of new subsections 43(2) and (3). This amendment applies after February 27, 1995.

**Related Provisions**: 43(3) — Where trust makes payment out of income or gains.

**(2) Ecological gifts** — For the purposes of subsection (1) and section 53, where at any time a taxpayer disposes of a servitude, covenant or easement to which land is subject in circumstances where subsection 110.1(5) or 118.1(12) applies,

(a) the portion of the adjusted cost base to the taxpayer of the land immediately before the disposition that can reasonably be regarded as attributable to the servitude, covenant or easement, as the case may be, is deemed to be equal to the amount determined by the formula

$$A \times B/C$$

where

A is the adjusted cost base to the taxpayer of the land immediately before the disposition,

B is the amount determined under subsection 110.1(5) or 118.1(12) in respect of the disposition, and

C is the fair market value of the land immediately before the disposition; and

(b) for greater certainty, the cost to the taxpayer of the land shall be reduced at the time of disposition by the amount determined under paragraph (a).

**Technical Notes**: New subsection 43(2) of the Act applies where the part of a property disposed of is a servitude, covenant or easement to which land is subject. The 1995 budget introduced enhanced incentives for the donation of ecologically sensitive land to the Government of Canada, a provincial government, a Canadian municipality or an approved registered charity established for the purpose of protecting Canada's environmental heritage. Donations from individuals are eligible for the charitable donations tax credit (section 118.1 of the Act), while those from corporations are eligible for deduction from income (section 110.1 of the Act). Besides transfers of title, landowners are able to donate covenants, easements and servitudes established under common law, the civil law of the province of Quebec, or the law of other provinces allowing for their establishment.

Normally the value of a donated property is determined to be the price that a purchaser would pay for the property on the open market. As there is no established market for covenants, easements and servitudes, the fair market value of such restrictions on land use is difficult to determine. To provide greater certainty in making these valuations, the 1997 budget introduced a measure to deem the value of these gifts to be not less than the resulting decrease in the value of the land. That measure was implemented with application to gifts made after February 27, 1995.

Like other capital property, the adjusted cost base (ACB) of a covenant, easement or servitude is also relevant in calculating the capital gain or loss that may arise on disposition. To provide taxpayers greater certainty in making this calculation, new subsection 43(2) ensures that a portion of the ACB of the land to which the covenant, easement or servitude relates is to be allocated to the donated covenant, easement or servitude. For this purpose, the allocation of the ACB of the land to the gift is calculated in proportion to the percentage decrease in the value of the land as a result of the donation.

This amendment applies in respect of gifts made after February 27, 1995.

**Department of Finance news release, June 3, 1999**: See under 118.1(12).

**Related Provisions**: 107(2), (2.1), (2.11) — No capital gain on disposition of capital interest.

**(3) Payments out of trust income, etc.** — Notwithstanding subsection (1), where part of a capital interest of a taxpayer in a trust would, but for paragraph (g) or (h) of the definition "disposition" in subsection 248(1), be disposed of solely because of the satisfaction of a right to enforce a payment of an amount by the trust, no part of the adjusted cost base to the taxpayer of the taxpayer's capital interest in the trust shall be allocated to that part of the capital interest.

**Technical Notes**: New subsection 43(3) applies where part of a capital interest in a trust would, but for paragraph (h) or (i) of the definition "disposition" in subsection 248(1), be disposed of solely because of a satisfaction by the trust of a right to enforce a payment from the trust. No portion of the ACB of the taxpayer's capital interest is allocated to such a right. Accordingly, the ACB to the taxpayer of the remaining part of the taxpayer's capital interest in the trust is not reduced after the satisfaction of such a right. This amendment applies to satisfactions of rights that occur after 1999.

*EXAMPLE*

Joseph buys 1,000 units of XYZ Mutual Fund on December 23, 2000 for $10,000. XYZ has not made an election under subsection 132.11(1) to have a December 15 year end. XYZ makes $400 of its income for its 2000 taxation year payable to Joseph on December 31, 2000. However, without making any cash distribution of the income, XYZ issues 42 additional units on that date in satisfaction of the $400 of income payable. In November 2001, Joseph disposes of his 1,042 units for $10,700.

Results:

1. Under subsection 104(13), Joseph is required to include $400 in computing his income for the 2000 taxation year.

2. The right to enforce the payment of the distribution is treated as part of Joseph's capital interest in the trust under subsection 108(1). However, under paragraphs (h) and (i) of the definition "disposition" in subsection 248(1), there is no disposition of that part of the capital interest on the satisfaction of the right.

3. Under subsection 43(3), no part of the ACB of the original interest is allocated to the right to the income payable when the right is satisfied. Without taking into account the identical properties rule in subsection 47(1), this ensures that the ACB of Joseph's original 1,000 units will remain $10,000 once the right to income is satisfied, notwithstanding that Joseph acquired the units late in the 2000 taxation year.

4. The 42 additional units issued in satisfaction of the right to income are acquired at a cost of $400 because new subsection 248(25.3) ensures that the cost of the units issued directly in satisfaction of the income payable is equal to that amount. Consequently, the total ACB of the 1,042 units at the time of the disposition is $10,400.

5. Consequently, the capital gain realized on the subsequent disposition of all of the units is $300.

The introduction of subsection 43(3) is part of a set of amendments designed to clarify the tax consequences of distributions from trusts to their beneficiaries after 1999. For the large part, the end results achieved under these rules are intended to accord with existing income tax practice. Other related amendments include the repeal of subsection 52(6), amendments to subsections 107(2) and (2.1), the amended definition of "capital interest" in subsection 108(1), paragraphs (d), (h) and (i) of the definition "disposition" in subsection 248(1) and new subsections 248(25.3) and (25.4). For further detail, see the commentary on those provisions.

**Application**: Bill C-43 (First Reading September 20, 2000), s. 15, will amend s. 43 to read as above, subsec. (1) applicable after February 27, 1995, subsec. (2) applicable in respect of gifts made after February 27, 1995, and subsec. (3) applicable to satisfactions of rights that occur after 1999.

**Related Provisions**: 53(2)(d) — Reduction in adjusted cost base; 98.2(c), 100(3)(c) — No application to transfer of partnership interest on death.

**Definitions [s. 43]**: "adjusted cost base" — 54, 248(1); "capital interest" — 108(1), 248(1); "disposition" — 54 [to be repealed], 248(1) [draft]; "property" — 248(1); "taxation year" — 249; "taxpayer" — 248(1); "trust" — 104(1), 248(1), (3).

**Interpretation Bulletins [s. 43]**: IT-200: Surface rentals and farming operations; IT-226R: Gift to a charity of a residual interest in real property or an equitable interest in a trust; IT-242R: Retired partners; IT-264R: Part dispositions; IT-278R2: Death of a partner or of a retired partner; IT-338R2: Partnership interests — changes in cost base resulting from the admission or retirement of a partner; IT-359R2: Premiums and other amounts re leases; IT-373R: Farm wood lots and tree farms; IT-418: Capital cost allowance — partial dispositions of property.

**43.1 (1) Life estates in real property** — Notwithstanding any other provision of this Act, where at any time a taxpayer disposes of a remainder interest in real property (except as a result of a transaction to which subsection 73(3) would otherwise apply or by way of a gift to a donee described in the definition "total charitable gifts" or "total Crown gifts" in subsection 118.1(1)) to a person or partnership and retains a life estate or an estate *pur autre vie* (in this section called the "life estate") in the property, the taxpayer shall be deemed

(a) to have disposed at that time of the life estate in the property for proceeds of disposition equal to its fair market value at that time; and

(b) to have reacquired the life estate immediately after that time at a cost equal to the proceeds of disposition referred to in paragraph (a).

**Related Provisions**: 248(4) — Interest in real property.

**Notes**: See Notes at end of 43.1.

**(2) Idem** — Where, as a result of an individual's death, a life estate to which subsection (1) applied is terminated,

(a) the holder of the life estate immediately before the death shall be deemed to have disposed of the life estate immediately before the death for proceeds of disposition equal to the adjusted cost base to that person of the life estate immediately before the death; and

(b) where a person who is the holder of the remainder interest in the real property immediately before the death was not dealing at arm's length with the holder of the life estate, there shall, after the death, be added in computing the adjusted cost base to that person of the real property an amount equal to the lesser of

(i) the adjusted cost base of the life estate in the property immediately before the death, and

(ii) the amount, if any, by which the fair market value of the real property immediately after the death exceeds the adjusted cost base to that person of the remainder interest immediately before the death.

**Related Provisions**: 53(1)(o) — Addition to adjusted cost base.

**Notes**: 43.1 added by 1992 technical bill (and amended retroactively by 1993 technical bill), effective for dispositions and terminations after December 20, 1991. The amendment broadened the exemption from the deemed disposition by changing "other than a registered charity that is a charitable organization described in subsection 149.1(1)" to "or by way of a gift to a donee described in the definition "total charitable gifts" or "total Crown gifts" in subsection 118.1(1)". The effect is to extend the exemption to donations to governments and certain other organizations.

## S. 43.1 — Income Tax Act, Part I, Division B

**Definitions [s. 43.1]**: "adjusted cost base" — 54, 248(1); "arm's length" — 251(1); "individual" — 248(1); "life estate" — 43.1(1); "person", "property", "registered charity", "taxpayer" — 248(1).

**44. (1) Exchanges of property** — Where at any time in a taxation year (in this subsection referred to as the "initial year") an amount has become receivable by a taxpayer as proceeds of disposition of a capital property (in this section referred to as the taxpayer's "former property") that is either

### Proposed Amendment — 44(1) opening words

**44. (1) Exchanges of property** — Where at any time in a taxation year (in this subsection referred to as the "initial year") an amount has become receivable by a taxpayer as proceeds of disposition of a capital property that is not a share of the capital stock of a corporation (which capital property is in this section referred to as the taxpayer's "former property") that is either

**Application**: Bill C-43 (First Reading September 20, 2000), s. 16, will amend the opening words of subsec. 44(1) to read as above, applicable to shares disposed of after April 15, 1999 other than shares disposed of after that date as a consequence of a public takeover bid or offer filed with a public authority before April 16, 1999.

**Technical Notes**: Section 44 allows a taxpayer to defer in certain circumstances the recognition of a capital gain in respect of property.

Subsection 44(1) allows a taxpayer who incurs a capital gain on the disposition of certain capital property to defer tax on the gain to the extent that the taxpayer reinvests the proceeds in a replacement property within a certain period of time.

Subsection 44(1) is amended to provide that the replacement property provisions do not apply to shares of the capital stock of a corporation.

**Department of Finance news release, April 15, 1999**: *Tax Rollover for Canadian Shareholders of Foreign Corporations*

[For the first portion of this news release, see under 85.1(6) — ed.]

Under the "replacement property rules" in section 44 of the *Income Tax Act*, a taxpayer can defer the recognition of a gain arising on an involuntary disposition of property to the extent that the proceeds of disposition for such property are used to purchase a replacement property. The replacement property rules are not intended to apply to the disposition of shares. Consequently, the rules are proposed to be amended to exclude, after today's date, the disposition of shares of a corporation. [However, 85(1), 85.1(1), 85.1(5), 86, 86.1 or 87 may be available in some cases — ed.]

For further information: Davine Roach, Tax Policy Branch, (613) 992-4852; Karl Littler, Secretary of State (International Financial Institutions), (613) 996-7861; Jean-Michel Catta, Public Affairs and Operations Division, (613) 992-1574.

(a) property the proceeds of disposition of which are described in paragraph (b), (c) or (d) of the definition "proceeds of disposition" in subsection 13(21) or paragraph (b), (c) or (d) of the definition "proceeds of disposition" in section 54, or

(b) a property that was, immediately before the disposition, a former business property of the taxpayer,

and the taxpayer has

(c) where the former property is described in paragraph (a), before the end of the second taxation year following the initial year, and

(d) in any other case, before the end of the first taxation year following the initial year,

acquired a capital property that is a replacement property for the taxpayer's former property and the replacement property has not been disposed of by the taxpayer before the time the taxpayer disposed of the taxpayer's former property, notwithstanding subsection 40(1), if the taxpayer so elects under this subsection in the taxpayer's return of income for the year in which the taxpayer acquired the replacement property,

(e) the gain for a particular taxation year from the disposition of the taxpayer's former property shall be deemed to be the amount, if any, by which

(i) where the particular year is the initial year, the lesser of

(A) the amount, if any, by which the proceeds of disposition of the former property exceed

(I) in the case of depreciable property, the lesser of the proceeds of disposition of the former property computed without reference to subsection (6) and the total of its adjusted cost base to the taxpayer immediately before the disposition and any outlays and expenses to the extent that they were made or incurred by the taxpayer for the purpose of making the disposition, and

(II) in any other case, the total of its adjusted cost base to the taxpayer immediately before the disposition and any outlays and expenses to the extent that they were made or incurred by the taxpayer for the purpose of making the disposition, and

(B) the amount, if any, by which the proceeds of disposition of the former property exceed the total of the cost to the taxpayer, or in the case of depreciable property, the capital cost to the taxpayer, determined without reference to paragraph (f), of the taxpayer's replacement property and any outlays and expenses to the extent that they were made or incurred by the taxpayer for the purpose of making the disposition, or

(ii) where the particular year is subsequent to the initial year, the amount, if any, claimed by the taxpayer under subparagraph (iii) in computing the taxpayer's gain for the immediately preceding year from the disposition of the former property,

exceeds

(iii) subject to subsection (1.1), such amount as the taxpayer claims,

(A) in the case of an individual (other than a trust), in prescribed form filed with the taxpayer's return of income under this Part for the particular year, and

(B) in any other case, in the taxpayer's return of income under this Part for the particular year,

as a deduction, not exceeding the lesser of

(C) a reasonable amount as a reserve in respect of such of the proceeds of disposition of the former property that are payable to the taxpayer after the end of the particular year as can reasonably be regarded as a portion of the amount determined under subparagraph (i) in respect of the property, and

(D) an amount equal to the product obtained when $1/5$ of the amount determined under subparagraph (i) in respect of the property is multiplied by the amount, if any, by which 4 exceeds the number of preceding taxation years of the taxpayer ending after the disposition of the property, and

(f) the cost to the taxpayer or, in the case of depreciable property, the capital cost to the taxpayer, of the taxpayer's replacement property at any time after the time the taxpayer disposed of the taxpayer's former property, shall be deemed to be

(i) the cost to the taxpayer or, in the case of depreciable property, the capital cost to the taxpayer of the taxpayer's replacement property otherwise determined,

minus

(ii) the amount, if any, by which the amount determined under clause (e)(i)(A) exceeds the amount determined under clause (e)(i)(B).

**Related Provisions**: 13(4) — Parallel rule for CCA recapture; 14(6) — Parallel rule for eligible capital property; 44(4) — Deemed election; 44(5) — Replacement property; 44(6) — Deemed proceeds of disposition; 72(1)(c) — No reserve for year of death; 72(2)(b) — Election by legal representative and transferee re reserves; 79.1(3), (6)(c) — Capital gains reserve where property repossessed by creditor; 87(2)(l.3) — Amalgamations — replacement property acquired by new corporation; 87(2)(m) — Amalgamations — proceeds not due until after end of year; 87(2)(ll) — Amalgamations — continuation of predecessor corporations; 88(1)(d)(i)(C) — Winding-up; 96(3) — Election by members of partnership; 220(3.2), Reg. 600(b) — Late filing of election or revocation.

**Notes**: 44(1) allows a rollover of the cost base of property, and deferral of accrued capital gain, where the property is replaced (see 44(5)) and was a "former business property" (as defined in 248(1)), was expropriated, or was stolen or destroyed and paid for by insurance. For the parallel rule preventing recapture of capital cost allowance (CCA), see 13(4).

The phrase "immediately before the disposition" in 44(1)(b) has been interpreted very liberally by the courts, so that it does not mean "immediately before" at all. See *Macklin*, [1993] 1 C.T.C. 21 (FCTD).

44(1) between (d) and (e) amended by 1995-97 technical bill, effective for dispositions of former properties after the 1993 taxation year. For earlier dispositions, since April 1977, read:

acquired a capital property (in this section referred to as the taxpayer's "replacement property") as a replacement for the taxpayer's former property and the taxpayer's replacement property has not been disposed of by the taxpayer prior to the time the taxpayer disposed of the taxpayer's former property, notwithstanding subsection 40(1), if the taxpayer so elects under this subsection in the taxpayer's return of income under this Part for the year in which the taxpayer acquired the replacement property,

The amendment was consequential on amendments to subsection 44(5). Generally, the condition requiring a taxpayer to acquire a property as a replacement for the taxpayer's former property was moved to 44(5).

44(1)(e)(iii) amended by 1991 technical bill, effective 1990, to add clause (A) requiring an individual to file a prescribed form to make this claim.

44(1)(e)(iii)(C) amended by 1994 tax amendments bill (Part I), effective for taxation years that end after February 21, 1994, to change "not due to the taxpayer until after" to "payable to the taxpayer after". The purpose of the amendment is to avoid penalizing creditors who exercise "acceleration" clauses pursuant to an agreement under which the creditor sold property and received, as part of the consideration, a note payable by the purchaser of the property. The acceleration clause would typically be exercised only if the purchaser defaulted on its obligations to a creditor.

The draft legislation of July 12, 1994 had proposed a formula for 44(1)(e)(iii)(C) that was the same as the calculation that Revenue Canada has always used on an administrative basis for calculating a "reasonable" reserve (see Interpretation Bulletin IT-236R3, para. 4). That calculation was not included in the 1994 tax amendments bill, however, so the determination of a "reasonable" reserve is still open to interpretation.

**Remission Orders**: *Telesat Canada Remission Order*, P.C. 1999-1335.

**Interpretation Bulletins**: IT-491: Former business property. See also list at end of s. 44.

**Information Circulars**: 92-1: Guidelines for accepting late, amended or revoked elections.

**Forms**: T1030: Election to allow individuals (other than trusts) the recognition of a capital gain re dispositions of capital property after 1990 *et seq.*; T2069: Election in respect of amounts not deductible as reserves for the year of death.

## (1.1) Farm property disposed of to child —
Where the former property referred to in subparagraph (1)(e)(iii) is real property in respect of the disposition of which the rules in subsection 73(3) apply, in computing the amount of any claim in respect of that property under that subparagraph, it shall be read as if the references therein to "$1/5$" and "4" were references to "$1/10$" and "9" respectively.

**Notes**: 44(1.1) added by 1981 Budget, effective with respect to dispositions occurring after November 12, 1981 otherwise than pursuant to the terms in existence on November 12, 1981 of an offer or agreement in writing made or entered into on or before that date or otherwise than by virtue of an event referred to in 54(h)(ii), (iii) or (iv) [now 54"proceeds of disposition"(b), (c) or (d)] that occurred on or before that date. Where it applies, it extends the capital gains reserve period from 5 years to 10 years.

**(2) Time of disposition and of receipt of proceeds** — For the purposes of this Act, the time at which a taxpayer has disposed of a property for which there are proceeds of disposition as described in paragraph (b), (c) or (d) of the definition "proceeds of disposition" in subsection 13(21) or paragraph (b), (c) or (d) of the definition "proceeds of disposition" in section 54, and the time at which an amount, in respect of those proceeds of disposition has become receivable by the taxpayer shall be deemed to be the earliest of

(a) the day the taxpayer has agreed to an amount as full compensation to the taxpayer for the property lost, destroyed, taken or sold;

(b) where a claim, suit, appeal or other proceeding has been taken before one or more tribunals or courts of competent jurisdiction, the day on which the taxpayer's compensation for the property is finally determined by those tribunals or courts;

(c) where a claim, suit, appeal or other proceeding referred to in paragraph (b) has not been taken before a tribunal or court of competent jurisdiction within two years of the loss, destruction or taking of the property, the day that is two years following the day of the loss, destruction or taking;

(d) the time at which the taxpayer is deemed by section 70 or paragraph 128.1(4)(b) to have disposed of the property, and

(e) where the taxpayer is a corporation other than a subsidiary corporation referred to in subsection 88(1), the time immediately before the winding-up of the corporation,

and the taxpayer shall be deemed to have owned the property continuously until the time so determined.

**Related Provisions**: 59.1 — Involuntary disposition of resource property; 70(10), (11) — Definitions.

**Notes**: 44(2)(d) amended by 1993 technical bill to change reference from s. 48 to 128.1(4)(b), effective 1993. Where a corporation continued before 1993 elects for new 250(5.1) to apply earlier (see Notes to 250(5.1)), the amendment is effective from the corporation's "time of continuation".

**Interpretation Bulletins**: IT-125R4: Dispositions of resource properties; IT-185R: Losses from theft, defalcation or embezzlement; IT-259R3: Exchanges of property; IT-271R: Expropriations — time and proceeds of disposition.

**(3) Where subsec. 70(3) does not apply** — Subsection 70(3) does not apply to compensation referred to in paragraph (b), (c) or (d) of the definition "proceeds of disposition" in subsection 13(21) or paragraph (b), (c) or (d) of the definition "proceeds of disposition" in section 54 that has been transferred or distributed to beneficiaries or other persons beneficially interested in an estate or trust.

**(4) Deemed election** — Where a former property of a taxpayer was a depreciable property of the taxpayer

(a) if the taxpayer has elected in respect of that property under subsection (1), the taxpayer shall be deemed to have elected in respect thereof under subsection 13(4); and

(b) if the taxpayer has elected in respect of that property under subsection 13(4), the taxpayer shall be deemed to have elected in respect thereof under subsection (1).

**(5) Replacement property** — For the purposes of this section, a particular capital property of a taxpayer is a replacement property for a former property of the taxpayer, if

(a) it is reasonable to conclude that the property was acquired by the taxpayer to replace the former property;

(a.1) it was acquired by the taxpayer and used by the taxpayer or a person related to the taxpayer for a use that is the same as or similar to the use to which the taxpayer or a person related to the taxpayer put the former property;

(b) where the former property was used by the taxpayer or a person related to the taxpayer for the purpose of gaining or producing income from a business, the particular capital property was acquired for the purpose of gaining or producing income from that or a similar business or for use by a person related to the taxpayer for such a purpose;

(c) where the former property was a taxable Canadian property of the taxpayer, the particular capital property is a taxable Canadian property of the taxpayer; and

(d) where the former property was a taxable Canadian property (other than treaty-protected property) of the taxpayer, the particular capital property is a taxable Canadian property (other than treaty-protected property) of the taxpayer.

**Notes**: To qualify for rollover as replacement property, the former property must have actually been used, not simply intended to be used: *Glaxo Wellcome Inc.*, [1999] 4 C.T.C. 371 (FCA). For an example of a farming property that was found to be "used" in the same manner as the former property, and thus qualified as "replacement property", see *Depaoli*, [1996] 3 C.T.C. 2640 (TCC), aff'd [2000] 1 C.T.C. 6 (FCA).

44(5)(c) amended and (d) added by 1998 Budget, effective for any disposition that occurs in a taxation year that end after 1997. For earlier dispositions, read:

(c) where the former property was taxable Canadian property (or would have been taxable Canadian property if the taxpayer were non-resident throughout the year in which the former property was disposed of and the former property were used in a business carried on by the taxpayer), the particular capital property was taxable Canadian property (or would have been taxable Canadian property if the taxpayer were non-resident throughout the year in which the particular capital property was acquired and the particular capital property were used in a business carried on by the taxpayer).

44(5)(a) replaced by new (a) and (a.1) by 1995-97 technical bill, effective for dispositions of former properties after the 1993 taxation year except that, where a taxpayer elects in respect of a former property that was disposed of before June 18, 1998 by notifying Revenue Canada in writing on or before the filing-due date for the taxpayer's first taxation year that ends after June 18, 1998, 44(5)(a.1) shall, for the purpose of determining whether a property is a replacement property of the former property, be read as follows:

(a.1) it was acquired by the taxpayer for a use that is the same as or similar to the use to which the taxpayer or a person related to the taxpayer put the former property;

Before the amendment (i.e., generally up to the 1993 taxation year), read:

(a) it was acquired by the taxpayer for the same or a similar use as the use to which the taxpayer or a person related to the taxpayer put the former property;

New 44(5)(a) was formerly 44(1) between (d) and (e); the former para. (a) is now (a.1), but was expanded to allow use by a related person (e.g., where a taxpayer rents the acquired property to a subsidiary corporation which uses it in the same or similar business).

44(5)(a) to (c) amended by 1991 technical bill, paras. (a) [now (a.1)] and (b) effective for dispositions of former properties after July 13, 1990, and para. (c) effective for property acquired as a replacement for a former property disposed of after April 2, 1990, other than a former property disposed of

(a) under an agreement in writing entered into before April 3, 1990; or

(b) pursuant to a written notice of an intention to take the property under statutory authority given before April 3, 1990 or for the sale price of the property sold to a person by whom such a notice was given before April 3, 1990.

For earlier cases, read:

(a) it was acquired by the taxpayer for the same or a similar use as the use to which the taxpayer put the former property;

(b) where the former property was used by the taxpayer for the purpose of gaining or producing income from a business, the particular capital property was acquired for the purpose of gaining or producing income from that or a similar business; and

(c) where the taxpayer was not resident in Canada at the time the taxpayer acquired the particular capital property, in addition to the requirements in paragraphs (a) and (b), the particular capital property was taxable Canadian property.

**Interpretation Bulletins**: IT-259R3: Exchanges of property; IT-271R: Expropriations — time and proceeds of disposition.

**(6) Deemed proceeds of disposition** — Where a taxpayer has disposed of property that was a former business property and was in part a building and in part the land (or an interest therein) subjacent to, or immediately contiguous to and necessary for the use of, the building, for the purposes of this subdivision, the amount if any, by which

(a) the proceeds of disposition of one such part determined without regard to this subsection

exceed

(b) the adjusted cost base to the taxpayer of that part

shall, to the extent that the taxpayer so elects in the taxpayer's return of income under this Part for the year in which the taxpayer acquired a replacement property for the former business property, be deemed not to be proceeds of disposition of that part and to be proceeds of disposition of the other part.

**Related Provisions**: 96(3) — Election by members of partnership; 220(3.2), Reg. 600(b) — Late filing of election or revocation; 248(4) — Interest in real property.

**Notes**: Opening words of 44(6) amended by 1993 technical bill, effective for dispositions after December 21, 1992, to change "subjacent to or necessary" to "subjacent to, or immediately contiguous to and necessary"; and to change "for the purposes of subsection (1)" to "for the purposes of this subdivision". The second change means that the reallocated proceeds of disposition in respect of the land and building apply for purposes of the capital gains determination under 40(1) as well as for 44(1).

**Interpretation Bulletins**: IT-271R: Expropriations — time and proceeds of disposition; IT-259R3: Exchanges of property.

**Information Circulars**: 92-1: Guidelines for accepting late, amended or revoked elections.

**(7) Where subpara. (1)(e)(iii) does not apply** — Subparagraph (1)(e)(iii) does not apply to permit a taxpayer to claim any amount under that subparagraph in computing a gain for a taxation year where

(a) the taxpayer, at the end of the year or at any time in the immediately following year, was not resident in Canada or was exempt from tax under any provision of this Part; or

(b) the person to whom the former property of the taxpayer was disposed of was a corporation that, immediately after the disposition,

(i) was controlled, directly or indirectly in any manner whatever, by the taxpayer,

(ii) was controlled, directly or indirectly in any manner whatever, by a person or group of persons by whom the taxpayer was controlled, directly or indirectly in any manner whatever, or

(iii) controlled the taxpayer, directly or indirectly in any manner whatever, where the taxpayer is a corporation.

**Related Provisions**: 256(5.1), (6.2) — Controlled directly or indirectly — control in fact.

**(8) Application of subsec. 70(10)** — The definitions in subsection 70(10) apply to this section.

**Notes**: 44(8) added in the R.S.C. (5th Supp.) consolidation, effective for taxation years ending after November 1991. This rule was formerly in the opening words to subsec. 70(10).

**Definitions [s. 44]**: "amount" — 248(1); "adjusted cost base" — 54, 248(1); "beneficially interested" — 248(25); "business" — 248(1); "capital property" — 54, 248(1); "child" — 44(8), 70(10), 252(1); "controlled directly or indirectly" — 256(5.1), (6.2); "corporation" — 248(1), *Interpretation Act* 35(1); "depreciable property" — 13(21), 248(1); "disposition" — 54 [to be repealed], 248(1) [draft]; "farming" — 248(1); "former business property" — 248(1); "former property" — 44(1); "individual" — 248(1); "interest" — (in real property) 248(4); "prescribed" — 248(1); "proceeds of disposition" — 54; "property" — 248(1); "resident in Canada" — 250; "replacement property" — 44(5); "share", "taxable Canadian property" — 248(1); "taxation year" — 249; "taxpayer", "treaty-protected property" — 248(1); "trust" — 104(1), 248(1), (3).

**Interpretation Bulletins [s. 44]**: IT-259R3: Exchanges of property; IT-271R: Expropriations — time and proceeds of disposition.

Part I                                    Income Tax Act, Part I, Division B

## Proposed Addition — 44.1 — Small Business Share Rollover

**Technical Notes**: New section 44.1 permits an individual to defer, in certain circumstances, the recognition for income tax purposes of all or a portion of a capital gain arising on a disposition of an eligible small business investment.

This new section applies to disposition that occur after February 27, 2000.

### 44.1 (1) [Small business share rollover] Definitions — The definitions in this subsection apply in this section.

**"ACB reduction"** of an individual in respect of a replacement share of the individual in respect of a qualifying disposition of the individual means the amount determined by the formula

$$D \times (E/F)$$

where

- D  is the permitted deferral of the individual in respect of the qualifying disposition;
- E  is the qualifying cost to the individual of the replacement share; and
- F  is the qualifying cost to the individual of all the replacement shares of the individual in respect of the qualifying disposition.

**Technical Notes**: The term "ACB reduction" is relevant for the purpose of new paragraph 44.1(2)(b). An individual's ACB reduction in respect of a replacement share of an individual in respect of a qualifying disposition is determined as that proportion of the permitted deferral of the individual in respect of the qualifying disposition that the qualifying cost to the individual of the replacement share is of the qualifying cost to the individual of all replacement shares. The ACB reduction reduces the adjusted cost base to the individual of the replacement share under paragraph 44.1(2)(b) and subparagraph 53(2)(b)(i).

**"active business corporation"** at any time means, subject to subsection (10), a corporation that is, at that time, a taxable Canadian corporation all or substantially all of the fair market value of the assets of which at that time is attributable to assets of the corporation that are

(a) assets used principally in an active business carried on by the corporation or by an active business corporation that is related to the corporation;

(b) shares issued by or debt owing by other active business corporations that are related to the corporation; or

(c) a combination of assets described in paragraphs (a) and (b).

**Technical Notes**: The term "active business corporation" is relevant for the purposes of the term "qualifying disposition" and new subsection 44.1(6). An active business corporation at any time is a taxable Canadian corporation all or substantially all of the fair market value of the assets of which, at that time, is attributable to assets of the corporation that are

- used principally in an active business carried on by the corporation or by an active business corporation related to it,
- shares or debt of other active business corporations related to the corporation, or
- a combination of those types of assets.

Pursuant to new subsection 44.1(10), a professional corporation, a specified financial institution, a corporation that the principal business of which is the leasing, rental, development of sale or any combination thereof of real property owned by it, or a corporation that more than 50 per cent of the fair market value of the property of which is attributable to real property are excluded from this definition.

**Related Provisions**: 44.1(8) — Special rule re carrying on an active business; 44.1(10) — Exclusions to definition.

**"carrying value"** of the assets of a corporation at any time means the amount at which the assets of the corporation would be valued for the purpose of the corporation's balance sheet as of that time if that balance sheet were prepared in accordance with generally accepted accounting principles used in Canada at that time, except that an asset of a corporation that is a share or debt issued by a related corporation is deemed to have a carrying value of nil.

**Technical Notes**: The term "carrying value" is relevant for the purpose of the term "eligible small business corporation share". The carrying value of the assets of a corporation at any time is the amount at which its assets would be valued for the purpose of its balance sheet if that balance sheet were prepared in accordance with generally accepted accounting principles used in Canada. An exception is that an asset of the corporation that is a share or a debt issued by a related corporation is deemed to have a carrying value of nil.

**Related Provisions**: 248(24) — Equity and consolidation methods of accounting not to be used.

**Regulations**: 6204 (prescribed share).

**"common share"** means a share prescribed for the purpose of paragraph 110(1)(d).

**Technical Notes**: The term "common share" is relevant for the purposes of the definition "eligible small business corporation share" and new subsection 44.1(7). A common share is a share prescribed by subsection 6204(1) of the *Income Tax Regulations* for the purpose of paragraph 110(1)(d).

**"eligible pooling arrangement"** in respect of an individual means an agreement in writing made between the individual and another person or partnership (which other person or partnership is referred to in this definition and subsection (3) as the "investment manager") where the agreement provides for

(a) the transfer of funds or other property by the individual to the investment manager for the purpose of making investments on behalf of the individual;

(b) the purchase of eligible small business corporation shares with those funds, or the proceeds of a disposition of the other property, within 60 days after receipt of those funds or the other property by the investment manager; and

(c) the provision of a statement of account to the individual by the investment manager at the end of each month that ends after the transfer disclosing the details of the investment portfolio held by the investment manager on behalf of the individual at the end of that month and the details of the transactions made by the investment manager on behalf of the individual during the month.

**Technical Notes**: The term "eligible pooling arrangement" is relevant for the purpose of new subsection 44.1(3). An eligible pooling arrangement is an agreement in writing made between an individual and another person or partnership (the investment manager) where the terms and conditions of the agreement provide

- for the transfer of funds or other property by the individual to the investment manager,
- the use of the funds or proceeds from the sale of the property by the investment manager to purchase eligible small business corporation shares on behalf of the individual within 60 days of the receipt of the funds or property, and
- a monthly reporting to the individual by the investment manager of the securities transactions made on behalf of the individual.

**"eligible small business corporation"** at any time means, subject to subsection (10), a corporation that, at that time, is a Canadian-controlled private corporation all or substantially all of the fair market value of the assets of which at that time is attributable to assets of the corporation that are

(a) assets used principally in an active business carried on primarily in Canada by the corporation or by an eligible small business corporation that is related to the corporation;

(b) shares issued by or debt owing by other eligible small business corporations that are related to the corporation; or

(c) a combination of assets described in paragraphs (a) and (b).

**Technical Notes**: The term "eligible small business corporation" is relevant for the purposes of the term "eligible small business corporation share". An eligible small business corporation, at a particular time, means a Canadian-controlled private corporation all or substantially all of the fair market value of the assets of which is, at that time, attributable to assets of the corporation that are

- assets used principally in an active business carried on primarily in Canada by the corporation or an eligible small business corporation related to it,
- shares of or debt issued by other eligible small business corporations related to the corporation, or
- a combination of those two types of assets.

An exception is that an asset of the corporation that is a share or a debt issued by a related corporation is deemed to have a carrying value of nil.

**Related Provisions**: 44.1(8) — Special rule re carrying on an active business; 44.1(10) — Exclusions to definition.

**"eligible small business corporation share"** of an individual means a common share issued by a corporation to the individual if

(a) at the time the share was issued, the corporation was an eligible small business corporation; and

(b) immediately before and after the share was issued, the total carrying value of the assets of the corporation and corporations related to it did not exceed $50,000,000.

**Technical Notes**: The term "eligible small business corporation share" of an individual is relevant for the purposes of the term "qualifying disposition" of an individual and new subsections 44.1(6) and (7). An eligible small business corporation share of an individual is a common share issued by a corporation to the individual where at the time the share is issued the corporation was an eligible small business corporation and immediately before and after that time it's the total carrying value carrying value of its assets and the assets of corporations related to it does not exceed $50 million.

**"permitted deferral"** of an individual in respect of a qualifying disposition of the individual means the amount determined by the formula

$$(G/H) \times I$$

where

G is the lesser of the amount included in the description of H and the total of all amounts each of which is the qualifying cost to the individual of a replacement share in respect of the qualifying disposition;

H is the qualifying portion of the individual's proceeds of disposition from the qualifying disposition; and

I is the qualifying portion of the individual's capital gain from the qualifying disposition.

**Technical Notes**: An individual's "permitted deferral" in respect of a qualifying disposition is the amount of a capital gain from the disposition that can be deferred. It reduces the gain otherwise determined of the individual for the qualifying disposition. It is determined as that portion of the qualifying portion of the capital gain of the individual from a qualifying disposition of the individual that the total of the qualifying cost to the individual of replacement shares in respect of the disposition is of the qualifying proceeds of disposition of the individual in respect of the disposition.

**Related Provisions**: 44.1(12) — Anti-avoidance — permitted deferral deemed nil.

**"qualifying cost"** to an individual of particular replacement shares of the individual in respect of a qualifying disposition of the individual that are shares of the capital stock of a particular eligible small business corporation means the lesser of

(a) the total of all amounts each of which is the cost to the individual of such a replacement share; and

(b) the amount by which $2,000,000 exceeds the total of all amounts each of which is the cost to the individual of a share that was a share of the capital stock of the particular eligible small business corporation or of a corporation related to it at the time the particular replacement shares were acquired and that was a replacement share of the individual in respect of another qualifying disposition.

**Technical Notes**: The term "qualifying cost" of an individual of replacement shares of the individual in respect of a particular qualifying disposition of the individual is relevant in computing the individual's permitted deferral in respect of the qualifying disposition. The qualifying cost is the lesser of two amounts. The first is the cost of the replacement shares issued by the particular eligible small business corporation. The second is the amount by which $2,000,000 exceeds the total of the cost of all other replacement shares in respect of other qualifying dispositions of the individual at or before the time of the qualifying disposition that were shares of the particular eligible small business corporation or an eligible small business corporation related to it at the time the share was acquired.

**"qualifying disposition"** of an individual (other than a trust) means, subject to subsection (9), a disposition of shares of the capital stock of a corporation where each such share disposed of was,

(a) an eligible small business corporation share of the individual;

(b) throughout the period during which the individual owned the share, a common share of an active business corporation; and

(c) throughout the 185-day period that ended immediately before the disposition of the share, owned by the individual.

**Technical Notes**: The term "qualifying disposition" of an individual is relevant for the purposes of the term "permitted deferral" and subsection 44.1(2). An individual can have a capital gain deferral only in respect a gain arising on a qualifying disposition of the individual. A qualifying disposition of an individual is a disposition of common shares of the capital stock of a corporation owned by the individual where each such share was a an eligible small business corporation share of the individual, was a common share of the capital stock of an active business corporation throughout the time it was owned by the individual and was owned by the individual throughout the 185-day period that ended immediately before the disposition. Pursuant to new subsection 44.1(9), the active business of the corporation referred to in the definition "active business corporation" has to be carried on primarily in Canada, at all times in the period that began when the individual last acquired the share and ended when the disposition occurred (the "ownership period"), if that period is less than 730 days. In any other case that active business has to be carried on primarily in Canada for at least 730 days during the ownership period.

**Related Provisions**: 44.1(9) — Special rule re qualifying disposition.

**"qualifying portion of a capital gain"** of an individual from a particular qualifying disposition of the individual means the amount determined by the formula

$$J \times (1 - (K/L))$$

where

J is the individual's capital gain from the particular qualifying disposition, determined without reference to this section;

K is the amount, if any, by which the total of

(a) the total of all amounts each of which is the adjusted cost base to the individual of a share of the particular corporation that was the subject of the particular qualifying disposition (which adjusted cost base shall be determined immediately before the share was disposed of and without reference to this section), and

(b) the total of all amounts each of which is the adjusted cost base to the individual of a share of the particular corporation or a corporation related to it at the time of the particular qualifying disposition that was the subject of another qualifying disposition (in respect of which a permitted deferral was deducted under this section by the individual) that occurred at or before the time of the particular qualifying disposition (which adjusted cost base shall be determined immediately before the share was disposed of and without reference to this section)

exceeds

(c) $ 2,000,000; and

L is the total of all amounts each of which is the adjusted cost base to the individual of a share of the particular corporation that was the subject of the particular qualifying disposition (which adjusted cost base shall be determined immediately before the share was disposed of and without reference to this section).

**Technical Notes**: The term "qualifying portion of a capital gain" of an individual from a qualifying disposition of the individual is relevant for the purpose of the term "permitted deferral". An individual's portion of a capital gain from a particular qualifying disposition of shares of the capital stock of a particular eligible small business corporation is determined as that proportion the capital gain (determined without reference to section 44.1) of the individual from that disposition that can be attributed to the amount of adjusted cost base of shares disposed of that does not exceed the $2,000,000 investment limit. This amount of adjusted cost base is determined by reference to the adjusted cost bases of shares (determined without reference to new section 44.1) of the particular corporation or corporations related to it disposed of in qualifying dispositions of the individual at or before the time of the particular qualifying disposition.

For example, if the individual had a capital gain from a particular qualifying disposition in which the individual sold shares with a total adjusted cost base of $3,000,000, because of the $2,000,000 investment limit, only 2/3 of the gain otherwise determined the capital would be included in the qualifying portion of the capital gain.

**Related Provisions**: 257 — Formula cannot calculate to less than zero.

**"qualifying portion of the proceeds of disposition"** of an individual from a qualifying disposition means the amount determined by the formula

$$M \times (N/O)$$

where

M is the individual's proceeds of disposition from the qualifying disposition;

N is the individual's qualifying portion of the capital gain from the qualifying disposition; and

O is the individual's capital gain from the qualifying disposition, determined without reference to this section.

**Technical Notes**: The term "qualifying portion of the proceeds of disposition" of an individual from a qualifying disposition is relevant for the purposes of the term "permitted deferral". It is determined by multiplying the individual's proceeds of disposition by the fraction that is determined by dividing the individual's qualifying portion of the capital gain from the disposition by the individual's capital gain from the disposition determined without reference to section 44.1. The individual's qualifying portion of the proceeds of disposition represents the maximum amount that the individual can include as the qualifying cost of replacement shares when calculating the permitted deferral of the individual in respect of the qualifying disposition.

**"replacement share"** of an individual in respect of a qualifying disposition of the individual in a taxation year means an eligible small business corporation share, of the individual, that is

(a) acquired by the individual in the year or within 60 days after the end of the year, but not later than 120 days after the qualifying disposition occurred; and

(b) designated by the individual, in the individual's return of income for the year, to be a replacement share in respect of the qualifying disposition.

**Technical Notes**: The term "replacement share" of an individual is relevant for the purposes of the term "permitted deferral". A replacement share of an individual in respect of a particular qualifying disposition of the individual in a taxation year means an eligible small business corporation share that was designated by the individual in the individual's return of income to be a replacement share of the individual in respect of the qualifying disposition and that was acquired by the individual within the year or within 60 days after the year but no later than 120 days after the qualifying disposition.

**(2) Capital gain deferral** — Where an individual has made a qualifying disposition in a taxation year,

(a) the individual's capital gain for the year from the qualifying disposition is deemed to be the amount by which the individual's capital gain for the year from the qualifying disposition, determined without reference to this section, exceeds the individual's permitted deferral in respect of the qualifying disposition;

(b) in computing the adjusted cost base to the individual of a replacement share of the individual in respect of the qualifying disposition at any time after its acquisition, there shall be deducted the amount of the ACB reduction of the individual in respect of the replacement share; and

(c) where the qualifying disposition was a disposition of a share that was a taxable Canadian property of the individual, the replacement share of the individual in respect of the qualifying disposition is deemed to be taxable Canadian property of the individual.

**Technical Notes**: New subsection 44.1(2) permits an individual that has a capital gain, determined without reference to section 44.1, from a qualifying disposition in a taxation year to claim the permitted deferral of the individual in determining the individual's capital gain for the year from the disposition. Where the individual has a permitted deferral in respect of a qualifying disposition, the capital gain from the disposition is deemed to be the amount by which the individual's capital gain (determined without reference to section 44.1) exceeds the permitted deferral. The individual can establish a permitted deferral less than the maximum amount available by designating a lesser amount of replacement shares.

Under the subsection, the adjusted cost base to the individual, determined without reference to section 44.1, of the replacement shares of the individual in respect of the disposition is reduced by the amount of the individual's ACB reduction in respect of such replacement shares.

**Related Provisions**: 53(2)(a)(v) — Reduction in ACB of replacement share as per 44.1(2)(b).

**(3) Special rule — re: eligible pooling arrangements** — Except for the purpose of the definition "eligible pooling arrangement" in this section, any transaction entered into by an investment manager under an eligible pooling arrangement on behalf of an individual is deemed to be a transaction of the individual and not a transaction of the investment manager.

**Technical Notes**: New subsection 44.1(3) provides that any transaction entered into by an investment manager on behalf of an individual under an eligible pooling arrangement is deemed to be a transaction of the individual and not a transaction of the investment manager, except for the purpose of the definition "eligible pooling arrangement".

**Related Provisions**: 44.1(1)"eligible pooling arrangement" — Meaning of "investment manager".

**(4) Special rule — re: acquisitions on death** — For the purpose of this section, a share of the capital stock of a corporation, acquired by an individual as a consequence of the death of a person who is the individual's spouse, common-law partner or parent, is deemed to be a share that was acquired by the individual at the time it was acquired by that person and owned by the individual throughout the period that it was owned by that person, if

(a) where the person was the spouse or common-law partner of the individual, the share was an eligible small business share of the person and subsection 70(6) applied to the individual in respect of the share; or

(b) where the person was the individual's parent, the share was an eligible small business share of the parent and subsection 70(9.2) applied to the individual in respect of the share.

**Technical Notes**: New subsection 44.1(4) provides a special rule in cases where eligible small business corporation shares are acquired by an individual as a consequence of the death of a person who is a spouse, common-law partner or a parent of the individual. Where subsection 70(6) or 70(9.2) applies to the individual in respect of such shares, the individual shall, for the purposes of section 44.1, be deemed to have acquired and owned the shares when they were acquired and owned by the spouse, common-law partner or parent. This rule permits the individual to be in the same position to claim a permitted deferral as the spouse, common-law partner or parent in respect of a capital gain arising on the disposition of such shares.

**(5) Special rule — re: breakdown of relationships** — For the purpose of this section, a share of the capital stock of a corporation, acquired by an individual from a person who was the individual's former spouse or common-law partner as a consequence of the settlement of rights arising out of their marriage or common-law partnership, is deemed to be a share that was acquired by the individual at the time it was acquired by that person and owned by the individual throughout the period that it was owned by that person if the share was an eligible small business share of the person and subsection 73(1) applied to the individual in respect of the share.

**Technical Notes**: New subsection 44.1(5) provides a special rule in cases where eligible small business corporation shares of a former spouse or common-law partner of an individual are acquired by the individual as the consequence of the settlement of rights arising out of their marriage or common-law partnership. Where subsection 73(1) applied to the individual in respect of such shares, the individual is, for the purposes of section 44.1, deemed to have acquired and owned the shares when they were acquired and owned by the former spouse or common-law partner. This rule puts the individual in the same position to claim a permitted deferral as the former spouse or common-law partner in respect of a capital gain arising on the disposition of such shares.

**(6) Special rule — re: eligible small business corporation share exchanges** — For the purpose of this section, where an individual receives shares of the capital stock of a corporation that are eligible small business corporation shares of the individual (in this subsection referred to as the "new shares") as the sole consideration for the disposition of shares issued by another corporation that were eligible small business corporation shares of the individual (in this subsection referred to as the "exchanged shares"), the new shares are deemed to have been owned by the individual throughout the period that the exchanged shares were owned by the individual if

(a) paragraph 85(1)(g) or subsection 85.1(3) or 87(4) applied to the individual in respect of the new shares; and

(b) the individual's total proceeds of disposition of the exchanged shares was equal to the total of all amounts each of which was the individual's adjusted cost base of an exchanged share immediately before the disposition.

**Technical Notes**: New subsection 44.1(6) provides special rules where an individual exchanges an eligible small business corporation share for new eligible small business corporation shares and the only consideration received on the exchange is the new eligible small business corporation shares. Where the individual's proceeds of disposition of the exchanged shares equals the adjusted cost base to the individual of the exchanged shares and paragraph 85(1)(g) or subsection 85.1(3) or 87(4) applies to the individual in respect of the new shares, the new shares are deemed to have been owned by the individual throughout the period that the exchanged shares were owned by the individual. The individual's eligibility to claim a permitted deferral with respect to a gain arising on a disposition of the exchanged shares is rolled over to new shares.

**(7) Special rule — re: active business corporation share exchanges** — For the purpose of this section, where an individual receives common shares of the capital stock of a corporation (in this subsection referred to as the "new shares") as the sole consideration for the disposition of common shares of another corporation (in this subsection referred to as the "exchanged shares"), the new shares are deemed to be eligible small business corporation shares of the individual and shares of the capital stock of an active business corporation that were owned by the individual throughout the period that the exchanged shares were owned by the individual, if

(a) paragraph 85(1)(g) or subsection 85.1(3) or 87(4) applied to the individual in respect of the new shares;

(b) the total of the individual's proceeds of disposition in respect of the disposition of the exchanged shares was equal to the total of the individual's adjusted cost bases immediately before the disposition of such shares; and

(c) the disposition of the exchanged shares was a qualifying disposition of the individual.

**Technical Notes**: New subsection 44.1(7) provides special rules where an individual, in a qualifying disposition, disposes of common shares of an active business corporation for consideration consisting only of new common shares of another active business corporation issued to the individual. Where the individual's proceeds of disposition for the exchanged shares equals the individual's adjusted cost base of those shares and paragraph 85(1)(g) or subsection 85.1(3) or 87(4) applies to the individual in respect of the new shares, the new shares are deemed to be eligible small business shares of the individual that were owned by the individual throughout the period that the exchanged shares were owned by the individual and the new shares are deemed to be shares of an active business corporation that were owned by the individual throughout the period that the exchanged shares were owned by the individual. In effect, the individual's eligibility to claim a permitted deferral with respect to a capital gain arising on a disposition of the exchanged shares is rolled over to new shares.

**(8) Special rule — re: carrying on an active business** — For the purpose of the definitions in subsection (1), a property held at any particular time by a corporation that would, if this Act were read without reference to this subsection, be considered to carry on an active business at that time, is deemed to be used or held by the corporation in the course of carrying on that active business if the property (or other property for which the property is substituted property) was acquired by the corporation, at any time in the 36 month period ending at the particular time, because the corporation

(a) issued a debt or a share of a class of its capital stock in order to acquire money for the purpose of acquiring property to be used in or held in the course of, or making expenditures for the purpose of, earning income from an active business carried on by it;

(b) disposed of property used or held by it in the course of carrying on an active business in order to acquire money for the purpose of acquiring property to be used in or held in the course of, or making expenditures for the purpose of, earning income from an active business carried on by it; or

(c) accumulated income derived from an active business carried on by it in order to acquire property to be used in or held in the course of, or to make expenditures for the purpose of, earning income from an active business carried on by it.

**Technical Notes**: New subsection 44.1(8) is relevant in determining whether a property held by a corporation is considered to be used or held in the course of carrying on an active business (active business property). Property held by a corporation at any particular time will be treated as active business property where that property or property for which that property is substituted property (special purpose property) was acquired by the corporation because it issued a debt or a share of a class of its capital stock, it disposed of property used or held in the course of carrying on an active business or it accumulated its active business earnings in order to acquire money for the purpose of acquiring property to be used in or held in the course of or making expenditures for the purpose of earning income from an active business carried on by the corporation. This rule will apply only where the corporation carries on an active business and the property was acquired within 36 months after the particular time.

**Related Provisions**: 248(12) — Substituted property.

**(9) Special rule — re: qualifying disposition** — A disposition of a common share of an active business corporation (in this subsection referred to as the "subject share") by an individual that, but for this subsection, would be a qualifying disposition of the individual is deemed not to be a qualifying disposition of the individual unless the active business of the corporation referred to in paragraph (a) of the definition "active business corporation" in subsection (1) was carried on primarily in Canada

(a) at all times in the period that began at the time the individual last acquired the subject share and ended at the time of disposition, if that period is less than 730 days; or

(b) in any other case, for at least 730 days in the period referred to in paragraph (a).

**Technical Notes**: New subsection 44.1(9) is relevant in determining whether a disposition is a qualifying disposition. A disposition of a common share of an active business corporation by an individual that would otherwise be a qualifying disposition is deemed not to be a qualifying disposition unless the active business of the corporation referred to in paragraph (a) of the definition "active business corporation" was carried on primarily in Canada, at all times in the period that began when the individual last acquired the share and ended when the disposition occurred (the "ownership period"), if that period is less than 730 days. In any other case that active business has to be carried on primarily in Canada for at least 730 days during the ownership period.

**(10) Special rule — re: exceptions** — For the purpose of this section, an eligible small business corporation and an active business corporation at any time does not include a corporation that is at that time,

(a) a professional corporation;

(b) a specified financial institution;

(c) a corporation the principal business of which is the leasing, rental, development or sale, or any combination of those activities, of real property owned by it; or

(d) a corporation more than 50 per cent of the fair market value of the property of which (net of debts incurred to acquire the property) is attributable to real property.

**Technical Notes**: New subsection 44.1(10) is relevant in determining whether a corporation can qualify as an eligible small business corporation or as an active business corporation. A professional corporation, a specified financial institution, a corporation that the principal business of which is the leasing, rental, development of sale or any combination thereof of real property owned by it, or a corporation more than 50 per cent of the fair market value of the property of which is attributable to real property cannot qualify as an eligible small business corporation or as an active business corporation.

**(11) Determination rule** — In determining whether a share owned by an individual is an eligible small business corporation share of the individual, this Act shall be read without reference to section 48.1.

**Technical Notes**: New subsection 44.1(11) is relevant in determining whether a share is an eligible small business corporation share of an individual for the purpose of section 48.1.

Section 48.1 permits a taxpayer, under certain circumstances, to elect to be treated as having disposed of a share and as having reacquired it at the same amount. Its purpose is to permit the individual to report an accrued gain on a small business share in respect of which the taxpayer would be eligible to claim a capital gains exemption under section 110.6. The deemed reacquisition of the share under section 48.1 prevents the share from qualifying as an eligible small business corporation share of the individual because the share is not deemed to have been acquired from the corporation that issued the share.

New subsection 44.1(11) provides that in determining if a share is an eligible small business corporation, the Act is to be read without reference to section 48.1.

**(12) Anti-avoidance rule** — The permitted deferral of an individual in respect of a qualifying disposition of shares issued by a corporation (in this subsection referred to as "new shares") is deemed to be nil where

(a) the new shares (or shares for which the new shares are substituted property) were issued to the individual or a person related to the individual as part of a series of transactions or events in which

(i) shares of the capital stock of a corporation (in this subsection referred to as the "old shares") were disposed of by the individual or a person related to the individual, or

(ii) the paid-up capital of old shares or the adjusted cost base to the individual or to a person related to the individual of the old shares was reduced;

(b) the new shares (or shares for which the new shares are substituted property) were issued by the corporation that issued the old shares or were issued by a corporation that, at or immediately after the time of issue of those shares, was a corporation that was not dealing at arm's length with the corporation that issued the old shares; and

(c) it is reasonable to conclude that one of the main reasons for the series of transactions or events or a transaction in the series was to permit the individual, persons related to the individual, or the individual and persons related to the individual to become eligible to deduct under subsection (2) permitted deferrals in respect of qualifying dispositions of new shares (or shares substituted for the new shares) the total of which would exceed the total that those persons would have been eligible to deduct under subsection (2) in respect of permitted deferrals in respect of qualifying dispositions of old shares.

**Technical Notes**: New subsection 44.1(12) is an anti-avoidance rule. It applies where an individual or persons related to the individual dispose of shares of a particular corporation (which would normally result in the use of the corporate reorganisation rules or a return of paid-up capital of shares of the corporation) and acquire new shares of the particular corporation or a corporation that does not deal at arm's length with the particular corporation principally for the purpose of increasing the total amount of permitted deferrals with respect to qualifying dispositions of the individual and the related persons. Where the rule applies, the permitted deferral with respect to qualifying dispositions of the new shares is deemed to be nil.

For example, the rule will apply in cases where:

- a corporation reorganises its capital using section 86 in order to give its shareholders small business shares in exchange for its shares that did not qualify as small business shares in order to increase the amount of permitted deferrals in respect of qualifying dispositions of the shareholders;

- a corporate reorganisation is undertaken by a particular corporation principally in order to reduce the adjusted cost base of shares in order to increase the amount of permitted deferral of its shareholders with respect to qualifying dispositions of the shareholders;

- paid-up capital of shares of a particular corporation is returned to its shareholders followed by a subscription by the shareholders of shares issued by the particular corporation or a related corporation in order to increase the amount of permitted deferrals of the shareholders in respect of qualifying dispositions.

**Related Provisions**: 248(12) — Substituted property.

**Application**: The December 21, 2000 draft legislation, s. 17, will add s. 44.1, applicable to dispositions that occur after February 27, 2000 except that, for dispositions that occurred after February 27, 2000 and before October 18, 2000,

(a) the definition "active business corporation" shall be read without reference to the words "subject to subsection (10)" and as if the reference to the words "carried on" in para. (a) of that definition were read as a reference to "carried on primarily in Canada";

(b) the definition "eligible small business corporation" shall be read without reference to the words "subject to subsection (10)";

(c) the definition "eligible small business corporation share" shall be read as follows:

"'eligible small business corporation share" of an individual means a common share issued by a corporation to the individual if

(a) at the time the share was issued, the corporation was an eligible small business corporation;

(b) immediately before the share was issued, the total carrying value of the assets of the corporation and corporations related to it did not exceed $2,500,000; and

(c) immediately after the share was issued, the total carrying value of the assets of the corporation and corporations related to it did not exceed $10,000,000;"

(d) the definition "qualifying cost" shall be read as if the reference to "$2,000,000" in para. (b) of that definition were read as a reference to "$500,000";

(e) the definition "qualifying disposition" shall be read without reference to the words "subject to subsection (9)";

(f) the definition "qualifying portion of a capital gain" shall be read as if the reference to "$2,000,000" in para. (c) of the description of K in that definition were read as a reference to "$500,000"; and

(g) s. 44.1 shall be read without reference to subsecs. 44.1(9) and (10).

**Technical Notes**: New section 44.1 applies to dispositions after February 27, 2000 except that, for dispositions after February 27, 2000 and before October 18, 2000,

- the definition "active business corporation" in subsection 44.1(1), is to be read without reference to the words "subject to subsection (10)" and as if the reference to the words "carried on" were read as reference to the words "carried on primarily in Canada",

- the definition "eligible small business corporation" in subsection 44.1(1) is to be read without reference to the words "subject to subsection (10)",

- the definition "eligible small business corporation share" in subsection 44.1(1), is to be read as:

    "eligible small business corporation share" of an individual means a common share issued by a corporation to the individual if

    (a) at the time the share was issued, the corporation was an eligible small business corporation;

    (b) immediately before the share was issued, the total carrying value of the assets of the corporation and corporations related to it did not exceed $2,500,000; and

    (c) immediately after the share was issued, the total carrying value of the assets of the corporation and corporations related to it did not exceed $10,000,000,

- the definition "qualifying cost" in subsection 44.1(1), is to be read as if the reference to "$2,000,000" in subparagraph (b) thereof were read as a reference "$500,000",

- the definition "qualifying disposition" in subsection 44.1(1), is to be read without reference to the words "subject to subsection (9)",

- the definition "qualifying portion of a capital gain" in subsection 44.1(1), is to be read as if the reference to "$2,000,000" in paragraph (c) in the description of K in that definition were read as a reference to "$500,000" and section 44.1, is to be read without reference to subsections (9) and (10) thereof, and

- section 44.1 is to be read without reference to subsections (9) and (10).

*Example 1*

The following example demonstrates the determinations required under section 44.1 for dispositions after October 17, 2000.

*Facts*

An individual makes a qualifying disposition of shares of corporation A with an adjusted cost base of $3,000,000 for proceeds of disposition of $4,500,000.

The individual purchases replacement shares in corporations B with a cost of $2,200,000 and in corporation C with a cost of $2,300,000.

*Determinations*

The capital gain of the individual otherwise determined is $1,500,000 ($4,500,000 − $3,000,000).

The qualifying portion of the capital gain of the individual from the disposition is determined to be $1,000,000 by the formula $J \times (1 - (K/L))$ found in the definition of that expression in section 44.1(1) ($1,500,000 × (1 − $1,000,000/$3,000,000) = $1,000,000) and represents the maximum amount of capital gain that can be deferred.

The qualifying portion of the proceeds of disposition of the individual from the disposition is determined to be $3,000,000 by the formula $M \times (N/O)$ found in the definition of that expression in section 44.1(1) ($4,500,000 × ($1,000,000/$1,500,000) = $3,000,000) and represents the maximum amount of replacement share investments that can be used to determined the maximum permitted deferral in respect of the disposition.

The qualifying cost (subject to the $2,000,000 limit per related group of corporations) of the replacement shares in corporation B is $2,000,000 and in corporation C is $2,000,000 for a total of $4,000,000.

The permitted deferral of the individual in respects of the disposition is determined to be $1,000,000 by the formula $(G/H) \times I$ found in the definition of that expression in section 44.1(1). ($3,000,000/$3,000,000 × $1,000,000 = $1,000,000.)

The capital gain from the disposition after deducting the permitted deferral in respect of the disposition is determined as $1,500,000 − $1,000,000 = $500,000.

The ACB reduction, which is determined by the formula $D \times (E/F)$ found in the definition of that expression in section 44.1(1), of the individual in respect of the replacement shares in corporation B is determined as $1,000,000 × (2,000,000/$4,000,000) = $500,000 and in respect of the replacement shares in corporation C is determined as $1,000,000 × (2,000,000/$4,000,000) = $500,000.

The adjusted cost base to the individual of the replacement shares in Corporation B is determined as ($2,2000,000 − $500,000) = $1,700,000 and of the replacement shares in corporation C ($2,300,000 − $500,000) = $1,800,000.

*Example 2*

The following example demonstrates the determinations required under section 44.1 for dispositions after February 27, 2000 and before October 18, 2000.

*Facts*

An individual makes a qualifying disposition of shares of corporation A with an adjusted cost base of $800,000 for proceeds of disposition of $1,600,000.

The individual purchases replacement shares in corporations B with a cost of $700,000 and in corporation C with a cost of $900,000.

*Determinations*

The capital gain of the individual otherwise determined is $800,000 ($1,600,000 − $800,000).

The qualifying portion of the capital gain of the individual from the disposition is determined to be $500,000 by the formula $J \times (1 − (K/L))$ found in the definition of that expression in section 44.1(1) ($800,000 × (1 − $300,000/$800,000) = $500,000) and represents the maximum amount of capital gain that can be deferred.

The qualifying portion of the proceeds of disposition of the individual from the disposition is determined to be $1,000,000 by the formula $M \times (N/O)$ found in the definition of that expression in section 44.1(1) ($1,600,000 × ($500,000/$800,000) = $1,000,000) and represents the maximum amount of replacement share investments that can be used to determined the maximum permitted deferral in respect of the disposition.

The qualifying cost (subject to the $500,000 limit per related group of corporations) of the replacement shares in corporation B is $500,000 and in corporation C is $500,000 for a total of $1,000,000.

The permitted deferral of the individual in respects of the disposition is determined to be $500,000 by the formula $(G/H) \times I$ found in the definition of that expression in section 44.1(1). ($1,000,000/$1,000,000 × $500,000 = $500,000.)

The capital gain from the disposition after deducting the permitted deferral in respect of the disposition is determined as $800,000 − $500,000 = $300,000.

The ACB reduction, which is determined by the formula $D \times (E/F)$ found in the definition of that expression in section 44.1(1), of the individual in respect of the replacement shares in corporation B is determined as $500,000 × (500,000/$1,000,000) = $250,000 and in respect of the replacement shares in corporation C is determined as $500,000 × (500,000/$1,000,000) = $250,000.

The adjusted cost base to the individual of the replacement shares in Corporation B is determined as ($7000,000 − $250,000) = $450,000 and of the replacement shares in corporation C ($900,000 − $250,000) = $650,000.

**Notice of Ways and Means Motion, Economic Statement, October 18, 2000**: *Capital Gains Deferral*

(15) That, in respect of dispositions that occur after October 17, 2000, the mechanism described in paragraph (11) of the 2000 Budget Notice to allow individuals (other than trusts) to defer the recognition of capital gains in respect of eligible small business investments be applied as if

(a) the investment limit for an eligible small business investment in a corporation or a related group were increased to $2,000,000,

(b) the amount of investment in a corporation or related group in respect of which capital gains deferrals are permitted were increased to $2,000,000,

(c) for the purpose of determining if a treasury share issued by the corporation is an eligible small business investment, the carrying value of assets that a small business corporation can hold immediately before and after an investment were $50 million,

(d) the reference to the word "primarily" in the requirement that all or substantially all of an eligible active business corporation's assets be used in an active business carried on primarily in Canada, or be shares of other related eligible active business corporations, applied only throughout the period that the individual owned the investment (or, if that period is greater than 24 months, during at least 24 months of the period), and

(e) an eligible small business corporation and an eligible active business corporation did not include

(i) a professional corporation,

(ii) a specified financial institution,

(iii) a corporation the principal business of which is the leasing, rental, development or sale or any combination thereof of real property owned by it, or

(iv) a corporation more than 50 per cent of the value of the property of which (net of debts incurred to acquire the property) is attributable to real property.

**Supplementary Information, Economic Statement, October 18, 2000**: *Capital Gains Rollovers for Small Business Investors*

To improve access to capital for small businesses with high growth potential, the 2000 budget introduced a measure that permits individuals to defer limited amounts of capital gains on eligible small business investments to the extent that the proceeds are reinvested in another eligible small business investment.

Currently, the rollover is available on the first $500,000 invested in an eligible small business, which can have no more than $2.5 million in assets immediately before the investment is made and $10 million immediately after the investment. The investment must be in newly issued treasury shares.

Effective immediately, the capital gains rollover measure for small business will be expanded as follows:

- the amount of the original investment on which the deferral will be available will be increased to $2 million from $500,000;

- the amount that can be reinvested in shares of an eligible small business that will qualify for the deferral will be increased to $2 million from $500,000;

- the size of businesses eligible for the rollover will be increased from $10 million to include corporations with no more than $50 million in assets immediately after the investment (the $2.5 million restriction will be eliminated); and

- the eligible business will be required to be primarily carried on in Canada for 24 months while the investor holds the shares.

These changes will expand the small business rollover measure to encompass later-stage financings and help facilitate the growth of small, new-economy companies.

Given that this measure is intended to improve access to capital for small businesses with high growth potential, especially in the fast-growing high-tech industries, specified financial institutions, professional corporations and corporations with significant real estate holdings will not qualify as eligible small businesses.

**Notice of Ways and Means Motion, federal budget, February 28, 2000**: *Capital Gains Deferral*

(11) That a mechanism be introduced to allow individuals (other than trusts) to defer the recognition of capital gains in respect of certain small business investments, in accordance with proposals described in the budget documents tabled by the Minister of Finance in the House of Commons on February 28, 2000.

**Federal budget, supplementary information, February 28, 2000**: *Capital Gain Rollover for Investment in Small Business*

To improve access to capital for small business corporations, the budget proposes to permit individuals a rollover of capital gains on the disposition of a small business investment where the proceeds of disposition are used to make other small business investments. The cost base of the new investment will be reduced by the capital gain deferred in respect of the initial investment.

*Eligible Small Business Investment*

An eligible small business investment will have the following characteristics:

- the investment is in ordinary common shares issued from treasury to the investor;
- the corporation is, at the time the shares are issued, an eligible small business corporation — which will generally be defined as a Canadian-controlled private corporation all or substantially all of the assets of which (measured by value) are used in an active business carried on primarily in Canada, or are shares of other related eligible small business corporations;
- the total carrying value of the assets of the corporation and related corporations does not exceed $2.5 million immediately before the investment is made, and does not exceed $10 million immediately after the investment. There will be look-through rules to account for assets held by the corporation through partnerships and trusts; and
- while the investor holds the shares, the issuing corporation is an eligible active business corporation — which will generally be defined as a taxable Canadian corporation all or substantially all of the assets of which (measured by value) are used in an active business carried on primarily in Canada, or are shares of other related eligible active business corporations.

The measure is designed to accommodate rollovers of gains irrespective of the company's size at the time of sale or the fact that it may have gone public before the sale.

The eligible small business investment must be held for more than six months from the time of acquisition before a gain can be deferred. The replacement eligible investment must be purchased after the beginning of the year of disposition of the original small business investment, and before the earlier of the 120th day following the disposition and the 60th day after the end of the year.

*Eligible Investor*

The measure will be available to individuals (other than trusts). Further, an individual who acquires shares from a related individual on a rollover basis currently provided under the *Income Tax Act* (e.g., on death or marriage breakdown) will be considered for the purpose of this measure to have acquired the shares at the time and under the same circumstances that they were acquired by that related individual.

The measure will also be available to individuals in respect of their capital gains on eligible small business investments that are held through a qualifying pooling arrangement. It is contemplated that such an arrangement will be a special-purpose partnership that is treated for the purpose of these rules as a joint venture — effectively allowing the investment vehicle to act as the investment agent for a number of investors, and to pool investments for those investors, while treating each investor as having his or her own share portfolio within the vehicle.

The issues related to the application of the measure to capital gains realized through a qualifying pooling arrangement will be the subject of consultations with stakeholders and other interested parties.

*Eligible Gains*

The deferral will be available in respect of capital gains realized after February 27, 2000, on up to $500,000 of eligible small business investments (by reference to adjusted cost base) in any particular corporation (or related group) made by an eligible investor or by a qualifying pooling arrangement on behalf of the investor.

*Investment Limit*

A capital gain from the disposition of an eligible investment can be deferred to the extent that the proceeds are reinvested in one or more other eligible small business investments. There are no limits on the total amount of proceeds that can be reinvested, but no amount reinvested in excess of $500,000 in shares of a particular corporation or related group will qualify for additional capital gain deferral.

*Calculation of Capital Gain Deferral*

The maximum capital gain that can be deferred in respect of an eligible capital gain from the disposition of an eligible small business investment is determined by the following formula:

$$(A/B) \times C$$

where:

A = the total cost of all replacement eligible small business investments (not exceeding $500,000 in any particular corporation or related group);

B = the proceeds of disposition that relate to the eligible gain; and

C = the eligible gain from the disposition.

This measure will apply to eligible small business investments disposed of after February 27, 2000.

*Example 1*

On March 31, 2000, Harold sells his shares in Corporation A which are eligible small business investments. His proceeds of disposition are $100,000 and his capital gain is $60,000. On July 1, 2000, Harold invests $90,000 in shares of Corporation B which are new eligible small business investments.

Since Harold reinvests only nine tenths of the proceeds in replacement small business investments, he can defer only nine tenths of the gain ($54,000). He therefore has a $6,000 capital gain from the disposition for the year.

**S. 44.1**      Income Tax Act, Part I, Division B

Harold's adjusted cost base of the Corporation B shares is reduced from $90,000 to $36,000 because of the capital gains deferral of $54,000.

*Example 2*

On November 30, 2000, Kate disposes of shares in Corporation C which are eligible small business investments. Her proceeds of disposition are $1,000,000 and she realizes a capital gain of $600,000. On February 1, 2001, Kate acquires shares in Corporation D at a cost of $1,000,000 which are new eligible small business investments.

Since the investment limit in respect of a corporation or a related group of corporations is $500,000, Kate can defer capital gains on up to one half of her eligible capital gains of $600,000 (i.e., $300,000). After the deferral, she has a capital gain from the disposition for the year of $300,000.

Kate's adjusted cost base of the Corporation D shares is reduced by the $300,000 deferred gain, from $1,000,000 to $700,000.

If Kate had instead reinvested $500,000 each in shares of two unrelated corporations that were eligible small business investments, she would have been able to defer all of the $600,000 eligible gain. In this case, the adjusted cost base of each of the two new investments would have been reduced by $300,000.

*Example 3*

Robert has shares in Corporation X which are eligible small business investments having an adjusted cost base of $1,000,000. He sells the shares for proceeds of disposition of $3,000,000 and realizes a capital gain of $2,000,000. Because of the $500,000 investment limit, only the capital gains relating to $500,000 of the original investment are eligible for a deferral. Robert purchases replacement eligible small business investments in six other unrelated corporations of $500,000 each for a total reinvestment of $3,000,000.

While Robert's cost of the replacement eligible small business investment is $3,000,000, the maximum amount he can use to calculate his capital gains deferral is $1,500,000, which is equal to the proceeds of disposition that relate to the eligible gain.

The maximum capital gains deferral that Robert can claim is $1,000,000.

**Definitions**: "ACB reduction" — 44.1(1); "active business" — 248(1); "active business corporation" — 44.1(1), (10); "adjusted cost base" — 54, 248(1); "amount" — 248(1); "arm's length" — 251(1); "business" — 248(1); "Canada" — 255, *Interpretation Act* 35(1); "Canadian-controlled private corporation" — 125(7), 248(1); "capital gain" — 39(1)(a), 248(1); "carrying value", "common share" — 44.1(1); "common-law partner", "common-law partnership" — 248(1); "corporation" — 248(1), *Interpretation Act* 35(1); "disposition" — 248(1); "eligible pooling arrangement" — 44.1(1); "eligible small business corporation" — 44.1(1), (10); "eligible small business corporation share" — 44.1(1), (11); "individual" — 248(1); "investment manager" — 44.1(1) "eligible pooling arrangement"; "month" — *Interpretation Act* 35(1); "paid-up capital" — 89(1), 248(1); "parent" — 252(2)(a); "partnership" — see Notes to 96(1); "permitted deferral" — 44.1(1); "person", "prescribed", "professional corporation", "property" — 248(1); "qualifying cost" — 44.1(1); "qualifying disposition" — 44.1(1), (9); "qualifying portion of a capital gain", "qualifying portion of the proceeds" — 44.1(1); "related" — 251(2)–(6); "replacement share" — 44.1(1); "share" —

"small business corporation", "specified financial institution" — 248(1); "substituted property" — 248(5); "taxable Canadian corporation" — 89(1), 248(1); "taxable Canadian property" — 248(1); "taxation year" — 249; "trust" — 104(1), 248(1), (3); "writing" — *Interpretation Act* 35(1).

**45. (1) Property with more than one use [change in use]** — For the purposes of this subdivision the following rules apply:

(a) where a taxpayer,

(i) having acquired property for some other purpose, has commenced at a later time to use it for the purpose of gaining or producing income, or

(ii) having acquired property for the purpose of gaining or producing income, has commenced at a later time to use it for some other purpose,

the taxpayer shall be deemed to have

(iii) disposed of it at that later time for proceeds equal to its fair market value at that later time, and

(iv) immediately thereafter reacquired it at a cost equal to that fair market value;

(b) where property has, since it was acquired by a taxpayer, been regularly used in part for the purpose of gaining or producing income and in part for some other purpose, the taxpayer shall be deemed to have acquired, for that other purpose, the proportion of the property that the use regularly made of the property for that other purpose is of the whole use regularly made of the property at a cost to the taxpayer equal to the same proportion of the cost to the taxpayer of the whole property, and, if the property has, in such a case, been disposed of, the proceeds of disposition of the proportion of the property deemed to have been acquired for that other purpose shall be deemed to be the same proportion of the proceeds of disposition of the whole property; and

(c) where, at any time after a taxpayer has acquired property, there has been a change in the relation between the use regularly made by the taxpayer of the property for gaining or producing income and the use regularly made of the property for other purposes,

(i) if the use regularly made of the property for those other purposes has increased, the taxpayer shall be deemed to have

(A) disposed of the property at that time for proceeds equal to the proportion of the fair market value of the property at that time that the amount of the increase in the use regularly made by the taxpayer of the property for those other purposes is of the whole use regularly made of the property, and

(B) immediately thereafter reacquired the property so disposed of at a cost equal to the proceeds referred to in clause (A), and

(ii) if the use regularly made of the property for those other purposes has decreased, the taxpayer shall be deemed to have

(A) disposed of the property at that time for proceeds equal to the proportion of the fair market value of the property at that time that the amount of the decrease in use regularly made by the taxpayer of the property for those other purposes is of the whole use regularly made of the property, and

(B) immediately thereafter reacquired the property so disposed of at a cost equal to the proceeds referred to in clause (A).

**Proposed Addition — 45(1)(d)**

(d) in applying this subsection in respect of a non-resident taxpayer, a reference to "gaining or producing income" shall be read as a reference to gaining or producing income from a source in Canada.

**Application**: Bill C-43 (First Reading September 20, 2000), s. 17, will add para. 45(1)(d), applicable after October 1, 1996.

**Technical Notes**: Subsection 45(1) of the Act provides for a deemed disposition and reacquisition of property where its use is altered, wholly or in part, from a personal to an income-earning or income-producing use, or vice versa. This "change in use" rule applies for the purpose of the subdivision of the Act that deals with taxable capital gains and allowable capital losses.

New paragraph 45(1)(d) provides that, in applying subsection 45(1) in respect of a non-resident taxpayer, any reference to "gaining or producing income" is to be read as a reference to gaining or producing income from a source in Canada. As a result, a non-resident who ceases to use a property to earn income in Canada and begins to use it instead to earn income outside Canada will be treated as having disposed of the property.

New paragraph 45(1)(d) applies after October 1, 1996.

**Related Provisions**: 13(7)(a), (b), (d) — Change in use rules — depreciable property; 54"superficial loss"(c) — Superficial loss rule does not apply.

**Notes**: 45(1)(c) amended by 1991 technical bill, retroactive to 1972, to correct technical errors.

**Interpretation Bulletins**: IT-83R3: Non-profit organizations — taxation of income from property; IT-120R5: Principal residence; IT-160R3: Personal use of aircraft; IT-218R: Profit, capital gains and losses from the sale of real estate, including farmland and inherited land and conversion of real estate from capital property to inventory and vice versa.

**(2) Election where change of use** — For the purposes of this subdivision and section 13, where subparagraph (1)(a)(i) or paragraph 13(7)(b) would otherwise apply to any property of a taxpayer for a taxation year and the taxpayer so elects in respect of the property in the taxpayer's return of income for the year under this Part, the taxpayer shall be deemed not to have begun to use the property for the purpose of gaining or producing income except that, if in the taxpayer's return of income under this Part for a subsequent taxation year the taxpayer rescinds the election in respect of the property, the taxpayer shall be deemed to have begun so to use the property on the first day of that subsequent year.

**Related Provisions**: 13(1) — Recapture of depreciation; 54"principal residence"(b) — Effect of election on principal residence; 220(3.2), Reg. 600(b) — Late filing of election or revocation.

**Notes**: 45(2) amended by 1993 technical bill, effective for 1992 and later taxation years. The amendment clarifies that an election may be made in respect of non-depreciable capital property, such as land; and, by deleting reference to gaining or producing income "from a business", makes 45(2) no longer apply (just as 45(1) no longer applies, since 1988) to a change from one kind of income-producing use to another (e.g., from property income to business income).

**Interpretation Bulletins**: IT-120R5: Principal residence.

**Information Circulars**: 92-1: Guidelines for accepting late, amended or revoked elections.

**(3) Election concerning principal residence** — Where at any time a property that was acquired by a taxpayer for the purpose of gaining or producing income ceases to be used for that purpose and becomes the principal residence of the taxpayer, subsection (1) shall not apply to deem the taxpayer to have disposed of the property at that time and to have reacquired it immediately thereafter if the taxpayer so elects by notifying the Minister in writing on or before the earlier of

(a) the day that is 90 days after a demand by the Minister for an election under this subsection is sent to the taxpayer, and

(b) the taxpayer's filing-due date for the taxation year in which the property is actually disposed of by the taxpayer.

**Related Provisions**: 45(4) — Where election cannot be made; 54"principal residence"(b), (d) — Effect of election and parallel rule when moving out of principal residence; 220(3.2), Reg. 600(b) — Late filing of election or revocation.

**Notes**: 45(3)(b) amended by 1995 Budget, effective 1995. For 1985–94, read: "(b) April 30 following the year in which...". The change results from the filing deadline for individuals carrying on business (and their spouses) having been extended from April 30 to June 15 (see 150(1)(d)).

**Interpretation Bulletins**: IT-120R5: Principal residence.

**Information Circulars**: 92-1: Guidelines for accepting late, amended or revoked elections.

**(4) Where election cannot be made** — Notwithstanding subsection (3), an election described in that subsection shall be deemed not to have been made in respect of a change in use of property if any deduction in respect of the property has been allowed for any taxation year ending after 1984 and on or before the change in use under regulations made under paragraph 20(1)(a) to the taxpayer, the taxpayer's spouse or common-law partner or a trust under which the taxpayer or the taxpayer's spouse or common-law partner is a beneficiary.

**Notes**: 45(4) amended by 2000 same-sex partners bill to add reference to "common-law partner", effective for the 2001 and later taxation years, or earlier by election (see Notes to 248(1)"common-law partner").

**Interpretation Bulletins**: IT-120R5: Principal residence.

**Definitions [s. 45]**: "amount", "business", "common-law partner" — 248(1); "filing-due date" — 150(1), 248(1); "gaining or producing income" — 45(1)(d); "Minister" — 248(1); "principal residence", "proceeds of disposition" — 54; "property", "regulation" — 248(1); "taxation year" — 249; "taxpayer", "writing" — *Interpretation Act* 35(1).

**Interpretation Bulletins [s. 45]**: IT-102R2: Conversion of property, other than real property, from or to inventory.

**46. (1) Personal-use property** — Where a taxpayer has disposed of any personal-use property of the taxpayer, for the purposes of this subdivision

> **Proposed Amendment — 46(1) opening words**
>
> **46. (1) Personal-use property** — Where a taxpayer has disposed of a personal-use property (other than an excluded property disposed of in circumstances to which subsection 110.1(1), or the definition "total charitable gifts", "total cultural gifts" or "total ecological gifts" in subsection 118.1(1), applies) of the taxpayer, for the purposes of this subdivision
>
> **Application**: The December 21, 2000 draft legislation, subsec. 18(1), will amend the opening words of subsec. 46(1) to read as above, applicable to property acquired after February 27, 2000.
>
> **Technical Notes**: Section 46 provides rules that apply to personal-use property (which is defined in section 54). The effect of these rules is to ensure that no gain or loss is recognized in respect of the first $1,000 of proceeds or cost of a personal-use property.
>
> Subsection 46(2) provides related rules that apply where only part of a personal-use property is disposed of.
>
> Subsections 46(1) and (2) are amended to exclude from their application "excluded property" that is disposed of in circumstances to which the charitable gift deduction in subsection 110.1(1) applies, or the definition "total charitable gifts", "total cultural gifts" or "total ecological gifts" in subsection 118.1(1) applies.

(a) the adjusted cost base to the taxpayer of the property immediately before the disposition shall be deemed to be the greater of $1,000 and the amount otherwise determined to be its adjusted cost base to the taxpayer at that time; and

(b) the taxpayer's proceeds of disposition of the property shall be deemed to be the greater of $1,000 and the taxpayer's proceeds of disposition of the property otherwise determined.

**Related Provisions**: 40(2)(g)(iii) — No loss allowed on most personal-use property; 46(3) — Properties ordinarily disposed of as a set; 46(5) — Excluded property; 50(2) — Personal-use property debts.

**Notes**: The effect of the minimum $1,000 to both cost and proceeds of personal-use property is that, if such property is sold for proceeds not greater than $1,000, no gain or loss will result and there will be no tax consequences. Note that losses on personal-use property cannot be used anyway (see 40(2)(g)(iii)), except for listed-personal-property losses, which can only be used against listed-personal-property gains (see 3(b)(ii) and 41(2)). For art flips, see 46(5).

**Interpretation Bulletins**: IT-332R: Personal Use Property.

**(2) Where part only of property disposed of** — Where a taxpayer has disposed of part of a personal-use property owned by the taxpayer and has retained another part of the property, for the purposes of this subdivision

> **Proposed Amendment — 46(2) opening words**
>
> **(2) Where part only of property disposed of** — Where a taxpayer has disposed of part of a personal-use property (other than a part of an excluded property disposed of in circumstances to which subsection 110.1(1), or the definition "total charitable gifts", "total cultural gifts" or "total ecological gifts" in subsection 118.1(1), applies) owned by the taxpayer and has retained another part of the property, for the purposes of this subdivision
>
> **Application**: The December 21, 2000 draft legislation, subsec. 18(2), will amend the opening words of subsec. 46(2) to read as above, applicable to property acquired after February 27, 2000.
>
> **Technical Notes**: See under 46(1).

(a) the adjusted cost base to the taxpayer, immediately before the disposition, of the part so disposed of shall be deemed to be the greater of

(i) the adjusted cost base to the taxpayer at that time of that part otherwise determined, and

(ii) that proportion of $1,000 that the amount determined under subparagraph (i) is of the adjusted cost base to the taxpayer at that time of the whole property; and

(b) the proceeds of disposition of the part so disposed of shall be deemed to be the greater of

(i) the proceeds of disposition of that part otherwise determined, and

(ii) the amount determined under subparagraph (a)(ii).

**(3) Properties ordinarily disposed of as a set** — For the purposes of this subdivision, where a number of personal-use properties of a taxpayer that would, if the properties were disposed of, ordinarily be disposed of in one disposition as a set,

(a) have been disposed of by more than one disposition so that all of the properties have been acquired by one person or by a group of persons not dealing with each other at arm's length, and

(b) had, immediately before the first disposition referred to in paragraph (a), a total fair market value greater than $1,000,

the properties shall be deemed to be a single personal-use property and each such disposition shall be deemed to be a disposition of a part of that property.

Subdivision c — Taxable Capital Gains    S. 47(1)(a)

**(4) Decrease in value of personal-use property of corporation, etc.** — Where it may reasonably be regarded that, by reason of a decrease in the fair market value of any personal-use property of a corporation, partnership or trust,

(a) a taxpayer's gain, if any, from the disposition of a share of the capital stock of a corporation, an interest in a trust or an interest in a partnership has become a loss, or is less than it would have been if the decrease had not occurred, or

(b) a taxpayer's loss, if any, from the disposition of a share or interest described in paragraph (a) is greater than it would have been if the decrease had not occurred,

the amount of the gain or loss, as the case may be, shall be deemed to be the amount that it would have been but for the decrease.

### Proposed Addition — 46(5)

**(5) Excluded property** — For the purpose of this section, "excluded property" of a taxpayer means property acquired by the taxpayer, or by a person with whom the taxpayer does not deal at arm's length, in circumstances in which it is reasonable to conclude that the acquisition of the property relates to an arrangement, plan or scheme that is promoted by another person or partnership and under which it is reasonable to conclude that the property will be the subject of a gift to which subsection 110.1(1), or the definition "total charitable gifts", "total cultural gifts" or "total ecological gifts" in subsection 118.1(1), applies.

**Application**: The December 21, 2000 draft legislation, subsec. 18(3), will add subsec. 46(5), applicable to property acquired after February 27, 2000.

**Technical Notes**: New subsection 46(5) defines excluded property of a taxpayer to mean, in general terms, property acquired by the taxpayer in circumstances in which it is reasonable to conclude that the acquisition relates to an arrangement, plan or scheme that is promoted by another person or partnership in circumstances where it is reasonable to conclude that the property will be the subject of a gift to which a charitable deduction or credit will be claimed under the Act.

**Notice of Ways and Means Motion, federal budget, February 28, 2000**: *Personal-Use Property*

(20) That the provisions of the Act relating to the deemed proceeds of disposition and adjusted cost base applicable to personal-use property not apply to property of a taxpayer that is acquired by the taxpayer after February 27, 2000 as part of an arrangement under which the property is gifted to a qualified donee.

**Federal budget, supplementary information, February 28, 2000**: *Personal-Use Property*

Currently, the adjusted cost base and proceeds of disposition of personal-use property are deemed to be at least $1,000 for capital gains purposes. This rule is designed to ease the compliance and administrative burden associated with the reporting of dispositions of personal-use property. Personal-use property is generally property that is used primarily for the personal use or enjoyment of an individual and includes jewellery, works of art, furniture and clothing.

Certain charitable donation arrangements have been designed to exploit the $1,000 deemed adjusted cost base for personal-use property and to create a scheme under which taxpayers attempt to achieve an after-tax profit from such gifts. For example, arrangements have been designed under which a promoter acquires a number of objects for less than $50 each, invites taxpayers to purchase the objects for $250 each, and arranges for their appraisal at $1,000 each and their donation to a charity.

[These arrangements are known as "art flips" and have been successfully challenged by the CCRA on various grounds, including valuation. See Notes to 118.1(1)"total charitable gifts". See also the civil penalties for third parties in 163.2 — ed.]

Based on the $1,000 appraised value, there would be a $750 capital gain per item to the donor but for the $1,000 deemed adjusted cost base for the gift. However, with the deemed adjusted cost base there is no gain for tax purposes. As a result, the cost to governments of the "$1,000 gift" is approximately $500 (i.e., the federal and provincial tax savings associated with a $1,000 charitable donation), which in many cases exceeds the amount that the charity can realize from the donated property. Such an arrangement intends that the "donor" achieve a tax-free profit of $250.

The budget proposes to amend the *Income Tax Act* so that the $1,000 deemed adjusted cost base and deemed proceeds of disposition for personal-use property will not apply if the property is acquired after February 27, 2000, as part of an arrangement in which the property is donated as a charitable gift. [The condition that there also be a third-party promoter was added later — ed.]

**Related Provisions**: 163.2 — Penalties for third-party promoters and valuators.

**Definitions [s. 46]**: "adjusted cost base" — 54, 248(1); "amount" — 248(1); "arm's length" — 251(1); "corporation" — 248(1), *Interpretation Act* 35(1); "disposition" — 54 [to be repealed], 248(1) [draft]; "excluded property" — 46(5); "partnership" — see Notes to 96(1); "person" — 248(1); "personal-use property" — 54, 248(1); "proceeds of disposition" — 54; "property", "share", "taxpayer" — 248(1); "trust" — 104(1), 248(1), (3).

**Interpretation Bulletins [s. 46]**: IT-332R: Personal-use property.

**47. (1) Identical properties [averaging rule]** — Where at any particular time after 1971 a taxpayer who owns one property that was or two or more identical properties each of which was, as the case may be, acquired by the taxpayer after 1971, acquires one or more other properties (in this subsection referred to as "newly-acquired properties") each of which is identical to each such previously-acquired property, for the purposes of computing, at any subsequent time, the adjusted cost base of the taxpayer of each such identical property,

(a) the taxpayer shall be deemed to have disposed of each such previously-acquired property immediately before the particular time for proceeds equal to its adjusted cost base to the taxpayer immediately before the particular time;

## S. 47(1)(b)  Income Tax Act, Part I, Division B

(b) the taxpayer shall be deemed to have acquired the identical property at the particular time at a cost equal to the quotient obtained when

(i) the total of the adjusted cost bases to the taxpayer immediately before the particular time of the previously-acquired properties, and the cost to the taxpayer (determined without reference to this section) of the newly-acquired properties

is divided by

(ii) the number of the identical properties owned by the taxpayer immediately after the particular time;

(c) there shall be deducted, after the particular time, in computing the adjusted cost base to the taxpayer of each such identical property, the amount determined by the formula

$$\frac{A}{B}$$

where

A is the total of all amounts deducted under paragraph 53(2)(g.1) in computing immediately before the particular time the adjusted cost base to the taxpayer of the previously-acquired properties, and

B is the number of such identical properties owned by the taxpayer immediately after the particular time or, where subsection (2) applies, the quotient determined under that subsection in respect of the acquisition; and

(d) there shall be added, after the particular time, in computing the adjusted cost base to the taxpayer of each such identical property the amount determined under paragraph (c) in respect of the identical property.

**Related Provisions**: 7(1.3) — Order of disposition of securities acquired under stock-option agreement; 47(2) — Where identical properties are bonds, etc.; 47(3) — Certain securities acquired by employee deemed not identical; 53(1)(q) — Addition to ACB for amount under 47(1)(d); 53(2)(g.1) — Reduction in ACB under 47(1)(c); 80.03(2)(a) — Deemed gain on disposition following debt forgiveness; 138(11.1) — Properties of life insurance corporation; 248(12) — Meaning of "identical properties".

**Notes**: Shares held in escrow (such as where a company has recently gone public) have been held not to be identical to shares that can be freely disposed of, for purposes of this rule: *Taylor*, [1988] 2 C.T.C. 2227 (TCC).

Note also the extended definition of "identical" in 248(12) for debt obligations.

47(1)(c) and (d) added by 1994 tax amendments bill (Part I), effective for taxation years that end after February 21, 1994. They effectively preserve the history of deductions in computing ACB under 53(2)(g.1), which relates to reductions in ACB under the debt forgiveness rules in s. 80. The only relevance of 47(1)(c) and (d) is for the potential future application of 80.03. Similar amendments were made at 49(3.01), 51(1), 53(4)–(6), 86(4), 87(5.1) and 87(6.1). See also Notes to 53(2)(g.1).

**I.T. Application Rules**: 26(8)–(8.5) (property owned since before 1972).

**I.T. Technical News**: No. 19 (Disposition of identical properties acquired under a section 7 securities option; Change in position in respect of GAAR — section 7).

**(2) Where identical properties are bonds, etc.** — For the purposes of subsection (1), where a group of identical properties referred to in that subsection is a group of identical bonds, debentures, bills, notes or similar obligations issued by a debtor, subparagraph (1)(b)(ii) shall be read as follows:

"(ii) the quotient obtained when the total of the principal amounts of all such identical properties owned by the taxpayer immediately after the particular time is divided by the principal amount of the identical property."

**Related Provisions**: 248(12) — Whether bonds, etc., are identical properties.

**(3) [Repealed under former Act]**

**Notes**: 47(3), which defined "identical properties", repealed in 1987 and moved to 248(12).

### Proposed Addition — 47(3)

**(3) Securities acquired by employee** — For the purpose of subsection (1), a security (within the meaning assigned by subsection 7(7)) acquired by a taxpayer after February 27, 2000 is deemed not to be identical to any other security acquired by the taxpayer if

(a) the security is acquired in circumstances to which any of subsections 7(1.1), (1.5) or (8) or 147(10.1) applies; or

(b) the security is a security to which subsection 7(1.31) applies.

**Application**: The December 21, 2000 draft legislation, s. 19, will add subsec. 47(3), applicable after 1999.

**Technical Notes**: Subsection 47(1) requires that the cost of identical properties acquired by a taxpayer be averaged over all such properties. Generally, this results in each of the properties having the same adjusted cost base (ACB), thus ensuring that the capital gain or loss on the disposition of any one of the properties can be determined without having to identify a particular property as the property that has been disposed of.

New subsection 47(3) exempts certain securities acquired after February 27, 2000 from the cost-averaging rule by deeming such securities not to be identical to any other securities acquired by the taxpayer for the purposes of subsection 47(1). The specific securities to which subsection 47(3) applies are as follows:

- Securities (i.e., shares of a corporation and units of a mutual fund trust) acquired under an employee option agreement for which a deferral is provided under existing subsection 7(1.1) or new subsection 7(8), and securities acquired in exchange for such securities under circumstances to which subsection 7(1.5) applied.

- Securities acquired under an employee option agreement where the securities are designated by the taxpayer and deemed by new subsection 7(1.31) to be the securities that are the subject of a disposition of identical securities occurring within 30 days after the acquisition.

314

- Employer shares received by an employee as part of a lump sum payment on withdrawing from a deferred profit sharing plan (DPSP), where the employee filed an election in respect of those shares under subsection 147(10.1). Such an election allows the taxpayer to defer taxation on the growth of the shares while they were held by the plan until such time as the employee disposes of the shares.

The effect of a security being exempted from the cost-averaging rule in subsection 47(1) is that the ACB of the security, and thus the capital gain or loss on its disposition, is determined without regard to the ACB of any other securities owned by the taxpayer. In other words, each security to which subsection 47(3) applies has its own unique ACB.

It should be noted that, under amended subsection 7(1.3) and new subsection 7(1.31), it is possible to determine when each security which is exempted from the cost averaging rule by subsection 47(3) is disposed of by the taxpayer. As noted above, subsection 7(1.31) deals with situations in which there is an acquisition of an employee option security and a disposition of an identical security within 30 days. Amended subsection 7(1.3) deals with securities for which a deferral is provided under subsection 7(1.1) or (8) or 147(10.1) (referred to in these notes as "deferral securities"). In general terms, subsection 7(1.3) deems a taxpayer to dispose of deferral securities only after having disposed of non-deferral securities, and then to dispose of deferral securities in the order in which they were acquired. Since it is possible to determine exactly when a particular security to which subsection 47(3) applies is disposed of, the fact that the security has its own unique ACB is not problematic.

It should also be noted that, where an employee acquires a security after February 27, 2000 under circumstances to which subsection 7(1.1) or (8) apply, the deferred employment benefit is added, pursuant to amended paragraph 53(1)(j), to the ACB of the security at the time it is acquired even though the benefit is not subject to taxation until the security is disposed of.

The following examples illustrate the effect of subsection 47(3), in conjunction with the rules in subsections 7(1.3) and 7(1.31) for determining the order of disposition of identical securities and the amended ACB rule for employee option securities in paragraph 53(1)(j).

### Example 1

*On March 1, 1998, Simon acquires 50 shares of his corporate employer on the open market for $5 each. The ACB of each share is $5. On March 1, 1999, Simon acquires another 50 shares on the open market for $15 each. By virtue of subsection 47(1), the ACB of each of the 100 shares is $10 (= ((50 × $5) + (50 × $15)) divided by 100).*

*On March 1, 2001, Simon exercises two different employee stock options and acquires two additional company shares. The fair market value (FMV) at that time is $100 per share. One of the options was granted on July 1, 1999 and has an exercise price of $25. The other option was granted on July 1, 2000 and has an exercise price of $30.*

*Simon elects under subsection 7(8) to defer recognition of the employment benefit of $75 (= $100 − $25) associated with the option granted in 1999 as well as the employment benefit of $70 (= $100 − $30) associated with the option granted in 2000. Because of the election, subsection 47(3) excludes the shares from the cost-averaging rule in subsection 47(1). Thus, the ACB of the share acquired under the option granted in 1999 is $100 (= $25 cost amount + $75 deferred employment benefit added pursuant to amended paragraph 53(1)(j)). The ACB for the other stock option share is also $100 (= $30 cost amount + $70 deferred employment benefit added pursuant to paragraph 53(1)(j)).*

*Because of the application of subsection 47(3), the acquisition of the stock option shares does not affect the ACB of the previously-acquired 100 shares, which remains at $10 a share.*

*On March 1, 2002, Simon acquires an additional stock option share. The option was also granted on July 1, 2000 and has an exercise price of $30. The FMV of the share is $150. He elects, under subsection 7(8), to defer recognition of the employment benefit of $120 (= $150 − $30). Because of the election, the share is excluded from the cost-averaging rule. Thus, the ACB of the share is $150 (= $30 cost amount + $120 deferred employment benefit added pursuant to paragraph 53(1)(j)).*

*Because of the application of subsection 47(3), the ACB of the 100 market shares remains unchanged at $10 a share. Similarly, the ACB of each of the stock option shares acquired on March 1, 2001 remains unchanged at $100.*

*On December 1, 2003, Simon sells 60 shares for $160 a share. By virtue of subsection 7(1.3), Simon is deemed to have sold the 50 shares that he acquired on the open market on March 1, 1998, and 10 of the 50 shares that he acquired on the open market on March 1, 1999. The capital gain on each share is $150 (= $160 proceeds of disposition − $10 ACB), and the total capital gain is $9,000 (= $150 × 60).*

*In 2004, Simon sells another 40 shares for $180 a share. By virtue of subsection 7(1.3), he is deemed to have sold the remaining shares that he acquired on the open market. The capital gain on each share is $170 (= $180 proceeds of disposition − $10 ACB), and the total capital gain is $6,800 (= $170 × 40).*

*In 2005, Simon sells another share for $220. By virtue of subsection 7(1.3), he is deemed to have sold the stock option share that he acquired on March 1, 2001 under the option that was granted on July 1, 1999. In his tax return for 2005, he reports the employment benefit of $75 and the capital gain of $120 (= $220 − $100).*

*In 2006, he sells another share for $190. By virtue of subsection 7(1.3), he is deemed to have sold the stock option share that he acquired on March 1, 2001 under the option that was granted on July 1, 2000. In his tax return for 2006, he reports the employment benefit of $70 and the capital gain of $90 (= $190 − $100).*

*In 2007, Simon sells the one remaining share for $245. By virtue of subsection 7(1.3), he is deemed to have sold the stock option share that he acquired on March 1, 2002. In his tax return for that year, he reports the employment benefit of $120 and the capital gain of $95 (= $245 − $150).*

*If we were to assume that, in 2007, Simon acquired an additional share on the open market and later that year disposed of only one of the two shares in his possession, subsection 7(1.3) would deem the newly-acquired market share, rather than the one remaining stock option share, to be the share that is the subject of the disposition.*

**Example 2**

*Margaret owns 100 shares of her corporate employer. The shares have an ACB of $6 each. In July 2001, Margaret acquires another share under an employee stock option. The exercise price is $50 and the FMV is $150. As a result of the acquisition, she is deemed to have received a benefit from employment equal to $100, and is entitled to deduct 1/2 of the employment benefit under paragraph 110(1)(d). The share is publicly listed.*

*Margaret immediately donates an identical share to a qualifying charity. Under subsection 7(1.31), she identifies the newly-acquired share as the share being donated and, thus, is entitled to deduct another 1/4 of the employment benefit under paragraph 110(1)(d.01).*

*Because of the specific identification under subsection 7(1.31), the donated share is deemed not to be identical to the other shares for purposes of the cost-averaging rule in subsection 47(1). As a result, the ACB of the donated share is $150 (= $50 exercise price + $100 employment benefit). Under subsection 69(1), Margaret is deemed to have received proceeds of disposition for the donated share equal to its FMV at the time of donation, which is also $150. Therefore, there is no capital gain or loss determined in connection with the donated share. Furthermore, because of the application of subsection 47(3), the $6 ACB of the previously-acquired shares is unaffected by the acquisition of the donated share.*

**Related Provisions**: 7(1.3) — Order of disposition of securities.

**(4)** [Repealed under former Act]

**Notes**: 47(4), repealed by 1985 Budget, excluded indexed securities from "property". Indexed security investment plans no longer exist.

**Definitions [s. 47]**: "adjusted cost base" — 54, 248(1); "identical" — 138(11.1), 248(12); "principal amount", "property" — 248(1); "security" — 7(7); "taxpayer" — 248(1).

**Interpretation Bulletins [s. 47]**: IT-78: Capital property owned on December 31, 1971 — identical properties; IT-88R2: Stock dividends; IT-115R2: Fractional interest in shares; IT-199: Identical properties acquired in non-arm's length transactions; IT-387R2: Meaning of "identical properties".

## 47.1 Indexed Security Investment Plans —

**(1)–(26)** [Repealed under former Act]

**Notes**: 47.1(1)–(26), repealed by 1985 Budget, implemented indexed security investment plans (ISIPs), which existed only from 1983 to 1985 and were discarded with the introduction of the capital gains exemption in 110.6.

**(26.1) Application of section 47.1 of R.S.C., 1952, c. 148** — Words and expressions used in subsections (27) and (28) have the meanings assigned to them by subsections 47.1(1) to (26) of the *Income Tax Act*, chapter 148 of the Revised Statutes of Canada, 1952, as the latter subsections read on July 1, 1986 and in so far as they are not inconsistent with subsections (27) and (28).

**Notes**: 47.1(26.1) added in R.S.C. 1985 (5th Supp.) consolidation.

**I.T. Application Rules**: 69 (meaning of "*Income Tax Act*, chapter 148 of the Revised Statutes of Canada, 1952").

**(27)** [No longer relevant]

**Notes**: 47.1(27) not formally repealed, but it merely provided for capital losses in 1986 from ISIPs.

**(28) Transition for 1986** — Where a taxpayer was a participant under a Plan on January 1, 1986, the following rules apply:

(a) each indexed security owned under the Plan by the taxpayer on that date shall be deemed to have been disposed of under the Plan on that date for proceeds of disposition determined by the formula

$$A \times \frac{B}{C}$$

where

A is the indexing base of the Plan on that date determined as if subparagraph 47.1(3)(a)(i) of the *Income Tax Act*, chapter 148 of the Revised Statutes of Canada, 1952, were read as "the fair market value of all indexed securities owned by the taxpayer under the Plan at the end of the preceding taxation year",

B is the fair market value of the security on that date, and

C is the fair market value of all indexed securities owned under the Plan by the taxpayer on that date;

(b) each indexed security deemed under paragraph (a) to have been disposed of under the Plan shall be deemed to have been reacquired outside the Plan by the taxpayer immediately after that date at a cost equal to the amount deemed under paragraph (a) to be the proceeds of the disposition of that security;

(c) each put or call option referred to in clause 47.1(4)(a)(iv)(B) or (C) of the *Income Tax Act*, chapter 148 of the Revised Statutes of Canada, 1952, as that clause read on January 1, 1986, outstanding under the Plan on that date shall be deemed to have been closed out under the Plan on that date at a cost equal to the amount that the taxpayer would have had to pay on that date if the taxpayer had actually closed out the option on a prescribed stock exchange in Canada on that date;

(d) each put or call option deemed under paragraph (c) to have been closed out shall be deemed to be written outside the Plan immediately after that date for proceeds equal to the amount deemed under paragraph (c) to be the cost at which the option was closed out; and

(e) for greater certainty, the taxpayer's indexed gain or loss, as the case may be, for the 1986 taxation year from the Plan and unindexed gain or loss, as the case may be, for that year from the Plan shall be nil.

**I.T. Application Rules**: 69 (meaning of *"Income Tax Act*, chapter 148 of the Revised Statutes of Canada, 1952").

**Definitions [s. 47.1]**: "amount" — 248(1); "capital loss" — 39(1)(b), 248(1); "corporation" — 248(1), *Interpretation Act* 35(1); "prescribed stock exchange in Canada" — Reg. 3200; "proceeds of disposition" — 54; "taxation year" — 249; "taxpayer" — 248(1).

**Regulations [s. 47.1]**: 3200 (prescribed stock exchange).

## 48. [Repealed]

**Notes**: 48 repealed by 1993 technical bill, effective 1993. Where a corporation continued before 1993 elects for 250(5.1) to apply earlier (see Notes to 250(5.1)), the repeal is effective from the corporation's "time of continuation". In either case, once the repeal takes effect, 128.1 applies instead, and generally incorporates the rules that were in 48.

Where 48 applies, read:

48. (1) **Deemed disposition of property where taxpayer has ceased to be resident in Canada** — For the purposes of this subdivision, where a taxpayer has ceased, at any particular time in a taxation year and after 1971, to be resident in Canada, the taxpayer shall be deemed to have disposed, immediately before the particular time, of each property other than

(a) any property that would be taxable Canadian property if at no time in the year the taxpayer had been resident in Canada except where the taxpayer is an individual other than a trust and the taxpayer has elected in prescribed manner and within a prescribed time to be deemed to have disposed of such property owned by the taxpayer immediately before the particular time,

(b) a right to receive any payment described in paragraph 212(1)(h), in any of paragraphs 212(1)(j) to (q) and a right to receive any payment of a benefit under the *Canada Pension Plan* or a provincial pension plan as defined in section 3 of that Act, or

(c) where the taxpayer is an individual other than a trust or was, immediately before the particular time, a Canadian corporation, any property not described in paragraph (a) or (b) in respect of which the taxpayer has elected in prescribed manner and within prescribed time and has furnished the Minister with security acceptable to the Minister for the payment of the additional tax under this Part that would have been payable by the taxpayer if the taxpayer had not so elected,

that was owned by the taxpayer immediately before the particular time for proceeds of disposition equal to the fair market value of the property immediately before the particular time and to have reacquired the property immediately after the taxpayer so ceased to be resident in Canada at a cost equal to that fair market value, except that where the taxpayer has made an election under paragraph (a) or (c), the total of the taxpayer's allowable capital losses for the year from dispositions under this subsection of such of those properties as were not listed personal property of the taxpayer shall be deemed to be the lesser of that total otherwise determined and the total of the taxpayer's taxable capital gains for the year from the dispositions under this subsection of such of those properties as were not listed personal property of the taxpayer.

(2) **Property in respect of which election made deemed to be taxable Canadian property** — Any property of a taxpayer described in paragraph (1)(c) in respect of which the taxpayer has made an election under that paragraph shall be deemed to be taxable Canadian property of the taxpayer from the time immediately after the taxpayer ceased to be resident in Canada until the time immediately after the taxpayer

(a) disposes of it, or

(b) next becomes resident in Canada,

whichever first occurs.

(3) **Deemed acquisition of property on becoming a resident of Canada** — For the purposes of this subdivision, where a taxpayer has become, at any particular time in a taxation year and after 1971, resident in Canada, the taxpayer shall be deemed to have acquired at the particular time each property owned by the taxpayer at that time, other than

(a) property that would be taxable Canadian property if the taxpayer had disposed of it immediately before the particular time, or

(b) property described in paragraph (1)(c) in respect of which the taxpayer had previously made an election under that paragraph in respect of the last preceding time the taxpayer ceased to be resident in Canada,

at a cost equal to its fair market value at the particular time.

(4) **Exception where taxpayer resident in Canada for short term only** — Subsection (1) does not apply in respect of any property owned by an individual other than a trust at the particular time immediately before the individual ceased to be resident in Canada, if

(a) the property was

(i) owned by the individual immediately before the individual last became resident in Canada, or

(ii) acquired by the individual by inheritance or bequest at any time after the individual last became resident in Canada; and

(b) during the 10 years immediately preceding the particular time, the individual was resident in Canada for a period or periods the total of which was 60 months or less.

(5) **Where corporation becomes resident in Canada** — Where at any time a corporation becomes resident in Canada and immediately before that time the corporation was a foreign affiliate of a taxpayer resident in Canada, for the purposes of subdivision i, the following rules apply:

(a) the taxation year of the corporation that would otherwise have included that time shall be deemed to have ended immediately before that time and a new taxation year shall be deemed to have commenced at that time;

(b) the corporation shall be deemed to have been a controlled foreign affiliate (within the meaning assigned by subsection 95(1)) of the taxpayer at the end of the taxation year that is deemed by paragraph (a) to have ended immediately before that time; and

(c) such amount as is prescribed shall be included in the foreign accrual property income (within the meaning assigned by subsection 95(1)) of the foreign affiliate for the taxation year that is deemed by paragraph (a) to have ended immediately before that time.

## 48.1 (1) Gain when small business corporation becomes public[ly listed] — Where

(a) at any time in a taxation year an individual owns capital property that is a share of a class of the capital stock of a corporation that,

(i) at that time, is a small business corporation, and

(ii) immediately after that time, ceases to be a small business corporation because a class of its shares is listed on a prescribed stock exchange, and

### Proposed Amendment — 48.1(1)(a)(ii)

(ii) immediately after that time, ceases to be a small business corporation because a class of its or another corporation's shares is listed on a prescribed stock exchange, and

**Application**: Bill C-43 (First Reading September 20, 2000), s. 18, will amend subpara. 48.1(1)(a)(ii) to read as above, applicable to corporations that cease to be small business corporations after 1999.

Where a corporation ceases to be a Canadian-controlled private corporation in a taxation year solely because of the application of the amendment to 125(7)"Canadian-controlled private corporation", an election under subsec. 48.1(1), as amended, that is made by an individual in respect of the 2000 taxation year is deemed to have been made on time if the election is made on or before the individual's filing-due date for the taxation year in which the amending legislation is assented to.

**Technical Notes**: Section 48.1 allows the owner of qualified small business corporation shares to access the capital gains exemption under subsection 110.6(2.1) of the Act in respect of those shares when the corporation lists its shares on a prescribed stock exchange in Canada or outside of Canada. The listing of the shares on a prescribed stock exchange results in the shares losing their status as qualified small business corporation shares. Such a shareholder may elect to be treated as having disposed of the shares immediately before the change in the corporation's status, in order to realize all or any part of any latent capital gain on the shares. The shareholder is then treated as having reacquired the shares at a cost equal to their deemed proceeds of disposition.

Subsection 48.1(1) is amended as a consequence of amendments to the definition of "Canadian-controlled private corporation" (CCPC) in subsection 125(7) of the Act. In order to be a small business corporation as defined in subsection 248(1) of the Act, a corporation must, among other things, be a CCPC. The amended definition of CCPC will, however, deny CCPC status to a corporation controlled by a Canadian resident corporation with shares listed on a prescribed stock exchange outside of Canada. Such a corporation will, therefore, no longer qualify as a small business corporation, and, in the absence of a rule allowing the shareholder to trigger a capital gain that had accrued before the change of the corporation's status, its shares would not be eligible for the capital gains exemption. Subparagraph 48.1(1)(a)(ii) of the Act is amended to ensure that the election under section 48.1 is available to realize a capital gain in such a case.

Not only will shareholders of subsidiaries controlled by corporations that have newly listed their shares on a prescribed foreign exchange qualify to make the election, but also those subsidiaries controlled by a corporation the shares of which were already listed on a prescribed foreign exchange on January 1, 2000, when the revised CCPC definition takes effect. If a subsidiary's parent corporation's shares were listed on that date, and the subsidiary was a small business corporation on December 31, 1999, an election under section 48.1 by an individual shareholder of the subsidiary will be treated as having been made in a timely manner provided it is made on or before the individual's filing-due date for the taxation year in which the Bill implementing this amendment receives Royal Assent.

(b) the individual elects in prescribed form to have this section apply,

the individual shall be deemed, except for the purposes of sections 7 and 35 and paragraph 110(1)(d.1),

(c) to have disposed of the share at that time for proceeds of disposition equal to the greater of

(i) the adjusted cost base to the individual of the share at that time, and

(ii) the lesser of the fair market value of the share at that time and such amount as is designated in the prescribed form by the individual in respect of the share, and

(d) to have reacquired the share immediately after that time at a cost equal to those proceeds of disposition.

**Related Provisions**: 44.1(11) — 48.1 inapplicable in determining eligible small business corporation share for small business investment rollover; 53(4) — Effect on adjusted cost base where para. 48.1(1)(c) applies; 110.6(2.1) — Capital gains deduction — qualified small business corporation shares.

**Notes**: See Notes at end of 48.1 for an explanation of the purpose of this section.

48.1(1)(a)(ii) amended by 1995-97 technical bill, effective for corporations that cease to be a small business corporation after 1995. However, an election made under amended 48.1(1) for the 1995 taxation year is deemed to have been made on time, if

(a) a class of the shares of the capital stock of the corporation was, on January 1, 1996, listed on a stock exchange listed in Reg. 3201;

(b) the corporation was a small business corporation on December 31, 1995; and

(c) the election is made by September 30, 1998.

Previously read, since 1991:

(ii) immediately after that time, becomes a public corporation because of the listing of a class of its shares on a prescribed stock exchange in Canada, and

**Regulations**: 3200, 3201 (prescribed stock exchanges for 48.1(1)(a)(ii)).

**Forms**: T2101: Election for gains on shares of a corporation becoming public.

**(2) Time for election** — An election made under subsection (1) by an individual for a taxation year shall be made on or before the individual's filing-due date for the year.

**(3) Late filed election** — Where the election referred to in subsection (2) was not made on or before the day referred to therein, the election shall be deemed for the purposes of subsections (1) and (2) to have been made on that day if, on or before the day that is 2 years after that day,

(a) the election is made in prescribed form; and

(b) an estimate of the penalty in respect of that election is paid by the individual when the election is made.

**(4) Penalty for late filed election** — For the purposes of this section, the penalty in respect of an election referred to in paragraph (3)(a) is an amount equal to the lesser of

(a) ¼ of 1% of the amount, if any, by which

(i) the proceeds of disposition determined under subsection (1)

exceed

(ii) the amount referred to in subparagraph (1)(c)(i)

for each month or part of a month during the period commencing on the day referred to in subsection (2) and ending on the day the election is made, and

(b) an amount equal to the product obtained by multiplying $100 by the number of months each of which is a month all or part of which is during the period referred to in paragraph (a).

**(5) Unpaid balance of penalty** — The Minister shall, with all due dispatch, examine each election referred to in paragraph (3)(a), assess the penalty payable and send a notice of assessment to the individual, who shall pay forthwith to the Receiver General the amount, if any, by which the penalty so assessed exceeds the total of all amounts previously paid on account of that penalty.

**Notes [s. 48.1]**: 48.1 added by 1991 Budget, effective 1991. It allows the owner of qualified small business corporation shares (as defined in 110.6(1)) to crystallize the accrued capital gain for purposes of the $500,000 capital gains exemption in 110.6(2.1) without having to actually sell the shares before the corporation has its shares listed on a stock exchange. (Once the shares are listed the corporation no longer qualifies as a small business corporation.)

See Gordon Funt, "Section 48.1 — Going Public and the Lifetime Capital Gains Exemption", VI(3) *Business Vehicles* (Federated Press) 305-307 (2000).

The CCRA takes the view that an election under 48.1 cannot be revoked: VIEWS doc #9916575. Thus, if an error is made in determining the availability of the exemption, there is no way to undo the election. The CBA/CICA Joint Committee on Taxation has submitted to the Dept. of Finance (Dec. 2/99) that this should be changed.

48.1(2) amended by 1995 Budget, effective 1995. For 1991-94, read "balance-due day" instead of "filing-due date" (see definitions of both terms in 248(1)). The change results from the filing deadline for individuals carrying on business (and their spouses) having been extended from April 30 to June 15 (see 150(1)(d)).

**Definitions [s. 48.1]**: "adjusted cost base" — 54, 248(1); "amount" — 248(1); "capital property" — 54, 248(1); "class of shares" — 248(6); "corporation" — 248(1), *Interpretation Act* 35(1); "filing-due date" — 150(1), 248(1); "individual", "Minister", "prescribed" — 248(1); "prescribed stock exchange" — Reg. 3200, 3201; "share", "small business corporation" — 248(1); "taxation year" — 11(2), 249.

**49. (1) Granting of options** — Subject to subsections (3) and (3.1), for the purposes of this subdivision, the granting of an option, other than

(a) an option to acquire or to dispose of a principal residence,

(b) an option granted by a corporation to acquire shares of its capital stock or bonds or debentures to be issued by it, or

(c) an option granted by a trust to acquire units of the trust to be issued by the trust,

is a disposition of a property the adjusted cost base of which to the grantor immediately before the grant is nil.

**Related Provisions**: 13(5.3) — Disposition of option on depreciable property or real property; 49(2), (2.1) — Where option expires; 49(5) — Extension or renewal of options.

**Notes**: 49(1)(c) added by 1991 technical bill, and "(2), (3) and (3.1)" in opening words changed to "(3) and (3.1)", effective for options granted after 1989.

49(1) amended by 1985 Budget to add reference to 45(3.1), effective for dispositions of property under options granted, extended or renewed after November 21, 1985.

**Interpretation Bulletins**: IT-96R6: Options granted by corporations to acquire shares, bonds or debentures and by trusts to acquire trust units; IT-403R: Options on real estate.

**(2) Where option expires** — Where at any time an option described in paragraph (1)(b) (other than an option to acquire shares of the capital stock of a corporation in consideration for the incurring, pursuant to an agreement described in paragraph (e) of the definition "Canadian exploration and development expenses" in subsection 66(15), paragraph (i) of the definition "Canadian exploration expense" in subsection 66.1(6), paragraph (g) of the definition "Canadian development expense" in subsection 66.2(5) or paragraph (c) of the definition "Canadian oil and gas property expense" in subsection 66.4(5), of any expense described in whichever of those paragraphs is applicable) that has been granted by a corporation after 1971 expires,

(a) the corporation shall be deemed to have disposed of capital property at that time for proceeds equal to the proceeds received by it for the granting of the option; and

(b) the adjusted cost base to the corporation of that capital property immediately before that time shall be deemed to be nil.

**Related Provisions**: 49(5) — Extension or renewal of options; 54 "superficial loss"(d) — Superficial loss rule does not apply; 87(2)(o) — Amalgamations — expiry of options previously granted.

**Interpretation Bulletins**: IT-96R6: Options granted by corporations to acquire shares, bonds or debentures and by trusts to acquire trust units; IT-98R2: Investment corporations.

**(2.1) Idem** — Where at any time an option referred to in paragraph (1)(c) expires,

(a) the trust shall be deemed to have disposed of capital property at that time for proceeds equal to the proceeds received by it for the granting of the option; and

(b) the adjusted cost base to the trust of that capital property immediately before that time shall be deemed to be nil.

**Related Provisions**: 49(5) — Extension or renewal; 54 "superficial loss"(d) — Superficial loss rule does not apply.

**Notes**: 49(2.1) added by 1991 technical bill, effective for options granted after 1989.

**Interpretation Bulletins**: IT-96R6: Options granted by corporations to acquire shares, bonds or debentures and by trusts to acquire trust units.

**(3) Where option to acquire exercised** — Where an option to acquire property is exercised so that property is disposed of by a taxpayer (in this subsection referred to as the "vendor") or so that property is acquired by another taxpayer (in this subsection referred to as the "purchaser"), for the purpose of computing the income of each such taxpayer the granting and the exercise of the option shall be deemed not to be dispositions of property and there shall be included

(a) in computing the vendor's proceeds of disposition of the property, the consideration received by the vendor for the option; and

(b) in computing the cost to the purchaser of the property,

(i) where paragraph 53(1)(j) applied to the acquisition of the property by the purchaser because a person who did not deal at arm's length with the purchaser was deemed because of the acquisition to have received a benefit under section 7, the adjusted cost base to that person of the option immediately before that person last disposed of the option, and

(ii) in any other case, the adjusted cost base to the purchaser of the option.

**Related Provisions**: 49(3.2) — Election to have 49(3) not apply where option granted before Feb. 23/94; 49(5) — Extension or renewal of option; 164(5)(c), 164(5.1)(c) — Effect of carryback of loss.

**Notes**: 49(3)(b)(i) added by 1991 technical bill, effective July 14, 1990.

**Interpretation Bulletins**: IT-96R6: Options granted by corporations to acquire shares, bonds or debentures and by trusts to acquire trust units; IT-403R: Options on real estate.

**(3.01) Option to acquire specified property exercised** — Where at any time a taxpayer exercises an option to acquire a specified property,

(a) there shall be deducted after that time in computing the adjusted cost base to the taxpayer of the specified property the total of all amounts deducted under paragraph 53(2)(g.1) in computing, immediately before that time, the adjusted cost base to the taxpayer of the option; and

(b) the amount determined under paragraph (a) in respect of that acquisition shall be added after that time in computing the adjusted cost base to the taxpayer of the specified property.

**Related Provisions**: 53(1)(q) — Addition to adjusted cost base for amount under 49(3.01)(b); 53(2)(g.1) — Reduction in adjusted cost base under 49(3.01)(a); 80.03(2)(a) — Deemed gain on disposition following debt forgiveness.

**Notes**: 49(3.01) added by 1994 tax amendments bill (Part I), effective for taxation years that end after February 21, 1994. See Notes to 47(1).

**Interpretation Bulletins**: IT-96R6: Options granted by corporations to acquire shares, bonds or debentures and by trusts to acquire trust units.

**(3.1) Where option to dispose exercised** — Where an option to dispose of property is exercised so that property is disposed of by a taxpayer (in this subsection referred to as the "vendor") or so that property is acquired by another taxpayer (in this subsection referred to as the "purchaser"), for the purpose of computing the income of each such taxpayer the granting and the exercise of the option shall be deemed not to be dispositions of property and there shall be deducted

(a) in computing the vendor's proceeds of disposition of the property, the adjusted cost base to the vendor of the option; and

(b) in computing the cost to the purchaser of the property, the consideration received by the purchaser for the option.

**Related Provisions**: 49(5) — Extension or renewal of option.

**Notes**: 49(3.1) added by 1985 Budget, effective for dispositions of property under options granted, extended or renewed after November 21, 1985.

**Interpretation Bulletins**: IT-96R6: Options granted by corporations to acquire shares, bonds or debentures and by trusts to acquire trust units; IT-403R: Options on real estate.

**(3.2) Option granted before February 23, 1994** — Where an individual (other than a trust) who disposes of property pursuant to the exercise of an option that was granted by the individual before February 23, 1994 so elects in the individual's return of income for the taxation year in which the disposition occurs, subsection (3) does not apply in respect of the disposition in computing the income of the individual.

**Notes**: 49(3.2) added by 1994 Budget, effective for dispositions after February 22, 1994. It is consequential on the elimination of the $100,000 capital gains exemption. It allows the grantor of an option granted before February 23, 1994 to elect not to have 49(3) apply to the option. Thus, the gain arising on the granting of the option can be a gain from a disposition before February 23, 1994, and eligible for the exemption under 110.6(3).

**Interpretation Bulletins**: IT-96R6: Options granted by corporations to acquire shares, bonds or debentures and by trusts to acquire trust units.

**(4) Reassessment where option exercised in subsequent year** — Where

(a) an option granted by a taxpayer in a taxation year (in this subsection referred to as the "initial year") is exercised in a subsequent taxation year (in this subsection referred to as the "subsequent year"),

(b) the taxpayer has filed a return of the taxpayer's income for the initial year as required by section 150, and

(c) on or before the day on or before which the taxpayer was required by section 150 to file a return of the taxpayer's income for the subsequent year, the taxpayer has filed an amended return for the initial year excluding from the taxpayer's income the proceeds received by the taxpayer for the granting of the option,

such reassessment of the taxpayer's tax, interest or penalties for the year shall be made as is necessary to give effect to the exclusion.

**Related Provisions**: 49(5) — Extension or renewal of option; 161(7)(b)(iii) — Effect of carryback of loss, etc.

**Interpretation Bulletins**: IT-96R6: Options granted by corporations to acquire shares, bonds or debentures and by trusts to acquire trust units. See also list at end of s. 49; IT-384R: Reassessment where option exercised in subsequent year.

**(5) [Extension or renewal of option]** — Where a taxpayer has granted an option (in this subsection referred to as the "original option") to which subsection (1), (2) or (2.1) applies, and grants one or more extensions or renewals of that original option,

(a) for the purposes of subsections (1), (2) and (2.1), the granting of each extension or renewal shall be deemed to be the granting of an option at the time the extension or renewal is granted;

(b) for the purposes of subsections (2) to (4) and subparagraph (b)(iv) of the definition "disposition" in section 54, the original option and each extension or renewal thereof shall be deemed to be the same option; and

**Proposed Amendment — 49(5)(b)**

(b) for the purposes of subsections (2) to (4) and subparagraph (b)(iv) of the definition "disposition" in subsection 248(1), the original option and each extension or renewal of it is deemed to be the same option; and

**Application**: Bill C-43 (First Reading September 20, 2000), s. 19, will amend para. 49(5)(b) to read as above, applicable to options granted after December 23, 1998.

**Technical Notes**: Subsection 49(5) sets out rules dealing with extensions or renewals of an option.

Subsection 49(5) is amended to change a cross-reference in the subsection to the definition "disposition" in section 54 to a corresponding cross-reference to the new definition "disposition" in subsection 248(1).

(c) subsection (4) shall be read as if the year in which the original option was granted and each year in which any extension or renewal thereof was granted were all initial years.

**Notes**: 49(5)(b) amended by 1985 Budget to add reference to 45(3.1), effective for dispositions of property under options granted, extended or renewed after November 21, 1985.

References to 49(2.1) in 49(5) added by 1991 technical bill, effective for options granted, extended or renewed after 1989.

**Interpretation Bulletins**: IT-96R6: Options to acquire shares, bonds or debentures and by trusts to acquire trust units.

**Definitions [s. 49]**: "adjusted cost base" — 54, 248(1); "arm's length" — 251(1); "assessment" — 248(1); "capital property" — 54, 248(1); "corporation" — 248(1), *Interpretation Act* 35(1); "disposition" — 54 [to be repealed], 248(1) [draft]; "person" — 248(1); "principal residence" — 54; "property", "share" — 248(1); "specified property" — 54; "taxation year" — 249; "taxpayer" — 248(1); "trust" — 104(1), 248(1), (3).

**Interpretation Bulletins [s. 49]**: IT-334R2: Miscellaneous receipts; IT-403R: Options on real estate; IT-479R: Transactions in securities.

**49.1 No disposition where obligation satisfied** — For greater certainty, where a taxpayer acquires a particular property in satisfaction of an absolute or contingent obligation of a person or partnership to provide the particular property pursuant to a contract or other arrangement one of the main objectives of which was to establish a right, whether absolute or contingent, to the particular property and that right was not under the terms of a trust, partnership agreement, share or debt obligation, the satisfaction of the obligation is not a disposition of that right.

**Notes**: 49.1 added by 1999 Budget bill, effective for obligations satisfied after December 15, 1998. It is relevant to the demutualization of insurance corporations (see 139.1) as it clarifies that there are no tax consequences from satisfying of an undertaking to issue shares. It is also generally intended to apply in connection with property acquired as a result of the execution of a contract.

**Definitions**: "disposition" — 248(1); "partnership" — see Notes to 96(1); "person", "property", "share", "taxpayer" — 248(1); "trust" — 104(1), 248(1), (3).

**50. (1) Debts established to be bad debts and shares of bankrupt corporation** — For the purposes of this subdivision, where

(a) a debt owing to a taxpayer at the end of a taxation year (other than a debt owing to the taxpayer in respect of the disposition of personal-use property) is established by the taxpayer to have become a bad debt in the year, or

(b) a share (other than a share received by a taxpayer as consideration in respect of the disposition of personal-use property) of the capital stock of a corporation is owned by the taxpayer at the end of a taxation year and

(i) the corporation has during the year become a bankrupt (within the meaning of subsection 128(3)),

(ii) the corporation is a corporation referred to in section 6 of the *Winding-up and Restructuring Act* that is insolvent (within the meaning of that Act) and in respect of which a winding-up order under that Act has been made in the year, or

(iii) at the end of the year,

(A) the corporation is insolvent,

(B) neither the corporation nor a corporation controlled by it carries on business,

(C) the fair market value of the share is nil, and

(D) it is reasonable to expect that the corporation will be dissolved or wound up and will not commence to carry on business and the taxpayer elects in the taxpayer's return of income for the year to have this subsection apply in respect of the debt or the share, as the case may be, the taxpayer shall be deemed to have disposed of the debt or the share, as the case may be, at the end of the year for proceeds equal to nil and to have reacquired it immediately after the end of the year at a cost equal to nil.

**Related Provisions**: 39(1)(c) — Business investment loss; 40(2)(e.2), (g)(ii) — Restrictions on capital losses on debt; 50(1.1) — Where insolvent corporation begins carrying on business again; 54"superficial loss"(c) — Superficial loss rule does not apply; 79.1(8) — No bad debt deduction where property seized by creditor; 80.01(6)(b) — Debt deemed a specified obligation after subsec. 50(1) applies; 80.01(8) — Deemed settlement after debt parking; 96(3) — Election by members of partnership; 111(5.3) — Limitation on bad debt deduction after change in control of corporation; 220(3.2), Reg. 600(b) — Late filing of election or revocation.

**Notes**: The deemed disposition on bad debt, bankruptcy or insolvency triggers a capital loss under 39(1)(b). If the corporation was a "small business corporation" (as defined in 248(1)), the loss will be a business investment loss under 39(1)(c), and ½ of the loss will be an allowable business investment loss (38(c)), which can be applied under 3(d) against income from other sources rather than just against taxable capital gains.

For the CCRA's views on when a debt becomes bad, see Interpretation Bulletin IT-442R.

The draft legislation of July 12, 1994 (debt forgiveness) proposed turning 50(1)(a) into two paragraphs, (a) and (a.1). However, that amendment was not included in the 1994 tax amendments bill.

50(1)(b)(iii) and closing words of 50(1) amended by 1994 tax amendments bill (Part I), effective for taxation years that end after February 21, 1994. For earlier years, read:

> (iii) at the end of the year, the corporation is insolvent and neither the corporation nor a corporation controlled by it carries on business, and
>> (A) at the end of the year, the fair market value of the share is nil and it is reasonable to expect that the corporation will be dissolved or wound up and will not begin to carry on business, and
>> (B) in the taxpayer's return of income under this Part for the year the taxpayer elects to have this subsection apply in respect of the share,
>
> the taxpayer shall be deemed to have disposed of the debt or the share, as the case may be, at the end of the year for proceeds equal to nil and to have reacquired it immediately thereafter at a cost equal to nil.

The essence of the amendment was to have 50(1) apply, in the case of a debt payable to the taxpayer, only where the taxpayer elects. One might not elect if electing would result in 80.01(8) applying to a non-arm's length debtor or a debtor in which the taxpayer has a significant interest. See 80.01(6)–(8).

50(1)(b)(iii) amended by 1991 technical bill, effective

> (a) for 1990 and later taxation years; and
>
> (b) where the taxpayer so elects in respect of a share of the capital stock of a corporation by notifying Revenue Canada in writing by December 10, 1993 (deadline extended by 1992 technical bill, s. 159), for each of the taxpayer's 1985 to 1989 taxation years in respect of the share owned by the taxpayer at the end of the year (except that the amended subsec. is not applicable in respect of any such taxation year in respect of the share where the corporation or a corporation controlled by it carries on business during the 24-month period immediately following the end

of the year); and, where a taxpayer makes such an election in respect of a share of the capital stock of a corporation,

> (i) the taxpayer shall be deemed to have elected, in the taxpayer's returns of income under Part I for each of those years, to have subsec. 50(1), as amended, apply in respect of the share, and
>
> (ii) notwithstanding subsecs. 152(4) to (5), such assessments of tax, interest and penalties shall be made as are necessary to give effect to the election.

For earlier cases, read:

> (iii) the corporation ceased to carry on all of its businesses and was insolvent during the year, and
>> (A) at the end of the year, the fair market value of the share is nil and it is reasonable to expect that the corporation will be dissolved or wound up and will not commence to carry on any business, and
>> (B) the corporation did not commence to carry on any business in the year or within 24 months following the end of the year,

S. 6 of the *Winding-up and Restructuring Act*, R.S.C. 1985, c. W-11, (as amended by 1996, c. 6, s. 136) provides:

> **6. Application** — This Act applies to all corporations incorporated by or under the authority of an Act of Parliament, of the former Province of Canada or of the Province of Nova Scotia, New Brunswick, British Columbia, Prince Edward Island or Newfoundland, and whose incorporation and affairs are subject to the legislative authority of Parliament, and to incorporate banks and savings banks, trust companies, insurance companies, loan companies having borrowing powers, building societies having a capital stock and incorporated trading companies doing business in Canada wherever incorporated where any such body
>
>> (a) is insolvent;
>> (b) is in liquidation or in process of being wound up and, on petition by any of its shareholders or creditors, assignees or liquidators, asks to be brought under this Act; or
>> (c) if it is a financial institution, is under the control, or its assets are under the control, of the Superintendent and is the subject of an application for a winding-up order under section 10.1.

S. 3 of the *Winding-Up and Restructuring Act* defines "insolvent" as follows:

> **3. When company deemed insolvent** — A company is deemed insolvent
>
>> (a) if it is unable to pay its debts as they become due;
>> (b) if it calls a meeting of its creditors for the purpose of compounding with them;
>> (c) if it exhibits a statement showing its inability to meet its liabilities;
>> (d) if it has otherwise acknowledged its insolvency;
>> (e) if it assigns, removes or disposes of, or attempts or is about to assign, remove or dispose of, any of its property, with intent to defraud, defeat or delay its creditors, or any of them;
>> (f) if, with the intent referred to in paragraph (e), it has procured its money, goods, chattels, land or property to be seized, levied on or taken, under or by any process of execution;
>> (g) if it has made any general conveyance or assignment of its property for the benefit of its creditors, or if, being unable to meet its liabilities in full, it makes any sale or conveyance of the whole or the main part of its stock in trade or assets without the consent of its creditors or without satisfying their claims; or

(h) if it permits any execution issued against it, under which any of its goods, chattels, land or property are seized, levied on or taken in execution, to remain unsatisfied until within four days of the time fixed by the sheriff or other officer for the sale thereof, or for fifteen days after the seizure.

**Interpretation Bulletins**: IT-159R3: Capital debts established to be bad debts; IT-188R: Sale of accounts receivable; IT-220R2: Capital cost allowance — proceeds of disposition of depreciable property; IT-239R2: Deductibility of capital losses from guaranteeing loans for inadequate consideration and from loaning funds at less than a reasonable rate of interest in non-arm's length circumstances; IT-442R: Bad debts and reserves for doubtful debts; IT-484R2: Business investment losses.

**(1.1) Idem** — Where

(a) a taxpayer is deemed because of subparagraph (1)(b)(iii) to have disposed of a share of the capital stock of a corporation at the end of a taxation year, and

(b) the taxpayer or a person with whom the taxpayer is not dealing at arm's length owns the share at the earliest time, during the 24-month period immediately following the disposition, that the corporation or a corporation controlled by it carries on business,

the taxpayer or the person, as the case may be, shall be deemed to have disposed of the share at that earliest time for proceeds of disposition equal to its adjusted cost base to the taxpayer determined immediately before the time of the disposition referred to in paragraph (a) and to have reacquired it immediately after that earliest time at a cost equal to those proceeds.

**Notes**: 50(1.1) added by 1991 technical bill, effective 1990. It effectively eliminates the capital loss triggered by 50(1)(b)(iii) if the corporation begins to carry on business again within 2 years.

**(2) Where debt a personal-use property** — Where at the end of a taxation year a debt that is a personal-use property of a taxpayer is owing to the taxpayer by a person with whom the taxpayer deals at arm's length and is established by the taxpayer to have become a bad debt in the year,

(a) the taxpayer shall be deemed to have disposed of it at the end of the year for proceeds equal to the amount, if any, by which

(i) its adjusted cost base to the taxpayer immediately before the end of the year

exceeds

(ii) the amount of the taxpayer's gain, if any, from the disposition of the personal-use property the proceeds of disposition of which included the debt; and

(b) the taxpayer shall be deemed to have reacquired the debt immediately after the end of the year at a cost equal to the amount of the proceeds determined under paragraph (a).

**Related Provisions**: 46 — Disposition of personal-use property; 54"superficial loss"(c) — Superficial loss rule does not apply.

**Interpretation Bulletins**: IT-159R3: Capital debts established to be bad debts.

**(3) Disposal of RHOSP properties** — Each trust that was at the end of 1985 governed by a registered home ownership savings plan (within the meaning assigned by paragraph 146.2(1)(h) of the *Income Tax Act*, chapter 148 of the Revised Statutes of Canada, 1952, as it read in its application to the 1985 taxation year) shall be deemed to have disposed, immediately before 1986, of each property it holds at that time for proceeds of disposition equal to the fair market value of the property at that time and to have reacquired it immediately after 1985 at a cost equal to that fair market value.

**I.T. Application Rules**: 69 (meaning of "*Income Tax Act*, chapter 148 of the Revised Statutes of Canada, 1952").

**Definitions [s. 50]**: "adjusted cost base" — 54, 248(1); "amount" — 248(1); "carrying on business" — 253; "controlled" — 256(6), (6.1); "corporation" — 248(1), *Interpretation Act* 35(1); "disposition" — 54 [to be repealed], 248(1) [draft]; "personal-use property" — 54, 248(1); "share" — 248(1); "taxation year" — 249; "taxpayer" — 248(1).

**51. (1) Convertible property** — Where a share of the capital stock of a corporation is acquired by a taxpayer from the corporation in exchange for

(a) a capital property of the taxpayer that is another share of the corporation (in this section referred to as a "convertible property"), or

(b) a capital property of the taxpayer that is a bond, debenture or note of the corporation the terms of which confer on the holder the right to make the exchange (in this section referred to as a "convertible property")

and no consideration other than the share is received by the taxpayer for the convertible property,

(c) except for the purpose of subsection 20(21), the exchange shall be deemed not to be a disposition of the convertible property,

(d) the cost to the taxpayer of all the shares of a particular class acquired by the taxpayer on the exchange shall be deemed to be the amount determined by the formula

$$A \times \frac{B}{C}$$

where

A is the adjusted cost base to the taxpayer of the convertible property immediately before the exchange,

B is the fair market value, immediately after the exchange, of all the shares of the particular class acquired by the taxpayer on the exchange, and

C is the fair market value, immediately after the exchange, of all the shares acquired by the taxpayer on the exchange,

(d.1) there shall be deducted, after the exchange, in computing the adjusted cost base to the taxpayer of a share acquired by the taxpayer on the exchange, the amount determined by the formula

$$A \times \frac{B}{C}$$

where

A is the total of all amounts deducted under paragraph 53(2)(g.1) in computing, immediately before the exchange, the adjusted cost base to the taxpayer of the convertible property,

B is the fair market value, immediately after the exchange, of that share, and

C is the fair market value, immediately after the exchange, of all the shares acquired by the taxpayer on the exchange,

(d.2) the amount determined under paragraph (d.1) in respect of a share shall be added, after the exchange, in computing the adjusted cost base to the taxpayer of the share,

(e) for the purposes of sections 74.4 and 74.5, the exchange shall be deemed to be a transfer of the convertible property by the taxpayer to the corporation, and

(f) where the convertible property is taxable Canadian property of the taxpayer, the share acquired by the taxpayer on the exchange shall be deemed to be taxable Canadian property of the taxpayer.

**Related Provisions**: 51(2) — Where benefit conferred on related person; 51(3) — Computation of paid-up capital after exchange of shares; 51.1 — Conversion of debt obligation; 53(1)(q) — Addition to adjusted cost base for amount under 51(1)(d.2); 53(2)(g.1) — Reduction in adjusted cost base under 51(1)(d.1); 77 — Bond conversion; 80(2)(g) — Shares issued in settlement of debt; 80.03(2)(a) — Deemed gain on disposition following debt forgiveness; 84(1)(c.3) — Contributed surplus; 86(2) — Exchange of shares; 86(3) — Exchange of shares — reorganization of capital; 107(2)(d.1)(iii), 107.4(3)(f) — Deemed taxable Canadian property retains status when rolled out of trust or into trust; 112(7) — Application of stop-loss rule where shares exchanged.

**Notes**: Opening words of 51(1) amended to add "from the corporation" by 1995-97 technical bill, effective for exchanges occurring after June 20, 1996, other than exchanges occurring before 1997 under agreements in writing made by June 20, 1996.

51(1) amended by 1993 technical bill, effective for exchanges occurring, and reorganizations that begin, after December 21, 1992. For earlier cases, read:

51. (1) Where shares of the capital stock of a corporation have been acquired by a taxpayer in exchange for a capital property of the taxpayer that was a share, bond, debenture or note of the corporation (in this section referred to as a "convertible property") the terms of which conferred on the holder the right to make the exchange and no consideration was received by the taxpayer for the convertible property other than those shares, the following rules apply:

(a) the exchange shall be deemed not to have been a disposition of property;

(b) the cost to the taxpayer of all the shares of a particular class acquired by the taxpayer on the exchange shall be deemed to be that proportion of the adjusted cost base to the taxpayer of the convertible property immediately before the exchange that

(i) the fair market value, immediately after the exchange, of all the shares of the particular class acquired by the taxpayer on the exchange

is of

(ii) the fair market value, immediately after the exchange, of all the shares acquired by the taxpayer on the exchange; and

(c) for the purposes of sections 74.4 and 74.5, the exchange shall be deemed to be a transfer of the convertible property by the taxpayer to the corporation.

Aside from the cosmetic redrafting of the formula, the amendment provides that where a share (rather than debt) is exchanged for new shares, the rollover is available even though the terms and conditions of the share do not provide a right of exchange or conversion. This is accomplished by limiting the requirement of "the terms of which confer..." to para. (b) in the amended version, rather than having it in the opening words of the subsection.

51(1)(d.1) and (d.2) added by 1994 tax amendments bill (Part I), effective for taxation years that end after February 21, 1994. See Notes to 47(1).

**I.T. Application Rules**: 26(28).

**Interpretation Bulletins**: IT-115R2: Fractional interest in shares. See also list at end of s. 51.

**(2) Idem** — Notwithstanding subsection (1), where

(a) shares of the capital stock of a corporation have been acquired by a taxpayer in exchange for a convertible property in circumstances such that, but for this subsection, subsection (1) would have applied,

(b) the fair market value of the convertible property immediately before the exchange exceeds the fair market value of the shares immediately after the exchange, and

(c) it is reasonable to regard any portion of the excess (in this subsection referred to as the "gift portion") as a benefit that the taxpayer desired to have conferred on a person related to the taxpayer,

the following rules apply:

(d) the taxpayer shall be deemed to have disposed of the convertible property for proceeds of disposition equal to the lesser of

(i) the total of its adjusted cost base to the taxpayer immediately before the exchange and the gift portion, and

(ii) the fair market value of the convertible property immediately before the exchange,

(e) the taxpayer's capital loss from the disposition of the convertible property shall be deemed to be nil, and

(f) the cost to the taxpayer of all the shares of a particular class acquired in exchange for the convertible property shall be deemed to be that proportion of the lesser of

(i) the adjusted cost base to the taxpayer of the convertible property immediately before the exchange, and

(ii) the total of the fair market value immediately after the exchange of all the shares acquired by the taxpayer in exchange for the convertible property and the amount that, but for paragraph (e), would have been the taxpayer's capital loss on the disposition of the convertible property,

that

(iii) the fair market value, immediately after the exchange, of all the shares of the particular class acquired by the taxpayer on the exchange

is of

(iv) the fair market value, immediately after the exchange, of all the shares acquired by the taxpayer on the exchange.

**Related Provisions**: 112(7) — Application of stop-loss rule where shares exchanged.

**(3) Computation of paid-up capital** — Where subsection (1) applies to the exchange of convertible property described in paragraph (1)(a) (referred to in this subsection as the "old shares"), in computing the paid-up capital in respect of a particular class of shares of the capital stock of the corporation at any particular time that is the time of, or any time after, the exchange

(a) there shall be deducted the amount determined by the formula

$$(A - B) \times \frac{C}{A}$$

where

A is the total of all amounts each of which is the amount of the increase, if any, as a result of the exchange, in the paid-up capital in respect of a class of shares of the capital stock of the corporation, computed without reference to this subsection as it applies to the exchange,

B is the paid-up capital immediately before the exchange in respect of the old shares, and

C is the increase, if any, as a result of the exchange, in the paid-up capital in respect of the particular class of shares, computed without reference to this subsection as it applies to the exchange; and

(b) there shall be added an amount equal to the lesser of

(i) the amount, if any, by which

(A) the total of all amounts deemed by subsection 84(3), (4) or (4.1) to be a dividend on shares of that class paid by the corporation before the particular time

exceeds

(B) the total that would be determined under clause (A) if this Act were read without reference to paragraph (a), and

(ii) the total of all amounts required by paragraph (a) to be deducted in respect of that particular class of shares before the particular time.

**Related Provisions**: 257 — Formula cannot calculate to less than zero.

**Notes**: 51(3) added by 1993 technical bill, effective for exchanges occurring after August 1992. However, for exchanges from September 1 through December 20, 1992, it will not apply if the corporation issuing the new shares filed a written election with Revenue Canada by December 31, 1994.

The effect of 51(3), which reduces the paid-up capital (PUC) of the new shares, is to permit a PUC deficiency on the old shares (such as may have arisen where 85(2.1) applied to reduce PUC following a rollover under 85(1)) to flow through to the new shares. Thus, the 51(1) exchange will not result in an increase in PUC to which 84(1) would apply; and the amount received for the old shares for purposes of 84(3) will be equal to the PUC of the old shares (see 84(5)). 86(2.1) applies the same rule to share exchanges under s. 86.

**(4) Application** — Subsections (1) and (2) do not apply to any exchange to which subsection 85(1) or (2) or section 86 applies.

**Related Provisions**: 86(3) — Application of section 86.

**Notes**: 51(4) added by 1993 technical bill, effective for exchanges occurring, and reorganizations that begin, after December 21, 1992.

**Interpretation Bulletins**: IT-115R2: Fractional interest in shares.

**Definitions [s. 51]**: "adjusted cost base" — 54, 248(1); "capital loss" — 39(1)(b), 248(1); "capital property" — 54, 248(1); "class of shares" — 248(6); "convertible property" — 51(1) (draft 51(1)(b)); "corporation" — 248(1), *Interpretation Act* 35(1); "disposition" — 54; "paid-up capital" — 89(1), 248(1); "property", "share" — 248(1); "taxable Canadian property" — 248(1); "taxpayer" — 248(1).

**Interpretation Bulletins [s. 51]**: IT-96R6: Options to acquire shares, bonds or debentures and by trusts to acquire trust units; IT-146R4: Shares entitling shareholders to choose taxable or capital dividends; IT-243R4: Dividend refund to private corporations.

**51.1 Conversion of debt obligation** — Where

(a) a taxpayer acquires a bond, debenture or note of a debtor (in this section referred to as the "new obligation") in exchange for a capital property of the taxpayer that is another bond, debenture or note of the same debtor (in this section referred to as the "convertible obligation"),

(b) the terms of the convertible obligation conferred on the holder the right to make the exchange, and

(c) the principal amount of the new obligation is equal to the principal amount of the convertible obligation,

the cost to the taxpayer of the new obligation and the proceeds of disposition of the convertible obligation shall be deemed to be equal to the adjusted cost base to the taxpayer of the convertible obligation immediately before the exchange.

**Notes**: 51.1 added by 1994 tax amendments bill (Part III), effective for exchanges occurring after October 1994. For earlier exchanges, see former s. 77.

**Definitions [s. 51.1]**: "adjusted cost base" — 54, 248(1); "amount" — 248(1); "capital property" — 54, 248(1); "convertible obligation", "new obligation" — 51.1(a); "principal amount" — 248(1); "proceeds of disposition" — 54; "taxpayer" — 248(1).

**I.T. Application Rules**: 26(25) (where old bond owned since before 1972).

**52. (1) Cost of certain property value of which included in income** — For the purposes of this subdivision, where a taxpayer has acquired property after 1971 (other than an annuity contract or property acquired as described in subsection (2), (3) or (6)) and an amount in respect of the value thereof was included in computing the taxpayer's income otherwise than under section 7, the amount so included shall be added in computing the cost to the taxpayer of that property, except to the extent that the amount was otherwise added to the cost or included in computing the adjusted cost base to the taxpayer of the property.

### Proposed Amendment — 52(1), (1.1)

**52. (1) Cost of certain property the value of which included in income** — Where

(a) a taxpayer acquired property after 1971 (other than an annuity contract, a right as a beneficiary under a trust to enforce payment of an amount by the trust to the taxpayer, property acquired in circumstances to which subsection (2) or (3) applies or property acquired from a trust in satisfaction of all or part of the taxpayer's capital interest in the trust), and

(b) an amount in respect of its value was

(i) included, otherwise than under section 7, in computing

(A) the taxpayer's taxable income or taxable income earned in Canada, as the case may be, for a taxation year during which the taxpayer was non-resident, or

(B) the taxpayer's income for a taxation year throughout which the taxpayer was resident in Canada, or

(ii) for the purpose of computing the tax payable under Part XIII by the taxpayer, included in an amount that was paid or credited to the taxpayer,

for the purposes of this subdivision, the amount so included shall be added in computing the cost to the taxpayer of the property, except to the extent that the amount was otherwise added to the cost or included in computing the adjusted cost base to the taxpayer of the property.

**(1.1) [Repealed]**

**Application**: Bill C-43 (First Reading September 20, 2000), subsec. 20(1), will amend subsec. 52(1) to read as above, and repeal subsec. 52(1.1), applicable after 1999 except that, in respect of property acquired before 2000 and disposed of before March 2000, para. 52(1)(a), shall be read as follows:

(a) a taxpayer acquired property after 1971 (other than an annuity contract or property acquired as described in subsection (2), (3) or (6)), and

**Technical Notes**: Subject to a number of exceptions, subsection 52(1) provides that, where an amount in respect of the value of a property has been included in computing a taxpayer's income, that amount is added in determining the cost to the taxpayer of the property for the purposes of determining capital gains and losses in respect of the property. Subsection 52(1.1) provides a similar rule in respect of taxable Canadian property of non-residents, except that it refers to a taxpayer's taxable income earned in Canada (as well as any amount subject to Part XIII withholding tax) instead of a taxpayer's income. These subsections do not apply to rights to enforce payments from a trust that are described in subsection 52(6).

Subsection 52(1) is amended and subsection 52(1.1) is repealed so that subsection 52(1) applies to all taxpayers, whether resident in Canada or not. Amended subsection 52(1) generally applies where a taxpayer acquired property and an amount in respect of its value was included in computing the taxpayer's income for a taxation year throughout which the taxpayer was resident in Canada (or in computing a non-resident taxpayer's taxable income earned in Canada under section 115, taxable income under section 114 or an amount from which tax is withheld under Part XIII).

The exceptions in existing subsection 52(1) also generally apply for the purposes of amended subsection 52(1). However, the exception relating to subsection 52(6) is eliminated because of the repeal of that subsection (as described in the commentary below). Instead, amended subsection 52(1) excepts property that is a beneficiary's right to enforce payments by a trust or that is acquired in satisfaction of a beneficiary's "capital interest" in the trust (as defined in amended subsection 108(1)).

**Related Provisions**: 69(5)(c) — No application to property appropriated by shareholder on winding-up.

**Notes**: 52(1) amended by 1992 technical bill, effective October 17, 1991, to add the closing words beginning "except to the extent", in order to eliminate double-counting.

**Interpretation Bulletins**: IT-96R6: Options to acquire shares, bonds or debentures and by trusts to acquire trust units; IT-432R2: Benefits conferred on shareholders.

**(1.1) Idem, where owner non-resident** — For the purposes of this subdivision, where a non-resident person has acquired property after 1971 (other than property acquired as described in subsection (2), (3) or (6)) that would, if that person disposed of it, be taxable Canadian property of that person and

(a) an amount in respect of the value thereof has been included, otherwise than under section 7, in computing that person's taxable income earned in Canada, or

(b) an amount in respect of the value thereof has, for the purposes of computing the tax payable by that person under Part XIII, been included in an amount that has been paid or credited to that person,

the amount so included shall be added in computing the cost to that person of that property.

### Proposed Repeal — 52(1.1)

See under 52(1).

**Related Provisions**: 69(5)(c) — No application to property appropriated by shareholder on winding-up.

**Interpretation Bulletins**: IT-432R2: Benefits conferred on shareholders.

**(2) Cost of property received as dividend in kind** — Where any property has, after 1971, been received by a shareholder of a corporation at any time as, on account or in lieu of payment of, or in satisfaction of, a dividend payable in kind (other than a stock dividend) in respect of a share owned by the shareholder of the capital stock of the corporation, the shareholder shall be deemed to have acquired the property at a cost to the shareholder equal to its fair market value at that time, and the corporation shall be deemed to have disposed of the property at that time for proceeds equal to that fair market value.

**Related Provisions**: 69(5)(c) — No application to property appropriated by shareholder on winding-up; 80.1(4) — Assets acquired from foreign affiliate of taxpayer as dividend in kind or as benefit to taxpayer; 86.1(1)(b) — No application to eligible distribution (foreign spin-off).

**I.T. Technical News**: No. 11 (U.S. spin-offs (divestitures) — dividends in kind).

**(3) Cost of stock dividend** — Where a shareholder of a corporation has, after 1971, received a stock dividend in respect of a share owned by the shareholder of the capital stock of the corporation, the shareholder shall be deemed to have acquired the share or shares received by the shareholder as a stock dividend at a cost to the shareholder equal to the total of

(a) where the stock dividend is a dividend, the amount of the stock dividend,

(a.1) where the stock dividend is not a dividend, nil, and

(b) where an amount is included in the shareholder's income in respect of the stock dividend under subsection 15(1.1), the amount so included.

**Related Provisions**: 95(3) — Stock dividends from foreign affiliates.

**Notes**: 52(3) amended by 1991 technical bill, effective for stock dividends paid after May 23, 1985. For earlier dividends, ignore the words "where the stock dividend is a dividend" in 52(3)(a) and ignore 52(3)(a.1). The changes tie in to amendments to the definition of "dividend" in 248(1).

**Interpretation Bulletins**: IT-88R2: Stock dividends.

**(4) Cost of property acquired as prize** — Where any property has been acquired by a taxpayer at any time after 1971 as a prize in connection with a lottery scheme, the taxpayer shall be deemed to have acquired the property at a cost to the taxpayer equal to its fair market value at that time.

**Related Provisions**: 40(2)(f) — No gain or loss on disposition of chance to win or right to receive a prize.

**Interpretation Bulletins**: IT-213R: Prizes from lottery schemes and giveaway contests.

**(5)** [Repealed under former Act]

**Notes**: 52(5) repealed in 1973, retroactive to 1972.

**(6) Cost of right to receive from trust** — Notwithstanding subsection (1), where a beneficiary under a trust acquires a right to enforce payment by the trust of an amount out of a capital gain or the income of the trust (determined without reference to the provisions of this Act) for the taxation year of the trust in which the right was acquired by the beneficiary, for the purposes of this subdivision, the cost to the beneficiary of the right shall be deemed to be the amount that became so payable.

### Proposed Repeal — 52(6)

**Application**: Bill C-43 (First Reading September 20, 2000), subsec. 20(2), will repeal subsec. 52(6), applicable after 1999, but not to rights that were acquired before 2000 and disposed of before March 2000.

**Technical Notes**: Subsection 52(6) provides that, where a right to enforce payment by a trust of an amount out of the trust's capital gains or income (determined without reference to the provisions of the Act) for the trust's taxation year is acquired by a trust beneficiary in the year, the beneficiary's cost of the right is the amount that became so payable. This ensures that there is generally no capital gain realized where a payment is made in satisfaction of such a right.

Subsection 52(6) is being repealed. Instead, rights to which subsection 52(6) apply are now generally treated as part of a taxpayer's "income interest" or "capital interest" in a trust (as those expressions are defined in subsection 108(1)). Because of new paragraphs (h) and (i) of the definition "disposition" in subsection 248(1), where the right is part of a taxpayer's capital interest in a trust, the satisfaction of the right by way of a distribution by the trust will generally not constitute a disposition of that interest. In addition, under existing paragraph 53(2)(h), a distribution in satisfaction of such a right generally will not result in a reduction of the adjusted cost base of that interest. In the event that such a right is capitalized by way of the issue of new trust units, new subsection 248(25.3) expressly provides for the cost of the new units. Where a taxpayer's right to enforce payment of an amount is disposed of to a third party prior to the right being satisfied by the trust, new subsection 248(25.4) provides, where the requirements of that subsection are met, an increase in the cost of the taxpayer's capital interest in the trust.

The repeal of subsection 52(6) and the related amendments (described above) are designed to clarify the tax consequences of distributions from trusts to their beneficiaries after 1999. For the large part, the end results achieved under these rules are intended to accord with existing income tax practice.

**Related Provisions**: 107(2.1) — Distribution of trust property; 132.11(4) — Amounts paid from December 16-31 by mutual fund trust to beneficiary; 132.11(6)(c) — Designation or allocation by mutual fund trust.

**Notes**: 52(6) amended by 1988 tax reform, effective for rights acquired in a trust in the 1988 and later taxation years of the trust. For rights acquired earlier, read:

(6) Cost of right received from unit trust — Where a beneficiary under a unit trust has, after 1971, acquired a right to enforce payment of an amount by the unit trust out of its capital gains or income from property for its taxation year in which the right was acquired by him, notwithstanding subsection (1), he shall be deemed to have acquired the right at a cost to him equal to the amount that became so payable minus such portion of that amount as was deductible in computing his income by virtue of subsection 65(1) or 104(16).

**Interpretation Bulletins**: IT-286R2: Trusts — amounts payable; IT-390: Unit trusts — cost of rights and adjustments to cost base.

**(7) Cost of shares of subsidiary** — Notwithstanding any other provision of this Act, where a corporation disposes of property to another corporation in a transaction to which paragraph 219(1)(l) applies, the cost to it of any share of a particular class of the capital stock of the other corporation received by it as consideration for the property is deemed to be the lesser of the cost of the share to the corporation otherwise determined immediately after the disposition and the amount by which the paid-up capital in respect of that class increases because of the issuance of the share.

**Notes**: 52(7) amended by 1995-97 technical bill, effective for taxation years that begin after 1995. For earlier years generally since 1980, read:

> (7) Notwithstanding any other provision of this Act, where a corporation has disposed of property to its subsidiary wholly-owned corporation in a transaction to which paragraph 219(1)(k) applies, the cost to it of any share of a particular class of the capital stock of the subsidiary corporation received by it as consideration for the property shall be deemed to be equal to the lesser of the cost of the share to the corporation otherwise determined immediately after the disposition and the amount, if any, by which the paid-up capital of that class increased by virtue of the issuance of that share.

**Interpretation Bulletins**: IT-137R3: Additional tax on certain corporations carrying on business in Canada.

**(8) Cost of shares of immigrant corporation** — Notwithstanding any other provision of this Act, where at any time a corporation becomes resident in Canada, the cost to any shareholder who is not at that time resident in Canada of any share of the corporation's capital stock, other than a share that was taxable Canadian property immediately before that time, is deemed to be equal to the fair market value of the share at that time.

**Related Provisions**: 53(1)(b.1), (c) — Additions to ACB of share; 128.1(1)–(3) — Effect of corporation's immigration; 250(4), (5) — Residence of corporation.

**Notes**: 52(8) amended by 1998 Budget, effective for corporations that become resident in Canada after February 23, 1998. Before the amendment, read:

> (8) Cost of shares on immigration — Notwithstanding any other provision of this Act, where at any time a corporation becomes resident in Canada, the cost to any shareholder that is not at that time resident in Canada of any share of the capital stock of the corporation shall be deemed to be equal to the lesser of that cost otherwise determined and the paid-up capital in respect of the share immediately after that time.

52(8) added by 1993 technical bill, effective for dispositions in 1993 or later. Where a corporation becomes resident in Canada, 52(8) drops the cost of the corporation's shares to any non-resident shareholder to the paid-up capital of the share. There may thus be a higher capital gain on a subsequent disposition of the share by the non-resident (see 115(1)(b)(iii) and (iv)).

**Definitions [s. 52]**: "adjusted cost base" — 54, 248(1); "amount" — 95(7), 248(1); "annuity" — 248(1); "Canada" — 255; "capital gain" — 39(1)(a), 248(1); "capital interest" — 108(1), 248(1); "class of shares" — 248(6); "corporation" — 248(1), *Interpretation Act* 35(1); "disposition" — 54 [to be repealed], 248(1) [draft]; "dividend" — 248(1); "employees profit sharing plan" — 144(1), 248(1); "non-resident" — 248(1); "paid-up capital" — 89(1), 248(1); "person", "property" — 248(1); "resident in Canada" — 250; "share", "shareholder", "stock dividend", "subsidiary wholly-owned corporation" — 248(1); "taxable Canadian property" — 248(1); "taxable income", "taxable income earned in Canada" — 248(1); "taxation year" — 249; "taxpayer" — 248(1); "trust" — 104(1), 248(1), (3); "unit trust" — 108(2), 248(1).

**53. (1) Adjustments to cost base [additions to ACB]** — In computing the adjusted cost base to a taxpayer of property at any time, there shall be added to the cost to the taxpayer of the property such of the following amounts in respect of the property as are applicable:

**Notes**: Additions to ACB are good for the taxpayer since they result in a lower capital gain. For deductions from ACB, see 53(2).

(a) **[negative ACB]** — any amount deemed by subsection 40(3) to be a gain of the taxpayer for a taxation year from a disposition before that time of the property;

**Notes**: Under 40(3), a negative ACB normally triggers an immediate capital gain, except in respect of partnership interests of active partners. This provision then resets the ACB to zero.

(b) **[share, where 84(1) applied]** — where the property is a share of the capital stock of a corporation resident in Canada, the amount of any dividend on the share deemed by subsection 84(1) to have been received by the taxpayer before that time;

**Notes**: 84(1) generally deems a dividend to have been paid if the paid-up capital of a share is increased.

(b.1) **[share of immigrant corporation]** — where the property is a share of the capital stock of a corporation, the amount of any dividend deemed by paragraph 128.1(1)(c.2) to have been received in respect of the share by the taxpayer before that time and while the taxpayer was resident in Canada;

**Related Provisions**: 52(8) — Cost of share to non-resident.

**Notes**: 53(1)(b.1) added by 1998 Budget, effective February 24, 1998.

(c) **[share, where contribution of capital made]** — where the property is a share of the capital stock of a corporation and the taxpayer has, after 1971, made a contribution of capital to the corporation otherwise than by way of a loan, by way of a disposition of shares of a foreign affiliate of the taxpayer to which subsection 85.1(3) or paragraph 95(2)(c) applies or, subject to subsection (1.1), a disposition of property in respect of which the taxpayer and the corporation have made an election under section 85, that proportion of such part of the amount of the contribution as cannot reasonably be regarded as a benefit conferred by the taxpayer on a person (other than the corporation) who was related to the taxpayer that

(i) the amount that may reasonably be regarded as the increase in the fair market value, as a result of the contribution, of the share

is of

(ii) the amount that may reasonably be regarded as the increase in the fair market value, as a result of the contribution, of all shares of

Subdivision c — Taxable Capital Gains        S. 53(1)(e)(i)(A.2)

the capital stock of the corporation owned by the taxpayer immediately after the contribution;

**Related Provisions**: 52(8) — Cost to non-resident of share of corporation that becomes resident in Canada; 53(1)(j) — Addition to ACB of share on which stock option benefit received; 53(1.1) — Deemed contribution of capital.

**Notes**: 53(1)(c) amended by 1979 Budget, effective for contributions of capital made after December 11, 1979. For earlier contributions, read "other shareholder of the corporation" in place of "person (other than the corporation)".

Amended by 1988 tax reform, effective for contributions of capital made after June 1988. For contributions made from December 12, 1979 through June 30, 1988, read "a gift made to or for the benefit of a person (other than the corporation)" in place of "a benefit conferred by the taxpayer on a person (other than the corporation)".

**Interpretation Bulletins**: IT-291R2: Transfer of property to a corporation under subsection 85(1); IT-456R: Capital property — some adjustments to cost base; IT-527: Distress preferred shares.

(d) **[share of foreign affiliate]** — where the property is a share of the capital stock of a foreign affiliate of the taxpayer, any amount required by paragraph 92(1)(a) to be added in computing the adjusted cost base to the taxpayer of the share;

**Related Provisions**: 91(6) — Amounts deductible in respect of dividends received.

(d.01) **[share of demutualized insurer]** — where the property is a share of the capital stock of a corporation, any amount required by paragraph 139.1(16)(l) to be added in computing the adjusted cost base to the taxpayer of the share;

**Notes**: 53(1)(d.01) added by 1999 Budget, effective December 16, 1998.

(d.1) **[capital interest in trust]** — where the property is a capital interest of the taxpayer in a trust to which paragraph 94(1)(d) applies, any amount required by paragraph 94(5)(a) to be added in computing the adjusted cost base to the taxpayer of the interest;

> **Proposed Amendment — 53(1)(d.1)**
>
> (d.1) where the property is a capital interest of the taxpayer in a trust to which paragraph 94(1)(d) applied (as that paragraph read in its application before 2001), any amount required by paragraph 94(5)(a) (as that paragraph read in its application before 2001) to be added in computing the adjusted cost base to the taxpayer of the interest;
>
> **Application**: The June 22, 2000 draft legislation, subsec. 4(1), will amend para. 53(1)(d.1) to read as above, applicable after 2000.
>
> **Technical Notes**: Paragraph 53(1)(d.1), applied together with existing paragraph 94(5)(a), provides for an addition in computing the adjusted cost base (ACB) to a taxpayer of the taxpayer's capital interest in a trust to which existing paragraph 94(1)(d) applies. It is amended to ensure that historical ACB additions are maintained, notwithstanding the replacement of the rules in existing section 94.

**Related Provisions**: 53(2)(h), (i), (j) — Deductions from adjusted cost base — interest in a trust.

(d.2) **[unit in mutual fund trust]** — where the property is a unit in a mutual fund trust, any amount required by subsection 132.1(2) to be added in computing the adjusted cost base to the taxpayer of the unit;

(d.3) **[share]** — where the property is a share of the capital stock of a corporation of which the taxpayer was, at any time, a specified shareholder, any expense incurred by the taxpayer in respect of land or a building of the corporation that was by reason of subsection 18(2) or (3.1) not deductible by the taxpayer in computing the taxpayer's income for any taxation year commencing before that time;

**Related Provisions**: 10(1.1) — Effect of 53(1)(d.3) on cost of land inventory; 53(1)(h) — Where land owned directly by taxpayer.

**Interpretation Bulletins**: IT-153R3: Land developers — subdivision and development costs and carrying charges on land.

(e) **[partnership interest]** — where the property is an interest in a partnership,

(i) an amount in respect of each fiscal period of the partnership ending after 1971 and before that time, equal to the total of all amounts each of which is the taxpayer's share (other than a share under an agreement referred to in subsection 96(1.1)) of the income of the partnership from any source for that fiscal period, computed as if this Act were read without reference to

(A) the fractions set out in subsection 14(5), paragraph 38(a) and subsection 41(1),

(A.1) paragraph 18(1)(l.1), and

> **Proposed Amendment — 53(1)(e)(i)(A)–(A.2)**
>
> (A) the fractions set out in subsection 14(5), paragraphs 38(a) to (a.2), subsection 41(1) and in the formula in paragraph 14(1)(b),
>
> (A.1) paragraph 18(1)(l.1),
>
> (A.2) the description of C in the formula in paragraph 14(1)(b), and
>
> **Application**: The December 21, 2000 draft legislation, subsec. 20(1), will amend cls. 53(1)(e)(i)(A) and (A.1) to read as above, and add cl. (A.2), applicable in respect of fiscal periods that end after February 27, 2000 and, for fiscal periods that ended after February 18, 1997 and before February 28, 2000, cl. 53(1)(e)(i)(A) shall be read as follows:
>
> "(A) the fractions set out in subsection 14(5), paragraphs 38(a) and (a.1) and subsection 41(1),"
>
> **Technical Notes**: Section 53 sets out rules for determining the adjusted cost base of capital property for the purposes of calculating any capital gain or loss on its disposition. Certain adjustments to cost are made under this section. Subsection 53(1) provides for additions to cost and subsection 53(2) for deductions from cost.

Paragraph 53(1)(e) provides additions to a taxpayer's cost of a partnership interest for the purpose of determining its adjusted cost base. Clause (i)(A) thereof provides an addition to the cost base for each fiscal period of the partnership equal to the amount that would be the taxpayer's share of the income of the partnership for that fiscal period if any amounts included in income in respect of eligible capital property, taxable capital gains and taxable net gains on listed personal property for that fiscal period were computed without reference to the fractions referred to in those provisions.

Paragraph 53(2)(c) provides deductions from the taxpayer's cost of a partnership interest for the purpose of determining its adjusted cost base. Clause (i)(A) thereof provides for a deduction from the cost base for each fiscal period of the partnership equal to the amount that would be the taxpayer's share of any loss of the partnership for that fiscal period if any amounts deducted in respect of eligible capital property and allowable capital losses of the partnership were computed without the references to the fractions referred to in those provisions.

Clauses 53(1)(e)(i)(A) and 53(2)(c)(i)(A) are amended to add the references to the fraction in the formula in paragraph 14(1)(b) (as amended) and the variable C in that formula. These changes are consequential on the changes to the inclusion rates for the inclusion in income from business under subsection 14(1). Clause 53(1)(e)(i)(A) is also amended to correct an oversight in 1997 about the fraction in paragraph 38(a.1) concerning the taxable portion of a capital gain arising from certain donations.

    (B) paragraph (i), paragraphs 12(1)(o) and (z.5), 18(1)(m), 20(1)(v.1) and 29(1)(b) and (2)(b), section 55, subsections 69(6) and (7) and paragraph 82(1)(b) of this Act and paragraphs 20(1)(gg) and 81(1)(r) and (s) of the *Income Tax Act*, chapter 148 of the Revised Statutes of Canada, 1952, and the provisions of the *Income Tax Application Rules* relating to income from the operation of new mines,

(ii) the taxpayer's share of any capital dividends and any life insurance capital dividends received by the partnership before that time on shares of the capital stock of a corporation that were partnership property,

(iii) the taxpayer's share of the amount, if any, by which

    (A) any proceeds of a life insurance policy received by the partnership after 1971 and before that time in consequence of the death of any person whose life was insured under the policy,

exceeds

    (B) the adjusted cost basis (within the meaning assigned by subsection 148(9)) of the policy to the partnership immediately before that person's death,

(iv) where the taxpayer has, after 1971, made a contribution of capital to the partnership otherwise than by way of loan, such part of the amount of the contribution as cannot reasonably be regarded as a benefit conferred on any other member of the partnership who was related to the taxpayer,

(v) where the time is immediately before the taxpayer's death and the taxpayer was at that time a member of a partnership, the value, at the time of the taxpayer's death, of the rights or things referred to in subsection 70(2) in respect of a partnership interest held by the taxpayer immediately before the taxpayer's death, other than an interest referred to in subsection 96(1.5),

(vi) any amount deemed by subsection 40(3.1) to be a gain of the taxpayer for a taxation year from a disposition before that time of the property,

(vii) any amount deemed by paragraph 98(1)(c) or 98.1(1)(c) to be a gain of the taxpayer for a taxation year from a disposition before that time of the property,

(vii.1) a share of the taxpayer's Canadian development expense or Canadian oil and gas property expense that was deducted at or before that time in computing the adjusted cost base to the taxpayer of the interest because of subparagraph (2)(c)(ii) and in respect of which the taxpayer elected under paragraph (f) of the definition "Canadian development expense" in subsection 66.2(5) or paragraph (b) of the definition "Canadian oil and gas property expense" in subsection 66.4(5), as the case may be,

(viii) an amount deemed, before that time, by subsection 66.1(7), 66.2(6) or 66.4(6) to be an amount referred to in the description of G in the definition "cumulative Canadian exploration expense" in subsection 66.1(6), paragraph (a) of the description of F in the definition "cumulative Canadian development expense" in subsection 66.2(5) or the description of G in that definition, or paragraph (a) of the description of F in the definition "cumulative Canadian oil and gas property expense" in subsection 66.4(5) or the description of G in that definition in respect of the taxpayer,

(ix) the amount, if any, by which

    (A) the taxpayer's share of the amount of any assistance or benefit that the partnership received or became entitled to receive after 1971 and before that time from a government, municipality or other public authority, whether as a grant, subsidy, forgivable loan, deduction from royalty or tax, investment allowance or any other form of assistance or benefit, in respect of or related to a Canadian resource property or an exploration or development expense incurred in Canada

Subdivision c — Taxable Capital Gains    S. 53(1)(f.1)(i)

exceeds

(B) the part, if any, of the amount included in clause (A) in respect of the interest that was repaid before that time by the taxpayer under a legal obligation to repay all or any part of the amount,

(x) any amount required by section 97 to be added before that time in computing the adjusted cost base to the taxpayer of the interest,

(xi) of which the taxpayer's share of any income or loss of the partnership was, at any time, 10% or more, any expense incurred by the taxpayer in respect of land or a building of the partnership that was by reason of subsection 18(2) or (3.1) not deductible by the taxpayer in computing the taxpayer's income for any taxation year commencing before that time,

(xii) any amount required by paragraph 110.6(23)(a) to be added at that time in computing the adjusted cost base to the taxpayer of the interest, and

(xiii) any amount required by subsection 127(30) to be added to the taxpayer's tax otherwise payable under this Part for a taxation year that ended before that time;

**Related Provisions**: 10(1.1) — Cost of land inventory; 40(3.13) — Artificial transactions affecting partnership capital; 53(2)(c) — Reduction in adjusted cost base — partnership interest; 70(6)(d.1)(iii) — Where transfer or distribution to spouse or trust; 70(9.2)(c)(iii) — Transfer of family farm corporations and partnerships; 70(9.3)(e)(iii) — Transfer of family farm corporation or partnership from spouse's trust to children of settlor; 87(2)(e.1) — Amalgamations — cost of partnership interest; 96(1.9) — Foreign trusts and other foreign investment entities; 248(8) — Occurrences as a consequence of death; 248(16) — GST input tax credit and rebate deemed to be assistance; 248(18) — GST — repayment of input tax credit.

**Notes**: See also Notes to 53(2)(c).

53(1)(e)(i)(B) amended by 1996 Budget, effective for computing the ACB of property after 1996, to add reference to 12(1)(z.5).

53(1)(e)(iii)(B) amended by 1977 Budget, effective for life insurance proceeds received after March 1977. For proceeds received before April 1977 read:

(B) all amounts paid as or on account of premiums under the policy,

53(1)(e)(iv) amended by 1988 tax reform, effective for contributions of capital made after June 1988. For earlier contributions, read "a gift made to or for the benefit of any other member" in place of "a benefit conferred on any other member".

53(1)(e)(vi) added by 1994 Budget, effective February 22, 1994.

53(1)(e)(vii.1) added by 1992 technical bill, effective August 1990.

53(1)(e)(ix) amended by 1991 technical bill, effective February 1990. For computing the ACB of an interest in a partnership before that time, read:

(ix) the taxpayer's share of the amount of any assistance or benefit that the partnership has received or has become entitled to receive after 1971 and before that time from a government, municipality or other public authority, whether as a grant, subsidy, forgivable loan, deduction from royalty or tax, investment allowance or any other form of assistance or benefit, in respect of

or related to a Canadian resource property or an exploration or development expense incurred in Canada,

53(1)(e)(xi) added by 1988 tax reform, effective for 1988 and later taxation years.

53(1)(e)(xii) added by 1994 Budget, effective 1994.

53(1)(e)(xiii) added by 1998 Budget, effective for 1998 and later taxation years.

**I.T. Application Rules**: 26(9)–(9.4) (where taxpayer became partner before 1972); 69 (meaning of "*Income Tax Act*", chapter 148 of the Revised Statutes of Canada, 1952" in cl. 53(1)(e)(i)(B)).

**Interpretation Bulletins**: IT-138R: Computation and flow-through of partnership income; IT-153R3: Land developers — subdivision and development costs and carrying charges on land; IT-242R: Retired partners; IT-278R2: Death of a partner or of a retired partner; IT-338R2: Partnership interests — effects on ACB of admission or retirement of a partner; IT-353R2: Partnership interests — some adjustments to cost base; IT-358: Partnerships — deferment of fiscal year-end; IT-430R3: Life insurance proceeds received by a private corporation or a partnership as a consequence of death; IT-471R: Merger of partnerships.

**I.T. Technical News**: No. 5 (adjusted cost base of partnership interest); No. 9 (calculation of ACB of a partnership interest); No. 12 (adjusted cost base of partnership interest — subparagraph 53(1)(e)(viii)).

**Forms**: T2065: Determination of adjusted cost base of a partnership interest; T5015: Reconciliation of partner's capital account; T5016: Partner's share of partnership capital.

(f) **[substituted property]** — where the property is substituted property (within the meaning assigned by paragraph (a) of the definition "superficial loss" in section 54) of the taxpayer, the amount, if any, by which

(i) the amount of the loss that was, because of the acquisition by the taxpayer of the property, a superficial loss of any taxpayer from a disposition of a property

exceeds

(ii) where the property disposed of was a share of the capital stock of a corporation, the amount that would, but for paragraph 40(2)(g), be deducted under subsection 112(3), (3.1) or (3.2) in computing the loss of any taxpayer in respect of the disposition of the share;

**Related Provisions**: 40(2)(g)(i) — Superficial loss denied; 40(2)(h) — Loss on disposition of share of controlled corporation; 142.4(1)"tax basis"(h) — Disposition of specified debt obligation by financial institution.

**Notes**: 53(1)(f)(ii) added by 1991 technical bill, effective July 14, 1990.

**Interpretation Bulletins**: IT-456R: Capital property — some adjustments to cost base.

(f.1) **[property disposed of at loss by other corporation]** — where the taxpayer is a taxable Canadian corporation and the property was disposed of by another taxable Canadian corporation to the taxpayer in circumstances such that

(i) paragraph (f.2) does not apply to increase the adjusted cost base to the other corporation of shares of the capital stock of the taxpayer, and

331

(ii) the capital loss from the disposition was deemed by paragraph 40(2)(e.1) (or, where the property was acquired by the taxpayer before 1996, by paragraph 40(2)(e) or 85(4)(a) as those paragraphs read in their application to property acquired before April 26, 1995) to be nil,

the amount that would otherwise have been the capital loss from the disposition;

**Related Provisions**: 53(1)(f.11) — Alternative addition to ACB on dispositions subject to para. 40(2)(e.1); 142.4(1)"tax basis"(h) — Disposition of specified debt obligation by financial institution.

**Notes**: 53(1)(f.1) amended by 1995-97 technical bill, effective (subject to the grandfathering rule reproduced after s. 260) for dispositions of property after April 26, 1995, to split up the last part of the para. into subparas. (i) and (ii), and to add reference to 40(2)(e) and 85(4) having been repealed. Previously read:

(f.1) where the taxpayer is a taxable Canadian corporation and the property was disposed of by another taxable Canadian corporation to the taxpayer in circumstances such that paragraph (f.2) does not apply so as to increase the adjusted cost base to the other corporation of shares of the capital stock of the taxpayer and the capital loss from the disposition was deemed by paragraph 40(2)(e) or (e.1) or 85(4)(a) to be nil, the amount that would otherwise have been the capital loss from the disposition;

53(1)(f.1) amended by 1994 tax amendments bill (Part I), effective for taxation years that end after February 21, 1994, to add reference to 40(2)(e.1) and to change reference from 85(4)(b) to 53(1)(f.2). (Other changes made at the same time were cosmetic.)

**Advance Tax Rulings**: ATR-57: Transfer of property for estate planning purposes; ATR-66: Non-arm's length transfer of debt followed by a winding-up and a sale of shares.

(f.11) **[property disposed of at loss by other person]** — where the property was disposed of by a person (other than a non-resident person or a person exempt from tax under this Part on the person's taxable income) or by an eligible Canadian partnership (as defined in subsection 80(1)) to the taxpayer in circumstances such that

(i) paragraph (f.1) does not apply to increase the adjusted cost base to the taxpayer of the property,

(ii) paragraph (f.2) does not apply to increase the adjusted cost base to that person of shares of the capital stock of the taxpayer, and

(iii) the capital loss from the disposition was deemed by paragraph 40(2)(e.1) (or, where the property was acquired by the taxpayer before 1996, by paragraph 85(4)(a) as it read in its application to property acquired before April 26, 1995) to be nil,

the amount that would otherwise be the capital loss from the disposition;

**Notes**: 53(1)(f.11) amended by 1995-97 technical bill, effective (subject to the grandfathering rule reproduced after s. 260) for dispositions of property after April 26, 1995, to split up the last part of the para. into subparas. (i)-(iii), and to add reference to 85(4) having been repealed. Previously read:

(f.11) where the property was disposed of by a person (other than a non-resident person or a person exempt from tax under this Part on the person's taxable income) or by an eligible Canadian partnership (within the meaning assigned by subsection 80(1)) to the taxpayer in circumstances such that paragraph (f.1) does not apply so as to increase the adjusted cost base to the taxpayer of the property, paragraph (f.2) does not apply so as to increase the adjusted cost base to that person of shares of the capital stock of the taxpayer and the capital loss from the disposition was deemed by paragraph 40(2)(e.1) or 85(4)(a) to be nil, the amount that would otherwise be the capital loss from the disposition;

53(1)(f.11) added by 1994 tax amendments bill (Part I), effective for taxation years that end after February 21, 1994.

(f.12) **[commercial obligation owing to taxpayer]** — where the property is a particular commercial obligation (in this paragraph having the meaning assigned by subsection 80(1)) payable to the taxpayer as consideration for the settlement or extinguishment of another commercial obligation payable to the taxpayer and the taxpayer's loss from the disposition of the other obligation was reduced because of paragraph 40(2)(e.2), the proportion of the reduction that the principal amount of the particular obligation is of the total of all amounts each of which is the principal amount of a commercial obligation payable to the taxpayer as consideration for the settlement or extinguishment of that other obligation;

**Notes**: 53(1)(f.12) added by 1994 tax amendments bill (Part I), effective for taxation years that end after February 21, 1994.

(f.2) **[share, after transfer of other shares to corporation]** — where the property is a share, any amount required by paragraph 40(3.6)(b) (or, where the property was acquired by the taxpayer before 1996, by paragraph 85(4)(b) as it read in its application to property disposed of before April 26, 1995) to be added in computing the adjusted cost base to the taxpayer of the share;

**Related Provisions**: 53(1)(f.1), (f.11) — Para. (f.2) takes precedence over (f.1) and (f.11).

**Notes**: 53(1)(f.2) amended by 1995-97 technical bill, effective (subject to the grandfathering rule reproduced after s. 260) for dispositions of property after April 26, 1995. Previously read:

(f.2) where the property is a share of the capital stock of a corporation, any amount required by paragraph 85(4)(b) to be added in computing the adjusted cost base to the taxpayer of the share;

**Interpretation Bulletins**: IT-456R: Capital property — some adjustments to cost base.

(g) **[bond, mortgage, etc.]** — where the property is a bond, debenture, bill, note, mortgage or similar obligation, the amount, if any, by which the principal amount of the obligation exceeds the amount for which the obligation was issued, if such excess was required by subsection 16(2) or (3) to be included in computing the income of the taxpayer for a taxation year commencing before that time;

**Notes**: The term "bond, debenture, bill, note, mortgage or similar obligation" may not include bankers' acceptances. See *Federated Cooperatives Ltd.*, [2000] 2 C.T.C. 2382 (TCC).

(g.1) **[indexed debt obligation]** — where the property is an indexed debt obligation, any amount determined under subparagraph 16(6)(a)(i) in respect of the obligation and required to be included in computing the taxpayer's income for a taxation year beginning before that time;

**Related Provisions**: 53(2)(l.1) — Reduction in adjusted cost base — indexed debt obligation.

**Notes**: 53(1)(g.1) added by 1992 technical bill, effective for indexed debt obligations issued after October 16, 1991.

(h) **[land]** — where the property is land of the taxpayer, any amount paid by the taxpayer or by another taxpayer in respect of whom the taxpayer was a person, corporation or partnership described in subparagraph (b)(i), (ii) or (iii) of the definition "interest on debt relating to the acquisition of land" in subsection 18(3), after 1971 and before that time pursuant to a legal obligation to pay

(i) interest on debt relating to the acquisition of land (within the meaning assigned by subsection 18(3)), or

(ii) property taxes (not including income or profits taxes or taxes imposed by reference to the transfer of property) paid by the taxpayer in respect of the property to a province or to a Canadian municipality

to the extent that the amount was, because of subsection 18(2),

(iii) not deductible in computing the taxpayer's income from the land or from a business for any taxation year beginning before that time, or

(iv) not deductible in computing the income of the other taxpayer and was not included in or added to the cost to the other taxpayer of any property otherwise than because of subparagraph (d.3) or subparagraph (e)(xi);

**Related Provisions**: 43.1(2) — Life estates in real property; 53(1)(d.3) — Where land owned through a corporation.

**Notes**: 53(1)(h) amended by 1991 technical bill, effective for taxation years ending after 1987, to make minor technical corrections.

**Interpretation Bulletins**: IT-456R: Capital property — some adjustments to cost base.

(i) **[land used in farming]** — where the property is land used in a farming business carried on by the taxpayer, an amount in respect of each taxation year ending after 1971 and commencing before that time, equal to the taxpayer's loss, if any, for that year from the farming business, to the extent that the loss

(i) was not, by virtue of section 31, deductible in computing the taxpayer's income for that year,

(ii) was not deducted in computing the taxpayer's taxable income for the taxation year in which the taxpayer disposed of the property or any preceding taxation year,

(iii) did not exceed the total of

(A) taxes (other than income or profits taxes or taxes imposed by reference to the transfer of the property) paid by the taxpayer in that year or payable by the taxpayer in respect of that year to a province or a Canadian municipality in respect of the property, and

(B) interest, paid by the taxpayer in that year or payable by the taxpayer in respect of that year, pursuant to a legal obligation to pay interest on borrowed money used to acquire the property or on any amount as consideration payable for the property,

to the extent that those taxes and interest were included in computing the loss, and

(iv) did not exceed the remainder obtained when

(A) the total of each of the taxpayer's losses from the farming business for taxation years preceding that year (to the extent that they are required by this paragraph to be added in computing the taxpayer's adjusted cost base of the property),

is deducted from

(B) the amount, if any, by which the taxpayer's proceeds of disposition of the property exceed the adjusted cost base to the taxpayer of the property immediately before that time, determined without reference to this paragraph;

**Related Provisions**: 96(1)(e) — Partnerships — gains to be computed without reference to para. 53(1)(i); 101 — Corresponding rule for partnerships; 111(1)(c), (d) — Farming loss carryovers; 111(3) — Limitations on deductibility of loss carryover; 111(6) — Limitation.

**Interpretation Bulletins**: IT-232R2: Non-capital losses, net capital losses, restricted farm losses, farm losses and limited partnership losses — their composition and deductibility in computing taxable income.

(j) **[share or fund unit taxed as stock option benefit]** — if the property is a share or unit and, in respect of its acquisition by the taxpayer, a benefit was deemed by section 7 to have been received in any taxation year that ends after 1971 and begins before that time by the taxpayer or by a person that did not deal at arm's length with the taxpayer, the amount of the benefit so deemed to have been received;

**Proposed Amendment — 53(1)(j)**

(j) **share or fund unit taxed as stock option benefit** — if the property is a security (within the meaning assigned by subsection 7(7)) and, in respect of its acquisition by the taxpayer, a benefit was deemed by section 7 to have been received in any taxation year that ends after 1971 and begins before that time by the taxpayer or by a person that did not deal at arm's length with the taxpayer or, if the security was acquired after February 27, 2000, would have been so deemed if section 7 were read without reference to subsections 7(1.1) and (8), the amount of the benefit that was, or would have been, so deemed to have been received;

**Application**: The December 21, 2000 draft legislation, subsec. 20(2), will amend para. 53(1)(j), applicable after 1999.

**Technical Notes**: Paragraph 53(1)(j) provides for an addition to the ACB of a security (i.e., a share of a corporation or a unit of a mutual fund trust) acquired by a taxpayer under an employee option agreement. The amount that is added to the ACB is the amount of the employment benefit that the taxpayer (or a non-arm's length person) is deemed by subsection 7(1) to have received in connection with the acquisition of the security. The amount is generally equal to the excess of the fair market value of the security at the time it is acquired over the amount paid to acquire the security under the option. The amount is added to the ACB in the year in which the benefit is deemed to have been received, which is generally the year in which the taxpayer acquires the security. However, in the case of an option granted by a Canadian-controlled private corporation (CCPC) to an arm's length person, subsection 7(1.1) applies to defer recognition of the benefit to the year in which the taxpayer disposes of the security.

Paragraph 53(1)(j) is amended to provide that, for all employee option securities acquired after February 27, 2000, the employment benefit is included in the ACB of the security from the time of acquisition, even if recognition of the employment benefit is deferred, for tax purposes, until the taxpayer disposes of the security. This will be primarily relevant where securities for which a deferral is provided under either subsection 7(1.1), or new subsection 7(8) (which applies to publicly-listed shares and units of a fund trust), are exchanged for new securities in accordance with subsection 7(1.5), but in circumstances in which there is no rollover available, in respect of the disposition of the old securities, for capital gains purposes. The immediate inclusion in the ACB of the old securities ensures that the determination of the capital gain or loss on the disposition of those securities is not distorted by the exclusion of the deferred employment benefit associated with the acquisition of those securities.

**Related Provisions**: 7(1.6), 128.1(4)(d.1) — Effect of emigration on disposition of share or fund unit; 49(3)(b) — Where option to acquire exercised.

**Notes**: 53(1)(j) amended to add "or unit" by 1998 Budget, effective in computing the ACB of a unit acquired after February 1998. This was consequential on extending the rules in s. 7 to mutual fund units (see Notes to 7(1)).

There does not appear to be an offsetting reduction in ACB for the deduction allowed by 110(1)(d) or (d.1).

53(1)(j) amended by 1985 technical bill, effective for shares acquired after 1984, to add the reference to a person that did not deal at arm's length with the taxpayer. For shares acquired before 1985, only the amount of a benefit deemed received by the taxpayer is added to the adjusted cost base.

**Interpretation Bulletins**: IT-96R6: Options to acquire shares, bonds or debentures and by trusts to acquire trust units; IT-113R4: Benefits to employees — stock options.

**I.T. Technical News**: No. 19 (Disposition of identical properties acquired under a section 7 securities option).

(k) **[expropriation asset]** — where the property is an expropriation asset of the taxpayer (within the meaning assigned by section 80.1) or an asset of the taxpayer assumed for the purposes of that section to be an expropriation asset thereof, any amount required by paragraph 80.1(2)(b) to be added in computing the adjusted cost base to the taxpayer of the asset;

**Related Provisions**: 53(2)(n) — Reduction in ACB of expropriation asset.

(l) **[interest in related segregated fund trust]** — where the property is an interest in a related segregated fund trust referred to in section 138.1,

(i) each amount deemed by paragraph 138.1(1)(f) to be an amount payable to the taxpayer before that time in respect of that interest,

(ii) each amount required by subparagraph 138.1(1)(g)(ii) to be added before that time in respect of that interest,

(iii) each amount in respect of that interest that is a capital gain deemed to have been allocated under subsection 138.1(4) to the taxpayer before that time, and

(iv) each amount in respect of that interest that before that time was deemed by subsection 138.1(3) to be a capital gain of the taxpayer;

**Related Provisions**: 53(2)(q) — Deductions from ACB of related segregated fund trust; 138.1(5) — ACB of property in related segregated fund trust.

**I.T. Application Rules**: 26(4) (where property owned since before 1972).

(m) **[offshore investment fund property]** — where the property is an offshore investment fund property (within the meaning assigned by subsection 94.1(1)),

(i) any amount included in respect of the property by virtue of subsection 94.1(1) in computing the taxpayer's income for a taxation year commencing before that time, or

(ii) where the taxpayer is a controlled foreign affiliate (within the meaning of subsection 95(1)), of a person resident in Canada, any amount included in respect of the property in computing the foreign accrual property income of the controlled foreign affiliate by reason of the description of C in the definition "foreign accrual property income" in subsection 95(1) for a taxation year commencing before that time;

Subdivision c — Taxable Capital Gains    S. 53(1)(r)

### Proposed Amendment — 53(1)(m), (m.1)

(m) **[offshore investment fund property]** — where the property is an offshore investment fund property (within the meaning assigned by subsection 94.1(1) as that subsection read in its application before 2001),

(i) any amount included in respect of the property under subsection 94.1(1) (as that subsection read in its application before 2001) in computing the taxpayer's income for a taxation year that began both before that time and before 2001, and

(ii) where the taxpayer is a controlled foreign affiliate of a person resident in Canada, any amount included in respect of the property in computing the foreign accrual property income of the controlled foreign affiliate because of the description of C in the definition "foreign accrual property income" in subsection 95(1) for a taxation year of the controlled foreign affiliate that began both before that time and before 2001;

(m.1) **[interest in foreign investment entity]** — any amount required by subsection 94.1(9) or 94.2(11) to be added at or before that time in computing the adjusted cost base to the taxpayer of the property;

**Application**: The June 22, 2000 draft legislation, subsec. 4(2), will amend para. 53(1)(m) to read as above, and add para. (m.1), applicable after 2000.

**Technical Notes**: Paragraph 53(1)(m) of the Act provides for an addition in computing the ACB to a taxpayer of "offshore investment fund property" to which existing section 94.1 applies. It is amended to ensure that the historical ACB additions are maintained, notwithstanding the replacement of the rules in existing section 94.1.

Paragraph 53(1)(m.1) is introduced to provide for the ACB additions contemplated by new subsections 94.1(9) and 94.2(11). For more detail, see the commentary on those subsections.

(n) **[surveying and valuation costs]** — the reasonable costs incurred by the taxpayer, before that time, of surveying or valuing the property for the purpose of its acquisition or disposition (to the extent that those costs are not deducted by the taxpayer in computing the taxpayer's income for any taxation year or attributable to any other property);

**Related Provisions**: 20(1)(dd) — Deduction for site investigation expenses; 40(1)(a)(i), (b)(i) — Expenses incurred in making disposition deductible in computing gain or loss.

**Notes**: 53(1)(n) added by 1985 technical bill, effective for costs incurred after 1984.

**Interpretation Bulletins**: IT-407R4: Dispositions of cultural property to designated Canadian institutions.

(o) **[real property — remainder interest]** — where the property is real property of the taxpayer, any amount required by paragraph 43.1(2)(b) to be added in computing the adjusted cost base to the taxpayer of the property;

**Notes**: 53(1)(o) added by 1992 technical bill, effective December 21, 1991.

(p) **[flow-through entity after 2004]** — where the time is after 2004 and the property is an interest in or a share of the capital stock of a flow-through entity (within the meaning assigned by subsection 39.1(1)), the amount determined by the formula

$$A \times \frac{B}{C}$$

where

A is the amount, if any, that would, if the definition "exempt capital gains balance" in subsection 39.1(1) were read without reference to "that ends before 2005", be the taxpayer's exempt capital gains balance in respect of the entity for the taxpayer's 2005 taxation year,

B is the fair market value at that time of the property, and

C is the fair market value at that time of all the taxpayer's interests in or shares of the capital stock of the entity;

**Related Provisions**: 53(1)(r) — Increase in ACB before 2005.

**Notes**: 53(1)(p) added by 1994 Budget, effective 1994. See Notes to 39.1(1) "exempt capital gains balance" and "flow-through entity".

(q) **[history preservation rules — debt forgiveness]** — any amount required under paragraph (4)(b), (5)(b), (6)(b), 47(1)(d), 49(3.01)(b), 51(1)(d.2), 86(4)(b) or 87(5.1)(b) or (6.1)(b) to be added in computing the adjusted cost base to the taxpayer of the property; and

**Notes**: 53(1)(q) added by 1994 tax amendments bill (Part I), effective for taxation years that end after February 21, 1994. See Notes to 47(1).

(r) **[flow-through entity before 2005]** — where the time is before 2005, the property is an interest in, or a share of the capital stock of, a flow-through entity described in any of paragraphs (a) to (f) of the definition "flow-through entity" in subsection 39.1(1) and immediately after that time the taxpayer disposed of all of the taxpayer's interests in, and shares of the capital stock of, the entity, the amount determined by the formula

$$A \times \frac{B}{C}$$

where

A is the amount, if any, by which the taxpayer's exempt capital gains balance (as defined in subsection 39.1(1)) in respect of the entity for the taxpayer's taxation year that includes that time exceeds the total of all amounts each of which is

(i) the amount by which a capital gain is reduced under section 39.1 for the year because of the taxpayer's exempt capital gains balance in respect of the entity, or

(ii) 4/3 of an amount by which a taxable capital gain, or the income from a business, is reduced under section 39.1 for the year because of the taxpayer's exempt capital gains balance in respect of the entity,

**Proposed Amendment — 53(1)(r)A(ii)**

**Application**: The December 21, 2000 draft legislation, subsec. 20(3), will amend subpara. (ii) of the description of A in para. 53(1)(r) by replacing the reference to the expression "4/3 of" with a reference to the word "twice", applicable to taxation years that end after February 27, 2000 except that, in applying para. 53(1)(r) for those years in respect of a taxpayer's interest in an entity, where a taxation year of the entity that includes either February 28, 2000 or October 17, 2000 ends in the taxpayer's taxation year, the reference to the word "twice" shall be read as a reference to the expression "the fraction that is the reciprocal of the fraction in para. 38(a), as amended [by the December 21, 2000 draft legislation], that applies in respect of the entity for its taxation year, multiplied by".

**Technical Notes**: Paragraph 53(1)(r) increases an individual's adjusted cost base of each interest in, or share of the capital stock of, a flow-through entity described in any of paragraphs (a) to (f) of the definition "flow-through entity" by a pro-rata portion of the amount of the individual's unused exempt capital gains balance in respect of the entity where the individual disposes of all interests in and shares of the capital stock of the entity.

For the purpose of determining the unused portion of the individual's exempt capital gains balance in respect of the entity, the balance for the year is reduced by the total of all reductions in the year in capital gains because of the balance and 4/3 of the total of all reductions in the year of taxable capital gains or business income because of the balance.

Subparagraph (ii) of the description of A in paragraph 53(1)(r) is amended to replace the expression "4/3 of" with the word "twice". The amendment is consequential on the reduction of the inclusion rates for capital gains from 3/4 to 1/2 [see 38(a) — ed.].

The amendment applies to taxation years that end after February 27, 2000 except that, for a taxation a taxpayer's taxation year that includes either February 28, 2000 or October 17, 2000, the reference to the word "twice" in that subparagraph is to be read as reference to the expression "the fraction that is the reciprocal of the fraction in paragraph 38(a) that applies in respect of the entity for its taxation year, multiplied by". These modifications are required in order to reflect the capital gains/losses rate for the year.

B   is the fair market value at that time of the property, and

C   is the fair market value at that time of all the taxpayer's interests in, and shares of the capital stock of, the entity.

**Related Provisions**: 39.1(7) — Nil exempt capital gains balance; 53(1)(p) — Increase in ACB after 2004.

**Notes**: 53(1)(r) added by 1995-97 technical bill, effective for 1994 and later taxation years. See Notes to 39.1(7). 53(1)(r) will benefit individuals whose interests in or shares of a flow-through entity have declined in value since February 22, 1994. 53(1)(r) is available only in respect of dispositions before 2005. After 2004, 53(1)(p) increases the ACB of any remaining interests in, or shares of the capi-

tal stock of, a flow-through entity by the unused portion of the individual's exempt capital gains balance in respect of the entity at that time.

**(1.1) Deemed contribution of capital** — For the purposes of paragraph (1)(c), where there has been a disposition of property before May 7, 1974, and

(a) the taxpayer and the corporation referred to in that paragraph have made an election under section 85 in respect of that property, and

(b) the consideration received by the taxpayer for the property did not include shares of the capital stock of the corporation,

the disposition of property shall be deemed to be a contribution of capital equal to the amount, if any, by which

(c) the amount that the taxpayer and the corporation have agreed on in the election

exceeds

(d) the fair market value at the time of the disposition of any consideration received by the taxpayer for the property so disposed of.

**Interpretation Bulletins**: IT-456R: Capital property — some adjustments to cost base.

**(2) Amounts to be deducted [from ACB]** — In computing the adjusted cost base to a taxpayer of property at any time, there shall be deducted such of the following amounts in respect of the property as are applicable:

**Notes**: See Notes to opening words of 53(1).

(a) **[share]** — where the property is a share of the capital stock of a corporation resident in Canada,

(i) any amount received by the taxpayer after 1971 and before that time as, on account or in lieu of payment of, or in satisfaction of, a dividend on the share (other than a taxable dividend or a dividend in respect of which the corporation paying the dividend has elected in accordance with subsection 83(2) or (2.1) in respect of the full amount thereof),

(ii) any amount received by the taxpayer after 1971 and before that time on a reduction of the paid-up capital of the corporation in respect of the share, except to the extent that the amount is deemed by subsection 84(4) or (4.1) to be a dividend received by the taxpayer,

(iii) any amount required to be deducted before that time under section 84.1 of the *Income Tax Act*, chapter 148 of the Revised Statutes of Canada, 1952, as it applied before May 23, 1985 in computing the adjusted cost base to the taxpayer of the share, and

(iv) any amount, to the extent that such amount is not proceeds of disposition of a share, received by the taxpayer before that time that would, but for subsection 84(8), be deemed by subsection 84(2) to be a dividend received by the taxpayer;

### Proposed Addition — 53(2)(a)(v)

(v) any amount required by paragraph 44.1(2)(b) to be deducted in computing the adjusted cost base to the taxpayer of the share;

**Application**: The December 21, 2000 draft legislation, subsec. 20(4), will add para. 53(2)(a)(v), applicable to dispositions that occur after February 27, 2000.

**Technical Notes**: Subparagraph 53(2)(a) provides for a reduction in the adjusted cost base of a share of an individual provided for under various provisions of the Act. The amendment to that subparagraph adds a reference to new paragraph 44.1(2)(b) which requires a reduction in the adjusted cost base of a replacement share of an individual as defined in new section 44.1.

**Related Provisions**: 40(2)(h), (i) — Limitation on capital loss on certain shares; 52(8) — Cost to non-resident of share of corporation that becomes resident in Canada; 91(6) — Amounts deductible in respect of dividends received.

**Notes**: Reference to 84(4.1) in 53(2)(a)(ii) added by 1991 technical bill, effective 1990.

**I.T. Application Rules**: 69 (meaning of "*Income Tax Act*, chapter 148 of the Revised Statutes of Canada, 1952").

**Interpretation Bulletins**: IT-456R: Capital property — some adjustments to cost base.

**Advance Tax Rulings**: ATR-54: Reduction of paid-up capital.

(b) **[share of non-resident corporation]** — where the property is a share of the capital stock of a corporation not resident in Canada,

(i) any amount required by paragraph 80.1(4)(d) or section 92 to be deducted in computing the adjusted cost base to the taxpayer of the share, and

(ii) any amount received by the taxpayer after 1971 and before that time on a reduction of the paid-up capital of the corporation in respect of the share;

**Related Provisions**: 52(8) — Cost to non-resident of share of corporation that becomes resident in Canada; 56(6)–(9) — Whether control acquired.

(b.1) **[capital interest in non-resident trust]** — where the property is a capital interest of the taxpayer in a trust to which paragraph 94(1)(d) applies, any amount required by paragraph 94(5)(b) to be deducted in computing the adjusted cost base to the taxpayer of the interest;

(b.2) **[property of corporation after change in control]** — where the property is property of a corporation control of which was acquired by a person or group of persons at or before that time, any amount required by paragraph 111(4)(c) to be deducted in computing the adjusted cost base of the property;

**Related Provisions**: 142.4(1)"tax basis"(q) — Disposition of specified debt obligation by financial institution; 256(6)–(9) — Whether control acquired.

(c) **[partnership interest]** — where the property is an interest in a partnership,

(i) an amount in respect of each fiscal period of the partnership ending after 1971 and before that time, equal to the total of amounts each of which is the taxpayer's share (other than a share under an agreement referred to in subsection 96(1.1)) of any loss of the partnership from any source for that fiscal period, computed as if this Act were read without reference to

(A) the fractions set out in subsection 14(5) and paragraph 38(b),

(A.1) paragraph 18(1)(l.1),

### Proposed Amendment — 53(2)(c)(i)(A)–(A.2)

(A) the fractions set out in subsection 14(5), paragraph 38(b) and in the formula in paragraph 14(1)(b),

(A.1) paragraph 18(1)(l.1),

(A.2) the description of C in the formula in paragraph 14(1)(b),

**Application**: The December 21, 2000 draft legislation, subsec. 20(5), will amend cls. 53(2)(c)(i)(A) and (A.1) to read as above, and add cl. (a.2), applicable in respect of fiscal periods that end after February 27, 2000.

**Technical Notes**: See under 53(1)(e)(i)(A).

(B) paragraphs 12(1)(o) and (z.5), 18(1)(m) and 20(1)(v.1), section 31, subsection 40(2), section 55 and subsections 69(6) and (7) of this Act and paragraphs 20(1)(gg) and 81(1)(r) and (s) of the *Income Tax Act*, chapter 148 of the Revised Statutes of Canada, 1952, and

(C) subsections 100(4) and 112(3.1), and subsection 112(4.2) as it read in its application to dispositions of property that occurred before April 27, 1995,

except to the extent that all or a portion of such a loss may reasonably be considered to have been included in the taxpayer's limited partnership loss in respect of the partnership for the taxpayer's taxation year in which that fiscal period ended,

(i.1) an amount in respect of each fiscal period of the partnership ending before that time that is the taxpayer's limited partnership loss in respect of the partnership for the taxation year in which that fiscal period ends to the extent that such loss was deducted by the taxpayer in computing the taxpayer's taxable income for any taxation year that commenced before that time,

(i.2) any amount deemed by subsection 40(3.12) to be a loss of the taxpayer for a tax-

S. 53(2)(c)(i.2)     Income Tax Act, Part I, Division B

ation year from a disposition before that time of the property,

(i.3) if at that time the property is not a tax shelter investment as defined by section 143.2 and the taxpayer would be a member, described in subsection 40(3.1), of the partnership if the fiscal period of the partnership that includes that time ended at that time, the unpaid principal amount of any indebtedness of the taxpayer for which recourse is limited, either immediately or in the future and either absolutely or contingently, and that can reasonably be considered to have been used to acquire the property,

(i.4) if the taxpayer is a member of the partnership who was a specified member of the partnership at all times since becoming a member of the partnership or the taxpayer is at that time a limited partner of the partnership for the purposes of subsection 40(3.1), the amount

(A) deducted under subsection 34.2(4) in computing the taxpayer's income for the taxation year in respect of the interest, where that time is in the taxpayer's first taxation year in which a qualifying fiscal period (within the meaning assigned by subsection 34.2(1)) of the business carried on by the taxpayer as a member of the partnership ends and is after the end of that period, and

(B) where that time is in any other taxation year, deducted under subsection 34.2(4) in respect of the interest in computing the taxpayer's income for the taxation year preceding that other year

unless

(C) that time is immediately before a disposition of the interest and no amount is deductible under subsection 34.2(4) in respect of the interest in computing the taxpayer's income for the taxation year following the taxation year that includes that time,

(D) the taxpayer has December 31, 1995 income in respect of the business because of section 34.1, or

(E) the taxpayer's partnership interest was held by the taxpayer on February 22, 1994 and is an excluded interest (within the meaning assigned by subsection 40(3.15)) at the end of the fiscal period of the partnership that includes that time,

(ii) an amount in respect of each fiscal period of the partnership ending after 1971 and before that time, other than a fiscal period after the fiscal period in which the taxpayer ceased to be a member of the partnership, equal to the taxpayer's share of the total of

(A) amounts that, but for paragraph 96(1)(d), would be deductible in computing the income of the partnership for the fiscal period by virtue of the provisions of the *Income Tax Application Rules* relating to exploration and development expenses,

(B) the Canadian exploration and development expenses and foreign exploration and development expenses, if any, incurred by the partnership in the fiscal period,

---

**Proposed Amendment — 53(2)(c)(ii)(B)**

(B) the Canadian exploration and development expenses and foreign resource pool expenses, if any, incurred by the partnership in the fiscal period,

**Application**: The December 21, 2000 draft legislation, subsec. 20(6), will amend cl. 53(2)(c)(ii)(B) to read as above, applicable to taxation years that begin after 2000.

**Technical Notes**: Paragraph 53(2)(c) provides for certain amounts that must be deducted in computing the adjusted cost base to a taxpayer of a partnership interest. Under subparagraph 53(2)(c)(ii), the deducted amounts at any time include the taxpayer's share of specified resource expenses (including foreign exploration and development expenses) for each fiscal period of the partnership that ends before that time. This treatment is provided because a taxpayer's share of each specified resource expense enters directly into the calculation of a taxpayer's resource deductions under sections 66 to 66.4. Under subsection 96(1), the specified resource expenses are ignored in computing partnership income.

Clause 53(2)(c)(ii)(B) is amended so that the specified resource expenses include foreign resource expenses, as defined in the definition "foreign resource expense" in new subsection 66.21(1). (The new expression "foreign resource pool expenses", as defined in subsection 248(1), refers to both foreign resource expenses and foreign exploration and development expenses.)

---

(C) the Canadian exploration expense, if any, incurred by the partnership in the fiscal period,

(D) the Canadian development expense, if any, incurred by the partnership in the fiscal period, and

(E) the Canadian oil and gas property expense, if any, incurred by the partnership in the fiscal period,

(iii) any amount deemed by subsection 110.1(4) or 118.1(8) to have been a gift made, or by subsection 127(4.2) to have been an amount contributed, by the taxpayer by reason of the taxpayer's membership in the partnership at the end of a fiscal period of the partnership ending before that time,

(iv) any amount required by section 97 to be deducted before that time in computing the

Subdivision c — Taxable Capital Gains    S. 53(2)(d)

adjusted cost base to the taxpayer of the interest,

(v) any amount received by the taxpayer after 1971 and before that time as, on account or in lieu of payment of, or in satisfaction of, a distribution of the taxpayer's share (other than a share under an agreement referred to in subsection 96(1.1)) of the partnership profits or partnership capital,

(vi) an amount equal to that portion of all amounts deducted under subsection 127(5) in computing the tax otherwise payable by the taxpayer under this Part for the taxpayer's taxation years ending before that time that may reasonably be attributed to amounts added in computing the investment tax credit of the taxpayer by virtue of subsection 127(8),

(vii) any amount added pursuant to subsection 127.2(4) in computing the taxpayer's share-purchase tax credit for a taxation year ending before or after that time,

(viii) an amount equal to 50% of the amount deemed to be designated pursuant to subsection 127.3(4) before that time in respect of each share, debt obligation or right acquired by the partnership and deemed to have been acquired by the taxpayer under that subsection,

(ix) the amount of all assistance received by the taxpayer before that time that has resulted in a reduction of the capital cost of a depreciable property to the partnership by virtue of subsection 13(7.2),

(x) any amount deductible by the taxpayer under subparagraph 20(1)(e)(vi) in respect of the partnership for a taxation year of the taxpayer ending at or after that time,

(xi) any amount required by paragraph 110.6(23)(b) to be deducted at that time in computing the adjusted cost base to the taxpayer of the interest, and

(xii) any amount payable by the partnership, to the extent that the amount is deductible under subsection 20.01(1) in computing the taxpayer's income for a taxation year that began before that time;

**Related Provisions**: 40(3) — Deemed gain when ACB becomes negative; 40(3.13) — Artificial transactions affecting partnership capital; 53(1)(e) — Addition to adjusted cost base — partnership interest; 66.8(1) — Resource expenses of limited partner; 70(6)(d.1) — Where transfer or distribution to spouse or trust; 70(9.2)(c)(iii) — Transfer of family farm corporations and partnerships; 70(9.3)(e)(iii) — Transfer of family farm corporation or partnership from spouse's trust to children of settlor; 80(1)"excluded obligation"(a)(iii) — Debt forgiveness rules do not apply where amount deducted in computing ACB (e.g., under 53(2)(c)(i.3)); 87(2)(e.1) — Amalgamations — partnership interest; 87(2)(j.6) — Amalgamations — continuing corporation; 96(1.9) — Foreign trusts and other foreign investment entities; 96(2.2)(c) — At-risk amount — amount deducted under 53(2)(c)(i.3); 98(1)(c) — Disposition of partnership property; 100(2) — Gain from disposition of interest in partnership; 127(12.2) — Interpretation; 248(16) — GST — input tax credit and rebate; 248(18) — GST — repayment of input tax credit.

**Notes**: Unlike every other reduction that takes ACB below zero, 53(2)(c) does not necessarily trigger an immediate capital gain. The ACB of an active partner's partnership interest may be allowed to remain negative if the partner is an active partner (see 40(3)–(3.2)) unless the partnership ceases to exist (see 98(1)(c)). Simplified, the ACB of a partnership interest is the original investment plus the partner's share of the profits (53(1)(e)(i)) plus contributions of capital (53(1)(e)(iv)), minus the taxpayer's share of partnership losses (53(2)(c)(i)) and partnership drawings (53(2)(c)(v)).

53(2)(c)(i)(B) amended by 1996 Budget, effective for computing the ACB of property after 1996, to add reference to 12(1)(z.5).

53(2)(c)(i)(C) amended by 1995-97 technical bill, effective April 27, 1995, to add reference to 100(4) and reflect 112(4.2) having been repealed.

53(2)(c)(i.2) added by 1994 Budget, effective February 22, 1994.

53(2)(c)(i.3) added by 1994 Budget (and amended retroactively by 1995-97 technical bill to add exclusion for a tax shelter investment), effective for debts entered into by a taxpayer on or after September 26, 1994 other than such a debt entered into pursuant to an agreement in writing entered into by the taxpayer before that date. (See *Interpretation Act* 35(1) for meaning of "writing".)

53(2)(c)(i.4) added by 1995 Budget, effective 1995. It reduces the cost base of a taxpayer's passive partnership interest to the extent the taxpayer claimed a reserve in respect of 1995 "stub-period" income (see Notes to 34.2) from the partnership.

53(2)(c)(iii) amended by 1976 Budget, effective for amounts contributed after June 23, 1975, to add the reference to subsection 127(4.2).

53(2)(c)(iii) amended by 1988 tax reform, effective for gifts made and amounts contributed by partners in fiscal periods of partnerships ending after 1987. For earlier gifts or amounts contributed, read "subsection 110(5)" in place of "subsection 110.1(4) or 118.1(8)"; and "the fiscal period" in place of "a fiscal period".

53(2)(c)(vi) added by 1981 Budget, effective for investment tax credits deducted for 1982 and subsequent years.

53(2)(c)(ix) added by 1985 technical bill, effective for property acquired after May 9, 1985.

53(2)(c)(xi) added by 1994 Budget, effective 1994.

53(2)(c)(xii) added by 1998 Budget, effective 1998.

**I.T. Application Rules**: 26(9)–(9.4) (where taxpayer became partner before 1972); 69 (meaning of "*Income Tax Act*, chapter 148 of the Revised Statutes of Canada, 1952").

**Interpretation Bulletins**: IT-138R: Computation and flow-through of partnership income; IT-242R: Retired partners; IT-278R2: Death of a partner or of a retired partner; IT-338R2: Partnership interests — effects on ACB of admission or retirement of a partner; IT-341R3: Expenses of issuing or selling shares, units in a trust, interests in a partnership or syndicate, and expenses of borrowing money; IT-353R2: Partnership interests — some adjustments to cost base; IT-358: Partnerships — deferment of fiscal year-end.

**I.T. Technical News**: No. 5 (adjusted cost base of partnership interest); 9 (calculation of ACB of a partnership interest).

**Forms**: T2065: Determination of adjusted cost base of a partnership interest; T5015: Reconciliation of partner's capital account; T5016: Partner's share of partnership capital.

(d) **[part of property retained]** — where the property is such that the taxpayer has, after 1971 and before that time, disposed of a part of it while retaining another part of it, the amount determined under section 43 to be the adjusted cost base to the taxpayer of the part so disposed of;

**Interpretation Bulletins**: IT-200: Surface rentals and farming operations.

(e) **[share]** — where the property is a share, or an interest in or a right to a share, of the capital stock of a corporation acquired before August, 1976, an amount equal to any expense incurred by the taxpayer in consideration therefor, to the extent that the expense was, by virtue of

(i) paragraph (e) of the definition "Canadian exploration and development expenses" in subsection 66(15), a Canadian exploration and development expense,

(ii) paragraph (i) of the definition "Canadian exploration expense" in subsection 66.1(6), a Canadian exploration expense,

(iii) paragraph (g) of the definition "Canadian development expense" in subsection 66.2(5), a Canadian development expense, or

(iv) paragraph (c) of the definition "Canadian oil and gas property expense" in subsection 66.4(5), a Canadian oil and gas property expense

incurred by the taxpayer;

**Notes**: 53(2)(e)(iii) amended by 1976 Budget, effective for amounts paid or payable and the fair market of property paid or payable after May 6, 1974.

(f) **[consideration from joint exploration corporation]** — where the property was received by the taxpayer as consideration for any payment or loan

(i) made before April 20, 1983 by the taxpayer as a shareholder corporation (within the meaning assigned by subsection 66(15)) to a joint exploration corporation of the shareholder, and

(ii) described in paragraph (a) of the definition "agreed portion" in subsection 66(15),

or the property was substituted for such a property, such portion of the payment or loan as may reasonably be considered to be related to an agreed portion (within the meaning assigned by subsection 66(15)) of the joint exploration corporation's

(iii) Canadian exploration and development expenses,

(iv) Canadian exploration expense,

(v) Canadian development expense, or

(vi) Canadian oil and gas property expense,

as the case may be;

**Related Provisions**: 248(5) — Substituted property.

(f.1) **[share of joint exploration corporation]** — where the property is a share of the capital stock of a joint exploration corporation resident in Canada and the taxpayer has, after 1971, made a contribution of capital to the corporation otherwise than by way of a loan, which contribution was included in computing the adjusted cost base of the property by virtue of paragraph (1)(c), such portion of the contribution as may reasonably be considered to be part of an agreed portion (within the meaning assigned by subsection 66(15)) of the corporation's

(i) Canadian exploration and development expenses,

(ii) Canadian exploration expense,

(iii) Canadian development expense, or

(iv) Canadian oil and gas property expense,

as the case may be;

(f.2) **[resource expenses renounced by joint exploration corporation]** — any amount required by paragraph 66(10.4)(a) to be deducted before that time in computing the adjusted cost base to the taxpayer of the property;

**Notes**: 53(2)(f.2) added by 1983 Budget, effective with respect to any property received by a taxpayer with respect to payments or loans made after April 19, 1983.

**Advance Tax Rulings**: ATR-60: Joint exploration corporations.

(g) **[debt forgiveness]** — where section 80 is applicable in respect of the taxpayer, the amount, if any, by which the adjusted cost base to the taxpayer of the property is required in prescribed manner to be reduced before that time;

**Regulations**: 5400(1)(c)–(e) (prescribed manner).

(g.1) **[history preservation rules — debt forgiveness]** — any amount required under paragraph (4)(a), (5)(a), (6)(a), 47(1)(c), 49(3.01)(a), 51(1)(d.1), 86(4)(a) or 87(5.1)(a) or (6.1)(a) to be deducted in computing the adjusted cost base to the taxpayer of the property or any amount by which that adjusted cost base is required to be reduced because of subsection 80(9), (10) or (11);

**Related Provisions**: 80.03(2), (3) — Gain on subsequent "surrender" of property; 107(1)(a) — Reduction in gain on disposition of capital interest in trust.

**Notes**: The provisions listed in 53(2)(g.1) are referred to informally as the "history preservation rules", since under 80.03(2)(a) they may result in a subsequent deemed capital gain.

53(2)(g.1) added by 1994 tax amendments bill (Part I), effective for taxation years that end after February 21, 1994. See Notes to 47(1).

**Interpretation Bulletins**: IT-96R6: Options to acquire shares, bonds or debentures and by trusts to acquire trust units.

(h) **[capital interest in trust]** — where the property is a capital interest of the taxpayer in a trust (other than an interest in a personal trust acquired by the taxpayer for no consideration or an interest of the taxpayer in a trust described in any of paragraphs (a) to (d) of the definition "trust" in subsection 108(1)),

### Proposed Amendment — 53(2)(h) opening words

(h) **[capital interest in trust]** — where the property is a capital interest of the taxpayer in a trust (other than an interest in a personal trust that has never been acquired for consideration or an interest of a taxpayer in a trust described in any of paragraphs (a) to (e.1) of the definition "trust" in subsection 108(1)),

**Application**: Bill C-43 (First Reading September 20, 2000), subsec. 21(1), will amend the opening words of para. 53(2)(h) to read as above, applicable to amounts that become payable after 1999.

**Technical Notes**: Under paragraph 53(2)(h), certain amounts are deducted in computing the adjusted cost base (ACB) to a beneficiary of the beneficiary's capital interest in a trust (other than an interest in a personal trust acquired for no consideration or an interest in a trust described in any of paragraphs (a) to (d) of the definition "trust" in subsection 108(1)). Trusts described in these paragraphs are generally those deemed to exist for income tax purposes and those that relate to employee compensation and retirement savings. Among the deducted amounts (as described in subparagraph 53(2)(h)(i.1)) are certain amounts payable to a trust beneficiary in respect of the beneficiary's capital interest in a trust, otherwise than as proceeds of disposition.

Paragraph 53(2)(h) is amended to ensure that it does not apply to interests in trusts described in paragraphs (e) and (e.1) of the definition "trust" in subsection 108(1). Trusts referred to in these two paragraphs are cemetery care trusts, trusts governed by eligible funeral arrangements and trusts each of the beneficiaries of which is an employee compensation trust, retirement savings trust or related segregated fund trust. This amendment corrects a legislative oversight.

Paragraph 53(2)(h) is also amended so that it does not apply to an interest in a personal trust that has never been acquired for consideration. New paragraph 108(6)(c) and new subsection 108(7) are relevant for the purpose of determining when an interest in a trust is considered to have been acquired for consideration.

(i) any amount paid to the taxpayer by the trust after 1971 and before that time as a distribution or payment of capital by the trust (otherwise than as proceeds of disposition of the interest or part thereof), to the extent that the amount became payable before 1988,

(i.1) any amount that has become payable to the taxpayer by the trust after 1987 and before that time in respect of the interest (otherwise than as proceeds of disposition of the interest or part thereof), except to the extent of the portion thereof

(A) that was included in the taxpayer's income by reason of subsection 104(13) or from which an amount of tax was deducted under Part XIII by reason of paragraph 212(1)(c), or

(B) where the trust was resident in Canada throughout its taxation year in which the amount became payable

(I) that is equal to $1/3$ of the amount designated by the trust under subsection 104(21) in respect of the taxpayer, or

### Proposed Amendment — 53(2)(h)(i.1)(B)(I)

**Application**: The December 21, 2000 draft legislation, subsec. 20(7), will amend subcl. 53(2)(h)(i.1)(B)(I) by replacing the reference to the fraction "1/3" with a reference to the fraction "1/2", applicable to taxation years that end after February 27, 2000 except that, in applying the subcl. for those years in respect of a taxpayer's interest in a trust, where a taxation year of the trust that includes either February 28, 2000 or October 17, 2000 ends in the taxpayer's taxation year, the reference to the fraction "1/2" shall be read as a reference to the expression "the fraction that is equal to the fraction obtained when 1 is subtracted from the reciprocal of the fraction in para. 38(a), as amended [by the December 21, 2000 draft legislation], that applies to the trust for its taxation year, multiplied by".

**Technical Notes**: Subparagraph 53(2)(h) reduces the adjusted cost base to a taxpayer of a capital interest in a trust in respect of amounts set out in subparagraphs 53(2)(h)(i) to (v). Subparagraph 53(2)(h)(i.1) refers to certain payments made by the trust after 1987 other than payments out of income of the trust or the non-taxable portion of the capital gains of the trust. The amendment to subclause 53(2)(h)(i.1)(B)(I) replaces the fraction "1/3" with the fraction "1/2" and is consequential on the reduction of the inclusion rate for capital gains from 3/4 to 1/2.

The amendment applies to taxation years that end after February 27, 2000 except that, where the trust's taxation year that ends in the taxation year of the taxpayer includes either February 28, 2000 or October 17, 2000, the reference to the fraction "1/2" is to be read as reference to the fraction obtained when 1 is subtracted from the reciprocal of the fraction in amended paragraph 38(a) that applies to the trust for its taxation year. These modifications are required in order to reflect the capital gains/losses rate for the year.

(II) that was designated by the trust under subsection 104(20) in respect of the taxpayer,

(ii) an amount equal to that portion of all amounts deducted under subsection 127(5) in computing the tax otherwise payable by the taxpayer under this Part for the taxpayer's taxation years ending before that time that may reasonably be attributed to amounts added in computing the investment tax credit of the taxpayer by virtue of subsection 127(7),

(iii) any amount added pursuant to subsection 127.2(3) in computing the taxpayer's share-purchase tax credit for a taxation year ending before or after that time,

(iv) an amount equal to 50% of the amount deemed to be designated pursuant to subsection 127.3(3) before that time in respect of each share, debt obligation or right acquired by the trust and deemed to have been acquired by the taxpayer under that subsection, and

(v) an amount equal to the amount of all assistance received by the taxpayer before that time that has resulted in a reduction of the capital cost of a depreciable property to the trust by virtue of subsection 13(7.2);

**Related Provisions**: 53(1)(d.1) — Additions to adjusted cost base — capital interest in a trust; 53(2)(i), (j) — further deduction from ACB of interest in a trust; 87(2)(j.6) — Amalgamations — continuing corporation; 94(3)(a) [proposed] — Application to trust deemed resident in Canada; 104(20) — Designation re non-taxable dividends; 104(24) — Whether amount payable to beneficiary; 108(6) — Where terms of trust are varied; 108(7) — Meaning of "acquired for consideration"; 127(12.2) — Interpretation; 206(1)"cost amount" — Cost amount of capital interest in a trust

## S. 53(2)(h)

that is foreign property; 248(1)"personal trust" — Where interest deemed acquired for no consideration; 248(25.3) — Deemed cost of trust interest; 250(6.1) — Trust that ceases to exist deemed resident throughout year.

**Notes:** 53(2)(h)(ii) added by 1981 Budget, effective for investment tax credits deducted for 1982 and subsequent years.

53(2)(h)(v) added by 1985 technical bill, effective for property acquired after May 9, 1985.

53(2)(h) amended by 1988 tax reform, effective for amounts that become payable by trusts after 1987. For earlier amounts, read the first part of the paragraph as:

(h) where the property is a capital interest in a trust that was purchased by the taxpayer or a unit of a unit trust,

(i) any amount paid to the taxpayer by the trust after 1971 and before that time as, on account or in lieu of payment of, or in satisfaction of a distribution or payment of capital, otherwise than as proceeds of disposition of the interest or unit, as the case may be, or of a part thereof,

The 1988 amendments are, as noted, effective for amounts that become payable by trusts after 1987, except that

(a) with respect to amounts payable by trusts before 1990, the reference to "1/3" in 53(2)(h)(i.1)(B)(I) shall be read as a reference to "1/2"; and

(b) 53(2)(h)(i.1) does not apply with respect to that portion of an amount that becomes payable in a taxation year of the trust ending before 1990 to a taxpayer by a trust (other than a unit trust) created before October 2, 1987, that may reasonably be considered to be out of an amount that has been deducted under 20(16) or regulations made under 20(1)(a) or 65(1) in computing the income of the trust for the year, where

(i) such portion is designated by the trust in respect of the taxpayer and not in respect of any other beneficiary under the trust and does not exceed the proportion of the aggregate of amounts that the trust so designates in respect of all beneficiaries for the year that

(A) the taxpayer's share of the income of the trust for the year computed without reference to the amending legislation

is of

(B) the income of the trust for the year computed without reference to the amending legislation,

(ii) no beneficial interest in the trust is created before the end of the year and after October 1, 1987 (other than pursuant to the terms of a prospectus, preliminary prospectus, registration statement, offering memorandum or notice filed before October 2, 1987 with a public authority in Canada, where such document was required by law to be so filed before trading in the securities can commence), and

(iii) there has not been a substantial increase in the indebtedness of the trust before the end of the year and after October 1, 1987 (other than as a consequence of an agreement entered into in writing before October 2, 1987).

**Interpretation Bulletins:** IT-342R: Trusts: Income payable to beneficiaries; IT-381R3: Trusts — capital gains and losses and the flow-through of taxable capital gains to beneficiaries; IT-390: Unit trusts — cost of rights and adjustments to cost base; IT-456R: Capital property — some adjustments to cost base.

(i) **[capital interest in non-resident trust]** — where the property is a capital interest in a trust (other than a unit trust) not resident in Canada that was purchased after 1971 by the taxpayer from a non-resident person at a time when the fair market value of such of the trust property as was

---

Income Tax Act, Part I, Division B

> **Proposed Amendment — 53(2)(i) opening words**
>
> (i) **[capital interest in non-resident trust]** — where the property is a capital interest in a trust (other than a unit trust) not resident in Canada that was purchased after 1971 and before that time by the taxpayer from a non-resident person at a time (in this paragraph referred to as the "purchase time") when the property was not taxable Canadian property and the fair market value of such of the trust property as was
>
> **Application:** Bill C-43 (First Reading September 20, 2000), subsec. 21(2), will amend the opening words of para. 53(2)(i) to read as above, applicable for the purpose of computing the adjusted cost base of property after April 26, 1995.
>
> **Technical Notes:** Paragraphs 53(2)(i) and (j) set out certain reductions required to be made in determining the adjusted cost base (ACB) of a capital interest in a non-resident trust (including a unit of a non-resident unit trust) acquired by a purchaser. The ACB reduction in respect of a capital interest in such a trust occurs, in general terms, where the purchaser acquired the interest from a non-resident person and assets of the trust consist primarily of any combination of taxable Canadian properties, Canadian resource properties, timber resource properties and income interests in trusts resident in Canada. The ACB reduction reduces the overall tax advantages associated with the sale of such capital interests by reducing the ACB to the purchaser of the capital interest. The ACB reduction takes into account the deferral of the recognition of gains on such properties that used to result when a capital interest in a trust holding such properties (rather than the underlying properties) was sold by a non-resident person.
>
> Paragraphs 53(2)(i) and (j) are amended so that such ACB reductions are no longer required in connection with purchases of a capital interest in a trust, where the interest is taxable Canadian property to the non-resident vendor. This amendment, which is relevant to purchases after April 26, 1995, is consequential to the extension of taxable Canadian property (under former subsection 115(1) and the new definition "taxable Canadian property" in subsection 248(1)) to include capital interests in a non-resident trust in cases where the trust's assets consist primarily of taxable Canadian properties and other properties described above.

(i) a Canadian resource property,

(ii) [Repealed under former Act]

(iii) an income interest in a trust resident in Canada,

(iv) taxable Canadian property, or

(v) a timber resource property

was not less than 50% of the total of

(vi) the fair market value of all the trust property, and

(vii) the amount of any money of the trust on hand,

that proportion of the amount, if any, by which

(viii) the fair market value at that time of such of the trust property as was property described in subparagraphs (i) to (v)

Subdivision c — Taxable Capital Gains    S. 53(2)(k)(i)(A)

exceeds

(ix) the total of the cost amounts to the trust at that time of such of the trust properties as were properties described in subparagraphs (i) to (v),

that the fair market value at that time of the interest is of the fair market value at that time of all capital interests in the trust;

### Proposed Amendment — 53(2)(i)

was not less than 50% of the fair market value of all the trust property, that proportion of the amount, if any, by which

(vi) the fair market value at the purchase time of such of the trust properties as were properties described in any of subparagraphs (i) to (v)

exceeds

(vii) the total of the cost amounts to the trust at the purchase time of such of the trust properties as were properties described in any of subparagraphs (i) to (v),

that the fair market value at the purchase time of the interest is of the fair market value at the purchase time of all capital interests in the trust;

**Application**: Bill C-43 (First Reading September 20, 2000), subsec. 21(3), will amend the portion of para. 53(2)(i) after subpara. (v) to read as above, applicable for the purpose of computing the adjusted cost base of property after April 26, 1995.

**Technical Notes**: See under 53(2)(i) opening words.

**Related Provisions**: 53(3) — Application of 53(2)(i) and (j).

(j) **[unit of non-resident unit trust]** — where the property is a unit of a unit trust not resident in Canada that was purchased after 1971 by the taxpayer from a non-resident person at a time when the fair market value of such of the trust property as was

### Proposed Amendment — 53(2)(j) opening words

(j) **[unit of non-resident unit trust]** — where the property is a unit of a unit trust not resident in Canada that was purchased after 1971 and before that time by the taxpayer from a non-resident person at a time (in this paragraph referred to as the "purchase time") when the property was not taxable Canadian property and the fair market value of such of the trust property as was

**Application**: Bill C-43 (First Reading September 20, 2000), subsec. 21(4), will amend the opening words of para. 53(2)(j) to read as above, applicable for the purpose of computing the adjusted cost base of property after April 26, 1995.

**Technical Notes**: See under 53(2)(i) opening words.

(i) a Canadian resource property,

(ii) [Repealed under former Act]

(iii) an income interest in a trust resident in Canada,

(iv) taxable Canadian property, or

(v) a timber resource property

was not less than 50% of the total of

(vi) the fair market value of all the trust property, and

(vii) the amount of any money of the trust on hand,

that proportion of the amount, if any, by which

(viii) the fair market value at that time of such of the trust property as was property described in subparagraphs (i) to (v),

exceeds

(ix) the total of the cost amounts to the trust at that time of such of the trust properties as were properties described in subparagraphs (i) to (v),

that the fair market value at that time of the unit is of the fair market value at that time of all of the issued units of the trust;

### Proposed Amendment — 53(2)(j)

was not less than 50% of the fair market value of all the trust property, that proportion of the amount, if any, by which

(vi) the fair market value at the purchase time of such of the trust properties as were properties described in any of subparagraphs (i) to (v)

exceeds

(vii) the total of the cost amounts to the trust at the purchase time of such of the trust properties as were properties described in any of subparagraphs (i) to (v),

that the fair market value at the purchase time of the unit is of the fair market value at the purchase time of all the issued units of the trust;

**Application**: Bill C-43 (First Reading September 20, 2000), subsec. 21(5), will amend the portion of para. 53(2)(j) after subpara. (v) to read as above, applicable for the purpose of computing the adjusted cost base of property after April 26, 1995.

**Technical Notes**: See under 53(2)(i) opening words.

**Related Provisions**: 53(3) — Application of 53(2)(i) and (j).

(k) **[assistance received or receivable]** — where the property was acquired by the taxpayer after 1971, the amount, if any, by which the total of

(i) the amount of any assistance which the taxpayer has received or is entitled to receive before that time from a government, municipality or other public authority, in respect of, or for the acquisition of, the property, whether as a grant, subsidy, forgivable loan, deduction from tax not otherwise provided for under this paragraph, investment allowance or as any other form of assistance other than

(A) an amount described in paragraph 37(1)(d),

(B) an amount deducted as an allowance under section 65,

(C) the amount of prescribed assistance that the taxpayer has received or is entitled to receive in respect of, or for the acquisition of, shares of the capital stock of a prescribed venture capital corporation or a prescribed labour-sponsored venture capital corporation or shares of the capital stock of a taxable Canadian corporation that are held in a prescribed stock savings plan, or

(D) an amount included in income by virtue of paragraph 12(1)(u) or 56(1)(s), and

(ii) all amounts deducted under subsection 127(5) or (6) in respect of the property before that time,

exceeds such part, if any, of the assistance referred to in subparagraph (i) as has been repaid before that time by the taxpayer pursuant to an obligation to repay all or any part of that assistance;

**Related Provisions**: 39(13) — Repaid assistance deemed a capital loss; 125.4(5) — Canadian film/video credit is deemed to be assistance; 125.5(5) — Film/video production services credit is deemed to be assistance; 127(12.2) — Interpretation; 127.4(1)"net cost"(b) — Labour-sponsored venture capital corporation; 248(16) — GST input tax credit and rebate deemed to be assistance; 248(18) — GST — repayment of input tax credit.

**Notes**: 53(2)(k) amended by 1976 Budget, effective for acquisitions of property occurring after November 18, 1974 and in respect of the repayment on or after December 31, 1971 of grants, subsidies or other assistance. For property acquired before November 19, 1974, read:

(k) any grant, subsidy or other assistance from a government, municipality or other public authority received by the taxpayer for or in respect of the acquisition by him after 1971 of the property.

In other words, the exclusions in 53(2)(k)(i)(A) to (D) do not apply, and the paragraph is limited to a "grant, subsidy or other assistance ... received" rather than the broader wording now used. However, due to the application rule, amounts repaid may be excluded from the deduction from adjusted cost base, pursuant to subpara. (k)(ii) as it appeared under the 1976 amendment, *viz.*:

"(ii) such part, if any, of the assistance referred to in subparagraph (i) as has been repaid before that time by him pursuant to an obligation to repay all or any part of that assistance".

53(2)(k)(i)(A) amended by 1988 tax reform, effective for expenditures made after April 1988. For earlier expenditures, instead of the reference to an amount described in para. 37(1)(d), read:

"(A) an amount authorized to be paid under an *Appropriation Act* and on terms and conditions approved by the Treasury Board in respect of scientific research and experimental development expenditures incurred for the purpose of advancing or sustaining the technological capability of Canadian manufacturing or other industry".

53(2)(k)(i)(C) amended by 1993 technical bill, effective for 1991 and later taxation years, to change "has been provided" to "that the taxpayer has received or is entitled to receive". Thus, prescribed assistance (Reg. 6702) receivable (as well as received) in respect of a share does not reduce the ACB of the share. 40(2)(i)(ii) provides that such assistance reduces any capital loss on disposition of the share.

**Regulations**: 6700, 6700.1 (prescribed venture capital corporation); 6701 (prescribed labour-sponsored venture capital corporation); 6702 (prescribed assistance); 6705 (prescribed stock savings plan).

**Interpretation Bulletins**: IT-273R2: Government assistance — general comments.

(l) **[debt obligation]** — where the property is a debt obligation, any amount that was deductible by virtue of subsection 20(14) in computing the taxpayer's income for any taxation year commencing before that time in respect of interest on that debt obligation;

(l.1) **[indexed debt obligation]** — where the property is an indexed debt obligation,

(i) any amount determined under subparagraph 16(6)(a)(ii) in respect of the obligation and deductible in computing the income of the taxpayer for a taxation year beginning before that time, and

(ii) the amount of any payment that was received or that became receivable by the taxpayer at or before that time in respect of an amount that was added under paragraph (1)(g.1) to the cost to the taxpayer of the obligation;

**Related Provisions**: 53(1)(g.1) — Addition to adjusted cost base — indexed debt obligation.

**Notes**: 53(2)(l.1) added by 1992 technical bill, effective for indexed debt obligations issued after October 16, 1991.

(m) **[amounts deducted from income]** — such part of the cost to the taxpayer of the property as was deductible (otherwise than by virtue of this subdivision) in computing the taxpayer's income for any taxation year commencing before that time and ending after 1971;

**Interpretation Bulletins**: IT-350R: Investigation of site; IT-456R: Capital property — some adjustments to cost base.

(n) **[expropriation asset]** — where the property is an expropriation asset of the taxpayer (within the meaning assigned by section 80.1) or an asset of the taxpayer assumed for the purposes of that section to be an expropriation asset thereof, any amount required by paragraph 80.1(2)(b) to be deducted in computing the adjusted cost base to the taxpayer of the asset;

**Related Provisions**: 53(1)(k) — Addition to ACB of expropriation asset.

(o) **[right to receive partnership property]** — where the property is a right to receive partnership property within the meaning assigned by paragraph 98.2(a) or 100(3)(a), any amount received by the taxpayer in full or partial satisfaction of that right;

(p) **[debt owing by corporation]** — where the property is a debt owing to the taxpayer by a corporation, any amount required to be deducted before that time under section 84.1 of the *Income Tax Act*, chapter 148 of the Revised Statutes of Canada, 1952, as it applied before May 23, 1985

## Subdivision c — Taxable Capital Gains — S. 53(2)

or subsection 84.2(2) in computing the adjusted cost base to the taxpayer of the debt;

**I.T. Application Rules**: 69 (meaning of "*Income Tax Act*, chapter 148 of the Revised Statutes of Canada, 1952").

(q) **[interest in related segregated fund trust]** — where the property is an interest in a related segregated fund trust referred to in section 138.1,

(i) each amount in respect of that interest that is a capital loss deemed to have been allocated under subsection 138.1(4) to the taxpayer before that time, and

(ii) each amount in respect of that interest that before that time was deemed by subsection 138.1(3) to be a capital loss of the taxpayer;

**Related Provisions**: 53(1)(l) — Addition to ACB of interest in related segregated fund trust; 138.1(5) — ACB of property in related segregated fund trust.

(r) **[Repealed under former Act]**

**Notes**: 53(2)(r) repealed by 1986 Budget, effective for dividends paid after May 23, 1985.

53(2)(r) added by 1980 Budget and amended by 1981 Budget. With respect to windups commencing after 1983, for dividends paid before May 24, 1985, read:

(r) where the property is

(i) a share of a class of the capital stock of a corporation, which share was acquired (otherwise than by way of purchase) by the taxpayer as a consequence of the death of a person, or another share of the same class acquired by that taxpayer after the death of that person, or

(ii) a share substituted for a share referred to in subparagraph (i), the aggregate of all amounts each of which is a dividend thereon received by the taxpayer on or before that time, or deemed to have been received after that time by virtue of subsection 84(2) or (3), that can reasonably be considered to be as, on account or in lieu of proceeds of a disposition and in respect of which the corporation has made an election under subsection 83(2.1)

the aggregate of all amounts each of which is a dividend thereon received by the taxpayer on or before that time, or deemed to have been received after that time by virtue of subsection 84(2) or (3), that can reasonably be considered to be as, on account or in lieu of proceeds of a disposition and in respect of which the corporation has made an election under subsection 83(2.1).

With respect to windups commencing before 1984, read the closing words of 53(2)(r) as:

the aggregate of all amounts each of which is a dividend thereon received by the taxpayer (otherwise than pursuant to a transaction described in subsection 84(2)) on or before that time that can reasonably be considered to be as, on account or in lieu of proceeds of a disposition and in respect of which the corporation has made an election under subsection 83(2.1).

(s) **[government assistance — amount elected under 53(2.1)]** — the amount, if any, by which

(i) the amount elected by the taxpayer before that time under subsection (2.1)

exceeds

(ii) any repayment before that time by the taxpayer of an amount received by the taxpayer

as described in subsection (2.1) that may reasonably be considered to relate to the amount elected where the repayment is made pursuant to a legal obligation to repay all or any part of the amount so received;

**Related Provisions**: 12(1)(t) — Income inclusion — investment tax credit; 12(1)(x) — Payments as inducement or as reimbursement etc.; 39(13) — Repayment of assistance; 40(3) — Deemed capital gain when ACB goes negative; 53(2.1) — Election; 87(2)(j.6) — Amalgamations — continuing corporation.

**Interpretation Bulletins**: IT-273R2: Government assistance — general comments.

(t) **[right to acquire shares or fund units]** — if the property is a right to acquire shares or units under an agreement, any amount required by paragraph 164(6.1)(b) to be deducted in computing the adjusted cost base to the taxpayer of the right;

**Notes**: 53(2)(t) amended to add "or units" by 1998 Budget, effective March 1998. This was consequential on extending the rules in s. 7 to mutual fund units (see Notes to 7(1)).

53(2)(t) added by 1992 technical bill, effective July 14, 1990.

**I.T. Application Rules**: 26(3).

**Interpretation Bulletins**: IT-456R: Capital property — some adjustments to cost base.

(u) **[non-qualifying real property]** — where the property was at the end of February 22, 1994 a non-qualifying real property (within the meaning assigned by subsection 110.6(1) as that subsection applies to the 1994 taxation year) of a taxpayer, any amount required by paragraph 110.6(21)(b) to be deducted in computing the adjusted cost base to the taxpayer of the property; and

**Notes**: 53(2)(u) added by 1994 Budget, effective 1994.

(v) **[excessive capital gains election]** — where the taxpayer elected under subsection 110.6(19) in respect of the property, any amount required by subsection 110.6(22) to be deducted in computing the adjusted cost base to the taxpayer of the property at that time.

**Notes**: 53(2)(v) added by 1994 Budget, effective 1994.

---

**Proposed Addition — 53(2)(w)**

(w) **[interest in foreign investment entity]** — any amount required by subsection 94.1(9), 94.2(11) or 94.3(2) to be deducted at or before that time in computing the adjusted cost base to the taxpayer of the property.

**Application**: The June 22, 2000 draft legislation, subsec. 4(3), will add para. 53(2)(w), applicable after 2000.

**Technical Notes**: Paragraph 53(2)(w) is introduced to provide for the ACB reductions contemplated by new subsections 94.1(9), 94.2(11) and 94.3(2). For more detail, see the commentary on those subsections.

New paragraph 53(2)(w) applies after 2000.

---

**Notes [subsec. 53(2)]**: Subsec. 4(4) of the *Western Grain Transition Payments Act* (1995, c. 17, Sch. II), as amended by 1995-97 technical bill (s. 303), provides, effective for payments made after June 22, 1995:

4. (4) **Tax treatment** — For the purposes of the *Income Tax Act*, ...

(b) a transition payment received in respect of farmland that was, immediately before its disposition by the applicant, capital property of the applicant shall, where the farmland is disposed of before the payment is received, be considered to be an amount required by subsection 53(2) of that Act to be deducted in computing the adjusted cost base of the farmland to the applicant immediately before the disposition;

(c) a transition payment to which neither paragraph (a) nor (b) applies, received by the applicant, shall be considered to be assistance received in the course of earning income from a business or property in respect of the cost of the property or in respect of an outlay or an expense; and

(d) where, pursuant to an equitable arrangement referred to in paragraph 6(c), a portion of a transition payment received by an applicant is paid to a person or partnership that is leasing farmland from the applicant, that portion paid to the person or partnership is required to be included in computing the income of the person or partnership from a business for the taxation year of the person or partnership in which it is received and the amount so paid is deemed not to be a transition payment received by the applicant for the purposes of paragraphs (a) to (c).

See also Notes at end of 12(1)(x) re payments in respect of farmland that is not capital property.

**I.T. Technical News**: No. 5 (western grain transition payments).

**(2.1) Election** — For the purpose of paragraph (2)(s), where in a taxation year a taxpayer receives an amount that would, but for this subsection, be included in the taxpayer's income under paragraph 12(1)(x) in respect of the cost of a property (other than depreciable property) acquired by the taxpayer in the year, in the 3 taxation years preceding the year or in the taxation year following the year, the taxpayer may elect under this subsection on or before the date on or before which the taxpayer's return of income under this Part for the year is required to be filed or, where the property is acquired in the following year, for that following year, to reduce the cost of the property by such amount as the taxpayer specifies, not exceeding the least of

(a) the adjusted cost base, determined without reference to paragraph (2)(s), at the time the property was acquired,

(b) the amount so received by the taxpayer, and

(c) where the taxpayer has disposed of the property before the year, nil.

**Related Provisions**: 87(2)(j.6) — Amalgamations — continuing corporation; 220(3.2), Reg. 600(b) — Late filing of election or revocation.

**Notes**: Opening words of 53(2.1) amended by 1992 technical bill, effective 1991, to introduce the exclusion "(other than depreciable property)".

**Interpretation Bulletins**: IT-273R2: Government assistance — general comments; IT-456R: Capital property — some adjustments to cost base.

**(3) Application of paras. (2)(i) and (j)** — For the purposes of paragraphs (2)(i) and (j), where any property of a trust would, at a particular time, have been a taxable Canadian property of the trust if it had been disposed of by the trust at that time, the property shall be deemed to have been a taxable Canadian property of the trust at that time.

### Proposed Repeal — 53(3)

**Application**: Bill C-43 (First Reading September 20, 2000), subsec. 21(6), will repeal subsec. 53(3), applicable after October 1, 1996.

**Technical Notes**: Subsection 53(3) provides that, for the purposes of certain deductions required to be made in determining the adjusted cost base of interests in non-resident trusts, property of a trust is taxable Canadian property (TCP) at a particular time if the property would be TCP if the trust had disposed of the property at that time.

Subsection 53(3) is repealed with effect after October 1, 1996. This amendment is strictly consequential to changes in the definition of TCP (described in the commentary on subsection 248(1) of the Act) and does not represent any change in tax policy.

**Interpretation Bulletins [subsec. 53(3)]**: IT-138R: Computation and flow-through of a partnership income.

**(4) Recomputation of adjusted cost base on transfers and deemed dispositions** — Where at any time in a taxation year a person or partnership (in this subsection referred to as the "vendor") disposes of a specified property and the proceeds of disposition of the property are determined under paragraph 48.1(1)(c), section 70 or 73, subsection 85(1), paragraph 87(4)(a) or (c) or 88(1)(a), subsection 97(2) or 98(2), paragraph 98(3)(f) or (5)(f), subsection 104(4), paragraph 107(2)(a), (2.1)(a), (4)(d) or (5)(a) or 111(4)(e) or section 128.1,

### Proposed Amendment — 53(4) opening words

**(4) Recomputation of adjusted cost base on transfers and deemed dispositions** — Where at any time in a taxation year a person or partnership (in this subsection referred to as the "vendor") disposes of a specified property and the proceeds of disposition of the property are determined under paragraph 48.1(1)(c), section 70 or 73, subsection 85(1), paragraph 87(4)(a) or (c) or 88(1)(a), subsection 97(2) or 98(2), paragraph 98(3)(f) or (5)(f), subsection 104(4), paragraph 107(2)(a), (2.1)(a), (4)(d) or (5)(a), 107.4(3)(a) or 111(4)(e) or section 128.1,

**Application**: Bill C-43 (First Reading September 20, 2000), subsec. 21(7), will amend the opening words of subsec. 53(4) to read as above, applicable to 1998 *et seq.*

**Technical Notes**: Subsection 53(4) provides rules that affect the computation of the adjusted cost base (ACB) to a taxpayer of any "specified property". As defined in section 54, "specified property" is capital property that is a share, a capital interest in a trust, a partnership interest or an option to acquire any such property. The rules in subsection 53(4) apply where the proceeds of disposition of a specified property are determined under any one of a number of provisions in the Act set out in the subsection. Where this is the case and the ACB of the specified property was reduced under paragraph 53(2)(g.1) as a consequence of a forgiveness of debt, the ACB continues to be reduced under that paragraph as a consequence of the operation of subsection 53(4). The only significance of this reduction is with respect to the potential future application of section 80.03 which, in certain cases, recaptures reductions previously made under paragraph 53(2)(g.1) in computing the ACB of specified property on a future disposition of such property.

Subsection 53(4) is amended to add a reference in the subsection to paragraph 107.4(3)(a). Subsection 107.4(3) provides for a rollover on certain transfers of property that do not involve any change in the beneficial ownership of the property. As a result, the ACB of a property transferred to a trust that was subject to a reduction because of the forgiveness of debt rules continues to be reduced on the same basis if the property is transferred in circumstances where proceeds of disposition are determined under paragraph 107.4(3)(a).

(a) there shall be deducted after that time in computing the adjusted cost base to the person or partnership (in this subsection referred to as the "transferee") who acquires or reacquires the property at or immediately after that time the amount, if any, by which

(i) the total of all amounts deducted under paragraph (2)(g.1) in computing, immediately before that time, the adjusted cost base to the vendor of the property,

exceeds

(ii) the amount that would be the vendor's capital gain for the year from that disposition if this Act were read without reference to subparagraph 40(1)(a)(iii) and subsection 100(2); and

(b) the amount determined under paragraph (a) in respect of that disposition shall be added after that time in computing the adjusted cost base to the transferee of the property.

**Related Provisions**: 53(1)(q) — Addition to adjusted cost base for amount under 53(4)(b); 53(2)(g.1) — Reduction in adjusted cost base under 53(4)(a); 53(5) — Recomputation of ACB on other transfers; 80.03(2)(a) — Deemed gain on disposition following debt forgiveness; 251(1) — Arm's length.

**Notes**: 53(4) applies only to "specified property" as defined in 54 (shares, partnership or trust interests, or options on any of these), and its only significance is for the future application of 80.03. See Notes to 47(1). 53(4) added by 1994 tax amendments bill (Part I), effective for taxation years that end after February 21, 1994, and opening words amended retroactive to its introduction by 1995-97 technical bill to delete a reference to 85.1(1)(a).

### (5) Recomputation of adjusted cost base on other transfers — Where

(a) at any time in a taxation year a person or partnership (in this subsection referred to as the "vendor") disposes of a specified property to another person or partnership (in this subsection referred to as the "transferee"),

(b) immediately before that time, the vendor and the transferee do not deal with each other at arm's length or would not deal with each other at arm's length if paragraph 80(2)(j) applied for the purpose of this subsection,

(c) paragraph (b) would apply in respect of the disposition if each right referred to in paragraph 251(5)(b) that is a right of the transferee to acquire the specified property from the vendor or a right of the transferee to acquire other property as part of a transaction or event or series of transactions or events that includes the disposition were not taken into account, and

(d) the proceeds of the disposition are not determined under any of the provisions referred to in subsection (4),

the following rules apply:

(e) there shall be deducted after that time in computing the adjusted cost base to the transferee of the property the amount, if any, by which

(i) the total of all amounts deducted under paragraph (2)(g.1) in computing the adjusted cost base to the vendor of the property immediately before that time

exceeds

(ii) the amount that would be the vendor's capital gain for the year from that disposition if this Act were read without reference to subparagraph 40(1)(a)(iii) and subsection 100(2), and

(f) the amount determined under paragraph (e) in respect of that disposition shall be added after that time in computing the adjusted cost base to the transferee of the property.

**Related Provisions**: 53(1)(q) — Addition to ACB for amount under 53(5)(b); 53(2)(g.1) — Reduction in ACB under 53(5)(a); 80.03(2)(a) — Deemed gain on disposition following debt forgiveness.

**Notes**: 53(5) added by 1994 tax amendments bill (Part I), effective for taxation years that end after February 21, 1994, and amended retroactive to its introduction by 1995-97 technical bill. The version before the amendment, now deemed never to have been in force, read:

(5) Where at any time in a taxation year a person or partnership (in this subsection referred to as the "vendor") disposes of a specified property to another person or partnership (in this subsection referred to as the "transferee"), the vendor and the transferee do not deal with each other at arm's length (or would not deal with each other at arm's length if paragraph 80(2)(j) applied for the purpose of this subsection) and the proceeds of disposition of the property at that time are not determined under any of the provisions referred to in subsection (4),

(a) there shall be deducted after that time in computing the adjusted cost base to the transferee of the property the amount, if any, by which

(i) the total of all amounts deducted under paragraph (2)(g.1) in computing, immediately before that time, the adjusted cost base to the vendor of the property

exceeds

(ii) the amount that would be the vendor's capital gain for the year from that disposition if this Act were read without reference to subparagraph 40(1)(a)(iii) and subsection 100(2); and

(b) the amount determined under paragraph (a) in respect of that disposition shall be added after that time in computing the adjusted cost base to the transferee of the property.

See Notes to 47(1).

## (6) Recomputation of adjusted cost base on amalgamation
— Where a capital property that is a specified property is acquired by a new corporate entity at any time as a result of the amalgamation or merger of 2 or more predecessor corporations,

(a) there shall be deducted after that time in computing the adjusted cost base to the new entity of the property the total of all amounts deducted under paragraph (2)(g.1) in computing, immediately before that time, the adjusted cost base to a predecessor corporation of the property, unless those amounts are otherwise deducted under that paragraph in computing the adjusted cost base to the new entity of the property; and

(b) the amount deducted under paragraph (a) in respect of the acquisition shall be added after that time in computing the adjusted cost base to the new entity of the property.

**Related Provisions**: 53(1)(q) — Addition to ACB for amount under 53(6)(b); 53(2)(g.1) — Reduction in ACB under 53(6)(a); 80.03(2)(a) — Deemed gain on disposition following debt forgiveness.

**Notes**: 53(6) added by 1994 tax amendments bill (Part I), effective for taxation years that end after February 21, 1994. See Notes to 47(1).

**Definitions [s. 53]**: "acquired" — 256(7)–(9); "adjusted cost base" — 54, 248(1); "amount" — 248(1); "arm's length" — 251(1); "assistance" — 79(4), 125.4(5), 248(16), 248(18); "business" — 248(1); "Canada" — 255; "Canadian development expense" — 66.2(5), 248(1); "Canadian exploration and development expense" — 66(15), 248(1); "Canadian exploration expense" — 66.1(6), 248(1); "Canadian oil and gas property expense" — 66.4(5), 248(1); "Canadian resource property" — 66(15), 248(1); "capital dividend" — 83(2), 248(1); "capital interest" — 108(1), 248(1); "consequence of the death" — 248(8); "consideration" — 108(1); "control" — 256(6)–(9); "controlled foreign affiliate" — 95(1), 248(1); "corporation" — 248(1), Interpretation Act 35(1); "cost amount" — 248(1); "disposition" — 54 [to be repealed], 248(1) [draft]; "dividend" — 248(1); "expropriation asset" — 80.1(1); "farming" — 248(1); "fiscal period" — 249(2)(b), 249.1; "foreign accrual property income" — 95(1), (2), 248(1); "foreign affiliate" — 95(1), 248(1); "foreign exploration and development expense" — 66(15), 248(1); "foreign resource pool expense" — 248(1); "income bond", "income debenture" — 248(1); "income interest in a trust" — 108(1), 248(1); "indexed debt obligation" — 248(1); "joint exploration corporation" — 66(15); "life insurance capital dividend" — 83(2.1), 248(1); "life insurance policy" — 138(12), 248(1); "limited partnership loss" — 248(1); "mutual fund trust" — 132(6)–(7), 132.2(1)(q), 248(1); "non-qualifying real property" — 110.6(1); "non-resident" — 248(1); "partnership" — see Notes to 96(1); "person", "personal trust", "prescribed" — 248(1); "prescribed labour-sponsored venture capital corporation" — Reg. 6701; "prescribed venture capital corporation" — Reg. 6700, 6700.1, 6700.2; "principal amount", "property" — 248(1); "province" — Interpretation Act 35(1); "related" — 251(2); "resident in Canada" — 250; "security" — 7(7); "share", "shareholder", "specified member" — 248(1); "specified property" — 54; "specified shareholder" — 248(1); "superficial loss" — 54; "taxable Canadian corporation" — 89(1), 248(1); "taxable dividend" — 89(1), 248(1); "taxable income" — 2(2), 248(1); "taxation year" — 249; "taxpayer" — 248(1); "timber resource property" — 13(21), 248(1); "trust" — 104(1), 248(1), (3); "unit trust" — 108(2), 248(1); "vendor" — 53(4), (5).

## 54. Definitions — In this subdivision,

**"adjusted cost base"** to a taxpayer of any property at any time means, except as otherwise provided,

(a) where the property is depreciable property of the taxpayer, the capital cost to the taxpayer of the property as of that time, and

(b) in any other case, the cost to the taxpayer of the property adjusted, as of that time, in accordance with section 53,

except that

(c) for greater certainty, where any property (other than an interest in or a share of the capital stock of a flow-through entity within the meaning assigned by subsection 39.1(1) that was last reacquired by the taxpayer as a result of an election under subsection 110.6(19)) of the taxpayer is property that was reacquired by the taxpayer after having been previously disposed of by the taxpayer, no adjustment to the cost to the taxpayer of the property that was required to be made under section 53 before its reacquisition by the taxpayer shall be made under that section to the cost to the taxpayer of the property as reacquired property of the taxpayer, and

(d) in no case shall the adjusted cost base to a taxpayer of any property at any time be less than nil;

**Related Provisions**: 40(3), (3.1) — Deemed capital gain where ACB is negative; 43 — ACB on partial disposition; 47(1) — ACB of identical properties; 49(1) — Granting of options; 49(2) — Where option expires; 69(1)(c) — Deemed acquisition at fair market value in certain circumstances; 84.1(2) — Non-arm's length sale of shares; 91(6) — Amounts deductible in respect of dividends received; 92 — ACB of share of foreign affiliate; 93(4)(b) — Loss on disposition of shares of foreign affiliate; 110.6(19)(a)(ii) — Increase in cost base on capital gains exemption election; 139.1(4)(d) — Cost of share acquired on insurance demutualization deemed nil; 142.4(1)"tax basis" — cost base for securities held by financial institutions; 143.2(6) — Deemed cost reduction of tax shelter investment; 248(1)"adjusted cost base" — Definition applies to entire Act.

**Notes**: In simple terms, ACB is the cost of (capital) property, adjusted up by 53(1) and down by 53(2).

Paras. (c), (d) amended by 1994 Budget, effective 1994. For taxation years ending from December 1, 1991 through December 31, 1993, ignore the parenthesized "(other than...)" in para. (c), and read para. (d) as "in no case shall the adjusted cost base to a taxpayer of any property at any time be less than nil".

54"adjusted cost base" was 54(a) before consolidation in R.S.C. 1985 (5th Supp.), effective for taxation years ending after November 1991. See Table of Concordance.

**Regulations**: 4400, Sch. VII (ACB of publicly-traded shares at end of 1971).

**I.T. Application Rules**: 26(3)–(27) (where property owned since before 1972).

**Interpretation Bulletins**: IT-65: Stock splits and consolidations; IT-102R2: Conversion of property, other than real property, from or to inventory; IT-218R: Profit, capital gains and losses from the sale of real estate, including farmland and inherited land and conversion of real estate from capital property to inventory and vice versa; IT-418: Partial disposition of property.

**I.T. Technical News**: No. 9 (calculation of ACB of a partnership interest).

**Advance Tax Rulings**: ATR-67: Increase in the cost of property on the winding-up of a wholly-owned subsidiary.

**Forms**: T2065: Determination of adjusted cost base of a partnership interest.

**"capital property"** of a taxpayer means

(a) any depreciable property of the taxpayer, and

(b) any property (other than depreciable property), any gain or loss from the disposition of which would, if the property were disposed of, be a capital gain or a capital loss, as the case may be, of the taxpayer;

**Related Provisions**: 39(1) — Determination of capital gain and capital loss; 39(4) — Election to treat Canadian securities as capital property; 54.2 — Shares deemed to be capital property where all assets of business transferred; 66.3(1)(a)(i) — Certain exploration and development shares deemed not to be capital property; 96(1.4) — Certain rights to share in income or loss of partnership deemed not to be capital property; 142.5(1) — Mark-to-market rules for financial institutions; 248(1)"capital property" — Definition applies to entire Act.

**Notes**: This definition looks somewhat circular. The full technical definition is actually in 39(1)(a), which defines capital property, in effect, by excluding everything else.

Capital property is distinguished from property that, when disposed of, leads to a full income gain as income from business (inventory). All property is one or the other: *Friesen*, [1995] 2 C.T.C. 369 (SCC). "Business" is defined in 248(1) to include an "adventure in the nature of trade". There has been extensive case law determining whether gains (or losses) are on income or capital account. While each case depends on its facts, the general principle is that property purchased with the intention (including a secondary intention) of selling it at a profit is normally considered inventory, while property purchased to generate income (such as dividends or rent) is considered capital property. See Interpretation Bulletins IT-218R and IT-459. See also Notes to 10(1.01). Gains on capital property are only half-taxed; see 38(a).

54"capital property" was 54(b) before consolidation in R.S.C. 1985 (5th Supp.), effective for taxation years ending after November 1991. See Table of Concordance.

**I.T. Application Rules**: 26(5), (6) and (7).

**Interpretation Bulletins**: IT-102R2: Conversion of property, other than real property, from or to inventory; IT-143R2: Meaning of "eligible capital expenditure"; IT-218R: Profit, capital gains and losses from the sale of real estate, including farmland and inherited land and conversion of real estate from capital property to inventory and vice versa; IT-325R2: Property transfers after separation, divorce and annulment; IT-442R: Bad debts and reserves for doubtful debts; IT-459: Adventure or concern in the nature of trade.

**I.T. Technical News**: No. 7 (rollovers of capital property — *Mara Properties*); No. 12 ("millennium bug" expenditures).

**Advance Tax Rulings**: ATR-59: Financing exploration and development through limited partnerships.

**"disposition"** of any property, except as expressly otherwise provided, includes

(a) any transaction or event entitling a taxpayer to proceeds of disposition of property,

(b) any transaction or event by which

(i) any property of a taxpayer that is a share, bond, debenture, note, certificate, mortgage, agreement of sale or similar property, or an interest therein, is redeemed in whole or in part or is cancelled,

(ii) any debt owing to a taxpayer or any other right of a taxpayer to receive an amount is settled or cancelled,

(iii) any share owned by a taxpayer is converted by virtue of an amalgamation or merger, or

(iv) any option held by a taxpayer to acquire or dispose of property expires, and

(c) any transfer of property to a trust, or any transfer of property of a trust to any beneficiary under the trust, except as provided in paragraph (e),

but, for greater certainty, does not include

(d) any transfer of property for the purpose only of securing a debt or a loan, or any transfer by a creditor for the purpose only of returning property that had been used as security for a debt or a loan,

(e) any transfer of property by virtue of which there is a change in the legal ownership of the property without any change in the beneficial ownership thereof, other than a transfer by a trust resident in Canada to a trust not resident in Canada or a transfer to a trust governed by

(i) a registered retirement savings plan,

(ii) a deferred profit sharing plan,

(iii) an employees profit sharing plan, or

(iv) a registered retirement income fund

by a person who is, immediately after the transfer, a beneficiary under the plan or fund, or a transfer by any such trust governed by a plan or fund to a beneficiary thereunder,

(f) any issue by a corporation of a bond, debenture, note, certificate or mortgage of the corporation, or

(g) any issue by a corporation of a share of its capital stock, or any other transaction that, but for this paragraph, would be a disposition by a corporation of a share of its capital stock;

### Proposed Repeal — 54"disposition"

**Application**: Bill C-43 (First Reading September 20, 2000), subsec. 22(1), will repeal the definition "disposition" in s. 54, applicable to transactions and events that occur after December 23, 1998.

**Technical Notes**: The expression "disposition" is defined, for the purposes of the capital gains rules, in section 54.

The definition is repealed strictly as a consequence of the introduction of the new definition "disposition" in subsection 248(1).

**Related Provisions**: 48.1(1) — Gain when small business corporation becomes public; 49(5) — Extension or renewal of option; 49.1 — Satisfaction of obligation is not a disposition of property; 51(1) — Convertible property; 70(5) — Deemed disposition of property on death; 80.03(2), (4) — Deemed capital gain on disposi-

## S. 54 dis — Income Tax Act, Part I, Division B

tion of property following debt forgiveness; 87(4) — Shares of predecessor corporation; 104(5.3) — Election by trust to postpone deemed disposition; 107(2.1) — Distribution of trust property; 128.1(1)(b) — Deemed disposition of property on becoming resident in Canada; 128.1(4)(b) — Deemed disposition of property on ceasing to be resident in Canada.

**Notes**: 54"disposition" was 54(c) before consolidation in R.S.C. 1985 (5th Supp.), effective for taxation years ending after November 1991. See Table of Concordance.

See Notes to 248(1)"disposition".

**Interpretation Bulletins**: IT-65: Stock splits and consolidations; IT-96R6: Options to acquire shares, bonds or debentures and by trusts to acquire trust units; IT-102R2: Conversion of property, other than real property, from or to inventory; IT-124R6: Contributions to registered retirement savings plans; IT-125R4: Dispositions of resource properties; IT-126R2: Meaning of "winding-up"; IT-133: Stock exchange transactions — date of disposition of shares; IT-146R4: Shares entitling shareholders to choose taxable or capital dividends; IT-170R: Sale of property — when included in income computation; IT-218R: Profit, capital gains and losses from the sale of real estate, including farmland and inherited land and conversion of real estate from capital property to inventory and vice versa; IT-220R2: Capital cost allowance — proceeds of disposition of depreciable property; IT-334R2: Miscellaneous receipts; IT-444R: Corporations — involuntary dissolutions; IT-448: Dispositions — changes in terms of securities; IT-488R2: Winding-up of 90%-owned taxable Canadian corporations; IT-505: Mortgage foreclosures and conditional sales repossessions.

**I.T. Technical News**: No. 3 (loss utilization within a corporate group); No. 7 (revocable living trusts, protective trusts, bare trusts); No. 14 (changes in terms of debt obligations); No. 15 (tax consequences of the adoption of the "euro" currency).

**Advance Tax Rulings**: ATR-1: Transfer of legal title in land to bare trustee corporation — mortgagee's requirements sole reason for transfer; ATR-54: Reduction of paid-up capital.

**"eligible capital property"** of a taxpayer means any property, a part of the consideration for the disposition of which would, if the taxpayer disposed of the property, be an eligible capital amount in respect of a business;

**Related Provisions**: 14(3) — Non-arm's length acquisition of eligible capital property; 87(2)(f) — Amalgamations — security or debt obligation; 98(3)(b) — Rules applicable where partnership ceases to exist; 248(1)"eligible capital property" — Definition applies to entire Act.

**Notes**: The definition of "eligible capital property" is tortuous and somewhat circular. In essence, it is goodwill and other purchased intangibles, including incorporation expenses. See Notes to 20(1)(b).

54"eligible capital property" was 54(d) before consolidation in R.S.C. 1985 (5th Supp.), effective for taxation years ending after November 1991.

**Interpretation Bulletins**: IT-123R4: Disposition of eligible capital property; IT-123R5: Transactions involving eligible capital property; IT-143R2: Meaning of "eligible capital expenditure".

**"listed personal property"** of a taxpayer means the taxpayer's personal-use property that is all or any portion of, or any interest in or right to, any

(a) print, etching, drawing, painting, sculpture, or other similar work of art,

(b) jewellery,

(c) rare folio, rare manuscript, or rare book,

(d) stamp, or

(e) coin;

**Related Provisions**: 40(2)(g)(iii) — Limitations; 41 — Gain from listed personal property; 248(1)"listed personal property" — Definition applies to entire Act.

**Notes**: Listed personal property (LPP) typically appreciates rather than depreciates in value. See Notes to 41(1) re use of LPP losses.

Note that Reg. 1102(1)(e) generally prohibits CCA claims on art, except for Canadian art. Of course, listed personal property is, by definition, personal-use property and thus ineligible for CCA anyway because its use is personal and not for business or property income (see Reg. 1102(1)(c)).

54"listed personal property" was 54(e) before consolidation in R.S.C. 1985 (5th Supp.), effective for taxation years ending after November 1991. See Table of Concordance.

**Interpretation Bulletins**: IT-159R3: Capital debts established to be bad debts.

**"personal-use property"** of a taxpayer includes

(a) property owned by the taxpayer that is used primarily for the personal use or enjoyment of the taxpayer or for the personal use or enjoyment of one or more individuals each of whom is

(i) the taxpayer,

(ii) a person related to the taxpayer, or

(iii) where the taxpayer is a trust, a beneficiary under the trust or any person related to the beneficiary,

(b) any debt owing to the taxpayer in respect of the disposition of property that was the taxpayer's personal-use property, and

(c) any property of the taxpayer that is an option to acquire property that would, if the taxpayer acquired it, be personal-use property of the taxpayer,

and "personal-use property" of a partnership includes any partnership property that is used primarily for the personal use or enjoyment of any member of the partnership or for the personal use or enjoyment of one or more individuals each of whom is a member of the partnership or a person related to such a member;

**Related Provisions**: 3(b)(ii), 40(2)(g)(iii) — No capital loss on personal-use property; 46 — Disposition of personal-use property; 50(2) — Where debt personal-use property; 248(1)"personal-use property" — Definition applies to entire Act.

**Notes**: 54"personal-use property" was 54(f) before consolidation in R.S.C. 1985 (5th Supp.), effective for taxation years ending after November 1991. See Table of Concordance.

**Interpretation Bulletins**: IT-159R3: Capital debts established to be bad debts; IT-218R: Profit, capital gains and losses from the sale of real estate, including farmland and inherited land and conversion of real estate from capital property to inventory and vice versa; IT-332R: Personal-use property.

**"principal residence"** of a taxpayer for a taxation year means a particular property that is a housing unit, a leasehold interest in a housing unit or a share of the capital stock of a co-operative housing corporation acquired for the sole purpose of acquiring the right to inhabit a housing unit owned by the corporation and that is owned, whether jointly with another person or otherwise, in the year by the taxpayer, if

(a) where the taxpayer is an individual other than a personal trust, the housing unit was ordinarily inhabited in the year by the taxpayer, by the taxpayer's spouse or common-law partner or former spouse or common-law partner or by a child of the taxpayer,

(a.1) where the taxpayer is a personal trust, the housing unit was ordinarily inhabited in the calendar year ending in the year by a specified beneficiary of the trust for the year, by the spouse or common-law partner or former spouse or common-law partner of such a beneficiary or by a child of such a beneficiary, or

(b) where the taxpayer is a personal trust or an individual other than a trust, the taxpayer

(i) elected[1] under subsection 45(2) that relates to the change in use of the particular property in the year or a preceding taxation year, other than an election rescinded under subsection 45(2) in the taxpayer's return of income for the year or a preceding taxation year, or

(ii) elected[1] under subsection 45(3) that relates to a change in use of the particular property in a subsequent taxation year,

except that, subject to section 54.1, a particular property shall be considered not to be a taxpayer's principal residence for a taxation year

(c) where the taxpayer is an individual other than a personal trust, unless the particular property was designated by the taxpayer in prescribed form and manner to be the taxpayer's principal residence for the year and no other property has been designated for the purposes of this definition for the year by the taxpayer, by a person who was throughout the year the taxpayer's spouse or common-law partner (other than a spouse or common-law partner who was throughout the year living apart from, and was separated under a judicial separation or written separation agreement from, the taxpayer), by a person who was the taxpayer's child (other than a child who was during the year a married person or a person who is in a common-law partnership or 18 years or over) or, where the taxpayer was not during the year a married person or a person who is in a common-law partnership or a person 18 years or over, by a person who was the taxpayer's

(i) mother or father, or

(ii) brother or sister, where that brother or sister was not during the year a married person or a person who is in a common-law partnership or a person 18 years or over,

### Proposed Amendment — 54 "principal residence"(c)

(c) where the taxpayer is an individual other than a personal trust, unless the particular property was designated by the taxpayer in prescribed form and manner to be the taxpayer's principal residence for the year and no other property has been designated for the purposes of this definition for the year

(i) where the year is before 1982, by the taxpayer, or

(ii) where the year is after 1981,

(A) by the taxpayer,

(B) by a person who was throughout the year the taxpayer's spouse or common-law partner (other than a spouse or common-law partner who was throughout the year living apart from, and was separated under a judicial separation or written separation agreement from, the taxpayer),

(C) by a person who was the taxpayer's child (other than a child who was at any time in the year a married person, a person who is in a common-law partnership or 18 years of age or older), or

(D) where the taxpayer was not at any time in the year a married person or 18 years of age or older, by a person who was the taxpayer's

(I) mother or father, or

(II) brother or sister, where that brother or sister was not at any time in the year a married person, a person who is in a common-law partnership or 18 years of age or older,

**Application**: Bill C-43 (First Reading September 20, 2000), subsec. 22(2), will amend para. (c) of the definition "principal residence" in s. 54 to read as above, applicable to dispositions that occur after 1990 except that cls. (c)(ii)(B) to (D) of the definition shall be read without reference to "or common-law partner" and "a person who is in a common-law partnership" in their application to dispositions made by a taxpayer that occur in a taxation year that is before 2001 and

(a) before 1998; or

(b) after 1997, unless a valid election is made by the taxpayer under section 144 of the *Modernization of Benefits and Obligations Act*, c. 12 of S.C. 2000 [see Notes to 248(1)"common-law partner"], that that Act apply to the taxpayer in respect of one or more taxation years that include the year.

**Technical Notes**: Section 54 defines a number of expressions for the purpose of subdivision c of Division B of Part I, which deals with taxable capital gains and allowable capital losses. The definition "principal residence" in section 54 provides criteria for the classification of a dwelling as the principal residence of a taxpayer for the purposes of the exemption of such property from capital gains taxation.

Under existing rules, a family unit may treat only one housing unit as its principal residence for a taxation year. For

---

[1] *Sic.* Should read "made an election" — ed.

years before 1982, it was possible in the case of a married couple for each spouse to designate a principle residence for the purpose of capital gains exemption. However, as a result of an intervening amendment applicable to dispositions occurring after 1990, a strict interpretation of the definition would deny a taxpayer the benefit of the pre-1982 rules. This result is clearly unintended and the amendment reconfirms the benefit of the pre-1982 rules.

This amendment also reflects changes [re common-law partners — ed.] proposed under Bill C-23, the *Modernization of Benefits and Obligations Act*.

(c.1) where the taxpayer is a personal trust, unless

(i) the particular property was designated by the trust in prescribed form and manner to be the taxpayer's principal residence for the year,

(ii) the trust specifies in the designation each individual (in this definition referred to as a "specified beneficiary" of the trust for the year) who, in the calendar year ending in the year,

(A) is beneficially interested in the trust, and

(B) except where the trust is entitled to designate it for the year solely because of paragraph (b), ordinarily inhabited the housing unit or has a spouse or common-law partner, former spouse or common-law partner or child who ordinarily inhabited the housing unit,

(iii) no corporation (other than a registered charity) or partnership is beneficially interested in the trust at any time in the year, and

(iv) no other property has been designated for the purpose of this definition for the calendar year ending in the year by any specified beneficiary of the trust for the year, by a person who was throughout that calendar year such a beneficiary's spouse or common-law partner (other than a spouse or common-law partner who was throughout that calendar year living apart from, and was separated pursuant to a judicial separation or written separation agreement from, the beneficiary), by a person who was a beneficiary's child (other than a child who was during that calendar year a married person or a person who is in a common-law partnership or a person 18 years or over) or, where such a beneficiary was not during that calendar year a married person or a person who is in a common-law partnership or a person 18 years or over, by a person who was such a beneficiary's

(A) mother or father, or

(B) brother or sister, where that brother or sister was not during that calendar year a married person or a person who is in a common-law partnership or a person 18 years or over, or

(d) because of paragraph (b), if solely because of that paragraph the property would, but for this paragraph, have been a principal residence of the taxpayer for 4 or more preceding taxation years,

and, for the purpose of this definition,

(e) the principal residence of a taxpayer for a taxation year shall be deemed to include, except where the particular property consists of a share of the capital stock of a co-operative housing corporation, the land subjacent to the housing unit and such portion of any immediately contiguous land as can reasonably be regarded as contributing to the use and enjoyment of the housing unit as a residence, except that where the total area of the subjacent land and of that portion exceeds $1/2$ hectare, the excess shall be deemed not to have contributed to the use and enjoyment of the housing unit as a residence unless the taxpayer establishes that it was necessary to such use and enjoyment, and

(f) a particular property designated under paragraph (c.1) by a trust for a year shall be deemed to be property designated for the purposes of this definition by each specified beneficiary of the trust for the calendar year ending in the year;

**Related Provisions**: 40(2)(b), 40(4)–(6) — Principal residence rules; 40(7) — Property in satisfaction of interest in trust; 45(3), (4) — Election where change in use; 54.1 — Exception to principal residence rules; 107(2.01) — Principal residence distribution by spousal trust; 248(25) — Beneficially interested; 252(2) — Mother, father, etc..

**Notes**: "Ordinarily inhabited" in para. (a) does not mean that the taxpayer must spend most of his or her time in the residence. A cottage or other vacation property may be designated under 40(2)(b) as one's principal residence if one wishes (see IT-120R5, para. 5). However, due to para. (c), each family unit can have only one principal residence effective 1982. Where two spouses owned different principal residences for years before 1982, a partial exemption for both is still available under 40(6).

Paras. (a) and (c) amended by 2000 same-sex partners bill to add reference to "common-law partner" and "common-law partnership", effective for the 2001 and later taxation years, or earlier by election (see Notes to 248(1)"common-law partner").

"Principal residence" amended by 1992 technical bill, effective for dispositions after 1990.

54"principal residence" was 54(g) before consolidation in R.S.C. 1985 (5th Supp.), effective for taxation years ending after November 1991. See Table of Concordance.

54(g)(iii) (now"principal residence"(c)) amended by 1981 Budget, effective for designations made in respect of 1982 and later years. For designations in respect of years before 1982, read:

"(iii) unless it has been designated by him in prescribed manner to be his principal residence for that year and no other property has been so designated by him for that year, or"

**Regulations**: 2301 (prescribed manner of designation).

**I.T. Application Rules**: 26.1(1) (change of use of property before 1972).

**Interpretation Bulletins**: IT-120R5: Principal residence; IT-218R: Profit, capital gains and losses from the sale of real estate, including farmland and inherited land and conversion of real estate from capital property to inventory and vice versa; IT-268R3: *Inter vivos* transfer of farm property to child; IT-366R: Principal resi-

## Subdivision c — Taxable Capital Gains

dence: transfer to spouse or spouse trust; IT-437R: Ownership of property (principal residence).

**I.T. Technical News**: No. 7 (principal residence and the capital gains election).

**Forms**: T1079: Designation of a property as a principal residence by a personal trust; T1079-WS: Principal residence worksheet; T2091: Designation of a property as a principal residence by an individual; T2091(IND) WS: Principal residence worksheet.

**"proceeds of disposition"** of property includes,

(a) the sale price of property that has been sold,

(b) compensation for property unlawfully taken,

(c) compensation for property destroyed, and any amount payable under a policy of insurance in respect of loss or destruction of property,

(d) compensation for property taken under statutory authority or the sale price of property sold to a person by whom notice of an intention to take it under statutory authority was given,

(e) compensation for property injuriously affected, whether lawfully or unlawfully or under statutory authority or otherwise,

(f) compensation for property damaged and any amount payable under a policy of insurance in respect of damage to property, except to the extent that such compensation or amount, as the case may be, has within a reasonable time after the damage been expended on repairing the damage,

(g) an amount by which the liability of a taxpayer to a mortgagee is reduced as a result of the sale of mortgaged property under a provision of the mortgage, plus any amount received by the taxpayer out of the proceeds of the sale,

(h) any amount included in computing a taxpayer's proceeds of disposition of the property because of section 79, and

(i) in the case of a share, an amount deemed by subparagraph 88(2)(b)(ii) not to be a dividend on that share,

but notwithstanding any other provision of this Part, does not include

(j) any amount that would otherwise be proceeds of disposition of a share to the extent that the amount is deemed by subsection 84(2) or (3) to be a dividend received and is not deemed by paragraph 55(2)(a) or subparagraph 88(2)(b)(ii) not to be a dividend, or

(k) any amount that would otherwise be proceeds of disposition of property of a taxpayer to the extent that the amount is deemed by subsection 84.1(1), 212.1(1) or 212.2(2) to be a dividend paid to the taxpayer;

**Related Provisions**: 13(21)"proceeds of disposition" — Parallel definition for depreciable property; 13(21.1) — Disposition of a building; 43.1 — Life estates in real property; 44(6) — Deemed proceeds of disposition on replacement of land and building; 48.1(1) — Optional gain when small business corporation becomes public; 49.1 — Satisfaction of obligation is not a disposition of property; 50(1) — Debts established to be bad debts and shares of bankrupt corporation; 51.1 — Deemed proceeds on conversion of convertible bond; 55(2) — Deemed proceeds or capital gain; 59(5), 66.4(5) — Definition applies to 59 and 66.4; 69(1)(b) — Inadequate considerations — taxpayer deemed to have received proceeds of disposition; 69(4) — Shareholder appropriation — deemed proceeds of disposition to corporation; 69(11) — Deemed proceeds of disposition; 70(5) — Deemed disposition on death; 79(3) — Deemed proceeds to debtor on surrender of property to creditor; 79.1(5) — Deemed proceeds where property sold and repossessed in same taxation year; 85(1)(a) — Transfer of property to corporation by shareholders; 85.1(1)(a)(i) — Share for share exchange; 86(1)(c) — Exchange of shares by a shareholder in course of reorganization of capital; 87(4)(a), (c) — Shares of predecessor corporation; 88(1)(a), (b) — Winding-up; 128.1(4)(b) — Deemed disposition of property on ceasing to be resident in Canada; 128.1(8) — Retroactive adjustment to proceeds for deemed disposition on emigration where taxpayer returns to Canada; 132.2(1)(c), (f), (i), (j) — Deemed proceeds of disposition on mutual fund reorganization; 248(1) — Definition of "disposition".

**Notes**: 54"proceeds of disposition"(k) amended by 1999 Budget, effective for taxation years that end after December 15, 1998, to add reference to 212.2(2).

Reference to 79(c) in para. (h) changed to "section 79" by 1994 tax amendments bill (Part I), effective for taxation years that end after February 21, 1994.

54"proceeds of disposition" was 54(h) before consolidation in R.S.C. 1985 (5th Supp.), effective for taxation years ending after November 1991. See Table of Concordance.

**Interpretation Bulletins**: IT-125R4: Dispositions of resource properties; IT-149R4: Winding-up dividend; IT-170R: Sale of property — when included in income computation; IT-185R: Losses from theft, defalcation or embezzlement; IT-200: Surface rentals and farming operations; IT-220R2: Capital cost allowance — proceeds of disposition of depreciable property; IT-259R3: Exchanges of property; IT-271R: Expropriations; IT-444R: Corporations — involuntary dissolutions; IT-460: Dispositions — absence of consideration; IT-505: Mortgage foreclosures and conditional sales repossessions.

**Advance Tax Rulings**: ATR-28: Redemption of capital stock of family farm corporation; ATR-35: Partitioning of assets to get specific ownership — "butterfly".

**"specified property"** of a taxpayer is capital property of the taxpayer that is

(a) a share,

(b) a capital interest in a trust,

(c) an interest in a partnership, or

(d) an option to acquire specified property of the taxpayer;

**Notes**: 54"specified property" added by 1994 tax amendments bill (Part I), effective for taxation years that end after February 21, 1994. The term is used in 49(3.01) and 53(4)–(6).

**"superficial loss"** of a taxpayer means the taxpayer's loss from the disposition of a particular property where

(a) during the period that begins 30 days before and ends 30 days after the disposition, the taxpayer or a person affiliated with the taxpayer acquires a property (in this definition referred to as the "substituted property") that is, or is identical to, the particular property, and

(b) at the end of that period, the taxpayer or a person affiliated with the taxpayer owns or had a right to acquire the substituted property, except where the disposition was

(c) a disposition deemed by paragraph 33.1(11)(a), subsection 45(1), section 48 as it read in its application before 1993, section 50 or 70, subsection 104(4), section 128.1, paragraph 132.2(1)(f), subsection 138(11.3) or 142.5(2), paragraph 142.6(1)(b) or subsection 144(4.1) or (4.2) or 149(10) to have been made,

(d) the expiry of an option,

(e) a disposition to which paragraph 40(2)(e.1) applies,

(f) a disposition by a corporation the control of which was acquired by a person or group of persons within 30 days after the disposition,

(g) a disposition by a person that, within 30 days after the disposition, became or ceased to be exempt from tax under this Part on its taxable income, or

(h) a disposition to which subsection 40(3.4) or 69(5) applies,

and, for the purpose of this definition, a right to acquire a property (other than a right, as security only, derived from a mortgage, agreement for sale or similar obligation) is deemed to be a property that is identical to the property.

**Related Provisions**: 13(21.2) — Superficial loss rule for depreciable property; 18(13)–(16) — Superficial loss in moneylending business or adventure in nature of trade; 40(2)(g)(i) — Superficial loss deemed to be nil; 40(3.3), (3.4) — Limitation on loss where property acquired by affiliated person; 53(1)(f) — Addition to ACB of substituted property; 139.1(18) — Holding corporation deemed not to acquire control of insurer on demutualization; 248(12) — Identical properties; 251.1 — Affiliated persons; 256(5.1) — Controlled directly or indirectly — control in fact; 256(6)–(9) — Whether control acquired.

**Notes**: Under 40(2)(g)(i), a superficial loss is disallowed. There is no parallel rule preventing the recognition of a capital gain when the property disposed of is immediately reacquired. See Notes to 13(21.2) for more on the rules for superficial losses and transfers of pregnant losses.

Definition amended and extended by 1995-97 technical bill, effective (subject to the grandfathering rule reproduced after s. 260) for dispositions of property after April 26, 1995. Previously read:

"superficial loss" of a taxpayer means the taxpayer's loss from the disposition of a property in any case where

(a) the same or identical property (in this definition referred to as "substituted property") was acquired, during the period beginning 30 days before the disposition and ending 30 days after the disposition, by the taxpayer, the taxpayer's spouse or a corporation controlled, directly or indirectly in any manner whatever, by the taxpayer, and

(b) at the end of the period referred to in paragraph (a) the taxpayer, the taxpayer's spouse or the corporation, as the case may be, owned, in any manner whatever, the substituted property,

except that a loss otherwise described in this definition shall be deemed not to be a superficial loss if the disposition giving rise to the loss

(c) was a disposition deemed by paragraph 33.1(11)(a), subsection 45(1), section 48 as it read in its application before 1993, section 50 or 70, subsection 104(4), section 128.1, paragraph 132.2(1)(f), subsection 138(11.3) or 142.5(2), paragraph 142.6(1)(b) or subsection 144(4.1) or (4.2) or 149(10) to have been made,

(d) was the expiration of an option, or

(e) was a disposition of property by the taxpayer to which paragraph 40(2)(e.1) or subsection 85(4) applies.

*Pre-1995 amendments*

"Superficial loss"(a) amended by 1991 technical bill, effective for taxation years commencing after 1988, to change "controlled, whether directly" to "controlled, directly", so as to clarify that 256(5.1) applies in determining control.

Para. (c) amended by 1993 technical bill to add reference to 128.1 (and make reference to s. 48 be "as it read ... before 1993"), effective 1993. Where a corporation continued before 1993 elects for new 250(5.1) to apply earlier (see Notes to 250(5.1)), the amendment is effective from the corporation's "time of continuation".

Reference to 132.2(1)(f) added to para. (c) by 1994 tax amendments bill (Part IX), effective July 1994.

Reference to 142.5(2) and 142.6(1)(b) added to para. (c) by 1994 tax amendments bill (Part IX), effective for dispositions that occur after February 22, 1994.

Reference to 40(2)(e.1) added to para. (e) by 1994 tax amendments bill (Part I), effective for taxation years that end after February 21, 1994.

54"superficial loss" was 54(i) before consolidation in R.S.C. 1985 (5th Supp.), effective for taxation years ending after November 1991. See Table of Concordance.

**I.T. Application Rules**: 26(6) (superficial loss where disposition from June 19 to December 31, 1971).

**Interpretation Bulletins**: IT-159R3: Capital debts established to be bad debts; IT-325R2: Property transfers after separation, divorce and annulment; IT-387R2: Meaning of "identical properties".

**I.T. Technical News**: No. 7 (control by a group — 50/50 arrangement (re para. (f))).

**Definitions [s. 54]**: "acquired" — 256(7)–(9); "affiliated" — 251.1; "amount" — 248(1); "beneficially interested" — 248(25); "brother" — 252(2); "business" — 248(1); "calendar year" — *Interpretation Act* 37(1)(a); "Canada" — 255; "capital gain" — 39(1)(a), 248(1); "capital interest" — in a trust 108(1), 248(1); "capital loss" — 39(1)(b), 248(1); "capital property" — 54, 248(1); "child" — 252(1); "common-law partner", "common-law partnership" — 248(1); "control" — 256(5.1), (6.2); "corporation" — 248(1), *Interpretation Act* 35(1); "deferred profit sharing plan" — 147(1), 248(1); "depreciable property" — 13(21), 248(1); "disposition" — 54; "dividend" — 248(1); "eligible capital amount" — 14(1), 248(1); "eligible capital property" — 54, 248(1); "employees profit sharing plan" — 144(1), 248(1); "father" — 252(2); "identical" — 248(12); "individual" — 248(1); "mother" — 252(2); "partnership" — see Notes to 96(1); "person", "personal trust" — 248(1); "personal-use property" — 54, 248(1); "prescribed", "property" — 248(1); "registered charity" — 248(1); "registered retirement income fund" — 146.3(1), 248(1); "registered retirement savings plan" — 146(1), 248(1); "resident in Canada" — 250; "separation agreement" — 248(1); "share" — 248(1); "sister" — 252(2); "specified beneficiary" — 54"principal residence"(c.1)(ii); "substituted property" — 54"superficial loss"(a); "taxation year" — 249; "taxpayer" — 248(1); "trust" — 104(1), 248(1), (3); "written" — *Interpretation Act* 35(1)"writing".

## 54.1 (1) Exception to principal residence rules — A taxation year in which a taxpayer does not ordinarily inhabit the taxpayer's property as a consequence of the relocation of the taxpayer's or the taxpayer's spouse's or common-law partner's place of employment while the taxpayer or the spouse, as the case may be, is employed by an em-

ployer who is not a person to whom the taxpayer or the spouse is related shall be deemed not to be a previous taxation year referred to in paragraph (d) of the definition "principal residence" in section 54 if

(a) the property subsequently becomes ordinarily inhabited by the taxpayer during the term of the taxpayer's or the taxpayer's spouse's or common-law partner's employment by that employer or before the end of the taxation year immediately following the taxation year in which the taxpayer's or the spouse's or common-law partner's employment by that employer terminates; or

(b) the taxpayer dies during the term of the taxpayer's or the spouse's or common-law partner's employment by that employer.

**(2) Definition of "property"** — In this section, "property", in relation to a taxpayer, means a housing unit

(a) owned by the taxpayer,

(b) in respect of which the taxpayer has a leasehold interest, or

(c) in respect of which the taxpayer owned a share of the capital stock of a co-operative housing corporation if the share was acquired for the sole purpose of acquiring the right to inhabit a housing unit owned by the corporation

whether jointly with another person or otherwise in the year and that at all times was at least 40 kilometres farther from the taxpayer's or the taxpayer's spouse's or common-law partner's new place of employment than was the taxpayer's subsequent place or places of residence.

**Related Provisions**: 40(2)(b), 40(4)–(6) — Principal residence rules.

**Notes**: 54.1 amended by 2000 same-sex partners bill to add reference to "common-law partner's", effective for the 2001 and later taxation years, or earlier by election (see Notes to 248(1)"common-law partner").

**Definitions [s. 54.1]**: "common-law partner" — 248(1); "corporation" — 248(1), Interpretation Act 35(1); "employed", "employer", "employment", "person" — 248(1); "property" — 54.1(2); "share" — 248(1); "taxation year" — 249; "taxpayer" — 248(1).

**Interpretation Bulletins [s. 54.1]**: IT-120R5: Principal residence.

**54.2 Certain shares deemed to be capital property** — Where any person has disposed of property that consisted of all or substantially all of the assets used in an active business carried on by that person to a corporation for consideration that included shares of the corporation, the shares shall be deemed to be capital property of the person.

**Related Provisions**: 39(4) — Election re disposition of Canadian securities; 85(1) — Rollovers of property to corporation; 110.6(14)(f)(ii) — Shares qualify for capital gains exemption without waiting for 2-year holding period; 248(1) — "Business" does not include adventure or concern in the nature of trade.

**Notes**: 54.2 introduced by 1988 tax reform. It ensures that when a proprietor's business assets are rolled into a corporation under 85(1) and the corporation's shares are sold, the gain will be a capital gain even though the shares have been held for only a short time, and can qualify for the $500,000 capital gains exemption for small business shares under 110.6(2.1).

The CCRA takes the position that "all or substantially all" means 90% or more.

Note that 110.6(14)(f)(ii)(A) provides an exception from the 2-year share holding requirement for the capital gains exemption, for the situation covered by 54.2.

**Definitions [s. 54.2]**: "active business", "business" — 248(1); "capital property" — 54, 248(1); "corporation" — 248(1), Interpretation Act 35(1); "disposition" — 54 [to be repealed], 248(1) [draft]; "person", "property", "share" — 248(1).

**Information Circulars**: 88-2 Supplement, para. 7: General anti-avoidance rule — section 245 of the Income Tax Act.

**55. (1) Definitions** — In this section,

**"distribution"** means a direct or indirect transfer of property of a corporation (referred to in this section as the "distributing corporation") to one or more corporations (each of which is referred to in this section as a "transferee corporation") where, in respect of each type of property owned by the distributing corporation immediately before the transfer, each transferee corporation receives property of that type the fair market value of which is equal to or approximates the amount determined by the formula

$$A \times \frac{B}{C}$$

where

A is the fair market value, immediately before the transfer, of all property of that type owned at that time by the distributing corporation,

B is the fair market value, immediately before the transfer, of all the shares of the capital stock of the distributing corporation owned at that time by the transferee corporation, and

C is the fair market value, immediately before the transfer, of all the issued shares of the capital stock of the distributing corporation;

**Related Provisions**: 55(3.02) — Where distributing corporation is a specified corporation; 88(1)(c)(iv) — Winding-up.

**Notes**: In simple terms, a distribution is a divisive reorganization whereby each corporate shareholder of the corporation that receives property on the distribution receives its *pro rata* share of each type of property owned by the distributing corporation immediately before the distribution.

Definition "distribution" added by 1994 Budget, effective for dividends received after February 21, 1994, other than dividends received before 1995 in the course of a reorganization that was required on February 22, 1994 to be carried out pursuant to a written agreement entered into before February 22, 1994.

**"permitted acquisition"**, in relation to a distribution by a distributing corporation, means an acquisition of property by a person or partnership on, or as part of,

(a) a distribution, or

(b) a permitted exchange or permitted redemption in relation to a distribution by another distributing corporation;

**Notes**: Definition "permitted acquisition" added by 1994 Budget, effective on the same basis as 55(1)"distribution" (see Notes thereto).

**"permitted exchange"**, in relation to a distribution by a distributing corporation, means

(a) an exchange of shares for shares of the capital stock of the distributing corporation to which subsection 51(1) or 86(1) applies or would, if the shares were capital property to the holder thereof, apply, other than an exchange that resulted in an acquisition of control of the distributing corporation by any person or group of persons, and

(b) an exchange of shares of the capital stock of the distributing corporation by one or more shareholders of the distributing corporation (each of whom is referred to in this paragraph as a "participant") for shares of the capital stock of another corporation (referred to in this paragraph as the "acquiror") in contemplation of the distribution where

(i) no share of the capital stock of the acquiror outstanding immediately after the exchange (other than directors' qualifying shares) is owned at that time by any person or partnership other than a participant,

and either

(ii) the acquiror owns, immediately before the distribution, all the shares each of which is a share of the capital stock of the distributing corporation that was owned immediately before the exchange by a participant, or

(iii) the fair market value, immediately before the distribution, of each participant's shares of the capital stock of the acquiror is equal to or approximates the amount determined by the formula

$$\left(A \times \frac{B}{C}\right) + D$$

where

A is the fair market value, immediately before the distribution, of all the shares of the capital stock of the acquiror then outstanding (other than shares issued to participants in consideration for shares of a specified class all the shares of which were acquired by the acquiror on the exchange),

B is the fair market value, immediately before the exchange, of all the shares of the capital stock of the distributing corporation (other than shares of a specified class none or all of the shares of which were acquired by the acquiror on the exchange) owned at that time by the participant,

C is the fair market value, immediately before the exchange, of all the shares (other than shares of a specified class none or all of the shares of which were acquired by the acquiror on the exchange and shares to be redeemed, acquired or cancelled by the distributing corporation pursuant to the exercise of a statutory right of dissent by the holder of the share) of the capital stock of the distributing corporation outstanding immediately before the exchange, and

D is the fair market value, immediately before the distribution, of all the shares issued to the participant by the acquiror in consideration for shares of a specified class all of the shares of which were acquired by the acquiror on the exchange;

**Related Provisions**: 139.1(18) — Holding corporation deemed not to acquire control of insurer on demutualization; 256(6)–(9) — Whether control acquired.

**Notes**: Definition "permitted exchange" added by 1994 Budget, effective on the same basis as 55(1)"distribution" (see Notes thereto).

The definition covers two types of share-for-share exchanges. The first is an exchange of shares to which 51(1) or 86(1) applies (or would apply if the shares were held as capital property), except where the exchange results in an acquisition of control of the distributing corporation. The second is an exchange of shares of the capital stock of the distributing corporation for shares of the capital stock of another corporation (the acquiror) made in contemplation of the tax-deferred distribution of property by the distributing corporation to one or more of its corporate shareholders. In order for the second type to qualify as a permitted exchange, each participating shareholder must receive their pro rata share of shares of the capital stock of the acquiror on the exchange and, immediately after the exchange, all of the issued shares of the capital stock of the acquiror must be owned by those who participated in the exchange. In addition, where not all of the shares of the capital stock of the distributing corporation owned by a participant immediately before the exchange are transferred to the acquiror on the exchange, all of the shareholders of the distributing corporation (other than shareholders holding only shares of a "specified class", defined below) must participate in the exchange on a pro rata basis. Where a participant holds shares of a specified class before the exchange and none or all of the shares of that class are transferred on the exchange, the shares of that class will be ignored in determining whether the participants have participated in the exchange on a pro rata basis.

The requirements of the definition generally limit the use of the butterfly exemption to two basic types of butterfly reorganization:

- the spin-off, in which some of each type of property owned by the distributing corporation is transferred to a new corporation having the same shareholders as the distributing corporation; and

- the split-up, in which one or more of the existing shareholders of the distributing corporation cease to be shareholders of the distributing corporation and, in so doing, receive their pro rata share of each type of property owned by the distributing corporation.

The requirements of the definition must be satisfied whenever a person acquires a share of the capital stock of the distributing corporation in contemplation of the distribution from another person to whom the acquiror is not related. For this purpose, the acquiror will be considered not to be related to the other person unless

- the acquiror acquires all of the shares of the distributing corporation that are owned by the other person,

- the acquiror is related, after the reorganization that includes the distribution, to the distributing corporation (see 55(3.2)(c)), or

- the acquiror acquired the share on a capital distribution by a personal trust (see 55(3.2)(d)).

Subdivision c — Taxable Capital Gains    S. 55(1) spe

**"permitted redemption"**, in relation to a distribution by a distributing corporation, means

(a) a redemption or purchase for cancellation by the distributing corporation, as part of the reorganization in which the distribution was made, of all the shares of its capital stock that were owned, immediately before the distribution, by a transferee corporation in relation to the distributing corporation,

(b) a redemption or purchase for cancellation by a transferee corporation in relation to the distributing corporation, or by a corporation that, immediately after the redemption or purchase, was a subsidiary wholly-owned corporation of the transferee corporation, as part of the reorganization in which the distribution was made, of all of the shares of the capital stock of the transferee corporation or the subsidiary wholly-owned corporation that were acquired by the distributing corporation in consideration for the transfer of property received by the transferee corporation on the distribution, and

(c) a redemption or purchase for cancellation by the distributing corporation, in contemplation of the distribution, of all the shares of its capital stock each of which is

(i) a share of a specified class the cost of which, at the time of its issuance, to its original owner was equal to the fair market value at that time of the consideration for which it was issued, or

(ii) a share that was issued, in contemplation of the distribution, by the distributing corporation in exchange for a share described in subparagraph (i);

Notes: Definition "permitted redemption" added by 1994 Budget, effective on the same basis as 55(1)"distribution" (see Notes thereto).

Paras. (a) and (b) amended by 1995-97 technical bill, effective for dividends received after February 21, 1994. (This appears to override the grandfathering originally provided when the definition was enacted.) The former version, now deemed never to have been in force, read:

(a) a redemption or purchase for cancellation by the distributing corporation, as part of the reorganization in which the distribution was made, of all the shares of its capital stock owned by a transferee corporation in relation to the distributing corporation,

(b) a redemption or purchase for cancellation by a transferee corporation in relation to the distributing corporation, as part of the reorganization in which the distribution was made, of all of the shares of its capital stock owned by the distributing corporation, and

**"safe-income determination time"** for a transaction or event or a series of transactions or events means the time that is the earlier of

(a) the time that is immediately after the earliest disposition or increase in interest described in any of subparagraphs (3)(a)(i) to (v) that resulted from the transaction, event or series, and

(b) the time that is immediately before the earliest time that a dividend is paid as part of the transaction, event or series;

Notes: Definition "safe-income determination time" added by 1995-97 technical bill, effective for dividends received after June 20, 1996.

**"specified class"** means a class of shares of the capital stock of a distributing corporation where

(a) the paid-up capital in respect of the class immediately before the beginning of the series of transactions or events that includes a distribution by the distributing corporation was not less than the fair market value of the consideration for which the shares of that class then outstanding were issued,

(b) under neither the terms and conditions of the shares nor any agreement in respect of the shares are the shares convertible into or exchangeable for shares other than shares of a specified class or shares of the capital stock of a transferee corporation in relation to the distributing corporation, and

(c) under neither the terms and conditions of the shares nor any agreement in respect of the shares is any holder of the shares entitled to receive on the redemption, cancellation or acquisition of the shares by the corporation or by any person with whom the corporation does not deal at arm's length (excluding any premium for early redemption) an amount greater than the total of the fair market value of the consideration for which the shares were issued and the amount of any unpaid dividends thereon.

Notes: Definition "specified class" added by 1994 Budget, effective on the same basis as 55(1)"distribution" (see Notes thereto).

### Proposed Addition — 55(1)"specified corporation"

**"specified corporation"** in relation to a distribution means a distributing corporation

(a) that is a public corporation or a specified wholly-owned corporation of a public corporation,

(b) shares of the capital stock of which are exchanged for shares of the capital stock of another corporation (referred to in this definition and subsection (3.02) as an "acquiror") in an exchange to which the definition "permitted exchange" in this subsection would apply if that definition were read without reference to paragraph (a) and subparagraph (b)(ii) of that definition,

(c) that does not make a distribution, to a corporation that is not an acquiror, after 1998 and before the day that is three years after the day on which the shares of the capital stock of the distributing corporation are exchanged in a transaction described in paragraph (b), and

(d) no acquiror in relation to which makes a distribution after 1998 and before the day that is three years after the day on which the shares of the capital stock of the distributing corporation are exchanged in a transaction described in paragraph (b),

and, for the purposes of paragraphs (c) and (d),

(e) a corporation that is formed by an amalgamation of two or more other corporations is deemed to be the same corporation as, and a continuation of, each of the other corporations, and

(f) where there has been a winding-up of a corporation to which subsection 88(1) applies, the parent is deemed to be the same corporation as, and a continuation of, the subsidiary;

**Application**: Bill C-43 (First Reading September 20, 2000), subsec. 23(1), will add the definition "specified corporation" to subsec. 55(1), applicable to transfers that occur after 1998.

**Technical Notes**: Subsection 55(2) is an anti-avoidance provision directed against certain arrangements designed to use the inter-corporate dividend exemption to unduly reduce a capital gain on the sale of shares. It treats the dividend in these situations either as proceeds from the sale of the shares or as a capital gain, and not as a dividend received by the corporation.

Subsection 55(3) sets out circumstances in which subsection 55(2) does not apply to dividends.

Paragraph 55(3)(b) provides an exemption from the application of subsection 55(2) for dividends received in the course of a reorganization (commonly referred to as divisive or butterfly reorganizations) in which a distribution is made by a distributing corporation to one or more transferee corporations. Because of the meaning of "distribution" in subsection 55(1), each transferee corporation must receive its pro rata share of each type of property owned by the distributing corporation immediately before the distribution.

As a result of the new definitions "specified corporation" and "specified wholly-owned corporation" in subsection 55(1) and new subsection 55(3.02), the requirement that each transferee corporation must receive its pro rata share of each type of property owned by the distributing corporation on a butterfly reorganization will no longer apply in the case of certain public corporation butterflies. In particular, the type of property requirement will no longer apply for butterfly reorganizations of specified corporations that occur after 1998.

In order for a distributing corporation to qualify as a "specified corporation":

1) it must be a public corporation or specified wholly-owned corporation of a public corporation (specified wholly-owned corporation is a new expression and it is defined in subsection 55(1));

2) shares of the distributing corporation must be exchanged for shares of another corporation (an "acquiror") in an exchange to which the definition "permitted exchange" in subsection 55(1) would apply if the definition "permitted exchange" were read without reference to paragraph (a) and subparagraph (b)(ii) thereof;

3) the distributing corporation must not make a distribution to a corporation other than an acquiror after 1998 and before the day that is three years after the day on which the distributing corporation shares were exchanged in a transaction referred to in 2) above; and

4) no acquiror in relation to the distributing corporation may make a distribution after 1998 and before the day that is three years after the day on which the distributing corporation shares were exchanged in a transaction referred to in 2) above.

Reading the definition of "permitted exchange" without reference to paragraph (a) and subparagraph (b)(ii) ensures that the exchange of shares of the capital stock of the distributing corporation for shares of the acquiror is effected in the course of what is commonly referred to a "spin-off" reorganization. In a spin-off reorganisation, property owned by the distributing corporation is transferred to a new corporation having the same shareholders as the distributing corporation.

The new definition of specified corporation also sets out the consequences of an amalgamation of corporations or a winding-up of a subsidiary corporation to which subsection 88(1) applies. Paragraph (e) of the definition provides that a corporation formed on an amalgamation is treated as a continuation of each of its predecessors. Paragraph (f) of the definition provides that, in the case of a winding-up of a subsidiary corporation into its parent to which subsection 88(1) applies, the parent corporation is treated as a continuation of the subsidiary.

### Proposed Addition — 55(1)"specified wholly-owned corporation"

"specified wholly-owned corporation" of a public corporation means a corporation all of the outstanding shares of the capital stock of which (other than directors' qualifying shares and shares of a specified class) are held by

(a) the public corporation,

(b) a specified wholly-owned corporation of the public corporation, or

(c) any combination of corporations described in paragraph (a) or (b).

**Application**: Bill C-43 (First Reading September 20, 2000), subsec. 23(1), will add the definition "specified wholly-owned corporation" to subsec. 55(1), applicable to transfers that occur after 1998.

**Technical Notes**: The new definition of specified wholly-owned corporation of a public corporation is relevant for the purpose of the new definition "specified corporation". A specified wholly-owned corporation of a public corporation means a corporation all of the outstanding shares of the capital stock of which (other than directors' qualifying shares and shares of a specified class) are held by a public corporation, a specified wholly-owned corporation or any combination of the two. The meaning of a specified class is set out in subsection 55(1).

**Notes [subsec. 55(1)]**: Former 55(1), an anti-avoidance rule dealing with artificial reduction of a gain, repealed by 1988 tax reform, effective for transactions entered into after September 12, 1988, except for limited grandfathering on the same basis as the introduction of new 245(2) (see Notes thereto).

**(2) Deemed proceeds or capital gain** — Where a corporation resident in Canada has received a taxable dividend in respect of which it is entitled to a deduction under subsection 112(1) or (2) or 138(6) as part of a transaction or event or a series of transactions or events, one of the purposes of which (or, in the case of a dividend under subsection 84(3), one of the results of which) was to effect a significant reduction in the portion of the capital gain that, but for the dividend, would have been realized on a disposition at fair market value of any share of capital stock immediately before the dividend and that could reasonably be considered to be attributable to anything other than income earned or realized by any corporation after 1971 and before the safe-income determination time for the transaction, event or series, notwithstanding any other section of this Act, the amount of the dividend (other than the portion of it, if any, subject to tax under Part IV that is not refunded as a consequence of the payment of a dividend to a corporation where the payment is part of the series)

(a) shall be deemed not to be a dividend received by the corporation;

(b) where a corporation has disposed of the share, shall be deemed to be proceeds of disposition of the share except to the extent that it is otherwise included in computing such proceeds; and

(c) where a corporation has not disposed of the share, shall be deemed to be a gain of the corporation for the year in which the dividend was received from the disposition of a capital property.

**Related Provisions**: 54"proceeds of disposition"(j) — Effect of 55(2) on proceeds of disposition; 55(3) — Exception; 55(4) — Arm's length dealings; 55(5) — Applicable rules; 110.6(7)(a) — Capital gains exemption disallowed on butterfly; 112(3) — Stop-loss rule denying capital loss after dividends received on share; 248(10) — Series of transactions; 256(7) — Where control deemed not to be acquired; 256(8) — Where rights acquired rather than shares in order to avoid 55(2).

**Notes**: 55(2) is an anti-avoidance rule aimed at "capital gains stripping", whereby a capital gain would be turned into an intercorporate dividend that would be tax-free because of 112(1) or (2). Where 55(2) applies, it triggers a capital gain. See also the various stop-loss rules in s. 112, which can prevent the intercorporate dividend from being deductible in the first place.

The words "any corporation" in 55(2) include a foreign non-affiliate: *Lamont Management Ltd.*, [2000] 3 C.T.C. 18 (FCA).

For a detailed discussion of 55(2), see Mark Brender, "Subsection 55(2): Part 1", Taxation of Corporation Reorganizations column, 45(2) *Canadian Tax Journal* 343–373 (1997); and "... Part 2", 45(4) 806–843 (1997). See also Notes to 55(3.1).

Opening words of 55(2) amended by 1995-97 technical bill, effective for dividends received after June 20, 1996. For earlier dividends, since 1985, read:

(2) Where a corporation resident in Canada has after April 21, 1980 received a taxable dividend in respect of which it is entitled to a deduction under subsection 112(1) or 138(6) as part of a transaction or event or a series of transactions or events (other than as part of a series of transactions or events that commenced before April 22, 1980), one of the purposes of which (or, in the case of a dividend under subsection 84(3), one of the results of which) was to effect a significant reduction in the portion of the capital gain that, but for the dividend, would have been realized on a disposition at fair market

value of any share of capital stock immediately before the dividend and that could reasonably be considered to be attributable to anything other than income earned or realized by any corporation after 1971 and before the transaction or event or the commencement of the series of transactions or events referred to in paragraph (3)(a), notwithstanding any other section of this Act, the amount of the dividend (other than the portion thereof, if any, subject to tax under Part IV that is not refunded as a consequence of the payment of a dividend to a corporation where the payment is part of the series of transactions or events)

**Information Circulars**: 88-2, paras. 7, 13: General anti-avoidance rule — section 245 of the *Income Tax Act*.

**I.T. Technical News**: No. 3 (loss utilization within a corporate group; butterfly reorganizations); No. 7 (subsection 55(2) — recent cases).

**Advance Tax Rulings**: ATR-22R: Estate freeze using share exchange; ATR-27: Exchange and acquisition of interests in capital properties through rollovers and winding-up ("butterfly"); ATR-35: Partitioning of assets to get specific ownership — "butterfly"; ATR-47: Transfer of assets to Realtyco; ATR-56: Purification of a family farm corporation; ATR-57: Transfer of property for estate planning purposes; ATR-58: Divisive reorganization.

**(3) Application** — Subsection (2) does not apply to any dividend received by a corporation (in this subsection and subsection (3.01) referred to as the "dividend recipient")

(a) if, as part of a transaction or event or a series of transactions or events as a part of which the dividend was received, there was not at any particular time

(i) a disposition of property, other than

(A) money disposed of on the payment of a dividend or on a reduction of the paid-up capital of a share, and

(B) property disposed of for proceeds that are not less than its fair market value,

to a person or partnership that was an unrelated person immediately before the particular time,

(ii) a significant increase (other than as a consequence of a disposition of shares of the capital stock of a corporation for proceeds of disposition that are not less than their fair market value) in the total direct interest in any corporation of one or more persons or partnerships that were unrelated persons immediately before the particular time,

(iii) a disposition, to a person or partnership who was an unrelated person immediately before the particular time, of

(A) shares of the capital stock of the corporation that paid the dividend (referred to in this paragraph and subsection (3.01) as the "dividend payer"), or

(B) property more than 10% of the fair market value of which was, at any time during the course of the series, derived from shares of the capital stock of the dividend payer,

S. 55(3)(a)(iii)      Income Tax Act, Part I, Division B

### Proposed Amendment — 55(3)(a)(iii)
**Letter from Department of Finance, December 23, 1998**:

Dear [xxx],

This is in response to your letter of September 9, 1998 regarding the application of subparagraph 55(3)(a)(iii) of the *Income Tax Act* (the "Act") to the circumstances described in your letter.

We agree that, from a tax policy perspective, subsection 55(2) of the Act should not apply to Target in respect of the dividend it receives on the redemption of the SubCo shares as part of the transactions described in your letter and example 5 of the explanatory notes for subclause 96(4) of Bill C-28. The scope of subparagraph 55(3)(a)(iii) of the Act is too broad and should not capture the dividend paid on the Subco shares merely because the SubCo shares acquired by Target in exchange for the T2SubCo shares have a value greater than 10% of the value of the Target's shares.

We will recommend to the Minister of Finance that an amendment be made to subparagraph 55(3)(a)(iii) of the Act to ensure that it does not apply to the acquisition of the shares of Target by Buyerco in the circumstances described in your letter. We will recommend that an amendment be effective for dividends received by a corporation after February 21, 1994. If the recommendation is acted upon, I would anticipate that such an amendment would be included in the next technical bill.

Yours sincerely,

Brian Ernewein
Director, Tax Legislation Division, Tax Policy Branch

    (iv) after the time the dividend was received, a disposition, to a person or partnership that was an unrelated person immediately before the particular time, of

        (A) shares of the capital stock of the dividend recipient, or

        (B) property more than 10% of the fair market value of which was, at any time during the course of the series, derived from shares of the capital stock of the dividend recipient, and

    (v) a significant increase in the total of all direct interests in the dividend payer of one or more persons or partnerships who were unrelated persons immediately before the particular time; or

### Proposed Amendment — 55(3)(a)
**Letter from Department of Finance, February 19, 1999**:

Dear [xxx]

This is in reply to your letter of December 1, 1998 to Len Farber regarding an anomaly that results from the interaction of section 55 and 93 of the *Income Tax Act* (the "Act"). You ask that a technical amendment be made to the Act to remove this anomaly.

Based on our understanding of the facts set out in your letter, Parentco/Canco undertakes a series of transactions to utilize losses within its related group. As part of this series of transactions, Forco sells its shares of Forco2 to an arm's length third party for proceeds of disposition equal to the fair market value of the shares. On the disposition, section 93 of the Act applies to treat proceeds realized by Forco as a dividend with the result that, for the purposes of the Act, Forco is considered not to have received fair market value proceeds. As part of the series, Canco transfers on a tax-deferred basis under subsection 85(1) of the Act its shares of Forco to Sisterco in exchange for preferred shares of Sisterco. Sisterco redeems its preferred shares held by Canco and Canco receives a dividend (the "Sisterco Dividend"). The Sisterco Dividend is subject to subsection 55(2) of the Act only because section 93 applies to treat Forco's proceeds of disposition to be less than the fair market value of the Forco2 shares.

We agree that, in the above circumstances, the Sisterco Dividend should be exempt from the application of subsection 55(2) because of paragraph 55(3)(a) of the Act. Section 93 should not, in and by itself, cause an intercorporate dividend received by a corporation in the course of certain related-corporate transactions to be subject to subsection 55(2). Inter-corporate dividends that would, but for the application of section 93 which reduces the proceeds of disposition of a property to less than the fair market value of the property, have been exempt from the application of subsection 55(2) because of paragraph 55(3)(a) should remain exempt from the application of subsection 55(2).

We are prepared therefore to recommend to the Minister of Finance that the Act be amended to ensure the appropriate results in the circumstances described above. We will recommend that the amendment be effective for dividends received by a corporation after February 21, 1994. If the recommendation is acted upon, I would anticipate that such an amendment would be included in the next technical bill.

Yours sincerely,

Brian Ernewein
Director, Tax Legislation Division, Tax Policy Branch

  (b) if the dividend was received

    (i) in the course of a reorganization in which

        (A) a distributing corporation made a distribution to one or more transferee corporations, and

        (B) the distributing corporation was wound up or all of the shares of its capital stock owned by each transferee corporation immediately before the distribution were redeemed or cancelled otherwise than on an exchange to which subsection 51(1), 85(1) or 86(1) applies, and

    (ii) on a permitted redemption in relation to the distribution or on the winding-up of the distributing corporation.

**Related Provisions**: 13(30) — Transfers of property; 55(3.01) — Rules of interpretation for 55(3)(a). 55(3.1), (3.2) — Exception for purchase butterfly; 88(1)(d) — Winding-up; 88(1)(c)(iii), 88(1)(c.2) — Cost base of property after windup; 110.6(7)(a) — Capital gains exemption disallowed on butterfly; 248(10) — Series of transactions; Reg. 1100(2.2), 1102(14)(a) — Depreciable property acquired on reorganization.

**Notes**: The divisive reorganization allowed by 55(3)(b) is known as a "butterfly" transaction, because of the way it looks when the corporate holdings and transactions are drawn on paper. See Notes to 55(2) and (3.1).

55(3) amended by 1995-97 technical bill, effective for dividends received by a corporation after February 21, 1994, except that,

(a) in respect of such dividends received before June 20, 1996, or received under an arrangement substantially advanced, as evidenced in writing, before June 20, 1996, read 55(3)(a)(ii) and (v), if para. (b) below does not apply, as follows:

(ii) a significant increase (other than as a consequence of a disposition of shares of the capital stock of a corporation for proceeds of disposition that are not less than their fair market value) in the interest in any corporation of one or more persons or partnerships that were unrelated persons immediately before the particular time,

. . . . .

(v) a significant increase in the interest in the dividend payer of one or more persons or partnerships that were unrelated persons immediately before the particular time; or

and

(b) in respect of such dividends, where they are received on shares issued before June 20, 1996, and the corporation so elects in writing by October 31, 1998 or in its Part I return for the year in which it received the dividends, ignore 55(3.01) and read 55(3)(a) as:

(a) unless the dividend was received as part of a transaction or event or a series of transactions or events that resulted in

(i) a disposition of any property to a person with whom the dividend recipient was dealing at arm's length, or

(ii) a significant increase in the interest in any corporation of any person with whom the dividend recipient was dealing at arm's length; or

Where a corporation elects under para. (b) of the application rule above, in respect of dividends received after February 21, 1994,

(a) read 55(4) in respect of those dividends as:

(4) Where it can reasonably be considered that the principal purpose of one or more transactions or events was to cause 2 or more persons to be related or to not deal with each other at arm's length, or to cause one corporation to control another corporation, so as to make subsection (2) inapplicable, for the purposes of this section, those persons are deemed not to be related or are deemed to deal with each other at arm's length, or the corporation is deemed not to control the other corporation, as the case may be.

and

(b) read 55(5)(e) in respect of those dividends as:

(e) in determining whether 2 or more persons deal with each other at arm's length,

(i) a person is deemed to deal with another person at arm's length and not to be related to the other person if the person is the brother or sister of the other person, and

(ii) persons who are otherwise related to each other solely because of a right referred to in paragraph 251(5)(b) are deemed not to be related to each other; and

Before the 1995-97 technical bill amendment, 55(3) read:

(3) **Exception** — Subsection (2) does not apply to any dividend received by a corporation,

(a) unless the dividend was received as part of a transaction or event or a series of transactions or events that resulted in

(i) a disposition of property to a person (other than the corporation) to whom that corporation was not related, or

(ii) a significant increase in the interest in any corporation of any person (other than the corporation that received the dividend) to whom the corporation that received the dividend was not related; or

(b) if the dividend was received

(i) in the course of a reorganization in which

(A) a distributing corporation made a distribution to one or more transferee corporations, and

(B) the distributing corporation was wound up or all of the shares of its capital stock owned by each transferee corporation immediately before the distribution were redeemed or cancelled otherwise than on an exchange to which subsection 51(1), 85(1) or 86(1) applies, and

(ii) on a permitted redemption in relation to the distribution or on the winding-up of the distributing corporation.

55(3)(a)(i) and (ii) amended by 1994 Budget, effective for dividends received after February 21, 1994, other than dividends received as part of a transaction or event or a series of transactions or events that was required on February 22, 1994 to be carried out pursuant to a written agreement entered into before February 22, 1994. For earlier dividends since 1985, read:

(i) a disposition of any property to a person with whom that corporation was dealing at arm's length, or

(ii) a significant increase in the interest in any corporation of any person with whom the corporation that received the dividend was dealing at arm's length; or

55(3)(b) amended by 1994 Budget, effective on the same basis as 55(1)"distribution" (see Notes thereto). For earlier dividends since 1985, read:

(b) if the dividend was received in the course of a reorganization in which property of a particular corporation was transferred, directly or indirectly, to one or more corporations (each of which is in this paragraph referred to as a "transferee") and, in respect of each type of property so transferred, the fair market value of the property so received by each transferee was equal to or approximated the proportion of the fair market value of all property of that type owned by the particular corporation immediately before the transfer that

(i) the total of the fair market value immediately before the transfer of all shares of the capital stock of the particular corporation owned by the transferee at that time

is of

(ii) the fair market value immediately before the transfer of all the issued shares of the capital stock of the particular corporation at that time,

except that this paragraph does not apply in respect of a transfer where, in contemplation of and before the transfer, property has become property of the particular corporation, a corporation controlled by the particular corporation or a predecessor of any such corporation otherwise than as a result of

(iii) an amalgamation of corporations each of which was related to the particular corporation,

(iv) the winding-up of a corporation that was related to the particular corporation,

(v) a transaction to which subsection (2) would, but for this subsection, apply,

(vi) a disposition of property by the particular corporation or a corporation controlled by it to another corporation controlled by the particular corporation,

(vii) a disposition of property by the particular corporation or a predecessor thereof for consideration that consists only of money or indebtedness that is not convertible into other property, or of any combination thereof, or

(viii) a prescribed transaction.

**Information Circulars**: 88-2, para. 7: General anti-avoidance rule — section 245 of the *Income Tax Act*.

**I.T. Technical News**: No. 3 (butterfly reorganizations); No. 16 (*Parthenon Investments* case).

**Advance Tax Rulings**: ATR-22R: Estate freeze using share exchange; ATR-27: Exchange and acquisition of interests in capital properties through rollovers and winding-up ("butterfly"); ATR-35: Partitioning of assets to get specific ownership — "butterfly"; ATR-47: Transfer of assets to Realtyco; ATR-56: Purification of a family farm corporation; ATR-57: Transfer of property for estate planning purposes; ATR-58: Divisive reorganization.

**(3.01) Interpretation for para. (3)(a)** — For the purposes of paragraph (3)(a),

(a) an unrelated person means a person (other than the dividend recipient) to whom the dividend recipient is not related or a partnership any member of which (other than the dividend recipient) is not related to the dividend recipient;

(b) a corporation that is formed by an amalgamation of 2 or more other corporations is deemed to be the same corporation as, and a continuation of, each of the other corporations;

(c) where there has been a winding-up of a corporation to which subsection 88(1) applies, the parent is deemed to be the same corporation as, and a continuation of, the subsidiary;

(d) proceeds of disposition shall be determined without reference to "paragraph 55(2)(a) or" in paragraph (j) of the definition "proceeds of disposition" in section 54; and

(e) notwithstanding any other provision of this Act, where a non-resident person disposes of a property in a taxation year and the gain or loss from the disposition is not included in computing the person's taxable income earned in Canada for the year, the person is deemed to have disposed of the property for proceeds of disposition that are less than its fair market value unless, under the income tax laws of the country in which the person is resident, the gain or loss is computed as if the property were disposed of for proceeds of disposition that are not less than its fair market value and the gain or loss so computed is recognized for the purposes of those laws.

**Notes**: 55(3.01) added by 1995-97 technical bill, on the same basis as the amendments to 55(3) and subject to the same application and transitional rules (see Notes to 55(3)).

**Proposed Addition — 55(3.02)**

**(3.02) Distribution by a specified corporation** — For the purposes of the definition "distribution" in subsection (1), where the transfer referred to in that definition is by a specified corporation to an acquiror described in the definition "specified corporation" in subsection (1), the references in the definition "distribution" to

(a) "each type of property" shall be read as "property"; and

(b) "property of that type" shall be read as "property".

**Notes**: The introduction of 55(3.02) enabled BCE Inc. to spin off common shares of Nortel Networks Corp. in 1999-2000. See Christopher Steeves, "The BCE-Nortel Spin-Off and the New Public Company Butterfly", VI(2) *Corporate Structures and Groups* 312-315 (2000).

**Application**: Bill C-43 (First Reading September 20, 2000), subsec. 23(2), will add subsec. 55(3.02), applicable to transfers that occur after 1998.

**Technical Notes**: New subsection 55(3.02) provides that where the distribution is by a "specified corporation" to an acquiror described in the definition "specified corporation" in subsection 55(1), the definition "distribution" in subsection 55(1) is to be read as if the reference in that definition to "each type of property" were read as "property" and to "property of that type" were read as "property". These changes ensure that divisive reorganizations, commonly known as "butterfly reorganizations", of specified corporations will be required to effect a proportionate distribution of the overall property of the corporation undergoing the divisive reorganization rather than of each type of property. Subsection 55(3.02) applies to transfers of property that occur after 1998.

**(3.1) Where para. (3)(b) not applicable** — Notwithstanding subsection (3), a dividend to which subsection (2) would, but for paragraph (3)(b), apply is not excluded from the application of subsection (2) where

(a) in contemplation of and before a distribution made in the course of the reorganization in which the dividend was received, property became property of the distributing corporation, a corporation controlled by it or a predecessor corporation of any such corporation otherwise than as a result of

(i) an amalgamation of corporations each of which was related to the distributing corporation,

(ii) an amalgamation of a predecessor corporation of the distributing corporation and one or more corporations controlled by that predecessor corporation,

(iii) a reorganization in which a dividend was received to which subsection (2) would, but for paragraph (3)(b), apply, or

(iv) a disposition of property by

(A) the distributing corporation, a corporation controlled by it or a predecessor corporation of any such corporation to a corporation controlled by the distributing corporation or a predecessor corporation of the distributing corporation,

(B) a corporation controlled by the distributing corporation or by a predecessor corporation of the distributing corporation to the distributing corporation or predecessor corporation, as the case may be, or

(C) the distributing corporation, a corporation controlled by it or a predecessor corporation of any such corporation for consideration that consists only of money or indebtedness that is not convertible into other property, or of any combination thereof,

(b) the dividend was received as part of a series of transactions or events in which

(i) a person or partnership (referred to in this subparagraph as the "vendor") disposed of property and

(A) the property is

(I) a share of the capital stock of a distributing corporation that made a distribution as part of the series or of a transferee corporation in relation to the distributing corporation, or

(II) property 10% or more of the fair market value of which was, at any time during the course of the series, derived from one or more shares described in subclause (I),

(B) the vendor was, at any time during the course of the series, a specified shareholder of the distributing corporation or of the transferee corporation, and

(C) the property or any other property (other than property received by the transferee corporation on the distribution) acquired by any person or partnership in substitution therefor was acquired (otherwise than on a permitted acquisition, permitted exchange or permitted redemption in relation to the distribution) by a person (other than the vendor) who was not related to the vendor or, as part of the series, ceased to be related to the vendor or by a partnership,

(ii) control of a distributing corporation that made a distribution as part of the series or of a transferee corporation in relation to the distributing corporation was acquired (otherwise than as a result of a permitted acquisition, permitted exchange or permitted redemption in relation to the distribution) by any person or group of persons, or

(iii) in contemplation of a distribution by a distributing corporation, a share of the capital stock of the distributing corporation was acquired (otherwise than on a permitted acquisition or permitted exchange in relation to the distribution or on an amalgamation of 2 or more predecessor corporations of the distributing corporation) by

(A) a transferee corporation in relation to the distributing corporation or by a person or partnership with whom the transferee corporation did not deal at arm's length from a person to whom the acquiror was not related or from a partnership,

(B) a person or any member of a group of persons who acquired control of the distributing corporation as part of the series,

(C) a particular partnership any interest in which is held, directly or indirectly through one or more partnerships, by a person referred to in clause (B), or

(D) a person or partnership with whom a person referred to in clause (B) or a particular partnership referred to in clause (C) did not deal at arm's length,

(c) the dividend was received by a transferee corporation from a distributing corporation that, immediately after the reorganization in the course of which a distribution was made and the dividend was received, was not related to the transferee corporation and the total of all amounts each of which is the fair market value, at the time of acquisition, of a property that

(i) was acquired, as part of the series of transactions or events that includes the receipt of the dividend, by a person (other than the transferee corporation) who was not related to the transferee corporation or, as part of the series, ceased to be related to the transferee corporation or by a partnership, otherwise than

(A) as a result of a disposition in the ordinary course of business,

(B) on a permitted acquisition in relation to a distribution, or

(C) as a result of an amalgamation of 2 or more corporations that were related to each other immediately before the amalgamation, and

(ii) is a property (other than money, indebtedness that is not convertible into other property, a share of the capital stock of the transferee corporation and property more than 10% of the fair market value of which is attributable to one or more such shares)

(A) that was received by the transferee corporation on the distribution,

(B) more than 10% of the fair market value of which was, at any time after the distribution and before the end of the series, attributable to property (other than money and indebtedness that is not convertible into other property) described in clause (A) or (C), or

(C) to which, at any time during the course of the series, the fair market value of property described in clause (A) was wholly or partly attributable

is greater than 10% of the fair market value, at the time of the distribution, of all the property (other than money and indebtedness that is not convertible into other property) received by the transferee corporation on the distribution, or

(d) the dividend was received by a distributing corporation that, immediately after the reorganization in the course of which a distribution was made and the dividend was received, was not related to the transferee corporation that paid the dividend and the total of all amounts each of which is the fair market value, at the time of acquisition, of a property that

(i) was acquired, as part of the series of transactions or events that includes the receipt of the dividend, by a person (other than the distributing corporation) who was not related to the distributing corporation or, as part of the series, ceased to be related to the distributing corporation or by a partnership, otherwise than

(A) as a result of a disposition in the ordinary course of business,

(B) on a permitted acquisition in relation to a distribution, or

(C) as a result of an amalgamation of 2 or more corporations that were related to each other immediately before the amalgamation, and

(ii) is a property (other than money, indebtedness that is not convertible into other property, a share of the capital stock of the distributing corporation and property more than 10% of the fair market value of which is attributable to one or more such shares)

(A) that was owned by the distributing corporation immediately before the distribution and not disposed of by it on the distribution,

(B) more than 10% of the fair market value of which was, at any time after the distribution and before the end of the series, attributable to property (other than money and indebtedness that is not convertible into other property) described in clause (A) or (C), or

(C) to which, at any time during the course of the series, the fair market value of property described in clause (A) was wholly or partly attributable

is greater than 10% of the fair market value at the time of the distribution, of all the property (other than money and indebtedness that is not convertible into other property) owned immediately before that time by the distributing corporation and not disposed of by it on the distribution.

**Related Provisions**: 55(3.2) — Interpretation; 88(1)(c)(iv), 88(1)(c.2) — Limitation of cost base of property on winding-up; 139.1(18) — Holding corporation deemed not to acquire control of insurer on demutualization; 256(6)–(9) — Whether control acquired.

**Notes**: 55(3.1), in general, prohibits the use of the butterfly exception in 55(3)(b) on a so-called "purchase butterfly". See Notes to 55(1)"permitted exchange".

For a detailed discussion of 55(3.1), see Brian Carr & Siobhan Monaghan, "Today's Butterfly", Canadian Tax Foundation 1994 annual conference report, pp. 4:1–4:68. See also Notes to 55(2).

See also Notes to 125(7)"Canadian-controlled private corporation" re the meaning of "control".

55(3.1)(c)(ii)(B) and (C) and 55(3.1)(d)(ii)(B) and (C) amended by 1995-97 technical bill, effective for dividends received after April 26, 1995 except that, with respect to acquisitions of property that occur before June 20, 1996 or under a written agreement made before June 20, 1996, read both 55(3.1)(c)(ii)(B) and 55(3.1)(d)(ii)(B) as:

(B) more than 10% of the fair market value of which was, at any time after the distribution and before the end of the series, attributable to property (other than money and indebtedness that is not convertible into other property) described in clause (A), or

55(3.1) amended by 1994 Budget, effective for dividends received after February 21, 1994, other than dividends received before 1995 in the course of a reorganization that was required on February 22, 1994 to be carried out pursuant to a written agreement entered into before February 22, 1994. However, for dividends received before June 23, 1994 to which this version of 55(3.1) applies, ignore 55(3.1)(c) and (d) and read 55(3.1)(b) as follows:

(b) the dividend was received as part of a series of transactions or events in which

(i) a person or partnership (referred to in this subparagraph as the "vendor") disposed of property and

(A) the property is

(I) a share of the capital stock of a distributing corporation that made a distribution as part of the series or of a transferee corporation in relation to the distributing corporation, or

(II) property 10% or more of the fair market value of which was, at any time during the course of the series, derived from one or more shares described in subclause (I),

(B) the property or any other property (other than property received by the transferee corporation on the distribution) acquired by any person or partnership in substitution therefor was acquired (otherwise than on a permitted acquisition, permitted exchange or permitted redemption in relation to the distribution) by a person (other than the vendor) who was not related to the vendor or, as part of the series, ceased to be related to the vendor or by a partnership, and

(C) either

(I) control of the distributing corporation or of a transferee corporation in relation to the distributing corporation was acquired (otherwise than as a result of a permitted acquisition, permitted exchange or permitted redemption in relation to the distribution) by any person or group of persons, or

(II) the vendor was, at any time during the course of the series, a specified shareholder of the distributing corporation or a transferee corporation in relation to the distributing corporation, or

(ii) a share of the capital stock of a distributing corporation was acquired (otherwise than on a permitted acquisition or permitted exchange in relation to a distribution by the distributing corporation or on an amalgamation of 2 or more predecessor corporations of the distributing corporation), in contemplation of a distribution by the distributing corporation, by

(A) a transferee corporation in relation to the distributing corporation, or by any person or partnership with whom the transferee corporation did not deal at arm's length from a person to whom the acquiror was not related,

(B) a person or any member of a group of persons who acquired control of the distributing corporation as part of the series,

(C) a particular partnership any interest in which is held, directly or indirectly through one or more partnerships, by a person referred to in clause (B), or

(D) a person or partnership with whom a person referred to in clause (B) or a particular partnership referred to in clause (C) did not deal at arm's length, or

For dividends before this version of 55(3.1), former 55(3.1) below added by 1993 technical bill, effective for dividends received after May 4, 1993. However, it does not apply to dividends received as part of a series of transactions or events in which a foreign vendor was obliged on May 4, 1993 to dispose of property described in former 55(3.1)(a) under a written agreement entered into by that date. Former 55(3.1) read:

(3.1) **Idem** — Notwithstanding subsection (3), a dividend to which subsection (2) would, but for paragraph (3)(b), otherwise apply is not excluded from the application of subsection (2) where the dividend is received as part of a series of transactions or events in which

(a) a person or partnership (in this subsection referred to as the "foreign vendor") who, or any member of which, is resident in a country other than Canada disposes of property that is

(i) a share of the capital stock of the particular corporation referred to in paragraph (3)(b) or of a transferee (within the meaning assigned by that paragraph) in relation to the particular corporation that is taxable Canadian property of the foreign vendor or, where the foreign vendor is a partnership, would be taxable Canadian property of the foreign vendor if the foreign vendor were non-resident, or

(ii) property the fair market value of which, at any time during the course of the series of transactions or events, is derived principally from one or more shares which, if owned by the foreign vendor, would be shares described in subparagraph (i); and

(b) the property disposed of by the foreign vendor or any other property acquired by any person or partnership in substitution for it is acquired by a person (other than the particular corporation) or partnership that, at any time during the course of the series of transactions or events, deals at arm's length with the foreign vendor.

This earlier 55(3.1) prohibited the use of the butterfly exception in 55(3)(b) on a so-called "cross-border butterfly". The current 55(3.1) is much more restrictive.

**I.T. Technical News**: No. 3 (butterfly reorganizations); No. 9 (the backdoor butterfly rule); No. 16 (*Parthenon Investments* case).

**(3.2) Interpretation of para. (3.1)(b)** — For the purpose of paragraph (3.1)(b),

(a) in determining whether the vendor referred to in subparagraph (3.1)(b)(i) is at any time a specified shareholder of a transferee corporation or of a distributing corporation, the references in the definition "specified shareholder" in subsection 248(1) to "taxpayer" shall be read as "person or partnership";

(b) a corporation that is formed by the amalgamation of 2 or more corporations (each of which is referred to in this paragraph as a "predecessor corporation") shall be deemed to be the same corporation as, and a continuation of, each of the predecessor corporations;

(c) subject to paragraph (d), each particular person who acquired a share of the capital stock of a distributing corporation in contemplation of a distribution by the distributing corporation shall be deemed, in respect of that acquisition, not to be related to the person from whom the particular person acquired the share unless

(i) the particular person acquired all the shares of the capital stock of the distributing corporation that were owned, at any time during the course of the series of transactions or events that included the distribution and before the acquisition, by the other person, or

(ii) immediately after the reorganization in the course of which the distribution was made, the particular person was related to the distributing corporation;

(d) where a share is acquired by an individual from a personal trust in satisfaction of all or a part of the individual's capital interest in the trust, the individual shall be deemed, in respect of that acquisition, to be related to the trust;

(e) subject to paragraph (f), where at any time a share of the capital stock of a corporation is redeemed or cancelled (otherwise than on an amalgamation where the only consideration received or receivable for the share by the shareholder on the amalgamation is a share of the capital stock of the corporation formed by the amalgamation), the corporation shall be deemed to have acquired the share at that time;

(f) where a share of the capital stock of a corporation is redeemed, acquired or cancelled by the corporation pursuant to the exercise of a statutory right of dissent by the holder of the share, the corporation shall be deemed not to have acquired the share;

(g) control of a corporation shall be deemed not to have been acquired by a person or group of persons where it is so acquired solely because of

(i) the incorporation of the corporation, or

(ii) the acquisition by an individual of one or more shares for the sole purpose of qualifying as a director of the corporation; and

(h) each corporation that is a shareholder and specified shareholder of a distributing corporation at any time during the course of a series of transactions or events, a part of which includes a distribution made by the distributing corporation, is deemed to be a transferee corporation in relation to the distributing corporation.

**Related Provisions**: 88(1)(c)(iv), 88(1)(c.2) — Winding-up; 139.1(18) — Holding corporation deemed not to acquire control of insurer on demutualization; 256(6)–(9) — Whether control acquired.

**Notes**: 55(3.2)(h) added by 1995-97 technical bill, effective for dividends received after June 20, 1996 other than dividends received in the course of a reorganization carried out under a series of transactions or events substantially advanced, as evidenced in writing, before June 21, 1996 or that was required on June 20, 1996 to be carried out under a written agreement made before June 21, 1996; and for the purpose of this rule, a reorganization is deemed not to be required to be carried out if the parties to that agreement can be relieved of that requirement if there is a change to the Act.

55(3.2) added by 1994 Budget, effective on the same basis as new 55(3.1) (see Notes above). However, for dividends received before June 23, 1994 to which 55(3.2) applies, ignore 55(3.2)(c) and (e).

**(3.3) Interpretation of "specified shareholder" changed** — In determining whether a person is a specified shareholder of a corporation for the purposes of subparagraph (3.1)(b)(i) and paragraph (3.2)(h), the reference in the definition "specified shareholder" in subsection 248(1) to "or of any other corporation that is related to the corporation" shall be read as "or of any other corporation that is related to the corporation and that has a significant direct or indirect interest in any issued shares of the capital stock of the corporation".

**Proposed Amendment — 55(3.3)**

**Letter from Department of Finance, May 15, 2000**:

Dear [xxx]

This is in response to your letter of April 14, 2000 and further to your telephone conversation with Davine Roach of this Division regarding a proposed butterfly reorganisation in which [xxx], a Canadian public corporation, proposes to distribute some of its assets to Newco. You are concerned that the current wording of the definition "specified shareholder" in subsection 55(3.3) of the *Income Tax Act* (the "Act") inappropriately applies to cause paragraph 55(3.1)(b) of the Act to apply to the butterfly reorganization transaction rendering it taxable. You ask that the Act be amended to address this concern.

Our understanding of the facts of the proposed transaction is that MBC proposes to transfer on a tax-deferred-basis to Newco, in the course of a butterfly reorganization to which paragraph 55(3)(b) of the Act applies, 80% of the net fair market value of [xxx] total property. Newco will be owned by the shareholders of [xxx] for the purpose of acquiring the distributed assets. As part of the series of transactions that includes the butterfly reorganization, [xxx] will redeem the first preference shares (Series B). These shares are shares of a "specified class" within the meaning of the definition "specified class" in subsection 55(1) of the Act. Mr.

X owns more than 10% of the first preference shares. Consequently, Mr. X is a specified shareholder of [xxx] within the meaning of "specified shareholder" in subsection 55(3.3). Mr. X also owns common shares of [xxx] but would not be a specified shareholder of [xxx] if he did not own more than 10% of the first preference shares.

Immediately after the butterfly reorganization, a company wholly-owned by [xxx] ("Acquisition Co.") will acquire for cash all of [xxx] outstanding shares including those held by Mr. X. [xxx] is the controlling shareholder of [xxx]. Mr. X is unrelated to [xxx]. Because Mr. X is a "specified shareholder" of [xxx] and unrelated to Acquisition Co., paragraph 55(3.1)(b) of the Act will apply to the share acquisition by Acquisition Co. to cause the butterfly reorganization to be subject to the application of subsection 55(2) of the Act. You believe that the restrictions in paragraph 55(3.1)(b) should not apply to a person who is a specified shareholder because the person holds shares of a "specified class" as defined in subsection 55(1) of the Act.

We agree that, from a policy perspective, shareholders holding shares of a specified class should not be subject to all specified shareholder restrictions in paragraph 55(3.1)(b) of the Act. Consequently, we are prepared to recommend to the Minister of Finance that the Act be amended to provide that, for the purposes of subparagraph 55(3.1)(b)(i) and paragraph 55(3.2)(h) of the Act as it applies for the purposes of subparagraph 55(3.1)(b)(iii), a shareholder will not be treated as a specified shareholder only because the shareholder holds shares of a "specified class" as defined by subsection 55(1) of the Act and the shares are otherwise non-voting. It would also be recommended that such an amendment be effective for dividends received after 1999.

If the above recommendations are acted upon, I would anticipate that such amendments would be included in a future income tax technical bill.

Yours sincerely,
Brian Ernewein
Director, Tax Legislation Division

**Notes**: 55(3.3) added by 1995-97 technical bill, effective for dividends received after 1996.

**(4) Avoidance of subsec. (2)** — For the purposes of this section, where it can reasonably be considered that one of the main purposes of one or more transactions or events was to cause 2 or more persons to be related to each other or to cause a corporation to control another corporation, so that subsection (2) would, but for this subsection, not apply to a dividend, those persons shall be deemed not to be related to each other or the corporation shall be deemed not to control the other corporation, as the case may be.

**Related Provisions**: 55(5)(e) — Determination of "related" and "arm's length"; 139.1(18) — Holding corporation deemed not to acquire control of insurer on demutualization.

**Notes**: 55(4) amended by 1994 Budget, effective for dividends received after February 21, 1994, other than dividends received as part of a transaction or event or a series of transactions or events that was required on February 22, 1994 to be carried out pursuant to a written agreement entered into before February 22, 1994. For earlier dividends since 1985, read:

(4) **Arm's length dealings** — Where it may reasonably be considered that the principal purpose of one or more transac-

tions or events was to cause two or more persons to be related or to not deal with each other at arm's length, or to cause one corporation to control another corporation, so as to make subsection (2) inapplicable, for the purposes of this section, those persons shall be deemed not to be related or shall be deemed to deal with each other at arm's length, or the corporation shall be deemed not to control the other corporation, as the case may be.

**(5) Applicable rules** — For the purposes of this section,

(a) where a dividend referred to in subsection (2) was received by a corporation as part of a transaction or event or a series of transactions or events, the portion of a capital gain attributable to any income expected to be earned or realized by a corporation after the safe-income determination time for the transaction, event or series is deemed to be a portion of a capital gain attributable to anything other than income;

(b) the income earned or realized by a corporation for a period throughout which it was resident in Canada and not a private corporation shall be deemed to be the total of

(i) its income for the period otherwise determined on the assumption that no amounts were deductible by the corporation by reason of section 37.1 of this Act or paragraph 20(1)(gg) of the *Income Tax Act*, chapter 148 of the Revised Statutes of Canada, 1952,

(ii) the amount, if any, by which

(A) the amount, if any, by which the total of the capital gains of the corporation for the period exceeds the total of the taxable capital gains of the corporation for the period

exceeds

(B) the amount, if any, by which the total of the capital losses of the corporation for the period exceeds the total of the allowable capital losses of the corporation for the period, and

(iii) the total of all amounts each of which is an amount in respect of a business carried on by the corporation at any time in the period, equal to the amount, if any, by which the total of

(A) where the period commenced before the corporation's adjustment time, the amount, if any, by which

(I) the total of the amounts in respect of the business required to be included in the calculation of the corporation's cumulative eligible capital by reason of the description of E in the definition "cumulative eligible capital" in subsection 14(5) with respect to that portion of the period preceding its adjustment time

exceeds the total of

(II) the cumulative eligible capital of the corporation in respect of the business at the commencement of the period,

(III) $1/2$ of the total of the eligible capital expenditures in respect of the business that were made or incurred by the corporation during that portion of the period preceding its adjustment time, and

(IV) to the extent that the amount determined under subclause (I) exceeds the total of the amounts determined under subclauses (II) and (III), $1/2$ of the total of the eligible capital expenditures in respect of the business that were made or incurred by the corporation during that portion of the period following its adjustment time,

(B) $1/3$ of the total of the amounts in respect of the business required to be included in the calculation of the corporation's cumulative eligible capital by reason of the description of E in the definition "cumulative eligible capital" in subsection 14(5) with respect to that portion of the period following its adjustment time, and

(C) $1/3$ of all amounts received in the period that were required to be included in the corporation's income by reason of paragraph 12(1)(i.1)

exceeds the total of

(D) where the period commenced after the corporation's adjustment time, $1/3$ of the cumulative eligible capital of the corporation in respect of the business at the commencement of the period,

(E) $1/4$ of the total of the eligible capital expenditures in respect of the business made or incurred by the corporation with respect to that portion of the period after its adjustment time and a portion of which were not included in subclause (A)(IV),

(F) where the period commenced before the corporation's adjustment time, $1/2$ of the amount, if any, by which the total of the amounts determined in respect of the corporation under subclauses (A)(II) and (III) exceeds the amount determined in respect of the corporation under subclause (A)(I), and

(G) $1/3$ of all amounts deducted by the corporation under subsection 20(4.2) in respect of debts established by it to have become bad debts during the period;

**S. 55(5)(b)(iii)**     Income Tax Act, Part I, Division B

### Proposed Amendment — 55(5)(b)(iii)–(v)

(iii) the total of all amounts each of which is an amount required to have been included under this subparagraph as it read in its application to a taxation year that ended before February 28, 2000, and

(iv) the amount, if any, by which

(A) ½ of the total of all amounts each of which is an amount required by paragraph 14(1)(b) to be included in computing the corporation's income in respect of a business carried on by the corporation for a taxation year that is included in the period and that ended after February 27, 2000 and before October 18, 2000,

exceeds

(B) where the corporation has deducted an amount under subsection 20(4.2) in respect of a debt established by it to have become a bad debt in a taxation year that is included in the period and that ended after February 27, 2000 and before October 18, 2000, or has an allowable capital loss for such a year because of the application of subsection 20(4.3), the amount determined by the formula

$$V + W$$

V is ½ of the value determined for A under subsection 20(4.2) in respect of the corporation for the last such taxation year that ended in the period, and

W is ⅓ of the value determined for B under subsection 20(4.2) in respect of the corporation for the last such taxation year that ended in the period, and

(C) in any other case, nil; and

(v) the amount, if any, by which

(A) the total of all amounts each of which is an amount required by paragraph 14(1)(b) to be included in computing the corporation's income in respect of a business carried on by the corporation for a taxation year that is included in the period and that ends after October 17, 2000,

exceeds

(B) where the corporation has deducted an amount under subsection 20(4.2) in respect of a debt established by it to have become a bad debt in a taxation year that is included in the period and that ends after October 17, 2000, or has an allowable capital loss for such a year because of the application of subsection 20(4.3), the amount determined by the formula

$$X + Y$$

X is the value determined for A under subsection 20(4.2) in respect of the corporation for the last such taxation year that ended in the period, and

Y is ⅓ of the value determined for B under subsection 20(4.2) in respect of the corporation for the last such taxation year that ended in the period, and

(C) in any other case, nil;

**Application**: The December 21, 2000 draft legislation, s. 21, will amend subpara. 55(5)(b)(iii) to read as above and add subparas. (iv) and (v), applicable in respect of taxation years that end after February 27, 2000.

**Technical Notes**: Subsection 55(2) deals with intercorporate dividends that are ordinarily tax-free.

In order to prevent the conversion of capital gains on arm's length dispositions of property into tax-free intercorporate dividends, subsection 55(2) treats, in certain circumstances, all or a portion of such a dividend to be either as proceeds of disposition of shares or as a capital gain and not as a dividend. Subsection 55(2) does not apply where the dividend can reasonably be considered to be attributed to what is known as "safe income" — income earned by a corporation after 1971 and before "safe-income determination time" (defined in subsection 55(1)), calculated according to the rules in paragraph 55(5)(b). Safe income is protected from the application of subsection 55(2) because this income has been subject to corporate income tax (or it represents the non-taxable portion of capital gains) and should therefore be permitted to be paid as a tax-free dividend to other Canadian corporations.

Paragraph 55(5)(b) provides rules for the calculation of income for the purposes of section 55. Subparagraph 55(5)(b)(iii) adds to income otherwise determined the "untaxed portion" of gains in respect of eligible capital property. Because, under existing paragraph 14(1)(b), a corporation's gain in respect of eligible capital property was previously aggregated with a recapture of the paragraph 20(1)(b) deductions that were previously claimed, subparagraph 55(5)(b)(iii) describes the untaxed portion of gains in respect of eligible capital property by reference to the corporation's cumulative eligible capital, eligible capital expenditures and variable E in the definition "cumulative eligible capital".

Amended paragraph 14(1)(b) identifies the taxable (2/3 for taxation years that end after February 27, 2000 and before October 18, 2000 and 1/2 for taxation years that end after October 17, 2000) portion of gains in respect of eligible capital property. Consequently it is possible to simplify the description of the untaxed (1/3) portion of gains in respect of eligible capital property for taxation years that end after February 27, 2000 and before October 18, 2000 and (1/2) portion for taxation years that end after October 17, 2000. Subparagraph 55(5)(b)(iii) is, therefore, amended to describe deemed income as calculated under that provision as it applied to taxation years that ended before February 28, 2000.

New subparagraph 55(5)(b)(iv) generally requires the inclusion in the calculation of income under paragraph 55(5)(b) of 1/2 of all amounts required by amended paragraph 14(1)(b) to be included in the corporation's income for taxation years that end after February 27, 2000 and before October 18, 2000.

> New subparagraph 55(5)(b)(v) requires the inclusion of the amount required by paragraph 14(1)(b) to be included for taxation years that end after October 17, 2000.
>
> Both these amounts are reduced to take into account the appropriate portion of bad debts in respect of dispositions of eligible capital property. The calculation of the reduction for bad debts is complicated by the interaction of different inclusion rates for capital gains that may be relevant during the period. New subparagraphs 55(5)(b)(iv) and (v) recognize both the deduction under subsection 20(4.2) and the deemed allowable capital loss under subsection 20(4.3) as amounts that reduce safe income. For further detail, see the commentary to subsections 20(4.2) and (4.3).

(c) the income earned or realized by a corporation for a period throughout which it was a private corporation is deemed to be its income for the period otherwise determined on the assumption that no amounts were deductible by the corporation under section 37.1 of this Act, as that section applies for taxation years that ended before 1995, or paragraph 20(1)(gg) of the *Income Tax Act*, chapter 148 of the Revised Statutes of Canada, 1952;

(d) the income earned or realized by a corporation for a period ending at a time when it was a foreign affiliate of another corporation shall be deemed to be the total of the amount, if any, that would have been deductible by that other corporation at that time by virtue of paragraph 113(1)(a) and the amount, if any, that would have been deductible by that other corporation at that time by virtue of paragraph 113(1)(b) if that other corporation

(i) owned all of the shares of the capital stock of the foreign affiliate immediately before that time,

(ii) had disposed at that time of all of the shares referred to in subparagraph (i) for proceeds of disposition equal to their fair market value at that time, and

(iii) had made an election under subsection 93(1) in respect of the full amount of the proceeds of disposition referred to in subparagraph (ii);

(e) in determining whether 2 or more persons are related to each other, in determining whether a person is at any time a specified shareholder of a corporation and in determining whether control of a corporation has been acquired by a person or group of persons,

(i) a person shall be deemed to be dealing with another person at arm's length and not to be related to the other person if the person is the brother or sister of the other person,

(ii) where at any time a person is related to each beneficiary (other than a registered charity) under a trust who is or may (otherwise than by reason of the death of another beneficiary under the trust) be entitled to share in the income or capital of the trust, the person and the trust shall be deemed to be related at that time to each other and, for this purpose, a person shall be deemed to be related to himself, herself or itself,

(iii) a trust and a person shall be deemed not to be related to each other unless they are deemed by paragraph (3.2)(d) or subparagraph (ii) to be related to each other or the person is a corporation that is controlled by the trust, and

(iv) persons who are related to each other solely because of a right referred to in paragraph 251(5)(b) shall be deemed not to be related to each other; and

### Proposed Amendment — 55(5)(e)(iv)

(iv) this Act shall be read without reference to subsection 251(3) and paragraph 251(5)(b); and

**Application**: Bill C-43 (First Reading September 20, 2000), subsec. 23(4), will amend para. 55(5)(e)(iv) to read as above, applicable to dividends that are received after November 1999, other than dividends received as part of a transaction or event, or a series of transactions or events, that was required before December 1, 1999 to be carried out pursuant to a written agreement made before that day.

**Technical Notes**: Subparagraph 55(5)(e)(iv) provides that in determining, for the purposes of section 55, whether persons are related to each other or whether control of a corporation has been acquired, persons will be treated as not being related to each other if they are related to each other only because of a right referred to in paragraph 251(5)(b). Amended subparagraph 55(5)(e)(iv) provides that, for the purposes of determining, for the purposes of section 55, whether persons are related to each other or whether control of a corporation has been acquired, the Act is to be read without reference to paragraph 251(5)(b) and section 251(3). This will have the effect of ensuring that corporations will not be considered to be related to each other by reason only that they are each related to a third corporation.

(f) where a corporation has received a dividend any portion of which is a taxable dividend,

(i) the corporation may designate in its return of income under this Part for the taxation year during which the dividend was received any portion of the taxable dividend to be a separate taxable dividend, and

(ii) the amount, if any, by which the portion of the dividend that is a taxable dividend exceeds the portion designated under subparagraph (i) shall be deemed to be a separate taxable dividend.

**Related Provisions [subsec. 55(5)]**: 141.1 — Insurance corporation deemed not to be private corporation; 256(6)–(9) — Whether control acquired.

**Notes**: 55(5) does not define the term "any corporation" and thus does not prevent 55(2) from applying to a foreign non-affiliate: *Lamont Management Ltd.*, [2000] 3 C.T.C. 18 (FCA).

Late designations under 55(5)(f) were permitted by the Courts in *Administration Gilles Leclair*, [1997] 3 C.T.C. 3053 (TCC), and *Nassau Walnut Investments*, [1998] 1 C.T.C. 33 (FCA).

55(5)(a) amended by 1995-97 technical bill, effective for dividends received after June 20, 1996. For earlier dividends since April 22, 1980, read:

> (a) the portion of any capital gain attributable to any income that is expected to be earned or realized by a corporation after the time of receipt of the dividend referred to in subsection (2) shall, for greater certainty, be deemed to be a portion of the capital gain attributable to anything other than income;

55(5)(b) amended by 1988 tax reform; with respect to amounts included in the calculation of a corporation's income by reason of 12(1)(i.1) or 20(4.2) relating to an amount owing in respect of a disposition of property occurring in a taxation year of the corporation commencing before July 1988, read 55(5)(b)(iii)(C) and (G) without the words "⅓ of".

55(5)(c) amended by 1995-97 technical bill, effective for 1995 and later taxation years. For earlier years, since April 22, 1980, read:

> (c) the income earned or realized by a corporation for a period throughout which it was a private corporation shall be deemed to be its income for the period otherwise determined on the assumption that no amounts were deductible by the corporation by reason of section 37.1 of this Act or paragraph 20(1)(gg) of the *Income Tax Act*, chapter 148 of the Revised Statutes of Canada, 1952;

55(5)(e) amended by 1994 Budget, effective for dividends received after February 21, 1994, other than dividends received as part of a transaction or event or a series of transactions or events that was required on February 22, 1994 to be carried out pursuant to a written agreement entered into before February 22, 1994. For earlier dividends since April 22, 1980, read:

> (e) in determining whether two or more persons are dealing with each other at arm's length, persons shall be deemed to be dealing with each other at arm's length and not to be related to each other if one is the brother or sister of the other; and

**I.T. Application Rules**: 69 (meaning of "*Income Tax Act*, chapter 148 of the Revised Statutes of Canada, 1952").

**I.T. Technical News**: No. 7 (subsection 55(2) — recent cases); No. 16 (*Brelco Drilling* case).

**Definitions [s. 55]**: "acquired" — 55(3.2)(e), (f), 139.1(18), 256(7); "acquiror" — 55(1)"permitted exchange"(b); "acquisition of control" — 55(3.2)(g), 55(5)(e), 256(7), (8); "adjustment time" — 14(5), 248(1); "allowable capital loss" — 38(b), 248(1); "amount" — 248(1); "arm's length" — 55(4), 55(5)(e), 251(1); "brother" — 252(2); "business" — 248(1); "Canada" — 255; "capital gain", "capital loss" — 39(1), 248(1); "capital property" — 54, 248(1); "class of shares" — 248(6); "control", "controlled" — 55(3.2)(g), 55(5)(e), 139.1(18), 256(6)–(9); "corporation" — 55(3.2)(b), 248(1), *Interpretation Act* 35(1); "cumulative eligible capital" — 14(5), 248(1); "disposition" — 54 [to be repealed], 248(1) [draft]; "distributing corporation" — 55(1) (under "distribution"); "distribution" — 55(1); "dividend" — 248(1); "dividend payer" — 55(3)(a)(iii)(A); "dividend recipient" — 55(3); "eligible capital property" — 54, 248(1); "foreign vendor" — 55(3.1)(a); "income earned or realized…" — 55(5)(b), (c); "individual", "non-resident" — 248(1); "participant" — 55(1) [under "permitted exchange"(b)]; "partnership" — see Notes to 96(1); "permitted acquisition", "permitted exchange", "permitted redemption" — 55(1); "person" — 248(1); "proceeds of disposition" — 55(3.01)(d); "property" — 248(1); "public corporation" — 89(1), 248(1); "qualifying share" — 192(6), 248(1) [*not intended to apply to s. 55*]; "related" — 55(3.2)(c), (d), 55(5)(e), 251(2); "resident in Canada" — 250; "safe-income determination time" — 55(1); "series of transactions" — 248(10); "share", "shareholder" — 248(1); "sister" — 252(2); "specified class", "specified corporation" — 55(1); "specified shareholder" — 55(3.2)(a), 55.3.3, 248(1); "specified wholly-owned corporation" — 55(1); "subsidiary wholly-owned corporation" — 248(1); "taxable Canadian corporation" — 89(1), 248(1); "taxable Canadian property" — 248(1); "taxable capital gain" — 38(a), 248(1); "taxable dividend" — 89(1), 248(1); "taxpayer" — 248(1); "transferee" — 55(1)"distribution"; "transferee corporation" — 55(1)"distribution", 55(3.2)(h); "trust" — 104(1), 248(1), (3); "unrelated" — 55(3.01)(a) "vendor" — 55(3.1)(b)(i).

## Subdivision d — Other Sources of Income

**56. (1) Amounts to be included in income for year** — Without restricting the generality of section 3, there shall be included in computing the income of a taxpayer for a taxation year,

(a) **pension benefits, unemployment insurance benefits, etc.** — any amount received by the taxpayer in the year as, on account or in lieu of payment of, or in satisfaction of,

> (i) a superannuation or pension benefit including, without limiting the generality of the foregoing,
>
>> (A) the amount of any pension, supplement or spouse's or common-law partner's allowance under the *Old Age Security Act* and the amount of any similar payment under a law of a province,
>>
>> (B) the amount of any benefit under the *Canada Pension Plan* or a provincial pension plan as defined in section 3 of that Act,
>>
>> (C) the amount of any payment out of or under a prescribed provincial pension plan, and
>>
>> (C.1) the amount of any payment out of or under a foreign retirement arrangement established under the laws of a country, except to the extent that the amount would not, if the taxpayer were resident in the country, be subject to income taxation in the country,

> **Proposed Amendment — 56(1)(a)(i)(C.1) — Income inclusion on conversion to Roth IRA**
>
> **Department of Finance press release, December 18, 1998**: See under 248(1)"foreign retirement arrangement".

but not including

>> (D) the portion of a benefit received out of or under an employee benefit plan that is required by paragraph 6(1)(g) to be included in computing the taxpayer's income for the year, or would be required to be so included if that paragraph were read without reference to subparagraph 6(1)(g)(ii),
>>
>> (E) the portion of an amount received out of or under a retirement compensation arrangement that is required by paragraph

Subdivision d — Other Sources of Income    S. 56(1)(a.1)

(x) or (z) to be included in computing the taxpayer's income for the year, and

(F) a benefit received under section 71 of the *Canada Pension Plan* or under a similar provision of a provincial pension plan as defined in section 3 of that Act,

(ii) a retiring allowance, other than an amount received out of or under an employee benefit plan, a retirement compensation arrangement or a salary deferral arrangement,

(iii) a death benefit,

(iv) a benefit under the *Unemployment Insurance Act*, other than a payment relating to a course or program designed to facilitate the re-entry into the labour force of a claimant under that Act, or a benefit under Part I, VIII or VIII.1 of the *Employment Insurance Act*,

(v) a benefit under regulations made under an appropriation Act providing for a scheme of transitional assistance benefits to persons employed in the production of products to which the Canada-United States Agreement on Automotive Products, signed on January 16, 1965 applies, or

(vi) except to the extent otherwise required to be included in computing the taxpayer's income, a prescribed benefit under a government assistance program;

(vii) [Repealed]

**Related Provisions**: 56(8) — CPP/QPP benefits for previous years; 57 — Certain superannuation or pension benefits; 60(j) — Transfer of superannuation benefits; 60(j.03), (j.04) — Deduction for repayments of pension benefits; 60(j.1) — Transfer of retiring allowances; 60(j.2) — Transfer to spousal RRSP; 60(n)(iii) — Deduction for repayment of pension or benefits; 60(v.1) — UI/EI benefit repayment; 60.2(1) — Refund of undeducted past service AVCs; 78(4) — Unpaid remuneration and other amounts; 81(1)(d)–(g) — Certain pensions exempt from tax; 104(27) — Testamentary trust — income included under subpara. 56(1)(a)(i); 104(28) — Death benefit flowed through trust; 110(1)(f) — Deductions for certain payments; 110.2(1)"qualifying amount" — Retroactive spreading of certain lump-sum payments over prior years; 118.7 — Credit for UI/EI premium and CPP contributions; 128.1(10)"excluded right or interest"(a)(viii), (d), (g), (h) — Emigration — no deemed disposition of right to pension or retiring allowance; 139.1(12) — Conversion benefit on demutualization of insurance corporation; 147.4(4) — Amount deemed received when converting pension rights before 1997 to annuity contract commencing after age 69; 153(1) — Withholding of tax at source; 212(1)(h), (j) — Pension and benefit payments to non-residents — withholding tax; 254 — Contract under pension plan; Canada-U.S. tax treaty, Art. XVIII — Pensions and annuities; Art. XXIX:7 — exemption for half of old age security paid to citizen of U.S. resident in Canada.

**Notes**: 56(1)(a) amended by 2000 same-sex partners bill to add reference to "common-law partner's", effective for the 2001 and later taxation years, or earlier by election (see Notes to 248(1)"common-law partner").

56(1)(a)(i)(C.1) added by 1991 technical bill, effective for payments received after July 13, 1990. It deals with payments from U.S. Individual Retirement Accounts (IRAs). See Notes to 248(1)"foreign retirement arrangement".

56(1)(a)(i)(F) added by 1997 Budget, effective for 1997 and later taxation years, but it does not apply to benefits received before August 1997 by a taxpayer in respect of the death of an individual if the taxpayer is an estate that arose on or as a consequence of the death of the individual. It means that a CPP/QPP death benefit is ignored under 56(1)(a). Instead, it will be included in the estate's income under 56(1)(a.1).

56(1)(a)(iv) amended by 1991 technical bill, effective 1988, to add the words beginning "other than"; and amended by 1996 Employment Insurance bill and 1995-97 technical bill, both effective June 30, 1996, to reflect the replacement of the *Unemployment Insurance Act* with the *Employment Insurance Act*.

56(1)(a)(vi) amended by 1993 technical bill, effective for benefits received after October 1991, replacing 56(1)(a)(vi) and (vii), which formerly read:

(vi) a benefit under the *Labour Adjustment Benefits Act*, or

(vii) an income assistance payment made pursuant to an agreement under section 5 of the *Department of Labour Act*;

56(1)(a)(vii) added by 1991 technical bill, effective September 15, 1989, to deal with income assistance for eligible workers under the Program for Older Worker Adjustment. It was repealed because it is now covered under 56(1)(a)(vi) as a "prescribed benefit".

56(1)(a)(viii) added and then repealed by 1978 Budget and 1981 Budget; for amounts received (in any year) in respect of a termination of an office or employment after November 16, 1978 and before November 13, 1981, read:

(viii) a termination payment.

See "termination payment" as defined effective for that time period in 248(1). Termination payments (severance payments and wrongful dismissal awards) are now included in the definition of "retiring allowance" and taxed under 56(1)(a)(ii).

**Regulations**: 100(1)"remuneration"(b), (c), (d), (g) (withholding at source); 103(4), (6)(e) (withholding required for retiring allowance); 200(2)(e) (information return); 5502 (prescribed benefits for 56(1)(a)(vi)); 7800(1) (prescribed provincial pension plan).

**Interpretation Bulletins**: IT-75R3: Scholarships, fellowships, bursaries, prizes, and research grants; IT-91R4: Employment at special work sites or remote work locations; IT-122R2: U.S. social security taxes and benefits; IT-167R6: Registered pension plans — employee's contributions; IT-247: Employer's contribution to pensioners' premiums under provincial medical and hospital services plans; IT-337R3: Retiring allowances; IT-365R2: Damages, settlements and similar receipts; IT-397R: Amounts excluded from income — statutory exemptions and certain service or RCMP pensions, allowances and compensation; IT-499R: Superannuation or pension benefits; IT-508R: Death benefits; IT-528: Transfers of funds between registered plans; IT-529: Flexible employee benefit programs.

**Information Circulars**: 79-8R3: Forms to use to directly transfer funds to or between plans, or to purchase an annuity.

**Advance Tax Rulings**: ATR-12: Retiring allowance; ATR-21: Pension benefit from an unregistered pension plan.

**Forms**: RC4157(E): Employers' Guide: Filing the T4A Slip and Summary Form; T4A(OAS) Supp: Statement of old age security; T4A(P): Statement of Canada Pension Plan benefits.

(a.1) **benefits under CPP/QPP** — where the taxpayer is an estate that arose on or as a consequence of the death of an individual, each benefit received under section 71 of the *Canada Pension Plan*, or under a similar provision of a provincial pension plan as defined in section 3 of that Act, after July 1997 and in the year in respect of the death of the individual;

**Related Provisions**: 56(8) — CPP/QPP benefits for previous years.

**Notes**: 56(1)(a.1) added by 1997 Budget, effective for 1997 and later taxation years. These amounts are now excluded from 56(1)(a)(i) by 56(1)(a)(i)(F).

(b) **support** — the total of all amounts each of which is an amount determined by the formula

$$A - (B + C)$$

where

A is the total of all amounts each of which is a support amount received after 1996 and before the end of the year by the taxpayer from a particular person where the taxpayer and the particular person were living separate and apart at the time the amount was received,

B is the total of all amounts each of which is a child support amount that became receivable by the taxpayer from the particular person under an agreement or order on or after its commencement day and before the end of the year in respect of a period that began on or after its commencement day, and

C is the total of all amounts each of which is a support amount received after 1996 by the taxpayer from the particular person and included in the taxpayer's income for a preceding taxation year;

**Related Provisions**: 56.1 — Support payments; 56.1(4) — Definitions of "commencement day", "support amount" and "child support amount"; 60(b) — Parallel deduction for payer; 60(c.2) — Repayment of support payments; 110.2(1)"qualifying amount" — Retroactive spreading of lump-sum payments over prior years; 122.64(3) — Disclosure of name and address for enforcement of support payments; 146(1)"earned income" — RRSP — earned income includes amounts under 56(1)(b); 212(1)(f) — No withholding tax on support paid to non-resident; 248(1)"exempt income" — Support amount is not exempt income; 252(3) — Extended meaning of "spouse" and "former spouse"; Canada–U.S. tax treaty, Art. XVIII:6 — Child support exempt if paid by U.S. resident.

**Notes**: The 2000 same-sex partners bill (Royal Assent June 29, 2000), which extended references to "spouse" to add "common-law partner" throughout the Act, provides:

145. Paragraphs 56(1)(b) and 60(b) of the *Income Tax Act* do not apply to amounts paid or payable by a person for the maintenance of a taxpayer pursuant to an order or a written agreement, made before the coming into force of this section, unless the person and the taxpayer jointly elect to have those paragraphs apply to those amounts for the 2001 and following taxation years by notifying the Minister of National Revenue in prescribed manner on or before their filing due date for the year in which this Act receives royal assent.

Although the amendment dealt only with the addition of "common-law partner", the wording of s. 145 above, on its face, prevents *all* spousal support from being includable and deductible unless an election is filed.

Where an amount is included in income by 56(1)(b), an offsetting deduction is normally allowed to the payer by 60(b).

Note that amounts taxable under 56(1)(b) are deemed by 56.1(1) to be received as soon as they are *paid*, even if they are not actually received until the next year (e.g., by being delayed in the bureaucracy of the Ontario Family Support Plan).

See also Notes to 56.1(3) re prior payments, and 110.2 re averaging of a payment received as a lump sum.

56(1)(b) rewritten by 1996 Budget (and amended retroactively by 1995-97 technical bill to add the words "on or" near the end of 56(1)(b)B), effective for amounts received after 1996. For amounts received before 1997, read:

(b) **alimony** — an amount received by the taxpayer in the year as alimony or other allowance payable on a periodic basis for the maintenance of the taxpayer, children of the taxpayer or both the taxpayer and the children if the taxpayer, because of the breakdown of the taxpayer's marriage, was living separate and apart from the spouse or former spouse who was required to make the payment at the time the payment was received and throughout the remainder of the year and the amount was received under a decree, order or judgment of a competent tribunal or under a written agreement;

Although the structure of the legislation is very different from the pre-1997 version (see the definitions in 56.1(4)), the essence of the change is that child support, but not spousal support, is no longer taxable to the recipient and deductible to the payer, if the order or agreement was made or varied after April 30, 1997 (see 56.1(4)"commencement day"). Spousal support that meets the conditions continues to be deductible to the payer under 60(b) and included in the recipient's income under 56(1)(b). Note that any amount that was "outside" the inclusion/deduction system before the amendments, due to not meeting the conditions (e.g., certain pre-1993 agreements) remains outside the system due to the in-force application rule for 56.1(4)"support amount" (see Notes thereto).

In *Thibaudeau*, [1995] 1 C.T.C. 382, the Supreme Court of Canada ruled 5–2 that former 56(1)(b) did not violate s. 15 of the Charter of Rights in its application to child support. For a discussion of these issues, see Durnford and Toope, "Spousal Support in Family Law and Alimony in the Law of Taxation", 42(1) *Canadian Tax Journal* 1-107 (1994). The changes introduced by the 1996 Budget are the response to concerns about unfairness of the rules to women, although they deal only with child support and not spousal support.

Former 56(1)(b) and (c) consolidated into 56(1)(b) by 1992 technical bill, effective for breakdown of a "marriage" after 1992. "Marriage" is not specifically defined in the amending bill, but the drafters intended it to mean a marriage under the extended definition in 252(4)(b); this is supported by subsection 42(3) of the *Interpretation Act*, reproduced at the end of this book. For earlier breakdowns, read:

(b) **alimony** — any amount received by the taxpayer in the year, pursuant to a decree, order or judgment of a competent tribunal or pursuant to a written agreement, as alimony or other allowance payable on a periodic basis for the maintenance of the recipient thereof, children of the marriage, or both the recipient and children of the marriage, if the recipient was living apart from, and was separated pursuant to a divorce, judicial separation or written separation agreement from, the spouse or former spouse required to make the payment at the time the payment was received and throughout the remainder of the year;

(c) **maintenance** — any amount received by the taxpayer in the year, pursuant to an order of a competent tribunal, as an allowance payable on a periodic basis for the maintenance of the taxpayer, children of the taxpayer, or both the taxpayer and children of the taxpayer, if, at the time the payment was received and throughout the remainder of the year, the taxpayer was living apart from the taxpayer's spouse required to make the payment;

Former 56(1)(c) amended by 1979 Budget and 1981 Budget, effective (a) for all orders made after December 11, 1979, and (b) for earlier orders, where the payer and the taxpayer agree in writing at any time in a taxation year, for that year and all subsequent years. For earlier cases, read:

(c) **maintenance where recipient living apart from spouse** — any amount received by the taxpayer in the year, pursuant to an order of a competent tribunal, as an allowance payable on a periodic basis for the maintenance of the recipient thereof, children of the marriage, or both the recipient and children of the marriage, if the recipient was living apart from the spouse required to make the payment at the time the payment was received and throughout the remainder of the year;

**Interpretation Bulletins**: IT-99R5: Legal and accounting fees; IT-118R3: Alimony and maintenance; IT-325R2: Property transfers after separation, divorce and annulment; IT-530: Support payments.

**Forms**: T1157: Election for child support payments; T1158: Registration of family support payments; P102: Support payments (pamphlet).

(c), (c.1) [Repealed]

**Notes**: 56(1)(c) repealed by 1996 Budget, effective for amounts received after 1996. See now 56(1)(b). For amounts received before 1997, read:

(c) maintenance — an amount received by the taxpayer in the year as an allowance payable on a periodic basis for the maintenance of the taxpayer, children of the taxpayer or both the taxpayer and the children if

(i) at the time the amount was received and throughout the remainder of the year the taxpayer was living separate and apart from the person who was required to make the payment,

(ii) the person who was required to make the payment is the natural parent of a child of the taxpayer, and

(iii) the amount was received under an order made by a competent tribunal in accordance with the laws of a province;

Former 56(1)(c.1) amended and renumbered as 56(1)(c) by 1992 technical bill, effective for orders made after 1992.

Former 56(1)(c.1) added by 1981 Budget, effective (a) for all orders made after December 11, 1979, and (b) for earlier orders, where the taxpayer and the person agree in writing at any time in a taxation year, for that year and all subsequent years. In other words, for orders made before December 11, 1979, the amendment does not apply unless the parties elect (or have ever previously elected) for it to apply.

Former 56(1)(c.1) amended by 1988 tax reform, except that for orders made after December 11, 1979 under the laws of Ontario, read "December 11, 1979" and "December 12, 1979" in place of "February 10, 1988" and "February 11, 1988" respectively.

**Interpretation Bulletins**: IT-118R3: Alimony and maintenance; IT-325R2: Property transfers after separation, divorce and annulment.

(c.2) **reimbursement of support payments** — an amount received by the taxpayer in the year under a decree, order or judgment of a competent tribunal as a reimbursement of an amount deducted under paragraph 60(b) or (c), or under paragraph 60(c.1) as it applies, in computing the taxpayer's income for the year or a preceding taxation year to decrees, orders and judgments made before 1993;

**Related Provisions**: 60(c.2) — Repayment of support payments; 146(1)"earned income"(b) — Amount under 56(1)(c.2) included in RRSP earned income.

**Notes**: 56(1)(c.2) added by 1992 technical bill, effective for payments received after 1990.

**Interpretation Bulletins**: IT-530: Support payments.

(d) **annuity payments** — any amount received by the taxpayer in the year as an annuity payment other than an amount

(i) otherwise required to be included in computing the taxpayer's income for the year, or

(ii) with respect to an interest in an annuity contract to which subsection 12.2(1) applies (or would apply if the contract had an anniversary day in the year at a time when the taxpayer held the interest);

**Related Provisions**: 56(1.1) — Definitions in 12.2(11) apply; 58 — Government annuities and like annuities; 60(a) — Deduction of capital element; 94.2(10)(a)(ii) — No application to foreign insurance policy of foreign investment entity; 128.1(10)"excluded right or interest"(f)(i) — Emigration — no deemed disposition of right to annuity contract; 153(1)(f) — Withholding at source; 212(1)(o) — Withholding tax on annuity payment to non-resident.

**Notes**: 56(1)(d) amended by 1989 Budget, effective (per 1991 technical bill) for contracts last acquired after 1989.

For contracts last acquired before 1990, read the following in place of subpara. (ii):

(ii) with respect to an interest in an annuity contract to which subsection 12.2(1) applies or would apply if the interest had been last acquired after December 19, 1980 and before December 2, 1982 (other than a contract to which subsection 12.2(1) does not apply in the year by virtue of subsection 12.2(6)),

(iii) with respect to an interest in an annuity contract to which subsection 12.2(3) applies or would apply if the contract had a third anniversary in the year, or

(iv) with respect to an interest in an annuity contract to which subsection 12.2(4) applies;

**Interpretation Bulletins**: IT-85R2: Health and welfare trusts for employees; IT-111R2: Annuities purchased from charitable organizations; IT-365R2: Damages, settlements and similar receipts.

**Advance Tax Rulings**: ATR-40: Taxability of receipts under a structured settlement; ATR-50: Structured settlement; ATR-68: Structured settlement.

(d.1) [Repealed under former Act]

**Notes**: 56(1)(d.1) repealed by 1989 Budget, effective (per 1991 technical bill) for contracts last acquired after 1989.

For contracts last acquired before 1990, read:

(d.1) [annuity payments] — any amount paid in the year as an annuity payment with respect to

(i) an interest in an annuity contract (other than a contract to which subsection 12.2(3) does not apply in the year by virtue of subsection 12.2(7)) to which subsection 12.2(3) does not apply but would apply if the contract had a third anniversary in the year, or

(ii) an interest in an annuity contract (other than a contract to which subsection 12.2(1) does not apply in the year by virtue of subsection 12.2(6)) to which subsection 12.2(1) does not apply but would apply if the interest had been last acquired after December 19, 1980 and before December 2, 1982

where such interest was held by the taxpayer at the time of the payment, except to the extent that the aggregate of such amounts with respect to such an interest in a particular annuity contract exceeds the amount by which the accumulating fund at the end of the calendar year ending in the year, as determined in prescribed manner, with respect to the interest exceeds the aggregate of its adjusted cost basis at the end of that calendar year and the amount at the end of that calendar year of unallocated income accrued in respect of the interest before 1982, as determined in prescribed manner;

**Interpretation Bulletins**: IT-365R2: Damages, settlements and similar receipts.

(d.2) **idem [annuity payments]** — any amount received out of or under, or as proceeds of disposition of, an annuity the payment for which was

(i) deductible in computing the taxpayer's income because of paragraph 60(l) or because of subsection 146(5.5) of the *Income Tax Act*, Chapter 148 of the Revised Statutes of Canada, 1952,

(ii) made in circumstances to which subsection 146(21) applied, or

(iii) made pursuant to or under a deferred profit sharing plan by a trustee under the plan to purchase the annuity for a beneficiary under the plan;

**Related Provisions**: 60.2(1) — Refund of undeducted past service AVCs; 147(2)(k)(vi) — Purchase of annuity by DPSP; 147(10.6) — Purchase of annuity by DPSP before 1997.

**Notes**: 56(1)(d.2)(ii) added by 1993 technical bill, effective 1992. 146(21) applies to transfers from the Saskatchewan Pension Plan.

56(1)(d.2)(iii) added by 1996 Budget, effective for 1996 and later taxation years.

**I.T. Application Rules**: 69 (meaning of "*Income Tax Act*, chapter 148 of the Revised Statutes of Canada, 1952").

**Interpretation Bulletins**: IT-517R: Pension tax credit.

(e) **disposition of income-averaging annuity contract** — any amount received by the taxpayer in the year as, on account or in lieu of payment of, or in satisfaction of, proceeds of the surrender, cancellation, redemption, sale or other disposition of an income-averaging annuity contract;

**Related Provisions**: 153(1)(k) — Withholding of tax at source; Canada-U.S. tax treaty, Art. XVIII:3 — Pension income excludes payment from IAAC.

**Notes**: See Notes to 61(1).

**Regulations**: 208 (information return).

(f) **idem** — any amount deemed by subsection 61.1(1) to have been received by the taxpayer in the year as proceeds of the disposition of an income-averaging annuity contract;

**Related Provisions**: 212(1)(n), 214(3)(b) — Non-resident withholding tax.

**Regulations**: 208 (information return).

(g) **supplementary unemployment benefit plan** — amounts received by the taxpayer in the year from a trustee under a supplementary unemployment benefit plan as provided by section 145;

**Related Provisions**: 6(1)(a)(i) — Employer-paid premiums not a taxable benefit; 145(3) — Amounts received taxable; 146(1)"earned income"(b) — Amount under 56(1)(g) included in RRSP earned income; 153(1)(e) — Withholding of tax at source.

**Regulations**: 100(1)"remuneration"(e) (withholding at source).

(h) **registered retirement savings plan, etc. [RRSP or RRIF]** — amounts required by section 146 in respect of a registered retirement savings plan or a registered retirement income fund to be included in computing the taxpayer's income for the year;

**Related Provisions**: 56(1)(t) — RRIF inclusion under 146.3; 60.2(1) — Refund of undeducted past service AVCs; 139.1(12) — Conversion benefit on demutualization of insurance corporation; 146(8) — Benefits taxable; 148(8.1) — *Inter vivos* transfer to spouse; 153(1)(j) — Withholding of tax at source.

**Regulations**: 214 (information return).

**Interpretation Bulletins**: IT-307R3: Spousal registered retirement savings plans.

**Advance Tax Rulings**: ATR-37: Refund of premiums transferred to spouse.

(h.1) **Home Buyers' Plan** — amounts required by section 146.01 to be included in computing the taxpayer's income for the year;

**Related Provisions**: 146.01(4), (5), (6) — Income inclusions.

**Notes**: 56(1)(h.1) added by 1992 technical bill, effective 1992.

(h.2) **Lifelong Learning Plan** — amounts required by section 146.02 to be included in computing the taxpayer's income for the year;

**Related Provisions**: 146.02(4), (5), (6) — Income inclusions.

**Notes**: 56(1)(h.2) added by 1998 Budget, effective for 1999 and later taxation years.

(i) **deferred profit sharing plan** — amounts received by the taxpayer in the year under a deferred profit sharing plan as provided by section 147;

**Related Provisions**: 60(j.2) — Transfer to spousal RRSP; 139.1(11), (12) — Conversion benefit on demutualization of insurance corporation; 147(10) — Amounts received from DPSP taxable; 153(1)(h) — Withholding of tax at source; 212(1)(m) — DPSP payments to non-residents.

**Regulations**: 100(1)"remuneration"(f) (withholding at source).

**Interpretation Bulletins**: IT-281R2: Elections on single payments from a deferred profit-sharing plan.

**Advance Tax Rulings**: ATR-31: Funding of divorce settlement amount from DPSP.

(j) **life insurance policy proceeds** — any amount required by subsection 148(1) or (1.1) to be included in computing the taxpayer's income for the year;

**Related Provisions**: 94.2(10)(a)(ii) — No application to foreign insurance policy of foreign investment entity; 148(9)"adjusted cost basis"C — increase in adjusted cost basis.

**Regulations**: 217 (information return).

**Interpretation Bulletins**: IT-87R2: Policyholders' income from life insurance policies.

**Forms**: T5 Segment; T5 Summ: Return of investment income; T5 Supp: Statement of investment income.

(k) [Repealed under former Act]

**Notes**: 56(1)(k), repealed in 1977, dealt with allocations under insurance policies as provided by 148(1)(b). These are now covered by 56(1)(j).

(l) **legal expenses [awarded or reimbursed]** — amounts received by the taxpayer in the year as

(i) legal costs awarded to the taxpayer by a court on an appeal in relation to an assessment of any tax, interest or penalties referred to in paragraph 60(o),

(ii) reimbursement of costs incurred in relation to a decision of the Canada Employment

Subdivision d — Other Sources of Income    S. 56(1)(n)

and Immigration Commission, the Canada Employment and Insurance Commission, a board of referees or an umpire under the *Unemployment Insurance Act* or the *Employment Insurance Act*, or

(iii) reimbursement of costs incurred in relation to an assessment or a decision under the *Canada Pension Plan* or a provincial pension plan as defined in section 3 of that Act,

if with respect to that assessment or decision, as the case may be, an amount has been deducted or may be deductible under paragraph 60(o) in computing the taxpayer's income;

**Related Provisions**: 60(o) — Expense of objection or appeal; 152(1.2) — Rule applies to determination of losses as well as assessment.

**Notes**: 56(1)(l) amended by 1979 Budget to extend the scope of costs and reimbursements recognized. For an award or reimbursement of costs that were incurred before December 12, 1979, delete subpara. (iii) and, in subpara. (i), read "under this Act" in place of "referred to in paragraph 60(o)".

56(1)(l)(ii) amended by 1996 EI bill, effective July 12, 1996, to change "Unemployment Insurance" to "Employment Insurance"; and then recorrected by 1995-97 technical bill, effective June 30, 1996, to add *Unemployment Insurance Act* back (since procedures under the old UI Act are still ongoing).

**Interpretation Bulletins**: IT-99R5: Legal and accounting fees.

(l.1) **idem** — amounts received by the taxpayer in the year as an award or a reimbursement in respect of legal expenses (other than those relating to a division or settlement of property arising out of, or on a breakdown of, a marriage or common-law partnership) paid to collect or establish a right to a retiring allowance or a benefit under a pension fund or plan (other than a benefit under the *Canada Pension Plan* or a provincial pension plan as defined in section 3 of that Act) in respect of employment;

**Related Provisions**: 60(o.1) — Deductions in computing income — legal expenses in respect of retiring allowances and pension benefits.

**Notes**: 56(1)(l.1) amended by 2000 same-sex partners bill to add reference to "common-law partnership", effective for the 2001 and later taxation years, or earlier by election (see Notes to 248(1)"common-law partner").

Previously amended by 1992 technical bill, effective 1993, due to the new definition of "marriage" in 252(4)(b). For 1986 to 1992, read "arising from a marriage or other conjugal relationship" instead of "arising out of, or on a breakdown of, a marriage".

56(1)(l.1) added by 1989 Budget, effective for amounts received in 1986 or later years, other than amounts received as an award or reimbursement in respect of legal expenses paid before 1986. This parallels the application of 60(o.1).

**Interpretation Bulletins**: IT-99R5: Legal and accounting fees.

(m) [Repealed]

**Related Provisions**: 60(n) — Deduction of overpayment of pension or benefits; 153(1)(i) — Withholding of tax at source; 248(1) — Extended meaning of "personal or living expenses".

**Notes**: 56(1)(m) repealed by 1996 employment insurance bill, effective 1998. From August 2, 1982 through 1997, read:

(m) training allowance — amounts received by the taxpayer in the year as or on account of a training allowance paid to the taxpayer under the *National Training Act*, except to the extent that they were paid to the taxpayer as or on account of an allowance for the taxpayer's personal or living expenses while the taxpayer was away from home;

**Regulations**: 200(2)(c) (information return).

**Interpretation Bulletins**: IT-75R3: Scholarships, fellowships, bursaries, prizes, and research grants; IT-337R3: Retiring allowances.

(n) **scholarships, bursaries, etc.** — the amount, if any, by which

(i) the total of all amounts (other than amounts described in paragraph (q), amounts received in the course of business, and amounts received in respect of, in the course of or by virtue of an office or employment) received by the taxpayer in the year, each of which is an amount received by the taxpayer as or on account of a scholarship, fellowship or bursary, or a prize for achievement in a field of endeavour ordinarily carried on by the taxpayer (other than a prescribed prize),

exceeds the greater of $500 and the total of all amounts each of which is the lesser of

(ii) the amount included under subparagraph (i) for the year in respect of a scholarship, fellowship, bursary or prize that is to be used by the taxpayer in the production of a literary, dramatic, musical or artistic work, and

(iii) the total of all amounts each of which is an expense incurred by the taxpayer in the year for the purpose of fulfilling the conditions under which the amount described in subparagraph (ii) was received, other than

(A) personal or living expenses of the taxpayer (except expenses in respect of travel, meals and lodging incurred by the taxpayer in the course of fulfilling those conditions and while absent from the taxpayer's usual place of residence for the period to which the scholarship, fellowship, bursary or prize, as the case may be, relates),

(B) expenses for which the taxpayer was reimbursed, and

(C) expenses that are otherwise deductible in computing the taxpayer's income;

exceeds

**Proposed Amendment — 56(1)(n) closing words**

(ii) the taxpayer's scholarship exemption for the year computed under subsection (3);

**Application**: The December 21, 2000 draft legislation, subsec. 22(1), will amend the closing words of para. 56(1)(n), applicable to 2000 *et seq.*

**Technical Notes**: Paragraph 56(1)(n) provides for the inclusion in a taxpayer's income for a year of certain scholarships, fellowships, bursaries and prizes for achievement, to the extent that the total of such amounts received in the year exceeds $500. The addition of subparagraph 56(1)(n)(ii) and subsection 56(3) provide for an additional $2,500 exemption for scholarships, fellow-

S. 56(1)(n) — Income Tax Act, Part I, Division B

ships and bursaries received by a taxpayer in connection with the taxpayer's enrolment in a program in respect of which the taxpayer may claim the education tax credit.

**Related Provisions**: 56(1)(p) — Amounts to be included in income — refund of scholarships, bursaries and research grants; 56(3) — Amount of scholarship exemption; 60(q) — Refund of income payments; 62(1) — Moving expenses; 63(3)"earned income"(b), 64(b)(i)(A) — Amount under 56(1)(n) is earned income for child care expenses and for attendant deduction; 115(2)(a)–(b.1), 115(2)(e)(ii) — Non-resident's taxable income earned in Canada; 248(1) — Extended meaning of "personal or living expenses"; Canada-U.S. tax treaty, Art. XX — Students.

**Notes**: 56(1)(n)(ii) and (iii), allowing an artist who receives a project grant to deduct expenses against it, added by 1991 technical bill, effective 1987.

**Regulations**: 200(2)(a) (information return); 7700 (prescribed prize).

**Interpretation Bulletins**: IT-75R3: Scholarships, fellowships, bursaries, prizes and research grants; IT-178R3: Moving expenses; IT-257R: Canada Council grants; IT-340R: Scholarships, fellowships, bursaries and research grants — forgivable loans, repayable awards, etc.; IT-515R2: Education tax credit; IT-516R2: Tuition tax credit.

(o) **research grants** — the amount, if any, by which any grant received by the taxpayer in the year to enable the taxpayer to carry on research or any similar work exceeds the total of expenses incurred by the taxpayer in the year for the purpose of carrying on the work, other than

(i) personal or living expenses of the taxpayer except travel expenses (including the entire amount expended for meals and lodging) incurred by the taxpayer while away from home in the course of carrying on the work,

(ii) expenses in respect of which the taxpayer has been reimbursed, or

(iii) expenses that are otherwise deductible in computing the taxpayer's income for the year;

**Related Provisions**: 60(q) — Refund of income payments; 62(1) — Moving expenses; 63(3)"earned income"(b), 64(b)(i)(A) — Amount under 56(1)(o) is earned income for child care expenses and for attendant deduction; 115(2)(b.1), 115(2)(e)(ii) — Non-resident's taxable income earned in Canada; 146(1)"earned income"(b) — Amount under 56(1)(o) is earned income for RRSP; 248(1) — Extended meaning of "personal or living expenses"; Canada-U.S. tax treaty, Art. XX — Students.

**Regulations**: 200(2)(b) (information return).

**Interpretation Bulletins**: IT-75R3: Scholarships, fellowships, bursaries, prizes and research grants; IT-178R3: Moving expenses; IT-257R: Canada Council grants; IT-340R: Scholarships, fellowships, bursaries, business and research grants — forgivable loans and repayable awards, etc.

(p) **refund of scholarships, bursaries and research grants** — amounts as described in paragraph 60(q) received by the taxpayer in the year from an individual;

**Related Provisions**: 56(1)(n) — Scholarships, bursaries, etc.; 60(q) — Refund of income payments.

**Interpretation Bulletins**: IT-340R: Scholarships, fellowships, bursaries, and research grants — forgivable loans and repayable awards.

(q) **education savings plan payments** — amounts in respect of a registered education savings plan required by section 146.1 to be included in computing the taxpayer's income for the year;

**Related Provisions**: 146.1(7) — Amounts to be included in beneficiary's income; 212(1)(r) — RESP payments to non-residents.

**Interpretation Bulletins**: IT-75R3: Scholarships, fellowships, bursaries, prizes and research grants.

(r) **financial assistance** — amounts received in the year by the taxpayer as

(i) earnings supplements provided under a project sponsored by a government or government agency in Canada to encourage individuals to obtain or keep employment,

(ii) financial assistance under a program established by the Canada Employment Insurance Commission under Part II of the *Employment Insurance Act*, or

(iii) financial assistance under a program that is

(A) established by a government or government agency in Canada or by an organization,

(B) similar to a program established under Part II of that Act, and

(C) the subject of an agreement between the government, government agency or organization and the Canada Employment Insurance Commission because of section 63 of that Act;

**Related Provisions**: 56(1)(u) — Inclusion of social assistance payments generally (subject to offsetting deduction); 60(n)(iii) — "Deduction for amounts repaid"; 63(3)"earned income"(b), 64(b)(i)(A) — Amount under 56(1)(n) is earned income for child care expenses and for attendant deduction; 153(1)(s) — Withholding of tax at source.

**Notes**: 56(1)(r) added by 1995-97 technical bill, subpara. (i) effective for 1993 and later taxation years, and subparas. (ii) and (iii) effective July 1996.

Former 56(1)(r), repealed by 1985 Budget, dealt with amounts received from a registered home ownership savings plan (RHOSP, former 146.2).

**Regulations**: 100(1)"remuneration"(h) (withholding at source).

(s) **grants under prescribed programs** — the amount of any grant received in the year under a prescribed program of the Government of Canada relating to home insulation or energy conversion by

(i) the taxpayer, other than a married taxpayer or a taxpayer who is in a common-law partnership who resided with the taxpayer's spouse or common-law partner at the time the grant was received and whose income for the year is less than the taxpayer's spouse's or common-law partner's income for the year, or

(ii) the spouse or common-law partner of the taxpayer with whom the taxpayer resided at the time the grant was received, if the spouse's or common-law partner's income for the year is less than the taxpayer's income for the year to the extent that the amount is not required by paragraph 12(1)(u) to be included in computing the taxpayer's or the taxpayer's spouse's or common-law partner's income for the year or a subsequent year;

**Related Provisions**: 56(9) — Definition of "income for the year"; 13(7.1)(b.1) — Deemed capital cost of certain property.

**Notes**: There is no tax on grants relating to the 1998 ice storm, for personal losses or where the amounts were spent to replace destroyed rental or business properties. See Revenue Canada news release, March 11, 1999. See also the *Ice Storm Employee Benefits Remission Order*.

56(1)(s) amended by 2000 same-sex partners bill to add reference to "common-law partner" and "common-law partnership", effective for the 2001 and later taxation years, or earlier by election (see Notes to 248(1)"common-law partner").

**Regulations**: 224 (information return); 5500, 5501 (prescribed program).

**Interpretation Bulletins**: IT-273R2: Government assistance — general comments.

**(t) registered retirement income fund** — amounts in respect of a registered retirement income fund required by section 146.3 to be included in computing the taxpayer's income for the year;

**Related Provisions**: 60.2(1) — Refund of undeducted past service AVCs; 139.1(11), (12) — Conversion benefit on demutualization of insurance corporation; 146.3(5), (5.1), (7) — Benefits taxable; 153(1)(l) — Withholding of tax at source; 212(1)(q) — RRIF payments to non-residents.

**Regulations**: 215 (information return).

**Forms**: T2205: Calculation of amounts from a spousal RRSP or RRIF to be included in income.

**(u) social assistance [welfare] payments** — a social assistance payment made on the basis of a means, needs or income test and received in the year by

(i) the taxpayer, other than a married taxpayer or a taxpayer who is in a common-law partnership who resided with the taxpayer's spouse or common-law partner at the time the payment was received and whose income for the year is less than the spouse's or common-law partner's income for the year, or

(ii) the taxpayer's spouse or common-law partner, if the taxpayer resided with the spouse or common-law partner at the time the payment was received and if the spouse's or common-law partner's income for the year is less than the taxpayer's income for the year,

except to the extent that the payment is otherwise required to be included in computing the income for a taxation year of the taxpayer or the taxpayer's spouse or common-law partner;

**Related Provisions**: 56(1)(r) — Inclusion of social assistance payments intended to supplement employment income (with no offsetting deduction); 56(9) — Definition of "income for the year"; 81(1)(h) — Exemption for payments to foster care givers; 110(1)(f) — Offsetting deduction.

**Notes**: 56(1)(u) covers not only welfare (social assistance) payments from government and municipalities, but also payments by charities to poor people. See "Payments for Relief of Poverty" in Drache, 7(4) *Canadian Not-For-Profit News* (Carswell), 29-30 (April 1999); and VIEWS doc. # 9825265.

Although an amount is included in income under 56(1)(u), an offsetting deduction in computing taxable income is available under 110(1)(f). Thus, the only effect is on net income, which affects various things such as the Child Tax Benefit, the GST credit, the medical expense credit and the ability of another person to claim the taxpayer as a dependant.

The CCRA requires amounts to be reported on the return as required by 56(1)(u), and the offsetting deduction claimed. Before 1992, the policy as set out in the T1 General tax return and guide was that such amounts should not be included in income (except on certain forms) even though the Act required it.

56(1)(u) amended by 2000 same-sex partners bill to add reference to "common-law partner" and "common-law partnership", effective for the 2001 and later taxation years, or earlier by election (see Notes to 248(1)"common-law partner").

Closing words of 56(1)(u) amended by 1995-97 technical bill, effective for 1993 and later taxation years, to delete the words "from a business or property" after "taxation year".

56(1)(u) amended by 1991 technical bill, retroactive to 1982. Payments related to foster care are now excluded by 81(1)(h), and so do not enter the "net income" calculation.

**Regulations**: 233 (information return).

**Forms**: T4115: T5007 guide — return of benefits [guide]; T5007 Summ: Return of benefit payments — summary; T5007 Supp: Statement of benefit payments.

**(v) workers' compensation** — compensation received under an employees' or workers' compensation law of Canada or a province in respect of an injury, a disability or death;

**Related Provisions**: 110(1)(f) — Offsetting deduction.

**Notes**: Although an amount is included in income under 56(1)(v), an offsetting deduction in computing taxable income is available under 110(1)(f). Thus, the only effect is on net income, which affects various things such as the Child Tax Benefit, the GST credit, medical expense credit and the ability of another person to claim the taxpayer as a dependant.

The CCRA requires amounts to be reported on the return under 56(1)(v), and the offsetting deduction claimed. Before 1992, the policy as set out in the T1 General tax return and guide was that such amounts should not be included in income (except on certain forms) even though the Act required it.

In *Hepburn*, 77 D.T.C. 29 (TRB), payments from the Toronto Fire Dept. Superannuation and Benefit Fund to an injured fireman were considered to be a substitution for a provincial workers' compensation plan, and thus were exempt under the predecessor to 56(1)(v) (former 81(1)(h)).

For detailed CCRA policy on the circumstances when an amount paid by an employer (keeping the employee on salary while waiting for a decision on a claim) may be considered to be a workers' compensation payment, see Revenue Canada notice "Workers' Compensation Awards", Sept. 9, 1999 (in PITA 17th or 18th ed., or search on www.ccra-adrc.gc.ca).

The CCRA announced the following on November 3, 2000 (*Employers' Guide — Taxable Benefits*):

*Workers' compensation awards — Top-up amount*

There have been changes in how to treat top-up amounts paid while an employee is waiting for a workers' compensation award and top-up amounts funded by sick leave credits.

A top-up amount is an amount you pay your employee, in addition to the amount of a workers' compensation award the employee is paid by a workers' compensation board.

Exclude a top-up amount (even if it is paid as sick leave) from insurable earnings if you pay it after the claim is accepted by the workers' compensation board. However, the top-up amount is subject to CPP contributions and income tax, and you have to report it on a T4 slip at year end.

An amount you pay in addition to an advance or a loan is not a top-up amount if you pay it while waiting for a decision on a workers' compensation board claim. This amount is considered employment income, and you have to withhold CPP contributions, EI premiums, and income tax.

For withholding purposes, these changes will take effect on January 1, 2001.

**Regulations**: 232 (information return).

**Interpretation Bulletins**: IT-202R2: Employees' or workers' compensation.

**Forms**: T4115: T5007 guide — return of benefits [guide]; T5007 Summ: Return of benefit payments — summary; T5007 Supp: Statement of benefit payments.

(w) **salary deferral arrangement** — the total of all amounts each of which is an amount received by the taxpayer as a benefit (other than an amount received by or from a trust governed by a salary deferral arrangement) in the year out of or under a salary deferral arrangement in respect of a person other than the taxpayer except to the extent that the amount, or another amount that may reasonably be considered to relate thereto, has been included in computing the income of that other person for the year or for any preceding taxation year;

**Related Provisions**: 6(1)(i) — Inclusions — salary deferral arrangement payments; 6(11) — Salary deferral arrangement.

(x) **retirement compensation arrangement** — any amount, including a return of contributions, received in the year by the taxpayer or another person, other than an amount required to be included in that other person's income for a taxation year under paragraph 12(1)(n.3), out of or under a retirement compensation arrangement that can reasonably be considered to have been received in respect of an office or employment of the taxpayer;

**Related Provisions**: 56(11) — Disposition of property by RCA trust; 60(j.1) — Transfer of retiring allowances; 60(t) — Deductions — amount included under 56(1)(x); 149(1)(q.1) — RCA trust — exempt from Part I tax; 107.2 — Distribution by RCA to beneficiary; 153(1)(q) — Withholding of tax at source; 160.3 — Liability in respect of amounts received out of or under RCA trust; 207.6(7) — Transfer from RCA to another RCA; 212(1)(j) — Non-resident withholding tax.

**Notes**: See Notes to 248(1)"retirement compensation arrangement".

**Regulations**: 100(1)"remuneration"(b.1) (withholding at source).

**Interpretation Bulletins**: IT-499R: Superannuation or pension benefits.

**Forms**: T4A-RCA Summ: Return of distributions from an RCA; T4A-RCA Supp: Statement of amounts paid from an RCA; T4041: Retirement compensation arrangements guide.

(y) **idem** — any amount received or that became receivable in the year by the taxpayer as proceeds from the disposition of an interest in a retirement compensation arrangement;

**Related Provisions**: 60(u) — Deductions — amount included under 56(1)(y); 153(1)(r) — Withholding of tax at source; 214(3)(b.1) — Non-resident withholding tax — deemed payments.

**Forms**: T4A-RCA Summ: Return of distributions from an RCA; T4A-RCA Supp: Statement of amounts paid from an RCA; T4041: Retirement compensation arrangements guide.

(z) **idem** — the total of all amounts, including a return of contributions, each of which is an amount received in the year by the taxpayer out of or under a retirement compensation arrangement that can reasonably be considered to have been received in respect of an office or employment of a person other than the taxpayer, except to the extent that the amount was required

(i) under paragraph 12(1)(n.3) to be included in computing the taxpayer's income for a taxation year, or

(ii) under paragraph (x) or subsection 70(2) to be included in computing the income for the year of a person resident in Canada other than the taxpayer; and

**Related Provisions**: 56(11) — Disposition of property by RCA trust; 60(t) — Deductions — amount included under 56(1)(z); 153(1)(q) — Withholding of tax at source; 212(1)(j) — Non-resident withholding tax.

**Regulations**: 100(1)"remuneration"(b.1) (withholding at source).

**Forms**: T4A-RCA Summ: Return of distributions from an RCA; T4A-RCA Supp: Statement of amounts paid from an RCA; T4041: Retirement compensation arrangements guide.

**Interpretation Bulletins**: IT-499R: Superannuation or pension benefits.

(aa) **[benefit from registered national arts service organization]** — the value of benefits received or enjoyed by any person in the year in respect of workshops, seminars, training programs and similar development programs because of the taxpayer's membership in a registered national arts service organization.

**Related Provisions [para. 56(1)(aa)]**: 149.1(6.4) — National arts service organizations.

**Notes**: 56(1)(aa) added by 1991 technical bill, effective July 14, 1990.

**(1.1) Application of subsec. 12.2(11)** — The definitions in subsection 12.2(11) apply to paragraph (1)(d).

**Notes**: 56(1.1) added in the R.S.C. 1985 (5th Supp.) consolidation, effective for taxation years beginning after November 1991. This rule was formerly in the opening words of 12.2(11).

**(2) Indirect payments** — A payment or transfer of property made pursuant to the direction of, or with the concurrence of, a taxpayer to some other person for the benefit of the taxpayer or as a benefit that the taxpayer desired to have conferred on the other person (other than by an assignment of any portion of a retirement pension pursuant to section 65.1 of the *Canada Pension Plan* or a comparable provision of a provincial pension plan as defined in section 3 of that Act or of a prescribed provincial pension plan) shall be included in computing the taxpayer's income to the extent that it would be if the payment or transfer had been made to the taxpayer.

**Related Provisions**: 56(5) — 56(2) does not apply to income subject to income-splitting tax; 74.1–74.5 — Attribution rules; 80.04(5.1) — No benefit conferred where debtor transfers property to eligible transferee under 80.04; 135(4)"payment"(c) — Patronage dividend payments; 212(2), 214(3)(a) — Non-resident withholding tax; 246 — Benefit conferred on a person.

**Notes**: In *Neuman*, [1998] 3 C.T.C. 177, the Supreme Court of Canada ruled that 56(2) could not apply to dividends in a family income-splitting situation. Specifically, a shareholder need not contribute any services to the corporation to be entitled to a dividend; and a dividend, had it not been declared, would not otherwise have been included in any other taxpayer's income (since the dividend belongs to the corporation until it is declared).

Revenue Canada confirmed at the 1998 Canadian Tax Foundation annual conference (p. 52:3) that it accepts the *Neuman* decision and will not apply GAAR to such cases. The person directing a payment must have a pre-existing entitlement to the funds for 56(2) to apply. Note however that 74.4 can apply to some income-splitting done through a corporation. (See Income Tax Technical News No. 16.)

**Regulations**: 7800(1) (prescribed provincial pension plan).

**Interpretation Bulletins**: IT-75R3: Scholarships, fellowships, bursaries, prizes, and research grants; IT-335R: Indirect payments; IT-362R: Patronage dividends; IT-385R2: Disposition of an income interest in a trust; IT-415R2: Deregistration of registered retirement savings plans; IT-432R: Benefits conferred on shareholders.

**I.T. Technical News**: No. 16 (*Neuman* case).

**Advance Tax Rulings**: ATR-3: Winding-up of an estate; ATR-14: Non-arm's length interest charges; ATR-15: Employee stock option plan; ATR-17: Employee benefit plan — purchase of company shares; ATR-22R: Estate freeze using share exchange; ATR-27: Exchange and acquisition of interests in capital properties through rollovers and winding-up ("butterfly"); ATR-29: Amalgamation of social clubs; ATR-35: Partitioning of assets to get specific ownership ("butterfly"); ATR-36: Estate freeze.

**(3)** [Repealed under former Act]

### Proposed Addition — 56(3)

**(3) Exemption for scholarships, fellowships, bursaries and prizes** — For the purpose of subparagraph (1)(n)(ii), a taxpayer's scholarship exemption for a taxation year is the greatest of

(a) $500,

(b) the lesser of

(i) $3,000 and

(ii) the total of all amounts each of which is the amount included under subparagraph (1)(n)(i) in computing the taxpayer's income for the year in respect of a scholarship, fellowship or bursary received in connection with the taxpayer's enrolment in an educational program in respect of which an amount may be deducted under subsection 118.6(2) in computing the taxpayer's tax payable under this Part for the year, and

(c) the total of all amounts each of which is the lesser of

(i) the amount included under subparagraph (1)(n)(i) in computing the taxpayer's income for the year in respect of a scholarship, fellowship, bursary or prize that is to be used by the taxpayer in the production of a literary, dramatic, musical or artistic work, and

(ii) the total of all amounts each of which is an expense incurred by the taxpayer in the year for the purpose of fulfilling the conditions under which the amount described in subparagraph (i) was received, other than

(A) personal or living expenses of the taxpayer (except expenses in respect of travel, meals and lodging incurred by the taxpayer in the course of fulfilling those conditions and while absent from the taxpayer's usual place of residence for the period to which the scholarship, fellowship, bursary or prize, as the case may be, relates),

(B) expenses for which the taxpayer is entitled to be reimbursed, and

(C) expenses that are otherwise deductible in computing the taxpayer's income.

**Application**: The December 21, 2000 draft legislation, subsec. 22(2), will add subsec. 56(3), applicable to 2000 *et seq*.

**Technical Notes**: See under 56(1)(n) closing words.

**Notice of Ways and Means Motion, federal budget, February 28, 2000**: *Scholarships, Fellowships and Bursaries*

(25) That, for the 2000 and subsequent taxation years, the $500 exemption in respect of the total of all amounts received in the year by an individual on account of scholarships, fellowships, bursaries and certain prizes be increased by $2,500 for scholarships, fellowships and bursaries received by the individual in connection with the individual's enrolment at a designated educational institution in a program in respect of which the individual may claim the education tax credit.

**Federal budget, supplementary information, February 28, 2000**: *Partial Exemption for Scholarships, Fellowships and Bursaries*

The first $500 of scholarship, fellowship or bursary income received in a year has been excluded from income for tax purposes since 1972.

In order to provide additional assistance to students, the budget proposes to increase the annual exemption to $3,000, beginning with the 2000 taxation year. The $2,500 increase in the exemption will apply only to amounts received by a student where that student enrols in a program which entitles the student to claim the education tax credit. Generally, this includes programs at a post-secondary level and programs at educational institutions certified by the Minister of Human Resources Development that furnish or improve skills in an occupation.

**Notes**: Note the extended definition of "personal and living expenses" in 248(1).

**Notes**: Former 56(3) repealed by 1988 tax reform, except for any one or more transactions, one of which was entered into before April 13, 1988, that were entered into by a taxpayer in the course of an arrangement and in respect of which the taxpayer received from Revenue Canada, before April 13, 1988, a confirmation or opinion in writing with respect to the tax consequences thereof. (This parallels the introduction of the general anti-avoidance rule in s. 245.) It deemed certain undistributed amounts to have been received by the taxpayer.

**(4) Transfer of rights to income** — Where a taxpayer has, at any time before the end of a taxation year, transferred or assigned to a person with whom the taxpayer was not dealing at arm's length the right to an amount (other than any portion of a retirement pension assigned by the taxpayer under section 65.1 of the *Canada Pension Plan* or a comparable provision of a provincial pension plan as defined in section 3 of that Act) that would, if the right had not been so transferred or assigned, be included in computing the taxpayer's income for the taxation year, the part of the amount that relates to the period in the year throughout which the taxpayer is resident in Canada shall be included in computing the taxpayer's income for the year unless the income is from property and the taxpayer has also transferred or assigned the property.

**Related Provisions**: 56(5) — 56(4) does not apply to income subject to income-splitting tax; 82(2) — Dividends deemed received by taxpayer; 212(12) — No non-resident withholding tax where income attributed.

**Notes**: 56(4) amended by 1993 technical bill, effective for 1992 and later taxation years.

**Regulations**: 7800(1) (prescribed provincial pension plan).

**Interpretation Bulletins**: IT-440R2: Transfer of rights to income; IT-499R: Superannuation or pension benefits.

**(4.1) Interest free or low interest loans** — Where

(a) a particular individual (other than a trust) or a trust in which the particular individual is beneficially interested has, directly or indirectly by means of a trust or by any means whatever, received a loan from or become indebted to

(i) another individual (in this subsection referred to as the "creditor") who

(A) does not deal at arm's length with the particular individual, and

(B) is not a trust, or

(ii) a trust (in this subsection referred to as the "creditor trust") to which another individual (in this subsection referred to as the "original transferor") who

(A) does not deal at arm's length with the particular individual,

(B) was resident in Canada at any time in the period during which the loan or indebtedness is outstanding, and

(C) is not a trust,

has, directly or indirectly by means of a trust or by any means whatever, transferred property, and

(b) it can reasonably be considered that one of the main reasons for making the loan or incurring the indebtedness was to reduce or avoid tax by causing income from

(i) the loaned property,

(ii) property that the loan or indebtedness enabled or assisted the particular individual, or the trust in which the particular individual is beneficially interested, to acquire, or

(iii) property substituted for property referred to in subparagraph (i) or (ii)

to be included in the income of the particular individual,

the following rules apply:

(c) any income of the particular individual for a taxation year from the property referred to in paragraph (b) that relates to the period or periods in the year throughout which the creditor or the creditor trust, as the case may be, was resident in Canada and the particular individual was not dealing at arm's length with the creditor or the original transferor, as the case may be, shall be deemed,

(i) where subparagraph (a)(i) applies, to be income of the creditor for that year and not of the particular individual except to the extent that

(A) section 74.1 applies or would, but for subsection 74.5(3), apply, or

(B) subsection 75(2) applies

to that income, and

(ii) where subparagraph (a)(ii) applies, to be income of the creditor trust for that year and not of the particular individual except to the extent that

(A) subparagraph (i) applies,

(B) section 74.1 applies or would, but for subsection 74.5(3), apply, or

(C) subsection 75(2) applies (otherwise than because of paragraph (d))

to that income; and

(d) where subsection 75(2) applies to any of the property referred to in paragraph (b) and subparagraph (c)(ii) applies to income from the property, subsection 75(2) applies after subparagraph (c)(ii) is applied.

**Related Provisions**: 56(4.2) — Loans for value; 56(5) — 56(4.1) does not apply to income subject to income-splitting tax; 74.4(2) — Transfers and loan to corporation; 82(2) — Dividends deemed received by taxpayer; 96(1.8) — Transfer or loan of partnership interest; 212(12) — No non-resident withholding tax where income attributed; 248(5) — Substituted property; 248(25) — Meaning of "beneficially interested"; 250(6.1) — Creditor trust that ceases to exist deemed resident throughout year.

**Notes**: 56(4.1) is an attribution rule of more limited application than 74.1–74.5. It applies only to loans (not transfers), and only where income-splitting is one of the main reasons for the loan (or indebtedness). However, it applies to income-splitting with adult taxpayers, whereas 74.1 to 74.5 apply only in respect of spouses and minor children.

The phrase "beneficially interested" used in 56(4.1)(a), is defined in 248(25). Before 1991, 56(4.1)(a) referred explicitly to 74.5(10), which provided the same definition.

56(4.1) amended by 1991 technical bill, effective for income relating to periods beginning in 1991. For income relating to 1989 and 1990, it was much simpler.

56(4.1)(b)(ii) amended by 1993 technical bill, effective for income relating to periods that begin after December 21, 1992, to add the words "or the trust in which the particular individual is beneficially interested".

**Interpretation Bulletins**: IT-394R2: Preferred beneficiary election; IT-511R: Interspousal and certain other transfers and loans of property.

**(4.2) Exception** — Notwithstanding any other provision of this Act, subsection (4.1) does not apply to any income derived in a particular taxation year where

(a) interest was charged on the loan or indebtedness at a rate equal to or greater than the lesser of

(i) the prescribed rate of interest in effect at the time the loan was made or the indebtedness arose, and

(ii) the rate that would, having regard to all the circumstances, have been agreed on, at the time the loan was made or the indebtedness arose, between parties dealing with each other at arm's length;

(b) the amount of interest that was payable in respect of the particular year in respect of the loan or indebtedness was paid not later than 30 days after the end of the particular year; and

(c) the amount of interest that was payable in respect of each taxation year preceding the particular year in respect of the loan or indebtedness was paid not later than 30 days after the end of each of those preceding taxation years.

**Notes**: 56(4.2) amended by 1991 technical bill, effective for income relating to periods beginning in 1991, in consequence of changes to 56(4.1).

**Regulations**: 4301(c) (prescribed rate of interest).

**Interpretation Bulletins**: IT-511R: Interspousal and certain other transfers and loans of property.

**(4.3) Repayment of existing indebtedness** — For the purposes of subsection (4.1), where at any time a particular property is used to repay, in whole or in part, a loan or indebtedness that enabled or assisted an individual to acquire another property, there shall be included in computing the income from the particular property that proportion of the income or loss, as the case may be, derived after that time from the other property or from property substituted therefor that the amount so repaid is of the cost to the individual of the other property, but for greater certainty nothing in this subsection shall affect the application of subsection (4.1) to any income or loss derived from the other property or from property substituted therefor.

**Related Provisions**: 248(5) — Substituted property.

**Notes**: 56(4.3) amended by 1991 technical bill, effective for income relating to periods beginning in 1991, in consequence of changes to 56(4.1).

**Interpretation Bulletins**: IT-511R: Interspousal and certain other transfers and loans of property.

**(5) Exception for split income** — Subsections (2), (4) and (4.1) do not apply to any amount that is included in computing a specified individual's split income for a taxation year.

**Notes**: 56(5) added by 1999 Budget, effective for 2000 and later taxation years. For former 56(5) see Notes to 56(6), (7) below.

**(6), (7)** [Repealed]

**Notes**: Former 56(5), (6) and (7) repealed by 1992 Child Benefit bill, effective 1993. They provided that family allowance payments were included in the income of the higher-income spouse. Family allowances were discontinued as of January 1993, and replaced with non-taxable Child Tax Benefit payments under 122.61.

56(7)(a) previously amended by 1991 technical bill, retroactive to 1988, to correct an unintended result where one (unmarried) parent receives family allowances for a child and the other parent claimed the equivalent-to-married credit for the same child.

**(8) CPP/QPP benefits for previous years** — Notwithstanding subsection (1), where

(a) one or more amounts are received by an individual (other than a trust) in a taxation year as, on account of, in lieu of payment of or in satisfaction of, any benefit under the *Canada Pension Plan* or a provincial pension plan as defined in section 3 of that Act, and

(b) a portion, not less than $300, of the total of those amounts relates to one or more preceding taxation years,

that portion shall, at the option of the individual, not be included in the individual's income.

**Related Provisions**: 120.2 — General deferral rule for lump-sum payments; 120.3 — CPP/QPP benefits for previous years; 146(1)"earned income"(b.1) — RRSP — earned income includes amount under 56(8)(a).

**Notes**: 56(8) allows CPP/QPP benefits relating to an earlier year to be taxed in the current year at the earlier year's marginal rate, under 120.3, so that a lump sum received in one year will not push a lower-income individual into a higher bracket if it otherwise would have been taxed at lower rates over several years. Although the closing words of 56(8) say "at the option of the individual", there is no election to make; the CCRA calculates and applies this option automatically if it will result in less tax. (T1 General Income Tax Guide, Line 114.)

A more general retroactive averaging rule for lump-sum payments is now found in 120.2.

56(8) added by 1991 Budget, effective 1990, and para. (a) amended by 1997 Budget to change "a disability pension" to "any benefit", effective for amounts received after 1994, except by an individual to whom a tax has been remitted under subsec. 23(2) of the *Financial Administration Act* in respect of the amounts in question (i.e., a remission order has been granted).

**(9) Meaning of "income for the year"** — For the purposes of paragraphs (1)(s) and (u), "income for the year" of a person means the amount that would, but for those paragraphs, paragraphs 60(v.1) and (w) and section 63, be the income of that person for the year.

**Notes**: 56(9) amended by 1992 Child Benefit bill, effective 1993 (See Notes to repealed 56(5)). For 1989 through 1992, read:

(9) Definition of "income for the year" — For the purposes of paragraphs (1)(s) and (u) and subsection (6), "income for the year" of a person means the amount that would, but for

those paragraphs, subsection (5), paragraphs 60(v.1) and (w) and section 63, be the income of that person for the year.

**(10) Severability of retirement compensation arrangement** — Where a retirement compensation arrangement is part of a plan or arrangement (in this subsection referred to as the "plan") under which amounts not related to the retirement compensation arrangement are payable or provided, for the purposes of this Act, other than this subsection,

(a) the retirement compensation arrangement shall be deemed to be a separate arrangement independent of other parts of the plan of which it is a part; and

(b) subject to subsection 6(14), amounts paid out of or under the plan shall be deemed to have first been paid out of the retirement compensation arrangement unless a provision in the plan otherwise provides.

**(11) Disposition of property by RCA trust** — For the purposes of paragraphs (1)(x) and (z), where, at any time in a year, a trust governed by a retirement compensation arrangement

(a) disposes of property to a person for consideration less than the fair market value of the property at the time of the disposition, or for no consideration,

(b) acquires property from a person for consideration greater than the fair market value of the property at the time of the acquisition, or

(c) permits a person to use or enjoy property of the trust for no consideration or for consideration less than the fair market value of such use or enjoyment,

the amount, if any, by which such fair market value differs from the consideration or, if there is no consideration, the amount of the fair market value shall be deemed to be an amount received at that time by the person out of or under the arrangement that can reasonably be considered to have been received in respect of an office or employment of a taxpayer.

**Related Provisions**: 69(1) — General rule deeming disposition to be at fair market value.

**Notes**: This rule is similar to 69(1) but does not require that the disposition be to a non-arm's length person.

**(12) [Repealed]**

**Notes**: 56(12) repealed by 1996 Budget, effective for amounts received after 1996. This rule is now included in the opening words of 56.1(4)"support amount". For amounts received before 1997, read:

(12) Definition of "allowance" — Subject to subsections 56.1(2) and 60.1(2), for the purposes of paragraphs (1)(b), (c) and (c.1) (in this subsection referred to as the "former paragraphs") and 60(b), (c) and (c.1) (in this subsection referred to as the "latter paragraphs"), "allowance" does not include any amount that is received by a person, referred to in the former paragraphs as "the taxpayer" and in the latter paragraphs as "the recipient", unless that person has discretion as to the use of the amount.

56(12) added by 1988 tax reform, effective for decrees, orders, judgments and written agreements made or entered into before March 28, 1986 or after 1987. For those made or entered into from March 29, 1986 through the end of 1987, where amounts were paid before 1997, 56(12) did not apply. See the 1986 Supreme Court of Canada decision of *Gagnon*, [1986] 1 C.T.C. 410, instead.

**Definitions [s. 56]**: "allowance" — 56(12); "amount" — 248(1); "anniversary day" — 12.2(11), 56(1.1); "annuity" — 248(1); "arm's length" — 251(1); "assessment" — 248(1); "beneficially interested" — 248(25); "borrowed money", "business" — 248(1); "Canada" — 255; "child" — 252(1); "child support amount", "commencement day" — 56.1(4); "common-law partner", "common-law partnership" — 248(1); "consequence of the death" — 248(8); "death benefit" — 248(1); "deferred profit sharing plan" — 147(1), 248(1); "employee benefit plan", "employment" — 248(1); "estate" — 104(1), 248(1); "foreign retirement arrangement" — 248(1); "income for the year" — 56(9); "income-averaging annuity contract" — 61(4), 248(1); "individual", "insurer" — 248(1); "office" — 248(1); "parent" — 252(2); "person", "personal or living expenses", "prescribed" — 248(1); "prescribed rate" — Reg. 4301; "property" — 248(1); "province" — *Interpretation Act* 35(1); "received" — 248(7); "registered education savings plan" — 146.1(1), 248(1); "registered retirement income fund" — 146.3(1), 248(1); "registered retirement savings plan" — 146(1), 248(1); "regulation" — 248(1); "related" — 251(2); "resident in Canada" — 250; "retirement compensation arrangement", "retiring allowance", "salary deferral arrangement" — 248(1); "scholarship exemption" — 56(3); "specified individual", "split income" — 120.4(1), 248(1); "superannuation or pension benefit" — 248(1); "supplementary unemployment benefit plan" — 145(1), 248(1); "support amount" — 56.1(4); "taxation year" — 249; "taxpayer" — 248(1); "trust" — 104(1), 248(1), (3); "writing" — *Interpretation Act* 35(1).

**Interpretation Bulletins [s. 56]**: IT-495R2: Child care expenses.

**56.1 (1) Support** — For the purposes of paragraph 56(1)(b) and subsection 118(5), where an order or agreement, or any variation thereof, provides for the payment of an amount to a taxpayer or for the benefit of the taxpayer, children in the taxpayer's custody or both the taxpayer and those children, the amount or any part thereof

(a) when payable, is deemed to be payable to and receivable by the taxpayer; and

(b) when paid, is deemed to have been paid to and received by the taxpayer.

**Related Provisions**: 60.1(1) — Parallel rule for payer.

**Notes**: Where an amount is included in income by 56.1(1), an offsetting deduction is normally allowed to the payor by 60.1(1).

56.1(1) amended by 1996 Budget, effective for amounts received after 1996. For amounts received before 1997, read:

56.1 (1) Maintenance — Where a decree, order, judgment or written agreement described in paragraph 56(1)(b) or (c), or any variation thereof, provides for the periodic payment of an amount

(a) to a taxpayer by a person who is

(i) the taxpayer's spouse or former spouse, or

(ii) where the amount is paid under an order made by a competent tribunal in accordance with the laws of a province, an individual of the opposite sex who is the natural parent of a child of the taxpayer, or

(b) for the benefit of the taxpayer, children in the custody of the taxpayer or both the taxpayer and those children,

the amount or any part thereof, when paid, shall be deemed for the purposes of paragraphs 56(1)(b) and (c) to have been paid to and received by the taxpayer.

**Interpretation Bulletins**: IT-118R3: Alimony and maintenance; IT-530: Support payments.

**(2) Agreement** — For the purposes of section 56, this section and subsection 118(5), the amount determined by the formula

$$A - B$$

where

A is the total of all amounts each of which is an amount (other than an amount that is otherwise a support amount) that became payable by a person in a taxation year, under an order of a competent tribunal or under a written agreement, in respect of an expense (other than an expenditure in respect of a self-contained domestic establishment in which the person resides or an expenditure for the acquisition of tangible property that is not an expenditure on account of a medical or education expense or in respect of the acquisition, improvement or maintenance of a self-contained domestic establishment in which the taxpayer described in paragraph (a) or (b) resides) incurred in the year or the preceding taxation year for the maintenance of a taxpayer, children in the taxpayer's custody or both the taxpayer and those children, where the taxpayer is

(a) the person's spouse or common-law partner or former spouse or common-law partner, or

(b) where the amount became payable under an order made by a competent tribunal in accordance with the laws of a province, an individual who is the parent of a child of whom the person is a natural parent,

and

B is the amount, if any, by which

(a) the total of all amounts each of which is an amount included in the total determined for A in respect of the acquisition or improvement of a self-contained domestic establishment in which the taxpayer resides, including any payment of principal or interest in respect of a loan made or indebtedness incurred to finance, in any manner whatever, such acquisition or improvement

exceeds

(b) the total of all amounts each of which is an amount equal to $1/5$ of the original principal amount of a loan or indebtedness described in paragraph (a),

is, where the order or written agreement, as the case may be, provides that this subsection and subsection 60.1(2) shall apply to any amount paid or payable thereunder, deemed to be an amount payable to and receivable by the taxpayer as an allowance on a periodic basis, and the taxpayer is deemed to have discretion as to the use of that amount.

**Related Provisions**: 60.1(2) — Parallel rule for payer; 252(3) — Extended meaning of "spouse" and "former spouse".

**Notes**: 56.1(2) amended by 2000 same-sex partners bill to add reference to "common-law partner", effective for the 2001 and later taxation years, or earlier by election (see Notes to 248(1)"common-law partner").

56.1(2) opening words, description of "A" and closing words amended by 1996 Budget, effective for amounts received after 1996. For amounts received before 1997, read:

(2) For the purposes of paragraphs 56(1)(b) and (c), the amount determined by the formula

$$A - B$$

where

A is the total of all amounts each of which is an amount (other than an amount to which paragraph 56(1)(b) or (c) otherwise applies) paid by a person in a taxation year, under a decree, order or judgment of a competent tribunal or under a written agreement, in respect of an expense (other than an expenditure in respect of a self-contained domestic establishment in which the person resides or an expenditure for the acquisition of tangible property that is not an expenditure on account of a medical or education expense or in respect of the acquisition, improvement or maintenance of a self-contained domestic establishment in which the taxpayer described in paragraph (a) or (b) resides) incurred in the year or the preceding taxation year for the maintenance of a taxpayer who is

(a) that person's spouse or former spouse, or

(b) where the amount is paid under an order made by a competent tribunal in accordance with the laws of a province, an individual of the opposite sex who is the natural parent of a child of the person,

or for the maintenance of children in the taxpayer's custody or both the taxpayer and those children if, at the time the expense was incurred and throughout the remainder of the year, the taxpayer was living separate and apart from that person, and

B is the amount, if any, by which

(a) the total of all amounts each of which is an amount included in the total determined for A in respect of the acquisition or improvement of a self-contained domestic establishment in which the taxpayer resides, including any payment of principal or interest in respect of a loan made or indebtedness incurred to finance, in any manner whatever, such acquisition or improvement

exceeds

(b) the total of all amounts each of which is an amount equal to $1/5$ of the original principal amount of a loan or indebtedness described in paragraph (a),

shall, where the decree, order, judgment or written agreement, as the case may be, provides that this subsection and subsection 60.1(2) shall apply to any payment made thereunder, be deemed to be an amount paid by that person and received by the taxpayer as an allowance payable on a periodic basis.

See also Notes at end of 56.1 and Notes to 60.1(2).

**Interpretation Bulletins**: IT-118R3: Alimony and maintenance; IT-530: Support payments.

**(3) Prior payments** — For the purposes of this section and section 56, where a written agreement or order of a competent tribunal made at any time in a taxation year provides that an amount received before that time and in the year or the preceding taxation year is to be considered to have been paid and received thereunder,

(a) the amount is deemed to have been received thereunder; and

(b) the agreement or order is deemed, except for the purpose of this subsection, to have been made on the day on which the first such amount was received, except that, where the agreement or order is made after April 1997 and varies a child support amount payable to the recipient from the last such amount received by the recipient before May 1997, each varied amount of child support received under the agreement or order is deemed to have been receivable under an agreement or order the commencement day of which is the day on which the first payment of the varied amount is required to be made.

**Related Provisions**: 60.1(3) — Parallel rule for payer.

**Notes**: 56.1(3) amended by 1996 Budget, effective for amounts received after 1996. For amounts received before 1997, read:

(3) For the purposes of this section and section 56, where a decree, order or judgment of a competent tribunal or a written agreement made at any time in a taxation year provides that an amount received before that time and in the year or the preceding taxation year is to be considered to have been paid and received thereunder, the amount shall be deemed to have been received thereunder.

The amended version of 56.1(3) has an unusual effect. If an agreement is entered into in, for example, October 1997, it normally would be subject to the new non-deductibility/non-taxability treatment for the child support portion. However, if prior payments began in, for example, August 1996, and the agreement provides that the prior payments are under the agreement (which normally will be done in order to ensure that the spousal portion is deductible to the payer), and the amount of support is not varied, then 56.1(3) deems the agreement to be made in August 1996, and the child support becomes deductible and taxable! If the amount of support is varied, then a new agreement is deemed to be made, and the child support is not deductible or taxable.

**Interpretation Bulletins**: IT-118R3: Alimony and maintenance; IT-530: Support payments.

**(4) Definitions** — The definitions in this subsection apply in this section and section 56.

**"child support amount"** means any support amount that is not identified in the agreement or order under which it is receivable as being solely for the support of a recipient who is a spouse or common-law partner or former spouse or common-law partner of the payer or who is a parent of a child of whom the payer is a natural parent.

**Related Provisions**: 60.1(4) — Definition applies to sections 60 and 60.1; 252(3) — Extended meaning of "spouse" and "former spouse".

**Notes**: 56.1(4)"child support amount" amended by 2000 same-sex partners bill to add reference to "common-law partner", effective for the 2001 and later taxation years, or earlier by election (see Notes to 248(1)"common-law partner").

Definition "child support amount" added by 1996 Budget, effective for amounts received after 1996. A child support amount payable under an agreement made or varied after April 1997 is generally non-taxable and non-deductible, while other (i.e., spousal) support is generally taxable to the recipient and deductible to the payer. See Notes to 56(1)(b).

**Interpretation Bulletins**: IT-530: Support payments.

**"commencement day"** at any time of an agreement or order means

(a) where the agreement or order is made after April 1997, the day it is made; and

(b) where the agreement or order is made before May 1997, the day, if any, that is after April 1997 and is the earliest of

(i) the day specified as the commencement day of the agreement or order by the payer and recipient under the agreement or order in a joint election filed with the Minister in prescribed form and manner,

(ii) where the agreement or order is varied after April 1997 to change the child support amounts payable to the recipient, the day on which the first payment of the varied amount is required to be made,

(iii) where a subsequent agreement or order is made after April 1997, the effect of which is to change the total child support amounts payable to the recipient by the payer, the commencement day of the first such subsequent agreement or order, and

(iv) the day specified in the agreement or order, or any variation thereof, as the commencement day of the agreement or order for the purposes of this Act.

**Related Provisions**: 60.1(4) — Definition applies to sections 60 and 60.1.

**Notes**: Even a minor change to a pre-May/97 agreement or order, such as a change in the date on which child support will terminate several years down the road, may create a "commencement day" and thus put the agreement into the new non-inclusion non-deduction system. See VIEWS doc. 9829185 for a technical interpretation on this point.

Where a court order is made before May 1997 and then varied on appeal, the date of the varied order should still be considered to be before May 1997: *Dennis v. Wilson*, [1999] 2 C.T.C. 175 (Ont. CA).

Definition "commencement day" added by 1996 Budget, effective for amounts received after 1996.

**Interpretation Bulletins**: IT-530: Support payments.

**"support amount"** means an amount payable or receivable as an allowance on a periodic basis for the maintenance of the recipient, children of the recipient or both the recipient and children of the recipient, if the recipient has discretion as to the use of the amount, and

(a) the recipient is the spouse or common-law partner or former spouse or common-law partner of the payer, the recipient and payer are living separate and apart because of the breakdown of their marriage or common-law partnership and the amount is receivable under an order of a competent tribunal or under a written agreement; or

(b) the payer is a natural parent of a child of the recipient and the amount is receivable under an order made by a competent tribunal in accordance with the laws of a province.

## Subdivision d — Other Sources of Income — S. 56.1

**Related Provisions**: 60.1(4) — Definition applies to ss. 60 and 60.1; 118(5) — No personal credit in respect of person to whom support amount payable; 248(1)"exempt income" — Support amount is not exempt income; 252(3) — Extended meaning of "spouse" and "former spouse".

**Notes**: 56.1(4)"support amount" amended by 2000 same-sex partners bill to add reference to "common-law partner" and "common-law partnership", effective for the 2001 and later taxation years, or earlier by election (see Notes to 248(1)"common-law partner").

Definition "support amount" added by 1996 Budget, effective (per amendment to 1996 Budget bill made by 1995-97 technical bill, s. 307) after 1996, except that

    (a) a "support amount" does not include an amount

        (i) that was received under a decree, order or judgment of a competent tribunal, or under a written agreement, that does not have a commencement day (as defined in 56.1(4)), and

        (ii) that if paid and received would, but for the 1996 Budget bill, not be included in computing the income of the recipient of the amount; and

    (b) with respect to an amount payable or receivable under a decree, order or judgment of a competent tribunal, or under a written agreement, made after March 27, 1986 and before 1988, delete the words "the recipient has discretion as to the use of the amount, and" in the opening words of the definition.

The application rules ensure that the tax treatment of support payments triggered by events that occurred before the new regime is unchanged. This includes certain amounts payable under court orders or written agreements entered into or last amended after March 27, 1987 and before 1988 and which, following the *Gagnon* decision ([1986] 1 C.T.C. 410 (SCC)), were ruled deductible by the payers (even though the recipients had no discretion as to their use). Despite their deductibility from a payer's standpoint, those amounts were not required to be included in the recipients' incomes (see Notes to repealed 56(12)).

Also, with respect to marriage breakdowns that occurred before 1993, in order for a recipient to be taxed on support amounts received, the payer and the recipient had to live apart pursuant to their divorce, judicial separation or written separation agreement. The application rules ensure that the new regime does not tax amounts that were exempt because this requirement was not met in the hands of the recipients.

(Thus, for example, the grandfathering provided by former 56(12) is preserved, as is the grandfathering under former 56(1)(b) for certain pre-1993 agreements.) The reference to discretion in the opening words was formerly in 56(12). See also Notes to 56.1(4)"child support amount" and 56(1)(b).

See also Notes at end of 56.1.

**Interpretation Bulletins**: IT-530: Support payments.

**Forms**: T1157: Election for child support payments; T1158: Registration of family support payments.

**Notes [s. 56.1]**: For a thorough review of 56.1 and 60.1 as they applied before May 1997, see Durnford and Toope, "Spousal Support in Family Law and Alimony in the Law of Taxation", 42(1) *Canadian Tax Journal* 1-107 (1994).

56.1 amended by 1992 technical bill, effective for decrees, orders and judgments made after 1992 and agreements entered into after 1992, except where the marriage breakdown occurred before 1993 (this exception added by 1993 technical bill, s. 134). The changes were not substantive: they reflect the new definition of "spouse" in 252(4), the consolidation of 56(1)(b) and (c) into 56(1)(b) and the renumbering of 56(1)(c.1) as 56(1)(c). The descriptive formula in 56.1(2) was also redrafted in algebraic form. For decrees, orders and judgments made, and agreements entered into, before 1993, or where the marriage breakdown occurred before 1993, read:

    56.1 (1) Maintenance — Where, after May 6, 1974, a decree, order, judgment or written agreement described in paragraph 56(1)(b), (c) or (c.1), or any variation thereof, has been made providing for the periodic payment of an amount

    (a) to a taxpayer by a person who is

        (i) the taxpayer's spouse or former spouse, or

        (ii) where the amount is paid pursuant to an order made by a competent tribunal after February 10, 1988 in accordance with the laws of a province, an individual of the opposite sex who

            (A) before the date of the order cohabited with the taxpayer in a conjugal relationship, or

            (B) is the natural parent of a child of the taxpayer, or

    (b) for the benefit of the taxpayer, children in the custody of the taxpayer or both the taxpayer and those children,

the amount or any part thereof, when paid, shall be deemed, for the purposes of paragraphs 56(1)(b), (c) and (c.1), to have been paid to and received by the taxpayer.

(2) **Agreement** — For the purposes of paragraphs 56(1)(b), (c) and (c.1), the amount, if any, by which

    (a) the total of all amounts each of which is an amount (other than an amount to which paragraph 56(1)(b), (c) or (c.1) otherwise applies) paid by a person in a taxation year, pursuant to a decree, order or judgment of a competent tribunal or pursuant to a written agreement, in respect of an expense (other than an expenditure in respect of a self-contained domestic establishment in which the person resides or an expenditure for the acquisition of tangible property that is not an expenditure on account of a medical or educational expense or in respect of the acquisition, improvement or maintenance of a self-contained domestic establishment in which the taxpayer described in subparagraph (i) or (ii) resides) incurred in the year or the immediately preceding taxation year for maintenance of a taxpayer who is

        (i) that person's spouse or former spouse, or

        (ii) where the amount is paid pursuant to an order made by a competent tribunal after February 10, 1988 in accordance with the laws of a province, an individual of the opposite sex who

            (A) before the date of the order cohabited with the person in a conjugal relationship, or

            (B) is the natural parent of a child of the person,

or for the maintenance of children in the taxpayer's custody or both the taxpayer and those children if, at the time the expense was incurred and throughout the remainder of the year, the taxpayer was living apart from that person

exceeds

    (b) the amount, if any, by which

        (i) the total of all amounts each of which is an amount included in the aggregate determined under paragraph (a) in respect of the acquisition or improvement of a self-contained domestic establishment in which the taxpayer resides, including any payment of principal or interest in respect of a loan made or indebtedness incurred to finance, in any manner whatever, such acquisition or improvement

exceeds

        (ii) the total of all amounts each of which is an amount equal to $1/5$ of the original principal amount of a loan or indebtedness described in subparagraph (i)

shall, where the decree, order, judgment or written agreement, as the case may be, provides that this subsection and subsection 60.1(2) shall apply to any payment made pursuant thereto, be deemed to be an amount paid by that person and received by the taxpayer as an allowance payable on a periodic basis.

(3) **Prior payments** — For the purposes of this section and section 56, where a decree, order or judgment of a competent tribunal or a written agreement made at any time in a taxation year provides that an amount received before that time and in the year or the immediately preceding taxation year is to be considered as having been paid and received pursuant thereto, the following rules apply:

(a) the amount shall be deemed to have been received pursuant thereto; and

(b) the person who made the payment shall be deemed to have been separated pursuant to a divorce, judicial separation or written separation agreement from that person's spouse or former spouse at the time the payment was made and throughout the remainder of the year.

56.1(1) amended by 1988 tax reform, except that for orders made after May 6, 1974 under the laws of Ontario, read "May 6, 1974" in place of "February 10, 1988" in 56.1(1)(a)(ii).

See also Notes to 56(1)(b) and 60.1(2).

**Definitions [s. 56.1]**: "amount" — 248(1); "child" — 252(1); "child support amount", "commencement day" — 56.1(4); "common-law partner", "common-law partnership" — 248(1); "corporation" — 248(1), *Interpretation Act* 35(1); "employee benefit plan" — 248(1); "former spouse" — 252(3); "individual" — 248(1); "Minister" — 248(1); "parent" — 252(2); "person", "prescribed", "principal amount", "property" — 248(1); "province" — *Interpretation Act* 35(1); "received" — 248(7); "self-contained domestic establishment", "share" — 248(1); "spouse" — 252(3); "superannuation or pension benefit" — 248(1); "support amount" — 56.1(4); "taxation year" — 249; "taxpayer" — 248(1); "written" — *Interpretation Act* 35(1) [writing].

## 56.2 Reserve claimed for debt forgiveness —
There shall be included in computing an individual's income for a taxation year during which the individual was not a bankrupt the amount, if any, deducted under section 61.2 in computing the individual's income for the preceding taxation year.

**Notes**: 56.2 added by 1994 tax amendments bill (Part I), effective for taxation years that end after February 21, 1994. See Notes to 61.2.

**Definitions [s. 56.2]**: "amount", "bankrupt", "individual" — 248(1); "taxation year" — 249.

## 56.3 Reserve claimed for debt forgiveness —
There shall be included in computing a taxpayer's income for a taxation year during which the taxpayer was not a bankrupt the amount, if any, deducted under section 61.4 in computing the taxpayer's income for the preceding taxation year.

**Related Provisions**: 61.4(a)B(ii) — Effect on reserve for subsequent year; 87(2)(g) — Amalgamations — carryover of reserve; 115(1)(a)(iii.21) — Non-resident's taxable income earned in Canada.

**Notes**: 56.3 added by 1994 tax amendments bill (Part I), effective for taxation years that end after February 21, 1994. See Notes to 61.4.

**Definitions [s. 56.3]**: "amount", "bankrupt" — 248(1); "taxation year" — 249; "taxpayer" — 248(1).

## 57. (1) Certain superannuation or pension benefits — Notwithstanding subparagraph 56(1)(a)(i), there shall be included in computing the income of a taxpayer in respect of a payment received by the taxpayer out of or under a superannuation or pension fund or plan the investment income of which has at some time been exempt from taxation under the *Income War Tax Act* by reason of an election for such exemption by the trustees or corporation administering the fund or plan, only that part of the payment that remains after deducting the proportion thereof

(a) that the total of the amounts paid by the taxpayer into or under the fund or plan during the period when its income was exempt by reason of that election is of the total of all amounts paid by the taxpayer into or under the fund or plan, or

(b) that the total of the amounts paid by the taxpayer into or under the fund or plan during the period when its income was exempt by reason of that election together with simple interest on each amount so paid from the end of the year of payment thereof to the commencement of the superannuation allowance or pension at 3% per annum is of the total of all amounts paid by the taxpayer into or under the fund or plan together with simple interest, computed in the same manner, on each amount so paid,

whichever is the greater.

**Related Provisions**: 57(2)–(4) — Exceptions and limitations; 212(1)(h)(iv) — Parallel exemption from non-resident withholding tax.

(2) **Exception** — This section does not apply in respect of a payment received by a taxpayer out of or under a superannuation or pension fund or plan if the taxpayer made no payment into or under the fund or plan.

(3) **Limitation** — Where a payment, to which subsection (1) would otherwise be applicable, is received by a taxpayer out of or under a superannuation or pension fund or plan in respect of a period of service for part only of which the taxpayer made payments into or under the fund or plan, subsection (1) is applicable only to that part of the payment which may reasonably be regarded as having been received in respect of the period for which the taxpayer made payments into or under the fund or plan and any part of the payment which may reasonably be regarded as having been received in respect of a period for which the taxpayer made no payments into or under the fund or plan shall be included in computing the taxpayer's income for the year without any deduction whatever.

(4) **Certain payments from pension plan** — Where a taxpayer, during the period from August 15, 1944 to December 31, 1945, made a contribution in excess of $300 to or under a registered pension plan in respect of services rendered by the taxpayer before the taxpayer became a contributor, there shall be included in computing the taxpayer's income in respect of a payment received by the taxpayer out of

or under the plan only that part of the payment that remains after deducting the proportion thereof that the contribution so made minus $300 is of the total of the amounts paid by the taxpayer to or under the plan.

**Related Provisions**: 212(1)(h)(iv) — Parallel benefits — non-residents.

**(5) Payments to widow, etc., of contributor** — Where, in respect of the death of a taxpayer who was a contributor to or under a superannuation or pension fund or plan described in subsection (1) or (4), a payment is received by a person in a taxation year out of or under the fund or plan, there shall be included in computing the income of that person for the year in respect thereof only that part of the payment that would, if the payment had been received by the taxpayer in the year out of or under the fund or plan, have been included by virtue of this section in computing the income of the taxpayer for the year.

**Definitions [s. 57]**: "amount" — 248(1); "corporation" — 248(1), *Interpretation Act* 35(1); "registered pension plan", "superannuation or pension benefit" — 248(1); "taxation year" — 249; "taxpayer" — 248(1).

**Interpretation Bulletins [s. 57]**: IT-499R: Superannuation or pension benefits.

**58. (1) Government annuities and like annuities** — In determining the amount that shall be included in computing the income of a taxpayer in respect of payments received by the taxpayer in a taxation year under contracts entered into before May 26, 1932 with the Government of Canada or annuity contracts like those issued under the *Government Annuities Act* entered into before that day with the government of a province or a corporation incorporated or licensed to carry on an annuities business in Canada, there may be deducted from the total of the payments received the lesser of

(a) the total of the amounts that would have been so received if the contracts had continued in force as they were immediately before June 25, 1940, without the exercise of any option or contractual right to enlarge the annuity by the payment of additional sums or premiums unless those additional sums or premiums had been paid before that day, and

(b) $5,000.

**Related Provisions**: 58(3) — Limitation; 58(4) — Capital element.

**(2) Annuities before 1940** — In determining the amount that shall be included in computing the income of a taxpayer in respect of payments received by the taxpayer in a taxation year under annuity contracts entered into after May 25, 1932, and before June 25, 1940, with the Government of Canada or annuity contracts like those issued under the *Government Annuities Act* entered into during that period with the government of a province or a corporation incorporated or licensed to carry on an annuities business in Canada, there may be deducted from the total of the payments received the lesser of

(a) the total of the amounts that would have been received under the contracts if they had continued in force as they were immediately before June 25, 1940, without the exercise of any option or contractual right to enlarge the annuity by the payment of additional sums or premiums unless such additional sums or premiums had been paid before that day, and

(b) $1,200.

**Related Provisions**: 58(3) — Limitation; 58(4) — Capital element.

**(3) Limitation** — Where a taxpayer has received annuity payments in respect of which the taxpayer would otherwise be entitled to make deductions under both subsection (1) and subsection (2),

(a) if the amount deductible under subsection (1) is $1,200 or more, [the taxpayer] may not make a deduction under subsection (2); and

(b) if the amount deductible under subsection (1) is less than $1,200, the taxpayer may make one deduction computed as though subsection (2) applied to all contracts entered into before June 25, 1940.

**Related Provisions**: 58(4) — Capital element.

**(4) Capital element** — The amount remaining after deducting from the total of the annuity payments to which this section applies received in a taxation year the deductions permitted by subsection (1), (2) or (3) shall be deemed to be the annuity payment in respect of which the capital element is deductible under paragraph 60(a).

**(5) Spouses [or common-law partners]** — Where a taxpayer and the taxpayer's spouse or common-law partner each received annuity payments in respect of which they may deduct amounts under this section, the amount deductible shall be computed as if their annuities belonged to one person and may be deducted by either of them or be apportioned between them in such manner as is agreed to by them or, in case of disagreement, as the Minister determines.

**Notes**: 58(5) amended by 2000 same-sex partners bill to add reference to "common-law partner", effective for the 2001 and later taxation years, or earlier by election (see Notes to 248(1) "common-law partner").

**(6) Pension benefits** — This section does not apply to superannuation or pension benefits received out of or under a registered pension plan.

**(7) Enlargement of annuity** — For the purpose of this section, an annuity shall be deemed to have been enlarged on or after June 25, 1940, if what is payable under the contract has, at any such time, been increased whether by increasing the amount of each periodic payment, by increasing the number of payments or otherwise.

**Definitions [s. 58]:** "amount", "annuity", "business", "common-law partner" — 248(1); "corporation" — 248(1), *Interpretation Act* 35(1); "Minister" — 248(1); "province" — *Interpretation Act* 35(1); "registered pension plan" — 248(1); "superannuation or pension benefit" — 248(1); "taxation year" — 249; "taxpayer" — 248(1).

**59. (1) Consideration for foreign resource property** — Where a taxpayer has disposed of a foreign resource property, the amount, if any, by which the taxpayer's proceeds of disposition therefrom exceed any outlays or expenses made or incurred by the taxpayer for the purpose of making the disposition and that were not otherwise deductible for the purposes of this Part shall be included in computing the taxpayer's income for a taxation year to the extent that the proceeds become receivable in that year.

### Proposed Amendment — 59(1)

**59. (1) Consideration for foreign resource property** — Where a taxpayer has disposed of a foreign resource property, there shall be included in computing the taxpayer's income for a taxation year the amount, if any, by which

(a) the portion of the taxpayer's proceeds of disposition from the disposition of the property that becomes receivable in the year

exceeds

(b) the total of

(i) all amounts each of which is an outlay or expense made or incurred by the taxpayer for the purpose of making the disposition that was not otherwise deductible for the purposes of this Part, and

(ii) where the property is a foreign resource property in respect of a country, the amount designated under this subparagraph in prescribed form filed with the taxpayer's return of income for the year in respect of the disposition.

**Application:** The December 21, 2000 draft legislation, subsec. 23(1), will amend subsec. 59(1) to read as above, applicable to taxation years that begin after 2000.

**Technical Notes:** Subsection 59(1) applies where a taxpayer has disposed of a foreign resource property. In computing the taxpayer's income for a taxation year, the proceeds of disposition that become receivable in the year are included in computing the taxpayer's income (net of outlays and expenses incurred for the purpose of making the disposition).

Subsection 59(1) is amended so that, to the extent that the taxpayer so designates, there is no income inclusion under subsection 59(1) in connection with the disposition of a foreign resource property of the taxpayer in respect of a country. Instead, the amount so designated reduces the taxpayer's "cumulative foreign resource expense" pursuant to paragraph (a) of the description of F in the definition "cumulative foreign resource expense" in new subsection 66.21(1). This amendment applies to taxation years that begin after 2000.

**Related Provisions:** 59(1.1) — Look-through rule for partnerships; 66.21(1)"cumulative foreign resource expense"F(a) — Amount under 59(1)(b)(ii); 72(2) — Election by legal representative and transferee re reserves; 87(2)(p) — Consideration for resource property disposition; 96(1)(d)(i) — Partnerships — no deduction for resource expenses; 104(5.2) — Trusts — 21-year deemed disposition; 248(1)"foreign resource property" — Meaning of foreign resource property in respect of a country.

**Interpretation Bulletins:** IT-125R4: Dispositions of resource property.

### Proposed Addition — 59(1.1)

**59. (1.1) Partnerships [look-through rule]** — Where a taxpayer is a member of a partnership in a fiscal period of the partnership, the taxpayer's share of the amount that would be included under subsection (1) in respect of a disposition of a foreign resource property in computing the partnership's income for a taxation year if the partnership were a person, the fiscal period were a taxation year, subsection (1) were read without reference to subparagraph (1)(b)(ii) and section 96 were read without reference to paragraph 96(1)(d) is deemed to be proceeds of disposition that become receivable by the taxpayer at the end of the fiscal period in respect of a disposition of the property by the taxpayer.

**Application:** The December 21, 2000 draft legislation, subsec. 23(1), will add subsec. 59(1.1), applicable to fiscal periods that begin after 2000.

**Technical Notes:** New subsection 59(1.1) provides a look-through rule so that members of a partnership can avail themselves of a designation under subsection 59(1). Subsection 59(1.1) is similar to the existing rules for partnership members in subsections 66.2(6) and 66.4(6). A related change to paragraph 96(1)(d) provides that a member's share of partnership income is computed without reference to subsection 59(1). New subsection 59(1.1) applies to fiscal periods of partnerships that begin after 2000.

**(2) Deduction under former section 64 in preceding year** — There shall be included in computing a taxpayer's income for a taxation year any amount that has been deducted as a reserve under subsection 64(1), (1.1) or (1.2) of the *Income Tax Act*, chapter 148 of the Revised Statutes of Canada, 1952, in computing the taxpayer's income for the immediately preceding taxation year.

**Related Provisions:** 66(5) — Dealers; 85(1) — Transfer of property to corporation by shareholder; 85(2) — Transfer of property to corporation from partnership; 88 — Winding-up; 115(4) — Non-resident's income earned on Canadian resource property.

**Notes:** 59(2) refers to a version of s. 64 that was repealed by the 1981 Budget. See Notes to 64.

**I.T. Application Rules:** 69 (meaning of "*Income Tax Act*, chapter 148 of the Revised Statutes of Canada, 1952").

**(3), (3.1) [Repealed under former Act]**

**Notes:** 59(3) and (3.1), repealed by 1985 technical bill, dealt with disposition of a resource property acquired before 1972. They became ineffective after 1984.

Subdivision d — Other Sources of Income  S. 59(3.3)(c)(i)

**(3.2) Recovery of exploration and development expenses** — There shall be included in computing a taxpayer's income for a taxation year

(a) any amount referred to in paragraph 66(12.4)(b);

(b) any amount referred to in subsection 66.1(1);

(c) any amount referred to in subsection 66.2(1);

### Proposed Addition — 59(3.2)(c.1)

(c.1) any amount referred to in subsection 66.21(3);

**Application**: The December 21, 2000 draft legislation, subsec. 23(2), will add para. 59(3.2)(c.1), applicable to taxation years that begin after 2000.

**Technical Notes**: Subsection 59(3.2) provides for the inclusion in a taxpayer's income of specified amounts. For this purpose, new paragraph 59(3.2)(c.1) specifies amounts determined under new subsection 66.21(3), relating to "negative" FRE balances. For further detail, see the commentary on new subsection 66.21(3).

(d) any amount referred to in subparagraph 66(10.4)(b)(ii); and

(e) any amount referred to in paragraph 66(10.4)(c).

**Related Provisions**: 66(5) — Dealers; 66.21(1)"cumulative foreign resource expense"B — Amount under 59(3.2)(c.1); 66.21(3) — Amount to be included in income; 96(1)(d)(i) — Partnerships — no deduction for resource expenses; 104(5.2) — Trusts — 21-year deemed disposition; 110.6(1) — "investment income"; 115(1)(a)(iii.1) — Non-resident's taxable income earned in Canada.

**I.T. Application Rules**: 29(11)(b)(iv); 29(12)(b)(iv) (undeducted expenses incurred before 1972).

**Interpretation Bulletins**: IT-125R4: Dispositions of resource property.

**(3.3) Amounts to be included in income** — There shall be included in computing a taxpayer's income for a taxation year

(a) $33^1/_3\%$ of the total of all amounts, each of which is the stated percentage of

(i) an amount that became receivable by the taxpayer after December 31, 1983 and in the year (other than an amount that would have been a Canadian oil and gas exploration expense if it had been an expense incurred by the taxpayer at the time it became receivable),

(ii) an amount that became receivable by the taxpayer after December 31, 1983 and in the year that would have been a Canadian oil and gas exploration expense described in paragraph (c) or (d) of the definition "Canadian exploration expense" in subsection 66.1(6) in respect of a qualified tertiary oil recovery project if it had been an expense incurred by the taxpayer at the time it became receivable, or

(iii) 30% of an amount that became receivable by the taxpayer in the year and in 1984 that would have been a Canadian oil and gas exploration expense (other than an expense described in paragraph (c) or (d) of the definition "Canadian exploration expense" in subsection 66.1(6) in respect of a qualified tertiary oil recovery project) incurred in respect of non-conventional lands if it had been an expense incurred by the taxpayer at the time it became receivable

and in respect of which the consideration given by the taxpayer was a property (other than a share, depreciable property of a prescribed class or a Canadian resource property) or services the cost of which may reasonably be regarded as having been an expenditure that was added in computing the earned depletion base of the taxpayer or in computing the earned depletion base of a predecessor where the taxpayer is a successor corporation to the predecessor;

(b) $33^1/_3\%$ of the total of all amounts, each of which is the stated percentage of an amount in respect of a disposition of depreciable property of a prescribed class (other than a disposition of such property that had been used by the taxpayer to any person with whom the taxpayer was not dealing at arm's length) of the taxpayer after December 11, 1979 and in the year, the capital cost of which was added in computing the earned depletion base of the taxpayer or of a person with whom the taxpayer was not dealing at arm's length or in computing the earned depletion base of a predecessor where the taxpayer is a successor corporation to the predecessor, that is equal to the lesser of

(i) the proceeds of disposition of the property, and

(ii) the capital cost of the property to the taxpayer, the person with whom the taxpayer was not dealing at arm's length or the predecessor, as the case may be, computed as if no amount had been added thereto by virtue of paragraph 21(1)(b) or subsection 21(3);

(c) $33^1/_3\%$ of the total of all amounts, each of which is an amount in respect of a disposition of depreciable property of a prescribed class that is bituminous sands equipment (other than a disposition of such property that had been used by the taxpayer to any person with whom the taxpayer was not dealing at arm's length) of the taxpayer after December 11, 1979 and before 1990 and in the year, the capital cost of which was added in computing the supplementary depletion base of the taxpayer or of a person with whom the taxpayer was not dealing at arm's length or in computing the supplementary depletion base of a predecessor where the taxpayer is a successor corporation to the predecessor, that is equal to the lesser of

(i) the proceeds of disposition of the property, and

(ii) the capital cost of the property to the taxpayer, the person with whom the taxpayer was not dealing at arm's length or the predecessor, as the case may be, computed as if no amount had been added thereto by virtue of paragraph 21(1)(b) or subsection 21(3);

(d) 50% of the total of all amounts, each of which is an amount in respect of a disposition of depreciable property of a prescribed class that is enhanced recovery equipment (other than a disposition of such property that had been used by the taxpayer to any person with whom the taxpayer was not dealing at arm's length) of the taxpayer after December 11, 1979 and before 1990 and in the year, the capital cost of which was added in computing the supplementary depletion base of the taxpayer or of a person with whom the taxpayer was not dealing at arm's length or in computing the supplementary depletion base of a predecessor where the taxpayer is a successor corporation to the predecessor, that is equal to the lesser of

(i) the proceeds of disposition of the property, and

(ii) the capital cost of the property to the taxpayer, the person with whom the taxpayer was not dealing at arm's length or the predecessor, as the case may be, computed as if no amount had been added thereto by virtue of paragraph 21(1)(b) or subsection 21(3);

(e) 66⅔% of the total of all amounts, each of which is an amount that became receivable by the taxpayer after December 11, 1979 and before 1990 and in the year and in respect of which the consideration given by the taxpayer was a property (other than a share or a Canadian resource property) or services the cost of which may reasonably be regarded as having been an expenditure in connection with an oil or gas well in respect of which an amount was included in computing the taxpayer's frontier exploration base or in computing the frontier exploration base of a predecessor where the taxpayer is a successor corporation to the predecessor; and

(f) 33⅓% of the total of all amounts, each of which is the stated percentage of an amount that became receivable by the taxpayer after April 19, 1983 and in the year and in respect of which the consideration given by the taxpayer was a property (other than a share, depreciable property of a prescribed class or a Canadian resource property) or services the cost of which may reasonably be regarded as having been an expenditure that was included in computing the mining exploration depletion base of the taxpayer or in computing the mining exploration depletion base of a specified predecessor of the taxpayer.

**Related Provisions**: 66(5) — Dealers; 66.1(2) — Deduction for principal business corporation; 87(1.2) — Amalgamation — contin-

uing corporation; 88(1.5) — Winding-up — Parent deemed continuation of subsidiary.

**Regulations**: 1105 (classes in Schedule II are prescribed).

**(3.4) Definitions** — For the purposes of this subsection and subsection (3.3),

"**specified predecessor**" of a taxpayer means a person who is a predecessor of

(a) the taxpayer, or

(b) a person who is a specified predecessor of the taxpayer;

**Notes**: 59(3.4)"specified predecessor" was 59(3.4)(c) before consolidation in R.S.C. 1985 (5th Supp.), effective for taxation years ending after November 1991. See Table of Concordance.

"**stated percentage**" means

(a) in respect of an amount described in paragraph (3.3)(a) or (f) that became receivable by a taxpayer,

(i) 100% where the amount became receivable before July, 1988,

(ii) 50% where the amount became receivable after June, 1988 and before 1990, and

(iii) 0% where the amount became receivable after 1989, and

(b) in respect of the disposition described in paragraph (3.3)(b) of a depreciable property of a taxpayer,

(i) 100% where the property was disposed of before July, 1988,

(ii) 50% where the property was disposed of after June, 1988 and before 1990, and

(iii) 0% where the property was disposed of after 1989;

**Related Provisions**: 59(3.5) — Variation of stated percentage.

**Notes**: 59(3.4)"stated percentage" was 59(3.4)(b) before consolidation in R.S.C. 1985 (5th Supp.), effective for taxation years ending after November 1991. See Table of Concordance.

"**successor corporation**" means a corporation that has at any time after November 7, 1969 acquired, by purchase, amalgamation, merger, winding-up or otherwise (other than pursuant to an amalgamation that is described in subsection 87(1.2) or a winding-up to which the rules in subsection 88(1) apply), from another person (in this subsection and subsection (3.3) referred to as the "predecessor") all or substantially all of the Canadian resource properties of the predecessor in circumstances in which any of subsection 29(25) of the *Income Tax Application Rules* and subsections 66.7(1) and (3) to (5) apply to the corporation.

**Notes**: 59(3.4)"successor corporation" was 59(3.4)(a) before consolidation in R.S.C. 1985 (5th Supp.), effective for taxation years ending after November 1991.

The CCRA takes the position that "all or substantially all" means 90% or more.

**(3.5) Variation of stated percentage** — Notwithstanding the definition "stated percentage" in subsection (3.4), where

(a) an amount became receivable by a taxpayer within 60 days after the end of 1989 in respect of a disposition of property or services, and

(b) the person to whom the disposition was made is a corporation that, before the end of 1989, had issued, or had undertaken to issue, a flow-through share and the corporation renounces under subsection 66(12.66), effective on December 31, 1989, an amount in respect of Canadian exploration expenses that includes an expenditure in respect of the amount referred to in paragraph (a),

the stated percentage in respect of the amount described in paragraph (a) shall be 50%.

**(4)** [Repealed under former Act]

**Notes**: 59(4), repealed by 1985 technical bill, defined "relevant percentage", a term no longer used.

**(5) Definitions of "disposition" and "proceeds of disposition"** — In this section, "disposition" and "proceeds of disposition" have the meanings assigned by section 54.

---
**Proposed Amendment — 59(5)**

**(5) Definition of "proceeds of disposition"** — In this section, "proceeds of disposition" has the meaning assigned by section 54.

**Application**: Bill C-43 (First Reading September 20, 2000), s. 24, will amend subsec. 59(5) to read as above, applicable to transactions and events that occur after December 23, 1998.

**Technical Notes**: Subsections 59(5) and 66.4(5) define the expressions "disposition" and "proceeds of disposition" for the purposes of sections 59 and 66.4. These expressions are defined in the same way as they are defined in section 54.

Subsections 59(5) and 66.4(5) are amended to eliminate the references to the expression "disposition", as this expression is now defined in subsection 248(1).

---

**Interpretation Bulletins**: IT-125R4: Dispositions of resource property.

**(6) Definitions in regulations under section 65** — In this section, "bituminous sands equipment", "Canadian oil and gas exploration expense", "earned depletion base", "enhanced recovery equipment", "frontier exploration base", "mining exploration depletion base", "non-conventional lands", "qualified tertiary oil recovery project" and "supplementary depletion base" have the meanings assigned by regulations made for the purposes of section 65.

**Regulations [subsec. 59(6)]**: Part XII (Reg. 1206(1) and others).

**Definitions [s. 59]**: "amount" — 248(1); "bituminous sands equipment" — 59(6); "arm's length" — 251(1); "Canada" — 255; "Canadian exploration expense" — 66.1(6), 248(1); "Canadian oil and gas exploration expense" — 59(6); "Canadian resource property" — 66(15), 248(1); "corporation" — 248(1), *Interpretation Act* 35(1); "depreciable property" — 13(21), 248(1); "disposition" — 54, 59(5) [to be repealed], 248(1) [draft]; "earned depletion base"; "enhanced recovery equipment" — 59(6); "fiscal period" — 249.1; "flow-through share", "foreign resource property" — 66(15), 248(1); "foreign resource property in respect of a country" — 248(1); "frontier exploration base", "mining exploration depletion base", "non-conventional lands" — 59(6); "oil or gas well" — 248(1); "partnership" — see Notes to 96(1); "person", "prescribed" — 248(1); "proceeds of disposition" — 54, 59(5); "property", "share" — 248(1); "qualified tertiary oil recovery project" — 59(6); "specified predecessor" — 59(3.4); "stated percentage" — 59(3.4); "successor corporation" — 59(3.4); "supplementary depletion base" — 59(6); "taxation year" — 249; "taxpayer" — 248(1).

**59.1 Involuntary disposition of resource property** — Where in a particular taxation year an amount is deemed by subsection 44(2) to have become receivable by a taxpayer as proceeds of disposition described in paragraph (d) of the definition "proceeds of disposition" in section 54 of any Canadian resource property and the taxpayer elects, in the taxpayer's return of income under this Part for the year, to have this section apply to those proceeds of disposition,

(a) there shall be deducted in computing the taxpayer's income for the particular year such amount as the taxpayer may claim, not exceeding the least of,

(i) the total of all those proceeds so becoming receivable in the particular year by the taxpayer to the extent that they have been included in the amount referred to in paragraph (a) of the description of F in the definition "cumulative Canadian development expense" in subsection 66.2(5) or in paragraph (a) of the description of F in the definition "cumulative Canadian oil and gas property expense" in subsection 66.4(5) in respect of the taxpayer,

(ii) the amount required to be included in computing the taxpayer's income for the particular year by virtue of paragraph 59(3.2)(c), and

(iii) the taxpayer's income for the particular year determined without reference to this section;

(b) the amount, if any, by which

(i) the amount deducted under paragraph (a)

exceeds

(ii) the total of such of the Canadian exploration expenses, Canadian development expenses and Canadian oil and gas property expenses made or incurred by the taxpayer in the taxpayer's ten taxation years immediately following the particular year as were designated by the taxpayer in the taxpayer's return of income for the year in which the expense was made or incurred,

shall be included in computing the taxpayer's income for the particular year and, notwithstanding subsections 152(4) and (5), such reassessment of the taxpayer's tax, interest or penalties for any year shall be made as is necessary to give effect to such inclusion; and

(c) any Canadian exploration expense, Canadian development expense or Canadian oil and gas property expense made or incurred by the taxpayer and designated in the taxpayer's return of income in accordance with subparagraph (b)(ii) shall (except for the purposes of subsections 66(12.1), (12.2), (12.3) and (12.5) and for the purpose of computing the taxpayer's earned depletion base within the meaning assigned by regulations made for the purposes of section 65) be deemed not to be a Canadian exploration expense, a Canadian development expense or a Canadian oil and gas property expense, as the case may be, of the taxpayer.

**Related Provisions:** 66(18) — Members of partnerships.

**Definitions [s. 59.1]:** "amount" — 248(1); "Canadian development expense" — 66.2(5), 248(1); "Canadian exploration expense" — 66.1(6), 248(1); "Canadian oil and gas property expense" — 66.4(5), 248(1); "Canadian resource property" — 66(15), 248(1); "Minister", "property", "regulations" — 248(1); "taxation year" — 249; "taxpayer" — 248(1).

**Interpretation Bulletins [s. 59.1]:** IT-125R4: Dispositions of resource properties.

## Subdivision e — Deductions in Computing Income

**60. Other deductions** — There may be deducted in computing a taxpayer's income for a taxation year such of the following amounts as are applicable:

**Notes:** 60 provides miscellaneous deductions in computing net income. For deductions in computing employment income, see 8; for deductions in computing income from business or property, see 9(1) and 20–37. For deductions from net income in computing taxable income, see 110–114.2.

(a) **capital element of annuity payments** — the capital element of each annuity payment included by virtue of paragraph 56(1)(d) in computing the taxpayer's income for the year, that is to say,

(i) if the annuity was paid under a contract, an amount equal to that part of the payment determined in prescribed manner to have been a return of capital, and

(ii) if the annuity was paid under a will or trust, such part of the payment as can be established by the recipient not to have been paid out of the income of the estate or trust;

**Related Provisions:** 58(4) — Government and similar annuities; 94.2(10)(a)(ii) — No application to foreign insurance policy of foreign investment entity; 110.6(1) — "investment income"; 147.4(4) — Deemed annuity on conversion of pension rights before 1997 to annuity contract commencing after age 69; 148(9)"adjusted cost basis"K — Reduction in adjusted cost basis. See additional Related Provisions and Definitions at end of s. 60.

**Regulations:** 300 (prescribed manner).

**Interpretation Bulletins:** IT-85R2: Health and welfare trusts for employees; IT-111R2: Annuities purchased from charitable organizations; IT-415R2: Deregistration of registered retirement savings plans.

**Advance Tax Rulings:** ATR-68: Structured settlement.

(b) **support** — the total of all amounts each of which is an amount determined by the formula

$$A - (B + C)$$

where

A is the total of all amounts each of which is a support amount paid after 1996 and before the end of the year by the taxpayer to a particular person, where the taxpayer and the particular person were living separate and apart at the time the amount was paid,

B is the total of all amounts each of which is a child support amount that became payable by the taxpayer to the particular person under an agreement or order on or after its commencement day and before the end of the year in respect of a period that began on or after its commencement day, and

C is the total of all amounts each of which is a support amount paid by the taxpayer to the particular person after 1996 and deductible in computing the taxpayer's income for a preceding taxation year;

**Related Provisions:** 4(3) — Deductions applicable; 56(1)(b) — Parallel income inclusion for recipient; 56(1)(c.2) — Reimbursement of support payments; 56.1(4), 60.1(4) — Definitions of "commencement day", "support amount" and "child support amount"; 60.1(1), (2) — Payments to third parties; 60.1(3) — Payments made before agreement signed or court order made; 118(5) — No personal credits in respect of person to whom support paid; 146(1)"earned income"(f) — Amount under 60(b) reduces RRSP earned income; 212(1)(f) — No withholding tax on support paid to non-resident; 252(3) — Extended meaning of "spouse" and "former spouse"; 257 — Formula cannot calculate to less than zero; Canada-U.S. Tax Convention Art. XVIII:6 — Exemptions for cross-border alimony and support. See additional Related Provisions and Definitions at end of s. 60.

**Notes:** The 2000 same-sex partners bill (Royal Assent June 29, 2000), which extended references to "spouse" to add "common-law partner" throughout the Act, provides:

145. Paragraphs 56(1)(b) and 60(b) of the *Income Tax Act* do not apply to amounts paid or payable by a person for the maintenance of a taxpayer pursuant to an order or a written agreement, made before the coming into force of this section, unless the person and the taxpayer jointly elect to have those paragraphs apply to those amounts for the 2001 and following taxation years by notifying the Minister of National Revenue in prescribed manner on or before their filing due date for the year in which this Act receives royal assent.

Where an amount is deductible under 60(b), a parallel amount is normally included in the recipient's income by 56(1)(b). However, if the recipient is not resident in Canada there is no Canadian tax payable (see repealed 212(1)(f)).

60(b) rewritten by 1996 Budget, effective for amounts received after 1996, and amended retroactively (for amounts paid after 1996) by 1995-97 technical bill, to add the words "on or" near the end of 60(b)B). For amounts paid and received before 1997, read:

(b) **alimony payments** — an amount paid by the taxpayer in the year as alimony or other allowance payable on a periodic basis for the maintenance of the recipient, children of the recipient or both the recipient and the children, if the taxpayer, because of the breakdown of the taxpayer's marriage, was living separate and apart from the spouse or former spouse to whom the taxpayer was required to make the payment at the time the payment was made and throughout the remainder of the year and the amount was paid under a decree, order or judgment of a competent tribunal or under a written agreement;

See Notes to 56(1)(b) regarding this change.

Former 60(b) and (c) consolidated into 60(b) by 1992 technical bill, effective for breakdown of a "marriage" after 1992. "Marriage" is not defined in the amending bill, but the drafters intended it to mean a marriage under the extended definition in 252(4)(b); see subsec. 42(3) of the *Interpretation Act*. For earlier breakdowns, read:

(b) **alimony payments** — an amount paid by the taxpayer in the year, pursuant to a decree, order or judgment of a competent tribunal or pursuant to a written agreement, as alimony or other allowance payable on a periodic basis for the maintenance of the recipient thereof, children of the marriage, or both the recipient and children of the marriage, if the taxpayer was living apart from, and was separated pursuant to a divorce, judicial separation or written separation agreement from, the taxpayer's spouse or former spouse to whom the taxpayer was required to make the payment at the time the payment was made and throughout the remainder of the year;

(c) **maintenance payments** — an amount paid by the taxpayer in the year, pursuant to an order of a competent tribunal, as an allowance payable on a periodic basis for the maintenance of the recipient thereof, children of the recipient, or both the recipient and children of the recipient if, at the time the payment was made and throughout the remainder of the year, the taxpayer was living apart from the taxpayer's spouse to whom the taxpayer was required to make the payment;

Former 60(c) amended by 1979 Budget and 1981 Budget, effective (a) for all orders made after December 11, 1979, and (b) for earlier orders, where the recipient and the taxpayer agree in writing at any time in a taxation year, for that year and all subsequent years. For earlier cases, read:

(c) an amount paid by the taxpayer in the year, pursuant to an order of a competent tribunal, as an allowance payable on a periodic basis for the maintenance of the recipient thereof, children of the marriage, or both the recipient and children of the marriage, if he was living apart from his spouse to whom he was required to make the payment at the time the payment was made and throughout the remainder of the year;

**Regulations**: 100(3)(d) (payroll deduction of employee contribution reduces source withholding if required by pre-May 1997 court order).

**Interpretation Bulletins**: IT-118R3: Alimony and maintenance; IT-325R2: Property transfers after separation, divorce and annulment; IT-513R: Personal tax credits; IT-530: Support payments.

**Forms**: T1157: Election for child support payments; T1158: Registration of family support payments; P102: Support payments (pamphlet).

### (c), (c.1) [Repealed]

**Notes**: 60(c) repealed by 1996 Budget, effective for amounts received after 1996. See now 60(b). For amounts received before 1997, read:

(c) **maintenance** — an amount paid by the taxpayer in the year as an allowance payable on a periodic basis for the maintenance of the recipient, children of the recipient or both the recipient and the children, if

(i) at the time the amount was paid and throughout the remainder of the year the taxpayer was living separate and apart from the recipient,

(ii) the taxpayer is the natural parent of a child of the recipient, and

(iii) the amount was received under an order made by a competent tribunal in accordance with the laws of a province;

Former 60(c.1) amended and renumbered as 60(c) by 1992 technical bill, effective for orders made after 1992.

Former 60(c.1) added by 1981 Budget, effective (a) for all orders made after December 11, 1979, and (b) for earlier orders, where the taxpayer and the person agree in writing at any time in a taxation year, for that year and all subsequent years. In other words, for orders made before December 12, 1979, the amendment does not apply unless the parties elect (or have ever previously elected) for it to apply.

Former 60(c.1) amended by 1988 tax reform, except that for orders made after December 11, 1979 under the laws of Ontario, read "December 11, 1979" and "December 12, 1979" in place of "February 10, 1988" and "February 11, 1988" respectively (see 60.001). For provinces other than Ontario, the same relief is available by applying for remission pursuant to the *Maintenance Payments Remission Order*, Order in Council P.C. 1991-256, February 14, 1991 (reproduced in the "Remission Orders" section).

(c.2) **repayment of support payments** — an amount paid by the taxpayer in the year or one of the 2 preceding taxation years under a decree, order or judgment of a competent tribunal as a repayment of an amount included under paragraph 56(1)(b) or (c), or under paragraph 56(1)(c.1) (as it applies, in computing the taxpayer's income for the year or a preceding taxation year, to decrees, orders and judgments made before 1993) to the extent that it was not so deducted for a preceding taxation year;

**Related Provisions**: 56(1)(c.2) — Reimbursement of support payments; 146(1)"earned income"(f) — Amount deducted under 60(c.2) reduces RRSP earned income.

**Notes**: 60(c.2) added by 1992 technical bill, effective for payments made after 1990.

**Interpretation Bulletins**: IT-530: Support payments.

(d) **interest on death duties** — an amount equal to annual interest accruing within the taxation year in respect of succession duties, inheritance taxes or estate taxes;

**Related Provisions**: 4(3) — Deductions applicable. See additional Related provisions and Definitions at end of s. 60.

**Notes**: At present, neither Canada nor any of the provinces imposes succession duties, inheritance taxes or estate taxes, although the provinces impose probate fees, now called estate administration taxes in some provinces including Ontario. This provision could apply to interest on U.S. estate taxes, however.

**Interpretation Bulletins**: IT-203: Interest on death duties.

### (e)–(h) [Repealed under former Act]

### Proposed Addition — 60(e)

(e) **CPP/QPP contributions on self-employed earnings** — ½ of the lesser of

(i) the total of all amounts each of which is an amount payable by the taxpayer in respect of self-employed earnings for the year as a contribution under the *Canada Pension Plan* or under a provincial pension plan within the meaning assigned by section 3 of that Act, and

(ii) the maximum amount of such contributions payable by the taxpayer for the year under the plan;

**Application**: The December 21, 2000 draft legislation, s. 24, will add para. 60(e), applicable to 2001 et seq.

**Technical Notes**: Section 60 provides for various deductions in computing income, including deductions in respect of certain payments to deferred income plans.

New paragraph 60(e) provides for the deduction of one-half of a taxpayer's contributions to the Canada or Quebec Pension Plan payable on the taxpayer's self-employed earnings, subject to one-half of the maximum of such contributions payable by the taxpayer under the plan. The appropriate percentage (generally the lowest marginal tax rate) of the other half of those contributions continues to be deductible under 118.7 (see the commentary on that section) in computing the taxpayer's tax payable.

**Notice of Ways and Means Motion, Economic Statement, October 18, 2000**: (8) That, with respect to fiscal periods that end after 2000,

(a) one-half of any contribution payable by an individual under the Canada Pension Plan or the Quebec Pension Plan in respect of the individual's self-employed earnings for the period be deductible in computing the individual's income for the taxation year in which the period ends, and

(b) the remainder continue to qualify for the tax credit provided under section 118.7 of the Act.

**Minister's Speech, Economic Statement, October 18, 2000**: Next, at the moment, self-employed Canadians get a 17% credit on both the employer's and employee's contributions to the Canada and Quebec Pension Plans. This puts them at a disadvantage with incorporated businesses, which can deduct the employer's portion of these contributions. To remove this disadvantage for self-employed Canadians, effective January 1, 2001, the employer's portion of the contributions to these plans will be 100% deductible.

[For a self-employed person, the CPP/QPP contribution is double that of an employee, since there is no parallel amount paid by an employer. This puts self-employed persons on the same footing as employers in being able to deduct the notional "employer's" half of the CPP contribution, which is deductible under 8(1)(l.1) or 9(1) — ed.]

**Related Provisions**: 118.7 — Credit for 16% of other half of contributions.

**Notes**: Former 60(e), (f), (g) and (h) repealed by 1988 tax reform. The deduction for tuition fees paid to a university outside Canada is now a credit under 118.5(1)(b). The deduction for tuition fees paid in Canada is now a credit under 118.5(1)(a). The deduction for tuition fees for commuting students is now a credit under 118.5(1)(c). The deduction for Canada Pension Plan contributions is now a credit under 118.7.

(i) **premium or payment under RRSP or RRIF** — any amount that is deductible under section 146 or subsection 147.3(13.1) in computing the income of the taxpayer for the year;

**Related Provisions**: 4(3) — Deductions applicable; 127.52(1)(a) — Limitation on deduction for minimum tax purposes; 146(5), (5.1), (6), (6.1), (8.2) — RRSP payments and premiums deductible; 152(6) — Reassessment. See additional Related provisions and Definitions at end of s. 60.

**Notes**: 60(i) amended by 1992 technical bill, effective 1992, to add reference to 147.3(13.1).

**Regulations**: 100(3)(c) (payroll deduction of RRSP contribution reduces source withholding).

**Interpretation Bulletins**: IT-124R6: Contributions to registered retirement savings plans.

(j) **transfer of superannuation benefits [to RRSP]** — such part of the total of all amounts each of which is

(i) a superannuation or pension benefit (other than any amount in respect of the benefit that is deducted in computing the taxable income of the taxpayer for a taxation year because of subparagraph 110(1)(f)(i) or a benefit that is part of a series of periodic payments) payable out of or under a pension plan that is not a registered pension plan, attributable to services rendered by the taxpayer or a spouse or common-law partner or former spouse or common-law partner of the taxpayer in a period throughout which that person was not resident in Canada, and included in computing the income of the taxpayer for the year because of subparagraph 56(1)(a)(i), or

(ii) an eligible amount in respect of the taxpayer for the year under section 60.01, subsection 104(27) or (27.1) or paragraph 147(10.2)(d),

as

(iii) is designated by the taxpayer in the taxpayer's return of income under this Part for the year, and

(iv) does not exceed the total of all amounts each of which is an amount paid by the taxpayer in the year or within 60 days after the end of the year

(A) as a contribution to or under a registered pension plan for the taxpayer's benefit, other than the portion thereof deductible under paragraph 8(1)(m) in computing the taxpayer's income for the year, or

(B) as a premium (within the meaning assigned by subsection 146(1)) under a registered retirement savings plan under which the taxpayer is the annuitant (within the meaning assigned by subsection 146(1)), other than the portion thereof designated for a taxation year for the purposes of paragraph (l),

to the extent that the amount was not deducted in computing the taxpayer's income for a preceding taxation year;

**Related Provisions**: 60(j.01) — Transfer of surplus; 60.2(1) — Refund of undeducted past service AVCs; 104(27) — Pension benefits; 104(27.1) — DPSP benefits; 127.52(1)(a) — Limitation on deduction for minimum tax purposes; 146(5) — Amount of RRSP premiums deductible; 146(6.1) — Recontribution of certain withdrawals; 146(8.2) — Amount deductible; 147(10) — Amounts received taxable; 146(16) — RRSP deduction on transfer of funds; 147(10.2) — Single payment on retirement etc.; 147(21) — Restric-

## Subdivision e — Deductions in Computing Income   S. 60(j.04)

tion re transfers; 147.1(3)(a) — Deemed registration; 147.3 — Transfer from RPP; 147.3(12) — Restriction re transfers; 204.2(1)(b)(i)(A) — Excess amount for a year in respect of RRSP; 212(1)(h)(iii.1) — Pension benefits; 252(3) — Extended meaning of "spouse" and "former spouse". See additional Related Provisions and Definitions at end of s. 60.

**Notes:** 60(j) amended by 2000 same-sex partners bill to add reference to "common-law partner", effective for the 2001 and later taxation years, or earlier by election (see Notes to 248(1)"common-law partner").

60(j) amended by 1990 pension bill and 1991 technical bill, this version effective 1991.

60(j)(i) amended by 1992 technical bill, effective 1993, to delete a reference to "spouse" having the meaning assigned by 146(1.1); this change was generally not substantive, since a common-law spouse is now a spouse for all purposes under 252(4). However, the definition in 252(4) is slightly different than former 146(1.1).

**I.T. Application Rules:** 40(3), 40(6).

**Interpretation Bulletins:** IT-124R6: Contributions to registered retirement savings plans; IT-528: Transfers of funds between registered plans.

**Information Circulars:** 79-8R3: Forms to use to directly transfer funds to or between plans, or to purchase an annuity.

**Advance Tax Rulings:** ATR-31: Funding of divorce settlement amount from DPSP.

**Forms:** TD2: Tax deduction waiver for a direct transfer of an eligible retiring allowance.

**(j.01) [No longer relevant]**

**Notes:** 60(j.01) added by 1990 pension bill, effective for 1988 only. It allowed a rollover of an actuarial surplus under an RPP defined benefit provision, received before March 28, 1988, to an RRSP.

**Interpretation Bulletins:** IT-124R6: Contributions to registered retirement savings plans; IT-528: Transfers of funds between registered plans.

**(j.02) payment to registered pension plan** — an amount equal to the lesser of

  (i) the total of

    (A) all contributions made in the year by the taxpayer to registered pension plans in respect of eligible service of the taxpayer before 1990 under the plans, where the taxpayer was obliged under the terms of an agreement in writing entered into before March 28, 1988 to make the contributions, and

    (B) all amounts each of which is an amount paid in the year by the taxpayer to a registered pension plan as

      (I) a repayment under a prescribed statutory provision of an amount received from the plan that was included under subsection 56(1) in computing the taxpayer's income for a taxation year ending before 1990, where the taxpayer was obliged as a consequence of a written election made before March 28, 1988 to make the repayment, or

      (II) interest in respect of a repayment referred to in subclause (I),

other than the portion of that total that is deductible under paragraph 8(1)(m) or paragraph (j.03) in computing the taxpayer's income for the year, and

  (ii) the total of all amounts each of which is an amount paid out of or under a registered pension plan as part of a series of periodic payments and included under subsection 56(1) in computing the taxpayer's income for the year, other than the portion of that total that can reasonably be considered to have been designated by the taxpayer for the purpose of paragraph (j.2);

**Related Provisions:** 60(j.04) — Repayments of post-1989 pension benefits; 127.52(1)(a) — Limitation on deduction for minimum tax purposes.

**Notes:** 60(j.02) added by 1992 technical bill, effective 1990. It provides transitional relief where an agreement to acquire past service benefits under a registered pension plan may have been entered into with the expectation that payments under the agreement would be deductible under 60(j). It continues the deduction formerly provided by 60(j) for payments made under agreements entered into before March 28, 1988, which was the day the amendments to 60(j) made by the 1990 pension bill were announced.

**Regulations:** 6503 (prescribed statutory provisions for 60(j.02)(i)(B)(I)).

**(j.03) repayments of pre-1990 pension benefits** — an amount equal to the lesser of

  (i) the total of all amounts each of which is an amount paid in the year or a preceding taxation year by the taxpayer to a registered pension plan that was not deductible in computing the taxpayer's income for a preceding taxation year and that was paid as

    (A) a repayment under a prescribed statutory provision of an amount received from the plan that was included under subsection 56(1) in computing the taxpayer's income for a taxation year ending before 1990, or

    (B) interest in respect of a repayment referred to in clause (A), and

  (ii) the amount, if any, by which $3,500 exceeds the amount deducted under paragraph 8(1)(m) in computing the taxpayer's income for the year;

**Related Provisions:** 60(j.02) — Payments to registered pension plan; 127.52(1)(a) — Limitation on deduction for minimum tax purposes.

**Notes:** 60(j.03) added by 1992 technical bill, effective 1991.

**Regulations:** 6503 (prescribed statutory provisions for 60(j.03)(i)(A)).

**(j.04) repayments of post-1989 pension benefits** — the total of all amounts each of which is an amount paid in the year by the taxpayer to a registered pension plan as

(i) a repayment under a prescribed statutory provision of an amount received from the plan that

(A) was included under subsection 56(1) in computing the taxpayer's income for a taxation year ending after 1989, and

(B) can reasonably be considered not to have been designated by the taxpayer for the purpose of paragraph (j.2), or

(ii) interest in respect of a repayment referred to in subparagraph (i),

except to the extent that the total was deductible under paragraph 8(1)(m) in computing the taxpayer's income for the year;

**Related Provisions**: 127.52(1)(a) — Limitation on deduction for minimum tax purposes.

**Notes**: 60(j.04) added by 1992 technical bill, effective 1990.

**Regulations**: 6503 (prescribed statutory provisions for 60(j.04)(i)).

(j.1) **transfer of retiring allowances [to RRSP]** — such part of the total of all amounts each of which is an amount paid to the taxpayer by an employer, or under a retirement compensation arrangement to which the employer has contributed, as a retiring allowance and included in computing the taxpayer's income for the year by virtue of subparagraph 56(1)(a)(ii) or paragraph 56(1)(x) as

(i) is designated by the taxpayer in the taxpayer's return of income under this Part for the year,

(ii) does not exceed the amount, if any, by which the total of

(A) $2,000 multiplied by the number of years before 1996 during which the employee or former employee in respect of whom the payment was made (in this paragraph referred to as the "retiree") was employed by the employer or a person related to the employer, and

(B) $1,500 multiplied by the number by which the number of years before 1989 described in clause (A) exceeds the number that can reasonably be regarded as the equivalent number of years before 1989 in respect of which employer contributions under either a pension plan or a deferred profit sharing plan of the employer or a person related to the employer had vested in the retiree at the time of the payment

exceeds the total of

(C) all amounts deducted under this paragraph in respect of amounts paid before the year in respect of the retiree

(I) by the employer or a person related to the employer, or

(II) under a retirement compensation arrangement to which the employer or a person related to the employer has contributed,

(C.1) all other amounts deducted under this paragraph for the year in respect of amounts paid in the year in respect of the retiree

(I) by a person related to the employer, or

(II) under a retirement compensation arrangement to which a person related to the employer has contributed, and

(D) all amounts deducted under paragraph (t) in computing the retiree's income for the year in respect of a retirement compensation arrangement to which the employer or a person related to the employer has contributed, and

(iii) does not exceed the total of all amounts each of which is an amount paid by the taxpayer in the year or within 60 days after the end of the year in respect of the amount so designated

(A) as a contribution to or under a registered pension plan, other than the portion thereof deductible under paragraph (j) or 8(1)(m) in computing the taxpayer's income for the year, or

(B) as a premium (within the meaning assigned by section 146) under a registered retirement savings plan under which the taxpayer is the annuitant (within the meaning assigned by section 146), other than the portion thereof that has been designated for the purposes of paragraph (j) or (l),

to the extent that it was not deducted in computing the taxpayer's income for a preceding taxation year

and for the purposes of this paragraph, "person related to the employer" includes

(iv) any person whose business was acquired or continued by the employer, and

(v) a previous employer of the retiree whose service therewith is recognized in determining the retiree's pension benefits;

**Related Provisions**: 60(j.01) — Transfer of surplus; 127.52(1)(a) [repealed] — Limitation on deduction for minimum tax purposes; 146(5) — Amount of RRSP premiums deductible; 146(6.1) — Recontribution of certain withdrawals; 147.3 — Transfer from RPP; 204.2(1)(b)(i)(A) — Excess amount in respect of RRSP. See additional Related Provisions and Definitions at end of s. 60.

**Notes**: In general, 60(j.1) allows a rollover to an RRSP of part of a "retiring allowance" (which includes a wrongful dismissal settlement and severance pay). The limit is $2,000 for each calendar year (or part year) of employment before 1996, plus $1,500 for each such year before 1989 for which the employer's pension contributions (if any) have not vested (the CCRA's interpretation of "vested" is found in Income Tax Technical News No. 7). If form TD2 (direct transfer) is used, the employer is not required to withhold tax at source on the portion of the retiring allowance being transferred to the RRSP. Otherwise, lump-sum withholding is required under Reg. 103(4).

Due to the repeal of 127.52(1)(a) effective 1998, RRSP rollovers under 60(j.1) are no longer added back into income for alternative minimum tax (AMT) purposes.

The words "before 1996" added to 60(j.1)(ii)(A) by 1995 Budget, effective 1996. This change has the effect of phasing out the rollover of retiring allowances, as departing employees will have relatively fewer years of employment before 1996 as time passes.

60(j.1)(ii)(B) amended by 1990 pension bill: "before 1989" was added in two places, effective 1989.

60(j.1)(ii)(C.1) added, and (ii)(D) and (iii) amended by 1991 technical bill, effective 1990, to deal with retiring allowances from two or more related employers.

**Regulations**: 100(3)(c) (no source withholding where amount is paid by employer directly to RRSP); 100(3.1) (limitation on extent to which payroll deduction of employee contribution reduces source withholding).

**Interpretation Bulletins**: IT-124R6: Contributions to registered retirement savings plans; IT-337R3: Retiring allowances.

**Information Circulars**: 79-8R3: Forms to use to directly transfer funds to or between plans, or to purchase an annuity.

**I.T. Technical News**: No. 7 (retiring allowances); No. 19 (Retiring allowances — clarification to Interpretation Bulletin IT-337R3 — (d): Deductions at source).

**Advance Tax Rulings**: ATR-12: Retiring allowance; ATR-48: Transfer of retiring allowance to an RRSP.

**Forms**: NRTA1: Authorization for non-resident tax exemption; TD2: Tax deduction waiver in respect of funds to be transferred.

(j.2) **transfer to spousal RRSP [before 1995]** — for taxation years ending after 1988 and before 1995, such part of the total of all amounts (other than amounts paid out of or under a registered retirement savings plan or a registered retirement income fund that by reason of section 254 are considered to be amounts paid out of or under a registered pension plan) paid on a periodic basis out of or under a registered pension plan or a deferred profit sharing plan and included, by reason of subsection 56(1), in computing the taxpayer's income for the year as

(i) is designated by the taxpayer in the taxpayer's return of income under this Part for the year, and

(ii) does not exceed the least of

(A) $6,000,

(B) the amount, if any, by which that total exceeds the part of that total designated for the year for the purposes of paragraph (j) of this Act or deducted under paragraph 60(k) of the *Income Tax Act*, chapter 148 of the Revised Statutes of Canada, 1952, in computing the taxpayer's income for the year, and

(C) the total of all amounts each of which is paid by the taxpayer in the year or

within 60 days after the end of the year as a premium (within the meaning assigned by subsection 146(1)) under a registered retirement savings plan under which the taxpayer's spouse or common-law partner (or, where the taxpayer died in the year or within 60 days after the end of the year, an individual who was the taxpayer's spouse or common-law partner immediately before the death) is the annuitant (within the meaning assigned by subsection 146(1)), to the extent that the amount was not deducted in computing the taxpayer's income for a preceding taxation year;

**Related Provisions**: 60(j.02) — Payment to registered pension plan; 60(j.04) — Repayments of post-1989 pension benefits; 118(3) — Pension income credit; 127.52(1)(a) [repealed] — Limitation on deduction for minimum tax purposes; 146(1) — "earned income"; 146(5.1) — Amount of spousal RRSP premiums deductible; 146(8.3) — Spousal RRSP payments; 146(16) — RRSP — deduction on transfer of funds; 146.3(5.1) — Amount included in income; 147(21) — Restriction re transfers; 147.1(3)(a) — Deemed registration; 147.3(12)(b)(i) — RPP — restriction re transfers; 204.2(1)(b)(i)(A) — Excess amount in respect of RRSP; 212(1)(h)(iii.1)(B), 212(1)(m)(ii) — Exemption on payment to non-resident.

**Notes**: 60(j.2) amended by 2000 same-sex partners bill to add reference to "common-law partner", effective for the 2001 and later taxation years, or earlier by election (see Notes to 248(1)"common-law partner").

60(j.2)(ii)(C) amended by 1993 technical bill, effective for 1992 and later taxation years, to add the parenthesized words beginning "(or, where the taxpayer died in the year...". The change means that where an individual dies in the year or within 60 days after the end of the year, a deduction under 60(j.2) can be claimed for the deceased for RRSP premiums paid on the deceased's behalf to an RRSP whose annuitant is the widow or widower (including a common-law spouse). A parallel change was made to 146(5.1).

60(j.2) added by 1990 pension bill, effective 1989.

**Interpretation Bulletins**: IT-307R3: Spousal registered retirement savings plans.

**Information Circulars**: 79-8R3: Forms to use to directly transfer funds to or between plans, or to purchase an annuity.

(k) [Repealed under former Act]

**Notes**: 60(k) repealed by 1990 pension bill, effective 1990. It allowed transfers of amounts from one DPSP to another. For such transfers, now limited to lump-sum amounts, see 147(19)–(21).

(l) **transfer of refund of premium under RRSP [on death]** — the total of all amounts each of which is an amount paid by or on behalf of the taxpayer in the year or within 60 days after the end of the year (or within such longer period after the end of the year as is acceptable to the Minister)

(i) as a premium under a registered retirement savings plan under which the taxpayer is the annuitant,

(ii) to acquire, from a person licensed or otherwise authorized under the laws of Canada or a province to carry on in Canada an annuities business, an annuity

(A) under which the taxpayer is the annuitant

(I) for the taxpayer's life, or for the lives jointly of the taxpayer and the taxpayer's spouse or common-law partner either without a guaranteed period, or with a guaranteed period that is not greater than 90 years minus the lesser of the age in whole years of the taxpayer and the age in whole years of the taxpayer's spouse or common-law partner at the time the annuity was acquired, or

(II) for a term equal to 90 years minus the age in whole years of the taxpayer or the age in whole years of the taxpayer's spouse or common-law partner, at the time the annuity was acquired, or

(B) under which the taxpayer, or a trust under which the taxpayer is the sole person beneficially interested in amounts payable under the annuity, is the annuitant for a term not exceeding 18 years minus the age in whole years of the taxpayer at the time the annuity was acquired

that does not provide for any payment thereunder except

(C) the single payment by or on behalf of the taxpayer,

(D) annual or more frequent periodic payments

(I) beginning not later than one year after the date of the payment referred to in clause (C), and

(II) each of which is equal to all other such payments or not equal to all other such payments solely because of an adjustment that would, if the annuity were an annuity under a retirement savings plan, be in accordance with subparagraphs 146(3)(b)(iii) to (v), and

(E) payments in full or partial commutation of the annuity and, where the commutation is partial,

(I) equal annual or more frequent periodic payments thereafter, or

(II) annual or more frequent periodic payments thereafter that are not equal solely because of an adjustment that would, if the annuity were an annuity under a retirement savings plan, be in accordance with subparagraphs 146(3)(b)(iii) to (v),

or

(iii) to a carrier as consideration for a registered retirement income fund under which the taxpayer is the annuitant

where that total

(iv) is designated by the taxpayer in the taxpayer's return of income under this Part for the year,

(v) does not exceed the total of

(A) the amount included in computing the taxpayer's income for the year as a refund of premiums out of or under a registered retirement savings plan under which the taxpayer's spouse or common-law partner was the annuitant,

(B) the amount included in computing the taxpayer's income for the year as a refund of premiums out of or under a registered retirement savings plan where the taxpayer was dependent by reason of physical or mental infirmity on the annuitant under the plan,

(B.1) the least of

(I) the amount paid by or on behalf of the taxpayer to acquire an annuity that would be described in subparagraph (ii) if that subparagraph were read without reference to clause (A) thereof,

(II) the amount (other than any portion thereof included in the amount determined under clause (B) or (B.2)) included in computing the taxpayer's income for the year as

1. a payment (other than a payment that is part of a series of periodic payments or that relates to an actuarial surplus) received by the taxpayer out of or under a registered pension plan,

2. a refund of premiums out of or under a registered retirement savings plan, or

3. a designated benefit in respect of a registered retirement income fund (in this clause having the meaning assigned by subsection 146.3(1))

as a consequence of the death of an individual of whom the taxpayer is a child or grandchild, and

(III) the amount, if any, by which the amount determined for the year under subclause (II) in respect of the taxpayer exceeds the amount, if any, by which

1. the total of all designated benefits of the taxpayer for the year in respect of registered retirement income funds

exceeds

Subdivision e — Deductions in Computing Income  S. 60(l)

2. the total of all amounts that would be eligible amounts of the taxpayer for the year in respect of those funds (within the meaning that would be assigned by subsection 146.3(6.11) if the taxpayer were described in paragraph (b) thereof), and

(B.2) all eligible amounts of the taxpayer for the year in respect of registered retirement income funds (within the meaning assigned by subsection 146.3(6.11)),

and, where the amount is paid by a direct transfer from the issuer of a registered retirement savings plan or a carrier of a registered retirement income fund,

(C) the amount included in computing the taxpayer's income for the year as a consequence of a payment described in subparagraph 146(2)(b)(ii), and

(D) the amount, if any, by which

(I) the amount received by the taxpayer out of or under a registered retirement income fund under which the taxpayer is the annuitant and included because of subsection 146.3(5) in computing the taxpayer's income for the year

exceeds

(II) the amount, if any, by which the minimum amount (within the meaning assigned by subsection 146.3(1)) under the fund for the year exceeds the total of all amounts received out of or under the fund in the year by an individual who was an annuitant under the fund before the taxpayer became the annuitant under the fund and that were included because of subsection 146.3(5) in computing that individual's income for the year, and

(vi) was not deducted in computing the taxpayer's income for a preceding taxation year;

**Related Provisions**: 56(1)(d.2) — Income inclusion; 60(j) — Transfer of superannuation benefits; 60(j.01) — Transfer of surplus; 104(27) — Pension benefits; 127.52(1)(a) — Minimum tax — adjusted taxable income determined; 146(2), (3) — Acceptance of plan for registration; 146(5) — Amount of RRSP premiums deductible; 146(6.1) — Recontribution of certain withdrawals; 146(8.1) — RRSP — deemed receipt of refund of premiums; 146(8.2) — RRSP — amount deductible; 146(16) — RRSP — deduction on transfer of funds; 146(16)(d) — RRSP — transfer of funds; 146(21) — Transfer from prescribed provincial pension plan; 146.3(5.1) — Amount included in income; 146.3(6.11) — Transfer of designated benefit; 147.3 — Transfer from RPP; 148(1)(e) — Amounts included in computing policyholder's income; 204.2(1)(b)(i)(A) — Excess amount for a year in respect of RRSP; 212(1)(q)(i)(B) — Exemption from non-resident withholding tax; 248(8) — Occurrences as a consequence of death; 252(3) — Extended meaning of "spouse". See additional Related Provisions and Definitions at end of s. 60.

**Notes**: A "refund of premiums", as defined in 146(1), is paid on the death of the annuitant. 60(l) allows it to be rolled into the RRSP of the deceased's spouse, child or grandchild, subject to various conditions.

60(l) amended by 2000 same-sex partners bill to add reference to "common-law partner", effective for the 2001 and later taxation years, or earlier by election (see Notes to 248(1)"common-law partner").

60(l) opening words amended by 1999 Budget to add "(or within such longer period after the end of the year as is acceptable to the Minister)", effective for 1999 and later taxation years and, where an amount is included in computing a taxpayer's income for a taxation year as a result of an election under subsection 42(4) of the 1999 Budget bill (see Notes to 146(1)"refund of premiums"), 60(l) applies to the taxpayer for the year and each later taxation year that ends before 1999 as if

(a) the words "in the year or within 60 days after the end of the year" were read as "in the period that begins at the beginning of the year and ends on February 29, 2000 or on such later day as is acceptable to the Minister"; and

(b) 60(l)(iv) were read as follows:

(iv) is designated in prescribed form filed with the Minister before May 2000 (or before such later day as is acceptable to the Minister),

60(l) amended by 1990 pension bill, effective 1989, and 60(l)(ii)(A) and (B) amended retroactive to 1989 by 1995-97 technical bill, to make the wording consistent with 146(1)"qualified investment"(c.1). For 1988, ignore 60(l)(ii)(A)(II).

60(l)(ii)(D) and (E) amended by 1992 technical bill, effective 1990, to allow the acquisition of annuities that provide for payments that are cost-of-living adjusted or that otherwise fluctuate in ways permitted by 146(3)(b)(iii) to (v). For 1989, read:

(D) equal annual or more frequent periodic payments commencing not later than one year after the date of the payment referred to in clause (C), and

(E) payments in full or partial commutation of the annuity and, where the commutation is partial, equal annual or more frequent periodic payments thereafter,

60(l)(v)(B.1)(II)3, (B.1)(III) and reference to (B.2) in opening words of 60(l)(v)(B.1)(II) added by 1993 technical bill, effective for 1993 and later taxation years.

Former 60(l)(v)(B.2) added by 1991 technical bill and repealed by 1993 technical bill. It permitted a rollover of an amount received from the Saskatchewan Pension Plan on the death of the taxpayer's spouse or common-law spouse. This is now covered by 146(21). For the 1990 and 1991 taxation years, and for the 1992 taxation year if the taxpayer elects by notifying Revenue Canada in writing, read:

(B.2) the amount included in computing the taxpayer's income for the year that was received by the taxpayer, as a consequence of the death of the taxpayer's spouse, out of or under a provincial pension plan prescribed for the purposes of paragraph (v),

Current 60(l)(v)(B.2) added by 1993 technical bill, effective for 1993 and later taxation years. It allows a deduction for a transfer to an RRSP or RRIF or to acquire a life annuity described in 60(l)(ii).

60(l)(v)(D) amended by 1993 technical bill, effective for 1993 and later taxation years. For 1993 through 1996, read, after "the annuitant":

"(or, where the taxpayer's spouse died before 1993, under which the spouse was the annuitant)"

**Interpretation Bulletins**: IT-124R6: Contributions to registered retirement savings plans; IT-307R3: Spousal registered retirement savings plans; IT-500R: RRSPs — death of an annuitant; IT-517R: Pension tax credit; IT-528: Transfers of funds between registered plans.

**Information Circulars**: 79-8R3: Forms to use to directly transfer funds to or between plans, or to purchase an annuity.

**Advance Tax Rulings**: ATR-37: Refund of premiums transferred to spouse.

**Forms**: T2030: Direct transfer under subpara. 60(l)(v).

(m) **estate tax applicable to certain property** — that proportion of any superannuation or pension benefit, death benefit, benefit under a registered retirement savings plan or benefit under a deferred profit sharing plan, received by the taxpayer in the year, on or after the death of a predecessor, in payment of or on account of property to which the taxpayer is the successor, that

(i) such part of any tax payable under the *Estate Tax Act*, chapter E-9 of the Revised Statutes of Canada, 1970, in respect of the death of the predecessor as is determined under that Act to be the part thereof applicable to the property in payment of or on account of which the benefit was so received,

is of

(ii) the value of the property in payment of or on account of which the benefit was so received, computed as provided for the purpose of subsection 62(4) of the *Estate Tax Act*, chapter E-9 of the Revised Statutes of Canada, 1970;

**Notes**: The *Estate Tax Act* was repealed effective 1972. Canada does not impose an estate tax at present. See also Notes to 70(5).

(m.1) **succession duties applicable to certain property** — that proportion of any superannuation or pension benefit, death benefit, benefit under a registered retirement savings plan, benefit under a deferred profit sharing plan or benefit that is a payment under an income-averaging annuity contract, received by the taxpayer in the year, on or after the death of a predecessor, in payment of or on account of property to which the taxpayer is the successor, that

(i) such part of any succession duties payable under a law of a province in respect of the death of the predecessor as may reasonably be regarded as attributable to the property in payment of or on account of which the benefit was so received,

is of

(ii) the value of the property in payment of or on account of which the benefit was so received, as computed for the purposes of the law referred to in subparagraph (i);

**Notes**: At present, none of the provinces imposes succession duties. They do impose probate fees (called estate administration taxes in some provinces including Ontario), but those do not appear to be covered by 60(m.1). See also Notes to 70(5).

(n) **repayment of pension or benefits** — the amount of

(i) any pension described in clause 56(1)(a)(i)(A),

(i.1) any amount described in subparagraph 56(1)(a)(ii),

(ii) any benefit described in clause 56(1)(a)(i)(B),

(ii.1) any benefit described in subparagraph 56(1)(a)(vi), or

(iii) any amount or benefit described in subparagraph 56(1)(a)(iv) or paragraph 56(1)(r),

received by the taxpayer and included in computing the taxpayer's income for the year or a preceding taxation year, to the extent of the amount or benefit repaid by the taxpayer in the year otherwise than because of Part VII of the *Unemployment Insurance Act* or Part VII of the *Employment Insurance Act*;

**Notes**: Opening words of 60(n) changed from "the amount of any overpayment of" to "the amount of" by 1995-97 technical bill, effective June 30, 1996.

60(n)(i.1) added by 1993 technical bill, effective for repayments made in 1991 or later, to allow a deduction for retiring allowances repaid to the employer.

60(n)(ii.2) added by 1991 technical bill, effective for repayments made after September 14, 1989, and repealed by 1993 technical bill, effective for repayments made after October 1991. It read: "any amount described in subparagraph 56(1)(a)(vii)". The change is non-substantive, as such benefits and repayments are now covered by 56(1)(a)(vi) and 60(n)(ii.1); see Notes to 56(1)(a)(vi) and (vii).

60(n)(iii) amended by 1996 employment insurance bill and then by 1995-97 technical bill, both effective June 30, 1996. Before that date it read "any benefit under the *Unemployment Insurance Act*"; this was first changed to "*Employment Insurance Act*", then changed back to both Acts since procedures under the old UI Act are still ongoing.

60(n)(iv) repealed by 1996 employment insurance bill, effective 1998. It read: "any amount described in paragraph 56(1)(m)".

Closing words of 60(n) amended by 1996 employment insurance bill and then by 1995-97 technical bill, both effective June 30, 1996. The reference to the *Unemployment Insurance Act* was first changed to *Employment Insurance Act*, then changed back to both Acts since procedures under the old UI Act are still ongoing.

**Forms**: PD24: Statement of overpayment and application for refund; T2204: Employee overpayment of CPP contributions and EI premiums.

(o) **legal [or other] expenses [of objection or appeal]** — amounts paid by the taxpayer in the year in respect of fees or expenses incurred in preparing, instituting or prosecuting an objection to, or an appeal in relation to,

(i) an assessment of tax, interest or penalties under this Act or an Act of a province that imposes a tax similar to the tax imposed under this Act,

(ii) a decision of the Canada Employment and Immigration Commission, the Canada Employment and Insurance Commission, a board of referees or an umpire under the *Unemployment Insurance Act* or the *Employment Insurance Act*,

(iii) an assessment of any income tax deductible by the taxpayer under section 126 or any interest or penalty with respect thereto, or

Subdivision e — Deductions in Computing Income    S. 60(q)(iii)

(iv) an assessment or a decision made under the *Canada Pension Plan* or a provincial pension plan as defined in section 3 of that Act;

**Related Provisions**: 56(1)(l) — Reimbursed costs included in income; 152(1.2) — Rule applies to determination of losses as well as assessment. See additional Related Provisions and Definitions at end of s. 60.

**Notes**: The CCRA administratively permits 60(o)(i) to apply not only to fees for objecting to an assessment or reassessment, but also to fees for dealing with CCRA auditors upon being advised that one is under audit or review (i.e., fees for preventing a reassessment from being issued in the first place): IT-99R5, para. 7.

Note also that 60(o)(i) does not say "an assessment *of the taxpayer*". Therefore, amounts paid by a major shareholder to contest a corporation's assessment should still be deductible. See *Theodore Sherman (Walbi Trust)*, [1976] C.T.C. 2207 (TRB).

Legal fees may also be deductible from business or property income under generally accepted accounting principles. See Notes to 9(1). For other provisions allowing deduction of (or credit for) specific legal costs, see 8(1)(b), 8(1)(f), 20(1)(e), 20(1)(cc), 60(o.1), 62(3)(f), 118.2(2)(l.1)(i) and 152(1.2). See Interpretation Bulletin IT-99R5.

60(o)(ii) amended by 1996 Dept. of Human Resources bill, effective July 12, 1996, to change "Canada Employment and Immigration Commission" to "Canada Employment Insurance Commission". Amended by 1996 EI bill and then by 1995-97 technical bill, both effective June 30, 1996. The reference to the *Unemployment Insurance Act* was first changed to *Employment Insurance Act*, then changed back to both Acts since procedures under the old UI Act are still ongoing.

**Interpretation Bulletins**: IT-99R5: Legal and accounting fees; IT-337R3: Retiring allowances.

(o.1) **legal expenses** — the amount, if any, by which the lesser of

(i) the total of all legal expenses (other than those relating to a division or settlement of property arising out of, or on a breakdown of, a marriage or common-law partnership) paid by the taxpayer in the year or in any of the 7 preceding taxation years to collect or establish a right to an amount of

(A) a benefit under a pension fund or plan (other than a benefit under the *Canada Pension Plan* or a provincial pension plan as defined in section 3 of that Act) in respect of the employment of the taxpayer or a deceased individual of whom the taxpayer was a dependant, relation or legal representative, or

(B) a retiring allowance of the taxpayer or a deceased individual of whom the taxpayer was a dependant, relation or legal representative, and

(ii) the amount, if any, by which the total of all amounts each of which is

(A) an amount described in clause (i)(A) or (B)

(I) that is received after 1985,

(II) in respect of which legal expenses described in subparagraph (i) were paid, and

(III) that is included in computing the income of the taxpayer for the year or a preceding taxation year, or

(B) an amount included in computing the income of the taxpayer under paragraph 56(1)(l.1) for the year or a preceding taxation year,

exceeds the total of all amounts each of which is an amount deducted under paragraph (j), (j.01), (j.1) or (j.2) in computing the income of the taxpayer for the year or a preceding taxation year, to the extent that the amount may reasonably be considered to have been deductible as a consequence of the receipt of an amount referred to in clause (A),

exceeds

(iii) the portion of the total described in subparagraph (i) in respect of the taxpayer that may reasonably be considered to have been deductible under this paragraph in computing the income of the taxpayer for a preceding taxation year;

**Related Provisions**: 56(1)(l.1) — Amounts included in income — amounts received as award or in reimbursement of legal expenses paid to collect or establish a right to retiring allowance, etc. See additional Related Provisions and Definitions at end of s. 60.

**Notes**: 60(o.1) amended by 2000 same-sex partners bill to add reference to "common-law partnership", effective for the 2001 and later taxation years, or earlier by election (see Notes to 248(1)"common-law partner").

60(o.1) added by 1989 Budget, effective 1986, and amended by 1992 technical bill due to the new definition of "marriage", in 252(4)(b), effective 1993. For 1986 to 1992, it referred to "marriage or other conjugal relationship".

See also Notes to 60(o).

**Interpretation Bulletins**: IT-99R5: Legal and accounting fees.

(p) [Repealed]

**Notes**: 60(p) amended by 1992 Child Benefit bill for 1990–1994, and repealed effective 1995. It provided a deduction for repayment of an overpaid (pre-1993) family business.

(q) **refund of income payments** — where the taxpayer is an individual, an amount paid by the taxpayer in the year to a person with whom the taxpayer was dealing at arm's length (in this paragraph referred to as the "payer") if

(i) the amount has been included in computing the income of the taxpayer in a preceding taxation year as an amount described in subparagraph 56(1)(n)(i) or paragraph 56(1)(o) paid to the taxpayer by the payer,

(ii) at the time the amount was paid by the payer to the taxpayer a condition was stipulated for the taxpayer to fulfil,

(iii) as a result of the failure of the taxpayer to fulfil the condition referred to in subparagraph (ii) the taxpayer was required to repay the amount to the payer,

**S. 60(q)(iv)**     Income Tax Act, Part I, Division B

(iv) during the period for which the amount referred to in subparagraph (i) was paid the taxpayer did not provide other than occasional services to the payer as an officer or under a contract of employment, and

(v) the amount was paid to the taxpayer for the purpose of enabling the taxpayer to further the taxpayer's education;

**Related Provisions**: 56(1)(p) — Refund of scholarships, bursaries and research grants. See additional Related Provisions and Definitions at end of s. 60.

**Interpretation Bulletins**: IT-75R3: Scholarships, fellowships, bursaries, prizes, and research grants; IT-340R: Scholarships, fellowships, bursaries and research grants.

(r) **amounts included under subsec. 146.2(6) [RHOSP]** — where an amount has been included in computing the income of the taxpayer by virtue of subsection 146.2(6) of the *Income Tax Act*, chapter 148 of the Revised Statutes of Canada, 1952 (as it read in its application to the 1985 taxation year) for any of the taxpayer's three immediately preceding taxation years, the taxpayer may deduct the lesser of

(i) the amount that had been so included in computing the taxpayer's income, and

(ii) the total of all amounts used by the taxpayer to acquire in the year the taxpayer's owner-occupied home (within the meaning assigned by paragraph 146.2(1)(f) of the *Income Tax Act*, chapter 148 of the Revised Statutes of Canada, 1952, as it read in its application to the 1985 taxation year),

except that no amount may be deducted by the taxpayer for the year under this paragraph if an amount has been deducted

(iii) under subsection 146.2(6.1) of the *Income Tax Act*, chapter 148 of the Revised Statutes of Canada, 1952 (as it read in its application to taxation years before 1986) in computing the taxpayer's income for any taxation year ending before 1986, or

(iv) under this paragraph for any preceding taxation year ending after 1985;

**Related Provisions**: See Related Provisions and Definitions at end of s. 60.

**Notes**: 60(r) relates to registered home ownership savings plans (RHOSPs) under 146.2, which were eliminated in 1985.

**I.T. Application Rules**: 69 (meaning of "*Income Tax Act*, chapter 148 of the Revised Statutes of Canada, 1952").

(s) **repayment of policy loan** — the total of all repayments made by the taxpayer in the year in respect of a policy loan (within the meaning assigned by subsection 148(9) made under a life insurance policy, not exceeding the amount, if any, by which

(i) the total of all amounts required by subsection 148(1) to be included in computing the taxpayer's income for the year or a preceding taxation year from a disposition described in paragraph (b) of the definition "disposition" in subsection 148(9) in respect of that policy

exceeds

(ii) the total of all repayments made by the taxpayer in respect of the policy loan that were deductible in computing the taxpayer's income for a preceding taxation year;

**Related Provisions**: 94.2(10)(a)(ii) — No application to foreign insurance policy of foreign investment entity; 148(9) — "value". See additional Related provisions and Definitions at end of s. 60.

**Notes**: Opening words of 60(s) amended by 1992 technical bill, effective for repayments made after December 20, 1991, to change "payments" to "repayments". The amendment was intended to clarify that the deductible portion will not include any amount in respect of interest paid on such a loan.

(t) **RCA distributions** — where an amount in respect of a particular retirement compensation arrangement is required by paragraph 56(1)(x) or (z) or subsection 70(2) to be included in computing the taxpayer's income for the year, an amount equal to the lesser of

(i) the total of all amounts in respect of the particular arrangement so required to be included in computing the taxpayer's income for the year, and

(ii) the amount, if any, by which the total of all amounts each of which is

(A) an amount (other than an amount deductible under paragraph 8(1)(m.2) or transferred to the particular arrangement under circumstances in which subsection 207.6(7) applies) contributed under the particular arrangement by the taxpayer while it was a retirement compensation arrangement and before the end of the year,

(A.1) an amount transferred in respect of the taxpayer before the end of the year to the particular arrangement from another retirement compensation arrangement under circumstances in which subsection 207.6(7) applies, to the extent that the amount would have been deductible under this paragraph in respect of the other arrangement in computing the taxpayer's income if it had been received by the taxpayer out of the other arrangement,

(B) an amount paid by the taxpayer before the end of the year and at a time when the taxpayer was resident in Canada to acquire an interest in the particular arrangement, or

(C) an amount that was received or became receivable by the taxpayer before the end of the year and at a time when the taxpayer was resident in Canada as proceeds from the disposition of an interest in the particular arrangement, exceeds the total of all amounts each of which is

(D) an amount deducted under this paragraph or paragraph (u) in respect of the particular arrangement in computing the taxpayer's income for a preceding taxation year, or

(E) an amount transferred in respect of the taxpayer before the end of the year from the particular arrangement to another retirement compensation arrangement under circumstances in which subsection 207.6(7) applies, to the extent that the amount would have been deductible under this paragraph in respect of the particular arrangement in computing the taxpayer's income if it had been received by the taxpayer out of the particular arrangement;

**Related Provisions**: 107.2 — Distribution by retirement compensation arrangement. See additional Related Provisions and Definitions at end of s. 60.

**Notes**: 60(t) amended by 1995-97 technical bill, effective for 1996 and later taxation years. For 1989-95, read:

(t) amount included under para. 56(1)(x) or (z) or subsec. 70(2) — where an amount in respect of a retirement compensation arrangement is required by paragraph 56(1)(x) or (z) or subsection 70(2) to be included in computing the taxpayer's income for the year, an amount equal to the lesser of

(i) the total of all amounts in respect of the arrangement so required to be included in the taxpayer's income for the year, and

(ii) the amount, if any, by which the total of

(A) all amounts, other than amounts deductible under paragraph 8(1)(m.2), contributed under the arrangement by the taxpayer while it was a retirement compensation arrangement and before the end of the year,

(B) all amounts paid by the taxpayer before the end of the year and at a time when the taxpayer was resident in Canada to acquire an interest in the arrangement, and

(C) all amounts that were received or became receivable by the taxpayer before the end of the year and at a time when the taxpayer was resident in Canada as proceeds from the disposition of an interest in the arrangement,

exceeds the total of all amounts deducted under this paragraph or paragraph (u) in respect of the arrangement in computing the taxpayer's income for a preceding taxation year;

(u) **RCA dispositions** — where an amount in respect of a particular retirement compensation arrangement is required by paragraph 56(1)(y) to be included in computing the taxpayer's income for the year, an amount equal to the lesser of

(i) the total of all amounts in respect of the particular arrangement so required to be included in computing the taxpayer's income for the year, and

(ii) the amount, if any, by which the total of all amounts each of which is

(A) an amount (other than an amount deductible under paragraph 8(1)(m.2) or transferred to the particular arrangement under circumstances in which subsection 207.6(7) applies) contributed under the particular arrangement by the taxpayer while it was a retirement compensation arrangement and before the end of the year,

(A.1) an amount transferred in respect of the taxpayer before the end of the year to the particular arrangement from another retirement compensation arrangement under circumstances in which subsection 207.6(7) applies, to the extent that the amount would have been deductible under paragraph (t) in respect of the other arrangement in computing the taxpayer's income if it had been received by the taxpayer out of the other arrangement, or

(B) an amount paid by the taxpayer before the end of the year and at a time when the taxpayer was resident in Canada to acquire an interest in the particular arrangement

exceeds the total of all amounts each of which is

(C) an amount deducted under paragraph (t) in respect of the particular arrangement in computing the taxpayer's income for the year or a preceding taxation year,

(D) an amount deducted under this paragraph in respect of the particular arrangement in computing the taxpayer's income for a preceding taxation year, or

(E) an amount transferred in respect of the taxpayer before the end of the year from the particular arrangement to another retirement compensation arrangement under circumstances in which subsection 207.6(7) applies, to the extent that the amount would have been deductible under paragraph (t) in respect of the particular arrangement in computing the taxpayer's income if it had been received by the taxpayer out of the particular arrangement;

**Related Provisions**: 56(1)(y) — Retirement compensation arrangements; 107.2 — Distribution by a retirement compensation arrangement. See additional Related Provisions and Definitions at end of s. 60.

**Notes**: 60(u) amended by 1995-97 technical bill, effective for 1996 and later taxation years. For 1989-95, read:

(u) amount included under para. 56(1)(y) — where an amount in respect of a retirement compensation arrangement is required by paragraph 56(1)(y) to be included in computing the taxpayer's income for the year, an amount equal to the lesser of

(i) the total of all amounts in respect of the arrangement so required to be included in the taxpayer's income for the year, and

(ii) the amount, if any, by which the total of

(A) all amounts, other than amounts deductible under paragraph 8(1)(m.2), contributed under the arrangement by the taxpayer while it was a retirement compensation arrangement and before the end of the year, and

(B) all amounts paid by the taxpayer before the end of the year and at a time when the taxpayer was resident in Canada to acquire an interest in the arrangement

exceeds the total of

(C) the total of all amounts deducted under paragraph (t) in respect of the arrangement in computing the taxpayer's income for the year or a preceding taxation year, and

(D) the total of all amounts deducted under this paragraph in respect of the arrangement in computing the taxpayer's income for a preceding taxation year;

(v) **contribution to a provincial pension plan** — the least of

(i) the amount, if any, by which

(A) the total of all amounts each of which is a contribution made in the year, or within 60 days after the end of the year, by the taxpayer to the account of the taxpayer, or of the taxpayer's spouse or common-law partner, under a prescribed provincial pension plan

exceeds

(B) the portion of the total described in clause (A) that was deducted in computing the taxpayer's income for the preceding taxation year,

(ii) the prescribed amount for the year in respect of the plan, and

(iii) the amount by which the taxpayer's RRSP deduction limit for the year exceeds the total of the amounts deducted under subsections 146(5) and (5.1) in computing the taxpayer's income for the year;

**Related Provisions**: 18(11)(g) — No deduction for interest paid on money borrowed to make contribution; 60(l)(v)(B.2) — Transfer of premium under RRSP; 60.02 — 60(v)(iii) applicable since 1991; 118(3) — Pension tax credit; 128.1(10)"excluded right or interest"(g)(iii) — Emigration of individual — no deemed disposition of right to pension; 146(1)"unused RRSP deduction room"D — reduction in room; 146(21) — Transfer from prescribed provincial pension plan. See additional Related Provisions and Definitions at end of s. 60.

**Notes**: 60(v)(i)(a) amended by 2000 same-sex partners bill to add reference to "common-law partner", effective for the 2001 and later taxation years, or earlier by election (see Notes to 248(1)"common-law partner").

60(v)(i) amended by 1998 Budget, effective for 1998 and later taxation years, effectively to expand it to cover contributions to a spousal Saskatchewan Pension Plan account. For earlier years, read:

(i) the amount contributed by the taxpayer to the taxpayer's account under a prescribed provincial pension plan in the year or within 60 days after the end of the year to the extent that the amount has not been deducted in computing the taxpayer's income for a preceding taxation year,

60(v)(iii) amended by 1990 pension bill, effective 1991. (See 60.02.) For 1990 and earlier years, read:

(iii) the amount by which the amount determined in respect of the taxpayer for the year under paragraph 146(5)(a) or (b) (whichever is applicable in respect of the taxpayer) exceeds the aggregate of the amounts deducted under subsections 146(5) and (5.1) in computing his income for the year.

**Regulations**: 7800(1) (prescribed provincial pension plan is the Saskatchewan Pension Plan); 7800(2) (prescribed amount).

**Interpretation Bulletins**: IT-124R6: Contributions to registered retirement savings plans.

(v.1) **UI and EI benefit repayment** — any benefit repayment payable by the taxpayer under Part VII of the *Unemployment Insurance Act* or Part VII of the *Employment Insurance Act* on or before April 30 of the following year, to the extent that the amount was not deductible in computing the taxpayer's income for any preceding taxation year;

**Related Provisions**: 56(1)(a)(iv) — Unemployment insurance/employment insurance benefits taxable; 56(9) — Meaning of "income for the year"; 60(n)(iii) — Deduction for repayment under other Parts of the UI/EI Act; 63(2) — Child care expenses — income exceeding income of supporting person.

**Notes**: Employment insurance benefits are partially repayable when the taxpayer's net income exceeds a given threshold. The repayment is administered through the T1 General income tax return (line item 232). Such repayments, which reflect income that was originally subject to tax under 56(1)(a)(iv), are deductible under 60(v.1) to prevent taxation of income that was not kept by the recipient. They were formerly deductible in computing taxable income (rather than net income), under 110(1)(i).

See Notes to 180.2(1) re the legality of the EI benefit repayment requirement where the income threshold is exceeded due to income exempted under a tax treaty.

60(v.1) added by 1991 technical bill, effective 1989, and amended by 1996 EI bill and then by 1995-97 technical bill, both effective June 30, 1996. The reference to the *Unemployment Insurance Act* was first changed to *Employment Insurance Act*, then changed back to both Acts since procedures under the old UI Act are still ongoing.

(w) **tax under Part I.2** — the amount of the taxpayer's tax payable under Part I.2 for the year; and

**Related Provisions**: 56(9) — Meaning of "income for the year"; 180.2 — OAS benefits clawback. See additional Related Provisions and Definitions at end of s. 60.

**Notes**: 60(w) added by 1989 Budget, effective 1989. Part I.2 (180.2) imposes a "clawback" tax on old age security payments (and pre-1993 family allowance payments) received by taxpayers with high incomes. Where the clawback applies, the payment is partially or fully repaid under 180.2(1). Since it has also been brought into income under 56(1)(a)(i) for Part I tax purposes, the amount repaid under 180.2 is allowed as a deduction by 60(w) for Part I tax purposes to avoid double taxation.

(x) **CESG repayment** — the total of all amounts each of which is an amount paid by the taxpayer in the year as a repayment under Part III.1 of the *Department of Human Resources Development Act* of an amount included because of subsection 146.1(7) in computing the taxpayer's income for the year or a preceding taxation year.

**Notes**: Part III.1 of the DHRD Act provides the Canada Education Student Grant (CESG), a 20% grant on the first $2,000 of annual contributions made to a RESP (see 146.1). RESP trustees must limit

## Subdivision e — Deductions in Computing Income — S. 60.1(1)

CESG payments to $7,200 per beneficiary. However, if an individual is a beneficiary under more than one RESP, the total grants could exceed this limit, and the individual must repay the excess. Since the grants would have been included in income as educational assistance payments, 60(x) allows an offsetting deduction for the repayment.

60(x) added by 1998 Budget, effective for 1998 and later taxation years.

**Related Provisions [s. 60]:** 4(2), (3) — Whether deductions under s. 60 are applicable to a particular source.

**Definitions [s. 60]:** "allowance" — 56(12); "amount" — 248(1); "annuitant" — 146(1), 146.3(1); "annuity" — 248(1); "beneficially interested" — 248(25); "benefit under a deferred profit sharing plan", "business" — 248(1); "Canada" — 255; "child" — 252(1); "child support amount", "commencement day" — 56.1(4), 60.1(4); "common-law partner", "common-law partnership" — 248(1); "consequence of the death" — 248(8); "death benefit" — 248(1); "deferred profit sharing plan" — 147(1), 248(1); "eligible amount" — 60.01; "employee", "employee benefit plan", "employer", "employment" — 248(1); "estate" — 104(1), 248(1); "former spouse" — 252(3); "income-averaging annuity contract" — 61(4), 248(1); "individual" — 248(1); "life insurance policy" — 138(12), 248(1); "Minister" — 248(1); "parent" — 252(2); "person", "prescribed", "property" — 248(1); "province" — *Interpretation Act* 35(1); "registered pension plan" — 248(1); "registered retirement income fund" — 146.3(1), 248(1); "registered retirement savings plan", "RRSP deduction limit" — 146(1), 248(1); "related" — 251(2); "resident in Canada" — 250; "retirement compensation arrangement", "retiring allowance" — 248(1); "spouse" — 252(3); "superannuation or pension benefit" — 248(1); "support amount" — 56.1(4), 60.1(4); "taxable income" — 2(2), 248(1); "taxation year" — 249; "taxpayer" — 248(1); "trust" — 104(1), 248(1), (3); "writing" — *Interpretation Act* 35(1).

### 60.001 Application of subpara. 60(c.1)(i) — 
In the application of subparagraph 60(c.1)(i) in respect of amounts received pursuant to orders made after December 11, 1979 under the laws of Ontario, the references in that subparagraph to "February 10, 1988" and "February 11, 1988" shall be read as references to "December 11, 1979" and "December 12, 1979", respectively.

**Notes:** 60.001 added in the R.S.C. 1985 (5th Supp.) consolidation. This rule was formerly contained in the application rule to the 1988 tax reform amendment to 60(c.1). The reference to the subparagraph is to 60(c.1)(i) as it read before being amended by the 1992 technical bill (see Notes to 60(c), (c.1)).

**Definitions:** "amount" — 248(1).

### 60.01 Eligible amount — 
For the purpose of paragraph 60(j), the amount, if any, by which

(a) the amount of any payment received by a taxpayer in a taxation year out of or under a foreign retirement arrangement and included in computing the taxpayer's income because of clause 56(1)(a)(i)(C.1) (other than any portion thereof that is included in respect of the taxpayer for the year under subparagraph 60(j)(i) or that is part of a series of periodic payments)

exceeds

(b) the portion, if any, of the payment included under paragraph (a) that can reasonably be considered to derive from contributions to the foreign retirement arrangement made by a person other than the taxpayer or the taxpayer's spouse or common-law partner or former spouse or common-law partner,

is an eligible amount in respect of the taxpayer for the year.

**Notes:** See Notes to 248(1)"foreign retirement arrangement".

60.01(b) amended by 2000 same-sex partners bill to add reference to "common-law partner", effective for the 2001 and later taxation years, or earlier by election (see Notes to 248(1)"common-law partner").

60.01 added by 1991 technical bill, effective July 14, 1990. Amended by 1992 technical bill, effective 1993, to delete a reference to "spouse" having the meaning assigned by 146(1.1); this change is generally not substantive, since a common-law spouse became a spouse for all purposes under 252(4). However, the definition of "spouse" in (now-repealed) 252(4) differs slightly from that in former 146(1.1).

**Definitions [s. 60.01]:** "amount", "common-law partner" — 248(1); "foreign retirement arrangement" — 248(1); "former spouse" — 252(3); "person" — 248(1); "spouse" — 252(3); "taxation year" — 249; "taxpayer" — 248(1).

**Interpretation Bulletins:** IT-124R6: Contributions to registered retirement savings plans; IT-528: Transfers of funds between registered plans.

### 60.02 Application of subpara. 60(v)(iii) — 
Subparagraph 60(v)(iii) is applicable to the 1991 and subsequent taxation years.

**Notes:** 60.02 added in the R.S.C. 1985 (5th Supp.) consolidation. This rule was formerly part of the application rule in the 1990 pension bill amendment to 60(v)(iii).

**Definitions:** "taxation year" — 249.

### 60.1 (1) Support — 
For the purposes of paragraph 60(b) and subsection 118(5), where an order or agreement, or any variation thereof, provides for the payment of an amount by a taxpayer to a person or for the benefit of the person, children in the person's custody or both the person and those children, the amount or any part thereof

(a) when payable, is deemed to be payable to and receivable by that person; and

(b) when paid, is deemed to have been paid to and received by that person.

**Related Provisions:** 56.1(1) — Parallel rule for recipient; 60.11 — Application to orders made in Ontario after May 6, 1974.

**Notes:** Where an amount is deductible under 60.1(1), a parallel amount is normally included in the recipient's income by 56.1(1).

60.1(1) amended by 1996 Budget, effective for amounts received after 1996. For amounts received before 1997, read:

> 60.1 (1) Maintenance payments — Where a decree, order, judgment or written agreement described in paragraph 60(b) or (c), or any variation thereof, provides for the periodic payment of an amount by a taxpayer
>
> (a) to a person who is
>
> (i) the taxpayer's spouse or former spouse, or
>
> (ii) where the amount is paid under an order made by a competent tribunal in accordance with the laws of a province, an individual of the opposite sex who is the natural parent of a child of the taxpayer, or
>
> (b) for the benefit of the person, children in the custody of the person or both the person and those children,

**S. 60.1(1)**      Income Tax Act, Part I, Division B

the amount or any part thereof, when paid, shall be deemed for the purposes of paragraphs 60(b) and (c) to have been paid to and received by that person.

See also Notes at end of 60.1.

**Interpretation Bulletins:** IT-118R3: Alimony and maintenance; IT-530: Support payments.

**(2) Agreement** — For the purposes of section 60, this section and subsection 118(5), the amount determined by the formula

$$A - B$$

where

A   is the total of all amounts each of which is an amount (other than an amount that is otherwise a support amount) that became payable by a taxpayer in a taxation year, under an order of a competent tribunal or under a written agreement, in respect of an expense (other than an expenditure in respect of a self-contained domestic establishment in which the taxpayer resides or an expenditure for the acquisition of tangible property that is not an expenditure on account of a medical or education expense or in respect of the acquisition, improvement or maintenance of a self-contained domestic establishment in which the person described in paragraph (a) or (b) resides) incurred in the year or the preceding taxation year for the maintenance of a person, children in the person's custody or both the person and those children, where the person is

    (a) the taxpayer's spouse or common-law partner or former spouse or common-law partner, or

    (b) where the amount became payable under an order made by a competent tribunal in accordance with the laws of a province, an individual who is a parent of a child of whom the taxpayer is a natural parent,

and

B   is the amount, if any, by which

    (a) the total of all amounts each of which is an amount included in the total determined for A in respect of the acquisition or improvement of a self-contained domestic establishment in which that person resides, including any payment of principal or interest in respect of a loan made or indebtedness incurred to finance, in any manner whatever, such acquisition or improvement

exceeds

    (b) the total of all amounts each of which is an amount equal to $1/5$ of the original principal amount of a loan or indebtedness described in paragraph (a),

is, where the order or written agreement, as the case may be, provides that this subsection and subsection 56.1(2) shall apply to any amount paid or payable thereunder, deemed to be an amount payable by the taxpayer to that person and receivable by that person as an allowance on a periodic basis, and that person is deemed to have discretion as to the use of that amount.

**Related Provisions:** 56.1(2) — Parallel rule for recipient; 252(3) — Extended meaning of "spouse" and "former spouse".

**Notes:** As an alternative to payments to third parties qualifying under 60.1(2), a payment to a third party may be deductible if the payor is directed by the recipient to pay the third party, so that the recipient is still considered to have "discretion as to the use of the amount" (56.1(4)"support amount" and former 56(12)). See *Arsenault*, [1999] 4 C.T.C. 174 (FCA).

Although 60.1(2) purports to require that the court order or agreement specifically refer to 56.1(2) and 60.1(2) by number, the Courts may allow the reference to be implied: *Larsson*, [1996] 3 C.T.C. 2430 (TCC); *Pelchat*, [1998] 1 C.T.C. 2741 (TCC). Not always, however: *Paré*, [1994] 2 C.T.C. 2384 (TCC); *Armstrong*, [1996] 2 C.T.C. 266 (FCA); *Minicozzi*, [1998] 2 C.T.C. 2618 (TCC).

60.1(2)A(a) amended by 2000 same-sex partners bill to add reference to "common-law partner", effective for the 2001 and later taxation years, or earlier by election (see Notes to 248(1)"common-law partner").

60.1(2) opening words, description of "A" and closing words amended by 1996 Budget, effective for amounts received after 1996. For amounts received before 1997, read:

    (2) For the purposes of paragraphs 60(b) and (c), the amount determined by the formula

$$A - B$$

    where

    A   is the total of all amounts each of which is an amount (other than an amount to which paragraph 60(b) or (c) otherwise applies) paid by a taxpayer in a taxation year, under a decree, order or judgment of a competent tribunal or under a written agreement, in respect of an expense (other than an expenditure in respect of a self-contained domestic establishment in which the taxpayer resides or an expenditure for the acquisition of tangible property that is not an expenditure on account of a medical or education expense or in respect of the acquisition, improvement or maintenance of a self-contained domestic establishment in which the person described in paragraph (a) or (b) resides) incurred in the year or the preceding taxation year for maintenance of a person who is

        (a) the taxpayer's spouse or former spouse, or

        (b) where the amount is paid under an order made by a competent tribunal in accordance with the laws of a province, an individual of the opposite sex who is the natural parent of a child of the taxpayer,

    or for the maintenance of children in the person's custody or both the person and those children if, at the time the expense was incurred and throughout the remainder of the year, the taxpayer was living separate and apart from that person, and

    B   is the amount, if any, by which

        (a) the total of all amounts each of which is an amount included in the total determined for A in respect of the acquisition or improvement of a self-contained domestic establishment in which that person resides, including any payment of principal or interest in respect of a loan made or indebtedness incurred to finance, in any manner whatever, such acquisition or improvement

    exceeds

        (b) the total of all amounts each of which is an amount equal to $1/5$ of the original principal amount of a loan or indebtedness described in paragraph (a), shall, where the decree, order, judgment or written agreement, as the case may be, provides that this subsection and subsection 56.1(2) shall apply to any payment made thereunder, be deemed to be an amount paid by the taxpayer and received by that person as an allowance payable on a periodic basis.

See also Notes at end of 60.1.

**Interpretation Bulletins**: IT-118R3: Alimony and maintenance; IT-530: Support payments.

**(3) Prior payments** — For the purposes of this section and section 60, where a written agreement or order of a competent tribunal made at any time in a taxation year provides that an amount paid before that time and in the year or the preceding taxation year is to be considered to have been paid and received thereunder,

(a) the amount is deemed to have been paid thereunder; and

(b) the agreement or order is deemed, except for the purpose of this subsection, to have been made on the day on which the first such amount was paid, except that, where the agreement or order is made after April 1997 and varies a child support amount payable to the recipient from the last such amount paid to the recipient before May 1997, each varied amount of child support paid under the agreement or order is deemed to have been payable under an agreement or order the commencement day of which is the day on which the first payment of the varied amount is required to be made.

**Related Provisions**: 56.1(3) — Parallel rule for recipient.

**Notes**: 60.1(3) amended by 1996 Budget, effective for amounts received after 1996. For amounts paid before 1997, read:

(3) For the purposes of this section and section 60, where a decree, order or judgment of a competent tribunal or a written agreement made at any time in a taxation year provides that an amount paid before that time and in the year or the preceding taxation year is to be considered to have been paid and received thereunder, the amount shall be deemed to have been paid thereunder.

The amended version of 60.1(3) has a very strange side effect. See Notes to 56.1(3).

**Interpretation Bulletins**: IT-118R3: Alimony and maintenance; IT-530: Support payments.

**(4) Definitions** — The definitions in subsection 56.1(4) apply in this section and section 60.

**Notes [s. 60.1]**: See Notes to 56.1.

60.1 amended by 1992 technical bill, effective for decrees, orders and judgments made after 1992 and agreements entered into after 1992, except where the marriage breakdown occurred before 1993 (this exception added by 1993 technical bill, s. 135). The changes were not substantive: they reflect the new definition of "spouse" in 252(4), the consolidation of 60(b) and (c) into 60(b), and the renumbering of 60(c.1) as 60(c). The descriptive formula in 60.1(2) was redrafted in algebraic form. For decrees, orders and judgments made, and agreements entered into, before 1993 or where the marriage breakdown occurred before 1993, read:

60.1 (1) **Maintenance payments** — Where, after May 6, 1974, a decree, order, judgment or written agreement described in paragraph 60(b), (c) or (c.1), or any variation thereof, has been made providing for the periodic payment of an amount by a taxpayer

(a) to a person who is

(i) the taxpayer's spouse or former spouse, or

(ii) where the amount is paid pursuant to an order made by a competent tribunal after February 10, 1988 in accordance with the laws of a province, an individual of the opposite sex who

(A) before the date of the order cohabited with the taxpayer in a conjugal relationship, or

(B) is the natural parent of a child of the taxpayer, or

(b) for the benefit of the person or children in the custody of the person, or both the person and those children,

the amount or any part thereof, when paid, shall be deemed, for the purposes of paragraphs 60(b), (c) and (c.1), to have been paid to and received by that person.

(2) **Agreement** — For the purposes of paragraphs 60(b), (c) and (c.1), the amount, if any, by which

(a) the total of all amounts each of which is an amount (other than an amount to which paragraph 60(b), (c) or (c.1) otherwise applies) paid by a taxpayer in a taxation year, pursuant to a decree, order or judgment of a competent tribunal or pursuant to a written agreement, in respect of an expense (other than an expenditure in respect of a self-contained domestic establishment in which the taxpayer resides or an expenditure for the acquisition of tangible property that is not an expenditure on account of a medical or educational expense or in respect of the acquisition, improvement or maintenance of a self-contained domestic establishment in which the person described in subparagraph (i) or (ii) resides) incurred in the year or the immediately preceding taxation year for maintenance of a person who is

(i) the taxpayer's spouse or former spouse, or

(ii) where the amount is paid pursuant to an order made by a competent tribunal after February 10, 1988 in accordance with the laws of a province, an individual of the opposite sex who

(A) before the date of the order cohabited with the taxpayer in a conjugal relationship, or

(B) is the natural parent of a child of the taxpayer,

or for the maintenance of children in the person's custody or both the person and those children if, at the time the expense was incurred and throughout the remainder of the year, the taxpayer was living apart from that person

exceeds

(b) the amount, if any, by which

(i) the total of all amounts each of which is an amount included in the total determined under paragraph (a) in respect of the acquisition or improvement of a self-contained domestic establishment in which that person resides, including any payment of principal or interest in respect of a loan made or indebtedness incurred to finance, in any manner whatever, the acquisition or improvement

exceeds

(ii) the total of all amounts each of which is an amount equal to $1/5$ of the original principal amount of a loan or indebtedness described in subparagraph (i)

shall, where the decree, order, judgment or written agreement, as the case may be, provides that this subsection and subsection 56.1(2) shall apply to any payment made pursuant thereto, be deemed to be an amount paid by the taxpayer and received by that person as an allowance payable on a periodic basis.

(3) **Prior payments** — For the purposes of this section and section 60, where a decree, order or judgment of a competent tribunal or a written agreement made at any time in a taxation year provides that an amount paid before that time and in the year or the immediately preceding taxation year is to be considered as having been paid and received pursuant thereto, the following rules apply:

(a) the amount shall be deemed to have been paid pursuant thereto; and

(b) the person who made the payment shall be deemed to have been separated pursuant to a divorce, judicial separation or written separation agreement from the person's spouse or former spouse at the time the payment was made and throughout the remainder of the year.

60.1(1) amended by 1988 tax reform, except that for orders made after May 6, 1974 under the laws of Ontario, read "May 6, 1974" in place of "February 10, 1988" in subpara. (ii). (See s. 60.11).

**Definitions [s. 60.1]:** "amount" — 248(1); "child" — 252(1); "child support amount", "commencement day" — 56.1(4), 60.1(4); "former spouse" — 252(3); "housing unit" — 56.1(4); "individual" — 248(1); "parent" — 252(2); "person", "prescribed", "principal amount", "property" — 248(1); "province" — *Interpretation Act* 35(1); "received" — 248(7); "self-contained domestic establishment" — 248(1); "spouse" — 252(3); "support amount" — 56.1(4), 60.1(4); "taxation year" — 249; "taxpayer" — 248(1); "written" — *Interpretation Act* 35(1) [writing].

**60.11 Application of subpara. 60.1(1)(a)(ii)** — In the application of subparagraph 60.1(1)(a)(ii) in respect of amounts paid pursuant to orders made after May 6, 1974 under the laws of Ontario, the reference in that subparagraph to "February 10, 1988" shall be read as a reference to "May 6, 1974".

**Notes:** 60.11 added in the R.S.C. 1985 (5th Supp.) consolidation. This rule was formerly in the application rule in the tax reform amendment to 60.1(1) (1988, c. 55, s. 38(1)).

**Definitions:** "amount" — 248(1).

**60.2 (1) Refund of undeducted past service AVCs** — There may be deducted in computing a taxpayer's income for a taxation year an amount equal to the total of

(a) where the taxation year ends before 1991, the total of all amounts each of which is that portion of an amount paid to the taxpayer before 1991 and included by reason of subparagraph 56(1)(a)(i) or paragraph 56(1)(h) or (t) in computing the taxpayer's income for the year or a preceding taxation year that can reasonably be considered to be a refund of additional voluntary contributions made by the taxpayer before October 9, 1986 to a registered pension plan for the taxpayer's benefit in respect of services rendered by the taxpayer before the year in which the contributions were made, to the extent that the contributions were not deducted in computing the taxpayer's income for any taxation year; and

(b) the least of

(i) $3,500,

(ii) the total of all amounts each of which is an amount included after 1986 by reason of subparagraph 56(1)(a)(i) or paragraph 56(1)(d.2), (h) or (t) in computing the taxpayer's income for the year, and

(iii) the balance of the annuitized voluntary contributions of the taxpayer at the end of the year.

**Related Provisions:** 8(1)(m) — Employee's RRP contributions; 60(j.01) — Transfer of surplus.

**(2) Definition of "balance of the annuitized voluntary contributions"** — For the purposes of subsection (1), "balance of the annuitized voluntary contributions" of a taxpayer at the end of a taxation year means the amount, if any, by which

(a) such part of the total of all amounts each of which is an additional voluntary contribution made by the taxpayer to a registered pension plan before October 9, 1986 in respect of services rendered by the taxpayer before the year in which the contribution was made, to the extent that the contribution was not deducted in computing the taxpayer's income for any taxation year, as may reasonably be considered as having been

(i) used before October 9, 1986 to acquire or provide an annuity for the taxpayer's benefit under a registered pension plan or registered retirement savings plan, or

(ii) transferred before October 9, 1986 to a registered retirement income fund under which the taxpayer was the annuitant (within the meaning assigned by subsection 146.3(1)) at the time of the transfer

exceeds

(b) the total of all amounts each of which is

(i) an amount deducted under paragraph (1)(b) in computing the taxpayer's income for a preceding taxation year, or

(ii) an amount deducted under paragraph (1)(a) in computing the taxpayer's income for the year or a preceding taxation year, to the extent that the amount can reasonably be considered to be in respect of a refund of additional voluntary contributions included in determining the total under paragraph (a).

**Notes [s. 60.2]:** 60.2 added by 1990 pension bill, effective 1986.

**Definitions [s. 60.2]:** "additional voluntary contribution", "amount", "annuity" — 248(1); "balance" — 60.2(2); "registered pension plan" — 248(1); "registered retirement income fund" — 146.3(1), 248(1); "registered retirement savings plan" — 146(1), 248(1); "taxation year" — 249; "taxpayer" — 248(1).

**61. (1) Payment made as consideration for income-averaging annuity** — In computing the income for a taxation year of an individual resident

Subdivision e — Deductions in Computing Income    S. 61(2)(d)

in Canada, there may be deducted an amount equal to the lesser of

(a) such amount as the individual may claim, not exceeding the total of amounts each of which is a single payment

(i) made by the individual in the year or within 60 days after the end of the year as consideration for an income-averaging annuity contract of the individual, and

(ii) in respect of which no amount has been deducted in computing the individual's income for the immediately preceding taxation year, and

(b) the amount, if any, by which the total of

(i) the remainder obtained when the total of the amounts deductible in computing the individual's income for the year by reason of paragraphs 60(j) and (l) of this Act and paragraph 60(k) of the *Income Tax Act*, chapter 148 of the Revised Statutes of Canada, 1952, is deducted from the total of amounts described in subsection (2) in respect of the individual for the year,

(ii) the amount, if any, by which the amount determined under paragraph 3(b) in respect of the individual for the year exceeds the total of amounts each of which is an allowable business investment loss of the individual for the year,

(iii) the individual's income for the year from the production of a literary, dramatic, musical or artistic work,

(iv) the individual's income for the year from the individual's activities as an athlete, a musician or a public entertainer such as a theatre, motion picture, radio or television artist, and

(iv.1) the amount, if any, by which the amount included in computing the income of the individual for the year by virtue of section 59 exceeds the total of amounts deducted in computing the individual's income for the year under sections 64, 66, 66.1, 66.2 and 66.4 and under section 29 of the *Income Tax Application Rules*,

exceeds

(v) the total of amounts each of which is the annual annuity amount of the individual in respect of an income-averaging annuity contract in respect of the consideration for which any amount has been deducted under this subsection in computing the individual's income for the year.

**Notes**: Deductions for income-averaging annuity contracts (IAACs) were eliminated by the 1981 Budget. See the definition of "qualifying payment" in 61(4). This section has been maintained in the Act because it defines IAACs. Amounts received from an IAAC by a taxpayer are included in income by 56(1)(e) and (f).

Reference to s. 64 in 61(1)(b)(iv.1) should be to s. 64 of R.S.C. 1952, c. 148, meaning the version repealed by 1981 Budget. See Notes to 64.

Taxpayers with large fluctuations in their income may be able to use RRSPs for income-averaging purposes. See 146(5) and (8) and Notes to 146(10). See also Notes to 15(2). Forward averaging under 110.4 was eliminated in 1988.

**I.T. Application Rules**: 69 (meaning of "*Income Tax Act*, chapter 148 of the Revised Statutes of Canada, 1952").

**(2) Idem** — For the purposes of subsection (1), an amount described in this subsection in respect of an individual for a taxation year is any following amount:

(a) any single payment received by the individual in the year

(i) out of or under a superannuation or pension fund or plan

(A) on the death, withdrawal or retirement from employment of an employee or former employee,

(B) on the winding-up of the fund or plan in full satisfaction of all rights of the payee in or under the fund or plan, or

(C) to which the payee is entitled by virtue of an amendment to the plan although the payee continues to be an employee to whom the plan is applicable,

(ii) on retirement as an employee in recognition of long service and not made out of or under a superannuation fund or plan,

(iii) pursuant to an employees profit sharing plan in full satisfaction of all the individual's rights in or under the plan, to the extent that the amount thereof is required to be included in computing the individual's income for the year in which the payment was received, or

(iv) pursuant to a deferred profit sharing plan on the death, withdrawal or retirement from employment of an employee or former employee, to the extent that the amount thereof is required to be included in computing the individual's income for the year;

(b) a payment or payments made by an employer to the individual as an employee or former employee on or after retirement in respect of loss of office or employment, if made in the year of retirement or within one year after that year;

(c) a payment or payments paid to the individual as a death benefit, if paid in the year of death or within one year after that year;

(d) any amount included in computing the individual's income for the year by virtue of subsection 146(8), to the extent that the amount is a refund of premiums, as defined by section 146, under a registered retirement savings plan received by the individual under the plan on or after the death of the person who was, immediately before the person's death, the annuitant thereunder;

(e) any amount included in computing the individual's income for the year by virtue of section 13, 14 or 23, subsection 28(4) or (5) or paragraph 106(2)(a) of this Act or subparagraph 56(1)(a)(viii) of the *Income Tax Act*, chapter 148 of the Revised Statutes of Canada, 1952;

(f) any amount deemed by section 7 to be a benefit received by the individual in the year by virtue of the individual's employment;

(g) the amount, if any, by which any amount received by the individual in the year as or on account of a prize for achievement in a field of endeavour ordinarily carried on by the individual exceeds $500;

(h) any amount included in computing the individual's income for the year by virtue of subsection 146.2(6) of the *Income Tax Act*, chapter 148 of the Revised Statutes of Canada, 1952;

(i) a payment made in the year to an individual by virtue of paragraph 51(2)(b) of the *Judges Act*;

(j) except where the individual claimed a deduction under paragraph 23(3)(a) of the *Income Tax Application Rules* in computing the individual's income for the year, any amount included in computing that income by virtue of paragraph 23(3)(c) of that Act; and

(k) where the individual ceased to be a member of a partnership in the year or the preceding year and paragraph 34(a) applied in computing the individual's income therefrom in the preceding year, the amount included in the individual's income for the year by virtue of paragraph 3(a) to the extent that, having regard to all the circumstances including the proportion in which the members of the partnership have agreed to share the profits of the partnership, it can reasonably be considered to be in respect of the individual's share of the work in progress of the partnership at the time the individual ceased to be a member thereof, if, during the remainder of the year in which the individual ceased to be a member and in the following year, the individual did not

(i) become employed in the business that had been carried on by the partnership,

(ii) carry on a business that is a profession, or

(iii) become a member of a partnership that carries on a business that is a profession.

**Related Provisions**: 128.1(10)"excluded right or interest"(f)(ii) — Emigration — no deemed disposition of right to IAAC.

**I.T. Application Rules**: 69 (meaning of "*Income Tax Act*, chapter 148 of the Revised Statutes of Canada, 1952").

**(3)** [Repealed under former Act]

**Notes**: 61(3) moved to 61.1 in 1976.

**(4) Definitions** — In this section,

"**annual annuity amount**" of an individual in respect of an income-averaging annuity contract means the total of the equal payments described in paragraph (c) of the definition "income-averaging annuity contract" in this subsection that, under the contract, are receivable by the individual in the twelve month period commencing on the day that the first such payment under the contract becomes receivable by the individual;

"**income-averaging annuity contract**" of an individual means a contract between the individual and a person licensed or otherwise authorized under the laws of Canada or a province to carry on in Canada an annuities business or a corporation licensed or otherwise authorized under the laws of Canada or a province to carry on in Canada the business of offering to the public its services as trustee, under which

(a) in consideration of a qualifying payment as consideration under the contract, that person agrees to pay to the individual, commencing at a time not later than 10 months after the individual has made the qualifying payment,

(i) an annuity to the individual for the individual's life, with or without a guaranteed term not exceeding the number of years that is the lesser of

(A) 15, and

(B) 85 minus the age of the individual at the time the annuity payments commence, or

(ii) an annuity to the individual for a guaranteed term described in subparagraph (i), or

(b) in consideration of a single payment in respect of the individual's 1981 taxation year, other than a qualifying payment, made by the individual as consideration under the contract, that person makes all payments provided for under the contract to the individual before 1983

and under which no payments are provided except the single payment by the individual and,

(c) in respect of a contract referred to in paragraph (a), equal annuity payments that are to be made annually or at more frequent periodic intervals, or

(d) in respect of a contract referred to in paragraph (b), payments described therein to the individual;

"**qualifying payment**" means a single payment made before November 13, 1981 (or made on or after November 13, 1981 pursuant to an agreement in writing entered into before that date to make such a payment in respect of the individual's 1981 taxation year, or pursuant to an arrangement in writing made before that date to have funds withheld before 1982 from any of the individual's remuneration described in paragraph (1)(b) earned or received before November 13, 1981 and paid by or on behalf of the individual).

Subdivision e — Deductions in Computing Income   S. 61.3(1)(a)(i)

**Notes**: 61(4)"annual annuity amount", "income averaging annuity contract" and "qualifying payment" were 61(4)(a), (b) and (c) respectively, before consolidation in R.S.C. 1985 (5th Supp.), effective for taxation years ending after November 1991. See Table of Concordance.

**Definitions [s. 61]**: "amount", "annuity", "business" — 248(1); "Canada" — 255; "corporation" — 248(1), *Interpretation Act* 35(1); "death benefit" — 248(1); "deferred profit sharing plan" — 147(1), 248(1); "employee" — 248(1); "employees profit sharing plan" — 144(1), 248(1); "employment", "individual", "office", "person" — 248(1); "province" — *Interpretation Act* 35(1); "registered retirement savings plan" — 146(1), 248(1); "resident in Canada" — 250; "taxation year" — 249; "taxpayer" — 248(1); "writing" — *Interpretation Act* 35(1).

**61.1 (1) Where income-averaging annuity contract ceases to be such** — Where a contract that was at any time an income-averaging annuity contract of an individual has, at a subsequent time, ceased to be an income-averaging annuity contract otherwise than by virtue of the surrender, cancellation, redemption, sale or the disposition thereof, the individual shall be deemed to have received at that subsequent time as proceeds of the disposition of an income-averaging annuity contract an amount equal to the fair market value of the contract at that subsequent time and to have acquired the contract, as another contract not being an income-averaging annuity contract, immediately thereafter at a cost to the individual equal to that fair market value.

**Related Provisions**: 56(1)(f) — Disposition of income-averaging annuity contracts; 61 — Payment made as consideration for income-averaging annuity; 212(1)(n) — Withholding tax on payment to non-resident.

**(2) Where annuitant dies and payments continued** — Where an individual who was an annuitant under an income-averaging annuity contract has died and payments are subsequently made under that contract, the payments shall be deemed to be payments under an income-averaging annuity contract.

**Interpretation Bulletins [subsec. 61.1(2)]**: IT-212R3: Income of deceased persons — rights or things.

**Definitions [s. 61.1]**: "income-averaging annuity contract" — 61(4), 248(1); "individual" — 248(1).

**61.2 Reserve for debt forgiveness for resident individuals** — There may be deducted in computing the income for a taxation year of an individual (other than a trust) resident in Canada throughout the year such amount as the individual claims not exceeding the amount determined by the formula

$$A + B - 0.2(C - \$40{,}000)$$

where

A is the amount, if any, by which

(a) the total of all amounts each of which is an amount that, because of the application of section 80 to an obligation payable by the individual (or a partnership of which the individual was a member) was included under subsection 80(13) in computing the income of the individual for the year or the income of the partnership for a fiscal period that ends in the year (to the extent that, where the amount was included in computing income of a partnership, it relates to the individual's share of that income)

exceeds

(b) the total of all amounts deducted because of paragraph 80(15)(a) in computing the individual's income for the year,

B is the amount, if any, included under section 56.2 in computing the individual's income for the year, and

C is the greater of $40,000 and the individual's income for the year, determined without reference to this section, paragraph 20(1)(ww), section 56.2, paragraph 60(w), subsection 80(13) and paragraph 80(15)(a).

**Related Provisions**: 56.2 — Inclusion into income in following year; 61.3, 61.4 — Alternative deductions for corporations, non-residents and trusts; 80(16) — Designation by CCRA to reduce reserve under 61.2; 114(a) — No deduction under 61.2 for part-year residents; 257 — Formula cannot calculate to less than zero.

**Notes**: 61.2C amended by 1999 Budget, effective for 2000 and later taxation years, to add reference to 20(1)(ww).

61.2 added by 1994 tax amendments bill (Part I), effective for taxation years that end after February 21, 1994. It allows individuals with modest incomes a deferral of the income inclusion required by the debt forgiveness rules in 80(13). For individuals with net income not exceeding $40,000 per year, the income inclusion can be deferred indefinitely. Each year the amount deducted under 61.2 the previous year is included back into income under 56.2, but an offsetting reserve can be claimed again (see B in the formula) if the taxpayer qualifies. If the reserve is still being claimed by the year the taxpayer dies, the income will never be taxed. (For corporations, non-residents and trusts, see 61.3 and 61.4 instead.)

**Definitions [s. 61.2]**: "amount" — 248(1); "fiscal period" — 249(2)(b), 249.1; "individual" — 248(1); "partnership" — see Notes to 96(1); "resident in Canada" — 250; "taxation year" — 249; "trust" — 104(1), 248(1), (3).

**61.3 (1) Deduction for insolvency with respect to resident corporations** — There shall be deducted in computing the income for a taxation year of a corporation resident in Canada throughout the year that is not exempt from tax under this Part on its taxable income, the lesser of

(a) the amount, if any, by which

(i) the total of all amounts each of which is an amount that, because of the application of section 80 to a commercial obligation (in this section having the meaning assigned by subsection 80(1)) issued by the corporation (or a partnership of which the corporation was a member) was included under subsection 80(13) in computing the income of the corporation for the year or the income of the partnership for a fiscal period that ends in the year (to the extent that the amount, where it was included in computing income of a partner-

411

ship, relates to the corporation's share of that income)

exceeds

(ii) the total of all amounts deducted because of paragraph 80(15)(a) in computing the corporation's income for the year, and

(b) the amount determined by the formula

$$A - 2(B - C - D - E)$$

where

A is the amount determined under paragraph (a) in respect of the corporation for the year,

B is the total of

(i) the fair market value of the assets of the corporation at the end of the year,

(ii) the amounts paid before the end of the year on account of the corporation's tax payable under this Part or any of Parts I.3, II, VI and XIV for the year or on account of a similar tax payable for the year under an Act of a province, and

(iii) all amounts paid by the corporation in the 12-month period preceding the end of the year to a person with whom the corporation does not deal at arm's length

(A) as a dividend (other than a stock dividend),

(B) on a reduction of paid-up capital in respect of any class of shares of its capital stock,

(C) on a redemption, acquisition or cancellation of its shares, or

(D) as a distribution or appropriation in any manner whatever to or for the benefit of the shareholders of any class of its capital stock, to the extent that the distribution or appropriation cannot reasonably be considered to have resulted in a reduction in the amount otherwise determined for C in respect of the corporation for the year,

C is the total liabilities of the corporation at the end of the year (determined without reference to the corporation's liabilities for tax payable under this Part or any of Parts I.3, II, VI and XIV for the year or for a similar tax payable for the year under an Act of a province) and, for this purpose,

(i) the equity and consolidation methods of accounting shall not be used, and

(ii) subject to subparagraph (i) and except as otherwise provided in this description, the total liabilities of the corporation shall

(A) where the corporation is not an insurance corporation or a bank to which clause (B) or (C) applies and the balance sheet as of the end of the year was presented to the shareholders of the corporation and was prepared in accordance with generally accepted accounting principles, be considered to be the total liabilities shown on that balance sheet,

(B) where the corporation is a bank or an insurance corporation that is required to report to the Superintendent of Financial Institutions and the balance sheet as of the end of the year was accepted by the Superintendent, be considered to be the total liabilities shown on that balance sheet,

(C) where the corporation is an insurance corporation that is required to report to the superintendent of insurance or other similar officer or authority of the province under whose laws the corporation is incorporated and the balance sheet as of the end of the year was accepted by that officer or authority, be considered to be the total liabilities shown on that balance sheet, and

(D) in any other case, be considered to be the amount that would be shown as total liabilities of the corporation at the end of the year on a balance sheet prepared in accordance with generally accepted accounting principles,

D is the total of all amounts each of which is the principal amount at the end of the year of a distress preferred share (within the meaning assigned by subsection 80(1)) issued by the corporation, and

E is 50% of the amount, if any, by which

(i) the amount that would be the corporation's income for the year if that amount were determined without reference to this section and section 61.4

exceeds

(ii) the amount determined under paragraph (a) in respect of the corporation for the year.

**Related Provisions**: 37(1)(f.1) — Reduction in claim allowed for R&D expenditures; 61.2 — Reserve for individuals; 61.3(3) — Anti-avoidance; 61.4 — Additional reserve; 80(16) — Designation by CCRA to reduce reserve under 61.3; 80.01(8), (9) — Deemed settlement on debt parking or debt becoming statute-barred; 80.04(4)(j) — Agreement to transfer forgiven amount; 87(2)(1.21) — Amalgamations — continuing corporation; 257 — Formula cannot calculate to less than zero.

**Notes**: 61.3(1) added by 1994 tax amendments bill (Part I), effective for taxation years that end after February 21, 1994, and amended retroactive to its introduction by 1995-97 technical bill to remove a reference to 80(17) at the end of 61.3(1)(b)E(i). It allows an offset (not a "reserve", since there is no later inclusion back into income) against the income inclusion under 80(13). The effect is that a corporation is required to recognize income under 80(13) only to the extent of twice the corporation's net assets. Therefore, if the combined federal/provincial income tax rate of a corporation does not exceed 50%, the income inclusion under 80(13) should not result in the corporation's liabilities exceeding the fair market value of its assets (which could make the corporation insolvent under corporate law). Note, however, that 80(17) can bring an amount deducted under 61.3 back into income in certain cases.

61.3(1)(b)C(i) is redundant. See 248(24).

**(2) Reserve for insolvency with respect to non-resident corporations** — There shall be deducted in computing the income for a taxation year of a corporation that is non-resident at any time in the year, the lesser of

(a) the amount, if any, by which

(i) the total of all amounts each of which is an amount that, because of the application of section 80 to a commercial obligation issued by the corporation (or a partnership of which the corporation was a member) was included under subsection 80(13) in computing the corporation's taxable income or taxable income earned in Canada for the year or the income of the partnership for a fiscal period that ends in the year (to the extent that, where the amount was included in computing income of a partnership, it relates to the corporation's share of the partnership's income added in computing the corporation's taxable income or taxable income earned in Canada for the year)

exceeds

(ii) the total of all amounts deducted because of paragraph 80(15)(a) in computing the corporation's taxable income or taxable income earned in Canada for the year, and

(b) the amount determined by the formula

$$A - 2(B - C - D - E)$$

where

A is the amount determined under paragraph (a) in respect of the corporation for the year,

B is the total of

(i) the fair market value of the assets of the corporation at the end of the year,

(ii) the amounts paid before the end of the year on account of the corporation's tax payable under this Part or any of Parts I.3, II, VI and XIV for the year or on account of a similar tax payable for the year under an Act of a province, and

(iii) all amounts paid in the 12-month period preceding the end of the year by the corporation to a person with whom the corporation does not deal at arm's length

(A) as a dividend (other than a stock dividend),

(B) on a reduction of paid-up capital in respect of any class of shares of its capital stock,

(C) on a redemption, acquisition or cancellation of its shares, or

(D) as a distribution or appropriation in any manner whatever to or for the benefit of the shareholders of any class of its capital stock, to the extent that the distribution or appropriation cannot reasonably be considered to have resulted in a reduction of the amount otherwise determined for C in respect of the corporation for the year,

C is the total liabilities of the corporation at the end of the year (determined without reference to the corporation's liabilities for tax payable under this Part or any of Parts I.3, II, VI and XIV for the year or for a similar tax payable for the year under an Act of a province), determined in the manner described in the description of C in paragraph (1)(b),

D is the total of all amounts each of which is the principal amount at the end of the year of a distress preferred share (within the meaning assigned by subsection 80(1)) issued by the corporation, and

E is 50% of the amount, if any, by which

(i) the amount that would be the corporation's taxable income or taxable income earned in Canada for the year if that amount were determined without reference to this section and section 61.4

exceeds

(ii) the amount determined under paragraph (a) in respect of the corporation for the year.

**Related Provisions**: 37(1)(f.1) — Reduction in claim allowed for R&D expenditures; 61.3(3) — Anti-avoidance; 61.4 — Additional reserve; 80(16) — Designation by CCRA to reduce reserve under 61.3; 80.01(8), (9) — Deemed settlement on debt parking or debt becoming statute-barred; 80.04(4)(j) — Agreement to transfer forgiven amount; 87(2)(l.21) — Amalgamations — continuing corporation; 257 — Formula cannot calculate to less than zero.

**Notes**: 61.3(2) added by 1994 tax amendments bill (Part I), effective for taxation years that end after February 21, 1994, and amended retroactive to its introduction by 1995-97 technical bill to remove a reference to 80(17) at the end of 61.3(2)(b)E(i). It is similar to 61.3(1) but applies to non-resident corporations. See Notes to 61.3(1).

**(3) Anti-avoidance** — Subsections (1) and (2) do not apply to a corporation for a taxation year where property was transferred in the 12-month period preceding the end of the year or the corporation became indebted in that period and it can reasonably be considered that one of the reasons for the transfer or the indebtedness was to increase the amount that the corporation would, but for this subsection, be entitled to deduct under subsection (1) or (2).

**Related Provisions**: 160.4 — Joint liability of transferee where property transferred so that 61.3(3) applies.

**Notes**: 61.3(3) added by 1994 tax amendments bill (Part I), effective for taxation years that end after February 21, 1994.

**Definitions [s. 61.3]**: "Act" — *Interpretation Act* 35(1); "amount" — 248(1); "arm's length" — 251(1); "bank" — 248(1),

*Interpretation Act* 35(1); "class of shares" — 248(6); "commercial obligation" — 61.3(1)(a)(i), 80(1); "corporation" — 248(1), *Interpretation Act* 35(1); "dividend" — 248(1); "fiscal period" — 249(2)(b), 249.1; "insurance corporation", "non-resident" — 248(1); "officer" — 248(1)"office"; "paid-up capital" — 89(1), 248(1); "partnership" — see Notes to 96(1); "principal amount", "property" — 248(1); "province" — *Interpretation Act* 35(1); "resident in Canada" — 250; "share", "shareholder", "stock dividend" — 248(1); "taxable income" — 2(2), 248(1); "taxable income earned in Canada" — 115(1), 248(1); "taxation year" — 249.

## 61.4 Reserve for debt forgiveness for corporations and others

— There may be deducted as a reserve in computing the income for a taxation year of a taxpayer that is a corporation or trust resident in Canada throughout the year or a non-resident person who carried on business through a fixed placed of business in Canada at the end of the year such amount as the taxpayer claims not exceeding the least of

(a) the amount determined by the formula

$$A - B$$

where

A is the amount, if any, by which

(i) the total of all amounts each of which is an amount that, because of the application of section 80 to a commercial obligation (within the meaning assigned by subsection 80(1)) issued by the taxpayer (or a partnership of which the taxpayer was a member) was included under subsection 80(13) in computing the income of the taxpayer for the year or a preceding taxation year or of the partnership for a fiscal period that ends in that year or preceding year (to the extent that, where the amount was included in computing income of a partnership, it relates to the taxpayer's share of that income)

exceeds the total of

(ii) all amounts each of which is an amount deducted under paragraph 80(15)(a) in computing the taxpayer's income for the year or a preceding taxation year, and

(iii) all amounts deducted under section 61.3 in computing the taxpayer's income for the year or a preceding taxation year, and

B is the amount, if any, by which the amount determined for A in respect of the taxpayer for the year exceeds the total of

(i) the amount that would be determined for A in respect of the taxpayer for the year if that value did not take into account amounts included or deducted in computing the taxpayer's income for any preceding taxation year, and

(ii) the amount, if any, included under section 56.3 in computing the taxpayer's income for the year,

(b) the total of

(i) $4/5$ of the amount that would be determined for A in paragraph (a) in respect of the taxpayer for the year if that value did not take into account amounts included or deducted in computing the taxpayer's income for any preceding taxation year,

(ii) $3/5$ of the amount that would be determined for A in paragraph (a) in respect of the taxpayer for the year if that value did not take into account amounts included or deducted in computing the taxpayer's income for the year or any preceding taxation year (other than the last preceding taxation year),

(iii) $2/5$ of the amount that would be determined for A in paragraph (a) in respect of the taxpayer for the year if that value did not take into account amounts included or deducted in computing the taxpayer's income for the year or any preceding taxation year (other than the second last preceding taxation year), and

(iv) $1/5$ of the amount that would be determined for A in paragraph (a) in respect of the taxpayer for the year if that value did not take into account amounts included or deducted in computing the taxpayer's income for the year or any preceding taxation year (other than the third last preceding taxation year), and

(c) where the taxpayer is a corporation that commences to wind up in the year (otherwise than in circumstances to which the rules in subsection 88(1) apply), nil.

**Related Provisions**: 56.3 — Inclusion into income in following year; 61.2 — Reserve for resident individuals; 61.3 — Additional reserve for insolvent corporation; 80.04(4)(j) — Agreement to transfer forgiven amount; 87(2)(g), (h.1) — Amalgamations — carryover of reserve; 250(6.1) — Trust that ceases to exist deemed resident throughout year.

**Notes**: 61.4 added by 1994 tax amendments bill (Part I), effective for taxation years that end after February 21, 1994. Together with 56.3 it allows the income inclusion required by the debt forgiveness rules in 80(13) to be spread over 5 years. The taxpayer must be a corporation or trust resident in Canada, or a non-resident person that carries on business through a fixed place of business in Canada. No reserve is allowed for partnerships because of the special rules for partners under 80(15). A reserve is also not allowed under 61.4 for corporations that are winding up in circumstances to which 88(1) does not apply (see 61.4(c)). (Individuals resident in Canada can claim a reserve under 61.2. Some corporations may also claim a deduction under 61.3.)

**Definitions [s. 61.4]**: "amount", "business" — 248(1); "carrying on business in Canada" — 253; "corporation" — 248(1), *Interpretation Act* 35(1); "fiscal period" — 249(2)(b), 249.1; "non-resident" — 248(1); "partnership" — see Notes to 96(1); "resident in Canada" — 250; "taxation year" — 249; "taxpayer" — 248(1); "trust" — 104(1), 248(1), (3).

## 62. (1) Moving expenses

— There may be deducted in computing a taxpayer's income for a taxation year amounts paid by the taxpayer as or on account of moving expenses incurred in respect of an eligible relocation, to the extent that

(a) they were not paid on the taxpayer's behalf in respect of, in the course of or because of, the taxpayer's office or employment;

(b) they were not deductible because of this section in computing the taxpayer's income for the preceding taxation year;

(c) the total of those amounts does not exceed

(i) in any case described in subparagraph (a)(i) of the definition "eligible relocation" in subsection 248(1), the taxpayer's income for the year from the taxpayer's employment at a new work location or from carrying on the business at the new work location, as the case may be, and

(ii) in any case described in subparagraph (a)(ii) of the definition "eligible relocation" in subsection 248(1), the total of amounts included in computing the taxpayer's income for the year because of paragraphs 56(1)(n) and (o); and

(d) all reimbursements and allowances received by the taxpayer in respect of those expenses are included in computing the taxpayer's income.

**Related Provisions**: 4(2) — Deductions under s. 62 not applicable to any particular source; 64.1 — Individuals absent from Canada; 115(2)(f) — Deduction for non-resident; 118.2(2)(l.5) — Medical expense credit for moving expenses.

**Notes**: The determination of whether one has moved 40 km or more is based on road distance. See *Giannakopoulos*, [1995] 2 C.T.C. 316 (FCA), which overturned a string of Tax Court decisions that had ruled that the distance must be measured "as the crow flies". The CCRA agrees; see Income Tax Technical News No. 6.

In *Templeton*, [1998] 3 C.T.C. 207 (TCC), the Federal Court–Trial Division allowed a deduction under 62(1) for an individual with a home office, who moved to a new work location that was in the same location as his new residence.

The terms "old residence", "new residence" and "new work location" are all defined within the definition of "eligible relocation" in 248(1).

62(1) amended by 1998 Budget, effective 1998. Before 1998, read:

62. (1) Where a taxpayer has, at any time, commenced

(a) to carry on a business or to be employed at a location in Canada (in this subsection referred to as "the new work location"), or

(b) to be a student in full-time attendance at an educational institution (in this subsection referred to as "the new work location") that is a university, college or other educational institution providing courses at a post-secondary school level,

and by reason thereof has moved from the residence in Canada at which, before the move, the taxpayer ordinarily resided (in this section referred to as "the old residence") to a residence in Canada at which, after the move, the taxpayer ordinarily resided (in this section referred to as "the new residence"), so that the distance between the old residence and the new work location is not less than 40 kilometres greater than the distance between the new residence and the new

work location, in computing the taxpayer's income for the taxation year in which the taxpayer moved from the old residence to the new residence or for the immediately following taxation year, there may be deducted amounts paid by the taxpayer as or on account of moving expenses incurred in the course of moving from the old residence to the new residence, to the extent that

(c) they were not paid on the taxpayer's behalf by the taxpayer's employer,

(d) they were not deductible by virtue of this section in computing the taxpayer's income for the preceding taxation year,

(e) they would not, but for this section, be deductible in computing the taxpayer's income,

(f) the total of those amounts does not exceed

(i) in any case described in paragraph (a), the taxpayer's income for the year from the taxpayer's employment at the new work location or from carrying on the new business at the new work location, as the case may be, or

(ii) in any case described in paragraph (b), the total of amounts required to be included in computing the taxpayer's income for the year by virtue of paragraphs 56(1)(n) and (o), and

(g) any reimbursement or allowance received by the taxpayer in respect of those expenses is included in computing the taxpayer's income.

**Interpretation Bulletins**: See list at end of s. 62.

**I.T. Technical News**: No. 6 (road distance to be used instead of "as the crow flies").

**Forms**: T1-M: Moving expenses deduction.

**(2) Moving expenses of students** — There may be deducted in computing a taxpayer's income for a taxation year the amount, if any, that the taxpayer would be entitled to deduct under subsection (1) if the definition "eligible relocation" in subsection 248(1) were read without reference to subparagraph (a)(i) of that definition and if the word "both" in paragraph (b) of that definition were read as "either or both".

**Related Provisions**: 64.1 — Individuals absent from Canada; 115(2) — Non-resident's taxable income earned in Canada; 118.2(2)(l.5) — Medical expense credit for moving expenses.

**Notes**: 62(2) means that students (but not others) can claim moving expenses in respect of moves to or from outside Canada.

62(2) amended by 1998 Budget, effective 1998. Before 1998, read:

(2) Application of subsec. (1) to certain students — Where a taxpayer would, if subsection (1) were read without reference to paragraph (a) thereof and

(a) if the reference therein to "moved from the residence in Canada at which" were read as a reference to "moved from the residence at which", or

(b) if the reference therein to "to a residence in Canada at which" were read as a reference to "to a residence at which",

be entitled to deduct an amount by virtue of that subsection in computing the taxpayer's income for a taxation year, that amount may be deducted in computing the taxpayer's income for the year.

**Interpretation Bulletins**: See list at end of s. 62.

**S. 62(3)**      Income Tax Act, Part I, Division B

**(3) Definition of "moving expenses"** — In subsection (1), "moving expenses" includes any expense incurred as or on account of

(a) travel costs (including a reasonable amount expended for meals and lodging), in the course of moving the taxpayer and members of the taxpayer's household from the old residence to the new residence,

(b) the cost to the taxpayer of transporting or storing household effects in the course of moving from the old residence to the new residence,

(c) the cost to the taxpayer of meals and lodging near the old residence or the new residence for the taxpayer and members of the taxpayer's household for a period not exceeding 15 days,

(d) the cost to the taxpayer of cancelling the lease by virtue of which the taxpayer was the lessee of the old residence,

(e) the taxpayer's selling costs in respect of the sale of the old residence,

(f) where the old residence is sold by the taxpayer or the taxpayer's spouse or common-law partner as a result of the move, the cost to the taxpayer of legal services in respect of the purchase of the new residence and of any tax, fee or duty (other than any goods and services tax or value-added tax) imposed on the transfer or registration of title to the new residence,

(g) interest, property taxes, insurance premiums and the cost of heating and utilities in respect of the old residence, to the extent of the lesser of $5,000 and the total of such expenses of the taxpayer for the period

    (i) throughout which the old residence is neither ordinarily occupied by the taxpayer or by any other person who ordinarily resided with the taxpayer at the old residence immediately before the move nor rented by the taxpayer to any other person, and

    (ii) in which reasonable efforts are made to sell the old residence, and

(h) the cost of revising legal documents to reflect the address of the taxpayer's new residence, of replacing drivers' licenses and non-commercial vehicle permits (excluding any cost for vehicle insurance) and of connecting or disconnecting utilities,

but, for greater certainty, does not include costs (other than costs referred to in paragraph (f)) incurred by the taxpayer in respect of the acquisition of the new residence.

**Related Provisions:** 56(1)(n) — Scholarships, bursaries, etc.; 56(1)(o) — Research grants; 64.1 — Individuals absent from Canada; 115(2) — Non-resident's taxable income earned in Canada; 118.2(2)(l.5) — Medical expense credit for moving expenses.

**Notes:** Per a December 1999 CCRA Fact Sheet, travel expenses under 62(3)(a) can optionally be calculated using a simplified calculation without receipts: $11/meal (up to $33/day); and vehicle expenses per qualifying km (to cover both ownership and operating expenses) driven as follows:

| Province or territory | Cents/kilometre |
| --- | --- |
| British Columbia | 37.5 |
| Alberta | 35.0 |
| Saskatchewan | 34.5 |
| Manitoba | 37.0 |
| Ontario | 38.0 |
| Quebec | 41.0 |
| New Brunswick | 37.0 |
| Prince Edward Island | 36.0 |
| Nova Scotia | 36.5 |
| Newfoundland | 38.5 |
| NWT, Yukon, Nunavut | 42.5 |

See Notes to 60(o) re legal fees under 62(3)(f).

62(3)(f) amended by 2000 same-sex partners bill to add reference to "common-law partner", effective for the 2001 and later taxation years, or earlier by election (see Notes to 248(1)"common-law partner").

62(3)(f) amended by 1995-97 technical bill, effective for costs incurred after 1990 (i.e., retroactive to the introduction of the GST), to deny deductibility for GST paid on the purchase of a new home. From 1977 to 1990, read:

    (f) where the old residence is being or has been sold by the taxpayer or the taxpayer's spouse as a result of the move, the cost to the taxpayer of legal services in respect of the purchase of the new residence and of any taxes imposed on the transfer or registration of title to the new residence,

The amendment was described by Finance as "clarifying", but it reverses retroactively two decisions of the Tax Court, *Lachman*, [1995] 2 C.T.C. 2944D and *Mann*, [1995] 2 C.T.C. 2049; but see also *Johnson (H. & M.)*, [1995] 2 C.T.C. 2110, which went the other way.

62(3)(g) and (h) added by 1998 Budget, effective for expenses incurred after 1997.

**Definitions [s. 62]:** "amount", "business" — 248(1); "Canada" — 64.1, 255; "carrying on business" — 253; "common-law partner", "eligible relocation", "employed", "employer", "employment", "goods and services tax" — 248(1); "moving expenses" — 62(3); "new residence" — 248(1)"eligible relocation"(b); "new work location" — 248(1)"eligible relocation"(a); "office" — 248(1); "old residence" — 248(1)"eligible relocation"(b); "person", "property" — 248(1); "taxation year" — 249; "taxpayer" — 248(1).

**Interpretation Bulletins [s. 62]:** IT-178R3: Moving expenses; IT-193 SR: Taxable income of individuals resident in Canada during part of a year (Special Release); IT-518R: Food, beverages and entertainment expenses.

**Forms [s. 62]:** T1-M: Claim for moving expenses.

**63. (1) Child care expenses** — Subject to subsection (2), where a prescribed form containing prescribed information is filed with a taxpayer's return of income (other than a return filed under subsection 70(2) or 104(23), paragraph 128(2)(e) or subsection 150(4)) under this Part for a taxation year, there may be deducted in computing the taxpayer's income for the year such amount as the taxpayer claims not exceeding the total of all amounts each of which is an amount paid, as or on account of child care expenses incurred for services rendered in the year in respect of an eligible child of the taxpayer,

    (a) by the taxpayer, where the taxpayer is a taxpayer described in subsection (2) and the supporting person of the child for the year is a person described in subparagraph (2)(b)(vi)[2], or

> **Proposed Amendment — 63(1)(a)**
>
> (a) by the taxpayer, where the taxpayer is described in subsection (2) and the supporting person of the child for the year is a person described in clause (i)(D) of the description of C in the formula in that subsection, or
>
> **Application**: The December 21, 2000 draft legislation, subsec. 25(1), will amend para. 63(1)(a) to read as above, applicable to 1998 *et seq.*
>
> **Technical Notes**: Subsection 63(1) allows, subject to certain conditions, the deduction of child care expenses paid in a calendar year in respect of an eligible child, whether the expenses are paid by the taxpayer or by a supporting person of the child for the year. This amendment replaces an incorrect reference in paragraph 63(1)(a) to "subparagraph (2)(b)(vi)" with a reference to "paragraph 63(2)(b)" in order to reflect an amendment made in 1998.

(b) by the taxpayer or a supporting person of the child for the year, in any other case,

to the extent that

(c) the amount is not included in computing the amount deductible under this subsection by an individual (other than the taxpayer), and

(d) the amount is not an amount (other than an amount that is included in computing the taxpayer's income and that is not deductible in computing the taxpayer's taxable income) in respect of which any taxpayer is or was entitled to a reimbursement or any other form of assistance,

and the payment of which is proven by filing with the Minister one or more receipts each of which was issued by the payee and contains, where the payee is an individual, that individual's Social Insurance Number, but not exceeding the amount, if any, by which

(e) the lesser of

(i) $2/3$ of the taxpayer's earned income for the year, and

(ii) the total of

(A) the product obtained when $7,000 is multiplied by the number of eligible children of the taxpayer for the year each of whom

(I) is under 7 years of age at the end of the year, or

(II) is a person in respect of whom an amount may be deducted under section 118.3 in computing a taxpayer's tax payable under this Part for the year, and

(B) the product obtained when $4,000 is multiplied by the number of eligible chil-

dren of the taxpayer for the year (other than children referred to in clause (A))

> **Proposed Amendment — 63(1)(e)(ii)**
>
> (ii) the total of all amounts each of which is the annual child care expense amount in respect of an eligible child of the taxpayer for the year
>
> **Application**: The December 21, 2000 draft legislation, subsec. 25(2), will amend subpara. 63(1)(e)(ii) to read as above, applicable to 2000 *et seq.*
>
> **Technical Notes**: Paragraph 63(1)(e) provides for the computation of a taxpayer's deduction in respect of child care expenses. The annual maximum amount of child care expenses that may be claimed for a year in respect of an eligible child depends on the child's age and whether or not a disability tax credit may be claimed in respect of the child. Subparagraph 63(1)(e)(ii) is amended to refer to the annual child care expense amount that is relevant to a particular eligible child. The new expression "annual child care expense amount" is defined in subsection 63(3) (see the commentary on that subsection).

exceeds

(f) the total of all amounts each of which is an amount that is deducted, in respect of the taxpayer's eligible children for the year, under this section in computing the income for the year of an individual (other than the taxpayer) to whom subsection (2) applies for the year.

**Related Provisions**: 4(2) — Deductions under s. 63 not applicable to any particular source; 63(2.2) — Deduction for person attending school or university; 64.1 — Individuals absent from Canada; 220(2.1) — Waiver of filing of documents.

**Notes**: Although 63(1) requires receipts to be filed (see the words between paras. (d) and (e)), the CCRA's practice is not to request such receipts with the return. See forms T778 and T1065. See also 220(2.1). Furthermore, in *Senger-Hammond*, [1997] 1 C.T.C 2728, *Wells*, [1997] 3 C.T.C. 2581 and *Dominguez*, [1998] 4 C.T.C. 2222, the Tax Court ruled that the words requiring filing of receipts are "directory rather than imperative", and that receipts need not be filed provided the payment can be proven. The Quebec Court of Appeal reached a similar conclusion in *Letarte*, 97 DTC 5515.

A deduction for child-care expenses as business expenses, beyond the dollar limits provided under 63(1), will not be allowed. See *Symes*, [1994] 1 C.T.C. 40 (SCC).

Opening words of 63(1) amended by 1992 technical bill, effective 1992, to allow a claim for less than all child-care expenses incurred ("such amount as the taxpayer claims") and to base the claim on amounts paid for services rendered in the year rather than on amounts paid in the year. For 1988 to 1991, read as:

> (1) Subject to subsection (2), where a taxpayer who has an eligible child for a taxation year files with the taxpayer's return of income (other than a return of income filed under subsection 70(2) or 104(23), paragraph 128(2)(e) or subsection 150(4)) under this Part for the year a prescribed form containing prescribed information, there may be deducted in computing the income of the taxpayer for the year the total of all amounts each of which is an amount paid in the year as or on account of child care expenses in respect of an eligible child of the taxpayer for the year

Dollar limits in 63(1)(e)(ii)(A) and (B) increased by 1992 Budget, effective 1993, and by 1998 Budget, effective 1998. For 1988 to

---

[2] *Sic.* Reference should now be to 63(2)(b)C(i)(D) — ed.

## S. 63(1) — Income Tax Act, Part I, Division B

1992 these figures were $4,000 and $2,000, and from 1993 to 1997 they were $5,000 and $3,000.

63(1)(e)(ii)(A)(II) amended by 1991 technical bill, effective 1991, to correspond to changes in 118.3.

63(1)(f) amended by 1996 Budget, effective for 1996 and later taxation years. The change in wording was consequential on the introduction of 63(2.2). For 1983 through 1995, read:

(f) the total of all amounts each of which is an amount deducted, in respect of the eligible children of the taxpayer that are referred to in subparagraph (e)(ii), under this subsection for the year by an individual (other than the taxpayer) to whom subsection (2) is applicable for the year.

**Interpretation Bulletins**: See list at end of s. 63.

**Information Circulars**: 82-2R2: SIN legislation that relates to the preparation of information slips.

**Forms**: T778: Child care expenses deduction; T1065: Child care expenses information sheet.

**(2) Income exceeding income of supporting person** — Where the income for a taxation year of a taxpayer who has an eligible child for the year exceeds the income for that year of a supporting person of that child (on the assumption that both incomes are computed without reference to this section and paragraphs 60(v.1) and (w)), the amount that may be deducted by the taxpayer under subsection (1) for the year as or on account of child care expenses shall not exceed the lesser of

(a) the amount that would, but for this subsection, be deductible by the taxpayer for the year under subsection (1); and

(b) the amount determined by the formula

$$(A + B) \times C$$

### Proposed Amendment — 63(2)(b) formula

$$A \times C$$

**Application**: The December 21, 2000 draft legislation, subsec. 25(3), will amend the formula in para. 63(2)(b) to read as above, applicable to 2000 et seq.

**Technical Notes**: Subsections 63(2) to (2.3) provide for the calculation of the child care expense deduction where the claimant is the higher-income supporting person, or where the claimant is a student. In such circumstances, the claim is subject to a specific maximum which is computed by reference to the number of weeks (or months for part-time education) during which the lower-income supporting person is separated, infirm, confined to a bed or wheelchair, in prison or in attendance at school. This specific maximum referred to in the formulas used in paragraphs 63(2)(b) and (2.3)(c) is amended to refer to the "periodic child care expense amount" in respect of a child. This new expression is defined in subsection 63(3) (see the commentary on that subsection).

where

A is the product obtained when $175 is multiplied by the number of eligible children of the taxpayer for the year each of whom

(i) is under 7 years of age at the end of the year, or

(ii) is a person in respect of whom an amount may be deducted under section 118.3 in computing a taxpayer's tax payable under this Part for the year,

B is the product obtained when $100 is multiplied by the number of the taxpayer's eligible children for the year (other than children referred to in the description of A), and

### Proposed Amendment — 63(2)(b)A, B

A is the total of all amounts each of which is the periodic child care expense amount in respect of an eligible child of the taxpayer for the year, and

**Application**: The December 21, 2000 draft legislation, subsec. 25(4), will amend the description of A to read as above, and repeal the description of B, applicable to 2000 et seq.

**Technical Notes**: See under 63(2)(b) formula.

C is the total of

(i) the number of weeks in the year during which the child care expenses were incurred and throughout which the supporting person was

(A) a student in attendance at a designated educational institution or a secondary school and enrolled in a program of the institution or school of not less than 3 consecutive weeks duration that provides that each student in the program spend not less than 10 hours per week on courses or work in the program,

(B) a person certified by a medical doctor to be a person who

(I) was incapable of caring for children because of the person's mental or physical infirmity and confinement throughout a period of not less than 2 weeks in the year to bed, to a wheelchair or as a patient in a hospital, an asylum or other similar institution, or

(II) was in the year, and is likely to be for a long, continuous and indefinite period, incapable of caring for children, because of the person's mental or physical infirmity,

(C) a person confined to a prison or similar institution throughout a period of not less than 2 weeks in the year, or

(D) a person who, because of a breakdown of the person's marriage or common-law partnership, was living separate and apart from the taxpayer at the end of the year and for a period of at least 90 days that began in the year, and

(ii) the number of months in the year (other than a month that includes all or part of a week included in the number of weeks referred to in subparagraph (i)), each of which is a month during which the child care expenses were incurred and the supporting person was a student in attendance at a designated educational institution or a secondary school and enrolled in a program of the institution or school that is not less than 3 consecutive weeks duration and that provides that each student in the program spend not less than 12 hours in the month on courses in the program.

**Related Provisions**: 3(f) — Nil income is deemed to be $0 income for comparative purposes; 118.4(2) — Reference to medical practitioners.

**Notes**: Opening words of 63(2) amended by 1989 Budget, effective 1989, to replace references to 56(1)(s) and (u) with the present reference to 60(w).

63(2)(b)C(i)(D) amended by 2000 same-sex partners bill to add reference to "common-law partnership", effective for the 2001 and later taxation years, or earlier by election (see Notes to 248(1)"common-law partner").

63(2)(b) amended by 1998 Budget, effective for 1998 and later taxation years. The para. was restructured as a formula, but the substantive changes were to increase $150 to $175 and $90 to $100, and to relax the educational requirement for the lower-income spouse (entitling the higher-income spouse to claim the expenses) from 10 hours per week to 12 hours per month. Before 1998, read:

(b) the product obtained when the total of

(i) the product obtained when $150 is multiplied by the number of eligible children of the taxpayer for the year each of whom

(A) is under 7 years of age at the end of the year, or

(B) is a person in respect of whom an amount may be deducted under section 118.3 in computing a taxpayer's tax payable under this Part for the year, and

(ii) the product obtained when $90 is multiplied by the number of eligible children of the taxpayer for the year (other than those referred to in subparagraph (i))

is multiplied by the number of weeks in the year during which the child care expenses were incurred and throughout which the supporting person was

(iii) a student in attendance at a designated educational institution (as defined in subsection 118.6(1)) or a secondary school and enrolled in a program of the institution or school of not less than 3 consecutive weeks duration that provides that each student in the program spend not less than 10 hours per week on courses or work in the program,

(iv) a person certified by a medical doctor to be a person who

(A) by reason of mental or physical infirmity and confinement throughout a period of not less than 2 weeks in the year to bed or to a wheelchair or as a patient in a hospital, an asylum or other similar institution, was incapable of caring for children, or

(B) by reason of mental or physical infirmity, was in the year, and is likely to be for a long-continued period of indefinite duration, incapable of caring for children,

(v) a person confined to a prison or similar institution throughout a period of not less than 2 weeks in the year, or

(vi) a person who, because of a breakdown of the person's marriage, was living separate and apart from the taxpayer at the end of the year and for a period of at least 90 days beginning in the year.

63(2)(b)(i)(B) amended by 1991 technical bill, effective 1991, to correspond to changes in 118.3.

Dollar limits in 63(2)(b)(i) and (ii) raised by 1992 technical bill, effective 1993. For 1988 to 1992 these figures were $120 and $60.

63(2)(b)(iii) amended by 1996 Budget, effective for 1996 and later taxation years. For 1988 through 1995, read:

(iii) a person in full-time attendance at a designated educational institution (within the meaning assigned by subsection 118.6(1)),

63(2)(b)(vi) amended by 1992 technical bill, effective 1993, due to the new definition of "marriage" in 252(4)(b). For 1988 to 1992, in place of "marriage", read "marriage or similar domestic relationship".

**Interpretation Bulletins**: See list at end of s. 63.

**(2.1) Taxpayer and supporting person with equal incomes** — For the purposes of this section, where in any taxation year the income of a taxpayer who has an eligible child for the year and the income of a supporting person of the child are equal (on the assumption that both incomes are computed without reference to this section and paragraphs 60(v.1) and (w)), no deduction shall be allowed under this section to the taxpayer and the supporting person in respect of the child unless they jointly elect to treat the income of one of them as exceeding the income of the other for the year.

**Notes**: 63(2.1) amended by 1989 Budget, effective 1989, to replace references to 56(1)(s) and (u) with reference to 60(w). Reference to 60(v.1) added by 1991 technical bill, effective 1989.

**Interpretation Bulletins**: See list at end of s. 63.

**(2.2) Expenses while at school** — There may be deducted in computing a taxpayer's income for a taxation year such part of the amount determined under subsection (2.3) as the taxpayer claims, where

(a) the taxpayer is, at any time in the year, a student in attendance at a designated educational institution or a secondary school and enrolled in a program of the institution or school of not less than 3 consecutive weeks duration that provides that each student in the program spend not less than

(i) 10 hours per week on courses or work in the program, or

(ii) 12 hours per month on courses in the program;

(b) there is no supporting person of an eligible child of the taxpayer for the year or the income of the taxpayer for the year exceeds the income for the year of a supporting person of the child (on the assumption that both incomes are computed without reference to this section and paragraphs 60(v.1) and (w)); and

**S. 63(2.2)(c)**      Income Tax Act, Part I, Division B

(c) a prescribed form containing prescribed information is filed with the taxpayer's return of income (other than a return filed under subsection 70(2) or 104(23), paragraph 128(2)(e) or subsection 150(4)) for the year.

**Notes**: 63(2.2) allows a deduction for child care expenses for periods during which a taxpayer is a student and is either the sole supporting person of an eligible child or, if there is another supporting person, is the supporting person with the higher income. See also 63(3)"child care expense"(a)(v).

63(2.2)(a)(ii) added by 1998 Budget, effective for 1998 and later taxation years.

63(2.2) added by 1996 Budget, effective for 1996 and later taxation years.

**(2.3) Amount deductible** — For the purpose of subsection (2.2), the amount determined in respect of a taxpayer for a taxation year is the least of

(a) the amount by which the total of all amounts, each of which is an amount paid as or on account of child care expenses incurred for services rendered in the year in respect of an eligible child of the taxpayer, exceeds the amount that is deductible under subsection (1) in computing the taxpayer's income for the year,

(b) ²/₃ of the taxpayer's income for the year computed without reference to this section and paragraphs 60(v.1) and (w),

(c) the amount determined by the formula

$$(A + B) \times C$$

> **Proposed Amendment — 63(2.3)(c) formula**
>
> $$A \times C$$
>
> **Application**: The December 21, 2000 draft legislation, subsec. 25(5), will amend the formula in para. 63(2.3)(c) to read as above, applicable to 2000 et seq.
> **Technical Notes**: See under 63(2)(b) formula.

where

A is the product obtained when $175 is multiplied by the number of eligible children of the taxpayer for the year each of whom is

    (i) under 7 years of age at the end of the year, or

    (ii) a person in respect of whom an amount may be deducted under section 118.3 in computing a taxpayer's tax payable under this Part for the year,

B is the product obtained when $100 is multiplied by the number of the taxpayer's eligible children for the year, (other than children referred to in the description of A), and

> **Proposed Amendment — 63(2.3)(c)A, B**
>
> A is the total of all amounts each of which is the periodic child care expense amount in respect of an eligible child of the taxpayer for the year, and
>
> **Application**: The December 21, 2000 draft legislation, subsec. 25(6), will amend the description of A to read as above, and repeal the description of B, applicable applicable to 2000 et seq.
> **Technical Notes**: See under 63(2)(b) formula.

C is

    (i) if there is a supporting person of an eligible child of the taxpayer for the year,

        (A) the number of weeks, in the year, in which both the taxpayer and the supporting person were students who would be described in paragraph (2.2)(a) if that paragraph were read without reference to subparagraph (ii), and

        (B) the number of months in the year (other than a month that includes all or part of a week included in the number of weeks referred to in clause (A)), in which both the taxpayer and the supporting person were students described in paragraph (2.2)(a), and

    (ii) in any other case,

        (A) the number of weeks, in the year, in which the taxpayer was a student who would be described in paragraph (2.2)(a) if that paragraph were read without reference to subparagraph (ii), and

        (B) the number of months in the year (other than a month that includes all or part of a week included in the number of weeks referred to in clause (A)), in which the taxpayer was a student described in paragraph (2.2)(a),

(d) the amount by which the total calculated under subparagraph (1)(e)(ii) in respect of eligible children of the taxpayer for the year exceeds the amount that is deductible under subsection (1) in computing the taxpayer's income for the year, and

(e) where there is a supporting person of an eligible child of the taxpayer for the year, the amount by which the amount calculated under paragraph (2)(b) for the year in respect of the taxpayer exceeds ²/₃ of the taxpayer's earned income for the year.

**Notes**: 63(2.3)(c)A and B amended by 1998 Budget to change "$150" and "$90" to "$175" and "$100" respectively, and to add both "if that paragraph were read without reference to subparagraph (ii)" and cl. (B) in each of C(i) and (ii), effective for 1998 and later taxation years.

63(2.3) added by 1996 Budget, effective for 1996 and later taxation years.

**(3) Definitions** — In this section,

Subdivision e — Deductions in Computing Income     S. 63(3) chi

### Proposed Addition — 63(3) "annual child care expense amount"

**"annual child care expense amount"** in respect of an eligible child of a taxpayer for a taxation year means

(a) $10,000, where the child is a person in respect of whom an amount may be deducted under section 118.3 in computing a taxpayer's tax payable under this Part for the year, and

(b) where the child is not a person referred to in paragraph (a),

(i) $7,000, where the child is under 7 years of age at the end of the year, and

(ii) $4,000, in any other case;

**Application**: The December 21, 2000 draft legislation, subsec. 25(8), will add the definition "annual child care expense amount" to subsec. 63(3), applicable to 2000 et seq.

**Technical Notes**: This new definition sets out the overall maximum amount that may be deducted for a year in respect of child care expenses for an eligible child. In the case of a child in respect of whom the disability tax credit may be claimed, the annual child care expense amount is increased to $10,000. For other eligible children, the deductible amount remains at $7,000 for children under 7 years of age at the end of the relevant year, and $4,000 for children aged 7 to 16 (or over if they are infirm).

**Notice of Ways and Means Motion, federal budget, February 28, 2000**: *Child Care Expense Deduction*

(19) That, for the 2000 and subsequent taxation years, the maximum annual amount deductible for child care expenses be increased from $7,000 to $10,000 for each eligible child in respect of whom a disability tax credit may be claimed.

**Federal budget, supplementary information, February 28, 2000**: *The Child Care Expense Deduction for Persons Eligible for the DTC*

A child care expense deduction of up to $7,000 annually is currently available in respect of persons eligible for the DTC [disability tax credit under 118.3 — ed.]. The budget proposes to increase this limit to $10,000.

**"child care expense"** means an expense incurred in a taxation year for the purpose of providing in Canada, for an eligible child of a taxpayer, child care services including baby sitting services, day nursery services or services provided at a boarding school or camp if the services were provided

(a) to enable the taxpayer, or the supporting person of the child for the year, who resided with the child at the time the expense was incurred,

(i) to perform the duties of an office or employment,

(ii) to carry on a business either alone or as a partner actively engaged in the business,

(iii) [Repealed]

(iv) to carry on research or any similar work in respect of which the taxpayer or supporting person received a grant, or

(v) to attend a designated educational institution or a secondary school, where the taxpayer is enrolled in a program of the institution or school of not less than three consecutive weeks duration that provides that each student in the program spend not less than

(A) 10 hours per week on courses or work in the program, or

(B) 12 hours per month on courses in the program, and

(b) by a resident of Canada other than a person

(i) who is the father or the mother of the child,

(ii) who is a supporting person of the child or is under 18 years of age and related to the taxpayer, or

(iii) in respect of whom an amount is deducted under section 118 in computing the tax payable under this Part for the year by the taxpayer or by a supporting person of the child,

except that

(c) any such expenses paid in the year for a child's attendance at a boarding school or camp to the extent that the total thereof exceeds the product obtained when

(i) in the case of a child of the taxpayer who

(A) is under 7 years of age at the end of the year, or

(B) is a person in respect of whom an amount may be deducted under section 118.3 in computing a taxpayer's tax payable under this Part for the year,

$175, and

(ii) in any other case, $100

is multiplied by the number of weeks in the year during which the child attended the school or camp, and

### Proposed Amendment — 63(3) "child care expense" (c)

(c) any such expenses paid in the year for a child's attendance at a boarding school or camp to the extent that the total of those expenses exceeds the product obtained when the periodic child care expense amount in respect of the child for the year is multiplied by the number of weeks in the year during which the child attended the school or camp, and

**Application**: The December 21, 2000 draft legislation, subsec. 25(7), will amend para. (c) of the definition "child care expense" in subsec. 63(3) to read as above, applicable to 2000 et seq.

**Technical Notes**: Paragraph (c) of this definition provides for a specific maximum for expenses paid for an eligible child's attendance at a boarding school or camp. The maximum amount is computed by reference to the number of weeks of attendance at the school or camp. This paragraph is amended to refer to the "periodic child care expense amount" in respect of the child. This new expression is defined in subsection 63(3) (see the commentary on that subsection).

(d) for greater certainty, any expenses described in subsection 118.2(2) and any other expenses that are paid for medical or hospital care, clothing, transportation or education or for board and lodging, except as otherwise expressly provided in this definition,

are not child care expenses;

**Related Provisions**: 64.1 — Individuals absent from Canada.

**Notes**: The words "in Canada" in the opening words of the definition are effectively ignored for a resident of Canada while working outside Canada. See 64.1(a).

Subpara. (a)(v) added to the definition by 1996 Budget, effective for 1996 and later taxation years. See 63(2.2).

Cl. (a)(v)(B) added by 1998 Budget, effective for 1998 and later taxation years.

Subpara. (b)(ii) amended by 1991 technical bill, effective 1990, to lower the minimum age of a related caregiver from 21 to 18 years. One may now deduct child care expenses paid to one's 19-year-old sister or daughter, for example.

Para. (c) amended to change "$150" to "$175" and "$90" to $100" by 1998 Budget, effective for 1998 and later taxation years.

Cl. (c)(i)(B) amended by 1991 technical bill, effective 1991, to correspond to changes in 118.3.

Dollar limits in (c)(i) and (ii) raised by 1992 technical bill, effective 1993. For 1988 to 1992 these figures were $120 and $60.

63(3)"child care expense" was 63(3)(a) before consolidation in R.S.C. 1985 (5th Supp.), effective for taxation years ending after November 1991. See Table of Concordance.

**Interpretation Bulletins**: See list at end of s. 63.

"**earned income**" of a taxpayer means the total of

(a) all salaries, wages and other remuneration, including gratuities, received by the taxpayer in respect of, in the course of, or because of, offices and employments,

(b) all amounts that are included, or that would, but for paragraph 81(1)(a), be included, because of section 6 or 7 or paragraph 56(1)(n), (o) or (r), in computing the taxpayer's income,

**Proposed Amendment — 63(3)"earned income"(b)**

(b) all amounts that are included, or that would, but for paragraph 81(1)(a) or subsection 81(4), be included, because of section 6 or 7 or paragraph 56(1)(n), (o) or (r), in computing the taxpayer's income,

**Application**: Bill C-43 (First Reading September 20, 2000), s. 25, will amend para. (b) of the definition "earned income" in subsec. 63(3) to read as above, applicable to 1998 *et seq.*

**Technical Notes**: Subsection 63(3) contains the definition "earned income" for the purpose of the child care expense deduction. In any year, an individual is allowed to deduct child care expenses of up to two thirds of the individual's earned income for that year. The amendment to the definition "earned income" is strictly consequential on the replacement of the volunteers' deduction under paragraph 81(1)(a) with an equivalent exemption under subsection 81(4). The amendment ensures that an individual is entitled to the same child care expense deduction as would have been available if the volunteer's exempt income had been required to be included in income. For information on the exemption, see the commentary on new subsection 81(4).

(c) all the taxpayer's incomes or the amounts that would, but for paragraph 81(1)(a), be the taxpayer's incomes from all businesses carried on either alone or as a partner actively engaged in the business, and

(d) all amounts received by the taxpayer as, on account of, in lieu of payment of or in satisfaction of, a disability pension under the *Canada Pension Plan* or a provincial pension plan as defined in section 3 of that Act;

**Related Provisions**: 122.6"earned income" — definition in 63(3) applies to Child Tax Benefit.

**Notes**: "Earned income"(b) amended by 1995-97 technical bill, to add reference to 56(1)(n) and (r) effective 1993 and to remove the reference to 56(1)(m) effective 1998.

Para. (d) amended by 1997 Budget, effective for amounts received after 1994; formerly read "all amounts described in paragraph 56(8)(a) received by the taxpayer in the year". The change was non-substantive; since 56(8) was changed to apply to all CPP benefits rather than just disability benefits, para. (d) was amended so that it continues to apply only to disability benefits.

"Earned income" amended by 1992 Child Benefit bill, effective 1993, effectively to add para. (d) and the references to 81(1)(a) and 56(1)(r), and to delete a reference to 56(1)(m) (training allowances).

63(3)"earned income" was 63(3)(b) before consolidation in R.S.C. 1985 (5th Supp.), effective for taxation years ending after November 1991. See Table of Concordance.

**Interpretation Bulletins**: IT-434R: Rental of real property by individual. See also list at end of s. 63.

"**eligible child**" of a taxpayer for a taxation year means

(a) a child of the taxpayer or of the taxpayer's spouse or common-law partner, or

(b) a child dependent on the taxpayer or the taxpayer's spouse or common-law partner for support and whose income for the year does not exceed the amount used under paragraph (c) of the description of B in subsection 118(1) for the year

if, at any time during the year, the child

(c) is under 16 years of age, or

(d) is dependent on the taxpayer or on the taxpayer's spouse or common-law partner and has a mental or physical infirmity;

**Notes**: 63(3)"eligible child" amended by 2000 same-sex partners bill to add reference to "common-law partner", effective for the 2001 and later taxation years, or earlier by election (see Notes to 248(1)"common-law partner").

63(3)"eligible child"(b) amended by 1999 Budget, this version effective for 2000 and later taxation years. For the 1999 taxation year, in place of "the amount used under paragraph (c) of the description of B in subsection 118(1) for the year", read "$7,044". For 1998, read "the total of $500 and the amount used under paragraph (c) of the description of B in subsection 118(1) for the year".

Para. (b) amended by 1998 Budget to add "the total of $500 and", effective for 1998 and later taxation years. This reflects the $500 supplementary credit in 118(1)B(b.1), which effectively increased the income that can be earned tax-free from $6,456 to $6,956 for 1998.

## Subdivision e — Deductions in Computing Income — S. 64(a)

Para. (c) amended to change "14" to "16" by 1996 Budget, effective for 1996 and later taxation years. This means that $4,000 per child up to the age of 16 is counted towards the child-care expense limit. The change was stated in the budget as responding to concerns raised by single parents who must be away from home at night for their work, such as airline attendants, nurses and other shift workers. However, it also benefits families with children 14 and 15 who also have younger children whose child-care costs exceed the allowable limits. (There is no requirement that the $4,000 available for a 14- or 15-year old be spent on care for that child.)

Para. (b) amended by 1992 Child Benefit bill, effective 1993, due to the elimination of the credit for dependent children under 18 (in 118(1)B(d)) and its replacement with the child tax benefit in 122.61.

63(3)"eligible child" was 63(3)(c) before consolidation in R.S.C. 1985 (5th Supp.), effective for taxation years ending after November 1991. See Table of Concordance.

### Proposed Addition — 63(3)"periodic child care expense amount"

**"periodic child care expense amount"** in respect of an eligible child of a taxpayer for a taxation year means 1/40 of the annual child care expense amount in respect of the child for the year;

**Application**: The December 21, 2000 draft legislation, subsec. 25(8), will add the definition "periodic child care expense amount" to subsec. 63(3), applicable to 2000 et seq.

**Technical Notes**: This new definition sets out the maximum that may be claimed on a monthly or weekly basis, which is relevant when a claim is made by the higher-income supporting person. In all cases, the periodic child care expense amount in respect of an eligible child is equal to 1/40 of the annual child care expense amount in respect of that child.

**Notes**: The periodic limits are:
- Disabled child ($10,000) — $250 per week
- Child under 7 ($7,000) — $175 per week
- Child over 7 ($4,000) — $100 per week

**"supporting person"** of an eligible child of a taxpayer for a taxation year means a person, other than the taxpayer, who is

(a) a parent of the child,

(b) the taxpayer's spouse or common-law partner, or

(c) an individual who deducted an amount under section 118 for the year in respect of the child,

if the parent, spouse or common-law partner or individual, as the case may be, resided with the taxpayer at any time during the year and at any time within 60 days after the end of the year.

**Notes**: 63(3)"supporting person" amended by 2000 same-sex partners bill to add reference to "common-law partner", effective for the 2001 and later taxation years, or earlier by election (see Notes to 248(1)"common-law partner").

Opening words of the definition amended to add the words "a person, other than the taxpayer, who is", retroactive to 1983. This change corrects an error that was possibly open to abuse.

63(3)"supporting person" was 63(3)(d) before consolidation in R.S.C. 1985 (5th Supp.), effective for taxation years ending after November 1991. See Table of Concordance.

**(4) Commuter's child care expense** — Where in a taxation year a person resides in Canada near the boundary between Canada and the United States and while so resident incurs expenses for child care services that would be child care expenses if

(a) the definition "child care expense" in subsection (3) were read without reference to the words "in Canada", and

(b) the reference in paragraph (b) of the definition "child care expense" in subsection (3) to "resident of Canada" were read as "person",

those expenses (other than expenses paid for a child's attendance at a boarding school or camp outside Canada) shall be deemed to be child care expenses for the purpose of this section if the child care services are provided at a place that is closer to the person's principal place of residence by a reasonably accessible route, having regard to the circumstances, than any place in Canada where such child care services are available and, in respect of those expenses, subsection (1) shall be read without reference to the words "and contains, where the payee is an individual, that individual's Social Insurance Number".

**Notes**: 63(4) added by 1993 technical bill, effective for 1992 and later taxation years. It permits a deduction for child-care services provided in the U.S. if all of the conditions therein are met.

63(4), repealed by 1983 Budget, dealt with whether a child was in the custody of the taxpayer, a concept that no longer applies.

**Definitions [s. 63]**: "amount" — 248(1); "annual child care expense amount" — 63(3); "business" — 248(1); "Canada" — 64.1, 255; "child" — 252(1); "child care expense" — 63(3); "common-law partner", "common-law partnership" — 248(1); "designated educational institution" — 118.6(1); "earned income", "eligible child" — 63(3); "employment" — 248(1); "father" — 252(2); "individual" — 248(1); "medical doctor" — 118.4(2); "Minister" — 248(1); "month" — Interpretation Act 35(1); "mother" — 252(2); "office" — 248(1); "parent" — 252(2); "periodic child care expense amount" — 63(3); "person", "prescribed" — 248(1); "supporting person" — 63(3); "taxable income" — 2(2), 248(1); "taxation year" — 249; "taxpayer" — 248(1).

**Interpretation Bulletins [s. 63]**: IT-193 SR: Taxable income of individuals resident in Canada during part of a year (Special Release); IT-495R2: Child care expenses; IT-518R: Food, beverages and entertainment expenses.

**63.1** [See s. 64.1]

**64. Attendant care expenses** — If a taxpayer in respect of whom an amount may be deducted because of section 118.3 for a taxation year files with the taxpayer's return of income (other than a return of income filed under subsection 70(2), paragraph 104(23)(d) or 128(2)(e) or subsection 150(4)) for the year a prescribed form containing prescribed information, there may be deducted in computing the taxpayer's income for the year the lesser of

(a) the amount determined by the formula

$$A - B$$

where

**S. 64(a)** — Income Tax Act, Part I, Division B

A is the total of all amounts each of which is an amount that was

(i) paid in the year by the taxpayer to a person who, at the time of the payment, is neither the taxpayer's spouse or common-law partner nor under 18 years of age as or on account of attendant care provided in Canada to the taxpayer to enable the taxpayer to

(A) perform the duties of an office or employment,

(B) carry on a business either alone or as a partner actively engaged in the business, or

### Proposed Addition — 64(a)(C)

(C) attend a designated educational institution or a secondary school at which the taxpayer is enrolled in an educational program, or

**Application**: The December 21, 2000 draft legislation, subsec. 26(1), will add cl. 64(a)(C), applicable to 2000 *et seq.*

**Technical Notes**: Section 64 permits the deduction, in computing the income of an individual who has a severe and prolonged mental or physical impairment, of expenses paid to an attendant (other than the individual's spouse) who is at least 18 years of age that are incurred to enable the individual to work. Such an individual is allowed to deduct the lesser of the actual amount of expenses for attendant care provided in Canada and 2/3 of the individual's income from specific sources. This includes income from business, gross employment income, net research grants and the taxable portion of scholarships, fellowships, bursaries and similar awards.

Section 64 is amended to expand the list of eligible sources of income to include certain earnings supplements and financial assistance included in income under paragraph 56(1)(r). It is also amended to extend the deduction (up to a maximum of $10,000) to an individual who incurs attendant care expenses to attend a designated educational institution (see the commentary on subsection 118.6(1)) or high school.

(D) carry on research or any similar work in respect of which the taxpayer received a grant,

the payment of which is proven by filing with the Minister one or more receipts each of which was issued by the payee and contains, where the payee is an individual, that individual's Social Insurance Number, and

(ii) not included in computing a deduction under section 118.2 for any taxation year, and

B is the total of all amounts each of which is the amount of a reimbursement or any other form of assistance (other than prescribed assistance or an amount that is included in computing a taxpayer's income and that is not deductible in computing the taxpayer's taxable income)

that any taxpayer is or was entitled to receive in respect of an amount included in computing the value of A, and

(b) 2/3 of the total of all amounts each of which is

(i) an amount included under any of sections 5, 6 and 7 in computing the taxpayer's income for the year from an office or employment,

(ii) an amount included by reason of paragraph 56(1)(n) or (o) in computing a taxpayer's income for the year, or

(iii) the taxpayer's income for the year from a business carried on either alone or as a partner actively engaged in the business.

### Proposed Amendment — 64(b)

(b) 2/3 of the total of

(i) the total of all amounts each of which is

(A) an amount included under section 5, 6 or 7 or paragraph 56(1)(n), (o) or (r) in computing the taxpayer's income for the year, or

(B) the taxpayer's income for the year from a business carried on either alone or as a partner actively engaged in the business, and

(ii) where the taxpayer is in attendance at a designated educational institution or a secondary school at which the taxpayer is enrolled in an educational program, the least of

(A) $15,000,

(B) $375 times the number of weeks in the year during which the taxpayer is in attendance at the institution or school, and

(C) the amount, if any, by which the amount that would, if this Act were read without reference to this section, be the taxpayer's income for the year exceeds the total determined under subparagraph (i) in respect of the taxpayer for the year.

**Application**: The December 21, 2000 draft legislation, subsec. 26(2), will amend para. 64(b) to read as above, applicable to 2000 *et seq.*

**Technical Notes**: See under 64(a)(C).

**Notice of Ways and Means Motion, federal budget, February 28, 2000**: *Attendant Care Expenses*

(18) That, for the 2000 and subsequent taxation years,

(a) the attendant care expense deduction allowed in computing an individual's income be extended to an individual who incurs such expenses to attend a designated educational institution or a secondary school at which the individual is enrolled in an educational program, and

(b) the maximum amount of the deduction allowed for the year to such an individual for all eligible attendant care expenses be 2/3 of the total of

(i) the individual's earned income for the year, and

## Subdivision e — Deductions in Computing Income — S. 64.1

    (ii) the least of

        (A) the amount by which the individual's income otherwise determined for the year exceeds the individual's earned income for the year,

        (B) $15,000, and

        (C) $375 multiplied by the number of weeks in the year during which the individual attends the institution or school.

**Federal budget, supplementary information, February 28, 2000**: *The Deduction for Attendant Care and Students*

The current attendant care provisions allow a deduction in respect of a person with a severe disability for the cost of an attendant required in order for the person to be employed, carry on business or carry on funded research. The budget proposes expanding this deduction to include the cost of an attendant required in order to attend school. The deduction will be subject to a maximum of 2/3 of earned income plus, where the taxpayer attends a designated educational institution or a secondary school, 2/3 of the lesser of (a) the taxpayer's income from other sources (up to a maximum of $15,000) and (b) $375 times the number of weeks of attendance at the institution or school.

  (c) [Repealed]

**Related Provisions**: 4(2) — Deductions under s. 64 not applicable to any particular source; 64.1 — Individuals absent from Canada; 118.2(2)(b), (b.1), (c) — Medical expense — attendant care; 257 — Formula cannot calculate to less than zero.

**Notes**: 64 allows a deduction for the cost of an attendant, where a person eligible for the disability credit (118.3) earns business or employment income or attends school. Like s. 63, it is tied to such income, but since 1997 it no longer has a fixed dollar limit. A taxpayer with a full-time attendant can choose to claim a medical expense credit instead under 118.2(2)(b), which also does not have a dollar limit but which effectively is a deduction only against the low rate (16% federal) of tax. An alternative medical expense claim for an attendant can be made under 118.2(2)(b.1) or (c). For further discussion see David M. Sherman, *Taxes, Health & Disabilities* (Carswell, 1995), at §3.7.6.

64(a)A(i) amended by 2000 same-sex partners bill to add reference to "common-law partner", effective for the 2001 and later taxation years, or earlier by election (see Notes to 248(1)"common-law partner").

64 amended by 1997 Budget, effective for 1997 and later taxation years, to change "the least of" to "the lesser of" in the opening words, delete para. (c) ("$5,000"), and change 104(23) in the opening words to 104(23)(d). The amendment removes the former $5,000 per year limit on this claim.

64(a)A(i)(C) repealed by 1996 EI bill, effective 1998. For 1989-97, read:

    (C) undertake an occupational training course in respect of which the taxpayer received a training allowance under the *National Training Act*, or

This version of 64 added by 1989 Budget, effective 1989, and amended by 1991 technical bill, effective 1989, but for 1989 and 1990, read the opening words of 64(a)A(i) as follows:

    (i) paid in the year by the taxpayer to a person (other than a person related to the taxpayer or a person under 18 years of age) as or on account of attendant care provided in Canada to the taxpayer to enable the taxpayer to

The previous version of 64, repealed by 1981 Budget but still referred to (as, in some but not all cases, s. 64 of R.S.C. 1952, c. 148, as amended) in 59(2), 61(1)(b)(iv.1), 66(4)(b)(ii)(C)(II), 66(5), 66(15)"reserve amount"B, 66.4(1), 72(1)(d) and (e), 72(2)(a)(iii)(D), 72(2)(c)(iii), 87(2)(p) and 88(1)(d)(i)(C), was titled "Reserve in respect of consideration for disposition of resource property not receivable until subsequent year." It still applies to any dispositions pursuant to the terms in existence on November 12, 1981 of an offer or agreement in writing made or entered into on or before that date.

**Definitions [s. 64]**: "amount", "business" — 248(1); "Canada" — 64.1, 255; "common-law partner" — 248(1); "designated educational institution " — 118.6(1); "employment", "individual", "Minister", "office", "person", "prescribed" — 248(1); "taxable income" — 2(2), 248(1); "taxation year" — 249; "taxpayer" — 248(1).

**Regulations**: No assistance prescribed to date for 64(a)B.

**Interpretation Bulletins**: IT-519R2: Medical expense and disability tax credits and attendant care expense deduction.

**Information Circulars**: 82-2R2: SIN legislation that relates to the preparation of information slips.

**Forms**: RC4064: Information concerning people with disabilities [guide]; T929: Attendant care expenses.

## 64.1 Individuals absent from Canada

— In applying sections 63 and 64 in respect of a taxpayer who is, throughout all or part of a taxation year, absent from but resident in Canada, the following rules apply for the year or that part of the year, as the case may be:

  (a) the definition "child care expense" in subsection 63(3), and section 64, shall be read without reference to the words "in Canada";

  (b) subsection 63(1) and section 64 shall be read without reference to the words "and contains, where the payee is an individual, that individual's Social Insurance Number", if the payment referred to in that subsection or section, as the case may be, is made to a person who is not resident in Canada; and

  (c) paragraph (b) of the definition "child care expense" in subsection 63(3) shall be read as if the word "person" were substituted for the words "resident of Canada" where they appear therein.

**Notes**: 64.1 amended by 1998 Budget to change "62, 63 and 64" to "63 and 64" in the opening words and to delete opening words "subsection 62(1)," from para. (a), effective 1998. The rule still applies for moving expenses but is now in the closing words of 248(1)"eligible relocation".

64.1 effectively states that as long as the taxpayer is absent from Canada, there is no requirement that child care and certain other expenses be incurred in Canada. However, the "in Canada" rule applies while the taxpayer is in Canada (due to the words "that part of the year"). Thus, if one takes one's child on a business trip, a deduction for child care in the foreign country may be available; but if one stays home working and sends the child to summer camp outside Canada, no deduction is available.

64.1 was originally enacted as 63.1. Redrafted and renumbered by 1989 Budget, effective 1989, when 64 was enacted.

64.1 also covers deemed residents under 250(1) such as diplomats working abroad, who are physically outside Canada for all or part of the year, but are resident in Canada for tax purposes.

**Definitions [s. 64.1]**: "Canada" — 255; "person" — 248(1); "resident" — 250; "taxation year" — 249; "taxpayer" — 248(1).

**Remission Orders**: *Child Care Expense and Moving Expense Remission Order*, P.C. 1991-257 (same relief as section 64.1 for 1984-88, can be applied for retroactively).

**Interpretation Bulletins**: IT-178R3: Moving expenses; IT-495R2: Child care expenses; IT-519R2: Medical expense and disability tax credits and attendant care expense deduction.

## 65. (1) Allowance for oil or gas well, mine or timber limit — There may be deducted in computing a taxpayer's income for a taxation year such amount as an allowance, if any, in respect of

(a) a natural accumulation of petroleum or natural gas, oil or gas well, mineral resource or timber limit,

(b) the processing of ore (other than iron ore or tar sands) from a mineral resource to any stage that is not beyond the prime metal stage or its equivalent,

(c) the processing of iron ore from a mineral resource to any stage that is not beyond the pellet stage or its equivalent, or

(d) the processing of tar sands from a mineral resource to any stage that is not beyond the crude oil stage or its equivalent

as is allowed to the taxpayer by regulation.

**Related Provisions**: 20(1)(v.1) — Resource allowance; 53(2) — Amounts to be deducted; 65(3) — Allocation of allowance for coal mine; 66(1) — Exploration and development expenses of principal-business corporations; 66.7 — Successor rules; 96(1)(d) — No deduction at partnership level; 104(17) — Trusts — depletion allowance; 127.52(1)(e) — Limitation on deduction for minimum tax purposes; 133(1)(b) — No deduction allowed to non-resident-owned investment corporation; 209 — Tax on carved-out income.

**Regulations**: 1200.

**I.T. Application Rules**: 29(1)–(4), (11)–(14), (16), (24).

**(2) Regulations** — For greater certainty it is hereby declared that, in the case of a regulation made under subsection (1) allowing to a taxpayer an amount in respect of a natural accumulation of petroleum or natural gas, an oil or gas well or a mineral resource or in respect of the processing of ore,

(a) there may be allowed to the taxpayer by that regulation an amount in respect of any or all

(i) natural accumulations of petroleum or natural gas, oil or gas wells or mineral resources in which the taxpayer has any interest, or

(ii) processing operations described in any of paragraphs (1)(b), (c) or (d) that are carried on by the taxpayer; and

(b) notwithstanding any other provision contained in this Act, the Governor in Council may prescribe the formula by which the amount that may be allowed to the taxpayer by that regulation shall be determined.

**Related Provisions**: 20(1)(v) — Deduction for mining taxes; 59(6) — Definitions in regulations apply for purposes of s. 59; 66(1) — Exploration and development expenses of principal-business corporations; 66.7 — Successor rules; 221 — Rules applicable to regulations generally.

**Regulations**: Part XII.

**I.T. Application Rules**: 29(1)–(4), (11)–(14), (16), (24).

**(3) Lessee's share of allowance** — Where a deduction is allowed under subsection (1) in respect of a coal mine operated by a lessee, the lessor and lessee may agree as to what portion of the allowance each may deduct and, in the event that they cannot agree, the Minister may fix the portions.

**I.T. Application Rules**: 29(1)–(4), (11)–(14), (16), (24).

**Definitions [s. 65]**: "amount", "mineral resource", "Minister", "oil or gas well", "regulation", "tar sands" — 248(1); "taxation year" — 249; "taxpayer" — 248(1).

## 66. (1) Exploration and development expenses of principal-business corporations — A principal-business corporation may deduct, in computing its income for a taxation year, the lesser of

(a) the total of such of its Canadian exploration and development expenses as were incurred by it before the end of the taxation year, to the extent that they were not deductible in computing income for a previous taxation year, and

(b) of that total, an amount equal to its income for the taxation year if no deduction were allowed under this subsection, section 65 or subsection 66.1(2), minus the deductions allowed for the year by sections 112 and 113.

**Related Provisions**: 66(10) — Joint exploration corporation; 87(6), (7) — Obligations of predecessor corporation. See additional Related Provisions and Definitions at end of s. 66.

**I.T. Application Rules**: 29.

**Interpretation Bulletins**: IT-400: Exploration and development expenses — meaning of principal-business corporation.

**(2) Expenses of special product corporations** — A corporation (other than a principal-business corporation the principal business of which is described in paragraph (a) or (b) of the definition "principal-business corporation" in subsection (15)), whose principal business is the production or marketing of sodium chloride or potash or whose business includes manufacturing products the manufacturing of which involves processing sodium chloride or potash, may deduct, in computing its income for a taxation year, the drilling and exploration expenses incurred by it in the year and before May 7, 1974 on or in respect of exploring or drilling for halite or sylvite.

**Related Provisions**: See additional Related Provisions and Definitions at end of s. 66.

**I.T. Application Rules**: 29.

**(3) Expenses of other taxpayers** — A taxpayer other than a principal-business corporation may deduct, in computing the taxpayer's income for a taxation year, the total of the taxpayer's Canadian exploration and development expenses to the extent that they were not deducted in computing the taxpayer's income for a preceding taxation year.

## Subdivision e — Deductions in Computing Income

**Related Provisions**: 66(5) — Dealers; 66(10) — Joint exploration corporation. See additional Related Provisions and Definitions at end of s. 66.

**I.T. Application Rules**: 29.

**(4) Foreign exploration and development expenses** — A taxpayer who is resident throughout a taxation year in Canada may deduct, in computing the taxpayer's income for that taxation year, the lesser of

(a) the amount, if any, by which

(i) the total of the foreign exploration and development expenses incurred by the taxpayer before the end of the year

> **Proposed Amendment — 66(4)(a)(i)**
>
> (i) the total of the foreign exploration and development expenses incurred by the taxpayer before the end of the year and at a time at which the taxpayer was resident in Canada
>
> **Application**: Bill C-43 (First Reading September 20, 2000), subsec. 26(1), will amend subpara. 66(4)(a)(i) to read as above, applicable to 1999 et seq.
>
> **Technical Notes**: Subsection 66(4) sets out the deduction that may be claimed for foreign exploration and development expenses (FEDE) incurred by a taxpayer resident in Canada. A taxpayer's minimum deduction for a taxation year under this subsection is 10% of the taxpayer's undeducted FEDE balance at the end of the year. An additional portion of a taxpayer's undeducted FEDE balance may be deducted by a taxpayer for a taxation year, essentially to the extent of the taxpayer's foreign resource income in excess of that minimum amount.
>
> Subparagraph 66(4)(a)(i) is amended so that a taxpayer's FEDE balance takes into account only expenses incurred while the taxpayer was resident in Canada. As a result, a taxpayer who becomes resident in Canada cannot deduct FEDE that was incurred before becoming resident in Canada.
>
> The amendment to subparagraph 66(4)(a)(i) does not prevent the creation of FEDE as a consequence of a taxpayer becoming resident [in] Canada. In these circumstances, there is a deemed acquisition of the taxpayer's foreign resource properties at fair market value pursuant to paragraph 128.1(1)(c). The deemed cost of the foreign resource properties qualifies as FEDE under paragraph (c) of the FEDE definition in subsection 66(15).

> **Proposed Amendment — 66(4)(a)(i)**
>
> (i) the total of the foreign exploration and development expenses incurred by the taxpayer
>
> (A) before the end of the year,
>
> (B) at a time at which the taxpayer was resident in Canada, and
>
> (C) where the taxpayer became resident in Canada before the end of the year, after the last time (before the end of the year) that the taxpayer became resident in Canada,

**Application**: The December 21, 2000 draft legislation, subsec. 27(1), will amend subpara. 66(4)(a)(i) to read as above, applicable to 2000 et seq.

**Technical Notes**: Subparagraph 66(4)(a)(i) provides that the amount deductible by a taxpayer under subsection 66(4) must relate to foreign exploration and development expenses (FEDE) incurred while the taxpayer was resident in Canada.

Subparagraph 66(4)(a)(i) is amended to cover the unusual situation where a taxpayer with FEDE had ceased to reside in Canada and then becomes resident in Canada again. In these circumstances,

- the FEDE incurred during the taxpayer's prior periods of residence is not taken into account once the taxpayer subsequently becomes resident in Canada (amended subparagraph 66(4)(a)(i)), and
- there is a deemed acquisition at fair market value of the taxpayer's foreign resource properties on becoming resident in Canada (subsection 128.1(1)).

exceeds the total of

(ii) such of the expenses described in subparagraph (i) as were deductible in computing the taxpayer's income for a preceding taxation year, and

(iii) all amounts by which the amount described in this paragraph in respect of the taxpayer is required because of subsection 80(8) to be reduced at or before the end of the year, and

(b) of that total, the greater of,

(i) such amount as the taxpayer may claim not exceeding 10% of the total determined under paragraph (a), and

> **Proposed Amendment — 66(4)(b)**
>
> (b) of that total, the greatest of,
>
> (i) such amount as the taxpayer claims not exceeding 10% of the amount determined under paragraph (a) in respect of the taxpayer for the year,
>
> (i.1) if the taxpayer ceased to be resident in Canada immediately after the end of the year, such amount as the taxpayer claims not exceeding the amount determined under paragraph (a) in respect of the taxpayer for the year, and

**Application**: Bill C-43 (First Reading September 20, 2000), subsec. 26(2), will amend the portion of para. 66(4)(b) before subpara. (ii) to read as above, applicable to 1995 et seq.

**Technical Notes**: New subparagraph 66(4)(b)(i.1) is introduced to allow the full amount of a taxpayer's undeducted FEDE balance to be deducted in the event that the taxpayer ceases to be resident in Canada. This measure is consistent with existing income tax rules which allow emigrating taxpayers to claim a terminal loss on depreciable property as a consequence of deemed dispositions under paragraph 128.1(4)(b).

The amendment, which applies to the 1995 and subsequent taxation years, will allow the FEDE deduction to be claimed for the last taxation year throughout which a taxpayer is resident in Canada. (Under paragraph 128.1(4)(a), a new taxation year for a corporate taxpayer starts at the time that the taxpayer ceases to be resident in Canada.)

**Letter from Department of Finance, September 20, 1995**:

Dear [xxx]

I am writing further to your recent meeting with Brian Ernewein, Simon Thompson and Lawrence Purdy of this Division regarding the effect of the recently-signed Protocol to the Canada-U.S. tax Convention (the Treaty) on a corporation continued to the United States. I understand that your meeting followed some months of intermittent discussion, and I appreciate your patience in working through the issue with us.

In essence, the case you describe is as follows. A corporation incorporated in Canada continued into the U.S. some years ago. Because it had been created in Canada, the corporation remained resident here under the Treaty, and thus under the *Income Tax Act* as well, even after the enactment of subsection 250(5) of the Act (which effectively denies resident status under the Act to a corporation that is a non-resident under a treaty). The corporation is also, I gather, a Canadian corporation as defined in subsection 89(1).

The Protocol includes a rule that would treat a corporation that continues into either country as having been incorporated in that country. In this case, the rule will mean that the corporation will be treated as having been incorporated in the U.S., and not in Canada. This will make it resident in the U.S. under the Treaty and, by virtue of subsection 250(5) of the Act, no longer resident in Canada.

The consequences of thus ceasing to be resident in Canada will be significant. You have expressed particular concern about the effect on the corporation's foreign exploration and development expenses (FEDE). To the extent that the corporation's FEDE is represented in its foreign resource properties, the deemed disposition of those properties at fair market value on leaving Canada will give rise to an income inclusion under subsection 59(1) of the Act, and may correspondingly increase the amount deductible under subsection 66(4) for the corporation's last year in Canada. Any FEDE in excess of the fair market value of those properties will, however, cease to be available: as a non-resident, the corporation will not be taxable in Canada on its foreign-source income, and will not be able to deduct any amount in respect of FEDE.

You have suggested that this result is inappropriate, since it limits the recognition for Canadian tax purposes of expenses incurred by the corporation to earn revenue that has been subject to Canadian tax. Just as an emigrating taxpayer's deemed disposition may give rise to a terminal loss on a depreciable property used to earn foreign-source income, you suggest, a loss should be recognized in respect of FEDE amounts that become unusable on emigration.

I agree that the corporation in the case you describe ought, as a matter of tax policy, to get some recognition on emigration for FEDE amounts in excess of the amount the corporation can deduct under subsection 66(4) for its last year in Canada. That recognition should probably take the form of a loss for that year from a foreign business or property. [This was done in 66(4)(b)(i.1); but for the future see 115(1)(e.1) — ed.] As such, the loss would be available to offset income earned in that year, or could be applied in computing taxable income for any of the previous three years (assuming the corporation was resident in Canada throughout those years). The loss could not be carried forward for use against income earned while a non-resident, since paragraph 115(1)(d) of the Act allows a non-resident to deduct only Canadian-source losses.

Although further work will need to be done to determine its exact form, I expect that we will recommend including a provision along the lines I have described in a future package of draft technical amendments. I can, as you know, give no assurance that either the Minister or Parliament will endorse such a recommendation, but I have no reason to believe that it would present any special difficulty.

I trust these comments are of some assistance, and thank you for having brought this issue to our attention.

Yours sincerely,

Len Farber
Director, Tax Legislation Division

### Proposed Amendment — 66(4)(b) before (ii)

(b) of that total, the greater of

(i) the amount, if any, claimed by the taxpayer not exceeding 10% of the amount determined under paragraph (a) in respect of the taxpayer for the year, and

**Application**: The December 21, 2000 draft legislation, subsec. 27(2), will amend the portion of para. 66(4)(b) before subpara. (ii) to read as above, applicable to taxation years that end after February 27, 2000, except that the portion of the para. shall read as follows in respect of cessations of residence that occurred before February 28, 2000:

"(b) of that total, the greatest of

(i) the amount, if any, claimed by the taxpayer not exceeding 10% of the amount determined under paragraph (a) in respect of the taxpayer for the year,

(i.1) if the taxpayer ceased to be resident in Canada immediately after the end of the year, the amount, if any, claimed by the taxpayer not exceeding the amount determined under paragraph (a) in respect of the taxpayer for the year, and"

**Technical Notes**: Paragraph 66(4)(b) generally limits a taxpayer's deduction under subsection 66(4) for a taxation year to the greater of 10% of the taxpayer's undeducted foreign exploration and development expenses (FEDE) at the end of the year and an amount, determined under subparagraph 66(4)(b)(ii), representing the taxpayer's foreign resource income for the year. However, subparagraph 66(4)(b)(i.1) provides for the deduction of the full FEDE balance in the event that the taxpayer is a corporation or trust that ceases to reside in Canada immediately after the end of the year even if there is not sufficient supporting foreign resource income.

Paragraph 66(4)(b) is amended to eliminate the relief provided under subparagraph 66(4)(b)(i.1) for taxpayers who cease to reside in Canada. Instead, pursuant to new paragraph 115(1)(e.1), the unused FEDE balance can be applied to offset taxable income earned in Canada on a declining balance basis (10% per year). This amendment applies to cessations of residence that occur after February 27, 2000. As to the treatment of individuals who cease to reside in Canada, see the commentary to new subsection 66(4.3).

(ii) the total of

(A) such part of the taxpayer's income for the taxation year as may reasonably be regarded as attributable to the production of petroleum or natural gas from natural accumulations thereof outside Canada or from oil or gas wells outside Canada or to the production of minerals from mines outside Canada,

(B) the taxpayer's income for the taxation year from royalties in respect of a natural accumulation of petroleum or natural gas outside Canada, an oil or gas well outside Canada or a mine outside Canada, and

(C) the total of amounts each of which is an amount, in respect of a foreign resource property that has been disposed of by the taxpayer, equal to the amount, if any, by which

(I) the amount included in computing the taxpayer's income for the year by virtue of section 59 in respect of the disposition of the property,

exceeds

(II) the amount deducted under section 64 in respect of the property in computing the taxpayer's income for the year,

determined as if no deductions were allowed under this subsection, subsections (1) and (3), section 65 and subsections 66.1(2) and (3).

**Proposed Amendment — 66(4)(b)(ii)**

(ii) the total of

(A) the part of the taxpayer's income for the year, determined without reference to this subsection and subsection 66.21(4), that can reasonably be regarded as attributable to

(I) the production of petroleum or natural gas from natural accumulations outside Canada or from oil or gas wells outside Canada, or

(II) the production of minerals from mines outside Canada,

(B) the taxpayer's income for the year from royalties in respect of a natural accumulation of petroleum or natural gas outside Canada, an oil or gas well outside Canada or a mine outside Canada, determined without reference to this subsection and subsection 66.21(4), and

(C) all amounts each of which is an amount, in respect of a foreign resource property that has been disposed of by the taxpayer, equal to the amount, if any, by which

(I) the amount included in computing the taxpayer's income for the year by reason of subsection 59(1) in respect of the disposition

exceeds

(II) the total of all amounts each of which is that portion of an amount deducted under subsection 66.7(2) in computing the taxpayer's income for the year that

1. can reasonably be considered to be in respect of the foreign resource property, and

2. cannot reasonably be considered to have reduced the amount otherwise determined under clause (A) or (B) in respect of the taxpayer for the year.

**Application**: The December 21, 2000 draft legislation, subsec. 27(3), will amend subpara. 66(4)(b)(ii) to read as above, applicable to taxation years that begin after 2000.

**Technical Notes**: Subparagraph 66(4)(b)(ii) is amended so that deductions claimed under new subsection 66.21(4), which provides for the tax treatment of certain resource expenses that would be FEDE if they were incurred before 2001, do not result in any reduction of the foreign resource income determined under subparagraph 66(4)(b)(ii). This amendment is consequential on the introduction of section 66.21. This amendment applies to taxation years that begin after 2000.

Clause 66(4)(b)(ii)(C) is amended to clarify that deductions claimed by a taxpayer under subsection 66.7(2) (successor FEDE) will always result in a reduction of the taxpayer's foreign resource income determined under subparagraph 66(4)(b)(ii). Amended clause 66(4)(b)(ii)(C) also eliminates a reference to former section 64 that is no longer of any relevance. These amendments apply to taxation years that begin after 2000.

Reference should also be made to amendments being made to the definition of "foreign exploration and development expenses" in subsection 66(15). In general, FEDE balances will cease to be generated in taxation years that begin after 2000. Instead, new section 66.21 will apply with regard to expenses that are a "foreign resource expense" (FRE), as defined in subsection 66.21(1).

**Notice of Ways and Means Motion, federal budget, February 28, 2000**: *Foreign Exploration and Development Expenses*

(34) That an outlay made after February 27, 2000 by a person or partnership not be treated as a foreign exploration and development expense (FEDE) unless

(a) the outlay was made pursuant to an agreement in writing made by the person or partnership before February 28, 2000,

(b) the outlay was for the acquisition of foreign resource property by the person or partnership, or

(c) the outlay can reasonably be considered to have been incurred for the purpose of enhancing the value of foreign resource property owned or to be owned by the person or partnership.

(35) That, for outlays made in taxation years that begin after 2000, separate FEDE balances for a taxpayer be determined in respect of each country to which the taxpayer's FEDE relates.

(36) That, for FEDE incurred in a taxation year that begins after 2000, a taxpayer's FEDE deduction in respect of a country for the year be limited to the total of

(a) the greater of 10 per cent of the taxpayer's FEDE balance in respect of the country at the end of the year and the lesser of

(i) where the year is the taxpayer's last taxation year of residence in Canada, that FEDE balance and, in any other case, 30 per cent of that FEDE balance, and

(ii) the lesser of

(A) the amount, if any, by which the taxpayer's foreign resource income in respect of the country for the year (determined in accordance with subparagraph 66(4)(b)(ii) of the Act) exceeds the taxpayer's FEDE deduction for the year in respect of the country that relates to FEDE incurred in taxation years that begin before 2001, and

(B) the amount, if any, by which the taxpayer's total foreign resource income in respect of all countries for the year (determined in accordance with subparagraph 66(4)(b)(ii) of the Act) exceeds the taxpayer's total FEDE deduction for the year that relates to FEDE incurred in taxation years that begin before 2001, and

(b) the lesser of

(i) the amount, if any, by which that FEDE balance exceeds the amount determined under subparagraph (a), and

(ii) such portion of the taxpayer's specified foreign resource income as is designated by the taxpayer in respect of the country and no other country.

(37) That a taxpayer's specified foreign resource income for a taxation year be equal to the lesser of

(a) the amount, if any, by which the taxpayer's total foreign resource income for the year in respect of all countries (determined in accordance with subparagraph 66(4)(b)(ii) of the Act) exceeds the total of

(i) the maximum total FEDE deductions, in respect of all countries, that would be permitted in computing the taxpayer's income for the year in respect of FEDE incurred in taxation years that begin after 2000 if the taxpayer's specified foreign resource income for the year were nil, and

(ii) the amount deducted by the taxpayer for the year under subsection 66(4) of the Act in computing the taxpayer's income for the year in respect of FEDE incurred in taxation years that begin before 2001, and

(b) the amount, if any, by which

(i) 30 per cent of the taxpayer's total FEDE balances at the end of the year in respect of all countries in respect of expenses incurred in taxation years that begin after 2000,

exceeds

(ii) the maximum total FEDE deductions, in respect of all countries, that would be permitted in computing the taxpayer's income for the year in respect of FEDE incurred in taxation years that begin after 2000 if the taxpayer's specified foreign resource income for the year were nil.

(38) That, where a taxpayer ceases after February 27, 2000 to reside in Canada,

(a) the taxpayer's FEDE deduction for the taxpayer's last year of residence in Canada in respect of expenses incurred in taxation years that began before 2001 be limited to the greater of the taxpayer's foreign resource income for that year and 10 per cent of the taxpayer's FEDE balance at the end of that year, and

(b) the taxpayer be permitted for each subsequent taxation year of residence outside Canada to deduct up to 10 per cent of the taxpayer's FEDE balance at the end of that subsequent year in computing the taxpayer's taxable income earned in Canada.

(39) That, for taxation years that begin after the earlier of December 31, 1999 and the date selected by the taxpayer for the application of the rule described in paragraph (32) [reproduced under 126(7)"business-income tax" — ed.], all FEDE deductions claimed by a taxpayer be allocated, wherever relevant for the purposes of the Act, on a country-by-country basis.

(40) That, for taxation years that begin after 2000, the successor rules in section 66.7 of the Act reflect the 30 per cent FEDE balance deduction limit.

(41) That section 79.1 of the Act not apply in respect of acquisitions after February 27, 2000 of foreign resource property from a person (other than a person resident in Canada) or a partnership (other than a partnership each member of which is resident in Canada).

**Federal budget, supplementary information, February 28, 2000**: *Foreign Exploration and Development Expenses*

A Canadian oil and gas or mining company that incurs foreign exploration and development expenses (FEDE) may claim a minimum 10 per cent of its FEDE balance against its income from any source. A greater claim is permitted if a taxpayer's foreign resource income exceeds the 10 per cent minimum.

*Issues*

The existing regime for FEDE raises a number of concerns.

First, there is no explicit requirement under the existing rules that FEDE be incurred by a taxpayer for the purpose of entitling the taxpayer to profits or gains in respect of any foreign resource property of the taxpayer. For example, some taxpayers have claimed FEDE even though a foreign affiliate of the taxpayer owns the foreign resource property to which the FEDE relates.

In addition, there are circumstances where FEDE expenses have been generated by virtue of a taxpayer resident in Canada acquiring resource property of little value from a debtor of the taxpayer in circumstances to which section 79.1 of the *Income Tax Act* applies. The general effect of section 79.1 is that a creditor acquires property seized from a debtor in default of a payment of a debt at a cost equal to the principal amount of the debt, but is not entitled to claim a capital loss or bad debt expense with regard to that debt. The application of section 79.1 in this context is a particular concern where the debtor is not resident in Canada. This is because the parallel rules in section 79, under which the debtor is generally deemed to have proceeds of disposition from the resource property equal to the principal amount of the debt, will not have any effect on the debtor's Canadian income tax.

Second, existing FEDE rules allow taxpayers to claim a FEDE deduction of up to the full amount of foreign resource income earned. In this respect, the FEDE rules are more generous than the rules permitting the deduction of Canadian development expenses and Canadian oil and gas property expenses. The FEDE rules also result in similar treatment for foreign exploration expenses as compared to Canadian exploration expenses, even though the 100 per cent write-off is an accelerated incentive rate designed to encourage exploration activities in Canada.

Third, existing FEDE rules do not expressly apply on a country-by-country basis. Thus, it is difficult to source FEDE deductions to a particular country in cases where a taxpayer incurs FEDE in connection with more than one country outside Canada. This issue is of particular significance with regard to the calculation of a taxpayer's entitlement to foreign tax credits pursuant to the proposed new rules for production sharing agreements.

Also, the discretionary nature of the FEDE deduction may provide overly generous opportunities for maximizing foreign tax credit claims. This is because a FEDE deduction might be claimed in a taxation year for which little or no foreign business income taxes are paid, and not claimed in a taxation year for which large amounts of foreign business income taxes are paid. This action might be taken either to minimize the impact of the proposed 40 per cent limit with regard to production sharing agreements, or to minimize the effect of income-based restrictions in the existing foreign tax credit rules.

*Proposals*

The budget proposes to introduce amendments to address all of these concerns.

*Proposed Restrictions on FEDE Definition*

With regard to outlays made by a person or partnership after February 27, 2000 (other than any outlay made pursuant to an agreement in writing entered into before February 28, 2000), FEDE must

- relate to the acquisition of foreign resource property by the person or partnership, or
- be made for the purpose of enhancing the value of foreign resource property owned or to be owned by the person or partnership.

Consistent with this new measure, section 79.1 will not apply in connection with foreign resource property acquired after February 27, 2000, from a person (other than a person resident in Canada) or a partnership (other than a partnership each member of which is resident in Canada). These measures are aimed at ensuring that FEDE incurred by a taxpayer has the potential of directly generating income for the taxpayer that is subject to tax in Canada.

*Proposed Restrictions on Claiming of Post-2000 FEDE*

Post-2000 FEDE expenses will be allocated to separate pools on a country-by-country basis. Foreign resource income will be applied first to support global FEDE claims (i.e., FEDE claims generated under existing rules) and then, subject to a new limit equal to 30 per cent of the FEDE balance in respect of a country, to support FEDE deductions in respect of the country to which the income relates. However, to the extent that the country-by-country limitation would cause a taxpayer's overall maximum FEDE deductions for a taxation year to be less than 30 per cent of total FEDE balances, the taxpayer will be permitted to augment the portion of a FEDE balance for a taxation year that may be claimed. The augmentations to FEDE deductions for specific countries in these circumstances will be structured so that a taxpayer will be allowed in aggregate to claim FEDE deductions for a taxation year totalling not more than the lesser of

- 30 per cent of the total FEDE balances, and
- the taxpayer's total foreign resource income for the year.

It is proposed to provide taxpayers with maximum flexibility as to which FEDE balance a deduction is claimed against. This is consistent with the approach taken with regard to the undepreciated capital cost of depreciable property. However, it is only after determining the amount of deduction against an FEDE balance generated by pre-2001 expenses that it will be possible to determine deductions against FEDE balances generated by post-2000 expenses.

The new 30 per cent restriction for new FEDE balances necessitates consequential changes to the successor rules for foreign resource properties in section 66.7 of the *Income Tax Act*.

All of these measures apply to taxation years that begin after 2000.

*Taxpayers Ceasing to Reside in Canada*

Consistent with the proposed approach for the treatment of post-2000 FEDE, the budget proposes that the FEDE deduction that a taxpayer who ceases to reside in Canada may claim, be limited to the taxpayer's foreign resource income (including foreign resource income arising from the deemed disposition of foreign resource property on the taxpayer ceasing to reside in Canada). However, the taxpayer will be permitted to deduct annually up to 10 per cent of the taxpayer's FEDE balance while non-resident against taxable income earned in Canada while a non-resident.

This measure will apply to taxpayers who cease to reside in Canada after February 27, 2000.

*Allocation of FEDE for Foreign Tax Credit and Other Purposes*

An FEDE deduction claimed for a taxation year that begins after December 31, 1999 (or after such earlier date as the taxpayer has elected to have the new production sharing agreement rules apply), will be explicitly required to be allocated to a specific country where the FEDE deduction relates to a pre-2001 FEDE balance. This rule is intended to apply primarily for the purpose of computing a taxpayer's foreign tax credit.

A taxpayer will be permitted to make reasonable assumptions as to which country or countries a particular deduction from a pre-2001 FEDE balance relates, provided that those assumptions apply consistently from year to year. If a taxpayer fails to make reasonable assumptions in this regard, the Minister of National Revenue will make reasonable assumptions that will be binding on the taxpayer.

It will be assumed for the purpose of the foreign tax credit calculation that a taxpayer's FEDE deduction for a taxation year in respect of a country is generally the greater of

- the taxpayer's FEDE deduction for the year, and

**S. 66(4)(b)(ii)**      Income Tax Act, Part I, Division B

- the maximum FEDE deduction for the year that the taxpayer could claim if the augmentation of FEDE deductions (as described above in *Proposed Restrictions on Claiming of Post-2000 FEDE*) were not taken into account.

**Related Provisions**: 66(4.1) — Country-by-country FEDE allocations; 66(4.3) — Individuals who cease to be resident in Canada; 66(5) — Dealers; 66(11.4) — Change of control; 66(13.1) — Short taxation year; 66.21(1)"global foreign resource limit" — Determination of limit; 66.21(4) — Deduction for cumulative foreign resource expense; 66.7(2)(a) — Successor of foreign exploration and development expenses; 66.7(2.3) — Successor of foreign resource expenses; 80(8)(e) — Reduction of FEDE on debt forgiveness; 87(7) — Obligations of predecessor corporation; 104(5.2) — Trusts — 21-year deemed disposition; 110.6(1)"investment expense"(d) — effect of claim under 66(4) on capital gains exemption; 115(1)(e.1) — Deduction for unused FEDE balance against taxable income earned in Canada of non-resident; 115(4.1) — Taxable income earned in Canada — foreign resource pool expenses. See additional Related provisions and Definitions at end of s. 66.

**Notes**: 66(4)(a) amended effectively to add subpara. (iii) by 1994 tax amendments bill (Part I), effective for taxation years that end after February 21, 1994.

Reference to s. 64 in 66(4)(b)(ii)(C)(II) should be to s. 64 of R.S.C. 1952, c. 148, meaning the version repealed by 1981 Budget. See Notes to 64.

Closing words of 66(4)(b) moved to become closing words of 66(4)(b)(ii) by 1995-97 technical bill, retroactive to taxation years that end after May 6, 1974.

**I.T. Application Rules**: 29.

### Proposed Addition — 66(4.1)–(4.3)

**(4.1) Country-by-country FEDE allocations** — For greater certainty, the portion of an amount deducted under subsection (4) in computing a taxpayer's income for a taxation year that can reasonably be considered to be in respect of specified foreign exploration and development expenses of the taxpayer in respect of a country is considered to apply to a source in that country.

**Related Provisions**: 66(4.2) — Method of allocation; 66.7(2.1) — Parallel rule for successor corporation.

**(4.2) Method of allocation** — For the purpose of subsection (4.1), where a taxpayer has incurred specified foreign exploration and development expenses in respect of two or more countries, an allocation to each of those countries for a taxation year shall be determined in a manner that is

(a) reasonable having regard to all the circumstances, including the level and timing of

    (i) the taxpayer's specified foreign exploration and development expenses in respect of the country, and

    (ii) the profits or gains to which those expenses relate; and

(b) not inconsistent with the allocation made under subsection (4.1) for the preceding taxation year.

**Technical Notes**: Under existing subsection 66(4), FEDE in respect of one country is not distinct from FEDE in respect of any other country.

New subsection 66(4.1) provides that, to the extent that a FEDE deduction under subsection 66(4) can reasonably be considered to be in respect of "specified foreign exploration and development expenses" (as newly defined in subsection 66(15)) in respect of a country, for greater certainty that portion of the FEDE deduction is deemed to apply to a source in that country. As a consequence, that portion of the FEDE deduction can result in a reduction of the limit for the taxpayer's foreign tax credit under section 126 in respect of the country and, pursuant to subparagraph 66.21(4)(a)(ii)(C), can also result in a reduction of the limit for the taxpayer's deduction of foreign resource expenses under new section 66.21.

New subsection 66(4.2) elaborates how an allocation to a country is made under subsection 66(4.1). The method of allocation must be reasonable in the circumstances and be consistently applied from year to year.

These amendments apply to taxation years that begin after 1999. However, in the event that a taxpayer elects to have the new foreign tax credit provisions in section 126 apply to taxation years that begin after a date (no earlier than December 31, 1994) designated by the taxpayer, these amendments apply on the same basis.

**Related Provisions**: 66.7(2.2) — Parallel rule for successor corporation.

**(4.3) FEDE deductions where change of individual's residence** — Where at any time in a taxation year an individual becomes or ceases to be resident in Canada,

(a) subsection (4) applies to the individual as if the year were the period or periods in the year throughout which the individual was resident in Canada; and

(b) for the purpose of applying subsection (4), subsection (13.1) does not apply to the individual for the year.

**Technical Notes**: New subsection 66(4.3) applies where an individual becomes, or ceases to be, resident in Canada in a taxation year.

Under section 128.1, the immigration or emigration of an individual (other than a trust) has no impact on an individual's taxation year. Consequently, the individual would be resident in Canada for part of the taxation year and not resident in Canada for another part, with the result that, absent subsection 66(4.3), the individual would not be permitted to deduct an amount for the year under subsection 66(4). (This is because subsection 66(4) provides that, for a taxpayer to claim a deduction under that subsection for a taxation year, the taxpayer must be resident in Canada throughout the year.) Furthermore, the wording of section 114 that applies to the 1998 and subsequent taxation years would, absent subsection 66(4.3), preclude an individual who is resident in Canada for only part of a taxation year from obtaining a deduction in the year in respect of foreign exploration and development expenses (FEDE).

Consequently, subsection 66(4.3) provides that, for the purposes of subsection 66(4), a part-year resident's taxation year is treated as being the part of the taxation year throughout which the individual is resident in Canada and that, for these purposes, subsection 66(13.1) (which provides a rule relating to proration of deductions for short taxation years) does not apply to the individual for the year. As a result, an individual who is resident in Canada for only part of a taxation year can claim a non-prorated deduction under subsection 66(4). The deduction determined in this manner enters into the calculation of the individual's taxable income pursuant to section 114.

Given that section 128.1 operates to create new taxation years for trusts or corporations that become or cease to be resident in Canada, this measure has no relevance to trusts and there is no need to extend this measure to apply to corporations. Subsection 66(4.3) is parallel to new subsection 66.21(5), described in the commentary below.

**Application**: The December 21, 2000 draft legislation, subsec. 27(4), will add subsecs. 66(4.1) to (4.3), subsecs. (4.1) and (4.2) applicable to taxation years of a taxpayer that begin after the earlier of

(a) December 31, 1999; and

(b) where, for the purposes of subsec. 72(9), a date is designated in writing by the taxpayer and the designation is filed with the Minister of National Revenue on or before the taxpayer's filing-due date for the taxpayer's taxation year that includes the day on which the amending legislation receives Royal Assent, the later of

(i) the date so designated, and

(ii) December 31, 1994; and

subsec. 66(4.3) applicable to 1998 *et seq.*

**Notice of Ways and Means Motion, federal budget, and supplementary information, February 28, 2000**: See under 66(4)(b)(ii).

**(5) Dealers** — Subsections (3) and (4) and sections 59, 64[3], 66.1, 66.2, 66.4 and 66.7 do not apply in computing the income for a taxation year of a taxpayer (other than a principal-business corporation) whose business includes trading or dealing in rights, licences or privileges to explore for, drill for or take minerals, petroleum, natural gas or other related hydrocarbons.

### Proposed Amendment — 66(5)

**(5) Dealers** — Subsections (3) and (4) and sections 59, 64, 66.1, 66.2, 66.21, 66.4 and 66.7 do not apply in computing the income for a taxation year of a taxpayer (other than a principal-business corporation) whose business includes trading or dealing in rights, licences or privileges to explore for, drill for or take minerals, petroleum, natural gas or other related hydrocarbons.

**Application**: The December 21, 2000 draft legislation, subsec. 27(5), will amend subsec. 66(5) to read as above, applicable to taxation years that begin after 2000.

**Technical Notes**: Subsection 66(5) provides that most of the special provisions with regard to the treatment of resource expenses do not apply in computing the income for a taxation year of a taxpayer (other than a principal-business corporation, as defined in subsection 66(15)) whose business includes trading or dealing in specified resource-related properties.

Subsection 66(5) is amended so that the subsection similarly limits the application of new section 66.21.

**Related Provisions**: 253 — Extended meaning of "carrying on business". See additional Related Provisions and Definitions at end of s. 66.

**Notes**: Reference to s. 64 in 66(5) should be to s. 64 of R.S.C. 1952, c. 148, meaning the version repealed by 1981 Budget. See Notes to 64.

**I.T. Application Rules**: 29.

**Interpretation Bulletins**: IT-291R2: Transfer of property to a corporation under subsection 85(1); IT-314: Income of dealers in oil and gas leases; IT-400: Exploration and development expenses — meaning of principal-business corporation.

**(6)–(9) [Repealed under former Act]**

**Notes**: 66(6)–(9), repealed in 1987, were titled "Successor corporation's Canadian exploration and development expenses", "Second successor corporation's CEDE", "Successor corporation's foreign exploration and development expenses" and "Second successor corporation's FEDE" respectively. The successor corporation rules are now in 66.7.

**(10) [Repealed effective 2007]**

**Related Provisions**: 66(15)"agreed portion" — Reduction for amounts previously renounced; 79(3)F(b)(ii) — Where property surrendered to creditor; 80(1)"forgiven amount"B(e) — Debt forgiveness rules do not apply to amount renounced. See additional Related provisions and Definitions at end of s. 66.

**Notes**: 66(10) repealed by 1996 Budget, effective for renunciations made

(a) after 2006, in respect of a payment or loan received by a joint exploration corporation before March 6, 1996;

(b) after 2006, in respect of a payment or loan received by a joint exploration corporation after March 5, 1996 under an agreement in writing made

(i) by the corporation before March 6, 1996, or

(ii) by another corporation before March 6, 1996, where

(A) the other corporation controlled the corporation at the time the agreement was made, or

(B) the other corporation undertook, at the time the agreement was made, to form the corporation; and

(c) after March 5, 1996, in any other case.

It read:

(10) **Joint exploration corporation** — A joint exploration corporation may, in any particular taxation year or within 6 months from the end of that year, elect in prescribed form to renounce in favour of another corporation an agreed portion of the total of such of the joint exploration corporation's Canadian exploration and development expenses as were incurred by it during a period, after 1971 and before the end of the particular taxation year, throughout which the other corporation was a shareholder corporation, to the extent that the total of those expenses exceeds any amount deductible under subsection (1) in respect thereof by the joint exploration corporation in computing its income for any taxation year previous to the particular year and, on the election, that agreed portion

(a) shall be deemed, for the purpose of subsection (1) or (3), as the case may be, to be Canadian exploration and development expenses incurred by the other corporation during its taxation year in which the particular taxation year ends; and

(b) shall be subtracted from the total described in paragraph (1)(a) in determining the amount deductible by the

---

[3]The reference should be to s. 64 of R.S.C. 1952, c. 148 (the pre-RSC 1985 version) — ed.

## S. 66(10) — Income Tax Act, Part I, Division B

joint exploration corporation under subsection (1) in computing its income.

The elimination of the joint exploration corporation rules was announced in the 1996 budget after the government determined, through tax shelter reporting, that the JEC rules were being used primarily to dispose of resource properties in a tax-advantageous manner, rather than significantly assisting in the pooling of capital and expertise. 10 years of grandfathering is provided as indicated above.

**I.T. Application Rules**: 29.

**Forms**: T2035: Election to renounce exploration, development and oil and gas property expenses.

### (10.1) [Repealed effective 2007]

**Related Provisions**: 66(3) — Expenses of other taxpayers; 79(3)F(b)(ii) — Where property surrendered to creditor; 80(1)"forgiven amount"B(e) — Debt forgiveness rules do not apply to amount renounced; 163(2.2) — False statement or omissions — penalty; 248(16) — GST — input tax credit and rebate; 248(18) — GST — repayment of input tax credits. See additional Related Provisions and Definitions at end of s. 66.

**Notes**: 66(10.1) repealed by 1996 Budget, effective on the same basis as the repeal of 66(10). It read:

(10.1) Idem — A joint exploration corporation may, in any particular taxation year or within 6 months from the end of that year, elect in prescribed form in respect of that year to renounce in favour of another corporation an agreed portion of the total of such of the joint exploration corporation's Canadian exploration expenses as were incurred by it during a period (ending before the end of the particular taxation year) throughout which the other corporation was a shareholder corporation, to the extent that the total of those expenses exceeds the total of all amounts each of which is

(a) an amount deducted or required to be deducted under subsection 66.1(2) in respect of those expenses by the joint exploration corporation in computing its income for any taxation year preceding the particular taxation year, or

(b) assistance that any person has received, is entitled to receive or, at any time, becomes entitled to receive in respect of those expenses incurred during the period or that can reasonably be regarded as relating to Canadian exploration activities of the joint exploration corporation during the period, other than that portion of the assistance arising because of section 127 or 127.1 in respect of a shareholder corporation of the joint exploration corporation,

and, on the making of the election, that agreed portion

(c) shall be deemed, for the purposes of the definitions "Canadian exploration expense" and "cumulative Canadian exploration expense" in subsection 66.1(6), to be a Canadian exploration expense incurred by the other corporation during its taxation year in which the particular taxation year ends or, if it has no such year, its last taxation year, and

(d) shall be included in the amount determined for F in the definition "cumulative Canadian exploration expense" in subsection 66.1(6) by the joint exploration corporation in computing its cumulative Canadian exploration expense, at the time the election is made or, where the election is made after the end of the particular taxation year, immediately before the end of that year.

See Notes to 66(10).

66(10.1)(a) amended by 1992 Economic Statement, effective for taxation years ending after December 2, 1992, to change "deductible" to "deducted or required to be deducted", in consequence of the CCEE deduction for principal-business corporations in 66.1(2) becoming optional.

66(10.1)(b) amended by 1991 technical bill, retroactive to 1985, to add the words from "other than" to the end. This avoids a problem of circularity since the amount renounced and investment tax credit would otherwise depend on each other.

66(10.1)(d) amended by 1992 Economic Statement, effective for taxation years ending after December 2, 1992. For earlier expenses, read:

(d) shall be included in the amount determined for F in the definition "cumulative Canadian exploration expense" in subsection 66.1(6) by reason of its being deducted or deductible, as the case may be, by the joint exploration corporation in computing that corporation's cumulative Canadian exploration expense, at the time that the election is made or, where the election is made after the end of the particular taxation year, immediately before the end of that year.

**I.T. Application Rules**: 29.

**Advance Tax Rulings**: ATR-60: Joint exploration corporations.

**Forms**: T2035: Election to renounce exploration, development and oil and gas property expenses.

### (10.2) [Repealed effective 2007]

**Related Provisions**: 66.1(6)"restricted expense"(c) — inclusion of renounced expense; 79(3)F(b)(ii) — Where property surrendered to creditor; 80(1)"forgiven amount"B(e) — Debt forgiveness rules do not apply to amount renounced; 163(2.2) — False statement or omissions — penalty; 248(16) — GST input tax credit and rebate deemed to be assistance; 248(18) — GST — repayment of input tax credit. See additional Related Provisions and Definitions at end of s. 66.

**Notes**: 66(10.2) repealed by 1996 Budget, effective on the same basis as the repeal of 66(10). It read:

(10.2) Idem — A joint exploration corporation may, in any particular taxation year or within 6 months from the end of that year, elect in prescribed form in respect of that year to renounce in favour of another corporation an agreed portion of the total of such of the joint exploration corporation's Canadian development expenses as were incurred by it during a period (ending before the end of the particular taxation year) throughout which the other corporation was a shareholder corporation, to the extent that the total of those expenses exceeds the total of all amounts each of which is

(a) an amount deducted under subsection 66.2(2) in respect of those expenses by the joint exploration corporation in computing its income for any taxation year preceding the particular taxation year, or

(b) assistance that any person has received, is entitled to receive or, at any time, becomes entitled to receive in respect of those expenses incurred during the period or that can reasonably be related to Canadian development activities of the joint exploration corporation during the period,

and, on the making of the election, that agreed portion

(c) shall be deemed, for the purposes of the definitions "Canadian development expense" and "cumulative Canadian development expense" in subsection 66.2(5), to be a Canadian development expense incurred by the other corporation during its taxation year in which the particular taxation year ends or, if it has no such year, its last taxation year, and

(d) shall be included in the amount determined for E in the definition "cumulative Canadian development expense" in subsection 66.2(5) by reason of its being deducted by the joint exploration corporation in computing that corporation's cumulative Canadian development expense, at the time the election is made or, where the election is made after the end of the particular taxation year, immediately before the end of that year.

**Forms:** T2035: Election to renounce exploration, development and oil and gas property expenses.

**(10.3)** [Repealed effective 2007]

**Related Provisions:** 79(3)F(b)(ii) — Where property surrendered to creditor; 80(1)"forgiven amount"B(e) — Debt forgiveness rules do not apply to amount renounced; 163(2.2) — False statement or omission — penalty; 248(16) — GST input tax credit and rebate deemed to be assistance; 248(18) — GST — repayment of input tax credits. See additional Related Provisions and Definitions at the end of s. 66.

**Notes:** 66(10.3) repealed by 1996 Budget, effective on the same basis as the repeal of 66(10). It read:

(10.3) **Idem** — A joint exploration corporation may, in any particular taxation year or within 6 months from the end of that year, elect in prescribed form in respect of that year to renounce in favour of another corporation an agreed portion of the total of such of the joint exploration corporation's Canadian oil and gas property expenses as were incurred by it during a period (ending before the end of the particular taxation year) throughout which the other corporation was a shareholder corporation, to the extent that the total of those expenses exceeds the total of all amounts each of which is

(a) an amount deducted under subsection 66.4(2) in respect of those expenses by the joint exploration corporation in computing its income for any taxation year preceding the particular taxation year, or

(b) assistance that any person has received, is entitled to receive or, at any time, becomes entitled to receive in respect of those expenses incurred during the period or that can reasonably be related to those expenses during the period,

and, on the making of the election, that agreed portion

(c) shall be deemed, for the purposes of the definitions "Canadian oil and gas property expense" and "cumulative Canadian oil and gas property expense" in subsection 66.4(5), to be a Canadian oil and gas property expense incurred by the other corporation during its taxation year in which the particular taxation year ends or, if it has no such year, its last taxation year, and

(d) shall be included in the amount determined for E in the definition "cumulative Canadian oil and gas property expense" in subsection 66.4(5) by reason of its being deducted by the joint exploration corporation in computing that corporation's cumulative Canadian oil and gas property expense, at the time the election is made or, where the election is made after the end of the particular taxation year, immediately before the end of that year.

**I.T. Application Rules:** 29.

**Forms:** T2035: Election to renounce exploration, development and oil and gas property expenses.

**(10.4) Idem** — Where a taxpayer has, after April 19, 1983, made a payment or loan described in paragraph (a) of the definition "agreed portion" in subsection (15) to a joint exploration corporation in respect of which the corporation has at any time renounced in favour of the taxpayer any Canadian exploration expenses, Canadian development expenses or Canadian oil and gas property expenses (in this subsection referred to as "resource expenses") under subsection (10.1), (10.2) or (10.3), the following rules apply:

(a) where the taxpayer receives as consideration for the payment or loan property that is capital property to the taxpayer,

(i) there shall be deducted in computing the adjusted cost base to the taxpayer of the property at any time the amount of any resource expenses renounced by the corporation in the taxpayer's favour in respect of the loan or payment at or before that time,

(ii) there shall be deducted in computing the adjusted cost base to the taxpayer at any time of any property for which the property, or any property substituted therefor, was exchanged the amount of any resource expenses renounced by the corporation in the taxpayer's favour in respect of the loan or payment at or before that time (except to the extent such amount has been deducted under subparagraph (i)), and

(iii) the amount of any resource expenses renounced by the corporation in favour of the taxpayer in respect of the loan or payment at any time, except to the extent that the renunciation of those expenses results in a deduction under subparagraph (i) or (ii), shall, for the purposes of this Act, be deemed to be a capital gain of the taxpayer from the disposition by the taxpayer of property at that time;

(b) where the taxpayer receives as consideration for the payment or loan property that is not capital property to the taxpayer,

(i) there shall be deducted in computing the cost to the taxpayer of the property at any time the amount of any resource expenses renounced by the corporation in the taxpayer's favour in respect of the loan or payment at or before that time, and

(ii) there shall be included in computing the amount referred to in paragraph 59(3.2)(d) for a taxation year the amount of any resource expenses renounced by the corporation in the taxpayer's favour in respect of the loan or payment at any time in the year, except to the extent that the amount has been deducted under subparagraph (i); and

(c) where the taxpayer does not receive any property as consideration for the payment, there shall be included in computing the amount referred to in paragraph 59(3.2)(e) for a taxation year the amount of any resource expenses renounced by the corporation in the taxpayer's favour in respect of the payment in the year, except to the extent that the amount has been deducted from the adjusted cost base to the taxpayer of shares of the corporation under paragraph 53(2)(f.1) in respect of the payment.

**Related Provisions**: 53(2)(f)–(f.2) — Deductions from adjusted cost base — renounced expenses; 59(3.2)(d), (e) — Recovery of exploration and development expenses; 59(3.3)(f) — Resource property — amounts included in income; 248(5) — Substituted property. See additional Related Provisions and Definitions at the end of s. 66.

**Advance Tax Rulings**: ATR-60: Joint exploration corporations.

**(11) Acquisition of control** — Where after March 31, 1977 and before November 13, 1981 control of a corporation has been acquired by a person or persons who did not control the corporation at the time when it last ceased to carry on active business,

(a) the amount by which the Canadian exploration and development expenses incurred by the corporation before it last ceased to carry on active business exceeds the total of all amounts otherwise deductible by the corporation in respect of Canadian exploration and development expenses in computing its income for taxation years ending before control was so acquired, shall be deemed to have been deductible under this section by the corporation in computing its income for taxation years ending before control was so acquired;

(b) the amount by which the cumulative Canadian exploration expense of the corporation at the time it last ceased to carry on active business exceeds the total of amounts otherwise deducted under section 66.1 in computing its income for taxation years ending after that time and before control was so acquired, shall be deemed to have been deducted under that section by the corporation in computing its income for taxation years ending before control was so acquired;

(c) the amount by which the cumulative Canadian development expense of the corporation at the time it last ceased to carry on active business exceeds the total of amounts otherwise deducted under section 66.2 in computing its income for taxation years ending after that time and before control was so acquired, shall be deemed to have been deducted under that section by the corporation in computing its income for taxation years ending before control was so acquired;

(d) the amount by which the cumulative Canadian oil and gas property expense of the corporation at the time it last ceased to carry on active business exceeds the total of amounts otherwise deducted under section 66.4 in computing its income for taxation years ending after that time and before control was so acquired, shall be deemed to have been deducted under that section by the corporation in computing its income for taxation years ending before control was so acquired; and

(e) the amount by which the foreign exploration and development expenses incurred by the corporation before it last ceased to carry on active business exceeds the total of all amounts otherwise deductible by the corporation in respect of foreign exploration and development expenses in computing its income for taxation years ending before control was so acquired, shall be deemed to have been deductible under this section by the corporation in computing its income for taxation years ending before control was so acquired.

**Related Provisions**: 66(11.3) — Acquisition of control before 1983; 139.1(18) — Holding corporation deemed not to acquire control of insurer on demutualization; 249(4) — Deemed year end where change of control occurs; 256(6)–(9) — Whether control acquired. See additional Related Provisions and Definitions at end of s. 66.

**I.T. Application Rules**: 29.

**I.T. Technical News**: No. 7 (control by a group — 50/50 arrangement).

**(11.1), (11.2)** [Repealed under former Act]

**Notes**: 66(11.1) and (11.2), repealed in 1987, dealt with the application of the successor rules on change in control or change in tax-exempt status of a corporation. This is now dealt with in 66.7(10) and (11).

**(11.3) Control** — For the purposes of subsections (11) and 66.7(10), where a corporation acquired control of another corporation after November 12, 1981 and before 1983 by reason of the acquisition of shares of the other corporation pursuant to an agreement in writing concluded on or before November 12, 1981, it shall be deemed to have acquired that control on or before November 12, 1981.

**Related Provisions**: See Related Provisions and Definitions at end of s. 66.

**I.T. Application Rules**: 29.

**(11.4) Change of control** — Where,

(a) at any time, control of a corporation has been acquired by a person or group of persons,

(b) within the 12-month period that ended immediately before that time, the corporation or a partnership of which it was a majority interest partner acquired a Canadian resource property or a foreign resource property (other than a property that was owned by the corporation or partnership or a person that would, if section 251.1 were read without reference to the definition "controlled" in subsection 251.1(3), be affiliated with the corporation throughout the period that began immediately before the 12-month period began and ended at the time the property was acquired by the corporation or partnership), and

(c) immediately before the twelve month period commenced, the corporation was not a principal-business corporation and the partnership, if it were a corporation, would not be a principal-business corporation,

for the purposes of subsection (4) and sections 66.2 and 66.4, except as those provisions apply for the purposes of section 66.7, the property shall be deemed not to have been acquired by the corporation or partnership before that time and shall be deemed to have been acquired by it at that time, except that, where the property has been disposed of by it before that time and not reacquired by it before that time, the property shall be deemed to have been acquired by the corporation or partnership immediately before it disposed of the property.

> **Proposed Amendment — 66(11.4) closing words**
>
> for the purposes of subsection (4) and sections 66.2, 66.21 and 66.4, except as those provisions apply for the purposes of section 66.7, the property is deemed not to have been acquired by the corporation or partnership before that time and is deemed to have been acquired by it at that time, except that, where the property has been disposed of by it before that time and not reacquired by it before that time, the property is deemed to have been acquired by the corporation or partnership immediately before it disposed of the property.
>
> **Application**: The December 21, 2000 draft legislation, subsec. 27(6), will amend the closing words of subsec. 66(11.4) to read as above, applicable to taxation years that begin after 2000.
>
> **Technical Notes**: Subsection 66(11.4) applies where there is an acquisition of control of a corporation that was not a principal-business corporation immediately before the 12-month period preceding that acquisition of control. Any Canadian or foreign resource property acquired by the corporation (or a partnership of which it was a majority interest partner) in that period is (except for the purposes of applying the successor rules in section 66.7, notably the acquisition of control rule in subsection 66.7(10)) considered to have been acquired at the time control is acquired, for the purpose of subsection 66(4) (FEDE), section 66.2 (Canadian development expenses) and section 66.4 (Canadian oil and gas property expenses). Consequently, the corporation is prevented from claiming deductions under subsection 66(4) and sections 66.2 and 66.4 in respect of the property so acquired until after the acquisition of control. An exception to this treatment generally applies where the property in question was owned before that 12-month period described above by the corporation, the partnership or a person that was affiliated with the corporation.
>
> Subsection 66(11.4) is amended so that it also applies for the purpose of section 66.21 (foreign resource expenses).

**Related Provisions**: 66(11.5) — Where control changed within 12 months of incorporation; 87(2)(j.6) — Amalgamations — continuing corporation; 139.1(18) — Holding corporation deemed not to acquire control of insurer on demutualization; 256(6)–(9) — Whether control acquired. See additional Related Provisions and Definitions at end of s. 66.

**Notes**: 66(11.4)(b) amended by 1995-97 technical bill, effective April 27, 1995. From 1988 to April 26, 1995, read:

> (b) within the twelve month period ending immediately before that time, the corporation, or a partnership of which it was a majority interest partner (within the meaning assigned by subsection 97(3.1)) acquired a Canadian resource property or a foreign resource property (other than a property that was owned by the corporation, partnership or a person or persons related to the corporation throughout the period commencing immediately before the twelve month period and ending at the time the property was acquired by the corporation or partnership), and

**I.T. Technical News**: No. 7 (control by a group — 50/50 arrangement).

**(11.5) Early change of control** — For the purpose of subsection (11.4), where the corporation referred to in that subsection was incorporated or otherwise formed in the 12-month period referred to in that subsection, the corporation is deemed to have been, throughout the period that began immediately before the 12-month period and ended immediately after it was incorporated or otherwise formed,

(a) in existence; and

(b) affiliated with every person with whom it was affiliated (otherwise than because of a right referred to in paragraph 251(5)(b)) throughout the period that began when it was incorporated or otherwise formed and ended immediately before its control was acquired.

**Related Provisions**: 139.1(18) — Holding corporation deemed not to acquire control of insurer on demutualization; 256(6)–(9) — Whether control acquired. See additional Related Provisions and Definitions at end of s. 66.

**Notes**: 66(11.5) amended by 1995-97 technical bill, effective for acquisitions of control that occur after April 26, 1995. For earlier acquisition since 1988, read:

> (11.5) Change of control within 12 months of incorporation — For the purposes of subsection (11.4), where the corporation referred to in that subsection was incorporated or otherwise formed within the twelve month period referred to in that subsection, it shall be deemed to have been, throughout the period commencing immediately before the twelve month period and ending immediately after it was incorporated or otherwise formed,
>
> (a) in existence; and
>
> (b) related to the person or persons to whom it was related (otherwise than by virtue of a right referred to in paragraph 251(5)(b)) throughout the period commencing when it was incorporated or otherwise formed and ending immediately before control of the corporation was acquired.

**(12) Computation of exploration and development expenses** — In computing a taxpayer's Canadian exploration and development expenses,

(a) there shall be deducted any amount paid to the taxpayer before May 7, 1974

(i) and after 1971 under the *Northern Mineral Exploration Assistance Regulations* made under an appropriation Act that provides for payments in respect of the Northern Mineral Grants Program, or

(ii) pursuant to any agreement entered into between the taxpayer and Her Majesty in right of Canada under the Northern Mineral Grants Program or the Development Program of the Department of Indian Affairs and Northern Development, to the extent that the amount has been expended by the taxpayer as or on account of Canadian exploration and development expenses incurred by the taxpayer; and

(b) there shall be included any amount, except an amount in respect of interest, paid by the taxpayer after 1971 and before May 7, 1974 under the Regulations referred to in subparagraph (a)(i) to Her Majesty in right of Canada.

**Related Provisions**: 66(12.1) — Limitations. See additional Related provisions and Definitions at end of s. 66.

**I.T. Application Rules**: 29.

## (12.1) Limitations of Canadian exploration and development expenses — Except as expressly otherwise provided in this Act,

(a) where as a result of a transaction occurring after May 6, 1974 an amount has become receivable by a taxpayer at a particular time in a taxation year and the consideration given by the taxpayer therefor was property (other than a share or a Canadian resource property, or an interest therein or a right thereto) or services, the original cost of which to the taxpayer may reasonably be regarded as having been primarily Canadian exploration and development expenses of the taxpayer (or would have been so regarded if they had been incurred by the taxpayer after 1971 and before May 7, 1974) or a Canadian exploration expense, there shall at that time be included in the amount determined for G in the definition "cumulative Canadian exploration expense" in subsection 66.1(6) in respect of the taxpayer the amount that became receivable by the taxpayer at that time; and

(b) where as a result of a transaction occurring after May 6, 1974 an amount has become receivable by a taxpayer at a particular time in a taxation year and the consideration given by the taxpayer therefor was property (other than a share or a Canadian resource property, or an interest therein or a right thereto) or services, the original cost of which to the taxpayer may reasonably be regarded as having been primarily a Canadian development expense, there shall at that time be included in the amount determined for G in the definition "cumulative Canadian development expense" in subsection 66.2(5) in respect of the taxpayer the amount that became receivable by the taxpayer at that time.

**Related Provisions**: 59(1) — Amounts received as consideration for disposition of resource property; 66(15) — Definitions. See additional Related provisions and Definitions at end of s. 66.

**I.T. Application Rules**: 29.

**Interpretation Bulletins**: IT-125R4: Dispositions of resource properties.

**Advance Tax Rulings**: ATR-59: Financing exploration and development through limited partnerships.

## (12.2) Unitized oil or gas field in Canada —
Where, pursuant to an agreement between a taxpayer and another person to unitize an oil or gas field in Canada, an amount has become receivable by the taxpayer at a particular time after May 6, 1974 from that other person in respect of Canadian exploration expense incurred by the taxpayer or Canadian exploration and development expenses incurred by the taxpayer (or expenses that would have been Canadian exploration and development expenses if they had been incurred by the taxpayer after 1971 and before May 7, 1974) in respect of that field or any part thereof, the following rules apply:

(a) there shall, at that time, be included by the taxpayer in the amount determined for G in the definition "cumulative Canadian exploration expense" in subsection 66.1(6) the amount that became receivable by the taxpayer; and

(b) there shall, at that time, be included by the other person in the amount referred to in paragraph (c) of the definition "Canadian exploration expense" in subsection 66.1(6) the amount that became payable by that person.

**Related Provisions**: 66(15) — Definitions. See additional Related provisions and Definitions at end of s. 66.

**I.T. Application Rules**: 29.

**Interpretation Bulletins**: IT-273R2: Government assistance — general comments; IT-125R4: Dispositions of resource properties.

## (12.3) Idem — Where, pursuant to an agreement between a taxpayer and another person to unitize an oil or gas field in Canada, an amount has become receivable by the taxpayer at a particular time after May 6, 1974 from that other person in respect of Canadian development expense incurred by the taxpayer in respect of that field or any part thereof, the following rules apply:

(a) there shall, at that time, be included by the taxpayer in the amount determined for G in the definition "cumulative Canadian development expense" in subsection 66.2(5) the amount that became receivable by the taxpayer; and

(b) there shall, at that time, be included by the other person in the amount referred to in paragraph (a) of the definition "Canadian development expense" in subsection 66.2(5) the amount that became payable by that person.

**Related Provisions**: See Related Provisions and Definitions at end of s. 66.

**I.T. Application Rules**: 29.

**Interpretation Bulletins**: IT-273R2: Government assistance — general comments; IT-125R4: Dispositions of resource properties.

## (12.4) Limitation of foreign exploration and development expenses — Where, as a result of a transaction occurring after May 6, 1974, an amount has become receivable by a taxpayer at a particular time in a taxation year and the consideration given by the taxpayer therefor was property (other than a foreign resource property) or services, the original cost of which to the taxpayer may reasonably be regarded as having been primarily foreign exploration and development expenses of the taxpayer (or would have been so regarded if they had been incurred by the taxpayer after 1971), the following rules apply:

### Proposed Amendment — 66(12.4) opening words

**(12.4) Limitation of FEDE** — Where, as a result of a transaction that occurs after May 6, 1974, an amount becomes receivable by a taxpayer at a particular time in a taxation year and the consideration given by the taxpayer for the amount receivable is property (other than a foreign resource property) or services, the original cost of which to the taxpayer can reasonably be regarded as having been primarily foreign exploration and development expenses of the taxpayer (or would have been so regarded if they had been incurred by the taxpayer after 1971 and the definition "foreign exploration and development expenses" in subsection (15) were read without reference to paragraph (k) of that definition), the following rules apply:

**Application**: The December 21, 2000 draft legislation, subsec. 27(7), will amend the opening words of subsec. 66(12.4) to read as above, applicable to taxation years that begin after 2000.

**Technical Notes**: Subsection 66(12.4) provides special rules that apply where an amount (referred to below as a "specified amount receivable") becomes receivable by a taxpayer as a consequence of consideration, given by the taxpayer, the original cost of which was FEDE. The subsection does not apply where the consideration given is foreign resource property, given that an income inclusion resulting from the disposition of a foreign resource property is provided under subsection 59(1). Where subsection 66(12.4) applies, a taxpayer's FEDE balance is reduced by the specified amount receivable. If the specified amount receivable exceeds the FEDE balance, the excess is included in income.

Subsection 66(12.4) is amended so that it also applies in connection with consideration the original cost of which is excluded from FEDE because of new paragraph (k) of the FEDE definition in subsection 66(15). That paragraph excludes amounts from FEDE that form part of a taxpayer's foreign resource expenses (as defined in the definition "foreign resource expense" in new section 66.21).

Subsection 66(12.4) is also amended so that a designated portion of a specified amount receivable is, to the extent that it is primarily in respect of specified FEDE in respect of a country (as newly defined in subsection 66(15)) or a foreign resource expense in respect of a country (as newly defined in subsection 66.21(1)), not taken into account under subsection 66(12.4). Instead, the amount so designated will be taken into account under new subsection 66(12.41). The intended effect of this amendment is to permit a taxpayer to elect out of the tax consequences under subsection 66(12.4).

(a) in computing the taxpayer's foreign exploration and development expenses at that time, there shall be deducted the amount receivable by the taxpayer;

(b) where the amount receivable exceeds the total of the taxpayer's foreign exploration and development expenses incurred before that time to the extent that those expenses were not deducted or deductible, as the case may be, in computing the taxpayer's income for a previous taxation year, there shall be included in the amount referred to in paragraph 59(3.2)(a) the amount by which

   (i) the amount receivable

exceeds

   (ii) the total of the taxpayer's foreign exploration and development expenses incurred by the taxpayer before that time to the extent that those expenses were not deducted or deductible, as the case may be, in computing the taxpayer's income for a previous taxation year; and

**Proposed Amendment — 66(12.4)(b)**

(b) where the amount receivable exceeds the total of the taxpayer's foreign exploration and development expenses incurred before that time to the extent that those expenses were not deducted or deductible, as the case may be, in computing the taxpayer's income for a preceding taxation year, there shall be included in the amount referred to in paragraph 59(3.2)(a) the amount, if any, by which the amount receivable exceeds the total of

   (i) the taxpayer's foreign exploration and development expenses incurred before that time to the extent that those expenses were not deducted or deductible, as the case may be, in computing the taxpayer's income for a preceding taxation year, and

   (ii) the amount, designated by the taxpayer in prescribed form filed with the taxpayer's return of income for the year, not exceeding the portion of the amount receivable for which the consideration given by the taxpayer was property (other than a foreign resource property) or services, the original cost of which to the taxpayer can reasonably be regarded as having been primarily

      (A) specified foreign exploration and development expenses in respect of a country, or

      (B) foreign resource expenses in respect of a country; and

**Application**: The December 21, 2000 draft legislation, subsec. 27(8), will amend para. 66(12.4)(b) to read as above, applicable to taxation years that begin after 2000.

**Technical Notes**: See under 66(12.4) opening words.

(c) where an amount is included in the amount referred to in paragraph 59(3.2)(a) by virtue of paragraph (b), the total of the taxpayer's foreign exploration and development expenses at that time shall be deemed to be nil.

**Related Provisions**: 59(3.2)(a) — Income inclusion; 66(12.41), (12.42) — Limitations of foreign resource expenses; 95(1) — "foreign affiliate". See additional Related Provisions and Definitions at end of s. 66.

**I.T. Application Rules**: 29.

**Proposed Addition — 66(12.41)**

**(12.41) Limitations of foreign resource expenses** — Where a particular amount described in subsection (12.4) becomes receivable by a taxpayer at a particular time, there shall at that time be included in the value determined for G in the definition "cumulative foreign resource expense" in subsection 66.21(1) in respect of the taxpayer and a country the amount designated under subparagraph

(12.4)(b)(ii) by the taxpayer in respect of the particular amount and the country.

**Application**: The December 21, 2000 draft legislation, subsec. 27(9), will add subsec. 66(12.41), applicable to taxation years that begin after 2000.

**Technical Notes**: Subsection 66(12.41) is introduced so that the designated portion of a specified amount receivable by a taxpayer in respect of a country results in a reduction of the "cumulative foreign resource expense" of the taxpayer in respect of that country.

**Related Provisions**: 66(12.42) — Partnerships; 66.21(1)"cumulative foreign resource expense"G.

### Proposed Addition — 66(12.42)

**(12.42) Partnerships** — For the purposes of subsections (12.4) and (12.41), where a person or partnership is a member of a particular partnership and a particular amount described in subsection (12.4) becomes receivable by the particular partnership in a fiscal period of the particular partnership,

(a) the member's share of the particular amount is deemed to be an amount that became receivable by the member at the end of the fiscal period; and

(b) the amount deemed by paragraph (a) to be an amount receivable by the member is deemed to be an amount

(i) that is described in subsection (12.4) in respect of the member, and

(ii) that has the same attributes for the member as it did for the particular partnership.

**Application**: The December 21, 2000 draft legislation, subsec. 27(9), will add subsec. 66(14.2), applicable to fiscal periods that begin after 2000.

**Technical Notes**: Subsection 66(12.42) is introduced so that, where a partnership has a specified amount receivable, each partner of the partnership is considered for the purposes of subsections 66(12.4) and (12.41) to have had the partner's share of that amount become receivable. New subsection 66(12.42) is consistent with the fact that a partner's share of FEDE and foreign resource expenses qualifies as such.[1] In addition, subsection 66(12.42) is consistent with the existing treatment of amounts receivable by partnerships in connection with the calculation of "cumulative Canadian exploration expense"[2], "cumulative Canadian development expense"[3] and "cumulative Canadian oil and gas property expense".[4]

[1] Existing paragraph (d) of the definition "foreign exploration and development expenses" in subsection 66(15) and paragraph (e) of the definition "foreign resource expenses" in new subsection 66.21(1).

[2] See reference to the description of G in that definition in subsection 66.1(7).

[3] See reference to the description of G in that definition in subsection 66.2(6).

[4] See reference to the description of G in that definition in subsection 66.4(6).

**(12.5) Unitized oil or gas field in Canada** — Where, pursuant to an agreement between a taxpayer and another person to unitize an oil or gas field in Canada, an amount has become receivable by the taxpayer at a particular time from that other person in respect of Canadian oil and gas property expense incurred by the taxpayer in respect of that field or any part thereof, the following rules apply:

(a) there shall, at that time, be included by the taxpayer in the amount determined for G in the definition "cumulative Canadian oil and gas property expense" in subsection 66.4(5) the amount that became receivable by the taxpayer; and

(b) there shall, at that time, be included by the other person in the amount referred to in paragraph (a) of the definition "Canadian oil and gas property expense" in subsection 66.4(5) the amount that became payable by that person.

**Related Provisions**: See Related Provisions and Definitions at end of s. 66.

**I.T. Application Rules**: 29.

**Interpretation Bulletins**: IT-125R4: Dispositions of resource properties.

**(12.6) Canadian exploration expenses to flow-through shareholder** — Where a person gave consideration under an agreement to a corporation for the issue of a flow-through share of the corporation and, in the period that begins on the day the agreement was made and ends 24 months after the end of the month that includes that day, the corporation incurred Canadian exploration expenses, the corporation may, after it complies with subsection (12.68) in respect of the share and before March of the first calendar year that begins after the period, renounce, effective on the day on which the renunciation is made or on an earlier day set out in the form prescribed for the purposes of subsection (12.7), to the person in respect of the share the amount, if any, by which the part of those expenses that was incurred on or before the effective date of the renunciation (which part is in this subsection referred to as the "specified expenses") exceeds the total of

(a) the assistance that the corporation has received, is entitled to receive or can reasonably be expected to receive at any time, and that can reasonably be related to the specified expenses or to Canadian exploration activities to which the specified expenses relate (other than assistance that can reasonably be related to expenses referred to in paragraph (b) or (b.1)),

(b) all specified expenses that are prescribed Canadian exploration and development overhead expenses of the corporation,

(b.1) all specified expenses each of which is a cost of, or for the use of, seismic data

(i) that had been acquired (otherwise than as a consequence of performing work that resulted in the creation of the data) by any other person before the cost was incurred,

(ii) in respect of which a right to use had been acquired by any other person before the cost was incurred, or

(iii) all or substantially all of which resulted from work performed more than one year before the cost was incurred, and

(c) the total of amounts that are renounced on or before the date on which the renunciation is made by any other renunciation under this subsection in respect of those expenses,

but not in any case

(d) exceeding the amount, if any, by which the consideration for the share exceeds the total of other amounts renounced under this subsection or subsection (12.601) or (12.62) in respect of the share on or before the day on which the renunciation is made, or

(e) exceeding the amount, if any, by which the cumulative Canadian exploration expense of the corporation on the effective date of the renunciation computed before taking into account any amounts renounced under this subsection on the date on which the renunciation is made, exceeds the total of all amounts renounced under this subsection in respect of any other share

(i) on the date on which the renunciation is made, and

(ii) effective on or before the effective date of the renunciation.

**Related Provisions**: 66(12.601), (12.602) — Flow-through share rules for first $2 million of Canadian development expenses; 66(12.61) — Effect of renunciation of Canadian exploration expense; 66(12.62)(d) — Canadian development expenses to flow-through shareholder; 66(12.64)(c) — Canadian oil and gas property expenses to flow-through shareholder; 66(12.66) — Expense in the first 60 days of the year; 66(12.67) — Restriction on renunciation; 66(12.68) — Filing selling instruments; 66(12.69) — Filing re partners; 66(12.7) — Filing; 66(12.71) — Restriction on renunciation; 66(12.72) — Application of sections 231 to 231.2; 66(12.73) — Adjustment in renunciation; 66(12.741) — Late renunciation; 66(16) — Partnership deemed to be a person; 66(19) — Renunciation by member of partnership, etc.; 66.3(3) — Cost of flow-through shares; 66.3(4)(a)(ii)(B) — Paid-up capital; 87(4.4) — Amalgamations — flow-through shares; 110.6(1)"investment expense"(d) — effect of renunciation on capital gains exemption; 127(9)"investment tax credit"(a.2), 127(9)"flow-through mining expenditure"(c), (d) — Investment tax credit; 163(2.2) — False statement or omissions — penalty; 211.91 — Tax on issuer using one-year look-back rule; 248(1)"specified future tax consequence"(b) — Reduction under 66(12.73) is a specified future tax consequence; 248(16) — GST — input tax credit and rebate; 248(18) — GST — repayment of input tax credit. See additional Related Provisions and Definitions at end of s. 66.

**Notes**: 66(12.6) and (12.601) allow a corporation to "renounce" expenses that it could not otherwise claim, and pass them to the shareholders of its flow-through shares. Thus, the shareholders can claim the deductions as if they had incurred them directly. This is particularly useful for corporations that are not yet profitable, as it allows the fast write-offs available for resource expenditures to be used by the shareholders against their income. What makes the share a flow-through share is simply the agreement between the investor and the corporation, not any characteristic of the share itself; see 66(15)"flow-through share".

For a detailed discussion, see Department of Finance, *Flow-Through Shares: An Evaluation Report* (October 1994, 276 pp.).

66(12.6) opening words and paras. (a) and (b) amended by 1996 Budget, effective for expenses incurred after February 1996. For earlier expenses, read:

(12.6) Where a person gave consideration under an agreement to a corporation for the issue of a flow-through share of the corporation and, during the period beginning on the day the agreement was entered into and ending 24 months after the end of the month that included that day, the corporation incurred Canadian exploration expenses, the corporation may, after it complies with subsection (12.68) in respect of the share and before March of the first calendar year beginning after that period, renounce, effective on the date on which the renunciation is made or on an earlier date set out in the form prescribed for the purposes of subsection (12.7), to the person in respect of the share the amount, if any, by which those expenses incurred by it during that period and on or before the effective date of the renunciation exceed the total of

(a) the assistance that it has received, is entitled to receive, or may reasonably be expected to receive at any time, and that may reasonably be related to those expenses or to Canadian exploration activities to which those expenses relate (other than assistance that may reasonably be attributable to expenses referred to in paragraph (b)),

(b) any of those expenses that are prescribed Canadian exploration and development overhead expenses of the corporation, and

Opening words of 66(12.6) amended by 1992 Economic Statement, effective for expenses incurred after February 1986, to change "within that period or within 30 days thereafter" to "before March of the first calendar year beginning after that period", to extend the time for the renunciation of Canadian exploration expenses.

66(12.6)(b.1) added by 1996 Budget, effective for costs incurred after March 5, 1996, other than costs incurred under an agreement in writing made by that date. It prevents renunciation under 66(12.66) on the basis of costs of, or for the use of, "off-the-shelf" seismic data.

66(12.6)(d) amended by 1996 Budget, effective for renunciations made in 1999 or later, to delete reference to 66(12.64).

66(12.6)(d) amended by 1992 Economic Statement, effective for expenses incurred after December 2, 1992, to add reference to 66(12.601).

**Regulations**: 228 (information return); 1206(1), (4.1), (4.2) (prescribed Canadian exploration and development overhead expenses, for 66(12.6)(b)).

**Forms**: T101: Flow-through share — Summary of renunciation, reduction of amount previously renounced, allocation of assistance and calculation of Part XII.6 tax; T101 Supp: Statement — Renunciation of resource expense, reduction of amount previously renounced and allocation of assistance; T102 Summ: Allocation to members of a partnership of renounced resource expenses, reduction of amounts previously renounced and amount of assistance; T102 Supp: Statement of renounced resource expense, reduction of amount previously renounced and assistance allocation to member of partnership.

**(12.601) Flow-through share rules for first $1 million of Canadian development expenses** — Where

(a) a person gave consideration under an agreement to a corporation for the issue of a flow-through share of the corporation, (a.1) the corporation's taxable capital amount at the time the consideration was given was not more than $15,000,000, and

(b) during the period beginning on the later of December 3, 1992 and the particular day the agreement was entered into and ending on the day that is 24 months after the end of the month that included that particular day, the corporation incurred Canadian development expenses described in paragraph (a) or (b) of the definition "Canadian development expense" in subsection 66.2(5) or that would be described in paragraph (f) of that definition if the words "paragraphs (a) to (e)" in that paragraph were read as "paragraphs (a) and (b)",

the corporation may, after it complies with subsection (12.68) in respect of the share and before March of the first calendar year that begins after that period, renounce, effective on the day on which the renunciation is made or on an earlier day set out in the form prescribed for the purposes of subsection (12.7), to the person in respect of the share the amount, if any, by which the part of those expenses that was incurred on or before the effective date of the renunciation (which part is in this subsection referred to as the "specified expenses") exceeds the total of

(c) the assistance that the corporation has received, is entitled to receive, or can reasonably be expected to receive at any time, and that can reasonably be related to the specified expenses or Canadian development activities to which the specified expenses relate (other than assistance that can reasonably be related to expenses referred to in paragraph (d)),

(d) all specified expenses that are prescribed Canadian exploration and development overhead expenses of the corporation, and

(e) all amounts that are renounced on or before the day on which the renunciation is made by any other renunciation under this subsection or subsection (12.62) in respect of those expenses.

**Related Provisions**: 66(12.6011) — Meaning of "taxable capital amount" for 66(12.601)(a.1); 66(12.602) — Restriction; 66(12.62)(c), (d) — Canadian development expenses to flow-through shareholder; 66(12.64)(c) — Canadian oil and gas property expenses to flow-through shareholder; 66(12.66) — Expenses in first 60 days of following year; 66(12.67) — Restrictions on renunciation; 66(12.69) — Filing re partners; 66(12.7) — Filing; 66(12.71) — Restriction on renunciation; 66(12.72) — Application of sections 231 to 231.3; 66(12.73) — Adjustment in renunciation; 66(12.741) — Late renunciation; 66(16) — Partnership deemed to be a person; 66(19) — Renunciation by member of partnership, etc.; 66.1(6)"restricted expense"(c) — inclusion of renounced expenses; 66.3(4)(a)(ii)(B) — Paid-up capital; 87(4.4) — Amalgamations; 110.6(1)"investment expense"(d) — Effect of renunciation on capital gains exemption; 163(2.2) — False statements or omissions — penalty; 211.91 — Tax on issuer using one-year look-back rule; 248(1)"specified future tax consequence"(b) — Reduction under 66(12.73) is a specified future tax consequence.

**Notes**: See Notes to 66(12.6). 66(12.601) added by 1992 Economic Statement and paras. (c) and (d) amended retroactively by 1996 Budget, both effective for expenses incurred after December 2, 1992. It permits a corporation to renounce up to $1 million (see 66(12.602)) of Canadian development expenses (CDE), normally claimed at 30% per year, to flow-through shareholders, who can then claim that amount as Canadian exploration expenses (CEE), fully deductible in the year.

66(12.601)(a.1) added by 1996 Budget, effective for renunciations made after March 5, 1996, other than a renunciation made before 1999 in respect of consideration given

(a) before March 6, 1996; or

(b) under an agreement in writing made before March 6, 1996 or under the terms of a prospectus, preliminary prospectus, registration statement, offering memorandum or notice filed before March 6, 1996 with a public authority in Canada in accordance with securities legislation of a province.

**Regulations**: 1206(1), (4.1), (4.2) (prescribed Canadian exploration and development overhead expenses, for 66(12.601)(d)).

**Forms**: T101: Flow-through share — Summary of renunciation, reduction of amount previously renounced, allocation of assistance and calculation of Part XII.6 tax; T101 Supp: Statement — Renunciation of resource expense, reduction of amount previously renounced and allocation of assistance; T102 Summ: Allocation to members of a partnership of renounced resource expenses, reduction of amounts previously renounced and amount of assistance; T102 Supp: Statement of renounced resource expense, reduction of amount previously renounced and assistance allocation to member of partnership.

**(12.6011) Taxable capital amount** — For the purpose of subsection (12.601), a particular corporation's taxable capital amount at any time is the total of

(a) its taxable capital employed in Canada for its last taxation year that ended more than 30 days before that time, and

(b) the total of all amounts each of which is the taxable capital employed in Canada of another corporation associated at that time with the particular corporation for the other corporation's last taxation year that ended more than 30 days before that time.

**Related Provisions**: 66(12.6012) — Meaning of taxable capital employed in Canada; 66(12.6013) — Effect of amalgamation or merger; 256 — Associated corporations.

**Notes**: 66(12.6011) added by 1996 Budget, effective March 6, 1996, except that the amount determined under 66(12.6011) in respect of a renunciation by a corporation shall be determined as if each other corporation associated with the corporation were not so associated where the renunciation was made before 1999 in respect of consideration given

(a) before December 6, 1996; or

(b) under an agreement in writing made before December 6, 1996 or under the terms of a prospectus, preliminary prospectus, registration statement, offering memorandum or notice filed before December 7, 1996 with a public authority in Canada in accordance with securities legislation of a province.

**(12.6012) Taxable capital employed in Canada** — For the purpose of determining a corporation's taxable capital amount at a particular time under subsection (12.6011) and for the purpose of subsection (12.6013), a particular corporation's taxable capital employed in Canada for a taxation year is the amount that would be its taxable capital employed in Canada for the year, determined in accordance with subsection 181.2(1) and without reference to the portion of its investment allowance (as determined under subsection 181.2(4)) that is attributable to shares of the capital stock of, dividends payable by, or indebtedness of, another corporation that

(a) was not associated with the particular corporation at the particular time; and

(b) was associated with the particular corporation at the end of the particular corporation's last taxation year that ended more than 30 days before that time.

**Related Provisions**: 256 — Associated corporations.

**Notes**: 66(12.6012) added by 1996 Budget, effective March 6, 1996.

**(12.6013) Amalgamations and mergers** — For the purpose of determining the taxable capital amount at a particular time under subsection (12.6011) of any corporation and for the purpose of this subsection, a particular corporation that was created as a consequence of an amalgamation or merger of other corporations (each of which is in this subsection referred to as a "predecessor corporation"), and that does not have a taxation year that ended more than 30 days before the particular time, is deemed to have taxable capital employed in Canada for a taxation year that ended more than 30 days before the particular time equal to the total of all amounts each of which is the taxable capital employed in Canada of a predecessor corporation for its last taxation year that ended more than 30 days before the particular time.

**Notes**: 66(12.6013) added by 1996 Budget, effective March 6, 1996.

**(12.602) Idem** — A corporation shall be deemed not to have renounced any particular amount under subsection (12.601) in respect of a share where

(a) the particular amount exceeds the amount, if any, by which the consideration for the share exceeds the total of other amounts renounced in respect of the share under subsection (12.6), (12.601) or (12.62) on or before the day on which the renunciation is made;

(b) the particular amount exceeds the amount, if any, by which

(i) the cumulative Canadian development expense of the corporation on the effective date of the renunciation, computed before taking into account any amounts renounced under subsection (12.601) on the day on which the renunciation is made,

exceeds

(ii) the total of all amounts renounced under subsection (12.601) by the corporation in respect of any other share

(A) on the day on which the renunciation is made, and

(B) effective on or before the effective date of the renunciation; or

(c) the particular amount relates to Canadian development expenses incurred by the corporation in a calendar year and the total amounts renounced, on or before the day on which the renunciation is made, under subsection (12.601) in respect of

(i) Canadian development expenses incurred by the corporation in that calendar year, or

(ii) Canadian development expenses incurred in that calendar year by another corporation associated with the corporation at the time the other corporation incurred such expenses

exceeds $1,000,000.

**Related Provisions**: 66(12.66) — Expenses in first 60 days of following year.

**Notes**: 66(12.602) added by 1992 Economic Statement, effective for expenses incurred after December 2, 1992. See Notes to 66(12.601).

66(12.602)(a) amended by 1996 Budget, effective for renunciations made in 1999 or later, to delete reference to 66(12.64).

Closing words of 66(12.602)(c) amended by 1996 Budget to change "$2 million" to "$1 million", effective for renunciations made after March 5, 1996, other than a renunciation made before 1999 in respect of consideration given

(a) before March 6, 1996; or

(b) under an agreement in writing made before March 6, 1996 or under the terms of a prospectus, preliminary prospectus, registration statement, offering memorandum or notice filed before March 6, 1996 with a public authority in Canada in accordance with securities legislation of a province.

**(12.61) Effect of renunciation** — Subject to subsections (12.69) to (12.702), where under subsection (12.6) or (12.601) a corporation renounces an amount to a person,

(a) the Canadian exploration expenses or Canadian development expenses to which the amount relates shall be deemed to be Canadian exploration expenses incurred in that amount by the person on the effective date of the renunciation; and

(b) the Canadian exploration expenses or Canadian development expenses to which the amount relates shall, except for the purposes of that renunciation, be deemed on and after the effective date of the renunciation never to have been Canadian exploration expenses or Canadian development expenses incurred by the corporation.

**Related Provisions**: 66(16) — Partnership deemed to be a person; 66(17) — Non-arm's length partnerships; 127(9)"investment tax credit"(a.2), 127(9)"flow-through mining expenditure" — Investment tax credit. See additional Related Provisions and Definitions at end of s. 66.

**Notes**: 66(12.61) amended by 1992 Economic Statement, effective for expenses incurred after December 2, 1992, to add references to 66(12.601) and Canadian development expenses.

Opening words of 66(12.61) amended by 1991 technical bill, effective July 14, 1990, to add the words "Subject to subsections (12.69) to (12.701)". Amended by 1996 Budget, effective for renunciations made after 1998, to change "(12.701)" to "(12.702)".

**(12.62) Canadian development expenses to flow-through shareholder** — Where a person gave consideration under an agreement to a corporation for the issue of a flow-through share of the corporation and, in the period that begins on the day the agreement was made and ends 24 months after the end of the month that includes that day, the corporation incurred Canadian development expenses, the corporation may, after it complies with subsection (12.68) in respect of the share and before March of the first calendar year that begins after the period, renounce, effective on the day on which the renunciation is made or on an earlier day set out in the form prescribed for the purposes of subsection (12.7), to the person in respect of the share the amount, if any, by which the part of those expenses that was incurred on or before the effective date of the renunciation (which part is in this subsection referred to as the "specified expenses") exceeds the total of

(a) the assistance that the corporation has received, is entitled to receive, or can reasonably be expected to receive at any time, and that can reasonably be related to the specified expenses or to Canadian development activities to which the specified expenses relate (other than assistance that can reasonably be related to expenses referred to in paragraph (b) or (b.1)),

(b) all specified expenses that are prescribed Canadian exploration and development overhead expenses of the corporation,

(b.1) all specified expenses that are described in paragraph (e) of the definition "Canadian development expense" in subsection 66.2(5) or that are described in paragraph (f) of that definition because of the reference in the latter paragraph to paragraph (e), and

(c) the total of amounts that are renounced on or before the day on which the renunciation is made by any other renunciation under this subsection or subsection (12.601) in respect of those expenses,

but not in any case

(d) exceeding the amount, if any, by which the consideration for the share exceeds the total of other amounts renounced in respect of the share under this subsection or subsection (12.6) or (12.601) on or before the day on which the renunciation is made, or

(e) exceeding the amount, if any, by which the cumulative Canadian development expense of the corporation on the effective date of the renunciation computed before taking into account any amounts renounced under this subsection on the date on which the renunciation is made, exceeds the total of all amounts renounced under this subsection in respect of any other share

(i) on the date on which the renunciation is made, and

(ii) effective on or before the effective date of the renunciation.

**Related Provisions**: 66(12.601), (12.602) — Flow-through share rules for first $2 million of Canadian development expenses; 66(12.63) — Effect of renunciation of Canadian development expense; 66(12.64)(c) — Canadian oil and gas property expenses to flow-through shareholder; 66(12.67) — Restriction on renunciation; 66(12.68) — Filing selling instruments; 66(12.69) — Filing re partners; 66(12.7) — Filing; 66(12.71) — Restriction on renunciation; 66(12.72) — Application of sections 231 to 231.3; 66(12.73) — Adjustment in renunciation; 66(12.741) — Late renunciation; 66(16) — Partnership deemed to be a person; 66(19) — Renunciation by member of partnership, etc.; 66.1(6)"restricted expense"(c) — Inclusion of amount renounced; 66.2(5) — Definitions; 66.3(3) — Cost of flow-through shares; 66.3(4)(a)(ii)(B) — Paid-up capital; 87(4.4) — Flow-through shares; 110.6(1)"investment expense"(d) — effect of renunciation on capital gains exemption; 163(2.2) — False statement or omissions — penalty; 248(16) — GST input tax credit and rebate deemed to be assistance; 248(18) — GST — repayment of input tax credit. See additional Related Provisions and Definitions at end of s. 66.

**Notes**: Opening words of 66(12.62) amended by 1992 Economic Statement, effective for expenses incurred after February 1986, to change "within that period or within 30 days thereafter" to "before March of the first calendar year beginning after that period", to extend the time for the renunciation of Canadian development expenses. See also Notes to 66(12.6).

Opening words and paras. (a) and (b) amended by 1996 Budget, effective for expenses incurred after February 1996. The changes clarify that assistance in respect of CDE incurred after the effective date of a renunciation, as well as overhead expenses incurred after that date, do not reduce the CDE that can be flowed through under the renunciation. For earlier expenses, read:

> (12.62) Where a person gave consideration under an agreement to a corporation for the issue of a flow-through share of the corporation and, during the period beginning on the day the agreement was entered into and ending 24 months after the end of the month that included that day, the corporation incurred Canadian development expenses, the corporation may, after it complies with subsection (12.68) in respect of the share and before March of the first calendar year beginning after that period, renounce, effective on the date on which the renunciation is made or on an earlier date set out in the form prescribed for the purposes of subsection (12.7), to the person in respect of the share the amount, if any, by which those expenses incurred by it during that period and on or before the effective date of the renunciation exceed the total of
>
> (a) the assistance that it has received, is entitled to receive, or may reasonably be expected to receive at any time, and that may reasonably be related to those expenses or to Canadian development activities to which those expenses relate (other than assistance that may reasonably be attributable to expenses referred to in paragraph (b)),
>
> (b) any of those expenses that are prescribed Canadian exploration and development overhead expenses of the corporation, and

66(12.62)(b.1) added by 1996 Budget, effective on the same basis as 66(12.601)(a.1).

66(12.62)(d) amended by 1996 Budget, effective for renunciations made in 1999 or later, to delete reference to 66(12.64).

66(12.62)(c) and (d) amended by 1992 Economic Statement, effective for expenses incurred after December 2, 1992, to add references to 66(12.601).

**Regulations**: 228 (information return); 1206(1), (4.1), (4.2) (prescribed Canadian exploration and development overhead expenses, for 66(12.62)(b)).

**Forms**: T101: Flow-through share — Summary of renunciation, reduction of amount previously renounced, allocation of assistance and calculation of Part XII.6 tax; T101 Supp: Statement — Renunciation of resource expense, reduction of amount previously renounced and allocation of assistance; T102 Summ: Allocation to members of a partnership of renounced resource expenses, reduction of amounts previously renounced and amount of assistance; T102 Supp: Statement of renounced resource expense, reduction of amount previously renounced and assistance allocation to member of partnership.

**(12.63) Effect of renunciation** — Subject to subsections (12.691) to (12.702), where under subsection (12.62) a corporation renounces an amount to a person,

(a) the Canadian development expenses to which the amount relates shall be deemed to be Canadian development expenses incurred in that amount by the person on the effective date of the renunciation; and

(b) the Canadian development expenses to which the amount relates shall, except for the purposes of that renunciation, be deemed on and after the effective date of the renunciation never to have been Canadian development expenses incurred by the corporation.

**Related Provisions**: 66(16) — Partnership deemed to be a person; 66.2(5) — Definitions. See additional Related provisions and Definitions at end of s. 66.

**Notes**: Opening words of 66(12.63) amended by 1991 technical bill, effective July 14, 1990, to add the words "Subject to subsections (12.69) to (12.701)". Amended by 1996 Budget, effective for renunciations made after 1998, to change "(12.69) to (12.701)" to "(12.691) to (12.702)".

**(12.64)** [Repealed]

**Related Provisions**: 66(12.602) — Flow-through share rules for first $2 million of Canadian development expense; 66(12.62)(d) — Canadian development expenses to flow-through shareholder; 66(12.65) — Effect of renunciation of Canadian oil and gas property expenses; 66(12.67) — Restriction on renunciation; 66(12.68) — Filing selling instruments; 66 (12.69) — Filing re partners; 66(12.7) — Filing; 66(12.71) — Restriction on renunciation; 66(12.72) — Application of sections 231 to 231.3; 66(12.73) — Adjustment in renunciation; 66(12.741) — Late renunciation; 66(16) — Partnership deemed to be a person; 66(19) — Renunciation by member of partnership, etc.; 66.3(3) — Cost of flow-through shares; 66.3(4)(a)(ii)(B) — Paid-up capital; 87(4.4) — Flow-through shares; 110.6(1)"investment expense"(d) — effect of renunciation on capital gains exemption; 163(2.2) — False statement or omissions — penalty; 248(16) — GST input tax credit and rebate deemed to be assistance; 248(18) — GST — repayment of input tax credit. See additional Related Provisions and Definitions at end of s. 66.

**Notes**: 66(12.64) repealed by 1996 Budget, effective for renunciations made after March 5, 1996, other than a renunciation made before 1999 in respect of consideration given

(a) before March 6, 1996; or

(b) under an agreement in writing made before March 6, 1996 or under the terms of a prospectus, preliminary prospectus, registration statement, offering memorandum or notice filed before March 6, 1996 with a public authority in Canada in accordance with securities legislation of a province.

Thus, COGPE is no longer an eligible flow-through share expenditure. 66(12.64) previously read:

(12.64) **Canadian oil and gas property expenses to flow-through shareholder** — Where a person gave consideration under an agreement to a corporation for the issue of a flow-through share of the corporation and, during the period beginning on the day the agreement was entered into and ending 24 months after the end of the month that included that day, the corporation incurred Canadian oil and gas property expenses, the corporation may, after it complies with subsection (12.68) in respect of the share and before March of the first calendar year beginning after that period, renounce, effective on the date on which the renunciation is made or on an earlier date set out in the form prescribed for the purposes of subsection (12.7), to the person in respect of the share the amount, if any, by which those expenses incurred by it during that period and on or before the effective date of the renunciation exceed the total of

(a) the assistance that it has received, is entitled to receive, or may reasonably be expected to receive at any time, and that may reasonably be related to those expenses, and

(b) the total of amounts that are renounced on or before the date on which the renunciation is made by any other renunciation under this subsection in respect of those expenses,

but not in any case

(c) exceeding the amount, if any, by which the consideration for the share exceeds the total of other amounts renounced in respect of the share under this subsection or subsection (12.6), (12.601) or (12.62) on or before the date on which the renunciation is made, or

(d) exceeding the amount, if any, by which the cumulative Canadian oil and gas property expense of the corporation on the effective date of the renunciation computed before taking into account any amounts renounced under this subsection on the date on which the renunciation is made, exceeds the total of all amounts renounced under this subsection in respect of any other share

(i) on the date on which the renunciation is made, and

(ii) effective on or before the effective date of the renunciation.

Opening words of 66(12.64) amended by 1992 Economic Statement, effective for expenses incurred after February 1986, to change "within that period or within 30 days thereafter" to "before March of the first calendar year beginning after that period", to extend the time for the renunciation of Canadian oil and gas property expenses. See also Notes to 66(12.6).

66(12.64)(c) amended by 1992 Economic Statement, effective for expenses incurred after December 2, 1992, to add reference to 66(12.601).

**Regulations**: 228 (information return).

**Forms**: T101: Flow-through share — Summary of renunciation, reduction of amount previously renounced, allocation of assistance and calculation of Part XII.6 tax; T101 Supp: Statement — Renunciation of resource expense, reduction of amount previously renounced and allocation of assistance; T102 Summ: Allocation to members of a partnership of renounced resource expenses, reduction of amounts previously renounced and amount of assistance; T102 Supp: Statement of renounced resource expense, reduction of amount previously renounced and assistance allocation to member of partnership.

**(12.65)** [Repealed]

**Notes**: 66(12.65) repealed by 1996 Budget, effective on the same basis as the repeal of 66(12.64). It read:

> (12.65) **Effect of renunciation** — Subject to subsections (12.69) to (12.701), where under subsection (12.64) a corporation renounces an amount to a person,
>
>> (a) the Canadian oil and gas property expenses to which the amount relates shall be deemed to be Canadian oil and gas property expenses incurred in that amount by the person on the effective date of the renunciation; and
>>
>> (b) the Canadian oil and gas property expense to which the amount relates shall, except for the purposes of that renunciation, be deemed on and after the effective date of the renunciation never to have been Canadian oil and gas property expenses incurred by the corporation.

66(12.65) amended by 1991 technical bill, effective July 14, 1990, to add the words "Subject to subsections (12.69) to (12.701)".

**(12.66) Expenses in the first 60 days of year [or throughout next calendar year]** — Where

(a) a corporation that issues a flow-through share to a person under an agreement incurs, in a particular calendar year, Canadian exploration expenses or Canadian development expenses,

(a.1) the agreement was made in the preceding calendar year,

(b) the expenses

(i) are described in paragraph (a), (d) or (f) of the definition "Canadian exploration expense" in subsection 66.1(6) or paragraph (a) or (b) of the definition "Canadian development expense" in subsection 66.2(5),

(ii) would be described in paragraph (h) of the definition "Canadian exploration expense" in subsection 66.1(6) if the words "paragraphs (a), (b), (c), (d), (f) and (g)" were read as "paragraphs (a), (d) and (f)", or

(iii) would be described in paragraph (f) of the definition "Canadian development expense" in subsection 66.2(5) if the words "any of paragraphs (a) to (e)" were read as "paragraph (a) or (b)",

(c) before the end of that preceding year the person paid the consideration in money for the share to be issued,

(d) the corporation and the person deal with each other at arm's length throughout the particular year, and

(e) in January, February or March of the particular year, the corporation renounces an amount in respect of the expenses to the person in respect of the share in accordance with subsection (12.6) or (12.601) and the effective date of the renunciation is the last day of that preceding year,

the corporation is for the purpose of subsection (12.6) or for the purposes of subsection (12.601) and paragraph (12.602)(b), as the case may be, deemed to have incurred the expenses on the last day of the year.

**Related Provisions**: 66(12.6) — Canadian exploration expenses to flow-through shareholder; 66(16) — Partnership deemed to be a person; 66(17) — Non-arm's length partnerships; 87(4.4) — Amalgamations; 127(9)"investment tax credit"(a.2), 127(9)"flow-through mining expenditure"(e) — Investment tax credit; 163(2.21), (2.22) — Penalty for false statement or omission; 211.91 — Tax on issuer using one-year look-back rule; 248(1)"specified future tax consequence"(b) — Reduction under 66(12.73) is a specified future tax consequence. See additional Related provisions and Definitions at end of s. 66.

**Notes**: 66(12.66)(a) amended to change "within 60 days after the end of a calendar year" to "in a particular calendar year", and (a.1) added, by 1996 Budget, effective for expenses incurred after 1996, except expenses incurred in January or February 1997 in respect of an agreement made in 1995; and when applying para. (a.1) to expenses incurred in 1998, any agreement made in 1996 is deemed to have been made in 1997.

66(12.66)(a.1) was introduced so that, in order for the look-back rule to deem expenditures to be incurred at the end of a calendar year, the flow-through share agreement to which those expenditures relate must have been made in that year. This amendment is intended to simplify the operation of the new look-back rule while ensuring that the 24-month limit for the incurring of expenses under a flow-through share agreement is respected.

66(12.66)(b) amended by 1996 Budget, effective for expenses incurred after 1992.

66(12.66)(c), (d) and (e) amended by 1996 Budget, effective for expenses incurred after 1996, except expenses incurred in January or February 1997 in respect of an agreement made in 1995. For earlier expenses, read:

> (c) before the end of the year, the agreement was entered into between the corporation and the person and the person paid the consideration for the share in money,
>
> (d) the corporation and the person deal with each other at arm's length throughout the 60 days, and
>
> (e) within 90 days after the end of the year, the corporation renounces an amount in respect of the expenses to the person in respect of the share in accordance with subsection (12.6) or (12.601) and the effective date of the renunciation is the last day of the year,

66(12.66) amended by 1992 Economic Statement, effective for expenses incurred after 1992, to add references to Canadian development expenses and 66(12.601). See Notes to 66(12.601).

Closing words of 66(12.66) amended by 1995-97 technical bill, effective for expenses after 1992. Previously read:

> the corporation shall for the purpose of subsection (12.6) or (12.601) be deemed to have incurred the expenses on the effective date of the renunciation.

**(12.67) Restrictions on renunciation** — A corporation shall be deemed

(a) not to have renounced under any of subsections (12.6), (12.601) and (12.62) any expenses that are deemed to have been incurred by it because of a renunciation under this section by another corporation that is not related to it;

(b) not to have renounced under subsection (12.601) to a trust, corporation or partnership any Canadian development expenses (other than expenses renounced to another corporation that renounces under subsection (12.6) any Canadian exploration expense deemed to have been incurred by it because of the renunciation under subsection (12.601)) if, in respect of the renunciation under subsection (12.601), it has a prohibited relationship with the trust, corporation or partnership;

(c) not to have renounced under subsection (12.601) any Canadian development expenses deemed to have been incurred by it because of a renunciation under subsection (12.62); and

(d) not to have renounced under subsection (12.6) to a particular trust, corporation or partnership any Canadian exploration expenses (other than expenses ultimately renounced by another corporation under subsection (12.6) to an individual (other than a trust) or to a trust, corporation or partnership with which that other corporation does not have, in respect of that ultimate renunciation, a prohibited relationship) deemed to be incurred by it because of a renunciation under subsection (12.601) if, in respect of the renunciation under subsection (12.6), it has a prohibited relationship with the particular trust, corporation or partnership.

**Related Provisions**: 66(12.671) — Prohibited relationship. See additional Related Provisions and Definitions at end of s. 66.

**Notes**: 66(12.67)(a) amended by 1996 Budget, effective for renunciations made in 1999 or later, to delete reference to 66(12.64).

66(12.67) amended by 1992 Economic Statement, effective for expenses incurred after December 2, 1992, as a result of the addition of 66(12.601). For earlier expenses, read:

> (12.67) **Restriction on renunciation** — A corporation shall not renounce under any of subsections (12.6), (12.62) and (12.64) any expenses that are deemed to have been incurred by it by virtue of a renunciation under this section by another corporation that is not related to it.

**(12.671) Prohibited relationship** — For the purposes of subsection (12.67), where a trust, corporation (in paragraph (b) referred to as the "shareholder corporation") or partnership, as the case may be, gave consideration under a particular agreement for the issue of a flow-through share of a particular corporation, the particular corporation has, in respect of a renunciation under subsection (12.6) or (12.601) in respect of the share, a prohibited relationship

(a) with the trust if, at any time after the particular agreement was entered into and before the share is issued to the trust, the particular corporation or any corporation related to the particular corporation is beneficially interested in the trust;

(b) with the shareholder corporation if, immediately before the particular agreement was entered into, the shareholder corporation was related to the particular corporation; or

(c) with the partnership if any part of the amount renounced would, but for subsection (12.7001), be included, because of paragraph (h) of the definition "Canadian exploration expense" in subsection 66.1(6), in the Canadian exploration expense of

(i) the particular corporation, or

(ii) any other corporation that, at any time

(A) after the particular agreement was entered into, and

(B) before that part of the amount renounced would, but for this paragraph, be incurred,

would, if flow-through shares issued by the particular corporation under agreements entered into at the same time as or after the time the particular agreement was entered into were disregarded, be related to the particular corporation.

**Notes**: Opening words of 66(12.671)(c) amended by 1996 Budget, effective for renunciations made in 1999 or later, to change "subsection (12.7)" to "subsection (12.7001)".

66(12.671) added by 1992 Economic Statement, effective for expenses incurred after December 2, 1992.

**(12.68) Filing selling instruments** — A corporation that agrees to issue or prepares a selling instrument in respect of flow-through shares shall file with the Minister a prescribed form together with a copy of the selling instrument or agreement to issue the shares on or before the last day of the month following the earlier of

(a) the month in which the agreement to issue the shares is entered into, and

(b) the month in which the selling instrument is first delivered to a potential investor,

and the Minister shall thereupon assign an identification number to the form and notify the corporation of the number.

**Related Provisions**: 66(12.61) — Effect of renunciation; 66(12.74) — Late filed forms; 87(4.4) — Flow-through shares. See additional Related Provisions and Definitions at end of s. 66; 163.2(1)"excluded activity"(a)(i) — No good-faith reliance defence for advisor assessed third-party penalty.

**Forms**: T100: Flow-through share information.

**(12.69) Filing re partners** — Where, in a fiscal period of a partnership, an expense is incurred by the partnership as a consequence of a renunciation of an amount under subsection (12.6), (12.601) or (12.62), the partnership shall, before the end of the third month that begins after the end of the period, file with the Minister a prescribed form identifying the share of the expense attributable to each member of the partnership at the end of the period.

**Related Provisions**: 66(12.61) — Effect of renunciation; 66(12.6901) — Consequences of partnership failing to file; 66(12.74) — Late filed forms; 66(15) — Definitions. See additional Related provisions and Definitions at end of s. 66.

**Notes**: 66(12.69) amended by 1996 Budget, effective for renunciations made in 1999 or later. The substantive change was the elimination of a reference to 66(12.64), and moving the last part of the subsec. to new 66(12.6901). The rest of the changes were non-substantive wording changes. For renunciations made before 1999, read:

> (12.69) Where, in a fiscal period of a partnership, an expense is or, but for this subsection, would be incurred by the partnership as a consequence of a renunciation of an amount under subsection (12.6), (12.601), (12.62) or (12.64), the partnership shall, on or before the last day of the third month following the end of that period, file with the Minister a prescribed form indicating the share of the expense attributable to each member of the partnership at the end of the period

and, where the prescribed form is not so filed, the partnership shall be deemed not to have incurred the expense.

66(12.69) amended by 1992 Economic Statement, effective for expenses incurred after December 2, 1992, to add reference to 66(12.601).

66(12.69) amended by 1991 technical bill, effective for fiscal periods ending after July 13, 1990.

**Forms:** T5016: Summary information for tax shelters that are partnerships or for partnerships that allocated renounced resource expenses to their members.

**(12.6901) Consequences of failure to file** — Where a partnership fails to file a prescribed form as required under subsection (12.69) in respect of an expense, except for the purpose of subsection (12.69) the partnership is deemed not to have incurred the expense.

**Notes:** 66(12.6901) added by 1996 Budget, effective for renunciations made in 1999 or later. For earlier renunciations, the same rule applied in the last few words of 66(12.69). See Notes to 66(12.69).

**(12.691) Filing re assistance** — Where a partnership receives or becomes entitled to receive assistance as an agent for its members or former members at a particular time in respect of any Canadian exploration expense or Canadian development expense that is or, but for paragraph (12.61)(b) or (12.63)(b), would be incurred by a corporation, the following rules apply:

(a) where the entitlement of any such member or former member to any part of the assistance is known by the partnership as of the end of the partnership's first fiscal period ending after the particular time and that part of the assistance was not required to be reported under paragraph (b) in respect of a calendar year ending before the end of that fiscal period, the partnership shall, on or before the last day of the third month following the end of that fiscal period, file with the Minister a prescribed form indicating the share of that part of the assistance paid to each of those members or former members before the end of that fiscal period or to which each of those members or former members is entitled at the end of that fiscal period;

(b) where the entitlement of any of those members or former members to any part of the assistance is known by the partnership as of the end of a calendar year that ends after the particular time and that part of the assistance was not required to be reported under paragraph (a) in respect of a fiscal period ending at or before the end of that calendar year, or under this paragraph in respect of a preceding calendar year, the partnership shall, on or before the last day of the third month following the end of that calendar year, file with the Minister a prescribed form indicating the share of that part of the assistance paid to each of those members or former members before the end of that fiscal period or to which each of those members or former members is entitled at the end of that calendar year; and

(c) where a prescribed form required to be filed under paragraph (a) or (b) is not so filed, the part of that expense relating to the assistance required to be reported in the prescribed form shall be deemed not to have been incurred by the partnership.

**Related Provisions:** 163(2.3) — False statement or omissions.

**Notes:** Opening words of 66(12.691) amended by 1996 Budget, effective for renunciations made in 1999 or later, to delete reference to Canadian oil and gas property expense and to 66(12.65)(b).

66(12.691) added by 1991 technical bill, effective for assistance that a partnership receives or becomes entitled to receive that is both after 1989 and in a fiscal period of the partnership ending after July 13, 1990.

**(12.7) Filing re renunciation** — Where a corporation renounces an amount in respect of Canadian exploration expenses or Canadian development expenses under subsection (12.6), (12.601) or (12.62), the corporation shall file a prescribed form in respect of the renunciation with the Minister before the end of the first month after the month in which the renunciation is made.

**Related Provisions:** 66(12.7001) — Consequences of corporation failing to file; 66(12.74) — Late filed forms. See additional Related provisions and Definitions at end of s. 66.

**Notes:** 66(12.7) amended by 1996 Budget, effective for renunciations made in 1999 or later. The substantive change was the elimination of references to Canadian oil and gas property expense and 66(12.64), and moving the last part of the subsec. to new 66(12.7001). For renunciations made before 1999, read:

(12.7) Filing — Where a corporation renounces an amount in respect of Canadian exploration expenses, Canadian development expenses or Canadian oil and gas property expenses under subsection (12.6), (12.601), (12.62) or (12.64), the corporation shall file a prescribed form in respect of the renunciation with the Minister before the end of the first month following the month in which the renunciation is made and, where the prescribed form is not so filed, subsections (12.61), (12.63) and (12.65) do not apply in respect of the amount so renounced.

66(12.7) amended by 1992 Economic Statement, effective for renunciations made after December 2, 1992, to add reference to 66(12.601).

66(12.7) amended by 1991 technical bill, effective for renunciations made after July 13, 1990. For earlier renunciations, read:

(12.7) Filing — Where a corporation renounces an amount in respect of Canadian exploration expenses, Canadian development expenses or Canadian oil and gas property expenses under subsection (12.6), (12.62) or (12.64), the corporation shall file a prescribed form in respect of the renunciation with the Minister on or before the last day of the month following the month in which the renunciation was made.

**Forms:** T101: Flow-through share — Summary of renunciation, reduction of amount previously renounced, allocation of assistance and calculation of Part XII.6 tax; T101 Supp: Statement — Renunciation of resource expense, reduction of amount previously renounced and allocation of assistance; T102 Summ: Allocation to members of a partnership of renounced resource expenses, reduction of amounts previously renounced and amount of assistance; T102 Supp: Statement of renounced resource expense, reduction of amount previously renounced and assistance allocation to member of partnership.

**(12.7001) Consequences of failure to file** — Where a corporation fails to file a prescribed form as required under subsection (12.7) in respect of a renunciation of an amount, subsections (12.61) and (12.63) do not apply in respect of the amount.

**Notes**: 66(12.7001) added by 1996 Budget, effective for renunciations made in 1999 or later. For earlier renunciations, the same rule applied in the last few words of 66(12.7), and included a reference to subsec. (12.65). See Notes to 66(12.7).

**(12.701) Filing re assistance** — Where a corporation receives or becomes entitled to receive assistance as an agent in respect of any Canadian exploration expense or Canadian development expense that is or, but for paragraph (12.61)(b) or (12.63)(b), would be incurred by the corporation, the corporation shall, before the end of the first month after the particular month in which it first becomes known to the corporation that a person that holds a flow-through share of the corporation is entitled to a share of any part of the assistance, file with the Minister a prescribed form identifying the share of the assistance to which each of those persons is entitled at the end of the particular month.

**Related Provisions**: 66(12.702) — Consequences of corporation failing to file; 66(16) — Partnership deemed to be a person; 163(2.3) — False statement or omissions.

**Notes**: 66(12.701) amended by 1996 Budget, effective for renunciations made in 1999 or later. The substantive change was the elimination of references to Canadian oil and gas property expense and 66(12.65)(b), and moving the last part of the subsec. to new 66(12.702). For renunciations made before 1999, read:

> (12.701) **Idem** — Where at a particular time a corporation receives or becomes entitled to receive assistance as an agent in respect of any Canadian exploration expense, Canadian development expense or Canadian oil and gas property expense that is or, but for paragraph (12.61)(b), (12.63)(b) or (12.65)(b), would be incurred by the corporation, the corporation shall, before the end of the first month following the particular month in which it first becomes known that a person or partnership that holds a flow-through share of the corporation is entitled to a share of any part of the assistance, file with the Minister a prescribed form indicating the share of that part of the assistance to which each of those persons or partnerships is entitled at the end of the particular month and, where the prescribed form is not so filed, the part of the expense relating to the assistance required to be reported in the prescribed form shall be deemed not to have been incurred by the corporation.

66(12.701) added by 1991 technical bill, effective for assistance that a corporation receives or is entitled to receive after July 13, 1990.

**(12.702) Consequences of failure to file** — Where a corporation fails to file a prescribed form as required under subsection (12.701) in respect of assistance, except for the purpose of subsection (12.701) the Canadian exploration expense or Canadian development expense to which the assistance relates is deemed not to have been incurred by the corporation.

**Notes**: 66(12.702) added by 1996 Budget, effective for renunciations made in 1999 or later. For earlier renunciations, the same rule applied in the last few words of 66(12.701), and effectively covered COGPE as well. See Notes to 66(12.701).

**(12.71) Restriction on renunciation** — A corporation may renounce an amount under subsection (12.6), (12.601) or (12.62) in respect of Canadian exploration expenses or Canadian development expenses incurred by it only to the extent that, but for the renunciation, it would be entitled to a deduction in respect of the expenses in computing its income.

**Notes**: 66(12.71) amended by 1996 Budget, effective for renunciations made in 1999 or later. The substantive change was the elimination of references to Canadian oil and gas property expense and 66(12.64). For renunciations made before 1999, read:

> (12.71) A corporation may renounce an amount under subsection (12.6), (12.601), (12.62) or (12.64) in respect of Canadian exploration expenses, Canadian development expenses or Canadian oil and gas property expenses incurred by it only to the extent that, but for the renunciation, it would be entitled to claim a deduction in respect of the expenses in computing its income for the purposes of this Part.

66(12.71) amended by 1992 Economic Statement, effective for renunciations made after December 2, 1992, to add reference to 66(12.601).

**(12.72)** [Repealed]

**Notes**: 66(12.72) repealed by 1996 Budget, effective April 25, 1997 (Royal Assent). It gave Revenue Canada authority to verify or ascertain various expenses. Given the authority provided by 231–231.3, it was considered unnecessary. Before April 25, 1997, it read:

> (12.72) **Application of sections 231 to 231.3** — Without restricting the generality of sections 231 to 231.3, where a corporation renounces an amount under subsection (12.6), (12.601), (12.62) or (12.64), sections 231 to 231.3 apply, with such modifications as the circumstances require, for the purpose of permitting the Minister to verify or ascertain the Canadian exploration expenses, Canadian development expenses or Canadian oil and gas property expenses of the corporation in respect of which the amount is renounced, the amounts renounced in respect of those expenses, any information in respect of those expenses or the amounts renounced and the amount of, or information relating to, any assistance in respect of those expenses.

66(12.72) amended by 1992 Economic Statement, effective December 3, 1992, to add reference to 66(12.601).

**(12.73) Reductions in renunciations** — Where an amount that a corporation purports to renounce to a person under subsection (12.6), (12.601) or (12.62) exceeds the amount that it can renounce to the person under that subsection,

(a) the corporation shall file a statement with the Minister in prescribed form where

(i) the Minister sends a notice in writing to the corporation demanding the statement, or

(ii) the excess arose as a consequence of a renunciation purported to be made in a calendar year under subsection (12.6) or (12.601) because of the application of subsection (12.66) and, at the end of the year, the corporation knew or ought to have known of all or part of the excess;

(b) where subparagraph (a)(i) applies, the statement shall be filed not later than 30 days after the Minister sends a notice in writing to the corporation demanding the statement;

(c) where subparagraph (a)(ii) applies, the statement shall be filed before March of the calendar year following the calendar year in which the purported renunciation was made;

(d) except for the purpose of Part XII.6, any amount that is purported to have been so renounced to any person is deemed, after the statement is filed with the Minister, to have always been reduced by the portion of the excess identified in the statement in respect of that purported renunciation; and

(e) where a corporation fails in the statement to apply the excess fully to reduce one or more purported renunciations, the Minister may at any time reduce the total amount purported to be renounced by the corporation to one or more persons by the amount of the unapplied excess in which case, except for the purpose of Part XII.6, the amount purported to have been so renounced to a person is deemed, after that time, always to have been reduced by the portion of the unapplied excess allocated by the Minister in respect of that person.

**Related Provisions**: 66(16) — Partnership deemed to be a person; 152(4)(b)(v) — Three-year extension to normal reassessment period; 163(2.21), (2.22) — Penalty for false statement or omission; 248(1)"specified future tax consequence"(b) — Reduction is a specified future tax consequence. See also Related Provisions and Definitions at end of s. 66.

**Notes**: 66(12.73) amended by 1996 Budget, effective for purported renunciations made in 1997 or later, except that the reference to 66(12.64) in the opening words is only deleted for purported renunciations in 1999 or later. For renunciations made through the end of 1996, read:

(12.73) Adjustment in renunciation — Where the total of all amounts that a corporation purports to renounce to persons under subsection (12.6), (12.601), (12.62) or (12.64) in respect of expenses incurred by it in any period ending on the effective date of the purported renunciation exceeds the total amount of those expenses in respect of which it may renounce amounts under that subsection, it shall

(a) reduce the amount so renounced to one or more persons to effect a reduction in the total of the amounts so purported to be renounced by the amount of the excess, and

(b) file a statement with the Minister indicating the adjustments made in the renunciations,

and if the corporation does not so reduce the amounts and file that statement with the Minister within 30 days after notice in writing by the Minister is forwarded to the corporation that such a reduction is or will be required for the purposes of any assessment of tax under this Part, the Minister may, for the purposes of this section, reduce the amounts purported to be renounced by the corporation to one or more persons to effect a reduction in the total of the amounts so purported to be renounced by the amount of the excess, and in any such case, notwithstanding subsections (12.61), (12.63) and (12.65), the amount renounced to each of the persons shall be deemed to be the amount as reduced by the corporation or the Minister, as the case may be.

The 1996 Budget amendments make 66(12.73) apply to excess renounced amounts on a renunciation-by-renunciation basis, in light of the special treatment of renunciations of anticipated expenditures under 66(12.66). This special treatment is necessary because there are expected to be cases where an issuing corporation fails to incur amounts that have been renounced by it under the new rules.

The 1996 Budget amendments also deal explicitly with renunciations that can be made, under the look-back rule in 66(12.66), of expenditures that will be incurred after the renunciation is made. Where renunciations using the look-back rule are made, the issuing corporation must file the statement with Revenue Canada without any demand for it. The statement must be filed before March of the year following the calendar year of the renunciation. Note that adjustments under 66(12.73) will not affect the issuing corporation's liability under new Part XII.6 (see 211.91).

66(12.73) amended by 1992 Economic Statement, effective for renunciations made after December 2, 1992, to add reference to 66(12.601).

**(12.74) Late filed forms** — A corporation or partnership may file with the Minister a document referred to in subsection (12.68), (12.69), (12.691), (12.7) or (12.701) after the particular day on or before which the document is required to be filed under the applicable subsection and the document shall, except for the purposes of this subsection and subsection (12.75), be deemed to have been filed on the day on or before which it was required to be filed if

(a) if it is filed

(i) on or before the day that is 90 days after the particular day, or

(ii) after that day that is 90 days after the particular day where, in the opinion of the Minister, the circumstances are such that it would be just and equitable to permit the document to be filed; and

(b) the corporation or partnership, as the case may be, pays to the Receiver General at the time of filing a penalty in respect of the late filing.

**Related Provisions**: 66(12.75) — Penalty.

**Notes**: 66(12.74)(a)(ii) added by 1991 technical bill, effective for documents filed after June 1988. Reference to 66(12.691) and (12.701) added by 1991 technical bill, effective July 14, 1990.

**(12.741) Late renunciation** — Where a corporation purports to renounce an amount under subsection (12.6), (12.601) or (12.62) after the period in which the corporation was entitled to renounce the amount, the amount is deemed, except for the purposes of this subsection and subsections (12.7) and (12.75), to have been renounced at the end of the period if

(a) the corporation purports to renounce the amount

(i) on or before the day that is 90 days after the end of that period, or

(ii) after the day that is 90 days after the end of that period where, in the opinion of the Minister, the circumstances are such that it would be just and equitable that the amount be renounced; and

(b) the corporation pays to the Receiver General a penalty in respect of the renunciation not more than 90 days after the renunciation.

**Related Provisions**: 66(12.75) — Penalty.

**Notes**: 66(12.741) amended by 1996 Budget, effective for renunciations made in 1999 or later. The substantive change was the elimination of a reference to 66(12.64). For renunciations made before 1999, read:

> (12.741) Where a corporation purports to renounce an amount under subsection (12.6), (12.601), (12.62) or (12.64) after the period during which the corporation would otherwise be entitled to renounce the amount, the amount shall, except for the purposes of this subsection and subsections (12.7) and (12.75), be deemed to have been renounced at the end of the period if

66(12.741) added by 1992 Economic Statement, effective for renunciations purported to be made after February 1993.

**(12.75) Penalty** — For the purposes of subsections (12.74) and (12.741), the penalty in respect of the late filing of a document referred to in subsection (12.68), (12.69), (12.691), (12.7) or (12.701) or in respect of a renunciation referred to in subsection (12.741) is the lesser of $15,000 and

(a) where the penalty is in respect of the late filing of a document referred to in subsection (12.68), (12.69) or (12.7), the greater of

   (i) $100, and

   (ii) ¼ of 1% of the maximum amount in respect of the Canadian exploration expenses and Canadian development expenses renounced or attributed or to be renounced or attributed as set out in the document;

(b) where the penalty is in respect of the late filing of a document referred to in subsection (12.691) or (12.701), the greater of

   (i) $100, and

   (ii) ¼ of 1% of the assistance reported in the document; and

(c) where the penalty is in respect of a renunciation referred to in subsection (12.741), the greater of

   (i) $100, and

   (ii) ¼ of 1% of the amount of the renunciation.

**Notes**: 66(12.75)(a)(ii) amended by 1996 Budget, effective for renunciations made in 1999 or later, to delete reference to Canadian oil and gas property expenses.

Opening words of 66(12.75) amended to add reference to 66(12.741), and 66(12.75)(c) added, by 1992 Economic Statement, effective for renunciations purported to be made after February 1993. 66(12.75)(c) then amended retroactively by 1995-97 technical bill, retroactive to its introduction, to correct reference from (12.74) to (12.741).

66(12.75) amended by 1991 technical bill, effective December 18, 1991. For documents filed from July 14, 1990 through December 17, 1991, the penalty in respect of the late filing of a document referred to in subsection (12.691) or (12.701) is nil.

From July 1, 1988 through December 17, 1991, the penalty in respect of the late filing of a document referred to in 66(12.68), (12.69) or (12.7) is the lesser of

(a) $15,000, and

(b) ¼ of 1% of the maximum amount in respect of the Canadian exploration expenses, Canadian development expenses and Canadian oil and gas property expenses renounced, to be renounced, attributed or to be attributed as set out in the document.

**(13) Limitation** — Where a taxpayer has incurred an outlay or expense in respect of which a deduction from income is authorized under more than one provision of this section or section 66.1, 66.2 or 66.4, the taxpayer is not entitled to make the deduction under more than one provision but is entitled to select the provision under which to make the deduction.

**Related Provisions**: See Related Provisions and Definitions at end of s. 66.

**I.T. Application Rules**: 29(1)–(4), (6)–(34).

**(13.1) Short taxation years** — Where a taxpayer has a taxation year that is less than 51 weeks, the amount determined in respect of the year under any of subparagraph 66(4)(b)(i) and paragraphs 66.2(2)(c), 66.4(2)(b) and 66.7(4)(a) and (5)(a) shall not exceed that proportion of the amount otherwise determined thereunder that the number of days in the year is of 365.

---

**Proposed Amendment — 66(13.1)**

**(13.1) Short taxation year** — Where a taxpayer has a taxation year that is less than 51 weeks, the amount determined in respect of the year under each of subparagraph (4)(b)(i), paragraph 66.2(2)(c), subparagraph (b)(i) of the definition "global foreign resource limit" in subsection 66.21(1), subparagraph 66.21(4)(a)(i), clause 66.21(4)(a)(ii)(B) and paragraphs 66.4(2)(b) and 66.7(2.3)(a), (4)(a) and (5)(a) shall not exceed that proportion of the amount otherwise determined that the number of days in the year is of 365.

**Application**: The December 21, 2000 draft legislation, subsec. 27(10), will amend subsec. 66(13.1) to read as above, applicable to taxation years that begin after 2000.

**Technical Notes**: Subsection 66(13.1) limits the amount of FEDE, Canadian development expenses and Canadian oil and gas property expenses that a taxpayer may deduct in computing income where the amount is based on a percentage of the unclaimed balance. For a taxation year that is less than 51 weeks, the amount that may be deducted cannot exceed that portion of the amount otherwise determined that the number of days in the taxation year is of 365.

Subsection 66(13.1) is amended to similarly apply in determining the amount of foreign resources expenses deductible under new subsection 66.21(4) and successor foreign resource expenses deductible under new subsection 66.7(2.3).

---

**Related Provisions**: 20(1)(mm) — Deductions — injection substances; 66(4.3)(b), 66.21(5)(b) — No application to individual part-year resident. See additional Related Provisions and Definitions at end of s. 66.

**(14) Amounts deemed deductible under this subdivision** — For the purposes of section 3, any amount deductible under the *Income Tax Application Rules* in respect of this subsection shall be deemed to be deductible under this subdivision.

**S. 66(14)**      Income Tax Act, Part I, Division B

**Related Provisions**: See Related Provisions and Definitions at end of s. 66.

**I.T. Application Rules**: 29, 30(3).

**(14.1) Designation respecting Canadian exploration expense** — A corporation may designate for a taxation year, by filing a designation in prescribed form with the Minister on or before the day on or before which it is required to file a return of its income for the year under section 150, a particular amount not exceeding the lesser of

(a) its prescribed Canadian exploration expense for the year, and

(b) its cumulative Canadian exploration expense at the end of the year,

and the particular amount shall be added in computing its cumulative offset account immediately before the end of the year and deducted in computing its cumulative Canadian exploration expense at any time after the end of the year.

**Related Provisions**: 66.1(3)(a) — Expenses of other taxpayers; 66.1(6) "cumulative Canadian exploration expense" K — Reduction in CCEE; 66.5(1) — Deduction from income — cumulative offset account. See additional Related Provisions and Definitions at end of s. 66.

**Regulations**: 1217 (prescribed Canadian exploration expense).

**Forms**: T2098: Designation by a corporation to increase its cumulative offset account.

**(14.2) Designation respecting cumulative Canadian development expense** — A corporation may designate for a taxation year, by filing a designation in prescribed form with the Minister on or before the day on or before which it is required to file a return of its income for the year under section 150, a particular amount not exceeding

(a) where a deduction has been made under subsection 66.2(2) in computing its income for the year, the lesser of

(i) 30% of its prescribed Canadian development expense for the year, and

(ii) the amount, if any, by which 30% of its cumulative Canadian development expense at the end of the year exceeds the amount, if any, deducted for the year under subsection 66.2(2) in computing its income for the year, or

(b) where a deduction has not been made under subsection 66.2(2) in computing its income for the year, the lesser of

(i) 30% of its prescribed Canadian development expense for the year, and

(ii) 30% of the amount, if any, of its adjusted cumulative Canadian development expense at the end of the year,

and the particular amount shall be added in computing its cumulative offset account immediately before the end of the year and deducted in computing its cumulative Canadian development expense at any time after the end of the year.

**Related Provisions**: 66(14.3) — Meaning of "adjusted cumulative Canadian development expense"; 66.2(5) "cumulative Canadian development expense" N — Reduction in CCDE; 66.5(1) — Deduction from income — cumulative offset account. See additional Related Provisions and Definitions at end of s. 66.

**Regulations**: 1218 (prescribed Canadian development expense).

**Forms**: T2098: Designation by a corporation to increase its cumulative offset account.

**(14.3) Definition of "adjusted cumulative Canadian development expense"** — For the purposes of paragraph (14.2)(b), "adjusted cumulative Canadian development expense" of a corporation at the end of a taxation year means the amount, if any, that would be its cumulative Canadian development expense at the end of the year, if no Canadian resource property were disposed of by it in the year.

**Related Provisions**: See Related Provisions and Definitions at end of s. 66.

**(14.4) Special cases** — Where, in the opinion of the Minister, the circumstances of a case are such that it would be just and equitable

(a) to permit a designation under subsection (14.1) or (14.2) to be filed after the day on or before which it is required by that subsection to be filed, or

(b) to permit a designation filed under subsection (14.1) or (14.2) to be amended,

the Minister may permit the designation to be filed or amended, as the case may be, after that day, and where the designation or amendment is filed pursuant to that permission, it shall be deemed to have been filed on the day on or before which it was required to be filed if

(c) it is filed with the Minister in prescribed form, and

(d) the corporation filing it pays to the Receiver General at the time of filing the penalty in respect of it,

and where a designation is amended under this subsection, the designation to which the amendment is made shall be deemed not to have been effective.

**Related Provisions**: See Related Provisions and Definitions at end of s. 66.

**(14.5) Penalty for late designation** — For the purposes of this section, the penalty in respect of a designation or amended designation referred to in paragraph (14.4)(a) or (b) is the lesser of

(a) an amount determined by the formula

$$.0025 \times A \times B$$

where

A is

(i) in the case of a late-filed designation, the amount designated therein, and

(ii) in the case of an amended designation, the amount, if any, by which the amount designated in the designation being amended differs from the amount designated in the amended designation, and

B is the number of months each of which is included in whole or in part in the period commencing on the day on or before which the designation was required to be filed under subsection (14.1) or (14.2), as the case may be, and ending on the day the late-filed designation or amended designation, as the case may be, is filed, and

(b) an amount, not exceeding $8,000, equal to the product obtained by multiplying $100 by the number of months each of which is included in whole or in part in the period referred to in the description of B in paragraph (a).

**Related Provisions**: See Related Provisions and Definitions at the end of s. 66.

### (14.6) Deduction of carved-out income — A taxpayer may deduct in computing the taxpayer's income under this Part for a taxation year, an amount equal to the total of the taxpayer's carved-out incomes for the year within the meaning assigned by subsection 209(1).

**Related Provisions**: See Related Provisions and Definitions at end of s. 66.

### (15) Definitions — In this section,

**Related Provisions**: 66.1(6.1) — Application to section 66.1; 66.2(5.1) — Application to section 66.2; 66.4(5.1) — Application to section 66.4; 66.7(18) — Application to section 66.7.

**Notes**: Before R.S.C. 1985 (5th Supp.) consolidation, effective for taxation years ending after November 1991, the opening words of 66(15) also referred to 66, 66.2, 66.4 and 66.7. That application is now provided by 66.1(6.1), 66.2(5.1), 66.4(5.1) and 66.7(18).

**"agreed portion"** in respect of a corporation that was a shareholder corporation of a joint exploration corporation means such amount as may be agreed on between the joint exploration corporation and the shareholder corporation not exceeding

(a) the total of all amounts each of which is a payment or loan referred to in paragraph (b) of the definition "shareholder corporation" in this subsection (except to the extent that the payment or loan was made by a shareholder corporation that was not a Canadian corporation and was used by the joint exploration corporation to acquire a Canadian resource property after December 11, 1979 from a shareholder corporation that was not a Canadian corporation) made by the shareholder corporation to the joint exploration corporation during the period it was a shareholder corporation of the joint exploration corporation,

minus

(b) the total of the amounts, if any, previously renounced by the joint exploration corporation under any of subsections (10) to (10.3) in favour of the shareholder corporation;

**Related Provisions**: 53(2)(f.1) — Deduction from ACB.

**Notes**: 66(15)"agreed portion" was 66(15)(a) before consolidation in R.S.C. 1985 (5th Supp.), effective for taxation years ending after November 1991. See Table of Concordance.

**Advance Tax Rulings**: ATR-60: Joint exploration corporations.

**"assistance"** means any amount, other than a prescribed amount, received or receivable at any time from a person or government, municipality or other public authority whether the amount is by way of a grant, subsidy, rebate, forgivable loan, deduction from royalty or tax, rebate of royalty or tax, investment allowance or any other form of assistance or benefit;

**Related Provisions**: 66(16) — Partnership deemed to be a person; 248(16) — GST input tax credit and rebate deemed to be government assistance.

**Notes**: 66(15)"assistance" was 66(15)(a.1) before consolidation in R.S.C. 1985 (5th Supp.), effective for taxation years ending after November 1991.

**"Canadian exploration and development expenses"** incurred by a taxpayer means any expense incurred before May 7, 1974 that is

(a) any drilling or exploration expense, including any general geological or geophysical expense, incurred by the taxpayer after 1971 on or in respect of exploring or drilling for petroleum or natural gas in Canada,

(b) any prospecting, exploration or development expense incurred by the taxpayer after 1971 in searching for minerals in Canada,

(c) the cost to the taxpayer of any Canadian resource property acquired by the taxpayer after 1971,

(d) the taxpayer's share of the Canadian exploration and development expenses incurred after 1971 by any association, partnership or syndicate in a fiscal period thereof, if at the end of that fiscal period the taxpayer was a member or partner thereof,

(e) any expense incurred by the taxpayer after 1971 pursuant to an agreement with a corporation under which the taxpayer incurred the expense solely in consideration for shares of the capital stock of the corporation issued to the taxpayer by the corporation or any interest in such shares or right thereto, to the extent that the expense was incurred as or on account of the cost of

(i) drilling or exploration activities, including any general geological or geophysical activities, in or in respect of exploring or drilling for petroleum or natural gas in Canada,

(ii) prospecting, exploration or development activities in searching for minerals in Canada, or

(iii) acquiring a Canadian resource property, and

(f) any annual payment made by the taxpayer for the preservation of a Canadian resource property, but, for greater certainty, does not include

(g) any consideration given by the taxpayer for any share or any interest therein or right thereto, except as provided by paragraph (e), or

(h) any expense described in paragraph (e) incurred by another taxpayer to the extent that the expense was, by virtue of that paragraph, a Canadian exploration and development expense of that other taxpayer;

**Related Provisions**: 49(2) — Where option expires; 53(2)(e)(i) — Deduction from ACB of shares; 66.7(1) — Deduction to successor corporation; 248(1)"Canadian exploration and development expenses" — Definition applies to entire Act. See additional Related provisions and Definitions at end of s. 66.

**Notes**: For expenses incurred now, see the definitions of "Canadian exploration expense" (66.1(6) — 100% deductible); "Canadian development expense" (66.2(5) — 30% deductible); and "Canadian oil and gas property expense" (66.4(5) — 10% deductible).

Para. (c) amended to add "after 1971" by 1995-97 technical bill, retroactive to taxation years that begin after 1984. The amendment was needed because of the broadening of 66(15)"Canadian resource property" in 1985 to include specified property acquired before 1972.

66(15)"Canadian exploration and development expenses" was 66(15)(b) before consolidation in R.S.C. 1985 (5th Supp.), effective for taxation years ending after November 1991. See Table of Concordance.

**Interpretation Bulletins**: IT-109R2: Unpaid amounts.

**"Canadian resource property"** of a taxpayer means any property of the taxpayer that is

(a) any right, licence or privilege to explore for, drill for or take petroleum, natural gas or related hydrocarbons in Canada,

(b) any right, licence or privilege to

(i) store underground petroleum, natural gas or related hydrocarbons in Canada, or

(ii) prospect, explore, drill or mine for minerals in a mineral resource in Canada,

(c) any oil or gas well in Canada or any real property in Canada the principal value of which depends on its petroleum or natural gas content (but not including any depreciable property used or to be used in connection with the extraction or removal of petroleum or natural gas therefrom),

### Proposed Amendment — 66(15)"Canadian resource property"(c)

(c) any oil or gas well in Canada or any real property in Canada the principal value of which depends on its petroleum or natural gas content (but not including any depreciable property),

**Application**: The December 21, 2000 draft legislation, subsec. 27(11), will amend para. (c) of the definition "Canadian resource property" in subsec. 66(15) to read as above, applicable to taxation years that begin after 2000.

**Technical Notes**: Paragraph (c) of that definition covers "any oil or gas well in Canada or any real property in Canada the principal value of which depends on its petroleum or natural gas content (but not including any depreciable property used or to be used in connection with the extraction or removal of petroleum or natural gas therefrom)". This paragraph is amended to delete the words "used or to be used in connection with the extraction or removal of petroleum or natural gas therefrom" following the words "depreciable property". This amendment parallels new paragraph (c) of the amended definition "foreign resource property" in subsection 248(1), as described in the commentary below. This amendment applies to taxation years that begin after 2000.

(d) any rental or royalty computed by reference to the amount or value of production from an oil or gas well in Canada or from a natural accumulation of petroleum or natural gas in Canada,

(e) any rental or royalty computed by reference to the amount or value of production from a mineral resource in Canada,

(f) any real property in Canada the principal value of which depends upon its mineral resource content (but not including any depreciable property used or to be used in connection with the extraction or removal of minerals therefrom), or

### Proposed Amendment — 66(15)"Canadian resource property"(f)

(f) any real property in Canada the principal value of which depends on its mineral resource content (but not including any depreciable property), or

**Application**: The December 21, 2000 draft legislation, subsec. 27(12), will amend para. (f) of the definition "Canadian resource property" in subsec. 66(15) to read as above, applicable to taxation years that begin after 2000.

**Technical Notes**: Paragraph (f) of that definition covers "any real property in Canada the principal value of which depends on its mineral resource content (but not including any depreciable property used or to be used in connection with the extraction or removal of minerals therefrom)". This paragraph is amended to delete the words "used or to be used in connection with the extraction or removal of minerals therefrom" following the words "depreciable property". This amendment parallels new paragraph (f) of the amended definition "foreign resource property" in subsection 248(1), as described in the commentary below. This amendment applies to taxation years that begin after 2000.

(g) any right to or interest in any property described in any of paragraphs (a) to (f), other than such a right or interest that the taxpayer has by virtue of being a beneficiary of a trust;

**Related Provisions**: 18.1(1)"right to receive production" — Canadian resource property excluded from matchable expenditure rules; 59(1) — Disposition of resource property; 66(5) — Dealers; 69 — Inadequate consideration and fair market value; 128.1(4)(b)(i) — Canadian resource property excluded from deemed disposition on emigration; 209 — Tax on carved-out income; 248(1)"Canadian resource property" — Definition applies to entire Act; *Interpretation Act* 8(2.1), (2.2) — Application to exclusive economic zone and continental shelf. See additional Related provisions and Definitions at end of s. 66.

**Notes**: 66(15)"Canadian resource property" was 66(15)(c) before consolidation in R.S.C. 1985 (5th Supp.), effective for taxation years ending after November 1991. See Table of Concordance.

**Interpretation Bulletins**: IT-125R4: Dispositions of resource properties; IT-273R2: Government assistance — general comments;

IT-291R2: Transfer of property to a corporation under subsection 85(1).

**I.T. Technical News**: No. 10 (net profits interests and proposed section 18.1).

**"drilling or exploration expense"** incurred on or in respect of exploring or drilling for petroleum or natural gas includes any expense incurred on or in respect of

(a) drilling or converting a well for the disposal of waste liquids from a petroleum or natural gas well,

(b) drilling for water or gas for injection into a petroleum or natural gas formation, or

(c) drilling or converting a well for the injection of water or gas to assist in the recovery of petroleum or natural gas from another well;

**Related Provisions**: 66(16) — Partnerships — person — taxation year; 87(4.4) — Flow-through shares.

**Notes**: 66(15)"drilling or exploration expense" was 66(15)(d) before consolidation in R.S.C. 1985 (5th Supp.), effective for taxation years ending after November 1991. See Table of Concordance.

**Regulations**: 6202, 6202.1 (prescribed share).

**Interpretation Bulletins**: IT-273R2: Government assistance — general comments; IT-400: Exploration and development expenses — meaning of principal-business corporation.

**"expense"**, incurred before a particular time by a taxpayer,

(a) includes an amount designated by the taxpayer at that time under paragraph 98(3)(d) or (5)(d) of the *Income Tax Act*, chapter 148 of the Revised Statutes of Canada, 1952, as a cost in respect of property that is a Canadian resource property or a foreign resource property,

but

(b) for greater certainty, does not include any amount paid or payable

(i) as consideration for services to be rendered after that time, or

(ii) as, on account or in lieu of payment of, or in satisfaction of, rent in respect of a period after that time;

**Related Provisions**: 66(15)"outlay" — same meaning as "expense".

**Notes**: 66(15)"expense" was 66(15)(g.2) and (g.3) before consolidation in R.S.C. 1985 (5th Supp.), effective for taxation years ending after November 1991. See Table of Concordance.

**I.T. Application Rules**: 69 (meaning of "*Income Tax Act*, chapter 148 of the Revised Statutes of Canada, 1952").

**Interpretation Bulletins**: IT-273R2: Government assistance — general comments; IT-503: Exploration and development shares.

**"flow-through share"** means a share (other than a prescribed share) of the capital stock of a principal-business corporation that is issued to a person under an agreement in writing entered into between the person and the corporation after February 1986, under which the corporation agrees for consideration that does not include property to be exchanged or transferred by the person under the agreement in circumstances in which section 51, 85, 85.1, 86 or 87 applies

(a) to incur, in the period that begins on the day the agreement was made and ends 24 months after the end of the month that includes that day, Canadian exploration expenses or Canadian development expenses in an amount not less than the consideration for which the share is to be issued, and

(b) to renounce, before March of the first calendar year that begins after that period, in prescribed form to the person in respect of the share, an amount in respect of the Canadian exploration expenses or Canadian development expenses so incurred by it not exceeding the consideration received by the corporation for the share,

and includes a right of a person to have such a share issued to that person and any interest acquired in such a share by a person pursuant to such an agreement;

**Related Provisions**: 66(12.6), (12.601) — Flow-through of expenditures to shareholder; 66(16) — Partnership deemed to be a person; 127.52(1)(e), (e.1) — Minimum tax; 248(1)"flow-through share" — Definition applies to entire Act.

**Notes**: See Notes to 66(12.6).

Opening words of "flow-through share" amended by 1991 technical bill. For shares issued pursuant to an agreement in writing entered into before July 14, 1990, ignore the words "for consideration that does not include property to be exchanged or transferred by the person under the agreement in circumstances in which section 51, 85, 85.1, 86 or 87 applies".

Paras. (a) and (b) amended by 1996 Budget, effective for renunciations made in 1999 or later. The substantive change was the elimination of references to COGPE. The other changes are purely cosmetic. For earlier renunciations, read:

(a) to incur, during the period commencing on the day the agreement was entered into and ending 24 months after the end of the month that includes that day, Canadian exploration expenses, Canadian development expenses or Canadian oil and gas property expenses in an amount not less than the consideration for which the share is to be issued, and

(b) to renounce, before March of the first calendar year beginning after that period, in prescribed form to the person in respect of the share, an amount in respect of the Canadian exploration expenses, Canadian development expenses or Canadian oil and gas property expenses so incurred by it not exceeding the consideration received by the corporation for the share,

Para. (b) amended by 1992 Economic Statement, effective for shares issued pursuant to an agreement entered into after February 1986, to change "within that period or within 30 days thereafter" to "before March of the first calendar year beginning after that period". See Notes to 66(12.6).

66(15)"flow-through share" was 66(15)(d.1) before consolidation in R.S.C. 1985 (5th Supp.), effective for taxation years ending after November 1991. See Table of Concordance.

**Regulations**: 6202(1), (2) (prescribed share).

**"foreign exploration and development expenses"** incurred by a taxpayer means

(a) any drilling or exploration expense, including any general geological or geophysical expense, incurred by the taxpayer after 1971 on or in respect of exploring or drilling for petroleum or natural gas outside Canada,

(b) any prospecting, exploration or development expense incurred by the taxpayer after 1971 in searching for minerals outside Canada,

---

**Proposed Amendment — 66(15)"foreign exploration and development expenses"(b)**

(b) any expense incurred by the taxpayer for the purpose of determining the existence, location, extent or quality of a mineral resource outside Canada, including any expense incurred in the course of

(i) prospecting,

(ii) carrying out geological, geophysical or geochemical surveys,

(iii) drilling by rotary, diamond, percussion or other method, or

(iv) trenching, digging test pits and preliminary sampling,

**Application**: The December 21, 2000 draft legislation, subsec. 27(13), will amend para. (b) of the definition "foreign exploration and development expenses" in subsec. 66(15) to read as above, applicable to expenses incurred after December 21, 2000, other than expenses incurred pursuant to an agreement in writing made before December 22, 2000.

**Technical Notes**: The definition "foreign exploration and development expenses" (FEDE) is set out in subsection 66(15). FEDE balances are deductible to the extent provided under subsection 66(4). Paragraph (b) of the definition includes in FEDE any prospecting, exploration or development expenses incurred by a taxpayer in searching for minerals outside Canada. A number of explicit exclusions from FEDE are provided under paragraphs (f) to (i) of the definition.

Paragraph (b) of the definition is amended so that prospecting, exploration and development expenses covered by that paragraph must be incurred for the purpose of determining the existence, location, extent or quality of a "mineral resource" (as defined in subsection 248(1)) outside Canada. This amendment makes paragraph (b) of the FEDE definition more consistent with paragraph (f) of the definition "Canadian exploration expense" in subsection 66.1(6). This amendment applies to expenses incurred after December 21, 2000, other than expenses incurred pursuant to an agreement in writing made before December 22, 2000.

---

(c) the cost to the taxpayer of any foreign resource property acquired by [the taxpayer],

(d) subject to section 66.8, the taxpayer's share of the foreign exploration and development expenses incurred after 1971 by a partnership in a fiscal period thereof, if at the end of that period the taxpayer was a member of the partnership, and

(e) any annual payment made by the taxpayer for the preservation of a foreign resource property,

but does not include

(f) any amount included at any time in the capital cost to the taxpayer of any depreciable property of a prescribed class,

(g) an expenditure incurred at any time after the commencement of production from a foreign resource property of the taxpayer in order to evaluate the feasibility of a method of recovery of petroleum, natural gas or related hydrocarbons from the portion of a natural reservoir to which the foreign resource property relates,

(h) an expenditure (other than a drilling expense) incurred at any time after the commencement of production from a foreign resource property of the taxpayer in order to assist in the recovery of petroleum, natural gas or related hydrocarbons from the portion of a natural reservoir to which the foreign resource property relates, or

(i) an expenditure incurred at any time relating to the injection of any substance to assist in the recovery of petroleum, natural gas or related hydrocarbons from a natural reservoir;

---

**Proposed Addition — 66(15)"foreign exploration and development expenses"(j)–(l)**

(j) an expenditure that is the cost, or any part of the cost, to the taxpayer of any depreciable property of a prescribed class that was acquired after December 21, 2000,

**Technical Notes**: Paragraph (j) of the definition is introduced to ensure that an expenditure that is the cost, or any part of the cost, to the taxpayer of depreciable property of a prescribed class is excluded from FEDE. This measure, which complements existing paragraph (f) of the definition, is provided for greater certainty and is consistent with similar language in the exclusions within the definitions "Canadian exploration expense" in subsection 66.1(6) and "Canadian development expense" in subsection 66.2(5). This amendment applies to property acquired after December 21, 2000.

(k) foreign resource expenses in respect of a country, or

**Technical Notes**: New paragraph (k) of the definition excludes foreign resource expense (as defined in the definition "foreign resource expense" in subsection 66.21(1)) from FEDE. Foreign resource expense (FRE) covers the same expenditures as FEDE (as amended), except that FRE expenditures are incurred in taxation years that begin after 2000 and FRE expenditures are explicitly linked to a particular country. This amendment applies to taxation years that begin after 2000.

(l) an expenditure made after February 27, 2000 by the taxpayer unless the expenditure was made

(i) pursuant to an agreement in writing made by the taxpayer before February 28, 2000,

(ii) for the acquisition of foreign resource property by the taxpayer, or

(iii) for the purpose of

(A) enhancing the value of foreign resource property that the taxpayer owned at the time the expenditure was incurred or that the taxpayer had a reasonable expectation of owning after that time, or

(B) assisting in evaluating whether a foreign resource property is to be acquired by the taxpayer;

**Technical Notes**: New paragraph (l) of the definition excludes expenditures made by a taxpayer after February 27, 2000 unless:

- the expenditure was made pursuant to an agreement in writing made by the taxpayer before February 28, 2000,
- the expenditure was for the acquisition of foreign resource property by the taxpayer, or
- the expenditure was incurred for the purpose of
  - enhancing the value of foreign resource property that the taxpayer owned at the time the expenditure was incurred or that the taxpayer had a reasonable expectation of owning after that time, or
  - assisting in evaluating whether a foreign resource property is to be acquired by the taxpayer.

**Application**: The December 21, 2000 draft legislation, subsec. 27(14), will add paras. (j) to (l) to the definition "foreign exploration and development expenses" in subsec. 66(15), para. (j) applicable after 2000, para. (k) applicable to taxation years that begin after 2000, and para. (l) applicable after February 27, 2000.

**Notice of Ways and Means Motion, federal budget, February 28, 2000**: [See Resolutions (34) and (35) under 66(4)(b)(ii) — ed.]

**Related Provisions**: 66(4) — Deduction for FEDE; 66.7(2) — Deduction to successor corporation; 80(8)(e) — Reduction of FEDE on debt forgiveness; 248(1)"foreign exploration and development expenses" — Definition applies to entire Act.

**Notes**: Paras. (f) through (i) added by 1996 Budget, effective for taxation years that end after December 5, 1996. These exclusions from FEDE are consistent with parallel changes to 66.1(6)"Canadian exploration expense".

66(15)"foreign exploration and development expenses" was 66(15)(e) before consolidation in R.S.C. 1985 (5th Supp.), effective for taxation years ending after November 1991. See Table of Concordance.

**Interpretation Bulletins**: IT-109R2: Unpaid amounts; IT-273R2: Government assistance — general comments.

**"foreign resource property"** of a taxpayer means any property that would be a Canadian resource property of the taxpayer if the definition "Canadian resource property" in this subsection were read as if the references therein to "in Canada" were read as references to "outside Canada";

**Related Provisions**: 18.1(1)"right to receive production" — foreign resource property excluded from matchable expenditure rules; 66.7(2.3) — Successor corporation rules; 248(1)"foreign resource property" — Definition applies to entire Act, and definition of FRP in respect of a country.

**Notes**: 66(15)"foreign resource property" was 66(15)(f) before consolidation in R.S.C. 1985 (5th Supp.), effective for taxation years ending after November 1991.

**Interpretation Bulletins**: IT-125R4: Dispositions of resource properties; IT-273R2: Government assistance — general comments.

**"joint exploration corporation"** means a principal-business corporation that has not at any time since its incorporation had more than 10 shareholders, not including any individual holding a share for the sole purpose of qualifying as a director;

**Related Provisions**: 248(1)"Joint exploration corporation" — Definition applies to entire Act.

**Notes**: 66(15)"joint exploration corporation" was 66(15)(g) before consolidation in R.S.C. 1985 (5th Supp.), effective for taxation years ending after November 1991.

**Interpretation Bulletins**: IT-400: Exploration and development expenses — meaning of principal-business corporation; IT-273R2: Government assistance — general comments.

**Advance Tax Rulings**: ATR-60: Joint exploration corporations.

**"oil or gas well [para. 66(15)(g.1)]"** — [Repealed under former Act]

**Notes**: 66(15)(g.1), repealed by 1985 technical bill, defined "oil or gas well". The definition was changed and moved to 248(1).

**"original owner"** of a Canadian resource property or a foreign resource property means a person

(a) who owned the property and disposed of it to a corporation that acquired it in circumstances in which subsection 29(25) of the *Income Tax Application Rules* or subsection 66.7(1), (2), (3), (4) or (5) applies, or would apply if the corporation had continued to own the property, to the corporation in respect of the property, and

(b) who would, but for subsection 66.7(12), (13) or (17), as the case may be, be entitled in computing that person's income for a taxation year ending after that person disposed of the property to a deduction under section 29 of the *Income Tax Application Rules* or subsection (2), (3) or (4), 66.1(2) or (3), 66.2(2) or 66.4(2) of this Act in respect of expenses described in subparagraph 29(25)(c)(i) or (ii) of that Act, Canadian exploration and development expenses, foreign exploration and development expenses, Canadian exploration expenses, Canadian development expenses or Canadian oil and gas property expenses incurred by the person before the person disposed of the property;

**Proposed Amendment — 66(15)"original owner"**

**"original owner"** of a Canadian resource property or a foreign resource property means a person

(a) who owned the property and disposed of it to a corporation that acquired it in circumstances in which subsection 29(25) of the *Income Tax Application Rules* or subsection 66.7(1), (2), (2.3), (3), (4) or (5) applies, or would apply if the corporation had continued to own the property, to the corporation in respect of the property, and

(b) who would, but for subsection 66.7(12), (13), (13.1) or (17), as the case may be, be entitled in computing that person's income for a taxation year that ends after that person disposed of the property to a deduction under section 29 of the *Income Tax Application Rules* or subsection (2), (3) or (4), 66.1(2) or (3), 66.2(2), 66.21(4) or 66.4(2) of this Act in respect of expenses described in subparagraph 29(25)(c)(i) or (ii) of that Act, Canadian exploration and development expenses, foreign resource pool expenses, Canadian exploration expenses, Canadian development expenses or Canadian oil and gas property expenses incurred by the person before the person disposed of the property;

**Application**: The December 21, 2000 draft legislation, subsec. 27(15), will amend the definition "original owner" in subsec. 66(15) to read as above, applicable to taxation years that begin after 2000.

**Technical Notes**: An "original owner" of a resource property for the purposes of the successor rules in section 66.7 is defined as a person

- who owned the resource property and disposed of it to a corporation in circumstances where the successor rules apply to the corporation in respect of the property, and
- who would, but for that disposition and the resulting reduction of resource pools available to the person, be entitled in computing income for a taxation year that ends after the disposition to a deduction in respect of the resource expenses incurred by the person prior to the disposition.

This definition is amended to add cross-references to the new rules governing the treatment of foreign resource expenses under subsections 66.21(4) and 66.7(2.3) and (13.1). Similarly, the existing reference to "foreign exploration and development expenses" (as defined in subsection 66(15)) is replaced by a more general reference to "foreign resource pool expenses" (as defined in subsection 248(1)).

**Notes**: 66(15)"original owner" was 66(15)(g.11) before consolidation in R.S.C. 1985 (5th Supp.), effective for taxation years ending after November 1991. See Table of Concordance.

**"outlay"** made before a particular time by a taxpayer, has the meaning assigned to the expression "expense" by this subsection;

**Notes**: 66(15)"outlay" was included in the definitions of "expense" in 66(15)(g.2) and (g.3) before consolidation in R.S.C. 1985 (5th Supp.), effective for taxation years ending after November 1991.

**Interpretation Bulletins**: IT-273R2: Government assistance — general comments; IT-503: Exploration and development shares.

**"predecessor owner"** of a Canadian resource property or a foreign resource property means a corporation

(a) that acquired the property in circumstances in which subsection 29(25) of the *Income Tax Application Rules* or subsection 66.7(1), (2), (3), (4) or (5) applies, or would apply if the corporation had continued to own the property, to the corporation in respect of the property,

(b) that disposed of the property to another corporation that acquired it in circumstances in which subsection 29(25) of the *Income Tax Application Rules* or subsection 66.7(1), (2), (3), (4) or (5) applies, or would apply if the other corporation had continued to own the property, to the other corporation in respect of the property, and

(c) that would, but for subsection 66.7(14), (15) or (17), as the case may be, be entitled in computing its income for a taxation year ending after it disposed of the property to a deduction under subsection 29(25) of the *Income Tax Application Rules* or subsection 66.7(1), (2), (3), (4) or (5) in respect of expenses incurred by an original owner of the property;

**Proposed Amendment — 66(15)"predecessor owner"**

**"predecessor owner"** of a Canadian resource property or a foreign resource property means a corporation

(a) that acquired the property in circumstances in which subsection 29(25) of the *Income Tax Application Rules* or subsection 66.7(1), (2), (2.3), (3), (4) or (5) applies, or would apply if the corporation had continued to own the property, to the corporation in respect of the property,

(b) that disposed of the property to another corporation that acquired it in circumstances in which subsection 29(25) of the *Income Tax Application Rules* or subsection 66.7(1), (2), (2.3), (3), (4) or (5) applies, or would apply if the other corporation had continued to own the property, to the other corporation in respect of the property, and

(c) that would, but for subsection 66.7(14), (15), (15.1) or (17), as the case may be, be entitled in computing its income for a taxation year ending after it disposed of the property to a deduction under subsection 29(25) of the *Income Tax Application Rules* or subsection 66.7(1), (2), (2.3), (3), (4) or (5) in respect of expenses incurred by an original owner of the property;

**Application**: The December 21, 2000 draft legislation, subsec. 27(15), will amend the definition "predecessor owner" in subsec. 66(15) to read as above, applicable to taxation years that begin after 2000.

**Technical Notes**: A "predecessor owner" of a resource property for the purposes of the successor rules in section 66.7 is defined as a corporation

- that acquired the resource property in circumstances where the successor rules apply to it in respect of the property,
- that disposed of the property to another corporation in circumstances where the successor rules apply to the other corporation in respect of the property, and
- that would, but for the disposition and resulting reduction of successor pools available to the corporation, be entitled in computing its income from the property for a taxation year ending after the disposi-

Subdivision e — Deductions in Computing Income       S. 66(15) pro

> tion to a deduction in respect of the resource expenses incurred by an original owner of the property.
> This definition is amended to add cross-references to the new rules governing the treatment of foreign resource expenses under new subsections 66.7(2.3) and (15.1).

**Notes**: 66(15)"predecessor owner" was 66(15)(g.4) before consolidation in R.S.C. 1985 (5th Supp.), effective for taxation years ending after November 1991. See Table of Concordance.

**"principal-business corporation"** means a corporation the principal business of which is any of, or a combination of,

(a) the production, refining or marketing of petroleum, petroleum products or natural gas,

(a.1) exploring or drilling for petroleum or natural gas,

(b) mining or exploring for minerals,

(c) the processing of mineral ores for the purpose of recovering metals or minerals from the ores,

(d) the processing or marketing of metals or minerals that were recovered from mineral ores and that include metals or minerals recovered from mineral ores processed by the corporation,

(e) the fabrication of metals,

(f) the operation of a pipeline for the transmission of oil or gas,

(f.1) the production or marketing of calcium chloride, gypsum, kaolin, sodium chloride or potash,

(g) the manufacturing of products, where the manufacturing involves the processing of calcium chloride, gypsum, kaolin, sodium chloride or potash,

(h) the generation of energy using property described in Class 43.1 of Schedule II to the *Income Tax Regulations*, and

(i) the development of projects for which it is reasonable to expect that at least 50% of the capital cost of the depreciable property to be used in each project would be the capital cost of property described in Class 43.1 of Schedule II to the *Income Tax Regulations*,

or a corporation all or substantially all of the assets of which are shares of the capital stock or indebtedness of one or more principal-business corporations that are related to the corporation (otherwise than because of a right referred to in paragraph 251(5)(b));

**Related Provisions**: 66(2) — Expenses of special products corporations; 66.1(2) — Deduction for principal-business corporation; 66.1(3) — Deduction for corporation that is a principal-business corporation solely under paras. (h) and (i); 115(4) — Non-resident's income from Canadian resource property. See additional Related Provisions at end of s. 66.

**Notes**: Paras. (h) and (i) added by 1996 Budget, effective December 6, 1996. See 66.1(6)"Canadian renewable and conservation expense".

Definition "principal-business corporation" amended by 1993 technical bill, effective for 1993 and later taxation years, except for transactions and events that occurred before the 1993 taxation year. As well, a corporation could elect for the new version not to apply to its 1993 to 1996 taxation years by notifying Revenue Canada in writing by December 31, 1994. Where the old version applies, read:

"principal-business corporation" means a corporation whose principal business is

(a) production, refining or marketing of petroleum, petroleum products or natural gas, or exploring or drilling for petroleum or natural gas,

(b) mining or exploring for minerals,

(c) processing mineral ores for the purpose of recovering metals therefrom,

(d) a combination of

(i) processing mineral ores for the purpose of recovering metals therefrom, and

(ii) processing metals recovered from the ores so processed,

(e) fabricating metals,

(f) operating a pipeline for the transmission of oil or natural gas, or

(g) production or marketing of sodium chloride or potash, or whose business includes manufacturing products the manufacturing of which involves processing sodium chloride or potash,

or a corporation all or substantially all of the assets of which are shares of the capital stock of one or more other corporations that are related to the corporation (otherwise than by reason of a right referred to in paragraph 251(5)(b)) and whose principal business is described in any of paragraphs (a) to (g);

66(15)"principal-business corporation" was 66(15)(h) before consolidation in R.S.C. 1985 (5th Supp.), effective for taxation years ending after November 1991. See Table of Concordance.

The CCRA takes the position that "all or substantially all", used in the closing words of the definition, means 90% or more.

For the administrative definition of "pipeline", used in para. (f), see Interpretation Bulletin IT-482.

**Interpretation Bulletins**: IT-273R2: Government assistance — general comments; IT-400: Exploration and development expenses — meaning of principal-business corporation; IT-482: CCA — Pipelines.

**Advance Tax Rulings**: ATR-60: Joint exploration corporations.

**"production"** from a Canadian resource property or a foreign resource property means

(a) petroleum, natural gas and related hydrocarbons produced from the property,

(b) heavy crude oil produced from the property processed to any stage that is not beyond the crude oil stage or its equivalent,

(c) ore (other than iron ore or tar sands) produced from the property processed to any stage that is not beyond the prime metal stage or its equivalent,

(d) iron ore produced from the property processed to any stage that is not beyond the pellet stage or its equivalent,

(e) tar sands produced from the property processed to any stage that is not beyond the crude oil stage or its equivalent, and

(f) any rental or royalty from the property computed by reference to the amount or value of the production of petroleum, natural gas or related hydrocarbons or ore;

**Notes**: 66(15)"production" was 66(15)(h.01), before consolidation in R.S.C. 1985 (5th Supp.), effective for taxation years ending after November 1991. See Table of Concordance.

**"reserve amount"** of a corporation for a taxation year in respect of an original owner or predecessor owner of a Canadian resource property means the amount determined by the formula

$$A - B$$

where

A is the total of all amounts that are

(a) required by subsection 59(2) to be included in computing the corporation's income for the year, and

(b) in respect of a reserve, deducted in computing the income of the original owner or predecessor owner and deemed by paragraph 87(2)(g) or by virtue of that paragraph and paragraph 88(1)(e.2) to have been deducted by the corporation as a reserve in computing its income for a preceding taxation year, and

B is the total of amounts deducted in computing the corporation's income for the year by virtue of subsection 64(1), (1.1) or (1.2) in respect of dispositions by the original owner or predecessor owner, as the case may be;

**Related Provisions**: 257 — Formula cannot calculate to less than zero.

**Notes**: 66(15)"reserve amount" was 66(15)(h.02) before consolidation in R.S.C. 1985 (5th Supp.), effective for taxation years ending after November 1991. See Table of Concordance.

Reference to s. 64 in 66(15)"reserve amount" should be to s. 64 of R.S.C. 1952, c. 148, meaning the version repealed by 1981 Budget. See Notes to 64.

**"selling instrument"** in respect of flow-through shares means a prospectus, registration statement, offering memorandum, term sheet or other similar document that describes the terms of the offer (including the price and number of shares) pursuant to which a corporation offers to issue flow-through shares;

**Notes**: 66(15)"selling instrument" was 66(15)(h.1) before consolidation in R.S.C. 1985 (5th Supp.), effective for taxation years ending after November 1991.

**"shareholder corporation"** of a joint exploration corporation means a corporation that for the period in respect of which the expression is being applied

(a) was a shareholder of the joint exploration corporation, and

(b) made a payment or loan to the joint exploration corporation in respect of Canadian exploration and development expenses, a Canadian exploration expense, a Canadian development expense or a Canadian oil and gas property expense incurred or to be incurred by the joint exploration corporation.

**Notes**: 66(15)"shareholder corporation" was 66(15)(i) before consolidation in R.S.C. 1985 (5th Supp.), effective for taxation years ending after November 1991. See Table of Concordance.

**Advance Tax Rulings**: ATR-60: Joint exploration corporations.

### Proposed Addition — 66(15)"specified foreign exploration and development expense"

**"specified foreign exploration and development expense"** of a taxpayer in respect of a country (other than Canada) means an amount that is included in the taxpayer's foreign exploration and development expenses and that is

(a) a drilling or exploration expense, including any general geological or geophysical expense, incurred by the taxpayer on or in respect of exploring or drilling for petroleum or natural gas in that country,

(a.1) an expense incurred by the taxpayer after December 21, 2000 (otherwise than pursuant to an agreement in writing made before December 22, 2000) for the purpose of determining the existence, location, extent or quality of a mineral resource in that country, including any expense incurred in the course of

(i) prospecting,

(ii) carrying out geological, geophysical or geochemical surveys,

(iii) drilling by rotary, diamond, percussion or other methods, or

(iv) trenching, digging test pits and preliminary sampling,

(b) a prospecting, exploration or development expense incurred by the taxpayer before December 22, 2000 (or after December 21, 2000 pursuant to an agreement in writing made before December 22, 2000) in searching for minerals in that country,

(c) the cost to the taxpayer of the taxpayer's foreign resource property in respect of that country,

(d) an annual payment made by the taxpayer in a taxation year of the taxpayer for the preservation of a foreign resource property in respect of that country,

(e) an amount deemed by subsection 21(2) or (4) to be a foreign exploration and development expense incurred by the taxpayer, to the extent that it can reasonably be considered to relate to an amount that, without reference to this paragraph and paragraph (f), would be a specified foreign exploration and development expense in respect of that country, or

(f) subject to section 66.8, the taxpayer's share of the specified foreign exploration and development expenses of a partnership incurred in respect of that country in a fiscal period of the partnership if, at the end of that period, the taxpayer was a member of the partnership.

**Application**: The December 21, 2000 draft legislation, subsec. 27(16), will add the definition "specified foreign exploration and development expense" to subsec. 66(15), applicable after 1994.

**Technical Notes**: The new definition "specified foreign exploration and development expense" in subsection 66(15) provides for a subcategory of FEDE. The definition explicitly links FEDE (determined with reference to the amendments to the definition "foreign exploration and development expenses", described above) to the particular country in which the foreign resource property that relates to a given expenditure is situated. The definition is used in new subsections 66(4.1) and (4.2), amended subsection 66(12.4) and new subsections 66(12.41) and 66.7(2.1) and (2.2). For more detail, see the commentary on subsections 66(4.1) and (4.2).

This definition applies after 1994, given that those subsections can apply from as early as January 1, 1995.

**Related Provisions**: 66(4.1), (4.2) — Country-by-country allocation of specified FEDE; 248(1)"foreign resource property" — Meaning of foreign resource property in respect of a country.

**(15.1) Application of subsecs. 66.1(6), 66.2(5), 66.4(5) and 66.5(2)** — The definitions in subsections 66.1(6), 66.2(5), 66.4(5) and 66.5(2) apply to this section.

### Proposed Amendment — 66(15.1)

**(15.1) Other definitions** — The definitions in subsections 66.1(6), 66.2(5), 66.21(1), 66.4(5) and 66.5(2) apply in this section.

**Application**: The December 21, 2000 draft legislation, subsec. 27(17), will amend subsec. 66(15.1) to read as above, applicable after 2000.

**Technical Notes**: Subsection 66(15.1) provides that the definitions in sections 66.1, 66.2, 66.4 and 66.5 apply for the purposes of section 66.

Subsection 66(15) is amended so that this measure also applies with regard to the definitions in new section 66.21.

**Notes**: 66(15.1) added in the R.S.C. 1985 (5th Supp.) consolidation, effective for taxation years ending after November 1991. Formerly contained in the opening words to 66.1(6), 66.2(5), 66.4(5) and 66.5(2).

**(16) Partnerships** — For the purposes of subsections (12.6) to (12.73), the definitions "assistance" and "flow-through share" in subsection (15) and subsections (18), (19) and 66.3(3) and (4), a partnership is deemed to be a person and its taxation year is deemed to be its fiscal period.

**Notes**: Reference in 66(16) to 66(18) and (19) added by 1991 technical bill, retroactive to fiscal periods ending after February 1986. Reference to 66(12.6)–(12.66) changed to 66(12.6)–(12.73) by 1996 Budget, effective for fiscal periods that end after 1995.

**(17) Non-arm's length partnerships** — Where an expense would, but for paragraph (12.61)(b), be incurred during the first 60 days of a calendar year by a corporation and the expense is deemed by subsection (12.61) to be incurred by a partnership, the partnership and the corporation shall be deemed not to deal with each other at arm's length throughout that period for the purposes of paragraph (12.66)(d) only where a share of the expense of the partnership is included because of paragraph (h) of the definition "Canadian exploration expense" in subsection 66.1(6) in the Canadian exploration expense of the corporation or a member of the partnership with whom the corporation does not deal at arm's length at any time during that period.

**Notes**: 66(17) amended by 1991 technical bill, retroactive to fiscal periods ending after February 1986.

**(18) Members of partnerships** — For the purposes of this section, subsection 21(2), sections 59.1 and 66.1 to 66.7, paragraph (d) of the definition "investment expense" in subsection 110.6(1) and the descriptions of C and D in subsection 211.91(1), where a person's share of an outlay or expense made or incurred by a partnership in a fiscal period of the partnership is included in respect of the person under paragraph (d) of the definition "foreign exploration and development expenses" in subsection (15), paragraph (h) of the definition "Canadian exploration expense" in subsection 66.1(6), paragraph (f) of the definition "Canadian development expense" in subsection 66.2(5) or paragraph (b) of the definition "Canadian oil and gas property expense" in subsection 66.4(5), the portion of the outlay or expense so included is deemed, except for the purposes of applying the definitions "foreign exploration and development expenses", "Canadian exploration expense", "Canadian development expense" and "Canadian oil and gas property expense" in respect of the person, to be made or incurred by the person at the end of that fiscal period.

### Proposed Amendment — 66(18)

**(18) Members of partnerships** — For the purposes of this section, subsection 21(2), sections 59.1 and 66.1 to 66.7, paragraph (d) of the definition "investment expense" in subsection 110.6(1) and the descriptions of C and D in subsection 211.91(1), where a person's share of an outlay or expense made or incurred by a partnership in a fiscal period of the partnership is included in respect of the person under paragraph (d) of the definition "foreign exploration and development expenses" in subsection (15), paragraph (h) of the definition "Canadian exploration expense" in subsection 66.1(6), paragraph (f) of the definition "Canadian development expense" in subsection 66.2(5), paragraph (e) of the definition "foreign resource expenses" in subsection 66.21(1) or paragraph (b) of the definition "Canadian oil and gas property expense" in subsection 66.4(5), the portion of the outlay or expense so included is deemed, except for the purposes of applying the definitions "foreign exploration and development expenses", "Canadian exploration expense", "Canadian development expense", "foreign resource expense" and "Canadian oil and gas property expense" in respect of the person, to be made or incurred by the person at the end of that fiscal period.

**Application**: The December 21, 2000 draft legislation, subsec. 27(18), will amend subsec. 66(18) to read as above, applicable to fiscal periods that begin after 2000.

**Technical Notes**: Existing subsection 66(18) clarifies the tax treatment of a person (including a partnership) who is a member of a partnership involved in mining or oil and gas. Where a resource expenditure is attributed by the partnership to the member, the member is treated under this provision as having incurred the attributed expenditure at the end of the fiscal period in which that expenditure is incurred by the partnership to the extent that such attributed expenditure is included in the member's foreign exploration and development expense (FEDE), Canadian exploration expense (CEE), Canadian development expense (CDE) or Canadian oil and gas property expense (COGPE).

Subsection 66(18) is amended to provide the same tax treatment with regard to expenses that are a foreign resource expense, as defined in new subsection 66.21(1).

**Related Provisions**: 6(16) — Partnership deemed to be a person; 66.1(7) — Canadian exploration expense — share of partner; 66.2(6) — Canadian development expense — share of partner; 66.4(6) — Canadian oil and gas property expense — share of partner; 96(1)(d) — Partnerships — no deduction at partnership level; 127(9)"investment tax credit"(a.2), 127(9)"flow-through mining expenditure" — Investment tax credit.

**Notes**: 66(18) amended by 1996 Budget, effective for fiscal periods that end after 1996. The substantive change was to add reference to 211.91(1)C and D. The other changes were cosmetic. For fiscal periods ending before 1997, read:

(18) For the purposes of this section, subsection 21(2), sections 59.1 and 66.1 to 66.7 and paragraph (d) of the definition "investment expense" in subsection 110.6(1), where a person's share of an outlay or expense incurred by a partnership in a fiscal period thereof is included in respect of the person under paragraph (d) of the definition "foreign exploration and development expenses" in subsection (15), paragraph (h) of the definition "Canadian exploration expense" in subsection 66.1(6), paragraph (f) of the definition "Canadian development expense" in subsection 66.2(5) or paragraph (b) of the definition "Canadian oil and gas property expense" in subsection 66.4(5), the portion of the outlay or expense so included shall be deemed, except for the purposes of applying the definitions "foreign exploration and development expenses", "Canadian exploration expense", "Canadian development expense" and "Canadian oil and gas property expense" in respect of the person, to be made or incurred by the person at the end of that fiscal period.

66(18) added by 1991 technical bill, effective for fiscal periods ending after February 1986.

## (19) Renunciation by corporate partner, etc.
— A corporation is not entitled to renounce under subsection (12.6), (12.601) or (12.62) to a person a specified amount in respect of the corporation where the corporation would not be entitled to so renounce the specified amount if

(a) the expression "end of that fiscal period" in subsection (18) were read as "time the outlay or expense was made or incurred by the partnership"; and

(b) the expression "on the effective date of the renunciation" in each of paragraphs (12.61)(a) and (12.63)(a) were read as "at the earliest time that any part of such expense was incurred by the corporation".

**Related Provisions**: 66(16) — Partnership deemed to be a person; 66(20) — Meaning of "specified amount".

**Notes**: 66(19) amended by 1996 Budget, effective for renunciations made in 1999 or later. The substantive change was the elimination of references to 66(12.64) and (12.65)(b), and moving part of the subsec. to new 66(20). For renunciations made before 1999, read:

(19) Renunciation by member of partnership, etc. — Notwithstanding subsections (12.6), (12.601), (12.62) and (12.64), where at any time a corporation

(a) would, but for this subsection, be entitled to renounce under subsection (12.6), (12.601), (12.62) or (12.64) to another person

(i) all or part of the corporation's share of an outlay or expense made or incurred by a partnership of which the corporation is a member or former member at that time, or

(ii) all or part of an amount renounced to the corporation under subsection (12.6), (12.601), (12.62) or (12.64), and

(b) would not be entitled to so renounce the amount described in subparagraph (a)(i) or (ii) to the other person if

(i) the expression "end of that fiscal period" in subsection (18) were read as "time the outlay or expense was made or incurred by the partnership", and

(ii) the expression "on the effective date of the renunciation" in each of paragraphs (12.61)(a), (12.63)(a) and (12.65)(a) were read as "at the earliest time that any part of such expense was incurred by the corporation",

the corporation is not entitled to renounce that amount under subsection (12.6), (12.601), (12.62) or (12.64), as the case may be, at that time to the other person.

66(19) amended by 1992 Economic Statement, effective for renunciations of outlays or expenses made or incurred after December 2, 1992, to add references to 66(12.601).

66(19) added by 1991 technical bill, effective for renunciations after July 13, 1990, other than renunciation of outlays or expenses made or incurred pursuant to an agreement in writing entered into before July 14, 1990.

## (20) Specified amount
— For the purpose of subsection (19), a specified amount in respect of a corporation is an amount that represents

(a) all or part of the corporation's share of an outlay or expense made or incurred by a partnership of which the corporation is a member or former member; or

(b) all or part of an amount renounced to the corporation under subsection (12.6), (12.601) or (12.62).

**Notes**: 66(20) added by 1996 Budget, effective for renunciations made in 1999 or later. This rule was formerly part of 66(19), where it also applied to COGPE (i.e., included references to 66(12.64) and 66(12.65)(b)). For renunciations made before 1999, see former 66(19).

**Related Provisions [s. 66]**: 35(1)(e) — Prospectors and grubstakers; 66.1(6), 66.2(5), 66.4(5) — Definitions; 66.7 — Successor rules; 66.8(1) — Resource expenses of limited partner; 87(1.2) — Amalgamations — new corporation deemed continuation of predecessor; 88(1.5) — Winding-up — parent deemed continuation of subsidiary; 127.52(1)(e) — Addition to adjusted taxable income for minimum tax purposes; 209 — Tax on carved-out income; 248(16) — GST — input tax credit and rebate; 248(18) — GST — repayment of input tax credit.

**Definitions [s. 66]**: "acquired" — 256(7)–(9); "adjusted cost base" — 54, 248(1); "adjusted cumulative Canadian development expense" — 66(14.3); "affiliated" — 66(11.5), 251.1; "agreed portion" — 66(15); "amount" — 248(1); "arm's length" — 251(1); "assessment" — 248(1); "assistance" — 66(15), 79(4), 125.4(5), 248(16), 248(18); "associated" — 256; "beneficially interested" — 248(25); "business" — 248(1); "calendar year" — *Interpretation Act* 37(1)(a); "Canada" — 255, *Interpretation Act* 8(2.1), (2.2); "Canadian corporation" — 89(1), 248(1); "Canadian development expense" — 66.2(5), 248(1); "Canadian exploration and development expenses" — 66(15), 248(1); "Canadian exploration expense" — 66.1(6), 248(1); "Canadian oil and gas property expense" — 66.4(5), 248(1); "Canadian resource property" — 66(15), 248(1); "capital gain" — 39(1), 248(1); "capital property" — 54, 248(1); "control" — 256(6)–(9); "corporation" — 248(1), *Interpretation Act* 35(1); "cumulative Canadian development expense" — 66(15.1), 66.2(5); "cumulative Canadian exploration expense" — 66(15.1), 66.1(6); "cumulative Canadian oil and gas property expense" — 66(15.1), 66.4; "cumulative foreign resource expense" — 66.21(1); "cumulative offset account" — 66(15.1), 66.5(2); "depreciable property" — 13(21), 248(1); "disposition" — 54, 66.4(5), 248(1); "drilling or exploration expense", "expense" — 66(15); "fiscal period" — 66(16), 249(2), 249.1; "flow-through share" — 66(15); "foreign exploration and development expenses" — 66(15), 248(1); "foreign resource expense" — 66.21(1), 248(1); "foreign resource pool expense" — 66(15); "foreign resource property" — 66(15), 248(1); "global foreign resource limit" — 66.21(1); "Her Majesty" — *Interpretation Act* 35(1); "individual" — 248(1); "in respect of that country" — 248(1)"foreign resource property"; "joint exploration corporation" — 66(15); "majority interest partner", "mineral", "mineral resource", "Minister", "oil or gas well" — 248(1); "original owner", "outlay" — 66(15); partnership — see Notes to 96(1); "person" — 66(16), 248(1); "predecessor owner" — 66(15); "prescribed" — 248(1); "principal-business corporation", "production" — 66(15); "prohibited relationship" — 66(12.671); "property" — 248(1); "related" — 66(11.5), 251(2); "reserve amount" — 66(15); "resident in Canada" — 250; "restricted expense" — 66(15.1), 66.1(6); "selling instrument" — 66(15); "share", "shareholder" — 248(1); "shareholder corporation" — 66(15); "specified amount" — 66(20); "specified foreign exploration and development expense" — 66(15); "specified purpose" — 66(15.1), 66.1(6); "tar sands" — 248(1); "taxable capital amount" — 66(12.6011); "taxable capital employed in Canada" — 66(12.6012); "taxation year" — 66(16), 249; "taxpayer" — 248(1); "writing" — *Interpretation Act* 35(1).

**I.T. Application Rules [s. 66]**: 29, 30.

**Interpretation Bulletins [s. 66]**: IT-143R2: Meaning of "eligible capital expenditure"; IT-273R2: Government assistance — general comments.

**66.1 [Canadian exploration expenses] — (1) Amount to be included in income** — There shall be included in computing the amount referred to in paragraph 59(3.2)(b) in respect of a taxpayer for a taxation year the amount, if any, by which

(a) the total of all amounts referred to in the descriptions of F to M in the definition "cumulative Canadian exploration expense" in subsection (6) that are deducted in computing the taxpayer's cumulative Canadian exploration expense at the end of the year

exceeds the total of

(b) all amounts referred to in the descriptions of A to E.1 in the definition "cumulative Canadian exploration expense" in subsection (6) that are included in computing the taxpayer's cumulative Canadian exploration expense at the end of the year, and

(c) the total determined under subparagraph 66.7(12.1)(a)(i) in respect of the taxpayer for the year.

**Related Provisions**: 59(3.2)(b) — Income inclusion; 66.7(1) — Successor of Canadian exploration and development expenses; 87(1.3) — Amalgamations — shareholder corporation. See additional Related Provisions and Definitions at end of s. 66.1.

**Notes**: 66.1(1)(c) added by 1991 technical bill, effective for taxation years ending after February 17, 1987, except that for taxation years commencing before February 18, 1987, read "(iv)" in place of "(iv.2)" in 66.1(1)(b).

**(2) Deduction for certain principal-business corporations** — In computing the income for a taxation year of a principal-business corporation (other than a corporation that would not be a principal-business corporation if the definition "principal-business corporation" in subsection 66(15) were read without reference to paragraphs (h) and (i) of that definition, there may be deducted any amount that the corporation claims not exceeding the lesser of

(a) the total of

(i) the amount, if any, by which its cumulative Canadian exploration expense at the end of the year exceeds the amount, if any, designated by it for the year under subsection 66(14.1), and

(ii) the amount, if any, by which

(A) the total determined under subparagraph 66.7(12.1)(a)(i) in respect of the corporation for the year

exceeds

(B) the amount that would be determined under subsection (1) in respect of the corporation for the year, if that subsection were read without reference to paragraph (c) thereof, and

(b) the amount, if any, by which

(i) the amount that would be its income for the year if no deduction (other than a prescribed deduction) were allowed under this subsection or section 65

exceeds

(ii) the total of all amounts each of which is an amount deducted by the corporation under section 112 or 113 in computing its taxable income for the year.

**Related Provisions**: 20(1)(hh) — Repayments of inducements, etc.; 65 — Allowance for oil or gas well, mine or timber limit; 66 — Exploration and development expenses; 66.1(3) — Deduction for other taxpayers; 66.7(1) — Successor of Canadian exploration and development expenses; 127.52(1)(e) — Add-back of deduction

S. 66.1(2) — Income Tax Act, Part I, Division B

for minimum tax purposes; 209 — Tax on carved-out income. See additional Related Provisions and Definitions at end of s. 66.1.

**Notes**: Opening words of 66.1(2) amended by 1996 Budget to add the exclusion for a corporation described in 66(15)"principal-business corporation"(h) and (i), effective for taxation years that end after December 5, 1996. See 66.1(6)"Canadian renewable and conservation expense".

66.1(2) amended by 1992 Economic Statement, effective for taxation years ending after December 2, 1992, to add references to 66(12.601) to make the deduction of CCEE by a principal-business corporation optional rather than mandatory.

66.1(2) amended by 1991 technical bill, effective for taxation years ending after February 17, 1987.

**Regulations**: 1213 (prescribed deduction).

**Interpretation Bulletins**: IT-400: Exploration and development expenses — meaning of principal-business corporation.

**Advance Tax Rulings**: ATR-59: Financing exploration and development through limited partnerships.

**(3) Expenses of other taxpayer** — In computing the income for a taxation year of a taxpayer that is not a principal-business corporation, or that is a corporation that would not be a principal-business corporation if the definition "principal-business corporation" in subsection 66(15) were read without reference to paragraphs (h) and (i) of that definition, there may be deducted such amount as the taxpayer claims not exceeding the total of

(a) the amount, if any, by which the taxpayer's cumulative Canadian exploration expense at the end of the year exceeds the amount, if any, designated by the taxpayer for the year under subsection 66(14.1), and

(b) the amount, if any, by which

(i) the total determined under subparagraph 66.7(12.1)(a)(i) in respect of the taxpayer for the year

exceeds

(ii) the amount that would, but for paragraph (1)(c), be the amount determined under subsection (1) in respect of the taxpayer for the year.

**Related Provisions**: 66.1(2) — Deduction for principal-business corporation; 110.6(1)"investment expense"(d) — effect of claim under 66.1(3) on capital gains exemption; 127.52(1)(e) — Addback of deduction for minimum tax purposes. See additional Related Provisions and Definitions at end of s. 66.1.

**Notes**: Opening words of 66.1(3) amended by 1996 Budget to add the reference to 66(15)"principal-business corporation"(h) and (i), effective for taxation years that end after December 5, 1996. See 66.1(6)"Canadian renewable and conservation expense".

66.1(3) amended by 1991 technical bill, effective for taxation years ending after February 17, 1987.

**Advance Tax Rulings**: ATR-59: Financing exploration and development through limited partnerships.

**(4), (5)** [Repealed under former Act]

**Notes**: 66.1(4) and (5), repealed in 1987, dealt with a successor corporation's Canadian exploration expenses. The successor corporation rules are now in 66.7.

**(6) Definitions** — In this section,

**Notes**: Before consolidation in the R.S.C. 1985 (5th Supp.), effective for taxation years ending after November 1991, the opening words also referred to 66, 66.2 and 66.4. This application rule is now in 66(15.1), 66.2(5.1) and 66.4(5.1).

**"Canadian exploration expense"** of a taxpayer means any expense incurred after May 6, 1974 that is

(a) any expense including a geological, geophysical or geochemical expense incurred by the taxpayer (other than an expense incurred in drilling or completing an oil or gas well or in building a temporary access road to, or preparing a site in respect of, any such well) for the purpose of determining the existence, location, extent or quality of an accumulation of petroleum or natural gas (other than a mineral resource) in Canada,

(b) any expense (other than an expense incurred in drilling or completing an oil or gas well or in building a temporary access road to, or preparing a site in respect of, any such well) incurred by the taxpayer after March, 1985 for the purpose of bringing a natural accumulation of petroleum or natural gas (other than a mineral resource) in Canada into production and incurred prior to the commencement of the production (other than the production from an oil or gas well) in reasonable commercial quantities from such accumulation, including

(i) clearing, removing overburden and stripping, and

(ii) sinking a shaft or constructing an adit or other underground entry,

(c) any expense incurred before April, 1987 in drilling or completing an oil or gas well in Canada or in building a temporary access road to, or preparing a site in respect of, any such well,

(i) incurred by the taxpayer in the year, or

(ii) incurred by the taxpayer in any previous year and included by the taxpayer in computing the taxpayer's Canadian development expense for a previous taxation year,

if, within six months after the end of the year, the drilling of the well is completed and

(iii) it is determined that the well is the first well capable of production in commercial quantities from an accumulation of petroleum or natural gas (other than a mineral resource) not previously known to exist, or

(iv) it is reasonable to expect that the well will not come into production in commercial quantities within twelve months of its completion,

(d) any expense incurred by the taxpayer after March, 1987 and in a taxation year of the taxpayer in drilling or completing an oil or gas well in Canada or in building a temporary access road to, or preparing a site in respect of, any such well if

(i) the well resulted in the discovery of a natural accumulation of petroleum or natural gas and the discovery occurred at any time before six months after the end of the year,

### Proposed Amendment — 66.1(6)"Canadian exploration expense"(d)(i)

(i) the drilling or completing of the well resulted in the discovery that a natural underground reservoir contains petroleum or natural gas, where

(A) before the time of the discovery, no person or partnership had discovered that the reservoir contained either petroleum or natural gas, and

(B) the discovery occurred at any time before six months after the end of the year,

**Application**: Bill C-43 (First Reading September 20, 2000), subsec. 27(1), will amend subpara. (d)(i) of the definition "Canadian exploration expense" to read as above, applicable to expenses incurred after March 1987.

**Technical Notes**: Subsections 66.1(2) and (3) allow a taxpayer a deduction for a taxation year of up to 100 per cent of its cumulative Canadian exploration expense (cumulative CEE) at the end of the year. The definitions of CEE and cumulative CEE are contained in subsection 66.1(6).

Under subparagraph (d)(i) of the CEE definition, CEE includes a taxpayer's expenses incurred in a taxation year in drilling or completing an oil or gas well in Canada, provided that the well resulted in the discovery of a natural accumulation of petroleum or natural gas and the discovery occurred within six months after the end of the year. If such a discovery occurs later, subsection 66.1(9) generally allows for the expenditure to be treated as CEE incurred at the time of the discovery.

Subparagraph (d)(i) of the CEE definition was reviewed in the decision of the Tax Court of Canada in Resman Holdings Limited and *Dex Resources Limited v. Her Majesty the Queen*, [1998] 4 C.T.C. 2289, 98 DTC 1999. The Tax Court's decision stood for the proposition that the costs of a step-out well can qualify as CEE under this subparagraph, even though the well was being drilled merely to establish the extent of an already-known pool of oil. The result in the case was surprising, given that the consistent practice of the industry was that the cost of step-out wells was treated as Canadian development expense rather than CEE. The Tax Court's decision was reversed by the Federal Court of Appeal in a judgment delivered on May 24, 2000.

Subparagraph (d)(i) of the CEE definition and paragraph 66.1(9)(a) are amended to confirm that the costs of drilling or completing a well qualify as CEE under those provisions only in the event that the drilling or completing of the well resulted in the initial discovery that a natural underground reservoir contains petroleum or natural gas. These amendments apply to expenses incurred after March 1987.

These amendments apply, with necessary minor technical modifications to take into account the restructuring of subsection 66.1(6), to the version of the CEE definition in force prior to the enactment of the Revised Statutes of Canada, 1985, Fifth Supplement. Subsection 79(1) of the *Income Tax Application Rules* contains a rule to this effect.

**Department of Finance news release, July 23, 1999**: See under para. (k.1) below.

(ii) the well is abandoned in the year or within six months after the end of the year without ever having produced otherwise than for specified purposes,

(iii) the period of 24 months commencing on the day of completion of the drilling of the well ends in the year, the expense was incurred within that period and in the year and the well has not within that period produced otherwise than for specified purposes, or

(iv) there has been filed with the Minister, on or before the day that is 6 months after the end of the taxation year of the taxpayer in which the drilling of the well was commenced, a certificate issued by the Minister of Natural Resources certifying that, on the basis of evidence submitted to that Minister, that Minister is satisfied that

(A) the total of expenses incurred and to be incurred in drilling and completing the well, in building a temporary access road to the well and in preparing the site in respect of the well will exceed $5,000,000, and

(B) the well will not produce, otherwise than for a specified purpose, within the period of 24 months commencing on the day on which the drilling of the well is completed,

(e) any expense deemed by subsection (9) to be a Canadian exploration expense incurred by the taxpayer,

(f) any expense incurred by the taxpayer (other than an expense incurred in drilling or completing an oil or gas well or in building a temporary access road to, or preparing a site in respect of, any such well) for the purpose of determining the existence, location, extent or quality of a mineral resource in Canada including any expense incurred in the course of

(i) prospecting,

(ii) carrying out geological, geophysical or geochemical surveys,

(iii) drilling by rotary, diamond, percussion or other methods, or

(iv) trenching, digging test pits and preliminary sampling,

but not including

(v) any Canadian development expense, or

(vi) any expense that may reasonably be considered to be related to a mine that has come into production in reasonable commercial quantities or to be related to a potential or actual extension thereof,

(g) any expense incurred by the taxpayer after November 16, 1978 for the purpose of bringing a new mine in a mineral resource in Canada into production in reasonable commercial quantities and incurred before the coming into production of the new mine, including

(i) clearing, removing overburden and stripping, and

(ii) sinking a mine shaft, constructing an adit or other underground entry,

(g.1) any Canadian renewable and conservation expense incurred by the taxpayer,

(h) subject to section 66.8, the taxpayer's share of any expense referred to in any of paragraphs (a) to (d) and (f) to (g.1) incurred by a partnership in a fiscal period thereof, if at the end of the period the taxpayer is a member of the partnership, or

(i) any expense referred to in any of paragraphs (a) to (g) incurred by the taxpayer pursuant to an agreement in writing with a corporation, entered into before 1987, under which the taxpayer incurred the expense solely as consideration for shares, other than prescribed shares, of the capital stock of the corporation issued to the taxpayer or any interest in such shares or right thereto,

but, for greater certainty, shall not include

(j) any consideration given by the taxpayer for any share or any interest therein or right thereto, except as provided by paragraph (i),

(k) any expense described in paragraph (i) incurred by any other taxpayer to the extent that the expense was,

(i) by virtue of that paragraph, a Canadian exploration expense of that other taxpayer,

(ii) by virtue of paragraph (g) of the definition "Canadian development expense" in subsection 66.2(5), a Canadian development expense of that other taxpayer, or

(iii) by virtue of paragraph (c) of the definition "Canadian oil and gas property expense" in subsection 66.4(5), a Canadian oil and gas property expense of that other taxpayer,

### Proposed Addition — 66.1(6) "Canadian exploration expense"(k.1)

(k.1) an expense that is the cost, or any part of the cost, to the taxpayer of any depreciable property of a prescribed class that was acquired after 1987.

**Application**: Bill C-43 (First Reading September 20, 2000), subsec. 27(2), will add para. (k.1) to the definition "Canadian exploration expense", applicable to 1988 *et seq.*

**Technical Notes**: Paragraph (k.1) of the CEE definition is introduced to clarify that a taxpayer's CEE does not include the cost to the taxpayer of any depreciable property of a prescribed class. This amendment, as well as the related amendment to the definition "Canadian development expense", is for greater certainty. It responds to an issue raised by the decision of the Tax Court of Canada in *Robert Phénix v. Her Majesty the Queen*, [1998] 1 C.T.C. 2379, 97 DTC 1228, which is currently under appeal. [Appeal dismissed by FCA, Sept. 14, 2000, A-667-97 — ed.] This amendment applies to property acquired after 1987. Paragraph (k.1) complements the wording in existing paragraph (l) of the CEE definition, with the result that both paragraphs provide for the same exclusions with regard to property acquired after December 5, 1996.

It should be noted that new paragraph (k.1), unlike existing paragraph (l), does not explicitly exempt a "Canadian renewable and conservation expense" (CRCE) from being excluded from CEE. The explicit exemption is not considered necessary, since proposed paragraph 1102(1)(a.1) of the *Income Tax Regulations* results in any CRCE not being considered to be included in the capital cost of depreciable property.

These amendments apply, with necessary minor technical modifications to take into account the restructuring of subsection 66.1(6), to the version of the CEE definition in force prior to the enactment of the Revised Statutes of Canada, 1985, Fifth Supplement. Subsection 79(1) of the *Income Tax Application Rules* contains a rule to this effect.

**Department of Finance news release, July 23, 1999**: *Clarifying Amendments Regarding Tax Treatment of Resource Expenditures*

Finance Minister Paul Martin today released proposed amendments regarding the tax treatment of certain resource expenditures.

The proposed amendments are designed to deal with two related issues. First, they would ensure that taxpayers cannot obtain unintended tax relief by reclassifying certain Canadian development expenses (CDE), which qualify for a 30-per-cent annual write-off, as Canadian exploration expenses (CEE) qualifying for full deductibility in the year in which they were incurred. Second, these changes would prevent the reclassification, as CDE or CEE, of expenditures that have consistently been treated by taxpayers in the resource sector as relating to depreciable property, the cost of which is deducted as capital cost allowance (CCA) within the limits specified in the *Income Tax Act*.

Allowing these expenditures to be reclassified would result in a windfall for taxpayers. The windfall is due to the 100 per cent rate of write-off for CEE, as opposed to lower rates of write-offs for CDE and CCA. In the case of the reclassification of depreciable property, an additional unintended benefit would occur because, unlike CCA claims, CEE and CDE claims do not result in a reduction of the resource allowance deduction available to taxpayers in the resource sector.

The proposed amendments are intended to clarify the policy underlying the income tax law. Any necessary action will be taken to ensure that the right of parties involved in outstanding court cases to make arguments on the basis of the existing income tax law is not affected. However, the changes would prevent other taxpayers from seeking to benefit from the perceived deficiency in the existing law.

More detailed information on the proposed amendments is contained in the attached draft legislation and explanatory notes.

For further information: Victor Pietrow, Tax Policy Branch, (613) 992-3031; Karl Littler, Executive Assistant, to the Secretary of State, (613) 996-7861; Jean-Michel Catta, Public Affairs and Operations Division, (613) 996-8080.

(l) any amount (other than a Canadian renewable and conservation expense) included at any time in the capital cost to the taxpayer of any depreciable property of a prescribed class,

(m) an expenditure incurred at any time after the commencement of production from a Canadian resource property of the taxpayer in order to evaluate the feasibility of a method of recovery of, or to assist in the recovery of, petroleum, natural gas or related hydrocarbons from the portion of a natural reservoir to which the Canadian resource property relates,

(n) an expenditure incurred at any time relating to the injection of any substance to assist in the recovery of petroleum, natural gas or related hydrocarbons from a natural reservoir, or

(o) the taxpayer's share of any consideration, expense, cost or expenditure referred to in any of paragraphs (j) to (n) given or incurred by a partnership,

but any assistance that a taxpayer has received or is entitled to receive after May 25, 1976 in respect of or related to the taxpayer's Canadian exploration expense shall not reduce the amount of any of the expenses described in any of paragraphs (a) to (i);

**Related Provisions**: 13(7.5) — Depreciable property treatment for costs associated with building roads and similar projects; 66.1(8) — Expenses in first 60 days of year; 66.1(9)(a) — Past CDE deemed to be CEE; 66.1(10) — Certificate ceasing to be valid; 66.2(2) — Deduction — Canadian development expenses; 66.3 — Exploration and development shares; 127(9)"investment tax credit"(a.2), 127(9)"flow-through mining expenditure"(a), (b) — Investment tax credit; 248(1)"Canadian exploration expense" — Definition applies to entire Act; 248(16) — GST input tax credit and rebate deemed to be assistance; 248(18) — GST — repayment of input tax credit; *Interpretation Act* 8(2.1), (2.2) — Application to exclusive economic zone and continental shelf. See additional Related Provisions and Definitions at end of s. 66.1.

**Notes**: Para. (g.1), and reference to it in para. (h), added by 1996 Budget, effective December 6, 1996.

Paras. (l) to (o) added by 1996 Budget, effective for taxation years that end after December 5, 1996. Paras. (l) and (o) were (l) and (m) in the draft legislation of March 6, 1996.

66.1(6)"Canadian exploration expense" was 66.1(6)(a), before consolidation in R.S.C. 1985 (5th Supp.), effective for taxation years ending after November 1991. See Table of Concordance.

*Pre-1991 amendments*

In 66.1(6)(a)(iii) (now "Canadian exploration expense"(f)), parenthetical exclusion "(other than ... such well)" added by 1985 technical bill, effective for expenses incurred after May 9, 1985.

66.1(6)(a)(iii.1) (now "Canadian exploration expense"(g)) amended by 1985 technical bill, effective for expenses incurred after May 9, 1985, to add the reference to a "new mine". For earlier expenses, read:

> (iii.1) any expense incurred by him after November 16, 1978 for the purpose of bringing a mineral resource in Canada into production and incurred prior to the commencement of production from the resource in reasonable commercial quantities, including

Closing words of 66.1(6)(a) (now 66.1(6)"Canadian exploration expense" amended by 1986 Budget, effective for expenses incurred after December 19, 1986. For earlier expenses, read:

> but no amount of assistance or benefit that a taxpayer has received or is entitled to receive after May 25, 1976 from a government, municipality or other public authority in respect of or related to his Canadian exploration expense, whether as a grant, subsidy, forgivable loan, deduction from royalty or tax, investment allowance or any other form of assistance or benefit, shall reduce the amount of any of the expenses described in any of subparagraphs (i) to (v); and

For expenses incurred before 1981, an earlier edition of the Act should be consulted.

**Regulations**: 1215 (prescribed frontier exploration area); 6202 (prescribed share).

**Interpretation Bulletins**: IT-109R2: Unpaid amounts; IT-273R2: Government assistance — general comments; IT-503: Exploration and development shares.

**Advance Tax Rulings**: ATR-59: Financing exploration and development through limited partnerships.

**"Canadian renewable and conservation expense"** has the meaning assigned by regulation, and for the purpose of determining whether an outlay or expense meets the criteria set out in the Regulations in respect of Canadian renewable and conservation expenses, the *Technical Guide to Canadian Renewable and Conservation Expenses*, as amended from time to time and published by the Department of Natural Resources, shall apply conclusively with respect to engineering and scientific matters;

**Related Provisions**: 241(4)(d)(vi.1) — Communication with Dept. of Natural Resources permitted for purpose of determining whether an expense is a CRCE; Reg. 1102(1)(a.1) — CRCE ineligible for capital cost allowance.

**Notes**: Definition "Canadian renewable and conservation expense" added by 1996 Budget, effective December 6, 1996. In general terms, CRCE is certain intangible development costs associated with projects for which the required equipment primarily consists of Class 43.1 assets. See Reg. 1219. CRCE is fully deductible by being included in CEE: see 66.1(6)"Canadian exploration expense"(g.1) and 66.1(3). CRCE can be renounced under 66(12.6) by a principal-business corporation to investors in flow-through shares issued by it. See 66(15)"principal-business corporation"(h) and (i).

**Regulations**: 1219 (meaning of Canadian renewable and conservation expense).

**"cumulative Canadian exploration expense"** of a taxpayer at any time in a taxation year means the amount determined by the formula

$$(A + B + C + D + E + E.1) - (F + G + H + I + J + J.1 + K + L + M)$$

where

A  is the total of all Canadian exploration expenses made or incurred by the taxpayer before that time,

B  is the total of all amounts required by subsection (1) to be included in computing the amount referred to in paragraph 59(3.2)(b) for the taxpayer's taxation years ending before that time,

C  is the total of all amounts, except amounts in respect of interest, paid by the taxpayer after May 6, 1974 and before that time to Her Majesty in right of Canada in respect of amounts paid to the taxpayer before May 25, 1976 under the regulations referred to in paragraph (a) of the description of H,

D is the total of all amounts referred to in the description of G that are established by the taxpayer to have become bad debts before that time,

E is such part, if any, of the amount determined for J as has been repaid before that time by the taxpayer pursuant to a legal obligation to repay all or any part of that amount, and

E.1 is the total of all specified amounts determined under paragraph 66.7(12.1)(a) in respect of the taxpayer for taxation years ending before that time,

F is the total of all amounts deducted or required to be deducted in computing the taxpayer's income for a taxation year ending before that time in respect of the taxpayer's cumulative Canadian exploration expense,

G is the total of all amounts that became receivable by the taxpayer before that time that are to be included in the amount determined under this description by virtue of paragraph 66(12.1)(a) or (12.2)(a),

H is the total of all amounts paid to the taxpayer after May 6, 1974 and before May 25, 1976

(a) under the *Northern Mineral Exploration Assistance Regulations* made under an appropriations Act that provides for payments in respect of the Northern Mineral Grants Program, or

(b) pursuant to any agreement entered into between the taxpayer and Her Majesty in right of Canada under the Northern Mineral Grants Program or the Development Program of the Department of Indian Affairs and Northern Development,

to the extent that the amounts have been expended by the taxpayer as or on account of Canadian exploration and development expenses or Canadian exploration expense incurred by the taxpayer,

I is the total of all amounts each of which is an amount received before that time on account of any amount referred to in the description of D,

J is the total amount of assistance that the taxpayer has received or is entitled to receive in respect of any Canadian exploration expense incurred after 1980 or that can reasonably be related to Canadian exploration activities after 1980, to the extent that the assistance has not reduced the taxpayer's Canadian exploration expense by virtue of paragraph (9)(g),

J.1 is the total of all amounts by which the cumulative Canadian exploration expense of the taxpayer is required because of subsection 80(8) to be reduced at or before that time,

K is the total of all amounts that are required to be deducted before that time under subsection 66(14.1) in computing the taxpayer's cumulative Canadian exploration expense,

L is that portion of the total of all amounts deducted by the taxpayer under subsection 127(5) or (6) for a taxation year ending before that time that may reasonably be attributed to a qualified Canadian exploration expenditure (within the meaning assigned by subsection 127(9)) made in a preceding taxation year, and

### Proposed Amendment — 66.1(6) "cumulative Canadian exploration expense" L

L is that portion of the total of all amounts each of which was deducted by the taxpayer under subsection 127(5) or (6) for a taxation year that ended before that time and that can reasonably be attributed to a qualified Canadian exploration expenditure or a flow-through mining expenditure (within the meaning assigned by subsection 127(9)) made in a preceding taxation year, and

**Application**: The December 21, 2000 draft legislation, s. 28, will amend the description of L in the definition "cumulative Canadian exploration expense" in subsec. 66.1(6) to read as above, applicable after October 17, 2000.

**Technical Notes**: The description of L, in the formula in the definition "cumulative Canadian exploration expense", provides that the investment tax credit claimed by a taxpayer under subsection 127(5) or (6), in a year preceding the taxpayer's taxation year, in respect of a qualified Canadian exploration expenditure reduces the taxpayer's cumulative Canadian exploration expense (CCEE) pool in the taxation year. (The expression "qualified Canadian exploration expense" was previously defined in subsection 127(9). The definition of that expression was repealed by S.C. 1996, c. 21, subsection 30(9), applicable to taxation years that begin after 1995.)

The description of L is amended, after October 17, 2000, to provide that a taxpayer's CCEE is reduced by any investment tax credit claimed by the taxpayer in respect of a flow-through mining expenditure of the taxpayer. (See the commentary on the new definition "flow-through mining expenditure" in subsection 127(9) for further details.) Because the investment tax credit calculation can become circular if the credit were to reduce CCEE in the same year in which the credit is claimed, the description of L requires a reduction of the CCEE in the taxation year following the year in which the credit is claimed.

M is the total of all amounts that are required to be deducted before that time under paragraph 66.7(12)(b) in computing the taxpayer's cumulative Canadian exploration expense;

**Related Provisions**: 12(1)(t) — Investment tax credit; 20(1)(kk) — Exploration & development grants; 50(1)(a) — Deemed disposition where debt becomes bad debt; 59(3.2) — Recovery of exploration & development expenses; 66(10.1)(b) — Joint exploration corporation; 66(12.1) — Limitations of Canadian exploration & development expenses; 66(12.2) — Unitized oil or gas field in Canada; 66(15) — Definitions; 66.1(1) — Amount to be included in income; 66.1(7) — Share of partner; 66.7(3) — Deduction to successor corporation; 79(4)(c) — Subsequent payment by debtor following surrender of property deemed to be repayment of assistance; 79.1(8) — No claim for principal amount of bad debt where property seized by creditor; 80(8)(b) — Reduction of CCEE on debt forgiveness; 87(2)(j.6) — Amalgamations — continuing corporation; 96(2.2)(d) — At-risk amount; 127(12.3) — Reduction of cumulative Canadian exploration expense of trust; 248(16) — GST input tax credit and rebate deemed to be assistance; 248(18) — GST — repayment of input tax credit; 257 — Formula cannot calculate to less than zero. See additional Related Provisions and Definitions at end of s. 66.1.

**Notes**: 66.1(6)(b)(iv.1) (now formula element E) added by 1990 GST, effective for amounts repaid after January 1990.

66.1(6)(b)(iv.2) (now formula element E.1) added by 1991 technical bill, effective for taxation years commencing after February 17, 1987.

Description of F amended by 1992 Economic Statement, effective for taxation years ending after December 2, 1992, to change "deducted or deductible" to "deducted or required to be deducted".

66.1(6)(b)(ix) (now formula element J) amended by 1986 Budget, effective for expenses incurred after March 1987. For expenses incurred from December 20, 1986 through March 31, 1987, ignore everything after the comma (i.e., the entire reference to paragraph (9)(g)). For expenses incurred before December 20, 1986, read:

> (ix) any amount of assistance or benefit that he has received or is entitled to receive from a government, municipality or other public authority in respect of any Canadian exploration expense made or incurred after December 31, 1980 or that can reasonably be related to Canadian exploration activities after that date, whether such amount is by way of a grant, subsidy, forgiveable loan, deduction from royalty or tax, investment allowance or any other form of assistance or benefit, or

Formula element J.1 added by 1994 tax amendments bill (Part I), effective for taxation years that end after February 21, 1994.

66.1(6)(b)(xi) (now formula element L) added by 1986 Budget, effective for expenditures made after November 1985.

66.1(6)"cumulative Canadian exploration expense" was 66.1(6)(b) before consolidation in R.S.C. 1985 (5th Supp.), effective for taxation years ending after November 1991. The previous version, identical in meaning, read:

> (b) "cumulative Canadian exploration expense" of a taxpayer at any time shall be the amount, if any, by which the aggregate of
>
> (i) the aggregate of all Canadian exploration expenses made or incurred by him before that time,
>
> (ii) the aggregate of all amounts required by virtue of subsection (1) to be included in computing the amount referred to in paragraph 59(3.2)(b) for his taxation years ending before that time,
>
> (iii) the aggregate of amounts, except amounts in respect of interest, paid by him after May 6, 1974 and before that time to Her Majesty in right of Canada in respect of amounts paid to him before May 25, 1976 under the regulations referred to in clause (vii)(A),
>
> (iv) any amount referred to in subparagraph (vi) that is established by him to have become a bad debt before that time, and
>
> (iv.1) such part, if any, of the amount included in subparagraph (ix) as has been repaid before that time by the taxpayer pursuant to a legal obligation to repay all or any part of that amount
>
> exceeds the aggregate of all amounts each of which is
>
> (v) any amount deducted or deductible, as the case may be, in computing his income for a taxation year ending before that time in respect of his cumulative Canadian exploration expense,
>
> (vi) any amount that became receivable by him before that time that is to be included in the amount determined under this subparagraph by virtue of paragraph 66(12.1)(a) or (12.2)(a),
>
> (vii) the aggregate of all amounts paid to him after May 6, 1974 and before May 25, 1976
>
>> (A) under the *Northern Mineral Exploration Assistance Regulations* made under an *Appropriations Act* that provides for payments in respect of the Northern Mineral Grants Program, or
>>
>> (B) pursuant to any agreement entered into between the taxpayer and Her Majesty in right of Canada under the Northern Mineral Grants Program or the Development Program of the Department of Indian Affairs and Northern Development,
>
> to the extent that the amounts have been expended by the taxpayer as or on account of Canadian exploration and development expenses or Canadian exploration expense incurred by him,
>
> (viii) any amount received before that time on account of any amount referred to in subparagraph (iv),
>
> (ix) any assistance that he has received or is entitled to receive in respect of any Canadian exploration expense incurred after 1980 or that can reasonably be related to Canadian exploration activities after 1980, to the extent that the assistance has not reduced his Canadian exploration expense by virtue of paragraph (9)(g),
>
> (x) any amount that is required to be deducted before that time under subsection 66(14.1) in computing his cumulative Canadian exploration expense,
>
> (xi) that portion of the aggregate of all amounts deducted by the taxpayer under subsection 127(5) or (6) for a taxation year ending before that time that may reasonably be attributed to a qualified Canadian exploration expenditure (within the meaning assigned by subsection 127(9)) made in a preceding taxation year, or
>
> (xii) any amount that is required to be deducted before that time under paragraph 66.7(12)(b) in computing his cumulative Canadian exploration expense;

**"restricted expense"** of a taxpayer means an expense

(a) incurred by the taxpayer before April, 1987,

(b) that is deemed by paragraph 66(10.2)(c) to have been incurred by the taxpayer, or included by the taxpayer in the amount referred to in paragraph (a) of the definition "Canadian development expense" in subsection 66.2(5) by virtue of paragraph 66(12.3)(b), to the extent that the expense was originally incurred before April, 1987,

(c) that was renounced by the taxpayer under subsection 66(10.2), (12.601) or (12.62),

(d) in respect of which an amount referred to in subsection 66(12.3) becomes receivable by the taxpayer,

(e) deemed to be a Canadian exploration expense of the taxpayer or any other taxpayer by virtue of subsection (9), or

(f) where the taxpayer is a corporation, that was incurred by the corporation before the time control of the corporation was last acquired by a person or persons;

**Related Provisions**: 256(6)–(9) — Whether control acquired.

**S. 66.1(6) res**      Income Tax Act, Part I, Division B

**Notes**: Reference to 66(12.601) in para. (c) added by 1992 Economic Statement, effective for expenses incurred after December 2, 1992.

66.1(6)"restricted expense" was 66.1(6)(c) before consolidation in R.S.C. 1985 (5th Supp.), effective for taxation years ending after November 1991. See Table of Concordance.

**"specified purpose"** means

    (a) the operation of an oil or gas well for the sole purpose of testing the well or the well head and related equipment, in accordance with generally accepted engineering practices,

    (b) the burning of natural gas and related hydrocarbons to protect the environment, and

    (c) prescribed purposes.

**Notes**: 66.1(6)"specified purpose" was 66.1(6)(d) before consolidation in R.S.C. 1985 (5th Supp.), effective for taxation years ending after November 1991. See Table of Concordance.

66.1(6)(d) (now "specified purpose") added by 1986 Budget, effective for expenses incurred after March 1987.

**(6.1) Application of subsecs. 66(15), 66.2(5) and 66.4(5)** — The definitions in subsections 66(15), 66.2(5) and 66.4(5) apply to this section.

**Notes**: 66.1(6.1) added in the R.S.C. 1985 (5th Supp.) consolidation, effective for taxation years ending after November 1991. This rule was formerly contained in the opening words of 66(15), 66.2(5) and 66.4(5).

**(7) Share of partner** — Where a taxpayer is a member of a partnership, the taxpayer's share of any amount that would be an amount referred to in the description of E, G or J in the definition "cumulative Canadian exploration expense" in subsection (6) in respect of the partnership for a taxation year of the partnership if section 96 were read without reference to paragraph 96(1)(d) shall, for the purposes of this Act, be deemed to be an amount referred to in the description of E, G or J, as the case may be, in that definition in respect of the taxpayer for the taxation year of the taxpayer in which the partnership's taxation year ends.

**Related Provisions**: 87(1.2) — Amalgamations — new corporation deemed continuation of predecessor; 88(1.5) — Windup — parent corporation deemed to be continuation of subsidiary. See additional Related Provisions and Definitions at end of s. 66.1.

**Notes**: References to "cumulative Canadian exploration expense"E (formerly 66.1(6)(b)(iv.1)) added to 66.1(7) by 1991 technical bill, effective February 1990.

**Interpretation Bulletins**: IT-273R2: Government assistance — general comments; IT-353R2: Partnership interests — some adjustments to cost base.

**I.T. Technical News**: No. 12 (adjusted cost base of partnership interest — subparagraph 53(1)(e)(viii)).

**(8)** [Repealed]

**Notes**: 66.1(8) repealed by 1996 Budget, effective March 7, 1996. See now 66(12.66).

**(9) Canadian development expenses for preceding years** — Where at any time in a taxpayer's taxation year

    (a) an oil or gas well resulted in the discovery of a natural accumulation of petroleum or natural gas,

> **Proposed Amendment — 66.1(9)(a)**
>
> (a) the drilling or completing of an oil or gas well resulted in the discovery that a natural underground reservoir contains petroleum or natural gas and, before the time of the discovery, no person or partnership had discovered that the reservoir contained either petroleum or natural gas,
>
> **Application**: Bill C-43 (First Reading September 20, 2000), subsec. 27(3), will amend para. 66.1(9)(a) to read as above, applicable to expenses incurred after March 1987.
>
> **Technical Notes**: See under 66.1(6)"Canadian exploration expense"(d)(i).

    (b) the period of 24 months commencing on the day of completion of the drilling of an oil or gas well ends and the well has not, within that period, produced otherwise than for specified purposes, or

    (c) an oil or gas well that has never produced, otherwise than for specified purposes, is abandoned,

the amount, if any, by which the total of

    (d) all Canadian development expenses (other than restricted expenses) described in subparagraph (a)(ii) of the definition "Canadian development expense" in subsection 66.2(5) in respect of the well that are deemed by subsection 66(10.2) or (12.63) to have been incurred by the taxpayer in the year or a preceding taxation year,

    (e) all Canadian development expenses (other than restricted expenses) described in subparagraph (a)(ii) of the definition "Canadian development expense" in subsection 66.2(5) in respect of the well that are required by paragraph 66(12.3)(b) to be included by the taxpayer in the amount referred to in paragraph (a) of that definition for the year or a preceding taxation year, and

    (f) all Canadian development expenses (other than expenses referred to in paragraph (d) or (e) and restricted expenses) described in subparagraph (a)(ii) of the definition "Canadian development expense" in subsection 66.2(5) incurred by the taxpayer in respect of the well in a taxation year preceding the year,

exceeds

    (g) any assistance that the taxpayer or a partnership of which the taxpayer is a member has received or is entitled to receive in respect of the expenses referred to in any of paragraphs (d) to (f), shall, for the purposes of this Act, be deemed to be a Canadian exploration expense referred to in paragraph (e) of the definition "Canadian exploration expense" in subsection (6) incurred by the taxpayer at that time.

**Related Provisions**: 66.2(5)"cumulative Canadian development expense"I, M — Reduction in CCDE; 66.7(9) — CDE becoming CEE; 248(16) — GST input tax credit and rebate deemed to be government assistance; 248(18) — GST — repayment of input tax credit. See additional Related Provisions and Definitions at end of s. 66.1.

**Notes**: 66.1(9) added by 1986 Budget, effective for expenses incurred after March 1987.

**(10) Certificate ceasing to be valid** — A certificate in respect of an oil or gas well issued by the Minister of Natural Resources for the purposes of paragraph (d)(iv) of the definition "Canadian exploration expense" in subsection (6) shall be deemed never to have been issued and never to have been filed with the Minister where

(a) the well produces, otherwise than for a specified purpose, within the period of 24 months commencing on the day on which the drilling of the well was completed; or

(b) in applying for the certificate, the applicant, in any material respect, provided any incorrect information or failed to provide information.

**(11) [Repealed under former Act]**

**Notes**: 66.1(11), repealed in 1987, dealt with successor corporations, now covered in 66.7.

**Related Provisions [s. 66.1]**: 66(5) — Dealers; 66(18) — Members of partnerships; 66.7 — Successor rules; 66.8(1) — Resource expenses of limited partner; 88(1.5) — Winding-up — parent deemed continuation of subsidiary.

**Definitions [s. 66.1]**: "acquired" — 256(7)–(9); "amount" — 248(1); "assistance" — 66(15), 66.1(6.1), 79(4), 125.4(5), 248(16), 248(18); "Canada" — 255, *Interpretation Act* 8(2.1), (2.2); "Canadian development expense" — 66.2(5), 248(1); "Canadian exploration expense" — 66.1(6), 248(1); "Canadian exploration and development expenses" — 66(15), 66.1(6.1); "Canadian oil and gas property expense" — 66.4(5), 248(1); "Canadian renewable and conservation expense" — 66.1(6); "control" — 256(6)–(9); "corporation" — 248(1), *Interpretation Act* 35(1); "cumulative Canadian development expense" — 66.1(6.1), 66.2(5); "expense" — 66(15), 66.1(6.1); "fiscal period" — 249(2), 249.1; "flow-through mining expenditure" — 127(9), (11.1)(c.2); "Her Majesty" — *Interpretation Act* 35(1); "mineral resource", "Minister" — 248(1); "oil or gas well" — 248(1); "outlay" — 66(15), 66.1(6.1); "person", "prescribed" — 248(1); "principal-business corporation" — 66(15), 66.1(6.1); "property", "regulation", "share" — 248(1); "taxation year" — 249; "taxpayer" — 248(1); "writing" — *Interpretation Act* 35(1); IT-273R2: Government assistance — general comments.

**Interpretation Bulletins [s. 66.1]**: IT-273R2: Government assistance — general comments.

**66.2 [Canadian development expenses] — (1) Amount to be included in income** — There shall be included in computing the amount referred to in paragraph 59(3.2)(c) in respect of a taxpayer for a taxation year the amount, if any, by which the total of

(a) all amounts referred to in the descriptions of E to O in the definition "cumulative Canadian development expense" in subsection (5) that are deducted in computing the taxpayer's cumulative Canadian development expense at the end of year, and

(b) the amount that is designated by the taxpayer for the year under subsection 66(14.2)

exceeds the total of

(c) all amounts referred to in the descriptions of A to D.1 in the definition "cumulative Canadian development expense" in subsection (5) that are included in computing the taxpayer's cumulative Canadian development expense at the end of the year, and

(d) the total determined under subparagraph 66.7(12.1)(b)(i) in respect of the taxpayer for the year.

**Related Provisions**: 59(3.2)(c) — Income inclusion; 66(11.4) — Change of control; 66.7(12) — Reduction of Canadian resource expenses; 104(5.2) — Trusts — 21-year deemed disposition; 115(1)(a)(iii.1) — Non-resident's taxable income earned in Canada. See additional Related Provisions and Definitions at end of s. 66.2.

**Notes**: 66.2(1)(d) added by 1991 technical bill, effective for taxation years ending after February 17, 1987, except that for taxation years commencing before February 18, 1987, read "(iii)" in place of "(iii.2)" in 66.2(1)(c).

**Interpretation Bulletins**: IT-125R4: Dispositions of resource properties; IT-273R2: Government assistance — general comments.

**(2) Deduction for cumulative Canadian development expenses** — A taxpayer may deduct, in computing the taxpayer's income for a taxation year, such amount as the taxpayer may claim not exceeding the total of

(a) the lesser of

(i) the total of

(A) the taxpayer's cumulative Canadian development expense at the end of the year, and

(B) the amount, if any, by which

(I) the total determined under subparagraph 66.7(12.1)(b)(i) in respect of the taxpayer for the year

exceeds

(II) the amount that would, but for paragraph (1)(d), be determined under subsection (1) in respect of the taxpayer for the year, and

(ii) the amount, if any, by which the amount determined under subparagraph 66.4(2)(a)(ii) exceeds the amount determined under subparagraph 66.4(2)(a)(i),

(b) the lesser of

(i) the amount, if any, by which the amount determined under subparagraph (a)(i) exceeds the amount determined under subparagraph (a)(ii), and

(ii) the amount, if any, by which the total of all amounts each of which is

(A) an amount included in the taxpayer's income for the year by virtue of a disposition in the year of inventory described in section 66.3 that was a share, any interest therein or right thereto, acquired by the taxpayer under circumstances described in paragraph (g) of the definition "Canadian development expense" in subsection (5) or paragraph (i) of the definition "Canadian exploration expense" in subsection 66.1(6), or

(B) an amount included by virtue of paragraph 12(1)(e) in computing the taxpayer's income for the year to the extent that it relates to inventory described in clause (A)

exceeds

(C) the total of all amounts deducted as a reserve by virtue of paragraph 20(1)(n) in computing the taxpayer's income for the year to the extent that the reserve relates to inventory described in clause (A), and

(c) 30% of the amount, if any, by which the amount determined under subparagraph (b)(i) exceeds the amount determined under subparagraph (b)(ii).

**Related Provisions**: 20(1)(hh) — Repayments of inducements, etc.; 66(13.1) — Short taxation year; 110.6(1)"investment expense"(d) — effect of claim under 66.2(2) on capital gains exemption; 127.52(1)(e) — Add-back of deduction for minimum tax purposes. See additional Related provisions and Definitions at end of s. 66.2.

**Notes**: 66.2(2) amended by 1991 technical bill, effective for taxation years ending after February 17, 1987.

**Interpretation Bulletins**: IT-273R2: Government assistance — general comments; IT-438R2: Crown charges — resource properties in Canada.

**Advance Tax Rulings**: ATR-59: Financing exploration and development through limited partnerships.

**(3), (4) [Repealed under former Act]**

**Notes**: 66.2(3) and (4), repealed in 1987, dealt with a successor corporation's Canadian development expenses. The successor corporation rules are now in 66.7

**(5) Definitions** — In this section,

**Related Provisions**: 66(15.1) — Application to s. 66; 66.1(6.1) — Application to s. 66.1.

**Notes**: Before the R.S.C. 1985 (5th Supp.), effective for taxation years ending after November 1991, the opening words of 66.2(5) also referred to 66 and 66.1. This application rule is now in 66(15.1) and 66.1(6.1).

**"Canadian development expense"** of a taxpayer means any cost or expense incurred after May 6, 1974 that is

(a) any expense incurred by the taxpayer in

(i) drilling or converting a well in Canada for the disposal of waste liquids from an oil or gas well,

(ii) drilling or completing an oil or gas well in Canada, building a temporary access road to the well or preparing a site in respect of the well, to the extent that the expense was not a Canadian exploration expense of the taxpayer in the taxation year in which it was incurred,

(iii) drilling or converting a well in Canada for the injection of water, gas or any other substance to assist in the recovery of petroleum or natural gas from another well,

(iv) drilling for water or gas in Canada for injection into a petroleum or natural gas formation, or

(v) drilling or converting a well in Canada for the purposes of monitoring fluid levels, pressure changes or other phenomena in an accumulation of petroleum or natural gas,

(b) any expense incurred by the taxpayer in drilling or recompleting an oil or gas well in Canada after the commencement of production from the well,

(c) any expense incurred by the taxpayer before November 17, 1978 for the purpose of bringing a mineral resource in Canada into production and incurred prior to the commencement of production from the resource in reasonable commercial quantities, including

(i) clearing, removing overburden and stripping, and

(ii) sinking a mine shaft, constructing an adit or other underground entry,

(d) any expense (other than an amount included in the capital cost of depreciable property) incurred by the taxpayer after 1987

(i) in sinking or excavating a mine shaft, main haulage way or similar underground work designed for continuing use, for a mine in a mineral resource in Canada built or excavated after the mine came into production, or

(ii) in extending any such shaft, haulage way or work,

(e) notwithstanding paragraph 18(1)(m), the cost to the taxpayer of any property described in paragraph (b), (e) or (f) of the definition "Canadian resource property" in subsection 66(15) or any right to or interest in such property (other than such a right or interest that the taxpayer has by virtue of being a beneficiary of a trust) but not including any payment made to any of the persons referred to in any of subparagraphs

18(1)(m)(i) to (iii) for the preservation of a taxpayer's rights in respect of a Canadian resource property nor a payment to which paragraph 18(1)(m) applied by virtue of subparagraph 18(1)(m)(v),

(f) subject to section 66.8, the taxpayer's share of any expense referred to in any of paragraphs (a) to (e) incurred by a partnership in a fiscal period thereof at the end of which the taxpayer was a member of the partnership, unless the taxpayer elects in respect of the share in prescribed form and manner on or before the day that is 6 months after the taxpayer's taxation year in which that period ends, or

(g) any cost or expense referred to in any of paragraphs (a) to (e) incurred by the taxpayer pursuant to an agreement in writing with a corporation, entered into before 1987, under which the taxpayer incurred the cost or expense solely as consideration for shares, other than prescribed shares, of the capital stock of the corporation issued to the taxpayer or any interest in such shares or right thereto,

but, for greater certainty, shall not include

(h) any consideration given by the taxpayer for any share or any interest therein or right thereto, except as provided by paragraph (g),

(i) any expense described in paragraph (g) incurred by any other taxpayer to the extent that the expense was,

(i) by virtue of that paragraph, a Canadian development expense of that other taxpayer,

(ii) by virtue of paragraph (i) of the definition "Canadian exploration expense" in subsection 66.1(6), a Canadian exploration expense of that other taxpayer, or

(iii) by virtue of paragraph (c) of the definition "Canadian oil and gas property expense" in subsection 66.4(5), a Canadian oil and gas property expense of that other taxpayer,

**Proposed Addition — 66.2(5)"Canadian development expense"(i.1)**

(i.1) an expense that is the cost, or any part of the cost, to the taxpayer of any depreciable property of a prescribed class that was acquired after 1987,

**Application:** Bill C-43 (First Reading September 20, 2000), s. 28, will add para. (i.1) to the definition "Canadian development expense", applicable to 1988 et seq.

**Technical Notes:** Subsection 66.2(2) generally allows a taxpayer a deduction for a taxation year of up to 30 per cent of its cumulative Canadian development expense (cumulative CDE) at the end of the year. The definitions of CDE and cumulative CDE are contained in subsection 66.2(5).

Paragraph (i.1) of the CDE definition is introduced to clarify that a taxpayer's CDE does not include the cost to the taxpayer of any depreciable property of a prescribed class. This amendment, as well as the related amendment to the definition "Canadian exploration expense", is for greater certainty. It responds to an issue raised by the decision of the Phénix case referred to above.

This amendment applies to property acquired after 1987. Paragraph (i.1) complements the wording in existing paragraph (j) of the CDE definition, with the result that both paragraphs provide for the same exclusion with regard to property acquired after December 5, 1996.

This amendment applies, with necessary minor technical modifications to take into account the restructuring of subsection 66.2(5), to the version of the CDE definition in force prior to the enactment of the Revised Statutes of Canada, 1985, Fifth Supplement. Subsection 79(1) of the *Income Tax Application Rules* contains a rule to this effect.

(j) any amount included at any time in the capital cost to the taxpayer of any depreciable property of a prescribed class, or

(k) the taxpayer's share of any consideration, expense, cost or expenditure referred to in any of paragraphs (h) to (j) given or incurred by a partnership,

but any assistance that a taxpayer has received or is entitled to receive after May 25, 1976 in respect of or related to the taxpayer's Canadian development expense shall not reduce the amount of any of the expenses described in any of paragraphs (a) to (g);

**Related Provisions:** 13(7.5) — Depreciable property treatment for costs associated with building roads and similar projects; 18(1)(m) — Royalties, etc.; 53(1)(e)(vii.1) — Addition to ACB — partnership interest; 66.2(2) — Deduction for cumulative CDE; 66.2(8) — Presumption; 66.3 — Exploration and development shares; 248(1)"Canadian development expense" — Definition applies to entire Act; 248(16) — GST input tax credit and rebate deemed to be government assistance; 248(18) — GST — repayment of input tax credit; *Interpretation Act* 8(2.1), (2.2) — Application to exclusive economic zone and continental shelf. See additional Related Provisions and Definitions at end of s. 66.2.

**Notes:** Paras. (j) and (k) added by 1996 Budget, effective for taxation years that end after December 5, 1996. They are parallel to 66.1(6)"Canadian exploration expense"(l) and (o).

66.2(5)"Canadian development expense" was 66.2(5)(a) before consolidation in R.S.C. 1985 (5th Supp.), effective for taxation years ending after November 1991. See Table of Concordance.

66.2(5)(a)(i)(C) (now "Canadian development expense"(a)(iii)) amended by 1983 Budget, effective for expenses incurred after 1980, to change "water or gas" to "water, gas or any other substance".

66.2(5)(a)(i)(E) (now "Canadian development expense"(a)(v)) added by 1985 technical bill, effective for expenses incurred after 1981.

"Canadian development expense"(f) amended by 1992 technical bill, effective for partnership fiscal periods ending after 1990, to add the exception beginning "unless the taxpayer elects". (See 53(1)(e)(vii.1) for the offsetting addition to ACB.) An election for past years may be filed until December 10, 1993.

The exclusion of prescribed shares in 66.2(5)(a)(v) (now "Canadian development expense"(g)) was added by 1981 Budget, effective for any outlay or expense made or incurred after 1982.

Closing words of 66.2(5)(a) (now 66.2(5)"Canadian development expense") amended by 1986 Budget, effective for expenses incurred after December 19, 1986. For earlier expenses read:

but no amount of assistance or benefit that a taxpayer has received or is entitled to receive after May 25, 1976 from a government, municipality or other public authority in respect of or related to his Canadian development expense, whether as a grant, subsidy, forgivable loan, deduction from royalty or tax, investment allowance or any other form of assistance or benefit, shall reduce the amount of any of the expenses described in any of subparagraphs (i) to (v); and

For expenses incurred before 1981, an earlier edition of the Act should be consulted.

**Regulations**: 6202 (prescribed share).

**Interpretation Bulletins**: IT-109R2: Unpaid amounts; IT-273R2: Government assistance — general comments; IT-438R2: Crown charges — resource properties in Canada; IT-503: Exploration and development shares.

**Advance Tax Rulings**: ATR-59: Financing exploration and development through limited partnerships.

**Forms**: T1086: Election by a partner waiving Canadian development expenses or oil and gas property expenses.

**"cumulative Canadian development expense"** of a taxpayer at any time in a taxation year means the amount determined by the formula

$$(A + B + C + D + D.1) - (E + F + G + H + I + J + K + L + M + M.1 + N + O)$$

where

A is the total of all Canadian development expenses made or incurred by the taxpayer before that time,

B the total of all amounts required by virtue of subsection (1) to be included in computing the amount referred to in paragraph 59(3.2)(c) for taxation years ending before that time,

C is the total of all amounts referred to in the description of F or G that are established by the taxpayer to have become a bad debt before that time,

D is such part, if any, of the amount determined for M as has been repaid before that time by the taxpayer pursuant to a legal obligation to repay all or any part of that amount,

D.1 is the total of all specified amounts determined under paragraph 66.7(12.1)(b) in respect of the taxpayer for taxation years ending before that time,

E is the total of all amounts deducted in computing the taxpayer's income for a taxation year ending before that time in respect of the taxpayer's cumulative Canadian development expense,

F is the total of all amounts each of which is an amount in respect of a property described in paragraph (b), (e) or (f) of the definition "Canadian resource property" in subsection 66(15) or a right to or interest in such a property, other than such a right or interest that the taxpayer has by virtue of being a beneficiary of a trust, (in this description referred to as the "particular property") disposed of by the taxpayer before that time equal to the amount, if any, by which

(a) the amount, if any, by which the proceeds of disposition in respect of the particular property that became receivable by the taxpayer after May 6, 1974 and before that time exceed any outlays or expenses that were made or incurred by the taxpayer after May 6, 1974 and before that time for the purpose of making the disposition and that were not otherwise deductible for the purposes of this Part

exceeds

(b) the amount, if any, by which

(i) the total of all amounts that would be determined under paragraph 66.7(4)(a), immediately before the time (in this paragraph referred to as the "relevant time") when such proceeds of disposition became receivable, in respect of the taxpayer and an original owner of the particular property (or of any other property acquired by the taxpayer with the particular property in circumstances in which subsection 66.7(4) applied and in respect of which the proceeds of disposition became receivable by the taxpayer at the relevant time) if

(A) amounts that became receivable at or after the relevant time were not taken into account,

(B) each designation made under subparagraph 66.7(4)(a)(iii) in respect of an amount that became receivable before the relevant time were made before the relevant time,

(C) paragraph 66.7(4)(a) were read without reference to "30% of", and

(D) no reduction under subsection 80(8) at or after the relevant time were taken into account

exceeds the total of

(ii) all amounts that would be determined under paragraph 66.7(4)(a) at the relevant time in respect of the taxpayer and an original owner of the particular property (or of that other property) if

(A) amounts that became receivable after the relevant time were not taken into account,

(B) each designation made under subparagraph 66.7(4)(a)(iii) in respect of an amount that became receivable at or before the relevant time were made before the relevant time,

(C) paragraph 66.7(4)(a) were read without reference to "30% of",

(D) amounts described in subparagraph 66.7(4)(a)(iii) that became receivable at the relevant time were not taken into account, and

(E) no reduction under subsection 80(8) at or after the relevant time were taken into account, and

Subdivision e — Deductions in Computing Income    S. 66.2(5) cum

(iii) such portion of the amount otherwise determined under this paragraph as was otherwise applied to reduce the amount otherwise determined under this description,

G is the total of all amounts that became receivable by the taxpayer before that time that are to be included in the amount determined under this description by virtue of paragraph 66(12.1)(b) or (12.3)(a),

H is the total of all amounts each of which is an amount included by the taxpayer as an expense under paragraph (a) of the definition "Canadian development expense" in this subsection in computing the taxpayer's Canadian development expense for a previous taxation year that has become a Canadian exploration expense of the taxpayer by virtue of subparagraph (c)(ii) of the definition "Canadian exploration expense" in subsection 66.1(6),

I is the total of all amounts each of which is an amount that before that time has become a Canadian exploration expense of the taxpayer by virtue of subsection 66.1(9),

J is the total of all amounts each of which is an amount received before that time on account of any amount referred to in the description of C,

K is the total of all amounts paid to the taxpayer after May 6, 1974 and before May 25, 1976

(a) under the *Northern Mineral Exploration Assistance Regulations* made under an appropriation Act that provides for payments in respect of the Northern Mineral Grants Program, or

(b) pursuant to any agreement, entered into between the taxpayer and Her Majesty in right of Canada under the Northern Mineral Grants Program or the Development Program of the Department of Indian Affairs and Northern Development,

to the extent that the amounts have been expended by the taxpayer as or on account of Canadian development expense incurred by the taxpayer,

L is the amount by which the total of all amounts determined under subsection 66.4(1) in respect of a taxation year of the taxpayer ending at or before that time exceeds the total of all amounts each of which is the least of

(a) the amount that would be determined under paragraph 66.7(4)(a), at a time (hereafter in this description referred to only as the "particular time") that is the end of the latest taxation year of the taxpayer ending at or before that time, in respect of the taxpayer as successor in respect of a disposition (in this description referred to as the "original disposition") of Canadian resource property by a person who is an original owner of the property because of the original disposition, if

(i) that paragraph were read without reference to "30% of",

(ii) where the taxpayer has disposed of all or part of the property in circumstances in which subsection 66.7(4) applied, that subsection continued to apply to the taxpayer in respect of the original disposition as if subsequent successors were the same person as the taxpayer, and

(iii) each designation made under subparagraph 66.7(4)(a)(iii) in respect of an amount that became receivable before the particular time were made before the particular time,

(b) the amount, if any, by which the total of all amounts each of which became receivable at or before the particular time and before 1993 by the taxpayer and is included in computing the amount determined under subparagraph 66.7(5)(a)(ii) in respect of the original disposition exceeds the amount, if any, by which

(i) where the taxpayer disposed of all or part of the property before the particular time in circumstances in which subsection 66.7(5) applied, the amount that would be determined at the particular time under subparagraph 66.7(5)(a)(i) in respect of the original disposition if that subparagraph continued to apply to the taxpayer in respect of the original disposition as if subsequent successors were the same person as the taxpayer, and

(ii) in any other case, the amount determined at the particular time under subparagraph 66.7(5)(a)(i) in respect of the original disposition

exceeds

(iii) the amount that would be determined at the particular time under subparagraph 66.7(5)(a)(ii) in respect of the original disposition if that subparagraph were read without reference to the words "or the successor", wherever they appear therein, and if amounts that became receivable after 1992 were not taken into account, and

(c) where

(i) after the original disposition and at or before the particular time, the taxpayer disposed of all or part of the property in circumstances in which subsection 66.7(4) applied, otherwise than by way of an amalgamation or merger or solely because of the application of paragraph 66.7(10)(c), and

475

(ii) the winding-up of the taxpayer began at or before that time or the taxpayer's disposition referred to in subparagraph (i) (other than a disposition under an agreement in writing entered into before December 22, 1992) occurred after December 21, 1992,

nil,

M is the total amount of assistance that the taxpayer has received or is entitled to receive in respect of any Canadian development expense (including an expense that has become a Canadian exploration expense of the taxpayer by virtue of subsection 66.1(9)) incurred after 1980 or that can reasonably be related to Canadian development activities after 1980,

M.1 is the total of all amounts by which the cumulative Canadian development expense of the taxpayer is required because of subsection 80(8) to be reduced at or before that time,

N is the total of all amounts that are required to be deducted before that time under subsection 66(14.2) in computing the taxpayer's cumulative Canadian development expense, and

O is the total of all amounts that are required to be deducted before that time under paragraph 66.7(12)(c) in computing the taxpayer's cumulative Canadian development expense.

**Related Provisions**: 35(1)(c) — Prospectors and grubstakers; 50(1)(a) — Deemed disposition where debt becomes bad debt; 59(3.2) — Recovery of exploration & development expenses; 66(12.1) — Limitations of Canadian exploration & development expenses; 66(12.3) — Unitized oil or gas field in Canada; 66.2(7) — Exception; 66.4(1) — Recovery of costs; 66.7(4) — Deduction to successor corporation; 70(5.2)(a) — Resource properties and land inventories of deceased; 79(4)(c) — Subsequent payment by debtor following surrender of property deemed to be repayment of assistance; 79.1(8) — No claim for principal amount of bad debt where property seized by creditor; 80(8)(c) — Reduction of CCDE on debt forgiveness; 96(2.2)(d) — at-risk amount; 104(5.2) — Trusts — 21-year deemed disposition; 248(16) — GST input tax credit and rebate deemed to be government assistance; 248(18) — GST — repayment of input tax credit; 257 — Formula cannot calculate to less than zero. See additional Related Provisions and Definitions at end of s. 66.2.

**Notes**: 66.2(5)(b)(iii.1) (now formula element D) added by 1990 GST, effective for amounts repaid after January 1990.

66.2(5)(b)(iii.2) (now formula element D.1) added by 1991 technical bill, effective for taxation years commencing after February 17, 1987.

Description of F amended by 1993 technical bill, retroactive to taxation years that end after February 17, 1987. The main effect of the amendments is that an offset in respect of a disposition of Canadian mining property is not determined with reference to the current amounts of the taxpayer's successored CCDE balances. Rather, the offset is determined with reference to the successored CCDE balances immediately before the proceeds became receivable. In effect, the proceeds of disposition of Canadian mining property acquired on a succession are applied first to reduce any successored CCDE balance before reducing the taxpayer's own CCDE.

F(b)(i)(D) and F(b)(ii)(E) added by 1994 tax amendments bill (Part I), effective for taxation years that end after February 21, 1994.

Description of L amended by 1993 technical bill, effective for taxation years that end after December 21, 1992. However, where a taxpayer elects by notifying Revenue Canada in writing by December 31, 1994, the new version applies to taxation years that end after February 17, 1987, and in such case, notwithstanding 152(4) to (5), such assessments and determinations in respect of any taxation year shall be made as are necessary to give effect to the election. The old version reads:

L is the amount by which the total of all amounts each of which is an amount determined under subsection 66.4(1) in respect of a taxation year of the taxpayer ending at or before that time exceeds the total of all amounts each of which is the lesser of

(a) the amount that would be determined at that time under paragraph 66.7(4)(a) in respect of the acquisition of property from a particular original owner or predecessor owner of the property by the taxpayer if that paragraph were read without reference to "30% of", and

(b) the amount, if any, by which the total of the amounts that became receivable at or before that time by the taxpayer and that are described in subparagraph 66.7(5)(a)(ii) in respect of the disposition of property acquired from the particular original owner or predecessor owner exceeds the amount determined in subparagraph 66.7(5)(a)(i) in respect of the acquisition of that property,

66.2(5)(b)(xi) (now formula element M) amended by 1986 Budget, effective for expenses incurred after March 1987. For expenses incurred from December 20, 1986 through March 31, 1987, ignore the parenthetical reference to 66.1(9). For expenses incurred before December 20, 1986, read:

(xi) any amount of assistance or benefit that he has received or is entitled to receive from a government, municipality or other public authority in respect of any Canadian development expense made or incurred after December 31, 1980 or that can reasonably be related to Canadian development activities after that date, whether such amount is by way of a grant, subsidy, forgiveable loan, deduction from royalty or tax, investment allowance or any other form of assistance or benefit, or

Formula element M.1 added by 1994 tax amendments bill (Part I), effective for taxation years that end after February 21, 1994.

66.2(5)"cumulative Canadian development expense" was 66.2(5)(b) before consolidation in R.S.C. 1985 (5th Supp.), effective for taxation years ending after November 1991. The previous version, identical in meaning, read;

(b) "cumulative Canadian development expense" of a taxpayer at any time in a taxation year means the amount, if any, by which the aggregate of

(i) the aggregate of all Canadian development expenses made or incurred by him before that time,

(ii) the aggregate of all amounts required by virtue of subsection (1) to be included in computing the amount referred to in paragraph 59(3.2)(c) for taxation years ending before that time,

(iii) any amount referred to in subparagraph (v) or (vi) that is established by him to have become a bad debt before that time, and

(iii.1) such part, if any, of the amount included in subparagraph (xi) as has been repaid before that time by the taxpayer pursuant to a legal obligation to repay all or any part of that amount

exceeds the aggregate of all amounts each of which is

(iv) any amount deducted in computing his income for a taxation year ending before that time in respect of his cumulative Canadian development expense,

(v) the aggregate of all amounts each of which is an amount in respect of a property described in subparagraph 66(15)(c)(ii), (v) or (vi) or a right to or interest in such property, other than such a right or interest that he has by virtue of being a beneficiary of a trust, (in this subparagraph referred to as the "particular property") disposed of by the taxpayer before that time equal to the amount, if any, by which

(A) the amount, if any, by which the proceeds of disposition in respect of the particular property that became receivable by him after May 6, 1974 and before that time exceeds any outlays or expenses that were made or incurred by him after May 6, 1974 and before that time for the purpose of making the disposition and that were not otherwise deductible for the purposes of this Part

exceeds the amount equal to

(B) where the proceeds of disposition referred to in clause (A) may reasonably be attributed to the disposition of a property that was acquired by the taxpayer in circumstances in which subsection 66.7(4) applies to the taxpayer as successor, the lesser of

(I) the amount determined under clause (A) in respect of the property, and

(II) the aggregate of all amounts each of which is an amount that would be determined at that time under paragraph 66.7(4)(a) in respect of the acquisition of the property by the taxpayer if that paragraph were read without reference to "30% of", and

(C) in any other case, nil,

(vi) any amount that became receivable by him before that time that is to be included in the amount determined under this subparagraph by virtue of paragraph 66(12.1)(b) or 66(12.3)(a),

(vii) any amount included by him as an expense under subparagraph (a)(i) in computing his Canadian development expense for a previous taxation year that has become a Canadian exploration expense of the taxpayer by virtue of clause 66.1(6)(a)(ii)(B),

(vii.1) any amount that before that time has become a Canadian exploration expense of the taxpayer by virtue of subsection 66.1(9),

(viii) any amount received before that time on account of any amount referred to in subparagraph (iii),

(ix) the aggregate of all amounts paid to him after May 6, 1974 and before May 25, 1976

(A) under the *Northern Mineral Exploration Assistance Regulations* made under an *Appropriation Act* that provides for payments in respect of the Northern Mineral Grants Program, or

(B) pursuant to any agreement, entered into between the taxpayer and Her Majesty in right of Canada under the Northern Mineral Grants Program or the Development Program of the Department of Indian Affairs and Northern Development,

to the extent that the amounts have been expended by the taxpayer as or on account of Canadian development expense incurred by him,

(x) the amount by which the aggregate of all amounts each of which is an amount determined under subsection 66.4(1) in respect of a taxation year of the taxpayer ending at or before that time exceeds the aggregate of all amounts each of which is the lesser of

(A) the amount that would be determined at that time under paragraph 66.7(4)(a) in respect of the acquisition of property from a particular original owner or predecessor owner of the property by the taxpayer if that paragraph were read without reference to "30% of", and

(B) the amount, if any, by which the aggregate of the amounts that became receivable at or before that time by the taxpayer and that are described in subparagraph 66.7(5)(a)(ii) in respect of the disposition of property acquired from the particular original owner or predecessor owner exceeds the amount determined in subparagraph 66.7(5)(a)(i) in respect of the acquisition of such property,

(xi) any assistance that he has received or is entitled to receive in respect of any Canadian development expense (including an expense that has become a Canadian exploration expense of the taxpayer by virtue of subsection 66.1(9)) incurred after 1980 or that can reasonably be related to Canadian development activities after 1980,

(xii) any amount that is required to be deducted before that time under subsection 66(14.2) in computing his cumulative Canadian development expense, or

(xiii) any amount that is required to be deducted before that time under paragraph 66.7(12)(c) in computing his cumulative Canadian development expense.

**Interpretation Bulletins**: IT-109R2: Unpaid amounts; IT-125R4: Dispositions of resource properties; IT-273R2: Government assistance — general comments.

**(5.1) Application of subsecs. 66(15), 66.1(6) and 66.4(5)** — The definitions in subsections 66(15), 66.1(6) and 66.4(5) apply to this section.

**Notes**: 66.2(5.1) added in the R.S.C. 1985 (5th Supp.) consolidation, effective for taxation years ending after November 1991 (formerly contained in the opening words of subsecs. 66(15), 66.1(6) and 66.4(5)).

**(6) Presumption** — Except as provided in subsection (7), where a taxpayer is a member of a partnership, the taxpayer's share of any amount that would be an amount referred to in the description of D in the definition "cumulative Canadian development expense" in subsection (5), in paragraph (a) of the description of F in that definition or in the description of G or M in that definition in respect of the partnership for a taxation year of the partnership if section 96 were read without reference to paragraph 96(1)(d) shall, for the purposes of this Act, be deemed to be an amount referred to in the description of D in the definition "cumulative Canadian development expense" in subsection (5), in paragraph (a) of the description of F in that definition or in the description of G or M in that definition, whichever is applicable, in respect of the taxpayer for the taxation year of the taxpayer in which the partnership's taxation year ends.

**Notes**: References to "cumulative Canadian development expense"D (formerly 66.2(5)(b)(iii.1)) added to 66.2(6) by 1991 technical bill, effective February 1990.

**Interpretation Bulletins**: IT-125R4: Dispositions of resource properties; IT-273R2: Government assistance — general comments; IT-353R2: Partnership interest — some adjustments to cost base.

**I.T. Technical News**: No. 12 (adjusted cost base of partnership interest — subparagraph 53(1)(e)(viii)).

**(7) Exception** — Where a non-resident person is a member of a partnership that is deemed under paragraph 115(4)(b) to have disposed of any Canadian resource property, the person's share of any amount that would be an amount referred to in the description of D in the definition "cumulative Canadian development expense" in subsection (5), in paragraph (a) of the description of F in that definition or in the description of G or M in that definition in respect of the partnership for a taxation year of the partnership if section 96 were read without reference to paragraph 96(1)(d) shall, for the purposes of this Act, be deemed to be an amount referred to in the description of D in the definition "cumulative Canadian development expense" in subsection (5), in paragraph (a) of the description of F in that definition or in the description of G or M in that definition, whichever is applicable, in respect of the person for the taxation year of the person that is deemed under paragraph 115(4)(a) to have ended.

**Notes**: References to "cumulative Canadian development expense" D (formerly 66.2(5)(b)(iii.1)) added to 66.2(7) by 1991 technical bill, effective February 1990.

**Interpretation Bulletins**: IT-125R4: Dispositions of resource properties; IT-273R2: Government assistance — general comments.

**(8) Presumption** — Where pursuant to the terms of an arrangement in writing entered into before December 12, 1979 a taxpayer acquired a property described in paragraph (a) of the definition "Canadian oil and gas property expense" in subsection 66.4(5), for the purposes of this Act, the cost of acquisition shall be deemed to be a Canadian development expense incurred at the time the taxpayer acquired the property.

**Related Provisions [s. 66.2]**: 66(5) — Dealers; 66(18) — Members of partnerships; 66.7 — Successor rules; 66.8(1) — Resource expenses of limited partner; 87(1.2) — New corporation deemed continuation of predecessor; 88(1.5) — Winding-up — parent deemed continuation of subsidiary.

**Definitions [s. 66.2]**: "amount" — 248(1); "assistance" — 66(15), 66.2(5.1), 79(4), 125.4(5), 248(16), 248(18); "Canada" — 255, *Interpretation Act* 8(2.1), (2.2); "Canadian development expense" — 66.2(5), (8), 248(1); "Canadian exploration expense" — 66.1(6), 248(1); "Canadian exploration and development expense" — 66(15), 66.2(5.1); "Canadian exploration expense" — 66.1(6), 248(1); "Canadian oil and gas property expense" — 66.4(5), 248(1); "Canadian resource property" — 66(15), 248(1); "corporation" — 248(1), *Interpretation Act* 35(1); "disposition" — 54, 66.2(5.1), 66.4(5); "expense" — 66(15), 66.2(5.1); "fiscal period" — 249(2)(b), 249.1; "Her Majesty" — *Interpretation Act* 35(1); "mineral resource", "non-resident", "oil or gas well", "person", "prescribed" — 248(1); "proceeds of disposition" — 54, 66.2(5.1), 66.4(5); "property", "share" — 248(1); "taxation year" — 11(2), 249; "taxpayer" — 248(1); "writing" — *Interpretation Act* 35(1).

**Interpretation Bulletins [s. 66.2]**: IT-273R2: Government assistance — general comments.

### Proposed Addition — 66.21

**Technical Notes**: New section 66.21 sets out the rules governing foreign resource expenses (FRE). The expression "foreign resource expense" in subsection 66.21(1) is defined essentially in the same way as FEDE, except that there are separate FRE accounts in respect of each country to which FRE relates. FRE applies to expenses incurred in taxation years that begin after 2000, although a partner's FRE is determined with reference to partnership fiscal periods that begin after 2000. FRE is explicitly excluded from the amended FEDE definition in subsection 66(15). Section 66.21 is structured as follows:

- subsections 66.21(1) and (2) provide definitions used in section 66.21;
- subsection 66.21(3), in conjunction with paragraph 59(3.2)(c.1), provides for an amount to be included in income where there is a "negative" FRE balance;
- subsection 66.21(4) provides for a deduction in respect of the FRE balance for a taxation year. Generally, the deduction cannot exceed 30% of the balance at the end of the year; and
- subsection 66.21(5) provides a special rule for individuals who cease to reside in Canada.

New section 66.21 applies to taxation years that begin after 2000. The structure of section 66.21 and related successor rules in section 66.7 is similar to parallel rules for Canadian development expenses.

**66.21 (1) Definitions** — The definitions in this subsection apply in this section.

**"adjusted cumulative foreign resource expense"** of a taxpayer in respect of a country at the end of a taxation year means the total of

(a) the cumulative foreign resource expense of the taxpayer in respect of that country at the end of the year; and

(b) the amount, if any, by which

(i) the total determined under paragraph 66.7(13.2)(a) in respect of that country and the taxpayer for the year

exceeds

(ii) the amount that would, but for paragraph (3)(c), be determined under subsection (3) in respect of that country and the taxpayer for the year.

**Technical Notes**: The "adjusted cumulative foreign resource expense" of a taxpayer in respect of a country at the end of a taxation year is the taxpayer's cumulative foreign resource expense at the end of the year, plus an adjustment that applies in the event that the taxpayer disposes of foreign resource properties in the year in circumstances to which the successor rules in section 66.7 apply. The purpose of this adjustment is to permit a taxpayer to claim deductions for a taxation year of a succession in respect of foreign resource expenses incurred before the succession occurs, despite the taxpayer's cumulative FRE being reduced to nil under the description of J of the definition "cumulative foreign resource expense" as a consequence of a succession.

This definition is used in subsection 66.21(4). Its effect is illustrated in the example contained in the commentary on new subsections 66.7(13.1) and (13.2).

**"cumulative foreign resource expense"** of a taxpayer in respect of a country other than Canada at a particular time means the amount determined by the formula

$$(A + B + C + D) - (E + F + G + H + I + J)$$

Subdivision e — Deductions in Computing Income   S. 66.21(1) cum

where

A is the total of all foreign resource expenses, in respect of that country, made or incurred by the taxpayer

    (a) before the particular time, and

    (b) at a time (in this definition referred to as a "resident time")

        (i) at which the taxpayer was resident in Canada, and

        (ii) where the taxpayer became resident in Canada before the particular time, that is after the last time (before the particular time) that the taxpayer became resident in Canada;

B is the total of all amounts required to be included in computing the amount referred to in paragraph 59(3.2)(c.1) in respect of that country for taxation years that ended before the particular time and at a resident time;

C is the total of all amounts referred to in the description of F or G that are established by the taxpayer to have become a bad debt before the particular time and at a resident time;

D is the total of all specified amounts determined under subsection 66.7(13.2) in respect of the taxpayer and that country for taxation years that ended before the particular time and at a resident time;

E is the total of all amounts deducted, in computing the taxpayer's income for a taxation year that ended before the particular time and at a resident time, in respect of the taxpayer's cumulative foreign resource expense in respect of that country;

F is the total of all amounts each of which is an amount in respect of a foreign resource property in respect of that country (in this description referred to as the "particular property") disposed of by the taxpayer equal to the amount, if any, by which

    (a) the amount designated under subparagraph 59(1)(b)(ii) by the taxpayer in respect of the portion of the proceeds of that disposition that became receivable before the particular time and at a resident time

exceeds

    (b) the amount, if any, by which

        (i) the total of all amounts that would be determined under paragraph 66.7(2.3)(a), immediately before the time (in this paragraph referred to as the "relevant time") when such proceeds of disposition became receivable, in respect of the taxpayer, that country and an original owner of the particular property (or of any other property acquired by the taxpayer with the particular property in circumstances to which subsection 66.7(2.3) applied and in respect of which the proceeds of disposition became receivable by the taxpayer at the relevant time) if

        (A) amounts that became receivable at or after the relevant time were not taken into account,

        (B) paragraph 66.7(2.3)(a) were read without reference to "30% of", and

        (C) no reduction under subsection 80(8) at or after the relevant time were taken into account,

exceeds the total of

        (ii) all amounts that would be determined under paragraph 66.7(2.3)(a) at the relevant time in respect of the taxpayer, that country and an original owner of the particular property (or of that other property) if

        (A) amounts that became receivable after the relevant time were not taken into account,

        (B) paragraph 66.7(2.3)(a) were read without reference to "30% of", and

        (C) no reduction under subsection 80(8) at or after the relevant time were taken into account, and

        (iii) the portion of the amount otherwise determined under this paragraph that was otherwise applied to reduce the amount otherwise determined under this description;

G is the total of all amounts, in respect of that country, each of which is an amount included in the amount determined under this description by reason of subsection 66(12.41) that became receivable by the taxpayer before the particular time and at a resident time;

H is the total of all amounts each of which is an amount received before the particular time and at a resident time on account of any amount referred to in the description of C;

I is the total of all amounts each of which is an amount by which the cumulative foreign resource expense of the taxpayer in respect of that country is required, by reason of subsection 80(8), to be reduced at or before the particular time and at a resident time; and

J is the total of all amounts each of which is an amount that is required to be deducted, before the particular time and at a resident time, under paragraph 66.7(13.1)(a) in computing the taxpayer's cumulative foreign resource expense.

**Technical Notes**: The definition "cumulative foreign resource expense" is essentially the balance of unused FRE, determined as of a particular time. The FRE deduction under subsection 66.21(4) for a taxation year is determined with reference to cumulative FRE at the end of the year. In general, cumulative FRE at any time for a taxpayer in respect of a country is determined as follows:

- [A] ADD the taxpayer's FRE incurred in respect of the country before that time;
- [B] ADD "negative" FRE balances in respect of the country previously included in computing the taxpayer's income;
- [C] ADD bad debt amounts in respect of amounts receivable previously deducted in computing cumulative FRE under the descriptions of F or G (described below);
- [D] ADD specified amounts under subsection 66.7(13.2), representing cumulative FRE in respect of the country not available to a successor after there has been a disposition of foreign resource properties by the taxpayer in circumstance to which the successor rules in section 66.7 applies (See, in this regard, the example in the commentary on subsections 66.7(13.1) and (13.2).);
- [E] SUBTRACT the taxpayer's previous FRE claims in respect of the country;
- [F] SUBTRACT previous proceeds from the disposition of foreign resource properties in respect of the country, to the extent allocated under new subparagraph 59(1)(b)(ii). However, in cases where those properties were acquired by the taxpayer in circumstances to which the successor rules apply, proceeds are applied first to reduce unused successor FRE balances under new subsection 66.7(2.3);
- [G] SUBTRACT amounts receivable that enter into the calculation of cumulative FRE in respect of the country because of new subsection 66(12.41);
- [H] SUBTRACT recoveries of bad debts previously reflected as an addition under the description of C;
- [I] SUBTRACT adjustment provided because of the debt forgiveness rules in section 80; and
- [J] where the taxpayer previously disposed of foreign resource properties in circumstances to which the successor rules applied, SUBTRACT the taxpayer's cumulative FRE in respect of the country as of the time of the succession.

In calculating cumulative FRE at any time, the amounts that would otherwise be included in [A] to [J] and that relate to periods of time during which the taxpayer was not resident in Canada are ignored. If a taxpayer had previously been a resident of Canada, ceased to reside in Canada and subsequently becomes a resident in Canada, amounts that would otherwise be included in [A] to [J] and that relate to the previous periods of residence in Canada are likewise ignored.

**Related Provisions**: 104(5.2) — Trusts — 21-year deemed disposition; 248(1)"foreign resource property" — Meaning of foreign resource property in respect of a country; 257 — Formula cannot calculate to less than zero.

**"foreign resource expense"** of a taxpayer in respect of a country other than Canada means

(a) any drilling or exploration expense, including any general geological or geophysical expense, incurred by the taxpayer on or in respect of exploring or drilling for petroleum or natural gas in that country,

(b) any expense incurred by the taxpayer for the purpose of determining the existence, location, extent or quality of a mineral resource in that country, including any expense incurred in the course of

(i) prospecting,

(ii) carrying out geological, geophysical or geochemical surveys,

(iii) drilling by rotary, diamond, percussion or other methods, or

(iv) trenching, digging test pits and preliminary sampling,

(c) the cost to the taxpayer of any of the taxpayer's foreign resource property in respect of that country,

(d) any annual payment made by the taxpayer for the preservation of a foreign resource property in respect of that country, and

(e) subject to section 66.8, the taxpayer's share of an expense, cost or payment referred to in any of paragraphs (a) to (d) that is made or incurred by a partnership in a fiscal period of the partnership that begins after 2000 if, at the end of that period, the taxpayer was a member of the partnership

but does not include

(f) an expenditure that is the cost, or any part of the cost, to the taxpayer of any depreciable property of a prescribed class,

(g) an expenditure incurred at any time after the commencement of production from a foreign resource property of the taxpayer in order to evaluate the feasibility of a method of recovery of petroleum, natural gas or related hydrocarbons from the portion of a natural reservoir to which the foreign resource property relates,

(h) an expenditure (other than a drilling expense) incurred at any time after the commencement of production from a foreign resource property of the taxpayer in order to assist in the recovery of petroleum, natural gas or related hydrocarbons from the portion of a natural reservoir to which the foreign resource property relates,

(i) an expenditure, incurred at any time, that relates to the injection of any substance to assist in the recovery of petroleum, natural gas or related hydrocarbons from a natural reservoir,

(j) an expenditure incurred by the taxpayer, unless the expenditure was made

(i) for the acquisition of foreign resource property by the taxpayer, or

(ii) for the purpose of

(A) enhancing the value of foreign resource property that the taxpayer owned at the time the expenditure was incurred or that the taxpayer had a reasonable expectation of owning after that time, or

(B) assisting in evaluating whether a foreign resource property is to be acquired by the taxpayer, or

(k) the taxpayer's share of any cost or expenditure referred to in any of paragraphs (f) to (j) that is incurred by a partnership.

**Technical Notes**: See at the beginning of 66.21.

**Related Provisions**: 66(18) — Expenses of partnerships; 66.7(2.3) — Successor of foreign resource expenses; 248(1)"foreign resource expense" — Definition applies to entire Act; 248(1)"foreign resource property" — Meaning of foreign resource property in respect of a country.

**"foreign resource income"** of a taxpayer for a taxation year in respect of a country other than Canada means the total of

(a) that part of the taxpayer's income for the year, determined without reference to subsections (4) and 66(4), that is reasonably attributable to

(i) the production of petroleum or natural gas from natural accumulations of petroleum or natural gas in that country or from oil or gas wells in that country, or

(ii) the production of minerals from mines in that country;

(b) the taxpayer's income for the year from royalties in respect of a natural accumulation of petroleum or natural gas in that country, an oil or gas well in that country or a mine in that country, determined without reference to subsections (4) and 66(4); and

(c) all amounts each of which is an amount, in respect of a foreign resource property in respect of that country that has been disposed of by the taxpayer, equal to the amount, if any, by which

(i) the amount included in computing the taxpayer's income for the year by reason of subsection 59(1) in respect of that disposition,

exceeds

(ii) the total of all amounts each of which is that portion of an amount deducted under subsection 66.7(2) in computing the taxpayer's income for the year that

(A) can reasonably be considered to be in respect of the foreign resource property, and

(B) cannot reasonably be considered to have reduced the amount otherwise determined under paragraph (a) or (b) in respect of the taxpayer for the year.

**Technical Notes**: The new definition "foreign resource income" is structured in a manner similar to that of the foreign resource income limitation provided under amended subparagraph 66(4)(b)(ii), except that the new definition applies on a country-by-country basis while subparagraph 66(4)(b)(ii) applies to world-wide income. In general terms, the definition refers to a taxpayer's mineral, oil and gas production and royalty income in respect of a country, as well as income from the disposition of foreign resource property in respect of the country. In computing foreign resource income, deductions under subsections 66(4) and 66.21(4) are not taken into account. (However, successor deductions under subsections 66.7(2) and (2.3) are taken into account and can result in a decrease of foreign resource income.)

**Related Provisions**: 248(1)"foreign resource property" — Meaning of foreign resource property in respect of a country.

**"foreign resource loss"** of a taxpayer for a taxation year in respect of a country other than Canada means the taxpayer's loss for the year in respect of the country determined in accordance with the definition "foreign resource income" with such modifications as the circumstances require.

**Technical Notes**: The "foreign resource loss" of a taxpayer for a taxation year in respect of a country (other than Canada) is defined as the taxpayer's loss for a taxation year in respect of the country determined in accordance with the definition "foreign resource income", with such modifications as the circumstances require.

The expression "foreign resource loss" is used in new clause 66.21(4)(a)(ii)(D).

**"global foreign resource limit"** of a taxpayer for a taxation year means the amount that is the lesser of

(a) the amount, if any, by which

(i) the amount determined under subparagraph 66(4)(b)(ii) in respect of the taxpayer for the year

exceeds the total of

(ii) the total of all amounts each of which is the maximum amount that the taxpayer would be permitted to deduct, in respect of a country, under subsection (4) in computing the taxpayer's income for the year if, in its application to the year, subsection (4) were read without reference to paragraph (4)(b), and

(iii) the amount deducted for the year under subsection 66(4) in computing the taxpayer's income for the year; and

(c) the amount, if any, by which

(i) 30% of the total of all amounts each of which is, at the end of the year, the taxpayer's adjusted cumulative foreign resource expense in respect of a country,

exceeds

(ii) the total described in subparagraph (a)(ii).

**Technical Notes**: A taxpayer's deduction limit for FRE under new subsection 66.21(4) is determined with reference to the taxpayer's "global foreign resource limit". Without reference to the "global foreign resource limit", a taxpayer cannot deduct in respect of a country more than 30% of the taxpayer's cumulative FRE in respect of the country. In general terms, the definition "global foreign resource limit" and paragraph 66.21(4)(b) are structured to permit a taxpayer to deduct a higher amount of the taxpayer's cumulative FRE in respect of a country, provided that on an overall basis the taxpayer claims no more than the lesser of:

- 30% of the taxpayer's total cumulative FRE in respect of all countries; and
- the taxpayer's global foreign resource income determined under subparagraph 66(4)(b)(ii), other than the portion of it used to support the taxpayer's deduction under subsection 66(4) or to support total deductions otherwise available under subsection 66.21(4).

**Related Provisions**: 66(13.1) — Short taxation year.

**(2) Application of subsection 66(15)** — The definitions in subsection 66(15) apply in this section.

**Technical Notes**: Subsection 66.21(2) provides that the definitions in subsection 66(15) apply for the purposes of section 66.21. The relevant definitions include the expressions "foreign resource property", "production" and "drilling or exploration expense".

**(3) Amount to be included in income** — For the purpose of paragraph 59(3.2)(c.1), the amount referred to in this subsection in respect of a taxpayer for a taxation year is the amount, if any, by which

(a) the total of all amounts referred to in the descriptions of E to J in the definition "cumulative foreign resource expense" in subsection (1) that are deducted in computing the taxpayer's cumulative foreign resource expense at the end of the year in respect of a country

exceeds the total of

(b) the total of all amounts referred to in the descriptions of A to D in the definition "cumulative foreign resource expense" in subsection (1) that are included in computing the taxpayer's cumulative foreign resource expense at the end of the year in respect of the country, and

(c) the total determined under paragraph 66.7(13.2)(a) for the year in respect of the taxpayer and the country.

**Technical Notes**: Subsection 66.21(3) provides for an amount to be included in computing a taxpayer's income for a taxation year where there is a "negative" FRE balance. In the event that the taxpayer disposes of foreign resource properties in the year in circumstances in which the successor rules apply, the income inclusion is offset by the taxpayer's FRE balance immediately before the succession (other than the portion of the balance that the taxpayer has made exclusively available to the successor because of a designation under subparagraph 66.7(13.2)(a)(ii)).

**Related Provisions**: 59(3.2)(c.1) — Income inclusion; 66(5) — No application to certain dealers; 66(11.4)(c) — Change of control; 66.8(1) — Resource expenses of limited partner; 70(5.2)(a) — Death of taxpayer; 87(1.2) — Amalgamation — continuing corporation; 88(1.5) — Windup — parent continuation of subsidiary.

**(4) Deduction for cumulative foreign resource expense** — In computing a taxpayer's income for a taxation year throughout which the taxpayer is resident in Canada, the taxpayer may deduct the amount claimed by the taxpayer, in respect of a country other than Canada, not exceeding the total of

(a) the greater of

(i) 10% of a particular amount equal to the taxpayer's adjusted cumulative foreign resource expense in respect of the country at the end of the year, and

(ii) the least of

(A) if the taxpayer ceased to be resident in Canada immediately after the end of the year, the particular amount,

(B) if clause (A) does not apply, 30% of the particular amount,

(C) the amount, if any, by which the taxpayer's foreign resource income for the year in respect of the country exceeds the portion of the amount, deducted under subsection 66(4) in computing the taxpayer's income for the year, that applies to a source in the country, and

(D) the amount, if any, by which

(I) the total of all amounts each of which is the taxpayer's foreign resource income for the year in respect of a country

exceeds the total of

(II) all amounts each of which is the taxpayer's foreign resource loss for the year in respect of a country, and

(III) the amount deducted under subsection 66(4) in computing the taxpayer's income for the year, and

(b) the lesser of

(i) the amount, if any, by which the particular amount exceeds the amount determined for the year under paragraph (a) in respect of the taxpayer, and

(ii) that portion of the taxpayer's global foreign resource limit for the year that is designated for the year by the taxpayer, in respect of that country and no other country, in prescribed form filed with the Minister with the taxpayer's return of income for the year.

**Technical Notes**: Subsection 66.21(4) permits a deduction in respect of a taxpayer's cumulative FRE in respect of each country. The deduction for a taxation year is generally available only to persons resident in Canada throughout the year. See, however, subsection 66.21(5) (application of subsection 66.21(4) to part-year residents) and new paragraph 115(1)(e.1) (FRE deduction for non-residents).

The limit of the permitted deduction is determined in accordance with subsection 66.21(4). The limit is not less than 10% of the taxpayer's cumulative FRE in respect of the country at the end of a taxation year and, in all cases, is not more than the full amount of the balance. Cumulative FRE for this purpose is adjusted, as explained in the commentary on the definition "adjusted cumulative foreign resource expense".

Subject to paragraph 66.21(4)(b) and the 10% minimum limit, the maximum that a taxpayer may deduct in computing income for a taxation year in respect of a country is generally an amount that does not exceed the least of

- the amount of the taxpayer's "foreign resource income" in respect of the country,
- 30% of the taxpayer's adjusted cumulative FRE at the end of the year,
- the amount determined by clause 66.21(4)(a)(ii)(C), and
- the amount determined by clause 66.21(4)(a)(ii)(D).

In connection with clause 66.21(4)(a)(ii)(C), see the commentary on new subsections 66(4.1) and (4.2).

With regard to the defined expression "foreign resource income", see the commentary on the expression "foreign resource income" in subsection 66.21(1).

Paragraph 66.21(4)(b) permits, in some cases, a taxpayer to deduct a higher amount from the taxpayer's cumulative FRE in respect of a country than would otherwise be the case. The additional deduction is equal to the lesser of:

- the amount by which the taxpayer's cumulative FRE in respect of the country at the end of the year exceeds the portion of it that would otherwise be deductible under subsection 66.21(4) in computing the taxpayer's income for the year; and
- the portion of the taxpayer's "global foreign resource limit" designated by the taxpayer in respect of the country.

The effect of paragraph 66.21(4)(b) is to permit a taxpayer to deduct an additional amount of the taxpayer's cumulative FRE in respect of a country beyond the 10% or 30% limit set out in paragraph 66.21(4)(a). The additional amount is determined with reference to a taxpayer's "global foreign resource limit" (as described in the commentary above), which is intended to allow additional deductions in order to permit a taxpayer to use, in aggregate, up to 30% of the taxpayer's total cumulative FRE in respect of all countries to the extent that there is sufficient supporting global foreign resource income.

As provided in subsection 66.21(4), FEDE claims by a taxpayer may affect the amount of permitted deduction in respect of cumulative FRE.

**Notice of Ways and Means Motion, federal budget, and supplementary information, February 28, 2000**: See under 66(4)(b)(ii).

**Related Provisions**: 20(1)(hh) — Repayments of inducements, etc.; 66(5) — No application to certain dealers; 66(11.4)(c) — Change of control; 66(13.1) — Short taxation year; 66.8(1) — Resource expenses of limited partner; 70(5.2)(a) — Death of taxpayer; 87(1.2) — Amalgamation — continuing corporation; 88(1.5) — Windup — parent continuation of subsidiary; 96(1)(d)(ii) — Partnerships — no deduction for resource expenses; 110.6(1)"investment expense"(d) — Effect of claim under 66.21(4) on capital gains exemption; 115(4.1) — Taxable income earned in Canada — foreign resource pool expenses; 127.52(1)(e) — Add-back of deduction for minimum tax purposes.

**(5) Individual changing residence** — Where at any time in a taxation year an individual becomes or ceases to be resident in Canada,

(a) subsection (4) applies to the individual as if the year were the period or periods in the year throughout which the individual was resident in Canada; and

(b) for the purpose of applying this section, subsection 66(13.1) does not apply to the individual for the year.

**Technical Notes**: Subsection 66.21(5) applies where an individual becomes, or ceases to be, resident in Canada in a taxation year.

Under section 128.1, the immigration or emigration of an individual (other than a trust) has no impact on an individual's taxation year. Consequently, the individual would be resident in Canada for part of the taxation year and not resident in Canada for another part, with the result that, absent subsection 66.21(5), the individual would otherwise not be permitted to deduct an amount for the year under subsection 66.21(4). (This is because subsection 66.21(4) provides that, for a taxpayer to claim a deduction under that subsection for a taxation year, the taxpayer must be resident in Canada throughout the year.) Furthermore, the wording of section 114 that applies to the 1998 and subsequent taxation years would, absent subsection 66.21(5), preclude an individual who is resident in Canada for only part of a taxation year from obtaining a deduction in the year in respect of cumulative FRE.

Consequently, subsection 66.21(5) provides that, for the purposes of subsection 66.21(4), a part-year resident's taxation year is treated as being the part of the taxation year throughout which the individual is resident in Canada and that, for these purposes, subsection 66(13.1) (which provides a rule relating to proration of deductions for short taxation years) does not apply to the individual for the year. As a result, an individual who is resident in Canada for only part of a taxation year can claim a non-prorated deduction under subsection 66.21(4). The deduction determined in this manner enters into the calculation of the individual's taxable income pursuant to section 114.

Given that section 128.1 operates to create new taxation years for trusts or corporations that become or cease to be resident in Canada, this measure has no relevance to trusts and there is no need to extend this measure to apply to corporations. Subsection 66.21(5) is parallel to new subsection 66(4.3), described in the commentary above.

Subsection 66.21(5) provides that, in this case, the individual's taxation year for the purposes of subsection 66.21(4) is considered to be the period or periods throughout which the individual is resident in Canada. The deduction determined in this manner enters into the calculation of the individual's taxable income pursuant to section 114.

**Application**: The December 21, 2000 draft legislation, s. 29, will add s. 66.21, applicable to taxation years that begin after 2000.

**Definitions [s. 66.21]**: "adjusted cumulative foreign resource expense" — 66.21(1); "amount" — 248(1); "Canada" — 255, *Interpretation Act* 35(1); "commencement" — *Interpretation Act* 35(1); "cumulative foreign resource expense" — 66.21(1); "depreciable property" — 13(21), 248(1); "disposition" — 248(1);

"drilling or exploration expense", "expense" — 66(15), 66.21(2); "fiscal period" — 249.1; "foreign resource expense" — 66.21(1), 248(1); "foreign resource income", "foreign resource loss" — 66.21(1); "foreign resource property" — 66(15), 248(1); "global foreign resource limit" — 66.21(1); "in respect of that country" — 248(1)"foreign resource property"; "individual", "mineral", "mineral resource", "Minister", "oil or gas well" — 248(1); "original owner" — 66(15), 66.21(2); "partnership" — see Notes to 96(1); "prescribed" — 248(1); "production" — 66(15), 66.21(2); "property" — 248(1); "related" — 251(2)–(6); "resident", "resident in Canada" — 250; "share" — 248(1); "taxation year" — 249; "taxpayer" — 248(1).

**66.3 (1) Exploration and development shares** — Any shares of the capital stock of a corporation or any interest in any such shares or right thereto acquired by a taxpayer under circumstances described in paragraph (i) of the definition "Canadian exploration expense" in subsection 66.1(6), paragraph (g) of the definition "Canadian development expense" in subsection 66.2(5) or paragraph (c) of the definition "Canadian oil and gas property expense" in subsection 66.4(5)

(a) shall, if acquired before November 13, 1981, be deemed

(i) not to be a capital property of the taxpayer,

(ii) subject to subsection 142.6(3), to be inventory of the taxpayer, and

(iii) to have been acquired by the taxpayer at a cost to the taxpayer of nil; and

(b) shall, if acquired after November 12, 1981, be deemed to have been acquired by the taxpayer at a cost to the taxpayer of nil.

**Notes**: Reference to 142.6(3) in 66.3(1)(a) added by 1994 tax amendments bill (Part III), effective for taxation years that begin after October 1994.

66.3(1) originally enacted as 66.3, effective for property acquired after July 1976. A subsequent amendment to this provision by 1979 Budget, and its being changed to 66.3(1), have apparently not preserved this original date of application. It is therefore possible that 66.3(1)(a) applies for shares acquired before August 1976.

**(2) Deductions from paid-up capital** — Where, at any time after May 23, 1985, a corporation has issued a share of its capital stock under circumstances described in paragraph (i) of the definition "Canadian exploration expense" in subsection 66.1(6), paragraph (g) of the definition "Canadian development expense" in subsection 66.2(5) or paragraph (c) of the definition "Canadian oil and gas property expense" in subsection 66.4(5) or has issued a share of its capital stock on the exercise of an interest in or right to such a share granted under circumstances described in any of those paragraphs, in computing, at any particular time after that time, the paid-up capital in respect of the class of shares of the capital stock of the corporation that included that share

(a) there shall be deducted the amount, if any, by which

(i) the increase as a result of the issue of the share in the paid-up capital, determined without reference to this subsection as it applies to the share, in respect of all of the shares of that class

exceeds

(ii) the amount, if any, by which

(A) the total amount of consideration received by the corporation in respect of the share, including any consideration for the interest or right in respect of the share

exceeds

(B) 50% of the amount of the expense referred to in paragraph (i) of the definition "Canadian exploration expense" in subsection 66.1(6), paragraph (g) of the definition "Canadian development expense" in subsection 66.2(5) or paragraph (c) of the definition "Canadian oil and gas property expense" in subsection 66.4(5) that was incurred by a taxpayer who acquired the share or the interest or right on the exercise of which the share was issued, as the case may be, pursuant to an agreement with the corporation under which the taxpayer incurred the expense solely as consideration for the share, interest or right, as the case may be; and

(b) there shall be added an amount equal to the lesser of

(i) the amount, if any, by which

(A) the total of all amounts each of which is an amount deemed by subsection 84(3), (4) or (4.1) to be a dividend on shares of that class paid by the corporation after May 23, 1985 and before the particular time

exceeds

(B) the total that would be determined under clause (A) if this Act were read without reference to paragraph (a), and

(ii) the total of all amounts each of which is an amount required by paragraph (a) to be deducted in computing the paid-up capital in respect of that class of shares after May 22, 1985 and before the particular time.

**(3) Cost of flow-through shares** — Any flow-through share (within the meaning assigned by subsection 66(15)) of a corporation acquired by a person who was a party to the agreement pursuant to which it was issued shall be deemed to have been acquired by the person at a cost to the person of nil.

**(4) Paid-up capital** — Where, at any time after February, 1986, a corporation has issued a flow-through share (within the meaning assigned by subsection 66(15)), in computing, at any particular time after that time, the paid-up capital in respect of the class of shares of the capital stock of the corporation that included that share

(a) there shall be deducted the amount, if any, by which

(i) the increase as a result of the issue of the share in the paid-up capital, determined without reference to this subsection as it applies to the share, in respect of all of the shares of that class

exceeds

(ii) the amount, if any, by which

(A) the total amount of consideration received by the corporation in respect of the share

exceeds

(B) 50% of the total of the expenses that were renounced by the corporation under subsection 66(12.6), (12.601), (12.62) or (12.64) in respect of the share; and

(b) there shall be added an amount equal to the lesser of

(i) the amount, if any, by which

(A) the total of all amounts each of which is an amount deemed by subsection 84(3), (4) or (4.1) to be a dividend on shares of that class paid by the corporation after February, 1986 and before the particular time

exceeds

(B) the total that would be determined under clause (A) if this Act were read without reference to paragraph (a), and

(ii) the total of all amounts each of which is an amount required by paragraph (a) to be deducted in computing the paid-up capital in respect of that class of shares after February, 1986 and before the particular time.

**Notes**: Reference to 66(12.601) in 66.3(4)(a)(ii)(B) added by 1992 Economic Statement, effective December 3, 1992.

**Related Provisions [s. 66.3]**: 66(16) — Partnerships — person — taxation year; 66.4(2) — Deduction — Canadian oil and gas property expenses; 66.7 — Successor rules.

**Definitions [s. 66.3]**: "amount" — 248(1); "capital property" — 54, 248(1); "class of shares" — 248(6); "corporation" — 248(1), *Interpretation Act* 35(1); "dividend", "inventory" — 248(1); "paid-up capital" — 89(1), 248(1); "person" — 66(16), 248(1); "share", "taxpayer" — 248(1).

**Interpretation Bulletins [s. 66.3]**: IT-503: Exploration and development shares.

## 66.4 [Canadian oil and gas property expenses] — (1) Recovery of costs
— For the purposes of the description of B in the definition "cumulative Canadian oil and gas property expense" in subsection (5) and the description of L in the definition "cumulative Canadian development expense" in subsection 66.2(5) and for the purpose of subparagraph 64(1.2)(a)(ii) of the *Income Tax Act*, chapter 148 of the Revised Statutes of Canada, 1952, as it applies to dispositions occurring before November 13, 1981, the amount determined under this subsection in respect of a taxpayer for a taxation year is the amount, if any, by which

(a) the total of all amounts referred to in the descriptions of E to J in the definition "cumulative Canadian oil and gas property expense" in subsection (5) that are deducted in computing the taxpayer's cumulative Canadian oil and gas property expense at the end of the year

exceeds the total of

(b) all amounts referred to in the descriptions of A to D.1 in the definition "cumulative Canadian oil and gas property expense" in subsection (5) that are included in computing the taxpayer's cumulative Canadian oil and gas property expense at the end of the year, and

(c) the total determined under subparagraph 66.7(12.1)(c)(i) in respect of the taxpayer for the year.

**Related Provisions**: 66(11) — Acquisition of control; 66(11.4) — Change of control; 66(13) — Limitation; 104(5.2) — Trusts — 21-year deemed disposition. See additional Related provisions and Definitions at end of s. 66.4.

**Notes**: 66.4(1)(c) added by 1991 technical bill, effective for taxation years ending after February 17, 1987, except that for taxation years commencing before February 18, 1987, read "C" in place of "D.1" in 66.4(1)(b). Opening words amended by 1993 technical bill, retroactive to taxation years ending after February 17, 1987, to correct a cross-referencing error and other minor drafting errors.

**I.T. Application Rules**: 69 (meaning of "*Income Tax Act*, chapter 148 of the Revised Statutes of Canada, 1952").

**(2) Deduction for cumulative Canadian oil and gas property expense** — A taxpayer may deduct, in computing the taxpayer's income for a taxation year, such amount as the taxpayer may claim not exceeding the total of

(a) the lesser of

(i) the total of

(A) the taxpayer's cumulative Canadian oil and gas property expense at the end of the year, and

(B) the amount, if any, by which

(I) the total determined under subparagraph 66.7(12.1)(c)(i) in respect of the taxpayer for the year

exceeds

(II) the amount that would, but for paragraph (1)(c), be determined under subsection (1) in respect of the taxpayer for the year, and

(ii) the amount, if any, by which the total of all amounts each of which is

(A) an amount included in the taxpayer's income for the year by virtue of a disposition in the year of inventory described in section 66.3 that was a share, any interest therein or right thereto acquired by the taxpayer under circumstances described in paragraph (c) of the definition "Canadian oil and gas property expense" in subsection (5), or

(B) an amount included by virtue of paragraph 12(1)(e) in computing the taxpayer's income for the year to the extent that it relates to inventory described in clause (A)

exceeds

(C) the total of all amounts deducted as a reserve by virtue of paragraph 20(1)(n) in computing the taxpayer's income for the year to the extent that the reserve relates to inventory described in clause (A); and

(b) 10% of the amount, if any, by which the amount determined under subparagraph (a)(i) exceeds the amount determined under subparagraph (a)(ii).

**Related Provisions**: 20(1)(hh) — Repayments of inducements, etc.; 66(10.3) — Joint exploration corporation; 66(13.1) — Short taxation year; 66.2(2) — Deduction for cumulative CDE; 110.6(1)"investment expense"(d) — effect of claim under 66.4(2) on capital gains exemption; 127.52(1)(e) — Add-back of deduction for minimum tax purposes. See additional Related provisions and Definitions at end of s. 66.4.

**Notes**: 66.4(2) amended by 1991 technical bill, effective for taxation years ending after February 17, 1987.

**Interpretation Bulletins**: IT-273R2: Government assistance — general comments; IT-438R2: Crown charges — resource properties in Canada.

**(3), (4)** [Repealed under former Act]

**Notes**: 66.4(3) and (4), repealed in 1987, dealt with a successor corporation's Canadian oil and gas property expenses. The successor corporation rules are now in 66.7.

**(5) Definitions** — In this section

**Related Provisions**: 66(15.1) — Application to s. 66; 66.1(6.1) — Application to s. 66.1; 66.2(5.1) — Application to s. 66.2.

**Notes**: Before consolidation in the R.S.C. 1985 (5th Supp.), the opening words of 66.4(5) referred to ss. 66, 66.1 and 66.2. See now 66(15.1), 66.1(6.1) and 66.2(5.1).

**"Canadian oil and gas property expense"** of a taxpayer means any cost or expense incurred after December 11, 1979 that is

(a) notwithstanding paragraph 18(1)(m), the cost to the taxpayer of any property described in paragraph (a), (c) or (d) of the definition "Canadian resource property" in subsection 66(15) or a right to or interest in such property (other than such a right or interest that the taxpayer has by reason of being a beneficiary of a trust) or an amount paid or payable to Her Majesty in right of the Province of Saskatchewan as a net royalty payment pursuant to a net royalty petroleum and natural gas lease that was in effect on March 31, 1977 to the extent that it can reasonably be regarded as a cost of acquiring the lease, but not including any payment made to any of the persons referred to in any of subparagraphs 18(1)(m)(i) to (iii) for the preservation of a taxpayer's rights in respect of a Canadian resource property nor a payment (other than a net royalty payment referred to in this paragraph) to which paragraph 18(1)(m) applied by virtue of subparagraph 18(1)(m)(v),

(b) subject to section 66.8, the taxpayer's share of any expense referred to in paragraph (a) incurred by a partnership in a fiscal period thereof at the end of which the taxpayer was a member of the partnership, unless the taxpayer elects in respect of the share in prescribed form and manner on or before the day that is 6 months after the taxpayer's taxation year in which that period ends, or

(c) any cost or expense referred to in paragraph (a) incurred by the taxpayer pursuant to an agreement in writing with a corporation, entered into before 1987, under which the taxpayer incurred the cost or expense solely as consideration for shares, other than prescribed shares, of the capital stock of the corporation issued to the taxpayer or any interest in such shares or right thereto,

but, for greater certainty, shall not include

(d) any consideration given by the taxpayer for any share or any interest therein or right thereto, except as provided by paragraph (c), or

(e) any expense described in paragraph (c) incurred by any other taxpayer to the extent that the expense was,

(i) by virtue of that paragraph, a Canadian oil and gas property expense of that other taxpayer,

(ii) by virtue of paragraph (i) of the definition "Canadian exploration expense" in subsection 66.1(6), a Canadian exploration expense of that other taxpayer, or

(iii) by virtue of paragraph (g) of the definition "Canadian development expense" in subsection 66.2(5), a Canadian development expense of that other taxpayer,

but any amount of assistance that a taxpayer has received or is entitled to receive in respect of or related to the taxpayer's Canadian oil and gas property expense shall not reduce the amount of any of the expenses described in any of paragraphs (a) to (c);

**Related Provisions**: 49(2) — Where option expires; 53(1)(e)(vii.1) — Addition to ACB — partnership interest; 66(10.3) — Joint exploration corporation; 66(12.5) — Unitized oil or gas field in Canada; 66.2(8) — Presumption; 66.3 — Exploration and development shares; 66.4(1) — Recovery of costs; 66.4(2) — Deduction for cumulative COGPE; 248(1)"Canadian oil and gas property expense" — Definition applies to entire Act; 248(16) — GST input tax credit and rebate deemed to be assistance; 248(18) — GST — repayment of input tax credit; *Interpretation Act* 8(2.1), (2.2) — Application to exclusive economic zone and continental shelf. See additional Related Provisions and Definitions at end of s. 66.4.

**Notes**: 66.4(5)"Canadian oil and gas property expense" was 66.4(5)(a) before consolidation in R.S.C. 1985 (5th Supp.), effective for taxation years ending after November 1991. See Table of Concordance.

66.4(5)(a)(ii) (now "Canadian oil and gas property expense"(b)) amended by 1992 technical bill, effective for partnership fiscal periods ending after July 1990, to add the exception beginning "unless the taxpayer elects". (See 53(1)(e)(vii.1) for the offsetting addition to ACB.) An election for past years may be filed until December 10, 1993.

The exclusion, in 66.4(5)(a)(iii) (now "Canadian oil and gas property expense"(c)), of prescribed shares was added by 1981 Budget, effective for any outlay or expense made or incurred after 1982.

**Regulations**: 6202 (prescribed share).

**Interpretation Bulletins**: IT-109R2: Unpaid amounts; IT-273R2: Government assistance — general comments; IT-438R2: Crown charges — resource properties in Canada; IT-503: Exploration and development shares.

**Forms**: T1086: Election by a partner waiving Canadian development expenses or oil and gas property expenses.

**"cumulative Canadian oil and gas property expense"** of a taxpayer at any time in a taxation year means the amount determined by the formula

$$(A + B + C + D + D.1) - (E + F + G + H + I + I.1 + J)$$

where

A is the total of all Canadian oil and gas property expenses made or incurred by the taxpayer before that time,

B is the total of all amounts determined under subsection (1) in respect of the taxpayer for taxation years ending before that time,

C is the total of all amounts referred to in the description of F or G that are established by the taxpayer to have become bad debts before that time,

D is such part, if any, of the amount determined for I as has been repaid before that time by the taxpayer pursuant to a legal obligation to repay all or any part of that amount,

D.1 is the total of all specified amounts, determined under paragraph 66.7(12.1)(c) in respect of the taxpayer for taxation years ending before that time,

E is the total of all amounts deducted in computing the taxpayer's income for a taxation year ending before that time in respect of the taxpayer's cumulative Canadian oil and gas property expense,

F is the total of all amounts each of which is an amount in respect of a property described in paragraph (a), (c) or (d) of the definition "Canadian resource property" in subsection 66(15) or a right to or interest in such a property, other than such a right or interest that the taxpayer has by reason of being a beneficiary of a trust, (in this description referred to as "the particular property") disposed of by the taxpayer before that time equal to the amount, if any, by which

   (a) the amount, if any, by which the proceeds of disposition in respect of the particular property that became receivable by the taxpayer

before that time exceed any outlays or expenses made or incurred by the taxpayer before that time for the purpose of making the disposition and that were not otherwise deductible for the purposes of this Part

exceeds the total of

   (b) the amount, if any, by which

      (i) the total of all amounts that would be determined under paragraph 66.7(5)(a), immediately before the time (in this paragraph and paragraph (c) referred to as the "relevant time") when such proceeds of disposition became receivable, in respect of the taxpayer and an original owner of the particular property (or of any other property acquired by the taxpayer with the particular property in circumstances in which subsection 66.7(5) applied and in respect of which the proceeds of disposition became receivable by the taxpayer at the relevant time) if

         (A) amounts that became receivable at or after the relevant time were not taken into account,

         (B) each designation made under subparagraph 66.7(4)(a)(iii) in respect of an amount that became receivable before the relevant time were made before the relevant time,

         (C) paragraph 66.7(5)(a) were read without reference to "10% of", and

         (D) no reduction under subsection 80(8) at or after the relevant time were taken into account

exceeds the total of

      (ii) all amounts that would be determined under paragraph 66.7(5)(a) at the relevant time in respect of the taxpayer and an original owner of the particular property (or of that other property described in subparagraph (i)) if

         (A) amounts that became receivable after the relevant time were not taken into account,

         (B) each designation made under subparagraph 66.7(4)(a)(iii) in respect of an amount that became receivable at or before the relevant time were made before the relevant time,

         (C) paragraph 66.7(5)(a) were read without reference to "10% of", and

         (D) no reduction under subsection 80(8) at or after the relevant time were taken into account, and

      (iii) such portion of the amount determined under this paragraph as was otherwise applied to reduce the amount otherwise determined under this description, and

(c) the amount, if any, by which

(i) the total of all amounts that would be determined under paragraph 66.7(4)(a), immediately before the relevant time, in respect of the taxpayer and an original owner of the particular property (or of any other property acquired by the taxpayer with the particular property in circumstances in which subsection 66.7(4) applied and in respect of which the proceeds of disposition became receivable by the taxpayer at the relevant time) if

(A) amounts that became receivable at or after the relevant time were not taken into account,

(B) each designation made under subparagraph 66.7(4)(a)(iii) in respect of an amount that became receivable before the relevant time were made before the relevant time,

(C) paragraph 66.7(4)(a) were read without reference to "30% of", and

(D) no reduction under subsection 80(8) at or after the relevant time were taken into account

exceeds the total of

(ii) all amounts that would be determined under paragraph 66.7(4)(a) at the relevant time in respect of the taxpayer and an original owner of the particular property (or of that other property described in subparagraph (i)) if

(A) amounts that became receivable after the relevant time were not taken into account,

(B) each designation made under subparagraph 66.7(4)(a)(iii) in respect of an amount that became receivable at or before the relevant time were made before the relevant time,

(C) paragraph 66.7(4)(a) were read without reference to "30% of",

(D) amounts described in subparagraph 66.7(4)(a)(ii) that became receivable at the relevant time were not taken into account, and

(E) no reduction under subsection 80(8) at or after the relevant time were taken into account, and

(iii) such portion of the amount otherwise determined under this paragraph as was otherwise applied to reduce the amount otherwise determined under this description,

G is the total of all amounts that became receivable by the taxpayer before that time that are to be included in the amount determined under this description by virtue of paragraph 66(12.5)(a),

H is the total of all amounts each of which is an amount received before that time on account of any amount referred to in the description of C,

I is the total amount of assistance that the taxpayer has received or is entitled to receive in respect of any Canadian oil and gas property expense incurred after 1980 or that can reasonably be related to any such expense after 1980,

I.1 is the total of all amounts by which the cumulative Canadian oil and gas property expense of the taxpayer is required because of subsection 80(8) to be reduced at or before that time, and

J is the total of all amounts that are required to be deducted before that time under paragraph 66.7(12)(d) in computing the taxpayer's cumulative Canadian oil and gas property expense;

**Related Provisions**: 20(1)(kk) — Exploration and development grants; 50(1)(a) — Deemed disposition where debt becomes bad debt; 66(10.3) — Joint exploration corporation; 66(12.5) — Unitized oil or gas field in Canada; 66.7(5) — Deduction to successor corporation; 70(5.2) — Resource properties and land inventories of deceased taxpayer; 79(4)(c) — Subsequent payment by debtor following surrender of property deemed to be repayment of assistance; 79.1(8) — No claim for principal amount of bad debt where property seized by creditor; 80(8)(d) — Reduction of CCOGPE on debt forgiveness; 96(2.2)(d) — At-risk amount; 104(5.2) — Trusts — 21-year deemed disposition; 248(16) — GST — input tax credit and rebate; 248(18) — GST — repayment of input tax credit; 257 — Formula cannot calculate to less than zero. See additional Related Provisions and Definitions at end of s. 66.4.

**Notes**: 66.4(5)"cumulative Canadian oil and gas property expense" was 66.4(5)(b) before consolidation in R.S.C. 1985 (5th Supp.), effective for taxation years ending after November 1991. The previous version, identical in meaning, read:

(b) "cumulative Canadian oil and gas property expense" of a taxpayer at any time in a taxation year means the amount, if any, by which the aggregate of

(i) the aggregate of all Canadian oil and gas property expenses made or incurred by him before that time,

(ii) the aggregate of all amounts determined under subsection (1) in respect of the taxpayer for taxation years ending before that time,

(iii) any amount referred to in subparagraph (v) or (vi) that is established by him to have become a bad debt before that time, and

(iii.1) such part, if any, of the amount included in subparagraph (viii) as has been repaid before that time by the taxpayer pursuant to a legal obligation to repay all or any part of that amount

exceeds the aggregate of all amounts each of which is

(iv) an amount deducted in computing his income for a taxation year ending before that time in respect of his cumulative Canadian oil and gas property expense,

(v) the aggregate of all amounts each of which is an amount in respect of a property described in subparagraph 66(15)(c)(i), (iii) or (iv) or a right to or interest in such property, other than such a right or interest that he has by reason of being a beneficiary of a trust, (in this subparagraph referred to as "the particular property") disposed of by the taxpayer before that time equal to the amount, if any, by which

(A) the amount, if any, by which the proceeds of disposition in respect of the particular property that became receivable by him before that time exceeds any outlays or expenses made or incurred by him before that time for the purpose of making the disposition and that were not otherwise deductible for the purposes of this Part

exceeds the amount equal to

(B) where the proceeds of disposition referred to in clause (A) may reasonably be attributed to the disposition of a property that was acquired by the taxpayer in circumstances in which subsection 66.7(5) applies to the taxpayer as successor, the lesser of

(I) the amount determined under clause (A) in respect of the property, and

(II) the aggregate of all amounts each of which is an amount that would be determined at that time under paragraph 66.7(5)(a) in respect of the acquisition of the property by the taxpayer if that paragraph were read without reference to "10% of", and

(C) in any other case, nil,

(vi) an amount that became receivable by him before that time that is to be included in the amount determined under this subparagraph by virtue of paragraph 66(12.5)(a),

(vii) an amount received before that time on account of any amount referred to in subparagraph (iii),

(viii) any assistance that he has received or is entitled to receive in respect of any Canadian oil and gas property expense incurred after 1980 or that can reasonably be related to any such expense after 1980, or

(ix) any amount that is required to be deducted before that time under paragraph 66.7(12)(d) in computing his cumulative Canadian oil and gas property expense;

66.4(5)(b)(iii).1 (now formula element D) added by 1990 GST, effective for amounts repaid after January 1990.

Formula element D.1 (formerly 66.4(5)(b)(iii).2)) added by 1991 technical bill, effective for taxation years commencing after February 17, 1987.

Description of F amended by 1993 technical bill, retroactive to taxation years that end after February 17, 1987. This amendment was parallel to the amendment to 66.2(5)"cumulative Canadian development expense"F.

F(b)(i)(D), F(b)(ii)(D), F(c)(i)(D) and F(c)(ii)(E) added by 1994 tax amendments bill (Part I), effective for taxation years that end after February 21, 1994.

Formula element I.1 added by 1994 tax amendments bill (Part I), effective for taxation years that end after February 21, 1994.

**Interpretation Bulletins**: IT-125R4: Dispositions of resource properties; IT-273R2: Government assistance — general comments.

**"disposition"** and **"proceeds of disposition"** have the meanings assigned by section 54.

#### Proposed Amendment — 66.4(5)"disposition" and "proceeds of disposition"

**"proceeds of disposition"** has the meaning assigned by section 54.

**Application**: Bill C-43 (First Reading September 20, 2000), s. 29, will amend the definitions "disposition" and "proceeds of disposition" in subsec. 66.4(5) to read as above, applicable to transactions and events that occur after December 23, 1998.

**Technical Notes**: See under 59(5).

**Notes**: 66.4(5)"disposition" and "proceeds of disposition" were 66.4(5)(c) before consolidation in R.S.C. 1985 (5th Supp.), effective for taxation years ending after November 1991.

### (5.1) Application of subsecs. 66(15) and 66.1(6) — The definitions in subsections 66(15) and 66.1(6) apply to this section.

**Notes**: 66.4(5.1) added in the R.S.C. 1985 (5th Supp.) consolidation, effective for taxation years ending after November 1991 (formerly contained in the opening words of subsecs. 66(15) and 66.1(6)).

### (6) Share of partner — Except as provided in subsection (7), where a taxpayer is a member of a partnership, the taxpayer's share of any amount that would be an amount referred to in the description of D in the definition "cumulative Canadian oil and gas property expense" in subsection (5), in paragraph (a) of the description of F in that definition or in the description of G or I in that definition in respect of the partnership for a taxation year of the partnership if section 96 were read without reference to paragraph 96(1)(d) shall, for the purposes of this Act, be deemed to be an amount referred to in the description of D in the definition "cumulative Canadian oil and gas property expense" in subsection (5), in paragraph (a) of the description of F in that definition or in the description of G or I in that definition, whichever is applicable, in respect of the taxpayer for the taxation year of the taxpayer in which the partnership's taxation year ends.

**Notes**: References to "cumulative Canadian oil and gas property expense"D (formerly 66.4(5)(b)(iii).1)) added to 66.4(6) by 1991 technical bill, effective February 1990.

**Interpretation Bulletins**: IT-125R4: Dispositions of resource properties; IT-273R2: Government assistance — general comments; IT-353R2: Partnership interests — some adjustments to cost base.

**I.T. Technical News**: No. 12 (adjusted cost base of partnership interest — subparagraph 53(1)(e)(viii)).

### (7) Exception — Where a non-resident person is a member of a partnership that is deemed under paragraph 115(4)(b) to have disposed of any Canadian resource property, the person's share of any amount that would be an amount referred to in the description of D in the definition "cumulative Canadian oil and gas property expense" in subsection (5), in paragraph (a) of the description of F in that definition or in the description of G or I in that definition in respect of the partnership for a taxation year of the partnership if section 96 were read without reference to paragraph 96(1)(d) shall, for the purposes of this Act, be deemed to be an amount referred to in the description of D in the definition "cumulative Canadian oil and gas property expense" in subsection (5), in paragraph (a) of the description of F in that definition or in the description of G or I in that definition, whichever is applicable, in respect of the person for the taxation year of the person that is deemed under paragraph 115(4)(a) to have ended.

**Notes**: References to "cumulative Canadian oil and gas property expense"D (formerly 66.4(5)(b)(iii.1)) added to 66.4(7) by 1991 technical bill, effective for partnerships' taxation years beginning after 1984.

**Interpretation Bulletins**: IT-125R4: Dispositions of resource properties; IT-273R2: Government assistance — general comments.

**Related Provisions [s. 66.4]**: 66(5) — Dealers; 66(18) — Members of partnerships; 66.7 — Successor rules; 66.8(1) — Resource expenses of limited partner; 87(1.2) — New corporation deemed continuation of predecessor.

**Definitions [s. 66.4]**: "amount" — 248(1); "assistance" — 66(15), 66.4(5.1), 79(4), 125.4(5), 248(16), 248(18); "Canada" — 255, *Interpretation Act* 8(2.1), (2.2); "Canadian exploration expense" — 66.1(6), 66.4(5.1), 248(1); "Canadian oil and gas property expense" — 66.4(5), 248(1); "Canadian resource property" — 66(15), 66.4(5.1), 248(1); "corporation" — 248(1), *Interpretation Act* 35(1); "disposition" — 54, 66.4(5); "expense" — 66(15), 66.4(5.1); "fiscal period" — 249.1; "inventory", "mineral", "non-resident", "oil or gas well", "prescribed" — 248(1); "proceeds of disposition" — 54, 66.4(5); "property", "share" — 248(1); "taxation year" — 11(2), 249; "taxpayer" — 248(1); "writing" — *Interpretation Act* 35(1).

**Interpretation Bulletins [s. 66.4]**: IT-273R2: Government assistance — general comments.

### 66.5 (1) Deduction from income
— In computing its income for a taxation year that ends before 1995, a corporation that has not made a designation for the year under subsection 66(14.1) or (14.2) may deduct such amount as it may claim not exceeding its cumulative offset account at the end of the year.

**Related Provisions**: 66.7 — Successor rules; 66.8(1) — Resource expenses of limited partner; 196 — Tax on deduction under s. 66.5.

**Forms**: T2099: Part IX tax return in respect of amounts deducted under subsection 66.5(1).

### (2) Definition of "cumulative offset account"
— In this section, "cumulative offset account" of a corporation at any time means the amount, if any, by which

(a) the total of all amounts required to be added under subsections 66(14.1) and (14.2) in computing its cumulative offset account before that time,

exceeds

(b) the total of all amounts deducted under subsection (1) in computing its income for taxation years ending before that time.

**Related Provisions**: 87(2)(pp) — Amalgamation — cumulative offset account computation.

### (3) Change of control
— Where at any time after June 5, 1987 control of a corporation has been acquired by a person or group of persons, the amount deductible under subsection (1) by the corporation in computing its income for a taxation year ending after that time shall not exceed the amount, if any, by which

(a) the part of its income for the year that may reasonably be regarded as attributable to production from Canadian resource properties owned by it immediately before that time

exceeds

(b) the total of all amounts deducted under subsection 29(25) of the *Income Tax Application Rules* and subsections 66.7(1), (3), (4) and (5) by it in respect of its income for the year in computing its income for the year.

**Related Provisions [subsec. 66.5(3)]**: 139.1(18) — Holding corporation deemed not to acquire control of insurer on demutualization; 249(4) — Deemed year end where change of control occurs; 256(6)–(9) — Whether control acquired.

**Definitions [s. 66.5]**: "acquired" — 256(7)–(9); "amount" — 248(1); "control" — 256(6)–(9); "corporation" — 248(1), *Interpretation Act* 35(1); "cumulative offset account" — 66.5(2); "person" — 248(1); "taxation year" — 249.

### 66.6 Acquisition from tax-exempt [person]
— Where a corporation acquires, by purchase, amalgamation, merger, winding-up or otherwise, all or substantially all of the Canadian resource properties or foreign resource properties of a person whose taxable income is exempt from tax under this Part, subsection 29(25) of the *Income Tax Application Rules* and subsections 66.7(1) to (5) do not apply to the corporation in respect of the acquisition of the properties.

**Related Provisions**: 66.7 — Successor rules; 66.8(1) — Resource expenses of limited partner.

**Notes**: 66.6 amended by 1995-97 technical bill, effective for acquisitions after April 26, 1995, other than an acquisition before 1996 that was required by an agreement in writing entered into before April 27, 1995. For earlier acquisitions since 1987-88, read:

> **66.6 (1) Where subsec. 29(25) of ITAR and subsecs. 66.7(1), (2), etc. do not apply** — Where a particular corporation has at any time after July 19, 1985 acquired by purchase, amalgamation, merger, winding-up or otherwise, from another person who is exempt from tax under this Part on that person's taxable income (other than a corporation that is referred to in paragraph 149(1)(d) and that is a principal-business corporation within the meaning assigned by subsection 66(15)) all or substantially all of the person's Canadian resource properties, subsection 29(25) of the *Income Tax Application Rules* and subsections 66.7(1), (2), (3) and (4) do not apply to the particular corporation in respect of the acquisition of the properties except to the extent that the properties were acquired by it before 1987 pursuant to an agreement in writing made by it before July 20, 1985.
>
> **(2) Where subsec. 66.7(5) does not apply** — Where a particular corporation has at any time after July 19, 1985 acquired by purchase, amalgamation, merger, winding-up or otherwise, from another person who is exempt from tax under this Part on that person's taxable income all or substantially all of the person's Canadian resource properties, subsection 66.7(5) does not apply to the particular corporation in respect of the acquisition of the properties except to the extent that the properties were acquired by it before 1987 pursuant to an agreement in writing made by it before July 20, 1985.

The CCRA takes the position that "all or substantially all" means 90% or more.

**Definitions [s. 66.6]**: "business" — 248(1); "corporation" — 248(1), *Interpretation Act* 35(1); "person", "property" — 248(1); "taxable income" — 2(2), 248(1); "writing" — *Interpretation Act* 35(1).

**Interpretation Bulletins**: IT-126R2: Meaning of "winding-up".

**66.7 (1) Successor of Canadian exploration and development expenses** — Subject to subsections (6) and (7), where after 1971 a corporation (in this subsection referred to as the "successor") acquired a particular Canadian resource property (whether by way of a purchase, amalgamation, merger, winding-up or otherwise), there may be deducted by the successor in computing its income for a taxation year an amount not exceeding the total of all amounts each of which is an amount determined in respect of an original owner of the particular property that is the lesser of

(a) the Canadian exploration and development expenses incurred by the original owner before the original owner disposed of the particular property to the extent that those expenses were not otherwise deducted in computing the income of the successor for the year, were not deducted in computing the income of the successor for a preceding taxation year and were not deductible under subsection 66(1) or deducted under subsection 66(2) or (3) by the original owner, or deducted by any predecessor owner of the particular property, in computing income for any taxation year, and

(b) the amount, if any, by which

(i) the part of the successor's income for the year that may reasonably be regarded as attributable to

(A) the amount included in computing its income for the year under paragraph 59(3.2)(c) that may reasonably be regarded as attributable to the disposition by it in the year or a preceding taxation year of any interest in or right to the particular property to the extent that the proceeds of the disposition have not been included in determining an amount under clause 29(25)(d)(i)(A) of the *Income Tax Application Rules*, this clause, clause (3)(b)(i)(A) or paragraph (10)(g) for a preceding taxation year,

(B) its reserve amount for the year in respect of the original owner and each predecessor owner, if any, of the particular property, or

(C) production from the particular property,

computed as if no deduction were allowed under section 29 of the *Income Tax Application Rules*, this section or any of sections 65 to 66.5,

exceeds the total of

(ii) all other amounts deducted under subsection 29(25) of the *Income Tax Application Rules*, this subsection and subsections (3), (4) and (5) for the year that can reasonably be regarded as attributable to the part of its income

for the year described in subparagraph (i) in respect of the particular property, and

(iii) all amounts added because of subsection 80(13) in computing the amount determined under subparagraph (i).

**Related Provisions**: 66(1) — Exploration and development expenses; 66.6(1) — Application; 66.7(2.3) — Income deemed not attributable to production from Canadian resource property; 66.7(6), (7) — Application rules; 66.7(10) — Change of control; 66.7(11) — Change of control — anti-avoidance rule; 66.7(12) — Reduction of Canadian resource expenses; 66.7(14) — Disposal of Canadian resource properties; 66.7(16) — Non-successor acquisitions; 66.7(17) — Restriction on deductions. See additional Related Provisions and Definitions at end of s. 66.7.

**Notes**: 66.7(1)(a) amended by 1991 technical bill, effective for taxation years ending after February 17, 1987.

66.7(1)(b)(iii) added by 1994 tax amendments bill (Part I), effective for taxation years that end after February 21, 1994, and amended retroactive to its introduction by 1995-97 technical bill to delete reference to 80(17).

See also Notes at end of 66.7.

**Forms**: T2010: Election to deduct resource expenses upon acquisition of resource property by a corporation.

**(2) Successor of foreign exploration and development expenses** — Subject to subsections (6) and (8), where after 1971 a corporation (in this subsection referred to as the "successor") acquired a particular foreign resource property (whether by way of a purchase, amalgamation, merger, winding-up or otherwise), there may be deducted by the successor in computing its income for a taxation year an amount not exceeding the total of all amounts each of which is an amount determined in respect of an original owner of the particular property that is the lesser of

(a) the amount, if any, by which

(i) the foreign exploration and development expenses incurred by the original owner before the original owner disposed of the particular property to the extent that those expenses were not otherwise deducted in computing the successor's income for the year, were not deducted in computing the successor's income for a preceding taxation year and were not deductible by the original owner, or deducted by any predecessor owner of the particular property, in computing income for any taxation year

### Proposed Amendment — 66.7(2)(a)(i)

(i) the foreign exploration and development expenses incurred by the original owner before the original owner disposed of the particular property to the extent that those expenses were incurred when the original owner was resident in Canada, were not otherwise deducted in computing the successor's income for the year, were not deducted in computing the successor's income for a preceding taxation year and were not de-

S. 66.7(2)(a)(i)  Income Tax Act, Part I, Division B

ductible by the original owner, nor deducted by any predecessor owner of the particular property, in computing income for any taxation year

**Application**: Bill C-43 (First Reading September 20, 2000), subsec. 30(1), will amend subpara. 66.7(2)(a)(i) to read as above, applicable to 1999 et seq.

**Technical Notes**: Section 66.7 includes what are commonly known as the "successor rules" with respect to resource properties and expenditures.

Subsection 66.7(2) allows a corporation to claim deductions with respect to foreign exploration and development expenses (FEDE) incurred by one or more original owners, where property has been acquired in circumstances to which the successor rules apply.

Subparagraph 66.7(2)(a)(i) is amended so that the successor FEDE that may be deducted by a successor corporation in respect of an original owner's FEDE is limited to FEDE incurred while the original owner was resident in Canada. This change is parallel to the amendment described above, to subparagraph 66(4)(a)(i).

This amendment applies to the 1999 and subsequent taxation years.

exceeds

(ii) the total of all amounts each of which is an amount by which the amount described in this paragraph is required because of subsection 80(8) to be reduced at or before the end of the year, and

(b) the amount, if any, by which the total of

(i) the part of the successor's income for the year that can reasonably be regarded as attributable to

(A) the amount included under subsection 59(1) in computing its income for the year that can reasonably be regarded as attributable to the disposition by it of any interest in or right to the particular property, or

(B) production from the particular property,

computed as if no deduction were allowed under sections 65 to 66.5 and this section, and

(ii) the lesser of

(A) the total of all amounts each of which is the amount designated by the successor for the year in respect of a Canadian resource property owned by the original owner immediately before being acquired with the particular property by the successor or a predecessor owner of the particular property, not exceeding the amount included in the successor's income for the year, computed as if no deduction were allowed under section 29 of the *Income Tax Application Rules*, this section or any of sections 65 to 66.5, that can reasonably be regarded as being attributable to the production after 1988 from the Canadian resource property, and

(B) the amount, if any, by which 10% of the amount described in paragraph (a) for the year in respect of the original owner exceeds the total of all amounts each of which would, but for this subparagraph, clause (iii)(B) and subparagraph (10)(h)(vi), be determined under this paragraph for the year in respect of the particular property or other foreign resource property owned by the original owner immediately before being acquired with the particular property by the successor or a predecessor owner of the particular property

exceeds the total of

(iii) all other amounts deducted under this subsection for the year that can reasonably be regarded as attributable to

(A) the part of its income for the year described in subparagraph (i) in respect of the particular property, or

(B) a part of its income for the year described in clause (ii)(A) in respect of which an amount is designated by the successor under clause (ii)(A), and

(iv) all amounts added because of subsection 80(13) in computing the amount determined under subparagraph (i),

and income in respect of which an amount is designated under clause (b)(ii)(A) shall, for the purposes of clause 29(25)(d)(i)(B) of the *Income Tax Application Rules*, clauses (1)(b)(i)(C), (3)(b)(i)(C), (4)(b)(i)(B) and (5)(b)(i)(B) and subparagraph (10)(g)(iii), be deemed not to be attributable to production from a Canadian resource property.

**Related Provisions**: 66(4) — Foreign exploration and development expenses; 66.6(1) — Application; 66.7(2.1), (2.2) — Country-by-country successor FEDE allocations; 66.7(2.3) — Income deemed not attributable to production from Canadian resource property; 66.7(6), (8) — Application rules; 66.7(10) — Change of control; 66.7(11) — Change of control — anti-avoidance rule; 66.7(13) — Reduction of foreign resource expenses; 66.7(15) — Disposal of foreign resource properties; 66.7(16) — Non-successor acquisitions; 66.7(17) — Restriction on deductions; 80(1)"successor pool" — Debt forgiveness; 80(8)(a) — Reduction of undeducted balances on debt forgiveness. See additional Related Provisions and Definitions at end of s. 66.7.

**Notes**: 66.7(2)(a)(ii) and (b)(iv) added by 1994 tax amendments bill (Part I), effective for taxation years that end after February 21, 1994; and (b)(iv) amended retroactive to its introduction by 1995-97 technical bill to delete reference to 80(17).

66.7(2)(a) and (b) amended by 1991 technical bill (and reference in 66.7(2)(b)(ii)(B) corrected retroactively by 1993 technical bill), effective for taxation years ending after February 17, 1987, except that, where 66.7(2) applies to a successor by reason of 66.7(10), ignore the words "after 1988" in 66.7(2)(b)(ii)(A).

See also Notes at end of 66.7.

**Forms**: T2010: Election to deduct resource expenses upon acquisition of resource property by a corporation.

## Proposed Addition — 66.7(2.1)–(2.3)

**(2.1) Country-by-country successor FEDE allocations** — For greater certainty, the portion of an amount deducted under subsection (2) in computing a taxpayer's income for a taxation year that can reasonably be considered to be in respect of specified foreign exploration and development expenses of the taxpayer in respect of a country is considered to apply to a source in that country.

**Related Provisions**: 66(4.1) — Parallel rule for predecessor; 66.7(2.2) — Method of allocation.

**(2.2) Method of allocation** — For the purpose of subsection (2.1), where a taxpayer has incurred specified foreign exploration and development expenses in respect of two or more countries, an allocation to each of those countries for a taxation year shall be determined in a manner that is

(a) reasonable having regard to all the circumstances, including the level and timing of

(i) the taxpayer's specified foreign exploration and development expenses in respect of the country, and

(ii) the profits or gains to which those expenses relate; and

(b) not inconsistent with the allocation made under subsection (2.1) for the preceding taxation year.

**Technical Notes**: Under existing subsection 66.7(2), successor FEDE in respect of one country is not distinct from successor FEDE in respect of another country.

New subsection 66.7(2.1) provides that, to the extent that a successor FEDE deduction under subsection 66.7(2) can reasonably be considered to be in respect of "specified foreign exploration and development expenses" (as newly defined in subsection 66(15)) in respect of a country, for greater certainty that portion of the successor FEDE deduction is considered to apply to a source in that country. As a consequence, that portion of the successor FEDE deduction can result in a reduction of the limit for the taxpayer's foreign tax credit under section 126 in respect of the country and, pursuant to clause 66.21(4)(a)(ii)(C) or (D), can also result in a reduction of the limit for the taxpayer's deduction of foreign resource expenses under new section 66.21.

New subsection 66.7(2.2) elaborates on how an allocation to a country is made under subsection 66.7(2.1). The method of allocation must be reasonable in the circumstances and be consistently applied from year to year.

New subsections 66.7(2.1) and (2.2) are analogous to new subsections 66(4.1) and (4.2), described in the commentary above.

These amendments apply to taxation years that begin after 1999. However, in the event that a taxpayer elects to have the new foreign tax credit provisions under section 126 apply to taxation years that begin after an earlier date (not earlier than December 31, 1994) designated by the taxpayer, these amendments apply on the same basis.

**Related Provisions**: 66(4.2) — Parallel rule for predecessor.

**(2.3) Successor of foreign resource expenses** — Subject to subsections (6) and (8), where a corporation (in this subsection referred to as the "successor") acquired a particular foreign resource property in respect of a country (whether by way of a purchase, amalgamation, merger, winding-up or otherwise), there may be deducted by the successor in computing its income for a taxation year an amount not exceeding the total of all amounts each of which is an amount determined in respect of an original owner of the particular property that is the lesser of

(a) 30% of the amount, if any, by which

(i) the cumulative foreign resource expense, in respect of the country, of the original owner determined immediately after the disposition of the particular property by the original owner to the extent that it has not been

(A) deducted by the original owner or any predecessor owner of the particular property in computing income for any taxation year,

(B) otherwise deducted in computing the income of the successor for the year, or

(C) deducted by the successor in computing its income for any preceding taxation year

exceeds the total of

(ii) all amounts each of which is an amount (other than any portion of the amount that can reasonably be considered to result in a reduction of the amount otherwise determined under this paragraph in respect of another original owner of a relevant resource property who is not a predecessor owner of a relevant resource property or who became a predecessor owner of a relevant resource property before the original owner became a predecessor owner of a relevant resource property) that became receivable by a predecessor owner of the particular property, or by the successor in the year or a preceding taxation year, and that

(A) was included by the predecessor owner or the successor in computing an amount determined under paragraph (a) of the description of F in the definition "cumulative foreign resource expense" in subsection 66.21(1) at the end of the year, and

(B) can reasonably be regarded as attributable to the disposition of a property (in this subparagraph referred to as a "relevant resource property") that is

(I) the particular property, or

(II) another foreign resource property in respect of the country that was acquired from the original owner with the particular property by the successor or a predecessor owner of the particular property, and

(iii) all amounts each of which is an amount by which the amount described in this paragraph is required by reason of subsection 80(8) to be reduced at or before the end of the year, and

(b) the amount, if any, by which the total of

(i) the part of the successor's income for the year that can reasonably be regarded as attributable to production from the particular property, computed as if no deduction were permitted under this section or any of sections 65 to 66.5, except that, where the successor acquired the particular property from the original owner at any time in the year (otherwise than by way of an amalgamation or merger or solely by reason of the application of paragraph (10)(c)) and did not deal with the original owner at arm's length at that time, the amount determined under this subparagraph is deemed to be nil, and

(ii) unless the amount determined under subparagraph (i) is nil by reason of the exception provided under that subparagraph, the lesser of

(A) the total of all amounts each of which is the amount designated by the successor for the year in respect of a Canadian resource property owned by the original owner immediately before being acquired with the particular property by the successor or a predecessor owner of the particular property, not exceeding the amount included in the successor's income for the year, computed as if no deduction were permitted under section 29 of the *Income Tax Application Rules*, this section or any of sections 65 to 66.5, that can reasonably be regarded as being attributable to the production from the Canadian resource property, and

(B) the amount, if any, by which 10% of the amount described in paragraph (a) for the year, in respect of the original owner, exceeds the total of all amounts each of which would, but for this subparagraph, clause (2)(b)(iii)(B) and subparagraph (10)(h)(vi), be determined under this paragraph for the year in respect of the particular property or other foreign resource property, in respect of the country, owned by the original owner immediately before being acquired with the particular property by the successor or by a predecessor owner of the particular property

exceeds the total of

(iii) all other amounts each of which is an amount deducted for the year under this subsection or subsection (2) that can reasonably be regarded as attributable to

(A) the part of its income for the year described in subparagraph (i) in respect of the particular property, or

(B) a part of its income for the year described in clause (ii)(A) in respect of which an amount is designated by the successor under clause (ii)(A), and

(iv) all amounts added by reason of subsection 80(13) in computing the amount determined under subparagraph (i),

and income in respect of which an amount is designated under clause (b)(ii)(A) is, for the purposes of clause 29(25)(d)(i)(B) of the *Income Tax Application Rules*, clauses (1)(b)(i)(C), (3)(b)(i)(C), (4)(b)(i)(B) and (5)(b)(i)(B) and subparagraph (10)(g)(iii), deemed not to be attributable to production from a Canadian resource property.

**Technical Notes**: New subsection 66.7(2.3) provides for the transfer of an original owner's unused foreign resource expense (FRE) balance, on an acquisition of foreign resource properties from the original owner in circumstances to which the successor rules apply. Subsection 66.7(2.3) is structured much like the deduction for successor Canadian development expense in subsection 66.7(4), in that proceeds from the disposition of such foreign resource properties are generally applied to reduce the successor FRE balance. The amount by which a successor FRE balance is reduced offsets the amount of reduction otherwise required under subsection 66.21(1) to the successor's own cumulative FRE.

The unused amount of a successor FRE balance may be deducted against "streamed income" (as determined under subparagraph 66.7(2.3)(b)(i)) in respect of the foreign resource properties acquired on the succession. This subparagraph refers only to income from production, not to proceeds of disposition, given the treatment of proceeds described immediately above. Under subparagraph 66.7(2.3)(b)(ii), any "streamed income" from Canadian resource properties acquired with such foreign resource properties on a succession can be used to support additional successor FRE deductions required in order for the successor to claim up to 10% of the successor FRE balance in a taxation year. Subparagraph 66.7(2.3)(b)(ii) is consistent with subparagraph 66.7(2)(b)(ii), and ensures that the 10% minimum relating to maximum deductions with regard to FEDE or FRE is not lost on a succession involving a mixture of Canadian and foreign resource properties if there is sufficient overall foreign and Canadian resource income to support the 10% minimum. However, any "streamed income" can only be used once in determining the level of deductions to which a taxpayer is entitled under subsection 66.7(2) or (2.3). In addition, deductions under those subsections can limit the extent to which a taxpayer can claim deductions under subsections 66(4) and 66.21(4).

The operation of subsection 66.7(2.3) and related provisions are illustrated in the example below.

*Example*

ABC Corp. has an outstanding successor FEDE pool of $30,000, an outstanding successor FRE pool of $20,000, a FEDE balance in its own right of $70,000 and cumulative FRE of $40,000. In 2001, ABC disposes of all its foreign resource properties acquired on the succession for $145,000. ABC designates $60,000 under subparagraph 59(1)(b)(ii), so that the amount included in its income under subsection 59(1) is $85,000. There are no relevant transactions or events after the succession, and no relevant production income in 2001. ABC uses calendar years as its taxation years.

*Results:*

1. ABC is permitted to deduct the full amount ($30,000) of its successor pool under subsection 66.7(2) for its 2001 taxation year. For this purpose, ABC's streamed income is equal to the $85,000 included under subsection 59(1) in computing ABC's income.

2. No deduction is permitted under subsection 66.7(2.3), because the $60,000 designated amount reduces the successor FRE pool under subparagraph 66.7(2.3)(a)(ii). Instead, under paragraph (b) of the description of F in the definition "cumulative foreign resource expense" in subsection 66.21(1), the resulting $20,000 grind to the successor FRE pool offsets the amount by which ABC's own cumulative FRE is required to be reduced.

3. ABC will therefore not be entitled to deduct any amount under subsection 66.21(4) for its 2001 taxation year because its cumulative FRE is nil (i.e., ($40,000 − ($60,000 − $20,000)) at the end of the year. For the same reason, ABC's income inclusion under subsection 66.21(3) for the year is nil.

4. The amount deductible by ABC under subsection 66(4) for the year is equal to $55,000, which is the lesser of:
- 70,000 (subparagraph 66(4)(b)(i)), and
- $85,000 (subsection 59(1) and subclause 66(4)(b)(ii)(C)(I)), minus $30,000 (subclause 66(4)(b)(ii)(C)(II)).

5. As a consequence, $15,000 of FEDE remains available for deduction in a subsequent year or years.

6. The following table summarizes these results

| A. Pool | B. Pool Amount | C. Portion of "B" used |
|---|---|---|
| successor FEDE | $30,000 | $30,000 |
| successor FRE | $20,000 | $20,000 |
| FEDE balance | $70,000 | $55,000 |
| cumulative FRE | $40,000 | $40,000 |
| TOTAL | $160,000 | $145,000 |

**Related Provisions**: 66(13.1) — Short taxation year; 66.21(1) "cumulative foreign resource expense" F(b)(i); 66.7(8) — Application; 66.7(10)(h)(v), (vi), 66.7(10)(j)(ii) — Change of control; 66.7(13.1) — Reduction of foreign resource expenses; 66.7(15.1) — Disposal of foreign resource properties; 80(8)(a) — Debt forgiveness; 248(1) "foreign resource property" — Meaning of foreign resource property in respect of a country.

**Application**: The December 21, 2000 draft legislation, subsec. 30(1), will add subsecs. 66.7(2.1) to (2.3), subsecs. (2.1) and (2.2) applicable to taxation years of a taxpayer that begin after the earlier of

(a) December 31, 1999; and

(b) where, for the purposes of subsec. 72(9), a date is designated in writing by the taxpayer and the designation is filed with the Minister of National Revenue on or before the taxpayer's filing-due date for the taxpayer's taxation year that includes the day on which the amending legislation receives Royal Assent, the later of

(i) the date so designated, and

(ii) December 31, 1994; and

subsec. (2.3) applicable to taxation years that begin after 2000.

**Notice of Ways and Means Motion, federal budget, February 28, 2000**: (40) That, for taxation years that begin after 2000, the successor rules in section 66.7 of the Act reflect the 30 per cent FEDE balance deduction limit.

**Federal budget, supplementary information, February 28, 2000**: [See under 66(4)(b)(ii) — ed.]

**(3) Successor of Canadian exploration expense** — Subject to subsections (6) and (7), where after May 6, 1974 a corporation (in this subsection referred to as the "successor") acquired a particular Canadian resource property (whether by way of a purchase, amalgamation, merger, winding-up or otherwise), there may be deducted by the successor in computing its income for a taxation year an amount not exceeding the total of all amounts each of which is an amount determined in respect of an original owner of the particular property that is the lesser of

(a) the amount, if any, by which

(i) the total of

(A) the cumulative Canadian exploration expense of the original owner determined immediately after the disposition of the particular property by the original owner, and

(B) all amounts required to be added under paragraph (9)(f) to the cumulative Canadian exploration expense of the original owner in respect of a predecessor owner of the particular property, or the successor, as the case may be, at any time after the disposition of the particular property by the original owner and before the end of the year,

to the extent that an amount in respect of that total was not

(C) deducted or required to be deducted under subsection 66.1(2) or (3) by the original owner or deducted by any predecessor owner of the particular property in computing income for any taxation year,

(D) otherwise deducted in computing the successor's income for the year,

(E) deducted in computing the successor's income for a preceding taxation year, or

(F) designated by the original owner pursuant to subsection 66(14.1) for any taxation year,

exceeds

(ii) the total of all amounts each of which is an amount by which the amount described in this paragraph is required because of subsection 80(8) to be reduced at or before the end of the year, and

(b) the amount, if any, by which

(i) the part of the successor's income for the year that may reasonably be regarded as attributable to

(A) the amount included in computing its income for the year under paragraph 59(3.2)(c) that may reasonably be regarded as being attributable to the disposition by it in the year or a preceding taxation year of any interest in or right to the particular property to the extent that the proceeds have not been included in determining an amount under clause 29(25)(d)(i)(A) of the *Income Tax Application Rules*, this clause, clause (1)(b)(i)(A) or paragraph (10)(g) for a preceding taxation year,

(B) its reserve amount for the year in respect of the original owner and each predecessor owner, if any, of the particular property, or

(C) production from the particular property,

computed as if no deduction were allowed under section 29 of the *Income Tax Application Rules*, this section or any of sections 65 to 66.5,

exceeds the total of

(ii) all other amounts deducted under subsection 29(25) of the *Income Tax Application Rules*, this subsection and subsections (1), (4) and (5) for the year that can reasonably be regarded as attributable to the part of its income for the year described in subparagraph (i) in respect of the particular property, and

(iii) all amounts added because of subsection 80(13) in computing the amount determined under subparagraph (i).

**Related Provisions**: 66.6(1) — Application; 66.7(2.3) — Income deemed not attributable to production from Canadian resource property; 66.7(6), (7), (9) — Application rules; 66.7(10), (11) — Change of control; 66.7(12) — Reduction of Canadian resource expenses; 66.7(14) — Disposal of Canadian resource properties; 66.7(16) — Non-successor acquisitions; 66.7(17) — Restriction on deductions; 80(1)"successor pool" — Debt forgiveness; 80(8)(a) — Reduction of undeducted balances on debt forgiveness. See additional Related Provisions and Definitions at end of s. 66.7.

**Notes**: 66.7(3)(a)(ii) and (b)(iii) added (and provisions renumbered to accommodate) by 1994 tax amendments bill (Part I), effective for taxation years that end after February 21, 1994; and (b)(iii) amended retroactive to its introduction by 1995-97 technical bill to delete reference to 80(17).

66.7(3)(a)(iii) amended by 1992 Economic Statement, effective for taxation years ending after December 2, 1992, to change "deductible under subsection 66.1(2) or deducted under subsection 66.1(3)" to "deducted or required to be deducted under subsection 66.1(2) or (4)".

66.7(3)(a)(iii.1) added by 1991 technical bill, effective for taxation years ending after February 17, 1987.

See also Notes at end of 66.7.

**Forms**: T2010: Election to deduct resource expenses upon acquisition of resource property by a corporation.

### (4) Successor of Canadian development expense
— Subject to subsections (6) and (7), where after May 6, 1974 a corporation (in this subsection referred to as the "successor") acquired a particular Canadian resource property (whether by way of a purchase, amalgamation, merger, winding-up or otherwise), there may be deducted by the successor in computing its income for a taxation year an amount not exceeding the total of all amounts each of which is an amount determined in respect of an original owner of the particular property that is the lesser of

(a) 30% of the amount, if any, by which

(i) the amount, if any, by which

(A) the cumulative Canadian development expense of the original owner determined immediately after the disposition of the particular property by the original owner to the extent that it has not been

(I) deducted by the original owner or any predecessor owner of the particular property in computing income for any taxation year,

(I.1) otherwise deducted in computing the income of the successor for the year,

(II) deducted by the successor in computing its income for any preceding taxation year, or

(III) designated by the original owner pursuant to subsection 66(14.2) for any taxation year,

exceeds

(B) any amount required to be deducted under paragraph (9)(e) from the cumulative Canadian development expense of the original owner in respect of a predecessor owner of the particular property or the successor, as the case may be, at any time after the disposition of the particular property by the original owner and before the end of the year,

exceeds the total of

(ii) all amounts each of which is an amount (other than any portion thereof that can reasonably be considered to result in a reduction of the amount otherwise determined under this paragraph in respect of another original owner of a relevant mining property who is not a predecessor owner of a relevant mining property or who became a predecessor owner of a relevant mining property before the original owner became a predecessor owner of a relevant mining property) that became receivable by a predecessor owner of the particular property or the successor in the year or a preceding taxation year and that

(A) was included by the predecessor owner or the successor in computing an amount determined under paragraph (a) of the description of F in the definition "cumulative Canadian development expense" in subsection 66.2(5) at the end of the year, and

(B) can reasonably be regarded as attributable to the disposition of a property (in this subparagraph referred to as a "relevant mining property") that is the particular property or another Canadian resource property that was acquired from the original owner with the particular property by the successor or a predecessor owner of the particular property,

(iii) all amounts each of which is an amount (other than any portion thereof that can reasonably be considered to result in a reduction of the amount otherwise determined under paragraph (5)(a) in respect of the original owner or under this paragraph or paragraph (5)(a) in respect of another original owner of a relevant oil and gas property who is not a predecessor owner of a relevant oil and gas property or who became a predecessor owner of a relevant oil and gas property before the original owner became a predecessor owner of a relevant oil and gas property) that became receivable by a predecessor owner of the particular property or the successor after 1992 and in the year or a preceding taxation year and that

(A) is designated in respect of the original owner by the predecessor owner or the successor, as the case may be, in prescribed form filed with the Minister within 6 months after the end of the taxation year in which the amount became receivable,

(B) was included by the predecessor owner or the successor in computing an amount determined under paragraph (a) of the description of F in the definition "cumulative Canadian oil and gas property expense" in subsection 66.4(5) at the end of the year, and

(C) can reasonably be regarded as attributable to the disposition of a property (in this subparagraph referred to as a "relevant oil and gas property") that is the particular property or another Canadian resource property that was acquired from the original owner with the particular property by the successor or a predecessor owner of the particular property, and

(iv) all amounts each of which is an amount by which the amount described in this paragraph is required because of subsection 80(8) to be reduced at or before the end of the year, and

(b) the amount, if any, by which

(i) the part of the successor's income for the year that can reasonably be regarded as attributable to

(A) its reserve amount for the year in respect of the original owner and each predecessor owner of the particular property, or

(B) production from the particular property,

computed as if no deduction were allowed under section 29 of the *Income Tax Application Rules*, this section or any of sections 65 to 66.5, except that, where the successor acquired the particular property from the original owner at any time in the year (otherwise than by way of an amalgamation or merger or solely because of the application of paragraph (10)(c)) and did not deal with the original owner at arm's length at that time, the amount determined under this subparagraph shall be deemed to be nil,

exceeds the total of

(ii) all other amounts deducted under subsection 29(25) of the *Income Tax Application Rules*, this subsection and subsections (1), (3) and (5) for the year that can reasonably be regarded as attributable to the part of its income for the year described in subparagraph (i) in respect of the particular property, and

(iii) all amounts added because of subsection 80(13) in computing the amount determined under subparagraph (i).

**Related Provisions**: 66(13.1) — Short taxation year; 66.6(1) — Application; 66.7(6), (7), (9) — Application rules; 66.7(10) — Change of control; 66.7(11) — Change of control — anti-avoidance rule; 66.7(12) — Reduction of Canadian resource expenses; 66.7(12.1) — Canadian resource properties — Specified amount; 66.7(14) — Disposal of Canadian resource properties; 66.7(16) — Non-successor acquisitions; 66.7(17) — Restriction on deductions; 80(1)"successor pool" — Debt forgiveness; 80(8)(a) — Reduction of undeducted balances on debt forgiveness. See additional Related Provisions and Definitions at end of s. 66.7.

**Notes**: 66.7(4) redrafted in R.S.C. 1985 (5th Supp.) consolidation, effective for taxation years ending after November 1991. See Table of Concordance.

66.7(4)(a)(i)(A)(I.1) added by 1991 technical bill, effective for taxation years ending after February 17, 1987.

66.7(4)(a)(ii) amended by 1993 technical bill, retroactive to taxation years that end after February 17, 1987. The amendments ensure that, in computing a successor CCDE balance of an original owner in respect of a particular property, there are deducted other proceeds of disposition with respect to other Canadian mining property owned by the original owner because of being acquired with the particular property by a successor; and where there is more than one original owner of a particular Canadian mining property, the proceeds of disposition are applied to reduce the successored CCDE balance of the first original owner before those of subsequent original owners.

66.7(4)(a)(iii) added by 1993 technical bill, retroactive to taxation years that end after February 17, 1987. The prescribed form in 66.7(4)(a)(iii)(A) may be filed for any year up to the end of the sixth month beginning after the end of the taxation year that includes June 15, 1994.

66.7(4)(a)(iv) added by 1994 tax amendments bill (Part I), effective for taxation years that end after February 21, 1994.

66.7(4)(b)(i) amended by 1991 technical bill, effective for dispositions in taxation years commencing after December 16, 1991. Also effective for a disposition in an earlier taxation year that ends after February 17, 1987, where

(a) the taxpayer, and

(b) each corporation that, before the end of the taxpayer's taxation year that includes December 17, 1991, acquired the property or any other property that was disposed of by the taxpayer in a taxation year ending after February 17, 1987 as part of a transaction or an event as a consequence of which that corporation was or, but for those subsecs., would be entitled to deduct an amount under subsec. 66.7(3), (4) or (5) in respect of an expense incurred by the taxpayer,

so elected by notice in writing filed with the Minister of National Revenue on or before the day that was 180 days after the end of the taxpayer's taxation year that included December 17, 1991; and,

(c) notwithstanding subsecs. 152(4) to (5), such assessments of tax, interest and penalties shall be made as are necessary to give effect to the election, and

(d) where the taxpayer so elected in respect of a disposition, a designation under cl. 66.7(12.1)(a)(i)(B), (b)(i)(B) or (c)(i)(B) in respect of the disposition shall be deemed to have been filed as required if it was filed with the Minister of National Revenue on or before the day that was 180 days after the end of the taxpayer's taxation year that included December 17, 1991.

For cases where the new version does not apply, read 66.7(4)(b)(i) as:

(i) the part of the successor's income for the year that may reasonably be regarded as attributable to

(A) its reserve amount for the year in respect of the original owner and each predecessor owner of the particular property, or

(B) production from the particular property,

computed as if no deduction were allowed under section 29 of the *Income Tax Application Rules, 1971*, this section or any of sections 65 to 66.5.

66.7(4)(b)(iii) added by 1994 tax amendments bill (Part I), effective for taxation years that end after February 21, 1994; and (b)(iii) amended retroactive to its introduction by 1995-97 technical bill to delete reference to 80(17).

See also Notes at end of 66.7.

**Forms**: T2010: Election to deduct resource expenses upon acquisition of resource property by a corporation.

**(5) Successor of Canadian oil and gas property expense** — Subject to subsections (6) and (7), where after December 11, 1979 a corporation (in this subsection referred to as the "successor") acquired a particular Canadian resource property (whether by way of a purchase, amalgamation, merger, winding-up or otherwise), there may be deducted by the successor in computing its income for a taxation year an amount not exceeding the total of all amounts each of which is an amount determined in respect of an original owner of the particular property that is the lesser of

(a) 10% of the amount, if any, by which

(i) the cumulative Canadian oil and gas property expense of the original owner determined immediately after the disposition of the particular property by the original owner to the extent it has not been

(A) deducted by the original owner or any predecessor owner of the particular property in computing income for any taxation year,

(A.1) otherwise deducted in computing the income of the successor for the year, or

(B) deducted by the successor in computing its income for any preceding taxation year

exceeds the total of

(ii) the total of all amounts each of which is an amount (other than any portion thereof that can reasonably be considered to result in a reduction of the amount otherwise determined under this paragraph or paragraph (4)(a) in respect of another original owner of a relevant oil and gas property who is not a predecessor owner of a relevant oil and gas property or who became a predecessor owner of a relevant oil and gas property before the original owner became a predecessor owner of a relevant oil and gas property) that became receivable by a predecessor owner of the particular property or the successor in the year or a preceding taxation year and that

(A) was included by the predecessor owner or the successor in computing an amount determined under paragraph (a) of the description of F in the definition "cumulative Canadian oil and gas property expense" in subsection 66.4(5) at the end of the year, and

(B) can reasonably be regarded as attributable to the disposition of a property (in this subparagraph referred to as a "relevant oil and gas property") that is the particular property or another Canadian resource property that was acquired from the original owner with the particular property by the successor or a predecessor owner of the particular property, and

(iii) the total of all amounts each of which is an amount by which the amount described in this paragraph is required because of subsection 80(8) to be reduced at or before the end of the year, and

(b) the amount, if any, by which

(i) the part of the successor's income for the year that can reasonably be regarded as attributable to

(A) its reserve amount for the year in respect of the original owner and each predecessor owner of the particular property, or

(B) production from the particular property,

computed as if no deduction were allowed under section 29 of the *Income Tax Application Rules*, this section or any of sections 65 to 66.5, except that, where the successor acquired the particular property from the original owner at any time in the year (otherwise than by way of an amalgamation or merger or solely because of the application of paragraph (10)(c)) and did not deal with the original owner at arm's length at that time, the amount determined under this subparagraph shall be deemed to be nil,

exceeds the total of

(ii) all other amounts deducted under subsection 29(25) of the *Income Tax Application Rules*, this subsection and subsections (1), (3) and (4) for the year that can reasonably be regarded as attributable to the part of its income for the year described in subparagraph (i) in respect of the particular property, and

(iii) all amounts added because of subsection 80(13) in computing the amount determined under subparagraph (i).

**Related Provisions**: 66(13.1) — Short taxation year; 66.6(2) — Application; 66.7(2.3) — Income deemed not attributable to production from Canadian resource property; 66.7(6), (7) — Application rules; 66.7(10) — Change of control; 66.7(11) — Change of control — anti-avoidance rule; 66.7(12) — Reduction of Canadian resource expenses; 66.7(14) — Disposal of Canadian resource properties; 66.7(16) — Non-successor acquisitions; 66.7(17) — Restriction on deductions; 80(1)"successor pool" — Debt forgiveness; 80(8)(a) — Reduction of undeducted balances on debt forgiveness. See additional Related Provisions and Definitions at end of s. 66.7.

**Notes**: 66.7(5) redrafted in R.S.C. 1985 (5th Supp.) consolidation, effective from taxation years ending after November 1991. See Table of Concordance.

66.7(5)(a)(i)(A.1) added by 1991 technical bill, effective for taxation years ending after February 17, 1987.

66.7(5)(a)(ii) amended by 1993 technical bill, retroactive to taxation years that end after February 17, 1987. The amendments parallel those to 66.7(4)(a)(ii) (see Notes thereto).

66.7(5)(a)(iii) added by 1994 tax amendments bill (Part I), effective for taxation years that end after February 21, 1994.

66.7(5)(b)(i) amended by 1991 technical bill, effective for dispositions in taxation years commencing after December 16, 1991. Also effective for a disposition in an earlier taxation year that ends after February 17, 1987, where an election was filed by 180 days after the end of the taxation year that included December 17, 1991.

66.7(5)(b)(iii) added by 1994 tax amendments bill (Part I), effective for taxation years that end after February 21, 1994; and (b)(iii) amended retroactive to its introduction by 1995-97 technical bill to delete reference to 80(17).

See also Notes at end of 66.7.

**Forms**: T2010: Election to deduct resource expenses upon acquisition of resource property by a corporation.

**(6) Where subsec. 29(25) of ITAR and subsecs. (1) to (5) do not apply** — Subsection 29(25) of the *Income Tax Application Rules* and subsections (1) to (5) do not apply

(a) in respect of a Canadian resource property or a foreign resource property acquired by way of an amalgamation to which subsection 87(1.2) applies or a winding-up to which subsection 88(1.5) applies; or

(b) to permit, in respect of the acquisition by a corporation before February 18, 1987 of a Canadian resource property or a foreign resource property, a deduction by the corporation of an amount that the corporation would not have been entitled to deduct under section 29 of the *Income Tax Application Rules* or section 66, 66.1, 66.2 or 66.4 if those sections, as they read in their application to taxation years ending before February 18, 1987, applied to taxation years ending after February 17, 1987.

**Related Provisions**: See Related Provisions and Definitions at end of s. 66.7.

**(7) Application of subsec. 29(25) of ITAR and subsecs. (1), (3), (4) and (5)** — Subsection 29(25) of the *Income Tax Application Rules* and subsections (1), (3), (4) and (5) apply only to a corporation that has acquired a particular Canadian resource property

(a) where it acquired the particular property in a taxation year commencing before 1985 and, at the time it acquired the particular property, the corporation acquired all or substantially all of the property used by the person from whom it acquired the particular property in carrying on in Canada such of the businesses described in paragraphs (a) to (g) of the definition "principal-business corporation" in subsection 66(15) as were carried on by the person;

(b) where it acquired the particular property in a taxation year commencing after 1984 and, at the time it acquired the particular property, the corporation acquired all or substantially all of the Canadian resource properties of the person from whom it acquired the particular property;

(c) where it acquired the particular property after June 5, 1987 by way of an amalgamation or winding-up and it has filed an election in prescribed form with the Minister on or before the day on or before which the corporation is required to file a return of income pursuant to section 150 for its taxation year in which it acquired the particular property;

(d) where it acquired the particular property after November 16, 1978 and in a taxation year ending before February 18, 1987 by any means other than by way of an amalgamation or winding-up and it and the person from whom it acquired the particular property, have filed with the Minister a joint election under and in accordance with any of subsection 29(25) of the *Income Tax Application Rules*, subsection 29(29) of the *Income Tax Application Rules, 1971*, Part III of chapter 63 of the Statutes of Canada, 1970-71-72, and subsections 66(6) and (7), 66.1(4) and (5), 66.2(3) and (4) and 66.4(3) and (4) of the *Income Tax Act*, chapter 148 of the Revised Statutes of Canada, 1952, as all of those subsections read in their application to that year; and

(e) where it acquired the particular property in a taxation year ending after February 17, 1987 by any means other than by way of an amalgamation or winding-up and it and the person from whom it acquired the particular property have filed a joint election in prescribed form with the Minister on or before the earlier of the days on or before which either of them is required to file a return of income pursuant to section 150 for its or the person's taxation year in which the corporation acquired the particular property.

**Related Provisions**: 220(3.2), Reg. 600(c) — Late filing of election or revocation under 66.7(7)(c), (d) or (e). See additional Related Provisions and Definitions at end of s. 66.7.

**Notes**: The CCRA takes the position that "all or substantially all", used in 66.7(7)(a) and (b), means 90% or more.

**I.T. Application Rules**: 69 (meaning of "*Income Tax Act*, chapter 148 of the Revised Statutes of Canada, 1952"; meaning of "*Income Tax Application Rules, 1971*, Part III of chapter 63 of the Statutes of Canada, 1970-71-72").

**Information Circulars**: 92-1: Guidelines for accepting late, amended or revoked elections.

**Forms**: T2010: Election to deduct resource expenses upon acquisition of resource property by a corporation.

**(8) Application of subsec. (2)** — Subsection (2) applies only to a corporation that has acquired a particular foreign resource property

> **Proposed Amendment — 66.7(8) opening words**
>
> **(8) Application of ss. (2) and (2.3)** — Subsections (2) and (2.3) apply only to a corporation that has acquired a particular foreign resource property
>
> **Application**: The December 21, 2000 draft legislation, subsec. 30(2), will amend the opening words of subsec. 66.7(8) to read as above, applicable to taxation years that begin after 2000.
>
> **Technical Notes**: Subsection 66.7(8) generally provides a restriction under which the successor rules for FEDE in subsection 66.7(2) apply only with regard to acquisitions by a corporation of all or substantially all of the foreign resource properties of another person.
>
> Subsection 66.7(8) is amended to include a reference to new subsection 66.7(2.3), so that the same restriction applies with regard to the successor rules for FRE in new subsection 66.7(2.3).

(a) where it acquired the particular property in a taxation year commencing before 1985 and, at the time it acquired the particular property, the corporation acquired all or substantially all of the property used by the person from whom it acquired the particular property in carrying on outside Canada such of the businesses described in paragraphs (a) to (g) of the definition "principal-business corporation" in subsection 66(15) as were carried on by that person;

(b) where it acquired the particular property in a taxation year commencing after 1984 and, at the time it acquired the particular property, the corporation acquired all or substantially all of the foreign resource properties of the person from whom it acquired the particular property;

(c) where it acquired the particular property after June 5, 1987 by way of an amalgamation or winding-up and it has filed an election in prescribed form with the Minister on or before the day on or before which the corporation is required to file a return of income pursuant to section 150 for its taxation year in which it acquired the particular property;

(d) where it acquired the particular property after November 16, 1978 and in a taxation year ending before February 18, 1987 by any means other than by way of an amalgamation or winding-up and it and the person from whom it acquired the particular property, have filed with the Minister a joint election under and in accordance with subsection 66(6) or (7) (as modified by subsections 66(8) and (9), respectively) of the *Income Tax Act*, chapter 148 of the Revised Statutes of Canada, 1952, as those subsections read in their application to that year; and

(e) where it acquired the particular property in a taxation year ending after February 17, 1987 by any means other than by way of an amalgamation or winding-up and it and the person from whom it acquired the particular property have filed a joint election in prescribed form with the Minister on or before the earlier of the days on or before which either of them is required to file a return of income pursuant to section 150 for its or the person's taxation year in which the corporation acquired the particular property.

**Related Provisions**: 220(3.2), Reg. 600(c) — Late filing of election or revocation under 66.7(8)(c), (d) or (e). See additional Related Provisions and Definitions at end of s. 66.7.

**Notes**: The CCRA takes the position that "all or substantially all", used in 66.7(8)(a) and (b), means 90% or more.

**I.T. Application Rules**: 69 (meaning of "*Income Tax Act*, chapter 148 of the Revised Statutes of Canada, 1952").

**Information Circulars**: 92-1: Guidelines for accepting late, amended or revoked elections.

**Forms**: T2010: Election to deduct resource expenses upon acquisition of resource property by a corporation.

**(9) Canadian development expense becoming Canadian exploration expense** — Where

(a) a corporation acquires a Canadian resource property,

(b) subsection (4) applies in respect of the acquisition, and

(c) the cumulative Canadian development expense of an original owner of the property determined under clause (4)(a)(i)(A) in respect of the corporation includes a Canadian development expense incurred by the original owner in respect of an oil or gas well that would, but for this subsection, be deemed by subsection 66.1(9) to be a Canadian exploration expense incurred in respect of the well by the original owner at any particular time after the acquisition by the corporation and before it disposed of the property,

the following rules apply:

(d) subsection 66.1(9) does not apply in respect of the Canadian development expense incurred in respect of the well by the original owner,

(e) an amount equal to the lesser of

(i) the amount that would be deemed by subsection 66.1(9) to be a Canadian exploration expense incurred in respect of the well by the original owner at the particular time if that subsection applied in respect of the expense, and

(ii) the cumulative Canadian development expense of the original owner as determined under clause (4)(a)(i)(A) in respect of the corporation immediately before the particular time

shall be deducted at the particular time from the cumulative Canadian development expense of the original owner in respect of the corporation for the purposes of subparagraph (4)(a)(i), and

(f) the amount required by paragraph (e) to be deducted shall be added at the particular time to the cumulative Canadian exploration expense of the original owner in respect of the corporation for the purpose of paragraph (3)(a).

**Related Provisions**: See Related Provisions and Definitions at end of s. 66.7.

**Notes**: 66.7(9)(f) amended by 1994 tax amendments bill (Part I), effective for taxation years that end after February 21, 1994, to change "subparagraph (3)(a)(ii)" to "paragraph (3)(a)".

**(10) Change of control** — Where at any time after November 12, 1981

(a) control of a corporation has been acquired by a person or group of persons, or

(b) a corporation ceased on or before April 26, 1995 to be exempt from tax under this Part on its taxable income,

for the purposes of the provisions of the *Income Tax Application Rules* and this Act (other than subsections 66(12.6), (12.601), (12.602), (12.62) and (12.71)) relating to deductions in respect of drilling and exploration expenses, prospecting, exploration and development expenses, Canadian exploration and development expenses, foreign exploration and development expenses, Canadian exploration expenses, Canadian development expenses and Canadian oil and gas property expenses (in this subsection referred to as "resource expenses") incurred by the corporation before that time, the following rules apply:

### Proposed Amendment — 66.7(10)

for the purposes of the provisions of the *Income Tax Application Rules* and this Act (other than subsections 66(12.6), (12.601), (12.602), (12.62) and (12.71)) relating to deductions in respect of drilling and exploration expenses, prospecting, exploration and development expenses, Canadian exploration and development expenses, foreign resource pool expenses, Canadian exploration expenses, Canadian development expenses and Canadian oil and gas property expenses (in this subsection referred to as "resource expenses") incurred by the corporation before that time, the following rules apply:

**Application**: The December 21, 2000 draft legislation, subsec. 30(3), will amend the portion of subsec. 66.7(10) after para. (b) and before para. (c) to read as above, applicable to taxation years that begin after 2000.

**Technical Notes**: Under subsection 66.7(10), a corporation is treated as a successor for the purposes of the successor rules in section 66.7 after an acquisition of control (or a change in the tax-exempt status) of the corporation.

This subsection is amended to replace a reference to foreign exploration and development expenses with a more general reference to foreign resource pool expenses, as defined in subsection 248(1).

(c) the corporation shall be deemed after that time to be a successor (within the meaning assigned by subsection 29(25) of the *Income Tax Application Rules* or any of subsections (1) to (5)) that had, at that time, acquired all the properties owned by the corporation immediately before that time from an original owner thereof,

(c.1) where the corporation did not own a foreign resource property immediately before that time, the corporation is deemed to have owned a foreign resource property immediately before that time,

(d) a joint election shall be deemed to have been filed in accordance with subsections (7) and (8) in respect of the acquisition,

(e) the resource expenses incurred by the corporation before that time shall be deemed to have been incurred by an original owner of the properties and not by the corporation,

(f) [Repealed]

S. 66.7(10)(f)      Income Tax Act, Part I, Division B

> **Proposed Addition — 66.7(10)(f)**
>
> (f) the original owner is deemed to have been resident in Canada before that time while the corporation was resident in Canada,
>
> **Application**: Bill C-43 (First Reading September 20, 2000), subsec. 30(2), will add para. 66.7(10)(f), applicable to 1999 et seq.
>
> **Technical Notes**: Under subsection 66.7(10), a corporation is treated as a successor for the purposes of the successor rules in section 66.7 after an acquisition of control of the corporation. Under paragraph 66.7(10)(e), resource expenses incurred by the corporation prior to the change of control are deemed to have been incurred by an original owner of resource properties owned at the time of the acquisition of control.
>
> New paragraph 66.7(10)(f) ensures that the deemed original owner had the same status with regard to residence in Canada before the acquisition of control of a corporation as the corporation itself. This amendment is consequential to an amendment, described above, to subparagraph 66.7(2)(a)(i) affecting successor FEDE claims.
>
> This amendment applies to the 1999 and subsequent taxation years.

(g) where the corporation (in this paragraph referred to as the "transferee") was, immediately before and at that time,

    (i) a parent corporation (within the meaning assigned by subsection 87(1.4)), or

    (ii) a subsidiary wholly-owned corporation (within the meaning assigned by subsection 87(1.4))

of a particular corporation (in this paragraph referred to as the "transferor"), if both corporations agree to have this paragraph apply to them in respect of a taxation year of the transferor ending after that time and notify the Minister in writing of the agreement in the return of income under this Part of the transferor for that year, the transferor may, if throughout that year the transferee was such a parent corporation or subsidiary wholly-owned corporation of the transferor, designate in favour of the transferee, in respect of that year, for the purpose of making a deduction under subsection 29(25) of the *Income Tax Application Rules* or this section in respect of resource expenses incurred by the transferee before that time and when it was such a parent corporation or subsidiary wholly-owned corporation of the transferor, an amount not exceeding such portion of the amount that would be its income for the year, if no deductions were allowed under any of section 29 of the *Income Tax Application Rules*, this section and sections 65 to 66.5, that may reasonably be regarded as being attributable to

    (iii) the production from Canadian resource properties owned by the transferor immediately before that time, and

    (iv) the disposition in the year of any Canadian resource properties owned by the transferor immediately before that time,

to the extent that such portion of the amount so designated is not designated under this paragraph in favour of any other taxpayer, and the amount so designated shall be deemed, for the purposes of determining the amount under paragraph 29(25)(d) of the *Income Tax Application Rules* and paragraphs (1)(b), (3)(b), (4)(b) and (5)(b),

    (v) to be income from the sources described in subparagraph (iii) or (iv), as the case may be, of the transferee for its taxation year in which that taxation year of the transferor ends, and

    (vi) not to be income from the sources described in subparagraph (iii) or (iv), as the case may be, of the transferor for that year,

(h) where the corporation (in this paragraph referred to as the "transferee") was, immediately before and at that time,

    (i) a parent corporation (within the meaning assigned by subsection 87(1.4)), or

    (ii) a subsidiary wholly-owned corporation (within the meaning assigned by subsection 87(1.4))

of a particular corporation (in this paragraph referred to as the "transferor"), if both corporations agree to have this paragraph apply to them in respect of a taxation year of the transferor ending after that time and notify the Minister in writing of the agreement in the return of income under this Part of the transferor for that year, the transferor may, if throughout that year the transferee was such a parent corporation or subsidiary wholly-owned corporation of the transferor, designate in favour of the transferee, in respect of that year, for the purpose of making a deduction under this section in respect of resource expenses incurred by the transferee before that time and when it was such a parent corporation or subsidiary wholly-owned corporation of the transferor, an amount not exceeding such portion of the amount that would be its income for the year, if no deductions were allowed under this section and sections 65 to 66.5, that may reasonably be regarded as being attributable to

    (iii) the production from foreign resource properties owned by the transferor immediately before that time, and

    (iv) the disposition of any foreign resource properties owned by the transferor immediately before that time,

to the extent that such portion of the amount so designated is not designated under this paragraph in favour of any other taxpayer, and the amount so designated shall be deemed,

    (v) for the purposes of determining the amounts under paragraph (2)(b), to be income from the sources described in subparagraph (iii) or (iv), as the case may be, of the transferee for its taxation year in which that taxation year of the transferor ends, and

(vi) for the purposes of determining the amount under paragraph (2)(b), not to be income from the sources described in subparagraph (iii) or (iv), as the case may be, of the transferor for that year,

### Proposed Amendment — 66.7(10)(h)(v), (vi)

(v) for the purposes of determining the amounts under paragraphs (2)(b) and (2.3)(b), to be income from the sources described in subparagraph (iii) or (iv), as the case may be, of the transferee for its taxation year in which that taxation year of the transferor ends, and

(vi) for the purposes of determining the amount under paragraphs (2)(b) and (2.3)(b), not to be income from the sources described in subparagraph (iii) or (iv), as the case may be, of the transferor for that year,

**Application**: The December 21, 2000 draft legislation, subsec. 30(4), will amend subparas. 66.7(10)(h)(v) and (vi) to read as above, applicable to taxation years that begin after 2000.

**Technical Notes**: Where control of a parent corporation is acquired at a time when it owns foreign resource property, and a subsidiary wholly-owned corporation of the parent had incurred foreign resource expenses before that time, paragraph 66.7(10)(h) generally allows the parent to designate in favour of the subsidiary any portion of its income for the year attributable to the production from such foreign resource properties. After the designation, the amount designated will, for the purpose only of claiming a deduction under the successor rules, be treated as production income of the subsidiary and not of the parent from foreign properties owned by it before the acquisition of control. In the situation where the subsidiary, rather than the parent, owns the foreign resource property after an acquisition of control this paragraph also allows the subsidiary to designate amounts in favour of its parent.

Paragraph 66.7(10)(h) is amended to permit designations of foreign production income to enable greater deductions to be claimed under new subsection 66.7(2.3) by the subsidiary or the parent, as the case may be.

(i) where, immediately before and at that time, the corporation (in this paragraph referred to as the "transferee") and another corporation (in this paragraph referred to as the "transferor") were both subsidiary wholly-owned corporations (within the meaning assigned by subsection 87(1.4)) of a particular parent corporation (within the meaning assigned by subsection 87(1.4)), if the transferee and the transferor agree to have this paragraph apply to them in respect of a taxation year of the transferor ending after that time and notify the Minister in writing of the agreement in the return of income under this Part of the transferor for that year, paragraph (g) or (h), or both, as the agreement provides, shall apply for that year to the transferee and transferor as though

one were the parent corporation (within the meaning of subsection 87(1.4)) of the other, and

(j) where that time is after January 15, 1987 and at that time the corporation was a member of a partnership that owned a Canadian resource property or a foreign resource property at that time

(i) for the purpose of paragraph (c), the corporation shall be deemed to have owned immediately before that time that portion of the property owned by the partnership at that time that is equal to its percentage share of the total of amounts that would be paid to all members of the partnership if it were wound up at that time, and

(ii) for the purposes of clause 29(25)(d)(i)(B) of the *Income Tax Application Rules* and clauses (1)(b)(i)(C), (2)(b)(i)(B), (3)(b)(i)(C), (4)(b)(i)(B) and (5)(b)(i)(B) for a taxation year ending after that time, the lesser of

### Proposed Amendment — 66.7(10)(j)(ii) opening words

(ii) for the purposes of clause 29(25)(d)(i)(B) of the *Income Tax Application Rules* and clauses (1)(b)(i)(C) and (2)(b)(i)(B), subparagraph (2.3)(b)(i) and clauses (3)(b)(i)(C), (4)(b)(i)(B) and (5)(b)(i)(B) for a taxation year ending after that time, the lesser of

**Application**: The December 21, 2000 draft legislation, subsec. 30(5), will amend the opening words of subpara. 66.7(10)(j)(ii) to read as above, applicable to taxation years that begin after 2000.

**Technical Notes**: Where control of a corporation is acquired and, at the time of the acquisition of control, the corporation was a member of a partnership, paragraph 66.7(10)(j) treats the corporation as owning, immediately before the acquisition of control, a portion of the resource property owned by the partnership at the time of the acquisition of control. The portion is equal to the corporation's percentage share of all amounts that would be paid to all members of the partnership if the partnership were wound up at the time of the acquisition of control. In the event of a sale of these properties, the corporation would treat the proceeds as being from a disposition of resource properties owned before the acquisition of control. As a consequence, the corporation can have higher levels of "streamed income" against which to claim specified successor deductions under section 66.7.

Paragraph 66.7(10)(j) is amended so that successor deductions under new subsection 66.7(2.3) are likewise specified for this purpose. This amendment is consequential on the introduction of new rules for the deduction of foreign resource expenses and successor foreign resource expenses under new subsections 66.21(4) and 66.7(2.3).

(A) its share of the part of the income of the partnership for the fiscal period of the partnership ending in the year that may reasonably be regarded as being attributable to the production from the property, and

(B) an amount that would be determined under clause (A) for the year if its share of the income of the partnership for the fiscal period of the partnership ending in the year were determined on the basis of the percentage share referred to in subparagraph (i),

shall be deemed to be income of the corporation for the year that may reasonably be attributable to production from the property.

**Related Provisions**: 66(11.3) — Control; 66.7(2.3) — Income deemed not attributable to production from Canadian resource property; 139.1(18) — Holding corporation deemed not to acquire control of insurer on demutualization; 149(10) — Ceasing to be exempt after April 26, 1995; 249(4) — Deemed year end where change of control occurs; 256(6)–(9) — Whether control acquired. See additional Related Provisions and Definitions at end of s. 66.7.

**Notes**: 66.7(10)(b) amended by 1995-97 technical bill, effective April 27, 1995. (See now 149(10).) From 1987-88 to April 26, 1995, read:

(b) a corporation ceases to be exempt from tax under this Part on its taxable income,

66.7(10) between (b) and (c) amended by 1996 Budget, effective for taxation years that begin after 1998, to delete reference to 66(12.64) and to make a non-substantive wording change (changing "with respect to" to "in respect of").

66.7(10) between (b) and (c) amended by 1992 Economic Statement, effective December 3, 1992, to add references to 66(12.601) and (12.602).

66.7(10)(c.1) added by 1995-97 technical bill, retroactive to taxation years that end after February 17, 1987.

Former 66.7(10)(f) repealed, and reference to 66.7(10)(f)(ii) in 66.7(10)(h)(v) deleted, by 1991 technical bill, effective for taxation years ending after February 17, 1987.

66.7(10)(j) amended to change reference to 66.7(4)(b)(i)(B) to (4)(b)(i)(A)(II), and reference to 66.7(5)(b)(i)(B) to (5)(b)(I)(A)(II) by 1991 technical bill, effective on the same basis as the amendments to those subsection (see Notes thereto).

**I.T. Technical News**: No. 7 (control by a group — 50/50 arrangement).

**Advance Tax Rulings**: ATR-19: Earned depletion base and cumulative Canadian development expense.

**(11) Idem** — Where, at any time,

(a) control of a taxpayer that is a corporation has been acquired by a person or group of persons, or

(b) a taxpayer has disposed of all or substantially all of the taxpayer's Canadian resource properties or foreign resource properties,

and, before that time, the taxpayer or a partnership of which the taxpayer was a member acquired a property that is a Canadian resource property, a foreign resource property or an interest in a partnership and it may reasonably be considered that one of the main purposes of the acquisition was to avoid any limitation provided in subsection 29(25) of the *Income Tax Application Rules* or any of subsections (1) to (5) on the deduction in respect of any expenses incurred by the taxpayer or a corporation referred to as a transferee in paragraph (10)(g) or (h), the taxpayer or the partnership, as the case may be, shall be deemed, for the purposes of applying those subsections to or in respect of the taxpayer, not to have acquired the property.

**Related Provisions**: 87(2)(j.6) — Amalgamations — continuing corporation; 139.1(18) — Holding corporation deemed not to acquire control of insurer on demutualization; 249(4) — Deemed year end where change of control occurs; 256(6)–(9) — Whether control acquired. See additional Related Provisions and Definitions at end of s. 66.7.

**Notes**: The CCRA takes the position that "all or substantially all" means 90% or more.

See also Notes at end of 66.7.

**I.T. Technical News**: No. 7 (control by a group — 50/50 arrangement).

**(12) Reduction of Canadian resource expenses** — Where in a taxation year an original owner of Canadian resource properties disposes of all or substantially all of the original owner's Canadian resource properties to a particular corporation in circumstances in which subsection 29(25) of the *Income Tax Application Rules* or subsection (1), (3), (4) or (5) applies,

(a) the Canadian exploration and development expenses incurred by the original owner before that owner so disposed of the properties shall, for the purposes of this subdivision, be deemed after the disposition not to have been incurred by the original owner except for the purposes of making a deduction under subsection 66(1) or (2) for the year and of determining the amount that may be deducted under subsection (1) by the particular corporation or by any other corporation that subsequently acquires any of the properties;

(b) in determining the cumulative Canadian exploration expense of the original owner at any time after the time referred to in subparagraph (3)(a)(i), there shall be deducted the amount thereof determined immediately after the disposition;

(b.1) for the purposes of paragraph (3)(a), the cumulative Canadian exploration expenses of the original owner determined immediately after the disposition that was deducted or required to be deducted under subsection 66.1(2) or (3) in computing the original owner's income for the year shall be deemed to be equal to the lesser of

(i) the amount deducted under paragraph (b) in respect of the disposition, and

(ii) the amount, if any, by which

(A) the specified amount determined under paragraph (12.1)(a) in respect of the original owner for the year

exceeds

(B) the total of all amounts each of which is an amount determined under this paragraph in respect of any disposition made by the original owner before the disposition and in the year;

(b.2) for greater certainty, any amount (other than the amount determined under paragraph (b.1)) that was deducted or required to be deducted under subsection 66.1(2) or (3) by the original owner for the year or a subsequent taxation year shall, for the purposes of paragraph (3)(a), be deemed not to be in respect of the cumulative Canadian exploration expense of the original owner determined immediately after the disposition;

(c) in determining the cumulative Canadian development expense of the original owner at any time after the time referred to in clause (4)(a)(i)(A), there shall be deducted the amount thereof determined immediately after the disposition;

(c.1) for the purpose of paragraph (4)(a), the cumulative Canadian development expense of the original owner determined immediately after the disposition that was deducted under subsection 66.2(2) in computing the original owner's income for the year shall be deemed to be equal to the lesser of

(i) the amount deducted under paragraph (c) in respect of the disposition, and

(ii) the amount, if any, by which

(A) the specified amount determined under paragraph (12.1)(b) in respect of the original owner for the year

exceeds

(B) the total of all amounts determined under this paragraph in respect of any dispositions made by the original owner before the disposition and in the year;

(c.2) for greater certainty, any amount (other than the amount determined under paragraph (c.1)) that was deducted under subsection 66.2(2) by the original owner for the year or a subsequent taxation year shall, for the purpose of paragraph (4)(a), be deemed not to be in respect of the cumulative Canadian development expense of the original owner determined immediately after the disposition;

(d) in determining the cumulative Canadian oil and gas property expense of the original owner at any time after the time referred to in subparagraph (5)(a)(i), there shall be deducted the amount thereof determined immediately after the disposition;

(d.1) for the purpose of paragraph (5)(a), the cumulative Canadian oil and gas property expense of the original owner determined immediately after the disposition that was deducted under subsection 66.4(2) in computing the original owner's income for the year shall be deemed to be equal to the lesser of

(i) the amount deducted under paragraph (d) in respect of the disposition, and

(ii) the amount, if any, by which

(A) the specified amount determined under paragraph (12.1)(c) in respect of the original owner for the year

exceeds

(B) the total of all amounts determined under this paragraph in respect of any dispositions made by the original owner before the disposition and in the year;

(d.2) for greater certainty, any amount (other than the amount determined under paragraph (d.1)) that was deducted under subsection 66.4(2) by the original owner for the year or a subsequent taxation year shall, for the purpose of paragraph (5)(a), be deemed not to be in respect of the cumulative Canadian oil and gas property expense of the original owner determined immediately after the disposition; and

(e) the drilling and exploration expenses, including all general geological and geophysical expenses, incurred by the original owner before 1972 on or in respect of exploring or drilling for petroleum or natural gas in Canada and the prospecting, exploration and development expenses incurred by the original owner before 1972 in searching for minerals in Canada shall, for the purposes of section 29 of the *Income Tax Application Rules*, be deemed after the disposition not to have been incurred by the original owner except for the purposes of making a deduction under that section for the year and of determining the amount that may be deducted under subsection 29(25) of that Act by the particular corporation or any other corporation that subsequently acquires any of the properties.

**Related Provisions**: 66.1(6)"cumulative Canadian exploration expense"M — Reduction in CCEE; 66.2(5)"cumulative Canadian development expense"O — Reduction in CCDE; 66.4(5)"cumulative Canadian oil and gas property expense"J — Reduction in CCOGPE. See Related Provisions and Definitions at end of s. 66.7.

**Notes**: 66.7(12)(b.1) and (b.2) amended by 1992 Economic Statement, effective for taxation years ending after December 2, 1992, to change "deductible under subsection 66.1(2) or deducted under subsection 66.1(3)" to "deducted or required to be deducted under subsection 66.1(2) or (4)".

66.7(12)(b.1), (b.2), (c.1), (c.2), (d.1) and (d.2) added by 1991 technical bill, effective for dispositions in taxation years commencing after December 16, 1991. Also effective for a disposition in an earlier taxation year that ends after February 17, 1987, where

(a) the taxpayer, and

(b) each corporation that, before the end of the taxpayer's taxation year that includes December 17, 1991, acquired the property or any other property that was disposed of by the taxpayer in a taxation year ending after February 17, 1987 as part of a transaction or an event as a consequence of which that corporation was or, but for those subsecs., would be entitled to deduct an amount under subsec. 66.7(3), (4) or (5) in respect of an expense incurred by the taxpayer, so elected by notice in writing filed with the Minister of National Revenue on or before the day that was 180 days after the end of the taxpayer's taxation year that included December 17, 1991; and,

(c) notwithstanding subsecs. 152(4) to (5), such assessments of tax, interest and penalties shall be made as are necessary to give effect to the election, and

(d) where the taxpayer so elected in respect of a disposition, a designation under cl. 66.7(12.1)(a)(i)(B), (b)(i)(B) or (c)(i)(B) in respect of the disposition shall be deemed to have been filed as required if it was filed with the Minister of National Revenue on or before the day that was 180 days after the end of the taxpayer's taxation year that included December 17, 1991.

The CCRA takes the position that "all or substantially all", used in the opening words of 66.7(12), means 90% or more.

**(12.1) Specified amount** — Where in a taxation year an original owner of Canadian resource properties disposes of all or substantially all of the original owner's Canadian resource properties in circumstances in which subsection (3), (4) or (5) applies,

(a) the lesser of

(i) the total of all amounts each of which is the amount, if any, by which

(A) an amount deducted under paragraph (12)(b) in respect of a disposition in the year by the original owner

exceeds

(B) the amount, if any, designated by the original owner in prescribed form filed with the Minister within 6 months after the end of the year in respect of an amount determined under clause (A), and

(ii) the total of

(A) the amount claimed under subsection 66.1(2) or (3) by the original owner for the year, and

(B) the amount that would, but for paragraph 66.1(1)(c), be determined under subsection 66.1(1) in respect of the original owner for the year

is the specified amount in respect of the original owner for the year for the purposes of clause (12)(b.1)(ii)(A) and of determining the value of E.1 in the definition "cumulative Canadian exploration expense" in subsection 66.1(6);

(b) the lesser of

(i) the total of all amounts each of which is the amount, if any, by which

(A) an amount deducted under paragraph (12)(c) in respect of a disposition in the year by the original owner

exceeds

(B) the amount, if any, designated by the original owner in prescribed form filed with the Minister within 6 months after the end of the year in respect of an amount determined under clause (A), and

(ii) the total of

(A) the amount claimed under subsection 66.2(2) by the original owner for the year, and

(B) the amount that would, but for paragraph 66.2(1)(d), be determined under subsection 66.2(1) in respect of the original owner for the year

is the specified amount in respect of the original owner for the year for the purposes of clause (12)(c.1)(ii)(A) and of determining the value of D.1 in the definition "cumulative Canadian development expense" in subsection 66.2(5); and

(c) the lesser of

(i) the total of all amounts each of which is the amount, if any, by which

(A) an amount deducted under paragraph (12)(d) in respect of a disposition in the year by the original owner

exceeds

(B) the amount, if any, designated by the original owner in prescribed form filed with the Minister within 6 months after the end of the year in respect of an amount determined under clause (A), and

(ii) the total of

(A) the amount claimed under subsection 66.4(2) by the original owner for the year, and

(B) the amount that would, but for paragraph 66.4(1)(c), be determined under subsection 66.4(1) in respect of the original owner for the year

is the specified amount in respect of the original owner for the year for the purposes of clause (12)(d.1)(ii)(A) and of determining the value of D.1 in the definition "cumulative Canadian oil and gas property expense" in subsection 66.4(5).

**Related Provisions**: 66.1(1) — Amount to be included in income; 66.1(2)(b) — Deduction for principal-business corporation; 66.1(3)(b) — Expenses of other taxpayers; 66.1(6)"cumulative Canadian exploration expense"E.1 — addition to CCEE; 66.2(2)(a) — Deduction for CCDE; 66.2(5)"cumulative Canadian development expense"D.1 — Addition to CCDE; 66.4(1)(c) — Recovery of costs; 66.4(2)(a)(i) — Deduction for CCOGPE; 66.4(5)"cumulative Canadian oil and gas property expense"D.1 — addition to CCOGPE.

**Notes**: 66.7(12.1) added by 1991 technical bill, effective for dispositions in taxation years commencing after December 16, 1991. Also effective for a disposition in an earlier taxation year that ends after February 17, 1987, where

(a) the taxpayer, and

(b) each corporation that, before the end of the taxpayer's taxation year that includes December 17, 1991, acquired the property or any other property that was disposed of by the taxpayer in a taxation year ending after February 17, 1987 as part of a transaction or an event as a consequence of which that corporation was or, but for those subsecs., would be entitled to deduct an amount under subsec. 66.7(3), (4) or (5) in respect of an expense incurred by the taxpayer, so elected by notice in writing filed with the Minister of National Revenue on or before the day that was 180 days after the end of the taxpayer's taxation year that included December 17, 1991; and,

(c) notwithstanding subsecs. 152(4) to (5), such assessments of tax, interest and penalties shall be made as are necessary to give effect to the election, and

(d) where the taxpayer so elected in respect of a disposition, a designation under cl. 66.7(12.1)(a)(i)(B), (b)(i)(B) or (c)(i)(B) in respect of the disposition shall be deemed to have been filed as required if it was filed with the Minister of National Revenue on or before the day that was 180 days after the end of the taxpayer's taxation year that included December 17, 1991.

The CCRA takes the position that "all or substantially all", used in the opening words of 66.7(12.1), means 90% or more.

**Forms**: T1046: Designation of resource amount by an original owner.

**(13) Reduction of foreign resource expenses** — Where after June 5, 1987 an original owner of foreign resource properties disposes of all or substantially all of the original owner's foreign resource properties to a particular corporation in circumstances in which subsection (2) applies, the foreign exploration and development expenses incurred by the original owner before that owner so disposed of the properties shall be deemed after the disposition not to have been incurred by the original owner except for the purposes of determining the amounts that may be deducted under that subsection by the particular corporation or any other corporation that subsequently acquires any of the properties.

**Related Provisions**: See Related Provisions and Definitions at end of s. 66.7.

**Notes**: The CCRA takes the position that "all or substantially all" means 90% or more.

### Proposed Addition — 66.7(13.1), (13.2)

**(13.1) Reduction of foreign resource expenses** — Where in a taxation year an original owner of foreign resource properties in respect of a country disposes of all or substantially all of the original owner's foreign resource properties in circumstances to which subsection (2.3) applies,

(a) in determining the cumulative foreign resource expense of the original owner in respect of the country at any time after the time referred to in subparagraph (2.3)(a)(i), there shall be deducted the amount of that cumulative foreign resource expense determined immediately after the disposition; and

(b) for the purpose of paragraph (2.3)(a), the cumulative foreign resource expense of the original owner in respect of the country determined immediately after the disposition that was deducted under subsection 66.21(4) in computing the original owner's income for the year is deemed to be equal to the lesser of

(i) the amount deducted under paragraph (a) in respect of the disposition, and

(ii) the amount, if any, by which

(A) the specified amount determined under subsection (13.2) in respect of the original owner and the country for the year

exceeds

(B) the total of all amounts determined under this paragraph in respect of another disposition of foreign resource property in respect of the country made by the original owner before the disposition and in the year.

**Related Provisions**: 66.21(1)"cumulative foreign resource expense"J; 66.7(15.1) — Parallel rule for predecessor owner; 248(1)"foreign resource property" — Meaning of foreign resource property in respect of a country.

**(13.2) Specified amount — foreign resource expenses** — Where in a taxation year an original owner of foreign resource properties in respect of a country disposes of all or substantially all of the original owner's foreign resource properties in circumstances to which subsection (2.3) applies, the specified amount in respect of the country and the original owner for the year for the purposes of clause (13.1)(b)(ii)(A) and of determining the value of D in the definition "cumulative foreign resource expense" in subsection 66.21(1) is the lesser of

(a) the total of all amounts each of which is the amount, if any, by which

(i) an amount deducted under paragraph (13.1)(a) in respect of a disposition in the year by the original owner of foreign resource property in respect of the country

exceeds

(ii) the amount, if any, designated by the original owner in prescribed form filed with the Minister within six months after the end of the year in respect of an amount described under subparagraph (i); and

(b) the total of

(i) the amount claimed under subsection 66.21(4) by the original owner in respect of the country for the year, and

(ii) the amount that would, but for paragraph 66.21(3)(c), be determined under subsection 66.21(3) in respect of the country and the original owner for the year.

**Application**: The December 21, 2000 draft legislation, subsec. 30(6), will add subsecs. 66.7(13.1) and (13.2), applicable to taxation years that begin after 2000.

**Technical Notes**: New subsection 66.7(13.1) sets out the tax consequences to an original owner of foreign resource properties who disposes of the properties in circumstances to which new subsection 66.7(2.3) applies. This subsection is structured in a manner similar to paragraphs 66.7(12)(c) and (c.1), both of which relate to successor Canadian development expense. For the purposes of the commentary below it is assumed that an original owner is party to only one transaction in a taxation year as a consequence of which its cumulative FRE is subject to the successor rules.

Under paragraph 66.7(13.1)(a), the original owner's cumulative FRE is reduced immediately after the succession to nil. See also in this regard the description of J in the definition "cumulative foreign resource expense" in subsection 66.21(1).

The part of the successor FRE balance considered to have been deducted by the original owner (and, as a consequence, not available to the successor) in connection with a transfer, to which new subsection 66.7(2.3) applies, at any time by the original owner is generally the specified amount determined under subsection 66.7(13.2). That subsection is parallel to paragraph 66.7(12.1)(b), which relates to Canadian development expenses. The specified amount determined under subsection 66.7(13.2) represents the portion of the successor FRE balance that the original owner:

- used under paragraph 66.21(3)(c) in order to offset an income inclusion under paragraph 59(3.2)(c.1); or
- deducted under subsection 66.21(4), because of the adjustments provided under the definition "adjusted cumulative foreign resource expense" in subsection 66.21(1).

Under subparagraph 66.7(13.2)(a)(ii), the original owner can elect to reduce or eliminate its specified amount so that the full amount of (or a higher portion of) the original owner's cumulative FRE at the time of a succession is available to the successor.

The example below illustrates the operation of subsections 66.7(13.1) and (13.2) and related provisions.

*Example*

*XYZ Corp. transfers all of its foreign resource properties in 2003 to Newco in circumstances to which the successor rules in section 66.7 apply. Before the transfer, XYZ's cumulative foreign resource expense (cumulative FRE) is $100,000. The proceeds of disposition of the foreign resource properties are $40,000. XYZ wants to deduct the maximum amount it can under subsection 66.21(4) for the year of the succession. XYZ incurs no further FRE after the succession, has no foreign resource production income in the year of succession and, after the succession, disposes of no foreign resource properties.*

*Results:*

*1. The potential successor FRE pool available to Newco is $60,000 (i.e., $100,000 minus $40,000). See, in this regard, the description of F in the definition "cumulative foreign resource expense" in subsection 66.21(1) and subparagraph 66.7(2.3)(a)(i). However, this potential FRE pool is reduced to the extent that XYZ claims a deduction in respect of the pool for the year of the succession.*

*2. XYZ's deduction under subsection 66.21(4) for the year of succession is computed with reference to its adjusted cumulative FRE under subsection 66.21 (1). This amount is computed by totalling:*

- *XYZ's cumulative FRE at the end of the succession year (i.e. $100,000 (A, E) − $40,000 (F) − $60,000 (J)), which is nil; and*

- *the amount determined under paragraph 66.7(13.2)(a), which is $60,000. (It is assumed that XYZ designates no amount under subparagraph 66.7(13.2)(a)(ii). XYZ would only designate an amount under that subparagraph if it is willing to limit its ability to claim FEDE in the succession year.)*

*3. XYZ claims $6,000 under subsection 66.21(4) for the year of succession.*

*4. Immediately after the end of the year of succession, XYZ's cumulative FRE is nil. This is equal to nil (balance at end of the year of the succession), plus $6,000 (D — which is equal to the amount determined under subsection 66.7(13.2)), minus $6,000 (E — representing deductions under subsection 66.21(4)).*

*5. As a consequence of XYZ's claim, clause 66.7(2.3)(a)(i)(A) and paragraph 66.7(13.1)(b), the successor FRE pool actually available to Newco is $54,000.*

**Related Provisions**: 66.21(1) "adjusted cumulative foreign resource expense"; 66.21(1) "cumulative foreign resource expense" D; 66.21(3)(c) — Deduction.

**(14) Disposal of Canadian resource properties** — Where in a taxation year a predecessor owner of Canadian resource properties disposes of Canadian resource properties to a corporation in circumstances in which subsection 29(25) of the *Income Tax Application Rules* or subsection (1), (3), (4) or (5) applies,

(a) for the purposes of applying any of those subsections to the predecessor owner in respect of its acquisition of any Canadian resource property owned by it immediately before the disposition, it shall be deemed, after the disposition, never to have acquired any such properties except for the purposes of

(i) determining an amount deductible under subsection (1) or (3) for the year,

(ii) where the predecessor owner and the corporation dealt with each other at arm's length at the time of the disposition or the disposition was by way of an amalgamation or merger, determining an amount deductible under subsection (4) or (5) for the year, and

(iii) determining the amount for F in the definition "cumulative Canadian development expense" in subsection 66.2(5), the amounts for paragraphs (a) and (b) in the description of L in that definition and the amount for F in the definition "cumulative Canadian oil and gas property expense" in subsection 66.4(5); and

(b) where the corporation or another corporation acquires any of the properties on or after the disposition in circumstances in which subsection (4) or (5) applies, amounts that become receivable by the predecessor owner after the disposition in respect of Canadian resource properties retained by it at the time of the disposition shall, for the purposes of applying subsection (4) or (5) to the corporation or the other corporation in respect of the

Subdivision e — Deductions in Computing Income   S. 66.7(17)

acquisition, be deemed not to have become receivable by the predecessor owner.

**Related Provisions**: 66.6 — Canadian resource properties acquired from exempt person. See additional Related Provisions and Definitions at end of s. 66.7.

**Notes**: 66.7(14) amended by 1991 technical bill and 1993 technical bill, both amendments retroactive to dispositions in taxation years that end after February 17, 1987.

The CCRA takes the position that "all or substantially all" means 90% or more.

**(15) Disposal of foreign resource properties** — Where after June 5, 1987 a predecessor owner of foreign resource properties disposes of all or substantially all of its foreign resource properties to a corporation in circumstances in which subsection (2) applies, for the purpose of applying that subsection to the predecessor owner in respect of its acquisition of any of those properties (or other foreign resource properties retained by it at the time of the disposition which were acquired by it in circumstances in which subsection (2) applied), it shall be deemed, after the disposition, never to have acquired the properties.

**Related Provisions**: See Related Provisions and Definitions at end of s. 66.7.

**Notes**: 66.7(15) amended by 1993 technical bill, retroactive to taxation years that end after February 17, 1987.

The CCRA takes the position that "all or substantially all" means 90% or more.

---

**Proposed Addition — 66.7(15.1)**

**(15.1) Disposal of foreign resource properties — ss. (2.3)** — Where in a taxation year a predecessor owner of foreign resource properties disposes of foreign resource properties to a corporation in circumstances to which subsection (2.3) applies,

(a) for the purpose of applying that subsection to the predecessor owner in respect of its acquisition of any foreign resource properties owned by it immediately before the disposition, it is deemed, after the disposition, never to have acquired any such properties except for the purposes of

(i) where the predecessor owner and the corporation dealt with each other at arm's length at the time of the disposition or the disposition was by way of an amalgamation or merger, determining an amount deductible under subsection (2.3) for the year, and

(ii) determining the value of F in the definition "cumulative foreign resource expense" in subsection 66.21(1); and

(b) where the corporation or another corporation acquires any of the properties on or after the disposition in circumstances to which subsection (2.3) applies, amounts that become receivable by the predecessor owner after the disposition in respect of foreign resource properties retained by it at the time of the disposition are, for the purposes of applying subsection (2.3) to the corporation or the other corporation in respect of the acquisition, deemed not to have become receivable by the predecessor owner.

**Application**: The December 21, 2000 draft legislation, subsec. 30(7), will add subsec. 66.7(15.1), applicable to taxation years that begin after 2000.

**Technical Notes**: New subsection 66.7(15.1) provide rules for predecessor owners similar to those in subsections 66.7(13.1) and (13.2) that apply to original owners. (A "predecessor owner" of resource properties is a corporation that acquires resource properties in circumstances to which the successor rules apply and subsequently disposes of resource properties in circumstances to which the successor rules apply.) Under paragraph 66.7(15.1)(a), where a predecessor owner of foreign resource properties disposes of all or substantially all of its foreign resource properties in circumstances in which the successor rules apply, it is generally treated after the disposition as never having acquired the properties in respect of which the successor rule applied. As a consequence, the predecessor is generally precluded from claiming successor FRE deductions after the subsequent succession. Subsection 66.7(15.1) is structured in a manner that is similar to that of subsection 66.7(14).

In the case of arm's length dispositions or dispositions by way of amalgamation or merger, notwithstanding the general rule in paragraph 66.7(15.1)(a) the predecessor owner is allowed to claim deductions under subsection 66.7(2.3) (dealing with an original owner's foreign resource expenses) for the taxation year of the disposition. In addition, subparagraph 66.7(15.1)(a)(ii) ensures that paragraph 66.7(15.1)(a) does not have a retrospective negative impact on the value of F in the definition "cumulative foreign resource expense" in subsection 66.21(1) in respect of the predecessor owner.

Paragraph 66.7(15.1)(b) ensures that proceeds that subsequently become receivable by a predecessor owner will not affect the calculation of the portion of an original owner's cumulative FRE available to a subsequent successor.

**Related Provisions**: 66.7(13.1) — Parallel rule for original owner.

---

**(16) Non-successor acquisitions** — Where at any time a Canadian resource property or a foreign resource property is acquired by a person in circumstances in which none of subsection 29(25) of the *Income Tax Application Rules* and subsections (1) to (5) apply, every person who was an original owner or predecessor owner of the property by reason of having disposed of the property before that time shall, for the purpose of applying those subsections to or in respect of the person or any other person who after that time acquires the property, be deemed after that time not to be an original owner or predecessor owner of the property by reason of having disposed of the property before that time.

**Related Provisions**: See Related Provisions and Definitions at end of s. 66.7.

**(17) Restriction on deductions** — Where in a particular taxation year and before June 6, 1987 a person disposed of a Canadian resource property or a foreign resource property in circumstances in which any of subsection 29(25) of the *Income Tax Application Rules* and subsections (1) to (5) applies, no deduction in respect of an expense incurred before the property was disposed of may be made under this section or section 66, 66.1, 66.2 or 66.4 by the person in computing the person's income for a taxation year subsequent to the particular taxation year.

**(18) Application of subsec. 66(15)** — The definitions in subsection 66(15) apply to this section.

---

**Proposed Amendment — 66.7(18)**

**(18) Application of interpretation provisions** — The definitions in subsection 66(15) and sections 66.1 to 66.4 apply in this section.

**Application**: The December 21, 2000 draft legislation, subsec. 30(8), will amend subsec. 66.7(18) to read as above, applicable to taxation years that begin after 2000.

**Technical Notes**: Subsection 66.7(18) provides that the definitions in subsection 66(15) apply to section 66.7.

Subsection 66.7(18) is amended to clarify that the definitions in sections 66.1 to 66.4, including new section 66.21, also apply to section 66.7.

---

**Notes [66.7(18)]**: 66.7(18) added in the R.S.C. 1985 (5th Supp.) consolidation, effective for taxation years ending after November 1991. This rule was formerly contained in the opening words to 66(15).

**Related Provisions [s. 66.7]**: 66(5) — Dealers; 66(18) — Members of partnerships; 66.1(6) — Canadian exploration expense; 66.8(1) — Resource expenses of limited partners; 87(1.2) — Amalgamation — new corporation deemed continuation of predecessor; 88(1.5) — Windup — parent continuation of subsidiary.

**Notes [s. 66.7]**: 66.7 added by 1987 Budget. However, with respect to property acquired before January 15, 1987, or acquired before 1988 where the person acquiring the property was obliged on that date to acquire the property pursuant to the terms of an agreement in writing entered into on or before that date,

(a) clauses 66.7(1)(b)(i)(C), (2)(b)(i)(B), (3)(b)(i)(C), (4)(b)(i)(B) and (5)(b)(i)(B) shall be read as follows:

where the particular property was an interest in or a right to take or remove petroleum or natural gas or a right to take or remove minerals from a property, the production from that property, and

(b) subsection 66.7(11) is not applicable.

For this purpose, the amending legislation provides that "a person shall be considered not to be obliged ... to acquire ... property ... if the person may be excused from performing the obligation as a result of changes to the *Income Tax Act* affecting acquisitions or dispositions of property or acquisitions of control of corporations".

**Definitions [s. 66.7]**: "acquired" — 256(7)–(9); "amount" — 248(1); "arm's length" — 251(1); "business" — 248(1); "Canada" — 255; "Canadian development expense" — 66.2(5), 248(1); "Canadian exploration and development expense" — 66(15), 248(1); "Canadian exploration expense" — 66.1(6), 248(1); "Canadian oil and gas property expense" — 66.4(5), 248(1); "Canadian resource property" — 66(15), 66.7(18), 248(1); "carrying on business" — 253; "control" — 256(6)–(9); "corporation" — 248(1), *Interpretation Act* 35(1); "cumulative foreign resource expense" — 66.21(1), 66.7(18); "disposition" — 248(1); "expense" — 66(15), 66.7(18); "fiscal period" — 249(2), 249.1; "foreign exploration and development expenses" — 66(15), 248(1); "foreign resource expense" — 66.21(1), 248(1); "foreign resource pool expense" — 248(1); "foreign resource property" — 66(15), 248(1); "foreign re-

source property in respect of", "mineral", "Minister" — 248(1); "month" — *Interpretation Act* 35(1); "oil or gas well", "person", "prescribed", "property" — 248(1); "resident in Canada" — 250; "specified amount" — 66.7(12.1); "specified foreign exploration and development expense" — 66(15); "subsidiary wholly-owned corporation" — 248(1); "taxable income" — 2(2), 248(1); "taxation year" — 249; "taxpayer" — 248(1); "writing" — *Interpretation Act* 35(1).

**Interpretation Bulletins [s. 66.7]**: IT-126R2: Meaning of "winding-up".

**66.8 (1) Resource expenses of limited partner** — Where a taxpayer is a limited partner of a partnership at the end of a fiscal period of the partnership, the following rules apply:

(a) determine the amount, if any, by which

(i) the total of all amounts each of which is the taxpayer's share of

(A) the Canadian oil and gas property expenses (in this subsection referred to as "property expenses"),

(B) the Canadian development expenses (in this subsection referred to as "development expenses"),

(C) the Canadian exploration expenses (in this subsection referred to as "exploration expenses"), or

(D) the foreign exploration and development expenses (in this subsection referred to as "foreign expenses"),

---

**Proposed Amendment — 66.8(1)(a)(i)(D), (E)**

(D) the foreign resource expenses in respect of a country (in this subsection referred to as "country-specific foreign expenses"), or

(E) the foreign exploration and development expenses (in this subsection referred to as "global foreign expenses")

**Application**: The December 21, 2000 draft legislation, subsec. 31(1), will amend cl. 66.8(1)(a)(i)(D) to read as above, and add cl. (E), applicable to fiscal periods that begin after 2000.

**Technical Notes**: Subsection 66.8(1) provides for the reduction of a taxpayer's share of a partnership's resource expenditures incurred in a fiscal period in certain cases where the taxpayer's share of such resource expenditures exceeds the taxpayer's "at-risk amount" at the end of the fiscal period in respect of the partnership. Where there is such a reduction, subsection 66.8(2) allows the amount of the reduction to be carried forward and treated as if it were a resource expenditure incurred in the following fiscal period. The reduction of the taxpayer's resource expenditures occurs in a specified order, with a taxpayer's share of foreign exploration and development expenses being the last type of resource expenditure that is reduced.

Subsection 66.8(1) is amended so that a taxpayer's share of expenses that are a foreign resource expense in respect of a country (as defined in new section 66.21) is likewise reduced. Given the greater restrictions on the use of such expenses, the reduction is applied first to such expenses before being applied to foreign exploration and development expenses. In the event that the partnership incurred foreign resource expenses in respect of more than one country, the taxpayer can choose which country's foreign resource expenses are reduced. The Minister of National Revenue chooses the order in the event that no specification is made by the taxpayer on a timely basis.

      incurred by the partnership in the fiscal period determined without reference to this subsection

exceeds

      (ii) the amount, if any, by which

           (A) the taxpayer's at-risk amount at the end of the fiscal period in respect of the partnership

      exceeds

           (B) the total of

                (I) the amount required by subsection 127(8) in respect of the partnership to be added in computing the investment tax credit of the taxpayer in respect of the fiscal period, and

                (II) the taxpayer's share of any losses of the partnership for the fiscal period from a farming business;

(b) the amount determined under paragraph (a) shall be applied

      (i) first to reduce the taxpayer's share of property expenses,

      (ii) if any remains unapplied, then to reduce the taxpayer's share of development expenses,

      (iii) if any remains unapplied, then to reduce the taxpayer's share of exploration expenses, and

      (iv) if any remains unapplied, then to reduce the taxpayer's share of foreign expenses,

**Proposed Amendment — 66.8(1)(b)(iv), (v)**

(iv) if any remains unapplied, then to reduce (in the order specified by the taxpayer in writing filed with the Minister on or before the taxpayer's filing-due date for the taxpayer's taxation year in which the fiscal period ends or, where no such specification is made, in the order determined by the Minister) the taxpayer's share of country-specific foreign expenses, and

(v) if any remains unapplied, then to reduce the taxpayer's share of global foreign expenses,

**Application**: The December 21, 2000 draft legislation, subsec. 31(2), will amend subpara. 66.8(1)(b)(iv) to read as above and add subpara. (v), applicable to fiscal periods that begin after 2000.

**Technical Notes**: See under 66.8(1)(a)(i)(D), (E).

incurred by the partnership in the fiscal period; and

(c) for the purposes of subparagraph 53(2)(c)(ii), sections 66 to 66.7, subsection 96(2.1) and section 111, the taxpayer's share of each class of expenses described in subparagraph (a)(i) incurred by the partnership in the fiscal period shall be deemed to be the amount by which the taxpayer's share of that class of expenses as determined under subparagraph (a)(i) exceeds the amount, if any, that was applied under paragraph (b) to reduce the taxpayer's share of that class of expenses.

**(2) Expenses in following fiscal period** — For the purposes of subparagraph (1)(a)(i), the amount by which a taxpayer's share of a class of expenses incurred by a partnership is reduced under paragraph (1)(b) in respect of a fiscal period of the partnership shall be added to the taxpayer's share, otherwise determined, of that class of expenses incurred by the partnership in the immediately following fiscal period of the partnership.

**(3) Interpretation** — In this section,

(a) the expressions "at-risk amount" of a taxpayer in respect of a partnership and "limited partner" of a partnership have the meanings assigned by subsections 96(2.2) and (2.4), respectively, except that, with respect to the definition "limited partner", the definition "exempt interest" in subsection 96(2.5) shall be read as though the reference therein to

      (i) "February 25, 1986" were a reference to "June 17, 1987",

      (ii) "February 26, 1986" were a reference to "June 18, 1987",

      (iii) "January 1, 1987" were a reference to "January 1, 1988",

      (iv) "June 12, 1986" were a reference to "June 18, 1987", and

      (v) "prospectus, preliminary prospectus or registration statement" were read as "prospectus, preliminary prospectus, registration statement, offering memorandum or notice that is required to be filed before any distribution of securities may commence";

(b) a reference to a taxpayer who is a member of a particular partnership shall include a reference to another partnership that is a member of the particular partnership; and

(c) a taxpayer's share of Canadian development expenses or Canadian oil and gas property expenses incurred by a partnership in a fiscal period in respect of which the taxpayer has elected in respect of the share under paragraph (f) of the definition "Canadian development expense" in subsection 66.2(5) or paragraph (b) of the definition "Canadian oil and gas property expense" in subsection 66.4(5), as the case may be, shall be deemed to be nil.

**S. 66.8**     Income Tax Act, Part I, Division B

**Definitions [s. 66.8]**: "amount", "business" — 248(1); "Canadian development expense" — 66.2(5), 248(1); "Canadian exploration expense" — 66.1(6), 248(1); "Canadian oil and gas property expense" — 66.4(5), 248(1); "country-specific foreign expenses" — 66.8(1)(a)(i)(D); "farming", "filing-due date" — 248(1); "fiscal period" — 249(2), 249.1; "foreign exploration and development expenses" — 66(15), 248(1); "global foreign expenses" — 66.8(1)(a)(i)(E); "investment tax credit" — 127(9), 248(1); "Minister", "share", "property" — 248(1); "taxation year" — 249; "taxpayer" — 248(1); "writing" — *Interpretation Act* 35(1). See also 66.8(3).

## Subdivision f — Rules Relating to Computation of Income

**67. General limitation re expenses** — In computing income, no deduction shall be made in respect of an outlay or expense in respect of which any amount is otherwise deductible under this Act, except to the extent that the outlay or expense was reasonable in the circumstances.

**Related Provisions**: 8(9) — Employee's aircraft costs must be reasonable; 18(1)(a) — Expense not deductible unless for purpose of earning income; 18(1)(h) — Personal or living expenses disallowed; 20(1)(c) closing words — Interest deduction limited to reasonable amount; 247(8) — Transfer pricing rules take priority over s. 67.

**Notes [s. 67]**: A corporation can generally deduct an unlimited salary or bonus payable to its owner-manager, on the principle that the corporation's profits are attributable to the owner's work. See *Safety Boss Ltd.*, [2000] 3 C.T.C. 2497 (TCC). This has long been accepted by the CCRA; see 1981 Canadian Tax Foundation annual conference report, Revenue Canada Round Table, p. 757, q. 42. An April 10/00 technical interpretation (VIEWS doc 2000-0013085) suggests this will not apply when the owners' shareholdings are indirect. However, this may be wrong in light of *Safety Boss*.

**Definitions [s. 67]**: "amount" — 248(1).

**I.T. Application Rules**: 31.

**Interpretation Bulletins**: IT-75R3: Scholarships, fellowships, bursaries, prizes, and research grants; IT-131R2: Convention expenses; IT-178R3: Moving expenses; IT-357R2: Expenses of training; IT-467R: Damages, settlements and similar payments; IT-468R: Management or administration fees paid to non-residents; IT-521R: Motor vehicle expenses claimed by self-employed individuals; IT-525R: Performing artists.

**Information Circulars**: 87-2R: International transfer pricing.

**I.T. Technical News**: No. 12 (meals and beverages at golf clubs); No. 15 (Christmas parties and employer-paid special events); No. 16 (*Shell* case).

**Advance Tax Rulings**: ATR-12: Retiring allowance; ATR-45: Share appreciation rights plan.

**67.1 (1) Expenses for food, etc.** — For the purposes of this Act, other than sections 62, 63 and 118.2, an amount paid or payable in respect of the human consumption of food or beverages or the enjoyment of entertainment shall be deemed to be 50% of the lesser of

(a) the amount actually paid or payable in respect thereof, and

(b) an amount in respect thereof that would be reasonable in the circumstances.

**Related Provisions**: 8(4) — Limitation on meals of employee.

**Notes**: The 50% limitation is the same as applies in the United States (Internal Revenue Code subsec. 274(n)). It also applies to GST input tax credits (except for charities and public institutions), under s. 236 of the *Excise Tax Act*.

Opening words of 67.1(1) amended by 1994 Budget to change "80%" to "50%", effective for food and beverages consumed and entertainment enjoyed after February 1994, unless the expense was incurred before February 22, 1994.

**Interpretation Bulletins**: IT-504R2: Visual artists and writers; IT-518R: Food beverages and entertainment expenses; IT-525R: Performing artists.

**Information Circulars**: 73-21R7: Away from home expenses.

**I.T. Technical News**: No. 12 (meals and beverages at golf clubs); No. 16 (*Scott* case).

**(2) Exceptions** — Subsection (1) does not apply to an amount paid or payable by a person in respect of the consumption of food or beverages or the enjoyment of entertainment where the amount

(a) is paid or payable for food, beverages or entertainment provided for, or in expectation of, compensation in the ordinary course of a business carried on by that person of providing the food, beverages or entertainment for compensation;

(b) relates to a fund-raising event the primary purpose of which is to benefit a registered charity;

(c) is an amount for which the person is compensated and the amount of the compensation is reasonable and specifically identified in writing to the person paying the compensation;

(d) is required to be included in computing any taxpayer's income because of the application of section 6 in respect of food or beverages consumed or entertainment enjoyed by the taxpayer or a person with whom the taxpayer does not deal at arm's length, or would be so required but for subparagraph 6(6)(a)(ii);

(e) is an amount that

(i) is not paid or payable in respect of a conference, convention, seminar or similar event,

(ii) would, but for subparagraph 6(6)(a)(i), be required to be included in computing any taxpayer's income for a taxation year because of the application of section 6 in respect of food or beverages consumed or entertainment enjoyed by the taxpayer or a person with whom the taxpayer does not deal at arm's length, and

(iii) is paid or payable in respect of the taxpayer's duties performed at a work site in Canada that is

(A) outside any urban area, as defined by the last Census Dictionary published by Statistics Canada before the year, that has a population of at least 40,000 individuals as determined in the last census published by Statistics Canada before the year, and

(B) at least 30 kilometres from the nearest point on the boundary of the nearest such urban area; or

(f) is in respect of one of six or fewer special events held in a calendar year at which the food, beverages or entertainment is generally available to all individuals employed by the person at a particular place of business of the person and consumed or enjoyed by those individuals.

**Notes**: To determine whether a given place is within 30 km of an urban area under 67.1(2)(e)(iii)(B), see http://www.ccra-adrc.gc.ca/tax/business/smallbusiness/searchmap-e.html for a "Meal and entertainment expenses search map" on the CCRA's Web site.

67.1(2)(d) amended by 1998 Budget, retroactive to its introduction (1987), to refer to "any taxpayer's income". The amendment ensures that the exemption applies when a person incurs meal or entertainment expenses that give rise to a taxable benefit for employees of another person.

67.1(2)(e) amended and (f) added by 1998 Budget, effective for expenses incurred after February 23, 1998. For earlier years, read:

(e) is incurred by the person for food, beverages or entertainment generally available to all individuals employed by the person at a particular place of business of the person and consumed or enjoyed by such individuals.

67.1(2)(e) amended by 1991 technical bill, effective for taxation years ending after July 13, 1990. For earlier years, read "... generally available to all employees of the person at a particular location".

**I.T. Technical News**: No. 15 (Christmas parties and employer-paid special events).

**(3) Fees for convention, etc.** — For the purposes of this section, where a fee paid or payable for a conference, convention, seminar or similar event entitles the participant to food, beverages or entertainment (other than incidental beverages and refreshments made available during the course of meetings or receptions at the event) and a reasonable part of the fee, determined on the basis of the cost of providing the food, beverages and entertainment, is not identified in the account for the fee as compensation for the food, beverages and entertainment, $50 or such other amount as may be prescribed shall be deemed to be the actual amount paid or payable in respect of food, beverages and entertainment for each day of the event on which food, beverages or entertainment is provided and, for the purposes of this Act, the fee for the event shall be deemed to be the actual amount of the fee minus the amount deemed by this subsection to be the actual amount paid or payable for the food, beverages and entertainment.

**Related Provisions**: 20(10) — Deduction for convention expenses.

**Regulations**: No amount other than $50 has been prescribed for purposes of 67.1(3).

**Interpretation Bulletins**: IT-131R2: Convention expenses.

**(4) Interpretation** — For the purposes of this section,

(a) no amount paid or payable for travel on an airplane, train or bus shall be considered to be in respect of food, beverages or entertainment consumed or enjoyed while travelling thereon; and

(b) "entertainment" includes amusement and recreation.

**Definitions [s. 67.1]**: "amount", "business", "employee" — 248(1); "entertainment" — 67.1(4)(b); "individual", "person", "prescribed", "registered charity" — 248(1); "writing" — *Interpretation Act* 35(1).

**Interpretation Bulletins**: IT-518R: Food, beverages and entertainment expenses; IT-522R: Vehicle, travel and sales expenses of employees.

**67.2 Interest on money borrowed for passenger vehicle** — For the purposes of this Act, where an amount is paid or payable for a period by a person in respect of interest on borrowed money used to acquire a passenger vehicle or on an amount paid or payable for the acquisition of such a vehicle, in computing the person's income for a taxation year, the amount of interest so paid or payable shall be deemed to be the lesser of the actual amount paid or payable and the amount determined by the formula

$$\frac{A}{30} \times B$$

where

A is $250 or such other amount as may be prescribed; and

B is the number of days in the period in respect of which the interest was paid or payable, as the case may be.

**Related Provisions**: 8(1)(j) — Automobile and aircraft costs; 20(1)(c) — Interest deductible; 20(1)(d) — Compound interest deductible; 67.4 — More than one owner or lessor.

**Notes**: The limitation on deductible interest depends on the date of acquisition of the automobile, as follows (see Reg. 7307(2)):

| Acquisition date | Limit on monthly interest |
| --- | --- |
| June 18/87–Aug. 31/89 | $250 |
| Sept. 1/89–Dec. 31/96 | $300 |
| 1997–2000 | $250 |
| 2001 | $300 |

67.2 amended by 1991 technical bill, retroactive to the introduction of the section (taxation years and fiscal periods commencing after June 17, 1987 that end after 1987). The new version deals with cash-basis taxpayers by using the words "paid or payable" rather than just "payable".

See also Notes to 13(7)(g).

**Definitions [s. 67.2]**: "amount", "borrowed money", "passenger vehicle", "prescribed" — 248(1); "taxation year" — 11(2), 249.

**Regulations**: 7307(2) (prescribed amount).

**Interpretation Bulletins**: IT-355R2: Interest on loans to buy life insurance policies and annuity contracts, and interest on policy loans; IT-521R: Motor vehicle expenses claimed by self-employed individuals; IT-522R: Vehicle, travel and sales expenses of employees; IT-525R: Performing artists.

**I.T. Technical News**: No. 10 (1997 deduction limits and benefit rates for automobiles).

**67.3 Limitation re cost of leasing passenger vehicle** — Notwithstanding any other section of this Act, where

(a) in a taxation year all or part of the actual lease charges in respect of a passenger vehicle are paid

**S. 67.3(a)**      Income Tax Act, Part I, Division B

or payable, directly or indirectly, by a taxpayer, and

(b) in computing the taxpayer's income for the year an amount may be deducted in respect of those charges,

in determining the amount that may be so deducted, the total of those charges shall be deemed not to exceed the lesser of

(c) the amount determined by the formula

$$\left(A \times \frac{B}{30}\right) - C - D - E$$

where

A  is $600 or such other amount as is prescribed,

B  is the number of days in the period commencing at the beginning of the term of the lease and ending at the earlier of the end of the year and the end of the lease,

C  is the total of all amounts deducted in computing the taxpayer's income for preceding taxation years in respect of the actual lease charges in respect of the vehicle,

D  is the amount of interest that would be earned on the part of the total of all refundable amounts in respect of the lease that exceeds $1,000 if interest were

    (i) payable on the refundable amounts at the prescribed rate, and

    (ii) computed for the period before the end of the year during which the refundable amounts were outstanding, and

E  is the total of all reimbursements that became receivable before the end of the year by the taxpayer in respect of the lease, and

(d) the amount determined by the formula

$$\left(\frac{A \times B}{0.85C}\right) - D - E$$

where

A  is the total of the actual lease charges in respect of the lease incurred in respect of the year or the total of the actual lease charges in respect of the lease paid in the year (depending on the method regularly followed by the taxpayer in computing income),

B  is $20,000 or such other amount as is prescribed,

C  is the greater of $23,529 (or such other amount as is prescribed) and the manufacturer's list price for the vehicle,

D  is the amount of interest that would be earned on that part of the total of all refundable amounts paid in respect of the lease that exceeds $1,000 if interest were

    (i) payable on the refundable amounts at the prescribed rate, and

    (ii) computed for the period in the year during which the refundable amounts are outstanding, and

E  is the total of all reimbursements that became receivable during the year by the taxpayer in respect of the lease.

**Related Provisions**: 67.4 — More than one owner or lessor; 257 — Formula cannot calculate to less than zero.

**Notes**: The limitation on deductible leasing cost for an automobile depends on the date of the lease, as follows (see Reg. 7307(3)):

| Lease date | Limit on monthly lease expense |
|---|---|
| June 18/87–Aug. 31/89 | $600 |
| Sept. 1/89–Dec. 31/96 | $650 |
| 1997 | $550 |
| 1998–1999 | $650 |
| 2000 | $700 |
| 2001 | $800 |

Note, however, the alternative limitation in 67.3(d).

67.3 amended by 1991 technical bill, effective for taxation years and fiscal periods commencing after June 17, 1987 that end after 1987, except that with respect to amounts paid or payable as a reimbursement in respect of a lease expense, it is applicable to taxation years that end after July 13, 1990; and with respect to leases entered into before 1991 the description of C in para. (d) shall be read as follows:

    C  is the greater of $23,529 (or such other amount as may be prescribed) and the total of

        (i) the manufacturer's list price for the vehicle, and

        (ii) the provincial sales tax, if any, that would have been payable by a purchaser of the vehicle if it had been purchased at the manufacturer's list price for the vehicle at the time the first lease of the vehicle was entered into and in the province under the laws of which the vehicle was registered for the greatest part of the year,

The section did not apply to persons making reimbursement of lease costs before July 14, 1990.

See also Notes to 13(7)(g).

**Definitions [s. 67.3]**: "amount", "borrowed money", "motor vehicle", "passenger vehicle", "prescribed" — 248(1); "prescribed rate" — Reg. 4301; "taxation year" — 11(2), 249; "taxpayer" — 248(1); "trust" — 104(1), 248(1), (3).

**Regulations**: 4301(c) (prescribed rate of interest); 7307(1), (3), (4) (prescribed amounts).

**Interpretation Bulletins**: IT-521R: Motor vehicle expenses claimed by self-employed individuals; IT-522R: Vehicle, travel and sales expenses of employees; IT-525R: Performing artists.

**I.T. Technical News**: No. 10 (1997 deduction limits and benefit rates for automobiles); No. 12 (1998 deduction limits and benefit rates for automobiles).

## 67.4 More than one owner or lessor

— Where a person owns or leases a motor vehicle jointly with one or more other persons, the reference in paragraph 13(7)(g) to the amount of $20,000, in section 67.2 to the amount of $250 and in section 67.3 to the amounts of $600, $20,000 and $23,529 shall be read as a reference to that proportion of each of those amounts or such other amounts as may be prescribed for the purposes thereof that the fair market value of the first-mentioned person's interest in the vehicle is of the fair market value of the interests in the vehicle of all those persons.

**Definitions [s. 67.4]**: "amount", "motor vehicle", "person" — 248(1).

**Regulations**: 7307 (prescribed amounts).

**Interpretation Bulletins**: IT-521R: Motor vehicle expenses claimed by self-employed individuals; IT-522R: Vehicle, travel and sales expenses of employees; IT-525R: Performing artists.

**I.T. Technical News**: No. 10 (1997 deduction limits and benefit rates for automobiles).

## 67.5 (1) Non-deductibility of illegal payments

— In computing income, no deduction shall be made in respect of an outlay made or expense incurred for the purpose of doing anything that is an offence under section 3 of the *Corruption of Foreign Public Officials Act* or under any of sections 119 to 121, 123 to 125, 393 and 426 of the *Criminal Code*, or an offence under section 465 of the *Criminal Code* as it relates to an offence described in any of those sections.

**Notes**: See Notes at end of 67.5.

**(2) Reassessments** — Notwithstanding subsections 152(4) to (5), the Minister may make such assessments, reassessments and additional assessments of tax, interest and penalties and such determinations and redeterminations as are necessary to give effect to subsection (1) for any taxation year.

**Related Provisions**: 165(1.1) — Limitation of right to object to assessment; 169(2)(a) — Limitation of right to appeal.

**Notes [s. 67.5]**: Section 119 of the *Criminal Code* deals with bribery of judges, members of Parliament and members of a provincial legislature. Section 120 deals with bribery of officers involved in the administration of criminal law, such as police officers, justices and officers of a juvenile court. Section 121 deals with payments to government employees or officials in order to obtain contracts or other benefits. Section 123 deals with attempts to influence municipal officials through bribery, threats, deceit, etc. Section 124 deals with selling or paying for an appointment to an office. Section 125 deals with influencing or negotiating appointments and dealing in offices. Section 393 deals with paying off a collector who fails to collect a fare or admission fee. Section 426 deals with secretly paying an agent a commission and deceiving the agent's principal. Section 465 sets out the offence of conspiracy to commit an act that is an offence under the *Criminal Code*.

Fines and penalties, except those paid under the ITA, are deductible if incurred in the course of business. See Notes to 18(1)(t).

67.5 amended by the *Corruption of Foreign Public Officials Act* (S.C. 1998, c. 34), proclaimed into force February 14, 1999, to add reference to s. 3 of that Act. That section provides:

> 3. (1) Bribing a foreign public official — Every person commits an offence who, in order to obtain or retain an advantage in the course of business, directly or indirectly gives, offers or agrees to give or offer a loan, reward, advantage or benefit of any kind to a foreign public official or to any person for the benefit of a foreign public official
>
> (a) as consideration for an act or omission by the official in connection with the performance of the official's duties or functions; or
>
> (b) to induce the official to use his or her position to influence any acts or decisions of the foreign state or public international organization for which the official performs duties or functions.

(2) Punishment — Every person who contravenes subsection (1) is guilty of an indictable offence and liable to imprisonment for a term not exceeding five years.

(3) Saving provision — No person is guilty of an offence under subsection (1) if the loan, reward, advantage or benefit

(a) is permitted or required under the laws of the foreign state or public international organization for which the foreign public official performs duties or functions; or

(b) was made to pay the reasonable expenses incurred in good faith by or on behalf of the foreign public official that are directly related to

(i) the promotion, demonstration or explanation of the person's products and services, or

(ii) the execution or performance of a contract between the person and the foreign state for which the official performs duties or functions.

(4) Facilitation payments — For the purpose of subsection (1), a payment is not a loan, reward, advantage or benefit to obtain or retain an advantage in the course of business, if it is made to expedite or secure the performance by a foreign public official of any act of a routine nature that is part of the foreign public official's duties or functions, including

(a) the issuance of a permit, licence or other document to qualify a person to do business;

(b) the processing of official documents, such as visas and work permits;

(c) the provision of services normally offered to the public, such as mail pick-up and delivery, telecommunication services and power and water supply; and

(d) the provision of services normally provided as required, such as police protection, loading and unloading of cargo, the protection of perishable products or commodities from deterioration or the scheduling of inspections related to contract performance or transit of goods.

(5) Greater certainty — For greater certainty, an "act of a routine nature" does not include a decision to award new business or to continue business with a particular party, including a decision on the terms of that business, or encouraging another person to make any such decision.

Section 2 of that Act defines "foreign public official" as

(a) a person who holds a legislative, administrative or judicial position of a foreign state;

(b) a person who performs public duties or functions for a foreign state, including a person employed by a board, commission, corporation or other body or authority that is established to perform a duty or function on behalf of the foreign state, or is performing such a duty or function; and

(c) an official or agent of a public international organization that is formed by two or more states or governments, or by two or more such public international organizations.

67.5 added by 1991 technical bill, effective for outlays or expenses after July 13, 1990.

**Definitions [s. 67.5]**: "assessment", "Minister" — 248(1); "taxation year" — 249.

**Interpretation Bulletins**: IT-525R: Performing artists.

## 68. Allocation of amounts in consideration for disposition of property

— Where an amount received or receivable from a person can reasonably be regarded as being in part the consideration for the disposition of a particular property of a taxpayer or

**S. 68**      Income Tax Act, Part I, Division B

as being in part consideration for the provision of particular services by a taxpayer,

(a) the part of the amount that can reasonably be regarded as being the consideration for the disposition shall be deemed to be proceeds of disposition of the particular property irrespective of the form or legal effect of the contract or agreement, and the person to whom the property was disposed of shall be deemed to have acquired it for an amount equal to that part; and

(b) the part of the amount that can reasonably be regarded as being consideration for the provision of particular services shall be deemed to be an amount received or receivable by the taxpayer in respect of those services irrespective of the form or legal effect of the contract or agreement, and that part shall be deemed to be an amount paid or payable to the taxpayer by the person to whom the services were rendered in respect of those services.

**Related Provisions**: 12(1)(a) — Services, etc. to be rendered; 12(1)(b) — Amounts receivable in respect of services, etc, rendered; 13(33) — Consideration given for depreciable capital; 247(8) — Transfer pricing rules take priority over s. 68.

**Notes**: 68(b) added by 1988 tax reform, effective for amounts received or receivable after June 1988 otherwise than pursuant to agreements entered into in writing before May 1988.

**Definitions [s. 68]**: "amount", "person", "property" — 248(1); "received" — 248(7); "taxpayer" — 248(1).

**Interpretation Bulletins**: IT-143R2: Meaning of "eligible capital expenditure"; IT-220R2: Capital cost allowance — proceeds of disposition of depreciable property.

**69. (1) Inadequate considerations** — Except as expressly otherwise provided in this Act,

(a) where a taxpayer has acquired anything from a person with whom the taxpayer was not dealing at arm's length at an amount in excess of the fair market value thereof at the time the taxpayer so acquired it, the taxpayer shall be deemed to have acquired it at that fair market value;

(b) where a taxpayer has disposed of anything

(i) to a person with whom the taxpayer was not dealing at arm's length for no proceeds or for proceeds less than the fair market value thereof at the time the taxpayer so disposed of it, or

(ii) to any person by way of gift *inter vivos*,

**Proposed Addition — 69(1)(b)(iii)**

(iii) to a trust because of a disposition of a property that does not result in a change in the beneficial ownership of the property,

**Application**: Bill C-43 (First Reading September 20, 2000), subsec. 31(1), will add subpara. 69(1)(b)(iii), applicable to dispositions that occur after December 23, 1998.

**Technical Notes**: Subsection 69(1) of the Act provides rules that deal with gifts and non-arm's length dispositions of property, except where such transactions are covered by other express provisions in the Act (e.g., section 85, subsections 107(2) and (2.1) and new subsection 107.4(3)). Under paragraph 69(1)(b), a taxpayer is deemed to receive proceeds of disposition equal to the fair market value of the property disposed of where the taxpayer disposed of the property by way of gift or to a non-arm's length person for proceeds less than the fair market value of the property. Under paragraph 69(1)(c), a taxpayer who has acquired property by way of gift, bequest or inheritance is deemed by paragraph 69(1)(c) to have acquired the property at its fair market value.

Paragraph 69(1)(b) is amended to ensure that, subject to subsection 107.4(3), it applies to a disposition to a trust of a property where no change in the beneficial ownership of the property is involved.

the taxpayer shall be deemed to have received proceeds of disposition therefor equal to that fair market value; and

(c) where a taxpayer has acquired property by way of gift, bequest or inheritance, the taxpayer shall be deemed to have acquired the property at its fair market value at the time the taxpayer so acquired it.

**Proposed Amendment — 69(1)(c)**

(c) where a taxpayer acquires a property by way of gift, bequest or inheritance or because of a disposition that does not result in a change in the beneficial ownership of the property, the taxpayer is deemed to acquire the property at its fair market value.

**Application**: Bill C-43 (First Reading September 20, 2000), subsec. 31(2), will amend para. 69(1)(c) to read as above, applicable to acquisitions that occur after December 23, 1998.

**Technical Notes**: Paragraph 69(1)(c) is amended so that a taxpayer, where subsection 69(1) applies, is also considered to acquire property at its fair market value where the acquisition is because of a disposition that does not result in any change in the beneficial ownership of the property.

For a description of circumstances where a transfer without any change in beneficial ownership is not a "disposition", reference should be made to the commentary on the new definition "disposition" in subsection 248(1).

**Related Provisions**: 13(33) — Consideration given for depreciable capital; 15(1) — Benefit conferred on shareholder; 28(1.1) — Farming or fishing business — acquisition of inventory; 38(a.1) — Gift of publicly traded shares to charity; 53(5) — Recomputation of ACB on non-arm's length disposition; 56(11) — Disposition of interest in retirement compensation; 69(1.1) — Idem; 69(6) — Inadequate considerations; 73(1) — Rollover at cost on transfer to spouse; 73(3) — Rollover of farm property on transfer to child or grandchild; 79(3)E(a) — Where property surrendered to a creditor; 97(1) — Contribution of property by partner to partnership deemed to be at fair market value; 106(1.1) — Cost of income interest in a trust; 107(1.1) — Cost of capital interest in a trust; 107.4(3) — Tax consequences of qualifying disposition to a trust; 107.4(4) — Fair market value of vested interest in trust; 110.1(5) — Determination of value on donation of servitude, covenant or easement for ecologically sensitive land; 118.1(10.1) — Determination of value by Canadian Cultural Property Export Review Board; 118.1(12) — Determination of value on donation of servitude, covenant or easement for ecologically sensitive land; 127(11.8)(b) — Ignore 69(1)(c) for certain non-arm's length costs re investment tax credit; 146(9) — Disposition or acquisition of property by RRSP; 146.3(4) — Disposition or acquisition of property by RRIF; 206(4) — Deemed fair

## Subdivision f — Rules Relating to Computation of Income  S. 69(2)

market value for purposes of tax on foreign property held by RRSPs etc.; 247(8) — Transfer pricing rules take priority over subsec. 69(1); 251 — Arm's length; Canada-U.S. tax treaty, Art. IX — Adjustments for transactions between related persons.

**Notes**: 69(1)(b)(ii) has a counterpart in 69(1)(c). However, 69(1)(b)(i) has no counterpart. If X and Y are related and X sells Y a piece of land for $1, X will be deemed to have disposed of the land for fair market value but Y will have acquired it for a cost base of $1, leading to double taxation when Y eventually disposes of it. No such double taxation occurs if X gives the land to Y.

If the price under a non-arm's length agreement is the fair market value (FMV) at the time the agreement is entered into, but is not the FMV at the time the property is transferred, the CCRA takes the position that 69(1) will apply to change the cost or proceeds of disposition. See Revenue Canada Round Table, Canadian Tax Foundation 1993 annual conference report, Q. 39. However, it could be argued that the agreement affects the FMV, so that the FMV is set by what is provided under the agreement; see Interpretation Bulletin IT-140R3.

A transfer to a "bare trust" is not a disposition and will not trigger 69(1). See proposed 69(1)(b)(iii) and Notes to 104(1).

**Regulations**: 1102(14) — Class of depreciable property preserved on non-arm's length acquisition.

**I.T. Application Rules**: 20(1.3), 32.

**Interpretation Bulletins**: IT-125R4: Dispositions of resource properties; IT-140R3: Buy-sell agreements; IT-188R: Sale of accounts receivable; IT-212R3: Income of deceased persons — rights or things; IT-213R: Prizes from lottery schemes and giveaway contests; IT-226R: Gift to a charity of a residual interest in real property or an equitable interest in a trust; IT-288R2: Gifts of capital properties to a charity and others; IT-297R2: Gifts in kind to charity and others; IT-385R2: Disposition of an income interest in a trust; IT-403R: Options on real estate; IT-405: Inadequate considerations — acquisitions and dispositions; IT-427R: Livestock of farmers; IT-432R2: Benefits conferred on shareholders; IT-433R: Farming or fishing — use of cash method; IT-442R: Bad debts and reserves for doubtful debts; IT-504R2: Visual artists and writers. See also list at end of s. 69.

**Information Circulars**: 87-2R: International transfer pricing; 89-3: Policy statement on business equity valuations.

**Advance Tax Rulings**: ATR-1: Transfer of legal title in land to bare trustee corporation — mortgagee's requirements sole reason for transfer; ATR-9: Transfer of personal residence from corporation to its controlling shareholder; ATR-36: Estate freeze.

**(1.1) Idem, where subsec. 70(3) applies** — Where a taxpayer has acquired property that is a right or thing to which subsection 70(3) applies, the following rules apply:

(a) paragraph (1)(c) is not applicable to that property; and

(b) the taxpayer shall be deemed to have acquired the property at a cost equal to the total of

(i) such part, if any, of the cost thereof to the taxpayer who has died as had not been deducted by the taxpayer in computing the taxpayer's income for any year, and

(ii) any expenditures made or incurred by the taxpayer to acquire the property.

**Notes**: 69(1.1) added by 1974 Budget, effective for appropriations, dispositions or acquisitions of property after May 6, 1974.

**Interpretation Bulletins**: IT-212R3: Income of deceased persons — rights or things; IT-427R: Livestock of farmers. See also list at end of s. 69.

**(1.2) Idem** — Where, at any time,

(a) a taxpayer disposed of property for proceeds of disposition (determined without reference to this subsection) equal to or greater than the fair market value at that time of the property, and

(b) there existed at that time an agreement under which a person with whom the taxpayer was not dealing at arm's length agreed to pay as rent, royalty or other payment for the use of or the right to use the property an amount less than the amount that would have been reasonable in the circumstances if the taxpayer and the person had been dealing at arm's length at the time the agreement was entered into,

the taxpayer's proceeds of disposition of the property shall be deemed to be the greater of

(c) those proceeds determined without reference to this subsection, and

(d) the fair market value of the property at the time of the disposition, determined without reference to the existence of the agreement.

**Related Provisions**: 247(8) — Transfer pricing rules take priority over subsec. 69(1.2).

**Notes**: 69(1.2) added by 1992 technical bill, effective for dispositions after December 20, 1991.

**(2) [Repealed]**

**Notes**: 69(2) repealed by 1995-97 technical bill, effective for taxation years that begin after 1997. It and 69(3) were replaced by a new transfer-pricing rule in 247(2). It read:

(2) **Unreasonable consideration** — Where a taxpayer has paid or agreed to pay to a non-resident person with whom the taxpayer was not dealing at arm's length as price, rental, royalty or other payment for or for the use or reproduction of any property, or as consideration for the carriage of goods or passengers or for other services, an amount greater than the amount (in this subsection referred to as "the reasonable amount") that would have been reasonable in the circumstances if the non-resident person and the taxpayer had been dealing at arm's length, the reasonable amount shall, for the purpose of computing the taxpayer's income under this Part, be deemed to have been the amount that was paid or is payable therefor.

69(2) and (3) addressed transfer pricing within multinational groups. 69(2) limited deductions for non-arm's length payments to non-residents to a reasonable amount. 69(3) required non-arm's length payments from non-residents to be at least a reasonable amount. Revenue Canada announced in July 1993 that it will enter into Advance Pricing Agreements (APAs) with taxpayers (and in conjunction with the IRS, where the related person is in the U.S.), to confirm beforehand that transfer pricing amounts are acceptable to the Department. See also Department of Finance news release 94-003 (January 7, 1994), in which the Canadian government clarified its position re acceptable methods of transfer pricing. For detailed discussion of APA policy at both Revenue Canada and the IRS, see the papers by Bergquist, Gouin-Toussaint and Tillinghast in sections 5 to 7 of the 1993 Corporate Management Tax Conference proceedings (Canadian Tax Foundation), and Information Circular 94-4.

Revenue Canada announced on October 28, 1994 that it had reached agreement with the U.S., Japan and Australia on bilateral APAs, whereby two governments will agree on a particular company's transfer pricing methodology.

Note that Competent Authority assistance can be sought under tax treaties where an adjustment is made under 69(2) or (3), so that the resulting higher Canadian tax can be offset by lower tax in the other jurisdiction. See 115.1. See also Article IX of the Canada-U.S. tax treaty.

For a discussion of calculating management fees that will withstand a transfer-pricing audit, see Emma Purdy & Jeffrey Zanchelli, "Calculating and Supporting Management Fees", 44(1) *Canadian Tax Journal* 157–187 (1996).

See also Notes to 247(2).

**Interpretation Bulletins:** IT-468R: Management or administration fees paid to non-residents. See also list at end of s. 69.

**Information Circulars:** 87-2R: International transfer pricing; 94-4: International transfer pricing — advance pricing agreements (APA).

**(3)** [Repealed]

**Notes:** 69(3) repealed by 1995-97 technical bill, effective for taxation years that begin after 1997. See Notes to 69(2). For taxation years beginning before 1998, read:

> (3) **Idem** — Where a non-resident person has neither paid nor agreed to pay to a taxpayer with whom the person was not dealing at arm's length as price, rental, royalty or other payment for or for the use or reproduction of any property or as consideration for the carriage of goods or passengers or for other services, an amount equal to or greater than the amount that would have been a reasonable amount in the circumstances if the non-resident person and the taxpayer had been dealing at arm's length, that reasonable amount shall, for the purpose of computing the taxpayer's income under this Part, be deemed to have been received or receivable by the taxpayer therefor.

69(3) amended by 1991 technical bill, effective July 14, 1990, to clarify that it would applied only where the amount paid by the related non-resident is nil or insufficient.

See also Notes to former 69(2).

**(4) Shareholder appropriations** — Where at any time property of a corporation has been appropriated in any manner whatever to or for the benefit of a shareholder of the corporation for no consideration or for consideration that is less than the property's fair market value and a sale of the property at its fair market value would have increased the corporation's income or reduced a loss of the corporation, the corporation shall be deemed to have disposed of the property, and to have received proceeds of disposition therefor equal to its fair market value, at that time.

**Related Provisions:** 15(1) — Benefit conferred on shareholder.

**Notes:** 69(4) amended by 1993 technical bill, effective for appropriations after December 21, 1992, to extend to cases where a sale would have reduced a loss of the corporation.

**Interpretation Bulletins:** See list at end of s. 69.

**(5) Idem** — Where in a taxation year of a corporation property of the corporation has been appropriated in any manner whatever to, or for the benefit of, a shareholder, on the winding-up of the corporation, the following rules apply:

> (a) the corporation is deemed, for the purpose of computing its income for the year, to have disposed of the property immediately before the winding-up for proceeds equal to its fair market value at that time;

(b) the shareholder shall be deemed to have acquired the property at a cost equal to its fair market value immediately before the winding-up;

(c) subsections 52(1), (1.1) and (2) are not applicable for the purposes of determining the cost to the shareholder of the property; and

---

**Proposed Amendment — 69(5)(c)**

(c) subsections 52(1) and (2) do not apply for the purposes of determining the cost to the shareholder of the property; and

**Application:** Bill C-43 (First Reading September 20, 2000), subsec. 31(3), will amend para. 69(5)(c) to read as above, applicable to dispositions that occur after 1999.

**Technical Notes:** Subsection 69(5) ensures that where property is appropriated by a shareholder on the winding-up of a corporation, the property is treated as having been transferred at its fair market value with the consequent recognition on the transfer of any resulting income or loss. For this purpose, paragraph 69(5)(c) provides that subsections 52(1), (1.1) and (2) do not apply for the purposes of determining the cost to the shareholder of the property transferred.

Paragraph 69(5)(c) is amended to remove the reference to subsection 52(1.1), strictly consequential on the repeal of that subsection.

---

(d) subsections 13(21.2), 14(12), 18(15) and 40(3.4) and (3.6) do not apply in respect of any property disposed of on the winding-up.

(e) [Repealed]

**Related Provisions:** 15(1) — Benefit conferred on shareholder; 54"superficial loss"(h) — Superficial loss rule inapplicable when 69(5) applies; 84(2) — Distribution on winding-up, etc.

**Notes:** 69(5)(a) and (d) amended, and (e) repealed, by 1995-97 technical bill, effective for windups that begin after 1995. For windups that begin from April 27 to December 31, 1995, read in references to 85(4) and (5.1) in para. (d). The changes were in consequence of the new regime dealing with transfers of pregnant losses (see Notes to 13(21.2) and 40(3.4)).

For appropriations after November 12, 1981 until the above amendments, read:

> (a) for the purpose of computing the corporation's income for the year,
>
>> (i) it shall be deemed to have sold each such property immediately before the winding-up and to have received therefor the fair market value thereof at that time, and
>>
>> (ii) paragraph 40(2)(e) shall not apply in computing the loss, if any, from the sale of any such property;
>
> .....
>
> (d) subsections 85(4) and (5.1) shall not apply in respect of the winding-up; and
>
> (e) paragraph 40(2)(e) does not apply in computing the loss, if any, of the shareholder from the disposition of a share of the capital stock of the corporation to the corporation on the winding-up.

69(5) amended by 1974, 1979 and 1981 Budgets; resulting version effective for appropriations occurring after November 12, 1981 (but see below regarding 69(5)(e)).

For appropriations, dispositions of acquisitions of property before May 7, 1974, read:

> (5) Where property of a corporation has been appropriated in any manner whatever to, or for the benefit of, a shareholder,

on the winding-up of the corporation, if the sale thereof at the fair market value immediately prior to the winding-up would have increased the corporation's income for a taxation year, for the purpose of determining the corporation's income for the year, it shall be deemed to have sold the property during the year and to have received therefor the fair market value thereof.

For appropriations, dispositions or acquisitions from May 7, 1974 through November 16, 1978, read as now enacted but without para. (d).

For appropriations, dispositions or acquisitions from November 17, 1978 through November 12, 1981, read as now enacted, but without the reference to 85(5.1) in para. (d).

69(5)(e) added by 1991 technical bill, effective for dispositions of shares after 1985.

**Interpretation Bulletins**: IT-444R: Corporations — involuntary dissolutions; IT-488R2: Winding-up of 90%-owned taxable Canadian corporations. See also list at end of s. 69.

**Information Circulars**: 89-3: Policy statement on business equity valuations.

**(6) Idem** — Where a taxpayer who is an operator with respect to a natural accumulation of petroleum or natural gas in Canada, an oil or gas well in Canada or a mineral resource in Canada disposes by virtue of an obligation imposed by statute or a contractual obligation substituted for an obligation imposed by statute of any petroleum, natural gas or related hydrocarbons or metal or minerals produced in the operation to

(a) Her Majesty in right of Canada or a province,

(b) an agent of Her Majesty in right of Canada or a province, or

(c) a corporation, commission or association that is controlled by Her Majesty in right of Canada or a province or by an agent of Her Majesty in right of Canada or a province

for no proceeds of disposition or for proceeds of disposition less than the fair market value thereof at the time the taxpayer so disposes of it, the taxpayer shall be deemed to have received proceeds of disposition therefor equal to that fair market value determined, in circumstances where the taxpayer is required by a law or contract to so dispose thereof, without regard to that law or contract.

**Related Provisions**: 69(7) — Unreasonable consideration; 104(29) — Amounts deemed to be payable to beneficiaries; 219(1)(k) — Reduction in branch tax.

**Remission Orders**: *Syncrude Remission Order*, C.R.C. 1978, c. 794 (P.C. 1976-1026) (remission of tax on royalties etc. relating to the Syncrude Project).

**Interpretation Bulletins**: IT-438R2: Crown charges — resource properties in Canada. See also list at end of s. 69.

**(7) Idem** — Where a taxpayer who is an operator with respect to a natural accumulation of petroleum or natural gas in Canada, an oil or gas well in Canada or a mineral resource in Canada acquires any petroleum, natural gas or related hydrocarbons or metal or minerals produced in the operation from

(a) Her Majesty in right of Canada or a province,

(b) an agent of Her Majesty in right of Canada or a province, or

(c) a corporation, commission or association that is controlled by Her Majesty in right of Canada or a province or by an agent of Her Majesty in right of Canada or a province

for an amount in excess of the fair market value thereof at the time the taxpayer so acquired the petroleum, natural gas or related hydrocarbons or metal or minerals, the taxpayer shall be deemed to have acquired the petroleum, natural gas or related hydrocarbons or metal or minerals at that fair market value determined, in circumstances where the taxpayer is required by a law or contract to so acquire the petroleum, natural gas or related hydrocarbons or metal or minerals, without regard to that law or contract.

**Related Provisions**: 69(9) — Fair market value of resource output acquired from Crown; 104(29) — Amounts deemed to be payable to beneficiaries; 219(1)(k) — Reduction in branch tax.

**Notes**: 69(7) added by 1974 Budget effective May 7, 1974; minor amendments made by 1978 and 1985 Budgets and 1988 tax reform.

**Remission Orders**: *Syncrude Remission Order*, C.R.C. 1978, c. 794 (P.C. 1976-1026) (remission of tax on royalties etc. relating to the Syncrude Project).

**Interpretation Bulletins**: IT-438R2: Crown charges — resource properties in Canada. See also list at end of s. 69.

**(7.1)** [Repealed under former Act]

**Notes**: 69(7.1), repealed by 1983 Budget, dealt with the disposition of aviation turbine fuel.

**(8) Fair market value of resource output disposed of to Crown** — For the purposes of subsection (6), the fair market value at the time of disposition of a unit of any particular quantity of petroleum, natural gas or related hydrocarbons or metal or minerals disposed of by the taxpayer referred to in that subsection to a person referred to in any of paragraphs (6)(a) to (c) shall be deemed to be the amount by which

(a) the average proceeds of disposition that became receivable in the month that included that time by that person for the disposition of a like unit from a person other than a person referred to in any of paragraphs (6)(a) to (c)

exceed the total of

(b) the average total of all expenses (including depreciation) incurred by that person in respect of that month for each like unit that may reasonably be attributed to transmitting, transporting, marketing or processing thereof to the extent that those expenses are reasonable and necessary and do not include any cost of acquisition thereof, and

(c) in respect of the unit disposed of by the taxpayer, the amount that may reasonably be attributed as being an amount paid to, an amount that became payable to or an amount that became receivable by, Her Majesty in Right of Canada for the use and benefit of a band or bands as defined in the *Indian Act*.

**Related Provisions**: 69(10) — Certain persons deemed to be same person.

**Remission Orders**: *Syncrude Remission Order*, C.R.C. 1978, c. 794 (P.C. 1976-1026) (remission of tax on royalties etc. relating to the Syncrude Project).

**Interpretation Bulletins**: IT-438R2: Crown charges — resource properties in Canada. See also list at end of s. 69.

**(9) Fair market value of resource output acquired from Crown** — For the purposes of subsection (7), the fair market value of a unit of any particular quantity of petroleum, natural gas or related hydrocarbons or metals or minerals acquired by the taxpayer referred to in that subsection from a person referred to in any of paragraphs (7)(a) to (c) shall be deemed to be equal to the total of

(a) the amount, if any, paid or payable to the taxpayer by that person in respect of that unit, and

(b) the amount, if any, in respect of that unit paid or payable to Her Majesty in right of Canada by that person for the use and benefit of a band or bands as defined in the *Indian Act*.

**Remission Orders**: *Syncrude Remission Order*, C.R.C. 1978, c. 794 (P.C. 1976-1026) (remission of tax on royalties etc. relating to the Syncrude Project).

**Interpretation Bulletins**: IT-438R2: Crown charges — resource properties in Canada. See also list at end of s. 69.

**(10) Certain persons deemed to be same person** — For the purposes of subsection (8), where a person referred to in any of paragraphs (6)(a) to (c) disposes of a unit of any particular quantity of petroleum, natural gas or related hydrocarbons or metal or minerals to another person referred to in any of those paragraphs, those persons shall be deemed to be the same person.

**Remission Orders**: *Syncrude Remission Order*, C.R.C. 1978, c. 794 (P.C. 1976-1026) (remission of tax on royalties etc. relating to the Syncrude Project).

**Interpretation Bulletins**: IT-438R2: Crown charges — resource properties in Canada. See also list at end of s. 69.

**(11) Deemed proceeds of disposition** — Where, at any particular time as part of a series of transactions or events, a taxpayer disposes of property for proceeds of disposition that are less than its fair market value and it can reasonably be considered that one of the main purposes of the series is

(a) to obtain the benefit of

(i) any deduction (other than a deduction under subsection 110.6(2.1) in respect of a capital gain from a disposition of a share acquired by the taxpayer in an acquisition to which subsection 85(3) or 98(3) applied) in computing income, taxable income, taxable income earned in Canada or tax payable under this Act, or

(ii) any balance of undeducted outlays, expenses or other amounts

available to a person (other than a person that would be affiliated with the taxpayer immediately before the series began, if section 251.1 were read without reference to the definition "controlled" in subsection 251.1(3)) in respect of a subsequent disposition of the property or property substituted for the property, or

(b) to obtain the benefit of an exemption available to any person from tax payable under this Act on any income arising on a subsequent disposition of the property or property substituted for the property,

notwithstanding any other provision of this Act, where the subsequent disposition occurs, or arrangements for the subsequent disposition are made, before the day that is 3 years after the particular time, the taxpayer is deemed to have disposed of the property at the particular time for proceeds of disposition equal to its fair market value at the particular time.

**Related Provisions [subsec. 69(11)]**: 69(12) — Reassessment to give effect to 69(11); 69(13) — Amalgamation or merger; 69(14) — Where corporation incorporated during series of transactions; 87 — Amalgamations; 88(1) — Winding-up; 160(1.1) — Joint liability of vendor and specified person; 248(5) — Substituted property.

**Notes**: 69(11) is an anti-avoidance rule that prevents a vendor from disposing of property on a tax-deferred basis in order to obtain the benefit of tax deductions or other entitlements available to a non-"affiliated" person (see 251.1) on a subsequent disposition of the property within 3 years of the original disposition. 69(11) denies the benefit of the rollover on the original disposition by deeming the vendor's proceeds of disposition to be equal to the fair market value of the property disposed of.

For further discussion see Marc Ton-That, "Unexpected Problems under Subsection 69(11)", V(3) *Corporate Structures and Groups* (Federated Press) 268-273 (1999); and David Williamson and Michael Manly, "Subsection 69(11) — Unexpected Problems from Inappropriate Positions", V(4) *Corporate Structures and Groups* 285-289 (1999).

69(11) amended by 1995-97 technical bill, effective for each disposition that is part of a series of transactions or events that begins after April 26, 1995, other than a disposition that occurred before 1996 to a person who was obliged on that day to acquire the property under the terms of an agreement in writing entered into on or before that day; and for the purpose of this rule, a person is considered not to be obliged to acquire property if the person can be excused from the obligation if there is a change to the Act or if there is an adverse assessment under the Act. From January 16, 1987 (subject to old grandfathering) until the amendment, read (note that "specified person" was defined in 69(12)):

(11) Where, at any time as part of a series of transactions, a person or partnership (in this subsection and subsection (12) referred to as the "vendor") has disposed of property for proceeds of disposition that are less than its fair market value and it may reasonably be considered that one of the main purposes of the series was to obtain the benefit of

(a) any deduction in computing income, taxable income, taxable income earned in Canada or tax payable under this Act, or

(b) any balance of undeducted outlays, expenses or other amounts

available to a specified person in respect of a subsequent disposition of the property or property substituted for the property, notwithstanding any other provision of this Act, the vendor shall, where the subsequent disposition occurs within three years after that time, be deemed to have disposed of the property at that time for proceeds of disposition equal to its fair market value at that time.

**Interpretation Bulletins**: IT-488R2: Winding-up of 90%-owned taxable Canadian corporations. See also list at end of s. 69.

**Information Circulars**: 88-2, para. 9: General anti-avoidance rule — section 245 of the *Income Tax Act*.

**I.T. Technical News**: No. 9 (loss consolidation within a corporate group).

**(12) Reassessments** — Notwithstanding subsections 152(4) to (5), the Minister may at any time make such assessments or reassessments of the tax, interest and penalties payable by the taxpayer as are necessary to give effect to subsection (11).

**Notes**: 69(12) replaced by 1995-97 technical bill, effective on the same basis as the amendment to 69(11). Previously read:

(12) Definition of "specified person" — For the purposes of subsection (11), a "specified person" is

(a) a person that was not (otherwise than by virtue of a right referred to in paragraph 251(5)(b)) related to the vendor immediately before the series of transactions commenced;

(b) a partnership of which neither the vendor nor a person who was (otherwise than by virtue of a right referred to in paragraph 251(5)(b)) related to the vendor immediately before the series commenced was a majority interest partner (within the meaning assigned by subsection 97(3.1)) immediately before the series commenced; or

(c) where the vendor is a partnership, a person who was neither

(i) a majority interest partner (within the meaning assigned by subsection 97(3.1)) of the partnership immediately before the series commenced, nor

(ii) a person who was (otherwise than by virtue of a right referred to in paragraph 251(5)(b)) related to a person described in subparagraph (i) immediately before the series commenced.

**Interpretation Bulletins**: See list at end of s. 69.

**(12.1), (12.2) [Repealed]**

**Notes**: 69(12.1), (12.2) repealed by 1995-97 technical bill, effective on the same basis as the amendment to 69(11). They were added in the R.S.C. 1985 (5th Supp.) consolidation, effective for taxation years ending after November 1991, and were originally an application rule in S.C. 1987, c. 46, s. 24. Where they apply, read:

(12.1) Application of subsecs. (11) and (12) — Subsections (11) and (12) are applicable with respect to property disposed of after January 15, 1987 except where the person or partnership disposing of the property after that date was obliged on that date to dispose of it pursuant to an agreement in writing entered into on or before that date or where the person or partnership disposed of the property as part of a series of transactions that commenced on or before that date.

(12.2) Obligation to acquire property, etc. — For the purposes of subsection (12.1), a person shall be considered not to be obliged either to acquire or dispose of property if the person may be excused from performing the obligation as a result of changes to this Act affecting acquisitions or dispositions of property.

**(13) Amalgamation or merger** — Where there is an amalgamation or merger of a corporation with one or more other corporations to form one corporate entity (in this subsection referred to as the "new corporation"), each property of the corporation that becomes property of the new corporation as a result of the amalgamation or merger is deemed, for the purpose of determining whether subsection (11) applies to the amalgamation or merger, to have been disposed of by the corporation immediately before the amalgamation or merger for proceeds equal to

(a) in the case of a Canadian resource property or a foreign resource property, nil; and

(b) in the case of any other property, the cost amount to the corporation of the property immediately before the amalgamation or merger.

**Related Provisions**: 87(2)(e) — Rules applicable — capital property.

**Notes**: 69(13) amended by 1995-97 technical bill, effective for amalgamations and mergers that occur after April 26, 1995. The changes were purely cosmetic (e.g., changing "is applicable" to "applies"), except that para. (c) was renumbered as (b), (b) having being previously repealed.

69(13)(b), which applied a $4/3$ multiplier to the cost amount of eligible capital property, was repealed by 1992 technical bill, retroactive to the amalgamation or merger of a corporation after the commencement of its first taxation year beginning after June 1988. Amended 248(1)"cost amount"(d) now multiplies the prorated cumulative eligible capital by $4/3$ to account for the $3/4$ inclusion rate in 14(5)"cumulative eligible capital" on eligible capital property.

**(14) New taxpayer** — For the purpose of subsection (11), where a taxpayer is incorporated or otherwise comes into existence at a particular time during a series of transactions or events, the taxpayer is deemed

(a) to have existed at the time that was immediately before the series began; and

(b) to have been affiliated at that time with every person with whom the taxpayer is affiliated (otherwise than because of a right referred to in paragraph 251(5)(b)) at the particular time.

**Notes**: 69(14) added by 1995-97 technical bill, effective on the same basis as the amendment to 69(11). It is a relieving rule that prevents inappropriate effects where, because a taxpayer came into existence as part of the series of transactions described in 69(11), the taxpayer might not be considered to meet the affiliation test in 251.1 because it didn't exist immediately before the series began.

**Definitions [s. 69]**: "amount" — 248(1); "affiliated" — 69(14), 251.1; "arm's length" — 251; "assessment" — 248(1); "business" — 248(1); "Canada" — 255; "Canadian resource property" — 66(15), 248(1); "controlled" — 256(6), (6.1); "corporation" — 248(1), *Interpretation Act* 35(1); "eligible capital property" — 54, 248(1); "foreign resource property" — 66(15), 248(1); "Her Majesty" — *Interpretation Act* 35(1); "non-resident", "oil or gas well", "person", "prescribed" — 248(1); "proceeds of disposition" — 54 [technically does not apply to s. 69]; "property" — 248(1); "province" — *Interpretation Act* 35(1); "series of transactions or events" — 248(10); "shareholder" — 248(1); "substituted property" — 248(5); "tax payable" — 248(2); "taxable income" — 2(2), 248(1); "taxable income earned in Canada" — 115(1), 248(1); "taxation year" — 11(2), 249; "taxpayer" — 248(1).

**Interpretation Bulletins [s. 69]**: IT-169: Price adjustment clauses; IT-209R: *Inter vivos* gifts of capital property to individuals directly or through trusts; IT-268R4: *Inter vivos* transfer of farm property to child; IT-490: Barter transactions.

**70. (1) Death of a taxpayer** — In computing the income of a taxpayer for the taxation year in which the taxpayer died,

(a) an amount of interest, rent, royalty, annuity (other than an amount with respect to an interest in an annuity contract to which paragraph 148(2)(b) applies), remuneration from an office or employment, or other amount payable periodically, that was not paid before the taxpayer's death, shall be deemed to have accrued in equal daily amounts in the period for or in respect of which the amount was payable, and the value of the portion thereof so deemed to have accrued to the day of death shall be included in computing the taxpayer's income for the year in which the taxpayer died; and

(b) paragraph 12(1)(t) shall be read as follows:

"(t) the amount deducted under subsection 127(5) or (6) in computing the taxpayer's tax payable for the year or a preceding taxation year to the extent that it was not included in computing the taxpayer's income for a preceding taxation year under this paragraph or is not included in an amount determined under paragraph 13(7.1)(e) or 37(1)(e) or subparagraph 53(2)(c)(vi) or (h)(ii) or for I in the definition "undepreciated capital cost" in subsection 13(21) or L in the definition "cumulative Canadian exploration expense" in subsection 66.1(6);"

**Related Provisions**: 7(1)(e) — Stock option benefit where employee has died; 28(1) — Farming or fishing business; 61.2 — Deduction of debt forgiveness reserve for year of death; 70(5) — Capital property of deceased; 80(2)(p), (q) — Debt forgiveness rules — debt obligation settled by estate; 118.1(1)"total gifts"(a)(ii); 118.1(5) — Unlimited claim for charitable donations after death; 146(8.8) — RRSP — effect of death; 146.01(6) — RRSP Home Buyers' Plan — income inclusions; 146.02(6) — RRSP Lifelong Learning Plan — income inclusions; 146.3(6) — RRIF — effect of death; 147.2(6) — Additional deductible pension contributions for year of death; 148.1(2)(b)(i) — No tax on provision of funeral or cemetary services from eligible funeral arrangement; 156.1(3) — Instalments not required after death; 164(6) — Election by executor to carry back losses of estate to year of death.

**Notes**: See Notes to 70(5).

**Interpretation Bulletins**: IT-210R2: Income of deceased persons — periodic payments and investment tax credit; IT-212R3: Income of deceased persons — rights or things; IT-234: Income of deceased persons — farm crops; IT-396R: Interest income; IT-410R: Debt obligations — accrued interest on transfer.

**Forms**: RC4111(E): What to do following a death [guide]; T4011: Preparing returns for deceased persons [guide].

**(2) Amounts receivable** — Where a taxpayer who has died had at the time of death rights or things (other than any capital property or any amount included in computing the taxpayer's income by virtue of subsection (1)), the amount of which when realized or disposed of would have been included in computing the taxpayer's income, the value thereof at the time of death shall be included in computing the taxpayer's income for the taxation year in which the taxpayer died, unless the taxpayer's legal representative has, not later than the day that is one year after the date of death of the taxpayer or the day that is 90 days after the mailing of any notice of assessment in respect of the tax of the taxpayer for the year of death, whichever is the later day, elected otherwise, in which case the legal representative shall file a separate return of income for the year under this Part and pay the tax for the year under this Part as if

(a) the taxpayer were another person;

(b) that other person's only income for the year were the value of the rights or things; and

(c) subject to sections 114.2 and 118.93, that other person were entitled to the deductions to which the taxpayer was entitled under sections 110, 118 to 118.7 and 118.9 for the year in computing the taxpayer's taxable income or tax payable under this Part, as the case may be, for the year.

**Related Provisions**: 28(1) — Farming or fishing business; 53(1)(e)(v) — Adjustments to cost base; 60(t) — Deductions — amount included under 70(2); 70(3) — Rights or things transferred to beneficiaries; 70(4) — Revocation of election; 110.4(5) — Exception; 114.2 — Deductions in separate returns; 118.93 — Credits in separate returns; 120.2(4)(a) — No minimum tax carryover on special return; 127.1(1)(a) — No refundable investment tax credit on special return; 127.55 — Minimum tax not applicable; 150(1)(b) — Filing deadline for deceased's return; 159(5) — Election where certain provisions applicable.

**Notes**: A "right or thing" must be brought into the deceased's income on death, but may be recorded on a separate return on which personal credits may be claimed (thus, as a minimum, the first $7,375 of income (in 2001) will effectively be exempt). Alternatively, see 70(3). Rights or things include: dividends declared but unpaid; unused vacation leave credits; work in progress of a professional who elected under 34(a); inventory of a farmer who reported on a cash basis; and a right to payment for grain marketed through the Canadian Wheat Board. See IT-212R3 for more detail, including a list of various items (such as a NISA Fund No. 2, an RRSP, and land inventory) that are *not* considered rights or things.

**Interpretation Bulletins**: IT-210R2: Income of deceased persons — periodic payments and investment tax credit; IT-212R3: Income of deceased persons — rights or things; IT-234: Farm crops; IT-278R2: Death of a partner or of a retired person; IT-326R3: Returns of deceased persons as "another person"; IT-337R3: Retiring allowances; IT-382: Debts bequeathed or forgiven on death; IT-427R: Livestock of farmers; IT-457R: Election by professionals to exclude work in progress from income; IT-502: Employee benefit plans and employee trusts.

**Forms**: T4011: Preparing returns for deceased persons [guide].

**(3) Rights or things transferred to beneficiaries** — Where before the time for making an election under subsection (2) has expired, a right or thing to which that subsection would otherwise apply has been transferred or distributed to beneficiaries or other persons beneficially interested in the estate or trust,

(a) subsection (2) is not applicable to that right or thing; and

(b) an amount received by one of the beneficiaries or persons on the realization or disposition of the right or thing shall be included in comput-

Subdivision f — Rules Relating to Computation of Income     S. 70(5)(d)(i)

ing the income of the beneficiary or person for the taxation year in which the beneficiary or person received it.

**Related Provisions**: 44(3) — Where subsec. 70(3) not to apply; 69(1.1) — Deemed cost of property to beneficiary; 70(3.1) — Exception; 118.1(7)(b), 118.1(7.1)(b) — Donation of art or cultural property on death.

**Notes**: 70(3)(b) amended by 1995-97 technical bill, retroactive to taxation years that end after November 1991 (the in-force date for the R.S.C. 1985 5th Supp. consolidation), changing "taxpayer" to "beneficiary or person", to correct an error made in the consolidation when the text was made gender-neutral.

**Interpretation Bulletins**: IT-210R2: Income of deceased persons — periodic payments and investment tax credit; IT-212R3: Income of deceased persons — rights or things; IT-278R2: Death of a partner or of a retired partner; IT-427R: Livestock of farmers.

**(3.1) Exception** — For the purposes of this section, "rights or things" do not include an interest in a life insurance policy (other than an annuity contract of a taxpayer where the payment therefor was deductible in computing the taxpayer's income because of paragraph 60(l) or was made in circumstances in which subsection 146(21) applied), eligible capital property, land included in the inventory of a business, a Canadian resource property or a foreign resource property.

---
**Proposed Amendment — 70(3.1)**

**(3.1) Exception** — For the purposes of this section, "rights or things" in respect of an individual do not include an interest in a life insurance policy (other than an annuity contract where the payment for the contract was deductible in computing the individual's income under paragraph 60(l) or was made in circumstances in which subsection 146(21) applied), eligible capital property, land included in the inventory of a business, a Canadian resource property, a foreign resource property or property in respect of which subsection 94.2(3) applied to the individual immediately before the individual's death.

**Application**: The June 22, 2000 draft legislation, subsec. 5(1), will amend subsec. 70(3.1) to read as above, applicable to 2001 et seq.

**Technical Notes**: Under subsection 70(2) of the Act, the value of certain "rights or things" owned by an individual at death is required to be included in the individual's income for the year of death. Subsection 70(3) provides that this rule does not apply in connection with "rights or things" transferred to beneficiaries of the deceased within a specified time. Subsection 70(3.1) provides that certain property does not constitute a "right or thing" for this purpose.

Subsection 70(3.1) is amended so that a "right or thing" also does not include property in respect of which new subsection 94.2(3) applied to the deceased immediately before death. New subsection 94.2(3) sets out the conditions for the application of the mark-to-market taxation regime under subsection 94.2(4) for participating interests in foreign investment entities.

---

**Notes**: 70(3.1) amended by 1993 technical bill, effective for 1992 and later taxation years, to add reference to 146(21) (transfers from Saskatchewan Pension Plan).

**Interpretation Bulletins**: IT-212R3: Income of deceased persons — rights or things; IT-313R2: Eligible capital property — rules where a taxpayer has ceased carrying on a business or has died.

**(4) Revocation of election** — An election made under subsection (2) may be revoked by a notice of revocation signed by the legal representative of the taxpayer and filed with the Minister within the time that an election under that subsection may be made.

**Interpretation Bulletins**: IT-212R3: Income of deceased persons — rights or things.

**(5) Capital property of a deceased taxpayer** — Where in a taxation year a taxpayer dies,

(a) the taxpayer shall be deemed to have, immediately before the taxpayer's death, disposed of each capital property of the taxpayer and received proceeds of disposition therefor equal to the fair market value of the property immediately before the death;

(b) any person who as a consequence of the taxpayer's death acquires any property that is deemed by paragraph (a) to have been disposed of by the taxpayer shall be deemed to have acquired it at the time of the death at a cost equal to its fair market value immediately before the death;

(c) where any depreciable property of the taxpayer of a prescribed class that is deemed by paragraph (a) to have been disposed of is acquired by any person as a consequence of the taxpayer's death (other than where the taxpayer's proceeds of disposition of the property under paragraph (a) are redetermined under subsection 13(21.1)) and the amount that was the capital cost to the taxpayer of the property exceeds the amount determined under paragraph (b) to be the cost to the person thereof, for the purposes of sections 13 and 20 and any regulations made for the purpose of paragraph 20(1)(a),

(i) the capital cost to the person of the property shall be deemed to be the amount that was the capital cost to the taxpayer of the property, and

(ii) the excess shall be deemed to have been allowed to the person in respect of the property under regulations made for the purpose of paragraph 20(1)(a) in computing income for taxation years that ended before the person acquired the property; and

(d) where a property of the taxpayer that was deemed by paragraph (a) to have been disposed of is acquired by any person as a consequence of the taxpayer's death and the taxpayer's proceeds of disposition of the property under paragraph (a) are redetermined under subsection 13(21.1), notwithstanding paragraph (b),

(i) where the property was depreciable property of a prescribed class and the amount that was the capital cost to the taxpayer of the

523

property exceeds the amount so redetermined under subsection 13(21.1), for the purposes of sections 13 and 20 and any regulations made for the purpose of paragraph 20(1)(a),

(A) its capital cost to the person shall be deemed to be the amount that was its capital cost to the taxpayer, and

(B) the excess shall be deemed to have been allowed to the person in respect of the property under regulations made for the purpose of paragraph 20(1)(a) in computing income for taxation years that ended before the person acquired the property, and

(ii) where the property is land (other than land to which subparagraph (i) applies), its cost to the person shall be deemed to be the amount that was the taxpayer's proceeds of disposition of the land as redetermined under subsection 13(21.1).

**Related Provisions**: 38(a.1)(ii) — Reduced capital gain on gift on death of publicly-traded securities to charity; 43.1(2) — Life estates in real property; 44(2) — Exchanges of property; 53(4) — Effect on ACB of share, partnership interest or trust interest; 54"superficial loss"(c) — Superficial loss rule does not apply; 70(5.3) — Value of property that depends on life insurance policy; 70(6) — Where transfer or distribution to spouse or trust; 70(6.2) — Election; 70(9) — Transfer of farm property to taxpayer's child; 70(9.2) — Transfer of family farm corporations and partnerships; 70(12) — Capital cost of certain depreciable property; 70(13) — Order of disposal of depreciable property; 80(2)(p), (q) — Debt forgiveness rules — debt obligation settled by estate; 110.6(14)(g) — Related persons, etc.; 118.1(5) — Gift by will deemed made immediately before death; 118.1(10.1) — Determination of value by Canadian Cultural Property Export Review Board; 139.1(5) — Value of ownership rights in insurer during demutualization; 143.1(4) — Death of beneficiary of amateur athlete trust; 159(5) — Election where certain provisions applicable; 164(6) — Election by executor to carry back losses of estate to year of death; 248(8) — Occurrences as a consequence of death; 256(7)(a)(i)(D) — Control of corporation deemed not acquired; Canada-U.S. tax treaty, Art. XXIX B:6, 7 — Credit for U.S. estate taxes.

**Notes**: 70(5) generally triggers a deemed disposition of property at fair maket value at death, thus triggering tax in the deceased's final return on accrued capital gains. It is thus known informally as a "death tax". Neither Canada nor any of the provinces has estate taxes or succession duties at present (although the provinces impose probate fees or estate administration taxes for processing a deceased's will, which can reach 1.5% of the value of the estate. In Ontario, see the *Estate Administration Tax Act*, reproduced in *The Practitioner's Ontario Taxes Annotated*). The principal exception to the tax triggered by 70(5) is in 70(6), where property is left to the deceased's spouse or a "spousal trust" that meets certain conditions.

For a good overview of the tax consequences of death including 70(5), see Jane Kirby Donahue & Sheila Crummey, "Tax Issues in Will Planning: Part 1", 48(4) *Canadian Tax Journal* 1299-1320 (2000).

70(5) amended and restructured by 1992 technical bill and 1993 technical bill, effective 1993, to delete the rule that depreciable property was deemed disposed of at the average of fair market value and undepreciable capital cost; to ensure that the fair market value of the property is determined immediately before death; and to introduce new 70(5)(d) for cases where 13(21.1) applied. For deaths from 1982 through 1992, read:

(5) Depreciable and other capital property of deceased taxpayer — Where in a taxation year a taxpayer has died, the following rules apply:

(a) the taxpayer shall be deemed to have disposed, immediately before the taxpayer's death, of each property owned by the taxpayer at that time that was a capital property of the taxpayer (other than depreciable property of a prescribed class) and to have received proceeds of disposition therefor equal to the fair market value of the property at that time;

(b) the taxpayer shall be deemed to have disposed, immediately before the taxpayer's death, of all depreciable property of a prescribed class owned by the taxpayer at that time and to have received proceeds of disposition therefor equal to,

(i) where the fair market value of that property at that time exceeds the undepreciated capital cost thereof to the taxpayer at that time, the amount of that undepreciated capital cost plus ½ of the amount of the excess, and

(ii) in any other case, the fair market value of that property at that time plus ½ of the amount, if any, by which the undepreciated capital cost thereof to the taxpayer at that time exceeds that fair market value;

(c) any person who, as a consequence of the death of the taxpayer, has acquired any particular capital property of the taxpayer (other than depreciable property of a prescribed class) that is deemed by paragraph (a) to have been disposed of by the taxpayer at any time shall be deemed to have acquired it immediately after that time at a cost equal to its fair market value immediately before the death of the taxpayer;

(d) any person who, as a consequence of the death of the taxpayer, has acquired any particular depreciable property of the taxpayer of a prescribed class that is deemed by paragraph (b) to have been disposed of by the taxpayer at any time shall be deemed to have acquired it immediately after that time at a cost equal to that proportion of the proceeds of disposition of all depreciable property of that class deemed by paragraph (b) to have been received by the taxpayer that the fair market value immediately before the death of the taxpayer of the particular property is of the fair market value at that time of all of that property of that class; and

(e) where any depreciable property of the taxpayer of a prescribed class that is deemed by paragraph (b) to have been disposed of by the taxpayer has been acquired by any person as a consequence of the death of the taxpayer and the amount that was the capital cost to the taxpayer of that property exceeds the amount determined under paragraph (d) to be the cost to that person thereof, for the purposes of sections 13 and 20 and any regulations made under paragraph 20(1)(a),

(i) the capital cost to that person of the property shall be deemed to be the amount that was the capital cost to the taxpayer of the property, and

(ii) the excess shall be deemed to have been allowed to that person in respect of the property under regulations made under paragraph 20(1)(a) in computing income for taxation years before the acquisition by that person of the property.

From 1972 to 1981, read as above, but with "by virtue of" instead of "as a consequence of" the death of the taxpayer.

**I.T. Application Rules**: 20(1.2) (where depreciable property owned since before 1972 is transferred on death).

Subdivision f — Rules Relating to Computation of Income   S. 70(5.1)

**Interpretation Bulletins**: IT-140R3: Buy-sell agreements; IT-242R: Retired partners; IT-217R: Depreciable property owned on December 31, 1971; IT-259R3: Exchanges of property; IT-278R2: Death of a partner or of a retired partner; IT-288R2: Gifts of capital properties to a charity and others; IT-305R4: Testamentary spouse trusts; IT-325R2: Property transfers after separation, divorce and annulment; IT-382: Debts bequeathed or forgiven on death; IT-349R3: Intergenerational transfers of farm property on death; IT-416R3: Valuation of shares of a corporation receiving life insurance proceeds on death of a shareholder; IT-504R2: Visual artists and writers; IT-522R: Vehicle, travel and sales expenses of employees.

**Information Circulars**: 89-3: Policy statement on business equity valuations.

**Forms**: RC4111(E): What to do following a death [guide]; T4011: Preparing returns for deceased persons [guide].

**(5.1) Eligible capital property of deceased** — Notwithstanding subsection 24(1), where at any time a taxpayer dies and any person (in this subsection referred to as the beneficiary), as a consequence of the taxpayer's death, acquires an eligible capital property of the taxpayer in respect of a business carried on by the taxpayer immediately before that time (otherwise than by way of a distribution of property by a trust that claimed a deduction under paragraph 20(1)(b) in respect of the property or in circumstances to which subsection 24(2) applies),

(a) the taxpayer shall be deemed to have disposed of the property, immediately before the taxpayer's death, for proceeds equal to $4/3$ of that proportion of the cumulative eligible capital of the taxpayer in respect of the business that the fair market value immediately before that time of the property is of the fair market value immediately before that time of all of the eligible capital property of the taxpayer in respect of the business;

(b) subject to paragraph (c), the beneficiary shall be deemed to have acquired a capital property at the time of the taxpayer's death at a cost equal to the proceeds referred to in paragraph (a);

(c) where the beneficiary continues to carry on the business previously carried on by the taxpayer, the beneficiary shall be deemed to have, at the time of the taxpayer's death, acquired an eligible capital property and made an eligible capital property expenditure at a cost equal to the total of

(i) the proceeds referred to in paragraph (a), and

(ii) $4/3$ of that proportion of the amount, if any, determined for F in the definition "cumulative eligible capital" in subsection 14(5) in respect of the business of the taxpayer at that time that the fair market value immediately before that time of the particular property is of the fair market value immediately before that time of all eligible capital property of the taxpayer in respect of the business,

and, for the purposes of determining at any time the beneficiary's cumulative eligible capital in respect of the business, an amount equal to $3/4$ of the amount determined under subparagraph (ii) shall be added to the amount otherwise determined, in respect of the business, for P in the definition "cumulative eligible capital" in subsection 14(5); and

(d) for the purposes of determining, after that time,

(i) the amount deemed by subparagraph 14(1)(a)(v) to be the beneficiary's taxable capital gain, and

(ii) the amount to be included under subparagraph 14(1)(a)(v) or paragraph 14(1)(b) in computing the beneficiary's income

in respect of any subsequent disposition of the property of the business, there shall be added to the amount determined for Q in the definition "cumulative eligible capital" in [subsection] 14(5) the amount determined by the formula

**Proposed Amendment — 70(5.1)(d)**

(d) for the purpose of determining, after that time, the amount required by paragraph 14(1)(b) to be included in computing the income of the beneficiary in respect of any subsequent disposition of the property of the business, there shall be added to the amount determined for Q in the definition "cumulative eligible capital" in subsection 14(5) the amount determined by the formula

**Application**: The December 21, 2000 draft legislation, subsec. 32(1), will amend the portion of para. 70(5.1)(d) before the formula to read as above, applicable in respect of taxation years that end after February 27, 2000.

**Technical Notes**: Subsection 70(5.1) deals with the transfer of a taxpayer's eligible capital property to a beneficiary on death.

Paragraph 70(5.1)(d), which deals with the beneficiary's gains in respect of the eligible capital property after the death of the taxpayer, is amended consequential on the re-numbering of subsection 14(1), which is described in further detail in the commentary to that subsection.

$$A \times \frac{B}{C}$$

where

A is the amount, if any, determined for Q in that definition in respect of the business of the taxpayer immediately before that time,

B is the fair market value immediately before that time of the particular property, and

C is the fair market value immediately before that time of all eligible capital property of the taxpayer in respect of the business.

**Related Provisions**: 14(1) — Inclusion in income from business; 24(1) — Ceasing to carry on business; 24(2) — Where business carried on by spouse or controlled corporation; 110.6(1) "qualified farm property"(d)(ii) — Capital gains exemption; 248(8) — Occurrences as a consequence of death.

**Notes**: 70(5.1) amended by 1991 technical bill and para. (d) added by 1992 technical bill, both effective for acquisitions occurring as a result of the death of a taxpayer after the commencement of the first fiscal period of the taxpayer's business commencing after 1987, except that in applying 70(5.1) to acquisitions before July 13, 1990, ignore the words "(otherwise than under a distribution of property by a trust that has claimed a deduction under paragraph 20(1)(b) in respect of the property or in circumstances to which subsection 24(2) applies)".

70(5.1)(b) and opening words of (c) amended by 1993 technical bill, effective for dispositions and acquisitions in 1993 or later. For earlier cases, read:

(b) subject to paragraph (c), the beneficiary shall be deemed to have acquired a capital property, immediately after the death of the taxpayer, at a cost equal to the proceeds referred to in paragraph (a);

(c) where the beneficiary continues to carry on the business previously carried on by the taxpayer, the beneficiary shall be deemed to have acquired an eligible capital property and to have made an eligible capital expenditure at a cost equal to the total of

The draft legislation of July 12, 1994 (debt forgiveness) proposed an amendment to 70(5.1)(c)(ii) to refer to "F and G" instead of "F". However, that amendment was not included in the December 20, 1994 revision of the draft legislation. See now 14(5)"cumulative eligible capital"F:P.1.

Reference to 14(1)(a)(v) added to 70(5.1)(d)(ii) by 1994 Budget, effective for dispositions and acquisitions after February 22, 1994.

**Interpretation Bulletins**: IT-313R2: Eligible capital property — rules where a taxpayer has ceased carrying on a business or has died.

**(5.2) Resource properties and land inventories of a deceased taxpayer** — Where in a taxation year a taxpayer dies,

(a) for the purposes of subsection 59(1), paragraph (a) of the description of F in the definition "cumulative Canadian development expense" in subsection 66.2(5) and paragraph (a) of the description of F in the definition "cumulative Canadian oil and gas property expense" in subsection 66.4(5), the taxpayer shall be deemed to have, immediately before the taxpayer's death, disposed of each Canadian resource property and foreign resource property of the taxpayer and received proceeds of disposition therefor equal to its fair market value immediately before the death;

**Proposed Amendment — 70(5.2)(a), (a.1)**

(a) the taxpayer is deemed to have, immediately before the taxpayer's death, disposed of each Canadian resource property and foreign resource property of the taxpayer and received proceeds of disposition for that property equal to its fair market value immediately before the death;

(a.1) subject to subparagraph (b)(ii), any particular person who as a consequence of the taxpayer's death acquires any property that is deemed by paragraph (a) to have been disposed of by the taxpayer is deemed to have acquired the property at the time of the death at a cost equal to the fair market value of the property immediately before the death;

**Application**: The December 21, 2000 draft legislation, subsec. 32(2), will amend para. 70(5.2)(a) to read as above, and add para. (a.1), para. (a) applicable to taxation years that begin after 2000, and para. (a.1) applicable to acquisitions that occur after 1992.

**Technical Notes**: Subsection 70(5.2) provides rules in respect of the disposition of resource properties and land inventories on death. Under paragraph 70(5.2)(a), foreign resource properties and Canadian resource properties are deemed for specified purposes to have been disposed of at fair market value immediately before the taxpayer's death. However, paragraph 70(5.2)(b) generally overrides paragraph 70(5.2)(a) in connection with property transferred or distributed to a spouse, a common-law partner or a joint spousal or common-law partner trust. Where this is the case, the taxpayer's legal representative can elect that an amount be the proceeds of disposition (to the taxpayer), and the acquisition cost (to the spouse, common-law partner or trust) of such a property. The elected amount cannot exceed the property's fair market value immediately before death. The elected amount is considered to be the proceeds of disposition and acquisition cost, respectively, of the property, to the extent that the elected amount is reflected in an amount included in computing the taxpayer's income under subsection 59(1) (in the case of foreign resource property) or in an amount that reduces the taxpayer's cumulative Canadian development expense (in the case of Canadian mining property) or the taxpayer's cumulative Canadian oil and gas property expense (in the case of Canadian oil and gas property).

Paragraph 70(5.2)(a) is amended so that it applies for all purposes, including new section 66.21 which deals with the calculation of a taxpayer's deductions and income inclusions in respect of foreign resource expenses.

Paragraph 70(5.2)(a.1) is introduced to ensure that, subject to paragraph 70(5.2)(b), the acquisition cost, to a taxpayer, of a resource property acquired by the taxpayer on the death of an individual, is considered to be equal to the fair market value of the property at the time of death. This amendment applies to acquisitions that occur after 1992 and is consistent with the wording in paragraph 70(5)(b).

(b) notwithstanding paragraph (a), where the taxpayer was resident in Canada immediately before the taxpayer's death, any Canadian resource property or foreign resource property of the taxpayer that is, on or after the death and as a consequence of the death, transferred or distributed to a spouse or common-law partner of the taxpayer described in paragraph (6)(a) or a trust described in paragraph (6)(b) and it can be shown within the period ending 36 months after the death or, where written application therefor has been made to the Minister by the taxpayer's legal representative within that period, within such longer period as the Minister considers reasonable in the circumstances, that the property vested indefeasibly in the spouse or common-law partner or trust, as the case may be,

(i) the taxpayer shall be deemed to have, immediately before the death, disposed of the property and received proceeds of disposition therefor equal to such amount as is specified by the taxpayer's legal representative in the return of income of the taxpayer filed under paragraph 150(1)(b), not exceeding its fair market value immediately before the death, and

(ii) the spouse or common-law partner or trust, as the case may be, shall be deemed to have acquired the property at the time of the death at a cost equal to the amount included in the taxpayer's income under subsection 59(1) or included in the amount determined under paragraph (a) of the description of F in the definition "cumulative Canadian development expense" in subsection 66.2(5) or paragraph (a) of the description of F in the definition "cumulative Canadian oil and gas property expense" in subsection 66.4(5), as the case may be, in respect of the property;

### Proposed Amendment — 70(5.2)(b)(ii)

(ii) the spouse, common-law partner or trust, as the case may be, is deemed to have acquired the property at the time of the death at a cost equal to the amount determined in respect of the disposition under subparagraph (i);

**Application**: The December 21, 2000 draft legislation, subsec. 32(3), will amend subpara. 70(5.2)(b)(ii) to read as above, applicable to taxation years that begin after 2000.

**Technical Notes**: Subparagraph 70(5.2)(b)(ii) is amended so that the acquisition cost determined under paragraph 70(5.2)(b) is equal to the elected amount determined under subparagraph 70(5.2)(b)(i). The existing restriction with regard to foreign resource property is not appropriate in light of new subparagraph 59(1)(b)(ii). This amendment applies to taxation years that begin after 2000.

(c) the taxpayer shall be deemed to have, immediately before the taxpayer's death, disposed of each property that was land included in the inventory of a business of the taxpayer and received proceeds of disposition therefor equal to its fair market value immediately before the death; and

(d) notwithstanding paragraph (c), where the taxpayer was resident in Canada immediately before the taxpayer's death, any property that is land included in the inventory of a business of the taxpayer is, on or after the death and as a consequence of the death, transferred or distributed to a spouse or common-law partner of the taxpayer described in paragraph (6)(a) or a trust described in paragraph (6)(b) and it can be shown within the period ending 36 months after the death of the taxpayer or, where written application therefor has been made to the Minister by the taxpayer's legal representative within that period, within such longer period as the Minister considers reasonable in the circumstances, that the property vested indefeasibly in the spouse or common-law partner or trust, as the case may be,

(i) the taxpayer shall be deemed to have, immediately before the death, disposed of the land and received proceeds of disposition therefor equal to its cost amount to the taxpayer immediately before the death, and

(ii) the spouse or common-law partner or trust, as the case may be, shall be deemed to have acquired the property at the time of the death at a cost equal to those proceeds.

### Proposed Addition — 70(5.2)(e)

(e) where subsection 94.2(3) applies to the taxpayer in respect of the property immediately before the taxpayer's death,

(i) the taxpayer is deemed to have disposed of the property at that time for proceeds equal to the fair market value of the property at that time,

(ii) for the purposes of subsection 94.2(4), the taxpayer is deemed not to hold the property after that time, and

(iii) any person who acquires the property as a consequence of the taxpayer's death is deemed to acquire the property at the time of the taxpayer's death at a cost equal to the proceeds referred to in subparagraph (i).

**Application**: The June 22, 2000 draft legislation, subsec. 5(2), will add para. 70(5.2)(e), applicable to 2001 et seq.

**Technical Notes**: Subsection 70(5.2) of the Act provides rules with respect to the disposition of resource properties and land inventories on death.

Paragraph 70(5.2)(e) is introduced to provide for a deemed disposition, on the death of an individual, of an interest in a foreign investment entity held by the individual. Paragraph 70(5.2)(e) applies only to interests in foreign investment entities in respect of which new subsection 94.2(3) applied to the deceased immediately before death. (New subsection 94.2(3) sets out the conditions for the application of the mark-to-market taxation regime under subsection 94.2(4) for participating interests in foreign investment entities.)

A disposition under paragraph 70(5.2)(e) is deemed to occur at the fair market value of an interest in a foreign investment entity and to be acquired for the same amount by a person who acquires the interest as a consequence of the individual's death. The proceeds of disposition are included in the value of A in the formula in paragraph 94.2(4)(a) in computing the deceased's income under subsection 94.2(4) for the taxation year of death. The deceased is treated as not having held the interest after death.

**Related Provisions**: 104(4)(a)(i.1) — Deemed disposition of trust property; 159(5) — Election where certain provisions applicable; 248(8) — Occurrences as a consequence of death; 248(9.2) — Meaning of "vested indefeasibly".

**Notes**: 70(5.2)(b) and (d) amended by 2000 same-sex partners bill to add reference to "common-law partner", effective for the 2001 and later taxation years, or earlier by election (see Notes to 248(1)"common-law partner").

70(5.2) amended by 1993 technical bill, effective for dispositions and acquisitions in 1993 or later. The amendment ensures that the fair market value of the property is determined immediately before death. For deaths from 1985 to 1992, read:

(5.2) Where in a taxation year a taxpayer has died, the following rules apply:

(a) for the purposes of subsection 59(1), paragraph (a) of the description of F in the definition "cumulative Canadian development expense" in subsection 66.2(5) and paragraph (a) of the description of F in the definition "cumulative Canadian oil and gas property expense" in subsection 66.4(5), the taxpayer shall be deemed to have, immediately before the taxpayer's death, disposed of each property owned by the taxpayer at that time that was a Canadian resource property or a foreign resource property and to have received proceeds of disposition therefor equal to its fair market value at that time;

(b), (c) [Repealed under former Act]

(d) notwithstanding paragraph (a), where any property of a taxpayer who was resident in Canada immediately before the taxpayer's death that is a Canadian resource property or foreign resource property has, on or after the death of the taxpayer and as a consequence thereof, been transferred or distributed to the taxpayer's spouse referred to in paragraph (6)(a) or a trust referred to in paragraph (6)(b), if it can be shown, within the period ending 36 months after the death of the taxpayer or, where written application therefor has been made to the Minister by the taxpayer's legal representative within that period, within such longer period as the Minister considers reasonable in the circumstances, that the property has become vested indefeasibly in the spouse or trust, as the case may be, the following rules apply:

(i) the taxpayer shall be deemed to have disposed of the property immediately before the taxpayer's death and to have received proceeds of disposition therefor equal to such amount as is specified by the taxpayer's legal representative in the return of income of the taxpayer referred to in paragraph 150(1)(b), not exceeding the fair market value of the property immediately before the taxpayer's death, and

(ii) the spouse or trust, as the case may be, shall be deemed to have acquired the property for an amount equal to the amount included in the taxpayer's income by virtue of subsection 59(1) or included in the amount determined under paragraph (a) of the description of F in the definition "cumulative Canadian development expense" in subsection 66.2(5) or paragraph (a) of the description of F in the definition "cumulative Canadian oil and gas property expense" in subsection 66.4(5), as the case may be, in respect of the property;

(e) the taxpayer shall be deemed to have disposed, immediately before the taxpayer's death, of each property that was land included in the inventory of a business of the taxpayer and to have received proceeds of disposition therefor equal to the fair market value of the property at that time; and

(f) notwithstanding paragraph (e), where any property of a taxpayer who was resident in Canada immediately before the taxpayer's death that is land included in the inventory of a business has, on or after the taxpayer's death and as a consequence thereof, been transferred or distributed to the taxpayer's spouse referred to in paragraph (6)(a) or a trust referred to in paragraph (6)(b), if it can be shown within the period ending 36 months after the death of the taxpayer or, where written application therefor has been made to the Minister by the taxpayer's legal representative within that period, within such longer period as the Minister considers reasonable in the circumstances, that the property has become vested indefeasibly in the spouse or trust, as the case may be, the taxpayer shall be deemed to have disposed of the land immediately before the taxpayer's death and to have received proceeds of disposition therefor equal to the cost amount thereof immediately before the taxpayer's death and the spouse or trust, as the case may be, shall be deemed to have acquired the property for an amount equal to those proceeds.

**Interpretation Bulletins**: IT-125R4: Dispositions of resource properties; IT-212R3: Income of deceased persons — rights or things; IT-449R: Meaning of "vested indefeasibly".

**(5.3) Fair market value** — For the purposes of subsection (5) of this section and subsections 70(9.4) and (9.5) of the *Income Tax Act*, chapter 148 of the Revised Statutes of Canada, 1952, the fair market value, immediately before the death of the taxpayer referred to in any of those subsections, of any share of the capital stock of a corporation deemed to have been disposed of as a consequence of the taxpayer's death shall be determined as though the fair market value at that time of any life insurance policy under which the taxpayer was the person whose life was insured were the cash surrender value (within the meaning assigned by subsection 148(9)) of the policy at that time.

### Proposed Amendment — 70(5.3)

**(5.3) Fair market value** — For the purposes of subsections (5) and 104(4) and section 128.1, the fair market value at any time of any property deemed to have been disposed of at that time as a consequence of a particular individual's death or as a consequence of the particular individual becoming or ceasing to be resident in Canada shall be determined as though the fair market value at that time of any life insurance policy, under which the particular individual (or any other individual not dealing at arm's length with the particular individual at that time or at the time the policy was issued) was a person whose life was insured, were the cash surrender value (as defined in subsection 148(9)) of the policy immediately before the particular individual died or became or ceased to be resident in Canada, as the case may be.

**Application**: Bill C-43 (First Reading September 20, 2000), subsec. 32(1), will amend subsec. 70(5.3) to read as above, applicable to dispositions that occur after October 1, 1996.

**Technical Notes**: Subsection 70(5) provides for the deemed disposition of a taxpayer's capital property on the taxpayer's death for proceeds equal to the property's fair market value immediately before the death. In the event that the property includes shares and there was a life insurance policy under which the taxpayer's life was insured, the fair market value of the shares is determined under subsection 70(5.3) as if the value of the policy were the policy's cash surrender value immediately before the taxpayer's death. The purpose of subsection 70(5.3) is to ensure that life insurance proceeds payable as a consequence of death are not reflected in share value and therefore do not give rise to a capital gain on death.

Existing subsection 104(4) provides, in certain cases specified, for a deemed disposition of capital property (which includes shares) on the death of a taxpayer for proceeds equal to the property's fair market value. Existing section 128.1 also provides, in certain cases, that property (including shares) is deemed to be disposed of by an individual for its fair market value in the event that the individual becomes or ceases to be resident in Canada.

Subsection 70(5.3) is amended so that it applies for the purposes of subsection 104(4) and section 128.1.

Subsection 70(5.3) is also amended so that it applies in respect of property deemed to be disposed of as a consequence of a particular individual's death or change of residence where the relevant insurance policy insures the life of another individual (e.g., the spouse of the particular individual) with whom the particular individual does not deal at arm's length.

As a consequence of these amendments, where property is deemed by subsection 104(4) to have been disposed of by a trust as a consequence of the death of a particular individual and there is a life insurance policy under which the particular individual's life (or the life of an individual with whom the particular individual does not deal at arm's length) is insured, the fair market value of the property is determined for the purposes of subsection 104(4) as if the value of the policy were the policy's cash surrender value immediately before the death. Similarly, where property is deemed by section 128.1 to have been disposed of by a particular individual as a consequence of the particular individual becoming or ceasing to be resident in Canada, and there is a life insurance policy under which the particular individual's life (or the life of an individual with whom the particular individual does not deal at arm's length) is insured, the fair market value of the property is determined for the purposes of section 128.1 as if the value of the policy were the policy's cash surrender value immediately before the particular individual became or ceased to be resident in Canada.

Subsection 70(5.3) is also amended so that it applies in determining the fair market value of any property (e.g., an interest in a trust or a partnership), not just shares.

Subsection 70(5.3) is further amended to remove references to former subsections 70(9.4) and (9.5), given that these subsections have been repealed.

**Related Provisions**: 139.1(5) — Value of ownership rights in insurer during demutualization; 248(8) — Occurrences as a consequence of death; 251 — Arm's length.

**Notes**: The reference to R.S.C. 1952, c. 148, is to repealed subsections 70(9.4) and (9.5). See Notes to those repealed provisions.

**I.T. Application Rules**: 69 (meaning of "*Income Tax Act*, chapter 148 of the Revised Statutes of Canada, 1952").

**Interpretation Bulletins**: IT-416R3: Valuation of shares of a corporation receiving life insurance proceeds on death of a shareholder.

**Information Circulars**: 89-3: Policy statement on business equity valuations.

**(5.4) NISA on death** — Where a taxpayer who dies has at the time of death a net income stabilization account, all amounts held for or on behalf of the taxpayer in the taxpayer's NISA Fund No. 2 shall be deemed to have been paid out of that fund to the taxpayer immediately before that time.

**Related Provisions**: 12(10.2) — NISA receipts; 248(9.1) — Whether trust created by taxpayer's will.

**Notes**: 70(5.4) added by 1992 technical bill, effective 1991. See Notes to 70(2).

**Interpretation Bulletins**: IT-212R3: Income of deceased persons — rights or things; IT-305R4: Testamentary spouse trusts.

**(6) Where transfer or distribution to spouse [or common-law partner] or spouse trust** — Where any property of a taxpayer who was resident in Canada immediately before the taxpayer's death that is a property to which subsection (5) would otherwise apply is, as a consequence of the death, transferred or distributed to

(a) the taxpayer's spouse or common-law partner who was resident in Canada immediately before the taxpayer's death, or

(b) a trust, created by the taxpayer's will, that was resident in Canada immediately after the time the property vested indefeasibly in the trust and under which

(i) the taxpayer's spouse or common-law partner is entitled to receive all of the income of the trust that arises before the spouse's or common-law partner's death, and

(ii) no person except the spouse or common-law partner may, before the spouse's or common-law partner's death, receive or otherwise obtain the use of any of the income or capital of the trust,

if it can be shown, within the period ending 36 months after the death of the taxpayer or, where written application therefor has been made to the Minister by the taxpayer's legal representative within that period, within such longer period as the Minister considers reasonable in the circumstances, that the property has become vested indefeasibly in the spouse or common-law partner or trust, as the case may be, the following rules apply:

(c) paragraphs (5)(a) and (b) do not apply in respect of the property,

(d) subject to paragraph (d.1), the taxpayer shall be deemed to have, immediately before the taxpayer's death, disposed of the property and received proceeds of disposition therefor equal to

(i) where the property was depreciable property of a prescribed class, the lesser of the capital cost and the cost amount to the taxpayer of the property immediately before the death, and

(ii) in any other case, its adjusted cost base to the taxpayer immediately before the death,

and the spouse or common-law partner or trust, as the case may be, shall be deemed to have acquired the property at the time of the death at a cost equal to those proceeds,

**S. 70(6)(d.1)**  Income Tax Act, Part I, Division B

(d.1) where the property is an interest in a partnership (other than an interest in a partnership to which subsection 100(3) applies),

    (i) the taxpayer shall, except for the purposes of paragraph 98(5)(g), be deemed not to have disposed of the property as a consequence of the taxpayer's death,

    (ii) the spouse or common-law partner or the trust, as the case may be, shall be deemed to have acquired the property at the time of the death at a cost equal to its cost to the taxpayer, and

    (iii) each amount added or deducted in computing the adjusted cost base to the taxpayer of the property shall be deemed to be required by subsection 53(1) or (2) to be added or deducted, as the case may be, in computing the adjusted cost base to the spouse or common-law partner or the trust, as the case may be, of the property; and

(e) where the property was depreciable property of the taxpayer of a prescribed class, paragraph (5)(c) applies as if the references therein to "paragraph (a)" and to "paragraph (b)" were read as references to "paragraph (6)(d)".

**Related Provisions**: 40(3.18)(a) — Grandfathering of partnership interest transferred under 70(6)(d.1); 40(4) — Where principal residence disposed of to spouse or spouse trust; 44.1(4) — Treatment of small business investment rollover on death; 70(6.2) — Election; 70(7) — Special rules applicable re spouse trust; 70(9.1), (9.3) — Transfer of farm property from spouse trust to settlor's children; 72(2) — Election by legal representative and transferee re reserves; 73(1)(c) — *Inter vivos* transfer of property of spouse, etc., or trust; 104(4)(a)(i.1) — Trust — deemed disposition on death of spouse; 108(3) — Income of trust; 108(4) — Trust not disqualified by reason only of payment of certain duties and taxes; 148(8.2) — Rollover of life insurance policy to spouse on death; 248(8) — Occurrences as a consequence of death; 248(9.1) — Whether trust created by taxpayer's will; 248(9.2) — Meaning of "vested indefeasibly"; 248(23.1) — Transfer under provincial family law after death; 252(3) — Extended meaning of "spouse"; 256(7)(a)(i)(D) — Control of corporation deemed not acquired; Canada-U.S. tax treaty, Art. XXVI:3(g) — Relief from double taxation; Art. XXIX B:5, 6 — Credit for U.S. estate taxes.

**Notes**: For the *inter vivos* spouse trust which parallels 70(6) but is created during the taxpayer's life, see 73(1)(c). For discussion see Pearl Schusheim, "Spouse Trusts: Tips and Trips — Part 1", 47(6) *Canadian Tax Journal* 1525-1544 (1999), and Roanne Bratz, "...Part 2", 48(2) *CTJ* 477-497 (2000). Part 2 deals with cases where one spouse is a US citizen.

70(6) amended by 2000 same-sex partners bill to add reference to "common-law partner", effective for the 2001 and later taxation years, or earlier by election (see Notes to 248(1)"common-law partner").

70(6)(d.1) added, and (d) amended to refer to it, by 1991 technical bill, effective for transfers, distributions and acquisitions after January 15, 1987.

70(6) opening words, (c) and (e) amended by 1992 technical bill, to match cross-references to amended 70(5). For dispositions after 1981 and before 1993, read:

    (6) Where any property of a taxpayer who was resident in Canada immediately before his death that is a property to which paragraphs (5)(a) and (c), or paragraphs (5)(b) and (d), as the case may be, would otherwise apply has, on or after his death and as a consequence thereof been transferred or distributed to

.....

    (c) paragraphs (5)(a) to (d) are not applicable to the property;

.....

    (e) where the property was depreciable property of the taxpayer of a prescribed class, paragraph (5)(e) is applicable as if the reference therein to "paragraph (b)" and to "paragraph (d)" were read as references to "paragraph (6)(d)".

70(6)(d) and (d.1)(ii) amended by 1993 technical bill, effective for dispositions and acquisitions in 1993 or later. For dispositions and acquisitions from January 16, 1987 through the end of 1992, read:

    (d) subject to paragraph (d.1), the taxpayer shall be deemed to have disposed of the property immediately before the taxpayer's death and to have received proceeds of disposition therefor equal to,

        (i) where the property was depreciable property of the taxpayer of a prescribed class, that proportion of the undepreciated capital cost to the taxpayer immediately before the taxpayer's death of all of the depreciable property of the taxpayer of that class that the fair market value at that time of the property is of the fair market value at that time of all of the depreciable property of the taxpayer of that class, and

        (ii) in any other case, the adjusted cost base to the taxpayer of the property immediately before the taxpayer's death,

and the spouse or trust, as the case may be, shall be deemed to have acquired the property for an amount equal to those proceeds,

.....

    (ii) the spouse or the trust, as the case may be, shall be deemed to have acquired the property for an amount equal to the cost thereof to the taxpayer, and

**I.T. Application Rules**: 20(1.1)(a) (property owned since before 1972).

**Interpretation Bulletins**: IT-125R4: Dispositions of resource properties; IT-236R4: Reserves — disposition of capital property; IT-242R: Retired partners; IT-259R3: Exchange of property; IT-278R2: Death of a partner or of a retired partner; IT-305R4: Testamentary spouse trusts; IT-321R: Insurance agents and brokers — unearned commissions; IT-325R2: Property transfers after separation, divorce and annulment; IT-382: Debts bequeathed or forgiven on death; IT-449R: Meaning of "vested indefeasibly"; IT-522R: Vehicle, travel and sales expenses of employees.

**Advance Tax Rulings**: ATR-37: Refund of premiums transferred to spouse.

**Forms**: T4011: Preparing returns for deceased persons [guide].

**(6.1) Transfer or distribution of NISA to spouse [or common-law partner] or trust** — Where a property that is a net income stabilization account of a taxpayer is, on or after the taxpayer's death and as a consequence thereof, transferred or distributed to

    (a) the taxpayer's spouse or common-law partner, or

    (b) a trust, created by the taxpayer's will, under which

        (i) the taxpayer's spouse or common-law partner is entitled to receive all of the income of the trust that arises before the spouse's or common-law partner's death, and

(ii) no person except the spouse or common-law partner may, before the spouse's or common-law partner's death, receive or otherwise obtain the use of any of the income or capital of the trust,

subsections (5.4) and 73(5) do not apply in respect of the taxpayer's NISA Fund No. 2 if it can be shown, within the period ending 36 months after the death of the taxpayer or, where written application therefor has been made to the Minister by the taxpayer's legal representative within that period, within such longer period as the Minister considers reasonable in the circumstances, that the property has vested indefeasibly in the spouse or common-law partner or trust, as the case may be.

**Related Provisions**: 12(10.2) — NISA receipts; 70(6.2) — Election; 70(7) — Special rules applicable in respect of trust for benefit of spouse; 104(5.1) — NISA Fund No. 2 held by spousal trust; 104(6) — Deduction in computing income of trust; 104(14.1) — NISA election; 108(3) — Meaning of "income" of trust; 108(4) — Trust not disqualified by reason only of payment of certain duties and taxes; 248(8) — Occurrences as a consequence of death; 248(9.1) — Whether trust created by taxpayer's will; 248(9.2) — Meaning of "vested indefeasibly"; 252(3) — Extended meaning of "spouse".

**Notes**: 70(6.1) amended by 2000 same-sex partners bill to add reference to "common-law partner", effective for the 2001 and later taxation years, or earlier by election (see Notes to 248(1)"common-law partner").

70(6.1) added by 1992 technical bill, effective 1991.

Former 70(6.1), repealed by 1992 technical bill effective 1990, provided the rule now found in 248(9.1).

**Interpretation Bulletins**: IT-212R3: Income of deceased persons — rights or things; IT-305R4: Testamentary spouse trusts.

**(6.2) Election** — Subsection (6) or (6.1) does not apply to any property of a deceased taxpayer in respect of which the taxpayer's legal representative elects, in the taxpayer's return of income under this Part (other than a return of income filed under subsection (2) or 104(23), paragraph 128(2)(e) or subsection 150(4)) for the year in which the taxpayer died, to have subsection (5) or (5.4), as the case may be, apply.

**Related Provisions**: 220(3.2), Reg. 600(b) — Late filing of election or revocation.

**Notes**: 70(6.2) amended by 1992 technical bill, effective 1991, to add references to subsecs. (6.1) and (5.4) and the parenthetical exclusion beginning "(other than...)".

**Interpretation Bulletins**: IT-305R4: Testamentary spouse trusts.

**Information Circulars**: 92-1: Guidelines for accepting late, amended or revoked elections.

**(7) Special rules applicable in respect of trust for benefit of spouse [or common-law partner]** — Where a trust created by a taxpayer's will would, but for the payment of, or provision for payment of, any particular testamentary debts in respect of the taxpayer, be a trust to which subsection (6) or (6.1) applies,

(a) for the purpose of determining the day on or before which a return (in this subsection referred to as the "taxpayer's return") of the taxpayer's income for the taxation year in which the taxpayer died is required to be filed by the taxpayer's legal representatives, subsection 150(1) shall be read without reference to paragraph 150(1)(b) and as if paragraph 150(1)(d) read as follows:

"(d) in the case of any other person, by the person's legal representative within 18 months after the person's death; or"; and

(b) where the taxpayer's legal representative so elects in the taxpayer's return (other than a return of income filed under subsection (2) or 104(23), paragraph 128(2)(e) or subsection 150(4)) and lists therein one or more properties (other than a net income stabilization account) that were, on or after the taxpayer's death and as a consequence thereof, transferred or distributed to the trust, the total fair market value of which properties immediately after the taxpayer's death was not less than the total of the non-qualifying debts in respect of the taxpayer,

(i) subsection (6) does not apply in respect of the properties so listed, and

(ii) notwithstanding the payment of, or provision for payment of, any such particular testamentary debts, the trust shall be deemed to be a trust described in subsection (6),

except that, where the fair market value, immediately after the taxpayer's death, of all of the properties so listed exceeds the total of the non-qualifying debts in respect of the taxpayer (the amount of which excess is referred to in this subsection as the "listed value excess") and the taxpayer's legal representative designates in the taxpayer's return one property so listed (other than money) that is capital property other than depreciable property,

(iii) the amount of the taxpayer's capital gain or capital loss, as the case may be, from the disposition of that property deemed by subsection (5) to have been made by the taxpayer is that proportion of that capital gain or capital loss otherwise determined that

(A) the amount, if any, by which the fair market value of that property immediately after the taxpayer's death exceeds the listed value excess,

is of

(B) the fair market value of that property immediately after the taxpayer's death, and

(iv) the cost to the trust of that property is

(A) where the taxpayer has a capital gain from the disposition of that property deemed by subsection (5) to have been made by the taxpayer, the total of

(I) its adjusted cost base to the taxpayer immediately before the taxpayer's death, and

(II) the amount determined under subparagraph (iii) to be the taxpayer's capital gain from the disposition of that property, or

(B) where the taxpayer has a capital loss from the disposition of that property deemed by subsection (5) to have been made by the taxpayer, the amount by which

(I) its adjusted cost base to the taxpayer immediately before the taxpayer's death

exceeds

(II) the amount determined under subparagraph (iii) to be the taxpayer's capital loss from the disposition of that property.

**Related Provisions**: 70(8) — Meaning of certain expressions; 248(8) — Occurrences as a consequence of death; 248(9.1) — Whether trust created by taxpayer's will.

**Notes**: Opening words of 70(7) amended by 1992 technical bill, effective 1991, to add reference to subsec. (6.1).

70(7)(a) amended by 1991 technical bill, effective 1990, in consequence of amendments to 150(1)(b). The amendment ensures that the legal representatives can still file the taxpayer's terminal return up to 18 months after death.

70(7)(a) amended by 1995 Budget, effective 1995, consequential on amendments to 150(1)(d). For earlier years, read:

... and the reference in paragraph 150(1)(d) to "on or before April 30 in the next year" shall be read as a reference to "within 18 months after the person's death"

70(7)(b) amended by 1992 technical bill, effective 1991. For 1977 to 1990, read:

(b) where the taxpayer's legal representative has so elected in the taxpayer's return and has listed therein one or more specified properties (including any money) that have, on or after the taxpayer's death and as a consequence thereof, been transferred or distributed to the trust, the aggregate fair market value of which properties immediately after the taxpayer's death was not less than the aggregate of the non-qualifying debts in respect of the taxpayer,

(i) subsection (6) does not apply in respect of the specified properties so listed, and

(ii) notwithstanding the payment of, or provision for payment of, any such particular testamentary debts, the trust shall be deemed to be a trust described in subsection (6),

except that where the fair market value, immediately after the taxpayer's death, of all of the specified properties so listed exceeds the aggregate of the non-qualifying debts in respect of the taxpayer (the amount of which excess is referred to in this subsection as the "listed value excess") and the taxpayer's legal representative has designated in the taxpayer's return one specified property so listed (other than money) that is a capital property other than depreciable property,

**Interpretation Bulletins**: IT-305R4: Testamentary spouse trusts.

**(8) Meaning of certain expressions in subsec. (7)** — In subsection (7),

(a) the **"fair market value"** at any time of any property subject to a mortgage is the amount, if any, by which the fair market value at that time of the property otherwise determined exceeds the amount outstanding at that time of the debt secured by the mortgage, as the case may be[4];

(b) **"non-qualifying debt"** in respect of a taxpayer who has died and by whose will any trust has been created that would, but for the payment of, or provision for payment of, any particular testamentary debts in respect of the taxpayer, be a trust described in subsection (6), means any such particular testamentary debt in respect of the taxpayer other than

(i) any estate, legacy, succession or inheritance duty payable, in consequence of the taxpayer's death, in respect of any property of, or interest in, the trust, or

(ii) any debt secured by a mortgage on property owned by the taxpayer immediately before the taxpayer's death; and

(c) **"testamentary debt"**, in respect of a taxpayer who has died, means

(i) any debt owing by the taxpayer, or any other obligation of the taxpayer to pay an amount, that was outstanding immediately before the taxpayer's death, and

(ii) any amount payable (other than any amount payable to any person as a beneficiary of the taxpayer's estate) by the taxpayer's estate in consequence of the taxpayer's death,

including any income or profits tax payable by or in respect of the taxpayer for the taxation year in which the taxpayer died or for any previous taxation year, and any estate, legacy, succession or inheritance duty payable in consequence of the taxpayer's death.

**Related Provisions**: 248(8) — Occurrences as a consequence of death.

**Interpretation Bulletins**: IT-305R4: Testamentary spouse trusts.

**(9) Transfer of farm property to child** — Where any land in Canada or depreciable property in Canada of a prescribed class of a taxpayer to which subsection (5) would otherwise apply was, before the taxpayer's death, used principally in the business of farming in which the taxpayer, the taxpayer's spouse or common-law partner or any of the taxpayer's children was actively engaged on a regular and continuous basis and the property is, as a consequence of the death, transferred or distributed to a child of the taxpayer who was resident in Canada immediately

---

[4]*Sic.* Disregard the words "as the case may be": they should have been deleted along with "or hypothec" in the R.S.C. 1985 consolidation. (That change was non-substantive.) — ed.

before the death and it can be shown, within the period ending 36 months after the death or, where written application therefor has been made to the Minister by the taxpayer's legal representative within that period, within such longer period as the Minister considers reasonable in the circumstances, that the property has vested indefeasibly in the child,

(a) paragraphs (5)(a) and (b) do not apply in respect of the property,

(b) the taxpayer shall be deemed to have, immediately before the taxpayer's death, disposed of the property and received proceeds of disposition therefor equal to

(i) where the property was depreciable property of a prescribed class, the lesser of the capital cost and the cost amount to the taxpayer of the property immediately before the death, and

(ii) where the property is land (other than land to which subparagraph (i) applies), its adjusted cost base to the taxpayer immediately before the death,

and the child shall be deemed to have acquired the property at the time of the death at a cost equal to those proceeds, and

(c) where the property was depreciable property of a prescribed class, paragraphs (5)(c) and (d) apply as if the references therein to "paragraph (a)" and "paragraph (b)" were read as "paragraph (9)(b)",

except that, where the taxpayer's legal representative so elects in the taxpayer's return of income under this Part for the year in which the taxpayer died, paragraph (b) shall be read as follows:

"(b) the taxpayer shall be deemed to have, immediately before the taxpayer's death, disposed of the property and received proceeds of disposition therefor equal to such amount as the legal representative elects in the taxpayer's return of income under this Part for the year in which the taxpayer died, not greater than the greater of nor less than the lesser of

(i) where the property was depreciable property of a prescribed class,

(A) its fair market value immediately before the death, and

(B) the lesser of the capital cost and the cost amount to the taxpayer of the property immediately before the death, and

(ii) where the property is land (other than land to which subparagraph (i) applies),

(A) its fair market value immediately before the death, and

(B) its adjusted cost base to the taxpayer immediately before the death,

and the child shall be deemed to have acquired the property at the time of the death at a cost equal to those proceeds, except that for the purpose of this paragraph, where the elected amount exceeds the greater of the amounts determined under clauses (i)(A) and (B) or (ii) (A) and (B), as the case may be, it shall be deemed to be equal to the greater thereof, and where the elected amount is less than the lesser of the amounts determined under clauses (i)(A) and (B) or (ii) (A) and (B), as the case may be, it shall be deemed to be equal to the lesser thereof, and".

**Related Provisions**: 70(9.6) — Transfer to parent; 70(9.8) — Leased farm property; 70(10) — Definitions; 70(12) — Capital cost of certain depreciable property; 73(3) — *Inter vivos* transfer of farm property by farmer to his child; 220(3.2), Reg. 600(b) — Late filing of election or revocation; 248(8) — Occurrences as a consequence of death; 248(9.2) — Meaning of "vested indefeasibly".

**Notes**: 70(9) opening words amended by 2000 same-sex partners bill to add reference to "common-law partner", effective for the 2001 and later taxation years, or earlier by election (see Notes to 248(1)"common-law partner").

70(9) amended by 1992 technical bill and 1993 technical bill, effective for dispositions and acquisitions in 1993 or later, to correspond to changes to 70(5) and to clarify the required extent of the use of the property and the involvement of the taxpayer, spouse or children in the farming business. For dispositions and acquisitions from 1985 through 1992, read:

(9) Where any land in Canada or depreciable property in Canada of a prescribed class of a taxpayer to which paragraphs (5)(a) and (c) or (5)(b) and (d), as the case may be, would otherwise apply was, immediately before the taxpayer's death, used by the taxpayer, the taxpayer's spouse or any of the taxpayer's children in the business of farming and the property has, on or after the death of the taxpayer and as a consequence thereof, been transferred or distributed to a child of the taxpayer who was resident in Canada immediately before the death of the taxpayer and it can be shown, within the period ending 36 months after the death of the taxpayer or, where written application therefor has been made to the Minister by the taxpayer's legal representative within that period, within such longer period as the Minister considers reasonable in the circumstances, that the property has become vested indefeasibly in the child, the following rules apply:

(a) paragraphs (5)(a) to (d) are not applicable to the property;

(b) the taxpayer shall be deemed to have disposed of the property immediately before the taxpayer's death and to have received proceeds of disposition therefor equal to,

(i) where the property was depreciable property of the taxpayer of a prescribed class, that proportion of the undepreciated capital cost to the taxpayer immediately before the taxpayer's death of all of the depreciable property of the taxpayer of that class that the fair market value at that time of the property was of the fair market value at that time of all of the depreciable property of the taxpayer of that class, and

(ii) where the property was land, its adjusted cost base to the taxpayer immediately before the taxpayer's death,

and the child shall be deemed to have acquired the property for an amount equal to those proceeds, and

(c) where the property was depreciable property of the taxpayer of a prescribed class, paragraph (5)(e) is applicable as if the reference therein to "paragraph (b)" and to "paragraph (d)" were read as references to "paragraph (9)(b)", except that, where the legal representative of the taxpayer has so elected in the taxpayer's return of income under this Part for the year in which the taxpayer died, paragraph (b) shall be read as follows:

"(b) the taxpayer shall be deemed to have disposed of the property immediately before the taxpayer's death and to have received proceeds of disposition therefor equal to such amount as the legal representative has elected, not greater than the greater of or less than the lesser of

(i) where the property was depreciable property of a prescribed class,

(A) the fair market value of the property immediately before the death of the taxpayer, and

(B) that portion of the undepreciated capital cost to the taxpayer immediately before the taxpayer's death of all the depreciable property of that class of the taxpayer that the fair market value at that time of the property disposed of was of the fair market value at that time of all of the depreciable property of that class of the taxpayer, and

(ii) where the property was land not described in subparagraph (i),

(A) the fair market value of the land immediately before the taxpayer's death, and

(B) the adjusted cost base to the taxpayer of the land immediately before the taxpayer's death,

and the child shall be deemed to have acquired the property for an amount equal to those proceeds, except that for the purposes of this paragraph, where the elected amount exceeds the greater of the amounts determined under subparagraphs (i) and (ii), it shall be deemed to be equal to the greater thereof, and where the elected amount is less than the lesser of the amounts determined under those subparagraphs, it shall be deemed to be equal to the lesser thereof; and"

**I.T. Application Rules**: 26(18) (farmland owned since before 1972).

**Interpretation Bulletins**: IT-349R3: Intergenerational transfers of farm property on death; IT-382: Debts bequeathed or forgiven on death; IT-449R: Meaning of "vested indefeasibly".

**Information Circulars**: 92-1: Guidelines for accepting late, amended or revoked elections.

**(9.1) Transfer of farm property from spouse's [or common-law partner's] trust to settlor's children** — Where any property in Canada of a taxpayer that is land or depreciable property of a prescribed class has been transferred or distributed to a trust described in subsection (6) or subsection 73(1) and the property or a replacement property therefor in respect of which the trust has made an election under subsection 13(4) or 44(1) was, immediately before the death of the taxpayer's spouse or common-law partner who was a beneficiary under the trust, used in the business of farming and has, on the death of the spouse or common-law partner and as a consequence thereof, been transferred or distributed to and become vested indefeasibly in a child of the taxpayer who was resident in Canada immediately before the death of the spouse or common-law partner, the following rules apply:

**Proposed Amendment — 70(9.1) opening words**

**(9.1) Transfer of farm property from trust to settlor's children** — Where any property in Canada of a taxpayer that is land or depreciable property of a prescribed class has been transferred or distributed to a trust described in subsection (6) or subsection 73(1) (as that subsection applied to transfers before 2000) or a trust to which subparagraph 73(1.01)(c)(i) applies and the property or a replacement property for that property in respect of which the trust has made an election under subsection 13(4) or 44(1) was, immediately before the death of the taxpayer's spouse or common-law partner who was a beneficiary under the trust, used in the business of farming and has, on the death of the spouse or common-law partner and as a consequence of the death, been transferred or distributed to and vested indefeasibly in an individual who was a child of the taxpayer and who was resident in Canada immediately before the death of the spouse or common-law partner, the following rules apply:

**Application**: Bill C-43 (First Reading September 20, 2000), subsec. 32(2), will amend the opening words of subsec. 70(9.1) to read as above, applicable to transfers and distributions from trusts that occur after 1999.

Where a particular transfer or distribution to a trust referred to in amended subsec. 70(9.1) occurred before 2001, in applying that subsec. to a transfer or distribution from the trust that occurs after 1997, it shall be read without reference to the words "or common-law partner" and to the *Modernization of Benefits and Obligations Act*, c. 12 of S.C. 2000 [see Notes to 248(1)"common-law partner"], unless

(a) the particular transfer or distribution occurred after 1997;

(b) the death referred to in that subsec. occurs after 1997; and

(c) either

(i) at the time of the particular transfer or distribution referred to in para. (a), the taxpayer was a spouse of the individual whose death is referred to in para. (b), or

(ii) because of an election under s. 144 of the *Modernization of Benefits and Obligations Act* [see Notes to 248(1)"common-law partner"], sections 130 to 142 of that Act applied, at the time of the particular transfer or distribution referred to in para. (a), to the taxpayer and the individual whose death is referred to in para. (b).

**Technical Notes**: Subsections 70(9.1) and (9.3) of the Act permit farm property (including shares of, or interests in, family farm corporations and family farm partnerships) to be disposed of on a rollover basis from a spousal trust to the children of the settlor of the spousal trust.

Subsections 70(9.1) and (9.3) are amended to preserve the existing rollover. These amendments are strictly consequential to changes to the rules in subsection 73(1) that govern rollovers to spousal trusts.

These amendments apply to dispositions after 1999.

These amendments also reflect changes [re common-law partners — ed.] proposed under Bill C-23, the *Modernization of Benefits and Obligations Act*.

(a) subsections 104(4) and (5) do not apply to the trust in respect of the property,

(b) the trust shall be deemed to have, immediately before the spouse's or common-law partner's death, disposed of the property and received proceeds of disposition therefor equal to

(i) where the property was depreciable property of a prescribed class, the lesser of the capital cost and the cost amount to the trust of the property immediately before the death, and

(ii) where the property is land (other than land to which subparagraph (i) applies), its adjusted cost base to the trust immediately before the death,

and the child shall be deemed to have acquired the property at the time of the death at a cost equal to those proceeds,

(c) where any depreciable property of a prescribed class that is deemed by paragraph (b) to have been disposed of by the trust is acquired by a child of the taxpayer as a consequence of the spouse's or common-law partner's death (other than where the trust's proceeds of disposition of the property under paragraph (b) are redetermined under subsection 13(21.1)) and the amount that was the capital cost to the trust of the property exceeds the amount determined under paragraph (b) to be the cost to the child of the property, for the purposes of sections 13 and 20 and any regulations made for the purpose of paragraph 20(1)(a),

(i) its capital cost to the child shall be deemed to be the amount that was its capital cost to the trust, and

(ii) the excess shall be deemed to have been allowed to the child in respect of the property under regulations made for the purpose of paragraph 20(1)(a) in computing income for taxation years that ended before the child acquired the property, and

(d) where the property of the trust that is deemed by paragraph (b) to have been disposed of is acquired by a child of the taxpayer as a consequence of the spouse's or common-law partner's death and the trust's proceeds of disposition of the property under paragraph (b) are redetermined under subsection 13(21.1), notwithstanding paragraph (b),

(i) where the property was depreciable property of a prescribed class and the amount that was its capital cost to the trust exceeds the amount so redetermined under subsection 13(21.1), for the purposes of sections 13 and 20 and any regulations made for the purpose of paragraph 20(1)(a),

(A) its capital cost to the child shall be deemed to be the amount that was its capital cost to the trust, and

(B) the excess shall be deemed to have been allowed to the child in respect of the property under regulations made for the purpose of paragraph 20(1)(a) in computing income for taxation years that ended before the child acquired the property, and

(ii) where the property is land (other than land to which subparagraph (i) applies), its cost to the child shall be deemed to be the amount that was the trust's proceeds of disposition as redetermined under subsection 13(21.1),

except that, where the trust so elects in its return of income under this Part for its taxation year in which the spouse or common-law partner died, paragraph (b) shall be read as follows:

"(b) the trust shall be deemed to have, immediately before the spouse's or common-law partner's death, disposed of the property and received proceeds of disposition therefor equal to such amount as the trust elects in its return of income under this Part for the year in which the spouse or common-law partner died, not greater than the greater of nor less than the lesser of

(i) where the property was depreciable property of a prescribed class,

(A) its fair market value immediately before the death, and

(B) the lesser of the capital cost and the cost amount to the trust of the property immediately before the death, and

(ii) where the property is land (other than land to which subparagraph (i) applies),

(A) its fair market value immediately before the death, and

(B) its adjusted cost base to the trust immediately before the death,

and the child shall be deemed to have acquired the property at the time of the death at a cost equal to those proceeds, except that for the purpose of this paragraph, where the elected amount exceeds the greater of the amounts determined under clauses (i)(A) and (B) or (ii)(A) and (B), as the case may be, it shall be deemed to be equal to the greater thereof, and where the elected amount is less than the lesser of the amounts determined under clauses (i)(A) and (B) or (ii)(A) and (B), as the case may be, it shall be deemed to be equal to the lesser thereof,".

**Related Provisions**: 70(9.6) — Transfer to parent; 70(10) — Definitions; 70(12) — Capital cost of certain depreciable property; 70(13) — Order of disposal of depreciable property; 73(4) — *Inter vivos* transfer of family farm corporations and partnerships; 220(3.2); 248(8) — Occurrences as a consequence of death; 248(9.2) — Meaning of "vested indefeasibly"; Reg. 600(b) — Late filing of election or revocation.

**Notes**: 70(9.1) amended by 2000 same-sex partners bill to add reference to "common-law partner", effective for the 2001 and later taxation years, or earlier by election (see Notes to 248(1)"common-law partner").

70(9.1) amended by 1993 technical bill, effective for dispositions and acquisitions in 1993 or later. For earlier dispositions and acquisitions, read:

(9.1) Where any property in Canada of a taxpayer that is land or depreciable property of a prescribed class has been transferred or distributed to a trust described in subsection (6) or subsection 73(1) and the property or a replacement property therefor in respect of which the trust has made an election under subsection 13(4) or 44(1) was, immediately before the death of the taxpayer's spouse who was a beneficiary under the trust, used in the business of farming and has, on the death of the spouse and as a consequence thereof, been transferred or distributed to and become vested indefeasibly in a child of the taxpayer who was resident in Canada immediately before the death of the spouse, the following rules apply:

(a) subsections 104(4) and (5) do not apply to the trust in respect of the property,

(b) the trust shall be deemed to have disposed of the property immediately before the death of the taxpayer's spouse and to have received proceeds of disposition therefor equal to,

(i) where the property was depreciable property of the trust of a prescribed class, that proportion of the undepreciated capital cost to the trust immediately before the death of the spouse of all of the depreciable property of the trust of that class that the fair market value at that time of the property was of the fair market value at that time of all of the depreciable property of the trust of that class, and

(ii) where the property was land, its adjusted cost base to the trust immediately before the death of the spouse,

and the child shall be deemed to have acquired the property for an amount equal to those proceeds, and

(c) where any depreciable property of the trust of a prescribed class that is deemed by paragraph (b) to have been disposed of by the trust has been acquired by a child of the taxpayer by virtue of the death of the taxpayer's spouse and the amount that was the capital cost to the trust of that property exceeds the amount determined under paragraph (b) to be the cost to the child of that property, for the purposes of sections 13 and 20 and any regulations made under paragraph 20(1)(a),

(i) the capital cost to the child of the property shall be deemed to be the amount that was the capital cost to the trust of the property, and

(ii) the excess shall be deemed to have been allowed to the child in respect of the property under regulations made under paragraph 20(1)(a) in computing income for taxation years before the acquisition by the child of the property,

except that, where the trust has so elected in its return of income under this Part for its taxation year in which the taxpayer's spouse died, paragraph (b) shall be read as follows:

"(b) the trust shall be deemed to have disposed of the property immediately before the death of the taxpayer's spouse and to have received proceeds of disposition therefor equal to such amount as the trust has elected, not greater than the greater of or less than the lesser of

(i) where the property was depreciable property of a prescribed class,

(A) the fair market value of the property immediately before the death of the spouse, and

(B) that proportion of the undepreciated capital cost to the trust immediately before the death of the spouse of all the depreciable property of that class of the trust that the fair market value at that time of the property disposed of was of the fair market value at that time of all the depreciable property of that class of the trust, and

(ii) where the property was land not described in subparagraph (i),

(A) the fair market value of the land immediately before the death of the spouse, and

(B) the adjusted cost base to the trust of the land immediately before the death of the spouse,

and the child shall be deemed to have acquired the property for an amount equal to those proceeds, except that for the purposes of this paragraph, where the elected amount exceeds the greater of the amounts determined under subparagraphs (i) and (ii), it shall be deemed to be equal to the greater thereof, and where the elected amount is less than the lesser of the amounts determined under those subparagraphs, it shall be deemed to be equal to the lesser thereof; and".

The above amendment made four changes. First, as with 70(5), it ensures that fair market value is determined immediately before death. Second, the formula in 70(9.1)(b)(i), which determines proceeds of depreciable property, was amended so that a rollover to a child of the taxpayer results on the death of the taxpayer's spouse unless an election is filed by the trust. (See 248(1)"cost amount".) Third, 70(9.1)(b)(ii) now excludes land that is depreciable property (e.g., land described in 13(5.2)). Fourth, 70(9.1)(c) was amended so that new 70(9.1)(d) applies where the trust's proceeds of disposition are redetermined under 13(21.1).

70(9.1)(a) amended by 1992 technical bill, effective December 21, 1991, to read "do not apply to the trust in respect of the property" instead of "are not applicable to the property".

**Interpretation Bulletins**: IT-349R3: Intergenerational transfers of farm property; IT-449R: Meaning of "vested indefeasibly".

**Information Circulars**: 92-1: Guidelines for accepting late, amended or revoked elections.

## (9.2) Transfer of family farm corporations and partnerships
— Where at any time property of a taxpayer that was, immediately before the taxpayer's death, a share of the capital stock of a family farm corporation of the taxpayer or an interest in a family farm partnership of the taxpayer to which subsection (5) would otherwise apply is, as a consequence of the death, transferred or distributed to a child of the taxpayer who was resident in Canada immediately before the death and it can be shown, within the period ending 36 months after the death or, where written application therefor has been made to the Minister by the taxpayer's legal representative within that period, within such longer period as the Minister considers reasonable in the circumstances, that the property has vested indefeasibly in the child,

(a) subsection (5) does not apply in respect of the property, and

(b) where the property is a share of the capital stock of a family farm corporation, the taxpayer shall be deemed to have, immediately before the taxpayer's death, disposed of the property and received proceeds of disposition therefor equal to its adjusted cost base to the taxpayer immediately before the death, and the child shall be deemed to have acquired the property at the time of the death at a cost equal to those proceeds, and

(c) where the property is an interest in a family farm partnership (other than an interest in a partnership to which subsection 100(3) applies),

(i) the taxpayer shall, except for the purpose of paragraph 98(5)(g), be deemed not to have disposed of the property as a consequence of the taxpayer's death,

(ii) the child shall be deemed to have acquired the property at the time of the death at a cost equal to the cost to the taxpayer of the interest, and

(iii) each amount added or deducted in computing the adjusted cost base to the taxpayer of the property shall be deemed to be required by subsection 53(1) or (2) to be added or deducted, as the case may be, in computing its adjusted cost base to the child,

except that, where the taxpayer's legal representative so elects in the taxpayer's return of income under this Part for the year in which the taxpayer died, paragraph (c) does not apply and paragraph (b) shall be read as follows:

"(b) the taxpayer shall be deemed to have, immediately before the taxpayer's death, disposed of the property and received proceeds of disposition therefor equal to such amount as the legal representative elects in the taxpayer's return of income under this Part for the year in which the taxpayer died, not greater than the greater of nor less than the lesser of

(i) its fair market value immediately before the death, and

(ii) its adjusted cost base to the taxpayer immediately before the death,

and the child shall be deemed to have acquired the property at the time of the death at a cost equal to those proceeds, except that for the purpose of this paragraph, where the elected amount exceeds the greater of the amounts determined under subparagraphs (i) and (ii), it shall be deemed to be equal to the greater thereof, and where the elected amount is less than the lesser of the amounts determined under subparagraphs (i) and (ii), it shall be deemed to be equal to the lesser thereof, and,".

**Related Provisions**: 40(3.18)(b) — Grandfathering of partnership interest transferred under 70(9.2)(c); 44.1(4) — Treatment of small business investment rollover on death; 70(9.6) — Transfer to parent; 70(10) — Definitions; 220(3.2) — Late, amended or revoked elections; 220(3.2); 248(8) — Occurrences as a consequence of death; 248(9.2) — Meaning of "vested indefeasibly"; Reg. 600(b) — Late filing of election or revocation.

**Notes**: 70(9.2) amended by 1992 technical bill and 1993 technical bill, effective for dispositions and acquisitions after 1992, to correspond to changes made to 70(5). For earlier dispositions and acquisitions, since January 15, 1987, read:

(9.2) Where at any particular time after April 10, 1978 property of a taxpayer that was, immediately before the taxpayer's death, a share of the capital stock of a family farm corporation of the taxpayer or an interest in a family farm partnership of the taxpayer to which paragraphs (5)(a) and (c) would otherwise apply has, on or after the death of the taxpayer and as a consequence thereof, been transferred or distributed to a child of the taxpayer who was resident in Canada immediately before the death of the taxpayer and it can be shown, within the period ending 36 months after the death of the taxpayer or, where written application therefor has been made to the Minister by the taxpayer's legal representative within that period, within such longer period as the Minister considers reasonable in the circumstances, that the property has become vested indefeasibly in the child, the following rules apply:

(a) paragraphs (5)(a) and (c) are not applicable to the property;

70(9.2) amended by 1991 technical bill, effective for transfers, distributions and acquisitions after January 15, 1987.

**Interpretation Bulletins**: IT-349R3: Intergenerational transfers of farm property on death; IT-449R: Meaning of "vested indefeasibly".

**(9.3) Transfer of family farm corporation or partnership from spouse's [or common-law partner's] trust to children of settlor** — Where property of a taxpayer has been transferred or distributed to a trust described in subsection (6) or 73(1) and the property was,

---

**Proposed Amendment — 70(9.3) opening words**

**(9.3) Transfer of family farm corporation or partnership from trust to children of settlor** — Where property of a taxpayer has been transferred or distributed to a trust described in subsection (6) or 73(1) (as that subsection applied to transfers before 2000) or a trust to which subparagraph 73(1.01)(c)(i) applies and the property was,

**Application**: Bill C-43 (First Reading September 20, 2000), subsec. 32(3), will amend the opening words of subsec. 70(9.3) to read as above, applicable to transfers and distributions from trusts that occur after 1999.

Where a particular transfer or distribution to a trust referred to in subsec. 70(9.3), as amended, occurred before 2001, in applying that subsec. to a transfer or distribution from the trust that occurs after 1997, that subsec. shall be read without reference to the words "or common-law partner" and to the *Modernization of Benefits and Obligations Act*, c. 12 of S.C. 2000 [see Notes to 248(1) "common-law partner"], unless

(a) the particular transfer or distribution occurred after 1997;

(b) the death referred to in that subsec. occurs after 1997; and

(c) either

(i) at the time of the particular transfer or distribution referred to in para. (a), the taxpayer was a spouse of the individual whose death is referred to in para. (b), or

(ii) because of an election under s. 144 of the *Modernization of Benefits and Obligations Act* [see Notes to 248(1) "common-law partner"], sections 130 to 142 of that Act applied, at the time of the particular transfer or distribution referred to in para. (a), to the taxpayer and the individual whose death is referred to in para. (b).

**Technical Notes**: See under 70(9.1) opening words.

(a) immediately before the transfer or distribution, a share of the capital stock of a family farm corporation of the taxpayer or an interest in a family farm partnership of the taxpayer, and

(b) immediately before the death of the taxpayer's spouse or common-law partner who was a beneficiary under the trust,

(i) a share in the capital stock of a Canadian corporation that would be a share in the capital stock of a family farm corporation if paragraph (a) of the definition "share of the capital stock of a family farm corporation" in subsection (10) were read without the words "in which the person or a spouse, common-law partner, child or parent of the person was actively engaged on a regular and continuous basis", or

(ii) an interest in a partnership that carried on the business of farming in Canada in which it used all or substantially all of its property,

and has, at any time after April 10, 1978, on the death of the spouse or common-law partner and as a consequence thereof, been transferred or distributed to and become vested indefeasibly in a child of the taxpayer who was resident in Canada immediately before the death of the spouse or common-law partner, the following rules apply:

(c) subsection 104(4) does not apply to the trust in respect of the property,

(d) where the property is a share of the capital stock of a family farm corporation, the trust shall be deemed to have disposed of the share immediately before the death of the spouse or common-law partner and to have received proceeds of disposition therefor equal to its adjusted cost base to the trust immediately before the death of the spouse or common-law partner, and the child shall be deemed to have acquired the property for an amount equal to those proceeds, and

(e) where the property is an interest in a family farm partnership (other than an interest in a partnership to which subsection 100(3) applies),

(i) the trust shall, except for the purposes of paragraph 98(5)(g), be deemed not to have disposed of the property as a consequence of the death of the spouse or common-law partner,

(ii) the child shall be deemed to have acquired the property for an amount equal to the cost thereof to the trust, and

(iii) each amount added or deducted in computing the adjusted cost base to the trust of the property shall be deemed to be required by subsection 53(1) or (2) to be added or deducted, as the case may be, in computing the adjusted cost base to the child of the property,

except that, where the trust so elects in its return of income under this Part for its taxation year in which the spouse or common-law partner died, paragraph (e) shall not apply and paragraph (d) shall be read as follows:

"(d) the trust shall be deemed to have disposed of the property immediately before the death of the spouse or common-law partner and to have received proceeds of disposition therefor equal to such amount as the trust elects, not greater than the greater of or less than the lesser of

(i) the fair market value of the property immediately before the death of the spouse or common-law partner, and

(ii) the adjusted cost base to the trust of the property immediately before the death of the spouse or common-law partner,

and the child shall be deemed to have acquired the property for an amount equal to those proceeds, except that for the purposes of this paragraph, where the elected amount exceeds the greater of the amounts determined under subparagraphs (i) and (ii), it shall be deemed to be equal to the greater thereof, and where the elected amount is less than the lesser of the amounts determined under those subparagraphs, it shall be deemed to be equal to the lesser thereof,".

**Related Provisions**: 40(3.18)(c) — Grandfathering of partnership interest transferred under 70(9.3)(e); 70(9.6) — Transfer to parent; 70(10) — Definitions; 220(3.2) — Late, amended or revoked elections; 220(3.2); 248(8) — Occurrences as a consequence of death; 248(9.2) — Meaning of "vested indefeasibly"; Reg. 600(b) — Late filing of election or revocation.

**Notes**: 70(9.3) amended by 2000 same-sex partners bill to add reference to "common-law partner", effective for the 2001 and later taxation years, or earlier by election (see Notes to 248(1)"common-law partner").

70(9.3) amended by 1991 technical bill, effective for transfers, distributions and acquisitions after January 15, 1987.

70(9.3)(b)(i) amended by 1992 technical bill, effective 1992, to correspond to changes in 70(10)(b). For earlier years, read:

(i) a share in the capital stock of a Canadian corporation that would be a share in the capital stock of a family farm corporation if subparagraph (10)(b)(i) were read without the words "and in which that person, his spouse or his child was actively engaged" and clause (10)(b)(ii)(B) were read without the words "in which that person, his spouse or his child was actively engaged", or

70(9.3)(c) amended by 1992 technical bill, effective December 21, 1991, to read "does not apply to the trust in respect of the property" instead of "is not applicable to the property".

The CCRA takes the position that "all or substantially all", used in 70(9.3)(b)(ii), means 90% or more.

**Interpretation Bulletins**: IT-349R3: Intergenerational transfers of farm property on death; IT-449R: Meaning of "vested indefeasibly".

**Information Circulars**: 92-1: Guidelines for accepting late, amended or revoked elections.

## (9.4), (9.5) [Repealed under former Act]

**Notes**: 70(9.4) and (9.5), repealed by 1985 Budget (due to the introduction of the capital gains exemption in 110.6), provided rollovers, respectively, on the transfer of shares of a small business corporation to the taxpayer's child and from a spousal trust to the children of the settlor. See now 110.6(2.1).

### (9.6) Transfer to parent — Where

(a) any property has been acquired by a taxpayer in circumstances where any of subsections (9), (9.1), (9.2), (9.3) and 73(3) and (4) applied,

(b) as a consequence of the death of the taxpayer after 1983 the property has been transferred or distributed to a parent of the taxpayer, and

(c) the taxpayer's legal representative has so elected in the taxpayer's return of income under this Part for the year in which the taxpayer died,

subsection (9) or (9.2), as the case may be, shall apply in respect of the transfer or distribution as if the references therein to "child" were read as references to "parent".

**Related Provisions**: 248(8) — Occurrences as a consequence of death.

**Interpretation Bulletins**: IT-268R4: *Inter vivos* transfer of farm property to child.

### (9.7) [Repealed under former Act]

**Notes**: 70(9.7), repealed by 1985 Budget (due to the introduction of the capital gains exemption in 110.6), dealt with retransfer to a parent, on the death of a child, of shares of a small business corporation that had been rolled over to the child under 70(9.4), 70(9.5) or 73(5).

### (9.8) Leased farm property — For the purposes of subsections (9) and 14(1), paragraph 20(1)(b), subsection 73(3) and paragraph (d) of the definition "qualified farm property" in subsection 110.6(1), where at any time any property of the taxpayer was used by

(a) a corporation a share of the capital stock of which is a share of the capital stock of a family farm corporation of the taxpayer, the taxpayer's spouse or common-law partner or any of the taxpayer's children, or

(b) a partnership an interest in which is an interest in a family farm partnership of the taxpayer, the taxpayer's spouse or common-law partner or any of the taxpayer's children

in the course of carrying on the business of farming in Canada, the property shall be deemed to have been used at that time by the taxpayer in the business of farming.

**Notes**: 70(9.8) amended by 2000 same-sex partners bill to add reference to "common-law partner", effective for the 2001 and later taxation years, or earlier by election (see Notes to 248(1)"common-law partner").

Opening words of 70(9.8) amended by 1991 technical bill, effective 1986, to refer to 14(1), 20(1)(b) and 110.6(1)"qualified farm property"(d).

**Interpretation Bulletins**: IT-268R4: *Inter vivos* transfer of farm property to child.

### (10) Definitions — In this section,

**Related Provisions**: 40(8), 44(8), 73(6) — Definitions in 70(10) apply to ss. 40, 44 and 73.

**Notes**: Before consolidation in R.S.C. 1985 (5th Supp.), the opening words of 70(10) also referred to 40, 44, 73, 146(5.3) and 146(5.4). These rules of application are now in 40(8), 44(8) and 73(6); 146(5.3) and (5.4) have been repealed.

Opening words of 70(10) amended by 1990 pension bill, effective 1989, to restrict the scope of 70(10) from all of 146 to only 146(5.3) and (5.4).

**"child"** of a taxpayer includes

(a) a child of the taxpayer's child,

(b) a child of the taxpayer's child's child, and

(c) a person who, at any time before the person attained the age of 19 years, was wholly dependent on the taxpayer for support and of whom the taxpayer had, at that time, in law or in fact, the custody and control;

**Related Provisions**: 84.1(2.2)(a)(i), 212.1(3)(b)(i) — Extended meaning of "child" applies for dividend stripping rules; 110.6(1)"child" — Extended meaning applies for capital gains exemption; 148(9)"child" — Extended meaning applies for life insurance policy rules; 252(1) — Additional extended meaning of "child".

**Notes**: 70(10)"child" was 70(10)(a) before consolidation in R.S.C. 1985 (5th Supp.), effective for taxation years ending after November 1991. See Table of Concordance.

**Interpretation Bulletins**: IT-489R: Non-arm's length sale of shares to a corporation.

**"interest in a family farm partnership"** of a person at a particular time means an interest owned by the person at that time in a partnership where, at that time, all or substantially all of the fair market value of the property of the partnership was attributable to

(a) property that has been used by

(i) the partnership,

(ii) the person,

(iii) a spouse, common-law partner, child or parent of the person, or

(iv) a corporation a share of the capital stock of which was a share of the capital stock of a family farm corporation of the person or of a spouse, common-law partner, child or parent of the person,

principally in the course of carrying on the business of farming in Canada in which the person or a spouse, common-law partner, child or parent of the person was actively engaged on a regular and continuous basis,

(b) shares of the capital stock or indebtedness of one or more corporations all or substantially all of the fair market value of the property of which was attributable to property described in paragraph (c), or

(c) properties described in paragraph (a) or (b);

**Notes**: Para. (a) amended by 2000 same-sex partners bill to add reference to "common-law partner", effective for the 2001 and later taxation years, or earlier by election (see Notes to 248(1)"common-law partner").

70(10)"interest in a family farm partnership" was 70(10)(c) before consolidation in R.S.C. 1985 (5th Supp.), effective for taxation years ending after November 1991. See Table of Concordance. See also Notes to "share of the capital stock ..." below.

**"share of the capital stock of a family farm corporation"** of a person at a particular time means a share of the capital stock of a corporation owned by the person at that time where, at that time, all or substantially all of the fair market value of the property owned by the corporation was attributable to

(a) property that has been used by

(i) the corporation or any other corporation, a share of the capital stock of which was a share of the capital stock of a family farm corporation of the person or of a spouse, common-law partner, child or parent of the person,

(i.1) a corporation controlled by a corporation referred to in subparagraph (i),

(ii) the person,

(iii) a spouse, common-law partner, child or parent of the person, or

(iv) a partnership, an interest in which was an interest in a family farm partnership of the person or of a spouse, common-law partner, child or parent of the person,

principally in the course of carrying on the business of farming in Canada in which the person or a spouse, common-law partner, child or parent of the person was actively engaged on a regular and continuous basis,

(b) shares of the capital stock or indebtedness of one or more corporations all or substantially all of the fair market value of the property of which was attributable to property described in paragraph (c), or

(c) properties described in paragraph (a) or (b).

**Related Provisions**: 70(12) — Value of NISA deemed nil; 256(6), (6.1) — Meaning of "controlled".

**I.T. Application Rules**: 20(1.11), 26(20).

**Interpretation Bulletins**: IT-236R4: Reserves — disposition of capital property; IT-349R3: Intergenerational transfers of farm property on death.

**Advance Tax Rulings**: ATR-28: Redemption of capital stock of family farm corporation; ATR-56: Purification of a family farm corporation.

**Notes**: Para. (a) amended by 2000 same-sex partners bill to add reference to "common-law partner", effective for the 2001 and later taxation years, or earlier by election (see Notes to 248(1)"common-law partner").

Subpara. (a)(i.1) added by 1995-97 technical bill, effective for 1994 and later taxation years. It allows property used in the qualifying farm business of a corporation to be held by a controlled subsidiary of the corporation.

70(10)"share of the capital stock of a family farm corporation" was 70(10)(b) before consolidation in R.S.C. 1985 (5th Supp.), effective for taxation years ending after November 1991. See Table of Concordance.

"interest in a family farm partnership" and "share of the capital stock of a family farm corporation" amended by 1992 technical bill, effective 1992, so that: the share or interest must be owned by the person at the relevant time; the property need not be being used in farming at the relevant time; the "property" that the corporation or partnership may own includes indebtedness; all or substantially all of the fair market value of the corporation's or partnership's property must be attributable to property that has been used principally in carrying on a farming business in Canada; and the list of qualifying users of farming property includes the taxpayer's parent.

The CCRA takes the position that "all or substantially all" means 90% or more.

**Interpretation Bulletins**: IT-268R4: *Inter vivos* transfer of farm property to child.

**(11) Application of subsec. 138(12)** — The definitions in subsection 138(12) apply to this section.

**Notes**: 70(11) added in the R.S.C. 1985 (5th Supp.) consolidation, effective for taxation years ending after November 1991. This rule was formerly in the opening words of 138(12).

Former 70(11), repealed by 1985 Budget, provided definitions for "cumulative small business gains account" (no longer necessary, owing to the repeal of other provisions) and "small business corporation" (moved to 248(1)).

**(12) Value of NISA** — For the purpose of the definition "share of the capital stock of a family farm corporation" in subsection (10), the fair market value of a net income stabilization account shall be deemed to be nil.

**Notes**: 70(12) added by 1992 technical bill, effective 1992.

**(13) Capital cost of certain depreciable property** — For the purposes of this section and, where a provision of this section (other than this subsection) applies, for the purposes of sections 13 and 20 (but not for the purposes of any regulation made for the purpose of paragraph 20(1)(a)),

(a) the capital cost to a taxpayer of depreciable property of a prescribed class disposed of immediately before the taxpayer's death, or

(b) the capital cost to a trust, to which subsection (9.1) applies, of depreciable property of a prescribed class disposed of immediately before the death of the spouse or common-law partner described in that subsection,

shall, in respect of property that was not disposed of by the taxpayer or the trust before that time, be the amount that it would be if subsection 13(7) were read without reference to

(c) the expression "the lesser of" in paragraph (b) and clause (d)(i)(A) thereof, and

(d) subparagraph (b)(ii), subclause (d)(i)(A)(II), clause (d)(i)(B) and paragraph (e) thereof.

**Related Provisions**: 13(7) — Change in use of depreciable property.

**Notes**: 70(13)(b) amended by 2000 same-sex partners bill to add reference to "common-law partner", effective for the 2001 and later taxation years, or earlier by election (see Notes to 248(1)"common-law partner").

70(13) added by 1993 technical bill, effective for dispositions and acquisitions in 1993 or later. It readjusts the capital cost of depreciable property for purposes of 70(6)(d), 70(9)(b) and 70(9.1)(b). The readjusted capital cost is used for determining undepreciated capital cost (UCC) and the amount by which UCC is reduced on a disposition, but does not affect CCA claims under 20(1)(a).

**Interpretation Bulletins**: IT-349R3: Intergenerational transfers of farm property on death.

**(14) Order of disposal of depreciable property** — Where 2 or more depreciable properties of a prescribed class are disposed of at the same time as a consequence of a taxpayer's death, this section and paragraph (a) of the definition "cost amount" in subsection 248(1) apply as if each property so disposed of were separately disposed of in the order designated by the taxpayer's legal representative or, in the case of a trust described in subsection (9.1), by the trust and, where the taxpayer's legal representative or the trust, as the case may be, does not designate an order, in the order designated by the Minister.

**Notes**: 70(14) added by 1993 technical bill, effective for dispositions and acquisitions in 1993 or later.

**Interpretation Bulletins**: IT-349R3: Intergenerational transfers of farm property on death.

**Definitions [s. 70]**: "active business" — 248(1); "adjusted cost base" — 54, 248(1); "amount", "annuity" — 248(1); "arm's length" — 251; "business" — 248(1); "Canada" — 255; "Canadian resource property" — 66(15), 248(1); "capital cost" — 70(12); "capital gain", "capital loss" — 39(1), 248(1); "capital property" — 54, 248(1); "carrying on business" — 253; "child" — 70(10), 252(1); "common-law partner" — 248(1); "consequence" — 248(8); "controlled" — 256(6), (6.1); "corporation" — 248(1), *Interpretation Act* 35(1); "cost amount" — 248(1); "created by the taxpayer's will" — 248(9.1); "cumulative eligible capital" — 14(5), 248(1); "depreciable property" — 13(21), 248(1); "eligible capital expenditure" — 14(5), 248(1); "eligible capital property" — 54, 248(1); "employment" — 248(1); "estate" — 104(1), 248(1); "fair market value" — 70(8), 70(12), 139.1(5); "family farm corporation", "family farm partnership" — 70(10); "farming" — 248(1); "foreign resource property" — 66(15), 248(1); "income" — of trust 108(3); "individual" — 248(1); "interest in a family farm partnership" — 70(10); "inventory" — 248(1); "life insurance policy" — 138(12), 248(1); "Minister", "net income stabilization account", "NISA Fund No. 2", "office" — 248(1); "non-qualifying debt" — 70(8); "parent" — 252(2); "person", "prescribed", "property", "regulation" — 248(1); "related" — 251(2); "resident in Canada" — 250; "rights or things" — 70(3.1); "share" — 248(1); "share in the capital stock of a family farm corporation" — 70(10); "specified investment business" — 125(7); "spouse" — 252(3); "tax payable" — 248(2); "taxable income" — 2(2), 248(1); "taxation year" — 11(2), 249; "taxpayer" — 248(1); "testamentary debt" — 70(8); "trust" — 104(1), 248(1), (3); "undepreciated capital cost" — 13(21), 248(1); "vested indefeasibly" — 248(9.2).

**Interpretation Bulletins [s. 70]**: IT-226R: Gift to a charity of a residual interest in real property or an equitable interest in a trust.

## 71. [Repealed under former Act]

**Notes**: 71, repealed by 1985 Budget, allowed unlimited use of previous years' allowable capital losses to offset income in the year of death. It was replaced by 111(2).

## 72. (1) Reserves, etc., for year of death — Where in a taxation year a taxpayer has died,

(a) paragraph 20(1)(n) does not apply to allow, in computing the income of the taxpayer for the year from a business, the deduction of any amount as a reserve in respect of property sold in the course of the business;

(b) no amount is deductible under subsection 32(1) as a reserve in respect of unearned commissions in computing the taxpayer's income for the year;

(c) no amount may be claimed under subparagraph 40(1)(a)(iii), paragraph 40(1.01)(c) or subparagraph 44(1)(e)(iii) in computing any gain of the taxpayer for the year;

(d) subsection 64(1) does not apply to allow, in computing the income of the taxpayer for the year, the deduction of any amount as a reserve in respect of the disposition of any property; and

(e) subsection 64(1.1) does not apply to allow, in computing the income of the taxpayer for the year, the deduction of any amount as a reserve in respect of the disposition of any property.

**Related Provisions**: 61.2 — Deduction of debt forgiveness reserve for year of death; 72(2) — Election by legal representative and transferee re reserves.

**Notes**: 72(1)(c) amended by 1991 technical bill, effective 1990, to add the reference to 44(1)(e)(iii); and by 1997 Budget, effective for 1997 and later taxation years, to add reference to 40(1.01)(c).

72(1)(d) and (e) refer to a version of s. 64 that was repealed by the 1981 Budget, not the current s. 64. See Notes to 64.

**Interpretation Bulletins**: IT-152R3: Special reserves — sale of land; IT-154R: Special reserves; IT-236R4: Reserves — disposition of capital property; IT-321R: Insurance agents and brokers — unearned commissions.

**(2) Election by legal representative and transferee re reserves** — Where property of a taxpayer that is a right to receive any amount has, on or after the death of the taxpayer and as a consequence thereof, been transferred or distributed to the taxpayer's spouse or common-law partner described in paragraph 70(6)(a) or to a trust described in paragraph 70(6)(b) (in this subsection referred to as the "transferee"), if the taxpayer was resident in Canada immediately before the taxpayer's death and the taxpayer's legal representative and the transferee have executed jointly an election in respect of the property in prescribed form,

(a) any amount in respect of the property that would, but for paragraph (1)(a), (b), (d) or (e), as the case may be, have been deductible as a reserve in computing the taxpayer's income for the taxation year in which the taxpayer died, shall,

(i) notwithstanding subsection (1), be deducted in computing the taxpayer's income for the taxation year in which the taxpayer died,

(ii) be included in computing the transferee's income for the transferee's first taxation year ending after the death of the taxpayer, and

(iii) be deemed to be

(A) an amount that has been included in computing the transferee's income from a business for a previous year in respect of property sold in the course of the business,

(B) an amount that has been included in computing the transferee's income for a previous year as a commission in respect of an insurance contract, other than a life insurance contract,

**S. 72(2)(a)(iii)(C)**      Income Tax Act, Part I, Division B

(C) an amount that by virtue of subsection 59(1) has been included in computing the transferee's income for a preceding taxation year, or

(D) for the purposes of subsection 64(1.1), an amount that by virtue of paragraph 59(3.2)(c) has been included in computing the transferee's income for a preceding taxation year and to be an amount deducted by the transferee pursuant to paragraph 64(1.1)(a)[5] in computing the transferee's income for the transferee's last taxation year ending before the death,

as the case may be;

(b) any amount in respect of the property that could, but for paragraph (1)(c), have been claimed under subparagraph 40(1)(a)(iii) or 44(1)(e)(iii) in computing the amount of any gain of the taxpayer for the year shall,

(i) notwithstanding paragraph (1)(c), be deemed to have been so claimed, and

(ii) for the purpose of computing the transferee's income for the transferee's first taxation year ending after the death of the taxpayer and any subsequent taxation year, be deemed to have been

(A) proceeds of the disposition of capital property disposed of by the transferee in that first taxation year, and

(B) the amount determined under subparagraph 40(1)(a)(i) or 44(1)(e)(i), as the case may be, in respect of the capital property referred to in clause (A); and

(c) notwithstanding paragraphs (a) and (b), where any property had been disposed of by the taxpayer, in computing the income of the transferee for any taxation year ending after the death of the taxpayer,

(i) the amount of the transferee's deduction under paragraph 20(1)(n) as a reserve in respect of the property sold in the course of business,

(ii) the amount of the transferee's claim under subparagraph 40(1)(a)(iii) or 44(1)(e)(iii) in respect of the disposition of the property, and

(iii) the amount of the transferee's deduction under section 64[5] as a reserve in respect of the disposition of the property

shall be computed as if the transferee were the taxpayer who had disposed of the property and as if the property were disposed of by the transferee at the time it was disposed of by the taxpayer.

**Related Provisions**: 220(3.2), Reg. 600(b) — Late filing of election or revocation; 248(8) — Occurrences as a consequence of death.

**Notes**: 72(2) amended by 2000 same-sex partners bill to add reference to "common-law partner", effective for the 2001 and later taxation years, or earlier by election (see Notes to 248(1)"common-law partner").

72(2)(b) and (c) amended by 1991 technical bill, effective 1990, to add references to 44(1)(e)(iii).

The references in 72(2)(a)(iii)(D) and (c)(iii) to 64(1.1) are to a version of 64 that has been repealed. See Notes to 64.

**Interpretation Bulletins [subsec. 72(2)]**: IT-152R3: Special reserves — sale of land; IT-236R4: Reserves — disposition of capital property.

**Information Circulars [subsec. 72(2)]**: 92-1: Guidelines for accepting late, amended or revoked elections.

**Forms [subsec. 72(2)]**: T2069: Election in respect of amounts not deductible as reserves for the year of death; T4011: Preparing returns for deceased persons [guide].

**Definitions [s. 72]**: "amount", "business" — 248(1); "Canada" — 255; "capital property", "common-law partner" — 54, 248(1); "consequence" — 248(8); "prescribed", "property" — 248(1); "resident in Canada" — 250; "taxation year" — 11(2), 249; "taxpayer" — 248(1); "trust" — 104(1), 248(1), (3).

**73. (1) *Inter vivos* transfer of property of spouse, etc., or trust** — For the purposes of this Part, where at any time after 1977 any particular capital property of a taxpayer has been transferred to

(a) the taxpayer's spouse or common-law partner,

(b) a former spouse or common-law partner of the taxpayer in settlement of rights arising out of their marriage or common-law partnership, or

(c) a trust created by the taxpayer under which

(i) the taxpayer's spouse or common-law partner is entitled to receive all of the income of the trust that arises before the spouse's or common-law partner's death, and

(ii) no person except the spouse or common-law partner may, before the spouse's or common-law partner's death, receive or otherwise obtain the use of any of the income or capital of the trust,

(d) [Repealed]

and both the taxpayer and the transferee were resident in Canada at that time, unless the taxpayer elects in the taxpayer's return of income under this Part for the taxation year in which the property was transferred not to have the provisions of this subsection apply, the particular property shall be deemed to have been disposed of at that time by the taxpayer for proceeds equal to,

(e) where the particular property is depreciable property of a prescribed class, that proportion of the undepreciated capital cost to the taxpayer immediately before that time of all property of that class that the fair market value immediately before that time of the particular property is of the fair market value immediately before that time of all of that property of that class, and

---

[5]The section 64 meant to be referred to is s. 64 of R.S.C. 1952, c. 148 — ed.

(f) in any other case, the adjusted cost base to the taxpayer of the particular property immediately before that time,

and to have been acquired at that time by the transferee for an amount equal to those proceeds.

### Proposed Amendment — 73(1), (1.01), (1.02)

**73. (1) *Inter vivos* transfers by individuals —** For the purposes of this Part, where at any time any particular capital property of an individual (other than a trust) has been transferred in circumstances to which subsection (1.01) applies and both the individual and the transferee are resident in Canada at that time, unless the individual elects in the individual's return of income under this Part for the taxation year in which the property was transferred that the provisions of this subsection not apply, the particular property is deemed

(a) to have been disposed of at that time by the individual for proceeds equal to,

(i) where the particular property is depreciable property of a prescribed class, that proportion of the undepreciated capital cost to the individual immediately before that time of all property of that class that the fair market value immediately before that time of the particular property is of the fair market value immediately before that time of all of that property of that class, and

(ii) in any other case, the adjusted cost base to the individual of the particular property immediately before that time; and

(b) to have been acquired at that time by the transferee for an amount equal to those proceeds.

**(1.01) Qualifying transfers —** Subject to subsection (1.02), property is transferred by an individual in circumstances to which this subsection applies where it is transferred to

(a) the individual's spouse or common-law partner;

(b) a former spouse or common-law partner of the individual in settlement of rights arising out of their marriage or common-law partnership; or

(c) a trust created by the individual under which

(i) the individual's spouse or common-law partner is entitled to receive all of the income of the trust that arises before the spouse's or common-law partner's death and no person except the spouse or common-law partner may, before the spouse's or common-law partner's death, receive or otherwise obtain the use of any of the income or capital of the trust,

(ii) the individual is entitled to receive all of the income of the trust that arises before the individual's death and no person except the individual may, before the individual's death, receive or otherwise obtain the use of any of the income or capital of the trust, or

(iii) either

(A) the individual or the individual's spouse is, in combination with the other, entitled to receive all of the income of the trust that arises before the later of the death of the individual and the death of the spouse and no other person may, before the later of those deaths, receive or otherwise obtain the use of any of the income or capital of the trust, or

(B) the individual or the individual's common-law partner is, in combination with the other, entitled to receive all of the income of the trust that arises before the later of the death of the individual and the death of the common-law partner and no other person may, before the later of those deaths, receive or otherwise obtain the use of any of the income or capital of the trust.

**Related Provisions:** 73(1.02) — Limitation on transfers to trusts; 108(3) — Calculation of income of trust; 108(4) — Trust not disqualified by reason only of payment of certain duties and taxes; 248(1) "alter ego trust" — Trust for individual during own lifetime.

**Notes:** A trust under 73(1.01)(c)(i) is a spouse trust or spousal trust; under (c)(ii) is an "alter ego trust"; under (c)(iii) is a "joint partner trust" (see 248(1)).

**(1.02) Exception for transfers —** Subsection (1.01) applies to a transfer of property by an individual to a trust the terms of which satisfy the conditions in subparagraph (1.01)(c)(ii) or (iii) only where

(a) the trust was created after 1999;

(b) either

(i) the individual has attained 65 years of age at the time the trust was created, or

(ii) no person (other than the individual) or partnership has any absolute or contingent right as a beneficiary under the trust (determined with reference to subsection 104(1.1));

(c) unless subparagraph (b)(ii) applies in respect of the transfer, the transfer is not part of a series of transactions or events

(i) that includes a transfer of property to the individual (or the spouse or common-law partner or former spouse or common-law partner, as the case may be, of the individual) from a trust (other than a testamentary trust) in circumstances to which subsection 107(2) applied, and

(ii) one of the main purposes of which can reasonably be considered to be to avoid the application of subsection 104(4) or (5) on a day determined under paragraph 104(4)(b) or (c); and

(d) in the case of a trust the terms of which satisfy the conditions in subparagraph (1.01)(c)(ii), the trust does not make an election under subparagraph 104(4)(a)(ii.1).

**Related Provisions:** 104(1.1) — Restricted meaning of "beneficiary".

**Application:** Bill C-43 (First Reading September 20, 2000), s. 33, will amend subsec. 73(1) to read as above, and add subsecs. (1.01) and (1.02), applicable to transfers that occur after 1999 except that, in respect of transfers that occur in 2000,

(a) for the purpose of subsec. 73(1), the residence of a transferee trust shall be determined without reference to sec. 94, as it read before 2001;

(b) subject to para. (c),

(i) subsecs 73(1.01) and (1.02) shall be read without reference to the words "or common-law partner", "or common-law partner's" and "or common-law partnership", and

(ii) subpara. 73(1.01)(c)(iii) shall be read as follows:

(iii) the individual or the individual's spouse is, in combination with the other, entitled to receive all of the income of the trust that arises before the later of the death of the individual and the death of the spouse and no other person may, before the later of those deaths, receive or otherwise obtain the use of any of the income or capital of the trust,

(c) para. (b) does not apply to a transfer at any time by an individual to or for the benefit of another individual where, because of an election under sec. 144 of the *Modernization of Benefits and Obligations Act*, c. 12, of S.C. 2000 [see Notes to 248(1)"common-law partner"], ss. 130 to 142 of that Act applied at that time to those individuals.

**Technical Notes:** Subsection 73(1) of the Act generally provides for a tax-free disposition of capital property where it is transferred by an individual to the individual's spouse or to a spousal trust (i.e., essentially a trust for the exclusive benefit of the spouse during the spouse's lifetime). For subsection 73(1) to apply, the transferor and transferee must both be resident in Canada (determined without reference to subsection 94(1) as it read before 2001) at the time of the transfer. Provision is made to elect out of the rollover rule, in which case the proceeds of disposition for the transferor would be deemed by subsection 69(1) to be not less than the fair market value of the property transferred. Where there has been a transfer to a spousal trust, subsections 104(4) and 107(4) ensure that capital gains are appropriately recognized by a deemed disposition of trust property at the time of the beneficiary spouse's death (or, where applicable, at the time of any earlier distribution to another beneficiary).

Subsection 73(1) is amended, in conjunction with the introduction of subsection 73(1.01), so that the current rules in subsection 73(1) for transfers by an individual to a trust are extended to similarly allow for a tax-free disposition where:

- the individual transfers property to a trust for the exclusive benefit of the individual during the individual's own lifetime (such a trust will generally be an "*alter ego*" trust, as defined in subsection 248(1), in the event that the individual is at least 65 years of age), or

- the individual transfers the property for the joint benefit of the individual and the individual's spouse during their lifetimes (such a trust will generally be a "joint partner trust", as defined in subsection 248(1), in the event that the individual is at least 65 years of age). This can involve either equal or unequal entitlements of the two spouses to trust income (as defined in subsection 108(3)).

However, new subsection 73(1.02) limits the application of subsection 73(1.01). It provides that, in order for subparagraphs 73(1.01)(c)(ii) and (iii) to apply to a transfer of property by an individual to a trust, the following conditions must be met:

- the trust was created after 1999;

- the individual has attained 65 years of age at the time the trust was created, except where no person (other than the individual) or partnership has any absolute or contingent right as a beneficiary under the trust (determined with reference to subsection 104(1.1));

- subject to the same exception, the transfer was not part of a series of transactions or events that includes a transfer of property to the transferor (or the spouse or former spouse of the transferor) from a trust (other than a testamentary trust) in circumstances to which subsection 107(2) applied, where one of the main purposes of that series can reasonably be considered to be to avoid the deemed disposition of trust property under subsection 104(4) or (5) on a day determined under paragraph 104(4)(b) or (c); and

- in the case of a trust to which the individual transfers property for the exclusive benefit of the individual during the individual's own lifetime, the trust does not make an election under subparagraph 104(4)(a)(ii.1). For more information on this election see the commentary below on amended paragraph 104(4)(a).

The purpose of the "age 65" condition (above and in amended subsection 104(4)) is to limit the opportunity to engage in tax planning involving trusts and the maximization of the deferral of the recognition of capital gains. For example, a 66 year old parent might arrange for common shares of a private corporation to be issued to his or her 27 year old child with the understanding that those common shares be transferred by the child into a trust effectively controlled by the parent that provides for beneficiaries after the child's death. The purpose of this arrangement may, in part, be to minimize capital gains otherwise recognized on the death of the parent. In these circumstances, the transfer by the child to the trust cannot be made on a rollover basis and subsection 104(4) generally provides for a deemed disposition on the 21st anniversary of the trust (rather than on the child's death).

The purpose of the third condition is consistent with the purpose of the "age 65" condition. Assume there is an upcoming 21-year anniversary for a trust the beneficiaries of which are a 66 year old parent and the adult children of the parent. Property is transferred to the parent alone (rather than to both the parent and the beneficiaries) on the understanding that the parent will transfer the property back to a trust with the same beneficiaries. In the absence of the third condition, the transactions described would result in an inappropriate extension of the 21-year rule for deemed dispositions of trust property.

Changes to subsections 104(4) and (6) and 107(4), as described in the commentary below, have been made so that the income tax regime for trusts to which transfers have been made under amended section 73 parallels the existing rules for spousal trusts.

These amendments apply to transfers that occur after 1999.

These amendments also reflect changes [re "common-law partners" — ed.] proposed under Bill C-23, the *Modernization of Benefits and Obligations Act*.

**Related Provisions**: 40(4) — Where principal residence disposed of to a spouse; 44.1(5) — Small business investment rollover on breakdown of relationship; 53(4) — Effect on ACB of share, partnership interest or trust interest; 56.1 — Maintenance payments; 70(6)(a) — Where transfer or distribution to spouse or trust; 70(9.1), (9.3) — Transfer of farm property from spouse trust to settlor's children before 2000; 73(1.1) — Interpretation; 74.1(1) — Attribution of income or loss on property transferred to spouse; 74.2(1) — Gain or loss deemed that of lender or transferor; 104(4)(a) — Deemed disposition by a trust; 104(4)(a.3) — Deemed disposition by trust on emigration of transferor; 107.4 — Qualifying disposition to a trust; 108(3) — Meaning of "income" of trust; 108(4) — Trust not disqualified by reason only of payment of certain taxes; 148(8) — Disposition at non-arm's length and similar cases; 148(8.1) — *Inter vivos* transfer to spouse; 220(3.2) — Late filing of election or revocation; 252(3) — Extended meaning of "spouse" and "former spouse"; Reg. 600(b) — Late filing of election or revocation.

**Notes**: For discussion of spouse trusts in 73(1)(c), see Notes to 70(6). See also 248(1)"alter ego trust" and "joint partner trust" for new extensions of the spousal-trust concept.

The ability to "elect out" of the application of 73(1), provided in the words between paras. (d) and (e) (to be moved to the opening words of 73(1)), was introduced effective for property transferred after 1979. There is no specific form required for the election. Note, however, that the election must be made "in" the return, not merely by the due date for the return. (This also means that if the return is filed late, the election can still be made "in" the return.)

Note that after a spousal transfer, whether or not the transferor has elected out of 73(1), future income or gains from the property will be attributed back to the transferor under 74.1(1) or 74.2(1), unless one of the exceptions in 74.5(1)–(3) applies.

For transfers before 1978, read:

> 73. (1) *Inter vivos* transfer of property to spouse or trust — For the purposes of this Part, where at any time after 1971 any particular capital property has been transferred by a taxpayer to his spouse, or to a trust created by him under which
>
> > (a) his spouse is entitled to receive all of the income of the trust that arises before the spouse's death, and
> >
> > (b) no person except the spouse may, before the spouse's death, receive or otherwise obtain the use of any of the income or capital of the trust,
>
> and both the taxpayer and the spouse or trust, as the case may be, were resident in Canada at that time, the particular property shall be deemed to have been disposed of at that time by the taxpayer for proceeds equal to,
>
> > (c) where the particular property is depreciable property of a prescribed class, that proportion of the undepreciated capital cost to the taxpayer immediately before that time of all property of that class that the fair market value immediately before that time of the particular property is of the fair market value immediately before that time of all of that property of that class, and
> >
> > (d) in any other case, the adjusted cost base to the taxpayer of the particular property immediately before that time,
>
> and to have been acquired at that time by the spouse or trust, as the case may be, for an amount equal to those proceeds.

73(1) amended by 2000 same-sex partners bill to add reference to "common-law partner" and "common-law partnership", effective for the 2001 and later taxation years, or earlier by election (see Notes to 248(1)"common-law partner").

73(1)(d) amended by 1991 technical bill and repealed by 1992 technical bill (due to the introduction of an extended definition of "spouse" in 252(4)). For transfers from 1979 through July 13, 1990, read:

> (d) an individual pursuant to a decree, order or judgment of a competent tribunal made in accordance with prescribed provisions of the law of a province if that individual either entered into a written agreement with the taxpayer in accordance with such provisions or is a person within a prescribed class of persons referred to in such provisions,

For transfers from July 14, 1990 through the end of 1992, read:

> (d) an individual of the opposite sex, pursuant to an order for the support or maintenance of the individual, made by a competent tribunal in accordance with the laws of a province, where the individual and the taxpayer cohabited in a conjugal relationship before the date of the order,

**I.T. Application Rules**: 20(1.1) (where property owned since before 1972).

**Interpretation Bulletins**: IT-209R: *Inter vivos* gifts of capital property to individuals directly or through trusts; IT-325R2: Property transfers after separation, divorce and annulment.

**Information Circulars**: 92-1: Guidelines for accepting late, amended or revoked elections.

**(1.1) Interpretation** — For greater certainty, where, under the laws of a province or because of a decree, order or judgment of a competent tribunal made in accordance with those laws, a person referred to in subsection (1)

> (a) acquires or is deemed to have acquired,
>
> (b) is deemed or declared to have or is awarded, or
>
> (c) has vested in that person,

property that was or would, but for those provisions, have been a capital property of the taxpayer referred to in subsection (1), that property shall, for the purposes of that subsection, be deemed to be capital property of the taxpayer that has been transferred to that person.

### Proposed Amendment — 73(1.1)

**(1.1) Interpretation** — For greater certainty, a property is, for the purposes of subsections (1) and (1.01), deemed to be property of the individual referred to in subsection (1) that has been transferred to a particular transferee where,

> (a) under the laws of a province or because of a decree, order or judgment of a competent tribunal made in accordance with those laws, the property
>
> > (i) is acquired or is deemed to have been acquired by the particular transferee,
> >
> > (ii) is deemed or declared to be property of, or is awarded to, the particular transferee, or
> >
> > (iii) has vested in the particular transferee;

(b) the property was or would, but for those laws, have been a capital property of the individual referred to in subsection (1).

**Application**: Bill C-43 (First Reading September 20, 2000), s. 33, will amend subsec. 73(1.1) to read as above, applicable to transfers that occur after 1999.

**Technical Notes**: Subsection 73(1.1) generally provides that one individual is considered to have transferred property to another individual where the other individual obtains the property under provincial law or because of a decree, order or judgment of a competent tribunal made in accordance with that law. The rule applies for the purpose of the rollover rule in subsection 73(1).

Subsection 73(1.1) is amended to change a number of cross-references, to reflect amended subsection 73(1) and new subsection 73(1.01) (described in the commentary above).

**Related Provisions**: 70(9.1), (9.3) — Transfer of farm property from spouse trust to settlor's children.

**Notes**: 73(1.1) added in 1978, effective 1978, and amended by 1993 technical bill. For 1978 through transfers up to July 13, 1990, read "by the operation of a prescribed provision of the law of a province" in place of "under the laws of a province".

**Regulations**: 6500(2) (prescribed provisions; no longer needed).

**I.T. Application Rules**: 20(1.1).

**Interpretation Bulletins**: IT-325R2: Property transfers after separation, divorce and annulment.

**(1.2)** [Repealed under former Act]

**Notes**: The rule in 73(1.2), extending the meaning of "spouse" and "former spouse" to include a party to a void or voidable marriage, was moved to 252(3) effective 1982.

**(2) Capital cost and amount deemed allowed to spouse, etc., or trust** — Where a transferee is deemed by subsection (1) to have acquired any particular depreciable property of a prescribed class of a taxpayer for an amount determined under paragraph (1)(e) and the capital cost to the taxpayer of the particular property exceeds the amount determined under that paragraph, for the purposes of sections 13 and 20 and any regulations made under paragraph 20(1)(a)

(a) the capital cost to the transferee of the particular property shall be deemed to be the amount that was the capital cost to the taxpayer thereof; and

(b) the excess shall be deemed to have been allowed to the transferee in respect of the particular property under regulations made under paragraph 20(1)(a) in computing income for taxation years before the acquisition thereof.

**Notes**: 73(2) amended effective 1978. For earlier transfers, read:

(2) Capital cost and amount deemed allowed to spouse or trust — Where a spouse or trust, as the case may be, is deemed by subsection (1) to have acquired any particular depreciable property of a prescribed class of a taxpayer for an amount determined under paragraph (1)(c) and the capital cost to the taxpayer of the particular property exceeds the amount determined under that paragraph, for the purposes of sections 13 and 20 and any regulations made under paragraph 20(1)(a)

(a) the capital cost to the spouse or trust, as the case may be, of the particular property shall be deemed to be the amount that was the capital cost to the taxpayer thereof, and

(b) the excess shall be deemed to have been allowed to the spouse or trust, as the case may be, in respect of the particular property under regulations made under paragraph 20(1)(a) in computing income for taxation years before the acquisition thereof.

**I.T. Application Rules**: 20(1.1) (where property owned since before 1972).

**Interpretation Bulletins**: IT-209R: *Inter vivos* gifts of capital property to individuals directly or through trusts; IT-325R2: Property transfers after separation, divorce and annulment.

**(3) *Inter vivos* transfer of farm property to child** — For the purposes of this Part, where at any time any land in Canada or depreciable property in Canada of a prescribed class of a taxpayer or any eligible capital property in respect of a business carried on in Canada by a taxpayer is transferred by the taxpayer to a child of the taxpayer who was resident in Canada immediately before the transfer, and the property was, before the transfer, used principally in the business of farming in which the taxpayer, the taxpayer's spouse or common-law partner or any of the taxpayer's children was actively engaged on a regular and continuous basis,

(a) where the property transferred was depreciable property of a prescribed class, the taxpayer shall be deemed to have disposed of the property at the time of the transfer for proceeds of disposition equal to,

(i) in any case to which neither subparagraph (ii) nor (iii) applies, the proceeds of disposition otherwise determined,

(ii) if the proceeds of disposition otherwise determined exceeded the greater of

(A) the fair market value of the property immediately before the time of the transfer, and

(B) that proportion of the undepreciated capital cost to the taxpayer immediately before the time of the transfer of all of the depreciable property of the taxpayer of that class that the fair market value at that time of the property so transferred was of the fair market value at that time of all of the depreciable property of the taxpayer of that class,

the greater of the amounts referred to in clauses (A) and (B), or

(iii) if the proceeds of disposition otherwise determined were less than the lesser of the amounts referred to in clauses (ii)(A) and (B), the lesser of those amounts;

(b) where the property transferred was land, the taxpayer shall be deemed to have disposed of the

Subdivision f — Rules Relating to Computation of Income   S. 73(3)(d.2)

property at the time of the transfer for proceeds of disposition equal to,

(i) in any case to which neither subparagraph (ii) nor (iii) applies, the proceeds of disposition otherwise determined,

(ii) if the proceeds of disposition otherwise determined exceeded the greater of

(A) the fair market value of the land immediately before the time of the transfer, and

(B) the adjusted cost base to the taxpayer of the land immediately before the time of the transfer,

the greater of the amounts referred to in clauses (A) and (B), or

(iii) if the proceeds of disposition otherwise determined were less than the lesser of the amounts referred to in clauses (ii)(A) and (B), the lesser of those amounts;

(b.1) where the property transferred was eligible capital property, the taxpayer shall be deemed to have disposed of the property at the time of the transfer for proceeds of disposition equal to,

(i) in any case to which neither subparagraph (ii) nor (iii) applies, the proceeds of disposition otherwise determined,

(ii) if the proceeds of disposition otherwise determined exceeded the greater of

(A) the fair market value of the property immediately before the time of the transfer, and

(B) the amount determined by the formula

$$\frac{4}{3}\left(A \times \frac{B}{C}\right)$$

where

A is the cumulative eligible capital of the taxpayer in respect of the business,

B is the fair market value of the property immediately before the transfer, and

C is the fair market value immediately before that time of all eligible capital property of the taxpayer in respect of the business,

the greater of the amounts referred to in clauses (A) and (B), or

(iii) if the proceeds of disposition otherwise determined were less than the lesser of the amounts referred to in clauses (ii)(A) and (B), the lesser of those amounts;

(c) section 69 does not apply in determining the proceeds of disposition of the depreciable property, the land or the eligible capital property;

(d) the child shall be deemed to have acquired the depreciable property or the land, as the case may be, for an amount equal to the proceeds of disposition determined under paragraph (a) or (b), respectively;

(d.1) where the property transferred was eligible capital property of the taxpayer, the child shall be deemed to have acquired a capital property, immediately after the transfer, at a cost equal to the proceeds of disposition determined under paragraph (b.1), except that, where the child continues to carry on the business previously carried on by the taxpayer, the taxpayer's spouse or common-law partner or any of the taxpayer's children, the taxpayer shall be deemed to have acquired an eligible capital property and to have made an eligible capital expenditure at a cost equal to the total of

(i) the proceeds of disposition referred to in paragraph (b.1), and

(ii) $4/3$ of the amount determined by the formula

$$\left(A \times \frac{B}{C}\right) - D$$

where

A is the amount, if any, determined for F in the definition "cumulative eligible capital" in subsection 14(5) in respect of the business of the taxpayer immediately before the time of the transfer,

B is the fair market value of the property immediately before that time,

C is the fair market value immediately before that time of all eligible capital property of the taxpayer in respect of the business, and

D is the amount, if any, included under subparagraph 14(1)(a)(iv) in computing the income of the taxpayer as a result of the disposition,

and, for the purpose of determining at any subsequent time the child's cumulative eligible capital in respect of the business, an amount equal to $3/4$ of the amount determined under subparagraph (ii) shall be added to the amount otherwise determined in respect thereof for P in the definition "cumulative eligible capital" in subsection 14(5);

(d.2) for the purposes of determining after the time of the transfer

(i) the amount deemed by subparagraph 14(1)(a)(v) to be the child's taxable capital gain, and

(ii) the amount to be included under subparagraph 14(1)(a)(v) or paragraph 14(1)(b) in computing the child's income

in respect of any subsequent disposition of the property of the business, there shall be added to the amount otherwise determined for Q in the definition "cumulative eligible capital" in subsection 14(5) the amount determined by the formula

$$A \times \frac{B}{C}$$

where

A is the amount, if any, determined for Q in that definition in respect of the business of the taxpayer immediately before the time of the transfer,

B is the fair market value immediately before that time of the property transferred, and

C is the fair market value immediately before that time of all eligible capital property of the taxpayer in respect of the business; and

(e) where the child is deemed to have acquired depreciable property of a prescribed class of the taxpayer for an amount determined under paragraph (d) and the capital cost to the taxpayer of the property exceeds the amount determined under that paragraph, for the purposes of sections 13 and 20 and any regulations made under paragraph 20(1)(a),

(i) the capital cost to the child of the property shall be deemed to be the amount that was the capital cost to the taxpayer thereof, and

(ii) the excess shall be deemed to have been allowed to the child in respect of the property under regulations made under paragraph 20(1)(a) in computing income for taxation years before the acquisition thereof.

**Related Provisions**: 44(1.1) — Farm property disposed of to child; 70(9) — Transfer of farm property by farmer to child; 70(9.6) — Transfer to parent; 70(9.8) — Leased farm property; 75.1 — Gain or loss deemed that of transferor; 110.6(1) "qualified farm property"(d)(ii) — Property to which 73(3)(d.1) applies eligible for capital gains exemption; 110.6(2) — Capital gains exemption on farm property; 257 — Formula cannot calculate to less than zero.

**Notes**: 73(3) amended by 2000 same-sex partners bill to add reference to "common-law partner", effective for the 2001 and later taxation years, or earlier by election (see Notes to 248(1) "common-law partner").

Opening words of 73(3) amended by 1978 Budget to apply to transfers of eligible capital property after April 10, 1978, and amended by 1992 technical bill, effective 1993, to delete a requirement that the property have been used in farming *immediately* before the transfer and to add the requirement that it have been used *principally* in farming and that the business have been actively engaged in on a regular and continuous basis. From 1972 through 1992, read the last part of the opening words as:

and the property was, immediately before the transfer, used by the taxpayer, the taxpayer's spouse or any of the taxpayer's children in the business of farming, the following rules apply:

73(3)(b.1) added by 1978 budget, effective for transfers of eligible capital property after April 10, 1978. Cl. (b.1)(ii)(B) amended by 1988 tax reform and, retroactively, by 1992 technical bill (to clarify the treatment of multiple eligible capital properties), effective for transfers after the beginning of the taxpayer's business's first fiscal period that begins after 1987. For earlier transfers, read:

(B) 2 times the taxpayer's cumulative eligible capital in respect of the business immediately before the time of the transfer,

73(3)(c) amended and (d.1) added by 1978 budget, effective for transfers of eligible capital property after April 10, 1978; (d.1) amended by 1988 tax reform and 1992 technical bill, effective for transfers after the beginning of the taxpayer's business's first fiscal period that begins after 1987. For earlier transfers, delete everything from "the aggregate of" to the end of the para., and read "those proceeds".

73(3)(d.2) added by 1992 technical bill, effective for transfers after the beginning of the taxpayer's business's first fiscal period that begins after 1987, to prevent an overstatement of the deemed taxable gain or amount to be included in income on the subsequent disposition of eligible capital property by the child.

The draft legislation of July 12, 1994 (debt forgiveness) proposed an amendment to 73(3)(d.1)(ii)A to refer to "F and G" instead of "F". However, that amendment was not included in the December 20, 1994 revision of the draft legislation. See now 14(5) "cumulative eligible capital" F:P.1.

Reference to 14(1)(a)(v) added to 73(3)(d.2)(ii) by 1994 Budget, effective for transfers after February 22, 1994.

**I.T. Application Rules**: 26(19) (property owned since before 1972).

**Interpretation Bulletins**: IT-268R4: *Inter vivos* transfer of farm property to child.

**(4) *Inter vivos* transfer of family farm corporations and partnerships** — For the purposes of this Part, where at any particular time after April 10, 1978 a taxpayer has transferred property to a child of the taxpayer who was resident in Canada immediately before the transfer, and the property was, immediately before the transfer, a share of the capital stock of a family farm corporation of the taxpayer or an interest in a family farm partnership of the taxpayer (within the meaning assigned by subsection 70(10)), the following rules apply:

(a) the taxpayer shall be deemed to have disposed of the property at the time of the transfer for proceeds of disposition equal to,

(i) in any case to which neither subparagraph (ii) nor (iii) applies, the proceeds of disposition otherwise determined,

(ii) if the proceeds of disposition otherwise determined exceeded the greater of

(A) the fair market value of the property immediately before the time of the transfer, and

(B) the adjusted cost base to the taxpayer of the property immediately before the time of the transfer,

the greater of the amounts referred to in clauses (A) and (B), or

(iii) if the proceeds of disposition otherwise determined were less than the lesser of the amounts referred to in clauses (ii)(A) and (B), the lesser of those amounts;

(b) section 69 does not apply in determining the proceeds of disposition of the property; and

(c) the child shall be deemed to have acquired the property for an amount equal to the proceeds of disposition determined under paragraph (a).

**Related Provisions**: 53(4) — Effect on ACB of share or partnership interest; 70(9.2) — Transfer of family farm corporations and partnerships; 70(9.6) — Transfer to parent; 70(10) — "child"; 75.1 — Gain or loss deemed that of transfer.

**I.T. Application Rules**: 20(1.1).

**Interpretation Bulletins**: IT-268R4: *Inter vivos* transfer of farm property to child.

**Advance Tax Rulings**: ATR-56: Purification of a family farm corporation.

**(5) Disposition of a NISA** — Where at any time a taxpayer disposes of an interest in the taxpayer's NISA Fund No. 2, an amount equal to the balance in the fund so disposed of shall be deemed to have been paid out of the fund at that time to the taxpayer except that,

(a) where the interest is disposed of to the taxpayer's spouse or common-law partner, former spouse or common-law partner or an individual referred to in paragraph (1)(d) (as it applies to transfers of property that occurred before 1993) in settlement of rights arising out of their marriage or common-law partnership, on or after the breakdown of the marriage or common-law partnership, that amount shall not be deemed to have been paid to the taxpayer if

(i) the disposition is made under a decree, order or judgment of a competent tribunal or, in the case of a spouse or common-law partner or former spouse or common-law partner, a written separation agreement, and

(ii) the taxpayer elects in the taxpayer's return of income under this Part for the taxation year in which the property was disposed of to have this paragraph apply to the disposition; and

(b) where the interest is disposed of to a taxable Canadian corporation in a transaction in respect of which an election is made under section 85, an amount equal to the proceeds of disposition in respect of that interest shall be deemed to be paid, at that time, to the taxpayer out of the taxpayer's NISA Fund No. 2.

**Related Provisions**: 252(3) — Extended meaning of "spouse" and "former spouse".

**Notes**: 73(5)(a) amended by 2000 same-sex partners bill to add reference to "common-law partner" and "common-law partnership", effective for the 2001 and later taxation years, or earlier by election (see Notes to 248(1)"common-law partner").

73(5) added by 1992 technical bill, effective for dispositions after 1990. However, before 1993 read "marriage or other conjugal relationship" in place of "marriage". (From 1992–2000, "marriage" was given an extended meaning by 252(4)(b).)

Former 73(5), repealed by 1985 Budget (due to the introduction of the capital gains exemption in 110.6), provided for a limited rollover of shares of a small business corporation to a taxpayer's child.

**Interpretation Bulletins**: IT-268R3: *Inter vivos* transfer of farm property to child.

**(6) Application of subsec. 70(10)** — The definitions in subsection 70(10) apply to this section.

**Notes**: 73(6) added in the R.S.C. 1985 (5th Supp.) consolidation, effective for taxation years ending after November 1991. This rule was formerly contained in the opening words of 70(10).

**Interpretation Bulletins**: IT-268R4: *Inter vivos* transfer of farm property to child.

**Definitions [s. 73]**: "adjusted cost base" — 54, 248(1); "amount" — 248(1); "beneficiary" — 104(1.1); "business" — 248(1); "Canada" — 255; "capital property" — 54, 73(1.1), 248(1); "carrying on business" — 253; "child" — 70(10), 73(6), 252(1); "common-law partner", "common-law partnership" — 248(1); "cumulative eligible capital" — 14(5), 248(1); "depreciable property" — 13(21), 248(1); "eligible capital property" — 54, 248(1); "farming" — 248(1); "former spouse" — 252(3); "income" — of trust 108(3); "individual" — 248(1); "interest in a family farm partnership" — 70(10), 73(6); "NISA Fund No. 2" — 248(1); "partnership" — see Notes to 96(1); "person", "prescribed" — 248(1); "proceeds of disposition" — 54; "property" — 248(1); "province" — *Interpretation Act* 35(1); "regulation" — 248(1); "resident in Canada" — 250; "separation agreement" — 248(1); "share of the capital stock of a family farm corporation" — 70(10), 73(6); "spouse" — 252(3); "taxable Canadian corporation" — 89(1), 248(1); "taxation year" — 11(2), 249; "taxpayer" — 248(1); "testamentary trust" — 108(1), 248(1); "transfer" — 73(1.1); "trust" — 104(1), 248(1), (3); "undepreciated capital cost" — 13(21), 248(1).

**74. [Repealed under former Act]**

**Notes**: 74 repealed by 1985 Budget, generally effective for transfers after May 22, 1985, in conjunction with the introduction of new attribution rules in 74.1 through 74.5. For property transferred before May 23, 1985, read:

74. (1) **Transfers to spouse** — Where a person has on or after August 1, 1917, transferred property either directly or indirectly by means of a trust or by any other means whatever to his spouse, or to a person who has since become his spouse, any income or loss, as the case may be, for a taxation year from the property or from property substituted therefor shall, during the lifetime of the transferor while he is resident in Canada and the transferee is his spouse, be deemed to be income or a loss, as the case may be, of the transferor and not of the transferee.

(2) **Gain or loss deemed that of transferor** — Where a person has, after 1971, transferred property either directly or indirectly by means of a trust or by any other means whatever to his spouse, or to a person who has since become his spouse, (which property is referred to in this subsection as "transferred property"), the following rules apply:

(a) the amount, if any, by which

(i) the aggregate of the transferee's taxable capital gains for the year from dispositions of transferred property other than listed personal property and from dispositions of property (other than listed personal property) substituted for transferred property

exceeds

(ii) the aggregate of the transferee's allowable capital losses for the year from dispositions of transferred property other than listed personal property and from dispositions of property (other than listed personal property) substituted for transferred property,

shall, during the lifetime of the transferor while the transferor is resident in Canada and the transferee is his spouse, be deemed to be a taxable capital gain of the transferor for the year from the disposition of property other than listed personal property;

(b) the amount, if any, by which the aggregate determined under subparagraph (a)(ii) exceeds the aggregate determined under subparagraph (a)(i) shall, during the lifetime of the transferor while the transferor is resident in Canada and the transferee is his spouse, be deemed to be an allowable capital loss of the transferor for the year from the disposition of property other than listed personal property;

(c) the amount, if any, by which

(i) the amount that the aggregate of the transferee's gains for the year from dispositions of listed personal property would be if the transferee had at no time owned listed personal property other than listed personal property that was transferred property or property substituted therefor

exceeds

(ii) the amount that the aggregate of the transferee's losses for the year from dispositions of listed personal property would be if the transferee had at no time owned listed personal property other than listed personal property that was transferred property or property substituted therefor,

shall during the lifetime of the transferor while the transferor is resident in Canada and the transferee is his spouse, be deemed to be a gain of the transferor for the year from the disposition of listed personal property;

(d) the amount, if any, by which the aggregate determined under subparagraph (c)(ii) exceeds the aggregate determined under subparagraph (c)(i) shall, during the lifetime of the transferor while the transferor is resident in Canada and the transferee is his spouse, be deemed to be a loss of the transferor for the year from the disposition of listed personal property;

(e) any taxable capital gain or allowable capital loss or any gain or loss taken into account in computing an amount described in paragraph (a), (b), (c) or (d) shall, except for the purposes of those paragraphs, to the extent that the amount so described is deemed by virtue of this subsection to be a taxable capital gain or an allowable capital loss or a gain or loss of the transferor, be deemed not to be a taxable capital gain or an allowable capital loss or a gain or loss, as the case may be, of the transferee; and

(f) such part of the capital gain or capital loss of the transferee for the year from an indexed security investment plan as may reasonably be considered to be derived from the transferred property or property substituted therefor shall, during the lifetime of the transferor while he is resident in Canada and the transferee is his spouse, be deemed to be a capital gain or capital loss, as the case may be, of the transferor for the year from an indexed security investment plan and shall be deemed not to be included in the capital gain or capital loss, as the case may be, of the transferee from his plan.

(3)–(5) [Repealed. These subsections dealt with remuneration of one's spouse as an employee before 1980.]

(6) **Application** — This section does not apply in respect of a transfer by a taxpayer of property

(a) as a payment of a premium under a registered retirement savings plan under which the taxpayer's spouse is, immediately after the transfer, the annuitant (within the meanings of subsection 146(1)); or

(b) as or on account of an amount paid by the taxpayer to his spouse in a taxation year that is deductible in computing his income for the year and is required to be included in computing the income of his spouse.

(7) **Spouse living apart** — Notwithstanding subsections (1) and (2), where a person has transferred property either directly or indirectly by means of a trust or by any other means whatever to his spouse or to a person who has since become his spouse,

(a) subsection (1) does not apply with respect to any income or loss from the property, or property substituted therefor, that relates to the period during which the person is living apart and is separated from his spouse pursuant to a decree, order or judgment of a competent tribunal or a written separation agreement; and

(b) subsection (2) does not apply with respect to a disposition of the property, or property substituted therefor, during the period the person is living apart and is separated from his spouse pursuant to a decree, order or judgment of a competent tribunal or a written separation agreement, or to any part of a capital gain or capital loss of the spouse from an indexed security investment plan that may reasonably be considered to relate to that period or any part thereof, if the person files with his return of income under this Part for the taxation year during which he commenced to so live apart and be so separated from his spouse an election completed jointly with his spouse not to have that subsection apply.

(8) **Exception** — Subsection (7) does not apply where a person who is separated from his spouse pursuant to a written separation agreement ceases to live apart from that spouse within 12 months from the date on which the agreement was entered into.

74(2)(f) above, however, applied for transfers of property from October 1, 1983 through the end of 1985.

74(7) and (8), as reproduced above, applied from December 12, 1979 through May 22, 1985. For transfers of property from May 23 through December 31, 1985, 74(7) reads differently, with respect to indexed security investment plans only.

For transfers of property made before 1980, read 74(1) and (2) as above, and also:

(6) **Transfer to RRSP** — This section does not apply in respect of a transfer of property by a taxpayer as a payment under a registered retirement savings plan under which the taxpayer's spouse is, immediately after the transfer, an annuitant, where that payment would be a premium as described in paragraph 146(1)(f) had the transferor been the annuitant under the plan.

In reading 74(7)(b), as reproduced above, where a decree, order or judgment was made, or a written separation agreement entered into, before 1981, read "for the 1980 or 1981 taxation year" in place of "for the taxation year during which he commenced to so live apart and be so separated from his spouse".

## 74.1 (1) Transfers and loans to spouse [or common-law partner] 
— Where an individual has transferred or lent property (otherwise than by an assignment of any portion of a retirement pension pursuant to section 65.1 of the *Canada Pension Plan* or a comparable provision of a provincial pension plan as defined in section 3 of that Act or of a prescribed provincial pension plan), either directly or indirectly, by means of a trust or by any other means whatever, to or for the benefit of a person who is the individual's spouse or common-law partner or who has since become the individual's spouse or common-law partner, any income or loss, as the case may be, of that person for a taxation year from the property or from property substituted therefor, that relates to the period in the year throughout which the individual is resident in Canada and that person is the individual's spouse or common-law partner, shall

be deemed to be income or a loss, as the case may be, of the individual for the year and not of that person.

**Related Provisions**: 56(2) — Indirect payments; 56(4.1) — Interest free or low interest loans; 73(1) — Transfer to spouse deemed at cost; 74.1(3) — Repayment of existing indebtedness; 74.2(1) — Gain or loss deemed that of lender or transferor; 74.3 — Transfers or loans to a trust; 74.4(4) — Benefit not granted to a designated person; 74.5(1) — Transfers for fair market value consideration; 74.5(2) — Loans for value; 74.5(3) — Spouses living apart; 74.5(6) — Back-to-back loans and transfers; 74.5(7) — Guarantees; 74.5(9) — Transfers or loans to a trust; 74.5(11) — Artificial transactions; 74.5(12) — Attribution rules — exemption; 74.5(13) — No attribution of split income subject to kiddie tax; 82(2) — Attributed dividends deemed received by taxpayer; 96(1.8) — Transfer or loan of partnership interest; 212(12) — No non-resident withholding tax where income attributed; 248(5) — Substituted property.

**Notes**: 74.1 to 74.5 are known as the "attribution" rules, since they attribute income of a transferee or borrower back to the transferor or lender of property, so as to prevent income splitting. They apply to transfers made and loans outstanding after May 22, 1985. For earlier transfers (but not loans), see repealed s. 74, which still applies to attribute income from such transferred property.

Where the loan or indebtedness is repaid with property other than the property loaned or property substituted therefor, Revenue Canada takes the position that the attribution of income under 74.1 continues. See Revenue Canada Round Table, Canadian Tax Foundation 1993 annual conference report, Q. 36.

Note that the attribution rules apply to income on the property transferred, but not to income on *that* income ("secondary" income). They also do not apply to income earned with business assets transferred or loaned, since such income is business income and not income from property.

See also 56(4.1), which provides an alternative attribution rule for loans; and Notes at end of 74.1.

74.1(1) amended by 2000 same-sex partners bill to add reference to "common-law partner", effective for the 2001 and later taxation years, or earlier by election (see Notes to 248(1)"common-law partner").

**Regulations**: 7800(1) (prescribed provincial pension plan is the Saskatchewan Pension Plan).

**Interpretation Bulletins**: IT-295R4: Taxable dividends received after 1987 by a spouse; IT-325R2: Property transfers after separation, divorce and annulment; IT-385R2: Disposition of an income interest in a trust; IT-394R2: Preferred beneficiary election; IT-434R: Rental of real property by individual; IT-511R: Interspousal and certain other transfers and loans of property; IT-531: Eligible funeral arrangements.

**(2) Transfers and loans to minors** — Where an individual has transferred or lent property, either directly or indirectly, by means of a trust or by any other means whatever, to or for the benefit of a person who was under 18 years of age (other than an amount received in respect of that person as a consequence of the operation of subsection 122.61(1)) and who

(a) does not deal with the individual at arm's length, or

(b) is the niece or nephew of the individual,

any income or loss, as the case may be, of that person for a taxation year from the property or from property substituted therefor, that relates to the period in the year throughout which the individual is resident in Canada, shall be deemed to be income or a loss, as the case may be, of the individual and not of that person unless that person has, before the end of the year, attained the age of 18 years.

**Related Provisions**: 56(2) — Indirect payments; 56(4.1) — Interest free or low interest loans; 69(1)(b) — Transfer not at arm's length deemed to be disposition at fair market value; 74.1(3) — Repayment of existing indebtedness; 74.3 — Transfers or loans to a trust; 74.4(4) — Benefit not granted to a designated person; 74.5(1) — Transfers for fair market value consideration; 74.5(2) — Loans for value; 74.5(3) — Spouses living apart; 74.5(6) — Back-to-back loans and transfers; 74.5(7) — Guarantees; 74.5(9) — Transfers or loans to a trust; 74.5(11) — Artificial transactions; 74.5(12) — Attribution rules — exemption; 74.5(13) — No attribution of split income subject to kiddie tax; 75(1) — Transfers before May 23, 1985; 82(2) — Attributed dividends deemed received by taxpayer; 96(1.8) — Transfer or loan of partnership interest; 212(12) — No non-resident withholding tax where income attributed; 248(5) — Substituted property.

**Notes**: See Notes at end of 74.1. 74.1(2) attributes income on property transferred or loaned to minors (this rule was formerly in 75(1)). There is no attribution of capital gains, however, so "growth" shares (or mutual fund units) can be given to children (directly or through a trust) for income-splitting purposes as well as for purposes of multiplying the capital gains exemption under 110.6(2.1). See also Notes to 74.1(1).

Parenthetical exclusion in the opening words of 74.1(2) added by 1992 Child Benefit bill, effective 1993. The change means that Child Tax Benefit payments may be given to the children in respect of whom they were paid, and allowed to earn income that will not be attributed back to the parents. This was already Revenue Canada's long-standing administrative policy with respect to pre-1993 family allowance payments (Information Circular 79-9R, para. 16).

**Interpretation Bulletins**: IT-268R4: *Inter vivos* transfer of farm property to child; IT-325R2: Property transfers after separation, divorce and annulment; IT-385R2: Disposition of an income interest in a trust; IT-394R2: Preferred beneficiary election; IT-434R: Rental of real property by individual; IT-510: Transfers and loans of property made after May 22, 1985 to a related minor; IT-531: Eligible funeral arrangements.

**(3) Repayment of existing indebtedness** — For the purposes of subsections (1) and (2), where, at any time, an individual has lent or transferred property (in this subsection referred to as the "lent or transferred property") either directly or indirectly, by means of a trust or by any other means whatever, to or for the benefit of a person, and the lent or transferred property or property substituted therefor is used

(a) to repay, in whole or in part, borrowed money with which other property was acquired, or

(b) to reduce an amount payable for other property,

there shall be included in computing the income from the lent or transferred property, or from property substituted therefor, that is so used, that proportion of the income or loss, as the case may be, derived after that time from the other property or from property substituted therefor that the fair market value at that time of the lent or transferred property, or property substituted therefor, that is so used is of the cost to that person of the other property at the time of its acquisition, but for greater certainty nothing in this subsection shall affect the application of subsections (1) and (2) to any income or loss derived from the other property or from property substituted therefor.

**Interpretation Bulletins [subsec. 74.1(3)]**: IT-325R2: Property transfers after separation, divorce and annulment; IT-394R2: Preferred beneficiary election; IT-510: Transfers and loans of property made after May 22, 1985 to a related minor.

**Notes [s. 74.1]**: 74.1 added by 1985 Budget, effective for property transferred after May 22, 1985 and (after 1987) for all loans. For earlier transfers, see former 74 and 75(1).

**Definitions [s. 74.1]**: "amount" — 248(1); "arm's length" — 251(1); "borrowed money" — 248(1); "Canada" — 255; "common-law partner", "individual" — 248(1); "nephew", "niece" — 252(2)(g); "person", "property" — 248(1); "resident in Canada" — 250; "substituted property" — 248(5); "taxation year" — 249; "trust" — 104(1), 248(1), (3).

**74.2 (1) Gain or loss deemed that of lender or transferor** — Where an individual has lent or transferred property (in this section referred to as "lent or transferred property"), either directly or indirectly, by means of a trust or by any other means whatever, to or for the benefit of a person (in this subsection referred to as the "recipient") who is the individual's spouse or common-law partner or who has since become the individual's spouse or common-law partner, the following rules apply for the purposes of computing the income of the individual and the recipient for a taxation year:

(a) the amount, if any, by which

(i) the total of the recipient's taxable capital gains for the year from dispositions of property (other than listed personal property) that is lent or transferred property or property substituted therefor occurring in the period (in this subsection referred to as the "attribution period") throughout which the individual is resident in Canada and the recipient is the individual's spouse or common-law partner

exceeds

(ii) the total of the recipient's allowable capital losses for the year from dispositions occurring in the attribution period of property (other than listed personal property) that is lent or transferred property or property substituted therefor

shall be deemed to be a taxable capital gain of the individual for the year from the disposition of property other than listed personal property;

(b) the amount, if any, by which the total determined under subparagraph (a)(ii) exceeds the total determined under subparagraph (a)(i) shall be deemed to be an allowable capital loss of the individual for the year from the disposition of property other than listed personal property;

(c) the amount, if any, by which

(i) the amount that the total of the recipient's gains for the year from dispositions occurring in the attribution period of listed personal property that is lent or transferred property or property substituted therefor would be if the recipient had at no time owned listed personal property other than listed personal property that was lent or transferred property or property substituted therefor

exceeds

(ii) the amount that the total of the recipient's losses for the year from dispositions of listed personal property that is lent or transferred property or property substituted therefor would be if the recipient had at no time owned listed personal property other than listed personal property that was lent or transferred property or property substituted therefor,

shall be deemed to be a gain of the individual for the year from the disposition of listed personal property;

(d) the amount, if any, by which the total determined under subparagraph (c)(ii) exceeds the total determined under subparagraph (c)(i) shall be deemed to be a loss of the individual for the year from the disposition of listed personal property; and

(e) any taxable capital gain or allowable capital loss or any gain or loss taken into account in computing an amount described in paragraph (a), (b), (c) or (d) shall, except for the purposes of those paragraphs and to the extent that the amount so described is deemed by virtue of this subsection to be a taxable capital gain or an allowable capital loss or a gain or loss of the individual, be deemed not to be a taxable capital gain or an allowable capital loss or a gain or loss, as the case may be, of the recipient.

**Related Provisions**: 73(1) — Transfer to spouse deemed at cost; 74.1(1) — Transfers and loans to spouse; 74.2(3) — Application to disposition on emigration; 74.3 — Transfers or loans to a trust; 74.4(4) — Benefit not granted to a designated person; 74.5(1) — Transfer for fair market value consideration; 74.5(2) — Loans for value; 74.5(3) — Spouses living apart; 74.5(6) — Back-to-back loans and transfers; 74.5(7) — Guarantees; 74.5(12) — Attribution rules — exemption; 248(5) — Substituted property.

**Notes**: 74.2(1) amended by 2000 same-sex partners bill to add reference to "common-law partner", effective for the 2001 and later taxation years, or earlier by election (see Notes to 248(1)"common-law partner").

74.2(1) added by 1985 Budget, effective for property transferred after May 22, 1985 and (after 1987) for all loans. For earlier transfers, see former 74. For transfers to minor children, see Notes to 74.1(2).

**Interpretation Bulletins**: IT-325R2: Property transfers after separation, divorce and annulment; IT-394R2: Preferred beneficiary election; IT-511R: Interspousal and certain other transfers and loans of property; IT-531: Eligible funeral arrangements.

**(2) Deemed gain or loss** — Where an amount is deemed by subsection (1) or 75(2) or section 75.1 of this Act, or subsection 74(2) of the *Income Tax Act*, chapter 148 of the Revised Statutes of Canada, 1952, to be a taxable capital gain or an allowable capital loss of an individual for a taxation year,

(a) for the purposes of sections 3 and 111, as they apply for the purposes of section 110.6, such portion of the gain or loss as may reasonably be con-

Subdivision f — Rules Relating to Computation of Income     S. 74.3(1)(b)(i)

sidered to relate to the disposition of a property by another person in the year shall be deemed to arise from the disposition of that property by the individual in the year; and

(b) for the purposes of section 110.6, that property shall be deemed to have been disposed of by the individual on the day on which it was disposed of by the other person.

**Notes**: Reference to 75(2) in opening words of 74.2(2) added by 1991 technical bill, effective 1987.

Final words of 74.2(2)(b) amended by 1994 Budget, effective 1994, to change "in the year" to "on the day on which it was disposed of by the other person". The change allows the disposition to be recorded either as before February 23, 1994 for purposes of the capital gains exemption in 110.6(3), or as after February 22, 1994, in which case that exemption is not available.

**I.T. Application Rules**: 69 (meaning of "*Income Tax Act*, chapter 148 of the Revised Statutes of Canada, 1952").

**Interpretation Bulletins [subsec. 74.2(2)]**: IT-369R: Attribution of trust income to settlor; IT-394R2: Preferred beneficiary election.

### Proposed Addition — 74.2(3), (4)

**(3) Election for subsection (1) to apply** — Subsection (1) does not apply to a disposition at any particular time (in this subsection referred to as the "emigration disposition") under paragraph 128.1(4)(b), by a taxpayer who is a recipient referred to in subsection (1), unless the recipient and the individual referred to in that subsection, in their returns of income for the taxation year that includes the first time, after the particular time, at which the recipient disposes of the property, jointly elect that subsection (1) apply to the emigration disposition.

**Related Provisions**: 74.2(4) — Application rule.

**(4) Application of subsection (3)** — For the purpose of applying subsection (3) and notwithstanding subsections 152(4) to (5), any assessment of tax payable under this Act by the recipient or the individual referred to in subsection (1) shall be made that is necessary to take an election under subsection (3) into account except that no such assessment shall affect the computation of

(a) interest payable under this Act to or by a taxpayer in respect of any period that is before the taxpayer's filing-due date for the taxation year that includes the first time, after the particular time referred to in subsection (3), at which the recipient disposes of the property referred to in that subsection; or

(b) any penalty payable under this Act.

**Application**: Bill C-43 (First Reading September 20, 2000), s. 34, will add subsecs. 74.2(3) and (4), applicable after October 1, 1996.

**Technical Notes**: Section 74.2 attributes to an individual taxable capital gains and allowable capital losses realized by the individual's spouse on the disposition of property that was loaned or transferred by the individual to or for the benefit of the individual's spouse, or someone who has since become the individual's spouse.

If the individual's spouse emigrates from Canada after having received the property, an accrued gain or loss on the property that is deemed to be realized by the spouse under paragraph 128.1(4)(b) could be attributed to the individual, resulting in anomalies in the application of the post-emigration loss rules under subsection 128.1(8) and the security rules under subsection 220(4.5). To prevent such anomalies, new subsection 74.2(3) provides that the attribution rule in subsection 74.2(1) does not apply to the deemed disposition under paragraph 128.1(4)(b) unless the individual and the individual's spouse jointly elect, in their tax returns for the taxation year during which the spouse disposes of the property for the first time after emigration, that the rule apply to the deemed disposition.

New subsection 74.2(4) allows any assessment of tax to be made that is necessary for the joint election to be taken into account, but provides that no such assessment shall affect the computation of interest or penalties payable.

**Definitions [s. 74.2]**: "allowable capital loss" — 38(b), 248(1); "amount", "assessment" — 248(1); "Canada" — 255; "common-law partner", "disposition", "filing-due date", "individual" — 248(1); "listed personal property" — 54, 248(1); "person", "property" — 248(1); "resident in Canada" — 250; "substituted property" — 248(5); "taxable capital gain" — 38(a), 248(1); "taxation year" — 249; "taxpayer" — 248(1); "trust" — 104(1), 248(1), (3).

**74.3 (1) Transfers or loans to a trust** — Where an individual has lent or transferred property (in this section referred to as "lent or transferred property"), either directly or indirectly, by means of a trust or by any other means whatever, to a trust in which another individual who is at any time a designated person in respect of the individual is beneficially interested at any time, the following rules apply:

(a) for the purposes of section 74.1, the income of the designated person for a taxation year from the lent or transferred property shall be deemed to be an amount equal to the lesser of

(i) the amount in respect of the trust that was included by virtue of paragraph 12(1)(m) in computing the income for the year of the designated person, and

(ii) that proportion of the amount that would be the income of the trust for the year from the lent or transferred property or from property substituted therefor if no deduction were made under subsections 104(6) or (12) that

(A) the amount determined under subparagraph (i) in respect of the designated person for the year

is of

(B) the total of all amounts each of which is an amount determined under subparagraph (i) for the year in respect of the designated person or any other person who is throughout the year a designated person in respect of the individual; and

(b) for the purposes of section 74.2, an amount equal to the lesser of

(i) the amount that was designated under subsection 104(21) in respect of the designated person in the trust's return of income for the year, and

(ii) the amount, if any, by which

(A) the total of all amounts each of which is a taxable capital gain for the year from the disposition by the trust of the lent or transferred property or property substituted therefor

exceeds

(B) the total of all amounts each of which is an allowable capital loss for the year from the disposition by the trust of the lent or transferred property or property substituted therefor,

shall be deemed to be a taxable capital gain of the designated person for the year from the disposition of property (other than listed personal property) that is lent or transferred property.

**Related Provisions**: 56(4.1) — Interest free or low-interest loans; 74.4(4) — Benefit not granted to a designated person; 74.5(5) — "Designated person"; 74.5(6) — Back to back loans and transfers; 74.5(7) — Guarantees; 74.5(12) — Attribution rules — exemption; 74.5(13) — No attribution of split income subject to kiddie tax; 75(2) — Reversionary trusts — attribution rules; 82(2) — Attributed dividends deemed received by individual; 96(1.8) — Transfer or loan of partnership interest; 212(12) — No non-resident withholding tax where income attributed; 248(5) — Substituted property; 248(25) — Beneficially interested.

**Interpretation Bulletins**: IT-394R2: Preferred beneficiary election; IT-510: Transfers and loans of property made after May 22, 1985 to a related minor; IT-511R: Interspousal and certain other transfers and loans of property.

**(2) Definition of "designated person"** — In this section, "designated person", in respect of an individual, has the meaning assigned by subsection 74.5(5).

**Notes**: 74.3(2) added in the R.S.C. 1985 (5th Supp.) consolidation, effective for taxation years ending after November 1991. This rule of application was formerly contained within 74.5(5).

**Notes [s. 74.3]**: 74.3 added by 1985 Budget, effective for property transferred after May 22, 1985 and (after 1987) for all loans. For earlier transfers, see former 74 and 75.

**Definitions [s. 74.3]**: "allowable capital loss" — 38(b), 248(1); "amount" — 248(1); "beneficially interested" — 248(25); "designated person" — 74.3(2), 74.5(5); "individual" — 248(1); "listed personal property" — 54, 248(1); "property" — 248(1); "substituted property" — 248(5); "taxable capital gain" — 38(a), 248(1); "taxation year" — 249; "trust" — 104(1), 248(1), (3).

**74.4 (1) Definitions** — In this section,

**"designated person"**, in respect of an individual, has the meaning assigned by subsection 74.5(5);

**Notes**: 74.4(1)"designated person" added in the R.S.C. 1985 (5th Supp.) consolidation, effective for taxation years ending after November 1991. This rule of application was formerly contained within 74.5(5).

**"excluded consideration"**, at any time, means consideration received by an individual that is

(a) indebtedness,

(b) a share of the capital stock of a corporation, or

(c) a right to receive indebtedness or a share of the capital stock of a corporation.

**(2) Transfers and loans to corporations** — Where an individual has transferred or lent property, either directly or indirectly, by means of a trust or by any other means whatever, to a corporation and one of the main purposes of the transfer or loan may reasonably be considered to be to reduce the income of the individual and to benefit, either directly or indirectly, by means of a trust or by any other means whatever, a person who is a designated person in respect of the individual, in computing the income of the individual for any taxation year that includes a period after the loan or transfer throughout which

(a) the person is a designated person in respect of the individual and would have been a specified shareholder of the corporation if the definition "specified shareholder" in subsection 248(1) were read without reference to paragraphs (a) and (d) of that definition and if the reference therein to "any other corporation that is related to the corporation" were read as a reference to "any other corporation (other than a small business corporation) that is related to the corporation",

(b) the individual was resident in Canada, and

(c) the corporation was not a small business corporation,

the individual shall be deemed to have received as interest in the year the amount, if any, by which

(d) the amount that would be interest on the outstanding amount of the loan or transferred property for such periods in the year if the interest were computed thereon at the prescribed rate of interest for such periods

exceeds the total of

(e) any interest received in the year by the individual in respect of the transfer or loan (other than amounts deemed by this subsection to be interest),

(f) $5/4$ of all taxable dividends received (other than dividends deemed by section 84 to have been received) by the individual in the year on shares that were received from the corporation as consideration for the transfer or as repayment for the loan that were excluded consideration at the time the dividends were received or on shares substituted therefor that were excluded consideration at that time, and

(g) where the designated person is a specified individual in relation to the year, the amount required to be included in computing the designated person's income for the year in respect of all taxable dividends received by the designated person that

(i) can reasonably be considered to be part of the benefit sought to be conferred, and

## Subdivision f — Rules Relating to Computation of Income — S. 74.4

(ii) are included in computing the designated person's split income for any taxation year.

**Related Provisions**: 56(4.1) — Interest free or low interest loan to individual; 74.4(4) — Benefit not granted to a designated person; 82(2) — Attributed dividends deemed received by individual; 248(5) — Substituted property. See additional Related Provisions and Definitions at end of s. 74.4.

**Notes**: Because of 74.4(2)(c), the shares of a small business corporation (as defined in 248(1)) can be used for income splitting (through a trust or otherwise) with one's spouse or children.

See also Notes to 56(2) regarding attempts to apply that provision to counter income-splitting that is done through corporations.

74.4(2)(a) amended by 1991 technical bill, effective (since 1988) for loans and transfers made after October 27, 1986 (which is the application for all of 74.4), to add the words from "and if the reference" to the end. The reason for the amendment is to ignore, in determining whether a designated person is a specified shareholder of a corporation, any shareholdings in a related small business corporation.

74.4(2)(g) added by 1999 Budget, effective for 2000 and later taxation years. (It applies to "split income" taxed under 120.4.)

**Regulations**: 4301(c) (prescribed rate of interest for 74.4(2)(d)).

**Interpretation Bulletins**: IT-394R2: Preferred beneficiary election.

**Information Circulars**: 88-2, para. 10: General anti-avoidance rule — section 245 of the *Income Tax Act*.

**I.T. Technical News**: No. 16 (*Neuman* case).

**Advance Tax Rulings**: ATR-25: Estate freeze; ATR-36: Estate freeze; ATR-47: Transfer of assets to Realtyco.

**(3) Outstanding amount** — For the purposes of subsection (2), the outstanding amount of a transferred property or loan at a particular time is

(a) in the case of a transfer of property to a corporation, the amount, if any, by which the fair market value of the property at the time of the transfer exceeds the total of

(i) the fair market value, at the time of the transfer, of the consideration (other than consideration that is excluded consideration at the particular time) received by the transferor for the property, and

(ii) the fair market value, at the time of receipt, of any consideration (other than consideration that is excluded consideration at the particular time) received by the transferor at or before the particular time from the corporation or from a person with whom the transferor deals at arm's length, in exchange for excluded consideration previously received by the transferor as consideration for the property or for excluded consideration substituted for such consideration;

(b) in the case of a loan of money or property to a corporation, the amount, if any, by which

(i) the principal amount of the loan of money at the time the loan was made, or

(ii) the fair market value of the property lent at the time the loan was made,

as the case may be, exceeds the fair market value, at the time the repayment is received by the lender, of any repayment of the loan (other than a repayment that is excluded consideration at the particular time).

**(4) Benefit not granted to a designated person** — For the purposes of subsection (2), one of the main purposes of a transfer or loan by an individual to a corporation shall not be considered to be to benefit, either directly or indirectly, a designated person in respect of the individual, where

(a) the only interest that the designated person has in the corporation is a beneficial interest in shares of the corporation held by a trust;

(b) by the terms of the trust, the designated person may not receive or otherwise obtain the use of any of the income or capital of the trust while being a designated person in respect of the individual; and

(c) the designated person has not received or otherwise obtained the use of any of the income or capital of the trust, and no deduction has been made by the trust in computing its income under subsection 104(6) or (12) in respect of amounts paid or payable to, or included in the income of, that person while being a designated person in respect of the individual.

**Related Provisions [s. 74.4]**: 51(1)(e) — Exchange deemed transfer of convertible property by taxpayer to corporation; 74.5(4) — Exemption where spouses are living separate and apart; 74.5(5) — "Meaning of designated person"; 74.5(6) — Back-to-back loans and transfers; 74.5(7) — Guarantees; 74.5(9) — Transfers or loans to a trust; 74.5(11) — Artificial transactions; 82(2) — Dividends deemed received; 87(2)(j.7) — Amalgamations — continuing corporation; 212(12) — No non-resident withholding tax where income attributed; 248(25) — Meaning of "beneficial interest".

**Notes [s. 74.4]**: 74.4 added in 1986, effective (since 1988) for loans and transfers made after October 27, 1986. For loans and transfers made from November 22, 1985 through October 27, 1986, read:

74.4 (1) Definitions — In this section,

"designated benefit", at any particular time, in respect of property loaned or transferred either directly or indirectly by means of a trust or by any other means whatever by an individual (in this definition referred to as the "transferor") to a corporation, means

(a) in the case of a loan of property that is money, the principal amount of the loan outstanding at the particular time,

(b) in the case of a loan of property other than money, the fair market value of the property at the time the loan was made, and

(c) in the case of a transfer of property, the amount, if any, by which

(i) the fair market value of the property at the time the transfer was made to the corporation

exceeds

(ii) the aggregate of

(A) the fair market value, at the time the transfer was made, of the consideration, other than consideration that is excluded consideration at the particular time, received by the transferor for the property, and

555

(B) the fair market value, at the time of receipt, of any consideration, other than consideration that is excluded consideration at the particular time, received by the transferor at or before the particular time from the corporation or from a person with whom the transferor deals at arm's length, in exchange for excluded consideration previously received by the transferor as consideration for the property;

"designated shareholder" of a subject corporation in respect of an individual means a shareholder of the subject corporation that is

(a) a person who is the individual's spouse,

(b) a person who is under 18 years of age,

(c) a partnership of which a person described in paragraph (a) or (b) is a member,

(d) a trust in which a person described in paragraph (a) or (b) is beneficially interested, or

(e) a corporation (other than a small business corporation) of which a person described in paragraph (a) or (b) is a specified shareholder;

"excluded consideration", at any time, means consideration received by an individual that is

(a) indebtedness,

(b) a share of the capital stock of a corporation, where the articles of the corporation provide for more than one class of shares at that time, or

(c) a right to receive a share described in paragraph (b);

"monthly designated benefit" in respect of a property, for a month or a portion thereof, means the greatest amount that the designated benefit in respect of the property is at any time in the month or the portion, as the case may be.

(2) **Transfers and loans to corporation for benefit of spouse or minor** — Where an individual has loaned or transferred property, either directly or indirectly, by means of a trust or by any other means whatever, to a corporation (in this section referred to as the "subject corporation") other than a small business corporation, in computing the income of the individual for a taxation year, with respect to the period (in this section referred to as the "relevant period") in the year and after the time of the loan or transfer and throughout which the individual is resident in Canada and any shareholder of the subject corporation is a designated shareholder in respect of the individual, an amount equal to the amount calculated under subsection (3) in respect of the property shall be deemed to be a taxable dividend received by the individual in the year from the subject corporation.

(3) **Calculation of amount** — For the purpose of subsection (2), the amount calculated under this subsection in respect of the property with respect to the relevant period in the year is the amount, if any, by which the lesser of

(a) the amount, if any, by which

(i) the aggregate of

(A) the aggregate of all amounts each of which is the product obtained when

(I) the monthly designated benefit in respect of the property for a month, or a portion thereof, in the relevant period

is multiplied by

(II) $2/3$ of the quotient obtained when the rate of interest prescribed for the purpose of subsection 161(1) that is in effect during that month is divided by 12, and

(B) the aggregate of all amounts each of which is an amount calculated under clause (A) in respect of the property with respect to a relevant period in a preceding taxation year

exceeds

(ii) the aggregate of

(A) the aggregate of all amounts each of which is a taxable dividend paid in the year or a preceding taxation year to the individual or to a taxable Canadian corporation that is wholly-owned by him, on a share that is excluded consideration received by him as consideration for the loan or transfer of the property or excluded consideration substituted therefor, and

(B) $2/3$ of the aggregate of all amounts each of which is an amount included in computing the income for the year or a preceding taxation year of the individual or a taxable Canadian corporation that is wholly-owned by him as interest on excluded consideration, received by him as consideration for the loan or transfer of the property or on excluded consideration substituted therefor, and

(b) the aggregate of all amounts each of which is

(i) a taxable dividend paid by the subject corporation in the relevant period or a relevant period in a preceding taxation year to a designated shareholder of the subject corporation in respect of the individual, or

(ii) a capital gain of the individual's spouse from a disposition of property occurring in the relevant period or in a relevant period in a preceding taxation year, to the extent that the gain may reasonably be attributed to an increase in the value of the property loaned or transferred or of property substituted therefor

exceeds

(c) the aggregate of all amounts each of which is an amount calculated under this subsection for the purpose of subsection (2) in respect of the property for a preceding taxation year.

(4) **Deduction permitted** — Where an individual has loaned or transferred property, either directly or indirectly, by means of a trust or by any other means whatever, to a corporation and as a consequence thereof an amount (in this subsection referred to as the "attributed amount") has, by virtue of subsection (2), been deemed to be a taxable dividend received from a subject corporation by an individual in a taxation year, the following rules apply:

(a) an amount equal to the lesser of

(i) the aggregate of all taxable dividends paid by the subject corporation in the year to a designated shareholder of the subject corporation in respect of the individual, and

(ii) that portion of the attributed amount that

(A) the amount determined under subparagraph (i) in respect of the designated shareholder for the year

is of

(B) the aggregate of all amounts each of which is an amount determined under subparagraph (i) for the year in respect of a designated shareholder of the subject corporation in respect of the individual

shall be deemed not to be a taxable dividend received from the subject corporation in the year by the designated shareholder; and

(b) an amount equal to the lesser of

(i) the amount that would have been the amount determined under subparagraph (3)(b)(ii) for the year in respect of the designated shareholder if that subparagraph were read without reference to the words "or in a relevant period in a preceding taxation year", and

(ii) the amount, if any, by which

(A) the attributed amount

exceeds

(B) the aggregate of all amounts each of which is an amount determined under paragraph (a) for the year in respect of a designated shareholder of the subject corporation in respect of the individual,

shall be deemed not to be a capital gain of the designated shareholder from the disposition of a property by him in the year.

**(5) Time of dividend** — For the purposes of this section, where one or more loans or transfers of property have been made as part of a series of transactions or events which includes the payment of a dividend, and it may reasonably be considered that the payment of the dividend was made in contemplation of such loans or transfers, the dividend shall be deemed to have been paid immediately after the first such loan or transfer, as the case may be.

For earlier transfers, see repealed 74 and 75(1).

**Definitions [s. 74.4]:** "amount" — 248(1); "arm's length" — 251(1); "Canada" — 255; "corporation" — 248(1), *Interpretation Act* 35(1); "designated person" — 74.4(1), 74.5(5); "dividend" — 248(1); "excluded consideration" — 74.4(1); "individual", "person", "prescribed" — 248(1); "prescribed rate" — Reg. 4301; "principal amount", "property" — 248(1); "received" — 248(7); "resident in Canada" — 250; "share" — 248(1), "small business corporation" — 248(1); "specified individual" — 120.4(1), 248(1); "specified shareholder" — 248(1); "split income" — 120.4(1), 248(1); "substituted" — 248(5); "taxable dividend" — 89(1), 248(1); "taxation year" — 249; "trust" — 104(1), 248(1), (3).

**74.5 (1) Transfers for fair market consideration** — Notwithstanding any other provision of this Act, subsections 74.1(1) and (2) and section 74.2 do not apply to any income, gain or loss derived in a particular taxation year from transferred property or from property substituted therefor if

(a) at the time of the transfer the fair market value of the transferred property did not exceed the fair market value of the property received by the transferor as consideration for the transferred property;

(b) where the consideration received by the transferor included indebtedness,

(i) interest was charged on the indebtedness at a rate equal to or greater than the lesser of

(A) the prescribed rate that was in effect at the time the indebtedness was incurred, and

(B) the rate that would, having regard to all the circumstances, have been agreed on, at the time the indebtedness was incurred, between parties dealing with each other at arm's length,

(ii) the amount of interest that was payable in respect of the particular year in respect of the indebtedness was paid not later than 30 days after the end of the particular year, and

(iii) the amount of interest that was payable in respect of each taxation year preceding the particular year in respect of the indebtedness was paid not later than 30 days after the end of each such taxation year; and

(c) where the property was transferred to or for the benefit of the transferor's spouse or common-law partner, the transferor elected in the transferor's return of income under this Part for the taxation year in which the property was transferred not to have the provisions of subsection 73(1) apply.

**Related Provisions:** 74.5(6) — Back-to-back loans and transfers. See additional Related Provisions and Definitions at end of s. 74.5.

**Notes:** 74.5(1)(c) amended by 2000 same-sex partners bill to add reference to "common-law partner", effective for the 2001 and later taxation years, or earlier by election (see Notes to 248(1) "common-law partner").

**Regulations:** 4301(c) (prescribed rate of interest for 74.5(1)(b)(i)(A)).

**Interpretation Bulletins:** IT-394R2: Preferred beneficiary election; IT-510: Transfers and loans of property made after May 22, 1985 to a related minor; IT-511R: Interspousal and certain other transfers and loans of property.

**(2) Loans for value** — Notwithstanding any other provision of this Act, subsections 74.1(1) and (2) and section 74.2 do not apply to any income, gain or loss derived in a particular taxation year from lent property or from property substituted therefor if

(a) interest was charged on the loan at a rate equal to or greater than the lesser of

(i) the prescribed rate that was in effect at the time the loan was made, and

(ii) the rate that would, having regard to all the circumstances, have been agreed on, at the time the loan was made, between parties dealing with each other at arm's length;

(b) the amount of interest that was payable in respect of the particular year in respect of the loan was paid not later than 30 days after the end of the particular year; and

(c) the amount of interest that was payable in respect of each taxation year preceding the particular year in respect of the loan was paid not later than 30 days after the end of each such taxation year.

**Related Provisions:** 74.5(7) — Guarantees. See additional Related provisions and Definitions at end of s. 74.5.

**Regulations:** 4301(c) (prescribed rate of interest for 74.5(2)(a)(i)).

**Interpretation Bulletins:** IT-394R2: Preferred beneficiary election; IT-510: Transfers and loans of property made after May 22, 1985 to a related minor; IT-511R: Interspousal and certain other transfers and loans of property.

**(3) Spouses [or common-law partners] living apart** — Notwithstanding subsection 74.1(1) and section 74.2, where an individual has lent or transferred property, either directly or indirectly, by means of a trust or by any other means whatever, to or for the benefit of a person who is the individual's spouse or common-law partner or who has since become the individual's spouse or common-law partner,

    (a) subsection 74.1(1) does not apply to any income or loss from the property, or property substituted therefor, that relates to the period throughout which the individual is living separate and apart from that person because of a breakdown of their marriage or common-law partnership; and

    (b) section 74.2 does not apply to a disposition of the property, or property substituted therefor, occurring at any time while the individual is living separate and apart from that person because of a breakdown of their marriage or common-law partnership, if an election completed jointly with that person not to have that section apply is filed with the individual's return of income under this Part for the taxation year that includes that time or for any preceding taxation year.

**Notes**: 74.5(3) amended by 2000 same-sex partners bill to add reference to "common-law partner" and "common-law partnership", effective for the 2001 and later taxation years, or earlier by election (see Notes to 248(1)"common-law partner").

74.5(3)(b) amended by 1991 technical bill, effective for transfers of property after May 22, 1985 and loans outstanding on or after May 22, 1985, to eliminate the requirement that the election be filed in the year of separation.

**Interpretation Bulletins**: IT-394R2: Preferred beneficiary election; IT-434R: Rental of real property by individual; IT-511R: Interspousal and certain other transfers and loans of property.

**(4) Idem** — No amount shall be included in computing the income of an individual under subsection 74.4(2) in respect of a designated person in respect of the individual who is the spouse or common-law partner of the individual for any period throughout which the individual is living separate and apart from the designated person by reason of a breakdown of their marriage or common-law partnership.

**Related Provisions**: See Related Provisions and Definitions at end of s. 74.5.

**Notes**: 74.5(4) amended by 2000 same-sex partners bill to add reference to "common-law partner" and "common-law partnership", effective for the 2001 and later taxation years, or earlier by election (see Notes to 248(1)"common-law partner").

**(5) Definition of "designated person"** — For the purposes of this section, "designated person" in respect of an individual, means a person

    (a) who is the spouse or common-law partner of the individual; or

    (b) who is under 18 years of age and who

        (i) does not deal with the individual at arm's length, or

        (ii) is the niece or nephew of the individual.

**Notes**: Before consolidation in the R.S.C. 1985 (5th Supp.), 74.5(5) explicitly applied for purposes of 74.3 and 74.4. Those rules of application are now in 74.3(2) and 74.4(1).

74.5(5)(a) amended by 2000 same-sex partners bill to add reference to "common-law partner", effective for the 2001 and later taxation years, or earlier by election (see Notes to 248(1)"common-law partner").

**Interpretation Bulletins**: IT-394R2: Preferred beneficiary election; IT-511R: Interspousal and certain other transfers and loans of property.

**(6) Back to back loans and transfers** — Where an individual has lent or transferred property

    (a) to another person and that property, or property substituted therefor, is lent or transferred by any person (in this subsection referred to as a "third party") directly or indirectly to or for the benefit of a specified person with respect to the individual, or

    (b) to another person on condition that property be lent or transferred by any person (in this subsection referred to as a "third party") directly or indirectly to or for the benefit of a specified person with respect to the individual,

the following rules apply:

    (c) for the purposes of sections 74.1, 74.2, 74.3 and 74.4, the property lent or transferred by the third party shall be deemed to have been lent or transferred, as the case may be, by the individual to or for the benefit of the specified person, and

    (d) for the purposes of subsection (1), the consideration received by the third party for the transfer of the property shall be deemed to have been received by the individual.

**Related Provisions**: 74.5(8) — "Specified person". See additional Related Provisions and Definitions at end of s. 74.5.

**Interpretation Bulletins**: IT-394R2: Preferred beneficiary election; IT-510: Transfers and loans of property made after May 22, 1985 to a related minor; IT-511R: Interspousal and certain other transfers and loans of property.

**(7) Guarantees** — Where an individual is obligated, either absolutely or contingently, to effect any undertaking including any guarantee, covenant or agreement given to ensure the repayment, in whole or in part, of a loan made by any person (in this subsection referred to as the "third party") directly or indirectly to or for the benefit of a specified person with respect to the individual or the payment, in whole or in part, of any interest payable in respect of the loan, the following rules apply:

    (a) for the purposes of sections 74.1, 74.2, 74.3 and 74.4, the property lent by the third party shall be deemed to have been lent by the individual to or for the benefit of the specified person; and

    (b) for the purposes of paragraphs (2)(b) and (c), the amount of interest that is paid in respect of the loan shall be deemed not to include any amount paid by the individual to the third party as interest on the loan.

Subdivision f — Rules Relating to Computation of Income    S. 74.5

**Related Provisions**: 74.5(8) — "Specified person". See additional Related Provisions and Definitions at end of s. 74.5.

**Interpretation Bulletins**: IT-394R2: Preferred beneficiary election; IT-510: Transfers and loans of property made after May 22, 1985 to a related minor; IT-511R: Interspousal and certain other transfers and loans of property.

**(8) Definition of "specified person"** — For the purposes of subsections (6) and (7), "specified person", with respect to an individual, means

(a) a designated person in respect of the individual; or

(b) a corporation, other than a small business corporation, of which a designated person in respect of the individual would have been a specified shareholder if the definition "specified shareholder" in subsection 248(1) were read without reference to paragraphs (a) and (d) of that definition.

**Interpretation Bulletins**: IT-394R2: Preferred beneficiary election; IT-510: Transfers and loans of property made after May 22, 1985 to a related minor; IT-511R: Interspousal and certain other transfers and loans of property.

**(9) Transfers or loans to a trust** — Where a taxpayer has lent or transferred property, either directly or indirectly, by means of a trust or by any other means whatever, to a trust in which another taxpayer is beneficially interested, the taxpayer shall, for the purposes of this section and sections 74.1 to 74.4, be deemed to have lent or transferred the property, as the case may be, to or for the benefit of the other taxpayer.

**Related Provisions**: 248(25) — Beneficially interested.

**Interpretation Bulletins**: IT-394R2: Preferred beneficiary election; IT-510: Transfers and loans of property made after May 22, 1985 to a related minor; IT-511R: Interspousal and certain other transfers and loans of property.

**(10)** [Repealed]

**Notes**: 74.5(10), repealed by 1992 technical bill, defined "beneficially interested" (in a trust), for purposes of 74.1–74.5. The definition was moved to 248(25), effective 1991.

**(11) Artificial transactions** — Notwithstanding any other provision of this Act, sections 74.1 to 74.4 do not apply to a transfer or loan of property where it may reasonably be concluded that one of the main reasons for the transfer or loan was to reduce the amount of tax that would, but for this subsection, be payable under this Part on the income and gains derived from the property or from property substituted therefor.

**Notes**: 74.5(11) prevents "reverse attribution" — using the attribution rules backwards with the intent of having them apply to reduce tax.

**Interpretation Bulletins**: IT-394R2: Preferred beneficiary election; IT-510: Transfers and loans of property made after May 22, 1985 to a related minor; IT-511R: Interspousal and certain other transfers and loans of property.

**(12) Where sections 74.1 to 74.3 do not apply** — Sections 74.1, 74.2 and 74.3 do not apply in respect of a transfer by an individual of property

(a) as a payment of a premium under a registered retirement savings plan under which the individual's spouse or common-law partner is, immediately after the transfer, the annuitant (within the meaning of subsection 146(1)) to the extent that the premium is deductible in computing the income of the individual for a taxation year;

(a.1) as an amount contributed under a provincial pension plan prescribed for the purposes of paragraph 60(v) under which the individual's spouse or common-law partner is, immediately after the transfer, the annuitant (within the meaning assigned by subsection 146(1)) or the owner of the account under the plan to the extent that the amount does not exceed the amount by which the amount prescribed for the purposes of subparagraph 60(v)(ii) for the year in respect of the plan exceeds the total of all other contributions to the plan for the year to the account of the spouse or common-law partner under the plan; or

(b) as or on account of an amount paid by the individual to another individual who is the individual's spouse or common-law partner or a person who was under 18 years of age in a taxation year and who

(i) does not deal with the individual at arm's length, or

(ii) is the niece or nephew of the individual,

that is deductible in computing the individual's income for the year and is required to be included in computing the income of the other individual.

**Related Provisions**: 146(5.1) — Amount of spousal RRSP premiums deductible; 146(8.3) — Attribution on spousal RRSP payments if withdrawn soon.

**Notes**: 74.5(12) amended by 2000 same-sex partners bill to add reference to "common-law partner", effective for the 2001 and later taxation years, or earlier by election (see Notes to 248(1)"common-law partner").

**Interpretation Bulletins [subsec. 74.5(12)]**: IT-394R2: Preferred beneficiary election; IT-510: Transfers and loans of property made after May 22, 1985 to a related minor; IT-511R: Interspousal and certain other transfers and loans of property.

**(13) Exception from attribution rules [kiddie tax]** — Subsections 74.1(1) and (2), 74.3(1) and 75(2) of this Act and section 74 of the *Income Tax Act*, chapter 148 of the Revised Statutes of Canada, 1952, do not apply to any amount that is included in computing a specified individual's split income for a taxation year.

**Notes**: 74.5(13) added by 1999 Budget, effective for 2000 and later taxation years. It provides that the attribution rules do not apply to income that is taxed at a high rate under the "kiddie tax" in 120.4.

**Related Provisions [s. 74.5]**: 51(1)(c) — Exchange deemed transfer of convertible property by taxpayer to corporation; 87(2)(j.7) — Amalgamations — continuing corporation; 248(5) — Substituted property.

## S. 74.5 — Income Tax Act, Part I, Division B

**Notes [s. 74.5]**: 74.5 added by 1985 Budget, effective for transfers of property after May 22, 1985 and (after 1987) for all loans.

**Definitions [s. 74.5]**: "amount" — 248(1); "arm's length" — 251(1); "beneficially interested" — 248(25); "capital gain" — 39(1)(a), 248(1); "common-law partner", "common-law partnership" — 248(1); "corporation" — 248(1), *Interpretation Act* 35(1); "designated person" — 74.5(5); "individual" — 248(1); "nephew", "niece" — 252(2)(g); "person", "prescribed" — 248(1); "prescribed rate" — Reg. 4301; "property" — 248(1); "registered retirement savings plan" — 146(1), 248(1); "shareholder", "small business corporation" — 248(1); "specified individual" — 120.4(1), 248(1); "specified person" — 74.5(8); "specified shareholder" — 248(1); "split income" — 120.4(1), 248(1); "substituted property" — 248(5); "taxable dividend" — 89(1), 248(1); "taxation year" — 249; "taxpayer" — 248(1); "trust" — 104(1), 248(1), (3).

### 75. (1) [Repealed under former Act]

**Notes**: 75(1) repealed by 1985 Budget (on the introduction of new attribution rules in 74.1 through 74.5), effective for transfers of property after May 22, 1985. See now 74.1(2). For earlier transfers, read:

> 75. (1) **Transfers to minors** — Where a taxpayer has, since 1930, transferred property to a person who was under 18 years of age, either directly or indirectly, by means of a trust or by any other means whatever, any income or loss, as the case may be, for a taxation year from the property or from property substituted therefor shall, during the lifetime of the transferor while he is resident in Canada, be deemed to be income or a loss, as the case may be, of the transferor and not of the transferee, unless the transferee has, before the end of the year, attained the age of 18 years.

**(2) Trusts** — Where, by a trust created in any manner whatever since 1934, property is held on condition

  (a) that it or property substituted therefor may

    (i) revert to the person from whom the property or property for which it was substituted was directly or indirectly received (in this subsection referred to as "the person"), or

    (ii) pass to persons to be determined by the person at a time subsequent to the creation of the trust, or

  (b) that, during the lifetime of the person, the property shall not be disposed of except with the person's consent or in accordance with the person's direction,

any income or loss from the property or from property substituted therefor, any taxable capital gain or allowable capital loss from the disposition of the property or of property substituted therefor, shall, during the lifetime of the person while the person is resident in Canada be deemed to be income or a loss, as the case may be, or a taxable capital gain or allowable capital loss, as the case may be, of the person.

#### Proposed Amendment — 75(2)

(b) that, during the existence of the person, the property shall not be disposed of except with the person's consent or in accordance with the person's direction,

any income or loss from the property or from property substituted for the property, and any taxable capital gain or allowable capital loss from the disposition of the property or of property substituted for the property, shall, during the existence of the person while the person is resident in Canada, be deemed to be income or a loss, as the case may be, or a taxable capital gain or allowable capital loss, as the case may be, of the person.

**Application**: Bill C-43 (First Reading September 20, 2000), subsec. 35(1), will amend the portion of subsec. 75(2) after para. (a) to read as above, applicable to taxation years that begin after 2000.

**Technical Notes**: Subsection 75(2) generally provides for the attribution of income from a trust property to a person resident in Canada where that property was received by the trust from the person and can revert to the person (or pass to other persons determined by that person).

Subsection 75(2) is amended to clarify that the reference to "person" in the provision includes a corporation.

**Related Provisions**: 56(4.1) — Interest free or low interest loans; 73(1) — Rollover of capital property to revocable living trust; 74.2(2) — Deemed gain or loss; 74.5(13) — No attribution of split income subject to kiddie tax; 75(3) — Exceptions; 82(2) — Dividends deemed received; 107(4.1) — Denial of rollover under subsec. 107(2); 107.4(1)(e) — No qualifying disposition where settlor can change beneficiaries of trust; 160(1) — Tax liability — non-arm's length property transfer; 212(12) — Deemed payments to spouse, etc; 248(5) — Substituted property; 256(1.2)(f)(iv) — Associated corporations — where shares owned by trust described in 75(2).

**Notes**: A trust described in 75(2)(a) is often referred to as a "reversionary trust" or a "revocable trust".

For a detailed discussion of 75(2), see John Saunders, "*Inter Vivos* Discretionary Family Trusts", 1993 Canadian Tax Foundation annual conference report, at 37:6–37:14.

See also Notes to 248(1)"disposition" regarding revocable living trusts.

**Interpretation Bulletins**: IT-325R2: Property transfers after separation, divorce and annulment; IT-394R2: Preferred beneficiary election; IT-369R: Attribution of trust income to settlor; IT-447: Residence of a trust or estate; IT-531: Eligible funeral arrangements.

**I.T. Technical News**: No. 7 (revocable living trusts; protective trusts).

**(3) Exceptions** — Subsection (2) does not apply to property held in a taxation year

  (a) by a trust governed by a registered pension plan, an employees profit sharing plan, a registered supplementary unemployment benefit plan, a registered retirement savings plan, a deferred profit sharing plan, a registered education savings plan, a registered retirement income fund or an employee benefit plan;

  (b) by an employee trust, a related segregated fund trust (within the meaning assigned by paragraph 138.1(1)(a)) or a trust described in paragraph 149(1)(y);

#### Proposed Amendment — 75(3)(a), (b)

(a) by a trust governed by a deferred profit sharing plan, an employee benefit plan, an employees profit sharing plan, a registered education

Subdivision f — Rules Relating to Computation of Income   S. 75.1(1)(b)

savings plan, a registered pension plan, a registered retirement income fund, a registered retirement savings plan, a registered supplementary unemployment benefit plan or a retirement compensation arrangement;

(b) by an employee trust, a related segregated fund trust (within the meaning assigned by paragraph 138.1(1)(a)), a trust described in paragraph (a.1) of the definition "trust" in subsection 108(1), or a trust described in paragraph 149(1)(y);

**Application**: Bill C-43 (First Reading September 20, 2000), subsec. 35(2), will amend paras. 75(3)(a) and (b) to read as above, para. (a) applicable to taxation years that end after October 8, 1986 and, notwithstanding subsecs. 152(4) to (5), the Minister of National Revenue shall make any assessments, reassessments and additional assessments of tax, interest and penalties that are necessary to give effect to the words "retirement compensation arrangement" in para. 75(3)(a); and para. (b) applicable to 1999 *et seq.*

**Technical Notes**: Subsection 75(3) exempts certain trusts from the application of subsection 75(2), which generally provides for the attribution of income from a trust property to a person resident in Canada where that property was received by the trust from the person and can revert to the person (or pass to other persons determined by that person).

Paragraph 75(3)(a) is amended to extend the exemption to trusts governed by retirement compensation arrangements (as defined in subsection 248(1)). These trusts are subject to tax in the hands of the trustee under Part XI.3. This amendment ensures that these trusts will not also be subject to tax under Part I in the hands of a person (typically an employer) who made contributions to the trust. This amendment applies to taxation years ending after October 8, 1986, the date on which the retirement compensation arrangement rules were originally announced.

Paragraph 75(3)(b) is amended to extend the exemption to a trust described in paragraph (a.1) of the definition "trust" in subsection 108(1). For additional information on new paragraph (a.1) of the definition "trust", see the commentary on that provision.

(c) by a trust that

(i) is not resident in Canada,

(ii) is resident in a country under the laws of which an income tax is imposed,

(iii) is exempt under the laws referred to in subparagraph (ii) from the payment of income tax to the government of the country of which the trust is a resident, and

(iv) was established principally in connection with, or the principal purpose of which is to administer or provide benefits under, one or more superannuation, pension or retirement funds or plans or any funds or plans established to provide employee benefits;

(c.1) by a qualifying environmental trust; or

**Proposed Addition — 75(3)(c.2)**

(c.2) by a trust that is non-resident for the purposes of computing its income for the year, notwithstanding that there is a person who is, at the end of the year, both resident in Canada and a contributor (as defined in section 94) to the trust; or

**Application**: The June 22, 2000 draft legislation, s. 6, will add para. 75(3)(c.2), applicable to trust taxation years that begin after 2000.

**Technical Notes**: Subsection 75(2) generally provides that, where a person transfers property to a trust under certain conditions, the income from the property is attributed to the person. Subsection 75(3) exempts certain trusts from this attribution rule.

Subsection 75(3) is amended so that it does not apply to a trust that is not resident in Canada for the purposes of computing its income, notwithstanding that there is a person who is, at the end of the year, both resident in Canada and a contributor (as defined in section 94) to the trust. In effect, this exception will generally apply to trusts in respect of which the contributors are recent immigrants to Canada (i.e., resident in Canada for not more than 60 months). The exception is consistent with similar 60-month exemptions in:

- section 94 (see the definition of "resident contributor" in subsection 94(1) and subsection 94(3)),
- section 94.1 (see paragraph 94.1(2)(a)), and
- section 94.2 (see subparagraph 94.2(3)(b)(i)).

(d) by a prescribed trust.

**Notes**: 75(3)(c.1) added by 1994 Budget, effective for taxation years that end after February 22, 1994; and amended retroactive to its introduction by 1997 Budget to change "mining reclamation trust" to "qualifying environmental trust". (The latter term has replaced the former throughout the Act.)

**Regulations [subsec. 75(3)]**: No trusts prescribed for purposes of 75(3)(d) to date.

**Definitions [s. 75]**: "allowable capital loss" — 38(b), 248(1); "Canada" — 255; "capital gain", "capital loss" — 39(1), 248(1); "deferred profit sharing plan" — 147(1), 248(1); "employee benefit plan" — 248(1); "employees profit sharing plan" — 144(1), 248(1); "employee trust", "person", "property" — 248(1); "qualifying environmental trust" — 248(1); "registered education savings plan" — 146.1(1), 248(1); "registered pension plan" — 248(1); "registered retirement income fund" — 146.3(1), 248(1); "registered retirement savings plan" — 146(1), 248(1); "registered supplementary unemployment benefit plan" — 145(1), 248(1); "resident in Canada" — 250; "retirement compensation arrangement" 248(1); "substituted property" — 248(5); "taxable capital gain" — 38(a), 248(1); "taxation year" — 249; "taxpayer" — 248(1); "trust" — 104(1), 248(1), (3).

**Interpretation Bulletins [s. 75]**: IT-268R3: *Inter vivos* transfer of farm property to child; IT-369R: Attribution of trust income to settlor.

## 75.1 (1) Gain or loss deemed that of transferor — Where

(a) subsection 73(3) or (4) applied to the transfer of property (in this subsection referred to as "transferred property") by a taxpayer to a child of the taxpayer,

(b) the transfer was made at less than the fair market value of the transferred property immediately before the time of the transfer, and

(c) in a taxation year, the transferee disposed of the transferred property and did not, before the end of that year, attain the age of 18 years,

the following rules apply:

(d) the amount, if any, by which

(i) the total of the transferee's taxable capital gains for the year from dispositions of transferred property

exceeds

(ii) the total of the transferee's allowable capital losses for the year from dispositions of transferred property,

shall, during the lifetime of the transferor while the transferor is resident in Canada, be deemed to be a taxable capital gain of the transferor for the year from the disposition of property,

(e) the amount, if any, by which the total determined under subparagraph (d)(ii) exceeds the total determined under subparagraph (d)(i) shall, during the lifetime of the transferor while the transferor is resident in Canada, be deemed to be an allowable capital loss of the transferor for the year from the disposition of property, and

(f) any taxable capital gain or allowable capital loss taken into account in computing an amount described in paragraph (d) or the amount described in paragraph (e) shall, except for the purposes of those paragraphs, to the extent that the amount so described is deemed by virtue of this subsection to be a taxable capital gain or an allowable capital loss of the transferor, be deemed not to be a taxable capital gain or an allowable capital loss, as the case may be, of the transferee.

**Related Provisions**: 38 — Taxable capital gain and allowable capital loss; 39(1) — Capital gain and capital loss; 74.2(2) — Deemed gain or loss.

**Notes**: 75.1(1)(a) amended by 1991 technical bill, effective for property transferred after 1989, to add the reference to 73(4).

**(2) Definition of "child"** — For the purposes of this section, "child" of a taxpayer includes a child of the taxpayer's child and a child of the taxpayer's child's child.

**Related Provisions**: 70(10) — Parallel definition for other purposes; 252(1) — Further extended meaning of "child".

**Definitions [s. 75.1]**: "allowable capital loss" — 38(b), 248(1); "amount" — 248(1); "Canada" — 255; "child" — 75.1(2), 252(1); "property" — 248(1); "resident in Canada" — 250; "taxable capital gain" — 38(a), 248(1); "taxation year" — 249; "taxpayer" — 248(1); "transferred property" — 75.1(1)(a).

**Interpretation Bulletins [s. 75.1]**: IT-268R4: *Inter vivos* transfer of farm property to child.

**76. (1) Security in satisfaction of income debt** — Where a person receives a security or other right or a certificate of indebtedness or other evidence of indebtedness wholly or partially as payment of, in lieu of payment of or in satisfaction of, a debt that is then payable, the amount of which debt would be included in computing the person's income if it were paid, the value of the security, right or indebtedness or the applicable portion thereof shall, notwithstanding the form or legal effect of the transaction, be included in computing the person's income for the taxation year in which it is received.

**Related Provisions**: 214(4) — Non-resident — securities.

**Advance Tax Rulings**: ATR-6: Vendor reacquires business assets following default by purchaser.

**(2) Idem** — Where a security or other right or a certificate of indebtedness or other evidence of indebtedness is received by a person wholly or partially as payment of, in lieu of payment of or in satisfaction of, a debt before the debt is payable, but is not itself payable or redeemable before the day on which the debt is payable, it shall, for the purpose of subsection (1), be deemed to be received by the person holding it at that time when the debt becomes payable.

**(3) Section enacted for greater certainty** — This section is enacted for greater certainty and shall not be construed as limiting the generality of the other provisions of this Part by which amounts are required to be included in computing income.

**(4) Debt deemed not to be income debt** — Where a cash purchase ticket or other form of settlement prescribed pursuant to the *Canada Grain Act* or by the Minister is issued to a taxpayer in respect of grain delivered in a taxation year of a taxpayer to a primary elevator or process elevator and the ticket or other form of settlement entitles the holder thereof to payment by the operator of the elevator of the purchase price, without interest, stated in the ticket for the grain at a date that is after the end of that taxation year, the amount of the purchase price stated in the ticket or other form of settlement shall, notwithstanding any other provision of this section, be included in computing the income of the taxpayer to whom the ticket or other form of settlement was issued for the taxpayer's taxation year immediately following the taxation year in which the grain was delivered and not for the taxation year in which the grain was delivered.

**Related Provisions**: 76(5) — Meaning of certain expressions.

**Interpretation Bulletins**: IT-184R: Deferred cash purchase tickets issued for grain; IT-433R: Farming or fishing — use of cash method.

**(5) Definitions of certain expressions** — In subsection (4), the expressions "cash purchase ticket", "operator", "primary elevator" and "process elevator" have the meanings assigned by the *Canada Grain Act* and "grain" means wheat, oats, barley, rye, flaxseed and rapeseed produced in the designated area defined by the *Canadian Wheat Board Act*.

**Related Provisions**: 24 — Ceasing to carry on business; 214(4) — Non-resident's tax on securities income.

**Definitions [s. 76]**: "amount" — 248(1); "cash purchase ticket", "grain" — 76(5); "Minister" — 248(1); "operator" — 76(5); "person" — 248(1); "primary elevator", "process elevator" — 76(5); "taxpayer" — 248(1); "taxation year" — 249.

Subdivision f — Rules Relating to Computation of Income S. 78(1)(b)(i)

**Interpretation Bulletins [s. 76]**: IT-77R: Securities in satisfaction of an income debt.

### Proposed Addition — 76.1

**76.1 (1) Non-resident moving debt from Canadian business** — If at any time a debt obligation of a non-resident taxpayer that is denominated in a foreign currency ceases to be an obligation of the taxpayer in respect of a business or part of a business carried on by the taxpayer in Canada immediately before that time (other than an obligation in respect of which the taxpayer ceased to be indebted at that time), for the purpose of determining the amount of any income, loss, capital gain or capital loss due to the fluctuation in the value of the foreign currency relative to Canadian currency, the taxpayer is deemed to have settled the debt obligation immediately before that time at the amount outstanding on account of its principal amount.

**(2) Non-resident assuming debt** — If at any time a debt obligation of a non-resident taxpayer that is denominated in a foreign currency becomes an obligation of the taxpayer in respect of a business or part of a business that the taxpayer carries on in Canada after that time (other than an obligation in respect of which the taxpayer became indebted at that time), the amount of any income, loss, capital gain or capital loss in respect of the obligation due to the fluctuation in the value of the foreign currency relative to Canadian currency shall be determined based on the amount of the obligation in Canadian currency at that time.

**Application**: The August 8, 2000 draft legislation (authorized foreign banks), s. 5, will add s. 76.1, applicable after June 27, 1999 in respect of an authorized foreign bank, and after August 8, 2000 in any other case.

**Technical Notes**: New section 76.1 sets out rules that apply where a debt obligation denominated in a foreign currency, of a non-resident taxpayer that carries on business in Canada, either ceases to be or becomes an obligation in respect of the business. These rules ensure that income, gains and losses due to currency fluctuations are appropriately measured.

New subsection 76.1(1) applies any time a foreign-currency debt obligation ceases to be an obligation of a non-resident's Canadian business (otherwise than because the non-resident ceased to be indebted under the obligation). The subsection treats the non-resident, for the purposes of determining any income, loss, capital gain or capital loss due to foreign exchange fluctuation, as having settled the debt immediately before that time for its principal amount. This ensures that any foreign currency gain or loss that accrued during the time the debt was associated with the Canadian business is captured when the debt is transferred out of the Canadian business.

Similarly, new subsection 76.1(2) applies where a non-resident taxpayer's Canadian business acquires a foreign-currency debt obligation that the non-resident formerly held outside the business. This subsection provides that the amount to be used for the purposes of calculating any income, loss, capital gain or capital loss with respect to the debt because of foreign exchange fluctuations is the amount of the debt obligation in Canadian dollars at the time the debt became an obligation of the Canadian business. This ensures that only currency fluctuations from the time the debt was assumed by the Canadian business are subsequently taken into account.

New section 76.1 applies after June 27, 1999 in respect of an authorized foreign bank, and after August 8, 2000 in any other case.

**Definitions [s. 76.1]**: "amount", "business" — 248(1); "Canada" — 255, *Interpretation Act* 35(1); "capital gain" — 39(1)(a), 248(1); "capital loss" — 39(1)(b), 248(1); "foreign currency", "non-resident", "principal amount", "taxpayer" — 248(1).

**Interpretation Bulletins [s. 76]**: IT-77R: Securities in satisfaction of an income debt.

**77.** [Repealed]

**Notes**: 77 repealed by 1994 tax amendments bill (Part III), effective for exchanges occurring after October 1994. See now 51.1 instead. For earlier exchanges, read:

77. Bond conversion — Where a bond of a debtor is acquired by a taxpayer in exchange for another bond of the same debtor and

(a) the terms of the bond for which it was exchanged conferred on the holder thereof the right to make the exchange, and

(b) the amount payable to the holder of the bond on its maturity is the same as the amount that would have been payable to the holder of the bond for which it was exchanged on the maturity of that bond,

the cost of the bond so acquired and the sale price of the bond for which it was exchanged shall be deemed to be,

(c) in the event that the bond that was exchanged was property described in an inventory of a business carried on by the taxpayer, the amount at which it had been valued at the end of the last complete fiscal period of the business preceding the exchange, or

(d) in any other event, the adjusted cost base to the taxpayer of the bond that was exchanged, immediately before the exchange.

**78. (1) Unpaid amounts** — Where an amount in respect of a deductible outlay or expense that was owing by a taxpayer to a person with whom the taxpayer was not dealing at arm's length at the time the outlay or expense was incurred and at the end of the second taxation year following the taxation year in which the outlay or expense was incurred, is unpaid at the end of that second taxation year, either

(a) the amount so unpaid shall be included in computing the taxpayer's income for the third taxation year following the taxation year in which the outlay or expense was incurred, or

(b) where the taxpayer and that person have filed an agreement in prescribed form on or before the day on or before which the taxpayer is required by section 150 to file the taxpayer's return of income for the third succeeding taxation year, for the purposes of this Act the following rules apply:

(i) the amount so unpaid shall be deemed to have been paid by the taxpayer and received by that person on the first day of that third

S. 78(1)(b)(i)  Income Tax Act, Part I, Division B

taxation year, and section 153, except subsection 153(3), is applicable to the extent that it would apply if that amount were being paid to that person by the taxpayer, and

(ii) that person shall be deemed to have made a loan to the taxpayer on the first day of that third taxation year in an amount equal to the amount so unpaid minus the amount, if any, deducted or withheld therefrom by the taxpayer on account of that person's tax for that third taxation year.

**Related Provisions**: 12(1)(b) — Income inclusion for certain amounts not received until after end of year; 78(3) — Late filing; 78(4), (5) — Unpaid remuneration; 80(1)"excluded obligation"(c) — Obligation not subject to debt forgiveness rules; 127(26) — Parallel rule for unpaid amounts re investment tax credit; 248(1)"salary deferral arrangement"(k) — No SDA where bonus paid within 3 years.

**Notes**: The provisions with respect to debt forgiveness apply after February 21, 1994 in the following order: s. 78; 6(15) for employee indebtedness; 15(1.2) for shareholder indebtedness; 9(1); s. 79 for foreclosures and repossessions; s. 80. See Notes to 80(2)(c).

**Interpretation Bulletins**: IT-109R2: Unpaid amounts; IT-152R3: Special reserves — sale of land.

**Information Circulars**: 88-2, para. 16: General anti-avoidance rule — section 245 of the *Income Tax Act*.

**Forms**: T2047: Agreement in respect of unpaid amounts.

**(2) Idem** — Where an amount in respect of a deductible outlay or expense that was owing by a taxpayer that is a corporation to a person with whom the taxpayer was not dealing at arm's length is unpaid at the time when the taxpayer is wound up, and the taxpayer is wound up before the end of the second taxation year following the taxation year in which the outlay or expense was incurred, the amount so unpaid shall be included in computing the taxpayer's income for the taxation year in which it is wound up.

**Related Provisions**: 80(1)"excluded obligation"(c) — Obligation not subject to debt forgiveness rules.

**Interpretation Bulletins**: IT-109R2: Unpaid amounts.

**(3) Late filing** — Where, in respect of an amount described in subsection (1) that was owing by a taxpayer to a person, an agreement in a form prescribed for the purposes of this section is filed after the day on or before which the agreement is required to be filed for the purposes of paragraph (1)(b), both paragraphs (1)(a) and (b) apply in respect of the said amount, except that paragraph (1)(a) shall be read and construed as requiring 25% only of the said amount to be included in computing the taxpayer's income.

**Interpretation Bulletins**: IT-109R2: Unpaid amounts.

**(4) Unpaid remuneration and other amounts** — Where an amount in respect of a taxpayer's expense that is a superannuation or pension benefit, a retiring allowance, salary, wages or other remuneration (other than reasonable vacation or holiday pay or a deferred amount under a salary deferral arrangement) in respect of an office or employment is unpaid on the day that is 180 days after the end of the taxation year in which the expense was incurred, for the purposes of this Act other than this subsection, the amount shall be deemed not to have been incurred as an expense in the year and shall be deemed to be incurred as an expense in the taxation year in which the amount is paid.

**Related Provisions**: 37(11) — SR&ED expense must be claimed as such even if not deductible due to 78(4); 78(5) — 78(4) takes priority over 78(1); 80(1)"excluded obligation"(c) — Obligation not subject to debt forgiveness rules; 127(9)"investment tax credit"(m) — investment tax credit must be claimed as such even if not deductible due to 78(4); 127(26) — Unpaid amounts re investment tax credit; 248(1)"salary deferral arrangement"(k) — No SDA where bonus paid within 3 years.

**Notes**: Under 78(4), if bonus is declared by an employer in a fiscal year, it must be paid by 180 days after the end of the year to be deductible. The employee pays tax on employment income only when it is received (see 5(1)); so a one-year deferral is possible if the employer corporation's fiscal year-end is July 5 or later and the payment is correctly timed.

78(4) amended by 1991 technical bill, effective for expenses incurred after July 1990, to extend to unfunded obligations in respect of pension benefits and retiring allowances (which include severance payments).

**Interpretation Bulletins**: IT-109R2: Unpaid amounts.

**(5) Where subsec. (1) does not apply** — Subsection (1) does not apply in any case where subsection (4) applies.

**Definitions [s. 78]**: "amount" — 248(1); "arm's length" — 251(1); "corporation" — 248(1), *Interpretation Act* 35(1); "deferred amount", "employment", "office", "person", "prescribed", "retiring allowance", "salary deferral arrangement", "salary or wages", "superannuation or pension benefit" — 248(1); "taxation year" — 11(2), 249; "taxpayer" — 248(1).

**Interpretation Bulletins [s. 78]**: IT-109R2: Unpaid amounts; IT-152R3: Special reserves — sale of land.

**79. (1) Definitions** — In this section,

**"creditor"** of a particular person includes a person to whom the particular person is obligated to pay an amount under a mortgage or similar obligation and, where property was sold to the particular person under a conditional sales agreement, the seller of the property (or any assignee with respect to the agreement) shall be deemed to be a creditor of the particular person in respect of that property;

**Related Provisions**: 79.1(1)"creditor" — Definition applies to s. 79.1.

**Notes**: See Notes at end of 79.

**"debt"** includes an obligation to pay an amount under a mortgage or similar obligation or under a conditional sales agreement;

**Related Provisions**: 79.1(1)"debt" — Definition applies to s. 79.1.

**"person"** includes a partnership;

**Related Provisions**: 79.1(1)"person" — Definition applies to s. 79.1.

**"property"** does not include

(a) money, or

564

Subdivision f — Rules Relating to Computation of Income S. 79(3)

(b) indebtedness owed by or guaranteed by the government of a country, or a province, state, or other political subdivision of that country;

**Related Provisions**: 79.1(1)"property" — Definition applies to s. 79.1.

**"specified amount"** at any time of a debt owed or assumed by a person means

(a) the unpaid principal amount of the debt at that time, and

(b) unpaid interest accrued to that time on the debt.

**Related Provisions**: 79.1(1)"specified amount" — Definition applies to s. 79.1.

**(2) Surrender of property** — For the purposes of this section, a property is surrendered at any time by a person to another person where the beneficial ownership of the property is acquired or reacquired at that time from the person by the other person and the acquisition or reacquisition of the property was in consequence of the person's failure to pay all or part of one or more specified amounts of debts owed by the person to the other person immediately before that time.

**Related Provisions**: 79.1(2) — Seizure of property by creditor; 180.2(1)"adjusted income" — No OAS clawback on gain to which 79(2) applies.

**(3) Proceeds of disposition for debtor** — Where a particular property is surrendered at any time by a person (in this subsection referred to as the "debtor") to a creditor of the debtor, the debtor's proceeds of disposition of the particular property shall be deemed to be the amount determined by the formula

$$(A + B + C + D + E - F) \times \frac{G}{H}$$

where

A is the total of all specified amounts of debts of the debtor that are in respect of properties surrendered at that time by the debtor to the creditor and that are owing immediately before that time to the creditor;

B is the total of all amounts each of which is a specified amount of a debt that is owed by the debtor immediately before that time to a person (other than the creditor), to the extent that the amount ceases to be owing by the debtor as a consequence of properties being surrendered at that time by the debtor to the creditor;

C is the total of all amounts each of which is a specified amount of a particular debt that is owed by the debtor immediately before that time to a person (other than a specified amount included in the amount determined for A or B as a consequence of properties being surrendered at that time by the debtor to the creditor), where

(a) any property surrendered at that time by the debtor to the creditor was security for

(i) the particular debt, and

(ii) another debt that is owed by the debtor immediately before that time to the creditor, and

(b) the other debt is subordinate to the particular debt in respect of that property;

D is

(a) where a specified amount of a debt owed by the debtor immediately before that time to a person (other than the creditor) ceases, as a consequence of the surrender at that time of properties by the debtor to the creditor, to be secured by all properties owned by the debtor immediately before that time, the lesser of

(i) the amount, if any, by which the total of all such specified amounts exceeds the portion of that total included in any of the amounts determined for B or C as a consequence of properties being surrendered at that time by the debtor to the creditor, and

(ii) the amount, if any, by which the total cost amount to the debtor of all properties surrendered at that time by the debtor to the creditor exceeds the total amount that would, but for this description and the description of F, be determined under this subsection as a consequence of the surrender, and

(b) in any other case, nil;

E is

(a) where the particular property is surrendered at that time by the debtor in circumstances in which paragraph 69(1)(b) would, but for this subsection, apply and the fair market value of all properties surrendered at that time by the debtor to the creditor exceeds the amount that would, but for this description and the description of F, be determined under this subsection as a consequence of the surrender, that excess, and

(b) in any other case, nil;

F is the total of all amounts each of which is the lesser of

(a) the portion of a particular specified amount of a particular debt included in the amount determined for A, B, C or D in computing the debtor's proceeds of disposition of the particular property, and

(b) the total of

(i) all amounts included under paragraph 6(1)(a) or subsection 15(1) in computing the income of any person because the particular debt was settled, or deemed by sub-

565

section 80.01(8) to have been settled, at or before the end of the taxation year that includes that time,

(ii) all amounts renounced under subsection 66(10), (10.1), (10.2) or (10.3) by the debtor in respect of the particular debt,

(iii) all amounts each of which is a forgiven amount (within the meaning assigned by subsection 80(1)) in respect of the debt at a previous time that the particular debt was deemed by subsection 80.01(8) to have been settled,

(iv) where the particular debt is an excluded obligation (within the meaning assigned by subsection 80(1)), the particular specified amount, and

(v) the lesser of

(A) the unpaid interest accrued to that time on the particular debt, and

(B) the total of

(I) the amount, if any, by which the total of all amounts included because of section 80.4 in computing the debtor's income for the taxation year that includes that time or for a preceding taxation year in respect of interest on the particular debt exceeds the total of all amounts paid before that time on account of interest on the particular debt, and

(II) such portion of that unpaid interest as would, if it were paid, be included in the amount determined under paragraph 28(1)(e) in respect of the debtor;

G is the fair market value at that time of the particular property; and

H is the fair market value at that time of all properties surrendered by the debtor to the creditor at that time.

**Related Provisions**: 13(21)"proceeds of disposition"(h) — Inclusion for depreciable property rules; 15(1.21)(b) — Inclusion under 79(3) ignored for calculating shareholder benefit from forgiven amount; 18(9.3) — Rule where debtor previously prepaid interest; 79(2) — Meaning of "surrendered"; 79(4) — Subsequent payment by debtor; 79(5) — Where amount included in consequence of properties being surrendered before the year; 79(7) — Where debt denominated in foreign currency; 80(1)"forgiven amount"B(f) — Debt forgiveness rules do not apply; 87(2)(h.1) — Amalgamations — continuing corporation; 118(2)B — Inclusion under s. 79 ignored for old age credit threshold; 122.5(1)"adjusted income" — Inclusion under s. 79 ignored for GST credit threshold; 122.6"adjusted income" — Inclusion under s. 79 ignored for Child Tax Benefit threshold; 257 — Formula cannot calculate to less than zero.

**Notes**: See Notes at end of 79.

**Interpretation Bulletins**: IT-505: Mortgage foreclosures and conditional sales repossessions.

**(4) Subsequent payment by debtor** — An amount paid at any time by a person as, on account of or in satisfaction of, a specified amount of a debt that can reasonably be considered to have been included in the amount determined for A, C or D in subsection (3) in respect of a property surrendered before that time by the person shall be deemed to be a repayment of assistance, at that time in respect of the property, to which

(a) subsection 39(13) applies, where the property was capital property (other than depreciable property) of the person immediately before its surrender;

(b) paragraph 20(1)(hh.1) applies, where the cost of the property to the person was an eligible capital expenditure;

(c) the description of E in the definition "cumulative Canadian exploration expense" in subsection 66.1(6), the description of D in the definition "cumulative Canadian development expense" in subsection 66.2(5) or the description of D in the definition "cumulative Canadian oil and gas property expense" in subsection 66.4(5), as the case may be, applies, where the cost of the property to the person was a Canadian exploration expense, a Canadian development expense or a Canadian oil and gas property expense; or

(d) paragraph 20(1)(hh) applies, in any other case.

**(5) Subsequent application with respect to employee or shareholder debt** — Any amount included under paragraph 6(1)(a) or subsection 15(1) in computing a person's income for a taxation year that can reasonably be considered to have been included in the amount determined for A, C or D in subsection (3) as a consequence of properties being surrendered before the year by the person shall be deemed to be a repayment by the person, immediately before the end of the year, of assistance to which subsection (4) applies.

**(6) Surrender of property not payment or repayment by debtor** — Where a specified amount of a debt is included in the amount determined at any time for A, B, C or D in subsection (3) in respect of a property surrendered at that time by a person to a creditor of the person, for the purpose of computing the person's income, no amount shall be considered to have been paid or repaid by the person as a consequence of the acquisition or reacquisition of the surrendered property by the creditor.

**Advance Tax Rulings**: ATR-6: Vendor reacquires business assets following default by purchaser.

**(7) Foreign exchange** — Where a debt is denominated in a currency (other than Canadian currency), any amount determined for A, B, C or D in subsection (3) in respect of the debt shall be determined with reference to the relative value of that currency and Canadian currency at the time the debt was issued.

**Notes [s. 79]:** 79 provides rules for debtors on foreclosures, conditional sale repossessions and similar transactions. For the effects on creditors, see 79.1.

Note that special GST rules will apply to the repossession and to the subsequent use or sale of the property by the creditor. See ss. 183 and 266 of the *Excise Tax Act*, reproduced in the *Practitioner's Goods and Services Tax, Annotated* and the *Canada GST Service*.

79 completely replaced by 1994 tax amendments bill (Part I), effective for property acquired or reacquired after February 21, 1994, other than property acquired or reacquired pursuant to a court order made before February 22, 1994. In addition, where a taxpayer elects in writing filed with Revenue Canada, former 79(f) applies to the taxpayer in respect of property reacquired by the taxpayer after 1991 and to which new 79 does not apply as if former 79(f) read as follows:

(e.1) where the property is capital property of the taxpayer and was disposed of by the taxpayer to the other person in the year and subsequently reacquired by the taxpayer in the year, the taxpayer's proceeds of disposition of the property shall be deemed to be the lesser of the proceeds of disposition of the property to the taxpayer (determined without reference to this paragraph) and the amount that is the greater of

(i) the amount, if any, by which such proceeds (determined without reference to this paragraph) exceeds such portion of the proceeds as is represented by the taxpayer's claim, and

(ii) the cost amount to the taxpayer of the property immediately before its disposition by the taxpayer;

(f) the taxpayer shall be deemed to have reacquired the property at the amount, if any, by which the cost at that time of the taxpayer's claim exceeds the amount described in subparagraph (e)(i) or (ii) in respect of that property or the amount, if any, by which the proceeds of disposition of the property are reduced because of paragraph (e.1), as the case may be;

For cases where the new 79 does not apply, read (subject to (f) being read as above where the taxpayer elects, as noted):

**79. Mortgage foreclosures and conditional sales repossessions** — Where, at any time in a taxation year, a taxpayer who

(a) was a mortgagee or other creditor of another person who had previously acquired property, or

(b) had previously sold property to another person under a conditional sales agreement,

has acquired or reacquired the beneficial ownership of the property in consequence of the other person's failure to pay all or any part of an amount (in this section referred to as the "taxpayer's claim") owing by that person to the taxpayer, the following rules apply:

(c) there shall be included, in computing the other person's proceeds of disposition of the property, the principal amount of the taxpayer's claim plus all amounts each of which is the principal amount of any debt that had been owing by the other person, to the extent that it has been extinguished by virtue of the acquisition or reacquisition, as the case may be,

(d) any amount paid by the other person after the acquisition or reacquisition, as the case may be, as, on account of or in satisfaction of the taxpayer's claim shall be deemed to be a loss of that person, for that person's taxation year in which payment of that amount was made, from the disposition of the property,

(e) in computing the income of the taxpayer for the year,

(i) the amount, if any, claimed by the taxpayer under subparagraph 40(1)(a)(iii) or 44(1)(e)(iii) in computing the taxpayer's gain for the immediately preceding taxation year from the disposition of the property, and

(ii) the amount, if any, deducted under paragraph 20(1)(n) in computing the income of the taxpayer for the immediately preceding year in respect of the property,

shall be deemed to be nil,

(f) the taxpayer shall be deemed to have acquired or reacquired, as the case may be, the property at the amount, if any, by which the cost at that time of the taxpayer's claim exceeds the amount described in subparagraph (e)(i) or (ii), as the case may be, in respect of the property,

(g) the adjusted cost base to the taxpayer of the taxpayer's claim shall be deemed to be nil, and

(h) in computing the taxpayer's income for the year or a subsequent year, no amount is deductible in respect of the taxpayer's claim by virtue of paragraph 20(1)(l) or (p).

Former 79(e) amended by 1991 technical bill to add reference to 44(1)(e)(iii), effective for property acquired or reacquired after July 12, 1990. However, where the taxpayer elects before July 1991, the amendment also applies to property in respect of which a taxpayer has claimed an amount under 44(1)(e)(iii) and that was reacquired by the taxpayer after 1985 and before July 13, 1990. (Notwithstanding 152(4) to (5), such assessments of tax, interest and penalties shall be made as are necessary to give effect to such an election.)

Former 79(f) amended by 1981 Budget. In respect of acquisitions and reacquisitions occurring before November 13, 1981, read "principal amount" in place of "cost".

**Definitions [s. 79]:** "amount" — 248(1); "assistance" — 79(4), 125.4(5), 248(16), (18); "Canadian exploration expense" — 66.1(6), 248(1); "Canadian development expense" — 66.2(5), 248(1); "Canadian oil and gas property expense" — 66.4(5), 248(1); "creditor", "debt" — 79(1); "debtor" — 79(3); "eligible capital expenditure" — 14(5), 248(1); "partnership" — see Notes to 96(1); "person" — 79(1), 248(1); "principal amount" — 248(1); "property" — 79(1), 248(1); "province" — *Interpretation Act* 35(1); "specified amount" — 79(1); "surrendered" — 79(2); "taxation year" — 249.

**79.1 (1) Definitions** — In this section,

**"creditor"** has the meaning assigned by subsection 79(1);

**Notes:** See Notes at end of 79.

**"debt"** has the meaning assigned by subsection 79(1);

**"person"** has the meaning assigned by subsection 79(1);

**"property"** has the meaning assigned by subsection 79(1);

**"specified amount"** has the meaning assigned by subsection 79(1);

**"specified cost"** to a person of a debt owing to the person means

(a) where the debt is capital property of the person, the adjusted cost base to the person of the debt, and

(b) in any other case, the amount, if any, by which

(i) the cost amount to the person of the debt

exceeds

    (ii) such portion of that cost amount as would be deductible in computing the person's income (otherwise than in respect of the principal amount of the debt) if the debt were established by the person to have become a bad debt or to have become uncollectable.

**Related Provisions**: 20(1)(p), 20(4)–(4.2), 50(1) — Provisions allowing deductions for bad debts.

**(2) Seizure of property** — For the purposes of this section, a property is seized at any time by a person in respect of a debt where the beneficial ownership of the property is acquired or reacquired at that time by the person and the acquisition or reacquisition of the property was in consequence of another person's failure to pay to the person all or part of the specified amount of the debt.

> **Proposed Amendment — 79.1(2), (2.1)**
>
> **(2) Seizure of property** — Subject to subsection (2.1) and for the purpose of this section, a property is seized at any time by a person in respect of a debt where
>
> (a) the beneficial ownership of the property is acquired or reacquired at that time by the person; and
>
> (b) the acquisition or reacquisition of the property is in consequence of another person's failure to pay to the person all or part of the specified amount of the debt.
>
> **(2.1) Exception** — For the purpose of this section, foreign resource property is deemed not to be seized at any time from
>
> (a) an individual or a corporation, if the individual or corporation is non-resident at that time; or
>
> (b) a partnership (other than a partnership each member of which is resident in Canada at that time).
>
> **Application**: The December 21, 2000 draft legislation, s. 33, will amend subsec. 79.1(2) to read as above and add subsec. (2.1), applicable in respect of property acquired or reacquired after February 27, 2000.
>
> **Technical Notes**: Section 79.1 provides the income tax consequences for creditors in connection with acquisitions and reacquisitions of property from debtors. The operative rules in section 79.1 apply only where property is seized by a creditor in respect of a debt. Under subsection 79.1(2), property is seized by a creditor in respect of a debt where the beneficial ownership of the property is acquired or reacquired by the creditor and the acquisition or reacquisition was in consequence of another person's failure to pay to the creditor all or part of the debt.
>
> Subsection 79.1(2) is amended so that it is subject to new subsection 79.1(2.1). Subsection 79.1(2.1) provides that, for the purpose of section 79.1, foreign resource property is deemed not to be seized from a non-resident individual or corporation or from a partnership (other than a partnership each member of which is resident in Canada).

> **Notice of Ways and Means Motion, federal budget, February 28, 2000**: (41) That section 79.1 of the Act not apply in respect of acquisitions after February 27, 2000 of foreign resource property from a person (other than a person resident in Canada) or a partnership (other than a partnership each member of which is resident in Canada).
>
> **Federal budget, supplementary information, February 28, 2000**: [See under 66(4)(b)(ii) — ed.]

**Related Provisions**: 50(1) — Deemed disposition of debt on bad debt, windup, insolvency or bankruptcy; 79(2) — Surrender of property by debtor; 79.1(2.1) — Exception — foreign resource property; 138(11.93)(a) — Section 79.1 does not apply to insurer.

**Notes**: See Notes at end of 79.1.

**(3) Creditor's capital gains reserves** — Where a property is seized at any time in a particular taxation year by a creditor in respect of a debt, for the purpose of computing the income of the creditor for the particular year, the amount claimed by the creditor under subparagraph 40(1)(a)(iii) or 44(1)(e)(iii) in computing the creditor's gain for the preceding taxation year from any disposition before the particular year of the property shall be deemed to be the amount, if any, by which the amount so claimed exceeds the total of all amounts each of which is an amount determined under paragraph (6)(a) or (b) in respect of the seizure.

**(4) Creditor's inventory reserves** — Where a property is seized at any time in a particular taxation year by a creditor in respect of a debt, for the purpose of computing the income of the creditor for the particular year, the amount deducted under paragraph 20(1)(n) in computing the income of the creditor for the preceding taxation year in respect of any disposition of the property before the particular year shall be deemed to be the amount, if any, by which the amount so deducted exceeds the total of all amounts each of which is an amount determined under paragraph (6)(a) or (b) in respect of the seizure.

**(5) Adjustment where disposition and reacquisition of capital property in same year** — Where a property is seized at any time in a taxation year by a creditor in respect of one or more debts and the property was capital property of the creditor that was disposed of by the creditor at a previous time in the year, the proceeds of disposition of the property to the creditor at the previous time shall be deemed to be the lesser of the amount of the proceeds (determined without reference to this subsection) and the amount that is the greater of

    (a) the amount, if any, by which the amount of such proceeds (determined without reference to this subsection) exceeds such portion of the proceeds as is represented by the specified amounts of those debts immediately before that time, and

    (b) the cost amount to the creditor of the property immediately before the previous time.

## Subdivision f — Rules Relating to Computation of Income S. 79.1(8)

**(6) Cost of seized properties for creditor** — Where a particular property is seized at any time in a taxation year by a creditor in respect of one or more debts, the cost to the creditor of the particular property shall be deemed to be the amount, if any, by which the total of

(a) that proportion of the total specified costs immediately before that time to the creditor of those debts that

(i) the fair market value of the particular property immediately before that time

is of

(ii) the fair market value of all properties immediately before that time that were seized by the creditor at that time in respect of those debts, and

(b) all amounts each of which is an outlay or expense made or incurred, or a specified amount at that time of a debt that is assumed, by the creditor at or before that time to protect the creditor's interest in the particular property, except to the extent the outlay or expense

(i) was included in the cost to the creditor of property other than the particular property,

(ii) was included before that time in computing, for the purposes of this Act, any balance of undeducted outlays, expenses or other amounts of the creditor, or

(iii) was deductible in computing the creditor's income for the year or a preceding taxation year

exceeds

(c) the amount, if any, claimed or deducted under paragraph 20(1)(n) or subparagraph 40(1)(a)(iii) or 44(1)(e)(iii), as the case may be, in respect of the particular property in computing the creditor's income or capital gain for the preceding taxation year or the amount by which the proceeds of disposition of the creditor of the particular property are reduced because of subsection (5) in respect of a disposition of the particular property by the creditor occurring before that time and in the year.

**Related Provisions**: 79.1(3) — Capital gains reserve; 79.1(4) — Inventory reserve.

**(7) Treatment of debt** — Where a property is seized at any time in a taxation year by a creditor in respect of a particular debt,

(a) the creditor shall be deemed to have disposed of the particular debt at that time;

(b) the amount received on account of the particular debt as a consequence of the seizure shall be deemed

(i) to be received at that time, and

(ii) to be equal to

(A) where the particular debt is capital property, the adjusted cost base to the creditor of the particular debt, and

(B) in any other case, the cost amount to the creditor of the particular debt;

(c) where any portion of the particular debt is outstanding immediately after that time, the creditor shall be deemed to have reacquired that portion immediately after that time at a cost equal to

(i) where the particular debt is capital property, nil, and

(ii) in any other case, the amount, if any, by which

(A) the cost amount to the creditor of the particular debt

exceeds

(B) the specified cost to the creditor of the particular debt; and

(d) where no portion of the particular debt is outstanding immediately after that time and the particular debt is not capital property, the creditor may deduct as a bad debt in computing the creditor's income for the year the amount described in subparagraph (c)(ii) in respect of the seizure.

**Related Provisions**: 79.1(8) — No deduction for principal amount of bad debt; 142.4(3)(a) — Disposition of specified debt obligation.

**(8) Claims for debts** — Where a property is seized at any time in a taxation year by a creditor in respect of a debt, no amount in respect of the debt

(a) is deductible in computing the creditor's income for the year or a subsequent taxation year as a bad, doubtful or impaired debt; or

(b) shall be included after that time in computing, for the purposes of this Act, any balance of undeducted outlays, expenses or other amounts of the creditor as a bad, doubtful or impaired debt.

**Related Provisions**: 50(1)(a) — Deemed disposition of bad debt; 79.1(7)(d) — Deduction by creditor for bad debt.

**Notes**: 79.1(8) amended by 1995-97 technical bill, effective

(a) for taxation years that end after September 1997; and

(b) for taxation years that end after 1995 and before October 1997, if the taxpayer files an election for amended 20(1)(l) to apply to such years (see Notes to 20(1)(l)).

For earlier taxation years, generally for property acquired after February 21, 1994, read:

(8) Claims for bad and doubtful debts — Where a property is seized at any time in a taxation year by a creditor in respect of a debt, no amount in respect of the principal amount of the debt shall be

(a) deductible in computing the creditor's income for the year or a subsequent taxation year as a bad or doubtful debt; or

(b) included after that time in computing, for the purposes of this Act, any balance of undeducted outlays, expenses or other amounts of the creditor as a bad or doubtful debt.

## S. 79.1(8) — Income Tax Act, Part I, Division B

79.1(8) enacted together with all of 79.1 (see below).

**Notes [s. 79.1]**: 79.1 provides the rules for creditors on foreclosures, conditional sale repossessions and similar transactions. (79 provides the rules for debtors.) Note that special GST rules will apply to the repossession and to the subsequent use or sale of the property by the creditor. See ss. 183 and 266 of the *Excise Tax Act*, reproduced in the *Practitioner's Goods and Services Tax Annotated* and the *Canada GST Service*.

79.1 added by 1994 tax amendments bill (Part I), effective for property acquired or reacquired after February 21, 1994, other than property acquired or reacquired pursuant to a court order made before February 22, 1994.

**Definitions [s. 79.1]**: "adjusted cost base" — 54, 248(1); "amount" — 248(1); "capital gain" — 39(1), 248(1); "capital property" — 54, 248(1); "corporation" — 248(1), *Interpretation Act* 35(1); "cost" — 79.1(6); "cost amount" — 248(1); "creditor"; "debt" — 79(1), 79.1(1); "disposition" — 50(1), 54; "foreign resource property" — 66(15), 248(1); "individual", "non-resident" — 248(1); "partnership" — see Notes to 96(1); "person" — 79(1), 79.1(1), 248(1); "principal amount" — 248(1); "proceeds of disposition" — 54; "property" — 79(1), 79.1(1), 248(1); "resident in Canada" — 250; "seized" — 79.1(2); "specified amount" — 79(1), 79.1(1); "specified cost" — 79.1(1); "taxation year" — 249.

## 80. (1) Definitions — In this section,

**"commercial debt obligation"** issued by a debtor means a debt obligation issued by the debtor

(a) where interest was paid or payable by the debtor in respect of it pursuant to a legal obligation, or

(b) if interest had been paid or payable by the debtor in respect of it pursuant to a legal obligation,

an amount in respect of the interest was or would have been deductible in computing the debtor's income, taxable income or taxable income earned in Canada, as the case may be, if this Act were read without reference to subsections 15.1(2) and 15.2(2), paragraph 18(1)(g), subsections 18(2), (3.1) and (4) and section 21;

**Related Provisions**: 80.01(1)"commercial debt obligation" — Definition applies to s. 80.01; 80.02(1) — Definition applies to s. 80.02; 80.03(1)(a) — Definition applies to s. 80.03; 80.03(7)(b)(i) — Commercial debt obligation deemed issued where amount designated; 80.04(1) — Definition applies to s. 80.04; 80.04(4)(e) — Commercial debt obligation deemed issued on agreement to transfer forgiven amount; 95(2)(g.1)(i) — Application to FAPI; 248(26) — Liability deemed to be obligation issued by debtor; 248(27) — Partial settlement of debt obligation.

**Notes**: See Notes at end of s. 80.

**"commercial obligation"** issued by a debtor means

(a) a commercial debt obligation issued by the debtor, or

(b) a distress preferred share issued by the debtor;

**Related Provisions**: 40(2)(e.2) — Disposition of commercial obligation in exchange for another obligation issued by same person; 80(2)(b) — Obligation to pay interest deemed to be a debt obligation; 80.01(1)"commercial obligation" — Definition applies to s. 80.01; 80.02(1) — Definition applies to s. 80.02; 80.03(1)(a) — Definition applies to s. 80.03; 80.04(1) — Definition applies to s. 80.04.

**"debtor"** includes any corporation that has issued a distress preferred share and any partnership;

**Related Provisions**: 80.01(1)"debtor" — Definition applies to s. 80.01; 80.04(1) — Definition applies to s. 80.04.

**"directed person"** at any time in respect of a debtor means

(a) a taxable Canadian corporation or an eligible Canadian partnership by which the debtor is controlled at that time, or

(b) a taxable Canadian corporation or an eligible Canadian partnership that is controlled at that time by

(i) the debtor,

(ii) the debtor and one or more persons related to the debtor, or

(iii) a person or group of persons by which the debtor is controlled at that time;

**Related Provisions**: 80.04(1) — Definition applies to s. 80.04; 256(6), (6.1) — Meaning of "controlled".

**"distress preferred share"** issued by a corporation means, at any time, a share issued after February 21, 1994 (other than a share issued pursuant to an agreement in writing entered into on or before that date) by the corporation that is a share described in paragraph (e) of the definition "term preferred share" in subsection 248(1) that would be a term preferred share at that time if that definition were read without reference to paragraphs (e) and (f);

**Related Provisions**: 61.3(1)(b)D, 61.3(2)(b)D — Deduction of principal amount of distress preferred share in determining debt forgiveness reserve; 80.01(1)"distress preferred share" — Definition applies to s. 80.01; 80.02(1) — Definition applies to s. 80.02; 80.03(1)(a) — Definition applies to s. 80.03.

**"eligible Canadian partnership"** at any time means a Canadian partnership none of the members of which is, at that time,

(a) a non-resident owned investment corporation,

(b) a person exempt, because of subsection 149(1), from tax under this Part on all or part of the person's taxable income,

(c) a partnership, other than an eligible Canadian partnership, or

(d) a trust, other than a trust in which no non-resident person and no person described in paragraph (a), (b) or (c) is beneficially interested;

**Related Provisions**: 80.04(1) — Definition applies to s. 80.04; 102(1) — Canadian partnership.

**"excluded obligation"** means an obligation issued by a debtor where

(a) the proceeds from the issue of the obligation

(i) were included in computing the debtor's income or, but for the expression "other than a prescribed amount" in paragraph 12(1)(x), would have been so included,

(ii) were deducted in computing, for the purposes of this Act, any balance of undeducted outlays, expenses or other amounts, or

(iii) were deducted in computing the capital cost or cost amount to the debtor of any property of the debtor,

(b) an amount paid by the debtor in satisfaction of the entire principal amount of the obligation would be included in the amount determined under paragraph 28(1)(e) or section 30 in respect of the debtor,

(c) section 78 applies to the obligation, or

(d) the principal amount of the obligation would, if this Act were read without reference to sections 79 and 80 and the obligation were settled without any amount being paid in satisfaction of its principal amount, be included in computing the debtor's income because of the settlement of the obligation;

**Related Provisions**: 79(3)F(b)(iv) — Proceeds of disposition for debtor; 80(1)"forgiven amount"B(j) — Debt forgiveness rules do not apply to principal amount of excluded obligation; 80(2)(a) — Debt forgiveness rules do not apply to obligation settled as consideration for share described in para. (c).

**"excluded property"** means property of a non-resident debtor that is treaty-protected property or that is not taxable Canadian property;

**Related Provisions**: 111(9) — Losses ignored while taxpayer is non-resident.

**Notes**: Definition amended by 1998 Budget, effective for 1998 and later taxation years. For earlier years, read:

"excluded property" at any time means property of a non-resident debtor that would not be taxable Canadian property of the debtor if it were disposed of at that time by the debtor;

See also Notes at end of s. 80.

**"excluded security"** issued by a corporation to a person as consideration for the settlement of a debt means

(a) a distress preferred share issued by the corporation to the person, or

(b) a share issued by the corporation to the person under the terms of the debt, where the debt was a bond, debenture or note listed on a prescribed stock exchange in Canada and the terms for the conversion to the share were not established or substantially modified after the later of February 22, 1994 and the time that the bond, debenture or note was issued;

**Regulations**: 3200 (prescribed stock exchange; not yet amended to apply for purposes of 80(1)).

**"forgiven amount"** at any time in respect of a commercial obligation issued by a debtor is the amount determined by the formula

$$A - B$$

where

A is the lesser of the amount for which the obligation was issued and the principal amount of the obligation, and

B is the total of

(a) the amount, if any, paid at that time in satisfaction of the principal amount of the obligation,

(b) the amount, if any, included under paragraph 6(1)(a) or subsection 15(1) in computing the income of any person because of the settlement of the obligation at that time,

(c) the amount, if any, deducted at that time under paragraph 18(9.3)(f) in computing the forgiven amount in respect of the obligation,

(d) the capital gain, if any, of the debtor resulting from the application of subsection 39(3) to the purchase at that time of the obligation by the debtor,

(e) such portion of the principal amount of the obligation as relates to an amount renounced under subsection 66(10), (10.1), (10.2) or (10.3) by the debtor,

(f) any portion of the principal amount of the obligation that is included in the amount determined for A, B, C or D in subsection 79(3) in respect of the debtor for the taxation year of the debtor that includes that time or for a preceding taxation year,

(g) the total of all amounts each of which is a forgiven amount at a previous time that the obligation was deemed by subsection 80.01(8) or (9) to have been settled,

(h) such portion of the principal amount of the obligation as can reasonably be considered to have been included under section 80.4 in computing the debtor's income for a taxation year that includes that time or for a preceding taxation year,

(i) where the debtor is a bankrupt at that time, the principal amount of the obligation,

(j) such portion of the principal amount of the obligation as represents the principal amount of an excluded obligation,

(k) where the debtor is a partnership and the obligation was, since the later of the creation of the partnership or the issue of the obligation, always payable to a member of the partnership actively engaged, on a regular, continuous and substantial basis, in those activities of the partnership that are other than the financing of the partnership business, the principal amount of the obligation, and

(l) the amount, if any, given at or before that time by the debtor to another person as consideration for the assumption by the other person of the obligation;

**Related Provisions**: 6(15.1) — Meaning of "forgiven amount" for employee benefits; 15(1.21) — Meaning of "forgiven amount" for shareholder benefits; 80(2)(k) — Determination of forgiven amount where obligation denominated in foreign currency; 80.01(1)"forgiven amount" — Application of definition to s. 80.01; 80.01(8)(b) — Determination of forgiven amount following debt parking; 80.02(3)–(6) — Distress preferred share — determination of amount paid in satisfaction of principal; 80.03(1)(a) — Definition applies to s. 80.03; 80.03(7)(b)(ii) — Deemed forgiven amount where amount designated following debt forgiveness; 80.04(1) — Definition applies to s. 80.04; 80.04(4)(f) — Agreement to transfer forgiven amount; 87(2)(h.1) — Amalgamations — continuing corporation; 137.1(10) — Settlement of debts by deposit insurance corporation; 248(26) — Liability deemed to be obligation issued by debtor; 248(27) — Partial settlement of debt obligation; 257 — Formula cannot calculate to less than zero.

**Notes**: 80(3)–(14) set out a scheme of rules for using up the forgiven amount. See Notes at end of 80.

**I.T. Application Rules**: 26(1.1) (debt outstanding since before 1972).

**Advance Tax Rulings**: ATR-27: Exchange and acquisition of interests in capital properties through rollovers and winding-up ("butterfly").

**I.T. Technical News**: No. 15 (tax consequences of the adoption of the "euro" currency).

**"person"** includes a partnership;

**Related Provisions**: 80(15)(c) — Where commercial debt obligation issued by partnership; 80.01(1)"person" — Definition applies to s. 80.01; 80.02(1) — Definition applies to s. 80.02; 80.03(1)(a) — Definition applies to s. 80.03; 80.04(1) — Definition applies to s. 80.04.

**"relevant loss balance"** at a particular time for a commercial obligation and in respect of a debtor's non-capital loss, farm loss, restricted farm loss or net capital loss, as the case may be, for a particular taxation year means the amount of such loss that would be deductible in computing the debtor's taxable income or taxable income earned in Canada, as the case may be, for the taxation year that includes that time if

(a) the debtor had sufficient incomes from all sources and sufficient taxable capital gains,

(b) subsections (3) and (4) did not apply to reduce such loss at or after that time, and

(c) paragraph 111(4)(a) and subsection 111(5) did not apply to the debtor,

except that, where the debtor is a corporation the control of which was acquired at a previous time by a person or group of persons and the particular year ended before the previous time, the relevant loss balance at the particular time for the obligation and in respect of such loss for the particular year shall be deemed to be nil unless

(d) the obligation was issued by the debtor before, and not in contemplation of, the acquisition of control, or

(e) all or substantially all of the proceeds from the issue of the obligation were used to satisfy the principal amount of another obligation to which paragraph (d) or this paragraph would apply if the other obligation were still outstanding;

**Related Provisions**: 80(15)(c)(iv)(B) — Application of para. (e) of definition where obligation issued by partnership; 80.04(4)(h)(ii) — Application of para. (e) of definition on agreement to transfer forgiven amount; 139.1(18) — Holding corporation deemed not to acquire control of insurer on demutualization; 256(6)–(9) — Whether control acquired; 256(8) — Deemed acquisition of shares.

**Notes**: The CCRA takes the position that "all or substantially all", used in para. (e), means 90% or more.

**I.T. Technical News**: No. 7 (control by a group — 50/50 arrangement).

**"successor pool"** at any time for a commercial obligation and in respect of an amount determined in relation to a debtor means such portion of that amount as would be deductible under subsection 66.7(2), (3), (4) or (5), as the case may be, in computing the debtor's income for the taxation year that includes that time, if

(a) the debtor had sufficient incomes from all sources,

(b) subsection (8) did not apply to reduce the amount so determined at that time,

(c) the year ended immediately after that time, and

(d) paragraphs 66.7(4)(a) and (5)(a) were read without reference to the expressions "30% of" and "10% of", respectively,

except that the successor pool at that time for the obligation shall be deemed to be nil unless

(e) the obligation was issued by the debtor before, and not in contemplation of, the event described in paragraph (8)(a) that gives rise to the deductibility under subsection 66.7(2), (3), (4) or (5), as the case may be, of all or part of that amount in computing the debtor's income, or

---

**Proposed Amendment — 80(1)"successor pool" pre (f)**

**"successor pool"** at any time for a commercial obligation and in respect of an amount determined in relation to a debtor means the portion of that amount that would be deductible under subsection 66.7(2), (2.3), (3), (4) or (5), as the case may be, in computing the debtor's income for the taxation year that includes that time, if

(a) the debtor had sufficient incomes from all sources,

(b) subsection (8) did not apply to reduce the amount so determined at that time,

(c) the year ended immediately after that time, and

(d) paragraphs 66.7(2.3)(a), (4)(a) and (5)(a) were read without reference to the expressions "30% of", "30% of" and "10% of", respectively,

except that the successor pool at that time for the obligation is deemed to be nil unless

(e) the obligation was issued by the debtor before, and not in contemplation of, the event described in paragraph (8)(a) that gives rise to the deductibility under subsection 66.7(2), (2.3), (3), (4) or (5), as the case may be, of all or part of that amount in computing the debtor's income, or

**Application**: The December 21, 2000 draft legislation, subsec. 34(1), will amend the portion of the definition "successor pool" in subsec. 80(1) before para. (f) to read as above, applicable to taxation years that begin after 2000.

**Technical Notes**: See under 80(8)(a) below.

(f) all or substantially all of the proceeds from the issue of the obligation were used to satisfy the principal amount of another obligation to which paragraph (e) or this paragraph would apply if the other obligation were still outstanding;

**Related Provisions**: 80(15)(c)(iv)(B) — Application of para. (f) of definition where obligation issued by partnership; 80.04(4)(h)(ii) — Application of para. (f) of definition on agreement to transfer forgiven amount; 256(8) — Deemed acquisition of shares.

**Notes**: The CCRA takes the position that "all or substantially all", used in para. (f), means 90% or more.

**"unrecognized loss"** at a particular time, in respect of an obligation issued by a debtor, from the disposition of a property means the amount that would, but for subparagraph 40(2)(g)(ii), be a capital loss from the disposition by the debtor at or before the particular time of a debt or other right to receive an amount, except that where the debtor is a corporation the control of which was acquired before the particular time and after the time of the disposition by a person or group of persons, the unrecognized loss at the particular time in respect of the obligation is deemed to be nil unless

(a) the obligation was issued by the debtor before, and not in contemplation of, the acquisition of control, or

(b) all or substantially all of the proceeds from the issue of the obligation were used to satisfy the principal amount of another obligation to which paragraph (a) or this paragraph would apply if the other obligation were still outstanding.

**Related Provisions**: 80(15)(c)(iv)(B) — Application of para. (b) of definition where obligation issued by partnership; 80.04(4)(h)(ii) — Application of para. (b) of definition on agreement to transfer forgiven amount; 87(2)(l.21) — Amalgamations — continuing corporation; 139.1(18) — Holding corporation deemed not to acquire control of insurer on demutualization; 256(6)–(9) — Whether control acquired; 256(8) — Deemed acquisition of shares.

**Notes**: Opening words of 80(1)"unrecognized loss" amended to add the words "by the debtor" by 1995-97 technical bill, retroactive to the introduction of the definition (taxation years ending after February 21, 1994 — see Notes at end of s. 80).

The CCRA takes the position that "all or substantially all", used in para. (b), means 90% or more.

**(2) Application of debt forgiveness rules** — For the purposes of this section,

(a) **[when obligation settled]** — an obligation issued by a debtor is settled at any time where the obligation is settled or extinguished at that time (otherwise than by way of a bequest or inheritance or as consideration for the issue of a share described in paragraph (b) of the definition "excluded security" in subsection (1));

**Related Provisions**: 6(15) — Forgiveness of debt owing by employee — taxable benefit; 15(1.2) — Forgiveness of debt owing by shareholder — taxable benefit; 80.01(2)(a) — Application to s. 80.01; 80.01(3)–(9) — Deemed settlement of debts; 80.02(2)(c) — Meaning of "settled" for distress preferred share; 80.02(7)(a) — Deemed settlement where share ceases to be distress preferred share; 80.03(7)(b)(i) — Deemed settlement where amount designated; 80.04(3) — Application to s. 80.04; 80.04(4)(e) — Deemed settlement on agreement to transfer forgiven amount.

(b) **[interest deemed to be obligation]** — an amount of interest payable by a debtor in respect of an obligation issued by the debtor shall be deemed to be an obligation issued by the debtor that

(i) has a principal amount, and

(ii) was issued by the debtor for an amount,

equal to the portion of the amount of such interest that was deductible or would, but for subsection 18(2) or (3.1) or section 21, have been deductible in computing the debtor's income for a taxation year;

**Related Provisions**: 6(15.1)(d), 15(1.21)(d) — 80(2)(b) ignored for employee and shareholder benefit purposes; 80.01(2)(a) — Application to s. 80.01; 80.04(3) — Application to s. 80.04.

**Notes**: With respect to interest accruing before July 14, 1990, read "was deductible" in 80(2)(b) as "was deducted" (1994 tax amendments bill, para. 27(2)(b).) See also Notes at end of 80.

(c) **[ordering of rules]** — subsections (3) to (5) and (7) to (13) apply in numerical order to the forgiven amount in respect of a commercial obligation;

**Related Provisions**: 80(15) — Deduction by member of partnership; 80.04(4)(b) — Transfer of forgiven amount to related person after maximum designations; 248(27)(b), (c) — Partial settlement of debt deemed to be proportional to entire amount.

**Notes**: The rules for debt forgiveness apply in the following order:

- 78 [see 79(3)F, 80(1)"excluded obligation"(c)]
- 6(1), 6(15) [see 79(3)F, 79(5), 80(1)"forgiven amount"B(b)]
- 15(1), (1.2) [see 79(3)F, 79(5), 80(1)"forgiven amount"B(b)]
- 9(1) [see 79(3)F, 80(1)"excluded obligation", 4(4), 248(28)]
- 79 [see 80(1)"forgiven amount"B(f)]
- 80 [per 80(2)(c); the unstated assumption is that the rules apply in *ascending* numerical order]

(d) **[applicable fraction]** — the applicable fraction of the unapplied portion of a forgiven amount at any time in respect of an obligation issued by a debtor is

(i) in respect of a loss for a taxation year that ends after 1989, $3/4$,

(ii) in respect of a loss for a taxation year that ended before 1988, $1/2$, and

(iii) in respect of a loss for any other taxation year, the fraction required to be used under section 38 for that year;

**Proposed Amendment — 80(2)(d)**

(d) **[applicable fraction]** — the applicable fraction of the unapplied portion of a forgiven amount at any time in respect of an obligation issued by the debtor is

[beginning of portion to be deleted (see Notes below) — ed.]

(i) in respect of a loss for a taxation year that begins after February 27, 2000, ⅔, and

(ii) in respect of a loss for any other taxation year, [end of portion to be deleted — ed.] the fraction required to be used under section 38 for that year;

**Application**: The December 21, 2000 draft legislation, subsec. 34(2), will amend para. 80(2)(d) to read as above, applicable to taxation years that end after February 27, 2000.

**Technical Notes**: Paragraphs 80(2)(d) defines the "applicable fraction" of an unapplied portion of a forgiven amount in respect of an obligation issued by a debtor in respect of a loss for a taxation year for the purposes of section 80.

Subparagraph 80(2)(d) is amended to provide that the applicable fraction of the unapplied portion of a forgiven amount in respect of an obligation issued by a debtor in respect of a loss for any taxation year, is the fraction required to be used by the taxpayer under amended section 38 for that year. The amendment is consequential on the reduction of the inclusion rate for capital gains from 3/4 to 1/2 [see 38(a) — ed.].

**Notes**: Proposed 80(2)(d)(i) is wrong, since gains are now half-taxed under 38(a) effective October 18, 2000. The Department of Finance has confirmed that subpara. (i) will be deleted.

(e) **[where applicable fraction reduces loss]** — where an applicable fraction (as determined under paragraph (d)) of the unapplied portion of a forgiven amount is applied under subsection (4) to reduce at any time a loss for a taxation year, the portion of the forgiven amount so applied shall, except for the purpose of reducing the loss, be deemed to be the quotient obtained when the amount of the reduction is divided by the applicable fraction;

(f) **[cumulative eligible capital]** — where ¾ of the unapplied portion of a forgiven amount is applied under subsection (7) to reduce cumulative eligible capital, except for the purpose of reducing the cumulative eligible capital, the portion of the forgiven amount so applied shall be deemed to be ⁴⁄₃ of the amount of the reduction;

(g) **[amount paid in satisfaction of debt]** — where a corporation issues a share (other than an excluded security) to a person as consideration for the settlement of a debt issued by the corporation and payable to the person, the amount paid in satisfaction of the debt because of the issue of the share is deemed to be equal to the fair market value of the share at the time it was issued;

**Related Provisions**: 51(1) — Conversion of convertible debt into shares.

**Notes**: 80(2)(g) amended by 1995-97 technical bill, retroactive to its introduction (taxation years ending after February 21, 1994 — see Notes at end of s. 80). It was split into two paras., (g) and (g.1). The main difference from the original version is that new (g) and (g.1) do not limit the amount that is considered to have been paid in satisfaction of a debt because of any non-share consideration that is given by a debtor. The original version, now deemed never to have been in force, read:

(g) the amount paid in satisfaction of a debt issued by a corporation and payable to a person shall

(i) where any part of the consideration given to the person for the settlement of the debt consists of a share (other than an excluded security) issued by the corporation to the person, be deemed to be equal to the total of

(A) the fair market value of the share at the time it was issued, and

(B) the amount, if any, that can reasonably be considered to be the increase, as a consequence of the settlement of the debt, in the fair market value of other shares of the capital stock of the corporation owned by the person, and

(ii) in any other case, be deemed to include the amount described in clause (i)(B);

(g.1) **[amount paid in satisfaction of debt]** — where a debt issued by a corporation and payable to a person is settled at any time, the amount, if any, that can reasonably be considered to be the increase, as a consequence of the settlement of the debt, in the fair market value of shares of the capital stock of the corporation owned by the person (other than any shares acquired by the person as consideration for the settlement of the debt) is deemed to be an amount paid at that time in satisfaction of the debt;

**Notes**: 80(2)(g.1) added by 1995-97 technical bill, effective for taxation years ending after February 21, 1994. See Notes to 80(2)(g).

(h) **[debt replaced with debt]** — where any part of the consideration given by a debtor to another person for the settlement at any time of a particular commercial debt obligation issued by the debtor and payable to the other person consists of a new commercial debt obligation issued by the debtor to the other person

(i) an amount equal to the principal amount of the new obligation shall be deemed to be paid by the debtor at that time, because of the issue of the new obligation, in satisfaction of the principal amount of the particular obligation, and

(ii) the new obligation shall be deemed to have been issued for an amount equal to the amount, if any, by which

(A) the principal amount of the new obligation

exceeds

(B) the amount, if any, by which the principal amount of the new obligation exceeds the amount for which the particular obligation was issued;

Subdivision f — Rules Relating to Computation of Income    S. 80(2)(o)

**Related Provisions**: 40(2)(e.2) — Limitation on capital loss; 80(2)(l) — Where debt replaced with debt to third party; 248(1)"principal amount" — Principal amount excludes amounts payable on account of interest.

**I.T. Technical News**: No. 15 (tax consequences of the adoption of the "euro" currency).

(i) **[multiple debts settled]** — where 2 or more commercial obligations issued by a debtor are settled at the same time, those obligations shall be treated as if they were settled at different times in the order designated by the debtor in a prescribed form filed with the debtor's return of income under this Part for the debtor's taxation year that includes that time or, if the debtor does not so designate any such order, in the order designated by the Minister;

**Related Provisions**: 220(3.21)(a) — Late filing, amendment or revocation of designation.

**Notes**: The prescribed form for 1994 could be filed with Revenue Canada up to the end of 1995. (1994 tax amendments bill, para. 27(2)(c).) See also Notes at end of 80.

**Forms**: T2153: Designations under para. 80(2)(i) for forgiven debts.

(j) **["related" and "controlled"]** — for the purpose of determining, at any time, whether 2 persons are related to each other or whether any person is controlled by any other person, it shall be assumed that

(i) each partnership and each trust is a corporation having a capital stock of a single class of voting shares divided into 100 issued shares,

(ii) each member of a partnership and each beneficiary under a trust owned at that time the number of issued shares of that class that is equal to the proportion of 100 that

(A) the fair market value at that time of the member's interest in the partnership or the beneficiary's interest in the trust, as the case may be

is of

(B) the fair market value at that time of all members' interests in the partnership or all beneficiaries' interests in the trust, as the case may be, and

(iii) where a beneficiary's share of the income or capital of a trust depends on the exercise by any person of, or the failure by any person to exercise, any discretionary power, the fair market value at any time of the beneficiary's interest in the trust is equal to

(A) where the beneficiary is not entitled to receive or otherwise obtain the use of any of the income or capital of the trust before the death after that time of one or more other beneficiaries under the trust, nil, and

(B) in any other case, the total fair market value at that time of all beneficiaries' interests under the trust;

**Related Provisions**: 40(2)(e.1) — Application to stop-loss rule; 80.01(2)(a) — Application to s. 80.01; 80.04(3) — Application to s. 80.04.

(k) **[foreign currency obligation]** — where an obligation is denominated in a currency (other than Canadian currency), the forgiven amount at any time in respect of the obligation shall be determined with reference to the relative value of that currency and Canadian currency at the time the obligation was issued;

**Related Provisions**: 79(7) — Parallel rule re proceeds of disposition where property surrendered to creditor; 80.01(11) — Debt parking and statute-barred debt rules ignored where currency fluctuates.

(l) **[debt replaced with debt to third party]** — where an amount is paid in satisfaction of the principal amount of a particular commercial obligation issued by a debtor and, as a consequence of the payment, the debtor is legally obliged to pay that amount to another person, the obligation to pay that amount to the other person shall be deemed to be a commercial obligation that was issued by the debtor at the same time and in the same circumstances as the particular obligation;

**Related Provisions**: 80(2)(h) — Where debt replaced with new debt; 80.01(2)(a) — Application to s. 80.01.

(m) **[amount reducible only to zero]** — for greater certainty, the amount that can be applied under this section to reduce another amount may not exceed that other amount;

**Related Provisions**: 257 — Formulas cannot calculate to less than zero.

(n) **[where debt owed by partnership]** — except for the purposes of this paragraph, where

(i) a commercial debt obligation issued by a debtor is settled at any time,

(ii) the debtor is at that time a member of a partnership, and

(iii) the obligation was, under the agreement governing the obligation, treated immediately before that time as a debt owed by the partnership,

the obligation shall be considered to have been issued by the partnership and not by the debtor;

**Related Provisions**: 80(2)(o) — Override rule where debtor jointly liable with others; 80(15) — Commercial debt obligation issued by partnership; 80.01(2)(a) — Application to s. 80.01; 80.04(3) — Application to s. 80.04.

(o) **[where joint liability for debt]** — notwithstanding paragraph (n), where a commercial debt obligation for which a particular person is jointly liable with one or more other persons is settled at any time in respect of the particular person but not in respect of all of the other persons, the portion of the obligation that can reasonably be considered to be the particular person's share of the obligation shall be considered to have been issued by the particular person and settled at that time and not at any subsequent time;

(p) **[death of debtor]** — a commercial debt obligation issued by an individual that is outstanding at the time of the individual's death and settled at a subsequent time shall, if the estate of the individual was liable for the obligation immediately before the subsequent time, be deemed to have been issued by the estate at the same time and in the same circumstances as the obligation was issued by the individual; and

**Related Provisions**: 80(2)(q) — Where debt settled within 6 months of death.

(q) **[death of debtor]** — where a commercial debt obligation issued by an individual would, but for this paragraph, be settled at any time in the period ending 6 months after the death of an individual (or within such longer period as is acceptable to the Minister and the estate of the individual) and the estate of the individual was liable immediately before that time for the obligation

(i) the obligation shall be deemed to have been settled at the beginning of the day on which the individual died and not at that time,

(ii) any amount paid at that time by the estate in satisfaction of the principal amount of the obligation shall be deemed to have been paid at the beginning of the day on which the individual died,

(iii) any amount given by the estate at or before that time to another person as consideration for assumption by the other person of the obligation shall be deemed to have been given at the beginning of the day on which the individual died, and

(iv) paragraph (b) shall not apply in respect of the settlement to interest that accrues within that period,

except that this paragraph does not apply in circumstances in which any amount is because of the settlement included under paragraph 6(1)(a) or subsection 15(1) in computing the income of any person or in which section 79 applies in respect of the obligation.

**Related Provisions**: 6(15.1)(d), 15(1.21)(d) — 80(2)(q) ignored for employee and shareholder benefit purposes; 80(2)(p) — Where debt not settled within 6 months of death.

(3) **Reductions of non-capital losses** — Where a commercial obligation issued by a debtor is settled at any time, the forgiven amount at that time in respect of the obligation shall be applied to reduce at that time, in the following order,

(a) the debtor's non-capital loss for each taxation year that ended before that time to the extent that the amount so applied

(i) does not exceed the amount (in subsection (4) referred to as the debtor's "ordinary non-capital loss at that time for the year") that would be the relevant loss balance at that time for the obligation and in respect of the debtor's non-capital loss for the year if the description of E in the definition "non-capital loss" in subsection 111(8) were read without reference to the expression "the taxpayer's allowable business investment loss for the year", and

(ii) does not, because of this subsection, reduce the debtor's non-capital loss for a preceding taxation year;

(b) the debtor's farm loss for each taxation year that ended before that time, to the extent that the amount so applied

(i) does not exceed the amount that is the relevant loss balance at that time for the obligation and in respect of the debtor's farm loss for the year, and

(ii) does not, because of this subsection, reduce the debtor's farm loss for a preceding taxation year; and

(c) the debtor's restricted farm loss for each taxation year that ended before that time, to the extent that the amount so applied

(i) does not exceed the amount that is the relevant loss balance at that time for the obligation and in respect of the debtor's restricted farm loss for the year, and

(ii) does not, because of this subsection, reduce the debtor's restricted farm loss for a preceding taxation year.

**Related Provisions**: 31(1.1)(b) — Reduction in restricted farm loss; 80(2)(c) — Order of application of rules; 80(2)(m) — Reduction cannot exceed the amount of losses; 80(4)(a) — Reduction of allowable business investment loss carryforward; 111(8)"farm loss"C — Reduction in farm loss; 111(8)"non-capital loss"D.2 — Reduction in non-capital loss.

**Notes**: 80(3)–(14) set out a scheme of rules for using up the "forgiven amount" as defined in 80(1). See Notes at end of 80.

(4) **Reductions of capital losses** — Where a commercial obligation issued by a debtor is settled at any time, the applicable fraction of the remaining unapplied portion of a forgiven amount at that time in respect of the obligation shall be applied to reduce at that time, in the following order,

(a) the debtor's non-capital loss for each taxation year that ended before that time to the extent that the amount so applied

(i) does not exceed the amount, if any, by which

(A) the relevant loss balance at that time for the obligation and in respect of the debtor's non-capital loss for the year

exceeds

(B) the debtor's ordinary non-capital loss (within the meaning assigned by subparagraph (3)(a)(i)) at that time for the year, and

(ii) does not, because of this subsection, reduce the debtor's non-capital loss for a preceding taxation year; and

Subdivision f — Rules Relating to Computation of Income  S. 80(8)(a)

(b) the debtor's net capital loss for each taxation year that ended before that time, to the extent that the amount so applied

(i) does not exceed the relevant loss balance at that time for the obligation and in respect of the debtor's net capital loss for the year, and

(ii) does not, because of this subsection, reduce the debtor's net capital loss for a preceding taxation year.

**Related Provisions**: 80(2)(c) — Order of application of rules; 80(2)(e) — Determination of applicable fraction; 80(2)(m) — Reduction cannot exceed the amount of losses; 111(8)"net capital loss"D — Reduction in net capital loss; 111(8)"non-capital loss"D.2 — Reduction in non-capital loss.

**(5) Reductions with respect to depreciable property** — Where a commercial obligation issued by a debtor is settled at any time, the remaining unapplied portion of the forgiven amount at that time in respect of the obligation shall be applied, in such manner as is designated by the debtor in a prescribed form filed with the debtor's return of income under this Part for the taxation year that includes that time, to reduce immediately after that time the following amounts:

(a) the capital cost to the debtor of a depreciable property that is owned by the debtor immediately after that time; and

(b) the undepreciated capital cost to the debtor of depreciable property of a prescribed class immediately after that time.

**Related Provisions**: 13(7.1)(g) — Reduction in capital cost of depreciable property; 13(21)"undepreciated capital cost"E.1 — Reduction in undepreciated capital cost; 80(2)(c) — Order of application of rules; 80(2)(m) — Reduction cannot exceed the capital cost or u.c.c.; 80(6) — Restriction with respect to depreciable property; 80(13)D(a) — Income inclusion of remaining balance; 80(16) — Designation by CCRA where debtor fails to designate; 80.04(4)(b) — Transfer of forgiven amount after maximum designations; 96(3) — Designation by members of partnership; 220(3.21)(a) — Late filing, amendment or revocation of designation.

**Notes**: The prescribed form for 1994 could be filed with Revenue Canada up to the end of 1995. (1994 tax amendments bill, para. 27(2)(c).) See also Notes at end of 80.

**Regulations**: 1105 (prescribed classes of depreciable property).

**Forms**: T2153: Designations under para. 80(2)(i) for forgiven debts; T2154: Application of designated forgiven debt under sec. 80.

**(6) Restriction with respect to depreciable property** — Where a commercial obligation issued by a debtor is settled at any time,

(a) an amount may be applied under subsection (5) to reduce, immediately after that time, the capital cost to the debtor of a depreciable property of a prescribed class only to the extent that

(i) the undepreciated capital cost to the debtor of depreciable property of that class at that time

exceeds

(ii) the total of all other reductions immediately after that time to that undepreciated capital cost; and

(b) an amount may be applied under subsection (5) to reduce, immediately after that time, the capital cost to the debtor of a depreciable property (other than a depreciable property of a prescribed class) only to the extent that

(i) the capital cost to the debtor of the property at that time

exceeds

(ii) the amount that was allowed to the debtor before that time under Part XVII of the *Income Tax Regulations* in respect of the property.

**Regulations**: 1105 (prescribed classes of depreciable property).

**(7) Reductions of cumulative eligible capital** — Where a commercial obligation issued by a debtor is settled at any time, ¾ of the remaining unapplied portion of the forgiven amount at that time in respect of the obligation shall be applied (to the extent designated in a prescribed form filed with the debtor's return of income under this Part for the taxation year that includes that time) to reduce immediately after that time the cumulative eligible capital of the debtor in respect of each business of the debtor (or, where the debtor is at that time non-resident, in respect of each business carried on in Canada by the debtor).

**Related Provisions**: 14(5)"cumulative eligible capital"F:P.1 — Reduction in cumulative eligible capital; 80(2)(c) — Order of application of rules; 80(2)(f) — Rule where cumulative eligible capital reduced; 80(2)(m) — Reduction cannot exceed the amount of cumulative eligible capital; 80(13)D(a) — Income inclusion of remaining balance; 80(16) — Designation by CCRA where debtor fails to designate; 80.04(4)(b) — Transfer of forgiven amount after maximum designations; 220(3.21)(a) — Late filing, amendment or revocation of designation; 253 — Extended meaning of carrying on business in Canada.

**Notes**: The prescribed form for 1994 could be filed with Revenue Canada up to the end of 1995. (1994 tax amendments bill, para. 27(2)(c).) See also Notes at end of 80.

**Forms**: T2153: Designations under para. 80(2)(i) for forgiven debts; T2154: Application of designated forgiven debt under sec. 80.

**(8) Reductions of resource expenditures** — Where a commercial obligation issued by a debtor is settled at any time, the remaining unapplied portion of the forgiven amount at that time in respect of the obligation shall be applied (to the extent designated in a prescribed form filed with the debtor's return of income under this Part for the taxation year that includes that time) to reduce immediately after that time the following amounts:

(a) where the debtor is a corporation resident in Canada throughout that year, each particular amount that would be determined in respect of the debtor under paragraph 66.7(2)(a), (3)(a), (4)(a) or (5)(a) if paragraphs 66.7(4)(a) and (5)(a) were read without reference to the expressions "30% of" and "10% of", respectively, as a consequence of the acquisition of control of the debtor by a person or group of persons, the debtor ceasing to be exempt from tax under this Part on its taxable income or the acquisition of properties by the debtor by way of an amalgamation or merger, where the amount so applied does not exceed the successor pool immediately after that time for the obligation and in respect of the particular amount;

### Proposed Amendment — 80(8)(a)

(a) where the debtor is a corporation resident in Canada throughout that year, each particular amount that would be determined in respect of the debtor under paragraph 66.7(2)(a), (2.3)(a), (3)(a), (4)(a) or (5)(a) if paragraphs 66.7(2.3)(a), (4)(a) and (5)(a) were read without reference to the expressions "30% of", "30% of" and "10% of", respectively, as a consequence of the acquisition of control of the debtor by a person or group of persons, the debtor ceasing to be exempt from tax under this Part on its taxable income or the acquisition of properties by the debtor by way of an amalgamation or merger, where the amount so applied does not exceed the successor pool immediately after that time for the obligation and in respect of the particular amount;

**Application**: The December 21, 2000 draft legislation, subsec. 34(3), will amend para. 80(8)(a) to read as above, applicable to taxation years that begin after 2000.

**Technical Notes**: The expression "forgiven amount" is defined in subsection 80(1). A forgiven amount is applied as required by subsections 80(3) to (7) to reduce various tax attributes of the taxpayer. Under subsection 80(8), the unapplied portion of a debtor's forgiven amount remaining after the application of subsections 80(3) to (7) may, to the extent designated by the debtor in a prescribed form filed with the debtor's income tax return, be applied to reduce specified resource expenditure pools.

Paragraph 80(8)(a) is amended so that the resource expenditure pools referred to include "successor" foreign resource expenses, as determined under new subsection 66.7(2.3). The definition "successor pool" in subsection 80(1) is similarly amended.

(b) the cumulative Canadian exploration expense (within the meaning assigned by subsection 66.1(6)) of the debtor;

(c) the cumulative Canadian development expense (within the meaning assigned by subsection 66.2(5)) of the debtor;

(d) the cumulative Canadian oil and gas property expense (within the meaning assigned by subsection 66.4(5)) of the debtor; and

(e) the total determined under paragraph 66(4)(a) in respect of the debtor, where

(i) the debtor is resident in Canada throughout that year, and

(ii) the amount so applied does not exceed such portion of the total of the debtor's foreign exploration and development expenses (within the meaning assigned by subsection 66(15)) as were incurred by the debtor before that time and would be deductible under subsection 66(4) in computing the debtor's income for that year if the debtor had sufficient income described in subparagraph 66(4)(b)(ii) and if that year ended at that time.

### Proposed Addition — 80(8)(f)

(f) the cumulative foreign resource expense (within the meaning assigned by subsection 66.21(1)) of the debtor in respect of a country.

**Application**: The December 21, 2000 draft legislation, subsec. 34(4), will add para. 80(8)(f), applicable to taxation years that begin after 2000.

**Technical Notes**: Paragraph 80(8)(f) is introduced to permit the forgiven amount to be applied against a debtor's cumulative foreign resource expense in respect of a country, as determined under new section 66.21.

**Related Provisions**: 66(4)(a)(iii) — Reduction in claim for foreign exploration and development expenses; 66.1(6)"cumulative Canadian exploration expense"J.1 — Reduction in CCEE; 66.2(5)"cumulative Canadian development expense"M.1 — Reduction in CCDE; 66.21(1)"cumulative foreign resource expense"I; 66.4(5)"cumulative Canadian oil and gas property expense"I.1 — Reduction in CCOGPE; 66.7(2)(a)(ii), 66.7(3)(a)(ii), 66.7(4)(a)(iv), 66.7(5)(a)(iii) — Reductions in successor pools; 80(2)(c) — Order of application of rules; 80(2)(m) — Reduction cannot exceed the resource expenditures reduced; 80(13)D(a) — Income inclusion of remaining balance; 80(16) — Designation by CCRA where debtor fails to designate; 80.04(4)(b) — Transfer of forgiven amount after maximum designations; 139.1(18) — Holding corporation deemed not to acquire control of insurer on demutualization; 220(3.21)(a) — Late filing, amendment or revocation of designation; 256(6)–(9) — Whether control acquired.

**Notes**: The prescribed form for 1994 could be filed with Revenue Canada up to the end of 1995. (1994 tax amendments bill, para. 27(2)(c).) See also Notes at end of 80.

**Forms**: T2153: Designations under para. 80(2)(i) for forgiven debts; T2154: Application of designated forgiven debt under sec. 80.

**(9) Reductions of adjusted cost bases of capital properties** — Where a commercial obligation issued by a debtor is settled at any time and amounts have been designated under subsections (5), (7) and (8) to the maximum extent permitted in respect of the settlement, subject to subsection (18)

(a) the remaining unapplied portion of the forgiven amount at that time in respect of the obligation shall be applied (to the extent designated in a prescribed form filed with the debtor's return of income under this Part for the taxation year that includes that time) to reduce immediately after that time the adjusted cost bases to the debtor of capital properties (other than shares of the capital stock of corporations of which the debtor is a specified shareholder at that time, debts issued by corporations of which the debtor is a specified shareholder at that time, interests in partnerships that are related to the debtor at that time, depreciable property that is not of a prescribed class, personal-use properties and excluded properties) that are owned by the debtor immediately after that time;

(b) an amount may be applied under this subsection to reduce, immediately after that time, the capital cost to the debtor of a depreciable property of a prescribed class only to the extent that

(i) the capital cost immediately after that time to the debtor of the property (determined without reference to the settlement of the obligation at that time)

exceeds

(ii) its capital cost immediately after that time to the debtor for the purposes of paragraphs 8(1)(j) and (p), sections 13 and 20 and any regulations made for the purpose of paragraph 20(1)(a) (determined without reference to the settlement of the obligation at that time); and

(c) for the purposes of paragraphs 8(1)(j) and (p), sections 13 and 20 and any regulations made for the purpose of paragraph 20(1)(a), no amount shall be considered to have been applied under this subsection.

**Related Provisions**: 53(2)(g.1) — Reduction in ACB; 80(2)(c) — Order of application of rules; 80(2)(m) — Reduction cannot exceed the adjusted cost base; 80(10), (11) — Reduction of ACB of certain shares, debt and partnership interests; 80(13)D(a) — Income inclusion of remaining balance; 80(16) — Designation by CCRA where debtor fails to designate; 80(18) — Limitation on designation by partnership; 80.04(4)(b) — Transfer of forgiven amount after maximum designations; 96(3) — Designation by members of partnership; 220(3.21)(a) — Late filing, amendment or revocation of designation.

**Notes**: The prescribed form for 80(9)(a) for 1994 could be filed with Revenue Canada up to the end of 1995. (1994 tax amendments bill, para. 27(2)(c).) See also Notes at end of 80.

**Regulations**: 1105 (prescribed classes of depreciable property).

**Forms**: T2153: Designations under para. 80(2)(i) for forgiven debts; T2154: Application of designated forgiven debt under sec. 80.

### (10) Reduction of adjusted cost bases of certain shares and debts

— Where a commercial obligation issued by a debtor is settled at any time in a taxation year and amounts have been designated by the debtor under subsections (5), (7), (8) and (9) to the maximum extent permitted in respect of the settlement, subject to subsection (18) the remaining unapplied portion of that forgiven amount shall be applied (to the extent that it is designated in a prescribed form filed with the debtor's return of income under this Part for the year) to reduce immediately after that time the adjusted cost bases to the debtor of capital properties, owned by the debtor immediately after that time, that are shares of the capital stock of corporations of which the debtor is a specified shareholder at that time and debts issued by corporations of which the debtor is a specified shareholder at that time (other than shares of the capital stock of corporations related to the debtor at that time, debts issued by corporations related to the debtor at that time and excluded properties).

**Related Provisions**: 53(2)(g.1) — Reduction in ACB; 80(2)(c) — Order of application of rules; 80(2)(m) — Reduction cannot exceed the adjusted cost base; 80(11) — Reduction of ACB of certain shares, debt and partnership interests; 80(13)D(a) — Income inclusion of remaining balance; 80(16) — Designation by CCRA where debtor fails to designate; 80(18) — Limitation on designation by partnership; 80.04(4)(b) — Transfer of forgiven amount after maximum designations; 96(3) — Designation by members of partnership; 220(3.21)(a) — Late filing, amendment or revocation of designation.

**Notes**: The prescribed form for 1994 could be filed with Revenue Canada up to the end of 1995. (1994 tax amendments bill, para. 27(2)(c).) See also Notes at end of 80. For gains on subsequent dispositions, see 80.03.

**Forms**: T2153: Designations under para. 80(2)(i) for forgiven debts; T2154: Application of designated forgiven debt under sec. 80.

### (11) Reduction of adjusted cost bases of certain shares, debts and partnership interests

— Where a commercial obligation issued by a debtor is settled at any time in a taxation year and amounts have been designated by the debtor under subsections (5), (7), (8), (9) and (10) to the maximum extent permitted in respect of the settlement, subject to subsection (18) the remaining unapplied portion of that forgiven amount shall be applied (to the extent that it is designated in a prescribed form filed with the debtor's return of income under this Part for the year) to reduce immediately after that time the adjusted cost bases to the debtor of

(a) shares and debts that are capital properties (other than excluded properties and properties the adjusted cost bases of which are reduced at that time under subsection (9) or (10)) of the debtor immediately after that time; and

(b) interests in partnerships that are related to the debtor at that time that are capital properties (other than excluded properties) of the debtor immediately after that time.

**Related Provisions**: 53(2)(g.1) — Reduction in ACB; 80(2)(c) — Order of application of rules; 80(2)(m) — Reduction cannot exceed the adjusted cost base; 80(13)B(a) — Income inclusion where reductions in ACB are excessive; 80(16) — Designation by CCRA where debtor fails to designate; 80(18) — Limitation on designation by partnership; 80.03 — Gains on subsequent dispositions; 96(3) — Designation by members of partnership; 220(3.21)(a) — Late filing, amendment or revocation of designation.

**Notes**: The prescribed form for 1994 could be filed with Revenue Canada up to the end of 1995. (1994 tax amendments bill, para. 27(2)(c).) See also Notes at end of 80. For gains on subsequent dispositions, see 80.03.

**Forms**: T2153: Designations under para. 80(2)(i) for forgiven debts; T2154: Application of designated forgiven debt under sec. 80.

### (12) Capital gain where current year capital loss

— Where a commercial obligation issued by a debtor (other than a partnership) is settled at any time in a taxation year and amounts have been designated by the debtor under subsections (5), (7), (8) and (9) to the maximum extent permitted in respect of the settlement,

(a) the debtor shall be deemed to have a capital gain for the year from the disposition of capital property (or, where the debtor is non-resident at the end of the year, taxable Canadian property), equal to the lesser of

(i) the remaining unapplied portion of the forgiven amount at that time in respect of the obligation, and

(ii) the amount, if any, by which the total of

(A) all of the debtor's capital losses for the year from the dispositions of properties (other than listed personal properties and excluded properties), and

(B) ⁴/₃ of the amount that would, because of subsection 88(1.2), be deductible under paragraph 111(1)(b) in computing the debtor's taxable income for the year, if the debtor had sufficient income and taxable capital gains for the year,

**Proposed Amendment — 80(12)(a)(ii)(B)**

**Application**: The December 21, 2000 draft legislation, subsec. 34(5), will amend cl. 80(12)(a)(ii)(B) by replacing the reference to the expression "4/3 of" with a reference to the word "twice", applicable to taxation years that end after February 27, 2000 except that, for a taxation year of a debtor that includes either February 28, 2000 or October 17, 2000 the reference to the word "twice" shall be read as a reference to the expression "the fraction that is the reciprocal of the fraction in para. 38(a), as amended [by the December 21, 2000 draft legislation], that applies to the debtor for the year, multiplied by".

**Technical Notes**: Subsection 80(12) treats the unapplied portion of a forgiven amount in respect of a commercial obligation of a debtor settled in a year as a capital gain of the debtor for the year from the disposition of capital property to the extent of the lesser of the amount of the remaining unapplied portion and the amount of the debtor's net capital losses for the year. In calculating the amount of the net capital losses of the debtor for the year, clause 80(12)(a)(ii)(B) includes 4/3 of certain deductible net capital losses of a subsidiary of the debtor that has been wound up into the debtor.

Clause 80(12)(a)(ii)(B) is amended to replace the expression "4/3 of" with the word "twice". The amendment is consequential on the reduction of the inclusion rate for capital gains from 3/4 to 1/2 [see 38(a) — ed.].

The amendment applies to taxation years that end after February 27, 2000 except that, for a debtor's taxation year that includes either February 28, 2000 or October 17, 2000, the reference to the word "twice" in clause 80(12)(a)(ii)(B) is to be read as a reference to the expression "the fraction that is the reciprocal of the fraction in paragraph 38(a) that applies to the debtor for the year, multiplied by". These modifications are required in order to reflect the capital gains/losses rate for the year.

exceeds the total of

(C) all of the debtor's capital gains for the year from the dispositions of such properties (determined without reference to this subsection), and

(D) all amounts each of which is an amount deemed by this subsection to be a capital gain of the debtor for the year as a consequence of the application of this subsection to other commercial obligations settled before that time; and

(b) the forgiven amount at that time in respect of the obligation shall be considered to have been applied under this subsection to the extent of the amount deemed by this subsection to be a capital gain of the debtor for the year as a consequence of the application of this subsection to the settlement of the obligation at that time.

**Related Provisions**: 80(2)(c) — Order of application of rules.

**(13) Income inclusion** — Where a commercial obligation issued by a debtor is settled at any time in a taxation year, there shall be added, in computing the debtor's income for the year from the source in connection with which the obligation was issued, the amount determined by the formula

$$(A + B - C - D) \times E$$

where

A is the remaining unapplied portion of the forgiven amount at that time in respect of the obligation,

B is the lesser of

(a) the total of all amounts designated under subsection (11) by the debtor in respect of the settlement of the obligation at that time, and

(b) the residual balance at that time in respect of the settlement of the obligation,

C is the total of all amounts each of which is an amount specified in an agreement filed under section 80.04 in respect of the settlement of the obligation at that time,

D is

(a) where the debtor has designated amounts under subsections (5), (7), (8), (9) and (10) to the maximum extent permitted in respect of the settlement, the amount, if any, by which

(i) the total of all amounts each of which is an unrecognized loss at that time, in respect of the obligation, from the disposition of a property

exceeds

(ii) ⁴/₃ of the total of all amounts each of which is an amount by which the amount determined before that time under this subsection in respect of a settlement of an obligation issued by the debtor has been reduced because of an amount determined under this paragraph, and

Subdivision f — Rules Relating to Computation of Income    S. 80(14)(c)(ii)

### Proposed Amendment — 80(13)D(a)(ii)

**Application**: The December 21, 2000 draft legislation, subsec. 34(6), will amend subpara. (a)(ii) of the description of D in subsec. 80(13) by replacing the reference to the expression "4/3 of" with a reference to the word "twice", applicable to taxation years that end after February 27, 2000 except that, for a taxation year of a debtor that includes either February 28, 2000 or October 17, 2000 the reference to the word "twice" shall be read as a reference to the expression "the fraction that is the reciprocal of the fraction in para. 38(a), as amended [by the December 21, 2000 draft legislation], that applies to the debtor for the year, multiplied by".

**Technical Notes**: Subsection 80(13) includes an amount in computing the income of a debtor for the taxation year in respect the remaining unapplied portion of the forgiven amount in respect of a commercial obligation settled in the year.

The descriptions of D and E (in subparagraph (a)(ii) of the description of D in subsection 80(13) and paragraph (b) in the description of E in that subsection) are amended to replace references to the fraction "3/4" and the decimal "0.75" with a reference to the fraction "1/2". The amendments are consequential on the reduction of the inclusion rate for capital gains from 3/4 to 1/2 [see 38(a) — ed.].

The amendments apply to taxation years that end after February 27, 2000 except that, for a debtor's taxation year that includes either February 28, 2000 or October 17, 2000, the references to "1/2" in the descriptions of D and E in subsection 80(13) are to be read as references to the fraction in amended paragraph 38(a) that applies to the debtor for the year. These modifications are required in order to reflect the capital gains/losses rate for the year.

**Notice of Ways and Means Motion, Economic Statement, October 18, 2000**: *Capital Gains Inclusion Rate*

(11) That, for the 2000 and subsequent taxation years,

 (c) in determining a taxpayer's inclusion rate [for capital gains under s. 38 — ed.] for the year

 ...

 (v) the amount that would be included in computing the taxpayer's income for the year because of subsection 80(13) of the Act, if the value of E in the formula in that subsection were 1, in respect of a commercial obligation that is settled at any time be treated as a capital gain of the taxpayer from a disposition of property at that time, ...

 (b) in any other case, nil, and

E is

 (a) where the debtor is a partnership, 1, and

 (b) in any other case, 0.75.

### Proposed Amendment — 80(13)E(b)

**Application**: The December 21, 2000 draft legislation, subsec. 34(7), will amend para. (b) of the description of E in subsec. 80(13) by replacing the reference to the number "0.75" with a reference to the fraction "1/2", applicable to taxation years that end after February 27, 2000 except that, for a taxation year of a debtor that includes either February 28, 2000 or October 17, 2000 the reference to the fraction "1/2" shall be read as a reference to the fraction in para. 38(a), as amended [by the December 21, 2000 draft legislation], that applies to the debtor for the year.

**Technical Notes**: See under 80(13)D(a)(ii).

**Related Provisions**: 4(1) — Income from a source; 12(1)(z.3) — Inclusion into income from business or property; 28(1)(d) — Inclusion in farming or fishing income when using cash method; 61.2–61.4 — Reserves to offset amount included under 80(13); 66.7(1)(b)(iii), 66.7(2)(b)(iv), 66.7(3)(b)(iii), 66.7(4)(b)(iii), 66.7(5)(b)(iii) — Resource expenditures — reduction in successor pools; 80(2)(c) — Order of application of rules; 80(14) — Determination of residual balance; 80(16) — Designation by CCRA to reduce reserve under 61.2; 80.04(8) — Where corporations become related in order to transfer forgiven amount; 95(1)"foreign accrual property income"A.1 — 4/3 inclusion in FAPI; 137.1(10) — Settlement of debts by deposit insurance corporation; 257 — Formula cannot calculate to less than zero.

**Notes**: If after applying the "forgiven amount" (defined in 80(1)) as set out in 80(3)–(12) there is still a residual balance (defined in 80(14)), it is included into income under 80(13) unless it can be transferred to another taxpayer under 80.04. See Notes at end of s. 80. However, there may be an offsetting deduction under 61.3 and/or a deferral of the income to later years under 61.2 and 61.4.

80(13)B(b) amended by 1995-97 technical bill, retroactive to its introduction (taxation years ending after February 21, 1994 — see Notes at end of s. 80). The amendment effectively deleted former subpara. (ii). The previous version, now deemed never to have been in force, read:

 (b) the total of

 (i) the residual balance at that time in respect of the settlement of the obligation, and

 (ii) the amount, if any, by which the amount determined for C in respect of the settlement exceeds the amount determined for A in respect of the settlement,

**Interpretation Bulletins**: See list at end of s. 80.

**Information Circulars**: See list at end of s. 80.

**Advance Tax Rulings**: ATR-27: Exchange and acquisition of interests in capital properties through rollovers and winding-up ("butterfly").

**(14) Residual balance** — For the purpose of subsection (13), the residual balance at any time in a taxation year in respect of the settlement of a particular commercial obligation issued by a debtor is the amount, if any, by which

 (a) the gross tax attributes of directed persons at that time in respect of the debtor

exceeds the total of

 (b) the value of A in subsection (13) in respect of the settlement of the particular obligation at that time,

 (c) all amounts each of which is

 (i) the amount, if any, by which the value of A in subsection (13) in respect of a settlement before that time and in the year of a commercial obligation issued by the debtor exceeds the value of C in that subsection in respect of the settlement,

 (ii) the value of A in subsection (13) in respect of a settlement of a commercial obligation that is deemed by paragraph 80.04(4)(e) to have been issued by a directed person in respect of the debtor because of the filing of an agreement under section 80.04 in respect of a settlement before that time and in the year of a commercial obligation issued by the debtor, or

(iii) the amount specified in an agreement (other than an agreement with a directed person in respect of the debtor) filed under section 80.04 in respect of the settlement before that time and in the year of a commercial obligation issued by the debtor, and

(d) all amounts each of which is an amount in respect of a settlement at a particular time before that time and in the year of a commercial obligation issued by the debtor equal to the least of

(i) the total of all amounts designated under subsection (11) in respect of the settlement,

(ii) the residual balance of the debtor at the particular time, and

(iii) the amount, if any, by which the sum of the values of A and B in subsection (13) in respect of the settlement exceeds the value of C in that subsection in respect of the settlement.

**Related Provisions**: 80(14.1) — Meaning of "gross tax attributes".

**Notes**: 80(14) amended by 1995-97 technical bill, retroactive to its introduction (taxation years ending after February 21, 1994 — see Notes at end of s. 80). 80(14.1) was introduced together with this amendment. The previous 80(14), now deemed never to have been in force, read:

(14) For the purpose of subsection (13), the residual balance at any time in a taxation year in respect of the settlement of a particular commercial obligation issued by a debtor is the amount, if any, by which the total of

(a) all amounts each of which is an amount that would be applied under any of subsections (3) to (10) and (12) in respect of the settlements of separate commercial obligations issued by directed persons at that time in respect of the debtor if

(i) those obligations were issued at that time by those directed persons and were settled immediately after that time,

(ii) an amount equal to the forgiven amount at that time in respect of the particular obligation were the forgiven amount immediately after that time in respect of each of those obligations,

(iii) amounts were designated under subsections (5), (7), (8), (9) and (10) by those directed persons to the maximum extent permitted in respect of the settlement of each of those obligations, and

(iv) no amounts were designated under subsection (11) by any of those directed persons in respect of the settlement of any of those obligations, and

(b) where the debtor is a partnership, all amounts each of which is ¼ of an amount deducted because of paragraph (c) or (d) in computing the residual balance at that time in respect of the settlement of the particular obligation,

exceeds the total of

(c) all amounts each of which is ⅔ of the amount that would be included under subsection (13) in computing the debtor's income for the year in respect of the settlement at or before that time of a commercial obligation issued by the debtor if the amounts determined for B and D in subsection (13) were nil,

(d) all amounts each of which is ⅔ of an amount that would, if the amount determined for D in subsection (13) were nil, be included under subsection (13) in computing

the income of any of those directed persons in respect of the settlement of an obligation that is deemed by paragraph 80.04(4)(e) to have been issued by the directed person because of the filing of an agreement under section 80.04 in respect of the settlement at or before that time and in the year of a commercial obligation issued by the debtor,

(e) all amounts each of which is an amount specified in an agreement (other than an agreement with any of those directed persons) filed under section 80.04 in respect of the settlement at or before that time and in the year of a commercial obligation issued by the debtor, and

(f) all amounts each of which is the lesser of

(i) the total of all amounts designated under subsection (11) in respect of the settlement before that time and in the year of another commercial obligation issued by the debtor, and

(ii) the residual balance of the debtor at that previous time.

**(14.1) Gross tax attributes** — The gross tax attributes of directed persons at any time in respect of a debtor means the total of all amounts each of which is an amount that would be applied under any of subsections (3) to (10) and (12) in respect of a settlement of a separate commercial obligation (in this subsection referred to as a "notional obligation") issued by directed persons at that time in respect of the debtor if the following assumptions were made:

(a) a notional obligation was issued immediately before that time by each of those directed persons and was settled at that time;

(b) the forgiven amount at that time in respect of each of those notional obligations was equal to the total of all amounts each of which is a forgiven amount at or before that time and in the year in respect of a commercial obligation issued by the debtor;

(c) amounts were designated under subsections (5), (7), (8), (9) and (10) by each of those directed persons to the maximum extent permitted in respect of the settlement of each of those notional obligations; and

(d) no amounts were designated under subsection (11) by any of those directed persons in respect of the settlement of any of the notional obligations.

**Notes**: 80(14.1) added by 1995-97 technical bill, effective for taxation years ending after February 21, 1994. See Notes to 80(14).

**(15) Members of partnerships** — Where a commercial debt obligation issued by a partnership (in this subsection referred to as the "partnership obligation") is settled at any time in a fiscal period of the partnership that ends in a taxation year of a member of the partnership,

(a) the member may deduct, in computing the member's income for the year, such amount as the member claims not exceeding the relevant limit in respect of the partnership obligation;

(b) for the purpose of paragraph (a), the relevant limit in respect of the partnership obligation is the amount that would be included in computing the member's income for the year as a consequence of the application of subsection (13) and section 96 to the settlement of the partnership obligation if the partnership had designated amounts under subsections (5), (7), (8), (9) and (10) to the maximum extent permitted in respect of each obligation settled in that fiscal period and if income arising from the application of subsection (13) were from a source of income separate from any other sources of partnership income; and

(c) for the purposes of this section and section 80.04,

(i) the member shall be deemed to have issued a commercial debt obligation that was settled at the end of that fiscal period,

(ii) the amount deducted under paragraph (a) in respect of the partnership obligation in computing the member's income shall be treated as if it were the forgiven amount at the end of that fiscal period in respect of the obligation referred to in subparagraph (i),

(iii) subject to subparagraph (iv), the obligation referred to in subparagraph (i) shall be deemed to have been issued at the same time at which, and in the same circumstances in which, the partnership obligation was issued,

(iv) where the member is a corporation the control of which was acquired at a particular time that is before the end of that fiscal period and before the corporation became a member of the partnership and the partnership obligation was issued before the particular time,

(A) subject to the application of this subparagraph to an acquisition of control of the corporation after the particular time and before the end of that fiscal period, the obligation referred to in subparagraph (i) shall be deemed to have been issued by the member after the particular time, and

(B) paragraph (e) of the definition "relevant loss balance" in subsection (1), paragraph (f) of the definition "successor pool" in that subsection and paragraph (b) of the definition "unrecognized loss" in that subsection do not apply in respect of that acquisition of control, and

(v) the source in connection with which the obligation referred to in subparagraph (i) was issued shall be deemed to be the source in connection with which the partnership obligation was issued.

**Related Provisions**: 4(1) — Income from a source; 20(1)(uu) — Deduction for amount allowed under para. 80(15)(a); 61.2:A(b) — Effect of para. 80(15)(a) on reserve for individuals; 61.2:A(b), 61.3(1)(a)(ii), 61.3(2)(a)(ii), 61.4(a)A(ii) — Reserve in respect of debt forgiven; 80(1) — "Person" includes a partnership; 80(2)(n) — Commercial debt obligation issued by partner — deemed issued by partnership; 80(13)E(a) — Income inclusion where debtor is partnership; 80(14)(b) — Residual balance where debtor is partnership;

80(18) — Limitation on designation by partnership; 96(3) — Designation by members of partnership; 139.1(18) — Holding corporation deemed not to acquire control of insurer on demutualization; 256(6)–(9) — Whether control acquired; 256(8) — Deemed acquisition of shares.

**Notes**: 80(15) provides relief for members of a partnership, since a partner may have undeducted loss carryforwards and resource expenditure pools that are attributable to partnership activities. Forgiveness of an obligation that is deemed to arise for a partner is treated the same as a forgiven amount in respect of an obligation issued by the debtor. Further relief for certain partnership obligations is provided under 80(1)"forgiven amount"B(k). Special rules for partnership obligations are also provided under 80(2)(n) and (o) and 80(18). See also Notes at end of 80.

**(16) Designations by Minister** — Where a commercial obligation issued by a debtor is settled at any time in a taxation year and, as a consequence of the settlement an amount would, but for this subsection, be deducted under section 61.2 or 61.3 in computing the debtor's income for the year and the debtor has not designated amounts under subsections (5) to (11) to the maximum extent possible in respect of the settlement,

(a) the Minister may designate amounts under subsections (5) to (11) to the extent that the debtor would have been permitted to designate those amounts; and

(b) the amounts designated by the Minister shall, except for the purpose of this subsection, be deemed to have been designated by the debtor as required by subsections (5) to (11).

**Notes**: 80(16) allows the CCRA to designate amounts under any of subsections 80(5)–(11), to the extent the debtor would have been permitted to have designated those amounts. However, this is only where an amount would otherwise be deducted under 61.2 or 61.3. Note that, in these circumstances, the CCRA can designate an amount under 80(11) even where that increase also results in an increase in the amount added in computing the debtor's income under 80(13) and, therefore, an increase in an offsetting amount deducted under section 61.3. See also Notes at end of 80.

**(17) [Repealed]**

**Notes**: 80(17) repealed by 1995-97 technical bill, retroactive to its introduction (taxation years ending after February 21, 1994 — see Notes at end of s. 80). It was repealed to reduce the complexity of the debt forgiveness rules. Now deemed never to have been in force, it read:

(17) **Income inclusion where residual balance a positive amount** — Where a commercial obligation issued by a corporation is settled at any time in a taxation year and, as a consequence of the settlement an amount is deducted under section 61.3 in computing the corporation's income for the year, unless the corporation has commenced to wind up on or before the day that is 12 months after the end of the year there shall be added in computing the corporation's income for the year from the source in connection with which the obligation was issued 50% of the lesser of

(a) the total of all amounts designated under subsection (11) by the corporation in respect of the settlement of the obligation at that time, and

(b) the amount, if any, by which the lesser of

(i) the residual balance (within the meaning assigned by subsection (14)) of the corporation at that time in respect of the settlement of the obligation, and

(ii) the amount, if any, by which the amount deducted under section 61.3 in computing the corporation's income for the year exceeds the amount, if any, deducted because of paragraph 37(1)(f.1) in determining the balance determined under subsection 37(1) in respect of the corporation after the year because of an amount deducted under section 61.3 in computing the corporation's income for the year

exceeds the total of all amounts included because of this subsection in computing the corporation's income for the year in respect of a settlement before that time of a commercial obligation issued by the corporation.

**(18) Partnership designations** — Where a commercial obligation issued by a partnership is settled at any time after December 20, 1994, the amount designated under subsection (9), (10) or (11) in respect of the settlement by the partnership to reduce the adjusted cost base of a capital property acquired shall not exceed the amount, if any, by which the adjusted cost base at that time to the partnership of the property exceeds the fair market value at that time of the property.

**Notes [subsec. 80(18)]**: The purpose of 80(18) is to prevent partnerships from acquiring capital properties in order to minimize the impact of s. 80. It is limited to partnerships because many tax attributes (e.g. loss carryforwards and resource expenditures) are allocated to partnership members and the forgiveness of a commercial obligation considered to have been issued by a partnership does not result in a reduction of those attributes, subject to the application of 80(15).

**Notes [s. 80]**: 80 sets out a series of rules for a debtor to apply the "forgiven amount" (defined in 80(1)) where a debt is forgiven. In general terms, the balance is applied first to non-capital losses (80(3)), then ABILs and net capital losses (80(4)), then depreciable property capital cost and UCC balances (80(5), (6)), then cumulative eligible capital (goodwill) (80(7)), then resource expenditure balances (80(8)), then ACB of certain capital property (80(9)–(11)), then current year net capital losses (80(12)). Any remaining balance may be transferable to another taxpayer under 80.04. If there is still a "residual balance" (as defined in 80(14)), it will be included in income under 80(13), possibly offset by a deduction or reserve under 61.2–61.4. See also the special rules in 80.01–80.04 and Notes to 80(15)–(18).

The debt forgiveness rules apply in the following order: 78 [see 80(1)"excluded obligation"(c)]; 6(1) and (15) [see 80(1)"forgiven amount"B(b)]; 15(1) and (1.2); 9(1) [e.g. if a trade account payable is settled]; 79 [see 80(1)"forgiven amount"(f)]; and finally, s. 80.

For a detailed discussion, see Barry Pickford & Wayne Tunney, "The Tax Treatment of Forgiveness of Debt and Foreclosures: The Proposed New Rules", 1994 Canadian Tax Foundation annual conference report, pp. 3:1-3:62.

80 completely replaced by 1994 tax amendments bill (Part I), effective for taxation years that end after February 21, 1994, except that the new version of 80, as well as 80.01 to 80.04, do not, other than for the purposes of 6(15), 6(15.1), 15(1.2), 15(1.21) and 79, apply to any obligation settled or extinguished

(i) before February 22, 1994,

(ii) after February 21, 1994

(A) under the terms of an agreement in writing entered into by that date, or

(B) under the terms of any amendment to such an agreement, where that amendment was entered into in writing before July 12, 1994 and the amount of the settlement or extinguishment was not substantially greater than the settlement or extinguishment provided under the terms of the agreement,

(iii) before 1996 pursuant to a restructuring of debt in connection with a proceeding commenced in a court in Canada before February 22, 1994,

(iv) before 1996 in connection with a proposal (or notice of intention to make a proposal) that was filed under the Bankruptcy and Insolvency Act, or similar legislation of a country other than Canada, before February 22, 1994, or

(v) before 1996 in connection with a written offer that was made by, or communicated to, the holder of the obligation before February 22, 1994.

See also Notes to 80(2)(b) re transitional rule for that provision.

Where the new version of 80 does not apply, read:

80. (1) **Debtor's gain on settlement of debts** — Where at any time in a taxation year a debt or other obligation of a taxpayer to pay an amount is settled or extinguished after 1971 without any payment by the taxpayer or by the payment of an amount less than the principal amount of the debt or obligation, as the case may be, the amount by which the lesser of the principal amount thereof and the amount for which the obligation was issued by the taxpayer exceeds the amount so paid, if any, shall be applied

(a) to reduce, in the following order, the taxpayer's

(i) non-capital losses,

(i.1) farm losses,

(ii) net capital losses, and

(iii) restricted farm losses,

for preceding taxation years, to the extent of the amount of those losses that would otherwise be deductible in computing the taxpayer's taxable income for the year or a subsequent year, and

(b) to the extent that the excess exceeds the portion thereof required to be applied as provided in paragraph (a), to reduce in prescribed manner the capital cost to the taxpayer of any depreciable property and the adjusted cost base to the taxpayer of any capital property,

unless

(c) the taxpayer is, at that time, a bankrupt within the meaning of section 128,

(d) the debt or obligation was such that

(i) where interest was paid or payable by the taxpayer in respect of it pursuant to a legal obligation, or

(ii) if interest had been paid or payable by the taxpayer in respect of it pursuant to a legal obligation,

no amount in respect of the interest was or would have been deductible under this Part in computing the taxpayer's income if this Act were read without reference to subsections 18(2), (3.1) and (4) and section 21,

(e) section 79 is applicable in respect of the debt or obligation,

(f) the excess is otherwise required to be included in computing the taxpayer's income for the year or a preceding taxation year or to be deducted in computing the capital cost to the taxpayer of any depreciable property, the adjusted cost base to the taxpayer of any capital property or the cost amount to the taxpayer of any other property,

(g) the excess would be deemed by subsection 39(3) to be a capital gain of the taxpayer for the year from the disposition of a capital property if this Act were read without reference to this subsection, or

(h) the debt or obligation is settled or extinguished by way of bequest or inheritance.

**(2) Deemed settlement on amalgamation** — Where a debt or other obligation of a corporation (in this subsection referred to as the "debtor") to pay an amount to another corporation (in this subsection referred to as the "creditor") is settled or extinguished on or by virtue of an amalgamation of the debtor and the creditor, the debt or obligation shall be deemed to have been settled or extinguished immediately before the time that is immediately before the amalgamation by a payment made by the debtor and received by the creditor of an amount equal to the amount that would have been the creditor's cost amount of the debt or obligation at that time if the definition "cost amount" in subsection 248(1) were read without reference to paragraph (e) of that definition.

**(3) Deemed settlement on winding-up** — Where

(a) there has been a winding-up to which the rules in subsection 88(1) applied and a debt or other obligation of the subsidiary to pay an amount to the parent or a debt or other obligation of the parent to pay an amount to the subsidiary is settled or extinguished on the winding-up without any payment or by the payment of an amount that is less than both the principal amount of the debt or obligation and the amount that would have been the cost amount to the parent or the subsidiary, as the case may be, of the debt or obligation immediately before the winding-up if the definition "cost amount" in subsection 248(1) were read without reference to paragraph (e) of that definition, and

(b) the parent so elects in prescribed form on or before the day on or before which the parent is required to file a return of income pursuant to section 150 for the taxation year in which the debt or obligation was settled or extinguished,

the debt or obligation shall be deemed to have been settled or extinguished on the winding-up by the payment of an amount equal to the amount that would have been the cost amount to the parent or the subsidiary, as the case may be, of the debt or obligation immediately before the winding-up if the definition "cost amount" in subsection 248(1) were read without reference to paragraph (e) of that definition.

**(4) Principal for interest payable** — For the purposes of subsections (1) and (3), an amount of interest in respect of a debt or other obligation of a taxpayer shall be deemed to be a debt or other obligation issued by the taxpayer that

(a) has a principal amount, and

(b) was issued by the taxpayer for an amount,

equal to the portion of the amount of the interest that is deductible, or would, but for subsection 18(2) or (3.1) or section 21, be deductible, in computing the taxpayer's income under this Part for a taxation year.

Former 80(4) amended by 1991 technical bill, retroactive to its introduction in 1985. However, with respect to interest accruing before July 14, 1990, read "was deducted" in place of "was deductible" in the closing words of the subsection.

**Definitions [s. 80]**: "acquired" — 256(7)–(9); "adjusted cost base" — 54, 248(1); "amount" — 248(1); "applicable fraction" — 80(2)(d); "bankrupt" — 248(1); "beneficially interested" — 248(25); "business" — 80.03(7)(b)(iii), 248(1); "Canada" — 255; "Canadian partnership" — 102(1), 248(1); "capital gain", "capital loss" — 39(1), 248(1); "capital property" — 54, 248(1); "carried on in Canada" — 253; "commercial debt obligation" — 80(1); "control" — 80(2)(j), 256(6)–(9); "controlled, directly or indirectly" — 256(5.1), (6.2); "corporation" — 248(1), *Interpretation Act* 35(1); "cost amount" — 248(1); "cumulative eligible capital" — 14(5), 248(1); "cumulative foreign resource expense" — 66.21(1); "debtor" — 80(1); "depreciable property" — 13(21), 248(1); "directed person" — 80(1); "distress preferred share", "eligible Canadian partnership", "excluded obligation", "excluded property", "ex-cluded security" — 80(1); "farm loss" — 111(8), 248(1); "fiscal period" — 249(2)(b), 249.1; "forgiven amount" — 80(1), 80.01(8)(b), 80.03(7)(b)(ii); "gross tax attributes" — 80(14.1) "listed personal property" — 54, 248(1); "Minister" — 248(1); "net capital loss", "non-capital loss" — 111(8), 248(1); "non-resident" — 248(1); "non-resident-owned investment corporation" — 133(8), 248(1); "ordinary non-capital loss" — 80(3)(a)(i); "partnership" — see Notes to 96(1); "partnership obligation" — 80(15); "person" — 80(1), 248(1); "personal-use property" — 54, 248(1); "prescribed" — 248(1); "prescribed stock exchange in Canada" — Reg. 3200; "principal amount", "property", "regulation" — 248(1); "related" — 80(2)(j), 251(2); "relevant limit" — 80(15)(b); "relevant loss balance" — 80(1); "residual balance" — 80(14); "resident in Canada" — 250; "restricted farm loss" — 31, 248(1); "settled" — 80(2)(a), 80.01(3)–(9), 80.02(2)(c), 80.02(7)(a), 80.03(7)(b)(i); "share" — 248(1); "source" — 4(1), 80.03(7)(b)(iv); "specified shareholder" — 248(1); "successor pool" — 80(1); "taxable Canadian corporation" — 89(1), 248(1); "taxable Canadian property" — 248(1); "taxable capital gain" — 38(a), 248(1); "taxable income" — 2(2), 248(1); "taxable income earned in Canada" — 115(1), 248(1); "taxation year" — 11(2), 249; "treaty-protected property" — 248(1); "trust" — 104(1), 248(1), (3); "undepreciated capital cost" — 13(21), 248(1); "unrecognized loss" — 80(1); "writing" — *Interpretation Act* 35(1).

**I.T. Application Rules [s. 80]**: 26(1.1) (debt outstanding since before 1972.).

**Interpretation Bulletins [s. 80]**: IT-109R2: Unpaid amounts; IT-142R3: Settlement of debts on the winding-up of a corporation; IT-143R2: Meaning of "eligible capital expenditure"; IT-232R3: Losses — their deductibility in the loss year or in other years; IT-262R2: Losses of non-residents and part-year residents; IT-268R3: *Inter vivos* transfer of farm property to child; IT-293R: Debtor's gain on settlement of debt; IT-382: Debts bequeathed or forgiven on death; IT-430R3: Life insurance proceeds received by a private corporation or a partnership as a consequence of death; IT-474R: Amalgamations of Canadian corporations; IT-488R2: Winding-up of 90%-owned taxable Canadian corporations.

**Information Circulars [s. 80]**: 88-2, para. 23: General anti-avoidance rule — section 245 of the *Income Tax Act*; 88-2 Supplement, para. 6: General anti-avoidance rule — section 245 of the *Income Tax Act*.

**80.01 (1) Definitions** — In this section,

**"commercial debt obligation"** has the meaning assigned by subsection 80(1);

**Notes**: See Notes at end of 80.01.

**"commercial obligation"** has the meaning assigned by subsection 80(1);

**"debtor"** has the meaning assigned by subsection 80(1);

**"distress preferred share"** has the meaning assigned by subsection 80(1);

**"forgiven amount"** has the meaning assigned by subsection 80(1) except that, where an amount would be included in computing a person's income under paragraph 6(1)(a) or subsection 15(1) as a consequence of the settlement of an obligation if the obligation were settled without any payment being made in satisfaction of its principal amount, "forgiven amount" in respect of that obligation has the meaning assigned by subsection 6(15.1) or 15(1.21), as the case may be;

"person" has the meaning assigned by subsection 80(1);

"specified cost" at any time to a person of an obligation means,

(a) where the obligation is capital property of the person at that time, the adjusted cost base at that time to the person of the obligation, and

(b) in any other case, the cost amount to the person of the obligation.

(2) **Application** — For the purposes of this section,

(a) paragraphs 80(2)(a), (b), (j), (l) and (n) apply; and

(b) a person has a significant interest in a corporation at any time if the person owned at that time

(i) shares of the capital stock of the corporation that would give the person 25% or more of the votes that could be cast under all circumstances at an annual meeting of shareholders of the corporation, or

(ii) shares of the capital stock of the corporation having a fair market value of 25% or more of the fair market value of all the issued shares of the capital stock of the corporation

and, for the purposes of this paragraph, a person shall be deemed to own at any time each share of the capital stock of a corporation that is owned, otherwise than because of this paragraph, at that time by another person with whom the person does not deal at arm's length.

**Notes**: See Notes at end of 80.01.

(3) **Deemed settlement on amalgamation** — Where a commercial obligation or another obligation (in this subsection referred to as the "indebtedness") of a debtor that is a corporation to pay an amount to another corporation (in this subsection referred to as the "creditor") is settled on an amalgamation of the debtor and the creditor, the indebtedness shall be deemed to have been settled immediately before the time that is immediately before the amalgamation by a payment made by the debtor and received by the creditor of an amount equal to the amount that would have been the creditor's cost amount of the indebtedness at that time if

(a) the definition "cost amount" in subsection 248(1) were read without reference to paragraph (e) of that definition; and

(b) that cost amount included amounts added in computing the creditor's income in respect of the portion of the indebtedness representing unpaid interest, to the extent those amounts have not been deducted in computing the creditor's income as bad debts in respect of that unpaid interest.

**Related Provisions**: 80(3)–(13) — Treatment of obligation deemed to have been settled.

(4) **Deemed settlement on winding-up** — Where there is a winding-up of a subsidiary to which the rules in subsection 88(1) apply and

(a) a debt or other obligation (in this subsection referred to as the "subsidiary's obligation") of the subsidiary to pay an amount to the parent, or

(b) a debt or other obligation (in this subsection referred to as the "parent's obligation") of the parent to pay an amount to the subsidiary

is, as a consequence of the winding-up, settled at a particular time without any payment of an amount or by the payment of an amount that is less than the principal amount of the subsidiary's obligation or the parent's obligation, as the case may be,

(c) where that payment is less than the amount that would have been the cost amount to the parent or subsidiary of the subsidiary's obligation or the parent's obligation immediately before the particular time if the definition "cost amount" in subsection 248(1) were read without reference to paragraph (e) of that definition and the parent so elects in a prescribed form on or before the day on or before which the parent is required to file a return of income pursuant to section 150 for the taxation year that includes the particular time, the amount paid at that time in satisfaction of the principal amount of the subsidiary's obligation or the parent's obligation shall be deemed to be equal to the amount that would be the cost amount to the parent or the subsidiary, as the case may be, of the subsidiary's obligation or the parent's obligation immediately before the particular time if

(i) the definition "cost amount" in subsection 248(1) were read without reference to paragraph (e) of that definition, and

(ii) that cost amount included amounts added in computing the parent's income or the subsidiary's income in respect of the portion of the indebtedness representing unpaid interest, to the extent that the parent or the subsidiary has not deducted any amounts as bad debts in respect of that unpaid interest, and

(d) for the purposes of applying section 80 to the subsidiary's obligation, where property is distributed at any time in circumstances to which paragraph 88(1)(a) or (b) applies and the subsidiary's obligation is settled as a consequence of the distribution, the subsidiary's obligation shall be deemed to have been settled immediately before the time that is immediately before the time of the distribution and not at any later time.

**Related Provisions**: 50(1)(b)(ii) — Deemed disposition of debt or shares on winding-up; 80(3)–(13) — Treatment of obligation deemed to have been settled; 80.01(5) — Where distress preferred share issued; 220(3.2), Reg. 600(b) — Late filing or revocation of election under 80.01(4)(c).

**Advance Tax Rulings**: ATR-66: Non-arm's length transfer of debt followed by a winding-up and a sale of shares.

**Forms**: T2027: Election to deem amount of settlement of a debt or obligation.

**(5) Deemed settlement on winding-up** — Where there is a winding-up of a subsidiary to which the rules in subsection 88(1) apply and, as a consequence of the winding-up, a distress preferred share issued by the subsidiary and owned by the parent (or a distress preferred share issued by the parent and owned by the subsidiary) is settled at any time without any payment of an amount or by the payment of an amount that is less than the principal amount of the share,

(a) where the payment was less than the adjusted cost base of the share to the parent or the subsidiary, as the case may be, immediately before that time, for the purposes of applying the provisions of this Act to the issuer of the share, the amount paid at that time in satisfaction of the principal amount of the share shall be deemed to be equal to its adjusted cost base to the parent or to the subsidiary, as the case may be; and

(b) for the purposes of applying section 80 to the share, where property is distributed at any time in circumstances to which paragraph 88(1)(a) or (b) applies and the share is settled as a consequence of the distribution, the share shall be deemed to have been settled immediately before the time that is immediately before the time of the distribution and not at any later time.

**Related Provisions**: 50(1)(b)(ii) — Deemed disposition of debt or shares on winding-up; 80(3)–(13) — Treatment of obligation deemed to have been settled; 80.02(2)(c) — Meaning of "settled" for distress preferred shares; 88(1)(b) — Determination of proceeds of disposition to parent.

**(6) Specified obligation in relation to debt parking** — For the purpose of subsection (7), an obligation issued by a debtor is, at a particular time, a specified obligation of the debtor where

(a) at any previous time (other than a time before the last time, if any, the obligation became a parked obligation before the particular time),

(i) a person who owned the obligation

(A) dealt at arm's length with the debtor, and

(B) where the debtor is a corporation, did not have a significant interest in the debtor, or

(ii) the obligation was acquired by the holder of the obligation from another person who was, at the time of that acquisition, not related to the holder or related to the holder only because of paragraph 251(5)(b); or

(b) the obligation is deemed by subsection 50(1) to be reacquired at the particular time.

**Related Provisions**: 80(2)(j), 80.01(2)(a) — Special rules for determining the meaning of "related" and "arm's length"; 80.01(7) — Meaning of "parked obligation".

**(7) Parked obligation** — For the purposes of this subsection and subsections (6), (8) and (10),

(a) an obligation issued by a debtor is a "parked obligation" at any time where at that time

(i) the obligation is a specified obligation of the debtor, and

(ii) the holder of the obligation

(A) does not deal at arm's length with the debtor, or

(B) where the debtor is a corporation and the holder acquired the obligation after July 12, 1994 (otherwise than pursuant to an agreement in writing entered into on or before July 12, 1994), has a significant interest in the debtor; and

(b) an obligation that is, at any time, acquired or reacquired in circumstances to which subparagraph (6)(a)(ii) or paragraph (6)(b) applies shall, if the obligation is a parked obligation immediately after that time, be deemed to have become a parked obligation at that time.

**Related Provisions**: 80(2)(j), 80.01(2)(a) — Special rules for determining the meaning of "related" and thence "arm's length"; 80.01(6) — Meaning of "specified obligation".

**(8) Deemed settlement after debt parking** — Where at any particular time after February 21, 1994 a commercial debt obligation that was issued by a debtor becomes a parked obligation (otherwise than pursuant to an agreement in writing entered into before February 22, 1994) and the specified cost at the particular time to the holder of the obligation is less than 80% of the principal amount of the obligation, for the purpose of applying the provisions of this Act to the debtor

(a) the obligation shall be deemed to have been settled at the particular time; and

(b) the forgiven amount at the particular time in respect of the obligation shall be determined as if the debtor had paid an amount at the particular time in satisfaction of the principal amount of the obligation equal to that specified cost.

**Related Provisions**: 40(2)(e.1), (e.2), (g)(ii) — Stop-loss rules on disposition of debt; 50(1)(a) — Deemed disposition of bad debt; 79(3)F(b)(i), (iii) — Where property surrendered to creditor; 80(1)"forgiven amount"B(g) — Debt forgiveness rules do not apply if parked obligation subsequently forgiven; 80(3)–(13) — Treatment of obligation deemed to have been settled; 80.01(7) — Meaning of "parked obligation"; 80.01(10) — Subsequent payments; 80.01(11) — Foreign currency fluctuation to be ignored.

**(9) Statute-barred debt** — Where at any particular time after February 21, 1994 a commercial debt obligation issued by a debtor that is payable to a person (other than a person with whom the debtor is related at the particular time) becomes unenforceable in a court of competent jurisdiction because of a statutory limitation period and the obligation would, but for this subsection, not have been settled or extinguished at the particular time, for the purpose of applying the provisions of this Act to the debtor, the obligation shall be deemed to have been settled at the particular time.

**Related Provisions**: 80(1)"forgiven amount"B(g) — Debt forgiveness rules do not apply; 80(2)(j), 80.01(2)(a) — Special rules for determining the meaning of "related"; 80(3)–(13) — Treatment of obligation deemed to have been settled; 80.01(10) — Subsequent payments; 80.01(11) — Foreign currency fluctuation to be ignored.

**(10) Subsequent payments in satisfaction of debt** — Where a commercial debt obligation issued by a debtor is first deemed by subsection (8) or (9) to have been settled at a particular time, at a subsequent time a payment is made by the debtor of an amount in satisfaction of the principal amount of the obligation and it cannot reasonably be considered that one of the reasons the obligation became a parked obligation or became unenforceable, as the case may be, before the subsequent time was to have this subsection apply to the payment, in computing the debtor's income for the taxation year (in this subsection referred to as the "subsequent year") that includes the subsequent time from the source in connection with which the obligation was issued, there may be deducted the amount determined by the formula

$$0.75(A - B) - C$$

where

A is the amount of the payment,

B is the amount, if any, by which

    (a) the principal amount of the obligation exceeds the total of

    (b) all amounts each of which is a forgiven amount at any time

        (i) in the period that began at the particular time and ended immediately before the subsequent time, and

        (ii) at which a particular portion of the obligation is deemed by subsection (8) or (9) to be settled

in respect of the particular portion, and

    (c) all amounts paid in satisfaction of the principal amount of the obligation in the period that began at the particular time and ended immediately before the subsequent time, and

C is the amount, if any, by which the total of

    (a) all amounts deducted under section 61.3 in computing the debtor's income for the subsequent year or a preceding taxation year,

    (b) all amounts added because of subsection 80(13) in computing the debtor's income for the subsequent year or a preceding taxation year in respect of a settlement under subsection (8) or (9) in a period during which the debtor was exempt from tax under this Part on its taxable income, and

    (c) all amounts added because of subsection 80(13) in computing the debtor's income for the subsequent year or a preceding taxation year in respect of a settlement under subsection (8) or (9) in a period during which the debtor was non-resident (other than any of those amounts added in computing the debtor's taxable income or taxable income earned in Canada)

exceeds the total of

    (d) the amount, if any, deducted because of paragraph 37(1)(f.1) in determining the balance determined under subsection 37(1) in respect of the debtor immediately after the subsequent year, and

    (e) all amounts by which the amount deductible under this subsection in respect of a payment made by the debtor before the subsequent time in computing the debtor's income for the subsequent year or a preceding year has been reduced because of this description.

**Proposed Amendment — 80.01(10)**

**Application**: The December 21, 2000 draft legislation, s. 35, will amend subsec. 80.01(10) by replacing the reference to the number "0.75" in the formula with a reference to the number "0.5", applicable to taxation years that end after February 27, 2000 except that, where a taxation year of a debtor includes either February 28, 2000 or October 17, 2000, the reference to the fraction "1/2" in the subsec. shall be read as a reference to the fraction in para. 38(a), as amended [by the December 21, 2000 draft legislation], that applies to the debtor for the year.

**Technical Notes**: Subsection 80.01(10) permits, in certain circumstances, a debtor to deduct an amount in computing income in respect of a payment made in respect of the principal amount of a commercial debt obligation that was previously settled.

The amendment to subsection 80.01(10) replaces the reference to the decimal "0.75" with a reference to the fraction "1/2". The amendment is consequential on the reduction of the inclusion rate for capital gains from 3/4 to 1/2 [see 38(a) — ed.].

The amendment applies to taxation years that end after February 27, 2000 except that, for a debtor's taxation year that includes either February 28, 2000 or October 17, 2000, the reference to "1/2" in subsection 80.01(10) is to be read as a reference to the fraction in amended paragraph 38(a) that applies to the debtor for the year. These modifications are required in order to reflect the capital gains/losses rate for the year.

**Related Provisions**: 3, 4(1) — Income from a source; 20(1)(uu) — Deduction for amount allowed under subsec. 80.01(10); 80.01(7) — Meaning of "parked obligation"; 87(2)(l.21) — Amalgamations — continuing corporation; 257 — Formula cannot calculate to less than zero.

**(11) Foreign currency gains and losses** — Where an obligation issued by a debtor is denominated in a currency (other than the Canadian currency) and the obligation is deemed by subsection (8) or (9) to have been settled, those subsections do not apply for the purpose of determining any gain or loss of the debtor on the settlement that is attributable to a fluctuation in the value of the currency relative to the value of Canadian currency.

**Related Provisions**: 39(2) — Gain or loss on fluctuation of foreign currency; 79(7) — Currency fluctuation where property surrendered to creditor; 80(2)(k) — Determination of forgiven amount where obligation denominated in foreign currency.

**I.T. Technical News**: No. 15 (tax consequences of the adoption of the "euro" currency).

**Notes [s. 80.01]**: 80.01 added by 1994 tax amendments bill (Part I), effective for taxation years that end after February 21, 1994, except where grandfathering applies (see Notes to end of s. 80). It provides that debts are deemed to be settled in a number of specific situations, thus leading to the application of the debt forgiveness rules in 80.

**Definitions [s. 80.01]**: "adjusted cost base" — 54, 248(1); "amount" — 248(1); "arm's length" — 80(2)(j), 80.01(2)(a), 251(1); "capital property" — 54, 248(1); "commercial debt obligation", "commercial obligation" — 80(1), 80.01(1); "corporation" — 248(1), *Interpretation Act* 35(1); "cost amount" — 248(1); "creditor" — 80.01(3); "debtor", "distress preferred share" — 80(1), 80.01(1); "forgiven amount" — 80(1), 80.01(1), 80.01(8)(b); "parent" — 88(1); "parked obligation" — 80.01(7); "person" — 80(1), 80.01(1); "prescribed", "principal amount" — 248(1); "related" — 80(2)(j), 80.01(2)(a), 251(2); "settled" — 80(2)(a), 80.01(3)–(9), 80.02(2)(c), 80.02(7)(a); "significant interest" — 80.01(2)(b); "source" — 4(1); "specified cost" — 248(1); "specified obligation" — 80.01(6); "specified shareholder" — 248(1); "subsidiary" — 88(1); "taxation year" — 249; "writing" — *Interpretation Act* 35(1).

**80.02 (1) Definitions** — In this section, "commercial debt obligation", "commercial obligation", "distress preferred share" and "person" have the meanings assigned by subsection 80(1).

**Notes**: See Notes at end of 80.02.

**(2) General rules for distress preferred shares** — For the purpose of applying the provisions of this Act to an issuer of a distress preferred share,

(a) the principal amount, at any time, of the share shall be deemed to be the amount (determined at that time) for which the share was issued;

(b) the amount for which the share was issued shall, at any time, be deemed to be the amount, if any, by which the total of

(i) the amount for which the share was issued, determined without reference to this paragraph, and

(ii) all amounts by which the paid-up capital in respect of the share increased after the share was issued and before that time

exceeds

(iii) the total of all amounts each of which is an amount paid before that time on a reduction of the paid-up capital in respect of the share, except to the extent that the amount is deemed by section 84 to have been paid as a dividend;

(c) the share shall be deemed to be settled at such time as it is redeemed, acquired or cancelled by the issuer; and

(d) a payment in satisfaction of the principal amount of the share is any payment made on a reduction of the paid-up capital in respect of the share to the extent that the payment would be proceeds of disposition of the share within the meaning that would be assigned by the definition "proceeds of disposition" in section 54 if that definition were read without reference to paragraph (j).

**Related Provisions**: 80.02(3)(b), 80.02(5)(b) — Deemed amounts for purposes of subpara. 80.02(2)(b)(i).

**Notes**: See Notes at end of 80.02.

**(3) Substitution of distress preferred share for debt** — Where any part of the consideration given by a corporation to another person for the settlement or extinguishment at any time of a commercial debt obligation that was issued by the corporation and owned immediately before that time by the other person consists of a distress preferred share issued by the corporation to the other person,

(a) for the purposes of section 80, the amount paid at that time in satisfaction of the principal amount of the obligation because of the issue of that share shall be deemed to be equal to the lesser of

(i) the principal amount of the obligation, and

(ii) the amount by which the paid-up capital in respect of the class of shares that include that share increases because of the issue of that share; and

(b) for the purpose of subparagraph (2)(b)(i), the amount for which the share was issued shall be deemed to be equal to the amount deemed by paragraph (a) to have been paid at that time.

**Related Provisions**: 80.02(2) — General rules.

**(4) Substitution of commercial debt obligation for distress preferred share** — Where any part of the consideration given by a corporation to another person for the settlement at any time of a distress preferred share that was issued by the corporation and owned immediately before that time by the other person consists of a commercial debt obligation issued by the corporation to the other person, for the purposes of section 80

(a) the amount paid at that time in satisfaction of the principal amount of the share because of the issue of that obligation shall be deemed to be equal to the principal amount of the obligation; and

(b) the amount for which the obligation was issued shall be deemed to be equal to its principal amount.

**Related Provisions**: 80.02(2) — General rules.

**(5) Substitution of distress preferred share for other distress preferred share** — Where any part of the consideration given by a corporation to another person for the settlement at any time of a particular distress preferred share that was issued by the corporation and owned immediately before that time by the other person consists of another distress preferred share issued by the corporation to the other person, for the purposes of section 80

(a) the amount paid at that time in satisfaction of the principal amount of the particular share because of the issue of the other share shall be deemed to be equal to the amount by which the paid-up capital in respect of the class of shares that includes the other share increases because of the issue of the other share; and

(b) for the purpose of subparagraph (2)(b)(i), the amount for which the other share was issued shall be deemed to be equal to the amount deemed by paragraph (a) to have been paid at that time.

**Related Provisions**: 80.02(2) — General rules.

**(6) Substitution of non-commercial obligation for distress preferred share** — Where any part of the consideration given by a corporation to another person for the settlement at any time of a distress preferred share that was issued by the corporation and owned immediately before that time by the other person consists of another share (other than a distress preferred share) or an obligation (other than a commercial obligation) issued by the corporation to the other person, for the purposes of section 80, the amount paid at that time in satisfaction of the principal amount of the distress preferred share because of the issue of the other share or obligation shall be deemed to be equal to the fair market value of the other share or obligation, as the case may be, at that time.

**Related Provisions**: 80.02(2) — General rules.

**(7) Deemed settlement on expiry of term** — Where at any time a distress preferred share becomes a share that is not a distress preferred share, for the purposes of section 80

(a) the share shall be deemed to have been settled immediately before that time; and

(b) a payment equal to the fair market value of the share at that time shall be deemed to have been made immediately before that time in satisfaction of the principal amount of the share.

**Related Provisions**: 80(1)"distress preferred share", 248(1)"term preferred share"(e) — Maximum term of distress preferred share is 5 years.

**Notes [s. 80.02]**: 80.02 added by 1994 tax amendments bill (Part I), effective for taxation years that end after February 21, 1994, except where grandfathering applies (see Notes to end of s. 80).

**Definitions [s. 80.02]**: "amount" — 80.02(2)(b), 248(1); "class of shares" — 248(6); "commercial debt obligation", "commercial obligation" — 80(1), 80.02(1); "corporation" — 248(1), *Interpretation Act* 35(1); "distress preferred share" — 80(1), 80.02(1); "dividend" — 248(1); "paid-up capital" — 89(1), 248(1); "payment in satisfaction" — 80.02(2)(d); "person" — 80(1), 80.02(1); "principal amount" — 80.02(2)(a), 248(1); "settled" — 80(2)(a), 80.01(5), 80.02(2)(c), 80.02(7)(a); "share" — 248(1).

**80.03 (1) [Definitions** — In this section, "commercial debt obligation", "commercial obligation", "distress preferred share", "forgiven amount" and "person" have the meanings assigned by subsection 80(1).]

**Notes**: The definitions in 80.03(1) were accidentally deleted in the English version on Third Reading of the 1995-97 technical bill (S.C. 1998, c. 19), when only "taxable dividend" should have been repealed. The French version is correct. Officials at the Department of Finance have confirmed that this will be corrected in an upcoming technical bill. "Taxable dividend" was defined to exclude capital gains dividends. The term is no longer used in 80.03.

Also see Notes at end of 80.03.

**(2) Deferred recognition of debtor's gain on settlement of debt** — Where at any time in a taxation year a person (in this subsection referred to as the "transferor") surrenders a particular capital property (other than a distress preferred share) that is a share, a capital interest in a trust or an interest in a partnership, the person shall be deemed to have a capital gain from the disposition at that time of another capital property (or, where the particular property is a taxable Canadian property, another taxable Canadian property) equal to the amount, if any, by which

(a) the total of all amounts deducted under paragraph 53(2)(g.1) in computing the adjusted cost base to the transferor of the particular property immediately before that time

exceeds the total of

(b) the amount that would be the transferor's capital gain for the year from the disposition of the particular property if this Act were read without reference to subsection 100(2), and

(c) where, at the end of the year, the transferor is resident in Canada or is a non-resident person who carries on business in Canada through a fixed place of business, the amount designated under subsection (7) by the transferor in respect of the disposition, at that time or immediately after that time, of the particular property.

**Related Provisions**: 80.03(3) — Meaning of "surrender"; 253 — Extended meaning of carrying on business in Canada.

**Notes**: See Notes at end of 80.03.

**(3) Surrender of capital property** — For the purpose of subsection (2), a person shall be considered to have surrendered a property at any time only where

(a) in the case of a share of the capital stock of a particular corporation,

(i) the person is a corporation that disposed of the share at that time and the proceeds of disposition of the share are determined under paragraph 88(1)(b), or

(ii) the person is a corporation that owned the share at that time and, immediately after that time, amalgamates or merges with the particular corporation;

(b) in the case of a capital interest in a trust, the person disposed of the interest at that time and the proceeds of disposition are determined under paragraph 107(2)(c); and

(c) in the case of an interest in a partnership, the person disposed of the interest at that time and the proceeds of disposition are determined under paragraph 98(3)(a) or (5)(a).

**(4)–(6)** [Repealed]

**Notes**: 80.03(4), (5) and (6) repealed by 1995-97 technical bill, retroactive to their introduction (taxation years ending after February 21, 1994 — see Notes at end of 80.03). These rules applied where a corporation disposed of capital property that was a share or a partnership or trust interest. In certain cases, there were tax consequences based on ACB adjustments arising because of section 80 and dividends received by the corporation. They were repealed to reduce the complexity of the debt forgiveness rules, although the general anti-avoidance rule in section 245 may apply to some of the cases where 80.03(4) applied. Now deemed never to have been in force, 80.03(4)–(6) provided:

(4) **Dispositions by corporations** — Where at any time in a taxation year a corporation (in this subsection referred to as the "vendor") disposes of a particular capital property that is a share, an interest in a partnership or a capital interest in a trust, otherwise than by way of a disposition to which subsection (2) or 53(6) applies, a disposition to another corporation in circumstances to which subsection 53(5) applies, or a disposition the proceeds from which are determined under subsection 47(1), section 86 or any of the provisions (other than subsection 97(2)) referred to in subsection 53(4), the vendor shall be deemed to have a capital gain from the disposition at that time of another capital property (or where the particular property is a taxable Canadian property, another taxable Canadian property) equal to the amount, if any, by which the lesser of

(a) all amounts deducted under paragraph 53(2)(g.1) in computing the adjusted cost base to the vendor of the particular property immediately before that time, and

(b) where the particular property

(i) is a share, the total of all amounts each of which is

(A) a taxable dividend on the share that was received in the specified period relating to the disposition of the share, to the extent that the dividend is deductible in computing taxable income of a holder of the share or a beneficiary under a trust that held the share, or

(B) a capital dividend on the share that was received in the specified period relating to the disposition of the share,

(ii) is an interest in a partnership, the total of all amounts each of which is

(A) the share of a taxable dividend relating to the interest that was received after July 12, 1994 and in a fiscal period of the partnership that ended in the specified period relating to the disposition of the interest, to the extent that such share is deductible in computing taxable income of a person holding the interest in the partnership or a beneficiary under a trust that held the interest in the partnership, or

(B) the share of a capital dividend relating to the interest that was received after July 12, 1994 and in a fiscal period of the partnership that ended in the specified period relating to the disposition of the interest, or

(iii) is a capital interest in a trust, the total of all amounts each of which is such portion of a taxable dividend that was received by the trust in the speci-

fied period relating to the disposition of the capital interest and that was deemed by subsection 104(19) to have been received in respect of the capital interest, to the extent that such portion was deductible in computing taxable income of a person holding the capital interest

exceeds the total of

(c) the amount that would be the vendor's capital gain for the year from the disposition of the particular property if this Act were read without reference to subparagraph 40(1)(a)(iii) and subsection 100(2), and

(d) where the vendor is resident in Canada at the end of the year or is a non-resident person who carries on business in Canada through a fixed place of business at the end of the year, the amount designated under subsection (7) by the vendor in respect of the disposition of the particular property.

(5) **Specified period** — For the purpose of subsection (4), the specified period relating to a disposition at a particular time of a property by a person is the period

(a) that began at or on the later of July 12, 1994 and the last time before the particular time that the person acquired the property, and

(b) that ended at the particular time.

(6) **When property acquired** — For the purposes of this subsection and subsection (5), where, as a consequence of the disposition at a particular time of a property to a person, an amount is deducted under paragraph 53(2)(g.1) in computing the adjusted cost base of the property after the particular time, the person shall be deemed not to have acquired the property at the particular time and to have acquired the property at the time it was last acquired before the particular time.

**(7) Alternative treatment** — Where at any time in a taxation year a person disposes of a property, for the purposes of subsection (2) and section 80

(a) the person may designate an amount in a prescribed form filed with the person's return of income under this Part for the year; and

(b) where an amount is designated by the person under paragraph (a) in respect of the disposition,

(i) the person shall be deemed to have issued a commercial debt obligation at that time that is settled immediately after that time,

(ii) the lesser of the amount so designated and the amount that would, but for this subsection, be a capital gain determined in respect of the disposition because of subsection (2) shall be treated as if it were the forgiven amount at the time of the settlement in respect of the obligation referred to in subparagraph (i),

(iii) the source in connection with which the obligation referred to in subparagraph (i) was issued shall be deemed to be the business, if any, carried on by the person at the end of the year, and

(iv) where the person does not carry on a business at the end of the year, the person shall be deemed to carry on an active business at the end of the year and the source in connection with which the obligation referred to in subparagraph (i) was issued shall be deemed to be the business deemed by this subparagraph to be carried on.

**Related Provisions**: 87(2)(h.1) — Amalgamations — continuing corporation; 220(3.21)(a) — Late filing, amendment or revocation of designation.

**Notes**: Opening words of 80.03(7) and 80.03(7)(b)(ii) both amended to delete reference to 80.03(4) (after "subsection (2)" in both cases), by 1995-97 technical bill, retroactive to their introduction (taxation years ending after February 21, 1994 — see Notes at end of 80.03). This was consequential on the repeal of 80.03(4).

The prescribed form could be filed with Revenue Canada up to the end of 1995. (1994 tax amendments bill, para. 27(2)(c).) See also Notes at end of 80.03.

**Forms**: T2155: Alternative treatment of capital gains under sec. 80.03 that arise from a forgiven debt.

**(8) Lifetime capital gains exemption** — Where, as a consequence of the disposition at any time by an individual of a property that is a qualified farm property of the individual or a qualified small business corporation share of the individual (within the meanings assigned by subsection 110.6(1)), the individual is deemed by subsection (2) to have a capital gain at that time from the disposition of another property, for the purposes of sections 3, 74.3 and 111, as they apply for the purpose of section 110.6, the other property shall be deemed to be a qualified farm property of the individual or a qualified small business corporation share of the individual, as the case may be.

**Notes [s. 80.03]**: 80.03 is designed to preserve the effectiveness of the debt forgiveness rules in 80, where 80 has resulted in a reduction of ACB of a share, partnership interest or trust interest (see 80(10) and (11)).

80.03 added by 1994 tax amendments bill (Part I), effective for taxation years that end after February 21, 1994, except where grandfathering applies (see Notes to end of s. 80). See also Notes to 80.03(7).

**Definitions [s. 80.03]**: "active business" — 248(1); "adjusted cost base" — 54, 248(1); "amount" — 248(1); "business" — 248(1); "capital dividend" — 83(2), 248(1); "capital gain" — 39(1)(a), 248(1); "capital interest" — in a trust 108(1), 248(1); "capital property" — 54, 248(1); "carried on business in Canada" — 253; "commercial debt obligation" — 80(1), 80.03(1)(a), 80.03(7)(b)(i); "commercial obligation" — 80(1), 80.03(1)(a); "corporation" — 248(1), *Interpretation Act* 35(1); "directed person" — 80(1), 80.04(1); "distress preferred share" — 80(1), 80.03(1)(a); "fiscal period" — 249(2)(b), 249.1; "forgiven amount" — 80(1), 80.03(1)(a), 80.03(7)(b)(ii); "individual", "non-resident" — 248(1); "partnership" — see Notes to 96(1); "person" — 80(1), 80.03(1)(a); "prescribed" — 248(1); "proceeds of disposition" — 54; "property" — 248(1); "resident in Canada" — 250; "settled" — 80.03(7)(b)(i); "share" — 248(1); "source" — 4(1), 80.03(7)(b)(iv); "surrender" — 80.03(3); "taxable Canadian property" — 248(1); "taxable income" — 2(2), 248(1); "taxation year" — 249; "transferor" — 80.03(2); "trust" — 104(1), 248(1), (3); "vendor" — 80.03(4).

**80.04 (1) Definitions** — In this section, "commercial debt obligation", "commercial obligation", "debtor", "directed person", "eligible Canadian partnership", "forgiven amount" and "person" have the meanings assigned by subsection 80(1).

**Notes**: See Notes at end of 80.04.

**(2) Eligible transferee** — For the purpose of this section, an "eligible transferee" of a debtor at any time is a directed person at that time in respect of the debtor or a taxable Canadian corporation or eligible Canadian partnership related (otherwise than because of a right referred to in paragraph 251(5)(b)) at that time to the debtor.

**Related Provisions**: 87(2)(h.1) — Amalgamations — continuing corporation.

**(3) Application** — Paragraphs 80(2)(a), (b), (j), (l) and (n) apply for the purpose of this section.

**(4) Agreement respecting transfer of forgiven amount** — Where

(a) a particular commercial obligation (other than an obligation deemed by paragraph (e) to have been issued) issued by a debtor is settled at a particular time,

(b) amounts have been designated by the debtor under subsections 80(5) to (10) to the maximum extent permitted in respect of the settlement of the particular obligation at the particular time,

(c) the debtor and an eligible transferee of the debtor at the particular time file under this section an agreement between them in respect of that settlement, and

(d) an amount is specified in that agreement

the following rules apply:

(e) except for the purposes of subsection 80(11), the transferee shall be deemed to have issued a commercial debt obligation that was settled at the particular time,

(f) the specified amount shall be deemed to be the forgiven amount at the particular time in respect of the obligation referred to in paragraph (e),

(g) subject to paragraph (h), the obligation referred to in paragraph (e) shall be deemed to have been issued at the same time (in paragraph (h) referred to as the "time of issue") at which, and in the same circumstances in which, the particular obligation was issued,

(h) where the transferee is a corporation the control of which was acquired by a person or group of persons after the time of issue and the transferee and the debtor were not related to each other immediately before that acquisition of control,

(i) the obligation referred to in paragraph (e) shall be deemed to have been issued after that acquisition of control, and

(ii) paragraph (e) of the definition "relevant loss balance" in subsection 80(1), paragraph (f) of the definition "successor pool" in that subsection and paragraph (b) of the definition "unrecognized loss" in that subsection do not apply in respect of that acquisition of control,

### Subdivision f — Rules Relating to Computation of Income    S. 80.04(6)(b)(iv)

(i) the source in connection with which the obligation referred to in paragraph (e) was issued shall be deemed to be the source in connection with which the particular obligation was issued, and

(j) for the purposes of sections 61.3 and 61.4, the amount included under subsection 80(13) in computing the income of the eligible transferee in respect of the settlement of the obligation referred to in paragraph (e) or deducted under paragraph 80(15)(a) in respect of such income shall be deemed to be nil.

**Related Provisions**: 80(13)C — Amount specified in agreement reduces income inclusion; 80(14)(c) — Calculation of residual balance for income inclusion; 80(15)(c) — Where commercial debt obligation issued by partnership; 80.04(5) — Where consideration given for entering into agreement; 80.04(6) — How and when agreement to be filed with CCRA; 87(2)(h.1) — Amalgamations — continuing corporation; 139.1(18) — Holding corporation deemed not to acquire control of insurer on demutualization; 256(6)–(9) — Whether control acquired; 256(8) — Deemed acquisition of shares.

**Notes**: See Notes at end of 80.04.

**(5) Consideration for agreement** — For the purposes of this Part, where property is acquired at any time by an eligible transferee as consideration for entering into an agreement with a debtor that is filed under this section

(a) where the property was owned by the debtor immediately before that time,

(i) the debtor shall be deemed to have disposed of the property at that time for proceeds equal to the fair market value of the property at that time, and

(ii) no amount may be deducted in computing the debtor's income as a consequence of the transfer of the property, except any amount arising as a consequence of the application of subparagraph (i);

(b) the cost at which the property was acquired by the eligible transferee at that time shall be deemed to be equal to the fair market value of the property at that time; and

(c) the eligible transferee shall not be required to add an amount in computing income solely because of the acquisition at that time of the property.

(d) [Repealed]

**Related Provisions**: 80.04(5.1) — No benefit conferred on debtor as a consequence of the agreement; 191.3(1.1) — Similar rule for purposes of Part VI.1 tax.

**Notes**: 80.04(5)(d) repealed by 1995-97 technical bill, retroactive to its introduction (taxation years ending after February 21, 1994 — see Notes at end of 80.03). This rule is now in 80.04(5.1), which is of more general application. Now deemed never to have been in force, para. (d) read:

(d) no benefit shall be considered to have been conferred on the debtor as a consequence of the debtor entering into an agreement filed under this section.

**(5.1) No benefit conferred** — For the purposes of this Part, where a debtor and an eligible transferee enter into an agreement that is filed under this section, no benefit shall be considered to have been conferred on the debtor as a consequence of the agreement.

**Notes**: 80.04(5.1) added by 1995-97 technical bill, effective for taxation years ending after February 21, 1994 (i.e., retroactive to the introduction of 80.04). This rule was formerly in 80.04(4)(d), but the new rule applies whether or not property is acquired by an eligible transferee as consideration for entering into an agreement filed under 80.04.

**(6) Manner of filing agreement** — Subject to subsection (7), a particular agreement between a debtor and an eligible transferee in respect of an obligation issued by the debtor that was settled at any time shall be deemed not to have been filed under this section

(a) where it is not filed with the Minister in a prescribed form

(i) on or before the later of

(A) the day on or before which the debtor's return of income under this Part is required to be filed for the taxation year or fiscal period, as the case may be, that includes that time (or would be required to be filed if tax under this Part were payable by the debtor for the year), and

(B) the day on or before which the transferee's return of income under this Part is required to be filed for the taxation year or fiscal period, as the case may be, that includes that time, or

(ii) within the period within which the debtor or the transferee may serve a notice of objection to an assessment of tax payable under this Part for a taxation year or fiscal period, as the case may be, described in clause (i)(A) or (B), as the case may be;

(b) where it is not accompanied by,

(i) where the debtor is a corporation and its directors are legally entitled to administer its affairs, a certified copy of their resolution authorizing the agreement to be made,

(ii) where the debtor is a corporation and its directors are not legally entitled to administer its affairs, a certified copy of the document by which the person legally entitled to administer its affairs authorized the agreement to be made,

(iii) where the transferee is a corporation and its directors are legally entitled to administer its affairs, a certified copy of their resolution authorizing the agreement to be made, and

(iv) where the transferee is a corporation and its directors are not legally entitled to administer its affairs, a certified copy of the document by which the person legally entitled to administer its affairs authorized the agreement to be made; or

(c) if an agreement amending the particular agreement has been filed in accordance with this section, except where subsection (8) applies to the particular agreement.

**Related Provisions**: 80.04(7) — Deemed due dates for partnership to file return and service notice of objection; 96(3) — Agreement of members of partnership; 150(1) — Due date for return; 165(1) — Deadline for serving notice of objection.

**Notes**: The prescribed form could be filed with Revenue Canada up to the end of 1995. (1994 tax amendments bill, para. 27(2)(c).) See also Notes at end of 80.04.

**Forms**: T2156: Transfer agreement for transferor of forgiven debt under s. 80.04.

**(7) Filing by partnership** — For the purpose of subsection (6), where an obligation is settled at any time in a fiscal period of a partnership, it shall be assumed that

(a) the partnership is required to file a return of income under this Part for the fiscal period on or before the latest day on or before which any member of the partnership during the fiscal period is required to file a return of income under this Part for the taxation year in which that fiscal period ends (or would be required to file such a return of income if tax under this Part were payable by the member for that year); and

(b) the partnership may serve a notice of objection described in subparagraph (6)(a)(ii) within each period within which any member of the partnership during the fiscal period may serve a notice of objection to tax payable under this Part for a taxation year in which that fiscal period ends.

**(8) Related corporations** — Where at any time a corporation becomes related to another corporation and it can reasonably be considered that the main purpose of the corporation becoming related to the other corporation is to enable the corporations to file an agreement under this section, the amount specified in the agreement shall be deemed to be nil for the purpose of the description of C in subsection 80(13).

**(9) Assessment of taxpayers in respect of agreement** — The Minister shall, notwithstanding subsections 152(4) to (5), assess or reassess the tax, interest and penalties payable under this Act by any taxpayer in order to take into account an agreement filed under this section.

**(10) Liability of debtor** — Without affecting the liability of any person under any other provision of this Act, where a debtor and an eligible transferee file an agreement between them under this section in respect of an obligation issued by the debtor that was settled at any time, the debtor is, to the extent of 30% of the amount specified in the agreement, liable to pay

(a) where the transferee is a corporation, all taxes payable under this Act by it for taxation years that end in the period that begins at that time and ends 4 calendar years after that time;

(b) where the transferee is a partnership, the total of all amounts each of which is the tax payable under this Act by a person for a taxation year

(i) that begins or ends in that period, and

(ii) that includes the end of a fiscal period of the partnership during which the person was a member of the partnership; and

(c) interest and penalties in respect of such taxes.

**Related Provisions**: 80.04(11) — Joint and several liability; 80.04(12) — Assessment; 80.04(14) — Where partnership is a member of a partnership; 87(2)(h.1) — Amalgamations — continuing corporation.

**Notes**: 80.04(10)(a) amended to change "10 years" to "4 years" by 1995-97 technical bill, retroactive to its introduction (taxation years ending after February 21, 1994 — see Notes at end of 80.03).

**(11) Joint liability** — Where taxes, interest and penalties are payable under this Act by a person for a taxation year and those taxes, interest and penalties are payable by a debtor because of subsection (10), the debtor and the person are jointly and severally liable to pay those amounts.

**Related Provisions**: 87(2)(h.1) — Amalgamations — continuing corporation.

**(12) Assessments in respect of liability** — Where a debtor and an eligible transferee file an agreement between them under this section in respect of an obligation issued by the debtor that was settled at a particular time,

(a) where the debtor is an individual or a corporation, the Minister may at any subsequent time assess the debtor in respect of taxes, interest and penalties for which the debtor is liable because of subsection (10); and

(b) where the debtor is a partnership, the Minister may at any subsequent time assess any person who has been a member of the partnership in respect of taxes, interest and penalties for which the partnership is liable because of subsection (10), to the extent that those amounts relate to taxation years of the transferee (or, where the transferee is another partnership, members of the other partnership) that end at or after

(i) where the person was not a member of the partnership at the particular time, the first subsequent time the person becomes a member of the partnership, and

(ii) in any other case, the particular time.

**Related Provisions**: 80.04(13) — Provisions applicable to assessment; 80.04(14) — Where partnership is a member of a partnership; 87(2)(h.1) — Amalgamations — continuing corporation.

**(13) Application of Division I** — The provisions of Division I apply to an assessment under subsection (12) as though it had been made under section 152.

**(14) Partnership members** — For the purposes of paragraphs (10)(b) and (12)(b) and this subsection, where at any time a member of a particular partnership is another partnership, each member of the other partnership shall be deemed to be a member of the particular partnership at that time.

**Notes [s. 80.04]**: 80.04 applies where a commercial debt obligation has been settled, but the "forgiven amount" (as defined in 80(1)) has not all been used up under 80(3)–(12). The remaining balance may be transferred, in certain cases, to another taxpayer to prevent it from being included in income under 80(13) or (17). The mechanism is similar to that under 191.3 for Part VI.1 tax.

80.04 added by 1994 tax amendments bill (Part I), effective for taxation years that end after February 21, 1994, except where grandfathering applies (see Notes to end of s. 80). See also Notes to 80.04(6).

**Definitions [s. 80.04]**: "acquired" — 256(7)–(9); "amount" — 80.04(5), 248(1); "benefit" — 80.04(5.1); "commercial debt obligation" — 80(1), 80.04(1), (4)(e); "commercial obligation" — 80(1), 80.04(1); "control" — 256(6)–(9); "corporation" — 248(1), *Interpretation Act* s. 35(1); "debtor", "directed person", "eligible Canadian partnership" — 80(1), 80.04(1); "eligible transferee" — 80.04(2); "fiscal period" — 249(2)(b), 249.1; "forgiven amount" — 80(1), 80.01(8)(b), 80.04(1); "individual", "Minister" — 248(1); "partnership" — see Notes to 96(1); "person" — 80(1), 80.04(1); "prescribed" — 248(1); "related" — 80(2)(j), 80.04(3), (8), 251(2); "settled" — 80(2)(a), 80.01(3)–(9), 80.02(2)(c), 80.02(7)(a), 80.04(4)(e); "specified amount" — 80.04(4)(d); "taxable Canadian corporation" — 89(1), 248(1); "taxation year" — 249; "time of issue" — 80.04(4)(g).

**80.1 (1) Expropriation assets acquired as compensation for or as consideration for sale of foreign property taken by or sold to foreign issuer** — Where in a taxation year ending coincidentally with or after December 31, 1971 a taxpayer resident in Canada has acquired any bonds, debentures, mortgages, notes or similar obligations (in this section referred to as "expropriation assets") issued by the government of a country other than Canada or issued by a person resident in a country other than Canada and guaranteed by the government of that country,

(a) as compensation for

(i) shares owned by the taxpayer of the capital stock of a foreign affiliate of the taxpayer that carried on business in that country, or

(ii) all or substantially all of the property used by the taxpayer in carrying on business in that country,

(which shares or property, as the case may be, are referred to in this section as "foreign property"), taken, after June 18, 1971, from the taxpayer by the issuer under the authority of a law of that country, or

(b) as consideration for the sale of foreign property sold, after June 18, 1971, by the taxpayer to the issuer, if

(i) the sale was, by a law of that country, expressly required to be made, or

(ii) the sale was made after notice or other manifestation of an intention to take the foreign property,

if the taxpayer has so elected, in prescribed form and within prescribed time, in respect of all of the expropriation assets so acquired by the taxpayer, the following rule applies, namely, an amount in respect of each such expropriation asset, equal to

(c) the principal amount of the asset, or

(d) where the taxpayer has designated in the taxpayer's election an amount in respect of the asset that is less than the principal amount thereof, the amount so designated,

shall be deemed to be

(e) the cost to the taxpayer of the asset, and

(f) for the purpose of computing the taxpayer's proceeds of disposition of the foreign property so taken or sold, the amount received by the taxpayer by virtue of the taxpayer's acquisition of the asset,

except that in no case may the taxpayer designate an amount in respect of any expropriation asset so that the taxpayer's proceeds of disposition of the foreign property so taken or sold (computed having regard to the provisions of paragraph (f)) are less than the cost amount to the taxpayer of the foreign property immediately before it was so taken or sold.

**Related Provisions**: 53(1)(k), 53(2)(n) — Adjustments to cost base; 90–95 — Shareholders of corporations not resident in Canada.

**Notes**: The CCRA takes the position that "all or substantially all", used in 80.1(1)(a)(ii), means 90% or more.

**Regulations**: 4500 (prescribed time).

**Forms**: T2079: Elections re expropriation assets.

**(2) Election re interest received or to be received on expropriation assets acquired by taxpayer** — Where a taxpayer has elected in prescribed form and within prescribed time in respect of all amounts (each of which is referred to in this subsection as an "interest amount") received or to be received by the taxpayer as or on account of interest on all expropriation assets acquired by the taxpayer as compensation for, or as consideration for the sale of, foreign property taken by or sold to any particular issuer as described in subsection (1), the following rules apply in respect of each such asset so acquired by the taxpayer:

(a) in computing the taxpayer's income for a taxation year from the asset, there may be deducted, in respect of each interest amount received by the taxpayer in the year on the asset, the lesser of the interest amount and the total of

(i) the amount required by paragraph (b) to be added, by virtue of the receipt by the taxpayer of the interest amount, in computing the adjusted cost base to the taxpayer of the asset, and

(ii) the greater of

(A) the adjusted cost base to the taxpayer of the asset immediately before the interest amount was so received by the taxpayer, and

(B) the adjusted principal amount to the taxpayer of the asset immediately before the interest amount was so received by the taxpayer,

and there shall be included, in respect of each amount (in this paragraph referred to as a "capital amount") received by the taxpayer in the year as, on account or in lieu of payment of, or in satisfaction of,

(iii) any proceeds of disposition of the asset, or

(iv) the principal amount of the asset,

the amount, if any, by which the capital amount exceeds the greater of the adjusted cost base to the taxpayer of the asset immediately before the capital amount was received by the taxpayer and its adjusted principal amount to the taxpayer at that time;

(b) in computing, at any particular time, the adjusted cost base to the taxpayer of the asset, there shall be added, in respect of each interest amount received by the taxpayer on the asset before the particular time, an amount equal to the lesser of

(i) any income or profits tax paid by the taxpayer to the government of a country other than Canada in respect of the interest amount, and

(ii) that proportion of the tax referred to in subparagraph (i) that the adjusted cost base to the taxpayer of the asset immediately before the interest amount was received by the taxpayer is of the amount, if any, by which the interest amount exceeds the tax referred to in that subparagraph,

and there shall be deducted

(iii) each interest amount received by the taxpayer on the asset before the particular time, and

(iv) each amount received by the taxpayer before the particular time on account of the principal amount of the asset;

(c) the receipt by the taxpayer of an amount described in subparagraph (b)(iv) in respect of the asset shall be deemed not to be a partial disposition thereof; and

(d) for the purposes of section 126, notwithstanding the definition "non-business-income tax" in subsection 126(7), the "non-business-income tax" paid by a taxpayer does not include any tax, or any portion thereof, the amount of which is required by paragraph (b) to be added in computing the adjusted cost base to the taxpayer of the asset.

**Related Provisions**: 53(1)(k), 53(2)(n) — Adjustments to cost base.

**Regulations**: 4500 (prescribed time).

**Forms**: T2079: Elections re expropriation assets.

**(3) Where interest amount and capital amount received at same time** — For the purposes of subsection (2), where an interest amount on an expropriation asset and a capital amount with respect to that asset are received by a taxpayer at the same time, the interest amount shall be deemed to have been received by the taxpayer immediately before the capital amount.

**(4) Assets acquired from foreign affiliate of taxpayer as dividend in kind or as benefit to shareholder** — Where a foreign affiliate of a taxpayer resident in Canada would, on the assumption that the foreign affiliate were resident in Canada and its only foreign affiliates were corporations that were foreign affiliates of the taxpayer, be entitled to make an election under subsection (1) in respect of assets acquired by it that would, on that assumption, be expropriation assets of the foreign affiliate, and all or any of those assets are subsequently acquired by the taxpayer from the foreign affiliate as a dividend payable in kind, or as a benefit received from the foreign affiliate that would otherwise be required by subsection 15(1) to be included in computing the income of the taxpayer, if the taxpayer has so elected, in prescribed form and within prescribed time, in respect of all of the assets so acquired by the taxpayer from the foreign affiliate, the following rules apply in respect of each such asset so acquired by the taxpayer:

(a) an amount equal to

(i) the principal amount of the asset, or

(ii) where the taxpayer has designated in the taxpayer's election an amount in respect of the asset that is less than the principal amount thereof, the amount so designated,

shall be deemed to be,

(iii) notwithstanding subsection 52(2), the cost to the taxpayer of the asset, and

(iv) the amount of the dividend or benefit, as the case may be, received by the taxpayer by virtue of the acquisition by the taxpayer of the asset;

(b) where the asset was so acquired as such a benefit and the taxpayer has designated in the election a class of shares as described in this paragraph in respect of the asset, the amount of the benefit shall be deemed

(i) to have been received by the taxpayer as a dividend from the foreign affiliate in respect of such class of shares of the capital stock thereof as the taxpayer has designated in the election, and

(ii) not to be an amount required by subsection 15(1) to be included in computing the taxpayer's income;

(c) in computing the taxable income of the taxpayer for the taxation year in which the taxpayer acquired the asset, there may be deducted from the taxpayer's income for the year the amount, if any, by which the amount received by the taxpayer as a dividend by virtue of the acquisition by the taxpayer of the asset exceeds the total of amounts deductible in respect of the dividend under sections 91 and 113 in computing the taxpayer's income or taxable income, as the case may be, for the year;

(d) there shall be deducted in computing the adjusted cost base to the taxpayer of each share of the capital stock of the foreign affiliate that is a share of a class in respect of which an amount was received by the taxpayer as a dividend by virtue of the acquisition by the taxpayer of the asset, the quotient obtained by dividing the amount, if any, deducted by the taxpayer under paragraph (c) in respect of the dividend by the number of shares of that class owned by the taxpayer immediately before that amount was received by the taxpayer as a dividend;

(e) any capital loss of the taxpayer from the disposition, after that time when the asset was so acquired by the taxpayer, of a share of the capital stock of the foreign affiliate shall be deemed to be nil; and

(f) where the taxpayer has so elected in prescribed form and within prescribed time, subsection (2) applies as if the asset were an expropriation asset acquired by the taxpayer as compensation for foreign property taken by a particular issuer as described in subsection (1).

**Related Provisions**: 53(2)(b) — Reduction in ACB; 220(3.2), Reg. 600(b) — Late filing or revocation of election.

**Regulations**: 4500 (prescribed time).

**Forms**: T2079: Elections re expropriation assets.

**(5) Assets acquired from foreign affiliate of taxpayer as consideration for settlement, etc., of debt** — Where a foreign affiliate of a taxpayer resident in Canada would, on the assumption that the foreign affiliate were resident in Canada and its only foreign affiliates were corporations that were foreign affiliates of the taxpayer, be entitled to make an election under subsection (1) in respect of assets acquired by it that would, on that assumption, be expropriation assets of the foreign affiliate, and all or any of those assets are subsequently acquired by the taxpayer from the foreign affiliate as consideration for the settlement or extinguishment of a capital property of the taxpayer that was a debt payable by the foreign affiliate to the taxpayer or any other obligation of the foreign affiliate to pay an amount to the taxpayer (which debt or other obligation is referred to in this subsection as the "obligation"), if the taxpayer has so elected, in prescribed form and within prescribed time, in respect of all of the assets so acquired by the taxpayer from the foreign affiliate, the following rules apply in respect of each such asset so acquired by the taxpayer,

(a) paragraph (4)(a) applies in respect of the asset as if subparagraph (4)(a)(iv) were read as follows:

"(iv) the taxpayer's proceeds of the disposition of the obligation settled or extinguished by virtue of the acquisition by the taxpayer of the asset;";

(b) where the taxpayer has designated in the taxpayer's election a class of shares as described in this paragraph in respect of the asset,

(i) the amount, if any, by which the cost to the taxpayer of the asset (computed having regard to paragraph (a) and paragraph (4)(a)) exceeds the amount of the obligation settled or extinguished by virtue of the acquisition by the taxpayer of the asset shall be deemed to have been received by the taxpayer as a dividend from the foreign affiliate in respect of such class of shares of the capital stock thereof as the taxpayer has designated in the election, and

(ii) the taxpayer's gain, if any, from the disposition of the obligation shall be deemed to be nil;

(c) the taxpayer's loss, if any, from the disposition of the obligation shall be deemed to be nil; and

(d) paragraphs (4)(c) to (f) apply in respect of the asset.

**Regulations**: 4500 (prescribed time).

**Forms**: T2079: Elections re expropriation assets.

**(6) Assets acquired from foreign affiliate of taxpayer on winding-up, etc.** — Where a foreign affiliate of a taxpayer resident in Canada would, on the assumption that the foreign affiliate were resident in Canada and its only foreign affiliates were corporations that were foreign affiliates of the taxpayer, be entitled to make an election under subsection (1) in respect of assets acquired by it that would, on that assumption, be expropriation assets of the foreign affiliate, and all or any of those assets are subsequently acquired by the taxpayer from the foreign affiliate,

(a) on the winding-up, discontinuance or reorganization of the business of the foreign affiliate, or

(b) as consideration for the redemption, cancellation or acquisition by the foreign affiliate of shares of its capital stock,

if the taxpayer has so elected, in prescribed form and within prescribed time,

(c) in respect of all of the assets so acquired by the taxpayer from the foreign affiliate, subsection (1) applies in respect of each such asset, or

(d) in respect of all amounts received or to be received by the taxpayer as or on account of interest on all of the assets so acquired by the taxpayer from the foreign affiliate, subsection (2) applies in respect of each such asset,

as if the assets were expropriation assets acquired by the taxpayer as consideration for the sale of foreign property that consisted of shares of the capital stock of the foreign affiliate owned by the taxpayer immediately before the assets were so acquired and that was sold to a particular issuer as described in subsection (1).

**Regulations**: 4500 (prescribed time).

**Forms**: T2079: Elections re expropriation assets.

**(7) Definition of "adjusted principal amount"** — In this section, "adjusted principal amount" to a taxpayer of an expropriation asset at any particular time means the amount, if any, by which

(a) the total of the principal amount of the asset and, in respect of each interest amount received by the taxpayer on the asset before the particular time, the lesser of the tax referred to in subparagraph (2)(b)(i) in respect of that interest amount and the proportion determined under subparagraph (2)(b)(ii) in respect thereof,

exceeds

(b) the total of each amount received by the taxpayer before the particular time as an interest amount on the asset and each amount received by the taxpayer before the particular time as, on account or in lieu of payment of, or in satisfaction of, the principal amount of the asset.

**(8) Currency in which adjusted principal amount to be computed or expressed** — For the purposes of this section, the adjusted principal amount, at any particular time, of an expropriation asset or of any asset assumed for the purposes of this section to be an expropriation asset shall be computed in the currency in which the principal amount of the asset is, under the terms thereof, payable, except that for greater certainty, for the purposes of paragraph (2)(a), the adjusted principal amount at any particular time of such an asset is its adjusted principal amount at that time computed as provided in this subsection but expressed in Canadian currency.

**(9) Election in respect of two or more expropriation assets acquired by taxpayer** — For the purposes of subdivision c and subsection (2), and in applying subsections (7) and (8) for those purposes, where two or more expropriation assets that were

(a) issued by the government of a country other than Canada, or

(b) issued by a person resident in a country other than Canada and guaranteed by the government of that country

at the same time, or as compensation for, or consideration for the sale of, the same foreign property, have been acquired by a taxpayer and the taxpayer has so elected, in prescribed form and within prescribed time, in respect of all of the expropriation assets that were so issued or guaranteed by the government of that country and acquired by the taxpayer before the making of the election, all of those expropriation assets shall be considered to be a single expropriation asset that was issued or guaranteed by the government of that country and acquired by the taxpayer.

**Notes**: Subdivision c deals with taxable capital gains and allowable capital losses (38–55).

**Regulations**: 4500 (prescribed time).

**Forms**: T2079: Elections re expropriation assets.

**Definitions [s. 80.1]**: "adjusted cost base" — 54, 248(1); "adjusted principal amount" — 80.1(7); "amount", "business" — 248(1); "Canada" — 255; "capital loss" — 39(1)(b), 248(1); "capital property" — 54, 248(1); "class of shares" — 248(6); "corporation" — 248(1), Interpretation Act 35(1); "cost amount", "dividend" — 248(1); "expropriation assets" — 80.1(1); "foreign affiliate" — 95(1), 248(1); "person", "prescribed", "principal amount", "property" — 248(1); "resident in Canada" — 250; "share" — 248(1); "taxable income" — 2(2), 248(1); "taxation year" — 11(2), 249; "taxpayer" — 248(1).

**80.2 Reimbursement by taxpayer [resource royalties]** — Where

(a) a taxpayer, under the terms of a contract, pays to another person an amount (in this subsection[6] referred to as the "specified payment") that may reasonably be considered to have been received by the other person as a reimbursement, contribution or allowance in respect of an amount (referred to in paragraph (b) as the "particular amount") paid or payable by the other person,

(b) the particular amount is included in the income of the other person or is denied as a deduction in computing the income of the other person by reason of paragraph 12(1)(o) or 18(1)(m), as the case may be, and

(c) the taxpayer was resident in Canada or carrying on business in Canada at the time the specified payment was made by the taxpayer,

the following rules apply for the purposes of this Act, other than this section:

(d) the taxpayer shall be deemed neither to have made nor to have become obligated to make the specified payment to the other person but to have paid an amount described in paragraph 18(1)(m) equal to the amount of the specified payment, and

(e) the other person shall be deemed neither to have received nor to have become entitled to receive the specified payment from the taxpayer.

---

[6] *Sic*. Should read "section" — ed.

## Subdivision f — Rules Relating to Computation of Income S. 80.3(5)

**Related Provisions**: 104(29) — Amounts deemed to be payable to beneficiaries.

**Notes**: 80.2 rephrased by 1990 GST, effective for payments made after January 1990.

**Definitions**: "amount", "person", "property" — 248(1); "resident in Canada" — 250; "specified payment" — 80.2(a); "taxpayer" — 248(1).

**Interpretation Bulletins**: IT-438R2: Crown charges — resource properties in Canada.

### 80.3 [Income deferrals — livestock] — (1) Definitions — In this section,

**"breeding animals"** means

(a) horses that are over 12 months of age and are kept for breeding in the commercial production of pregnant mares' urine, and

(b) deer, elk and other similar grazing ungulates, bovine cattle, bison, goats and sheep that are over 12 months of age and are kept for breeding;

**Notes**: Para. (b) of "breeding animals" amended by 1992 technical bill, effective for fiscal periods and taxation years ending after 1990, to add "deer, elk and other similar grazing ungulates".

**"breeding herd"** of a taxpayer at any time means the number determined by the formula

$$A - (B - C)$$

where

A  is the total number of the taxpayer's breeding animals held in the course of carrying on a farming business at that time,

B  is the total number of the taxpayer's breeding animals held in the business at that time that are female bovine cattle that have not given birth to calves, and

C  is the lesser of the number determined as the value of B and one-half the total number of the taxpayer's breeding animals held in the business at that time that are female bovine cattle that have given birth to calves.

**(2) Income deferral from the destruction of livestock** — Where a particular amount in respect of the forced destruction of livestock under statutory authority in a taxation year of a taxpayer is included in computing the income of the taxpayer for the year from a farming business, there may be deducted in computing that income such amount as the taxpayer claims not exceeding the particular amount.

**Related Provisions**: 28(1)(g) — Deduction for farmer using cash method; 80.3(3) — Inclusion of deferred amount; 80.3(6) — Where subsecs. (2) and (4) not to apply.

**(3) Inclusion of deferred amount** — The amount deducted under subsection (2) in computing the income of a taxpayer from a farming business for a taxation year shall be deemed to be income of the taxpayer from the business for the taxpayer's immediately following taxation year.

**Related Provisions**: 28(1)(d) — Amount under 80.3(3) to be added to income of farmer using cash method; 87(2)(tt) — Amalgamations — deferral of amounts received; 88(1)(e.2) — Winding-up — rules applicable.

**(4) Income deferral for sales in prescribed drought region** — Where in a taxation year a taxpayer carries on a farming business in a region that is a prescribed drought region at any time in the year and the taxpayer's breeding herd at the end of the year in respect of the business does not exceed 85% of the taxpayer's breeding herd at the beginning of the year in respect of the business, there may be deducted in computing the taxpayer's income from the business for the year such amount as the taxpayer claims, not exceeding the amount, if any, determined by the formula

$$(A - B) \times C$$

where

A  is the amount by which

(a) the total of all amounts included in computing the taxpayer's income for the year from the business in respect of the sale of breeding animals in the year

exceeds

(b) the total of all amounts deducted under paragraph 20(1)(n) in computing the taxpayer's income from the business for the year in respect of an amount referred to in paragraph (a) of this description;

B  is the total of all amounts deducted in computing the taxpayer's income from the business for the year in respect of the acquisition of breeding animals; and

C  is

(a) 30% where the taxpayer's breeding herd at the end of the year in respect of the business exceeds 70% of the taxpayer's breeding herd at the beginning of the year in respect of the business, and

(b) 90% where the taxpayer's breeding herd at the end of the year in respect of the business does not exceed 70% of the taxpayer's breeding herd at the beginning of the year in respect of the business.

**Related Provisions**: 28(1)(g) — Deduction for farmer using cash method; 80.3(5) — Inclusion of deferred amount; 80.3(6) — Where subsecs. (2) and (4) not to apply; 257 — Formula cannot calculate to less than zero.

**Regulations**: 7305, 7305.01 (prescribed drought region).

**(5) Inclusion of deferred amount** — The amount deducted under subsection (4) in computing the income of a taxpayer for a particular taxation year from a farming business carried on in a prescribed drought region may, to the extent that the taxpayer so elects, be included in computing the taxpayer's income from the business for a taxation year ending after the particular taxation year, and shall, except to the extent that the amount has been included under this subsection in computing the taxpayer's income from the business for a preceding taxation year after the particular year, be deemed to be income of the taxpayer from the business for the taxation year of the taxpayer that is the earliest of

(a) the first taxation year beginning after the end of the period or series of continuous periods, as the case may be, for which the region is a prescribed drought region,

(b) the first taxation year, following the particular taxation year, at the end of which the taxpayer is

   (i) non-resident, and

   (ii) not carrying on business through a fixed place of business in Canada, and

(c) the taxation year in which the taxpayer dies.

**Related Provisions**: 28(1)(d) — Inclusion in farming or fishing income when using cash method.

**Notes**: 80.3(5) amended by 1991 technical bill, effective for fiscal periods and taxation years ending after 1987.

**Regulations**: 7305 (prescribed drought regions for each year).

**(6) Where subsecs. (2) and (4) do not apply** — Subsections (2) and (4) do not apply to a taxpayer in respect of a farming business for a taxation year

(a) in which the taxpayer died; or

(b) where at the end of the year the taxpayer is non-resident and not carrying on the business through a fixed place of business in Canada.

**Notes [s. 80.3]**: 80.3(6)(b) amended by 1991 technical bill, effective for fiscal periods and taxation years ending after 1987.

80.3 completely revised by 1989 Budget, effective for fiscal periods and taxation years ending after 1987.

**Definitions [s. 80.3]**: "amount" — 248(1); "breeding animals", "breeding herd" — 80.3(1); "business" — 248(1); "Canada" — 255; "farming", "taxpayer" — 248(1); "taxation year" — 11(2), 249; "year" — 11(2).

**Interpretation Bulletins [s. 80.3]**: IT-425: Miscellaneous farm income.

**80.4 (1) Loans [to employees]** — Where a person or partnership receives a loan or otherwise incurs a debt because of or as a consequence of a previous, the current or an intended office or employment of an individual, or because of the services performed or to be performed by a corporation carrying on a personal services business, the individual or corporation, as the case may be, shall be deemed to have received a benefit in a taxation year equal to the amount, if any, by which the total of

(a) all interest on all such loans and debts computed at the prescribed rate on each such loan and debt for the period in the year during which it was outstanding, and

(b) the total of all amounts each of which is an amount of interest that was paid or payable in respect of the year on such a loan or debt by

   (i) a person or partnership (in this paragraph referred to as the "employer") that employed or intended to employ the individual,

   (ii) a person (other than the debtor) related to the employer, or

   (iii) a person or partnership to or for whom or which the services were or were to be provided or performed by the corporation or a person (other than the debtor) that does not deal at arm's length with that person or any member of such partnership,

exceeds the total of

(c) the amount of interest for the year paid on all such loans and debts not later than 30 days after the end of the year, and

(d) any portion of the total determined in respect of the year under paragraph (b) that is reimbursed in the year or within 30 days after the end of the year by the debtor to the person or entity who made the payment referred to in that paragraph.

**Related Provisions**: 6(9) — Inclusion as income from office or employment; 6(23) — Employer-provided mortgage subsidy is taxable; 12(1)(w) — Benefit from carrying on personal services business; 15(2) — Shareholder debt; 20(1)(c)(v) — Deductibility of interest; 79(3)F(b)(v)(B)(I) — Where property surrendered to creditor; 80(1)"forgiven amount"B(h) — Debt forgiveness rules do not apply; 80.4(1.1) — Interpretation; 80.4(3) — Loans — exceptions; 80.4(4) — Interest on loans for home purchase or relocation; 80.5 — Interest deemed paid; 110(1)(j) — Deduction — home relocation loan; 248(1)"home relocation loan"(c) — Definition based on application of 80.4(1).

**Notes**: The income inclusion under 80.4(1) can be offset by a deduction under 80.5 in some cases. See Notes to 80.5. However, a loan to the taxpayer in his/her capacity as a shareholder rather than as an employee may lead to full inclusion of the loan into income under 15(2).

Opening words of 80.4(1) amended by 1992 technical bill, effective for taxation years that begin after 1991, to extend to a "previous" office or employment, and to apply where the person receives a loan or incurs a debt "because of or as a consequence of" an office or employment or "because of" a corporation's services, rather than "by virtue of" in each case.

**Regulations**: 4301(c) (prescribed rate of interest for 80.4(1)(a)); but see also ITA 80.4(7)"prescribed rate".

**Interpretation Bulletins**: IT-171R2: Non-resident individuals — computation of taxable income earned in Canada and non-refundable tax credits; IT-421R2: Benefits to individuals, corporations and shareholders from loans or debt.

**I.T. Technical News**: No. 6 (payment of mortgage interest subsidy by employer).

**(1.1) Interpretation** — A loan or debt is deemed to have been received or incurred because of an individual's office or employment, or because of services performed by a corporation that carries on a personal services business, as the case may be, if it is reasonable to conclude that, but for an individual's previous, current or intended office or employment, or the services performed or to be performed by the corporation,

(a) the terms of the loan or debt would have been different; or

(b) the loan would not have been received or the debt would not have been incurred.

## Subdivision f — Rules Relating to Computation of Income    S. 80.4(7) hom

**Related Provisions**: 6(23) — Employer-provided mortgage subsidy is taxable; 248(1) "home relocation loan"(c) — Definition based on application of 80.4(1).

**Notes**: 80.4(1.1) is a response to *Siwik*, [1996] 2 C.T.C. 2417 (TCC). It was added by 1998 Budget, effective for loans received and debts incurred after February 23, 1998 except that, where the loan or debt is in respect of an eligible relocation in connection with which the individual begins employment at the new work location by September 30, 1998, it does not apply to taxation years that end before 2001.

**(2) Idem** — Where a person (other than a corporation resident in Canada) or a partnership (other than a partnership each member of which is a corporation resident in Canada) was

  (a) a shareholder of a corporation,

  (b) connected with a shareholder of a corporation, or

  (c) a member of a partnership, or a beneficiary of a trust, that was a shareholder of a corporation,

and by virtue of such shareholding that person or partnership received a loan from, or otherwise incurred a debt to, that corporation, any other corporation related thereto or a partnership of which that corporation or any corporation related thereto was a member, the person or partnership shall be deemed to have received a benefit in a taxation year equal to the amount, if any, by which

  (d) all interest on all such loans and debts computed at the prescribed rate on each such loan and debt for the period in the year during which it was outstanding

exceeds

  (e) the amount of interest for the year paid on all such loans and debts not later than 30 days after the later of the end of the year and December 31, 1982.

**Related Provisions**: 15(2) — Income inclusion for amount of loan; 15(9) — Deemed benefit to shareholder; 20(1)(c)(vi) — Deductibility of interest; 79(3)F(b)(v)(B)(I) — Where property surrendered to creditor; 80(1) "forgiven amount" B(h) — Debt forgiveness rules do not apply; 80.4(3) — Exceptions; 80.4(8) — Meaning of "connected"; 80.5 — Deemed interest; 95(1) "foreign accrual property income" A(d) — Definitions — "foreign accrual property income".

**Notes**: The income inclusion under 80.4(2) can be offset by a deduction under 80.5 in some cases. See Notes to 80.5.

**Regulations**: 4301(c) (prescribed rate of interest for 80.4(2)(d)); but see also ITA 80.4(7) "prescribed rate".

**Interpretation Bulletins**: IT-421R2: Benefits to individuals, corporations and shareholders from loans or debt.

**(3) Where subsecs. (1) and (2) do not apply** — Subsections (1) and (2) do not apply in respect of any loan or debt, or any part thereof,

  (a) on which the rate of interest was equal to or greater than the rate that would, having regard to all the circumstances (including the terms and conditions of the loan or debt), have been agreed on, at the time the loan was received or the debt was incurred, between parties dealing with each other at arm's length if

    (i) none of the parties received the loan or incurred the debt by virtue of an office or employment or by virtue of the shareholding of a person or partnership, and

    (ii) the ordinary business of the creditor included the lending of money,

except where an amount is paid or payable in any taxation year to the creditor in respect of interest on the loan or debt by a party other than the debtor; or

  (b) that was included in computing the income of a person or partnership under this Part.

**Notes**: 80.4(3)(b) will exclude 80.4 from applying where the amount was already fully included in income as a shareholder loan under 15(2) or a forgiven employee loan under 6(15).

**(4) Interest on loans for home purchase or relocation** — For the purpose of computing the benefit under subsection (1) in a taxation year in respect of a home purchase loan or a home relocation loan and for the purpose of paragraph 110(1)(j), the amount of interest determined under paragraph (1)(a) shall not exceed the amount of interest that would have been determined thereunder if it had been computed at the prescribed rate in effect at the time the loan was received or the debt was incurred, as the case may be.

**Related Provisions**: 80(14)(d) — Residual balance; 80.4(6) — Interest rate cap reset every 5 years; 110(1.4) — Replacement of home relocation loan.

**Regulations**: 4301(c) (prescribed rate of interest); but see also ITA 80.4(7) "prescribed rate".

**Interpretation Bulletins**: IT-421R2: Benefits to individuals, corporations and shareholders from loans or debt.

**(5)** [No longer relevant]

**Notes**: 80.4(5) affects the 1982 and 1983 taxation years.

**(6) Deemed new home purchase loans** — For the purposes of this section, other than paragraph (3)(a) and subsection (5), where a home purchase loan or a home relocation loan of an individual has a term for repayment exceeding five years, the balance outstanding on the loan on the date that is five years from the day the loan was received or was last deemed by this subsection to have been received shall be deemed to be a new home purchase loan received by the individual on that date.

**Related Provisions**: 110(1)(j) — Home relocation loan; 110(1.4) — Replacement of home relocation loan.

**Interpretation Bulletins**: IT-421R2: Benefits to individuals, corporations and shareholders from loans or debt.

**(7) Definitions** — In this section,

**"home purchase loan"** means that portion of any loan received or debt otherwise incurred by an individual in the circumstances described in subsection (1) that is used to acquire, or to repay a loan or debt that was received or incurred to acquire, a dwelling, or a share of the capital stock of a cooperative housing corporation acquired for the sole purpose of acquiring the right to inhabit a dwelling owned by the corporation, where the dwelling is for the habitation of

(a) the individual by virtue of whose office or employment the loan is received or the debt is incurred,

(b) a specified shareholder of the corporation by virtue of whose services the loan is received or the debt is incurred, or

(c) a person related to a person described in paragraph (a) or (b),

or that is used to repay a home purchase loan;

**Notes**: 80.4(7)"home purchase loan" was 80.4(7)(a) before consolidation in R.S.C. 1985 (5th Supp.), effective for taxation years ending after November 1991. See Table of Concordance.

Definition amended by 1991 technical bill, retroactive to 1985.

**Interpretation Bulletins**: IT-421R2: Benefits to individuals, corporations and shareholders from loans or debt.

**"prescribed rate"** of interest means

(a) 6% per annum before 1978,

(b) 8% per annum for 1978, and

(c) for any year, or part thereof, after 1978, such rate of interest as is prescribed therefor except that, for the purpose of computing the benefit under subsection (1) in a taxation year on a home purchase loan received after November 12, 1981 and before 1982, the prescribed rate of interest at the time the loan was received shall be deemed to be 16% per annum.

**Notes**: 80.4(7)"prescribed rate" was 80.4(7)(b) before consolidation in R.S.C. 1985 (5th Supp.), effective for taxation years ending after November 1991. See Table of Concordance.

**Regulations**: 4301(c) (prescribed rate of interest for para. (c)).

**(8) Persons connected with a shareholder** — For the purposes of subsection (2), a person is connected with a shareholder of a corporation if that person does not deal at arm's length with the shareholder and if that person is a person other than

(a) a foreign affiliate of the corporation; or

(b) a foreign affiliate of a person resident in Canada with which the corporation does not deal at arm's length.

**Definitions [s. 80.4]**: "amount" — 248(1); "arm's length" — 251(1); "because of" — 80.4(1.1); "Canada" — 255; "carrying on business" — 253; "common-law partner" — 248(1); "connected" — 80.4(8); "corporation" — 248(1), *Interpretation Act* 35(1); "employee" — 248(1); "employer" — 80.4(1)(b)(i); "employment" — 248(1); "foreign affiliate" — 95(1), 248(1); "home purchase loan" — 80.4(7); "home relocation loan", "individual", "office", "officer", "person" — 248(1); "personal services business" — 125(7), 248(1); "prescribed" — 80.4(7), 248(1); "prescribed rate" — Reg. 4301; "related" — 251(2); "resident in Canada" — 250; "share", "shareholder", "specified shareholder" — 248(1); "taxation year" — 249; "writing" — *Interpretation Act* 35(1).

**80.5 Deemed interest** — Where a benefit is deemed by section 80.4 to have been received in a taxation year by

(a) an individual or corporation under subsection 80.4(1), or

(b) a person or partnership under subsection 80.4(2),

the amount of the benefit shall, for the purposes of subparagraph 8(1)(j)(i) and paragraph 20(1)(c), be deemed to be interest paid in, and payable in respect of, the year by the debtor pursuant to a legal obligation to pay interest on borrowed money.

**Notes**: If the purpose for which the loan was used entitles the taxpayer to a deduction for interest expenses under 20(1)(c) or 8(1)(j), the effect of 80.5 will be to negate the effect of the income inclusion under 80.4 by allowing an offsetting deduction. Thus, for example, an interest-free loan to enable the taxpayer to acquire shares will normally have no net tax cost to the taxpayer (subject to the *Ludmer* case discussed in the Notes to 20(1)(c)). However, there may still be an income inclusion under 15(2) of the amount of the loan, subject to deduction under 20(1)(j) when it is repaid.

**Definitions [s. 80.5]**: "amount" — 248(1); "corporation" — 248(1), *Interpretation Act* 35(1); "individual", "person" — 248(1); "taxation year" — 249.

**Interpretation Bulletins**: IT-421R2: Benefits to individuals, corporations and shareholders from loans or debt.

## Subdivision g — Amounts Not Included in Computing Income

**81. (1) Amounts not included in income** — There shall not be included in computing the income of a taxpayer for a taxation year,

(a) **statutory exemptions** — an amount that is declared to be exempt from income tax by any other enactment of Parliament, other than an amount received or receivable by an individual that is exempt by virtue of a provision contained in a tax convention or agreement with another country that has the force of law in Canada;

### Proposed Amendment — First Nations taxation

**Federal budget, Supplementary Information, February 24, 1998**: *First Nations Taxation*

In the 1997 budget, the federal government indicated its willingness to put into effect taxation arrangements with interested First Nations. Since that time, Parliament has passed legislation that allows the Cowichan Tribes and the Westbank First Nation to levy taxes on tobacco products sold on their respective reserves. In the case of the Westbank First Nation, a tax collection agreement has been concluded under which Revenue Canada will collect Westbank's tax.

The federal government has also been working, this past year, with the self-governing First Nations in the Yukon to facilitate the exercise of taxation powers provided in their self-government agreements. The discussions have focused on the co-ordination of the First Nations tax system with that of Canada through the use of tax collection agreements. The successful conclusion of these first tax collection agreements will open a new and important revenue

Subdivision g — Amounts Not Included                                        S. 81(1)(d)

source for these communities. The first such agreements will address the co-ordination of our respective personal income tax systems. The government has also identified co-ordination of corporate income taxes and sales taxes as subjects for discussion in the next year.

Building on the work of the last year, the federal government is once again expressing its willingness to continue discussions and to put into effect taxation arrangements with the First Nations that indicate an interest in exercising taxation powers.

**Federal budget, Supplementary Information, February 16, 1999**: *First Nations taxation*

In the 1997 and 1998 budgets, the federal government indicated its willingness to put into effect taxation arrangements with interested First Nations. Since that time, Parliament has passed legislation that enables the Cowichan Tribes, the Westbank First Nation and the Kamloops Indian Band to levy a tax on sales of certain products on their reserves. In addition, personal income tax collection and sharing agreements with the seven self-governing Yukon First Nations came into effect on January 1, 1999. The federal government is once again expressing its willingness to discuss and to put into effect arrangements in respect of direct taxation with interested First Nations.

**Federal budget, supplementary Information, February 28, 2000**: *First Nations Taxation*

In the 1997, 1998 and 1999 budgets, the Government indicated its willingness to put into effect taxation arrangements with interested First Nations. Since that time, Parliament has passed legislation that enables the Cowichan Tribes, the Westbank First Nation, the Kamloops Indian Band and the Sliammon First Nation to levy a tax on sales of certain products on their reserves. In addition, personal income tax collection and sharing agreements with the seven self-governing Yukon First Nations came into effect on January 1, 1999. The Government is once again expressing its willingness to discuss and to put into effect arrangements in respect of direct taxation with interested First Nations.

**Notes**: In August 2000 similar arrangements were reached with the Chemainus First Nation.

**Related Provisions**: 110(1)(f)(i) — Deduction for amount exempted by treaty; 120(2.2) — Credit for persons subject to First Nations Tax; 126(3)(c) — Employees of international organizations; 150(1)(a)(ii) — Non-resident claiming treaty exemption must file tax return; 212(1)(h)(iii) — Exemption from non-resident withholding tax.

**Notes**: Section 87 of the *Indian Act* exempts status Indians from taxation of their "personal property situated on a reserve". The Supreme Court of Canada ruled in *Nowegijick*, [1983] C.T.C. 20, that income is personal property. There are no fixed rules for determining when income is "situated on a reserve"; in *Williams*, [1992] 1 C.T.C. 225, the Supreme Court ruled that there must be "sufficient connecting factors" to the reserve and that the purpose of the exemption is also relevant. See also *Clarke*, [1997] 3 C.T.C. 157 (FCA). In most cases, employment income of a status Indian who lives on a reserve and either works on the reserve or is paid by an employer resident on the reserve will be exempt. For a review of the recent jurisprudence, see Murray Marshall, "Business and Investment Income under Section 87 of the *Indian Act*: *Recalma v. Canada*", 77(3 & 4) *Canadian Bar Review* (Sept.-Dec. 1998), pp. 528-548.

Revenue Canada announced at the 1995 Canadian Tax Foundation annual conference that Interpretation Bulletin IT-62 has been withdrawn effective July 15, 1995. Specifically, the situs of interest earned by an Indian will depend on the facts of each case; the fact the bank account is on a reserve will no longer be sufficient to exempt the interest. See Income Tax Technical News No. 7.

Effective 1999, Indians in the Yukon are no longer entitled to exemption under the *Indian Act*, as a result of a treaty reached with the federal government. (See VIEWS docs 9821446 and 9806857.)

Amounts exempted by tax treaty are included in income and then granted an offsetting deduction under 110(1)(f)(i). The effect is to increase "income" (net income) without affecting taxable income. This can have a number of side effects, including eliminating another person's credits for the taxpayer as a dependent spouse (118(1)B(a)), increasing the taxpayer's threshold for medical expenses (118.2(1)C) and increasing the taxpayer's ability to claim charitable donations (118.1(1)"total gifts"(a)(ii)). Where the increase in net income results in increased tax, the treaty will override the increased tax if it is a real tax, but not if it is a clawback of social benefits. See *Peter*, [1997] 2 C.T.C. 2504 (TCC); *Swantje*, [1996] 1 C.T.C. 355 (SCC), aff'g [1994] 2 C.T.C. 382 (FCA) ; and Canada-U.S. tax treaty, Art. XXIV(10).

Certain income of members of armed forces of other countries in Canada may be exempt. See subsec. 22(2) of the *Visiting Forces Act*, reproduced in the Notes to 250(1).

**Remission Orders**: *Indian Settlements Remission Order*, P.C. 2000-1112 (remission of tax payable by taxpayer whose income is situated on an Indian Settlement); *Indian Income Tax Remission Order (Yukon Territory Lands)*, P.C. 1995-197 (certain lands in Yukon treated as Indian reserves for income tax purposes); *Indian Income Tax Remission Order*, P.C. 1993-523, P.C. 1993-1649 (remission of tax on income from an employer that resides on a reserve); *Indians and Bands on certain Indian Settlements Remission Orders*, P.C. 1992-1052 (remission of tax payable by Indians and Indian bands); *Indians and Bands on Certain Indian Settlements Remission Orders (1997)*, P.C. 1992-1529 (remission of tax payable by Indians and Indian bands).

**Interpretation Bulletins**: IT-62: Indians [withdrawn — under revision] see Notes; IT-397R: Amounts excluded from income — statutory exemptions and certain service or RCMP pensions, allowances and compensation.

**I.T. Technical News**: No. 2 (tax exemption for Indians); No. 5 (statutory exemptions — *Indian Act*); No. 7 (Indians: interest income — situs of savings accounts); No. 9 (taxation of Indians' investment income).

**Forms**: TD1-IN: Determination of exemption of an Indian's employment income.

(b) **War Savings Certificate** — an amount received under a War Savings Certificate issued by His Majesty in right of Canada or under a similar savings certificate issued by His Majesty in right of Newfoundland before April 1, 1949;

**Related Provisions**: 212(1)(h)(iii) — Exemption from non-resident withholding tax.

(c) **ship or aircraft of non-residents** — the income for the year of a non-resident person earned in Canada from the operation of a ship or aircraft in international traffic, if the country where that person resided grants substantially similar relief for the year to a person resident in Canada;

**Related Provisions**: 115(1)(b)(ii)(B) — Exclusion of ship or aircraft from taxable Canadian property; 250(6) — Residence of international shipping corporation; Canada–U.S. tax treaty, Art. VIII — Operation of ships or aircraft in international traffic.

**Interpretation Bulletins**: IT-494: Hire of ships and aircraft from non-residents.

(d) **service pension, allowance or compensation** — a pension payment, an allowance or compensation that is received under or is subject to the *Pension Act*, the *Civilian War-related Benefits Act* or the *War Veterans Allowance Act*, an amount received under the *Gallantry Awards Order* or compensation received under the regulations made under section 9 of the *Aeronautics Act*;

**Related Provisions**: 212(1)(h)(iii) — Exemption from non-resident withholding tax.

**Notes**: Reference to *Gallantry Awards Order* in 81(1)(d) added by 1991 technical bill, effective 1986. Reference to *Civilian War Pension and Allowances Act* changed to *Merchant Navy Veteran and Civilian War-related Benefits Act*, effective July 1, 1992, and changed back to *Civilian ...* by S.C. 1999, c. 10, effective May 1, 1999 (P.C. 1999-738).

**Interpretation Bulletins**: IT-397R: Amounts excluded from income — statutory exemptions and certain service or RCMP pensions, allowances and compensation.

(e) **war pensions** — a pension payment received on account of disability or death arising out of a war from a country that was an ally of Canada at the time of the war, if that country grants substantially similar relief for the year to a person receiving a pension referred to in paragraph (d);

**Related Provisions**: 212(1)(h)(iii) — Exemption from non-resident withholding tax.

**Notes**: 81(1)(e) amended by 1991 technical bill, effective 1988, to delete the phrase "war service" and thus exempt pensions paid to civilian war casualties, provided the other conditions are met.

**Interpretation Bulletins**: IT-397R: Amounts excluded from income — statutory exemptions and certain service or RCMP pensions, allowances and compensation.

(f) **Halifax disaster pensions, grants or allowances** — a pension payment, a grant or an allowance in respect of death or injury sustained in the explosion at Halifax in 1917 and received from the Halifax Relief Commission the incorporation of which was confirmed by *An Act respecting the Halifax Relief Commission*, chapter 24 of the Statutes of Canada, 1918, or received pursuant to the *Halifax Relief Commission Pension Continuation Act*, chapter 88 of the Statutes of Canada, 1974-75-76;

**Related Provisions**: 212(1)(h)(iii) — Exemption from non-resident withholding tax.

(g) **compensation by Federal Republic of Germany** — a payment made by the Federal Republic of Germany or by a public body performing a function of government within that country as compensation to a victim of National Socialist persecution, where no tax is payable in respect of that payment under a law of the Federal Republic of Germany that imposes an income tax;

**Notes**: 81(1)(g) exempts payments to Holocaust survivors made by Germany (formerly West Germany) on an ongoing basis as compensation for persecution by Nazi Germany during the years 1933–45. It also applies to payments under a new foundation ("Remembrance, Responsibility and Future") recently created by Germany to compensate Holocaust survivors: VIEWS doc. 2000-0051495 (October 31, 2000).

(g.1) **income from personal injury award property** — the income for the year from any property acquired by or on behalf of a person as an award of, or pursuant to an action for, damages in respect of physical or mental injury to that person, or from any property substituted therefor and any taxable capital gain for the year from the disposition of any such property,

(i) where the income was income from the property, if the income was earned in respect of a period before the end of the taxation year in which the person attained the age of 21 years, and

(ii) in any other case, if the person was less than 21 years of age during any part of the year;

**Related Provisions**: 81(1)(g.2) — Income from income exempt under paragraph (g.1); 81(5) — Election to increase ACB of capital property at age 21; 212(1)(h)(iii) — Exemption from non-resident holding tax; 248(5) — Substituted property.

**Interpretation Bulletins**: IT-365R2: Damages, settlements and similar receipts.

(g.2) **income from income exempt under para. (g.1)** — any income for the year from any income that is by virtue of this paragraph or paragraph (g.1) not required to be included in computing the taxpayer's income (other than any income attributable to any period after the end of the taxation year in which the person on whose behalf the income was earned attained the age of 21 years);

**Related Provisions**: 212(1)(h)(iii) — Exemption from non-resident withholding tax.

**Interpretation Bulletins**: IT-365R2: Damages, settlements and similar receipts.

(g.3) **hepatitis C trust** — the amount that, but for this paragraph, would be the income of the taxpayer for the year where

(i) the taxpayer is the trust established under the 1986-1990 Hepatitis C Settlement Agreement entered into by Her Majesty in right of Canada and Her Majesty in right of each of the provinces, and

(ii) the only contributions made to the trust before the end of the year are those provided for under the Agreement;

**Notes**: 81(1)(g.3) added by 1999 Budget, effective for 1999 and later taxation years.

Former 81(1)(g.3), repealed in 1985, dealt with property acquired as an award and held for the benefit of an injured person under 21. This rule is now covered by 81(1)(g.1).

(h) **social assistance** — where the taxpayer is an individual (other than a trust), a social assistance payment (other than a prescribed payment) ordinarily made on the basis of a means, needs or income test under a program provided for by an Act of Parliament or a law of a province, to the extent that it is received directly or indirectly by the taxpayer for the benefit of another individual (other than the taxpayer's spouse or common-law partner or a person who is related to the taxpayer or to the taxpayer's spouse or common-law partner), if

(i) no family allowance under the *Family Allowances Act* or any similar allowance under a law of a province that provides for payment of an allowance similar to the family allowance provided under that Act is payable in respect of the other individual for the period in respect of which the social assistance payment is made, and

(ii) the other individual resides in the taxpayer's principal place of residence, or the taxpayer's principal place of residence is maintained for use as the residence of that other individual, throughout the period referred to in subparagraph (i);

**Related Provisions**: 56(1)(u), 110(1)(f) — Income inclusion and deduction — social assistance payments; 212(1)(h)(iii) — Exemption from non-resident holding tax.

**Notes**: 81(1)(h) exempts social assistance payments related to foster children in the taxpayer's care. Such payments would otherwise be taxable under 56(1)(u), with an offsetting deduction under 110(1)(f).

81(1)(h) amended by 2000 same-sex partners bill to add reference to "common-law partner", effective for the 2001 and later taxation years, or earlier by election (see Notes to 248(1)"common-law partner").

Opening words of 81(1)(h) amended by 1992 technical bill, effective 1993, due to the extended definition of "spouse" in 252(4). For 1982 to 1992, read the parenthetical exclusion at the end of the opening words as:

(other than a person who is cohabiting in a conjugal relationship with the taxpayer or who is related to the taxpayer or to such a person)

81(1)(h) added by 1991 technical bill, retroactive to 1982.

Former 81(1)(h), repealed effective 1982, exempted workers' compensation payments from tax. They are now taxed under 56(1)(v) but subject to an offsetting deduction under 110(1)(f).

**Regulations**: No prescribed payments to date.

**I.T. Technical News**: No. 17 (application of para. 81(1)(h) to employment income).

(i) **RCMP pension or compensation** — a pension payment or compensation received under section 5, 31 or 45 of the *Royal Canadian Mounted Police Pension Continuation Act*, chapter R-10 of the Revised Statutes of Canada, 1970, or section 32 or 33 of the *Royal Canadian Mounted Police Superannuation Act*, in respect of an injury, disability or death;

**Related Provisions**: 212(1)(h)(iii) — Exemption from non-resident withholding tax.

**Interpretation Bulletins**: IT-397R: Amounts excluded from income — statutory exemptions and certain service or RCMP pensions, allowances and compensation.

(j) **[Repealed under former Act]**

**Notes**: 81(1)(j), repealed effective 1982, exempted social assistance payments (such as welfare) from tax. They are now taxed under 56(1)(u) but subject to an offsetting deduction under 110(1)(f).

(k) **employees profit sharing plan** — a payment or part of a payment from an employees profit sharing plan that section 144 provides is not to be included;

**Related Provisions**: 212(1)(h)(iii) — Exemption from non-resident withholding tax.

(l) **prospecting** — an amount in respect of the receipt of a share that section 35 provides is not to be included;

**Related Provisions**: 212(1)(h)(iii) — Exemption from non-resident withholding tax.

(m) **interest on certain obligations** — interest that accrued to, became receivable or was received by, a corporation resident in Canada (in this paragraph referred to as the "parent corporation") on a bond, debenture, bill, note, mortgage or similar obligation received by it as consideration for the disposition by it, before June 18, 1971, of

(i) a business carried on by it in a country other than Canada, or

(ii) all of the shares of a corporation that carried on a business in a country other than Canada, and such of the debts and other obligations of that corporation as were, immediately before the disposition, owing to the parent corporation,

if

(iii) the business was of a public utility or public service nature,

(iv) the business or the property described in subparagraph (ii), as the case may be, was disposed of to a person or persons resident in that country, and

(v) the obligation received by the parent corporation was issued by or guaranteed by the government of that country or any agent thereof;

**Related Provisions**: 40(2)(d) — Reduction in capital loss on bond to reflect exempt income; 87(2)(jj) — Amalgamations — continuation of predecessor corporations; 212(1)(h)(iii) — Exemption from non-resident withholding tax.

(n) **Governor General** — income from the office of Governor General of Canada;

**Notes**: The Governor General does not pay GST either. See the *Excise Tax Act*, Sch. VI, Part VIII, s. 1.

(o), (p) **[Repealed]**

**Notes**: 81(1)(o) and (p) repealed by 1997 Budget, effective for 1998 and later taxation years. For 1992 to 1997, read:

(o) **RESP refunds** — a refund of payments (within the meaning assigned by subsection 146.1(1));

(p) **educational assistance payments** — an educational assistance payment (within the meaning assigned by subsection 146.1(1)) received by a beneficiary under an education savings plan (within the meaning assigned by subsection 146.1(1)) that is not registered or the registration of which has been revoked pursuant to section 146.1;

81(1)(o) was unnecessary, since nothing in the Act would otherwise include a "refund of payments" in income. 81(1)(p) was repealed because 146.1(14) was repealed, and no amount is included in a subscriber's income on the revocation of a RESP.

(q) **provincial indemnities** — an amount paid to an individual as an indemnity under a prescribed provision of the law of a province; or

**Regulations**: 6501 (prescribed provisions — criminal injuries compensation and motor vehicle accident claims).

(r) **foreign retirement arrangements** — an amount that is credited or added to a deposit or account governed by a foreign retirement arrangement as interest or other income in respect of the deposit or account, where the amount would, but for this paragraph, be included in the taxpayer's income solely because of that crediting or adding.

**Proposed Amendment — Income Inclusion on Conversion to Roth IRA**
**Department of Finance press release, December 18, 1998**: [See under 248(1)"foreign retirement arrangement" — ed.]

**Related Provisions**: 56(1)(a)(i)(C.1) — Inclusion in income of payment from foreign retirement arrangement; 146(20) — Where amount credited or added deemed not received.

**Notes**: 81(1)(r) added by 1991 technical bill, effective 1990. It ensures that amounts accruing in a foreign retirement arrangement (a U.S. Individual Retirement Account, or IRA) are not taxed until they are paid out.

(s) [Repealed under former Act]

**Notes [paras. 81(1)(r), (s)]**: 81(1)(s) and former 81(1)(r), repealed in 1986, exempted certain amounts received under the *Petroleum and Gas Revenue Act*.

**(1.1)** [Repealed under former Act]

**Notes**: 81(1.1), repealed in 1986, defined terms for purposes of 81(1)(s) (repealed at the same time).

**(2) M.L.A.'s expense allowance** — Where an elected member of a provincial legislative assembly has, under an Act of the provincial legislature, been paid an allowance in a taxation year for expenses incident to the discharge of the member's duties in that capacity, the allowance shall not be included in computing the member's income for the year unless it exceeds ½ of the maximum fixed amount provided by law as payable to the member by way of salary, indemnity and other remuneration as a member in respect of attendance at a session of the legislature, in which event there shall be included in computing the member's income for the year only the amount by which the allowance exceeds ½ of that maximum fixed amount.

**Related Provisions**: 6(1)(b) — Allowances taxable, and exclusions.

**Notes**: 81(2) allows ⅓ of an MLA's remuneration to be tax-free as an unaccountable "allowance". There is no requirement that the MLA prove expenses equal to the amount of the allowance; additional reimbursements for actual expenses are also non-taxable.

"MLA", used in the heading to 81(2), stands for Member of the Legislative Assembly. Ontario members are called Members of Provincial Parliament, while those in Quebec are called Members of the National Assembly (Assemblée Nationale).

The rule in 81(2) applies to the territorial as well as the provincial legislatures. See the definitions of "Act", "legislative assembly" and "province" in subsec. 35(1) of the *Interpretation Act*, reproduced towards the end of the book.

The parallel rule for federal Members of Parliament is in 6(1)(b)(i)(A). See Notes to 6(1)(b). For municipal officials, see 81(3).

**Interpretation Bulletins**: IT-266: Taxation of members of provincial legislative assemblies.

**(3) Municipal officers' expense allowance** — Where a person who is

(a) an elected officer of an incorporated municipality,

(b) an officer of a municipal utilities board, commission or corporation or any other similar body, the incumbent of whose office as such an officer is elected by popular vote, or

(c) a member of a public or separate school board or similar body governing a school district,

has been paid by the municipal corporation or the body of which the person was such an officer or member (in this subsection referred to as the person's "employer") an amount as an allowance in a taxation year for expenses incident to the discharge of the person's duties as such an officer or member, the allowance shall not be included in computing the person's income for the year unless it exceeds ½ of the amount that was paid to the person in the year by the person's employer as salary or other remuneration as such an officer or member, in which event there shall be included in computing the person's income for the year only the amount by which the allowance exceeds ½ of the amount so paid to the person by way of salary or remuneration.

**Related Provisions**: 6(1)(b) — Allowances taxable, and exclusions.

**Notes**: See Notes to 81(2). In some provinces, ⅓ of municipal officers' remuneration is deemed by legislation to be an allowance so as to qualify under 81(3). See for example s. 255 of the Ontario *Municipal Act*.

**Interpretation Bulletins**: IT-292: Taxation of elected officers of incorporated municipalities, school boards, etc.

**(3.1) Travel expenses** — An amount received by an individual in respect of the individual's part-time employment by an employer with whom the individual was dealing at arm's length as an allowance for, or reimbursement of, travel expenses incurred during a period throughout which the individual had other employment or was carrying on a business shall not be included in computing the individual's income to the extent that it is paid by the employer and does not exceed a reasonable amount on account of travel expenses (other than expenses incurred in the performance of the duties of the individual's part-time employment) incurred by the individual in respect of that part-time employment, if the duties of the part-time employment are performed at a location not less than 80 kilometres from both the individual's ordi-

Subdivision g — Amounts Not Included S. 81(4)

nary place of residence and principal place of employment or business.

### Proposed Amendment — 81(3.1)

**(3.1) Travel expenses** — There shall not be included in computing an individual's income for a taxation year an amount (not in excess of a reasonable amount) received by the individual from an employer with whom the individual was dealing at arm's length as an allowance for, or reimbursement of, travel expenses incurred by the individual in the year in respect of the individual's part-time employment in the year with the employer (other than expenses incurred in the performance of the duties of the individual's part-time employment) if

(a) throughout the period in which the expenses were incurred,

(i) the individual had other employment or was carrying on a business, or

(ii) where the employer is a designated educational institution (as defined in subsection 118.6(1)), the duties of the individual's part-time employment were the provision in Canada of a service to the employer in the individual's capacity as a professor or teacher; and

(b) the duties of the individual's part-time employment were performed at a location not less than 80 kilometres from,

(i) where subparagraph (a)(i) applies, both the individual's ordinary place of residence and the place of the other employment or business referred to in that subparagraph, and

(ii) where subparagraph (a)(ii) applies, the individual's ordinary place of residence.

**Application**: Bill C-43 (First Reading September 20, 2000), s. 36, will amend subsec. 81(3.1) to read as above, applicable to 1995 *et seq.* and, notwithstanding subsecs. 152(4) to (5), any assessment of an individual's tax payable under the Act for any taxation year that ends before 2000 shall be made that is necessary to take into account the application of subsec. 81(3.1).

**Technical Notes**: Section 81 of the Act lists various amounts which are not included in computing a taxpayer's income.

Subsection 81(3.1) of the Act excludes from income certain amounts received by a part-time employee in respect of travel expenses. In order to benefit from the exemption, the part-time employee is required to carry on a business or to have another employment. Since one of the purposes of this exemption is to facilitate the recruiting of part-time teachers by universities and other educational institutions located outside the major metropolitan areas, the amendment waives this particular requirement for individuals who are employed as professors or teachers by designated educational institutions. The term "designated educational institution", which is also used for the purposes of the tuition fee and education tax credits, is defined in subsection 118.6(1).

**Interpretation Bulletins**: IT-522R: Vehicle, travel and sales expenses of employees.

**(4) [Repealed under former Act]**

**Notes**: Former 81(4), repealed effective 1979, provided a rule of interpretation relating to a previous version of 81(1)(g.1) to (g.3).

### Proposed Addition — 81(4)

**(4) Payments for volunteer [emergency] services** — Where

(a) an individual was employed or otherwise engaged in a taxation year by a government, municipality or public authority (in this subsection referred to as "the employer") and received in the year from the employer one or more amounts for the performance, as a volunteer, of the individual's duties as

(i) an ambulance technician,

(ii) a firefighter, or

(iii) a person who assists in the search or rescue of individuals or in other emergency situations, and

(b) if the Minister so demands, the employer has certified in writing that

(i) the individual was in the year a person described in paragraph (a), and

(ii) the individual was at no time in the year employed or otherwise engaged by the employer, otherwise than as a volunteer, in connection with the performance of any of the duties referred to in paragraph (a) or of similar duties,

there shall not be included in computing the individual's income derived from the performance of those duties the lesser of $1,000 and the total of those amounts.

**Application**: Bill C-43 (First Reading September 20, 2000), s. 36, will add subsec. 81(4), applicable to 1998 *et seq.*

**Technical Notes**: New subsection 81(4) of the Act provides for an exemption equivalent to the deduction available under paragraph 8(1)(a), which is being repealed. The exemption applies to the first $1,000 of amounts received by an individual from a government, municipality or public authority for the performance, as a volunteer, of the individual's duties as an ambulance technician, a firefighter or a person who assists in the search or rescue of individuals or in other emergency situations. The exemption is granted under the same conditions as was the deduction under paragraph 8(1)(a).

**CCRA news release, February 22, 2000**: *Tax Tips: What is changing for emergency volunteers this year?*

In 1999, you may have received an allowance from a government, municipality or other public authority as an emergency worker for performing as a volunteer ambulance technician, fire fighter, in search and rescue, or in some other emergency capacity.

If you received an allowance, the T4 slip issued by such an authority will generally show only the taxable part of the allowance. This is the part that is more than $1,000. However, it is important to remember that if you were employed by the same authority for work other than as a volunteer, for the same or similar duties, the whole allowance will be taxable.

## S. 81(4) — Income Tax Act, Part I, Division B

> **Related Provisions**: 63(3)"earned income"(b) — Exempted amount included in earned income for child-care expense deduction.
>
> **Notes**: The certification requirement in 81(4)(b) is similar to that in 8(10) for many employment expenses, but only applies if the CCRA asks for it.

**(5) Election** — Where a taxpayer or a person described in paragraph (1)(g.1) has acquired capital property under the circumstances described in that paragraph, the taxpayer or the person may, in the return of income of the taxpayer for the taxation year in which the taxpayer attains the age of 21 years, elect to treat any such capital property held by the taxpayer or person as having been disposed of on the day immediately preceding the day on which the taxpayer attained the age of 21 years for proceeds of disposition equal to the fair market value of the property on that day and the person or taxpayer making the election shall be deemed to have reacquired that property immediately thereafter at a cost equal to those proceeds.

**Definitions [s. 81]**: "Act" — *Interpretation Act* 35(1); "amount" — 248(1); "arm's length" — 251(1); "business" — 248(1); "Canada" — 255; "capital property" — 54, 248(1); "common-law partner" — 248(1); "corporation" — 248(1), *Interpretation Act* 35(1); "designated educational institution" — 118.6(1); "employees profit sharing plan" — 144(1), 248(1); "employed" — 248(1); "employer" — 81(4)(a), 248(1); "employment" — 248(1); "foreign retirement arrangement" — 248(1); "Her Majesty" — *Interpretation Act* 35(1); "individual", "international traffic" — 248(1); "legislative assembly" — *Interpretation Act* 35(1); "legislature" — *Interpretation Act* 35(1)"legislative assembly" — "Minister", "non-resident", "office", "person", "prescribed", "property" — 248(1); "province" — *Interpretation Act* 35(1); "regulation" — 248(1); "related" — 251(2); "resident in Canada" — 250; "share" — 248(1); "taxable capital gain" — 38(a), 248(1); "taxation year" — 249; "taxpayer" — 248(1); "trust" — 104(1), 248(1), (3); "writing" — *Interpretation Act* 35(1).

## Subdivision h — Corporations Resident in Canada and Their Shareholders

**82. (1) Taxable dividends received** — In computing the income of a taxpayer for a taxation year, there shall be included

(a) the total of

(i) all amounts each of which is a taxable dividend received by the taxpayer in the year as part of a dividend rental arrangement of the taxpayer from a corporation resident in Canada or a taxable dividend received by the taxpayer in the year from a corporation resident in Canada that is not a taxable Canadian corporation,

(i.1) where the taxpayer is a trust, all amounts each of which is all or part of a taxable dividend (other than a taxable dividend described in subparagraph (i)) that was received by the trust in the year on a share of the capital stock of a taxable Canadian corporation and that can reasonably be considered as having been included in computing the income of a beneficiary under the trust who was non-resident at the end of the year, and

(ii) the amount, if any, by which

(A) the total of all amounts received by the taxpayer in the year from corporations resident in Canada as, on account of, in lieu of payment of or in satisfaction of, taxable dividends, other than an amount included in computing the income of the taxpayer because of subparagraph (i) or (i.1)

exceeds

(B) where the taxpayer is an individual, the total of all amounts paid by the taxpayer in the year that are deemed by subsection 260(5) to have been received by another person as taxable dividends,

plus

(b) where the taxpayer is an individual, other than a trust that is a registered charity, $1/4$ of the amount determined under subparagraph (a)(ii) in respect of the taxpayer for the year.

**Related Provisions**: 12(1)(j) — Inclusion into income from business or property; 52(3) — Cost of stock dividend; 82(1.1) — Application of 82(1)(a)(i); 82(2) — Dividends included in income by attribution rules; 82(3) — Dividends received by spouse; 84 — Deemed dividends; 90 — Dividends received from non-resident corporation; 104(19) — Taxable dividend received by trust; 112(3)(b)(i) — Reduction in loss on subsequent disposition of share by corporate shareholder; 112(4)–(4.3) — Loss on share held as inventory; 120.4(1)"split income"(a)(i) — Dividends received by children subject to income splitting tax; 121 — Dividend tax credit; 127.52(1)(f) — Exclusion of gross-up for minimum tax purposes; 137(4.2) — Credit unions — deemed interest deemed not to be a dividend; 139.1(4)(f), (g) — Deemed dividend on demutualization of insurance corporation; 139.2 — Deemed dividend on distribution by mutual holding corporation; Canada–U.S. tax treaty, Art. X — Taxation of dividends.

**Notes**: 82(1) looks much more complex that it is. Where there is no dividend rental arrangement, securities lending arrangement or trust receiving dividends for a non-resident beneficiary, read only 82(1)(a)(ii)(A) and 82(1)(b) — the actual dividend plus, for individuals, a gross-up of $1/4$. The higher tax resulting from the gross-up is more than offset by the dividend tax credit in s. 121 and resulting lower provincial tax. The gross-up brings the income inclusion to the theoretical level of pre-tax corporate income (assuming combined corporate federal and provincial income tax of 20%, which approximates the actual rate when the small business deduction under 125 and parallel provincial deductions apply).

For corporations, the full dividend is included in income under 82(1)(a)(ii)(A), but an offsetting deduction in computing taxable income is generally allowed under 112(1), so there is no net tax cost. However, the deduction can be denied by several anti-avoidance rules (112(2.1)–(2.9)); and the dividend may be subject to Part IV tax (186(1)) even where the deduction is allowed. Also, a loss on the share may be denied after the deduction has been claimed: 112(3)–(4.22).

A dividend is considered a transfer of property, so if the corporation paying the dividend is unable to pay its debts to the CCRA, a non-arm's length shareholder can be assessed for the amount of the dividend. See Notes to 160(1). Liability may also arise under 159(2) if the corporation is insolvent when it pays the dividend and no clearance certificate is issued; see *L'Écuyer v. Québec (Sous-Ministre du Revenu)*, [1993] R.D.F.Q. 110 (Que. Ct.).

82(1)(a)(i.1) added, and 82(1)(a)(ii)(A) amended to refer to it, by 1995-97 technical bill, effective for taxation years that end after April 26, 1995. It provides that the gross-up does not apply to taxable dividends received by a trust in the year from a taxable Canadian corporation, to the extent such dividends are included in the income of a non-resident beneficiary (NRB). The trust's dividend tax credit (DTC) will thus not be affected by whether or not the trust designates amounts under 104(19) in respect of NRBs. The reason for the amendment is that the DTC is aimed at Canadian residents, whose income tax rates are generally higher than the withholding rates for non-residents. The amendment prevents trusts with NRBs from obtaining access to the DTC on income allocated to the NRBs that has not been flowed-out to them under 104(19).

82(1) amended by 1989 Budget, effective 1989, to add (a)(i) and (a)(ii)(B), dealing with dividend rental arrangements. Subpara. (a)(i) applies only to dividends received on a share acquired after April 1989 (see 82(1.1)). Cl. (a)(ii)(B) applies to amounts paid after May 1989.

**Regulations**: 201(1)(a) (information return).

**Interpretation Bulletins**: IT-67R3: Taxable dividends from corporations resident in Canada; IT-379R: Employees profit sharing plans — allocations to beneficiaries; IT-432R2: Benefits conferred on shareholders; IT-524: Trusts — flow-through of taxable dividends to a beneficiary — after 1987.

**I.T. Technical News**: No. 11 (U.S. spin-offs (divestitures) — dividends in kind).

**Forms**: T5 Segment; T5 Summary: Return of investment income; T5 Supplementary: Statement of investment income.

**(1.1) Limitations as to subpara. (1)(a)(i)** — An amount shall be included in the amounts described in subparagraph (1)(a)(i) in respect of a taxable dividend received at any time as part of a dividend rental arrangement only where that dividend was received on a share acquired before that time and after April, 1989.

**Notes**: 82(1.1) added in R.S.C. 1985 (5th Supp.) consolidation. Formerly an application rule in the 1989 Budget bill.

**(2) Certain dividends [deemed] received by taxpayer** — Where by reason of subsection 56(4) or (4.1) or sections 74.1 to 75 of this Act or section 74 of the *Income Tax Act*, chapter 148 of the Revised Statutes of Canada, 1952, there is included in computing a taxpayer's income for a taxation year a dividend received by another person, for the purposes of this Act, the dividend shall be deemed to have been received by the taxpayer.

**Notes**: This rule ensures that the dividend tax credit (s. 121) and other consequences of receiving a dividend all apply when dividend income is subject to the attribution rules.

**I.T. Application Rules**: 69 (meaning of "*Income Tax Act*, chapter 148 of the Revised Statutes of Canada, 1952").

**Interpretation Bulletins**: IT-440R2: Transfer of rights to income.

**(3) Dividends received by spouse [or common-law partner]** — Where the amount that would, but for this subsection, be deductible under subsection 118(1) by reason of paragraph 118(1)(a) in computing a taxpayer's tax payable under this Part for a taxation year is less than the amount that would be so deductible if no amount were required by subsection (1) to be included in computing the income for the year of the taxpayer's spouse or common-law partner and the taxpayer so elects in the taxpayer's return of income for the year under this Part, all amounts described in paragraph (1)(a) received in the year from taxable Canadian corporations by the taxpayer's spouse or common-law partner shall be deemed to have been so received by the taxpayer and not by the spouse or common-law partner.

**Related Provisions**: 220(3.2) — Late filing of election or revocation; Reg. 600(b) — Late filing of election or revocation.

**Notes**: As per the T1 General Income Tax Guide, dividends received by a spouse are simply reported on Schedule 4 and line 120 of the T1 General return, together with other dividends. There is no special form for this purpose.

82(3) amended by 2000 same-sex partners bill to add reference to "common-law partner", effective for the 2001 and later taxation years, or earlier by election (see Notes to 248(1)"common-law partner").

**Interpretation Bulletins [subsec. 82(3)]**: IT-295R4: Taxable dividends received after 1987 by a spouse; IT-513R: Personal tax credits.

**Definitions [s. 82]**: "amount" — 248(1); "Canada" — 255; "Canadian corporation" — 89(1), 248(1); "common-law partner" — 248(1); "corporation" — 248(1), *Interpretation Act* 35(1); "dividend", "dividend rental arrangement", "individual", "person" — 248(1); "received" — 248(7); "registered charity" — 248(1); "resident in Canada" — 250; "series of transactions" — 248(10); "tax payable" — 248(2); "taxable Canadian corporation", "taxable dividend" — 89(1), 248(1); "taxation year" — 249; "taxpayer" — 248(1); "trust" — 104(1), 248(1), (3).

**83. (1) Qualifying dividends** — Where a qualifying dividend has been paid by a public corporation to shareholders of a series of tax-deferred preferred shares of a class of the capital stock of the corporation that were outstanding on March 31, 1977, the following rules apply:

(a) no part of the qualifying dividend shall be included in computing the income of any shareholder of the corporation by virtue of this subdivision; and

(b) in computing the adjusted cost base to any shareholder of the corporation of any tax-deferred preferred share of the corporation owned by the shareholder, there shall be deducted in respect of the qualifying dividend an amount as provided by subparagraph 53(2)(a)(i).

**Related Provisions**: 83(3) — Late filed elections; 83(6) — "Qualifying dividend" defined; 89(3) — Simultaneous dividends; 184 — Tax on excessive elections.

**Notes**: Qualifying dividends have not been paid since 1991; see 83(6). Before 1979, 83(1) applied to dividends paid out of "tax-paid undistributed surplus" or "1971 capital surplus on hand", concepts that have been eliminated from the Act.

**Regulations**: 2107 (tax-deferred preferred series).

**Interpretation Bulletins**: IT-67R3: Taxable dividends from corporations resident in Canada; IT-379R: Employees profit sharing plans — allocations to beneficiaries; IT-465R: Non-resident beneficiaries of trusts.

**(2) Capital dividend** — Where at any particular time after 1971 a dividend becomes payable by a private corporation to shareholders of any class of shares of its capital stock and the corporation so elects in respect of the full amount of the dividend, in prescribed manner and prescribed form and at or before the particular time or the first day on which any part of the dividend was paid if that day is earlier than the particular time, the following rules apply:

(a) the dividend shall be deemed to be a capital dividend to the extent of the corporation's capital dividend account immediately before the particular time; and

(b) no part of the dividend shall be included in computing the income of any shareholder of the corporation.

**Related Provisions**: 83(2.1) — Capital dividend on certain shares disallowed; 83(3) — Late filed elections; 87(2)(z.1) — Amalgamations — capital dividend account; 88(2)(b) — Winding-up of a Canadian corporation; 89(1) — Capital dividend account; 89(1)"taxable dividend"(a) — Taxable dividend excludes capital dividend; 89(3) — Simultaneous dividends; 104(20) — Flow-through of capital dividend through trust; 108(3)(a) — "Income" of a trust; 112(3)(a), 112(3)(b)(ii) — Reduction in loss on disposition of share on which capital dividend paid; 112(3.1)(a), 112(3.1)(b)(ii) — Reduction in loss of partner on disposition of share by partnership; 112(3.2)(b) — Reduction in loss on disposition of share by trust; 112(5.2)B(b)(iv) — Adjustment for dividends received on mark-to-market property; 133(1)(e) — NRO investment corporations; 184, 185 — Tax on excessive elections; 212(1)(c)(ii) — Tax on payments to non-residents — estate or trust income derived from capital dividend; 212(2)(b) — Tax on capital dividend paid to non-resident; 220(3.2) — Late filing of election or revocation; 248(1)"capital dividend" — Definition applies to entire Act; Reg. 600(b) — Late filing of election or revocation.

**Notes**: The "capital dividend" mechanism allows the untaxed ½ of any capital gain realized by a private corporation (or ¾ for donations of publicly-traded securities to charities; see 38(a.1)) to be flowed out tax-free to the shareholders, either directly or through intermediate holding corporations, so that it remains untaxed. See Notes to 89(1)"capital dividend".

**Regulations**: 2101 (prescribed manner, prescribed form).

**Interpretation Bulletins**: IT-66R6: Capital dividends; IT-67R3: Taxable dividends from corporations resident in Canada; IT-146R4: Shares entitling shareholders to choose taxable or capital dividends; IT-149R4: Winding-up dividend; IT-430R3: Life insurance proceeds received by a private corporation or a partnership as a consequence of death.

**Information Circulars**: 92-1: Guidelines for accepting late, amended or revoked elections.

**I.T. Technical News**: No. 9 (life insurance policy used as security for indebtedness).

**Advance Tax Rulings**: ATR-54: Reduction of paid-up capital;.

**Forms**: T2054: Election for a capital dividend.

**(2.1) Idem** — Notwithstanding subsection (2), where a dividend that, but for this subsection, would be a capital dividend is paid on a share of the capital stock of a corporation and the share (or another share for which the share was substituted) was acquired by its holder in a transaction or as part of a series of transactions one of the main purposes of which was to receive the dividend,

(a) the dividend shall, for the purposes of this Act (other than for the purposes of Part III and computing the capital dividend account of the corporation), be deemed to be received by the shareholder and paid by the corporation as a taxable dividend and not as a capital dividend; and

(b) paragraph (2)(b) does not apply in respect of the dividend.

**Related Provisions**: 83(2.2)–(2.4) — Exceptions; 87(2)(z.1) — Amalgamations — capital dividend account; 112(3)(a)(i), 112(3)(b)(ii), 112(3.1)(a), 112(3.1)(b)(ii), 112(3.2)(b) — Taxable dividend under 83(2.1) excluded from stop-loss rule on disposition of share; 248(1)"life insurance capital dividend" — Definition applies to entire Act248(10) — Series of transactions.

**Notes**: This version of 83(2.1) added by 1988 tax reform, effective for dividends paid after 4:00 pm EDST, September 25, 1987. Former 83(2.1), repealed effective for dividends paid after May 23, 1985, permitted a corporation to elect for a dividend to be a "life insurance capital dividend". The normal capital dividend rules now apply to proceeds of disposition from life insurance: see 89(1)"capital dividend account"(d) and (e). However, life insurance capital dividends paid before May 24, 1985 are still taken into account for adjusted cost base purposes (see 53(1)(e)(ii)) and for purposes of limiting capital losses (112(3)–(3.2)), and are tracked through amalgamations (87(2)(x)) and windups (88(1)(d)(i.1)(B)). "Life insurance capital dividend" is still (erroneously) defined for purposes of the Act in 248(1) by reference to 83(2.1), even though it has been repealed.

**Interpretation Bulletins**: IT-66R6: Capital dividends.

**Advance Tax Rulings**: ATR-54: Reduction of paid-up capital;.

**(2.2) Where subsec. (2.1) does not apply** — Subsection (2.1) does not apply to a particular dividend, in respect of which an election is made under subsection (2), paid on a share of the capital stock of a particular corporation to an individual where it is reasonable to consider that all or substantially all of the capital dividend account of the particular corporation immediately before the particular dividend became payable consisted of amounts other than any amount

(a) added to that capital dividend account under paragraph (b) of the definition "capital dividend account" in subsection 89(1) in respect of a dividend received on a share of the capital stock of another corporation, which share (or another share for which the share was substituted) was acquired by the particular corporation in a transaction or as part of a series of transactions one of the main purposes of which was that the particular corporation receive the dividend, but not in respect of a dividend where it is reasonable to consider that the purpose of paying the dividend was to distribute an amount that was received by the other corporation and included in computing the other corporation's capital dividend account by reason of paragraph (d) of that definition;

(b) added to that capital dividend account under paragraph 87(2)(z.1) as a result of an amalgamation or winding-up or a series of transactions including the amalgamation or winding-up that would not have been so added had the amalgamation or winding-up occurred or the series of transactions been commenced after 4:00 p.m. Eastern Daylight Saving Time, September 25, 1987;

(c) added to that capital dividend account at a time when the particular corporation was controlled, directly or indirectly, in any manner whatever, by one or more non-resident persons; or

(d) in respect of a capital gain from a disposition of a property by the particular corporation or another corporation that may reasonably be considered as having accrued while the property (or another property for which it was substituted) was a property of a corporation that was controlled, directly or indirectly, in any manner whatever, by one or more non-resident persons.

**Related Provisions**: 248(5) — Substituted property; 248(10) — Series of transactions; 256(5.1), (6.2) — Controlled directly or indirectly — control in fact.

**Notes**: The CCRA takes the position that "all or substantially all", used in the opening words of 83(2.2), means 90% or more.

**Interpretation Bulletins**: IT-66R6: Capital dividends.

**(2.3) Idem** — Subsection (2.1) does not apply in respect of a dividend, in respect of which an election is made under subsection (2), paid on a share of the capital stock of a corporation where it is reasonable to consider that the purpose of paying the dividend was to distribute an amount that was received by the corporation and included in computing its capital dividend account by reason of paragraph (d) of the definition "capital dividend account" in subsection 89(1).

**Interpretation Bulletins**: IT-66R6: Capital dividends.

**(2.4) Idem** — Subsection (2.1) does not apply in respect of a particular dividend, in respect of which an election is made under subsection (2), paid on a share of the capital stock of a particular corporation to a corporation (in this subsection referred to as the "related corporation") related (otherwise than by reason of a right referred to in paragraph 251(5)(b)) to the particular corporation where it is reasonable to consider that all or substantially all of the capital dividend account of the particular corporation immediately before the particular dividend became payable consisted of amounts other than any amount

(a) added to that capital dividend account under paragraph (b) of the definition "capital dividend account" in subsection 89(1) in respect of a dividend received on a share of the capital stock of another corporation if it is reasonable to consider that any portion of the capital dividend account of that other corporation immediately before that dividend became payable consisted of amounts added to that account under paragraph 87(2)(z.1) or paragraph (b) of that definition as a result of a transaction or a series of transactions that would not have been so added had the transaction occurred or the series of transactions been commenced after 4:00 p.m. Eastern Daylight Saving Time, September 25, 1987;

(b) that represented the capital dividend account of a corporation before it became related to the related corporation;

(c) added to the capital dividend account of the particular corporation at a time when that corporation was controlled, directly or indirectly, in any manner whatever, by one or more non-resident persons;

(d) in respect of a capital gain from a disposition of a property by the particular corporation or another corporation that may reasonably be considered as having accrued while the property (or another property for which it was substituted) was a property of a corporation that was controlled, directly or indirectly, in any manner whatever, by one or more non-resident persons; or

(e) in respect of a capital gain from a disposition of a property (or another property for which it was substituted) that may reasonably be considered as having accrued while the property or the other property was a property of a person that was not related to the related corporation.

**Related Provisions**: 248(5) — Substituted property; 248(10) — Series of transactions; 256(5.1), (6.2) — Controlled directly or indirectly — control in fact.

**Notes**: The CCRA takes the position that "all or substantially all", used in the opening words of 83(2.4), means 90% or more.

**Interpretation Bulletins**: IT-66R6: Capital dividends.

**(3) Late filed elections** — Where at any particular time after 1974 a dividend has become payable by a corporation to shareholders of any class of shares of its capital stock, and subsection (1) or (2) would have applied to the dividend except that the election referred to therein was not made on or before the day on or before which the election was required by that subsection to be made, the election shall be deemed to have been made at the particular time or on the first day on which any part of the dividend was paid, whichever is the earlier, if

(a) the election is made in prescribed manner and prescribed form;

(b) an estimate of the penalty in respect of that election is paid by the corporation when that election is made; and

(c) the directors or other person or persons legally entitled to administer the affairs of the corporation have, before the time the election is made, authorized the election to be made.

**Related Provisions**: 83(3.1) — Request for late filed election; 83(4) — Penalty for late filed election; 83(5) — Unpaid balance of penalty.

**Regulations**: 2101(e) (prescribed manner, prescribed form).

**Forms**: T2054: Election for a capital dividend.

**(3.1) Request for election** — The Minister may at any time, by written request served personally or by registered mail, request that an election referred to in subsection (3) be made by a taxpayer, and where the taxpayer on whom such a request is served

**S. 83(3.1)**

does not comply therewith within 90 days of service thereof on the taxpayer, subsection (3) does not apply to such an election made by the taxpayer.

**Related Provisions**: 244(5), (6) — Proof of service; 248(7) — Mail deemed received on day mailed.

**(4) Penalty for late filed election** — For the purposes of this section, the penalty in respect of an election referred to in paragraph (3)(a) is an amount equal to the lesser of

(a) 1% per annum of the amount of the dividend referred to in the election for each month or part of a month during the period commencing with the time that the dividend became payable, or the first day on which any part of the dividend was paid if that day is earlier, and ending with the day on which that election was made, and

(b) the product obtained when $500 is multiplied by the proportion that the number of months or parts of months during the period referred to in paragraph (a) bears to 12.

**Related Provisions**: 83(5) — Unpaid balance of penalty.

**(5) Unpaid balance of penalty** — The Minister shall, with all due dispatch, examine each election referred to in paragraph (3)(a), assess the penalty payable and send a notice of assessment to the corporation and the corporation shall pay, forthwith to the Receiver General, the amount, if any, by which the penalty so assessed exceeds the total of all amounts previously paid on account of that penalty.

**(6) Definition of "qualifying dividend"** — For the purposes of subsection (1), "qualifying dividend" means a dividend on shares of a series of a class of the capital stock of a public corporation that is prescribed to be a tax-deferred preferred series that became payable by the corporation after 1978 and not later than

(a) where the terms as at March 31, 1977 of the shares of that series entitled the holder of any such share to exchange it after a particular date for a share or shares of another series or class of preferred shares of the capital stock of the corporation, that particular date,

(b) where the terms as at March 31, 1977 of the shares of that series required the corporation to offer to purchase at a time not later than a particular date all of the shares of that series from all of the holders of those shares, that particular date, and

(c) in any other case, October 1, 1991,

whichever is applicable in respect of that series of shares, except that a dividend on shares of such a series that would otherwise be a qualifying dividend shall be deemed not to be a qualifying dividend if

(d) at the time that the dividend became payable, the terms of the shares of that series differ from the terms as at March 31, 1977 of the shares of that series, or

(e) after March 31, 1977 the corporation issued additional shares of that series.

**Regulations**: 2107 (tax-deferred preferred series).

**(7) Amalgamation where there are tax-deferred preferred shares** — For the purposes of this section, where, after March 31, 1977, there has been an amalgamation within the meaning of section 87 and one or more of the predecessor corporations had a series of shares outstanding on March 31, 1977 that was prescribed to be a tax-deferred preferred series, the following rules apply:

(a) the series of shares of the capital stock of the predecessor corporation that was prescribed to be a tax-deferred preferred series shall be deemed to have been continued in existence in the form of the new shares; and

(b) the new corporation shall be deemed to be the same corporation as, and a continuation of, each such predecessor corporation.

**Regulations**: 2107 (tax-deferred preferred series).

**Definitions [s. 83]**: "adjusted cost base" — 54, 248(1); "amount", "assessment" — 248(1); "Canadian corporation" — 89(1), 248(1); "capital dividend" — 83(2), 248(1); "capital dividend account" — 89(1); "capital gain" — 39(1)(a), 248(1); "class of shares" — 248(6); "controlled directly or indirectly" — 256(5.1), (6.2); "corporation" — 248(1), *Interpretation Act* 35(1); "dividend", "individual", "Minister", "non-resident" — 248(1); "payable" — 84(7), 89(3); "person", "preferred share", "prescribed" — 248(1); "private corporation" — 89(1), 248(1); "property" — 248(1); "qualifying dividend" — 83(6); "received" — 248(7); "series of transactions or events" — 248(10); "share", "shareholder" — 248(1); "substituted property" — 248(5); "taxable dividend" — 89(1), 248(1).

**84. (1) Deemed dividend** — Where a corporation resident in Canada has at any time after 1971 increased the paid-up capital in respect of the shares of any particular class of its capital stock, otherwise than by

(a) payment of a stock dividend,

(b) a transaction by which

(i) the value of its assets less its liabilities has been increased, or

(ii) its liabilities less the value of its assets have been decreased,

by an amount not less than the amount of the increase in the paid-up capital in respect of the shares of the particular class,

(c) a transaction by which the paid-up capital in respect of the shares of all other classes of its capital stock has been reduced by an amount not less than the amount of the increase in the paid-up capital in respect of the shares of the particular class,

(c.1) where the corporation is an insurance corporation, any action by which it converts contributed surplus related to its insurance business into paid-up capital in respect of the shares of its capital stock, (c.2) where the corporation is a bank, any action by which it converts any of its contributed surplus that arose on the issuance of shares of its capital stock into paid-up capital in respect of shares of its capital stock, or

(c.3) where the corporation is neither an insurance corporation nor a bank, any action by which it converts into paid-up capital in respect of a class of shares of its capital stock any of its contributed surplus that arose after March 31, 1977

(i) on the issuance of shares of that class or shares of another class for which the shares of that class were substituted (other than an issuance to which section 51, 66.3, 84.1, 85, 85.1, 86 or 87, subsection 192(4.1) or 194(4.1) or section 212.1 applied),

(ii) on the acquisition of property by the corporation from a person who at the time of the acquisition held any of the issued shares of that class or shares of another class for which shares of that class were substituted for no consideration or for consideration that did not include shares of the capital stock of the corporation, or

(iii) as a result of any action by which the paid-up capital in respect of that class of shares or in respect of shares of another class for which shares of that class were substituted was reduced by the corporation, to the extent of the reduction in paid-up capital that resulted from the action,

the corporation shall be deemed to have paid at that time a dividend on the issued shares of the particular class equal to the amount, if any, by which the amount of the increase in the paid-up capital exceeds the total of

(d) the amount, if any, of the increase referred to in subparagraph (b)(i) or the decrease referred to in subparagraph (b)(ii), as the case may be,

(e) the amount, if any, of the reduction referred to in paragraph (c), and

(f) the amount, if any, of the increase in the paid-up capital that resulted from a conversion referred to in paragraph (c.1), (c.2) or (c.3),

and a dividend shall be deemed to have been received at that time by each person who held any of the issued shares of the particular class immediately after that time equal to that proportion of the dividend so deemed to have been paid by the corporation that the number of the shares of the particular class held by the person immediately after that time is of the number of the issued shares of that class outstanding immediately after that time.

**Related Provisions**: 15(1) — Benefit conferred on shareholder — income inclusion; 53(1)(b) — Addition to ACB; 82(1) — Income inclusion of dividend deemed received; 84(8) — Application; 84(10) — Reduction of contributed surplus; 84(11) — Computation of contributed surplus; 85(2.1) — Reduction in paid-up capital to prevent deemed dividend on s. 85 rollover; 86(2.1) — Adjustment to paid-up capital on internal reorganization; 87(2)(y) — Amalgamations — contributed surplus; 89(3) — Simultaneous dividends; 131(4) — S. 84 does not apply to mutual fund corporation; 131(11)(c) — Rules re prescribed labour-sponsored venture capital corporations; 138(11.9) — Computation of contributed surplus.

**Notes**: See Notes to 84(3) for explanation of the purpose of s. 84.

84(1)(c.3)(iii) amended by 1993 technical bill, this version effective for actions occurring after December 21, 1992. For actions from July 14, 1990 through December 20, 1992, read:

(iii) on the reduction by the corporation of the paid-up capital in respect of that class of shares or in respect of another class for which shares of that class were substituted,

84(1)(c.3) amended by 1991 technical bill, effective for actions occurring after July 13, 1990, effectively to add (c.3)(ii) and (iii).

84(1)(f) added by 1991 technical bill, effective 1986.

**Regulations**: 201(1)(a) (information return).

**Interpretation Bulletins**: IT-67R3: Taxable dividends from corporations resident in Canada; IT-243R4: Dividend refund to private corporations; IT-432R2: Benefits conferred on shareholders; IT-463R2: Paid-up capital.

**Information Circulars**: 76-19R3: Transfer of property to a corporation under section 85.

**Advance Tax Rulings**: ATR-33: Exchange of shares.

**Forms**: T5 Segment; T5 Summary: Return of investment income; T5 Supplementary: Statement of investment income.

**(2) Distribution on winding-up, etc.** — Where funds or property of a corporation resident in Canada have at any time after March 31, 1977 been distributed or otherwise appropriated in any manner whatever to or for the benefit of the shareholders of any class of shares in its capital stock, on the winding-up, discontinuance or reorganization of its business, the corporation shall be deemed to have paid at that time a dividend on the shares of that class equal to the amount, if any, by which,

(a) the amount or value of the funds or property distributed or appropriated, as the case may be,

exceeds

(b) the amount, if any, by which the paid-up capital in respect of the shares of that class is reduced on the distribution or appropriation, as the case may be,

and a dividend shall be deemed to have been received at that time by each person who held any of the issued shares at that time equal to that proportion of the amount of the excess that the number of the shares of that class held by the person immediately before that time is of the number of the issued shares of that class outstanding immediately before that time.

**Related Provisions**: 15(1) — Benefit conferred on shareholder; 54"proceeds of disposition"(j) — exclusion of deemed dividend; 55(1) — "Permitted redemption" for butterfly purposes; 69(5) — Unreasonable consideration; 84(5) — Amount distributed or paid where a share; 84(6), (8) — Application rules; 88(1) — Winding-up; 88(2)(b) — Winding up of a Canadian corporation; 89(3) — Simultaneous dividends; 131(4) — S. 84 does not apply to mutual fund corporation; 137(4.2) — No application to credit union.

## S. 84(2)

**Notes**: See Notes to 84(3).

If there is no true discontinuance of the corporation's business, 84(2) will not apply and 15(1) will apply instead to the appropriation of the corporation's property by the shareholders, resulting in income inclusion without the beneficial treatment given to dividend income under 112(1) and 121: *Felray Inc.*, [1998] 2 C.T.C. 4 (FCTD).

84(2) was found by the Tax Court to apply to a sale of shares that in substance constituted the extraction of corporate surplus, in *RMM Canadian Enterprises* (also known as *Equilease Corp.*), [1998] 1 C.T.C. 2300.

**Interpretation Bulletins**: IT-67R3: Taxable dividends from corporations resident in Canada; IT-126R2: Meaning of "winding-up"; IT-149R4: Winding-up dividend; IT-243R4: Dividend refund to private corporations; IT-409: Winding-up of a non-profit organization; IT-444R: Corporations — involuntary dissolutions; IT-488R2: Winding-up of 90%-owned taxable Canadian corporations.

**(3) Redemption, etc.** — Where at any time after December 31, 1977 a corporation resident in Canada has redeemed, acquired or cancelled in any manner whatever (otherwise than by way of a transaction described in subsection (2)) any of the shares of any class of its capital stock,

(a) the corporation shall be deemed to have paid at that time a dividend on a separate class of shares comprising the shares so redeemed, acquired or cancelled equal to the amount, if any, by which the amount paid by the corporation on the redemption, acquisition or cancellation, as the case may be, of those shares exceeds the paid-up capital in respect of those shares immediately before that time; and

(b) a dividend shall be deemed to have been received at that time by each person who held any of the shares of that separate class at that time equal to that portion of the amount of the excess determined under paragraph (a) that the number of those shares held by the person immediately before that time is of the total number of shares of that separate class that the corporation has redeemed, acquired or cancelled, at that time.

**Related Provisions**: 8(12) — Return of employee shares by trustee; 40(3.6) — Stop-loss rule on disposition of share of corporation to the corporation; 54 "proceeds of disposition"(j) — exclusion of deemed dividend; 55(1) — "Permitted redemption" for butterfly purposes; 55(2) — Deemed proceeds or capital gain on capital gains strip; 84(5) — Amount distributed or paid where a share; 84(6), (8) — Application rules; 84(9) — Shares disposed of on redemption; 89(3) — Simultaneous dividends; 128.1(3) — Addition to PUC of corporation that previously became resident in Canada; 131(4) — S. 84 does not apply to mutual fund corporation; 137(4.1) — Deemed interest on certain reductions of capital by credit union; 137(4.2) — No application to credit union; 191.1(1) — Application of Part VI.1 tax to corporation.

**Notes**: On a redemption of shares, 84(3) provides for a deemed dividend to the extent the amount paid on redemption exceeds the paid-up capital (PUC) of the shares. If the shareholder is a corporation, the deemed dividend will normally pass tax-free due to 82(1)(a) and 112(1); but 55(2) may deem the dividend to be a capital gain if the effect is to strip capital gains from the value of the redeeming corporation's shares; or the stop-loss rules in s. 112 may apply. If the shares are preferred shares, Part VI.1 tax may apply to the corporation.

Like the rest of s. 84, 84(3) ensures that the PUC can be returned to the shareholder free of tax but that any excess is treated as a dividend. However, 84.1, 85(2.1), 87(3) and numerous other provisions ensure that PUC cannot be artificially increased through corporate reorganizations.

PUC is calculated under 89(1) by class, not by individual shareholder, so issuance of new treasury shares can change existing shareholders' PUC. However, artificial averaging "up" of PUC using this technique may contravene the general anti-avoidance rule: *Nadeau*, [1999] 3 C.T.C. 2235 (TCC).

**Interpretation Bulletins**: IT-146R4: Shares entitling shareholders to choose taxable or capital dividends; IT-243R4: Dividend refund to private corporations; IT-269R3: Part IV tax on taxable dividends received by private corporation or subject corporation; IT-450R: Share for share exchange; IT-489R: Non-arm's length sale of shares to a corporation.

**Advance Tax Rulings**: ATR-28: Redemption of capital stock of family farm corporation; ATR-35: Partitioning of assets to get specific ownership — "butterfly"; ATR-54: Reduction of paid-up capital; ATR-57: Transfer of property for estate planning purposes; ATR-58: Divisive reorganization.

**(4) Reduction of paid-up capital** — Where at any time after March 31, 1977 a corporation resident in Canada has reduced the paid-up capital in respect of any class of shares of its capital stock otherwise than by way of a redemption, acquisition or cancellation of any shares of that class or a transaction described in subsection (2) or (4.1),

(a) the corporation shall be deemed to have paid at that time a dividend on shares of that class equal to the amount, if any, by which the amount paid by it on the reduction of the paid-up capital, exceeds the amount by which the paid-up capital in respect of that class of shares of the corporation has been so reduced; and

(b) a dividend shall be deemed to have been received at that time by each person who held any of the issued shares at that time equal to that proportion of the amount of the excess referred to in paragraph (a) that the number of the shares of that class held by the person immediately before that time is of the number of the issued shares of that class outstanding immediately before that time.

**Related Provisions**: 53(2)(a)(ii) — Reduction in ACB; 84(5) — Amount distributed or paid where a share; 84(8) — Application; 89(3) — Simultaneous dividends; 128.1(3) — Addition to PUC of corporation that previously became resident in Canada; 131(4) — S. 84 does not apply to mutual fund corporation; 137(4.1) — Deemed interest on certain reductions of capital by credit union; 137(4.2) — No application to credit union.

**Notes**: See Notes to 84(3).

In a letter dated June 9, 1997 to the chair of the CICA Taxation Committee, Revenue Canada's Assistant Deputy Minister, VECR (Barry Lacombe) pointed out that 84(4) may apply when a corporation returns a portion of its share capital to shareholder following the comprehensive revaluation of its assets and liabilities under *CICA Handbook* section 1625. A comprehensive revaluation occurs following a financial reorganization where there has been a substantial realignment of the equity and non-equity interest of an enterprise, or where its assets and liabilities are revised after its purchase.

**Interpretation Bulletins**: IT-67R3: Taxable dividends from corporations resident in Canada; IT-243R4: Dividend refund to private corporations; IT-450R: Share for share exchange.

**(4.1) Deemed dividend on reduction of paid-up capital** — Where at any time after April 10, 1978, a public corporation has reduced the paid-up capital in respect of any class of shares of its capital stock otherwise than by way of a redemption, acquisition or cancellation of any shares of that class or a transaction described in subsection (2) or section 86, any amount paid by it on the reduction of the paid-up capital shall be deemed to have been paid by the corporation and received by the person to whom it was paid, as a dividend.

### Proposed Amendment — 84(4.1)
**Letter from Department of Finance, July 2, 1998:**

Dear [xxx]

This is in reply to your letter of June 30, 1998 to Davine Roach of the Department regarding the application of subsection 84(4.1) of the *Income Tax Act* to your client.

As you know, we are prepared to recommend to the Minister of Finance that subsection 84(4.1) of the *Income Tax Act* be amended. The amendment would provide that subsection 84(4.1) apply only in respect of a reduction in the paid-up capital of a class of shares to the extent that a previous increase in the paid-up capital of that class resulted in a dividend in respect of which the taxpayer elected to treat the dividend as having been paid out of the taxpayer's 1971 CSOH.

It would be recommended that such an amendment be effective for paid-up capital reductions occurring after 1996. If the recommendation is acted upon, I would anticipate that such an amendment would be included in a future technical bill.

Yours sincerely,

Len Farber
Director General
Tax Legislation Division

**Notes**: Judith Harris, in "Paid-Up Capital and Return of Capital Public Corporations", VI(2) *Business Vehicles* (Federated Press) 290-291, notes at p. 291 re the above letter: "The proposed amendment has not yet materialized. At a meeting sponsored by the Canadian Tax Foundation in 1999, it was revealed that the publication of the above mentioned comfort letter resulted in a number of requests for similar comfort letters applicable to a variety of situations, some of which the Department thought might warrant "deemed dividend" treatment. Accordingly, it is likely that the proposed amendment to subsection 84(4.1), when it appears, will be somewhat more restricted than as suggested by the 1998 comfort letter. For example, the proposed amendment may not preclude the application of subsection 84(4.1) where a public corporation uses a reduction in capital to replace what would otherwise be actual dividends paid to shareholders in the ordinary course. Similarly, capital reductions adopted to accommodate non-resident investors (who would otherwise pay Canadian withholding tax on actual dividends) might also fall outside the more lenient approach to be taken in the amended subsection 84(4.1).

**Letter from Department of Finance, May 12, 1999:**

Dear [xxx]

This is in reply to your letter of April 23, 1999 regarding subsection 84(4.1) of the *Income Tax Act* as it applies to your client, [xxx].

Based on our understanding of the facts described in your letter, [xxx] has been refocusing its business activity in an effort to improve profitability. To this end, [xxx] has been disposing of businesses that are inconsistent with its aviation services business. The last disposition was scheduled to close by the end of [xxx]. As a result of these dispositions, [xxx] has capital in excess of its future business requirements. Consequently, [xxx] may want to reduce the stated capital of its common shares with a payment of cash to its shareholders in an amount equal to the reduction. The amount of any such reduction has not been determined.

As you know, we believe that subsection 84(2) of the *Income Tax Act* may apply to this proposed reduction in stated capital. While the Department of National Revenue would determine the applicability of subsection 84(2) in the circumstances, it is our understanding that the Department has ruled in circumstances where they have been satisfied that the conditions set out in subsection 84(2) have been met. Given that subsection 84(2) of the *Income Tax Act* would appear to render the appropriate tax results on the proposed reduction of stated capital, your concerns about subsection 84(4.1) of the *Income Tax Act* may not be warranted.

However, as you are aware, we are prepared to recommend to the Minister of Finance that subsection 84(4.1) of the *Income Tax Act* be amended so that it applies only in respect of certain reductions of the paid-up capital of a class of shares of a corporation. Based on our understanding of the facts associated with [xxx]'s proposed reduction of the stated capital of its common shares, we do not regard the distribution as a substitution for an ordinary-course dividend and therefore are prepared to recommend that such a reduction be excluded from the application of subsection 84(4.1). If the recommendation were acted upon, I would anticipate that such an amendment would be included in the next technical bill.

Yours sincerely,

Brian Ernewein
Director General, Tax Legislation Division, Tax Policy Branch

**Notes**: The Department has subsequently cautioned that the amendment to be made may not be as broad as the above letter implies. See Notes above.

**Related Provisions**: 53(2)(a) — Reduction in ACB; 84(4) — Reduction of paid-up capital; 89(3) — Simultaneous dividends; 128.1(3) — Addition to PUC of corporation that previously became resident in Canada; 131(4) — S. 84 does not apply to mutual fund corporation.

**Interpretation Bulletins**: IT-243R4: Dividend refund to private corporations; IT-450R: Share for share exchange.

**(4.2) Deemed dividend on term preferred share** — Where, at any time after November 16, 1978, the paid-up capital in respect of a term preferred share owned by a shareholder that is

(a) a specified financial institution, or

(b) a partnership or trust of which a specified financial institution or a person related to such an institution was a member or a beneficiary,

was reduced otherwise than by way of a redemption, acquisition or cancellation of the share or of a transaction described in subsection (2) or (4.1), the amount received by the shareholder on the reduction of the paid-up capital in respect of the share shall be deemed to be a dividend received by the shareholder at that time unless the share was not acquired in the ordinary course of the business carried on by the shareholder.

**Related Provisions**: 89(3) — Simultaneous dividends; 131(4) — S. 84 does not apply to mutual fund corporation; 248(13) — Interests in trusts or partnerships.

**(4.3) Deemed dividend on guaranteed share** — Where at any time after 1987 the paid-up capital in respect of a share of the capital stock of a particular corporation owned

(a) by a shareholder that is another corporation to which subsection 112(2.2) or (2.4) would, if the particular corporation were a taxable Canadian corporation, apply to deny the deduction under subsection 112(1) or (2) or 138(6) of a dividend received on the share, or

(b) by a partnership or trust of which such other corporation is a member or beneficiary, as the case may be,

was reduced otherwise than by way of a redemption, acquisition or cancellation of the share or of a transaction described in subsection (2) or (4.1), the amount received by the shareholder on the reduction of the paid-up capital in respect of the share shall be deemed to be a dividend received by the shareholder at that time.

**Related Provisions**: 89(3) — Simultaneous dividends; 131(4) — S. 84 does not apply to mutual fund corporation; 248(13) — Interests in trusts or partnerships.

**(5) Amount distributed or paid where a share** — Where

(a) the amount of property distributed by a corporation or otherwise appropriated to or for the benefit of its shareholders as described in paragraph (2)(a), or

(b) the amount paid by a corporation as described in paragraph (3)(a) or (4)(a),

includes a share of the capital stock of the corporation, for the purposes of subsections (2) to (4) the following rules apply:

(c) in computing the amount referred to in paragraph (a) at any time, the share shall be valued at an amount equal to its paid-up capital at that time, and

(d) in computing the amount referred to in paragraph (b) at any time, the share shall be valued at an amount equal to the amount by which the paid-up capital in respect of the class of shares to which it belongs has increased by virtue of its issue.

**Related Provisions**: 51(3), 86(2.1) — Computation of paid-up capital after share exchange.

**(6) Where subsec. (2) or (3) does not apply** — Subsection (2) or (3), as the case may be, is not applicable

(a) in respect of any transaction or event, to the extent that subsection (1) is applicable in respect of that transaction or event; and

(b) in respect of any purchase by a corporation of any of its shares in the open market, if the corporation acquired those shares in the manner in which shares would normally be purchased by any member of the public in the open market.

**(7) When dividend payable** — A dividend that is deemed by this subsection or section 84.1, 128.1 or 212.1 to have been paid at a particular time is deemed, for the purposes of this subdivision and sections 131 and 133, to have become payable at that time.

**Related Provisions**: 15(1) — Appropriation of property to a shareholder.

**Notes**: 84(7) amended by 1998 Budget to add reference to 128.1, effective February 24, 1998.

Amended by 1991 technical bill, effective for dividends paid after 1988, to add references to sections 84.1, 131 and 133.

**(8) Where subsec. (3) does not apply** — Subsection (3) does not apply to deem a dividend to have been received by a shareholder of a public corporation where the shareholder is an individual resident in Canada who deals at arm's length with the corporation and the shares redeemed, acquired or cancelled are prescribed shares of the capital stock of the corporation.

**Regulations**: 6206 (prescribed shares — Class I shares of Reed Stenhouse).

**(9) Shares disposed of on redemptions, etc.** — For greater certainty it is declared that where a shareholder of a corporation has disposed of a share of the capital stock of the corporation as a result of the redemption, acquisition or cancellation of the share by the corporation, the shareholder shall, for the purposes of this Act, be deemed to have disposed of the share to the corporation.

**Interpretation Bulletins**: IT-243R4: Dividend refund to private corporations; IT-444R: Corporations — involuntary dissolutions; IT-484R2: Business investment losses.

**(10) Reduction of contributed surplus** — For the purpose of paragraph (1)(c.3), there shall be deducted in determining at any time a corporation's contributed surplus that arose after March 31, 1977 in any manner described in that paragraph the lesser of

(a) the amount, if any, by which the amount of a dividend paid by the corporation at or before that time and after March 31, 1977 and when it was a public corporation exceeded its retained earnings immediately before the payment of the dividend, and

(b) the amount of its contributed surplus immediately before the payment of the dividend referred to in paragraph (a) that arose after March 31, 1977.

**Related Provisions**: 84(11) — Computation of contributed surplus; 87(2)(y) — Amalgamations — contributed surplus.

**Notes**: 84(10) added by 1991 technical bill, effective July 14, 1990.

**Interpretation Bulletins**: IT-463R2: Paid-up capital.

**(11) Computation of contributed surplus** — For the purpose of subparagraph (1)(c.3)(ii), where the property acquired by the corporation (in this subsection referred to as the "acquiring corporation") consists of shares (in this subsection referred to as the "subject shares") of any class of the capital stock of another corporation resident in Canada (in this subsection referred to as the "subject corporation") and, immediately after the acquisition of the subject shares, the subject corporation would be connected (within the meaning that would be assigned by subsection 186(4) if the references in that subsection to "payer corporation" and "particular corporation" were read as "subject corporation" and "acquiring corporation", respectively) with the acquiring corporation, the contributed surplus of the acquiring corporation that arose on the acquisition of the subject shares shall be deemed to be the lesser of

(a) the amount added to the contributed surplus of the acquiring corporation on the acquisition of the subject shares, and

(b) the amount, if any, by which the paid-up capital in respect of the subject shares at the time of the acquisition exceeded the fair market value of any consideration given by the acquiring corporation for the subject shares.

**Related Provisions**: 84(10) — Reduction of contributed surplus.

**Notes**: 84(11) is intended to prevent circumvention of the anti-surplus-stripping rules in 84.1 and 212.1. It was added by 1993 technical bill, effective for actions occurring after December 20, 1992.

**Interpretation Bulletins**: IT-463R2: Paid-up capital.

**Definitions [s. 84]**: "amount" — 248(1); "arm's length" — 251(1); "bank" — 248(1), *Interpretation Act* 35(1); "business" — 248(1); "Canada" — 255; "class of shares" — 248(6); "contributed surplus" — 84(10), (11); "corporation" — 248(1), *Interpretation Act* 35(1); "dividend", "insurance corporation", "non-resident" — 248(1); "paid-up capital" — 89(1), 248(1); "payable" — 84(7), 89(3); "person", "prescribed" — 248(1); "private corporation", "public corporation" — 89(1), 248(1); "property" — 248(1); "received" — 248(7); "resident in Canada" — 250; "share", "shareholder", "specified financial institution" — 248(1); "taxable Canadian corporation" — 89(1), 248(1); "taxable income" — 2(2), 248(1); "term preferred share" — 248(1); "trust" — 104(1), 248(1), (3).

**84.1 (1) Non-arm's length sale of shares** — Where after May 22, 1985 a taxpayer resident in Canada (other than a corporation) disposes of shares that are capital property of the taxpayer (in this section referred to as the "subject shares") of any class of the capital stock of a corporation resident in Canada (in this section referred to as the "subject corporation") to another corporation (in this section referred to as the "purchaser corporation") with which the taxpayer does not deal at arm's length and, immediately after the disposition, the subject corporation would be connected (within the meaning assigned by subsection 186(4) if the references therein to "payer corporation" and to "particular corporation" were read as "subject corporation" and "pur-

chaser corporation" respectively) with the purchaser corporation,

(a) where shares (in this section referred to as the "new shares") of the purchaser corporation have been issued as consideration for the subject shares, in computing the paid-up capital, at any particular time after the issue of the new shares, in respect of any particular class of shares of the capital stock of the purchaser corporation, there shall be deducted an amount determined by the formula

$$(A - B) \times \frac{C}{A}$$

where

A is the increase, if any, determined without reference to this section as it applies to the acquisition of the subject shares, in the paid-up capital in respect of all shares of the capital stock of the purchaser corporation as a result of the issue of the new shares,

B is the amount, if any, by which the greater of

(i) the paid-up capital, immediately before the disposition, in respect of the subject shares, and

(ii) subject to paragraphs (2)(a) and (a.1), the adjusted cost base to the taxpayer, immediately before the disposition, of the subject shares,

exceeds the fair market value, immediately after the disposition, of any consideration (other than the new shares) received by the taxpayer from the purchaser corporation for the subject shares, and

C is the increase, if any, determined without reference to this section as it applies to the acquisition of the subject shares, in the paid-up capital in respect of the particular class of shares as a result of the issue of the new shares; and

(b) for the purposes of this Act, a dividend shall be deemed to be paid to the taxpayer by the purchaser corporation and received by the taxpayer from the purchaser corporation at the time of the disposition in an amount determined by the formula

$$(A + D) - (E + F)$$

where

A is the increase, if any, determined without reference to this section as it applies to the acquisition of the subject shares, in the paid-up capital in respect of all shares of the capital stock of the purchaser corporation as a result of the issue of the new shares,

D is the fair market value, immediately after the disposition, of any consideration (other than the new shares) received by the taxpayer from the purchaser corporation for the subject shares,

## S. 84.1(1)(b) — Income Tax Act, Part I, Division B

E is the greater of

(i) the paid-up capital, immediately before the disposition, in respect of the subject shares, and

(ii) subject to paragraphs (2)(a) and (a.1), the adjusted cost base to the taxpayer, immediately before the disposition, of the subject shares, and

F is the total of all amounts each of which is an amount required to be deducted by the purchaser corporation under paragraph (a) in computing the paid-up capital in respect of any class of shares of its capital stock by virtue of the acquisition of the subject shares.

**Related Provisions**: 53(2)(a)(iii), 53(2)(p) — Reductions in adjusted cost base; 54"proceeds of disposition"(k) — Exclusion of deemed dividend from proceeds; 84(7) — When dividend payable; 84.1(2) — Non-arm's length sale of shares; 85(2.1) — Alternative reduction in paid-up capital of new shares; 89(1) — Definitions; 212.1 — Similar rule for non-residents; 257 — Formula amounts cannot calculate to less than zero.

**Notes**: 84.1(1)(a) ensures that where shares with a low paid-up capital (PUC) are transferred to a corporation (whether under s. 85 or not), the PUC of the acquiring corporation is not increased beyond the PUC of the shares transferred in (except to the extent the adjusted cost base exceeds that PUC). This is consistent with the general scheme of the Act to permit the PUC of a corporation to be extracted at any time as a return of capital. 85(2.1) and the other provisions listed in 89(1)"paid-up capital"(b)(iii) have the same objective. See Notes to 84(3). 84.1(1)(b) creates a deemed dividend out of any "boot" (non-share consideration) that exceeds both the paid-up capital and the adjusted cost base.

The reference in the opening words of 84.1(1) to "connected" as defined in 186(4) has been held not to incorporate the meaning of "control" which applies for purposes of s. 186: *Olsen*, [2000] 3 C.T.C. 2299 (TCC).

84.1(1) amended by 1985 Budget and by 1991 technical bill, effective for dispositions after May 22, 1985.

For dispositions from November 13, 1981 through May 22, 1985, read:

84.1 (1) Where, at any particular time in a taxation year and after April 10, 1978, a taxpayer resident in Canada (other than a corporation) disposes of shares that are capital property of the taxpayer (in this section referred to as the "subject shares") of any class of the capital stock of a corporation resident in Canada (in this section referred to as the "subject corporation") to another corporation (in this section referred to as the "purchaser corporation"), with which the taxpayer does not deal at arm's length and, immediately after the disposition, the subject corporation is connected (within the meaning of subsection 186(4) on the assumption that the references therein to "payer corporation" and to "particular corporation" were read as "subject corporation" and "purchaser corporation" respectively) with the purchaser corporation,

(a) an amount equal to the amount, if any, by which the lesser of

(i) the adjusted cost base to the taxpayer of the subject shares immediately before the disposition, and

(ii) the fair market value of any consideration (other than any debt owing by, or share of the capital stock of, the purchaser corporation) received by the taxpayer for the subject shares from the purchaser corporation,

exceeds

(iii) the paid-up capital in respect of the subject shares immediately before the disposition

shall be deemed to be a capital gain of the taxpayer for the taxation year from the disposition of a capital property; and

(b) in computing the adjusted cost base to the taxpayer at any time after the particular time of any property received by the taxpayer as consideration for the subject shares that was any particular debt owing by the purchaser corporation or any particular share of the capital stock of the purchaser corporation, there shall be deducted from the adjusted cost base of that property to the taxpayer otherwise determined, an amount equal to that proportion of the amount, if any, by which the lesser of

(i) the adjusted cost base referred to in subparagraph (a)(i), and

(ii) the aggregate of the fair market value referred to in subparagraph (a)(ii), the principal amounts of all such particular debts and the amount, if any, by which the paid-up capital in respect of all the shares of the capital stock of the purchaser corporation is increased by virtue of the issue of all such particular shares,

exceeds

(iii) the greater of the fair market value referred to in subparagraph (a)(ii) and the paid-up capital referred to in subparagraph (a)(iii),

that the cost to the taxpayer of the particular debt or share, as the case may be, is of the aggregate of the costs to him of all such particular debts and particular shares so received as consideration for the subject shares.

For dispositions from April 11, 1978 through November 12, 1981, read as immediately above, except that (b)(ii) should be read as follows:

(ii) the aggregate of the fair market value referred to in subparagraph (a)(ii) and the principal amounts of all such particular debts and the paid-up capital in respect of all such particular shares,

For dispositions from April 1, 1977 through April 10, 1978, read as immediately above, except that the opening portion of 84.1(1) reads as follows:

84.1 (1) Where, at any particular time in a taxation year and after March 31, 1977, a taxpayer resident in Canada (other than a corporation) disposes of shares that are capital property of the taxpayer (in this section referred to as the "subject shares") of any class of the capital stock of a corporation resident in Canada (in this section referred to as the "subject corporation") to another corporation (in this section referred to as the "purchaser corporation"), that, immediately after the disposition, does not deal at arm's length with the taxpayer, and immediately after the disposition the purchaser corporation controls (within the meaning of subsection 186(2)) the subject corporation,

For payments from November 19, 1974 through March 31, 1977, read as follows:

84.1 (1) Where, at any time before a particular time and after November 18, 1974, a corporation incurred any debt as consideration for the purchase of shares of the capital stock of a second corporation and,

(a) at any time before the debt was incurred, any particular person, or the group of persons to whom the debt was owed at the time it was incurred,

(i) controlled the second corporation, directly or indirectly in any manner whatever, or

(ii) beneficially owned shares of the capital stock of the second corporation representing more than 50% of its paid-up capital, and

(b) at any time before the particular time, the particular person or group of persons referred to in paragraph (a)

(i) controlled the corporation, directly or indirectly in any manner whatever,

(ii) beneficially owned shares of the capital stock of the corporation representing more than 50% of its paid-up capital, or

(iii) held an amount of debt payable by the corporation that exceeded the paid-up capital of the corporation, at a time when shares of the capital stock of the corporation representing more than 50% of its paid-up capital were beneficially owned by

(A) that particular person,

(B) that group of persons,

(C) persons related to the particular person or any member of the group of persons, or

(D) any combination of persons referred to in clause (A), (B) or (C),

the following rules apply:

(c) where the corporation has, at the particular time, made any payment on account of that debt, or any other debt substituted for that debt

(i) a dividend shall be deemed to have been paid by the corporation at the particular time equal to the lesser of

(A) the amount of that payment, and

(B) the amount, if any, by which

(I) the aggregate of the payment referred to in clause (A) and all payments made before the particular time on account of that debt, or any other debt substituted therefor,

exceeds

(II) the debt limit of the corporation in respect of that debt,

(ii) a dividend shall be deemed to have been received at the particular time, by each person who received any portion of that payment, equal to that proportion of the dividend so deemed to have been paid by the corporation at that time that the portion of that payment received by that person is of the amount of that payment, and

(iii) section 83 (except paragraph 83(1)(d)) shall be applicable to the dividend referred to in subparagraph (i) as though the persons referred to in subparagraph (ii) were shareholders of a class of shares of the capital stock of the corporation, and

(d) where any portion of that debt, or any debt substituted for that debt, is converted into shares of the capital stock of the corporation, an amount equal to the lesser of

(i) the portion of that debt, or any debt substituted for that debt, that was so converted, and

(ii) the amount, if any, by which

(A) the amount of the debt owed by the corporation at the time it was incurred,

exceeds

(B) debt limit of the corporation in respect of that debt

shall be added to the aggregate of the amounts determined under subparagraph 89(1)(d)(iv.1) at any time after the time of the conversion.

84.1 did not apply before November 19, 1974.

**Interpretation Bulletins**: IT-67R3: Taxable dividends from corporations resident in Canada; IT-489R: Non-arm's length sale of shares to a corporation.

**Information Circulars**: 88-2 Supplement, paras. 4, 9: General anti-avoidance rule — section 245 of the *Income Tax Act*.

**Advance Tax Rulings**: ATR-27: Exchange and acquisition of interests in capital properties through rollovers and winding-up ("butterfly"); ATR-32: Rollover of fixed assets from Opco into Holdco; ATR-35: Partitioning of assets to get specific ownership — "butterfly"; ATR-36: Estate freeze; ATR-42: Transfer of shares; ATR-55: Amalgamation followed by sale of shares; ATR-57: Transfer of property for estate planning purposes.

**(2) Idem** — For the purposes of this section,

(a) where a share disposed of by a taxpayer was acquired by a taxpayer before 1972, the adjusted cost base to the taxpayer of the share at any time shall be deemed to be the total of

(i) the amount that would be its adjusted cost base to the taxpayer if the *Income Tax Application Rules* were read without reference to subsections 26(3) and (7) of that Act, and

(ii) the total of all amounts each of which is an amount received by the taxpayer after 1971 and before that time as a dividend on the share and in respect of which the corporation that paid the dividend has made an election under subsection 83(1);

(a.1) where a share disposed of by a taxpayer was acquired by the taxpayer after 1971 from a person with whom the taxpayer was not dealing at arm's length, was a share substituted for such a share or was a share substituted for a share owned by the taxpayer at the end of 1971, the adjusted cost base to the taxpayer of the share at any time shall be deemed to be the amount, if any, by which its adjusted cost base to the taxpayer, otherwise determined, exceeds the total of

(i) where the share or a share for which the share was substituted was owned at the end of 1971 by the taxpayer or a person with whom the taxpayer did not deal at arm's length, the amount in respect of that share equal to the amount, if any, by which

(A) the fair market value of the share or the share for which it was substituted, as the case may be, on valuation day (within the meaning assigned by section 24 of the *Income Tax Application Rules*)

exceeds the total of

(B) the actual cost (within the meaning assigned by subsection 26(13) of that Act) of the share or the share for which it was substituted, as the case may be, on January 1, 1972, to the taxpayer or the person with whom the taxpayer did not deal at arm's length, and

(C) the total of all amounts each of which is an amount received by the taxpayer or the person with whom the taxpayer did not deal at arm's length after 1971 and before that time as a dividend on the share or the share for which it was substituted and in respect of which the corporation that paid the dividend has made an election under subsection 83(1), and

(ii) the total of all amounts each of which is an amount determined after 1984 under subparagraph 40(1)(a)(i) in respect of a previous disposition of the share or a share for which the share was substituted (or such lesser amount as is established by the taxpayer to be the amount in respect of which a deduction under section 110.6 was claimed) by the taxpayer or an individual with whom the taxpayer did not deal at arm's length;

(a.2) [Repealed]

(b) in respect of any disposition described in subsection (1) by a taxpayer of shares of the capital stock of a subject corporation to a purchaser corporation, the taxpayer shall, for greater certainty, be deemed not to deal at arm's length with the purchaser corporation if the taxpayer

(i) was, immediately before the disposition, one of a group of fewer than 6 persons that controlled the subject corporation, and

(ii) was, immediately after the disposition, one of a group of fewer than 6 persons that controlled the purchaser corporation, each member of which was a member of the group referred to in subparagraph (i); and

(c) [Repealed]

(d) a trust and a beneficiary of the trust or a person related to a beneficiary of the trust shall be deemed not to deal with each other at arm's length.

(e) [Repealed]

**Related Provisions**: 84.1(2.01) — Rules for 84.1(2)(a.1); 84.1(2.1) — Where capital gains reserve claimed; 84.1(2.2) — Rules for 84.1(2)(b); 256(6), (6.1) — Meaning of "controlled".

**Notes**: 84.1(2)(a.2) repealed by 1995-97 technical bill, effective for 1994 and later taxation year. This rule was moved to new 84.1(2.01)(a). It read:

(a.2) for the purposes of paragraph (a.1), where a corporation (in this paragraph referred to as the "issuing corporation") issues previously unissued shares of a class of its capital stock (in this paragraph referred to as the "new shares") to a taxpayer, the taxpayer and the issuing corporation shall be deemed not to have been dealing with each other at arm's length at the time the new shares were acquired by the taxpayer;

84.1(2)(c) and (e) repealed by 1995-97 technical bill, effective June 18, 1998. These rules were moved to new 84.1(2.2). They read:

(c) for the purposes of determining whether or not a taxpayer referred to in paragraph (b) was a member of a group of fewer than 6 persons that controlled a corporation at any time, any shares of the capital stock of that corporation owned at that time by

(i) the taxpayer's child (within the meaning assigned by subsection 70(10)), who is under 18 years of age, or the taxpayer's spouse,

(ii) a trust of which the taxpayer, a person described in subparagraph (i) or a corporation described in subparagraph (iii), is a beneficiary, or

(iii) a corporation controlled by the taxpayer, by a person described in subparagraph (i), by a trust described in subparagraph (ii) or by any combination thereof

shall be deemed to be owned at that time by the taxpayer and not by the person who actually owned the shares at that time;

. . . . .

(e) for the purpose of paragraph (b),

(i) a group of persons in respect of a corporation means any 2 or more persons each of whom owns shares of the capital stock of the corporation,

(ii) a corporation that is controlled by one or more members of a particular group of persons in respect of that corporation shall be considered to be controlled by that group of persons, and

(iii) a corporation may be controlled by a person or a particular group of persons notwithstanding that the corporation is also controlled or deemed to be controlled by another person or group of persons.

84.1(2) amended by 1985 Budget and by 1988 tax reform, effective for dispositions after May 22, 1985; by 1991 technical bill, effective for dispositions after July 14, 1990; and by 1992 technical bill, effective for dispositions after December 20, 1991.

For dispositions from July 14, 1990 through December 20, 1991, delete 84.1(2)(e).

For dispositions from May 23, 1985 through July 13, 1990, ignore 84.1(2)(d), and read 84.1(2)(c)(i) to (iii) as follows:

(i) the taxpayer's spouse,

(ii) an *inter vivos* trust of which the taxpayer, the spouse, a corporation described in subparagraph (iii) or any combination thereof is a beneficiary, or

(iii) a corporation controlled by the taxpayer, the spouse, a trust described in subparagraph (ii) or any combination thereof.

For dispositions from April 11, 1978 through May 22, 1985, delete 84.1(2)(a.1) and (a.2), and read 84.1(2)(a) as follows:

(a) where after 1971 a taxpayer (other than a corporation) has acquired any share from a person with whom he did not deal at arm's length, for the purposes of computing the taxpayer's adjusted cost base of the share,

(i) he shall be deemed to have acquired it at a cost equal to its adjusted cost base to that person immediately before the acquisition thereof by the taxpayer, and

(ii) subsection 26(5) of the *Income Tax Application Rules, 1971* shall be read without reference to paragraph (c) thereof;

For dispositions from April 1, 1977 through April 10, 1978, read 84.1(2)(a) as immediately above, delete 84.1(2)(c), and read 84.1(2)(b) as follows:

(b) a taxpayer who is one of a group of less than 10 persons who act in concert to control a corporation shall be deemed not to deal with the corporation at arm's length.

For payments from November 19, 1974 through March 31, 1977, read as follows:

(2) **"Debt limit" defined** — For the purpose of this section, the "debt limit" of a corporation in respect of any debt incurred by it as consideration for the purchase of shares of the

capital stock of a second corporation shall be the amount, if any, by which

    (a) the amount of the debt owed by the corporation at the time it was incurred

exceeds

    (b) the amount if any, by which the aggregate of

        (i) the amount of the debt owed by the corporation at the time it was incurred, and

        (ii) the fair market value, at the time the debt was incurred, of any other consideration (other than shares of the capital stock of the corporation) given by the corporation for the purchase of the shares of the capital stock of the second corporation,

exceeds the lesser of

        (iii) the paid-up capital limit of the second corporation at the time the debt was incurred, and

        (iv) the paid-up capital, at the time the debt was incurred, of the shares of the capital stock of the second corporation so purchased.

84.1 did not apply before November 19, 1974.

**Interpretation Bulletins**: IT-67R3: Taxable dividends from corporations resident in Canada; IT-489R: Non-arm's length sale of shares to a corporation.

**Advance Tax Rulings**: ATR-42: Transfer of shares; ATR-55: Amalgamation followed by sale of shares.

**(2.01) Rules for para. 84.1(2)(a.1)** — For the purpose of paragraph (2)(a.1),

    (a) where at any time a corporation issues a share of its capital stock to a taxpayer, the taxpayer and the corporation are deemed not to be dealing with each other at arm's length at that time;

    (b) where a taxpayer is deemed by paragraph 110.6(19)(a) to have reacquired a share, the taxpayer is deemed to have acquired the share at the beginning of February 23, 1994 from a person with whom the taxpayer was not dealing at arm's length; and

    (c) where a share owned by a particular person, or a share substituted for that share, has by one or more transactions or events between persons not dealing at arm's length become vested in another person, the particular person and the other person are deemed at all times not to be dealing at arm's length with each other whether or not the particular person and the other person coexisted.

**Notes**: 84.1(2.01) added by 1995-97 technical bill, effective for 1994 and later taxation years, except that 84.1(2.01)(c) applies in respect of the determination of the adjusted cost base of a share after June 20, 1996. Para. (a) was previously in 84.1(2)(a.1).

**(2.1) Idem** — For the purposes of subparagraph (2)(a.1)(ii), where the taxpayer or an individual with whom the taxpayer did not deal at arm's length (in this subsection referred to as the "transferor") disposes of a share in a taxation year and claims an amount under subparagraph 40(1)(a)(iii) in computing the gain for the year from the disposition, the amount in respect of which a deduction under section 110.6 was claimed in respect of the transferor's gain from the disposition shall be deemed to be equal to the lesser of

    (a) the total of

        (i) the amount claimed under subparagraph 40(1)(a)(iii) by the transferor for the year in respect of the disposition, and

        (ii) $4/3$ of the amount deducted under section 110.6 in computing the taxable income of the transferor for the year in respect of the taxable capital gain from the disposition, and

    (b) $4/3$ of the maximum amount that could have been deducted under section 110.6 in computing the taxable income of the transferor for the year in respect of the taxable capital gain from the disposition if

        (i) no amount had been claimed by the transferor under subparagraph 40(1)(a)(iii) in computing the gain for the year from the disposition, and

        (ii) all amounts deducted under section 110.6 in computing the taxable income of the transferor for the year in respect of taxable capital gains from dispositions of property to which this subsection does not apply were deducted before determining the maximum amount that could have been deducted under section 110.6 in respect of the taxable capital gain from the disposition,

and, for the purposes of subparagraph (ii), $3/4$ of the total of all amounts determined under this subsection for the year in respect of other property disposed of before the disposition of the share shall be deemed to have been deducted under section 110.6 in computing the taxable income of the transferor for the year in respect of the taxable capital gain from the disposition of property to which this subsection does not apply,

and, for the purposes of this subsection, where more than one share to which this subsection applies is disposed of in the year, each such share shall be deemed to have been separately disposed of in the order designated by the taxpayer in the taxpayer's return of income under this Part for the year.

**Proposed Amendment — 84.1(2.1)**

**Application**: The December 21, 2000 draft legislation, s. 36, will amend subsec. 84.1(2.1) by replacing the references to the expression "4/3 of" with references to the word "twice" and by replacing the reference to the fraction "3/4" with a reference to the fraction "1/2", applicable to taxation years that end after February 27, 2000 except that, for a taxation year of a taxpayer that includes either February 28, 2000 or October 17, 2000, the references to the word "twice" shall be read as references to the expression "the fraction that is the reciprocal of the fraction in para. 38(a), as amended [by the December 21, 2000 draft legislation], that applies to the taxpayer for the year multiplied by" and the reference to the fraction "1/2" shall be read as a reference to the fraction in para. 38(a), as amended [by the December 21, 2000 draft legislation], that applies to the taxpayer for the year.

**Technical Notes**: Subsection 84.1(2.1) provides a special rule that applies for the purpose of subparagraph

84.1(2)(a.1)(ii). Paragraph 84.1(2)(a.1) provides a rule for the purpose of determining the adjusted cost base to a taxpayer of a share for the purposes of section 84.1.

Subsection 84.1(2.1) is amended by replacing the references to the expressions "4/3 of" with references to the word "twice" and by replacing the reference to the fraction "3/4" with a reference to the fraction "1/2". The amendments are consequential on the reduction of the inclusion rate for capital gains from 3/4 to 1/2 [see 38(a) — ed.].

The amendments apply to taxation years that end after February 27, 2000 except that, for a taxpayer's taxation year that includes either February 28, 2000 or October 17, 2000, the reference to the word "twice" in subsection 84.1(2.1) is to be read as a reference to the expression "the fraction that is the reciprocal of the fraction in paragraph 38(a) that applies to the taxpayer for the year, multiplied by" and the reference to the fraction "1/2" is to be read as a reference to the fraction in amended paragraph 38(a) that applies to the taxpayer for the year. These modifications are required in order to reflect the capital gains/losses rate for the year.

**Notes**: 84.1(2.1) added by 1991 technical bill, effective for dispositions after July 13, 1990.

**(2.2) Rules for para. 84.1(2)(b)** — For the purpose of paragraph (2)(b),

  (a) in determining whether or not a taxpayer referred to in that paragraph was a member of a group of fewer than 6 persons that controlled a corporation at any time, any shares of the capital stock of that corporation owned at that time by

    (i) the taxpayer's child (as defined in subsection 70(10)), who is under 18 years of age, or the taxpayer's spouse or common-law partner,

    (ii) a trust of which the taxpayer, a person described in subparagraph (i) or a corporation described in subparagraph (iii), is a beneficiary, or

    (iii) a corporation controlled by the taxpayer, by a person described in subparagraph (i) or (ii) or by any combination of those persons or trusts

are deemed to be owned at that time by the taxpayer and not by the person who actually owned the shares at that time;

  (b) a group of persons in respect of a corporation means any 2 or more persons each of whom owns shares of the capital stock of the corporation;

  (c) a corporation that is controlled by one or more members of a particular group of persons in respect of that corporation is considered to be controlled by that group of persons; and

  (d) a corporation may be controlled by a person or a particular group of persons even though the corporation is also controlled or deemed to be controlled by another person or group of persons.

**Related Provisions**: 256(6), (6.1) — Extended meaning of "controlled".

**Notes**: 84.1(2.2)(a)(i) amended by 2000 same-sex partners bill to add reference to "common-law partner", effective for the 2001 and later taxation years, or earlier by election (see Notes to 248(1)"common-law partner").

84.1(2.2) added by 1995-97 technical bill, effective June 18, 1998. These rules were formerly in 84.1(2)(c) and (e).

**(3) Addition to paid-up capital** — In computing the paid-up capital at any time after May 22, 1985 in respect of any class of shares of the capital stock of a corporation, there shall be added an amount equal to the lesser of

  (a) the amount, if any, by which

    (i) the total of all amounts each of which is an amount deemed by subsection 84(3), (4) or (4.1) to be a dividend on shares of the class paid after May 22, 1985 and before that time by the corporation

  exceeds

    (ii) the total of such dividends that would be determined under subparagraph (i) if this Act were read without reference to paragraph (1)(a), and

  (b) the total of all amounts required by paragraph (1)(a) to be deducted in computing the paid-up capital in respect of that class of shares after May 22, 1985 and before that time.

**Notes**: 84.1(3) added by 1985 Budget, effective for dispositions made after May 22, 1985.

**Interpretation Bulletins**: IT-67R3: Taxable dividends from corporations resident in Canada; IT-489R: Non-arm's length sale of shares to a corporation.

**Definitions [s. 84.1]**: "adjusted cost base" — 54, 248(1); "amount" — 248(1); "arm's length" — 84.1(2)(b), (d), 84.1(2.01)(a), (c), 251(1); "child" — 70(10), 252(1); "class of shares" — 248(6); "common-law partner" — 248(1); "control" — 84.1(2.2)(c), (d); "controlled" — 256(6), (6.1); "corporation" — 248(1), *Interpretation Act* 35(1); "dividend" — 248(1); "group" — 84.1(2.2)(a), (b); "individual" — 248(1); "paid-up capital" — 84.1(3), 89(1), 248(1); "person" — 248(1); "private corporation" — 89(1), 248(1); "resident in Canada" — 250; "share" — 248(1); "taxable income" — 2(2), 248(1); "taxation year" — 249; "taxpayer" — 248(1); "trust" — 104(1), 248(1), (3).

**84.2 (1) Computation of paid-up capital in respect of particular class of shares** — In computing the paid-up capital in respect of any particular class of shares of the capital stock of a corporation at any particular time after March 31, 1977,

  (a) there shall be deducted that proportion of the amount, if any, by which the paid-up capital in respect of all of the issued shares of the capital stock of the corporation on April 1, 1977, determined without reference to this section, exceeds the greater of

    (i) the amount that the paid-up capital limit of the corporation would have been on March 31, 1977 if paragraph 89(1)(d) of the *Income Tax Act*, chapter 148 of the Revised Statutes of Canada, 1952, as it read at that date, were read without reference to clause 89(1)(d)(iv.1)(F) of that Act and without reference to all subparagraphs of paragraph 89(1)(d) of that Act except subparagraphs 89(1)(d)(iv.1) and (vii) of that Act, and

(ii) the paid-up capital limit of the corporation on March 31, 1977,

that the paid-up capital on April 1, 1977, determined without reference to this section, in respect of the particular class of shares is of the paid-up capital on April 1, 1977, determined without reference to this section, in respect of all of the issued and outstanding shares of the capital stock of the corporation; and

(b) there shall be added an amount equal to the lesser of

(i) the amount, if any, by which

(A) the total of all amounts each of which is an amount deemed by subsection 84(3) or (4) to be a dividend on shares of the particular class paid by the corporation after March 31, 1977 and before the particular time

exceeds

(B) the total that would be determined under clause (A) if this Act were read without reference to paragraph (a), and

(ii) the amount required by paragraph (a) to be deducted in computing the paid-up capital of shares of the particular class.

**Related Provisions**: 84.1 — Non-arm's length sale of shares.

**I.T. Application Rules**: 69 (meaning of "*Income Tax Act*, chapter 148 of the Revised Statutes of Canada, 1952").

**(2) Debt deficiency** — In computing, after March 31, 1977, the adjusted cost base to an individual of a debt that was owing to the individual by a corporation on March 31, 1977, there shall be deducted the amount of any dividend that would have been deemed to have been received by the individual on that day if the corporation had paid the debt in full on that day.

**Related Provisions**: 53(2)(p) — Deduction from ACB; 84.2(3) — Where debt converted to shares.

**(3) Idem** — Where, after March 31, 1977 and before 1979, any debt referred to in subsection (2) owing by a corporation and held by an individual on March 31, 1977 and continuously after that date until conversion, is converted into shares of a particular class of the capital stock of the corporation,

(a) subsection (2) shall not apply in respect of the debt; and

(b) in computing the paid-up capital in respect of the shares of the particular class at any particular time after the conversion,

(i) there shall be deducted the amount by which the adjusted cost base to the taxpayer of the debt would, but for paragraph (a), have been reduced by virtue of subsection (2), and

(ii) there shall be added an amount equal to the lesser of

(A) the amount, if any, by which

(I) the total of all amounts deemed by subsection 84(3), (4) or (4.1) to be a dividend on shares of the particular class paid by the corporation after the conversion and before the particular time,

exceeds

(II) the total that would be determined under subclause (I) if this Act were read without reference to subparagraph (i), and

(B) the amount required by subparagraph (i) to be deducted in computing the paid-up capital of shares of the particular class.

**Definitions [s. 84.2]**: "adjusted cost base" — 54, 248(1); "amount" — 248(1); "class of shares" — 248(6); "corporation" — 248(1), *Interpretation Act* 35(1); "dividend" — 248(1); "paid-up capital" — 89(1), 248(1); "share" — 248(1); "taxation year" — 249; "taxpayer" — 248(1).

**85. (1) Transfer of property to corporation by shareholders [rollover]** — Where a taxpayer has, in a taxation year, disposed of any of the taxpayer's property that was eligible property to a taxable Canadian corporation for consideration that includes shares of the capital stock of the corporation, if the taxpayer and the corporation have jointly elected in prescribed form and in accordance with subsection (6), the following rules apply:

(a) the amount that the taxpayer and the corporation have agreed on in their election in respect of the property shall be deemed to be the taxpayer's proceeds of disposition of the property and the corporation's cost of the property;

(b) subject to paragraph (c), where the amount that the taxpayer and the corporation have agreed on in their election in respect of the property is less than the fair market value, at the time of the disposition, of the consideration therefor (other than any shares of the capital stock of the corporation or a right to receive any such shares) received by the taxpayer, the amount so agreed on shall, irrespective of the amount actually so agreed on by them, be deemed to be an amount equal to that fair market value;

(c) where the amount that the taxpayer and the corporation have agreed on in their election in respect of the property is greater than the fair market value, at the time of the disposition, of the property so disposed of, the amount so agreed on shall, irrespective of the amount actually so agreed on, be deemed to be an amount equal to that fair market value;

(c.1) where the property was inventory, capital property (other than depreciable property of a prescribed class), a NISA Fund No. 2 or a property that is eligible property because of paragraph (1.1)(g) or (g.1), and the amount that the taxpayer and corporation have agreed on in their election in respect of the property is less than the lesser of

(i) the fair market value of the property at the time of the disposition, and

(ii) the cost amount to the taxpayer of the property at the time of the disposition,

the amount so agreed on shall, irrespective of the amount actually so agreed on by them, be deemed to be an amount equal to the lesser of the amounts described in subparagraphs (i) and (ii);

(c.2) subject to paragraphs (b) and (c) and notwithstanding paragraph (c.1), where the taxpayer carries on a farming business the income from which is computed in accordance with the cash method and the property was inventory owned in connection with that business immediately before the particular time the property was disposed of to the corporation,

(i) the amount that the taxpayer and the corporation agreed on in their election in respect of inventory purchased by the taxpayer shall be deemed to be equal to the amount determined by the formula

$$\left(A \times \frac{B}{C}\right) + D$$

where

A is the amount that would be included because of paragraph 28(1)(c) in computing the taxpayer's income for the taxpayer's last taxation year beginning before the particular time if that year had ended immediately before the particular time,

B is the value (determined in accordance with subsection 28(1.2)) to the taxpayer immediately before the particular time of the purchased inventory in respect of which the election is made,

C is the value (determined in accordance with subsection 28(1.2)) of all of the inventory purchased by the taxpayer that was owned by the taxpayer in connection with that business immediately before the particular time, and

D is such additional amount as the taxpayer and the corporation designate in respect of the property,

(ii) for the purpose of subparagraph 28(1)(a)(i), the disposition of the property and the receipt of proceeds of disposition therefor shall be deemed to have occurred at the particular time and in the course of carrying on the business, and

(iii) where the property is owned by the corporation in connection with a farming business and the income from that business is computed in accordance with the cash method, for the purposes of section 28,

(A) an amount equal to the cost to the corporation of the property shall be deemed to have been paid by the corporation, and

(B) the corporation shall be deemed to have purchased the property for an amount equal to that cost,

at the particular time and in the course of carrying on that business;

(d) where the property was eligible capital property in respect of a business of the taxpayer and the amount that, but for this paragraph, would be the proceeds of disposition of the property is less than the least of

(i) ⁴/₃ of the taxpayer's cumulative eligible capital in respect of the business immediately before the disposition,

(ii) the cost to the taxpayer of the property, and

(iii) the fair market value of the property at the time of the disposition,

the amount agreed on by the taxpayer and the corporation in their election in respect of the property shall, irrespective of the amount actually so agreed on by them, be deemed to be the least of the amounts described in subparagraphs (i) to (iii);

(d.1) for the purpose of determining after the time of the disposition the amount to be included under paragraph 14(1)(b) in computing the corporation's income, there shall be added to the amount otherwise determined for Q in the definition "cumulative eligible capital" in subsection 14(5) the amount determined by the formula

$$\left(A \times \frac{B}{C}\right) - 2(D - E)$$

where

A is the amount, if any, determined for Q in that definition in respect of the taxpayer's business immediately before the time of the disposition,

B is the fair market value immediately before that time of the eligible capital property disposed of to the corporation by the taxpayer,

C is the fair market value immediately before that time of all eligible capital property of the taxpayer in respect of the business,

D is the amount, if any, that would be included under subsection 14(1) in computing the taxpayer's income as a result of the disposition if

(i) the amounts determined for C and D in subparagraph 14(1)(a)(v) were zero, and

(ii) paragraph 14(1)(b) were read as follows:

"(b) in any other case, the excess shall be included in computing the taxpayer's income from that business for that year.", and

E is the amount, if any, that would be included under subsection 14(1) in computing the taxpayer's income as a result of the disposition if the amount determined for D in subparagraph 14(1)(a)(v) were zero;

**Proposed Amendment — 85(1)(d.1)D, E**

D is the amount, if any, that would be included under subsection 14(1) in computing the taxpayer's income as a result of the disposition if the values determined for C and D in paragraph 14(1)(b) were zero, and

E is the amount, if any, that would be included under subsection 14(1) in computing the taxpayer's income as a result of the disposition if the value determined for D in paragraph 14(1)(b) were zero;

**Application:** The December 21, 2000 draft legislation, subsec. 37(1), will amend the descriptions of D and E in para. 85(1)(d.1) to read as above, applicable in respect of taxation years that end after February 27, 2000.

**Technical Notes:** Subsection 85(1) provides a tax deferral for the transfer of various types of property by a taxpayer to a taxable Canadian corporation for consideration that includes shares of the corporation's capital stock. Paragraph 85(1)(d.1) provides specific rules to ensure that the tax accounts relating to eligible capital property in respect of a business are carried through from the transferor to the transferee. Descriptions D and E in paragraph 85(1)(d.1) are amended consequential on the renumbering of subsection 14(1), which is described in further detail in the commentary to that subsection.

(e) where the property was depreciable property of a prescribed class of the taxpayer and the amount that, but for this paragraph, would be the proceeds of disposition thereof is less than the least of

(i) the undepreciated capital cost to the taxpayer of all property of that class immediately before the disposition,

(ii) the cost to the taxpayer of the property, and

(iii) the fair market value of the property at the time of the disposition,

the amount agreed on by the taxpayer and the corporation in their election in respect of the property shall, irrespective of the amount actually so agreed on by them, be deemed to be the least of the amounts described in subparagraphs (i) to (iii);

(e.1) where two or more properties, each of which is a property described in paragraph (d) or each of which is a property described in paragraph (e), are disposed of at the same time, paragraph (d) or (e), as the case may be, applies as if each property so disposed of had been separately disposed of in the order designated by the taxpayer before the time referred to in subsection (6) for the filing of an election in respect of those properties or, if the taxpayer does not so designate any such order, in the order designated by the Minister;

(e.2) where the fair market value of the property immediately before the disposition exceeds the greater of

(i) the fair market value, immediately after the disposition, of the consideration received by the taxpayer for the property disposed of by the taxpayer, and

(ii) the amount that the taxpayer and the corporation have agreed on in their election in respect of the property, determined without reference to this paragraph,

and it is reasonable to regard any part of the excess as a benefit that the taxpayer desired to have conferred on a person related to the taxpayer (other than a corporation that was a wholly owned corporation of the taxpayer immediately after the disposition), the amount that the taxpayer and the corporation agreed on in their election in respect of the property shall, regardless of the amount actually so agreed on by them, be deemed (except for the purposes of paragraphs (g) and (h)) to be an amount equal to the total of the amount referred to in subparagraph (ii) and that part of the excess;

(e.3) where, under any of paragraphs (c.1), (d) and (e), the amount that the taxpayer and the corporation have agreed on in their election in respect of the property (in this paragraph referred to as "the elected amount") would be deemed to be an amount that is greater or less than the amount that would be deemed, subject to paragraph (c), to be the elected amount under paragraph (b), the elected amount shall be deemed to be the greater of

(i) the amount deemed by paragraph (c.1), (d) or (e), as the case may be, to be the elected amount, and

(ii) the amount deemed by paragraph (b) to be the elected amount;

(e.4) where

(i) the property is depreciable property of a prescribed class of the taxpayer and is a passenger vehicle the cost to the taxpayer of which was more than $20,000 or such other amount as may be prescribed, and

(ii) the taxpayer and the corporation do not deal at arm's length,

the amount that the taxpayer and the corporation have agreed on in their election in respect of the property shall be deemed to be an amount equal to the undepreciated capital cost to the taxpayer of the class immediately before the disposition, except that, for the purposes of subsection 6(2), the cost to the corporation of the vehicle shall be deemed to be an amount equal to its fair market value immediately before the disposition;

(f) the cost to the taxpayer of any particular property (other than shares of the capital stock of the corporation or a right to receive any such shares) received by the taxpayer as consideration for the disposition shall be deemed to be an amount equal to the lesser of

(i) the fair market value of the particular property at the time of the disposition, and

(ii) that proportion of the fair market value, at the time of the disposition, of the property disposed of by the taxpayer to the corporation that

(A) the amount determined under subparagraph (i)

is of

(B) the fair market value, at the time of the disposition, of all properties (other than shares of the capital stock of the corporation or a right to receive any such shares) received by the taxpayer as consideration for the disposition;

(g) the cost to the taxpayer of any preferred shares of any class of the capital stock of the corporation receivable by the taxpayer as consideration for the disposition shall be deemed to be the lesser of the fair market value of those shares immediately after the disposition and that proportion of the amount, if any, by which the proceeds of the disposition exceed the fair market value of the consideration (other than shares of the capital stock of the corporation or a right to receive any such shares) received by the taxpayer for the disposition, that

(i) the fair market value, immediately after the disposition, of those preferred shares of that class,

is of

(ii) the fair market value, immediately after the disposition, of all preferred shares of the capital stock of the corporation receivable by the taxpayer as consideration for the disposition;

(h) the cost to the taxpayer of any common shares of any class of the capital stock of the corporation receivable by the taxpayer as consideration for the disposition shall be deemed to be that proportion of the amount, if any, by which the proceeds of the disposition exceed the total of the fair market value, at the time of the disposition, of the consideration (other than shares of the capital stock of the corporation or a right to receive any such shares) received by the taxpayer for the disposition and the cost to the taxpayer of all preferred shares of the capital stock of the corporation receivable by the taxpayer as consideration for the disposition, that

(i) the fair market value, immediately after the disposition, of those common shares of that class,

is of

(ii) the fair market value, immediately after the disposition, of all common shares of the capital stock of the corporation receivable by the taxpayer as consideration for the disposition; and

(i) where the property so disposed of is taxable Canadian property of the taxpayer, all of the shares of the capital stock of the Canadian corporation received by the taxpayer as consideration for the property shall be deemed to be taxable Canadian property of the taxpayer.

**Related Provisions**: 13(7)(e) — Deemed maximum capital cost on non-arm's length transfer; 13(7)(g), (h) — Maximum capital cost of passenger vehicles; 13(21.2)(d) — No election allowed on certain transfers of depreciable property where u.c.c. exceeds fair market value; 40(3.3), (3.4) — Limitation on loss where share acquired by affiliated person; 44.1(6), (7) — Small business investment rollover on exchange of shares; 51(4) — Application of 85(1) to exchange of convertible property; 53(4) — Effect on ACB of share, partnership interest or trust interest; 54.2 — Certain shares deemed to be capital property; 55(1) — "Permitted redemption" for butterfly purposes; 55(3.1)(b) — Rules where foreign vendor's capital gain exempted by treaty; 69(11) — Where corporation later sells transferred property and shelters gain; 85(1.1) — "Eligible property"; 85(2) — Rollover of property to corporation from partnership; 85(5) — Rules on transfers of depreciable property; 85(6) — Time for election; 86(3) — 85(1) takes precedence over s. 86; 97(2)(a) — Rollover of property to a partnership; 107(2)(d.1)(iii), 107.4(3)(f) — Deemed taxable Canadian property retains status when rolled out of trust or into trust; 138(11.5) — Transfer of insurance business by non-resident insurer; 139.1(4)(c) — No election allowed re ownership rights on demutualization of insurer; 142.5(9) — Transitional rule — mark-to-market property acquired by financial institution on rollover; 142.7(3) — Application on conversion of foreign bank affiliate to branch; 256(7)(c), (d) — Whether control of corporation acquired on rollover; 257 — Formula cannot calculate to less than zero; Reg. 5301(8) — Effect of transfer on instalment base of transferee; Canada-U.S. tax treaty, Art. XIII:8 — Deferral of tax for U.S. resident transferor.

**Notes**: The "section 85 rollover" can be used whenever the opening words of 85(1) are satisfied and the property being transferred to a corporation is "eligible property" under 85(1.1). The amount elected will become the deemed proceeds of disposition of the property as well as its deemed cost to the corporation. However, the elected amount cannot be less than the non-share consideration or "boot" (85(1)(b)); nor can it exceed the value of the property transferred (85(1)(c)); nor can it be less than both the cost and the value of the property transferred (85(1)(c.1), (d), (e)). The amount elected is then allocated for cost purposes, first to boot, then to preferred shares and finally (if there is anything left) to common shares (85(1)(f), (g), (h)). (The above explanation is simplified.)

The CCRA generally considers that where capital property is rolled into a corporation by a controlling shareholder, it remains capital property even if the corporation sells it immediately. See Income Tax Technical News No. 7, as well as Revenue Canada's statements at the 1983, 1984 and 1995 Canadian Tax Foundation annual conference round tables. See also *Hickman Motors Ltd.*, [1997] 1

C.T.C. 213 (SCC) and *Mara Properties Ltd.*, [1996] 2 C.T.C. 54 (SCC), where the Courts have essentially come to the same conclusion.

It is extremely important, when both a lawyer and an accountant are advising on a transaction, that it be well documented as to who has the responsibility for filing the 85(1) election under 85(6). Where the deadline is missed, see 85(7)–(9).

Because section 85 rollovers undertaken years ago still affect the cost of property today, the changes to the section are tracked in detail below.

*Opening words of 85(1)*

Amended by 1988 tax reform, effective for dispositions in 1987 or later.

For dispositions in 1984 through 1986, read:

85. (1) Where a taxpayer has after May 6, 1974 disposed of any of his property that was a capital property (other than real property, an interest therein or an option in respect thereof, owned by a non-resident person), a Canadian resource property, a foreign resource property, an eligible capital property or an inventory (other than real property) to a taxable Canadian corporation for consideration that includes shares of the capital stock of the corporation, if the taxpayer and the corporation have jointly so elected in prescribed form and within the time referred to in subsection (6), the following rules apply:

For dispositions from August 29, 1980 through 1983, read:

85. (1) Where a taxpayer has after May 6, 1974 disposed of any of his property that was a capital property (other than real property, an interest therein or an option in respect thereof, owned by a non-resident), a property referred to in subsection 59(2), an eligible capital property or an inventory (other than real property) to a taxable Canadian corporation for consideration that includes shares of the capital stock of the corporation, if the taxpayer and the corporation have jointly so elected in prescribed form and within the time referred to in subsection (6), the following rules apply:

For dispositions from December 12, 1979 through August 28, 1980, read:

85. (1) Where a taxpayer has after May 6, 1974 disposed of any of his property that was a capital property (other than real property, or an option in respect thereof, owned by a non-resident), a property referred to in subsection 59(2), an eligible capital property or an inventory (other than real property) to a taxable Canadian corporation for consideration that includes shares of the capital stock of the corporation, if the taxpayer and the corporation have jointly so elected in prescribed form and within the time referred to in subsection (6), the following rules apply:

For dispositions from May 7, 1974 through December 11, 1979, read:

85. (1) Where a taxpayer has, after May 6, 1974, disposed of any property that was a capital property (other than real property or an option in respect thereof owned by a non-resident), an eligible capital property, an inventory other than real property or a property referred to in subsection 59(2) of the taxpayer to a Canadian corporation for consideration including shares of the capital stock of the corporation, if the taxpayer and the corporation have jointly so elected in prescribed form and within the time referred to in subsection (6), the following rules apply:

For dispositions from 1972 through May 6, 1974, read:

85. (1) Transfer of property to corporation by controlling shareholder — Where a taxpayer has, after 1971, disposed of any property that was a capital property or eligible capital property of the taxpayer or a property referred to in subsection 59(2) of the taxpayer to a Canadian corporation, and immediately after the disposition owned not less than 80% of the issued shares of each class of the capital stock of the corporation, if the taxpayer and the corporation have jointly so elected in prescribed form and within prescribed time the following rules apply:

*85(1)(c.1)*

Amended by 1994 tax amendments bill (Part III). For dispositions before February 23, 1994, in place of "a property that is eligible property because of paragraph (1.1)(g) or (g.1)", read:

a property (other than capital property or an inventory) of the taxpayer that is a security or debt obligation used in the year in, or held in the year in the course of, carrying on the business of insurance or lending money

Amended by 1988 tax reform, effective 1987, and by 1992 technical bill, effective 1991. For dispositions in 1987 through 1990, ignore the words "a NISA Fund No. 2". For dispositions from May 7, 1974 through the end of 1986, read the opening words of para. (c.1) as:

(c.1) where the property was inventory or capital property (other than depreciable property of a prescribed class) of the taxpayer and the amount that the taxpayer and the corporation have agreed upon in their election in respect of the property is less than the lesser of

*85(1)(c.2)*

Added by 1991 technical bill, effective for dispositions after July 13, 1990.

*85(1)(d)*

Amended by 1988 tax reform, effective, for corporations, for taxation years beginning after June 1988, and for other taxpayers, for business fiscal periods beginning in 1988 or later. For dispositions from May 7, 1974 until that cutoff, read "2 times" in place of "⁴/₃ of" in subpara. (d)(i).

For dispositions from 1972 to May 6, 1974, read:

(d) where the property was eligible capital property in respect of a business of the taxpayer and the amount that, but for this paragraph, would be the proceeds of disposition thereof is less than the least of

(i) 2 times the taxpayer's cumulative eligible capital in respect of the business immediately before the disposition,

(ii) the cost to the taxpayer of the property, and

(iii) the fair market value of the property at the time of the disposition, the amount agreed upon by the taxpayer and the corporation in their election in respect of the property shall, irrespective of the amount actually so agreed upon by them, and notwithstanding paragraphs (b) and (c), be deemed to be the least of the amounts described in subparagraphs (i) to (iii);

*85(1)(d.1)*

This para. prevents an overstatement of the corporation's income under 14(1)(b) resulting from a later disposition of eligible property.

Amended by 1994 Budget, deleting formula elements F and G, adding D(i), and changing E, effective for dispositions of property in respect of a business that occur in a fiscal period of the business that ends after February 22, 1994 otherwise than because of an election under 25(1). For earlier dispositions, read:

(d.1) for the purpose of determining after the time of the disposition the amount to be included under paragraph 14(1)(b) in computing the corporation's income, there shall be added to the amount otherwise determined for Q in the definition "cumulative eligible capital" in subsection 14(5) the amount determined by the formula

$$\left(A \times \frac{B}{C}\right) - 2[(D + E) - (F + G)]$$

**S. 85(1)**      Income Tax Act, Part I, Division B

where

A    is the amount, if any, determined for Q in that definition in respect of the taxpayer's business immediately before the time of the disposition,

B    is the fair market value immediately before that time of the eligible capital property disposed of to the corporation by the taxpayer,

C    is the fair market value immediately before that time of all eligible capital property of the taxpayer in respect of the business,

D    is the amount, if any, that would be included under subsection 14(1) in computing the taxpayer's income as a result of the disposition if paragraph 14(1)(b) were read as follows:

"(b) in any other case, the excess shall be included in computing the taxpayer's income from that business for that year.",

E    is the amount, if any, that would be deemed under subsection 14(1) to be a taxable capital gain of the taxpayer as a result of the disposition if clause 14(1)(a)(v)(B) were read as follows:

"(B) zero"

F    is the amount, if any, included under subsection 14(1) in computing the taxpayer's income as a result of the disposition, and

G    is the amount, if any, deemed under subsection 14(1) to be a taxable capital gain of the taxpayer as a result of the disposition;

Added by 1992 technical bill and amended retroactively by 1993 technical bill (adding formula elements D, E, F and G), effective for dispositions to a corporation after the beginning of its first taxation year that begins after June 1988.

*85(1)(e)*

Amended by 1974 Budget, effective May 7, 1974. For dispositions from 1972 through May 6, 1974, read:

(e) where the property was depreciable property of a prescribed class of the taxpayer and the amount that, but for this paragraph, would be the proceeds of disposition thereof is less than the least of

(i) the undepreciated capital cost to the taxpayer of all property of that class immediately before the disposition,

(ii) the cost to the taxpayer of the property, and

(iii) the fair market value of the property at the time of the disposition,

the amount agreed upon by the taxpayer and the corporation in their election in respect of the property shall, irrespective of the amount actually so agreed upon by them, and notwithstanding paragraphs (b) and (c), be deemed to be the least of the amounts described in subparagraphs (i) to (iii);

*85(1)(e.2)*

Amended by 1988 tax reform and 1991 technical bill, effective July 1988. For dispositions from May 7, 1974 through June 30, 1988, read:

(e.2) where the fair market value of the property at the time of the disposition exceeds the greater of

(i) the fair market value at the time of the disposition of the consideration received by the taxpayer for the property disposed of by him, and

(ii) the amount that the taxpayer and the corporation have agreed upon in their election in respect of the property, determined without reference to this paragraph,

and it is reasonable to regard any portion of such excess as a gift made by the taxpayer to or for the benefit of any other shareholder of the corporation, the amount that the taxpayer and the corporation have agreed upon in their election in respect of the property shall, irrespective of the amount actually so agreed upon by them, be deemed (except for the purposes of paragraphs (g) and (h)) to be an amount equal to the aggregate of

(iii) the amount referred to in subparagraph (ii), and

(iv) the portion of such excess that may reasonably be regarded as a gift made by the taxpayer to or for the benefit of any other shareholder of the corporation;

For dispositions before May 7, 1974, para. (e.2) has no application.

*85(1)(e.3)*

Applies only to dispositions after May 6, 1974.

*85(1)(e.4)*

Added by 1988 tax reform, effective for taxation years and fiscal periods beginning after June 17, 1987 that end after 1987.

*85(1)(i)*

Amended by 1974 Budget, effective May 7, 1974. For dispositions from 1972 through May 6, 1974, read:

(i) for greater certainty, where the application of this subsection results in a capital loss of the taxpayer from the disposition of any property, subsection (4) is applicable.

**Regulations**: 7307(1) (prescribed amount for 85(1)(e.4)(i)).

**I.T. Application Rules**: 20(1.2) (transfer of depreciable property by person who owned it before 1972).

**Interpretation Bulletins**: IT-188R: Sale of accounts receivable; IT-217R: Depreciable property owned on December 31, 1971; IT-243R4: Dividend refund to private corporations; IT-291R2: Transfer of property to a corporation under subsection 85(1); IT-427R: Livestock of farmers; IT-433R: Farming or fishing — use of cash method; IT-457R: Election by professionals to exclude work in progress from income; IT-489R: Non-arm's length sale of shares to a corporation; IT-521R: Motor vehicle expenses claimed by self-employed individuals; IT-522R: Vehicle, travel and sales expenses of employees.

**Information Circulars**: 76-19R3: Transfer of property to a corporation under section 85; 88-2, paras. 9, 10, 13, 14, 22: General anti-avoidance rule — section 245 of the *Income Tax Act*; 88-2 Supplement, paras. 3, 8: General anti-avoidance rule — section 245 of the *Income Tax Act*; 89-3: Policy statement on business equity valuations.

**I.T. Technical News**: No. 3 (section 85 — *Dale* case); No. 7 (rollovers of capital property — *Mara Properties*); No. 10 (1997 deduction limits and benefit rates for automobiles (for 85(1)(e.4)(i)).

**Advance Tax Rulings**: ATR-6: Vendor reacquires business assets following default by purchaser; ATR-7: Amalgamation involving losses and control; ATR-19: Earned depletion base and cumulative Canadian development expense; ATR-25: Estate freeze; ATR-27: Exchange and acquisition of interests in capital properties through rollovers and winding-up ("butterfly"); ATR-28: Redemption of capital stock of family farm corporation; ATR-32: Rollover of fixed assets from Opco into Holdco; ATR-35: Partitioning of assets to get specific ownership — "butterfly"; ATR-36: Estate freeze; ATR-42: Transfer of shares; ATR-55: Amalgamation followed by sale of shares; ATR-57: Transfer of property for estate planning purposes; ATR-58: Divisive reorganization; ATR-70: Distribution of taxable Canadian property by a trust to a non-resident.

**Forms**: T2057: Election on disposition of property by a taxpayer to a taxable Canadian corporation.

**(1.1) Definition of "eligible property"** — For the purposes of subsection (1), "eligible property" means

(a) a capital property (other than real property, or an interest in or an option in respect of real property, owned by a non-resident person);

(b) a capital property that is real property, or an interest in or an option in respect of real property, owned by a non-resident insurer where that property and the property received as consideration for that property are designated insurance property for the year;

(c) a Canadian resource property;

(d) a foreign resource property;

(e) an eligible capital property;

(f) an inventory (other than real property, an interest in real property or an option in respect of real property);

(g) a property that is a security or debt obligation used by the taxpayer in the year in, or held by it in the year in the course of, carrying on the business of insurance or lending money, other than

(i) a capital property,

(ii) inventory, or

### Proposed Addition — 85(1.1)(g)(ii.1)

(ii.1) a property held by the taxpayer if subsection 94.2(3) applies to the taxpayer in respect of the property, or

**Application**: The June 22, 2000 draft legislation, s. 7, will add subpara. 85(1.1)(g)(ii.1), applicable after 2000.

**Technical Notes**: Subsection 85(1.1) of the Act describes the types of property (which are referred to as "eligible property") that may be transferred to a corporation under subsection 85(1). Eligible property includes certain capital property described in the subsection, as well as additional property.

Subsection 85(1.1) is amended so that eligible property for a taxpayer, in all cases, excludes property in respect of which new subsection 94.2(3) applies to the taxpayer. New subsection 94.2(3) sets out the conditions for the application of the mark-to-market taxation regime under subsection 94.2(4) for participating interests in foreign investment entities.

This amendment applies after 2000.

(iii) where the taxpayer is a financial institution in the year, a mark-to-market property for the year;

(g.1) where the taxpayer is a financial institution in the year, a specified debt obligation (other than a mark-to-market property of the taxpayer for the year);

(h) a capital property that is real property, an interest in real property or an option in respect of real property, owned by a non-resident person (other than a non-resident insurer) and used in the year in a business carried on in Canada by that person; or

(i) a NISA Fund No. 2.

**Related Provisions**: 85(1.11) — Exception — foreign resource property; 85(1.2) — Limitation on 85(1.1)(h); 248(4) — Interest in real property includes a leasehold interest but not a security interest.

**Notes**: Farm inventory, and Canadian resource property that is real property, are considered by the CCRA to be eligible property even though they might not technically qualify. See Interpretation Bulletin IT-291R2, paras. 4, 5 and 6.

85(1.1) added by 1988 tax reform, effective for dispositions after 1986.

85(1.1)(b) amended by 1996 Budget, effective for dispositions that occur in an insurer's 1997 or later taxation year (changed from 1996 at Second Reading of the Budget bill), to use the term "designated insurance property" in place of an older term. For earlier years since 1987, read:

> (b) a capital property that is real property or an interest in or an option in respect of real property, owned by a non-resident insurer where that property and the property received as consideration for that property are property used by it in the year in, or held by it in the year in the course of (within the meaning assigned by subsection 138(12)), carrying on an insurance business in Canada;

85(1.1)(f) amended by 1992 technical bill, effective for dispositions after December 20, 1991. For dispositions from 1987 through that date, read as "in inventory (other than real property)".

85(1.1)(g)(iii) added by 1994 tax amendments bill (Part III), effective for dispositions occurring in taxation years that begin after October 1994.

85(1.1)(g.1) added by 1994 tax amendments bill (Part III), effective for dispositions occurring after February 22, 1994.

85(1.1)(h) added by 1991 technical bill, effective

(a) for dispositions after 1989, and

(b) for dispositions from 1985 through 1989, where the taxpayer is resident in a country with which Canada has a tax treaty, and a provision of that treaty that was prescribed for the purposes of section 115.1 was effective at the time of the disposition. (Paragraphs XIII(8) of the Canada-U.S. treaty and 13(6) of the Canada-Netherlands treaty are prescribed by Reg. 7400).

85(1.1)(i) added by 1992 technical bill, effective for dispositions after 1990.

For dispositions of property from 1972 through February 15, 1984, an earlier version of 85(1.1) provided:

> (1.1) Exception to subsection (1) — Subsection (1) does not apply with respect to any disposition by a taxpayer of any of his property referred to in subsection 59(2) if the corporation to which the property was disposed of has carried on any business before the disposition.

**Interpretation Bulletins**: IT-291R2: Transfer of property to a corporation under subsection 85(1).

### Proposed Addition — 85(1.11)

**(1.11) Exception** — Notwithstanding subsection (1.1), a foreign resource property, or an interest in a partnership that derives all or part of its value from one or more foreign resource properties, is not an eligible property of a taxpayer in respect of a disposition by the taxpayer to a corporation where

(a) the taxpayer and the corporation do not deal with each other at arm's length; and

(b) it is reasonable to conclude that one of the purposes of the disposition, or a series of transactions or events of which the disposition is a part, is to increase the extent to which any person may claim a deduction under section 126.

**Application**: The December 21, 2000 draft legislation, subsec. 37(2), will add subsec. 85(1.11), applicable to dispositions that occur after December 21, 2000 other than a disposition by a tax-

**S. 85(1.11)**     Income Tax Act, Part I, Division B

payer that occurs pursuant to an agreement in writing made by the taxpayer on or before that date.

**Technical Notes**: Subsection 85(1.1) describes the types of property (referred to in the Act as "eligible property") that may be transferred to a corporation under subsection 85(1).

New subsection 85(1.11) provides that a foreign resource property (or an interest in a partnership that derives all or part of its value from one or more foreign resource properties) is not an "eligible property" of a taxpayer in respect of a transfer to a corporation where:

- the taxpayer and the corporation do not deal with each other at arm's length; and
- it is reasonable to conclude that one of the purposes of the disposition, or a series of transactions or events of which the disposition is a part, is to increase the extent to which any person may claim a deduction under section 126. (An increase of a deduction under section 126 could arise as a consequence of a reduction of an amount that the person deducts, or is entitled to deduct, under any combination of subsections 66(4), 66.21(4) and 66.7(2) and (2.3).)

This provision is intended to counter the avoidance of income-based limits on the foreign tax credit in section 126 that might be achieved through the sale of direct or indirect interests in foreign resource property at less than fair market value. In general terms, under subsection 126(2) the level of a foreign tax credit for a taxpayer in respect of a business carried on in a foreign country cannot exceed a specified percentage of the taxpayer's Canadian income tax. The specified percentage is essentially the percentage that the taxpayer's "qualifying income" from that business is of the taxpayer's world-wide income. (New subsection 126(9) reinforces the "qualifying income" limit for foreign tax credits by generally requiring a taxpayer to maximize foreign exploration and development expense deductions and foreign resource deductions for the purpose of computing qualifying income.)

**(1.2) Application of subsec. (1)** — Subsection (1) does not apply to a disposition by a taxpayer to a corporation of a property referred to in paragraph (1.1)(h) unless

(a) immediately after the disposition, the corporation is controlled by the taxpayer, a person or persons related (otherwise than because of a right referred to in paragraph 251(5)(b)) to the taxpayer or the taxpayer and a person or persons so related to the taxpayer;

(b) the disposition is part of a transaction or series of transactions in which all or substantially all of the property used in the business referred to in paragraph (1.1)(h) is disposed of by the taxpayer to the corporation; and

(c) the disposition is not part of a series of transactions that result in control of the corporation being acquired by a person or group of persons after the time that is immediately after the disposition.

**Related Provisions**: 139.1(18) — Holding corporation deemed not to acquire control of insurer on demutualization; 256(6)–(9) — Whether control acquired.

**Notes**: 85(1.2) added by 1991 technical bill, effective

(a) for dispositions after 1989, and

(b) for dispositions from 1985 through 1989, where the taxpayer is resident in the United States or the Netherlands (countries prescribed under Reg. 7400).

The CCRA takes the position that "all or substantially all", used in 85(1.2)(b), means 90% or more.

**(1.3) Meaning of "wholly owned corporation"** — For the purposes of this subsection and paragraph (1)(e.2), "wholly owned corporation" of a taxpayer means a corporation all the issued and outstanding shares of the capital stock of which (except directors' qualifying shares) belong to

(a) the taxpayer;

(b) a corporation that is a wholly owned corporation of the taxpayer; or

(c) any combination of persons described in paragraph (a) or (b).

**Notes**: 85(1.3) added by 1991 technical bill, effective for dispositions after June 1988.

**(1.4) Definitions** — For the purpose of subsection (1.1), "financial institution", "mark-to-market property" and "specified debt obligation" have the meanings assigned by subsection 142.2(1).

**Notes**: 85(1.4) added by 1994 tax amendments bill (Part III), effective for dispositions occurring after February 22, 1994.

**(2) Transfer of property to corporation from partnership** — Where

(a) a partnership has disposed, to a taxable Canadian corporation for consideration that includes shares of the corporation's capital stock, of any partnership property that was

(i) a capital property (other than real property, or an interest in or an option in respect of real property, where the partnership was not a Canadian partnership at the time of the disposition),

(ii) a property described in any of paragraphs (1.1)(c) to (f), or

(iii) a property that would be described in paragraph (1.1)(g) or (g.1) if the references in those paragraphs to "taxpayer" were read as "partnership", and

(b) the corporation and all the members of the partnership have jointly so elected, in prescribed form and within the time referred to in subsection (6),

paragraphs (1)(a) to (i) are applicable, with such modifications as the circumstances require, in respect of the disposition as if the partnership were a taxpayer resident in Canada who had disposed of the property to the corporation.

**Related Provisions**: 13(21.2)(d) — No election allowed on certain transfers of depreciable property where u.c.c. exceeds fair market value; 40(3.3), (3.4) — Limitation on loss where share acquired by affiliated person; 51(4) — Application of 85(2) to exchange of convertible property; 54.2 — Certain shares deemed to be capital property; 69(11) — Where corporation later sells transferred property and shelters gain; 85(3) — Where partnership wound up; 85(5) — Rules on transfers of depreciable property; 85(6) — Time for election; 86(3) — Section 86 does not apply where 85(2) applies; 139.1(4)(c) — No election allowed re ownership rights on demutualization of insurer; 248(4) — Interest in real property; Reg. 5301(8) — Effect of transfer on instalment base of transferee; Canada-U.S. tax treaty, Art. XIII:8 — Deferral of tax for U.S. resident transferor.

**Notes**: 85(2) deals with rollovers from a Canadian partnership (see 102(1)) to a corporation. For rollovers from an individual to a partnership, see 97(2).

*Opening words*

Opening words amended from "Where, after May 6, 1974" to "Where" by 1995-97 technical bill, effective for dispositions after June 20, 1996 (i.e., no substantive change).

*85(2)(a)*

85(2)(a) amended by 1995-97 technical bill, effective for dispositions after June 20, 1996. For dispositions from January 1987 through June 20, 1996, read:

(a) a partnership has disposed of any partnership property that was a capital property (other than real property, or an interest in or an option in respect of real property, owned by a partnership that was not a Canadian partnership at the time of the disposition), a Canadian resource property, a foreign resource property, an eligible capital property, an inventory (other than real property) or a property (other than a capital property or an inventory) that is a security or debt obligation used by it in the year in, or held by it in the year in the course of, carrying on the business of insurance or lending money to a taxable Canadian corporation for consideration that includes shares of the capital stock of the corporation, and

85(2)(a) amended by 1988 tax reform, effective for dispositions in 1987 or later. For taxation years beginning in 1985, and dispositions to the end of 1986, read:

(a) a partnership has disposed of any partnership property that was a capital property (other than real property, an interest therein or an option in respect thereof, owned by a partnership that was not a Canadian partnership at the time of the disposition), a Canadian resource property, a foreign resource property, an eligible capital property or an inventory (other than real property) to a taxable Canadian corporation for consideration that includes shares of the capital stock of the corporation, and

For dispositions from August 29, 1980, for taxation years beginning before 1985, read:

(a) a partnership has disposed of any partnership property that was a capital property (other than real property, an interest therein or an option in respect thereof, owned by a partnership that was not a Canadian partnership at the time of the disposition), a property referred to in subsection 59(2), an eligible capital property or an inventory (other than real property) to a taxable Canadian corporation for consideration that includes shares of the capital stock of the corporation, and

For dispositions from December 12, 1979 through August 28, 1980, read as for 1980-84 above, but ignore the words "an interest therein".

For dispositions from May 7, 1974 through December 11, 1979, read:

(a) a partnership has disposed of any partnership property that was a capital property (other than real property or an interest therein owned by a partnership that was not a Canadian partnership at the time of the disposition), an eligible capital property, an inventory other than real property or a property referred to in subsection 59(2) of the partnership to a Canadian corporation for consideration, including shares of the capital stock of the corporation, and

*Closing words*

For dispositions from May 7, 1974 through February 15, 1984, the closing words of the subsec. made subsec. (1.1) applicable, as well as paras. (1)(a) to (i).

*Before May 7, 1974*

For dispositions from 1972 through May 6, 1974, in place of subsec. (2), read subsecs. (2) and (2.1) as:

(2) Where, after 1971,

(a) any partnership property that was a capital property or eligible capital property of a partnership or a property referred to in subsection 59(2) of a partnership has been disposed of to a Canadian corporation,

(b) immediately after the disposition, not less than 80% of the issued shares of each class of the capital stock of the corporation was partnership property, and

(c) the corporation and all the members of the partnership have so elected in respect of the disposition, in prescribed form and within prescribed time,

paragraphs (1)(a) to (i) are applicable in respect of the disposition *mutatis mutandis* as if the partnership were a taxpayer resident in Canada who had disposed of the property to the corporation.

(2.1) Subsection (2) does not apply with respect to any disposition by a partnership of any partnership property referred to in subsection 59(2) if the corporation to which the property was disposed of has carried on any business before the disposition.

**I.T. Application Rules**: 20(1.2) (transfer of depreciable property by person who owned it before 1972).

**Interpretation Bulletins**: IT-217R: Depreciable property owned on December 31, 1971; IT-378R: Winding-up of a partnership; IT-457R: Election by professionals to exclude work in progress from income.

**Information Circulars**: 76-19R3: Transfer of property to a corporation under section 85.

**Forms**: T2058: Election on disposition of property by a partnership to a taxable Canadian corporation.

**(2.1) Computing paid-up capital** — Where subsection (1) or (2) applies to a disposition of property (other than a disposition of property to which section 84.1 or 212.1 applies) to a corporation by a person or partnership (in this subsection referred to as the "taxpayer"),

(a) in computing the paid-up capital in respect of any particular class of shares of the capital stock of the corporation at the time of, and at any time after, the issue of shares of the capital stock of the corporation in consideration for the disposition of the property, there shall be deducted an amount determined by the formula

$$(A - B) \times \frac{C}{A}$$

where

A is the increase, if any, determined without reference to this section as it applies to the disposition of the property, in the paid-up capital in respect of all the shares of the capital stock of the corporation as a result of the acquisition by the corporation of the property,

B is the amount, if any, by which the corporation's cost of the property, immediately after the acquisition, determined under subsection

**S. 85(2.1)(a)**     Income Tax Act, Part I, Division B

(1) or (2), as the case may be, exceeds the fair market value, immediately after the acquisition, of any consideration (other than shares of the capital stock of the corporation) received by the taxpayer from the corporation for the property, and

C is the increase, if any, determined without reference to this section as it applies to the disposition of the property, in the paid-up capital in respect of the particular class of shares as a result of the acquisition by the corporation of the property; and

(b) in computing the paid-up capital, at any time after November 21, 1985, in respect of any class of shares of the capital stock of a corporation, there shall be added an amount equal to the lesser of

(i) the amount, if any, by which

(A) the total of all amounts each of which is an amount deemed by subsection 84(3), (4) or (4.1) to be a dividend on shares of that class paid after November 21, 1985 and before that time by the corporation

exceeds

(B) the total of such dividends that would be determined under clause (A) if the Act were read without reference to paragraph (a), and

(ii) the total of all amounts required by paragraph (a) to be deducted in computing the paid-up capital in respect of that class of shares after November 21, 1985 and before that time.

**Related Provisions**: 257 — Formula cannot calculate to less than zero.

**Notes**: See Notes to 84(3).

Opening words of 85(2.1) and of (a) (before the formula) amended by 1993 technical bill, effective for dispositions occurring after November 21, 1985. Notwithstanding 152(4) and (5), such assessments and determinations in respect of any taxation year may be made as are consequential on the application of this amendment to dispositions occurring before 1993. These provisions formerly read:

(2.1) **Computation of paid-up capital** — Where subsection (1) or (2) has been applicable in respect of a disposition to a corporation, after November 21, 1985, of property (other than a disposition of property in respect of which section 84.1 or 212.1 applies) by a person or partnership (in this subsection referred to as the "taxpayer"), the following rules apply:

(a) in computing the paid-up capital, at any time after the disposition of the property, in respect of any particular class of shares of the capital stock of the corporation, there shall be deducted an amount determined by the formula

**Interpretation Bulletins**: IT-291R2: Transfer of property to a corporation under subsection 85(1).

**Advance Tax Rulings**: ATR-28: Redemption of capital stock of family farm corporation; ATR-32: Rollover of fixed assets from Opco into Holdco; ATR-35: Partitioning of assets to get specific ownership — "butterfly"; ATR-36: Estate freeze;.

(3) **Where partnership wound up** — Where,

(a) in respect of any disposition of partnership property of a partnership to a corporation, subsection (2) applies,

(b) the affairs of the partnership were wound up within 60 days after the disposition, and

(c) immediately before the winding-up there was no partnership property other than money or property received from the corporation as consideration for the disposition,

the following rules apply:

(d) the cost to any member of the partnership of any property (other than shares of the capital stock of the corporation or a right to receive any such shares) received by the member as consideration for the disposition of the member's partnership interest on the winding-up shall be deemed to be the fair market value of the property at the time of the winding-up,

(e) the cost to any member of the partnership of any preferred shares of any class of the capital stock of the corporation receivable by the member as consideration for the disposition of the member's partnership interest on the winding-up shall be deemed to be

(i) where any common shares of the capital stock of the corporation were also receivable by the member as consideration for the disposition of the interest, the lesser of

(A) the fair market value, immediately after the winding-up, of the preferred shares of that class so receivable by the member, and

(B) that proportion of the amount, if any, by which the adjusted cost base to the member of the member's partnership interest immediately before the winding-up exceeds the total of the fair market value, at the time of the winding-up, of the consideration (other than shares of the capital stock of the corporation or a right to receive any such shares) received by the member for the disposition of the interest, that

(I) the fair market value, immediately after the winding-up, of the preferred shares of that class so receivable by the member,

is of

(II) the fair market value, immediately after the winding-up, of all preferred shares of the capital stock of the corporation receivable by the member as consideration for the disposition, and

(ii) in any other case, the amount determined under clause (i)(B),

(f) the cost to any member of the partnership of any common shares of any class of the capital stock of the corporation receivable by the member as consideration for the disposition of the member's partnership interest on the winding-up shall be deemed to be that proportion of the amount, if any, by which the adjusted cost base to the member of the member's partnership interest immediately before the winding-up exceeds the total of the fair market value, at the time of the winding-up, of the consideration (other than shares of the capital stock of the corporation or a right to receive any such shares) received by the member for the disposition of the interest and the cost to the member of all preferred shares of the capital stock of the corporation receivable by the member as consideration for the disposition of the interest, that

(i) the fair market value, immediately after the winding-up, of the common shares of that class so receivable by the member,

is of

(ii) the fair market value, immediately after the winding-up, of all common shares of the capital stock of the corporation so receivable by the member as consideration for the disposition,

(g) the proceeds of disposition of the partnership interest of any member of the partnership shall be deemed to be the cost to the member of all shares and property receivable or received by the member as consideration for the disposition of the interest plus the amount of any money received by the member as consideration for the disposition, and

(h) where the partnership has distributed partnership property referred to in paragraph (c) to a member of the partnership, the partnership shall be deemed to have disposed of that property for proceeds equal to the cost amount to the partnership of the property immediately before its distribution.

**Related Provisions**: 69(11)(a)(i) — Exception to rule deeming proceeds at FMV where capital gains exemption claimed after incorporation of partnership; 98(2) — Deemed proceeds; 98(4) — Winding-up of partnership.

**I.T. Application Rules**: 20(1.2) (transfer of depreciable property by person who owned it before 1972).

**Interpretation Bulletins**: IT-217R: Depreciable property owned on December 31, 1971; IT-242R: Retired partners; IT-338R2: Partnership interests — effects on adjusted cost base resulting from the admission or retirement of a partner; IT-378R: Winding-up of a partnership; IT-457R: Election by professionals to exclude work in progress from income.

**(4) [Repealed]**

**Related Provisions**: 40(2)(e), (g) — Other limitations on capital loss; 40(2)(e.1) — Loss on disposition of debt owing by related person deemed nil; 53(1)(f.1), (f.2) — Additions to ACB; 54"superficial loss"(e) — Superficial loss rule does not apply; 69(5)(d) — No application where property appropriated by shareholder on winding-up; 80.01(8) — Deemed settlement after debt parking; 93(2) — Loss limitation on disposition of share; 97(3), (3.1) — Property acquired from majority interest partner; 112(3), (3.1) — Loss on share that is capital property; 256(5.1) — Controlled directly or indirectly — control in fact.

**Notes**: 85(4) repealed by 1995-97 technical bill, effective (subject to grandfathering rule reproduced after s. 260) for dispositions of property after April 26, 1995. See Notes to 13(21.2) and 40(3.4) re the "suspended pregnant loss" regime, and 40(3.6) for the loss denial rule that has replaced it. Before its repeal, from 1987-88 (see below) until April 26, 1995, read:

(4) **Loss from disposition to controlled corporation** — Where a taxpayer or a partnership (in this subsection referred to as the "taxpayer") disposes of any capital property (other than depreciable property of a prescribed class) of the taxpayer or eligible capital property in respect of a business of the taxpayer in respect of which the taxpayer would, but for this subsection, be permitted a deduction under paragraph 24(1)(a), to a corporation that immediately after the disposition is controlled, directly or indirectly in any manner whatever, by the taxpayer, by the spouse of the taxpayer or by a person or group of persons by whom the taxpayer is controlled, directly or indirectly in any manner whatever,

(a) notwithstanding any other provision of this Act,

(i) the capital loss therefrom, and

(ii) any deduction under paragraph 24(1)(a) in respect of the business in computing the taxpayer's income for the taxation year in which the taxpayer ceased to carry on the business

shall be deemed to be nil; and

(b) except where the property so disposed of was, immediately after the disposition, an obligation that was payable to the corporation by another corporation that is related to the corporation or by a corporation or a partnership that would be related to the corporation if paragraph 80(2)(j) applied for the purpose of this paragraph, in computing the adjusted cost base to the taxpayer of all shares of any particular class of the capital stock of the corporation owned by the taxpayer immediately after the disposition, there shall be added that proportion of the amount, if any, by which

(i) the cost amount to the taxpayer immediately before the disposition of the property so disposed of,

exceeds the total of

(ii) the taxpayer's proceeds of disposition of the property or, where the property is an eligible capital property, 4/3 of the taxpayer's eligible capital amount resulting from the disposition of the property, and

(ii.1) where the property disposed of by the taxpayer is a share of the capital stock of a corporation, the total of all amounts each of which is an amount that, but for paragraphs (a) and 40(2)(e), would be deducted

(A) under subsection 93(2) or 112(3) or (3.2) in computing a loss of the taxpayer from the disposition, or

(B) where the taxpayer is a partnership, by a corporation that is a member of the partnership under subsection 112(3.1) in computing its share of the loss of the partnership from the disposition,

that

(iii) the fair market value, immediately after the disposition, of all shares of that class so owned by the taxpayer,

is of

(iv) the fair market value, immediately after the disposition, of all shares of the capital stock of the corporation so owned by the taxpayer.

85(4)(b)(ii) amended before its repeal by 1995-97 technical bill to add the words "4/3 of", effective

(a) for a corporation, for dispositions by it of property after the beginning of its first taxation year that begins after June 1988; and

(b) in any other case, to dispositions of property in respect of a business after the beginning of the first fiscal period of the business that begins after 1987.

See also Notes to 13(21.2).

Opening words of 85(4)(b) amended by 1994 tax amendments bill (Part I) to add everything before "in computing", effective for dispositions that occur after July 12, 1994, other than pursuant to agreements in writing entered into by that date. Where the exception in the opening words of 85(4)(b) applies, the denied capital loss is added to ACB under 53(1)(f.1) or (f.11). The amendment ensures balance between the rules in 85(4) for creditors and the debt parking rules in 80.01 for debtors.

85(4) amended by 1991 technical bill, effective for dispositions after July 13, 1990, and by 1993 technical bill, effective as of the 1988 tax reform cutoff (see below). For dispositions after the 1988 tax reform cutoff through July 13, 1990, read:

(4) Where loss from disposition of property to controlled corporation — Where a taxpayer or a partnership (hereinafter referred to as the taxpayer) has, after May 6, 1974, disposed of any capital property or eligible capital property of the taxpayer to a corporation that, immediately after the disposition, was controlled, directly or indirectly in any manner whatever, by the taxpayer, by the spouse of the taxpayer or by a person or group of persons by whom the taxpayer was controlled, directly or indirectly in any manner whatever, and, but for this subsection, subsection 24(2) and paragraphs 40(2)(e) and (g), the taxpayer would have had a capital loss therefrom or a deduction pursuant to paragraph 24(1)(a) in computing his income for the taxation year in which he ceased to carry on a business, as the case may be, the following rules apply:

(a) notwithstanding section 24 and paragraphs 40(2)(e) and (g), his capital loss therefrom, or his deduction pursuant to paragraph 24(1)(a) in computing his income for the taxation year in which he ceased to carry on the business, as the case may be, otherwise determined shall be deemed to be nil; and

(b) in computing the adjusted cost base to the taxpayer of all shares of any particular class of the capital stock of the corporation owned by him immediately after the disposition, there shall be added that proportion of the amount, if any, by which

(i) the cost amount to him, immediately before the disposition, of the property so disposed of,

exceeds

(ii) his proceeds of disposition of the property or where the property was an eligible capital property, his eligible capital amount, within the meaning assigned by section 14, as a result of the disposition of the property

that

(iii) the fair market value, immediately after the disposition, of all shares of that class so owned by him,

is of

(iv) the fair market value, immediately after the disposition, of all shares of the capital stock of the corporation so owned by him.

85(4) amended by 1988 tax reform, effective, for corporations, for taxation years beginning after June 1988, and for other taxpayers, for business fiscal periods beginning in 1988 or later.

For dispositions from May 7, 1974 until the above cutoff, read, in the opening words of para. (b), beginning at "there shall be added":

... there shall be added, in the case of capital property, the amount that is equal to, and in the case of eligible capital property, twice the amount that is equal to, that proportion of the amount, if any by which

For dispositions from 1972 through May 6, 1974, read 85(4) as follows:

(4) Where capital loss from disposition of property to controlled corporation — Where a taxpayer has, after 1971, disposed of any capital property of the taxpayer to a corporation that, immediately after the disposition, was controlled, directly or indirectly in any manner whatever, by the taxpayer or by a person or group of persons by whom the taxpayer was controlled directly or indirectly in any manner whatever, and, but for this subsection, the taxpayer would have had a capital loss therefrom, the following rules apply:

(a) his capital loss therefrom otherwise determined shall be deemed to be nil;

(b) where, immediately after the disposition, the taxpayer owned any common shares of any class of the capital stock of the corporation, in computing the adjusted cost base to him of all common shares of that class owned by him immediately after the disposition there shall be added that proportion of the amount, if any, by which the adjusted cost base to him, immediately before the disposition, of the property so disposed of exceeds his proceeds of the disposition, that

(i) the fair market value, immediately after the disposition, of all common shares of that class so owned by him,

is of

(ii) the fair market value, immediately after the disposition, of all common shares of the capital stock of the corporation owned by him immediately after the disposition; and

(c) where, immediately after the disposition, the taxpayer owned no common shares of any class of the capital stock of the corporation, in computing the adjusted cost base to him of all preferred shares of any class of the capital stock of the corporation owned by him at that time, there shall be added that proportion of the amount, if any, by which the adjusted cost base to him, immediately before the disposition, of the property so disposed of exceeds his proceeds of the disposition, that

(i) the fair market value, immediately after the disposition, of all preferred shares of that class so owned by him,

is of

(ii) the fair market value, immediately after the disposition, of all preferred shares of the capital stock of the corporation owned by him immediately after the disposition.

**I.T. Application Rules:** 26(5)(c)(ii)(A) (where property owned since June 18, 1971).

**Interpretation Bulletins:** IT-291R2: Transfer of property to a corporation under subsection 85(1).

**Advance Tax Rulings:** ATR-57: Transfer of property for estate planning purposes; ATR-66: Non-arm's length transfer of debt followed by a winding-up and a sale of shares.

## (5) Rules on transfers of depreciable property — Where subsection (1) or (2) has applied to a

Subdivision h — Corporations Resident in Canada    S. 85(7)(b)

disposition at any time of depreciable property to a person (in this subsection referred to as the "transferee") and the capital cost to the transferor of the property exceeds the transferor's proceeds of disposition of the property, for the purposes of sections 13 and 20 and any regulations made for the purpose of paragraph 20(1)(a),

(a) the capital cost to the transferee of the property is deemed to be the amount that was its capital cost to the transferor; and

(b) the excess is deemed to have been deducted by the transferee under paragraph 20(1)(a) in respect of the property in computing income for taxation years that ended before that time.

**Related Provisions**: 13(7)(e) — Similar rule on non-arm's length transfer of depreciable property; 132.2(1)(d) — Parallel rule on mutual fund reorganization.

**Notes**: 85(5) amended by 1995-97 technical bill, effective on the same basis as the repeal of 85(5.1), to delete reference to (5.1) at the beginning. (Other wording changes were cosmetic.)

85(5) amended by 1981 Budget, effective for dispositions after November 12, 1981, other than those pursuant to an agreement in writing entered into on or before that date. For earlier dispositions, read the opening words as follows:

(5) **Rules where depreciable property transferred to controlled corporation** — Where subsection (1) or (2) has been applicable in respect of any disposition of any depreciable property to a corporation (in this subsection referred to as "the transferee") and the capital cost to the transferor of the property exceeds the transferor's proceeds of the disposition, for the purposes of sections 13 and 20 and any regulations made under paragraph 20(1)(a)

**Interpretation Bulletins**: IT-291R2: Transfer of property to a corporation under subsection 85(1).

**(5.1) [Repealed]**

**Related Provisions**: 13(7)(e) — Limitation on capital cost on non-arm's length transfer; 69(5)(d) — No application where property appropriated by shareholder on winding-up; 88(1)(d.1) — Winding-up; 256(5.1) — Controlled directly or indirectly — control in fact.

**Notes**: 85(5.1) repealed by 1995-97 technical bill, effective (subject to grandfathering rule reproduced after s. 260) for dispositions of property after April 26, 1995. See Notes to 13(21.2) and 40(3.4) re the "suspended pregnant loss" regime that has replaced it. Before its repeal, generally from November 13, 1981 (see below) until April 26, 1995, read:

(5.1) **Idem** — Where a person or a partnership (in this subsection referred to as the "taxpayer") has disposed of any depreciable property of a prescribed class of the taxpayer to a transferee that was

(a) a corporation that, immediately after the disposition, was controlled, directly or indirectly in any manner whatever, by the taxpayer, by the spouse of the taxpayer or by a person, group of persons or partnership by whom or which the taxpayer was controlled, directly or indirectly in any manner whatever,

(b) a person, spouse of a person, member of a group of persons or partnership who or that immediately after the disposition controlled the taxpayer, directly or indirectly in any manner whatever, or

(c) a partnership and, immediately after the disposition, the taxpayer's interest in the partnership as a member thereof is as described in paragraph 97(3.1)(a) or (b),

and the fair market value of the property at the time of the disposition is less than both the cost to the taxpayer of the property and the amount (in this subsection referred to as the "proportionate amount") that is the proportion of the undepreciated capital cost to the taxpayer of all property of that class immediately before the disposition that the fair market value of the property at the time of the disposition is of the fair market value of all property of that class at the time of disposition, the following rules apply:

(d) subsections (1) and (2) and section 97 are not applicable with respect to the disposition,

(e) the lesser of the cost to the taxpayer of the property and the proportionate amount in respect of the property shall be deemed to be the taxpayer's proceeds of disposition and the transferee's cost of the property,

(f) where two or more depreciable properties of a prescribed class of the taxpayer are disposed of at the same time, paragraph (e) applies as if each property so disposed of had been separately disposed of in the order designated by the taxpayer or, if the taxpayer does not so designate any such order, in the order designated by the Minister, and

(g) the cost to the taxpayer of any particular property received by the taxpayer as consideration for the disposition shall be deemed to be an amount equal to the lesser of

(i) the fair market value of the particular property at the time of the disposition, and

(ii) that proportion of the fair market value, at the time of the disposition, of the property disposed of by the taxpayer that

(A) the amount determined under subparagraph (i)

is of

(B) the fair market value, at the time of the disposition, of all properties received by the taxpayer as consideration for the disposition.

85(5.1) added by 1981 Budget, effective for dispositions after November 12, 1981, other than those pursuant to an agreement in writing entered into on or before that date.

**Interpretation Bulletins**: IT-291R2: Transfer of property to a corporation under subsection 85(1); IT-338R2: Partnership interests — effects on adjusted cost base resulting from the admission or retirement of a partner.

**(6) Time for election** — Any election under subsection (1) or (2) shall be made on or before the day that is the earliest of the days on or before which any taxpayer making the election is required to file a return of income pursuant to section 150 for the taxation year in which the transaction to which the election relates occurred.

**Related Provisions**: 85(7)–(9) — Late-filed election.

**(7) Late filed election** — Where the election referred to in subsection (6) was not made on or before the day on or before which the election was required by that subsection to be made and that day is after May 6, 1974, the election shall be deemed to have been made on that day if, on or before the day that is 3 years after that day,

(a) the election is made in prescribed form; and

(b) an estimate of the penalty in respect of that election is paid by the taxpayer or the partnership, as the case may be, when that election is made.

**Related Provisions**: 85(8), (9) — Penalty for late-filed election.

**Information Circulars**: 76-19R3: Transfer of property to a corporation under section 85.

**(7.1) Special cases** — Where, in the opinion of the Minister, the circumstances of a case are such that it would be just and equitable

(a) to permit an election under subsection (1) or (2) to be made after the day that is 3 years after the day on or before which the election was required by subsection (6) to be made, or

(b) to permit an election made under subsection (1) or (2) to be amended,

the election or amended election shall be deemed to have been made on the day on or before which the election was so required to be made if

(c) the election or amended election is made in prescribed form, and

(d) an estimate of the penalty in respect of the election or amended election is paid by the taxpayer or partnership, as the case may be, when the election or amended election is made,

and where this subsection applies to the amendment of an election, that election shall be deemed not to have been effective.

**Related Provisions**: 85(8), (9) — Penalty for late-filed election.

**Information Circulars**: 76-19R3: Transfer of property to a corporation under section 85; 92-1: Guidelines for accepting late, amended or revoked elections.

**(8) Penalty for late filed election** — For the purposes of this section, the penalty in respect of an election or an amended election referred to in paragraph (7)(a) or (7.1)(c) is an amount equal to the lesser of

(a) ¼ of 1% of the amount, if any, by which

(i) the fair market value of the property in respect of which that election or amended election was made, at the time the property was disposed of,

exceeds

(ii) the amount agreed on in the election or amended election by the taxpayer or partnership, as the case may be, and the corporation,

for each month or part of a month during the period commencing with the day on or before which the election is required by subsection (6) to be made and ending on the day the election or amended election is made, and

(b) an amount, not exceeding $8,000, equal to the product obtained by multiplying $100 by the number of months each of which is a month all or part of which is during the period referred to in paragraph (a).

**Related Provisions**: 220(3.1) — Waiver of penalty by CCRA.

**(9) Unpaid balance of penalty** — The Minister shall, with all due dispatch, examine each election and amended election referred to in paragraph (7)(a) or (7.1)(c), assess the penalty payable and send a notice of assessment to the taxpayer or partnership, as the case may be, and the taxpayer or partnership, as the case may be, shall pay forthwith to the Receiver General the amount, if any, by which the penalty so assessed exceeds the total of all amounts previously paid on account of that penalty.

**Definitions [s. 85]**: "acquired" — 256(7)–(9); "adjusted cost base" — 54, 248(1); "amount" — 248(1); "arm's length" — 251(1); "assessment", "business" — 248(1); "Canada" — 255; "Canadian corporation" — 89(1), 248(1); "Canadian partnership" — 102(1), 248(1); "Canadian resource property" — 66(15), 248(1); "capital loss" — 39(1)(b), 248(1); "capital property" — 54, 248(1); "cash method" — 28(1), 248(1); "class of shares" — 248(6); "common share" — 248(1); "control" — 256(6)–(9); "controlled" — 256(6), (6.1); "corporation" — 248(1), *Interpretation Act* 35(1); "cumulative eligible capital" — 14(5), 248(1); "depreciable property" — 13(21), 248(1); "designated insurance property" — 138(12), 248(1); "disposition" — 248(1); "eligible capital property" — 54, 248(1); "eligible property" — 85(1.1), (1.11); "farming" — 248(1); "financial institution" — 85(1.4), 142.2(1); "foreign affiliate" — 95(1), 248(1); "foreign resource property" — 66(15), 248(1); "insurer" — 248(1); "interest" — in real property 248(4); "inventory" — 248(1); "mark-to-market property" — 85(1.4), 142.2(1); "Minister", "NISA Fund No. 2", "non-resident" — 248(1); "partnership" — see Notes to 96(1); "paid-up capital" — 89(1), 248(1); "passenger vehicle", "person", "preferred share", "prescribed", "property" — 248(1); "qualifying share" — 192(6), 248(1) [*not intended to apply to s. 85*]; "regulation" — 248(1); "related" — 251(2); "resident in Canada" — 250; "share", "shareholder" — 248(1); "specified debt obligation" — 85(1.4), 142.2(1); "taxable Canadian corporation" — 89(1), 248(1); "taxable Canadian property" — 248(1); "taxable dividend" — 89(1), 248(1); "taxation year" — 249; "taxpayer" — 248(1); "undepreciated capital cost" — 13(21), 248(1); "wholly owned corporation" — 85(1.3).

**Interpretation Bulletins [s. 85]**: IT-188R: Sale of accounts receivable.

**Information Circulars [s. 85]**: 76-19R3: Transfer of property to a corporation under section 85.

**85.1 (1) Share for share exchange** — Where shares of any particular class of the capital stock of a Canadian corporation (in this section referred to as the "purchaser") are issued to a taxpayer (in this section referred to as the "vendor") by the purchaser in exchange for a capital property of the vendor that is shares of any particular class of the capital stock (in this section referred to as the "exchanged shares") of another corporation that is a taxable Canadian corporation (in this section referred to as the "acquired corporation"), subject to subsection (2),

(a) except where the vendor has, in the vendor's return of income for the taxation year in which the exchange occurred, included in computing the vendor's income for that year any portion of the gain or loss, otherwise determined, from the disposition of the exchanged shares, the vendor shall be deemed

(i) to have disposed of the exchanged shares for proceeds of disposition equal to the adjusted cost base to the vendor of those shares immediately before the exchange, and

(ii) to have acquired the shares of the purchaser at a cost to the vendor equal to the adjusted cost base to the vendor of the exchanged shares immediately before the exchange,

and where the exchanged shares were taxable Canadian property of the vendor, the shares of the purchaser so acquired by the vendor shall be deemed to be taxable Canadian property of the vendor; and

(b) the cost to the purchaser of each exchanged share, at any time up to and including the time the purchaser disposed of the share, shall be deemed to be the lesser of

(i) its fair market value immediately before the exchange, and

(ii) its paid-up capital immediately before the exchange.

**Related Provisions**: 7(1.5) — Shares acquired through employee stock option; 85.1(2) — Where rollover not to apply; 85.1(3)–(6) — Exchange of foreign share for foreign share; 107(2)(d.1)(iii), 107.4(3)(f) — Deemed taxable Canadian property retains status when rolled out of trust or into trust; 112(7) — Application of stop-loss rule where shares exchanged; 219.1 — Corporate emigration; 256(7)(c), (d) — Whether control of corporation acquired on rollover; Canada-U.S. tax treaty, Art. XIII:8 — Deferral of tax for U.S. resident transferor.

**Notes**: For a detailed discussion of 85.1, see Paul Cobb, "Share-for-Share Exchanges: Section 85.1", 43(6) *Canadian Tax Journal* 2230–2242 (1995).

Opening words of 85.1(1) amended by 1992 technical bill, effective for share exchanges after December 20, 1991, to require that the acquired corporation be a taxable Canadian corporation. For earlier exchanges it merely needed to be a corporation.

85.1(1) amended in 1987, effective for shares exchanged after June 5, 1987, other than shares exchanged after that date pursuant to

(a) an agreement in writing to do so entered into on or before that date; or

(b) the terms of a prospectus, preliminary prospectus, proxy statement, preliminary proxy statement or registration statement filed before June 6, 1987 with a public authority in a country or a political subdivision of that country in accordance with the securities legislation of that country or subdivision and, where required by law, accepted for filing by such public authority.

For shares exchanged from February 18, 1987 through June 5, 1987, read "acquired by a taxpayer ... from the purchaser" instead of "issued by a taxpayer ... to the purchaser" in the opening words of the subsec. The February 18, 1987 cutoff does not apply to shares exchanged after that date pursuant to

(a) an agreement in writing to do so entered into on or before that date; or

(b) the terms of a prospectus, preliminary prospectus, proxy statement, preliminary proxy statement or registration statement filed before February 18, 1987 with a public authority in a country or a political subdivision of that country in accordance with the securities legislation of that country or subdivision and, where required by law, accepted for filing by such public authority.

For shares exchanged from May 7, 1974 through February 17, 1987, or those grandfathered as indicated above, read:

"(b) the cost to the purchaser of each exchanged share, at any particular time up to and including the time he disposed of such share, shall be deemed to be

(i) its fair market value immediately before the exchange if, at the particular time or at any earlier time after the exchange, the purchaser owned shares of the capital stock of the acquired corporation

(A) to which are attached not less than 10% of all the votes that could then be cast for any and all purposes by holders of all shares of the capital stock of the acquired corporation, and

(B) that represent not less than 10% of the fair market value of all issued and outstanding shares of the capital stock of the acquired corporation, and

(ii) in any other case, nil."

85.1(1) did not apply to share exchanges before May 7, 1974.

**I.T. Application Rules**: 26(26), (28).

**Interpretation Bulletins**: IT-243R4: Dividend refund to private corporations; IT-291R2: Transfer of property to a corporation under subsection 85(1); IT-450R: Share for share exchange.

**Advance Tax Rulings**: ATR-26: Share exchange.

**(2) Where subsec. (1) does not apply** — Subsection (1) does not apply where

(a) the vendor and purchaser were, immediately before the exchange, not dealing with each other at arm's length (otherwise than because of a right referred to in paragraph 251(5)(b) that is a right of the purchaser to acquire the exchanged shares);

(b) the vendor or persons with whom the vendor did not deal at arm's length, or the vendor together with persons with whom the vendor did not deal at arm's length,

(i) controlled the purchaser, or

(ii) beneficially owned shares of the capital stock of the purchaser having a fair market value of more than 50% of the fair market value of all of the outstanding shares of the capital stock of the purchaser,

immediately after the exchange;

(c) the vendor and the purchaser have filed an election under subsection 85(1) or (2) with respect to the exchanged shares; or

(d) consideration other than shares of the particular class of the capital stock of the purchaser was received by the vendor for the exchanged shares, notwithstanding that the vendor may have disposed of shares of the capital stock of the acquired corporation (other than the exchanged shares) to the purchaser for consideration other than shares of one class of the capital stock of the purchaser.

**Proposed Addition — 85.1(2)(e)**

(e) the vendor

(i) is a foreign affiliate of a taxpayer resident in Canada at the end of the taxation year of the vendor in which the exchange occurred, and

(ii) has included any portion of the gain or loss, otherwise determined, from the disposition of the exchanged shares in computing its foreign accrual property income for the taxation year of the vendor in which the exchange occurred.

**Application**: Bill C-43 (First Reading September 20, 2000), subsec. 37(1), will add para. 85.1(2)(e), applicable to exchanges that occur after 1995.

**Technical Notes**: Subsection 85.1(2) of the Act is amended to add new paragraph (e), consequential on the introduction of new subsection 85.1(5). New paragraph 85.1(2)(e) provides that subsection 85.1(1) will not apply to allow a tax-deferred rollover in respect of a Canadian share-for-share exchange where a vendor is a foreign affiliate and the vendor includes any portion of the gain or loss realized from the exchange in computing its foreign accrual property income for the year.

### Proposed Amendment — 85.1(2)

**Letter from Department of Finance, June 6, 2000**: See under 248(1)"taxable Canadian property".

**Related Provisions**: 256(6), (6.1) — Meaning of "controlled".

**Notes**: Parenthetical exclusion in 85.1(2)(a) added by 1993 technical bill, effective for exchanges occurring after December 21, 1992.

85.1(2)(b)(i) amended by 1988 tax reform. For exchanges before 1989, read:

(i) controlled, directly or indirectly in any manner whatever, the purchaser, or

(The change was made to avoid having 256(5.1), which was introduced in 1988, apply to this test.)

For transactions before April 1, 1977, read 85.1(2)(b)(ii) as follows:

(ii) beneficially owned shares of the capital stock of the purchaser representing more than 50% of its paid-up capital,

**Interpretation Bulletins**: IT-243R4: Dividend refund to private corporations; IT-291R2: Transfer of property to a corporation under subsection 85(1); IT-450R: Share for share exchange.

**Advance Tax Rulings**: ATR-26: Share exchange.

**(2.1) Computation of paid-up capital** — Where, at any time, a purchaser has issued shares of its capital stock as a result of an exchange to which subsection (1) applied, in computing the paid-up capital in respect of any particular class of shares of its capital stock at any particular time after that time

(a) there shall be deducted that proportion of the amount, if any, by which

(i) the increase, if any, as a result of the issue, in the paid-up capital in respect of all the shares of the capital stock of the purchaser, computed without reference to this subsection as it applies to the issue,

exceeds

(ii) the paid-up capital in respect of all of the exchanged shares received as a result of the exchange

that

(iii) the increase, if any, as a result of the issue, in the paid-up capital in respect of the particular class of shares, computed without reference to this subsection as it applies to the issue,

is of

(iv) the amount, if any, determined in subparagraph (i) in respect of the issue; and

(b) there shall be added an amount equal to the lesser of

(i) the amount, if any, by which

(A) the total of all amounts each of which is an amount deemed by subsection 84(3), (4) or (4.1) to be a dividend on shares of that class paid by the purchaser before the particular time

exceeds

(B) the total that would be determined under clause (A) if this Act were read without reference to paragraph (a), and

(ii) the total of all amounts required by paragraph (a) to be deducted in respect of that particular class of shares before the particular time.

**Related Provisions**: 219.1 — Corporate emigration; 256(6), (6.1) — Meaning of "controlled".

**Notes**: 85.1(2.1) added in 1987, effective for shares exchanged after June 5, 1987, other than shares exchanged after that date pursuant to

(a) an agreement in writing to do so entered into on or before that date; or

(b) the terms of a prospectus, preliminary prospectus, proxy statement, preliminary proxy statement or registration statement filed before June 6, 1987 with a public authority in a country or a political subdivision of that country in accordance with the securities legislation of that country or subdivision and, where required by law, accepted for filing by such public authority.

**Interpretation Bulletins**: IT-243R4: Dividend refund to private corporations; IT-291R2: Transfer of property to a corporation under subsection 85(1); IT-450R: Share for share exchange.

**(3) Disposition of shares of foreign affiliate** — Where a taxpayer has disposed of capital property that was shares of the capital stock of a foreign affiliate of the taxpayer to any corporation that was, immediately following the disposition, a foreign affiliate of the taxpayer (in this subsection referred to as the "acquiring affiliate") for consideration including shares of the capital stock of the acquiring affiliate,

(a) the cost to the taxpayer of any property (other than shares of the capital stock of the acquiring affiliate) receivable by the taxpayer as consideration for the disposition shall be deemed to be the fair market value of the property at the time of the disposition;

(b) the cost to the taxpayer of any shares of any class of the capital stock of the acquiring affiliate receivable by the taxpayer as consideration for the disposition shall be deemed to be that proportion of the amount, if any, by which the total of the adjusted cost bases to the taxpayer, immediately before the disposition, of the shares disposed of exceeds the fair market value at that time of the consideration receivable for the disposition (other than shares of the capital stock of the acquiring affiliate) that

(i) the fair market value, immediately after the disposition, of those shares of the acquiring affiliate of that class

is of

(ii) the fair market value, immediately after the disposition, of all shares of the capital stock of the acquiring affiliate receivable by the taxpayer as consideration for the disposition;

(c) the taxpayer's proceeds of disposition of the shares shall be deemed to be an amount equal to the cost to the taxpayer of all shares and other property receivable by the taxpayer from the acquiring affiliate as consideration for the disposition; and

(d) the cost to the acquiring affiliate of the shares acquired from the taxpayer shall be deemed to be an amount equal to the taxpayer's proceeds of disposition referred to in paragraph (c).

**Related Provisions**: 44.1(6), (7) — Small business investment rollover on exchange of shares; 53(1)(c) — Addition to ACB of share; 85.1(4) — Exception.

**(4) Exception** — Subsection (3) is not applicable in respect of a disposition at any time by a taxpayer of a share of the capital stock of a foreign affiliate, all or substantially all of the property of which at that time was excluded property (within the meaning assigned by subsection 95(1)), to another foreign affiliate of the taxpayer where the disposition is part of a series of transactions or events for the purpose of disposing of the share to a person who, immediately after the series of transactions or events, was a person (other than a foreign affiliate of the taxpayer) with whom the taxpayer was dealing at arm's length.

**Related Provisions**: 248(10) — Series of transactions.

**Notes**: 85.1(4) added by 1981 Budget, effective for dispositions after November 12, 1981.

The CCRA takes the position that "all or substantially all" means 90% or more.

**Interpretation Bulletins**: IT-243R4: Dividend refund to private corporations; IT-291R2: Transfer of property to a corporation under subsection 85(1).

### Proposed Addition — 85.1(5), (6)

**(5) Foreign share for foreign share exchange** — Subject to subsections (3) and (6) and 95(2), where a corporation resident in a country other than Canada (in this section referred to as the "foreign purchaser") issues shares of its capital stock (in this section referred to as the "issued foreign shares") to a vendor in exchange for shares of the capital stock of another corporation resident in a country other than Canada (in this section referred to as the "exchanged foreign shares") that were immediately before the exchange capital property of the vendor, except where the vendor has, in the vendor's return of income for the taxation year in which the exchange occurred, included in computing the vendor's income for that year any portion of the gain or loss, otherwise determined, from the disposition of the exchanged foreign shares, the vendor is deemed

(a) to have disposed of the exchanged foreign shares for proceeds of disposition equal to the adjusted cost base to the vendor of those shares immediately before the exchange, and

(b) to have acquired the issued foreign shares at a cost to the vendor equal to the adjusted cost base to the vendor of the exchanged foreign shares immediately before the exchange,

and where the exchanged foreign shares were taxable Canadian property of the vendor, the issued foreign shares so acquired by the vendor are deemed to be taxable Canadian property of the vendor.

**Related Provisions**: 85.1(6) — Where rollover does not apply.

**(6) Where subsec. (5) does not apply** — Subsection (5) does not apply where

(a) the vendor and foreign purchaser were, immediately before the exchange, not dealing with each other at arm's length (otherwise than because of a right referred to in paragraph 251(5)(b) that is a right of the foreign purchaser to acquire the exchanged foreign shares);

(b) immediately after the exchange the vendor, persons with whom the vendor did not deal at arm's length or the vendor together with persons with whom the vendor did not deal at arm's length,

(i) controlled the foreign purchaser, or

(ii) beneficially owned shares of the capital stock of the foreign purchaser having a fair market value of more than 50% of the fair market value of all of the outstanding shares of the capital stock of the foreign purchaser; or

(c) consideration other than issued foreign shares was received by the vendor for the exchanged foreign shares, notwithstanding that the vendor may have disposed of shares of the capital stock of the other corporation referred to in subsection (5) (other than the exchanged foreign shares) to the foreign purchaser for consideration other than shares of the capital stock of the foreign purchaser;

(d) the vendor

(i) is a foreign affiliate of a taxpayer resident in Canada at the end of the taxation year of

**S. 85.1(6)(d)(i)**     Income Tax Act, Part I, Division B

the vendor in which the exchange occurred, and

(ii) has included any portion of the gain or loss, otherwise determined, from the disposition of the exchanged foreign shares in computing its foreign accrual property income for the taxation year of the vendor in which the exchange occurred; or

(e) the vendor is a foreign affiliate of a taxpayer resident in Canada at the end of the taxation year of the vendor in which the exchange occurred and the exchanged foreign shares are excluded property (within the meaning assigned by subsection 95(1)) of the vendor.

**Application**: Bill C-43 (First Reading September 20, 2000), subsec. 37(2), will add subsecs. 85.1(5) and (6), applicable to exchanges that occur after 1995.

**Technical Notes**: Section 85.1 of the Act permits a tax-deferred rollover for shareholders who exchange shares of a taxable Canadian corporation for shares of a Canadian purchaser corporation in the course of an arm's length sale of the acquired corporation's shares. Subsection 85.1(1) provides, amongst other things, that the shareholder's tax cost of the old shares becomes the tax cost of the new shares with the result that any capital gain is deferred. If, however, the shareholder recognizes, in the shareholder's tax return for the year in which the exchange occurred, any portion of the gain or loss realized on the share exchange, subsection 85.1(1) provides that the rollover will not apply to the shares. Subsection 85.1(2) of the Act sets out other circumstances where the rollover will not be available. These include circumstances where the purchaser corporation and the shareholder are not dealing at arm's length immediately before the exchange or where the shareholder controls the purchaser immediately after the exchange.

New subsection 85.1(5) of the Act provides a similar tax-deferred rollover for shareholders who exchange shares of a foreign corporation for shares of another foreign corporation to that provided in subsection 85.1(1) in respect of exchanges of shares of Canadian corporations. The application of subsection 85.1(5) is subject to the rollover for foreign shares contained in subsection 85.1(3) and 95(2) of the Act.

New subsection 85.1(6) of the Act describes the circumstances where new subsection 85.1(5) will not apply to a foreign share-for-share exchange. The rules in subsection 85.1(6) are similar to those in subsection 85.1(2), except that paragraph 85.1(6)(e) provides that subsection 85.1(5) will not apply where the vendor is a foreign affiliate and the exchanged foreign shares are excluded property (within the meaning assigned by subsection 95(1) of the Act) of the vendor. In other words, excluded property is not eligible for the foreign share-for-foreign share rollover in new subsection 85.1(5).

New subsections 85.1(2), (5) and (6) apply to foreign share-for-share exchanges that occur after 1995. Taxpayers may request a reassessment of their 1996, 1997 and 1998 taxation years in cases where they have disposed of shares in the relevant year in circumstances in which subsections 85.1(5) and (6) of the Act may apply to the disposition. These requests should be made in writing to the Canada Customs and Revenue Agency Tax Centre which serves the area in which the taxpayer lives.

**Revenue Canada Question and Answers, April 28, 1999**: *Tax Rollover for Canadian Shareholders of Foreign Corporations*

*Background*

On April 15, 1999, Finance Minister Paul Martin announced proposed changes to the "rollover" provisions of the *Income Tax Act* dealing with the disposition of shares of foreign corporations. (Press Release number 99-035)

Under the current rollover provisions in sections 85.1 and 87 of the *Income Tax Act*, a taxpayer who disposes of shares of one taxable Canadian corporation and receives shares of another, on a "share-for-share" exchange or with a merger of such corporations, may defer the recognition of any gain or loss arising on the disposition. The gain or loss will ultimately be recognized when the shares received on the exchange are sold in a taxable transaction.

The proposed changes will extend this tax-deferral treatment to taxpayers who dispose of shares of one foreign corporation for shares of another on share-for-share exchange or with the merger of foreign corporations. The foreign corporations would not have to be residents of the same foreign jurisdiction. These changes would apply to share exchanges that occur after 1997. They would also apply to share exchanges that occurred after 1995 and before 1998 where the taxpayer elects by notifying the Department in writing.

A taxpayer would also be able to elect, for the year in which the exchange occurs, not to have these proposed tax-deferral changes apply in respect of the disposition. In this case, any gain or loss realized by the taxpayer on the exchange of the shares of the foreign corporation would be included in computing the taxpayer's income for tax purposes in the year of the exchange.

Questions and Answers

*Q1. Can I take advantage of these proposed changes when I file my 1998 income tax return?*

A1. Yes. This proposal takes effect immediately. Unless you want to include the gain or loss in your income for 1998, the rollover provisions of subsection 85.1(1) apply automatically to the exchange and no election is required to be filed. In this transaction, you are deemed to have disposed of the original shares at their adjusted cost base and to have acquired the new shares at a cost equal to the adjusted cost base of the original shares immediately before the exchange.

*Q2. I want to elect to include the capital gain or loss in 1998. What do I do?*

A2. If you have yet to file your 1998 return and you wish to include the gain or loss for 1998, you must elect to do so by reporting the details of the transaction on your 1998 Schedule 3.

*Q3. I have already filed my 1998 income tax return and I included the capital gain from such a transaction. Can I have my return corrected to recognize this change?*

A3. Yes. You can elect to exclude the capital gain from this transaction by requesting a reassessment of your 1998 income tax return to delete this capital gain. This election must be made in writing and you should refer to the Press Release. Be sure to provide your name, Social Insurance Number and the tax year involved.

*Q4. What other information is required to elect to include or exclude a capital gain from such a transaction?*

A4. To assist us in identifying the reported gain, please provide the details of the transaction including the following:
- the name of the corporation;
- the number of shares disposed of;
- the adjusted cost base of these shares;
- the proceeds of disposition; and,
- the capital gain reported.

Q5. *I included the capital gain from this transaction on my 1998 income tax return but I have no tax owing for 1998. Do I need to do anything further?*

A5. If you have already filed your 1998 income tax return, there is no need to supply any additional information to leave the capital gain on your 1998 return.

Q6. *I included the capital gain from such a transaction on my 1996 and/or 1997 return(s). How can I request that these returns be corrected to recognize this modification?*

A6. You can elect to exclude the capital gain from these transactions by requesting a reassessment of your 1996 and/or 1997 income tax return(s) to delete such a capital gain. This election must be made in writing and you should refer to the Press Release. In addition, you should supply the information listed in Question 4. This election must be forwarded to the tax centre which serves the area where you live.

Q7. *I included the capital gain from such a transaction on my 1996 or 1997 return and I would prefer it to remain there. Is there anything I need to do?*

A7. No. The requirement to elect to include such income applies to 1998 returns yet to be filed and to subsequent tax years. Therefore, you are not required to complete any particular forms or letters requesting the inclusion of such an income.

**Department of Finance news release, April 15, 1999**: *Tax Rollover for Canadian Shareholders of Foreign Corporations*

Finance Minister Paul Martin today proposed changes to the "rollover" and "replacement property" provisions of the *Income Tax Act* dealing with the disposition of shares of a foreign corporation.

Under the current rollover provisions in sections 85.1 and 87 of the *Income Tax Act*, a taxpayer who disposes of shares of one taxable Canadian corporation and receives shares of another, on a "share-for-share" exchange or a merger of such corporations, may defer the recognition of any gain or loss arising on the disposition. The gain or loss will ultimately be recognized when the shares received on the exchange are sold in a taxable transaction.

The announcement today would extend this tax-deferral treatment to taxpayers who dispose of shares of one foreign corporation for shares of another on a share-for-share exchange [85.1(5), (6) — ed.] or foreign merger [87(8), (8.1) — ed.]. The foreign corporations would not have to be residents of the same foreign jurisdiction. These changes would apply to share exchanges that occur after 1997. They would also apply to share exchanges that occurred after 1995 and before 1998 where the taxpayer elects by notifying the Minister of National Revenue in writing.

A taxpayer would also be able to elect, for the year in which a share exchange occurs, not to have these proposed tax-deferral changes apply in respect of the disposition. In this case, any gain or loss realized by the taxpayer on the exchange of the shares of the foreign corporation would be included in computing the taxpayer's income for tax purposes in the year of the exchange.

[For the change affecting the replacement property rules, see under 44(1), which will no longer apply to shares — ed.]

For further information: Davine Roach, Tax Policy Branch, (613) 992-4852; Karl Littler, Secretary of State (International Financial Institutions), (613) 996-7861; Jean-Michel Catta, Public Affairs and Operations Division, (613) 992-1574.

## Proposed Amendment — Canadian/foreign share-for-share exchange

**Supplementary information, Economic Statement, October 18, 2000**: *Canadian/Foreign Share-for-Share Exchanges*

Under the *Income Tax Act*, certain share-for-share exchanges can be effected on a tax-deferred basis where the corporations involved are all resident in Canada or are all non-residents. These rules do not apply, however, to a Canadian resident shareholder who exchanges shares of a domestic corporation for shares of a foreign corporation (or vice versa).

It is intended that a share-for-share exchange rollover rule be developed in consultation with the private sector to apply to cross-border share-for-share exchanges where a Canadian resident shareholder receives only share consideration on the exchange. To ensure the preservation of the Canadian income tax base, rules must be developed to provide for, among other things, cost base adjustments, paid-up capital adjustments, the preservation of taxable Canadian property status, and adjustments for tax benefits that could potentially arise because of the conversion of capital gains into dividends (or vice versa). Any such rollover rule would not take effect before the release of draft legislation for public discussion.

**Definitions [s. 85.1]**: "acquired corporation" — 85.1(1); "adjusted cost base" — 54, 248(1); "amount" — 248(1); "arm's length" — 251(1); "Canadian corporation" — 89(1), 248(1); "capital property" — 54, 248(1); "class of shares" — 248(6); "controlled" — 256(6), (6.1); "corporation" — 248(1), *Interpretation Act* 35(1); "disposition" — 248(1); "dividend" — 248(1); "exchanged foreign shares" — 85.1(5); "exchanged share" — 85.1(1); "foreign accrual property income" — 95(1); "foreign affiliate" — 95(1), 248(1); "foreign purchaser", "issued foreign shares" — 85.1(5); "paid-up capital" — 89(1), 248(1); "person", "property" — 248(1); "purchaser" — 85.1(1); "resident", "resident in Canada" — 250; "series of transactions" — 248(10); "share" — 248(1); "taxable Canadian corporation" — 89(1), 248(1); "taxable Canadian property" — 248(1); "taxation year" — 249; "taxpayer" — 248(1).

## 86. (1) Exchange of shares by a shareholder in course of reorganization of capital —

Where, at a particular time after May 6, 1974, in the course of a reorganization of the capital of a corporation, a taxpayer has disposed of capital property that was all the shares of any particular class of the capital stock of the corporation that were owned by the taxpayer at the particular time (in this section referred to as the "old shares"), and property is receivable from the corporation therefor that includes other shares of the capital stock of the corporation (in this section referred to as the "new shares"), the following rules apply:

(a) the cost to the taxpayer of any property (other than new shares) receivable by the taxpayer for the old shares shall be deemed to be its fair market value at the time of the disposition;

(b) the cost to the taxpayer of any new shares of any class of the capital stock of the corporation receivable by the taxpayer for the old shares shall be deemed to be that proportion of the amount, if any, by which the total of the adjusted cost bases to the taxpayer, immediately before the disposition, of the old shares exceeds the fair market value at that time of the consideration receivable for the old shares (other than new shares) that

(i) the fair market value, immediately after the disposition, of those new shares of that class,

is of

(ii) the fair market value, immediately after the disposition, of all new shares of the capital stock of the corporation receivable by the taxpayer for the old shares; and

(c) the taxpayer shall be deemed to have disposed of the old shares for proceeds of disposition equal to the cost to the taxpayer of all new shares and other property receivable by the taxpayer for the old shares.

**Related Provisions**: 7(1.5) — Exchange of shares; 51(1), (2) — Conversion of debt to shares; 51(4) — Application of s. 86 to exchange of convertible property; 55(1) — "Permitted redemption" for butterfly purposes; 85(1)–(3) — Transfer of property to corporation; 86(2.1) — Computation of paid-up capital; 86(3) — Application; 86(4) — Debt forgiveness — reduction in adjusted cost base of new shares; 112(7) — Application of stop-loss rule where shares exchanged; Canada-U.S. tax treaty, Art. XIII:8 — Deferral of tax for U.S. resident transferor.

**Notes**: See Notes at end of s. 86 for pre-1980 reorganizations.

**I.T. Application Rules**: 26(27), (28).

**Interpretation Bulletins**: IT-146R4: Shares entitling shareholders to choose taxable or capital dividends.

**Advance Tax Rulings**: ATR-22R: Estate freeze using share exchange; ATR-33: Exchange of shares.

**(2) Idem** — Notwithstanding paragraphs (1)(b) and (c), where a taxpayer has disposed of old shares in circumstances described in subsection (1) and the fair market value of the old shares immediately before the disposition exceeds the total of

(a) the cost to the taxpayer of the property (other than new shares) receivable by the taxpayer for the old shares as determined under paragraph (1)(a), and

(b) the fair market value of the new shares, immediately after the disposition,

and it is reasonable to regard any portion of the excess (in this subsection referred to as the "gift portion") as a benefit that the taxpayer desired to have conferred on a person related to the taxpayer, the following rules apply:

(c) the taxpayer shall be deemed to have disposed of the old shares for proceeds of disposition equal to the lesser of

(i) the total of the cost to the taxpayer of the property as determined under paragraph (1)(a) and the gift portion

and

(ii) the fair market value of the old shares immediately before the disposition,

(d) the taxpayer's capital loss from the disposition of the old shares shall be deemed to be nil, and

(e) the cost to the taxpayer of any new shares of any class of the capital stock of the corporation receivable by the taxpayer for the old shares shall be deemed to be that proportion of the amount, if any, by which the total of the adjusted cost bases to the taxpayer, immediately before the disposition, of the old shares exceeds the total determined under subparagraph (c)(i) that

(i) the fair market value, immediately after the disposition, of the new shares of that class,

is of

(ii) the fair market value, immediately after the disposition, of all new shares of the capital stock of the corporation receivable by the taxpayer for the old shares.

**Related Provisions**: 86(3) — Application.

**I.T. Application Rules**: 26(27), (28) (where shares or property owned since before 1972).

**Advance Tax Rulings**: ATR-22R: Estate freeze using share exchange; ATR-33: Exchange of shares.

**(2.1) Computation of paid-up capital** — Where subsection (1) applies to a disposition of shares of the capital stock of a corporation (in this subsection referred to as the "exchange"), in computing the paid-up capital in respect of a particular class of shares of the capital stock of the corporation at any particular time that is the time of, or any time after, the exchange,

(a) there shall be deducted the amount determined by the formula

$$(A - B) \times \frac{C}{A}$$

where

A  is the total of all amounts each of which is the increase, if any, as a result of the exchange, in the paid-up capital in respect of a class of shares of the capital stock of the corporation, computed without reference to this subsection as it applies to the exchange,

B  is the amount, if any, by which the paid-up capital in respect of the old shares exceeds the fair market value of the consideration (other than shares of the capital stock of the corporation) given by the corporation for the old shares on the exchange, and

C is the increase, if any, as a result of the exchange, in the paid-up capital in respect of the particular class of shares, computed without reference to this subsection as it applies to the exchange; and

(b) there shall be added an amount equal to the lesser of

(i) the amount, if any, by which

(A) the total of all amounts deemed by subsection 84(3), (4) or (4.1) to be a dividend on shares of that class paid by the corporation before the particular time

exceeds

(B) the total that would be determined under clause (A) if this Act were read without reference to paragraph (a), and

(ii) the total of all amounts required by paragraph (a) to be deducted in respect of that particular class of shares before the particular time.

**Related Provisions**: 257 — Formula cannot calculate to less than zero.

**Notes**: 86(2.1) added by 1993 technical bill, effective for exchanges occurring after August 1992. However, for exchanges from September 1 through December 20, 1992, it will not apply if the corporation issuing the new shares filed a written election with Revenue Canada by December 31, 1994.

The effect of 86(2.1), which reduces the paid-up capital (PUC) of the new shares, is to permit a PUC deficiency on the old shares (such as may have arisen where 85(2.1) applied to reduce PUC following a rollover under 85(1)) to flow through to the new shares. Thus, the 86(1) exchange will not result in an increase in PUC to which 84(1) would apply; and the amount received for the old shares for purposes of 84(3) will be equal to the PUC of the old shares (see 84(5)). 51(3) applies the same rule to share exchanges that fall under s. 51.

See also Notes at end of s. 86 for pre-1980 reorganizations.

**(3) Application** — Subsections (1) and (2) do not apply in any case where subsection 85(1) or (2) applies.

**Related Provisions**: 51(4) — Application of section 51.

**Notes**: 86(3) amended by 1993 technical bill, effective for reorganizations that begin after December 21, 1992, to remove reference to section 51. Under the old rules 86 did not apply if 51 applied. Now 86 takes precedence, and 51 does not apply if 86 can apply (see 51(4)).

**(4) Computation of adjusted cost base** — Where a taxpayer has disposed of old shares in circumstances described in subsection (1),

(a) there shall be deducted after the disposition in computing the adjusted cost base to the taxpayer of each new share the amount determined by the formula

$$A \times \frac{B}{C}$$

where

A is the amount, if any, by which

(i) the total of all amounts deducted under paragraph 53(2)(g.1) in computing the adjusted cost base to the taxpayer of the old shares immediately before the disposition

exceeds

(ii) the amount that would be the taxpayer's capital gain for the taxation year that includes the time of the disposition from the disposition of the old shares if paragraph 40(1)(a) were read without reference to subparagraph (iii) of that paragraph,

B is the fair market value of the new share at the time it was acquired by the taxpayer in consideration for the disposition of the old shares, and

C is the total of all amounts each of which is the fair market value of a new share at the time it was acquired by the taxpayer in consideration for the disposition of the old shares; and

(b) the amount determined under paragraph (a) in respect of the acquisition shall be added in computing the adjusted cost base to the taxpayer of the new share after the disposition.

**Related Provisions**: 53(1)(q) — Addition to ACB for amount under 86(4)(b); 53(2)(g.1) — Reduction in ACB under 86(4)(a); 80.03(2)(a) — Deemed gain on disposition following debt forgiveness.

**Notes**: 86(4) added by 1994 tax amendments bill (Part I), effective for taxation years that end after February 21, 1994. See Notes to 47(1).

**Notes [s. 86]**: 86 amended by 1979 Budget. For reorganizations from May 7, 1974 through December 11, 1979, read:

86. (1) Where, at a particular time after May 6, 1974, in the course of reorganization of the capital of a corporation, a taxpayer has disposed of capital property that was all the shares of any particular class of the capital stock of the corporation that were owned by him at the particular time (in this section referred to as the "old shares"), and property is receivable from the corporation therefor that includes other shares of the capital stock of the corporation (in this section referred to as the "new shares"), the following rules apply:

(a) the cost to the taxpayer of any property (other than shares of the capital stock of the corporation) receivable by him for the old shares shall be deemed to be its fair market value at the time of the disposition;

(b) the cost to the taxpayer of any new shares of any class of the capital stock of the corporation receivable by him for the old shares shall be deemed to be that proportion of the amount, if any, by which the aggregate of the adjusted cost bases to him, immediately before the disposition, of the old shares exceeds the fair market value at that time of the consideration receivable therefor (other than shares of the capital stock of the corporation) that

(i) the fair market value, immediately after the disposition, of those new shares of that class,

is of

(ii) the fair market value, immediately after the disposition, of all new shares of the capital stock of the corporation receivable by him for the old shares; and

(c) the taxpayer shall be deemed to have disposed of the old shares for proceeds of disposition equal to the cost to him of all new shares and other property receivable by him for the old shares.

(2) **Application** — This section is not applicable in any case where section 51 or any of subsections 85(1) to (3) is applicable.

For dispositions from 1972 through May 6, 1974, read:

86. (1) **Disposition of shares by a shareholder in course of reorganization of capital** — Where in the course of a reorganization of the capital of a corporation, a taxpayer has, after 1971, disposed of, and the corporation has acquired, category A shares of any class of the capital stock of the corporation, the following rules apply:

(a) the cost to the taxpayer of any property (other than shares of the capital stock of the corporation or a right to receive any such shares) received by him as consideration for the disposition shall be deemed to be its fair market value at the time of the disposition;

(b) the cost to the taxpayer of any category B shares of any class of the capital stock of the corporation receivable by him as consideration for the disposition shall be deemed to be,

(i) where category A shares were also receivable by him as consideration for the disposition, the lesser of

(A) the fair market value, immediately after the disposition, of those category B shares of that class, and

(B) that proportion of the amount, if any, by which the adjusted cost base to him, immediately before the disposition, of the category A shares so disposed of exceeds the fair market value of the consideration for the disposition (other than shares of the capital stock of the corporation or a right to receive any such shares) received by him from the corporation, that

(I) the fair market value, immediately after the disposition, of those category B shares of that class,

is of

(II) the fair market value, immediately after the disposition, of all category B shares of the capital stock of the corporation receivable by him as consideration for the disposition, and

(ii) in any other case, the amount determined under clause (i)(B);

(c) the cost to the taxpayer of any category A shares of any class of the capital stock of the corporation receivable by him as consideration for the disposition shall be deemed to be that proportion of the amount, if any, by which the adjusted cost base to him, immediately before the disposition, of the category A shares so disposed of exceeds the aggregate of the fair market value of the consideration (other than shares of the capital stock of the corporation or a right to receive any such shares) received by him from the corporation as consideration for the disposition and the cost to him of all category B shares of the capital stock of the corporation receivable by him as consideration for the disposition, that

(i) the fair market value, immediately after the disposition, of the category A shares of that class receivable by him as consideration for the disposition,

is of

(ii) the fair market value, immediately after the disposition, of all category A shares of the capital stock

of the corporation receivable by him as consideration for the disposition; and

(d) his proceeds of the disposition of the shares shall be deemed to be the cost to him of all shares and other property receivable or received by him as consideration for the disposition of the shares plus the amount of any money received by him on the disposition.

(2) **Definitions** — For the purposes of this section,

(a) "category A share" means a common share where the taxpayer has disposed of a common share in the course of a reorganization, and means a preferred share where the taxpayer has disposed of a preferred share in the course of a reorganization; and

(b) "category B share" means a preferred share where a category A share means a common share, and means a common share where a category A share means a preferred share.

(3) **Application** — This section is not applicable in any case where any of subsections 85(1) to (3) is applicable.

**Definitions [s. 86]**: "adjusted cost base" — 54, 248(1); "amount" — 248(1); "capital loss" — 39(1)(b), 248(1); "capital property" — 54, 248(1); "class of shares" — 248(6); "common share" — 248(1); "corporation" — 248(1), *Interpretation Act* 35(1); "person", "preferred share", "property", "share", "taxpayer" — 248(1).

**I.T. Application Rules [s. 86]**: 26(27) (where old shares owned since before 1972).

**Interpretation Bulletins [s. 86]**: IT-146R4: Shares entitling shareholders to choose taxable or capital dividends; IT-243R4: Dividend refund to private corporations.

### Proposed Addition — 86.1 — Foreign Spin-offs

**Technical Notes**: New section 86.1 allows for a tax deferral, generally on an elective basis, in respect of certain foreign distributions of spin-off shares by a foreign corporation that are received by Canadian resident shareholders of the foreign corporation. The rules in new section 86.1 are described below and may be applied to otherwise taxable distributions received after 1997.

**86.1 Foreign Spin-offs — (1) Eligible distribution not included in income** — Notwithstanding any other provision of this Part,

(a) the amount of an eligible distribution received by a taxpayer shall not be included in computing the income of the taxpayer; and

(b) subsection 52(2) does not apply to the eligible distribution received by the taxpayer.

**Technical Notes**: New subsection 86.1(1) provides that an amount in respect of an "eligible distribution" of spin-off shares received by a taxpayer is not to be included in computing the taxpayer's income. Further, the cost of those shares to the taxpayer is not their fair market value as otherwise provided by subsection 52(2). Rather, the cost of the original share which generated the distribution of the spin-off share will be allocated amongst the two.

New subsection 86.1(2) defines an "eligible distribution". A distribution of spin-off shares to a taxpayer is an "eligible distribution" only if a number of conditions are met. First, the distribution to the taxpayer must be because the taxpayer owns common shares in the distributing corporation (i.e., the "original shares").

644

Second, the distribution to the taxpayer must consist solely of common shares of the capital stock of another corporation owned by the distributing corporation (i.e., the "spin-off shares") — the distribution to the taxpayer must not include non-share consideration.

Third, in the case of a distribution made by a corporation in the United States,

- both the distributing corporation and the spun-off corporation (the issued shares of which are being spun-off) must be resident of the United States at the time of the distribution and must never have been resident in Canada,
- the taxpayer's original shares must be included in a class of stock that is widely held and actively traded on a prescribed stock exchange (section 3201 of the Regulations) in the United States at the time of the distribution, and
- the shareholders of the distributing corporation that are resident in the United States must not be taxable in respect of the distribution under the United States Internal Revenue Code.

Fourth, in the case of a distribution that is not in the United States and that is prescribed by regulation,

- both the distributing corporation and the spun-off corporation (the issued shares of which are being spun-off) must be resident of the same foreign country, other than the United States, with which Canada has a tax treaty and those corporations must never have been resident in Canada,
- the taxpayer's original shares must be included in a class of stock that is widely held and actively traded on a prescribed stock exchange (section 3201 of the Regulations) at the time of the distribution,
- under the law of the country in which the distributing corporation is resident, the shareholders of the distributing corporation must not be taxable in respect of the distribution, and
- such terms and conditions as are considered appropriate in the circumstances with respect to the prescription must be met.

Fifth, the distributing corporation must provide the Minister of National Revenue, within six months of the distribution, evidence satisfactory to the Minister of certain matters including the type and fair market value of each property distributed to residents of Canada and the name and address of each resident of Canada that received property because of the distribution. Property that is distributed to residents of Canada includes, for example, property that is distributed to investment dealers resident in Canada as well as individual and corporate shareholders.

Sixth, generally the taxpayer acquiring the spin-off shares must elect in writing (filed with the taxpayer's return of income for the year in which the distribution occurs) to have section 86.1 apply to the distribution and provide evidence satisfactory to the Minister of National Revenue of certain matters relating to the distribution and the taxpayer.

The information submitted to the Minister must establish, for example, the number, cost amount and fair market value of the taxpayer's original shares immediately before the distribution, and the number, and the fair market value, of the spin-off shares immediately after the distribution. Furthermore, in the case of a distribution received before October 18, 2000, while the election must be filed in writing with the Minister, it need not be included in the taxpayer's return of income for the year in which the distribution occurs.

Information filed by the corporation or the taxpayer under paragraph 86.1(2)(e) or (f) in respect of a distribution that occurred before these provisions receive Royal Assent will be considered to have been filed on time if it is filed within 90 days of that Royal Assent.

However, if the taxpayer acquiring the spin-off shares is a taxpayer to which Part XI applies, no election is required and the cost adjustment rules will apply automatically where the conditions of subsections 86.1(2) and (3) are satisfied. Part XI provides that certain deferred income trusts, pension trusts and corporations, registered investments and persons exempt from Part I tax (e.g., an employees profit sharing plan) will generally be subject to a special tax on foreign property or certain rights to acquire shares. For more detail on the foreign property rule, see the commentary on Part XI.

A trust or corporation referred to in Part L of the *Income Tax Regulations* is also subject to foreign property limits. However, because Part XI does not apply in respect of such a trust or corporation, the trust or corporation must meet all of the requirements of section 86.1, including the requirement to file an election, in order for that section to apply for the purposes of Part I and the foreign property limits in Part L of the Regulations.

**Related Provisions**: 86.1(2) — Eligible distribution.

**(2) Eligible distribution** — For the purposes of this section and Part XI, a distribution by a particular corporation that is received by a taxpayer is an eligible distribution if

(a) the distribution is with respect to all of the taxpayer's common shares of the capital stock of the particular corporation (in this section referred to as the "original shares");

(b) the distribution consists solely of common shares of the capital stock of another corporation that were owned by the particular corporation immediately before their distribution to the taxpayer (in this section referred to as the "spin-off shares");

(c) in the case of a distribution that is not prescribed,

(i) at the time of the distribution, both corporations are resident in the United States and were never resident in Canada,

(ii) at the time of the distribution, the shares of the class that includes the original shares are widely held and actively traded on a prescribed stock exchange in the United States, and

(iii) under the United States Internal Revenue Code applicable to the distribution, the shareholders of the particular corporation who are resident in the United States are not taxable in respect of the distribution;

(d) in the case of a distribution that is prescribed,

    (i) at the time of the distribution, both corporations are resident in the same country, other than the United States, with which Canada has a tax treaty (in this section referred to as the "foreign country") and were never resident in Canada,

    (ii) at the time of the distribution, the shares of the class that includes the original shares are widely held and actively traded on a prescribed stock exchange,

    (iii) under the law of the foreign country, those shareholders of the particular corporation who are resident in that country are not taxable in respect of the distribution, and

    (iv) the distribution is prescribed subject to such terms and conditions as are considered appropriate in the circumstances;

(e) before the end of the sixth month following the day on which the particular corporation first distributes a spin-off share in respect of the distribution, the particular corporation provides to the Minister information satisfactory to the Minister establishing

    (i) that, at the time of the distribution, the shares of the class that includes the original shares are widely held and actively traded on a prescribed stock exchange,

    (ii) that the particular corporation and the other corporation referred to in paragraph (b) were never resident in Canada,

    (iii) the date of the distribution,

    (iv) the type and fair market value of each property distributed to residents of Canada,

    (v) the name and address of each resident of Canada that received property with respect to the distribution,

    (vi) in the case of a distribution that is not prescribed, that the distribution is not taxable under the United States Internal Revenue Code applicable to the distribution,

    (vii) in the case of a distribution that is prescribed, that the distribution is not taxable under the law of the foreign country, and

    (viii) such other matters that are required, in prescribed form; and

(f) except where Part XI applies in respect of the taxpayer, the taxpayer elects in writing filed with the taxpayer's return of income for the taxation year in which the distribution occurs (or, in the case of a distribution received before October 18, 2000, filed with the Minister before July 2001) that this section apply to the distribution and provides information satisfactory to the Minister

    (i) of the number, cost amount (determined without reference to this section) and the fair market value of the taxpayer's original shares immediately before the distribution,

    (ii) of the number, and fair market value, of the spin-off shares immediately after the distribution of those shares to the taxpayer,

    (iii) except where the election is filed with the taxpayer's return of income for the year in which the distribution occurs, concerning the amount of the distribution, the manner in which the distribution was reported by the taxpayer and the details of any subsequent disposition of original shares or spin-off shares for the purpose of determining any gains or losses from those dispositions, and

    (iv) of such other matters that are required, in prescribed form.

**Technical Notes**: See under 86.1(1).

**Related Provisions**: 86.1(5) — Reassessments beyond limitation period; 95(2)(g.2) — Foreign accrual property income.

**(3) Cost adjustments** — Where a spin-off share is distributed by a corporation to a taxpayer pursuant to an eligible distribution with respect to an original share of the taxpayer,

(a) there shall be deducted for the purpose of computing the cost amount to the taxpayer of the original share at any time the amount determined by the formula

$$A \times B/C$$

where

A is the cost amount to the taxpayer of the original share, determined without reference to this section,

B is the fair market value of the spin-off share immediately after its distribution to the taxpayer, and

C is the total of

    (i) the fair market value of the original share immediately after the distribution of the spin-off share to the taxpayer, and

    (ii) the fair market value of the spin-off share immediately after its distribution to the taxpayer; and

(b) the cost to the taxpayer of the spin-off share is the amount by which the cost amount of the taxpayer's original share was reduced as a result of paragraph (a).

**Technical Notes**: New subsection 86.1(3) provides two rules that adjust the cost amount of a taxpayer's original shares, and spin-off shares received on an eligible distribution.

New paragraph 86.1(3)(a) provides a formula for computing the amount that is to be deducted from the cost amount of a taxpayer's original share. The amount to be deducted from the cost amount of each original share is determined by the formula:

$$A \times (B/C)$$

where

A is the cost amount to the taxpayer of the original share (determined without reference to section 86.1),

B is the fair market value of the spin-off share immediately after its distribution to the taxpayer,

C is the total of
- the fair market value of the original share immediately after the distribution of the spin-off share to the taxpayer, and
- the fair market value of spin-off share immediately after its distribution to the taxpayer.

New paragraph 86.1(3)(b) provides that the cost of a taxpayer's spin-off share is equal to the amount deducted from the cost amount of the taxpayer's original share.

*Example:*

*Assume:*

*John owns one original common share of DC Ltd. (resident in the U.S.), which distributes one spin-off share of SO Ltd. (also resident in the U.S.) on a per share basis to holders of common shares of DC Ltd. The cost amount of John's original share of DC Ltd. is $10 immediately before the distribution and its fair market value immediately after the distribution is $70. The fair market value of the SO Ltd. spin-off share is $30 immediately after the distribution.*

*Application of subsection 86.1(3):*

- *The cost amount of John's original share in DC Ltd. is reduced to $7 — i.e., the $10 cost amount less the $3 amount deducted because of paragraph 86.1(3)(a).*
    - *$10 − (A × (B/C))*
    - *A = $10.*
    - *B = $30.*
    - *C = $100 (= $70 + $30).*
- *The cost of John's spin-off share in SO Ltd. is $3 because of paragraph 86.1(3)(b).*

The adjustments in subsection 86.1(3) to the cost amount of an original share and spin-off share apply for all purposes of the Act, including the foreign property rule contained in Part XI. The application for purposes of the foreign property rule in Part XI will ensure that the level of foreign property held by a taxpayer subject to that rule is not affected solely because of an eligible distribution.

**(4) Inventory** — For the purpose of calculating the value of the property described in an inventory of a taxpayer's business,

(a) an eligible distribution to the taxpayer of a spin-off share that is included in the inventory is deemed not to be an acquisition of property in the fiscal period of the business in which the distribution occurs; and

(b) for greater certainty, the value of the spin-off share is to be included in computing the value of the inventory at the end of that fiscal period.

**Technical Notes**: New subsection 86.1(4) provides rules that apply for the purpose of calculating the value of property (an original share and a spin-off share) described in an inventory of a taxpayer's business. New paragraph 86.1(4)(a) provides that a spin-off share that is included in such an inventory is deemed not to be an acquisition of property in the fiscal period of the business in which the distribution occurs. This rule is intended to exclude the cost of the spin-off share from the cost of inventory acquired the year, as the cost of the spin-off shares will normally be reflected in the cost of the original share.

New paragraph 86.1(4)(b) provides that, for greater certainty, the value of the spin-off share is to be included in computing the value of that inventory at the end of the fiscal period.

**(5) Reassessments** — Notwithstanding subsections 152(4) to (5), the Minister may make at any time such assessments, reassessments, determinations and redeterminations that are necessary where information is obtained that the conditions in subparagraph (2)(c)(iii) or (d)(iii) are not, or are no longer, satisfied.

**Technical Notes**: New subsection 86.1(5) allows the Minister of National Revenue to make such reassessments, determinations and redeterminations as are necessary where information is obtained that the conditions in subparagraph 86.1(2)(c)(iii) or (2)(d)(iii) are not, or are no longer, satisfied. Those conditions are more fully described in the commentary to new subsection 86.1(2).

**Application**: The December 21, 2000 draft legislation, s. 38 will add s. 86.1, applicable to distributions received after 1997, except that

(a) information referred to in para. 86.1(2)(e) is deemed to be provided to the Minister of National Revenue on a timely basis if it is provided to that Minister before the day that is 90 days after the day on which the amending legislation receives Royal Assent; and

(b) the election referred to in para. 86.1(2)(f) is deemed to be filed on a timely basis if it is filed with the Minister of National Revenue before the day that is 90 days after the day on which the amending legislation receives Royal Assent.

**Notice of Ways and Means Motion, Economic Statement, October 18, 2000**:

(17) That

(a) eligible distributions and prescribed distributions received at any time after 1997 not be taxable,

(b) in respect of any such distribution, there be deducted in computing the cost amount of each original share owned by a taxpayer the amount determined by the formula

$$A \times (B/C)$$

where

A is the cost amount at that time, otherwise determined, to the taxpayer of the original share,

B is the fair market value at that time of the spin-off share received by the taxpayer in respect of the original share, and

C is the total of

(i) the fair market value at that time of the taxpayer's original share, and

(ii) the fair market value at that time of the spin-off share received by the taxpayer in respect of the original share,

(c) the cost of a spin-off share acquired by the taxpayer in respect of an original share be the amount by which the cost amount of the original share is reduced by subparagraph (b), and

(d) for the purpose of calculating the value of an inventory of a business, the acquisition of a spin-off share on such a distribution not be considered to be an acquisition of property in the year in which the distribution occurred but the value of the spin-off share be included in the value of the inventory at the end of the year.

(18) For the purposes of paragraph (17) and this paragraph,

(a) an "eligible distribution" be a distribution, with respect to all the common shares of a particular corporation owned by a taxpayer immediately before the distribution (in paragraph (17) and this paragraph referred to as the "original shares") to the taxpayer by the particular corporation, that consists solely of common shares of another corporation (in paragraph (17) and this paragraph referred to as the "spin-off shares") where

(i) at the time of the distribution, the particular corporation is a foreign corporation and both corporations are resident in the United States and were never resident in Canada,

(ii) under the Internal Revenue Code of the United States, the particular corporation and its shareholders resident in the United States are not taxable in respect of the distribution,

(iii) before the later of June 30, 2001 and the end of the sixth month following the day on which the particular corporation first distributes a spin-off share in respect of the distribution, the particular corporation provides to the Minister of National Revenue information satisfactory to the Minister establishing

(A) the date of the distribution and the type and fair market value of the property distributed to residents of Canada,

(B) the name and address of each resident of Canada that received property with respect to the distribution, and

(C) that the distribution is not taxable under the Internal Revenue Code of the United States, and

(iv) the taxpayer elects in the taxpayer's return of income for the taxation year in which the distribution occurs (or in the case of a distribution received by a taxpayer after 1997 and before October 18, 2000, by notifying the Minister in writing before July 2001) to treat the distribution as an eligible distribution and provides satisfactory evidence

(A) of the number, cost amount otherwise determined and fair market value of the original shares owned by the taxpayer at the time of the distribution,

(B) of the number and fair market value of the spin-off shares at the time those shares were received by the taxpayer, and

(C) except where the election is filed with the taxpayer's return of income for the year in which the distribution occurs, concerning the amount of the distribution and the manner in which it was reported by the taxpayer, and details of subsequent dispositions of original shares and spin-off shares as required to determine gains and losses on those dispositions,

(b) a "foreign corporation" in relation to a distribution be a corporation the common shares of which (that were original shares) were, throughout the 24-month period preceding the distribution, widely held and actively traded on a prescribed stock exchange in the United States (referred to in Income Tax Regulation 3201),

(c) a "prescribed distribution" be a distribution that would be an eligible distribution if

(i) clauses (i) and (ii) of the definition "eligible distribution" in subparagraph (a) were read as follows:

(i) at the time of the distribution, the particular corporation is a foreign corporation and both corporations are resident in the same country, other than Canada and the United States, (in this subparagraph referred to as the "foreign country") with which Canada has a tax treaty,

(ii) under the law of the foreign country, the particular corporation and its shareholders resident in that country are not taxable in respect of the distribution and the distribution is prescribed with such terms and conditions as are prescribed,

(ii) that definition were read without reference to subclause (iii)(C), and

(iii) the definition "foreign corporation" in subparagraph (b) were read without reference to the words "in the United States", and

(d) the Minister of National Revenue be permitted to reassess, after the normal reassessment period, where information is obtained by the Minister that the conditions in subparagraph (ii) of the definition "eligible distribution" or such conditions as May be prescribed in respect of a prescribed distribution are not, or are no longer, satisfied.

**Supplementary information, Economic Statement, October 18, 2000**: *Foreign Spin-offs*

In the last three years, Canadian and U.S. corporations have been undergoing corporate reorganizations on a regular basis to rationalize their business activities. These reorganizations are complex because of, amongst other things, corporate, securities and tax law requirements.

Canada has, as other countries do, its own set of detailed tax rules that allow for the tax-deferred reorganization of a corporation's business structure. A divisive reorganization (spin-off) can occur on a tax-deferred or taxable basis, depending on the facts and on the law of the jurisdiction in which the spin-off occurs and the shareholders reside. The appropriate corporate and tax law that applies to a corporation that is the subject of a reorganization is specific to the particular jurisdiction in which the corporation is incorporated and in which it is undergoing the reorganization. However, shareholders of the corporation

May not reside in that jurisdiction and, therefore, the tax law applicable to those shareholders can differ from that applicable in the country in which the corporation is reorganized.

A tax-deferred corporate divisive reorganization in the U.S. is generally not a tax-deferred transaction for shareholders who reside in Canada. Similarly, a tax-deferred divisive reorganization in Canada is generally not a tax-deferred transaction for U.S. shareholders of a reorganizing Canadian corporation. This disparity for Canadian shareholders who participate in a U.S. spin-off has been under review.

It is proposed that the *Income Tax Act* be amended, effective for distributions received after 1997, to allow a tax deferral, on an elective basis, in respect of certain distributions by foreign corporations of spin-off shares to Canadian resident shareholders. Applying the change for distributions after 1997 takes into account the three-year reassessment period when year 2000 is accounted for. In general terms, to be eligible the distribution to a Canadian resident must be made by a widely held and actively traded U.S. public corporation, of shares only. Further, the U.S. tax law must provide tax-deferred treatment to the distributing corporation and its U.S. resident shareholders.

In the case of spin-off distributions undertaken by corporations resident in other foreign countries, provision will be made to allow similar tax deferrals on a prescriptive basis.

### Proposed Amendment — Canadian/foreign share-for-share exchange

**Supplementary Information, Economic Statement, October 18, 2000**: See after 85.1.

**87. (1) Amalgamations** — In this section, an amalgamation means a merger of two or more corporations each of which was, immediately before the merger, a taxable Canadian corporation (each of which corporations is referred to in this section as a "predecessor corporation") to form one corporate entity (in this section referred to as the "new corporation") in such a manner that

    (a) all of the property (except amounts receivable from any predecessor corporation or shares of the capital stock of any predecessor corporation) of the predecessor corporations immediately before the merger becomes property of the new corporation by virtue of the merger,

    (b) all of the liabilities (except amounts payable to any predecessor corporation) of the predecessor corporations immediately before the merger become liabilities of the new corporation by virtue of the merger, and

    (c) all of the shareholders (except any predecessor corporation), who owned shares of the capital stock of any predecessor corporation immediately before the merger, receive shares of the capital stock of the new corporation because of the merger,

otherwise than as a result of the acquisition of property of one corporation by another corporation, pursuant to the purchase of that property by the other corporation or as a result of the distribution of that property to the other corporation on the winding-up of the corporation.

### Proposed Amendment — Amalgamation of Farmers' and Fishermen's Insurers

**Letter from Department of Finance, February 21, 2000:**

Dear [xxx]

Thank you for your letter of November 8, 1999 regarding section 87 of the *Income Tax Act* (the "Act") and the treatment accorded thereunder to insurance corporations earning premium income in respect of the insurance of property used in farming or fishing.

In your letter you express concern that an amalgamation of insurers of farmers and fishermen partially, or totally, exempt from tax under paragraph 149(1)(t) of the Act could trigger significant tax consequences. You ask that I consider amending the Act so that insurers of farmers and fishermen can, on amalgamation, benefit from the tax rollover provisions contained in section 87.

There does not appear to be a policy reason for not allowing subsection 87(1) of the Act to apply to an amalgamation of two or more farmers' and fishermen's insurers described in paragraph 149(1)(t) of the Act. Consequently, I am prepared to support an amendment to the Act to provide that subsection 87(1) of the Act apply to amalgamations of insurers exempt, or partially exempt, from tax under paragraph 149(1)(t) occurring after 1999.

Thank you for your helpful advice on this matter.

Sincerely,

The Honourable Paul Martin, P.C., M.P.
Minister of Finance

**Related Provisions**: 53(6) — Effect of amalgamation or merger on adjusted cost base of share, partnership interest or trust interest; 69(13) — Amalgamation or merger — deemed proceeds of disposition; 80.03(1), (3)(a)(ii) — Capital gain on amalgamation following debt forgiveness; 87(1.1) — Shares deemed to have been received by virtue of merger; 87(8) — Foreign mergers; 87(9) — Triangular amalgamations; 89(1) "Canadian corporation" — Whether amalgamated corporation is a Canadian corporation; 89(2) — Where corporation is beneficiary under life insurance policy; 112(7) — Application of stop-loss rule following amalgamation; 128.2 — Predecessor corporations taken on residence status of amalgamated corporation; 137(4.3) — Determination of preferred-rate amount; 139.1(3)(g) — Where insurance corporation merges causing demutualization; 204.85(3) — Rules on amalgamation of LSVCCs; 251(3.1), (3.2) — Amalgamated corporation deemed related to predecessor. See additional Related Provisions and Definitions at end of s. 87.

**Notes**: 87(2) provides extensive rules for rollovers and carryforwards of amounts on an amalgamation. See Notes to 248(1) "business number" re whether a new BN must be obtained.

87(1)(c) amended by 1992 technical bill, effective for amalgamations after 1989, to add "who owned shares of the capital stock". The change clarifies that shareholders who did not actually own shares (such as a policyholder of a mutual insurance corporation) do not have to receive shares of the new corporation for the merger to qualify as an amalgamation.

**I.T. Application Rules**: 26(28).

**Interpretation Bulletins**: IT-302R3: Losses of a corporation — the effect that acquisitions of control, amalgamations, and windings-up have on their deductibility — after January 15, 1987. See also list at end of s. 87.

**Information Circulars**: 88-2, paras. 20, 28: General anti-avoidance rule — section 245 of the *Income Tax Act*; 88-2 Supplement, para. 9: General anti-avoidance rule — section 245 of the *Income Tax Act*.

**Advance Tax Rulings**: ATR-29: Amalgamation of social clubs; ATR-55: Amalgamation followed by sale of shares; ATR-59: Financing exploration and development through limited partnerships.

**(1.1) Shares deemed to have been received by virtue of merger** — For the purposes of paragraph (1)(c) and the *Income Tax Application Rules*, where there is a merger of

(a) a corporation and one or more of its subsidiary wholly-owned corporations, or

(b) two or more corporations each of which is a subsidiary wholly-owned corporation of the same corporation,

any shares of the capital stock of a predecessor corporation owned by a shareholder (except any predecessor corporation) immediately before the merger that were not cancelled on the merger shall be deemed to be shares of the capital stock of the new corporation received by the shareholder by virtue of the merger as consideration for the disposition of the shares of the capital stock of the predecessor corporations.

**Related Provisions**: 87(1.4) — Subsidiary wholly-owned corporation. See additional Related Provisions and Definitions at end of s. 87.

**Interpretation Bulletins**: See list at end of s. 87.

**(1.2) New corporation continuation of a predecessor** — Where there has been an amalgamation of corporations described in paragraph (1.1)(a) or of 2 or more corporations each of which is a subsidiary wholly-owned corporation of the same person, the new corporation shall, for the purposes of section 29 of the *Income Tax Application Rules*, subsection 59(3.3) and sections 66, 66.1, 66.2, 66.4 and 66.7, be deemed to be the same corporation as, and a continuation of, each predecessor corporation, except that this subsection shall not affect the determination of any predecessor corporation's fiscal period, taxable income or tax payable.

**Proposed Amendment — 87(1.2)**

**(1.2) New corporation continuation of a predecessor** — Where there has been an amalgamation of corporations described in paragraph (1.1)(a) or of two or more corporations each of which is a subsidiary wholly-owned corporation of the same person, the new corporation is, for the purposes of section 29 of the *Income Tax Application Rules*, subsection 59(3.3) and sections 66, 66.1, 66.2, 66.21, 66.4 and 66.7, deemed to be the same corporation as, and a continuation of, each predecessor corporation, except that this subsection does not affect the determination of any predecessor corporation's fiscal period, taxable income or tax payable.

**Application**: The December 21, 2000 draft legislation, s. 39, will amend subsec. 87(1.2) to read as above, applicable to amalgamations that occur after 2000.

**Technical Notes**: Section 87 sets out rules that apply where there has been an amalgamation of two or more taxable Canadian corporations to form a new corporation.

Where there has been an amalgamation of two or more corporations, the successor rules in section 66.7 generally provide that unclaimed resource expenditures of a predecessor corporation may be deducted by the new corporation only within the limitations of the successor rules (i.e., against "streamed income" related to the predecessor corporation's resource properties). However, under subsection 87(1.2) the successor rules do not apply where there has been an amalgamation of a corporation and one or more of its subsidiary wholly-owned corporations (as defined by subsection 87(1.4)) or an amalgamation of two or more corporations which are subsidiary wholly-owned corporations of the same corporation.

Subsection 87(1.2) is amended so that the same exception applies in respect of foreign resource expenses calculated under new section 66.21.

**Related Provisions**: 87(1.4) — Subsidiary wholly-owned corporation. See additional Related Provisions and Definitions at end of s. 87.

**Notes**: 87(1.2) amended by 1993 technical bill, effective for amalgamations occurring after December 21, 1992, to extend its application to two subsidiary wholly-owned corporations of any "person" (i.e., including an individual, not just of a corporation). For earlier amalgamations since 1983, read simply "Where there has been an amalgamation of corporations described in paragraph (1.1)(a) or (b), the new corporation shall...".

**Regulations**: 1214 (resource and processing allowances — purposes for which amalgamated corporation deemed to be continuation of predecessors).

**Interpretation Bulletins**: IT-125R4: Dispositions of resource properties. See also list at end of s. 87.

**(1.3)** [Repealed under former Act]

**Notes**: 87(1.3), repealed in 1985, dealt with an amalgamation of a "shareholder corporation" (under the joint exploration corporation rules) with its subsidiary. This case is now covered by 87(1.2).

**(1.4) Definition of "subsidiary wholly-owned corporation"** — Notwithstanding subsection 248(1), for the purposes of this subsection and subsections (1.1), (1.2) and (2.11), "subsidiary wholly-owned corporation" of a person (in this subsection referred to as the "parent") means a corporation all the issued and outstanding shares of the capital stock of which belong to

(a) the parent;

(b) a corporation that is a subsidiary wholly-owned corporation of the parent; or

(c) any combination of persons each of which is a person described in paragraph (a) or (b).

**Related Provisions**: See Related Provisions and Definitions at end of s. 87.

**Notes**: Application of 87(1.4) extended to 87(2.11) by 1992 technical bill, effective for amalgamations after 1989. 87(1.4) amended by 1993 technical bill, effective for amalgamations occurring after December 21, 1992, to change "corporation(s)" to "person(s)" in three places; see Notes to 87(1.2).

**Interpretation Bulletins**: See list at end of s. 87.

**(1.5) Definitions** — For the purpose of this section, "financial institution", "mark-to-market property" and "specified debt obligation" have the meanings assigned by subsection 142.2(1).

**Notes**: 87(1.5) added by 1994 tax amendments bill (Part III), effective for taxation years that end after February 22, 1994.

**(2) Rules applicable** — Where there has been an amalgamation of two or more corporations after 1971 the following rules apply:

**Notes**: See Notes to 248(1)"business number" re whether a new BN must be obtained.

(a) **taxation year** — for the purposes of this Act, the corporate entity formed as a result of the amalgamation shall be deemed to be a new corporation the first taxation year of which shall be deemed to have commenced at the time of the amalgamation, and a taxation year of a predecessor corporation that would otherwise have ended after the amalgamation shall be deemed to have ended immediately before the amalgamation;

**Notes**: For some of the effects of the deemed year-end, see Notes to 249(4).

This rule can cause loss carryforwards (see 87(2.1)) to expire a year earlier than they otherwise would, even where they are still deductible after the amalgamation.

**Interpretation Bulletins**: IT-179R: Change of fiscal period. See also list at end of s. 87.

**Information Circulars**: 88-2, para. 21: General anti-avoidance rule — section 245 of the *Income Tax Act*.

(b) **inventory** — for the purpose of computing the income of the new corporation, where the property described in the inventory, if any, of the new corporation at the beginning of its first taxation year includes property that was described in the inventory of a predecessor corporation at the end of the taxation year of the predecessor corporation that ended immediately before the amalgamation (which taxation year of a predecessor corporation is referred to in this section as its "last taxation year"), the property so included shall be deemed to have been acquired by the new corporation at the beginning of its first taxation year for an amount determined in accordance with section 10 as the value thereof for the purpose of computing the income of the predecessor corporation for its last taxation year, except that where the income of the predecessor corporation for its last taxation year from a farming business was computed in accordance with the cash method, the amount so determined in respect of inventory owned in connection with that business shall be deemed to be the total of all amounts each of which is an amount included because of paragraph 28(1)(b) or (c) in computing that income for that year and, where the income of the new corporation from a farming business is computed in accordance with the cash method, for the purpose of section 28,

(i) an amount equal to that total shall be deemed to have been paid by the new corporation, and

(ii) the new corporation shall be deemed to have purchased the property for an amount equal to that total,

in its first taxation year and in the course of carrying on that business;

**Notes**: 87(2)(b) amended by 1991 technical bill, effective for amalgamations occurring after 1988, except that, in its application with respect to property acquired from a predecessor corporation the last taxation year of which commenced before 1989, ignore the reference to 28(1)(c).

**Interpretation Bulletins**: IT-427R: Livestock of farmers. See also list at end of s. 87.

(c) **method adopted for computing income** — in computing the income of the new corporation for a taxation year from a business or property

(i) there shall be included any amount received or receivable (depending on the method followed by the new corporation in computing its income for that year) by it in that year that would, if it had been received or receivable (depending on the method followed by the predecessor corporation in computing its income for its last taxation year) by the predecessor corporation in its last taxation year, have been included in computing the income of the predecessor corporation for that year, and

(ii) there may be deducted any amount paid or payable (depending on the method followed by the new corporation in computing its income for that year) by it in that year that would, if it had been paid or payable (depending on the method followed by the predecessor corporation in computing its income for its last taxation year) by the predecessor corporation in its last taxation year, have been deductible in computing the income of the predecessor corporation for that year;

**Related Provisions**: 88(1)(e.2) — Winding-up. See additional Related Provisions and Definitions at end of s. 87.

**Interpretation Bulletins**: See list at end of s. 87.

(d) **depreciable property** — for the purposes of sections 13 and 20 and any regulations made under paragraph 20(1)(a),

(i) where depreciable property of a prescribed class has been acquired by the new corporation from a predecessor corporation, the capital cost of the property to the new corporation shall be deemed to be the amount that was the capital cost of the property to the predecessor corporation, and

(ii) in determining the undepreciated capital cost to the new corporation of depreciable property of a prescribed class at any time,

(A) there shall be added to the capital cost to the new corporation of depreciable property of the class acquired before that time the cost amount, immediately before the amalgamation, to a predecessor corporation of each property included in that class by the new corporation,

(B) there shall be subtracted from the capital cost to the new corporation of depreciable property of that class acquired before that time the capital cost to the new corporation of property of that class acquired by virtue of the amalgamation,

(C) a reference in subparagraph 13(5)(b)(ii) to amounts that would have been deducted in respect of property in computing a taxpayer's income shall be construed as including a reference to amounts that would have been deducted in respect of that property in computing a predecessor corporation's income, and

(D) where depreciable property that is deemed by subsection 37(6) to be a separate prescribed class has been acquired by the new corporation from a predecessor corporation, the property shall continue to be deemed to be of that same separate prescribed class;

**Notes:** 87(2)(d)(ii)(A) amended by 1988 tax reform. For amalgamations before 1988, read:

(A) there shall be added to the capital cost to the new corporation of depreciable property of that class acquired before that time the undepreciated capital cost to each of the predecessor corporations of property of that class immediately before the amalgamation,

87(2)(d)(ii)(C) amended by 1991 technical bill, effective for taxation years beginning after June 17, 1987 that end after 1987, to change reference from 13(5)(a)(ii) to 13(5)(b)(ii). Amended by 1996 Budget, effective for taxation years that begin after 1996, to reflect minor wording changes in 13(5)(b)(ii). Before the 1996 Budget amendment, read:

(C) a reference in subparagraph 13(5)(b)(ii) to amounts that would have been deducted by a taxpayer in respect of transferred property shall be construed as including a reference to amounts that would have been deducted by a predecessor corporation in respect of that property, and

**I.T. Application Rules:** 20(1.2) (transfer of depreciable property by person who owned it before 1972).

**Interpretation Bulletins:** See list at end of s. 87.

(d.1) **depreciable property acquired from predecessor corporation** — for the purposes of this Act, where depreciable property (other than property of a prescribed class) has been acquired by the new corporation from a predecessor corporation, the new corporation shall be deemed to have acquired the property before 1972 at an actual cost equal to the actual cost of the property to the predecessor corporation, and the new corporation shall be deemed to have been allowed the total of all amounts allowed to the predecessor corporation in respect of the property, under regulations made under paragraph 20(1)(a), in computing the income of the predecessor corporation;

**Related Provisions:** 88(1)(e.2) — Winding-up. See additional Related Provisions and Definitions at end of s. 87.

**I.T. Application Rules:** 20(1.2) (transfer of depreciable property by person who owned it before 1972).

**Interpretation Bulletins:** See list at end of s. 87.

(e) **capital property** — subject to paragraph (e.4) and subsection 142.6(5), where a capital property (other than depreciable property or an interest in a partnership) has been acquired by the new corporation from a predecessor corporation, the cost of the property to the new corporation shall be deemed to be the amount that was the adjusted cost base of the property to the predecessor corporation immediately before the amalgamation;

**Related Provisions:** 53(6) — Effect of amalgamation on ACB of share, partnership interest or trust interest; 69(13) — Amalgamation or merger. See additional Related Provisions and Definitions at end of s. 87.

**Notes:** References to 87(2)(e.4) and 142.6(5) added to 87(2)(e) by 1994 tax amendments bill (Part III), effective for taxation years that end after February 22, 1994.

87(2)(e) amended in 1987. For amalgamations before January 16, 1987, delete the words "or an interest in a partnership".

**Interpretation Bulletins:** See list at end of s. 87.

(e.1) **partnership interest** — where a partnership interest that is capital property has been acquired from a predecessor corporation to which the new corporation was related, for the purposes of this Act, the cost of that partnership interest to the new corporation shall be deemed to be the amount that was the cost of that interest to the predecessor corporation and, in respect of that partnership interest, the new corporation shall be deemed to be the same corporation as and a continuation of the predecessor corporation;

**Related Provisions:** 53(1)(e), 53(2)(c) — ACB — partnership interest; 88(1)(c), 88(1)(e.2) — Winding-up; 100(2.1) — Gain from disposition of partnership interest on amalgamation. See additional Related Provisions and Definitions at end of s. 87.

**Notes:** 87(2)(e.1) added in 1987, effective for amalgamations after January 15, 1987.

**Interpretation Bulletins:** See list at end of s. 87.

(e.2) **security or debt obligation** — subject to paragraphs (e.3) and (e.4) and subsection 142.6(5), where a property that is a security or debt obligation (other than a capital property or an inventory) of a predecessor corporation used by it in the year in, or held by it in the year in the course of, carrying on the business of insurance or lending money in the taxation year ending immediately before the amalgamation has been acquired by the new corporation from the predecessor corporation, the cost of the property to the new corporation shall be deemed to be the amount that was the cost amount of the property to the predecessor corporation immediately before the amalgamation;

**Notes**: References to 87(2)(e.3), (e.4) and 142.6(5) added to 87(2)(e.2) by 1994 tax amendments bill (Part III), effective for taxation years that end after February 22, 1994.

87(2)(e.2) added by 1988 tax reform, effective for amalgamations after December 15, 1987.

**Interpretation Bulletins**: See list at end of s. 87.

(e.3) **financial institutions — specified debt obligation** — where the new corporation is a financial institution in its first taxation year, it shall be deemed, in respect of a specified debt obligation (other than a mark-to-market property) acquired from a predecessor corporation that was a financial institution in its last taxation year, to be the same corporation as, and a continuation of, the predecessor corporation;

**Related Provisions**: 87(1.5) — Interpretation; 88(1)(e.2) — Winding-up; 142.6(5) — Parallel rule for rollover transactions generally. See additional Related Provisions and Definitions at end of s. 87.

**Notes**: 87(2)(e.3) added by 1994 tax amendments bill (Part III), effective for amalgamations occurring, and windups beginning, after February 22, 1994.

(e.4) **financial institutions — mark-to-market property** — where

(i) the new corporation is a financial institution in its first taxation year and a property acquired by the new corporation from a predecessor corporation is a mark-to-market property of the new corporation for the year, or

(ii) a predecessor corporation was a financial institution in its last taxation year and a property acquired by the new corporation from the predecessor corporation was a mark-to-market property of the predecessor corporation for the year,

the cost of the property to the new corporation shall be deemed to be the amount that was the fair market value of the property immediately before the amalgamation;

**Related Provisions**: 87(1.5) — Interpretation; 87(2)(e), (e.2) — Rule overrides normal rules for capital property, securities and debt obligations; 87(2)(g.2), 142.6(1)(b) — Predecessor non-financial institution deemed to have disposed of property before amalgamation; 142.5(2) — Predecessor financial institution deemed to have disposed of property before amalgamation; 142.6(5), (6) — Acquisition of specified debt obligation by financial institution in rollover transaction. See additional Related Provisions and Definitions at end of s. 87.

**Notes**: 87(2)(e.4) added by 1994 tax amendments bill (Part III), effective for amalgamations occurring after October 1994.

(e.5) **financial institutions — mark-to-market property** — for the purposes of subsections 112(5) to (5.2) and (5.4) and the definition "mark-to-market property" in subsection 142.2(1), the new corporation shall be deemed to be the same corporation as, and a continuation of, each predecessor corporation;

**Related Provisions**: 87(1.5) — Interpretation; 88(1)(h) — Parallel rule on windup; 142.7(6)(a) — Parallel rule on conversion of foreign bank affiliate to branch. See additional Related Provisions and Definitions at end of s. 87.

**Notes**: 87(2)(e.5) added by 1994 tax amendments bill (Part III), effective for amalgamations occurring at any time (including those before Royal Assent to the amendments bill).

(f) **eligible capital property** — for the purposes of determining under this Act any amount relating to cumulative eligible capital, an eligible capital amount, an eligible capital expenditure or eligible capital property, the new corporation shall be deemed to be the same corporation as, and a continuation of, each predecessor corporation;

**Notes**: 87(2)(f) amended by 1992 technical bill, effective for amalgamations after June 1988. For amalgamations from 1972 through June 1988, read:

(f) cumulative eligible capital — for the purposes of computing the cumulative eligible capital of the new corporation at any time in respect of a business, where a predecessor corporation carried on a business that is carried on by the new corporation, the amount of the cumulative eligible capital of the predecessor corporation immediately before the amalgamation in respect of that business shall be added to the amount determined for A in the definition "cumulative eligible capital" in subsection 14(5) in respect of that business;

**Interpretation Bulletins**: See list at end of s. 87.

(f.1) [Repealed]

**Notes**: 87(2)(f.1) repealed by 1992 technical bill, retroactive to its introduction, in conjunction with the amendment to 87(2)(f) above.

(g) **reserves** — for the purpose of computing the income of the new corporation for a taxation year,

(i) any amount that has been deducted as a reserve in computing the income of a predecessor corporation for its last taxation year shall be deemed to have been deducted as a reserve in computing the income of the new corporation for a taxation year immediately preceding its first taxation year, and

(ii) any amount deducted under paragraph 20(1)(p) in computing the income of a predecessor corporation for its last taxation year or a previous taxation year shall be deemed to have been deducted under that paragraph in computing the income of the new corporation for a taxation year immediately preceding its first taxation year;

**Related Provisions**: 88(1)(e.2) — Winding-up.

(g.1) **continuation** — for the purposes of sections 12.3 and 12.4, subsection 20(26) and section 26, the new corporation shall be deemed to be the same corporation as, and a continuation of, each predecessor corporation;

**Related Provisions**: 88(1)(e.2) — Winding-up. See additional Related Provisions and Definitions at end of s. 87.

**Notes**: 87(2)(g.1) added by 1986 Budget, effective 1980.

**Interpretation Bulletins**: See list at end of s. 87.

(g.2) **financial institution rules** — for the purposes of paragraphs 142.4(4)(c) and (d) and subsections 142.5(5) and (7) and 142.6(1), the new corporation shall be deemed to be the same corporation as, and a continuation of, each predecessor corporation;

**Related Provisions**: 88(1)(e.2) — Winding-up; 142.6(1)(b) — Deemed disposition of specified debt obligations and mark-to-market properties on becoming a financial institution. See additional Related Provisions and Definitions at end of s. 87.

**Notes**: 87(2)(g.2) added by 1994 tax amendments bill (Part III), effective for taxation years that end after February 22, 1994.

(g.3) **superficial losses** — for the purposes of applying subsections 13(21.2), 14(12), 18(15) and 40(3.4) to any property that was disposed of by a predecessor corporation before the amalgamation, the new corporation is deemed to be the same corporation as, and a continuation of, each predecessor corporation;

**Related Provisions**: 88(1)(e.2) — Winding-up. See additional Related Provisions and Definitions at end of s. 87.

**Notes**: 87(2)(g.3) added by 1995-97 technical bill, effective for amalgamations occurring (and, by 88(1)(e.2), for windups beginning) after April 26, 1995.

(g.4) **superficial losses — capital property** — for the purpose of applying paragraph 40(3.5)(c) in respect of any share that was acquired by a predecessor corporation, the new corporation is deemed to be the same corporation as, and a continuation of, each predecessor corporation;

**Related Provisions**: 88(1)(e.2) — Winding-up. See additional Related Provisions and Definitions at end of s. 87.

**Notes**: 87(2)(g.4) added by 1995-97 technical bill, effective for amalgamations occurring (and, by 88(1)(e.2), for windups beginning) after April 26, 1995.

(h) **debts** — for the purpose of computing a deduction from the income of the new corporation for a taxation year under paragraph 20(1)(l), (l.1) or (p)

(i) any debt owing to a predecessor corporation that was included in computing the income of the predecessor corporation for its last taxation year or a preceding taxation year,

(ii) where a predecessor corporation was an insurer or a corporation the ordinary business of which included the lending of money, any loan or lending asset made or acquired by the predecessor corporation in the ordinary course of its business of insurance or the lending of money, or

(iii) where a predecessor corporation was an insurer or a corporation the ordinary business of which included the lending of money, any instrument or commitment described in paragraph 20(1)(l.1) that was issued, made or assumed by the predecessor corporation in the ordinary course of its business of insurance or the lending of money,

and that by reason of the amalgamation, has been acquired by the new corporation, shall be deemed to be a debt owing to the new corporation that was included in computing its income for a preceding taxation year, a loan or lending asset made or acquired or an instrument or commitment that was issued, made or assumed by the new corporation in a preceding taxation year in the ordinary course of its business of insurance or the lending of money, as the case may be;

**Related Provisions**: 80(2) — Deemed settlement on amalgamation; 88(1)(e.2) — Winding-up. See additional Related Provisions and Definitions at end of s. 87.

**Interpretation Bulletins**: See list at end of s. 87.

(h.1) **debts** — for the purposes of section 61.4, the description of F in subsection 79(3), the definition "forgiven amount" in subsection 80(1), subsection 80.03(7) and section 80.04, the new corporation shall be deemed to be the same corporation as, and a continuation of, each predecessor corporation;

**Related Provisions**: 88(1)(e.2) — Winding-up. See additional Related Provisions and Definitions at end of s. 87.

**Notes**: 87(2)(h.1) added by 1994 tax amendments bill (Part I), effective for taxation years that end after February 21, 1994. It covers various rules relating to debt forgiveness (see also 87(2)(l.21) for others). It does not refer to 56.3 because 87(2)(g) provides for reserves claimed by a predecessor (including reserves under 61.4) to be added back to the amalgamated corporation's income.

(i) **special reserve** — for the purpose of computing a deduction from the income of the new corporation for a taxation year under paragraph 20(1)(n), any amount included in computing the income of a predecessor corporation from a business for its last taxation year or a previous taxation year in respect of property sold in the course of the business shall be deemed to have been included in computing the income of the new corporation from the business for a previous year in respect of that property;

**Related Provisions**: 88(1)(e.2) — Winding-up. See additional Related Provisions and Definitions at end of s. 87.

**Interpretation Bulletins**: IT-154R: Special reserves. See also list at end of s. 87.

(j) **special reserves** — for the purposes of paragraphs 20(1)(m), (m.1) and (m.2), subsection 20(24) and section 34.2, the new corporation is deemed to be the same corporation as, and a continuation of, each predecessor corporation;

**Related Provisions**: 88(1)(e.2) — Winding-up. See additional Related Provisions and Definitions at end of s. 87.

**Notes**: 87(2)(j) reworded by 1992 technical bill, effective for amalgamations occurring (and, by 88(1)(e.2), for windings-up beginning) after 1990. The substantive change was to delete reference to s. 32 and add reference to 20(24).

Reference to 34.2 added to 87(2)(j) by 1995 Budget, effective for amalgamations that occur, and (per 88(1)(e.2)) windups that begin, after 1994.

**Interpretation Bulletins**: IT-154R: Special reserves. See also list at end of s. 87.

(j.1) **inventory adjustment** — for the purposes of paragraph 20(1)(ii), an amount required by paragraph 12(1)(r) to be included in computing the income of a predecessor corporation for its last taxation year shall be deemed to be an amount required by paragraph 12(1)(r) to be included in computing the income of the new corporation for a taxation year immediately preceding its first taxation year;

**Related Provisions**: 88(1)(e.2) — Winding-up. See additional Related Provisions and Definitions at end of s. 87.

**Interpretation Bulletins**: See list at end of s. 87.

(j.2) **prepaid expenses and matchable expenditures** — for the purposes of subsections 18(9) and (9.01), section 18.1 and paragraph 20(1)(mm), the new corporation is deemed to be the same corporation as, and a continuation of, each predecessor corporation;

**Related Provisions**: 88(1)(e.2) — Winding-up. See additional Related Provisions and Definitions at end of s. 87.

**Notes**: Reference in 87(2)(j.2) to 18(9.01) added by 1994 Budget, effective 1994. Reference to 18.1 added by 1995-97 technical bill, effective November 18, 1996.

**Interpretation Bulletins**: See list at end of s. 87.

(j.3) **employee benefit plans, etc. [SDAs, RCAs]** — for the purposes of paragraphs 12(1)(n.1), (n.2) and (n.3) and 20(1)(r), (oo) and (pp), section 32.1, paragraph 104(13)(b) and Part XI.3, the new corporation shall be deemed to be the same corporation as, and a continuation of, each predecessor corporation;

**Related Provisions**: 88(1)(e.2) — Winding-up. See additional Related Provisions and Definitions at end of s. 87.

**Notes**: Reference to 20(1)(pp) in 87(2)(j.3) added by 1991 technical bill, retroactive to 1986. Reference to 12(1)(n.1) and 104(13)(b) added by 1993 technical bill, effective for taxation years that end after December 21, 1992.

**Interpretation Bulletins**: IT-502: Employee benefit plans and employee trusts. See also list at end of s. 87.

(j.4) **accrual rules** — for the purposes of subsections 12(3) and (9), section 12.2, subsection 20(19) and the definition "adjusted cost basis" in subsection 148(9) of this Act, and subsections 12(5) and (6) and paragraph 56(1)(d.1) of the *Income Tax Act*, chapter 148 of the Revised Statutes of Canada, 1952, the new corporation shall be deemed to be the same corporation as, and a continuation of, each predecessor corporation;

**Related Provisions**: 88(1)(e.2) — Winding-up. See additional Related Provisions and Definitions at end of s. 87.

**I.T. Application Rules**: 69 (meaning of "*Income Tax Act*, chapter 148 of the Revised Statutes of Canada, 1952").

**Interpretation Bulletins**: See list at end of s. 87.

(j.5) **cancellation of lease** — for the purposes of paragraphs 20(1)(z) and (z.1), the new corporation shall be deemed to be the same corporation as, and a continuation of, each predecessor corporation;

**Related Provisions**: 88(1)(e.2) — Winding-up. See additional Related Provisions and Definitions at end of s. 87.

**Interpretation Bulletins**: See list at end of s. 87.

(j.6) **continuing corporation** — for the purposes of paragraphs 12(1)(t) and (x), subsections 12(2.2) and 13(7.1), (7.4) and (24), paragraphs 13(27)(b) and (28)(c), subsections 13(29) and 18(9.1), paragraphs 20(1)(e), (e.1) and (hh), sections 20.1 and 32, paragraph 37(1)(c), subsection 39(13), subparagraphs 53(2)(c)(vi) and (h)(ii), paragraph 53(2)(s), subsections 53(2.1), 66(11.4) and 66.7(11), section 139.1, subsection 152(4.3), the determination of D in the definition "undepreciated capital cost" in subsection 13(21) and the determination of L in the definition "cumulative Canadian exploration expense" in subsection 66.1(6), the new corporation is deemed to be the same corporation as, and a continuation of, each predecessor corporation;

**Related Provisions**: 55(3.2)(b) — Continuation for purposes of butterfly reorganizations and capital gains stripping; 88(1)(e.2) — Winding-up. See additional Related Provisions and Definitions at end of s. 87.

**Notes**: 87(2)(j.6) amended by 1999 Budget, effective for amalgamations that occur (and, by 88(1)(e.2), for windups that begin), after December 15, 1998, to add reference to 139.1 (demutualization of insurance companies).

87(2)(j.6) amended by 1993 technical bill, to add reference to 20(1)(e.1) effective 1988, and reference to 20.1 effective 1994.

Amended by 1992 technical bill, effective February 1990, to add references to 12(2.2), 39(13) and 152(4.3).

Amended by 1991 technical bill, effective 1990, to add references to 13(27)(b), 13(28)(c), 13(29), 18(9.1) and 32.

Amended by 1988 tax reform, effective 1988, to add reference to 20(1)(e).

**Interpretation Bulletins**: See list at end of s. 87.

(j.7) **certain transfers and loans [attribution rules]** — for the purposes of sections 74.4 and 74.5, the new corporation shall be deemed to be the same corporation as, and a continuation of, each predecessor corporation;

**Related Provisions**: 88(1)(e.2) — Winding-up. See additional Related Provisions and Definitions at end of s. 87.

**Notes**: 87(2)(j.7) added by 1985 Budget bill, effective for amalgamations after November 21, 1985.

**Interpretation Bulletins**: See list at end of s. 87.

(j.8) **international banking centre business** — for the purposes of section 33.1, the new corporation shall be deemed to be the same corporation as, and a continuation of, each predecessor corporation;

**Related Provisions**: 88(1)(e.2) — Winding-up. See additional Related Provisions and Definitions at end of s. 87.

**Interpretation Bulletins**: See list at end of s. 87.

(j.9) **Part VI and Part I.3 tax [pre-1992]** — for the purposes of determining the amount deductible by the new corporation for any taxation year under section 125.2 or 125.3, the new corporation shall be deemed to be the same corporation as, and a continuation of, each predecessor corporation;

**Related Provisions**: 88(1)(e.2) — Winding-up. See additional Related Provisions and Definitions at end of s. 87.

**Interpretation Bulletins**: See list at end of s. 87.

(j.91) **Part I.3 and Part VI tax** — for the purpose of determining the amount deductible under subsection 181.1(4) or 190.1(3) by the new corporation for any taxation year, the new corporation is deemed to be the same corporation as, and a continuation of, each predecessor corporation, except that this paragraph does not affect the determination of the fiscal period of any corporation or the tax payable by any predecessor corporation;

**Related Provisions**: 88(1)(e.2) — Winding-up. See additional Related Provisions and Definitions at end of s. 87.

**Notes**: All the words beginning "except that..." added by 1995-97 technical bill, effective for amalgamations occurring (and, by 88(1)(e.2), for windups beginning) after April 26, 1995.

87(2)(j.91) added by 1992 technical bill, effective for amalgamations occurring (and, by 88(1)(e.2), for windings-up beginning) after 1990.

(j.92) **subsec. 125(5.1) [small business deduction]** — for the purposes of subsection 125(5.1), the new corporation shall be deemed to be the same corporation as, and a continuation of, each predecessor corporation;

**Related Provisions**: 88(1)(e.2) — Winding-up. See additional Related Provisions and Definitions at end of s. 87.

**Notes**: 87(2)(j.92) added by 1994 Budget, effective for taxation years that end after June 1994.

(j.93) **mining reclamation trusts [and qualifying environmental trusts]** — for the purposes of paragraphs 12(1)(z.1) and (z.2) and 20(1)(ss) and (tt) and sections 107.3 and 127.41, the new corporation shall be deemed to be the same corporation as, and a continuation of, each predecessor corporation;

**Related Provisions**: 88(1)(e.2) — Winding-up. See additional Related Provisions and Definitions at end of s. 87.

**Notes**: 87(2)(j.93) added by 1994 Budget, effective for amalgamations that occur and windups (by 88(1)(e.2)) that begin after February 22, 1994.

(j.94) **film or video productions** — for the purposes of sections 125.4 and 125.5, the new corporation is deemed to be the same corporation as, and a continuation of, each predecessor corporation;

**Related Provisions**: 88(1)(e.2) — Winding-up. See additional Related Provisions and Definitions at end of s. 87.

**Notes**: Reference to 125.5 added by 1995-97 technical bill, effective for amalgamations occurring (and, by 88(1)(e.2), for windups beginning) after October 1997.

87(2)(j.94) added by 1995 Budget, effective for amalgamations that occur, and (per 88(1)(e.2)) windups that begin, after 1994.

### Proposed Addition — 87(2)(j.95)

(j.95) **non-resident trusts and foreign investment entities** — for the purposes of sections 94 to 94.3, the new corporation is deemed to be the same corporation as, and a continuation of, each predecessor corporation;

**Application**: The June 22, 2000 draft legislation, s. 8, will add para. 87(2)(j.95), applicable after 2000.

**Technical Notes**: Section 87 of the Act sets out rules that apply on the amalgamation of two or more taxable Canadian corporations. The amalgamated corporation is generally treated as a continuation of the predecessor corporations for the purposes of the Act.

New paragraph 87(2)(j.95) provides that, where there has been an amalgamation of two or more taxable Canadian corporations, the amalgamated corporation is deemed to be a continuation of its predecessor corporations for the purposes of sections 94 to 94.3, which relate to foreign trusts and foreign investment entities. Thus, for example, an amalgamated corporation will be considered to be a "contributor" to a trust (as defined in subsection 94(1)) if any predecessor corporation was a contributor to the trust. In addition, the new corporation's "deferral amount" under paragraph 94.2(1)(b) in respect of an interest in a foreign investment entity will be determined in the same manner as a predecessor's "deferral amount" in respect of the same interest.

Because of the operation of paragraph 88(1)(e.2), new paragraph 87(2)(j.95) also applies to windings-up to which section 88 applies.

**Related Provisions**: 88(1)(e.2) — Winding-up. See additional Related Provisions and Definitions at end of s. 87.

(k) **certain payments to employees** — for the purpose of subsection 6(3), any amount received by a person from the new corporation that would, if received by the person from a predecessor corporation, be deemed for the purpose of section 5 to be remuneration for that person's services rendered as an officer or during a period of employment, shall be deemed for the purposes of section 5 to be remuneration for services so rendered by the person;

**Related Provisions**: 88(1)(e.2) — Winding-up. See additional Related Provisions and Definitions at end of s. 87.

(l) **scientific research and experimental development** — for the purposes of section 37 and Part VIII, the new corporation shall be deemed to be the same corporation as, and a continuation of, each predecessor corporation;

**Related Provisions**: 88(1)(e.2) — Winding-up. See additional Related Provisions and Definitions at end of s. 87.

**Interpretation Bulletins**: See list at end of s. 87.

(l.1) **idem** — for the purposes of this paragraph, paragraph (l.2) and section 37.1,

(i) the base period for a particular taxation year of a new corporation that has fewer than 3 preceding taxation years shall be deemed to be the period

(A) commencing on the day that

(I) is the earliest of all days each of which is a day immediately before the commencement of a taxation year of a predecessor corporation in respect of the new corporation that ended after 1976, and

(II) is in the 3 year period ending on the day immediately before the commencement of the particular year, and

(B) ending immediately before the first day of the particular taxation year,

(ii) where subparagraph (i) applies,

(A) in determining the qualified expenditures made by the new corporation in its base period, there shall be included the total of all amounts each of which is the qualified expenditure made by a predecessor corporation in a taxation year that commenced in the base period of the new corporation, and

(B) in determining the total of the amounts paid to the new corporation by persons referred to in subparagraphs (b)(i) to (iii) of the definition "expenditure base" in subsection 37.1(5) in its base period, there shall be included the total of all such amounts paid to a predecessor corporation by a person referred to in those subparagraphs in a taxation year that commenced in the base period of the new corporation,

(iii) the capital cost to the new corporation of any property that was a research property of a predecessor corporation acquired by it from the predecessor corporation shall be deemed to be the capital cost thereof to the predecessor corporation and the property shall be deemed to be a research property of the new corporation, and

(iv) each amount determined in respect of the new corporation under subparagraph 37.1(3)(b)(i) or (iii), as the case may be, shall be deemed to be the total of the amount otherwise determined and the total of amounts each of which is the amount determined under subparagraph 37.1(3)(b)(i) or (iii), as the case may be, in respect of a predecessor corporation;

(l.2) **definition of "predecessor corporation"** — for the purposes of this paragraph and paragraph (l.1), "predecessor corporation" includes any corporation in respect of which a predecessor corporation was a new corporation;

(l.21) **[debt forgiveness rules]** — for the purposes of section 61.3, the definition "unrecognized loss" in subsection 80(1) and subsection 80.01(10), the new corporation is deemed to be the same corporation as, and a continuation of, each predecessor corporation;

**Notes**: 87(2)(l.21) added by 1994 tax amendments bill (Part I), effective for taxation years that end after February 21, 1994; and amended by 1995-97 technical bill retroactive to its introduction to add reference to 80(1)"unrecognized loss". It covers various rules relating to debt forgiveness (see also 87(2)(h.1) for others).

(l.3) **replacement property** — where before the amalgamation property of a predecessor corporation was unlawfully taken, lost, destroyed or taken under statutory authority, or was a former business property of the predecessor corporation, for the purposes of applying sections 13 and 44 and the definition "former business property" in subsection 248(1) to the new corporation in respect of the property and any replacement property acquired therefor, the new corporation shall be deemed to be the same corporation as, and a continuation of, the predecessor corporation;

**Related Provisions**: 88(1)(e.2) — Winding-up. See additional Related Provisions and Definitions at end of s. 87.

**Notes**: 87(2)(l.3) reworded by 1992 technical bill, effective for amalgamations occurring (and, by 88(1)(e.2), for windings-up beginning) after 1989, to apply to voluntary dispositions of former business property. For earlier amalgamations, read:

(l.3) property lost, destroyed or taken — if the amalgamation was after May 6, 1974 and a property of a predecessor corporation was unlawfully taken, lost, destroyed or taken under statutory authority prior to the amalgamation, sections 13 and 44 apply to the new corporation as though

(i) the new corporation had been in existence and owned that property at the time it was so lost, destroyed or taken,

(ii) the cost or capital cost, as the case may be, of that property to the new corporation were its cost or capital cost, as the case may be, to the predecessor corporation, and

(iii) where the predecessor corporation had acquired a replacement property for that property before the amalgamation, the new corporation had acquired that replacement property immediately after the amalgamation;

**Interpretation Bulletins**: IT-259R3: Exchanges of property. See also list at end of s. 87.

(m) **reserves** — for the purpose of computing the income of the new corporation for a taxation year, any amount claimed under subparagraph 40(1)(a)(iii) or 44(1)(e)(iii) in computing a predecessor corporation's gain for its last taxation year from the disposition of any property shall be deemed

(i) to have been claimed under subparagraph 40(1)(a)(iii) or 44(1)(e)(iii), as the case may be, in computing the new corporation's gain for a taxation year immediately preceding its first taxation year from the disposition of that property by it before its first taxation year, and

(ii) to be the amount determined under subparagraph 40(1)(a)(i) or 44(1)(e)(i), as the case may be, in respect of that property;

**Related Provisions**: 88(1)(e.2) — Winding-up. See additional Related Provisions and Definitions at end of s. 87.

**Notes**: 87(2)(m) amended by 1991 technical bill, effective 1990, to add references to 44(1)(e).

(m.1) **[charitable] gift of non-qualifying security** — for the purpose of computing the new corporation's gain under subsection 40(1.01) for any taxation year from the disposition of a property, the new corporation is deemed to be the same corporation as, and a continuation of, each predecessor corporation;

**Related Provisions**: 88(1)(e.2) — Winding-up. See additional Related Provisions and Definitions at end of s. 87.

**S. 87(2)(m.1)**     Income Tax Act, Part I, Division B

**Notes**: 87(2)(m.1) added by 1997 Budget, effective for 1997 and later taxation years.

(n) **outlays made pursuant to warranty** — for the purpose of section 42, any outlay or expense made or incurred by the new corporation in a taxation year, pursuant to or by virtue of an obligation described in that section incurred by a predecessor corporation, that would, if the outlay or expense had been made or incurred by the predecessor corporation in that year, have been deemed to be a loss of the predecessor corporation for that year from the disposition of a capital property shall be deemed to be a loss of the new corporation for that year from the disposition of a capital property;

**Related Provisions**: 88(1)(e.2) — Winding-up. See additional Related Provisions and Definitions at end of s. 87.

**Interpretation Bulletins**: IT-330R: Disposition of capital property subject to warranty, covenant, etc. See also list at end of s. 87.

(o) **expiration of options previously granted** — for the purpose of subsection 49(2), any option granted by a predecessor corporation that expires after the amalgamation shall be deemed to have been granted by the new corporation, and any proceeds received by the predecessor corporation for the granting of the option shall be deemed to have been received by the new corporation therefor;

**Related Provisions**: 88(1)(e.2) — Winding-up. See additional Related Provisions and Definitions at end of s. 87.

(p) **consideration for resource property disposition** — for the purpose of computing a deduction from the income of the new corporation for a taxation year under section 64 of the *Income Tax Act*, chapter 148 of the Revised Statutes of Canada, 1952, any amount that has been included in computing the income of a predecessor corporation for its last taxation year or a previous taxation year by virtue of subsection 59(1) or paragraph 59(3.2)(c) of this Act, of subsection 59(3) of the *Income Tax Act*, chapter 148 of the Revised Statutes of Canada, 1952, or of subsection 83A(5ba) or (5c) of that Act as it read in its application to a taxation year before the 1972 taxation year, shall be deemed to have been included in computing the income of the new corporation for a previous year by virtue thereof;

**Related Provisions**: 88(1)(e.2) — Winding-up. See additional Related Provisions and Definitions at end of s. 87.

**Notes**: The version of s. 64 referred to was repealed by the 1981 Budget. See Notes to s. 64.

**I.T. Application Rules**: 69 (meaning of "*Income Tax Act*, chapter 148 of the Revised Statutes of Canada, 1952").

(q) **registered [pension] plans [and DPSPs]** — for the purposes of sections 147, 147.1 and 147.2 and any regulations made under subsection 147.1(18), the new corporation shall be deemed to be the same corporation as, and a continuation of, each predecessor corporation;

**Related Provisions**: 88(1)(e.2) — Winding-up. See additional Related Provisions and Definitions at end of s. 87.

**Interpretation Bulletins**: See list at end of s. 87.

(r)–(s.1) [Repealed under former Act]

**Notes**: 87(2)(r), (s) and (s.1), repealed in 1978, dealt with "1971 capital surplus on hand" and "paid-up capital deficiency".

(t) **pre-1972 capital surplus on hand** — for the purpose of subsection 88(2.1), any capital property owned by a predecessor corporation on December 31, 1971 that was acquired by the new corporation by virtue of the amalgamation shall be deemed to have been acquired by the new corporation before 1972 at an actual cost to it equal to the actual cost of the property to the predecessor corporation;

**Related Provisions**: 88(1)(e.2) — Winding-up. See additional Related Provisions and Definitions at end of s. 87.

**Interpretation Bulletins**: See list at end of s. 87.

(u) **shares of foreign affiliate** — where one or more shares of the capital stock of a foreign affiliate of a predecessor corporation have, by virtue of the amalgamation, been acquired by the new corporation and as a result of the acquisition the affiliate has become a foreign affiliate of the new corporation,

(i) for the purposes of subsection 91(5) and paragraph 92(1)(b), any amount required by section 92 to be added or deducted, as the case may be, in computing the adjusted cost base of any such share to the predecessor corporation before the amalgamation shall be deemed to have been so required to be added or deducted, as the case may be, in computing the adjusted cost base of the share to the new corporation, and

(ii) for the purpose of subsection 93(2), any exempt dividend received by the predecessor corporation on any such share shall be deemed to be an exempt dividend received by the new corporation on the share;

**Proposed Amendment — 87(2)(u)(ii)**

(ii) for the purposes of subsections 93(2) to (2.3), any exempt dividend received by the predecessor corporation on any such share is deemed to be an exempt dividend received by the new corporation on the share;

**Application**: Bill C-43 (First Reading September 20, 2000), subsec. 38(1), will amend subpara. 87(2)(u)(ii) to read as above, applicable after November 1999.

**Technical Notes**: Section 87 of the Act provides rules that apply where there has been a merger of two or more corporations to form a new corporation.

Paragraph 87(2)(u) of the Act applies where two or more taxable Canadian corporations (referred to as "predecessor corporations") amalgamate to form a new corporation. Subparagraph 87(2)(u)(ii) provides that any dividend received by a predecessor corporation on a share that is an exempt dividend is considered for the purposes of subsection 93(2) to be an exempt dividend received by the new corporation. Subparagraph 87(2)(u)(ii) of the Act is amended to refer to subsections 93(2) to (2.3), effective after November 30, 1999, to refer to new subsections 93(2) to (2.3) which limit the losses arising on the disposition of shares of a foreign affiliate.

**Related Provisions**: 88(1)(e.2) — Winding-up. See additional Related Provisions and Definitions at end of s. 87.

**Notes**: 87(2)(u)(i) amended by 1974 Budget. For amalgamations before May 7, 1974, read:

(i) for the purposes of subsection 90(2), paragraph 92(1)(b) and subsection 93(1), any amount required by section 92 to be added or deducted, as the case may be, in computing the adjusted cost base of any such share to the predecessor corporation before the amalgamation shall be deemed to have been so required to be added or deducted, as the case may be, in computing the adjusted cost base of the share to the new corporation, and

**Interpretation Bulletins**: See list at end of s. 87.

(v) **gifts [charitable donations]** — for the purposes of section 110.1, the new corporation shall be deemed to be the same corporation as, and a continuation of, each predecessor corporation with respect to gifts;

**Interpretation Bulletins**: See list at end of s. 87.

(w) [Repealed under former Act]

**Notes**: 87(2)(w), repealed in 1983, prevented unclaimed restricted farm losses from being carried through an amalgamation. Such losses can now be carried through under 87(2.1).

(x) **taxable dividends** — for the purposes of subsections 112(3) to (4.22),

(i) any taxable dividend received on a share that was deductible from the predecessor corporation's income for a taxation year under section 112 or subsection 138(6) is deemed to be a taxable dividend received on the share by the new corporation that was deductible from the new corporation's income under section 112 or subsection 138(6), as the case may be,

(ii) any dividend (other than a taxable dividend) received on a share by the predecessor corporation is deemed to have been received on the share by the new corporation, and

(iii) a share acquired by the new corporation from a predecessor corporation is deemed to have been owned by the new corporation throughout any period of time throughout which it was owned by a predecessor corporation;

**Related Provisions**: 88(1)(e.2) — Winding-up. See additional Related Provisions and Definitions at end of s. 87.

**Notes**: 87(2)(x) amended by 1995-97 technical bill, this version effective for dispositions of shares after April 26, 1995. For earlier dispositions, for the 1994 and later taxation years, read:

(x) for the purposes of subsections 112(3) to (4.3),

(i) any taxable dividend received on a share that was deductible from the predecessor corporation's income for a taxation year under section 112 or subsection 138(6) is deemed to be a taxable dividend received on the share by the new corporation that was deductible from the new corporation's income under section 112 or 138(6), as the case may be,

(ii) any capital dividend or life insurance capital dividend received on a share by the predecessor corporation is deemed to be a capital dividend or life insurance capital dividend, as the case may be, received on the share by the new corporation, and

(iii) a share acquired by the new corporation from a predecessor corporation is deemed to have been owned by the new corporation throughout any period of time throughout which it was owned by a predecessor corporation;

For amalgamations after June 5, 1987 until the 1993 taxation year, read:

(x) for the purposes of subsections 112(3) to (4.3),

(i) any taxable dividend received on a share that was deductible from the predecessor corporation's income for a taxation year under section 112 or subsection 138(6) shall be deemed to be a taxable dividend received on the share by the new corporation that was deductible from the new corporation's income for a taxation year under section 112 or subsection 138(6), as the case may be, and

(ii) any capital dividend or life insurance capital dividend received on a share by the predecessor corporation shall be deemed to be a capital dividend or life insurance capital dividend, as the case may be, received on the share by the new corporation;

**Interpretation Bulletins**: See list at end of s. 87.

(y) **contributed surplus** — for the purposes of subsections 84(1) and (10), the new corporation shall be deemed to be the same corporation as, and a continuation of, each predecessor corporation;

**Notes**: 87(2)(y) added by 1991 technical bill, effective July 14, 1990.

(y.1) [Repealed]

**Notes**: 87(2)(y.1) repealed by 1995-97 technical bill, effective for taxes payable for taxation years that begin after 1986. It provided a rule for computing the "preferred-earnings amount" under former 181(2). These rules were eliminated with the repeal of former Part II, which imposed a special 12.5% tax from 1982-86 on dividends paid by corporations out of income subject to the small business deduction.

**Interpretation Bulletins**: See list at end of s. 87.

(z) **foreign tax carryover** — for the purposes of determining the new corporation's unused foreign tax credit (within the meaning of subsection 126(7)) in respect of a country for any taxation year and determining the extent to which subsection 126(2.3) applies to reduce the amount that may be claimed by the new corporation under paragraph 126(2)(a) in respect of an unused foreign tax credit in respect of a country for a taxation year, the new corporation shall be deemed to be the same corporation as, and a continuation of, each predecessor corporation, except that this paragraph shall in no respect affect the determination of

(i) the fiscal period of the new corporation or any of its predecessor corporations, or

(ii) the tax payable under this Act by any predecessor corporation;

**Interpretation Bulletins**: IT-520: Unused foreign tax credits — carryforward and carryback. See also list at end of s. 87.

(z.1) **capital dividend account** — for the purposes of computing the capital dividend account of the new corporation, it shall be deemed to be the same corporation as, and a continuation of, each predecessor corporation, other than a predecessor corporation to which subsection 83(2.1) would, if a dividend were paid immediately before the amalgamation and an election were made under subsection 83(2) in respect of the full amount of that dividend, apply to deem any portion of the dividend to be paid by the predecessor corporation as a taxable dividend;

**Related Provisions**: 88(1)(e.2) — Winding-up. See additional Related Provisions and Definitions at end of s. 87.

**Notes**: 87(2)(z.1) amended by 1991 technical bill, effective for amalgamations that occur, and (per 88(1)(e.2)) windups that begin, after July 13, 1990, to ensure that a negative balance in a predecessor's capital dividend account effectively flows through to the new corporation. For earlier amalgamations, read:

(z.1) for the purpose of computing at any particular time after the amalgamation the capital dividend account of a new corporation that has been a private corporation continuously from the time of the amalgamation to the particular time, there shall be added the amount of the capital dividend account of each predecessor corporation immediately before the amalgamation, except that the amount of the capital dividend account of any predecessor corporation immediately before the amalgamation shall be deemed to be nil where, had a dividend been paid by the predecessor corporation immediately before the amalgamation and an election been made under subsection 83(2) in respect of that dividend, subsection 83(2.1) would have applied to deem all or any portion of the dividend to be a taxable dividend;

87(2)(z.1) amended by 1988 tax reform, effective for amalgamations after 4 p.m. EDST, September 25, 1987. For amalgamations before that date, read:

(z.1) for the purpose of computing, at any particular time after the amalgamation, the capital dividend account or the life insurance capital dividend account for a new corporation that has been a private corporation continuously from the time of the amalgamation to the particular time, there shall be added the amount of the capital dividend account or the life insurance capital dividend account, as the case may be, of each predecessor corporation immediately before the amalgamation;

**Interpretation Bulletins**: IT-66R6: Capital dividends. See also list at end of s. 87.

(z.2) **application of Part III** — for the purposes of Part III, the new corporation shall be deemed to be the same corporation as, and a continuation of, each predecessor corporation;

**Related Provisions**: 88(1)(e.2) — Winding-up. See additional Related Provisions and Definitions at end of s. 87.

**Notes**: 87(2)(z.2) added by 1988 tax reform, effective for amalgamations after April 1988.

**Interpretation Bulletins**: See list at end of s. 87.

(aa) **refundable dividend tax on hand** — where the new corporation was a private corporation immediately after the amalgamation, for the purpose of computing the refundable dividend tax on hand (within the meaning assigned by subsection 129(3)) of the new corporation at the end of its first taxation year there shall be added to the total determined under subsection 129(3) in respect of the new corporation for the year the total of all amounts each of which is the amount, if any, by which the refundable dividend tax on hand of a predecessor corporation at the end of its last taxation year exceeds its dividend refund (within the meaning assigned by subsection 129(1)) for its last taxation year, except that no amount shall be added under this paragraph in respect of a predecessor corporation

(i) that was not a private corporation at the end of its last taxation year, or

(ii) where subsection 129(1.2) would have applied to deem a dividend paid by the predecessor corporation immediately before the amalgamation not to be a taxable dividend for the purpose of subsection 129(1);

**Related Provisions**: 88(1)(e.2) — Winding-up. See additional Related Provisions and Definitions at end of s. 87; 131(5) — Dividend refund to mutual fund corporation; 186(5) — Deemed private corporation. See additional Related Provisions and Definitions at end of subsec. 87(9).

**Notes**: 87(2)(aa) amended by 1995 Budget, effective for amalgamations that occur, and (per 88(1)(e.2)) windups that begin, after June 1995. (Earlier windups were dealt with by 88(1)(e.5).) The amendment reflects changes in the calculation of RDTOH under 129(3). For earlier amalgamations since the 1993 taxation year, read:

(aa) where the new corporation was a private corporation continuously from the time of the amalgamation until the time immediately after the beginning of any taxation year, for the purpose of computing the refundable dividend tax on hand (within the meaning assigned by subsection 129(3)) of the new corporation at the end of that year there shall be added to the total determined under subsection 129(3) for that year, from which the total of amounts determined under paragraphs 129(3)(c) to (e) is subtracted, the total of all amounts each of which is the amount, if any, by which the refundable dividend tax on hand immediately before the amalgamation of a predecessor corporation that was a private corporation at that time exceeds its dividend refund (within the meaning assigned by subsection 129(1)) for its taxation year ending at that time, except that no amount shall be so added in respect of a predecessor corporation where subsection 129(1.2) would have applied to deem a dividend paid by the predecessor corporation immediately before the amalgamation not to be a taxable dividend for the purpose of subsection 129(1);

Amended by 1992 technical bill, effective as of the 1993 taxation year, to require that the new corporation be a private corporation only until after the beginning of a new taxation year. For earlier years, read:

(aa) in the case of a new corporation that has been a private corporation continuously from the time of the amalgamation to the end of any taxation year, for the purposes of computing the refundable dividend tax on hand (within the meaning assigned by subsection 129(3)), of the new corporation at the end of the taxation year, where a predecessor corporation had refundable dividend tax on hand immediately before the amalgamation, the amount by which the refundable dividend tax on hand at that time exceeds any dividend refund (within the meaning assigned by subsection 129(1)) of the predecessor corporation for its taxation year ending immediately before the amalgamation shall be added to the total determined under subsection 129(3) from which the new corporation's dividend refunds are to be subtracted, except that the amount to be added to the total determined under subsection 129(3) shall be deemed to be nil where, had a dividend been paid by the predecessor corporation immediately before the amalgamation, subsection 129(1.2) would have applied to deem the dividend not to be a taxable dividend;

Amended by 1988 tax reform, effective for amalgamations after 4 p.m. EDST, September 25, 1987. For amalgamations from May 7, 1974 until that time, 87(2)(aa) ends at "are to be subtracted".

For amalgamations from 1972 through May 6, 1974, read:

(aa) in the case of a new corporation that is a private corporation, for the purpose of computing the refundable dividend tax on hand (within the meaning assigned by subsection 129(3)) of the new corporation at the end of any taxation year, where a predecessor corporation had refundable dividend tax on hand immediately before the amalgamation, the amount by which the refundable dividend tax on hand at that time exceeds any dividend refund (within the meaning assigned by subsection 129(1)) of the predecessor corporation for its taxation year ending immediately before the amalgamation shall be added to the aggregate determined under subsection 129(3) from which the new corporation's dividend refunds are to be subtracted;

**Interpretation Bulletins**: See list at end of s. 87.

(bb) **mutual fund and investment corporations** — where the new corporation is a mutual fund corporation or an investment corporation, there shall be added to

(i) the amount determined under each of paragraphs (a) and (b) of the definition "capital gains dividend account" in subsection 131(6), and

(ii) the values of A and B in the definition "refundable capital gains tax on hand" in that subsection

in respect of the new corporation at any time the amounts so determined and the values of those factors immediately before the amalgamation in respect of each predecessor corporation that was, immediately before the amalgamation, a mutual fund corporation or an investment corporation;

**Notes**: 87(2)(bb) amended by 1995-97 technical bill, this version effective for amalgamations that occur after February 22, 1994. For amalgamations from January 1992 to February 22, 1994, read "(a) to (g)" instead of "(a) and (b)" in 87(2)(bb)(i).

From July 14, 1990 to amalgamations occurring to the end of 1991, read:

(bb) where the new corporation is a mutual fund corporation or an investment corporation, there shall be added to the amount determined for each of A, B, C and D in the definition "capital gains dividend account" and A and B in the definition "refundable capital gains tax on hand" in subsection 131(6) in respect of the new corporation at any time the amount so determined immediately before the amalgamation in respect of each predecessor corporation that was a mutual fund corporation or an investment corporation;

87(2)(bb) amended by 1991 technical bill, effective July 14, 1990 and, where the corporation elected by notifying Revenue Canada in writing by the end of 1992, for amalgamations after 1986. For earlier amalgamations, read:

(bb) mutual fund corporation — in the case of a new corporation that is a mutual fund corporation,

(i) for the purpose of computing its capital gains dividend account at any time, where a predecessor mutual fund corporation had a capital gains dividend account immediately before the amalgamation the amount thereof shall be added to the amount determined for A in the definition "capital gains dividend account" in subsection 131(6), and

(ii) for the purpose of computing its refundable capital gains tax on hand at the end of any taxation year, where a predecessor mutual fund corporation had refundable capital gains tax on hand immediately before the amalgamation the amount thereof shall be added to the amount determined for A in the definition "refundable capital gains [tax] on hand" in subsection 131(6);

(bb.1) **flow-through entities** — where a predecessor corporation was, immediately before the amalgamation, an investment corporation, a mortgage investment corporation or a mutual fund corporation and the new corporation is an investment corporation, a mortgage investment corporation or a mutual fund corporation, as the case may be, for the purpose of section 39.1, the new corporation is deemed to be the same corporation as, and a continuation of, the predecessor corporation;

**Notes**: 87(2)(bb.1) added by 1995-97 technical bill, effective for amalgamations that occur after 1993.

(cc) **non-resident-owned investment corporation** — in the case of a new corporation that is a non-resident-owned investment corporation,

(i) for the purpose of computing its allowable refundable tax on hand (within the meaning assigned by subsection 133(9)) at any time, where a predecessor corporation had allowable refundable tax on hand immediately before the amalgamation, the amount thereof shall be added to the total determined for A in the definition "allowable refundable tax on hand" in subsection 133(9),

(ii) for the purpose of computing its capital gains dividend account (within the meaning assigned by subsection 133(8)) at any time, where a predecessor corporation had an amount in its capital gains dividend account immediately before the amalgamation, that amount shall be added to the amount determined under paragraph (a) of the description of A in the definition "capital gains dividend account" in subsection 133(8), and

(iii) for the purpose of computing its cumulative taxable income (within the meaning assigned by subsection 133(9)) at any time, where a predecessor corporation had cumulative taxable income immediately before the amalgamation, the amount thereof shall be added to the total determined for A in the definition "cumulative taxable income" in subsection 133(9);

**Related Provisions**: 88(1)(e.2) — Winding-up. See additional Related Provisions and Definitions at end of s. 87.

**Interpretation Bulletins**: See list at end of s. 87.

(dd)–(hh) [Repealed under former Act]

(ii) **public corporation** — where a predecessor corporation was a public corporation immediately before the amalgamation, the new corporation shall be deemed to have been a public corporation at the commencement of its first taxation year;

**Interpretation Bulletins**: See list at end of s. 87.

(jj) **interest on certain obligations** — for the purposes of paragraph 81(1)(m), the new corporation shall be deemed to be the same corporation as, and a continuation of, each predecessor corporation;

**Interpretation Bulletins**: See list at end of s. 87.

(kk) **disposition of shares of controlled corporation** — for the purposes of paragraph 40(2)(h),

(i) where a corporation was controlled, directly or indirectly in any manner whatever, by a predecessor corporation immediately before the amalgamation and has, by reason of the amalgamation, become controlled, directly or indirectly in any manner whatever, by the new corporation, the new corporation shall be deemed to have acquired control of the corporation so controlled at the time control thereof was acquired by the predecessor corporation, and

(ii) where a predecessor corporation was immediately before the amalgamation controlled, directly or indirectly in any manner whatever, by a corporation that, immediately after the amalgamation, controlled, directly or indirectly in any manner whatever, the new corporation, the new corporation shall be deemed to be the same corporation as, and a continuation of, each predecessor corporation;

**Related Provisions**: 256(5.1), (6.2) — Controlled directly or indirectly — control in fact. See additional Related Provisions and Definitions at end of s. 87.

**Interpretation Bulletins**: See list at end of s. 87.

(ll) **para. 20(1)(n) and subpara. 40(1)(a)(iii) amounts** — notwithstanding any other provision of this Act, where any property was disposed of by a predecessor corporation, the new corporation shall, in computing

(i) the amount of any deduction under paragraph 20(1)(n) as a reserve in respect of the property sold in the course of business, and

(ii) the amount of its claim under subparagraph 40(1)(a)(iii) or 44(1)(e)(iii) in respect of the disposition of the property,

be deemed to be the same corporation as, and a continuation of, the predecessor corporation;

**Related Provisions**: 88(1)(e.2) — Winding-up. See additional Related Provisions and Definitions at end of s. 87.

**Notes**: 87(2)(ll) amended by 1991 technical bill, effective for amalgamations occurring after 1989, to add reference to 44(1)(e)(iii).

(mm) **idem** — for the purposes of section 126.1, the new corporation shall be deemed to be the same corporation as, and a continuation of, each predecessor corporation;

**Related Provisions**: 126.1(5) — UI premium tax credit — "specified employer" defined. See additional Related Provisions and Definitions at end of s. 87.

**Notes**: 87(2)(mm) added by 1992 Economic Statement, effective for amalgamations occurring, and windups beginning, after 1991.

(nn) **refundable Part VII tax on hand** — for the purpose of computing the refundable Part VII tax on hand of the new corporation at the end of any taxation year, there shall be added to the total determined under paragraph 192(3)(a) the total of all amounts each of which is the amount, if any, by which

(i) a predecessor corporation's refundable Part VII tax on hand at the end of its last taxation year

exceeds

(ii) the predecessor corporation's Part VII refund for its last taxation year;

**Related Provisions**: 88(1)(e.2) — Winding-up. See additional Related Provisions and Definitions at end of s. 87.

**Interpretation Bulletins**: See list at end of s. 87.

(oo) **investment tax credit** — for the purpose of applying subsection 127(10.2) to any corporation, the new corporation is deemed to have had

(i) a particular taxation year that

(A) where it was associated with another corporation in the new corporation's first taxation year, ended in the calendar year that precedes the calendar year in which that first year ends, and

(B) in any other case, immediately precedes that first year, and

(ii) taxable income for the particular year (determined before taking into consideration the specified future tax consequences for the particular year) equal to the total of all amounts each of which is a predecessor corporation's taxable income for its taxation year that ended immediately before the amalgamation (determined before taking into consideration the specified future tax consequences for that year);

**Notes**: 87(2)(oo) amended by 1996 Budget, this version effective for amalgamations occurring after 1996. For amalgamations in 1996, read "the new corporation" in place of "any corporation". For amalgamations from May 24, 1985 through the end of 1995 (taking into account a retroactive amendment made by the 1996 Budget bill), read:

(oo) for the purposes of applying subsection 127(10.1) in respect of the first taxation year of the new corporation, the new corporation shall be deemed to have had a taxation year immediately preceding its first taxation year and to have had

(i) taxable income for that preceding taxation year equal to the total of amounts each of which is the taxable income of a predecessor corporation for its taxation year ending immediately before the amalgamation, and

(ii) a business limit for that preceding taxation year equal to the total of amounts each of which is the business limit of a predecessor corporation for its taxation year ending immediately before the amalgamation;

**Interpretation Bulletins**: See list at end of s. 87.

**(oo.1) refundable investment tax credit and balance-due day** — for the purpose of applying subparagraph 157(1)(b)(i) and the definition "qualifying corporation" in subsection 127.1(2) to any corporation, the new corporation is deemed to have had

(i) a particular taxation year that

(A) where it was associated with another corporation in the new corporation's first taxation year, ended in the calendar year that precedes the calendar year in which that first year ends, and

(B) where clause (A) does not apply, immediately precedes that first year,

(ii) taxable income for the particular year (determined before taking into consideration the specified future tax consequences for the particular year) equal to the total of all amounts each of which is a predecessor corporation's taxable income for its taxation year that ended immediately before the amalgamation (determined before taking into consideration the specified future tax consequences for that year), and

(iii) a business limit for the particular year equal to the total of all amounts each of which is a predecessor corporation's business limit for its taxation year that ended immediately before the amalgamation;

**Notes**: 87(2)(oo.1) added by 1996 Budget, effective for amalgamations occurring after May 23, 1985, except that,

(a) for amalgamations before 1997, read "any corporation" as "the new corporation";

(b) when applying it for the purpose of 127.1(2)"qualifying corporation", the business limits referred to in 87(2)(oo.1), for taxation years that ended after June 1994 and began before 1996, shall be determined under s. 125 as that section read in its application to taxation years that ended before July 1994; and

(c) 87(2)(oo.1)(i)(A) does not apply

(i) when applying 127.1(2)"qualifying corporation" to taxation years that ended before July 1994, and

(ii) when applying 157(1)(b)(i) to taxation years that end before 1998.

**(pp) cumulative offset account computation** — for the purpose of computing the cumulative offset account (within the meaning assigned by subsection 66.5(2)) of the new corporation at any time, there shall be added to the total otherwise determined under paragraph 66.5(2)(a) the total of all amounts each of which is the amount, if any, by which

(i) a predecessor corporation's cumulative offset account at the end of its last taxation year

exceeds

(ii) the amount deducted under subsection 66.5(1) in computing the predecessor corporation's income for its last taxation year;

**Related Provisions**: 88(1)(e.2) — Winding-up. See additional Related Provisions and Definitions at end of s. 87.

**Interpretation Bulletins**: See list at end of s. 87.

**(qq) continuation of corporation [investment tax credit]** — for the purpose of computing the new corporation's investment tax credit at the end of any taxation year, the new corporation is deemed to be the same corporation as, and a continuation of, each predecessor corporation, except that this paragraph does not affect the determination of the fiscal period of any corporation or the tax payable by any predecessor corporation;

**Related Provisions**: See Related Provisions and Definitions at end of s. 87.

**Notes**: 87(2)(qq) amended by 1995-97 technical bill, effective for amalgamations occurring after April 26, 1995. For amalgamations from May 24, 1985 to April 26, 1995, read:

(qq) for the purpose of computing the new corporation's investment tax credit and employment tax credit at the end of any taxation year, the new corporation shall be deemed to be the same corporation as, and a continuation of, each predecessor corporation;

87(2)(qq) added by 1985 Budget, effective for amalgamations occurring after May 23, 1985.

**Interpretation Bulletins**: See list at end of s. 87.

**(rr) tax on taxable preferred shares** — for the purposes of subsections 112(2.9), 191(4), and 191.1(2) and (4), the new corporation shall be deemed to be the same corporation as, and a continuation of, each predecessor corporation;

**Related Provisions**: 88(1)(e.2) — Winding-up. See additional Related Provisions and Definitions at end of s. 87.

**(ss) transferred liability for Part VI.1 tax** — for the purposes of section 191.3, the new corporation shall be deemed to be the same corporation as, and a continuation of, each predecessor corporation;

**(tt) livestock — inclusion of deferred amount** — for the purposes of subsections 80.3(3) and (5), the new corporation shall be deemed to be the same corporation as, and a continuation of, each predecessor corporation; and

**Related Provisions**: 88(1)(e.2) — Winding-up. See additional Related Provisions and Definitions at end of s. 87.

**(uu) fuel tax rebates** — for the purposes of paragraph 12(1)(x.1), the description of D.1 in the definition "non-capital loss" in subsection 111(8), and subsections 111(10) and (11), the new corporation is deemed to be the same corporation as, and a continuation of, each predecessor corporation.

**Related Provisions**: 88(1)(e.2) — Winding-up; 93(2)–(2.3) — Loss limitation on disposition of share. See additional Related Provisions and Definitions at end of s. 87.

**Notes**: 87(2)(uu) tracks fuel tax rebates and the use of the 1992 Loss Offset Program, and the 1997–2000 aviation fuel rebate program, through an amalgamation. See Notes to 12(1)(x.1).

87(2)(uu) added by 1992 transportation industry assistance bill, effective for amalgamations in 1992 or later, and amended by 1997 Budget (first bill), effective for 1997 and later taxation years, to change reference to 111(10)(a)(i)(B) to 111(10). That subsection has been reworded to use a formula.

**Interpretation Bulletins**: See list at end of s. 87.

### (2.01) Application of subsec. 37.1(5) — The definitions in subsection 37.1(5) apply to subsection (2).

**Notes**: 87(2.01) added in the R.S.C. 1985 (5th Supp.) consolidation, effective for taxation years ending after November 1991. This rule was formerly in the opening words of 37.1(5). Section 37.1, which provided an additional R&D allowance, has been repealed.

### (2.1) Non-capital losses, etc., of predecessor corporations — Where there has been an amalgamation of two or more corporations, for the purposes only of

(a) determining the new corporation's non-capital loss, net capital loss, restricted farm loss, farm loss or limited partnership loss, as the case may be, for any taxation year, and

(b) determining the extent to which subsections 111(3) to (5.4) and paragraph 149(10)(c) apply to restrict the deductibility by the new corporation of any non-capital loss, net capital loss, restricted farm loss, farm loss or limited partnership loss, as the case may be,

the new corporation shall be deemed to be the same corporation as, and a continuation of, each predecessor corporation, except that this subsection shall in no respect affect the determination of

(c) the fiscal period of the new corporation or any of its predecessors,

(d) the income of the new corporation or any of its predecessors, or

(e) the taxable income of, or the tax payable under this Act by, any predecessor corporation.

**Related Provisions**: 87(2)(a) — Taxation year-end; 87(2.11) — Losses, etc., on amalgamation with subsidiary wholly-owned corporation; 256(7) — Where control deemed not acquired. See additional Related Provisions and Definitions at end of s. 87.

**Notes**: See Notes to 87(2)(a). 87(2.1)(d) and (e) allow losses to be carried forward through an amalgamation (subject to the change-of-control rule in 111(4) and (5)), since they are deducted in computing the *taxable* income of the new corporation. Losses can only be carried back under a vertical amalgamation; see 87(2.11).

The reference in 87(2.1)(b) to 149(10)(d) was added in 1987, effective for amalgamations after June 5, 1987; and changed from 149(10)(d) to 149(10)(c) by 1995-97 technical bill, effective for a corporation that becomes or ceases to be exempt from tax under Part I after April 26, 1995.

For amalgamations from April 1, 1977 through the end of 1982, 87(2.1) as applied only for purposes of determining non-capital losses and net capital losses, and 111(3), (4) and (5).

87(2.1) has no application to amalgamations before April 1977.

**Interpretation Bulletins**: IT-302R3: Losses of a corporation — the effect that acquisitions of control, amalgamations, and windings-up have on their deductibility — after January 15, 1987. See also list at end of s. 87.

### (2.11) Vertical amalgamations — Where a new corporation is formed by the amalgamation of a particular corporation and one or more of its subsidiary wholly-owned corporations, the new corporation is deemed to be the same corporation as, and a continuation of, the particular corporation for the purposes of applying sections 111 and 126, subsections 127(5) to (26) and 181.1(4) to (7), Part IV and subsections 190.1(3) to (6) in respect of the particular corporation.

**Related Provisions**: 87(1.4) — Definition of "subsidiary wholly-owned corporation"; 87(2.1) — Non-capital losses, etc., of predecessor corporations; 87(11) — Vertical amalgamation — effects; 256(7) — Where control deemed not acquired.

**Notes**: 87(2.11) effectively permits losses of the amalgamated corporation to be carried back to the predecessor parent (under the rules in 111) on a vertical short-form amalgamation or other amalgamation of a corporation with a subsidiary wholly-owned corporation (see 87(1.4)).

Revenue Canada indicated, at the 1994 Canadian Tax Foundation annual conference, that the purpose of 87(2.11) is to put vertical amalgamations on an equal footing with 88(1) windups re the ability to carry back losses to the parent. 87(2.11) does not permit an application of a subsidiary's prior year losses to be carried back against the parent's prior year's income. This is consistent with the rules in 88(1.1).

87(2.11) added by 1992 technical bill, effective for amalgamations after 1989, and amended by 1995-97 technical bill, effective for amalgamations that occur after April 26, 1995. For amalgamations from 1990 through April 25, 1995, read:

(2.11) Losses, etc., on amalgamation with subsidiary wholly-owned corporation — Where a new corporation is formed by the amalgamation of a particular corporation and one or more of its subsidiary wholly-owned corporations, the new corporation shall, for the purposes of applying section 111 and Part IV in respect of the particular corporation, be deemed to be the same corporation as, and a continuation of, the particular corporation.

**I.T. Technical News**: No. 3 (subsection 87(2.11)).

### (2.2) Amalgamation of insurers — Where there has been an amalgamation and one or more of the predecessor corporations was an insurer, the new corporation is, notwithstanding subsection (2), deemed, for the purposes of paragraphs 12(1)(d), (e), (e.1), (i) and (s) and 20(1)(l), (l.1), (p) and (jj) and 20(7)(c), subsection 20(22), sections 138, 138.1, 140, 142 and 148 and Part XII.3, to be the same corporation as, and a continuation of, each of those predecessor corporations.

**Related Provisions**: 139.1(3)(g) — Where merger causes demutualization of insurer. See also Related Provisions and Definitions at end of s. 87.

**Notes**: 87(2.2) amended by 1996 Budget, effective for amalgamations that occur after 1995, to add reference to 12(1)(e.1) and

20(22), and to make cosmetic changes in the wording. For earlier amalgamations, read:

(2.2) **Amalgamation of insurance corporations** — Where there has been an amalgamation of two or more corporations and one or more of the predecessor corporations was an insurance corporation, the new corporation shall, notwithstanding subsection (2), be deemed, for the purposes of paragraphs 12(1)(d), (e), (i) and (s) and 20(1)(l), (l.1), (p) and (jj) and 20(7)(c), sections 138, 138.1, 140, 142 and 148 and Part XII.3 of this Act and section 33 of the *Income Tax Act*, chapter 148 of the Revised Statutes of Canada, 1952, to be the same corporation as, and a continuation of, each such predecessor corporation.

87(2.2) amended by 1988 tax reform, effective for amalgamations after December 15, 1987. For amalgamations from 1978 through December 15, 1987, read:

(2.2) **Amalgamation of life insurance corporations** — Where there has been an amalgamation of two or more life insurance corporations after 1977, the new corporation shall be deemed, for purposes of section 138, to be the same corporation as, and a continuation of, each predecessor corporation except that this subsection shall in no respect affect the determination of

(a) the fiscal period of the new corporation or any of its predecessors; or

(b) the taxable income of, or the tax payable under this Act by, any predecessor corporation.

**I.T. Application Rules**: 69 (meaning of "*Income Tax Act*, chapter 148 of the Revised Statutes of Canada, 1952").

**Interpretation Bulletins**: See list at end of s. 87.

**(3) Computation of paid-up capital** — Subject to subsection (3.1), where there is an amalgamation or a merger of 2 or more Canadian corporations, in computing at any particular time the paid-up capital in respect of any particular class of shares of the capital stock of the new corporation,

(a) there shall be deducted that proportion of the amount, if any, by which the paid-up capital, determined without reference to this subsection, in respect of all the shares of the capital stock of the new corporation immediately after the amalgamation or merger exceeds the total of all amounts each of which is the paid-up capital in respect of a share (except a share held by any other predecessor corporation) of the capital stock of a predecessor corporation immediately before the amalgamation or merger, that

(i) the paid-up capital, determined without reference to this subsection, of the particular class of shares of the capital stock of the new corporation immediately after the amalgamation or merger

is of

(ii) the paid-up capital, determined without reference to this subsection, in respect of all of the issued and outstanding shares of the capital stock of the new corporation immediately after the amalgamation or merger; and

(b) there shall be added an amount equal to the lesser of

(i) the amount, if any, by which

(A) the total of all amounts each of which is an amount deemed by subsection 84(3), (4) or (4.1) to be a dividend on shares of the particular class paid by the new corporation before the particular time

exceeds

(B) the total that would be determined under clause (A) if this Act were read without reference to paragraph (a), and

(ii) the amount required by paragraph (a) to be deducted in computing the paid-up capital of shares of the particular class.

**Related Provisions**: 87(3.1) — Election for 87(3) not to apply. See additional Related Provisions and Definitions at end of s. 87.

**Notes**: See Notes to 84(3).

Opening words of 87(3) amended by 1992 technical bill, effective for amalgamations after 1990, to make it subject to 87(3.1).

For amalgamations and mergers before April 1977, read 87(3) as follows:

(3) **Where share of predecessor corporation owned by another such corporation** — Where there has been an amalgamation of two or more corporations after 1971 and, immediately before the amalgamation, one of the predecessor corporations (in this subsection referred to as the "owner corporation") owned any share of the capital stock of another of the predecessor corporations, the following rules apply:

(a) for the purpose of computing the paid-up capital deficiency of the new corporation at any time, the amount, if any, by which the paid-up capital in respect of the share immediately before the amalgamation exceeds the adjusted cost base of the share to the owner corporation immediately before the amalgamation shall be added to the aggregate of the amounts determined under subparagraph 89(1)(d)(iii); and

(b) for the purpose of computing the post-1971 undistributed surplus on hand (within the meaning assigned by subsection 192(15)) of the new corporation at any time, the amount, if any, by which the adjusted cost base of the share to the owner corporation immediately before the amalgamation exceeds the paid-up capital in respect of the share immediately before the amalgamation shall be added to the aggregate of the amounts determined under paragraphs 192(15)(a) to (d).

**Interpretation Bulletins**: See list at end of s. 87.

**(3.1) Election for non-application of subsec. (3)** — Where,

(a) there is an amalgamation of 2 or more corporations,

(b) all of the issued shares, immediately before the amalgamation, of each class of shares (other than a class of shares all of the issued shares of which were cancelled on the amalgamation) of the capital stock of each predecessor corporation (in this subsection referred to as the "exchanged class") are converted into all of the issued shares, immediately after the amalgamation, of a separate class of shares of the capital stock of the new corporation (in this subsection referred to as the "substituted class"),

(c) immediately after the amalgamation, the number of shareholders of each substituted class, the number of shares of each substituted class owned by each shareholder, the number of issued shares of each substituted class, the terms and conditions of each share of a substituted class, and the paid-up capital of each substituted class determined without reference to the provisions of this Act are identical to the number of shareholders of the exchanged class from which the substituted class was converted, the number of shares of each such exchanged class owned by each shareholder, the number of issued shares of each such exchanged class, the terms and conditions of each share of such exchanged class, and the paid-up capital of each such exchanged class determined without reference to the provisions of this Act, respectively, immediately before the amalgamation, and

(d) the new corporation elects in its return of income filed in accordance with section 150 for its first taxation year to have the provisions of this subsection apply,

for the purpose of computing at any particular time the paid-up capital in respect of any particular class of shares of the capital stock of the new corporation,

(e) subsection (3) does not apply in respect of the amalgamation, and

(f) each substituted class shall be deemed to be the same as, and a continuation of, the exchanged class from which it was converted.

**Notes**: 87(3.1) added by 1992 technical bill, effective for amalgamations after 1990.

**(4) Shares of predecessor corporation** — Where there has been an amalgamation of two or more corporations after May 6, 1974, each shareholder (except any predecessor corporation) who, immediately before the amalgamation, owned shares of the capital stock of a predecessor corporation (in this subsection referred to as the "old shares") that were capital property to the shareholder and who received no consideration for the disposition of those shares on the amalgamation, other than shares of the capital stock of the new corporation (in this subsection referred to as the "new shares"), shall be deemed

(a) to have disposed of the old shares for proceeds equal to the total of the adjusted cost bases to the shareholder of those shares immediately before the amalgamation, and

(b) to have acquired the new shares of any particular class of the capital stock of the new corporation at a cost to the shareholder equal to that proportion of the proceeds described in paragraph (a) that

(i) the fair market value, immediately after the amalgamation, of all new shares of that particular class so acquired by the shareholder,

is of

(ii) the fair market value, immediately after the amalgamation, of all new shares so acquired by the shareholder,

except that, where the fair market value of the old shares immediately before the amalgamation exceeds the fair market value of the new shares immediately after the amalgamation and it is reasonable to regard any portion of the excess (in this subsection referred to as the "gift portion") as a benefit that the shareholder desired to have conferred on a person related to the shareholder, the following rules apply:

(c) the shareholder shall be deemed to have disposed of the old shares for proceeds of disposition equal to the lesser of

(i) the total of the adjusted cost bases to the shareholder, immediately before the amalgamation, of the old shares and the gift portion, and

(ii) the fair market value of the old shares immediately before the amalgamation,

(d) the shareholder's capital loss from the disposition of the old shares shall be deemed to be nil,

(e) the cost to the shareholder of any new shares of any class of the capital stock of the new corporation acquired by the shareholder on the amalgamation shall be deemed to be that proportion of the lesser of

(i) the total of the adjusted cost bases to the shareholder, immediately before the amalgamation, of the old shares, and

(ii) the total of the fair market value, immediately after the amalgamation, of all new shares so acquired by the shareholder and the amount that, but for paragraph (d), would have been the shareholder's capital loss from the disposition of the old shares

that

(iii) the fair market value, immediately after the amalgamation, of the new shares of that class so acquired by the shareholder

is of

(iv) the fair market value, immediately after the amalgamation, of all new shares so acquired by the shareholder,

and where the old shares were taxable Canadian property of the shareholder, the new shares shall be deemed to be taxable Canadian property of the shareholder.

**Related Provisions**: 44.1(6), (7) — Small business investment rollover on exchange of shares; 7(1.5) — Shares acquired through employee stock option; 53(4) — Effect on ACB of shares; 87(5) —

Option to acquire share of predecessor corporation; 87(8) — Merger of foreign affiliate; 87(9) — Rules applicable in respect of certain mergers; 95(2)(d) — Merger of foreign affiliate; 107(2)(d.1)(iii), 107.4(3)(f) — Deemed taxable Canadian property retains status when rolled out of trust or into trust. See additional Related Provisions and Definitions at end of s. 87.

**Notes**: 87(4) amended by 1974 and 1979 Budgets. For amalgamations from May 7, 1974 through December 11, 1979, jump from the end of (b)(ii) to the portion following (e)(iv).

For amalgamations from 1972 through May 6, 1974, a different version of 87(4) applied, entitled "Rules applicable for computing income of shareholder of predecessor corporation".

**Interpretation Bulletins**: IT-113R: Benefits to employees — stock options. See also list at end of s. 87.

**(4.1) Exchanged shares** — For the purposes of the definition "term preferred share" in subsection 248(1), where there has been an amalgamation of two or more corporations after November 16, 1978 and a share of any class of the capital stock of the new corporation (in this subsection referred to as the "new share") was issued in consideration for the disposition of a share of any class of the capital stock of a predecessor corporation (in this subsection referred to as the "exchanged share") and the terms and conditions of the new share were the same as, or substantially the same as, the terms and conditions of the exchanged share,

(a) the new share shall be deemed to have been issued at the time the exchanged share was issued;

(b) if the exchanged share was issued under an agreement in writing, the new share shall be deemed to have been issued under that agreement; and

(c) the new corporation shall be deemed to be the same corporation as, and a continuation of, each such predecessor corporation.

**Related Provisions**: 87(9)(a.1) — Rules applicable in respect of certain mergers. See additional Related Provisions and Definitions at end of s. 87.

**Interpretation Bulletins**: See list at end of s. 87.

**(4.2) Idem** — Where there has been an amalgamation or merger of two or more corporations after November 27, 1986 and a share of any class of the capital stock of the new corporation (in this subsection referred to as the "new share") was issued to a shareholder in consideration for the disposition of a share by that shareholder of any class of the capital stock of a predecessor corporation (in this subsection referred to as the "exchanged share") and the terms and conditions of the new share were the same as, or substantially the same as, the terms and conditions of the exchanged share, for the purposes of applying the provisions of this subsection, subsections 112(2.2) and (2.4), Parts IV.1 and VI.1, section 258 and the definitions "grandfathered share", "short-term preferred share", "taxable preferred share" and "taxable RFI share" in subsection 248(1) to the new share, the following rules apply:

(a) the new share shall be deemed to have been issued at the time the exchanged share was issued;

(b) where the exchanged share was a share described in paragraph (a), (b), (c) or (d) of the definition "grandfathered share" in subsection 248(1), the new share shall be deemed to be the same share as the exchanged share for the purposes of that definition;

(c) the new share shall be deemed to have been acquired by the shareholder at the time the exchanged share was acquired by the shareholder;

(d) the new corporation shall be deemed to be the same corporation as, and a continuation of, each predecessor corporation;

(e) an election made under subsection 191.2(1) by a predecessor corporation with respect to the class of shares of its capital stock to which the exchanged share belonged shall be deemed to be an election made by the new corporation with respect to the class of shares of its capital stock to which the new share belongs; and

(f) where the terms or conditions of the exchanged share or an agreement in respect of the exchanged share specify an amount in respect of the exchanged share for the purposes of subsection 191(4) and an amount equal to the amount so specified in respect of the exchanged share is specified in respect of the new share for the purposes of subsection 191(4),

(i) for the purposes of subparagraphs 191(4)(d)(i) and (e)(i), the new share shall be deemed to have been issued for the same consideration as that for which the exchanged share was issued and to have been issued for the purpose for which the exchanged share was issued,

(ii) for the purposes of subparagraphs 191(4)(d)(ii) and (e)(ii), the new share shall be deemed to be the same share as the exchanged share and to have been issued for the purpose for which the exchanged share was issued, and

(iii) where the shareholder received no consideration for the disposition of the exchanged share other than the new share, for the purposes of subsection 191(4),

(A) in the case of an exchanged share to which subsection 191(4) applies because of paragraph 191(4)(a), the new share shall be deemed to have been issued for consideration having a fair market value equal to the consideration for which the exchanged share was issued, and

(B) in the case of an exchanged share to which subsection 191(4) applies because of an event described in paragraph 191(4)(b) or (c), the consideration for which the new share was issued shall be deemed to have a fair market value equal to the fair market value of the exchanged share immediately before the time that event occurred.

**Related Provisions**: 87(9)(a.1) — Rules applicable in respect of certain mergers.

**Notes**: 87(4.2)(f) added by 1991 technical bill, effective 1988.

**Interpretation Bulletins**: See list at end of s. 87.

**(4.3) Exchanged rights** — Where there has been an amalgamation or merger of two or more corporations after June 18, 1987 and a right listed on a prescribed stock exchange to acquire a share of any class of the capital stock of the new corporation (in this subsection referred to as the "new right") was acquired by a shareholder in consideration for the disposition of a right described in paragraph (d) of the definition "grandfathered share" in subsection 248(1) to acquire a share of any class of the capital stock of a predecessor corporation (in this subsection referred to as the "exchanged right"), the new right shall be deemed to be the same right as the exchanged right for the purposes of paragraph (d) of the definition "grandfathered share" in subsection 248(1) where the terms and conditions of the new right were the same as, or substantially the same as, the terms and conditions of the exchanged right and the terms and conditions of the share receivable on an exercise of the new right were the same as, or substantially the same as, the terms and conditions of the share that would have been received on an exercise of the exchanged right.

**Related Provisions**: 87(9)(a.2) — Rules applicable in respect of certain mergers. See additional Related Provisions and Definitions at end of s. 87.

**Regulations**: 3200 (prescribed stock exchange).

**Interpretation Bulletins**: See list at end of s. 87.

**(4.4) Flow-through shares** — Where

(a) there is an amalgamation of two or more corporations each of which is a principal-business corporation (within the meaning assigned by subsection 66(15)) or a corporation that at no time carried on business,

(b) a predecessor corporation entered into an agreement with a person at a particular time for consideration given by the person to the predecessor corporation,

(c) a share of the predecessor corporation

(i) that was a flow-through share (in this subsection having the meaning that would be assigned by subsection 66(15) if the definition "flow-through share" in that subsection were read without reference to the portion after paragraph (b) of that definition) was issued to the person before the amalgamation, or

(ii) that would (if it were issued) be a flow-through share, was to be issued to the person

for the consideration under the agreement, and

(d) the new corporation

(i) issues a share (in this subsection referred to as a "new share") of any class of its capital stock on the amalgamation to the person in consideration for the disposition of the flow-through share of the predecessor corporation and the terms and conditions of the new share are the same as, or substantially the same as, the terms and conditions of the flow-through share, or

(ii) is obliged after the amalgamation to issue a new share of any class of its capital stock to the person under the obligation of the predecessor corporation to issue a flow-through share of the predecessor corporation to the person and the new share would not, if issued, be a prescribed share referred to in the definition "flow-through share" in subsection 66(15),

for the purposes of subsection 66(12.66) and Part XII.6 and for the purposes of renouncing an amount under subsection 66(12.6), (12.601) or (12.62) in respect of Canadian exploration expenses or Canadian development expenses that would, but for the renunciation, be incurred by the new corporation after the amalgamation,

(e) the person shall be deemed to have given the consideration under the agreement to the new corporation for the issue of the new share,

(f) the agreement shall be deemed to have been entered into between the new corporation and the person at the particular time,

(g) the new share shall be deemed to be a flow-through share of the new corporation, and

(h) the new corporation shall be deemed to be the same corporation as, and a continuation of, the predecessor corporation.

**Notes**: Words between (d) and (e) amended by 1992 Economic Statement, effective for amalgamations occurring after December 2, 1992, to add reference to 66(12.601), and amended by 1996 Budget (with the in-force rule corrected by 1995-97 technical bill, s. 308) to add reference to Part XII.6, effective for amalgamations that occur after 1995; and to delete references to 66(12.64) and Canadian oil and gas property expense, effective for amalgamations that occur after 1998.

87(4.4) added by 1991 technical bill, effective March 1986.

**(5) Options to acquire shares of predecessor corporation** — Where there has been an amalgamation of two or more corporations after May 6, 1974, each taxpayer (except any predecessor corporation) who immediately before the amalgamation owned a capital property that was an option to acquire shares of the capital stock of a predecessor corporation (in this subsection referred to as the "old option") and who received no consideration for the disposition of that option on the amalgamation, other than an option to acquire shares of the capital stock of the new corporation (in this subsection referred to as the "new option"), shall be deemed

(a) to have disposed of the old option for proceeds equal to the adjusted cost base to the taxpayer of that option immediately before the amalgamation, and

(b) to have acquired the new option at a cost to the taxpayer equal to the proceeds described in paragraph (a),

and where the old option was taxable Canadian property of the taxpayer, the new option shall be deemed to be taxable Canadian property of the taxpayer.

**Related Provisions**: 7(1.4) — Employee stock options; 87(5.1) — ACB of option; 87(8) — Merger of foreign affiliate; 87(9)(a.3) — Rules applicable in respect of certain mergers; 107(2)(d.1)(iii), 107.4(3)(f) — Deemed taxable Canadian property retains status when rolled out of trust or into trust. See additional Related Provisions and Definitions at end of s. 87.

**Interpretation Bulletins**: See list at end of s. 87.

**(5.1) Adjusted cost base of option** — Where the cost to a taxpayer of a new option is determined at any time under subsection (5),

(a) there shall be deducted after that time in computing the adjusted cost base to the taxpayer of the new option the total of all amounts deducted under paragraph 53(2)(g.1) in computing, immediately before that time, the adjusted cost base to the taxpayer of the old option; and

(b) the amount determined under paragraph (a) shall be added after that time in computing the adjusted cost base to the taxpayer of the new option.

**Related Provisions**: 53(1)(q) — Addition to ACB for amount under 87(5.1)(b); 53(2)(g.1) — Reduction in ACB under 87(5.1)(a); 80.03(2)(a) — Deemed gain on disposition following debt forgiveness.

**Notes**: 87(5.1) added by 1994 tax amendments bill (Part I), effective for taxation years that end after February 21, 1994. See Notes to 47(1).

**(6) Obligations of predecessor corporation** — Notwithstanding subsection (7), where there has been an amalgamation of two or more corporations after May 6, 1974, each taxpayer (except any predecessor corporation) who, immediately before the amalgamation, owned a capital property that was a bond, debenture, mortgage, note or other similar obligation of a predecessor corporation (in this subsection referred to as the "old property") and who received no consideration for the disposition of the old property on the amalgamation other than a bond, debenture, mortgage, note or other similar obligation respectively, of the new corporation (in this subsection referred to as the "new property") shall, if the amount payable to the holder of the new property on its maturity is the same as the amount that would have been payable to the holder of the old property on its maturity, be deemed

(a) to have disposed of the old property for proceeds equal to the adjusted cost base to the taxpayer of that property immediately before the amalgamation; and

(b) to have acquired the new property at a cost to the taxpayer equal to the proceeds described in paragraph (a).

**Related Provisions**: 80(2) — Deemed settlement on amalgamation; 87(6.1) — ACB of property; 88(1)(e.2) — Application to winding-up. See additional Related Provisions and Definitions at end of s. 87.

**Notes**: The term "bond, debenture, bill, note, mortgage or other similar obligation" may not include bankers' acceptances. See *Federated Cooperatives Ltd.*, [2000] 2 C.T.C. 2382 (TCC).

**I.T. Application Rules**: 26(23) (where taxpayer owned the old property since before 1972).

**Interpretation Bulletins**: See list at end of s. 87.

**(6.1) Adjusted cost base** — Where the cost to a taxpayer of a particular property that is a bond, debenture or note is determined at any time under subsection (6) and the terms of the bond, debenture or note conferred upon the holder the right to exchange that bond, debenture or note for shares,

(a) there shall be deducted after that time in computing the adjusted cost base to the taxpayer of the bond, debenture or note the total of all amounts deducted under paragraph 53(2)(g.1) in computing, immediately before that time, the adjusted cost base to the taxpayer of the property for which the particular property was exchanged at that time; and

(b) the amount determined under paragraph (a) in respect of the particular property shall be added after that time in computing the adjusted cost base to the taxpayer of the particular property.

**Related Provisions**: 53(1)(q) — Addition to ACB for amount under 87(6.1)(b); 53(2)(g.1) — Reduction in ACB under 87(6.1)(a); 80.03(2)(a) — Deemed gain on disposition following debt forgiveness.

**Notes**: 87(6.1) added by 1994 tax amendments bill (Part I), effective for taxation years that end after February 21, 1994. See Notes to 47(1).

**(7) [Obligations of predecessor corporation]** — Where there has been an amalgamation of two or more corporations after May 6, 1974 and

(a) a debt or other obligation of a predecessor corporation that was outstanding immediately before the amalgamation became a debt or other obligation of the new corporation on the amalgamation, and

(b) the amount payable by the new corporation on the maturity of the debt or other obligation, as the case may be, is the same as the amount that would have been payable by the predecessor corporation on its maturity, the provisions of this Act

(c) shall not apply in respect of the transfer of the debt or other obligation to the new corporation, and

(d) shall apply as if the new corporation had incurred or issued the debt or other obligation at the time it was incurred or issued by the predecessor corporation under the agreement made on the day on which the predecessor corporation made an agreement under which the debt or other obligation was issued,

except that, for the purposes of the definition "income bond" or "income debenture" in subsection 248(1), paragraph (d) shall not apply to any debt or other obligation of the new corporation unless the terms and conditions thereof immediately after the amalgamation are the same as, or substantially the same as, the terms and conditions of the debt or obligation that was an income bond or income debenture of the predecessor corporation immediately before the amalgamation.

**Related Provisions**: 87(6) — Obligations of predecessor corporation; 88(1)(e.2) — Application to winding-up. See additional Related Provisions and Definitions at end of s. 87.

**Notes**: 87(7)(a) amended by 1992 technical bill, effective June 10, 1993, to delete the exclusion (after the first nine words) "other than any such debt or other obligation owed to any other predecessor corporation". The exclusion was superfluous because such debts are extinguished on amalgamation.

**Interpretation Bulletins**: See list at end of s. 87.

**(8) Foreign merger** — Where there has been a foreign merger in which a taxpayer's shares or options to acquire shares of the capital stock of a corporation that was a predecessor foreign corporation immediately before the merger were exchanged for or became shares or options to acquire shares of the capital stock of the new foreign corporation or the foreign parent corporation, unless the taxpayer elects in the taxpayer's return of income under this Part for the taxation year in which the foreign merger took place not to have this subsection apply, subsections (4) and (5) apply to the taxpayer as if the references in those subsections to

### Proposed Amendment — 87(8) opening words

**(8) Foreign merger** — Subject to subsection 95(2), where there has been a foreign merger in which a taxpayer's shares or options to acquire shares of the capital stock of a corporation that was a predecessor foreign corporation immediately before the merger were exchanged for or became shares or options to acquire shares of the capital stock of the new foreign corporation or the foreign parent corporation, unless the taxpayer elects in the taxpayer's return of income for the taxation year in which the foreign merger took place not to have this subsection apply, subsections (4) and (5) apply to the taxpayer as if the references in those subsections to

**Notes**: This proposal is known informally as the "Chrysler amendment". It was triggered by the merger of (U.S.) Chrysler with (German) Daimler-Benz in 1998, and will allow Canadian shareholders of either pre-merger company to defer capital gains that the merger would have triggered. Before this amendment, the replacement-property rule in 44(1) might have applied; that provision will be amended to eliminate its application to shares.

**Application**: Bill C-43 (First Reading September 20, 2000), subsec. 38(2), will amend the opening words of subsec. 87(8) to read as above, applicable to mergers and combinations that occur after 1995 and, where a taxpayer notifies the Minister of National Revenue in writing before the taxpayer's filing-due date for the taxation year in which the amending legislation is assented to that the taxpayer makes the election referred to in subsec. 87(8), as amended, in respect of a merger or combination that occurred before 1999, the election is deemed to have been validly made in respect of the merger or combination.

**Technical Notes**: Subsections 87(8) and (8.1) of the Act provide tax-deferred rollover treatment to a shareholder of a foreign corporation (a predecessor) in respect of a disposition of shares of the predecessor where the predecessor undergoes a merger with one or more other foreign corporations. It also provides a shareholder with a similar rollover in respect of the disposition of shares of the predecessor in the case of a three-way or "triangular" foreign merger. The rollover is only available where the predecessor corporations, the new corporation formed on the merger and, in the case of a triangular merger, the corporation that controls the new corporation formed on the merger, are resident in the same foreign jurisdiction.

Subsections 87(8) and (8.1) are amended to remove the requirement that all of the corporations be resident in the same foreign jurisdiction. Consequently, the tax-deferred rollover will be available under subsection 87(8) in cases where the foreign corporations are resident in the same or different foreign jurisdictions.

New subsections 87(8) and (8.1) apply to mergers that occur after 1995. Where subsection 87(8) would otherwise apply to a taxpayer in respect of a merger that occurred in 1996, 1997 or 1998, the taxpayer can notify the Minister of National Revenue in writing, before the taxpayer's filing-due date for the taxation year in which subsections 87(8) and (8.1) receive Royal Assent, that the taxpayer elects not to have the subsection apply. Where the taxpayer so elects, the election will be considered to have been made in accordance with new subsection 87(8) of the Act.

**Dept. of Finance news release, April 15, 1999**: See under 85.1(5), (6).

**Letter from Department of Finance, October 8, 1997**:

Dear [xxx]

This is in response to your letters of May 18 and June 20, 1997 and further to your telephone conversations with Davine Roach of the Department regarding the income tax treatment granted a Canadian shareholder of a foreign corporation which has been the subject of a so-called triangular foreign merger. You suggest that the Canadian income tax provisions are deficient in that they do not provide rollover treatment to the Canadian shareholder in such a merger.

As you indicate, the income tax provisions provide in certain circumstances for the tax deferred exchange by a Canadian shareholder of a share of a "predecessor foreign corporation" for a share of the "new foreign corporation" formed on the merger of the predecessor foreign corporation and another "predecessor foreign corporation" (a "foreign merger"). The provisions do not however provide for such a tax-deferred exchange where such a shareholder exchanges a share of the foreign predecessor corporation for a share of the foreign corporation that controls, immediately after the merger, the new foreign corporation (a "triangular foreign merger"). You believe this is unintended because the Canadian shareholder should be treated the same in respect of an exchanged share under both the foreign merger and the triangular foreign merger.

From a tax policy perspective, we agree that it would be appropriate for a Canadian shareholder of a predecessor foreign corporation to receive rollover tax treatment in the case of a triangular foreign merger. Therefore, we are prepared to recommend to the Minister of Finance that the *Income Tax Act* be amended to accommodate such mergers. In particular, such amendments would provide that a Canadian shareholder of a predecessor foreign corporation would receive rollover treatment in respect of the adjusted cost base of a share of the predecessor foreign corporation owned by the shareholder and exchanged for a share of the foreign corporation that controls, immediately after the merger, the new foreign corporation formed as a result of the merger of the predecessor foreign corporation and another predecessor foreign corporation where such predecessor corporations and controlling corporation are all resident of the same country.

We would recommend that such amendments apply in respect of triangular foreign mergers that occur after 1996. If this recommendation is acted upon, I would anticipate that such an amendment would be included in a future technical bill.

Yours sincerely,

Len Farber
Director General, Tax Legislation Division

(a) "amalgamation" were read as "foreign merger";

(b) "predecessor corporation" were read as "predecessor foreign corporation"; and

(c) "new corporation" were read as "new foreign corporation or the foreign parent corporation".

**Related Provisions**: 87(8.1) — Definition of "foreign merger"; 95(2)(d) — Effect of foreign merger on FAPI. See additional Related Provisions and Definitions at end of s. 87.

**Notes**: 87(8) amended by 1998 Budget to add "or options to acquire shares" (two places), to add reference to 87(5), and to delete subpara. (d), effective for a taxpayer in respect of a merger or combination of foreign corporations

(a) that occurs after February 24, 1998, or

(b) that occurred

(i) before February 25, 1998 and in a taxation year for which the taxpayer's normal reassessment period, as defined in 152(3.1), has not ended before 1999, or

(ii) after 1994 and before February 25, 1998 and in a taxation year in which the taxpayer was exempt under section 149,

unless the taxpayer elects by notifying Revenue Canada in writing, by the end of 1999, that the amendments to 87(8) and (8.1) not apply to the taxpayer in respect of the merger or combination. Before the amendment, read 87(8)(d) as:

(d) "May 6, 1974" were read as "November 12, 1981".

87(8) amended by 1981 Budget, effective for foreign mergers after November 12, 1981. For earlier mergers, read:

(8) Where there has been a merger of a foreign affiliate of a taxpayer (in this subsection referred to as a "predecessor affiliate") and one or more other corporations to form one corporate entity (in this subsection referred to as a "new affiliate") that, immediately after the merger, is a foreign affiliate of the taxpayer and such merger is not as a result of the acquisition of property of one corporation by another corporation, pursuant to the purchase of such property by the other corporation, or as a result of the distribution of such property to another corporation upon the winding-up of the predecessor affiliate, subsection (4) applies to the taxpayer as if the references therein to

(a) "amalgamation" were read as "merger";

(b) "predecessor corporation" were read as "predecessor affiliate";

(c) "new corporation" were read as "new affiliate"; and

(d) "May 6, 1974" were read as "1971".

**Interpretation Bulletins**: See list at end of s. 87.

**(8.1) Definition of "foreign merger"** — For the purposes of this section, "foreign merger" means a merger or combination of two or more corporations each of which was, immediately before the merger or combination, resident in a country other than Canada (each of which is in this section referred to as a "predecessor foreign corporation") to form one corporate entity resident in the country in which all the predecessor foreign corporations were resident (in this section referred to as the "new foreign corporation") in such manner that

(a) all or substantially all the property (except amounts receivable from any predecessor foreign corporation or shares of the capital stock of any predecessor foreign corporation) of the predecessor foreign corporations immediately before the merger or combination becomes property of the new foreign corporation by virtue of the merger or combination,

(b) all or substantially all the liabilities (except amounts payable to any predecessor foreign corporation) of the predecessor foreign corporations immediately before the merger or combination become liabilities of the new foreign corporation by virtue of the merger or combination, and

(c) all or substantially all of the shares of the capital stock of the predecessor foreign corporations (except any shares or options owned by any predecessor foreign corporation) are exchanged for or become, because of the merger or combination,

(i) shares of the capital stock of the new foreign corporation, or

(ii) if, immediately after the merger, the new foreign corporation was controlled by another foreign corporation (in this section referred to as the "foreign parent corporation") that was resident in the same country as the new foreign corporation, shares of the capital stock of the foreign parent corporation, otherwise than as a result of the distribution of property to one corporation on the winding-up of another corporation.

### Proposed Amendment — 87(8.1)

**(8.1) Definition of "foreign merger"** — For the purposes of this section, "foreign merger" means a merger or combination of two or more corporations each of which was, immediately before the merger or combination, resident in a country other than Canada (each of which is in this section referred to as a "predecessor foreign corporation") to form one corporate entity resident in a country other than Canada (in this section referred to as the "new foreign corporation") in such a manner that, and otherwise than as a result of the distribution of property to one corporation on the winding-up of another corporation,

(a) all or substantially all the property (except amounts receivable from any predecessor foreign corporation or shares of the capital stock of any predecessor foreign corporation) of the predecessor foreign corporations immediately before the merger or combination becomes property of the new foreign corporation as a consequence of the merger or combination;

(b) all or substantially all the liabilities (except amounts payable to any predecessor foreign corporation) of the predecessor foreign corporations immediately before the merger or combination become liabilities of the new foreign corporation as a consequence of the merger or combination; and

(c) all or substantially all of the shares of the capital stock of the predecessor foreign corporations (except any shares or options owned by any predecessor foreign corporation) are exchanged for or become, because of the merger or combination,

(i) shares of the capital stock of the new foreign corporation, or

(ii) if, immediately after the merger, the new foreign corporation was controlled by another corporation (in this section referred to as the "foreign parent corporation") that was resident in a country other than Canada, shares of the capital stock of the foreign parent corporation.

**Application**: Bill C-43 (First Reading September 20, 2000), subsec. 38(3), will amend subsec. 87(8.1) to read as above, applicable to mergers and combinations that occur after 1995.

**Technical Notes and Letter from Department of Finance**: See under 87(8).

**Related Provisions**: 95(4.1) — Application to FAPI; 256(6), (6.1) — Meaning of "controlled". See Related provisions and Definitions at end of s. 87.

**Notes**: 87(8.1)(c) amended by 1998 Budget to add "or options" and subpara. (ii), effective on same basis as the amendments to 87(8).

87(8.1) added by 1981 Budget, effective for foreign mergers after November 12, 1981.

Before re-enactment in R.S.C. 1985, (5th Supp.), 87(8.1) explicitly applied for purposes of section 95. This rule of application is now in 95(4.1).

The CCRA takes the position that "all or substantially all" means 90% or more.

**Interpretation Bulletins**: See list at end of s. 87.

**(9) Rules applicable in respect of certain mergers [triangular amalgamation]** — Where there has been a merger of two or more taxable Canadian corporations to form a new corporation that was controlled, immediately after the merger, by a taxable Canadian corporation (in this subsection referred to as the "parent") and, on the merger, shares of the capital stock of the parent (in this subsection referred to as "parent shares") were issued by the parent to persons who were, immediately before the merger, shareholders of a predecessor corporation, the following rules apply:

(a) for the purposes of paragraph (1)(c), subsection (4) and the *Income Tax Application Rules*, any parent shares received by a shareholder of a predecessor corporation shall be deemed to be shares of the capital stock of the new corporation received by the shareholder by virtue of the merger;

(a.1) for the purposes of subsections (4.1) and (4.2), a parent share issued to a shareholder in consideration for the disposition of a share of a class of the capital stock of a predecessor corporation shall be deemed to be a share of a class of the capital stock of the new corporation that was issued in consideration for the disposition of a share of a class of the capital stock of a predecessor corporation by that shareholder;

(a.2) for the purposes of subsection (4.3), a right listed on a prescribed stock exchange to acquire a share of a class of the capital stock of the parent shall be deemed to be a right listed on a prescribed stock exchange to acquire a share of a class of the capital stock of the new corporation;

(a.3) for the purpose of applying subsection (5) in respect of the merger, the reference in that subsection to "the new corporation" shall be read as a reference to "the parent";

(a.4) for the purpose of paragraph (c), any shares of the new corporation acquired by the parent on the merger shall be deemed to be new shares;

(a.5) for the purpose of applying subsection (10) in respect of the merger,

(i) the reference in paragraph (10)(b) to "the new corporation" shall be read as a reference to "the new corporation or the parent, within the meaning assigned by subsection (9)", and

(ii) the references in paragraphs (10)(c) and (f) to "the new corporation" shall be read as references to "the public corporation described in paragraph (b)".

(b) in computing, at any particular time, the paid-up capital in respect of any particular class of shares of the capital stock of the parent that included parent shares immediately after the merger

(i) there shall be deducted that proportion of the amount, if any, by which the paid-up capital, determined without reference to this paragraph, in respect of all the shares of the capital stock of the parent immediately after the merger exceeds the total of all amounts each of which is the paid-up capital in respect of a share of the capital stock of the parent or a predecessor corporation (other than any share of a predecessor corporation owned by the parent or by another predecessor corporation and any share of a predecessor corporation owned by a shareholder other than the parent or another predecessor corporation that was not exchanged on the merger for parent shares) immediately before the merger that

(A) the paid-up capital, determined without reference to this paragraph, in respect of that particular class of shares of the capital stock of the parent immediately after the merger

is of

(B) the paid-up capital, determined without reference to this paragraph, in respect of all the issued and outstanding shares of the classes of the capital stock of the parent that included parent shares immediately after the merger, and

(ii) there shall be added an amount equal to the lesser of

(A) the amount, if any, by which

(I) the total of all amounts each of which is an amount deemed by subsection 84(3), (4) or (4.1) to be a dividend on shares of the particular class paid by the parent before the particular time

exceeds

(II) the total that would be determined under subclause (I) if this Act were read without reference to subparagraph (i), and

(B) the amount required by subparagraph (i) to be deducted in computing the paid-up capital of shares of the particular class; and

(c) notwithstanding paragraph (4)(b), the parent shall be deemed to have acquired the new shares of any particular class of the capital stock of the new corporation at a cost equal to the total of

(i) the amount otherwise determined under paragraph (4)(b) to be the cost of those shares, and

(ii) in any case where the parent owned, immediately after the merger, all of the issued shares of the capital stock of the new corporation, such portion of

(A) the amount, if any, by which

(I) the amount by which the total of the money on hand of the new corporation and all amounts each of which is the cost amount to the new corporation of a property owned by it, immediately after the merger, exceeds the total of all amounts each of which is the amount of any debt owing by the new corporation, or of any other obligation of the new corporation to pay any amount, that was outstanding immediately after the merger,

exceeds

(II) the total of the adjusted cost bases to the parent of all shares of the capital stock of each predecessor corporation beneficially owned by it immediately before the merger

as is designated by the parent in respect of the shares of that particular class in its return of income under this Part for its taxation year in which the merger occurred, except that

(B) in no case shall the amount so designated in respect of the shares of a particular class exceed the amount, if any, by which the total fair market value, immediately after the merger, of the shares of that particular class issued by virtue of the merger exceeds the cost of those shares to the parent determined without reference to this paragraph, and

(C) in no case shall the total of the amounts so designated in respect of the shares of each class of the capital stock of the new corporation exceed the amount determined under clause (A).

**Related Provisions**: 88(4) — Amalgamation deemed not to be acquisition of control; 256(6), (6.1) — Meaning of "controlled". See also Related provisions and Definitions at end of s. 87.

**Notes**: The merger described in 87(9) is generally referred to as a "triangular amalgamation".

87(9) added by 1978 Budget, effective for amalgamations after November 16, 1978.

87(9)(a.1) and (a.2) added by 1991 technical bill, effective for amalgamations and mergers after 1986.

87(9)(a.3) and (a.4) added by 1992 technical bill, effective for amalgamations and mergers after December 20, 1991.

87(9)(a.5) added by 1995-97 technical bill, this version effective for amalgamations that occur after 1997. For amalgamations from April 27, 1995 to the end of 1997, read:

(a.5) for the purpose of applying subsection (10) in respect of the merger,

(i) any share issued by the parent on the merger is deemed to have been issued by the new corporation, and

## S. 87(9) — Income Tax Act, Part I, Division B

(ii) the reference in paragraph (10)(f) to "the new corporation" shall be read as a reference to "the corporation that issued the share";

**Regulations**: 3200 (prescribed stock exchange).

### (10) Share deemed listed — Where

(a) a new corporation is formed as a result of an amalgamation,

(b) the new corporation is a public corporation,

(c) the new corporation issues a share (in this subsection referred to as the "new share") of its capital stock,

(d) the new share is issued in exchange for a share (in this subsection referred to as the "old share") of the capital stock of a predecessor corporation,

(e) immediately before the amalgamation, the old share was listed on a prescribed stock exchange, and

(f) the new share is redeemed, acquired or cancelled by the new corporation within 60 days after the amalgamation,

the new share is deemed, for the purposes of subsections 115(1) and 116(6) and the definitions "qualified investment" in subsections 146(1), 146.1(1) and 146.3(1) and in section 204, to be listed on the exchange until the earliest time at which it is so redeemed, acquired or cancelled.

> **Proposed Amendment — 87(10) closing words**
>
> the new share is deemed, for the purposes of subsection 116(6), the definitions "qualified investment" in subsections 146(1), 146.1(1), and 146.3(1) and in section 204, and the definition "taxable Canadian property" in subsection 248(1), to be listed on the exchange until the earliest time at which it is so redeemed, acquired or cancelled.
>
> **Application**: Bill C-43 (First Reading September 20, 2000), subsec. 38(4), will amend the closing words of subsec. 87(10) to read as above, applicable after October 1, 1996.
>
> **Technical Notes**: Section 87 of the Act sets out rules that apply where there has been an amalgamation of two or more taxable Canadian corporations to form a new corporation.
>
> Subsection 87(10) of the Act treats certain shares issued as part of an "amalgamation squeeze-out" as being listed on a prescribed stock exchange. The subsection is amended, with application after October 1, 1996, to replace its reference to subsection 115(1) of the Act with a reference to the new definition "taxable Canadian property" in subsection 248(1) of the Act. This consequential change is not intended to have any substantive effect on the operation of subsection 87(10).

**Notes**: 87(10) added by 1995-97 technical bill, this version effective for amalgamations that occur after June 1996. For amalgamations occurring from April 27, 1995 to June 30, 1996, ignore para. (b).

Closing words of 87(10) amended by 1998 Budget to add reference to 146.1(1), effective 1998.

**Regulations**: 3200, 3201 (prescribed stock exchanges; expected to be amended to cover 87(10)).

### (11) Vertical amalgamations — 
Where at any time there is an amalgamation of a corporation (in this subsection referred to as the "parent") and one or more other corporations (each of which in this subsection is referred to as the "subsidiary") each of which is a subsidiary wholly-owned corporation of the parent,

(a) the shares of the subsidiary are deemed to have been disposed of by the parent immediately before the amalgamation for proceeds equal to the proceeds that would be determined under paragraph 88(1)(b) if subsections 88(1) and (1.7) applied, with any modifications that the circumstances require, to the amalgamation; and

(b) the cost to the new corporation of each capital property of the subsidiary acquired on the amalgamation is deemed to be the amount that would have been the cost to the parent of the property if the property had been distributed at that time to the parent on a winding-up of the subsidiary and subsections 88(1) and (1.7) had applied to the winding-up.

**Related Provisions**: 87(2.11) — Vertical amalgamation — carryback of losses; 87(9)(a.5) — Application on triangular amalgamation.

**Notes**: 87(11) added by 1995-97 technical bill, effective for amalgamations occurring after 1994. However:

- For the purpose of 87(11)(b), a designation by a new corporation of an amount under 88(1)(d) that was filed with Revenue Canada by Sept. 30, 1998 is deemed to have been made by the new corporation in its Part I return for its first taxation year;

- Where the new corporation formed on an amalgamation before June 20, 1996 elects in writing, filed with Revenue Canada with the return for the parent's taxation year that ended immediately before the amalgamation, or within 90 days after any assessment or reassessment of tax payable under Part I for the year, 87(11) does not apply to the amalgamation. (1995-97 technical bill, subsec. 117(27).)

**Related Provisions [s. 87]**: 66.7 — Resource taxation — successor corporation rules; 89(1)"Canadian corporation" — Whether amalgamated corporation is a Canadian corporation; 128.2 — Predecessor corporations take on residence status of amalgamated corporation; 134 — Status of non-resident-owned investment corporation for purposes of s. 87; 142.6(5), (6) — Acquisition of specified debt obligation by financial institution in rollover transaction; 251(3.1), (3.2) — Amalgamated corporation — whether related to predecessor.

**Definitions [s. 87]**: "adjusted cost base" — 54, 248(1); "amalgamation" — 87(1); "amount" — 248(1); "business" — 248(1); "business limit" — 125(2)–(5.1), 248(1); "calendar year" — *Interpretation Act* 37(1)(a); "Canada" — 255; "Canadian corporation" — 89(1), 248(1); "Canadian development expense" — 66.2(5), 248(1); "Canadian exploration expense" — 66.1(6), 248(1); "Canadian oil and gas property expense" — 66.4(5), 248(1); "capital dividend" — 83(2), 248(1); "capital gain", "capital loss" — 39(1), 248(1); "capital property" — 54, 248(1); "carrying on business" — 253; "cash method" — 248(1); "class of shares" — 248(6); "common share" — 248(1); "controlled directly or indirectly" — 256(5.1), (6.2); "corporation" — 248(1), *Interpretation Act* 35(1); "cost amount" — 248(1); "cumulative eligible capital" — 14(5), 248(1); "depreciable property" — 13(21), 248(1); "dividend" — 248(1); "eligible capital amount" — 14(1), 248(1); "eligible capital expenditure" — 14(5), 248(1); "eligible capital property" — 54, 248(1); "employment" — 248(1); "farming" — 248(1); "farm loss" — 111(8), 248(1); "financial institution" — 87(1.5), 142.2(1); "fiscal period" — 249(2)(b), 249.1; "flow-through share" — 66(15), 87(4.4), 248(1); "foreign affiliate" — 95(1), 248(1); "foreign merger" — 87(8.1); "foreign parent corporation" — 87(8.1)(c); "former business property" — 248(1); "grandfathered share", "income bond", "insurance corporation", "insurer", "inventory" — 248(1); "investment corporation" — 130(3), 248(1); "investment tax credit" — 127(9), 248(1); "lending asset" — 248(1); "life insurance capital dividend" — 83(2.1), 248(1); "life insurance corporation", "limited partnership loss" — 248(1); "mark-to-market property" — 87(1.5), 142.2(1); "mineral" — 248(1); "mutual fund corporation" — 131(8), 248(1); "net capital loss" — 111(8), 248(1); "new corporation" — 87(1); "new foreign corporation" — 87(8.1); "non-capital loss" — 111(8), 248(1); "paid-up capital" — 89(1), 248(1); "person" — 248(1); "predecessor corporation" — 87(1); "predecessor foreign corporation" — 87(8.1); "preferred share", "prescribed" — 248(1); "prescribed stock exchange" — Reg. 3200, 3201; "private corporation" — 89(1), 248(1); "property" — 248(1); "public corporation" — 89(1), 248(1); "qualified expenditure" — 37.1(5), 87(2.01); "regulation" — 248(1); "research property" — 37.1(5), 87(2.01); "restricted farm loss" — 31, 248(1); "share", "shareholder", "short-term preferred share" — 248(1); "specified debt obligation" — 87(1.5), 142.2(1); "specified future tax consequence" — 248(1); "subsidiary wholly-owned corporation" — 87(1.4), 248(1); "tax payable" — 248(2); "taxable Canadian corporation" — 89(1), 248(1); "taxable Canadian property" — 248(1); "taxable dividend" — 89(1), 248(1); "taxable income" — 2(2), 248(1); "taxable preferred share", "taxable RFI share" — 248(1); "taxation year" — 87(2)(a), 249; "taxpayer", "term preferred share" — 248(1); "writing" — *Interpretation Act* 35(1).

**I.T. Application Rules [s. 87]**: 20(1.2), 26(21)–(23), 34(4), (7), 58(3.3).

**Interpretation Bulletins [s. 87]**: IT-52R4: Income bonds and income debentures; IT-121R3: Election to capitalize cost of borrowed money; IT-151R5: Scientific research and experimental development expenditures; IT-243R4: Dividend refund to private corporations; IT-315: Interest expense incurred for the purpose of winding-up or amalgamation; IT-474R: Amalgamations of Canadian corporations; IT-488R2: Winding-up of 90%-owned taxable Canadian corporations.

**Information Circulars [s. 87]**: 88-2, para. 20: General anti-avoidance rule — section 245 of the *Income Tax Act*.

## 88. (1) Winding-up [of subsidiary] — Where a taxable Canadian corporation (in this subsection referred to as the "subsidiary") has been wound up after May 6, 1974 and not less than 90% of the issued shares of each class of the capital stock of the subsidiary were, immediately before the winding-up, owned by another taxable Canadian corporation (in this subsection referred to as the "parent") and all of the shares of the subsidiary that were not owned by the parent immediately before the winding-up were owned at that time by persons with whom the parent was dealing at arm's length, notwithstanding any other provision of this Act other than subsection 69(11), the following rules apply:

**Related Provisions**: See at end of subsec. 88(1).

**Notes**: Where the conditions in the opening words of 88(1) are satisfied (an "88(1) windup"), there is a general rollover of most properties and tax accounts, as set out in the rest of 88(1) (see especially 88(1)(e.2)). Otherwise, 88(2) applies. See also 84(2) and 69(5).

Opening words of 88(1) amended by 1979 Budget, effective for windups commencing on January 13, 1981 or later, to add the restriction that shares not owned by the parent be owned by persons dealing at arm's length with the parent. However, the opening words were substituted in 1987, effective January 16, 1987, to add the words "other than subsection 69(11)"; theoretically, the fact the opening words were substituted for all purposes effective that date means that 88(1), to the extent that it still applies to pre-1981 windups (e.g., to determine the cost of property), contains the indicated restriction even for such windups.

For windups ending before November 16, 1978, the opening words applied only in the case of 100% ownership of the subsidiary, and applied to any Canadian corporations (parent and subsidiary), not just taxable Canadian corporations.

(a) **[property of subsidiary]** — subject to paragraphs (a.1) and (a.3), each property (other than an interest in a partnership) of the subsidiary that was distributed to the parent on the winding-up shall be deemed to have been disposed of by the subsidiary for proceeds equal to

(i) in the case of a Canadian resource property, a foreign resource property or a right to receive production (as defined in subsection 18.1(1)) to which a matchable expenditure (as defined in subsection 18.1(1)) relates, nil, and

(ii) [Repealed]

(iii) in the case of any other property, the cost amount to the subsidiary of the property immediately before the winding-up;

**Related Provisions**: 53(4) — Effect on ACB of share or trust interest; 84(2) — Deemed dividend on distribution of assets; 88(2) — Windup of other corporation.

**Notes**: The phrase "(other than an interest in a partnership)" added to the opening words of 88(1)(a) by 1987 Budget, effective for windups after January 15, 1987.

Reference to 88(1)(a.3) added to opening words of 88(1)(a) by 1994 tax amendments bill (Part III), effective for windups that begin after February 22, 1994.

88(1)(a)(i) amended by 1995-97 technical bill, effective November 18, 1996, to add reference to a right to receive production to which a matchable expenditure relates.

88(1)(a)(ii) amended by 1991 technical bill but repealed retroactively by 1992 technical bill, both effective for windings-up in a subsidiary's taxation year that begins after June 1988. (Amended 248(1)"cost amount"(d) now multiplies the prorated cumulative eligible capital by $4/3$ to account for the $3/4$ inclusion rate in 14(5)"cumulative eligible capital" on eligible capital property.) For earlier windings-up, read:

(ii) in the case of any eligible capital property, an amount equal to twice the cost amount to the subsidiary of that property immediately before the winding-up, and

**Interpretation Bulletins**: IT-259R3: Exchanges of property.

**Advance Tax Rulings**: ATR-67: Increase in the cost of property on the winding-up of a wholly-owned subsidiary.

(a.1) **[property of subsidiary]** — each property of the subsidiary that was distributed to the parent on the winding-up shall, for the purpose of paragraph (2.1)(b) or (e), be deemed not to have been disposed of;

(a.2) **[partnership interest]** — each interest of the subsidiary in a partnership that was distributed to the parent on the winding-up shall, except for the purpose of paragraph 98(5)(g), be deemed not to have been disposed of by the subsidiary;

**S. 88(1)(a.2)**   Income Tax Act, Part I, Division B

**Notes**: 88(1)(a.2) amended by 1991 technical bill, effective for windups beginning after January 15, 1987, so as not to apply for purposes of 98(5)(g).

(a.3) **[specified debt obligation]** — where

(i) the subsidiary was a financial institution in its taxation year in which its assets were distributed to the parent on the winding up, and

(ii) the parent was a financial institution in its taxation year in which it received the assets of the subsidiary on the winding up,

each specified debt obligation (other than a mark-to-market property) of the subsidiary that was distributed to the parent on the winding-up shall, except for the purpose of subsection 69(11), be deemed not to have been disposed of, and for the purpose of this paragraph, "financial institution", "mark-to-market property" and "specified debt obligation" have the meanings assigned by subsection 142.2(1);

**Related Provisions**: Reg. 8103(3) — Mark-to-market — transition inclusion; Reg. 9204(2) — Residual portion of specified debt obligation.

**Notes**: 88(1)(a.3) added by 1994 tax amendments bill (Part III), effective for windups that begin after February 22, 1994.

(b) **[shares of subsidiary]** — the shares of the capital stock of the subsidiary owned by the parent immediately before the winding-up shall be deemed to have been disposed of by the parent on the winding-up for proceeds equal to the greater of

(i) the lesser of the paid-up capital in respect of those shares immediately before the winding-up and the amount determined under subparagraph (d)(i), and

(ii) the total of all amounts each of which is an amount in respect of any share of the capital stock of the subsidiary so disposed of by the parent on the winding-up, equal to the adjusted cost base to the parent of the share immediately before the winding-up;

**Related Provisions**: 80.01(5) — Determination of proceeds of disposition of distress preferred share to subsidiary; 80.03(1), (3)(a)(i) — Capital gain where para. 88(1)(b) applies to share on disposition following debt forgiveness; 87(11) — Application to vertical amalgamation. See additional Related Provisions at end of 88(1).

(c) **[cost to parent]** — subject to paragraph 87(2)(e.3) (as modified by paragraph (e.2)), and notwithstanding paragraph 87(2)(e.1) (as modified by paragraph (e.2)), the cost to the parent of each property of the subsidiary distributed to the parent on the winding-up shall be deemed to be

(i) in the case of a property that is an interest in a partnership, the amount that but for this paragraph would be the cost to the parent of the property, and

(ii) in any other case, the amount, if any, by which

(A) the amount that would, but for subsection 69(11), be deemed by paragraph (a) to be the proceeds of disposition of the property

exceeds

(B) any reduction of the cost amount to the subsidiary of the property made because of section 80 on the winding-up,

plus, where the property was a capital property (other than an ineligible property) of the subsidiary at the time that the parent last acquired control of the subsidiary and was owned by the subsidiary thereafter without interruption until such time as it was distributed to the parent on the winding-up, the amount determined under paragraph (d) in respect of the property and, for the purposes of this paragraph, "ineligible property" means

(iii) depreciable property,

(iv) property transferred to the parent on the winding-up where the transfer is part of a distribution (within the meaning assigned by subsection 55(1)) made in the course of a reorganization in which a dividend was received to which subsection 55(2) would, but for paragraph 55(3)(b), apply,

(v) property acquired by the subsidiary from the parent or from any person or partnership that was not (otherwise than because of a right referred to in paragraph 251(5)(b)) dealing at arm's length with the parent, or any other property acquired by the subsidiary in substitution for it, where the acquisition was part of the series of transactions or events in which the parent last acquired control of the subsidiary, and

**Letter from Department of Finance, October 8, 1997**:

Dear [xxx]

This is in response to your letter of October 7, 1997 to Davine Roach of this Department, on behalf of your client, [xxx], regarding subparagraph 88(1)(c)(v) of the *Income Tax Act*. In particular, you ask if we could confirm our intention to recommend to the Minister of Finance that a particular amendment be made to subparagraph 88(1)(c)(v).

We can confirm that we are prepared to recommend to the Minister of Finance that subparagraph 88(1)(c)(v) of the *Income Tax Act* be amended to refer to property transferred to the subsidiary by the parent or a person or partnership that was not (otherwise than because of a right referred to in paragraph 251(5)(b)) dealing at arm's length with the parent where the transfer was made as part of the series of transactions or events in which the parent last acquired control of the subsidiary. It will be recommended that such an amendment be effective for windings-up that begin after 1996.

If the recommendation is acted upon, I would anticipate that such an amendment would be included in a future technical bill.

Yours sincerely,

Len Farber
Director General, Tax Legislation Division

(vi) property distributed to the parent on the winding-up where, as part of the series of transactions or events that includes the winding-up,

(A) the parent acquired control of the subsidiary, and

(B) any property distributed to the parent on the winding-up or any other property acquired by any person in substitution therefor is acquired by

(I) a particular person (other than a specified person) that, at any time during the course of the series and before control of the subsidiary was last acquired by the parent, was a specified shareholder of the subsidiary,

(II) 2 or more persons (other than specified persons), if a particular person would have been, at any time during the course of the series and before control of the subsidiary was last acquired by the parent, a specified shareholder of the subsidiary if all the shares that were then owned by those 2 or more persons were owned at that time by the particular person, or

(III) a corporation (other than a specified person)

### Proposed Amendment — 88(1)(c)(vi)(B)(III) opening words

(III) a corporation (other than a specified person or the subsidiary)

**Application**: Bill C-43 (First Reading September 20, 2000), subsec. 39(1), will amend the opening words of subcl. 88(1)(c)(vi)(B)(III) to read as above, applicable to windings-up that begin after November 1994.

**Technical Notes**: Section 88 of the Act deals with the tax consequences arising from the winding-up of a corporation. Subsection 88(1) provides rules that apply where a subsidiary has been wound up into its parent corporation where both corporations are taxable Canadian corporations and the parent owns at least 90% of the issued shares of each class of the subsidiary's capital stock.

Paragraph 88(1)(c) of the Act provides that the cost to a parent corporation of each property distributed to it on the winding-up of a subsidiary is equal to the subsidiary's proceeds of disposition of the property plus, where the property is not an "ineligible property", an amount determined under paragraph 88(1)(d) of the Act in respect of the property. An ineligible property is defined in paragraph 88(1)(c) and consists of four types of property. Subparagraph 88(1)(c)(vi) describes the fourth type of ineligible property.

Subclause 88(1)(c)(vi)(B)(III) of the Act provides that property will be an ineligible property for the purposes of paragraph 88(1)(c) where the property distributed to the parent on the winding-up is acquired as part of the series of transactions or events that includes the winding-up by a person described in subclause 88(1)(c)(vi)(B)(III).

A person described in subclause 88(1)(c)(vi)(B)(III) of the Act is

A. a corporation (other than a specified person) of which any person who was a specified shareholder of the subsidiary is a specified shareholder, or

B. a corporation (other than a specified person) in which persons described in subclause 88(1)(c)(vi)(B)(II) owns shares that, if owned by one person, would have made that person a specified shareholder of the corporation.

Subclause 88(1)(c)(vi)(B)(III) of the Act is amended to also exclude from persons described therein the subsidiary itself. This amendment will ensure that where a target/subsidiary corporation transfers some of its property to a subsidiary of the target prior to the parent's acquisition of control of the target, the transfer, in and by itself, will not cause property distributed to the parent on the winding-up of the target/subsidiary to be ineligible property.

### Letter from Department of Finance, June 19, 1998:

Dear [xxx]

This is in reply to your letter of May 28, 1998 to Davine Roach of the Department regarding the application of proposed subclause 88(1)(c)(vi)(B)(III) of the *Income Tax Act* (the "Act") to the proposed takeover transaction described in your letter. You believe this application gives rise to unintended tax consequences and ask that consideration be given to amending the subclause to ensure the appropriate tax results.

Based on our understanding of the facts of the proposed transaction, proposed subclause 88(1)(c)(vi)(B)(III) will cause the Opco shares to be "ineligible property" for the purpose of paragraph 88(1)(c) of the Act and therefore ineligible for a step-up in tax basis. The Opco shares will be rendered "ineligible property" because of the fact that as part of the series of transactions or events in which PCo acquired control of TCo and in which Amalco was wound-up into PCo, Holdco acquired the shares of Opco.

In these circumstances, we agree that the Opco shares should not be "ineligible property" for the purposes of the step-up in tax basis under paragraph 88(1)(c) of the Act. Consequently, we will recommend to the Minister of Finance that an amendment to paragraph 88(1)(c)(vi) of the Act be introduced to ensure that, in the circumstances described in your letter, the Opco shares will not be "ineligible property". We will recommend that such an amendment be effective for windings-up that occur after November 1994. If the recommendation is acted upon, I would anticipate that such an amendment would be included in the government's next technical bill.

Yours sincerely,

Len Farber
Director General, Tax Legislation Division

### Letter from Department of Finance, October 8, 1997:

Dear [xxx]

This is in response to your letter of September 24, 1997 to Davine Roach of the Department regarding amended subparagraph 88(1)(c)(vi) of the *Income Tax Act* as contained in Bill C-69. You ask if we would reconsider the appropriateness of the application of this subparagraph in view of the transaction described in your letter.

Based on our understanding of your transaction, the Newco shares will be considered to be substituted property for the purposes of subparagraph 88(1)(c)(vi) of the *Income Tax Act*. As a result, the partnership interests distributed to Buyco on the winding-up of Newco will be considered to be ineligible property for the purposes of the step-up in cost under paragraph 88(1)(c) of the *Income Tax Act*.

We are prepared to recommend to the Minister of Finance that the income tax provisions be amended so that in the transaction you describe the Newco shares will not be considered to be substituted property for the purposes of subparagraph 88(1)(c)(vi) of the *Income Tax Act*. It will be recommended that such an amendment have the same effective date as currently provided for proposed paragraph 88(1)(c.3) of the *Income Tax Act* included in former Bill C-69.

If the recommendation is acted upon, I would anticipate that the amendment would be included in either the bill that replaces former Bill C-69 or a future technical bill.

Yours sincerely,

Len Farber
Director General, Tax Legislation Division

### Letter from Department of Finance, August 28, 1997:

Dear [xxx]

This is in response to your letter of August 26, 1997 regarding proposed paragraph 88(1)(c.3) of the *Income Tax Act*. You state that the current wording of proposed paragraph 88(1)(c.3) is too restrictive thereby rendering a capital property that would otherwise qualify for the step-up in cost under paragraph 88(1)(c) of the *Income Tax Act* to be an ineligible property for this purpose.

Based on our understanding of the facts of the so-called Dual Offer and the Amalgamation Squeeze Out described in your letter, certain capital property owned by the subsidiary since the Parent last acquired control of the subsidiary and distributed to the Parent on the winding-up of the subsidiary does not technically qualify for the step-up in cost under paragraph 88(1)(c) of the *Income Tax Act*. This is as a consequence of certain transitory transactions which were facilitating in nature and which may be considered to have occurred during the series of transactions or events that included the acquisition of control of the subsidiary by the Parent and the winding-up of the subsidiary into the Parent.

Under the Dual Offer, shares of the Parent, a taxable Canadian corporation, (the "Dual Shares"), were issued as consideration for the acquisition of the shares of the subsidiary by a wholly-owned subsidiary corporation of the Parent.

Under the Amalgamation Squeeze Out, shares of the subsidiary, (the "Amalco Shares"), which subsidiary was formed on the amalgamation of two or more corporations one of which was a wholly-owned subsidiary corporation of the Parent, were issued on the amalgamation in exchange for the shares of a predecessor corporation and were redeemed immediately after the amalgamation for money or shares of the Parent.

From a tax policy perspective, the Dual Shares and the Amalco Shares should not, in and by themselves, cause the capital property distributed to the parent on the winding-up of the subsidiary to be ineligible property for the purposes of the step-up in cost under paragraph 88(1)(c) of the *Income Tax Act*. While Revenue Canada's strict application of the law is that the issue of the Dual Shares and the Amalco Shares is part of the series of transactions that includes the acquisition of control by the Parent of the subsidiary and the winding-up of the subsidiary, we believe that there is scope to interpret these provisions in a manner consistent with the policy intent underlying the provisions. We intend to pursue this approach further with Revenue Canada.

Should Revenue Canada continue to maintain its position with respect to the Dual Shares and the Amalco Shares we are prepared to recommend to the Minister of Finance that a technical amendment be made to the income tax provisions to ensure that the tax policy intent of those provisions is more properly reflected in the law. In this context, we would recommend that paragraph 88(1)(c.3) of the *Income Tax Act* be amended to provide that such shares will not be considered to be substituted property for the purposes of clause 88(1)(c)(vi)(B) of the *Income Tax Act*. It would be recommended that such an amendment have the same effective date as is currently provided for proposed paragraph 88(1)(c.3) of the *Income Tax Act* in former Bill C-69. If the recommendation is acted upon, I would anticipate that such an amendment would be included in either the bill that replaces Bill C-69 or a future technical bill.

Yours sincerely,

Len Farber
Director General, Tax Legislation Division

### Letter from Department of Finance, June 19, 1997:

Dear [xxx]

This letter is in response to the letters to Ms. Davine Roach of the Department of Finance dated June 6 and 9, 1997 that were written by [xxx] on behalf of [xxx] and [xxx] [regarding the] proposed public takeover offer by [xxx] of [xxx]. These letters request an amendment to the *Income Tax Act* that would eliminate the negative effect subparagraph 88(1)(c)(vi) of the *Income Tax Act* has on the proposed takeover.

Based on our understanding of the facts as set out in the letters, [xxx] and his personal holding company [xxx] own shares of [xxx]. Prior to the sale of the [xxx] shares to [xxx], [xxx] will transfer his [xxx] shares to [xxx] and [xxx] will then transfer the [xxx] shares to a newly incorporated company (Newco). The adjusted cost base and paid-up capital of the Newco shares will be increased by an amount equal to the so-called "safe income" that [xxx] had in [xxx] at the time of the transfer. [xxx] will then sell the Newco shares to Acquisico. Newco will be wound up into (or amalgamated with) Acquisico and the cost of the [xxx] shares acquired on the winding-up (or amalgamation) will be stepped-up in accordance with subsection 88(1) (or proposed subsection 87(11)) of the *Income Tax Act*. The acquisition of the shares of Newco by [xxx] will however cause the [xxx] shares to be ineligible property for the purpose of paragraph 88(1)(c) of the *Income Tax Act* with the result that on the winding-up (or [xxx] amalgamation) of Newco, Acquisico will be denied the step-up in the cost of the [xxx] shares.

We are prepared to recommend to the Minister of Finance that the income tax provisions be amended so that in the circumstances described herein the [xxx] shares will not be considered to be ineligible property of Newco for the purpose of paragraph 88(1)(c) of the *Income Tax Act*. It will be recommended that such an amendment have the same ef-

> fective date as currently provided for proposed paragraph 88(1)(c.3) of the *Income Tax Act* included in former Bill C-69. If the recommendation is acted upon, I would anticipate that such an amendment would be included in either the bill that replaces former Bill C-69 or a future technical bill.
>
> Yours sincerely,
> David A. Dodge
> Deputy Minister

1. of which a particular person referred to in subclause (I) is, at any time during the course of the series and after control of the subsidiary was last acquired by the parent, a specified shareholder, or

2. of which a particular person would be, at any time during the course of the series and after control of the subsidiary was last acquired by the parent, a specified shareholder if all the shares then owned by persons (other than specified persons) referred to in subclause (II) and acquired by those persons as part of the series were owned at that time by the particular person;

**Related Provisions**: 88(1)(c.2) — Specified person for 88(1)(c)(vi); 88(1)(c.3) — Property acquired in substitution, for purpose of 88(1)(c)(vi)(B); 88(1)(c.7) — Extended meaning of depreciable property; 88(1)(d.2) — When taxpayer last acquired control; 88(1)(d.3) — Where control acquired because of death; 88(1.7) — Where parent did not deal at arm's length; 88(4) — Amalgamation deemed not to be acquisition of control; 248(10) — Series of transactions or events; 256(6)–(9) — Whether control acquired. See additional Related Provisions at end of 88(1).

**Notes**: 88(1)(c)(vi) implements a "back-door butterfly" rule for certain specific circumstances. See Judith Woods, "The Bump Denial Rule in Subparagraph 88(1)(c)(vi)", 1998 Canadian Tax Foundation annual conference report, pp. 14:1-40.

88(1)(c)(v) amended by 1995-97 technical bill, effective for windups that begin after 1996. For earlier windups, read:

> (v) property transferred to the subsidiary by the parent or by any person or partnership that was not, otherwise than because of a right referred to in paragraph 251(5)(b), dealing at arm's length with the parent, and

88(1)(c)(vi) opening words and 88(1)(c)(vi)(B) opening words amended by 1995-97 technical bill, effective for windups that begin after June 20, 1996, other than windups that are part of an arrangement that was substantially advanced, as evidenced in writing, before June 21, 1996. For earlier windups, read:

> (vi) property disposed of by the parent as part of the series of transactions or events that includes the winding-up where, as part of the series,
>
> (A) the parent acquired control of the subsidiary, and
>
> (B) the property or any other property acquired by any person in substitution therefor is acquired by

88(1)(c)(vi)(B)(III)2 amended by 1995-97 technical bill, effective for windups that begin after November 1994, to add the words "and acquired by those persons as part of the series".

In opening words of 88(1)(c), the words "notwithstanding the reference to paragraph 87(2)(e.1) in paragraph (e.2)" changed to "subject to paragraph 87(2)(e.3) (as modified by paragraph (e.2)), and notwithstanding paragraph 87(2)(e.1) (as modified by paragraph (e.2))" by 1994 tax amendments bill, effective for windups that begin after February 22, 1994.

88(1)(c) amended by 1994 Budget, this version effective for windups that begin after November 1994. For windups that begin after February 21, 1994 and before December 1994, read 88(1)(c)(vi)(B) as:

> (B) the property or any other property acquired by any person in substitution therefor is acquired by
>
> (I) [7] a particular person (other than a specified person) that, at any time during the course of the series and before control of the subsidiary was last acquired by the parent, was a specified shareholder of the subsidiary, or
>
> (II) any person (other than a specified person) that at any time during the course of the series did not deal at arm's length with a particular person (other than a specified person) referred to in subclause (I);

For windups that begin before February 22, 1994, read everything after 88(1)(c)(ii)(B) as simply:

> plus, where the property was a capital property (other than depreciable property) owned by the subsidiary at the time that the parent last acquired control of the subsidiary and thereafter without interruption until such time as it was distributed to the parent on the winding-up, the amount determined under paragraph (d) in respect thereof;

88(1)(c)(ii)(A) amended by 1992 technical bill, effective for windings-up that begin after December 20, 1991, to add "that would, but for subsection 69(11), be".

88(1)(c)(ii)(B) added by 1991 technical bill, and cross-reference to 80(1)(b) changed to s. 80 retroactively by 1994 tax amendments bill (Part I), both effective for windups beginning after July 13, 1990.

88(1)(c) amended in 1987. For windups commencing before January 16, 1987, delete the opening "notwithstanding" phrase and all of subpara. (i).

Amended by 1977 Budget. For windups commencing before April 1, 1977, delete also the phrase "owned by the subsidiary ... on the winding-up".

**Advance Tax Rulings**: ATR-67: Increase in the cost of property on the winding-up of a wholly-owned subsidiary.

**I.T. Technical News**: No. 9 (the backdoor butterfly rule).

(c.1) **[eligible capital property]** — for the purpose of determining after the winding-up the amount to be included under paragraph 14(1)(b) in computing the parent's income in respect of the business carried on by the subsidiary immediately before the winding-up, there shall be added to the amount otherwise determined for Q in the definition "cumulative eligible capital" in subsection 14(5) the amount, if any, determined for Q in that definition in respect of that business immediately before the disposition;

**Notes**: 88(1)(c.1) added by 1992 technical bill, effective for distributions of property on a winding-up in a subsidiary's taxation year that begins after June 1988.

(c.2) **["specified person" and "specified shareholder"]** — for the purposes of this paragraph and subparagraph (c)(vi),

> (i) "specified person" at any time means the parent and each person that would, if this Act were read without reference to paragraph

---

[7] This appeared in the enacting legislation as "(II)", but clearly should have been "(I)" — ed.

251(5)(b), be related to the parent at that time and, for this purpose, a person shall be deemed not to be related to the parent where it can reasonably be considered that one of the main purposes of one or more transactions or events was to cause the person to be related to the parent so as to prevent a property that was distributed to the parent on the winding-up from being an ineligible property for the purpose of paragraph (c),

(ii) where at any time a property is owned or acquired by a partnership or a trust,

(A) the partnership or the trust, as the case may be, shall be deemed to be a person that is a corporation having one class of issued shares, which shares have full voting rights under all circumstances,

(B) each member of the partnership or beneficiary under the trust, as the case may be, shall be deemed to own at that time the proportion of the number of issued shares of the capital stock of the corporation that

(I) the fair market value at that time of that member's interest in the partnership or that beneficiary's interest in the trust, as the case may be,

is of

(II) the fair market value at that time of all the members' interests in the partnership or beneficiaries' interests in the trust, as the case may be, and

(C) the property shall be deemed to have been owned or acquired at that time by the corporation, and

(iii) in determining whether a person is a specified shareholder of a corporation,

(A) the reference in the definition "specified shareholder" in subsection 248(1) to "or of any other corporation that is related to the corporation" shall be read as "or of any other corporation that is related to the corporation and that has a significant direct or indirect interest in any issued shares of the capital stock of the corporation", and

**Proposed Amendment — 88(1)(c.2)(iii)(A)**

(A) the reference in the definition "specified shareholder" in subsection 248(1) to "the issued shares of any class of the capital stock of the corporation or of any other corporation that is related to the corporation" shall be read as "the issued shares of any class (other than a specified class) of the capital stock of the corporation or of any other corporation that is related to the corporation and that has a significant direct or indirect interest in

any issued shares of the capital stock of the corporation", and

**Application**: Bill C-43 (First Reading September 20, 2000), subsec. 39(2), will amend cl. 88(1)(c.2)(iii)(A) to read as above, applicable to windings-up that begin after November 1994.

**Technical Notes**: Subparagraph 88(1)(c.2)(iii) of the Act provides, for the purposes of paragraph 88(1)(c.2) and subparagraph 88(1)(c)(vi) of the Act, that an expanded definition of "specified shareholder" in subsection 248(1) of the Act is to be used. In particular, clause 88(1)(c.2)(iii)(A) provides that the definition of specified shareholder is to be read as including a reference to "or of any other corporation that is related to the corporation and that has a significant direct or indirect interest in any issued shares of any class of the capital stock of the corporation" rather than the reference to "or of any corporation that is related to the corporation".

Amended clause 88(1)(c.2)(iii)(A) provides for a new modification to the expanded definition "specified shareholder" in subsection 248(1) of the Act. In particular, for the purposes of paragraph 88(1)(c.2) and subparagraph 88(1)(c)(vi), the definition of specified shareholder is to be read as including a reference to "the issued shares of any class (other than a specified class) of the capital stock of the corporation or of any other corporation that is related to the corporation and that has a significant direct or indirect interest in any issued shares of any class of the capital stock of the corporation" rather than the reference to "or of any corporation that is related to the corporation". Proposed clause 88(1)(c.2)(iii)(A) ensures that in determining whether a person is a specified shareholder of a particular corporation, for the purposes of paragraph 88(1)(c.2) and subparagraph 88(1)(c)(vi), the person does not have to account for shares of a specified class. Specified class is a new expression and is defined in new paragraph 88(1)(c.8) of the Act.

(B) a corporation is deemed not to be a specified shareholder of itself;

**Related Provisions**: 88(1)(c.8) — Meaning of "specified class" for 88(1)(c.2)(iii)(A); 88(4) — Amalgamation deemed not to be acquisition of control.

**Notes**: 88(1)(c.2) added by 1994 Budget, effective for windups that begin after February 21, 1994; subpara. (iii) added by 1995-97 technical bill, effective for windups that begin after November 1994.

(c.3) **[substituted property]** — for the purpose of clause (c)(vi)(B), property acquired by any person in substitution for particular property or properties distributed to the parent on the winding-up includes

(i) property (other than a specified property) owned by the person at any time after the acquisition of control referred to in clause (c)(vi)(A) the fair market value of which is, at that time, wholly or partly attributable to the particular property or properties, and

(ii) property owned by the person at any time after the acquisition of control referred to in clause (c)(vi)(A) the fair market value of which is, at that time, determinable primarily by reference to the fair market value of, or to any proceeds from a disposition of, the particular property or properties

but does not include

(iii) money,

(iv) property that was not owned by the person at any time after the acquisition of control referred to in clause (c)(vi)(A), or

(v) property described in subparagraph (i) if the only reason the property is described in that subparagraph is because a specified property described in any of subparagraphs (c.4)(i) to (iv) was received as consideration for the acquisition of a share of the capital stock of the subsidiary in the circumstances described in subparagraphs (c.4)(i) to (iv);

**Related Provisions**: 88(1)(c.4) — Meaning of specified property; 88(1)(c.6) — Where control acquired by way of articles of arrangement; 88(1)(c.7) — Extended meaning of depreciable property; 88(4) — Amalgamation deemed not to be acquisition of control; 248(5) — Substituted property; 256(6)–(9) — Whether control acquired.

**Notes**: 88(1)(c.3) added by 1995-97 technical bill, this version effective for windups that begin after June 20, 1996 (except windups that are part of an arrangement that was substantially advanced, as evidenced in writing, by that date). For windups that began after February 21, 1994 and before June 21, 1996 (or were grandfathered as above), read:

(c.3) for the purpose of clause (c)(vi)(B), property acquired by any person in substitution for particular property or properties

(i) includes property owned by the person at any time after the acquisition of control referred to in clause (c)(vi)(A) the fair market value of which is, at that time, determinable primarily by reference to the fair market value of the particular property or properties or by reference to any proceeds from a disposition of the particular property or properties, but

(ii) does not include property that is money received as consideration for a disposition of the particular property or properties;

88(1)(c.3) does not apply to windups that began before February 22, 1994.

**I.T. Technical News**: No. 9 (the backdoor butterfly rule).

(c.4) **["specified property"]** — for the purposes of subparagraphs (c.3)(i) and (v), a specified property is

(i) a share of the capital stock of the parent that was received as consideration for the acquisition of a share of the capital stock of the subsidiary by the parent or by a corporation that was a specified subsidiary corporation of the parent immediately before the acquisition,

(ii) an indebtedness that was issued by the parent as consideration for the acquisition of a share of the capital stock of the subsidiary by the parent,

(iii) a share of the capital stock of a taxable Canadian corporation that was received as consideration for the acquisition of a share of the capital stock of the subsidiary by the taxable Canadian corporation or by the parent where the parent was a specified subsidiary corporation of the taxable Canadian corporation immediately before the acquisition,

(iv) an indebtedness of a taxable Canadian corporation that was issued by it as consideration for the acquisition of a share of the capital stock of the subsidiary by the taxable Canadian corporation or by the parent where the parent was a specified subsidiary corporation of the taxable Canadian corporation immediately before the acquisition,

(v) where the subsidiary was formed on the amalgamation of 2 or more predecessor corporations at least one of which was a subsidiary wholly-owned corporation of the parent, a share of the capital stock of the subsidiary

(A) that was issued on the amalgamation in exchange for a share of the capital stock of a predecessor corporation, and

(B) that was, immediately after the amalgamation, redeemed, acquired or cancelled by the subsidiary for money, and

(vi) where the subsidiary was formed on the amalgamation of 2 or more predecessor corporations at least one of which was a subsidiary wholly-owned corporation of the parent, a share of the capital stock of the parent

(A) that was issued on the amalgamation in exchange for a share of the capital stock of a predecessor corporation, and

(B) that was, immediately after the amalgamation, redeemed, acquired or cancelled by the parent for money;

**Proposed Amendment — 88(1)(c.4)**
**Letter from Department of Finance, September 28, 2000:**

Dear [xxx]

This is in response to your letters of September 15 and 20, 2000, and further to your conversations with Davine Roach, regarding the application of the "specified property" rule in paragraph 88(1)(c.4) of the *Income Tax Act* (the "Act") to the proposed transactions described in your letter. You believe this application gives rise to unintended tax consequences and ask that consideration be given to amending the paragraph to ensure the appropriate tax results in the circumstances.

Based on our understanding of the facts of the proposed transactions as described in your letter, JB1 and JB2 will make a joint bid through Bidco to acquire all the shares of Target for cash. JB1 is a specified shareholder of the Target and JB2 is not a specified shareholder of Target. JB1 will, amongst other things, contribute cash to Bidco, which will issue shares to JB1 in consideration for that cash. JB1 will not control Bidco at the time Bidco acquires control of Target. Target will be wound-up into Bidco and Bidco will seek to bump the cost of certain non-depreciable capital property distributed to Bidco on the wind-up of Target pursuant to paragraph 88(1)(c) of the Act. Bidco shares acquired by JB1 as consideration for the cash contribution will not qualify as "specified property" for the purposes of 88(1)(c)(vi) and consequently the so called "bump denial rule" in 88(l)(c)(vi) will cause the property distributed to Bidco on the winding up of Target to be an "ineligible property" for the purposes of the 88(1)(c) bump.

As you know, paragraph 88(l)(c.4) of the Act excludes property that is "specified property" from the extended definition of substituted property in subparagraph 88(l)(c.3)(i), which applies for the purpose of the bump denial rule in subparagraph 88(1)(c)(vi) of the Act. The statutory exclusions from the bump denial rule do not, however, anticipate joint takeover bids by a specified shareholder of the subsidiary and a third party, where such bids result in the acquisition of a non-controlling interest in the parent by the specified shareholder who acquired shares of the parent for cash prior to the acquisition of control of the subsidiary by the parent.

In these circumstances, we agree that the bump denial rule in subparagraph 88(1)(c)(vi) of the Act should not apply. Consequently, we will recommend to the Minister of Finance that an amendment be introduced to the Act to ensure that, in the circumstances described in your letter, the bump denial rule does not apply solely because JB1 acquired shares of Bidco for consideration consisting only of cash prior to Bidco acquiring control of Target. We would also recommend that such an amendment be effective for windings-up that begin after 1999.

If the recommendation is acted upon, I would anticipate that such an amendment would be included in a future technical bill.

Yours sincerely,
Len Farber
General Director, Tax Legislation Division, Tax Policy Branch

**Related Provisions**: 88(1)(c.5) — Meaning of specified subsidiary corporation; 88(4) — Amalgamation deemed not to be acquisition of control.

**Notes**: 88(1)(c.4) added by 1995-97 technical bill, effective for windups that begin after February 21, 1994.

(c.5) **["specified subsidiary corporation"]** — for the purpose of paragraph (c.4), a corporation is a specified subsidiary corporation of another corporation, at any time, where the other corporation holds, at that time, shares of the corporation

   (i) that give the shareholder 90% or more of the votes that could be cast under all circumstances at an annual meeting of shareholders of the corporation, and

   (ii) having a fair market value of 90% or more of the fair market value of all the issued shares of the capital stock of the corporation;

**Related Provisions**: 88(4) — Amalgamation deemed not to be acquisition of control.

**Notes**: 88(1)(c.5) added by 1995-97 technical bill, effective for windups that begin after February 21, 1994.

(c.6) **[control acquired by way of articles of arrangement]** — for the purpose of paragraph (c.3) and notwithstanding subsection 256(9), where control of a corporation is acquired by way of articles of arrangement, that control is deemed to have been acquired at the end of the day on which the arrangement becomes effective;

**Related Provisions**: 88(4) — Amalgamation deemed not to be acquisition of control.

**Notes**: 88(1)(c.6) added by 1995-97 technical bill, effective for windups that begin after February 21, 1994.

(c.7) **[depreciable property]** — for the purpose of subparagraph (c)(iii), a leasehold interest in a depreciable property and an option to acquire a depreciable property are depreciable properties;

**Related Provisions**: 88(4) — Amalgamation deemed not to be acquisition of control.

**Notes**: 88(1)(c.7) added by 1995-97 technical bill, effective for windups that begin after June 20, 1996.

### Proposed Addition — 88(1)(c.8)

(c.8) **["specified class"]** — for the purpose of clause (c.2)(iii)(A), a specified class of the capital stock of a corporation is a class of shares of the capital stock of the corporation where

   (i) the paid-up capital in respect of the class was not, at any time, less than the fair market value of the consideration for which the shares of that class then outstanding were issued,

   (ii) the shares are non-voting in respect of the election of the Board of Directors of the corporation, except in the event of a failure or default under the terms or conditions of the shares,

   (iii) under neither the terms and conditions of the shares nor any agreement in respect of the shares are the shares convertible into or exchangeable for shares other than shares of a specified class of the capital stock of the corporation, and

   (iv) under neither the terms and conditions of the shares nor any agreement in respect of the shares is any holder of the shares entitled to receive on the redemption, cancellation or acquisition of the shares by the corporation or by any person with whom the corporation does not deal at arm's length an amount (excluding any premium for early redemption) greater than the total of the fair market value of the consideration for which the shares were issued and the amount of any unpaid dividends on the shares;

**Related Provisions**: 88(4) — Amalgamation deemed not to be acquisition of control.

**Application**: Bill C-43 (First Reading September 20, 2000), subsec. 39(3), will add para. 88(1)(c.8), applicable to windings-up that begin after November 1994.

**Technical Notes**: New paragraph 88(1)(c.8) of the Act is relevant in determining whether a person is a specified shareholder for the purposes of a divisive reorganization commonly known as a "backdoor butterfly" described in subparagraph 88(1)(c)(vi) of the Act. (See the commentary on subclause 88(1)(c)(vi)(B)(III) of the Act re the significance of specified shareholder status.) Shares of a specified class are considered to be financing or debt-like shares and consequently need not be counted in determining whether a person is a specified shareholder of a corporation.

New paragraph 88(1)(c.8) provides that shares of the capital stock of a corporation will qualify as shares of a specified class where

1) the paid-up capital in respect of the class was not at any time less than the fair market value of the consideration for which the shares of that class then outstanding were issued;

2) the shares are non-voting in respect of the election of the Board of Directors of the corporation, except in the event of a failure or default under the terms or conditions of the shares;

3) the shares are not convertible into or exchangeable for any other shares (other than shares of a specified class) of the capital stock of the corporation; and

4) the holder of the share is not entitled to receive on the redemption, cancellation or acquisition of the share by the corporation or any person who does not deal at arm's length with the corporation, an amount (excluding any premium for early redemption) greater than the fair market value of the consideration for which the share was issued plus the amount of any unpaid dividends on the share.

(d) **[increase in cost amounts (bump)]** — the amount determined under this paragraph in respect of each property of the subsidiary distributed to the parent on the winding-up is such portion of the amount, if any, by which the total determined under subparagraph (b)(ii) exceeds the total of

(i) the amount, if any, by which

(A) the total of all amounts each of which is an amount in respect of any property owned by the subsidiary immediately before the winding-up, equal to the cost amount to the subsidiary of the property immediately before the winding-up, plus the amount of any money of the subsidiary on hand immediately before the winding-up,

exceeds the total of

(B) all amounts each of which is the amount of any debt owing by the subsidiary, or of any other obligation of the subsidiary to pay any amount, that was outstanding immediately before the winding-up, and

(C) the amount of any reserve (other than a reserve referred to in paragraph 20(1)(n), subparagraph 40(1)(a)(iii) or 44(1)(e)(iii) of this Act or in subsection 64(1) or (1.1) of the *Income Tax Act*, chapter 148 of the Revised Statutes of Canada, 1952, as those two provisions read immediately before November 3,[8] 1981) deducted in computing the subsidiary's income for its taxation year during which its assets were distributed to the parent on the winding-up, and

(i.1) the total of all amounts each of which is an amount in respect of any share of the capital stock of the subsidiary disposed of by the parent on the winding-up or in contemplation of the winding-up, equal to the total of all amounts received by the parent or by a corporation with which the parent was not dealing at arm's length (otherwise than because of a right referred to in paragraph 251(5)(b) in respect of the subsidiary) in respect of

(A) taxable dividends on the share or on any share (in this subparagraph referred to as a "replaced share") for which the share or a replaced share was substituted or exchanged to the extent that the amounts thereof were deductible from the recipient's income for any taxation year by virtue of section 112 or subsection 138(6) and were not amounts on which the recipient was required to pay tax under Part VII of the *Income Tax Act*, chapter 148 of the Revised Statutes of Canada, 1952, as it read on March 31, 1977, or

(B) capital dividends and life insurance capital dividends on the share or on any share (in this subparagraph referred to as a "replaced share") for which a share or a replaced share was substituted or exchanged,

as is designated by the parent in respect of that capital property in its return of income under this Part for its taxation year in which the subsidiary was so wound up, except that

(ii) in no case shall the amount so designated in respect of any such capital property exceed the amount, if any, by which the fair market value of the property at the time the parent last acquired control of the subsidiary exceeds the cost amount to the subsidiary of the property immediately before the winding-up, and

(iii) in no case shall the total of amounts so designated in respect of all such capital properties exceed the amount, if any, by which the total determined under subparagraph (b)(ii) exceeds the total of the amounts determined under subparagraphs (i) and (i.1).

**Related Provisions**: 88(1)(d.2) — When taxpayer last acquired control; 88(1)(d.3) — Where control acquired because of death; 88(1.7) — Where parent did not deal at arm's length; 88(4) — Amalgamation deemed not to be acquisition of control; 256(6)–(9) — Whether control acquired. See additional Related Provisions at end of 88(1).

**Notes**: The increase in cost amounts of assets that arises under 88(1)(d) is often referred to as a "bump". It is implemented by 88(1)(c), between subparas. (ii) and (iii). See also Notes to 125(7)"Canadian-controlled private corporation" re the meaning of "control".

Closing words of 88(1)(d) repealed by 1995-97 technical bill, effective for windups that begin after February 21, 1994. This interpreta-

---

[8]*Sic*. The date should be November 13, although in practice it makes no difference. See Notes to s. 64 — ed.

**S. 88(1)(d)**      Income Tax Act, Part I, Division B

tion provision was moved to 88(1.7). For windups beginning from November 17, 1978 to February 21, 1994, read:

> and for the purposes of this paragraph, where a parent corporation has been incorporated or otherwise formed after the time any other corporation (other than a corporation acquired by it from a person with whom it was dealing at arm's length) with which it did not deal at arm's length at any time prior to the winding-up was incorporated or otherwise formed, the parent corporation shall be deemed to have been in existence from the time of formation of the other corporation and to have been not dealing at arm's length with the other corporation from that time;

Opening words of 88(1)(d) amended by 1994 Budget, effective for windups that begin after February 21, 1994, to delete certain restrictions; they are now found in 88(1)(c) under "ineligible property". For earlier windups, read:

> (d) the amount determined under this paragraph in respect of each property that was a capital property (other than property transferred in the course of a reorganization described in paragraph 55(3)(b) in the course of which a dividend was received by a corporation to which subsection 55(2) would, but for paragraph 55(3)(b), apply where the winding-up of the subsidiary was part of a transfer, directly or indirectly, of property of a particular corporation to a transferee, within the meaning assigned by paragraph 55(3)(b), property transferred to the subsidiary by the parent or by any person or partnership that was not, otherwise than by reason of a right referred to in paragraph 251(5)(b), dealing at arm's length with the parent, or a depreciable property) owned by the subsidiary at the time that the parent last acquired control of the subsidiary and thereafter without interruption until such time as it was distributed to the parent on the winding-up, is such portion of the amount, if any, by which the total determined under subparagraph (b)(ii) exceeds the total of

Opening words of 88(1)(d) amended by 1982 Budget and 1991 technical bill. For distributions before June 29, 1982, ignore the exclusion in parentheses, which deals with butterfly reorganizations. For windups that begin before October 1988, read the exclusion as "(other than property transferred in the course of a series of transactions or events to which subsection 55(2) would, but for paragraph 55(3)(b), apply or a depreciable property)". For windups that begin from October 1988 through July 13, 1990, read the exclusion as now enacted, but ignore the words "property transferred to the subsidiary by the parent or by any person or partnership that was not, otherwise than by reason of a right referred to in paragraph 251(5)(b), dealing at arm's length with the parent".

88(1)(d)(i)(C) amended by 1991 technical bill, effective for windups that begin after 1989, to refer to 44(1)(e)(iii) and to correct an inaccurate reference to 64(1) and (1.1).

88(1)(d)(i.1) amended by 1988 tax reform, to add the words "or in contemplation of the winding-up", effective for windups commencing in July 1988 or later. Also amended by 1991 technical bill, effective for windups commencing after 1986, to add the parenthetical exclusion referring to 251(5)(b).

For windups commencing after March 1977 and ending before November 17, 1978, read 88(1)(d) as:

> (d) the amount determined under this paragraph in respect of each property that was a capital property (other than a depreciable property) owned by the subsidiary at the time that the parent last acquired control of the subsidiary and thereafter without interruption until such time as it was distributed to the parent on the winding-up, is such portion of the amount, if any, by which the aggregate determined under subparagraph (b)(ii) exceeds
>
>> (i) the amount, if any, by which
>>
>>> (A) the aggregate of amounts each of which is an amount in respect of any property owned by the subsidiary immediately before the winding-up, equal to the cost amount to the subsidiary of the property immediately before the winding-up, plus the amount of any money of the subsidiary on hand immediately before the winding-up,
>>
>> exceeds the aggregate of
>>
>>> (B) all amounts each of which is the amount of any debt owing by the subsidiary, or of any other obligation of the subsidiary to pay any amount, that was outstanding immediately before the winding-up, and
>>>
>>> (C) the amount of any reserve (other than a reserve referred to in paragraph 20(1)(n), subparagraph 40(1)(a)(iii) or subsection 64(1) or (1.1)), deducted in computing the subsidiary's income for its taxation year during which its assets were distributed to the parent on the winding-up,
>
> as is designated by the parent in respect of that capital property in its return of income under this Part for its taxation year in which the subsidiary was so wound up, except that
>
>> (ii) in no case shall the amount so designated in respect of any such capital property exceed the amount, if any, by which the fair market value of the property at the time the parent last acquired control of the subsidiary exceeds the cost amount to the subsidiary of the property immediately before the winding-up, and
>>
>> (iii) in no case shall the aggregate of amounts so designated in respect of all such capital properties exceed the amount, if any, by which the aggregate determined under subparagraph (b)(ii) exceeds the amount determined under subparagraph (i);

For earlier windups commencing before April 1977, read as for 1977-78, but delete also the phrase in the opening portion, "owned by the subsidiary ... on the winding-up". Also delete the reference to 64(1.1) in clause (i)(C), and add in subparas. (i.1) and (i.2), reading:

> (i.1) the amount of the subsidiary's tax-paid undistributed surplus on hand at the time it was wound up, and
>
> (i.2) the amount of the subsidiary's 1971 capital surplus on hand at the time it was wound up.

**I.T. Application Rules:** 26(5)(c)(i)(C) (where property owned since before 1972); 69 (meaning of "*Income Tax Act*, chapter 148 of the Revised Statutes of Canada, 1952").

**I.T. Technical News:** No. 16 (*Parthenon Investments* case).

**Advance Tax Rulings:** ATR-67: Increase in the cost of property on the winding-up of a wholly-owned subsidiary.

(d.1) **[rules not applicable]** — subsection 84(2) and section 21 of the *Income Tax Application Rules* do not apply to the winding-up of the subsidiary, and subsections 13(21.2) and 14(12) do not apply to the winding-up of the subsidiary with respect to property acquired by the parent on the winding-up;

**Notes:** 88(1)(d.1) amended by 1995-97 technical bill to add references to 13(21.2) and 14(12) effective for windups that begin after April 26, 1995; and to delete a reference to 85(5.1), effective for windups that begin after 1995.

(d.2) **[when control acquired]** — in determining, for the purposes of this paragraph and paragraphs (c) and (d), the time at which a person or group of persons (in this paragraph and paragraph (d.3) referred to as the "acquirer") last acquired control of the subsidiary, where control of the subsidiary was acquired from another person or group of persons (in this paragraph referred to as the "vendor") with whom the acquirer was not (otherwise than solely because of a right referred to in paragraph 251(5)(b)) dealing at arm's length, the acquirer is deemed to have last acquired control of the subsidiary at the earlier of

(i) the time at which the vendor last acquired control (within the meaning that would be assigned by subsection 186(2) if the reference in that subsection to "another corporation" were read as "a person" and the references in that subsection to "the other corporation" were read as "the person") of the subsidiary, and

(ii) the time at which the vendor was deemed for the purpose of this paragraph to have last acquired control of the subsidiary;

**Related Provisions**: 88(1)(d.3) — Where control acquired because of death; 88(4) — Amalgamation deemed not to be acquisition of control; 256(6)–(9) — Whether control acquired. See additional Related Provisions at end of 88(1).

**Notes**: 88(1)(d.2) amended by 1992 technical bill, 1993 technical bill and 1995-97 technical bill, all effective for windups that begin after December 20, 1991. For earlier windups that began after November 12, 1981, read:

(d.2) in determining, for the purposes of this paragraph and paragraphs (c) and (d), the time that a taxpayer last acquired control of the subsidiary, where control of the subsidiary was acquired (otherwise than by way of bequest or inheritance) from a person or group of persons (in this paragraph referred to as the "vendor") with whom the taxpayer was not (otherwise than because of a right referred to in paragraph 251(5)(b)) dealing at arm's length, the taxpayer shall be deemed to have last acquired control at the earlier of the time that the vendor last acquired control (within the meaning that would be assigned by subsection 186(2) if the reference therein to "another corporation" were read as "a person" and the references therein to "the other corporation" were read as "the person") of the subsidiary and the time that the vendor was deemed by this subsection to have last acquired control;

88(1)(d.2) amended by 1981 Budget (and amended retroactively by 1983 Budget), effective for windups commencing on November 13, 1981 or later. For windups ending after November 16, 1978 and commencing by November 12, 1981, delete the reference to a group of persons and delete the exclusion for control by virtue of 251(5)(b).

88(1)(d.2) has no application to windups ending before November 17, 1978.

(d.3) **[control acquired due to death]** — for the purposes of paragraphs (c), (d) and (d.2), where at any time control of a corporation is last acquired by an acquirer because of an acquisition of shares of the capital stock of the corporation as a consequence of the death of an individual, the acquirer is deemed to have last acquired control of the corporation immediately after the death from a person who dealt at arm's length with the acquirer;

**Related Provisions**: 88(4) — Amalgamation deemed not to be acquisition of control; 256(6)–(9) — Whether control acquired. See additional Related Provisions at end of 88(1).

**Notes**: 88(1)(d.3) added by 1995-97 technical bill, effective for windups that begin after December 20, 1991.

(e) [Repealed under former Act]

(e.1) **[reserves]** — the subsidiary may, for the purposes of computing its income for its taxation year during which its assets were transferred to, and its obligations were assumed by, the parent on the winding-up, claim any reserve that would have been allowed under this Part if its assets had not been transferred to, or its obligations had not been assumed by, the parent on the winding-up and notwithstanding any other provision of this Part, no amount shall be included in respect of any reserve so claimed in computing the income of the subsidiary for its taxation year, if any, following the year in which its assets were transferred to or its obligations were assumed by the parent;

(e.2) **[rules applicable]** — paragraphs 87(2)(c), (d.1), (e.1), (e.3), (g) to (l), (l.3) to (u), (x), (z.1), (z.2), (aa), (cc), (ll), (nn), (pp), (rr), (tt) and (uu), subsection 87(6) and, subject to section 78, subsection 87(7) apply to the winding-up as if the references in those provisions to

(i) "amalgamation" were read as "winding-up",

(ii) "predecessor corporation" were read as "subsidiary",

(iii) "new corporation" were read as "parent",

(iv) "its first taxation year" were read as "its taxation year during which it received the assets of the subsidiary on the winding-up",

(v) "its last taxation year" were read as "its taxation year during which its assets were distributed to the parent on the winding-up",

(vi) "predecessor corporation's gain" were read as "subsidiary's gain",

(vii) "predecessor corporation's income" were read as "subsidiary's income",

(viii) "new corporation's income" were read as "parent's income",

(ix) [Repealed under former Act]

(x) "any predecessor private corporation" were read as "the subsidiary (if it was a private corporation at the time of the winding-up)",

(xi), (xii) [Repealed]

(xiii) "two or more corporations" were read as "a subsidiary",

(xiv), (xv) [Repealed]

(xvi) "the life insurance capital dividend account of any predecessor corporation immediately before the amalgamation" were read as "the life insurance capital dividend account of the subsidiary at the time the subsidiary was wound-up",

(xvii) "predecessor corporation's refundable Part VII tax on hand" were read as "subsidiary's refundable Part VII tax on hand",

(xviii) "predecessor corporation's Part VII refund" were read as "subsidiary's Part VII refund",

(xix) "predecessor corporation's refundable Part VIII tax on hand" were read as "subsidiary's refundable Part VIII tax on hand",

(xx) "predecessor corporation's Part VIII refund" were read as "subsidiary's Part VIII refund", and

(xxi) "predecessor corporation's cumulative offset account" were read as "subsidiary's cumulative offset account";

**Related Provisions**: 88(1)(g) — Where subsidiary was insurance corporation; 126.1(5) — UI premium tax credit — specified employer defined. See additional Related Provisions at end of 88(1).

**Notes**: Where provisions of 87(2) were amended by 1991 technical bill as of July 14, 1990, any amendments that also apply for purposes of 88(1)(e.2) apply to windups *beginning* after July 13, 1990.

Opening words of 88(1)(e.2) amended as follows:

Reference to 87(2)(e.1) added in 1987, effective for windups commencing on January 16, 1987 or later.

A reference to 87(2)(e.2), added by 1988 tax reform, was retroactively deleted by 1991 technical bill, since 88(1)(a)(iii) and (c)(ii) deal with the properties described in 87(2)(e.2).

Reference to 87(2)(e.3) added by 1994 tax amendments bill (Part III), effective for windups that begin after February 22, 1994.

Reference to 87(2)(y.1) deleted by 1995-97 technical bill, effective for windups that begin after June 1995.

Reference to 87(2)(z.2) added by 1988 tax reform, effective (per 1991 technical bill) for windups commencing in May 1988 or later.

Reference to 87(2)(aa) added by 1995 Budget, effective for windups that begin after June 1995. RDTOH on windup was formerly dealt with by 88(1)(e.5).

Reference to 87(2)(rr) added by 1988 tax reform, effective for windups ending on June 19, 1987 or later.

Reference to 87(2)(tt) added by 1989 Budget, effective for windups commencing in 1988 or later.

Reference to 87(2)(uu) added by 1992 transportation industry assistance bill, effective for windups commencing in 1992 or later.

88(1)(e.2)(xi) and (xii) repealed by 1991 technical bill, effective July 14, 1990. For computing capital dividend accounts before that date, read:

(xi) "predecessor corporation's capital dividend account" were read as "subsidiary's capital dividend account",

(xii) "the capital dividend account of any predecessor corporation immediately before the amalgamation" were read as "the capital dividend account of the subsidiary at the time the subsidiary was wound up".

88(1)(e.2)(xiv) and (xv) repealed by 1995-97 technical bill, effective for windups that begin after June 1995. They dealt with the "preferred-earnings amount", a concept used in 87(2)(y.1) and old Part II and repealed in 1986.

**Interpretation Bulletins**: IT-66R6: Capital dividends; IT-330R: Dispositions of capital property subject to warranty, covenant, etc.; IT-502: Employee benefit plans and employee trusts. See also lists at end of subsec. 88(1) and s. 88.

(e.3) **[investment tax credit]** — for the purpose of computing the parent's investment tax credit at the end of any particular taxation year ending after the subsidiary was wound up,

(i) property acquired or expenditures made by the subsidiary or an amount included in the investment tax credit of the subsidiary by virtue of paragraph (b) of the definition "investment tax credit" in subsection 127(9) in a taxation year (in this paragraph referred to as the "expenditure year") shall be deemed to have been acquired, made or included, as the case may be, by the parent in its taxation year in which the expenditure year of the subsidiary ended, and

(ii) there shall be added to the amounts otherwise determined for the purposes of paragraphs (f) to (k) of the definition "investment tax credit" in subsection 127(9) in respect of the parent for the particular year

(A) the amounts that would have been determined in respect of the subsidiary for the purposes of paragraph (f) of the definition "investment tax credit" in subsection 127(9) for its taxation year in which it was wound up if the reference therein to "a preceding taxation year" were read as a reference to "the year or a preceding taxation year",

(B) the amounts determined in respect of the subsidiary for the purposes of paragraphs (g) to (i) and (k) of the definition "investment tax credit" in subsection 127(9) for its taxation year in which it was wound up, and

(C) the amount determined in respect of the subsidiary for the purposes of paragraph (j) of the definition "investment tax credit" in subsection 127(9) for its taxation year in which it was wound up except that, for the purpose of the calculation in this clause, where control of the subsidiary has been acquired by a person or group of persons (each of whom is referred to in this clause as the "purchaser") at any time (in this clause referred to as "that time") before the end of the taxation year in which the subsidiary was wound up, there may be added to the amount determined under subparagraph 127(9.1)(d)(i) in respect of the subsidiary the amount, if any, by which that proportion of the amount that, but for subsections 127(3) and (5) and sections 126, 127.2 and 127.3, would be the parent's tax payable under this Part for the particular year, that,

(I) where the subsidiary carried on a particular business in the course of which a property was acquired, or an expenditure was made, before that time in respect of which an amount was included in computing the subsidiary's investment tax credit for its taxation year in which it was wound up, and the parent carried on the particular business throughout the particular year, the amount, if any, by which the total of all amounts each of which is the parent's income for the particular year from the particular business, or the parent's income for the particular year from any other business substantially all the income of which was derived from the sale, leasing, rental or development of properties or the rendering of services similar to the properties sold, leased, rented or developed, or the services rendered, as the case may be, by the subsidiary in carrying on the particular business before that time, exceeds the total of the amounts, if any, deducted for the particular year under paragraph 111(1)(a) or (d) by the parent in respect of a non-capital loss or a farm loss, as the case may be, for a taxation year in respect of the particular business

is of the greater of

(II) the amount determined under subclause (I), and

(III) the parent's taxable income for the particular year

exceeds the amount, if any, calculated under subparagraph 127(9.1)(d)(i) in respect of the particular business or the other business, as the case may be, in respect of the parent at the end of the particular year

to the extent that such amounts determined in respect of the subsidiary may reasonably be considered to have been included in computing the parent's investment tax credit at the end of the particular year by virtue of subparagraph (i),

and, for the purposes of the definitions "first term shared-use-equipment" and "second term shared-use-equipment" in subsection 127(9), the parent shall be deemed to be the same corporation as, and a continuation of, the subsidiary;

**Related Provisions**: 88(1.3) — Rules relating to computation of income and tax of parent; 256(6)–(9) — Whether control acquired. See additional Related Provisions at end of 88(1).

**Notes**: The CCRA takes the position that "substantially all", used in 88(1)(e.3)(ii)(C)(I), means 90% or more.

88(1)(e.3)(ii)(C)(I) amended by 1993 technical bill, effective for windups that begin after December 21, 1992, to add the words "and the parent carried on the particular business throughout the particular year". Thus, the flow-through of ITCs restricted by the change-of-control rules (127(9.1)) on an 88(1) windup is conditional on the parent carrying on the business of the subsidiary throughout the year in which the flowed-through ITC is claimed.

88(1)(e.3) amended in 1987, effective retroactively for windups commencing on May 24, 1985 or later. However, with respect to acquisitions of control occurring on or before January 15, 1987, or before 1988 where the persons acquiring the control were obliged on that date to acquire the control pursuant to the terms of agreements in writing entered into on or before that date, read subclause (ii)(C)(I) as follows:

(I) where the subsidiary carried on a particular business in the course of which a property was acquired, or an expenditure was made, before that time in respect of which an amount was included in computing the subsidiary's investment tax credit for its taxation year in which it was wound up, the amount, if any, by which the aggregate of all amounts each of which is the parent's income for the particular year from the particular business, the parent's income for the particular year from any other business substantially all the income of which was derived from the sale, leasing, rental or development of properties or the rendering of services similar to the properties sold, leased, rented or developed, or the services rendered, as the case may be, by the subsidiary in carrying on the particular business before that time, or the amount, if any, by which,

1. the aggregate of the parent's taxable capital gains for the particular year from the disposition of property owned by the subsidiary at that time, other than property that was acquired from the purchaser or a person who did not deal at arm's length with the purchaser,

exceeds

2. the aggregate of the parent's allowable capital losses for the particular year from the disposition of such property

exceeds, in the case of a winding-up commencing after June 5, 1987, the aggregate of the amounts, if any, deducted by the parent under paragraph 111(1)(a) or (d) for the particular year in respect of a non-capital loss or a farm loss, as the case may be, for a taxation year in respect of the particular business.

For this purpose, the amending legislation provides that "a person shall be considered not to be obliged ... to acquire control of a corporation ... if the person may be excused from performing the obligation as a result of changes to the [*Income Tax Act*] affecting acquisitions or dispositions of property or acquisitions of control of corporations".

Closing words of 88(1)(e.3), beginning "and, for the purposes...", added by 1992 Economic Statement, effective for taxation years ending after December 2, 1992.

88(1)(e.3) has no application for windups commencing before May 24, 1985.

(e.4) **[employment tax credit]** — [No longer relevant]

**Notes**: 88(1)(e.4) added by 1985 Budget, effective for windups commencing on May 24, 1985 or later. However, the employment tax credit (former 127(13)–(16)) was repealed effective 1989.

(e.5) **[refundable dividend tax on hand]** — [Repealed]

**Notes**: 88(1)(e.5) repealed by 1995 Budget, effective for windups that begin after June 1995. RDTOH is now dealt with by reference to 87(2)(aa) in 88(1)(e.2). For earlier windups since the 1993 taxation year, read:

(e.5) for the purpose of computing the refundable dividend tax on hand (within the meaning assigned by subsection 129(3)) of the parent at the end of any particular taxation year ending after the subsidiary was wound up, the amount, if any, by which

(i) the subsidiary's refundable dividend tax on hand at the end of its taxation year during which it was wound up

exceeds

(ii) the subsidiary's dividend refund (within the meaning assigned by subsection 129(1)) for its taxation year referred to in subparagraph (i) shall, if

    (iii) the subsidiary was a private corporation at the end of the year during which it was wound up, and

    (iv) the parent was a private corporation

        (A) where the subsidiary was wound up in the particular year, at the time immediately after the winding-up, and

        (B) in any other case, continuously from the time of the winding-up until the time immediately after the beginning of the particular year,

be added to the total determined for the particular year under subsection 129(3) from which the total of amounts determined under paragraphs 129(3)(c) to (e) is subtracted, except that no amount shall be so added in respect of the subsidiary where subsection 129(1.2) would have applied to deem a dividend paid by the subsidiary immediately before the winding-up not to be a taxable dividend for the purpose of subsection 129(1);

88(1)(e.5) amended by 1992 technical bill, effective for computing RDTOH for the 1993 and later taxation years, to require the parent to be a private corporation only until after the beginning of the year. For earlier years, read everything after subpara. (ii) as:

"shall, if the parent has been a private corporation continuously from the time of the winding-up to the end of the taxation year, be added to the total determined under subsection 129(3) from which the parent's dividend refunds are to be subtracted, except that the amount to be added to the total determined under subsection 129(3) shall be deemed to be nil where, had a dividend been paid by the subsidiary immediately before the winding-up, subsection 129(1.2) would have applied to deem the dividend not to be a taxable dividend;"

In the earlier version, everything following "are to be subtracted," added by 1988 tax reform, effective for windups occurring after 4 p.m. EDST, September 15, 1987.

(e.6) **[charitable donations]** — where a subsidiary has made a gift in a taxation year (in this section referred to as the "gift year"), for the purposes of computing the amount deductible under section 110.1 by the parent for its taxation years ending after the subsidiary was wound up, the parent shall be deemed to have made a gift in each of its taxation years in which a gift year of the subsidiary ended equal to the amount, if any, by which the total of all gifts made by the subsidiary in the gift year exceeds the total of all amounts deducted by the subsidiary under section 110.1 of this Act or paragraph 110(1)(a), (b) or (b.1) of the *Income Tax Act*, chapter 148 of the Revised Statutes of Canada, 1952, in respect of those gifts;

**I.T. Application Rules**: 69 (meaning of *"Income Tax Act*, chapter 148 of the Revised Statutes of Canada, 1952").

(e.61) **[donation of non-qualifying securities]** — the parent is deemed for the purpose of section 110.1 to have made any gift deemed by subsection 118.1(13) to have been made by the subsidiary after the subsidiary ceased to exist;

**Notes**: 88(1)(e.61) added by 1997 Budget, effective August 1997.

(e.7) **[foreign tax credit]** — for the purposes of

    (i) determining the amount deductible by the parent under subsection 126(2) for any taxation year commencing after the commencement of the winding-up, and

    (ii) determining the extent to which subsection 126(2.3) applies to reduce the amount that may be claimed by the parent under paragraph 126(2)(a),

any unused foreign tax credit (within the meaning of subsection 126(7)) of the subsidiary in respect of a country for a particular taxation year (in this section referred to as the "foreign tax year"), to the extent that it exceeds the total of all amounts each of which is claimed in respect thereof under paragraph 126(2)(a) in computing the tax payable by the subsidiary under this Part for any taxation year, shall be deemed to be an unused foreign tax credit of the parent for its taxation year in which the subsidiary's foreign tax year ended;

**Related Provisions**: 88(1.3) — Rules relating to computation of income and tax of parent. See additional Related Provisions at end of 88(1).

(e.8) **[investment tax credit — expenditure limit]** — for the purpose of applying subsection 127(10.2) to any corporation (other than the subsidiary)

    (i) where the parent is associated with another corporation in a taxation year (in this paragraph referred to as the "current year") of the parent that begins after the parent received an asset of the subsidiary on the winding-up and that ends in a calendar year,

        (A) the parent's taxable income for its last taxation year that ended in the preceding calendar year (determined before taking into consideration the specified future tax consequences for that last year) is deemed to be the total of

            (I) its taxable income for that last year (determined before applying this paragraph to the winding-up and before taking into consideration the specified future tax consequences for that last year), and

            (II) the total of the subsidiary's taxable incomes for its taxation years that ended in that preceding calendar year (determined without reference to clause (B) and before taking into consideration the specified future tax consequences for those years), and

        (B) the subsidiary's taxable income for each of its taxation years that ends after the first time that the parent receives an asset of the subsidiary on the winding-up of the subsidiary is deemed to be nil, and

    (ii) where the parent received an asset of the subsidiary on the winding-up before the current year and is not associated with any corporation in the current year, the parent's taxable income for its immediately preceding taxation year (determined before taking into consideration the specified future tax consequences for that preceding year) is deemed to be the total of

(A) its taxable income for that preceding taxation year (determined before applying this paragraph to the winding-up and before taking into consideration the specified future tax consequences for that preceding taxation year), and

(B) the total of the subsidiary's taxable incomes for its taxation years that ended in the calendar year in which that preceding taxation year ended (determined before taking into consideration the specified future tax consequences for those years);

**Notes**: 88(1)(e.8) amended by 1996 Budget, this version effective for the purpose of applying 127(10.1) and (10.2) to taxation years that begin in 1997. For taxation years that begin in 1996, read "the parent" in place of "any corporation (other than the subsidiary)" in the opening words. For earlier windups that begin after May 23, 1985 through the end of 1995 (taking into account retroactive amendments made by the 1991 technical bill and by the 1996 Budget bill), read:

(e.8) for the purposes of subsection 127(10.1), the definition "qualifying corporation" in subsection 127.1(2) and subparagraph 157(1)(b)(i),

(i) the taxable income of the parent for its taxation year during which it received the assets of the subsidiary on the winding-up shall be deemed to be the total of its taxable income for that year as otherwise determined and the taxable incomes of the subsidiary for its taxation years ending in the calendar year in which that year ended, and

(ii) the business limit of the parent for that year shall be deemed to be the total of its business limit for that year as otherwise determined and the business limits of the subsidiary for its taxation years ending in the calendar year in which that year ended;

For 127.1(2) "qualifying corporation" and 157(1)(b)(i), which were previously covered by 88(1)(e.8) until the 1996 Budget bill retroactive amendment, see now 88(1)(e.9).

(e.9) **[instalments and refundable ITCs]** — for the purpose of applying subparagraph 157(1)(b)(i) and the definition "qualifying corporation" in subsection 127.1(2) to any corporation (other than the subsidiary)

(i) where the parent is associated with another corporation in a taxation year (in this paragraph referred to as the "current year") of the parent that begins after the parent received an asset of the subsidiary on the winding-up and ends in a calendar year,

(A) the parent's taxable income for its last taxation year that ended in the preceding calendar year (determined before taking into consideration the specified future tax consequences for that last year) is deemed to be the total of

(I) its taxable income for that last year (determined before applying this paragraph to the winding-up and before taking into consideration the specified future tax consequences for that last year), and

(II) the total of the subsidiary's taxable incomes for its taxation years that ended in that preceding calendar year (determined without reference to subparagraph (iii) and before taking into consideration the specified future tax consequences for those years), and

(B) the parent's business limit for that last year is deemed to be the total of

(I) its business limit (determined before applying this paragraph to the winding-up) for that last year, and

(II) the total of the subsidiary's business limits (determined without reference to subparagraph (iii)) for its taxation years that ended in that preceding calendar year,

(ii) where the parent received an asset of the subsidiary on the winding-up before the current year and subparagraph (i) does not apply,

(A) the parent's taxable income for its immediately preceding taxation year (determined before taking into consideration the specified future tax consequences for that preceding year) is deemed to be the total of

(I) its taxable income for that preceding taxation year (determined before applying this paragraph to the winding-up and before taking into consideration the specified future tax consequences for that preceding taxation year), and

(II) the total of the subsidiary's taxable incomes for the subsidiary's taxation years that end in the calendar year in which that preceding taxation year ended (determined before taking into consideration the specified future tax consequences for those years), and

(B) the parent's business limit for that preceding taxation year is deemed to be the total of

(I) its business limit (determined before applying this paragraph to the winding-up) for that preceding taxation year, and

(II) the total of the subsidiary's business limits (determined without reference to subparagraph (iii)) for the subsidiary's taxation years that end in the calendar year in which that preceding taxation year ended, and

(iii) where the parent and the subsidiary are associated with each other in the current year, the subsidiary's taxable income and the subsidiary's business limit for each taxation year that ends after the first time that the parent receives an asset of the subsidiary on the winding-up are deemed to be nil;

**Notes:** 88(1)(e.9) amended by 1996 Budget, effective for windups that begin after May 23, 1985, except that

(a) for windups that begin before 1997, read "any corporation (other than the subsidiary)" in the opening words as "the parent";

(b) for the purpose of applying para. (e.9) for the purpose of 127.1(2)"qualifying corporation", the business limits referred to in para. (e.9), for taxation years that ended after June 1994 and began before 1996, shall be determined under s. 125 as that section read in its application to taxation years that ended before July 1994; and

(c) 88(1)(e.9)(i) does not apply

(i) in applying 127.1(2)"qualifying corporation" to taxation years that ended before July 1994, and

(ii) in applying 157(1)(b)(i) to taxation years that end before 1998.

The rules for 127.1(1)"qualifying corporation" and 157(1)(b)(i) were in 88(1)(e.8) until being moved to here, retroactive to 1985, by the 1996 Budget bill. See Notes to 88(1)(e.8).

(f) **[depreciable property]** — where property that was depreciable property of a prescribed class of the subsidiary has been distributed to the parent on the winding-up and the capital cost to the subsidiary of the property exceeds the amount deemed by paragraph (a) to be the subsidiary's proceeds of disposition of the property, for the purposes of sections 13 and 20 and any regulations made under paragraph 20(1)(a),

(i) notwithstanding paragraph (c), the capital cost to the parent of the property shall be deemed to be the amount that was the capital cost of the property to the subsidiary, and

(ii) the excess shall be deemed to have been allowed to the parent in respect of the property under regulations made under paragraph 20(1)(a) in computing income for taxation years before the acquisition by the parent of the property;

**I.T. Application Rules:** 20(1.2) (transfer of depreciable property by person who owned it before 1972).

(g) **[insurance corporation]** — where the subsidiary was an insurance corporation,

(i) for the purposes of paragraphs 12(1)(d), (e), (e.1), (i) and (s) and 20(1)(l), (l.1), (p) and (jj) and 20(7)(c), subsection 20(22), sections 138, 138.1, 140, 142 and 148 and Part XII.3, the parent is deemed to be the same corporation as, and a continuation of, the subsidiary, and

(ii) for the purpose of determining the amount of the gross investment revenue required to be included under subsection 138(9) in the income of the subsidiary and the parent and the amount of gains and losses of the subsidiary and the parent from property used by them in the year or held by them in the year in the course of carrying on an insurance business in Canada

(A) the subsidiary and the parent shall, in addition to their normal taxation years, be deemed to have had a taxation year ending immediately before the time when the property of the subsidiary was transferred to, and the obligations of the subsidiary were assumed by, the parent on the winding-up, and

(B) for the taxation years of the subsidiary and the parent following the time referred to in clause (A), the property transferred to, and the obligations assumed by, the parent on the winding-up shall be deemed to have been transferred or assumed, as the case may be, on the last day of the taxation year ending immediately before that time and the parent shall be deemed to be the same corporation as and a continuation of the subsidiary with respect to that property, those obligations and the insurance businesses carried on by the subsidiary;

**Notes:** 88(1)(g)(i) amended by 1996 Budget, effective for windups that begin after 1995, to add references to 12(1)(e.1) and 20(22), and to remove an obsolete reference to s. 33 of the pre-RSC 1985 (5th Supp.) Act.

88(1)(g) added by 1988 tax reform, effective for windups commencing on December 16, 1987 or later.

**I.T. Application Rules:** 69 (meaning of "*Income Tax Act*, chapter 148 of the Revised Statutes of Canada, 1952").

(h) **[financial institution — mark-to-market property]** — for the purposes of subsections 112(5) to (5.2) and (5.4) and the definition "mark-to-market property" in subsection 142.2(1), the parent shall be deemed, in respect of each property distributed to it on the winding-up, to be the same corporation as, and a continuation of, the subsidiary; and

**Notes:** 88(1)(h) added by 1994 tax amendments bill (Part III), effective for windups that begin at any time (including those before Royal Assent to the amendments bill).

(i) **[financial institution — mark-to-market property]** — for the purpose of subsection 142.5(2), the subsidiary's taxation year in which its assets were distributed to the parent on the winding-up shall be deemed to have ended immediately before the time when the assets were distributed.

**Notes:** 88(1)(i) added by 1994 tax amendments bill (Part III), effective for windups that begin after October 1994.

**Related Provisions [subsec. 88(1)]:** 69(5) — Deemed distribution of corporation's property before windup; 69(13) — Amalgamation or merger; 80.01(4) — Deemed settlement of debt on winding-up; 80.01(5) — Deemed settlement of distress preferred share on winding-up; 84(2) — Distribution on winding-up, etc.; 89(3) — Ordering of simultaneous dividends; 98(5)(a)(i) — Where partnership business carried on as sole proprietorship; 137(4.3) — Determination of preferred-rate amount; 142.6(5), (6) — Acquisition of specified debt obligation by financial institution in rollover transaction; 186(5) — Presumption; Reg. 8101(3) — Windup of insurer.

**Interpretation Bulletins [subsec. 88(1)]:** IT-109R2: Unpaid amounts; IT-121R3: Election to capitalize cost of borrowed money; IT-126R2: Meaning of "winding-up"; IT-142R3: Settlement of debts on the winding-up of a corporation; IT-151R5: Scientific research and experimental development expenditures; IT-154R: Special reserves; IT-321R: Insurance agents and brokers — unearned commissions; IT-488R2: Winding-up of 90%-owned taxable Canadian corporations. See also list at end of s. 88.

**Information Circulars [subsec. 88(1)]**: 88-2 Supplement, para. 8: General anti-avoidance rule — section 245 of the *Income Tax Act*.

**I.T. Technical News**: No. 16 (*Continental Bank* case).

### (1.1) Non-capital losses, etc., of subsidiary —
Where a Canadian corporation (in this subsection referred to as the "subsidiary") has been wound up and not less than 90% of the issued shares of each class of the capital stock of the subsidiary were, immediately before the winding-up, owned by another Canadian corporation (in this subsection referred to as the "parent") and all the shares of the subsidiary that were not owned by the parent immediately before the winding-up were owned at that time by a person or persons with whom the parent was dealing at arm's length, for the purpose of computing the taxable income of the parent under this Part and the tax payable under Part IV by the parent for any taxation year commencing after the commencement of the winding-up, such portion of any non-capital loss, restricted farm loss, farm loss or limited partnership loss of the subsidiary as may reasonably be regarded as its loss from carrying on a particular business (in this subsection referred to as the "subsidiary's loss business") and any other portion of any non-capital loss or limited partnership loss of the subsidiary as may reasonably be regarded as being derived from any other source or being in respect of a claim made under section 110.5 for any particular taxation year of the subsidiary (in this subsection referred to as "the subsidiary's loss year"), to the extent that it

(a) was not deducted in computing the taxable income of the subsidiary for any taxation year of the subsidiary, and

(b) would have been deductible in computing the taxable income of the subsidiary for any taxation year beginning after the commencement of the winding-up, on the assumption that it had such a taxation year and that it had sufficient income for that year,

shall, for the purposes of this subsection, paragraphs 111(1)(a), (c), (d) and (e), subsection 111(3) and Part IV,

(c) in the case of such portion of any non-capital loss, restricted farm loss, farm loss or limited partnership loss of the subsidiary as may reasonably be regarded as its loss from carrying on the subsidiary's loss business, be deemed, for the taxation year of the parent in which the subsidiary's loss year ended, to be a non-capital loss, restricted farm loss, farm loss or limited partnership loss, respectively, of the parent from carrying on the subsidiary's loss business, that was not deductible by the parent in computing its taxable income for any taxation year that commenced before the commencement of the winding-up,

(d) in the case of any other portion of any non-capital loss or limited partnership loss of the subsidiary as may reasonably be regarded as being derived from any other source, be deemed, for the taxation year of the parent in which the subsidiary's loss year ended, to be a non-capital loss or a limited partnership loss, respectively, of the parent that was derived from the source from which the subsidiary derived the loss and that was not deductible by the parent in computing its taxable income for any taxation year that commenced before the commencement of the winding-up, and

(d.1) in the case of any other portion of any non-capital loss of the subsidiary as may reasonably be regarded as being in respect of a claim made under section 110.5, be deemed, for the taxation year of the parent in which the subsidiary's loss year ended, to be a non-capital loss of the parent in respect of a claim made under section 110.5 that was not deductible by the parent in computing its taxable income for any taxation year that commenced before the commencement of the winding-up,

except that

(e) where at any time control of the parent or subsidiary has been acquired by a person or group of persons, no amount in respect of the subsidiary's non-capital loss or farm loss for a taxation year ending before that time is deductible in computing the taxable income of the parent for a particular taxation year ending after that time, except that such portion of the subsidiary's non-capital loss or farm loss as may reasonably be regarded as its loss from carrying on a business and, where a business was carried on by the subsidiary in that year, such portion of the non-capital loss as may reasonably be regarded as being in respect of an amount deductible under paragraph 110(1)(k) in computing its taxable income for the year is deductible only

(i) if that business is carried on by the subsidiary or the parent for profit or with a reasonable expectation of profit throughout the particular year, and

(ii) to the extent of the total of the parent's income for the particular year from that business and, where properties were sold, leased, rented or developed or services rendered in the course of carrying on that business before that time, from any other business substantially all of the income of which was derived from the sale, leasing, rental or development, as the case may be, of similar properties or the rendering of similar services,

and, for the purpose of this paragraph, where this subsection applied to the winding-up of another corporation in respect of which the subsidiary was the parent and this paragraph applied in respect of losses of that other corporation, the subsidiary shall be deemed to be the same corporation as, and a continuation of, that other corporation with respect to those losses, and

(f) any portion of a loss of the subsidiary that would otherwise be deemed by paragraph (c), (d) or (d.1) to be a loss of the parent for a particular taxation year beginning after the commencement of the winding-up shall be deemed, for the purpose of computing the parent's taxable income for taxation years beginning after the commencement of the winding-up, to be such a loss of the parent for its immediately preceding taxation year and not for the particular year, where the parent so elects in its return of income under this Part for the particular year.

**Related Provisions**: 10(11) — Adventure in the nature of trade deemed to be business carried on by corporation; 88(1.3) — Rules relating to computation of income and tax of parent; 139.1(18) — Holding corporation deemed not to acquire control of insurer on demutualization; 256(6)–(9) — Whether control acquired.

**Notes**: 88(1.1)(b) amended by 1991 technical bill, retroactive to 1985, to read "any taxation year" instead of "its first taxation year".

Closing words of 88(1.1)(e), beginning "and, for the purposes ...", added by 1991 technical bill, effective 1990.

Opening words of 88(1.1)(e) were amended by 1988 tax reform, effective for non-capital losses and farm losses for 1988 and later years. For earlier losses, jump from "its loss from carrying on a business" to "is deductible".

88(1.1)(e) amended in 1987, effective for acquisitions of control occurring after January 15, 1987, other than acquisitions of control before 1988 where the persons acquiring control were obliged to do so pursuant to the terms of agreements in writing entered into by January 15, 1987. For this purpose, the amending legislation provides that "a person shall be considered not to be obliged ... to acquire control of a corporation ... if the person may be excused from performing the obligation as a result of changes to the [*Income Tax Act*] affecting acquisitions or dispositions of property or acquisitions of control of corporations".

For acquisitions of control from May 10, 1985 to the above date, read:

(e) where, at any time, control of the parent or subsidiary has been acquired by a person or persons (each of whom is in this section referred to as the "purchaser") such portion of the subsidiary's non-capital loss or farm loss for a taxation year ending before that time as may reasonably be regarded as its loss from carrying on a particular business is deductible by the parent for a particular taxation year ending after that time

(i) only if that business was carried on by the subsidiary or parent for profit or with a reasonable expectation of profit

(A) throughout the part of the particular year that is after that time, where control of the parent or subsidiary was acquired in the particular year, and

(B) throughout the particular year, in any other case, and

(ii) only to the extent of the aggregate of

(A) the parent's income for the particular year from that business and, where properties were sold, leased, rented or developed or services rendered in the course of carrying on that business before that time, from any other business substantially all the income of which was derived from the sale, leasing, rental or development, as the case may be, of similar properties or the rendering of similar services, and

(B) the amount, if any, by which

(I) the aggregate of the parent's taxable capital gains for the particular year from dispositions of property owned by the corporation at or before that time, other than property that was acquired by the subsidiary within the two-year period ending at that time from the purchaser or a person who did not deal at arm's length with the purchaser,

exceeds

(II) the aggregate of the parent's allowable capital losses for the particular year from dispositions described in subclause (I).

For acquisitions of control from January 1, 1984 to May 9, 1985, read as above, but read subclause (e)(ii)(B)(II) as follows:

(II) the amount, if any, by which the aggregate of the parent's allowable capital losses for the particular year from the disposition of property described in subclause (I) exceeds the aggregate of its allowable business investment losses for the particular year from the disposition of that property.

Amendments from before 1984 are generally no longer relevant for claiming business losses.

The CCRA takes the position that "all or substantially all", used in 88(1.1)(e)(ii), means 90% or more.

88(1.1)(f) added by 1991 technical bill, effective for parent corporations as of 1985. However, a parent could elect for any of taxation years 1985 through 1991 by notifying Revenue Canada in writing by June 17, 1992.

**Interpretation Bulletins**: IT-302R3: Losses of a corporation — the effect that acquisitions of control, amalgamations, and windings-up have on their deductibility — after January 15, 1987. See also list at end of s. 88.

**(1.2) Net capital losses of subsidiary** — Where the winding-up of a Canadian corporation (in this subsection referred to as the "subsidiary") commenced after March 31, 1977 and not less than 90% of the issued shares of each class of the capital stock of the subsidiary were, immediately before the winding-up, owned by another Canadian corporation (in this subsection referred to as the "parent") and all of the shares of the subsidiary that were not owned by the parent immediately before the winding-up were owned at that time by persons with whom the parent was dealing at arm's length, for the purposes of computing the taxable income of the parent for any taxation year commencing after the commencement of the winding-up, any net capital loss of the subsidiary for any particular taxation year of the subsidiary (in this subsection referred to as the "subsidiary's loss year"), to the extent that it

(a) was not deducted in computing the taxable income of the subsidiary for any taxation year of the subsidiary, and

(b) would have been deductible in computing the taxable income of the subsidiary for any taxation year beginning after the commencement of the winding-up, on the assumption that it had such a taxation year and that it had sufficient income and taxable capital gains for that year,

shall, for the purposes of this subsection, paragraph 111(1)(b) and subsection 111(3), be deemed to be a net capital loss of the parent for its taxation year in which the particular taxation year of the subsidiary ended, except that

(c) where at any time control of the parent or subsidiary has been acquired by a person or group of persons, no amount in respect of the subsidiary's net capital loss for a taxation year ending before that time is deductible in computing the parent's taxable income for a taxation year ending after that time, and

(d) any portion of a net capital loss of the subsidiary that would otherwise be deemed by this subsection to be a loss of the parent for a particular taxation year beginning after the commencement of the winding-up shall be deemed, for the purposes of computing its taxable income for taxation years beginning after the commencement of the winding-up, to be a net capital loss of the parent for its immediately preceding taxation year and not for the particular year, where the parent so elects in its return of income under this Part for the particular year.

**Related Provisions**: 80(12)(a)(ii)(B) — Application of subsidiary's capital losses against capital gain from forgiveness of debt; 88(1.3) — Computation of income and tax of parent; 111(5.4) — Non-capital loss; 139.1(18) — Holding corporation deemed not to acquire control of insurer on demutualization; 256(6)–(9) — Whether control acquired.

**Notes**: 88(1.2) amended by 1991 technical bill, effective for parents' 1985 and later taxation years. However, a corporation could elect for any of taxation years 1985 through 1991 by notifying Revenue Canada in writing by June 17, 1992.

88(1.2)(a) amended by 1983 Budget. For windups commencing before 1983, read "deductible" in place of "deducted".

Opening words of 88(1.2) amended by 1979 Budget. For windups commencing from December 12, 1979 through January 12, 1981, delete the requirement that shares not owned by the parent have been owned by a person dealing at arm's length with the parent.

For windups commencing from April 1, 1977 to December 11, 1979, the requirement was that 100% of the subsidiary's shares be owned by the parent.

**Interpretation Bulletins**: IT-302R3: Losses of a corporation — the effect that acquisitions of control, amalgamations, and windings-up have on their deductibility — after January 15, 1987. See also list at end of s. 88.

### (1.3) Computation of income and tax of parent

— For the purpose of paragraphs (1)(e.3), (e.6) and (e.7), subsections (1.1) and (1.2), section 110.1, subsections 111(1) and (3) and Part IV, where a parent corporation has been incorporated or otherwise formed after the end of an expenditure year, gift year, foreign tax year or loss year, as the case may be, of a subsidiary of the parent, for the purpose of computing the taxable income of, and the tax payable under this Part and Part IV by, the parent for any taxation year,

(a) it shall be deemed to have been in existence during the particular period beginning immediately before the end of the subsidiary's first expenditure year, gift year, foreign tax year or loss year, as the case may be, and ending immediately after it was incorporated or otherwise formed;

(b) it shall be deemed to have had, throughout the particular period, fiscal periods ending on the day of the year on which its first fiscal period ended; and

(c) it shall be deemed to have been controlled, throughout the particular period, by the person or persons who controlled it immediately after it was incorporated or otherwise formed.

**Related Provisions**: 256(6), (6.1) — Meaning of "controlled".

**Notes**: 88(1.3)(a) amended by 1992 technical bill, effective for windings-up that begin after 1988, to add reference to "expenditure year".

**Interpretation Bulletins**: IT-302R3: Losses of a corporation — the effect that acquisitions of control, amalgamations, and windings-up have on their deductibility — after January 15, 1987.

### (1.4) Qualified expenditure of subsidiary

— For the purposes of this subsection and section 37.1, where the rules in subsection (1) applied to the winding-up of a subsidiary, for the purpose of computing the income of its parent for any taxation year commencing after the subsidiary has been wound up, the following rules apply:

(a) where the parent's base period consists of fewer than three taxation years, its base period shall be determined on the assumption that it had taxation years in each of the calendar years preceding the year in which it was incorporated, each of which commenced on the same day of the year as the day of its incorporation;

(b) the qualified expenditure made by the parent in a particular taxation year in its base period shall be deemed to be the total of the amount thereof otherwise determined and the qualified expenditure made by the subsidiary in its taxation year ending in the same calendar year as the particular year;

(c) the total of the amounts paid to the parent by persons referred to in subparagraphs (b)(i) to (iii) of the definition "expenditure base" in subsection 37.1(5) in a particular taxation year in its base period shall be deemed to be the total otherwise determined and all those amounts paid to the subsidiary by a person referred to in those subparagraphs in the subsidiary's taxation year ending in the same calendar year as the particular year; and

(d) there shall be added to the total of the amounts otherwise determined in respect of the parent under subparagraphs 37.1(3)(b)(i) and (iii) respectively, the total of the amounts determined under those subparagraphs in respect of the subsidiary.

### (1.41) Application of subsec. 37.1(5)

— The definitions in subsection 37.1(5) apply to subsection (1.4).

**Notes**: 88(1.41) added in the R.S.C. 1985 (5th Supp.) consolidation, effective for taxation years ending after November 1991. This rule of application was formerly in the opening words of 37.1(5).

Section 37.1, which provided an additional R&D allowance, has been repealed.

**(1.5) Parent continuation of subsidiary** — For the purposes of section 29 of the *Income Tax Application Rules*, subsection 59(3.3) and sections 66, 66.1, 66.2, 66.4 and 66.7, where the rules in subsection (1) applied to the winding-up of a subsidiary, its parent shall be deemed to be the same corporation as, and a continuation of, the subsidiary.

> **Proposed Amendment — 88(1.5)**
>
> **(1.5) Parent continuation of subsidiary** — For the purposes of section 29 of the *Income Tax Application Rules*, subsection 59(3.3) and sections 66, 66.1, 66.2, 66.21, 66.4 and 66.7, where the rules in subsection (1) applied to the winding-up of a subsidiary, its parent is deemed to be the same corporation as, and a continuation of, the subsidiary.
>
> **Application**: The December 21, 2000 draft legislation, s. 40, will amend subsec. 88(1.5) to read as above, applicable to windings-up that occur after 2000.
>
> **Technical Notes**: Section 88 deals with the tax consequences arising from the winding-up of a corporation. Where there has been a winding-up of a subsidiary into a parent corporation that owned at least 90% of the subsidiary's shares, subsection 88(1.5) provides that the parent is considered to be the same corporation as the subsidiary for the purpose of the provisions dealing with the deduction of exploration, development and resource property expenses. This effectively removes the restrictions of the successor corporation rules that would otherwise apply with respect to the deduction by the parent of the unclaimed resource expenses of the subsidiary following its winding-up.
>
> Subsection 88(1.5) is amended so that the same rule also applies in respect of foreign resource expenses calculated under new section 66.21.

**Interpretation Bulletins**: IT-125R4: Dispositions of resource properties; IT-488R2: Winding-up of 90%-owned taxable Canadian corporations.

**(1.6) Idem** — Where a corporation that carries on a farming business and computes its income from that business in accordance with the cash method is wound up in circumstances to which subsection (1) applies and, at the time that is immediately before the winding-up of the corporation, owned inventory that was used in connection with that business,

(a) for the purposes of subparagraph (1)(a)(iii), the cost amount to the corporation at that time of property purchased by it that is included in that inventory shall be deemed to be the amount determined by the formula

$$\left(A \times \frac{B}{C}\right) + D$$

where

A is the amount, if any, that would be included under paragraph 28(1)(c) in computing the corporation's income for its last taxation year beginning before that time if that year had ended at that time,

B is the value (determined in accordance with subsection 28(1.2)) to the corporation at that time of the purchased inventory that is distributed to the parent on the winding-up,

C is the value (determined in accordance with subsection 28(1.2)) of all of the inventory purchased by the corporation that was owned by it in connection with that business at that time, and

D is the lesser of

(i) such additional amount as the corporation designates in respect of the property, and

(ii) the amount, if any, by which the fair market value of the property at that time exceeds the amount determined for A in respect of the property;

(b) for the purpose of subparagraph 28(1)(a)(i), the disposition of the inventory and the receipt of the proceeds of disposition therefor shall be deemed to have occurred at that time and in the course of carrying on the business; and

(c) where the parent carries on a farming business and computes its income therefrom in accordance with the cash method, for the purposes of section 28,

(i) an amount equal to the cost to the parent of the inventory shall be deemed to have been paid by it, and

(ii) the parent shall be deemed to have purchased the inventory for an amount equal to that cost,

in the course of carrying on that business and at the time it acquired the inventory.

**Notes**: 88(1.6) added by 1991 technical bill, effective for windups commencing after July 13, 1990.

**Interpretation Bulletins**: IT-427R: Livestock of farmers.

**(1.7) Interpretation** — For the purposes of paragraphs (1)(c) and (d), where a parent of a subsidiary did not deal at arm's length with another person (other than a corporation the control of which was acquired by the parent from a person with whom the parent dealt at arm's length) at any time before the winding-up of the subsidiary, the parent and the other person are deemed never to have dealt with each other at arm's length, whether or not the parent and the other person coexisted.

**Related Provisions**: 87(11) — Application to vertical amalgamation; 256(6)–(9) — Whether control acquired.

**Notes**: 88(1.7) added by 1995-97 technical bill, effective for windups that begin after February 21, 1994. This rule was formerly in the closing words of 88(1)(d).

**(2) Winding-up of [other] Canadian corporation** — Where a Canadian corporation (other than a subsidiary to the winding-up of which the rules in subsection (1) applied) has been wound up after 1978 and, at a particular time in the course of the winding-up, all or substantially all of the property owned by the corporation immediately before that time was distributed to the shareholders of the corporation,

(a) for the purposes of computing the corporation's

(i) capital dividend account,

(i.1) capital gains dividend account (within the meaning assigned by subsection 131(6)), where the corporation is an investment corporation,

(ii) capital gains dividend account (within the meaning assigned by section 133, and

(iii) pre-1972 capital surplus on hand,

at the time (in this paragraph referred to as the "time of computation") immediately before the particular time,

(iv) the taxation year of the corporation that otherwise would have included the particular time shall be deemed to have ended immediately before the time of computation, and a new taxation year shall be deemed to have commenced at that time, and

(v) each property of the corporation that was so distributed at the particular time shall be deemed to have been disposed of by the corporation immediately before the end of the taxation year so deemed to have ended for proceeds equal to the fair market value of the property immediately before the particular time;

(vi) [Repealed]

(b) where the corporation is, by virtue of subsection 84(2), deemed to have paid at the particular time a dividend (in this paragraph referred to as the "winding-up dividend") on shares of any class of its capital stock, the following rules apply:

(i) such portion of the winding-up dividend as does not exceed the corporation's capital dividend account immediately before that time or capital gains dividend account immediately before that time, as the case may be, shall be deemed, for the purposes of an election in respect thereof under subsection 83(2), 131(1) (as that subsection applies for the purposes of section 130) or 133(7.1), as the case may be, and where the corporation has so elected, for all other purposes, to be the full amount of a separate dividend,

(i.1) [Repealed under former Act]

(ii) the portion of the winding-up dividend equal to the lesser of the corporation's pre-1972 capital surplus on hand immediately before that time and the amount by which the winding-up dividend exceeds

(A) the portion thereof in respect of which the corporation has made an election under subsection 83(2), or

(B) the portion thereof in respect of which the corporation has made an election under subsection 133(7.1),

as the case may be, shall be deemed not to be a dividend,

(iii) notwithstanding the definition "taxable dividend" in subsection 89(1), the winding-up dividend, to the extent that it exceeds the total of the portion thereof deemed by subparagraph (i) to be a separate dividend for all purposes and the portion deemed by subparagraph (ii) not to be a dividend, shall be deemed to be a separate dividend that is a taxable dividend, and

(iv) each person who held any of the issued shares of that class at the particular time shall be deemed to have received that proportion of any separate dividend determined under subparagraph (i) or (iii) that the number of shares of that class held by the person immediately before the particular time is of the number of issued shares of that class outstanding immediately before that time; and

(c) for the purpose of computing the income of the corporation for its taxation year that includes the particular time, paragraph 12(1)(t) shall be read as follows:

"(t) the amount deducted under subsection 127(5) or (6) in computing the taxpayer's tax payable for the year or a preceding taxation year to the extent that it was not included under this paragraph in computing the taxpayer's income for a preceding taxation year or is not included in an amount determined under paragraph 13(7.1)(e) or 37(1)(e) or subparagraph 53(2)(c)(vi) or (h)(ii) or the amount determined for I in the definition "undepreciated capital cost" in subsection 13(21) or L in the definition "cumulative Canadian exploration expense" in subsection 66.1(6);".

**Related Provisions**: 69(5) — Property appropriated by shareholder on winding-up of corporation; 84(2) — Distribution of property on winding-up of corporation; 88(2.1) — "Pre-1972 capital surplus on hand" defined; 89(3) — Ordering of simultaneous dividends; 134 — Status of non-resident-owned investment corporation for 88(2).

**Notes**: The CCRA takes the position that "all or substantially all", used in the opening words to 88(2), means 90% or more.

88(2)(a)(i.1) added by 1991 technical bill, effective for windups commencing after 1988.

88(2)(a)(vi) repealed by 1991 technical bill, effective for windups commencing after 1987. For earlier windups, read:

> (vi) in calculating the income of the corporation for the taxation year so deemed to have ended, paragraph 12(1)(t) shall be read as follows:
>
>> "(t) the amount deducted under subsection 127(5) or (6) in computing the taxpayer's tax payable for the year or a preceding taxation year to the extent that it was not included in computing the taxpayer's income for a preceding taxation year under this paragraph or is not included in an amount determined under paragraph 13(7.1)(e) or 37(1)(e), or subparagraph 53(2)(c)(vi) or (h)(ii) or for I in the definition "undepreciated capital cost" in subsection 13(21) or L in the definition "cumulative Canadian exploration expense" in subsection 66.1(6);" and

88(2)(b)(i) amended by 1991 technical bill, effective for windups beginning after 1988, to add reference to 131(1).

88(2)(c) added by 1991 technical bill (replacing 88(2)(a)(vi)), effective for windups beginning after 1987.

**Interpretation Bulletins**: IT-126R2: Meaning of "winding-up"; IT-149R4: Winding-up dividend. See also list at end of s. 88.

## (2.1) Definition of "pre-1972 capital surplus on hand"
— For the purposes of subsection (2), "pre-1972 capital surplus on hand" of a particular corporation at a particular time means the amount, if any, by which the total of

(a) the corporation's 1971 capital surplus on hand on December 31, 1978 within the meaning of the *Income Tax Act*, chapter 148 of the Revised Statutes of Canada, 1952, as it read on that date,

(b) the total of all amounts each of which is an amount in respect of a capital property of the corporation owned by it on December 31, 1971 and disposed of by it after 1978 and before the particular time, equal to the amount, if any, by which the lesser of its fair market value on valuation day (within the meaning assigned by section 24 of the *Income Tax Application Rules*) and the corporation's proceeds of disposition of that capital property exceeds its actual cost to the corporation determined without reference to the *Income Tax Application Rules* other than subsections 26(15), (17) and (21) to (27) of that Act,

(c) where before the particular time a subsidiary (to the winding-up of which the rules in subsection (1) applied) of the particular corporation has been wound up after 1978, an amount equal to the pre-1972 capital surplus on hand of the subsidiary immediately before the commencement of the winding-up, and

(d) where the particular corporation is a new corporation formed as a result of an amalgamation (within the meaning of section 87) after 1978 and before the particular time, the total of all amounts each of which is an amount in respect of a predecessor corporation, equal to the predecessor corporation's pre-1972 capital surplus on hand immediately before the amalgamation

exceeds

(e) the total of all amounts each of which is an amount in respect of a capital property (other than depreciable property) of the corporation owned by it on December 31, 1971 and disposed of by it after 1978 and before the particular time equal to the amount, if any, by which its actual cost to the corporation determined without reference to the *Income Tax Application Rules*, other than subsections 26(15), (17) and (21) to (27) of that Act, exceeds the greater of the fair market value of the property on valuation day (within the meaning assigned by section 24 of that Act) and the corporation's proceeds of disposition of the property.

**Related Provisions**: 84(2) — Distribution on winding-up, etc.; 87(2)(t) — Deemed date of acquisition; 88(2.2) — Determination of pre-1972 CSOH; 88(2.3) — Actual cost of certain depreciable property.

**I.T. Application Rules**: 26(15), (17), (21)–(27); 69 (meaning of "*Income Tax Act*, chapter 148 of the Revised Statutes of Canada, 1952").

**Interpretation Bulletins**: IT-488R2: Winding-up of 90%-owned taxable Canadian corporations. See also list at end of s. 88.

## (2.2) Determination of pre-1972 capital surplus on hand
— For the purposes of determining the pre-1972 capital surplus on hand of any corporation at a particular time after 1978, the following rules apply:

(a) an amount referred to in paragraphs (2.1)(b) and (e) in respect of the corporation shall be deemed to be nil, where the property disposed of is

(i) a share of the capital stock of a subsidiary, within the meaning of subsection (1), that was disposed of on the winding-up of the subsidiary where that winding-up commenced after 1978,

(ii) a share of the capital stock of another Canadian corporation that was controlled, within the meaning assigned by subsection 186(2), by the corporation immediately before the disposition and that was disposed of by the corporation after 1978 to a person with whom the corporation was not dealing at arm's length immediately after the disposition, other than by a disposition referred to in paragraph (b), or

(iii) subject to subsection 26(21) of the *Income Tax Application Rules*, a share of the capital stock of a particular corporation that was disposed of by the corporation after 1978, on an amalgamation, within the meaning assigned by subsection 87(1), where the corporation controlled, within the meaning assigned by subsection 186(2), both the particular corporation immediately before the amalgamation and the new corporation immediately after the amalgamation; and

(b) where another corporation that is a Canadian corporation owned a capital property on December 31, 1971 and subsequently disposed of it to the corporation in a transaction to which section 85 applied, the other corporation shall be deemed not to have disposed of that property in the transaction and the corporation shall be deemed to have owned that property on December 31, 1971 and to have acquired it at an actual cost equal to the actual cost of that property to the other corporation.

**Interpretation Bulletins**: IT-488R2: Winding-up of 90%-owned taxable Canadian corporations. See also list at end of s. 88.

**(2.3) Actual cost of certain depreciable property** — For the purpose of subsection (2.1), the actual cost of the depreciable property that was acquired by a corporation before the commencement of its 1949 taxation year that is capital property referred to in that subsection shall be deemed to be the capital cost of that property to the corporation (within the meaning assigned by section 144 of the *Income Tax Act*, chapter 148 of the Revised Statutes of Canada, 1952, as it read in its application to the 1971 taxation year).

**I.T. Application Rules**: 69 (meaning of "*Income Tax Act*, chapter 148 of the Revised Statutes of Canada, 1952").

**(3) Dissolution of foreign affiliate** — Where on the dissolution of a controlled foreign affiliate (within the meaning assigned by subsection 95(1)) of a taxpayer (in this subsection referred to as the "disposing affiliate") one or more shares of the capital stock of another foreign affiliate of the taxpayer have been disposed of to the taxpayer,

(a) the disposing affiliate's proceeds of disposition of each such share and the cost thereof to the taxpayer shall be deemed to be an amount equal to the adjusted cost base to the disposing affiliate of the share immediately before the dissolution, or such greater amount as the taxpayer claims not exceeding the fair market value of the share immediately before the dissolution; and

(b) the taxpayer's proceeds of disposition of the shares of the disposing affiliate shall be deemed to be the amount, if any, by which the total of

(i) the cost to the taxpayer of the shares of the other foreign affiliate, as determined in paragraph (a), and

(ii) the fair market value of any property (other than the shares referred to in subparagraph (i)) disposed of by the disposing affiliate to the taxpayer on the dissolution,

exceeds

(iii) the total of all debts owing by the disposing affiliate, and of all amounts of other obligations of the disposing affiliate to pay amounts, otherwise than as or on account of a dividend owing by the disposing affiliate to the taxpayer or to persons with whom the taxpayer was not dealing at arm's length, that were outstanding immediately before the dissolution and that were assumed or cancelled by the taxpayer on the dissolution.

**Related Provisions**: 95(2)(f) — Determination of certain components of foreign accrual property income.

**Notes**: 88(3) amended by 1981 Budget, effective for dissolutions after November 12, 1981, other than a dissolution that was part of a reorganization that was substantially advanced by November 12, 1981. For such earlier (and grandfathered) dissolutions, read the opening words as follows:

(3) Where on the dissolution of a foreign affiliate of a taxpayer (in this subsection referred to as the "disposing affiliate") one or more shares of the capital stock of another foreign affiliate of the taxpayer have been disposed of to the taxpayer,

88(3)(b)(iii) amended by 1991 technical bill, effective July 14, 1990. For earlier dissolutions, ignore the words "otherwise than as or on account of a dividend owing by the disposing affiliate to the taxpayer or to a person with whom the taxpayer was not dealing at arm's length".

**(4) Amalgamation deemed not to be acquisition of control** — For the purposes of paragraphs (1)(c), (d) and (d.2),

**Proposed Amendment — 88(4) opening words**

**(4) Amalgamation deemed not to be acquisition of control** — For the purposes of paragraphs (1)(c), (c.2), (d) and (d.2) and, for greater certainty, paragraphs (c.3) to (c.8) and (d.3),

**Application**: Bill C-43 (First Reading September 20, 2000), subsec. 39(4), will amend the opening words of para. 88(4) to read as above, applicable to windings-up that begin after November 1994.

**Technical Notes**: Subsection 88(4) of the Act sets out for the purposes of paragraphs 88(1)(c), (d) and (d.2) the circumstances in which, among other things, a corporation formed on an amalgamation will be considered to be a continuation of its predecessor corporations. Subsection 88(4) is amended to also apply for the purpose of paragraph 88(1)(c.2), and for greater certainty, subsection 88(4) is amended to clarify that it also applies for the purposes of paragraphs 88(1)(c.3) to (c.8) and (d.3) of the Act.

(a) subject to paragraph (c), control of any corporation shall be deemed not to have been acquired because of an amalgamation;

(b) any corporation formed as a result of an amalgamation shall be deemed to be the same corporation as, and a continuation of, each predecessor corporation; and

(c) in the case of an amalgamation described in subsection 87(9), control of a predecessor corporation that was not controlled by the parent before the amalgamation shall be deemed to have been acquired by the parent immediately before the amalgamation.

**Notes**: 88(4) added by 1977 Budget and amended by 1978 Budget and 1991 technical bill, effective for windups commencing after March 1977.

**Interpretation Bulletins**: IT-488R2: Winding-up of 90%-owned taxable Canadian corporations.

**Definitions [s. 88]**: "acquired" — 88(1)(c.6), (d.2), 88(4), 256(7)–(9); "acquirer" — 88(1)(d.2); "adjusted cost base" — 54, 248(1); "allowable business investment loss", "allowable capital loss" — 38, 248(1); "amount" — 248(1); "arm's length" — 88(1.7), 251(1); "business" — 248(1); "business limit" — 125(2)–(5.1), 248(1); "calendar year" — *Interpretation Act* 37(1)(a); "Canadian corporation" — 89(1), 248(1); "Canadian resource property" — 66(15), 248(1); "capital property" — 54, 248(1); "carrying on business" — 253; "cash method" — 28(1), 248(1); "class of shares" — 248(6); "consequence of the death" — 248(8); "control" — 88(1)(c.6), (d.2), 88(4), 256(6)–(9); "controlled" — 256(6), (6.1); "controlled foreign affiliate" — 95(1), 248(1); "corporation" — 248(1), *Interpretation Act* 35(1); "cost amount" — 248(1); "depreciable property" — 13(21), 88(1)(c.7), 248(1); "dividend" — 248(1); "expenditure year" — 88(1)(e.3); "farm loss" — 111(8); "farming" — 248(1); "fiscal period" — 249(2)(b), 249.1; "foreign affiliate" — 95(1), 248(1); "foreign resource property" — 66(15), 248(1); "ineligible property" — 88(1)(c) [before (iii)]; "investment tax credit" — 127(9), 248(1); "life insurance capital dividend" — 83(2.1), 248(1); "limited partnership loss" — 248(1); "net capital loss", "non-capital loss" — 111(8), 248(1); "paid-up capital" — 89(1), 248(1); "parent" — 88(1), (1.1), (1.2); "partnership" — see Notes to 96(1); "payable" — 84(7), 89(3); "person" — 248(1); "pre-1972 capital surplus on hand" — 88(2.1), (2.2); "prescribed", "property" — 248(1); "qualified expenditure" — 37.1(5), 88(1.41); "restricted farm loss" — 31, 248(1); "series of transactions" — 248(10); "share", "shareholder" — 248(1); "specified class" — 88(1)(c.8); "specified future tax consequence" — 248(1); "specified person" — 88(1)(c.2)(i); "specified property" — 88(1)(c.4); "specified shareholder" — 88(1)(c.2)(iii), 248(1); "specified subsidiary corporation" — 88(1)(c.5); "subsidiary" — 88(1), (1.1), (1.2); "substitution" — 88(1)(c.3); "tax payable" — 248(2); "taxable Canadian corporation" — 89(1), 248(1); "taxable capital gain" — 38, 248(1); "taxable dividend" — 89(1), 248(1); "taxable income" — 2(2), 248(1); "taxation year" — 249; "taxpayer" — 248(1); "trust" — 104(1), 108(1).

**I.T. Application Rules [s. 88]**: 20(1.2).

**Interpretation Bulletins [s. 88]**: IT-188R: Sale of accounts receivable; IT-243R4: Dividend refund to private corporations; IT-474R: Amalgamations of Canadian corporations.

## 88.1 [Repealed]

**Notes**: 88.1 repealed by 1993 technical bill, effective 1993. Where a corporation continued before 1993 elects for new 250(5.1) to apply earlier (see Notes to 250(5.1)), the repeal is effective from the corporation's "time of continuation". Where a corporation continued in 1993 or the first 6 months of 1994 had arrangements for the continuation substantially advanced by December 21, 1992 and elects for new 250(5.1) not to apply to the continuation, the repeal is effective only after the corporation was granted the articles of continuance or similar constitutional documents in respect of which the election was made. (The repeal dovetails with 250(5.1) taking effect; once 88.1 is repealed, 250(5.1) applies instead.) See also 219.1.

Where 88.1 continues to apply, read:

> **88.1 Corporate emigration** — Where at any particular time after August 28, 1980 a corporation that was incorporated in Canada, other than a corporation that was not at any time resident in Canada,
>
> (a) has been granted articles of continuance, or similar corporate constitutional documents, in a jurisdiction outside Canada, or
>
> (b) has become resident in a jurisdiction outside Canada and would, as a consequence thereof, be exempt from tax under this Part on income from any source outside Canada derived by it after the particular time by virtue of any Act of Parliament or anything approved, made or declared to have the force of law under any Act of Parliament,
>
> the following rules apply:
>
> (c) the corporation's taxation year that would otherwise have included the particular time shall be deemed to have ended immediately before the particular time and a new taxation year of the corporation shall be deemed to have commenced at the particular time,
>
> (d) the corporation shall be deemed not to be a Canadian corporation at the particular time and all subsequent times,
>
> (e) each property owned by the corporation immediately before the particular time shall be deemed to have been disposed of by it immediately before that time for proceeds of disposition equal to its fair market value at that time and those proceeds shall be deemed to have become receivable and to have been received by it immediately before that time,
>
> (f) section 48 does not apply to the corporation for the taxation year in which it is deemed by paragraph (e) to have disposed of its property, and
>
> (g) each property deemed by paragraph (e) to have been disposed of by the corporation shall be deemed to have been reacquired by it immediately after the particular time at a cost equal to the proceeds of disposition of the property as determined in that paragraph.

**Interpretation Bulletins**: IT-451R: Deemed disposition and acquisition on ceasing to be or becoming resident in Canada.

## 89. (1) Definitions — In this subdivision,

**"Canadian corporation"** at any time means a corporation that is resident in Canada at that time and was

(a) incorporated in Canada, or

(b) resident in Canada throughout the period that began on June 18, 1971 and that ends at that time,

and, for greater certainty, a corporation formed at any particular time by the amalgamation or merger of, or by a plan of arrangement or other corporate reorganization in respect of, 2 or more corporations (otherwise than as a result of the acquisition of property of one corporation by another corporation, pursuant to the purchase of the property by the other corporation or as a result of the distribution of the property to the other corporation on the winding-up of the corporation) is a Canadian corporation because of paragraph (a) only if

(c) that reorganization took place under the laws of Canada or a province, and

(d) each of those corporations was, immediately before the particular time, a Canadian corporation;

**Related Provisions**: 134 — NRO not a Canadian corporation; 219 — Additional tax on corporations (other than Canadian corporations) carrying on business in Canada; 219.1 — Tax when corporation ceases to be Canadian corporation; 248(1)"Canadian corporation" — Definition applies to entire Act; 248(1)"corporation" — meaning of "incorporated in Canada"; 250 — Resident in Canada.

## Subdivision h — Corporations Resident in Canada    S. 89(1) cap

**Notes**: Definition "Canadian corporation" amended by 1993 technical bill to add everything after para. (b) (i.e., beginning "and, for greater certainty"), effective June 15, 1994.

**Interpretation Bulletins**: IT-98R2: Investment corporations; IT-320R2: Registered retirement savings plan — qualified investments; IT-458R2: Canadian-controlled private corporation.

**"capital dividend account"** of a corporation at any particular time means the amount, if any, by which the total of

(a) the amount, if any, by which

(i) the total of all amounts each of which is the amount if any, by which

(A) the amount of the corporation's capital gain from a disposition (other than a disposition that is the making of a gift after December 8, 1997 that is not a gift described in subsection 110.1(1)[)] of a property in the period beginning at the beginning of its first taxation year (that began after the corporation last became a private corporation and that ended after 1971) and ending immediately before the particular time

---

**Proposed Amendment — 89(1)"capital dividend account"(a)(i)(A)**

(A) the amount of the corporation's capital gain from a disposition (other than a disposition that is the making of a gift after December 8, 1997 that is not a gift described in subsection 110.1(1)) of a property in the period beginning at the beginning of its first taxation year (that began after the corporation last became a private corporation and that ended after 1971) and ending immediately before the particular time

**Application**: Bill C-43 (First Reading September 20, 2000), s. 40, will amend cl. (a)(i)(A) of the definition "capital dividend account" in subsec. 89(1) to read as above, applicable to dispositions made after December 8, 1997, other than a disposition made under a written agreement made before December 9, 1997.

**Technical Notes**: Subsection 89(1) defines certain terms that apply to corporations and their shareholders.

Clause (a)(i)(A) of the definition "capital dividend account" is amended to add a bracket that was omitted when the provision was amended by S.C. 1998, c. 19, ss. 17(1) [formerly Bill C-28] [1997 Budget bill — ed.].

The current amendment applies to dispositions made after December 8, 1997, other than a disposition made under a written agreement made before December 9, 1997 — the same coming-into-force provision as the 1998 amendment.

---

exceeds the total of

(B) the portion of the capital gain referred to in clause (A) that is the corporation's taxable capital gain, and

(C) the portion of the amount, if any, by which the amount determined under clause (A) exceeds the amount determined under clause (B) from the disposition by it of a property that can reasonably be regarded as having accrued while the property, or a property for which it was substituted,

(I) except in the case of a disposition of a designated property, was a property of a corporation (other than a private corporation, an investment corporation, a mortgage investment corporation or a mutual fund corporation),

(II) where, after November 26, 1987, the property became a property of a Canadian-controlled private corporation (otherwise than by reason of a change in the residence of one or more shareholders of the corporation), was a property of a corporation controlled directly or indirectly in any manner whatever by one or more non-resident persons, or

(III) where, after November 26, 1987, the property became a property of a private corporation that was not exempt from tax under this Part on its taxable income, was a property of a corporation exempt from tax under this Part on its taxable income,

exceeds

(ii) the total of all amounts each of which is the amount, if any, by which

(A) the amount of the corporation's capital loss from a disposition (other than a disposition that is the making of a gift after December 8, 1997 that is not a gift described in subsection 110.1(1) of a property in that period

exceeds the total of

(B) the part of the capital loss referred to in clause (A) that is the corporation's allowable capital loss, and

(C) the portion of the amount, if any, by which the amount determined under clause (A) exceeds the amount determined under clause (B) from the disposition by it of a property that can reasonably be regarded as having accrued while the property, or a property for which it was substituted,

(I) except in the case of a disposition of a designated property, was a property of a corporation (other than a private corporation, an investment corporation, a mortgage investment corporation or a mutual fund corporation),

(II) where, after November 26, 1987, the property became a property of a Canadian-controlled private corporation (otherwise than by reason of a change in the residence of one or more shareholders of the corporation), was a property of a corporation controlled directly or indirectly in any manner whatever by one or more non-resident persons, or

(III) where, after November 26, 1987, the property became a property of a private corporation that was not exempt from tax under this Part on its taxable income, was a property of a corporation exempt from tax under this Part on its taxable income,

(b) all amounts each of which is an amount in respect of a dividend received by the corporation on a share of the capital stock of another corporation in the period, which amount was, by virtue of subsection 83(2), not included in computing the income of the corporation,

(c) all amounts each of which is an amount in respect of a business carried on by the corporation at any time in the period, equal to the amount, if any, by which the total of

(i) where the period commenced before the corporation's adjustment time, the amount, if any, by which

(A) the total of the amounts in respect of the business required to be included in the calculation of the corporation's cumulative eligible capital by reason of the description of E in the definition "cumulative eligible capital" in subsection 14(5) with respect to that portion of the period preceding its adjustment time

exceeds the total of

(B) the cumulative eligible capital of the corporation in respect of the business at the commencement of the period, and

(C) ½ of the total of the eligible capital expenditures in respect of the business that were made or incurred by the corporation during that portion of the period preceding its adjustment time,

(ii) ⅓ of the total of the amounts in respect of the business required to be included in the calculation of the corporation's cumulative eligible capital by reason of the description of E in the definition "cumulative eligible capital" in subsection 14(5) with respect to that portion of the period following its adjustment time, and

(iii) ⅓ of all amounts received in the period that were required to be included in the corporation's income by reason of paragraph 12(1)(i.1)

exceeds the total of

(iv) where the period commenced after the corporation's adjustment time, ⅓ of its cumulative eligible capital in respect of the business at the commencement of the period,

(v) ¼ of the total of the eligible capital expenditures in respect of the business made or incurred by the corporation with respect to that portion of the period after its adjustment time,

(vi) where the period commenced before the corporation's adjustment time, ½ of the amount, if any, by which the total of the amounts determined in respect of the corporation under clauses (i)(B) and (C) exceeds the amount determined in respect of the corporation under clause (i)(A), and

(vii) ⅓ of all amounts deducted by the corporation under subsection 20(4.2) in respect of debts established by it to have become bad debts during the period,

**Proposed Amendment — 89(1)"capital dividend account"(c)–(c.2)**

(c) the total of all amounts each of which is an amount required to have been included under this paragraph as it read in its application to a taxation year that ended before February 28, 2000,

(c.1) the amount, if any, by which

(i) ½ of the total of all amounts each of which is an amount required by paragraph 14(1)(b) to be included in computing the corporation's income in respect of a business carried on by the corporation for a taxation year that is included in the period and that ended after February 27, 2000 and before October 18, 2000,

exceeds

(ii) where the corporation has deducted an amount under subsection 20(4.2) in respect of a debt established by it to have become a bad debt in a taxation year that is included in the period and that ended after February 27, 2000 and before October 18, 2000, or has an allowable capital loss for such a year because of the application of subsection 20(4.3), the amount determined by the formula:

$$V + W$$

where

V is ½ of the value determined for A under subsection 20(4.2) in respect of the corporation for the last such taxation year that ended in the period, and

W is ⅓ of the value determined for B under subsection 20(4.2) in respect of the corporation for the last such taxation year that ended in the period, and

(iii) in any other case, nil,

(c.2) the amount, if any, by which

(i) the total of all amounts each of which is an amount required by paragraph 14(1)(b) to be included in computing the corporation's income in respect of a business carried on by the corporation for a taxation year that is included in the period and that ends after October 17, 2000,

exceeds

(ii) where the corporation has deducted an amount under subsection 20(4.2) in respect of a debt established by it to have become a bad debt in a taxation year that is included in the period and that ends after October 17, 2000, or has an allowable capital loss for such a year because of the application of subsection 20(4.3), the amount determined by the formula

$$X + Y$$

where

X is the value determined for A under subsection 20(4.2) in respect of the corporation for the last such taxation year that ended in the period, and

Y is $1/3$ of the value determined for B under subsection 20(4.2) in respect of the corporation for the last such taxation year that ended in the period, and

(iii) in any other case, nil,

**Application**: The December 21, 2000 draft legislation, s. 41, will amend para. (c) of the definition "capital dividend account" in subsec. 89(1) to read as above, and add paras. (c.1) and (c.2), applicable in respect of taxation years that end after February 27, 2000.

**Technical Notes**: Where the appropriate elections have been made by a private corporation, dividends paid out of its capital dividend account are received tax-free by the corporation's shareholders who are resident in Canada. A corporation's capital dividend account includes the untaxed portion of gains in respect of dispositions of capital property.

Paragraph (c) of the definition "capital dividend account" describes the "untaxed portion" of gains in respect of eligible capital property. Because, under existing paragraph 14(1)(b), a corporation's gain in respect of eligible capital property was previously aggregated with a recapture of the paragraph 20(1)(b) deductions that were previously claimed, paragraph (c) of the definition "capital dividend account" describes the untaxed portion of gains in respect of eligible capital property by reference to the corporation's cumulative eligible capital, eligible capital expenditures and variable E in the definition "cumulative eligible capital".

Amended paragraph 14(1)(b) identifies the taxable (2/3 for taxation years that end after February 27, 2000 and before October 18, 2000 and 1/2 for taxation years that end after October 17, 2000) portion of gains in respect of eligible capital property. Accordingly it is possible to simplify the description of the untaxed (1/3) portion of gains in respect of eligible capital property for taxation years that end after February 27, 2000 and before October 18, 2000 and (1/2) portion for taxation years that end after October 17, 2000. Paragraph (c) of the definition "capital dividend account" is therefore amended to describe amounts determined under that provision as it applied to taxation years that ended before February 28, 2000.

New paragraph (c.1) of the definition "capital dividend account" generally requires the inclusion in the capital dividend account of 1/2 of all amounts required by amended paragraph 14(1)(b) to be included in the corporation's income for taxation years that end after February 27, 2000 and before October 18, 2000.

New paragraph (c.2) of the definition requires the inclusion of the amount required by paragraph 14(1)(b) (as amended) to be included for taxation years that end after October 17, 2000.

Both these amounts are reduced to take into account the appropriate portion of bad debts in respect of dispositions of eligible capital property. The calculation of the reduction for bad debts is complicated by the interaction of different inclusion rates for capital gains that may be relevant during the period. New paragraphs (c.1) and (c.2) of the definition "capital dividend account" recognize both the deduction under subsection 20(4.2) and the deemed allowable capital loss under subsection 20(4.3) as amounts that reduce the capital dividend account. For further detail, see the commentary on subsections 20(4.2) and (4.3).

**Notice of Ways and Means Motion, Economic Statement, October 18, 2000**: (12) That the amount required by subsection 14(1) of the Act to be included in computing a taxpayer's income from business (other than in respect of recaptured deductions)

(a) reflect a 2/3 inclusion rate for taxation years that end after February 27, 2000 and before October 18, 2000, and

(b) reflect a 1/2 inclusion rate for taxation years that end after October 17, 2000,

and that the rules for calculating a corporation's capital dividend account be modified to take into account these changes to the inclusion rate.

**Supplementary Information, Economic Statement, October 18, 2000**: See under 14(1) and s. 38.

(d) the amount, if any, by which the total of

(i) all amounts each of which is the proceeds of a life insurance policy of which the corporation was a beneficiary on or before June 28, 1982 received by the corporation in the period and after 1971 in consequence of the death of any person, and

(ii) all amounts each of which is the proceeds of a life insurance policy of which the corporation was not a beneficiary on or before June 28, 1982 received by the corporation in the period and after May 23, 1985 in consequence of the death of any person

exceeds the total of all amounts each of which is the adjusted cost basis (within the meaning assigned by subsection 148(9)) of a policy referred to in subparagraph (i) or (ii) to the corporation immediately before that person's death, and

(e) the amount of the corporation's life insurance capital dividend account immediately before May 24, 1985, exceeds the total of all capital dividends that became payable by the corporation after the commencement of the period and before the particular time;

**Related Provisions**: 83(2) — Election to pay capital dividend out of capital dividend account; 83(2.3) — Life insurance proceeds included under 89(1)"capital dividend account"(d); 87(2)(z.1) — Amalgamations — rules applicable — capital dividend account; 88(2)(a) — Winding-up of a Canadian corporation; 89(1.1) — Capital dividend account where control acquired; 89(1.2) — Capital dividend account where corporation ceases to be exempt; 89(2) — Where corporation is beneficiary; 104(20) — Flow-through of capital dividend through trust; 131(11)(e) — Rules re prescribed labour-sponsored venture capital corporations; 141.1 — Insurance corporation deemed not to be private corporation; 248(5) — Substituted property; 248(8) — Occurrences as a consequence of death; 256(5.1), (6.2) — Controlled directly or indirectly — control in fact.

**Notes**: The capital dividend account (CDA) is used to pay out tax-free capital dividends under 83(2). Although the definition is horrendously complex, the basic concept is that the CDA is the "untaxed ½" (¼ before February 28, 2000, ⅓ from then through October 17, 2000) of capital gains (see cls. (a)(i)(A) and (B) of the definition). Capital dividends paid out by a corporation go into the recipient corporation's CDA to preserve the flow-through of the "untaxed ½" of capital gains; see para. (b) of the definition.

Note that for publicly listed securities donated to a charity in circumstances where 38(a.1) applies and only ¼ of the gain is taxed (instead of ⅓), the effect of subpara. (a)(i) of this definition is that the capital dividend account is the "untaxed ¼", rather than the "untaxed ½"! This offers an extra bonus to corporations to donate listed shares or mutual fund units.

Problems may arise in determining who is entitled to the increase in CDA from life insurance proceeds where there has been a collateral assignment of corporate-owned life insurance. See Interpretation Bulletin IT-430R3, para. 6, and J. Milan Legris, "Crediting the Capital Dividend Account", 7(5) *Tax Law Update* (Canadian Bar Association — Ontario Taxation Law Section) pp. 15–19 (June 1997).

See also Notes to 104(21) re where capital gains are flowed through a mutual fund trust or corporation.

89(1)"capital dividend account" was 89(1)(b) before consolidation in R.S.C. 1985 (5th Supp.), applicable to taxation years ending after November 1991. See Table of Concordance.

"Capital dividend account"(a) (formerly 89(1)(b)(i)) amended by 1991 technical bill, effective for taxation years ending after November 26, 1987, to provide that capital gains on designated property will be excluded in calculating the capital dividend account to the extent the gain accrued while the property was owned by a corporation controlled by non-residents or by an exempt corporation.

Cls. (a)(i)(A) and (a)(ii)(A) amended by 1997 Budget bill (amended before Third Reading as per Finance news release, December 22, 1997), effective for dispositions made after December 8, 1997, other than a disposition made under a written agreement made before December 9, 1997. This gives effect to the 1997 Budget change but also eliminates additions to the CDA for gifts other than charitable donations. For earlier dispositions, read:

(a)(i)(A) the amount of a capital gain of the corporation realized in the period commencing on the first day of the first taxation year commencing after the time the corporation last became a private corporation and ending after 1971, and ending immediately before the particular time

. . . . .

(a)(ii)(A) the amount of a capital loss of the corporation realized in that period

**I.T. Application Rules**: 32.1(4) (where dividend paid or payable before May 7, 1974).

**Interpretation Bulletins**: IT-66R6: Capital dividends IT-123R4: Disposition of eligible capital property; IT-123R6: Transactions involving eligible capital property; IT-138R: Computation and flow-through of partnership income; IT-149R4: Winding-up dividend; IT-430R3: Life insurance proceeds received by a private corporation or a partnership as a consequence of death; IT-484R2: Business investment losses.

**I.T. Technical News**: No. 9 (life insurance policy used as security for indebtedness).

**Advance Tax Rulings**: ATR-54: Reduction of paid-up capital.

**"designated property" means**

(a) any property of a private corporation that last became a private corporation before November 13, 1981 and that was acquired by it

(i) before November 13, 1981, or

(ii) after November 12, 1981 pursuant to an agreement in writing entered into on or before that date,

(b) any property of a private corporation that was acquired by it from another private corporation with whom the private corporation was not dealing at arm's length (otherwise than by virtue of a right referred to in paragraph 251(5)(b)) at the time the property was acquired, where the property was a designated property of the other private corporation,

(c) a share acquired by a private corporation in a transaction to which section 51, subsection 85(1) or section 85.1, 86 or 87 applied in exchange for another share that was a designated property of the corporation, or

(d) a replacement property (within the meaning assigned by section 44) for a designated property disposed of by virtue of an event referred to in paragraph (b), (c) or (d) of the definition "proceeds of disposition" in section 54;

**Related Provisions**: 89(1)"capital dividend account"(a)(i)(C)(I), 89(1)"capital dividend account"(a)(ii)(C)(I) — Application to capital dividend account; 129(4.3) — Application of definition to s. 129.

**Notes**: 89(1)"designated property" was 89(1)(b.1) before consolidation in R.S.C. 1985 (5th Supp.), applicable to taxation years ending after November 1991. See Table of Concordance.

**Interpretation Bulletins**: IT-66R6: Capital dividends; IT-243R4: Dividend refund to private corporations.

**"life insurance capital dividend account [para. 89(1)(b.2)]"** — [Repealed under former Act]

**Notes**: 89(1)(b.2), repealed by 1985 Budget, defined "life insurance capital dividend account". The proceeds of life insurance are now dealt with in 89(1)"capital dividend account"(d) and (e). See Notes to 83(2.1).

**"paid-up capital"** at any particular time means,

(a) in respect of a share of any class of the capital stock of a corporation, an amount equal to the paid-up capital at that time, in respect of the class of shares of the capital stock of the corporation to which that share belongs, divided by the number of issued shares of that class outstanding at that time,

Subdivision h — Corporations Resident in Canada S. 89(1) pri

(b) in respect of a class of shares of the capital stock of a corporation,

(i) where the particular time is before May 7, 1974, an amount equal to the paid-up capital in respect of that class of shares at the particular time, computed without reference to the provisions of this Act,

(ii) where the particular time is after May 6, 1974, and before April 1, 1977, an amount equal to the paid-up capital in respect of that class of shares at the particular time, computed in accordance with the *Income Tax Act*, chapter 148 of the Revised Statutes of Canada, 1952, as it read on March 31, 1977, and

(iii) where the particular time is after March 31, 1977, an amount equal to the paid-up capital in respect of that class of shares at the particular time, computed without reference to the provisions of this Act except subsections 51(3) and 66.3(2) and (4), sections 84.1 and 84.2, subsections 85(2.1), 85.1(2.1), 86(2.1), 87(3) and (9), 128.1(2) and (3), 138(11.7), 139.1(6) and (7), 192(4.1) and 194(4.1) and section 212.1,

except that, where the corporation is a cooperative corporation (within the meaning assigned by subsection 136(2)) or a credit union and the statute by or under which it was incorporated does not provide for paid-up capital in respect of a class of shares, the paid-up capital in respect of that class of shares at the particular time, computed without reference to the provisions of this Act, shall be deemed to be the amount, if any, by which

(iv) the total of the amounts received by the corporation in respect of shares of that class issued and outstanding at that time

exceeds

(v) the total of all amounts each of which is an amount or part thereof described in subparagraph (iv) repaid by the corporation to persons who held any of the issued shares of that class before that time, and

(c) in respect of all the shares of the capital stock of a corporation, an amount equal to the total of all amounts each of which is an amount equal to the paid-up capital in respect of any class of shares of the capital stock of the corporation at the particular time;

**Related Provisions**: 51(3) — Exchange of convertible property; 66.3(2) — Exploration and development shares — deductions from PUC; 66.3(4) — PUC of flow-through share; 84.1 — Non-arm's length sales of shares; 84.2 — Computation of PUC in respect of particular class of shares; 85(2.1) — Transfer of property to corporation by shareholders — computation of PUC; 85.1(2.1) — Share for share exchange — computation of PUC; 86(2.1) — Internal reorganization; 87(3), (3.1) — Amalgamation — computation of PUC; 87(9)(b) — Rules applicable re certain mergers; 128.1(2), (3) — Corporation becoming resident in Canada; 138(11.7) — Insurance corporations — computation of PUC; 139.1(6), (7) — PUC after demutualization of insurer; 192(4.1), 194(4.1) — Computing PUC after SPTC or SRTC designation; 212.1 — Non-arm's length sales of shares by non-residents; 248(1)"paid-up capital" — Definition applies to entire Act; 248(6) — Series of shares.

**Notes**: The definition of paid-up capital in terms of paid-up capital, in subpara. (b)(iii), is a reference to paid-up capital (or "stated capital") as determined for corporate law purposes under the applicable business corporations legislation (federal or provincial). See sections 26, 38 and 39 of the *Canada Business Corporations Act*, for example. From that starting point, paid-up capital is modified for tax purposes by the specific provisions listed in subpara. (b)(iii).

PUC can generally be extracted by a shareholder tax-free, while increases in PUC will trigger a deemed dividend. See 84(1) and Notes to 84(3).

89(1)"paid-up capital"(b)(iii) amended by 1999 Budget, effective December 16, 1998, to add reference to 139.1(6) and (7).

Reference to 51(3) and 86(2.1) added to subpara. (b)(iii) by 1993 technical bill, effective for determinations of paid-up capital after August 1992. Reference to 128.1(2) and (3) added by 1993 technical bill, effective 1993.

"Paid-up capital"(b) amended by 1991 technical bill, effective 1989, to add everything after subpara. (iii) (i.e., from "except that" through to and including subpara. (v)).

89(1)"paid-up capital" was 89(1)(c) before consolidation in R.S.C. 1985 (5th Supp.), effective for taxation years ending after November 1991. See Table of Concordance.

**I.T. Application Rules**: 69 (meaning of "*Income Tax Act*, chapter 148 of the Revised Statutes of Canada, 1952").

**Interpretation Bulletins**: IT-88R2: Stock dividends; IT-463R2: Paid-up capital; IT-489R: Non-arm's length sale of shares to a corporation.

**Advance Tax Rulings**: ATR-27: Exchange and acquisition of interests in capital properties through rollovers and winding-up ("butterfly"); ATR-28: Redemption of capital stock of family farm corporation; ATR-35: Partitioning of assets to get specific ownership — "butterfly"; ATR-54: Reduction of paid-up capital.

**"paid-up capital deficiency [para. 89(1)(d)]" and "paid-up capital limit [para. 89(1)(e)]"** — [Repealed under former Act]

**Notes**: 89(1)(d) and (e), repealed in 1977, defined "paid-up capital deficiency" and "paid-up capital limit", terms no longer used.

**"private corporation"** at any particular time means a corporation that, at the particular time, is resident in Canada, is not a public corporation and is not controlled by one or more public corporations (other than prescribed venture capital corporations) or prescribed federal Crown corporations or by any combination thereof and, for greater certainty, for the purposes of determining at any particular time when a corporation last became a private corporation,

(a) a corporation that was a private corporation at the commencement of its 1972 taxation year and thereafter without interruption until the particular time shall be deemed to have last become a private corporation at the end of its 1971 taxation year, and

(b) a corporation incorporated after 1971 that was a private corporation at the time of its incorporation and thereafter without interruption until the particular time shall be deemed to have last become a private corporation immediately before the time of its incorporation;

**S. 89(1) pri**   Income Tax Act, Part I, Division B

**Related Provisions**: 27(2) — Crown corporations; 134 — NRO deemed not private corporation; 136(1) — Cooperative corporation not private corporation; 137(7) — Credit union not private corporation; 137.1(6) — Deposit insurance corporation not private corporation; 141.1 — Insurance corporation not private corporation for certain purposes; 186(5) — Subject corporation deemed private corporation for certain purposes; 227(16) — Municipal or provincial corporation deemed not private corporation for Part IV tax; 248(1)"private corporation" — Definition applies to entire Act; 250 — Resident in Canada; 256(6), (6.1) — Meaning of "controlled".

**Notes**: 89(1)"private corporation" was 89(1)(f) before consolidation in R.S.C. 1985 (5th Supp.), applicable to taxation years ending after November 1991. See Table of Concordance.

Opening words of the definition amended by 1991 technical bill, effective July 14, 1990, to add references to prescribed venture capital corporations and prescribed federal Crown corporations.

Note that a corporation controlled by a public corporation is not a private corporation, although it is not a public corporation either. For most purposes it is treated similarly to a public corporation. Note also that to be *either* a private or a public corporation, a corporation must first be resident in Canada (see 250(4), (5)).

**Regulations**: 6700 (prescribed venture capital corporation); 7100 (prescribed federal Crown corporation; intended to apply to 89(1), but has not been amended to do so).

**I.T. Application Rules**: 50(1) (status of corporation in 1972 taxation year).

**Interpretation Bulletins**: IT-243R4: Dividend refund to private corporations; IT-391R: Status of corporations; IT-458R2: Canadian-controlled private corporation.

**"public corporation"** at any particular time means

(a) a corporation that is resident in Canada at the particular time if at that time a class of shares of the capital stock of the corporation is listed on a prescribed stock exchange in Canada,

(b) a corporation (other than a prescribed labour-sponsored venture capital corporation) that is resident in Canada at the particular time if at any time after June 18, 1971 and

(i) before the particular time, it elected in prescribed manner to be a public corporation, and at the time of the election it complied with prescribed conditions relating to the number of its shareholders, the dispersal of ownership of its shares and the public trading of its shares, or

(ii) before the day that is 30 days before the day that includes the particular time it was, by notice in writing to the corporation, designated by the Minister to be a public corporation and at the time it was so designated it complied with the conditions referred to in subparagraph (i),

unless, after the election or designation, as the case may be, was made and before the particular time, it ceased to be a public corporation because of an election or designation under paragraph (c), or

(c) a corporation (other than a prescribed labour-sponsored venture capital corporation) that is resident in Canada at the particular time if, at any time after June 18, 1971 and before the particular time it was a public corporation, unless after the time it last became a public corporation and

(i) before the particular time, it elected in prescribed manner not to be a public corporation, and at the time it so elected it complied with prescribed conditions relating to the number of its shareholders, the dispersal of ownership of its shares and the public trading of its shares, or

(ii) before the day that is 30 days before the day that includes the particular time, it was, by notice in writing to the corporation, designated by the Minister not to be a public corporation and at the time it was so designated it complied with the conditions referred to in subparagraph (i),

and where a corporation has, on or before its filing-due date for its first taxation year, become a public corporation, it is, if it so elects in its return of income for the year, deemed to have been a public corporation from the beginning of the year until the time when it so became a public corporation;

**Related Provisions**: 13(27)(f) — Restriction on deduction before available for use; 87(2)(ii) — Amalgamations — public corporation; 130.1(5) — Mortgage investment corporation deemed to be public corporation; 141(2) — Life insurance corporation deemed to be public corporation; 141(3) — Life insurance holding corporation deemed to be public corporation; 248(1)"public corporation" — Definition applies to entire Act; 250 — Resident in Canada.

**Notes**: A corporation listed on Tier 3 of the Canadian Venture Exchange is not a public corporation. See Notes to Reg. 3200.

Definition "public corporation" rewritten by 1997 Budget, effective for 1995 and later taxation years. Although many changes were made to the wording, the substantive change was to provide that a prescribed labour-sponsored venture capital corporation is not a public corporation unless a class of its shares becomes listed on a prescribed stock exchange in Canada. (For this purpose, it is intended that Reg. 6701 will be amended to add a cross reference to this definition.) For taxation years before 1995, read:

"public corporation" at any particular time means a corporation that was resident in Canada at the particular time, if

(a) at the particular time, a class or classes of shares of the capital stock of the corporation were listed on a prescribed stock exchange in Canada,

(b) at any time after June 18, 1971 and

(i) before the particular time, it elected in prescribed manner to be a public corporation, and at the time of the election it complied with prescribed conditions relating to the number of its shareholders, dispersal of ownership of its shares, public trading of its shares and size of the corporation, or

(ii) before a day 30 days before the particular time, it was, by notice in writing to the corporation, designated by the Minister to be a public corporation, and at the time it was so designated it complied with the conditions referred to in subparagraph (i),

unless subsequent to the election or designation, as the case may be, and before the particular time, it ceased to be a public corporation by virtue of paragraph (c), or

(c) at any time after June 18, 1971 and before the particular time, it was a public corporation, unless after the time it last became a public corporation and

(i) before the particular time, it elected in prescribed manner not to be a public corporation, and at the time it so elected it complied with prescribed conditions relating to the number of its shareholders, dispersal of ownership of its shares and public trading of its shares, or

(ii) before a day 30 days before the particular time, it was, by notice in writing to the corporation, designated by the Minister not to be a public corporation, and at the time it was so designated it complied with the conditions referred to in subparagraph (i),

in which case it shall be deemed thereupon to have ceased to be a public corporation,

except that where a corporation's first taxation year ended after 1971 and the corporation has, after 1971 and on or before the day on or before which it was required by section 150 to file its return of income for that year, become a public corporation, it shall, if it so elected in that return, be deemed to have been a public corporation from the commencement of that year until the day on which it so became a public corporation;

89(1)"public corporation" was 89(1)(g) before consolidation in R.S.C. 1985 (5th Supp.), applicable to taxation years ending after November 1991. See Table of Concordance.

See Notes to 89(1)"private corporation".

**Regulations**: 3200 (prescribed stock exchange); 4800, 4803 (prescribed conditions); 6701 (prescribed labour-sponsored venture capital corporation).

**I.T. Application Rules**: 50 (status of corporation in 1972 taxation year).

**Interpretation Bulletins**: IT-98R2: Investment corporations; IT-176R2: Taxable Canadian property — interests in and options on real property and shares; IT-320R2: Registered retirement savings plan — qualified investments; IT-391R: Status of corporations; IT-458R2: Canadian-controlled private corporation.

**Forms**: T2067: Election not to be a public corporation; T2073: Election to be a public corporation.

### "tax equity [para. 89(1)(h)]" — [Repealed under former Act]

**Notes**: 89(1)(h), repealed effective 1979, defined the "tax equity" of a corporation at the end of its 1971 taxation year, a concept no longer used.

### "taxable Canadian corporation" means a corporation that, at the time the expression is relevant,

(a) was a Canadian corporation, and

(b) was not, by virtue of a statutory provision, exempt from tax under this Part;

**Related Provisions**: 134 — NRO deemed not taxable Canadian corporation; 149 — Statutory provisions exempting taxpayers from tax under this Part; 248(1)"taxable Canadian corporation" — Definition applies to entire Act.

**Notes**: 89(1)"taxable Canadian corporation" was 89(1)(i) before consolidation in R.S.C. 1985 (5th Supp.), applicable to taxation years ending after November 1991. See Table of Concordance.

### "taxable dividend" means a dividend other than

(a) a dividend in respect of which the corporation paying the dividend has elected in accordance with subsection 83(1) as it read prior to 1979 or in accordance with subsection 83(2), and

(b) a qualifying dividend paid by a public corporation to shareholders of a prescribed class of tax-deferred preferred shares of the corporation within the meaning of subsection 83(1).

**Related Provisions**: 15.1(1) — Small business development bond interest deemed taxable dividend; 15.2(1) — Small business bond interest deemed taxable dividend; 82(1) — Inclusion of taxable dividend in income; 88(2) — Winding-up of a Canadian corporation; 129(1.2) — Dividends paid to create dividend refund deemed not to be taxable dividends for purposes of s. 129; 129(7) — Capital gains dividend is not a taxable dividend for purposes of dividend refund (s. 129); 142.7(10)(a) — Branch-establishment dividend to foreign entrant bank deemed not to be taxable dividend; 248(1)"taxable dividend" — Definition applies to entire Act; 260(5) — Deemed taxable dividend on securities lending arrangement.

**Notes**: 89(1)"taxable dividend" was 89(1)(j) before consolidation in R.S.C. 1985 (5th Supp.), applicable to taxation years ending after November 1991. See Table of Concordance.

For practical purposes, a taxable dividend now means a dividend other than a capital dividend. Note that "dividend", as defined in 248(1), includes certain stock dividends. See also Notes to 82(1).

**Regulations**: 2107 (tax-deferred preferred series).

**Interpretation Bulletins**: IT-52R4: Income bonds and income debentures. IT-67R3: Taxable dividends from corporations resident in Canada; IT-146R4: Shares entitling shareholders to choose taxable or capital dividends.

### "tax-paid undistributed surplus on hand [para. 89(1)(k)]" — [Repealed under former Act]

### "1971 capital surplus on hand [para. 89(1)(l)]" — [Repealed under former Act]

**Notes**: 89(1)(k) and (l), repealed effective 1979, defined "tax-paid undistributed surplus on hand" and "1971 capital surplus on hand", terms no longer used. From 1972 through 1978 these represented amounts that pre-dated the introduction of capital gains tax and could be extracted from a corporation tax-free in certain circumstances.

**(1.01) Application of subsec. 138(12)** — The definitions in subsection 138(12) apply to this section.

**Notes**: 89(1.01) added in the R.S.C. (5th Supp.) consolidation, effective for taxation years ending after November 1991. This rule was formerly contained in the opening words of 138(12).

**(1.1) Capital dividend account where control acquired** — Where at any particular time after March 31, 1977 a corporation that was, at a previous time, a private corporation controlled directly or indirectly in any manner whatever by one or more non-resident persons becomes a Canadian-controlled private corporation (otherwise than by reason of a change in the residence of one or more of its shareholders), in computing the corporation's capital dividend account at and after the particular time there shall be deducted the amount of the corporation's capital dividend account immediately before the particular time.

**Related Provisions**: 256(5.1), (6.2) — Controlled directly or indirectly — control in fact; 256(7) — Where control deemed not acquired.

**Interpretation Bulletins**: IT-66R6: Capital dividends.

**(1.2) Capital dividend account of tax-exempt corporation** — Where at any particular time after November 26, 1987 a corporation ceases to be exempt from tax under this Part on its taxable income, in computing the corporation's capital dividend account at and after the particular time there shall be deducted the amount of the corporation's capital dividend account (computed without reference to this subsection) immediately after the particular time.

**Interpretation Bulletins**: IT-66R6: Capital dividends.

**(2) Where corporation is beneficiary** — For the purposes of this section,

(a) where a corporation was a beneficiary under a life insurance policy on June 28, 1982, it shall be deemed not to have been a beneficiary under such a policy on or before June 28, 1982 where at any time after December 1, 1982 a prescribed premium has been paid under the policy or there has been a prescribed increase in any benefit on death under the policy; and

(b) where a corporation becomes a beneficiary under a life insurance policy by virtue of an amalgamation or a winding-up to which subsection 87(1) or 88(1) applies, it shall be deemed to have been a beneficiary under the policy throughout the period during which its predecessor or subsidiary, as the case may be, was a beneficiary under the policy.

**Regulations**: 309 (prescribed increase, prescribed premium).

**(3) Simultaneous dividends** — Where a dividend becomes payable at the same time on more than one class of shares of the capital stock of a corporation, for the purposes of sections 83, 84 and 88, the dividend on any such class of shares shall be deemed to become payable at a different time than the dividend on the other class or classes of shares and to become payable in the order designated

(a) by the corporation on or before the day on or before which its return of income for its taxation year in which such dividends become payable is required to be filed; or

(b) in any other case, by the Minister.

**(4)–(6)** [Repealed under former Act]

**Notes**: 89(4)–(6), repealed in 1977, provided additional rules relating to the definitions in 89(1) for paid-up capital deficiency and 1971 capital surplus on hand, concepts that no longer exist.

**Definitions [s. 89]**: "adjustment time" — 14(5), 248(1); "allowable capital loss" — 38(b), 248(1); "amount" — 248(1); "arm's length" — 251(1); "business" — 248(1); "Canada" — 255; "Canadian-controlled private corporation" — 125(7), 248(1); "Canadian corporation" — 89(1), 248(1); "capital dividend" — 83(2), 248(1); "capital gain" — 39(1)(a), 248(1); "capital loss" — 39(1)(b), 248(1); "capital property" — 54, 248(1); "class of shares" — 248(6); "consequence of the death" — 248(8); "controlled" — 256(6), (6.1); "controlled directly or indirectly" — 256(5.1), (6.2); "corporation" — 248(1), *Interpretation Act* 35(1); "credit union" — 137(6), 248(1); "cumulative eligible capital" — 14(5), 248(1); "depreciable property" — 13(21), 248(1); "designated property" — 89(1); "dividend" — 248(1); "eligible capital amount" — 14(1), 248(1); "eligible capital expenditure" — 14(5), 248(1); "foreign affiliate" — 95(1), 248(1); "incorporated in Canada" — 248(1) "corporation incorporated in Canada"; "inventory" — 248(1); "investment corporation" — 130(3), 248(1); "life insurance corporation" — 248(1); "life insurance policy" — 138(12), 248(1); "Minister" — 248(1); "mortgage investment corporation" — 130.1(6), 248(1); "mutual fund corporation" — 131(8), 248(1); "non-resident" — 248(1); "paid-up capital" — 89(1), 248(1); "payable" — 84(7); "person", "prescribed" — 248(1); "prescribed labour-sponsored venture capital corporation" — Reg. 6701; "prescribed stock exchange in Canada" — Reg. 3200; "prescribed venture capital corporation" — Reg. 6700; "private corporation" — 89(1), 248(1); "property" — 248(1); "province" — *Interpretation Act* 35(1); "public corporation" — 89(1), 248(1); "resident in Canada" — 250; "share", "shareholder" — 248(1); "substituted property" — 248(5); "taxable capital gain" — 38(a), (a.1), 248(1); "taxable income" — 2(2), 248(1); "taxation year" — 249; "taxpayer" — 248(1); "writing" — *Interpretation Act* 35(1).

**Regulations [s. 89]**: 3200 (prescribed stock exchange).

**89.1** [Repealed under former Act]

**Notes**: 89.1, repealed in 1977, provided special rules for the determination of paid-up capital under 89(1)(c), the former definition of "paid-up capital".

## Subdivision i — Shareholders of Corporations Not Resident in Canada

**90. Dividends received from non-resident corporation** — In computing the income for a taxation year of a taxpayer resident in Canada, there shall be included any amounts received by the taxpayer in the year as, on account or in lieu of payment of, or in satisfaction of, dividends on a share owned by the taxpayer of the capital stock of a corporation not resident in Canada.

**Related Provisions**: 82(1) — Dividends received from corporation resident in Canada; 113(1) — Deduction for dividend received from foreign affiliate; 139.1(4)(f), (g) — Deemed dividend on demutualization of insurance corporation; 139.2 — Deemed dividend on distribution by mutual holding corporation.

**Notes**: The inclusion in income of dividends from non-resident corporations can be offset by a deduction under 113(1), depending on the country of source (see Reg. 5907(11)) and whether the dividend is considered paid out of the foreign affiliate's taxable surplus, exempt surplus or pre-acquisition surplus.

**Definitions [s. 90]**: "amount" — 248(1); "Canada" — 255; "corporation" — 248(1), *Interpretation Act* 35(1); "dividend" — 248(1); "resident in Canada" — 250; "share" — 248(1); "taxation year" — 249; "taxpayer" — 248(1).

**Interpretation Bulletins**: IT-451R: Deemed disposition and acquisition on ceasing to be or becoming resident in Canada.

**91. (1) Amounts to be included in respect of share of foreign affiliate** — In computing the income for a taxation year of a taxpayer resident in Canada, there shall be included, in respect of each share owned by the taxpayer of the capital stock of a controlled foreign affiliate of the taxpayer, as income from the share, the percentage of the foreign accrual property income of any controlled foreign affiliate of the taxpayer, for each taxation year of the affiliate ending in the taxation year of the taxpayer, equal to that share's participating percentage in respect of the

Subdivision i — Shareholders of Non-Resident Corporations    S. 91(4)(a)

affiliate, determined at the end of each such taxation year of the affiliate.

### Proposed Amendment — 91(1)

**91. (1) Amounts to be included in respect of share of foreign affiliate** — In computing the income for a taxation year of a taxpayer resident in Canada, there shall be included, in respect of each share owned by the taxpayer of the capital stock of a controlled foreign affiliate of the taxpayer, as income from the share, the percentage of the foreign accrual property income of any controlled foreign affiliate of the taxpayer, for each taxation year of the affiliate that ends in the taxation year of the taxpayer, equal to the amount that would be that share's participating percentage in respect of the affiliate, determined at the end of each such taxation year of the affiliate if paragraph (a) of the definition "equity percentage" in subsection 95(4) did not take into account each share that would be subject to subsection 94.2(9) in respect of the taxpayer for the year if the taxpayer held the share throughout the year.

**Application**: The June 22, 2000 draft legislation, subsec. 9(1), will amend subsec. 91(1) to read as above, applicable to taxation years that begin after 2000.

**Technical Notes**: Subsection 91(1) of the Act provides that a taxpayer who is resident in Canada must include in computing income an amount in respect of each share owned by the taxpayer in the capital stock of a controlled foreign affiliate of the taxpayer.

Subsection 91(1) is amended so that it does not result in additional income for a taxpayer arising because of the ownership by the taxpayer (or a controlled foreign affiliate of the taxpayer) of shares that are "tracked interests" subject to the mark-to-market regime in section 94.2 by reason of the application of subsection 94.2(9). Note that, because of paragraph (a) of the definition "exempt interest" in subsection 94.1(1), a share of the capital stock of a controlled foreign affiliate is otherwise not subject to the regime for foreign investment entities in sections 94.1 and 94.2.

This amendment applies to trust taxation years that begin after 2000.

**Related Provisions**: 17(1)(b)(iii) — Amount included as FAPI not taxed under rule for loan to non-resident; 94.1(16), (17) — Where demand for information not satisfied; 152(6.1) — Reassessment to apply FAPI loss carryback. See also Related Provisions and Definitions at end of s. 91.

**Notes**: The FAPI (foreign accrual property income) rules seek to prevent Canadian resident taxpayers from avoiding tax by earning passive (investment) income earned in holding companies in offshore jurisdictions. For any resident taxpayer, FAPI (as defined in 95(1)) of a controlled foreign affiliate (as defined in 95(1)) is brought into income by 91(1) on a current basis. Although the concept is straightforward, the rules are highly complex. For example, certain payments made by a Canadian resident to its controlled foreign affiliate for services are FAPI (95(2)(b)), and most real estate income is FAPI unless the affiliate has 6 or more employees (95(1)"active business", "investment business"). See 95 and Reg. 5900-5907.

For a thorough discussion of FAPI, see Sandra Jack, "The Foreign Affiliate Rules: The 1995 Amendments", 43(2) *Canadian Tax Journal* 347-400 (1995), and especially the flowcharts on pp. 396–398 which allow one to determine the characterization of income as FAPI or not.

See also Eric Lockwood & Michael Maikawa, "Foreign Affiliates and FAPI: Problems and Tax-Planning Opportunities Resulting from the 1995 Changes", 46(2) *Canadian Tax Journal* 377-414 (1998); and Melanie Huynh & Eric Lockwood, "Foreign Accrual Property Income: A Practical Perspective", 48(3) *Canadian Tax Journal* 752-777 (2000).

**Interpretation Bulletins**: IT-392: Meaning of the term "share"; IT-451R: Deemed disposition and acquisition on ceasing to be or becoming resident in Canada.

**I.T. Application Rules**: 35(1) (ITAR 26 does not apply to gains and losses of foreign affiliates for FAPI purposes).

**Information Circulars**: 77-9R: Books, records and other requirements for taxpayers having foreign affiliates.

**(2) Reserve where foreign exchange restriction** — Where an amount in respect of a share has been included in computing the income of a taxpayer for a taxation year by virtue of subsection (1) or (3) and the Minister is satisfied that, by reason of the operation of monetary or exchange restrictions of a country other than Canada, the inclusion of the whole amount with no deduction for a reserve in respect thereof would impose undue hardship on the taxpayer, there may be deducted in computing the taxpayer's income for the year such amount as a reserve in respect of the amount so included as the Minister deems reasonable in the circumstances.

**Interpretation Bulletins**: IT-392: Meaning of the term "share".

**(3) Reserve for preceding year to be included** — In computing the income of a taxpayer for a taxation year, there shall be included each amount in respect of a share that was deducted by virtue of subsection (2) in computing the taxpayer's income for the immediately preceding year.

**(4) Amounts deductible in respect of foreign taxes** — Where, by virtue of subsection (1), an amount in respect of a share has been included in computing the income of a taxpayer for a taxation year or for any of the 5 immediately preceding taxation years (in this subsection referred to as the "income amount"), there may be deducted in computing the taxpayer's income for the year the lesser of

(a) the product obtained when

(i) the portion of the foreign accrual tax applicable to the income amount that was not deductible under this subsection in any previous year

is multiplied by

(ii) the relevant tax factor, and

### Proposed Amendment — 91(4)(a)(ii)

(ii) the taxpayer's relevant tax factor for the year, and

**Application**: The June 22, 2000 draft legislation, subsec. 9(2), will amend subpara. 91(4)(a)(ii) to read as above, applicable after 2000.

**Technical Notes**: Subsection 91(4) of the Act provides for a deduction in computing the income of a taxpayer resident in Canada. The deduction is available to a taxpayer where the taxpayer has included an amount under subsection 91(1) in computing income in respect of a share of the capital stock of a controlled foreign affiliate of the taxpayer. The deduction is generally determined with reference to foreign taxes payable by the affiliate and a "relevant tax factor". The "relevant tax factor" for a resident taxpayer is designed to permit a deduction for the resident taxpayer to result in tax relief that is representative of foreign taxes payable by a controlled foreign affiliate of the resident taxpayer.

Subsection 91(4) is amended to explicitly link the "relevant tax factor" to the resident taxpayer and the taxation year for which the deduction under subsection 91(4) is claimed. This is consistent with the more explicit definition of "relevant tax factor" described below in the commentary on subsection 95(1).

(b) the amount, if any, by which the income amount exceeds the total of the amounts in respect of that share deductible under this subsection in any of the 5 immediately preceding taxation years in respect of the income amount.

**(5) Amounts deductible in respect of dividends received** — Where in a taxation year a taxpayer resident in Canada has received a dividend on a share of the capital stock of a corporation that was at any time a controlled foreign affiliate of the taxpayer, there may be deducted, in respect of such portion of the dividend as is prescribed to have been paid out of the taxable surplus of the affiliate, in computing the taxpayer's income for the year, the lesser of

(a) the amount by which that portion of the dividend exceeds the amount, if any, deductible in respect thereof under paragraph 113(1)(b), and

(b) the amount, if any, by which

(i) the total of all amounts required by paragraph 92(1)(a) to be added in computing the adjusted cost base to the taxpayer of the share before the dividend was so received by the taxpayer

exceeds

(ii) the total of all amounts required by paragraph 92(1)(b) to be deducted in computing the adjusted cost base to the taxpayer of the share before the dividend was so received by the taxpayer.

**Related Provisions**: 20(13) — Dividend on share from foreign affiliate of taxpayer; 91(6) — Amounts deductible re dividends received; 91(7) — Where share acquired by partner from partnership; 94.3(2)(a)(i)(B)(I) — Prevention of double taxation. See additional Related Provisions and Definitions at end of s. 91.

**Regulations**: 5900(1)(b), 5900(3) (portion of dividend prescribed to be paid out of taxable surplus).

**Interpretation Bulletins**: IT-392: Meaning of the term "share".

**Information Circulars**: 77-9R: Books, records and other requirements for taxpayers having foreign affiliates.

**(6) Idem** — Where a share of the capital stock of a foreign affiliate of a taxpayer that is a taxable Canadian corporation is acquired by the taxpayer from another corporation resident in Canada with which the taxpayer is not dealing at arm's length, for the purpose of subsection (5), any amount required by section 92 to be added or deducted, as the case may be, in computing the adjusted cost base to the other corporation of the share shall be deemed to have been so required to be added or deducted, as the case may be, in computing the adjusted cost base to the taxpayer of the share.

**Related Provisions**: 20(13) — Dividend on share from foreign affiliate of taxpayer; 80.1(4)(c) — Assets acquired from foreign affiliate as dividend in kind or benefit to shareholder; 87(2)(u) — Amalgamations; 92(1) — ACB of share in foreign affiliate; 94(1)(d) — Application of certain provisions to trusts not resident in Canada; 113(1) — Deduction for dividend received from foreign affiliate; 233.2–233.5 — Disclosure of foreign property.

**Notes**: 91(6) added by 1991 technical bill, effective 1990.

**Interpretation Bulletins**: IT-392: Meaning of the term "share".

### Proposed Addition — 91(7)

**(7) Shares acquired from a partnership** — For the purpose of subsection (5), where a taxpayer resident in Canada acquires a share of the capital stock of a corporation that is immediately after the acquisition a foreign affiliate of the taxpayer from a partnership of which the taxpayer, or a corporation resident in Canada with which the taxpayer was not dealing at arm's length at the time the share was acquired, was a member (each such person is referred to in this subsection as the "member") at any time during any fiscal period of the partnership that began before the acquisition,

(a) that portion of any amount required by subsection 92(1) to be added to the adjusted cost base to the partnership of the share of the capital stock of the foreign affiliate equal to the amount included in the income of the member because of subsection 96(1) in respect of the amount that was included in the income of the partnership because of subsection (1) or (3) in respect of the foreign affiliate and added to that adjusted cost base, and

(b) that portion of any amount required by subsection 92(1) to be deducted from the adjusted cost base to the partnership of the share of the capital stock of the foreign affiliate equal to the amount by which the income of the member from the partnership under subsection 96(1) was reduced because of the amount deducted in computing the income of the partnership under subsection (2), (4) or (5) and deducted from that adjusted cost base

is deemed to be an amount required by subsection 92(1) to be added or deducted, as the case may be, in computing the adjusted cost base to the taxpayer of the share.

**Interpretation Bulletins**: IT-392: Meaning of the term "share".

**Application**: Bill C-43 (First Reading September 20, 2000), s. 41, will add subsec. 91(7), applicable to shares acquired after November 1999.

**Technical Notes**: Section 91 of the Act sets out rules for determining amounts that a taxpayer resident in Canada is to include in computing its income for a particular year as income from a share of a controlled foreign affiliate of the taxpayer.

New subsection 91(7) of the Act applies where a taxpayer that is a taxable Canadian corporation acquires a share of the capital stock of a corporation that is, immediately after the acquisition, a foreign affiliate of the taxpayer, from a partnership of which the taxpayer or a corporation resident in Canada with which the taxpayer was not dealing at arm's length at the time the share was acquired was a member (the "member"). Where, after the acquisition, the taxpayer receives a dividend on such a share out of the foreign affiliate's taxable surplus, subsection 91(7) allows the taxpayer to make a deduction under subsection 91(5) of the Act in respect of the net foreign accrual property income in respect of the share that was previously included in the income of the member from the partnership from which the taxpayer acquired the share. Subsection 91(7) allows the deduction under subsection 91(5) by deeming the taxpayer's adjusted cost base of the share to have been adjusted under subsection 92(1) of the Act by the member's share of any additions to, or deductions from, the adjusted cost base of the share to the partnership under subsection 92(1).

New paragraph 91(7)(a) provides that the member's share of the increase to the partnership's adjusted cost base of the share is the amount included in the member's income under subsection 96(1) in respect of the affiliate's foreign accrual property income included in the partnership's income under subsections 91(1) or (3) of the Act. New paragraph 91(7)(b) provides that the member's share of the decrease to the partnership's adjusted cost base of the share is the amount by which the member's share of the partnership's income determined under subsection 96(1) decreased as a result of an amount deducted in computing the partnership's income under subsections 91(2), (4) or (5) of the Act.

**Definitions [s. 91]**: "adjusted cost base" — 54, 248(1); "amount" — 248(1); "arm's length" — 251(1); "Canada" — 255; "controlled foreign affiliate" — 94(1)(d), 95(1), 248(1); "corporation" — 248(1), *Interpretation Act* 35(1); "dividend" — 248(1); "fiscal period" — 249.1; "foreign accrual property income" — 95(1), (2), 248(1); "foreign accrual tax" — 95(1); "foreign affiliate" — 94(1)(d), 95(1), 248(1); "Minister" — 248(1); "participating percentage" — 95(1); "partnership" — see Notes to 96(1); "person" — 248(1); "relevant tax factor" — 95(1); "resident in Canada" — 250; "share" — 248(1); "taxable Canadian corporation" — 89(1), 248(1); "taxable surplus" — 113(1)(b)(i), Reg. 5907(1); "taxation year" — 95(1) (for foreign affiliate only), 249; "taxpayer" — 248(1).

## 92. (1) Adjusted cost base of share of foreign affiliate
— In computing, at any time in a taxation year, the adjusted cost base to a taxpayer resident in Canada of any share owned by the taxpayer of the capital stock of a foreign affiliate of the taxpayer,

(a) there shall be added any amount required to be included in respect of that share by reason of subsection 91(1) or (3) in computing the taxpayer's income for the year or any preceding taxation year (or that would have been so required to be included but for subsection 56(4.1) and sections 74.1 to 75 of this Act and section 74 of the *Income Tax Act*, chapter 148 of the Revised Statutes of Canada, 1952); and

(b) there shall be deducted in respect of that share

(i) any amount deducted by the taxpayer by reason of subsection 91(2) or (4), and

(ii) any dividend received by the taxpayer before that time to the extent of the amount deducted by the taxpayer in respect thereof by reason of subsection 91(5)

in computing the taxpayer's income for the year or any preceding taxation year (or that would have been deductible by the taxpayer but for subsection 56(4.1) and sections 74.1 to 75 of this Act and section 74 of the *Income Tax Act*, chapter 148 of the Revised Statutes of Canada, 1952).

**Related Provisions**: 53(1)(d) — ACB — additions; 53(2)(b) — ACB — deductions; 87(2)(u) — Shares of foreign affiliate; 91(6) — Amounts deductible re dividends received.

**I.T. Application Rules**: 69 (meaning of "*Income Tax Act*, chapter 148 of the Revised Statutes of Canada, 1952").

**Interpretation Bulletins**: IT-392: Meaning of the term "share".

## (2) Deduction in computing adjusted cost base
— In computing, at any time in a taxation year,

(a) the adjusted cost base to a corporation resident in Canada (in this subsection referred to as an "owner") of any share of the capital stock of a foreign affiliate of the corporation, or

(b) the adjusted cost base to a foreign affiliate (in this subsection referred to as an "owner") of a person resident in Canada of any share of the capital stock of another foreign affiliate of that person,

there shall be deducted, in respect of any dividend received on the share before that time by the owner of the share, an amount equal to the amount, if any, by which

(c) such portion of the amount of the dividend so received as was deductible by virtue of paragraph 113(1)(d) from the income of the owner for the year in computing the owner's taxable income for the year or as would have been so deductible if the owner had been a corporation resident in Canada,

exceeds

(d) such portion of any income or profits tax paid by the owner to the government of a country other than Canada as may reasonably be regarded as having been paid in respect of the portion described in paragraph (c).

**Related Provisions**: 53(2)(b) — ACB — deductions; 91(6) — Amounts deductible re dividends received.

**Interpretation Bulletins**: IT-392: Meaning of the term "share".

## (3) Idem
— In computing, at any time in a taxation year, the adjusted cost base to a corporation resident in Canada of any share of the capital stock of a foreign affiliate of the corporation, there shall be deducted an amount in respect of any dividend received on the share by the corporation before that time equal to such portion of the amount so received

as was deducted under subsection 113(2) from the income of the corporation for the year or any preceding year in computing its taxable income.

**Related Provisions**: 53(2)(b) — ACB — deductions.

**Interpretation Bulletins**: IT-392: Meaning of the term "share".

### Proposed Addition — 92(4)–(6)

**(4) Disposition of a partnership interest** — Where a corporation resident in Canada or a foreign affiliate of a corporation resident in Canada has at any time disposed of all or a portion of an interest in a partnership of which it was a member, there shall be added, in computing the proceeds of disposition of that interest, the amount determined by the formula

$$(A - B) \times C/D$$

where

A is the amount, if any, by which

(a) the total of all amounts each of which is an amount that was deductible under paragraph 113(1)(d) by the member from its income in computing its taxable income for any taxation year of the member that began before that time in respect of any portion of a dividend received by the partnership, or would have been so deductible if the member were a corporation resident in Canada,

exceeds

(b) the total of all amounts each of which is the portion of any income or profits tax paid by the partnership or the member of the partnership to a government of a country other than Canada that can reasonably be considered as having been paid in respect of the member's share of the dividend described in paragraph (a);

B is the total of

(a) the total of all amounts each of which was an amount added under this subsection in computing the member's proceeds of a disposition before that time of another interest in the partnership, and

(b) the total of all amounts each of which was an amount deemed by subsection (5) to be a gain of the member from a disposition before that time of a share by the partnership;

C is the adjusted cost base, immediately before that time, of the portion of the member's interest in the partnership disposed of by the member at that time; and

D is the adjusted cost base, immediately before that time, of the member's interest in the partnership immediately before that time.

**Technical Notes**: Section 92 of the Act provides for adjustments to be made to the adjusted cost base of a share in a foreign affiliate with respect to certain amounts included or deducted in computing income of the owner of the share.

New subsection 92(4) of the Act applies where a member of a partnership that is a corporation resident in Canada or a foreign affiliate of a corporation resident in Canada disposes of all or any portion of its interest in the partnership. New subsection 92(4) ensures that prior dividends received by the partnership out of the affiliate's pre-acquisition surplus, to the extent that they exceed related foreign withholding taxes, are included in calculating the member's proceeds of disposition on the partnership interest. Subsection 92(4) increases the member's proceeds of disposition by the amount that was deductible (or would have been deductible if it were a corporation resident in Canada) by the member under paragraph 113(1)(d) of the Act net of foreign withholding taxes. The amount added to the member's proceeds does not include amounts previously added under this subsection, or amounts that were previously deemed to be a gain under new subsection 92(5) of the Act. Where the member does not dispose of all of its interests in the partnership, the deemed proceeds under new subsection 92(4) are reduced in proportion to the interests that were retained.

New subsection 92(4) applies to dispositions that occur after November 30, 1999.

**Related Provisions**: 257 — Formula cannot calculate to less than zero.

**(5) Deemed gain from the disposition of a share** — Where a partnership has, at any time in a fiscal period of the partnership at the end of which a corporation resident in Canada or a foreign affiliate of a corporation resident in Canada was a member, disposed of a share of the capital stock of a corporation, the amount determined under subsection (6) in respect of such a member is deemed to be a gain of the member from the disposition of the share by the partnership for the member's taxation year in which the fiscal period of the partnership ends.

**(6) Formula** — The amount determined for the purposes of subsection (5) is the amount determined by the formula

$$A - B$$

where

A is the amount, if any, by which

(a) the total of all amounts each of which is an amount that was deductible under paragraph 113(1)(d) by the member from its income in computing its taxable income for a taxation year in respect of any portion of a dividend received by the partnership on the share in a fiscal period of the partnership that began before the time referred to in subsection (5) and ends in the member's taxation year, or would have been so deductible if the member were a corporation resident in Canada,

exceeds

(b) the total of all amounts each of which is the portion of any income or profits tax paid

## Subdivision i — Shareholders of Non-Resident Corporations — S. 93(1)

by the partnership or the member to a government of a country other than Canada that can reasonably be considered as having been paid in respect of the member's share of the dividend described in paragraph (a), and

B is the total of all amounts each of which is an amount that was added under subsection (4) in computing the member's proceeds of a disposition before the time referred to in subsection (5) of an interest in the partnership.

**Application**: Bill C-43 (First Reading September 20, 2000), s. 42, will add subsecs. 92(4) to (6), applicable to dispositions that occur after November 1999.

**Technical Notes**: New subsections 92(5) and (6) of the Act apply where a partnership disposes of a share of corporation. Where a corporation resident in Canada or a foreign affiliate of a corporation resident in Canada is a member of the partnership (the "member"), new subsections 92(5) and (6) treat the member as having a gain on the disposition of the share equal to the amount that was deductible (or would have been deductible by the member if it were a corporation resident in Canada) by the member under paragraph 113(1)(d) of the Act in respect of dividends (net of foreign withholding taxes) received by the partnership on the share that were paid out of pre-acquisition surplus. The gain in this subsection is reduced by any amount that was added to the member's proceeds of disposition of a partnership interest under subsection 92(4).

**Related Provisions**: 257 — Formula cannot calculate to less than zero.

**Definitions [s. 92]**: "adjusted cost base" — 54, 248(1); "amount" — 248(1); "Canada" — 255; "corporation" — 248(1), *Interpretation Act* 35(1); "disposition", "dividend" — 248(1); "fiscal period" — 249.1; "foreign affiliate" — 95(1), 248(1); "partnership" — see Notes to 96(1); "person" — 248(1); "resident in Canada" — 250; "share" — 248(1); "taxable income" — 2(2), 248(1); "taxation year" — 95(1) (for foreign affiliate only), 249; "taxpayer" — 248(1).

**93. (1) Election re disposition of share in foreign affiliate** — For the purposes of this Act, where a corporation resident in Canada so elects, in prescribed manner and within the prescribed time, in respect of any share of the capital stock of a foreign affiliate of the corporation disposed of by it or by another foreign affiliate of the corporation,

(a) the amount (in this subsection referred to as the "elected amount") designated by the corporation in its election not exceeding the proceeds of disposition of the share shall be deemed to have been a dividend received on the share from the affiliate by the disposing corporation or disposing affiliate, as the case may be, immediately before the disposition and not to have been proceeds of disposition; and

(b) where subsection 40(3) applies to the disposing corporation or disposing affiliate, as the case may be, in respect of the share,

(i) the amount deemed by that subsection to be the gain of the disposing corporation or disposing affiliate, as the case may be, from the disposition of the share shall, except for the purposes of paragraph 53(1)(a), be deemed to be equal to the amount, if any, by which

(A) the amount deemed by that subsection to be the gain from the disposition of the share determined without reference to this subparagraph

exceeds

(B) the elected amount, and

(ii) for the purposes of determining the exempt surplus, exempt deficit, taxable surplus, taxable deficit and underlying foreign tax of the affiliate in respect of the corporation resident in Canada (within the meanings assigned by the regulations for the purpose of section 95), the affiliate shall be deemed at the time of disposition to have redeemed shares of a class of its capital stock.

### Proposed Amendment — 93(1)(b)(ii)

(ii) for the purposes of determining the exempt surplus, exempt deficit, taxable surplus, taxable deficit and underlying foreign tax of the affiliate in respect of the corporation resident in Canada (within the meanings assigned by Part LIX of the *Income Tax Regulations*), the affiliate is deemed to have redeemed at the time of disposition shares of a class of its capital stock.

**Application**: Bill C-43 (First Reading September 20, 2000), subsec. 43(1), will amend subpara. 93(1)(b)(ii) to read as above, applicable to dispositions that occur after November 1999.

**Technical Notes**: Section 93 of the Act contains a number of rules relating to the disposition of shares of a foreign affiliate of a taxpayer resident in Canada.

Subsection 93(1) of the Act permits a corporation resident in Canada that disposes of a share of a foreign affiliate of the corporation to treat the proceeds of disposition of the share as a dividend.

In such circumstances, subparagraph 93(1)(b)(ii) provides that the foreign affiliate of the corporation will be considered to have redeemed shares of a class of its capital stock for the purposes of calculating certain of its surplus accounts in respect of the corporation. Subparagraph 93(1)(b)(ii) is amended to clarify that those accounts take their meaning from those meanings assigned for the purpose of Part LIX of the Regulations. New subparagraph 93(1)(b)(ii) applies to dispositions that occur after November 30, 1999.

**Related Provisions**: 40(3) — Deemed gain where amounts to be deducted from ACB exceed cost plus amounts to be added to adjusted cost base; 93(1.1) — Election re share in foreign affiliate; 93(5) — Late filed elections; 95(2)(f) — Determination of certain components of foreign accrual property income; Reg. 5900(2) — No election for dividend to have been paid out of taxable surplus; Reg. 5905(2) — Where shares of foreign affiliate are redeemed or cancelled.

**Notes**: 93(1)(b) added by 1991 technical bill, effective 1987.

**Regulations**: 5902 (prescribed manner, prescribed time).

**Interpretation Bulletins**: See at end of s. 93.

**Information Circulars**: 76-19R3: Transfer of property to a corporation under section 85; 77-9R: Books, records and other requirements for taxpayers having foreign affiliates.

**Forms**: T2107: Election for a disposition of shares in a foreign affiliate.

**(1.1) Idem** — Where at any time shares of the capital stock of a foreign affiliate of a corporation resident in Canada that are excluded property are disposed of by another foreign affiliate of the corporation (other than a disposition to which paragraph 95(2)(c), (d) or (e) applies), the corporation shall be deemed to have made an election at that time under subsection (1) in respect of each such share disposed of and in the election to have designated an amount equal to such amount as is prescribed.

**Related Provisions**: 95(2)(f) — Determination of certain components of foreign accrual property income.

**Regulations**: 5902(6) (prescribed amount).

### Proposed Addition — 93(1.2), (1.3)

**(1.2) Disposition of a share of a foreign affiliate held by a partnership** — Where a particular corporation resident in Canada or a foreign affiliate of the particular corporation (each of which is referred to in this subsection as the "disposing corporation") would, but for this subsection, have a taxable capital gain from a disposition by a partnership, at any time, of a share of the capital stock of a foreign affiliate of the particular corporation and the particular corporation so elects in prescribed manner in respect of the disposition,

(a) 4/3 of

(i) the amount designated by the particular corporation (which amount shall not exceed the amount of the disposing corporations's[9] taxable capital gain from the disposition of the share), or

(ii) where subsection (1.3) applies, the amount prescribed for the purpose of that subsection

in respect of the share is deemed to have been a dividend received on the share by the disposing corporation from the affiliate immediately before that time;

(b) notwithstanding section 96, the disposing corporation's taxable capital gain from the disposition of the share is deemed to be the amount, if any, by which the disposing corporation's taxable capital gain from the disposition of the share otherwise determined exceeds the amount designated by the particular corporation in respect of the share;

(c) for the purpose of any regulation made under this subsection, the disposing corporation is deemed to have disposed of the share at that time and to have had a capital gain from the disposition of the share equal to 4/3 of the disposing corporation's taxable capital gain from the disposition of the share;

(d) for the purpose of section 113 in respect of the dividend referred to in paragraph (a), the disposing corporation is deemed to have owned the share on which that dividend was received; and

(e) where the disposing corporation has a taxable capital gain from the partnership because of the application of subsection 40(3) to the partnership in respect of the share, for the purposes of this subsection, the share is deemed to have been disposed of by the partnership.

**Technical Notes**: New subsection 93(1.2) of the Act provides that, where a particular corporation resident in Canada or a foreign affiliate of the particular corporation (referred to as "disposing corporation") would, but for this subsection, have a taxable capital gain from a partnership from the disposition by the partnership of a share of a foreign affiliate of the corporation, and the particular corporation elects in prescribed manner in respect of the gain, the amount designated will reduce the taxable capital gain and will be grossed-up and recharacterized as a dividend received on the share by the disposing corporation.

New paragraph 93(1.2)(a) provides that 4/3 of the amount designated by the particular corporation in respect of the share (the amount designated cannot exceed the disposing corporation's taxable capital gain), or where proposed subsection 93(1.3) applies 4/3 of the amount determined under that subsection, will be treated as a dividend received on the share by the disposing corporation from the foreign affiliate.

New paragraph 93(1.2)(b) provides that, notwithstanding section 96, the disposing corporation's taxable capital gain from the disposition of the share is considered to be the amount by which the disposing corporation's taxable capital gain from the disposition of the share otherwise determined exceeds the amount designated by the particular corporation.

New paragraph 93(1.2)(c) provides that, for the purpose of any regulation made under subsection 93(1.2), the disposing corporation is treated as having disposed of the share and to have had a capital gain from the disposition equal to 4/3 of the disposing corporation's taxable capital gain.

New paragraph 93(1.2)(d) provides that, for the purpose of section 113 in respect of the dividend referred to in new paragraph 93(1.2)(a), the disposing corporation is considered to have owned the share on which the dividend is paid.

New paragraph 93(1.2)(e) provides that, where the disposing corporation has a taxable capital gain from the disposition of the share because of the application of subsection 40(3) of the Act to the partnership in respect of the share, the partnership is treated for the purposes of this subsection as having disposed of the share.

**Related Provisions**: 93(1.3) — Deemed election; Reg. 5900(2) — No election for dividend to have been paid out of tax-

---

[9] Sic.

Subdivision i — Shareholders of Non-Resident Corporations    S. 93(2)

able surplus; Reg. 5905(2) — Where shares of foreign affiliate are redeemed or cancelled.

**Regulations**: 5902 (prescribed manner, prescribed time).

**(1.3) Deemed election** — Where a foreign affiliate of a particular corporation resident in Canada has a gain from the disposition by a partnership at any time of shares of the capital stock of a foreign affiliate of the particular corporation that are excluded property, the particular corporation is deemed to have made an election under subsection (1.2) in respect of each such share disposed of by the partnership and to have designated in the election an amount equal to a prescribed amount.

**Technical Notes**: New subsection 93(1.3) of the Act provides that, where a foreign affiliate of a particular corporation resident in Canada has a gain from the disposition by a partnership of a share of a foreign affiliate of the particular corporation and the share is excluded property, the particular corporation will treated as having made the election under new subsection 93(1.2) and to have designated the prescribed amount.

**Related Provisions**: Reg. 5902(6) — Deemed amount designated.

**Application**: Bill C-43 (First Reading September 20, 2000), subsec. 43(2), will add subsecs. 93(1.2) and (1.3), applicable to dispositions that occur after November 1999.

**(2) Loss limitation on disposition of share** — Where

(a) a corporation resident in Canada has disposed of a share of the capital stock of any foreign affiliate of the corporation, or

(b) a foreign affiliate of a corporation resident in Canada has disposed of a share of the capital stock of another foreign affiliate of the corporation,

the amount of the loss of the disposing corporation from the disposition of the share shall be deemed to be the amount, if any, by which

(c) the amount that would be the loss of the disposing corporation therefrom if this Act were read without reference to this subsection

exceeds

(d) the amount, if any, by which

(i) the total of all amounts received before the disposition of the share in respect of exempt dividends on the share or a share for which the share was substituted by

(A) the disposing corporation,

(B) a corporation related to the disposing corporation,

(C) a foreign affiliate of the disposing corporation, or

(D) a foreign affiliate of a corporation related to the disposing corporation

exceeds

(ii) the total of all amounts each of which is the amount by which a loss from a previous disposition of the share or a share for which the share was substituted by a corporation referred to in any of clauses (i)(A) to (D) has been reduced because of this subsection.

**Proposed Amendment — 93(2)**

**(2) Loss limitation on disposition of share** — Where

(a) a corporation resident in Canada has a loss from the disposition by it at any time of a share of the capital stock of a foreign affiliate of the corporation (in this subsection referred to as the "affiliate share"), or

(b) a foreign affiliate of a corporation resident in Canada has a loss from the disposition by it at any time of a share of the capital stock of another foreign affiliate of the corporation resident in Canada that is not excluded property (in this subsection referred to as the "affiliate share"),

the amount of the loss is deemed to be the amount determined by the formula

$$A - (B - C)$$

where

A is the amount of the loss determined without reference to this subsection,

B is the total of all amounts each of which is an amount received before that time, in respect of an exempt dividend on the affiliate share or on a share for which the affiliate share was substituted, by

(a) the corporation resident in Canada,

(b) a corporation related to the corporation resident in Canada,

(c) a foreign affiliate of the corporation resident in Canada, or

(d) a foreign affiliate of a corporation related to the corporation resident in Canada,

C is the total of

(a) the total of all amounts each of which is the amount by which a loss (determined without reference to this section), from another disposition at or before that time by a corporation or foreign affiliate described in the description of B of the affiliate share or a share for which the affiliate share was substituted, was reduced under this subsection in respect of the exempt dividends referred to in the description of B,

(b) the total of all amounts each of which is 4/3 of the amount by which an allowable capital loss (determined without reference to this section), of a corporation or foreign affiliate described in the description of B from a previous disposition by a partnership of the affiliate share or a share for which the affiliate share was substituted, was reduced

**S. 93(2)**      Income Tax Act, Part I, Division B

under subsection (2.1) in respect of the exempt dividends referred to in the description of B,

(c) the total of all amounts each of which is the amount by which a loss (determined without reference to this section), from a disposition at or before that time by a corporation or foreign affiliate described in the description of B of an interest in a partnership, was reduced under subsection (2.2) in respect of the exempt dividends referred to in the description of B, and

(d) the total of all amounts each of which is 4/3 of the amount by which an allowable capital loss (determined without reference to this section), of a corporation or foreign affiliate described in the description of B from a disposition at or before that time by a partnership of an interest in another partnership, was reduced under subsection (2.3) in respect of the exempt dividends referred to in the description of B.

**Application**: Bill C-43 (First Reading September 20, 2000), subsec. 43(3), will amend subsec. 93(2) to read as above, applicable to dispositions that occur after November 1999.

**Technical Notes**: Subsection 93(2) is an anti-avoidance rule. It reduces a loss arising on a disposition of a share of the capital stock of a foreign affiliate of a corporation resident in Canada by exempt dividends received on the share before the disposition. The rule applies to the corporation resident in Canada and any foreign affiliate of such a corporation in respect of a share of a foreign affiliate of the corporation resident in Canada.

Subsection 93(2) of the Act is repealed and replaced by new subsections 93(2) to (2.3) of the Act because of the introduction of new section 93.1 of the Act.

Subsection 93(2) of the Act applies where a corporation resident in Canada or a foreign affiliate of such a corporation has a loss from the disposition of a share of a foreign affiliate of the corporation resident in Canada. Where the foreign affiliate has the loss from the disposition of a share of another foreign affiliate of the taxpayer, the rule does not apply where that affiliate share is excluded property of the disposing affiliate.

Where the rule applies, the loss arising on the disposition of the affiliate share is reduced by the exempt dividends received on the share by the particular corporation resident in Canada, a foreign affiliate of the particular corporation, another corporation related to the particular corporation or a foreign affiliate of a corporation resident in Canada that is related to the particular corporation, to the extent that those exempt dividends have not already reduced a capital loss or an allowable capital loss under subsections 93(2) to 93(2.3) arising on other dispositions of property. The term "exempt dividend" is defined in subsection 93(3) of the Act and is modified consequential on the introduction of section 93.1 of the Act.

### Proposed Amendment — 93(2)

**Application**: The December 21, 2000 draft legislation, subsec. 42(1), will amend subsec. 93(2) by replacing the references to the expression "4/3 of" with references to the word "twice", applicable to taxation years that end after February 27, 2000 except that, for a taxation year of a taxpayer that includes either February 28, 2000 or October 17, 2000, the references to the word "twice" shall be read as references to the expression "the fraction that is the reciprocal of the fraction in para. 38(a), as amended [by the December 21, 2000 draft legislation], that applies to the taxpayer for the year, multiplied by".

**Technical Notes**: Subsection 93(2) provides a rule for the purpose of determining a loss of a corporation resident in Canada or a foreign affiliate of such a corporation from the disposition of a share of another foreign affiliate of the corporation. The loss is reduced by exempt dividends received on the share.

The amendment to subsection 93(2) replaces the reference to the expression "4/3 of" with a reference to the word "twice", as a consequence of the reduction of the inclusion rate for capital gains from 3/4 to 1/2 [see 38(a) — ed.]

The amendment generally applies to taxation years that end after February 27, 2000. For a taxation year of a corporation that includes either February 28, 2000 or October 17, 2000, the reference to the word "twice" in subsection 93(2) is to be read as reference to the expression "the fraction that is the reciprocal of the fraction in paragraph 38(a) that applies to the taxpayer for the year, multiplied by". These modifications are required in order to reflect the capital gains/losses rate for the year.

**Related Provisions**: 40(3) — Deemed gain where amounts to be deducted from ACB exceed cost plus amounts to be added; 40(3.3), (3.4) — Limitation on loss where share acquired by affiliated person; 87(2)(u)(ii) — Amalgamation; 93(3) — Exempt dividends; 93(4) — Loss on disposition of shares of foreign affiliate; 93.1(2) — Dividend on shares of foreign affiliate held by partnership; 257 — Formula amounts cannot calculate to less than zero.

**Notes**: 93(2) amended by 1991 technical bill, this version effective for the determination of losses arising from dispositions after July 12, 1990. For earlier dispositions, for determination of losses arising in 1985 and later taxation years, read 93(2)(d) as follows:

(d) the total of all amounts in respect of exempt dividends received by the disposing corporation on the share at any time before the disposition.

**Interpretation Bulletins**: See at end of s. 93.

### Proposed Addition — 93(2.1)

**(2.1) Loss limitation — disposition of share by partnership** — Where

(a) a corporation resident in Canada has an allowable capital loss from a disposition at any time by a partnership of a share of the capital stock of a foreign affiliate of the corporation (in this subsection referred to as the "affiliate share"), or

(b) a foreign affiliate of a corporation resident in Canada has an allowable capital loss from a disposition at any time by a partnership of a share of the capital stock of another foreign affiliate of the corporation resident in Canada that would not be excluded property of the affiliate if the affiliate owned the share immediately before it was disposed of (in this subsection referred to as the "affiliate share"),

the amount of the allowable capital loss is deemed to be the amount determined by the formula

$$A - (B - C)$$

where

A is the amount of the allowable capital loss determined without reference to this subsection,

B is 3/4 of the total of all amounts each of which was received before that time, in respect of an exempt dividend on the affiliate share or on a share for which the affiliate share was substituted, by

    (a) the corporation resident in Canada,

    (b) a corporation related to the corporation resident in Canada,

    (c) a foreign affiliate of the corporation resident in Canada, or

    (d) a foreign affiliate of a corporation related to the corporation resident in Canada, and

C is the total of

    (a) the total of all amounts each of which is the amount by which an allowable capital loss (determined without reference to this section,) of a corporation or foreign affiliate described in the description of B from a disposition at or before that time by a partnership of the affiliate share or a share for which the affiliate share was substituted, was reduced under this subsection in respect of the exempt dividends referred to in the description of B,

    (b) the total of all amounts each of which is 3/4 of the amount by which a loss (determined without reference to this section), of a corporation or foreign affiliate described in the description of B from another disposition at or before that time of the affiliate share or a share for which the affiliate share was substituted, was reduced under subsection (2) in respect of the exempt dividends referred to in the description of B,

    (c) the total of all amounts each of which is 3/4 of the amount by which a loss (determined without reference to this section), from a disposition at or before that time by a corporation or foreign affiliate described in the description of B of an interest in a partnership, was reduced under subsection (2.2) in respect of the exempt dividends referred to in the description of B, and

    (d) the total of all amounts each of which is the amount by which an allowable capital loss (determined without reference to this section), of a corporation or foreign affiliate described in the description of B from a disposition at or before that time by a partnership of an interest in another partnership, was reduced under subsection (2.3) in respect of exempt dividends referred to in the description of B.

**Application**: Bill C-43 (First Reading September 20, 2000), subsec. 43(3), will add subsec. 93(2.1), applicable to dispositions that occur after November 1999.

**Technical Notes**: New subsection 93(2.1) applies where a corporation resident in Canada or a foreign affiliate of such a corporation has an allowable capital loss from a partnership arising on the disposition by the partnership of a share of a foreign affiliate of the corporation resident in Canada. Where the foreign affiliate has the allowable capital loss, the rule does not apply where that affiliate share would be excluded property of the disposing affiliate if the affiliate owned the share.

Where the rule applies, the allowable capital loss from the partnership arising on the disposition of the affiliate share is reduced by 3/4 of the exempt dividends received on the share by the particular corporation resident in Canada, a foreign affiliate of the particular corporation, another corporation related to the particular corporation or a foreign affiliate of a corporation resident in Canada that is related to the particular corporation, to the extent that those exempt dividends have not already reduced a capital loss or an allowable capital loss under subsections 93(2) to 93(2.3) arising on other dispositions of property. The term "exempt dividend" is defined in subsection 93(3) and is modified consequential on the introduction of section 93.1.

**Related Provisions**: 87(2)(u)(ii) — Amalgamation; 93(3) — Exempt dividends; 93.1(2) — Dividend on shares of foreign affiliate held by partnership; 257 — Formula amounts cannot calculate to less than zero.

## Proposed Amendment — 93(2.1)

**Application**: The December 21, 2000 draft legislation, subsec. 42(2), will amend subsec. 93(2.1) by replacing the references to the fraction "3/4" with references to the fraction "1/2", applicable to taxation years that end after February 27, 2000 except that, for a taxation year of a taxpayer that includes either February 28, 2000 or October 17, 2000, the references to the fraction "1/2" shall be read as references to the fraction in para. 38(a), as amended [by the December 21, 2000 draft legislation], that applies to the taxpayer for the year.

**Technical Notes**: New subsection 93(2.1) provides a rule for the purpose of determining a loss of a corporation resident in Canada or a foreign affiliate of such a corporation from the disposition by a partnership of a share of another foreign affiliate of the corporation. The loss is reduced by exempt dividends received on the share.

The amendment to subsection 93(2.1) replaces the reference to the fraction "3/4" with a reference to the fraction "1/2", as a consequence of the reduction of the inclusion rate for capital gains from 3/4 to 1/2 [see 38(a) — ed.].

The amendment generally applies to taxation years that end after February 27, 2000. For a taxation year of a corporation that includes either February 28, 2000 or October 17, 2000, the reference to the fraction "1/2" in subsection 93(2) is to be read as reference to the fraction in amended paragraph 38(a) that applies to the taxpayer for the year. These modifications are required in order to reflect the capital gains/losses rate for the year.

## Proposed Addition — 93(2.2)

**(2.2) Loss limitation — disposition of partnership interest** — Where

(a) a corporation resident in Canada has a loss from the disposition by it at any time of an interest in a partnership (in this subsection referred to as the "partnership interest"), which has a direct or indirect interest in shares of the capital stock of a foreign affiliate of the corporation resident in Canada (in this subsection referred to as "affiliate shares"), or

(b) a foreign affiliate of a corporation resident in Canada has a loss from the disposition by it at any time of an interest in a partnership (in this subsection referred to as the "partnership interest"), which has a direct or indirect interest in shares of the capital stock of another foreign affiliate of the corporation resident in Canada that would not be excluded property if the shares were owned by the affiliate (in this subsection referred to as "affiliate shares")

the amount of the loss is deemed to be the amount determined by the formula

$$A - (B - C)$$

where

A is the amount of the loss determined without reference to this subsection,

B is the total of all amounts each of which was received before that time, in respect of an exempt dividend on affiliate shares or on shares for which affiliate shares were substituted, by

(a) the corporation resident in Canada,

(b) a corporation related to the corporation resident in Canada,

(c) a foreign affiliate of the corporation resident in Canada, or

(d) a foreign affiliate of a corporation related to the corporation resident in Canada, and

C is the total of

(a) the total of all amounts each of which is the amount by which a loss (determined without reference to this section), from another disposition at or before that time by a corporation or foreign affiliate described in the description of B of affiliate shares or shares for which affiliate shares were substituted, was reduced under subsection (2) in respect of the exempt dividends referred to in the description of B,

(b) the total of all amounts each of which is 4/3 of the amount by which an allowable capital loss (determined without reference to this section), of a corporation or foreign affiliate described in the description of B from another disposition at or before that time by a partnership of affiliate shares or shares for which affiliate shares were substituted, was reduced under subsection (2.1) in respect of the exempt dividends referred to in the description of B,

(c) the total of all amounts each of which is the amount by which a loss (determined without reference to this section), from a disposition at or before that time by a corporation or foreign affiliate described in the description of B of an interest in a partnership, was reduced under this subsection in respect of the exempt dividends referred to in the description of B, and

(d) the total of all amounts each of which is 4/3 of the amount by which an allowable capital loss (determined without reference to this section), of a corporation or foreign affiliate described in the description of B from a disposition at or before that time by a partnership of an interest in another partnership, was reduced under subsection (2.3) in respect of the exempt dividends referred to in the description of B.

**Application**: Bill C-43 (First Reading September 20, 2000), subsec. 43(3), will add subsec. 93(2.2), applicable to dispositions that occur after November 1999.

**Technical Notes**: New subsection 93(2.2) applies where a corporation resident in Canada or a foreign affiliate of such a corporation has a loss on the disposition of an interest in a partnership that has a direct or indirect interest in shares of a foreign affiliate of the corporation resident in Canada. Where the foreign affiliate has the loss, the rule does not apply where those affiliate shares in which the partnership has an interest would be excluded property of the affiliate with the loss if the affiliate owned them immediately before the disposition.

Where the rule applies, the loss arising on the disposition of the partnership interest is reduced by the exempt dividends received before the disposition on the affiliate shares (in which the partnership has the interest) by the particular corporation resident in Canada, a foreign affiliate of the particular corporation, another corporation related to the particular corporation or a foreign affiliate of a corporation resident in Canada that is related to the particular corporation, to the extent that those exempt dividends have not already reduced a capital loss or an allowable capital loss under subsections 93(2) to 93(2.3) arising on other dispositions of property. The term exempt dividend is defined in subsection 93(3) and is modified consequentially on the introduction of section 93.1.

**Related Provisions**: 87(2)(u)(ii) — Amalgamation; 93(3) — Exempt dividends; 93.1(2) — Dividend on shares of foreign affiliate held by partnership; 257 — Formula amounts cannot calculate to less than zero.

## Proposed Amendment — 93(2.2)

**Application**: The December 21, 2000 draft legislation, subsec. 42(3), will amend subsec. 93(2.2) by replacing the references to the expression "4/3 of" with references to the word "twice", applicable to taxation years that end after February 27, 2000 except that, for a taxation year of a taxpayer that includes either February 28, 2000 or October 17, 2000, the references to the word "twice" shall be read as references to the expression "the fraction that is the reciprocal of the fraction in para. 38(a), as amended [by the December 21, 2000 draft legislation], that applies to the taxpayer for the year, multiplied by".

**Technical Notes**: Subsection 93(2.2) provides a rule for the purpose of determining a loss of a corporation resident in Canada or a foreign affiliate of such a corporation from the disposition of an interest in a partnership owning a share of another foreign affiliate of the corporation. The loss is reduced by exempt dividends received on the share.

The amendment to subsection 93(2.2) replaces the reference to the expression "4/3 of" with a reference to the word "twice", as a consequence of the reduction of the inclusion rate for capital gains from 3/4 to 1/2 [see 38(a) — ed.].

The amendment generally applies to taxation years that end after February 27, 2000. For a taxation year of a corporation that includes either February 28, 2000 or October 17, 2000, the reference to the word "twice" in subsection 93(2.2) is to be read as reference to the expression "the fraction that is the reciprocal of the fraction in paragraph 38(a) that applies to the taxpayer for the year, multiplied by". These modifications are required in order to reflect the capital gains/losses rate for the year.

### Proposed Addition — 93(2.3)

**(2.3) Loss limitation — disposition of partnership interest** — Where

(a) corporation resident in Canada has an allowable capital loss from a partnership from a disposition at any time of an interest in another partnership that has a direct or indirect interest in shares of the capital stock of a foreign affiliate of the corporation resident in Canada (in this subsection referred to as "affiliate shares"), or

(b) a foreign affiliate of a corporation resident in Canada has an allowable capital loss from a partnership from a disposition at any time by a partnership of an interest in another partnership which has a direct or indirect interest in shares of the capital stock of a foreign affiliate of the corporation resident in Canada that would not be excluded property of the affiliate if the affiliate owned the shares immediately before the disposition (in this subsection referred to as "affiliate shares"),

the amount of the allowable capital loss is deemed to be the amount determined by the formula

$$A - (B - C)$$

where

A is the amount of the allowable capital loss determined without reference to this subsection,

B is 3/4 of the total of all amounts each of which was received before that time, in respect of an exempt dividend on affiliate shares or on shares for which affiliate shares were substituted, by

(a) the corporation resident in Canada,

(b) a corporation related to the corporation resident in Canada,

(c) a foreign affiliate of the corporation resident in Canada, or

(d) a foreign affiliate of a corporation related to the corporation resident in Canada, and

C is the total of

(a) the total of all amounts each of which is 3/4 of the amount by which a loss (determined without reference to this section), of a corporation or foreign affiliate described in the description of B from another disposition at or before that time of affiliate shares or shares for which affiliate shares were substituted, was reduced under subsection (2) in respect of the exempt dividends referred to in the description of B,

(b) the total of all amounts each of which is the amount by which an allowable capital loss (determined without reference to this section), of a corporation or foreign affiliate described in the description of B from a disposition at or before that time by a partnership of affiliate shares or shares for which affiliate shares were substituted, was reduced under subsection (2.1) in respect of the exempt dividends referred to in the description of B,

(c) the total of all amounts each of which is 3/4 of the amount by which a loss (determined without reference to this section), from a disposition at or before that time by a corporation or foreign affiliate described in the description of B of an interest in a partnership, was reduced under subsection (2.2) in respect of the exempt dividends referred to in the description of B, and

(d) the total of all amounts each of which is the amount by which an allowable capital loss (determined without reference to this section), of a corporation or foreign affiliate described in the description of B from a disposition at or before that time by a partnership of an interest in another partnership, was reduced under this subsection in respect of the exempt dividends referred to in the description of B.

**Application**: Bill C-43 (First Reading September 20, 2000), subsec. 43(3), will add subsec. 93(2.3), applicable to dispositions that occur after November 1999.

**Technical Notes**: New subsection 93(2.3) of the Act applies where a corporation resident in Canada or a foreign affiliate of such a corporation has an allowable capital loss from a partnership arising on the disposition of an interest in a partnership where that partnership (the interest in which is disposed of) has a direct or indirect interest in shares of a foreign affiliate of the corporation resident in Canada. Where the foreign affiliate has the allowable capital loss, the rule does not apply where the affiliate shares in which the partnership (the interest in which was disposed of) has the interest would be excluded property of the affiliate (with the allowable capital loss) if the affiliate had owned the shares.

Where the rule applies, the allowable capital loss from the partnership arising on the disposition of an interest in another partnership which has a direct or indirect interest in the affiliate shares is reduced by 3/4 of the exempt dividends received on the affiliate shares before the time of the disposition by the particular corporation resident in Canada, a foreign affiliate of the particular corporation, another corporation related to the particular corporation or a foreign affiliate of a corporation resident in Canada that is related to the particular corporation, to the extent that those exempt dividends have not already reduced a capital loss or an allowable capital loss under subsections 93(2) to 93(2.3) arising on other dispositions of property. The term exempt dividend is defined in subsection 93(3) and is modified consequential on the introduction of section 93.1.

**Related Provisions**: 87(2)(u)(ii) — Amalgamation; 93(3) — Exempt dividends; 93.1(2) — Dividend on shares of foreign affiliate held by partnership; 257 — Formula amounts cannot calculate to less than zero.

### Proposed Amendment — 93(2.3)

**Application**: The December 21, 2000 draft legislation, subsec. 42(4), will amend subsec. 93(2.3) by replacing the references to the fraction "3/4" with references to the fraction "1/2", applicable to taxation years that end after February 27, 2000 except that, for a taxation year of a taxpayer that includes either February 28, 2000 or October 17, 2000, the references to the fraction "1/2" shall be read as references to the fraction in para. 38(a), as amended [by the December 21, 2000 draft legislation], that applies to the taxpayer for the year.

**Technical Notes**: Subsection 93(2.3) provides a rule for the purpose of determining a loss of a corporation resident in Canada or a foreign affiliate of such a corporation from the disposition by a partnership of a share of another foreign affiliate of the corporation. The loss is reduced by exempt dividends received on the share.

The amendment to subsection 93(2.3) replaces the reference to the fraction "3/4" with a reference to the fraction "1/2", as a consequence of the reduction of the inclusion rate for capital gains from 3/4 to 1/2 [see 38(a) — ed.].

The amendment generally applies to taxation years that end after February 27, 2000. For a taxation year of a corporation that includes either February 28, 2000 or October 17, 2000, the reference to the fraction "1/2" in subsection 93(2.3) is to be read as reference to the fraction in amended paragraph 38(a) that applies to the taxpayer for the year. These modifications are required in order to reflect the capital gains/losses rate for the year.

**(3) Exempt dividends** — For the purposes of subsection (2),

(a) a dividend received by a corporation resident in Canada is an exempt dividend to the extent of the amount in respect of the dividend that is deductible from the income of the corporation in computing its taxable income by virtue of paragraph 113(1)(a), (b) or (c); and

(b) a dividend received by a foreign affiliate of a corporation resident in Canada from another foreign affiliate of that corporation is an exempt dividend to the extent of the amount, if any, by which the portion of the dividend that was not prescribed to have been paid out of the pre-acquisition surplus of that other affiliate exceeds such portion of any income or profits tax paid by the first-mentioned affiliate as may reasonably be regarded as having been paid in respect of that portion of the dividend.

### Proposed Amendment — 93(3)

**(3) Exempt dividends** — For the purposes of subsections (2) to (2.3),

(a) a dividend received by a corporation resident in Canada is an exempt dividend to the extent of the amount in respect of the dividend that is deductible from the income of the corporation for the purpose of computing the taxable income of the corporation because of paragraph 113(1)(a), (b) or (c); and

(b) a dividend received by a particular foreign affiliate of a corporation resident in Canada from another foreign affiliate of the corporation is an exempt dividend to the extent of the amount, if any, by which the portion of the dividend that was not prescribed to have been paid out of the pre-acquisition surplus of the other affiliate exceeds the total of such portion of income or profits tax that can reasonably be considered to have been paid in respect of that portion of the dividend by the particular affiliate or by a partnership in which the particular affiliate had, at the time of the payment of the income or profits tax, a partnership interest, either directly or indirectly.

**Application**: Bill C-43 (First Reading September 20, 2000), subsec. 43(4), will amend subsec. 93(3) to read as above, applicable to dispositions that occur after November 1999.

**Technical Notes**: Subsection 93(3) of the Act defines the term "exempt dividend" for the purpose of subsection 93(2) of the Act. A dividend received by a Canadian corporation is an exempt dividend to the extent it is deductible under paragraphs 113(1)(a), (b) or (c) of the Act. A dividend received by a foreign affiliate of a Canadian corporation is an exempt dividend to the extent that the portion of the dividend that was not paid out of pre-acquisition surplus exceeds the income or profits tax paid by the affiliate.

Subsection 93(3) is amended to also apply for the purposes of new subsections 93(2.1) to (2.3) of the Act. In addition, the subsection is amended to apply in respect of shares of foreign affiliates that are owed by partnerships. For information on the treatment of foreign affiliate shares owned by partnerships, see the commentary on new section 93.1.

**Regulations**: 5900(1)(c) (amount prescribed to have been paid out of pre-acquisition surplus).

**(4) Loss on disposition of shares of foreign affiliate** — Where a taxpayer resident in Canada or a foreign affiliate of the taxpayer (in this subsection referred to as the "vendor") has acquired shares of a foreign affiliate of the taxpayer (in this subsection referred to as the "acquired affiliate") on the disposition of shares of any other foreign affiliate of the taxpayer (other than a disposition to which subsection 40(3.4) applies),

(a) the capital loss therefrom otherwise determined shall be deemed to be nil; and

(b) in computing the adjusted cost base to the vendor of all shares of any particular class of the capital stock of the acquired affiliate owned by the vendor immediately after the disposition, there shall be added an amount determined by the formula

$$(A - B) \times \frac{C}{D}$$

where

A is the cost amount to the vendor immediately before the disposition of the shares disposed of,

B is the total of

(i) the proceeds of disposition of the shares disposed of, and

(ii) the total of all amounts deducted under paragraph (2)(d) in computing losses of the vendor from the dispositions of the shares disposed of,

C is the fair market value, immediately after the disposition, of all shares of that particular class owned by it at that time, and

D is the fair market value, immediately after the disposition, of all shares of the capital stock of the acquired affiliate owned by it at that time.

**Related Provisions**: 93(2) — Loss limitation on disposition of share; 257 — Formula cannot calculate to less than zero.

**Notes**: Opening words of 93(4) amended by 1995-97 technical bill to change "85(4)" to "40(3.4)", effective (subject to grandfathering rule reproduced after s. 260) for dispositions of property after April 26, 1995.

93(4)(b) amended by 1991 technical bill, effective July 14, 1990, to ensure that only the portion of a capital loss on a share that is not attributable to exempt dividends received on the share will be added to the ACB to the vendor of the acquired affiliate's shares. For earlier dispositions of shares, read:

(b) in computing the adjusted cost base to the vendor of all shares of any particular class of the capital stock of the acquired affiliate owned by it immediately after the disposition there shall be added the amount that is equal to that proportion of the amount, if any, by which

(i) the cost amount to it immediately before the disposition of the shares disposed of

exceeds

(ii) the proceeds of the disposition

that

(iii) the fair market value, immediately after the disposition, of all shares of that class owned by it at that time,

is of

(iv) the fair market value, immediately after the disposition, of all shares of the capital stock of the acquired affiliate owned by it at that time.

**Interpretation Bulletins**: See at end of s. 93.

**(5) Late filed elections** — Where the election referred to in subsection (1) was not made on or before the day on or before which the election was required by that subsection to be made, the election shall be deemed to have been made on that day if, on or before the day that is 3 years after that day,

(a) the election is made in prescribed manner; and

(b) an estimate of the penalty in respect of that election is paid by the corporation when that election is made.

**Regulations**: 5902 (prescribed manner).

**Forms**: T2107: Election for a disposition of shares in a foreign affiliate.

**(5.1) Special cases** — Where, in the opinion of the Minister, the circumstances of a case are such that it would be just and equitable

(a) to permit an election under subsection (1) to be made after the day that is 3 years after the day on or before which the election was required by that subsection to be made, or

(b) to permit an election made under subsection (1) to be amended,

the election or amended election shall be deemed to have been made on the day on or before which the election was so required to be made if

(c) the election or amended election is made in prescribed form, and

(d) an estimate of the penalty in respect of the election or amended election is paid by the corporation when the election or amended election is made,

and where this subsection applies to the amendment of an election, that election shall be deemed not to have been effective.

**Forms**: T2107: Election for a disposition of shares in a foreign affiliate.

**(6) Penalty for late filed election** — For the purposes of this section, the penalty in respect of an election or amended election referred to in paragraph (5)(a) or (5.1)(c) is an amount equal to the lesser of

(a) $\frac{1}{4}$ of 1% of the amount designated in the election or amended election for each month or part of a month during the period commencing with the day on or before which the election is required by subsection (1) to be made and ending on the day the election is made, and

(b) an amount, not exceeding $8,000, equal to the product obtained by multiplying $100 by the number of months each of which is a month all or part of which is during the period referred to in paragraph (a).

**Related Provisions**: 93(7) — Assessment of penalty; 220(3.1) — Waiver of penalty by CCRA.

**(7) Unpaid balance of penalty** — The Minister shall, with all due dispatch, examine each election and amended election referred to in paragraph (5)(a) or (5.1)(c), assess the penalty payable and send a notice of assessment to the corporation, and the corporation shall pay forthwith to the Receiver General the amount, if any, by which the penalty so assessed exceeds the total of all amounts previously paid on account of that penalty.

**Definitions [s. 93]**: "adjusted cost base" — 54, 248(1); "allowable capital loss" — 38(b), 248(1); "amount" — 248(1); "Canada" — 255; "capital gain", "capital loss" — 39(1), 248(1); "class" — of shares 248(6); "corporation" — 248(1), *Interpretation Act* 35(1); "cost amount", "disposition", "dividend" — 248(1); "excluded property" — 95(1); "exempt surplus" — 113(1)(a), Reg. 5907(1)(d); "foreign affiliate" — 93.1(1), 95(1), 248(1); "Minister" — 248(1); "partnership" — see Notes to 96(1); "pre-acquisition surplus" — Reg. 5900(1)(c); "prescribed" — 248(1); "proceeds of disposition" — 54; "property", "regulation" — 248(1); "related" — 251(2)–(6); "resident in Canada" — 250; "share" — 248(1); "taxable capital gain" — 38(a), 248(1); "taxable income" — 248(1); "taxable surplus" — 113(1)(b)(i), Reg. 5907(1)(k); "taxation year" — 95(1) (for foreign affiliate only), 249; "taxpayer" — 248(1).

**Interpretation Bulletins [s. 93]**: IT-392: Meaning of the term "share"; IT-451R: Deemed disposition and acquisition on ceasing to be or becoming resident in Canada.

### Proposed Addition — 93.1

**93.1 (1) Shares held by a partnership** — For the purpose of determining whether a non-resident corporation is a foreign affiliate of a corporation resident in Canada for the purposes of subsections (2) and 20(12), sections 93 and 113 (and any regulations made for the purposes of those sections), section 95 (to the extent that that section is applied for the purposes of those provisions) and section 126, where at any time shares of a class of the capital stock of a corporation are owned by a partnership or are deemed under this subsection to be owned by a partnership, each member of the partnership is deemed to own at that time that number of those shares that is equal to the proportion of all those shares that

(a) the fair market value of the member's interest in the partnership at that time

is of

(b) the fair market value of all members' interests in the partnership at that time.

**Technical Notes**: New subsection 93.1(1) of the Act applies for the purpose of determining whether a non-resident corporation is a foreign affiliate of a corporation resident in Canada for the purposes of new subsection 93.1(2), subsection 20(12), sections 93 and 113 and any regulations made for the purposes of those sections and the rules in section 95 that are required to be applied to a foreign affiliate of a corporation resident in Canada in applying sections 93 and 113 of the Act and section 126.

For this purpose, new subsection 93.1(1) deems a member of a partnership to own its proportionate number of shares of a corporation held by a partnership. The number of shares owned by a member at any particular time is equal to the proportion of the total number of shares owned by the partnership that the fair market value of the member's interest in the partnership at that time is of the fair market value of all members' interests in the partnership at that time.

Subsection 93.1(1) applies at any time after November 30, 1999 in determining whether a non-resident corporation is a foreign affiliate of a taxpayer and, where the taxpayer elects in writing and files the election with Minister before 2002, the subsection also applies after 1972 and before December 1999 in determining whether a non-resident corporation is a foreign affiliate of a taxpayer (other than for the purposes of subsection 20(12) and section 126 of the Act).

**Regulations**: 5905(14) (where number of shares deemed owned increases or decreases).

**(2) Where dividends received by a partnership** — Where at any time shares of a class of the capital stock of a foreign affiliate of a corporation resident in Canada (in this subsection referred to as "affiliate shares") are owned by a partnership and at that time the affiliate pays a dividend on affiliate shares to the partnership (in this subsection referred to as the "partnership dividend"),

(a) for the purposes of sections 93 and 113 and any regulations made for the purposes of those sections, each member of the partnership is deemed to have received the proportion of the partnership dividend that

(i) the fair market value of the member's interest in the partnership at that time

is of

(ii) the fair market value of all members' interests' in the partnership at that time;

(b) for the purposes of sections 93 and 113 and any regulations made for the purposes of those sections, the proportion of the partnership dividend deemed by paragraph (a) to have been received by a member of the partnership at that time is deemed to have been received by the member in equal proportions on each affiliate share that is property of the partnership at that time;

(c) for the purpose of applying section 113, in respect of the dividend referred to in paragraph (a), each affiliate share referred to in paragraph (b) is deemed to be owned by each member of the partnership; and

(d) notwithstanding paragraphs (a) to (c),

(i) where the corporation resident in Canada is a member of the partnership, the amount deductible by it under section 113 in respect of the dividend referred to in paragraph (a) shall not exceed the portion of the amount of the dividend included in its income pursuant to subsection 96(1), and

(ii) where another foreign affiliate of the corporation resident in Canada is a member of the partnership, the amount included in that other affiliate's income in respect of the dividend referred to in paragraph (a) shall not exceed the amount that would be included in its income pursuant to subsection 96(1) in respect of the partnership dividend received by the partnership if the value for H in the definition "foreign accrual property income" in subsection 95(1) were nil and this Act were read without reference to this subsection.

**Technical Notes**: New subsection 93.1(2) of the Act applies where a partnership receives a dividend from a foreign affiliate of the corporation resident in Canada.

Paragraph 93.1(2)(a) provides that, for the purposes of sections 93 and 113 of the Act and any regulations made for the purposes of those sections, a member of a partnership is treated as having received its proportionate share of a dividend received by the partnership from a foreign affiliate of the member. That proportionate share is determined as that proportion of the partnership dividend that the fair market value of the member's interest in the partnership is of the fair market value of all members' interests in the partnership.

Paragraph 93.1(2)(b) provides that, for the purposes of sections 93 and 113 and any regulations made for the purposes of those sections, a dividend that is treated as having been received by a member of a partnership under paragraph 93.1(2)(a) is treated as having been received in equal proportions on each affiliate share held by the partnership at that time.

Paragraph 93.1(2)(c) provides that, for the purpose of section 113, each affiliate share referred to in paragraph 93.1(2)(b) is treated as having been owned by each member of the partnership.

Subparagraph 93.1(2)(d)(i) provides that, notwithstanding paragraphs 93.1(2)(a), (b) and (c), where a member of the partnership is a corporation resident in Canada, the maximum amount that the member may deduct under section 113 is restricted to the amount of the dividend received by the partnership that is included in its income under subsection 96(1) of the Act.

Subparagraph 93.1(2)(d)(ii) provides that, notwithstanding paragraphs 93.1(2)(a), (b) and (c), where the member is another foreign affiliate of the corporation resident in Canada, the amount included in the other affiliate's income in respect of the dividend referred to in paragraph 93.1(2)(a) shall not exceed the amount that would have been included in the other affiliate's income under subsection 96(1) if the value of H in the formula in the definition "foreign accrual property income" in subsection 95(1) were nil and the Act were read without reference to subsection 93.1(2). In effect, the maximum amount that an affiliate can deduct in computing its foreign accrual property income in respect of the dividend referred to in paragraph 93.1(2)(a) is restricted to the amount of the dividend included in the affiliate's foreign accrual property income under subsection 96(1).

New subsection 93.1(2) applies to dividends received after November 30, 1999.

**Related Provisions**: 92(4)–(6) — Dividend from pre-acquisition surplus; 95(1)"foreign accrual property income"H — Exclusion from FAPI.

**Notes**: For discussion of 93.1(1) and (2), see Eric Lockwood, Michael Maikawa & Nick Pantaleo, "Proposed Technical Amendments to the FAPI and Foreign Affiliate Rules" 48(2) *Canadian Tax Journal* 456-476 (2000).

**Application**: Bill C-43 (First Reading September 20, 2000), s. 44, will add s. 93.1, subsec. 93.1(1) applicable in determining whether a non-resident corporation is, at any time after November 1999, a foreign affiliate of a taxpayer and, where a taxpayer so elects and notifies the Minister of National Revenue in writing before 2002 of its election, that subsection also applies in determining (other than for the purposes of subsec. 20(12) and s. 126) whether a non-resident corporation is, at any time after 1972 and before December 1999, a foreign affiliate of the taxpayer; subsec. 93.1(2) applicable in respect of dividends received after November 1999.

**Letter from Department of Finance, July 29, 1997**:

Dear [xxx]

I am writing in response to your letter of July 21, 1997, requesting confirmation that our Department intends to recommend an amendment to the *Income Tax Act* (the "Act") to accommodate the holding of foreign affiliates through partnerships. You have noted that Revenue Canada has expressed the view that a foreign corporation ("FA") is not a foreign affiliate of a Canadian corporation ("Canco") where FA's shares are property of a partnership in which Canco is a partner. As a result, dividends paid by FA to the partnership and distributed by the partnership to Canco do not qualify for deductions under section 113 of the Act.

Our Department is prepared to recommend to the Minister of Finance that amendments to the Act be made in a future technical bill to accommodate the holding of shares of foreign corporations in a partnership. Such amendments to the Act would ensure that, in the appropriate circumstances, dividends paid by a foreign corporation to a partnership and distributed by the partnership to a Canadian corporation would qualify for deductions under section 113 of the Act. The appropriate circumstances would encompass the circumstances set out in the example in your letter.

I trust that you will find these comments helpful.

Yours sincerely,

Len Farber
Director General, Tax Legislation Division

**Definitions [s. 93.1]**: "amount" — 248(1); "corporation" — 248(1), *Interpretation Act* 35(1); "dividend" — 248(1); "foreign accrual property income" — 95(1), (2), 248(1); "foreign affiliate" — 93.1(1), 95(1), 248(1); "non-resident" — 248(1); "partnership" — see Notes to 96(1); "property", "regulation" — 248(1); "resident in Canada" — 250; "share" — 248(1).

## 94. (1) Application of certain provisions to trusts not resident in Canada — Where,

(a) at any time in a taxation year of a trust that is not resident in Canada or that, but for paragraph (c), would not be so resident, a person beneficially interested in the trust (in this section referred to as a "beneficiary") was

(i) a person resident in Canada,

(ii) a corporation or trust with which a person resident in Canada was not dealing at arm's length, or

(iii) a controlled foreign affiliate of a person resident in Canada, and

(b) at any time in or before the taxation year of the trust,

(i) the trust, or a non-resident corporation that would, if the trust were resident in Canada, be a controlled foreign affiliate of the trust, has, other than in prescribed circumstances, ac-

**S. 94(1)(b)(i)**      Income Tax Act, Part I, Division B

quired property, directly or indirectly in any manner whatever, from

  (A) a particular person who

    (I) was the beneficiary referred to in paragraph (a), was related to that beneficiary or was the uncle, aunt, nephew or niece of that beneficiary,

    (II) was resident in Canada at any time in the 18 month period before the end of that year or, in the case of a person who has ceased to exist, was resident in Canada at any time in the 18 month period before the person ceased to exist, and

    (III) in the case of an individual, had before the end of that year been resident in Canada for a period of, or periods the total of which is, more than 60 months, or

  (B) a trust or corporation that acquired the property, directly or indirectly in any manner whatever, from a particular person described in clause (A) with whom it was not dealing at arm's length

and the trust was not

  (C) an *inter vivos* trust created at any time before 1960 by a person who at that time was a non-resident person,

  (D) a testamentary trust that arose as a consequence of the death of an individual before 1976, or

  (E) governed by a foreign retirement arrangement, or

(ii) all or any part of the interest of the beneficiary in the trust was acquired directly or indirectly by the beneficiary by way of

  (A) purchase,

  (B) gift, bequest or inheritance from a person referred to in clause (i)(A) or (B), or

  (C) the exercise of a power of appointment by a person referred to in clause (i)(A) or (B),

the following rules apply for that taxation year of the trust:

(c) where the amount of the income or capital of the trust to be distributed at any time to any beneficiary of the trust depends on the exercise by any person of, or the failure by any person to exercise, any discretionary power,

  (i) the trust is deemed for the purposes of this Part and sections 233.3 and 233.4 to be a person resident in Canada no part of whose taxable income is exempt because of section 149 from Part I tax and whose taxable income for the taxation year is the total of

    (A) the amount, if any, that would but for this subparagraph be its taxable income earned in Canada for that year,

    (B) the amount that would, if it were a trust to which paragraph (d) applies, be its foreign accrual property income for that year, and

    (C) the amount, if any, by which the amount required by section 91 to be included in computing its income for the year exceeds the amount deducted for that year by virtue of subsections 91(2), (4) and (5), and

  (ii) for the purposes of section 126,

    (A) the amounts referred to in clauses (i)(B) and (C) shall be deemed to be income of the trust from sources in the country other than Canada in which the trust would, but for subparagraph (i), be resident, and

    (B) such part of any income or profits tax paid by the trust for the year (other than any tax paid by virtue of this section) that may reasonably be regarded as having been paid in respect of that income shall be deemed to be the non-business-income tax paid by the trust to the government of that country, and

**Proposed Amendment — 94(1)(c)(i), (ii)**

(i) the trust is deemed for the purposes of this Part and sections 233.3 and 233.4 to be a person resident in Canada no part of whose taxable income is exempt because of section 149 from tax under this Part and whose taxable income for the year is the amount, if any, by which the total of

  (A) the amount, if any, that would but for this subparagraph be its taxable income earned in Canada for the year,

  (B) the amount that would be its foreign accrual property income for the year if

    (I) except for the purpose of applying subsections 104(4) to (5.2) to days after 1998 that are determined under subsection 104(4), the trust were a non-resident corporation all the shares of which were owned by a person who was resident in Canada,

    (II) the description of A in the definition "foreign accrual property income" in subsection 95(1) were, in respect of dividends received after 1998, read without reference to paragraph (b) of that description,

(III) the descriptions of B and E in that definition were, in respect of dispositions that occur after 1998, read without reference to "other than dispositions of excluded property to which none of paragraphs (2)(c), (d) and (e) apply",

(IV) the value of C in that definition were nil, and

(V) for the purpose of computing the trust's foreign accrual property income, the consequences of the application of subsections 104(4) to (5.2) applied in respect of days after 1998 that are determined under subsection 104(4),

(C) the amount, if any, by which the total of all amounts each of which is an amount required by subsection 91(1) or (3) to be included in computing its income for the year exceeds the total of all amounts each of which is an amount deducted by it for that year under subsection 91(2), (4) or (5), and

(D) the amount, if any, required by section 94.1 to be included in computing its income for the year,

exceeds

(E) the amount, if any, by which the total of all amounts each of which is an amount deducted by it under subsection 91(2), (4) or (5) in computing its income for the year exceeds the total of all amounts each of which is an amount included in computing its income for the year because of subsection 91(1) or (3), and

(ii) for the purposes of section 126,

(A) the amount that would be determined under subparagraph (i) in respect of the trust for the year, if that subparagraph were read without reference to clause (i)(A), is deemed to be income of the trust for the year from sources in the country other than Canada in which the trust would, but for subparagraph (i), be resident, and

(B) any income or profits tax paid by the trust for the year (other than any tax paid because of this section), to the extent that it can reasonably be regarded as having been paid in respect of that income, is deemed to be non-business income tax paid by the trust to the government of that country, and

**Application**: Bill C-43 (First Reading September 20, 2000), s. 45, will amend subparas. 94(1)(c)(i) and (ii) to read as above, applicable to 1999 *et seq.*

**Technical Notes**: Where certain conditions are met, a non-resident discretionary trust to which existing section 94 of the Act applies is generally treated as a trust resident in Canada for the purposes of Part I and sections 233.3 and 233.4 of the Act. Under existing subparagraph 94(1)(c)(i), the taxable income of such a trust is the total of its taxable income earned in Canada (computed on the assumption that the trust is non-resident) and two additional amounts. The first additional amount for a taxation year is described in clause 94(1)(c)(i)(B) as the amount that would be the trust's foreign accrual property income for the year if paragraph 94(1)(d) applied. Under clause 94(1)(c)(i)(C), the second additional amount for a taxation year is the net amount included under section 91 in computing the trust's income for the year.

Clause 94(1)(c)(i)(B) is amended so that the amount determined under that clause in respect of a trust for a taxation year is generally the trust's foreign accrual property income for the year, determined on the assumptions that the trust is a non-resident corporation and that all of the shares of the capital stock of that corporation are owned by a person resident in Canada. Exceptions to this general rule are described below.

Clause 94(1)(c)(i)(B) is also amended to clarify that the 21-year deemed disposition rule for trusts applies for the purpose of computing the amount determined under clause 94(1)(c)(i)(B), notwithstanding the fact that the rule applies to trusts and not to corporations. This clarification applies to disposition dates determined after 1998.

Subclauses 94(1)(c)(i)(B)(II) and (III) are introduced so that, after 1998, dividends from foreign affiliates, and taxable capital gains and allowable losses that relate to "excluded property" (as defined in subsection 95(1)), are included in the trust's foreign accrual property income determined under clause 94(1)(c)(i)(B). Because trust income can be distributed as trust capital, it is appropriate to remove the exclusions from foreign accrual property income for dividends and capital gains from excluded property.

Subclause 94(1)(c)(i)(B)(IV) is introduced so that section 94.1 is no longer relevant for the purposes of determining the amount under clause 94(1)(c)(i)(B). Instead, new clause 94(1)(c)(i)(D) adds the amount determined under that section in respect of a trust in computing the trust's taxable income under subparagraph 94(1)(c)(i).

Clause 94(1)(c)(i)(C) is amended to clarify that the second additional amount added in computing a trust's taxable income under paragraph 94(1)(c) is determined by subtracting the amounts deducted in computing income under subsections 91(2), (4) and (5) from the amount added in computing income under subsections 91(1) and (3). This amendment applies to the 1999 and subsequent taxation years.

Clause 94(1)(c)(i)(E) (in conjunction with a change to the opening words of subparagraph 94(1)(c)(i)) is introduced to provide for a deduction in computing the taxable income for a taxation year of a trust under subparagraph 94(1)(c)(i). This deduction is equal to the amount, if any, by which the total of the amounts deducted under subsections 91(2), (4) and (5) in computing the trust's income for the year exceeds the total amount included in computing the trust's income for the year because of subsections 91(1) and (3). Clause 94(1)(c)(i)(E) will apply, for example, where an amount was included in computing a trust's taxable income because of clause 94(1)(c)(i)(C) and there is subsequently a

**S. 94(1)(c)**      Income Tax Act, Part I, Division B

distribution of dividends to which that amount relates. Clause 94(1)(c)(i)(E) is meant to avoid the double taxation of the same income that might otherwise arise. The example below illustrates the operation of clause 94(1)(c)(i)(E).

*EXAMPLE*

Trust X is a non-resident trust to which paragraph 94(1)(c) applies. Trust X owns 100% of the shares in Foreignco. In year 1, Foreignco's only income is $20,000 of interest income on government bonds. In year 2, Foreignco pays a dividend of $7,000 to Trust X. In year 3, Foreignco pays a dividend of $15,000 to Trust X. Foreignco had no other relevant income in years 2 and 3.

*Results:*

1. The taxable income of Trust X for year 1 is calculated under subparagraph 94(1)(c)(i) as follows:

- ADD the amount that would be Trust X's "foreign accrual property income" if a number of assumptions were made. Trust X's own foreign accrual property income for year 1 is nil. [Clause 94(1)(c)(i)(B), in conjunction with definition of "foreign accrual property income" in subsection 95(1)]
- ADD the net amount required by section 91 to be included in Trust X's income. This amount is $20,000. [Clause 94(1)(c)(i)(C), in conjunction with subsection 91(1)]

As a result, the taxable income of Trust X for year 1 is $20,000.

2. The taxable income of Trust X for year 2 is calculated as follows:

- ADD the amount that would be Trust X's "foreign accrual property income" if a number of assumptions were made. Because of subclause 94(1)(c)(i)(B)(II), dividends received by affiliates are included in computing Trust X's foreign accrual property income for this purpose. Consequently, Trust X's "foreign accrual property income" is $7,000.
- SUBTRACT the net amount deducted under section 91 in computing the trust's income. [Clause 94(1)(c)(i)(E)] The deduction available is equal to the lesser of the amount of the dividend ($7,000) and the net adjusted cost base adjustments ($20,000) up to the time the $10,000 dividend is paid. [Subsection 91(5)] Consequently, the full $7,000 is deducted because of clause 94(1)(c)(i)(E).

As a result, the taxable income of Trust X for year 2 is nil.

3. The taxable income of Trust X for year 3 is calculated as follows:

- ADD the amount that would be Trust X's "foreign accrual property income" if a number of assumptions were made. Because of subclause 94(1)(c)(i)(B)(II), dividends received by affiliates are included in computing Trust X's foreign accrual property income for this purpose. Consequently, Trust X's "foreign accrual property income" is $15,000.
- SUBTRACT the net amount deducted under section 91 in computing the trust's income. [Clause 94(1)(c)(i)(E)] The deduction available is equal to the lesser of the amount of the dividend ($15,000) and the net adjusted cost base adjustments ($20,000-$7,000) up to the time the $15,000 dividend is paid. [Subsection 91(5)] Consequently, $13,000 is deducted because of clause 94(1)(c)(i)(E).

As a result, the taxable income of Trust X for year 2 is $2,000.

These amendments come into effect in the manner indicated in the commentary above and apply to the 1999 and subsequent taxation years. However, as announced in the 1999 budget, further amendments to this section are contemplated.

Subparagraph 94(1)(c)(ii) of the Act is relevant for the purpose of determining the foreign tax credit of a trust to which paragraph 94(1)(c) applies. For this purpose, the trust's income is generally deemed to be from sources in the country in which the trust would be resident if that paragraph did not apply. However, subparagraph 94(1)(c)(ii) does not apply in connection with taxable income calculated under clause 94(1)(c)(i)(A) (taxable income earned in Canada).

Subparagraph 94(1)(c)(ii) is amended strictly to reflect the amendments to subparagraph 94(1)(c)(i). Under amended subparagraph 94(1)(c)(ii), the portion of the taxable income sourced for the purposes of the foreign tax credit is equal to amount that would be the trust's taxable income calculated under subparagraph 94(1)(c)(i) if the trust's taxable income earned in Canada were not taken into account.

This amendment applies to the 1999 and subsequent taxation years. However, as announced in the 1999 budget, further amendments to section 94 are contemplated.

(d) in any other case, for the purposes of subsections 91(1) to (4) and sections 95 and 233.4,

(i) the trust shall, with respect to any beneficiary under the trust the fair market value of whose beneficial interest in the trust is not less than 10% of the aggregate fair market value of all beneficial interests in the trust, be deemed to be a non-resident corporation that is controlled by the beneficiary,

(ii) the trust shall be deemed to be a non-resident corporation having a capital stock of a single class divided into 100 issued shares, and

(iii) each beneficiary under the trust shall be deemed to own at any time the number of the issued shares that is equal to the proportion of 100 that

(A) the fair market value at that time of the beneficiary's beneficial interest in the trust

is of

(B) the fair market value at that time of all beneficial interests in the trust.

### Proposed Amendment — 94(1)

[See at end of s. 94.]

**Related Provisions**: 94(2) — Rights and obligations; 94(3) — Deduction in computing taxable income; 94(4) — Deduction from foreign accrual property income; 94(5) — ACB of capital interest in trust; 94(6) — Where financial assistance given; 94.1(2) — Trust covered by 94(1)(c) or (d) is a "non-resident entity"; 126 — Foreign tax credit; 248(8) — Occurrences as a consequence of death; 248(25) — Beneficially interested.

**Notes**: 94(1)(b)(i)(A)(III) effectively gives non-residents who move to Canada up to 5 years to keep assets in a properly structured trust (sometimes called an "immigration trust"). (In the new s. 94

below, this will be 94(1)"resident contributor" and "connected contributor".) In order to have the maximum time for the trust to escape Canadian tax, it should be set up before the person becomes resident in Canada. Some of the concerns when setting up an immigration trust include 75(2) (reversionary trust); 74.1-74.4 (attribution rules); 94.1 (offshore investment funds); 56(4.1) (attribution on loan); U.S. grantor trust rules; and U.K. gift and inheritance taxes.

94(1)(b)(i)(E) added by 1991 technical bill, effective 1990.

Opening words of 94(1)(c)(i) amended by 1996 Budget to add reference to 233.3 and 233.4 and to make a minor wording change, effective 1996. From 1972 through 1995, read:

> (i) the trust shall be deemed for the purposes of this Part to be a person resident in Canada not exempt from tax under section 149 whose taxable income for the taxation year is the total of

94(1)(d) amended by 1996 Budget, effective 1996, to add reference to 233.4.

**Regulations**: 5909 (prescribed circumstances for 94(1)(b)(i)).

**Interpretation Bulletins**: IT-447: Residence of a trust or estate; IT-451R: Deemed disposition and acquisition on ceasing to be or becoming resident in Canada.

**Information Circulars**: 77-9R: Books, records and other requirements for taxpayers having foreign affiliates.

**(2) Rights and obligations** — Where paragraph (1)(c) is applicable to a trust, each person described in clause (1)(b)(i)(A) or (B) shall jointly and severally with the trust have the rights and obligations of the trust by virtue of Divisions I and J and shall be subject to the provisions of Part XV, but no amount in respect of taxes, penalties, costs and other amounts payable under this Act shall be recoverable from any such person except to the extent of

(a) amounts paid to the person by the trust or the payment of which from the trust the person is entitled to enforce; and

(b) amounts received by the person on the disposition of an interest in the trust.

**(3) Deduction in computing taxable income** — In computing the amount of taxable income of a trust to which paragraph (1)(c) applies for any taxation year, there may be deducted such portion of the amount that would, but for this subsection, be included in computing the taxable income of the trust for the year by virtue of clauses (1)(c)(i)(B) and (C) as may reasonably be considered as having become an amount payable in the year within the meaning of subsection 104(24) to a beneficiary.

**Interpretation Bulletins**: IT-342R: Trusts — income payable to beneficiaries; IT-451R: Deemed disposition and acquisition on ceasing to be or becoming resident in Canada.

**(4) Deduction from foreign accrual property income** — In computing the foreign accrual property income of a trust to which paragraph (1)(d) applies for any taxation year, there may be deducted such portion of the amount that would, but for this subsection, be the foreign accrual property income of the trust as may reasonably be considered as having become an amount payable in the year within the meaning of subsection 104(24) to a beneficiary.

**Interpretation Bulletins**: IT-342R: Trusts — income payable to beneficiaries; IT-451R: Deemed disposition and acquisition on ceasing to be or becoming resident in Canada.

**(5) Adjusted cost base of capital interest in trust** — In computing, at any time in a taxation year, the adjusted cost base to a taxpayer resident in Canada of a capital interest in a trust to which paragraph (1)(d) applies,

(a) there shall be added any amount required by subsection 91(1) or (3) to be included in computing the taxpayer's income for the year or any preceding taxation year (or that would have been so required to be included but for subsection 56(4.1) and sections 74.1 to 75 of this Act and section 74 of the *Income Tax Act*, chapter 148 of the Revised Statutes of Canada, 1952) in respect of that interest; and

(b) there shall be deducted any amount deducted by the taxpayer by reason of subsection 91(2) or (4) in computing the taxpayer's income for the year or any preceding taxation year (or that would have been so deductible by the taxpayer but for subsection 56(4.1) and sections 74.1 to 75 of this Act and section 74 of the *Income Tax Act*, chapter 148 of the Revised Statutes of Canada, 1952) in respect of that interest.

**Related Provisions**: 53(1)(d.1) — Addition to ACB; 53(2)(b.1) — Reduction in ACB.

**(6) Where financial assistance given** — For the purposes of paragraph (1)(b), a trust or a non-resident corporation shall be deemed to have acquired property from any person who has given a guarantee on its behalf or from whom it has received any other financial assistance whatever.

**(7) [Repealed]**

**Notes**: The rule in 94(7), defining "beneficially interested", was moved to 248(25) by 1992 technical bill, effective 1991.

**Definitions [s. 94]**: "adjusted cost base" — 54, 248(1); "allowable capital loss" — 38(b), 248(1); "amount", "annuity" — 248(1); "arm's length" — 251(1); "aunt" — 252(2)(e); "beneficially interested" — 248(25); "beneficiary" — 94(1)(a); "business" — 248(1); "Canada" — 255; "capital interest" — 108(1), 248(1); "consequence of the death" — 248(8); "controlled foreign affiliate" — 95(1), 248(1); "corporation" — 248(1), *Interpretation Act* 35(1); "dividend" — 248(1); "fiscal period" — 249(2)(b), 249.1; "foreign accrual property income", "foreign affiliate" — 95(1), 248(1); "foreign retirement arrangement" — 248(1); "nephew", "niece" — 252(2)(g); "non-resident" — 248(1); "non-resident-owned investment corporation" — 133(8), 248(1); "person", "prescribed", "property" — 248(1); "resident in Canada" — 94(1)(c)(i), 250; "share" — 248(1); "taxable capital gain" — 38(a), 248(1); "taxable dividend" — 89(1), 248(1); "taxable income" — 2(2), 248(1); "taxation year" — (of foreign affiliate) 95(1); "taxpayer" — 248(1); "testamentary trust" — 108(1), 248(1); "trust" — 104(1), 248(1), (3); "uncle" — 252(2)(e).

**Interpretation Bulletins [s. 94]**: IT-451R: Deemed disposition and acquisition on ceasing to be or becoming resident in Canada.

### Proposed Amendment — 94

**Technical Notes**: *OVERVIEW*

*Existing Rules*

Section 94 of the Act sets out rules that tax the passive income earned by certain non-resident trusts. Section 94 generally applies if a person resident in Canada has transferred or loaned property to a non-resident trust that has one or more beneficiaries who are resident in Canada.

Section 94 uses two different methods to impose tax, depending on whether or not the trust is discretionary. A discretionary trust is a trust under which a person has a discretionary power to determine the amount of the income or capital of the trust that one or more beneficiaries will receive.

If the non-resident trust is discretionary, paragraph 94(1)(c) deems the trust to be resident in Canada for the purposes of Part I of the Act and deems its income for tax purposes to be the total of its Canadian source income and its foreign accrual property income, if any. Each beneficiary is jointly and severally liable to pay the Canadian tax of the trust. However, the liability can be enforced against a particular beneficiary only to the extent that the beneficiary has received a distribution from the trust or proceeds from the sale of an interest in the trust.

If the non-resident trust is not a discretionary trust, paragraph 94(1)(d) provides that it is to be treated in much the same manner that a non-resident corporation is treated. If a Canadian resident beneficiary holds an interest in the trust with a fair market value equal to 10% or more of the total fair market value of all interests in the trust, the trust is deemed to be a controlled foreign affiliate of the beneficiary. Consequently, the foreign accrual property income rules apply to the trust and the beneficiary, requiring the beneficiary to include a portion of the foreign accrual property income of the trust in income. On the other hand, beneficiaries that do not have 10% or greater interests in the trust may be subject to tax under the offshore investment fund rules in section 94.1. If section 94.1 does not apply, such beneficiaries are taxed only if trust income becomes payable to them in the year that it arises.

*New Rules*

New section 94 takes a different approach to the taxation of non-resident trusts (NRTs) that bears some similarity to the grantor trust approach used by the United States, New Zealand and Australia. In general, if a Canadian resident contributes property to a non-resident trust, the contributor, the non-resident trust and certain Canadian resident beneficiaries of the trust may all become liable to pay Canadian tax on the world-wide income of the trust.

Except as indicated otherwise, the amendments to section 94 apply to taxation years of trusts that begin after 2000. The table below briefly summarizes section 94 and related rules.

| Issue | Summary | References |
|---|---|---|
| 1. Which trusts are subject to the new NRT rules? | A. In general, a trust (other than an exempt foreign trust) will be subject to tax for a taxation year as a trust resident in Canada if a contribution was made to the trust by a person who is resident in Canada at the end of the year (other than a recent immigrant to Canada). | S. 94(3) "exempt foreign trust" — s. 94(1) "contribution" — s. 94(1) and (2) "resident contributor" — s. 94(1) |
| | | As to 60-month test for new immigrants, see definition "resident contributor" in s. 94(1). |
| | B. In addition, a trust (other than an exempt foreign trust) will generally be subject to Canadian tax for a taxation year if<br>• the contribution was made by a person when the person was resident in Canada (or within a 60-month period before the person became resident in Canada or within a 60-month period after the person ceased to be resident in Canada),<br>• by the end of the year that person had been resident in Canada for more than 60 months, and<br>• at the end of the year there is a person resident in Canada who is beneficially interested in the trust. | S. 94(3) "contribution" — s. 94(1) "connected contributor" — s. 94(1) "resident beneficiary" — s. 94(1) |

Subdivision i — Shareholders of Non-Resident Corporations  S. 94(1) arm

| Issue | Summary | References |
|---|---|---|
| 2. Who is responsible for the tax payable an NRT? | The trust is required to pay tax. If it fails to do so, each contributor referred to in 1(A) and/or each beneficiary referred to in 1(B) is jointly and severally liable with the trust for the tax. However, the amount recoverable from a person who is simply a beneficiary is limited to benefits received by the beneficiary from the trust. Relief is also available in some cases for a contributor whose contribution to the trust is insignificant relative to other contributions made to the trust. | Joint liability: paragraph 94(3)(d) Relief from joint liability: s. 94(7) 10% and $10,000 tests for significant contribution: paragraph 94(7)(b). |
| 3. Where the NRT rules do apply for a taxation year to a trust, how will the trust's tax liabilities be calculated? | A. Canadian rules apply to the trust as if the trust were resident in Canada throughout the year for the purpose of computing the trust's income. | s. 94(3) |
|  | B. Explicit rule treats the trust as becoming resident in Canada, with resulting adjustment to cost amount of property under section 128.1. | s. 94(3)(c) |
|  | C. Parts XII.2 and XIII do not apply to the trust. Explicit exemption from Part XIII tax on amounts distributed to the trust, although payer must still withhold. | s. 94(3)(a)(iii) and (4)(d) |
|  | D. Flow-through of income to resident and non-resident beneficiaries permitted, subject to special rules in the event that Canadian-source income is distributed to non-residents. | s. 104(7.01) — special rules |

**Notes**: For discussion of proposed s. 94 see Edward Heakes, "Detailed Legislative Proposals on Offshore Trusts", IX(3) *International Tax Planning* (Federated Press) 656-660 (2000).

**94. Treatment of Trusts with Canadian Contributors — (1) Definitions —** The definitions in this subsection apply in this section.

**"accounting profit"** of a trust for a taxation year of the trust means

(a) where the trust prepares financial statements in accordance with accounting principles substantially similar to generally accepted accounting principles used in Canada, the trust's profit for the year (determined before taking into account income or profits tax) reflected in the trust's financial statements; and

(b) in any other case, the amount that would be the trust's total profit for the year (determined before taking into account income or profits tax) from businesses carried on by the trust, properties owned by the trust, or any combination of those businesses and properties, if that amount were calculated in accordance with generally accepted accounting principles used in Canada.

**Technical Notes**: New subsection 94(1) of the Act defines a number of expressions that apply for the purpose of section 94.

The "accounting profit" of a trust for a taxation year refers to the trust's profit for the year (determined before taking into account income or profits tax) reflected in its financial statements, on the assumption that the financial statements were prepared in accordance with accounting principles substantially similar to generally accepted accounting principles used in Canada. Where such financial statements have not been prepared, a trust's "accounting profit" for a taxation year is the amount that would be the trust's total profit (determined before taking into account income or profits tax) for the year, from businesses carried on by the trust and properties owned by the trust, if that amount were calculated in accordance with generally accepted accounting principles used in Canada.

This definition is used only in paragraph (d) of the definition "exempt foreign trust", as described in the commentary below.

**"arm's length transfer"** at any time by a person or partnership (in this definition referred to as the "transferor") in respect of a trust means a particular transfer or loan of property at that time by the transferor to a particular person or partnership (in this definition referred to as the "recipient") where

(a) one of the following applies, namely,

(i) in exchange for the particular transfer or loan, the recipient transfers or loans property, or becomes obligated to transfer or loan property, and it is reasonable to conclude, having regard only to the particular transfer or loan and the property transferred or loaned, or obligated to be transferred or loaned, by the recipient to the transferor in exchange, that

(A) the exchange is one that the transferor would have been willing to carry out if the transferor had dealt at arm's length with the recipient, and

(B) the terms and conditions made or imposed in respect of the exchange would have been acceptable to the transferor if the transferor had dealt at arm's length with the recipient,

(ii) the particular transfer or loan is a payment of interest, a dividend, rent, a royalty or any similar return on investment, or any substitute for such a return on investment, in respect of a particular property owned by the recipient immediately before that time, if the fair market value at that time of the property so transferred does not exceed the fair market value of property that the transferor would have been willing to transfer at that time in respect of the particular property to the recipient if the transferor had dealt at arm's length with the recipient,

(iii) the particular transfer or loan

(A) is in satisfaction of an obligation that arose because of a transfer to which subparagraph (i) applied, and

(B) is one that the transferor would have been willing to carry out if the transferor had dealt at arm's length with the recipient,

(iv) the particular transfer or loan was made in the ordinary course of the business of the transferor, or

(v) it is reasonable to conclude that none of the reasons for the particular transfer or loan was to permit or facilitate, directly or indirectly, the conferral, in the future, of a benefit in respect of the trust on

(A) the transferor,

(B) a descendant of the transferor, or

(C) any person with whom the transferor or descendant does not deal at arm's length; and

(b) it is reasonable to conclude that the reasons for which the property was transferred or loaned to the recipient did not include the relationship between the transferor and

(i) any person or partnership that was

(A) beneficially interested in the trust,

(B) a trustee of the trust,

(C) a person having influence over the operation of the trust or the enforcement of its terms, or

(D) a person having influence over the selection or appointment of any person or partnership referred to in any of clauses (A) to (C) or this clause, or

(ii) any group at least one of the members of which is described in subparagraph (i).

**Technical Notes**: An "arm's length transfer" does not result in any person or partnership being considered to be a "contributor" to a trust. Accordingly, subsection 94(3) does not apply to a non-resident trust as a consequence only of an arm's length transfer.

An "arm's length transfer" is, in general terms:

- a transfer or loan that is part of an arm's length exchange [Subparagraph (a)(i) of the definition.],
- an arm's length return on an investment, conferred by the entity in which the investment is made [Subparagraph (a)(ii) of the definition.],
- a repayment of an arm's length loan [Subparagraph (a)(iii) of the definition.],
- a transfer or loan made in the ordinary course of business [Subparagraph (a)(iv) of the definition.], or
- a transfer or loan that was not undertaken to allow for the conferral, in the future, of a benefit on the transferor, on a descendant of the transferor or on any person with whom the transferor or descendant does not deal at arm's length [Subparagraph (a)(v) of the definition.].

However, a transfer or loan qualifies as an "arm's length transfer" in respect of a trust only where it is reasonable to conclude that none of reasons for the transfer or loan included the relationship between the maker of the transfer or loan and any person or partnership that was

- beneficially interested in the trust,
- a trustee of the trust,
- a person having influence over the operation of the trust or the enforcement of its terms, or
- a person having influence over the selection or appointment of other persons so described.

It should be noted that, under amended subsection 233.2(4) and new subsection 233.2(4.1), an "arm's length transfer" covered by subparagraph (a)(v) of the definition cannot be used as a basis for an exemption from the reporting requirements under those subsections. Reporting requirements under those subsections are structured in this way so that claims for relief on the basis of paragraph (a)(v) of the definition "arm's length transfer" can be carefully scrutinized by the Canada Customs and Revenue Agency (CCRA).

Reference should also be made to new subsection 94(2), which provides various rules that have the effect of broadening the meaning of a "transfer" of property.

**Related Provisions**: 87(2)(j.95) — Amalgamations — continuing corporation; 94(2) [proposed] — Deemed transfers in various situations; 94(3) [proposed] — No application to non-resident trust on arm's length transfer.

**"connected contributor"** to a trust at any time means a person (including any person who has ceased to exist) who is a contributor to the trust at that time, other than

(a) an individual (other than a trust) who was, at or before that time, resident in Canada for a period of, or periods the total of which is, not more than 60 months, and

(b) a person who would not be a contributor to the trust at that time if

(i) the transfers and loans referred to in paragraph (a) of the definition "contribution" made by the person at a non-resident time of the person were not taken into account,

(ii) the particular transfers and loans referred to in paragraph (b) of that definition made by the person at a non-resident time of the person were not taken into account, and

(iii) each obligation referred to in paragraph (c) of that definition arising at a non-resident time of the person were not taken into account,

and, for the purpose of this definition, a "non-resident time" of a person means a particular time at which the person is non-resident, where the person was non-resident or not in existence throughout the period that began 60 months before the particular time (or, where the particular time is before June 23, 2000 or the trust arose on and as a consequence of the death of the person, 18 months before the particular time) and ends 60 months after the particular time.

**Technical Notes**: Where a person is a "connected contributor" to a trust, it can result in another person being a "resident beneficiary" under a non-resident trust. A "resident beneficiary" under a non-resident trust can, to an extent, be liable for the trust's income tax, as set out in greater detail on the commentary on subsections 94(3) and (7).

A "connected contributor" at any time is any person, living or deceased, who is a "contributor" to the trust (as defined in new subsection 94(1)) at that time, provided that the person:

- is not, or at the time of death was not, a recent immigrant to Canada (i.e., an individual who was resident in Canada for a period of, or periods the total of which is, not more than 60 months), or
- is not a person who is a "contributor" only because of one or more transactions that occurred at a "non-resident time" of the contributor.

For these purposes, a "non-resident time" is defined within the definition "connected contributor" as being a particular time at which a contributor is non-resident, provided that the contributor is also non-resident (or not in existence) throughout the period that began 60 months before the particular time and ends 60 months after the particular time. However, if the particular time occurs before June 23, 2000 or the trust arose on and as a consequence of the death of the person, the period begins 18 months (rather than 60 months) before the particular time, consistent with existing subclause 94(1)(b)(i)(A)(II).

**"contribution"** at any time to a trust by a particular person or partnership means

(a) a transfer or loan at that time of property to the trust by the particular person or partnership (other than an arm's length transfer);

(b) where a particular transfer or loan of property is made by the particular person or partnership (other than an arm's length transfer by the particular person or partnership in respect of the trust) as part of a series of transactions or events that includes another transfer or loan of a property that is made at that time to the trust by another person or partnership, that other transfer or loan to the extent that it can reasonably be considered to have been enabled by the particular transfer or loan; and

(c) where the particular person or partnership becomes obligated to make a particular transfer or loan (other than an arm's length transfer by the particular person or partnership in respect of the trust) as part of a series of transactions or events that includes a transfer or loan of a property that is made at that time by another person or partnership, that transfer or loan to the extent that it can reasonably be considered to have been enabled by that obligation.

**Technical Notes**: Where a "contribution" is made to a non-resident trust by a person, that person is a "contributor" who, in certain cases, can be jointly and severally liable under subsection 94(3) for the trust's income taxes.

A transferor is considered to make a "contribution" to a trust where a property is transferred or loaned to the trust and any one of three alternative sets of conditions is satisfied. The three sets of conditions are described below.

First, a transfer or loan of a particular property at any time to a trust is considered to be a contribution at that time by a person or partnership to a trust where:

- the particular property is, at that time, transferred, or loaned, directly to the trust by the person or partnership; and
- the transfer or loan is not an "arm's length transfer" (as described in the commentary above).

The second and third alternate sets of conditions deal with cases where a particular person or partnership can be viewed as indirectly contributing property to a trust because of a loan or transfer of property (or an obligation to transfer or loan property) to another person or partnership (other than the trust). In such circumstances, property contributed at a particular time in the same series of transactions and events by another person or partnership to a trust will be treated as having been contributed at the particular time by the particular person or partnership to the trust.

More specifically, the second alternate set of conditions deals with the case where a particular transfer or loan of a property (other than an arm's length transfer) is made by a particular person or partnership as part of a series of transactions or events that includes another transfer or loan of any property, to the particular trust, by another person or partnership. The other transfer or loan is a considered to be a "contribution" to the particular trust by the particular person or partnership to the extent that the other transfer or loan can reasonably be considered to have been enabled by the particular transfer or loan. The contribution is considered to be made at the time of the other transfer or loan.

The third alternate set of conditions deals with the case where a particular person or partnership becomes obligated to make a particular transfer or loan of a property (other than in an arm's length transfer) as part of a series of transactions or events that includes another transfer or loan of any property, to the particular trust, by another person or partnership. The other transfer or loan is considered to be a "contribution" by the particular person or partnership to the particular trust to the extent that the other transfer or loan can reasonably be considered to have been enabled by the particular person's obligation to make the particular loan or transfer. The contribution is considered to be made at the time of the other transfer or loan.

Under new subsection 94(2), there are a number of rules that have the effect of applying the definition "contribution" more broadly than would otherwise be the case. For example, the rendering of services is generally treated as a transfer of property. An obligation to render services is likewise treated as an obligation to transfer property. For more details, see the commentary on subsection 94(2).

As noted earlier, this definition applies to taxation years of trusts that begin after 2000, whether or not a relevant transfer or loan occurred before that time. However, in order to provide for transition between the existing and new rules, a contribution does not include:

- a payment to a trust before 2002 in satisfaction of any amount payable to the trust, or
- the repayment made before 2005, in accordance with terms of repayment established before June 23, 2000, to a trust of a loan made by the trust. (This exception is consistent with existing section 5909 of the Income Tax Regulations.)

**"contributor"** to a trust at any time means a person or partnership that, at or before that time, has made a contribution to the trust.

**Technical Notes**: A "contributor" to a trust is any person or partnership that has made a "contribution" to the trust. See, in this regard, the commentary on the definition "contribution". The definition "contributor" is significant primarily for the purposes of the definitions "resident contributor" and "connected contributor".

Reference should also be made in this context to new paragraphs 94(2)(k) to (o), under which "look-through" rules are provided to deal with cases where trusts, partnerships or corporations are contributors.

**Related Provisions**: 75(3)(c.2) — Reversionary trust rules do not apply to non-resident trust even with Canadian resident contributor; 233.2(4) — Annual information return by contributor to non-resident trust.

**"exempt foreign trust"** at a particular time means

(a) a non-resident trust, where

  (i) each beneficiary of the trust at the particular time is

    (A) an individual who, at the time that the trust was created, was, because mental or physical infirmity, dependent on an individual who is a contributor to the trust or on an individual related to such a contributor (which beneficiary is in this paragraph referred to as an "infirm beneficiary"), or

    (B) a person who is entitled, only after the particular time, to receive or otherwise obtain the use of any of the trust's income or capital,

  (ii) at least one infirm beneficiary suffers at the particular time from a mental or physical infirmity that causes the beneficiary to be dependent on any person,

  (iii) each infirm beneficiary is non-resident at any time in the trust's taxation year that includes the particular time (in this definition referred to as the trust's "current year"), and

  (iv) each contribution to the trust made at or before the particular time can reasonably be considered to have been, at the time that the contribution was made, made to provide for the maintenance of an infirm beneficiary during the expected period of the beneficiary's infirmity;

(b) a non-resident trust, where

  (i) the trust was created after the breakdown of a marriage or common-law partnership of two individuals to provide for the maintenance of a beneficiary under the trust who is a child of one of those individuals (which beneficiary is in this paragraph referred to as a "child beneficiary"),

  (ii) each beneficiary of the trust at the particular time is

    (A) a child beneficiary under 21 years of age at the particular time,

    (B) a child beneficiary under 31 years of age at the particular time who is enroled at any time in the trust's current year at an educational institution that is described in clause (v)(A) or (B), or

    (C) a person who is entitled, only after the particular time, to receive or otherwise obtain the use of any of the trust's income or capital,

  (iii) each child beneficiary is non-resident at any time in the trust's current year,

  (iv) each contributor to the trust at the particular time was one of those individuals or a person related to one of those individuals, and

  (v) each contribution to the trust, at the time that the contribution was made, was made to provide for the maintenance of a child beneficiary, while the child was either under 21 years of age, or was under 31 years of age and enroled at an educational institution located outside Canada that is

    (A) a university, college or other educational institution that provides courses at a post-secondary school level, or

    (B) an educational institution that provides courses that furnish a person with skills for, or improve a person's skills in, an occupation;

(c) a non-resident trust where

  (i) at the particular time, the trust is an agency of the United Nations,

Subdivision i — Shareholders of Non-Resident Corporations   S. 94(1) res

(ii) at the particular time, the trust owns and administers a university described in paragraph (f) of the definition "total charitable gifts" in subsection 118.1(1), or

(iii) at any time in the calendar year that includes the particular time or at any time in the preceding calendar year, Her Majesty in right of Canada has made a gift to the trust;

(d) a non-resident trust that has a taxation year that ends at or before the particular time where

(i) the trust was created exclusively for charitable purposes and has been operated, throughout the period that began at the time it was created and ends at the particular time, exclusively for charitable purposes,

(ii) where the particular time is more than 24 months after the day on which the trust was created, there is a group of at least 20 persons (other than trusts) at the particular time who are all contributors to the trust and who all deal with each other at arm's length,

(iii) the accounting profit of the trust for each such taxation year would, if the profit were not distributed and the laws described in subparagraph (iv) did not apply, be subject to an income or profits tax in a particular country other than Canada, and

(iv) for each such taxation year, the laws of the particular country exempted the trust from the payment of any income or profits tax to the government of that country in recognition of the charitable purposes for which the trust is operated;

(e) a non-resident trust that is, or but for any of paragraphs (a) to (n) of the definition "retirement compensation arrangement" in subsection 248(1) would be, governed by a retirement compensation arrangement;

(f) a non-resident trust that is governed by a foreign retirement arrangement;

(g) a non-resident trust that is governed by an employees profit sharing plan;

(h) a non-resident trust that is a trust described in paragraph (c) of the definition "exempt trust" in subsection 233.2(1); or

(i) a prescribed trust.

**Technical Notes**: An "exempt foreign trust" includes a number of different types of non-resident trusts that are exempt from the application of new subsection 94(3). The expression refers to the following types of non-resident trusts:

- (a) a non-resident trust the current income (determined with reference to amended subsection 108(3)) or capital from which can be provided only to one or more physically or mentally infirm dependent individuals, provided that these individuals are non-resident and that any property settled on the trust could reasonably be considered, at the time it was settled, to be necessary for the maintenance of those individuals;

- (b) a non-resident trust created after the breakdown of a marriage or common-law partnership of two individuals, the current income (determined with reference to amended subsection 108(3)) or capital from which can be provided only to non-resident children of one of the individuals, if the children are under 21 years of age (or under 31 years of age and enrolled in a specified educational institution) and each "contribution" to the trust (as defined in subsection 94(1)) was to provide for the maintenance of those children;

- (c) certain non-resident trusts that could qualify under the definition "total charitable gifts" in subsection 118.1(1) as a recipient permitted for the purposes of the tax credit for charitable gifts;

- (d) certain non-resident trusts established exclusively for charitable purposes;

- (e) non-resident trusts set up to administer certain types of retirement or pension plans or arrangements;

- (f) a non-resident trust that is governed by a "foreign retirement arrangement", as defined in subsection 248(1);

- (g) a non-resident trust that is governed by an "employees profit sharing plan", as defined in subsection 248(1);

- (h) a non-resident trust that is described in paragraph (c) of the definition "exempt trust" in subsection 233.2(1) (i.e., certain foreign unit trusts which are dealt with under the foreign investment entity rules in new sections 94.1 and 94.2); and

- (i) a prescribed trust. (Presently, it is not anticipated that any trusts will be prescribed for this purpose.)

**Related Provisions**: 94(6) [proposed] — Becoming or ceasing to be an exempt foreign trust; 94.1(1)"foreign investment entity"(a) — Exclusion from foreign investment entity rules; 108(3) — Meaning of "income" of trust; 233.2(4)(a) — Exclusion from reporting requirements.

**Notes**: For a list of the foreign charities that qualify under subpara. (c)(iii) because Canada has donated to them recently, contact the CCRA's Charities Division, 613-954-0410 or 1-800-267-2384 (fax 613-952-6020), or check www.ccra-adrc.gc.ca/charities (Information Circular 84-3R5). This list also applies for purposes of 118.1(1)"total charitable gifts"(g).

**Information Circulars**: 84-3R5: Gifts to certain charitable organizations outside Canada.

**Regulations**: The Department of Finance technical notes (June 22, 2000) state that it is not currently anticipated that any trusts will be prescribed under para. (h).

**"resident beneficiary"** at any time under a trust means a person resident in Canada where, at that time,

(a) there is a connected contributor to the trust; and

(b) the person is a beneficiary under the trust whose interest as a beneficiary under the trust is not solely contingent on the subsequent death of an individual who

(i) is related at that time to a contributor to the trust, or

(ii) would have been related at that time to a contributor to the trust if every individual who existed before that time had existed at that time.

**Technical Notes**: A "resident beneficiary" at a particular time under a trust is a person resident in Canada at the particular time, where:

- at the particular time, there is a "connected contributor" to the trust (as defined in new subsection 94(1)), and
- the person is a beneficiary under the trust and the person's interest in the trust is not solely contingent on the death of a individual who is related at that time to a contributor to the trust (or who would have been related at any earlier time to a contributor to the trust if the individual and every person related at the particular time to the individual had existed at that earlier time).

Under new subsection 94(3), a trust is generally treated as resident in Canada for a particular taxation year if there is a "resident beneficiary" under the trust at the end of the particular year. Under new paragraph 94(3)(d), each "resident beneficiary" can be jointly and severally liable with the trust for the trust's income tax liabilities for the particular year under the Act.

**Related Provisions**: 94(3)(a) — Trust with resident beneficiary deemed resident in Canada for certain purposes; 94(3)(d)(i) — Liability of resident beneficiary for trust's tax; 104(1.1) — Restricted meaning of "beneficiary".

**"resident contributor"** to a trust at any time means a person who is, at that time, both resident in Canada and a contributor to the trust, but does not include an individual (other than a trust) who has not, at that time, been resident in Canada for a period of, or periods the total of which is, more than 60 months.

**Technical Notes**: A "resident contributor" at any time is a person resident in Canada at that time who is a "contributor" to the trust at that time. However, an exemption is provided in this context for new immigrants to Canada (i.e., individuals who have been resident in Canada for a period of, or periods the total of which is, 60 months or less).

Under new subsection 94(3), a trust is generally treated as resident in Canada for a particular taxation year if there is a "resident contributor" to the trust at the end of the particular year. Under new paragraph 94(3)(d), a "resident contributor" can be jointly and severally liable with the trust for the trust's income tax liabilities for the particular year under the Act.

**Letter from Department of Finance, September 22, 2000**:

Dear [xxx]

I am responding to your faxed memo to me dated August 25, 2000 concerning the Legislative Proposals and Explanatory Notes on Taxation of Non-Resident Trusts and Foreign Investment Entities (the "Legislative Proposals") released by the Department of Finance by way of Finance Canada News Release number 2000-050, dated June 22, 2000.

In your memo, you referred to the grandfathering provision in existing clause 94(1)(b)(i)(D) of the *Income Tax Act* in relation to *inter vivos* trusts created at any time before 1960 by a person who at that time was a non-resident person. In this connection, you have suggested that a grandfathering rule be introduced in the Legislative Proposals. In particular, you have suggested that the definition "resident contributor" in new proposed subsection 94(1) of the Act be revised to exclude from that definition an individual, in the case of a particular trust, where

(i) the particular trust is an *inter vivos* trust that was created at any time before 1960 by a person who at that time was a non-resident person, and

(ii) no contribution is made to the particular trust by the individual at any time after 1959.

We are prepared to recommend to the Minister your suggested revision to that definition.

We confirm that the effect of this revision would be to save a non-resident trust from the application of the rule in proposed paragraph 94(3)(a) (which deems the trust to be resident in Canada for tax purposes) in any particular trust taxation year only if all the following conditions are met:

1. the trust is an *inter vivos* trust that was created at any time before 1960 by a person who at that time was a non-resident person,

2. no contribution is made to the trust at any time after 1959 by any individual who, at the end of the particular year, is both resident in Canada and a contributor to the trust (except an individual (other than a trust) who has not, at the end of the particular year, been resident in Canada for a period of, or periods the total of which is, more than 60 months), and

3. there are no resident beneficiaries (as defined in the Legislative Proposals) under the trust at the end of the particular year.

Thank you for writing.

Yours sincerely,

Len Farber
General Director, Tax Legislation Division,
Tax Policy Branch

**Related Provisions**: 94(1) "connected contributor"(a) — 60-month limit; 94(3)(a) — Trust with resident beneficiary deemed resident in Canada for certain purposes; 94(3)(d)(i) — Liability of resident beneficiary for trust's tax.

**(2) Rules of application** — For the purposes of this section,

(a) property is deemed to be transferred by a person or partnership at any time to a trust where, because of a transfer or loan (other than an arm's length transfer) at that time of property to another person or partnership,

(i) the fair market value of one or more properties held at that time by the trust increases, or

(ii) a liability or potential liability of the trust decreases;

(b) property is deemed to be transferred by a particular person or partnership at any time to a trust where

(i) at that time, the trust holds property the fair market value of which is derived in whole or in part, directly or indirectly, from properties held by another person or partnership (in this paragraph referred to as the "recipient"),

(ii) property is transferred or loaned at that time by the particular person or partnership (in subparagraph (iii) referred to as the "transferor") to the recipient, and

(iii) it is reasonable to conclude that one of the reasons for which the property was transferred or loaned to the recipient included the relationship between the transferor and

   (A) any person or partnership that was

      (I) beneficially interested in the trust,

      (II) a trustee of the trust,

      (III) a person having influence over the operation of the trust or the enforcement of its terms, or

      (IV) a person having influence over the selection or appointment of any person or partnership referred to in any of subclauses (I) to (III) or this subclause, or

   (B) any group at least one of the members of which is described in clause (A);

(c) the fair market value, at the time of the transfer, of property deemed by paragraph (a) or (b) to have been transferred to the trust is deemed to be the total of all amounts each of which is an amount by which

   (i) the fair market value of a property of the trust increased at that time because of the other transfer or loan referred to in paragraph (a) or (b), or

   (ii) a liability or potential liability of the trust decreased at that time because of the transfer or loan referred to in paragraph (a) or (b);

(d) where a property is acquired at any time by a person or partnership as a consequence of the death of an individual, the individual is deemed to have transferred, at that time, the property to the person or partnership;

(e) where, at any time, a person or partnership has given a guarantee on behalf of, or has provided any other financial assistance to, another person or partnership, the person or partnership is deemed to have transferred, at that time, property to that other person or partnership;

(f) where, at any time after June 22, 2000, a person or partnership renders (otherwise than in the person's capacity as an employee or in the person's or partnership's capacity as agent) any service to, for or on behalf of, another person or partnership (other than any service rendered to a trust that is related to the administration of the trust), the person or partnership is deemed to have transferred, at that time, property to that other person or partnership;

(g) where, at any time after June 22, 2000, a particular person or partnership acquires

   (i) a share of the capital stock of a corporation from the corporation,

   (ii) a beneficial interest in a trust (otherwise than as a consequence of a disposition of the interest by a beneficiary under the trust),

   (iii) an interest in a partnership (otherwise than as a consequence of a disposition of the interest by a member of the partnership), or

   (iv) indebtedness owing by a corporation, trust or partnership from the corporation, trust or partnership,

the corporation, trust or partnership referred to in subparagraph (i), (ii), (iii) or (iv), as the case may be, is deemed to have transferred, at that time, the share, interest or debt to the particular person or partnership;

(h) where, at any time after June 22, 2000, a particular person or partnership grants to another person or partnership a right to acquire or to be loaned property, the particular person or partnership is deemed to have transferred property at that time to that other person or partnership;

(i) the fair market value of property deemed by paragraph (e), (f) or (h) to have been transferred is the fair market value, at the time of the transfer, of the assistance, service or right to which the property relates;

(j) for greater certainty, where at any time a particular person or partnership becomes obligated to do an act that would constitute the transfer of a property to another person or partnership if the act occurred, the particular person or partnership is deemed to have become obligated at that time to transfer property to that other person or partnership;

(k) where, at a particular time, a particular trust makes a contribution to another trust, the contribution is deemed to have been made jointly by the particular trust and by each person or partnership that, at the particular time, is a contributor to the particular trust;

(l) were a particular trust makes a contribution to another trust, the contribution is made at the direction, or with the concurrence, of another person and it is reasonable to conclude that one of the reasons the contribution is made to the other trust is to enable that other person to avoid liability under paragraph (3)(d) in respect of the other trust, the contribution is deemed to be made jointly by the particular trust and by that other person;

(m) where, at a particular time, a particular partnership makes a contribution to a trust, the contribution is deemed to have been made jointly by the particular partnership and by each person or partnership that, at the particular time, is a member of the particular partnership (other than a member of the particular partnership where, by operation of any law governing the partnership arrangement, the liability of the member as a member of the particular partnership is limited);

(n) where a partnership makes a contribution to a trust, the contribution is made at the direction, or with the concurrence, of another person and it is reasonable to conclude that one of the reasons the contribution is made to the trust is to enable that other person to avoid liability under paragraph (3)(d) in respect of the trust, the contribution is deemed to be made jointly by the partnership and by that other person;

(o) where a corporation makes a contribution to a trust, the contribution is made at the direction, or with the concurrence, of another person, and it is reasonable to conclude that one of the reasons the contribution is made to the trust is to enable that other person to avoid liability under paragraph (3)(d) in respect of the trust, the contribution is deemed to be made jointly by the corporation and by that other person; and

(p) subject to subsection (9), the fair market value of a contribution to a trust at the time it was made is deemed to be the fair market value, at the time of the contribution, of the property that was the subject of the contribution.

**Technical Notes**: New subsection 94(2) of the Act sets out a number of rules for use in applying section 94. These rules are primarily relevant for the purposes of determining whether a transaction constitutes a "contribution" of property to a trust (as defined in subsection 94(1)). These rules are also relevant for the purposes of subsections 94(7) to (9) and the amended reporting rules in subsections 162(10.1) and 163(2.4) and section 233.2. These rules apply to taxation years of trusts that begin after 2000, but in some cases specified below relief is provided with regard to transactions or events that occur before June 23, 2000.

Paragraph 94(2)(a) deals with transfers or loans (other than a transfer or loan which is an "arm's length transfer" as defined in subsection 94(1)) that may be viewed as indirect transfers or loans of property to trusts, through transfers or loans to other persons or partnerships. A transfer or loan will be considered a direct transfer to a trust where, because of the transfer or loan to another person or partnership,

- the fair market value of one or more properties held by the trust increases, or
- a liability or potential liability of the trust decreases.

Paragraph 94(2)(b) deals with cases where a trust holds property the fair market value of which is derived from properties held by another person or partnership. Where this paragraph applies, property transferred or loaned to the other person or partnership is deemed to be transferred to the trust itself. Paragraph 94(2)(b) applies where it is reasonable to conclude that one of the reasons for the transfer or loan can reasonably be considered to be connected to the identity of the trust's beneficiaries or other specified persons.

Paragraph 94(2)(c) sets out a rule that applies for the purposes of determining the fair market value of property deemed to be transferred to a trust as a consequence of the application of paragraph 94(2)(a) or (b). This rule is relevant for the purposes of new subsections 94(7) and (8), as well as the penalty provisions for failure to report in subsections 162(10.1) and 163(2.4). The fair market value of the property deemed to have been transferred is considered to be equal to the amount by which the fair market value of the net assets of the trust increased (or the amount by which the liability or potential liability of the trust decreased) due to the transfer or loan that gave rise to the application of paragraph 94(2)(a) or (b).

Paragraph 94(2)(d) applies where property is acquired by a person or partnership as a consequence of the death of an individual. The deceased individual is deemed to have transferred the property to the person or partnership. The paragraph ensures that a person who was resident in Canada immediately before death is generally considered to be a "connected contributor" to the testamentary trust created as a consequence of the person's death. For more detail, see the definitions "connected contributor" and "resident beneficiary".

Paragraph 94(2)(e) deems a person or partnership that provides financial assistance to another person or partnership to have transferred property to that other person or partnership. Under paragraph 94(2)(i), the fair market value of the property deemed to have been transferred is considered to be equal to the fair market value of the assistance. A deemed transfer will be considered to be a contribution to a trust, by the person or partnership who gives the financial assistance, if the deemed transfer falls within the criteria of the definition "contribution" in subsection 94(1). In this regard, note that the definition contains an exception in respect of arm's length transfers.

Paragraph 94(2)(f) applies where services are rendered after June 22, 2000 to, for or on behalf of another person or partnership. In these circumstances, the party rendering the service is deemed to have transferred property to the other person or partnership. Paragraph 94(2)(f) contains an exception for services rendered in a person's capacity as agent or employee, in which case the paragraph will apply instead to the principal or employer of the agent or employee. Paragraph 94(2)(f) also contains an exception for services rendered to a trust that are related to the administration of the trust. Under paragraph 94(2)(i), the fair market value of the property deemed to have been transferred is considered to be equal to the fair market value of the services. A deemed transfer under paragraph 94(2)(f) will be considered a contribution to a trust, by the person or partnership who rendered the services, if the deemed transfer falls within the criteria of the definition "contribution" in subsection 94(1). In this regard, note that the definition contains an exception in respect of arm's length transfers.

Under paragraph 94(2)(g), a corporation is considered to transfer shares that it issues. Similar rules apply to trust and partnership interests, as well as to debt issued by any person or partnership. Paragraph 94(2)(g) applies to shares, debt and interests that are issued after June 22, 2000.

Paragraph 94(2)(h) deems a person or partnership that, after June 22, 2000, grants, to another person or partnership, a right to acquire or to be loaned property to have transferred property to that other person or partnership. Under paragraph 94(2)(i), the fair market value of the property deemed to have been transferred under paragraph 94(2)(h) is considered to be equal to the fair market value of the right.

As noted above, the fair market value of property deemed to have been transferred under paragraphs 94(2)(e), (f) or (h) is determined with reference to paragraph 94(2)(i). As is the case with a similar rule in paragraph 94(2)(c), paragraph 94(2)(i) is relevant for the purposes of new subsections 94(7) and (8), as well as the penalty provisions for failure to report in subsections 162(10.1) and 163(2.4).

Paragraph 94(2)(j) is included for greater certainty. It applies where a person or partnership becomes obligated to do an act (e.g., the rendering of a service) that would constitute the transfer of a property to another person or partnership if the act were to occur. Where this is the case, the person or partnership is deemed to become obligated to transfer property to the other person or partnership. This rule is relevant for the purposes of paragraph (c) of the definition "contribution" in subsection 94(1).

Paragraph 94(2)(k) applies where a particular trust makes a contribution to another trust. Where this is the case, the contribution is deemed to have been made jointly by the particular trust and each person or partnership who is a contributor to the particular trust.

Paragraph 94(2)(l) applies where a particular trust makes a contribution to another trust, the contribution is made at the direction (or with the concurrence) of another person and it is reasonable to consider that one of the reasons the contribution is made to the other trust is to enable that other person to avoid liability, as a resident contributor, under paragraph 94(3)(d) in respect of the other trust. In such a case, the contribution is deemed to have been made jointly by the particular trust and by that other person.

Paragraph 94(2)(m) applies where a partnership makes a contribution to a trust. Where this is the case, partnership members (other than limited partners) are considered to have made a contribution to the trust jointly with the partnership.

Paragraph 94(2)(n) applies where a partnership makes a contribution to a trust, the contribution is made at the direction (or with the concurrence) of another person and it is reasonable to consider that one of the reasons the contribution is made to the trust is to enable that other person to avoid liability, as a resident contributor, under paragraph 94(3)(d) in respect of the trust. In such a case, the contribution is deemed to have been made jointly by the partnership and by that other person. It should be noted that paragraph 94(2)(n) is not relevant to contributions made by a partnership at the direction (or with the concurrence) of a member of a partnership who is not a limited partner, given that paragraph 94(2)(m) also applies in this case.

Paragraph 94(2)(o) applies where a corporation makes a contribution to a trust, the contribution is made at the direction (or with the concurrence) of another person and it is reasonable to consider that one of the reasons the contribution is made to the trust is to enable that other person to avoid liability, as a resident contributor, under paragraph 94(3)(d) in respect of the trust. In such a case, the contribution is deemed to have been made jointly by the corporation and by that other person.

Paragraph 94(2)(p) provides that the fair market value of a contribution to a trust at the time it was made is deemed to be the fair market value of the property loaned or transferred that was the subject of the contribution. The rule is useful for the purposes of new subsections 94(7) and (8), as well as the reporting penalty provisions in amended subsections 162(10.1) and 163(2.4). The rule is relevant because a "contribution" is defined as being a transfer or loan, rather than as being the property that was the subject of the transfer or loan.

The examples below illustrate the operation of subsection 94(2) and the definition "contribution" in subsection 94(1).

*Example 1*

Donald is a long-term resident of Canada. In 2001, Donald pays higher than fair market value consideration for a property acquired from a corporation. A non-resident trust holds shares in the corporation. The fair market value of those shares increases because of the transaction.

*Results*

1. Under paragraph 94(2)(a), Donald is considered to have transferred property to the trust in these circumstances. The exception for "arm's length transfers" is not relevant.

2. As a consequence, Donald is considered to have made a "contribution" to the trust, which results in Donald being a "contributor" and a "resident contributor" to the trust.

*Example 2*

1. Lucie, who is a long-term resident of Canada, transfers property to Canco on condition that Canco direct Canco's wholly-owned foreign subsidiary (Foreignco-1) to transfer properties to another corporation (Foreignco-2) for consideration that is less than fair market value.

2. Shares of the capital stock of Foreignco-2 are held by a non-resident trust.

3. The fair market value of the Foreignco-2 shares increases as a result of the increase in the fair market value of the property owned by Foreignco-2.

*Results*

1. The transfers to Canco and to Foreignco-2 are part of the same series of transactions.

2. Because of paragraph 94(2)(a), the transfer to Foreignco-2 is considered to be a transfer by Foreignco-1 to the trust. The exception for "arm's length transfers" is not relevant.

3. As a consequence, Lucie is considered to have made a "contribution" to the trust under paragraph (b) of the definition "contribution" in subsection 94(1), which results in Lucie being a "contributor" and a "resident contributor" to the trust. Canco is also a "contributor" and a "resident contributor" to the trust.

4. Foreignco-1 is also a "contributor" to the trust, but this does not have any practical consequences because Foreignco-1 is non-resident.

**Related Provisions**: 87(2)(j.95) — Amalgamations — continuing corporation.

**(3) Liabilities of non-resident trust and others** — Where a trust (other than an exempt foreign trust) is non-resident at the end of a taxation year of the trust and, at that time, there is a resident contributor to the trust or a resident beneficiary under the trust,

    (a) subject to subsection (4), the trust is deemed to be resident in Canada throughout the year for the purposes of

        (i) applying section 2 and computing the trust's income for the year,

        (ii) applying subsection (5), clause 53(2)(h)(i.1)(B), the definition "non-resident entity" in subsection 94.1(1), subsections 104(13.1) to (29) and 107(5), section 115 and sections 233.3 and 233.4,

        (iii) determining the liability of the trust for tax under Part XIII on amounts paid or credited to the trust, and

        (iv) determining the rights and obligations of the trust under Divisions I and J;

**Letter from Department of Finance, September 22, 2000**: [See under 94(1)"resident contributor" above — ed.]

    (b) for the purposes of section 126

        (i) the trust's income for the year (other than the portion of the income that, but for this subsection, would be the trust's taxable income earned in Canada) is deemed to be income of the trust from sources in the country other than Canada in which the trust would, but for this subsection, be resident, and

        (ii) such part of any income or profits tax paid by the trust for the year (other than any tax paid because of this section) that can reasonably be regarded as having been paid in respect of the amount determined under subparagraph (i) is deemed to be the non-business-income tax paid by the trust to the government of that country;

    (c) where the trust was non-resident throughout the preceding taxation year for the purpose of computing its income for that preceding year, for the purpose of subsection 128.1(1) the trust is deemed to have become resident in Canada immediately after the end of that preceding year; and

    (d) subject to subsection (7),

        (i) each person who at any time in the year is a resident contributor to the trust or a resident beneficiary under the trust shall have, jointly and severally with the trust and with each other such person, the rights and obligations of the trust in respect of the year under Divisions I and J and subsection 180.1(4), and

        (ii) each such person shall be subject to the provisions of Part XV in respect of those rights and obligations.

**Technical Notes**: New subsection 94(3) of the Act applies to a non-resident trust (other than an "exempt foreign trust", defined in subsection 94(1)) for a taxation year where, at the end of the year, there is a "resident contributor" to the trust or a "resident beneficiary" under the trust. All of these definitions are explained in detail in the commentary on new subsection 94(1).

Where subsection 94(3) applies to a non-resident trust for a taxation year, the trust is deemed to have been resident in Canada throughout the year for the purposes specified in the subsection. Except to the extent otherwise provided by subsection 94(4), a trust is deemed to be resident in Canada for a taxation year under subsection 94(3):

- for the purposes of applying sections 2 and 115 and computing the trust's income for the year — with the result that the trust is subject to tax under Parts I and I.1 on its world-wide income for the year (Note: These trusts are viewed as resident in Canada for the purposes of tax treaties whether or not they are also considered to be resident in another country. However, subsection 94(3) is structured so that there is no tax arising under the Act for a trust subject to subsection 94(3) in the event that the trust earns only foreign-source income and makes full current distributions of the income to non-resident beneficiaries.);

- for the purpose of applying subsection 94(5) — with the result that, as contemplated by subsection 94(5), the tax consequences under subsection 128.1(4) for a trust that ceases to be resident in Canada apply to the trust (See also the note on paragraph 94(3)(c), below.);

- for the purpose of applying clause 53(2)(h)(i.1)(b) — with the result that the adjusted cost base to a beneficiary of the beneficiary's interest in a trust to which this clause applies is computed in the same way as for interests in trusts resident in Canada;

- for the purpose of applying the definition "non-resident entity" in subsection 94.1(1) — with the result that a beneficiary's interest in the trust is not treated as an interest of a beneficiary in a foreign investment entity for the purposes of new sections 94.1 and 94.2;

- for the purposes of applying subsections 104(13.1) to (29) and 107(5) — with the result that the tax treatment of beneficiaries under the trust accords with the tax treatment available to beneficiaries under trusts that are resident in Canada;

- for the purposes of applying sections 233.3 and 233.4 — with the result that the trust is required to file information returns under sections 233.3 (information return on a foreign property holdings that cost in excess of $100,000) and 233.4 (information return on foreign affiliates);

- for the purpose of determining the liability of the trust for tax under Part XIII — with the result that the trust is exempt from Part XIII tax on amounts paid or credited to it; and

- for the purpose of determining the rights and obligations of the trust under sections 150 to 180 — with the result that various administrative provisions in the Act apply in the same way as to other trusts resident in Canada. These provisions include those with regard

Subdivision i — Shareholders of Non-Resident Corporations  S. 94(4)

to the filing of returns, assessments, tax payments, arrears interest, refund interest, instalment interest, penalties, refunds and appeals.

Paragraph 94(3)(b) provides that a trust that is subject to subsection 94(3) is entitled to claim foreign tax credits against its Canadian income tax in accordance with the rules in section 126, except with regard to any taxable income earned in Canada (as would otherwise be determined under subsection 115(1)).

Paragraph 94(3)(c) clarifies that a non-resident trust that becomes subject to subsection 94(3) for a particular taxation year, after not being subject to either it or existing paragraph 94(1)(c) for the preceding year, is deemed to become resident in Canada at the beginning of the particular year. As a result, the cost amount of each of the properties (other than taxable Canadian properties) held by the trust at the beginning of the particular year is deemed by subsection 128.1(1) to be the fair market value of the property at the beginning of the particular year. Note, in this regard, that paragraph 94(3)(c) complements the rule in subsection 94(6) in the case where a non-resident trust ceases to be an "exempt foreign trust" (as defined in subsection 94(1)). In this case, subsection 94(6) establishes the beginning of a new "stub" taxation year to which subsection 94(3) may apply. If subsection 94(3) does apply for that "stub" year, subsection 128.1(1) would apply with regard to the properties (other than taxable Canadian properties) held by the trust at the beginning of that "stub" year.

Paragraph 94(3)(d) imposes liabilities for a taxation year on persons who, at the end of the year, are "resident contributors" or "resident beneficiaries". Where subsection 94(3) applies to a trust for a taxation year, each of these persons is jointly and severally liable with the trust in respect of the trust's obligations under sections 150 to 180, including its Part I.1 obligations that arise as a consequence of subsection 180.1(4). Typically, the most significant obligation in this context is the obligation to pay tax instalments pursuant to section 156. However, the extent of the joint liability imposed by paragraph 94(3)(d) is limited by new subsection 94(7) — which is explained in the commentary below.

Note, in particular, that subsection 94(3) does not result in the creation of any obligations for a trust that is subject to subsection 94(3) to withhold tax on distributions to non-resident beneficiaries under Part XIII or to pay any tax under Part XII.2. As noted above, one of the effects of subsection 94(3) is that the trust is not liable in connection with distributions of Canadian-source income to the non-resident trust. However, the rules in new subsection 104(7.01) are designed so that there will be a reasonable level of Part I tax in respect of Canadian-source income received by the trust in the event the trust also distributes income to non-resident beneficiaries.

**Related Provisions**: 75(3)(c.2) — Reversionary trust rules do not apply to non-resident trust; 94(4) [proposed] — Excluded provisions; 94(5) [proposed] — Trust deemed to cease being resident in Canada; 94(7) [proposed] — Limit to amount recoverable under 94(3)(d); 104(7.01) — Limit to trust's deduction under 104(6); 233.2(4) — Annual information return by contributor; 233.3(3) — Annual information return by holder of interest.

**Notes**: See Notes at beginning of proposed s. 94.

**(4) Excluded provisions** — Paragraph (3)(a) does not apply for the purposes of

(a) the definition "exempt foreign trust" in subsection (1);

(b) computing any income or loss from property, or any taxable capital gain or allowable loss, because of the application of subsection 75(2);

(c) paragraph 107.4(1)(c) (other than subparagraph 107.4(1)(c)(i)), paragraph (a) of the definition "mutual fund trust" in subsection 132(6), and subparagraph (f)(ii) of the definition "disposition" in subsection 248(1); and

(d) determining the liability of a person that arises because of the application of section 215, except as the Minister otherwise permits in writing.

**Technical Notes**: New subsection 94(4) of the Act provides that the rules in subsection 94(3) treating non-resident trusts as resident in Canada do not apply for certain limited purposes:

- the definition "exempt foreign trust" — thus ensuring that there is no circularity due to fact that the definition "exempt foreign trust" is used in subsection 94(3);

- computing income or loss from property, or any taxable capital gain or allowable capital loss, because of the application of subsection 75(2) — thus providing that income generated from a property transferred by a non-resident trust to a reversionary trust is not attributed back if the non-resident trust is deemed to be resident in Canada under subsection 94(3);

- proposed paragraph 107.4(1)(c), other than subparagraph 107.4(1)(c)(i), and proposed subparagraph (f)(ii) of the definition "disposition" in subsection 248(1) [The measures were contained in a detailed Notice of Ways and Means Motion tabled on June 5, 2000.] — thus ensuring that proposed rules allowing in some cases for a rollover of property on transfers involving no change in beneficial ownership generally do not apply to transfers to a trust deemed to be resident in Canada by subsection 94(3); and

- paragraph (a) of the definition "mutual fund trust" in subsection 132(6) — a reference which makes it clear that a trust deemed to be resident in Canada by subsection 94(3) will not be treated as a mutual fund trust for any purpose.

Furthermore, except as otherwise permitted in writing by the Minister of National Revenue, subsection 94(3) does not relieve a payer of Canadian-source income the obligation to withhold under section 215 in connection with amounts received by a trust deemed to be resident of Canada by subsection 94(3). This is so even though such a trust is not liable for Part XIII tax on amounts paid or credited to it, because of the application of subparagraph 94(3)(a)(iii). The trust would be expected to apply for a refund of such tax, which would be given unless there are any outstanding liabilities of the trust with regard to Part I tax.

**(5) Ceasing to reside in Canada** — A trust is deemed to have ceased to be resident in Canada at any time where

(a) that time is in a particular period that, but for this subsection and subsection 128.1(4), would be a taxation year of the trust that immediately follows a taxation year of the trust throughout which the trust was resident in Canada because of the application of subsection (3);

(b) the trust is non-resident at the end of the particular period;

(c) there was a resident contributor to the trust, or a resident beneficiary under the trust, at the beginning of the particular period; and

(d) that time is the earliest time in the particular period at which there is neither a resident contributor to the trust nor a resident beneficiary under the trust.

**Technical Notes**: New subsection 94(5) of the Act applies to a trust with regard to a particular period that (without reference to the combined application of subsections 94(5) and 128.1(4)) would be a taxation year of the trust that immediately follows a taxation year of the trust throughout which it is resident in Canada because of the application of subsection 94(3). If the trust is not resident in Canada at the end of the particular period (i.e., because the criteria in subsection 94(3) for deeming the trust to be resident in Canada are no longer satisfied), the trust is deemed to have ceased to reside in Canada at the earliest time in the particular period at which there is neither a "resident contributor" to the trust nor a "resident beneficiary" under the trust. These two definitions are explained in the commentary on subsection 94(1).

In such circumstances, the cessation of residence in Canada results in the application of paragraph 128.1(4)(a). As a consequence of that paragraph, a taxation year of the trust is considered to have ended immediately before the earliest time in the particular period described above. At the end of that taxation year, the criteria in subsection 94(3) are satisfied. Accordingly, the trust would be subject to tax under Parts I and I.1 on its world-wide income for that year because it is considered to be resident in Canada under subsection 94(3).

**Related Provisions**: 94(3)(a) [proposed] — Application to trust deemed resident in Canada.

**(6) Becoming or ceasing to be an exempt foreign trust** — Where at any time a trust becomes or ceases to be an exempt foreign trust (otherwise than because of becoming resident in Canada),

(a) the trust's taxation year that would otherwise include that time is deemed to have ended immediately before that time and a new taxation year of the trust is deemed to have begun at that time; and

(b) for the purpose of determining the trust's fiscal period after that time, the trust is deemed not to have established a fiscal period before that time.

**Technical Notes**: New subsection 94(6) of the Act generally provides that, if a trust becomes or ceases to be an exempt foreign trust at any time, the trust's taxation year is deemed to have ended immediately before that time, a new "stub" taxation year is deemed to have begun at that time and the trust is deemed not to have established a fiscal period before that time. However, subsection 94(6) does not apply where a trust ceases to be an exempt foreign trust because it becomes resident in Canada.

Subsection 94(3) may apply in respect of the later "stub" taxation year of the trust if the criteria set out in that subsection are satisfied at the end of that year. Where this is the case, the trust would be subject to tax under Parts I and I.1 on its world-wide income for that later "stub" year because it would be considered under subsection 94(3) to be resident in Canada for that year.

**(7) Limit to amount recoverable** — Notwithstanding subsection (3), the amount recoverable under paragraph (3)(d) at any time from a person in respect of a trust and a particular taxation year of the trust shall not exceed the recovery limit at that time of the person in respect of the trust and the particular year where

(a) except where subparagraph (b)(ii) would apply if the portion of that subparagraph after clause (b)(ii)(B) were read as "is not more than $10,000", the person has filed on a timely basis under section 233.2 all information returns required to be filed by the person before that time in respect of the trust (or within such later period as is acceptable to the Minister);

(b) either

(i) the person is liable under paragraph (3)(d) in respect of the trust and the particular year solely because the person was a resident beneficiary under the trust at the end of the particular year, or

(ii) at the end of the particular year, the total of all amounts each of which is the fair market value, at the time it was made, of a contribution to the trust before the end of the particular year by

(A) the person, or

(B) another person not dealing at arm's length with the person,

is not more than the greater of $10,000 and 10% of the total of all amounts each of which was the fair market value, at the time it was made, of a contribution to the trust before the end of the particular year; and

(c) it is reasonable to conclude that each transaction or event that occurred before the end of the particular year at the direction of, or with the concurrence of, the person satisfied the following conditions:

(i) none of the purposes of the transaction or event was to enable the person to minimize

## Subdivision i — Shareholders of Non-Resident Corporations  S. 94(8)(a)(i)

liability under paragraph (3)(d) in respect of the trust, and

(ii) the transaction or event was not part of a series of transactions or events any of the purposes of which was to enable the person to minimize liability under paragraph (3)(d) in respect of the trust.

**Technical Notes**: New subsection 94(7) of the Act allows for a limitation of the amount that may be recovered from a person who would otherwise be jointly and severally liable for the entire amount of the trust's tax obligations under the Act. Subsection 94(7) applies to a person in respect of a particular taxation year of a trust where three conditions are satisfied.

The first condition is that the person must have filed on a timely basis all information returns required to be filed by the person in respect of the trust under section 233.2 (or within such later period as is acceptable to the Minister of National Revenue). [Paragraph 94(7)(a).] However, the first condition need not be satisfied if the second condition (below) is satisfied because of the $10,000 contribution test referred to below.

The second condition is satisfied in respect of a particular taxation year of the trust:

- where the person is jointly and severally liable with the trust only because the person was a "resident beneficiary" under the trust at the end of the particular year, [Subparagraph 94(7)(b)(i).] or
- where, at the end of the particular year, the total fair market value (determined with reference to paragraphs 94(2)(c), (i) and (p) and subsection 94(9)) of contributions made to the trust by the person (or another person not dealing at arm's length with the person) is not more than the greater of $10,000 and 10% of the total fair market value of all contributions to the trust. [Subparagraph 94(7)(b)(ii).]

The third condition is satisfied in respect of a person and a particular taxation year of the trust where it is reasonable to conclude that each transaction or event that occurred before the end of the particular year at the direction of, or with the concurrence of, the person satisfied the following conditions:

- none of the purposes of the transaction or event was to enable the person to minimize liability under paragraph 94(3)(d) in respect of the trust, [Subparagraph 94(7)(c)(i).] and
- the transaction or event was not part of a series of transactions or events any of the purposes of which was to enable the person to minimize liability under paragraph 94(3)(d) in respect of the trust. [Subparagraph 94(7)(c)(ii).]

There are a number of transactions or events, or series of transactions or events, which may result in a failure to satisfy the third condition. For example, an artificial dilution of a person's relative contribution in the trust (i.e., below the 10% level) could well be impugned. Likewise, corporate distributions that have the effect of minimizing the impact of the three-year rule described in subsection 94(9) could also be offensive for these purposes.

Reference should be made in this context to the definition "contribution" in subsection 94(1), as well as to related rules in subsection 94(2).

Where subsection 94(7) applies to a person in respect of a taxation year of a trust, the amount recoverable at any time from the person in respect of the year is limited to the person's "recovery limit" in respect of the trust and the year. Under subsection 94(8), the amount of the recovery limit at any time is calculated as follows:

- ADD amounts payable and amounts previously paid by the trust to the person in respect of the person's beneficial interest in the trust;
- ADD previous proceeds from the disposition of the person's interest in the trust, not otherwise taken into account above;
- ADD the fair market value of benefits conferred by the trust on the person, not otherwise taken into account above;
- ADD the total fair market value (determined with reference to paragraphs 94(2)(c), (i) and (p) and subsection 94(9)) of contributions made to the trust by the person, to the extent that this amount exceeds the total of the first three amounts; and
- SUBTRACT previous recoveries by the CCRA under subsection 94(3) from the person in respect of the trust and the year or a preceding taxation year of the trust.

As indicated above, subsection 94(9) affects the calculation of the fair market value of a "contribution" to a trust. It applies where the contributed property is a share, a right to acquire a share, or other property primarily deriving its value from a share or a right to acquire a share.

For the purpose of determining whether the "recovery limit" limitation applies to a contributor to a trust in respect of a transfer to the trust and of determining the amount of the "recovery limit", the fair market value of contributed property is deemed by subsection 94(9) to be the greater of:

- its fair market value, otherwise determined, at the time it was transferred (see in this regard paragraph 94(2)(p)); and
- its fair market value (or the fair market value of substituted property) at the end of the third calendar year ending after its transfer to the trust.

Subsection 94(9) is intended to allow for a reasonable opportunity for recovery of tax by the CCRA in the context of a series of transactions involving the transfer of shares or similar property. For example, an estate freeze might occur under which common shares with a nominal initial fair market value are transferred directly or indirectly to a non-resident trust. In these circumstances, it would be inappropriate to limit a recovery of tax to the initial fair market value of the shares.

**Related Provisions**: 94(8) [proposed] — Recovery limit; 94(9) [proposed] — Determination of fair market value.

**(8) Recovery limit** — For the purpose of subsection (7), the recovery limit at a particular time of a person in respect of a trust and a particular taxation year of the trust is the amount, if any, by which the greater of

(a) the total of all amounts each of which is

(i) an amount paid before the particular time to the person by the trust because of the interest of the person as a beneficiary under the trust,

(ii) an amount the payment of which by the trust the person is at the particular time entitled to enforce because of the interest of the person as a beneficiary under the trust,

(iii) an amount (other than an amount described in subparagraph (i)) received before the particular time by the person on the disposition of an interest as a beneficiary under the trust, or

(iv) the fair market value of a benefit received or enjoyed by the person from or under the trust (other than a benefit described in any of subparagraphs (i) to (iii)), and

(b) the total of all amounts each of which is the fair market value, at the time it was made, of a contribution to the trust before the particular time by the person,

exceeds

(c) the total of all amounts each of which is an amount recovered before the particular time from the person in connection with a liability of the person arising under subsection (3) in respect of the trust and the particular year or a preceding taxation year of the trust.

**Technical Notes**: See under 94(7).

**Related Provisions**: 94(9) [proposed] — Determination of fair market value.

**(9) Determination of fair market value — special case** — For the purposes of applying subparagraph (7)(b)(ii) and determining the recovery limit under subsection (8), where a contribution is made at any time by a person or partnership to a trust as a consequence of a transaction that is, or as a consequence of a series of transactions or events that includes, the transfer at that time to the trust of a particular property that is a share, a right to acquire a share, or other property primarily deriving its value from a share or a right to acquire a share, the fair market value of the contribution at the time it is made is deemed to be the greater of

(a) the fair market value of the contribution at that time, determined without reference to this subsection, and

(b) the fair market value of the particular property, or property substituted for the particular property, at the end of the third calendar year that ends after that time.

**Technical Notes**: See under 94(7).

**Application**: The June 22, 2000 draft legislation, s. 10, will amend s. 94 to read as above, applicable to taxation years of trusts that begin after 2000 [to be changed to "that begin after 2001", per Sept. 7/00 news release reproduced after 94.3 — ed.], except that the definition "contribution" in subsec. 94(1) shall not apply to

(a) a payment made to a trust before 2002 in satisfaction of any amount payable to the trust; or

(b) a repayment made before 2005, in accordance with terms of repayment established before June 23, 2000, to a trust of a loan made by the trust.

**Notice of Ways and Means Motion, federal budget, February 16, 1999**: *Non-resident trusts and foreign-based investment funds*

(8) That the provisions of the Act governing the taxation of

(a) trust beneficiaries and non-resident trusts, and

(b) taxpayers resident in Canada who hold interests in foreign-based investment funds

be modified in accordance with proposals described in the budget documents tabled by the Minister of Finance in the House of Commons on February 16, 1999.

**Federal budget, Supplementary Information, February 16, 1999**: *Taxation of trusts — Background*

Trusts that are resident in Canada are subject to tax in Canada annually on their undistributed income.

Beneficiaries of resident trusts are taxable on distributions received from such trusts, to the extent that the distributions are made out of the income of the trust. Distributions made out of the capital of the trust are tax-free. As a result, the Canadian tax base is protected.

Generally, non-resident trusts are not taxable in Canada and income can be accumulated in such trusts on a tax-deferred basis. When such trusts pay little or no foreign tax on their accumulated income and capital gains, taxpayers making use of such trusts may benefit either from a deferral of tax or complete avoidance of tax. Avoidance occurs where the accumulated income is transformed into the capital of the trust, which is distributed to the Canadian beneficiaries tax-free.

*Issue*

The anti-avoidance rules in the Act attempt to tax income earned by non-resident trusts in certain circumstances in order to ensure that they are not used to defer Canadian tax on the income accumulating in the trusts. Current rules apply only to non-resident trusts with a Canadian beneficiary. However, these rules are not fully effective and relatively little of such income is taxed in Canada.

Canadian residents are able to transfer funds to non-resident trusts under circumstances designed to circumvent the application of existing anti-avoidance rules. The trust regimes in several tax-haven jurisdictions have been specifically modified in an attempt to permit Canadians to avoid the application of the anti-avoidance rules. A feature of such schemes is to disguise the fact that the non-resident trust has a Canadian resident beneficiary. A number of tax-haven jurisdictions have modified their trust laws so that no beneficiaries need to be designated, thus facilitating tax planning by Canadians in order to defer the taxation of the income accumulating in the non-resident trust. Arrangements between the Canadian transferors and the trustee ensure that the Canadian transferors retain effective control of the trust, or are able to designate who may ultimately receive capital of the trust, including its accumulated income.

Non-resident trusts can therefore offer higher-income Canadians the opportunity to defer or avoid Canadian tax on investment income that would otherwise be taxable in Canada.

[See also the portions reproduced under 94.1(1) — ed.]

Consultations will also be initiated on the following proposed modifications to the tax rules governing non-resident trusts:

- That where a Canadian resident transfers or loans property to a non-resident trust, the trust be treated as being resident in Canada and be taxed on all of its undistributed income, subject to a number of exceptions noted below. The Canadian resident transferor would be jointly (with the trust) liable for tax. Where a foreign income tax is imposed in respect of the undistributed income of the trust, a foreign tax credit would be provided. The proposed rules would apply whether or not the trust has a Canadian-resident beneficiary, since in practice it may not be possible to determine whether the property in the trust will be distributed to Canadian beneficiaries.

- That the proposed changes also deal with the distributions from trusts. Distributions out of current income of the trust would be taxed in the hands of the beneficiaries. As well, distributions out of any previously untaxed accumulated income of the trust would be subject to tax.

- That the following trusts be excluded from the application of the proposed rules:
  - trusts resident in the United States and subject to United States tax provisions;
  - non-resident trusts set up prior to immigrants' arrival in Canada, for a five-year period after immigration; and
  - non-resident trusts set up for the benefit of individuals with disabilities or children of divorced parents where the trust and beneficiaries are resident within the same country.

- Additional exceptions could be contemplated to remove from the rules non-resident trusts that are clearly not used to avoid or defer Canadian tax, such as *bona fide* foreign charitable trusts.

- The proposed rules would apply to any taxation year commencing after 1999, with respect to non-resident trusts to which a Canadian resident transfers or loans property on or after February 16, 1999, subject to the exceptions noted above. Other non-resident trusts to which a transfer or a loan of property was made by a Canadian resident before February 16, 1999, would be subject to the proposed rules for taxation years commencing after 2000.

The proposed changes are consistent with Revenue Canada devoting more resources to the audit of taxpayers whose investment activities extend beyond Canada.

Further details on the proposed legislative changes will be released soon to enhance the consultation process.

**Department of Finance news release, November 30, 1999**: *Update on Proposals for the Taxation of Non-Resident Trusts and Foreign Investment Funds*

The February 1999 budget announced that consultations would be initiated on proposed new approaches for the taxation of non-resident "family" trusts (NRTs) and foreign investment funds (FIFs).

The proposed approach for NRTs generally provides for them to be treated as resident in Canada during the period in which a contributor to the NRT was resident in Canada. The contributor would, in these circumstances, be jointly liable with the NRT for the NRT's resulting Canadian income tax liability on its worldwide income.

The proposed approach for FIFs provides for an annual allocation of a FIF's income to a Canadian unitholder. If insufficient information is available for a unitholder to adopt this approach, the unitholder is to be taxed on an annual basis on any increases in the fair market value of the unitholder's interest in the FIF.

The February 1999 budget also proposed that distributions from foreign trusts would generally be subject to an additional tax to the extent that the distributions represented income that had not been subject to Canadian income tax, and that the proposals would not apply to FIFs and NRTs based in the United States.

Further to consultations on these proposals and additional analysis within the Department, the following modifications to the package are proposed:

1. The additional tax on distributions from foreign trusts will not be implemented. The implementation of this tax would have raised concerns about fairness, double taxation and complexity. The strengthened taxation rules proposed for NRTs and FIFs will ensure that Canadian tax will generally be exigible whenever Canadian residents contribute to these vehicles.

2. The administrative advantages of an exemption for NRTs and FIFs based in the United States are reduced because of the elimination of the additional tax on distributions from foreign trusts. Moreover, there were concerns that this exemption would allow for structures that could have undermined the effectiveness of the rules. Consequently, a proposed exemption from the new rules for NRTs and FIFs based in the United States will not be implemented.

3. The proposed new rules for NRTs will apply in all cases to NRT taxation years that begin after 2000. The proposed rules for FIFs will apply in all cases to taxation years of Canadian investors that begin after 2000.

One technical question that has been frequently raised is that of the application of the five-year exemption under proposed rules for NRTs to trusts established after an emigrant becomes resident in Canada. It is proposed that this exemption be structured much like it is under the existing law, so that it is not restricted to trusts established before an emigrant becomes resident in Canada.

It is anticipated that draft legislation on NRTs and FIFs will be released early in 2000 in order to permit an additional period of consultation before it is incorporated in a bill.

**Department of Finance news release, September 7, 2000**: *Finance Minister Extends Consultation Period and Announces New Effective Date for Foreign Investment Entity and Trust Tax Proposals* [See after 94.3 — ed.]

**Definitions [s. 94]**: "accounting profit" — 94(1); "amount" — 248(1); "arm's length" — 251(1); "arm's length transfer" — 94(1); "beneficiary" — 104(1.1); "business" — 248(1); "Canada" — 255, *Interpretation Act* 35(1); "child" — 252(1); "common-law partnership" — 248(1); "connected contributor", "contribution", "contributor" — 94(1); "corporation" — 248(1), *Interpretation Act* 35(1); "disposition", "dividend", "employee" — 248(1); "employees profit sharing plan" — 144(1), 248(1); "exempt foreign trust" — 94(1); "fair market value" — 94(2)(c), 94(9); "fiscal period" — 249.1; "foreign retirement arrangement" — 248(1), Reg. 6803; "Her Majesty" — *Interpreta-*

*tion Act* 35(1); "individual", "Minister" — 248(1); "infirm beneficiary" — 94(1)"exempt foreign trust"(a)(i)(A); "month" — *Interpretation Act* 35(1); "non-resident" — 248(1); "partnership" — see Notes to 96(1); "person", "prescribed", "property" — 248(1); "recovery limit" — 94(8); "related" — 251(2)–(6); "resident" — 250; "resident beneficiary", "resident contributor" — 94(1); "resident in Canada" — 250; "retirement compensation arrangement", "share" — 248(1); "taxable capital gain" — 38(a), 248(1); "taxable income earned in Canada" — 248(1); "taxation year" — 249; "transfer" — 94(1); "trust" — 104(1), 248(1), (3); "writing" — *Interpretation Act* 35(1).

## 94.1 (1) Offshore investment fund property —
Where in a taxation year a taxpayer, other than a non-resident-owned investment corporation, holds or has an interest in property (in this section referred to as an "offshore investment fund property")

(a) that is a share of the capital stock of, an interest in, or a debt of, a non-resident entity (other than a controlled foreign affiliate of the taxpayer or a prescribed non-resident entity) or an interest in or a right or option to acquire such a share, interest or debt, and

(b) that may reasonably be considered to derive its value, directly or indirectly, primarily from portfolio investments of that or any other non-resident entity in

(i) shares of the capital stock of one or more corporations,

(ii) indebtedness or annuities,

(iii) interests in one or more corporations, trusts, partnerships, organizations, funds or entities,

(iv) commodities,

(v) real estate,

(vi) Canadian or foreign resource properties,

(vii) currency of a country other than Canada,

(viii) rights or options to acquire or dispose of any of the foregoing, or

(ix) any combination of the foregoing,

and it may reasonably be concluded, having regard to all the circumstances, including

(c) the nature, organization and operation of any non-resident entity and the form of, and the terms and conditions governing, the taxpayer's interest in, or connection with, any non-resident entity,

(d) the extent to which any income, profits and gains that may reasonably be considered to be earned or accrued, whether directly or indirectly, for the benefit of any non-resident entity are subject to an income or profits tax that is significantly less than the income tax that would be applicable to such income, profits and gains if they were earned directly by the taxpayer, and

(e) the extent to which the income, profits and gains of any non-resident entity for any fiscal period are distributed in that or the immediately following fiscal period,

that one of the main reasons for the taxpayer acquiring, holding or having the interest in such property was to derive a benefit from portfolio investments in assets described in any of subparagraphs (b)(i) to (ix) in such a manner that the taxes, if any, on the income, profits and gains from such assets for any particular year are significantly less than the tax that would have been applicable under this Part if the income, profits and gains had been earned directly by the taxpayer, there shall be included in computing the taxpayer's income for the year the amount, if any, by which

(f) the total of all amounts each of which is the product obtained when

(i) the designated cost to the taxpayer of the offshore investment fund property at the end of a month in the year

is multiplied by

(ii) the quotient obtained when the prescribed rate of interest for the period including that month is divided by 12

exceeds

(g) the taxpayer's income for the year (other than a capital gain) from the offshore investment fund property determined without reference to this subsection.

### Proposed Amendment — 94.1(1)
See at end of 94.1.

**Related Provisions**: 53(1)(m) — Addition to ACB; 94(1)(c)(i)(D) — Income under 94.1 included in income of offshore trust; 95(1)"foreign accrual property income"C — Application to determination of FAPI.

**Notes**: 94.1 generally applies to offshore investment funds which the taxpayer does not control. For controlled funds, see the offshore trust rules in 94(1). But see proposed 94.1–94.3 below. Note also the reporting rules in 233.2–233.7.

**Regulations**: 4301(c) (prescribed rate of interest for 94.1(1)(f)(ii)); to date, no prescribed non-resident entities prescribed for 94.1(1)(a).

**Interpretation Bulletins**: IT-451R: Deemed disposition and acquisition on ceasing to be or becoming resident in Canada.

**(2) Definitions** — In this section,

**"designated cost"** to a taxpayer at any time in a taxation year of an offshore investment fund property that the taxpayer holds or has an interest in means the amount determined by the formula

$$A + B + C + D$$

where

A is the cost amount to the taxpayer of the property at that time (determined without reference to paragraphs 53(1)(m) and (q), subparagraph 53(2)(c)(i.3), paragraphs 53(2)(g) and (g.1) and section 143.2),

B is, where an additional amount has been made available by a person to another person after 1984 and before that time, whether by way of gift, loan, payment for a share, transfer of property at less than its fair market value or otherwise, in circumstances such that it may reasonably be concluded that one of the main reasons for so making the additional amount available to the other person was to increase the value of the property, the total of all amounts each of which is the amount, if any, by which such an additional amount exceeds any increase in the cost amount to the taxpayer of the property by virtue of that additional amount,

C is the total of all amounts each of which is an amount included in respect of the offshore investment fund property by virtue of this section in computing the taxpayer's income for a preceding taxation year, and

D is

(a) where the taxpayer has held or has had the interest in the property at all times since the end of 1984, the amount, if any, by which the fair market value of the property at the end of 1984 exceeds the cost amount to the taxpayer of the property at the end of 1984, or

(b) in any other case, the total of

(i) the amount, if any, by which the fair market value of the property at the particular time the taxpayer acquired the property exceeds the cost amount to the taxpayer of the property at the particular time, and

(ii) the amount, if any, by which

(A) the total of all amounts each of which is an amount that would have been included in respect of the property because of this section in computing the taxpayer's income for a taxation year that began before June 20, 1996 if the cost to the taxpayer of the property were equal to the fair market value of the property at the particular time

exceeds

(B) the total of all amounts each of which is an amount that was included in respect of the property because of this section in computing the taxpayer's income for a taxation year that began before June 20, 1996,

except that the designated cost of an offshore investment fund property that is a prescribed offshore investment fund property is nil;

**Related Provisions**: 94.1(3) – Pre-Feb. 15/84 property.

**Notes**: 94.1(2)"designated cost"A amended by 1995-97 technical bill, to add references to 53(2)(c)(i.3) and 143.2 effective September 27, 1994, and to 53(1)(q), 53(2)(g) and 53(2)(g.1) effective for taxation years that end after April 26, 1995.

Para. D(b) added by 1995-97 technical bill, effective for taxation years that begin after June 20, 1996.

94.1(2)"designated cost" was 94.1(2)(a) before consolidation in R.S.C. 1985 (5th Supp.), effective for taxation years ending after November 1991. The previous version, identical in meaning, read:

(a) "designated cost" — "designated cost" to a taxpayer at any time in a taxation year of an offshore investment fund property that he holds or has an interest in means the aggregate of

(i) the cost amount to the taxpayer of the property at that time (determined without reference to paragraph 53(1)(m)),

(ii) where an additional amount has been made available by a person to another person after 1984 and before that time, whether by way of gift, loan, payment for a share, transfer of property at less than its fair market value or otherwise, in circumstances such that it may reasonably be concluded that one of the main reasons for so making the additional amount available to the other person was to increase the value of the property, the aggregate of all amounts each of which is the amount, if any, by which such an additional amount exceeds any increase in the cost amount to the taxpayer of the property by virtue of that additional amount,

(iii) the aggregate of all amounts each of which is an amount included in respect of the offshore investment fund property by virtue of this section in computing the taxpayer's income for a preceding taxation year, and

(iv) where the taxpayer held or had the interest in the property at the end of 1984, the amount, if any, by which the fair market value of the property at that time exceeds the cost amount to the taxpayer of the property at that time,

except that the designated cost of an offshore investment fund property that is a prescribed offshore investment fund property is nil; and

**Regulations**: 6900 (prescribed offshore investment fund property).

**"non-resident entity"** means a corporation that is not resident in Canada, a partnership, organization, fund or entity that is not resident or is not situated in Canada or a trust with respect to which the rules in paragraph 94(1)(c) or (d) apply.

**Notes**: 94.1(2)"non-resident entity" was 94.1(2)(b) before consolidation in R.S.C. 1985 (5th Supp.), effective for taxation years ending after November 1991.

**(3) Interpretation** — Where subsection (1) is applied with respect to an offshore investment fund property that was

(a) held by the taxpayer on February 15, 1984,

(b) received as a stock dividend in respect of a share of the capital stock of a non-resident entity held by the taxpayer on February 15, 1984,

(c) received as a stock dividend in respect of a share of the capital stock of a non-resident entity that the taxpayer had previously received as described in paragraph (b), or

(d) substituted for a property held by the taxpayer on February 15, 1984 pursuant to an arrangement that existed on that date,

the reference to "1984" in the descriptions of B and D in the definition "designated cost" in subsection (2) shall be read as a reference to "1985".

## S. 94.1(3)  Income Tax Act, Part I, Division B

**Definitions [s. 94.1]**: "amount", "annuity" — 248(1); "capital gain" — 39(1)(a), 248(1); "controlled foreign affiliate" — 95(1), 248(1); "corporation" — 248(1), *Interpretation Act* 35(1); "cost amount" — 248(1); "designated cost" — 94.1(2); "fiscal period" — 249(2), 249.1; "foreign affiliate" — 95(1), 248(1); "foreign resource property" — 66(15), 248(1); "investment corporation" — 130(3), 248(1); "non-resident" — 248(1); "non-resident entity" — 94.1(2); "offshore investment fund property" — 94.1(1); "prescribed" — 248(1); "prescribed rate" — Reg. 4301; "property", "share" — 248(1); "taxation year" — 249; "taxpayer" — 248(1); "trust" — 104(1), 248(1), (3).

### Proposed Amendment — 94.1, 94.2, 94.3

**Technical Notes**: Existing section 94.1 of the Act applies where a taxpayer has invested in an offshore investment fund and one of the main reasons for the investment is to reduce or defer the tax liability that would have applied to the income generated from the underlying assets of the fund if such income had been earned directly by the taxpayer. In these circumstances, existing section 94.1 generally requires an amount to be included in computing the taxpayer's income from the investment. This amount is determined, in general terms, by multiplying the cost amount of the taxpayer's investment by a factor based on interest rates prescribed under Part XLIII of the Regulations.

Section 94.1 is replaced by provisions in new sections 94.1 to 94.3, which contain rules governing the tax treatment of interests in foreign investment entities (FIEs). Under the new rules, a taxpayer's investment motives are no longer relevant. In computing a taxpayer's income for a taxation year, where a taxpayer so elects and has sufficient information to comply, new section 94.1 generally requires the inclusion of the taxpayer's share of FIE income for each FIE taxation year that ends in the taxpayer's taxation year. New section 94.2 applies in place of the rules in section 94.1 in all other cases. Under section 94.2, a taxpayer takes into account the annual increase or decrease in the fair market value of the taxpayer's interest in an FIE in computing the taxpayer's income from the FIE. Section 94.3 is designed to prevent double taxation with respect to amounts included in income under sections 94.1 and 94.2.

New section 94.1 applies to taxation years of Canadian investors that begin after 2000.

The table below provides an overview of new sections 94.1 to 94.3 and related provisions.

| Issue | Summary | References |
|---|---|---|
| 1. Which taxpayers are subject to the new FIE rules? | A. All taxpayers, except exempt taxpayers. Except as indicated in (C), below, FIE rules do not apply to non-resident taxpayers. | S. 94.1(2) to (4) and 94.2(3) and (4). "Exempt taxpayer" (s. 94.1(1)). Non-resident taxpayers: see also s. 94.1(3) and 94.2(5). |
| | B. Partnerships with members resident in Canada must allocate FIE income to those members. | Existing section 96, including exception in s. 96(1.9). See also s. 94.2(6) for application to cases where partnership members become resident in Canada. |
| | C. Controlled foreign affiliates. | New s. 95(2)(g.2). |
| 2. What property is subject to the new FIE rules? | A. Participating interests (other than exempt interests) in foreign investment entities. However, if no taxation year of an FIE has ended before the end of the taxpayer's taxation year, the FIE rules do not apply to the taxpayer for the taxpayer's year in respect of the FIE. | S. 94.1(2). The following definitions in s. 94.1(1): "entity", "non-resident entity", "foreign investment entity", "exempt interest" and "participating interest". |
| | B. Where property described in (A) is a right to acquire property or is not capital property, it is not subject to section 94.1 but it is subject to s. 94.2. | S. 94.1(4) and 94.2(3). |
| | C. Interests in non-resident entities, where those interests track returns in respect of investment property. This property is subject only to s. 94.2, not to s. 94.1. | S. 94.2(9). See also amended s. 91(1). |
| | D. Interests in certain foreign insurance policies. This property is subject only to s. 94.2, not s. 94.1. | S. 94.2(10). |
| 3. What is the difference in the tax treatment of FIE interests between s. 94.1 and s. 94.2? | A. Section 94.1. Taxes only investor's "share" of FIE's income (e.g., does not include FIE's share of unrealized gains). | S. 94.1(3). |
| | B. Section 94.2. Full appreciation/decline in fair market value recognized on an annual basis. | S. 94.2(4). |

Subdivision i — Shareholders of Non-Resident Corporations    S. 94.1(1) car

| Issue | Summary | References |
|---|---|---|
| 4. How will foreign affiliates of taxpayers resident in Canada be treated under new FIE rules? | Subject to s. 94.2(9) (tracked interests), a taxpayer's share of the capital stock of a controlled foreign affiliate is exempt from the new FIE rules. In certain cases, a taxpayer can elect to have a foreign affiliate treated as a controlled foreign affiliate. | Paragraph (a) of the definition "exempt interest". S. 94.1(12). |
| 5. If a non-resident corporation that is an FIE pays out dividends, how are these dividends taxed? | A. General principle: existing rules apply. | Existing s. 90 and 113. |
| | B. Relief provided to prevent double taxation. This relief extends to taxable distribution from other FIEs (e.g., trusts). | S. 94.3. |
| | C. Special rules in the event that the dividends paid to another FIE. | S. 94.1(5)A(g). |
| 6. In what circumstances is a taxpayer subject to sections 94.1 and 94.2, respectively? | A. S. 94.2 rule applies, except as expressly provided otherwise. | S. 94.1(2) to (4) and s. 94.1(3). |
| | B. Election to use s. 94.1 available. | S. 94.1(4) |
| | C. Requirement to use s. 94.2 where insufficient information to use s. 94.1. | S. 94.1(17) |
| | D. Requirement for FIEs to calculate own income with reference to s. 94.2. | S. 94.1(4)(e) |

| Issue | Summary | References |
|---|---|---|
| E. Requirement to use s. 94.2 in the case of properties described in 2(B), (C) and (D), above. | | See references in 2(B), (C) and (D). |

The table above reflects two main variations from the outline of the proposals put forward for consultation for foreign investment funds in the 1999 budget papers and the November 30, 1999 press release issued by the Minister of Finance. First, in recognition of the complexity associated with proposed section 94.1 and the likelihood that most investors will not have sufficient information to comply with the section, the simpler mark-to-market regime has been made the "default" regime. Second, there is no exemption provided for foreign investment funds that distribute their income annually for the following reasons:

- these distributions may not necessarily be subject to immediate Canadian income tax;
- such an exemption could inappropriately allow for the use of tiered structures under which a fund that distributes annually itself invests, directly or indirectly, in a foreign investment fund that does not distribute annually; and
- to provide equality of treatment between domestic and foreign investment funds, it would be necessary to use income for Canadian tax purposes for the purpose of such an exemption.

However, income of this nature is not generally calculated by foreign investment funds and would not normally be known by investors.

**94.1 Foreign Investment Entities — Accrual Treatment — (1) Definitions** — The definitions in this subsection apply in this section and sections 94.2 and 94.3.

**"carrying value"** at any time of property of an entity means [note also amendments announced in Sept. 7/00 news release and Backgrounder item #9 reproduced after 94.3 — ed.]

(a) where a balance sheet of the entity is prepared as of that time in accordance with accounting principles substantially similar to generally accepted accounting principles used in Canada, the balance sheet is distributed not later than three months after that time to holders of participating interests in the entity at that time and the property is valued in the balance sheet, the amount at which the property is valued in the balance sheet; and

(b) in any other case, the amount at which the property would be valued for the purpose of the entity's balance sheet as of that time if a balance sheet of the entity were prepared in accordance with generally accepted accounting principles used in Canada at that time.

**Technical Notes:** New subsection 94.1(1) of the Act defines a number of expressions for the purpose of section 94.1. These definitions are also relevant for the purposes of sections 94.2 and 94.3.

The "carrying value" of a property held by an entity at any time is the amount at which the property is valued as of that time for the purpose of the entity's balance sheet, except where

- the balance sheet was not prepared in accordance with accounting principles similar to generally accepted accounting principles used in Canada, or
- the balance sheet was not distributed within 3 months after that time.

The carrying value of a property is generally expected to be either the historical cost of the property or the fair market value of the property. In the event that a qualifying balance sheet is not prepared or distributed on a timely basis or the property is not expressly valued, a property's carrying value is the amount at which the property would have been valued using generally accepted accounting principles used in Canada.

The carrying value of property is relevant primarily for the purpose of determining whether a non-resident entity is an FIE. This determination is made at the end of the entity's taxation year. (For further detail, see the commentary on the definition "foreign investment entity".) However, it should be noted that the look-through rule in subsection 94.1(10) can affect the properties considered to be owned by an entity and the carrying values of the entity's properties. This look-through rule applies where the entity has a "significant interest" (defined in subsection 94.1(11)) in a corporation, partnership, or trust. For the purposes of the look-through rule, the time at which the determination of carrying value is made is the end of the taxation year of the first tier non-resident entity (whether or not lower tier entities share the same taxation year).

**Related Provisions**: 87(2)(j.95) — Amalgamations — continuing corporation; 94.1(10) — Deemed carrying value.

**"entity"** includes a trust, a corporation, an organization and a fund, but does not include a partnership unless a contrary intent is evident.

**Technical Notes**: An entity includes a trust, a corporation, an organization and a fund. Subject to the comments below, it does not include a partnership. The new rules are designed so that, in the case of partnerships, members' shares of incomes and losses are allocated in accordance with section 96 (including new subsection 96(1.9), described in the commentary below).

An "entity" does, however, include a partnership to the extent that this intent is evident in section 94.1. The intent is evident in the definition "carrying value" and paragraph 94.1(10)(c), as it may be necessary to determine the carrying value of the assets of a partnership because of the operation of subsection 94.1(10).

**Notes**: For a partnership, profits are flowed out to the partners through the rules in 96(1).

**"excluded investment business"** of a corporation in a period means an investment business of the corporation in the period where, throughout the part of the period during which the business was carried on, all or substantially all of the corporation's assets used or held in the business are participating interests or debt issued by one or more other corporations

(a) each of which is related to the corporation or is a corporation in which the corporation has a significant interest; and

(b) the principal business carried on by each of which in the period is not an investment business.

**Technical Notes**: An "excluded investment business" is a type of "investment business" (as described in the commentary below) that is provided favourable tax treatment. The favourable treatment arises because of the reference to "excluded investment business" in the definition "qualifying corporation". A publicly traded share issued by a "qualifying corporation" is generally an "exempt interest" to which the FIE regime in sections 94.1 and 94.2 does not apply. In addition, there is a reference to an "excluded investment business" in subsection 94.1(12) which permits an election to be made by a taxpayer to treat a foreign affiliate principally carrying on an excluded investment business as a controlled foreign affiliate of the taxpayer.

In general terms, an "excluded investment business" is a business of a corporation in which it finances the operations of related corporations that do not carry on investment businesses. Thus, an "excluded investment business" has a substantial link to active businesses (or, more precisely, to businesses that are not investment businesses).

More specifically, an "excluded investment business" of a particular corporation in a period is defined as an "investment business" of the particular corporation in the period where, throughout the part of the period throughout which the business was carried on, all or substantially all of the particular corporation's assets used or held in the business are participating interests or debt issued by one or more corporations:

- related to the particular corporation (or in which the particular corporation has a "significant interest", as defined in subsection 94.1(11)), and
- the principal businesses of which are not investment businesses.

**Related Provisions**: 94.1(11) — Significant interest.

**"exempt interest"** of a taxpayer in a foreign investment entity at any time means

(a) a participating interest held by the taxpayer at that time in a controlled foreign affiliate of the taxpayer;

(b) property held by the taxpayer at that time that is a share of a class of the capital stock of a particular corporation or a right to acquire a share of the class, where

(i) the class is, throughout the part of the taxpayer's taxation year that includes that time (which year is in this definition referred to as the "relevant year") during which shares of the class (or rights to acquire shares of the class) are held by the taxpayer, widely-held, actively traded on a regular basis and listed on a prescribed stock exchange, and

(ii) either

(A) the particular corporation's principal business was not an investment business in the period referred to in subparagraph (i), or

(B) the particular corporation is a qualifying corporation in the period referred to in subparagraph (i);

(c) where the taxpayer is a financial institution (within the meaning assigned by subsection 142.2(1)) in the relevant year, a participating interest that is a mark-to-market property (within the meaning assigned by subsection 142.2(1)) for that year; and

(d) a participating interest of the taxpayer in a testamentary trust that, before that time, has never been acquired for consideration.

**Technical Notes**: An "exempt interest" of a taxpayer in an FIE is each of the following properties:

- a participating interest held by the taxpayer in a controlled foreign affiliate of the taxpayer (including an affiliate that is a controlled foreign affiliate because of an election under new subsection 94.1(12)),
- as described in greater detail below, certain shares and options in respect of publicly traded corporations,
- where the taxpayer is a financial institution (as defined in subsection 142.2(1)), a participating interest held by the taxpayer that is mark-to-market property (as defined in that same subsection), and
- a participating interest in a testamentary trust, provided the interest has not been acquired for consideration.

The rules in sections 94.1 and 94.2 generally do not apply in respect of "exempt interests". In most cases, the time of determination for whether a property is an "exempt interest" in an entity is the end of a taxation year of the entity. See, in this regard, subsection 94.1(2).

As noted above, an exempt interest includes certain shares and options with respect to publicly traded FIEs. Given the definition "foreign investment entity", most non-resident financial institutions and real estate development companies, and some resource companies, are expected to be classified as FIEs. Consequently, shares issued by these entities (as well as options in respect of these shares) would be subject to the rules in section 94.1 or 94.2 if it were not for the definition "exempt interest". Under paragraph (b) of the definition "exempt interest", the FIE rules will not apply to a taxpayer's shares and rights to acquire shares of a class of the capital stock of a non-resident corporation held during a taxation year of the taxpayer where, in the period in the year during which the property was held:

- the class is widely held, actively traded and listed on a prescribed stock exchange (note: stock exchanges listed in section 3200 or 3201 of the Regulations are to be prescribed for this purpose), and
- either
  — the corporation's principal business was not an investment business (as defined in subsection 94.1(1) and described in the commentary below) in the period, or

— the corporation is a qualifying corporation in the period. (See commentary below on the definition "qualifying corporation".)

**Related Provisions**: 94.1(12) — Exemption by electing to use FAPI rules; 95(2)(g.2)(viii)(A) — Application to FAPI rules.

**"exempt taxpayer"** for a taxation year means

(a) an individual (other than a trust) who, before the end of the year, was resident in Canada for a period of, or periods the total of which is, not more than 60 months, but not including an individual who, before the end of the year, was never non-resident; and

(b) an entity the taxable income of which for a period any part of which occurs in the year is exempt from tax under this Part because of subsection 149(1) (otherwise than because of paragraph 149(1)(q.1), (t) or (z)).

**Technical Notes**: An individual is an "exempt taxpayer" for a taxation year where the individual, before the end of the year, was a resident of Canada for a period of, or periods the total of which is, 60 months or less. (Children who have always been resident in Canada cannot fall within the 60-month exception.)

The rules in new sections 94.1 and 94.2 do not apply in respect of periods during which a taxpayer qualifies as an exempt taxpayer, due to the reference to exempt taxpayers in paragraph 94.1(2)(a) and subsections 94.2(9) and (10). The 60-month exemption for new immigrants to Canada is similar to an exemption in the rules for non-resident trusts in existing section 94.

Tax-exempt entities to which subsection 149(1) applies are also included as exempt taxpayers. However, this inclusion does not apply to retirement compensation arrangements and qualifying environmental trusts for which alternative income tax rules are provided under Parts XI.3 and XII.4. The inclusion also does not apply to insurers to which paragraph 149(1)(t) applies, given the taxability of those insurers pursuant to subsection 149(4.1).

The express reference to tax-exempt entities is generally of significance for the purposes of calculating Part I tax only in the context of the narrow circumstances to which new subsection 94.2(16) applies. That subsection contemplates a case where a taxpayer ceases to be an "exempt taxpayer" and subsequently becomes an "exempt taxpayer". However, the reference to tax-exempt entities may also be of significance in the context of Part XI (foreign property limits), given that the application of sections 94.1 and 94.2 has an impact on the cost amount of participating interests in FIEs.

**Related Provisions**: 94.2(16) — Fresh start on change of status; 96(1.9) — Where exempt taxpayer is member of partnership.

**"foreign bank"** has the same meaning as in subsection 95(1).

**Technical Notes**: The definition "foreign bank" has the same meaning as in subsection 95(1). The expression is used in the definition "investment business".

**"foreign investment entity"** at any time means a non-resident entity at that time except where, at the end of its taxation year that includes that time,

(a) the entity would be an exempt foreign trust (within the meaning assigned by subsection

94(1)) if the definition "exempt trust" in subsection 233.2(1) were read without reference to paragraph (c) of that definition;

(b) the entity is

(i) a personal trust, and

(ii) not a non-discretionary trust; or

(c) the carrying value of all of the entity's investment property is not more than one-half of the carrying value of all of the entity's property.

**Technical Notes**: The new tax regime for FIEs in sections 94.1 and 94.2 generally applies only to participating interests in a foreign entity that is a "foreign investment entity".

A non-resident entity is generally a "foreign investment entity" throughout one of its taxation years where the total carrying value of its investment property is greater than 50% of the total carrying value of all of its property at the end of the year. In making this determination, the entity's property must be identified as either investment property or other property and it must be assigned a carrying value.

A foreign investment entity does not, however, include:

- an "exempt foreign trust" under subsection 94(1) (other than a widely-held mutual fund trust referred to in paragraph (c) of the definition "exempt trust" in existing subsection 233.2(1)), or

- a discretionary personal trust (or, more precisely, a trust that is not a "non-discretionary trust").

For more detail, see the commentary on the expressions "entity", "non-resident entity", "investment property" and "carrying value" in subsection 94.1(1). "Non-discretionary trust" is newly defined in subsection 248(1), with reference to the definition of the same expression in subsection 17(15).

Special rules in subsections 94.1(10) and (13) generally limit the circumstances in which a non-resident entity falls within the definition "foreign investment entity".

**Related Provisions**: 94.1(13) — Exception for qualifying dispositions and issues.

**"investment business"** of an entity in a period means a business carried on by the entity at any time in the period the principal purpose of which is to derive income from property (including interest, dividends, rents, royalties or any similar return on investment or any substitute for such a return), income from the insurance or reinsurance of risks, income from the factoring of trade accounts receivable, or profits from the disposition of indebtedness or properties described in any of paragraphs (a) to (d) or (f) to (l) of the definition "investment property", unless it is established that, throughout the part of the period during which the business was carried on by the entity, the business (other than any business conducted principally with persons with whom the entity does not deal at arm's length) is [note also exclusion announced in Sept. 7/00 news release and Backgrounder item #6 reproduced after 94.3 — ed.]

(a) a business carried on by the entity as a foreign bank, a trust company, a credit union or an insurance corporation, the activities of which are regulated under the laws of the country in which the business is principally carried on;

(b) the development of real estate for sale;

(c) the rental of real estate held by the entity if the management, maintenance, and other services in respect of the real estate are provided principally by the employees of the entity or of a corporation related to it; or

(d) the development of foreign resource property.

**Technical Notes**: The expression "investment business" is used in the definitions "exempt interest" and "investment property", as well as in subsection 94.1(12) (election to be a controlled foreign affiliate). The definition "investment business" is similar to the definition of the same expression in existing subsection 95(1). Note, however, that in this definition:

- there is no exception for traders and dealers in securities or for the lending of money, the leasing or licensing of property or the insurance or reinsurance of risks;

- there is a greater accommodation of real estate businesses and businesses involved in the development of foreign resource properties;

- there is no explicit requirement for a specific number of full-time employees for the exceptions to the definition to apply; and

- the supporting definitions and rules contained in subsections 95(1) to (2.4) are not relevant.

**Letter from Department of Finance, September 15, 2000**:

Dear [xxx]

We are responding to your letter dated July 26, 2000 concerning the draft legislation released by the Minister of Finance on June 22, 2000 dealing with foreign investment entities and non-residents trusts.

In particular, you are concerned that shares of a "high tech" corporation that derives its revenue from the licensing of its proprietary technology and software products would not be considered an exempt interest because the business of the corporation would be an investment business. Therefore, you are requesting confirmation that this result was not intended and that we would be prepared to recommend that the definition of investment business be amended to exclude such a business.

As you may be aware, the Minister of Finance announced on September 7, 2000, a number of modifications to the proposals. One of the proposed changes would modify the definition of investment business to exclude a business of developing or purchasing and developing of property for sale or licensing. This announcement should address your concerns.

Thank you for taking the time to express your views with respect to this matter.

Yours sincerely,

Brian Ernewein

Director, Tax Legislation Division, Tax Policy Branch

**Letter from Department of Finance, July 25, 2000**: See under 94.1(1) "participating interest".

## Subdivision i — Shareholders of Non-Resident Corporations   S. 94.1(1) par

**Related Provisions**: 87(2)(j.95) — Amalgamations — continuing corporation.

**"investment property"** of an entity includes property that is [note also exclusions announced in Sept. 7/00 news release and Backgrounder item #5 reproduced after 94.3 — ed.]

(a) a share of the capital stock of a corporation;

(b) an interest in a partnership;

(c) an interest in a trust;

(d) an interest in any other entity;

(e) indebtedness, other than accounts receivable that arose from the sale of tangible property or services in the ordinary course of a business of the entity that is not an investment business;

(f) an annuity;

(g) a commodity or commodity future purchased or sold, directly or indirectly in any manner whatever, on a commodities or commodities futures exchange (except a commodity manufactured, produced, grown, extracted or processed by the entity or a person to whom the entity is related, otherwise than because of a right referred to in paragraph 251(5)(b), or a commodity future in respect of such a commodity);

(h) real estate;

(i) a Canadian resource property or foreign resource property;

(j) currency;

(k) a derivative financial product (other than a commodity future to which the exception in paragraph (g) applies); or

(l) an interest, option, or right in respect of property included in any of paragraphs (a) to (k).

**Technical Notes**: The expression "investment property" includes a list of specified properties. Most of the specified properties (e.g., shares, partnership interests, real estate and resource properties) are also specified in the definition of the same expression in subsection 95(1). In addition to the properties also specified in the definition in subsection 95(1), "investment property" held by a particular entity includes:

- an interest in an organization, fund or other entity;
- most derivative financial products; and
- interests, options and rights in respect of the above properties.

It should be noted, however, that "investment property" in subsection 94.1(1) does not include accounts receivable that arise from the sale of tangible property or services in the ordinary course of a business (other than an "investment business", described above).

The definition is primarily relevant for purposes of the determining whether a non-resident entity is a "foreign investment entity".

**Related Provisions**: 94.1(12) — Election to use FAPI rules.

**Notes**: Since the opening words of 95(1) exclude that subsection from applying to 94–94.3, the definition of "investment property" in 95(1) does not apply even though this definition uses the word "includes" rather than "means".

**"non-resident entity"** at any time means

(a) a corporation or trust that is non-resident at that time; and

(b) any entity (other than a corporation or trust)

(i) organized under the laws of a jurisdiction outside Canada, or

(ii) the governance of which is provided at that time under the laws of a jurisdiction outside Canada.

**Technical Notes**: One of the requirements for an entity to be an FIE to which sections 94.1 and 94.2 apply is that the entity must be a "non-resident entity".

In addition to non-resident corporations and trusts, a "non-resident entity" includes any other type of entity

- organized under the laws of a jurisdiction outside Canada, or
- the governance of which is provided under the laws of a jurisdiction outside Canada.

**Related Provisions**: 94(3)(a) [proposed] — Application to trust deemed resident in Canada.

**Notes**: See Notes to 94.1(2).

**"participating interest"** in an entity means

(a) where the entity is a corporation,

(i) a share of the capital stock of the corporation, and

(ii) a right to acquire a share of the capital stock of the corporation;

(b) where the entity is a trust,

(i) a beneficial interest in the trust, and

(ii) a right to acquire a beneficial interest in the trust; and

(c) in any other case, an interest in the entity or a right to acquire an interest in the entity.

**Technical Notes**: A "participating interest" in an entity means a share of the capital stock of, or an interest in, the entity. It also includes a right to acquire such a share or interest. Section 94.1 or 94.2 generally applies to a taxpayer in respect of a participating interest in an FIE that is not an "exempt interest" of the taxpayer.

**Letter from Department of Finance, July 25, 2000**:

Dear [xxx]

I am responding to your letter dated July 17, 2000 concerning the draft legislation released by the Minister of Finance on June 22, 2000 on foreign investment entities and non-resident trusts. Your letter concerns the application of proposed new sections 94.1 and 94.2 of the *Income Tax Act* to the shareholders of [xxx] in respect of exchangeable shares that they are to receive as consideration for the disposition of shares of [Fxx] on the acquisition of control of [xxx].

We understand that [xxx] which is a corporation resident in the United States, is to incorporate a Canadian holding corporation (Holdco) to acquire the shares of [xxx] which is a corporation resident in Canada. We also understand that Holdco is to issue shares of its capital stock (Holdco shares) as consideration in respect of the acquisition by it of shares of the capital stock of [xxx] owned by the shareholders of [xxx] prior to the acquisition of control. The Holdco shares will provide the holder of the shares with a right to acquire shares issued by [xxx].

The proposed definition of "participating interest" in the June 22, 2000 draft legislation does not explicitly address shares issued by an entity that are exchangeable for the shares in the capital stock of a non-resident entity. However, it would be keeping with the policy intent underlying the legislation that shares issued by a Canadian entity which are exchangeable into the shares issued by a non-resident entity, generally be treated as a "participating interest" in the non-resident entity. This letter therefore makes the assumption that Holdco shares would be "participating interests" in [xxx] and that, for the purposes of the proposed definition "exempt interest", the right to acquire the [Qxx] shares has been exercised by the Holdco shareholders.

Based on these assumptions, the treatment of the holders of the Holdco shares under the proposed new rules will then depend on the status of [Qxx] as a foreign investment entity and the status of the [xxx] shares as an exempt interest in a foreign investment entity. If [xxx] is not a foreign investment entity or the [xxx] shares are an exempt interest, the rules in sections 94.1 and 94.2 (including proposed subsection 94.2(9)) would not be expected to apply to the holders of the Holdco shares.

You have told us that [xxx] has recently made two public offerings of shares and, as a consequence, more than 50% of the company's assets are cash and near cash, being "investment properties", as defined in proposed subsection 94.1(1). It is anticipated that the cash and near cash will be used in the next year to acquire active business property or fund active business operations. Because of proposed subsections 94.1(13) and (15), in general the cash or near cash raised in a taxation year can be ignored in determining if [xxx] is a foreign investment entity at the end of that year. In the event that the cash and near cash is not used as contemplated, we would expect that [xxx] would be a foreign investment entity at the end of its first taxation year that ends after the year in which the public offerings occurred.

If [xxx] a foreign investment entity, the question remains whether the [xxx] shares would be an "exempt interest". To qualify as an exempt interest, the [xxx] shares must be of a class that is widely held, actively traded and listed on a prescribed stock exchange and the [xxx] shares must satisfy one of two additional criteria. One of these criteria is that the principal business of [xxx] must not be an "investment business" as defined in proposed subsection 94.1(1). The proposed definition would include a business the principal purpose of which is to derive income from property including royalties.

It is understood that the gross revenue of [xxx] is derived principally from royalties paid in the respect of the use of software developed by [xxx]. Consequently, under the definition proposed, the business of [xxx] is an investment business. Therefore, the [xxx] shares would not qualify as an exempt interest under the June 22, 2000 draft legislation. We are of the view, however, that the treatment of such a business as an "investment business" is unintended from a policy perspective.

Consequently, we are prepared to recommend to the Minister of Finance that the definition of an investment business be modified. The proposed modification would provide that, where the principal purpose of a corporation's business is to earn income from property that is royalty income, that business will not be an investment business where the royalty income is derived principally from property that was developed, produced or created by the corporation. I trust that such a modification would address your concerns.

Yours sincerely,
Len Farber
General Director, Tax Legislation Division, Tax Policy Branch

**Related Provisions**: 94.2(12) — Cost of participating interest.

**"qualifying corporation"** in a period means a particular corporation all or substantially all of the assets of which are, throughout the period, any combination of

(a) properties (other than investment properties); and

(b) shares and debt issued by one or more other corporations each of which

(i) is, at any time in the period, a corporation all of the shares of which (other than directors' qualifying shares) are held by

(A) the particular corporation,

(B) a corporation related to the particular corporation, or

(C) any combination of corporations described in clauses (A) and (B), and

(ii) is either

(A) a corporation the principal business of which throughout the period is

(I) an excluded investment business, or

(II) a business that is not an investment business, or

(B) a qualifying corporation in the period.

**Technical Notes**: Shares issued by a qualifying corporation are generally exempt from the FIE regime in sections 94.1 and 94.2 because of the definition "exempt interest" (described in the commentary above), provided the shares are widely-held, actively traded and listed on a prescribed stock exchange.

In general terms, a "qualifying corporation" is a corporation that (directly or indirectly) finances the active business operations of related corporations.

More specifically, a "qualifying corporation" in a period is defined as a particular corporation all or substantially all of the assets of which are, throughout the period, any combination of:

• properties (other than investment properties), and

• shares or debt issued by one or more other corporations each of which

— is, at any time in the period, a corporation all of the shares of which (other than directors' qualifying shares) are held by any combination of the particular corporation and related corporations, and

— either

— has as its principal business an excluded investment business or a business (other than an investment business), or

— is itself a qualifying corporation in the period.

Reference should also be made to the commentary on the definition "excluded investment business".

**Related Provisions**: 87(2)(j.95) — Amalgamations — continuing corporation; 94.1(1)"exempt interest"(b)(ii)(B) — Share of qualifying corporation can be exempt interest.

**"taxation year"** of a non-resident entity means

(a) in the case of a corporation the accounts of which have ordinarily been made up for a period not exceeding 53 weeks, that period; and

(b) in any other case, a calendar year.

**Technical Notes**: The "taxation year" of a non-resident entity is a calendar year. However, if the entity is a corporation, its taxation year is the period, not exceeding 53 weeks, for which its accounts are ordinarily made up.

**(2) Conditions for application of tax regime for foreign investment entities** — [Note also amendments announced in Sept. 7/00 news release and Backgrounder items #1–3 reproduced after 94.3 — ed.] This subsection applies to a taxpayer for a particular taxation year in respect of a participating interest held in the particular year by the taxpayer in a non-resident entity where

(a) the taxpayer is not an exempt taxpayer for the particular year;

(b) a taxation year of the entity ended at or before the end of the particular year;

(c) at the end of the latest of the entity's taxation years referred to in paragraph (b), the entity was a foreign investment entity;

(d) if the interest or identical property to the interest was held by the taxpayer at the end of the latest of the entity's taxation years referred to in paragraph (b), none of the interest and each identical property was, at the end of that year, an exempt interest in respect of the taxpayer; and

(e) if neither the interest nor identical property to the interest was held by the taxpayer at the end of the latest of the entity's taxation years referred to in paragraph (b), none of the interest and each identical property was, at the latest time in the particular year at which the interest or identical property was held by the taxpayer, an exempt interest in respect of the taxpayer.

**Technical Notes**: New subsection 94.1(2) of the Act sets out the common conditions for the application of the FIE rules in section 94.1(3) (accrual regime) and 94.2(4) (mark-to-market regime). For the accrual or mark-to-market regimes to apply to a taxpayer for a particular taxation year in respect of a participating interest held in the particular year by the taxpayer in a non-resident entity, all of the following conditions set out in subsection 94.1(2) must be satisfied:

- the taxpayer is not an "exempt taxpayer" for the particular year; [Paragraph 94.12(2)(a).]

- a taxation year of the entity ended at or before the end of the particular year and, at the end of the latest such taxation year of the entity, the entity was an FIE; [Paragraphs 94.1(2)(b) and (c).]

- where the interest or identical property to the interest was held by the taxpayer at the end of the latest such year, the interest or the identical property was not an "exempt interest" in respect of the taxpayer; [Paragraph 94.1(2)(d).] and

- where neither the interest nor identical property to the interest were held by the taxpayer at the end of the latest such year, the interest and each identical property was not an exempt interest while held in the particular year by the taxpayer. [Paragraph 94.1(2)(e).]

**Related Provisions**: 87(2)(j.95) — Amalgamations — continuing corporation; 95(2)(g.2) — Application to FAPI rules.

**Notes**: If the non-resident trust rules in new s. 94 apply, the entity is deemed resident in Canada by 94(3)(a) and 94.1 does not apply since the entity is not a "non-resident entity"; thus 94 takes priority over 94.1.

**(3) Income inclusion and deduction** — Subject to subsection (4), where, at any time in a particular taxation year of a taxpayer, the taxpayer holds a participating interest, or two or more identical participating interests, in a non-resident entity and subsection (2) applies to the taxpayer for the particular year in respect of those interests, in computing the taxpayer's income for the particular year in respect of such of those interests that are held by the taxpayer at the end of a taxation year of the entity (in this subsection referred to as the "relevant interests") that ends in the particular year, except where the taxpayer is non-resident at the end of the entity's year,

(a) there shall be added the positive amount, if any, determined by the formula

$$A - B - C - D$$

where

A is the taxpayer's income allocation in respect of the relevant interests for the entity's year,

B is the taxpayer's loss allocation in respect of the relevant interests for the entity's year,

C is the specified tax allocation of the taxpayer for the entity's year in respect of the relevant interests, and

D is the amount, if any, by which

(i) the amount determined in respect of the taxpayer under subparagraph (b)(i) for the preceding taxation year of the entity in respect of the relevant interests or identical properties

exceeds

    (ii) the amount determined for that preceding year in respect of the taxpayer under subparagraph (b)(ii) in respect of the relevant interests or identical properties; and

(b) there may be deducted the lesser of

    (i) the absolute value of the negative amount, if any, determined by the formula in paragraph (a) in respect of the relevant interests for the entity's year, and

    (ii) the amount, if any, by which

        (A) the total of all amounts each of which is an amount added under paragraph (a) in computing the taxpayer's income in respect of the relevant interests or identical properties for a preceding taxation year of the entity

exceeds

        (B) the total of all amounts each of which is an amount deductible under this paragraph in computing the taxpayer's income in respect of the relevant interests or identical properties for a preceding taxation year of the entity.

**Technical Notes**: Where the accrual regime does apply to a taxpayer for a particular taxation year in connection with one or more of a taxpayer's identical participating interests in a non-resident entity, subsection 94.1(3) provides:

- The taxpayer's "income allocation" in respect of those interests for a taxation year of the entity ending in the particular year is added in computing the amount included in the taxpayer's income under subsection 94.1(3), to the extent that the taxpayer held those interests at the end of the entity's year. (However, in order to clarify the application of section 114 to part-year residents and to ensure that section 94.1 does not affect the taxability of non-resident taxpayers, subsection 94.1(3) does not apply to a taxpayer for a taxation year in respect of an FIE's taxation year that ends in the taxpayer's year where the taxpayer is not resident in Canada at the end of the FIE's year.)

- The taxpayer's "loss allocation" in respect of those participating interests is deductible to the extent that there has previously been a net cumulative positive balance determined under subsection 94.1(3) in respect of the taxpayer for such property in respect of preceding taxation years of the entity. An unused loss allocation is carried forward to offset the total amount otherwise required to be computing the taxpayer's income under subsection 94.1(3) in respect of identical participating interests for a subsequent taxation year of the entity.

- A taxpayer's specified tax allocation in respect of the entity's year is treated in the same way as a loss allocation. However, unlike a loss allocation, a specified tax allocation can arise for the same entity's year as an income allocation. Where this is the case, the specified tax allocation can directly offset the income allocation. A taxpayer's specified tax allocation, as determined under subsection 94.1(8), represents the taxpayer's grossed-up share or income of profits tax paid by the entity in the year on account of a liability for income or profits tax for the entity's year or an earlier year of the entity. The taxpayer's share of taxes in respect of the liability year is determined with reference to the taxpayer's position in the entity at the end of the liability year.

The examples after the commentary on subsections 94.1(5) and (6) illustrate the operation of subsection 94.1(3).

**Related Provisions**: 87(2)(j.95) — Amalgamations — continuing corporation; 94.1(4) — Exceptions; 94.1(5) — Income allocation; 94.1(7) — Loss allocation; 94.1(8) — Specified tax allocation; 94.3(2)(a)(ii) — Prevention of double taxation; 95(2)(g.2) — Application to FAPI rules.

**Notes**: The references to "positive amount" in (a) and "negative amount" in (b)(i) override the rule in s. 257.

**(4) Exceptions** — Subsection (3) applies to a taxpayer for a taxation year in respect of a participating interest held in the year by the taxpayer in a non-resident entity only where

(a) the taxpayer so elects in respect of the interest in prescribed form and files the election with the Minister not later than the taxpayer's filing-due date for the year;

(b) the taxpayer filed an election under paragraph (a) in respect of the interest (or property identical to it) for each preceding taxation year that began after 2000 and in which the interest or the identical property was held by the taxpayer;

(c) subsection (17) does not apply to the taxpayer for the year in respect of the interest;

(d) subsection 94.2(3) does not, because of subsection 94.2(9), apply to the taxpayer for the year or a preceding taxation year in respect of the interest or identical property to the interest;

(e) the taxpayer is not a foreign investment entity;

(f) the interest is not a right to acquire

    (i) shares of the capital stock of the entity, or

    (ii) an interest in the entity; and

(g) the interest would, if this Act were read without reference to subparagraph 39(1)(a)(ii.3) and section 94.2, be capital property.

**Technical Notes**: Notwithstanding the above, the mark-to-market regime, rather than the accrual regime, applies where the exceptions under subsection 94.1(4) apply. Subsection 94.1(4) provides that the accrual regime applies only to capital property and only where an election to use the accrual regime has been made at the earliest opportunity. Moreover, the accrual regime does not apply to a taxpayer for a taxation year in respect of a participating interest in a non-resident entity in the following cases:

- where section 94.1 does not apply because of the operation of subsection 94.1(17) (insufficient information),

- where, because of subsection 94.2(9) (tracked interests), subsection 94.2(3) applies or has applied to the taxpayer in respect of the interest or identical property,
- where the taxpayer is itself an FIE, [See commentary on paragraph 94.1(5)A(a) for more detail.] or
- where the interest is an option or similar right to acquire.

**Related Provisions**: 95(2)(g.2)(ix) — Application to FAPI rules; 96(3) — Election by members of partnership.

**(5) Income allocation** — For the purpose of subsection (3), the income allocation of a particular taxpayer in respect of a participating interest, or two or more identical participating interests, of the particular taxpayer in a foreign investment entity for a particular taxation year of the entity is the amount determined by the formula

$$A \times \frac{B}{C}$$

where

A is the amount that would be the income of the entity for the particular year if

(a) except for the purposes of section 91, paragraph (4)(e), subsection 107.4(1) and paragraph (f) of the definition "disposition" in subsection 248(1), the entity had been a taxpayer resident in Canada throughout the entity's existence,

(b) each property held by the entity at the beginning of the entity's fresh start year in respect of the particular taxpayer had been

(i) disposed of by the entity immediately before that time for proceeds equal to its fair market value at that time, and

(ii) reacquired by the entity at that time at a cost equal to that fair market value,

(c) for the entity's fresh start year in respect of the particular taxpayer and for each following taxation year of the entity, each deduction in computing the entity's income that is contingent on a claim by the entity had been claimed by the entity to the extent, and only to the extent, designated by the particular taxpayer in prescribed form filed with the Minister with the particular taxpayer's return of income for the particular taxpayer's taxation year in which that fresh start year or the following year, as the case may be, ends,

(d) the entity had deducted the greatest amounts that it could have claimed or deducted as a reserve under sections 20, 138 and 140 for its taxation year that precedes its fresh start year in respect of the particular taxpayer,

(e) for the purposes of applying sections 37, 65 to 66.4 and 66.7, the entity had not existed before the entity's fresh start year in respect of the particular taxpayer,

(f) this Act were read without reference to subsections 20(11) and (12) and 104(4) to (6),

(g) where the particular taxpayer is a corporation resident in Canada, dividends received by the entity in the particular year from a foreign affiliate of the particular taxpayer were included in computing the income of the entity for the particular year only where

(i) the particular taxpayer did not have a qualifying interest (within the meaning assigned by paragraph 95(2)(m)) in the affiliate at the time the dividends were received, or

(ii) taking into account the application of paragraphs (a) and (i), subsection 94.2(4) applied for the purpose of computing the entity's income for the particular year in respect of the entity's participating interest in the affiliate,

(h) where the entity holds at any time in the particular year a participating interest in a non-resident entity, the description of D in paragraph 94.2(4)(a) did not apply in respect of that interest, and

(i) the words "controlled foreign affiliate of the taxpayer" in paragraph (a) of the definition "exempt interest" referred to a controlled foreign affiliate of the particular taxpayer and not to a controlled foreign affiliate of the entity;

B is the fair market value of those interests at the end of the particular year; and

C is the fair market value of all participating interests in the entity (other than rights to acquire shares of the capital stock of, or interests in, the entity) at the end of the year.

**Technical Notes**: New subsection 94.1(5) of the Act provides for the calculation of a taxpayer's income allocation in respect of participating interests in an FIE. A taxpayer's income allocation in respect of one or more identical participating interest in an FIE held by the taxpayer at the end of the FIE's taxation year is included in computing the taxpayer's income under subsection 94.1(3). In general terms, a taxpayer's income allocation in respect of participating interests in an FIE is the proportion of the FIE's income for a taxation year that the fair market value of those interests is of the fair market value of all participating interests in the FIE.

The calculation of a taxpayer's income allocation in respect of an FIE depends on a calculation of income for the FIE in accordance with rules set out in paragraphs 94.1(5)A(a) to (i). The calculation for a particular taxpayer generally only takes into account an FIE's taxation years that end after the particular taxpayer first holds a participating interest in the FIE in a taxation year of the taxpayer that begins after 2000. The first such FIE taxation year in respect of a taxpayer is defined in subsection 94.1(6) as the "fresh start year" of the FIE in respect of the taxpayer. This permits taxpayers to make independent calculations of an FIE's income for the purpose of determining income allocations under section 94.1.

The special rules that apply in calculating an FIE's income in respect of an investor taxpayer for the FIE's fresh start year and subsequent years are as follows:

- Subject to three exceptions, the FIE is generally treated as having been a taxpayer resident of Canada throughout its existence. [Paragraph 94.1(5)A(a).] First, this rule does not apply for the purposes of proposed subsection 107.4(1) or proposed paragraph (f) of the definition "disposition" in subsection 248(1), [Proposed section 107.4 and a new definition "disposition" in subsection 248(1) are contained in a detailed Notice of Ways and Means Motion tabled on June 5, 2000.] with the result that property that is transferred to the FIE without there being any change in the beneficial ownership of the property is considered to have been transferred to the FIE under subsection 69(1) at the fair market value of the property. Second, this rule does not apply for the purposes of section 91 with the result that the FIE will not itself be required to include an amount in respect of foreign accrual property income in computing the FIE's income. Third, this rule does not apply for the purposes of paragraph 94.1(4)(e) with the result that section 94.2 (rather that section 94.1) potentially applies in the event that the FIE owns a participating interest in another FIE.

- Each property held by the FIE at the beginning of the fresh start year is deemed to have been disposed of for its fair market value immediately before that time and reacquired for the same amount at that time. [Paragraph 94.1(5)A(b). Compare paragraph 149(10)(b).]

- Each discretionary deduction permitted in computing the FIE's income for the FIE's fresh start year and subsequent taxation years is deemed to have been claimed to the extent designated by the investor taxpayer. Thus, in calculating an income allocation in respect of the FIE, the investor taxpayer will be permitted to claim deductions such as capital cost allowance. [Paragraph 94.1(5)A(c).]

- The FIE is assumed to have deducted the greatest amounts permissible, for its taxation year preceding the fresh start year, under sections 20, 138 and 140. [Paragraph 94.1(5)A(d). Compare paragraph 149(10)(a.1).] These amounts are added in computing the FIE's income for the fresh start year, but appropriate deductions under these sections can be claimed for the fresh start year and subsequent taxation years. In the context of the reserve for life insurers under subsection 138(3), it is intended to amend paragraph (c) of the definition "reported reserve" in subsection 1408(1) of the Regulations so that the FIE can have a "reported reserve".

- The FIE is deemed not to have been in existence before the fresh start year for the purposes of sections 37, 65 to 66.4 and 66.7. [Paragraph 94.1(5)A(e). Compare paragraph 149(10)(c).] As a consequence, the scientific research and resource expenditure pools to which these sections refer are ignored, to the extent that these pools were generated before the fresh start year.

- The FIE is not permitted to deduct any amount under subsection 20(11) or (12) in respect of its foreign tax. [Paragraph 94.1(5)A(f).] However, foreign tax will be taken into account because the FIE's specified tax allocation (as determined under new subsection 94.1(8)) can offset amounts otherwise included in income under subsection 94.1(3).

- If the FIE is a trust, no amount is considered deductible under subsection 104(6) in determining its income for the year. [Paragraph 94.1(5)A(f).] Double taxation for the investor taxpayer is avoided through the application of new subsection 94.3(2). In addition, no deemed disposition day under subsection 104(4) is determined in respect of the trust, whether or not the FIE falls outside the restricted meaning of "trust" for this purpose under subsection 108(1).

- If the investor taxpayer is a corporation resident in Canada and the FIE is a foreign affiliate of the taxpayer, any dividends received by the FIE from a foreign affiliate of the taxpayer in respect of which the taxpayer has a qualifying interest (as determined under paragraph 95(2)(m)) are not included in the FIE's income. [Paragraph 94.1(5)A(g).] Note, that this rule does not apply in the event that the FIE's interest in the foreign affiliate is subject to the mark-to-market regime in subsection 94.2(4). However, an income inclusion resulting from the application of subsection 94.2(4) for the FIE in some cases can, however, be offset by the deduction provided under new subsection 94.3(2).

- Where the FIE has an interest in another FIE, there is no "deferral amount" taken into account in computing the FIE's income pursuant to new subsection 94.2(4). [Paragraph 94.1(5)A(h).] (The fresh start rule described above eliminates the need for a "deferral amount".)

- Participating interests in controlled foreign affiliates of the investor taxpayer (rather than controlled foreign affiliates of the FIE) are treated as "exempt interests" of the FIE. [Paragraph 94.1(5)A(i).]

A taxpayer's income allocation in respect of a participating interest in a FIE is the proportion of an entity's income for a taxation year (determined in accordance with the special rules detailed above) that the fair market value at the end of the year of the participating interest is of the fair market value at that time of all participating interests in the entity (other than rights to acquire shares of the capital stock of, or to acquire interests in, the entity).

For further details, see the related commentary on the expressions "foreign investment entity", "exempt interest" in subsection 94.1(1), as well as the commentary on subsection 94.1(5) (income allocation), subsection 94.1(7) (loss allocation) and subsection 94.1(8) (specified tax allocation).

The examples below illustrate the operation of subsections 94.1(3) and (5). It should be noted in this context that any negative amount otherwise resulting from the formula in paragraph 94.1(3)(a) is deemed to be nil as a result of the application of section 257.

*Example 1*

Canco owns shares in the capital stock of FIE-1, which like Canco has a calendar taxation year. Canco's income (loss) allocations for 2001, 2002, 2003, 2004 and 2005 are (100), 25, 90, (20) and 50, respectively.

*Results*

1. The amount included under subsection 94.1(3) in Canco's income for 2001 is nil (B = 100). The amount determined under subparagraph 94.1(3)(b)(i) for 2001 is 100, which can be carried forward to 2002.
2. The amount included under paragraph 94.1(3)(a) in Canco's income for 2002 is nil (A = 25, D = 100). The amount determined under subparagraph 94.1(3)(b)(i) for 2002 is 75, which can be carried forward to 2003.
3. The amount included under paragraph 94.1(3)(a) in Canco's income for 2003 is 15 (A = 90, D = 75). The amount determined under subparagraph 94.1(3)(b)(i) for 2003 is nil.
4. The amount included under paragraph 94.1(3)(a) in Canco's income for 2004 is nil (B = 20, D = 0). The amount deductible under paragraph 94.1(3)(b) is 15 (= the lesser of 20 and 15). The remaining $5 unused loss allocation can be carried forward to 2005.
5. The amount included under paragraph 94.1(3)(a) in Canco's income for 2005 is $45 (A = 50, D = 5).

*Example 2*

Canco owns shares in the capital stock of FIE-1, which like Canco has a calendar taxation year. Canco's income (loss) allocations for 2001, 2002, 2003, 2004 and 2005 are: (100), (125), (175), 300 and 150.

*Results*

1. The amount included under subsection 94.1(3) in Canco's income for 2001 is nil (B = 100). The amount determined under subparagraph 94.1(3)(b)(i) for 2001 is 100 (= B), which can be carried forward to 2002.
2. The amount included under paragraph 94.1(3)(a) in Canco's income for 2002 is nil (B = 125, D = 100). The amount determined under subparagraph 94.1(3)(b)(i) for 2002 is 225 (= B+D), which can be carried forward to 2003.
3. The amount included under paragraph 94.1(3)(a) in Canco's income for 2003 is nil (B = 175, D = 225). The amount determined under subparagraph 94.1(3)(b)(i) for 2003 is 400 (= B+D).
4. The amount included under paragraph 94.1(3)(a) in Canco's income for 2004 is nil (A = 300, D = 400). The amount deductible under paragraph 94.1(3)(b) is nil (= the lesser of 100 and nil). The remaining $100 unused loss allocation (= D − A) can be carried forward to 2005.
5. The amount included under paragraph 94.1(3)(a) in Canco's income for 2005 is $50 (A = 150, D = 100).

*Example 3*

1. Canco, FIE-1 and ABC Inc. each have taxation years that coincide with calendar years and each issue only one class of shares.
2. Canco is a corporation resident in Canada that holds 20% of the shares of the capital stock of an FIE (FIE-1).
3. FIE-1 owns 75% of the shares of the capital stock of ABC Inc.
4. ABC Inc. is not an FIE, but would be a controlled foreign affiliate of FIE-1 if FIE-1 were resident in Canada. Although ABC Inc. is a foreign affiliate of Canco, it is not a controlled foreign affiliate of Canco.
5. FIE-1 earns $5,000 in interest income in 2001. It also receives a dividend of $1,000 from ABC Inc.
6. The fair market value of FIE-1's shares in ABC Inc. increases by $6,500 in 2001. This increase in value ignores the $1,000 dividend paid from ABC Inc. (i.e., the increase in value would have been about $1,000 higher if no such dividends had been paid).

*Results*

1. Under subsection 94.1(3), Canco is required to include in computing income its income allocation in respect of its shares in the capital stock of FIE-1. For this purpose, FIE-1's income is generally computed as if FIE-1 were resident in Canada.
2. FIE-1's income includes the $5,000 of interest income (as per paragraph 12(1)(c)). However, the $1,000 dividend from ABC Inc. is disregarded because of paragraph 94.1(5)A(g). Because of the reference to section 91 in paragraph 94.1(5)A(a), it is not necessary to make any foreign accrual property income calculation in respect of ABC Inc.
3. Canco must therefore include $1,000 (i.e., 20% × $5,000) in computing its income by virtue of subsection 94.1(3).

*Example 4*

Same facts as in example 3, except that ABC Inc. is itself an FIE.

*Results*

1. The mark-to-market rules in section 94.2 will apply in the calculation of FIE-1's income in respect of its interest in ABC Inc.. See, in this regard, paragraph 94.1(4)(e).
2. For the purpose of computing Canco's income allocation in respect of its shares in FIE-1, FIE-1's income would include the $5,000 of interest (as per example 3), but not include any share of foreign accrual property income (as per example 3). However, FIE-1's income would include the $1,000 dividend paid in addition to its gain determined under subsection 94.2(4) in respect of its participating interest in ABC Inc. This gain so determined is $7,500, which is equal to the $6,500 increase in the value of shares plus the $1,000 dividend paid. However, for the purposes of computing Canco's income allocation, a deduction for the $1,000 dividend is permitted for FIE-1 because subsection 94.3(2) would have permitted the deduction if FIE-1 had been resident in Canada.
3. Consequently, Canco's income allocation in respect of its shares of the capital stock of FIE-1 is equal to $2,500 [i.e., ($5,000 + $7,500 + $1,000 − $1,000) × 20%)]. This amount is required to be included in computing Canco's income under subsection 94.1(3).

**Related Provisions**: 94.1(6) — Fresh start year; 95(2)(g.2) — Application to FAPI rules; 96(3) — Election by members of partnership.

**(6) Fresh start year** — For the purpose of subsection (5), the fresh start year of a foreign investment entity in respect of a taxpayer is the first taxation year of the entity

(a) that ends in a taxation year of the taxpayer that begins after 2000; and

(b) any time in which the taxpayer holds a participating interest in the entity.

**Technical Notes**: See under 94.1(5).

**(7) Loss allocation** — For the purpose of subsection (3), the loss allocation of a taxpayer in respect of a participating interest, or two or more identical participating interests, of the taxpayer in a foreign investment entity for a taxation year of the entity is the amount that would, if paragraphs (a) to (i) of the description of A in subsection (4) applied, be determined by the formula

$$(A - B) \times \frac{C}{D}$$

where

A is the total of all amounts each of which is a loss of the entity for the year from business or property;

B is the amount determined under paragraph 3(c) in respect of the entity for the year;

C is the fair market value of those interests at the end of the year; and

D is the fair market value of all participating interests in the entity (other than rights to acquire shares of the capital stock of, or interests in, the entity) at the end of the year.

**Technical Notes**: A taxpayer's "loss allocation" in respect of the taxpayer's participating interest in an entity is relevant for the purposes of determining the amounts deductible and included in computing income under new subsection 94.1(3) of the Act. In general, a taxpayer's loss allocation in respect of an FIE is the proportion of the FIE's net loss for the year that the fair market value of the taxpayer's participating interest in the FIE is of the fair market value of all participating interests in the FIE. More specifically, a taxpayer's loss allocation in respect of a participating interest of a taxpayer in an entity for a taxation year of the entity is determined as follows:

- ADD the entity's total losses for the year from businesses and properties,
- SUBTRACT the amount determined under paragraph 3(c) for the entity for the year (i.e., the total amount of its income from business and property and taxable capital gains in excess of allowable capital losses for the year), and
- MULTIPLY any positive remainder by the percentage that the fair market value of the interest represents of the fair market value of all participating interests in the entity (other than rights to acquire participating interests).

The determination of a taxpayer's loss allocation is subject to the same special rules that apply for the purposes of computing a taxpayer's income allocation under subsection 94.1(5) (e.g., the entity is generally deemed to be resident in Canada).

**Related Provisions**: 257 — Formula cannot calculate to less than zero.

**(8) Specified tax allocation** — For the purpose of subsection (3), the **specified tax allocation** of a taxpayer for a particular taxation year of a non-resident entity in respect of a participating interest, or two or more identical participating interests, held by the taxpayer at the end of the particular year is the total of all amounts each of which is the amount determined, in respect of a taxation year of the entity (in this subsection referred to as the "liability year") that is the particular year or a preceding taxation year, by the formula

$$A \times (B/C) \times D$$

where

A is

(a) where the liability year ends in a taxation year of the taxpayer that begins after 2000, the income or profits tax paid in the particular year by the particular entity for the liability year, and

(b) in any other case, nil;

B is

(a) where the taxpayer did not hold those interests or identical properties at the end of the liability year, nil, and

(b) in any other case, the total fair market value of those interests and identical properties that are held by the taxpayer at the end of the liability year;

C is the fair market value of all participating interests in the entity (other than rights to acquire shares of the capital stock of, or interests in, the entity) at the end of the liability year; and

D is the taxpayer's relevant tax factor (within the meaning assigned by subsection 95(1)) for the particular year.

**Technical Notes**: Under new subsection 94.1(3) of the Act, a taxpayer is entitled to deduct the taxpayer's specified tax allocation in computing income, provided that sufficient amounts are otherwise included under subsection 94.1(3) in computing the taxpayer's income.

A taxpayer's specified tax allocation for an entity's taxation year in respect of a participating interest in an entity is determined under subsection 94.1(8). It represents the total of the taxpayer's shares of "grossed-up" taxes paid by the entity in the entity's year in respect of the entity's liability for income or profits taxes for the entity's year and preceding taxation years of the entity. The taxpayer's share is based on the taxpayer's percentage fair market value interest in the entity at the end of each of the entity's taxation years to which the tax liability relates. The gross-up available to a taxpayer is equal to 163% for corporations and 100% for individuals, as a result of the taxpayer's share of income profits being multiplied by the relevant tax factor (2.63 for corporations and 2 for individuals).

Income or profits tax is normally expected to be tax that is paid by an entity to a foreign government. However, it could also include income tax paid to the government of Canada or a province with respect to income earned by the entity from Canadian sources. In each case, only income or profits tax payable for taxation years of entities that end in a taxation year of a taxpayer that begins after 2000 is taken into account.

Subdivision i — Shareholders of Non-Resident Corporations  S. 94.1(10)(b)

The example below illustrates the operation of subsections 94.1(3) and (8).

*Example*

In 1998, Mireille (a resident of Canada) purchased a 30% participating interest in an entity (FIE-1) that is an FIE. The rate of foreign tax applicable to FIE-1's income is 20%. FIE-1's taxation years coincide with calendar years. For the purposes of computing Mireille's income allocation and loss allocation in respect of the interest, the income (loss) and the foreign tax of FIE-1 for taxation years 2001 to 2004 are as follows:

| Year | 2001 | 2002 | 2003 | 2004 | Total |
|---|---|---|---|---|---|
| Income (loss) | $100,000 | (120,000)** | $95,000 | $130,000 | $205,000 |
| Foreign tax paid* | $20,000 | Nil | Nil | $21,000 | $41,000 |

**Notes:**

\* Assume foreign tax paid in the same taxation year as liability arose.

\*\* Assume that an equivalent amount is carried forward under the laws of the relevant foreign jurisdiction to reduce FIE-1's tax liabilities after 2002.

*Results*

Mireille's income allocations, loss allocations and specified tax allocations are shown in the table below, as are the resulting income inclusions and deductions under subsection 94.1(3). The specified tax allocations in the table below are obtained by multiplying the related figures in the above table by 30% (Mireille's percentage interest) and 2 (specified tax factor for Mireille). For example, for 2001 Mireille's specified tax allocation is $12,000 ($20,000 × 30% × 2).

| Year | 2001 | 2002 | 2003 | 2004 |
|---|---|---|---|---|
| A. Income allocation | $30,000 | nil | $28,500 | $39,000 |
| B. Specified tax allocation | $12,000 | nil | nil | $12,600 |
| C. Loss allocation (used) | nil | $18,000 | nil | nil |
| D. Carry-forward offset used | nil | nil | $18,000 | nil |
| E. Loss allocation/ tax allocation to carryforward | nil | $18,000 | nil | nil |
| Amount included in income under subsection 94.1(3) (A - B - C - D) | $18,000 | nil | $10,500 | $26,400 |
| Amount deducted in computing income under subsection 94.1(3) (D + C + B - A) | nil | $18,000 | nil | nil |

**(9) Adjusted cost base** — In computing the adjusted cost base to a taxpayer of a participating interest in an entity at and after the end of a taxation year of the entity,

(a) there shall be added the amount, if any, added under subsection (3) in computing the taxpayer's income in respect of the interest for the entity's year (or that would have been so added if this Act were read without reference to subsection 56(4.1) and sections 74.1 to 75); and

(b) there shall be deducted the amount, if any, deducted under subsection (3) in computing the taxpayer's income in respect of the interest for the entity's year (or that would have been so deducted if this Act were read without reference to subsection 56(4.1) and sections 74.1 to 75).

**Technical Notes**: New subsection 94.1(9) of the Act provides for adjustments to the adjusted cost base (ACB) of a participating interest in an entity held by a taxpayer.

Paragraph 94.1(9)(a) provides for an addition to the ACB of a participating interest held by a taxpayer at the end of a taxation year of the entity, in respect of an amount included in computing the taxpayer's income under subsection 94.1(3) in respect of the interest and the year. Conversely, paragraph 94.1(9)(b) provides for a reduction to the ACB of a participating interest held by a taxpayer at the end of a taxation year of the entity, in respect of amounts deducted in computing the taxpayer's income under subsection 94.1(3) in respect of the interest and the year.

**Related Provisions**: 53(1)(m.1) — Addition to adjusted cost base; 53(2)(w) — Deduction from adjusted cost base; 87(2)(j.95) — Amalgamations — continuing corporation.

**(10) Property deemed owned by an entity** — Where at any time a particular entity has a significant interest in a corporation, a partnership or a non-discretionary trust, for the purposes of this section and section 94.2 [note also exclusion of debt owing to arm's length financial institutions announced in Sept. 7/00 news release and Backgrounder item #8 reproduced after 94.3 — ed.],

(a) the carrying value at that time of each participating interest held at that time by the particular entity in the corporation, partnership or trust (and of each debt owing to the particular entity by the corporation, partnership or trust that is investment property of the particular entity) is deemed to be nil;

(b) the property owned at that time by the corporation is deemed to be owned at that time by the particular entity and to have a carrying value at that time equal to the amount determined by the formula

$$A \times B/C$$

where

A is the carrying value of the property to the corporation at that time,

B  B is the total of

(i) the fair market value at that time of the shares of the corporation owned at that time by the particular entity, and

(ii) the fair market value at that time of debts (other than debts that are not investment properties) owing at that time to the particular entity by the corporation, and

C is the total of

    (i) the fair market value at that time of all the issued shares of the corporation outstanding at that time, and

    (ii) the fair market value at that time of debts owing at that time by the corporation (other than debts that are not investment properties);

(c) the property owned at that time by the partnership is deemed to be owned at that time by the particular entity and to have a carrying value at that time equal to the amount determined by the formula

$$D \times E/F$$

where

D is the carrying value of the property to the partnership at that time,

E is the total of

    (i) the fair market value of the interests in the partnership owned at that time by the particular entity, and

    (ii) the fair market value of debts (other than debts that are not investment properties) owing at that time to the particular entity by the partnership, and

F is the total of

    (i) the fair market value at that time of all interests in the partnership, and

    (ii) the fair market value at that time of debts owing by the partnership (other than debts that are not investment property); and

(d) the property owned at that time by the trust is deemed to be owned at that time by the particular entity and to have a carrying value at that time equal to the amount determined by the formula

$$G \times H/I$$

where

G is the carrying value of the property to the trust at that time,

H is the total of

    (i) the fair market value of the interests in the trust owned at that time by the particular entity, and

    (ii) the fair market value of debts (other than debts that are not investment properties) owing at that time to the particular entity by the trust, and

I is the total of

    (i) the fair market value at that time of all interests in the trust, and

    (ii) the fair market value at that time of debts owing by the trust (other than debts that are not investment properties).

**Technical Notes**: New subsections 94.1(10) and (11) of the Act are relevant in determining whether a non-resident entity is an FIE. A non-resident entity is generally an FIE at any time if the carrying value of all of the entity's "investment property" is more than 50% of the "carrying value" of all its property at the end of the entity's taxation year that includes that time.

Where at any time an entity has a "significant interest" (as described below) in a corporation, partnership or non-discretionary trust, in determining the carrying value at that time of the entity's property, the carrying values of the entity's "participating interests" (as described in the commentary above) in the corporation, trust or partnership are deemed to be nil. Debt that is investment property (and that is owing to the entity by the corporation, partnership or trust) is also deemed to have a carrying value to the entity of nil. Instead, the entity is deemed to own the property of the corporation, trust or partnership. Each such property is deemed to have a carrying value to the entity based on the product of the property's carrying value to the corporation, trust or partnership and a percentage based on:

- the entity's percentage relative ownership (determined with reference to fair market value) of shares or interests in the corporation, partnership or trust, as the case may be, and

- the entity's percentage relative ownership (determined with reference to fair market value) in debt issued by the corporation, partnership or trust (other than debts that are not investment property), as the case may be.

Subsection 94.1(10) is intended to operate on an iterative basis. Thus, if there are tiers of entities each of which has a significant interest in the other, the intended effect of subsection 94.1(10) is to deem higher tier entities to own properties of lower tier entities on an iterative basis. For example, assume a non-resident entity (Foreignco-1) owns 100% of the shares in Foreignco-2 which in turn only owns 100% of shares in Foreignco-3 and that Foreignco-1, Foreignco-2 and Foreignco-3 have identical taxation year ends. The carrying values from properties in Foreignco-3 would, under subsection 94.1(10), become the carrying values of properties in Foreignco-2. Because subsection 94.1(10) operates on an iterative basis, the carrying value of those properties would be considered to be the carrying values of properties held by Foreignco-1.

**Related Provisions**: 94.1(11) — Significant interest; 94.2(2)(b) — Application of rule to s. 94.2; 94.2(9) — Tracked interests.

**(11) Significant interest in an entity** — For the purposes of subsection (10) and section 94.2, an entity has a **significant interest** in [note also extension to related persons announced in Sept. 7/00 news release and Backgrounder item #7 reproduced after 94.3 — ed.]

    (a) a corporation at any time if at that time the entity holds shares of the capital stock of the corporation

        (i) that would give the entity 25% or more of the votes that could be cast under all circum-

Subdivision i — Shareholders of Non-Resident Corporations    S. 94.1(12)(f)

stances at an annual meeting of shareholders of the corporation, and

(ii) having a fair market value of 25% or more of the fair market value of all of the issued and outstanding shares of the corporation;

(b) a partnership at any time if at that time the entity holds an interest in the partnership having a fair market value of 25% or more of the fair market value of all interests in the partnership; and

(c) a non-discretionary trust at any time if at that time the entity holds interests in the trust having a fair market value of 25% or more of the fair market value of all interests in the trust.

**Technical Notes**: New subsection 94.1(11) sets out the circumstances in which an entity is considered to have a "significant interest" in a corporation, partnership or non-discretionary trust for the purposes of subsection 94.1(10). An entity is considered to have a significant interest in a corporation, partnership, or non-discretionary trust where it holds shares or interests in the corporation, partnership or trust that have a fair market value equal to 25% or more of the fair market value of all the shares or interests in the corporation, partnership or trust and, in the case of a corporation the entity has shares entitling the entity to cast at least 25% of votes at an annual shareholders' meeting of the corporation.

The example below illustrates the operation of subsection 94.1(10).

*Example*

1. Jean, who resides in Canada, holds a participating interest in Foreignco, a non-resident corporation that is not a controlled foreign affiliate of Jean. Foreignco's principal activity is the carrying on of investment activities on behalf of its shareholders. Foreignco prepares its financial statements in accordance with accounting principles substantially similar to generally accepted accounting principles used in Canada.

2. The carrying values of Foreignco's assets at the end of its taxation year ending in the taxpayer's year are as follows:

| | |
|---|---:|
| guaranteed investment certificate | $10,000 |
| shares of XYZ Inc. in which Foreignco has a significant interest | $20,000 |
| shares of ABC Inc. in which Foreignco does not have a significant interest | $ 5,000 |
| cash | $ 4,000 |
| Total assets | $39,000 |

3. XYZ Inc. owns assets at that time that are used in the course of carrying on an active business, with a carrying value of $80,000. It also has investment property with a carrying value of $15,000.

4. The fair market value of the shares of XYZ Inc. held by Foreignco is $40,000 while the fair market value of all the issued and outstanding shares of XYZ Inc. is $100,000 at that time.

*Results*

1. The guaranteed investment certificate, cash, and the shares of XYZ Inc. and ABC Inc. are all investment property by virtue of the definition "investment property" in subsection 94.1(1).

2. However, since Foreignco owns a significant interest in XYZ Inc., the special look-through rule in new subsection 94.1(10) applies. Under this look-through rule the carrying value of Foreignco's shares in XYZ Inc. is deemed to be nil. Instead, Foreignco is deemed to own the property that XYZ Inc. owns.

3. The carrying value of the XYZ property deemed to be owned by Foreignco is 40% of its carrying value to XYZ, since Foreignco's percentage ownership of shares is 40%.

4. Consequently, the carrying values of the investment property of Foreignco are:

| | |
|---|---:|
| guaranteed investment certificate | $10,000 |
| shares of XYZ Inc. | nil |
| shares of ABC Inc. | $ 5,000 |
| cash | $ 4,000 |
| investment property of XYZ Inc. (40% of $15,000) | $ 6,000 |
| Total | $25,000 |

5. The total carrying value of the assets of Foreignco is:

| | |
|---|---:|
| Investment property (see above) | $ 25,000 |
| assets of XYZ Inc. (other than investment property) (40% of $80,000) | $ 32,000 |
| Total | $ 57,000 |

6. As a result, Foreignco is not an FIE because less than 50% of the carrying value of its property is investment property.

**Related Provisions**: 94.2(2)(b) — Application of rule to s. 94.2.

**Notes**: This definition is intended to apply to 94.1(1)"excluded investment business"(a) as well, but technically it does not.

**(12) Entity treated as controlled foreign affiliate** — Where

(a) at a particular time in a particular taxation year of a taxpayer, the taxpayer, or a particular controlled foreign affiliate of the taxpayer, holds a participating interest in a non-resident entity,

(b) a taxation year of the entity ends at or before the end of the particular year,

(c) the principal business of the entity in the particular year is an excluded investment business or a business that is not an investment business,

(d) the entity is, at the end of the particular year, a foreign affiliate of the taxpayer in respect of which the taxpayer has a qualifying interest (as defined in paragraph 95(2)(m)),

(e) the taxpayer elects in prescribed form in the taxpayer's return of income for the particular year, and

(f) the taxpayer has not elected under this subsection in respect of the entity for any taxation year of the taxpayer that precedes the particular year, subject to subsection (17), the entity is deemed to be a controlled foreign affiliate of the taxpayer throughout the period

    (g) that begins at the earliest time in the particular year at which the entity is a foreign affiliate of the taxpayer, and

    (h) that ends at the earlier of

        (i) the earliest subsequent time at which the entity is not a foreign affiliate of the taxpayer, and

        (ii) the end of the first subsequent taxation year of the taxpayer in which the principal business of the entity is an investment business (other than an excluded investment business).

**Technical Notes**: New subsection 94.1(12) of the Act permits a taxpayer to make an irrevocable election to treat its foreign affiliate (including an affiliate the shares which are held by the taxpayer's controlled foreign affiliate) as a controlled foreign affiliate for a particular taxation year and subsequent taxation years. This one-time election is available only if:

- a taxation year of the affiliate ends at or before the end of the particular year,
- the taxpayer has a "qualifying interest" (as defined in paragraph 95(2)(m)) in the affiliate, and
- the principal business of the affiliate is an excluded investment business or a business that is not an investment business (as defined in subsection 94.1(1)).

The election must be made in prescribed form in the taxpayer's tax return for the year. However, under subsection 94.1(17), the election may be rendered invalid in the event that the taxpayer cannot provide sufficient information to the Minister of National Revenue for the Minister to be able to determine amounts required to be included in the taxpayer's income under section 91. In addition, the election no longer has any effect if the corporation ceases to be a foreign affiliate of the taxpayer or once the entity's principal business is an investment business (other than an excluded investment business).

In the period during which such an election is effective, a foreign affiliate of a taxpayer is deemed to be a controlled foreign affiliate of the taxpayer. As a result, a share issued by the affiliate to the taxpayer would be an "exempt interest" under the definition in subsection 94.1(1). Sections 94.1 and 94.2 generally would not apply to the taxpayer's participating interest in the affiliate. However, the foreign accrual property income (FAPI) rules would apply and the taxpayer would be required to include in income under section 91 a percentage of any FAPI derived by the affiliate in the year. Notwithstanding an election under subsection 94.1(12), section 94.2 may still apply in the event that a taxpayer's interest in a controlled foreign affiliate is a tracked interest to which subsection 94.2(9) applies.

**Related Provisions**: 17(15) — Subsec. 94.1(12) ignored for CFA definition under s. 17; 87(2)(j.95) — Amalgamations — continuing corporation; 94.1(16), (17) — Where demand for information not satisfied; 95(1)"controlled foreign affiliate" — CFA under 94.1(12) is a CFA for ss. 90–95; 96(3) — Election by members of partnership.

**(13) Exception for qualifying dispositions and issues** — For the purpose of determining whether an entity is a foreign investment entity at the end of a taxation year of the entity in which a qualifying disposition of that or another entity, or a qualifying issue of that or another entity, occurred, each investment property received by either entity as consideration for the qualifying disposition or the qualifying issue, and investment property substituted therefor, is deemed to have a carrying value of nil.

**Technical Notes**: New subsection 94.1(13) of the Act provides a special rule under which investment property is deemed to have a carrying value of nil.

Subsection 94.1(13) applies where there is a "qualifying disposition" (as defined in subsection 94.1(14)) or a "qualifying issue" (as defined in subsection 94.1(15)).

**Related Provisions**: 94.1(14) — Qualifying disposition; 94.1(15) — Qualifying issue.

**(14) Qualifying disposition** — For the purpose of subsection (13), a **qualifying disposition** of an entity is a transaction or part of a series of transactions or events as a consequence of which the entity disposes, to a person with whom the entity deals at arm's length, of all or substantially all of the assets used or held for the purpose of gaining or producing income from a business (other than an investment business) carried on by it.

**Technical Notes**: A "qualifying disposition" of an entity occurs where the entity disposes of all or substantially all of its assets used or held in a business (other than an investment business, as defined in the commentary above) in an arm's length transaction, either in a single transaction or as part of a series of transactions or events.

**(15) Qualifying issue** — For the purpose of subsection (13), a **qualifying issue** of an entity is an issue by the entity of a debt of, or a participating interest in, the entity to a person or partnership, otherwise than as part of a series of transactions or events that includes the disposition of a debt of, or a participating interest in, the entity (or another entity with which the entity does not deal at arm's length) by

    (a) the person or partnership (or another person or partnership with which the person or partnership does not deal at arm's length);

    (b) a trust in which the person or partnership (or another person or partnership with which the person or partnership does not deal at arm's length) is beneficially interested; or

    (c) a partnership in which the person or partnership (or another person or partnership with which the person or partnership does not deal at arm's length) has a direct or indirect interest.

**Technical Notes**: A "qualifying issue" of an entity is essentially an issue to a person or partnership of a debt or participating interest, but with the qualification that a qualifying issue does not arise if the issue is part of a series of transactions or events that also includes the disposition of a debt or participating interest in the entity (or another non-arm's length entity) by the same person or partnership (or certain other non-arm's length parties). This qualification is meant to prevent the circular flow of funds from and to an entity giving rise to a "qualifying issue".

Where an entity has a "qualifying disposition" or "qualifying issue", the consideration received by the entity (cash, shares, and debt) will in most cases be "investment property", as defined in subsection 94.1(1). As a result, the entity (or another entity that has a significant interest in the entity) might otherwise become an FIE. To allow a potential grace period before an entity is classified as an FIE, investment property received as consideration received on the sale of the business or on a qualifying issue (and each investment property substituted for the investment property so received) is deemed, at the end of the taxation year in which the qualifying disposition or qualifying issue took place, to have a carrying value of nil.

**(16) Demand for information** — Subsection (17) applies to a taxpayer for a taxation year of the taxpayer where

(a) the Minister demands, in writing, from the taxpayer additional information for the purpose of enabling the Minister to make a determination of an amount that, but for subsection (17), would be required to be added or deducted (otherwise than under subsection 104(13)) in computing the income of the taxpayer for the year

(i) because of the application of section 91 and an election under subsection (12), or

(ii) because of the application of subsection (3) to a participating interest in an entity; and

(b) sufficient information to make the determination is not delivered to the Minister within 60 days (or within such longer period as is acceptable to the Minister) after the Minister sends the demand.

**Technical Notes**: New subsections 94.1(16) and (17) of the Act provide for the application of the mark-to-market rules in section 94.2 to a participating interest in an FIE, if insufficient information is available to determine amounts required to be added or deducted in a taxpayer's income in respect of the interest under subsection 94.1(3). The information required for this purpose would include a calculation of taxable capital gains from dispositions, calculated in Canadian dollars and with reference to the assumptions for the calculation of income set out in subsection 94.1(5).

If this information is not made available to the Minister on a timely basis on demand in respect of a participating interest in an entity, subsection 94.1(17) effectively provides that the rules in section 94.2, rather than the rules in section 94.1, apply in respect of the entity.

Similar rules apply in the event that insufficient information is provided to enable the appropriate calculation of a taxpayer's income arising from an election under subsection 94.1(12). The latter election would otherwise permit an affiliate to be treated as a controlled foreign affiliate. If insufficient information is provided in this context, the mark-to-market rules in section 94.2 will generally apply to the taxpayer if the affiliate is an FIE.

**(17) Effect of insufficient information** — Where this subsection applies to a taxpayer for a taxation year because of subsection (16), for the purpose of computing the taxpayer's income for the year and following taxation years,

(a) where paragraph (16)(a) applies because of subparagraph (16)(a)(i),

(i) the election referred to in that subparagraph is deemed not to have been made, and

(ii) subsection (3) shall not apply in respect of the foreign affiliate that was the subject of the election; and

(b) where paragraph (16)(a) applies because of subparagraph (16)(a)(ii), subsection (3) shall not apply in respect of the entity referred to in that subparagraph.

**Technical Notes**: See under 94.1(16).

**Definitions [s. 94.1]**: "adjusted cost base" — 54, 248(1); "amount", "annuity" — 248(1); "arm's length" — 251(1); "business" — 248(1); "Canada" — 255, *Interpretation Act* 35(1); "Canadian resource property" — 66(15), 248(1); "capital property" — 54, 248(1); "carrying value" — 94.1(1), (10); "controlled foreign affiliate" — 94.1(12), 95(1), 248(1); "corporation" — 248(1), *Interpretation Act* 35(1); "credit union", "disposition", "dividend", "employee" — 248(1); "entity" — 94.1(1); "estate" — 104(1), 248(1); "excluded investment business", "exempt interest", "exempt taxpayer" — 94.1(1); "exempt foreign trust" — 94(1); "filing-due date" — 248(1); "foreign affiliate" — 95(1), 248(1); "foreign bank" — 94.1(1), 95(1); "foreign investment entity" — 94.1(1), (13); "foreign resource property" — 66(15), 248(1); "fresh start year" — 94.1(6); "income allocation" — 94.1(5); "individual", "insurance corporation" — 248(1); "investment business", "investment property" — 94.1(1); "loss allocation" — 94.1(7); "Minister" — 248(1); "month" — *Interpretation Act* 35(1); "non-discretionary trust" — 17(15), 248(1); "non-resident" — 248(1); "non-resident entity", "participating interest" — 94.1(1); "owned" — 94.1(10); "partnership" — see Notes to 96(1); "person", "personal trust", "prescribed" — 248(1); "prescribed stock exchange" — Reg. 3200, 3201; "property" — 248(1); "qualifying corporation" — 94.1(1); "qualifying disposition" — 94.1(14); "qualifying issue" — 94.1(15); "qualifying share" — 192(6), 248(1); "related" — 251(2)–(6); "relevant tax factor" — 95(1); "resident in Canada" — 250; "share", "shareholder" — 248(1); "significant interest" — 94.1(11); "specified tax allocation" — 94.1(8); "taxable income" — 248(1); "taxation year" — 94.1(1), 249; "taxpayer" — 248(1); "testamentary trust" — 108(1), 248(1); "trust" — 104(1), 248(1), (3); "writing" — *Interpretation Act* 35(1).

## 94.2 Foreign Investment Entities — Mark-to-market — (1) Definitions — In this section,

(a) the definitions in subsection 94.1(1) apply;

**Technical Notes**: New section 94.2 of the Act sets out new rules for the taxation of interests in FIEs.

Except as otherwise indicated, section 94.2 applies to taxation years of investors that begin after 2000.

New subsection 94.2(1) of the Act provides that the definitions in subsection 94.1(1) apply for the purposes of section 94.2.

(b) subject to subsections (6) and (13) to (17), **"deferral amount"** of a taxpayer in respect of a participating interest in an entity means the positive or negative amount determined by the formula

$$A \times (B - C)$$

where

A is

(i) if on June 22, 2000 the interest was capital property held by the taxpayer, 2/3, and

(ii) in any other case, 1 [to be changed to 2/3; see Sept. 7/00 news release and Backgrounder item #4 reproduced after 94.3 — ed.],

B is

(i) the fair market value of the interest at the first time in a particular taxation year of the taxpayer at which the taxpayer was resident in Canada where

(A) the taxpayer held the interest at the end of the preceding taxation year,

(B) at the end of that preceding year, the taxpayer was resident in Canada or the interest was taxable Canadian property,

(C) subsection (4) did not apply to the taxpayer for the purpose of computing the taxpayer's income in respect of the interest for any preceding taxation year, and

(D) subsection (4) applies to the taxpayer for the purpose of computing the taxpayer's income in respect of the interest for the particular year, and

(ii) nil in any other case, and

C is

(i) if subparagraph (i) of the description of B applies in respect of the interest, the cost amount of the property immediately before the first time in the particular year at which the taxpayer was resident in Canada, and

(ii) nil in any other case; and

**Technical Notes**: Subsection 94.2(1) also sets out the definitions "deferral amount" and "gross-up factor".

The deferral amount of a taxpayer generally represents the gain or loss (or, in the event that the interest was capital property held by the taxpayer on June 22, 2000, two-thirds of the gain or loss) in respect of the interest accrued to the time when the interest first became subject to the operation of the rules in section 94.2. The expression "deferral amount" in respect of a participating interest in an entity applies principally for the purpose of determining the value of D in the formula set out in subsection 94.2(4). Subsection 94.2(4) generally provides for the recognition of a deferral amount in respect of a participating interest on the disposition of the interest. Because of subsection 94.2(2), identical participating interests are considered to be disposed of in the order in which they were acquired.

For participating interests in FIEs acquired after 2000, each deferral amount will be nil in the typical cases where the rules in section 94.2 apply to a taxpayer's interest in an FIE for the year in which the interests were acquired.

The deferral amount is calculated, in conjunction with subsections 94.2(5) and subsection 128.1(4), so that gains and losses accruing while a taxpayer is not resident in Canada are ignored for the purposes of section 94.2, except in the unusual case where an interest in an FIE is taxable Canadian property.

Additional rules affecting the calculation of the deferral amount are contained in subsections 94.2(6) and (13) to (17), as described in the commentary below.

**Related Provisions [para. 94.2(1)(b)]**: 94.2(16)(c) — Deferral amount on fresh start re tax-exempt entity; 94.2(17) — Deferral amount on superficial disposition.

**Notes**: The reference to "positive or negative amount" before the formula overrides the rule in s. 257.

(c) **"gross-up factor"** for a deferral amount is

(i) if the amount determined for A in respect of the deferral amount is 2/3, 3/2, and

(ii) in any other case, 1.

**Technical Notes**: The "gross-up factor" for a deferral amount is 1, except where the 2/3 factor is relevant in computing the deferral amount. In the latter case, the "gross-up factor" is the reciprocal of the 2/3 factor (i.e., 3/2). For detail on the relevance of this definition, see the commentary on subsection 94.2(11).

(2) **Rules of application** — For the purposes of this section

(a) identical participating interests held by a taxpayer are deemed to be disposed of in the order in which they were acquired by the taxpayer, determined without reference to any other provision of this Act; and

(b) subsections 94.1(10) and (11) apply.

**Technical Notes**: New subsection 94.2(2) of the Act provides rules of application for the purpose of section 94.2.

Paragraph 94.2(2)(a) provides that identical properties held by a taxpayer are deemed to be disposed of in the order in which they were acquired by the taxpayer. For this purpose, paragraph 94.2(2)(a) makes it clear that the various acquisitions that are deemed to occur under the Act (e.g., section 47) are not to be taken into account. This measure is relevant primarily for the purpose of determining the amount added or deducted from a taxpayer's income under subsection 94.2(4), especially with reference to the "deferral amount" referred to in the description of D in paragraph 94.2(4)(a).

Paragraph 94.2(2)(b) provides that the rules in subsections 94.1(10) and (11) (look-through rule for significant interests) also apply for the purposes of section 94.2. This measure is significant for the purposes of applying subsection 94.2(9) (tracked interests).

**Related Provisions**: 94.3(1) — Rule in 94.2(2)(a) applies to s. 94.3; 95(2)(g.2)(xi), (xii) — Application to FAPI rules;

Subdivision i — Shareholders of Non-Resident Corporations    S. 94.2(4)(a)

104(4.1) — Mark-to-market property can be capital property for trust's 21-year deemed disposition.

**(3) Where mark-to-market method applies** — Subject to paragraph (5)(b), this subsection applies to a taxpayer throughout a taxation year in respect of a participating interest held in the year by the taxpayer in a non-resident entity where

(a) subsection (9) or (10) applies to the taxpayer for the year in respect of the interest; or

(b) both

(i) subsection 94.1(2) applies to the taxpayer for the year in respect of the interest, and

(ii) because of subsection 94.1(4), subsection 94.1(3) does not apply to the taxpayer for the year in respect of the interest.

**Technical Notes**: Subsection 94.2(3) of the Act sets out those circumstances where, subject to paragraph 94.2(5)(b), subsection 94.2(3) applies to a taxpayer in respect of a participating interest in a non-resident entity. For the mark-to-market regime in subsection 94.2(4) to apply for a taxation year, subsection 94.2(3) must apply for the year.

For subsection 94.2(3) to apply to a taxpayer throughout a taxation year in respect of a participating interest in a non-resident entity, either:

- Subsection 94.1(2) applies to the taxpayer for the year in respect of the interest, but not result in the application of the accrual regime under subsection 94.1(3) because of the application of subsection 94.1(4). (For details, see the commentary on subsections 94.1(2) and (4).); or

- Subsections 94.2(9) (tracked interests) or 94.2(10) (foreign insurance policies) apply to the taxpayer for the year in respect of the interest.

**Related Provisions**: 39(1)(a)(ii.3) — Property excluded from capital gain calculation; 70(3.1) — Property excluded from "rights or things" calculation on death; 70(5.2)(e) — Deemed disposition on death; 85(1.1)(g)(ii.1) — Property excluded from s. 85 rollover eligibility; 94.2(4) — Application of mark-to-market rule; 94.2(9) — Tracked interests; 94.2(10) — Treatment of foreign insurance policies; 104(4.1) — Mark-to-market property can be capital property for trust's 21-year deemed disposition; 248(1)'inventory" — Property under 94.2(3) excluded from definition of inventory.

**(4) Mark-to-market** — Where subsection (3) applies to a taxpayer throughout a taxation year in respect of a participating interest in a non-resident entity, in computing the taxpayer's income for the year in respect of the interest

(a) there shall be added the positive amount, if any, determined by the formula

$$(A + B + C + D) - (E + F + G)$$

where

A is the total of all amounts each of which is the taxpayer's proceeds from a disposition of the interest in the year (other than a disposition deemed to arise because of subsection 128.1(4) or 149(10)),

B is

(i) if the taxpayer held the interest at the end of the year, the fair market value of the interest at that time (determined before taking into account any amount payable at the end of the year from the entity in respect of the interest), and

(ii) in any other case, nil,

C is the total of all amounts (other than an amount to which the description of A applies) received by the taxpayer in the year from the entity in respect of the interest,

D is

(i) the taxpayer's deferral amount in respect of the interest, if

(A) the deferral amount is a positive amount,

(B) the interest was not disposed of by the taxpayer in the year, and

(C) the taxpayer elects in respect of the interest in prescribed form filed with the Minister not later than the taxpayer's filing-due date for the year,

(ii) the taxpayer's deferral amount in respect of the interest if

(A) the taxpayer disposed of the interest in the year, and

(B) no election was made under subparagraph (i) in respect of the interest by the taxpayer for a preceding taxation year, and

(iii) in any other case, nil,

E is the total of all amounts each of which is the cost at which the taxpayer acquired the interest in the year (otherwise than because of an acquisition deemed to arise because of subsection 128.1(4) or 149(10)),

F is

(i) if the taxpayer held the interest at the beginning of the year, the fair market value of the interest at that time (determined before taking into account any amount payable at that time from the entity in respect of the interest), and

(ii) in any other case, nil, and

G is

(i) if the interest was deemed by paragraph (10)(a) to be a participating interest in an entity for the preceding taxation year of the taxpayer, the amount that would be deductible under paragraph (b) in computing the taxpayer's income for that preceding year in respect of the interest if this subsection were read without reference to subparagraph (b)(i), and

## S. 94.2(4)(a) — Income Tax Act, Part I, Division B

(ii) in any other case, nil; and

(b) there may be deducted

(i) if the interest was deemed by paragraph (10)(a) to be a participating interest in an entity for the year, nil, and

(ii) in any other case, the absolute value of the negative amount, if any, determined by the formula in paragraph (a).

**Technical Notes**: Where subsection 94.2(3) applies to a participating interest in an FIE, paragraph 94.2(4)(a) requires a taxpayer to include in computing income, in respect of the interest, any positive amount resulting from the operation of the formula set out in paragraph 94.2(4)(a). Under paragraph 94.2(4)(b), the absolute value of any negative amount resulting from the operation of the same formula may be deducted in computing the taxpayer's income. (Note, however, that losses in respect of foreign insurance polices are denied because of subparagraph 94.2(4)(b)(i). Instead, as described below, the denied losses are carried forward to offset later income inclusions.)

The amount determined under the formula for a taxpayer's taxation year in respect of a participating interest in an FIE is computed as follows:

- [A] ADD the proceeds of disposition in the year from any disposition by the taxpayer in the year of the interest (other than a disposition arising from the application of subsection 128.1(4) or 149(10), given that the value of B would take into account the fair market value of the interest at the time of such deemed dispositions);

- [B] where the taxpayer held the interest at the end of the year, ADD the fair market value of the interest at that time (determined before taking into account the FIE's liability in respect of any amount payable from the FIE in respect of the interest);

- [C] ADD the total payments received by the taxpayer in the year from the FIE, other than payments included in the value of A;

- [D] where the taxpayer so elects for a year during which the taxpayer did not dispose of the interest, ADD any positive deferral amount in respect of the interest;

- [D] where the taxpayer disposed of the interest in the year and the election referred to above has not been previously made, ADD the deferral amount in respect of the interest; [The value of D will reduce the amount determined under the formula in the event that the deferral amount is a negative amount.]

- [E] SUBTRACT the cost of the interest on any acquisition in the year of the interest (disregarding acquisitions arising because of the application of subsection 128.1(4) or 149(10), given that these acquisitions are taken into account in the value of F);

- [F] where the taxpayer held the interest at the beginning of the year, SUBTRACT the fair market value of the interest; and

- [G] in the case of a foreign insurance policy to which subsection 94.2(3) applies because of the operation of new subsection 94.2(10), SUBTRACT any loss denied for the preceding year because of the operation of subparagraph 94.2(4)(b)(i).

Ignoring the descriptions of D and G, the formula in paragraph 94.2(4)(a) in effect determines the net increase or decrease in the fair market value of a taxpayer's participating interest in an FIE for a taxation year.

The value of D represents a taxpayer's accrued gain or loss when a participating interest first becomes subject to section 94.2. The amount of this accrued gain or loss (or two-thirds of it, in the event so provided in the definition "deferral amount" in paragraph 94.2(1)(b)) is included in computing income under the description of D, but only for the taxation year in which the interest is disposed of unless the taxpayer elects for earlier recognition of a positive deferral amount. (An earlier recognition of a positive deferral amount may be beneficial for a taxpayer, particularly where section 94.3 applies.) Where the taxpayer is a trust, a disposition may occur as a consequence of the application of the 21-year deemed disposition rule. See, in this regard, new subsection 104(4.1).

The example below illustrates the operation of subsection 94.2(4).

*Example*

1. Leonard acquires a 1% interest in ABC Inc. in 1999 for $500. On June 22, 2000, it is capital property to Leonard. ABC Inc. is not an FIE in respect of the taxpayer at any time before 2003.

2. ABC Inc. becomes an FIE during 2003 and Leonard does not elect under subsection 94.1(4) to have the rules in section 94.1 apply. Leonard's interest in ABC Inc. does not qualify as an "exempt interest".

3. The fair market values of Leonard's participating interest at the beginning and at the end of year 2003 are $800 and $1,000 respectively.

4. Leonard disposes of his shares just before the end of 2004 for $1,200. ABC Inc. does not make any distributions to Leonard during his period of ownership.

*Results*

1. No amount is included in Leonard's income for 2001 and 2002 under either section 94.1 or 94.2. For 2003, Leonard is required to include $200 in income under the formula in paragraph 94.2(4)(a).

2. The $200 inclusion is determined as follows:
   - "A" is nil, since no participating interest in ABC Inc. is disposed of in 2003,
   - "B" is $1,000, the fair market value of the participating interest at the end of 2003,
   - "C" is nil since no payments are received in 2003,
   - "D" is nil since no participating interest is disposed of in 2003 and no election was otherwise made,
   - "E" is nil since no participating interest in ABC Inc. is acquired in 2003, and
   - "F" is $800, the fair market value of the participating interest at the beginning of 2003.

3. Although Leonard's participating interest has appreciated by $500 since the time of its acquisition, only $200 is required to be included in income under section 94.2 for 2003.

4. For 2004, the amount included in income under subsection 94.2(4) is $400, computed as follows:
   - "A" is $1,200, the proceeds of disposition of the participating interest,

- "B" is nil since Leonard does not own any participating interest in ABC Inc. at the end of 2004,
- "C" is nil since no payments or distributions were received in 2004,
- "D" is $200, the deferral amount in respect of the interest — the "deferral amount" is two-thirds [The two-third factor applies because Leonard's interest in ABC Inc. is capital property held by Leonard on June 22, 2000.] of the amount by which $800 (the fair market value of the interest at the beginning of 2003 which is the first year in respect of which section 94.2 applies to the interest) exceeds $500 (the cost amount of the interest),
- "E" is nil since no participating interest in ABC Inc. is acquired in 2004, and
- "F" is $1,000, the fair market value of the participating interest at the beginning of 2004.

**Related Provisions**: 70(5.2)(e)(ii) — Taxpayer deemed not to hold property on death; 94.2(5) — Non-resident periods excluded; 94.2(10) — Treatment of foreign insurance policies; 94.2(11) — Change of status of entity; 94.2(12) — Cost of participating interest; 94.2(15) — Fresh start after emigration; 94.3(2)(a)(ii) — Prevention of double taxation; 96(3) — Election by members of partnership; 257 — Formula cannot calculate to less than zero.

**Notes**: The references to "positive amount" in (a) and "negative amount" in (b)(ii) override the rule in s. 257.

**(5) Non-resident periods excluded** — Where a taxpayer is non-resident at any time in a taxation year

(a) for the purpose of subsection (4) (other than the description of D in paragraph (4)(a)), the year is deemed to be the period, if any, that begins at the first time in the year at which the taxpayer is resident in Canada and ends at the last time in the year at which the taxpayer is resident in Canada;

(b) except for the purposes of subsection (4) and paragraph (c), subsection (3) does not apply to the taxpayer at that time; and

(c) if the taxpayer is an individual who was non-resident throughout a particular period that is within the period described in paragraph (a), at any time in the particular period, the individual holds a participating interest in a non-resident entity and subsection (3) applies to the individual throughout the particular period in respect of the interest,

(i) for the purposes of section 114, the income or loss of the individual in respect of the interest for the particular period shall be determined without reference to this section, and

(ii) in computing the amount determined under paragraph 114(a) in respect of the individual for the year

(A) there shall be deducted any amount that would be included under paragraph (4)(a) in computing the individual's income in respect of the interest for the particular period if

(I) the value of D in paragraph (4)(a) were nil, and

(II) the particular period were a taxation year, and

(B) there shall be added any amount that would be deductible under paragraph (4)(b) in computing the individual's income in respect of the interest for the particular period if

(I) the value of D in paragraph (4)(a) were nil, and

(II) the particular period were a taxation year.

**Technical Notes**: New subsection 94.2(5) of the Act provides special rules dealing with the application of section 94.2 for a taxation year to persons who are not resident in Canada throughout the year.

Under paragraph 94.2(5)(a), the amounts determined under section 94.2 are generally determined as if the taxation year of such a taxpayer excludes the period in the year during which the taxpayer is not resident in Canada. This rule, in conjunction with section 128.1, generally ensures that the increases and decreases in fair market values that are relevant in determining income inclusions and deductions under section 94.2 are the increases and decreases occurring while the taxpayer is resident in Canada. However, this rule does not affect the calculation of the taxpayer's deferral amount: paragraph 94.2(1)(b) (in conjunction with subsection 128.1(1)) already ensures that gains or losses accruing prior to becoming resident in Canada are not taken into account for the purposes of computing a taxpayer's deferral amount in respect of a participating interest in an FIE, except in the unusual case where the FIE interest is taxable Canadian property.

Paragraph 94.2(5)(a) also ensures that subsection 94.2(4) does not apply to a taxpayer for a taxation year throughout which the taxpayer is not resident in Canada.

Under paragraph 94.2(5)(b), subsection 94.2(3) generally does not apply to a taxpayer at a particular time if the taxpayer is not resident in Canada at the particular time. This has relevance for the purposes of a number of new provisions, including subparagraph 39(1)(a)(ii.3). This subparagraph has the effect of excluding, from a taxpayer's capital property, a property in respect of which subsection 94.2(3) applies and is intended to ensure that there is no double taxation with respect to the same economic gain. Paragraph 94.2(5)(b) thus ensures that a non-resident taxpayer cannot claim that a taxable Canadian property consisting of an FIE interest is not capital property on the basis of subparagraph 39(1)(a)(ii.3). (Note: non-resident taxpayers are generally subject to tax on taxable capital gains from their dispositions of taxable Canadian properties.)

Paragraph 94.2(5)(c) applies in the unusual case where an individual changes his or her Canadian residence status more than once in the same calendar year. For example, an individual might leave Canada near the beginning of a calendar year but return later in the same year. In the event that such an individual is considered not to reside in Canada during a period in the calendar year, the individual's period of non-residence would be included within the individual's taxation year and the rule in paragraph 94.2(5)(a) would have no effect. In order to not tax gains accrued while an individual was non-resident and to not provide relief for losses accrued during the same period, paragraph 94.2(5)(c) provides:

- for the purposes of section 114, the individual's income or loss from the individual's period of non-residence is determined without reference to section 94.2, and
- in computing the individual's taxable income under section 114,
  - there is deducted the fair market value appreciation of an interest in an FIE to which subsection 94.2(4) applies during the non-resident period (this fair market value appreciation would be reflected in the amount determined under subsection 94.2(4) in computing the taxpayer's income), and
  - there is added the fair market value decline of an interest in an FIE to which subsection 94.2(4) applies during the non-resident period (this fair market value decline would be reflected in the amount determined under subsection 94.2(4) in computing the taxpayer's income).

The example below illustrates the operation of paragraph 94.2(5)(c).

*Example*

Bernard emigrates from Canada on February 1, 2001 in order to start permanent employment elsewhere. After the position does not work out, he returns to Canada on December 1, 2001. Bernard owns an interest in an FIE to which section 94.2 applies. The fair market value of the interest in 2001 is $100 (January 1, 2001), $105 (February 1, 2001), $108 (December 1, 2001) and $107 (December 31, 2001). It is assumed that Bernard establishes that he did not reside in Canada from February 1, 2001 to December 1, 2001.

*Results*

1. Under section 94.2(4), the amount included in computing Bernard's income for 2001 is equal to $7 (B = 107, F = 100).
2. Paragraph 94.2(5)(c) permits a deduction for the purposes of paragraph 114(a) equal to $3 (i.e., $108 – $105) equal to the appreciation in the fair market value of the interest while Bernard was not resident in Canada. As a consequence, Bernard's taxable income in respect of the FIE interest for 2001 is equal to $4 (i.e., $7 minus $3).

**Related Provisions**: 95(2)(g.2)(x) — Application to FAPI rules.

**(6) Foreign partnership — member becoming resident** — Where, at a particular time in a fiscal period of a partnership, a person resident in Canada becomes a member of the partnership, or a person who is a member of the partnership becomes resident in Canada and immediately before the particular time no member of the partnership is resident in Canada,

(a) all amounts determined under this section shall be determined as if that period began at the first time in that period at which a member of the partnership was resident in Canada;

(b) for the purpose of the definition "deferral amount" in paragraph (1)(b), as it applies in respect of dispositions that occur after the particular time and before the first subsequent time to which this subsection applies in respect of the partnership, subsection (4) is deemed not to have applied to the partnership for any preceding fiscal period; and

(c) where, but for this paragraph, a negative deferral amount would be determined in respect of a participating interest held by the partnership immediately before the particular time, the deferral amount in respect of the interest is deemed to be nil.

**Technical Notes**: New subsections 94.2(6) to (8) of the Act provide special rules for partnerships having non-resident members. These subsections are analogous to rules in existing subsections 96(8) and (9) and are designed, in general terms, to prevent partnership losses that accrue while no partnership member is resident in Canada from being used in Canada. A further rule for partnership members is set out in new subsection 96(1.9).

More specifically, subsection 94.2(6) applies where a partnership begins to have members who reside in Canada. Under subsection 94.2(7), a corresponding rule applies in a similar fashion where a partnership ceases to have members who reside in Canada. In either case, for the purposes of determining amounts under section 94.2 portions of the fiscal period of the partnership in which no member is resident in Canada will generally be disregarded.

Where subsection 94.2(6) applies to a partnership at any time, the deferral amount for an FIE interest held by the partnership immediately before that time is computed with reference to the fair market value and the cost amount of the interest. However, if a negative deferral amount is otherwise determined with respect to the interest, the deferral amount is deemed to be nil.

**Related Provisions**: 94.2(8) — Application — anti-avoidance and partnership look-through rules.

**(7) Foreign partnership — members ceasing to be resident** — Where, at a particular time in a fiscal period of a partnership, a person resident in Canada ceases to be a member of the partnership, or a person who is a member of the partnership ceases to be resident in Canada and immediately after the particular time no member of the partnership is resident in Canada, all amounts determined under this section shall be determined as if that period ended at the last time in that period at which a member of the partnership was resident in Canada.

**Technical Notes**: As a consequence of subsections 94.2(6) and (7), amounts added or deductible under subsection 94.2(4) for a partnership in respect of an FIE interest will generally reflect increases or decreases in fair market value while the partnership has members resident in Canada. However, once the interest is disposed of, an amount reflecting gains accruing before any member became resident in Canada will be recognized because of the application of subsection 94.2(4).

**Related Provisions**: 94.2(8) — Application — anti-avoidance and partnership look-through rules.

**(8) Application of subsecs. (6) and (7)** — For the purposes of applying subsections (6) and (7) and this subsection,

(a) where it can reasonably be considered that one of the main reasons that a member of a partnership is resident in Canada is to avoid the application of subsection (6) or (7), the member is deemed not to be resident in Canada; and

(b) where a particular partnership is a member of another partnership at any time,

(i) each person or partnership that is at that time a member of the particular partnership is deemed to be a member of the other partnership at that time,

(ii) each person or partnership that becomes at that time a member of the particular partnership is deemed to become a member of the other partnership at that time, and

(iii) each person or partnership that ceases at that time to be a member of the particular partnership is deemed to cease to be a member of the other partnership at that time.

**Technical Notes**: Subsection 94.2(8) contains an anti-avoidance rule, which is aimed at preventing the insertion of nominal Canadian resident partners for tax planning purposes. This rule is parallel to the rule in existing subsection 96(9).

Subsection 94.2(8) also contains a look-through rule. It allows for the look-through of one or more tiers of partnerships for the purposes of determining whether a person is a member of a partnership.

**Related Provisions**: 96(9) — Parallel rule for foreign partnerships.

**(9) Tracked interests** — Subject to paragraph (5)(b), subsection (3) applies to a taxpayer throughout a particular taxation year of the taxpayer in respect of a participating interest in a non-resident entity where

(a) the taxpayer holds the interest at any time in the particular year;

(b) a taxation year of the entity ends at or before the end of the particular year;

(c) the taxpayer is not an exempt taxpayer for the particular year;

(d) the entitlement to receive payments from the entity in respect of the interest (or its fair market value) is determined primarily by reference to production, revenue, profit or cash flow from, the fair market value or the use of, or any similar criterion in respect of, a property or group of properties (each of which is referred to in paragraphs (e) and (f) as a "tracked property");

(e) at the end of the latest of the entity's taxation years described in paragraph (b), the tracked properties

(i) are not all of the properties that would be owned by the entity if this Act were read without reference to subsection 94.1(10), or

(ii) include properties that would not be owned by the entity if this Act were read without reference to subsection 94.1(10); and

(f) either

(i) at the end of the latest of the entity's taxation years described in paragraph (b), the total of all amounts each of which is

(A) the carrying value of an investment property that is a tracked property owned at the end of that year by the entity, or

(B) an amount that would, if this Act were read without reference to paragraph 94.1(10)(a), be the carrying value of a tracked property that is

(I) owned at the end of the year by the entity,

(II) deemed by paragraph 94.1(10)(a) to have a carrying value of nil, and

(III) either a participating interest in a foreign investment entity or indebtedness owing by a foreign investment entity,

exceeds one-half of the total of

(C) all amounts each of which is the entity's carrying value of a tracked property owned by it at the end of that year, and

(D) the carrying value (determined without reference to paragraph 94.1(10)(a)) of a tracked property to which subclauses (B)(I) to (III) apply, or

(ii) at the end of the latest of the entity's taxation years described in paragraph (b)

(A) the entity, or another non-resident entity, owns an investment property (other than a tracked property owned by the entity), and

(B) it is reasonable to conclude that the production, revenue, profit or cash flow from the investment property, the increase in the fair market value of the investment property, or any other return on the investment property based on a similar criterion, is intended to enable the entity to satisfy all or part of an entitlement referred to in paragraph (d).

**Technical Notes**: New subsection 94.2(9) of the Act is an anti-avoidance rule intended to prevent the circumvention of sections 94.1 and 94.2 through the creation of "tracked interests" in entities that are not FIEs or through the creation of an interest in an FIE that would otherwise be an "exempt interest". Where subsection 94.2(9) applies with regard to a "tracked interest" for a taxation year, the mark-to-market regime in section 94.2(4) applies to a taxpayer for that year.

A participating interest held by a taxpayer in a particular non-resident entity in a taxation year is a "tracked interest" in the particular entity for a particular taxation year of the taxpayer where:

- a taxation year of the particular entity ended at or before the end of the particular year (the latest of which taxation years is referred to below as the "specified year"); [Paragraph 94.2(9)(b).]
- the taxpayer is not an exempt taxpayer for the particular year (see commentary on definition "exempt taxpayer" in subsection 94.1(1)); [Paragraph 94.2(9)(c).]
- the entitlement to receive payments from the particular entity in respect of the participating interest (or its fair market value) is determined primarily by reference to production, revenue, profit or cash flow from, the fair market value or the use of, or any other similar criterion in respect of, a property or group of properties (referred to below as the "tracked properties"); [Paragraph 94.2(9)(d).]
- in the event that all of the tracked properties are properties owned by the particular entity, they do not comprise the totality of the entity's properties. [Paragraph 94.2(9)(e).] (Note: the deemed ownership rule in subsection 94.1(10) is ignored for the purpose of determining whether this condition is satisfied.);
- either
  — the entity (or any other non-resident entity) owns an investment property (other than a tracked property owned by the entity) and it is reasonable to conclude that the production, revenue, profit or cash flow from that investment property, the increase in the fair market value of that investment property or any other return based on a similar criterion is intended to enable the entity to satisfy all or part of an entitlement in respect of a tracked interest. [Paragraph 94.2(9)(f)(ii).]] or
  — in general terms, the total carrying value of investment property owned by the entity that is included in the tracked properties is more than one-half of the total carrying value of all property owned by the entity that is included in the tracked properties. [Paragraph 94.2(9)(f)(i).]

More specifically, for the purpose of determining the above totals, the carrying value of investment property owned by an entity included in the tracked properties as of the end of the specified year is determined as follows:

- ADD the carrying value of investment property included in the tracked properties and owned by the particular entity (determined with reference to the definition "investment property" and the deemed ownership rule in subsection 94.1(10)); and
- ADD the carrying value (determined without reference to subsection 94.1(10)) of specified investment property owned by the particular entity and included in the tracked properties. The investment property so specified is the property that would otherwise have a deemed cost of nil under paragraph 94.1(10)(a) and that is either a participating interest in an FIE or indebtedness owing by an FIE. (The specified investment property represents debt or equity interests in entities in which the particular entity has a "significant interest", as defined by subsection 94.1(11).)

For the same purpose, the total carrying value of the total property included in the tracked properties is determined as of the end of the specified taxation year of the particular entity in the following manner:

- ADD the carrying value of each property owned by the particular entity that is included in the tracked properties. (This determination is made with reference to the look-through rule in subsection 94.1(10).); and
- ADD the carrying value (determined without reference to subsection 94.1(10)) of specified investment property referred to above.

It should be noted that tracked properties can include any property, whether or not owned by a taxpayer or a related group of which the taxpayer is a part. For example, if the fair market value of shares issued by a non-resident entity is tracked to the world-wide price of gold bullion, the tracked properties in question would be the world-wide supply of gold bullion. Whether subsection 94.2(9) applies or not in this case would typically depend on whether subparagraph 94.2(9)(f)(ii) applies to the non-resident entity.

It should also be noted that there is no exemption under subsection 94.2(9) with regard to an "exempt interest" (as defined in subsection 94.1(1)) in a non-resident entity. Thus, the mark-to-market rules can apply to a taxpayer in respect of shares of the capital stock of a controlled foreign affiliate of the taxpayer.

**Letter from Department of Finance, July 6, 2000:**

Dear [xxx]

I am responding to your letters of June 26 and 29, 2000 regarding proposed section 94.2 of the *Income Tax Act* (the Act) and your request for an amendment to the section to limit the scope of those mark-to-market rules.

Proposed subsection 94.2(9) of the Act describes a "tracking share" which is subject to the mark-to-market rules in proposed section 94.2 of the Act. The result of the application of the section to the shareholder in respect of a tracking share is that the shareholder will be required to include in income for a taxation year, the growth in the market value of the share during the year.

Proposed subsection 94.2(9) of the Act is an anti-avoidance rule. It is intended to apply to tracking shares in circumstances where the value of and return on the tracking shares tracks the value of and return on investment property (as defined for that section) or interests in foreign investment entities (as defined for that section). It is not intended to apply to shares owned by a Canadian corporation where, directly or indirectly, the value of and return on the shares track the value of and return on shares of the capital stock of a foreign affiliate of the Canadian corporation, and where such shares would be a qualifying interest (as defined in paragraph 95(2)(m) of the Act) in the foreign affiliate of the corporation if owned by the corporation and the foreign affiliate is a qualifying corporation (as defined for that section).

In your letter, you describe a corporate structure in which a corporation resident in Canada holds tracking shares that track the value of and return on shares of a foreign affiliate (that is a qualifying corporation) of the corporation which represent a qualifying interest in the foreign affiliate. You have concluded that the mark-to-market rules in proposed section 94.2 of the Act apply inappropriately to the corporation in respect of the tracking shares. The result is that the growth in the market value of the tracking shares for a year must be included in the corporation's income for that year. Consequently, you are asking that the proposed section be amended to correct this anomaly.

We agree with your conclusion in the circumstances described in your letters. Consequently, we are prepared to recommend to the Minister of Finance that the legislation in proposed section 94.2 of the Act be modified. The change would ensure that section 94.2 would not apply to require a corporation resident in Canada to include in computing income for a year the increase or decrease in the market value of tracking shares for the year where the following conditions are met. First, all or substantially all of the value and return on those tracking shares must track, directly or indirectly, the value and return on shares of a foreign affiliate of the corporation. Second, if those shares of that foreign affiliate of the corporation were owned by the corporation those shares would be a qualifying interest in the foreign affiliate (as defined in paragraph 95(2)(m) of the Act) of the corporation. Third, that foreign affiliate (the value of and return on the shares of which are tracked) must be a qualifying corporation (as defined for the purposes of section 94.2 of the Act). Finally, no other tracking shares may track those shares of the foreign affiliate.

I trust that this letter satisfies your concerns and meets requirements.

> Yours sincerely,
> Len Farber
> General Director, Tax Legislation Division, Tax Policy Branch

**Related Provisions**: 91(1) — Tracked shares ignored for FAPI income inclusion.

**(10) Treatment of foreign insurance policies** — Where, in a particular taxation year of a taxpayer (other than an exempt taxpayer for the particular year), the taxpayer holds a particular interest in an insurance policy that was neither issued in the course of carrying on an insurance business in Canada, the income from which is subject to tax under this Part, nor entered into solely in respect of risks that relate to activities occurring outside Canada or losses in respect of tangible property ordinarily situated outside Canada,

(a) subject to paragraph (b),

(i) for the purposes of applying subsections (3) and (4) and paragraph (d.1) of the definition "specified foreign property" in subsection 233.3(1) to the taxpayer in respect of the particular interest for the particular year,

(A) the particular interest is deemed at each time throughout the particular year that it is held by the taxpayer to be a participating interest in a non-resident entity,

(B) subject to paragraph (5)(b), subsection (3) is deemed to apply to the taxpayer throughout the particular year in respect of the particular interest, and

(C) the value of D in paragraph (4)(a) is deemed to be nil, and

(ii) section 12.2, paragraphs 56(1)(d) and (j) and 60(a) and (s) and sections 138 and 138.1 do not apply in respect of the particular interest for the purpose of computing the taxpayer's income for the year;

(b) paragraph (a) does not apply to an individual for a taxation year in respect of a policy an interest in which was acquired by the individual more than five years before the individual became resident in Canada unless, after the day that is five years before the day that the individual became resident in Canada, the individual paid premiums in respect of the policy that are in excess of the level that can reasonably be considered to have been contemplated at the time the first interest in the policy was acquired;

(c) an interest in an insurance policy is deemed to have been disposed of by a person at the end of a taxation year of the person for proceeds of disposition equal to its fair market value at that time where

(i) paragraph (a) did not apply to the person in respect of the interest for the year,

(ii) the person held the interest at the end of the year, and

(iii) paragraph (a) applies to the person in respect of the interest for the person's following taxation year;

(d) an interest in an insurance policy is deemed to have been acquired by a person at the beginning of a taxation year of the person at a cost equal to its fair market value at that time where

(i) paragraph (a) does not apply to the person in respect of the interest for the year,

(ii) the person held the interest at the beginning of the year, and

(iii) paragraph (a) applied to the person in respect of the interest for the person's preceding taxation year; and

(e) for the purposes of this subsection and subsection (4), the fair market value of an interest in an insurance policy, the proceeds of disposition of an interest in an insurance policy and amounts paid to a beneficiary in respect of an interest in an insurance policy shall each be determined without reference to benefits paid, payable or anticipated to be payable, under the policy as a consequence only of a death, sickness, disability or prescribed event.

**Technical Notes**: New subsection 94.2(10) of the Act sets out the treatment under section 94.2 of an interest in a foreign insurance policy. For this purpose, a foreign insurance policy is one that is neither

- issued by an insurer in the course of carrying on business in Canada the income from which is subject to tax under Part I, nor

**S. 94.2(10)** — Income Tax Act, Part I, Division B

- entered into solely in respect of risks that relate to activities occurring outside Canada or losses in respect of tangible property ordinarily situated outside Canada.

Paragraph 94.2(10)(a) generally provides that, where a taxpayer (other than an exempt taxpayer) holds an interest in such an insurance policy, for the purposes of subsections 94.2(3) and (4) (and a corresponding foreign property reporting rule in subsection 233.3(1)) the particular interest is deemed to be a participating interest in a non-resident entity to which the mark-to-market rules in subsection 94.2(4) apply. However, the mark-to-market regime under subsection 94.2(4) applies differently to insurance policies in two respects. First, no deferral amount is calculated with regard to insurance policies. Second, losses are not deductible, but instead can be used to offset future income amounts otherwise arising under subsection 94.2(4). (As to the treatment of losses, see the commentary on subsection 94.2(4).) Paragraph 94.2(10)(a) also provides that, where the mark-to-market rules apply to an insurance policy, the other rules in the Act with regard to the taxation of insurance products do not apply.

Under paragraph 94.2(10)(b), paragraph 94.2(10)(a) does not apply in connection with a policy an interest in which was acquired more than five years before a taxpayer became resident in Canada. However, this exception does not apply if premiums in excess of the level originally contemplated under the policy have been paid within 5 years of the policyholder becoming resident in Canada or while the policyholder was resident in Canada.

In the event that an insurance policy is subject to paragraph 94.2(10)(a) for one taxation year but not subject to that paragraph for the preceding year, paragraph 94.2(10)(c) provides that the taxpayer is deemed, at the end of the preceding year, to have disposed of the taxpayer's interest in the insurance policy at its fair market value (determined with reference to paragraph 94.2(10)(e)).

In the event that an insurance policy is subject to paragraph 94.2(10)(a) for one taxation year but not subject to that paragraph for the following year, paragraph 94.2(10)(d) provides that the taxpayer is deemed, at the beginning of the following year, to have acquired the taxpayer's interest in the insurance policy at its fair market value (determined with reference to paragraph 94.2(10)(e)).

Paragraph 94.2(10)(e) provides that the fair market value of an interest in an insurance policy and other relevant amounts are determined without reference to benefits paid, payable and anticipated to be payable under the policy only as a consequence of a death, sickness, disability or other prescribed event. (Note: Presently, it is not anticipated that events will be prescribed for this purpose.)

*Example*

Assume that David, a long-term resident of Canada, pays premiums of $10,000 to an offshore insurer for a life insurance policy. The policy's cash surrender value is $9,000 and $10,700 at the end of 2002 and 2003 (respectively).

*Results*

1. For 2002, no amount is determined under paragraph 94.2(4)(a) because the cost of the policy exceeds the fair market value at the end of 2002.

2. No loss is permitted to be claimed under paragraph 94.2(4)(b). The amount of the denied loss is equal to $1,000.

3. For 2003, the amount included in income under paragraph 94.2(4)(a) is $700 (= $10,700 ("B"), minus $9,000 ("F"), minus $1,000 ("G")).

4. It should be noted, however, that it is possible that the fair market value could be higher that a policy's cash surrender value. This might be the case, for example, if cash surrender values under a policy were not provided on a consistent basis over time. If this were the case, the fair market value of a policy would be a question of fact.

Subsection 94.2(10), unlike the rest of section 94.2, is to apply to taxation years that begin after 2001.

**Related Provisions**: 233.3(1)"specified foreign property"(d.1) — Annual information reporting re interest in insurance policy.

**(11) Change of status of entity** — Where a participating interest is held by a taxpayer at the beginning of a taxation year, subsection (4) applied for the purpose of computing the taxpayer's income in respect of the interest for the preceding taxation year and that subsection does not apply for the purpose of computing the taxpayer's income in respect of the interest for the year (otherwise than because the taxpayer became an exempt taxpayer or ceased to reside in Canada),

(a) subject to paragraph (c), the taxpayer is deemed to have acquired the interest at the beginning of the year at a cost equal to its fair market value at that time;

(b) where the interest is capital property at the beginning of the year, in computing the adjusted cost base after that time to the taxpayer of the interest

(i) except where the taxpayer has made an election in respect of the interest under clause (i)(C) of the description of D in paragraph (4)(a), there shall be deducted the product of any positive deferral amount in respect of the interest and the gross-up factor for the deferral amount, and

(ii) there shall be added the product of the absolute value of any negative deferral amount in respect of the interest and the gross-up factor for the deferral amount; and

(c) where paragraph (b) does not apply,

(i) except where the taxpayer has made an election in respect of the interest under clause (i)(C) of the description of D in paragraph (4)(a), there shall be deducted in computing the cost to the taxpayer of the interest the lesser of

(A) the product of any positive deferral amount in respect of the interest and the gross-up factor for the deferral amount, and

(B) the cost to the taxpayer of the interest, determined without reference to this subparagraph,

(ii) there shall be included in computing the taxpayer's income for the year in respect of the interest the amount, if any, by which

(A) the amount determined under clause (i)(A) in respect of the interest

exceeds

(B) the amount determined under clause (i)(B) in respect of the interest, and

(iii) there shall be added in computing the cost to the taxpayer of the interest the product of the absolute value of any negative deferral amount in respect of the interest and the gross-up factor for the deferral amount.

**Technical Notes:** New subsection 94.2(11) of the Act sets out rules that apply where a taxpayer holding a participating interest in an entity was subject to subsection 94.2(4) for a taxation year but is not subject, in respect of the interest, to subsection 94.2(4) for the following taxation year (otherwise than because the taxpayer ceased to reside in Canada or became an "exempt taxpayer", as defined in subsection 94.1(1)).

Where subsection 94.2(11) applies, the taxpayer is deemed to have acquired the particular interest at the beginning of the following taxation year at a cost equal to the fair market value of the particular interest at that time.

The subsection could apply, for example, where a taxpayer holds a share of the capital stock of a non-resident corporation and the share is not an "exempt interest", as defined in subsection 94.1(1). Assume that the taxpayer made no election under subsection 94.1(4) for section 94.1 to apply. If the entity subsequently becomes a controlled foreign affiliate of the taxpayer, subsection 94.2(4) would cease to apply.

Since the taxpayer is deemed to have acquired the property at its fair market value at the beginning of the following year, all increases and decreases in the value of the interest from the time of its acquisition are reflected in the taxpayer's cost of the interest for tax purposes. However, only the gain or loss accruing while it was subject to subsection 94.2(4) has been brought into income. The gain or loss in value for the period from the time of acquisition to the time it became subject to subsection 94.2(4) has not been taken into consideration for tax purposes.

Accordingly, paragraph 94.2(10)(b) provides for a negative or positive adjustment to the adjusted cost base (ACB) of a participating interest held as capital property. Any positive "deferral amount" (as defined in subsection 94.2(1)) in respect of the interest is deducted in computing the ACB of the interest, but the deduction is grossed-up by one-half in the event that the deferral amount was calculated with reference to two-thirds of the accrued gains. The ACB deduction does not, however, apply in the event that a positive deferral amount has already been taken into account because of an election under the description of D in paragraph 94.2(4)(a). The absolute value of any negative deferral amount (or three-halves of it where the 2/3 factor was used in computing the negative deferral amount) is added in computing the ACB of the interest. Where capital property is not involved, a corresponding decrease or increase in cost (rather than adjusted cost basis) is provided under paragraph 94.2(11)(c). To the extent that the decrease would otherwise result in a negative cost, the decrease is brought into the taxpayer's income under paragraph 94.2(11)(c).

**Related Provisions:** 53(1)(m.1) — Addition to adjusted cost base; 53(2)(w) — Deduction from adjusted cost base; 94.2(14) — Fresh start re change of status of entity.

**(12) Cost of participating interest** — Where a taxpayer's participating interest in a non-resident entity is disposed of by the taxpayer at a particular time in a taxation year and subsection (4) applies for the purpose of computing the taxpayer's income for the year in respect of the interest, for the purpose of determining the taxpayer's cost of the interest immediately before the particular time

(a) if the interest was held by the taxpayer at the beginning of the year, its cost to the taxpayer immediately before the particular time is deemed to be equal to the fair market value of the interest at the beginning of the year; and

(b) in any other case, its cost to the taxpayer immediately before the particular time is deemed to be equal to the amount that would be its cost to the taxpayer at the particular time if this Act were read without reference to this section (other than subsection (2)).

**Technical Notes:** New subsection 94.2(12) of the Act provides a rule for determining the cost at a particular time of a participating interest in an entity for a taxation year in the event that the interest is disposed of by the taxpayer in the year.

The cost to the taxpayer immediately before the disposition of the property is deemed to be its fair market value at the beginning of the taxpayer's taxation year. In the event that the property was not held by the taxpayer at that time, its cost immediately before the disposition is its cost determined without reference to subsections 94.2(4) and (12). In identifying property for these purposes, identical properties of a taxpayer are considered to be disposed of on a "first in, first out" basis, as a consequence of the application of subsection 94.2(2).

Under new paragraph (c.2) of the definition "cost amount" in subsection 248(1), the cost determined at a particular time for a property under subsection 94.2 (12) is also the "cost amount" of the property at the particular time.

**Related Provisions:** 248(1)"cost amount"(c.2) — Cost amount applies for entire Act.

**(13) Deferral amount where same interest reacquired** — Subject to subsections (14) to (17), where a taxpayer disposes of a participating interest in an entity at any time in a taxation year of the taxpayer and subsection (4) applies for the purpose of computing the taxpayer's income for the year in respect of the interest, for the purpose of applying subsection (4) to dispositions after that time the deferral amount of the taxpayer in respect of the interest is nil.

**Technical Notes**: New subsection 94.2(13) of the Act generally provides that a "deferral amount" in respect of a property of a taxpayer is deemed to be nil, after the property has been disposed of by the taxpayer at a time when the mark-to-market rules in subsection 94.2(4) applied to the property. This is of relevance to property that is reacquired by a taxpayer. However, subsection 94.2(13) is subject to rules in subsections 94.2(14) to (17).

It should be noted that identical properties of a taxpayer are considered to be disposed of on a "first in, first out" basis as a consequence of the application of subsection 94.2(2).

**Related Provisions**: 87(2)(j.95) — Amalgamations — continuing corporation.

**(14) Fresh start re change of status of entity** — Where a participating interest is deemed by paragraph (11)(a) to have been acquired at a particular time by a taxpayer, for the purpose of applying subsection (4) to a subsequent disposition of the interest and a subsequent election in respect of the interest under clause (i)(C) of the description of D in paragraph (4)(a), the deferral amount of the taxpayer in respect of the interest shall

(a) for the purpose of clause (i)(C) of the description of B in the definition "deferral amount" in paragraph (1)(b), be determined as if subsection (4) had not applied to the taxpayer in respect of the interest for taxation years that began before the particular time; and

(b) be determined without reference to the application of subsection (13) with regard to dispositions that occurred before the particular time.

**Technical Notes**: New subsection 94.2(14) of the Act covers the case where a taxpayer's participating interest in an entity was initially subject to the rules in subsection 94.2(4) and ceases to be subject to those rules (otherwise than because of the taxpayer having become an "exempt taxpayer"). For example, subsection 94.2(14) could apply where an entity loses its status as an FIE.

In these circumstances, the deferral amount in respect of the participating interest is determined without reference to the past application of subsections 94.2(4) and (13). This rule is relevant only in the event that the same participating interest of the taxpayer again becomes subject to the rules in subsection 94.2(4).

Parallel "fresh start" rules are contained in subsection 94.2(15) and (16). All of these "fresh start" rules are expected to be only rarely invoked, given that more than one change in status of an investment or a taxpayer is required for the rules to become relevant. For further detail on the "deferral amount" defined in subsection 94.2(1), see the commentary on that definition.

**(15) Fresh start after emigration of taxpayer** — Where a taxpayer ceases at a particular time to be resident in Canada, for the purpose of applying subsection (4) to dispositions, and elections under clause (i)(C) of the description of D in paragraph (4)(a), that occur or that are made after the particular time, the deferral amount in respect of the taxpayer's participating interests shall

(a) for the purpose of clause (i)(C) of the description of B in the definition "deferral amount" in paragraph (1)(b), be determined as if subsection (4) had not applied to the taxpayer in respect of participating interests for taxation years that began before the particular time; and

(b) be determined without reference to the application of subsection (13) with regard to dispositions that occurred before the particular time.

**Technical Notes**: New subsection 94.2(15) of the Act affects the calculation of the "deferral amount" in respect of a participating interest in an entity for a taxpayer who has ceased to reside in Canada. It is relevant in the event that, at a subsequent time, the taxpayer becomes resident in Canada again.

In these circumstances, the deferral amounts in respect of the taxpayer's FIE interests are determined without reference to the past application of subsections 94.2(4) and (13).

For further context, see the commentary above on the related fresh start rule in subsection 94.2(14).

**(16) Fresh start re change of status of tax-exempt entity** — Where

(a) a taxpayer was not an exempt taxpayer for a particular taxation year, and

(b) the taxpayer is an exempt taxpayer for the following taxation year because of the application of paragraph (b) of the definition "exempt taxpayer" in subsection 94.1(1),

for the purpose of applying subsection (4) to dispositions, and elections under clause (i)(C) of the description of D in paragraph (4)(a), that occur or that are made after that following year, the deferral amount in respect of the taxpayer's participating interests shall

(c) for the purpose of clause (i)(C) of the description of B in the definition "deferral amount" in paragraph (1)(b), be determined as if subsection (4) had not applied to the taxpayer in respect of participating interests for taxation years that ended before that following year, and

(d) be determined without reference to the application of subsection (13) with regard to dispositions that occurred before that following year.

**Technical Notes**: New subsection 94.2(16) of the Act affects the calculation of the "deferral amount" in respect of an interest in an entity for a taxpayer that initially was not an "exempt taxpayer" under paragraph (b) of that definition and then subsequently both obtains and loses that status.

In these circumstances, the deferral amounts in respect of the FIE interests of the taxpayer are determined without reference to the past application of subsections 94.2(4) and (13).

For further context, see the commentary on the related fresh start rule in subsection 94.2(14). In addition, it should be noted that amended subsection 149(10) applies to changes of tax-exempt status for taxpayers that are corporations. Where subsection 149(10) applies, the rules in subsection 94.2(16) do not apply.

**(17) Superficial dispositions** — Where a taxpayer disposes of a particular participating interest in an entity, the deferral amount in respect of the particular interest would otherwise be a negative amount and the disposition would, if the particular interest were a capital property and a loss arose on the disposition, give rise to a superficial loss (within the meaning that would be assigned by section 54 if the definition "superficial loss" in that section were read without the reference to subsection 40(3.4) in paragraph (h) of that definition),

(a) except for the purpose of applying paragraph (b) in respect of the disposition, the deferral amount of the taxpayer in respect of the particular interest is deemed to be nil; and

(b) the deferral amount of the taxpayer in respect of the property that would be the substituted property referred to in that definition if the assumptions described in this subsection applied is deemed to be equal to the deferral amount of the taxpayer in respect of the particular interest.

**Technical Notes**: New subsection 94.2(17) of the Act applies where a taxpayer disposes of a participating interest in an entity in respect of which a negative amount is determined under the description of D in the formula in subsection 94.2(4). This would be the case where there is a negative deferral amount associated with the interest. In these circumstances, the deferral amount is instead generally deemed to be nil if, during the period beginning 30 days before the disposition and ending 30 days after the disposition, identical property is acquired by the taxpayer or certain related persons.

Subsection 94.2(17) operates in a manner similar to the "superficial loss" rules for capital properties and is intended to prevent the premature realization of losses in respect of a property in which a taxpayer effectively retains an economic interest. "Superficial loss" has the same meaning as assigned in section 54, except that the definition for the purposes of subsection 94.2(17) does not contain the exception for transactions covered by subsection 40(3.4).

Property substituted for the particular property is, in these circumstances, considered to have the deferral amount associated with the property disposed of.

**Definitions [s. 94.2]**: "adjusted cost base" — 54, 248(1); "amount", "business" — 248(1); "Canada" — 255, *Interpretation Act* 35(1); "capital property" — 54, 248(1); "carrying value" — 94.1(1), (10), 94.2(1)(a); "cost amount" — 248(1); "deferral amount" — 94.2(1)(b); "disposition" — 248(1); "entity", "exempt taxpayer" — 94.1(1), 94.2(1)(a); "foreign investment entity" — 94.1(1), (13), 94.2(1)(a); "filing-due date" — 248(1); "fiscal period" — 249.1; "gross-up factor" — 94.2(1)(c); "individual", "insurance policy" — 248(1); "investment property" — 94.1(1), 94.2(1)(a); "Minister" — 248(1); "non-resident" — 248(1); "non-resident entity" — 94.1(1), 94.2(1)(a); "owned" — 94.1(10); "participating interest" — 94.1(1), 94.2(1)(a); "partnership" — see Notes to 96(1); "person", "prescribed", "property" — 248(1); "resident", "resident in Canada" — 250; "significant interest" — 94.1(11); "taxation year" — 94.1(1), 94.2(1)(a), 249; "taxpayer" — 248(1); "tracked property" — 94.2(9)(d).

**94.3 (1) Definitions and rules of application** — The definitions in subsection 94.1(1), and paragraph 94.2(2)(a), apply in this section.

**(2) Prevention of double taxation** — Where at a particular time in a taxation year a taxpayer resident in Canada receives or becomes entitled to receive a payment from an entity in respect of a participating interest in the entity,

(a) there may be deducted in computing the taxpayer's income for the year the lesser of

(i) the amount, if any, by which

(A) the amount included (otherwise than because of subsection 94.2(4)) in computing the taxpayer's income for the year in respect of the payment,

exceeds

(B) the total of all amounts each of which is an amount deductible

(I) under subsection 91(5) in computing the taxpayer's income for the year in respect of the payment, or

(II) under section 113 in computing the taxpayer's taxable income for the year in respect of the payment, and

(ii) the amount, if any, by which

(A) the total of all amounts each of which is an amount added under subsection 94.1(3) or 94.2(4), in respect of the interest, in computing the taxpayer's income for the year or a preceding taxation year

exceeds the total of

(B) all amounts each of which is an amount deducted under subsection 94.1(3) or subsection 94.2(4), in respect of the interest, in computing the taxpayer's income for the year or a preceding taxation year, and

(C) all amounts each of which is an amount deducted under this paragraph, in respect of the interest, in computing the taxpayer's income in respect of a payment in respect of the interest that was received or became receivable before the particular time; and

(b) if the interest is capital property at the particular time, in computing the adjusted cost base to the taxpayer of the interest after the particular time there shall be deducted the amount deducted under paragraph (a) in computing the taxpayer's income.

**Related Provisions**: 53(2)(w) — Deduction from adjusted cost base; 87(2)(j.95) — Amalgamations — continuing corporation.

**Technical Notes**: Where a taxpayer resident in Canada has received a payment (a dividend, for example) in respect of a participating interest in an entity held by the taxpayer (otherwise than as consideration for the disposition of the interest), new section 94.3 of the Act permits a deduction designed to offset any net income inclusion resulting from the payment. The permitted deduction for a taxation year is equal to the lesser of:

- the amount included (otherwise than because of subsection 94.2(4)) in computing the taxpayer's income for the year in respect of the payment, less any increase in amounts deductible under subsection 91(5) or section 113 caused by the making of the payment, and
- the net amount included in computing the taxpayer's income under sections 94.1 and 94.2 in respect of the participating interest, less deductions for the taxpayer under subsection 94.3(2) in respect of previous payments in respect of the interest.

In the event that the participating interest is capital property, the amount deducted from income under subsection 94.3(2) in respect of the interest is also required to be deducted in computing the adjusted cost base of the interest. Note that this deduction is not of relevance to property to which the mark-to-market rules in section 94.2 apply, given that such property will not be capital property as a consequence of the application of subparagraph 39(1)(a)(ii.3) and section 94.2.

Section 94.3 also allows income inclusions in respect of amounts payable (for example, amounts payable by an FIE that is a trust) to be similarly treated.

The example below illustrates the operation of section 94.3.

*Example*

1. A taxpayer resident in Canada, Canco, purchases a 20% interest in Foreignco, a non-resident corporation. Foreignco is an FIE. Participating interests in Foreignco do not qualify as "exempt interests". Both Canco and Foreignco have taxation years that coincide with calendar years. Canco makes an election under subsection 94.1(4) to have section 94.1 apply.

2. Canco's income allocation in respect of its participating interest in Foreignco for 2001 is $100,000, which is added in computing Canco's income under subsection 94.1(3). This is partially offset by a specified tax allocation of $30,000. Foreignco pays a dividend of $50,000 to Canco in 2001. Canco includes the dividend in income pursuant to section 90 and claims a deduction of $20,000 in computing its taxable income pursuant to subsection 113(1).

*Results*

1. Canco's deduction from income under section 94.3 is equal to $35,000, being the lesser of the net income inclusion as a result of the payment (= $50,000 minus $20,000) and the amount of the net income inclusions under subsection 94.1(3) ($100,000 minus $30,000).

2. The result would generally be the same if the $50,000 dividend were instead paid in a subsequent year.

**Application**: The June 22, 2000 draft legislation, s. 11, will amend s. 94.1 to read as above, and add ss. 94.2 and 94.3, applicable to taxpayer's taxation years that begin after 2000 [to be changed to "that begin after 2001", per Sept. 7/00 news release below — ed.], except that subsec. 94.2(10) does not apply to taxation years that begin before 2002.

**Notice of Ways and Means Motion, federal budget, February 16, 1999**: *Non-resident trusts and foreign-based investment funds*

(8) That the provisions of the Act governing the taxation of

(a) trust beneficiaries and non-resident trusts, and

(b) taxpayers resident in Canada who hold interests in foreign-based investment funds

be modified in accordance with proposals described in the budget documents tabled by the Minister of Finance in the House of Commons on February 16, 1999.

**Federal budget, Supplementary Information, February 16, 1999**: *Non-resident trust and foreign-based investment fund rules*

Canadians have significantly increased their holdings of investments in foreign countries over the past ten years. This reflects the globalization of capital markets and recognizes the benefits of portfolio diversification. However, tax planning techniques have developed to create advantages from using foreign-based investment funds and non-resident trusts in comparison with Canadian-based investment vehicles.

The *Income Tax Act* contains provisions that are designed to prevent the use by taxpayers of foreign-based investment funds and non-resident trusts to avoid Canadian tax. The purpose of the rules is to ensure that an appropriate amount of Canadian tax is paid on the foreign investment income earned by taxpayers through such vehicles in order to provide a level playing field with Canadian-based investment vehicles.

There is growing evidence that the objectives of the current provisions of the Act are not being fully met and that high-income individuals are able, in some cases, to avoid Canadian tax by investing in foreign-based investment funds and by contributing property to non-resident trusts. Such an outcome is inconsistent with a fair and neutral tax system, erodes the Canadian tax base and is contrary to the policy intent of the current rules.

*Background*

Canadian investment funds are taxed annually on the income and capital gains accumulated in the funds but not allocated to investors. Investors in such funds are taxed annually on the income and capital gains of the funds allocated to them, as well as on any taxable capital gains arising on the disposition of their interest in the fund. As a result, the Canadian tax base is protected.

Investment funds located outside Canada are generally not subject to tax in Canada. Where such funds face little or no tax in their country of residence, Canadian investors holding interests in such vehicles may benefit from a significant deferral of tax on income and realized capital gains retained in the funds over the years. Furthermore, on the disposition of their interest in a foreign-based investment fund, investors may also be able to convert ordinary income to capital gains, which are taxed at a lower rate. These tax advantages have resulted in a growing number of Canadians investing in foreign-based funds.

*Issue*

The *Income Tax Act* contains rules that attempt to eliminate these tax advantages. Where a Canadian makes an investment in a foreign-based investment fund and one of the main reasons for acquiring, holding or having the interest in such property is to avoid Canadian tax, a notional annual allocation of income is imputed to the taxpayer and subject to tax. This notional amount is determined by multiplying the cost of the taxpayer's interest in the fund by a prescribed interest rate.

The current provision, however, has rarely been applied. Revenue Canada has had difficulty in enforcing this provision because of the frequent lack of information and the challenge of establishing that the interest in the foreign-based investment fund was acquired primarily to avoid Canadian tax. Although the provision may have been effective when first introduced in 1984, its impact has weakened over the years. When the provision has been applied, it has been criticized as subjecting to tax an arbitrary amount that may bear no relationship to the actual income accruing in the fund.

These deficiencies and the resulting erosion of the Canadian tax base necessitate the actions that the government is proposing in this budget.

[See also portions reproduced under 94 — ed.]

*Proposal*

The budget sets forth an approach to address the deficiencies in the current rules governing foreign-based investment funds and non-resident trusts. The objective of the proposals is to enhance fairness in the tax system in relation to the taxation of income earned from investing in foreign-based investment funds and contributing property to non-resident trusts on the one hand, and income earned from investing in similar entities resident in Canada. These proposals would not prevent Canadians from investing in foreign-based investment funds or from contributing property to non-resident trusts, but are intended to ensure that there is no tax advantage in doing so.

Consultations will be initiated on the following proposed modifications to the tax rules governing foreign-based investment funds:

- That the proposed rules apply to interests in a foreign-based investment fund, subject to a number of exceptions noted below. Taxpayers would be subject, annually, to tax on their pro-rata share of all the undistributed income of the foreign-based investment fund where they have access to sufficient information about the income of the fund (the income accrual approach that applies in respect of controlled foreign affiliates of Canadian taxpayers), subject to a foreign tax credit for foreign income taxes paid by the fund. Alternatively, taxpayers would be required to add to or deduct from their income, as the case may be, the annual increase or decrease in the market value of their interest in the fund (the "mark-to-market" approach). These rules would replace the tax motivation test that "one of the main reasons for the taxpayer acquiring, holding or having an interest in a foreign-based investment fund was to avoid Canadian taxation". The rules would not apply where the foreign-based investment fund annually distributes or allocates to Canadian investors all of the fund's income to which those investors are entitled.

- That a foreign-based investment fund be defined as any non-resident corporation, trust, fund or other entity where more than 50 per cent of the cost of the entity's assets are investment properties. Look-through rules would apply in respect of significant investments in other entities for the purpose of making this determination. Where trusts are subject to the proposed non-resident trust rules, such trusts would not be subject to these rules.

- That investment funds situated in the United States not be subject to these rules since tax avoidance and deferral opportunities are not a concern through the use of such vehicles.

- That a five-year exception for temporary residents and new immigrants apply. Additional exemptions could be contemplated to remove from the rules foreign- based investment funds that are clearly not used to avoid or defer Canadian tax.

- That the proposed rules apply to any taxation year commencing after 1999, with respect to any interest in a foreign-based investment fund (in which the taxpayer does not already own an interest) not covered by the exceptions, acquired by a Canadian resident on or after February 16, 1999. All interests in any foreign-based investment fund not covered by the exceptions would be subject to the proposed rules for taxation years commencing after 2000.

**Department of Finance news release, November 30, 1999**: *Update on Proposals for the Taxation of Non-Resident Trusts and Foreign Investment Funds*

[See under 94 — ed.]

**Department of Finance news release, September 7, 2000**: *Finance Minister Extends Consultation Period and Announces New Effective Date for Foreign Investment Entity and Trust Tax Proposals*

Finance Minister Paul Martin today announced that the period of consultation on draft legislation regarding the taxation of non-resident trusts and foreign investment entities will be extended from September 1, 2000, as previously announced, to December 31, 2000. In addition, the implementation date will be delayed by one year, to taxation years beginning after 2001.

Proposals affecting the taxation of non-resident trusts and foreign investment entities were released with the 1999 federal budget to limit opportunities for Canadians to avoid Canadian income tax by transferring funds to offshore trusts or accounts. On November 30, 1999, Minister Martin announced a number of revisions to the proposals. On June 22, 2000, the Department released draft legislation and invited the public to submit comments by September 1, 2000. Extending this deadline to the end of the year responds to a number of requests for more time to provide comments.

Minister Martin also announced that interests in certain U.S. investment funds would be excluded from the application of the foreign investment entity proposals. The backgrounder to this press release contains details on this change and on other changes that are being proposed in response to submissions received to date.

In view of the issues identified in these submissions and the extension of the consultation period on these proposals, it is now proposed to introduce the rules with effect for taxation years that begin after 2001 rather than for taxation years beginning after 2000, as previously proposed. This will allow the Department of Finance to consider fully all comments received before the end of this year and to release a revised draft of the proposals early in 2001.

Interested parties wishing to comment on the draft legislation are invited to send written submissions before the end of the year to the following address: Tax Legislation

Division, Department of Finance Canada, 17th Floor, East Tower, 140 O'Connor Street, Ottawa, Ontario K1A 0G5.

For further information:

Non-resident trusts: Victor Pietrow, Tax Legislation Division, (613) 992-3031; Karl Littler, Senior Advisor, Tax Policy (613) 996-7861.

Foreign investment entities: Marie-Claude Hébert, Tax Legislation Division, (613) 992-4859; Jean-Michel Catta, Public Affairs and Operations Division, (613) 996-8080.

## BACKGROUNDER

### Foreign Investment Entities

Further to the consultations to date on these proposals and additional analysis within the Department, the following modifications to the foreign investment entity (FIE) rules are proposed:

1. It is proposed that interests in United States investment funds that are considered "regulated investment companies" (RICs) for the purposes of the U.S. Internal Revenue Code be excluded from the application of the FIE rules. To qualify as a RIC, an investment fund must annually distribute 90 per cent or more of its income to its unitholders. It is understood that a number of U.S. funds (including those commonly referred to as DIAMONDS, SPDRs and NASDAQ-100) are RICs. As a result of this income distribution requirement, the policy underlying the FIE proposals — that of annual recognition of the FIE's income or growth — is largely met through the existing law. The Department is continuing to explore whether other foreign-based funds should be similarly exempted.

2. Modifications will be proposed to ensure that the cost amount of properties for the purposes of calculating the foreign content limit in registered pension plans and registered retirement savings plans is not impacted by the FIE rules.

3. Employee stock options held by taxpayers in respect of which subsection 7(1) of the *Income Tax Act* applies will not be subject to the proposed FIE rules.

4. Proposed paragraph 94.2(1)(b) of the *Income Tax Act* sets out the definition of "deferral amount". The deferral amount ensures that gains on a taxpayer's interest in a FIE that have accrued before the new rules are to come into effect are not taxed until the interest is disposed of by the taxpayer. The proposed rules released on June 22, 2000, ensure that these gains are taxed at a 2/3 inclusion rate in respect of capital property acquired on or before June 22, 2000. In view of concerns expressed, the 2/3 inclusion rate will be extended to apply to deferral amounts in respect of capital property acquired after June 22, 2000.

5. Under the proposals, a "foreign investment entity" is generally defined as a non-resident entity whose investment properties have a carrying value of more than 50 per cent of the total carrying value of all its property. Proposed paragraph 94.1(1) of the *Income Tax Act* sets out the definition of "investment property". It is proposed that the definition be modified to exclude property that is:

   - real estate used in a business (other than real estate principally used or held to derive rents or profits on its sale),
   - shares held by a corporation that are shares of its own capital stock (e.g., treasury shares),
   - a resource property used in a business (other than an investment business), and
   - indebtedness incurred in connection with a business (other than an investment business) and owing to a related person.

6. Generally speaking, where a taxpayer holds a share of a class of the capital stock of a corporation that is widely held and actively traded on a prescribed stock exchange and whose principal business is not an investment business, the taxpayer's interest in the share will not be subject to the proposed FIE rules. The term "investment business" is defined in proposed subsection 94.1(1) of the *Income Tax Act* as, generally, a business having a principal purpose of deriving income from property (interest, dividends, rents, royalties, etc.).

   However, the definition excludes certain businesses as investment businesses, and it is proposed that the definition be modified to also exclude a business of developing or purchasing and developing property (such as computer software and films but not investment property) for sale or licensing.

7. Proposed subsection 94.1(11) of the *Income Tax Act* sets out the circumstances in which an entity is considered to have a "significant interest" in a corporation, partnership or trust for the purposes of subsection 94.1(10). An entity is considered to have a significant interest in a corporation if it holds shares representing 25 per cent or more of the votes and value associated with all the corporation's shares. It is proposed that subsection 94.1(11) be modified to permit the shareholdings of an entity and persons related to the entity to be aggregated in determining whether the 25 per cent significant interest test has been satisfied. Similar changes are proposed in determining whether an entity has a significant interest in a partnership or trust.

8. An entity that has a "significant interest" in a corporation, partnership or non-discretionary trust is treated under proposed subsection 94.1(10) as owning its proportionate share of the property of the corporation, partnership or trust. The formula for determining this share is based on the relationship of the shares and debt owned by the entity to all the shares and debt issued by the corporation, partnership or trust. It is proposed to change this formula so that debts owing to arm's length financial institutions are excluded.

9. The term "carrying value" is defined in proposed subsection 94.1(1) of the *Income Tax Act*. The carrying value of property is, generally, the amount at which the property is valued for balance sheet purposes. The carrying value of a property is relevant primarily for the purpose of determining whether a non-resident entity is a foreign investment entity. The Department is reviewing the "carrying value" definition to ensure fair results and facilitate the use of the proposed rules by taxpayers. Particular consideration is being given to introducing an alternative method of valuing property in determining whether a non-resident entity is a foreign investment entity.

**Definitions [s. 94.3]:** "adjusted cost base" — 54, 248(1); "amount" — 248(1); "capital property" — 54, 248(1); "entity", "participating interest" — 94.1(1), 94.3(1); "resident in Canada" — 250; "taxable income" — 248(1); "taxation year" — 94.1(1), 94.3(1), 249; "taxpayer" — 248(1).

**95. (1) Definitions for this subdivision** — In this subdivision,

> **Proposed Amendment — 95(1)**
>
> **95. Definitions re foreign affiliates — (1)** In this subdivision (other than sections 94 to 94.3),
>
> **Application**: The June 22, 2000 draft legislation, subsec. 12(1), will amend the opening words of subsec. 95(1) to read as above, applicable to taxation years of foreign affiliates of taxpayers that begin after 2000.
>
> **Technical Notes**: Subsection 95(1) of the Act sets out definitions that are relevant for the purposes of sections 90 to 95.
>
> Subsection 95(1) is amended so that these definitions do not apply for the purposes of sections 94 to 94.3, except where the definition applies for the purposes of the Act as a whole because of subsection 248(1). This amendment applies to taxation years that begin after 2000.

**Notes**: This subdivision is sections 90-95.

**"active business"** of a foreign affiliate of a taxpayer means any business carried on by the affiliate other than

(a) an investment business carried on by the affiliate, or

(b) a business that is deemed by subsection (2) to be a business other than an active business carried on by the affiliate;

**Related Provisions**: 95(1)"income from an active business" — What income included; 248(1) — Meanings of "active business" and "business".

**Notes**: Definition "active business" added by 1994 tax amendments bill (Part II), effective on the same basis as 95(2.1) (see Notes thereto).

**"controlled foreign affiliate"**, at any time, of a taxpayer resident in Canada means a foreign affiliate of the taxpayer that was, at that time, controlled by

> **Proposed Amendment — 95(1)"controlled foreign affiliate" opening words**
>
> **"controlled foreign affiliate"**, at any time, of a taxpayer resident in Canada means a foreign affiliate of the taxpayer that is, at that time, a controlled foreign affiliate of the taxpayer because of subsection 94.1(12) or that is, at that time, controlled by
>
> **Application**: The June 22, 2000 draft legislation, subsec. 12(2), will amend the opening words of the definition "controlled foreign affiliate" in subsec. 95(1) to read as above, applicable to taxation years of foreign affiliates of taxpayers that begin after 2000.
>
> **Technical Notes**: As set out below, various definitions in subsection 95(1) are also being amended.
>
> The income for a taxation year of a taxpayer resident in Canada includes, pursuant to subsection 91(1) of the Act, a specified percentage of the foreign accrual property income (FAPI) of any controlled foreign affiliate of the taxpayer. In order to eliminate overlap between the FAPI rules and the rules for foreign investment entities in sections 94.1 and 94.2, the latter rules do not apply in respect of a taxpayer's interest in a controlled foreign affiliate of a taxpayer resident in Canada. An election is provided under new subsection 94.1(12) under which a foreign affiliate of a taxpayer can be treated as controlled foreign affiliate.
>
> The definition "controlled foreign affiliate" is amended to make a cross-reference to foreign affiliates that are deemed by subsection 94.1(12) to be controlled foreign affiliates. Given the wording in subsection 94.1(12), this reference is not technically necessary but is meant to serve as a useful clarification of the potential application of subsection 94.1(12).

(a) the taxpayer,

(b) the taxpayer and not more than four other persons resident in Canada,

(c) not more than 4 persons resident in Canada, other than the taxpayer,

(d) a person or persons with whom the taxpayer does not deal at arm's length, or

(e) the taxpayer and a person or persons with whom the taxpayer does not deal at arm's length;

**Related Provisions**: 17(15)"controlled foreign affiliate" — Definition applicable to loan by corporation to non-resident; 128.1(1)(d) — Foreign affiliate becoming resident in Canada deemed to have been controlled foreign affiliate; 233.4(4) — Reporting requirements; 248(1)"controlled foreign affiliate" — Definition applies to entire Act; 256(6), (6.1) — Meaning of "controlled".

**Notes**: 95(1)"controlled foreign affiliate" was 95(1)(a) before consolidation in R.S.C. 1985 (5th Supp.), effective for taxation years ending after November 1991. See Table of Concordance.

Para. (c) amended and paras. (d) and (e) added by 1991 technical bill, effective for taxation years beginning after July 13, 1990.

**"excluded property"** of a foreign affiliate of a taxpayer means any property of the foreign affiliate that is

(a) used or held by the foreign affiliate principally for the purpose of gaining or producing income from an active business,

(b) shares of the capital stock of another foreign affiliate of the taxpayer where all or substantially all of the property of the other foreign affiliate is excluded property, or

(c) an amount receivable the interest on which is, or would be if interest were payable thereon, income from an active business by virtue of subparagraph (2)(a)(ii),

and, for the purposes of the definitions "foreign affiliate" in this subsection and "direct equity percentage" in subsection (4) as they apply to this definition, where at any time a foreign affiliate of a taxpayer has an interest in a partnership,

(d) the partnership shall be deemed to be a non-resident corporation having capital stock of a single class divided into 100 issued shares, and

(e) the affiliate shall be deemed to own at that time that proportion of the issued shares of that class that

(i) the fair market value of the affiliate's interest in the partnership at that time

is of

(ii) the fair market value of all interests in the partnership at that time;

**Related Provisions**: 85.1(4) — Exception to share-for-share exchange rules where foreign affiliate's property is substantially all excluded property.

**Notes**: Amended by 1991 technical bill, effective 1990. From November 13, 1981 through 1989, the mechanics of what is now paras. (d) and (e) were different.

The CCRA takes the position that "all or substantially all", used in para. (b), means 90% or more.

95(1)"excluded property" was 95(1)(a.1) before consolidation in R.S.C. 1985 (5th Supp.), effective for taxation years ending after November 1991. See Table of Concordance.

**"foreign accrual property income"** of a foreign affiliate of a taxpayer, for any taxation year of the affiliate, means the amount determined by the formula

$$(A + A.1 + A.2 + B + C) - (D + E + F + G)$$

### Proposed Amendment — 95(1)"foreign accrual property income"

$$(A + A.1 + A.2 + B + C) - (D + E + F + G + H)$$

**Application**: Bill C-43 (First Reading September 20, 2000), subsec. 46(1), will amend the formula in the definition "foreign accrual property income" in subsec. 95(1) to read as above, applicable after November 1999.

**Technical Notes**: See under 95(1)"foreign accrual property income"H.

### Proposed Amendment — 95(1)"foreign accrual property income"

$$(A + A.1 + A.2 + B) - (D + E + F + G + H)$$

**Application**: The June 22, 2000 draft legislation, subsec. 12(3), will amend the formula in the definition "foreign accrual property income" in subsec. 95(1) to read as above, applicable to taxation years of foreign affiliates of taxpayers that begin after 2000.

**Technical Notes**: See under 95(1)"foreign accrual property income"C.

where

A is the amount that would, if section 80 did not apply to the affiliate for the year or a preceding taxation year, be the total of the affiliate's incomes for the year from property and businesses (other than active businesses) determined as if each amount described in clause (2)(a)(ii)(D) that was paid or payable, directly or indirectly, by the affiliate to another foreign affiliate of either the taxpayer or a person with whom the taxpayer does not deal at arm's length were nil where an amount in respect of the income derived by the other foreign affiliate from that amount that was paid or payable to it by the affiliate was added in computing its income from an active business, other than

(a) interest that would, by virtue of paragraph 81(1)(m), not be included in computing the income of the affiliate if it were resident in Canada,

(b) a dividend from another foreign affiliate of the taxpayer,

(c) a taxable dividend to the extent that the amount thereof would, if the dividend were received by the taxpayer, be deductible by the taxpayer under section 112, or

(d) any amount included because of subsection 80.4(2) in the affiliate's income in respect of indebtedness to another corporation that is a foreign affiliate of the taxpayer or of a person resident in Canada with whom the taxpayer does not deal at arm's length,

A.1 is $4/3$ of the total of all amounts included in computing the affiliate's income from property or businesses (other than active businesses) for the year because of subsection 80(13),

### Proposed Amendment — 95(1)"foreign accrual property income"A.1

**Application**: The December 21, 2000 draft legislation, subsec. 43(1), will amend the description of A.1 in the definition "foreign accrual property income" in subsec. 95(1) by replacing the reference to the expression "4/3 of" with a reference to the word "twice", applicable to taxation years that end after February 27, 2000 except that, where a taxation year of a foreign affiliate of a taxpayer includes either February 28, 2000 or October 17, 2000, the reference to the word "twice" shall be read as a reference to the expression "the fraction that is the reciprocal of the fraction in para. 38(a), as amended [by the December 21, 2000 draft legislation], that applies to the foreign affiliate for the year, multiplied by".

**Technical Notes**: The description of A.1 in the definition "foreign accrual property income" in subsection 95(1) includes in the foreign accrual property income of a foreign affiliate of a taxpayer 4/3 of the amount required in respect of a debt settlement to be added to the affiliate's income because of subsection 80(13).

The description of A.1 is amended to replace the reference to the expression "4/3 of" with a reference to the word "twice". The change is consequential on the reduction of the capital gains inclusion rate from 3/4 to 1/2 [see 38(a) — ed.].

The amendment generally applies to taxation years that end after February 27, 2000 except that, where the affiliate's taxation year includes either February 28, 2000 or October 17, 2000, the reference to the word "twice" in the description of A.1 in the definition "foreign accrual property income" in subsection 95(1) is to be read as a reference the expression "the fraction that is the reciprocal of the fraction in paragraph 38(a) that applies to the foreign affiliate for the year, multiplied by". These modifications are required in order to reflect the capital gains/losses rate for the year.

A.2 is the amount determined for G in respect of the affiliate for the preceding taxation year,

B is such portion of the affiliate's taxable capital gains for the year from dispositions of property, other than dispositions of excluded property to which none of paragraphs (2)(c), (d) and (e) apply, as may reasonably be considered to have accrued after its 1975 taxation year,

C is where the affiliate is a controlled foreign affiliate of the taxpayer, the amount that would be required to be included in computing its income for the year if

(a) subsection 94.1(1) were applicable in computing that income,

(b) the words "earned directly by the taxpayer" in that subsection were replaced by the words "earned by the person resident in Canada in respect of whom the taxpayer is a foreign affiliate",

(c) the words "other than a controlled foreign affiliate of the taxpayer or a prescribed non-resident entity" in paragraph 94.1(1)(a) were replaced by the words "other than a prescribed non-resident entity or a controlled foreign affiliate of a person resident in Canada of whom the taxpayer is a controlled foreign affiliate", and

(d) the words "other than a capital gain" in paragraph 94.1(1)(g) were replaced by the words "other than any income that would not be included in the taxpayer's foreign accrual property income for the year if the value of C in the definition "foreign accrual property income" in subsection 95(1) were nil and other than a capital gain",

### Proposed Repeal — 95(1)"foreign accrual property income"C

**Application**: The June 22, 2000 draft legislation, subsec. 12(4), will repeal the description of C in the definition "foreign accrual property income" in subsec. 95(1), applicable to taxation years of foreign affiliates of taxpayers that begin after 2000.

**Technical Notes**: The FAPI of a controlled foreign affiliate of a taxpayer resident in Canada is allocated to the taxpayer in accordance with subsection 91(1) of the Act. Under its definition in subsection 95(1), FAPI includes certain amounts that would be included in the affiliate's income under existing subsection 94.1(1) if that subsection were read in the manner specified in the description of C of the definition.

Existing section 94.1 is being repealed. Accordingly, the description of C in the definition "foreign accrual property income" is also repealed. There are, however, special rules in new paragraph 95(2)(g.2) with regard to the application of sections 94.1 to 94.3 for the purposes of computing FAPI.

D is the total of the affiliate's losses for the year from property and businesses (other than active businesses) determined as if there were not included in the affiliate's income any amount described in any of paragraphs (a) to (d) of the description of A and as if each amount described in clause (2)(a)(ii)(D) that was paid or payable, directly or indirectly, by the affiliate to another foreign affiliate of either the taxpayer or a person with whom the taxpayer does not deal at arm's length were nil where an amount in respect of the income derived by the other foreign affiliate from that amount that was paid or payable to it by the affiliate was added in computing its income from an active business,

E is such portion of the affiliate's allowable capital losses for the year from dispositions of property, other than dispositions of excluded property to which none of paragraphs (2)(c), (d) and (e) apply, as may reasonably be considered to have accrued after its 1975 taxation year,

F is the amount prescribed to be the deductible loss of the affiliate for the year and the five immediately preceding taxation years, and

### Proposed Amendment — 95(1)"foreign accrual property income"F

F is the amount prescribed to be the deductible loss of the affiliate for the year, and

**Application**: Bill C-43 (First Reading September 20, 2000), subsec. 46(2), will amend the description of F in the definition "foreign accrual property income" in subsec. 95(1) to read as above, applicable to foreign affiliates' taxation years that begin after November 1999.

**Technical Notes**: The description of F in the definition "foreign accrual property income" in subsection 95(1) of the Act and section 5903 of the Regulations establish the extent to which a foreign affiliate of a taxpayer is permitted to deduct amounts in computing its foreign accrual property income for the year in respect of foreign accrual property losses of other taxation years. Under the existing provisions such losses may be carried forward for five years.

The amendments to the description of F in the definition "foreign accrual property income" in subsection 95(1) of the Act and section 5903 of the Regulations provide that foreign accrual property losses may be carried back three years and forward seven years.

G is the amount, if any, by which

(a) the total of amounts determined for A.1 and A.2 in respect of the affiliate for the year

exceeds

(b) the total of all amounts determined for D to F in respect of the affiliate for the year;

### Proposed Addition — 95(1)"foreign accrual property income"H

H is

(a) where the affiliate was a member of a partnership at the end of the fiscal period of the partnership that ended in the year and the partnership received a dividend at a particular time in that fiscal period from a corporation that was, for the purposes of sections 93 and 113, a foreign affiliate of the taxpayer at that particular time, the portion of the amount of that dividend that is included in the value of A in respect of the affiliate for the year and that is deemed by paragraph 93.1(2)(a) to have been received by the affiliate for the purposes of sections 93 and 113, and

(b) in any other case, nil;

**Application**: Bill C-43 (First Reading September 20, 2000), subsec. 46(3), will add the description of H to the definition "foreign accrual property income" in subsec. 95(1), applicable after November 1999.

S. 95(1) for                Income Tax Act, Part I, Division B

**Technical Notes**: The amendment to the definition of "foreign accrual property income" in subsection 95(1) of the Act adds new description H to the formula in that definition. The description of H applies where the affiliate was a member of a partnership that received a dividend from another foreign affiliate of the taxpayer. In such a case, the amount for the description of H is equal to the portion of such dividend received by the partnership that is included in the description of A in the formula in respect of the affiliate for the year that is deemed by paragraph 93.1(2)(a) of the Act to have been a dividend received by the member affiliate from another foreign affiliate of the taxpayer. New description H ensures that inter-affiliate dividends are not included in foreign accrual property income of an affiliate of the taxpayer.

**Related Provisions**: 40(3)(d) — Deemed gain where ACB would become negative; 53(1)(m) — ACB of offshore investment fund property; 95(2) — Determination of certain components of FAPI; 152(6.1) — Reassessment to apply FAPI loss carryback; 248(1)"foreign accrual property income" — Definition applies to entire Act; 257 — Formula cannot calculate to less than zero.

**Notes**: See Notes to 91(1) for an overview of the FAPI rules. See also 95(2) for detailed rules affecting the calculation of FAPI.

Opening words of A amended by 1994 tax amendments bill (Part IX — general — combining both debt forgiveness and foreign affiliate amendments). The version shown applies on the same basis as 95(2.1) (see Notes thereto). Where the version above does not apply (i.e., generally for taxation years of foreign affiliates that begin before 1995), for taxation years that end after February 21, 1994, ignore everything from "determined as if each amount..." through to "income from an active business".

For taxation years that end before February 22, 1994, ignore the words "the amount that would, if section 80 did not apply to the affiliate for the year or a preceding taxation year", so the opening words of A read simply "the total of the affiliate's incomes for the year from property and businesses other than active businesses, other than".

Para. A(d) (formerly 95(1)(b)(i)(D)), and reference to it in D (formerly (b)(iii)), added by 1991 technical bill, effective 1987.

Formula elements A.1, A.2 and G added by 1994 tax amendments bill (Part I — debt forgiveness), effective for taxation years that end after February 21, 1994.

Para. C(c) added by 1995-97 technical bill, effective for taxation years that end after November 1991.

Para. C(d) added by 1995-97 technical bill, effective for taxation years that begin after June 19, 1996.

Description of D amended to add everything from "and as if each amount..." by 1994 tax amendments bill (Part II — foreign affiliates), effective on the same basis as 95(2.1) (see Notes thereto).

95(1)"foreign accrual property income" was 95(1)(b) before consolidation in R.S.C. 1985 (5th Supp.), effective for taxation years ending after November 1991. The previous version, identical in meaning, read:

(b) "foreign accrual property income" — "foreign accrual property income" of a foreign affiliate of a taxpayer, for any taxation year of the affiliate, means the amount, if any, by which the aggregate of

(i) the affiliate's incomes for the year from property and businesses other than active businesses, other than

(A) interest that would, by virtue of paragraph 81(1)(m), not be included in computing the income of the affiliate if it were resident in Canada,

(B) a dividend from another foreign affiliate of the taxpayer, or

(C) a taxable dividend to the extent that the amount thereof would, if the dividend were received by the taxpayer, be deductible by him under section 112, and

(ii) such portion of the affiliate's taxable capital gains for the year from dispositions of property, other than dispositions of excluded property to which none of paragraphs (2)(c), (d) and (e) apply, as may reasonably be considered to have accrued after its 1975 taxation year, and

(ii.1) where the affiliate is a controlled foreign affiliate of the taxpayer, the amount that would be required to be included in computing its income for the year if

(A) subsection 94.1(1) were applicable in computing such income, and

(B) the words "earned directly by the taxpayer" in that subsection were replaced by the words "earned by the person resident in Canada in respect of whom the taxpayer is a foreign affiliate"

exceeds the aggregate of

(iii) the affiliate's losses for the year from property and businesses other than active businesses determined as if there were not included in the affiliate's income any amount described in clause (i)(A), (B) or (C),

(iv) such portion of the affiliate's allowable capital losses for the year from dispositions of property, other than dispositions of excluded property to which none of paragraphs (2)(c), (d) and (e) apply, as may reasonably be considered to have accrued after its 1975 taxation year, and

(v) the amount prescribed to be the deductible loss of the affiliate for the year and the five immediately preceding taxation years;

**Regulations**: 5903 (prescribed deductible loss); 5907(2.8) (transfer of active business income between foreign affiliates).

**I.T. Application Rules**: 35(1) (ITAR 26 does not apply in determining gains and losses of foreign affiliates; 35(4) (where corporation deemed to be foreign affiliate before May 7, 1974 because of election).

**Interpretation Bulletins**: IT-451R: Deemed disposition and acquisition on ceasing to be or becoming resident in Canada.

**"foreign accrual tax"** applicable to any amount included in computing a taxpayer's income by virtue of subsection 91(1) for a taxation year in respect of a particular foreign affiliate of the taxpayer means

(a) the portion of any income or profits tax that was paid by

(i) the particular affiliate, or

(ii) any other foreign affiliate of the taxpayer in respect of a dividend received from the particular affiliate

and that may reasonably be regarded as applicable to that amount, and

(b) any amount prescribed in respect of the particular affiliate to be foreign accrual tax applicable to that amount;

**Notes**: 95(1)"foreign accrual tax" was 95(1)(c) before consolidation in R.S.C. 1985 (5th Supp.), effective for taxation years ending after November 1991. See Table of Concordance.

**Regulations**: 5907(1.3) (prescribed foreign accrual tax).

**"foreign affiliate"**, at any time, of a taxpayer resident in Canada means a non-resident corporation in which, at that time,

(a) the taxpayer's equity percentage is not less than 1%, and

(b) the total of the equity percentages in the corporation of the taxpayer and of each person related to the taxpayer (where each such equity percentage is determined as if the determinations under paragraph (b) of the definition "equity percentage" in subsection (4) were made without reference to the equity percentage of any person in the taxpayer or in any person related to the taxpayer) is not less than 10%,

except that a corporation is not a foreign affiliate of a non-resident-owned investment corporation;

**Related Provisions**: 87(8) — Merger of foreign affiliate; 93.1 — Shares held by a partnership; 95(4) — Equity percentage; 128.1(1)(d) — Foreign affiliate becoming resident in Canada; 233.4(4) — Reporting requirements; 248(1)"foreign affiliate" — Definition applies to entire Act.

**Notes**: Definition "foreign affiliate" amended by 1994 tax amendments bill (Part II), effective on the same basis as 95(2.1) (see Notes thereto). Previously read:

"foreign affiliate", at any time, of a taxpayer (other than a non-resident-owned investment corporation) resident in Canada means a corporation (other than a corporation resident in Canada), in which, at that time, the taxpayer's equity percentage was not less than 10%;

95(1)"foreign affiliate" was 95(1)(d) before consolidation in R.S.C. 1985 (5th Supp.), effective for taxation years ending after November 1991.

**I.T. Application Rules**: 35(4) (where corporation deemed to be foreign affiliate due to election made before May 6, 1974).

**Interpretation Bulletins**: IT-343R: Meaning of the term "corporation"; IT-451R: Deemed disposition and acquisition on ceasing to be or becoming resident in Canada.

**Information Circulars**: 77-9R: Books, records and other requirements for taxpayers having foreign affiliates.

**"foreign bank"** means an entity that would be a foreign bank within the meaning assigned by the definition of that expression in section 2 of the *Bank Act* if

(a) that definition were read without reference to the portion thereof after paragraph (g) thereof, and

(b) the entity had not been exempt under section 12 of that Act from being a foreign bank;

**Related Provisions**: 94.1(1)"foreign bank" — Definition applies to foreign investment entity rules.

**Notes**: Definition "foreign bank" added by 1994 tax amendments bill (Part II), effective on the same basis as 95(2.1) (see Notes thereto).

Section 2 of the *Bank Act*, S.C. 1991, c. 46, defines "foreign bank" as follows:

"foreign bank", subject to section 12, means an entity incorporated or formed by or under the laws of a country other than Canada that

(a) is a bank according to the laws of any foreign country where it carries on business,

(b) carries on a business in any foreign country that, if carried on in Canada, would be, wholly or to a significant extent, the business of banking,

(c) engages, directly or indirectly, in the business of providing financial services and employs, to identify or describe its business, a name that includes the word "bank", "banque", "banking" or "bancaire", either alone or in combination with other words, or any word or words in any language other than English or French corresponding generally thereto,

(d) engages in the business of lending money and accepting deposit liabilities transferable by cheque or other instrument,

(e) engages, directly or indirectly, in the business of providing financial services and is affiliated with another foreign bank,

(f) controls another foreign bank, or

(g) is a foreign institution, other than a foreign bank within the meaning of any of paragraphs (a) to (f), that controls a bank named in Schedule II,

but does not include a subsidiary of a bank named in Schedule I;

Note that the closing words do not apply for purposes of this definition, so a subsidiary of a Schedule I bank (Canadian bank) can be a foreign bank for purposes of the FAPI rules. Section 12 of the *Bank Act*, which also does not apply for FAPI purposes, provides that the Minister of Finance may, by order, and subject to such terms and conditions as the Minister deems appropriate, exempt any entity from being a foreign bank.

**"income from an active business"** of a foreign affiliate of a taxpayer for a taxation year includes, for greater certainty, any income of the affiliate for the year that pertains to or is incident to that business but does not include

(a) other income that is its income from property for the year, or

(b) its income for the year from a business that is deemed by subsection (2) to be a business other than an active business carried on by the affiliate;

**Related Provisions**: 95(1)"active business" — Businesses excluded; 95(1)"income from property" — Extended meaning of income from property.

**Notes**: Definition "income from an active business" added by 1994 tax amendments bill (Part II), effective on the same basis as 95(2.1) (see Notes thereto).

**"income from property"** of a foreign affiliate of a taxpayer for a taxation year includes its income for the year from an investment business and its income for the year from an adventure or concern in the nature of trade, but, for greater certainty, does not include its income for the year that is because of subsection (2) included in its income from an active business or in its income from a business other than an active business;

**Related Provisions**: 9(1) — Determination of income from property; 95(1)"investment business" — Meaning of investment business; 95(2)(l) — Income from trading or dealing in indebtedness.

**Notes**: Definition "income from property" added by 1994 tax amendments bill (Part II), effective on the same basis as 95(2.1) (see Notes thereto).

**"investment business"** of a foreign affiliate of a taxpayer means a business carried on by the affiliate in

**S. 95(1) inv**      Income Tax Act, Part I, Division B

a taxation year (other than a business deemed by subsection (2) to be a business other than an active business carried on by the affiliate) the principal purpose of which is to derive income from property (including interest, dividends, rents, royalties or any similar returns or substitutes therefor), income from the insurance or reinsurance of risks, income from the factoring of trade accounts receivable, or profits from the disposition of investment property, unless it is established by the taxpayer or the affiliate that, throughout the period in the year during which the business was carried on by the affiliate,

  (a) the business (other than any business conducted principally with persons with whom the affiliate does not deal at arm's length) is

    (i) a business carried on by it as a foreign bank, a trust company, a credit union, an insurance corporation or a trader or dealer in securities or commodities, the activities of which are regulated in the country in which the business is principally carried on, or

> **Proposed Amendment — 95(1)"investment business"(a)(i)**
>
> (i) a business carried on by it as a foreign bank, a trust company, a credit union, an insurance corporation or a trader or dealer in securities or commodities, the activities of which are regulated under the laws of the country in which the business is principally carried on, or
>
> **Application:** The June 22, 2000 draft legislation, subsec. 12(5), will amend subpara. (a)(i) of the definition "investment business" in subsec. 95(1) to read as above, applicable to taxation years of foreign affiliates of taxpayers that begin after 2000.
>
> **Technical Notes:** "Investment business" of a foreign affiliate means a business carried on by the foreign affiliate the principal purpose of which is to derive income from property. However, an arm's length business carried on by a foreign bank, trust company, credit union, insurance corporation or securities trader is excluded from the definition "investment business" where the business is regulated in the country in which the business is principally carried on and a 5-employee test is satisfied.
>
> The definition is amended to clarify that the regulation of the business must be under the laws of the country. This language corresponds to a similar definition of the same expression in new subsection 94.1(1).

    (ii) the development of real estate for sale, the lending of money, the leasing or licensing of property or the insurance or reinsurance of risks, and

  (b) the affiliate or, where the affiliate carries on the business as a member of a partnership (except where the affiliate is a specified member of the partnership in a fiscal period of the partnership that ends in the year), the partnership employs

    (i) more than 5 employees full time in the active conduct of the business, or

    (ii) the equivalent of more than 5 employees full time in the active conduct of the business taking into consideration only the services provided by its employees and the services provided outside Canada to the affiliate or the partnership by the employees of

      (A) a corporation related to the affiliate (otherwise than because of a right referred to in paragraph 251(5)(b)), or

      (B) members of the partnership (other than a member of the partnership that was a specified member of the partnership in a fiscal period of the partnership that ends in the year)

where the corporation or members referred to in clause (A) or (B) receive compensation from the affiliate or the partnership for the services provided to the affiliate or the partnership by those employees the value of which is not less than the cost to such corporation or members of the compensation paid or accruing to the benefit of those employees that performed the services during the time the services were performed by those employees;

**Related Provisions:** 95(1)"active business"(a) — Investment business excluded from active business; 95(2)(a.2) — Income from insurance business; 95(2.1) — Whether dealing with foreign affiliate at arm's length; 125(7) — Analogous definition of "specified investment business" for small business deduction purposes.

**Notes:** Definition "investment business" added by 1994 tax amendments bill (Part II), effective on the same basis as 95(2.1) (see Notes thereto).

The words "more than 5 full-time employees" mean 6 or more, not 5 plus a part-time person. See *Hughes & Co. Holdings Ltd.*, [1994] 2 C.T.C. 170 (FCTD). However, in appropriate cases even 4 hours per day could be "full-time": *Ben Raedarc Holdings Ltd.*, [1998] 1 C.T.C. 2774 (TCC).

**"investment property"** of a foreign affiliate of a taxpayer includes

  (a) a share of the capital stock of a corporation other than a share of another foreign affiliate of the taxpayer that is excluded property of the affiliate,

  (b) an interest in a partnership other than an interest in a partnership that is excluded property of the affiliate,

  (c) an interest in a trust other than an interest in a trust that is excluded property of the affiliate,

  (d) indebtedness or annuities,

  (e) commodities or commodities futures purchased or sold, directly or indirectly in any manner whatever, on a commodities or commodities futures exchange (except commodities manufactured, produced, grown, extracted or processed by the affiliate or a person to whom the affiliate is related (otherwise than because of a right referred to in paragraph 251(5)(b)) or commodities futures in respect of such commodities),

## Subdivision i — Shareholders of Non-Resident Corporations S. 95(1) rel

(f) currency,

(g) real estate,

(h) Canadian and foreign resource properties,

(i) interests in funds or entities other than corporations, partnerships and trusts, and

(j) interests or options in respect of property that is included in any of paragraphs (a) to (i);

**Notes**: Definition "investment property" added by 1994 tax amendments bill (Part II), effective on the same basis as 95(2.1) (see Notes thereto).

**"lease obligation"** of a person includes an obligation under an agreement that authorizes the use of or the production or reproduction of property including information or any other thing;

**Notes**: Definition "lease obligation" added by 1994 tax amendments bill (Part II), effective on the same basis as 95(2.1) (see Notes thereto).

**"lending of money"** by a person (for the purpose of this definition referred to as the "lender") includes

(a) the acquisition by the lender of trade accounts receivable (other than trade accounts receivable owing by a person with whom the lender does not deal at arm's length) from another person or the acquisition by the lender of any interest in any such accounts receivable,

(b) the acquisition by the lender of loans made by and lending assets (other than loans or lending assets owing by a person with whom the lender does not deal at arm's length) of another person or the acquisition by the lender of any interest in such a loan or lending asset,

(c) the acquisition by the lender of a foreign resource property (other than a foreign resource property that is a rental or royalty payable by a person with whom the lender does not deal at arm's length) of another person, and

(d) the sale by the lender of loans or lending assets (other than loans or lending assets owing by a person with whom the lender does not deal at arm's length) or the sale by the lender of any interest in such loans or lending assets;

and for the purpose of this definition, the definition "lending asset" in subsection 248(1) shall be read without the words "but does not include a prescribed property";

**Notes**: Definition "lending of money" added by 1994 tax amendments bill (Part II), effective on the same basis as 95(2.1) (see Notes thereto).

Closing words of definition added by 1995-97 technical bill, this version effective for taxation years of a foreign affiliate that ended after September 1997. For earlier years, retroactive to the introduction of the definition, read "security" in place of "property" as the last word of the definition.

**"licensing of property"** includes authorizing the use of or the production or reproduction of property including information or any other thing;

**Notes**: Definition "licensing of property" added by 1994 tax amendments bill (Part II), effective on the same basis as 95(2.1) (see Notes thereto).

**"participating percentage"** of a particular share owned by a taxpayer of the capital stock of a corporation in respect of any foreign affiliate of the taxpayer that was, at the end of its taxation year, a controlled foreign affiliate of the taxpayer is

(a) where the foreign accrual property income of the affiliate for that year is $5,000 or less, nil, and

(b) where the foreign accrual property income of the affiliate for that year exceeds $5,000,

(i) where the affiliate and each corporation that is relevant to the determination of the taxpayer's equity percentage in the affiliate has only one class of issued shares at the end of that taxation year of the affiliate, the percentage that would be the taxpayer's equity percentage in the affiliate at that time on the assumption that the taxpayer owned no shares other than the particular share (but in no case shall that assumption be made for the purpose of determining whether or not a corporation is a foreign affiliate of the taxpayer), and

(ii) in any other case, the percentage determined in prescribed manner;

**Related Provisions**: 95(1) — Foreign accrual property income; 95(1) — Foreign affiliate; 95(4) — Equity percentage.

**Notes**: 95(1)"participating percentage" was 95(1)(e) before consolidation in R.S.C. 1985 (5th Supp.), effective for taxation years ending after November 1991. See Table of Concordance.

**Regulations**: 5904 (prescribed manner).

**"relevant tax factor"** means

(a) where the taxpayer is an individual, 2, or

(b) where the taxpayer is a corporation, the quotient obtained when one is divided by the percentage set out in paragraph 123(1)(a);

### Proposed Amendment — 95(1)"relevant tax factor"

**"relevant tax factor"** of a person or partnership for a taxation year means

(a) in the case of a corporation (or a partnership all the members of which, other than non-resident persons, are corporations), the quotient obtained when 1 is divided by the percentage set out in paragraph 123(1)(a) in respect of the year, and

(b) in any other case, 2.

**Application**: The June 22, 2000 draft legislation, subsec. 12(6), will amend the definition "relevant tax factor" in subsec. 95(1) to read as above, applicable after 2000.

**Technical Notes**: The existing definition "relevant tax factor" provides that the "relevant tax factor" for an individual is 2 and for a corporation is the reciprocal of the basic corporate tax rate (i.e., 1/.38, or 2.63).

Under new section 94.1, the "relevant tax factor" is relevant in determining the extent to which relief is provided for investors in foreign investment entities in respect of income or profits taxes payable by those entities. (See, in this regard, subsection 94.1(8).) Partnerships may hold interests in such entities, in which case it may become necessary to compute a relevant tax factor in respect of a partnership.

The definition "relevant tax factor" is amended so that the relevant tax factor for a partnership is 2, except where its members consist entirely of corporations resident in Canada and non-resident persons. In the latter case, the "relevant tax factor" is 2.63.

This amendment applies after 2000.

**Notes**: 95(1)"relevant tax factor" was 95(1)(f) before consolidation in R.S.C. 1985 (5th Supp.), effective for taxation years ending after November 1991. See Table of Concordance.

**"surplus entitlement percentage"**, at any time, of a taxpayer in respect of a foreign affiliate has the meaning assigned by regulation; and

**Notes**: 95(1)"surplus entitlement percentage" was 95(1)(f.1) before consolidation in R.S.C. 1985 (5th Supp.), effective for taxation years ending after November 1991.

**Regulations**: 5905(13).

**"taxation year"** in relation to a foreign affiliate of a taxpayer means the period for which the accounts of the foreign affiliate have been ordinarily made up, but no such period may exceed 53 weeks.

**Related Provisions**: 95(1) — Foreign affiliate; 249 — Taxation year.

**Notes**: 95(1)"taxation year" was 95(1)(g) before consolidation in R.S.C. 1985 (5th Supp.), effective for taxation years ending after November 1991.

**"trust company"** includes a corporation that is resident in Canada and that is a loan company as defined in subsection 2(1) of the *Canadian Payments Association Act*.

**Notes**: Subsec. 2(1) of the *Canadian Payments Association Act* (as amended by S.C. 1991, c. 45, s. 546(1)) defines "loan company" as follows:

> "loan company" means a body corporate that accepts deposits transferable by order to a third party and that
>
> (a) is a company to which the *Trust and Loan Companies Act* applies and that is not a trust company pursuant to subsection 57(2) of that Act, or
>
> (b) carries on, under an Act of the legislature of a province or a constating instrument issued under provincial jurisdiction, a business substantially similar to the business of a company referred to in paragraph (a).

Definition "trust company" added by 1995-97 technical bill, effective on the same basis as the introduction of 95(2.1).

**(2) Determination of certain components of foreign accrual property income** — For the purposes of this subdivision,

(a) **[income related to active business]** — in computing the income from an active business for a taxation year of a particular foreign affiliate of a taxpayer in respect of which the taxpayer has a qualifying interest throughout the year there shall be included any income of the affiliate for that year from sources in a country other than Canada that would otherwise be income from property of the affiliate for the year to the extent that

(i) the income

(A) is derived by the particular affiliate from activities that can reasonably be considered to be directly related to the active business activities carried on in a country other than Canada by

(I) any other non-resident corporation to which the particular affiliate and the taxpayer are related throughout the year, or

(II) the taxpayer, where the taxpayer is a life insurance corporation resident in Canada throughout the year, and

(B) would be included in computing the amount prescribed to be the earnings or loss from an active business carried on in a country other than Canada of

(I) the non-resident corporation to which the particular affiliate and the taxpayer are related throughout the year, or

(II) the taxpayer, where the taxpayer is a life insurance corporation resident in Canada throughout the year

if it were a foreign affiliate of the taxpayer and the income were earned by it,

(ii) the income is derived from amounts that were paid or payable, directly or indirectly, to the particular affiliate or a partnership of which the particular affiliate was a member

(A) by

(I) a non-resident corporation to which the particular affiliate and the taxpayer are related throughout the year, or

(II) a partnership of which a non-resident corporation to which the particular affiliate and the taxpayer are related throughout the year is a member and of which that non-resident corporation is not a specified member at any time in a fiscal period of the partnership that ends in the year

to the extent that those amounts that were paid or payable are for expenditures that would, if the non-resident corporation or the partnership were a foreign affiliate of the taxpayer, be deductible by it in the year or a subsequent year in computing the amounts prescribed to be its earnings or loss from an active business, other than an active business carried on in Canada,

(B) by

(I) another foreign affiliate of the taxpayer in respect of which the taxpayer has a qualifying interest throughout the year, or

(II) a partnership of which another foreign affiliate of the taxpayer in respect of which the taxpayer has a qualifying interest throughout the year is a member and of which that other affiliate is not a specified member at any time in a fiscal period of the partnership that ends in the year

to the extent that those amounts that were paid or payable are for expenditures that were or would be, if the partnership were a foreign affiliate of the taxpayer, deductible in the year or a subsequent taxation year by the other affiliate or the partnership in computing the amounts prescribed to be its earnings or loss from an active business, other than an active business carried on in Canada,

(C) by a partnership of which the particular affiliate is a member and of which the particular affiliate is not a specified member at any time in a fiscal period of the partnership that ends in the year to the extent that those amounts that were paid or payable were for expenditures that would be, if the partnership were a foreign affiliate of the taxpayer, deductible in the year or a subsequent year in computing the amounts prescribed to be its earnings or loss from an active business carried on by it outside Canada,

(D) by another foreign affiliate of the taxpayer (in this clause referred to as the "second affiliate") to which the particular affiliate and the taxpayer are related throughout the year to the extent that the amounts are paid or payable by the second affiliate

(I) under a legal obligation to pay interest on borrowed money used for the purpose of earning income from property, or

(II) on an amount payable for property acquired for the purpose of gaining or producing income from property

where

(III) the property is excluded property of the second affiliate that is shares of a foreign affiliate (other than the particular affiliate) of the taxpayer in respect of which the taxpayer has a qualifying interest throughout the year (in this clause referred to as the "third affiliate"),

(IV) the second and third affiliates are resident in and subject to income taxation in the same country, and

(V) the amounts paid or payable are relevant in computing the liability for income taxes in that country of the members of a group of corporations composed of the second affiliate and one or more other foreign affiliates of the taxpayer (the shares of which are excluded property) that are resident and subject to income taxation in that country and in respect of which the taxpayer has a qualifying interest throughout the year, or

(E) by the taxpayer, where the taxpayer is a life insurance corporation resident in Canada (in this clause referred to as the "insurer"), to the extent that those amounts that were paid or payable were for expenditures that are deductible in the year or a subsequent taxation year by the insurer in computing its income or loss from carrying on its life insurance business outside Canada and are not deductible in the year or a subsequent taxation year in computing its income or loss from carrying on its life insurance business in Canada,

(iii) the income is derived by the particular affiliate from the factoring of trade accounts receivable acquired by the particular affiliate or a partnership of which the particular affiliate was a member from a non-resident corporation to which the particular affiliate and the taxpayer are related throughout the year to the extent that the accounts receivable arose in the course of an active business carried on in a country other than Canada by the non-resident corporation, or

(iv) the income is derived by the particular affiliate from loans or lending assets acquired by the particular affiliate or a partnership of which the particular affiliate was a member from a non-resident corporation to which the particular affiliate and the taxpayer are related throughout the year to the extent that the loans or lending assets arose in the course of an active business carried on in a country other than Canada by the non-resident corporation;

(a.1) **[income from sale of property]** — in computing the income from a business other than an active business for a taxation year of a foreign affiliate of a taxpayer there shall be included the income of the affiliate for the year from the sale of property (which, for the purposes of this paragraph, includes the income of the affiliate for the year from the performance of services as an agent in relation to a purchase or sale of property) where

(i) it is reasonable to conclude that the cost to any person of the property (other than property that was manufactured, produced, grown, extracted or processed in Canada by the taxpayer or a person with whom the taxpayer does not deal at arm's length in the course of carrying on a business in Canada and that was sold to non-resident persons other than the affiliate or sold to the affiliate for sale to non-resident persons) is relevant in computing the income from a business carried on by the taxpayer or a person resident in Canada with whom the taxpayer does not deal at arm's length or is relevant in computing the income from a business carried on in Canada by a non-resident person with whom the taxpayer does not deal at arm's length, and

(ii) the property was not manufactured, produced, grown, extracted or processed in the country under whose laws the affiliate was formed or continued and exists and is governed and in which the affiliate's business is principally carried on,

unless more than 90% of the gross revenue of the affiliate for the year from the sale of property is derived from the sale of such property (other than a property described in subparagraph (ii) the cost of which to any person is a cost referred to in subparagraph (i)) to persons with whom the affiliate deals at arm's length (which, for this purpose, includes a sale of property to a non-resident corporation with which the affiliate does not deal at arm's length for sale to persons with whom the affiliate deals at arm's length) and, where this paragraph applies to include income of the affiliate from the sale of property in the income of the affiliate from a business other than an active business,

(iii) the sale of such property shall be deemed to be a separate business, other than an active business, carried on by the affiliate, and

(iv) any income of the affiliate that pertains to or is incident to that business shall be deemed to be income from a business other than an active business;

(a.2) **[income from insurance]** — in computing the income from a business other than an active business for a taxation year of a foreign affiliate of a taxpayer there shall be included the income of the affiliate for the year from the insurance of a risk (which, for the purposes of this paragraph, includes income of the affiliate for the year from the reinsurance of a risk) where the risk was in respect of

(i) a person resident in Canada,

(ii) a property situated in Canada, or

(iii) a business carried on in Canada

unless more than 90% of the gross premium revenue of the affiliate for the year from the insurance of risks (net of reinsurance ceded) was in respect of the insurance of risks (other than risks in respect of a person, a property or a business described in subparagraphs (i) to (iii)) of persons with whom the affiliate deals at arm's length and, where this paragraph applies to include income of the affiliate from the insurance of risks in the income of the affiliate from a business other than an active business,

(iv) the insurance of those risks shall be deemed to be a separate business, other than an active business, carried on by the affiliate, and

(v) any income of the affiliate that pertains to or is incident to that business shall be deemed to be income from a business other than an active business;

(a.3) **[income from Canadian debt and lease obligations]** — in computing the income from a business other than an active business for a taxation year of a foreign affiliate of a taxpayer there shall be included the income of the affiliate for the year derived directly or indirectly from indebtedness (other than a specified deposit with a prescribed financial institution) and lease obligations (which, for the purposes of this paragraph, includes the income of the affiliate for the year from the purchase and sale of indebtedness and lease obligations on its own account)

(i) of persons resident in Canada, or

(ii) in respect of businesses carried on in Canada

unless more than 90% of the gross revenue of the affiliate derived directly or indirectly from indebtedness (other than a specified deposit with a prescribed financial institution) and lease obligations was derived directly or indirectly from indebtedness and lease obligations of non-resident persons with whom the affiliate deals at arm's length and, where this paragraph applies to include income of the affiliate for the year in the income of the affiliate from a business other than an active business,

**Proposed Amendment — 95(2)(a.3)**

(a.3) in computing the income from a business other than an active business for a taxation year of a foreign affiliate of a taxpayer there shall be included the income of the affiliate for the year derived directly or indirectly from indebtedness and lease obligations (which, for the purposes of this paragraph, includes the income of the affiliate for the year from the purchase and sale of indebtedness and lease obligations on its own account, but does not include income that is derived directly or indirectly from a specified deposit with a prescribed financial institution or that is included in computing the affiliate's income for the year from carrying on a business through a permanent establishment in Canada)

(i) of persons resident in Canada, or

(ii) in respect of businesses carried on in Canada

Subdivision i — Shareholders of Non-Resident Corporations    S. 95(2)(b)(i)(B)

unless more than 90% of the gross revenue of the affiliate derived directly or indirectly from indebtedness and lease obligations (other than revenue that is derived from a specified deposit with a prescribed financial institution or that is included in computing the affiliate's income for the year from carrying on a business through a permanent establishment in Canada) was derived directly or indirectly from indebtedness and lease obligations of non-resident persons with whom the affiliate deals at arm's length and, where this paragraph applies to include income of the affiliate for the year in the income of the affiliate from a business other than an active business,

**Application**: The August 8, 2000 draft legislation (authorized foreign banks), s. 6, will amend the portion of para. 95(2)(a.3) before subpara. (iii) to read as above, applicable to taxation years that begin after 1999.

**Technical Notes**: Subsection 95(2) of the Act provides rules for determining the income of a foreign affiliate of a taxpayer resident in Canada from a particular source. Paragraph 95(2)(a.3) includes in the income from a business other than an active business — and thus the foreign accrual property income — of a foreign affiliate of a taxpayer resident in Canada, the income of the affiliate derived directly or indirectly from most forms of indebtedness or lease obligations of persons resident in Canada or in respect of businesses carried on in Canada. Currently excluded from the income treated in this way is income that derives from specified deposits with a prescribed financial institution. Paragraph 95(2)(a.3) is amended to exclude as well any income that is earned in a business carried on by the affiliate through a permanent establishment in Canada. Such business income is already subject to full Canadian taxation, and need not be added to the affiliate's income under this provision.

(iii) those activities carried out to earn such income shall be deemed to be a separate business, other than an active business, carried on by the affiliate, and

(iv) any income of the affiliate that pertains to or is incident to that business shall be deemed to be income from a business other than an active business;

(a.4) **[income from partnership debt and lease obligations]** — in computing the income from a business other than an active business for a taxation year of a foreign affiliate of a taxpayer there shall be included (to the extent not included under paragraph (a.3) in such income of the affiliate for the year) that proportion of the income of the affiliate for the year derived directly or indirectly from indebtedness and lease obligations (which, for the purposes of this paragraph, includes the income of the affiliate for the year from the purchase and sale of indebtedness and lease obligations on its own account) in respect of a business carried on outside Canada by a partnership (any portion of the income or loss of which for fiscal periods of the partnership that end in the year is included or would, if the partnership had an income or loss for such fiscal periods, be included directly or indirectly in computing the income or loss of the taxpayer or a person resident in Canada with whom the taxpayer does not deal at arm's length) that

(i) the total of all amounts each of which is the income or loss of the partnership for fiscal periods of the partnership that end in the year that are included directly or indirectly in computing the income or loss of the taxpayer or a person resident in Canada with whom the taxpayer does not deal at arm's length

is of

(ii) the total of all amounts each of which is the income or loss of the partnership for fiscal periods of the partnership that end in the year

unless more than 90% of the gross revenue of the affiliate derived directly or indirectly from indebtedness and lease obligations was derived directly or indirectly from indebtedness and lease obligations of non-resident persons with whom the affiliate deals at arm's length (other than indebtedness and lease obligations of a partnership described in this paragraph) and where this paragraph applies to include a proportion of the income of the affiliate for the year in the income of the affiliate from a business other than an active business

(iii) those activities carried out to earn such income of the affiliate for the year shall be deemed to be a separate business, other than an active business, carried on by the affiliate, and

(iv) any income of the affiliate that pertains to or is incident to that business shall be deemed to be income from a business other than an active business

and for the purpose of this paragraph, where the income or loss of a partnership for a fiscal period that ends in the year is nil, the proportion of the income of the affiliate that is to be included in the income of the affiliate for the year from a business other than an active business shall be determined as if the partnership had income of $1,000,000 for that fiscal period;

(b) **[services deemed not active business]** — where a controlled foreign affiliate of a taxpayer provides services or an undertaking to provide services and

(i) the amount paid or payable in consideration therefor

(A) is deductible in computing the income from a business carried on in Canada by any person in relation to whom the affiliate is a controlled foreign affiliate or by a person related to that person, or

(B) was paid or payable by a person other than the taxpayer and can reasonably be considered to relate to an amount that was deductible by the taxpayer or a person related to the taxpayer in computing the income of that taxpayer or person from a business carried on in Canada, or

(ii) the services are performed or are to be performed by any person referred to in subparagraph (i) who is an individual resident in Canada,

the provision of those services or the undertaking to provide those services shall be deemed to be a separate business, other than an active business, carried on by the affiliate, and any income from that business or that pertains to or is incident to that business shall be deemed to be income from a business other than an active business;

(c) **[rollover of FA shares to another FA]** — where a foreign affiliate of a taxpayer (in this paragraph referred to as the "disposing affiliate") has disposed of capital property that was shares of the capital stock of another foreign affiliate of the taxpayer (in this paragraph referred to as the "shares disposed of") to any corporation that was, immediately following the disposition, a foreign affiliate of the taxpayer (in this paragraph referred to as the "acquiring affiliate") for consideration including shares of the capital stock of the acquiring affiliate,

(i) the cost to the disposing affiliate of any property (other than shares of the capital stock of the acquiring affiliate) receivable by the disposing affiliate as consideration for the disposition shall be deemed to be the fair market value of the property at the time of the disposition,

(ii) the cost to the disposing affiliate of any shares of any class of the capital stock of the acquiring affiliate receivable by the disposing affiliate as consideration for the disposition shall be deemed to be that proportion of the amount, if any, by which the total of the relevant cost bases to it, immediately before the disposition, of the shares disposed of exceeds the fair market value at that time of the consideration receivable for the disposition (other than shares of the capital stock of the acquiring affiliate) that

(A) the fair market value, immediately after the disposition, of those shares of the acquiring affiliate of that class

is of

(B) the fair market value, immediately after the disposition, of all shares of the capital stock of the acquiring affiliate receivable by the disposing affiliate as consideration for the disposition,

(iii) the disposing affiliate's proceeds of disposition of the shares shall be deemed to be an amount equal to the cost to it of all shares and other property receivable by it from the acquiring affiliate as consideration for the disposition, and

(iv) the cost to the acquiring affiliate of the shares acquired from the disposing affiliate shall be deemed to be an amount equal to the disposing affiliate's proceeds of disposition referred to in subparagraph (iii);

(d) **[foreign merger]** — where there has been a foreign merger in which the shares owned by a foreign affiliate of a taxpayer of the capital stock of a corporation that was a predecessor foreign corporation immediately before the merger were exchanged for or became shares of the capital stock of the new foreign corporation or the foreign parent corporation, subsection 87(4) applies to the foreign affiliate as if the references in that subsection to

(i) "amalgamation" were read as "foreign merger",

(ii) "predecessor corporation" were read as "predecessor foreign corporation",

(iii) "new corporation" were read as "new foreign corporation or the foreign parent corporation", and

(iv) "adjusted cost base" were read as "relevant cost base";

(d.1) **[foreign merger]** — where there has been a foreign merger of two or more predecessor foreign corporations, in respect of each of which a taxpayer's surplus entitlement percentage was not less than 90% immediately before the merger, to form a new foreign corporation in respect of which the taxpayer's surplus entitlement percentage immediately after the merger was not less than 90%, other than a foreign merger where, under the income tax law of the country in which the predecessor foreign corporations were resident immediately before the merger, a gain or loss was recognized in respect of any capital property of a predecessor foreign corporation that became capital property of the new foreign corporation in the course of the merger,

(i) each capital property of the new foreign corporation that was a capital property of a predecessor foreign corporation immediately before the merger shall be deemed to have been disposed of by the predecessor foreign corporation immediately before the merger for proceeds of disposition equal to the cost amount of the property to the predecessor foreign corporation at that time; and

(ii) for the purposes of this subsection and the definition "foreign accrual property income" in subsection (1), the new foreign corporation shall, with respect to any disposition by it of any capital property to which subparagraph (i) applied, be deemed to be the same corporation as, and a continuation of, the predecessor foreign corporation that owned the property immediately before the merger,

but for greater certainty nothing in this paragraph shall affect the determination of whether any property of a predecessor foreign corporation is disposed of on a foreign merger other than one to which this paragraph applies;

(e) **[windup of foreign affiliate]** — except as otherwise provided in paragraph (e.1), where on the dissolution of a foreign affiliate of a taxpayer (in this paragraph referred to as the "disposing affiliate") one or more shares of the capital stock of another foreign affiliate of the taxpayer have been disposed of to a shareholder that is another foreign affiliate of the taxpayer,

(i) the disposing affiliate's proceeds of disposition of each such share and the cost thereof to the shareholder shall be deemed to be an amount equal to the relevant cost base to the disposing affiliate of the share immediately before the dissolution, and

(ii) the shareholder's proceeds of disposition of the shares of the disposing affiliate shall be deemed to be the amount, if any, by which the total of

(A) the cost to the shareholder of the shares of the other foreign affiliate, as determined in subparagraph (i), and

(B) the fair market value of any property (other than the shares referred to in clause (A)) disposed of by the disposing affiliate to the shareholder on the dissolution,

exceeds

(C) the total of all amounts each of which is the amount of any debt owing by the disposing affiliate, or of any other obligation of the disposing affiliate to pay any amount, that was outstanding immediately before the dissolution and that was assumed or cancelled by the shareholder on the dissolution;

(e.1) **[windup of foreign affiliate]** — where there has been a liquidation and a dissolution of a foreign affiliate (in this paragraph referred to as the "disposing affiliate") of a taxpayer in respect of which, immediately before the liquidation, the taxpayer's surplus entitlement percentage was not less than 90%, other than a liquidation and a dissolution where, under the income tax law of the country in which the disposing affiliate was resident immediately before the liquidation, a gain or loss was recognized by the disposing affiliate in respect of any capital property distributed by it in the course of the liquidation to another foreign affiliate of the taxpayer resident in that country, the following rules apply:

(i) each capital property of the disposing affiliate that was so distributed to another foreign affiliate of the taxpayer shall be deemed to have been disposed of by the disposing affiliate for proceeds of disposition equal to the cost amount of the property to the disposing affiliate immediately before the distribution,

(ii) for the purposes of this subsection and the definition "foreign accrual property income" in subsection (1), the other affiliate shall, with respect to any disposition by it of capital property to which subparagraph (i) applied, be deemed to be the same corporation as, and a continuation of, the disposing affiliate, and

(iii) the other affiliate's proceeds of disposition of the shares of the capital stock of the disposing affiliate disposed of in the course of the liquidation shall be deemed to be the adjusted cost base of those shares to the other affiliate immediately before the disposition;

(f) **[capital gains and losses of foreign affiliate]** — except as otherwise provided in this subsection, each taxable capital gain and each allowable capital loss of a foreign affiliate of a taxpayer from the disposition of property shall be computed in accordance with Part I, read without reference to section 26 of the *Income Tax Application Rules*, as though the affiliate were resident in Canada

(i) where that gain or loss is the gain or loss of a controlled foreign affiliate from the disposition of property to which paragraph (c), (d) or (e) or 88(3)(a) applies or from any other disposition of property (other than excluded property), in Canadian currency, and

(ii) in any other case, on the assumption that the currency of the country in which the affiliate is resident or such other currency as is reasonable in the circumstances (in this subparagraph referred to as the "calculating currency") were the currency of Canada and, where subsection 39(2) is applicable, on the further assumptions that

(A) the reference in that subsection to "the currency or currencies of one or more countries other than Canada relative to Canadian currency" were read as a reference to "one or more currencies other than the calculating currency relative to the calculating currency", and

(B) the references therein to "of a country other than Canada" were read as references to "of a country other than the country of the calculating currency",

except that in computing any such gain or loss from the disposition of property owned by the affiliate at the time it last became a foreign affiliate of the taxpayer there shall not be included such portion of the gain or loss, as the case may be, as may reasonably be considered to have accrued during the period that the affiliate was not a foreign affiliate of

(iii) the taxpayer,

(iv) any person with whom the taxpayer was not dealing at arm's length,

(v) any person with whom the taxpayer would not have been dealing at arm's length if the person had been in existence after the taxpayer came into existence,

(vi) any predecessor corporation (within the meaning assigned by subsection 87(1)) of the taxpayer or of a person described in subparagraph (iv) or (v), or

(vii) any predecessor corporation (within the meaning assigned by paragraph 87(2)(l.2)) of the taxpayer or of a person described in subparagraph (iv) or (v);

(g) **[debt settlement — currency fluctuation]** — where, by virtue of a fluctuation in the value of the currency of a country other than Canada relative to the value of the Canadian dollar, a foreign affiliate of a taxpayer has realized a taxable capital gain or an allowable capital loss in a taxation year on the settlement of a debt that was owing to

(i) another foreign affiliate of the taxpayer or any other non-resident corporation with which the taxpayer does not deal at arm's length, or

(ii) the affiliate by another foreign affiliate of the taxpayer or any other non-resident corporation with which the taxpayer does not deal at arm's length,

such gain or loss, as the case may be, shall be deemed to be nil;

### Proposed Amendment — 95(2)(g)

(g) **[currency fluctuation]** — where, because of a fluctuation in the value of the currency of a country other than Canada relative to the value of the Canadian currency, a particular foreign affiliate of a taxpayer in respect of which the taxpayer has a qualifying interest throughout a taxation year of the particular affiliate has earned income or incurred a loss or realized a capital gain or a capital loss in the year, on

(i) the settlement of a debt obligation (other than a "specified debt obligation" as defined in subsection 142.2(1)), that was owing to

(A) another foreign affiliate of the taxpayer in respect of which the taxpayer has a qualifying interest throughout the year or any other non-resident corporation to which the particular affiliate and the taxpayer are related throughout the year (referred to in this paragraph as a "qualified foreign corporation"), or

(B) the particular affiliate by a qualified foreign corporation,

(ii) the redemption, cancellation or acquisition of a share of the capital stock of, or the reduction of the capital of, the particular affiliate or another foreign affiliate of the taxpayer in respect of which the taxpayer has a qualifying interest throughout the year (other than a "mark-to-market property" as defined in subsection 142.2(1)), or

(iii) the disposition to a qualified foreign corporation of a share of the capital stock of another foreign affiliate of the taxpayer in respect of which the taxpayer has a qualifying interest throughout the year (other than a "mark-to-market property" as defined in subsection 142.2(1)),

that income, gain or loss, as the case may be, is deemed to be nil;

**Application**: Bill C-43 (First Reading September 20, 2000), subsec. 46(4), will amend para. 95(2)(g) to read as above, applicable to taxation years of a foreign affiliate of a taxpayer that begin after November 1999 except that, where the taxpayer so elects in writing and files the election with the Minister of National Revenue before 2002, the amendment applies to taxation years, of all of its foreign affiliates, that began after 1994 and, notwithstanding subsecs. 152(4) to (5), any assessment of a taxpayer's tax payable under the Act for any of those taxation years shall be made that is necessary to take into account the application of the amendment.

**Technical Notes**: Paragraph 95(2)(g) provides that foreign currency gains or losses realized on the settlement of debts owing between foreign affiliates or between a foreign affiliate and a non-arm's length non-resident corporation are ignored for the purpose of determining foreign accrual property income ("FAPI"). Similarly, paragraph 95(2)(h) allows foreign currency gains or losses to be ignored for the purpose of determining FAPI when realized by a foreign affiliate as a result of the redemption, cancellation or acquisition of shares of, or on the reduction of capital of, another foreign affiliate of the taxpayer. Paragraph 95(2)(h) also allows foreign currency gains or losses to be ignored when realized on a non-arm's length sale of shares of another affiliate.

The amendment to paragraph 95(2)(g) incorporates the provisions of paragraphs 95(2)(g) and (h) into one paragraph. Also, the amendment allows paragraph 95(2)(g) to apply regardless of whether the foreign currency gains or losses are incurred on income or capital account. As well, paragraph 95(2)(g) applies in circumstances where the foreign affiliate redeems, cancels or acquires its own shares. Paragraph 95(2)(g) will not apply where the gain or loss is incurred on a "mark-to-market property" or a "specified debt obligation" as defined in subsection 142.2(1). In light of the foreign corporate group concept adopted in paragraph 95(2)(a) as part of the 1994 budget amendments, the relief in paragraph 95(2)(g) is restricted to circumstances where the taxpayer resident in Canada has a qualifying interest in each relevant foreign affiliate. In addition, each qualified non-resident corporation must be a corporation that is related to the taxpayer and the affiliate benefiting from the relief of paragraph 95(2)(g).

Amended paragraph 95(2)(g) applies to taxation years of a foreign affiliate that begin after November 30, 1999. However, if the taxpayer so elects and notifies the Minister of National Revenue in writing before 2001 of its election, paragraph 95(2)(g) applies to of all its foreign affiliates' taxation years that begin after 1994.

**Letter from Department of Finance, October 11, 2000**:

Mr. Angelo Nikolakakis
Stikeman Elliott
Toronto, Ontario

Dear Mr. Nikolakakis:

Thank you for your letter of September 15, 2000 concerning proposed paragraph 95(2)(g) of the *Income Tax Act*.

For the reasons identified in your letter, you have requested that the references to "specified debt obligation" and "mark-to-market property" be eliminated from proposed paragraph 95(2)(g). You also requested that we confirm our willingness to recommend such an amendment to the Minister of Finance.

We are sympathetic to your request and will recommend to the Minister of Finance that the references to "specified debt obligation" and "mark-to-market properties" be deleted. Such an amendment, if made, would be effective at the same time as the proposed new paragraph 95(2)(g) is effective.

Thank you for bringing this matter to our attention.

Yours sincerely,

Brian Ernewein
Director, Tax Legislation Division, Tax Policy Branch

(g.1) **[debt forgiveness rules]** — in computing the foreign accrual property income of a foreign affiliate of a taxpayer the Act shall be read

(i) as if the expression "income, taxable income or taxable income earned in Canada, as the case may be" in the definition "commercial debt obligation" in subsection 80(1) were read as "foreign accrual property income (within the meaning assigned by subsection 95(1))", and

(ii) without reference to subsections 80(3) to (12) and (15) and 80.01(5) to (11) and sections 80.02 to 80.04;

**Proposed Addition — 95(2)(g.2)**

(g.2) **[foreign spin-off election]** — for the purpose of computing the foreign accrual property income of a foreign affiliate of any taxpayer resident in Canada for a taxation year of the affiliate, an election made pursuant to paragraph 86.1(2)(f) in respect of a distribution received by the affiliate in a particular taxation year of the affiliate is deemed to have been filed under that paragraph by the affiliate if

(i) where there is only one taxpayer resident in Canada in respect of whom the affiliate is a controlled foreign affiliate, the election is filed by the taxpayer with the taxpayer's return of income for the taxpayer's taxation year in which the particular year of the affiliate ends, and

(ii) where there is more than one taxpayer resident in Canada in respect of whom the affiliate is a controlled foreign affiliate, all of those taxpayers jointly elect in writing and each of them files the joint election with the Minister with their return of income for their taxation year in which the particular year of the affiliate ends.

**Application**: The December 21, 2000 draft legislation, subsec. 43(2), will add para. 95(2)(g.2), applicable to distributions received after 1997 except that the election referred to in para. 95(2)(g.2) is deemed to be filed on a timely basis if it is filed with the Minister of National Revenue before the day that is 90 days after the day on which the amending legislation receives Royal Assent.

**Technical Notes**: Subsection 95(2) provides rules for determining the income of a foreign affiliate of a taxpayer resident in Canada. These rules apply for the purposes of sections 90 to 95.

New paragraph 95(2)(g.2) is added as a consequence of the introduction of the foreign spin-off tax-deferral rules in new section 86.1. Paragraph 95(2)(g.2) applies for the purpose of computing the foreign accrual property income of a foreign affiliate of any taxpayer resident in Canada for a taxation year of the affiliate. New paragraph 95(2)(g.2) deems an election pursuant to paragraph 86.1(2)(f) in respect of a distribution received by the foreign affiliate (in a particular taxation year of the affiliate) to have been filed under that paragraph in two cases.

First, where there is only one taxpayer resident in Canada in respect of whom the foreign affiliate is a controlled foreign affiliate, section 86.1 applies to the distribution received by the foreign affiliate if the election is filed by that taxpayer with the taxpayer's return of income for the taxpayer's taxation year in which the taxation year of the affiliate ends.

Second, where there is more than one taxpayer resident in Canada in respect of whom the affiliate is a controlled foreign affiliate, section 86.1 applies to the distribution received by the foreign affiliate if the election is filed by one such taxpayer and all such taxpayers so agree in writing and file that agreement and the election with the Minister in each of their returns of income for their taxation year in which the taxation year of the affiliate ends.

For more detail in respect of the foreign spin-off rules, see the commentary on new section 86.1.

**Proposed Addition — 95(2)(g.2) [*sic*; will be (g.3)]**

(g.2) **[application of foreign investment entity rules]** — in computing the foreign accrual property income of a particular foreign affiliate of a particular taxpayer for a particular taxation year of the particular affiliate, sections 94.1 to 94.3 shall apply as if

(i) the words "controlled foreign affiliate of the taxpayer" in paragraph (a) of the definition "exempt interest" in subsection 94.1(1) referred to a controlled foreign affiliate of the particular taxpayer and not to a controlled foreign affiliate of the particular affiliate,

(ii) subsection 94.1(3) were read without reference to the words "except where the

S. 95(2)(g.2)(ii) — Income Tax Act, Part I, Division B

taxpayer is non-resident at the end of the entity's year",

(iii) the form referred to in paragraph (c) of the description of A in subsection 94.1(5) in respect of participating interests in a foreign investment entity for a taxation year of the entity that ends in the particular year were required to be filed with, and only with, the particular taxpayer's return of income for the particular taxpayer's taxation year in which the particular year ends,

(iv) designations made by the particular taxpayer in the form referred to in subparagraph (iii) were made by the particular affiliate,

(v) the words "the particular taxpayer" in paragraph (g) of the description of A in subsection 94.1(5) referred to the particular taxpayer rather than to the particular affiliate,

(vi) each reference to "foreign affiliate" and "affiliate" in paragraph (g) of the description of A in subsection 94.1(5) were a reference to a foreign affiliate of the particular taxpayer and not to a foreign affiliate of the particular affiliate,

(vii) subsection 94.1(5) were read without reference to paragraph (i) of the description of A in subsection 94.1(5),

(viii) for the purpose of applying sections 94.1 and 94.2 in computing the income of a foreign investment entity in which the particular affiliate holds a participating interest,

(A) the words "controlled foreign affiliate of the taxpayer" in paragraph (a) of the definition "exempt interest" in subsection 94.1(1) referred to a controlled foreign affiliate of the particular taxpayer and not to a controlled foreign affiliate of the entity, and

(B) the fresh start year of the entity in respect of the particular affiliate were the first taxation year of the entity

(I) that ends in a taxation year of the particular affiliate that begins after 2000, and

(II) at any time in which both the particular affiliate holds a participating interest in the entity and the particular affiliate is a controlled foreign affiliate of the particular taxpayer,

(ix) an election under paragraph 94.1(4)(a) or clause (i)(C) of the description of D in paragraph 94.2(4)(a) for the particular year were required to be filed under that provision in respect of the particular affiliate, by, and only by, the particular taxpayer, with the Minister on or before the filing-due date of the particular taxpayer for the particular taxpayer's taxation year in which the particular year ends,

(x) section 94.2 were read without reference to subsection 94.2(5),

(xi) paragraph 94.2(1)(b) were read without reference to the words "at which the taxpayer was resident in Canada" and to clause (i)(B) of the description of B in that paragraph, and

(xii) the amount determined under paragraph 94.2(1)(b) did not include the portion of that amount that can reasonably be considered to have accrued during the period that the particular affiliate was not a foreign affiliate of any person described in any of subparagraphs (f)(iii) to (vii);

**Application**: The June 22, 2000 draft legislation, subsec. 12(7), will add para. 95(2)(g.2) [expected to change to (g.3)], applicable to taxation years of foreign affiliates of taxpayers that begin after 2000 [to be changed to "after 2001"; see Sept 7/00 news release after 94.3].

**Technical Notes**: Subsection 95(2) of the Act provides rules for determining the income of a foreign affiliate of a taxpayer resident in Canada. These rules apply for the purposes of sections 90 to 95.

The rules in new paragraph 95(2)(g.2) set out the manner in which sections 94.1 to 94.3 apply for the purpose of computing the FAPI of a particular foreign affiliate of a Canadian taxpayer for a particular taxation year of the affiliate:

- The exemption in the definition "exempt interest" for controlled foreign affiliates is treated as if it referred only to controlled foreign affiliates of the Canadian taxpayer (not of the particular affiliate). [Subparagraph 95(2)(g.2)(i).]

- The measures in sections 94.1 and 94.2 that would otherwise restrict their application to residents in Canada are ignored. [Subparagraph 95(2)(g.2)(ii), (x) and (xi).]

- The Canadian taxpayer, rather than the particular affiliate, claims deductions relevant in determining the particular affiliate's income allocation or loss allocation in respect of a participating interest in a foreign investment entity held by the particular affiliate. [Subparagraphs 95(2)(g.2)(iii) and (iv).] These claims are only relevant for taxation years of the particular affiliate that begin after 2000, once the particular affiliate holds an interest in the foreign investment entity and is a controlled foreign affiliate of the Canadian taxpayer. [Clause 95(2)(g.2)(viii)(B).]

- The exclusion of dividends under paragraph 94.1(5)A(g) applies only where the Canadian taxpayer is resident in Canada, in connection with dividends received by the particular affiliate from foreign affiliates of the Canadian taxpayer (not of the particular affiliate) in which the Canadian taxpayer (not the particular affiliate) has a qualifying interest (determined under paragraph 95(2)(m)). [Subparagraphs 95(2)(g.2)(v) and (vi).]

- In the event that the particular affiliate has a participating interest in a particular foreign investment entity and the particular entity has a participating interest in another non-resident entity, the application of sections 94.1 and 94.2 to the particular entity is determined as if the exclusion from the application of those sections for controlled foreign affiliates referred to in paragraph (a) of the definition "exempt interest" in subsection 94.1(1) were for controlled foreign affiliates of the Canadian taxpayer (not controlled foreign affiliates of the particular entity). [Clause 95(2)(g.2)(viii)(A).] This rule applies instead of the rule in paragraph 94.1(5)A(i). [Subparagraph 95(2)(g.2)(vii).]

- The Canadian taxpayer (rather than the particular affiliate) is permitted to make an election under subsection 94.1(4) or subparagraph 94.2(4)(a)D(i) in connection with the particular affiliate's participating interests in foreign investment entities. [Subparagraph 95(2)(g.2)(ix).]

- The particular affiliate's deferral amount determined under paragraph 94.2(1)(b) does not include the portion of the amount that can reasonably be considered to have accrued during the period that the particular affiliate was not a foreign affiliate of the Canadian taxpayer and certain other specified persons. [Subparagraph 95(2)(g.2)(xii).]

(h) **[share transactions — currency fluctuation]** — where, by virtue of a fluctuation in the value of the currency of a country other than Canada relative to the value of the Canadian dollar, a foreign affiliate of a taxpayer has realized a taxable capital gain or an allowable capital loss in a taxation year on

(i) the redemption, cancellation or acquisition of a share of the capital stock of, or the reduction of the capital of, another foreign affiliate of the taxpayer, or

(ii) the disposition to a person with whom the taxpayer does not deal at arm's length of a share of the capital stock of another foreign affiliate of the taxpayer,

that gain or loss, as the case may be, shall be deemed to be nil;

### Proposed Repeal — 95(2)(h)

**Application**: Bill C-43 (First Reading September 20, 2000), subsec. 46(5), will repeal para. 95(2)(h), applicable on the same basis as the amendment to 95(2)(g) above.

**Technical Notes**: See under 95(2)(g).

(i) **[settlement of debt relating to excluded property]** — any gain or loss of a foreign affiliate of a taxpayer from the settlement or extinguishment of a debt that related at all times to the acquisition of excluded property shall be deemed to be a gain or loss from the disposition of excluded property;

(j) **[ACB of partnership interest]** — the adjusted cost base to a foreign affiliate of a taxpayer of an interest in a partnership at any time shall be such amount as is prescribed by regulation;

(k) **[change in business — fresh start rule]** — where, in a particular taxation year, a foreign affiliate of a taxpayer

(i) carries on an investment business outside Canada and, in the preceding taxation year, that business was not an investment business of the affiliate (or the definition "investment business" in subsection (1) did not apply in respect of the business in the preceding taxation year), or

(ii) is deemed by paragraph (a.1), (a.2), (a.3) or (a.4) to carry on a separate business, other than an active business, and, in the preceding taxation year, that paragraph did not apply to deem the affiliate to be carrying on that separate business,

for the purpose of computing the income of the affiliate from the investment business or the separate business as the case may be (in this subsection referred to as the "foreign business") for the particular year and each subsequent taxation year in which the foreign business is carried on,

(iii) the affiliate shall be deemed

(A) to have begun to carry on the foreign business in Canada at the later of the time the particular year began or the time that it began to carry on the foreign business, and

(B) to have carried on the foreign business in Canada throughout that part of the particular year and each such subsequent taxation year in which the foreign business was carried on by it,

(iv) where the foreign business of the affiliate is a business in respect of which, if the foreign business were carried on in Canada, the affiliate would be required by law to report to a regulating authority in Canada such as the Superintendent of Financial Institutions or a similar authority of a province, the affiliate shall be deemed to have been required by law to report to and to have been subject to the supervision of such regulating authority, and

(v) paragraphs 138(11.91)(c) to (f) apply to the affiliate for the particular year in respect of the foreign business as if

(A) the affiliate were the insurer referred to in subsection 138(11.91),

(B) the particular year of the affiliate were the particular year of the insurer referred to in that subsection, and

(C) the foreign business of the affiliate were the business of the insurer referred to in that subsection;

(l) **[trading or dealing in debt]** — in computing the income from property for a taxation year of a foreign affiliate of a taxpayer there shall be included the income of the affiliate for the year from a business (other than an investment business of the affiliate) the principal purpose of which is to derive income from trading or dealing in indebtedness (which for the purpose of this paragraph includes the earning of interest on indebtedness) other than

    (i) indebtedness owing by persons with whom the affiliate deals at arm's length who are resident in the country in which the affiliate was formed or continued and exists and is governed and in which the business is principally carried on, or

    (ii) trade accounts receivable owing by persons with whom the affiliate deals at arm's length,

unless

    (iii) the business is carried on by the affiliate as a foreign bank, a trust company, a credit union, an insurance corporation or a trader or dealer in securities or commodities, the activities of which are regulated in the country under whose laws the affiliate was formed or continued and exists and is governed and in which the business is principally carried on, and

    (iv) the taxpayer is

        (A) a bank, a trust company, a credit union, an insurance corporation or a trader or dealer in securities or commodities resident in Canada, the business activities of which are subject by law to the supervision of a regulating authority such as the Superintendent of Financial Institutions or a similar authority of a province,

        (B) a subsidiary wholly-owned corporation of a corporation described in clause (A), or

        (C) a corporation of which a corporation described in clause (A) is a subsidiary wholly-owned corporation; and

(m) **["qualifying interest"]** — a taxpayer has a qualifying interest in respect of a foreign affiliate of the taxpayer at any time if, at that time, the taxpayer owned

    (i) not less than 10% of the issued and outstanding shares (having full voting rights under all circumstances) of the affiliate, and

    (ii) shares of the affiliate having a fair market value of not less than 10% of the fair market value of all the issued and outstanding shares of the affiliate

and for the purpose of this paragraph

    (iii) where, at any time, shares of a corporation are owned or are deemed for the purposes of this paragraph to be owned by another corporation (in this paragraph referred to as the "holding corporation"), those shares shall be deemed to be owned at that time by each shareholder of the holding corporation in a proportion equal to the proportion of all such shares that

        (A) the fair market value of the shares of the holding corporation owned at that time by the shareholder

is of

        (B) the fair market value of all the issued shares of the holding corporation outstanding at that time,

    (iv) where, at any time, shares of a corporation are property of a partnership or are deemed for the purposes of this paragraph to be property of a partnership, those shares shall be deemed to be owned at that time by each member of the partnership in a proportion equal to the proportion of all such shares that

        (A) the member's share of the income or loss of the partnership for its fiscal period that includes that time

is of

        (B) the income or loss of the partnership for its fiscal period that includes that time

and for the purpose of this subparagraph, where the income and loss of the partnership for its fiscal period that includes that time are nil, that proportion shall be computed as if the partnership had income for the period in the amount of $1,000,000, and

    (v) where, at any time, a person is a holder of convertible property issued by the affiliate before June 23, 1994 the terms of which confer on the holder the right to exchange the convertible property for shares of the affiliate and the taxpayer elects in its return of income for its first taxation year that ends after 1994 to have the provisions of this subparagraph apply to the taxpayer in respect of all the convertible property issued by the affiliate and outstanding at that time, each holder shall, in respect of the convertible property held by it at that time, be deemed to have, immediately before that time,

        (A) exchanged the convertible property for shares of the affiliate, and

        (B) acquired shares of the affiliate in accordance with the terms and conditions of the convertible property.

**Related Provisions**: 20(3) — Purpose for which borrowed money deemed to have been used; 53(1)(c) — Addition to ACB of share; 87(8.1) — Foreign merger; 94(1)(d) — Application of certain provisions to trusts not resident in Canada; 95(2.2)–(2.5) — Interpretation rules for 95(2)(a)–(a.3) and (g); 95(3) — "Services" defined; 95(6) — Anti-avoidance rules; 96(3) — Election under 95(2)(g.2) by members of partnership; 253 — Whether business carried on in Canada.

**Notes**: See Notes to 91(1).

95(2)(a) amended, and (a.1)–(a.4) added, by 1994 tax amendments bill (Part II — foreign affiliates), effective on the same basis as 95(2.1) (see Notes thereto). 95(2)(a) formerly read:

(a) in computing the income from an active business of a foreign affiliate of a taxpayer there shall be included

(i) any income from sources in a country other than Canada that would otherwise be income from property or a business other than an active business, to the extent that it pertains to or is incident to an active business carried on in a country other than Canada by the affiliate or any other non-resident corporation with which the taxpayer does not deal at arm's length, and

(ii) any amount paid or payable to the affiliate by, and, where the affiliate is a member of a partnership, the affiliate's share of any amount paid or payable to the partnership by,

(A) another foreign affiliate of the taxpayer, or

(B) any other non-resident corporation with which the taxpayer does not deal at arm's length

to the extent that, in computing the amount prescribed to be its earnings from an active business other than a business carried on by it in Canada, that amount is deductible or would be deductible if the non-resident corporation were a foreign affiliate of the taxpayer;

95(2)(a)(ii) amended by 1991 technical bill, effective 1987, to deal with the case where the affiliate is a member of a partnership.

Opening and closing words of 95(2)(b) amended by 1991 technical bill, effective for taxation years commencing after July 13, 1990, to clarify that, in computing income from an active business of a controlled foreign affiliate, investment income is to be excluded to the extent it pertains to or is incident to a business that is treated as not being an active business.

95(2)(d) amended by 1998 Budget to add "or the foreign parent corporation" in subpara. (iii) and to delete subpara. (v), effective for a taxpayer in respect of a merger or combination of foreign corporations

(a) that occurs after February 24, 1998, or

(b) that occurred

(i) before February 25, 1998 and in a taxation year for which the taxpayer's normal reassessment period, as defined in 152(3.1), has not ended before 1999, or

(ii) after 1994 and before February 25, 1998 and in a taxation year in which the taxpayer was exempt under s. 149,

unless the taxpayer elects by notifying Revenue Canada in writing, by the end of 1999, that the amendments to 95(2)(d) and 95(4.1) not apply to the taxpayer in respect of the merger or combination.

95(2)(d.1) and (e.1) amended by 1991 technical bill, effective for foreign mergers occurring (d.1) and liquidations commencing (e.1) after 1989, to extend to cases where the country of residence has no income tax law (rather than only cases where the income tax law of that country does not recognize the gain or loss).

95(2)(f)(i) amended by 1991 technical bill, effective July 13, 1990, so as to allow a disposing affiliate to transfer shares of another foreign affiliate at their original cost expressed in Canadian currency without having to report a gain or loss arising from currency fluctuation. For earlier dispositions, read:

(i) where that gain or loss is the gain or loss of a controlled foreign affiliate from the disposition of property other than excluded property, in Canadian currency, and

95(2)(g.1) added by 1994 tax amendments bill (Part I — debt forgiveness), effective for taxation years that end after February 21, 1994, and amended retroactive to its introduction by 1995-97 technical bill to delete a reference to 80(17). See Notes to 47(1).

95(2)(h)(i) amended by 1993 technical bill, effective for redemptions, cancellations, acquisitions and reductions occurring after December 21, 1992, to change "the affiliate or another foreign affiliate" to simply "another foreign affiliate". The change means that a foreign affiliate cannot realize a foreign exchange gain or loss on the redemption, cancellation or acquisition of a share of its own capital stock or a reduction of its own capital.

95(2)(k)–(m) added by 1994 tax amendments bill (Part II — foreign affiliates), effective on the same basis as 95(2.1) (see Notes thereto). See also 95(2.1)–(2.5) for certain provisions that were originally released as draft paragraphs of 95(2). 95(2)(k) is sometimes referred to as the "fresh start" provision.

**Regulations**: 5900–5908 (FAPI rules); 7900(1), (2) (prescribed financial institutions for 95(2)(a.3)); 8201 (meaning of "permanent establishment" for 95(2)(a.3)).

**I.T. Application Rules**: 35(2) (where corporation deemed to be foreign affiliate due to election made before May 6, 1974).

**Interpretation Bulletins**: IT-392: Meaning of term "share".

**Information Circulars**: 77-9R: Books, records and other requirements for taxpayers having foreign affiliates.

**I.T. Technical News**: No. 15 (tax consequences of the adoption of the "euro" currency).

**(2.1) Rule for definition "investment business"** — For the purposes of the definition "investment business" in subsection (1), a foreign affiliate of a taxpayer, the taxpayer and, where the taxpayer is a corporation all the issued shares of which are owned by a corporation described in subparagraph (a)(i), such corporation described in subparagraph (a)(i) shall be considered to be dealing with each other at arm's length in respect of the entering into of agreements that provide for the purchase, sale or exchange of currency and the execution of such agreements where

(a) the taxpayer is

(i) a bank, a trust company, a credit union, an insurance corporation or a trader or dealer in securities or commodities resident in Canada, the business activities of which are subject by law to the supervision of a regulating authority such as the Superintendent of Financial Institutions or a similar authority of a province, or

(ii) a subsidiary wholly-owned corporation of a corporation described in subparagraph (i);

(b) the agreements are swap agreements, forward purchase or sale agreements, forward rate agreements, futures agreements, options or rights agreements or similar agreements;

(c) the agreements are entered in the course of a business carried on by the affiliate principally with persons with whom the affiliate deals at arm's length in the country under whose laws the affiliate was formed or continued and exists and is governed and in which the business is principally carried on; and

(d) the terms and conditions of such agreements are substantially the same as the terms and conditions of similar agreements made by persons dealing at arm's length.

795

**Notes**: 95(2.1) added by 1994 tax amendments bill (Part II), effective for taxation years of foreign affiliates of taxpayers that begin after 1994 except that, where there has been a change in the taxation year of a foreign affiliate of a taxpayer from February 23 through December 31, 1994, it applies to taxation years of the foreign affiliate of the taxpayer that end after 1994, unless

(a) the foreign affiliate had requested that change in the taxation year in writing before February 22, 1994 from the income tax authority of the country in which it was resident and subject to income tax; or

(b) the first taxation year of the foreign affiliate that began after 1994 began at a time in 1995 that is earlier than the time that that taxation year would have begun if there had not been that change in the taxation year of the foreign affiliate.

This provision was 95(2)(p) in the draft legislation of January 23, 1995.

**(2.2) Rule for para. (2)(a)** — For the purpose of paragraph (2)(a),

> **Proposed Amendment — 95(2.2) opening words**
>
> **(2.2) Rule for subsec. (2)** — For the purpose of subsection (2),
>
> **Application**: Bill C-43 (First Reading September 20, 2000), subsec. 46(6), will amend the opening words of subsec. 95(2.2) to read as above, applicable to taxation years of a foreign affiliate of a taxpayer that begin after November 1999 except that, where the taxpayer so elects in writing and files the election with the Minister of National Revenue before 2002, the amendment applies to taxation years, of all of its foreign affiliates, that began after 1994 and, notwithstanding subsecs. 152(4) to (5), any assessment of a taxpayer's tax payable under the Act for any of those taxation years shall be made that is necessary to take into account the application of the amendment.
>
> **Technical Notes**: Subsection 95(2.2) of the Act provides rules for the purpose of paragraph 95(2)(a) of the Act. The subsection provides that in certain circumstances a non-resident corporation that was not a foreign affiliate of a taxpayer will be considered to be a foreign affiliate of the taxpayer. It also provides that in certain circumstances a non-resident corporation that was not related to a foreign affiliate of a taxpayer will be considered to be related to the foreign affiliate and the taxpayer.
>
> Subsection 95(2.2) is amended to apply to all of subsection 95(2), rather than merely paragraph 95(2)(a). This amendment ensures that subsection 95(2.2) will apply to the changes in paragraph 95(2)(g) of the Act and has the same effective date as those changes.

(a) a non-resident corporation that was not a foreign affiliate of a taxpayer in respect of which the taxpayer had a qualifying interest throughout a particular taxation year shall be deemed to be a foreign affiliate of a taxpayer in respect of which the taxpayer had a qualifying interest throughout that year where

(i) a person has, in that year, acquired or disposed of shares of that non-resident corporation or any other corporation and, because of that acquisition or disposition, that non-resident corporation became or ceased to be a foreign affiliate of the taxpayer in respect of which the taxpayer had a qualifying interest, and

(ii) at the beginning of that year or at the end of that year, the non-resident corporation was a foreign affiliate of the taxpayer in respect of which the taxpayer had a qualifying interest; and

(b) a non-resident corporation that was not related to a foreign affiliate of a taxpayer and the taxpayer throughout a particular taxation year shall be deemed to be related to the foreign affiliate of the taxpayer and that taxpayer throughout that year where

(i) a person has, in that year, acquired or disposed of shares of that non-resident corporation or any other corporation and, because of that acquisition or disposition, that non-resident corporation became or ceased to be a non-resident corporation that was related to the foreign affiliate of the taxpayer and the taxpayer, and

(ii) at the beginning of that year or at the end of that year, the non-resident corporation was related to the foreign affiliate of the taxpayer and the taxpayer.

**Notes**: 95(2.2) added by 1994 tax amendments bill (Part II), effective on the same basis as 95(2.1) (see Notes thereto). This provision was 95(2)(s) in the draft legislation of January 23, 1995.

**(2.3) Application of para. (2)(a.1)** — Paragraph (2)(a.1) does not apply to a foreign affiliate of a taxpayer in respect of a sale or exchange of property that is currency or a right to purchase, sell or exchange currency where

(a) the taxpayer is

(i) a bank, a trust company, a credit union, an insurance corporation or a trader or dealer in securities or commodities resident in Canada, the business activities of which are subject by law to the supervision of a regulating authority such as the Superintendent of Financial Institutions or a similar authority of a province, or

(ii) a subsidiary wholly-owned corporation of a corporation described in subparagraph (i);

(b) the sale or exchange was made in the course of a business carried on by the affiliate principally with persons with whom the affiliate deals at arm's length in the country under whose laws the affiliate was formed or continued and exists and is governed and in which the business is principally carried on by it; and

(c) the terms and conditions of the sale or exchange of such property are substantially the same as the terms and conditions of similar sales or exchanges of such property by persons dealing at arm's length.

**Notes**: 95(2.3) added by 1994 tax amendments bill (Part II), effective on the same basis as 95(2.1) (see Notes thereto). This provision was 95(2)(o) in the draft legislation of January 23, 1995.

**(2.4) Application of para. (2)(a.3)** — Paragraph (2)(a.3) does not apply to a foreign affiliate of a taxpayer in respect of its income derived directly or indirectly from indebtedness to the extent that

(a) the income is derived by the affiliate in the course of a business conducted principally with persons with whom the affiliate deals at arm's length carried on by it as a foreign bank, a trust company, a credit union, an insurance corporation or a trader or dealer in securities or commodities, the activities of which are regulated in the country under whose laws the affiliate was formed or continued and exists and is governed and in which the business is principally carried on, and

(b) the income is derived by the affiliate from trading or dealing in the indebtedness (which, for this purpose, consists of income from the actual trading or dealing in the indebtedness and interest earned by the affiliate during a short term holding period on indebtedness acquired by it for the purpose of the trading or dealing) with persons (in this subsection referred to as "regular customers") with whom it deals at arm's length who were resident in a country other than Canada in which it and any competitor (which is resident in the country in which the affiliate is resident and regulated in the same manner the affiliate is regulated in the country under whose laws the affiliate was formed or continued and exists and is governed and in which its business is principally carried on) compete and have a substantial market presence,

and, for the purpose of this subsection, an acquisition of indebtedness from the taxpayer shall be deemed to be part of the trading or dealing in indebtedness described in paragraph (b) where the indebtedness is acquired by the affiliate and sold to regular customers and the terms and conditions of the acquisition and the sale are substantially the same as the terms and conditions of similar acquisitions and sales made by the affiliate in transactions with persons with whom it deals at arm's length.

**Notes**: 95(2.4) added by 1994 tax amendments bill (Part II), effective on the same basis as 95(2.1) (see Notes thereto). This provision was 95(2)(l) in the draft legislation of January 23, 1995.

**(2.5) Definitions for para. (2)(a.3)** — For the purpose of paragraph (2)(a.3),

**"indebtedness"** does not include obligations of a person under agreements with non-resident corporations providing for the purchase, sale or exchange of currency where

(a) the agreements are swap agreements, forward purchase or sale agreements, forward rate agreements, futures agreements, options or rights agreements, or similar agreements,

(b) the person is a bank, a trust company, a credit union, an insurance corporation or a trader or dealer in securities or commodities resident in Canada, the business activities of which are subject by law to the supervision of a regulating authority in Canada such as the Superintendent of Financial Institutions or a similar authority of a province,

(c) the agreements are entered into by the non-resident corporation in the course of a business carried on by it principally with persons with which it deals at arm's length in the country under whose laws the non-resident corporation was formed or continued and exists and is governed and in which the business is principally carried on by it, and

(d) the terms and conditions of such agreements are substantially the same as the terms and conditions of similar agreements made by persons dealing at arm's length;

**Notes**: This provision was 95(2)(q) in the draft legislation of January 23, 1995.

**"specified deposit"** means a deposit of a foreign affiliate of a taxpayer resident in Canada with a prescribed financial institution resident in Canada where

(a) the income from the deposit is income of the affiliate for the year that would, but for paragraph (2)(a.3), be income from an active business carried on by it in a country other than Canada (other than a business the principal purpose of which is to derive income from property including interest, dividends, rents, royalties or similar returns or substitutes therefor or profits from the disposition of investment property), or

(b) the income from the deposit is income of the affiliate for the year that would, but for paragraph (2)(a.3), be income from an active business carried on by the affiliate principally with persons with whom the affiliate deals at arm's length in the country under whose laws the affiliate was formed or continued and exists and is governed and in which the business is principally carried on by it and the deposit was held by the affiliate in the course of carrying on that part of the business conducted with non-resident persons with whom the affiliate deals at arm's length or that part of the business conducted with a person with whom the affiliate was related where it can be demonstrated that the related person used or held the funds deposited in the course of a business carried on by the related person with non-resident persons with whom the related person and the affiliate deal at arm's length.

**Notes**: 95(2.5) added by 1994 tax amendments bill (Part II), effective on the same basis as 95(2.1) (see Notes thereto). This provision was 95(2)(n) in the draft legislation of January 23, 1995.

**Regulations**: 7900 (prescribed financial institution).

**(3) Definition of "services"** — For the purposes of paragraph (2)(b), "services" includes the insurance of Canadian risks but does not include

(a) the transportation of persons or goods; or

(b) services performed in connection with the purchase or sale of goods.

**(4) Definitions** — In this section,

**"direct equity percentage"** at any time of any person in a corporation is the percentage determined by the following rules:

(a) for each class of the issued shares of the capital stock of the corporation, determine the proportion of 100 that the number of shares of that class owned by that person at that time is of the total number of issued shares of that class at that time, and

(b) select the proportion determined under paragraph (a) for that person in respect of the corporation that is not less than any other proportion so determined for that person in respect of the corporation at that time,

and the proportion selected under paragraph (b), when expressed as a percentage, is that person's direct equity percentage in the corporation at that time;

**Notes:** 95(4) "direct equity percentage" was 95(4)(a) before consolidation in R.S.C. 1985 (5th Supp.), effective for taxation years ending after November 1991. See Table of Concordance.

**Interpretation Bulletins:** IT-392: Meaning of term "share".

**"equity percentage"** at any time of a person, in any particular corporation, is the total of

(a) the person's direct equity percentage at that time in the particular corporation, and

(b) all percentages each of which is the product obtained when the person's equity percentage at that time in any corporation is multiplied by that corporation's direct equity percentage at that time in the particular corporation

except that for the purposes of the definition "participating percentage" in subsection (1), paragraph (b) shall be read as if the reference to "any corporation" were a reference to "any corporation other than a corporation resident in Canada";

**Related Provisions:** 94(1)(d) — Deemed ownership in trust deemed to be corporation for FAPI purposes.

**Notes:** 95(4) "equity percentage" was 95(4)(b) before consolidation in R.S.C. 1985 (5th Supp.), effective for taxation years ending after November 1991. See Table of Concordance.

**"relevant cost base"** to a foreign affiliate of property at any time means the adjusted cost base to the affiliate of the property at that time or such greater amount as the taxpayer claims not exceeding the fair market value of the property at that time.

**Notes:** 95(4) "relevant cost base" was 95(4)(c) before consolidation in R.S.C. 1985 (5th Supp.), effective for taxation years ending after November 1991.

**(4.1) Application of subsec. 87(8.1)** — In this section, the expressions "foreign merger", "predecessor foreign corporation", "new foreign corporation" and "foreign parent corporation" have the meanings assigned by subsection 87(8.1).

**Notes:** 95(4.1) amended by 1998 Budget to add "foreign parent corporation", effective on same basis as the amendments to 95(2)(d).

95(4.1) added in the R.S.C. 1985 (5th Supp.) consolidation, effective for taxation years ending after November 1991. This rule was formerly in the opening words of 87(8.1).

**(5) Income bonds or debentures issued by foreign affiliates** — For the purposes of this subdivision, an income bond or income debenture issued by a corporation (other than a corporation resident in Canada) shall be deemed to be a share of the capital stock of the corporation unless any interest or other similar periodic amount paid by the corporation on or in respect of the bond or debenture was, under the laws of the country in which the corporation was resident, deductible in computing the amount for the year on which the corporation was liable to pay income or profits tax imposed by the government of that country.

**Interpretation Bulletins:** IT-388: Income bonds issued by foreign corporations.

**(6) Where rights or shares issued, acquired or disposed of to avoid tax** — For the purposes of this subdivision (other than section 90),

(a) where any person or partnership has a right under a contract, in equity or otherwise, either immediately or in the future and either absolutely or contingently, to, or to acquire, shares of the capital stock of a corporation and

---

**Proposed Amendment — 95(6)(a) opening words**

(a) where any person or partnership has a right under a contract, in equity or otherwise, either immediately or in the future and either absolutely or contingently, to, or to acquire, shares of the capital stock of a corporation or interests in a partnership and

**Application:** Bill C-43 (First Reading September 20, 2000), subsec. 46(7), will amend the opening words of para. 95(6)(a) to read as above, applicable after November 1999.

**Technical Notes:** Subsection 95(6) of the Act is an anti-avoidance rule that prevents the avoidance of tax through the use of rights to acquire shares or the issuance of shares. The amendments to this subsection clarify that the subsection is intended to prevent the avoidance of tax through the use of rights to acquire partnership interests or the issuance of partnership interests. [See 93.1 — ed.] Where applicable, paragraph 95(6)(b) treats an acquisition or disposition of shares or partnership interests to have not taken place. Where the shares or partnership interests were previously unissued, the paragraph deems the shares or partnership interests to have not been issued.

---

(i) it can reasonably be considered that the principal purpose for the existence of the right is to cause 2 or more corporations to be related for the purpose of paragraph (2)(a), those corporations shall be deemed not to be related for that purpose, or

(ii) it can reasonably be considered that the principal purpose for the existence of the right

Subdivision i — Shareholders of Non-Resident Corporations    S. 95

is to permit any person to avoid, reduce or defer the payment of tax or any other amount that would otherwise be payable under this Act, those shares shall be deemed to be owned by that person or partnership; and

**Proposed Amendment — 95(6)(a)(ii)**

(ii) it can reasonably be considered that the principal purpose for the existence of the right is to permit any person to avoid, reduce or defer the payment of tax or any other amount that would otherwise be payable under this Act, those shares or partnership interests, as the case may be, are deemed to be owned by that person or partnership; and

**Application**: Bill C-43 (First Reading September 20, 2000), subsec. 46(8), will amend subpara. 95(6)(a)(ii) to read as above, applicable after November 1999.

**Technical Notes**: See under 95(6)(a).

(b) where a person or partnership acquires or disposes of shares of the capital stock of a corporation, either directly or indirectly, and it can reasonably be considered that the principal purpose for the acquisition or disposition of the shares is to permit a person to avoid, reduce or defer the payment of tax or any other amount that would otherwise be payable under this Act, those shares shall be deemed not to have been acquired or disposed of, as the case may be, and where the shares were unissued by the corporation immediately prior to the acquisition, those shares shall be deemed not to have been issued.

**Proposed Amendment — 95(6)(b)**

(b) where a person or partnership acquires or disposes of shares of the capital stock of a corporation or interests in a partnership, either directly or indirectly, and it can reasonably be considered that the principal purpose for the acquisition or disposition is to permit a person to avoid, reduce or defer the payment of tax or any other amount that would otherwise be payable under this Act, that acquisition or disposition is deemed not to have taken place, and where the shares or partnership interests were unissued by the corporation or partnership immediately before the acquisition, those shares or partnership interests, as the case may be, are deemed not to have been issued.

**Application**: Bill C-43 (First Reading September 20, 2000), subsec. 46(9), will amend para. 95(6)(b) to read as above, applicable after November 1999.

**Technical Notes**: See under 95(6)(a).

**Related Provisions**: 17(14) — Similar rule re loans to non-residents; 256(5.1) — Controlled directly or indirectly — control in fact.

**Notes**: 95(6) amended by 1994 tax amendments bill (Part II), effective (as per amendment to in-force rule by 1995-97 technical bill, s. 305) for rights acquired and shares acquired or disposed of in taxation years of foreign affiliates of taxpayers that begin after 1994, subject to the same exception for changes in taxation years in 1994 as for the introduction of 95(2.1) (see Notes thereto). From 1972 until this amendment, read:

(6) **Where rights or shares issued to avoid tax** — For the purposes of this subdivision,

(a) where any person has a right under a contract, in equity or otherwise, either immediately or in the future and either absolutely or contingently, to, or to acquire, shares of the capital stock of a corporation, those shares shall, if one of the main reasons for the existence of the right may reasonably be considered to be the reduction or postponement of the amount of taxes that would otherwise be payable under this Act, be deemed to be owned by that person; and

(b) where any foreign affiliate of a taxpayer or any non-resident corporation controlled, directly or indirectly in any manner whatever, by the taxpayer or by a related group of which the taxpayer was a member has issued shares of a class of its capital stock and one of the main reasons for the existence or issuance of one or more of the shares of that class may reasonably be considered to be the reduction or postponement of the amount of taxes that would otherwise be payable under this Act, those shares shall be deemed not to have been issued.

**(7) Stock dividends from foreign affiliates** — For the purposes of this subdivision and subsection 52(3), the amount of any stock dividend paid by a foreign affiliate of a corporation resident in Canada shall, in respect of the corporation, be deemed to be nil.

**Interpretation Bulletins [subsec. 95(7)]**: IT-88R2: Stock dividends.

**Definitions [s. 95]**: "active business" — 95(1); "allowable capital loss" — 38(b), 248(1); "amount" — 95(7), 248(1); "annuity" — 248(1); "arm's length" — 95(2.1), 251(1); "bank" — 248(1), *Interpretation Act* 35(1); "business" — 248(1); "business carried on in Canada" — 253; "Canada" — 253, 255; "Canadian resource property" — 66(15), 248(1); "capital gain" — 39(1), 248(1); "capital loss" — 39(1)(b), 248(1); "capital property" — 54, 248(1); "class" — of shares 248(6); "controlled" — 256(6), (6.1); "controlled directly or indirectly" — 256(5.1), (6.2); "controlled foreign affiliate" — 94(1)(d), 95(1), 248(1); "corporation" — 94(1)(d), 248(1), *Interpretation Act* 35(1); "credit union" — 137(6), 248(1); "direct equity percentage" — 95(4); "disposition", "dividend", "employee" — 248(1); "equity percentage" — 95(4); "excluded property" — 95(1); "fiscal period" — 249(2)(b), 249.1; "foreign accrual property income" — 95(1), 95(2), 248(1); "foreign affiliate" — 93.1(1), 94(1)(d), 95(1), 248(1); "foreign bank" — 95(1); "foreign business" — 95(2)(k); "foreign merger", "foreign parent corporation" — 87(8.1), 95(4.1); "foreign resource property" — 66(15), 248(1); "fresh start year" — 94.1(6); "holding corporation" — 95(2)(m)(iii); "income bond", "income debenture" — 248(1); "income from an active business" — 95(1); "income from property" — 9(1), 95(1); "indebtedness" — 95(2.5); "insurance corporation" — 248(1); "investment business", "investment property", "lease obligation" — 95(1); "lending asset" — 95(1)"lending of money", 248(1); "lending of money", "licensing of property" — 95(1); "life insurance corporation", "Minister" — 248(1); "new foreign corporation" — 87(8.1), 95(4.1); "new foreign corporation" — 87(8.1), 95(4.1); "non-resident" — 248(1); "non-resident-owned investment corporation" — 133(8), 248(1); "partnership" — see Notes to 96(1); "permanent establishment" — Reg. 8201; "person" — 248(1); "predecessor foreign corporation" — 87(8.1), 95(4.1); "prescribed" — 248(1); "prescribed financial institution" — Reg. 7900(1), (2); "property" — 248(1); "province" — *Interpretation Act* 35(1); "qualifying interest" — 95(2)(m), 95(2.2); "related" — 95(2.2)(b), 95(6)(a)(i), 251(2); "related group" — 251(4); "relevant cost base" — 95(4); "resident in Canada" — 250; "services" — 95(3); "share" — 248(1); "specified deposit" — 95(2.5); "specified member" — 248(1); "subsidiary wholly-owned corporation" — 248(1); "surplus entitlement percentage" — 95(1); "taxable capital gain" — 38(a), 248(1); "taxable dividend" — 89(1), 248(1); "taxation year" — 95(1), 249; "taxpayer" — 248(1); "trust" — 104(1), 108(1); "trust company" — 95(1); "writing" — *Interpretation Act* 35(1).

## Subdivision j — Partnerships and Their Members

**96. (1) General rules** — Where a taxpayer is a member of a partnership, the taxpayer's income, non-capital loss, net capital loss, restricted farm loss and farm loss, if any, for a taxation year, or the taxpayer's taxable income earned in Canada for a taxation year, as the case may be, shall be computed as if

(a) the partnership were a separate person resident in Canada;

(b) the taxation year of the partnership were its fiscal period;

(c) each partnership activity (including the ownership of property) were carried on by the partnership as a separate person, and a computation were made of the amount of

(i) each taxable capital gain and allowable capital loss of the partnership from the disposition of property, and

(ii) each income and loss of the partnership from each other source or from sources in a particular place,

for each taxation year of the partnership;

(d) each income or loss of the partnership for a taxation year were computed as if this Act were read without reference to paragraphs 12(1)(z.5) and 20(1)(v.1), section 34.1 and subsections 66.1(1), 66.2(1) and 66.4(1) and as if no deduction were permitted under any of section 29 of the *Income Tax Application Rules*, subsections 34.2(4) and 65(1) and sections 66, 66.1, 66.2 and 66.4;

### Proposed Amendment — 96(1)(d)

(d) each income or loss of the partnership for a taxation year were computed as if

(i) this Act were read without reference to paragraphs 12(1)(z.5) and 20(1)(v.1), section 34.1, subsection 59(1), paragraph 59(3.2)(c.1) and subsections 66.1(1), 66.2(1) and 66.4(1), and

(ii) no deduction were permitted under any of section 29 of the *Income Tax Application Rules*, subsections 34.2(4) and 65(1) and sections 66, 66.1, 66.2, 66.21 and 66.4;

**Application**: The December 21, 2000 draft legislation, subsec. 44(1), will amend para. 96(1)(d) to read as above, applicable to fiscal periods that begin after 2000.

**Technical Notes**: Under subsection 96(1), the income earned and the losses incurred by a partnership are generally calculated at the partnership level and attributed to partners in accordance with their respective interests. However, under paragraph 96(1)(d) the income or loss of a partnership is computed without reference to a number of provisions including various provisions relating to resource income and expenditures.

Paragraph 96(1)(d) is amended so that income inclusions under subsection 59(1) (dispositions of foreign resource property) and paragraph 59(3.2)(c.1) are ignored for this purpose. Instead, under new subsections 59(1.1) and 66(12.42), there is a flow-through to a member of a partnership of the member's share of proceeds of disposition of foreign resource property and of other relevant amounts receivable.

Paragraph 96(1)(d) is also amended to ignore deductions under new section 66.21, given that a partner's share of foreign resource expenses qualifies under paragraph (e) of the definition "foreign resource expense" in subsection 66.21(1) as the partner's own foreign resource expenses.

(e) each gain of the partnership from the disposition of land used in a farming business of the partnership were computed as if this Act were read without reference to paragraph 53(1)(i);

(e.1) the amount, if any, by which

(i) the total of all amounts determined under paragraphs 37(1)(a) to (c.1) in respect of the partnership at the end of the taxation year

exceeds

(ii) the total of all amounts determined under paragraphs 37(1)(d) to (g) in respect of the partnership at the end of the year

were deducted under subsection 37(1) by the partnership in computing its income for the year;

(f) the amount of the income of the partnership for a taxation year from any source or from sources in a particular place were the income of the taxpayer from that source or from sources in that particular place, as the case may be, for the taxation year of the taxpayer in which the partnership's taxation year ends, to the extent of the taxpayer's share thereof; and

(g) the amount, if any, by which

(i) the loss of the partnership for a taxation year from any source or sources in a particular place,

exceeds

(ii) in the case of a specified member (within the meaning of the definition "specified member" in subsection 248(1) if that definition were read without reference to paragraph (b) thereof) of the partnership in the year, the amount, if any, deducted by the partnership by virtue of section 37 in calculating its income for the taxation year from that source or sources in the particular place, as the case may be, and

(iii) in any other case, nil

were the loss of the taxpayer from that source or from sources in that particular place, as the case

## Subdivision j — Partnerships and Their Members       S. 96(1.1)(a)(i)

may be, for the taxation year of the taxpayer in which the partnership's taxation year ends, to the extent of the taxpayer's share thereof.

**Related Provisions**: 12(1)(l) — Inclusion of partnership income; 12(1)(y) — Auto provided to partner; 33.1(2)(a) — "person" includes partnership for international banking centre rules; 39.1(2)B(b), 39.1(4), (5) — Election to trigger capital gains exemption; 53(1)(e), 53(2)(c) — ACB of partnership interest; 66(16) — "person" includes partnership for flow-through share rules; 66(18) — Resource expenditures claimed by members of partnerships; 66.1(7), 66.2(6), (7), 66.4(6), (7), 66.7(11) — Resource expenses; 79(1), 79.1(1) — "person" includes partnership for rules re seizure of property by creditor; 80(1)"forgiven amount"B(k) — Debt forgiveness rules do not apply to debt forgiven by partnership to active partner; 80(1), 80.01(1) — "person" includes partnership for debt forgiveness rules; 80(15) — Application of debt forgiveness rules to partners; 87(2)(e.1) — Amalgamations — partnership interest; 93(1.2) — Disposition of share of foreign affiliate; 93.1 — Shares of foreign affiliate held by partnership; 96(1.1) — Allocation of income share to retiring partner; 96(1.7) — Gains and losses; 96(1.9) — Foreign trusts and other foreign investment entities; 96(2.1) — Limited partnership losses; 100(2.1) — Disposition of an interest in a partnership; 107(1)(d) — Stop-loss rule on disposition by partnership of interest in trust that flowed out dividends; 111(1)(a)–(d) — Losses deductible; 112(3.1) — Stop-loss rule for partner on disposition by partnership of share on which dividends paid; 118.1(8) — Donations made by partnership; 120.4(1)"split income"(b) — Certain partnership income of children subject to income splitting tax; 127(8), (8.1) — Investment tax credit of partnership or limited partner; 127.52(1)(c.1) — Minimum tax — no deduction for losses of limited partner; 127.52(2) — Application of partnership income and loss for minimum tax purposes; 139.1(1) — "person" includes partnership for purposes of insurance demutualization; 152(1.4)–(1.8) — Determination by CCRA of partnership income or loss; 162(8.1) — Rules where partnership liable to penalty; 187.4(c) — "person" includes partnership for Part IV.1 tax; 209(6) — "person" includes partnership for tax on carved-out income; 210 — Partnership as designated beneficiary; 212(13.1) — Non-resident withholding tax where payer or payee is a partnership; 227(5.2) — Partnership liable for obligations re withholding tax; 227(15) — Assessment of partnership for Part XIII tax; 237.1(1) — "person" includes partnership for tax shelter identification rules; 244(20) — Notice to members of partnerships; 251.1(4)(b) — "person" includes partnership for definition of affiliated persons; *Income Tax Conventions Interpretation Act* 6.2 — Partnership with Canadian resident partner cannot be resident in another country.

**Notes**: Under 96(1), a partnership is not a person, but partnership income is calculated as though it were a person, and allocated to the partners for tax purposes. The partners report this income (or loss) regardless of actual distributions from the partnership. Distributions are counted as adjustments to the cost base of the partnership interest under 53(1)(e) and 53(2)(c) (see Notes to 53(2)(c)). A partnership does not file a tax return, but a partnership with six or more members must file an information return under Reg. 229. Partnership income or loss can effectively be assessed by the CCRA under 152(1.4)–(1.8).

Income from a partnership retains its character in the hands of the partner, e.g., as business income or dividends. See 96(1)(f) and 4(1). This is in contrast to a trust, where the character of the income disappears (see 108(5)), except for certain designations made by the trust under s. 104 (e.g., 104(19) and (21)).

Certain partnerships must use a calendar year-end, or, in effect, prepay the tax to December 31. See 34.1, 34.2 and 249.1.

A reference to a partnership by its firm name is deemed to be a reference to all the partners: see 244(20)(a).

"Partnership" is not defined; refer to the applicable provincial law (both common-law and legislation such as the provincial *Partnerships Act*). The standard test is "carrying on business in common with a view to profit". See *Continental Bank of Canada*, [1998] 4 C.T.C. 119 (SCC). In Quebec, see article 2186 of the *Civil Code of Quebec*. See also 98(6) re continuation of predecessor partnership as new partnership, and Interpretation Bulletin IT-90, *What is a Partnership?* See also GST Policy Statement P-171R, "Distinguishing between a Joint Venture and a Partnership" (February 24, 1999), in David M. Sherman, *GST Memoranda, Bulletins & Policies* (Carswell, annual).

The law is still developing in cases where a partnership interest is purchased in order to obtain tax losses. See Notes to 96(8).

96(1)(d) amended by 1996 Budget, effective for fiscal periods that begin after 1996, to add reference to 12(1)(z.5). The amount included under 12(1)(z.5), like the resource allowance under 20(1)(v.1) itself, is computed at the partner level rather than the partnership level.

96(1)(d) amended by 1995 Budget, effective 1995, to add reference to 34.1 and 34.2(4). Both of these (additional income inclusion for off-calendar year-ends, and reserve for 1995 stub-period income) are calculated at the individual partner level.

96(1)(d) amended by 1992 technical bill, effective for partnership fiscal periods that begin after December 20, 1991, to add reference to 20(1)(v.1). Reg. 1210 now allows a partner to claim a share of resource allowances disallowed as a deduction at the partnership level.

**Regulations**: 229 (partnership information return); 1101(1ab), 1102(1a) (depreciable property of partnership); 1210 (partner's share of resource allowances).

**I.T. Application Rules**: 20(3) (depreciable property of partnership held since before 1972).

**Interpretation Bulletins**: IT-123R6: Transactions involving eligible capital property; IT-183: Foreign tax credit — member of a partnership; IT-259R3: Exchanges of property; IT-278R2: Death of a partner or of a retired partner; IT-346R: Commodity futures and certain commodities; IT-353R2: Partnership interests — some adjustments to cost base; IT-406R2: Tax payable by an *inter vivos* trust. See also list at end of s. 96.

**Information Circulars**: 73-13: Investment clubs; 89-5R: Partnership information return.

**I.T. Technical News**: No. 3 (use of a partner's assets by a partnership); No. 6 (expenses paid personally by partner where fiscal years do not coincide — policy in para. 14 of IT-138R reversed).

**Advance Tax Rulings**: ATR-59: Financing exploration and development through limited partnerships; ATR-62: Mutual fund distribution limited partnership — amortization of selling commissions.

**Forms**: T2032: Statement of professional activities; T2121: Statement of fishing activities; T2124: Statement of business activities; T4068: Guide for the partnership information return; T5013 Summ: Partnership information return; T5014: Partnership capital cost allowance schedule; T5015: Reconciliation of partner's capital account; T5017: Calculation of deduction for cumulative eligible capital of a partnership.

## (1.1) Allocation of share of income to retiring partner

— For the purposes of subsection (1) and sections 34.1, 34.2, 101, 103 and 249.1,

(a) where the principal activity of a partnership is carrying on a business in Canada and its members have entered into an agreement to allocate a share of the income or loss of the partnership from any source or from sources in a particular place, as the case may be, to any taxpayer who at any time ceased to be a member of

(i) the partnership, or

(ii) a partnership that at any time has ceased to exist or would, but for subsection 98(1), have ceased to exist, and either

(A) the members of that partnership, or

(B) the members of another partnership in which, immediately after that time, any of the members referred to in clause (A) became members

have agreed to make such an allocation

or to the taxpayer's spouse, common-law partner, estate or heirs or to any person referred to in subsection (1.3), the taxpayer, spouse, common-law partner, estate, heirs or person, as the case may be, shall be deemed to be a member of the partnership; and

(b) all amounts each of which is an amount equal to the share of the income or loss referred to in this subsection allocated to a taxpayer from a partnership in respect of a particular fiscal period of the partnership shall, notwithstanding any other provision of this Act, be included in computing the taxpayer's income for the taxation year in which that fiscal period of the partnership ends.

**Related Provisions**: 53(2)(c) — ACB of partnership interest; 96(1.2) — Disposal of right to share in income; 96(1.3) — Deductions; 96(1.4) — Right deemed not to be capital property; 96(1.5) — Disposition by virtue of death of taxpayer; 96(1.6) — Deemed members of partnership are deemed to carry on business.

**Notes**: 96(1.1)(a) amended by 2000 same-sex partners bill to add reference to "common-law partner", effective for the 2001 and later taxation years, or earlier by election (see Notes to 248(1)"common-law partner").

Reference to 34.1 and 34.2 added to 96(1.1) by 1995 Budget, effective 1995. Thus, a taxpayer deemed to be a partner under 96(1.1) may be eligible to claim a reserve under 34.2 for 1995 stub-period income from a business carried on by the partnership.

**Interpretation Bulletins**: IT-278R2: Death of a partner or of a retired partner; IT-338R2: Partnership interests — effects on adjusted cost base resulting from the admission or retirement of a partner. See also list at end of s. 96.

**(1.2) Disposal of right to share in income, etc** — Where in a taxation year a taxpayer who has a right to a share of the income or loss of a partnership under an agreement referred to in subsection (1.1) disposes of that right,

(a) there shall be included in computing the taxpayer's income for the year the proceeds of the disposition; and

(b) for greater certainty, the cost to the taxpayer of each property received by the taxpayer as consideration for the disposition is the fair market value of the property at the time of the disposition.

**Related Provisions**: 96(1.3) — Deductions.

**Interpretation Bulletins**: See list at end of s. 96.

**(1.3) Deductions** — Where, by virtue of subsection (1.1) or (1.2), an amount has been included in computing a taxpayer's income for a taxation year, there may be deducted in computing the taxpayer's income for the year the lesser of

(a) the amount so included in computing the taxpayer's income for the year, and

(b) the amount, if any, by which the cost to the taxpayer of the right to a share of the income or loss of a partnership under an agreement referred to in subsection (1.1) exceeds the total of all amounts in respect of that right that were deductible by virtue of this subsection in computing the taxpayer's income for previous taxation years.

**Interpretation Bulletins**: IT-278R2: Death of a partner or of a retired partner; IT-338R2: Partnership interests — effects on adjusted cost base resulting from the admission or retirement of a partner. See also list at end of s. 96.

**(1.4) Right deemed not to be capital property** — For the purposes of this Act, a right to a share of the income or loss of a partnership under an agreement referred to in subsection (1.1) shall be deemed not to be capital property.

**Interpretation Bulletins**: IT-338R2: Partnership interests — effects on adjusted cost base resulting from the admission or retirement of a partner.

**(1.5) Disposition by virtue of death of taxpayer** — Where, at the time of a taxpayer's death, the taxpayer has a right to a share of the income or loss of a partnership under an agreement referred to in subsection (1.1), subsections 70(2) to (4) apply.

**Related Provisions**: 53(1)(e)(v) — Adjustments to cost base.

**Interpretation Bulletins**: IT-212R3: Income of deceased persons — rights or things; IT-278R2: Death of a partner or of a retired partner. See also list at end of s. 96.

**(1.6) Members of partnership deemed to be carrying on business in Canada** — Where a partnership carries on a business in Canada at any time, each taxpayer who is deemed by paragraph (1.1)(a) to be a member of the partnership at that time is deemed to carry on the business in Canada at that time for the purposes of subsection 2(3), sections 34.1 and 150 and (subject to subsection 34.2(7)) section 34.2.

**Notes**: References to 34.1, 34.2 and 150 added to 96(1.6) by 1995 Budget, effective 1994.

**Interpretation Bulletins**: See list at end of s. 96.

**(1.7) Gains and losses** — Notwithstanding subsection (1) or section 38, where in a particular taxation year of a taxpayer (other than an individual who is not a testamentary trust) commencing before 1990, the taxpayer is a member of a partnership with a fiscal period ending in the particular year, the amount of its taxable capital gain (other than that part of the amount that can be attributed to an amount deemed under subsection 14(1) to be a taxable capital gain of the partnership), allowable capital loss or allowable business investment loss for the particular year determined in respect of the partnership shall be the amount determined by the formula

## Proposed Amendment — 96(1.7) opening words

**(1.7) Gains and losses** — Notwithstanding subsection (1) or section 38, where in a particular taxation year of a taxpayer, the taxpayer is a member of a partnership with a fiscal period that ends in the particular year, the amount of a taxable capital gain (other than that part of the amount that can reasonably be attributed to an amount deemed under subsection 14(1) to be a taxable capital gain of the partnership), allowable capital loss or allowable business investment loss of the taxpayer for the particular year determined in respect of the partnership is the amount determined by the formula

**Application**: The December 21, 2000 draft legislation, subsec. 44(2), will amend the opening words of subsec. 96(1.7) to read as above, applicable to taxation years that end after February 27, 2000.

**Technical Notes**: Subsection 96(1.7) applies to a taxpayer other than an individual who is not a testamentary trust and adjusts the amount of a partnership's taxable capital gain or allowable capital loss included in a taxpayer's income where the taxpayer's capital gains inclusion rate for the taxpayer's taxation year in which the partnership's fiscal period ends is different from the partnership's inclusion rate used to calculate the partnership's taxable capital gain or allowable capital loss.

The adjusted taxable capital gain or allowable capital loss reflects the taxpayer's inclusion rate for the taxpayer's taxation year in which the fiscal period of the partnership ends. This is necessary since a taxpayer may have other taxable capital gains or allowable capital losses and all taxable capital gains and allowable capital losses should be calculated using the same inclusion rate

The subsection is amended to make the subsection apply in respect of all taxpayers.

$$A \times \frac{B}{C}$$

where

A is the amount of the taxpayer's taxable capital gain (other than that part of the amount that can be attributed to an amount deemed under subsection 14(1) to be a taxable capital gain of the partnership) allowable capital loss or allowable business investment loss, as the case may be, for the particular year otherwise determined under this section in respect of the partnership;

B is the fraction that would be used under section 38 for the particular year in respect of the taxpayer if the taxpayer had a capital gain for the particular year; and

C is the fraction that was used under section 38 for the fiscal period of the partnership.

**Interpretation Bulletins**: See list at end of s. 96.

**(1.8) Loan of property** — For the purposes of subsection 56(4.1) and sections 74.1 and 74.3, where an individual has transferred or lent property, either directly or indirectly, by means of a trust or by any other means whatever, to a person and the property or property substituted therefor is an interest in a partnership, the person's share of the amount of any income or loss of the partnership for a fiscal period in which the person was a specified member of the partnership shall be deemed to be income or loss, as the case may be, from the property or substituted property.

**Related Provisions**: 248(5) — Substituted property.

**Interpretation Bulletins**: IT-511R: Interspousal and certain other transfers and loans of property. See also list at end of s. 96.

## Proposed Addition — 96(1.9)

**(1.9) Application of sections 94.1 and 94.2** — Where an exempt taxpayer (as defined in subsection 94.1(1)) for a taxation year is a member of a partnership at any time in the year, for the purposes of applying paragraphs (1)(f) and (g) and 53(1)(e) and 2(c) to the taxpayer for a fiscal period of the partnership that ends in the year this Act shall be read without reference to sections 94.1 and 94.2.

**Application**: The June 22, 2000 draft legislation, subsec. 13(1), will add subsec. 96(1.9), applicable to fiscal periods that begin after June 22, 2000.

**Technical Notes**: New subsection 96(1.9) of the Act is relevant where an "exempt taxpayer" (in general, an individual who has been resident in Canada for fewer than 60 months) is a member of a partnership and the partnership invests in a foreign investment entity. In these circumstances, the exempt taxpayer's share of the partnership's income or loss is computed without regard to new sections 94.1 and 94.2. For further details on the application of section 94.2 to partnerships, see the commentary on new subsections 94.2(6) to (8).

**(2) Construction** — The provisions of this subdivision shall be read and construed as if each of the assumptions in paragraphs (1)(a) to (g) were made.

**(2.1) Limited partnership losses [at-risk rule]** — Notwithstanding subsection (1), where a taxpayer is, at any time in a taxation year, a limited partner of a partnership, the amount, if any, by which

(a) the total of all amounts each of which is the taxpayer's share of the amount of any loss of the partnership, determined in accordance with subsection (1), for a fiscal period of the partnership ending in the taxation year from a business (other than a farming business) or from property

exceeds

(b) the amount, if any, by which

(i) the taxpayer's at-risk amount in respect of the partnership at the end of the fiscal period

exceeds the total of

(ii) the amount required by subsection 127(8) in respect of the partnership to be added in computing the investment tax credit of the taxpayer for the taxation year,

(iii) the taxpayer's share of any losses of the partnership for the fiscal period from a farming business, and

(iv) the taxpayer's share of

(A) the foreign exploration and development expenses, if any, incurred by the partnership in the fiscal period,

> **Proposed Amendment — 96(2.1)(b)(iv)(A)**
>
> (A) the foreign resource pool expenses, if any, incurred by the partnership in the fiscal period,
>
> **Application**: The December 21, 2000 draft legislation, subsec. 44(3), will amend cl. 96(2.1)(b)(iv)(A) to read as above, applicable to fiscal periods that begin after 2000.
>
> **Technical Notes**: Subsection 96(2.1) deals with the losses of limited partnerships. That subsection generally limits the deduction by a limited partner of losses to an amount equal to the amount by which the limited partner's "at-risk amount" in respect of a partnership exceeds the partner's share of specified resource expenditures flowed-through to the partner. Under clause 96(2.1)(b)(iv)(A), the resource expenditures specified include foreign exploration and development expenses.
>
> Clause 96(2.1)(b)(iv)(A) is amended to specify "foreign resource pool expenses", as newly defined in subsection 248(1), rather than only foreign exploration and development expenses. The new definition "foreign resource pool expenses" includes both foreign exploration and development expenses (as defined in subsection 66.21(1)) and expenses that are a foreign resource expense (as defined in subsection 66.21(1)).

(B) the Canadian exploration expense, if any, incurred by the partnership in the fiscal period,

(C) the Canadian development expense, if any, incurred by the partnership in the fiscal period, and

(D) the Canadian oil and gas property expense, if any, incurred by the partnership in the fiscal period,

shall

(c) not be deducted in computing the taxpayer's income for the year,

(d) not be included in computing the taxpayer's non-capital loss for the year, and

(e) be deemed to be the taxpayer's limited partnership loss in respect of the partnership for the year.

**Related Provisions**: 66.8(1) — Resource expenses of limited partner; 87(2.1)(a) — Amalgamation — limited partnership loss carried forward; 96(2.2) — At-risk amount; 111(1)(e) — Carryforward of non-deductible limited partnership losses; 111(9) — Limited partnership loss where taxpayer not resident in Canada; 127.52(1)(i)(ii)(B) — Calculation of previous year's limited partnership loss for minimum tax purposes; 128.1(4)(f) — Limited partnership loss limitation on becoming non-resident; 152(1.1)–(1.3) — Determination of losses; 248(1)"limited partnership loss" — Definition applies to entire Act.

**Notes**: The essence of the "at-risk rules" is in 96(2.1)(b)(i) and 96(2.2)(a) — losses from a limited partnership can only be claimed against other income (i.e., used as a tax shelter) to the extent of the taxpayer's investment in the partnership that is "at risk" of being lost if the business venture of the partnership fails. The rest of the rules in 96(2.1)–(2.7) implement this rule and protect it from avoidance. Limited partnership losses (96(2.1)(e)) cannot be deducted against other sources of income, but can be carried forward indefinitely and claimed against limited partnership income under 111(1)(e).

See also 143.2 and 237.1, with respect to partnerships that are tax shelters.

Revenue Canada took the position that the at-risk rules applied even without being enacted, on general principles. However, the Federal Court of Appeal disagreed, in *Signum Communications Inc.*, [1992] 2 C.T.C. 31.

**Interpretation Bulletins**: IT-232R3: Losses — their deductibility in the loss year or in other years; IT-262R2: Losses of non-residents and part-year residents; IT-302R3: Losses of a corporation — the effect that acquisitions of control, amalgamations, and windings-up have on their deductibility — after January 15, 1987. See also list at end of s. 96.

**I.T. Technical News**: No. 5 (adjusted cost base of partnership interest).

**Advance Tax Rulings**: ATR-51: Limited partner at-risk rules; ATR-59: Financing exploration and development through limited partnerships.

**(2.2) At-risk amount** — For the purposes of this section and sections 111 and 127, the at-risk amount of a taxpayer, in respect of a partnership of which the taxpayer is a limited partner, at any particular time is the amount, if any, by which the total of

(a) the adjusted cost base to the taxpayer of the taxpayer's partnership interest at that time, computed in accordance with subsection (2.3) where applicable,

(b) where the particular time is the end of the fiscal period of the partnership, the taxpayer's share of the income of the partnership from a source for that fiscal period computed under the method described in subparagraph 53(1)(e)(i), and

(b.1) where the particular time is the end of the fiscal period of the partnership, the amount referred to in subparagraph 53(1)(e)(viii) in respect of the taxpayer for that fiscal period

exceeds the total of

(c) all amounts each of which is an amount owing at that time to the partnership, or to a person or partnership not dealing at arm's length with the partnership, by the taxpayer or by a person or partnership not dealing at arm's length with the taxpayer, other than any amount deducted under subparagraph 53(2)(c)(i.3) in computing the adjusted cost base, or under section 143.2 in computing the cost, to the taxpayer of the taxpayer's partnership interest at that time, and

(d) any amount or benefit that the taxpayer or a person not dealing at arm's length with the taxpayer is entitled, either immediately or in the future and either absolutely or contingently, to receive or to obtain, whether by way of reimbursement, compensation, revenue guarantee, proceeds of disposition, loan or any other form of indebtedness or in any other form or manner whatever, granted or to be granted for the purpose of reducing the impact, in whole or in part, of any loss that the taxpayer may sustain because the taxpayer is a member of the partnership or holds or disposes of an interest in the partnership, except to the extent that the amount or benefit is included in the determination of the value of J in the definition "cumulative Canadian exploration expense" in subsection 66.1(6), of M in the definition "cumulative Canadian development expense" in subsection 66.2(5) or of I in the definition "cumulative Canadian oil and gas property expense" in subsection 66.4(5) in respect of the taxpayer, or the entitlement arises

> (i) by virtue of a contract of insurance with an insurance corporation dealing at arm's length with each member of the partnership under which the taxpayer is insured against any claim arising as a result of a liability incurred in the ordinary course of carrying on the partnership business,
>
> (ii) [Repealed]
>
> (iii) as a consequence of the death of the taxpayer,
>
> (iv), (v) [Repealed]
>
> (vi) in respect of an amount not included in the at-risk amount of the taxpayer determined without reference to this paragraph, or
>
> (vii) because of an excluded obligation (as defined in subsection 6202.1(5) of the *Income Tax Regulations*) in relation to a share issued to the partnership by a corporation,

and, for the purposes of this subsection,

> (e) where the amount or benefit to which the taxpayer or the person is entitled at any time is provided by way of an agreement or other arrangement under which the taxpayer or the person has a right, either immediately or in the future and either absolutely or contingently (otherwise than as a consequence of the death of the taxpayer), to acquire other property in exchange for all or any part of the partnership interest, for greater certainty the amount or benefit to which the taxpayer or the person is entitled under the agreement or arrangement is considered to be not less than the fair market value of the other property at that time, and
>
> (f) where the amount or benefit to which the taxpayer or the person is entitled at any time is provided by way of a guarantee, security or similar indemnity or covenant in respect of any loan or other obligation of the taxpayer or the person, for greater certainty the amount or benefit to which the taxpayer or the person is entitled under the guarantee or indemnity at any particular time is considered to be not less than the total of the un-

paid amount of the loan or obligation at that time and all other amounts outstanding in respect of the loan or obligation at that time.

**Related Provisions**: 40(3.14)(b) — Meaning of "limited partner" re negative ACB of partnership interest; 66.8 — Resource expenses of limited partner; 96(2.3) — Computation of at-risk amount; 96(2.6) — Artificial transactions; 96(2.7) — Non-arm's length contribution of capital to partnership; 143.2(2), (6) — At-risk adjustment to tax shelter investment; 248(8) — Occurrences as a consequence of death.

**Notes**: 96(2.2)(c) amended by 1994 Budget, effective September 27, 1994, to add everything from "other than any such amount..."; and by 1995-97 technical bill to add the words "or under section 143.2 in computing the cost", effective December 1994.

Opening words of 96(2.2)(d) amended by 1995-97 technical bill, effective December 1994, primarily to add the words "or any other form of indebtedness", but also to restructure the wording and make minor wording changes. From 1986-87 (see below) to November 1994, read:

> (d) where the taxpayer or a person with whom the taxpayer does not deal at arm's length is entitled, either immediately or in the future and either absolutely or contingently, to receive or obtain any amount or benefit, whether by way of reimbursement, compensation, revenue guarantee or proceeds of disposition or in any other form or manner whatever, granted or to be granted for the purpose of reducing the impact, in whole or in part, of any loss that the taxpayer may sustain because the taxpayer is a member of the partnership or holds or disposes of an interest in the partnership, the amount or benefit, as the case may be, that the taxpayer or the person is or will be so entitled to receive or obtain, except to the extent that the amount or benefit is included in the determination of J in the definition "cumulative Canadian exploration expense" in subsection 66.1(6), of M in the definition "cumulative Canadian development expense" in subsection 66.2(5) or of I in the definition "cumulative Canadian oil and gas property expense" in subsection 66.4(5) in respect of the taxpayer or the entitlement arises

96(2.2)(d)(ii) repealed by 1995 Budget, effective for revenue guarantees granted after 1995. The exclusion from the at-risk rules for film productions has thus been removed, which eliminates films as tax shelters. Instead, a new Canadian film/video production credit is provided directly to film producers in 125.4. For revenue guarantees granted from February 26, 1986 through the end of 1995, read:

> (ii) by virtue of a prescribed revenue guarantee in respect of a prescribed film production

96(2.2)(d)(iv) and (v) repealed by 1995-97 technical bill, effective for partnership interests acquired by a taxpayer after April 26, 1995, except that they still apply (i.e., for grandfathered transactions) where:

> (a) the interest in the partnership is acquired by the taxpayer under the terms of an agreement in writing entered into by the taxpayer before April 27, 1995, or the interest was acquired by the taxpayer
>
> > (i) before 1996 where
> >
> > > (A) all or substantially all of the property of the partnership is
> > >
> > > > (I) a film production prescribed for the purpose of subpara. 96(2.2)(d)(ii), or
> > > >
> > > > (II) an interest in one or more partnerships all or substantially all of the property of which is a film production prescribed for the purpose of subpara. 96(2.2)(d)(ii),
> > >
> > > (B) the principal photography of the production began before 1996, or, in the case of a production that is a television series, the principal photography of one episode of the series began before 1996, and

## S. 96(2.2) — Income Tax Act, Part I, Division B

(C) the principal photography of the production was completed before March 1996,

(ii) before 1996 where it can reasonably be considered that the funds raised by the partnership through the issue of the interest were used by the partnership to acquire before 1996 property included in Class 24, 27 or 34 in Schedule II to the Income Tax Regulations and the property was

(A) acquired under an agreement in writing entered into by the partnership before April 27, 1995, or

(B) under construction by or on behalf of the partnership on April 26, 1995,

(iii) before July 1995 under the terms of a document that is a prospectus, preliminary prospectus or registration statement filed before April 27, 1995 with a public authority in Canada under and in accordance with the securities legislation of Canada or of any province and, where required by law, accepted for filing by the public authority, and the funds so raised were expended before 1996 on expenditures contemplated by the document, or

(iv) before July 1995 under the terms of an offering memorandum distributed as part of an offering of securities where

(A) the memorandum contained a complete or substantially complete description of the securities contemplated in the offering as well as the terms and conditions of the offering,

(B) the memorandum was distributed before April 27, 1995,

(C) solicitations in respect of the sale of the securities contemplated by the memorandum were made before April 27, 1995,

(D) the sale of the securities was substantially in accordance with the memorandum, and

(E) the funds were spent before 1996 in accordance with the memorandum; and

(b) the following conditions are met:

(i) in the case of an interest

(A) acquired by the taxpayer under the terms of an agreement in writing entered into by the taxpayer before April 27, 1995, or

(B) to which subparagraph (a)(iii) or (iv) applies

that is a tax shelter for which s. 237.1 requires an identification number to be obtained, an identification number was obtained before April 27, 1995, and

(ii) there is no agreement or other arrangement under which the taxpayer's obligations with respect to the interest can be changed, reduced or waived if there is a change to the Act or if there is an adverse assessment under the Act.

From February 26, 1986 (subject to certain grandfathering before 1987) until the above amendment, read:

(iv) by virtue of an agreement under which the taxpayer may dispose of the partnership interest for an amount not exceeding its fair market value, determined without reference to the agreement, at the time of the disposition,

(v) by virtue of a revenue guarantee or other agreement in respect of which gross revenue is earned by the partnership except to the extent that the revenue guarantee or other agreement may reasonably be considered to ensure that the taxpayer or person will receive a return of a portion of the taxpayer's investment,

96(2.2)(d) amended by 1991 technical bill, effective for taxation years ending after June 17, 1987, to add subpara. (vii) and to add references to 66.1, 66.2 and 66.4 in opening words.

Everything after 96(2.2)(d) (i.e., (e) and (f) and the words preceding (e)) amended by 1995-97 technical bill, effective for partnership interests acquired by a taxpayer after April 26, 1995, except that the new version does not apply where:

(a) the interest was acquired by the taxpayer

(i) under the terms of an agreement in writing entered into by the taxpayer before April 27, 1995,

(ii) before July 1995 under the terms of a document that is a prospectus, preliminary prospectus or registration statement filed before April 27, 1995 with a public authority in Canada under and in accordance with the securities legislation of Canada or of any province and, where required by law, accepted for filing by the public authority, and the funds so raised were expended before 1996 on expenditures contemplated by the document, or

(iii) before July 1995 under the terms of an offering memorandum distributed as part of an offering of securities where

(A) the memorandum contained a complete or substantially complete description of the securities contemplated in the offering as well as the terms and conditions of the offering,

(B) the memorandum was distributed before April 27, 1995,

(C) solicitations in respect of the sale of the securities contemplated by the memorandum were made before April 27, 1995,

(D) the sale of the securities was substantially in accordance with the memorandum, and

(E) the funds were spent before 1996 in accordance with the memorandum; and

(b) the following conditions are met:

(i) in the case of an interest that is a tax shelter for which s. 237.1 requires an identification number to be obtained, an identification number was obtained before April 27, 1995, and

(ii) there is no agreement or other arrangement under which the taxpayer's obligations with respect to the interest can be changed, reduced or waived if there is a change to the Act or if there is an adverse assessment under the Act.

From February 26, 1986 (subject to certain grandfathering before 1987) until their repeal, read:

and, for the purposes of this subsection, where the amount or benefit to which the taxpayer is at any time entitled is provided

(e) by way of an agreement or other arrangement under which the taxpayer has a right, either absolutely or contingently (otherwise than as a consequence of the death of the taxpayer), to acquire other property in exchange for all or any part of the partnership interest, for greater certainty the amount or benefit to which the taxpayer is entitled under the agreement or arrangement shall be not less than the fair market value of that other property at that time, or

(f) by way of a guarantee, security or similar indemnity or covenant in respect of any loan or other obligation of the taxpayer, by the partnership or a person or partnership with whom or which the partnership does not deal at arm's length, for greater certainty the amount or benefit to which the taxpayer is entitled under the guarantee or indemnity at any particular time shall not be less than the total of the unpaid amount of the loan or obligation at that time and all other amounts outstanding in respect of the loan or obligation at that time.

**Regulations**: 7500 (prescribed film production, prescribed revenue guarantee).

**Interpretation Bulletins**: IT-232R3: Losses — their deductibility in the loss year or in other years. See also list at end of s. 96.

## Subdivision j — Partnerships and Their Members  S. 96(2.4)(a)

**I.T. Technical News**: No. 5 (adjusted cost base of partnership interest); No. 12 (adjusted cost base of partnership interest).

**Advance Tax Rulings**: ATR-51: Limited partner at-risk rules; ATR-59: Financing exploration and development through limited partnerships.

**(2.3) Idem** — For the purposes of subsection (2.2), where a taxpayer has acquired the taxpayer's partnership interest at any time from a transferor other than the partnership, the adjusted cost base to the taxpayer of that interest shall be computed as if the cost to the taxpayer of the interest were the lesser of

(a) the taxpayer's cost otherwise determined, and

(b) the greater of

  (i) the adjusted cost base of that interest to the transferor immediately before that time, and

  (ii) nil,

and where the adjusted cost base of the transferor cannot be determined, it shall be deemed to be equal to the total of the amounts determined in respect of the taxpayer under paragraphs (2.2)(c) and (d) immediately after that time.

**(2.4) Limited partner** — For the purposes of this section and sections 111 and 127, a taxpayer who is a member of a partnership at a particular time is a limited partner of the partnership at that time if the member's partnership interest is not an exempt interest (within the meaning assigned by subsection (2.5)) at that time and if, at that time or within 3 years after that time,

(a) by operation of any law governing the partnership arrangement, the liability of the member as a member of the partnership is limited;

### Proposed Amendment — 96(2.4)(a)

(a) by operation of any law governing the partnership arrangement, the liability of the member as a member of the partnership is limited (except by operation of a provision of a statute of Canada or a province that limits the member's liability only for debts, obligations and liabilities of the partnership, or any member of the partnership, arising from negligent acts or omissions or misconduct that another member of the partnership or an employee, agent or representative of the partnership commits in the course of the partnership business while the partnership is a limited liability partnership);

**Application**: Bill C-43 (First Reading September 20, 2000), s. 47, will amend para. 96(2.4)(a) to read as above, applicable after 1997.

**Technical Notes**: Subsection 96(2.4) of the Act provides an extended definition of "limited partner" that is relevant for the purpose of applying the restrictions on partnership tax credits and losses.

Paragraph 96(2.4)(a) provides that a member of a partnership is a "limited partner" if, by operation of any law governing the partnership arrangement, the liability of the member as a member of the partnership is limited. Concern has been expressed that paragraph 96(2.4)(a) applies to a partner of a "limited liability partnership" in addition to a limited partner of a limited partnership. A limited liability partnership is a new type of partnership the form of which has only recently been permitted under some provincial statutes.

Unlike a limited partner of a limited partnership, a member of limited liability partnership can be liable for the general debts and obligations of a limited liability partnership. However, a member of a limited liability partnership is not liable for the debts, obligations and liabilities of the partnership, or any member of the partnership, arising from negligent acts or omissions that another member of the partnership or an employee, agent or representative of the partnership commits in the course of the partnership business while the partnership is a limited liability partnership [e.g., lawyers and chartered accountants in Ontario — ed.].

Paragraph 96(2.4)(a) is amended to exclude from its application cases where a member's liability is limited by operation of a statutory provision of Canada or a province that limits the member's liability only for the debts, obligations and liabilities of a limited liability partnership, or any member of the partnership, arising from negligent acts or omissions that another member of the partnership or an employee, agent or representative of the partnership commits in the course of the partnership business while the partnership is a limited liability partnership.

**Letter from Department of Finance re Limited Liability Partnerships, 1998**:

Mr. Joel Shafer
Blake, Cassels & Graydon
Toronto, Ontario

Dear Mr. Shafer:

Thank you for your facsimile transmission of July 14, 1998, in which you brought to my attention the introduction in the Ontario Legislature of Bill 6, *An Act to amend the law with respect to Partnerships*. You are concerned that the definition of "limited partner" in subsection 96(2.4) of the *Income Tax Act* might apply to a partner described in new subsection 10(2) of the *Partnerships Act* of Ontario.

It is my understanding that the amendments are intended to limit the liability of a member of a professional accounting partnership only in respect of obligations arising from negligent acts or omissions of another partner, employee, agent or other representative of the partnership. Moreover, this legislation only applies to a partnership for which the sole business is a professional accounting practice governed by statute.

From a tax policy perspective it would not be appropriate for such a partner to be subject to the *Income Tax Act* definition by reason only of a limitation of this nature. Accordingly, we will recommend to the Minister of Finance an amendment to the *Income Tax Act* to preclude a member of a partnership from being considered a limited partner by reason only of a law such as the new Ontario legislation. Further, we will recommend that the amendments be effective as of the date of coming into force of the Ontario legislation.

Thank you for bringing this matter to my attention.

Sincerely,
Len Farber
Director General, Tax Legislation Division

**Letter from Department of Finance, November 4, 1998**: Dear [xxx]

Re: *Limited Liability Partnerships*

Thank you for your facsimile transmission of September 15, 1998, in which you brought to my attention the introduction in the Ontario Legislature of Bill 53, *An Act to amend the Law Society Act*.

As you are aware, we propose to recommend amendments to the *Income Tax Act* to preclude a member of a partnership that carries on an accounting practice from being considered a limited partner by reason only of amendments to the Ontario *Chartered Accountants Act, 1956* that have recently been enacted. We are aware that subsection 10(2) of the Ontario *Partnerships Act* is not restricted to professional accounting practices governed by statute; indeed, it was that lack of restriction that prompted us to limit the scope of our September 8th correspondence with [xxx] to the particular profession with which that firm's submission was concerned. Your letter is the first to raise the issue of the application of the Ontario *Partnership Act* raised in relation to the legal profession.

While Ontario Bill 53 (1998) has received only second reading at this time, this is to confirm our intention to propose similar amendments concerning the legal profession to our Minister in the event that section 28 of Ontario Bill 53 (1998) is enacted by the Ontario legislature. Further, we will recommend that the amendments be effective as of the date of coming into force of the Ontario legislation.

Thank you for bringing this matter to my attention.

Yours sincerely,
Len Farber
Director General, Tax Legislation Division

    (b) the member or a person not dealing at arm's length with the member is entitled, either immediately or in the future and either absolutely or contingently, to receive an amount or to obtain a benefit that would be described in paragraph (2.2)(d) if that paragraph were read without reference to subparagraphs (ii) and (vi);

    (c) one of the reasons for the existence of the member who owns the interest

        (i) can reasonably be considered to be to limit the liability of any person with respect to that interest, and

        (ii) cannot reasonably be considered to be to permit any person who has an interest in the member to carry on that person's business (other than an investment business) in the most effective manner; or

    (d) there is an agreement or other arrangement for the disposition of an interest in the partnership and one of the main reasons for the agreement or arrangement can reasonably be considered to be to attempt to avoid the application of this subsection to the member.

**Related Provisions**: 40(3.14) — Definition of limited partner for purposes of negative ACB rules; 66.8 — Resource expenses of limited partner; 96(2.5) — Exempt interest in a partnership; 127.52(3) — Definition for minimum tax purposes; 143.2(1)"tax shelter investment"(b) — Whether limited partnership interest is tax shelter investment.

**Notes**: 96(2.4) amended by 1995-97 technical bill, effective for fiscal periods that end after November 1994. The substantive change was the addition of "either immediately or in the future and either absolutely or contingently" in para. (b); the other changes were cosmetic (e.g., "may reasonably be considered" to "can reasonably be considered").

**Interpretation Bulletins**: IT-232R3: Losses — their deductibility in the loss year or in other years. See also list at end of s. 96.

**(2.5) Exempt interest** — For the purposes of subsection (2.4), an exempt interest in a partnership at any time means a prescribed partnership interest or an interest in a partnership that was actively carrying on business on a regular and a continuous basis immediately before February 26, 1986 and continuously thereafter until that time or that was earning income from the rental or leasing of property immediately before February 26, 1986 and continuously thereafter until that time, where there has not after February 25, 1986 and before that time been a substantial contribution of capital to the partnership or a substantial increase in the indebtedness of the partnership and, for this purpose, an amount will not be considered to be substantial where

    (a) the amount was used by the partnership to make an expenditure required to be made pursuant to the terms of a written agreement entered into by it before February 26, 1986, or to repay a loan, debt or contribution of capital that had been received or incurred in respect of any such expenditure,

    (b) the amount was raised pursuant to the terms of a prospectus, preliminary prospectus or registration statement filed before February 26, 1986 with a public authority in Canada pursuant to and in accordance with the securities legislation of Canada or of any province, and, where required by law, accepted for filing by that public authority, or

    (c) the amount was used for the activity that was carried on by the partnership on February 25, 1986 but was not used for a significant expansion of the activity

and, for the purposes of this subsection,

    (d) a partnership in respect of which paragraph (b) applies shall be considered to have been actively carrying on a business on a regular and a continuous basis immediately before February 26, 1986 and continuously thereafter until the earlier of the closing date, if any, stipulated in the document referred to that paragraph and January 1, 1987, and

    (e) an expenditure shall not be considered to have been required to be made pursuant to the terms of an agreement where the obligation to make the expenditure is conditional in any way on the consequences under this Act relating to the expenditure and the condition has not been satisfied or waived before June 12, 1986.

**Regulations**: No prescribed partnership interests to date.

**(2.6) Artificial transactions** — For the purposes of paragraph (2.2)(c), where at any time an amount owing by a taxpayer or a person with whom the taxpayer does not deal at arm's length is repaid and it is established, by subsequent events or otherwise, that the repayment was made as part of a series of loans or other transactions and repayments, the amount owing shall be deemed not to have been repaid.

**Related Provisions**: 248(10) — Series of transactions.

**(2.7) Idem** — For the purposes of paragraph (2.2)(a), where at any time a taxpayer makes a contribution of capital to a partnership and the partnership or a person or partnership with whom or which the partnership does not deal at arm's length makes a loan to the taxpayer or to a person with whom the taxpayer does not deal at arm's length or repays the contribution of capital, and it is established, by subsequent events or otherwise, that the loan or repayment, as the case may be, was made as part of a series of loans or other transactions and repayments, the contribution of capital shall be deemed not to have been made to the extent of the loan or repayment, as the case may be.

**Related Provisions**: 248(10) — Series of transactions.
**Interpretation Bulletins**: See list at end of s. 96.

**(3) Agreement or election of partnership members** — Where a taxpayer who was a member of a partnership during a fiscal period has, for any purpose relevant to the computation of the taxpayer's income from the partnership for the fiscal period, made or executed an agreement, designation or an election under or in respect of the application of any of subsections 13(4), (15) and (16) and 14(6), section 15.2, subsections 20(9) and 21(1) to (4), section 22, subsection 29(1), section 34, clause 37(8)(a)(ii)(B), subsections 44(1) and (6), 50(1) and 80(5), (9), (10) and (11), section 80.04 and subsections 97(2), 139.1(16) and (17) and 249.1(4) and (6) that, but for this subsection, would be a valid agreement, designation or election,

---

**Proposed Amendment — 96(3) opening words**

**(3) Agreement or election of partnership members** — Where a taxpayer who was a member of a partnership at any time in a fiscal period has, for any purpose relevant to the computation of the taxpayer's income from the partnership for the fiscal period, made or executed an agreement, designation or election under or in respect of the application of any of subsections 13(4) and (16) and 14(6), section 15.2, subsections 20(9) and 21(1) to (4), section 22, subsection 29(1), section 34, clause 37(8)(a)(ii)(B), subsections 44(1) and (6), 50(1) and 80(5), (9), (10) and (11), section 80.04, subsections 94.1(4), (5) and (12), clause (i)(C) of the description of D in paragraph 94.2(4)(a), paragraph 95(2)(g.2) and subsections 97(2), 139.1(16) and (17) and 249.1(4) and (6) that, but for this subsection, would be a valid agreement, designation or election,

**Application**: The June 22, 2000 draft legislation, subsec. 13(2), will amend the opening words of subsec. 96(3) to read as above, applicable to fiscal periods that begin after June 22, 2000.

---

**Technical Notes**: Subsection 96(3) of the Act provides rules that apply if a member of a partnership makes an election under certain provisions of the Act for a purpose that is relevant to the computation of the member's income from the partnership. In such a case, the election will be valid only if it is made on behalf of all the members of the partnership and the member had authority to act for the partnership.

Subsection 96(3) is amended so that it applies for the purposes of elections under

- new paragraph 94.1(5)A(c) (election by taxpayer to use discretionary deductions on behalf of FIE);
- new subsection 94.1(12) (election to treat foreign affiliate as controlled foreign affiliate);
- new subsection 94.1(4) (election to have accrual regime for foreign investment entities apply);
- new subparagraph 94.2(4)(a)D(i) (election to recognize positive deferral amount before year of disposition); and
- new paragraph 95(2)(g.2) (elections and designations for the purposes of computing foreign accrual property income).

(a) the agreement, designation or election is not valid unless

(i) it was made or executed on behalf of the taxpayer and each other person who was a member of the partnership during the fiscal period, and

(ii) the taxpayer had authority to act for the partnership;

(b) unless the agreement, designation or election is invalid because of paragraph (a), each other person who was a member of the partnership during the fiscal period shall be deemed to have made or executed the agreement, designation or election; and

(c) notwithstanding paragraph (a), any agreement, designation or election deemed by paragraph (b) to have been made or executed by any person shall be deemed to be a valid agreement, designation or election made or executed by that person.

**Related Provisions**: 244(20) — Members of partnerships.

**Notes**: Opening words of 96(3) amended by 1999 Budget, effective for fiscal periods that end after December 15, 1998, to add reference to 139.1(16) and (17).

Amended by 1995 Budget, effective 1995, to add references to 249.1.

Amended by 1994 tax amendments bill (Part I), effective for fiscal periods that end after February 21, 1994, to change all references to "election" to "agreement, designation or election" and to add references to 80(5), (9), (10), (11) and 80.04.

Amended by 1992 technical bill, effective February 26, 1992, to add reference to 15.2. Reference to 37(8)(a)(ii)(B) added by 1992 Economic Statement, effective for fiscal periods that end after December 2, 1992. The 1992 Economic Statement bill unintentionally deleted the reference to 15.2, but it was retroactively restored by 1995-97 technical bill.

Amended by 1991 technical bill to remove a reference to 39(4), effective for dispositions after July 13, 1990, and to add the reference to 50(1). For elections under 50(1) for the 1985 to 1989 taxation years, notwithstanding 152(4) to (5), such assessments of tax, interest and penalties payable for the 1985 to 1989 taxation years shall be made as are necessary to give effect to such elections.

**Interpretation Bulletins**: IT-278R2: Death of a partner or of a retired partner; IT-413R: Election by members of a partnership under subsection 97(2); IT-457R: Election by professionals to exclude work in progress from income. See also list at end of s. 96.

**(4) Election** — Any election under subsection 97(2) or 98(3) shall be made on or before the day that is the earliest of the days on or before which any taxpayer making the election is required to file a return of income pursuant to section 150 for the taxpayer's taxation year in which the transaction to which the election relates occurred.

**Related Provisions**: 96(5) — Late filing; 96(6) — Penalty for late filing; 96(7) — Unpaid balance of penalty.

**Interpretation Bulletins**: IT-413R: Election by members of a partnership under subsection 97(2). See also list at end of s. 96.

**Forms**: T2060: Election for disposition of property upon cessation of partnership.

**(5) Late filing** — Where an election referred to in subsection (4) was not made on or before the day on or before which the election was required by that subsection to be made and that day was after May 6, 1974, the election shall be deemed to have been made on that day if, on or before the day that is 3 years after that day,

(a) the election is made in prescribed form; and

(b) an estimate of the penalty in respect of that election is paid by the taxpayer referred to in subsection 97(2) or by the persons referred to in subsection 98(3), as the case may be, when that election is made.

**Interpretation Bulletins**: IT-413R: Election by members of a partnership under subsection 97(2). See also list at end of s. 96.

**(5.1) Special cases** — Where, in the opinion of the Minister, the circumstances of a case are such that it would be just and equitable

(a) to permit an election under subsection 97(2) or 98(3) to be made after the day that is 3 years after the day on or before which the election was required by subsection (4) to be made, or

(b) to permit an election made under subsection 97(2) to be amended,

the election or amended election shall be deemed to have been made on the day on or before which the election was so required to be made if

(c) the election or amended election is made in prescribed form, and

(d) an estimate of the penalty in respect of the election or amended election is paid by the taxpayer referred to in subsection 97(2) or by the persons referred to in subsection 98(3), as the case may be, when the election or amended election is made;

and where this subsection applies to the amendment of an election, that election shall be deemed not to have been effective.

**Interpretation Bulletins**: IT-413R: Election by members of a partnership under subsection 97(2). See also list at end of s. 96.

**(6) Penalty for late-filed election** — For the purposes of this section, the penalty in respect of an election or an amended election referred to in paragraph (5)(a) or (5.1)(c) is

(a) where the election or amended election is made under subsection 97(2), an amount equal to the lesser of

(i) $1/4$ of 1% of the amount by which the fair market value of the property disposed of by the taxpayer referred to therein at the time of disposition exceeds the amount agreed on by the taxpayer and the members of the partnership in the election or amended election, for each month or part of a month during the period commencing with the day on or before which the election is required by subsection (4) to be made and ending on the day the election or amended election is made, and

(ii) an amount, not exceeding $8,000, equal to the product obtained by multiplying $100 by the number of months each of which is a month all or part of which is during the period referred to in subparagraph (i); and

(b) where the election is made under subsection 98(3), an amount equal to the lesser of

(i) $1/4$ of 1% of the amount by which

(A) the total of all amounts of money and the fair market value of partnership property received by the persons referred to therein as consideration for their interests in the partnership at the time that the partnership ceased to exist

exceeds

(B) the total of each such person's proceeds of disposition of that person's interest in the partnership as determined under paragraph 98(3)(a),

for each month or part of a month during the period commencing with the day on or before which the election is required by subsection (4) to be made and ending on the day the election or amended election is made, and

(ii) an amount, not exceeding $8,000, equal to the product obtained by multiplying $100 by the number of months each of which is a month all or part of which is during the period referred to in subparagraph (i).

**Related Provisions**: 96(7) — Assessment of penalty; 220(3.1) — Waiver of penalty by CCRA.

**Interpretation Bulletins**: IT-413R: Election by members of a partnership under subsection 97(2). See also list at end of s. 96.

**(7) Unpaid balance of penalty** — The Minister shall, with all due dispatch, examine each election and amended election referred to in paragraph (5)(a) or (5.1)(c), assess the penalty payable and send a notice of assessment to the taxpayer or persons, as the case may be, and the taxpayer or persons, as the case may be, shall pay forthwith to the Receiver General the amount, if any, by which the penalty so assessed exceeds the total of all amounts previously paid on account of that penalty.

**(8) Foreign partnerships** — For the purposes of this Act, where at a particular time a person resident in Canada becomes a member of a partnership, or a person who is a member of a partnership becomes resident in Canada, and immediately before the particular time no member of the partnership is resident in Canada, the following rules apply for the purpose of computing the partnership's income for fiscal periods ending after the particular time:

(a) where, at or before the particular time, the partnership held depreciable property of a prescribed class (other than taxable Canadian property),

(i) no amount shall be included in determining the amounts for any of A, C, D and F to I in the definition "undepreciated capital cost" in subsection 13(21) in respect of the acquisition or disposition before the particular time of the property, and

(ii) where the property is the partnership's property at the particular time, the property shall be deemed to have been acquired, immediately after the particular time, by the partnership at a capital cost equal to the lesser of its fair market value and its capital cost to the partnership otherwise determined;

(b) in the case of the partnership's property that is inventory (other than inventory of a business carried on in Canada) or non-depreciable capital property (other than taxable Canadian property) of the partnership at the particular time, its cost to the partnership shall be deemed to be, immediately after the particular time, equal to the lesser of its fair market value and its cost to the partnership otherwise determined;

(c) any loss in respect of the disposition of a property (other than inventory of a business carried on in Canada or taxable Canadian property) by the partnership before the particular time shall be deemed to be nil; and

(d) where 4/3 of the cumulative eligible capital in respect of a business carried on at the particular time outside Canada by the partnership exceeds the total of the fair market value of each eligible capital property in respect of the business at that time, the partnership shall be deemed to have, immediately after that time, disposed of an eligible capital property in respect of the business for proceeds equal to the excess and to have received those proceeds.

**Related Provisions**: 96(9) — Anti-avoidance.

**Notes**: 96(8)(a) ensures that CCA on a foreign partnership's depreciable property is based on capital costs that do not exceed the lesser of the value of the partnership's property and its capital cost at the time when the property becomes relevant for purposes of the Canadian tax system.

96(8)(b) ensures that a partnership that previously had no Canadian resident partners cannot import and allocate an unrealized loss to a Canadian partner.

96(8)(c) ensures that a loss on a disposition by the partnership before it acquires a Canadian resident partner is deemed to be nil, even if it is incurred in the same fiscal period in which 96(8) applies.

96(8)(d) provides that where 4/3 of the cumulative eligible capital (CEC) of a business carried outside Canada by the partnership at the time it acquires a Canadian resident partner is greater than the value of the related eligible capital property (ECP), the partnership is deemed to have disposed of and received proceeds for an ECP equal to the excess. This reduction in the CEC results in its being the lesser of the CEC otherwise determined and 3/4 of the total value of the business's ECP. Subsequent claims under 20(1)(b) are thus limited so that they are based on the value of the ECP.

The CCRA considers that 96(8) is largely clarifying, and that the same rules should apply in principle before the effective dates of the legislation. (See *Spire Freezers Ltd.*, [1999] 3 C.T.C. 476 (FCA), leave to appeal granted by SCC (April 10, 2000), File 27415, where the Court ruled the losses non-deductible on the basis that there was no real partnership.) Where necessary, the CCRA will consider using the general anti-avoidance rule in 245 for this purpose. Another case, *Backman*, [1999] 4 C.T.C. 177 (FCA), which also dealt with a taxpayer buying into a U.S. partnership that had previously created losses, is also under appeal to the Supreme Court of Canada (leave granted (June 8, 2000), File 27561).

96(8) added by 1993 technical bill, effective for a particular partnership where a person or partnership becomes a member of the particular partnership after December 21, 1992, or where a member of the particular partnership becomes resident in Canada after August 30, 1993. However, before May 1994, ignore 96(8)(d).

**(9) Idem** — For the purpose of applying subsection (8), where it can reasonably be considered that one of the main reasons that there is a member of the partnership who is resident in Canada is to avoid the application of that subsection, the member shall be deemed not to be resident in Canada.

### Proposed Amendment — 96(9)

**(9) Application of foreign partnership rule** — For the purposes of applying subsection (8) and this subsection,

(a) where it can reasonably be considered that one of the main reasons that a member of a partnership is resident in Canada is to avoid the application of subsection (8), the member is deemed not to be resident in Canada; and

(b) where at any time a particular partnership is a member of another partnership,

(i) each person or partnership that is, at that time, a member of the particular partnership is deemed to be a member of the other partnership at that time,

(ii) each person or partnership that becomes a member of the particular partnership at that time is deemed to become a member of the other partnership at that time, and

(iii) each person or partnership that ceases to be a member of the particular partnership at that time is deemed to cease to be a member of the other partnership at that time.

**Related Provisions**: 94.2(8) — Parallel rule for foreign investment entities.

**Application**: The June 22, 2000 draft legislation, subsec. 13(3), will amend subsec. 96(9) to read as above, applicable to fiscal periods that begin after June 22, 2000.

**Technical Notes**: Subsection 96(8) of the Act provides rules that apply where, at a particular time, a Canadian resident becomes a member of a partnership, or a person who is a member of such a partnership becomes a resident of Canada. Where, immediately before the particular time no member of the partnership was resident in Canada, these rules apply in computing the income of the partnership for fiscal periods ending after the particular time. In general terms, the rules in subsection 96(8) are designed to prevent losses accrued while a partnership had no Canadian resident partners from being used to reduce Canadian income tax liabilities.

Subsection 96(9) provides that, where one of the main reasons that there is a member of the partnership who is resident in Canada is to avoid the application of subsection 96(8), that member will, for the purpose of applying subsection 96(8), be considered not to be resident in Canada.

Subsection 96(9) is amended to provide an explicit look-through rule for the purposes of subsection 96(8) so that members of partnerships may be identified through one or more tiers of partnerships which are members of other partnerships. Amended subsection 96(9) is consistent with new subsection 94.2(8).

**Notes**: 96(9) added by 1993 technical bill, effective on the same basis as 96(8).

**Definitions [s. 96]**: "adjusted cost base" — 54, 248(1); "allowable business investment loss", "allowable capital loss" — 38, 248(1); "amount" — 248(1); "arm's length" — 251(1); "business" — 248(1); "Canada" — 250, 255; "Canadian development expense" — 66.2(5), 248(1); "Canadian exploration expense" — 66.1(6), 248(1); "Canadian oil and gas property expense" — 66.4(5), 248(1); "Canadian partnership" — 102(1); "capital cost" — of depreciable property 13(7); "capital property" — 54, 248(1); "carried on in Canada", "carrying on business" — 253; "common-law partner" — 248(1); "consequence of the death" — 248(8); "cost" — 96(8); "cumulative eligible capital" — 14(5), 248(1); "depreciable property" — 13(21), 248(1); "disposition" — 13(21), 248(1); "eligible capital property" — 54, 248(1); "employee" — 248(1); "farm loss" — 111(8), 248(1); "farming" — 248(1); "fiscal period" — 249(2)(b), 249.1; "foreign exploration and development expenses" — 66(15), 248(1); "foreign resource pool expense", "gross revenue", "insurance corporation", "inventory" — 248(1); "investment tax credit" — 127(9), 248(1); "limited partner" — 96(2.4); "limited partnership loss" — 96(2.1), 248(1); "member" — 102(2); "Minister" — 248(1); "net capital loss", "non-capital loss" — 111(8), 248(1); "partnership" — see Notes to 96(1); "person", "prescribed", "property" — 248(1); "province" — *Interpretation Act* 35(1); "resident in Canada" — 250; "restricted farm loss" — 31, 248(1); "series of transactions" — 248(10); "share", "specified member" — 248(1); "substituted property" — 248(5); "taxable Canadian property" — 248(1); "taxable capital gain" — 38(a), 248(1); "taxable income earned in Canada" — 115(1), 248(1); "taxation year" — 11(2), 96(1)(b), 249; "taxpayer" — 248(1); "testamentary trust" — 108(1), 248(1); "trust" — 104(1), 248(1), (3).

**Interpretation Bulletins [s. 96]**: IT-81R: Partnerships — income of non-resident partners; IT-90: What is a partnership?; IT-138R: Computation and flow-through of partnership income; IT-151R5: Scientific research and experimental development expenditures; IT-242R: Retired partners.

**97. (1) Contribution of property to partnership** — Where at any time after 1971 a partnership has acquired property from a taxpayer who was, immediately after that time, a member of the partnership, the partnership shall be deemed to have acquired the property at an amount equal to its fair market value at that time and the taxpayer shall be deemed to have disposed of the property for proceeds equal to that fair market value.

**Related Provisions**: 13(21.2)(d) — No application on certain transfers of depreciable property where u.c.c. exceeds fair market value; 96(2) — Construction; 97(2) — Election for rollover on transfer of property to partnership.

**Interpretation Bulletins**: IT-457R: Election by professionals to exclude work in progress from income; IT-471R: Merger of partnerships.

**I.T. Technical News**: No. 3 (use of a partner's assets by a partnership).

**(2) Rules where election by partners** — Notwithstanding any other provision of this Act other than subsection 13(21.2), where a taxpayer at any time disposes of any property that is a capital property, Canadian resource property, foreign resource property, eligible capital property or inventory of the taxpayer to a partnership that immediately after that time is a Canadian partnership of which the taxpayer is a member, if the taxpayer and all the other members of the partnership jointly so elect in prescribed form within the time referred to in subsection 96(4),

(a) the provisions of paragraphs 85(1)(a) to (f) apply to the disposition as if

(i) the reference therein to "corporation's cost" were read as a reference to "partnership's cost",

(ii) the references therein to "other than any shares of the capital stock of the corporation or a right to receive any such shares" and to "other than shares of the capital stock of the corporation or a right to receive any such shares" were read as references to "other than an interest in the partnership",

(iii) the references therein to "shareholder of the corporation" were read as references to "member of the partnership",

(iv) the references therein to "the corporation" were read as references to "all the other members of the partnership", and

(v) the references therein to "to the corporation" were read as references to "to the partnership";

(b) in computing, at any time after the disposition, the adjusted cost base to the taxpayer of the taxpayer's interest in the partnership immediately after the disposition,

(i) there shall be added the amount, if any, by which the taxpayer's proceeds of disposition of the property exceed the fair market value, at the time of the disposition, of the consideration (other than an interest in the partnership) received by the taxpayer for the property, and

(ii) there shall be deducted the amount, if any, by which the fair market value, at the time of the disposition, of the consideration (other than an interest in the partnership) received by the taxpayer for the property so disposed of by the taxpayer exceeds the fair market value of the property at the time of the disposition; and

(c) where the property so disposed of by the taxpayer to the partnership is taxable Canadian property of the taxpayer, the interest in the partnership received by the taxpayer as consideration therefor shall be deemed to be taxable Canadian property of the taxpayer.

**Related Provisions**: 13(21.2)(d) — No election allowed on certain transfers of depreciable property where u.c.c. exceeds fair market value; 40(3.3), (3.4) — Limitation on loss where share acquired by affiliated person; 53(4) — Effect on ACB of share, partnership interest or trust interest; 96(2) — Construction; 96(3) — Election by members; 96(4)–(7) Elections; 97(4) — Where capital cost to partner exceeds proceeds of disposition; 98.1(2) — Continuation of original partnership; 107(2)(d.1)(iii), 107.4(3)(f) — Deemed taxable Canadian property retains status when rolled out of trust or into trust; Canada-U.S. Tax Convention, Art. XIII:8 — Deferral of tax for U.S. resident transferor.

**Notes**: 97(2) provides a rollover of property into a partnership that parallels the rollover provided by 85(1) for transfers to a corporation. Without this rollover, 97(1) deems the transfer to take place at fair market value. For rollovers from a partnership to a corporation, see 85(2).

Opening words of 97(2) amended by 1995-97 technical bill, effective (subject to grandfathering rule reproduced after s. 260) for dispositions of property that occur after April 26, 1995, to change reference to 85(5.1) to 13(21.2). Numerous other changes were made, but they were cosmetic and non-substantive.

97(2) amended by 1981 Budget, effective for dispositions after November 12, 1981, other than dispositions before 1983 if the arrangements therefor were substantially advanced and evidenced in writing on November 12, 1981. For earlier dispositions, read:

(2) Notwithstanding any other provision of this Act, where at any time after 1971 a Canadian partnership has acquired property from a taxpayer who was, immediately after that time, a member of the partnership, if all the persons who immediately after that time were members of the partnership have jointly so elected in respect of the property in prescribed form and within the time referred to in subsection 96(4), the following rules apply:

(a) the amount that all of those persons have agreed upon in their election in respect of the property shall be deemed to be the taxpayer's proceeds of disposition of the property and the amount for which the partnership acquired the property;

(b) the amount, if any, by which the amount so elected in respect of the property exceeds the amount of the consideration (other than an interest in the partnership) received by the taxpayer for the property shall

(i) if immediately before that time the taxpayer was a member of the partnership, be included in computing the adjusted cost base to him of his interest in the partnership, and

(ii) in any other case, be included in computing the cost to him of his interest in the partnership;

(c) where the amount that all of those persons have agreed upon in their election in respect of the property is greater than the fair market value, at the time of the disposition, of the property so disposed of, the amount so agreed upon shall, irrespective of the amount actually so agreed upon, be deemed to be an amount equal to that fair market value; and

(d) notwithstanding paragraph (c), where the amount that all of those persons have agreed upon in their election in respect of the property is less than the amount of the consideration (other than an interest in the partnership) received by the taxpayer for the property, the amount so agreed upon shall, irrespective of the amount so agreed upon, be deemed to be an amount equal to the amount of that consideration.

**I.T. Application Rules**: 20(1.2) (where transferred depreciable property was owned by the transferor since before 1972).

**Interpretation Bulletins**: IT-338R2: Partnership interests — effects on adjusted cost base resulting from the admission or retirement of a partner; IT-413R: Election by members of a partnership under subsection 97(2); IT-457R: Election by professionals to exclude work in progress from income; IT-471R: Merger of partnerships.

**Information Circulars**: 76-19R3: Transfer of property to a corporation under section 85; 88-2, paras. 12, 22: General anti-avoidance rule — section 245 of the *Income Tax Act*.

**I.T. Technical News**: No. 16 (*Continental Bank* case).

**Forms**: T2059: Election on disposition of property by a taxpayer to a Canadian partnership.

**(3) [Repealed]**

**Notes**: 97(3) repealed by 1995-97 technical bill, effective (subject to grandfathering rule reproduced after s. 260) for dispositions of property that occur after April 26, 1995. Under 40(3.4), a loss arising on the transfer of property to a partnership of which the transferor is a majority interest partner continues to be denied. However, the loss is no longer added to the ACB of the taxpayer's partnership interest, but will instead be deferred, generally until the property is sold out of the affiliated group. See Notes to 40(3.4). Where 97(3) applies, read:

(3) **Where property acquired from majority interest partner** — Where, at any time after November 12, 1981, a taxpayer has disposed of any capital property to a partnership and, immediately after the disposition, the taxpayer was a majority interest partner of the partnership and, but for this subsection, the taxpayer would have had a capital loss therefrom, the following rules apply:

(a) notwithstanding any other provision of this Act, the taxpayer's capital loss therefrom shall be deemed to be nil; and

(b) except where the property so disposed of was, immediately after the disposition, an obligation that was payable to the partnership by a corporation that is related to the taxpayer or by a corporation or partnership that would be related to the taxpayer if paragraph 80(2)(j) applied for the purposes of this paragraph, in computing at any time after the disposition the adjusted cost base to the taxpayer of the taxpayer's interest in the partnership immediately after the disposition, there shall be added the amount, if any, by which

(i) the cost amount to the taxpayer, immediately before the disposition, of the property

exceeds

(ii) the taxpayer's proceeds of disposition of the property.

Opening words of 97(3)(b) amended by 1994 tax amendments bill (Part I) to add everything before "in computing", effective for property disposed of after July 12, 1994, other than pursuant to agreements in writing entered into by that date. Where the exception in the opening words of 97(3)(b) applies, the denied capital loss is added to ACB under 53(1)(f.1) or (f.11). The amendment ensures balance between the rules in 97(3) for creditors and the debt parking rules in 80.01 for debtors.

### (3.1) [Repealed]

**Notes**: 97(3.1) repealed by 1995-97 technical bill, effective (subject to grandfathering rule reproduced after s. 260) for dispositions of property that occur after April 26, 1995. The definition of "majority interest partner" now appears in 248(1). Where 97(3.1) applies, read:

> (3.1) **Deemed majority interest partner** — For the purposes of subsection (3), a taxpayer shall be deemed to be a majority interest partner of a partnership at any time if
>
>> (a) the total of the taxpayer's share, the share of the taxpayer's spouse and the share of a person or group of persons that, directly or indirectly in any manner whatever, controlled or was controlled by the taxpayer, of the income of the partnership from any source for the fiscal period of the partnership that includes that time exceeds $1/2$ of the income of the partnership from the source for that period; or
>>
>> (b) the total of the taxpayer's share, the share of the taxpayer's spouse and the share of a person or group of persons that, directly or indirectly in any manner whatever, controlled or was controlled by the taxpayer, of the total amount that would be paid to all members of the partnership (otherwise than as the share of any income of the partnership) if it were wound up at that time exceeds $1/2$ of that amount.

97(3.1) amended by 1981 Budget, effective for dispositions after November 12, 1981, other than dispositions before 1983 if the arrangements therefor were substantially advanced and evidenced in writing on November 12, 1981. For earlier dispositions, delete subsec. (3.1), and read the following in place of subsec. (3):

> (3) Where at any time after 1971 a partnership has acquired property from a taxpayer who was, immediately after the acquisition, a member of the partnership, and
>
>> (a) the taxpayer's share, as a member of the partnership, of the income of the partnership from any source for the taxation year of the partnership in which the property was acquired exceeds $1/2$ of the income of the partnership from that source for the year, or
>>
>> (b) the amount that would, if the partnership were wound up immediately after the acquisition, be paid to the taxpayer as a member of the partnership (otherwise than as his share of any income of the partnership) exceeds $1/2$ of the aggregate of all such amounts that would be so paid to all persons as members of the partnership,
>
> the loss, if any, of the taxpayer arising from the acquisition of the property by the partnership
>
>> (c) is, notwithstanding any other provision of this Act, not deductible in computing the income, net capital loss, non-capital loss or restricted farm loss, if any, of the taxpayer for any taxation year, and
>>
>> (d) shall,
>>
>>> (i) where immediately before that time the taxpayer was a member of the partnership, be included in computing the adjusted cost base to him of his interest in the partnership, and
>>>
>>> (ii) in any other case, be included in computing the cost to him of his interest in the partnership.

### (4) Where capital cost to partner exceeds proceeds of disposition — Where subsection (2) has been applicable in respect of the acquisition of any depreciable property by a partnership from a taxpayer who was, immediately after the taxpayer disposed of the property, a member of the partnership and the capital cost to the taxpayer of the property exceeds the taxpayer's proceeds of the disposition, for the purposes of sections 13 and 20 and any regulations made under paragraph 20(1)(a)

(a) the capital cost to the partnership of the property shall be deemed to be the amount that was the capital cost thereof to the taxpayer; and

(b) the excess shall be deemed to have been allowed to the partnership in respect of the property under regulations made under paragraph 20(1)(a) in computing income for taxation years before the acquisition by the partnership of the property.

**Related Provisions**: 13(7)(e) — Non-arm's length transfer of depreciable property.

**Definitions [s. 97]**: "adjusted cost base" — 54, 248(1); "amount" — 248(1); "Canadian partnership" — 102(1), 248(1); "Canadian resource property" — 66(15), 248(1); "depreciable property" — 13(21), 248(1); "fiscal period" — 249(2)(b), 249.1; "foreign resource property" — 66(15), 248(1); "majority interest partner" — 248(1); "member" — 102(2); "net capital loss", "non-capital loss" — 111(8), 248(1); "partnership" — see Notes to 96(1); "person", "prescribed", "property", "regulation" — 248(1); "restricted farm loss" — 31, 248(1); "taxable Canadian property" — 248(1); "taxation year" — 249; "taxpayer" — 248(1).

**Interpretation Bulletins [s. 97]**: IT-188R: Sale of accounts receivable.

## 98. (1) Disposition of partnership property — For the purposes of this Act, where, but for this subsection, at any time after 1971 a partnership would be regarded as having ceased to exist, the following rules apply:

(a) until such time as all the partnership property and any property substituted therefor has been distributed to the persons entitled by law to receive it, the partnership shall be deemed not to have ceased to exist, and each person who was a partner shall be deemed not to have ceased to be a partner,

(b) the right of each such person to share in that property shall be deemed to be an interest in the partnership, and

(c) notwithstanding subsection 40(3), where at the end of a fiscal period of the partnership, in respect of an interest in the partnership,

> (i) the total of all amounts required by subsection 53(2) to be deducted in computing the adjusted cost base to the taxpayer of the interest at that time

exceeds

> (ii) the total of the cost to the taxpayer of the interest determined for the purpose of computing the adjusted cost base to the taxpayer of that interest at that time and all amounts required by subsection 53(1) to be added to the cost to the taxpayer of the interest in computing the adjusted cost base to the taxpayer of that interest at that time,

the amount of the excess shall be deemed to be a gain of the taxpayer for the taxpayer's taxation year that includes that time from a disposition at that time of that interest.

**Related Provisions**: 20(1)(e)(vi) — Expenses re financing; 40(3.2) — Para. 98(1)(c) takes precedence over subsec. 40(3.1); 98(3) — Rules where partnership ceases to exist; 98.1(2) — Continuation of original partnership; 99(1) — Fiscal period of terminated partnership; 99(2) — Fiscal period for individual member of terminated partnership; 248(5) — Substituted property.

**Notes**: Closing words of 98(1)(c) amended by 1994 Budget, this version effective 1996. For 1994 and 1995, add to the end of 98(1)(c):

and, for the purposes of section 110.6, that interest shall be deemed to have been disposed of by the taxpayer at that time.

For 1985 through 1993, read as for 1994 and 1995 but ending in "in that year" instead of "at that time". The change for 1994 ensures that a gain will be eligible for the capital gains exemption under 110.6(3) only if the partnership ceased to exist before February 23, 1994.

Closing words of 98(1)(c) amended by 1991 technical bill, retroactive to 1985, to clarify that the gains described are treated as gains of the taxpayer for the taxation year that includes the end of the partnership's fiscal period.

**I.T. Application Rules**: 23(4.1)(a) (where professional business carried on in partnership since before 1972).

**Interpretation Bulletins**: IT-338R2: Partnership interests — effects on ACB resulting from admission or retirement of a partner; IT-358: Partnerships — deferment of fiscal year-end.

**(2) Deemed proceeds** — Subject to subsections (3) and (5) and 85(3), where at any time after 1971 a partnership has disposed of property to a taxpayer who was, immediately before that time, a member of the partnership, the partnership shall be deemed to have disposed of the property for proceeds equal to its fair market value at that time and the taxpayer shall be deemed to have acquired the property at an amount equal to that fair market value.

**Related Provisions**: 53(4) — Effect on ACB of share, partnership interest or trust interest.

**Interpretation Bulletins**: IT-338R2: Partnership interests — effects on ACB resulting from admission or retirement of a partner; IT-457R: Election by professionals to exclude work in progress from income.

**(3) Rules applicable where partnership ceases to exist [rollout]** — Where at any particular time after 1971 a Canadian partnership has ceased to exist and all of the partnership property has been distributed to persons who were members of the partnership immediately before that time so that immediately after that time each such person has, in each such property, an undivided interest that, when expressed as a percentage (in this subsection referred to as that person's "percentage") of all undivided interests in the property, is equal to the person's undivided interest, when so expressed, in each other such property, if each such person has jointly so elected in respect of the property in prescribed form and within the time referred to in subsection 96(4), the following rules apply:

(a) each such person's proceeds of the disposition of the person's interest in the partnership shall be deemed to be an amount equal to the greater of

(i) the adjusted cost base to the person, immediately before the particular time, of the person's interest in the partnership, and

(ii) the amount of any money received by the person on the cessation of the partnership's existence, plus the person's percentage of the total of amounts each of which is the cost amount to the partnership of each such property immediately before its distribution;

(b) the cost to each such person of that person's undivided interest in each such property shall be deemed to be an amount equal to the total of

(i) that person's percentage of the cost amount to the partnership of the property immediately before its distribution,

(i.1) where the property is eligible capital property, that person's percentage of $4/3$ of the amount, if any, determined for F in the definition "cumulative eligible capital" in subsection 14(5) in respect of the partnership's business immediately before the particular time, and

(ii) where the amount determined under subparagraph (a)(i) exceeds the amount determined under subparagraph (a)(ii), the amount determined under paragraph (c) in respect of the person's undivided interest in the property;

(c) the amount determined under this paragraph in respect of each such person's undivided interest in each such property that was a capital property (other than depreciable property) of the partnership is such portion of the excess, if any, described in subparagraph (b)(ii) as is designated by the person in respect of the property, except that

(i) in no case shall the amount so designated in respect of the person's undivided interest in any such property exceed the amount, if any, by which the person's percentage of the fair market value of the property immediately after its distribution exceeds the person's percentage of the cost amount to the partnership of the property immediately before its distribution, and

(ii) in no case shall the total of amounts so designated in respect of the person's undivided interests in all such capital properties (other than depreciable property) exceed the excess, if any, described in subparagraph (b)(ii);

(d) [Repealed under former Act]

(e) where the property so distributed by the partnership was depreciable property of the partnership of a prescribed class and any such person's percentage of the amount that was the capital cost to the partnership of that property exceeds the amount determined under paragraph (b) to be the cost to the person of the person's undivided interest in the property, for the purposes of sections 13 and 20 and any regulations made under paragraph 20(1)(a)

(i) the capital cost to the person of the person's undivided interest in the property shall be deemed to be the person's percentage of the amount that was the capital cost to the partnership of the property, and

(ii) the excess shall be deemed to have been allowed to the person in respect of the property under regulations made under paragraph 20(1)(a) in computing income for taxation years before the acquisition by the person of the undivided interest;

(f) the partnership shall be deemed to have disposed of each such property for proceeds equal to the cost amount to the partnership of the property immediately before its distribution; and

(g) where the property so distributed by the partnership was eligible capital property in respect of the business,

(i) for the purposes of determining under this Act any amount relating to cumulative eligible capital, an eligible capital amount, an eligible capital expenditure or eligible capital property, each such person shall be deemed to have continued to carry on the business, in respect of which the property was eligible capital property and that was previously carried on by the partnership, until the time that the person disposes of the person's undivided interest in the property,

(ii) for the purposes of determining the person's cumulative eligible capital in respect of the business, an amount equal to $3/4$ of the amount determined under subparagraph (b)(i.1) in respect of the business shall be added to the amount otherwise determined in respect thereof for P in the definition "cumulative eligible capital" in subsection 14(5), and

(iii) for the purposes of determining after the particular time

(A) the amount deemed under subparagraph 14(1)(a)(v) to be the person's taxable capital gain, and

(B) the amount to be included under subparagraph 14(1)(a)(v) or paragraph 14(1)(b) in computing the person's income

in respect of any subsequent disposition of the property of the business, the amount determined for Q in the definition "cumulative eligible capital" in subsection 14(5) shall be deemed to be the amount, if any, of that person's percentage of the amount determined under that clause in respect of the partnership's business immediately before the particular time.

**Proposed Amendment — 98(3)(g)(iii)**

(iii) for the purpose of determining after the particular time the amount required by paragraph 14(1)(b) to be included in computing the person's income in respect of any subsequent disposition of property of the business, the value determined for Q in the definition "cumulative eligible capital" in subsection 14(5) is deemed to be the amount, if any, of that person's percentage of the value determined for Q in that definition in respect of the partnership's business immediately before the particular time.

**Application**: The December 21, 2000 draft legislation, subsec. 45(1), will amend subpara. 98(3)(g)(iii) to read as above, applicable in respect of taxation years that end after February 27, 2000.

**Technical Notes**: Subsection 98(3) is an elective provision permitting property of a Canadian partnership which has ceased to exist to be distributed to its members, for proceeds to the partnership and at a cost to the members, equal to the cost amount of the property to the partnership, provided certain conditions are met. Where those conditions are met, this provision allows a special increase or "bump-up" in the tax value of the distributed partnership property where the adjusted cost base of a member's partnership interest exceeds the amount of any money and the cost amount to the partnership of the property which the member has received upon the dissolution.

Subparagraph 98(3)(g)(iii) prevents an overstatement of the income inclusions under existing subparagraph 14(1)(a)(v) and existing paragraph 14(1)(b). Subparagraph 98(3)(g)(iii) is amended consequential on the renumbering of subsection 14(1), which is described in further detail in the commentary to that subsection.

**Related Provisions**: 24(3) — Where partnership has ceased to exist; 53(4) — Effect on ACB of partnership interest; 69(11)(a)(i) — Exception to rule deeming proceeds at FMV where capital gains exemption claimed after dissolution of partnership; 80.03(1), (3)(c) — Capital gain where para. 98(3)(a) applies to partnership interest on disposition following debt forgiveness; 85(3) — Alternative provision where partnership wound up; 96(4) — Election; 96(6) — Penalty for late filed election; 98(2) — Deemed proceeds; 98(4) — Application.

**Notes**: Reference to 14(1)(a)(v) added to 98(3)(g)(iii)(B) by 1994 Budget, effective for acquisitions of property after February 22, 1994.

98(3)(b)(i.1) and 98(3)(g) added by 1992 technical bill, effective for acquisitions resulting from a partnership ceasing to exist after the beginning of its first fiscal period that begins after 1987.

98(3) amended in 1986, generally effective December 5, 1985 (see below) to repeal 98(3)(d) and change "under paragraph (c) or (d), as the case may be" in 98(3)(b)(ii) to "under paragraph (c)". For earlier transactions, read 98(3)(d) as follows:

(d) the amount determined under this paragraph in respect of each such person's undivided interest in each such property that was depreciable property or a property other than a capital property of the partnership is such portion of

(i) the amount, if any, by which the excess, if any, described in subparagraph (b)(ii) exceeds the aggregate of amounts designated by him under paragraph (c) in respect of his undivided interests in all such capital properties (other than depreciable property)

as is designated by him in respect of the property, except that

(ii) in no case shall the amount so designated in respect of his undivided interest in any such property exceed the amount, if any, by which his percentage of the fair market value of the property immediately after its distribution exceeds his percentage of the cost amount to the partnership of the property immediately before its distribution, and

(iii) in no case shall the aggregate of amounts so designated in respect of his undivided interests in all such properties that are depreciable property or properties other than capital properties, exceed ½ of the amount determined under subparagraph (i) in respect of him;

The repeal of 98(3)(d) applies with respect to property received by a member of a partnership where

(1) the property was acquired by the partnership after December 4, 1985, otherwise than pursuant to an agreement in writing entered into before that date;

(2) the property is received in satisfaction of an interest in the partnership acquired by the member after December 4, 1985, otherwise than

(a) pursuant to an agreement in writing entered into on or before that date, or

(b) from a person with whom the member was not dealing at arm's length, where the interest in the partnership has not been acquired in an arm's length transaction after December 4, 1985, otherwise than pursuant to an agreement in writing entered into on or before that date; or

(3) the property is received in satisfaction of an interest in the partnership that was owned by a corporation at a time when control thereof was acquired (otherwise than by virtue of an acquisition described in para. 256(7)(a)) after December 4, 1985, otherwise than pursuant to an agreement in writing entered into on or before that date,

and, for the purposes of (2)(b) above, the references to "arm's length" shall be interpreted as though the Act were read without reference to para. 251(5)(b), except that

(4) in respect of properties to which the repeal of para. 98(3)(d) does not apply, subpara. 98(3)(d)(iii) shall, in its application to taxation years and fiscal periods ending after 1987, be read as follows:

"(iii) in no case shall the aggregate of amounts so designated in respect of his undivided interests in all such properties that are depreciable property or properties other than capital properties, exceed ¾ of the amount determined under subparagraph (i) in respect of him;",

(5) where the person is an individual, for taxation years and fiscal periods ending after 1987 and before 1990, the reference in subpara. 98(3)(d)(iii) to "¾" shall be read as a reference to "⅔",

(6) where the person is a Canadian-controlled private corporation throughout its taxation year, for taxation years ending after 1987 and commencing before 1990 the reference to "¾" in subpara. 98(3)(d)(iii) shall, in respect of the corporation for the year, be read as a reference to the fraction determined as the aggregate of

(a) that proportion of ½ that the number of days in the year that are before 1988 is of the number of days in the year,

(b) that proportion of ⅔ that the number of days in the year that are after 1987 and before 1990 is of the number of days in the year, and

(c) that proportion of ¾ that the number of days in the year that are after 1989 is of the number of days in the year; and

(7) where the person is a corporation that was not a Canadian-controlled private corporation throughout its taxation year, for taxation years ending after 1987 and commencing before 1990, the reference to "¾" in subpara. 98(3)(d)(iii) shall, in respect of the corporation for the year, be read as a reference to the fraction determined as the aggregate of

(a) that proportion of ½ that the number of days in the year that are before July, 1988 is of the number of days in the year,

(b) that proportion of ⅔ that the number of days in the year that are after June, 1988 and before 1990 is of the number of days in the year, and

(c) that proportion of ¾ that the number of days in the year that are after 1989 is of the number of days in the year.

**I.T. Application Rules**: 20(1.2) (where transferred depreciable property was owned by transferor since before 1972).

**Interpretation Bulletins**: IT-338R2: Partnership interests — effects on ACB resulting from admission or retirement of a partner; IT-442R: Bad debts and reserves for doubtful debts; IT-457R: Election by professionals to exclude work in progress from income; IT-471R: Merger of partnerships.

**I.T. Technical News**: No. 12 (adjusted cost base of partnership interest).

**Information Circulars**: 76-19R3: Transfer of property to a corporation under section 85.

**Forms**: T2060: Election for disposition of property upon cessation of partnership.

**(4) Where subsec. (3) does not apply** — Subsection (3) is not applicable in any case in which subsection (5) or 85(3) is applicable.

**(5) Where partnership business carried on as sole proprietorship** — Where at any particular time after 1971 a Canadian partnership has ceased to exist and within 3 months after the particular time one, but not more than one, of the persons who were, immediately before the particular time, members of the partnership (which person is in this subsection referred to as the "proprietor", whether an individual, a trust or a corporation) carries on alone the business that was the business of the partnership and continues to use, in the course of the business, any property that was, immediately before the particular time, partnership property and that was received by the proprietor as proceeds of disposition of the proprietor's interest in the partnership, the following rules apply:

(a) the proprietor's proceeds of disposition of the proprietor's interest in the partnership shall be deemed to be an amount equal to the greater of

(i) the total of the adjusted cost base to the proprietor, immediately before the particular time, of the proprietor's interest in the partnership, and the adjusted cost base to the proprietor of each other interest in the partnership deemed by paragraph (g) to have been acquired by the proprietor at the particular time, and

(ii) the total of

(A) the cost amount to the partnership, immediately before the particular time, of each such property so received by the proprietor, and

(B) the amount of any other proceeds of the disposition of the proprietor's interest in the partnership received by the proprietor;

(b) the cost to the proprietor of each such property shall be deemed to be an amount equal to the total of

(i) the cost amount to the partnership of the property immediately before that time,

(i.1) where the property is eligible capital property, $^4/_3$ of the amount, if any, determined for F in the definition "cumulative eligible capital" in subsection 14(5) in respect of the partnership's business immediately before the particular time, and

(ii) where the amount determined under subparagraph (a)(i) exceeds the amount determined under subparagraph (a)(ii), the amount determined under paragraph (c) in respect of the property;

(c) the amount determined under this paragraph in respect of each such property so received by the proprietor that is a capital property (other than depreciable property) of the proprietor is such portion of the excess, if any, described in subparagraph (b)(ii) as is designated by the proprietor in respect of the property, except that

(i) in no case shall the amount so designated in respect of any such property exceed the amount, if any, by which the fair market value of the property immediately after the particular time exceeds the cost amount to the partnership of the property immediately before that time, and

(ii) in no case shall the total of amounts so designated in respect of all such capital properties (other than depreciable property) exceed the excess, if any, described in subparagraph (b)(ii);

(d) [Repealed under former Act]

(e) where any such property so received by the proprietor was depreciable property of a prescribed class of the partnership and the amount that was the capital cost to the partnership of that property exceeds the amount determined under paragraph (b) to be the cost to the proprietor of the property, for the purposes of sections 13 and 20 and any regulations made under paragraph 20(1)(a)

(i) the capital cost to the proprietor of the property shall be deemed to be the amount that was the capital cost to the partnership of the property, and

(ii) the excess shall be deemed to have been allowed to the proprietor in respect of the property under regulations made under paragraph 20(1)(a) in computing income for taxation years before the acquisition by the proprietor of the property;

(f) the partnership shall be deemed to have disposed of each such property for proceeds equal to the cost amount to the partnership of the property immediately before the particular time;

(g) where, at the particular time, all other persons who were members of the partnership immediately before that time have disposed of their interests in the partnership to the proprietor, the proprietor shall be deemed at that time to have acquired partnership interests from those other persons and not to have acquired any property that was property of the partnership; and

(h) where the property so received by the proprietor is eligible capital property in respect of the business,

(i) for the purpose of determining the proprietor's cumulative eligible capital in respect of the business, an amount equal to $^3/_4$ of the amount determined under subparagraph (b)(i.1) in respect of the business shall be added to the amount otherwise determined in respect thereof for P in the definition "cumulative eligible capital" in subsection 14(5), and

(ii) for the purposes of determining after the particular time

(A) the amount deemed under subparagraph 14(1)(a)(v) to be the proprietor's taxable capital gain, and

(B) the amount to be included under subparagraph 14(1)(a)(v) or paragraph 14(1)(b) in computing the proprietor's income

in respect of any subsequent disposition of property of the business, the amount determined for Q in the definition "cumulative eligible capital" in subsection 14(5) shall be deemed to be the amount, if any, determined for Q in that definition in respect of the partnership's business immediately before the particular time.

**Proposed Amendment — 98(5)(h)(ii)**

(ii) for the purpose of determining after the particular time the amount required by paragraph 14(1)(b) to be included in computing the proprietor's income in respect of any subsequent disposition of property of the business, the value determined for Q in the definition "cumulative eligible capital" in subsection 14(5) is deemed to be the value, if any, determined for Q in that definition in respect of the partnership's business immediately before the particular time.

**Application:** The December 21, 2000 draft legislation, subsec. 45(2), will amend subpara. 98(5)(h)(ii) to read as above, applicable in respect of taxation years that end after February 27, 2000.

**Technical Notes:** Subsection 98(5) contains rules which provide a tax-deferred transfer or "rollover" of a Canadian partnership's property where the partnership has ceased to exist and the transfer is to one member of the partnership who continues to carry on the business of the partnership as a sole proprietor.

Where the adjusted cost base of the member's partnership interest, including the interests acquired from other members, exceeds the amount of any money and the cost amount to the partnership of the property received by the proprietor upon the dissolution, the member may designate this excess to be added to the cost base of one or more particular properties.

Subparagraph 98(5)(h)(ii) prevents an overstatement of the income inclusions under subparagraph 14(1)(a)(v) or paragraph 14(1)(b). Subparagraph 98(5)(h)(ii) is amended consequential on the re-numbering of subsection 14(1), which is described in further detail in the commentary to that subsection.

**Related Provisions:** 24(3) — Where partnership has ceased to exist; 53(4) — Effect on ACB of partnership interest; 80.03(1), (3)(c) — Capital gain where para. 98(5)(a) applies to partnership interest on disposition following debt forgiveness; 88(1)(a.2) — Winding-up; 98(2) — Deemed proceeds; 98(4) — Subsec. 98(3) does not apply.

**Notes:** Reference to 14(1)(a)(v) added to 98(5)(h)(ii)(B) by 1994 Budget, effective for acquisitions of property after February 22, 1994.

98(5)(b)(i.1) and 98(5)(h) added by 1992 technical bill, effective for acquisitions resulting from a partnership ceasing to exist after the beginning of its first fiscal period that begins after 1987.

98(5)(a)(i) amended by 1991 technical bill, effective January 16, 1987, to refer to "adjusted cost base" rather than "cost", in order to deal with the case where a partnership ceases to exist because of the windup of a subsidiary into a parent under 88(1).

98(5) amended in 1986, generally effective December 5, 1985 (see below), to repeal para. (d) and change the words "under paragraph (c) or (d), as the case may be" in subpara. (b)(ii) to "under paragraph (c)". For earlier transactions, read para. (d) as follows:

"(d) the amount determined under this paragraph in respect of each such property so received by him that is depreciable property or a property other than a capital property of the proprietor is such portion of

(i) the amount, if any, by which the excess, if any, described in subparagraph (b)(ii) exceeds the aggregate of amounts designated by him under paragraph (c) in respect of all capital properties (other than depreciable property) as is designated by him in respect of the property, except that

(ii) in no case shall the amount so designated in respect of any such property exceed the amount, if any, by which the fair market value of the property immediately after the particular time exceeds the cost amount to the partnership of the property immediately before that time, and

(iii) in no case shall the aggregate of amounts so designated in respect of all such properties of the proprietor that are depreciable property or properties other than capital properties, exceed ½ of the amount determined under subparagraph (i) in respect of the proprietor;"

The repeal of 98(5)(d) applies with respect to property received by a member of a partnership where

(1) the property was acquired by the partnership after December 4, 1985, otherwise than pursuant to an agreement in writing entered into before that date;

(2) the property is received in satisfaction of an interest in the partnership acquired by the member after December 4, 1985, otherwise than

(a) pursuant to an agreement in writing entered into on or before that date, or

(b) from a person with whom the member was not dealing at arm's length, where the interest in the partnership has not been acquired in an arm's length transaction after December 4, 1985, otherwise than pursuant to an agreement in writing entered into on or before that date; or

(3) the property is received in satisfaction of an interest in the partnership that was owned by a corporation at a time when control thereof was acquired (otherwise than by virtue of an acquisition described in paragraph 256(7)(a)) after December 4, 1985, otherwise than pursuant to an agreement in writing entered into on or before that date,

and, for the purposes of 2(b) above, the references to "arm's length" shall be interpreted as though the Act were read without reference to para. 251(5)(b).

The purpose of repealing 98(5)(d) was to stop an avoidance technique known as the "Little Egypt bump".

**I.T. Application Rules:** 20(1.2) (where transferred depreciable property was owned by transferor since before 1972).

**Interpretation Bulletins:** IT-338R2: Partnership interests — effects on ACB resulting from admission or retirement of a partner; IT-457R: Election by professionals to exclude work in progress from income.

**Information Circulars:** 88-2, para. 22: General anti-avoidance rule — section 245 of the *Income Tax Act*.

**(6) Continuation of predecessor partnership by new partnership** — Where a Canadian partnership (in this subsection referred to as the "predecessor partnership") has ceased to exist at any particular time after 1971 and, at or before that time, all of the property of the predecessor partnership has been transferred to another Canadian partnership (in this subsection referred to as the "new partnership") the only members of which were members of the predecessor partnership, the new partnership shall be deemed to be a continuation of the predecessor partnership and any member's partnership interest in the new partnership shall be deemed to be a continuation of the member's partnership interest in the predecessor partnership.

**Related Provisions:** 53(4) — Effect on ACB of share, partnership interest or trust interest; Reg. 8103(5) — Mark-to-market transition — inclusion; Reg. 9204(4) — Residual portion of specified debt obligation.

**Interpretation Bulletins [subsec. 98(6)]:** IT-338R2: Partnership interests — effects on ACB resulting from admission or retirement of a partner; IT-358: Partnerships — deferment of fiscal year-end; IT-457R: Election by professionals to exclude work in progress from income.

**Definitions [s. 98]:** "adjusted cost base" — 54, 248(1); "amount", "business" — 248(1); "Canadian partnership" — 102(1), 248(1); "capital property" — 54, 248(1); "cost amount" — 248(1); "cumulative eligible capital" — 14(5), 248(1); "depreciable property" — 13(21), 248(1); "eligible capital amount" — 14(1), 248(1); "eligible capital expenditure" — 14(5), 248(1); "eligible capital property" —

54, 248(1); "member" — 102(2); "partnership" — see Notes to 96(1); "person", "property", "regulation" — 248(1); "substituted property" — 248(5); "taxation year" — 11(2), 249; "taxpayer" — 248(1).

## 98.1 (1) Residual interest in partnership —
Where, but for this subsection, at any time after 1971 a taxpayer has ceased to be a member of a partnership of which the taxpayer was a member immediately before that time, the following rules apply:

(a) until such time as all the taxpayer's rights (other than a right to a share of the income or loss of the partnership under an agreement referred to in subsection 96(1.1)) to receive any property of or from the partnership in satisfaction of the taxpayer's interest in the partnership immediately before the time at which the taxpayer ceased to be a member of the partnership are satisfied in full, that interest (in this section referred to as a "residual interest") is, subject to sections 70, 110.6 and 128.1 but notwithstanding any other section of this Act, deemed not to have been disposed of by the taxpayer and to continue to be an interest in the partnership;

(b) where all of the taxpayer's rights described in paragraph (a) are satisfied in full before the end of the fiscal period of the partnership in which the taxpayer ceased to be a member thereof, the taxpayer shall, notwithstanding paragraph (a), be deemed not to have disposed of the taxpayer's residual interest until the end of that fiscal period;

(c) notwithstanding subsection 40(3), where at the end of a fiscal period of the partnership, in respect of a residual interest in the partnership,

(i) the total of all amounts required by subsection 53(2) to be deducted in computing the adjusted cost base to the taxpayer of the residual interest at that time

exceeds

(ii) the total of the cost to the taxpayer of the residual interest determined for the purpose of computing the adjusted cost base to the taxpayer of that interest at that time and all amounts required by subsection 53(1) to be added to the cost to the taxpayer of the residual interest in computing the adjusted cost base to the taxpayer of that interest at that time

the amount of the excess shall be deemed to be a gain of the taxpayer, for the taxpayer's taxation year that includes that time, from a disposition at that time of that residual interest; and

(d) where a taxpayer has a residual interest

(i) by reason of paragraph (b), the taxpayer shall, except for the purposes of subsections 110.1(4), 118.1(8) and 127(4.2), be deemed not to be a member of the partnership, and

(ii) in any other case, the taxpayer shall, except for the purposes of subsection 85(3), be deemed not to be a member of the partnership.

**Related Provisions**: 40(3.2) — Para. 98.1(1)(c) takes precedence over subsec. 40(3.1); 98.1(2) — Continuation of original partnership; 98.2 — Transfer of interest on death.

**Notes**: 98.1(1)(a) amended by 1995-97 technical bill, effective for 1994 and later taxation years, to add reference to 110.6.

98.1(1)(a) amended by 1993 technical bill to change reference from s. 48 to 128.1, effective 1993. Where a corporation continued before 1993 elects for new 250(5.1) to apply earlier (see Notes to 250(5.1)), the amendment is effective from the corporation's "time of continuation".

98.1(1)(c) amended by 1991 technical bill, retroactive to 1985.

Closing words of 98.1(1)(c) amended by 1994 Budget, this version effective 1996. For 1994 and 1995, add to the end of 98.1(1)(c):

> and, for the purposes of section 110.6, the residual interest shall be deemed to have been disposed of by the taxpayer at that time.

For 1985 through 1993, read as for 1994 and 1995 but ending in "in that year" instead of "at that time". The change for 1994 ensures that a gain will be eligible for the capital gains exemption under 110.6(3) only if the taxpayer ceased to be a partner before February 23, 1994.

**I.T. Application Rules**: 23(4.1)(b) (where professional practice carried on in partnership since before 1972).

**Interpretation Bulletins**: IT-242R: Retired partners; IT-278R2: Death of a partner or of a retired partner.

## (2) Continuation of original partnership —
Where a partnership (in this subsection referred to as the "original partnership") has or would but for subsection 98(1) have ceased to exist at a time when a taxpayer had rights described in paragraph (1)(a) in respect of that partnership and the members of another partnership agree to satisfy all or part of those rights, that other partnership shall, for the purposes of that paragraph, be deemed to be a continuation of the original partnership.

**Interpretation Bulletins**: IT-278R2: Death of a partner or of a retired partner.

**Definitions [s. 98.1]**: "amount" — 248(1); "partnership" — see Notes to 96(1); "property" — 248(1); "residual interest" — 98.1(1)(a); "taxpayer" — 248(1).

## 98.2 Transfer of interest on death —
Where by virtue of the death of an individual a taxpayer has acquired a property that was an interest in a partnership to which, immediately before the individual's death, section 98.1 applied,

(a) the taxpayer shall be deemed to have acquired a right to receive partnership property and not to have acquired an interest in a partnership;

(b) the taxpayer shall be deemed to have acquired the right referred to in paragraph (a) at a cost equal to the amount determined to be the proceeds of disposition of the interest in the partnership to the deceased individual by virtue of paragraph 70(5)(a) or (6)(d), as the case may be; and

(c) section 43 is not applicable to the right.

**Related Provisions**: 53(2)(o) — Deductions from ACB; 248(8) — Occurrences as a consequence of death.

## Subdivision j — Partnerships and Their Members — S. 100(2)(b)(ii)

**Definitions [s. 98.2]:** "amount", "individual" — 248(1); "partnership" — see Notes to 96(1); "property", "taxpayer" — 248(1).

**Interpretation Bulletins [s. 98.2]:** IT-242R: Retired partners; IT-278R2: Death of a partner or of a retired partner; IT-349R3: Intergenerational transfers of farm property on death.

**99. (1) Fiscal period of terminated partnership** — Except as provided in subsection (2), where, at any time in a fiscal period of a partnership, the partnership would, but for subsection 98(1), have ceased to exist, the fiscal period shall be deemed to have ended immediately before that time.

**Related Provisions:** 127.52(1)(c.1), (c.2) — Exclusion from triggering minimum tax.

**(2) Fiscal period of terminated partnership for individual member** — Where an individual was a member of a partnership that, at any time in a fiscal period of a partnership, has or would have, but for subsection 98(1), ceased to exist, for the purposes of computing the individual's income for a taxation year the partnership's fiscal period may, if the individual so elects and subsection 249.1(4) does not apply in respect of the partnership, be deemed to have ended immediately before the time when the fiscal period of the partnership would have ended if the partnership had not so ceased to exist.

**Related Provisions:** 25(1) — Parallel rule for individuals; 99(3), (4) — Validity of election.

**Notes:** 99(2) amended by 1995 Budget, effective for fiscal periods that begin after 1994, to add "and subsection 249.1(4) does not apply in respect of the partnership".

**Interpretation Bulletins:** IT-179R: Change of fiscal period.

**Information Circulars:** 76-19R3: Transfer of property to a corporation under section 85.

**(3) Validity of election** — An election under subsection (2) is not valid unless the individual was resident in Canada at the time when the fiscal period of the partnership would, if the election were valid, be deemed to have ended.

**Related Provisions:** 96(4)–(7) — Elections.

**(4) Idem** — An election under subsection (2) is not valid if, for the individual's taxation year in which a fiscal period of the partnership would not, if the election were valid, be deemed to have ended but in which it would otherwise have ended, the individual elects to have applicable the rules set out in the *Income Tax Application Rules* that apply when two or more fiscal periods of a partnership end in the same taxation year.

**Definitions [s. 99]:** "Canada" — 255; "fiscal period" — 99(1), (2), 249.1; "individual" — 248(1); "member" — 102(2); "partnership" — see Notes to 96(1); "resident in Canada" — 250; "taxation year" — 11(2), 249; "taxpayer" — 248(1).

**Interpretation Bulletins [s. 99]:** IT-138R: Computation and flow-through of partnership income; IT-358: Partnerships — deferment of fiscal year-end.

**100. (1) Disposition of an interest in a partnership** — Notwithstanding paragraph 38(a), a taxpayer's taxable capital gain for a taxation year from the disposition of an interest in a partnership to any person exempt from tax under section 149 shall be deemed to be

(a) $3/4$ of such portion of the taxpayer's capital gain for the year therefrom as may reasonably be regarded as attributable to increases in the value of any partnership property of the partnership that is capital property other than depreciable property,

> **Proposed Amendment — 100(1)(a)**
>
> **Application:** The December 21, 2000 draft legislation, s. 46, will amend para. 100(1)(a) by replacing the reference to the fraction "3/4" with a reference to the fraction "1/2", applicable to taxation years that end after February 27, 2000 except that, where a taxation year of a taxpayer includes either February 28, 2000 or October 17, 2000, the reference to the fraction "1/2" shall be read as a reference to the fraction in para. 38(a), as amended [by the December 21, 2000 draft legislation], that applies to the taxpayer for the year.
>
> **Technical Notes:** Subsection 100(1) provides a rule for the purpose of determining a taxpayer's gain from the disposition of an interest in a partnership to a person part or all of whose taxable income is exempt from tax under section 149.
>
> Paragraph 100(1)(a) is amended to replace the reference to the fraction "3/4" with a reference to the fraction "1/2". The change is consequential on the reduction in the capital gains inclusion rate [see 38(a) — ed.].
>
> The amendment applies to taxation years that end after February 27, 2000 except that, for a taxation year of a taxpayer that includes either February 28, 2000 or October 17, 2000, the reference to the fraction "1/2" in paragraph 100(1)(a) is to be read as reference to the fraction in amended paragraph 38(a) that applies to the taxpayer for the year. These modifications are required in order to reflect the capital gains/losses rate for the year.

plus

(b) the whole of the remaining portion of that capital gain.

**(2) Gain from disposition of interest in partnership** — In computing a taxpayer's gain for a taxation year from the disposition of an interest in a partnership, there shall be included, in addition to the amount thereof determined under subsection 40(1), the amount, if any, by which

(a) the total of all amounts required by subsection 53(2) to be deducted in computing the adjusted cost base to the taxpayer, immediately before the disposition, of the interest in the partnership,

exceeds

(b) the total of

(i) the cost to the taxpayer of the interest in the partnership determined for the purpose of computing the adjusted cost base to the taxpayer of that interest at that time, and

(ii) all amounts required by subsection 53(1) to be added to the cost to the taxpayer of that interest in computing the adjusted cost base to the taxpayer of that interest at that time.

**Interpretation Bulletins**: IT-268R4: *Inter vivos* transfer of farm property to child; IT-278R2: Death of a partner or of a retired partner; IT-358: Deferment of fiscal year end.

**(2.1) Idem** — Where, as a result of an amalgamation or merger, an interest in a partnership owned by a predecessor corporation has become property of the new corporation formed as a result of the amalgamation or merger and the predecessor corporation was not related to the new corporation, the predecessor corporation shall be deemed to have disposed of the interest in the partnership to the new corporation immediately before the amalgamation or merger for proceeds of disposition equal to the adjusted cost base to the predecessor corporation of the interest in the partnership at the time of the disposition and the new corporation shall be deemed to have acquired the interest in the partnership from the predecessor corporation immediately after that time at a cost equal to the proceeds of disposition.

**Related Provisions**: 87(2)(e.1) — Partnership interest.

**Notes**: 100(2.1) added in 1987, effective for amalgamations and mergers occurring after January 15, 1987.

**(3) Transfer of interest on death** — Where by virtue of the death of an individual a taxpayer has acquired a property that was an interest in a partnership immediately before the individual's death (other than an interest to which, immediately before the individual's death, section 98.1 applied) and the taxpayer is not a member of the partnership and does not become a member of the partnership by reason of that acquisition,

(a) the taxpayer shall be deemed to have acquired a right to receive partnership property and not to have acquired an interest in a partnership;

(b) the taxpayer shall be deemed to have acquired the right referred to in paragraph (a) at a cost equal to the amount determined to be the proceeds of disposition of the interest in the partnership to the deceased individual by virtue of paragraph 70(5)(a) or (6)(d), as the case may be; and

(c) section 43 is not applicable to the right.

**Related Provisions**: 53(2)(o) — Deduction from ACB; 248(8) — Occurrences as a consequence of death.

**Interpretation Bulletins**: IT-278R2: Death of a partner or of a retired partner; IT-349R3: Intergenerational transfers of farm property on death.

**(4) Loss re interest in partnership** — Notwithstanding paragraph 39(1)(b), the capital loss of a taxpayer from the disposition at any time of an interest in a partnership is deemed to be the amount of the loss otherwise determined minus the total of all amounts each of which is the amount by which the taxpayer's share of the partnership's loss, in respect of a share of the capital stock of a corporation that was property of a particular partnership at that time, would have been reduced under subsection 112(3.1) if the fiscal period of every partnership that includes that time had ended immediately before that time and the particular partnership had disposed of the share immediately before the end of that fiscal period for proceeds equal to its fair market value at that time.

**Related Provisions**: 40(3.7) — Application to non-resident individual; 53(2)(c)(i)(C) — Reduction in ACB; 107.4(3)(b)(ii) — Application of stop-loss rule to qualifying disposition.

**Notes**: 100(4) amended by 1995-97 technical bill, effective for dispositions after April 26, 1995. The substantive changes were to add reference to 112(4.2) and to change "if the fiscal period of the partnership" to "if the fiscal period of every partnership that includes that time". Other changes were cosmetic and non-substantive.

**Definitions [s. 100]**: "adjusted cost base" — 54, 248(1); "amount" — 248(1); "capital gain" — 39(1)(a), 248(1); "capital loss" — 39(1)(b), 248(1); "capital property" — 54, 248(1); "corporation" — 248(1), *Interpretation Act* 35(1); "depreciable property" — 13(21), 248(1); "fiscal period" — 249(2)(b), 249.1; "member" — 102(2); "partnership" — see Notes to 96(1); "person" — 248(1); "property" — 248(1); "share" — 248(1); "taxable capital gain" — 38(a), 248(1); "taxation year" — 249; "taxpayer" — 248(1).

**101. Disposition of farmland by partnership** — Where a taxpayer was a member of a partnership at the end of a taxation year of the partnership in which the partnership disposed of land used in a farming business of the partnership, there may be deducted in computing the taxpayer's income for the taxpayer's taxation year in which the taxation year of the partnership ended, $3/4$ of the total of all amounts each of which is an amount in respect of that taxation year of the taxpayer or any preceding taxation year of the taxpayer ending after 1971, equal to the taxpayer's loss, if any, for the year from the farming business, to the extent that the loss

(a) was, by virtue of section 31, not deductible in computing the taxpayer's income for the year;

(b) was not deducted for the purpose of computing the taxpayer's taxable income for the taxpayer's taxation year in which the partnership's taxation year in which the land was disposed of ended, or for any preceding taxation year of the taxpayer;

(c) did not exceed that proportion of the total of

(i) taxes (other than income or profits taxes or taxes imposed by reference to the transfer of the property) paid by the partnership in its taxation year ending in the year or payable by it in respect of that taxation year to a province or a Canadian municipality in respect of the property, and

(ii) interest paid by the partnership in its taxation year ending in the year or payable by it in respect of that taxation year, pursuant to a legal obligation to pay interest on borrowed money used to acquire the property or on any amount as consideration payable for the property,

(to the extent that the taxes and interest were included in computing the loss of the partnership for that taxation year from the farming business), that

(iii) the taxpayer's loss from the farming business for the year

is of

(iv) the partnership's loss from the farming business for its taxation year ending in the year; and

(d) did not exceed the remainder obtained when

(i) the total of each of the taxpayer's losses from the farming business for taxation years preceding the year (to the extent that those losses are included in computing the amount determined under this section in respect of the taxpayer)

is deducted from

(ii) $4/3$ of the amount of the taxpayer's taxable capital gain from the disposition of the land.

**Proposed Amendment — 101**

**Application**: The December 21, 2000 draft legislation, s. 47, will amend s. 101 by replacing the reference to the fraction "3/4" with a reference to the fraction "1/2" and by replacing the reference to the expression "4/3 of" with a reference to the word "twice", applicable to taxation years that end after February 27, 2000 except that, in applying it to a taxpayer's taxation year that includes either February 28, 2000 or October 17, 2000,

(a) the reference to the fraction "1/2" shall be read as a reference to the fraction in para. 38(a), as amended [by the December 21, 2000 draft legislation], that applies to the taxpayer for the year; and

(b) the reference to the word "twice" shall be read as a reference to the expression "the fraction that is the reciprocal of the fraction in para. 38(a), as amended [by the December 21, 2000 draft legislation], that applies to the taxpayer for the year, multiplied by".

**Technical Notes**: Section 101 provides for a deduction in computing the income of a taxpayer for a taxation year of the taxpayer in which a fiscal period of a partnership ends where, in that fiscal period, the partnership has sold land used in farming. The deduction is equal to 3/4 of the farm losses that, because of section 31, were not deductible and that relate property taxes in respect of and interest on money borrowed to acquire the farmland sold. The amendments to subsection 101(1) replace the reference to the fraction "3/4" with a reference to the fraction "1/2" and the reference to the expression "4/3 of" with references to the word "twice". The changes are consequential on the reduction of the capital gains inclusion rate from 3/4 to 1/2 [see 38(a) — ed.].

The amendments apply to taxation years that end after February 27, 2000 except that, where the taxation year of the partnership that ends in the taxation year of the taxpayer includes either February 28, 2000 or October 17, 2000, the reference to the fraction "1/2" in subsection 101(1) is to be read as reference to the fraction in amended paragraph 38(a) that applies to the taxpayer for the taxpayer's taxation year in which the taxation year of the partnership ended. The reference to the word "twice" in subsection 101(1) is to be read as a reference to the expression "the fraction that is the reciprocal of the fraction in paragraph 38(a) that applies to the partnership for the fiscal period, multiplied by".

**Related Provisions**: 53(1)(i) — Corresponding rule for non-partnerships — addition to ACB; 96(1.1) — Allocation of share of income to retiring partner; 111(7) — Limitation.

**Definitions [s. 101]**: "amount", "borrowed money", "business", "farming" — 248(1); "member" — 102(2); "partnership" — see Notes to 96(1); "property" — 248(1); "province" — *Interpretation Act* 35(1); "taxable capital gain" — 38(a), 248(1); "taxable income" — 2(2), 248(1); "taxation year" — 249; "taxpayer" — 248(1).

**102. (1) Definition of "Canadian partnership"** — In this subdivision, "Canadian partnership" means a partnership all of the members of which were, at any time in respect of which the expression is relevant, resident in Canada.

**Related Provisions**: 80(1) — "Eligible Canadian partnership"; 96(8) — Anti-avoidance rules; 212(13.1)(b) — Non-Canadian partnership deemed non-resident for withholding tax purposes; 248(1)"Canadian partnership" — Definition applies to entire Act; *Income Tax Conventions Interpretation Act* 6.2 — Partnership with Canadian resident partner cannot be resident in another country.

**(2) Member of a partnership** — In this subdivision, a reference to a person or a taxpayer who is a member of a particular partnership shall include a reference to another partnership that is a member of the particular partnership.

**Notes**: 102(1) and (2) were 102(a) and (b) before consolidation in R.S.C. 1985 (5th Supp.), effective for taxation years ending after November 1991.

**Definitions [s. 102]**: "Canada" — 255;"partnership" — see Notes to 96(1); "person" — 248(1); "resident in Canada" — 250; "taxpayer" — 248(1).

**Interpretation Bulletins [s. 102]**: IT-123R6: Transactions involving eligible capital property; IT-338R2: Partnership interests — effects on adjusted cost base resulting from the admission or retirement of a partner; IT-413R: Election by members of a partnership under subsection 97(2); IT-417R: Merger of partnerships.

**103. (1) Agreement to share income, etc., so as to reduce or postpone tax otherwise payable** — Where the members of a partnership have agreed to share, in a specified proportion, any income or loss of the partnership from any source or from sources in a particular place, as the case may be, or any other amount in respect of any activity of the partnership that is relevant to the computation of the income or taxable income of any of the members thereof, and the principal reason for the agreement may reasonably be considered to be the reduction or postponement of the tax that might otherwise have been or become payable under this Act, the share of each member of the partnership in the income or loss, as the case may be, or in that other amount, is the amount that is reasonable having regard to all the circumstances including the proportions in which the members have agreed to share profits and losses of the partnership from other sources or from sources in other places.

**Related Provisions**: 103(2) — Meaning of "losses".

**(1.1) Agreement to share income, etc., in unreasonable proportions** — Where two or more members of a partnership who are not dealing with each other at arm's length agree to share any income or loss of the partnership or any other amount in respect of any activity of the partnership that is relevant to the computation of the income or taxable income of those members and the share of any such member of that income, loss or other amount is not reasonable in the circumstances having regard to the capital invested in or work performed for the partnership by the members thereof or such other factors as may be relevant, that share shall, notwithstanding any agreement, be deemed to be the amount that is reasonable in the circumstances.

**Interpretation Bulletins**: IT-231R2: Partnerships — partners not dealing at arm's length.

**(2) Definition of "losses"** — For the purposes of this section, the word "losses" when used in the expression "profits and losses" means losses determined without reference to other provisions of this Act.

**Related Provisions**: 96(1.1) — Allocation of share of income to retiring partner.

**Definitions [s. 103]**: "amount" — 248(1); "arm's length" — 251(1); "assessment" — 248(1); "losses" — 103(2); "member" — 102(2); "partnership" — see Notes to 96(1); "taxable income" — 2(2), 248(1).

**Interpretation Bulletins**: IT-338R2: Partnership interests — effects on adjusted cost base resulting from the admission or retirement of a partner.

## Subdivision k — Trusts and Their Beneficiaries

**104. (1) Reference to trust or estate** — In this Act, a reference to a trust or estate (in this subdivision referred to as a "trust") shall be read as a reference to the trustee or the executor, administrator, heir or other legal representative having ownership or control of the trust property.

### Proposed Amendment — 104(1)

**104. (1) Reference to trust or estate** — In this Act, a reference to a trust or estate (in this subdivision referred to as a "trust") shall, unless the context otherwise requires, be read to include a reference to the trustee, executor, administrator, liquidator of the succession, heir or other legal representative having ownership or control of the trust property, but, except for the purposes of this subsection, subsection (1.1) and paragraph (k) of the definition "disposition" in subsection 248(1), a trust is deemed to not include an arrangement under which the trust can reasonably be considered to act as agent for all the beneficiaries under the trust with respect to all dealings with all of the trust's property unless the trust is described in any of paragraphs (a) to (e.1) of the definition "trust" in subsection 108(1).

**Application**: Bill C-43 (First Reading September 20, 2000), subsec. 48(1), will amend subsec. 104(1) to read as above, applicable to 1998 et seq., except that in connection with transfers of property that occur before December 24, 1998, subsec. 104(1) shall be read as follows:

> 104. (1) Reference to trust or estate — In this Act, a reference to a trust or estate (in this subdivision referred to as a "trust") shall, unless the context otherwise requires, be read to include a reference to the trustee, executor, administrator, liquidator of the succession, heir or other legal representative having ownership or control of the trust property.

**Technical Notes**: Subsection 104(1) of the Act provides a rule under which a reference to a trust or estate is read in the Act as a reference to the trustee or the executor, administrator, heir or other legal representative having ownership or control over trust property.

Subsection 104(1) is amended to include a "liquidator of the succession" to the list of persons to which a trust or estate refers for the purposes of the Act. This amendment is made to ensure that the Act appropriately reflects both the civil law of the province of Quebec and the law of other provinces.

Subsection 104(1) is amended so that this rule does not apply where the context otherwise requires and to clarify that this rule is merely meant to be a convenient way of linking the trustees and others described in the subsection with a trust for the purposes of the Act. This amendment recognizes that there are references to "trust" in the Act that are meant to indicate a trust arrangement, rather than the persons who are responsible for the operation of the arrangement. The latter references include those found in subsections 74.4(4), 104(5.3) and (5.5), 108(6) and 127(7).

Subsection 104(1) is amended, in conjunction with 104(1.1), so that, except for the purposes of those two subsections and paragraph (k) of the definition "disposition" in subsection 248(1), references in the Act to trusts are not considered to include an arrangement where a trust can reasonably be considered to act as agent for its beneficiaries with respect to all dealings in all of the trust's property. These arrangements are generally known as "bare trusts". Trusts described in paragraphs (a) to (e.1) of the definition "trust" in subsection 108(1) are expressly not affected by this amendment.

**Related Provisions**: 75(2) — Revocable or reversionary trust; 94(3) — Non-resident trust deemed resident in Canada; 104(1.1) — Restricted meaning of "beneficiary"; 108(1) — Meaning of "trust"; 122(1) — High rate of tax for *inter vivos* trusts; 128(1)(b), 128(2)(b) — Estate of bankrupt deemed not to be a trust or estate; 146.1(1) "trust" — RESPs — meaning of "trust"; 233.2(4) — Reporting requirement re transfers to foreign trust; 233.6(1) — Reporting requirement re distributions from foreign trust; 248(1) "estate" — Definition applies to entire Act; 248(1) "trust" — Definition applies to entire Act; 248(3) — Deemed trusts in Quebec; 248(5.2) — Trust-to-trust transfers — deemed same trust; 248(25.1) — Trust-to-trust transfer — deemed continuation of trust; 251(1)(b) — Personal trust and beneficiary deemed not to deal at arm's length.

**Notes**: A trust is deemed to be an individual (see 104(2)) and thus files a return (T3; see 150(1)(c)) and pays tax as a separate person. When a person dies, the estate of the person (as represented by the executor or administrator) is treated as a trust for as long as it takes to wind up the affairs of the deceased and distribute the assets to the beneficiaries. However, if under the terms of the deceased's will a trust is created, that trust will be a separate person (a "testamentary trust" as defined in 108(1)) which can survive long beyond the winding-up of the estate and which must file its own annual returns.

Revenue Canada announced at the 1995 Canadian Tax Foundation annual conference that a revocable living trust and a protective trust

## Subdivision k — Trusts and Beneficiaries    S. 104(2)(a)

would henceforth be considered to be trusts. (This so-called protective trust may be what some people call a "blind trust".) A bare trust will continue to be considered a non-entity for tax purposes (i.e., the beneficiary is considered to deal directly with the property through the bare trustee as agent or nominee; see Interpretation Bulletin IT-216). (See Income Tax Technical News No. 7.) However, effective December 24, 1998 there are some legislated exceptions; see Notes to 248(1)"disposition". This position will be confirmed by the proposed amendment above and proposed 107.4.

For cases on a bare trust being a conduit or agent that is ignored for tax purposes, see *Brookview Investments*, [1963] C.T.C. 316 (Exch.); *Leowski*, [1996] G.S.T.C. 55 (TCC); *La Guercia Investments Ltd.*, [1996] G.S.T.C. 87 (TCC); *Cherny*, [1998] G.S.T.C. 97 (TCC); *Carnelian Investments Ltd.*, [1999] G.S.T.C. 92 (TCC); and *Szirtes*, [2000] G.S.T.C. 96 (TCC). See the commentary in the *Canada GST Service* to ETA 123(1)"person".

**Interpretation Bulletins**: IT-447: Residence of a trust or estate.

**I.T. Technical News**: No. 7 (revocable living trusts, protective trusts, bare trusts).

### Proposed Addition — 104(1.1)

**(1.1) Restricted meaning of "beneficiary"** — For the purposes of subsection (1), subparagraph 73(1.02)(b)(ii) and paragraph 107.4(1)(e), a person or partnership is deemed not to be a beneficiary under a trust at a particular time where the person or partnership is beneficially interested in the trust at the particular time solely because of

(a) a right that may arise as a consequence of the terms of the will or other testamentary instrument of an individual who, at the particular time, is a beneficiary under the trust;

(b) a right that may arise as a consequence of the law governing the intestacy of an individual;

(c) a right as a shareholder under the terms of the shares of the capital stock of a corporation that, at the particular time, is a beneficiary under the trust;

(d) a right as a member of a partnership under the terms of the partnership agreement, where, at the particular time, the partnership is a beneficiary under the trust; or

(e) any combination of rights described in paragraphs (a) to (d).

**Application**: Bill C-43 (First Reading September 20, 2000), subsec. 48(1), will add subsec. 104(1.1), applicable to 1998 *et seq.*

**Technical Notes**: New subsection 104(1.1) applies for the purpose of identifying beneficiaries under a trust for the purpose of subsection 104(1), as well as for the purposes of subparagraph 73(1.02)(b)(ii) and paragraph 107.4(1)(e). A person or partnership is deemed not to be a beneficiary under a trust at a particular time for these purposes where the person or partnership is beneficially interested in the trust at the particular time solely because of any one, or a combination of, the following:

- a right that may arise as a consequence of the terms of the will or other testamentary instrument of an individual who, at the particular time, is a beneficiary under the trust;

- a right that may arise as a consequence of the law governing the intestacy of an individual;

- a right as a shareholder under the terms of the shares of the capital stock of a corporation that, at the particular time, is a beneficiary under the trust; or

- a right as a member of a partnership under the terms of the partnership agreement, where, at the particular time, the partnership is a beneficiary under the trust.

These amendments generally apply to the 1998 and subsequent taxation years. However, in order to co-ordinate this amendment with changes to the replacement of the definition "disposition" in section 54 with the new definition of the same expression in subsection 248(1), it does not apply in connection with transfers of property that occurred before December 24, 1998.

### Proposed Amendment — 104(1.1) opening words

**(1.1) Restricted meaning of beneficiary** — For the purposes of subsection (1), subparagraph 73(1.02)(b)(ii), paragraph (b) of the definition "resident beneficiary" in subsection 94(1), and paragraph 107.4(1)(e), a person or partnership is deemed not to be a beneficiary under a trust at a particular time where the person or partnership is beneficially interested in the trust at the particular time solely because of

**Application**: The June 22, 2000 draft legislation, subsec. 14(1), will amend the opening words of subsec. 104(1.1) to read as above, applicable to trust taxation years that begin after 2000 [later Bill C-43, to be reintroduced early in 2001 — ed.].

**Technical Notes**: Proposed subsection 104(1.1) of the Act was one of the measures contained in a detailed Notice of Ways and Means Motion tabled on June 5, 2000.

Proposed subsection 104(1.1) of the Act applies for the purpose of identifying beneficiaries under a trust for the purpose of subsection 104(1), as well as for the purposes of proposed subparagraph 73(1.02)(b)(ii) and proposed paragraph 107.4(1)(e). Those provisions use the expression "beneficiary". Proposed subsection 104(1.1) deems a person or partnership not to be a "beneficiary" under a trust at a particular time for the purposes of those various provisions where the person or partnership is beneficially interested in the trust at the particular time solely because of a contingent right described in subsection 104(1.1).

It is proposed that subsection 104(1.1) be amended to also apply for the purpose of paragraph (b) of the definition "resident beneficiary" in new subsection 94(1), so that contingent rights described in subsection 104(1.1) will not result in a person being treated as a "resident beneficiary". For more detail on the implications of status as a resident beneficiary, see new subsection 94(3).

This amendment applies to trust taxation years that begin after 2000.

**(2) Taxed as individual** — A trust shall, for the purposes of this Act, and without affecting the liability of the trustee or legal representative for that person's own income tax, be deemed to be in respect of the trust property an individual, but where there is more than one trust and

(a) substantially all of the property of the various trusts has been received from one person, and

(b) the various trusts are conditioned so that the income thereof accrues or will ultimately accrue to the same beneficiary, or group or class of beneficiaries,

such of the trustees as the Minister may designate shall, for the purposes of this Act, be deemed to be in respect of all the trusts an individual whose property is the property of all the trusts and whose income is the income of all the trusts.

**Related Provisions**: 127.53(2), (3) — Multiple trusts must share minimum tax exemption; 248(1)"individual" — Trust is an individual.

**Notes**: 104(2) is designed to prevent creation of multiple testamentary trusts with the same beneficiaries in order to take advantage of the low rates of tax on low amounts of income. (This is not an issue for *inter vivos* trusts, since the top rate of tax applies to them: see 122(1).) 104(2) will not apply to separate testamentary trusts set up by the same will, each of which has a *different* beneficiary.

For more on multiple trusts, see Kathleen Cunningham, "The Creation of Multiple Trusts", VIII(1) *Goodman on Estate Planning* (Federated Press) 568-573 (1999).

The CCRA takes the position that "substantially all" means 90% or more.

**Regulations**: 204 (information return).

**Interpretation Bulletins**: IT-406R2: Tax payable by an *inter vivos* trust; IT-447: Residence of a trust or estate.

**Forms**: T3: Trust income tax and information return; T3 Summ: Summary of trust income allocations and designations; T3 Supp: Statement of trust income.

**(3) [Repealed under former Act]**

**Notes**: 104(3), repealed by 1988 tax reform, prohibited deductions for personal exemptions under 109, also repealed. Personal credits under 118 are now prohibited to trusts by 122(1.1).

**(4) Deemed disposition by trust** — Every trust shall, at the end of each of the following days, be deemed to have disposed of each property of the trust that was capital property (other than excluded property or depreciable property) or land included in the inventory of the trust for proceeds equal to its fair market value at the end of that day and to have reacquired the property immediately thereafter for an amount equal to that fair market value, and for the purposes of this Act those days are

**Proposed Amendment — 104(4) opening words**

**(4) Deemed disposition by trust** — Every trust is, at the end of each of the following days, deemed to have disposed of each property of the trust (other than exempt property) that was capital property (other than excluded property or depreciable property) or land included in the inventory of a business of the trust for proceeds equal to its fair market value (determined with reference to subsection 70(5.3)) at the end of that day and to have reacquired the property immediately after for an amount equal to that fair market value, and for the purposes of this Act those days are

**Application**: Bill C-43 (First Reading September 20, 2000), subsec. 48(2), will amend the opening words of subsec. 104(4) to read as above, applicable to days after December 23, 1998 that are determined in respect of a trust under subsec. 104(4), as amended, and for the purpose of determining the cost amount to a trust after December 23, 1998 of property to days after 1992 that are determined in respect of the trust under subsec. 104(4), as amended.

**Technical Notes**: Subsections 104(4) to (5.2) of the Act set out what is generally referred to as the "21-year deemed realization rule" for trusts. The purpose of the rule is to prevent the use of trusts to defer indefinitely the recognition for tax purposes of gains accruing on capital properties, resource properties and land inventories. These subsections generally treat such properties as having been disposed of and reacquired by trusts (other than spousal trusts) every 21 years at the properties' fair market value. The first deemed disposition day for post-1971 spousal trusts, as provided under paragraph 104(4)(a), is the day on which the spouse beneficiary dies. The fair market value of property that is deemed to be disposed of on a day determined under paragraph 104(4)(a) or (a.1), is determined with reference to the valuation rule for insurance policies in amended subsection 70(5.3) (see the commentary above on that provision).

Subsections 104(4) to (5.2) are amended so that the deemed realization rules do not apply to "exempt property" of a non-resident trust, as the expression is now defined in subsection 108(1). "Exempt property" is defined as property the income or gain from the disposition of which by a taxpayer is exempt from Canadian taxation for the taxpayer either because the taxpayer is not resident in Canada or because of a tax treaty. The purpose of this amendment is to prevent the deemed realization rules from being used to increase the cost of such property. The increased cost might be relevant in the event that a non-resident trust distributes such property to Canadian beneficiaries. These amendments apply to deemed disposition days that are after December 23, 1998. In the case of capital property (other than depreciable property), the amendments also apply to deemed disposition days that are after 1992, but only for the purpose of determining after December 23, 1998 the cost amount to a trust of property.

These amendments [re common-law partners — ed.] also reflect changes proposed under Bill C-23, the *Modernization of Benefits and Obligations Act*.

(a) where the trust

(i) is a trust that was created by the will of a taxpayer who died after 1971 and that, at the time it was created, was a trust,

(i.1) is a trust that was created by the will of a taxpayer who died after 1971 to which property was transferred in circumstances to which paragraph 70(5.2)(b) or (d) or (6)(d) applied and that, immediately after any such property vested indefeasibly in the trust as a consequence of the death of the taxpayer, was a trust, or

(ii) is a trust that was created after June 17, 1971 by a taxpayer during the taxpayer's lifetime that, at any time after 1971, was a trust

under which

(iii) the taxpayer's spouse or common-law partner was entitled to receive all of the income of the trust that arose before the spouse's or common-law partner's death, and

(iv) no person except the spouse or common-law partner could, before the spouse's or common-law partner's death, receive or otherwise obtain the use of any of the income or capital of the trust,

the day on which the spouse or common-law partner dies;

### Proposed Amendment — 104(4)(a)

(ii.1) is a trust (other than a trust the terms of which are described in clause (iv)(A) that elects in its return of income under this Part for its first taxation year that this subparagraph not apply) that was created after 1999 by a taxpayer during the taxpayer's lifetime that, at any time after 1999, was a trust

under which

(iii) the taxpayer's spouse or common-law partner was entitled to receive all of the income of the trust that arose before the spouse's or common-law partner's death and no person except the spouse or common-law partner could, before the spouse's or common-law partner's death, receive or otherwise obtain the use of any of the income or capital of the trust, or

(iv) in the case of a trust described in subparagraph (ii.1) created by a taxpayer who had attained 65 years of age at the time the trust was created,

(A) the taxpayer was entitled to receive all of the income of the trust that arose before the taxpayer's death and no person except the taxpayer could, before the taxpayer's death, receive or otherwise obtain the use of any of the income or capital of the trust, or

(B) the taxpayer or the taxpayer's spouse was, in combination with the spouse or the taxpayer, as the case may be, entitled to receive all of the income of the trust that arose before the later of the death of the taxpayer and the death of the spouse and no other person could, before the later of those deaths, receive or otherwise obtain the use of any of the income or capital of the trust,

(C) the taxpayer or the taxpayer's common-law partner was, in combination with the common-law partner or the taxpayer, as the case may be, entitled to receive all of the income of the trust that arose before the later of the death of the taxpayer and the death of the common-law partner and no other person could, before the later of those deaths, receive or otherwise obtain the use of any of the income or capital of the trust,

the day on which the death or the later death, as the case may be, occurs;

**Application**: Bill C-43 (First Reading September 20, 2000), subsec. 48(3), will amend the portion of para. 104(4)(a) after subpara. (ii) to read as above, applicable to 2000 *et seq.* except that, with regard to a trust created by a taxpayer at a particular time in 2000 for the benefit of another individual, subparas. 104(4)(a)(iii) and (iv) of the Act shall be read without reference to the words "or common-law partner" and "or common-law partner's" and to cl. 104(4)(a)(iv)(C), unless, because of an election under s. 144 of the *Modernization of Benefits and Obligations Act*, c. 12 of S.C. 2000 [see Notes to 248(1)"common-law partner"], ss. 130 to 142 of that Act applied at the particular time to the taxpayer and the other individual.

**Technical Notes**: Paragraph 104(4)(a) is amended to provide the first deemed disposition day in respect of an *inter vivos* trust created after 1999 that at any time after 1999 was a trust for the exclusive benefit of the settlor during the settlor's lifetime (i.e., an "*alter ego* trust", as newly defined in subsection 248(1)) or a trust for the joint benefit of the settlor and the settlor's spouse during their lifetimes (i.e., a "joint partner trust", as newly defined in subsection 248(1)). The first deemed disposition date in these circumstances, in the event that the settlor was at least 65 years of age at the time of the settlement, is generally the day on which the settlor dies (or, in the case of a trust for the joint benefit of the settlor and spouse, the day on which the survivor dies). However, where a trust that would otherwise be an alter ego trust so elects under subparagraph 104(4)(a)(ii.1), the first deemed disposition date of the trust will generally be the 21st anniversary of the creation of the trust, as determined under paragraph 104(4)(b). This amendment applies to the 2000 and subsequent taxation years. For an explanation of the age 65 restriction, see the commentary on new subsection 73(1.02).

(a.1) where the trust is a pre-1972 spousal trust on January 1, 1993 and the spouse or common-law partner referred to in the definition "pre-1972 spousal trust" in subsection 108(1) in respect of the trust was

(i) in the case of a trust created by the will of a taxpayer, alive on January 1, 1976, and

(ii) in the case of a trust created by a taxpayer during the taxpayer's lifetime, alive on May 26, 1976,

the day that is the later of

(iii) the day on which that spouse or common-law partner dies, and

(iv) January 1, 1993;

### Proposed Addition — 104(4)(a.2), (a.3)

(a.2) where the trust makes a distribution to a beneficiary in respect of the beneficiary's capital interest in the trust, it is reasonable to conclude that the distribution was financed by a liability of the trust and one of the purposes of incurring the liability was to avoid taxes otherwise payable under this Part as a consequence of the death of any individual, the day on which the distribution is made (determined as if a day ends for the trust immediately after the time at which each distribution is made by the trust to a beneficiary in respect of the beneficiary's capital interest in the trust);

(a.3) where property (other than property described in any of subparagraphs 128.1(4)(b)(i) to (iii)) has been transferred by a taxpayer after December 17, 1999 to the trust in circumstances to which subsection 73(1) applies, it is reasonable to conclude that the property was so transferred in anticipation that the taxpayer would subsequently cease to reside in Canada and the taxpayer subsequently ceases to reside in Canada, the first day after that transfer during which the taxpayer ceases to reside in Canada (determined as if a day ends for the trust immediately after each time at which the taxpayer ceases to be resident in Canada);

**Application**: Bill C-43 (First Reading September 20, 2000), subsec. 48(4), will add paras. 104(4)(a.2) and (a.3), applicable to days after December 17, 1999 that are determined under subsection 104(4), as amended.

**Technical Notes**: Paragraph 104(4)(a.2) is introduced to provide for a deemed disposition day for a trust that distributes property financed by a liability of the trust. This measure only applies, however, if one of the purposes of the transaction was to avoid taxes otherwise payable as a consequence of the death of an individual. The deemed disposition under this paragraph occurs immediately after the distribution of the property (as the determination is made as if a day had ended immediately after each distribution). This amendment applies to deemed disposition days determined after December 17, 1999.

Paragraph 104(4)(a.3) is introduced to provide for a deemed disposition day for a trust in the event that an individual, after December 17, 1999, has transferred property to the trust in circumstances to which subsection 73(1) applies, it is reasonable to conclude that the property was so transferred in anticipation that the taxpayer would subsequently cease to reside in Canada and the individual subsequently ceases to reside in Canada. This measure does not apply, however, to property transferred that is exempt under amended subparagraphs 128.1(4)(b)(i) to (iii) from a deemed disposition on the transferor's emigration. The deemed disposition under paragraph 104(4)(a.3) occurs immediately after the individual ceases to be resident in Canada.

(b) the day that is 21 years after the latest of

(i) January 1, 1972,

(ii) the day on which the trust was created, and

(iii) where applicable, the day determined under paragraph (a) or (a.1) as those paragraphs applied from time to time after 1971; and

(c) the day that is 21 years after any day (other than a day determined under paragraph (a) or (a.1)) that is, because of this subsection, a day on which the trust is deemed to have disposed of each such property.

**Proposed Amendment — 104(4)(c)**

(c) the day that is 21 years after any day (other than a day determined under paragraph (a), (a.1), (a.2) or (a.3)) that is, because of this subsection, a day on which the trust is deemed to have disposed of each such property.

**Application**: Bill C-43 (First Reading September 20, 2000), subsec. 48(5), will amend para. 104(4)(c) to read as above, applicable to 2000 et seq.

**Technical Notes**: Paragraph 104(4)(c) is amended so that there is not a deemed disposition day for a trust 21 years after any day determined under new paragraph 104(4)(a.2) or (a.3). This amendment applies to the 2000 and subsequent taxation years.

**Related Provisions**: 53(4) — Effect on ACB of share, partnership interest or trust interest; 54"superficial loss"(c) — Superficial loss rule does not apply; 70(5.3) — Value of property that depends on life insurance policy; 70(6)(a) — Where transfer or distribution to spouse or trust; 70(9.1) — Transfer of farm property from spouse's trust to settlor's children; 73(1)(c) — *Inter vivos* transfer of property to spouse trust; 73(1.02)(c)(ii) — Anti-avoidance rule; 94(1)(c)(i)(B) — Deemed disposition applies to non-resident trust after 1998; 104(4.1) — Mark-to-market property can be capital property for 104(4); 104(5) — Deemed disposition of depreciable property; 104(5.3) — Election to postpone deemed disposition to 1999; 104(5.8) — Trust transfers; 104(6) — Deduction in computing income of trust; 104(15)(a) — Allocable amount for preferred beneficiary election; 107(4) — Trust in favour of spouse; 107.4(3)(h) — Qualifying disposition to a trust; 108(1) — "accumulating income"; 108(1)"cost amount"(a.1) — Cost amount before death of taxpayer; 108(1)"trust" — Exclusions to meaning of "trust"; 108(3) — Meaning of "income" of trust; 108(4) — Trust payment of duties and taxes; 108(5) — Where terms of trust are varied; 127.55(e) — Application of minimum tax; 132.11(4) — Amounts paid from December 16-31 by mutual fund trust to beneficiary; 138.1(1) — Rules re segregated funds; 139.1(5) — Value of ownership rights in insurer during demutualization; 159(6.1) — Election to postpone payment of tax on deemed disposition; 248(1)"*alter ego* trust" — Name for trust described in 104(4)(a)(iv)(A); 248(1)"joint partner trust" — Name for trust described in 104(4)(a)(iv)(B); 248(8) — Occurrences as a consequence of death; 248(9.1) — Whether trust created by taxpayer's will; 248(9.2) — Meaning of "vested indefeasibly"; 252(3) — Extended meaning of "spouse".

**Notes**: 104(4) is the "21-year deemed disposition rule", designed to force trusts to recognize and pay tax on their accrued capital gains every 21 years. (A similar rule for depreciable property applies under 104(5), and for resource property under 104(5.2).) Under 104(5.3) the deemed disposition could be deferred until January 1, 1999 in certain cases.

See Wolfe Goodman, "Some Methods of Dealing with the 21-Year Deemed Disposition", VIII(3) *Goodman on Estate Planning* (Federated Press) 623–626 (1999).

104(4) amended by 2000 same-sex partners bill to add reference to "common-law partner", effective for the 2001 and later taxation years, or earlier by election (see Notes to 248(1)"common-law partner").

104(4)(a)(i.1) amended by 1995-97 technical bill, effective for acquisitions and dispositions after 1992, to change "70(5.2)(d) or (f)" to "70(5.2)(b) or (d)", consequential on amendments to 70(5.2) made by 1993 technical bill.

104(4)(a.1) amended by 1995 Budget, retroactive to trust taxation years that end after February 11, 1991. Since the amendments are retroactive, they supersede those made by 1992 technical bill. The amendments provide that a pre-1972 testamentary spousal trust is not subject to a deemed disposition unless the beneficiary spouse was alive on January 1, 1976; and that a pre-1972 *inter vivos* spousal trust is not subject to deemed disposition unless the beneficiary spouse was alive on May 26, 1976. These amendments recognize that, if a beneficiary spouse died after 1971 and before 1976 (or before May 26, 1976 for an *inter vivos* trust), a pre-1972 spousal trust would have already been subject to a deemed disposition on the day the beneficiary spouse died because of the former wording of 104(4)(a). 104(4)(b)(iii) amended by 1995 Budget, similarly retroactive, to add the words "as those paragraphs applied from time to time after 1971", thus clarifying that, in these circumstances, such a trust is subject to a further deemed disposition 21 years after the beneficiary spouse died.

104(4) amended by 1992 technical bill, effective for taxation years of trusts that end after February 11, 1991, in conjunction with the introduction of an election in 104(5.3) to postpone the deemed disposition. (However, amended 104(4)(a) does not apply to a trust described in 104(4)(a)(i.1) if the spouse who was the beneficiary died before December 21, 1991.) For earlier years:

(a) delete the reference to "excluded property" in the opening words;

(b) read "on that day" instead of "at the end of that day" in the opening words;

(c) delete subpara. (a)(i.1);

(d) delete "after June 17, 1971" in subpara. (a)(ii);

(e) delete para. (a.1) and the reference to it, as well as the words "as those paragraphs applied from time to time after 1971", in subpara. (b)(iii); and

(f) delete the parenthetical exclusion in para. (c).

104(4) amended by 1981 Budget and by 1985 technical bill. For taxation years of a trust commencing before 1985, the deemed disposition and reacquisition of property applied to certain resource properties as well as to the kinds of property specified in the opening words. See 104(5.2) for those rules now.

Before November 13, 1981, the deemed disposition and reacquisition applied only to "capital property (other than depreciable property)".

104(4)(a) amended in 1976, effective where the spouse who was the beneficiary died after May 25, 1976. Where the spouse died from January 1 through May 25, 1976, read as follows:

(a) where the trust is a trust created by the will of a taxpayer who died after December 31, 1971 or a trust created by a taxpayer during his lifetime, under which

(i) his spouse is entitled to receive all of the income of the trust that arises before the spouse's death, and

(ii) no person except the spouse may, before the spouse's death, receive or otherwise obtain the use of any of the income or capital of the trust,

the day on which the spouse dies;

Where the spouse died before January 1, 1976, read:

(a) where the trust is a trust created by a taxpayer, whether during his lifetime or by his will, under which

(i) his spouse is entitled to receive all of the income of the trust that arises before the spouse's death, and

(ii) no person except the spouse may, before the spouse's death, receive or otherwise obtain the use of any of the income or capital of the trust,

the day on which the spouse dies;

**Interpretation Bulletins**: IT-120R5: Principal residence; IT-286R2: Trusts — amounts payable; IT-325R2: Property transfers after separation, divorce and annulment; IT-349R3: Intergenerational transfers of farm property on death; IT-370: Trusts — capital property owned on December 31, 1971; IT-381R3: Trusts — capital gains and losses and the flow-through of taxable capital gains to beneficiaries; IT-394R2: Preferred beneficiary election; IT-449R: Meaning of "vested indefeasibly"; IT-465R — Non-resident beneficiaries of trusts.

**Advance Tax Rulings**: ATR-38: Distribution of all of the property of an estate.

**Forms**: T1055: Summary of deemed realizations.

### Proposed Addition — 104(4.1)

**(4.1) Mark-to-market property** — Notwithstanding any other provision of this Act, the determination of whether property is capital property for the purpose of subsection (4) shall be made without reference to subparagraph 39(1)(a)(ii.3) and section 94.2.

**Application**: The June 22, 2000 draft legislation, subsec. 14(2), will add subsec. 104(4.1), applicable to trust taxation years that begin after 2000.

**Technical Notes**: New subsection 104(4.1) of the Act provides that, for the purposes of the 21-year deemed disposition rule in subsection 104(4), a property's status as capital property is determined without reference to new subparagraph 39(1)(a)(ii.3) and new section 94.2. The latter provisions have the effect of providing that interests in foreign investment entities to which subsection 94.2 applies are not classified as capital property. In the event that such an interest is deemed to have been disposed of because of the application of subsection 104(4), there is a recognition of the "deferral amount" pursuant to subsection 94.2(4).

This amendment applies to trust taxation years that begin after 2000.

**(5) Idem [depreciable property]** — Every trust shall, at the end of each day determined under subsection (4) in respect of the trust, be deemed to have disposed of each property of the trust that was a depreciable property of a prescribed class of the trust for proceeds equal to its fair market value at the end of that day and to have reacquired the property immediately thereafter at a capital cost (in this subsection referred to as the "deemed capital cost") equal to that fair market value, except that

### Proposed Amendment — 104(5) opening words

**(5) Depreciable property [deemed disposition]** — Every trust is, at the end of each day determined under subsection (4) in respect of the trust, deemed to have disposed of each property of the trust (other than exempt property) that was a depreciable property of a prescribed class of the trust for proceeds equal to its fair market value at the end of that day and to have reacquired the property immediately after that day at a capital cost (in this subsection referred to as the "deemed capital cost") equal to that fair market value, except that

**Application**: Bill C-43 (First Reading September 20, 2000), subsec. 48(6), will amend the opening words of subsec. 104(5) to read as above, applicable to days after December 23, 1998 that are determined under subsection 104(4), as amended.

**Technical Notes**: See under 104(4) opening words.

(a) where the amount that was the capital cost to the trust of the property immediately before the end of the day (in this paragraph referred to as the "actual capital cost") exceeds the deemed capital

**S. 104(5)(a)**      Income Tax Act, Part I, Division B

cost to the trust of the property, for the purpose of sections 13 and 20 and any regulations made for the purpose of paragraph 20(1)(a) as they apply in respect of the property at any subsequent time,

    (i) the capital cost to the trust of the property on its reacquisition shall be deemed to be the amount that was the actual capital cost to the trust of the property, and

    (ii) the excess shall be deemed to have been allowed under paragraph 20(1)(a) to the trust in respect of the property in computing its income for taxation years that ended before the trust reacquired the property;

(b) for the purposes of this subsection, the reference to "at the end of a taxation year" in subsection 13(1) shall be read as a reference to "at the particular time a trust is deemed by subsection 104(5) to have disposed of depreciable property of a prescribed class"; and

(c) for the purpose of computing the excess, if any, referred to in subsection 13(1) at the end of the taxation year of a trust that included a day on which the trust is deemed by this subsection to have disposed of a depreciable property of a prescribed class, any amount that, on that day, was included in the trust's income for the year under subsection 13(1) as it reads because of paragraph (b), shall be deemed to be an amount included under section 13 in the trust's income for a preceding taxation year.

**Related Provisions**: 70(9.1) — Transfer of farm property from spouse's trust to settlor's children; 73(1.02)(c)(ii) — Anti-avoidance rule; 104(5.3) — Election by trust to postpone deemed disposition; 104(5.8) — Trust transfers; 104(6) — Deduction in computing income of trust; 108(1) — "accumulating income"; 108(1)"cost amount"(a.1) — Cost amount before death of taxpayer; 108(1)"trust" — Exclusions to meaning of "trust"; 108(6) — Where terms of trust are varied.

**Notes**: The deemed disposition of depreciable property may lead to recapture under 13(1) (where the undepreciated capital cost of the class goes negative), terminal loss under 20(16) (where no assets are left in the class), and/or a capital gain under 39(1) (where the current fair market value exceeds the adjusted cost base).

104(5) amended by 1992 technical bill and 1993 technical bill, effective for days determined under 104(4) that are after 1992. For days before 1993 but where the taxation year of the trust ends after February 11, 1991, read:

    (5) Every trust shall, at the end of each day determined under subsection (4) in respect of the trust, be deemed to have disposed of all depreciable property of a prescribed class of the trust for proceeds equal to

        (a) where the fair market value of that property at the end of the day exceeds the undepreciated capital cost thereof to the trust at the end of the day, the amount of that undepreciated capital cost plus ½ of the excess, and

        (b) in any other case, the fair market value of that property at the end of that day plus ½ of the amount, if any, by which the undepreciated capital cost thereof to the trust at the end of that day exceeds that fair market value,

and to have reacquired each such depreciable property of that class immediately thereafter at a capital cost (in this subsection referred to as the "deemed capital cost") equal to that proportion of the proceeds determined under paragraph (a) or (b), as the case may be, that the amount that was the fair market value of that property is of the total of the amounts that were the fair market values of all properties of that class at the end of that day, except that

    (c) where the amount that was the capital cost to the trust of any particular property of that class exceeds the deemed capital cost to the trust of the property, for the purposes of sedtions 13 and 20 and any regulations made under paragraph 20(1)(a) as they apply in respect of the property at any subsequent time,

        (i) the capital cost to the trust of the property shall be deemed to be the amount that was the capital cost to the trust of the property, and

        (ii) the excess shall be deemed to have been allowed to the trust in respect of the property under paragraph 20(1)(a) in computing income for taxation years before the reacquisition by the trust of the property, and any other amount allowed to the trust in respect of the property under that paragraph in computing income for those years shall be deemed to be nil,

    (d) for the purposes of this subsection, the words "at the end of a taxation year," in subsection 13(1) shall be deemed to read "at the particular time a trust is deemed by subsection 104(5) to have disposed of depreciable property of a prescribed class," and

    (e) for the purpose of computing the excess, if any, referred to in subsection 13(1) at the end of the taxation year of a trust that included a day on which the trust is deemed by this subsection to have disposed of all depreciable property of a prescribed class, any amount that, on that day, was included in the trust's income for the year by virtue of subsection 13(1) as it reads by virtue of paragraph (d), shall be deemed to be an amount included in the taxpayer's income by virtue of section 13 for a prior taxation year.

For taxation years of a trust that end before February 12, 1991, read as above but change "at the end of" to "on" in each case (i.e., "on each day", "on that day").

**Interpretation Bulletins**: IT-286R2: Trusts — amount payable; IT-349R3: Intergenerational transfers of farm property on death; IT-381R3: Trusts — capital gains and losses and the flow-through of taxable capital gains to beneficiaries; IT-394R2: Preferred beneficiary election; IT-465R: Non-resident beneficiaries of trusts.

**Forms**: T1055: Summary of deemed realizations.

### (5.1) Idem [NISA Fund No. 2] — Every trust that holds an interest in a NISA Fund No. 2 that was transferred to it in circumstances to which paragraph 70(6.1)(b) applied shall be deemed, at the end of the day on which the spouse or common-law partner referred to in that paragraph dies (in this subsection referred to as the "spouse or common-law partner"), to have been paid an amount out of the fund equal to the amount, if any, by which

    (a) the balance at the end of that day in the fund so transferred

exceeds

    (b) such portion of the amount described in paragraph (a) as is deemed by subsection (14.1) to have been paid to the spouse or common-law partner.

**Related Provisions**: 104(5.8) — Trust transfers; 104(6) — Deduction in computing income of trust; 252(3) — Extended meaning of "spouse".

**Notes**: 104(5.1) amended by 2000 same-sex partners bill to add reference to "common-law partner", effective for the 2001 and later taxation years, or earlier by election (see Notes to 248(1)"common-law partner").

104(5.1) added by 1992 technical bill, effective 1991.

**Forms**: T1055: Summary of deemed realizations.

### (5.2) Rules for trusts [resource property] —
Where on a day determined under subsection (4) in respect of a trust the trust owns a Canadian resource property or a foreign resource property, the following rules apply:

(a) for the purpose of determining the amounts under subsection 59(1), paragraph 59(3.2)(c), subsections 66(4) and 66.2(1), the definition "cumulative Canadian development expense" in subsection 66.2(5), subsection 66.4(1) and the definition "cumulative Canadian oil and gas property expense" in subsection 66.4(5), the trust shall be deemed

(i) to have a taxation year (in this subsection referred to as the "old taxation year") that ended on that day and a new taxation year (in this subsection referred to as the "new taxation year") that commenced immediately after that day, and

(ii) to have disposed, immediately before the end of the old taxation year, of each of its Canadian resource properties and foreign resource properties for proceeds that become receivable at that time equal to its fair market value at that time and to have reacquired, at the beginning of the new taxation year, each such property for an amount equal to that fair market value; and

### Proposed Amendment — 104(5.2)

**(5.2) Resource property** — Where at the end of a day determined under subsection (4) in respect of a trust the trust owns a Canadian resource property (other than an exempt property) or a foreign resource property (other than an exempt property),

(a) for the purpose of determining the amounts under subsection 59(1), paragraph 59(3.2)(c), subsections 66(4) and 66.2(1), the definition "cumulative Canadian development expense" in subsection 66.2(5), subsection 66.4(1) and the definition "cumulative Canadian oil and gas property expense" in subsection 66.4(5), the trust is deemed

(i) to have a taxation year (in this subsection referred to as the "old taxation year") that ended at the end of that day and a new taxation year that begins immediately after that day, and

(ii) to have disposed, immediately before the end of the old taxation year, of each of those properties for proceeds that became receivable at that time equal to its fair market value at that time and to have reacquired, at the

beginning of the new taxation year, each such property for an amount equal to that fair market value; and

**Application**: Bill C-43 (First Reading September 20, 2000), subsec. 48(7), will amend the portion of subsec. 104(5.2) before para. (b) to read as above, applicable to days after December 23, 1998 that are determined under subsec. 104(4), as amended.

**Technical Notes**: See under 104(4) opening words.

### Proposed Amendment — 104(5.2)(a) opening words

(a) for the purposes of determining the amounts under subsection 59(1), paragraphs 59(3.2)(c) and (c.1), subsections 66(4) and 66.2(1), the definition "cumulative Canadian development expense" in subsection 66.2(5), the definition "cumulative foreign resource expense" in subsection 66.21(1), subsection 66.4(1) and the definition "cumulative Canadian oil and gas property expense" in subsection 66.4(5), the trust is deemed

**Application**: The December 21, 2000 draft legislation, subsec. 48(1), will amend the opening words of para. 104(5.2)(a) to read as above, applicable to taxation years that begin after 2000.

**Technical Notes**: Subsection 104(5.2) provides that each Canadian resource property and foreign resource property of a trust is treated, for specified purposes, as having been disposed of immediately before the end of a day determined under subsection 104(4) for fair market value proceeds. For the purposes of specified resource provisions, the trust is treated as having a taxation year (referred below to as the "notional year") ending at the end of such a day for the purpose of computing the amount to be included in its income as a result of this disposition of the resource properties. The Canadian and foreign resource properties are deemed to be reacquired immediately after notional year for the same amount.

Paragraph 104(5.2)(a) is amended to include new paragraph 59(3.2)(c.1) and the new definition "cumulative foreign resource expense" in new section 66.21 in the resource provisions specified under subsection 104(5.2).

Paragraph 104(5.2)(b) is amended so that any resulting income inclusion under new paragraph 59(3.2)(c.1) with regard to the notional year is added in determining the trust's cumulative foreign resource expense at the end of the trust taxation year of which the notional year is part. This amendment ensures that there is no double taxation in respect of the same economic gain and is consistent with the treatment of resulting income inclusions with regard to Canadian resource properties.

The effect of these amendments is that the fair market value of a foreign resource property can, to the extent proceeds are designated under new subparagraph 59(1)(b)(ii), reduce a trust's cumulative foreign resource expense. If a negative balance results, the negative balance is included in income under paragraph 59(3.2)(c.1) and added in computing the trust's cumulative foreign resource expense after the end of the notional year.

(b) for the particular taxation year of the trust that included that day, the trust shall

(i) include in computing its income for the particular taxation year the amount, if any, determined under paragraph 59(3.2)(c) in respect of the old taxation year and the amount so included shall, for the purposes of the determination of B in the definition "cumulative Canadian development expense" in subsection 66.2(5), be deemed to have been included in computing its income for a preceding taxation year, and

#### Proposed Addition — 104(5.2)(b)(i.1)

(i.1) include in computing its income for the particular taxation year the amount, if any, determined under paragraph 59(3.2)(c.1) in respect of the old taxation year and the amount so included is, for the purpose of determining the value of B in the definition "cumulative foreign resource expense" in subsection 66.21(1), deemed to have been included in computing its income for a preceding taxation year, and

**Application**: The December 21, 2000 draft legislation, subsec. 48(2), will add subpara. 104(5.2)(b)(i.1), applicable to taxation years that begin after 2000.

**Technical Notes**: See under 104(5.2)(a) opening words.

(ii) deduct in computing its income for the particular taxation year the amount, if any, determined under subsection 66(4) in respect of the old taxation year and the amount so deducted shall, for the purposes of paragraph 66(4)(a), be deemed to have been deducted for a preceding taxation year.

**Related Provisions**: 104(5.3) — Election; 104(5.8) — Trust transfers; 104(6) — Deduction in computing income of trust; 108(1) — "accumulating income"; 108(1) — "trust"; 108(6) — Where terms of trust are varied.

**Notes**: 104(5.2) added by 1985 technical bill, effective for taxation years of a trust beginning in 1985 or later. For the deemed disposition and reacquisition in earlier years, see 104(4) as it applied to those years.

**Interpretation Bulletins**: IT-394R2: Preferred beneficiary election.

**(5.3) Election** — Where a trust files an election under this subsection in prescribed form with the Minister within 6 months after the end of a taxation year of the trust that includes a day before 1999 (in this subsection referred to as the "disposition day") that would, but for this subsection, be determined in respect of the trust under paragraph (4)(a.1) in the case of a trust described in that paragraph, or under paragraph (4)(b) in any other case, and there is an exempt beneficiary under the trust on the disposition day,

(a) for the purposes of subsections (4) to (5.2), paragraph (6)(b) and subsection 159(6.1), the day determined under paragraph (4)(a.1) or (b), as the case may be, in respect of the trust is deemed to be the earlier of

(i) January 1, 1999, and

(ii) the first day of the trust's first taxation year that begins after the first day after the disposition day throughout which there is no exempt beneficiary under the trust;

(b) subsection 107(2) does not apply to a distribution made by the trust during the period

(i) beginning immediately after the disposition day, and

(ii) ending at the end of the first day after the disposition day that is determined in respect of the trust under subsection (4)

to any beneficiary (other than an individual who is an exempt beneficiary under the trust immediately before the time of the distribution);

(b.1) where the trust filed the form before March 1995, paragraph (b) does not apply to distributions made by the trust after February 1995;

(c) subject to paragraph (d), paragraph (e) of the definition "disposition" in section 54 does not apply to a transfer by the trust after the disposition day during the period

#### Proposed Amendment — 104(5.3)(c) opening words

(c) subsection 107.4(3) does not apply to a disposition by the trust during the period

**Application**: Bill C-43 (First Reading September 20, 2000), subsec. 48(8), will amend the opening words of para. 104(5.3)(c) to read as above, applicable to transfers made after December 23, 1998.

**Technical Notes**: Subsection 104(5.3) allowed the deferral of the 21-year deemed disposition date (determined under paragraph 104(4)(a.1) or (b)) for certain family trusts. The measure has already been terminated under the existing rules, so that the deferred disposition date was no later than January 1, 1999.

Subject to paragraph 104(5.3)(d), paragraph 104(5.3)(c) ensures that the deemed disposition date cannot be deferred beyond January 1, 1999 (or an earlier date, where applicable) through a transfer of property from one trust to another that does not constitute a "disposition" because of existing paragraph (e) of the definition "disposition" in section 54. Any trust-to-trust transfer in the period (referred to below as the "relevant period") that is after the original date of the deemed disposition and before the date of the deferred deemed disposition is considered to be a "disposition" (i.e., a taxable event) for a trust that has made an election under subsection 104(5.3). Paragraph 104(5.3)(d) provides for relief from paragraph 104(5.3)(c) where, essentially, one trust is replaced by another trust with the same terms and beneficiaries. In this case, the new trust is deemed to be the same trust as, and a continuation of, the original trust.

Paragraph 104(5.3)(c) is amended to eliminate the reference to the existing definition of "disposition" in section 54, as a consequence of the repeal of that definition and its replacement by a new definition of "disposition" in subsection 248(1).

Paragraph 104(5.3)(c) is also amended so that it only applies where there is a "disposition" of property (as now defined in subsection 248(1)). The only relevant "trust-to-trust" transfer where there is no "disposition" is one to

Subdivision k — Trusts and Beneficiaries    S. 104(5.4)(b)(ii)(B)

which paragraph (f) of the new definition "disposition" applies. Where paragraph (f) of that definition applies, the transferee trust is considered under subsection 248(25.1) to be the same as and a continuation of the transferor trust.

   (i) beginning immediately after the disposition day, and

   (ii) ending at the end of the first day after the disposition day that is determined in respect of the trust under subsection (4); and

(d) where

   (i) property is transferred from the trust to another trust in circumstances to which paragraph (e) of the definition "disposition" in section 54 would, but for paragraph (c), apply,

   (ii) the other trust held no property immediately before the transfer, and

   (iii) the terms of the trust immediately before the transfer are identical to the terms of the other trust immediately after the transfer,

paragraph (e) of the definition "disposition" in section 54 applies to the transfer and the other trust shall be deemed to be the same trust as, and a continuation of, the trust.

**Proposed Repeal — 104(5.3)(d)**

**Application**: Bill C-43 (First Reading September 20, 2000), subsec. 48(9), will repeal para. 104(5.3)(d), applicable to transfers made after December 23, 1998.

**Technical Notes**: Paragraph 104(5.3)(d) is repealed, consequential on the introduction of paragraph (f) of the new definition "disposition" and new subsection 248(25.1).

**Related Provisions**: 104(5.31) — Revocation of election; 104(5.4) — Exempt beneficiary; 104(5.8) — Trust transfers; 107(2) — Rollout of property to beneficiaries where election not available; 108(1) — "trust"; 110.6(12) — Spousal trust deduction; 220(3.2), Reg. 600(b) — Late filing or revocation of election; 248(5.2) — Trust-to-trust transfers.

**Notes**: 104(5.3) added by 1992 technical bill, effective February 12, 1991. The impetus for its enactment was the existence of pre-1972 trusts that would have had to recognize and pay tax on their accrued capital gains due to a deemed disposition under 104(4)(b)(i) on January 1, 1993. However, it was eliminated as part of a political response to concerns about tax deferral through family trusts.

The elimination of 104(5.3) was implemented by amendments made by 1995 Budget, retroactive to February 12, 1991, adding "before 1999" in the opening words and adding subpara. (a)(i). Thus, the election is not available after 1998, and if it was made, the deemed disposition occurred on January 1, 1999.

104(5.3)(b.1) also added by 1995 Budget, retroactive to February 12, 1991, to ensure that trusts are not penalized by having made an election under 104(5.3). See also 104(5.31), which allows revocation until the end of 1996 of an election made before July 1995.

Now that 104(5.3) is no longer available, a "roll-out" of the trust assets to the beneficiaries under 107(2) may serve to defer recognition of gains on the assets.

**Interpretation Bulletins**: IT-381R3: Trusts — capital gains and losses and the flow-through of taxable capital gains to beneficiaries; IT-394R2: Preferred beneficiary election.

**Forms**: T1015: Election by a trust to defer the deemed realization day.

**(5.31) Revocation of election** — Where a trust that has filed an election under subsection (5.3) before July 1995 applies before 1997 to the Minister in writing for permission to revoke the election and the Minister grants permission to revoke the election,

(a) the election is deemed, otherwise than for the purposes of this subsection, never to have been made;

(b) the trust is not liable to any penalty under this Act to the extent that the liability would, but for this paragraph, have increased because of the revocation of the election; and

(c) notwithstanding subsections 152(4) to (5), such assessments of tax, interest and penalties under this Act shall be made as are necessary to take into account the consequences of the revocation of the election.

**Notes**: 104(5.31) added by 1995 Budget, effective June 20, 1996 (Royal Assent). See Notes to 104(5.3). The elimination of the indefinite deferral under 104(5.3) was announced in the February 1995 federal budget; hence trusts might have unwittingly made the election even shortly after the budget. As long as the revocation was filed by the end of 1996, an election made any time up to the end of June 1995 could be revoked.

**(5.4) Exempt beneficiary** — For the purpose of subsection (5.3), an "exempt beneficiary" under a trust at a particular time is an individual who is alive and a beneficiary under the trust at the particular time, where

(a) in the case of a trust that was created after February 11, 1991, the individual, or an individual who, otherwise than because of subsection 252(2), is the brother or sister of the individual, was alive at the earlier of

   (i) the time the trust was created, and

   (ii) the earliest of all times each of which is the time that another trust was created that, before the particular time and the end of the day that would, but for subsection (5.3), be determined in respect of the trust under paragraph (4)(a.1) or (b), transferred property to the trust either

      (A) directly, or

      (B) indirectly through one or more trusts,

in circumstances in which subsection (5.8) applies; and

(b) the individual or the individual's spouse or common-law partner or former spouse or common-law partner was

   (i) the designated contributor in respect of the trust, or

   (ii) a grandparent, parent, brother, sister, child, niece or nephew

      (A) of the designated contributor in respect of the trust, or

      (B) of the spouse or common-law partner or former spouse or common-law partner

833

S. 104(5.4)(b)(ii)(B)   Income Tax Act, Part I, Division B

of the designated contributor in respect of the trust.

**Related Provisions**: 104(5.5) — Beneficiary; 104(5.6) — Designated contributor; 252(3) — Extended meaning of "spouse".

**Notes**: 104(5.4)(b) amended by 2000 same-sex partners bill to add reference to "common-law partner", effective for the 2001 and later taxation years, or earlier by election (see Notes to 248(1)"common-law partner"). Since 104(5.3) was made ineffective as of 1999, the amendment can only be relevant for 1998.

104(5.4) added by 1992 technical bill, effective February 12, 1991.

**(5.5) Beneficiary** — For the purpose of subsection (5.4), a beneficiary under a trust is an individual who is beneficially interested in the trust, except that an individual shall be deemed not to be a beneficiary under a trust at a particular time

(a) where

(i) the interests in the trust at the particular time of all individuals who would, if this Act were read without reference to this paragraph, be exempt beneficiaries under the trust are conditional on or subject to the exercise of a discretionary power by a person,

(ii) by the exercise of (or the failure to exercise) such power under the terms of the trust after the particular time, all interests in the trust of

(A) those individuals, and

(B) other individuals who are children of deceased individuals who, if this Act were read without reference to this paragraph, would have been exempt beneficiaries under the trust at any time before the particular time

may terminate before the time at which the last of those individuals and the other individuals dies and without any of those individuals or the other individuals enjoying any benefit under the trust after the particular time, and

(iii) the trust was created after February 11, 1991 or subparagraph (ii) applies in respect of the trust because of a variation of the terms of the trust occurring after February 11, 1991; or

(b) where it is reasonable to consider that one of the main purposes for the creation of the interest of the individual in the trust was to defer the day determined under paragraph (4)(a.1) or (b) in respect of the trust.

**Related Provisions**: 248(25) — Beneficially interested.

**Notes**: 104(5.5) added by 1992 technical bill, effective February 12, 1991.

**(5.6) Designated contributor** — For the purpose of subsection (5.4), a designated contributor in respect of a trust is

(a) where the trust is described in paragraph (4)(a) or was, on December 20, 1991, a pre-1972 spousal trust, the individual who created (or whose will created) the trust;

(b) where paragraph (a) does not apply and the trust is a testamentary trust at the end of the taxation year for which it makes an election under subsection (5.3), the individual as a consequence of whose death the trust was created; and

(c) in the case of any other trust, the individual who was, or who was related to, an individual beneficially interested in the trust and who is designated by the trust in its election under subsection (5.3)

(i) where, at each time in the relevant period, the total amount of property transferred or loaned before that time by the designated individual (either directly or through another trust) to the trust

(A) exceeded the total amount of property so transferred or loaned before that time by each other individual who was born before the designated individual and who, at any time, was related to any individual beneficially interested in the trust, and

(B) was not less than the total amount of property so transferred or loaned before that time by each other individual who was born after the designated individual and who, at any time, was related to any individual beneficially interested in the trust,

(ii) where

(A) no individual may be designated in respect of the trust because of subparagraph (i),

(B) the designated individual transferred or loaned property (either directly or through another trust) to the trust at any time before the end of the relevant period, and

(C) the designated individual was born before all other individuals who

(I) at any time were related to any individual beneficially interested in the trust or to any individual who transferred or loaned property to the trust before the end of the relevant period, and

(II) transferred or loaned property (either directly or through another trust) to the trust at any time before the end of the relevant period, or

(iii) where throughout the relevant period the property of the trust consisted primarily of

(A) shares of the capital stock of a corporation

(I) controlled, on the day that the trust was created or at the beginning of the relevant period, by the designated individual or by the designated individual and one or more other individuals born after, and related to, the designated individual, or

(II) all or substantially all of the value of which throughout the relevant period derived from property transferred to the corporation by the designated individual or by the designated individual and one or more other individuals born after, and related to, the designated individual,

(B) shares of the capital stock of a corporation all or substantially all of the value of which, throughout the part of the relevant period throughout which the shares were held by the trust, derived from shares described in clause (A),

(C) property substituted for the shares described in clause (A) or (B),

(D) property attributable to profits, gains or distributions in respect of property described in clause (A), (B) or (C), or

(E) any combination of the properties described in clauses (A) to (D).

**Related Provisions**: 104(5.7) — Designated contributor; 248(5) — Substituted property; 248(9.1) — Trust created by taxpayer's will.

**Notes**: 104(5.6) added by 1992 technical bill, effective February 12, 1991.

**(5.7) Idem** — For the purposes of subsection (5.6),

(a) the relevant period in respect of a trust is the period that begins one year after the day on which the trust was created and ends at the end of the day that would, but for the election of the trust under subsection (5.3), be determined in respect of the trust under paragraph (4)(a.1) or (b), as the case may be;

(b) 2 individuals shall be deemed to be related to each other where one of them is the aunt, great aunt, uncle or great uncle of the other individual;

(c) an individual shall be deemed not to be a designated contributor in respect of a trust where it is reasonable to consider that one of the main purposes of a series of transactions or events that includes

(i) an individual becoming a trustee in respect of trust property, or

(ii) an acquisition of property or a borrowing by any individual

was to defer the day determined under paragraph (4)(b) in respect of the trust; and

(d) in determining whether all or substantially all of the value of shares of the capital stock of a corporation is derived from other property, the other property shall be deemed to include property substituted for the other property and property attributable to profits, gains or distributions in respect of the other property and the substituted property.

**Related Provisions**: 248(5) — Substituted property.

**Notes**: 104(5.7) added by 1992 technical bill, effective February 12, 1991.

**(5.8) Trust transfers** — Where capital property (other than excluded property), land included in inventory, Canadian resource property or foreign resource property is transferred at a particular time by a trust (in this subsection referred to as the "transferor trust") to another trust (in this subsection referred to as the "transferee trust") in circumstances in which paragraph (e) of the definition "disposition" in section 54 or subsection 107(2) applies,

### Proposed Amendment — 104(5.8) opening words

**(5.8) Trust transfers** — Where capital property (other than excluded property), land included in inventory, Canadian resource property or foreign resource property is transferred at a particular time by a trust (in this subsection referred to as the "transferor trust") to another trust (in this subsection referred to as the "transferee trust") in circumstances in which subsection 107(2) or 107.4(3) or paragraph (f) of the definition "disposition" in subsection 248(1) applies,

**Application**: Bill C-43 (First Reading September 20, 2000), subsec. 48(10), will amend the opening words of subsec. 104(5.8) to read as above, applicable to transfers made after February 11, 1991 except that, for transfers made before December 24, 1998, the opening words shall be read as follows:

(5.8) Where capital property (other than excluded property), land included in inventory, Canadian resource property or foreign resource property is transferred at a particular time by a trust (in this subsection referred to as the "transferor trust") to another trust (in this subsection referred to as the "transferee trust") in circumstances in which paragraph (e) of the definition "disposition" in section 54 or subsection 107(2) applies and the transferee trust is not described in paragraph (g) of the definition "trust" in subsection 108(1),

**Technical Notes**: Subsection 104(5.8) of the Act is a special rule designed to prevent the avoidance of the 21-year rule through the use of trust-to-trust transfers that do not involve dispositions of property at fair market value. Subsection 104(5.8) generally provides for a transferee trust to assume the next deemed disposition day of the transferor, if that day is earlier than the transferee's next deemed disposition day. In the case of spousal trusts under which the beneficiary spouse is still alive, subsection 104(5.8) provides a deemed disposition as soon as the transfer is completed unless relief is provided under paragraph 104(5.8)(b). Paragraph 104(5.8)(b) provides relief where both the transferor and transferee trusts are spousal trusts to which paragraph 104(4)(a) or (a.1) applies and under which the spouse beneficiary is alive.

Subsection 104(5.8) is amended to eliminate a reference to trust transfers under paragraph (e) of the definition "disposition" in section 54, as a consequence of the repeal of that definition. Subsection 104(5.8) is also amended so that it now covers transfers under new paragraph (f) of the definition "disposition" in subsection 248(1) and under new subsection 107.4(3). These amendments apply to transfers made after December 23, 1998.

Subsection 104(5.8) is amended so that it does not apply to transfers between trusts, if the transferee trust was, at the time of the transfer, described in paragraph (g) of the definition "trust" in subsection 108(1). This amendment, which is made as a consequence of the introduction of subparagraph (g)(iv) of that definition, applies only to transfers made after February 11, 1991 and before December 24, 1998. Subparagraph (g)(iv) of that definition has the effect of limiting an exemption from the 21-year deemed disposition rule for a trust in which interests are vested indefeasibly, in the event that non-resident beneficiaries own more than 20% of the interests in the trust.

These amendments also reflect changes [re common-law partners — ed.] proposed under Bill C-23, the *Modernization of Benefits and Obligations Act*.

(a) for the purposes of applying subsections (4) to (5.2) after the particular time,

(i) subject to paragraph (b), the first day (in this subsection referred to as the "disposition day") ending at or after the particular time determined under subsection (4) in respect of the transferee trust shall be deemed to be the earliest of

### Proposed Amendment — 104(5.8)(a)(i) opening words

(i) subject to paragraphs (b) to (b.2), the first day (in this subsection referred to as the "disposition day") that ends at or after the particular time that would, if this section were read without reference to paragraph (4)(a.2) and (a.3), be determined in respect of the transferee trust is deemed to be the earliest of

**Application**: Bill C-43 (First Reading September 20, 2000), subsec. 48(11), will amend the opening words of subpara. 104(5.8)(a)(i) to read as above, applicable to transfers made after December 17, 1999.

**Technical Notes**: Subparagraph 104(5.8)(a)(i) is amended to ensure that the determination of a deemed disposition day for a transferee trust will not preclude any earlier deemed disposition day under new paragraph 104(4)(a.2) or (a.3). This amendment applies to transfers made after December 17, 1999.

(A) the first day ending at or after the particular time that would be determined under subsection (4) in respect of the transferor trust without regard to the transfer and any transaction or event occurring after the particular time,

(B) the first day ending at or after the particular time that would otherwise be determined under subsection (4) in respect of the transferee trust without regard to any transaction or event occurring after the particular time,

(C) where the transferor trust is a trust that is described in paragraph (4)(a) or the definition "pre-1972 spousal trust" in subsection 108(1) and the spouse or common-law partner referred to in that paragraph or definition is alive at the particular time, the first day ending at or after the particular time, and

### Proposed Amendment — 104(5.8)(a)(i)(C)

(C) the first day that ends at or after the particular time, where

(I) the transferor trust is a joint partner trust, a post-1971 partner trust or a trust described in the definition "pre-1972 spousal trust" in subsection 108(1), and

(II) the spouse or common-law partner referred to in paragraph (4)(a) or in the definition "pre-1972 spousal trust" in subsection 108(1) is alive at the particular time,

(C.1) the first day that ends at or after the particular time, where

(I) the transferor trust is an *alter ego* trust or joint partner trust; and

(II) the taxpayer referred to in paragraph (4)(a) is alive at the particular time, and

**Application**: Bill C-43 (First Reading September 20, 2000), subsec. 48(12), will amend cl. 104(5.8)(a)(i)(C) to read as above, and add cl. (C.1), applicable to transfers made after 1999.

**Technical Notes**: Subsection 104(5.8) is further amended to extend its existing rules for transfers from spousal trusts to transfers from other specified trusts. The additional trusts so specified are those created after 1999 by a settlor (aged 65 years or more) for the exclusive benefit of the settlor during the settlor's lifetime (i.e., an "*alter ego* trust", as newly defined in subsection 248(1)) or for the joint benefit of the settlor and the settlor's spouse during their joint lifetimes (i.e., a "joint partner trust", as newly defined in subsection 248(1)). Where the settlor of an alter ego trust is still alive (or, in the case of a joint partner trust, where the settlor or the spouse is still alive), a deemed disposition day for the trust may occur once a transfer from the trust is completed. However, amended paragraph 104(5.8)(b) and new paragraphs 104(5.8)(b.1) and (b.2) provide for no deemed disposition day in the case of a transfer from one of the additional specified trusts where the transferee trust is also a specified trust to which paragraph 104(4)(a) applies and the settlor (or, in the case of a joint partner trust, either the settlor or that spouse) is alive. These amendments apply to transfers made after 1999. For further detail on new rules for alter ego trusts and joint partner trusts, see the commentary on amended subsection 73(1) and paragraph 104(4)(a).

(D) where

(I) the disposition day would, but for the application of this subsection to the transfer, be determined under paragraph (5.3)(a) in respect of the transferee trust, and

(II) the particular time is after the day that would, but for subsection (5.3), be determined under paragraph (4)(b) in respect of the transferee trust,

the first day ending at or after the particular time, and

Subdivision k — Trusts and Beneficiaries    S. 104(6)(a.2)

(ii) where the disposition day determined in respect of the transferee trust under subparagraph (i) is earlier than the day referred to in clause (i)(B) in respect of the transferee trust, subsections (4) to (5.2) do not apply to the transferee trust on the day referred to in clause (i)(B) in respect of the transferee trust;

(b) where the transferor trust is a trust (in this paragraph referred to as an "eligible trust") that is described in paragraph (4)(a) or the definition "pre-1972 spousal trust" in subsection 108(1) and the spouse or common-law partner referred to in that paragraph or definition is alive at the particular time, paragraph (a) does not apply in respect of the transfer where the transferee trust is an eligible trust; and

### Proposed Amendment — 104(5.8)(b)–(b.2)

(b) paragraph (a) does not apply in respect of the transfer where

(i) the transferor trust is a post-1971 partner trust or a trust described in the definition "pre-1972 spousal trust" in subsection 108(1),

(ii) the spouse or common-law partner referred to in paragraph (4)(a) or in the definition "pre-1972 spousal trust" in subsection 108(1) is alive at the particular time, and

(iii) the transferee trust is a post-1971 partner trust or a trust described in the definition "pre-1972 spousal trust" in subsection 108(1);

(b.1) paragraph (a) does not apply in respect of the transfer where

(i) the transferor trust is an *alter ego* trust,

(ii) the taxpayer referred to in paragraph (4)(a) is alive at the particular time, and

(iii) the transferee trust is an *alter ego* trust;

(b.2) paragraph (a) does not apply in respect of the transfer where

(i) the transferor trust is a joint partner trust,

(ii) either the taxpayer referred to in paragraph (4)(a), or the spouse or common-law partner referred to in that paragraph, is alive at the particular time, and

(iii) the transferee trust is a joint partner trust; and

**Application**: Bill C-43 (First Reading September 20, 2000), subsec. 48(13), will amend para. 104(5.8)(b) to read as above, and add paras. (b.1) and (b.2), applicable to transfers made after 1999.

**Technical Notes**: See under 104(5.8)(a)(i)(C).

(c) for the purposes of subsection (5.3), unless a day ending before the particular time has been determined under paragraph (4)(a.1) or (b) or would, but for subsection (5.3), have been so determined, a day determined under subparagraph (a)(i) shall be deemed to be a day determined under paragraph (4)(a.1) or (b), as the case may be, in respect of the transferee trust.

**Related Provisions**: 248(5.2) — Trust-to-trust transfers.

**Notes**: 104(5.8) amended by 2000 same-sex partners bill to add reference to "common-law partner", effective for the 2001 and later taxation years, or earlier by election (see Notes to 248(1)"common-law partner").

104(5.8) added by 1992 technical bill, effective for property transferred after December 20, 1991. For property transferred from February 12, 1991 through December 20, 1991, read (5.8)(b) as:

(b) where the transferor trust or the transferee trust is a trust that is described in paragraph (4)(a) or the definition "pre-1972 spousal trust" in subsection 108(1) and the spouse referred to therein is alive at the particular time, paragraph (a) does not apply in respect of the transfer; and

104(5.8) prevents the avoidance of the 21-year deemed realization rule through the use of trust transfers.

**(6) Deduction in computing income of trust** — For the purposes of this Part, there may be deducted in computing the income of a trust for a taxation year

### Proposed Amendment — 104(6) opening words

**(6) Deduction in computing income of trust** — Subject to subsections (7) and (7.01), for the purposes of this Part, there may be deducted in computing the income of a trust for a taxation year

**Application**: The June 22, 2000 draft legislation, subsec. 14(3), will amend the opening words of subsec. 104(6) to read as above, applicable to trust taxation years that begin after 2000.

**Technical Notes**: Subsection 104(6) of the Act generally permits a trust to deduct, in computing income for a taxation year, any income payable to a beneficiary under the trust.

Subsection 104(6) is amended so that it is expressly subject to subsection 104(7) and new subsection 104(7.01).

(a) in the case of an employee trust, the amount by which the amount that would, but for this subsection, be its income for the year exceeds the amount, if any, by which

(i) the total of all amounts each of which is its income for the year from a business

exceeds

(ii) the total of all amounts each of which is its loss for the year from a business;

(a.1) in the case of a trust governed by an employee benefit plan, such part of the amount that would, but for this subsection, be its income for the year as was paid in the year to a beneficiary;

(a.2) where the taxable income of the trust for the year is subject to tax under this Part because of paragraph 146(4)(c) or subsection 146.3(3.1), the part of the amount that, but for this subsection, would be the income of the trust for the year that was paid in the year to a beneficiary; and

### Proposed Addition — 104(6)(a.3)

(a.3) in the case of an *inter vivos* trust deemed by subsection 143(1) to exist in respect of a congregation that is a constituent part of a religious organization, such part of its income for the year as became payable in the year to a beneficiary; and

**Application**: Bill C-43 (First Reading September 20, 2000), subsec. 48(14), will add para. 104(6)(a.3), applicable to 1998 *et seq.*

**Technical Notes**: Subsection 104(6) of the Act generally allows a trust to deduct an amount for a taxation year not exceeding its income for the year that became payable to its beneficiaries. However, in the case of spousal trusts there are restrictions designed to ensure that a spousal trust cannot claim a deduction under subsection 104(6) in respect of income allocated to non-spouse beneficiaries to the extent the income accrues during the lifetime of the spouse beneficiary. (With regard to income for the year in which a spouse beneficiary dies, this restriction only applies in connection with income from dispositions of capital property, land inventory and Canadian and foreign resource property that occur before the end of the deemed disposition day caused by the spouse's death.) There is also a restriction in subsection 104(6) designed to limit the extent to which a trust can claim a deduction in respect of distributions by the trust of amounts paid to the trust from the trust's NISA Fund No. 2 (as defined in subsection 248(1)).

Paragraph 104(6)(a.3) is introduced so that the restrictions with regard to a trust's NISA Fund No. 2 do not apply to any trust deemed to exist because of the special rules for communal organizations in section 143.

    (b) in any other case, such amount as the trust claims not exceeding the amount, if any, by which

        (i) such part of the amount that, but for

            (A) this subsection,

            (B) subsections (5.1), (12), and 107(4),

            (C) the application of subsections (4), (5) and (5.2) in respect of a day determined under paragraph (4)(a), and

            (D) subsection 12(10.2), except to the extent that that subsection applies to amounts paid to a trust described in paragraph 70(6.1)(b) and before the death of the spouse or common-law partner referred to in that paragraph,

would be its income for the year as became payable in the year to a beneficiary or was included under subsection 105(2) in computing the income of a beneficiary

exceeds

        (ii) where the trust

            (A) is described in paragraph (4)(a) and was created after December 20, 1991, or

            (B) would be described in paragraph (4)(a) if the reference therein to "at the time it was created" were read as "on December 20, 1991"

### Proposed Amendment — 104(6)(b)(ii)(A), (B)

            (A) is a post-1971 partner trust that was created after December 20, 1991, or

            (B) would be a post-1971 partner trust if the reference in paragraph (4)(a) to "at the time it was created" were read as "on December 20, 1991",

**Application**: Bill C-43 (First Reading September 20, 2000), subsec. 48(15), will amend cls. 104(6)(b)(ii)(A) and (B) to read as above, applicable to 2000 *et seq.*

**Technical Notes**: Paragraph 104(6)(b) is amended to extend the restrictions for spousal trusts to other specified trusts created after 1999. The trusts so specified are those created after 1999 by a settlor (aged 65 years or more) for the exclusive benefit of the settlor during the settlor's lifetime (i.e., an "*alter ego* trust", as newly defined in subsection 248(1)) or for the joint benefit of the settlor and the settlor's spouse during their joint lifetimes (i.e., a "joint partner trust", as newly defined in subsection 248(1)). The restrictions for *alter ego* trusts apply until the death of the settlor. The restrictions for joint partner trusts apply until the later of the death of the settlor and the death of the spouse. For further detail on new rules for these specified trusts, see the commentary on amended subsection 73(1) and paragraph 104(4)(a). This amendment applies to the 2000 and subsequent taxation years.

Clauses 104(6)(b)(ii)(A) and (B) are amended to refer to a post-1971 partner trust, strictly as a consequence of the new definition of this term contained in subsection 248(1). For further detail, see the commentary on amended subsection 248(1). This amendment applies to the 2000 and subsequent taxation years.

and the spouse or common-law partner referred to in paragraph (4)(a) in respect of the trust is alive throughout the year, such part of the amount that, but for

            (C) this subsection,

            (D) subsections (12) and 107(4), and

            (E) subsection 12(10.2), except to the extent that that subsection applies to an amount paid to a trust described in paragraph 70(6.1)(b) and before the death of the spouse or common-law partner referred to in that paragraph,

would be its income for the year as became payable in the year to a beneficiary (other than the spouse or common-law partner) or was included under subsection 105(2) in computing the income of a beneficiary (other than the spouse or common-law partner) and

### Proposed Addition — 104(6)(b)(ii.1)

        (ii.1) where the trust is an *alter ego* trust or a joint partner trust and the death or later death, as the case may be, referred to in subparagraph (4)(a)(iv) has not occurred before the end of the year, such part of the amount that, but for this subsection and subsections (12), 12(10.2) and 107(4), would be its income as became payable in the year to a

## Subdivision k — Trusts and Beneficiaries — S. 104(6)

beneficiary (other than a taxpayer, spouse or common-law partner referred to in clause (4)(a)(iv)(A), (B) or (C)) or was included under subsection 105(2) in computing the income of a beneficiary (other than such a taxpayer, spouse or common-law partner), and

**Application**: Bill C-43 (First Reading September 20, 2000), subsec. 48(16), will add subpara. 104(6)(b)(ii.1), applicable to 2000 *et seq.*

**Technical Notes**: See under 104(6)(b)(iii).

(iii) where the trust is described in paragraph (4)(a) and the spouse or common-law partner referred to in paragraph (4)(a) in respect of the trust died on a day in the year, the part of the amount that, but for

(A) this subsection, and

(B) subsections (12) and 107(4)

would be the part of its income for the year that became payable in the year to a beneficiary (other than the spouse or common-law partner) and as is attributable to one or more dispositions by the trust before the end of that day of capital properties (other than excluded properties), land described in an inventory of the trust, Canadian resource properties or foreign resource properties.

### Proposed Amendment — 104(6)(b)(iii)

(iii) where the trust is an *alter ego* trust, a joint partner trust or a post-1971 partner trust and the death or the later death, as the case may be, referred to in paragraph (4)(a) in respect of the trust occurred on a day in the year, the amount, if any, by which

(A) the maximum amount that would be deductible under this subsection in computing the trust's income for the year if this subsection were read without reference to this subparagraph

exceeds the total of

(B) the amount that, but for this subsection and subsections (12), 12(10.2) and 107(4), would be its income as became payable in the year to the taxpayer, spouse or common-law partner referred to in subparagraph (4)(a)(iii) or clause (4)(a)(iv)(A), (B) or (C), as the case may be, and

(C) the amount that would be the trust's income for the year if that income were computed without reference to this subsection and subsection (12) and as if the year began immediately after the end of the day,

**Application**: Bill C-43 (First Reading September 20, 2000), subsec. 48(16), will amend subpara. 104(6)(b)(iii) to read as above, applicable to 2000 *et seq.*

**Technical Notes**: Subparagraph 104(6)(b)(iii) is amended to extend the restrictions for deductions under subsection 104(6) in the taxation year in which the relevant beneficiary dies. The intended effect of the new restrictions is that post-1971 partner trusts, *alter ego* trusts and joint partner trusts cannot deduct an amount under subsection 104(6) in respect of income accrued up to the end of the deemed disposition day caused by the death of the spouse or other relevant beneficiary. This amendment applies to the 2000 and subsequent taxation years.

These amendments also reflect changes [re common-law partners — ed.] proposed under Bill C-23, the *Modernization of Benefits and Obligations Act.*

*EXAMPLE*

The spouse beneficiary of a post-1971 partner trust dies in the 2001 taxation year of the trust. Before distribution to beneficiaries, the trust's total income for the year (determined without reference to any deemed disposition under subsection 104(4) and any deduction under subsection 104(6)) is $100, of which $20 is payable to the spouse prior to the spouse's death and of which the remaining $80 is payable to the surviving beneficiaries. $40 of the $100 income accrued before the spouse's death.

Results:

1. Under subparagraph 104(6)(b)(i) the trust's income for the year that became payable in the year to beneficiaries is $100.

2. The amount determined under subparagraph 104(6)(b)(iii) is $20 (i.e., [$100 − ($20 + $60)]).

3. The total amount deductible by the trust cannot exceed the amount by which the amount determined under subparagraph 104(6)(b)(i) exceeds the amount determined under subparagraph 104(6)(b)(iii).

4. Consequently, the trust's maximum deduction for the year is $80 (i.e., $100 − $20). The trust is not allowed a deduction in respect of the $20 portion of trust income accrued to the end of the deemed disposition day caused by the spouse's death but payable only after the death.

**Related Provisions**: 4(3)(b) — Whether deductions under 104(6) are applicable to a particular source; 104(5.3) — Election by trust to postpone deemed disposition; 104(7) — Non-resident beneficiary; 104(7.1) — Deduction denied — capital interest greater than income interest; 104(10) — Property owned for non-resident; 104(13) — Income inclusion to beneficiary; 104(13.1), (13.2) — Designation of income distributed to beneficiary; 104(18) — Trust for minor; 104(24) — Whether amount payable; 104(29) — Amounts deemed to be payable to beneficiaries; 107(2.11) — Election to not flow out gain on distribution to beneficiaries; 107.1 — Distribution by employee trust or benefit plan; 108(5) — Restriction on deduction for beneficiary; 132.11(6) — Additional income of mutual fund trust electing for December 15 year-end; 138.1(1) — Rules re segregated funds; 149.1(12) — Rules — charities; 210.2 — Tax on income of trust.

**Notes**: The essence of 104(6) for ordinary trusts is 104(6)(b)(i) closing words — a trust can deduct amounts of income payable to beneficiaries, who include such income under 104(13). (By making a preferred beneficiary election under 104(14), a trust can also deduct under 104(12) amounts allocated to disabled "preferred beneficiaries" that are included in those beneficiaries' income without actually being paid.) Once either the trust or the beneficiary has paid tax on the trust's income, that income is "capitalized" and can be paid to beneficiaries free of tax (just as a beneficiary can receive any capital of the trust).

The deduction under 104(6)(b) is for "such amount as the trust claims". A trust might claim less than the maximum in order to keep

S. 104(6)  Income Tax Act, Part I, Division B

income taxed at the trust level (for example, to use up loss carryforwards). It can then make a tax-free distribution to beneficiaries under 104(13.1) or (13.2).

104(6) amended by 2000 same-sex partners bill to add reference to "common-law partner", effective for the 2001 and later taxation years, or earlier by election (see Notes to 248(1)"common-law partner").

104(6)(a.2) added by 1995-97 technical bill, effective for 1996 and later taxation years. Once a trust governed by an RRSP or RRIF is no longer exempt from tax after the death of the annuitant, only trust income actually paid (not just payable) to a beneficiary in a taxation year is deductible from the trust's income. Because 104(13) does not apply to such trusts, such amounts paid are included in income under 146(8) or 146.3(5).

104(6)(b)(iii) added by 1995 Budget, effective for trust taxation years that end after July 19, 1995. It provides that, where the beneficiary spouse under a post-1971 spousal trust (see 104(4)(a)) died on a day in the trust's taxation year, the trust is not allowed to deduct income for that year that is payable to a beneficiary (other than the deceased spouse) that relates to any disposition by the trust, before the end of that day, of capital property (other than excluded properties), land described in an inventory of the trust, Canadian resource property or foreign resource property. The purpose is to ensure that the gains recognition for spousal trusts under 104(4), (5) and (5.2) cannot be avoided by actual dispositions by the trust before the beneficiary spouse dies.

104(6)(b) amended by 1992 technical bill, effective for trusts' taxation years that end after December 20, 1991.

**Interpretation Bulletins**: IT-85R2: Health and welfare trusts for employees; IT-286R2: Trusts — amount payable; IT-342R: Trusts — income payable to beneficiaries; IT-381R3: Trusts — capital gains and losses and the flow-through of taxable capital gains to beneficiaries; IT-394R2: Preferred beneficiary election; IT-465R — Non-resident beneficiaries of trusts; IT-493: Agency cooperative corporations; IT-500R: RRSPs — death of annuitant; IT-502: Employee benefit plans and employee trusts.

**I.T. Technical News**: No. 11 (payments made by a trust for the benefit of a minor beneficiary).

**Advance Tax Rulings**: ATR-65: Reduction to management fees for large investments in a mutual fund.

**(7) Non-resident beneficiary** — No deduction may be made under subsection (6) in computing the income for a taxation year of a trust in respect of such part of an amount that would otherwise be its income for the year as became payable in the year to a beneficiary who was, at any time in the year, a designated beneficiary of the trust (as that expression applies for the purposes of section 210.3) unless, throughout the year, the trust was resident in Canada.

**Related Provisions**: 104(24) — Whether amount payable; 212(1)(c) — Withholding tax on payment to non-resident beneficiary; 250(6.1) — Trust that ceases to exist deemed resident throughout year.

**Interpretation Bulletins**: IT-393R2: Election re tax on rents and timber royalties — non-residents.

### Proposed Addition — 104(7.01)

**(7.01) Trusts deemed to be resident in Canada** — Where a trust is deemed by subsection 94(3) to be resident in Canada for a taxation year for the purpose of computing the trust's income for the year, the maximum amount deductible under subsection (6) in computing its income for the year is deemed to be the amount, if any, by which

(a) the maximum amount that, but for this subsection, would be deductible under subsection (6) in computing its income for the year,

exceeds the lesser of

(b) the total of

(i) the designated income of the trust for the year (within the meaning assigned by subsection 210.2(2)), and

(ii) all amounts each of which is 50% of an amount paid or credited in the year to the trust that would, if this Act were read without reference to subparagraph 94(3)(a)(iii) and sections 216 and 217, be an amount as a consequence of the payment or crediting of which the trust would have been liable to tax under Part XIII, and

(c) the amount, if any, by which

(i) the maximum amount that, but for this subsection, would be deductible under subsection (6) in computing its income for the year

exceeds

(ii) the maximum amount that would be deductible in computing its income for the year if this section were read without reference to this subsection and if the only amounts that became payable in the year to a beneficiary were amounts that became payable in the year to

(A) a partnership (other than a partnership that is a Canadian partnership on the day that would be determined under paragraph 214(3)(f) in respect of the amount if the assumptions set out in subparagraph (b)(ii) applied), or

(B) a non-resident person on the day that would be determined under paragraph 214(3)(f) in respect of the amount if the assumptions set out in subparagraph (b)(ii) applied.

**Application**: The June 22, 2000 draft legislation, subsec. 14(4), will add subsec. 104(7.01), applicable to trust taxation years that begin after 2000.

**Technical Notes**: New subsection 104(7.01) of the Act restricts the amount that a trust, that is deemed by subsection 94(3) to be resident in Canada, can deduct in computing its income in the event that the trust has Canadian-source income and makes distributions to beneficiaries not resident in Canada.

Subsection 104(7.01) effectively acts as a proxy for taxes under Parts XII.2 and XIII. Trusts to which new subsection 94(3) applies are not subject to Part XII.2 because of an existing exemption for non-resident trusts in Part XII.2. They are also exempt from collecting Part XIII tax because they are not treated as resident in Canada for this purpose. Further, because of new subparagraph 94(3)(a)(iii), they are exempt from Part XIII tax on pay-

Subdivision k — Trusts and Beneficiaries    S. 104(10)

ments made to them. (The latter Part XIII exemption is new. Existing subparagraph 94(1)(c)(ii) allows a tax credit to be claimed under section 126 in connection with Part XIII tax.)

More specifically, the amount by which the maximum deduction under subsection 104(6) for a taxation year is reduced under subsection 104(7.01) is equal to the lesser of two amounts:

- the total of
  - the trust's "designated income" for the year (as defined in Part XII.2), which essentially consists of taxable capital gains from taxable Canadian property and income from businesses carried on in Canada, and
  - 50% of all amounts paid or credited in the year to the trust that would, disregarding express provisions to the contrary in the Act, be subject to Part XIII tax; and
- the portion of the maximum deduction under subsection 104(6) that is attributable to amounts that become payable in the year (determined with reference to subsection 104(24)) to non-resident persons and to partnerships (other than Canadian partnerships, referred to in section 102).

The example below illustrates the operation of new subsection 104(7.01).

*Example*

1. Trust X is an offshore trust established by Stefan, a long-term resident of Canada. The primary beneficiaries under the trust are Linda (a resident of Canada) and Bart (a resident of the United States).
2. Trust X receives $400 of dividends from a taxable Canadian corporation and has $1,200 of other income.
3. Trust income of $1,250 for 2001 is made payable to Bart. The remaining $350 is made payable to Linda.
4. Trust X is assumed to have designated $400 of dividends under subsection 104(19).

*Results*

1. Trust X is deemed by new subsection 94(3) to be resident in Canada for the purposes of computing its income.
2. Before taking into account subsection 104(6), Trust X's income is $1,600. Note, in this regard, that the dividends are included in computing the trust's income because of a proposed amendment to subsection 104(19). [This refers to an amendment to subsection 104(19) contained in a detailed Notice of Ways and Means Motion tabled on June 5, 2000.]
3. Before taking into account new subsection 104(7.01), the maximum deduction under subsection 104(6) is also $1,600.
4. Because of subsection 104(7.01), the maximum deduction under subsection 104(6) is reduced to $1,400 (i.e., $1,600 minus the lesser of: (50% × $400) and ($1,600 - $1,250)).
5. Assuming that the trust claims a deduction of $1,400, the trust would consequently have income of $200. If a tax rate of 50% were assumed, the trust would be liable for Canadian income tax of $100. (Note: The trust is expressly exempted from a Part XIII tax liability under new subparagraph 94(3)(a)(iii).) Disregard-ing this exemption, Part XIII tax liability would also have been $100 (i.e., 25% of $400).

New subsection 104(7.01) applies to trust taxation years that begin after 2000.

**Related Provisions**: 104(24) — Whether amount payable.

### (7.1) Capital interest greater than income interest
— Where it is reasonable to consider that one of the main purposes for the existence of any term, condition, right or other attribute of an interest in a trust (other than a personal trust) is to give a beneficiary a percentage interest in the property of the trust that is greater than the beneficiary's percentage interest in the income of the trust, no amount may be deducted under paragraph (6)(b) in computing the income of the trust.

**Related Provisions**: 104(7.2) — Anti-avoidance rule.

**Notes**: 104(7.1) added in 1986 and amended retroactively by 1988 tax reform. It does not apply to a trust created before November 26, 1985 in which no beneficial interest is issued after 5 p.m. EST on November 26, 1985 (other than an interest issued on account of a distribution of the income of the trust in accordance with the terms of the trust in effect on November 26, 1985).

**Interpretation Bulletins**: IT-381R3: Trusts — capital gains and losses and the flow-through of taxable capital gains to beneficiaries.

**Advance Tax Rulings**: ATR-65: Reduction to management fees for large investments in a mutual fund.

### (7.2) Avoidance of subsec. (7.1) — Notwithstanding any other provision of this Act, where

(a) a taxpayer has acquired a right to or to acquire an interest in a trust, or a right to or to acquire a property of a trust, and

(b) it is reasonable to consider that one of the main purposes of the acquisition was to avoid the application of subsection (7.1) in respect of the trust,

on a disposition of the right (other than pursuant to the exercise thereof), the interest or the property, there shall be included in computing the income of the taxpayer for the taxation year in which the disposition occurs the amount, if any, by which

(c) the proceeds of disposition of the right, interest or property, as the case may be,

exceed

(d) the cost amount to the taxpayer of the right, interest or property, as the case may be.

### (8), (9) [Repealed under former Act]

**Notes**: 104(8), repealed by 1988 tax reform (effective 1988), denied a deduction under 104(6) for distributions to designated beneficiaries. It has been replaced by the tax in Part XII.2 (210 to 210.2).

104(9) repealed effective 1974.

### (10) Where property owned for non-residents
— Where all the property of a trust is owned by the trustee for the benefit of non-resident persons or their unborn issue, in addition to the amount that may be deducted under subsection (6), there may be deducted in computing the income of the trust for a taxation year for the purposes of this

Part, such part of the dividends and interest received by the trust in a year from a non-resident-owned investment corporation as are not deductible under that subsection in computing the income of the trust for the year.

**Related Provisions**: 104(11) — Dividend received from non-resident-owned investment corporation; 212(9) — Exemptions from withholding tax.

**(11) Dividend received from non-resident-owned investment corporation** — Where any part of the dividends received in a taxation year by a trust described in subsection (10) from a non-resident-owned investment corporation are deductible under that subsection in computing the income of the trust for the year, for the purposes of Part XIII the trust shall be deemed to have paid to a non-resident person on the last day of the year an amount equal to that part, as income of the non-resident person from the trust.

**Related Provisions**: 212(1)(c) — Estate or trust income; 212(9) — Exemptions from non-resident withholding tax.

**(12) Deduction of amounts included in preferred beneficiaries' incomes** — There may be deducted in computing the income of a trust for a taxation year the lesser of

(a) the total of all amounts designated under subsection (14) by the trust in respect of the year, and

(b) the accumulating income of the trust for the year.

**Related Provisions**: 4(3)(b) — Whether deductions under 104(12) are applicable to a particular source; 104(6) — Deduction in computing trust income; 104(13) — Income payable to beneficiary; 108(1) — Accumulating income defined; 108(5) — Restriction on deduction for beneficiary; 149.1(12) — Rules — charities.

**Notes**: See Notes to 104(6) and 104(14).

104(12) amended by 1995 Budget, effective for trust taxation years that begin after 1995. The amendment, which is consequential on amendments to 104(14) and (15), ensures that the amount deductible in computing the trust's income for a taxation year does not exceed its "accumulating income" (see 108(1)) for the year. For earlier taxation years since 1972, read:

> (12) Deduction of part of accumulating income included in preferred beneficiary's income — For the purposes of this Part, there may be deducted in computing the income of a trust for a taxation year such part of its accumulating income for the year as was required by subsection (14) to be included in computing the income of a preferred beneficiary.

**Interpretation Bulletins**: IT-381R3: Trusts — capital gains and losses and the flow-through of taxable capital gains to beneficiaries; IT-394R2: Preferred beneficiary election; IT-465R: Non-resident beneficiaries of trusts; IT-500R: RRSPs — death of an annuitant.

**Advance Tax Rulings**: ATR-34: Preferred beneficiary's election.

**(13) Income of beneficiary** — There shall be included in computing the income for a taxation year of a beneficiary under a trust such of the following amounts as are applicable:

(a) in the case of a trust (other than a trust referred to in paragraph (a) of the definition "trust" in subsection 108(1)) that was resident in Canada throughout its particular taxation year that ended in the year, such part of the amount that, but for subsections (6) and (12), would be the trust's income for the particular year as became payable in the particular year to the beneficiary;

(b) in the case of a trust governed by an employee benefit plan to which the beneficiary has contributed as an employer, such part of the amount that, but for subsections (6) and (12), would be the income of the trust for its particular taxation year that ended in the year as was paid in the particular year to the beneficiary; and

(c) in the case of a trust (other than a trust referred to in paragraph (a) or paragraph (a) of the definition "trust" in subsection 108(1)), all amounts that became payable in the year by the trust to the beneficiary in respect of the beneficiary's interest in the trust, otherwise than

(i) as proceeds of disposition of the beneficiary's interest or part thereof, or

(ii) an amount paid as a distribution of capital by a personal trust.

**Proposed Amendment — 104(13)**

**(13) Income of beneficiary** — There shall be included in computing the income for a particular taxation year of a beneficiary under a trust such of the following amounts as are applicable:

(a) in the case of a trust (other than a trust referred to in paragraph (a) of the definition "trust" in subsection 108(1)), such part of the amount that, but for subsections (6) and (12), would be the trust's income for the trust's taxation year that ended in the particular year as became payable in the trust's year to the beneficiary; and

(b) in the case of a trust governed by an employee benefit plan to which the beneficiary has contributed as an employer, such part of the amount that, but for subsections (6) and (12), would be the trust's income for the trust's taxation year that ended in the particular year as was paid in the trust's year to the beneficiary.

**Application**: Bill C-43 (First Reading September 20, 2000), subsec. 48(17), will amend subsec. 104(13) to read as above, applicable to 2000 et seq.

**Technical Notes**: Subsection 104(13) of the Act sets out amounts included in computing the income of a beneficiary under a trust. Where a trust is not resident in Canada, paragraph 104(13)(c) provides that the beneficiary must include in computing income all amounts payable in respect of the beneficiary's interest in the trust, otherwise than as proceeds of disposition or amounts paid in satisfaction of the distribution of capital by a personal trust. There is uncertainty in this regard under the existing law, given that different types of distributions from a trust to a beneficiary might arguably be viewed as resulting in proceeds of disposition with respect to all or part of a beneficiary's interest in the trust.

Subsection 104(13) is amended so that it requires a beneficiary to include in income under that subsection only current income payable from a non-resident trust. For this purpose, a non-resident trust's income is intended to be determined in accordance with Canadian income tax rules. See also, in this regard, the commentary on new section 250.1.

**Related Provisions**: 6(1)(h) — Income from employee trust; 12(1)(m) — Income inclusion — benefits from trusts; 53(2)(h) — Reduction of ACB of beneficiary's interest re amount paid or payable by trust; 104(13.1), (13.2) — Designation of distributed income by trust; 104(18) — Trust for minor; 104(19) — Portion of taxable dividends deemed received by beneficiary; 104(21) — Portion of taxable capital gains deemed gain of beneficiary; 104(22)–(22.4) — Foreign tax credit allocation to beneficiary; 104(24) — Whether amount payable; 104(27) — Pension benefits; 104(29) — Flow-out of resource amounts; 104(31) — Amounts deemed payable to beneficiaries; 106(1) — Income interest in trust; 106(2)(a)(ii) — Reduction of income inclusion on disposition of income interest; 107(2.11) — Election to not flow out gain to beneficiaries on distribution; 107.1 — Distribution by employee trust or benefit plan; 107.3(4) — No application to qualifying environmental trusts; 108(5) — Amount deemed to be income from trust; 120.4(1)"split income"(c) — Certain trust income of children subject to income splitting tax; 132.11(4) — Amounts paid from December 16-31 by mutual fund trust to beneficiary; 132.11(6) — Additional income of MFT electing for December 15 year-end; 146(8.1) — RRSP — deemed receipt of refund of premiums; 210.2 — Tax on income of trust; 212(1)(c) — Non-resident withholding tax; 214(3)(f) — Non-resident withholding tax — deemed payments; 250(6.1) — Trust that ceases to exist deemed resident throughout year; 250.1(b) — Non-resident trust deemed to have income calculated under the Act.

**Interpretation Bulletins**: IT-75R3: Scholarships, fellowships, bursaries, prizes, and research grants; IT-201R2: Foreign tax credit — trust and beneficiaries; IT-243R4: Dividend refund to private corporations; IT-286R2: Trusts — amount payable; IT-342R: Trusts — income payable to beneficiaries; IT-381R3: Trusts — capital gains and losses and the flow-through of taxable capital gains to beneficiaries; IT-385R2: Disposition of an income interest in a trust; IT-465R: Non-resident beneficiaries of trusts; IT-500R: RRSPs — death of an annuitant; IT-502: Employee benefit plans and employee trusts; IT-524: Trusts — flow-through of taxable dividends to a beneficiary — after 1987; IT-531: Eligible funeral arrangements.

**I.T. Technical News**: No. 11 (payments made by a trust for the benefit of a minor beneficiary).

**Forms**: T4011: Preparing returns for deceased persons [guide].

**(13.1) Amounts deemed not paid** — Where a trust, in its return of income under this Part for a taxation year throughout which it was resident in Canada and not exempt from tax under Part I by reason of subsection 149(1), designates an amount in respect of a beneficiary under the trust, not exceeding the amount determined by the formula

$$\frac{A}{B} \times (C - D - E)$$

where

A is the beneficiary's share of the income of the trust for the year computed without reference to this Act,

B is the total of all amounts each of which is a beneficiary's share of the income of the trust for the year computed without reference to this Act,

C is the total of all amounts each of which is an amount that, but for this subsection or subsection (13.2), would be included in computing the income of a beneficiary under the trust by reason of subsection (13) or 105(2) for the year,

D is the amount deducted under subsection (6) in computing the income of the trust for the year, and

E is equal to the amount determined by the trust for the year and used as the value of C for the purposes of the formula in subsection (13.2) or, if no amount is so determined, nil,

the amount so designated shall be deemed, for the purposes of subsections (13) and 105(2), not to have been paid or to have become payable in the year to or for the benefit of the beneficiary or out of income of the trust.

**Related Provisions**: 94(3)(a) [proposed] — Application to trust deemed resident in Canada; 108(1) — "trust"; 250(6.1) — Trust that ceases to exist deemed resident throughout year; 257 — Formula cannot calculate to less than zero.

**Notes**: In *Lussier*, [2000] 2 C.T.C. 2147 (TCC), the Court allowed a letter from the taxpayer's accountant after the fact to amend the trust's income to designate an amount for 104(13.1), ruling that 104(13.1) did not prescribe any time period in which the designation had be made.

**Interpretation Bulletins**: IT-342R: Trusts — income payable to beneficiaries; IT-381R3: Trusts — capital gains and losses and the flow-through of taxable capital gains to beneficiaries; IT-394R2: Preferred beneficiary election.

**(13.2) Idem** — Where a trust, in its return of income under this Part for a taxation year throughout which it was resident in Canada and not exempt from tax under Part I by reason of subsection 149(1), designates an amount in respect of a beneficiary under the trust, not exceeding the amount determined by the formula

$$\frac{A}{B} \times C$$

where

A is the amount designated by the trust for the year in respect of the beneficiary under subsection (21),

B is the total of all amounts each of which has been designated for the year in respect of a beneficiary of the trust under subsection (21), and

C is the amount determined by the trust and used in computing all amounts each of which is designated by the trust for the year under this subsection, not exceeding the amount by which

(i) the total of all amounts each of which is an amount that, but for this subsection or subsection (13.1), would be included in computing the income of a beneficiary under the trust by reason of subsection (13) or 105(2) for the year

**S. 104(13.2)**     Income Tax Act, Part I, Division B

exceeds

   (ii) the amount deducted under subsection (6) in computing the income of the trust for the year,

the amount so designated shall

   (a) for the purposes of subsections (13) and 105(2) (except in the application of subsection (13) for the purposes of subsection (21)), be deemed not to have been paid or to have become payable in the year to or for the benefit of the beneficiaries or out of income of the trust; and

   (b) except for the purposes of subsection (21) as it applies for the purposes of subsections (21.1) and (21.2), reduce the amount of the taxable capital gains of the beneficiary otherwise included in computing the beneficiary's income for the year by reason of subsection (21).

**Related Provisions**: 94(3)(a) [proposed] — Application to trust deemed resident in Canada; 250(6.1) — Trust that ceases to exist deemed resident throughout year.

**Interpretation Bulletins**: IT-342R: Trusts — income payable to beneficiaries; IT-381R3: Trusts — capital gains and losses and the flow-through of taxable capital gains to beneficiaries.

**(14) Election by trust and preferred beneficiary** — Where a trust and a preferred beneficiary under the trust for a particular taxation year of the trust jointly so elect in respect of the particular year in prescribed manner, such part of the accumulating income of the trust for the particular year as is designated in the election, not exceeding the allocable amount for the preferred beneficiary in respect of the trust for the particular year, shall be included in computing the income of the preferred beneficiary for the beneficiary's taxation year in which the particular year ended and shall not be included in computing the income of any beneficiary of the trust for a subsequent taxation year.

**Related Provisions**: 12(1)(m) — Income inclusion — benefits from trusts; 94(3)(a) [proposed] — Application to trust deemed resident in Canada; 104(12) — Deduction for amount included in preferred beneficiary's income; 104(14.01), (14.02) — Late, amended or revoked election made with capital gains exemption election; 104(15) — Allocable amount; 104(19) — Portion of net taxable dividends deemed received by beneficiary; 104(21) — Portion of taxable capital gains deemed gain of beneficiary; 108(5) — Interpretation; 146(8.1) — RRSP — deemed receipt of refund premiums; 220(3.2), Reg. 600(b) — Late filing of election or revocation.

**Notes**: The preferred beneficiary election was, before 1996, a useful mechanism for splitting income by allocating income of a trust to certain beneficiaries. (The attribution rules in 74.1–74.5 must be considered, however.) After 1995 only a disabled person may be a "preferred beneficiary", although the 1997 budget relaxed slightly the definition of disabled persons who qualify (see 108(1)"preferred beneficiary"). Note also that if a person other than the settlor (including a beneficiary) contributes capital to the trust, the settlor may cease to be the "settlor" as defined in 108(1) and beneficiaries may thus cease to be "preferred beneficiaries" under 108(1).

Subsec. 220(3.2) and Reg. 600(b) permit the late filing of a preferred beneficiary election at the CCRA's discretion, but Agency officials do not often allow it.

104(14) amended by 1995 Budget, effective for trust taxation years that begin after 1995. For earlier taxation years since 1972, read:

   (14) Where a trust and a preferred beneficiary thereunder jointly so elect in respect of a taxation year in prescribed manner and within prescribed time, such part of the accumulating income of the trust for the year as is designated in the election, not exceeding the preferred beneficiary's share therein, shall be included in computing the income of the preferred beneficiary for the year, and shall not be included in computing the income of any beneficiary of the trust for a subsequent year in which it was paid.

The essence of the amendment was to change the reference to "preferred beneficiary's share" to "allocable amount" (see 104(15) for both terms). Note that the total allocable amounts for multiple preferred beneficiaries will typically exceed the trust's accumulating income. However, because of 104(12), there is no advantage to making elections under 104(14) in excess of the trust's accumulating income for the taxation year.

**Regulations**: 2800(1), (2) (prescribed manner, prescribed time).

**Interpretation Bulletins**: IT-201R2: Foreign tax credit — trust and beneficiaries; IT-243R4: Dividend refund to private corporations; IT-381R3: Trusts — capital gains and losses and the flow-through of taxable capital gains to beneficiaries; IT-394R2: Preferred beneficiary election; IT-500R: RRSPs — death of an annuitant; IT-524: Trusts — flow-through of taxable dividends to a beneficiary — after 1987.

**Information Circulars**: 92-1: Guidelines for accepting late, amended or revoked elections.

**Advance Tax Rulings**: ATR-30: Preferred beneficiary election on accumulating income of estate; ATR-34: Preferred beneficiary's election.

**(14.01) Late, amended or revoked election** — A trust and a preferred beneficiary under the trust may jointly make an election, or amend or revoke an election made, under subsection (14) where the election, amendment or revocation

   (a) is made solely because of an election or revocation to which subsection 110.6(25), (26) or (27) applies; and

   (b) is filed in prescribed manner with the Minister when the election or revocation referred to in paragraph (a) is filed.

**Related Provisions**: 104(14.02) — Effect of election.

**Notes**: 104(14.01) added by 1995-97 technical bill, effective for taxation years that include February 22, 1994.

**(14.02) Late, amended or revoked election** — Where a trust and a preferred beneficiary under the trust have made an election or amended or revoked an election in accordance with subsection (14.01),

   (a) the election or the amended election, as the case may be, is deemed to have been made on time for the purpose of subsection (14); and

   (b) the election that was revoked is deemed, otherwise than for the purposes of this subsection and subsection (14.01), never to have been made.

**Notes**: 104(14.02) added by 1995-97 technical bill, effective for taxation years that include February 22, 1994.

**(14.1) NISA election** — Where, at the end of the day on which a taxpayer dies and as a consequence of the death, an amount would, but for this subsection, be deemed by subsection (5.1) to have been paid to a trust out of the trust's interest in a NISA Fund No. 2 and the trust and the legal representative of the taxpayer so elect in prescribed manner, such portion of the amount as is designated in the election shall be deemed to have been paid to the taxpayer out of a NISA Fund No. 2 of the taxpayer immediately before the end of the day and, for the purpose of paragraph (a) of the description of B in subsection 12(10.2) in respect of the trust, the amount shall be deemed to have been paid out of the trust's NISA Fund No. 2 immediately before the end of the day.

**Related Provisions**: 248(8) — Occurrences as a consequence of death.

**Notes**: 104(14.1) added by 1992 technical bill, effective 1991.

**(15) Allocable amount for preferred beneficiary** — For the purpose of subsection (14), the allocable amount for a preferred beneficiary under a trust in respect of the trust for a taxation year is

(a) where the trust is a trust described in the definition "pre-1972 spousal trust" in subsection 108(1) at the end of the year or a trust described in paragraph (4)(a) and the taxpayer's spouse or common-law partner referred to in that definition or paragraph is alive at the end of the year, an amount equal to

(i) if the beneficiary is that spouse or common-law partner, the trust's accumulating income for the year, and

(ii) in any other case, nil;

(b) where paragraph (a) does not apply and the beneficiary's interest in the trust is not solely contingent on the death of another beneficiary who has a capital interest in the trust and who does not have an income interest in the trust, the trust's accumulating income for the year; and

**Proposed Amendment — 104(15)(a), (b)**

(a) where the trust is an *alter ego* trust, a joint partner trust, a post-1971 partner trust or a trust described in the definition "pre-1972 spousal trust" in subsection 108(1) at the end of the year and a beneficiary, referred to in paragraph (4)(a) or in that definition, is alive at the end of the year, an amount equal to

(i) if the preferred beneficiary is a beneficiary so referred to, the trust's accumulating income for the year, and

(ii) in any other case, nil;

(b) where paragraph (a) does not apply and the preferred beneficiary's interest in the trust is not solely contingent on the death of another beneficiary who has a capital interest in the trust and who does not have an income interest in the trust, the trust's accumulating income for the year; and

**Application**: Bill C-43 (First Reading September 20, 2000), subsec. 48(18), will amend paras. 104(15)(a) and (b) to read as above, applicable to 2000 *et seq.*

**Technical Notes**: Subsection 104(14) of the Act provides a mechanism under which a preferred beneficiary of a trust and the trust can elect to have a designated amount taxed in the hands of the beneficiary rather than at the trust level. Under the definition "preferred beneficiary" in subsection 108(1), a preferred beneficiary of a trust is generally a disabled person resident in Canada who is, or is closely related to, the settlor of the trust. Under paragraph 104(15)(a), if the preferred beneficiary is the living spouse beneficiary under a spousal trust, an "allocable amount" in respect of the beneficiary for a taxation year is the trust's "accumulating income" for the year (which, in general terms, is defined in subsection 108(1) as undistributed trust income).

Subsection 104(15) is amended so that the preferred beneficiary election in connection with allocations of income from an *alter ego* trust, a joint partner trust, a post-1971 partner trust or a trust described in the definition "pre-1972 spousal trust" in subsection 108(1) is available to the spouse or other beneficiary (i.e., the settlor) identified in paragraph 104(4)(a), only while the spouse or the other beneficiary is alive.

This amendment also reflects changes [re common-law partners — ed.] proposed under Bill C-23, the *Modernization of Benefits and Obligations Act*.

(c) in any other case, nil.

**Related Provisions**: 94(3)(a) [proposed] — Application to trust deemed resident in Canada; 108(1) — Trust defined; 138.1(1) — Rules re segregated funds; 250(6.1) — Trust that ceases to exist deemed resident throughout year.

**Notes**: 104(15)(a) amended by 2000 same-sex partners bill to add reference to "common-law partner", effective for the 2001 and later taxation years, or earlier by election (see Notes to 248(1)"common-law partner").

104(15) amended by 1995 Budget, effective for trust taxation years that begin after 1995. See Notes to 104(14). For earlier taxation years that end after December 20, 1991, read:

(15) Preferred beneficiary's share — The share of a particular preferred beneficiary under a trust in the accumulating income of the trust for a taxation year is,

(a) where the trust is a trust described in the definition "pre-1972 spousal trust" in subsection 108(1) at the end of the year or a trust described in paragraph (4)(a) and the taxpayer's spouse referred to in that definition or paragraph is alive at the end of the year, an amount equal to

(i) if the particular preferred beneficiary is the taxpayer's spouse, the trust's accumulating income for the year, and

(ii) in any other case, nil;

(b) in any case not referred to in paragraph (a), where the shares in which the accumulating income of the trust would be payable to the beneficiaries thereunder do not depend on the exercise by any person of, or the failure by any person to exercise, any discretionary power,

(i) if at the end of the year the particular beneficiary was a member of a class of beneficiaries under the trust each of whom was entitled, as a member of that class, to share equally in any income of the trust, the portion of the trust's accumulating income for the year that may reasonably be regarded as having been earned for the benefit of beneficiaries of that class, divided by the number of beneficiaries (other than registered charities) of that class in existence at the end of the year, and

(ii) in any other case, the portion of the trust's accumulating income for the year that may reasonably be regarded as having been earned for the benefit of the particular preferred beneficiary;

(c) in any case not referred to in paragraph (a) or (b), where each beneficiary under the trust whose share of the accumulating income of the trust depends on the exercise by any person of, or the failure by any person to exercise, any discretionary power, is a preferred beneficiary, or would be a preferred beneficiary if the beneficiary were resident in Canada, or is a registered charity, the portion of the trust's accumulating income for the year equal to the amount determined in prescribed manner to be the beneficiary's discretionary share of the trust's accumulating income for the year; and

(d) in any case not referred to in paragraph (a), (b) or (c), nil.

Opening words of 104(15) amended by 1992 technical bill, effective for taxation years of trusts that end after December 20, 1991. For earlier years, delete "a trust described in the definition "pre-1972 spousal trust" at the end of the year or".

**Regulations**: 2800(3), (4) (prescribed manner for 104(15)(c)).

**Interpretation Bulletins**: IT-394R2: Preferred beneficiary election.

**Advance Tax Rulings**: ATR-30: Preferred beneficiary election on accumulating income of estate; ATR-34: Preferred beneficiary's election.

**(16)–(17.2)** [Repealed under former Act]

**Notes**: 104(16) and (17), repealed by 1988 tax reform, allowed a beneficiary to claim capital cost allowance, terminal losses and depletion allowances, which can now be claimed only at the trust level under 104(13).

104(17.1) and (17.2), also repealed by 1988 tax reform, provided rules relating to 104(16) and (17).

**(18) Trust for minor** — Where any part of the amount that, but for subsections (6) and (12), would be the income of a trust for a taxation year throughout which it was resident in Canada

(a) has not become payable in the year,

(b) was held in trust for an individual who did not attain 21 years of age before the end of the year,

(c) the right to which vested at or before the end of the year otherwise than because of the exercise by any person of, or the failure of any person to exercise, any discretionary power, and

(d) the right to which is not subject to any future condition (other than a condition that the individual survive to an age not exceeding 40 years),

notwithstanding subsection (24), that part of the amount is, for the purposes of subsections (6) and (13), deemed to have become payable to the individual in the year.

**Related Provisions**: 94(3)(a) [proposed] — Application to trust deemed resident in Canada; 250(6.1) — Trust that ceases to exist deemed resident throughout year.

**Notes**: 104(18) amended by 1995 Budget, effective for trust taxation years that begin after 1995. For earlier taxation years since 1972, read:

(18) Where all or any part of the income of a trust for a taxation year has not become payable in the year and was held in trust for a minor whose right thereto has vested and the only reason that it has not become payable in the year was that the beneficiary was a minor, it shall, for the purposes of subsections (6) and (13) be deemed to have become payable to the minor in the year.

The new version makes it much more difficult (relative to the old version) to make amounts "payable" to a minor beneficiary of a discretionary trust for purposes of putting the income in that minor's hands (under 104(6)) for income-splitting purposes.

**Interpretation Bulletins**: IT-286R2: Trusts — amount payable; IT-342R: Trusts — income payable to beneficiaries; IT-381R3: Trusts — capital gains and losses and the flow-through of taxable capital gains to beneficiaries; IT-394R2: Preferred beneficiary election.

**I.T. Technical News**: No. 11 (payments made by a trust for the benefit of a minor beneficiary).

**(19) Taxable dividends** — Such portion of a taxable dividend received by a trust in a taxation year throughout which it was resident in Canada on a share of the capital stock of a taxable Canadian corporation as

(a) may reasonably be considered (having regard to all the circumstances including the terms and conditions of the trust arrangement) to be part of the amount that, by reason of subsection (13) or (14) or section 105, as the case may be, was included in computing the income for a particular taxation year of a beneficiary under the trust, and

(b) was not designated by the trust in respect of any other beneficiary under the trust

shall, if so designated by the trust in respect of the beneficiary in the return of its income for the year under this Part, be deemed, for the purposes of this Act, other than Part XIII, not to have been received by the trust and to be a taxable dividend on the share received by the beneficiary in the particular year from the corporation.

**Proposed Amendment — 104(19) closing words**

if so designated by the trust in respect of the beneficiary in its return of income for the year, is deemed, for the purposes of paragraphs 82(1)(b) and 107(1)(c) and (d) and section 112, not to have been received by the trust, and for the purposes of this Act (other than Part XIII), to be a taxable dividend on the share received by the beneficiary in the particular year from the corporation.

**Application**: Bill C-43 (First Reading September 20, 2000), subsec. 48(19), will amend the closing words of subsec. 104(19) to read as above, applicable to taxation years that end after 2000.

**Technical Notes**: Subsection 104(19) of the Act permits a trust to designate dividends received by it in a taxation year on shares of a taxable Canadian corporation to be taxable dividends received by a beneficiary of the trust, rather than by the trust itself, in the year from the corporation.

Subsection 104(19) of the Act is amended so that a trust will, except for the purposes of the dividend gross-up in paragraph 82(1)(b) and stop-loss rules in paragraphs 107(1)(c) and (d) and section 112, still be treated as having received the dividend even if it is designated in favour of a beneficiary. In most cases, the trust will be allowed a corresponding deduction under subsection 104(6) to offset the resulting income inclusion. However, as described in the commentary on amendments to subsection 104(6), there are certain restrictions under amended subsection 104(6) on the deduction of amounts made payable from *alter ego* trusts, joint partner trusts and post-1971 partner trusts.

This amendment applies to taxation years that end after 2000.

**Related Provisions**: 82(1) — Taxable dividends received; 94(3)(a) [proposed] — Application to trust deemed resident in Canada; 107(1)(c), (d) — Loss on disposition of capital interest in trust; 112(3.12) — Exclusion from stop-loss rule where beneficiary is partnership or trust; 112(3.2) — Stop-loss rule; 112(5.2)B(b)(iii) — Adjustment for dividends received on mark-to-market property; 250(6.1) — Trust that ceases to exist deemed resident throughout year.

**Notes**: 104(19) allows the character of dividend income to be preserved when flowed through to a beneficiary. Thus, the beneficiary, if an individual, can benefit from the gross-up and dividend tax credit (82(1)(b) and 121), and if a corporation, can benefit from the intercorporate dividend deduction (112(1)).

**Interpretation Bulletins**: IT-328R3: Losses on shares on which dividends have been received; IT-524: Trusts — flow-through of taxable dividends to a beneficiary — after 1987.

**(20) Designation in respect of non-taxable dividends** — The portion of the total of all amounts, each of which is the amount of a dividend (other than a taxable dividend) paid on a share of the capital stock of a corporation resident in Canada to a trust during a taxation year of the trust throughout which the trust was resident in Canada, that can reasonably be considered (having regard to all the circumstances including the terms and conditions of the trust arrangement) to be part of an amount that became payable in the year to a particular beneficiary under the trust shall be designated by the trust in respect of the particular beneficiary in the return of the trust's income for the year for the purposes of subclause 53(2)(h)(i.1)(B)(II), paragraphs 107(1)(c) and (d) and subsections 112(3.1), (3.2), (3.31) and (4.2).

**Related Provisions**: 83(2) — Capital dividends; 94(3)(a) [proposed] — Application to trust deemed resident in Canada; 107(1)(c) — Stop-loss rule where beneficiary is corporation; 104(24) — Whether amount payable; 112(3.2) — Stop-loss rule; 112(4.3) — Limitation on loss on disposition of share by trust; 132(3) — Application to a mutual fund trust; 248(1)"disposition"(i)(ii) — Payment in respect of capital interest in a trust; 250(6.1) — Trust that ceases to exist deemed resident throughout year.

**Notes**: 104(20) deals with capital dividends (see 83(2)), but applies only for the specific purposes stated. It does not provide for a general flow-through of the exemption to the beneficiary. However, 105(1)(b) provides, in effect, that capital dividends are not included in the income of a beneficiary of a commercial trust, since they are allowed as a deduction from the beneficiary's adjusted cost base under paragraph 53(2)(h). Also, for a personal trust, a capital dividend paid out to a beneficiary will not be included in income, since the income inclusion in 104(13)(a) applies only to amounts that would otherwise be income *of the trust*, and a capital dividend is not income of the trust in the first place.

Note that 104(20) uses the word "shall", and thus the designation of amounts as indicated is mandatory.

104(20) amended by 1995-97 technical bill, effective April 27, 1995, to add reference to 107(1)(d) and to change "112(3.2) and (4.3)" to "112(3.1), (3.2), (3.31) and (4.2)". Other changes made at the same time were cosmetic and non-substantive (e.g., "may reasonably" to "can reasonably").

**Interpretation Bulletins**: IT-328R3: Losses on shares on which dividends have been received.

**(21) Taxable capital gains** — Such portion of the net taxable capital gains of a trust for a taxation year throughout which it was resident in Canada as

(a) may reasonably be considered (having regard to all the circumstances including the terms and conditions of the trust arrangement) to be part of the amount that, by virtue of subsection (13) or (14) or section 105, as the case may be, was included in computing the income for the taxation year of

(i) a particular beneficiary under the trust, if the trust is a mutual fund trust, or

(ii) a particular beneficiary under the trust who is resident in Canada, if the trust is not a mutual fund trust, and

(b) was not designated by the trust in respect of any other beneficiary under the trust,

shall, if so designated by the trust in respect of the particular beneficiary in the return of its income for the year under this Part, be deemed, for the purposes of sections 3 and 111 except as they apply for the purposes of section 110.6, to be a taxable capital gain for the year of the particular beneficiary from the disposition by that beneficiary of capital property.

**Related Provisions**: 39.1(2)B(a), 39.1(3) — Reduction in gain to reflect capital gains exemption election; 94(3)(a) [proposed] — Application to trust deemed resident in Canada; 104(13.2) — Designation of amount by trust; 104(21.01), (21.02) — Late, amended or revoked designation made with capital gains exemption election; 104(21.1) — Beneficiary's taxable capital gain; 104(21.2) — Beneficiary's taxable capital gain from trust; 104(21.3) — Determination of net taxable capital gains; 104(21.4) — Deemed gain from Feb. 28 to Oct. 17, 2000; 110.6(19), (20) — Election to trigger capital gains exemption; 127.52(1)(d)(ii), 127.52(1)(g)(ii) — Adjusted taxable income (for minimum tax); 212(1)(c) — Estate or trust income — non-residents; 250(6.1) — Trust that ceases to exist deemed resident throughout year.

**Notes**: 104(21) allows the character of capital gains realized by the trust to be preserved when flowed through to a beneficiary. Thus, capital gains of the trust will only be ½ taxed in the beneficiary's hands (see 38(a)) and can be offset by the beneficiary's capital losses (see 3(b)(ii) and 111(1)(b)). However, they are not eligible for the capital gains exemption under 110.6 (see the closing words of 104(21)) unless a further designation is made by the trust under 104(21.2).

The CCRA has indicated that where taxable capital gains are designated by a mutual fund trust to a corporate beneficiary under 104(21), the non-taxable portion can *not* be added to the corporation's capital dividend account. However, a private corporation that receives a capital gains dividend from a mutual fund corporation can add the non-taxable portion to its CDA. See VIEWS doc 9830585 (June 1/99).

**Interpretation Bulletins**: IT-123R6: Transactions involving eligible capital property; IT-342R: Trusts — income payable to beneficiaries; IT-381R3: Trusts — capital gains and losses and the flow-through of taxable capital gains to beneficiaries; IT-394R2: Preferred beneficiary election; IT-465R: Non-resident beneficiaries of trusts; IT-493: Agency cooperative corporations.

**Advance Tax Rulings**: ATR-34: Preferred beneficiary's election.

**Forms**: RC4169: Tax treatment of mutual funds for individuals; T3 Sched. 3: Eligible taxable capital gains.

**(21.01) Late, amended or revoked designation** — A trust that has filed its return of income for its taxation year that includes February 22, 1994 may subsequently designate an amount under subsection (21), or amend or revoke a designation made under that subsection where the designation, amendment or revocation

(a) is made solely because of an increase or decrease in the net taxable capital gains of the trust for the year that results from an election or revocation to which subsection 110.6(25), (26) or (27) applies; and

(b) is filed with the Minister, with an amended return of income for the year, when the election or revocation referred to in paragraph (a) is filed with the Minister.

**Related Provisions**: 104(21.02) — Restriction; 104(21.03) — Effect of designation.

**Notes**: 104(21.01) added by 1995-97 technical bill, effective for taxation years that include February 22, 1994.

**(21.02) Late, amended or revoked designation** — A designation, amendment or revocation under subsection (21.01) that affects an amount determined in respect of a beneficiary under subsection (21.2) may be made only where the trust

(a) designates an amount, or amends or revokes a designation made, under subsection (21.2) in respect of the beneficiary; and

(b) files the designation, amendment or revocation referred to in paragraph (a) with the Minister when required by paragraph (21.01)(b).

**Notes**: 104(21.02) added by 1995-97 technical bill, effective for taxation years that include February 22, 1994.

**(21.03) Late, amended or revoked designation** — Where a trust designates an amount, or amends or revokes a designation, under subsection (21) or (21.2) in accordance with subsection (21.01),

(a) the designation or amended designation, as the case may be, is deemed to have been made in the trust's return of income for the trust's taxation year that includes February 22, 1994; and

(b) the designation that was revoked is deemed, other than for the purposes of this subsection and subsections (21.01) and (21.02), never to have been made.

**Notes**: 104(21.03) added by 1995-97 technical bill, effective for taxation years that include February 22, 1994.

**(21.1) Beneficiary's taxable capital gain** — Notwithstanding subsection (21) or section 38, where in a particular taxation year, commencing before 1990, of a taxpayer (other than an individual who is not a testamentary trust) the taxpayer is a beneficiary of a trust with a taxation year ending in the particular year, the amount (other than that part of the amount that can be attributed to an amount deemed under subsection 14(1) to be a taxable capital gain of the trust) deemed by subsection (21) to be a taxable capital gain of the taxpayer for the particular year in respect of the trust shall be the amount determined by the formula

$$A \times \frac{B}{C}$$

where

A is the amount, if any, by which the amount (other than that part of the amount that can be attributed to an amount deemed under subsection 14(1) to be a taxable capital gain of the trust) deemed by subsection (21) to be the taxpayer's taxable capital gain for the particular year in respect of the trust exceeds the amount (other than that part of the amount that can be attributed to an amount deemed under subsection 14(1) to be a taxable capital gain of the trust) designated by the trust for the particular year in respect of the taxpayer under subsection (13.2);

B is the fraction that would be used under section 38 for the particular year in respect of the taxpayer if the taxpayer had a capital gain for the particular year; and

C is the fraction that is used under section 38 for the year of the trust.

**Related Provisions**: 94(3)(a) [proposed] — Application to trust deemed resident in Canada.

**Notes**: 104(21.1) is a transitional provision to deal with the change in capital gains inclusion rates from $\frac{1}{2}$ (before 1988) to $\frac{2}{3}$ (1988 and 1989) to $\frac{3}{4}$ (1990–Feb. 27, 2000) to $\frac{2}{3}$ (since Feb. 28, 2000). It addresses the case where the trust has allocated capital gains to a beneficiary under 104(21) but the trust and beneficiary have different taxation years.

**(21.2) Beneficiaries' taxable capital gains** — Where, for the purposes of subsection (21), a personal trust designates an amount in respect of a beneficiary in respect of its net taxable capital gains for a taxation year (in this subsection referred to as the "designation year"),

### Proposed Amendment — 104(21.2) opening words

**(21.2) Beneficiaries' taxable capital gain** — Where, for the purposes of subsection (21), a personal trust or a trust referred to in subsection 7(2) designates an amount in respect of a beneficiary in respect of its net taxable capital gains for a taxation year (in this subsection referred to as the "designation year"),

**Application**: Bill C-43 (First Reading September 20, 2000), subsec. 48(20), will amend the opening words of subsec. 104(21.2) to read as above, applicable to trusts' taxation years that begin after February 22, 1994.

**Technical Notes**: Subsection 104(21.2) of the Act sets out the rules for allocating the net taxable capital gains of a trust to its beneficiaries for the purpose of section 110.6 of the Act. Personal trusts are the only trusts that can make designations of net taxable capital gains to beneficiaries. Subsection 104(21.2) is amended to provide that such designations can also be made by a trust described in subsection 7(2) of the Act. In general, those are trusts of which the trustee holds shares in trust for an employee and the employee is treated for the purposes of paragraphs 110(1)(d) and (d.1) of the Act as having acquired and disposed of the shares at the time that the trust acquired and disposed of them. This amendment ensures that a trust described in subsection 7(2) will be able to designate its net taxable capital gains arising from a disposition of "qualified farm property" or "qualified small business corporation shares" to its beneficiaries.

**Letter from Department of Finance, September 30, 1997:**

Dear [xxx]

This is in response to your letter of September 23, 1997 regarding the interaction of subsection 104(21.2) and section 110.6 of the *Income Tax Act*. In particular, you indicate that subsection 104(21.2) is technically deficient in that it does not apply to a trust described in paragraph 4800.1(a) of the Income Tax Regulations (an "employee trust").

As you indicate, subsection 104(21.2) of the *Income Tax Act* treats the net taxable capital gains realized by a personal trust and flowed through to its beneficiaries under subsection 104(21) of the *Income Tax Act* as a taxable capital gain of the beneficiaries for the purposes of the lifetime capital gains exemption under section 110.6 of the *Income Tax Act*. It also treats the beneficiaries as having disposed of the particular property that gave rise to that gain for the purposes of subsection 110.6. A personal trust may not necessarily include an employee trust. From a tax policy perspective, it would be appropriate for subsection 104(21.2) to apply to such net taxable capital gains realized by an employee trust and flowed through to its beneficiaries under subsection 104(21).

We are prepared therefore to recommend to the Minister of Finance that subsection 104(21.2) of the *Income Tax Act* be amended to ensure that it applies in respect of net taxable gains realized by a employee trust from the disposition of the particular property described in subsection 104(21.2). [The reference to "a trust referred to in subsection 7(2)" is intended to accomplish this — ed.] It will be recommended that such an amendment be effective for taxation years that end after 1996. If the recommendation is acted upon, I would anticipate that such an amendment would be included in a future technical bill.

Yours sincerely,

Len Farber
Director General, Tax Legislation Division

(a) the trust shall in its return of income under this Part for the designation year designate an amount in respect of its eligible taxable capital gains, if any, for the designation year in respect of the beneficiary equal to the amount determined in respect of the beneficiary under each of subparagraphs (b)(i) and (ii); and

(b) the beneficiary shall, for the purposes of sections 3, 74.3 and 111 as they apply for the purposes of section 110.6, be deemed to have a taxable capital gain for the beneficiary's taxation year in which the designation year ends

(i) from a disposition of capital property that is qualified farm property of the beneficiary equal to the amount determined by the formula

$$\frac{A \times B \times C}{D \times E}$$

and

(ii) from a disposition of capital property that is a qualified small business corporation share of the beneficiary equal to the amount determined by the formula

$$\frac{A \times B \times F}{D \times E}$$

where

A is the lesser of

(iii) the amount determined by the formula

$$G - H$$

where

G is the total of amounts designated under subsection (21) for the designation year by the trust, and

H is the total of amounts designated under subsection (13.2) for the designation year by the trust, and

(iv) the trust's eligible taxable capital gains for the designation year,

B is the amount, if any, by which the amount designated under subsection (21) for the designation year by the trust in respect of the beneficiary exceeds the amount designated under subsection (13.2) for the year by the trust in respect of the beneficiary,

C is the amount, if any, that would be determined under paragraph 3(b) for the designation year in respect of the trust's capital gains and capital losses if the only properties referred to in that paragraph were qualified farm properties of the trust disposed of by it after 1984,

D is the total of all amounts each of which is the amount determined for B for the designation year in respect of a beneficiary under the trust,

E is the total of the amounts determined for C and F for the designation year in respect of the beneficiary, and

F is the amount, if any, that would be determined under paragraph 3(b) for the designation year in respect of the trust's capital gains and capital losses if the only properties referred to in that paragraph were qualified small business corporation shares of the trust, other than qualified farm property, disposed of by it after June 17, 1987,

and for the purposes of section 110.6, those capital properties shall be deemed to have been disposed of by the beneficiary in that taxation year of the beneficiary.

## S. 104(21.2) — Income Tax Act, Part I, Division B

**Related Provisions**: 39(10) — Reduction of business investment loss; 94(3)(a) [proposed] — Application to trust deemed resident in Canada; 104(21.01), (21.02) — Late, amended or revoked designation made with capital gains exemption election; 104(21.3) — Determination of net taxable capital gains; 110.6(11) — No capital gains exemption allowed in certain cases; 110.6(12) — Spousal trust deduction; 110.6(14)(c) — Related persons, etc.; 110.6(20) — Election to trigger capital gains exemption; 257 — Formula amounts cannot calculate to less than zero.

**Notes**: 104(21.2) permits a beneficiary to claim the capital gains exemption under 110.6 in respect of a portion of the capital gains of a trust allocated to the beneficiary. See Notes to 104(21).

104(21.2) amended by 1994 Budget (as a result of the elimination of the $100,000 capital gains exemption in 110.6(3)), this version effective for trusts' taxation years that begin after February 22, 1994.

For taxation years that include February 22, 1994, read:

(21.2) Where, for the purposes of subsection (21), a trust (other than a mutual fund trust) designates an amount in respect of a beneficiary in respect of its net taxable capital gains for a taxation year (in this subsection referred to as the "designation year"),

(a) the trust shall in its return of income for the designation year designate an amount in respect of its eligible taxable capital gains for the designation year in respect of the beneficiary equal to the amount determined in respect of the beneficiary under each of subparagraphs (b)(i), (ii) and (iii), and

(b) the beneficiary shall, for the purposes of sections 3, 74.3 and 111 as they apply for the purposes of section 110.6, be deemed to have a taxable capital gain for the year

(i) from the disposition of capital property that is qualified farm property of the beneficiary equal to the amount determined by the formula

$$\left(A \times \frac{B}{C}\right) \times \frac{D}{G}$$

(ii) from the disposition of capital property that is a qualified small business corporation share of the beneficiary equal to the amount determined by the formula

$$\left(A \times \frac{B}{C}\right) \times \frac{E}{G}$$

and

(iii) from the disposition of capital property, other than properties referred to in subparagraphs (i) or (ii), equal to the amount determined by the formula

$$\left(A \times \frac{B}{C}\right) \times \frac{F}{G}$$

where

A is the lesser of

(i) the amount determined by the formula

$$H - I$$

where

H is the total of amounts designated under subsection (21) for the designation year by the trust, and

I is the total of amounts designated under subsection (13.2) for the designation year by the trust, and

(ii) the trust's eligible taxable capital gains for the designation year,

B is the amount, if any, by which the amount designated under subsection (21) for the designation year by the trust in respect of the beneficiary exceeds the amount designated under subsection (13.2) for the year by the trust in respect of the beneficiary,

C is the total of all amounts each of which is the amount determined for B for the designation year in respect of a beneficiary under the trust,

D is the amount, if any, that would be determined in respect of the trust for the designation year under paragraph 3(b) in respect of capital gains and capital losses if the only properties referred to in that paragraph were qualified farm properties of the trust disposed of by it after 1984,

E is the amount, if any, that would be determined in respect of the trust for the designation year under paragraph 3(b) in respect of capital gains and capital losses if the only properties referred to in that paragraph were qualified small business corporation shares of the trust, other than qualified farm property, disposed of by it after June 17, 1987,

F is the lesser of

(i) the amount, if any, that would be determined under paragraph 3(b) in respect of capital gains and capital losses in respect of the trust for the designation year if

(A) the only properties referred to in that paragraph were properties disposed of by it after 1984, other than qualified farm properties and other than qualified small business corporation shares disposed of by it after June 17, 1987, and

(B) the trust's capital gains and capital losses for the year from dispositions of non-qualifying real property of the trust were equal to its eligible real property gains and eligible real property losses, respectively, for the year from those dispositions, and

(ii) the amount that would be determined under subparagraph (i) if that subparagraph were read without reference to clause (i)(B), and

G is the total of the amounts used for D, E and F under this paragraph in respect of the beneficiary for the year,

and for the purposes of section 110.6, each such taxable capital gain of a beneficiary shall be deemed to be a taxable capital gain of the beneficiary for the beneficiary's taxation year in which the designation year ends from the disposition of a property that occurred on February 22, 1994.

For taxation years ending before February 22, 1994, read:

(21.2) **Beneficiary's taxable capital gain from trust** — Where a trust has, for the purposes of subsection (21), designated an amount (in this subsection referred to as the "designated amount") in respect of a beneficiary of the trust in respect of its net taxable capital gains for a taxation year (in this subsection referred to as the "designation year") and by virtue thereof the designated amount is deemed, for the purposes described in that subsection, to be a taxable capital gain for the year of the beneficiary from the disposition by the beneficiary of capital property,

(a) the trust shall in its return of income for the designation year designate an amount in respect of its eligible taxable capital gains for the designation year in respect of the beneficiary equal to the amount determined in respect of the beneficiary under each of subparagraphs (b)(i), (ii) and (iii), and

(b) the beneficiary shall, for the purposes of sections 3, 74.3 and 111 as they apply for the purposes of section 110.6, be deemed to have a taxable capital gain for the year

(i) from the disposition of capital property that is qualified farm property of the beneficiary equal to the amount determined by the formula

$$\left(A \times \frac{B}{C}\right) \times \frac{D}{G}$$

(ii) from the disposition of capital property that is a qualified small business corporation share of the beneficiary equal to the amount determined by the formula

$$\left(A \times \frac{B}{C}\right) \times \frac{E}{G}$$

and

(iii) from the disposition of capital property, other than properties referred to in subparagraphs (i) or (ii), equal to the amount determined by the formula

$$\left(A \times \frac{B}{C}\right) \times \frac{F}{G}$$

where

A   is the eligible taxable capital gains of the trust for the designation year,

B   is the amount, if any, by which the designated amount exceeds the amount designated in respect of the beneficiary for the designation year under subsection (13.2),

C   is the greater of

(i) the total of all amounts each of which is the amount used for B under this paragraph in respect of a beneficiary of the trust for the designation year, and

(ii) the amount, if any, by which the net taxable capital gains of the trust for the designation year exceed the amount, if any, by which

(A) the investment expense (within the meaning assigned by subsection 110.6(1) of the trust for the designation year

exceeds

(B) the investment income (within the meaning assigned by subsection 110.6(1) of the trust for the designation year,

D   is the amount, if any, that would be determined in respect of the trust for the designation year under paragraph 3(b) in respect of capital gains and capital losses if the only properties referred to in that paragraph were qualified farm properties of the trust disposed of by it after 1984,

E   is the amount, if any, that would be determined in respect of the trust for the designation year under paragraph 3(b) in respect of capital gains and capital losses if the only properties referred to in that paragraph were qualified small business corporation shares of the trust, other than qualified farm property, disposed of by it after June 17, 1987,

F   is the lesser of

(i) the amount, if any, that would be determined under paragraph 3(b) in respect of capital gains

and capital losses in respect of the trust for the designation year if

(A) the only properties referred to in that paragraph were properties disposed of by it after 1984, other than qualified farm properties and other than qualified small business corporation shares disposed of by it after June 17, 1987, and

(B) the trust's capital gains and capital losses for the year from dispositions of non-qualifying real property of the trust were equal to its eligible real property gains and eligible real property losses, respectively, for the year from those dispositions, and

(ii) the amount that would be determined under subparagraph (i) if that subparagraph were read without reference to clause (i)(B), and

G   is the total of the amounts used for D, E and F under this paragraph in respect of the beneficiary for the year,

and for the purposes of section 110.6, those capital properties shall be deemed to have been disposed of by the beneficiary in the year.

Description of C in 104(21.2)(b) amended by 1991 technical bill, retroactive to 1988.

Description of F amended by 1992 technical bill, effective for 1992 and later taxation years. For 1988 to 1991, ignore cl. (i)(B) and sub-para. (ii).

**Interpretation Bulletins**: IT-123R6: Transactions involving eligible capital property; IT-381R3: Trusts — capital gains and losses and the flow-through of taxable capital gains to beneficiaries.

**Advance Tax Rulings**: ATR-34: Preferred beneficiary's election.

**Forms**: T3 Sched. 3: Eligible taxable capital gains; T3 Sched. 4: Cumulative net investment loss.

### (21.3) Net taxable capital gains of trust determined

— For the purposes of this section, the net taxable capital gains of a trust for a taxation year is the amount, if any, by which the total of the taxable capital gains of the trust for the year exceeds the total of

(a) its allowable capital losses for the year, and

**Proposed Amendment — 104(21.3)(a)**

(a) the total of all amounts each of which is an allowable capital loss (other than an allowable business investment loss) of the trust for the year from the disposition of a capital property, and

**Application**: The June 22, 2000 draft legislation, subsec. 14(5), will amend para. 104(21.3)(a) to read as above, applicable to trust taxation years that begin after 2000.

**Technical Notes**: Subsection 104(21.3) of the Act defines the expression "net taxable capital gains". The expression is used in subsections 104(21) and (21.2), which permit a trust to flow its taxable capital gains realized in a year through to a beneficiary who has received a portion of the trust's income for the year. The trust can flow through its taxable capital gains to beneficiaries only to the extent of its net taxable capital gains for the year.

Under subsection 104(21.3), the net taxable capital gains of a trust for a taxation year equals the amount, if any, by

## S. 104(21.3)(a)

which its total taxable capital gains for the year exceeds the total of two amounts:

- its total allowable capital losses for the year, and
- the amount deducted by it under paragraph 111(1)(b) in computing its taxable income for the year (i.e., deduction of carried-over net capital losses for years preceding and the 3 years immediately following the year).

Subsection 104(21.3) is amended so that allowable business investment losses (ABILs) are disregarded for the purpose of the first of the two amounts. Accordingly, ABILs will not result in a reduction of taxable capital gains that may be flowed through to beneficiaries under trusts and against which allowable capital losses can be claimed.

This amendment applies to trust taxation years that begin after 2000.

(b) the amount, if any, deducted under paragraph 111(1)(b) in computing its taxable income for the year.

**Interpretation Bulletins**: IT-381R3: Trusts — capital gains and losses and the flow-through of taxable capital gains to beneficiaries.

**Forms**: T3 Sched. 3: Eligible taxable capital gains.

### Proposed Addition — 104(21.4)

**(21.4) Deemed gains** — Where an amount is designated in respect of a beneficiary by a trust for a particular taxation year of the trust that includes either February 28, 200[0] or October 17, 2000 and that amount is, because of subsection 104(21), deemed to be a taxable capital gain of the beneficiary from the disposition of capital property for the taxation year of the beneficiary in which the particular taxation year of the trust ends (in this subsection referred to as the "allocated gain"),

(a) the beneficiary is deemed to have realized capital gains (in this subsection referred to as the "deemed gains") from the disposition of capital property in the beneficiary's taxation year in which the particular taxation year ends equal to the amount, if any, by which

(i) the amount determined when the amount of the allocated gain is divided by the fraction in paragraph 38(a) that applies to the trust for the particular taxation year

exceeds

(ii) the amount claimed by the beneficiary not exceeding the beneficiary's exempt capital gains balance for the year in respect of the trust;

(b) notwithstanding subsection 104(21) and except as a consequence of the application of paragraph (a), the amount of the allocated gain shall not be included in computing the beneficiary's income for the beneficiary's taxation year in which the particular taxation year ends;

(c) the trust shall disclose to the beneficiary in prescribed form the portion of the deemed gains that are in respect of capital gains realized on dispositions of property that occurred before February 28, 2000, after February 27, 2000 and before October 18, 2000, and after October 17, 2000 and, if it does not do so, the deemed gains are deemed to be in respect of capital gains realized on dispositions of property that occurred before February 28, 2000; and

(d) where a trust so elects under this paragraph in its return of income for the year,

(i) the portion of the deemed gains that are in respect of capital gains realized on dispositions of property that occurred before February 28, 2000 is deemed to equal that proportion of the deemed gains that the number of days that are in the particular year and before February 28, 2000 is of the number of days that are in the particular year,

(ii) the portion of the deemed gains that are in respect of capital gains realized on dispositions of property that occurred in the year and in the period that began at the beginning of February 28, 2000 and ended at the end of October 17, 2000, is deemed to equal that proportion of the deemed gains that the number of days that are in the year and in that period is of the number of days that are in the particular year, and

(iii) the portion of the deemed gains that are in respect of capital gains realized on dispositions of property that occurred in the year and in the period that begins at the beginning of October 18, 2000 and ends at the end of the particular year, is deemed to equal that proportion of the deemed gains that the number of days that are in the year and in that period is of the number of days that are in the particular year; and

(e) no amount may be claimed by the beneficiary under subsection 39.1(3) in respect of the allocated gain.

**Application**: The December 21, 2000 draft legislation, subsec. 48(3), will add subsec. 104(21.4), applicable to taxation years that end after February 27, 2000.

**Technical Notes**: New subsection 104(21.4) provides a special rule that applies where a trust designates for its taxation year that includes either February 28, 2000 or October 17, 2000 an amount in respect of a beneficiary (the allocated gain) that is deemed because of subsection 104(21) to be a taxable capital gain of the beneficiary for the taxation year of the beneficiary in which the trust's year ends. The subsection provides that

- the beneficiary is deemed to have a capital gain (deemed gain) equal to the amount if any by which
  - (a) the amount determined when the allocated gain is divided by the fraction in amended paragraph 38(a) that applies to the trust for the year

  exceeds
  - (b) the amount claimed by the beneficiary, not exceeding the beneficiary's exempt capital gain balance for the year in respect of the trust, and

- notwithstanding subsection 104(21), the allocated gain is not included in the income of the beneficiary otherwise than because of the application of this subsection.

The trust is required to disclose to the beneficiary the portion of the deemed gain that is paid out of gains of the trust for each of the pre-February 28, 2000 period, the period that begins at the beginning of February 28, 2000 and ends at the end of October 17, 2000 and the period that begins after October 17, 2000 and, in the event that this is not done, the gains are deemed to be pre-February 28, 2000 gains. Where the trust elects, it can treat its gains as having been realized equally over the number of days in its taxation year, so that the gains in each of the periods will be equal that proportion of the deemed gains that the number of days in the year of the trust that are in each period is of the number of days in the year.

**(22) Designation of foreign source income by trust** — For the purposes of this subsection, subsection (22.1) and section 126, such portion of a trust's income for a taxation year (in this subsection referred to as "that year") throughout which it is resident in Canada from a source in a country other than Canada as

(a) can reasonably be considered (having regard to all the circumstances including the terms and conditions of the trust arrangement) to be part of the income that, because of subsection (13) or (14), was included in computing the income for a particular taxation year of a particular beneficiary under the trust, and

(b) is not designated by the trust in respect of any other beneficiary thereunder

shall, if so designated by the trust in respect of the particular beneficiary in its return of income under this Part for that year, be deemed to be the particular beneficiary's income for the particular year from that source.

**Related Provisions**: 4(3) — Whether deductions are applicable to a particular source; 94(3)(a) [proposed] — Application to trust deemed resident in Canada; 104(22.2), (22.3) — Recalculation of trust's foreign-source income and foreign tax; 250(6.1) — Trust that ceases to exist deemed resident throughout year.

**Notes**: 104(22) and (22.1) allow a trust to flow out to a beneficiary the foreign-source income of the trust, and to treat the beneficiary as having paid foreign tax paid by the trust on that income, so that the beneficiary can claim the foreign tax credit under 126 to offset Canadian taxes payable on the income of the beneficiary from the trust.

104(22) amended by 1993 technical bill, this version effective for taxation years of trusts that begin in 1988 or later.

**Interpretation Bulletins**: IT-201R2: Foreign tax credit — trust and beneficiaries; IT-506: Foreign income taxes as a deduction from income.

**(22.1) Foreign tax deemed paid by beneficiary** — Where a taxpayer is a beneficiary under a trust, for the purposes of this subsection and section 126, the taxpayer shall be deemed to have paid as business-income tax or non-business-income tax, as the case may be, for a particular taxation year in respect of a source the amount determined by the formula

$$A \times \frac{B}{C}$$

where

A is the amount that, but for subsection (22.3), would be the business-income tax or non-business-income tax, as the case may be, paid by the trust in respect of the source for a taxation year (in this subsection referred to as "that year") of the trust that ends in the particular year;

B is the amount deemed, because of a designation under subsection (22) for that year by the trust, to be the taxpayer's income from the source; and

C is the trust's income for that year from the source.

**Related Provisions**: 4(3) — Whether deductions are applicable to a particular source; 94(3)(a) [proposed] — Application to trust deemed resident in Canada; 126(2.22) — Foreign tax credit to trust on disposition of property by non-resident beneficiary.

**Notes**: 104(22.1) added by 1993 technical bill, effective for taxation years ending after November 12, 1981. It replaces former 104(22)(b). See Notes to 104(22).

**Interpretation Bulletins**: IT-201R2: Foreign tax credit — trust and beneficiaries.

**(22.2) Recalculation of trust's foreign source income** — For the purpose of section 126, there shall be deducted in computing a trust's income from a source for a taxation year the total of all amounts deemed, because of designations under subsection (22) by the trust for the year, to be income of beneficiaries under the trust from that source.

**Related Provisions**: 94(3)(a) [proposed] — Application to trust deemed resident in Canada.

**Notes**: 104(22.2) added by 1993 technical bill, effective for taxation years ending after November 12, 1981. It replaces former 104(22)(c). See Notes to 104(22).

**Interpretation Bulletins**: IT-201R2: Foreign tax credit — trust and beneficiaries.

**(22.3) Recalculation of trust's foreign tax** — For the purpose of section 126, there shall be deducted in computing the business-income tax or non-business-income tax paid by a trust for a taxation year in respect of a source the total of all amounts deemed, because of designations under subsection (22) by the trust for the year, to be paid by beneficiaries under the trust as business-income tax or non-business-income tax, as the case may be, in respect of the source.

**Related Provisions**: 94(3)(a) [proposed] — Application to trust deemed resident in Canada; 126(7)"non-business-income tax"(c.1) — Amount deducted under 104(22.3) from business-income tax excluded from non-business-income tax.

**Notes**: 104(22.3) added by 1993 technical bill, effective for taxation years ending after November 12, 1981. It replaces former 104(22)(d). See Notes to 104(22).

**Interpretation Bulletins**: IT-201R2: Foreign tax credit — trust and beneficiaries.

**(22.4) Definitions** — For the purposes of subsections (22) to (22.3), the expressions "business-income tax" and "non-business-income tax" have the meanings assigned by subsection 126(7).

**Notes**: 104(22.4) added by 1993 technical bill, effective for taxation years ending after November 12, 1981. See Notes to 104(22).

**Interpretation Bulletins**: IT-201R2: Foreign tax credit — trust and beneficiaries.

**(23) Testamentary trusts** — In the case of a testamentary trust, notwithstanding any other provision of this Act, the following rules apply:

(a) the taxation year of the trust is the period for which the accounts of the trust are made up for purposes of assessment under this Act, but no such period may exceed 12 months and no change in the time when such a period ends may be made for the purposes of this Act without the concurrence of the Minister;

(b) when a taxation year is referred to by reference to a calendar year, the reference is to the taxation year or years coinciding with, or ending in, that year;

(c) the income of a person for a taxation year from the trust shall be deemed to be the person's benefits from or under the trust for the taxation year or years of the trust that ended in the year determined as provided by this section and section 105;

(d) where an individual having income from the trust died after the end of a taxation year of the trust but before the end of the calendar year in which the taxation year ended, the individual's income from the trust for the period commencing immediately after the end of the taxation year and ending at the time of death shall be included in computing the individual's income for the individual's taxation year in which the individual died unless the individual's legal representative has elected otherwise, in which case the legal representative shall file a separate return of income for the period under this Part and pay the tax for the period under this Part as if

(i) the individual were another person,

(ii) the period were a taxation year,

(iii) that other person's only income for the period were the individual's income from the trust for that period, and

(iv) subject to sections 114.2 and 118.93, that other person were entitled to the deductions to which the individual was entitled under sections 110, 118 to 118.7 and 118.9 for the period in computing the individual's taxable income or tax payable under this Part, as the case may be, for the period; and

(e) in lieu of making the payments required by sections 155, 156 and 156.1, the trust shall pay to the Receiver General within 90 days after the end of each taxation year, the tax payable under this Part by it for the year.

**Related Provisions**: 94(3)(a) [proposed] — Application to trust deemed resident in Canada; 114.2 — Deductions in separate returns; 118.93 — Credits in separate returns; 120.2(4)(a) — No minimum tax carryover on special return under 104(23)(d); 127.1(1)(a) — No refundable investment tax credit on special return; 127.55 — Minimum tax not applicable.

**Notes**: In addition to the rules in 104(23), a testamentary trust is permitted to pay federal tax at the graduated rates (16%/22%/26%/29%) that apply to individuals under 117(2), while an *inter vivos* trust must pay at the top rate of 29% (see 122(1)).

104(23)(a) amended by 1995 Budget, effective 1995, consequential on the new definition of "fiscal period" in 249.1. From 1972 to the end of 1994, read:

(a) the taxation year of the trust is the period for which the accounts of the trust have been ordinarily made up and accepted for purposes of assessment under this Act and, in the absence of an established practice, the period adopted by the trust for that purpose (but no such period may exceed 12 months and a change in a usual and accepted period may not be made for the purpose of this Act without the concurrence of the Minister);

104(23)(e) amended by 1993 Budget, effective for 1994 and later taxation years. For 1972 through 1993, read:

(e) in lieu of making the payments required by section 156, the trust shall pay to the Receiver General within 90 days from the end of each taxation year, the tax for the year as estimated under section 151.

**Interpretation Bulletins**: IT-179R: Change of fiscal period; IT-326R3: Returns of deceased persons as "another person".

**(24) Amount payable** — For the purposes of subparagraph 53(2)(h)(i.1) and subsections (6), (7), (13) and (20), an amount shall be deemed not to have become payable to a beneficiary in a taxation year unless it was paid in the year to the beneficiary or the beneficiary was entitled in the year to enforce payment of the amount.

**Proposed Amendment — 104(24)**

**(24) Amount payable** — For the purposes of subparagraph 53(2)(h)(i.1) and subsections (6), (7), (7.01), (13) and (20), an amount is deemed not to have become payable to a beneficiary in a taxation year unless it was paid in the year to the beneficiary or the beneficiary was entitled in the year to enforce payment of it.

**Application**: The June 22, 2000 draft legislation, subsec. 14(6), will amend subsec. 104(24) to read as above, applicable to trust taxation years that begin after 2000.

**Technical Notes**: The determination of when an amount becomes payable in a taxation year is relevant for a number of purposes, including the determination of the amount deductible under subsection 104(6) of the Act. Under subsection 104(24), an amount (e.g., income payable to a beneficiary) is deemed not to have become payable in the year to a beneficiary unless it was paid in the year to the beneficiary or the beneficiary was entitled in the year to enforce payment of the amount.

Subsection 104(24) is amended so that it also applies for the purpose of new subsection 104(7.01), which is described in the commentary above.

**Related Provisions**: 94(3)(a) [proposed] — Application to trust deemed resident in Canada; 94(4) — FAPI does not include "amount payable" to beneficiary; 104(18) — Trust for person under age 21.

**Interpretation Bulletins**: IT-286R2: Trusts — amount payable; IT-342R: Trusts — income payable to beneficiaries; IT-381R3:

Trusts — capital gains and losses and the flow-through of taxable capital gains to beneficiaries.

**I.T. Technical News**: No. 11 (payments made by a trust for the benefit of a minor beneficiary).

**(25), (25.1), (26)** [Repealed under former Act]

Notes: 104(25) and (25.1), repealed by 1988 tax reform, provided rules to prevent the same income from being taxed in both the trust's and the beneficiaries' hands. Because of other amendments, these rules are no longer needed.

104(26), repealed by 1988 tax reform, preserved the character of a trust's interest income in the hands of a beneficiary for purposes of the $1,000 investment income deduction under former 110.1, repealed at the same time.

**(27) Pension benefits** — Where a testamentary trust has, in a taxation year throughout which it was resident in Canada, received a superannuation or pension benefit or a benefit out of or under a foreign retirement arrangement and has designated, in the return of its income for the year under this Part, an amount in respect of a beneficiary under the trust equal to such portion (in this subsection referred to as the "beneficiary's share") of the benefit as

(a) may reasonably be considered (having regard to all the circumstances including the terms and conditions of the trust arrangement) to be part of the amount that, by reason of subsection (13), was included in computing the income for a particular taxation year of the beneficiary, and

(b) was not designated by the trust in respect of any other beneficiary under the trust,

the following rules apply:

(c) where

(i) the benefit is an amount described in subparagraph (a)(i) of the definition "pension income" in subsection 118(7), and

(ii) the beneficiary was a spouse or common-law partner of the settlor of the trust,

the beneficiary's share of the benefit shall be deemed, for the purposes of subsections 118(3) and (7), to be a payment described in subparagraph (a)(i) of the definition "pension income" in subsection 118(7) that is included in computing the beneficiary's income for the particular year,

(d) where the benefit

(i) is a single amount (within the meaning assigned by subsection 147.1(1)), other than an amount that relates to an actuarial surplus, paid by a registered pension plan to the trust as a consequence of the death of the settlor of the trust who was, at the time of death, a spouse or common-law partner of the beneficiary, or

(ii) would be an amount included in the total determined under paragraph 60(j) in respect of the beneficiary for the taxation year of the beneficiary in which the benefit was received by the trust if the benefit had been received by the beneficiary at the time it was received by the trust,

the beneficiary's share of the benefit is, for the purposes of paragraph 60(j), an eligible amount in respect of the beneficiary for the particular year, and

(e) where the benefit is a single amount (within the meaning assigned by subsection 147.1(1)) paid by a registered pension plan to the trust as a consequence of the death of the settlor of the trust and the beneficiary was, at the time of the settlor's death, under 18 years of age and a child or grandchild of the settlor, the beneficiary's share of the benefit (other than any portion thereof that relates to an actuarial surplus) shall be deemed, for the purposes of paragraph 60(l), to be an amount from a registered pension plan included in computing the beneficiary's income for the particular year as a payment described in subclause 60(l)(v)(B.1)(II).

**Related Provisions**: 60(l)(v)(B.1) — Rollover of RRSP/RRIF designated benefits to child or grandchild on death; 94(3)(a) [proposed] — Application to trust deemed resident in Canada; 248(8) — Occurrences as a consequence of death; 250(6.1) — Trust that ceases to exist deemed resident throughout year.

Notes: 104(27) permits a trust to flow pension benefits through to a beneficiary, so that the income of the beneficiary from the trust has the status of pension income in the beneficiary's hands for purposes of the pension credit in 118(3), the rollover to an RRSP under 60(j) and the deduction under 60(l).

104(27)(c)(ii) and (d)(i) amended by 2000 same-sex partners bill to add reference to "common-law partner", effective for the 2001 and later taxation years, or earlier by election (see Notes to 248(1)"common-law partner").

104(27)(c) and (d) amended by 1992 technical bill, effective 1993. For earlier years, "spouse" in 104(27)(c)(ii) was defined by reference to 146(1.1); for 1993–2000, see 252(4). In 104(27)(d)(i), "at the time of death" formerly read "at the time of the settlor's death".

Opening words of 104(27) amended by 1991 technical bill, effective 1990, to apply to a benefit from a foreign retirement arrangement.

104(27) amended by 1990 pension bill, effective 1988.

**Interpretation Bulletins**: IT-124R6: Contributions to registered retirement savings plans; IT-528: Transfers of funds between registered plans.

**Forms**: T3 Sched. 7: Pension income allocations or designations.

**(27.1) DPSP benefits** — Where

(a) a testamentary trust has received in a taxation year (in this subsection referred to as the "trust year") throughout which it was resident in Canada an amount from a deferred profit sharing plan as a consequence of the death of the settlor of the trust,

(b) the settlor was an employee of an employer who participated in the plan on behalf of the settlor, and

(c) the amount is not part of a series of periodic payments, such portion of the amount as

(d) is included under subsection 147(10) in computing the income of the trust for the trust year,

(e) can reasonably be considered (having regard to all the circumstances including the terms and conditions of the trust arrangement) to be part of the amount that was included under subsection (13) in computing the income for a particular taxation year of a beneficiary under the trust who was, at the time of the settlor's death, a spouse or common-law partner of the settlor, and

(f) is designated by the trust in respect of the beneficiary in the trust's return of income under this Part for the trust year

is, for the purposes of paragraph 60(j), an eligible amount in respect of the beneficiary for the particular year.

**Related Provisions**: 94(3)(a) [proposed] — Application to trust deemed resident in Canada; 248(8) — Occurrences as a consequence of death; 250(6.1) — Trust that ceases to exist deemed resident throughout year.

**Notes**: 104(27.1)(e) amended by 2000 same-sex partners bill to add reference to "common-law partner", effective for the 2001 and later taxation years, or earlier by election (see Notes to 248(1)"common-law partner").

104(27.1)(e) amended by 1992 technical bill, effective 1993. For earlier years, "spouse" therein was defined by reference to 146(1.1); for 1993–2000, see 252(4).

104(27.1) added by 1990 pension bill, effective for amounts received in 1989 or later.

**Interpretation Bulletins**: IT-124R6: Contributions to registered retirement savings plans; IT-528: Transfers of funds between registered plans.

**(28) [Death benefit deemed received by beneficiary]** — Such portion of any amount received by a testamentary trust in a taxation year on or after the death of an employee in recognition of the employee's service in an office or employment as may reasonably be considered (having regard to all the circumstances including the terms and conditions of the trust arrangement) to be paid or payable at a particular time to a particular beneficiary under the trust shall be deemed to be an amount received by the particular beneficiary at the particular time on or after the death of the employee in recognition of the employee's service in an office or employment and not to have been received by the trust.

**Related Provisions**: 56(1)(a)(iii) — Death benefit included in income; 94(3)(a) [proposed] — Application to trust deemed resident in Canada; 250(6.1) — Trust that ceases to exist deemed resident throughout year.

**Notes**: 104(28) allows a death benefit to flow through a trust, so that the first $10,000 remains non-taxable in the beneficiary's hands. See the definition of "death benefit" in 248(1), and 56(1)(a)(iii).

**Interpretation Bulletins**: IT-508R: Death benefits.

**(29) Amounts deemed payable to beneficiaries [resource income]** — Where a trust, in its return of income under this Part for a taxation year throughout which it was resident in Canada, designates an amount not exceeding the proportion of the amount, if any, by which

(a) the total of all amounts each of which is an amount that would, but for paragraph 18(1)(l.1) or (m), be deductible in computing the income of the trust for the year or that is required to be included in computing its income for the year by reason of paragraph 12(1)(o) or subsection 69(6) or (7)

exceeds

(b) the total of all amounts each of which is an amount that is deductible (otherwise than because of the membership of the trust in a partnership) under paragraph 20(1)(v.1) in computing the income of the trust for the year or that would, but for section 80.2, be included in computing its income for the year,

that

(c) the total of all amounts each of which is a part of the income of the trust for the year computed without reference to the provisions of this Act (in this subsection referred to as the "trust-purpose income" for the year) that was payable in the year to a beneficiary of the trust or was included in computing the income of a beneficiary of the trust for the year by virtue of subsection 105(2)

is of

(d) the trust-purpose income of the trust for the year,

that designated amount shall, for the purposes of this section, be deemed to have become payable by the trust to particular beneficiaries of the trust in the year in such proportions as are designated by the trust in that return of income, provided that those proportions are reasonable having regard to the shares of the trust-purpose income of the trust for the year included in computing their incomes for the year.

**Related Provisions**: 94(3)(a) [proposed] — Application to trust deemed resident in Canada; 250(6.1) — Trust that ceases to exist deemed resident throughout year.

**Notes**: 104(29)(b) amended by 1992 technical bill, effective for taxation years that end after December 20, 1991, to add the parenthetical exclusion. The change is consequential on amendments to 96(1)(d) and Reg. 1210 under which the resource allowance is no longer claimed at the partnership level.

**Interpretation Bulletins**: IT-342R: Trusts — income payable to beneficiaries.

**(30) Tax under Part XII.2** — For the purposes of this Part, there shall be deducted in computing the income of a trust for a taxation year the tax paid by the trust for the year under Part XII.2.

**Related Provisions**: 18(1)(t) — Tax under Part XII.2 is deductible.

**(31) Idem** — The amount in respect of a taxation year of a trust that is deemed under subsection 210.2(3) to have been paid by a beneficiary under the trust on account of the beneficiary's tax under this Part shall, for the purposes of subsection (13), be

## Subdivision k — Trusts and Beneficiaries      S. 105

deemed to be an amount in respect of the income of the trust for the year that has become payable by the trust to the beneficiary at the end of the year.

**Interpretation Bulletins**: IT-342R: Trusts — income payable to beneficiaries.

**Definitions [s. 104]**: "accumulating income" — 108(1); "allocable amount" — 104(15); "allowable business investment loss" — 38(c), 248(1); "allowable capital loss" — 38(b), 248(1); *"alter ego trust"*, "amount", "assessment" — 248(1); "aunt" — 252(2)(e); "beneficially interested" — 248(25); "beneficiary" — 104(1.1), (5.5), 108(1); "brother" — 252(2); "business" — 248(1); "business-income tax" — 104(22.4), 126(7); "calendar year" — *Interpretation Act* 37(1)(a); "Canada" — 255, *Interpretation Act* 35(1); "Canadian resource property" — 66(15), 248(1); "capital gain" — 39(1), 248(1); "capital interest" — 108(1), 248(1); "capital loss" — 39(1), 248(1); "capital property" — 54, 104(4.1), 248(1); "child" — 252(1); "common-law partner" — 248(1); "consequence of the death", "consequence of whose death" — 248(8); "controlled" — 256(6), (6.1); "corporation" — 248(1), *Interpretation Act* 35(1); "cost amount" — 108(1); "created by the taxpayer's will" — 248(9.1); "deemed capital cost" — 104(5); "deferred profit sharing plan" — 147(1), 248(1); "depreciable property" — 13(21), 248(1); "designated beneficiary" — 210; "designated contributor" — 104(5.6), (5.7)(c); "designation year" — 104(21.2); "disposition" — 248(1); "disposition day" — 104(5.3), (5.8); "dividend" — 248(1); "eligible real property gain", "eligible real property loss", "eligible taxable capital gains" — 108(1); "employee", "employee benefit plan", "employer", "employment" — 248(1); "estate" — 104(1), 248(1); "excluded property" — 108(1); "exempt beneficiary" — 104(5.4); "exempt property" — 108(1); "foreign resource property" — 66(15), 248(1); "foreign retirement arrangement" — 248(1); "former spouse" — 252(3); "grandparent" — 252(2); "great-aunt", "great-uncle" — 252(2)(f); "income" — of trust 108(3); "income interest" — 108(1), 248(1); "individual" — 248(1); *"inter vivos* trust" — 108(1), 248(1); "inventory" — 248(1); "investment tax credit" — 127(9), 248(1); "joint partner trust", "legal representative", "Minister" — 248(1); "mutual fund trust" — 132(6)–(7), 132.2(1)(q), 248(1); "net taxable capital gains" — 104(21.3); "NISA Fund No. 2" — 248(1); "non-business-income tax" — 104(22.4), 126(7); "non-qualifying real property" — 108(1); "non-resident" — 248(1); "non-resident-owned investment corporation" — 133(8), 248(1); "office" — 248(1); "parent" — 252(2); "partnership" — see Notes to 96(1); "payable" — 104(24); "person", "personal trust", "post-1971 partner trust" — 248(1); "pre-1972 spousal trust", "preferred beneficiary" — 108(1); "preferred beneficiary's share" — 104(15); "prescribed", "property" — 248(1); "qualified farm property", "qualified small business corporation share" — 108(1), 110.6(1); "received" — 248(7); "registered charity", "registered pension plan" — 248(1); "related" — 104(5.7)(b), 251(2); "relevant period" — 104(5.7); "resident in Canada" — 250; "settlor" — 108(1); "share", "shareholder" — 248(1); "sister" — 252(2); "small business corporation" — 248(1); "spouse" — 252(3); "substituted property" — 248(5); "superannuation or pension benefit" — 248(1); "taxable Canadian corporation" — 89(1), 248(1); "taxable capital gain" — 38(a), 248(1); "taxable dividend" — 89(1), 248(1); "taxable income" — 2(2), 248(1); "taxation year" — 104(23), 249; "taxpayer" — 248(1); "testamentary trust" — 108(1), 248(1); "trust" — 104(1), (3), 108(1), 248(1); "trust-purpose income" — 104(29)(c); "uncle" — 252(2)(e); "vested indefeasibly" — 248(9.2).

**105. (1) Benefits under trust** — The value of all benefits to a taxpayer during a taxation year from or under a trust, irrespective of when created, shall, subject to subsection (2), be included in computing the taxpayer's income for the year except to the extent that the value

(a) is otherwise required to be included in computing the taxpayer's income for a taxation year; or

(b) has been deducted under paragraph 53(2)(h) in computing the adjusted cost base of the taxpayer's interest in the trust or would be so deducted if that paragraph

  (i) applied in respect of the taxpayer's interest in the trust, and

  (ii) were read without reference to clause 53(2)(h)(i.1)(B).

**Related Provisions**: 104(19) — Portion of dividends deemed received by beneficiary; 104(21) — Portion of capital gains deemed gain of beneficiary; 104(23) — Testamentary trusts; 107.3(4) — No application to qualifying environmental trusts; 108(5) — Interpretation.

**Notes**: 105(1) is not interpreted as broadly as it reads. Revenue Canada states (VIEWS doc 9707317): "although it is the Department's position that the use of trust property by a beneficiary of the trust constitutes a benefit for the purposes of subsection 105(1), in the case of personal-use property owned by a trust, the Department will generally not assess a benefit for the use of that property. In this regard, personal-use property of a trust will, in accordance with the definition in section 54, include property (such as homes, cottages, boats, cars, etc.) owned primarily for the personal use or enjoyment of a beneficiary of the trust or any person related to the beneficiary." (See also the 1988 and 1989 Canadian Tax Foundation annual conference Round Tables, qq. 69 and 31 respectively.)

**Interpretation Bulletins**: IT-75R3: Scholarships, fellowships, bursaries, prizes, and research grants; IT-243R4: Dividend refund to private corporations; IT-524: Trusts — flow-through of taxable dividends to a beneficiary — after 1987.

**I.T. Technical News**: No. 11 (payments made by a trust for the benefit of a minor beneficiary; taxable benefit for use of personal-use property).

**(2) Upkeep, etc.** — Such part of an amount paid by a trust out of income of the trust for the upkeep, maintenance or taxes of or in respect of property that, under the terms of the trust arrangement, is required to be maintained for the use of a tenant for life or a beneficiary as is reasonable in the circumstances shall be included in computing the income of the tenant for life or other beneficiary from the trust for the taxation year for which it was paid.

**Related Provisions**: 104(6) — Deduction in computing trust income; 104(13.1), (13.2) — Designation of distributed income by trust; 104(23) — Testamentary trusts; 104(29) — Amounts deemed to be payable to beneficiaries; 108(5) — Interpretation; 120.4(1)"split income"(c) — Certain trust income of children subject to income splitting tax.

**Interpretation Bulletins**: IT-243R4: Dividend refund to private corporations; IT-342R: Trusts — income payable to beneficiaries; IT-381R3: Trusts — capital gains and losses and the flow-through of taxable capital gains to beneficiaries; IT-465R: Non-resident beneficiaries of trusts; IT-524: Trusts — flow-through of taxable dividends to a beneficiary — after 1987.

**I.T. Technical News**: No. 11 (taxable benefit for use of personal-use property).

**Definitions [s. 105]**: "adjusted cost base" — 54, 248(1); "amount" — 248(1); "beneficiary" — 108(1); "property" — 248(1);

"taxation year" — 104(23)(a), 249; "taxpayer" — 248(1); "trust" — 104(1), 108(1), 248(1), (3).

**106. (1) Income interest in trust** — Where an amount in respect of a taxpayer's income interest in a trust has been included in computing the taxpayer's income for a taxation year by reason of subsection (2) or 104(13), except to the extent that an amount in respect of that income interest has been deducted in computing the taxpayer's taxable income pursuant to subsection 112(1) or 138(6), there may be deducted in computing the taxpayer's income for the year the lesser of

(a) the amount so included in computing the taxpayer's income for the year, and

(b) the amount, if any, by which the cost to the taxpayer of the income interest exceeds the total of all amounts in respect of the interest that were deductible under this subsection in computing the taxpayer's income for previous taxation years.

**Related Provisions**: 106(1.1) — Cost of income interest; 108(1) — Exclusions from definition of "trust"; 115(1)(a)(iv) — Non-residents' taxable income earned in Canada; 128.1(10) "excluded right or interest"(j), (k) — Emigration — whether a deemed disposition of income interest.

**Interpretation Bulletins**: IT-385R2: Disposition of an income interest in a trust.

**(1.1) Cost of income interest in a trust** — For the purposes of subsection (1) and notwithstanding paragraph 69(1)(c), the cost to a taxpayer of an income interest in a trust, other than an interest acquired by the taxpayer from a person who was the beneficiary in respect of the interest immediately before the acquisition thereof by the taxpayer, shall be deemed to be nil.

### Proposed Amendment — 106(1.1)

**(1.1) Cost of income interest in a trust** — The cost to a taxpayer of an income interest of the taxpayer in a trust is deemed to be nil unless

(a) any part of the interest was acquired by the taxpayer from a person who was the beneficiary in respect of the interest immediately before that acquisition; or

(b) the cost of any part of the interest would otherwise be determined not to be nil under paragraph 128.1(1)(c) or (4)(c).

**Application**: Bill C-43 (First Reading September 20, 2000), subsec. 49(1), will amend subsec. 106(1.1) to read as above, applicable to 2000 et seq.

**Technical Notes**: Subsection 106(1.1) of the Act provides that, for the purposes of determining the deduction available under subsection 106(1) in respect of a beneficiary's income interest in a trust, the cost to the beneficiary of the interest is nil except where the interest was acquired from a beneficiary under the trust.

Subsection 106(1.1) is amended so that the deemed nil cost also does not apply to a beneficiary's income interest in a trust where:

- any part of the interest was acquired from a person who was the beneficiary in respect of the interest immediately before that acquisition, or
- the cost of any part of the interest was ever determined not to be nil under the taxpayer migration rules in section 128.1.

Subsection 106(1.1) is also amended to ensure that it applies for the purposes of the Act, and not simply subsection 106(1).

**Related Provisions**: 108(1) — Exclusions from definition of "trust".

**Interpretation Bulletins**: IT-385R2: Disposition of an income interest in a trust.

**(2) Disposition by taxpayer of income interest** — Where in a taxation year a taxpayer disposes of an income interest in a trust,

(a) except where subsection (3) is applicable, there shall be included in computing the taxpayer's income for the year the proceeds of the disposition;

### Proposed Amendment — 106(2)(a)

(a) except where subsection (3) applies to the disposition, there shall be included in computing the taxpayer's income for the year the amount, if any, by which

(i) the proceeds of disposition

exceed

(ii) where that interest includes a right to enforce payment of an amount by the trust, the amount in respect of that right that has been included in computing the taxpayer's income for a taxation year because of subsection 104(13);

**Application**: Bill C-43 (First Reading September 20, 2000), subsec. 49(2), will amend para. 106(2)(a) to read as above, applicable to 2000 et seq.

**Technical Notes**: Subsection 106(2) of the Act applies where a taxpayer disposes of an income interest (as defined in subsection 108(1)) in a trust. Paragraph 106(2)(a) provides that unless the disposition results from a distribution of property by the trust, the taxpayer's proceeds of disposition are included in computing the taxpayer's income for the year that includes the disposition.

Paragraph 106(2)(a) is amended to ensure that where a taxpayer disposes of an income interest in a trust that includes a right to enforce payment by the trust, the proceeds of disposition of the income interest are offset by the amount that has been included in the taxpayer's income under subsection 104(13) because of that right. This measure is meant to ensure that there is no double taxation where such rights are disposed of.

(b) any taxable capital gain or allowable capital loss of the taxpayer from the disposition shall be deemed to be nil; and

(c) for greater certainty, the cost to the taxpayer of each property received by the taxpayer as con-

Subdivision k — Trusts and Beneficiaries  S. 107(1)(b)

sideration for the disposition is the fair market value of the property at the time of the disposition.

**Related Provisions**: 107.3(4) — No application to qualifying environmental trusts; 107.4(3)(n) — No disposition of income interest in trust on qualifying disposition; 108(1) — Exclusions from definition of "trust"; 115(1)(a)(iv) — Non-residents' taxable income earned in Canada.

**Notes**: Proposed amendments to 106(2) and (3) in the original version of the 1995–97 technical bill (Bill C-69) were not included when that bill was re-tabled and enacted as Bill C-28 (1998, c. 19) in December 1997. See instead the proposed amendments of December 23, 1998, later December 17, 1999, later June 5, 2000, later Bill C-43, to 108(1)"trust".

**Interpretation Bulletins**: IT-385R2: Disposition of an income interest in a trust.

**Advance Tax Rulings**: ATR-3: Winding-up of an estate.

**(3) Proceeds of disposition of income interest** — For greater certainty, where at any time any property of a trust has been distributed by the trust to a taxpayer who was a beneficiary under the trust in satisfaction of all or any part of the taxpayer's income interest in the trust, the trust shall be deemed to have disposed of the property for proceeds of disposition equal to the fair market value of the property at that time.

**Notes**: See Notes to 106(2).

**Interpretation Bulletins**: IT-385R2: Disposition of an income interest in a trust.

**Definitions [s. 106]**: "allowable capital loss" — 38(b), 248(1); "amount" — 248(1); "beneficiary" — 108(1); "cost" — 106(1.1); "income interest" — 108(1), 248(1); "person" — 248(1); "proceeds of disposition" — 54, 106(3); "property" — 248(1); "taxable capital gain" — 38(a), 248(1); "taxable income" — 2(2), 248(1); "taxation year" — 104(23)(a), 249; "taxpayer" — 248(1); "trust" — 104(1), 108(1), 248(1), (3).

**107. (1) Disposition by taxpayer of capital interest** — Where a taxpayer has disposed of all or any part of the taxpayer's capital interest in a trust,

(a) where the trust is a personal trust or a prescribed trust, for the purpose of computing the taxpayer's taxable capital gain, if any, from the disposition, the adjusted cost base to the taxpayer of the interest, or the part of the interest, as the case may be, immediately before the disposition shall be deemed to be the greater of

> **Proposed Amendment — 107(1)(a) opening words**
>
> (a) where the trust is a personal trust or a prescribed trust, for the purpose of computing the taxpayer's capital gain, if any, from the disposition, the adjusted cost base to the taxpayer of the interest or the part of the interest, as the case may be, immediately before the disposition is, unless any part of the interest has ever been acquired for consideration and, at the time of the disposition, the trust is non-resident, deemed to be the greater of
>
> **Application**: Bill C-43 (First Reading September 20, 2000), subsec. 50(1), will amend the opening words of para. 107(1)(a) to read as above, applicable to 2000 et seq., except that, in respect of transfers in 2000, for the purposes of subsec. 107(1), the residence of a transferee trust shall be determined without reference to s. 94, as it read before 2001.
>
> **Technical Notes**: Subsection 107(1) of the Act contains special rules that apply to the disposition of a capital interest in a trust.
>
> Paragraph 107(1)(a) applies for the purpose of computing a taxpayer's taxable capital gain from the disposition of a capital interest in a personal trust (or a prescribed trust described in section 4800.1 of the Regulations), except where the interest was an interest in a non-resident inter vivos trust purchased by the taxpayer and the disposition was not by way of a distribution to which subsection 107(2) applies. For this purpose the residency of the trust is to be determined without reference to section 94 as it read before 2001.
>
> Where paragraph 107(1)(a) applies, the adjusted cost base (ACB) to the taxpayer of a trust capital interest for capital gains purposes is generally equal to the greater of the ACB otherwise determined and the "cost amount" of the interest. Subsection 108(1) provides that, for this purpose, the "cost amount" of a capital interest at any time is based on the amount of the trust's money and the cost amount of the trust's other property. The "cost amount" mechanism in paragraph 107(1)(a) generally allows the flow-out from a personal or prescribed trust to a beneficiary of trust capital without adverse tax consequences. However, the concluding words in subsection 107(1) provide that paragraph 107(1)(a) generally does not apply with regard to certain purchased interests in non-resident trusts.
>
> Paragraph 107(1)(a) is amended, in conjunction with the repeal of the concluding wording in subsection 107(1), to ensure that paragraph 107(1)(a) never applies to dispositions of any capital interests in non-resident trusts acquired for consideration. New paragraph 108(6)(c) and new subsection 108(7) are relevant in determining where an interest in a trust has been acquired for consideration. Amended paragraph 107(1)(a) also provides that, for this purpose, a non-resident trust includes a trust deemed by subparagraph 94(1)(c)(i) to be resident in Canada.

(i) its adjusted cost base, otherwise determined, to the taxpayer immediately before the disposition, and

(ii) the amount, if any, by which

(A) its cost amount to the taxpayer immediately before the disposition

exceeds

(B) the total of all amounts deducted under paragraph 53(2)(g.1) in computing its adjusted cost base to the taxpayer immediately before the disposition;

(b) for greater certainty, for the purposes of computing the taxpayer's allowable capital loss, if any, from the disposition of the interest or part thereof, as the case may be, the adjusted cost base to the taxpayer of the interest or part thereof immediately before the disposition is the adjusted cost base to the taxpayer thereof immediately before that time as determined under this Act without reference to paragraph (a),

859

### Proposed Repeal — 107(1)(b)

**Application:** Bill C-43 (First Reading September 20, 2000), subsec. 50(2), will repeal para. 107(1)(b), applicable to 2000 *et seq.*

**Technical Notes:** Paragraph 107(1)(b) is repealed because it is unnecessary. Since paragraph 107(1)(a) applies only for the purposes of computing a taxpayer's capital gain, it is clear without paragraph 107(1)(b) that the ACB calculation in paragraph 107(1)(a) is not relevant for the purposes of computing a taxpayer's allowable capital loss.

(c) where the taxpayer is not a mutual fund trust, the taxpayer's loss from the disposition is deemed to be the amount, if any, by which the amount of that loss otherwise determined exceeds the amount, if any, by which

(i) the total of all amounts each of which was received or would, but for subsection 104(19), have been received by the trust on a share of the capital stock of a corporation before the disposition (and, where the trust is a unit trust, after 1987) and

(A) where the taxpayer is a corporation,

(I) was a taxable dividend designated under subsection 104(19) by the trust in respect of the taxpayer, to the extent of the amount of the dividend that was deductible under section 112 or subsection 115(1) or 138(6) in computing the taxpayer's taxable income or taxable income earned in Canada for any taxation year, or

(II) was an amount designated under subsection 104(20) by the trust in respect of the taxpayer,

(B) where the taxpayer is another trust, was an amount designated under subsection 104(19) or (20) by the trust in respect of the taxpayer, and

(C) where the taxpayer is not a corporation, trust or partnership, was an amount designated under subsection 104(20) by the trust in respect of the taxpayer

exceeds

(ii) the portion of the total determined under subparagraph (i) that can reasonably be considered to have resulted in a reduction, under this paragraph, of the taxpayer's loss otherwise determined from a previous disposition of an interest in the trust, and

(d) where the taxpayer is a partnership, the share of a person (other than another partnership or a mutual fund trust) of any loss of the partnership from the disposition is deemed to be the amount, if any, by which that loss otherwise determined exceeds the amount, if any, by which

(i) the total of all amounts each of which is a dividend that was received or would, but for subsection 104(19), have been received by the trust on a share of the capital stock of a corporation before the disposition (and, where the trust is a unit trust, after 1987) and

(A) where the person is a corporation,

(I) was a taxable dividend that was designated under subsection 104(19) by the trust in respect of the taxpayer, to the extent of the amount of the dividend that was deductible under section 112 or subsection 115(1) or 138(6) in computing the person's taxable income or taxable income earned in Canada for any taxation year, or

(II) was a dividend designated under subsection 104(20) by the trust in respect of the taxpayer and was an amount received by the person,

(B) where the person is an individual other than a trust, was a dividend designated under subsection 104(20) by the trust in respect of the taxpayer and was an amount received by the person, and

(C) where the person is another trust, was a dividend designated under subsection 104(19) or (20) by the trust in respect of the taxpayer and was an amount received by the person (or that would have been received by the person if this Act were read without reference to subsection 104(19)),

exceeds

(ii) the portion of the total determined under subparagraph (i) that can reasonably be considered to have resulted in a reduction, under this paragraph, of the person's loss otherwise determined from a previous disposition of an interest in the trust,

except that where the interest was an interest in an *inter vivos* trust not resident in Canada that was purchased by the taxpayer, paragraph (a) does not apply in respect of the disposition of all or any part thereof except where subsection (2) is applicable in respect of any distribution of property by the trust to the taxpayer in satisfaction of that interest or that part thereof, as the case may be.

### Proposed Repeal — 107(1) closing words

**Application:** Bill C-43 (First Reading September 20, 2000), subsec. 50(3), will repeal the portion of subsec. 107(1) after para. (d), applicable to 2000 *et seq.*

**Technical Notes:** See under 107(1)(a).

**Related Provisions:** 40(3.7) — Application to non-resident individual; 104(19) — Taxable dividends flowed through trust; 107(1.1) — Cost of capital interest; 107.3(4) — No application to qualifying environmental trusts; 107.4(3)(b)(ii) — Application of stop-loss rule to qualifying disposition; 108(6) — Where terms of trust are varied; 108(7) — Meaning of "acquired for consideration"; 128.1(10) "excluded right or interest"(j), (k) — Emigration — whether a deemed disposition of capital interest; 248(1) "disposition"(d), (h) — Whether transfer by trust is a disposition of capital interest; 248(25.4) — Addition to cost of capital interest in trust.

**Notes**: 107(1)(a)(ii)(B) added by 1994 tax amendments bill (Part I), effective for taxation years that end after February 21, 1994.

107(1) amended by 1988 tax reform and by 1991 technical bill. The phrase "where the trust is a personal trust" in 107(1)(a) does not apply to the disposition of a trust the units of which were listed on October 1, 1987 on a prescribed stock exchange, before 1991 (or before any date after October 1, 1987 on which a beneficial interest in the trust is issued, if such date is earlier than 1991).

107(1)(c) replaced with 107(1)(c) and (d) by 1995-97 technical bill, this version effective for dispositions after 1997. For dispositions from April 27, 1995 through the end of 1997, read the first reference to "loss" in 107(1)(c) as "capital loss". For dispositions before April 27, 1995, ignore 107(1)(d) and read:

(c) where the taxpayer is a corporation and the interest is not an interest in a prescribed trust, its capital loss from the disposition at any time of the interest or part thereof shall be deemed to be the amount, if any, by which the amount of its loss otherwise determined exceeds the amount, if any, by which

(i) the total of all amounts each of which was received by the trust before that time (and, where the trust is a unit trust, after 1987) and designated by it under subsection 104(19) or (20) in respect of the corporation

exceeds

(ii) such portion of the total referred to in subparagraph (i) as can reasonably be considered to have resulted in a reduction under this paragraph of its capital loss otherwise determined from the disposition before that time of an interest in the trust,

Former 107(1)(c) amended by 1993 technical bill, effective for 1988 and later taxation years, to add subpara. (ii) and the parenthesized words re unit trusts in subpara. (i).

**Regulations**: 3200 (prescribed stock exchange, for application before 1991; technically does not apply to the amending legislation [1994, c. 7, Sch. II (1991, c. 49, the 1991 technical bill), s. 76]); 4800.1 (prescribed trust).

**Advance Tax Rulings**: ATR-38: Distribution of all of the property of an estate.

**(1.1) Cost of capital interest in a trust** — For the purpose of subsection (1) and notwithstanding paragraph 69(1)(c), the cost to a taxpayer of a capital interest in a trust, other than an interest acquired by the taxpayer from a person who was the beneficiary in respect of the interest immediately before its acquisition by the taxpayer or an interest issued to the taxpayer for consideration paid by the taxpayer that is equal to the fair market value of the interest at the time of issuance, is deemed to be

(a) where the taxpayer elects under subsection 110.6(19) in respect of the interest and the trust does not elect under that subsection in respect of any property of the trust, the taxpayer's cost of the interest determined under paragraph 110.6(19)(a); and

(b) in any other case, nil.

### Proposed Amendment — 107(1.1)

**(1.1) Cost of capital interest in a trust** — The cost to a taxpayer of a capital interest of the taxpayer in a personal trust or a prescribed trust is deemed to be,

(a) where the taxpayer elected under subsection 110.6(19) in respect of the interest and the trust does not elect under that subsection in respect of any property of the trust, the taxpayer's cost of the interest determined under paragraph 110.6(19)(a); and

(b) in any other case, nil, unless

(i) any part of the interest was acquired by the taxpayer from a person who was the beneficiary in respect of the interest immediately before that acquisition, or

(ii) the cost of any part of the interest would otherwise be determined not to be nil under section 48 as it read in its application before 1993 or under paragraph 111(4)(e) or 128.1(1)(c) or (4)(c).

**Application**: Bill C-43 (First Reading September 20, 2000), subsec. 50(4), will amend subsec. 107(1.1) to read as above, applicable to 2000 et seq.

**Technical Notes**: Subsection 107(1.1) of the Act provides, for the purposes of subsection 107(1), that the cost of a capital interest in a trust is nil except where the interest is acquired from a previous capital beneficiary in the trust or where the interest is issued to the beneficiary for consideration equal to the fair market value of the interest at the time of issuance.

Subsection 107(1.1) is amended so that it applies only to trusts that are personal trusts or prescribed trusts. It is intended that trusts described in section 4800.1 of the Regulations be prescribed for this purpose.

Paragraph 107(1.1)(b) is amended to provide that the cost of the interest will not be deemed nil where:

- the cost of any part of the interest would otherwise be determined not to be nil under the taxpayer migration rules in section 128.1 or former section 48 or under paragraph 111(4)(e) (acquisition of control), or

- any part of the interest was acquired from a person who was the beneficiary in respect of the interest immediately before that acquisition.

Subsection 107(1.1) is also amended to ensure that it applies for the purposes of the Act, and not simply subsection 107(1).

**Related Provisions**: 107.4(3)(k)–(m) — Cost of capital interest in trust following qualifying disposition; 107.4(4) — Fair market value of capital interest in trust; 248(25.4) — Addition to cost of capital interest in trust.

**Notes**: 107(1.1)(a) added by 1995-97 technical bill, effective for 1994 and later taxation years.

**Regulations**: 4800.1 (prescribed trust; to be amended to apply to 107(1.1)).

**(2) Capital interest distribution by personal or prescribed trust** — Where at any time any property of a personal trust or a prescribed trust has been distributed by the trust to a taxpayer who was a beneficiary under the trust in satisfaction of all or any part of the taxpayer's capital interest in the trust, the following rules apply:

### Proposed Amendment — 107(2) opening words [temporary]

**(2) Distribution by personal trust** — Subject to subsection (2.001), where at any time a property of a personal trust or a prescribed trust is distributed by the trust to a taxpayer who was a beneficiary under the trust in satisfaction of all or any part of the taxpayer's capital interest in the trust,

**Application**: Bill C-43 (First Reading September 20, 2000), subsec. 50(5), will amend the opening words of subsec. 107(2) to read as above, applicable to distributions made after October 1, 1996 and before 2000 (see further amendment below).

**Technical Notes**: See under 107(2) below.

### Proposed Amendment — 107(2) opening words

**(2) Distribution by personal trust** — Subject to subsections (2.001), (2.002) and (4) to (5), where at any time a property of a personal trust or a prescribed trust is distributed by the trust to a taxpayer who was a beneficiary under the trust and there is a resulting disposition of all or any part of the taxpayer's capital interest in the trust,

**Application**: Bill C-43 (First Reading September 20, 2000), subsec. 50(6), will amend the opening words of subsec. 107(2) to read as above, applicable to distributions made after 1999.

**Technical Notes**: Subsection 107(2) of the Act applies where a personal trust or a trust described in section 4800.1 of the Regulations distributes property to a beneficiary in satisfaction of all or part of the beneficiary's capital interest in the trust. Under paragraphs 107(2)(a) and (b), the trust is deemed to have disposed of the property for proceeds of disposition equal to the property's cost amount and the property is deemed to have been acquired by the beneficiary for the same amount plus a "bump" equal to the specified percentage of any excess of the adjusted cost base to the beneficiary of the capital interest over its "cost amount" (as defined by subsection 108(1)) to the beneficiary of the interest. Under paragraph 107(2)(c), the beneficiary is deemed to have disposed of the capital interest for proceeds equal to the deemed acquisition cost (determined as if the specified percentage referred to above were 100 per cent) less a reduction equal to the amount of debt assumed by the beneficiary that is conditional upon the distribution of the property. Under subsection 107(3), the specified percentage is 100 per cent in the case of non-depreciable capital property (e.g., land and shares) and 50 per cent in any other case.

Subsection 107(2) is amended to clarify that it applies in connection with distributions in respect of a capital interest in a personal or prescribed trust only if the distribution results in a disposition of all or part of the capital interest. Where the distribution does not constitute a disposition of a capital interest in a trust because of new paragraph (i) of the definition "disposition" in subsection 248(1), the rules in amended subsection 107(2.1) apply.

Subsection 107(2) is amended so that it is expressly subject to amended subsections 107(4) to (5). This amendment is made for technical clarity and does not represent any change in policy. Amended subsections 107(4) to (5) describe trust distributions to which subsection 107(2.1) is to apply.

Subsection 107(2) also is amended so that it is subject to new subsections 107(2.001) and (2.002). New subsection 107(2.001) allows a trust to elect out of the rules in subsection 107(2) in respect of a distribution of property to a beneficiary in satisfaction of the beneficiary's capital interest in the trust where

- the trust is resident in Canada at the time of the distribution,
- the property is taxable Canadian property, or
- the property is capital property used in, eligible capital property in respect of, or property described in the inventory of, a business carried on by the trust through a permanent establishment (as defined by regulation) in Canada immediately before the time of the distribution.

If this election is made, the distribution is subject to the rules in amended subsection 107(2.1). An electing trust is generally required to file a prescribed form with the Minister with its tax return for the taxation year that includes the time of the distribution. This amendment applies to distributions made after October 1, 1996. For distributions made before the date of Royal Assent, the election is considered to have been made on a timely basis if it is filed by the filing-due date for the trust's taxation year that includes the date of Royal Assent.

New subsection 107(2.002) applies where a non-resident trust makes a distribution, after 1999, of a property (other than taxable Canadian property or business property connected with a Canadian permanent establishment) to a beneficiary of the trust in satisfaction of the beneficiary's capital interest in the trust. The beneficiary in these circumstances may elect out of the rules in subsection 107(2) in respect of the distribution, with the result that subsection 107(2.1) applies in respect of the distribution. The election is made by filing a prescribed form with the beneficiary's income tax return. Where the election is made, the cost amount of the beneficiary's interest also is deemed to be nil for the purposes of subparagraph 107(1)(a)(ii). This amendment applies to distributions made after 1999. For distributions made before the date of Royal Assent, the election is considered to have been made on a timely basis if it is filed by the filing-due date for the beneficiary's taxation year that includes the date of Royal Assent.

(a) the trust shall be deemed to have disposed of the property for proceeds of disposition equal to its cost amount to the trust immediately before that time;

(b) the taxpayer is, subject to subsection (2.2), deemed to have acquired the property at a cost equal to the total of its cost amount to the trust immediately before that time and the amount, if any, by which

(i) the adjusted cost base to the taxpayer of the capital interest or part thereof, as the case may be, immediately before that time as determined for the purposes of paragraph (1)(b)

exceeds

(ii) the cost amount to the taxpayer of the capital interest or part thereof, as the case may be, immediately before that time;

(c) the taxpayer shall be deemed to have disposed of all or part, as the case may be, of the capital interest for proceeds equal to the cost at which the taxpayer is deemed by paragraph (b) to have acquired the property, minus the amount of any debt assumed by the taxpayer or of any other legal obligation assumed by the taxpayer to pay any amount, if the distribution of the property to the taxpayer was conditional on the assumption by the taxpayer of the debt or obligation;

### Proposed Amendment — 107(2)(b)–(c)

(b) subject to subsection (2.2), the taxpayer is deemed to have acquired the property at a cost equal to the total of its cost amount to the trust immediately before that time and the specified percentage of the amount, if any, by which

  (i) the adjusted cost base to the taxpayer of the capital interest or part of it, as the case may be, immediately before that time (determined without reference to paragraph (1)(a))

exceeds

  (ii) the cost amount to the taxpayer of the capital interest or part of it, as the case may be, immediately before that time;

(b.1) for the purpose of paragraph (b), the specified percentage is,

  (i) where the property is capital property (other than depreciable property), 100%,

  (ii) where the property is eligible capital property in respect of a business of the trust, 100%, and

  (iii) in any other case, 75%;

(c) the taxpayer is deemed to have disposed of all or part, as the case may be, of the capital interest for proceeds equal to the amount, if any, by which

  (i) the cost at which the taxpayer would be deemed by paragraph (b) to have acquired the property if the specified percentage referred to in that paragraph were 100%

exceeds

  (ii) the total of all amounts each of which is an eligible offset at that time of the taxpayer in respect of the capital interest or the part of it;

**Application**: Bill C-43 (First Reading September 20, 2000), subsec. 50(7), will amend paras. 107(2)(b) and (c) to read as above, and add para. (b.1), applicable to distributions made after 1999.

**Technical Notes**: Paragraph 107(2)(b.1) is introduced (in conjunction with consequential amendments to paragraphs 107(2)(b) and (c) and the repeal of subsection 107(3)) so that the specified percentages referred to above are explicitly provided under subsection 107(2). This amendment is intended to clarify the operation of subsection 107(2). In addition, the specified percentage for property (other than non-depreciable capital property and eligible capital property) is being increased from 50 per cent to 75 per cent. The specified percentage for eligible capital property is increased from 50 per cent to 100 per cent in recognition that only a maximum of 75 per cent of the cost of eligible capital property can ultimately be deducted for income tax purposes. This amendment is intended to reduce the differential in the tax treatment of depreciable and non-depreciable property in this context, so that this differential corresponds more closely to that which prevailed before the increase in the capital gains inclusion rate from 50 per cent to 75 per cent.

Paragraph 107(2)(c) is amended so that the reduction, because of debt assumed by the beneficiary, to a beneficiary's proceeds of disposition of the beneficiary's capital interest is now provided under the new definition "eligible offset" in subsection 108(1).

(d) where the property so distributed was depreciable property of a prescribed class of the trust and the amount that was the capital cost to the trust of that property exceeds the cost at which the taxpayer is deemed by this section to have acquired the property, for the purposes of sections 13 and 20 and any regulations made under paragraph 20(1)(a)

  (i) the capital cost to the taxpayer of the property shall be deemed to be the amount that was the capital cost of the property to the trust, and

  (ii) the excess shall be deemed to have been allowed to the taxpayer in respect of the property under regulations made under paragraph 20(1)(a) in computing income for taxation years before the acquisition by the taxpayer of the property; and

### Proposed Addition — 107(2)(d.1)

(d.1) the property is deemed to be taxable Canadian property of the taxpayer where

  (i) the taxpayer is non-resident at that time,

  (ii) that time is before October 2, 1996, and

  (iii) the property was deemed by paragraph 51(1)(f), 85(1)(i) or 85.1(1)(a), subsection 87(4) or (5) or paragraph 97(2)(c) to be taxable Canadian property of the trust; and

**Application**: Bill C-43 (First Reading September 20, 2000), subsec. 50(8), will add para. 107(2)(d.1), applicable in determining after October 1, 1996 whether property is taxable Canadian property.

**Technical Notes**: Paragraph 107(2)(d.1) is amended to clarify the tax consequences of the disposition of taxable Canadian property by a trust to non-resident beneficiaries before October 2, 1996. In the event that the property was explicitly deemed to have been taxable Canadian property under a number of specified provisions of the Act, paragraph 107(2)(d.1) ensures that it continues to be taxable Canadian property of the beneficiary.

(e) [Repealed]

(f) where the property so distributed was eligible capital property of the trust in respect of a business of the trust,

  (i) where the eligible capital expenditure of the trust in respect of the property exceeds the cost at which the taxpayer is deemed by this subsection to have acquired the property, for the purposes of sections 14, 20 and 24,

    (A) the eligible capital expenditure of the taxpayer in respect of the property shall be deemed to be the amount that was the eligible capital expenditure of the trust in respect of the property, and

(B) ¾ of the excess shall be deemed to have been allowed under paragraph 20(1)(b) to the taxpayer in respect of the property in computing income for taxation years ending

(I) before the acquisition by the taxpayer of the property, and

(II) after the adjustment time of the taxpayer in respect of the business, and

(ii) for the purposes of determining after that time

(A) the amount deemed under subparagraph 14(1)(a)(v) to be the taxpayer's taxable capital gain, and

(B) the amount to be included under subparagraph 14(1)(a)(v) or paragraph 14(1)(b) in computing the taxpayer's income

in respect of any subsequent disposition of the property of the business, there shall be added to the amount otherwise determined for Q in the definition "cumulative eligible capital" in subsection 14(5) the amount determined by the formula

### Proposed Amendment — 107(2)(f)(ii) pre formula

(ii) for the purpose of determining after that time the amount required by paragraph 14(1)(b) to be included in computing the taxpayer's income in respect of any subsequent disposition of property of the business, there shall be added to the value otherwise determined for Q in the definition "cumulative eligible capital" in subsection 14(5) the amount determined by the formula

**Application**: The December 21, 2000 draft legislation, subsec. 49(1), will amend the portion of subpara. 107(2)(f)(ii) before the formula to read as above, applicable to taxation years that end after February 27, 2000.

**Technical Notes**: Subsection 107(2) provides a rollover on the distribution of property from a personal or prescribed trust to a beneficiary in satisfaction of all or part of the beneficiary's capital interest in such a trust.

Paragraph 107(2)(f) is intended to prevent an overstatement of the income inclusions under subparagraph 14(1)(a)(v) or paragraph 14(1)(b), on the subsequent disposition of eligible capital property by the beneficiary. Paragraph 107(2)(f) is amended consequential on the renumbering of subsection 14(1), which is described in further detail in the commentary to that subsection.

$$A \times \frac{B}{C}$$

where

A is the amount, if any, determined for Q in that definition in respect of the business of the trust immediately before the distribution,

B is the fair market value of the property so distributed immediately before the distribution, and

C is the fair market value immediately before the distribution of all eligible capital property of the trust in respect of the business.

**Related Provisions**: 43(2) — No capital loss on payment out of trust's income or gains; 53(4) — Effect on ACB of trust interest; 69(11) — Deemed proceeds of disposition; 73(1.02)(c)(i) — Where rollover under 73(1) disallowed; 80.03(1), (3)(b) — Capital gain where subsec. 107(2) applies to trust interest on disposition following debt forgiveness; 104(4)(a.2) — Anti-avoidance rule where trust distributes property before death; 104(5.8) — Trust transfers; 107(2.01) — Principal residence distribution by personal trust; 107(2.1) — Application where trust elects out of 107(2); 107(3) — Cost of certain property; 107(4) — Where trust in favour of spouse; 107(4.1) — Where subsec. 75(2) applicable to trust; 107(5) — Distribution to non-resident; 107.4(3) — Rollover of property to trust where no change in beneficial ownership; 107.4(4) — Fair market value of capital interest in trust; 126(2.22) — Foreign tax credit to trust on disposition of property by non-resident beneficiary; 220(4.6)–(4.63) — Security for tax on distribution of taxable Canadian property to non-resident beneficiary; 248(1)"disposition"(d), (h) — Whether transfer by trust is a disposition of capital interest.

**Notes**: 107(2) allows a "rollout" of a personal trust's property at cost to the beneficiaries in many circumstances. See, however, 107(4), (4.1) and (5) for various restrictions.

Opening words of 107(2)(b) amended by 1995-97 technical bill, effective for distributions made after 1993, to add "subject to subsection (2.2)". (Other changes were merely cosmetic.)

107(2)(e), added by 1991 technical bill, was repealed, retroactive to its introduction, by 1992 technical bill. 107(2)(f), added by 1992 technical bill effective for distributions after 1987, now deals with eligible capital property.

Reference to 14(1)(a)(v) added to 107(2)(f)(ii)(B) by 1994 Budget, effective for distributions of property made after February 22, 1994.

107(2) amended by 1988 tax reform. In the opening words of 107(2), read "trust" in place of "personal trust or a prescribed trust", in the case of the disposition of a trust the units of which were listed on October 1, 1987 on a prescribed stock exchange (see Regulations annotation to 107(1)), before 1991 (or before any date after October 1, 1987 on which a beneficial interest in the trust is issued, if such date is earlier than 1991).

**Regulations**: 3200 (prescribed stock exchange, for application before 1991 — see Notes); 4800.1 (prescribed trust).

**Interpretation Bulletins**: IT-120R5: Principal residence; IT-209R: *Inter vivos* gifts of capital property to individuals directly or through trusts; IT-349R3: Intergenerational transfers of farm property on death; IT-393R2: Election re tax on rents and timber royalties — non-residents.

**Advance Tax Rulings**: ATR-38: Distribution of all of the property of an estate; ATR-70: Distribution of taxable Canadian property by a trust to a non-resident.

### Proposed Addition — 107(2.001), (2.002)

**(2.001) No rollover on election by a trust** — Where a trust makes a distribution of a property to a beneficiary of the trust in full or partial satisfaction of the beneficiary's capital interest in the trust and so elects in prescribed form filed with the Minister with the trust's return of income for its taxation year in which the distribution occurred, subsection (2) does not apply to the distribution if

(a) the trust is resident in Canada at the time of the distribution;

(b) the property is taxable Canadian property; or

(c) the property is capital property used in, eligible capital property in respect of, or property described in the inventory of, a business carried on by the trust through a permanent establishment (as defined by regulation) in Canada immediately before the time of the distribution.

**Application**: Bill C-43 (First Reading September 20, 2000), subsec. 50(9), will add subsec. 107(2.001), applicable to distributions made after October 1, 1996, except that for distributions made from a trust before the particular day on which the amending legislation is assented to, an election under subsec. 107(2.001) is deemed to have been made in a timely manner if it is made on or before the trust's filing-due date for the taxation year that includes the particular day.

**Technical Notes**: See under 107(2).

**Related Provisions**: 107(2.002) — Election by beneficiary; 248(1)"taxable Canadian property"(m)–(q) — Extended meaning of TCP.

**(2.002) No rollover on election by a beneficiary** — Where a non-resident trust makes a distribution of a property (other than a property described in paragraph (2.001)(b) or (c)) to a beneficiary of the trust in full or partial satisfaction of the beneficiary's capital interest in the trust and the beneficiary makes an election under this subsection in prescribed form filed with the Minister with the beneficiary's return of income for the beneficiary's taxation year in which the distribution occurred,

(a) subsection (2) does not apply to the distribution; and

(b) for the purpose of subparagraph (1)(a)(ii), the cost amount of the interest to the beneficiary is deemed to be nil.

**Related Provisions**: 107(2.001) — Election by trust.

**Application**: Bill C-43 (First Reading September 20, 2000), subsec. 50(9), will add subsec. 107(2.002), applicable to distributions made after 1999, except that for distributions made to a beneficiary before the particular day on which the amending legislation is assented to, an election under subsec. 107(2.002) is deemed to have been made in a timely manner if it is made on or before the beneficiary's filing-due date for the taxation year that includes the particular day.

**Technical Notes**: See under 107(2).

**(2.01) Distribution of principal residence** — Where a property that would, if a personal trust had designated the property under paragraph (c.1) of the definition "principal residence" in section 54, be a principal residence (within the meaning of that definition) of the trust for a taxation year, is at any time (in this subsection referred to as "that time") distributed by the trust to a taxpayer in circumstances to which subsection (2) applies and subsection (4) does not apply and the trust so elects in its return of income under this Part for the taxation year that includes that time,

### Proposed Amendment — 107(2.01) opening words

**(2.01) Distribution of principal residence** — Where property that would, if a personal trust had designated the property under paragraph (c.1) of the definition "principal residence" in section 54, be a principal residence (within the meaning of that definition) of the trust for a taxation year, is at any time (in this subsection referred to as "that time") distributed by the trust to a taxpayer in circumstances to which subsection (2) applies and the trust so elects in its return of income for the taxation year that includes that time,

**Application**: Bill C-43 (First Reading September 20, 2000), subsec. 50(10), will amend the opening words of subsec. 107(2.01) to read as above, applicable to distributions made after 1999.

**Technical Notes**: Subsection 107(2.01) of the Act allows a personal trust to elect to be treated as if it had disposed of, and reacquired, a principal residence at its fair market value immediately before distributing the property to one of its beneficiaries under subsection 107(2). The rule does not apply to distributions of property by a post-1971 partner trust in circumstances to which subsection 107(4) applies. (Subsection 107(4) generally applies to distributions made by such a trust to a beneficiary, other than the beneficiary spouse, before the death of the beneficiary spouse.) Subsection 107(2.01) is designed to allow a personal trust to take advantage of the principal residence exemption. In this regard, reference can be made to the definition of "principal residence" in section 54.

Subsection 107(2.01) is amended to eliminate the reference to subsection 107(4), given that subsection 107(2.1) now applies to distributions to which amended subsection 107(4) applies.

(a) the trust shall be deemed to have disposed of the property immediately before the particular time that is immediately before that time for proceeds of disposition equal to the fair market value of the property at that time; and

(b) the trust shall be deemed to have reacquired the property at the particular time at a cost equal to that fair market value.

**Notes**: Opening words of 107(2.01) amended by 1992 technical bill, effective for distributions after 1990. An election by a trust (other than a spousal trust — i.e., a trust described in 70(6) or 73(1)) to have the amended 107(2.01) apply to a distribution after 1990 may be made by notifying Revenue Canada in writing by December 10, 1993. For distributions before 1991, read:

(2.01) Principal residence distribution by spousal trust — Where at any time (in this subsection referred to as "that time") a property has been distributed by a trust described in subsection 70(6) or 73(1) to a taxpayer in circumstances in which subsection (2) applies and subsection (4) does not apply and the property would, if the trust had designated the property under paragraph 54(g), be a principal residence (within the meaning assigned by that paragraph) of the trust for a taxation year, the following rules apply where the trust so elects in its return of income under this Part for the taxation year that includes that time:

107(2.01) added by 1991 technical bill, effective for distributions after May 9, 1985. An election to have 107(2.01) apply to a distribution by a trust before December 18, 1991 may be made by the trust by notifying Revenue Canada in writing before April 1992 and, notwithstanding 152(4) to (5), such assessments of tax, interest and penalties shall be made as are necessary to give effect to the election.

**Interpretation Bulletins**: IT-120R5: Principal residence.

**(2.1) Other distributions** — Where at any time any property of a trust is distributed by the trust to a beneficiary under the trust in satisfaction of all or any part of the beneficiary's capital interest in the trust or in satisfaction of a right described in subsection 52(6), and subsection (2) does not apply in respect of the distribution, notwithstanding any other provision of this Act other than section 132.2,

(a) the trust shall be deemed to have disposed of the property for proceeds equal to its fair market value at that time;

(b) the beneficiary shall be deemed to have acquired the property at a cost equal to that fair market value; and

(c) the beneficiary shall be deemed to have disposed of the interest or part thereof in the trust or the right, as the case may be, for proceeds of disposition equal to the cost at which the beneficiary is deemed by paragraph (b) to have acquired the property.

### Proposed Amendment — 107(2.1)

**(2.1) Other distributions** — Where at any time a property of a trust is distributed by the trust to a beneficiary under the trust, there would, if this Act were read without reference to paragraphs (h) and (i) of the definition "disposition" in subsection 248(1), be a resulting disposition of all or any part of the beneficiary's capital interest in the trust (which interest or part, as the case may be, is in this subsection referred to as the "former interest") and the rules in subsection (2) and section 132.2 do not apply in respect of the distribution,

(a) the trust is deemed to have disposed of the property for proceeds equal to its fair market value at that time;

(b) the beneficiary is deemed to have acquired the property at a cost equal to the proceeds determined under paragraph (a);

(c) the beneficiary's proceeds of disposition of the portion of the former interest disposed of by the beneficiary on the distribution are deemed to be equal to the amount, if any, by which

(i) the proceeds determined under paragraph (a) (other than the portion, if any, of the proceeds that is a payment to which paragraph (h) or (i) of the definition "disposition" in subsection 248(1) applies),

exceeds the total of

(ii) where the property is not a Canadian resource property or foreign resource property, the amount, if any, by which

(A) the fair market value of the property at that time

exceeds the total of

(B) the cost amount to the trust of the property immediately before that time, and

(C) the portion, if any, of the excess that would be determined under this subparagraph if this subparagraph were read without reference to this clause that represents a payment to which paragraph (h) or (i) of the definition "disposition" in subsection 248(1) applies, and

(iii) all amounts each of which is an eligible offset at that time of the taxpayer in respect of the former interest; and

(d) notwithstanding paragraphs (a) to (c), where the trust is non-resident at that time, the property is not described in paragraph (2.001)(b) or (c) and, if this Act were read without reference to this paragraph, there would be no income, loss, taxable capital gain or allowable capital loss of a taxpayer in respect of the property because of the application of subsection 75(2) to the disposition at that time of the property,

(i) the trust is deemed to have disposed of the property for proceeds equal to the cost amount of the property,

(ii) the beneficiary is deemed to have acquired the property at a cost equal to the fair market value of the property, and

(iii) the beneficiary's proceeds of disposition of the portion of the former interest disposed of by the beneficiary on the distribution are deemed to be equal to the amount, if any, by which

(A) the fair market value of the property

exceeds the total of

(B) the portion, if any, of the amount of the distribution that is a payment to which paragraph (h) or (i) of the definition "disposition" in subsection 248(1) applies, and

(C) all amounts each of which is an eligible offset at that time of the taxpayer in respect of the former interest.

**Application**: Bill C-43 (First Reading September 20, 2000), subsec. 50(11), will amend subsec. 107(2.1) to read as above, applicable to distributions made after 1999 (other than distributions made before March 2000 in satisfaction of rights described in subsec. 52(6) that were acquired before 2000).

**Technical Notes**: Where trust property is distributed by a trust to a beneficiary in satisfaction of the beneficiary's capital interest in the trust and subsection 107(2) of Act does not apply, the rules in subsection 107(2.1) apply. Subsection 107(2.1) also applies to a distribution by a trust in satisfaction of a right described in subsection 52(6). Under paragraphs 107(2.1)(a) to (c), the trust is deemed to have disposed of the distributed property for the property's fair market value and the beneficiary is deemed to have acquired the property, and disposed of the capital interest or right described in subsection 52(6), for the same amount. Notwithstanding the reference to subsection 52(6) (under which a cost is ascribed to the right to enforce payment out of a trust's capital gains and income), it is unclear that there is relief from double taxation on gains associated with the dispositions of the distributed property and the relinquished capital interest.

Subsection 107(2.1) is amended so that it no longer overrides every other provision of the Act. For example, subsection 107(2.1) no longer deems there to be a disposition of property where the existing law provides that there was no disposition because of paragraph (e) of the definition "disposition" in section 54. This amendment is consequential on the replacement of the existing definition "disposition" in section 54 with the new definition of the same expression in subsection 248(1) and new rules in section 107.4 to deal with acquisitions by trusts that do not involve any change in beneficial ownership.

Subsection 107(2.1) is amended so that it applies in connection with all distributions in respect of a capital interest in a trust, regardless of whether the distribution results in a disposition of all or part of the capital interest. This includes rights to which subsection 52(6) formerly applied, but which are now included as part of a capital interest in a trust under the amended definition of "capital interest" in subsection 108(1). Distributions in respect of amounts described in paragraph (h) and (i) of the definition "disposition" in subsection 248(1) need to be referred to in order to take into account the possibility that a distribution from a trust may consist only partly in respect of such amounts. In addition, even if a cash distribution is solely in respect of such an amount, it may not necessarily be denominated in Canadian dollars, in which case the trust may recognize a foreign currency gain or loss on the distribution. However, under amended paragraph 107(2.1)(c), proceeds of disposition are only determined with regard to the portion of a capital interest in a trust that is disposed of because of a distribution from the trust. No proceeds of disposition are determined in respect of rights to amounts to which paragraph (h) and (i) of that definition apply.

The proceeds of disposition for the portion of a capital interest in a trust that is disposed of because of a distribution (other than a distribution to which paragraph 107(2.1)(d) applies) are determined under paragraph 107(2.1)(c) as follows:

- ADD the proceeds of disposition determined in respect of the distribution (other than any portion of those proceeds that is a payment to which paragraph (h) or (i) of the definition "disposition" in subsection 248(1) applies). Note: paragraph (h) or (i) of that definition apply to a payment that represents a distribution of income or capital gains or to a payment from a unit trust that does not cause a reduction of the number of issued units of the trust;
- where the property distributed is not Canadian resource property or foreign resource property, SUBTRACT the amount (if any) by which the fair market value of the property exceeds the cost amount of the property (however, disregard this excess to the extent it represents a payment to which paragraph (h) or (i) of that definition applies); and
- SUBTRACT the "eligible offset" in respect of the distribution, as defined in subsection 108(1). (This is essentially debt assumed by the beneficiary on the distribution.)

Where there is no disposition of a capital interest because of paragraph (h) or (i) of the definition "disposition" in subsection 248(1), an amount distributed from the trust to a beneficiary generally results in a reduction of the beneficiary's adjusted cost base of the capital interest pursuant to paragraph 53(2)(h).

Paragraph 107(2.1)(d) applies to distributions of property (other than taxable Canadian property or business property connected to a Canadian permanent establishment) from a non-resident trust unless subsection 75(2) would, if the Act were read without reference to that paragraph, result in the attribution to a taxpayer of an income, loss, taxable capital gain or allowable capital loss in respect of the distribution. In these circumstances, new paragraph 107(2.1)(d) deems the beneficiary to acquire the property at its fair market value and to dispose of the corresponding portion of the capital interest in the trust for proceeds equal to the fair market value of the property less the total of two amounts. The first amount represents the portion of the distribution that is a payment to which paragraph (h) or (i) of the definition "disposition" in subsection 248(1) applies (i.e., a payment that represents a distribution of income or capital gains, or a payment from a unit trust that does not cause a reduction of the number of issued units of the trust). The second amount is the "eligible offset" (as defined in subsection 108(1)) in respect of the distribution (i.e., essentially debt assumed by the beneficiary on the distribution). Paragraph 107(2.1)(d) also ensures that there are no tax consequences to the trust in respect of the distribution of the property.

These amendments apply to distributions made after 1999 (other than distributions before March 2000 in connection with rights described in subsection 52(6) of the Act that were acquired before 2000).

The examples below illustrate the operation of amended subsection 107(2.1). Except as indicated otherwise, it is assumed that the trusts referred to below are all resident in Canada.

*EXAMPLE 1*

In 2000, a commercial trust distributes non-depreciable capital property (shares) to its beneficiary resident in Canada in satisfaction of the beneficiary's capital interest in the trust. The adjusted cost base of the shares is $40. The adjusted cost base of the beneficiary's capital interest is $20. The fair market value of the property is $100.

*Results:*

1. Subsection 107(2.1) applies to the distribution.

2. The trust is deemed by paragraph 107(2.1)(a) to have disposed of the property for $100 proceeds, so there is a capital gain of $60 on the resulting disposition and a taxable capital gain of $45.

3. The beneficiary is deemed by paragraph 107(2)(b) to have acquired the property at a $100 cost.

4. Because the distribution gives rise to a capital gain, the amount of the capital gain ($60) reduces the proceeds of

disposition of the beneficiary's capital interest under subparagraph 107(2.1)(c)(ii). The beneficiary is deemed to have disposed of the capital interest for $40 proceeds ($100 – $60). Alternatively, in the event that the payment of the gain were considered to be payment of the capital gains of the trust to which paragraph (i) of the definition "disposition" in subsection 248(1) applied, $40 would be determined under subparagraph 107(2.1)(c)(i) and no amount would be determined under subparagraph 107(2.1)(c)(ii). Consequently, under both of the alternative analyses, the beneficiary's proceeds of disposition of the beneficiary's capital interest in the trust are $40.

5. Consequently, the capital gain from the disposition of the capital interest is $20 ($40 – $20).

*EXAMPLE 2*

A personal trust distributes non-depreciable capital property (shares that are not taxable Canadian property) to its non-resident beneficiary in satisfaction of the beneficiary's capital interest in the trust. The adjusted cost base of the shares is $40. The adjusted cost base of the beneficiary's capital interest, determined before the application of paragraph 107(1)(a), is $0. The fair market value of the property is $100.

*Results:*

1. Subsection 107(2.1) applies to the distribution because of the application of amended subsection 107(5).

2. The trust is deemed by paragraph 107(2.1)(a) to have disposed of the property for $100 proceeds, so there is a capital gain of $60 from the resulting disposition and a taxable capital gain of $45.

3. The beneficiary is deemed by paragraph 107(2.1)(b) to have acquired the property at a $100 cost.

4. Because the distribution gives rise to a capital gain, the amount of the capital gain ($60) reduces the proceeds of the beneficiary's capital interest under subparagraph 107(2.1)(c)(ii). The beneficiary is deemed to have disposed of the capital interest for $40 proceeds ($100 – $60). The alternative analysis in paragraph 4 of Example 1 would likewise result in deemed proceeds of $40.

5. The capital interest in the trust constitutes taxable Canadian property for the non-resident beneficiary. For the purposes of computing capital gains, the adjusted cost base of the capital interest under subsection 107(1) is $40, being the greater of its adjusted cost base (nil) determined before the application of that subsection and the cost amount ($40) to the trust of the distributed property. Consequently, the taxable capital gain from the disposition of the capital interest is nil.

6. The allowable capital loss from the disposition of the capital interest is also nil.

**Related Provisions**: 43(2) — No capital loss on payment out of trust's income or gains; 53(2)(h)(i.2) — Reduction in ACB of interest in trust; 107(2.11) — Election not to flow out gains to beneficiaries; 107.4(4) — Fair market value of capital interest in trust; 248(1)"disposition"(d), (h) — Whether transfer by trust is a disposition of capital interest.

**Related Provisions**: 53(4) — Effect on ACB of share, partnership interest or trust interest.

**Notes**: Opening words of 107(2.1) amended by 1995-97 technical bill, effective for distributions made after June 1994, to add "other than section 132.2". (Other changes were cosmetic and non-substantive.)

107(2.1) added by 1988 tax reform, effective for dispositions of properties by trusts in 1988 or later.

### Proposed Addition — 107(2.11)

**(2.11) Gains not distributed to beneficiaries** — Where a trust makes one or more distributions of property in a taxation year in circumstances to which subsection (2.1) applies (or, in the case of property distributed after October 1, 1996 and before 2000, in circumstances to which subsection (5) applied)

(a) where the trust is resident in Canada at the time of each of those distributions and has so elected in prescribed form filed with the trust's return for the year or a preceding taxation year, the income of the trust for the year (determined without reference to subsection 104(6)) shall, for the purposes of subsections 104(6) and (13), be computed without regard to all of those distributions to non-resident persons (including a partnership other than a Canadian partnership); and

(b) where the trust is resident in Canada at the time of each of those distributions and has so elected in prescribed form filed with the trust's return for the year or a preceding taxation year, the income of the trust for the year (determined without reference to subsection 104(6)) shall, for the purposes of subsections 104(6) and (13), be computed without regard to all of those distributions.

**Application**: Bill C-43 (First Reading September 20, 2000), subsec. 50(11), will add subsec. 107(2.11), applicable to distributions made after October 1, 1996, except that for distributions made from a trust before the particular day on which the amending legislation is assented to, an election under subsec. 107(2.11) is deemed to have been made in a timely manner if it is made on or before the trust's filing-due date for the taxation year that includes the particular day.

**Technical Notes**: New subsection 107(2.11) of the Act provides a special rule that, for the purposes of subsections 104(6) and (13), allows income of a trust for a taxation year (computed without reference to subsection 104(6)) to be computed without regard to the tax consequences under subsection 107(2.1) (and former subsection 107(5)) of property distributed in kind to beneficiaries. This ensures that the gains, if any, that might arguably flow-out in some circumstances to beneficiaries as a consequence of the operation of subsections 107(2.1) and (5), will instead be included in income at the trust level.

More specifically, subsection 107(2.11) applies in two cases:

- where a trust resident in Canada distributes property to a non-resident beneficiary after October 1, 1996, the result described above applies in respect of distributions to non-resident beneficiaries if the trust so elects for the taxation year of the distribution or for a taxation year preceding the distribution. The election is considered to have been made on a timely basis if it is filed with the Minister before the trust's filing-due date for its taxation year that includes the date of Royal Assent; and

> • where a trust resident in Canada distributes property to a beneficiary after 1999, the result described above also applies in respect of all beneficiaries (including non-resident beneficiaries) if the trust so elects for the taxation year of the distribution or a taxation year that precedes the distribution. The election is considered to have been made on a timely basis if it is filed with the Minister before the trust's filing-due date for its taxation year that includes the date of Royal Assent.
>
> **Related Provisions**: 43(2) — No capital loss on payment out of trust's income or gains.
>
> **Notes**: An earlier version of this rule, applicable only to non-resident beneficiaries, appeared as 107(5.1) in the draft legislation of December 23, 1998.

**(2.2) Flow-through entity** — Where at any time before 2005 a beneficiary under a trust described in paragraph (h), (i) or (j) of the definition "flow-through entity" in subsection 39.1(1) received a distribution of property from the trust in satisfaction of all or a portion of the beneficiary's interests in the trust and the beneficiary files with the Minister on or before the beneficiary's filing-due date for the taxation year that includes that time an election in respect of the property in prescribed form, there shall be included in the cost to the beneficiary of a particular property (other than money) received by the beneficiary as part of the distribution of property the least of

(a) the amount, if any, by which the beneficiary's exempt capital gains balance (as defined in subsection 39.1(1)) in respect of the trust for the beneficiary's taxation year that includes that time exceeds the total of all amounts each of which is

(i) an amount by which a capital gain is reduced under section 39.1 in the year because of the beneficiary's exempt capital gains balance in respect of the trust,

(ii) 4/3 of an amount by which a taxable capital gain is reduced under section 39.1 in the year because of the beneficiary's exempt capital gains balance in respect of the trust, or

> **Proposed Amendment — 107(2.2)(a)(ii)**
>
> **Application**: The December 21, 2000 draft legislation, subsec. 49(2), will amend subpara. 107(2.2)(a)(ii) by replacing the reference to the expression "4/3 of" with a reference to the word "twice", applicable to taxation years that end after February 27, 2000 except that, for a beneficiary's taxation year that includes either February 28, 2000 or October 17, 2000, the reference to the word "twice" shall be read as a reference to the expression "the fraction that is the reciprocal of the fraction in para. 38(a), as amended [by the December 21, 2000 draft legislation], that applies to the beneficiary for the year, multiplied by".
>
> **Technical Notes**: Subsection 107(2.2) provides for an addition to the cost base of property received by a taxpayer from a trust in satisfaction of the taxpayer's interest in the trust where the exempt capital gains balance of the taxpayer in respect of the trust has not been fully utilised.
>
> The amendment to subparagraph 107(2.2)(a)(ii) replaces the reference to the expression "4/3 of" with a reference to the word "twice" and is consequential on the reduction of the inclusion rate for capital gains from 3/4 to 1/2 [see 38(a) — ed.].
>
> The amendment applies to taxation years that end after February 27, 2000 except that, for a taxation year of a taxpayer that includes either February 28, 2000 or October 17, 2000, the reference to the word "twice" in subparagraph 107(2)(a)(ii) is to be read as reference to the fraction that is the reciprocal of the fraction in amended paragraph 38(a) that applies to the taxpayer for the year. These modifications are required in order to reflect the capital gains/losses rate for the year.

(iii) an amount included in the cost to the beneficiary of another property received by the beneficiary at or before that time in the year because of this subsection,

(b) the amount by which the fair market value of the particular property at that time exceeds the adjusted cost base to the trust of the particular property immediately before that time, and

(c) the amount designated in respect of the particular property in the election.

**Related Provisions**: 39.1(1)"exempt capital gains balance"F(a) — Exempt capital gains balance of flow-through entity.

**Notes**: 107(2.2) added by 1995-97 technical bill, effective for dispositions made after 1993; and a prescribed form filed under 107(2.2) by the end of 1998 is deemed filed on time.

**(3) Cost of property other than non-depreciable capital property** — Where the property referred to in subsection (2) that was distributed by a trust to a taxpayer was property other than capital property that was not depreciable property, for the purpose of determining the cost to the taxpayer of the property under paragraph (2)(b) (except for the purposes of that paragraph as it applies to determine the taxpayer's proceeds of disposition of the taxpayer's capital interest under paragraph (2)(c)), the reference in paragraph (2)(b) to "the amount" shall be read as a reference to "$1/2$ of the amount".

> **Proposed Repeal — 107(3)**
>
> **Application**: Bill C-43 (First Reading September 20, 2000), subsec. 50(12), will repeal subsec. 107(3), applicable to distributions made after 1999.
>
> **Technical Notes**: Subsection 107(3) of the Act is repealed. See the commentary above on amendments to subsection 107(2).

**(4) Where trust in favour of spouse [or common-law partner]** — Where

(a) at any time property of a trust is distributed by the trust to a beneficiary in circumstances to which subsection (2) would, but for this subsection, apply,

(a.1) the trust is described in paragraph 104(4)(a),

(a.2) the property so distributed by the trust was capital property, a Canadian resource property, a foreign resource property or property that was land included in the inventory of the trust,

(b) the taxpayer to whom the property is so distributed is a person other than the spouse or common-law partner referred to in paragraph 104(4)(a) in respect of the trust, and

(c) that spouse or common-law partner is alive on the day the property is so distributed,

notwithstanding paragraphs (2)(a) to (c), the following rules apply:

(d) the trust shall be deemed to have disposed of the property and to have received proceeds of disposition therefor equal to its fair market value at that time,

(e) the taxpayer shall be deemed to have acquired the property at a cost equal to those proceeds, and

(f) the taxpayer shall be deemed to have disposed of all or part, as the case may be, of the taxpayer's capital interest in the trust for proceeds of disposition equal to the cost at which, but for this subsection, the taxpayer would be deemed by paragraph (2)(b) to have acquired the property, minus the amount of any debt assumed by the taxpayer or of any other legal obligation assumed by the taxpayer to pay any amount, if the distribution of the property to the taxpayer was conditional on the assumption by the taxpayer of the debt or obligation.

**Proposed Amendment — 107(4)**

**(4) Trusts in favour of spouse, common-law partner or self** — Subsection (2.1) applies at any time to property distributed to a beneficiary by a trust described in paragraph 104(4)(a) where

(a) the beneficiary is not

(i) in the case of a post-1971 partner trust, the partner or common-law partner referred to in paragraph 104(4)(a),

(ii) in the case of an *alter ego* trust, the taxpayer referred to in paragraph 104(4)(a), and

(iii) in the case of a joint partner trust, the taxpayer, spouse or common-law partner referred to in paragraph 104(4)(a); and

(b) a taxpayer, spouse or common-law partner referred to in subparagraph (a)(i), (ii), or (iii), as the case may be, is alive on the day of the distribution.

**Application**: Bill C-43 (First Reading September 20, 2000), subsec. 50(13), will amend subsec. 107(4) to read as above, applicable to distributions made after 1999.

**Technical Notes**: Subsection 107(4) of the Act applies where a post-1971 partner trust distributes capital property, resource property or land to a beneficiary other than the beneficiary spouse. When this occurs while the beneficiary spouse is alive, there is generally a deemed disposition of the property at its fair market value.

Subsection 107(4) is amended so that similar rules apply to *alter ego* trusts and joint partner trusts, as newly defined in subsection 248(1). Subsection 107(4) will apply to a distribution by these trusts where the individual (or, in the case of a joint partner trust, either the individual or the spouse) is alive on the day of the distribution and the distribution is made to a beneficiary other than the individual (or, in the case of a joint partner trust, the individual or the spouse). For more detail on these trusts, see the commentary on amended subsections 73(1) and 104(4).

Subsection 107(4) is amended so that the rules set out in amended subsection 107(2.1) apply to distributions covered by subsection 107(4).

These amendments also reflect changes [re common-law partners — ed.] proposed under Bill C-23, the *Modernization of Benefits and Obligations Act*.

**Related Provisions**: 53(4) — Effect on ACB of share, partnership interest or trust interest; 104(6) — Deduction in computing income of trust; 107(5) — Distribution to non-resident beneficiary; 108(1) — "accumulating income".

**Notes**: 107(4)(c), (d) amended by 2000 same-sex partners bill to add reference to "common-law partner", effective for the 2001 and later taxation years, or earlier by election (see Notes to 248(1)"common-law partner").

107(4) amended in 1976, by 1981 Budget, by 1985 technical bill, and by 1992 technical bill.

For distributions before 1993, read para. (d) as follows:

(d) the trust shall be deemed to have disposed of the property and to have received proceeds of disposition therefor equal to

(i) where the property was depreciable property of the trust of a prescribed class and the fair market value of that property at that time exceeds its cost amount to the trust at that time, the amount of that cost amount plus $\frac{1}{2}$ of the amount of the excess,

(ii) where the property was depreciable property of the trust of a prescribed class and the cost amount of that property to the trust at that time exceeds its fair market value at that time, the amount of that fair market value plus $\frac{1}{2}$ of the amount of the excess, and

(iii) in any other case, its fair market value at that time,

For distributions before December 21, 1991, read everything up to para. (d) as:

(4) Where trust in favour of spouse — Where the trust referred to in subsection (2) was a trust described in paragraph 104(4)(a) and

(a) the property so distributed by the trust was capital property, a Canadian resource property, a foreign resource property or property that was land included in the inventory of the trust,

(b) the taxpayer to whom the property was so distributed was a person other than the spouse, and

(c) the spouse was alive at the time the property was so distributed,

notwithstanding paragraphs (2)(a) to (c), the following rules apply:

For taxation years beginning before 1985 where the disposition occurred after November 12, 1981, read 107(4)(a) as follows:

(a) the property so distributed by the trust was capital property, property referred to in any of subparagraphs 59(2)(a) to (e) or property that was land included in the inventory of a business or the trust,

For dispositions from May 26, 1976 through November 12, 1981, read simply as:

(a) the property so distributed by the trust was capital property,

For dispositions before May 26, 1976, read 107(4) as follows:

(4) Where the trust referred to in subsection (2) was a trust described in paragraph 104(4)(a) and

(a) the property so distributed by the trust was capital property other than depreciable property,

## Subdivision k — Trusts and Beneficiaries     S. 107(5)

(b) the taxpayer to whom the property was so distributed was a person other than the spouse, and

(c) the spouse was alive at the time the property was so distributed,

notwithstanding paragraphs (2)(a) to (d), the following rules apply:

(d) the trust shall be deemed to have disposed of the property for proceeds equal to its fair market value at that time;

(e) the taxpayer shall be deemed to have acquired the property at a cost equal to that fair market value, and

(f) the taxpayer shall be deemed to have disposed of all or part, as the case may be, of his interest in the trust, for proceeds of disposition equal to that fair market value.

**Interpretation Bulletins**: IT-120R5: Principal residence; IT-286R2: Trusts — amount payable; IT-381R3: Trusts — capital gains and losses and the flow-through of taxable capital gains to beneficiaries; IT-465R: Non-resident beneficiaries of trusts.

**(4.1) Where subsec. 75(2) applicable to trust** — Where any property of a personal trust or a prescribed trust is distributed by the trust to a taxpayer who was a beneficiary under the trust in satisfaction of all or any part of the taxpayer's capital interest in the trust and

(a) subsection 75(2) was applicable at any time in respect of any property of the trust,

(b) the taxpayer was a person other than

(i) the person from whom the trust directly or indirectly received the property, or property for which the property was substituted, or

(ii) an individual in respect of whom subsection 73(1) would be applicable on the transfer of capital property from the person described in subparagraph (i), and

(c) the person described in subparagraph (b)(i) was alive at the time the property was distributed,

notwithstanding paragraphs (2)(a) to (c), the rules described in paragraphs (4)(d) to (f) apply.

### Proposed Amendment — 107(4.1) closing words

subsection (2.1) applies in respect of the distribution.

**Application**: Bill C-43 (First Reading September 20, 2000), subsec. 50(14), will amend the closing words of subsec. 107(4.1) to read as above, applicable to distributions made after 1999.

**Technical Notes**: Subsection 107(4.1) of the Act applies in certain cases where a reversionary trust distributes property to a specified beneficiary under the trust. When this occurs, there is a deemed disposition of the property at its fair market value.

Subsection 107(4.1) is amended so that, for distributions after 1999 in these cases, the rules set out in amended subsection 107(2.1) apply.

**Related Provisions**: 248(5) — Substituted property.

**Notes**: 107(4.1) added by 1988 tax reform, effective for distributions of properties by trusts in 1989 or later.

**Regulations**: 4800.1 (prescribed trust).

**(5) Distribution to non-resident** — Where subsection (2) applies to the distribution by a trust of any property (other than a Canadian resource property, excluded property or property that would, if at no time in the taxation year of the trust in which it is so distributed the trust is resident in Canada, be taxable Canadian property) to a non-resident taxpayer (including a partnership other than a Canadian partnership) who is a beneficiary under the trust, notwithstanding paragraphs (2)(a) to (c),

(a) the trust shall be deemed to have disposed of the property for proceeds equal to its fair market value at that time;

(b) the taxpayer shall be deemed to have acquired the property at a cost equal to that fair market value; and

(c) the taxpayer shall be deemed to have disposed of all or part, as the case may be, of the taxpayer's interest in the trust, for proceeds of disposition equal to the adjusted cost base to the taxpayer of the interest or part thereof, as the case may be, immediately before the property was so distributed.

### Proposed Amendment — 107(5)

**(5) Distribution to non-resident** — Subsection (2.1) applies in respect of a distribution of a property (other than a share of the capital stock of a non-resident-owned investment corporation or property described in any of subparagraphs 128.1(4)(b)(i) to (iii)) by a trust resident in Canada to a non-resident taxpayer (including a partnership other than a Canadian partnership) in satisfaction of all or part of the taxpayer's capital interest in the trust.

**Application**: Bill C-43 (First Reading September 20, 2000), subsec. 50(15), will amend subsec. 107(5) to read as above, applicable to distributions made after October 1, 1996, except that for distributions made after October 1, 1996 and before 2000, subsec. 107(5) shall be read as follows:

(5) Where subsection (2) applies to a distribution at any time by a trust resident in Canada of a property (other than a share of the capital stock of a non-resident-owned investment corporation or property described in any of subparagraphs 128.1(4)(b)(i) to (iii)) to a non-resident taxpayer (including a partnership other than a Canadian partnership) who is a beneficiary under the trust in satisfaction of the taxpayer's capital interest in the trust, notwithstanding paragraphs (2)(a) to (c),

(a) the trust is deemed to have disposed of the property for proceeds equal to its fair market value at that time;

(b) the taxpayer is deemed to have acquired the property at a cost equal to that fair market value; and

(c) the taxpayer is deemed to have disposed of all or part, as the case may be, of the taxpayer's capital interest in the trust, for proceeds of disposition equal to the adjusted cost base to the taxpayer of that interest or part of the interest, as the case may be, immediately before that time.

**Technical Notes**: Subsection 107(5) of the Act applies to the distribution of property (other than taxable Canadian property, Canadian resource property and shares in non-resident-owned investment corporations), where the distribution would otherwise be made to a non-resident beneficiary on a rollover basis under subsection 107(2). With regard to such distributions, subsection 107(5) provides for a deemed disposition of the distributed property at its fair market value and an acquisition by the beneficiary for the same amount. In addition, paragraph 107(5)(c) provides for proceeds of disposition of the relinquished capital interest equal to the adjusted cost base of that interest.

Subsection 107(5) is amended to replace existing exemptions with regard to taxable Canadian property and Canadian resource property with exemptions for property described in any of new subparagraphs 128.1(4)(b)(i) to (iii). This amendment applies to distributions made after October 1, 1996. For further detail on the enumerated subparagraphs, see the commentary on amended subsection 128.1(4).

Subsection 107(5) is also amended so that it only applies with regard to distributions by trusts resident in Canada. This amendment applies to distributions made after October 1, 1996 and recognizes that, if a distribution of property is made from a non-resident trust to a non-resident beneficiary, Canada's authority to ultimately collect tax on a future disposition of the property has not been compromised because of the distribution. This amendment is consistent with the policy with regard to distributions before October 2, 1996, as the type of property deemed to be disposed of before that date under subsection 107(5) would not have resulted in a non-resident trust being subject to Canadian tax.

Subsection 107(5) is amended so that, where it applies, the amended rules in subsection 107(2.1) provide for the corresponding tax consequences. This amendment applies with regard to distributions made after 1999.

**Related Provisions**: 53(4) — Effect on ACB of share, partnership interest or trust interest; 94(3)(a) [proposed] — Application to trust deemed resident in Canada; 107(2.11) — Election for gain not to be flowed out to beneficiary; 107(5.1) — Gain does not increase instalment requirements; 126(2.22) — Foreign tax credit to trust on disposition of property by non-resident beneficiary; 212(11) — Payment to non-resident beneficiary deemed paid as income of trust for withholding tax purposes; 220(4.6)–(4.63) — Security for tax on distribution of taxable Canadian property to non-resident beneficiary.

**Notes**: 107(5) amended by 1992 technical bill, effective for distributions after 1991, to add reference to "excluded property" (as defined in 108(1)"excluded property").

107(5) amended by 1988 tax reform, effective for distributions of properties by trusts in 1988 or later. For distributions from May 26, 1976 through 1987, read the opening words as follows:

> (5) **Distribution to non-resident beneficiary** — Where subsection (2) is applicable in respect of the distribution by a trust of any property of the trust to a non-resident taxpayer who was a beneficiary under the trust and the property was not taxable Canadian property or property that would be taxable Canadian property if at no time in the taxation year of the trust in which it was so distributed the trust had been resident in Canada, notwithstanding paragraphs (2)(a) to (c), the following rules apply:

For distributions before May 26, 1976, read 107(5) as follows:

> (5) Where subsection (2) is applicable in respect of the distribution by a trust of any property of the trust to a non-resident taxpayer who was a beneficiary under the trust and the property was not taxable Canadian property or property that would be taxable Canadian property if at no time in the taxation year of the trust in which it was so distributed the trust had been resident in Canada, notwithstanding paragraphs

(2)(a) to (c) the provisions of paragraphs (4)(d) to (f) are applicable in respect of the property as if the reference in paragraph (4)(f) to "that fair market value" were read as a reference to "the adjusted cost base to him of the interest or part thereof, as the case may be, immediately before the property was so distributed".

**Advance Tax Rulings**: ATR-70: Distribution of taxable Canadian property by a trust to a non-resident.

### Proposed Addition — 107(5.1)

**(5.1) Instalment interest** — Where, solely because of the application of subsection (5), paragraphs (2)(a) to (c) do not apply to a distribution in a taxation year of taxable Canadian property by a trust, in applying sections 155, 156 and 156.1 and subsections 161(2), (4) and (4.01) and any regulations made for the purpose of those provisions, the trust's total taxes payable under this Part and Part I.1 for the year are deemed to be the lesser of

(a) the trust's total taxes payable under this Part and Part I.1 for the year, determined before taking into consideration the specified future tax consequences for the year, and

(b) the amount that would be determined under paragraph (a) if subsection (5) did not apply to each distribution in the year of taxable Canadian property to which the rules in subsection (2) do not apply solely because of the application of subsection (5).

**Application**: Bill C-43 (First Reading September 20, 2000), subsec. 50(15), will add subsec. 107(5.1), applicable to distributions made after October 1, 1996.

**Technical Notes**: Subsection 107(5.1) of the Act is a special rule that applies for the purposes of computing instalment interest. The rule applies where

- there has been one or more distributions after October 1, 1996 of taxable Canadian property by a trust resident in Canada in a taxation year to non-resident beneficiaries, and
- paragraphs 107(2)(a) to (c) do not apply to such distributions solely because of subsection 107(5).

For the purposes of the measures pertaining to tax instalments or instalment interest in sections 155, 156, subsections 156.1(1) to (3) and subsections 161(2), (4) and (4.01), the trust's total taxes under Part I and Part I.1 are deemed in these circumstances to be the lesser of two amounts. The first amount is the trust's total taxes payable under those Parts for the distribution year, determined without taking into consideration the carryback of losses and other consequences described in the definition "specified future tax consequence" in subsection 248(1). The second amount is computed in the same manner, except that it is assumed that subsection 107(5) does not apply to each distribution of trust property in the distribution year that is described above. The general effect of subsection 107(5.1) is to ignore a trust's income tax liabilities arising from the distribution of taxable Canadian property to a non-resident beneficiary for the purpose of computing the trust's instalment interest obligations.

Subsection 107(5.1) is similar to new subsection 128.1(5). Both of these subsections should be read in conjunction with new subsections 220(4.5) and (4.6), under

Subdivision k — Trusts and Beneficiaries         S. 107.1(a)(i)

which the posting of security can result in a deferral of the accrual of arrears interest on unpaid taxes.

**Notes**: This was 107(5.2) in the draft legislation of December 23, 1998. Former proposed 107(5.1) was revised and appears as 107(2.11).

As well as applying to instalment obligations, this provision technically applies to 156.1(4), which is the obligation to pay the remaining balance by the balance-due day! This was doubtless not intended by the drafters.

**(6) Loss reduction** — Notwithstanding any other provision of this Act, where a person or partnership (in this subsection referred to as the "vendor") has disposed of property and would, but for this subsection, have had a loss from the disposition, the vendor's loss otherwise determined in respect of the disposition shall be reduced by such portion of that loss as may reasonably be considered to have accrued during a period in which

(a) the property or property for which it was substituted was owned by a trust; and

(b) neither the vendor nor a person that would, if section 251.1 were read without reference to the definition "controlled" in subsection 251.1(3), be affiliated with the vendor had a capital interest in the trust.

**Related Provisions**: 248(5) — Substituted property.

**Notes**: 107(6)(b) amended by 1995-97 technical bill, effective April 27, 1995, to use the new "affiliated person" concept in 251.1. Previously read:

(b) neither

(i) the vendor, nor

(ii) any person related to the vendor, nor

(iii) any partnership of which the vendor or a person related to the vendor was a majority interest partner (within the meaning assigned by subsection 97(3.1))

had a capital interest in the trust.

107(6) added in 1987, effective for property distributed to a beneficiary from a trust in satisfaction of all or part of a capital interest in the trust that was acquired by the beneficiary after January 15, 1987, except where the beneficiary acquiring the interest was obliged on that date to acquire it pursuant to an agreement in writing entered into on or before that date. For this purpose, the amending legislation provides that "a person shall be considered not to be obliged ... to acquire ... property ... if the person may be excused from performing the obligations as a result of changes to the *Income Tax Act* affecting acquisitions or dispositions of property or acquisitions of control of corporations".

**Definitions [s. 107]**: "acquired for consideration" — 108(7); "adjusted cost base" — 54, 248(1); "affiliated" — 251.1; "*alter ego* trust*" — 248(1); "allowable capital loss" — 38(b), 248(1); "amount" — 248(1); "beneficiary" — 108(1); "business" — 248(1); "Canada" — 255; "Canadian partnership" — 102(1), 248(1); "Canadian resource property" — 66(15), 248(1); "capital gain" — 39(1), 248(1); "capital interest" — 108(1), 248(1); "capital loss" — 39(1)(b), 107(1)(c), 248(1); "capital property" — 54, 248(1); "common-law partner" — 248(1); "corporation" — 248(1), *Interpretation Act* 35(1); "cost" — 107(1.1); "cost amount" — 108(1); "depreciable property" — 13(21), 248(1); "disposition" — 248(1); "eligible capital expenditure" — 14(5), 248(1); "eligible capital property" — 54, 248(1); "eligible offset", "excluded property" — 108(1); "fair market value" — 107.4(4); "foreign resource property" — 66(15), 248(1); "inventory", "insurance corporation" — 248(1); "*inter vivos* trust" — 108(1), 248(1); "inventory", "joint

partner trust" — 248(1); "Minister" — 248(1); "mutual fund trust" — 132(6)–(7), 132.2(1)(q), 248(1); "non-resident" — 248(1); "partnership" — see Notes to 96(1); "person", "personal trust", "post-1971 partner trust", "prescribed" — 248(1); "prescribed trust" — Reg. 4800.1; "property", "regulation" — 248(1); "related" — 251(2); "resident in Canada" — 250; "share", "specified future tax consequence" — 248(1); "specified percentage" — 107(2)(b.1); "substituted property" — 248(5); "taxable Canadian property" — 248(1); "taxable capital gain" — 38(a), 248(1); "taxation year" — 104(23)(a), 249; "taxpayer" — 248(1); "testamentary trust" — 108(1), 248(1); "trust" — 104(1), 108(1), 248(1), (3); "unit trust" — 108(2), 248(1).

**107.1 Distribution by employee trust or employee benefit plan** — Where at any time any property of an employee trust or a trust governed by an employee benefit plan has been distributed by the trust to a taxpayer who was a beneficiary under the trust in satisfaction of all or any part of the taxpayer's interest in the trust, the following rules apply:

(a) in the case of an employee trust,

---

**Proposed Amendment — 107.1 opening words**

**107.1 Distribution by employee trust, employee benefit plan or similar trust** — Where at any time any property of an employee trust, a trust governed by an employee benefit plan or a trust described in paragraph (a.1) of the definition "trust" in subsection 108(1) has been distributed by the trust to a taxpayer who was a beneficiary under the trust in satisfaction of all or any part of the taxpayer's interest in the trust, the following rules apply:

(a) in the case of an employee trust or a trust described in paragraph (a.1) of the definition "trust" in subsection 108(1),

**Application**: Bill C-43 (First Reading September 20, 2000), s. 51, will amend s. 107.1 before para. (b) to read as above, applicable to 1999 *et seq.*

**Technical Notes**: Section 107.1 provides rules to deal with a distribution to a taxpayer of a property by an employee trust or a trust governed by an employee benefit plan under which the taxpayer is a beneficiary. In the case of an employee trust, paragraph 107.1(a) requires the trust to recognize a gain or loss when it distributes trust property to a beneficiary by treating the trust as having disposed of the property at its fair market value immediately before the time of distribution. That paragraph also ensures that the beneficiary is considered to acquire the property at that fair market value.

Section 107.1 is amended so that paragraph 107.1(a) applies to a trust described in paragraph (a.1) of the definition "trust" in subsection 108(1). This is intended to ensure that, in the unusual circumstance that property other than cash is distributed by the trust, there is a recognition in the trust of any gain or loss in respect of the property. For more on new paragraph (a.1) of the definition "trust" in subsection 108(1), see the commentary on that subsection.

---

(i) the trust shall be deemed to have disposed of the property immediately before that time

873

for proceeds of disposition equal to its fair market value at that time, and

(ii) the taxpayer shall be deemed to have acquired the property at a cost equal to its fair market value at that time;

(b) in the case of a trust governed by an employee benefit plan,

(i) the trust shall be deemed to have disposed of the property for proceeds of disposition equal to its cost amount to the trust immediately before that time, and

(ii) the taxpayer shall be deemed to have acquired the property at a cost equal to the greater of

(A) its fair market value at that time, and

(B) the adjusted cost base to the taxpayer of the taxpayer's interest or part thereof, as the case may be, immediately before that time;

(c) the taxpayer shall be deemed to have disposed of the taxpayer's interest or part thereof, as the case may be, for proceeds of disposition equal to the adjusted cost base to the taxpayer of that interest or part thereof immediately before that time; and

(d) where the property was depreciable property of a prescribed class of the trust and the amount that was the capital cost to the trust of that property exceeds the cost at which the taxpayer is deemed by this section to have acquired the property, for the purposes of sections 13 and 20 and any regulations made under paragraph 20(1)(a),

(i) the capital cost to the taxpayer of the property shall be deemed to be the amount that was the capital cost of the property to the trust, and

(ii) the excess shall be deemed to have been allowed to the taxpayer in respect of the property under regulations made under paragraph 20(1)(a) in computing income for taxation years before the acquisition by the taxpayer of the property.

**Related Provisions**: 6(1)(g) — Income from employee benefit plan; 6(1)(h) — Income from employee trust; 18(1)(o) — No deduction for employee benefit plan contributions; 32.1 — Employee benefit plan deductions; 104(6) — Deduction in computing income of trust; 104(13) — Income payable to beneficiary.

**Notes**: 107.1 added by 1980 Budget, effective 1980.

**Definitions [s. 107.1]**: "adjusted cost base" — 54, 248(1); "amount" — 108(1), 248(1); "cost amount" — 108(1); "depreciable property" — 13(21), 248(1); "employee benefit plan", "employee trust", "prescribed", "property", "regulation" — 248(1); "taxation year" — 249; "taxpayer" — 248(1); "trust" — 104(1), 108(1), 248(1), (3).

**Interpretation Bulletins**: IT-502: Employee benefit plans and employee trusts.

**107.2 Distribution by a retirement compensation arrangement** — Where, at any time, any property of a trust governed by a retirement compensation arrangement has been distributed by the trust to a taxpayer who was a beneficiary under the trust in satisfaction of all or any part of the taxpayer's interest in the trust, for the purposes of this Part and Part XI.3, the following rules apply:

(a) the trust shall be deemed to have disposed of the property for proceeds of disposition equal to its fair market value at that time;

(b) the trust shall be deemed to have paid to the taxpayer as a distribution an amount equal to that fair market value;

(c) the taxpayer shall be deemed to have acquired the property at a cost equal to that fair market value;

(d) the taxpayer shall be deemed to have disposed of the taxpayer's interest or part thereof, as the case may be, for proceeds of disposition equal to the adjusted cost base to the taxpayer of that interest or part thereof immediately before that time; and

(e) where the property was depreciable property of a prescribed class of the trust and the amount that was the capital cost to the trust of that property exceeds the cost at which the taxpayer is deemed by this section to have acquired the property, for the purposes of sections 13 and 20 and any regulations made under paragraph 20(1)(a),

(i) the capital cost to the taxpayer of the property shall be deemed to be the amount that was the capital cost of the property to the trust, and

(ii) the excess shall be deemed to have been allowed to the taxpayer in respect of the property under regulations made under paragraph 20(1)(a) in computing the taxpayer's income for taxation years before the acquisition by the taxpayer of the property.

**Related Provisions**: 56(1)(x)–(z) — Benefits from retirement compensation arrangement; 60(t) — Amount included under para. 56(1)(x) or (z) or subsec. 70(2); 60(u) — Amount included under para. 56(1)(y); 153(1)(q) — Withholding required on distribution by RCA; Part XI.3 — Tax in respect of retirement compensation arrangements.

**Notes**: 107.2 added in 1987, effective October 9, 1986.

**Definitions [s. 107.2]**: "adjusted cost base" — 54, 248(1); "depreciable property" — 13(21), 248(1); "prescribed", "property", "regulation", "retirement compensation arrangement" — 248(1); "taxation year" — 249; "taxpayer" — 248(1); "trust" — 104(1), 108(1), 248(1), (3).

**107.3 (1) Treatment of beneficiaries under qualifying environmental trusts** — Where a taxpayer is a beneficiary under a qualifying environmental trust in a taxation year of the trust (in this subsection referred to as the "trust's year") that ends in a particular taxation year of the taxpayer,

(a) subject to paragraph (b), the taxpayer's income, non-capital loss and net capital loss for the particular year shall be computed as if the amount of the income or loss of the trust for the trust's year from any source or from sources in a particular place were the income or loss of the taxpayer from that source or from sources in that particular place for the particular year, to the extent of the portion thereof that can reasonably be considered to be the taxpayer's share of such income or loss; and

(b) if the taxpayer is non-resident at any time in the particular year and an income or loss described in paragraph (a) or an amount to which paragraph 12(1)(z.1) or (z.2) applies would not otherwise be included in computing the taxpayer's taxable income or taxable income earned in Canada, as the case may be, notwithstanding any other provision of this Act, the income, the loss or the amount shall be attributed to the carrying on of business in Canada by the taxpayer through a fixed place of business located in the province in which the site to which the trust relates is situated.

**Related Provisions**: 12(1)(z.1) — Inclusion in income of amount received from trust; 87(2)(j.93) — Amalgamations — continuing corporation; 107.3(2) — Where property transferred to beneficiary.

**Notes**: Qualifying environmental trusts (broadened from the earlier term "mining reclamation trusts") are exempt from tax under Part I (see 149(1)(z)), but are subject to tax under Part XII.4 (see 211.6). However, a beneficiary is entitled to a refundable tax credit under 127.41 for Part XII.4 tax payable by the trust. Under 107.3(1)(a), income or loss at the trust level is also treated as having been earned or realized by a trust beneficiary. Where there is a non-resident beneficiary, 107.3(1)(b) applies.

107.3(1) added by 1994 Budget, effective for taxation years that end after February 22, 1994; and amended by 1997 Budget, effective for taxation years that end after February 18, 1997, to change "mining reclamation trust" to "qualifying environmental trust" in the opening words, and to change "mine" to "site" at the end of 107.3(1)(b).

**(2) Transfers to beneficiaries** — Where property of a qualifying environmental trust is transferred at any time to a beneficiary under the trust in satisfaction of all or any part of the beneficiary's interest as a beneficiary under the trust,

(a) the trust shall be deemed to have disposed of the property at that time for proceeds of disposition equal to its fair market value at that time; and

(b) the beneficiary shall be deemed to have acquired the property at that time at a cost equal to its fair market value at that time.

**Related Provisions**: 87(2)(j.93) — Amalgamations — continuing corporation; 107.3(1) — Income or loss flowed through to beneficiaries.

**Notes**: Any income or loss resulting from this rule is flowed through to the beneficiaries under 107.3(1).

107.3(2) added by 1994 Budget, effective for taxation years that end after February 22, 1994; and amended by 1997 Budget, effective for taxation years that end after February 18, 1997, to change "mining reclamation trust" to "qualifying environmental trust".

**(3) Ceasing to be a qualifying environmental trust** — Where a trust ceases at any time to be a qualifying environmental trust,

(a) the taxation year of the trust that would otherwise have included that time is deemed to have ended immediately before that time and a new taxation year of the trust is deemed to have begun at that time;

(b) the trust shall be deemed to have disposed immediately before that time of each property held by the trust immediately after that time for proceeds of disposition equal to its fair market value at that time and to have reacquired immediately after that time each such property for an amount equal to that fair market value;

(c) each beneficiary under the trust immediately before that time shall be deemed to have received at that time from the trust an amount equal to the percentage of the fair market value of the properties of the trust immediately after that time that can reasonably be considered to be the beneficiary's interest in the trust; and

(d) each beneficiary under the trust shall be deemed to have acquired immediately after that time an interest in the trust at a cost equal to the amount deemed by paragraph (c) to have been received by the beneficiary from the trust.

**Related Provisions**: 87(2)(j.93) — Amalgamations — continuing corporation.

**Notes**: 107.3(3) added by 1994 Budget, effective for taxation years that end after February 22, 1994; and amended by 1997 Budget, effective for taxation years that end after February 18, 1997, to change "mining reclamation trust" to "qualifying environmental trust". See Notes to 107.3(1).

**(4) Application** — Subsection 104(13) and sections 105 to 107 do not apply to a trust with respect to a taxation year during which it is a qualifying environmental trust.

**Related Provisions**: 12(1)(z.1) — Income inclusion in lieu of application of 104(13); 75(3)(c.1) — Reversionary trust rules do not apply.

**Notes**: 107.3(4) added by 1994 Budget, effective for taxation years that end after February 22, 1994.

**Definitions [s. 107.3]**: "business" — 248(1), 253; "net capital loss", "non-capital loss" — 111(8), 248(1); "non-resident" — 248(1); "property" — 248(1); "province" — *Interpretation Act* 35(1); "qualifying environmental trust" — 248(1); "taxable income" — 2(2), 248(1); "taxable income earned in Canada" — 248(1); "taxation year" — 11(2), 107.3(3)(a), 249; "taxpayer" — 248(1); "trust's year" — 107.3(1).

### Proposed Addition — 107.4

**Technical Notes**: Subsection 107.4(3) of the Act applies where there has been a "qualifying disposition" of property. As set out in subsection 107.4(1), a qualifying disposition of property is a disposition that does not result in any change in the beneficial ownership of the property and that otherwise meets the conditions set out in that subsection. Subsection 107.4(3) generally provides for the rollover of property on the disposition.

**Part I**      Income Tax Act, Part I, Division B

To put new section 107.4 in context, the commentary below summarizes the tax consequences of transfers to bare trusts, protective trusts and revocable living trusts under the existing law before describing new section 107.4. Reference should also be made to the commentary on amended section 73 and subsection 104(1).

*Bare Trusts*

The stated interpretation of the existing law by the Canada Customs and Revenue Agency (CCRA) is that, where property is held by a bare trust, the trust is ignored for income tax purposes and the transferor/settlor is considered to be the owner of property held by the trustee in the trustee's capacity as an agent. [See Income Tax Technical News No. 7, Interpretation Bulletin IT-216 and GST Technical Information Bulletin B-068; see also Notes to 104(1) — ed.] Paragraph (e) of the definition "disposition" in section 54 is the current authority for the position that there is no "disposition" of property on its transfer to a "bare trust".

The CCRA has stated that it generally views a trust to be a bare trust when:

- the trustee has no significant powers or responsibilities, and can take no action without instructions from the settlor;
- the trustee's only function is to hold legal title to the property; and
- the settlor is the sole beneficiary and can cause the property to revert to him or her at any time.

The CCRA's position that transfers to bare trusts do not constitute "dispositions" has generally been reinforced because, under amended subsection 104(1), "bare trusts" are not treated as trusts. For this reason, the amended definition of "disposition" in subsection 248(1) will not apply because of the transfer by a settlor of a "bare trust" for the benefit of the settlor. In addition, it should be noted that it is possible that a settlor may establish a "bare trust" for another person. Where this is the case, the transfer of property to the "bare trust" by a settlor would be considered to be a disposition of property by the settlor to the person for whom the "bare trust" has been established.

*Revocable living trusts*

The CCRA has expressed the view [Income Tax Technical News No. 7 — ed.] that a "revocable living trust" should be fully recognized as a trust for income tax purposes. It is of the view that the transfer of property to such a trust involves a change in beneficial ownership of the property and is at the full fair market value of the property. A "revocable living trust" is an estate planning tool used, instead of a will, by individuals. The settlor of the trust is the trustee and, during his or her lifetime, is the sole income and capital beneficiary and retains the right to revoke, alter or amend the trust at any time. However, there is a change of beneficial ownership involved in a transfer to a "revocable living trust" because other beneficiaries under the trust have rights under the trust in the event that the settlor does not revoke the trust before his or her death.

The draft amendments to section 107.4 are generally consistent with the CCRA's present views in this regard. New subsection 107.4(3) is not intended to apply to transfers to revocable living trusts, on the basis that there is no qualifying disposition of property involved. However, for trusts created after 1999, it is generally possible for individuals who are at least 65 years of age to transfer capital property to a revocable living trust on a rollover basis pursuant to amended subsection 73(1).

*Protective trusts*

The CCRA considers the attributes of a "protective trust" to be as follows:

- The settlor is the sole beneficiary under the trust.
- The settlor is entitled to as much of the annual income and realized capital gains of the trust as he or she requests.
- The property of the trust will revert to the settlor if the trust is terminated prior to the settlor's death.
- The trust will terminate upon the death of the settlor unless it is terminated at an earlier date. (When the settlor dies, any property held by the trust will devolve in accordance with the terms of the settlor's will or, if the settlor dies intestate, the property of the trust will devolve in accordance with the laws of intestacy that are relevant to the estate.)

The CCRA considers that, under the existing law, a protective trust is fully recognized as a trust for income tax purposes and that there is no "disposition" of property where a settlor transfers it to a protective trust. Trust income and gains are attributed to the settlor in accordance with subsection 75(2).

New subsection 107.4(3) will apply to transfers to protective trusts, assuming that the requirements for a qualifying disposition are met. However, transfers of capital property to protective trusts created after 1999 will generally be covered by amended subsection 73(1).

The rules in subsection 107.4(3) (and subsection 73(1), where it is applicable) also bridge a gap in the existing law in the context of protective trusts by making it clear at what cost a transferee is considered to acquire property where there has been a transfer of property without any change in its beneficial ownership and the bare trust regime does not apply.

**107.4 (1) Qualifying disposition** — For the purpose of this section, a "qualifying disposition" of a property means a disposition of the property by a person or partnership (in this subsection referred to as the "contributor") as a result of a transfer of the property to a particular trust where

    (a) the disposition does not result in a change in the beneficial ownership of the property;

    (b) the proceeds of disposition would, if this Act were read without reference to this section and sections 69 and 73, not be determined under any provision of this Act;

    (c) if the particular trust is non-resident, the disposition is not

        (i) by a person resident in Canada or by a partnership (other than a partnership each member of which is non-resident), or

        (ii) a transfer of taxable Canadian property from a non-resident person who was resident in Canada in any of the ten calendar years preceding the transfer;

(d) the contributor is not a partnership, if the disposition is part of a series of transactions or events that begin after December 17, 1999 that includes the cessation of the partnership's existence and a subsequent distribution from a personal trust to a former member of the partnership in circumstances to which subsection 107(2) applies;

(e) unless the contributor is a trust, there is immediately after the disposition no absolute or contingent right of a person or partnership (other than the contributor or, where the property was co-owned, each of the joint contributors) as a beneficiary (determined with reference to subsection 104(1.1)) under the particular trust;

(f) the contributor is not an individual (other than a trust described in any of paragraphs (a) to (e.1) of the definition "trust" in subsection 108(1)), if the particular trust is described in any of paragraphs (a) to (e.1) of the definition "trust" in subsection 108(1);

(g) the disposition is not part of a series of transactions or events

(i) that begins after December 17, 1999 and that includes the subsequent acquisition, for consideration given to a personal trust, of a capital interest or an income interest in the trust,

(ii) that begins after December 17, 1999 and that includes the disposition of all or part of a capital interest or an income interest in a personal trust, other than a disposition solely as a consequence of a distribution from a trust to a person or partnership in satisfaction of all or part of that interest, or

(iii) that begins after June 5, 2000 and that includes the transfer to the particular trust of particular property as consideration for the acquisition of a capital interest in the particular trust, if the particular property can reasonably be considered to have been received by the particular trust in order to fund a distribution (other than a distribution that is proceeds of disposition of a capital interest in the particular trust);

(h) the disposition is not, and is not part of, a transaction

(i) that occurs after December 17, 1999, and

(ii) that includes the giving to the contributor, for the disposition, of any consideration (other than consideration that is an interest of the contributor as a beneficiary under the particular trust or that is the assumption by the particular trust of debt for which the property can, at the time of the disposition, reasonably be considered to be security);

(i) subsection 73(1) does not apply to the disposition and would not apply to the disposition if

(i) no election had been made under that subsection, and

(ii) section 73 were read without reference to subsection 73(1.02); and

(j) if the contributor is an amateur athlete trust, a cemetery care trust, an employee trust, an *inter vivos* trust deemed by subsection 143(1) to exist in respect of a congregation that is a constituent part of a religious organization, a related segregated fund trust (as defined by section 138.1), a trust described in paragraph 149(1)(o.4) or a trust governed by an eligible funeral arrangement, an employees profit sharing plan, a registered education savings plan or a registered supplementary unemployment benefit plan, the particular trust is the same type of trust.

**Technical Notes**: As discussed above, subsection 107.4(3) generally provides a rollover whenever there is a qualifying disposition of property to a trust. Under new subsection 107.4(1), a "qualifying disposition" of property is a "disposition" (as defined in subsection 248(1)) of the property as a result of a transfer to a particular trust where

- because of the disposition, there is no change in the beneficial ownership of the property,
- the proceeds would not, disregarding sections 69 and 73, be determined under any other provision of the Act (e.g., transfers from a trust to a beneficiary under the trust where the proceeds are determined under subsection 107(2)),
- the disposition is neither by a person resident in Canada to a non-resident trust nor a transfer of taxable Canadian property from a non-resident person who was resident in Canada in any of the ten calendar years preceding the transfer to a non-resident trust,
- the disposition is not by a partnership (other than a partnership each member of which is non-resident) to a non-resident trust,
- the disposition is not by a partnership, if the disposition is part of a series of transactions or events beginning after December 17, 1999 that includes the cessation of the partnership's existence and a subsequent distribution from a personal trust to a former member of the partnership in circumstances to which subsection 107(2) applies,
- immediately after the disposition, unless the contributor is a trust, there is no absolute or contingent right as a beneficiary under the particular trust for any beneficiary other than the contributor or joint contributors, as the case may be. (For this purpose, there is a restricted meaning under new subsection 104(1.1) associated with the expression "beneficiary".),
- the disposition does not occur after December 17, 1999 if the disposition is, or is part of, a transaction where the contributor receives for the disposition any consideration (other than consideration that is an interest of the contributor as a beneficiary under the particular trust or the assumption by the particular trust of debt for which the property may at the time of

the disposition reasonably be considered to be security),

- the disposition is not to a trust described in any of paragraphs (a) to (e.1) of the definition "trust" in subsection 108(1) (generally trusts relating to employee compensation and retirement savings and trusts deemed to exist for income tax purposes), except if it is a disposition by a trust so described,
- the disposition is not part of a series of transactions or events
  — that begins after December 17, 1999 and that includes the disposition of any interest in a personal trust (other than a disposition solely as a consequence of a distribution from the trust),
  — that begins after December 17, 1999 and that includes the subsequent acquisition, for consideration given to a personal trust, of any interest in the trust, or
  — that begins after June 5, 2000 and that includes the transfer to the particular trust of particular property as consideration for the acquisition of a capital interest in the particular trust, if the particular property can reasonably be considered to have been received in order to fund a distribution from the other trust (other than a distribution that is proceeds of disposition of a capital interest in the particular trust),
- subsection 73(1) would not apply to the disposition if no election were made under that subsection and there were no restrictions in subsection 73(1.02) as to the circumstances in which subsection 73(1) applies, and
- where the contributor is an amateur athlete trust, a cemetery care trust, an employee trust, an inter vivos trust deemed by subsection 143(1) to exist in respect of a congregation that is a constituent part of a religious organization, a related segregated fund trust (as defined in section 138.1), a trust described in paragraph 149(1)(o.4) or a trust governed by an eligible funeral arrangement, an employees profit sharing plan, a registered education savings plan or a registered supplementary unemployment benefit plan, the particular trust is the same type of trust. For example, if the contributor is a related segregated fund trust, the particular trust must also be a related segregated fund trust.

**Letter from Department of Finance, December 1, 1999**: [See under 248(1)"disposition" — ed.]

**Related Provisions**: 75(2) — Revocable or reversionary trust; 104(1.1) — Restricted meaning of "beneficiary"; 107.4(2) — Application of para. (1)(a); 107.4(3) — Tax consequences of qualifying dispositions; 248(1)"disposition" — Whether transfer to a trust is a disposition.

**(2) Application of paragraph (1)(a)** — For the purpose of paragraph (1)(a),

(a) where a trust (in this paragraph referred to as the "transferor trust"), in a period that does not exceed one day, disposes of one or more properties in the period to one or more other trusts, there is deemed to be no resulting change in the beneficial ownership of those properties if

  (i) the transferor trust receives no consideration for the disposition, and

  (ii) as a consequence of the disposition, the beneficial ownership at the beginning of the period of each beneficiary under the transferor trust in each particular property of the transferor trust is the same as the beneficiary's beneficial ownership at the end of the period in the particular property that relates to the beneficiary's combined interest in the transferor trust and in the other trust or trusts; and

(b) where a trust (in this paragraph referred to as the "transferor") governed by a registered retirement savings plan or by a registered retirement income fund transfers a property to a trust (in this paragraph referred to as the "transferee") governed by a registered retirement savings plan or by a registered retirement income fund, the transfer is deemed to not result in a change in the beneficial ownership of the property if the annuitant of the plan or fund that governs the transferor is also the annuitant of the plan or fund that governs the transferee.

**Technical Notes**: Subsection 107.4(2) provides a supplementary rule that applies for the purpose of paragraph 107.4(1)(a). Paragraph 107.4(2)(a) is designed to allow for the division of properties among trusts in certain cases. Consider, for example, the situation where 1,000 shares of ABC Corp. are held in trust A for beneficiaries X and Y. Assume that X has a 30 per cent interest in the trust and Y has the remaining 70 per cent interest. If 300 shares are transferred to trust B for X and the remaining 700 shares are transferred on the same day to trust C for Y, there has been no change in the economic interests of X and Y. Paragraph 107.4(2)(a) provides that, in these circumstances, the requirement in paragraph 107.4(1)(a) that there be no change in beneficial ownership is satisfied in the event that trust A receives no consideration. Consequently, assuming the other conditions under subsection 107.4(1) are satisfied, there would be a qualifying disposition of the 300 shares to trust B and another qualifying disposition of the 700 shares to trust C.

Paragraph 107.4(2)(b) deems there to be no change in beneficial ownership of a property where the property is transferred from a trust governed by an RRSP or RRIF to another trust governed by an RRSP or RRIF, provided that the annuitant of the transferor is the same as that of the transferee. The application of paragraph 107.4(2)(b) is illustrated in the following example.

*EXAMPLE*

Tom is the annuitant of an RRSP under which Laura is named as the beneficiary. The property is transferred from that RRSP trust to another trust governed by an RRSP under which Tom is the annuitant and under which Michelle is named as beneficiary. Assume that, because of an election or otherwise, neither paragraph (f) nor (g) of the definition "disposition" in subsection 248(1) of the Act applies.

*Results:*

1. In these circumstances, paragraph 107.4(2)(b) deems, for the purpose of paragraph 107.4(1)(a), there to be no change in beneficial ownership.

2. Consequently, there should be a qualifying disposition of the property.

Paragraph 107.4(2)(b) is part of a set of amendments intended to clarify the tax treatment of transfers of property involving RRSPs and RRIFs. For further detail, see the commentary on paragraphs 107.4(3)(c) and (f) and (g) of the new definition "disposition" (in subsection 248(1)) and subsections 206(4) and 248(25.1).

**(3) Tax consequences of qualifying dispositions** — Where at a particular time there is a qualifying disposition of a property by a person or partnership (in this subsection referred to as the "transferor") to a trust (in this subsection referred to as the "transferee trust"),

(a) the transferor's proceeds of disposition of the property are deemed to be

(i) where the transferor so elects in writing and files the election with the Minister on or before the transferor's filing-due date for its taxation year that includes the particular time, or at any later time that is acceptable to the Minister, the amount specified in the election that is not less than the cost amount to the transferor of the property immediately before the particular time and not more than the fair market value of the property at the particular time, and

(ii) in any other case, the cost amount to the transferor of the property immediately before the particular time;

(b) except as otherwise provided under paragraph (c), the transferee trust's cost of the property is deemed to be the amount, if any, by which

(i) the proceeds determined under paragraph (a) in respect of the qualifying disposition

exceed

(ii) the amount by which the transferor's loss otherwise determined from the qualifying disposition would be reduced because of subsection 100(4), paragraph 107(1)(c) or (d) or any of subsections 112(3) to (4.2), if the proceeds determined under paragraph (a) were equal to the fair market value of the property at the particular time;

(c) notwithstanding subsection 206(4), for the purposes of Part XI and regulations made for the purposes of that Part, the transferee trust's cost of the property is deemed to be

(i) the cost amount to the transferor immediately before the particular time where

(A) the particular time is before 2000,

(B) the transferor is a trust governed by a registered retirement savings plan or a registered retirement income fund,

(C) the transferee trust is governed by a registered retirement savings plan or a registered retirement income fund,

(D) the transferee trust files a written election with the Minister on or before the later of March 1, 2001 and its filing due-date for its taxation year that includes the particular time (or at such later date as is acceptable to the Minister) that this subparagraph apply, and

(E) it can reasonably be considered that the election was not made for the purpose of avoiding tax under Part XI,

(ii) the fair market value of the property at the particular time where

(A) subparagraph (iii) does not apply,

(B) the transferee trust files a written election with the Minister on or before the later of March 1, 2001 and its filing due-date for its taxation year that includes the particular time (or at such later date as is acceptable to the Minister) that this subparagraph apply, and

(C) it can reasonably be considered that the election was not made for the purpose of avoiding tax under Part XI,

(iii) the fair market value of the property at the particular time where

(A) subparagraph (i) does not apply to the qualifying disposition,

(B) the particular time is before 2000,

(C) the transferor is a trust governed by a registered retirement savings plan or a registered retirement income fund, and

(D) the transferee trust is governed by a registered retirement savings plan or a registered retirement income fund, and

(iv) the cost amount to the transferor of the property immediately before the particular time, in any other case;

(d) if the property was depreciable property of a prescribed class of the transferor and its capital cost to the transferor exceeds the cost at which the transferee trust is deemed by this subsection to have acquired the property, for the purposes of sections 13 and 20 and any regulations made for the purpose of paragraph 20(1)(a),

(i) the capital cost of the property to the transferee trust is deemed to be the amount that was the capital cost of the property to the transferor, and

(ii) the excess is deemed to have been allowed to the transferee trust in respect of the property under regulations made for the purpose of paragraph 20(1)(a) in computing income for taxation years that ended before the particular time;

(e) if the property was eligible capital property of the transferor in respect of a business of the transferor,

(i) where the eligible capital expenditure of the transferor in respect of the property exceeds the cost at which the transferee trust is deemed by this subsection to have acquired the property, for the purposes of sections 14, 20 and 24,

(A) the eligible capital expenditure of the transferee trust in respect of the property is deemed to be the amount that was the eligible capital expenditure of the transferor in respect of the property, and

(B) 3/4 of the excess is deemed to have been allowed under paragraph 20(1)(b) to the transferee trust in respect of the property in computing income for taxation years that ended

(I) before the particular time, and

(II) after the adjustment time of the transferee trust in respect of the business, and

(ii) for the purpose of determining after the particular time the amount to be included under subparagraph 14(1)(a)(v) or paragraph 14(1)(b) in computing the transferee trust's income in respect of any subsequent disposition of the property of the business, there shall be added to the value otherwise determined for Q in the definition "cumulative eligible capital" in subsection 14(5) the amount determined by the formula

$$A \times B/C$$

where

A is the amount, if any, determined for Q in that definition in respect of the business of the transferor immediately before the particular time,

B is the fair market value of the property immediately before the particular time, and

C is the fair market value immediately before the particular time of all eligible capital property of the transferor in respect of the business;

(f) if the property was deemed to be taxable Canadian property of the transferor by this paragraph or paragraph 51(1)(f), 85(1)(i) or 85.1(1)(a), subsection 87(4) or (5) or paragraph 97(2)(c) or 107(2)(d.1), the property is deemed to be taxable Canadian property of the transferee trust;

(g) where the transferor is a related segregated fund trust (in this paragraph having the meaning assigned by section 138.1),

(i) paragraph 138.1(1)(i) does not apply in respect of a disposition of an interest in the transferor that occurs in connection with the qualifying disposition, and

(ii) in computing the amount determined under paragraph 138.1(1)(i) in respect of a subsequent disposition of an interest in the transferee trust where the interest is deemed to exist in connection with a particular life insurance policy, the acquisition fee (as defined by subsection 138.1(6)) in respect of the particular policy shall be determined as if each amount determined under any of paragraphs 138.1(6)(a) to (d) in respect of the policyholder's interest in the transferor trust had been determined in respect of the policyholder's interest in the transferee trust;

(h) if the transferor is a trust to which property had been transferred by an individual (other than a trust),

(i) where subsection 73(1) applied in respect of the property so transferred and it is reasonable to consider that the property was so transferred in anticipation of the individual ceasing to be resident in Canada, for the purposes of paragraph 104(4)(a.3) and the application of this paragraph to a disposition by the transferee trust after the particular time, the transferee trust is deemed after the particular time to be a trust to which the individual had transferred property in anticipation of the individual ceasing to reside in Canada and in circumstances to which subsection 73(1) applied, and

(ii) for the purposes of paragraph (j) of the definition "excluded right or interest" in subsection 128.1(10) and the application of this paragraph to a disposition by the transferee trust after the particular time, where the property so transferred was transferred in circumstances to which this subsection would apply if subsection (1) were read without reference to paragraphs (1)(h) and (i), the transferee trust is deemed after the particular time to be a trust an interest in which was acquired by the individual as a consequence of a qualifying disposition;

(i) if the transferor is a trust (other than a personal trust or a trust prescribed for the purposes of subsection 107(2)), the transferee trust is deemed to be neither a personal trust nor a trust prescribed for the purposes of subsection 107(2);

(j) if the transferor is a trust and a taxpayer disposes of all or part of a capital interest in the transferor because of the qualifying disposition and, as a consequence, acquires a capital interest or part of it in the transferee trust

(i) the taxpayer is deemed to dispose of the capital interest or part of it in the transferor for proceeds equal to the cost amount to the taxpayer of that interest or part of it immediately before the particular time, and

(ii) the taxpayer is deemed to acquire the capital interest or part of it in the transferee trust at a cost equal to the amount, if any, by which

(A) that cost amount

exceeds

(B) the amount by which the taxpayer's loss otherwise determined from the disposition referred to in subparagraph (i) would be reduced because of paragraph 107(1)(c) or (d) if the proceeds under that subparagraph were equal to the fair market value of the capital interest or part of it in the transferor immediately before the particular time;

(k) where the transferor is a trust, a taxpayer's beneficial ownership in the property ceases to be derived from the taxpayer's capital interest in the transferor because of the qualifying disposition and no part of the taxpayer's capital interest in the transferor was disposed of because of the qualifying disposition, there shall, immediately after the particular time, be added to the cost otherwise determined of the taxpayer's capital interest in the transferee trust, the amount determined by the formula

$$A \times ((B-C)/B) - D$$

where

A is the cost amount to the taxpayer of the taxpayer's capital interest in the transferor immediately before the particular time,

B is the fair market value immediately before the particular time of the taxpayer's capital interest in the transferor,

C is the fair market value at the particular time of the taxpayer's capital interest in the transferor (determined as if the only property disposed of at the particular time were the particular property), and

D is the lesser of

(i) the amount, if any, by which the cost amount to the taxpayer of the taxpayer's capital interest in the transferor immediately before the particular time exceeds the fair market value of the taxpayer capital interest in the transferor immediately before the particular time, and

(ii) the maximum amount by which the taxpayer's loss from a disposition of a capital interest otherwise determined could have been reduced because of paragraph 107(1)(c) or (d) if the taxpayer's capital interest in the transferor had been disposed of immediately before the particular time;

(l) where paragraph (k) applies to the qualifying disposition in respect of a taxpayer, the amount that would be determined under that paragraph in respect of the qualifying disposition if the amount determined for D in that paragraph were nil shall, immediately after the particular time, be deducted in computing the cost otherwise determined of the taxpayer's capital interest in the transferor;

(m) where paragraphs (j) and (k) do not apply in respect of the qualifying disposition, the transferor is deemed to acquire the capital interest or part of it in the transferee trust that is acquired as a consequence of the qualifying disposition

(i) where the transferee trust is a personal trust, at a cost equal to nil, and

(ii) in any other case, at a cost equal to the excess determined under paragraph (b) in respect of the qualifying disposition; and

(n) if the transferor is a trust and a taxpayer disposes of all or part of an income interest in the transferor because of the qualifying disposition and, as a consequence, acquires an income interest or a part of an income interest in the transferee trust, for the purpose of subsection 106(2), the taxpayer is deemed not to dispose of any part of the income interest in the transferor at the particular time.

**Technical Notes**: Under paragraph 107.4(3)(a), the transferor's proceeds from the qualifying disposition are generally deemed to be the cost amount of the property. However, provision is made for the transferor to elect another amount, between the cost amount of the property and its fair market value, as proceeds.

Under paragraph 107.4(3)(b), the proceeds determined under paragraph (a) are also generally treated as the cost to the transferee trust of the property. However, this amount is reduced in some cases where the fair market value of the property is less than the cost amount. The reduction in these cases is equal to a hypothetical reduction in the transferor's loss on the disposition of the property. This hypothetical reduction is computed, using the stop-loss rules with regard to partnership interests (subsection 100(4)), trust interests (paragraphs 107(1)(c) and (d)) and shares (subsections 112(3) to (4.2)), on the assumption that the proceeds of disposition are the fair market value of the property rather than its cost amount.

Paragraph 107.4(3)(b) does not, however, apply for the purpose of the foreign property limit under Part XI. For this purpose, except for transfers before 2000 between RRSP trusts and RRIF trusts, the cost amount to the transferor under paragraph 107.4(3)(c) is the cost to the transferee of the same property unless the transferee elects that the cost be the fair market value of the property at the time of its transfer. (It is expected that this election will be used only if the transferee trust does not have information with regard to the cost amount of property from the transferor trust. If, on the other hand, the election is made for the purpose of avoiding Part XI tax, it is invalid.) With regard to the excepted transfers involving RRSPs and RRIFs, the transferee's cost of the property is its fair market value unless the transferee files the election described in subparagraph 107.4(3)(c)(i). (If this election is made for the purpose of avoiding Part XI tax, it is invalid.) For further detail on transfers involving RRSPs and RRIFs see the commentary, including examples, on paragraph (g) of the new definition "disposition" in subsection 248(1).

In addition, where the property is depreciable property or eligible capital property, there are rules in paragraphs 107.4(3)(d) and (e) designed, for the purposes of the capital cost allowance rules in the Act, to put the transferee in the same position as the transferor in the event that the transferee subsequently disposes of the property. These rules are parallel to existing rules in subsection 107(2) for trust distributions to beneficiaries.

Paragraph 107.4(3)(f) provides that, if the property was deemed to be taxable Canadian property of the transferor because of a number of specified provisions in the Act, the property retains that character in the hands of the transferee.

Paragraph 107.4(3)(g) provides that, where the transferor is a related segregated fund trust (as defined in section 138.1 of the Act), paragraph 138.1(1)(i) does not apply in respect of a disposition of an interest in the transferor that occurs in connection with the qualifying disposition. Consequently, no capital loss is provided on the qualifying disposition under paragraph 138.1(1)(i) in respect of load fees associated with a policyholder's interest in the transferor. Paragraph 107.4(3)(g) also ensures that such amounts can ultimately be recognized on a disposition of an interest in the transferee trust.

Paragraph 107.4(3)(h) applies if the transferor was a trust to which property was transferred by an individual (other than a trust) in anticipation of ceasing to reside in Canada and in circumstances to which subsection 73(1) applied. For the purposes of paragraph 104(4)(a.3), the transferee trust is likewise deemed to be a trust to which the individual had transferred property in circumstances to which subsection 73(1) applied and in anticipation of ceasing to reside in Canada. Thus, as a consequence of new paragraph 104(4)(a.3), there may be a deemed disposition by the transferee trust on the individual ceasing to reside in Canada. Paragraph 107.4(3)(h) also applies, where property was transferred by an individual (other than a trust) to the transferor trust in circumstances to which subsection 107.4(3) would apply if no exception under subsection 107.4(1) were made for either transfers to which subsection 73(1) applied or transfers that included the giving to the transferor of any consideration. In these circumstances, the transferee trust is deemed for the purposes of paragraph (j) of the definition "excluded right or interest" in subsection 128.1(10) to be a trust an interest in which was acquired by the individual as a consequence of a qualifying disposition. Thus, gains with regard to an interest in the transferee trust would be required to be recognized in the event that the individual subsequently ceases to reside in Canada.

Paragraph 107.4(3)(i) applies where the transferor was a trust that was neither a personal trust nor a trust prescribed for the purposes of subsection 107(2). In these circumstances, the transferee trust is likewise deemed to be neither a personal trust nor a trust prescribed for the purposes of subsection 107(2).

Paragraph 107.4(3)(j) applies where, as a result of a qualifying disposition from one trust to another trust, a taxpayer disposes of the taxpayer's capital interest in the transferor trust and acquires a capital interest in the transferee trust. In these circumstances, the taxpayer is deemed to dispose of the capital interest in the transferor trust for proceeds equal to the cost amount to the taxpayer of that interest. The taxpayer is also generally deemed to acquire the interest in the transferee trust at that same cost amount. However, the deemed cost amount to the taxpayer of the taxpayer's capital interest in the transferee trust is reduced in some cases where the fair market value of the taxpayer's capital interest in the transferee trust is less than its cost amount to the taxpayer. The reduction in these cases is equal to a hypothetical reduction in the transferor's loss on the disposition of the property. This hypothetical reduction is computed, using the stop-loss rules with regard to trust interests (paragraphs 107(1)(c) and (d)), on the assumption that the proceeds of disposition are the fair market value of the property rather than its cost amount.

Paragraph 107.4(3)(k) applies where the transferor is a trust and a taxpayer's beneficial ownership in property ceases because of a qualifying disposition to be derived from the taxpayer's capital interest in the transferor, but no part of the taxpayer's capital interest in the transferor was disposed of because of the qualifying disposition. In these circumstances, the taxpayer's cost of the taxpayer's capital interest in the transferee trust is increased to reflect the percentage change (attributable to the disposition) in value of the taxpayer's capital interest in the transferee trust. However, the cost amount of the taxpayer's interest in the transferee trust is reduced where the fair market value of the taxpayer's capital interest in the transferor is less than its cost amount to the taxpayer and, had the capital interest in the transferor trust been disposed of, the taxpayer's loss from that hypothetical disposition would have been reduced under the stop-loss rules for trust interests (paragraphs 107(1)(c) and (d)).

Paragraph 107.4(3)(l) generally provides that any amount added under that paragraph in computing the cost to a taxpayer of the taxpayer's capital interest in a transferee trust is deducted in computing the cost to a taxpayer of the taxpayer's capital interest in the transferor. However, the amount of the deduction does not take into account the reduction under paragraph 107.4(3)(k) in respect of the stop-loss rules for trust interests.

Where paragraphs 107.4(3)(j) and (k) do not apply, paragraph 107.4(3)(m) deems the cost to the transferor of the capital interest in the transferee trust acquired on the disposition to be

- where the transferee is a personal trust, nil, and
- in any other case, the excess determined under paragraph 107.4(3)(b).

Paragraph 107.4(3)(n) applies to a qualifying disposition that is a disposition of a property between two personal trusts. Where, because of the qualifying disposition, a taxpayer disposes of an income interest (as defined in subsection 108(1)) in the transferor trust and acquires an income interest in the transferee trust, for the purpose of subsection 106(2) the taxpayer is deemed not to dispose of any part of the income interest in the transferor trust. This measure is limited to personal trusts because an income interest only exists in respect of such trusts.

These amendments apply to dispositions that occur after December 23, 1998. However, in order to ensure that there will be a cost assigned in certain cases to property previously transferred, these amendments also apply, except for the purposes of Part XI of the Act and regulations made for the purpose of that Part, in simplified form to the 1993 and subsequent taxation years. The previous transfers to which the simplified rules apply are transfers (other than transfers to bare trusts) that were not dispositions of property because of paragraph (e) of the definition "disposition" in section 54. No proceeds of dispositions are ascribed to these previous transfers and the stop-loss rules in subsection 107.4(3) do not apply.

**Related Provisions**: 53(4) — Effect on ACB of trust interest; 104(5.3)(c) — No application where election in effect to postpone deemed disposition; 104(5.8) — Where property transferred from one trust to another; 107.4(4) — Fair market value of capital interest in trust; 257 — Formula cannot calculate to less than zero.

**Notes**: 107.4(3)(d), (e), (f), (j) and (m) were (c)–(g) in the draft legislation of December 23, 1998. Current (c), (g), (h), (i), (k), (l) and (n) were not in that version.

**(4) Fair market value of vested interest in trust** — Where

(a) a particular capital interest in a trust is held by a beneficiary at any time,

(b) the particular interest is vested indefeasibly at that time,

(c) the trust is not described in any of paragraphs (a) to (e.1) of the definition "trust" in subsection 108(1), and

(d) interests under the trust are not ordinarily disposed of for consideration that reflects the fair market value of the net assets of the trust,

the fair market value of the particular interest at that time is deemed to be not less than the amount determined by the formula

$$(A - B) \times (C/D)$$

where

A is the total fair market value at that time of all properties of the trust,

B is the total of all amounts each of which is the amount of a debt owing by the trust at that time or the amount of any other obligation of the trust to pay any amount that is outstanding at that time,

C is the fair market value at that time of the particular interest (determined without reference to this subsection), and

D is the total fair market value at that time of all interests as beneficiaries under the trust (determined without reference to this subsection).

**Technical Notes**: New subsection 107.4(4) of the Act provides a valuation rule with regard to vested capital interests in certain trusts.

For subsection 107.4(4) to apply at any time to a taxpayer's capital interest in a trust, the following additional conditions must be satisfied:

• the interest is vested indefeasibly at that time,

• the trust is not described in any of paragraphs (a) to (e.1) of the definition "trust" in subsection 108(1), (generally trusts relating to employee compensation and retirement savings and trusts deemed to exist for income tax purposes), and

• capital interests in the trust are not ordinarily disposed of for consideration that reflects the fair market value of the net assets of the trust.

In these circumstances, the fair market value of the capital interest is deemed to be not less than its "share" of the total net assets of the trust. More specifically, the fair market value of the capital interest is deemed to be not less than the product obtained by multiplying the fair market value of the net assets (i.e., assets minus liabilities) of the trust by the proportion of the fair market value of the particular interest (determined without reference to subsection 107.4(4)) to the total fair market value of all beneficial interests in the trust (determined without reference to subsection 107.4(4)).

These amendments apply to dispositions of capital interests that occur after December 23, 1998.

**Related Provisions**: 248(9.2) — Meaning of "vested indefeasibly"; 257 — Formula cannot calculate to less than zero.

**Application**: Bill C-43 (First Reading September 20, 2000), s. 52, will add s. 107.4, subsecs. (1) and (3) applicable

(a) to dispositions that occur after December 23, 1998, and

(b) re 1993 et seq., to transfers of capital property that occurred before December 24, 1998, except that, in its application to transfers before December 24, 1998,

(i) subsec. (1) shall be read as follows:

107.4 (1) For the purpose of this section, a "qualifying disposition" of a property means a transfer of the property to a particular trust that was not a disposition of the property for the purpose of subdivision c because of paragraph (e) of the definition "disposition" in section 54, except where

(a) if the transfer is from another trust to the particular trust,

(i) each trust can reasonably be considered to act as agent for the same beneficiary or beneficiaries in respect of the property transferred, or

(ii) the transferee trust can reasonably be considered to act as agent for the transferor trust in respect of the property transferred; and

(b) in any other case, it is reasonable to consider that the particular trust acts as agent in respect of the property transferred.

(ii) the opening words of subsec. (3) shall be read as follows:

(3) Where at a particular time there is a qualifying disposition of a property by a person or partnership (in this subsection referred to as the "transferor") to a trust (in this subsection referred to as the "transferee trust"), except for the purposes of Part XI and regulations made for the purposes of that Part

(iii) subsec. (3) shall be read without reference to paras. (a), (c), (g) and (h);

(iv) para. (3)(b) shall be read as follows:

(b) the transferee trust's cost of the property is deemed to be the cost amount to the transferor of the property immediately before the particular time;

(v) subsec. (3) shall be read as if each amount determined under cl. 107.4(3)(j)(ii)(B) and the description of D in paragraph 107.4(3)(k) were nil; and

(vi) subpara. 107.4(3)(m)(ii) shall be read as follows:

(ii) in any other case, at a cost equal to the amount determined under paragraph (b) in respect of the qualifying disposition.

Subsecs. (2) and (4) apply to dispositions that occur after December 23, 1998.

**Definitions [s. 107.4]**: "adjustment time" — 14(5), 248(1); "amateur athlete trust" — 143.1(1), 248(1); "amount" — 248(1); "beneficiary" — 104(1.1), 108(1); "business" — 248(1); "Canada" — 255, *Interpretation Act* 35(1); "capital interest" — 108(1), 248(1); "capital property" — 54, 248(1); "cemetery care trust" — 148.1(1), 248(1); "contributor" — 107.4(1); "cost amount" — 248(1); "depreciable property" — 13(21), 248(1); "disposition" — 248(1); "eligible capital expenditure" — 14(5), 248(1); "eligible capital property" — 54, 248(1); "eligible funeral arrangement" — 148.1(1), 248(1); "employee trust" — 248(1); "employees profit sharing plan" — 144(1), 248(1); "fair market value" — 107.4(4); "filing-due date" — 248(1); "income interest" — 108(1), 248(1); "individual" — 248(1); "*inter vivos* trust" — 108(1), 248(1); "life insurance policy" — 138(12), 248(1); "Minister", "non-resident" — 248(1); "partnership" — see Notes to 96(1); "person", "personal trust", "prescribed", "property" — 248(1); "registered education savings plan" — 146.1(1), 248(1); "registered supplementary unemployment benefit plan" — 145(1), 248(1); "regulation" — 248(1); "related" — 251(2)–(6); "resident in Canada" — 250; "security" — *Interpretation Act* 35(1); "taxable Canadian property" — 248(1); "taxation year" — 249; "taxpayer" — 248(1); "transferor trust" — 107.4(2); "trust" — 104(1), (3), 108(1), 248(1); "vested indefeasibly" — 248(9.2); "writing" — *Interpretation Act* 35(1).

### Proposed Amendment — 107.4(3)(e)(ii) pre formula

(ii) for the purpose of determining after the particular time the amount required by paragraph 14(1)(b) to be included in computing the transferee trust's income in respect of any subsequent disposition of the property of the business, there shall be added to the value otherwise determined for Q in the definition "cumulative eligible capital" in subsection 14(5) the amount determined by the formula

**Application**: The December 21, 2000 draft legislation, s. 50, will amend the portion of subpara. 107.4(3)(e)(ii) before the formula to read as above, applicable in respect of taxation years that end after February 27, 2000.

**Technical Notes**: Subsection 107.4(3) applies where there has been a "qualifying disposition" of property. As set out in subsection 107.4(1), a "qualifying disposition" of property is a disposition that does not result in any change in the beneficial ownership of the property and that otherwise meets the conditions set out in that subsection. Subsection 107.4(3) generally provides for the rollover of property on the disposition. Subparagraph 107.4(3)(e)(ii), which is intended to prevent an overstatement of the income inclusions required by subsection 14(1), is amended consequential on the re-numbering of

subsection 14(1), which is described in further detail in the commentary to that subsection.

**108. (1) Definitions** — In this subdivision,

**"accumulating income"** of a trust for a taxation year means the amount that would be the income of the trust for the year if that amount were

(a) computed without reference to subsections 104(5.1) and (12),

(b) computed as if the greatest amount that the trust was entitled to claim under subsection 104(6) in computing its income for the year were so claimed,

(c) where the trust

(i) is a pre-1972 spousal trust at the end of the year,

(ii) is described in paragraph 104(4)(a), or

(iii) elected under subsection 104(5.3) for a preceding taxation year,

computed without reference to subsections 104(4), (5) and (5.2) and 107(4),

(d) where the trust is described in paragraph 104(4)(a) and the taxpayer's spouse or common-law partner referred to in that paragraph died on a day in that year, computed as if any disposition by the trust before the end of that day of capital property, land described in an inventory of the trust, Canadian resource property or foreign resource property had not occurred, and

(e) computed without reference to subsection 12(10.2), except to the extent that that subsection applies to amounts paid to a trust to which paragraph 70(6.1)(b) applies and before the death of the spouse or common-law partner referred to in that paragraph;

### Proposed Amendment — 108(1)"accumulating income"

**"accumulating income"** of a trust for a taxation year means the amount that would be the income of the trust for the year if that amount were computed

(a) without reference to paragraphs 104(4)(a) and (a.1) and subsections 104(5.1), (5.2) and (12) and 107(4),

(b) as if the greatest amount that the trust was entitled to claim under subsection 104(6) in computing its income for the year were so claimed, and

(c) without reference to subsection 12(10.2), except to the extent that that subsection applies to amounts paid to a trust to which paragraph 70(6.1)(b) applies and before the death of the spouse or common-law partner referred to in that paragraph;

## Subdivision k — Trusts and Beneficiaries   S. 108(1) cap

**Application**: Bill C-43 (First Reading September 20, 2000), subsec. 53(1), will amend the definition "accumulating income" in subsec. 108(1) to read as above, applicable to 2000 et seq.

**Technical Notes**: The amount that may be allocated under subsection 104(15) of the Act to a disabled beneficiary for a trust taxation year is limited to the trust's accumulating income for the year. The trust's accumulating income is designed, in part, to ensure that the preferred beneficiary election cannot be used to allocate income and gains under a spousal trust to non-spouse beneficiaries. Under the existing definition, trust income arising from a deemed disposition of trust assets under subsection 104(4), (5) or (5.2) is not included in computing "accumulating income" and cannot be allocated to beneficiaries in the event that the trust is a spousal trust.

The definition "accumulating income" is amended so that the above restriction only applies in connection with the deemed disposition of trust assets that occurs on the death of the spouse beneficiary under a spousal trust. As a consequence of amendments to paragraph 104(4)(a), a similar restriction applies to *alter ego* trusts and joint partner trusts, as defined in subsection 248(1).

This amendment also reflects changes [re common-law partners — ed.] proposed under Bill C-23, the *Modernization of Benefits and Obligations Act*.

**Notes**: Para. (b) ensures that, if a trust fails to claim the maximum deduction under 104(6), "accumulating income" is computed as if the maximum claim had been made. (It may be advantageous not to claim the maximum under 104(6) in order to allow for a tax-free distribution to a beneficiary under 104(13.1) or (13.2).) The purpose of para. (d) (to be repealed) is to ensure that capital gains recognition for spousal trusts under 104(4) to (5.1) cannot be avoided by actual dispositions by the trust before the beneficiary spouse dies.

108(1)"accumulating income"(d) and (e) amended by 2000 same-sex partners bill to add reference to "common-law partner", effective for the 2001 and later taxation years, or earlier by election (see Notes to 248(1)"common-law partner").

Definition "accumulating income" amended by 1995 Budget, effective for trust taxation years that end after July 19, 1995, to add paras. (b) and (d) (renumbering former (b) as (c)).

Definition amended by 1992 technical bill, effective for 1991 and later taxation years. For earlier taxation years that begin after 1987, read:

> "accumulating income" of a trust for a taxation year means the amount that would, but for subsection 104(12) and, where the trust is a trust described in paragraph 104(4)(a), subsections 104(4), (5), (5.2) and 107(4), be its income for the year;

108(1)"accumulating income" was 108(1)(a) before consolidation in R.S.C. 1985 (5th Supp.), effective for taxation years ending after November 1991. See Table of Concordance.

**Interpretation Bulletins**: IT-381R3: Trusts — capital gains and losses and the flow-through of taxable capital gains to beneficiaries; IT-394R2: Preferred beneficiary election.

**Advance Tax Rulings**: ATR-34: Preferred beneficiary's election.

**"beneficiary"** under a trust includes a person beneficially interested therein;

**Related Provisions**: 104(5.5) — Meaning of "beneficiary" for purposes of election to postpone deemed disposition; 143.1(1)(e) — Deemed beneficiary of amateur athletes' reserve fund; 248(3) — Rules applicable in Quebec; 248(13) — Deemed beneficiary for certain purposes; 248(25) — Meaning of "beneficially interested".

**Notes**: 108(1)"beneficiary" was 108(1)(b) before consolidation in R.S.C. 1985 (5th Supp.), effective for taxation years ending after November 1991.

**"capital interest"** of a taxpayer in a trust means

(a) in the case of a personal trust or a prescribed trust, a right (whether immediate or future and whether absolute or contingent) of the taxpayer as a beneficiary under the trust to, or to receive, all or any part of the capital of the trust, and

(b) in any other case, a right of the taxpayer as a beneficiary under the trust;

### Proposed Amendment — 108(1)"capital interest"

**"capital interest"** of a taxpayer in a trust means all rights of the taxpayer as a beneficiary under the trust, and after 1999 includes a right (other than a right acquired before 2000 and disposed of before March 2000) to enforce payment of an amount by the trust that arises as a consequence of any such right, but does not include an income interest in the trust;

**Application**: Bill C-43 (First Reading September 20, 2000), subsec. 53(2), will amend the definition "capital interest" in subsec. 108(1) to read as above, applicable after 1999.

**Technical Notes**: Subsection 108(1) of the Act contains the definition "capital interest". In the case of a personal trust, a prescribed trust and certain "grandfathered" trusts, a taxpayer's capital interest encompasses all rights of the taxpayer to receive all or any part of the trust's capital. In any other case, a taxpayer's capital interest generally encompasses all rights of the taxpayer as a beneficiary under the trust.

The definition "capital interest" is amended to expressly provide that a capital interest does not include an income interest in the trust. With the exception of an income interest in a trust, a taxpayer's capital interest in a trust encompasses:

- all rights of the taxpayer as a beneficiary under any type of trust, and
- after 1999, a right (other than a right acquired before 2000 and disposed of before March 2000) to enforce payment by the trust that arises as a consequence of any such rights.

Note, in addition, that an amendment to subsection 104(1) has the effect of excluding a "bare trust" from the definition "trust" in the Act. One of the effects of this amendment is that there will be no capital interests in a "bare trust" for the purposes of the Act.

**Related Provisions**: 53(2)(h), (i) — Reduction in ACB of capital interest; 248(1)"capital interest" — Definition applies to entire Act; 248(1)"disposition"(d), (h) — Whether transfer by trust is a disposition of capital interest.

**Notes**: 108(1)"capital interest" was 108(1)(c) before consolidation in R.S.C. 1985 (5th Supp.), effective for taxation years ending after November 1991. See Table of Concordance.

Amended in 1987 (and retroactively by 1988 tax reform), effective for interests created or materially altered after January 31, 1987 that were acquired after 10:00 p.m. EST, February 6, 1987. For earlier interests, read:

> (c) "capital interest" of a taxpayer in a trust means a right (whether immediate or future and whether absolute or contingent) of the taxpayer as a beneficiary under the trust to, or to receive, all or any part of the capital of the trust;

**Regulations**: 4800.1 (prescribed trust).

885

**S. 108(1) cos** — Income Tax Act, Part I, Division B

"cost amount" to a taxpayer at any time of a capital interest or part thereof, as the case may be, in a trust (other than a trust that is a foreign affiliate of the taxpayer) means, notwithstanding the definition of "cost amount" in subsection 248(1),

### Proposed Amendment — 108(1) "cost amount" opening words

"cost amount" to a taxpayer at any time of a capital interest or part of the interest, as the case may be, in a trust (other than a trust that is a foreign affiliate of the taxpayer) means, except for the purposes of section 107.4 and notwithstanding subsection 248(1),

**Application**: Bill C-43 (First Reading September 20, 2000), subsec. 53(3), will amend the opening words of the definition "cost amount" in subsec. 108(1) to read as above, applicable to 1993 *et seq.*

**Technical Notes**: The calculation of the "cost amount" of a taxpayer's capital interest in a trust is primarily relevant for the purposes of determining a taxpayer's capital gain from the disposition of the taxpayer's capital interest in a personal trust. Under paragraph 107(1)(a) of the Act, for capital gains calculation purposes, the adjusted cost base (ACB) of a taxpayer's capital interest is generally the greater of the ACB otherwise determined and the cost amount of the taxpayer's interest determined under subsection 108(1).

Under the existing definition, the cost amount of a taxpayer's capital interest in a trust satisfied by way of a distribution of money is equal to the money distributed. The cost amount of a capital interest satisfied by way of the distribution of other property is equal to the sum of the cost amounts to the trust of those properties. In cases where a capital interest is disposed of without any distribution, the cost amount of a taxpayer's capital interest is considered to be the taxpayer's proportionate share of the trust's money on hand and the total cost amount of other trust property, offset by outstanding trust liabilities. The purpose of the existing definition is essentially to give beneficiaries of personal trusts recognition for cost amounts of trust assets, given that the cost of capital and income interests in such trusts will generally be nil because of the operation of subsections 106(1.1) and 107(1.1).

The definition is amended so that it does not apply for the purpose of section 107.4. This amendment applies to the 1993 and subsequent taxation years, in order to be consistent with the coming into force for section 107.4.

(a) where any money or other property of the trust has been distributed by the trust to the taxpayer in satisfaction of all or part of the taxpayer's capital interest (whether on the winding-up of the trust or otherwise), the total of

(i) the money so distributed, and

(ii) all amounts each of which is the cost amount to the trust, immediately before the distribution, of each such other property, and

(iii) [Repealed]

### Proposed Addition — 108(1) "cost amount" (a.1)

(a.1) where that time is immediately before the time of the death of the taxpayer and subsection 104(4) or (5) deems the trust to dispose of property at the end of the day that includes that time, the amount that would be determined under paragraph (b) if the taxpayer had died on a day that ended immediately before that time, and

**Application**: Bill C-43 (First Reading September 20, 2000), subsec. 53(4), will add para. (a.1) to the definition "cost amount" in subsec. 108(1), applicable to deaths that occur after 1999.

**Technical Notes**: New paragraph (a.1) of the definition is introduced to provide a special rule in the event that an individual is deemed to dispose of a capital interest in a trust immediately before the individual's death. If on the individual's death there is also a deemed disposition of trust assets and an immediate subsequent deemed reacquisition because of the operation of amended paragraph 104(4)(a), that deemed reacquisition is considered to occur immediately before the individual's death in order that the "cost amount" of the individual's capital interest reflects the deemed disposition of trust assets. This amendment is intended to prevent double taxation of the same economic gain in these circumstances.

(b) in any other case, the amount determined by the formula

$$(A - B) \times \frac{C}{D}$$

where

A is the total of

(i) all money of the trust on hand immediately before that time, and

(ii) all amounts each of which is the cost amount to the trust, immediately before that time, of each other property of the trust,

B is the total of all amounts each of which is the amount of any debt owing by the trust, or any other obligation of the trust to pay any amount, that was outstanding immediately before that time,

C is the fair market value at that time of the capital interest or part thereof, as the case may be, in the trust, and

D is the fair market value at that time of all capital interests in the trust;

**Related Provisions**: 206(1) "cost amount" — Meaning of cost amount of capital interest in a trust for foreign-property rules; 248(1) — Definition of "cost amount" for other purposes; 248(25.3) — Deemed cost of trust units; 257 — Formula cannot calculate to less than zero.

**Notes**: 108(1) "cost amount" was 108(1)(d) before consolidation in R.S.C. 1985 (5th Supp.), effective for taxation years ending after November 1991. See Table of Concordance.

"Cost amount" amended by 1991 technical bill and 1993 technical bill, effective July 14, 1990. The previous version was worded very differently, but the only new substantive provisions were (a)(iii) and (b)A(iii), which were added by 1991 technical bill but removed retroactively by 1993 technical bill. Before July 14, 1990, read (a) and (b) as:

(a) in any case where any money or property of the trust has been distributed by the trust to the taxpayer in satisfaction of the whole or part of the taxpayer's capital interest, as the case may be (whether on the winding-up of the trust or otherwise), the total of the money so distributed and all amounts each of which is the cost amount to the trust, immediately before the distribution, of a property so distributed to the taxpayer, and

(b) in any other case, that proportion of the amount, if any, by which the total of all money of the trust on hand immediately before that time and all amounts each of which is the cost amount to the trust, immediately before that time, of a property of the trust exceeds the total of all amounts each of which is the amount of a debt owing by the trust, or of any other obligation of the trust to pay any amount, that was outstanding immediately before that time, that

(i) the fair market value at that time of the capital interest or part thereof, as the case may be, in the trust,

is of

(ii) the fair market value at that time of all capital interests in the trust;

**Advance Tax Rulings**: ATR-38: Distribution of all of the property of an estate.

**"designated income [para. 108(1)(d.1)]"** — [Repealed under former Act]

**Notes**: Former 108(1)(d.1), which defined "designated income", repealed by 1988 tax reform effective 1988. The term is no longer used.

### Proposed Addition — 108(1) "eligible offset"

**"eligible offset"** at any time of a taxpayer in respect of all or part of the taxpayer's capital interest in a trust is the portion of any debt or obligation that is assumed by the taxpayer and that can reasonably be considered to be applicable to property distributed at that time in satisfaction of the interest or part of the interest, as the case may be, if the distribution is conditional upon the assumption by the taxpayer of the portion of the debt or obligation;

**Application**: Bill C-43 (First Reading September 20, 2000), subsec. 53(8), will add the definition "eligible offset" to subsec. 108(1), applicable after 1999.

**Technical Notes**: Subsection 108(1) of the Act is amended to introduce the expression "eligible offset".

A taxpayer's "eligible offset" in respect of all or part of a taxpayer's capital interest in a trust reduces the taxpayer's proceeds of disposition arising from the satisfaction of all or part of that interest, in the event there is a distribution to which amended subsection 107(2) or (2.1) applies. Where such a distribution was conditional upon the assumption by the taxpayer of a debt or obligation, the taxpayer's eligible offset at any time in respect of that interest is the portion of the debt or obligation assumed by the taxpayer that can reasonably be considered to be applicable to the property distributed at that time in satisfaction of that interest.

This amendment applies after 1999. For further detail on the effect of this amendment, see the notes on amendments to subsections 107(2) and (2.1).

**"eligible real property gain"** — [Repealed]

**Notes**: "Eligible real property gain" added by 1992 technical bill and amended retroactively by 1993 technical bill, effective for 1992 and later taxation years. Before redrafting to fit the R.S.C. 1985 (5th Supp.), it was para. 108(1)(d.1). It was repealed by 1994 Budget, effective for taxation years that begin after February 22, 1994, as a result of the elimination of the $100,000 capital gains exemption in 110.6(3). For 1992-95 taxation years that begin before February 23, 1994, read:

"eligible real property gain" of a trust has the meaning that would be assigned by the definition of that expression in subsection 110.6(1) if the reference in that definition to "non-qualifying real property" were read as "non-qualifying real property as defined in subsection 108(1)";

**"eligible real property loss"** — [Repealed]

**Notes**: "Eligible real property loss" added by 1992 technical bill and amended retroactively by 1993 technical bill, effective for 1992 and later taxation years. Before redrafting to fit the R.S.C. 1985 (5th Supp.), it was para. 108(1)(d.11). It was repealed by 1994 Budget, effective for taxation years that begin after February 22, 1994, as a result of the elimination of the $100,000 capital gains exemption in 110.6(3). For 1992-95 taxation years that begin before February 23, 1994, read:

"eligible real property loss" of a trust has the meaning that would be assigned by the definition of that expression in subsection 110.6(1) if the reference in that definition to "non-qualifying real property" were read as "non-qualifying real property as defined in subsection 108(1)";

**"eligible taxable capital gains"** of a personal trust for a taxation year means the lesser of

(a) its annual gains limit (within the meaning assigned by subsection 110.6(1)) for the year, and

(b) the amount determined by the formula

$$A - B$$

where

A is its cumulative gains limit (within the meaning assigned by subsection 110.6(1)) at the end of the year, and

B is the total of all amounts designated under subsection 104(21.2) by the trust in respect of beneficiaries for taxation years before that year;

**Related Provisions**: 257 — Formula cannot calculate to less than zero.

**Notes**: "Eligible taxable capital gains" added by 1992 technical bill and amended retroactively by 1993 technical bill, effective for 1992 and later taxation years. Before redrafting to fit the R.S.C. 1985 (5th Supp.), it was para. 108(1)(d.2). See Table of Concordance. It was amended by 1994 Budget, effective for taxation years that begin after February 22, 1994, to restrict its application to personal trusts as a result of the elimination of the $100,000 capital gains exemption in 110.6(3). For 1992-95 taxation years that begin before February 23, 1994, read:

"eligible taxable capital gains" of a trust for a taxation year means the lesser of

(a) its annual gains limit for the year (within the meaning that would be assigned by the definition of that expression in subsection 110.6(1) if the reference in that definition to "non-qualifying real property" were read as "non-qualifying real property as defined in subsection 108(1))", and

(b) the amount determined by the formula

A − B

where

A is its cumulative gains limit at the end of the year (within the meaning that would be assigned by the definition of that expression in subsection 110.6(1) if the reference in that definition to "non-qualifying real property" were read as "non-qualifying real property as defined in subsection 108(1))", and

B is the total of all amounts designated under subsection 104(21.2) by the trust in respect of beneficiaries in taxation years before that year;

**Interpretation Bulletins**: IT-381R3: Trusts — capital gains and losses and the flow-through of taxable capital gains to beneficiaries.

**Forms**: T3 Sched. 3: Eligible taxable capital gains.

**"excluded property"** means a share of the capital stock of a non-resident-owned investment corporation that is not taxable Canadian property;

**Notes**: 108(1)"excluded property" amended by 1995-97 technical bill, effective April 27, 1995. No substantive change was intended with the amendment. It previously read:

"excluded property" at a particular time means a share of the capital stock of a non-resident-owned investment corporation if, on the first day of the first taxation year of the corporation that ends at or after the particular time, the corporation does not own property referred to in any of clauses 115(1)(b)(v)(A) to (D);

108(1)"excluded property" added by 1992 technical bill, effective February 12, 1991. Before redrafting to fit the R.S.C. 1985 (5th Supp.), it was para. 108(1)(d.12).

### Proposed Addition — 108(1)"exempt property"

**"exempt property"** of a taxpayer at any time means property any income or gain from the disposition of which by the taxpayer at that time would, because the taxpayer is non-resident or because of a provision contained in a tax treaty, not cause an increase in the taxpayer's tax payable under this Part;

**Application**: Bill C-43 (First Reading September 20, 2000), subsec. 53(8), will add the definition "exempt property" to subsec. 108(1), applicable after 1992, except that before 1999, the words "tax treaty" shall be read as "convention or agreement with another country that has the force of law in Canada".

**Technical Notes**: Subsection 108(1) of the Act introduces the definition "exempt property". The expression is used in amended subsections 104(4) to (5.2). For further detail, see the notes above on those subsections.

**"income interest"** of a taxpayer in a trust means a right (whether immediate or future and whether absolute or contingent) of the taxpayer as a beneficiary under a personal trust to, or to receive, all or any part of the income of the trust;

### Proposed Amendment — 108(1)"income interest"

**"income interest"** of a taxpayer in a trust means a right (whether immediate or future and whether absolute or contingent) of the taxpayer as a beneficiary under a personal trust to, or to receive, all or any part of the income of the trust and, after 1999, includes a right (other than a right acquired before 2000 and disposed of before March 2000) to enforce payment of an amount by the trust that arises as a consequence of any such right;

**Application**: Bill C-43 (First Reading September 20, 2000), subsec. 53(5), will amend the definition "income interest" in subsec. 108(1) to read as above, applicable to in respect of interests created or materially altered after January 1987 that were acquired after 10 p.m. EST, February 6, 1987.

**Technical Notes**: Subsection 108(1) of the Act contains the definition "income interest". It is defined as a right as a beneficiary under a personal trust to income of the trust. Under subsection 108(3), "income" for this purpose is determined without reference to the provisions of the Act.

The definition is amended to provide that, after 1999, an income interest also includes a right (other than a right acquired before 2000 and disposed of before March 2000) to enforce payment by the trust that arises as a consequence of a right that is an income interest.

Except as noted above, these amendments apply in respect of interests created or materially altered after January 31, 1987 that were acquired after 10 p.m. EST, February 6, 1987.

**Related Provisions**: 108(3) — Meaning of "income" of trust; 248(1)"income interest" — Definition applies to entire Act.

**Notes**: 108(1)"income interest" was 108(1)(e) before consolidation in R.S.C. 1985 (5th Supp.), effective for taxation years ending after November 1991.

"Income interest" amended in 1987, effective for interests created or materially altered after January 1987 that were acquired after 10 p.m. EST, February 6, 1987. For earlier interests, read "under the trust" in place of "under a personal trust".

**Interpretation Bulletins**: IT-385R2: Disposition of an income interest in a trust.

**"inter vivos trust"** means a trust other than a testamentary trust;

**Related Provisions**: 143(1) — Communal religious congregation deemed to be *inter vivos* trust; 143.1(1)(a) — Amateur athletes' reserve fund deemed to be *inter vivos* trust; 146.1(11) — RESP deemed to be *inter vivos* trust for certain purposes; 149(5) — Exception re investment income of certain clubs; 207.6(1) — Retirement compensation arrangement deemed to be *inter vivos* trust; 248(1)"*inter vivos* trust" — Definition applies to entire Act.

**Notes**: 108(1)"*inter vivos* trust" was 108(1)(f) before consolidation in R.S.C. 1985 (5th Supp.), effective for taxation years ending after November 1991.

**"non-qualifying real property"** — [Repealed]

**Notes**: "Non-qualifying real property" added by 1992 technical bill, effective for 1992 and later taxation years. Before redrafting to fit the R.S.C. 1985 (5th Supp.), it was para. 108(1)(f.1).

Definition repealed by 1994 Budget, effective for taxation years that begin after February 22, 1994. It read:

"non-qualifying real property"

(a) of a trust that is a personal trust has the meaning assigned by subsection 110.6(1), and

(b) of a trust that is not a personal trust has the meaning assigned by subsection 131(6);

**"pre-1972 spousal trust"** at a particular time means a trust that was

(a) created by the will of a taxpayer who died before 1972, or

Subdivision k — Trusts and Beneficiaries    S. 108(1) qua

(b) created before June 18, 1971 by a taxpayer during the taxpayer's lifetime

that, throughout the period beginning at the time it was created and ending at the earliest of January 1, 1993, the day on which the taxpayer's spouse or common-law partner died and the particular time, was a trust under which the taxpayer's spouse or common-law partner was entitled to receive all of the income of the trust that arose before the spouse or common-law partner's death, unless a person other than the spouse or common-law partner received or otherwise obtained the use of any of the income or capital of the trust before the end of that period;

**Related Provisions**: 104(4)(a.1) — Deemed disposition by a trust; 104(15) — Preferred beneficiary's share; 104(15)(a) — Allocable amount for preferred beneficiary election; 108(3) — Meaning of "income" of trust; 108(4) — Trust not disqualified by reason only of payment of certain duties and taxes; 248(9.1) — Whether trust created by taxpayer's will; 252(3) — Extended meaning of "spouse".

**Notes**: 108(1)"pre-1972 spousal trust" amended by 2000 same-sex partners bill to add reference to "common-law partner", effective for the 2001 and later taxation years, or earlier by election (see Notes to 248(1)"common-law partner").

108(1)"pre-1972 spousal trust" added by 1992 technical bill, effective February 12, 1991. Before redrafting to fit the R.S.C. 1985 (5th Supp.), it was para. 108(1)(f.2).

**Interpretation Bulletins**: IT-381R3: Trusts — capital gains and losses and the flow-through of taxable capital gain to beneficiaries.

**"preferred beneficiary"** under a trust for a particular taxation year of the trust means a beneficiary under the trust at the end of the particular year who is resident in Canada at that time if

(a) the beneficiary is

(i) an individual in respect of whom paragraphs 118.3(1)(a) to (b) apply for the individual's taxation year (in this definition referred to as the "beneficiary's year") that ends in the particular year, or

(ii) an individual

(A) who attained the age of 18 years before the end of the beneficiary's year, was a dependant (within the meaning assigned by subsection 118(6)) of another individual for the beneficiary's year and was dependent on the other individual because of mental or physical infirmity, and

(B) whose income (computed without reference to subsection 104(14)) for the beneficiary's year does not exceed the amount used under paragraph (c) of the description of B in subsection 118(1) for the year, and

(b) the beneficiary is

(i) the settlor of the trust,

(ii) the spouse or common-law partner or former spouse or common-law partner of the settlor of the trust, or

(iii) a child, grandchild or great grandchild of the settlor of the trust or the spouse or common-law partner of any such person;

**Related Provisions**: 104(14) — Preferred beneficiary election.

**Notes**: Note that the "settlor" of a trust, as defined below, can lose his or her status as a result of the contribution of additional property to the trust by another person. Thus, a preferred beneficiary of a trust can cease to be a preferred beneficiary even though the terms of the trust are not changed.

108(1)"preferred beneficiary"(b) amended by 2000 same-sex partners bill to add reference to "common-law partner", effective for the 2001 and later taxation years, or earlier by election (see Notes to 248(1)"common-law partner").

108(1)"preferred beneficiary"(a)(ii)(B) amended by 1999 Budget, this version effective for 2000 and later taxation years. For the 1999 taxation year, read "the amount used under paragraph (c) of the description of B in subsection 118(1) for the year" as "$7,044", and for the 1998 taxation year, read "$6,956". Before the 1998 taxation year, read (B) as:

(B) whose income (computed without reference to subsection 104(14)) for the beneficiary's year does not exceed $6,456, and

Definition amended by 1997 Budget effective for trust taxation years that end after 1996. For taxation years that begin and end in 1996, read:

"preferred beneficiary" under a trust for a particular taxation year of the trust means an individual

(a) who is resident in Canada and a beneficiary under the trust at the end of the particular year,

(b) in respect of whom paragraphs 118.3(1)(a) to (b) apply for the individual's taxation year in which the particular year ends, and

(c) who is

(i) the settlor of the trust,

(ii) the spouse or former spouse of the settlor of the trust, or

(iii) a child, grandchild or great grandchild of the settlor of the trust, or the spouse of any such person;

Definition amended by 1995 Budget, effective for trust taxation years that begin in 1996. The substantive amendments were to add para. (b), thus restricting the preferred beneficiary election under 104(14) to severely disabled beneficiaries, and to require in para. (a) that the tests be "at the end of the particular year". See Notes to 104(14) and 118.3(1). For earlier taxation years since 1972, read:

"preferred beneficiary" under any trust means an individual resident in Canada who is a beneficiary under the trust and is

(a) the settlor of the trust,

(b) the spouse or former spouse of the settlor of the trust, or

(c) a child, grandchild or great grandchild of the settlor of the trust, or the spouse of any such person;

108(1)"preferred beneficiary" was 108(1)(g) before consolidation in R.S.C. 1985 (5th Supp.), effective for taxation years ending after November 1991. See Table of Concordance.

**Interpretation Bulletins**: IT-374: Meaning of "settlor"; IT-381R3: Trusts — capital gains and losses and the flow-through of taxable gains to beneficiaries; IT-394R2: Preferred beneficiary election.

**"qualified farm property"** of an individual has the meaning assigned by subsection 110.6(1);

**Notes**: 108(1)"qualified farm property" was 108(1)(g.1) before consolidation in R.S.C. 1985 (5th Supp.), effective for taxation years ending after November 1991.

"**qualified small business corporation share**" of an individual has the meaning assigned by subsection 110.6(1)

**Notes:** 108(1)"qualified small business corporation share" was 108(1)(g.2) before consolidation in R.S.C. 1985 (5th Supp.), effective for taxation years ending after November 1991.

"**settlor**",

(a) in relation to a testamentary trust, means the individual referred to in the definition "testamentary trust" in this subsection, and

(b) in relation to an *inter vivos* trust,

(i) if the trust was created by the transfer, assignment or other disposition of property thereto (in this paragraph referred to as property "contributed") by not more than one individual and the fair market value of such of the property of the trust as was contributed by the individual at the time of the creation of the trust or at any subsequent time exceeds the fair market value of such of the property of the trust as was contributed by any other person or persons at any subsequent time (such fair market values being determined at the time of the making of any such contribution), means that individual, and

(ii) if the trust was created by the contribution of property thereto jointly by an individual and the individual's spouse or common-law partner and by no other person and the fair market value of such of the property of the trust as was contributed by them at the time of the creation of the trust or at any subsequent time exceeds the fair market value of such of the property of the trust as was contributed by any other person or persons at any subsequent time (such fair market values being determined at the time of the making of any such contribution), means that individual and the spouse or common-law partner;

**Related Provisions:** 17(15)"settlor" — Alternate definition for purposes of loan by corporation to non-resident; 104(5.6) — Designated contributor.

**Notes:** 108(1)"settlor"(b)(ii) amended by 2000 same-sex partners bill to add reference to "common-law partner", effective for the 2001 and later taxation years, or earlier by election (see Notes to 248(1)"common-law partner").

108(1)"settlor" was 108(1)(h) before consolidation in R.S.C. 1985 (5th Supp.), effective for taxation years ending after November 1991. See Table of Concordance.

**Interpretation Bulletins:** IT-374: Meaning of "settlor"; IT-394R2: Preferred beneficiary election.

"**testamentary trust**" in a taxation year means a trust or estate that arose on and as a consequence of the death of an individual (including a trust referred to in subsection 248(9.1)), other than

(a) a trust created by a person other than the individual,

(b) a trust created after November 12, 1981 if, before the end of the taxation year, property has been contributed to the trust otherwise than by an individual on or after the individual's death and as a consequence thereof, and

(c) a trust created before November 13, 1981 if

(i) after June 28, 1982 property has been contributed to the trust otherwise than by an individual on or after the individual's death and as a consequence thereof, or

(ii) before the end of the taxation year, the total fair market value of the property owned by the trust that was contributed to the trust otherwise than by an individual on or after the individual's death and as a consequence thereof and the property owned by the trust that was substituted for such property exceeds the total fair market value of the property owned by the trust that was contributed by an individual on or after the individual's death and as a consequence thereof and the property owned by the trust that was substituted for such property, and for the purposes of this paragraph the fair market value of any property shall be determined as at the time it was acquired by the trust; and

**Related Provisions:** 210.1(a) — Part XII.2 does not apply to testamentary trust; 248(1)"testamentary trust" — Definition applies to entire Act; 248(8) — Occurrences as a consequence of death.

**Notes:** See Notes to 104(1).

108(1)"testamentary trust" amended by 1993 technical bill, effective for 1990 and later taxation years, to change reference to 70(6.1) to 248(9.1), which is where that provision was moved.

108(1)"testamentary trust" was 108(1)(i) before consolidation in R.S.C. 1985 (5th Supp.), effective for taxation years ending after November 1991. See Table of Concordance.

**Interpretation Bulletins:** IT-381R3: Trusts — capital gains and losses and the flow-through of taxable capital gains to beneficiaries.

"**trust**" includes an *inter vivos* trust and a testamentary trust but in subsections 104(4), (5), (5.2), (12), (13.1), (13.2), (14) and (15) and sections 105 to 107 does not include

(a) an amateur athlete trust, an employee trust, a trust described in paragraph 149(1)(o.4) or a trust governed by a deferred profit sharing plan, an employee benefit plan, an employees profit sharing plan, a foreign retirement arrangement, a registered education savings plan, a registered pension plan, a registered retirement income fund, a registered retirement savings plan or a registered supplementary unemployment benefit plan,

**Proposed Addition — 108(1)"trust"(a.1)**

(a.1) a trust, other than a trust described in paragraph (a) or (d), all or substantially all of the property of which is held for the purpose of providing benefits to individuals each of whom is provided with benefits in respect of, or because of, an office or employment or former office or employment of any individual,

## Subdivision k — Trusts and Beneficiaries

**Application**: Bill C-43 (First Reading September 20, 2000), subsec. 53(6), will add para. (a.1) to the definition "trust" in subsec. 108(1), applicable to 1999 *et seq.*

**Technical Notes**: Subsection 108(1) of the Act defines "trust", for the purposes of the 21-year deemed disposition rule and other specified measures, to exclude certain listed trusts. For these purposes, paragraph (f) of the definition excludes unit trusts (as defined in subsection 108(2)) and paragraph (g) of the definition excludes, except as specified, trusts all interests in which have vested indefeasibly and no interest in which may become effective in the future. One of the specified exceptions from the exclusion under paragraph (g) is for trusts described in paragraph 104(4)(a) (which, under the existing law, describes only spousal trusts).

Paragraph (a.1) is added to the definition so that the exclusion from the 21-year deemed disposition rule and other rules applies to a trust (other than a trust already described in paragraph (a) or (d) of the definition) all or substantially all of the property of which is held for the purpose of providing benefits to individuals each of whom is provided with benefits in respect of, or because of, an office or employment or former office or employment. It is generally intended that health and welfare trusts qualify for the exclusion, given that these trusts would not be expected to be described in paragraph (a) or (d) of the definition.

**Notes**: This is aimed at catching trusts that fall outside the definitions of "employee trust" and "employee benefit plan" in 248(1). See also 107.1 re distributions from such a trust.

(b) a related segregated fund trust (within the meaning assigned by section 138.1),

(c) an *inter vivos* trust deemed by subsection 143(1) to exist in respect of a congregation that is a constituent part of a religious organization,

(d) an RCA trust (within the meaning assigned by subsection 207.5(1)),

(e) a trust each of the beneficiaries under which was at all times after it was created a trust referred to in paragraph (a), (b) or (d) or a person who is a beneficiary of the trust only because of being a beneficiary under a trust referred to in any of those paragraphs, or

(e.1) a cemetery care trust or a trust governed by an eligible funeral arrangement,

and, in subsections 104(4), (5), (5.2), (12), (14) and (15), does not include

(f) a unit trust, or

(g) a trust (other than a trust described in paragraph 104(4)(a), a trust that has elected under subsection 104(5.3), or a trust that, in its return of income under this Part for its first taxation year ending after 1992, has elected that this subparagraph not apply) all interests in which have vested indefeasibly and no interest in which may become effective in the future.

**Proposed Amendment — 108(1) "trust"**

and, in applying subsections 104(4), (5), (5.2), (12), (14) and (15) and section 106 at any time, does not include

(f) a trust that, at that time, is a unit trust, or

(g) a trust all interests in which, at that time, have vested indefeasibly, other than

(i) an *alter ego* trust, a joint partner trust or a post-1971 partner trust,

(ii) a trust that has elected under subsection 104(5.3),

(iii) a trust that has, in its return of income under this Part for its first taxation year that ends after 1992, elected that this paragraph not apply,

(iv) a trust that is at that time resident in Canada where the total fair market value at that time of all interests in the trust held at that time by beneficiaries under the trust who at that time are non-resident is more than 20% of the total fair market value at that time of all interests in the trust held at that time by beneficiaries under the trust,

(v) a trust under the terms of which, at that time, all or part of a person's interest in the trust is to be terminated with reference to a period of time (including a period of time determined with reference to the person's death), otherwise than as a consequence of terms of the trust under which an interest in the trust is to be terminated as a consequence of a distribution to the person (or the person's estate) of property of the trust if the fair market value of the property to be distributed is required to be commensurate with the fair market value of that interest immediately before the distribution, or

(vi) a trust that, before that time and after December 17, 1999, has made a distribution to a beneficiary in respect of the beneficiary's capital interest in the trust, if the distribution can reasonably be considered to have been financed by a liability of the trust and one of the purposes of incurring the liability was to avoid taxes otherwise payable under this Part as a consequence of the death of any individual;

**Application**: Bill C-43 (First Reading September 20, 2000), subsec. 53(7), will amend the portion of the definition "trust" in subsec. 108(1) after para. (e.1) to read as above, applicable to 1998 *et seq.*, except that

(a) it does not apply for the purpose of applying subpara. (g)(iv) of the definition before December 24, 1998; and

(b) where the trust so elects in writing and files the election with the Minister of National Revenue on or before the trust's filing-due date for the taxation year of the trust that includes the day on which the amending legislation is assented to (or any later day that is acceptable to the Minister), subpara. (g)(v) of the definition, as it applies before 2001, shall be read as follows:

> (v) a trust any interest in which may become effective in the future, or

**Technical Notes**: The definition is also amended so that the exclusion under paragraphs (f) and (g) also apply for the purpose of the rules in section 106 governing the taxation of income interests.

Paragraph (g) of the definition is amended so that the exclusion can apply to a trust all interests in which have vested indefeasibly, without regard to whether an interest in the trust becomes effective in the future. However, under new subparagraph (g)(v), the exclusion generally does not apply to a trust under the terms of which all or part of any person's interest is to be terminated with reference to a period of time.

The elimination of the requirement that there be no future interest and its replacement by subparagraph (g)(v) applies to the 1998 and subsequent taxation years. However, where the trust so elects in writing before its filing-due date for its taxation year that includes the date of Royal Assent (or before such later day as is acceptable to the Minister of National Revenue), these amendments apply only after 2000.

*EXAMPLE*

A trust provides for beneficiary A to receive income from property for the lifetime of beneficiary A with the remainder interest to go beneficiary B (or the estate of beneficiary B, if beneficiary B does not survive beneficiary A). The above amendment clarifies that the above exclusion from the 21-year rule does not apply in this case. On the other hand, where new units in a trust can be issued by a commercial trust for fair market value consideration, the above amendment ensures that the trust is not precluded from qualifying for the exclusion.

New subparagraph (g)(iv) of the definition ensures that the above exclusion does not apply to a trust resident in Canada that has a non-resident beneficiary, unless the total fair market value of the interests of the non-resident beneficiaries is 20% or less of the total fair market value of the interests in the trust. This 20% level is meant to accommodate a limited level of foreign ownership of interests in the trust, given that gains in respect of those interests may not be subject to Canadian taxes because of income tax treaties. This amendment applies after December 23, 1998.

New subparagraph (g)(vi) of the definition ensures that the above exclusion does not apply to a trust that, after December 17, 1999, made a distribution to a beneficiary in respect of the beneficiary's capital interest in the trust, if the distribution may reasonably be considered to have been financed by a liability of the trust and one of the purposes of incurring the liability was to avoid taxes otherwise payable under Part I of the Act as a consequence of the death of any individual. This provision parallels new paragraph 104(4)(a.2), described in the notes above.

**Related Provisions**: 75(2) — Revocable or reversionary trust; 94(3) — Non-resident trust deemed resident in Canada; 104(1) — Reference to trust or estate; 107.4(4) — Fair market value of capital interest in trust; 146.1(1)"trust" — Meaning of "trust" for RESP; 210.1(d) — Certain trusts not subject to Part XII.2 tax; 233.2(4) — Reporting requirement re transfers to foreign trust; 233.6(1) — Reporting requirement re distributions from foreign trust; 248(1)"trust" — Definition outside subdiv. k is that in 104(1); 248(3) — Deemed trusts in Quebec; 248(5.2) — Trust-to-trust transfers — deemed same trust; 248(9.2) — Meaning of "vested indefeasibly"; 251(1)(b) — Personal trust and beneficiary deemed not to deal at arm's length.

**Notes**: See Notes to 104(1) re trusts generally.

"Trust" amended by 1992 technical bill to add reference to an amateur athlete trust in para. (a) (former 108(1)(j)(ii)) effective 1988, and to add paras. (e) and (g) (former 108(1)(j)(vi) and (i.1)) effective 1993.

Para. (e.1) added by 1994 tax amendments bill (Part IV), effective 1993, and amended by 1995-97 technical bill retroactive to its introduction to add reference to a cemetery care trust.

108(1)"trust" was 108(1)(j) before consolidation in R.S.C. 1985 (5th Supp.), effective for taxation years ending after November 1991. The order of the provisions was changed; paras. (a) to (e) were formerly subparas. (ii) to (vi), while paras. (f) and (g) were formerly subparas. (i) and (i.1). See Table of Concordance.

**Interpretation Bulletins [subsec. 108(1)"trust"]**: IT-394R2: Preferred beneficiary election; IT-449R: Meaning of "vested indefeasibly"; IT-502: Employee benefit plans and employee trusts; IT-531: Eligible funeral arrangements.

**Related Provisions [subsec. 108(1)]**: 104(4), (5), (5.2) — Exempt property excluded from 21-year deemed disposition.

**(2) Where trust is a unit trust** — For the purposes of this Act, a trust is a unit trust at any particular time if, at that time, it was an *inter vivos* trust the interest of each beneficiary under which was described by reference to units of the trust, and

(a) the issued units of the trust included

(i) units having conditions attached thereto that included conditions requiring the trust to accept, at the demand of the holder thereof and at prices determined and payable in accordance with the conditions, the surrender of the units, or fractions or parts thereof, that are fully paid, or

(ii) units qualified in accordance with prescribed conditions relating to the redemption of the units by the trust,

and the fair market value of such of the units as had conditions attached thereto that included such conditions or as were so qualified, as the case may be, was not less than 95% of the fair market value of all of the issued units of the trust (such fair market values being determined without regard to any voting rights attaching to units of the trust),

(b) throughout the taxation year in which the particular time occurred

(i) it was resident in Canada,

(ii) its only undertaking was

(A) the investing of its funds in property (other than real property or an interest in real property),

(B) the acquiring, holding, maintaining, improving, leasing or managing of any real property, or interest in real property, that is capital property of the trust, or

(C) any combination of the activities described in clauses (A) and (B),

(iii) at least 80% of its property consisted of any combination of

(A) shares,

(B) any property that, under the terms or conditions of which or under an agreement, is convertible into, is exchangeable for or confers a right to acquire, shares,

(C) cash,

(D) bonds, debentures, mortgages, notes and other similar obligations,

(E) marketable securities,

(F) real property situated in Canada and interests in such property, and

(G) rights to and interests in any rental or royalty computed by reference to the amount or value of production from a natural accumulation of petroleum or natural gas in Canada, from an oil or gas well in Canada or from a mineral resource in Canada,

(iv) not less than 95% of its income (determined without reference to subsections 49(2.1) and 104(6)) for the year was derived from, or from the disposition of, investments described in subparagraph (iii), and

(v) not more than 10% of its property consisted of bonds, securities or shares in the capital stock of any one corporation or debtor other than Her Majesty in right of Canada or a province or a Canadian municipality,

and, where the trust would not be a unit trust at the particular time if subparagraph (iii) were read without reference to the words "real property (or interests in real property) situated in Canada", the units of the trust are listed at any time in the year or in the following taxation year on a prescribed stock exchange in Canada, or

### Proposed Amendment — 108(2)(b)

(b) each of the following conditions was satisfied:

(i) throughout the taxation year that includes the particular time (in this paragraph referred to as the "current year"), the trust was resident in Canada,

(ii) throughout the period or periods (in this paragraph referred to as the "relevant periods") that are in the current year and throughout which the conditions in paragraph (a) are not satisfied in respect of the trust, its only undertaking was

(A) the investing of its funds in property (other than real property or an interest in real property),

(B) the acquiring, holding, maintaining, improving, leasing or managing of any real property or an interest in real property, that is capital property of the trust, or

(C) any combination of the activities described in clauses (A) and (B),

(iii) throughout the relevant periods at least 80% of its property consisted of any combination of

(A) shares,

(B) any property that, under the terms or conditions of which or under an agreement, is convertible into, is exchangeable for or confers a right to acquire, shares,

(C) cash,

(D) bonds, debentures, hypothecs, mortgages, notes and other similar obligations,

(E) marketable securities,

(F) real property situated in Canada and interests in real property situated in Canada, and

(G) rights to and interests in any rental or royalty computed by reference to the amount or value of production from a natural accumulation of petroleum or natural gas in Canada, from an oil or gas well in Canada or from a mineral resource in Canada,

(iv) either

(A) not less than 95% of its income for the current year (computed without regard to subsections 49(2.1) and 104(6)) was derived from, or from the disposition of, investments described in subparagraph (iii), or

(B) not less than 95% of its income for each of the relevant periods (computed without regard to subsections 49(2.1) and 104(6) and as though each of those periods were a taxation year) was derived from, or from the disposition of, investments described in subparagraph (iii),

(v) throughout the relevant periods, not more than 10% of its property consisted of bonds, securities or shares in the capital stock of any one corporation or debtor other than Her Majesty in right of Canada or a province or a Canadian municipality, and

(vi) where the trust would not be a unit trust at the particular time if this paragraph were read without reference to this subparagraph and subparagraph (iii) were read without reference to clause (F), the units of the trust are listed at any time in the current year or in the following taxation year on a prescribed stock exchange in Canada, or

**Application**: Bill C-43 (First Reading September 20, 2000), subsec. 53(9), will amend para. 108(2)(b) to read as above, applicable to 1998 *et seq.*

## S. 108(2)(b)

**Technical Notes**: Subsection 108(2) of the Act describes the requirements for a trust to be a "unit trust" (as defined in subsection 248(1)). A trust must be a unit trust to qualify as a "mutual fund trust" under subsection 132(6).

Paragraph 108(2)(b) is amended to allow a trust to qualify as a unit trust throughout a taxation year, provided that at all times throughout the year the trust meets the conditions set out in either paragraph 108(2)(a) or (b). This ensures that a trust will not lose its status as a unit trust only because it converts from a unit trust described in paragraph 108(2)(b) to a unit trust described in paragraph 108(2)(a) or *vice versa*.

Paragraph 108(2)(b) is intended, because of its closing words, to require a trust more than 20% of the assets of which consist of real property situated in Canada to qualify as a unit trust under paragraph 108(2)(b) only if its units are listed on a prescribed stock exchange in Canada. These closing words are replaced by subparagraph 108(2)(b)(vi). This subparagraph reflects past amendments to subsection 108(2).

Paragraph 108(2)(b) is also amended to add a reference to "hypothec" to the list of properties the combination of which must account for at least 80 per cent of a trust's total properties. This amendment is made to ensure that the Act appropriately reflects both the civil law of the province of Quebec and the law of other provinces.

These amendments apply to the 1998 and subsequent taxation years.

**Letter from Department of Finance, July 6, 1999**:

Dear [xxx]

This is in reply to your letter of June 23, 1999 to Simon Thompson concerning subsection 108(2) of the *Income Tax Act*.

We understand that your client currently meets the provision for closed-end unit trusts under paragraph 108(2)(b), and that your client expects, following the introduction of a redemption feature to its units, to meet the provision for open-end unit trusts under paragraph 108(2)(a). We understand that, as a result of its conversion from a closed-end to an open-end trust, your client will no longer have met, during the period before its conversion, the provision for closed-end trusts as it will not have met the requirements of paragraph 108(2)(b) throughout the taxation year.

We would agree that, in these circumstances, it would be appropriate to extend the application of subsection 108(2) to allow a trust to meet the definition of unit trust throughout a taxation year provided that at all times throughout the taxation year the trust meets the conditions set out in either paragraph 108(2)(a) or (b). We will recommend that this amendment apply after 1997. [See also 132(6.2) — ed.]

Thank you for writing.

Yours sincerely,

Brian Ernewein
Director, Tax Legislation Division, Tax Policy Branch

(c) the fair market value of the property of the trust at the end of 1993 was primarily attributable to real property (or an interest in real property), the trust was a unit trust throughout any calendar year that ended before 1994 and the fair market value of the property of the trust at the particular time is primarily attributable to property described in paragraph (a) or (b) of the definition "qualified investment" in section 204, real property (or an interest in real property) or any combination of those properties.

**Related Provisions**: 20(1)(e)(i) — Deduction for expenses relating to sale of units; 53(1)(d.1), 53(2)(h), (j) — ACB of units; 108(1)"trust"(f) — Unit trusts excluded from many trust rules; 132(6) — Meaning of "mutual fund trust"; 132(6.2) — Mutual fund trust — retention of status; 248(1)"unit trust" — Definition applies to entire Act; 250(6.1) — Trust that ceases to exist deemed resident throughout year; 253.1 — Deeming rule re investments in limited partnerships.

**Notes**: 108(2)(b)(ii)(A) and (B) and closing words of 108(2)(b) amended by 1995-97 technical bill, effective for 1994 and later taxation years, to add all references to "an interest in real property".

108(2)(b)(iii) amended and 108(2)(c) added by 1995-97 technical bill, effective for 1994 and later taxation years. For 1990-93, read 108(2)(b)(iii) as:

(iii) at least 80% of its property consisted of any combination of shares, bonds, mortgages, marketable securities, cash, real property situated in Canada or rights to or interests in any rental or royalty computed by reference to the amount or value of production from a natural accumulation of petroleum or natural gas in Canada, from an oil or gas well in Canada or from a mineral resource in Canada,

108(2)(b) amended by 1994 tax amendments bill (Part V), effective 1994. For earlier years since 1990, read:

(b) throughout the taxation year in which the particular time occurred it complied with the following conditions:

(i) it was resident in Canada,

(ii) its only undertaking was the investing of funds of the trust,

(iii) at least 80% of its property throughout the year consisted of shares, bonds, mortgages, marketable securities, cash or rights to or interests in any rental or royalty computed by reference to the amount or value of production from a natural accumulation of petroleum or natural gas in Canada, from an oil or gas well in Canada or from a mineral resource in Canada,

(iv) not less than 95% of its income (determined without reference to subsections 49(2.1) and 104(6)) for the year was derived from, or from dispositions of, investments described in subparagraph (iii),

(v) at no time in the year did more than 10% of its property consist of shares, bonds or securities of any one corporation or debtor other than Her Majesty in right of Canada or a province or a Canadian municipality, and

(vi) where there were prescribed for the purposes of this subparagraph conditions relating to the number of unit holders, dispersal of ownership of its units or public trading of its units, all holdings of and transactions in its units accorded with those conditions.

108(2)(b)(iv) amended by 1991 technical bill, effective 1990, to add the exclusion of 49(2.1) and 104(6).

**Regulations**: 3200 (prescribed stock exchange); not yet amended to apply for purposes of 108(2)(b)).

**I.T. Technical News**: No. 6 (mutual funds trading — meaning of "investing its funds in property" in 108(2)(b)(ii)(A)).

### (3) Income of a trust in certain provisions —

For the purposes of the definition "income interest" in subsection (1), the income of a trust is its income computed without reference to the provisions of this Act and, for the purposes of the definition "pre-1972 spousal trust" in subsection (1) and paragraphs 70(6)(b) and (6.1)(b), 73(1)(c) and 104(4)(a), the income of a trust is its income computed without reference to the provisions of this Act, minus any dividends included therein

> **Proposed Amendment — 108(3) opening words [temporary]**
>
> **(3) Income of a trust in certain provisions** — For the purposes of the definition "income interest" in subsection (1), the income of a trust is its income computed without reference to the provisions of this Act and, for the purposes of the definition "pre-1972 spousal trust" in subsection (1) and paragraphs 70(6)(b) and (6.1)(b), 73(1.01)(c) and 104(4)(a), the income of a trust is its income computed without reference to the provisions of this Act, minus any dividends included in that income
>
> **Application**: Bill C-43 (First Reading September 20, 2000), subsec. 53(10), will amend the opening words of subsec. 108(3) to read as above, applicable to 2000 *et seq.*, except for the purpose of applying s. 73 to transfers that occur before 2000.
>
> **Technical Notes**: Subsection 108(3) of the Act provides that a trust's income is generally its income computed without reference to the provisions of the Act. Subsection 108(3) applies for the purposes of the spousal trust rules in subsection 73(1), as well as other specified purposes.
>
> Subsection 108(3) is amended to change a cross-reference to paragraph 73(1)(c) to a cross-reference to new paragraph 73(1.01)(c). This is strictly a technical change consequential to amendments to section 73, described in the notes above.

> **Proposed Amendment — 108(3) opening words**
>
> **(3) Income of a trust in certain provisions** — For the purposes of the definition "income interest" in subsection (1) and the definition "exempt foreign trust" in subsection 94(1), the income of a trust is its income computed without reference to the provisions of this Act and, for the purposes of the definition "pre-1972 spousal trust" in subsection (1) and paragraphs 70(6)(b) and (6.1)(b), 73(1.01)(c) and 104(4)(a), the income of a trust is its income computed without reference to the provisions of this Act, minus any dividends included in that income
>
> **Application**: The June 22, 2000 draft legislation, s. 15, will amend the opening words of subsec. 108(3) to read as above, applicable to taxation years that begin after 2000.
>
> **Technical Notes**: Subsection 108(3) of the Act provides that, for the purposes of the definition "income interest" in subsection 108(1), the income of a trust is its income computed without reference to the provisions of the Act. Amendments to subsection 108(3) were contained in a detailed Notice of Ways and Means Motion tabled on June 5, 2000.
>
> It is proposed to further amend subsection 108(3) so that the rule described above also applies for the purposes of the definition "exempt foreign trust" in new subsection 94(1).

(a) that are amounts not included by reason of section 83 in computing the income of the trust for the purposes of the other provisions of this Act;

(b) that are described in subsection 131(1); or

(c) to which subsection 131(1) applies by reason of subsection 130(2).

**Related Provisions**: 108(5) — Interpretation.

**Notes**: Opening words of 108(3) amended by 1992 technical bill, effective 1991. For earlier years, instead of "paragraphs 70(6)(b) and (6.1)(b), 73(1)(c), 104(4)(a) and 108(1)(f.2)", read "subparagraphs 70(6)(b)(i), 73(1)(c)(i) and 104(4)(a)(iii)".

**Interpretation Bulletins**: IT-305R4: Testamentary spouse trusts; IT-385R2: Disposition of an income interest in a trust.

**(4) Trust not disqualified** — For the purposes of the definition "pre-1972 spousal trust" in subsection (1) and subparagraphs 70(6)(b)(ii) and (6.1)(b)(ii), 73(1)(c)(ii) and 104(4)(a)(iv), where a trust was created by a taxpayer whether by the taxpayer's will or otherwise, a person, other than the taxpayer's spouse or common-law partner, shall be deemed not to have received or otherwise obtained or to be entitled to receive or otherwise obtain the use of any income or capital of the trust solely because of the payment, or provision for payment, as the case may be, by the trust of

(a) any estate, legacy, succession or inheritance duty payable, in consequence of the taxpayer's death, in respect of any property of, or interest in, the trust; or

(b) any income or profits tax payable by the trust in respect of any income of the trust.

> **Proposed Amendment — 108(4)**
>
> **(4) Trust not disqualified** — For the purposes of the definition "pre-1972 spousal trust" in subsection (1), subparagraphs 70(6)(b)(ii) and (6.1)(b)(ii) and paragraphs 73(1.01)(c) and 104(4)(a), where a trust was created by a taxpayer whether by the taxpayer's will or otherwise, no person is deemed to have received or otherwise obtained or to be entitled to receive or otherwise obtain the use of any income or capital of the trust solely because of the payment, or provision for payment, as the case may be, by the trust of
>
> (a) any estate, legacy, succession or inheritance duty payable, in consequence of the death of the taxpayer or a spouse or common-law partner of the taxpayer who is a beneficiary under the trust, in respect of any property of, or interest in, the trust; or
>
> (b) any income or profits tax payable by the trust in respect of any income of the trust.
>
> **Application**: Bill C-43 (First Reading September 20, 2000), subsec. 53(11), will amend subsec. 108(4) to read as above, applicable to 2000 *et seq.*, except for the purpose of applying s. 73 to transfers that occur before 2000.
>
> **Technical Notes**: Subsection 108(4) of the Act provides that a trust is not disqualified as a spousal trust under a number of specified provisions in the Act merely because of the payment of estate, income or similar taxes.

**S. 108(4)**      Income Tax Act, Part I, Division B

Subsection 108(4) is amended so that this rule applies not only to spousal trusts but also to trusts established for the exclusive benefit of the settlor during the settlor's lifetime and to trusts established for the joint benefit of the settlor and the settlor's spouse during their lifetimes. This amendment is consequential to changes to section 73 that are described in the notes above.

This amendment applies to the 2000 and subsequent taxation years.

This provision is further amended to reflect changes [re common-law partners — ed.] proposed under Bill C-23, the *Modernization of Benefits and Obligations Act.*

**Related Provisions**: 248(8) — Occurrences as a consequence of death; 248(9.1) — Whether trust created by taxpayer's will.

**Notes**: Opening words of 108(4) amended by 2000 same-sex partners bill to add reference to "common-law partner", effective for the 2001 and later taxation years, or earlier by election (see Notes to 248(1)"common-law partner").

Opening words of 108(4) amended by 1992 technical bill, effective 1991, to add reference to 70(6.1)(b)(ii) and 108(1)"pre-1972 spousal trust".

**Interpretation Bulletins**: IT-305R4: Testamentary spouse trusts.

**(5) Interpretation** — Except as otherwise provided in this Part,

(a) an amount included in computing the income for a taxation year of a beneficiary of a trust under subsection 104(13) or (14) or section 105 shall be deemed to be income of the beneficiary for the year from a property that is an interest in the trust and not from any other source, and

(b) an amount deductible in computing the amount that would, but for subsections 104(6) and (12), be the income of a trust for a taxation year shall not be deducted by a beneficiary of the trust in computing the beneficiary's income for a taxation year,

but, for greater certainty, nothing in this subsection shall affect the application of subsection 56(4.1), sections 74.1 to 75 and 120.4 and subsection 160(1.2) of this Act and section 74 of the *Income Tax Act*, chapter 148 of the Revised Statutes of Canada, 1952.

**Related Provisions**: 3 — Calculation of income; 129(4) — "Canadian investment income" and "foreign investment income" defined.

**Notes**: 108(5) means that, in effect, income loses its character when flowed out to a beneficiary under 104(6) and (13). See 4(1) regarding the source of income. Note that certain kinds of distributions can be designated to retain their character in the beneficiary's hands — e.g., dividends under 104(19) and capital gains under 104(21). See Notes to 96(1) re income flowed through a partnership.

108(5) amended by 1999 Budget, effective for 2000 and later taxation years, to add reference to 120.4 and 160(1.2).

**I.T. Application Rules**: 69 (meaning of "*Income Tax Act*, chapter 148 of the Revised Statutes of Canada, 1952").

**Interpretation Bulletins**: IT-243R4: Dividend refund to private corporations.

**(6) Variation of trusts** — For the purposes of subsections 104(4), (5) and (5.2), where at any time the terms of a trust are varied, the trust shall at and after that time be deemed to be the same trust as, and a continuation of, the trust immediately before that time, but, for greater certainty, nothing in this subsection affects the application of paragraph 104(4)(a.1).

### Proposed Amendment — 108(6)

**(6) Variation of trusts** — Where at any time the terms of a trust are varied

(a) for the purposes of subsections 104(4), (5) and (5.2), subject to paragraph (b), the trust is, at and after that time, deemed to be the same trust as, and a continuation of, the trust immediately before that time;

(b) for greater certainty, paragraph (a) does not affect the application of paragraph 104(4)(a.1); and

(c) for the purposes of paragraph 53(2)(h), subsection 107(1), paragraph (j) of the definition "excluded right or interest" in subsection 128.1(10) and the definition "personal trust" in subsection 248(1), no interest of a beneficiary under the trust before it was varied is considered to be consideration for the interest of the beneficiary in the trust as varied.

**Application**: Bill C-43 (First Reading September 20, 2000), subsec. 53(12), will amend subsec. 108(6) to read as above, applicable to 2000 *et seq.*

**Technical Notes**: Subsection 108(6) of the Act applies where the terms of a trust are varied. It provides that the application of the 21-year deemed disposition rule is not affected by the variation.

Subsection 108(6) is amended to ensure that no interest of a beneficiary under the trust before it was varied is considered to be consideration for the interest of the beneficiary in the trust as varied. This rule is relevant for a number of specified provisions in the Act, which refer to trust interests being acquired for consideration.

This amendment applies to the 2000 and subsequent taxation years. The amendment is intended to extend to all trust variations, including variations that occurred before 2000.

**Notes**: 108(6) added by 1992 technical bill, effective February 12, 1991.

### Proposed Addition — 108(7)

**(7) Interests acquired for consideration** — For the purposes of paragraph 53(2)(h), subsection 107(1), paragraph (j) of the definition "excluded right or interest" in subsection 128.1(10) and the definition "personal trust" in subsection 248(1),

(a) an interest in a trust is deemed not to be acquired for consideration solely because it was acquired in satisfaction of any right as a beneficiary under the trust to enforce payment of an amount by the trust; and

(b) where all the beneficial interests in a particular *inter vivos* trust acquired by way of the transfer, assignment or other disposition of property to the particular trust were acquired by

(i) one person, or

(ii) two or more persons who would be related to each other if

(A) a trust and another person were related to each other, where the other person is a beneficiary under the trust or is related to a beneficiary under the trust, and

(B) a trust and another trust were related to each other, where a beneficiary under the trust is a beneficiary under the other trust or is related to a beneficiary under the other trust,

any beneficial interest in the particular trust acquired by such a person is deemed to have been acquired for no consideration.

**Application:** Bill C-43 (First Reading September 20, 2000), subsec. 53(12), will add subsec. 108(7), applicable after December 23, 1998.

**Technical Notes:** A "personal trust" is defined in subsection 248(1) of the Act as essentially a testamentary trust or an inter vivos trust in which no beneficial interest was acquired for consideration payable to the trust or to a contributor to the trust. An existing special rule within the definition generally ensures that one person (or two or more related persons) can make contributions to a trust and retain an interest under the trust without the prohibition on consideration being considered to apply. This existing rule also applies for the purposes of paragraph 53(2)(h), which deals with the calculation of the adjusted cost bases of certain trust interests.

The definition is amended so that this special rule is removed from the definition. Instead, the special rule is now provided in new subsection 108(7). The special rule also is to apply, under subsection 108(7), for the purposes of amended subsection 107(1), strictly as a consequence of the amendments to that provision and for the purposes of paragraph (j) of the new definition "excluded right or interest" in subsection 128.1(10).

New subsection 108(7) also ensures that, for the purposes of the above-noted provisions, an interest in a trust is deemed not to be acquired for consideration solely because of the acquisition of the interest in satisfaction of any right as a beneficiary under the trust to enforce payment from the trust.

**Definitions [s. 108]:** "*alter ego* trust" — 248(1); "amateur athlete trust" — 143.1(1)(a), 248(1); "amount" — 248(1); "beneficially interested" — 248(25); "beneficiary" — 108(1); "calendar year" — *Interpretation Act* 37(1)(a); "Canada" — 255, *Interpretation Act* 35(1); "capital interest" — 108(1), 248(1); "capital property" — 54, 248(1); "cemetery care trust", "common-law partner" — 248(1); "common-law partner" — 248(1); "consequence" — 248(8); "corporation" — 248(1), *Interpretation Act* 35(1); "cost amount" — 108(1); "created by the taxpayer's will" — 248(9.1); "deferred profit sharing plan" — 147(1), 248(1); "disposition" — 248(1); "dividend" — 248(1); "eligible capital property" — 54, 248(1); "eligible funeral arrangement" — 148.1(1), 248(1); "employee benefit plan", "employee trust" — 248(1); "estate" — 104(1), 248(1); "employees profit sharing plan" — 144(1), 248(1); "fair market value" — 107.4(4); "foreign affiliate" — 95(1), 248(1); "foreign retirement arrangement" — 248(1); "Her Majesty" — *Interpretation*

*Act* 35(1); "income of beneficiary" — 108(5); "income of trust" — 108(3); "income interest" — 108(1), 248(1); "individual" — 248(1); "*inter vivos* trust" — 108(1), 248(1); "joint partner trust", "mineral resource" — 248(1); "non-resident", "oil or gas well", "person", "personal trust" — 248(1); "post-1971 partner trust" — 248(1); "pre-1972 spousal trust" — 108(1); "prescribed" — 248(1); "prescribed stock exchange in Canada" — Reg. 3200; "prescribed trust" — Reg. 4800.1; "property" — 248(1); "province" — *Interpretation Act* 35(1); "registered education savings plan" — 146.1(1), 248(1); "registered pension plan" — 248(1); "registered retirement income fund" — 146.3(1), 248(1); "registered retirement savings plan" — 146(1), 248(1); "registered supplementary unemployment benefit plan" — 145(1), 248(1); "related" — 251(2)–(6); "relevant periods" — 108(2)(b)(ii); "resident in Canada" — 250; "retirement compensation arrangement", "share" — 248(1); "spouse" — 252(3); "tax treaty" — 248(1); "taxation year" — 104(23)(a), 249; "taxpayer" — 248(1); "testamentary trust" — 108(1), 248(1); "trust" — 104(1), (3), 108(1), 248(1); "undertaking" — 253.1(a); "unit trust" — 108(2), 248(1); "vested indefeasibly" — 248(9.2).

# DIVISION C — COMPUTATION OF TAXABLE INCOME

**109.** [Repealed under former Act]

**Notes:** 109, repealed by 1988 tax reform effective 1988, provided exemptions (deductions in calculating taxable income) for an individual's personal status and for dependants. These exemptions were replaced by the credits now found in 118.

**110. (1) Deductions permitted** — For the purpose of computing the taxable income of a taxpayer for a taxation year, there may be deducted such of the following amounts as are applicable:

(a)–(c) [Repealed under former Act]

**Notes:** 110(1)(a), (b) and (b.1), repealed by 1988 tax reform, provided deductions for charitable and similar donations. These have been moved to 118.1 (credit for individuals) and 110.1 (deduction for corporations).

110(1)(c), also repealed by 1988 tax reform, provided a deduction for medical expenses, now available as a credit under 118.2.

(d) **employee options** — an amount equal to 1/4 of the amount of the benefit deemed by subsection 7(1) to have been received by the taxpayer in the year in respect of a security that a particular qualifying person has agreed after February 15, 1984 to sell or issue under an agreement, or in respect of the transfer or other disposition of rights under the agreement, if

### Proposed Amendment — 110(1)(d) opening words

**Application:** The December 21, 2000 draft legislation, subsec. 51(1), will amend the opening words of para. 110(1)(d) to replace the reference to the fraction "1/4" with "1/2", applicable to 2000 *et seq.* except that, for the 2000 taxation year, the reference shall be read as a reference to

(a) the fraction "1/4", if the transaction, event or circumstance as a result of which a benefit is deemed by subsec. 7(1), as amended [by the December 21, 2000 draft legislation], to have been received by a taxpayer occurred before February 28, 2000, and

(b) the fraction "1/3", if the transaction, event or circumstance as a result of which a benefit is deemed by subsec. 7(1), as amended [by the December 21, 2000 draft legislation], to have been received by a taxpayer occurred after February 27, 2000 and before October 18, 2000.

**Technical Notes**: Paragraph 110(1)(d) provides a deduction in computing taxable income when an employee is deemed, by subsection 7(1), to have received a benefit from employment in connection with the exercise or disposition of rights under an employee option agreement. The deduction is equal to 1/4 of the amount of the employment benefit. The effect of the deduction is to have the benefit taxed at a rate equivalent to the capital gains inclusion rate [see 38(a) — ed.].

In order to qualify for the deduction under paragraph 110(1)(d), the following three conditions must be satisfied:

- The security that is the subject of the option must be either a prescribed share (as defined in section 6204 of the Regulations) or a unit of a widely-held class of units of a mutual fund trust. This condition is set out in subparagraph 110(1)(d)(i).
- The exercise price (that is, the amount payable by the employee to acquire the security under the option) must be at least equal to the fair market value of the security when the option was granted (less any amount paid by the employee to acquire the option). If the option being exercised or disposed of was acquired by the employee as a result of one or more exchanges of options to which subsection 7(1.4) applied, this condition applies to the original option. This condition is set out in clauses 110(1)(d)(ii)(A) and (iii)(A), and is referred to in these notes as the "exercise price test".
- At the time immediately after the option was granted, the employee must have been dealing at arm's length with the entity granting the option (the "grantor") and with each entity not dealing at arm's length with the grantor. If the option being exercised or disposed of was acquired by the employee as a result of one or more exchanges to which subsection 7(1.4) applied, this condition applies to each new option, but not to the original option. This condition is set out in clauses 110(1)(d)(ii)(B) and (iii)(B), and is referred to in these notes as the "arm's length test".

Paragraph 110(1)(d) is amended in the following ways.

*Amount of Deduction*

Paragraph 110(1)(d) is amended as a consequence of changes to the capital gains inclusion rate. Specifically, the deduction that an employee may claim under this paragraph is increased from 1/4 to 1/3 of the amount of the employment benefit that the employee is deemed, by subsection 7(1), to have received, if the transaction which results in the recognition of the employment benefit occurs after February 27, 2000 and before October 18, 2000. Similarly, if the transaction occurs after October 17, 2000, the deduction is increased to 1/2.

Where an employee acquires an option security under circumstances to which subsection 7(1.1) or (8) applies, it is the disposition of the security which results in the recognition of the employment benefit, and thus determines the amount of the deduction available under paragraph 110(1)(d). In all other cases, it is the exercise or disposition of the option which results in the recognition of the benefit, and thus determines the amount of the deduction available under paragraph 110(1)(d).

*Example*

A share acquired in June 2000 under an employee option granted by a Canadian-controlled private corporation (CCPC) is sold in November 2000. In accordance with subsection 7(1.1), the sale of the share results in the employee being deemed, by subsection 7(1), to have received a benefit from employment. Since the sale occurred after October 17, 2000, the deduction available under paragraph 110(1)(d) would be 1/2 of the employment benefit.

If the share were acquired under a non-CCPC option and there were no deferral under subsection 7(8), the acquisition of the share would result in the recognition of the benefit. Since the acquisition occurred after February 27 but before October 18, 2000, the deduction available under paragraph 110(1)(d) would be 1/3 of the employment benefit.

*Exercise Price Test*

Paragraph 110(1)(d) is amended to ensure that the condition relating to the exercise price under an employee option accommodates an exchange of options in accordance with subsection 7(1.4) and a subsequent repricing of the new option.

Specifically, subparagraph 110(1)(d)(iii) — which applies when the option being exercised or disposed of was acquired by the employee as a result of one or more exchanges of options in accordance with subsection 7(1.4) — is amended to require that the following conditions be satisfied:

- The closing exercise price under the original option (that is, the exercise price under the original option at the time it was exchanged) must not be less than the fair market value of the underlying security at the time the option was granted minus any amount paid by the employee to acquire the option. This condition is set out in new clause 110(1)(d)(iii)(C) and essentially replicates the condition currently set out in clause 110(1)(d)(iii)(A).
- For each subsequent exchange, the closing exercise price under the option being given up must be no less than the opening exercise price under that option (that is, the exercise price that was set under that option when it was granted). This condition is set out in new clause 110(1)(d)(iii)(D).
- For the option which is being exercised or disposed of (and which is, thus, giving rise to the deemed employment benefit under subsection 7(1)), the exercise price at the time of exercise or disposition, as the case may be, must not be less than the opening exercise price under that option. This condition is set out in amended clause 110(1)(d)(iii)(A).

In applying these conditions, reference must be made to subsection 7(1.4). That subsection provides that, where there is an exchange of employee security options within a related group (or on a corporate amalgamation or merger), the exchange is disregarded for the purposes of section 7 so long as the employee derives no economic gain from the exchange. As a consequence of the application of subsection 7(1.4), the disposition of the old options does not give rise to an employment benefit under subsection 7(1).

In determining whether or not an employee has derived an economic gain from an exchange of options, paragraph 7(1.4)(c) compares the potential benefit under the new options to the potential benefit under the old options.

- The potential benefit under the new options is determined by subtracting the total exercise price under those options immediately after the exchange (subparagraph 7(1.4)(c)(ii)) from the total value at that time of the securities underlying those options (subparagraph 7(1.4)(c)(i)). This is relevant for amended subparagraph 110(1)(d)(iii) in that the amount included in subparagraph 7(1.4)(c)(ii) on a per-security basis represents the opening exercise price under those options.

- The potential benefit under the old options is determined by subtracting the total exercise price under those options immediately before the exchange (subparagraph 7(1.4)(c)(iv)) from the total value at that time of the securities underlying those options (subparagraph 7(1.4)(c)(iii)). This is relevant for amended subparagraph 110(1)(d)(iii) in that the amount included in subparagraph 7(1.4)(c)(iv) on a per-security basis represents the closing exercise price under those options.

It should be noted that amended subsection 110(1.5) contains a number of provisions that affect the calculation of amounts for the purposes of paragraph 110(1)(d). Specifically, it provides for currency fluctuations to be disregarded in determining the exercise price under an option. (This is currently provided for in paragraph 110(1)(d), but is being moved to subsection 110(1.5).) It also provides for the fair market value of an employee option security, and the opening exercise price under an option acquired in an exchange of options, to be adjusted for structural changes (such as a split or consolidation of shares) occurring after the option is granted. (See the commentary on amended subsection 110(1.5) for further details.)

*Arm's Length Test*

The arm's length test is amended in two ways.

First, the entities with which the employee must be dealing at arm's length is narrowed. Rather than having to be at arm's length with the grantor and any entity not dealing at arm's length with the grantor, the employee must be at arm's length with the grantor, the employer and the entity whose securities can be acquired under the option. This is less restrictive than the existing condition in that an employee who is not dealing at arm's length with a particular entity which is not dealing at arm's length with the grantor will not be precluded from claiming the deduction under paragraph 110(1)(d) because of that relationship, so long as the particular entity is neither the employee's employer nor the entity whose securities can be acquired under the option.

Second, the arm's length test is amended so that, where there has been an exchange of options under subsection 7(1.4), the test is applied with respect to the original option and not with respect to any subsequent exchange of options.

The amendments to the arm's length test correct recent legislative changes that, inadvertently, had a tightening effect (extending the test to all persons not dealing at arm's length with the grantor) and a relieving effect (ceasing to apply the test to the original option after an exchange). They also further relax the test by restricting its application to the original option when there has been an exchange of options.

**Department of Finance news release Backgrounder, December 21, 2000:** *Stock Option Deduction*

Paragraph 110(1)(d) of the *Income Tax Act* allows a deduction in computing taxable income when an employee is deemed, by subsection 7(1), to have received a benefit from employment in connection with the exercise or disposition of rights under an employee stock option agreement. The effect of the deduction is to tax the benefit at a rate equivalent to the capital gains inclusion rate.

The proposed legislation amends paragraph 110(1)(d) in a number of ways. First, it is being amended to increase the stock option deduction as a consequence of the changes to the capital gains inclusion rate. As a result, the effective inclusion rate for qualifying stock option benefits is being significantly reduced — down from 75% before February 28, 2000, to 50% after October 17, 2000. These amendments are effective in respect of taxable events occurring after February 27, 2000.

The proposed legislation also contains amendments that were included in Bill C-43, as tabled in the House of Commons on September 20, 2000. The amendments are to correct the inadvertent effect of recent legislative changes made to implement the 1998 budget proposals extending the stock option rules to mutual fund trusts.

Further, one of the conditions that must be satisfied to qualify for the stock option deduction is that the exercise price under the option be not less than the fair market value of the share at the time the option was granted. Paragraph 110(1)(d) is being amended to clarify the application of this condition where there has been a qualifying exchange of options under subsection 7(1.4). Specifically, as amended, paragraph 110(1)(d) requires that, where an option is being exercised or disposed of, the exercise price at that time must be not less than the fair market value of the underlying share at the time the option was granted, in the case of the original option, and for each option subsequently acquired in a qualifying exchange, not less than the exercise price that was established at the time the option was acquired.

These amendments apply to the 1998 and subsequent taxation years.

**Notice of Ways and Means Motion, Economic Statement, October 18, 2000:**

(13) That, for the 2000 and subsequent taxation years, the deductions permitted under paragraphs 110(1)(d) to (d.3) of the Act in respect of amounts that are included in income for the year (other than amounts that would be included in income for the year if the year had ended at the end of October 17, 2000) be determined as 1/2 of the amounts so included in income.

[This parallels the changes in the capital gains inclusion rate. See under s. 38 — ed.]

(14) That the mechanism described in paragraph (24) of the 2000 Budget Notice to provide a deduction in respect of certain gifts of employee option securities be applied, when as a consequence of the application of paragraph (13) the fraction used to determine the deduction under paragraph 110(1)(d) of the Act is 1/2, as if the reference in that Notice to "1/3" were a reference to "1/4".

(i) the security

(A) is a prescribed share at the time of its sale or issue, as the case may be,

(B) would have been a prescribed share if it were issued or sold to the taxpayer at the time the taxpayer disposed of rights under the agreement,

(C) would have been a unit of a mutual fund trust at the time of its sale or issue if those units issued by the trust that were not

**S. 110(1)(d)(i)(C)**      Income Tax Act, Part I

identical to the security had not been issued, or

(D) would have been a unit of a mutual fund trust if

(I) it were issued or sold to the taxpayer at the time the taxpayer disposed of rights under the agreement, and

(II) those units issued by the trust that were not identical to the security had not been issued,

(ii) where rights under the agreement were not acquired by the taxpayer as a result of the disposition of rights to which subsection 7(1.4) applied,

(A) the amount payable by the taxpayer to acquire the security under the agreement (determined without reference to any change in the value of a currency of a country other than Canada relative to Canadian currency during the period between the time the agreement was made and the time the security was acquired) is not less than the amount by which

### Proposed Amendment — 110(1)(d)(ii)(A) opening words

(A) the amount payable by the taxpayer to acquire the security under the agreement (determined without reference to any change in the value of a currency of a country other than Canada relative to Canadian currency after the agreement was made) is not less than the amount by which

**Application**: Bill C-43 (First Reading September 20, 2000), subsec. 54(1), will amend the opening words of cl. 110(1)(d)(ii)(A) to read as above, applicable to 1998 *et seq.*

**Technical Notes**: Under subsection 7(1) of the Act, an individual who acquires a share of a corporation or a unit of a mutual fund trust (a "security") under an employee security option agreement (or disposes of rights under such an agreement) may be treated as having received a benefit from employment. Where certain conditions are met, paragraph 110(1)(d) allows the individual to deduct 1/4 of the amount included in income as a result of the application of subsection 7(1).

*Fair Market Value Test*

One of the conditions to be eligible for the 1/4 deduction is that the amount payable under the option for the security (the "option price") not be less than the fair market value of the security at the time the option was granted. Paragraph 110(1)(d) provides for the option price to be determined without reference to changes in the value of a foreign currency relative to Canadian currency during the period from the time the option is granted to the time the security is acquired. This is to eliminate the effect of foreign exchange fluctuations.

Paragraph 110(1)(d) is amended [110(1)(d)(ii)(A) — ed.] so that changes in the value of a foreign currency at any time after the option is granted are disregarded. This reflects the fact that, if there has been a disposition of rights

rather than a security acquisition, the period described above is indeterminable.

(I) the fair market value of the security at the time the agreement was made

exceeds

(II) the amount, if any, paid by the taxpayer to acquire the right to acquire the security, and

(B) immediately after the agreement was made, the taxpayer was dealing at arm's length with the particular person and with each qualifying person with which the particular person was not dealing at arm's length, and

(iii) where rights under the agreement were acquired by the taxpayer as a result of one or more dispositions to which subsection 7(1.4) applied,

(A) the amount payable by the taxpayer, to acquire the old security under the exchanged option in respect of the first of those dispositions (determined without reference to any change in the value of a currency of a country other than Canada relative to Canadian currency during the period between the time the agreement was made and the time the security was acquired), was not less than the amount by which

(I) the fair market value of the old security at the time the agreement in respect of the exchanged option was made

exceeds

(II) the amount, if any, paid by the taxpayer to acquire the right to acquire the old security, and

(B) immediately after each of those dispositions, the taxpayer was dealing at arm's length with

(I) the qualifying person with whom the taxpayer entered into an agreement to receive consideration in respect of the disposition, and

(II) each qualifying person with which the qualifying person described in subclause (I) did not deal at arm's length;

### Proposed Amendment — 110(1)(d)

(B) at the time immediately after the agreement was made, the taxpayer was dealing at arm's length with

(I) the particular qualifying person,

(II) each other qualifying person that, at that time, was an employer of the taxpayer and was not dealing at arm's

Division C — Computation of Taxable Income    S. 110(1)(d)(ii)(A)

length with the particular qualifying person, and

(III) each other qualifying person of which the taxpayer had, under the agreement, a right to acquire a security, and

(iii) where rights under the agreement were acquired by the taxpayer as a result of one or more dispositions to which subsection 7(1.4) applied, the requirements of clauses (ii)(A) and (B) would be satisfied if

(A) the agreement referred to in clauses (ii)(A) and (B) were the agreement (in this subparagraph referred to as the "original agreement") the rights under which were the subject of the first of those dispositions,

(B) the security referred to in clause (ii)(A) were a security that the taxpayer had a right to acquire under the original agreement, and

(C) the particular qualifying person referred to in clause (ii)(B) were the qualifying person that made the original agreement;

**Application**: Bill C-43 (First Reading September 20, 2000), subsec. 54(2), will amend the portion of para. 110(1)(d) after cl. (ii)(A) to read as above, applicable to 1998 *et seq.*

**Technical Notes**: *Arm's Length Test*

Another condition to be eligible for the 1/4 deduction is that the individual be dealing at arm's length, immediately after the option is granted, with the entity that granted the option (the "grantor") and with each entity not dealing at arm's length with the grantor. If the option under which the security is acquired (or rights are disposed of) was acquired as a result of one or more exchanges of options under subsection 7(1.4), the arm's length test must be satisfied after each such exchange but not after the granting of the original option.

The arm's length test [110(1)(d)(iii) — ed.] is amended in two ways. First, the requirement that the individual be dealing at arm's length with any entity not dealing at arm's length with the grantor is replaced with a requirement that the individual be dealing at arm's length with his or her employer and with the entity whose securities can be acquired under the option. There is no change to the requirement that the individual be dealing at arm's length with the grantor. Second, it is amended so that, if there has been an exchange of options under subsection 7(1.4), the arm's length test is applied with respect to the original option and not with respect to any subsequent exchange of options.

These amendments apply to the 1998 and subsequent taxation years. They undo recent legislative changes that had the unintended effect of both tightening the arm's length test (extending it to all entities not dealing at arm's length with the grantor) and relaxing the test (ceasing to apply it to the original option after an exchange). They also further relax the arm's length test by restricting its application to the original option when there has been an exchange of options.

**Letter from Department of Finance, September 14, 1999**:

Dear [xxx]

Thank you for your letter of July 26, 1999 concerning recent amendments made to paragraph 110(1)(d) of the *Income Tax Act*.

You express concern that these amendments have resulted in an expansion of the requirements which must be satisfied in order for an individual who exercises or disposes of a stock option to be eligible for the deduction provided for under paragraph 110(1)(d). In particular, the requirement that the individual be dealing at arm's length with certain corporations has been expanded to include any corporation with which the corporation granting the option (the "optionor") does not deal at arm's length, even if the corporation in question is neither the individual's employer nor the corporation whose shares are the subject of the option.

As you note, the intent of the arm's length test is to ensure that employees who are in a position of influence or control are not able to convert their ordinary employment income (which is fully taxable) into stock options which benefit from the deduction under paragraph 110(1)(d). We agree with your assessment that this objective can be achieved by limiting the application of the arm's length requirement to the employee's employer, the optionor and the corporation whose shares can be acquired under the option, and are prepared to recommend that the Act be amended accordingly.

You have also asked that consideration be given to amending paragraph 110(1)(d)[(iii) — ed.] so that, where there has been one or more exchanges of stock options to which subsection 7(1.4) applied, the arm's length test is applied only to the original option and not to each subsequent exchange. Again, we agree with your assessment that such a change should not provide any opportunity for abuse since the application of subsection 7(1.4) is limited to situations where there is a value for value exchange. We also appreciate the fact that such a change should achieve considerable simplification and provide greater certainty as to an individual's eligibility for a deduction under paragraph 110(1)(d). Therefore, we are prepared to recommend that the Act be amended accordingly.

We would recommend that these proposed amendments have the same coming-into-force as the recent amendments. In other words, we would recommend that paragraph 110(1)(d) as amended apply to the 1998 and subsequent taxation years.

We wish to thank you again for bringing these issues to our attention.

Yours sincerely,

Len Farber
Director General, Tax Legislation Division, Tax Policy Branch

**Proposed Amendment — 110(1)(d)(ii), (iii)**

(ii) where rights under the agreement were not acquired by the taxpayer as a result of a disposition of rights to which subsection 7(1.4) applied,

(A) the amount payable by the taxpayer to acquire the security under the agree-

## S. 110(1)(d)(ii)(A)   Income Tax Act, Part I

ment is not less than the amount by which

(I) the fair market value of the security at the time the agreement was made

exceeds

(II) the amount, if any, paid by the taxpayer to acquire the right to acquire the security, and

(B) at the time immediately after the agreement was made, the taxpayer was dealing at arm's length with

(I) the particular qualifying person,

(II) each other qualifying person that, at the time, was an employer of the taxpayer and was not dealing at arm's length with the particular qualifying person, and

(III) the qualifying person of which the taxpayer had, under the agreement, a right to acquire a security, and

(iii) where rights under the agreement were acquired by the taxpayer as a result of one or more dispositions to which subsection 7(1.4) applied,

(A) the amount payable by the taxpayer to acquire the security under the agreement is not less than the amount that was included, in respect of the security, in the amount determined under subparagraph 7(1.4)(c)(ii) with respect to the most recent of those dispositions,

(B) at the time immediately after the agreement the rights under which were the subject of the first of those dispositions (in this subparagraph referred to as the "original agreement") was made, the taxpayer was dealing at arm's length with

(I) the qualifying person that made the original agreement,

(II) each other qualifying person that, at the time, was an employer of the taxpayer and was not dealing at arm's length with the qualifying person that made the original agreement, and

(III) the qualifying person of which the taxpayer had, under the original agreement, a right to acquire a security,

(C) the amount that was included, in respect of each particular security that the taxpayer had a right to acquire under the original agreement, in the amount determined under subparagraph 7(1.4)(c)(iv) with respect to the first of those disposi-

tions was not less than the amount by which

(I) the fair market value of the particular security at the time the original agreement was made

exceeded

(II) the amount, if any, paid by the taxpayer to acquire the right to acquire the security, and

(D) for the purpose of determining if the condition in paragraph 7(1.4)(c) was satisfied with respect to each of the particular dispositions following the first of those dispositions,

(I) the amount that was included, in respect of each particular security that could be acquired under the agreement the rights under which were the subject of the particular disposition, in the amount determined under subparagraph 7(1.4)(c)(iv) with respect to the particular disposition

was not less than

(II) the amount that was included, in respect of the particular security, in the amount determined under subparagraph 7(1.4)(c)(ii) with respect to the last of those dispositions preceding the particular disposition;

**Application**: The December 21, 2000 draft legislation, subsec. 51(2), will amend subparas. 110(1)(d)(ii) and (iii) to read as above, applicable to 1998 *et seq.*

**Technical Notes**: See under 110(1)(d) opening words.

**Related Provisions**: 7(1.4) — Rules where options exchanged; 7(1.5) — Rules where securities exchanged; 7(2) — Securities held by trustee; 7(6)(a) — Sale to trustee for employees; 7(7) — Definitions; 7(14) — Deferral deemed valid at CCRA's discretion; 110(1)(d.01) — Deduction on donating employee stock-option shares to charity; 110(1)(d.1) — Alternative deduction; 110(1.5) — Determination of amounts; 111(8)"non-capital loss"A:E — Amount included in non-capital loss; 111.1 — Order of applying provisions; 114.2 — Deductions in separate returns; 127.52(1)(h) — Deduction disallowed for minimum tax purposes; 164(6.1) — Exercise or disposition of employee stock option by legal representative of deceased employee.

**Notes**: See Notes to 7(1) re inclusion of income from stock option benefit. This offsetting ½ (previously ¼ or ⅓) deduction is available in two ways. Simplified, if the share is a straightforward common share (see Reg. 6204) and the value of the share *when the stock option agreement was entered into* did not exceed the exercise price of the option, the deduction is available. Otherwise, if the corporation was a CCPC dealing at arm's length with the employee when the agreement was entered into, the deduction is available under 110(1)(d.1) provided that the employee holds the share (or a share it was exchanged for — see 7(1.5)) for at least two years. In both cases, the deduction leaves the "gain" on the shares taxed at the same rate as a capital gain (see 38(a)), but ineligible for the various special capital gains rules, such as the $500,000 exemption under 110.6(2) or (2.1) and the ability to offset the gain with capital losses under 3(b).

110(1)(d) amended by 1998 Budget, effective for 1998 and later taxation years. The substantive change was to extend the rule to mutual fund trust units (see Notes to 7(1)). (While shares are required to be "prescribed shares", trust units are instead required by 110(1)(d)(i)(C) or (D) to be of a widely-held class of units which permit the trust to satisfy the condition in 132(6)(c) for qualification as a mutual fund trust.) For earlier years, read:

   (d) **employee stock options** — where, after February 15, 1984,

      (i) a corporation has agreed to sell, issue or cause to be issued to the taxpayer a share of its capital stock or of the capital stock of another corporation with which it does not deal at arm's length,

      (ii) the share was a prescribed share at the time of its sale or issue, as the case may be, or, where the taxpayer has disposed of rights under the agreement, the share would have been a prescribed share if it were issued or sold to the taxpayer at the time the taxpayer disposed of such rights,

      (iii) the amount payable by the taxpayer to acquire the share under the agreement (determined without reference to any change in the value of a currency of a country other than Canada relative to Canadian currency during the period between the time the agreement was made and the time the share was acquired) is not less than the amount by which

         (A) the fair market value of the share at the time the agreement was made

      exceeds

         (B) the amount, if any, paid by the taxpayer to acquire the right to acquire the share,

or where the rights under the agreement were acquired by the taxpayer as a result of one or more dispositions of rights to which subsection 7(1.4) applied, the amount payable by the taxpayer to acquire the old share under the original option (determined without reference to any change in the value of a currency of a country other than Canada relative to Canadian currency during the period between the time the agreement was made and the time the share was acquired) that was disposed of in consideration for a new option in the first such disposition was not less than the amount by which

         (C) the fair market value of the old share at the time the agreement in respect of the original option was made

      exceeds

         (D) the amount, if any, paid by the taxpayer to acquire the right to acquire the old share, and

      (iv) at the time immediately after the agreement was made and, where the rights under the agreement were acquired by the taxpayer as a result of one or more dispositions to which subsection 7(1.4) applied, at the time the agreement in respect of the original option was made and at the time immediately after each disposition, the taxpayer was dealing at arm's length with the corporation, the other corporation and the corporation of which the taxpayer is an employee,

an amount equal to $\frac{1}{4}$ of the amount of the benefit deemed by subsection 7(1) to have been received by the taxpayer in the year in respect of the share or the transfer or other disposition of the rights under the agreement;

110(1)(d) added in 1984 and amended by 1985 Budget, in 1987 (a technical, retroactive amendment), by 1988 tax reform, by 1991 technical bill (retroactive to 1988) and by 1993 technical bill (effective 1992).

For taxation years before 1992, ignore the parenthesized words "(determined without reference to any change...)" in both places in 110(1)(d)(iii).

For shares acquired or rights in respect of shares transferred or otherwise disposed of in 1988 or 1989, read "$\frac{1}{3}$" in place of "$\frac{1}{4}$".

For shares acquired or rights in respect of shares transferred or otherwise disposed of from February 16, 1984 through the end of 1987, read "$\frac{1}{2}$" in place of "$\frac{1}{4}$".

For shares issued or sold or rights disposed of from February 16, 1984 through May 22, 1985 (or through the end of 1985 under the terms of an agreement in writing entered into by May 22, 1985), read subpara. (ii) as ending at "as the case may be".

**Regulations**: 6204 (prescribed share).

**Interpretation Bulletins**: IT-113R4: Benefits to employees — stock options; IT-151R5: Scientific research and experimental development expenditures.

**I.T. Technical News**: No. 7 (stock options plans — receipt of cash in lieu of shares); No. 19 (Securities option plan — disposal of securities option rights for shares).

### Proposed Addition — 110(1)(d.01)

**(d.01) charitable donation of employee option securities** — subject to subsection (2.1), where the taxpayer disposes of a security acquired in the year by the taxpayer under an agreement referred to in subsection 7(1) by making a gift of the security to a qualified donee (other than a private foundation), an amount in respect of the disposition of the security equal to $\frac{1}{4}$ of the lesser of the benefit deemed by paragraph 7(1)(a) to have been received by the taxpayer in the year in respect of the acquisition of the security and the amount that would have been that benefit had the value of the security at the time of its acquisition by the taxpayer been equal to the value of the security at the time of the disposition, if

   (i) the security is a security described in subparagraph 38(a.1)(i),

   (ii) the taxpayer acquired the security after February 27, 2000 and before 2002,

   (iii) the gift is made in the year and on or before the day that is 30 days after the day on which the taxpayer acquired the security, and

   (iv) the taxpayer is entitled to a deduction under paragraph (d) in respect of the acquisition of the security;

**Related Provisions**: 7(2) — Securities held by trustee; 7(6)(a) — Sale to trustee for employees; 38(a.1) — Parallel inclusion rate for capital gains on donated shares; 110(2.1) — Donation made with proceeds of sale; 111(8)"non-capital loss"A:E — Amount included in non-capital loss.

**Application**: The December 21, 2000 draft legislation, subsec. 51(3), will add para. 110(1)(d.01), applicable to 2000 et seq. except that, for the 2000 taxation year, the reference to the fraction "1/4" shall be read as a reference to the fraction "1/3" if the transaction, event or circumstance as a result of which a benefit is deemed by subsec. 7(1), as amended [by the December 21, 2000 draft legislation], to have been received by a taxpayer occurred after February 27, 2000 and before October 18, 2000.

**Technical Notes**: New paragraph 110(1)(d.01) allows an employee to deduct a portion of the employment benefit that the employee is deemed by subsection 7(1) to have received in connection with the acquisition of a security under an employee option agreement, if the employee donates the security to a qualified donee (other than a private foundation). For this purpose, a "security" (as defined in subsection 7(7)) means a share of the capital stock of a corporation or a unit of a mutual fund trust. A "qualified donee" (as defined in subsections 149.1(1) and 248(1)) means, in general terms, a person to whom gifts may be made that qualify for the charitable donations deduction or tax credit.

In order to qualify for a deduction under new paragraph 110(1)(d.01), the employee must also be eligible for the regular employee option deduction under paragraph 110(1)(d). (In general terms, this means that (i) the employee was dealing at arm's length, when the option was granted, with the employer, the grantor of the option and the person whose security was acquired under the option, (ii) the option was not issued at a discount and (iii) the security, if it is a share, is an ordinary common share.) The combined effect of the two deductions is to tax the employment benefit on the donated security at a rate that is comparable to the reduced capital gains inclusion rate provided under paragraph 38(a.1) for securities donated to a charity.

The additional deduction under paragraph 110(1)(d.01) is available for donated securities acquired after February 27, 2000 and before 2002. In order to qualify for the deduction, the donation must be made in the same year as the security was acquired and no later than 30 days after acquisition. If the security is a share, it must be of a class of shares listed on a Canadian or foreign stock exchange described in section 3200 or 3201 of the *Income Tax Regulations*.

The amount of the deduction under new paragraph 110(1)(d.01) depends on the amount of the regular deduction under paragraph 110(1)(d). If the regular deduction is 1/3 of the employment benefit, the additional deduction is also 1/3, and the net result is that only 1/3 of the employment benefit is subject to tax. If the regular deduction is 1/2, the additional deduction is 1/4, and the net result is that only 1/4 of the employment benefit is subject to tax. Generally, the 1/3 rate applies to securities acquired after February 27, 2000 and before October 18, 2000, and the 1/4 rate applies to securities acquired after October 17, 2000.

It should be noted that if the security is worth less when it is donated than when it was acquired, the additional deduction under paragraph 110(1)(d.01) is based on the employment benefit that the employee would have been deemed by subsection 7(1) to have received if the value of the security at the time of acquisition were that lesser value.

It should also be noted that, if the employee owns other securities that are identical to the security acquired under the employee option agreement, new subsection 7(1.31) may apply to deem the option security as the security being donated. In these circumstances, new subsection 47(3) also applies to exempt the security from the cost-averaging rule in subsection 47(1). Consequently, the adjusted cost base of the donated security, and thus the capital gain or loss on the disposition of the security, is determined without regard to the adjusted cost base of any other securities acquired by the employee.

Finally, it should be noted that, by virtue of new subsection 110(2.1), the deduction under paragraph 110(1)(d.01) may also be available where an employee sells an employee option security and donates all or part of the proceeds of the disposition to a qualifying charity. To qualify, certain conditions must be met regarding the acquisition and disposition of the security, and the donation of the proceeds of disposition to charity. Furthermore, the deduction will be prorated to reflect the proportion of the proceeds that are donated.

**Department of Finance news release Backgrounder, December 21, 2000**: *Charitable Donation of Stock Option Shares*

The February 2000 budget included a measure allowing those employees who donate certain stock option shares acquired after February 27, 2000, and before 2002 to a qualifying charity to deduct a portion of the taxable benefit that the employee is deemed to have received because of the exercise of the option.

Under the proposed legislation, this deduction is also available if the employee, through the administrator of a stock option plan, sells the shares immediately after exercising the option and donates all or part of the proceeds of disposition to a qualifying charity. The deduction will be prorated to reflect the proportion of the proceeds that are so donated. The expansion of the budget proposal in this way accommodates those situations in which employees sell their stock option shares immediately and use the proceeds from the disposition to cover the exercise price of the options. (See proposed paragraph 110(1)(d.01) and subsection 110(2.1) and related explanatory notes for further details.)

**Notice of Ways and Means Motion, Economic Statement, October 18, 2000**: (14) That the mechanism described in paragraph (24) of the 2000 Budget Notice to provide a deduction in respect of certain gifts of employee option securities be applied, when as a consequence of the application of paragraph (13) the fraction used to determine the deduction under paragraph 110(1)(d) of the Act is 1/2, as if the reference in that Notice to "1/3" were a reference to "1/4".

**Notice of Ways and Means Motion, federal budget, February 28, 2000**: *Donation of Stock Option Shares*

(24) That where

 (a) an individual acquires, after February 27, 2000 and before 2002, a security under an option that was granted to the individual as an employee of a corporation or mutual fund trust,

 (b) the individual disposes of the security, in the year it is acquired and not more than 30 days after its acquisition, by donating it to a qualified donee that is not a private foundation,

 (c) the individual is entitled to deduct an amount under paragraph 110(1)(d) of the Act in respect of the employment benefit determined under subsection 7(1) of the Act in connection with the acquisition of the security, and

 (d) if there were a capital gain determined in connection with the individual's disposition of the security, the gain would qualify for the reduced inclusion rate under paragraph 38(a.1) of the Act,

the individual be entitled to deduct, in computing taxable income for the year in which the security is acquired, an additional amount equal to 1/3 of the amount that would be the employment benefit if the fair market value of the security at the time of acquisition were the lesser of that value and the security's fair market value at the time of donation.

**Federal budget, supplementary information, February 28, 2000**: *Charitable Donations of Shares Acquired with Employee Stock Options*

The 1997 budget halved the inclusion rate on capital gains arising from charitable donations made before 2002 of listed securities, such as shares, bonds, bills, warrants and futures.

An individual who acquires a share under an employee stock option plan is required to include in income an employment benefit equal to the fair market value of the share, less any amounts paid to acquire the share. If certain conditions are satisfied, the individual is allowed to deduct part of the employment benefit in order to effectively tax the benefit at capital gains rates.

However, where the employee exercises the option in order to donate the share to a charity, there is no provision to reduce the tax burden on the employment benefit to parallel the reduced capital gains inclusion rate for donations of publicly-traded securities. The budget therefore proposes to introduce such a provision in order to provide parallel treatment between the two forms of gift-giving. In such circumstances, the individual will be allowed to deduct an additional third of the employment benefit. Taking into account the changes proposed in this budget to increase the existing stock option deduction from a quarter to a third, only a third of the employment benefit will be subject to tax.

If the value of the share at the time it is donated is less than when the option was exercised, the additional deduction will be reduced to provide the appropriate amount of tax assistance.

To be eligible for this measure, the share must be donated in the year and within 30 days of the option being exercised. Also, the share will have to meet the existing criteria for the reduced capital gains inclusion rate for donations of publicly-traded securities. The restrictions on eligible charities will also be the same. In addition, the conditions for the existing stock option deduction will have to be satisfied — principally, that the share be an ordinary common share and that amounts payable to acquire the share be no less than the fair market value of the share at the time the option is granted.

The measure will also apply to the donation of units of a mutual fund trust acquired under an employee option plan.

The measure will apply to securities acquired after February 27, 2000, and donated before 2002.

**Letter from Department of Finance, August 15, 2000:**

Dear [xxx]

This is further to your letters of July 19 and August 3, 2000 concerning the budget proposal to provide an additional deduction for stock option shares donated to charity.

I wish to confirm that we intend to recommend that the proposed amendments to the *Income Tax Act* accommodate the "cashless exercise" of stock options, and the donation of the net proceeds of disposition, as described in the material provided with your letter of August 3rd. The recommendation will clearly depend upon appropriate tracing mechanisms being developed to ensure that the donated proceeds can be tracked directly to the employee option, the exercise of the option, the issuance of the shares and the net proceeds being donated to the charity. As discussed, such a tracing mechanism is fundamental to the policy underlying the budget measure because of the fungibility of money and the identical nature of shares.

In addition, I wish to confirm that the additional deduction will be prorated to reflect the extent to which the proceeds of disposition are donated. The example set out in your letter of July 19th appropriately illustrates this proration. Finally, in accordance with the Budget Resolution, we intend to recommend that the additional deduction be available for shares acquired after February 27, 2000 and before 2002.

I welcome your input in developing this legislative proposal and appreciate you bringing this matter to my attention.

Yours sincerely,

Len Farber

General Director, Tax Legislation Division, Tax Policy Branch

(d.1) **idem** — where the taxpayer

(i) is deemed, under paragraph 7(1)(a) by virtue of subsection 7(1.1), to have received a benefit in the year in respect of a share acquired by the taxpayer after May 22, 1985,

(ii) has not disposed of the share (otherwise than as a consequence of the taxpayer's death) or exchanged the share within two years after the date the taxpayer acquired it, and

(iii) has not deducted an amount under paragraph (d) in respect of the benefit in computing the taxpayer's taxable income for the year,

an amount equal to $1/4$ of the amount of the benefit;

### Proposed Amendment — 110(1)(d.1)

**Application**: The December 21, 2000 draft legislation, subsec. 51(4), will amend para. 110(1)(d.1) to replace the reference to the fraction "1/4" with "1/2".

Para. 110(1)(d.1) is applicable to 2000 *et seq.* except that, for the 2000 taxation year, the reference shall be read as a reference to

(a) the fraction "1/4", if the transaction, event or circumstance as a result of which a benefit is deemed by subsec. 7(1), as amended [by the December 21, 2000 draft legislation], to have been received by a taxpayer occurred before February 28, 2000, and

(b) the fraction "1/3", if the transaction, event or circumstance as a result of which a benefit is deemed by subsec. 7(1), as amended [by the December 21, 2000 draft legislation], to have been received by a taxpayer occurred after February 27, 2000 and before October 18, 2000.

**Technical Notes**: Paragraph 110(1)(d.1) provides a deduction in computing the taxable income of a taxpayer where the taxpayer has included an amount in income for the year under paragraph 7(1)(a) in respect of a share acquired.

The paragraph is amended to replace the reference to the fraction "1/4" with a reference to the fraction "1/2", and is consequential on the reduction of the inclusion rate for capital gains from 3/4 to 1/2.

The amendment applies in respect of benefits which, as a result of transactions, events or circumstances that occur after February 27, 2000, are deemed by section 7 to have been received by a taxpayer except that, where the transaction, event or circumstances occurs after February 27, 2000 and before October 18, 2000, the reference to the fraction "1/2" is to be read as a reference to the fraction "1/3". These modifications are required in order to reflect the capital gains/losses rate for the year.

Paragraph 110(1)(d.2) provides a deduction in computing the taxable income of a taxpayer where the taxpayer has included an amount in income for the year under paragraph 35(1)(d) in respect of a share.

**S. 110(1)(d.1)**      Income Tax Act, Part I

The paragraph is amended to replace the reference to the fraction "1/4" with a reference to the fraction "1/2", and is consequential on the reduction of the inclusion rate for capital gains from 3/4 to 1/2.

The amendment applies with respect to dispositions and exchanges that occur after February 27, 2000 except that, for dispositions and exchanges that occur after February 27, 2000 and before October 18, 2000, the reference to the fraction "1/2" is to be read as a reference to the fraction "1/3". These modifications are required in order to reflect the capital gains/losses rate for the year.

Paragraph 110(1)(d.3) provides a deduction in computing the taxable income of a taxpayer where the taxpayer has included an amount in income for the year under subsection 147(10.4) in respect of a disposition of shares. Subsection 147(10.4) deals with the disposition of employer shares that had previously been received as part of a single payment from a deferred profit sharing plan.

The paragraph is amended to replace the reference to the fraction "1/4" with a reference to the fraction "1/2", and is consequential on the reduction of the inclusion rate for capital gains from 3/4 to 1/2.

The amendment applies in respect to dispositions and exchanges that occur after February 27, 2000 except that, for dispositions and exchanges that occur after February 27, 2000 and before October 18, 2000, the reference to the fraction "1/2" is to be read as a reference to the fraction "1/3". This modification is required in order to reflect the inclusion rate for capital gains realized during that period.

**Notice of Ways and Means Motions, Economic Statement, October 18, 2000 and federal budget, February 28, 2000**: [See under 110(1)(d).]

**Related Provisions**: 7(1.3) — Order of disposition of securities; 7(1.5) — Rules where securities exchanged; 7(1.6) — Emigration does not trigger disposition for purposes of 110(1)(d.1); 7(2) — Securities held by trustee; 7(6)(a) — Sale to trustee for employees; 110(1)(d) — Alternative deduction; 111(8)"non-capital loss"A:E — Amount included in non-capital loss; 111.1 — Order of applying provisions; 114.2 — Deductions in separate returns; 127.52(1)(h) — Deduction disallowed for minimum tax purposes; 248(8) — Occurrences as a consequence of death.

**Notes**: See Notes to 110(1)(d).

110(1)(d.1) added by 1985 Budget and amended by 1988 tax reform. For shares disposed of or exchanged in 1988 or 1989, read "1/3" in place of "1/4". For shares disposed of or exchanged from May 23, 1985 through the end of 1987, read "1/2" in place of "1/4".

110(1)(d.1) does not apply to shares acquired before May 23, 1985.

**Interpretation Bulletins**: IT-113R4: Benefits to employees — stock options.

(d.2) **prospector's and grubstaker's shares** — where the taxpayer has, under paragraph 35(1)(d), included an amount in the taxpayer's income for the year in respect of a share received after May 22, 1985, an amount equal to ¼ of that amount unless that amount is exempt from income tax in Canada by reason of a provision contained in a tax convention or agreement with another country that has the force of law in Canada;

**Proposed Amendment — 110(1)(d.2)**

**Application**: The December 21, 2000 draft legislation, subsec. 51(4), will amend para. 110(1)(d.2) to replace the reference to the fraction "1/4" with "1/2".

Para. 110(1)(d.2) is applicable in respect of dispositions and exchanges that occur after February 27, 2000 except that, for dispositions and exchanges that occurred after February 27, 2000 and before October 18, 2000, the reference to the fraction "1/2" shall be read as a reference to the fraction "1/3".

**Technical Notes**: [See under 110(1)(d.1).]

**Related Provisions**: 111(8)"non-capital loss"A:E — Amount included in non-capital loss; 111.1 — Order of applying provisions; 114.2 — Deductions in separate returns; 127.52(1)(h) — Deduction disallowed for minimum tax purposes.

**Notes**: 110(1)(d.2) added by 1985 Budget and amended by 1988 tax reform. For shares disposed of or exchanged in 1988 or 1989, read "1/3" in place of "1/4". For shares disposed of or exchanged from May 23, 1985 through the end of 1987, read "1/2" in place of "1/4".

110(1)(d.2) does not apply to shares acquired before May 23, 1985.

(d.3) **employer's shares [where election made re DPSP]** — where the taxpayer has, under subsection 147(10.4), included an amount in computing the taxpayer's income for the year, an amount equal to ¼ of that amount;

**Proposed Amendment — 110(1)(d.3)**

**Application**: The December 21, 2000 draft legislation, subsec. 51(4), will amend para. 110(1)(d.3) to replace the reference to the fraction "1/4" with "1/2".

Para. 110(1)(d.3) is applicable in respect of dispositions and exchanges that occur after February 27, 2000 except that, for dispositions and exchanges that occurred after February 27, 2000 and before October 18, 2000, the reference to the fraction "1/2" shall be read as a reference to the fraction "1/3".

**Technical Notes**: [See under 110(1)(d.1).]

**Related Provisions**: 111(8)"non-capital loss"A:E — Amount included in non-capital loss; 111.1 — Order of applying provisions; 114.2 — Deductions in separate returns; 127.52(1)(h) — Deduction disallowed for minimum tax purposes.

**Notes**: 110(1)(d.3) added by 1985 Budget and amended by 1988 tax reform. For shares disposed of or exchanged in 1988 or 1989, read "1/3" in place of "1/4". For shares disposed of or exchanged from May 24, 1985 through the end of 1987, read "1/2" in place of "1/4".

110(1)(d.3) does not apply to shares acquired on terminations of interests in deferred profit sharing plans before May 24, 1985.

**Interpretation Bulletins**: IT-281R2: Elections on single payments from a deferred profit-sharing plan.

(e)–(e.2) [Repealed under former Act]

**Notes**: 110(1)(e), (e.1) and (e.2), repealed by 1988 tax reform, provided deductions for disabled taxpayers and dependants. These have been replaced by credits in 118.3.

(f) **deductions for payments** — any social assistance payment made on the basis of a means, needs or income test and included because of clause 56(1)(a)(i)(A) or paragraph 56(1)(u) in computing the taxpayer's income for the year or any amount that is

(i) an amount exempt from income tax in Canada because of a provision contained in a tax convention or agreement with another country that has the force of law in Canada,

(ii) compensation received under an employees' or workers' compensation law of Canada or a province in respect of an injury, disability or death, except any such compensation received by a person as the employer or former

Division C — Computation of Taxable Income    S. 110(1.4)

employer of the person in respect of whose injury, disability or death the compensation was paid,

(iii) income from employment with a prescribed international organization, or

(iv) the taxpayer's income from employment with a prescribed international non-governmental organization, where the taxpayer

(A) was not, at any time in the year, a Canadian citizen,

(B) was a non-resident person immediately before beginning that employment in Canada, and

(C) if the taxpayer is resident in Canada, became resident in Canada solely for the purpose of that employment,

to the extent that it is included in computing the taxpayer's income for the year;

**Related Provisions**: 56(1)(u) — Social assistance payments; 56(1)(v) — Workers' compensation; 60(j) — Transfer of superannuation benefits; 81(1)(a) — Amounts not included in income; 111(8)"non-capital loss"A:E — Amount included in non-capital loss; 111.1 — Order of applying provisions; 114.2 — Deductions in separate returns; 126(7)"tax-exempt income" — Income exempted by tax treaty; 127.52(1)(h) — Application of deduction for minimum tax purposes; 146(1)"earned income"(c) — Income exempted by tax treaty is not earned income of a non-resident for RRSP purposes; 150(1)(a)(ii) — Requirement for non-resident corporation claiming treaty exemption to file tax return; 153(1.1) — Application for reduced source withholding where amount exempt from tax under treaty; 248(1)"treaty-protected business", "treaty-protected property" — Amounts exempted by tax treaty.

**Notes**: See Notes to 56(1)(u) and (v).

In *Creagh*, [1997] 1 C.T.C. 2392 (TCC), employees of Canadian Helicopter who worked on a United Nations peacekeeping mission were denied the deduction under 110(1)(f)(iv) because they were not employed directly by the UN (as prescribed in Reg. 8900).

110(1)(f) amended by 1991 technical bill, effective 1991, to clarify that social assistance payments will only be allowed as a deduction where they have been included in income under 56(1)(u).

110(1)(f)(iii) added by 1992 technical bill, effective 1991. The United Nations and certain UN agencies are prescribed under Reg. 8900(a) for this provision, which replaces the foreign tax credit formerly available under 126(3).

110(1)(f)(iv) added by 1993 technical bill, effective for 1993 and later taxation years.

**Regulations**: 232, 233 (information return); 8900(a) (prescribed international organization for 110(1)(f)(iii); 8900(b) (prescribed international non-governmental organization for 110(1)(f)(iv)).

**Interpretation Bulletins**: IT-122R2: United States social security taxes and benefits; IT-202R2: Employees' or workers' compensation; IT-499R: Superannuation or pension benefits; IT-528: Transfers of funds between registered plans.

(g)–(i) [Repealed under former Act]

**Notes**: 110(1)(g), repealed by 1988 tax reform, provided an exemption of $50 per month for full-time students, replaced by an education credit under 118.6.

110(1)(h), repealed by 1988 tax reform, provided for a deduction for a dependant who was a full-time student, replaced by rules in 118.8 and 118.9 permitting the transfer of education credits.

110(1)(i) repealed by 1991 technical bill, effective 1989. Unemployment Insurance (now Employment Insurance) benefits are partially repayable when the taxpayer's net income exceeds a given threshold. The repayment is administered through the T1 income tax return. Such repayments, which reflect income that was originally subject to tax under 56(1)(a)(iv), were formerly deductible under 110(1)(i). They are now deductible in computing net income (rather than taxable income), under 60(v.1).

(j) **home relocation loan** — where the taxpayer has, by virtue of section 80.4, included an amount in the taxpayer's income for the year in respect of a benefit received by the taxpayer in respect of a home relocation loan, the least of

(i) the amount of the benefit that would have been deemed to have been received by the taxpayer under section 80.4 in the year if that section had applied only in respect of the home relocation loan,

(ii) the amount of interest for the year that would be computed under paragraph 80.4(1)(a) in respect of the home relocation loan if that loan were in the amount of $25,000 and were extinguished on the earlier of

(A) the day that is five years after the day on which the home relocation loan was made, and

(B) the day on which the home relocation loan was extinguished, and

(iii) the amount of the benefit deemed to have been received by the taxpayer under section 80.4 in the year; and

**Related Provisions**: 80.4(4) — Interest on home relocation loan; 110(1.4) — Replacement of home relocation loan; 111(8)"non-capital loss"A:E — Amount included in non-capital loss; 111.1 — Order of applying provisions; 114.2 — Deductions in separate returns; 127.52(1)(h) — Deduction disallowed for minimum tax purposes.

**Interpretation Bulletins**: IT-421R2: Benefits to individuals, corporations and shareholders from loans or debt.

**I.T. Technical News**: No. 6 (payment of mortgage interest subsidy by employer).

(k) **Part VI.1 tax** — $9/4$ of the tax payable under subsection 191.1(1) by the taxpayer for the year.

**Related Provisions**: 111(5) — Change in control of corporation; 111(8)"non-capital loss"A:E — Amount included in non-capital loss; 191.3(4) — Related corporations.

**Notes**: 110(1)(k) amended by 1989 Budget, this version effective for taxation years ending December 31, 1990 or later. Transitional rules apply to a corporation's taxation year commencing before 1990 and ending after 1989, and to its 1989 taxation year.

**Interpretation Bulletins**: IT-302R3: Losses of a corporation — the effect that acquisitions of control, amalgamations, and windings-up have on their deductibility — after January 15, 1987.

**Forms**: T2 SCH 43: Calculation of Parts IV.1 and VI.1 taxes.

**(1.1)–(1.3)** [Repealed under former Act]

**Notes**: 110(1.1), (1.2) and (1.3), repealed by 1988 tax reform, provided special rules relating to medical expenses, gifts and the disabled; these have been moved to 118.2(4), 118.1(4) and 118.4(1) respectively.

**(1.4) Replacement of home relocation loan** — For the purposes of paragraph (1)(j), a loan received by a taxpayer that is used to repay a home relocation

**S. 110(1.4)** — Income Tax Act, Part I

loan shall be deemed to be the same loan as the relocation loan and to have been made on the same day as the relocation loan.

**Interpretation Bulletins**: IT-421R2: Benefits to individuals, corporations and shareholders from loans or debt.

**(1.5) Value of share under stock option** — For the purpose of subparagraph (1)(d)(iii), the fair market value of a share of the capital stock of a corporation at the time an agreement in respect of the share was made shall be determined on the assumption that

(a) any subdivision or consolidation of shares of the capital stock of the corporation,

(b) any reorganization of share capital of the corporation, and

(c) any stock dividend of the corporation

occurring after the agreement was made and before the share was acquired had taken place immediately before the agreement was made.

### Proposed Amendment — 110(1.5)–(1.7)

**(1.5) Determination of amounts relating to employee security options** — For the purpose of paragraph (1)(d),

(a) the amount payable by a taxpayer to acquire a security under an agreement referred to in subsection 7(1) shall be determined without reference to any change in the value of a currency of a country other than Canada, relative to Canadian currency, occurring after the agreement was made;

(b) the fair market value of a security at the time an agreement in respect of the security was made shall be determined on the assumption that all specified events associated with the security that occurred after the agreement was made and before the sale or issue of the security or the disposition of the taxpayer's rights under the agreement in respect of the security, as the case may be, had occurred immediately before the agreement was made; and

(c) in determining the amount that was included, in respect of a security that a qualifying person has agreed to sell or issue to a taxpayer, in the amount determined under subparagraph 7(1.4)(c)(ii) for the purpose of determining if the condition in paragraph 7(1.4)(c) was satisfied with respect to a particular disposition, an assumption shall be made that all specified events associated with the security that occurred after the particular disposition and before the sale or issue of the security or the taxpayer's subsequent disposition of rights under the agreement in respect of the security, as the case may be, had occurred immediately before the particular disposition.

**Technical Notes**: Subsection 110(1.5) contains a special rule that is relevant for purposes of determining eligibility for the deduction under paragraph 110(1)(d) in respect of certain stock option benefits.

Specifically, subsection 110(1.5) requires that, for the purposes of subparagraph 110(1)(d)(iii), certain changes in share structure that occur after a stock option is granted be considered in determining the fair market value of the shares at the time the option was granted. For example, where there is a one-for-two consolidation of stock option shares after the options are granted but before they are exercised, the fair market value of the shares at the time the options were granted would, for purposes of subparagraph 110(1)(d)(iii), be considered to be twice the actual value of the shares at that time.

Subsection 110(1.5) is amended in a number of ways.

First, it is amended so that it applies for all purposes of paragraph 110(1)(d), not just for the purposes of subparagraph 110(1)(d)(iii).

Second, it is amended so that it applies to units of a mutual fund trust as well as to shares of the capital stock of a corporation.

Third, it is amended to replace the detailed description of the specific structural changes that are to be taken into account in determining a security's fair market value with a simple reference to "specified events" (as defined in new subsection 110(1.6)).

Fourth, it is amended to provide that, in determining the opening exercise price of an option that has been received in exchange for another option under circumstances to which subsection 7(1.4) applies, all "specified events" (as defined in subsection 110(1.6)) that occur after the option is granted are to be taken into account. This is relevant in determining if the condition in clause 110(1)(d)(iii)(A) or (D), as the case may be, is satisfied when the new option is subsequently exercised or disposed of or exchanged for another option in accordance with subsection 7(1.4). This provision is set out in new paragraph 110(1.5)(c).

Finally, it is amended to provide for the exercise price under an employee option agreement to be determined without reference to changes in the value of a foreign currency relative to Canadian currency after the option is granted. This is currently provided for in paragraph 110(1)(d), but is being moved to amended paragraph 110(1.5)(a).

These changes, which apply to the 1998 and subsequent taxation years, are consequential on changes to paragraph 110(1)(d) (including changes previously made in the 1998 budget bill [S.C. 1999, c.22 (formerly Bill C-72)] to extend the application of that paragraph to mutual fund trust units and to improve its readability).

**(1.6) Meaning of "specified event"** — For the purpose of subsection (1.5), a specified event associated with a security is,

(a) where the security is a share of the capital stock of a corporation,

(i) a subdivision or consolidation of shares of the capital stock of the corporation,

(ii) a reorganization of share capital of the corporation, and

(iii) a stock dividend of the corporation; and

(b) where the security is a unit of a mutual fund trust,

(i) a subdivision or consolidation of the units of the trust, and

(ii) an issuance of units of the trust as payment, or in satisfaction of a person's right to enforce payment, out of the trust's income (determined before the application of subsection 104(6)) or out of the trust's capital gains.

**Technical Notes**: New subsection 110(1.6) defines "specified event", which is relevant for amended subsection 110(1.5). That subsection requires that, in determining either the fair market value of an employee option security at the time the option was granted or the opening exercise price to acquire a security under an option received in exchange for another option in accordance with subsection 7(1.4), all specified events associated with the security that occurred after the option was granted are to be taken into account. For this purpose, a security is defined by subsection 7(7) to be a share of the capital stock of a corporation or a unit of a mutual fund trust.

Paragraph 110(1.6)(a) describes the events that are considered to be specified events associated with a share of the capital stock of a corporation. The events, which were previously set out in subsection 110(1.5), include a split or consolidation of shares of the corporation, a reorganization of share capital of the corporation and a stock dividend.

Paragraph 110(1.6)(b) describes the events that are considered to be specified events associated with a unit of a mutual fund trust. The events, which are comparable to those identified for shares, include a split or consolidation of trust units and the issuance of new units out of the income or capital of the trust. The recognition of such events in the context of a mutual fund trust is consequential on changes previously made to section 7 and paragraph 110(1)(d) to extend the stock option rules to mutual fund trust units.

**Related Provisions**: 110(1.7) — Definitions in 7(7) apply.

**(1.7) Definitions in subsection 7(7)** — The definitions in subsection 7(7) apply for the purposes of subsections (1.5) and (1.6).

**Technical Notes**: New subsection 110(1.7) provides that the definitions "security" and "qualifying person" in subsection 7(7) apply for the purposes of amended subsection 110(1.5) and new subsection 110(1.6).

**Application**: The December 21, 2000 draft legislation, subsec. 51(5), will amend subsec. 110(1.5) to read as above and add subsecs. 110(1.6) and (1.7), applicable to 1998 et seq.

**Related Provisions**: 110(1.6) — Meaning of "specified event"; 110(1.7) — Definitions in 7(7) apply.

**Notes**: 110(1.5) added by 1991 technical bill, effective 1988.

**Interpretation Bulletins**: IT-113R4: Benefits to employees — stock options.

**(2) Charitable gifts** — Where an individual is, during a taxation year, a member of a religious order and has, as such, taken a vow of perpetual poverty, the individual may deduct in computing the individual's taxable income for the year an amount equal to the total of the individual's superannuation or pension benefits and the individual's earned income for the year (within the meaning assigned by section 63) if, of the individual's income, that amount is paid in the year to the order.

**Related Provisions**: 118.1(1) — "Total charitable gifts"; 118.1(3) — Deduction from tax.

**Interpretation Bulletins**: IT-86R: Vow of perpetual poverty.

**Information Circulars**: 78-5R3: Communal organizations.

**(2.1)–(9)** [Repealed under former Act]

### Proposed Addition — 110(2.1)

**(2.1) Charitable donation — proceeds of disposition of employee option securities** — Where a taxpayer, in exercising a right to acquire a security that a particular qualifying person has agreed to sell or issue to the taxpayer under an agreement referred to in subsection 7(1), directs a broker or dealer appointed or approved by the particular qualifying person (or by a qualifying person that does not deal at arm's length with the particular qualifying person) to immediately dispose of the security and pay all or a portion of the proceeds of disposition of the security to a qualified donee,

(a) if the payment is a gift, the taxpayer is deemed, for the purpose of paragraph (1)(d.01), to have disposed of the security by making a gift of the security to the qualified donee at the time the payment is made; and

(b) the amount deductible under paragraph (1)(d.01) by the taxpayer in respect of the disposition of the security is the amount determined by the formula

$$A \times B/C$$

where

A is the amount that would be deductible under paragraph (1)(d.01) in respect of the disposition of the security if this subsection were read without reference to this paragraph,

B is the amount of the payment, and

C is the amount of the proceeds of disposition of the security.

**Application**: The December 21, 2000 draft legislation, subsec. 51(6), will add subsec. 110(2.1), applicable to 2000 et seq.

**Technical Notes**: New subsection 110(2.1) allows an employee to claim a deduction under new paragraph 110(1)(d.01) where the employee, in exercising an option to acquire a security, directs the person administering the employee security option plan for the employer to sell the security immediately and donate all or part of the proceeds of the disposition to a qualifying charity. The deduction is equal to the amount that would have been deductible under new paragraph 110(1)(d.01) if the security had been so donated, prorated to reflect the proportion of the proceeds that are donated. This deduction applies to securities acquired after February 27, 2000.

*Example*

*In August 2001, Julie exercises options to acquire 100 shares of her corporate employer. The exercise price is $10 a share and the fair market value at the time of acquisition is $110 a share. At her direction, the administrator of the stock option plan for the employer*

**S. 110(2.1)**      Income Tax Act, Part I

*immediately sells all of the shares for proceeds of disposition equal to $11,000, pays $1,000 to the employer to cover the exercise price and pays the remaining $10,000 to a designated charity.*

*Subsection 7(1) deems Julie to have received a benefit equal to $10,000 (i.e., the fair market value of the shares at the time of acquisition less the exercise price). Julie is entitled to a deduction of $5,000 under paragraph 110(1)(d) (= 1/2 of $10,000). If she had donated the shares to a charity, she would have been entitled to an additional deduction of $2,500 under paragraph 110(1)(d.01) (= 1/4 of $10,000). Since she donated 90% of the proceeds from the disposition of the shares, she is entitled to deduct $2,250 under paragraph 110(1)(d.01) (= 90% of $2,500).*

**Notes**: Former 110(2.1)–(9), repealed by 1988 tax reform, provided special rules relating to charitable donations, medical expenses and the disability deduction. These have been integrated into the rules for credits in 118.1 through 118.4.

**Definitions [s. 110]**: "amount" — 248(1); "arm's length" — 251(1); "associated" — 256; "Canada" — 255; "capital gain" — 39(1)(a), 248(1); "consequence of the taxpayer's death" — 248(8); "corporation" — 248(1), *Interpretation Act* 35(1); "disposition", "employee", "employer" — 248(1); "exchanged option" — 7(1.4)(a); "home relocation loan" — 110(1.4), 248(1); "individual" — 248(1); "mutual fund trust" — 132(6)–(7), 132.2(1)(q), 248(1); "new option", "new share" — 7(1.4); "old share" — 7(1.4)(a); "person" — 248(1); "private foundation" — 149.1(1), 248(1); "province" — *Interpretation Act* 35(1); "qualified donee" — 149.1(1), 248(1); "qualifying person", "security" — 7(7); "share" — 248(1); "specified event" — 110(1.6); "stock dividend" — 248(1); "taxable income" — 2(2), 248(1); "taxation year" — 249; "taxpayer" — 248(1); "trust" — 104(1), 248(1), (3).

**Interpretation Bulletins**: IT-326R3: Returns of deceased persons as "another person".

**110.1 (1) Deduction for gifts** — For the purpose of computing the taxable income of a corporation for a taxation year, there may be deducted such of the following amounts as the corporation claims:

  (a) **charitable gifts** — the total of all amounts each of which is the fair market value of a gift (other than a gift described in paragraph (b), (c) or (d)) made by the corporation in the year or in any of the 5 preceding taxation years to

    (i) a registered charity,

    (ii) a registered Canadian amateur athletic association,

    (iii) a corporation resident in Canada and described in paragraph 149(l)(i),

    (iv) a municipality in Canada,

    (v) the United Nations or an agency thereof,

    (vi) a university outside Canada that is prescribed to be a university the student body of which ordinarily includes students from Canada,

    (vii) a charitable organization outside Canada to which Her Majesty in right of Canada has made a gift in the year or in the 12-month period preceding the year, or

    (viii) Her Majesty in right of Canada or a province,

not exceeding the lesser of the corporation's income for the year and the amount determined by the formula

$$0.75A + 0.25(B + C + D)$$

where

A   is the corporation's income for the year computed without reference to subsection 137(2),

B   is the total of all amounts each of which is a taxable capital gain of the corporation for the year from a disposition that is the making of a gift made by the corporation in the year and described in this paragraph,

C   is the total of all amounts each of which is a taxable capital gain of the corporation for the year, because of subsection 40(1.01), from a disposition of a property in a preceding taxation year, and

D   is the total of all amounts each of which is determined in respect of the corporation's depreciable property of a prescribed class and equal to the lesser of

    (A) the amount included under subsection 13(1) in respect of the class in computing the corporation's income for the year, and

    (B) the total of all amounts each of which is determined in respect of a disposition that is the making of a gift of property of the class made by the corporation in the year that is described in this paragraph and equal to the lesser of

      (I) the proceeds of disposition of the property minus any outlays and expenses to the extent that they were made or incurred by the corporation for the purpose of making the disposition, and

      (II) the capital cost to the corporation of the property;

  (b) **gifts to Her Majesty** — the total of all amounts each of which is the fair market value of a gift (other than a gift described in paragraph (c) or (d)) made by the corporation to Her Majesty in right of Canada or a province

    (i) in the year or in any of the 5 preceding taxation years, and

    (ii) before February 19, 1997 or under a written agreement made before that day;

  (c) **gifts to institutions** — the total of all amounts each of which is the fair market value of a gift (other than a gift described in paragraph (d)) of an object that the Canadian Cultural Property Export Review Board has determined meets the criteria set out in paragraphs 29(3)(b) and (c) of the *Cultural Property Export and Import Act*, which gift was made by the corporation in the

Division C — Computation of Taxable Income    S. 110.1(1)

year or in any of the 5 preceding taxation years to an institution or a public authority in Canada that was, at the time the gift was made, designated under subsection 32(2) of that Act either generally or for a specified purpose related to that object; and

(d) **ecological gifts** — the total of all amounts each of which is the fair market value of a gift of land, including a servitude for the use and benefit of a dominant land, a covenant or an easement, that is certified by the Minister of the Environment, or a person designated by that Minister, to be ecologically sensitive land, the conservation and protection of which is, in the opinion of that Minister, or that person, important to the preservation of Canada's environmental heritage, which gift was made by the corporation in the year or in any of the 5 preceding taxation years to

**Proposed Amendment — 110.1(1)(d) opening words**

(d) **ecological gifts** — the total of all amounts each of which is the fair market value of a gift of land, including a servitude for the use and benefit of a dominant land, a covenant or an easement, the fair market value of which is certified by the Minister of the Environment and that is certified by that Minister, or by a person designated by that Minister, to be ecologically sensitive land, the conservation and protection of which is, in the opinion of that Minister, or that person, important to the preservation of Canada's environmental heritage, which gift was made by the corporation in the year or in any of the five preceding taxation years to

**Application**: The December 21, 2000 draft legislation, subsec. 52(1), will amend the opening words of para. 110.1(1)(d) to read as above, applicable in respect of gifts made after February 27, 2000.

**Technical Notes**: Section 110.1 provides for the deductibility in computing income of charitable donations and certain other gifts.

Subsection 110.1(1) provides a deduction in computing taxable income in respect of gifts made by corporations to registered charities and to certain other entities. Paragraph 110.1(1)(d) provides an exemption from the annual 75% income limit for gifts of land (including a covenant, an easement or a servitude in respect of land) that is certified by the Minister of the Environment to be ecologically sensitive land, the conservation and protection of which is, in the opinion of that Minister, important to the preservation of Canada's environmental heritage. The beneficiary must be the federal government, a provincial or territorial government, a municipality or a registered charity approved by the Minister of the Environment.

Paragraph 110.1(1)(d) is amended to require that the fair market value of the gift [not just the existence of the gift — ed.] be certified by the Minister of the Environment. The fair market value is relevant to the calculation of the deduction available to the corporation under paragraph 110.1(1)(d) and of the taxable capital gain under section 38.

(i) Her Majesty in right of Canada or a province or a municipality in Canada, or

(ii) a registered charity one of the main purposes of which is, in the opinion of that Minister, the conservation and protection of Canada's environmental heritage, and that is approved by that Minister or that person in respect of the gift.

**Related Provisions**: 37(5) — Scientific research and experimental development expenditures; 46(1), (5) — Capital gain on certain donations of art and other property; 87(2)(v) — Amalgamations — gifts; 88(1)(e.6) — Gift by subsidiary; 88(1.3) — Winding-up — computation of income and tax payable by parent; 110.1(1.1)(a) — Gifts not deductible if previously deducted; 110.1(3) — Gifts of capital property; 110.1(5) — Fair market value of ecological servitude, covenant or easement; 118.1(10) — Cultural property — determination of fair market value; 118.1(10.1) — Determination of value by Canadian Cultural Property Export Review Board; 118.1(10.1)–(10.5) — Determination of fair market value of ecological gift by Minister of the Environment; 138(12) "surplus funds derived from operations" — Insurance operations — surplus funds; 149.1(6.4) — Donations to registered national arts service organization; 168 — Revocation of charitable registration; 207.3 — Tax on institution that disposes of cultural property; 207.31 — Tax if donee of ecological property disposes of it; 230(2) — Records of donations; Canada-U.S. tax treaty, Art. XXI:6 — Donations to U.S. charities..

**Notes**: 110.1 applies only to corporations. Charitable donations by individuals and trusts are eligible for a credit under 118.1, whose rules are generally parallel to 110.1. See Notes to 118.1(1) "total charitable gifts" and "total gifts".

As an alternative to a receipted donation under 110.1, a corporation can often deduct a donation, where some public recognition is given, as an advertising expense. If no receipt is requested, the donation does not increase the charity's disbursement quota (see Notes to 149.1(1) "disbursement quota").

110.1(1) amended by 1997 Budget, effective for taxation years that begin after 1996. The substantive change was that charitable gifts (formerly limited to 50% of net income) and Crown gifts (formerly 100%) are now both limited to 75% of net income, plus 25% of taxable capital gains on making the gifts, plus 25% of any 13(1) CCA recapture from making the gifts. Crown gifts made or agreed to in writing before February 19, 1997 (budget day) are grandfathered under 110.1(1)(b)(ii).

For taxation years beginning and ending in 1996, read:

(1) Deduction for gifts — For the purpose of computing the taxable income of a corporation for a taxation year, there may be deducted such of the following amounts as are applicable:

(a) charitable gifts — the total of all amounts each of which is the fair market value of a gift made by the corporation in the year (or in any of the 5 immediately preceding taxation years to the extent that the amount thereof was not deducted in computing its taxable income for any preceding taxation year) to

(i) a registered charity,

(ii) a registered Canadian amateur athletic association,

(iii) a housing corporation resident in Canada and exempt from tax under this Part because of paragraph 149(1)(i),

(iv) a Canadian municipality,

(v) the United Nations or an agency thereof,

911

(vi) a university outside Canada that is prescribed to be a university the student body of which ordinarily includes students from Canada, or

(vii) a charitable organization outside Canada to which Her Majesty in right of Canada has made a gift during the corporation's taxation year or the 12 months immediately preceding that taxation year,

not exceeding the amount determined by the formula

$$0.5(A + B)$$

where

A  is its income for the year computed without reference to subsection 137(2), and

B  is the total of all amounts each of which is the amount of a taxable capital gain from a gift of property made by it in the year to a donee described in this paragraph;

(b) **gifts to Her Majesty** — the total of all amounts each of which is the fair market value of a gift made by the corporation in the year (or in any of the 5 immediately preceding taxation years to the extent that the amount thereof was not deducted in computing its taxable income for any preceding taxation year) to Her Majesty in right of Canada or a province, not exceeding the amount remaining, if any, after the amount deducted for the year under paragraph (a) by the corporation is deducted in computing its taxable income for the year;

(c) **gifts to institutions** — the total of all amounts each of which is the fair market value of a gift (other than a gift in respect of which an amount is or was deducted under paragraph (a) or (b)) of an object that the Canadian Cultural Property Export Review Board has determined meets the criteria set out in paragraphs 29(3)(b) and (c) of the *Cultural Property Export and Import Act*, which gift was made by the corporation in the year (or in any of the 5 immediately preceding taxation years to the extent that the amount thereof was not deducted in computing its taxable income for any preceding taxation year) to an institution or a public authority in Canada that was, at the time the gift was made, designated under subsection 32(2) of that Act either generally or for a specified purpose related to that object, not exceeding the amount remaining, if any, after the amounts deducted for the year under paragraphs (a) and (b) by the corporation are deducted in computing its taxable income for the year; and

(d) **ecological gifts** — the total of all amounts each of which is the fair market value of a gift (other than a gift in respect of which an amount is or was deducted under paragraph (a), (b) or (c)) of land, including a servitude for the use and benefit of a dominant land, a covenant or an easement, that is certified by the Minister of the Environment, or a person designated by that Minister, to be ecologically sensitive land, the conservation and protection of which is, in the opinion of that Minister, or that person, important to the preservation of Canada's environmental heritage, which gift was made by the corporation in the year (or in any of the 5 immediately preceding taxation years to the extent that the amount was not deducted in computing its taxable income for any preceding taxation year) to

(i) a Canadian municipality, or

(ii) a registered charity one of the main purposes of which is, in the opinion of the Minister of the Environment, the conservation and protection of Canada's environmental heritage, and that is approved by that Minister, or that person, in respect of that gift,

and not exceeding the amount remaining, if any, after the amounts deducted for the year under paragraphs (a), (b) and (c) are deducted in computing the corporation's taxable income for the year.

This new limitation applies to gifts deducted in taxation years that begin after 1996, except that there is no limitation on Crown gifts made before February 19, 1997 nor on Crown gifts made pursuant to an agreement in writing made before that date.

Closing words of 110.1(1)(a) amended by 1996 Budget, effective for 1996 and later taxation years, effectively to change the limit from 20% to 50% and to add element B. These changes parallel the changes made for individuals in 118.1(1)"total gifts" (and note that the formula will change further as a result of the 1997 federal budget). For 1988 through 1995, read the closing words as:

> not exceeding 20% of its income for the year computed without reference to subsection 137(2);

110.1(1) amended by 1991 technical bill, effective December 11, 1988, to make the wording consistent with 118.1 and to update section references to the *Cultural Property Export and Import Act*.

110.1(1)(d) added by 1995 Budget, effective for gifts made after February 27, 1995. It harmonizes the federal law with a credit introduced in the May 1994 Quebec budget. Note that if the donee ever disposes of the land without authorization from the Minister of the Environment, a special 50% tax applies under 207.31.

**Regulations**: 3503, Sch. VIII (prescribed universities outside Canada).

**Interpretation Bulletins**: IT-110R3: Gifts and official donation receipts; IT-111R2: Annuities purchased from charitable organizations; IT-151R5: Scientific research and experimental development expenditures; IT-226R: Gift to a charity of a residual interest in real property or an equitable interest in a trust; IT-244R3: Gifts of life insurance policies as charitable donations; IT-288R2: Gifts of capital properties to a charity and others; IT-297R2: Gifts in kind to charity and others; IT-385R2: Disposition of an income interest in a trust; IT-407R4: Dispositions of cultural property to designated Canadian institutions.

**Information Circulars**: 84-3R5: Gifts to certain charitable organizations outside Canada.

**Advance Tax Rulings**: ATR-63: Donations to agents of the Crown.

**Forms**: RC4142: Tax advantages of donating to a charity [guide]; T2 SCH 2: Corporation's charitable donations and gifts.

**I.T. Technical News**: No. 17 (loan of property as a gift).

**Registered Charities Newsletters**: See under 118.1(1)"total charitable gifts".

## (1.1) Limitation on deductibility — For the purpose of determining the amount deductible under subsection (1) in computing a corporation's taxable income for a taxation year,

(a) an amount in respect of a gift is deductible only to the extent that it exceeds amounts in respect of the gift deducted under that subsection in computing the corporation's taxable income for preceding taxation years; and

(b) no amount in respect of a gift made in a particular taxation year is deductible under any of paragraphs (1)(a) to (d) until amounts deductible under that paragraph in respect of gifts made in taxation years preceding the particular year have been deducted.

**Related Provisions**: 118.1(2.1) — Ordering rule parallel to 110.1(1.1)(b).

Division C — Computation of Taxable Income       S. 110.1(3)

**Notes**: 110.1(1.1) added by 1997 Budget, effective for taxation years that begin after 1996. Its "first-in, first-out" assumption reflects Revenue Canada's previous assessing policy and is the assumption most favourable to taxpayers, since it allows the largest carryforward of unused donations.

**(2) Proof of gift** — A gift shall not be included for the purpose of determining a deduction under subsection (1) unless the making of the gift is proven by filing with the Minister a receipt therefor that contains prescribed information.

### Proposed Amendment — 110.1(2)

**(2) Proof of gift** — A gift shall not be included for the purpose of determining a deduction under subsection (1) unless the making of the gift is proven by filing with the Minister

(a) a receipt for the gift that contains prescribed information;

(b) in the case of a gift described in paragraph (1)(c), the certificate issued under subsection 33(1) of the *Cultural Property Export and Import Act*; and

(c) in the case of a gift described in paragraph (1)(d), both certificates referred to in that paragraph.

**Application**: The December 21, 2000 draft legislation, subsec. 52(2), will amend subsec. 110.1(2) to read as above, applicable in respect of gifts made after February 27, 2000, except that it shall be read without reference to para. (b) in respect of gifts made before December 21, 2000.

**Technical Notes**: Subsection 110.1(2) provides that no deduction may be made in respect of a charitable donation or a gift to the Crown unless the gift is evidenced by a receipt containing prescribed information. The subsection is amended to clarify that, in the case of a gift of certified cultural property or an ecological gift, certificates issued by the Cultural Property Export Review Board or the Minister of the Environment must also be submitted.

This amendment applies to gifts made after February 27, 2000, except that the amendment in respect of cultural property does not apply to gifts made before December 21, 2000.

**Related Provisions**: 118.1(2)"Parallel rule for individuals"; 149.1(1)"disbursement quota"A — Charity must spend 80% of gifts on charitable purposes; 188(1) — Revocation tax where registration of charity is revoked.

**Regulations**: 3500–3502 (prescribed information).

**Information Circulars**: 80-10R: Registered charities: operating a registered charity.

**Advance Tax Rulings**: ATR-63: Donations to agents of the Crown.

**Forms**: T2 SCH 2: Corporation's charitable donations and gifts.

**(3) Gifts of capital property** — Where at any time

(a) a corporation makes a gift of

(i) capital property to a donee described in paragraph (1)(a), (b) or (d), or

(ii) in the case of a corporation not resident in Canada, real property situated in Canada to a prescribed donee who provides an undertaking, in a form satisfactory to the Minister, to the effect that the property will be held for use in the public interest, and

(b) the fair market value of the property at that time exceeds its adjusted cost base to the corporation,

such amount, not greater than the fair market value and not less than the adjusted cost base to the corporation of the property at that time, as the corporation designates in its return of income under section 150 for the year in which the gift is made shall, if the making of the gift is proven by filing with the Minister a receipt containing prescribed information, be deemed to be its proceeds of disposition of the property and, for the purposes of subsection (1), the fair market value of the gift made by the corporation.

### Proposed Amendment — 110.1(3)

such amount, not greater than the fair market value otherwise determined and not less than the adjusted cost base to the corporation of the property at that time, as the corporation designates in its return of income under section 150 for the year in which the gift is made is, if the making of the gift is proven by filing with the Minister a receipt containing prescribed information, deemed to be its proceeds of disposition of the property and, for the purposes of subsection (1), the fair market value of the gift made by the corporation.

**Application**: Bill C-43 (First Reading September 20, 2000), subsec. 55(1), will amend the closing words of subsec. 110.1(3) to read as above, applicable in respect of gifts made after February 27, 1995.

**Technical Notes**: Section 110.1 of the Act provides for the deductibility in computing income of charitable donations and certain other gifts.

Subsection 110.1(3) of the Act provides that, if a corporation donates capital property to a charity, it may elect a value between the adjusted cost base and the fair market value of the donated property to be treated both as the proceeds of disposition for the purpose of calculating its capital gain and the amount of the gift for the purpose of the deduction allowed for charitable donations under subsection 110.1(1).

The amendment to subsection 110.1(3) is complementary to the amendment of subsection 110.1(5) of the Act, which provides that the fair market value of a gift of a covenant, easement or servitude in respect of ecologically sensitive land will not be considered to be less than the decrease in value of the subject land that resulted from the making of the gift. The amendments clarify that a corporate donor may nevertheless report a reduced amount as proceeds of disposition of such a gift, where the value of the gift for the purpose of the charitable donations deduction is reduced accordingly. This amendment applies in respect of gifts made after February 27, 1995.

**Dept. of Finance news release, June 3, 1999**: See under 118.1(12).

**Notes**: This measure was first announced in a news release on June 3, 1999.

**Related Provisions**: 118.1(6) — Parallel rule for individuals.

**S. 110.1(3)**      Income Tax Act, Part I

**Notes**: 110.1(3)(a)(i) amended to refer to para. (1)(d) by 1995 Budget, effective for gifts made after February 27, 1995 (see Notes to 110.1(1)).

Closing words of 110.1(3) amended by 1992 technical bill, effective for gifts made after December 11, 1988, to deem the proceeds of disposition of the property to be the "fair market value" of the gift for purposes of 110.1(1) rather than the "amount" of the gift, to fit with amendments made to 110.1(1) by 1991 technical bill.

See Notes to 118.1(6) re the usefulness of this designation as of 1996.

**Regulations**: 3500 to 3502 (prescribed information); 3504 (prescribed donee).

**Interpretation Bulletins**: IT-288R2: Gifts of capital properties to a charity and others.

**(4) Gifts made by partnership** — Where a corporation is, at the end of a fiscal period of a partnership, a member of the partnership, its share of any amount that would, if the partnership were a person, be a gift made by the partnership to any donee shall, for the purposes of this section, be deemed to be a gift made to that donee by the corporation in its taxation year in which the fiscal period of the partnership ends.

**Related Provisions**: 53(2)(c)(iii) — Deduction from ACB of partnership interest; 118.1(8) — Parallel rule for individuals.

**(5) Ecological gifts** — For the purposes of paragraph (1)(d) and section 207.31, the fair market value of a gift of a servitude, a covenant or an easement to which land is subject is deemed to be the greater of its fair market value otherwise determined and the amount by which the fair market value of the land is reduced as a consequence of the making of the gift.

### Proposed Amendment — 110.1(5) [temporary]

**(5) Ecological gifts** — For the purposes of applying subparagraph 69(1)(b)(ii), section 207.31 and this section in respect of a gift described in paragraph (1)(d) that is made by a taxpayer and that is a servitude, covenant or easement to which land is subject, the greater of

(a) the fair market value otherwise determined of the gift, and

(b) the amount by which the fair market value of the land is reduced as a result of the making of the gift

is deemed to be the fair market value (or, for the purpose of subsection (3), the fair market value otherwise determined) of the gift at the time the gift was made and, subject to subsection (3), to be the taxpayer's proceeds of disposition of the gift.

**Application**: Bill C-43 (First Reading September 20, 2000), subsec. 55(2), will amend subsec. 110.1(5) to read as above, applicable in respect of gifts made after February 27, 1995.

**Technical Notes**: Subsection 110.1(5) provides that the fair market value of a gift of a covenant, easement or servitude in respect of ecologically sensitive land will not be considered to be less than the decrease in value of the subject land that resulted from the making of the gift.

Subsection 110.1(5) is amended to clarify that such amount will also be, subject to the designation of an amount under subsection 110.1(3), the corporate donor's proceeds of disposition for the purposes of calculating income and capital gains.

**Dept. of Finance news release, June 3, 1999**: See under 118.1(12).

**Notes**: This measure was first announced in a news release on June 3, 1999.

### Proposed Amendment — 110.1(5)

**(5) Ecological gifts** — For the purposes of applying subparagraph 69(1)(b)(ii), this section and section 207.31 in respect of a gift described in paragraph (1)(d) that is made by a taxpayer, the amount that is the fair market value (or, for the purpose of subsection (3), the fair market value otherwise determined) of the gift at the time the gift was made and, subject to subsection (3), the taxpayer's proceeds of disposition of the gift, is deemed to be the amount determined by the Minister of the Environment to be

(a) where the gift is land, the fair market value of the gift; or

(b) where the gift is a servitude, covenant or easement to which land is subject, the greater of

(i) the fair market value otherwise determined of the gift, and

(ii) the amount by which the fair market value of the land is reduced as a result of the making of the gift.

**Application**: The December 21, 2000 draft legislation, subsec. 52(3), will amend subsec. 110.1(5) to read as above, applicable in respect of gifts made after February 27, 2000.

**Technical Notes**: Subsection 110.1(5) provides that the fair market value of a corporation's gift of a covenant, easement or servitude in respect of ecologically sensitive land will not be considered to be less than the decrease in value of the subject land that resulted from the making of the gift. That amount is also, subject to the designation of an amount under subsection 110.1(3), the corporate donor's proceeds of disposition for the purposes of calculating income and capital gains.

Subsection 110.1(5) is amended concurrently with paragraph 110.1(1)(d), to provide that the fair market value of ecologically sensitive land (including a covenant, an easement or a servitude) and, consequentially, the corporate donor's proceeds of disposition, is deemed to be the amount determined by the Minister of the Environment.

Administrative measures regarding the request for a determination of fair market value from the Minister of the Environment, including notification, determination and redetermination, are included in new subsections 118.1(10.2) to (10.5). Consequential assessments of tax are provided for in amended subsection 118.1(11). Appeals to the Tax Court of Canada are provided for in new subsection 169(1.1).

**Related Provisions**: 43(2) — calculation for 110.1(5) also applies for determining capital gain or loss on disposition; 118.1(12) — Parallel rule for individuals.

**Notes**: 110.1(5) added by 1997 Budget, effective for gifts made after February 27, 1995.

**(6) Non-qualifying securities** — Subsections 118.1(13), and (14) and (16) to (20) apply to a corporation as if the references in those subsections to an individual were read as references to a corporation and as if a non-qualifying security of a corporation included a share (other than a share listed on a prescribed stock exchange) of the capital stock of the corporation.

**Related Provisions**: 40(1.01) — Capital gains reserve on disposition of non-qualifying security; 88(1)(e.61) — Winding-up of subsidiary — gift deemed made by parent corporation; 110.1(7) — Where corporation ceases to exist after making donation of non-qualifying securities; 118.1(18) — Definition of non-qualifying security.

**Notes**: 110.1(6) added by 1997 Budget, effective August 1997.

**Regulations**: 3200 (prescribed stock exchange).

**(7) Corporation ceasing to exist** — If, but for this subsection, a corporation (other than a corporation that was a predecessor corporation in an amalgamation to which subsection 87(1) applied or a corporation that was wound up in a winding-up to which subsection 88(1) applied) would be deemed by subsection 118.1(13) to have made a gift after the corporation ceased to exist, for the purpose of this section, the corporation is deemed to have made the gift in its last taxation year, except that the amount of interest payable under any provision of this Act is the amount that it would be if this subsection did not apply to the gift.

**Notes**: 110.1(7) added by 1997 Budget, effective August 1997.

**Definitions [s. 110.1]**: "adjusted cost base" — 54, 248(1); "Canada" — 255; "capital property" — 54, 248(1); "corporation" — 248(1), *Interpretation Act* 35(1); "depreciable property" — 13(21), 248(1); "fair market value" — 110.1(5), 118.1(10); "fiscal period" — 249(2)(b), 249.1; "Minister", "prescribed", "property" — 248(1); "province" — *Interpretation Act* 35(1); "registered Canadian amateur athletic association", "registered charity" — 248(1); "resident in Canada" — 250; "taxable income" — 2(2), 248(1); "written" — *Interpretation Act* 35(1) ["writing"].

**110.2 Definitions [lump-sum averaging]** — (1) The definitions in this subsection apply in this section and section 120.31.

**"eligible taxation year"**, in respect of a qualifying amount received by an individual, means a taxation year

(a) that ended after 1977 and before the year in which the individual received the qualifying amount;

(b) throughout which the individual was resident in Canada;

(c) that did not end in a calendar year in which the individual became a bankrupt; and

(d) that was not included in an averaging period, within the meaning assigned by section 119 (as it read in its application to the 1987 taxation year), pursuant to an election that was made and not revoked by the individual under that section.

**Notes**: See Notes at end of 110.2.

**"qualifying amount"** received by an individual in a taxation year means an amount (other than the portion of the amount that can reasonably be considered to be received as, on account of, in lieu of payment of or in satisfaction of, interest) that is included in computing the individual's income for the year and is

(a) an amount

(i) that is received pursuant to an order or judgment of a competent tribunal, an arbitration award or a contract by which the payor and the individual terminate a legal proceeding, and

(ii) that is

(A) included in computing the individual's income from an office or employment, or

(B) received as, on account of, in lieu of payment of or in satisfaction of, damages in respect of the individual's loss of an office or employment,

(b) a superannuation or pension benefit (other than a benefit referred to in clause 56(1)(a)(i)(B)) received on account of, in lieu of payment of or in satisfaction of, a series of periodic payments (other than payments that would have otherwise been made in the year or in a subsequent taxation year),

(c) an amount described in paragraph 6(1)(f), subparagraph 56(1)(a)(iv) or paragraph 56(1)(b), or

(d) a prescribed amount or benefit,

except to the extent that the individual may deduct for the year an amount under paragraph 8(1)(b), (n) or (n.1), 60(n) or (o.1) or 110(1)(f) in respect of the amount so included.

**Notes**: See Notes at end of 110.2.

**"specified portion"**, in relation to an eligible taxation year, of a qualifying amount received by an individual means the portion of the qualifying amount that relates to the year, to the extent that the individual's eligibility to receive the portion existed in the year.

**Related Provisions**: 120.31(1) — Definitions apply to 120.31.

**(2) Deduction for lump-sum payments** — There may be deducted in computing the taxable income of an individual (other than a trust) for a particular taxation year the total of all amounts each of which is a specified portion of a qualifying amount received by the individual in the particular year, if that total is $3,000 or more.

**Related Provisions**: 120.31 — Tax payable for other years.

**Notes [s. 110.2]**: 110.2 provides a limited form of retroactive averaging of certain kinds of income (see 110.2(1)"qualifying amount"). It was introduced primarily to accommodate federal government pay equity settlements. It addresses taxpayers who are pushed into a higher bracket as a result of having all the income

## S. 110.2

lumped into the year in which it is received (see 5(1)). The deduction under 110.2(2) is offset by tax payable for the other years under 120.31. Note however that under 120.31(3)(b) an amount in lieu of interest must be paid for the earlier years. Where possible, the CCRA's computers will calculate and process the adjustment automatically.

See also CCRA, "Income Tax Information About Pay Equity Employment Income and Pay Equity Interest Payments Received in 2000" (Nov. 1, 2000), on the CCRA Web site and on *TaxPartner* under "Guides".

110.2 added by 1999 Budget, effective for amounts received by an individual after 1994 (other than an amount in respect of which tax has been remitted to the individual [by remission order] under subsec. 23(2) of the *Financial Administration Act*) and, notwithstanding 152(4) to (5), any assessment of the individual's tax payable for any taxation year that ended before 1999 shall be made as is necessary to take into account s. 110.2.

Former 110.2, repealed by 1988 tax reform, provided for a pension income deduction, replaced by a credit in 118(3).

**Definitions [s. 110.2]:** "amount", "bankrupt" — 248(1); "eligible taxation year" — 110.2(1); "employment", "individual", "office", "prescribed" — 248(1); "qualifying amount" — 110.2(1); "resident in Canada" — 250; "specified portion" — 110.2(1); "superannuation or pension benefit", "taxable income" — 248(1); "taxation year" — 249; "trust" — 104(1), 248(1), 248(3).

**Forms:** T1198: Statement of qualifying retroactive lump-sum payment.

## 110.3 [Repealed under former Act]

**Notes:** 110.3, repealed by 1988 tax reform, provided for a transfer to a spouse of certain unused deductions, replaced by a transfer of the pension credit under 118.8.

## 110.4 [Repealed]

**Related Provisions:** 111(8)"non-capital loss"C — Amount elected under 110.4(2) reduces non-capital loss; 111.1 — Order of applying provisions; 120.1 — Adjustments to tax payable; 220(3.2), Reg. 600(b) — Late filing of election or revocation.

**Notes:** 110.4 repealed by 1999 Budget, effective for 1998 and later taxation years. Until 1987, 110.4(1) permitted "forward averaging", under which a certain amount of income could be deferred to a later year, provided that the taxpayer prepaid a special amount under 120.1(2). Recovery of amounts forward-averaged before 1988 was available until 1997 under 110.4(2).

From 1988 to 1997, read 110.4(2), (4), (5), (6.1) and (8) as:

(2) Election — Where an individual files with the individual's return under this Part for a taxation year ending before 1998 and throughout which the individual was resident in Canada an election in prescribed form on or before the day on or before which the individual was, or would have been if tax had been payable under this Part by the individual for the year, required to file a return of income under this Part for the year, there shall be added in computing the individual's taxable income for the year the amount, if any, by which

(a) such portion of the individual's accumulated averaging amount at the end of the immediately preceding taxation year as is specified by the individual in the election

exceeds

(b) the total of amounts that would be the individual's farm loss or non-capital loss for the year if the amount determined for B in the definition "farm loss" or for C in the definition "non-capital loss" in subsection 111(8) were zero.

(4) Death of a taxpayer — For the purposes of subsection (2), where an individual was resident in Canada throughout the period beginning on the first day of the taxation year in which the individual died and ending at the time of the individual's death, the individual shall be deemed to have been resident in Canada throughout that year.

(5) Exception — Subsection (2) does not apply with respect to a return of income filed under subsection 70(2) or 150(4) or paragraph 104(23)(d).

(6.1) Revocation of election — An election filed by an individual under subsection (2) for a taxation year may be revoked,

(a) where the individual died in the year in which the election was filed, by the individual or the individual's legal representative filing with the Minister a notice of revocation in writing not later than the day on or before which the individual's return of income for the year of death is required to be filed, or would be required to be filed if tax under this Part were payable for the year of death; and

(b) in any other case, by the individual or the legal representative filing with the Minister a notice of revocation in writing not later than the 30th day following the day of mailing of a notice of assessment of an amount payable by the individual under this Part for the year.

(8) Accumulated averaging amount — In this section and section 120.1, the accumulated averaging amount of an individual

(a) at the end of any taxation year before 1998 (other than a taxation year in which the individual dies) is the product obtained when

(i) the amount, if any, by which

(A) the individual's accumulated averaging amount at the end of the immediately preceding taxation year

exceeds

(B) the amount specified under subsection (2) by the individual in the individual's election for the year

is multiplied by

(ii) the ratio (adjusted in such manner as may be prescribed and rounded to the nearest one-thousandth or, where the ratio is equidistant from two consecutive one-thousandths, to the higher thereof) that the Consumer Price Index of the 12 month period that ended on September 30 of that year bears to the Consumer Price Index for the 12 month period that ended on September 30 of the immediately preceding year;

(b) at the end of the taxation year before 1998 and in which the individuals dies is

(i) nil, where the individual's tax payable under this Part for the year is computed under section 119, or

(ii) the amount determined under subparagraph (a)(i) for the year, in any other case; and

(c) at any time after 1997 is nil.

Retroactive averaging of certain lump-sum payments is now available under 110.4 and 120.31. For taxpayers with fluctuating incomes, some income averaging may be possible through the use of RRSPs. See section 146. See also Notes to 15(2).

**Remission Orders [s. 110.4]:** *Prescribed Areas Forward Averaging Remission Order*, P.C. 1994-109 (remission for certain residents of prescribed areas who filed forward averaging elections for 1987).

**Interpretation Bulletins [s. 110.4]:** IT-212R3: Income of deceased persons — rights or things; IT-232R3: Losses — their deductibility in the loss year or in other years; IT-504R2: Visual artists and writers.

**Information Circulars [s. 110.4]**: 92-1: Guidelines for accepting late, amended or revoked elections.

**Forms [s. 110.4]**: T541: Forward averaging tax calculation — deceased individuals; T581: Forward averaging tax credits; T2203A: Forward averaging supplement — multiple jurisdictions.

## 110.5 Additions for foreign tax deductions —

There shall be added to a corporation's taxable income otherwise determined for a taxation year such amount as the corporation may claim to the extent that the addition thereof

(a) increases any amount deductible by the corporation under subsection 126(1) or (2) for the year; and

(b) does not increase an amount deductible by the corporation under any of sections 125, 125.1, 127, 127.2 and 127.3 for the year.

**Related Provisions**: 111(8)"non-capital loss"B — Carryforward of amount determined under 110.5; 115(1)(a)(vii) — Parallel rule for authorized foreign bank.

**Definitions [s. 110.5]**: "amount" — 248(1); "corporation" — 248(1), *Interpretation Act* 35(1); "taxable income" — 2(2), 248(1); "taxation year" — 249.

**Interpretation Bulletins [s. 110.5]**: IT-232R3: Losses — their deductibility in the loss year or in other years; IT-270R2: Foreign tax credit; IT-302R3: Losses of a corporation — the effect that acquisitions of control, amalgamations, and windings-up have on their deductibility — after January 15, 1987.

## 110.6 (1) [Capital gains exemption — ] Definitions — For the purposes of this section,

**"annual gains limit"** of an individual for a taxation year means the amount determined by the formula

$$A - B$$

where

A is the lesser of

(a) the amount determined in respect of the individual for the year under paragraph 3(b) in respect of capital gains and capital losses, and

(b) the amount that would be determined in respect of the individual for the year under paragraph 3(b) in respect of capital gains and losses if the only properties referred to in that paragraph were qualified farm properties disposed of by the individual after 1984 and qualified small business corporation shares disposed of by the individual after June 17, 1987, and

B is the total of

(a) the amount, if any, by which

(i) the individual's net capital losses for other taxation years deducted under paragraph 111(1)(b) in computing the individual's taxable income for the year

exceeds

(ii) the amount, if any, by which the amount determined in respect of the individual for the year under paragraph 3(b) in respect of capital gains and capital losses exceeds the amount determined for A in respect of the individual for the year, and

(b) all of the individual's allowable business investment losses for the year;

**Related Provisions**: 110.6(13) — Meaning of "amount determined under para. 3(b)"; 257 — Formula cannot calculate to less than zero. See also Related Provisions and Definitions at end of s. 110.6.

**Notes**: Para. B(b) prevents "double-dipping" by claiming both an allowable business investment loss (against other income) and the capital gains exemption. See Notes to 39(9).

Para. (b) of the description of A in "annual gains limit" amended by 1994 Budget, this version effective for 1996. For 1994 and 1995, read:

> (b) the amount that would be determined in respect of the individual for the year under paragraph 3(b) in respect of capital gains and capital losses if
>
> (i) the only properties referred to in paragraph 3(b) were properties disposed of by the individual after 1984 and, except where the property was at the time of the disposition a qualified small business corporation share or qualified farm property of the individual, before February 23, 1994,
>
> (i.1) no amount were included under paragraph 3(b) in respect of
>
>> (A) a taxable capital gain of the individual that resulted from an election made under subsection (19) by a personal trust unless the individual was a beneficiary under the trust on February 22, 1994, and
>>
>> (B) that portion of a taxable capital gain referred to in clause (A) that can reasonably be regarded as being in respect of an amount that is included in computing the individual's income because of an interest in the trust that was acquired by the individual after February 22, 1994,
>
> (i.2) except for the purpose of determining the individual's share of a taxable capital gain of a partnership for its fiscal period that includes February 22, 1994 or a taxable capital gain of the individual resulting from a designation made under section 104 by a trust for its taxation year that includes that day, in determining the individual's taxable capital gain for the 1995 taxation year from the disposition of a property (other than a qualified small business corporation share or qualified farm property), this Act were read without reference to subparagraphs 40(1)(a)(ii) and 44(1)(e)(ii), and
>
> (ii) the individual's capital gains and capital losses for the year from dispositions of non-qualifying real property of the individual were equal to the individual's eligible real property gains and eligible real property losses, respectively, for the year from those dispositions, and

Para. (b) of the description of A previously amended by 1992 technical bill and retroactively by 1993 technical bill. For 1992 and 1993, read:

> (b) the amount that would be determined in respect of the individual for the year under paragraph 3(b) in respect of capital gains and capital losses if
>
> (i) the only properties referred to in paragraph 3(b) were properties disposed of by the individual after 1984, and
>
> (ii) the individual's capital gains and capital losses for the year from dispositions of non-qualifying real property of the individual were equal to the individual's eligible real property gains and eligible real property losses, respectively, for the year from those dispositions, and

For 1988-1991, ignore A(b)(ii).

**Interpretation Bulletins**: IT-236R4: Reserves — disposition of capital property.

**Forms**: See list at end of s. 110.6.

**"child"** has the meaning assigned by subsection 70(10);

**"cumulative gains limit"** of an individual at the end of a taxation year means the amount, if any, by which

(a) the total of all amounts determined in respect of the individual for the year or preceding taxation years that end after 1984 for A in the definition "annual gains limit"

exceeds the total of

(b) all amounts determined in respect of the individual for the year or preceding taxation years that end after 1984 for B in the definition "annual gains limit",

(c) the amount, if any, deducted under paragraph 3(e) in computing the individual's income for the 1985 taxation year,

(d) all amounts deducted under this section in computing the individual's taxable incomes for preceding taxation years, and

(e) the individual's cumulative net investment loss at the end of the year;

**Notes**: Definition "cumulative gains limit" amended by 1992 technical bill and 1993 technical bill, this version effective 1985; and notwithstanding 152(4) to (5), such assessments and determinations in respect of any taxation years may be made as are necessary to give effect to the amendment.

See Notes to 110.6(1)"annual gains limit" and "cumulative net investment loss".

**"cumulative net investment loss"** of an individual at the end of a taxation year means the amount, if any, by which

(a) the total of all amounts each of which is the investment expense of the individual for the year or a preceding taxation year ending after 1987

exceeds

(b) the total of all amounts each of which is the investment income of the individual for the year or a preceding taxation year ending after 1987;

**Notes**: Cumulative net investment loss (CNIL, pronounced "senile") is used to limit the ability of a taxpayer to claim interest expense and other investment expenses that are deductible against income from other sources, while at the same time enjoying tax-free capital gains (possibly from the same investments) by virtue of the capital gains exemption. (The policy reason for this is less relevant since the repeal of the general $100,000 exemption in 110.6(3).)

All investment expenses since 1988 are pooled, and to the extent the total exceeds all investment income since 1988, there is a CNIL balance. The CNIL is used in para. (e) of the definition "cumulative gains limit" above, and effectively denies the exemption to the extent of the CNIL account. A CNIL account can be eliminated by earning sufficient investment income (which is, of course, taxed) in subsequent years.

**Forms**: T936: Calculation of cumulative net investment loss.

**"eligible real property gain"** — [Repealed]

**Notes**: Definition "eligible real property gain" added by 1992 Budget, effective 1992, and repealed by 1994 Budget effective 1996. It restricted the exemption for capital gains on most real estate investments (see repealed definition "non-qualifying real property") to the proportion of calendar months in which the property was owned before March 1992 (and since 1972) to the total number of calendar months in which the property was owned (since 1972). It was repealed because the general exemption under 110.6(3) was eliminated effective February 22, 1994. For 1992-95, read:

"eligible real property gain" of an individual for a taxation year from a disposition of a non-qualifying real property of the individual means the amount determined by the formula

$$A \times \frac{B}{C}$$

where

A   is the individual's capital gain for the year from the disposition,

B   is the number of calendar months in the period that begins with the later of the calendar month in which the property was last acquired by the individual and January 1972 and ends with February 1992, and

C   is the number of calendar months in the period that begins with the later of the calendar month in which the property was last acquired by the individual and January 1972 and ends with the calendar month in which the property was disposed of by the individual;

**"eligible real property loss"** — [Repealed]

**Notes**: Definition "eligible real property loss" added by 1992 Budget, effective 1992, and repealed by 1994 Budget effective 1996. It was the converse of "eligible real property gain" (see Notes to that repealed definition). For 1992-95, read:

"eligible real property loss" of an individual for a taxation year from a disposition of a non-qualifying real property of the individual means the amount determined by the formula

$$A \times \frac{B}{C}$$

where

A   is the individual's capital loss for the year from the disposition,

B   is the number of calendar months in the period that begins with the later of the calendar month in which the property was last acquired by the individual and January 1972 and ends with February 1992, and

C   is the number of calendar months in the period that begins with the later of the calendar month in which the property was last acquired by the individual and January 1972 and ends with the calendar month in which the property was disposed of by the individual;

**"interest in a family farm partnership"** of an individual (other than a trust that is not a personal trust) at any time means an interest owned by the individual at that time in a partnership where

(a) throughout any 24-month period ending before that time, more than 50% of the fair market value of the property of the partnership was attributable to

(i) property that was used by

(A) the partnership,

(B) the individual,

Division C — Computation of Taxable Income    S. 110.6(1) inv

(C) where the individual is a personal trust, a beneficiary of the trust,

(D) a spouse, common-law partner, child or parent of the individual or of a beneficiary referred to in clause (C), or

(E) a corporation a share of the capital stock of which was a share of the capital stock of a family farm corporation of the individual, a beneficiary referred to in clause (C) or a spouse, common-law partner, child or parent of the individual or of a beneficiary referred to in clause (C),

principally in the course of carrying on the business of farming in Canada in which the individual, a beneficiary referred to in clause (C) or a spouse, common-law partner, child or parent of the individual or of a beneficiary referred to in clause (C) was actively engaged on a regular and continuous basis,

(ii) shares of the capital stock or indebtedness of one or more corporations all or substantially all of the fair market value of the property of which was attributable to properties described in subparagraph (iii), or

(iii) properties described in either subparagraph (i) or (ii), and

(b) at that time, all or substantially all of the fair market value of the property of the partnership was attributable to

(i) property that was used principally in the course of carrying on the business of farming in Canada by the partnership or a person referred to in subparagraph (a)(i),

(ii) shares of the capital stock or indebtedness of one or more corporations described in subparagraph (a)(ii), or

(iii) properties described in subparagraph (i) or (ii).

**Related Provisions**: See Related Provisions and Definitions at end of s. 110.6.

**Notes**: This term is used in the definition of "qualified farm property" below (para. (c)).

Subpara. (a)(i) amended by 2000 same-sex partners bill to add reference to "common-law partner", effective for the 2001 and later taxation years, or earlier by election (see Notes to 248(1)"common-law partner").

Definition "interest in a family farm partnership" redrafted by 1992 technical bill, effective 1992. For 1988 to 1991, the substantive differences are: read "property used by" instead of "property that has been used by" in subpara. (a)(i) and delete subparas. (a)(ii) and (b)(ii).

Definition amended by 1991 technical bill, retroactive to the introduction of the definition in 1988. The principal change was to reduce the use-of-assets requirement over a 24-month period from "substantially all" to "more than 50% of the fair market value" of the property. The "all or substantially all" test, now in para. (b), now applies only at the time of the disposition. The CCRA takes the position that "all or substantially all" means 90% or more.

**"investment expense"** of an individual for a taxation year means the total of

(a) all amounts deducted in computing the individual's income for the year from property (except to the extent that the amounts were otherwise taken into account in computing the individual's investment expense or investment income for the year) other than any amounts deducted under

(i) paragraph 20(1)(c), (d), (e), or (e.1) of this Act or paragraph 20(1)(k) of the *Income Tax Act*, chapter 148 of the Revised Statutes of Canada, 1952, in respect of borrowed money that was used by the individual, or that was used to acquire property that was used by the individual,

(A) to make a payment as consideration for an income-averaging annuity contract,

(B) to pay a premium under a registered retirement savings plan, or

(C) to make a contribution to a registered pension plan or a deferred profit sharing plan, or

(ii) paragraph 20(1)(j) or subsection 65(1), 66(4), 66.1(3), 66.2(2) or 66.4(2),

> **Proposed Amendment — 110.6(1)"investment expense"(a)(ii)**
>
> (ii) paragraph 20(1)(j) or subsection 65(1), 66(4), 66.1(3), 66.2(2), 66.21(4) or 66.4(2),
>
> **Application**: The December 21, 2000 draft legislation, subsec. 53(1), will amend subpara. (a)(ii) of the definition "investment expense" in subsec. 110.6(1) to add a reference to subsec. 66.21(4), applicable to taxation years that begin after 2000.
>
> **Technical Notes**: Section 110.6 sets out the rules for calculating an individual's entitlement to the lifetime capital gains exemption. An individual's "investment expense" for a taxation year can result in a lower "cumulative gains limit", and can thereby reduce the individual's entitlement to a deduction under section 110.6. As a consequence of the application of subparagraph (a)(ii) and paragraph (d) of the definition "investment expense" in subsection 110.6(1), 50% of foreign exploration and development expenses deducted under subsection 66(4) in computing an individual's income for a taxation year is added in computing the individual's investment expense for the year in the event that the individual is a "specified member" of the partnership (as defined in subsection 248(1)).
>
> Subparagraph (a)(ii) and paragraph (d) of the definition "investment expense" are amended to extend this treatment of foreign exploration and development expenses to foreign resource expenses, as a consequence of the introduction of section 66.21.

(b) the total of

(i) all amounts deducted under paragraph 20(1)(c), (d), (e), (e.1), (f) or (bb) of this Act or paragraph 20(1)(k) of the *Income Tax Act*, chapter 148 of the Revised Statutes of Canada, 1952, in computing the individual's income for the year from a partnership of which the individual was a specified member in the fiscal period of the partnership ending in the year, and

(ii) all amounts deducted under subparagraph 20(1)(e)(vi) in computing the individual's income for the year in respect of an expense incurred by a partnership of which the individual was a specified member in the fiscal period of the partnership ending immediately before it ceased to exist,

(c) the total of

(i) all amounts (other than allowable capital losses) deducted in computing the individual's income for the year in respect of the individual's share of the amount of any loss of a partnership of which the individual was a specified member in the partnership's fiscal period ending in the year, and

(ii) all amounts each of which is an amount deducted under paragraph 111(1)(e) in computing the individual's taxable income for the year,

(d) 50% of the total of all amounts each of which is an amount deducted under subsection 66(4), 66.1(3), 66.2(2) or 66.4(2) in computing the individual's income for the year in respect of expenses incurred and renounced under subsection 66(12.6), (12.601), (12.62) or (12.64) by a corporation or incurred by a partnership of which the individual was a specified member in the fiscal period of the partnership in which the expense was incurred, and

### Proposed Amendment — 110.6(1) "investment expense" (d)

(d) 50% of the total of all amounts each of which is an amount deducted under subsection 66(4), 66.1(3), 66.2(2), 66.21(4) or 66.4(2) in computing the individual's income for the year in respect of expenses

(i) incurred and renounced under subsection 66(12.6), (12.601), (12.62) or (12.64) by a corporation, or

(ii) incurred by a partnership of which the individual was a specified member in the fiscal period of the partnership in which the expense was incurred, and

**Application**: The December 21, 2000 draft legislation, subsec. 53(2), will amend para. (d) of the definition "investment expense" in subsec. 110.6(1) to read as above, applicable to taxation years that begin after 2000.

**Technical Notes**: See under 110.6(1) "investment expense" (a)(ii).

(e) the total of all amounts each of which is the amount of the individual's loss for the year from

(i) property, or

(ii) renting or leasing a rental property (within the meaning assigned by subsection 1100(14) of the *Income Tax Regulations*) or a property described in Class 31 or 32 of Schedule II to the *Income Tax Regulations*

owned by the individual or by a partnership of which the individual was a member, other than a partnership of which the individual was a specified member in the partnership's fiscal period ending in the year, and

(f) the amount, if any, by which the total of the individual's net capital losses for other taxation years deducted under paragraph 111(1)(b) in computing the individual's taxable income for the year exceeds the amount determined in respect of the individual for the year under paragraph (a) of the description of B in the definition "annual gains limit";

**Notes**: See Notes to 110.6(1) "cumulative net investment loss".

Para. (d) of "investment expense" amended by 1992 Economic Statement, effective for 1992 and later taxation years, to add reference to 66(12.601).

Para. (f) added to "investment expense" by 1992 technical bill, effective 1992.

Definition "investment expense" extensively amended by 1991 technical bill, retroactive to 1988 (the introduction of the definition), with certain grandfathering for the 1988 and 1989 taxation years.

**I.T. Application Rules**: 69 (meaning of "*Income Tax Act*, chapter 148 of the Revised Statutes of Canada, 1952").

**"investment income"** of an individual for a taxation year means the total of

(a) all amounts included in computing the individual's income for the year from property (other than an amount included under subsection 15(2) or paragraph 56(1)(d) of this Act or paragraph 56(1)(d.1) of the *Income Tax Act*, chapter 148 of the Revised Statutes of Canada, 1952), including, for greater certainty, any amount so included under subsection 13(1) in respect of a property any income from which would be income from property (except to the extent that the amount was otherwise taken into account in computing the individual's investment income or investment expense for the year),

(b) all amounts (other than taxable capital gains) included in computing the individual's income for the year in respect of the individual's share of the income of a partnership of which the individual was a specified member in the partnership's fiscal period ending in the year, including, for greater certainty, the individual's share of all amounts included under subsection 13(1) in computing the income of the partnership,

(c) 50% of all amounts included under subsection 59(3.2) in computing the individual's income for the year,

(d) all amounts each of which is the amount of the individual's income for the year from

    (i) a property, or

    (ii) renting or leasing a rental property (within the meaning assigned by subsection 1100(14) of the *Income Tax Regulations*) or a property described in Class 31 or 32 of Schedule II to the *Income Tax Regulations*

owned by the individual or by a partnership of which the individual was a member (other than a partnership of which the individual was a specified member in the partnership's fiscal period ending in the year), including, for greater certainty, any amount included under subsection 13(1) in computing the individual's income for the year in respect of a rental property of the individual or the partnership or in respect of a property any income from which would be income from property,

(e) the amount, if any, by which

    (i) the total of all amounts (other than amounts in respect of income-averaging annuity contracts or annuity contracts purchased under deferred profit sharing plans or plans referred to in subsection 147(15) as revoked plans) included under paragraph 56(1)(d) of this Act or paragraph 56(1)(d.1) of the *Income Tax Act*, chapter 148 of the Revised Statutes of Canada, 1952, in computing the individual's income for the year

exceeds

    (ii) the total of all amounts deducted under paragraph 60(a) in computing the individual's income for the year, and

(f) the amount, if any, by which the total of all amounts included under paragraph 3(b) in respect of capital gains and capital losses in computing the individual's income for the year exceeds the amount determined in respect of the individual for the year for A in the definition "annual gains limit";

**Notes**: See Notes to 110.6(1)"cumulative net investment loss".

Para. (f) added to "investment income" by 1992 technical bill, effective 1992.

Definition "investment income" amended by 1991 technical bill, retroactive to 1988 (the introduction of the definition), with certain grandfathering for 1988 and 1989.

**I.T. Application Rules**: 69 (meaning of "*Income Tax Act*, chapter 148 of the Revised Statutes of Canada, 1952").

## "non-qualifying real property" — [Repealed]

**Notes**: Definition "non-qualifying real property" added by 1992 Budget and amended retroactively by 1993 technical bill, effective 1992, then repealed by 1994 Budget effective 1996. The exemption under 110.6(3) for gains on such property was restricted to the proportion of the gain that accrued in months before March 1992. It was repealed because the general exemption under 110.6(3) was eliminated effective February 22, 1994. For 1992-95, read:

"non-qualifying real property" of an individual (other than a trust that is not a personal trust) means property disposed of after February 1992 by the individual, or a partnership any of the income of which is required to be included in computing the income of the individual, that at the time of its disposition (in this definition referred to as the "determination time") is

    (a) real property, other than

        (i) qualified farm property of the individual,

        (ii) real property owned by the individual or the individual's spouse that was used

            (A) throughout that part of the 24-month period preceding the determination time during which it was owned by the individual or the individual's spouse, or

            (B) throughout all or substantially all of the time in the period preceding the determination time during which it was owned by the individual or the individual's spouse,

    principally in an active business carried on by

            (C) the individual (otherwise than as a member of a partnership),

            (D) where the individual is a personal trust, a preferred beneficiary (within the meaning assigned by subsection 108(1)) under the trust (otherwise than as a member of a partnership),

            (E) a spouse, child or parent of the individual or of a preferred beneficiary described in clause (D) (otherwise than as a member of a partnership),

            (F) a corporation (otherwise than as a member of a partnership) where shares representing all or substantially all of the fair market value of all the issued and outstanding shares of its capital stock were owned by one or more persons described in this subparagraph,

            (G) one or more persons as members of a partnership where interests representing all or substantially all of the fair market value of all partnership interests in the partnership were owned by one or more persons described in this subparagraph, or

            (H) a personal trust (otherwise than as a member of a partnership) where interests representing all or substantially all of the fair market value of all beneficial interests in the trust were owned by one or more persons described in this subparagraph, and

        (iii) real property of the partnership (except where the individual is a specified member of the partnership or, if a taxable capital gain of the individual's spouse from the disposition of property of the partnership would be a taxable capital gain of the individual, the individual's spouse is a specified member of the partnership) that was used

            (A) throughout that part of the 24-month period preceding the determination time during which it was property of the partnership, the individual or the individual's spouse, or

            (B) throughout all or substantially all of the time in the period preceding the determination time during which it was property of the partnership, the individual or the individual's spouse,

    principally in an active business carried on by

            (C) the individual,

            (D) where the individual is a personal trust, a preferred beneficiary (within the meaning assigned by subsection 108(1)) under the trust,

(E) a spouse, child or parent of the individual or of a preferred beneficiary described in clause (D),

(F) a corporation where shares representing all or substantially all of the fair market value of all the issued and outstanding shares of its capital stock were owned by one or more persons described in this subparagraph, or

(G) a personal trust where interests representing all or substantially all of the fair market value of all beneficial interests in the trust were owned by one or more persons described in this subparagraph,

(b) a share of the capital stock of a corporation (other than a qualified small business corporation share of the individual or a share of the capital stock of a family farm corporation of the individual) the fair market value of which is derived principally from real property, other than real property that was used

(i) throughout that part of the 24-month period preceding the determination time during which it was owned by the corporation or by persons described in any of clauses (a)(ii)(C) to (H), or

(ii) throughout all or substantially all of the time in the period preceding the determination time during which it was owned by the corporation or by persons described in any of clauses (a)(ii)(C) to (H),

principally in an active business carried on by the corporation or by persons described in any of clauses (a)(ii)(C) to (H), but not including a share of the capital stock of a corporation the fair market value of which is derived principally from real property owned by another corporation, a partnership or a trust, or any combination thereof, the shares of the capital stock of which, or the interests in which, as the case may be, would, if they were disposed of at the determination time by the individual, not be non-qualifying real property of the individual,

(c) an interest in a partnership (other than an interest in a family farm partnership of the individual) the fair market value of which is derived principally from real property, other than real property that was used

(i) throughout that part of the 24-month period preceding the determination time during which it was property of the partnership or persons described in any of clauses (a)(ii)(C) to (H), or

(ii) throughout all or substantially all of the time in the period preceding the determination time during which it was property of the partnership or persons described in any of clauses (a)(ii)(C) to (H),

principally in an active business carried on by one or more persons as members of the partnership or by persons described in any of clauses (a)(ii)(C) to (H), but not including an interest in a partnership the fair market value of which is derived principally from real property owned by another partnership, a corporation or a trust, or any combination thereof, the shares of the capital stock of which or the interests in which, as the case may be, would, if they were disposed of at the determination time by the individual, not be non-qualifying real property of the individual,

(d) an interest in a trust the fair market value of which is derived principally from real property, other than real property that was used

(i) throughout that part of the 24-month period preceding the determination time during which it was owned by the trust or persons described in any of clauses (a)(ii)(C) to (H), or

(ii) throughout all or substantially all of the time in the period preceding the determination time during which it was owned by the trust or persons described in any of clauses (a)(ii)(C) to (H),

principally in an active business carried on by the trust or by persons described in any of clauses (a)(ii)(C) to (H), but not including an interest in a trust the fair market value of which is derived principally from real property owned by another trust, a corporation or a partnership, or any combination thereof, the shares of the capital stock of which or the interests in which, as the case may be, would, if they were disposed of at the determination time by the individual, not be non-qualifying real property of the individual, or

(e) an interest or an option in respect of property described in any of paragraphs (a) to (d),

and, for the purposes of this definition, an "active business" carried on by a person at any time means any business carried on by the person at that time other than a business (other than a business carried on by a credit union or a business of leasing property that is not real property) the principal purpose of which is to derive income from property (including interest, dividends, rents or royalties), unless the person or, where the person carries on the business as a member of a partnership, the partnership

(f) employs in the business at that time more than 5 individuals on a full-time basis, or

(g) in the course of carrying on the business has managerial, administrative, financial, maintenance or other similar services provided to it at that time and the person or partnership could reasonably be expected to require more than 5 full-time employees if those services had not been so provided;

The CCRA takes the position that "all or substantially all" means 90% or more.

**"qualified farm property"** of an individual (other than a trust that is not a personal trust) at any particular time means a property owned at that time by the individual, the spouse or common-law partner of the individual or a partnership, an interest in which is an interest in a family farm partnership of the individual or the individual's spouse or common-law partner that is

(a) real property that was used by

(i) the individual,

(ii) where the individual is a personal trust, a beneficiary referred to in paragraph 104(21.2)(b) of the trust,

(iii) a spouse, common-law partner, child or parent of a person referred to in subparagraph (i) or (ii),

(iv) a corporation, a share of the capital stock of which is a share of the capital stock of a family farm corporation of an individual referred to in any of subparagraphs (i) to (iii), or

(v) a partnership, an interest in which is an interest in a family farm partnership of an individual referred to in any of subparagraphs (i) to (iii),

in the course of carrying on the business of farming in Canada and, for the purpose of this paragraph, property will not be considered to have been used in the course of carrying on the business of farming in Canada unless

(vi) the property or property for which the property was substituted (in this subparagraph referred to as "the property") was owned by a person who was the individual, a beneficiary referred to in subparagraph (ii) or a spouse, common-law partner, child or parent of the individual or of such a beneficiary, by a personal trust from which the individual acquired the property or by a partnership referred to in subparagraph (v) throughout the period of at least 24 months immediately preceding that time and

(A) in at least 2 years while the property was so owned the gross revenue of such a person, or of a personal trust from which the individual acquired the property, from the farming business carried on in Canada in which the property was principally used and in which such a person or, where the individual is a personal trust, a beneficiary of the trust was actively engaged on a regular and continuous basis exceeded the income of the person from all other sources for the year, or

(B) the property was used by a corporation referred to in subparagraph (iv) or a partnership referred to in subparagraph (v) principally in the course of carrying on the business of farming in Canada throughout a period of at least 24 months during which time the individual, a beneficiary referred to in subparagraph (ii) or a spouse, common-law partner, child or parent of the individual or of such a beneficiary was actively engaged on a regular and continuous basis in the farming business in which the property was used, or

(vii) where the property is a property last acquired by the individual or partnership before June 18, 1987, or after June 17, 1987 under an agreement in writing entered into before that date, the property or property for which the property was substituted (in this subparagraph referred to as "the property") was used by the individual, a beneficiary referred to in subparagraph (ii) or a spouse, common-law partner, child or parent of the individual or of such a beneficiary, a corporation referred to in subparagraph (iv) or a partnership referred to in subparagraph (v) or by a personal trust from which the individual acquired the property principally in the course of carrying on the business of farming in Canada

(A) in the year the property was disposed of by the individual, or

(B) in at least 5 years during which the property was owned by the individual, a beneficiary referred to in subparagraph (ii) or a spouse, common-law partner, child or parent of the individual or of such a beneficiary, by a personal trust from which the individual acquired the property or by a partnership referred to in subparagraph (v),

(b) a share of the capital stock of a family farm corporation of the individual or the individual's spouse or common-law partner,

(c) an interest in a family farm partnership of the individual or the individual's spouse or common-law partner, or

(d) an eligible capital property used by a person or partnership referred to in any of subparagraphs (a)(i) to (v), or by a personal trust from which the individual acquired the property, in the course of carrying on the business of farming in Canada and, for the purpose of this paragraph, eligible capital property

(i) will not be considered to have been used in the course of carrying on the business of farming in Canada unless the conditions set out in subparagraph (a)(vi) or (vii), as the case may be, are met, and

(ii) shall be deemed to include capital property to which paragraph 70(5.1)(b) or 73(3)(d.1) applies;

**Related Provisions**: 14(1.1) — Eligible capital property inclusion deemed to be taxable capital gain for exemption purposes; 80.03(8) — Deemed qualified farm property where capital gain deemed on disposition following debt forgiveness; 108(1)"qualified farm property" — Trusts — "qualified farm property"; 248(5) — Substituted property. See also Related Provisions and Definitions at end of s. 110.6.

**Notes**: Qualified farm property is eligible for the $500,000 exemption under 110.6(2). It was also excluded from the (now repealed) definition of "non-qualifying real property" (see subpara. (a)(i) thereof) and thus not subject to the restrictions on using the exemption in respect of real estate that applied from March 1992 to February 1994.

110.6(1)"qualified farm property" amended by 2000 same-sex partners bill to add reference to "common-law partner", effective for the 2001 and later taxation years, or earlier by election (see Notes to 248(1)"common-law partner").

Subparas. (a)(vi) and (vii) and para. (d) of the definition amended by 1991 technical bill, retroactive to 1988.

**Interpretation Bulletins**: IT-236R4: Reserves — disposition of capital property. See also list at end of s. 110.6.

**"qualified small business corporation share"** of an individual (other than a trust that is not a personal trust) at any time (in this definition referred to as the "determination time") means a share of the capital stock of a corporation that,

(a) at the determination time, is a share of the capital stock of a small business corporation owned by the individual, the individual's spouse or common-law partner or a partnership related to the individual,

(b) throughout the 24 months immediately preceding the determination time, was not owned by anyone other than the individual or a person or partnership related to the individual, and

(c) throughout that part of the 24 months immediately preceding the determination time while it was owned by the individual or a person or partnership related to the individual, was a share of the capital stock of a Canadian-controlled private corporation more than 50% of the fair market value of the assets of which was attributable to

(i) assets used principally in an active business carried on primarily in Canada by the corporation or by a corporation related to it,

(ii) shares of the capital stock or indebtedness of one or more other corporations that were connected (within the meaning of subsection 186(4) on the assumption that each of the other corporations was a "payer corporation" within the meaning of that subsection) with the corporation where

(A) throughout that part of the 24 months immediately preceding the determination time that ends at the time the corporation acquired such a share or indebtedness, the share or indebtedness was not owned by anyone other than the corporation, a person or partnership related to the corporation or a person or partnership related to such a person or partnership, and

(B) throughout that part of the 24 months immediately preceding the determination time while such a share or indebtedness was owned by the corporation, a person or partnership related to the corporation or a person or partnership related to such a person or partnership, it was a share or indebtedness of a Canadian-controlled private corporation more than 50% of the fair market value of the assets of which was attributable to assets described in subparagraph (iii), or

(iii) assets described in either of subparagraph (i) or (ii)

except that

(d) where, for any particular period of time in the 24-month period ending at the determination time, all or substantially all of the fair market value of the assets of a particular corporation that is the corporation or another corporation that was connected with the corporation cannot be attributed to assets described in subparagraph (c)(i), shares or indebtedness of corporations described in clause (c)(ii)(B), or any combination thereof, the reference in clause (c)(ii)(B) to "more than 50%" shall, for the particular period of time, be read as a reference to "all or substantially all" in respect of each other corporation that was connected with the particular corporation and, for the purpose of this paragraph, a corporation is connected with another corporation only where

(i) the corporation is connected (within the meaning of subsection 186(4) on the assumption that the corporation was a "payer corporation" within the meaning of that subsection) with the other corporation, and

(ii) the other corporation owns shares of the capital stock of the corporation and, for the purpose of this subparagraph, the other corporation shall be deemed to own the shares of the capital stock of any corporation that are owned by a corporation any shares of the capital stock of which are owned or are deemed by this subparagraph to be owned by the other corporation,

(e) where, at any time in the 24-month period ending at the determination time, the share was substituted for another share, the share shall be considered to have met the requirements of this definition only where the other share

(i) was not owned by any person or partnership other than a person or partnership described in paragraph (b) throughout the period beginning 24 months before the determination time and ending at the time of substitution, and

(ii) was a share of the capital stock of a corporation described in paragraph (c) throughout that part of the period referred to in subparagraph (i) during which such share was owned by a person or partnership described in paragraph (b), and

(f) where, at any time in the 24-month period ending at the determination time, a share referred to in subparagraph (c)(ii) is substituted for another share, that share shall be considered to meet the requirements of subparagraph (c)(ii) only where the other share

(i) was not owned by any person or partnership other than a person or partnership described in clause (c)(ii)(A) throughout the period beginning 24 months before the determination time and ending at the time of substitution, and

(ii) was a share of the capital stock of a corporation described in paragraph (c) throughout that part of the period referred to in subparagraph (i) during which the share was owned by a person or partnership described in clause (c)(ii)(A);

**Related Provisions**: 80.03(8) — Deemed qualified small business corporation share where capital gain deemed on disposition following debt forgiveness; 108(1)"qualified small business corporation share" — Trusts; 110.6(1.1) — Fair market value of net income stabilization account; 110.6(14) — Various rules of interpretation; 110.6(15) — Value of assets of corporation; 110.6(16) — Personal trust; 248(5) — Substituted property. See also Related Provisions and Definitions at end of s. 110.6.

Division C — Computation of Taxable Income    S. 110.6(1.1)

**Notes**: A qualified small business corporation share is eligible for the $500,000 exemption under 110.6(2.1). While the definition is complex, the basic concept is that: in para. (a), the corporation must be a Canadian-controlled private corporation using substantially all of its assets in carrying on an "active business" (see 248(1)) in Canada (see 248(1)"small business corporation" and 125(7)"Canadian-controlled private corporation"); and in para. (c), for the 2-year period preceding the disposition, more than 50% of the corporation's assets were used in carrying on an active business in Canada. For both tests, shares or debt of other corporations that meet the test can qualify as such assets. When valuing a corporation's assets for this purpose, see 110.6(15).

Under para. (b) of the definition, shares must generally have been held for 2 years to qualify for the exemption. See 110.6(14)(f), which deems new treasury shares to have been held by an unrelated person (and thus not to qualify) unless certain conditions are met.

An agreement to sell the shares to a public corporation or non-resident will not invalidate the shares' eligibility for the exemption. See 110.6(14)(b).

Where a corporation owns an interest in a limited partnership that carries on an active business in Canada, the CCRA will consider that the corporate partner uses its proportionate share of each asset of the partnership for purposes of this definition. See Revenue Canada Round Table, Canadian Tax Foundation 1993 annual conference report, Q. 58.

The CCRA takes the position that "all or substantially all", used in the opening words of para. (d), means 90% or more.

Para. (a) amended by 2000 same-sex partners bill to add reference to "common-law partner", effective for the 2001 and later taxation years, or earlier by election (see Notes to 248(1)"common-law partner").

Definition "qualified small business corporation share" extensively amended by 1991 technical bill, retroactive to dispositions of shares after June 17, 1987 (the introduction of the definition).

**Interpretation Bulletins**: See list at end of s. 110.6.

**Information Circulars**: 88-2, para. 15: General anti-avoidance rule — section 245 of the *Income Tax Act*; 88-2 Supplement, paras. 3, 4: General anti-avoidance rule — section 245 of the *Income Tax Act*.

**Advance Tax Rulings**: ATR-53: Purification of a small business corporation; ATR-55: Amalgamation followed by sale of shares.

**"share of the capital stock of a family farm corporation"** of an individual (other than a trust that is not a personal trust) at any time means a share of the capital stock of a corporation owned by the individual at that time where

(a) throughout any 24-month period ending before that time, more than 50% of the fair market value of the property owned by the corporation was attributable to

(i) property that was used by

(A) the corporation,

(B) the individual,

(C) where the individual is a personal trust, a beneficiary of the trust,

(D) a spouse, common-law partner, child or parent of the individual or of a beneficiary referred to in clause (C), or

(E) a partnership, an interest in which was an interest in a family farm partnership of the individual, a beneficiary referred to in clause (C) or a spouse, common-law partner, child or parent of the individual or of such a beneficiary,

principally in the course of carrying on the business of farming in Canada in which the individual, a beneficiary referred to in clause (C) or a spouse, common-law partner, child or parent of the individual or of such a beneficiary, was actively engaged on a regular and continuous basis,

(ii) shares of the capital stock or indebtedness of one or more corporations all or substantially all of the fair market value of the property of which was attributable to property described in subparagraph (iii), or

(iii) properties described in either subparagraph (i) or (ii), and

(b) at that time, all or substantially all of the fair market value of the property owned by the corporation was attributable to

(i) property that was used principally in the course of carrying on the business of farming in Canada by the corporation or a person or partnership referred to in subparagraph (a)(i),

(ii) shares of the capital stock or indebtedness of one or more corporations all or substantially all of the fair market value of the property of which was attributable to property described in subparagraph (iii), or

(iii) properties described in either subparagraph (i) or (ii).

**Notes**: Subpara. (a)(i) amended by 2000 same-sex partners bill to add reference to "common-law partner", effective for the 2001 and later taxation years, or earlier by election (see Notes to 248(1)"common-law partner").

This term is used in the definition of "qualified farm property" above (para. (b)).

Subpara. (a)(i) of "share of the capital stock of a family farm corporation" amended by 1992 technical bill, effective 1992. For 1988 to 1991, read "property used by" instead of "property that has been used by".

Definition extensively amended by 1991 technical bill, retroactive to 1988 (the introduction of the definition).

The CCRA takes the position that "all or substantially all" means 90% or more.

**Related Provisions [subsec. 110.6(1)]**: 110.6(1.1) — Fair market value of net income stabilization account; 110.6(15) — Value of assets of corporation; 257 — Formula cannot calculate to less than zero. See also Related Provisions and Definitions at end of s. 110.6.

**Advance Tax Rulings**: ATR-56: Purification of a family farm corporation.

**(1.1) Idem** — For the purposes of the definitions "qualified small business corporation share" and "share of the capital stock of a family farm corporation" in subsection (1), the fair market value of a net income stabilization account shall be deemed to be nil.

# S. 110.6(1.1) — Income Tax Act, Part I

**Notes:** 110.6(1.1) added by 1992 technical bill, effective 1991.

**(2) Capital gains deduction — qualified farm property** — In computing the taxable income for a taxation year of an individual (other than a trust) who was resident in Canada throughout the year and who disposed of qualified farm property in the year or a preceding taxation year ending after 1984, there may be deducted such amount as the individual may claim not exceeding the least of

(a) the amount, if any, by which $375,000 exceeds the total of

  (i) the total of all amounts each of which is an amount deducted by the individual under this section in computing the individual's taxable income for a preceding taxation year,

  (ii) where the taxation year ended after 1987, $1/3$ of the total of all amounts each of which is an amount deducted under this section in computing the individual's taxable income for a taxation year ending before 1988, and

  (iii) where the taxation year ended after 1989, $1/8$ of the total of

  (A) all amounts deducted under this section in computing the individual's taxable income for a taxation year ending before 1990 (other than amounts deducted under this section for a taxation year in respect of an amount that was included in computing the individual's income for that year because of subparagraph 14(1)(a)(v)), and

  (B) the amount determined under subparagraph (ii) in respect of the individual for the year,

---

**Proposed Amendment — 110.6(2)(a)**

(a) the amount determined by the formula

$$\$250{,}000 - (A + B + C + D)$$

where

A is the total of all amounts each of which is an amount deducted under this section in computing the individual's taxable income for a preceding taxation year that ended before 1988,

B is the total of all amounts each of which is

  (i) $3/4$ of an amount deducted under this section in computing the individual's taxable income for a preceding taxation year that ended after 1987 and before 1990 (other than amounts deducted under this section for a taxation year in respect of an amount that was included in computing an individual's income for that year because of subparagraph 14(1)(a)(v), or

  (ii) $3/4$ of an amount deducted under this section in computing the individual's taxable income for a preceding taxation

year that began after February 27, 2000 and ended before October 18, 2000,

C is $2/3$ of the total of all amounts each of which is an amount deducted under this section in computing the individual's taxable income

  (i) for a preceding taxation year that ended after 1989 and before February 28, 2000, or

  (ii) in respect of an amount that was included because of subparagraph 14(1)(a)(v) in computing the individual's income for a taxation year that began after 1987 and ended before 1990, and

D is equal to the product obtained when the reciprocal of the fraction in paragraph 38(a) that applied to the taxpayer for a preceding taxation year that began before and included either February 28, 2000 or October 17, 2000 is multiplied by $1/2$ of the amount deducted under this section in computing the individual's taxable income for that preceding year,

**Application:** The December 21, 2000 draft legislation, subsec. 53(3), will amend para. 110.6(2)(a) to read as above, applicable in respect of taxation years that end after February 27, 2000 except that, in computing an individual's taxable income for a taxation year that includes either February 28, 2000 or October 17, 2000, the amount determined by the formula in para. 110.6(2)(a), as amended, is deemed to be equal to the amount determined under that formula (without reference to this application) multiplied by twice the fraction in para. 38(a), as amended [by the December 21, 2000 draft legislation], that applies to the taxpayer for that year.

**Technical Notes:** Subsection 110.6(2) provides a deduction from income in computing the taxable income of taxpayer in respect of taxable capital gains from the disposition of qualified farm property.

Paragraph 110.6(2)(a) determines the unused portion of an individual's lifetime capital gains exemption limit in respect of capital gains realized on dispositions of qualified farm property. The paragraph is amended as a consequence of the reduction of the inclusion rate for capital gains from 3/4 to 1/2, and applies to taxation years that end after February 27, 2000.

Amended subsection 110.6(2)(a)

- decreases the lifetime taxable capital gains exemption limit from $375,000 to $250,000 to reflect the reduction of the inclusion rate for capital gains from 3/4 to 1/2,

- reduces the limit by the deductions claimed in prior years that ended before 1988, when the taxable capital gains inclusion rate was 1/2,

- reduces the limit by 3/4 of the deductions claimed in prior years that ended after 1987 and before 1988, and for taxation years that began after February 27, 2000 and ended before October 18, 2000 when the inclusion rate for capital gains was 2/3,

- reduces the limit by 8/9 of the deductions claimed in taxation years that ended after 1989 and before February 27, 2000, when the inclusion rate for capital gains was 3/4,

Division C — Computation of Taxable Income         S. 110.6(2)(d)

- reduces the limit by 8/9 of the deductions claimed in taxation years that ended after 1987 and before 1990 in respect of amounts included in income under subparagraph 14(1)(a)(v) when the inclusion rate was 3/4, and
- reduces the limit by the product obtained by multiplying the deductions claimed by the individual in the 2000 taxation year by the fraction obtained by multiplying 1/2 by the reciprocal of the fraction in amended paragraph 38(a) that applies to the taxpayer for the year.

These amendments apply in respect of taxation years that end after February 27, 2000 except that, in computing an individual's taxable income for the taxation year that includes either February 28, 2000 or October 17, 2000, the amount determined by the formula in paragraph 110.6(2)(a) is to equal the amount determined under that formula multiplied by twice the fraction in amended paragraph 38(a) that applies to the taxpayer for that year. These modifications are required in order to reflect the capital gains/losses rate for the year.

Example 1

Assume

Paul has in prior taxation years reported the following:

| Taxation Year | Capital Gain from the Disposition of Qualified Farm Property | Amount deducted under subsection 110.6(2) |
|---|---|---|
| 1985 | $50,000 | $25,000 |
| 1988 | $100,000 | $66,667 |
| 1991 | $100,000 | $75,000 |

No other amounts have been deducted by Paul under section 110.6.

In January, 2000, Paul realizes a $300,000 capital gain from the disposition of qualified farm property. The fraction required to be used by Paul under amended paragraph 38(a) for his 2000 taxation year is 3/4. What amount can be deducted by Paul under subsection 110.6(2) for his 2000 taxation year assuming paragraph 110.6(2)(a) applies?

Determination

Paragraph 110.6(2)(a) requires Paul to determine an amount using the formula $250,000 − (A + B + C + D)$.

Because Paul's 2000 taxation year includes either February 28, 2000 or October 17, 2000, the coming-into-force provision that applies to amended paragraph 110.6(2)(a) requires Paul to multiply the amount determined by the formula by 1.5 (i.e., twice the fraction that applies for the year: 3/4 × 2).

The amount of the unused deduction limit determined by the formula equals $125,000 since

$A = $25,000,

$B = $50,000 (i.e., 3/4 × 66,667),

$C = $50,000 (i.e., 2/3 × $75,000), and

$D = $0

For the taxation year that includes either February 28, 2000 or October 17, 2000, the unused capital gains exemption limit determined under the formula ($125,000) is multiplied by 1.5 to produce an unused deduction limit of $187,500.

The $187,500 is the amount determined for Paul under paragraph 110.6(2)(a) for his 2000 taxation year.

Example 2

Heather realized a $400,000 capital gain in her 2000 taxation year from the disposition of qualified farm property and deducted $300,000 in respect of that gain under section 110.6. The fraction in paragraph 38(a) that was applicable to Heather for her 2000 taxation year was 3/4. In 2001, Heather realizes a $100,000 capital gain from the disposition of another qualified farm property. Heather has not realized any other capital gains. How much is she entitled to deduct under subsection 110.6(2) assuming paragraph 110.6(2)(a) applies?

Determination

Paragraph 110.6(2)(a) requires Heather to determine an amount using the formula $250,000 − (A + B + C + D)$.

The amount determined by the formula equals $50,000 since

$A = $0,

$B = $0,

$C = $0, and

$D = $200,000 (4/3 × 1/2 × $300,000).

The deductions permitted under section 110.6 for Heather's 2000 and 2001 taxation years allow her to claim deductions in respect of taxable capital gains derived from $500,000 of capital gains realized from the disposition of qualified farm property.

**Notice of Ways and Means Motion, Economic Statement, October 18, 2000**: (11) That for the 2000 and subsequent taxation years,

. . .

(d) the halved inclusion rate for certain ecological gifts, the rules for determining the capital gains deduction under section 110.6 of the Act and any other rules of determination under the Act be modified to take into account the inclusion rate for the year.

**Notice of Ways and Means Motion, federal budget, February 28, 2000**: (9) That for the 2000 and subsequent taxation years,

. . .

(e) the rules for determining the capital gains deduction under section 110.6 of the Act and any other rules of determination under the Act take into account, where appropriate, the change in determination of a taxpayer's taxable capital gain and allowable capital loss from a disposition of a property.

(b) the individual's cumulative gains limit at the end of the year,

(c) the individual's annual gains limit for the year, and

(d) the amount that would be determined in respect of the individual for the year under paragraph 3(b) in respect of capital gains and capital losses if the only properties referred to in that

**S. 110.6(2)(d)**          Income Tax Act, Part I

paragraph were qualified farm properties disposed of by the individual after 1984.

**Related Provisions**: 14(1.1) — Eligible capital property inclusion deemed to be taxable capital gain for exemption purposes; 40(1.1) — extended capital gains reserve where farm property disposed of to child; 40(3.1) — Deemed disposition where negative ACB of partnership interest creates deemed gain; 73(3) — Intergenerational rollover of farm property; 110.6(4) — Maximum deduction; 110.6(5) — Individual deemed resident in Canada throughout year; 110.6(6) — Failure to report gain; 110.6(7)–(11) — Restrictions; 110.6(13) — Meaning of "amount determined under para. 3(b)"; 110.6(17) — Order of deduction; 257 — Formula cannot calculate to less than zero. See additional Related Provisions and Definitions at end of s. 110.6.

**Notes**: The $250,000 deduction offsets an underlying $500,000 of capital gains on qualified farm property, since ½ of the gain is included in income (see 38(a)).

The federal budget of February 22, 1994 announced that the $500,000 exemptions for small business shares and farms would be reviewed to determine whether replacement measures would be more appropriate. The budget of February 27, 1995 announced that this review had been completed and no changes would be made to these exemptions. The Mintz Committee report released in April 1998 recommended that they be eliminated.

Note that 73(3) and (4) provide a rollover that may be an alternative to this exemption when transferring a farm to one's children or grandchildren.

A taxpayer claiming a large deduction under 110.6(2.1) may run into Alternative Minimum Tax under 127.5–127.55, since 30% (formerly the untaxed 1/4) of the gain is considered a tax preference for AMT purposes (see 127.52(1)(d)(i)).

Parenthetical exclusion in 110.6(2)(a)(iii)(A) added by 1992 technical bill, effective 1990.

110.6(2)(d) amended by 1994 Budget, for 1994 and 1995 only, to add the words "otherwise than because of an election made under subsection (19)". The extra words ensure that the election to use the $100,000 capital gains exemption cannot trigger a gain against which the $500,000 exemption is claimed. Effective 1996, the quoted words are superfluous and are deleted.

See also Notes to 110.6(2.1).

**Interpretation Bulletins**: See list at end of s. 110.6.

**Advance Tax Rulings**: ATR-28: Redemption of capital stock of family farm corporation; ATR-56: Purification of a family farm corporation.

**Forms**: T657: Calculation of capital gains deduction on all capital property. See also list at end of s. 110.6.

**(2.1) Capital gains deduction — qualified small business corporation shares** — In computing the taxable income for a taxation year of an individual (other than a trust) who was resident in Canada throughout the year and who disposed of a share of a corporation in the year or a preceding taxation year and after June 17, 1987 that, at the time of disposition, was a qualified small business corporation share of the individual, there may be deducted such amount as the individual may claim not exceeding the least of

(a) the amount, if any, by which $375,000 exceeds the total of

(i) the total of all amounts each of which is an amount deducted by the individual under this section in computing the individual's taxable income for a preceding taxation year,

(ii) where the taxation year ended after 1987, the amount determined under subparagraph (2)(a)(ii) in respect of the individual for the year, and

(iii) where the taxation year ended after 1989, the amount determined under subparagraph (2)(a)(iii) in respect of the individual for the year,

> **Proposed Amendment — 110.6(2.1)(a)**
>
> (a) the amount determined by the formula in paragraph (2)(a) in respect of the individual for the year,
>
> **Application**: The December 21, 2000 draft legislation, subsec. 53(4), will amend para. 110.6(2.1)(a) to read as above, applicable to taxation years that end after February 27, 2000.
>
> **Technical Notes**: Subsection 110.6(2.1) provides a deduction in computing the taxable income of taxpayer in respect of taxable capital gains from the disposition of qualified small business corporation shares.
>
> Paragraph 110.6(2.1)(a) is amended as a consequence of the reduction of the inclusion rate for capital gains from 3/4 to 1/2, and applies to taxation years that end after February 27, 2000. Amended subsection 110.6(2.1)(a) refers to the amount referred to in proposed new paragraph 110.6(2)(a).
>
> **Notice of Ways and Means Motions, Economic Statement, October 18, 2000 and federal budget, February 28, 2000**: [See under 110.6(2)(a) — ed.]

(b) the amount, if any, by which the individual's cumulative gains limit at the end of the year exceeds the amount deducted under subsection (2) in computing the individual's taxable income for the year,

(c) the amount, if any, by which the individual's annual gains limit for the year exceeds the amount deducted under subsection (2) in computing the individual's taxable income for the year, and

(d) the amount that would be determined in respect of the individual for the year under paragraph 3(b) (other than an amount included in determining the amount in respect of the individual under paragraph (2)(d)) in respect of capital gains and capital losses if the only properties referred to in paragraph 3(b) were qualified small business corporation shares disposed of by the individual after June 17, 1987.

**Related Provisions**: 40(1.1)(c) — extended capital gains reserve where small business corporation disposed of to child; 48.1 — Deemed disposition to trigger exemption before small business corporation goes public; 69(11)(a)(i) — Exception to rule deeming proceeds at FMV where CG deduction claimed after incorporation or dissolution of partnership; 110.6(4) — Maximum deduction; 110.6(5) — Individual deemed resident in Canada throughout year; 110.6(6) — Failure to report gain; 110.6(7)–(11) — Restrictions; 110.6(13) — Meaning of "amount determined under para. 3(b)". See additional Related Provisions and Definitions at end of s. 110.6.

**Notes**: The $250,000 deduction offsets an underlying $500,000 of capital gains on qualified small business corporation shares, since ½ of the gain is included in income (see 38(a)).

See Notes to 110.6(1)"qualified small business corporation share" for the conditions that shares must meet to qualify for the exemption. Note also other conditions: not having CNIL (see Notes to 110.6(1)"cumulative net investment loss"); not having past ABILs (see Notes to 39(9)); being resident in Canada (but see 110.6(5)); reporting the gain and claiming the deduction (see 110.6(6)); and various others.

The federal budget of February 22, 1994 announced that the $500,000 exemptions for small business shares and farms would be reviewed to determine whether replacement measures would be more appropriate. The budget of February 27, 1995 announced that this review had been completed and no changes would be made to these exemptions. The Mintz Committee report released in April 1998 recommended that they be eliminated.

A taxpayer claiming a large deduction under 110.6(2.1) may run into Alternative Minimum Tax under 127.5–127.55, since 30% (formerly the untaxed 1/4) of the gain is considered a tax preference for AMT purposes (see 127.52(1)(d)(i)).

110.6(2.1)(d) amended by 1995-97 technical bill, effective for 1996 and later taxation years, to change "in that paragraph" to "in paragraph 3(b)". This change was made to eliminate a possible ambiguity.

110.6(2.1)(d) amended by 1994 Budget, for 1994 and 1995 only, to add the words "otherwise than because of an election made under subsection (19)". The extra words ensure that the election to use the $100,000 capital gains exemption cannot trigger a gain against which the $500,000 exemption is claimed. Effective 1996, the quoted words are superfluous and are deleted.

**Interpretation Bulletins**: See list at end of s. 110.6.

**Information Circulars**: 88-2, para. 15: General anti-avoidance rule — section 245 of the *Income Tax Act*; 88-2 Supplement, paras. 3, 4: General anti-avoidance rule — section 245 of the *Income Tax Act*.

**Advance Tax Rulings**: ATR-42: Transfer of shares; ATR-53: Purification of a small business corporation; ATR-55: Amalgamation followed by sale of shares.

**Forms**: T657: Calculation of capital gains deduction on all capital property. See also list at end of s. 110.6.

**(3) [Repealed]**

**Related Provisions**: 110.6(4) — Maximum deduction; 110.6(5) — Individual deemed resident in Canada throughout year; 110.6(6) — Failure to report gain; 110.6(7)–(11) — Restrictions; 110.6(17) — Order of deduction 110.6(19) — Election to trigger gains accrued to February 22/94. See additional Related Provisions and Definitions at end of s. 110.6.

**Notes**: 110.6(3) repealed by 1994 Budget, effective 1996. It provided a general exemption against up to $100,000 of capital gains, expressed as a $75,000 deduction against taxable capital gains (3/4 of a capital gain was then included in income — see 38(a)). It was usable to February 22, 1994 for regular gains, and for 1994 and 1995 for deemed gains due to an election under 110.6(19), which can be made up to 2 years late under 110.6(26). (The election normally applies to 1994, but in certain cases relating to a business, it applies to the taxation year that includes February 22, 1994, which for some taxpayers ends in 1995.)

For 1994 and 1995, read:

(3) Capital gains deduction — other property — In computing the taxable income for a taxation year of an individual (other than a trust) who was resident in Canada throughout the year and who disposed of property (other than property the capital gain or capital loss from the disposition of which is included in determining an amount under paragraph (2)(d)

or (2.1)(d) there may be deducted such amount as the individual claims, not exceeding the least of

(a) the amount, if any, by which $75,000 exceeds the total of

(i) the total of all amounts each of which is an amount deducted by the individual under this subsection in computing the individual's taxable income for a preceding taxation year,

(ii) where the taxation year ended after 1987, 1/3 of the total of all amounts each of which is an amount deducted under this subsection in computing the individual's taxable income for a taxation year ending before 1988, and

(iii) where the taxation year ended after 1989, 1/8 of the total of

(A) all amounts deducted under this subsection in computing the individual's taxable income for a taxation year ending before 1990 (other than amounts deducted under this subsection for a taxation year in respect of an amount that was included in computing the individual's income for that year because of subparagraph 14(1)(a)(v)), and

(B) the amount determined under subparagraph (ii) in respect of the individual for the year,

(b) the amount, if any, by which the individual's cumulative gains limit at the end of the year exceeds the total of all amounts each of which is an amount deducted under subsection (2) or (2.1) in computing the individual's taxable income for the year, and

(c) the amount, if any, by which the individual's annual gains limit for the year exceeds the total of all amounts each of which is an amount deducted under subsection (2) or (2.1) in computing the individual's taxable income for the year.

For 1990-1993, read the second parenthetical exclusion in the opening words as "(other than a disposition of property to which subsection (2) or (2.1) applies)".

Parenthetical exclusion in 110.6(3)(a)(iii)(A) added by 1992 technical bill, effective 1990.

**Advance Tax Rulings**: ATR-34: Preferred beneficiary's election.

**(4) Maximum capital gains deduction** — Notwithstanding subsections (2) and (2.1), the total amount that may be deducted under this section in computing an individual's taxable income for a taxation year shall not exceed the amount, if any, by which $375,000 exceeds the total of

(a) the total of all amounts each of which is an amount deducted by the individual under this section in computing the individual's taxable income for a preceding taxation year,

(b) where the taxation year ended after 1987, the amount determined under subparagraph (2)(a)(ii) in respect of the individual for the year, and

(c) where the taxation year ended after 1989, the amount determined under subparagraph (2)(a)(iii) in respect of the individual for the year.

**Proposed Amendment — 110.6(4)**

**(4) Maximum capital gains deduction** — Notwithstanding subsection (2) and (2.1), the total amount that may be deducted under this section in

**S. 110.6(4)**      Income Tax Act, Part I

computing an individual's income for a taxation year shall not exceed the amount determined by the formula in paragraph (2)(a) in respect of the individual for the year.

**Application**: The December 21, 2000 draft legislation, subsec. 53(5), will amend subsec. 110.6(4) to read as above, applicable to taxation years that end after February 27, 2000.

**Technical Notes**: Subsection 110.6(4) provides an overall lifetime taxable capital gains exemption limit for an individual.

The subsection is amended to adopt the limit provided for in paragraph 110.6(2)(a). Under that paragraph, the individual is limited to $250,000 of deductions in respect of taxable capital gains — which is determined by multiplying $500,000 of capital gains by the one-half inclusion rate for capital gains.

The amendment to subsection 110.6(4) is consequential on the reduction of the inclusion rate for capital gains from 3/4 to 1/2.

**Notes**: 110.6(4) ensures that the total of all exemptions claimed — $500,000 for farm property, $500,000 for small business shares and $100,000 generally until February 22, 1994 — cannot exceed $500,000.

Reference in opening words of 110.6(4) to "subsections (2), (2.1) and (3)" changed to "subsections (2) and (2.1)" by 1994 Budget, effective 1996. The change reflects the elimination of the general $100,000 exemption in 110.6(3).

**(5) Deemed resident in Canada** — Where an individual was resident in Canada at any time in a particular taxation year and throughout

    (a) the immediately preceding taxation year, or

    (b) the immediately following taxation year,

for the purposes of subsections (2) and (2.1) the individual shall be deemed to have been resident in Canada throughout the particular year.

**Related Provisions**: 14(8) — Parallel rule for cumulative eligible capital recapture. See additional Related Provisions and Definitions at end of s. 110.6.

**Notes**: See Notes to 14(8).

Reference in closing words of 110.6(5) to "subsections (2), (2.1) and (3)" changed to "subsections (2) and (2.1)" by 1994 Budget, effective 1996. The change reflects the elimination of the general $100,000 exemption in 110.6(3).

**(6) Failure to report capital gain** — Notwithstanding subsections (2) and (2.1), where an individual has a capital gain for a taxation year from the disposition of a capital property and knowingly or under circumstances amounting to gross negligence

    (a) fails to file a return of the individual's income for the year within one year after the day on or before which the individual is required to file a return of the individual's income for the year pursuant to section 150, or

    (b) fails to report the capital gain in the individual's return of income for the year required to be filed pursuant to section 150,

no amount may be deducted under this section in respect of the capital gain in computing the individual's taxable income for that or any subsequent taxation year and the burden of establishing the facts justifying the denial of such an amount under this section is on the Minister.

**Notes**: The "knowingly or gross negligence" test is the same wording as is used for penalties under 163(2), so there is extensive case law interpreting it.

Reference in opening words of 110.6(6) to "subsections (2), (2.1) and (3)" changed to "subsections (2) and (2.1)" by 1994 Budget, effective 1996. The change reflects the elimination of the general $100,000 exemption in 110.6(3).

**(7) Deduction not permitted** — Notwithstanding subsections (2) and (2.1), where an individual has a capital gain for a taxation year from the disposition of property as part of a series of transactions or events

    (a) to which subsection 55(2) would, but for paragraph 55(3)(b), apply, or

    (b) in which any property is acquired by a corporation or partnership for consideration that is significantly less than the fair market value of the property at the time of acquisition (other than an acquisition as the result of an amalgamation or merger of corporations or the winding-up of a corporation or partnership or a distribution of property of a trust in satisfaction of all or part of a corporation's capital interest in the trust),

no amount in respect of that capital gain shall be deducted under this section in computing the individual's taxable income for the year.

**Notes**: Reference in opening words of 110.6(7) to "subsections (2), (2.1) and (3)" changed to "subsections (2) and (2.1)" by 1994 Budget, effective 1996. The change reflects the elimination of the general $100,000 exemption in 110.6(3).

**Advance Tax Rulings**: ATR-56: Purification of a family farm corporation.

**(8) Deduction not permitted** — Notwithstanding subsections (2) and (2.1), where an individual has a capital gain for a taxation year from the disposition of a property and it can reasonably be concluded, having regard to all the circumstances, that a significant part of the capital gain is attributable to the fact that dividends were not paid on a share (other than a prescribed share) or that dividends paid on such a share in the year or in any preceding taxation year were less than 90% of the average annual rate of return thereon for that year, no amount in respect of that capital gain shall be deducted under this section in computing the individual's taxable income for the year.

**Related Provisions**: 110.6(9) — Average annual rate of return; 183.1(7) — Tax on corporate distributions — application of s. 110.6(8). See also Related Provisions and Definitions at end of s. 110.6.

**Notes**: For detailed analysis of this rule, see Mark Brender, "The *De Minimis* Dividend Test under Subsection 110.6(8)", 41(4) *Canadian Tax Journal* 808-827 and 41(5) 1034-1044 (1993).

Reference in 110.6(8) to "subsections (2), (2.1) and (3)" changed to "subsections (2) and (2.1)", and "may reasonably be concluded" changed to "can reasonably be concluded", by 1994 Budget, effective 1996. The change reflects the elimination of the general $100,000 exemption in 110.6(3).

Division C — Computation of Taxable Income                    S. 110.6(12)(b)

**Regulations**: 6205 (prescribed share).

**(9) Average annual rate of return** — For the purpose of subsection (8), the average annual rate of return on a share (other than a prescribed share) of a corporation for a taxation year is the annual rate of return by way of dividends that a knowledgeable and prudent investor who purchased the share on the day it was issued would expect to receive in that year, other than the first year after the issue, in respect of the share if

(a) there was no delay or postponement of the payment of dividends and no failure to pay dividends in respect of the share;

(b) there was no variation from year to year in the amount of dividends payable in respect of the share (other than where the amount of dividends payable is expressed as an invariant percentage of or by reference to an invariant difference between the dividend expressed as a rate of interest and a generally quoted market interest rate); and

(c) the proceeds to be received by the investor on the disposition of the share are the same amount the corporation received as consideration on the issue of the share.

**Regulations**: 6205 (prescribed share).

**(10)** [Repealed under former Act]

**Notes**: 110.6(10) repealed by 1988 tax reform, effective 1988. It prevented the use of extensions or renewal of options to defer capital gains during the phase-in of the exemption from 1985 to 1988.

**(11) Where deduction not permitted** — Where it is reasonable to consider that one of the main reasons for an individual acquiring, holding or having an interest in a partnership or trust (other than an interest in a personal trust) or a share of an investment corporation, mortgage investment corporation or mutual fund corporation, or for the existence of any terms, conditions, rights or other attributes of the interest or share, is to enable the individual to receive or have allocated to the individual a percentage of any capital gain or taxable capital gain of the partnership, trust or corporation that is larger than the individual's percentage of the income of the partnership, trust or corporation, as the case may be, notwithstanding any other provision of this Act,

(a) no amount may be deducted under this section by the individual in respect of any such gain allocated or distributed to the individual after November 21, 1985; and

(b) where the individual is a trust, any such gain allocated or distributed to it after November 21, 1985 shall not be included in computing its eligible taxable capital gain (within the meaning assigned by subsection 108(1)).

**(12) Spousal trust deduction** — Notwithstanding any other provision of this Act, a trust described in paragraph 104(4)(a) or (a.1) (other than a trust that elected under subsection 104(5.3)) may, in computing its taxable income for its taxation year that includes the day determined under paragraph 104(4)(a) or (a.1), as the case may be, in respect of the trust, deduct under this section an amount equal to the least of

**Proposed Amendment — 110.6(12) opening words**

**(12) Trust deduction** — Notwithstanding any other provision of this Act, a trust described in paragraph 104(4)(a) or (a.1) (other than a trust that elected under subsection 104(5.3), an *alter ego* trust or a joint partner trust) may, in computing its taxable income for its taxation year that includes the day determined under paragraph 104(4)(a) or (a.1), as the case may be, in respect of the trust, deduct under this section an amount equal to the least of

**Application**: Bill C-43 (First Reading September 20, 2000), s. 56, will amend the opening words of subsec. 110.6(12) to read as above, applicable to 2000 *et seq.*

**Technical Notes**: Subsection 110.6(12) of the Act generally allows spousal trusts access to the unused lifetime capital gains exemption of the beneficiary spouse, for the taxation year of the spousal trust in which the beneficiary spouse dies. Under paragraph 104(4)(a), there is generally a deemed disposition for a post-1971 partner trust once the beneficiary spouse dies.

Subsection 110.6(12) is amended to ensure that it does not apply to *alter ego* trusts or joint spousal trusts (as newly defined in subsection 248(1)). This amendment is consequential to the extension of paragraph 104(4)(a) to provide for deemed dispositions for *alter ego* trusts and joint partner trusts.

(a) the amount, if any, by which the eligible taxable capital gains (within the meaning assigned by subsection 108(1)) of the trust for that year exceeds the amount, if any, by which

(i) the total of all amounts each of which is the amount, if any, determined under paragraph (b) or (d) of the definition "cumulative gains limit" in subsection (1) in respect of the taxpayer's spouse or common-law partner at the end of the taxation year in which the spouse or common-law partner died

exceeds

(ii) the amount if any, determined under paragraph (a) of the definition "cumulative gains limit" in subsection (1) in respect of the taxpayer's spouse or common-law partner at the end of the taxation year in which the spouse or common-law partner died,

(b) the amount, if any, that would be determined in respect of the trust for that year under paragraph 3(b) in respect of capital gains and capital losses if the only properties referred to in that paragraph were qualified farm properties disposed of by it after 1984 and qualified small business corporation shares disposed of by it after June 17, 1987, and

(c) the amount, if any, by which $375,000 exceeds the total of

(i) the total of all amounts each of which is an amount deducted by the taxpayer's spouse or common-law partner under this section for the taxation year in which the spouse or common-law partner died or a preceding taxation year, and

(ii) the total of all amounts each of which is an amount determined under subparagraph (2)(a)(ii) or (iii) in respect of the taxpayer's spouse or common-law partner for the taxation year in which the spouse or common-law partner died.

**Proposed Amendment — 110.6(12)(c)**

(c) the amount, if any, by which the amount determined by the formula in paragraph (2)(a) in respect of the taxpayer's spouse or common-law partner for the taxation year in which that spouse or common-law partner died exceeds the amount deducted under this section for that taxation year by that spouse or common-law partner.

**Application**: The December 21, 2000 draft legislation, subsec. 53(6), will amend para. 110.6(12)(c) to read as above, applicable to taxation years that end after February 27, 2000, except that the amount determined under para. 110.6(12)(c), as amended, in computing a trust's taxable income for its particular taxation year that includes either February 28, 2000 or October 17, 2000 is deemed to be equal to the amount determined under that para. (without reference to this application) multiplied by the quotient obtained when the fraction in para. 38(a), as amended [by the December 21, 2000 draft legislation], that applies to the taxpayer's spouse or common-law partner for the taxation year in which the spouse or common-law partner died is divided by the fraction in para. 38(a), as amended, that applies to the trust for its particular taxation year.

**Technical Notes**: Subsection 110.6(12) generally provides for a deduction, in computing the taxable income of a trust for the benefit of a spouse or common-law partner for the year of the trust in which the spouse or common-law partner dies, of an amount equal to the lesser of the unused lifetime capital gains exemption limit of the deceased and the amount of the taxable gains of the trust determined under that subsection.

Paragraph 110.6(12)(c) is amended to adopt the limit provided for in paragraph 110.6(2)(a) in respect of the deceased spouse or common-law partner for the year of death, minus any amounts deducted by that person for the year of death.

The amendment to paragraph 110.6(12)(c) is consequential on the reduction of the inclusion rate for capital gains from 3/4 to 1/2 [see 38(a) — ed.].

The amendment applies to taxation years that end after February 27, 2000, except that the amount determined under amended paragraph 110.6(12)(c) in computing a trust's taxable income for a taxation year that includes either February 28, 2000 or October 17, 2000 is to equal to the amount determined under that paragraph multiplied by the quotient obtained when the fraction in amended paragraph 38(a) that applies to the taxpayer's spouse or common-law partner for the taxation year in which the spouse or common-law partner died is divided by the fraction in amended paragraph 38(a) that applies to the trust for its taxation year. These modifications are required in order to reflect the capital gains/losses rate for the year.

**Related Provisions**: 104(21.1) — Beneficiary's taxable capital gain from trust; 110.6(13) — Meaning of "amount determined under para. 3(b)". See additional Related Provisions and Definitions at end of s. 110.6.

**Notes**: 110.6(12)(a) and (c) amended by 2000 same-sex partners bill to add reference to "common-law partner", effective for the 2001 and later taxation years, or earlier by election (see Notes to 248(1)"common-law partner").

110.6(12)(b) amended by 1994 Budget, the current version effective for 1997 and later taxation years. For taxation years that end from February 22, 1994 through 1996, read:

(b) the total of

(i) the least of

(A) the amount, if any, determined in respect of the trust for that year under paragraph 3(b) in respect of capital gains and losses,

(A.1) the amount, if any, that would be determined in respect of the trust for that year under paragraph 3(b) in respect of capital gains and losses if

(I) the only properties referred to in that paragraph were properties (other than properties referred to in subparagraph (ii)) disposed of by it after 1984 and before February 23, 1994,

(II) the trust's capital gains and capital losses for the year from dispositions of non-qualifying real property of the trust were equal to its eligible real property gains and eligible real property losses, respectively, for that year from those dispositions,

(III) no amount were included under paragraph 3(b) in respect of a capital gain of the trust that resulted from an election made under subsection (19) by another trust unless the trust was a beneficiary under the other trust on February 22, 1994, and

(IV) except for the purpose of determining the trust's share of a taxable capital gain of a partnership for the partnership's fiscal period that includes February 22, 1994 or a taxable capital gain of the trust resulting from a designation made under section 104 by another trust for the other trust's taxation year that includes that day, in determining the trust's taxable capital gain for a taxation year that begins after that day from the disposition of a property (other than a qualified small business corporation share or qualified farm property), this Act were read without reference to subparagraphs 40(1)(a)(ii) and 44(1)(e)(ii), and

(B) the amount, if any, by which $75,000 exceeds the total of

(I) the total of all amounts each of which is an amount deducted under subsection (3) in computing the taxable income of the taxpayer's spouse for the taxation year in which the spouse died or a preceding taxation year, and

(II) the total of all amounts each of which is an amount determined under subparagraph (3)(a)(ii) or (iii) in respect of the taxpayer's spouse for the taxation year in which the spouse died, and

(ii) the amount, if any, that would be determined in respect of the trust for that year under paragraph 3(b) in respect of capital gains and losses if the only properties referred to in that paragraph were qualified farm properties disposed of by it after 1984 and qualified small business corporation shares disposed of by it after June 17, 1987; and

For previous taxation years since 1993, ignore 110.6(12)(b)(i)(A.1)(III) and (IV).

Opening words of 110.6(12) amended by 1992 technical bill, effective 1993, to reflect the addition of 104(4)(a.1) and 104(5.3).

110.6(12)(b)(i)(A) and (A.1)(II) added by 1992 technical bill, effective 1992. For 1988 to 1991, read subpara. (b)(i) as containing only subcl. (A.1)(I) and cl. (B).

**Forms:** T3 Sched. 5: Beneficiary spouse information and spousal trust's capital gains deduction.

**(13) Determination under para. 3(b)** — For the purposes of this section, the amount determined under paragraph 3(b) in respect of an individual for a period throughout which the individual was not resident in Canada is nil.

**Related Provisions:** 74.2(2) — Deemed gain or loss under attribution rules; 104(21), (21.2) — Beneficiary's taxable capital gain from trust. See additional Related Provisions and Definitions at end of s. 110.6.

**(14) Related persons, etc. [miscellaneous rules re shares]** — For the purposes of the definition "qualified small business corporation share" in subsection (1),

(a) a taxpayer shall be deemed to have disposed of shares that are identical properties in the order in which the taxpayer acquired them;

(b) in determining whether a corporation is a small business corporation or a Canadian-controlled private corporation at any time, a right referred to in paragraph 251(5)(b) shall not include a right under a purchase and sale agreement relating to a share of the capital stock of a corporation;

(c) a personal trust shall be deemed

(i) to be related to a person or partnership for any period throughout which the person or partnership was a beneficiary of the trust, and

(ii) in respect of shares of the capital stock of a corporation, to be related to the person from whom it acquired those shares where, at the time the trust disposed of the shares, all of the beneficiaries (other than registered charities) of the trust were related to that person or would have been so related if that person were living at that time;

(d) a partnership shall be deemed to be related to a person for any period throughout which the person was a member of the partnership;

(e) where a corporation acquires shares of a class of the capital stock of another corporation from any person, it shall be deemed in respect of those shares to be related to the person where all or substantially all the consideration received by that person from the corporation in respect of those shares was common shares of the capital stock of the corporation;

(f) shares issued after June 13, 1988 by a corporation to a particular person or partnership shall be deemed to have been owned immediately before their issue by a person who was not related to the particular person or partnership unless the shares were issued

(i) as consideration for other shares,

(ii) as part of a transaction or series of transactions in which the person or partnership disposed of property to the corporation that consisted of

(A) all or substantially all the assets used in an active business carried on by that person or the members of that partnership, or

(B) an interest in a partnership all or substantially all the assets of which were used in an active business carried on by the members of the partnership, or

(iii) as payment of a stock dividend; and

(g) where, immediately before the death of an individual, or, in the case of a deemed transfer under subsection 248(23), immediately before the time that is immediately before the death of an individual, a share would, but for paragraph (a) of the definition "qualified small business corporation share" in subsection (1), be a qualified small business corporation share of the individual, the share shall be deemed to be a qualified small business corporation share of the individual if it was a qualified small business corporation share of the individual at any time in the 12-month period immediately preceding the death of the individual.

**Related Provisions:** 54.2 — Sale of shares after incorporation of business; 110.6(16) — Personal trust; 248(1) — "business" does not include adventure or concern under 110.6(14)(f); 248(5)(b) — Effect of stock dividend; 248(12) — Identical properties. See additional Related Provisions and Definitions at end of 110.6.

**Notes:** The conditions in 110.6(14)(f)(ii)(A) are consistent with the rule in 54.2 that lets an individual incorporate a business, immediately sell the shares and claim the exemption under 110.6(2.1).

110.6(14)(c)(ii) and (g) added by 1991 technical bill, retroactive to 1988.

The CCRA takes the position that "all or substantially all", used in 110.6(14)(e) and (f)(ii), means 90% or more.

110.6(14)(f)(iii) added by 1995-97 technical bill, retroactive to dispositions of shares after June 17, 1987 (i.e., to the introduction of 110.6(14)).

**Advance Tax Rulings:** ATR-55: Amalgamation followed by sale of shares.

**(15) Value of assets of corporations** — For the purposes of the definitions "qualified small business corporation share" and "share of the capital stock of a family farm corporation" in subsection (1), the definition "share of the capital stock of a family farm corporation" in subsection 70(10) and the definition "small business corporation" in subsection 248(1),

(a) where a person (in this subsection referred to as the "insured"), whose life was insured under an insurance policy owned by a particular corporation, owned shares of the capital stock (in this subsection referred to as the "subject shares") of the particular corporation, any corporation connected with the particular corporation or with which the particular corporation is connected or any corporation connected with any such corporation or with which any such corporation is connected (within the meaning of subsection 186(4) on the assumption that the corporation referred to in this subsection was a payer corporation within the meaning of that subsection),

(i) the fair market value of the life insurance policy shall, at any time before the death of the insured, be deemed to be its cash surrender value (within the meaning assigned by subsection 148(9)) at that time, and

(ii) the total fair market value of assets (other than assets described in subparagraph (c)(i), (ii) or (iii) of the definition "qualified small business corporation share" in subsection (1), subparagraph (b)(i), (ii) or (iii) of the definition "share of the capital stock of a family farm corporation" in subsection (1) or paragraph (a), (b) or (c) of the definition "small business corporation" in subsection 248(1), as the case may be) of any of those corporations that are

(A) the proceeds, the right to receive the proceeds or attributable to the proceeds, of the life insurance policy of which the particular corporation was a beneficiary, and

(B) used, directly or indirectly, within the 24-month period beginning at the time of the death of the insured or, where written application therefor is made by the particular corporation within that period, within such longer period as the Minister considers reasonable in the circumstances, to redeem, acquire or cancel the subject shares owned by the insured immediately before the death of the insured,

not in excess of the fair market value of the assets immediately after the death of the insured, shall, until the later of

(C) the redemption, acquisition or cancellation, and

(D) the day that is 60 days after the payment of the proceeds under the policy,

be deemed not to exceed the cash surrender value (within the meaning assigned by subsection 148(9)) of the policy immediately before the death of the insured; and

(b) the fair market value of an asset of a particular corporation that is a share of the capital stock or indebtedness of another corporation with which the particular corporation is connected shall be deemed to be nil and, for the purpose of this paragraph, a particular corporation is connected with another corporation only where

(i) the particular corporation is connected (within the meaning assigned by paragraph (d) of the definition "qualified small business corporation share" in subsection (1)) with the other corporation, and

(ii) the other corporation is not connected (within the meaning of subsection 186(4) as determined without reference to subsection 186(2) and on the assumption that the other corporation is a payer corporation within the meaning of subsection 186(4)) with the particular corporation,

except that this paragraph applies only in determining whether a share of the capital stock of another corporation with which the particular corporation is connected is a qualified small business corporation share or a share of the capital stock of a family farm corporation and in determining whether the other corporation is a small business corporation.

**Notes**: 110.6(15)(b) added, and opening words of 110.6(15) amended to apply for purposes of 70(10), by 1993 technical bill, effective for dispositions in 1992 or later. The heading for 110.6(15) was formerly "Life insurance policy of corporation".

110.6(15) added by 1991 technical bill, effective for dispositions after June 17, 1987. However, for dispositions before July 13, 1990, instead of "within the 24-month period commencing at the time of the death of the insured or, where written application therefor is made by the particular corporation within that period, within such longer period" in 110.6(15)(b)(ii), read "before July 13, 1991 or, where written application therefor is made by the particular corporation before that date, before that date".

**(16) Personal trust** — For the purposes of the definition "qualified small business corporation share" in subsection (1) and of paragraph (14)(c), a personal trust shall be deemed to include a trust described in subsection 7(2).

**Notes**: 110.6(16) added by 1991 technical bill, effective for dispositions after June 17, 1987.

**(17) Order of deduction** — For the purpose of clause (2)(a)(iii)(A), amounts deducted under this section in computing an individual's taxable income for a taxation year that ended before 1990 shall be deemed to have first been deducted in respect of amounts that were included in computing the individual's income under this Part for the year because of subparagraph 14(1)(a)(v) before being deducted in respect of any other amounts that were included in computing the individual's income under this Part for the year.

**Notes**: 110.6(17) added by 1992 technical bill, effective 1990. It is intended to ensure that individuals who have not claimed the maximum exemption in 1990 and later years do not have their exemption inappropriately reduced as a result of the change in the capital gains inclusion rate after 1988-89.

Reference in 110.6(17) to "clauses (2)(a)(iii)(A) and (3)(a)(iii)(A)" changed to "clause (2)(a)(iii)(A)", and "under this Part" added in two places, by 1994 Budget, effective 1996. The change reflects the elimination of the general $100,000 exemption in 110.6(3).

**(18)** [Repealed]

**Notes**: 110.6(18) repealed by 1994 Budget, effective 1996, due to the elimination of the general $100,000 exemption in 110.6(3). For 1992–95, read:

> (18) Eligible real property gains and losses — For the purposes of the definitions "eligible real property gain" and "eligible real property loss" in subsection (1),
>
> (a) an individual shall be deemed to have disposed of identical properties in the order in which they were acquired;
>
> (b) where paragraph 74.2(2)(b) applies for the purposes of this section to deem a property disposed of by another person to have been disposed of by an individual in a taxation year, the individual shall be deemed to have last acquired that property at the time at which the other person last acquired it and to have disposed of it at the time at which the other person disposed of it;
>
> (c) where an individual is deemed by subsection 70(6), (9), (9.1), (9.2) or (9.3), 73(1), (3) or (4), 98(3) or (5) or 107(2) to have acquired property for an amount that is not greater than the adjusted cost base to the person or partnership from whom it was acquired, the individual shall be deemed to have acquired the property at the time it was last acquired by the person or partnership;
>
> (d) the number of calendar months in a period shall be determined without reference to any such month that is in a taxation year of the individual or the individual's spouse for which the property in respect of which the eligible real property gain or eligible real property loss is computed was a principal residence (within the meaning assigned by section 54) of the individual or the individual's spouse; and
>
> (e) where the eligible real property gain or eligible real property loss of an individual is computed in respect of a gain or loss from a disposition of property by a partnership, the individual shall be deemed to have last acquired the property at the time it was last acquired by the partnership and to have disposed of the property at the time it was disposed of by the partnership except that, where the individual had disposed of that property to the partnership and an election had been filed under subsection 97(2) in respect of that disposition, the individual shall be deemed to have last acquired the property at the time it was last acquired by the individual before that disposition if the amount agreed on in that election in respect of the property was not greater than the adjusted cost base to the individual of the property at the time of that disposition.

110.6(18) added by 1992 Budget/technical bill, effective 1992.

**(19) Election for property owned on February 22, 1994** — Subject to subsection (20), where an individual (other than a trust) or a personal trust (each of which is referred to in this subsection and subsections (20) to (29) as the "elector"), elects in prescribed form to have the provisions of this subsection apply in respect of

(a) a capital property (other than an interest in a trust referred to in any of paragraphs (f) to (j) of the definition "flow-through entity" in subsection 39.1(1)) owned at the end of February 22, 1994 by the elector, the property shall be deemed, except for the purposes of sections 7 and 35 and subparagraph 110(1)(d.1)(ii),

(i) to have been disposed of by the elector at that time for proceeds of disposition equal to the greater of

(A) the amount determined by the formula

$$A - B$$

where

A is the amount designated in respect of the property in the election, and

B is the amount, if any, that would, if the disposition were a disposition for the purpose of section 7 or 35, be included under that section as a result of the disposition in computing the income of the elector, and

(B) the adjusted cost base to the elector of the property immediately before the disposition, and

(ii) to have been reacquired by the elector immediately after that time at a cost equal to

(A) where the property is an interest in or a share of the capital stock of a flow-through entity (within the meaning assigned by subsection 39.1(1)) of the elector, the cost to the elector of the property immediately before the disposition referred to in subparagraph (i),

(B) where an amount would, if the disposition referred to in subparagraph (i) were a disposition for the purpose of section 7 or 35, be included under that section as a result of the disposition in computing the income of the elector, the lesser of

(I) the elector's proceeds of disposition of the property determined under subparagraph (i), and

(II) the amount determined by the formula

$$A - B$$

where

A is the amount, if any, by which the fair market value of the property at that time exceeds the amount that would, if the disposition referred to in subparagraph (i) were a disposition for the purpose of section 7 or 35, be included under that section as a result of the disposition in computing the income of the elector, and

B is the amount that would be determined by the formula in subclause (C)(II) in respect of the property if clause (C) applied to the property, and

(C) in any other case, the lesser of

(I) the designated amount, and

(II) the amount, if any, by which the fair market value of the property at that time exceeds the amount determined by the formula

$$A - 1.1B$$

where

A is the designated amount, and

B is the fair market value of the property at that time;

(b) a business carried on by the elector (otherwise than as a member of a partnership) on February 22, 1994,

(i) the amount that would be determined under subparagraph 14(1)(a)(v) at the end of that day in respect of the elector if

(A) all the eligible capital property owned at that time by the elector in respect of the business were disposed of by the elector immediately before that time for proceeds of disposition equal to the amount designated in the election in respect of the business, and

(B) the fiscal period of the business ended at that time

shall be deemed to be a taxable capital gain of the elector for the taxation year in which the fiscal period of the business that includes that time ends from the disposition of a particular property and, for the purposes of this section, the particular property shall be deemed to have been disposed of by the elector at that time, and

(ii) for the purpose of paragraph 14(3)(b), the amount of the taxable capital gain determined under subparagraph (i) shall be deemed to have been claimed, by a person who does not deal at arm's length with each person or partnership that does not deal at arm's length with the elector, as a deduction under this section in respect of a disposition at that time of the eligible capital property; and

(c) an interest owned at the end of February 22, 1994 by the elector in a trust referred to in any of paragraphs (f) to (j) of the definition "flow-through entity" in subsection 39.1(1), the elector shall be deemed to have a capital gain for the year from the disposition on February 22, 1994 of property equal to the lesser of

(i) the total of amounts designated in elections made under this subsection by the elector in respect of interests in the trust, and

(ii) $^4/_3$ of the amount that would, if all of the trust's capital properties were disposed of at the end of February 22, 1994 for proceeds of disposition equal to their fair market value at that time and that portion of the trust's capital gains and capital losses or its net taxable capital gains, as the case may be, arising from the dispositions as can reasonably be considered to represent the elector's share thereof were allocated to or designated in respect of the elector, be the increase in the annual gains limit of the elector for the 1994 taxation year as a result of the dispositions.

**Related Provisions**: 13(7)(e.1) — Depreciable capital property; 13(21)"undepreciated capital cost"F — No recapture of CCA on election; 14(1)(a)(v)D, 14(5)"cumulative eligible capital"B, 14(9) — Cumulative eligible capital; 39.1 — Holdings in flow-through entities; 40(2)(b)A, D, 40(7.1) — Principal residence; 49(3.2) — Options; 53(1)(r) — Increase in ACB immediately before disposing of all interests or shares of a flow-through entity; 54"adjusted cost base"(c) — ACB adjustment of flow-through entity preserved through disposition and reacquisition; 84.1(2.01)(a) — Share deemed acquired not at arm's length (cost base preserved) for purposes of later non-arm's length sale; 107(1.1)(a) — Cost of capital interest in a trust when election made; 110.6(20) — Application of election; 110.6(21) — Non-qualifying real property; 110.6(23) — Partnership interest; 110.6(24)–(30) — Time for election and late-filed elections; 257 — Formulas cannot calculate to less than zero; Reg. 2800(2) — Extended deadline for preferred beneficiary election. See additional Related Provisions and Definitions at end of s. 110.6.

**Notes**: 110.6(19) added by 1994 Budget, effective 1994. It provided a special election to crystallize accrued capital gains for purposes of using up one's $100,000 capital gains exemption, which was available under 110.6(3) only for dispositions by February 22, 1994. The election applies to the 1994 return in most cases, and thus was generally due by April 30, 1995. The election could be made up to 2 years late if a penalty was paid; see 110.6(26)–(30).

A list of share prices on Canadian stock exchanges on February 22, 1994, to facilitate making the election, appears at the beginning of the 6th and 7th editions of this book.

**I.T. Application Rules**: 20(1)(c) (where depreciable property owned since before 1972); 26(29) (following election, property deemed not owned at end of 1971 so ITAR 26(3) will not apply).

**Interpretation Bulletins**: IT-120R5: Principal residence; IT-217R: Depreciable property owned on December 31, 1971; IT-379R: Employees profit sharing plans — allocations to beneficiaries.

**I.T. Technical News**: No. 7 (principal residence and the capital gains election).

**Forms**: T4138: Capital gains election package [guide]; T4142: Capital gains election package for seniors [guide].

**(20) Application of subsec. (19)** — Subsection (19) applies to a property or to a business, as the case may be, of an elector only if

(a) where the elector is an individual (other than a trust),

(i) its application to all of the properties in respect of which elections were made under that subsection by the elector or a spouse or common-law partner of the elector and to all the

Division C — Computation of Taxable Income    S. 110.6(22)(b)

businesses in respect of which elections were made under that subsection by the elector

(A) would result in an increase in the amount deductible under subsection (3) in computing the taxable income of the elector or a spouse or common-law partner of the elector, and

(B) in respect of each of the 1994 and 1995 taxation years,

(I) where no part of the taxable capital gain resulting from an election by the elector is included in computing the income of a spouse or common-law partner of the elector, would not result in the amount determined under paragraph (3)(a) for the year in respect of the elector being exceeded by the lesser of the amounts determined under paragraphs (3)(b) and (c) for the year in respect of the elector, and

(II) where no part of the taxable capital gain resulting from an election by the elector is included in computing the income of the elector, would not result in the amount determined under paragraph (3)(a) for the year in respect of a spouse or common-law partner of the elector being exceeded by the lesser of the amounts determined under paragraphs (3)(b) and (c) for the year in respect of the spouse or common-law partner,

(ii) the amount designated in the election in respect of the property exceeds $^{11}/_{10}$ of its fair market value at the end of February 22, 1994, or

(iii) the amount designated in the election in respect of the business is $1.00 or exceeds $^{11}/_{10}$ of the fair market value at the end of February 22, 1994 of all the eligible capital property owned at that time by the elector in respect of the business; and

(b) where the elector is a personal trust, its application to all of the properties in respect of which an election was made under that subsection by the elector would result in

(i) an increase in the amount deemed by subsection 104(21.2) to be a taxable capital gain of an individual (other than a trust) who was a beneficiary under the trust at the end of February 22, 1994 and resident in Canada at any time in the individual's taxation year in which the trust's taxation year that includes that day ends, or

(ii) where subsection (12) applies to the trust for the trust's taxation year that includes that day, an increase in the amount deductible under that subsection in computing the trust's taxable income for that year.

**Notes**: 110.6(20) amended by 2000 same-sex partners bill to add reference to "common-law partner", effective for the 2001 and later taxation years, or earlier by election (see Notes to 248(1)"common-law partner"). (Since this subsection has not been operative since 1997, this amendment was pointless.)

110.6(20) added by 1994 Budget, effective 1994.

### (21) Effect of election on non-qualifying real property 
— Where an elector is deemed by subsection (19) to have disposed of a non-qualifying real property,

(a) in computing the elector's taxable capital gain from the disposition, there shall be deducted the amount determined by the formula

$$0.75(A - B)$$

where

A is the elector's capital gain from the disposition, and

B is the elector's eligible real property gain from the disposition; and

(b) in determining at any time after the disposition the capital cost to the elector of the property where it is a depreciable property and the adjusted cost base to the elector of the property in any other case (other than where the property was at the end of February 22, 1994 an interest in or a share of the capital stock of a flow-through entity within the meaning assigned by subsection 39.1(1)), there shall be deducted $^4/_3$ of the amount determined under paragraph (a) in respect of the property.

**Related Provisions**: 13(7)(e)(i)(B)(IV) — Reduction in capital cost reflected for CCA purposes; 53(2)(u) — Reduction in adjusted cost base; 127.52(1)(h.1) — Calculation for purposes of minimum tax; 257 — Formula cannot calculate to less than zero. See additional Related Provisions and Definitions at end of s. 110.6.

**Notes**: 110.6(21) added by 1994 Budget, effective 1994. It ensures that making the election under 110.6(19) on non-qualifying real property (investment real estate) will not require tax to be paid on the portion of the gain that is not eligible for the exemption (under the rules in effect since March 1992). Thus, the tax on the ineligible portion of the gain will be deferred until a later disposition of the property.

### (22) Adjusted cost base 
— Where an elector is deemed by paragraph (19)(a) to have reacquired a property, there shall be deducted in computing the adjusted cost base to the elector of the property at any time after the reacquisition the amount, if any, by which

(a) the amount determined by the formula

$$A - 1.1B$$

where

A is the amount designated in the election under subsection (19) in respect of the property, and

B is the fair market value of the property at the end of February 22, 1994

exceeds

(b) where the property is an interest in or a share of the capital stock of a flow-through entity

**S. 110.6(22)(b)**      Income Tax Act, Part I

(within the meaning assigned by subsection 39.1(1)), ⁴/₃ of the taxable capital gain that would have resulted from the election if the amount designated in the election were equal to the fair market value of the property at the end of February 22, 1994 and, in any other case, the fair market value of the property at the end of February 22, 1994.

**Related Provisions**: 14(9) — Further effects of excessive election; 53(2)(v) — Reduction in ACB; 110.6(19)(a)(ii)(C)(II), 110.6(28) — Further effects of excessive election; 257 — Formula cannot calculate to less than zero See additional Related Provisions and Definitions at end of s. 110.5.

**Notes**: 110.6(22) added by 1994 Budget, effective 1994. It grinds down the adjusted cost base of property where the amount designated under a 110.6(19) election exceeds 110% of the fair market value on February 22, 1994. This effectively imposes a penalty on guessing too high as to the value of the property.

**(23) Disposition of partnership interest** — Where an elector is deemed by subsection (19) to have disposed of an interest in a partnership, in computing the adjusted cost base to the elector of the interest immediately before the disposition

(a) there shall be added the amount determined by the formula

$$(A - B) \times \frac{C}{D} + E$$

where

A   is the total of all amounts each of which is the elector's share of the partnership's income (other than a taxable capital gain from the disposition of a property) from a source or from sources in a particular place for its fiscal period that includes February 22, 1994,

B   is the total of all amounts each of which is the elector's share of the partnership's loss (other than an allowable capital loss from the disposition of a property) from a source or from sources in a particular place for that fiscal period,

C   is the number of days in the period that begins the first day of that fiscal period and ends February 22, 1994,

D   is the number of days in that fiscal period, and

E   is ⁴/₃ of the amount that would be determined under paragraph 3(b) in computing the elector's income for the taxation year in which that fiscal period ends if the elector had no taxable capital gains or allowable capital losses other than those arising from dispositions of property by the partnership that occurred before February 23, 1994; and

(b) there shall be deducted the amount that would be determined under paragraph (a) if the formula in that paragraph were read as

$$(B - A) \times \frac{C}{D} - E$$

**Related Provisions**: 53(1)(e)(xii) — Addition to ACB; 53(2)(c)(xi) — Reduction in ACB; 257 — Formulas cannot calculate to less than zero. See additional Related Provisions and Definitions at end of s. 110.6.

**Notes**: 110.6(23) added by 1994 Budget, effective 1994. This provision was 110.6(22) in the draft legislation of August 8, 1994.

**(24) Time for election** — An election made under subsection (19) shall be filed with the Minister

(a) where the elector is an individual (other than a trust),

(i) if the election is in respect of a business of the elector, on or before the individual's filing-due date for the taxation year in which the fiscal period of the business that includes February 22, 1994 ends, and

(ii) in any other case, on or before the individual's balance-due day for the 1994 taxation year; and

(b) where the elector is a personal trust, on or before March 31 of the calendar year following the calendar year in which the taxation year of the trust that includes February 22, 1994 ends.

**Related Provisions**: 110.6(26)–(30) — Late and amended elections. See additional Related Provisions and Definitions at end of s. 110.6.

**Notes**: 110.6(24)(a)(i) amended by 1995 Budget, effective 1995. For 1994, read: "balance-due day" instead of "filing-due date" (see definitions of both terms in 248(1)). The change results from the filing deadline for individuals carrying on business (and their spouses) having been extended from April 30 to June 15 (see 150(1)(d)).

110.6(24) added by 1994 Budget, effective 1994. This provision was 110.6(23) in the draft legislation of August 8, 1994.

**(25) Revocation of election** — Subject to subsection (28), an elector may revoke an election made under subsection (19) by filing a written notice of the revocation with the Minister before 1998.

**Related Provisions**: 104(14.01) — Revocation of preferred beneficiary election at same time; 104(21.01) — Revocation of trust's taxable capital gains designation at same time. See additional Related Provisions and Definitions at end of s. 110.6.

**Notes**: 110.6(25) added by 1994 Budget, effective 1994. This provision was 110.6(24) in the draft legislation of August 8, 1994.

**I.T. Technical News**: No. 7 (principal residence and the capital gains election).

**(26) Late election** — Where an election made under subsection (19) is filed with the Minister after the day (referred to in this subsection and subsections (27) and (29) as the "election filing date") on or before which the election is required by subsection (24) to have been filed and on or before the day that is 2 years after the election filing date, the election shall be deemed for the purposes of this section (other than subsection (29)) to have been filed on the election filing date if an estimate of the penalty in respect of the election is paid by the elector when the election is filed with the Minister.

**Related Provisions**: 104(14.01) — Late preferred beneficiary election filed at same time; 104(21.01) — Late filing of trust's taxable capital gains designation at same time; 110.6(29) — Amount of penalty. See additional Related Provisions and Definitions at end of s. 110.6.

**Notes**: 110.6(26) added by 1994 Budget, effective 1994. This provision was 110.6(25) in the draft legislation of August 8, 1994.

**(27) Amended election** — Subject to subsection (28), an election under subsection (19) in respect of a property or a business is deemed to be amended and the election, as amended, is deemed for the purpose of this section (other than subsection (29)) to have been filed on the election filing date if

(a) an amended election in prescribed form in respect of the property or the business is filed with the Minister before 1998; and

(b) an estimate of the penalty, if any, in respect of the amended election is paid by the elector when the amended election is filed with the Minister.

**Related Provisions**: 104(14.01) — Amended preferred beneficiary election filed at same time; 104(21.01) — Amendment of trust's taxable capital gains designation at same time; 110.6(26) — Election filing date; 110.6(29) — Amount of penalty. See additional Related Provisions and Definitions at end of s. 110.6.

**Notes**: 110.6(27) added by 1994 Budget, effective 1994, and amended by 1995-97 technical bill retroactive to its introduction to add "for the purposes of this section (other than subsection (29))". This provision was 110.6(26) in the draft legislation of August 8, 1994.

**(28) Election that cannot be revoked or amended** — An election under subsection (19) cannot be revoked or amended where the amount designated in the election exceeds 11/10 of

(a) if the election is in respect of a property other than an interest in a partnership, the fair market value of the property at the end of February 22, 1994;

(b) if the election is in respect of an interest in a partnership, the greater of $1 and the fair market value of the property at the end of February 22, 1994; and

(c) if the election is in respect of a business, the greater of $1 and the fair market value at the end of February 22, 1994 of all the eligible capital property owned at that time by the elector in respect of the business.

**Related Provisions**: 14(9), 110.6(19)(a)(ii)(C)(II), 110.6(22)(a)B — Further effects of excessive election; 40(3)(a) — Partnership interest can have negative ACB. See additional Related Provisions and Definitions at end of s. 110.6.

**Notes**: 110.6(28) added by 1994 Budget, effective 1994, and amended by 1995-97 technical bill retroactive to its introduction, effectively to add what is now para. (b). (Para. (c) was formerly (b), and "other than an interest in a partnership" was not in para. (a).) This provision was 110.6(27) in the draft legislation of August 8, 1994.

**(29) Amount of penalty** — The penalty in respect of an election to which subsection (26) or (27) applies is the amount determined by the formula

$$\frac{A \times B}{300}$$

where

A is the number of months each of which is a month all or part of which is during the period that begins the day after the election filing date and ends the day the election or amended election is filed with the Minister; and

B is the total of all amounts each of which is the taxable capital gain of the elector or a spouse or common-law partner of the elector that results from the application of subsection (19) to the property or the business in respect of which the election is made less, where subsection (27) applies to the election, the total of all amounts each of which would, if the Act were read without reference to subsections (20) and (27), be the taxable capital gain of the elector or a spouse or common-law partner of the elector that resulted from the application of subsection (19) to the property or the business.

**Related Provisions**: 110.6(26) — Election filing date; 220(3.1) — Waiver of penalty by CCRA. See additional Related Provisions and Definitions at end of s. 110.6.

**Notes**: 110.6(29) amended by 2000 same-sex partners bill to add reference to "common-law partner", effective for the 2001 and later taxation years, or earlier by election (see Notes to 248(1)"common-law partner"). (Since this subsection has not been operative since 1997, this amendment was pointless.)

110.6(29) added by 1994 Budget, effective 1994. This provision was 110.6(28) in the draft legislation of August 8, 1994.

**(30) Unpaid balance of penalty** — The Minister shall, with all due dispatch, examine each election to which subsection (26) or (27) applies, assess the penalty payable and send a notice of assessment to the elector who made the election, and the elector shall pay forthwith to the Receiver General the amount, if any, by which the penalty so assessed exceeds the total of all amounts previously paid on account of that penalty.

**Notes**: 110.6(30) added by 1994 Budget, effective 1994. This provision was 110.6(29) in the draft legislation of August 8, 1994.

**Related Provisions [s. 110.6]**: 14(1)(a)(v) — Excess exceeding eligible capital amount deemed to be taxable capital gain; 39(9) — Reduction of business investment loss; 39(11) — Bad debt recovery; 39(13) — Repayment of assistance; 40(3) — Deemed gain when ACB adjusted below nil; 42 — Deemed loss on warranty; 70(2) — Rollovers on death; 98(1)(c) — Disposition of partnership property; 111(8)"non-capital loss"A:E — Carryforward of exemption deduction as non-capital loss; 111(8)"pre-1986 capital loss balance"C, D, E — Balance reduced by exemption claims; 111.1 — Order of applying provisions; 131(1)(b) — Election re capital gains dividend.

**Definitions [s. 110.6]**: "*alter ego*" trust", "active business" — 248(1); "adjusted cost base" — 54, 248(1); "allowable business investment loss" — 38(c), 248(1); "amount" — 248(1); "annual gains limit" — 110.6(1); "assessment" — 248(1); "borrowed money", "business" — 248(1); "calendar year" — *Interpretation Act* 37(1)(a); "Canada" — 255; "Canadian-controlled private corporation" — 125(7), 248(1); "capital gain" — 39(1)(a), 248(1); "capital interest" — in a trust 108(1), 248(1); "capital loss" — 39(1)(b), 248(1); "capital property" — 54, 248(1); "carrying on business" — 253; "child" — 70(10), 110.6(1), 252(1); "class of shares" — 248(6); "common-law partner", "common share" — 248(1); "corporation" — 248(1), *Interpretation Act* 35(1); "credit union" — 137(6), 248(1); "cumulative gains limit", "cumulative net investment loss" — 110.6(1); "deferred profit sharing plan" — 147(1),

248(1); "dividend" — 248(1); "election filing date" — 110.6(26); "elector" — 110.6(19); "eligible capital property" — 54, 248(1); "eligible real property loss" — 110.6(1); "employee", "farming" — 248(1); "filing-due date" — 150(1), 248(1); "fiscal period" — 249(2)(b), 249.1; "gross revenue" — 248(1); "identical" — 248(12); "income-averaging annuity contract" — 61(4), 248(1); "individual", "insurance policy" — 248(1); "interest in a family farm partnership" — 110.6(1); "investment corporation" — 130(3)(a), 248(1); "investment expense", "investment income" — 110.6(1); "joint partner trust", "Minister" — 248(1); "mortgage investment corporation" — 130.1(6), 248(1); "mutual fund corporation" — 131(8), 248(1); "mutual fund trust" — 132(6)–(7), 132.2(1)(q), 248(1); "net capital loss" — 111(8), 248(1); "net income stabilization account" — 110.6(1.1), 248(1); "non-qualifying real property" — 110.6(1), 248(1); "parent" — 252(2); "partnership" — see Notes to 96(1); "person" — 248(1); "personal trust" — 110.6(16), 248(1); "prescribed" — 248(1); "prescribed stock exchange" — Reg. 3200, 3201; "property" — 248(1); "qualified farm property", "qualified small business corporation share" — 110.6(1); "registered charity", "registered pension plan" — 248(1); "registered retirement savings plan" — 146(1), 248(1); "related" — 110.6(14)(c)–(e), 251(2); "related segregated fund trust" — 138.1(1)(a); "resident in Canada" — 110.6(5), 250; "series of transactions" — 248(10); "share" — 248(1); "share of the capital stock of a family farm corporation" — 110.6(1); "small business corporation" — 110.6(14)(b), 248(1); "specified member" — 248(1); "stock dividend" — 248(1); "substituted property" — 248(5); "taxable capital gain" — 38(a), 248(1); "taxable income" — 2(2), 248(1); "taxation year" — 249; "taxpayer" — 248(1); "testamentary trust" — 108(1), 248(1); "trust" — 104(1), 248(1), (3); "writing" — *Interpretation Act* 35(1).

**Interpretation Bulletins [s. 110.6]**: IT-120R5: Principal residence; IT-123R6: Transactions involving eligible capital property; IT-236R4: Reserves — disposition of capital property; IT-242R: Retired partners; IT-268R3: *Inter vivos* transfer of farm property to child; IT-268R4: *Inter vivos* transfer of farm property to child; IT-278R2: Death of a partner or of a retired partner; IT-281R2: Elections on single payments from a deferred profit-sharing plan; IT-330R: Dispositions of capital property subject to warranty, covenant, etc.; IT-369R: Attribution of trust income to settlor; IT-381R3: Trusts — capital gains and losses and the flow-through of taxable capital gains to beneficiaries; IT-395R: Foreign tax credit — foreign-source capital gains and losses; IT-442R: Bad debts and reserves for doubtful debts; IT-451R: Deemed disposition and acquisition on ceasing to be or becoming resident in Canada; IT-504R2: Visual artists and writers.

**Forms [s. 110.6]**: T1 Sched. 3: Capital gains (or losses); T3 Sched. 3: Eligible taxable capital gains; T657: Calculation of capital gains deduction (if disposed of farm property or small business shares); T657A: Calculation of capital gains deduction on other property; T936: Calculation of cumulative net investment loss; T1161: List of properties by an emigrant of Canada.

## 110.7 (1) Residing in prescribed zone [northern Canada deduction] — Where, throughout a period (in this section referred to as the "qualifying period") of not less than 6 consecutive months beginning or ending in a taxation year, a taxpayer who is an individual has resided in one or more particular areas each of which is a prescribed northern zone or prescribed intermediate zone for the year and files for the year a claim in prescribed form, there may be deducted in computing the taxpayer's taxable income for the year

(a) the total of all amounts each of which is the product obtained by multiplying the specified percentage for a particular area for the year in which the taxpayer so resided by an amount received, or the value of a benefit received or enjoyed, in the year by the taxpayer in respect of the taxpayer's employment in the particular area by a person with whom the taxpayer was dealing at arm's length in respect of travel expenses incurred by the taxpayer or another individual who was a member of the taxpayer's household during the part of the year in which the taxpayer resided in the particular area, to the extent that

(i) the amount received or the value of the benefit, as the case may be,

(A) does not exceed a prescribed amount in respect of the taxpayer for the period in the year in which the taxpayer resided in the particular area,

(B) is included and is not otherwise deducted in computing the taxpayer's income for the year or any other taxation year, and

(C) is not included in determining an amount deducted under subsection 118.2(1) for the year or any other taxation year,

(ii) the travel expenses were incurred in respect of trips made in the year by the taxpayer or another individual who was a member of the taxpayer's household during the part of the year in which the taxpayer resided in the particular area, and

(iii) neither the taxpayer nor a member of the taxpayer's household is at any time entitled to a reimbursement or any form of assistance (other than a reimbursement or assistance included in computing the income of the taxpayer or the member) in respect of travel expenses to which subparagraph (ii) applies; and

(b) the lesser of

(i) 20% of the taxpayer's income for the year, and

(ii) the total of all amounts each of which is the product obtained by multiplying the specified percentage for a particular area for the year in which the taxpayer so resided by the total of

(A) $7.50 multiplied by the number of days in the year included in the qualifying period in which the taxpayer resided in the particular area, and

(B) $7.50 multiplied by the number of days in the year included in that portion of the qualifying period throughout which the taxpayer maintained and resided in a self-contained domestic establishment in the particular area (except any day included in computing a deduction claimed under this paragraph by another person who resided on that day in the establishment).

Division C — Computation of Taxable Income    S. 111(1)

**Related Provisions**: 6(6) — Employment at special work site or remote area — non-taxable benefits; 111.1 — Order of applying provisions.

**Notes**: 110.7(1) requires a full 6 months, not parts of calendar months, despite the definition of "month" in the *Interpretation Act*. Thus, June 18–December 9 was not "6 consecutive months": *McCombie*, [2000] 4 C.T.C. 2251 (TCC).

Per a December 1999 CCRA Fact Sheet, travel expenses under 110.7 can optionally be calculated using a simplified calculation without receipts: $11/meal (up to $33/day); and vehicle expenses per qualifying km driven (to cover both ownership and operating expenses), using the table in the Notes to 62(3).

See also Notes at end of 110.7.

**Interpretation Bulletins**: IT-91R4: Employment at special work sites or remote work locations.

**Regulations**: 100(3.1) (deduction reduces source withholdings); 7303.1 (prescribed northern zone, prescribed intermediate zone).

**Forms**: RC4054: Ceiling amounts for housing benefits paid in prescribed zones [information sheet]; T2222: Northern residents deductions.

**(2) Specified percentage** — For the purpose of subsection (1), the specified percentage for a particular area for a taxation year is

(a) where the area is a prescribed northern zone for the year, 100%; and

(b) where the area is a prescribed intermediate zone for the year, 50%.

**Regulations**: 7303.1 (prescribed northern zone, prescribed intermediate zone).

**Interpretation Bulletins**: IT-91R4: Employment at special work sites or remote work locations.

**(3) Restriction** — The total determined under paragraph (1)(a) for a taxpayer in respect of travel expenses incurred in a taxation year in respect of an individual shall not be in respect of more than 2 trips made by the individual in the year, other than trips to obtain medical services that are not available in the locality in which the taxpayer resided.

**Related Provisions [s. 110.7(3)]**: 118.2(2)(g), (h) — Medical expense credit for travel expenses.

**(4) Board and lodging allowances, etc.** — The amount determined under subparagraph (1)(b)(ii) for a particular area for a taxpayer for a taxation year shall not exceed the amount by which the amount otherwise determined under that subparagraph for the particular area for the year exceeds the value of, or an allowance in respect of expenses incurred by the taxpayer for, the taxpayer's board and lodging in the particular area (other than at a work site described in paragraph 67.1(2)(e)) that

(a) would, but for subparagraph 6(6)(a)(i), be included in computing the taxpayer's income for the year; and

(b) can reasonably be considered to be attributable to that portion of the qualifying period that is in the year and during which the taxpayer maintained a self-contained domestic establishment as the taxpayer's principal place of residence in an area other than a prescribed northern zone or a prescribed intermediate zone for the year.

**Notes**: 110.7(4) amended by 1998 Budget to add "(other than at a work site described in paragraph 67.1(2)(e))" in the opening words, effective for 1998 and later taxation years.

**Regulations**: 7303.1 (prescribed northern zone, prescribed intermediate zone).

**Interpretation Bulletins**: IT-91R4: Employment at special work sites or remote work locations.

**Forms**: RC4054: Ceiling amounts for housing benefits paid in prescribed zones [information sheet].

**(5) Idem** — Where on any day an individual resides in more than one particular area referred to in subsection (1), for the purpose of that subsection, the individual shall be deemed to reside in only one such area on that day.

**Notes**: 110.7(1)(a)(iii) added by 1992 technical bill, effective 1992.

110.7 amended by 1991 technical bill, effective 1995. The version as enacted above applies as of 1991, but with the following transitional rules for 1991 through 1994:

(i) read the opening words of 110.7(1) as follows:

110.7 (1) Where, throughout a period (in this section referred to as the "qualifying period") of not less than 6 consecutive months beginning or ending in a taxation year, a taxpayer who is an individual has resided in one or more particular areas each of which is a prescribed area for the year or for one of the 2 preceding taxation years or a prescribed northern zone or prescribed intermediate zone for the year, and the taxpayer files for the year a claim in prescribed form, there may be deducted in computing the taxpayer's taxable income for the year,

(ii) read 110.7(2) as follows:

(2) For the purpose of subsection (1), the specified percentage for a particular area for a taxation year is

(a) where the area is a prescribed area for the year or a prescribed northern zone for the year, 100%;

(b) except as otherwise provided in paragraph (a), where the area was a prescribed area for the immediately preceding taxation year, 66⅔%;

(c) except as otherwise provided in paragraph (a) or (b), where the area is a prescribed intermediate zone for the year, 50%; and

(d) except as otherwise provided in paragraph (a), (b) or (c), where the area was a prescribed area for the second preceding taxation year, 33⅓%,

(iii) read 110.7(4)(b) as follows:

(b) can reasonably be considered to be attributable to that portion of the qualifying period that is in the year and during which the taxpayer maintained a self-contained domestic establishment as the taxpayer's principal place of residence in an area other than a prescribed area, prescribed northern zone or prescribed intermediate zone for the year.

**Definitions [s. 110.7]**: "amount" — 248(1); "arm's length" — 251(1); "employment", "individual", "person", "prescribed" — 248(1); "prescribed intermediate zone" — Reg. 7303.1(2); "prescribed northern zone" — Reg. 7303.1(1); "qualifying period" — 110.7(1); "self-contained domestic establishment" — 248(1); "specified percentage" — 110.7(2); "taxable income" — 2(2), 248(1); "taxation year" — 249.

**111. (1) Losses deductible** — For the purpose of computing the taxable income of a taxpayer for a

## S. 111(1) — Income Tax Act, Part I

taxation year, there may be deducted such portion as the taxpayer may claim of the taxpayer's

(a) **non-capital losses** — non-capital losses for the 7 taxation years immediately preceding and the 3 taxation years immediately following the year;

**Related Provisions**: 88(1.1) — Windup — non-capital losses of subsidiary; 88(1.3) — Windup — rules relating to computation of income and tax of parent; 111(7.2) — Non-capital loss of life insurer; 115(1)(c), (d) — Application of losses to non-resident; 127.52(1)(i)(i) — Limitation on deduction for minimum tax purposes; 186(1)(d)(i) — Application of non-capital loss to Part IV tax. See additional Related Provisions at end of subsec. 111(1) and s. 111.

**Notes**: The claim under 111(1)(a) for losses from the 7 taxation years *preceding* implements a 7-year carry*forward* of losses, since the legislation is written from the point of view of the year in which the loss is *claimed*. Similarly, the reference to the 3 taxation years *following* implements a carry*back* of losses for 3 years.

The losses covered by 111(1)(a) are business losses (excluding farm losses and limited partnership losses), property losses, employment losses and allowable business investment losses. See 111(8) "non-capital loss".

A formal determination of loss is necessary to start the statute-barred clock ticking, where a loss is left to carry over to a future year. See Notes to 152(1.1).

The CCRA generally accepts plans that involve a reorganization for the purpose of using losses within a corporate group as not violating the general anti-avoidance rule. See, for example, Information Circular 88-2, paras. 8 and 9; Income Tax Technical News No. 3; and the 1994 Canadian Tax Foundation annual conference (Conference Report, p. 47:2).

**Interpretation Bulletins**: IT-393R2: Election re tax on rents and timber royalties — non-residents; IT-484R2: Business investment losses. See also list at end of s. 111.

**Information Circulars**: 88-2, para. 8: General anti-avoidance rule — section 245 of the *Income Tax Act*.

**I.T. Technical News**: No. 3 (loss utilization within a corporate group).

**Advance Tax Rulings**: ATR-44: Utilization of deductions and credits within a related corporate group.

**Forms**: T3A: Request for loss carry-back by a trust.

(b) **net capital losses** — net capital losses for taxation years preceding and the three taxation years immediately following the year;

**Related Provisions**: 88(1.2) — Wind-up — net capital losses of subsidiary; 88(1.3) — Wind-up — rules relating to computation of income and tax of parent; 104(21)(a) — Trusts — portion of taxable capital gains deemed gain of beneficiary; 110.6(1) — "annual gains limit"; 111(1.1) — Net capital losses; 111(2) — Net capital losses when taxpayer dies; 115(1)(c), (d) — Application of losses to non-resident; 126(2.1) — Foreign tax credit — Amount determined for purpose of paragraph (2)(b); 127.52(1)(i)(i) — Limitation on deduction for minimum tax purposes; 129(3) — Refundable dividend tax on hand. See additional Related Provisions and Definitions at end of subsec. 111(1) and s. 111.

**Notes**: 111(1)(b) provides an indefinite carryforward, and 3-year carryback, of unused allowable capital losses. See 111(8) "net capital loss" and Notes to 111(1)(a).

**Interpretation Bulletins**: IT-98R2: Investment corporations; IT-243R4: Dividend refund to private corporations; IT-395R: Foreign tax credit — foreign-source capital gains and losses; IT-484R2: Business investment losses. See also list at end of s. 111.

**Forms**: T3A: Request for loss carry-back by a trust.

(c) **restricted farm losses** — restricted farm losses for the 10 taxation years immediately preceding and the 3 taxation years immediately following the year, but no amount is deductible for the year in respect of restricted farm losses except to the extent of the taxpayer's incomes for the year from all farming businesses carried on by the taxpayer;

**Related Provisions**: 31 — Loss from farming where chief source of income not from farming; 53(1)(i) — Addition to ACB of farmland; 88(1.3) — Winding-up — computation of income and tax payable by parent; 101 — Loss carryforward claimed on disposition of farmland by partnership; 115(1)(c), (d) — Application of losses to non-resident; 127.52(1)(i)(i) — Limitation on deduction for minimum tax purposes. See additional Related Provisions at end of subsec. 111(1) and s. 111.

**Notes**: 111(1)(c) provides a 10-year carryforward, and 3-year carryback, of unused restricted farm losses (as defined in 31(1.1)). See Notes to 111(1)(a) and to 31(1).

**Interpretation Bulletins**: See list at end of s. 111.

**Forms**: T3A: Request for loss carry-back by a trust.

(d) **farm losses** — farm losses for the 10 taxation years immediately preceding and the 3 taxation years immediately following the year; and

**Related Provisions**: 53(1)(i) — Addition to ACB of farmland; 101 — Claim of loss after disposition of farmland by partnership; 127.52(1)(i)(i) — Limitation on deduction for minimum tax purposes.

**Notes**: 111(1)(d) provides a 10-year carryforward, and 3-year carryback, of unused farm losses. See 111(8) "farm loss" and Notes to 111(1)(a) and to 31(1).

**Forms**: T3A: Request for loss carry-back by a trust.

(e) **limited partnership losses** — limited partnership losses in respect of a partnership for taxation years preceding the year, but no amount is deductible for the year in respect of a limited partnership loss except to the extent of the amount by which

(i) the taxpayer's at-risk amount in respect of the partnership (within the meaning assigned by subsection 96(2.2)) at the end of the last fiscal period of the partnership ending in the taxation year

exceeds

(ii) the total of all amounts each of which is

(A) the amount required by subsection 127(8) in respect of the partnership to be added in computing the investment tax credit of the taxpayer for the taxation year,

(B) the taxpayer's share of any losses of the partnership for that fiscal period from a business or property, or

(C) the taxpayer's share of

(I) the foreign exploration and development expenses, if any, incurred by the partnership in that fiscal period,

Division C — Computation of Taxable Income   S. 111(2)

> **Proposed Amendment — 111(1)(e)(ii)(C)(I)**
>
> (I) the foreign resource pool expenses, if any, incurred by the partnership in that fiscal period,
>
> **Application**: The December 21, 2000 draft legislation, subsec. 54(1), will amend subcl. 111(1)(e)(ii)(C)(I) to read as above, applicable to taxation years that begin after 2000.
>
> **Technical Notes**: To the extent provided by paragraph 111(1)(e), limited partnership losses (as defined in subsection 96(2.1)) for a taxation year in respect of a partnership may be carried forward for deduction in computing taxable income for a subsequent taxation year. The potential deduction in respect of a partnership is reduced to reflect the amount by which the taxpayer's "at-risk amount" in respect of the partnership exceeds the taxpayer's shares of specified resource expenditures (including foreign exploration and development expenses) incurred by the partnership.
>
> Subclause 111(1)(e)(ii)(C)(I) is amended so that "foreign resource pool expenses", as newly defined in subsection 248(1), are referred to instead of foreign exploration and development expenses. The new definition includes expenses that are a foreign resource expense, as defined in new section 66.21, in addition to foreign exploration and development expenses.

(II) the Canadian exploration expense, if any, incurred by the partnership in that fiscal period,

(III) the Canadian development expense, if any, incurred by the partnership in that fiscal period, and

(IV) the Canadian oil and gas property expense, if any, incurred by the partnership in that fiscal period.

**Related Provisions [para. 111(1)(e)]**: 88(1.1) — Wind-up — non-capital losses of subsidiary; 96(2.1) — Determination of limited partnership losses; 96(2.4) — Limited partner — extended definition; 127.52(1)(i)(i) — Limitation on deduction for minimum tax purposes. See additional Related Provisions at end of subsec. 111(1) and s. 111.

**Notes**: 111(1)(e) provides an indefinite carryforward of limited partnership losses (as defined in 96(2.1)(e)) that cannot be deducted because of the "at-risk" rules. See Notes to 96(2.1) and 111(1)(a).

**Related Provisions [subsec. 111(1)]**: 111(3) — Limitations on deductibility; 111(4), (5) — Limitations where change of control; 111(9) — Where taxpayer not resident in Canada; 152(6)(c) — CCRA required to reassess earlier year to allow carryback; 164(5), (5.1) — Effect of carryback of loss; 164(6) — Carryback of losses of estate to deceased's year of death; 256(7) — Where control deemed not to have been acquired; 256(8) — Where share deemed to have been acquired. See additional Related Provisions and Definitions at end of s. 111. For other carryovers, see under "carryforward" in Topical Index.

**Interpretation Bulletins [subsec. 111(1)]**: IT-151R5: Scientific research and experimental development expenditures; IT-232R3: Losses — their deductibility in the loss year or in other years; IT-262R2: Losses of non-residents and part-year residents; IT-302R3: Losses of a corporation — the effect that acquisitions of control, amalgamations, and windings-up have on their deductibility — after January 15, 1987. See also list at end of s. 111.

**Forms [subsec. 111(1)]**: T1A: Request for loss carryback; T2 SCH 4: Corporation loss and continuity application; T3A: Request for loss carry-back by a trust.

**(1.1) Net capital losses** — Notwithstanding paragraph (1)(b), the amount that may be deducted under that paragraph in computing a taxpayer's taxable income for a particular taxation year is the total of

(a) the lesser of

(i) the amount, if any, determined under paragraph 3(b) in respect of the taxpayer for the particular year, and

(ii) the total of all amounts each of which is an amount determined by the formula

$$A \times \frac{B}{C}$$

where

A is the amount claimed under paragraph (1)(b) for the particular year by the taxpayer in respect of a net capital loss for a taxation year (in this paragraph referred to as the "loss year"),

B is the fraction that would be used for the particular year under section 38 in respect of the taxpayer if the taxpayer had a capital loss for the particular year, and

C is the fraction required to be used under section 38 in respect of the taxpayer for the loss year; and

(b) where the taxpayer is an individual, the least of

(i) $2,000,

(ii) the taxpayer's pre-1986 capital loss balance for the particular year, and

(iii) the amount, if any, by which

(A) the amount claimed under paragraph (1)(b) in respect of the taxpayer's net capital losses for the particular year

exceeds

(B) the total of the amounts in respect of the taxpayer's net capital losses that, using the formula in subparagraph (a)(ii), would be required to be claimed under paragraph (1)(b) for the particular year to produce the amount determined under paragraph (a) for the particular year.

**Related Provisions**: 111(2) — Year of death. See additional Related provisions and Definitions at end of s. 111.

**Notes**: 111(1.1) amended by 1991 technical bill, retroactive to 1985, to ensure that the adjustment to net capital losses to reflect the various inclusion rates will not apply where the loss is a pre-May 23, 1985 loss of an individual that has been deducted against up to $2,000 of other income.

**Interpretation Bulletins**: IT-232R3: Losses — their deductibility in the loss year or in other years; IT-262R2: Losses of non-residents and part-year residents. See also list at end of s. 111.

**(2) Year of death** — Where a taxpayer dies in a taxation year, for the purpose of computing the taxpayer's taxable income for that year and the immediately preceding taxation year, the following rules apply:

(a) paragraph (1)(b) shall be read as follows:

"(b) the taxpayer's net capital losses for all taxation years not claimed for the purpose of computing the taxpayer's taxable income for any other taxation year;"; and

(b) paragraph (1.1)(b) shall be read as follows:

"(b) the amount, if any, by which

(i) the amount claimed under paragraph (1)(b) in respect of the taxpayer's net capital losses for the particular year

exceeds the total of

(ii) all amounts in respect of the taxpayer's net capital losses that, using the formula in subparagraph (a)(ii), would be required to be claimed under paragraph (1)(b) for the particular year to produce the amount determined under paragraph (a) for the particular year, and

(iii) all amounts each of which is an amount deducted under section 110.6 in computing the taxpayer's taxable income for a taxation year, except to the extent that, where the particular year is the year in which the taxpayer died, the amount, if any, by which the amount determined under subparagraph (i) in respect of the taxpayer for the immediately preceding taxation year exceeds the amount so determined under subparagraph (ii)."

**Notes**: 111(2) amended by 1991 technical bill, retroactive to 1985.
**Interpretation Bulletins**: IT-232R3: Losses — their deductibility in the loss year or in other years. See also list at end of s. 111.

**(3) Limitation on deductibility** — For the purposes of subsection (1),

(a) an amount in respect of a non-capital loss, restricted farm loss, farm loss or limited partnership loss, as the case may be, for a taxation year is deductible, and an amount in respect of a net capital loss for a taxation year may be claimed, in computing the taxable income of a taxpayer for a particular taxation year only to the extent that it exceeds the total of

(i) amounts deducted under this section in respect of that non-capital loss, restricted farm loss, farm loss or limited partnership loss in computing taxable income for taxation years preceding the particular taxation year,

(i.1) the amount that was claimed under paragraph (1)(b) in respect of that net capital loss for taxation years preceding the particular taxation year, and

(ii) amounts claimed in respect of that loss under paragraph 186(1)(c) for the year in which the loss was incurred or under paragraph 186(1)(d) for the particular taxation

year and taxation years preceding the particular taxation year, and

(b) no amount is deductible in respect of a non-capital loss, net capital loss, restricted farm loss, farm loss or limited partnership loss, as the case may be, for a taxation year until

(i) in the case of a non-capital loss, the deductible non-capital losses,

(ii) in the case of a net capital loss, the deductible net capital losses,

(iii) in the case of a restricted farm loss, the deductible restricted farm losses,

(iv) in the case of a farm loss, the deductible farm losses, and

(v) in the case of a limited partnership loss, the deductible limited partnership losses,

for preceding taxation years have been deducted.

**Related Provisions**: 87(2.1)(b) — Determining loss after amalgamation; 88(1.1) — Non-capital losses of subsidiary; 88(1.2) — Net capital losses of subsidiary; 88(1.3) — Winding-up — computation of income and tax payable by parent; 149(10)(c) — Restriction on carry-forward of losses on change of corporate tax status. See additional Related Provisions and Definitions at end of s. 111.

**Notes**: Opening words of 111(3)(a) amended by 1991 technical bill, retroactive to 1985, so as to refer to a net capital loss being "claimed" rather than "deducted", due to the operation of 111(1.1).

**Interpretation Bulletins**: IT-232R3: Losses — their deductibility in the loss year or in other years; IT-262R2: Losses of non-residents and part-year residents; IT-302R3: Losses of a corporation — the effect that acquisitions of control, amalgamations, and windings-up have on their deductibility — after January 15, 1987. See also list at end of s. 111.

**(4) Acquisition of control [capital losses]** — Notwithstanding subsection (1), where, at any time (in this subsection referred to as "that time"), control of a corporation has been acquired by a person or group of persons

(a) no amount in respect of a net capital loss for a taxation year ending before that time is deductible in computing the corporation's taxable income for a taxation year ending after that time, and

(b) no amount in respect of a net capital loss for a taxation year ending after that time is deductible in computing the corporation's taxable income for a taxation year ending before that time,

and where, at that time, the corporation neither became nor ceased to be exempt from tax under this Part on its taxable income,

(c) in computing the adjusted cost base to the corporation at and after that time of each capital property, other than a depreciable property, owned by the corporation immediately before that time, there shall be deducted the amount, if any, by which the adjusted cost base to the corporation of the property immediately before that time exceeds its fair market value immediately before that time,

Division C — Computation of Taxable Income    S. 111(4)

(d) each amount required by paragraph (c) to be deducted in computing the adjusted cost base to the corporation of a property shall be deemed to be a capital loss of the corporation for the taxation year that ended immediately before that time from the disposition of the property,

(e) each capital property owned by the corporation immediately before that time (other than a property in respect of which an amount would, but for this paragraph, be required by paragraph (c) to be deducted in computing its adjusted cost base to the corporation or a depreciable property of a prescribed class to which, but for this paragraph, subsection (5.1) would apply) as is designated by the corporation in its return of income under this Part for the taxation year that ended immediately before that time or in a prescribed form filed with the Minister on or before the day that is 90 days after the day on which a notice of assessment of tax payable for the year or notification that no tax is payable for the year is mailed to the corporation, shall be deemed to have been disposed of by the corporation immediately before the time that is immediately before that time for proceeds of disposition equal to the lesser of

(i) the fair market value of the property immediately before that time, and

(ii) the greater of the adjusted cost base to the corporation of the property immediately before the disposition and such amount as is designated by the corporation in respect of the property,

and shall be deemed to have been reacquired by it at that time at a cost equal to the proceeds of disposition thereof, except that, where the property is depreciable property of the corporation the capital cost of which to the corporation immediately before the disposition time exceeds those proceeds of disposition, for the purposes of sections 13 and 20 and any regulations made for the purpose of paragraph 20(1)(a),

(iii) the capital cost of the property to the corporation at that time shall be deemed to be the amount that was its capital cost immediately before the disposition, and

(iv) the excess shall be deemed to have been allowed to the corporation in respect of the property under regulations made for the purpose of paragraph 20(1)(a) in computing its income for taxation years ending before that time, and

(f) each amount that by virtue of paragraph (d) or (e) is a capital loss or gain of the corporation from a disposition of a property for the taxation year that ended immediately before that time shall, for the purposes of the definition "capital dividend account" in subsection 89(1), be deemed to be a capital loss or gain, as the case may be, of the corporation from the disposition of the property immediately before the time that a capital property of the corporation in respect of which paragraph (e) would be applicable would be deemed by that paragraph to have been disposed of by the corporation.

**Related Provisions**: 13(7)(f) — Rules applicable to depreciable property; 53(2)(b.2) — Reduction in ACB; 53(4) — Effect on ACB of share, partnership interest or trust interest; 87(2.1)(b) — Determining loss after amalgamation; 107(1.1)(b)(ii) — Deemed cost of income interest in trust; 139.1(18) — Holding corporation deemed not to acquire control of insurer on demutualization; 249(4) — Deemed year end where change of control occurs; 256(6)–(9) — Whether control acquired. See additional Related Provisions and Definitions at end of s. 111. See also under "Control of corporation: change of" in Topical Index.

**Notes**: See Notes to 111(5); the purpose of 111(4) is the same.

111(4) amended in 1984, 1987, and by 1991 technical bill. The current version applies to acquisitions of control after July 13, 1990, other than acquisitions of control where the persons acquiring control were obliged on that day to acquire control pursuant to the terms of agreements in writing entered into on or before that day.

For acquisitions of control from January 16, 1987 through July 13, 1990, or those grandfathered as above, read 111(4)(e) as follows:

(e) each capital property owned by the corporation immediately before that time, other than a property in respect of which an amount would, but for this paragraph, be required by paragraph (c) to be deducted in computing its adjusted cost base to the corporation, as is designated by the corporation in its return of income under this Part for the taxation year that ended immediately before that time or in a prescribed form filed with the Minister on or before the day that is 90 days after the day on which a notice of assessment of tax payable for the year or notification that no tax is payable for the year is mailed to the corporation, shall be deemed to have been disposed of by the corporation immediately before the time that is immediately before that time for proceeds of disposition equal to the greater of

(i) the adjusted cost base to the corporation of the property immediately before that time, and

(ii) the lesser of the fair market value of the property immediately before that time and such amount as is designated by the corporation in respect of the property

and shall be deemed to have been reacquired by it at that time at a cost equal to the proceeds of disposition thereof.

The version that applies to acquisitions of control after January 15, 1987 does not apply to acquisitions of control from January 16, 1987 through the end of 1987 where the persons acquiring the control were obliged on January 15, 1987 to acquire the control pursuant to the terms of agreements in writing entered into on or before that date. For this purpose, the amending legislation provides that "a person shall be considered not to be obliged ... to acquire control of a corporation ... if the person may be excused from performing the obligation as a result of changes to the *Income Tax Act* affecting acquisitions or dispositions of property or acquisitions of control of corporations".

For acquisitions of control before January 16, 1987, and those through the end of 1987 that are grandfathered as indicated above, read 111(4) as follows:

(4) **Application of subsec. (1) where change in control** — Subsection (1) does not apply to permit a corporation to deduct, for the purpose of computing its taxable income for a taxation year, any amount in respect of

(a) its net capital loss for a preceding year if, before the end of the year, control of the corporation has been ac-

945

## S. 111(4) — Income Tax Act, Part I

quired by a person or persons who did not, at the end of that preceding year, control the corporation; or

(b) its net capital loss for a subsequent year if, before the beginning of that subsequent year, control of the corporation has been acquired by a person or persons who did not, at the beginning of the taxation year, control the corporation.

**Interpretation Bulletins**: IT-302R3: Losses of a corporation — the effect that acquisitions of control, amalgamations, and windings-up have on their deductibility — after January 15, 1987. See also list at end of s. 111.

**I.T. Technical News**: No. 7 (control by a group — 50/50 arrangement); No. 9 (loss consolidation within a corporate group).

**Forms**: T2 SCH 6: Summary of dispositions of capital property.

**(5) Idem [business or property losses]** — Where, at any time, control of a corporation has been acquired by a person or group of persons, no amount in respect of its non-capital loss or farm loss for a taxation year ending before that time is deductible by the corporation for a taxation year ending after that time and no amount in respect of its non-capital loss or farm loss for a taxation year ending after that time is deductible by the corporation for a taxation year ending before that time except that

(a) such portion of the corporation's non-capital loss or farm loss, as the case may be, for a taxation year ending before that time as may reasonably be regarded as its loss from carrying on a business and, where a business was carried on by the corporation in that year, such portion of the non-capital loss as may reasonably be regarded as being in respect of an amount deductible under paragraph 110(1)(k) in computing its taxable income for the year is deductible by the corporation for a particular taxation year ending after that time

(i) only if that business was carried on by the corporation for profit or with a reasonable expectation of profit throughout the particular year, and

(ii) only to the extent of the total of the corporation's income for the particular year from that business and, where properties were sold, leased, rented or developed or services rendered in the course of carrying on that business before that time, from any other business substantially all the income of which was derived from the sale, leasing, rental or development, as the case may be, of similar properties or the rendering of similar services; and

(b) such portion of the corporation's non-capital loss or farm loss, as the case may be, for a taxation year ending after that time as may reasonably be regarded as its loss from carrying on a business and, where a business was carried on by the corporation in that year, such portion of the non-capital loss as may reasonably be regarded as being in respect of an amount deductible under paragraph 110(1)(k) in computing its taxable income

for the year is deductible by the corporation for a particular year ending before that time

(i) only if throughout the taxation year and in the particular year that business was carried on by the corporation for profit or with a reasonable expectation of profit, and

(ii) only to the extent of the corporation's income for the particular year from that business and, where properties were sold, leased, rented or developed or services rendered in the course of carrying on that business before that time, from any other business substantially all the income of which was derived from the sale, leasing, rental or development, as the case may be, of similar properties or the rendering of similar services.

**Related Provisions**: 10(11) — Adventure in the nature of trade deemed to be business carried on by corporation; 87(2.1)(b) — Determining loss after amalgamation; 111(4) — Parallel rule for capital losses; 139.1(18) — Holding corporation deemed not to acquire control of insurer on demutualization; 249(4) — Deemed year end when change of control occurs; 256(6)–(9) — Whether control acquired. See additional Related Provisions and Definitions at end of s. 111.

**Notes**: 111(5) is designed to limit "trading" in loss corporations, whereby a corporation would be acquired for its loss carryforwards, following which the assets of a profitable business would be rolled into it (e.g., under 85(1)), so that the losses could soak up the profits from the business. Shuffling losses *within* a corporate group (without a change in control) is generally permitted by the CCRA; see Notes to 111(1)(a).

In *Duha Printers (Western) Ltd.*, [1998] 3 C.T.C. 303 (SCC), the Court ruled that "control" under 111(5) means *de jure* control, so 111(5) was averted through a scheme that maintained technical control despite a shareholders' agreement that affected real control. The CCRA has indicated that it will apply GAAR to such schemes in the future (Canadian Tax Foundation 1998 annual conference report, p. 52:21; Income Tax Technical News # 16).

The CCRA takes the position that "substantially all", used in 111(5)(a)(ii) and (b)(ii), means 90% or more.

111(5) amended by 1981 and 1983 Budgets, 1985 technical bill, 1987 press release, and 1988 tax reform. The current version applies to acquisitions of control after January 15, 1987, and also to acquisitions of control from January 16, 1987 through the end of 1987 where the persons acquiring the control were obliged on January 15, 1987 to acquire the control pursuant to the terms of agreements in writing entered into on or before that date. For this purpose, the amending legislation provides that "a person shall be considered not to be obliged ... to acquire control of a corporation ... if the person may be excused from performing the obligation as a result of changes to the *Income Tax Act* affecting acquisitions or dispositions of property or acquisitions of control of corporations".

For acquisitions of control from May 10, 1985 though January 15, 1987 (or those through the end of 1987 that are grandfathered as indicated above), read:

(5) Where, at any time, control of a corporation has been acquired by a person or persons (each of whom is in this subsection referred to as the "purchaser")

(a) such portion of the corporation's non-capital loss or farm loss, as the case may be, for a taxation year commencing before that time as may reasonably be regarded as its loss from carrying on a business is deductible by the corporation for a particular taxation year ending after that time

(i) only if that business was carried on by the corporation for profit or a reasonable expectation of profit

(A) throughout the part of the particular year that is after that time, where control of the corporation was acquired in the particular year, and

(B) throughout the particular year, in any other case, and

(ii) only to the extent of the aggregate of

(A) the corporation's income for the particular year from that business and, where properties were sold, leased, rented or developed or services rendered in the course of carrying on that business before that time, from any other business substantially all the income of which was derived from the sale, leasing, rental or development, as the case may be, of similar properties or the rendering of similar services, and

(B) the amount, if any, by which

(I) the aggregate of the corporation's taxable capital gains for the particular year from dispositions of property owned by the corporation at or before that time, other than property that was acquired by the corporation within the two-year period ending at that time from the purchaser or a person who did not deal at arm's length with the purchaser, exceeds

(II) the aggregate of the corporation's allowable capital losses for the particular year from dispositions described in subclause (I); and

(b) such portion of the corporation's non-capital loss or farm loss, as the case may be, for a taxation year commencing after that time as may reasonably be regarded as its loss from carrying on a business is deductible by the corporation for a particular taxation year commencing before that time

(i) only if throughout the taxation year and in the particular year that business was carried on by the corporation for profit or with a reasonable expectation of profit, and

(ii) only to the extent of the corporation's income for the particular year from that business and, where properties were sold, leased, rented or developed or services rendered in the course of carrying on that business before that time, from any other business substantially all the income of which was derived from the sale, leasing, rental or development, as the case may be, of similar properties or the rendering of similar services.

**Interpretation Bulletins**: IT-206R: Separate businesses; IT-302R3: Losses of a corporation — the effect that acquisitions of control, amalgamations, and windings-up have on their deductibility — after January 15, 1987. See also list at end of s. 111.

**I.T. Technical News**: No. 7 (control by a group — 50/50 arrangement); No. 9 (loss consolidation within a corporate group); No. 16 (*Duha Printers* case).

**Advance Tax Rulings**: ATR-7: Amalgamation involving losses and control.

**(5.1) Computation of undepreciated capital cost** — Where, at any time, control of a corporation (other than a corporation that at that time became or ceased to be exempt from tax under this Part on its taxable income) has been acquired by a person or group of persons and, if this Act were read without reference to subsection 13(24), the undepreciated capital cost to the corporation of depreciable property of a prescribed class immediately before that time would have exceeded the total of

(a) the fair market value of all the property of that class immediately before that time, and

(b) the amount in respect of property of that class otherwise allowed under regulations made under paragraph 20(1)(a) or deductible under subsection 20(16) in computing the corporation's income for the taxation year ending immediately before that time,

the excess shall be deducted in computing the income of the corporation for the taxation year ending immediately before that time and shall be deemed to have been allowed in respect of property of that class under regulations made under paragraph 20(1)(a).

**Related Provisions**: 87(2.1)(b) — Determining loss after amalgamation; 139.1(18) — Holding corporation deemed not to acquire control of insurer on demutualization; 256(6)–(9) — Whether control acquired. See additional Related Provisions and Definitions at end of s. 111.

**Interpretation Bulletins**: IT-302R3: Losses of a corporation — the effect that acquisitions of control, amalgamations, and windings-up have on their deductibility — after January 15, 1987. See also list at end of s. 111.

**I.T. Technical News**: No. 7 (control by a group — 50/50 arrangement); No. 9 (loss consolidation within a corporate group).

**(5.2) Computation of cumulative eligible capital** — Where, at any time, control of a corporation (other than a corporation that at that time became or ceased to be exempt from tax under this Part on its taxable income) has been acquired by a person or group of persons and immediately before that time the corporation's cumulative eligible capital in respect of a business exceeded the total of

(a) $3/4$ of the fair market value of the eligible capital property in respect of the business, and

(b) the amount otherwise deducted under paragraph 20(1)(b) in computing the corporation's income from the business for the taxation year ending immediately before that time,

the excess shall be deducted under paragraph 20(1)(b) in computing the corporation's income from the business for the taxation year ending immediately before that time.

**Related Provisions**: 87(2.1)(b) — Determining loss after amalgamation; 139.1(18) — Holding corporation deemed not to acquire control of insurer on demutualization; 256(6)–(9) — Whether control acquired. See additional Related Provisions and Definitions at end of s. 111.

**Interpretation Bulletins**: IT-302R3: Losses of a corporation — the effect that acquisitions of control, amalgamations, and windings-up have on their deductibility — after January 15, 1987. See also list at end of s. 111.

**I.T. Technical News**: No. 7 (control by a group — 50/50 arrangement); No. 9 (loss consolidation within a corporate group).

**(5.3) Doubtful debts and bad debts** — Where, at any time, control of a corporation (other than a corporation that at that time became or ceased to be exempt from tax under this Part on its taxable income) has been acquired by a person or group of persons, no amount may be deducted under paragraph 20(1)(l) in computing the corporation's income for its taxation year ending immediately before that time and each amount that is the greatest amount that would, but for this subsection and subsection 26(2) of this Act and subsection 33(1) of the *Income Tax Act*, chapter 148 of the Revised Statutes of Canada, 1952, have been deductible under paragraph 20(1)(l) in respect of a debt owing to the corporation immediately before that time shall be deemed to be a separate debt and shall, notwithstanding any other provision of this Act, be deducted as a bad debt under paragraph 20(1)(p) in computing the corporation's income for the year and the amount by which the debt exceeds that separate debt shall be deemed to be a separate debt incurred at the same time and under the same circumstances as the debt was incurred.

**Related Provisions**: 50(1)(a) — Deemed disposition where debt becomes bad debt; 87(2.1)(b) — Determining loss after amalgamation; 88(1.1) — Non-capital losses, etc., of subsidiary; 139.1(18) — Holding corporation deemed not to acquire control of insurer on demutualization; 256(6)–(9) — Whether control acquired. See additional Related Provisions and Definitions at end of s. 111.

**I.T. Application Rules**: 69 (meaning of "*Income Tax Act*, chapter 148 of the Revised Statutes of Canada, 1952").

**Interpretation Bulletins**: IT-302R3: Losses of a corporation — the effect that acquisitions of control, amalgamations, and windings-up have on their deductibility — after January 15, 1987.

**I.T. Technical News**: No. 7 (control by a group — 50/50 arrangement); No. 9 (loss consolidation within a corporate group).

**(5.4) Non-capital loss** — Where, at any time, control of a corporation has been acquired by a person or persons, such portion of the corporation's non-capital loss for a taxation year ending before that time as

(a) was not deductible in computing the corporation's income for a taxation year ending before that time, and

(b) can reasonably be considered to be a non-capital loss of a subsidiary corporation (in this subsection referred to as the "former subsidiary corporation") from carrying on a particular business (in this subsection referred to as the "former subsidiary corporation's loss business") that was deemed by subsection 88(1.1) of the *Income Tax Act*, chapter 148 of the Revised Statutes of Canada, 1952, as it read on November 12, 1981 to be the non-capital loss of the corporation for the taxation year of the corporation in which the former subsidiary corporation's loss year ended

shall be deemed to be a non-capital loss of the corporation from carrying on the former subsidiary corporation's loss business.

**Related Provisions**: 87(2.1)(b) — Determining loss after amalgamation; 139.1(18) — Holding corporation deemed not to acquire control of insurer on demutualization; 256(6)–(9) — Whether control acquired. See additional Related Provisions and Definitions at end of s. 111.

**I.T. Application Rules**: 69 (meaning of "*Income Tax Act*, chapter 148 of the Revised Statutes of Canada, 1952").

**Interpretation Bulletins**: IT-302R3: Losses of a corporation — the effect that acquisitions of control, amalgamations, and windings-up have on their deductibility — after January 15, 1987. See also list at end of s. 111.

**I.T. Technical News**: No. 7 (control by a group — 50/50 arrangement); No. 9 (loss consolidation within a corporate group).

**(5.5) Restriction** — Where control of a corporation has been acquired by a person or group of persons and it may reasonably be considered that the main reason for the acquisition of control was to cause paragraph (4)(d) or subsection (5.1), (5.2) or (5.3) to apply with respect to the acquisition,

(a) that provision and paragraph (4)(e), and

(b) where that provision is paragraph (4)(d), paragraph (4)(c)

shall not apply with respect to the acquisition.

**Related Provisions**: 87(2.1)(b) — Determining loss after amalgamation; 139.1(18) — Holding corporation deemed not to acquire control of insurer on demutualization; 256(6)–(9) — Whether control acquired.

**Notes**: 111(5.5) added in 1987, effective for acquisitions of control after January 15, 1987, other than acquisitions of control before 1988 where the persons acquiring the control were obliged on January 15, 1987 to acquire the control pursuant to the terms of agreements in writing entered into on or before that date. For this purpose, the amending legislation provides that "a person shall be considered not to be obliged ... to acquire control of a corporation ... if the person may be excused from performing the obligation as a result of changes to the *Income Tax Act* affecting acquisitions or dispositions of property or acquisitions of control of corporations".

**Interpretation Bulletins**: IT-302R3: Losses of a corporation — the effect that acquisitions of control, amalgamations, and windings-up have on their deductibility — after January 15, 1987. See also list at end of s. 111.

**(6) Limitation** — For the purposes of this section and paragraph 53(1)(i), any loss of a taxpayer for a taxation year from a farming business shall, after the taxpayer disposes of the land used in that farming business and to the extent that the amount of the loss is required by paragraph 53(1)(i) to be added in computing the adjusted cost base to the taxpayer of the land immediately before the disposition, be deemed not to be a loss.

**(7) Idem** — For the purposes of this section, any loss of a taxpayer for a taxation year from a farming business shall, to the extent that the loss is included in the amount of any deduction permitted by section 101 in computing the taxpayer's income for any subsequent taxation year, be deemed not to be a loss of the taxpayer for the purpose of computing the taxpayer's taxable income for that subsequent year or any taxation year subsequent thereto.

**(7.1) Effect of election by insurer under subsec. 138(9) in respect of 1975 taxation year** — Where an insurer has made an election under subsection 138(9) in respect of its 1975 taxa-

Division C — Computation of Taxable Income S. 111(8) far

tion year, for the purpose of determining the amount deductible in computing its taxable income for its 1977 and subsequent taxation years in respect of the non-capital loss, if any, for the 1972 and each subsequent taxation year ending before 1977, a portion of the non-capital loss for each such year equal to the lesser of

(a) the portion of the non-capital loss for the year (determined without reference to this subsection) that would be deductible in computing the insurer's taxable income for its 1977 taxation year if the insurer had sufficient income for that year, and

(b) the amount, if any, by which

(i) its 1975 branch accounting election deficiency

exceeds

(ii) the total of

(A) the amount determined under subparagraph 138(4.1)(d)(ii) in respect of the insurer,

(B) the total of all amounts each of which is an amount determined under paragraph 13(22)(b) with respect to depreciable property of a prescribed class of the insurer, and

(C) the total of all amounts each of which is the portion determined under this subsection in respect of the non-capital loss for a taxation year after 1971 and preceding the year

shall, for the purposes of this section, be deemed to have been deductible under this section in computing the insurer's taxable income for a taxation year ending before 1977.

**Related Provisions**: 111(7.11) — Definitions in 138(12) apply. See also Related Provisions and Definitions at end of s. 111.

**Interpretation Bulletins**: See list at end of s. 111.

**(7.11) Application of subsec. 138(12)** — The definitions in subsection 138(12) apply to subsection (7.1).

**Notes**: 111(7.11) added in the R.S.C. 1985 (5th Supp.) consolidation, effective for taxation years ending after November 1991. This rule was formerly in the opening words of 138(12).

**(7.2) Non-capital loss of life insurer** — Notwithstanding paragraph (1)(a), in the case of a life insurer the amount deductible in computing its taxable income for its 1978 and subsequent taxation years,

(a) in respect of its non-capital loss for each taxation year ending before 1977 shall be deemed to be nil; and

(b) in respect of its non-capital loss for its 1977 taxation year shall be deemed to be the amount, if any, by which

(i) the amount referred to in subparagraph 138(4.2)(a)(iv)

exceeds the total of

(ii) the amount of the reserve determined for the purpose of subparagraph 138(4.2)(a)(i),

(iii) in any case where subparagraph 138(4.2)(a)(ii) applies, the total of amounts referred to in that subparagraph, and

(iv) in any case where subparagraph 138(4.2)(a)(iii) applies, the amount referred to in that subparagraph.

**Interpretation Bulletins**: See list at end of s. 111.

**(8) Definitions** — In this section,

**"farm loss"** of a taxpayer for a taxation year means the amount determined by the formula

$$A - C$$

where

A is the lesser of

(a) the amount, if any, by which

(i) the total of all amounts each of which is the taxpayer's loss for the year from a farming or fishing business

exceeds

(ii) the total of all amounts each of which is the taxpayer's income for the year from a farming or fishing business, and

(b) the amount that would be the taxpayer's non-capital loss for the year if each of the amounts determined for C and D in the definition "non-capital loss" in this subsection were zero, and

B [Repealed]

C is the total of all amounts by which the farm loss of the taxpayer for the year is required to be reduced because of section 80;

**Related Provisions**: 31(1), (1.1) — Restricted farm loss; 53(1)(i) — Addition to ACB of farmland; 80(3)(b) — Reduction in farm loss on debt forgiveness; 87(2.1)(a) — Amalgamation — farm loss carried forward; 96(1) — Farm loss of partner; 111(9) — Farm loss where taxpayer not resident in Canada; 127.52(1)(i)(ii)(B) — Calculation of previous year's farm loss for minimum tax purposes; 128.1(4)(f) — Farm loss limitation on becoming non-resident; 133(2) — Non-resident-owned investment corporations; 161(7) — Effect of carryback of loss; 248(1)"farm loss" — Definition applies to entire Act; 257 — Formula cannot calculate to less than zero. See additional Related Provisions and Definitions at end of s. 111.

**Notes**: 111(8)"farm loss" amended by 1999 Budget, effective for 1998 and later taxation years, to change formula "A − B − C" to "A − C". Before the 1998 taxation year, read B as:

B is the amount, if any, by which any amount specified by the taxpayer in the taxpayer's election for the year under subsection 110.4(2) exceeds the amount that would be the taxpayer's non-capital loss for the year if the amount determined for C in the definition "non-capital loss" in this subsection were zero, and

949

111(8)"farm loss" was 111(8)(b.1) before consolidation in R.S.C. 1985 (5th Supp.), effective for taxation years ending after November 1991. The previous version, identical in meaning, read:

(b.1) **"farm loss"** — "farm loss" of a taxpayer for a taxation year means the amount, if any, by which the lesser of

(i) the amount, if any, by which

(A) the aggregate of all amounts each of which is his loss for the year from a farming or fishing business

exceeds

(B) the aggregate of all amounts each of which is his income for the year from a farming or fishing business, and

(ii) the amount that would be the taxpayer's non-capital loss for the year if paragraph (b) were read without reference to subparagraphs (iii) and (iv) thereof

exceeds

(iii) the amount, if any, by which any amount specified by the taxpayer in his election for the year under subsection 110.4(2) exceeds the amount that would be his non-capital loss for the year if paragraph (b) were read without reference to subparagraph (iii) thereof;

Formula element C added by 1994 tax amendments bill (Part I), effective for taxation years that end after February 21, 1994.

See Notes to 111(1)(d) and 31(1).

**Interpretation Bulletins**: IT-302R3: Losses of a corporation — the effect that acquisitions of control, amalgamations, and windings-up have on their deductibility — after January 15, 1987; IT-322R: Farm losses. See also list at end of s. 111.

**"net capital loss"** of a taxpayer for a taxation year means the amount determined by the formula

$$A - B + C - D$$

where

A is the amount, if any, determined under subparagraph 3(b)(ii) in respect of the taxpayer for the year,

B is the lesser of the total determined under subparagraph 3(b)(i) in respect of the taxpayer for the year and the amount determined for A in respect of the taxpayer for the year,

C is the least of

(a) the amount of the allowable business investment losses of the taxpayer for the taxpayer's seventh preceding taxation year,

(b) the amount, if any, by which the amount of the non-capital loss of the taxpayer for the taxpayer's seventh preceding taxation year exceeds the total of all amounts in respect of that non-capital loss deducted in computing the taxpayer's taxable income or claimed by the taxpayer under paragraph 186(1)(c) or (d) for the year or for any preceding taxation year, and

(c) where the taxpayer is a corporation the control of which was acquired by a person or group of persons before the end of the year and after the end of the taxpayer's seventh preceding taxation year, nil, and

D is the total of all amounts by which the net capital loss of the taxpayer for the year is required to be reduced because of section 80;

**Related Provisions**: 80(4)(b) — Reduction in net capital loss on debt forgiveness; 87(2.1)(a) — Amalgamation — net capital loss carried forward; 96(1) — Net capital loss of partner; 96(8)(b) — Loss of partnership that previously had only non-resident partners; 96(8)(c) — Disposition of property by partnership that previously had only non-resident partners; 111(1)(b) — Application of net capital loss; 111(7.2) — Non-capital loss of life insurer; 111(9) — Net capital loss of non-resident; 127.52(1)(i)(ii) — Calculation of previous year's loss for minimum tax purposes; 128.1(4)(f) — Net capital loss limitation on becoming non-resident; 139.1(18) — Holding corporation deemed not to acquire control of insurer on demutualization; 142.7(12)(f) — Net capital loss on conversion of foreign bank affiliate to branch; 161(7) — Effect of carryback of loss; 248(1)"net capital loss" — Definition applies to entire Act; 256(6)–(9) — Whether control acquired; 257 — Formula cannot calculate to less than zero. See additional Related Provisions and Definitions at end of s. 111.

**Notes**: 111(8)"net capital loss" was 111(8)(a) before consolidation in R.S.C. 1985 (5th Supp.), effective for taxation years ending after November 1991. The previous version, identical in meaning, read:

(a) **"net capital loss"** — "net capital loss" of a taxpayer for a taxation year means the aggregate of

(i) the amount, if any, by which

(A) the amount, if any, determined under subparagraph 3(b)(ii) in respect of the taxpayer for the year

exceeds

(B) the aggregate determined under subparagraph 3(b)(i) in respect of the taxpayer for the year, and

(ii) the amount that is equal to the lesser of

(A) the amount of the allowable business investment losses of the taxpayer for his seventh preceding taxation year, and

(B) the amount, if any, by which the amount of the non-capital loss of the taxpayer for his seventh preceding taxation year exceeds the aggregate of amounts in respect of that non-capital loss deducted by the taxpayer in computing his taxable income or claimed by him under paragraph 186(1)(c) or (d) for the year or for any preceding taxation year

except that where the taxpayer is a corporation the control of which was acquired by a person or group of persons before the end of the year and after the end of the taxpayer's seventh preceding taxation year, the amount determined under this subparagraph in respect of the taxpayer for the year shall be deemed to be nil;

Formula elements C and D added, and description of B amended to be capped at the amount determined for A for the year, by 1994 tax amendments bill (Part I), effective for taxation years that end after February 21, 1994.

See Notes to 111(1)(b).

**Interpretation Bulletins**: IT-302R3: Losses of a corporation — the effect that acquisitions of control, amalgamations, and windings-up have on their deductibility — after January 15, 1987; IT-484R2: Business investment losses. See also list at end of s. 111.

**"non-capital loss"** of a taxpayer for a taxation year means the amount determined by the formula

$$(A + B) - (D + D.1 + D.2)$$

where

A is the amount determined by the formula

$$E - F$$

where

E is the total of all amounts each of which is the taxpayer's loss for the year from an office, employment, business or property, the taxpayer's allowable business investment loss for the year, an amount deducted under paragraph (1)(b) or section 110.6 in computing the taxpayer's taxable income for the year or an amount that may be deducted under paragraph 110(1)(d), (d.1), (d.2), (d.3), (f), (j) or (k), section 112 or subsection 113(1) or 138(6) in computing the taxpayer's taxable income for the year [, and]

### Proposed Amendment — 111(8)"non-capital loss"E

E is the total of all amounts each of which is the taxpayer's loss for the year from an office, employment, business or property, the taxpayer's allowable business investment loss for the year, an amount deducted under paragraph (1)(b) or section 110.6 in computing the taxpayer's taxable income for the year or an amount that may be deducted under any of paragraphs 110(1)(d) to (d.3), (f), (j) and (k), section 112 and subsections 113(1) and 138(6) in computing the taxpayer's taxable income for the year, and

**Application**: The December 21, 2000 draft legislation, subsec. 54(2), will amend the description of E in the definition "non-capital loss" in subsec. 111(8), applicable to 2000 et seq.

**Technical Notes**: The description of E in the definition "non-capital loss" lists certain amounts to be included in determining the amount of the loss to ensure that the loss is not understated.

The description of E is amended so that amounts deducted by a taxpayer under new paragraph 110(1)(d.01) are included in determining the taxpayer's non-capital loss. Paragraph 110(1)(d.01) allows a deduction where certain employee option securities (or proceeds from the disposition of such securities) are donated to a qualifying charity.

F is the amount determined under paragraph 3(c) in respect of the taxpayer for the year,

B is the amount, if any, determined in respect of the taxpayer for the year under section 110.5,

### Proposed Amendment — 111(8)"non-capital loss"B

B is the amount, if any, determined in respect of the taxpayer for the year under section 110.5 or subparagraph 115(1)(a)(vii),

**Application**: The August 8, 2000 draft legislation, s. 7, will amend the description of B in the definition "non-capital loss" in subsec. 111(8) to read as above, applicable after June 27, 1999.

**Technical Notes**: Section 111 of the Act establishes the extent to which a taxpayer is permitted to deduct amounts in computing the taxpayer's taxable income for the year in respect of losses of other taxation years.

Subsection 111(8) includes the definition "non-capital loss." The definition, which takes the form of a formula, includes in a corporation's non-capital loss for a taxation year any amount the corporation has added to its taxable income under section 110.5 of the Act — a rule that in certain circumstances permits a corporation to increase its taxable income in order to increase the corporation's foreign tax credit.

The definition "non-capital loss" is amended to add a reference to amounts determined under new subparagraph 115(1)(a)(vii) of the Act. That provision, which applies to authorized foreign banks, replicates the effect of section 110.5.

This amendment applies after June 27, 1999.

C [Repealed]

D is the amount that would be the taxpayer's farm loss for the year if the amount determined for B in the definition "farm loss" in this subsection were zero,

D.1 is the total of all amounts deducted under subsection (10) in respect of the taxpayer for the year, and

D.2 is the total of all amounts by which the non-capital loss of the taxpayer for the year is required to be reduced because of section 80;

**Related Provisions**: 80(3)(a), 80(4)(a) — Reduction in non-capital loss on debt forgiveness; 87(2.1)(a) — Amalgamation — non-capital loss carried forward; 96(1) — Non-capital loss of partner; 96(8)(b), (c) — Loss of partnership that previously had only non-resident partners; 111(1)(a) — Application of non-capital loss; 111(5.4) — Non-capital loss following change of control; 111(9) — Non-capital loss where taxpayer not resident in Canada; 111(10), (11) — Fuel tax rebate loss abatement; 127.52(1)(i)(ii)(B) — Calculation of previous year's non-capital loss for minimum tax purposes; 128.1(4)(f) — Non-capital loss limitation on becoming non-resident; 142.7(12)(d) — Non-capital loss on conversion of foreign bank affiliate to branch; 161(7) — Effect of carryback of loss; 248(1)"non-capital loss" — Definition applies to entire Act; 257 — Formula amounts cannot calculate to less than zero. See additional Related Provisions and Definitions at end of s. 111.

**Notes**: See Notes to 111(1)(a).

111(8)"non-capital loss"amended by 1999 Budget, effective for 1998 and later taxation years, to change formula (A + B) – (C + D + D.1 + D.2) to read (A + B) – (D + D.1 + D.2). Before the 1998 taxation year, read C as:

C is any amount specified by the taxpayer in the taxpayer's election for the year under subsection 110.4(2),

Description of "A" (formerly 111(8)(b)(i)(A)) amended by 1992 technical bill, effective 1991, to add reference to an amount deducted under 111(1)(b). Thus, business losses of a taxation year that have been used to reduce the amount of a taxable capital gain for that year may be reinstated where net capital losses of other taxation years are carried over to that year.

Formula element D.1 (formerly 111(8)(b)(v)) added by 1992 transportation industry assistance bill, effective for amounts received in 1992 or later. See Notes to 12(1)(x.1).

Formula element D.2 added by 1994 tax amendments bill (Part I), effective for taxation years that end after February 21, 1994.

111(8)"non-capital loss" was 111(8)(b) before consolidation in R.S.C. 1985 (5th Supp.). The previous version, identical in meaning, read:

> (b) "non-capital loss" of a taxpayer for a taxation year means the amount, if any, by which the aggregate of
>
> > (i) the amount, if any, by which
> >
> > > (A) the aggregate of all amounts each of which is the taxpayer's loss for the year from an office, employment, business or property, his allowable business investment loss for the year, an amount deducted under section 110.6 or an amount deductible under paragraph 110(1)(d), (d.1), (d.2), (d.3), (f), (j) or (k), section 112 or subsection 113(1) or 138(6) in computing his taxable income for the year
> >
> > exceeds
> >
> > > (B) the amount determined under paragraph 3(c) in respect of the taxpayer for the year, and
> >
> > (ii) the amount, if any, determined in respect of the taxpayer for the year under section 110.5
>
> exceeds the aggregate of
>
> > (iii) any amount specified by the taxpayer in his election for the year under subsection 110.4(2),
> >
> > (iv) the amount that would be his farm loss for the year if paragraph (b.1) were read without reference to subparagraph (iii) thereof;

**Interpretation Bulletins**: IT-302R3: Losses of a corporation — the effect that acquisitions of control, amalgamations, and windings-up have on their deductibility — after January 15, 1987; IT-484R2: Business investment losses. See also list at end of s. 111.

**"pre-1986 capital loss balance"** of an individual for a particular taxation year means the amount determined by the formula

$$(A + B) - (C + D + E)$$

> **Proposed Amendment — 111(8)"pre-1986 capital loss balance" first formula**
>
> $$(A + B) - (C + D + E + E.1)$$
>
> **Application**: The December 21, 2000 draft legislation, subsec. 54(3), will amend the first formula in the definition "pre-1986 capital loss balance" in subsec. 111(8) to read as above, applicable to taxation years that end after February 27, 2000.
>
> **Technical Notes**: See under 111(8)"pre-1986 capital loss balance"D–E.1.

where

A is the total of all amounts each of which is an amount determined by the formula

$$F - G$$

where

F is the individual's net capital loss for a taxation year ending before 1985, and

G is the total of all amounts claimed under this section by the individual in respect of that loss in computing the individual's taxable income for taxation years preceding the particular taxation year, and

B is the amount determined by the formula

$$H - I$$

where

H is the lesser of

> (a) the amount of the individual's net capital loss for the 1985 taxation year, and
>
> (b) the amount, if any, by which the amount determined under subparagraph 3(e)(ii) of the *Income Tax Act*, chapter 148 of the Revised Statutes of Canada, 1952, in respect of the individual for the 1985 taxation year exceeds the amount deductible by reason of paragraph 3(e) of that Act in computing the individual's taxable income for the 1985 taxation year, and

I is the total of all amounts claimed under this section by the individual in respect of the individual's net capital loss for the 1985 taxation year in computing the individual's taxable income for taxation years preceding the particular taxation year,

C is the total of all amounts deducted under section 110.6 in computing the individual's taxable income for taxation years preceding 1988,

D is ¾ of the total of all the amounts deducted under section 110.6 in computing the individual's taxable income for taxation years preceding the particular year and ending after 1987 and before 1990, and

E is ⅔ of the total of all the amounts deducted under section 110.6 in computing the individual's taxable income for taxation years preceding the particular year and ending after 1989.

> **Proposed Amendment — 111(8)"pre-1986 capital loss balance"D–E.1**
>
> D is ¾ of the total of all amounts each of which is an amount deducted under section 110.6 in computing the individual's taxable income for a taxation year, preceding the particular year, that
>
> > (a) ended after 1987 and before 1990, or
> >
> > (b) began after February 27, 2000 and ended before October 18, 2000,
>
> E is ⅔ of the total of all amounts deducted under section 110.6 in computing the individual's taxable income for taxation years, preceding the particular year, that ended after 1989 and before February 28, 2000, and
>
> E.1 is amount determined by the formula
>
> $$J \times (0.5/K)$$
>
> J is the amount deducted by the individual under section 110.6 for a taxation year of the individual, preceding the particular year, that includes either February 28, 2000 or October 17, 2000, and
>
> K is the fraction in paragraph 38(a) that applies to the individual for the individual's taxation year referred to in the description of J.
>
> **Application**: The December 21, 2000 draft legislation, subsec. 54(4), will amend the portion after the description of C in the def-

Division C — Computation of Taxable Income                S. 111(9)(a)

inition "pre-1986 capital loss balance" in subsec. 111(8) to read as above, applicable to taxation years that end after February 27, 2000.

**Technical Notes**: An individual's "pre-1986 capital loss balance" for a taxation year is relevant for the purposes of paragraph 111(1.1)(b) and represents the individual's unused pre-1986 capital losses that the individual can deduct, up to $2000 per year, from income other than capital gains of the individual.

The definition is amended as a consequence of the reduction of the inclusion rate for capital gains [see 38(a) — ed.], applicable to taxation years that end after February 27, 2000.

Under the current definition, because of the description of D in the formula, pre-1986 capital losses are reduced by 3/4 of the deductions claimed under section 110.6 for taxation years that ended after 1987 and before 1990. This description reflects the fact that the inclusion rate for those years was 2/3 rather than the 1/2-rate used for years prior to 1986 when the pre-1986 net capital losses were accumulated. The description of D in the formula is amended to provide for the deduction from the pre-1986 net capital losses of 3/4 of the section 110.6 deductions claimed by the individual in respect of taxable capital gains realized in taxation years that ended after 1987 and before 1990 or began after February 27, 2000 and ended before October 18, 2000, when the inclusion rate for capital gains was 2/3 rather than the 1/2 used for years prior to 1986 when the pre-1986 net capital losses were accumulated.

The description of E in the formula is amended to provide for the deduction from the pre-1986 net capital losses of 2/3 of the section 110.6 deductions claimed by the individual in respect of taxable capital gains realized in taxation years that ended after 1989 and before February 28, 2000, when the inclusion rate for capital gains was 3/4 rather than the 1/2 used for years prior to 1986 when the pre-1986 net capital losses were accumulated.

The description of E.1 in the formula provides for the deduction from the pre-1986 net capital losses of amounts in respect of deductions claimed under section 110.6 in the 2000 taxation year of the individual that includes either February 28, 2000 or October 17, 2000. The deduction is the product obtained by multiplying the total amounts of the individual's deductions claimed for the year by the fraction obtained by dividing 1/2 by the fraction in paragraph 38(a) that applies to the individual for the year.

**Related Provisions**: 161(7) — Effect of carryback of loss; 257 — Formula amounts cannot calculate to less than zero. See additional Related Provisions and Definitions at end of s. 111.

**Notes**: $2,000 per year of an individual's pre-1986 capital loss balance can be deducted against other sources of income each year. See 111(1.1)(b)(i).

111(8)"pre-1986 capital loss balance" was 111(8)(b.2) before consolidation in R.S.C. 1985 (5th Supp.), effective for taxation years ending after November 1991. The previous version, identical in meaning, read:

(b.2) "pre-1986 capital loss balance" of an individual for a particular taxation year means the amount, if any, by which the total of

(i) the aggregate of all amounts each of which is the amount, if any, by which

(A) his net capital loss for a taxation year ending before 1985

exceeds

(B) the aggregate of amounts deducted by him under this section in respect of that loss in computing his taxable income for taxation years preceding the particular taxation year, and

(ii) the amount, if any, by which the lesser of

(A) the amount of his net capital loss for the 1985 taxation year, and

(B) the amount, if any, by which the amount determined under subparagraph 3(e)(ii) in respect of the individual for the 1985 taxation year exceeds the amount deductible by virtue of paragraph 3(e) in computing his taxable income for the 1985 taxation year

exceeds

(C) the aggregate of amounts deducted by him under this section in respect of his net capital loss for the 1985 taxation year in computing his taxable income for taxation years preceding the particular taxation year,

exceeds the total of

(iii) the aggregate of amounts deducted under section 110.6 in computing his taxable income for taxation years preceding 1988,

(iv) 3/4 of the aggregate of amounts deducted under section 110.6 in computing his taxable income for taxation years preceding the particular year and ending after 1987 and before 1990, and

(v) 2/3 of the aggregate of amounts deducted under section 110.6 in computing his taxable income for taxation years preceding the particular year and ending after 1989; and

111(8)(b.2)(i)(B) and (ii)(C) (now 111(8)"pre-1986 capital loss balance"A and B) amended by 1991 technical bill, retroactive to 1985, to refer to amounts "claimed" rather than "deducted", due to the operation of 111(1.1).

**I.T. Application Rules**: 69 (meaning of "*Income Tax Act*, chapter 148 of the Revised Statutes of Canada, 1952").

**Interpretation Bulletins**: IT-232R3: Losses — their deductibility in the loss year or in other years; IT-262R2: Losses of non-residents and part-year residents. See also list at end of s. 111.

**(9) Exception** — In this section, a taxpayer's non-capital loss, net capital loss, restricted farm loss, farm loss and limited partnership loss for a taxation year during which the taxpayer was not resident in Canada shall be determined as if

(a) throughout the portion of the year referred to in paragraph 114(b), where section 114 applies to the taxpayer in respect of the year, and

### Proposed Amendment — 111(9)(a)

(a) in the part of the year throughout which the taxpayer was non-resident, if section 114 applies to the taxpayer in respect of the year, and

**Application**: Bill C-43 (First Reading September 20, 2000), s. 57, will amend para. 111(9)(a) to read as above, applicable to 1998 *et seq*.

**Technical Notes**: Section 111 establishes the extent to which a taxpayer is permitted to deduct amounts in computing taxable income for a taxation year in respect of losses of other years. Subsection 111(9) sets out special limits that apply to carryovers from taxation years during which a taxpayer is not resident in Canada.

> Subsection 111(9) is amended, for the 1998 and subsequent taxation years, as a consequence of changes to section 114 of the Act. The amendment replaces a reference to the portion of the year referred to in paragraph 114(b) with a reference to the part of the year throughout which the taxpayer was non-resident. This keeps the reference in step with the changes to section 114. For additional information, see the commentary on section 114.

(b) throughout the year, in any other case,

the taxpayer had no income other than income described in any of subparagraphs 115(1)(a)(i) to (vi), the taxpayer's only taxable capital gains, allowable capital losses and allowable business investment losses were from dispositions of taxable Canadian property (other than treaty-protected property) and the taxpayer's only other losses were losses from the duties of an office or employment performed by the taxpayer in Canada and businesses (other than treaty-protected businesses) carried on by the taxpayer in Canada.

**Related Provisions**: 80(1)"excluded property" — Properties to which debt forgiveness rules do not apply; 115(1)(b.1) — Treaty-protected property losses not usable against taxable Canadian property gains; 115(1)(c) — Treaty-protected business losses not usable against Canadian business profits; 161(7) — Effect of carryback of loss. See additional Related Provisions and Definitions at end of s. 111.

**Notes**: Closing words of 111(9) amended by 1998 Budget, effective for computing taxable income and taxable income earned in Canada for 1998 and later taxation years. For earlier years, read:

> the taxpayer had no income other than income described in subparagraphs 115(1)(a)(i) to (vi), the taxpayer's only taxable capital gains and allowable capital losses were taxable capital gains and allowable capital losses from the disposition of taxable Canadian property and the taxpayer's only losses were allowable business investment losses and losses from duties of an office or employment performed by the taxpayer in Canada and businesses carried on by the taxpayer in Canada.

111(9) was 111(8)(c) before consolidation in R.S.C. 1985 (5th Supp.), effective for taxation years ending after November 1991. See Table of Concordance.

Closing words of 111(9) (formerly 111(8)(c)) amended by 1992 technical bill, effective for 1991 and later taxation years and with respect to the computation of taxable income and taxable income earned in Canada for those years. For earlier years, delete the words "allowable business investment losses and losses from duties of an office or employment performed by the taxpayer in Canada and".

**Interpretation Bulletins**: IT-262R2: Losses of non-residents and part-year residents; IT-393R2: Election re tax on rents and timber royalties — non-residents.

**(10) Fuel tax rebate loss abatement** — Where in a particular taxation year a taxpayer received an amount (in this subsection referred to as a "rebate") as a fuel tax rebate under subsection 68.4(2) or (3.1) of the *Excise Tax Act*, in computing the taxpayer's non-capital loss for a taxation year (in this subsection referred to as the "loss year") that is one of the 7 taxation years preceding the particular year, there shall be deducted the lesser of

(a) the amount determined by the formula

$$10(A - B) - C$$

where

A is the total of all rebates received by the taxpayer in the particular year,

B is the total of all amounts, in respect of rebates received by the taxpayer in the particular year, repaid by the taxpayer under subsection 68.4(7) of that Act, and

C is the total of all amounts, in respect of rebates received in the particular year, deducted under this subsection in computing the taxpayer's non-capital losses for other taxation years; and

(b) such amount as the taxpayer claims, not exceeding that portion of the taxpayer's non-capital loss for the loss year (determined without reference to this subsection) that would be deductible in computing the taxpayer's taxable income for the particular year if the taxpayer had sufficient income for the particular year from businesses carried on by the taxpayer in the particular year.

**Related Provisions**: 12(1)(x.1) — Income inclusion — fuel tax rebates; 111(8)"non-capital loss"D.1 — Claim under 111(10) reduces non-capital loss; 111(11) — Fuel tax rebate loss abatement — partnerships; 257 — Formula cannot calculate to less than zero.

**Notes**: 111(10) amended by 1997 Budget (first bill), effective for 1997 and later taxation years, to add reference to 68.4(3.1) of the *Excise Tax Act* and to rewrite the subsec. using a formula. See Notes to 12(1)(x.1). For 1992–96, read:

> (10) Where, in a particular taxation year, a taxpayer received an amount (in this subsection referred to as a "rebate") as a fuel tax rebate under subsection 68.4(2) of the *Excise Tax Act*, in computing the amount of the taxpayer's non-capital loss for a taxation year (in this subsection referred to as the "loss year") that is one of the 7 taxation years preceding the particular year, there shall be deducted the lesser of
>
> (a) the amount, if any, by which
>
> (i) 10 times the amount, if any, by which
>
> (A) the total of all rebates received by the taxpayer in the particular year
>
> exceeds
>
> (B) the total of all amounts, in respect of rebates received by the taxpayer in the particular year, repaid by the taxpayer under subsection 68.4(7) of that Act
>
> exceeds
>
> (ii) the total of all amounts, in respect of rebates received in the particular year, deducted under this subsection in computing the taxpayer's non-capital losses for other taxation years, and

111(10) was 111(9) before consolidation in R.S.C. 1985 (5th Supp.), effective for taxation years ending after November 1991. The former 111(9) was added by 1992 transportation industry assistance bill, effective for amounts received in 1992 or later.

**Interpretation Bulletins**: IT-232R3: Losses — their deductibility in the loss year or in other years.

**(11) Fuel tax rebate — partnerships** — Where a taxpayer was a member of a partnership at any time in a fiscal period of the partnership during which it received a fuel tax rebate under subsection 68.4(2),

(3) or (3.1) of the *Excise Tax Act*, the taxpayer is deemed

(a) to have received at that time as a rebate under subsection 68.4(2), (3) or (3.1), as the case may be, of that Act an amount equal to that proportion of the amount of the rebate received by the partnership that the member's share of the partnership's income or loss for that fiscal period is of the whole of that income or loss, determined without reference to any rebate under section 68.4 of that Act; and

(b) to have paid as a repayment under subsection 68.4(7) of that Act an amount equal to that proportion of all amounts repaid under subsection 68.4(7) of that Act in respect of the rebate that the member's share of the partnership's income or loss for that fiscal period is of the whole of that income or loss, determined without reference to any rebate under section 68.4 of that Act.

**Related Provisions**: 12(1)(x.1) — Income inclusion — fuel tax rebates.

**Notes**: 111(11) amended by 1997 Budget (first bill), effective for 1997 and later taxation years, to add reference to 68.4(3.1) of the *Excise Tax Act*. See Notes to 12(1)(x.1).

111(11) was 111(10) before consolidation in R.S.C. 1985 (5th Supp.), effective for taxation years ending after November 1991.

111(11) (formerly 111(10)) added by 1992 transportation industry assistance bill, effective for amounts received in 1992 or later. See Notes to 12(1)(x.1).

**Related Provisions [s. 111]**: 31(1) — Loss from farming where chief source of income not farming; 66.8(1) — Resource expenses of limited partner; 87(2.1) — Non-capital loss, net capital loss, restricted farm loss and farm loss of predecessor corporation; 87(2.11) — Losses, etc., on amalgamation with subsidiary wholly-owned corporation; 88.1 — Non-capital loss, net capital loss, restricted farm loss, and farm loss of subsidiary; 96(2.2) — At-risk amount; 104(21) — Portion of taxable capital gains deemed gain of beneficiary; 111.1 — Ordering of applying provisions; 127.52(1) — Adjusted taxable income determined; 128(1)(g), 128(2)(g) — Where corporation or individual is bankrupt; 152(1.1)–(1.3) — Determination of losses; 152(6) — Reassessment; 164(6) — Where disposition of property by legal representative of deceased taxpayer; 256(8) — Deemed acquisition of shares.

**Definitions [s. 111]**: "acquired" — 256(7)–(9); "active business" — 248(1); "adjusted cost base" — 54, 248(1); "allowable business investment loss" — 38(c), 248(1); "allowable capital loss" — 38(b), 248(1); "amount" — 248(1); "arm's length" — 251(1); "assessment", "business" — 248(1); "Canada" — 255; "Canadian development expense" — 66.2(5), 248(1); "Canadian exploration expense" — 66.1(6), 248(1); "Canadian oil and gas property expense" — 66.4(5), 248(1); "capital loss" — 39(1)(b), 248(1); "capital property" — 54, 248(1); "carrying on business" — 253; "control" — 256(6)–(9); "corporation" — 248(1), *Interpretation Act* 35(1); "cumulative eligible capital" — 14(5), 248(1); "depreciable property" — 13(21), 248(1); "eligible capital property" — 54, 248(1); "employment", "farming" — 248(1); "farm loss" — 111(8), 248(1); "fiscal period" — 249(2)(b), 249.1; "fishing" — 248(1); "foreign exploration and development expenses" — 66(15), 248(1); "foreign resource pool expense", "individual", "insurer" — 248(1); "investment tax credit" — 127(9), 248(1); "life insurer" — 248(1); "limited partner" — 96(2.4); "limited partnership loss" — 96(2.1)(e), 248(1); "Minister" — 248(1); "net capital loss" — 111(8), 248(1); "1975 branch accounting election deficiency" — 111(7.11), 138(12); "non-capital loss" — 111(8), 248(1); "non-resident", "office", "person", "prescribed", "property", "regulation" — 248(1); "resident in Canada" — 250; "restricted farm loss" — 31,

248(1); "tax payable" — 248(2); "taxable capital gain" — 38, 248(1); "taxable income" — 2(2), 248(1); "taxation year" — 249; "taxpayer", "treaty-protected business", "treaty-protected property" — 248(1); "undepreciated capital cost" — 13(21), 248(1).

**Interpretation Bulletins [s. 111]**: IT-171R2: Non-resident individuals — computation of taxable income earned in Canada and non-refundable tax credits; IT-322R: Farm losses; IT-381R3: Trusts — capital gains and losses and the flow-through of taxable capital gains to beneficiaries; IT-474R: Amalgamations of Canadian corporations.

**111.1 Order of applying provisions** — In computing an individual's taxable income for a taxation year, the provisions of this Division shall be applied in the following order: sections 110, 110.2, 111, 110.6 and 110.7.

**Notes**: 111.1 amended by 1999 Budget, effective for 1998 and later taxation years, to add reference to 110.2, and to delete a reference to 110.4(2) from the beginning of the list.

**Definitions [s. 111.1]**: "individual" — 248(1); "taxable income" — 2(2), 248(1); "taxation year" — 249.

**Interpretation Bulletins**: IT-232R3: Losses — their deductibility in the loss year or in other years; IT-523: Order of provisions applicable in computing an individual's taxable income and tax payable.

**112. (1) Deduction of taxable dividends received by corporation resident in Canada** — Where a corporation in a taxation year has received a taxable dividend from

(a) a taxable Canadian corporation, or

(b) a corporation resident in Canada (other than a non-resident-owned investment corporation or a corporation exempt from tax under this Part) and controlled by it,

an amount equal to the dividend may be deducted from the income of the receiving corporation for the year for the purpose of computing its taxable income.

**Related Provisions**: 55(2) — Capital gains stripping; 104(19) — Taxable dividends flowed through trust; 111(8)"non-capital loss"A:E — Amount included in non-capital loss; 112(2) — Dividends received from non-resident corporation; 112(2.1)–(2.6) — Where no deduction permitted; 112(3)–(3.32) — Denial of capital loss on share where intercorporate dividend previously paid; 112(4)–(4.3) — Loss on share held as inventory; 112(5.2)B(b)(i), (ii) — Adjustment for dividends received on mark-to-market property; 115(1)(d.1) — Deduction from income of non-resident; 137(5.2) — Credit union — allocations of taxable dividends and capital gains; 138(6) — Life insurer; 186(1) — Tax payable on certain taxable dividends; 186(3)"assessable dividend" — Part IV tax; 219(1)(b) — Branch tax on non-resident corporations; 256(6), (6.1) — Meaning of "controlled". See additional Related Provisions and Definitions at end of s. 112.

**Notes**: 112(1) offsets 82(1)(a)(ii)(A), and thus allows many intercorporate dividends to be received tax-free. Conceptually, the same income, after being taxed once in the corporation that earns it, can be paid up as dividends through an arbitrarily long chain of holding companies without triggering tax until it reaches an individual.

The two major exceptions to the treatment of intercorporate dividends are 112(2.1)–(2.9) (exclusion for dividends on certain preferred shares and other shares used as financing vehicles to obtain the intercorporate dividend deduction) and Part IV (refundable tax under 186 on "portfolio" dividends and on dividends from a corporation receiving a dividend refund). As well, dividends deducted under 112(1) may trigger the stop-loss rules in 112(3)–(5.6).

For dividends from foreign corporations, see 113(1).

**Interpretation Bulletins**: IT-88R2: Stock dividends; IT-98R2: Investment corporations; IT-269R3: Part IV tax on dividends received by a private corporation or a subject corporation; IT-328R3: Losses on shares on which dividends have been received; IT-385R2: Disposition of an income interest in a trust; IT-524: Trusts — flow-through of taxable dividends to a beneficiary — after 1987.

**Information Circulars**: 88-2, para. 13: General anti-avoidance rule — section 245 of the *Income Tax Act*.

**Advance Tax Rulings**: ATR-16: Inter-company dividends and interest expense; ATR-18: Term preferred shares; ATR-22R: Estate freeze using share exchange; ATR-27: Exchange and acquisition of interests in capital properties through rollovers and winding-up ("butterfly"); ATR-32: Rollover of fixed assets from Opco into Holdco; ATR-35: Partitioning of assets to get specific ownership — "butterfly"; ATR-46: Financial difficulty; ATR-57: Transfer of property for estate planning purposes; ATR-58: Divisive reorganization.

**(2) Dividends received from non-resident corporation** — Where a taxpayer that is a corporation has, in a taxation year, received a dividend from a corporation (other than a foreign affiliate of the taxpayer) that was taxable under subsection 2(3) for the year and that has, throughout the period from June 18, 1971 to the time when the dividend was received, carried on a business in Canada through a permanent establishment as defined by regulation, an amount equal to that proportion of the dividend that the paying corporation's taxable income earned in Canada for the immediately preceding year is of the whole of the amount that its taxable income for that year would have been if it had been resident in Canada throughout that year, may be deducted from the income of the receiving corporation for the taxation year for the purpose of computing its taxable income.

**Related Provisions**: 55(2) — Capital gains stripping; 112(2.1)–(2.6) — Where no deduction permitted; 112(5.2)B(b)(i), (ii) — Adjustment for dividends received on mark-to-market property; 113(1) — Deduction for dividend from foreign affiliate; 115(1)(d.1) — Deduction from income of non-resident; 137(5.2) — Credit union — allocations of taxable dividends and capital gains; 186(3)"assessable dividend" — Part IV tax; 247(1) — Dividend stripping. See additional Related provisions and Definitions at end of s. 112.

**Regulations**: 400(2) (meaning of "permanent establishment" until April 26, 1989); 8201 (meaning of "permanent establishment" effective 10:00 p.m., April 26, 1989).

**(2.1) Where no deduction permitted** — No deduction may be made under subsection (1) or (2) in computing the taxable income of a specified financial institution in respect of a dividend received by it on a share that was, at the time the dividend was paid, a term preferred share, other than a dividend paid on a share of the capital stock of a corporation that was not acquired in the ordinary course of the business carried on by the institution, and for the purposes of this subsection, where a restricted financial institution received the dividend on a share of the capital stock of a mutual fund corporation or an investment corporation at any time after that mutual fund corporation or investment corporation has elected pursuant to subsection 131(10) not to be a restricted financial institution, the share shall be deemed to be a term preferred share acquired in the ordinary course of business.

**Related Provisions**: 84(4.2) — Deemed dividend where paid-up capital of term preferred share reduced; 191(4) — Subsection 112(2.1) deemed not to apply; 248(1) — "amount" of a stock dividend; 248(14) — Specified financial institution — corporations deemed related; 258(2) — Deemed dividend on term preferred share. See additional Related Provisions and Definitions at end of s. 112.

**Notes**: See Notes to 248(1)"term preferred share".

**Interpretation Bulletins**: IT-52R4: Income bonds and income debentures; IT-88R2: Stock dividends.

**Advance Tax Rulings**: ATR-10: Issue of term preferred shares; ATR-16: Inter-company dividends and interest expense; ATR-18: Term preferred shares; ATR-46: Financial difficulty.

**(2.2) Idem** — No deduction may be made under subsection (1), (2) or 138(6) in computing the taxable income of a particular corporation in respect of a dividend received on a share of the capital stock of a corporation that was issued after 8:00 p.m. Eastern Daylight Saving Time, June 18, 1987 where a person or partnership (other than the issuer of the share or an individual other than a trust) that is a specified financial institution or a specified person in relation to any such institution was, at or immediately before the time the dividend was paid, obligated, either absolutely or contingently and either immediately or in the future, to effect any undertaking (in this subsection referred to as a "guarantee agreement"), including any guarantee, covenant or agreement to purchase or repurchase the share and including the lending of funds to or the placing of amounts on deposit with, or on behalf of, the particular corporation or any specified person in relation to the particular corporation given to ensure that

(a) any loss that the particular corporation or a specified person in relation to the particular corporation may sustain by reason of the ownership, holding or disposition of the share or any other property is limited in any respect, or

(b) the particular corporation or a specified person in relation to the particular corporation will derive earnings by reason of the ownership, holding or disposition of the share or any other property,

and the guarantee agreement was given as part of a transaction or event or a series of transactions or events that included the issuance of the share, except that this subsection does not apply to a dividend received on

(c) a share that was at the time the dividend was received a share described in paragraph (e) of the definition "term preferred share" in subsection 248(1) during the applicable time period referred to in that paragraph,

(d) a grandfathered share, a taxable preferred share issued before December 16, 1987 or a prescribed share, or

(e) a taxable preferred share issued after December 15, 1987 and of a class of the capital stock of a corporation that is listed on a prescribed stock exchange where all guarantee agreements in respect of the share were given by the issuer of the share, by one or more persons that would be related to the issuer if this Act were read without reference to paragraph 251(5)(b) or by the issuer and one or more such persons unless at the time the dividend is received the shareholder or the shareholder and specified persons in relation to the shareholder receive dividends in respect of more than 10 per cent of the issued and outstanding shares to which the guarantee agreement applies,

and for the purposes of this subsection

(f) where a guarantee agreement in respect of a share is given at any particular time after 8:00 p.m. Eastern Daylight Saving Time, June 18, 1987, otherwise than pursuant to a written arrangement to do so entered into before 8:00 p.m. Eastern Daylight Saving Time, June 18, 1987, the share shall be deemed to have been issued at the particular time and the guarantee agreement shall be deemed to have been given as part of a series of transactions that included the issuance of the share, and

(g) "specified person" has the meaning assigned by paragraph (h) of the definition "taxable preferred share" in subsection 248(1).

### Proposed Amendment — 112(2.2)

**(2.2) Guaranteed shares** — No deduction may be made under subsection (1), (2) or 138(6) in computing the taxable income of a particular corporation in respect of a dividend received on a share of the capital stock of a corporation that was issued after 8:00 p.m. Eastern Daylight Saving Time, June 18, 1987 where

(a) a person or partnership (in this subsection and subsection (2.21) referred to as the "guarantor") that is a specified financial institution or a specified person in relation to any such institution, but that is not the issuer of the share or an individual other than a trust, is, at or immediately before the time the dividend is paid, obligated, either absolutely or contingently and either immediately or in the future, to effect any undertaking (in this subsection and subsections (2.21) and (2.22) referred to as a "guarantee agreement"), including any guarantee, covenant or agreement to purchase or repurchase the share and including the lending of funds to or the placing of amounts on deposit with, or on behalf of, the particular corporation or any specified person in relation to the particular corporation given to ensure that

(i) any loss that the particular corporation or a specified person in relation to the particular corporation may sustain by reason of the ownership, holding or disposition of the share or any other property is limited in any respect, or

(ii) the particular corporation or a specified person in relation to the particular corporation will derive earnings by reason of the ownership, holding or disposition of the share or any other property; and

(b) the guarantee agreement was given as part of a transaction or event or a series of transactions or events that included the issuance of the share.

**Application**: Bill C-43 (First Reading September 20, 2000), s. 58, will amend subsec. 112(2.2) to read as above, applicable in respect of dividends received after 1998.

**Technical Notes**: Section 112 of the Act deals with the treatment of dividends received by a corporation resident in Canada from another corporation.

Subsection 112(2.2) of the Act denies the intercorporate dividend deduction for dividends on certain shares that are guaranteed by a specified financial institution. This subsection is amended by dividing its provisions among three new subsections — (2.2), (2.21) and (2.22) — in order to improve readability. In addition, a new exception is set out in new paragraph 112(2.21)(d), described below.

Amended subsection (2.2) sets out the basic conditions under which a share is considered to be a guaranteed share.

**Related Provisions**: 84(4.3) — Deemed dividend where paid-up capital of guaranteed share reduced; 87(4.2) — Amalgamations; 112(2.21) — Exceptions; 112(2.22) — Interpretation; 248(1) — "amount" of a stock dividend; 248(10) — Series of transactions; 248(14) — Specified financial institution — corporations deemed related; 258(3) — Deemed interest on preferred shares. See additional Related Provisions and Definitions at end of s. 112.

**Notes**: 112(2.2) amended by 1988 tax reform, effective for dividends on shares issued (or deemed by para. (f) to have been issued) after 8 p.m. EDST, June 18, 1987. However, the subsection does not apply to "grandfathered shares", as defined in subsection 248(1).

For dividends on shares issued from May 24, 1985 until 8 p.m. EDST on June 17, 1987 (other than shares issued pursuant to an agreement in writing entered into on or before May 23, 1985 and shares distributed to the public in accordance with the terms of a prospectus, preliminary prospectus or registration statement filed before May 24, 1985 with a public authority in Canada pursuant to and in accordance with the securities legislation of Canada or of any province and, where required by law, accepted for filing by such authority), read:

(2.2) No deduction may be made under subsection (1) or (2) in computing the taxable income of a particular corporation in respect of a dividend received on a share of the capital stock of a corporation that was acquired after October 23, 1979, if a person (other than the issuer of the share) that is a specified financial institution or a person related thereto or a partnership or trust of which any such institution or a person related thereto is a member or beneficiary was obligated, either absolutely or contingently and either at or after the time the dividend was paid, to effect any undertaking (in this subsection referred to as a "guarantee agreement"), including any guarantee, covenant or agreement to purchase or repurchase the share, given to ensure that

(a) any loss that the particular corporation or any partnership or trust of which the particular corporation is a member or a beneficiary may sustain by virtue of the ownership, holding or disposition of the share is limited in any respect, or

(b) the particular corporation or any partnership or trust of which it is a member or a beneficiary will derive earnings by virtue of the ownership, holding or disposition of the share,

except that this subsection does not apply to a dividend received on

(c) a share described in paragraph (e) of the definition "term preferred share" in subsection 248(1),

(d) a share listed on a prescribed stock exchange in Canada that was issued after April 21, 1980 by

(i) a corporation described in paragraph (2.1)(a), or

(ii) a corporation that would be associated with a corporation referred to in subparagraph (i) if this Act were read without reference to paragraph 251(5)(b),

where all guarantee agreements in respect of the share were given by the issuer of the share, by one or more persons that would be associated with the issuer if this Act were read without reference to paragraph 251(5)(b) or by the issuer and one or more such persons,

(e) a share that is listed on a prescribed stock exchange in Canada and was issued before April 22, 1980 by a corporation described in any of paragraphs 39(5)(b) to (f) or by a corporation associated with any such corporation, or

(f) [Repealed]

(g) a share that is a prescribed share.

For dividends on shares issued before May 24, 1985 (or grandfathered with respect to that date as indicated above), read 112(2.2)(f) as:

(f) a share owned, at the time the dividend was paid, by a specified financial institution that acquired the share in the ordinary course of its business, or

For insurance corporations (other than life insurance corporations), subsection (2.2) applies only to dividends on shares acquired after October 23, 1979.

**Regulations**: 3200 (prescribed stock exchange); 6201(3) (prescribed share for 112(2.2)(g)); 6201(8) (prescribed share for 112(2.2)(d)).

**Advance Tax Rulings**: ATR-16: Inter-company dividends and interest expense; ATR-46: Financial difficulty.

### Proposed Addition — 112(2.21), (2.22)

**(2.21) Exceptions** — Subsection (2.2) does not apply to a dividend received by a particular corporation on

(a) a share that is at the time the dividend is received a share described in paragraph (e) of the definition "term preferred share" in subsection 248(1);

(b) a grandfathered share, a taxable preferred share issued before December 16, 1987 or a prescribed share;

(c) a taxable preferred share issued after December 15, 1987 and of a class of the capital stock of a corporation that is listed on a prescribed stock exchange where all guarantee agreements in respect of the share were given by one or more of the issuer of the share and persons that are related (otherwise than because of a right referred to in paragraph 251(5)(b)) to the issuer unless, at the time the dividend is paid to the particular corporation, dividends in respect of more than 10 per cent of the issued and outstanding shares to which the guarantee agreement applies are paid to the particular corporation, or the particular corporation and specified persons in relation to the particular corporation; or

(d) a share

(i) that was not acquired by the particular corporation in the ordinary course of its business,

(ii) in respect of which the guarantee agreement was not given in the ordinary course of the guarantor's business, and

(iii) the issuer of which is, at the time the dividend is paid, related (otherwise than because of a right referred to in paragraph 251(5)(b)) to both the particular corporation and the guarantor.

**Technical Notes**: New subsection 112(2.21) of the Act sets out exceptions specifying shares to which the guaranteed share rule in amended subsection 112(2.2) does not apply. Paragraphs 112(2.21)(a) to (c) set out the exceptions formerly contained in paragraphs 112(2)(c) to (e).

Paragraph 112(2.21)(d) sets out a new exception for certain shares held within a corporate group. The exception applies where two general conditions are met. First, the shares must not have been acquired by the holder in the ordinary course of its business, and the guarantee agreement must not have been given in the ordinary course of business of the party that gave it. Second, the issuer of the share must be related to both the holder and the guarantor, otherwise than because of an option or other right referred to in paragraph 251(5)(b) of the Act.

**Letter from Department of Finance, April 13, 1999**:

Dear [xxx]

SUBJECT: *Guaranteed Preferred Shares*

I am writing in reply to your letter of February 19, 1999 to Mr. Len Farber proposing a technical amendment to the *Income Tax Act* (the "Act") to provide an exception to the application of subsection 112(2.2), which deals with so-called "guaranteed preferred shares".

The special preferred share rules in the act were enacted in order to deal with various types of after-tax financing transactions in which a corporation that is not in a taxable position (as a result of losses, excess tax credits, etc.) effectively passes tax benefits on to other parties using preferentially-taxed shares.

The general policy behind the preferred share rules is to limit the tax benefits associated with structuring such financings using equity rather than debt. However, a number of provisions in the rules provide relief from this limitation of benefits in the case of certain transactions involving companies that are members of a single corporate group. As a result of these exceptions, certain types of after-tax financing are effectively permitted within a corporate group. Examples of such relief include the exemption in the "term preferred share" rules for shares not acquired in the ordinary course of business of the financial institution that holds the shares, and the exemption from the special issuer and holder taxes in the case of "taxable preferred shares" where the holder has a "substantial interest" in the issuer.

There is presently no such in-house financing exception in the guaranteed preferred share rules in subsection 112(2.2). The absence of similar relief in that case may be a result of the fact that one would not normally expect to see shares issued by one member in a corporate family to another member being subject to a guarantee given by a third member of the family. Your submission, however, illustrates a case where, because of minority shareholders, it might be reasonable for a corporation to require a guarantee from a related party.

Upon review of the matter, we are satisfied that it would be consistent with the overall scheme of the preferred share rules to provide a limited exception for certain intra-group financing transactions in the guaranteed share context. [This is now in 112(2.21)(d) — ed.] Specifically, the proposed exemption would provide that subsection 112(2.2) does not apply to a dividend received on a share if:

(a) the issuer was, at the time the dividend was received, related (otherwise than by reason of a right referred to in paragraph 251(5)(b) to both the holder of the share and party giving the guarantee agreement;

(b) the share was not acquired by the holder in the ordinary course of the business carried on by the holder; and

(c) the guarantee agreement was not given in the ordinary course of the business carried on by the guarantor.

The first requirement ensures that the transaction is between members of a corporate group. The requirements that the acquisition of the share and the granting of the guarantee not take place in the ordinary course of business maintain consistency with the term preferred share rules, of which the guaranteed share rules are an extension. These latter requirements ensure that the share transaction is not a substitute for a lending transaction that would otherwise be undertaken in the course of a business.

We will recommend that an amendment to the Act to introduce such an exception be included in a future package of amendments, probably the next technical bill. We will also recommend that the proposed exception apply with respect to dividends received after 1998, regardless of the date of issue of the share.

As you know, I cannot offer any assurance that either the Minister of Finance or Parliament will agree with the recommendations that we intend to make in this regard. Nonetheless, I hope that this statement of our position is helpful.

Yours sincerely,

Brian Ernewein
Director, Tax Legislation Division, Tax Policy Branch

**Related Provisions**: 112(2.22) — Interpretation. See additional Related Provisions and Definitions at end of s. 112.

**(2.22) Interpretation** — For the purposes of subsections (2.2) and (2.21),

(a) where a guarantee agreement in respect of a share is given at any particular time after 8:00 p.m. Eastern Daylight Saving Time, June 18, 1987, otherwise than under a written arrangement to do so entered into before 8:00 p.m. Eastern Daylight Saving Time, June 18, 1987, the share is deemed to have been issued at the particular time and the guarantee agreement is deemed to have been given as part of a series of transactions that included the issuance of the share; and

(b) "specified person" has the meaning assigned by paragraph (h) of the definition "taxable preferred share" in subsection 248(1).

**Technical Notes**: New subsection 112(2.22) of the Act sets out rules of interpretation that apply to the guaranteed share rules in subsections (2.2) and (2.21). These provisions were formerly contained in paragraphs 112(2.2)(f) and (g). This new subsection applies to dividends received after 1998.

**Application**: Bill C-43 (First Reading September 20, 2000), s. 58, will add subsecs. 112(2.21) and (2.22), applicable in respect of dividends received after 1998.

**Related Provisions**: 248(1)"grandfathered share" — Share deemed not to be grandfathered share; 258(3) — Deemed interest on preferred share. See additional Related Provisions and Definitions at end of s. 112.

**(2.3) Idem** — No deduction may be made under subsection (1) or (2) or 138(6) in computing the taxable income of a particular corporation in respect of a dividend received on a share of the capital stock of a corporation as part of a dividend rental arrangement of the particular corporation.

**Related Provisions**: 126(4.2) — No foreign tax credit on short-term securities acquisitions; 248(1)"dividend rental arrangement"(c) — Dividend rental arrangement includes arrangement where 112(2.3) applies; 260(6.1) — Deductible amount under securities lending arrangement. See additional Related Provisions and Definitions at end of s. 112.

**Notes**: 112(2.3) added by 1989 Budget, effective for dividends on shares acquired after April 1989. For explanation, see Notes to 248(1)"dividend rental arrangement".

Former subsection 112(2.3) repealed by 1988 tax reform, owing to the introduction of Part VI.1 tax in 191.1. For short-term preferred shares (as defined in subsection 248(1) at that time) issued before 8 p.m. EDST, June 18, 1987, read:

> (2.3) Idem — No deduction may be made under subsection (1) or (2) in computing the taxable income of a particular corporation in respect of a dividend received by it on a share that was, at the time the dividend was paid, a short-term preferred share of a corporation unless, at the time the dividend was paid, the corporation was not dealing at arm's length with the particular corporation (otherwise than by virtue of a right referred to in paragraph 251(5)(b)).

**Advance Tax Rulings**: ATR-16: Inter-company dividends and interest expense.

**(2.4) Where no deduction permitted** — No deduction may be made under subsection (1) or (2) or subsection 138(6) in computing the taxable income of a particular corporation in respect of a dividend received on a share (in this subsection referred to as the "subject share"), other than an exempt share, of the capital stock of another corporation where

(a) any person or partnership was obligated, either absolutely or contingently, to effect an undertaking, including any guarantee, covenant or agreement to purchase or repurchase the subject share, under which an investor is entitled, either immediately or in the future, to receive or obtain any amount or benefit for the purpose of reducing the impact, in whole or in part, of any loss that an investor may sustain by virtue of the ownership, holding or disposition of the subject share, and any property is used, in whole or in part, either directly or indirectly in any manner whatever, to secure the undertaking; or

(b) the consideration for which the subject share was issued or any other property received, either directly or indirectly, by an issuer from an investor, or any property substituted therefor, is or includes

(i) an obligation of an investor to make payments that are required to be included, in whole or in part, in computing the income of the issuer, other than an obligation of a corporation that, immediately before the subject share was issued, would be related to the corporation that issued the subject share if this Act were read without reference to paragraph 251(5)(b), or

(ii) any right to receive payments that are required to be included, in whole or in part, in computing the income of the issuer where that right is held on condition that it or property substituted therefor may revert or pass to an investor or a person or partnership to be determined by an investor,

where that obligation or right was acquired by the issuer as part of a transaction or event or a series of transactions or events that included the issuance or acquisition of the subject share, or a share for which the subject share was substituted.

**Related Provisions**: 87(4.2) — Amalgamations; 112(2.5) — Application of subsec. (2.4); 112(2.6) — Definitions; 112(2.8) — Loss sustained by investor; 112(2.9) — Related corporations; 248(1) — "amount" of a stock dividend; 248(5) — Substituted property; 248(10) — Series of transactions. See additional Related Provisions and Definitions at end of s. 112.

**Notes**: The shares described in 112(2.4) are generally referred to as "collateralized preferred shares".

**Interpretation Bulletins**: IT-88R2: Stock dividends.

**(2.5) Application of subsec. (2.4)** — Subsection (2.4) applies only in respect of a dividend on a share where, having regard to all the circumstances, it may reasonably be considered that the share was issued or acquired as part of a transaction or event or a series of transactions or events that enabled any corporation to earn investment income, or any income substituted therefor, and, as a result, the amount of its taxes payable under this Act for a taxation year is less than the amount that its taxes payable under this Act would be for the year if that investment income were the only income of the corporation for the year and all other taxation years and no amount were deductible under subsections 127(5) and 127.2(1) in computing its taxes payable under this Act.

**Related Provisions**: 248(10) — Series of transactions.

**(2.6) Definitions** — For the purposes of this subsection and subsection (2.4),

"**exempt share**" means

(a) a prescribed share,

(b) a share of the capital stock of a corporation issued before 5:00 p.m. Eastern Standard Time, November 27, 1986, other than a share held at that time

(i) by the issuer, or

(ii) by any person or partnership where the issuer may become entitled to receive any amount after that time by way of subscription proceeds or contribution of capital with respect to that share pursuant to an agreement made before that time, or

(c) a share that was, at the time the dividend referred to in subsection (2.4) was received, a share described in paragraph (e) of the definition "term preferred share" in subsection 248(1) during the applicable time period referred to in that paragraph;

"**investor**" means the particular corporation referred to in subsection (2.4) and a person with whom that corporation does not deal at arm's length and any partnership or trust of which that corporation, or a person with whom that corporation does not deal at arm's length, is a member or beneficiary, but does not include the other corporation referred to in that subsection;

"**issuer**" means the other corporation referred to in subsection (2.4) and a person with whom that corporation does not deal at arm's length and any partnership or trust of which that corporation, or a person with whom that corporation does not deal at arm's length, is a member or beneficiary, but does not include the particular corporation referred to in that subsection.

**Related Provisions**: 112(2.7) — Change in agreement or condition; 248(13) — Interests in trusts and partnerships. See additional Related Provisions and Definitions at end of s. 112.

**Notes**: Para. (c) of "exempt share" added by 1993 technical bill, effective December 22, 1992.

**(2.7) Change in agreement or condition** — For the purposes of the definition "exempt share" in subsection (2.6), where at any time after 5:00 p.m. Eastern Standard Time, November 27, 1986 the terms or conditions of a share of the capital stock of a corporation have been changed or any agreement in respect of the share has been changed or entered into by the corporation, the share shall be deemed to have been issued at that time.

**(2.8) Loss sustained by investor** — For the purposes of paragraph (2.4)(a), any loss that an investor may sustain by virtue of the ownership, holding or disposition of the subject share referred to in that paragraph shall be deemed to include any loss with respect to an obligation or share that was issued or acquired as part of a transaction or event or a series of transactions or events that included the issuance or acquisition of the subject share, or a share for which the subject share was substituted.

**Related Provisions**: 248(10) — Series of transactions.

**(2.9) Related corporations** — For the purposes of subparagraph (2.4)(b)(i), where it may reasonably be considered having regard to all the circumstances that a corporation has become related to any other corporation for the purpose of avoiding any limitation upon the deduction of a dividend under subsection (1), (2) or 138(6), the corporation shall be deemed not to be related to the other corporation.

**Related Provisions**: 87(2)(rr) — Amalgamations — tax on taxable preferred shares. See additional Related Provisions and Definitions at end of s. 112.

**(3) Loss on share that is capital property** — Subject to subsections (5.5) and (5.6), the amount of any loss of a taxpayer (other than a trust) from the disposition of a share that is capital property of the taxpayer (other than a share that is property of a partnership) is deemed to be the amount of the loss determined without reference to this subsection minus,

(a) where the taxpayer is an individual, the lesser of

(i) the total of all amounts each of which is a dividend received by the taxpayer on the share in respect of which an election was made under subsection 83(2) where subsection 83(2.1) does not deem the dividend to be a taxable dividend, and

(ii) the loss determined without reference to this subsection minus all taxable dividends received by the taxpayer on the share; and

(b) where the taxpayer is a corporation, the total of all amounts received by the taxpayer on the share each of which is

(i) a taxable dividend, to the extent of the amount of the dividend that was deductible under this section or subsection 115(1) or 138(6) in computing the taxpayer's taxable income or taxable income earned in Canada for any taxation year,

(ii) a dividend in respect of which an election was made under subsection 83(2) where subsection 83(2.1) does not deem the dividend to be a taxable dividend, or

(iii) a life insurance capital dividend.

**Related Provisions**: 40(2)(g) — Restriction on capital losses; 40(3.3), (3.4) — Limitation on loss where share acquired by affiliated person; 40(3.7) — Application to non-resident individual; 53(1)(f) — Addition to ACB; 87(2)(x) — Amalgamations — flow-through to new corporation; 107(1)(c), (d) — Parallel stop-loss rule on disposition of interest in trust that flowed dividends out to corporation; 107.4(3)(b)(ii) — Application of stop-loss rule to qualifying disposition; 112(3.01) — Exclusion for certain dividends; 112(3.1),

(3.2) — Loss on share that is capital property of partnership or trust; 112(4)–(4.22) — Shares held as inventory; 112(5.2)C(b) — Adjustment for dividends received on mark-to-market property; 112(7) — Rules where shares exchanged. See additional Related Provisions and Definitions at end of s. 112.

**Notes**: 112(3) is a "stop-loss" rule reducing the loss of a corporation in certain cases from a disposition of a share that is capital property, where the corporation received tax-free dividends on the share. Analogous rules to deal with shares held by partnerships and trusts, and shares held as inventory, appear throughout 112(3.1)–(4.22).

For discussion of 112(3)–(3.32), see T.R. Burpee, "The New Stop-Loss Rules: Grandfathered Shares", 46(3) *Canadian Tax Journal* (1998), pp. 678-695.

112(3) amended by 1995-97 technical bill, effective for dispositions after April 26, 1995, other than:

(a) a disposition pursuant to an agreement in writing made before April 27, 1995;

(b) a disposition of a share of the capital stock of a corporation that is made to the corporation if

(i) on April 26, 1995 the share was owned by an individual (other than a trust) or by a particular trust under which an individual (other than a trust) was a beneficiary,

(ii) on April 26, 1995 a corporation, or a partnership of which a corporation is a member, was a beneficiary of a life insurance policy that insured the life of the individual or the individual's spouse,

(iii) it was reasonable to conclude on April 26, 1995 that a main purpose of the life insurance policy was to fund, directly or indirectly, in whole or in part, a redemption, acquisition or cancellation of the share by the corporation that issued the share, and

(iv) the disposition is made by

(A) the individual or the individual's spouse,

(B) the estate of the individual or of the individual's spouse within the estate's first taxation year,

(C) the particular trust where it is a trust described in 104(4)(a) or (a.1) in respect of a spouse, the spouse is the beneficiary referred to in (i) above and the disposition occurs before the end of the trust's third taxation year that begins after the spouse's death, or

(D) a trust described in 73(1)(c) created by the individual in respect of the individual's spouse, or a trust described in 70(6)(b) created by the individual's will in respect of the individual's spouse, before the end of the trust's third taxation year that begins after the spouse's death;

(c) a disposition of a share of the capital stock of a corporation owned by an individual on April 26, 1995 that was made by the individual's estate before 1997;

(d) a disposition of a share of the capital stock of a corporation owned by an estate on April 26, 1995, the first taxation year of which ended after that day, that was made by the estate before 1997; or

(e) a disposition of a share of the capital stock of a corporation owned by an individual on April 26, 1995 where the individual is a trust described in para. 104(4)(a) or (a.1) of the Act in respect of a spouse, that was made by the trust after the spouse's death and before 1997.

For purposes of the above, subsec. 131(12) of the 1995-97 technical bill provides:

(12) For the purposes of paragraph [(b) above] and this subsection, a share of the capital stock of a corporation acquired in exchange for another share in a transaction to which section 51, 85, 86 or 87 of the Act applies is deemed to be the same share as the other share.

(In other words, the grandfathering provided continues to apply despite any number of rollovers under the indicated provisions.)

Before the amendment, since October 31, 1994, read:

(3) **Loss on share that is capital property** — Subject to subsections (5.5) and (5.6), where a corporation owns a share that is a capital property and receives a taxable dividend, a capital dividend or a life insurance capital dividend in respect of that share, the amount of any loss of the corporation arising from transactions with reference to the share on which the dividend was received shall, unless it is established by the corporation that

(a) the corporation owned the share 365 days or longer before the loss was sustained, and

(b) the corporation and persons with whom the corporation was not dealing at arm's length did not, at the time the dividend was received, own in the aggregate more than 5% of the issued shares of any class of the capital stock of the corporation from which the dividend was received,

be deemed to be the amount of that loss otherwise determined, minus the total of all amounts each of which is an amount received by the corporation in respect of

(c) a taxable dividend on the share to the extent that the amount of the dividend was deductible from the corporation's income for any taxation year by virtue of this section or subsection 138(6) and was not an amount on which the corporation was required to pay tax under Part VII of the *Income Tax Act*, chapter 148 of the Revised Statutes of Canada, 1952, as it read on March 31, 1977,

(d) a capital dividend on the share, or

(e) a life insurance capital dividend on the share.

Reference to 112(5.5) and (5.6) added to 112(3) by 1994 tax amendments bill (Part III), effective for dispositions occurring after October 30, 1994.

**I.T. Application Rules**: 69 (meaning of "*Income Tax Act*, chapter 148 of the Revised Statutes of Canada, 1952").

**Interpretation Bulletins**: IT-88R2: Stock dividends; IT-328R3: Losses on shares on which dividends have been received.

**I.T. Technical News**: No. 12 (stop-loss provisions — grandfathering).

**(3.01) Loss on share that is capital property — excluded dividends** — A dividend shall not be included in the total determined under subparagraph (3)(a)(i) or paragraph (3)(b) where the taxpayer establishes that

(a) it was received when the taxpayer and persons with whom the taxpayer was not dealing at arm's length did not own in total more than 5% of the issued shares of any class of the capital stock of the corporation from which the dividend was received; and

(b) it was received on a share that the taxpayer owned throughout the 365-day period that ended immediately before the disposition.

**Related Provisions**: 87(2)(x) — Amalgamations — flow-through to new corporation; 112(5.6) — Stop-loss rules restricted.

**Notes**: 112(3.01) added by 1995-97 technical bill, effective on the same basis as the amendments to 112(3) (i.e., generally April 27, 1995 but subject to extensive grandfathering).

**(3.1) Loss on share held by partnership** — Subject to subsections (5.5) and (5.6), where a taxpayer (other than a partnership or a mutual fund trust) is a member of a partnership, the taxpayer's share of any loss of the partnership from the disposition of a share that is held by a particular partnership as capital property is deemed to be that share of the loss determined without reference to this subsection minus,

(a) where the taxpayer is an individual, the lesser of

(i) the total of all amounts each of which is a dividend received by the taxpayer on the share in respect of which an election was made under subsection 83(2) where subsection 83(2.1) does not deem the dividend to be a taxable dividend, and

(ii) that share of the loss determined without reference to this subsection minus all taxable dividends received by the taxpayer on the share;

(b) where the taxpayer is a corporation, the total of all amounts received by the taxpayer on the share each of which is

(i) a taxable dividend, to the extent of the amount of the dividend that was deductible under this section or subsection 115(1) or 138(6) in computing the taxpayer's taxable income or taxable income earned in Canada for any taxation year,

(ii) a dividend in respect of which an election was made under subsection 83(2) where subsection 83(2.1) does not deem the dividend to be a taxable dividend, or

(iii) a life insurance capital dividend; and

(c) where the taxpayer is a trust, the total of all amounts each of which is

(i) a taxable dividend, or

(ii) a life insurance capital dividend

received on the share and designated under subsection 104(19) or (20) by the trust in respect of a beneficiary that was a corporation, partnership or trust.

**Related Provisions**: 40(3.3), (3.4) — Limitation on loss where share acquired by affiliated person; 40(3.7) — Application to non-resident individual; 53(1)(f) — Addition to ACB; 87(2)(x) — Amalgamations — flow-through to new corporation; 100(4) — Application of stop-loss rule to disposition of interest in partnership; 104(20) — Designation re non-taxable dividends; 107.4(3)(b)(ii) — Application of stop-loss rule to qualifying disposition; 112(3.11) — Exclusion for certain dividends; 112(3.12) — Amount designated by trust to beneficiary that is a partnership or trust; 112(5.2)C(c) — Adjustment for dividends received on mark-to-market property; 112(7) — Rules where shares exchanged. See additional Related Provisions and Definitions at end of s. 112.

**Notes**: 112(3.1) amended by 1995-97 technical bill, effective on the same basis as the amendments to 112(3) (i.e., generally April 27, 1995 but subject to extensive grandfathering).

Before the amendment, since October 31, 1994, read:

(3.1) **Loss on share that is capital property of partnership** — Subject to subsections (5.5) and (5.6), where a corporation is a member of a partnership and the corporation receives a taxable dividend, a capital dividend or a life

Division C — Computation of Taxable Income                S. 112(3.2)(a)(iii)

insurance capital dividend in respect of a share that is a capital property of the partnership, the corporation's share of any loss of the partnership arising with respect to the share on which the dividend was received shall, unless it is established by the corporation that

(a) the partnership held the share 365 days or longer before the loss was sustained, and

(b) the partnership, the corporation and persons with whom the corporation was not dealing at arm's length did not, at the time the dividend was received, hold in the aggregate more than 5% of the issued shares of any class of the capital stock of the corporation from which the dividend was received,

be deemed to be the amount of that loss otherwise determined, minus the total of all amounts each of which is an amount received by the corporation in respect of

(c) a taxable dividend on the share to the extent that the amount of the dividend was deductible from the corporation's income for any taxation year by virtue of this section or subsection 138(6) and was not an amount on which the corporation was required to pay tax under Part VII of the *Income Tax Act*, chapter 148 of the Revised Statutes of Canada, 1952, as it read on March 31, 1977,

(d) a capital dividend on the share, or

(e) a life insurance capital dividend on the share.

Reference to 112(5.5) and (5.6) added to 112(3.1) by 1994 tax amendments bill (Part III), effective for dispositions occurring after October 30, 1994.

**I.T. Application Rules**: 69 (meaning of "*Income Tax Act*, chapter 148 of the Revised Statutes of Canada, 1952").

**Interpretation Bulletins**: IT-88R2: Stock dividends; IT-328R3: Losses on shares on which dividends have been received.

**I.T. Technical News**: No. 12 (stop-loss provisions — grandfathering).

**(3.11) Loss on share held by partnership — excluded dividends** — A dividend shall not be included in the total determined under subparagraph (3.1)(a)(i) or paragraph (3.1)(b) or (c) where the taxpayer establishes that

(a) it was received when the particular partnership, the taxpayer and persons with whom the taxpayer was not dealing at arm's length did not hold in total more than 5% of the issued shares of any class of the capital stock of the corporation from which the dividend was received; and

(b) it was received on a share that the particular partnership held throughout the 365-day period that ended immediately before the disposition.

**Related Provisions**: 87(2)(x) — Amalgamations — flow-through to new corporation; 112(5.6) — Stop-loss rules restricted.

**Notes**: 112(3.11) added by 1995-97 technical bill, effective on the same basis as the amendments to 112(3) (i.e., generally April 27, 1995 but subject to extensive grandfathering).

**(3.12) Loss on share held by partnership — excluded dividends** — A taxable dividend received on a share and designated under subsection 104(19) by a particular trust in respect of a beneficiary that was a partnership or trust shall not be included in the total determined under paragraph (3.1)(c) where the particular trust establishes that the dividend was received by an individual (other than a trust).

**Notes**: 112(3.12) added by 1995-97 technical bill, effective on the same basis as the amendments to 112(3) (i.e., generally April 27, 1995 but subject to extensive grandfathering).

**(3.2) Loss on share held by trust** — Subject to subsections (5.5) and (5.6), the amount of any loss of a trust (other than a mutual fund trust) from the disposition of a share of the capital stock of a corporation that is capital property of the trust is deemed to be the amount of the loss determined without reference to this subsection minus the total of

(a) the amount, if any, by which the lesser of

(i) the total of all amounts each of which is a dividend received by the trust on the share in respect of which an election was made under subsection 83(2) where subsection 83(2.1) does not deem the dividend to be a taxable dividend, and

(ii) the loss determined without reference to this subsection minus the total of all amounts each of which is the amount of a taxable dividend

(A) received by the trust on the share,

(B) received on the share and designated under subsection 104(19) by the trust in respect of a beneficiary who is an individual (other than a trust), or

(C) received on the share and designated under subsection 104(19) by the trust in respect of a beneficiary that was a corporation, partnership or another trust where the trust establishes that

(I) it owned the share throughout the 365-day period that ended immediately before the disposition, and

(II) the dividend was received while the trust, the beneficiary and persons not dealing at arm's length with the beneficiary owned in total less than 5% of the issued shares of any class of the capital stock of the corporation from which the dividend was received

exceeds

(iii) where the trust is an individual's estate, the share was acquired as a consequence of the individual's death and the disposition occurs during the trust's first taxation year, 1/4 of the lesser of

(A) the loss determined without reference to this subsection, and

(B) the individual's capital gain from the disposition of the share immediately before the individual's death, and

**Proposed Amendment — 112(3.2)(a)(iii)**

**Application**: The December 21, 2000 draft legislation, s. 55, will amend subpara. 112(3.2)(a)(iii) to replace the reference to "1/4" with "1/2", applicable to dispositions that occur after February 27,

963

S. 112(3.2)(a)(iii)      Income Tax Act, Part I

> 2000 except that, for dispositions that occurred before October 18, 2000, the reference to "1/2" shall be read as a reference to "1/3".
>
> **Technical Notes**: Subsections 112(3.2) and (3.3) provide rules for the determination of a loss of a trust from a disposition of a share where the trust has received taxable dividends and capital dividends on the share.
>
> The amendments to these subsections, which apply to dispositions that occur after February 27, 2000, replace the reference to the fraction "1/4" with a reference to the fraction "1/2" and are consequential on the reduction of the inclusion rate for capital gains from 3/4 to 1/2 [see 38(a) — ed.].

(b) the total of all amounts each of which is

(i) a taxable dividend, or

(ii) a life insurance capital dividend

received on the share and designated under subsection 104(19) or (20) by the trust in respect of a beneficiary that was a corporation, partnership or trust.

**Related Provisions**: 40(3.7) — Application to non-resident individual; 53(1)(f) — Addition to ACB; 87(2)(x) — Amalgamations — flow-through to new corporation; 104(20) — Designation re non-taxable dividends; 107.4(3)(b)(ii) — Application of stop-loss rule to qualifying disposition; 112(3.3), (3.31) — Exceptions; 112(5.2)C(b) — Adjustment for dividends received on mark-to-market property; 112(5.6) — Stop-loss rules restricted; 112(7) — Rules where shares exchanged. See additional Related Provisions and Definitions at end of s. 112.

**Notes**: See Notes to 112(3). 112(3.2) will apply to an estate (as well as other trusts); the ½ allowance in 112(3.2)(a)(iii) allows a capital dividend, funded by corporate-owned life insurance, to reduce the tax payable on freeze shares (high value, low PUC) on death. See Joel Cuperfain, "Life Insurance and the Reduction of Tax Liability", VI(4) *Insurance Planning* (Federated Press) 398-401 (1999).

112(3.2) amended by 1995-97 technical bill, effective on the same basis as the amendments to 112(3) (i.e., generally April 27, 1995 but subject to extensive grandfathering).

Before the amendment, since October 31, 1994, read:

> (3.2) **Loss on share that is capital property of trust** — Subject to subsections (5.5) and (5.6), where a corporation is a beneficiary of a trust (other than a prescribed trust) that owns a share that is capital property and the corporation receives a taxable dividend in respect of that share pursuant to a designation under subsection 104(19) or the trust has made a designation under subsection 104(20) in respect of the corporation for a capital dividend or a life insurance capital dividend on that share, the amount of any loss of the trust arising with respect to the share on which the dividend was subject to a designation shall, unless it is established by the corporation that
>
> (a) the trust owned the share 365 days or longer before the loss was sustained, and
>
> (b) the trust, the corporation and persons with whom the corporation was not dealing at arm's length did not, at the time the dividend was received, own in the aggregate more than 5% of the issued shares of any class of the capital stock of the corporation from which the dividend was received,
>
> be deemed to be the amount of that loss otherwise determined, minus the total of all amounts each of which is a taxable dividend, a capital dividend or a life insurance capital dividend in respect of that share that was designated under subsection 104(19) or (20) in respect of a beneficiary that was a corporation.

Reference to 112(5.5) and (5.6) added to 112(3.2) by 1994 tax amendments bill (Part III), effective for dispositions occurring after October 30, 1994.

**Interpretation Bulletins**: IT-88R2: Stock dividends; IT-328R3: Losses on shares on which dividends have been received.

**I.T. Technical News**: No. 12 (stop-loss provisions — grandfathering).

**(3.3) Loss on share held by trust — special cases** — Notwithstanding subsection (3.2), where a trust has at any time acquired a share of the capital stock of a corporation because of subsection 104(4), the amount of any loss of the trust from a disposition after that time is deemed to be the amount of the loss determined without reference to subsection (3.2) and this subsection minus the total of

(a) the amount, if any, by which the lesser of

(i) the total of all amounts each of which is a dividend received after that time by the trust on the share in respect of which an election was made under subsection 83(2) where subsection 83(2.1) does not deem the dividend to be a taxable dividend, and

(ii) the loss determined without reference to subsection (3.2) and this subsection minus the total of all amounts each of which is the amount of a taxable dividend

(A) received by the trust on the share after that time,

(B) received on the share after that time and designated under subsection 104(19) by the trust in respect of a beneficiary who is an individual (other than a trust), or

(C) received on the share after that time and designated under subsection 104(19) by the trust in respect of a beneficiary that was a corporation, partnership or another trust where the trust establishes that

(I) it owned the share throughout the 365-day period that ended immediately before the disposition, and

(II) the dividend was received when the trust, the beneficiary and persons not dealing at arm's length with the beneficiary owned in total less than 5% of the issued shares of any class of the capital stock of the corporation from which the dividend was received

exceeds

(iii) 1/4 of the lesser of

(A) the loss from the disposition, determined without reference to subsection (3.2) and this subsection, and

(B) the trust's capital gain from the disposition immediately before that time of the share because of subsection 104(4), and

> **Proposed Amendment —
> 112(3.3)(a)(iii)**
>
> **Application**: The December 21, 2000 draft legislation, s. 55, will amend subpara. 112(3.3)(a)(iii) to replace the reference to "1/4" with "1/2", applicable to dispositions that occur after February 27, 2000 except that, for dispositions that occurred before October 18, 2000, the reference to "1/2" shall be read as "1/3".
>
> **Technical Notes**: See under 112(3.2)(a)(iii).

(b) the total of all amounts each of which is a taxable dividend received on the share after that time and designated under subsection 104(19) by the trust in respect of a beneficiary that was a corporation, partnership or trust.

**Related Provisions**: 40(3.7) — Application to non-resident individual; 87(2)(x) — Amalgamations — flow-through to new corporation; 107.4(3)(b)(ii) — Application of stop-loss rule to qualifying disposition; 112(3.31), (3.32) — Excluded dividends; 112(5.6) — Stop-loss rules restricted; 112(7) — Rules where shares exchanged.

**Notes**: 112(3.3) added by 1995-97 technical bill, effective on the same basis as the amendments to 112(3) (i.e., generally April 27, 1995 but subject to extensive grandfathering).

**(3.31) Loss on share held by trust — excluded dividends** — No dividend received by a trust shall be included under subparagraph (3.2)(a)(i) or (b)(ii) or (3.3)(a)(i) where the trust establishes that the dividend

(a) was received,

(i) in any case where the dividend was designated under subsection 104(19) or (20) by the trust, when the trust, the beneficiary and persons with whom the beneficiary was not dealing at arm's length did not own in total more than 5% of the issued shares of any class of the capital stock of the corporation from which the dividend was received, or

(ii) in any other case, when the trust and persons with whom the trust was not dealing at arm's length did not own in total more than 5% of the issued shares of any class of the capital stock of the corporation from which the dividend was received, and

(b) was received on a share that the trust owned throughout the 365-day period that ended immediately before the disposition.

**Related Provisions**: 87(2)(x) — Amalgamations — flow-through to new corporation; 104(20) — Designation re non-taxable dividends; 112(5.6) — Stop-loss rules restricted; 112(7) — Rules where shares exchanged.

**Notes**: 112(3.31) added by 1995-97 technical bill, effective on the same basis as the amendments to 112(3) (i.e., generally April 27, 1995 but subject to extensive grandfathering).

**(3.32) Loss on share held by trust — excluded dividends** — No taxable dividend received on the share and designated under subsection 104(19) by the trust in respect of a beneficiary that was a corporation, partnership or trust shall be included under paragraph (3.2)(b) or (3.3)(b) where the trust establishes that the dividend was received by an individual (other than a trust), or

(a) was received when the trust, the beneficiary and persons with whom the beneficiary was not dealing at arm's length did not own in total more than 5% of the issued shares of any class of the capital stock of the corporation from which the dividend was received; and

(b) was received on a share that the trust owned throughout the 365-day period that ended immediately before the disposition.

**Related Provisions**: 87(2)(x) — Amalgamations — flow-through to new corporation.

**Notes**: 112(3.32) added by 1995-97 technical bill, effective on the same basis as the amendments to 112(3) (i.e., generally April 27, 1995 but subject to extensive grandfathering).

**(4) Loss on share that is not capital property** — Subject to subsections (5.5) and (5.6), the amount of any loss of a taxpayer (other than a trust) from the disposition of a share of the capital stock of a corporation that is property (other than capital property) of the taxpayer is deemed to be the amount of the loss determined without reference to this subsection minus,

(a) where the taxpayer is an individual and the corporation is resident in Canada, the total of all dividends received by the individual on the share;

(b) where the taxpayer is a partnership, the total of all dividends received by the partnership on the share; and

(c) where the taxpayer is a corporation, the total of all amounts received by the taxpayer on the share each of which is

(i) a taxable dividend, to the extent of the amount of the dividend that was deductible under this section, section 113 or subsection 115(1) or 138(6) in computing the taxpayer's taxable income or taxable income earned in Canada for any taxation year, or

(ii) a dividend (other than a taxable dividend).

**Related Provisions**: 87(2)(x) — Amalgamations — flow-through to new corporation; 93(2)–(2.3) — Loss limitation on disposition of share; 112(4.01) — Exclusion for certain dividends; 112(5.2)C(b) — Adjustment for dividends received on mark-to-market property. See additional Related Provisions and Definitions at end of s. 112.

**Notes**: 112(4) amended by 1995-97 technical bill, effective for dispositions after April 26, 1995. From October 31, 1994 to dispositions on April 26, 1995, read:

> (4) Loss on share that is not capital property — Subject to subsections (5.5) and (5.6), where a taxpayer owns a share that is not a capital property and receives a dividend in respect of that share, the amount of any loss of the taxpayer arising from transactions with reference to the share on which the dividend was received shall, unless it is established by the taxpayer that
>
> (a) the taxpayer owned the share 365 days or longer before the loss was sustained, and
>
> (b) the taxpayer and persons with whom the taxpayer was not dealing at arm's length, did not, at the time the divi-

dend was received, own in the aggregate more than 5% of the issued shares of any class of the capital stock of the corporation from which the dividend was received,

be deemed to be the amount of that loss otherwise determined, minus

(c) where the taxpayer is an individual and the corporation is a taxable Canadian corporation, the total of all amounts each of which is a dividend (other than a capital gains dividend within the meaning assigned by subsection 131(1)) on the share received by the taxpayer,

(d) where the taxpayer is a corporation, the total of all amounts each of which is

(i) a taxable dividend, to the extent of the amount thereof that was deductible under this section or subsection 115(1) or 138(6) in computing the taxpayer's taxable income or taxable income earned in Canada for any taxation year, or

(ii) a dividend (other than a taxable dividend or a dividend deemed by subsection 131(1) to be a capital gains dividend),

on the share received by the taxpayer, and

(e) in any other case, nil.

Reference to 112(5.5) and (5.6) added to 112(4) by 1994 tax amendments bill (Part III), effective for dispositions occurring after October 30, 1994.

112(4) amended by 1991 technical bill and extended (to refer to capital gains dividends) by 1993 technical bill, both effective 1990, but also effective for 1985 to 1989, where the taxpayer elected by notifying Revenue Canada in writing by December 10, 1993 (deadline extended by 1992 technical bill, s. 159) (in which case, notwithstanding 152(4) to (5), such assessments of tax, interest and penalties shall be made as are necessary to give effect to the election). However, 112(4) as amended does not apply to a dividend on which the taxpayer was required to pay tax under Part VII of the Act as it read on March 31, 1977.

For years before 1990 where the taxpayer does not elect, read everything after 112(4)(b) to the end of 112(4) as follows:

be deemed to be the amount of that loss otherwise determined, minus the total of all amounts received by the taxpayer in respect of dividends (other than capital gains dividends within the meaning assigned by subsection 131(1)) on the share to the extent that the amounts of those dividends were not amounts on which the taxpayer was required to pay tax under Part VII of the *Income Tax Act*, chapter 148 of the Revised Statutes of Canada, 1952, as it read on March 31, 1977.

**Interpretation Bulletins**: IT-88R2: Stock dividends; IT-328R3: Losses on shares on which dividends have been received.

## (4.01) Loss on share that is not capital property — excluded dividends — A dividend shall not be included in the total determined under paragraph (4)(a), (b) or (c) where the taxpayer establishes that

(a) it was received when the taxpayer and persons with whom the taxpayer was not dealing at arm's length did not own in total more than 5% of the issued shares of any class of the capital stock of the corporation from which the dividend was received; and

(b) it was received on a share that the taxpayer owned throughout the 365-day period that ended immediately before the disposition.

**Related Provisions**: 87(2)(x) — Amalgamations — flow-through to new corporation; 112(5.6) — Stop-loss rules restricted.

**Notes**: 112(4.01) added by 1995-97 technical bill, effective for dispositions after April 26, 1995.

## (4.1) Fair market value of shares held as inventory — For the purpose of section 10, the fair market value at any time of a share of the capital stock of a corporation is deemed to be equal to the fair market value of the share at that time, plus

(a) where the shareholder is a corporation, the total of all amounts received by the shareholder on the share before that time each of which is

(i) a taxable dividend, to the extent of the amount of the dividend that was deductible under this section, section 113 or subsection 115(1) or 138(6) in computing the shareholder's taxable income or taxable income earned in Canada for any taxation year, or

(ii) a dividend (other than a taxable dividend);

(b) where the shareholder is a partnership, the total of all amounts each of which is a dividend received by the shareholder on the share before that time; and

(c) where the shareholder is an individual and the corporation is resident in Canada, the total of all amounts each of which is a dividend received by the shareholder on the share before that time (or, where the shareholder is a trust, that would have been so received if this Act were read without reference to subsection 104(19)).

**Related Provisions**: 87(2)(x) — Amalgamations — flow-through to new corporation; 112(4.11) — Exclusion for certain dividends. See additional Related Provisions and Definitions at end of s. 112.

**Notes**: 112(4.1) amended by 1995-97 technical bill, effective for taxation years that end after April 26, 1995. For earlier years since 1990, read:

(4.1) Fair market value of share that is not capital property — Where a taxpayer (other than a prescribed trust) or partnership (in this subsection referred to as the "holder") holds a share that is not a capital property and a dividend is received in respect of that share, for the purpose of subsection 10(1) and any regulations made under that subsection, the fair market value of the share at any particular time after November 12, 1981 shall, unless it is established by the holder that

(a) the holder held the share 365 days or longer before the particular time, and

(b) the holder and persons with whom the holder was not dealing at arm's length did not, at the time the dividend was received, hold in the aggregate more than 5% of the issued shares of any class of the capital stock of the corporation from which the dividend was received,

be deemed to be an amount equal to the fair market value of that share at the particular time otherwise determined, plus

(c) where the holder is an individual and the corporation is a taxable Canadian corporation, the total of all amounts each of which is a dividend (other than a capital gains dividend within the meaning assigned by subsection 131(1)) on the share received before the particular time by the holder or that would have been so received if this Act were read without reference to subsection 104(19),

Division C — Computation of Taxable Income     S. 112(4.21)

(d) where the holder is a corporation, the total of all amounts each of which is

   (i) a taxable dividend, to the extent of the amount thereof that was deductible under this section, section 113 or subsection 115(1) or 138(6) in computing the holder's taxable income or taxable income earned in Canada for any taxation year, or

   (ii) a dividend (other than a taxable dividend or a dividend deemed by subsection 131(1) to be a capital gains dividend),

on the share received before the particular time by the holder,

(e) where the holder is a partnership, the total of all amounts each of which is a dividend (other than a capital gains dividend within the meaning assigned by subsection 131(1)) on the share received before the particular time by the holder, and

(f) in any other case, nil.

112(4.1) amended by 1991 technical bill and extended (to refer to capital gains dividends) by 1993 technical bill, both effective 1990, but also effective for 1985 to 1989 where the taxpayer elected by notifying Revenue Canada in writing by December 10, 1993 (deadline extended by 1992 technical bill, s. 159) (in which case, notwithstanding 152(4) to (5), such assessments of tax, interest and penalties shall be made as are necessary to give effect to the election). However, 112(4.1) as amended does not apply to a dividend on which the taxpayer was required to pay tax under Part VII of the Act as it read on March 31, 1977.

**Interpretation Bulletins**: IT-88R2: Stock dividends; IT-328R3: Losses on shares on which dividends have been received.

### (4.11) Fair market value of shares held as inventory — excluded dividends — A dividend shall not be included in the total determined under paragraph (4.1)(a), (b) or (c) where the shareholder establishes that

(a) it was received while the shareholder and persons with whom the shareholder was not dealing at arm's length did not hold in total more than 5% of the issued shares of any class of the capital stock of the corporation from which the dividend was received; and

(b) it was received on a share that the shareholder held throughout the 365-day period that ended at the time referred to in subsection (4.1).

**Related Provisions**: 87(2)(x) — Amalgamations — flow-through to new corporation.

**Notes**: 112(4.11) added by 1995-97 technical bill, effective for taxation years that end after April 26, 1995.

### (4.2) Loss on share held by trust — Subject to subsections (5.5) and (5.6), the amount of any loss of a trust from the disposition of a share that is property (other than capital property) of the trust is deemed to be the amount of the loss determined without reference to this subsection minus

(a) the total of all amounts each of which is a dividend received by the trust on the share, to the extent that the amount was not designated under subsection 104(20) in respect of a beneficiary of the trust; and

(b) the total of all amounts each of which is a dividend received on the share that was designated under subsection 104(19) or (20) by the trust in respect of a beneficiary of the trust.

**Related Provisions**: 87(2)(x) — Amalgamations — flow-through to new corporation; 104(20) — Designation re non-taxable dividends; 112(3.2) — Stop-loss rule; 112(4.21), (4.22) — Exclusions for certain dividends; 112(5.2)C(b) — Adjustment for dividends received on mark-to-market property. See additional Related Provisions and Definitions at end of s. 112.

**Notes**: 112(4.2) amended by 1995-97 technical bill, effective for dispositions after April 26, 1995. From October 31, 1994 to April 26, 1995, read:

(4.2) Where no deduction permitted — Subject to subsections (5.5) and (5.6), where a taxpayer is a member of a partnership and the taxpayer receives a dividend in respect of a share that is not a capital property of the partnership, the taxpayer's share of any loss of the partnership arising with respect to the share on which the dividend was received shall, unless it is established by the taxpayer that

(a) the partnership held the share 365 days or longer before the loss was sustained, and

(b) the partnership, the taxpayer and persons with whom the taxpayer was not dealing at arm's length did not, at the time the dividend was received, hold in the aggregate more than 5% of the issued shares of any class of the capital stock of the corporation from which the dividend was received,

be deemed to be the amount of that loss otherwise determined, minus

(c) where the taxpayer is an individual and the corporation is a taxable Canadian corporation, the total of all amounts each of which is a dividend (other than a capital gains dividend within the meaning assigned by subsection 131(1)) on the share received by the taxpayer,

(d) where the taxpayer is a corporation, the total of all amounts each of which is

   (i) a taxable dividend, to the extent of the amount thereof that was deductible under this section or subsection 115(1) or 138(6) in computing the taxpayer's taxable income or taxable income earned in Canada for any taxation year, or

   (ii) a dividend (other than a taxable dividend or a dividend deemed by subsection 131(1) to be a capital gains dividend),

on the share received by the taxpayer, and

(e) in any other case, nil.

Reference to 112(5.5) and (5.6) added to 112(4.2) by 1994 tax amendments bill (Part III), effective for dispositions occurring after October 30, 1994.

112(4.2) amended by 1991 technical bill and extended (to refer to capital gains dividends) by 1993 technical bill, both effective 1990, but also effective for 1985 to 1989 where the taxpayer elected by notifying Revenue Canada in writing by December 10, 1993 (deadline extended by 1992 technical bill, s. 159) (in which case, notwithstanding 152(4) to (5), such assessments of tax, interest and penalties shall be made as are necessary to give effect to the election). However, 112(4.2) as amended does not apply to a dividend on which the taxpayer was required to pay tax under Part VII of the Act as it read on March 31, 1977.

**Interpretation Bulletins**: IT-88R2: Stock dividends; IT-328R3: Losses on shares on which dividends have been received.

### (4.21) Loss on share held by trust — excluded dividends — A dividend shall not be

included in the total determined under paragraph (4.2)(a) where the taxpayer establishes that

(a) it was received when the trust and persons with whom the trust was not dealing at arm's length did not own in total more than 5% of the issued shares of any class of the capital stock of the corporation from which the dividend was received; and

(b) it was received on a share that the trust owned throughout the 365-day period that ended immediately before the disposition.

**Related Provisions**: 87(2)(x) — Amalgamations — flow-through to new corporation; 112(5.6) — Stop-loss rules restricted.

**Notes**: 112(4.21) added by 1995-97 technical bill, effective for dispositions after April 26, 1995.

**(4.22) Loss on share held by trust — excluded dividends** — A dividend shall not be included in the total determined under paragraph (4.2)(b) where the taxpayer establishes that

(a) it was received when the trust, the beneficiary and persons with whom the beneficiary was not dealing at arm's length did not own in total more than 5% of the issued shares of any class of the capital stock of the corporation from which the dividend was received; and

(b) it was received on a share that the trust owned throughout the 365-day period that ended immediately before the disposition.

**Related Provisions**: 87(2)(x) — Amalgamations — flow-through to new corporation; 112(5.6) — Stop-loss rules restricted.

**Notes**: 112(4.22) added by 1995-97 technical bill, effective for dispositions after April 26, 1995.

**(4.3)** [Repealed]

**Notes**: 112(4.3) repealed by 1995-97 technical bill, effective for dispositions after April 26, 1995. From October 31, 1994 to April 26, 1995, read:

(4.3) **Idem** — Subject to subsections (5.5) and (5.6), where a taxpayer is a beneficiary of a trust (other than a prescribed trust) that owns a share that is not capital property and the taxpayer receives a taxable dividend in respect of that share pursuant to a designation under subsection 104(19) or the trust has made a designation under subsection 104(20) in respect of the taxpayer for a dividend other than a taxable dividend on that share, the amount of any loss of the trust arising with respect to the share on which the dividend was subject to a designation shall, unless it is established by the taxpayer that

(a) the trust owned the share 365 days or longer before the loss was sustained, and

(b) the trust, the taxpayer and persons with whom the taxpayer was not dealing at arm's length did not, at the time the dividend was received, own in the aggregate more than 5% of the issued shares of any class of the capital stock of the corporation from which the dividend was received,

be deemed to be the amount of that loss otherwise determined, minus the total of all amounts each of which is a dividend (other than a capital gains dividend within the meaning assigned by subsection 131(1)) in respect of that share that was designated under subsection 104(19) or (20) in respect of the taxpayer.

Reference to 112(5.5) and (5.6) added to 112(4.3) by 1994 tax amendments bill (Part III), effective for dispositions occurring after October 30, 1994.

**Interpretation Bulletins**: IT-88R2: Stock dividends; IT-328R3: Losses on shares on which dividends have been received.

**(5) Disposition of share by financial institution** — Subsection (5.2) applies to the disposition of a share by a taxpayer in a taxation year where

(a) the taxpayer is a financial institution in the year;

(b) the share is a mark-to-market property for the year; and

(c) the taxpayer received a dividend on the share at a time when the taxpayer and persons with whom the taxpayer was not dealing at arm's length held in total more than 5% of the issued shares of any class of the capital stock of the corporation from which the dividend was received.

**Related Provisions**: 87(2)(e.5) — Amalgamations — continuing corporation; 88(1)(h) — Windup — continuing corporation; 112(5.4) — Deemed dispositions and reacquisitions to be ignored; 138(11.5)(k.2) — Transfer of business by non-resident insurer.

**Notes**: 112(5) added by 1994 tax amendments bill (Part III), effective for dispositions in taxation years that begin after October 1994.

**(5.1) Share held for less than one year** — Subsection (5.2) applies to the disposition of a share by a taxpayer in a taxation year where

(a) the disposition is an actual disposition;

(b) the taxpayer did not hold the share throughout the 365-day period that ended immediately before the disposition; and

(c) the share was a mark-to-market property of the taxpayer for a taxation year that begins after October 1994 and in which the taxpayer was a financial institution.

**Related Provisions**: 87(2)(e.5) — Amalgamations — continuing corporation; 88(1)(h) — Windup — continuing corporation; 112(5.4) — Deemed dispositions and reacquisitions to be ignored; 138(11.5)(k.2) — Transfer of business by non-resident insurer.

**Notes**: 112(5.1)(b) amended by 1995-97 technical bill, effective for dispositions after April 26, 1995. For earlier dispositions, read:

(b) the taxpayer held the share for less than 365 days; and

112(5.1) added by 1994 tax amendments bill (Part III), effective for dispositions in taxation years that begin after October 1994.

**(5.2) Adjustment re dividends** — Subject to subsection (5.3), where subsection (5) or (5.1) provides that this subsection applies to the disposition of a share by a taxpayer at any time, the taxpayer's proceeds of disposition shall be deemed to be the amount determined by the formula

$$A + B - (C - D)$$

where

A is the taxpayer's proceeds determined without reference to this subsection,

B is the lesser of

(a) the loss, if any, from the disposition of the share that would be determined before the application of this subsection if the cost of the share to any taxpayer were determined without reference to

(i) paragraphs 87(2)(e.2) and (e.4), 88(1)(c), 138(11.5)(e) and 142.5(2)(b),

(ii) subsection 85(1), where the provisions of that subsection are required by paragraph 138(11.5)(e) to be applied, and

(iii) paragraph 142.6(1)(d), and

(b) the total of all amounts each of which is

(i) where the taxpayer is a corporation, a taxable dividend received by the taxpayer on the share, to the extent of the amount that was deductible under this section or subsection 115(1) or 138(6) in computing the taxpayer's taxable income or taxable income earned in Canada for any taxation year,

(ii) where the taxpayer is a partnership, a taxable dividend received by the taxpayer on the share, to the extent of the amount that was deductible under this section or subsection 115(1) or 138(6) in computing the taxable income or taxable income earned in Canada for any taxation year of members of the partnership,

(iii) where the taxpayer is a trust, an amount designated under subsection 104(19) in respect of a taxable dividend on the share, or

(iv) a dividend (other than a taxable dividend) received by the taxpayer on the share,

C is the total of all amounts each of which is the amount by which

(a) the taxpayer's proceeds of disposition on a deemed disposition of the share before that time were increased because of this subsection,

(b) where the taxpayer is a corporation or trust, a loss of the taxpayer on a deemed disposition of the share before that time was reduced because of subsection (3), (3.2), (4) or (4.2), or

(c) where the taxpayer is a partnership, a loss of a member of the partnership on a deemed disposition of the share before that time was reduced because of subsection (3.1) or (4.2), and

D is the total of all amounts each of which is the amount by which the taxpayer's proceeds of disposition on a deemed disposition of the share before that time were decreased because of this subsection.

**Related Provisions**: 87(2)(e.5) — Amalgamations — continuing corporation; 88(1)(h) — Windup — continuing corporation; 112(5.21) — Exclusion for certain dividends; 112(5.3), (5.4) — Application; 112(5.5), (5.6) — Stop-loss rules not applicable;

138(11.5)(k.2) — Transfer of business by non-resident insurer; 257 — Formula cannot calculate to less than zero.

**Notes**: 112(5.2)B(b)(iv) amended by 1995-97 technical bill to delete the words "or a dividend deemed by subsection 131(1) to be a capital gains dividend" after "taxable dividend"; and 112(5.2)C(b) amended to change reference from (4.3) to (4.2); both effective for dispositions after April 26, 1995.

112(5.2) added by 1994 tax amendments bill (Part III), effective for dispositions in taxation years that begin after October 1994.

**(5.21) Subsection (5.2) — excluded dividends** — A dividend shall not be included in the total determined under paragraph (b) of the description of B in subsection (5.2) unless

(a) the dividend was received when the taxpayer and persons with whom the taxpayer did not deal at arm's length held in total more than 5% of the issued shares of any class of the capital stock of the corporation from which the dividend was received; or

(b) the share was not held by the taxpayer throughout the 365-day period that ended immediately before the disposition.

**Notes**: 112(5.21) added by 1995-97 technical bill, effective for dispositions after April 26, 1995.

**(5.3) Adjustment not applicable** — For the purpose of determining the cost of a share to a taxpayer on a deemed reacquisition of the share after a deemed disposition of the share, the taxpayer's proceeds of disposition shall be determined without regard to subsection (5.2).

**Notes**: 112(5.3) added by 1994 tax amendments bill (Part III), effective for dispositions in taxation years that begin after October 1994.

**(5.4) Deemed dispositions** — Where a taxpayer disposes of a share at any time,

(a) for the purpose of determining whether subsection (5.2) applies to the disposition, the conditions in subsections (5) and (5.1) shall be applied without regard to a deemed disposition and reacquisition of the share before that time; and

(b) total amounts under subsection (5.2) in respect of the disposition shall be determined from the time when the taxpayer actually acquired the share.

**Related Provisions**: 87(2)(e.5) — Amalgamations — continuing corporation; 88(1)(h) — Windup — continuing corporation; 138(11.5)(k.2) — Transfer of business by non-resident insurer.

**Notes**: 112(5.4) added by 1994 tax amendments bill (Part III), effective for dispositions in taxation years that begin after October 1994.

**(5.5) Stop-loss rules not applicable** — Subsections (3) to (4) and (4.2) do not apply to the disposition of a share by a taxpayer in a taxation year that begins after October 1994 where

(a) the share is a mark-to-market property for the year and the taxpayer is a financial institution in the year; or

(b) subsection (5.2) applies to the disposition.

**Related Provisions**: 112(5.6) — Transitional rules.

**Notes**: Reference to 112(4.3) deleted from opening words of 112(5.5) by 1995-97 technical bill, effective for dispositions after April 26, 1995.

112(5.5) added by 1994 tax amendments bill (Part III), effective for dispositions in taxation years that begin after October 1994.

**(5.6) Stop-loss rules restricted** — In determining whether any of subsections (3) to (4) and (4.2) apply to reduce a loss of a taxpayer from the disposition of a share, this Act shall be read without reference to paragraphs (3.01)(b) and (3.11)(b), subclauses (3.2)(a)(ii)(C)(I) and (3.3)(a)(ii)(C)(I) and paragraphs (3.31)(b), (3.32)(b), (4.01)(b), (4.21)(b) and (4.22)(b) where

(a) the disposition occurs

(i) because of subsection 142.5(2) in a taxation year that includes October 31, 1994, or

(ii) because of paragraph 142.6(1)(b) after October 30, 1994; or

(b) the share was a mark-to-market property of the taxpayer for a taxation year that begins after October 1994 in which the taxpayer was a financial institution.

**Notes**: Opening words of 112(5.6) amended by 1995-97 technical bill, effective for dispositions after April 26, 1995. For dispositions from October 31, 1994 to April 26, 1995, read:

(5.6) Stop-loss rules restricted — In determining whether any of subsections (3) to (4), (4.2) and (4.3) apply to the disposition of a share by a taxpayer, each of those subsections shall be read without reference to paragraph (a) of the subsection where

112(5.6) added by 1994 tax amendments bill (Part III), effective for dispositions occurring after October 30, 1994.

**(6) Meaning of certain expressions** — For the purposes of this section,

(a) ["dividend", "taxable dividend"] — "dividend" and "taxable dividend" do not include a capital gains dividend (within the meaning assigned by subsection 131(1)) or any dividend received by a taxpayer on which the taxpayer was required to pay tax under Part VII of the *Income Tax Act*, chapter 148 of the Revised Statutes of Canada, 1952, as it read on March 31, 1977;

**Related Provisions**: 248(1) — Definitions of "dividend" and "taxable dividend".

**Notes**: 112(6)(a) amended by 1995-97 technical bill, effective April 27, 1995. From 1972 until the amendment, read:

(a) "taxable dividend" does not include a capital gains dividend within the meaning assigned by subsection 131(1); or

(b) ["control"] — one corporation is controlled by another corporation if more than 50% of its issued share capital (having full voting rights under all circumstances) belongs to the other corporation, to persons with whom the other corporation does not deal at arm's length, or to the other corporation and persons with whom the other corporation does not deal at arm's length; and

(c) ["financial institution", "mark-to-market property"] — "financial institution" and "mark-to-market property" have the meanings assigned by subsection 142.2(1).

**Related Provisions**: See Related Provisions and Definitions at end of s. 112.

**Notes**: 112(6)(c) added by 1994 tax amendments bill (Part III), effective for taxation years that begin after October 1994.

**(7) Rules where shares exchanged** — Where a share (in this subsection referred to as the "new share") has been acquired in exchange for another share (in this subsection referred to as the "old share") in a transaction to which section 51, 85.1, 86 or 87 applies, for the purposes of the application of any of subsections (3) to (3.32) in respect of a disposition of the new share, the new share is deemed to be the same share as the old share, except that

(a) any dividend received on the old share is deemed for those purposes to have been received on the new share only to the extent of the proportion of the dividend that

(i) the shareholder's adjusted cost base of the new share immediately after the exchange

is of

(ii) the shareholder's adjusted cost base of all new shares immediately after the exchange acquired in exchange for the old share; and

(b) the amount, if any, by which a loss from the disposition of the new share is reduced because of the application of this subsection shall not exceed the proportion of the shareholder's adjusted cost base of the old share immediately before the exchange that

(i) the shareholder's adjusted cost base of the new share immediately after the exchange

is of

(ii) the shareholder's adjusted cost base of all new shares, immediately after the exchange, acquired in exchange for the old share.

**Related Provisions**: 40(3.7) — Application to non-resident individual.

**Notes**: 112(7) amended by 1995-97 technical bill, effective for dispositions after April 26, 1995. Before then, read:

(7) Rules where shares exchanged — Where at a particular time a share (in this subsection referred to as the "new share") has been acquired by a corporation, partnership or trust (in this subsection referred to as the "holder") in exchange for another share (in this subsection referred to as the "old share") by means of a transaction to which section 51, 85.1, 86 or 87 applies, any reference in subsection (3), (3.1) or (3.2) to a share shall be deemed to include a reference to the new share and the old share as though they were the same share, except that the total of the amounts to be deducted from a loss otherwise determined on any new share of the holder, in respect of dividends received, or designated by the holder, in respect of the share, shall be deemed to be the total of

(a) the total of all amounts each of which is an amount that would be determined under subsection (3), (3.1) or (3.2) in respect of a taxable dividend, a capital dividend

Division C — Computation of Taxable Income    S. 113(1)(b)(i)(A)

or a life insurance capital dividend received or designated by the holder in respect of the new share only, and

(b) the amount determined by the formula

$$A \times \frac{B}{C}$$

where

A is the total of all amounts each of which is the amount determined in respect of an old share exchanged by the holder at the particular time equal to the lesser of

(i) the total of all amounts each of which is received or designated by the holder in respect of a taxable dividend, a capital dividend or a life insurance capital dividend on the old share, and

(ii) the adjusted cost base to the holder of the old share immediately before the particular time,

B is the adjusted cost base to the holder of the new share immediately after the exchange, and

C is the adjusted cost base to the holder of all new shares immediately after the exchange,

to the extent that those amounts were not amounts on which the holder was required to pay tax under Part VII of the *Income Tax Act*, chapter 148 of the Revised Statutes of Canada, 1952, as it read on March 31, 1977.

112(7)(b) amended by 1993 technical bill, effective for losses arising in 1992 and later taxation years. The substantive change was to add 112(7)(b)A(ii). For earlier losses, read:

(b) that proportion of the total of all amounts each of which is an amount received or designated by the holder in respect of a taxable dividend, a capital dividend or a life insurance capital dividend on all the old shares exchanged at the particular time that

(i) the adjusted cost base to the holder of the new share immediately after the exchange

is of

(ii) the adjusted cost base to the holder of all new shares immediately after the exchange

**I.T. Application Rules**: 69 (meaning of "*Income Tax Act*, chapter 148 of the Revised Statutes of Canada, 1952").

**Interpretation Bulletins [subsec. 112(7)]**: IT-88R2: Stock dividends; IT-269R3: Part IV tax on dividends received by a private corporation or a subject corporation; IT-328R3: Losses on shares on which dividends have been received.

**Related Provisions [s. 112]**: 66(1) — Exploration development expenses of principal-business corporations; 82(2) — Certain dividends deemed received by taxpayer; 138(6) — Insurance corporations — Deduction for dividends from taxable corporations; 187.2 — Tax on dividends on taxable preferred shares; 187.3 — Tax on dividends on taxable RFI shares.

**Definitions [s. 112]**: "adjusted cost base" — 54, 248(1); "amount" — 248(1); "arm's length" — 251(1); "business" — 248(1); "Canada" — 255; "capital dividend" — 83(2), 248(1); "capital property" — 54, 248(1); "class of shares" — 248(1); "consequence of the individual's death" — 248(8); "controlled" — 112(6)(b), 256(6), (6.1); "corporation" — 248(1), *Interpretation Act* 35(1); "disposition" — 248(1); "dividend" — 112(6)(a), 248(1); "dividend rental arrangement" — 248(1); "exempt share" — 112(2.6), (2.7); "financial institution" — 112(6)(c), 142.2(1); "foreign affiliate" — 95(1), 248(1); "grandfathered share" — 248(1); "guarantee agreement", "guarantor" — 112(2.2)(a); "individual", "insurance corporation" — 248(1); "investment corporation" — 130(3)(a), 248(1); "investor", "issuer" — 112(2.6); "life insurance capital dividend" — 248(1); "mark-to-market property" — 112(6)(c), 142.2(1); "mutual fund corporation" — 131(8), 248(1); "mutual fund trust" — 132(6)–(7), 132.2(1)(q), 248(1); "non-resi-

dent-owned investment corporation" — 133(8), 248(1); "partnership" — see Notes to 96(1); "permanent establishment" — Reg. 8201; "person", "prescribed" — 248(1); "prescribed stock exchange" — Reg. 3200, 3201; "property" — 248(1); "received" — 248(7); "regulation" — 248(1); "related" — 112(2.9), 251; "resident in Canada" — 250; "restricted financial institution" — 248(1); "series of transactions" — 248(10); "share" — 112(7), 248(1); "short-term preferred share" — 248(1); "specified financial institution" — 248(1), 248(14); "specified person" — 112(2.2)(g) [to be repealed], 112(2.22)(b) [draft]; "substituted property" — 248(5); "tax payable" — 248(2); "taxable Canadian corporation" — 89(1), 248(1); "taxable dividend" — 89(1), 112(6)(a), 248(1); "taxable income" — 2(2), 248(1); "taxable income earned in Canada" — 115(1), 248(1); "taxable preferred share" — 248(1); "taxation year" — 249; "taxpayer", "term preferred share" — 248(1); "trust" — 104(1), 248(1), (3); "written" — *Interpretation Act* 35(1)"writing".

### 113. (1) Deduction in respect of dividend received from foreign affiliate

Where in a taxation year a corporation resident in Canada has received a dividend on a share owned by it of the capital stock of a foreign affiliate of the corporation, there may be deducted from the income for the year of the corporation for the purpose of computing its taxable income for the year, an amount equal to the total of

(a) an amount equal to such portion of the dividend as is prescribed to have been paid out of the exempt surplus, as defined by regulation (in this Part referred to as "exempt surplus") of the affiliate,

(b) an amount equal to the lesser of

(i) the product obtained when the foreign tax prescribed to be applicable to such portion of the dividend as is prescribed to have been paid out of the taxable surplus, as defined by regulation (in this Part referred to as "taxable surplus") of the affiliate is multiplied by the amount by which

(A) the relevant tax factor

---

**Proposed Amendment — 113(1)(b)(i)(A)**

(A) the corporation's relevant tax factor for the year,

**Application**: The June 22, 2000 draft legislation, subsec. 16(1), will amend cl. 113(1)(b)(i)(A) to read as above, applicable after 2000.

**Technical Notes**: Subsection 113(1) of the Act permits a resident corporation to deduct specified amounts in respect of dividends received from a foreign affiliate out of the exempt, taxable and pre-acquisition surplus of the foreign affiliate. The amounts so deductible are determined largely with reference to Part LIX of the Regulations. The deductions under paragraphs 113(1)(b) and (c) with regard to dividends out of taxable surplus are also determined with reference to the resident corporation's "relevant tax factor".

Subsection 113(1) is amended to explicitly link the "relevant tax factor" to the resident corporation receiving the dividends and the taxation year in which the dividends are received. This is consistent with the more explicit defini-

tion of "relevant tax factor" described above in the commentary on subsection 95(1).
This amendment applies after 2000.

>    exceeds
>    (B) one, and
> (ii) that portion of the dividend,
> (c) an amount equal to the lesser of
>    (i) the product obtained when
>       (A) the non-business-income tax paid by the corporation applicable to such portion of the dividend as is prescribed to have been paid out of the taxable surplus of the affiliate
>    is multiplied by
>       (B) the relevant tax factor, and

**Proposed Amendment — 113(1)(c)(i)(B)**

(B) the corporation's relevant tax factor for the year,

**Application**: The June 22, 2000 draft legislation, subsec. 16(2), will amend cl. 113(1)(c)(i)(B) to read as above, applicable after 2000.

**Technical Notes**: See under 113(1)(b)(i)(A).

> (ii) the amount by which such portion of the dividend as is prescribed to have been paid out of the taxable surplus of the affiliate exceeds the deduction in respect thereof referred to in paragraph (b); and
> (d) an amount equal to such portion of the dividend as is prescribed to have been paid out of the pre-acquisition surplus of the affiliate,

and for the purposes of this subsection and subdivision i of Division B, the corporation may make such elections as may be prescribed.

**Related Provisions**: 20(13) — Deduction for dividend; 91(5) — Amounts deductible in respect of dividends received; 92(4)–(6) — Where dividend from pre-acquisition surplus received by partnership; 93(1.2) — Disposition of share of foreign affiliate held by partnership; 93(3) — Exempt dividends; 93.1(2) — Dividend on shares of foreign affiliate held by partnership; 94.3(2)(a)(i)(B)(II) — Prevention of double taxation; 111(8)"non-capital loss"A:E — Carryforward of dividend deduction as non-capital loss; 112(2) — Deduction for dividend received from corporation that is not a foreign affiliate; 113(4) — Dividend received before 1976; 186(1) — Part IV tax on certain taxable dividends; 186(3)"assessable dividend" — Part IV tax. See additional Related Provisions and Definitions at end of s. 113.

**Notes**: Dividends repatriated from foreign affiliates out of exempt surplus (as opposed to taxable surplus) are included in income under 82(1) and then deducted under 113(1)(a), resulting in no corporate tax. The dividend is presumed to be from income which bore foreign tax, and the dividend itself may have been subject to foreign withholding tax. Dividends from pre-acquisition surplus are similarly deductible under 113(1)(d). (For dividends from Canadian corporations, see 112(1).)

**Regulations**: 5900–5902, 5906, 5907 (prescribed portion, prescribed foreign tax, prescribed elections, definitions); 5900(1)(c) (pre-acquisition surplus); 5907(1.01) (exempt surplus, taxable surplus).

**Interpretation Bulletins**: IT-269R3: Part IV tax on taxable dividends received by a private corporation or a subject corporation; IT-328R3: Losses on shares on which dividends have been received.

**Information Circulars**: 77-9R: Books, records and other requirements for taxpayers having foreign affiliates.

**(2) Additional deduction** — Where, at any particular time in a taxation year ending after 1975, a corporation resident in Canada has received a dividend on a share owned by it at the end of its 1975 taxation year of the capital stock of a foreign affiliate of the corporation, there may be deducted from the income for the year of the corporation for the purpose of computing its taxable income for the year, an amount in respect of the dividend equal to the lesser of

(a) the amount, if any, by which the amount of the dividend so received exceeds the total of

(i) the deduction in respect of the dividend permitted by subsection 91(5) in computing the corporation's income for the year, and

(ii) the deduction in respect of the dividend permitted by subsection (1) from the income for the year of the corporation for the purpose of computing its taxable income, and

(b) the amount, if any, by which

(i) the adjusted cost base to the corporation of the share at the end of its 1975 taxation year

exceeds the total of

(ii) [Repealed under former Act]

(iii) such amounts in respect of dividends received by the corporation on the share after the end of its 1975 taxation year and before the particular time as are deductible under paragraph (1)(d) in computing the taxable income of the corporation for taxation years ending after 1975,

(iii.1) the total of all amounts received by the corporation on the share after the end of its 1975 taxation year and before the particular time on a reduction of the paid-up capital of the foreign affiliate in respect of the share, and

(iv) the total of all amounts deducted under this subsection in respect of dividends received by the corporation on the share before the particular time.

**Related Provisions**: 92 — ACB of share in foreign affiliate; 113(1) — Deduction in respect of dividend received from foreign affiliate; 186(3)"assessable dividend" — Part IV tax. See additional Related Provisions and Definitions at end of s. 113.

**Interpretation Bulletins**: IT-98R2: Investment corporations; IT-269R3: Part IV tax on taxable dividends received by a private corporation or a subject corporation.

**(3) Definitions** — In this section,

**"non-business-income tax"** paid by a taxpayer has the meaning assigned by subsection 126(7);

**"relevant tax factor"** has the meaning assigned by subsection 95(1).

**Notes:** 113(3)"non-business-income tax" was 113(3)(b) and 113(3)"relevant tax factor" was 113(3)(a) before consolidation in R.S.C. 1985 (5th Supp.), effective for taxation years ending after November 1991.

**(4) Portion of dividend deemed paid out of exempt surplus** — Such portion of any dividend received at any time in a taxation year by a corporation resident in Canada on a share owned by it of the capital stock of a foreign affiliate of the corporation, that was received after the 1971 taxation year of the affiliate and before the affiliate's 1976 taxation year, as exceeds the amount deductible in respect of the dividend under paragraph (1)(d) in computing the corporation's taxable income for the year shall, for the purposes of paragraph (1)(a), be deemed to be the portion of the dividend prescribed to have been paid out of the exempt surplus of the affiliate.

**Related Provisions**: 113(1) — Deduction in respect of dividend received from foreign affiliate. See additional Related Provisions and Definitions at end of s. 113.

**Related Provisions [s. 113]**: 66(1) — Exploration and development expenses of principal-business corporations; 80.1(4) — Assets acquired from foreign affiliate of taxpayer as dividend in kind or as benefit to shareholder; 82(2) — Dividend deemed received by taxpayer; 126(4) — Portion of foreign tax not included; 187.2 — Tax on dividends on taxable preferred shares; 187.3 — Tax on dividends on taxable RFI shares; 258(3) — Certain dividends on preferred shares deemed to be interest; 258(5) — Deemed interest on certain shares.

**Definitions [s. 113]**: "adjusted cost base" — 54; "amount" — 248(1); "Canada" — 255; "corporation" — 248(1), Interpretation Act 35(1); "dividend" — 248(1); "exempt surplus" — 113(1)(a), Reg. 5907(1); "foreign affiliate" — 93.1(1), 95(1), 248(1); "individual" — 248(1); "non-business-income tax" — 113(3), 126(7); "pre-acquisition surplus" — Reg. 5900(1)(c); "prescribed" — 248(1); "relevant tax factor" — 95(1), 113(3); "resident in Canada" — 250; "share" — 248(1); "taxable income" — 2(2), 248(1); "taxable surplus" — 113(1)(b)(i), Reg. 5907(1); "taxation year" — 249; "taxpayer" — 248(1).

**114. Individual resident in Canada for only part of year** — Notwithstanding subsection 2(2), where an individual is resident in Canada throughout part of a taxation year, and throughout another part of the year is non-resident, the individual's taxable income for the year is the amount, if any, by which the total of

(a) the individual's income for the period or periods in the year throughout which the individual is resident in Canada, computed without regard to section 61.2 and as though that period or those periods were the whole taxation year, and

(b) the amount that would be the individual's taxable income earned in Canada for the year if at no time in the year the individual had been resident in Canada, computed as though the part of the year that is not in the period or periods referred to in paragraph (a) were the whole taxation year,

exceeds

(c) the total of

(i) such of the deductions permitted for the purpose of computing taxable income as can reasonably be considered wholly applicable, and

(ii) such part of any other of those deductions as can reasonably be considered applicable

to the period or periods referred to in paragraph (a),

except that the total of all amounts included in computing the total determined under paragraph (c) and all amounts deducted because of paragraphs 115(1)(d) to (f) in respect of the individual for the year shall not exceed the total of the amounts that would have been deductible in computing the individual's taxable income for the year had the individual been resident in Canada throughout the year.

### Proposed Amendment — 114

**114. Individual resident in Canada for only part of year** — Notwithstanding subsection 2(2), the taxable income for a taxation year of an individual who is resident in Canada throughout part of the year and non-resident throughout another part of the year is the amount, if any, by which

(a) the amount that would be the individual's income for the year if the individual had no income or losses, for the part of the year throughout which the individual was non-resident, other than

(i) income or losses described in paragraphs 115(1)(a) to (c), and

(ii) income that would have been included in the individual's taxable income earned in Canada for the year under subparagraph 115(1)(a)(v) if the part of the year throughout which the individual was non-resident were the whole taxation year

exceeds the total of

(b) the deductions permitted by subsection 111(1) and, to the extent that they relate to amounts included in computing the amount determined under paragraph (a), the deductions permitted by any of paragraphs 110(1)(d), (d.1), (d.2) and (f), and

(c) any other deduction permitted for the purpose of computing taxable income to the extent that

(i) it can reasonably be considered to be applicable to the part of the year throughout which the individual was resident in Canada, or

(ii) if all or substantially all of the individual's income for the part of the year throughout which the individual was non-resident is included in the amount determined under paragraph (a), it can reasonably be considered to be applicable to that part of the year.

**Definitions**: "amount", "individual", "non-resident" — 248(1); "resident in Canada" — 250; "taxable income", "taxable income earned in Canada" — 248(1); "taxation year" — 249.

**Application**: Bill C-43 (First Reading September 20, 2000), s. 59, will amend s. 114 to read as above, applicable to 1998 et seq.

**Technical Notes**: Section 114 of the Act provides rules for computing the taxable income of an individual (often referred to as a "part-year resident") who is resident in Canada for some period or periods in a taxation year, and is non-resident for the rest of the year.

In its current form, section 114 in effect applies a two-stage computation. First, it adds the individual's income for the resident part of the year and the individual's taxable income earned in Canada (a term defined in subsection 115(1) of the Act) for the non-resident part of the year, in each case as though the part were the whole year. Second, it allows those deductions (or parts of deductions) in computing taxable income that can reasonably be considered to apply to the resident part of the year.

This division of the year into separate parts can produce unclear and perhaps inconsistent effects. For example, assume that an individual who emigrates from Canada on June 30 holds shares of a Canadian company that are not listed on a prescribed exchange, with an adjusted cost base of $100 and a fair market value of $160 on emigration. Under proposed amendments to section 128.1 of the Act, the individual is treated as having disposed of the shares and realized the $60 accrued gain before ceasing to be resident in Canada, and as having reacquired the shares, as a non-resident, at a cost of $160. Assume further that the individual actually disposes of the shares on September 30 of the same year, for $140.

On these facts, the individual has a gain of $60 in the resident part of the year, and a loss of $20 in the non-resident part. The result is an overall gain of $40, assuming that the post-departure loss can offset the pre-departure gain. However, the separate calculation under section 114 of the resident-period income and the non-resident period taxable income earned in Canada makes it uncertain that the two can be offset in this way.

Section 114 is amended to avoid such uncertainties, as well as to simplify the application of the rule. The starting-point for calculating a part-year resident's taxable income under amended section 114 is, in paragraph 114(a), the individual's income for the year, counting only those amounts of income and losses for the non-resident period that are included in computing taxable income earned in Canada under paragraphs 115(1)(a) to (c) of the Act.

Paragraphs 114(b) and (c) set out the deductions that the part-year resident may take in computing taxable income. Paragraph 114(b) allows the deduction of loss carryovers permitted by subsection 111(1) of the Act. It also allows the deductions permitted by paragraphs 110(1)(d), (d.1) and (d.2) (the non-taxable 1/4 of employee stock option and prospector's and grubstaker's share benefits) and paragraph 110(1)(f) (various social benefits, amounts exempt from Canadian tax under a tax treaty, and income from employment with certain international organizations), to the extent these relate to amounts that have been included in computing the paragraph 114(a) amount. Paragraph 114(c) allows any other deduction that the Act permits in computing taxable income. A deduction under paragraph 114(c) is allowed to the extent the deduction either can reasonably be considered to be applicable to the resident period or, if all or substantially all of the individual's income for the non-resident period is included in the paragraph 114(a) amount, can reasonably be considered to apply to the non-resident period.

In the example described above, amended section 114 will include both the resident-period gain and the non-resident-period loss in computing the single paragraph 114(a) income amount. The part-year resident will thus be treated as having realized a gain of $40 for the year as a whole.

Amended section 114 applies to the 1998 and subsequent taxation years. A number of consequential amendments ensure that these changes are reflected in other provisions of the Act that refer to section 114.

### Proposed Amendment — 114 opening words

**114. Individual resident in Canada for only part of year** — Notwithstanding subsection 2(2), subject to subsection 94.2(5) the taxable income for a taxation year of an individual who is resident in Canada throughout part of the year and non-resident throughout another part of the year is the amount, if any, by which

**Application**: The June 22, 2000 draft legislation, s. 17, will amend the opening words of s. 114 to read as above, applicable to 2001 et seq.

**Technical Notes**: Section 114 provides rules for computing the taxable income of an individual who is resident in Canada for a period or periods in a taxation year, and is non-resident for the rest of the year. Amendments to section 114 were contained in a detailed Notice of Ways and Means Motion tabled on June 5, 2000.

Section 114 is amended so that it is subject to paragraph 94.2(5)(c), a rule that applies in connection with interests in foreign investment entities that are subject to the mark-to-market regime under section 94.2. Paragraph 94.2(5)(c) is, however, only relevant to individuals who cease to be, and later become, resident in Canada in the same taxation year. For further detail, see the commentary on new subsection 94.2(5).

**Related Provisions**: 66(4.3) — Foreign exploration and development expenses of part-year resident; 111(9) — Losses where taxpayer not resident in Canada; 114.1 — Application of subsec. 115(2); 118.91 — Part-time resident — deductions from tax; 119 — Credit to former resident where stop-loss rule applies; 120(3)(a) — Effect of s. 114 where income earned in no province or in Quebec; 126(2.1) — Foreign tax credit where s. 114 applies; 128.1 — Change in residence.

**Notes**: An individual who is deemed resident under 250(1)(a), by "sojourning" in Canada for 183 days or more, is deemed resident *throughout* the year, and s. 114 does not apply. S. 114 applies only to someone who immigrates (becomes resident in Canada) or emigrates (ceases to be resident in Canada) during a taxation year. See 128.1 for the effect of immigration or emigration. See Notes to 250(1) re the meaning of "resident in Canada".

The words "without regard to section 61.2" added to 114(a) by 1994 tax amendments bill (Part I), effective for taxation years that end after February 21, 1994.

Opening words of 114 and 114(a) amended by 1993 technical bill, effective for 1992 and later taxation years. However, it does not apply to the 1992 taxation year if the taxpayer elected by notifying

Revenue Canada in writing by December 31, 1994. Where the old version applies, read:

> 114. Notwithstanding subsection 2(2), where an individual is resident in Canada during part of a taxation year, and during some other part of the year is not resident in Canada, is not employed in Canada and is not carrying on business in Canada, for the purposes of this Part, the individual's taxable income for the year is the amount, if any, by which the total of
>
> (a) the individual's income for the period or periods in the year throughout which the individual is resident in Canada, is employed in Canada or is carrying on business in Canada, computed as though that period or those periods were the whole taxation year and as though any disposition of property deemed by subsection 48(1) to have been made because the individual ceased to be resident in Canada were made in that period or those periods, and

The amendment ensures that an individual who becomes or ceases to be resident in a year is taxable, during his/her "non-resident" portion of the year, only on Canadian-source income.

114 amended by 1991 technical bill, retroactive to 1988, to clarify that an individual resident in Canada for only part of a year may not claim, in respect of deductions under 110 and 111, amounts greater than those available to individuals resident in Canada throughout the year.

**Definitions [s. 114]**: "amount", "business" — 248(1); "Canada" — 255; "capital gain", "capital loss" — 39(1), 248(1); "carrying on business" — 253; "employed", "individual", "non-resident", "property" — 248(1); "resident in Canada" — 250; "taxable income" — 2(2), 248(1); "taxable income earned in Canada" — 115(1), 248(1); "taxation year" — 249, 250.1(a); "taxpayer" — 248(1).

**Interpretation Bulletins [s. 114]**: IT-163R2: Election by non-resident individuals on certain Canadian source income; IT-193 SR: Taxable income of individuals resident in Canada during part of year (Special Release); IT-194: Foreign tax credit — part-time residents; IT-221R2: Determination of an individual's residence status; IT-262R2: Losses of non-residents and part-year residents; IT-497R3: Overseas employment tax credit.

**Forms**: T4056: Emigrants and income tax [guide]; T4058: Non-residents and temporary residents of Canada.

**114.1 Application of subsec. 115(2)** — In applying section 115 for the purposes of section 114, the references in paragraphs 115(2)(b), (b.1) and (c) to "who had, in any previous year, ceased to be resident in Canada" shall be read as references to "who has, in the year, or had, in any previous year, ceased to be resident in Canada".

### Proposed Repeal — 114.1

**Application**: Bill C-43 (First Reading September 20, 2000), s. 59, will repeal s. 114.1, applicable to 1998 *et seq.*

**Technical Notes**: Section 114.1 Act is a technical rule that applies a special reading of paragraphs 115(2)(b), (b.1) and (c) of the Act, for the purpose of applying section 114, to ensure that certain time references in those paragraphs accommodate cases to which section 114 applies. With the restructuring of section 114, this rule is no longer needed. Section 114.1 is repealed for the 1998 and subsequent taxation years.

**Definitions [s. 114.1]**: "resident in Canada" — 250.

**Interpretation Bulletins**: IT-193 SR: Taxable income of individuals resident in Canada during part of a year (Special Release).

**114.2 Deductions in separate returns** — Where a separate return of income with respect to a taxpayer is filed under subsection 70(2), 104(23) or 150(4) for a particular period and another return of income under this Part with respect to the taxpayer is filed for a period ending in the calendar year in which the particular period ends, for the purpose of computing the taxable income under this Part of the taxpayer in those returns, the total of all deductions claimed in all those returns under section 110 shall not exceed the total that could be deducted under that section for the year with respect to the taxpayer if no separate returns were filed under subsections 70(2), 104(23) and 150(4).

**Related Provisions**: 118.93 — Credits in separate returns.

**Definitions [s. 114.2]**: "calendar year" — *Interpretation Act* 37(1)(a); "taxable income" — 2(2), 248(1); "taxpayer" — 248(1).

**Interpretation Bulletins**: IT-326R3: Returns of deceased persons as "another person".

## DIVISION D — TAXABLE INCOME EARNED IN CANADA BY NON-RESIDENTS

**115. (1) Non-resident's taxable income [earned] in Canada [and taxable Canadian property]** — For the purposes of this Act, the taxable income earned in Canada for a taxation year of a person who at no time in the year is resident in Canada is the amount, if any, by which the amount that would be the non-resident person's income for the year under section 3 if

(a) the non-resident person had no income other than

(i) incomes from the duties of offices and employments performed by the non-resident person in Canada,

### Proposed Amendment — 115(1)(a)(i)

(i) incomes from the duties of offices and employments performed by the non-resident person in Canada and, if the person was resident in Canada at the time the person performed the duties, outside Canada,

**Application**: Bill C-43 (First Reading September 20, 2000), subsec. 60(1), will amend subpara. 115(1)(a)(i) to read as above, applicable to 1998 *et seq.* except that if an individual who ceased at any time after 1992 and before October 2, 1996 to be resident in Canada elects under clause 78(1) of Bill C-43 (see Proposed Amendment to 128.1(4)(b)) in respect of that cessation of residence, subpara. 115(1)(a)(i), as amended, applies to income received by the individual after that cessation of residence.

**Technical Notes**: Section 115 of the Act determines the amount of a non-resident person's income that is subject to tax under Part I of the Act. This amount is referred to as the non-resident's "taxable income earned in Canada".

Subsection 115(1) of the Act provides the general rules to be applied in calculating a non-resident's "taxable income earned in Canada". Paragraphs 115(1)(a) to (c) describe the conditions that apply in computing a non-resident's taxable income earned in Canada, while paragraphs 115(1)(d) to (f)

describe the deductions that are available for the purpose of that computation.

Paragraphs 115(1)(a) to (c) set out special assumptions that are applied in computing the taxable income earned in Canada of a non-resident taxpayer. The general effect of these paragraphs, in conjunction with the deduction provided for treaty-protected income because of the reference to paragraph 110(1)(f) in paragraph 115(1)(d), is to include in this computation only income and losses from sources in Canada, and of those only amounts that are not treaty-protected.

Subparagraph 115(1)(a)(i) includes in this computation income from the duties of offices and employments that the non-resident person in Canada performs in Canada. Subparagraph 115(1)(a)(i) is amended to include as well income from offices and employments performed by the non-resident person outside of Canada, if the person was resident in Canada at the time the duties were performed. This ensures that if an individual who is a former resident of Canada receives, as a non-resident, income relating to work the individual performed outside Canada at a time when the individual was resident in Canada, the income is subject to Canadian tax.

This amendment generally applies to the 1998 and subsequent taxation years. In addition, if an individual ceased to be resident in Canada after 1992 and before October 2, 1996, and the individual so elects [see under 128.1(4)(b) — ed.], this amendment applies to income received by the individual after that cessation of residence. The election in effect backdates the explicit exclusion of certain income rights and trust interests from the deemed disposition immediately before emigration. The basis for excluding the rights in question from the deemed disposition is that they generally represent entitlements to future income that will itself be subject to Canadian tax when it is received by a non-resident. Linking the application of amended subparagraph 115(1)(a)(i) to the election ensures that the Act does tax that income, where it relates to employment exercised abroad by a resident of Canada.

(ii) incomes from businesses carried on by the non-resident person in Canada,

(iii) taxable capital gains from dispositions described in paragraph (b),

(iii.1) the amount by which the amount required by paragraph 59(3.2)(c) to be included in computing the non-resident person's income for the year exceeds any portion of that amount that was included in computing the non-resident person's income from a business carried on by the non-resident person in Canada,

(iii.2) amounts required by section 13 to be included in computing the non-resident person's income for the year in respect of dispositions of properties to the extent that those amounts were not included in computing the non-resident person's income from a business carried on by the non-resident person in Canada,

(iii.21) the amount, if any, included under section 56.3 in computing the non-resident person's income for the year,

(iii.3) in any case where, in the year, the non-resident person carried on a business in Canada described in any of paragraphs (a) to (g) of the definition "principal-business corporation" in subsection 66(15), all amounts in respect of a Canadian resource property that would be required to be included in computing the non-resident person's income for the year under this Part if the non-resident person were resident in Canada at any time in the year, to the extent that those amounts are not included in computing the non-resident person's income by virtue of subparagraph (ii) or (iii.1),

(iv) the amount, if any, by which any amount required by subsection 106(2) to be included in computing the non-resident person's income for the year as proceeds of the disposition of an income interest in a trust resident in Canada exceeds the amount in respect of that income interest that would, if the non-resident person had been resident in Canada throughout the year, be deductible under subsection 106(1) in computing the non-resident person's income for the year,

(iv.1) the amount, if any, by which any amount required by subsection 96(1.2) to be included in computing the non-resident person's income for the year as proceeds of the disposition of a right to a share of the income or loss under an agreement referred to in paragraph 96(1.1)(a) exceeds the amount in respect of that right that would, if the non-resident person had been resident in Canada throughout the year, be deductible under subsection 96(1.3) in computing the non-resident person's income for the year,

(v) in the case of a non-resident person described in subsection (2), the total determined under paragraph (2)(e) in respect of the non-resident person, and

(vi) the amount that would have been required to be included in computing the non-resident person's income in respect of a life insurance policy in Canada by virtue of subsection 148(1) or (1.1) if the non-resident person had been resident in Canada throughout the year,

**Proposed Addition — 115(1)(a)(vii)**

(vii) in the case of an authorized foreign bank, the amount claimed by the bank to the extent that the inclusion of the amount in income

(A) increases any amount deductible by the bank under subsection 126(1) for the year, and

(B) does not increase an amount deductible by the bank under section 127 for the year,

Division D — Taxable Income Earned in Canada by Non-Residents  S. 115(1)(b)(x)

**Application**: The August 8, 2000 draft legislation, s. 8, will add subpara. 115(1)(a)(vii), applicable after June 27, 1999.

**Technical Notes**: Section 115 of the Act provides rules for the calculation of the "taxable income earned in Canada" of a non-resident person, which is subject to tax under Part I. This amount includes Canadian-source employment and business income, taxable capital gains on taxable Canadian property, and certain other income amounts.

Paragraph 115(1)(a) is amended to add new subparagraph (vii), which includes in the taxable income earned in Canada of an authorized foreign bank the amount claimed by the bank to the extent that the inclusion increases the bank's usable foreign tax credit under subsection 126(1) but does not increase any amount deductible by the bank under section 127 of the Act. This addition to taxable income earned in Canada parallels the addition to taxable income that is available to corporations resident in Canada under existing section 110.5 of the Act.

New subparagraph 115(1)(a)(vii) applies after June 27, 1999.

(b) the only taxable capital gains and allowable capital losses referred to in paragraph 3(b) were taxable capital gains and allowable capital losses from dispositions at any time in the year of property or an interest therein (in this Act referred to as "taxable Canadian property") that was

(i) real property situated in Canada,

(ii) a capital property used by the non-resident person in carrying on a business in Canada, other than

(A) property used in carrying on an insurance business, and

(B) ships and aircraft used principally in international traffic and personal property pertaining to their operation if the country in which the non-resident person is resident grants substantially similar relief for the year to persons resident in Canada,

(iii) where the non-resident person is an insurer, any capital property that is its designated insurance property for the year,

(iv) a share of the capital stock of a corporation (other than a mutual fund corporation) resident in Canada that is not listed on a prescribed stock exchange,

(v) a share of the capital stock of a non-resident corporation that is not listed on a prescribed stock exchange where, at any particular time during the 12-month period that ends at that time,

(A) the fair market value of all of the properties of the corporation each of which was

(I) a taxable Canadian property,

(II) a Canadian resource property,

(III) a timber resource property,

(IV) an income interest in a trust resident in Canada, or

(V) an interest in or option in respect of a property described in any of subclauses (II) to (IV), whether or not the property exists,

was more than 50% of the fair market value of all of its properties, and

(B) more than 50% of the fair market value of the share is derived directly or indirectly from one or any combination of

(I) real property situated in Canada,

(II) Canadian resource properties, and

(III) timber resource properties,

(vi) a share otherwise described in subparagraph (iv) or (v) that is listed on a prescribed stock exchange, or a share of the capital stock of a mutual fund corporation, if, at any time during the 5-year period that ends at that time, the non-resident person, persons with whom the non-resident person did not deal at arm's length, or the non-resident person together with all such persons owned 25% or more of the issued shares of any class of the capital stock of the corporation that issued the share,

(vii) an interest in a partnership where, at any particular time during the 12-month period that ends at that time, the fair market value of all of the properties of the partnership each of which was

(A) a taxable Canadian property,

(B) a Canadian resource property,

(C) a timber resource property,

(D) an income interest in a trust resident in Canada, or

(E) an interest in or option in respect of a property described in clauses (B) to (D), whether or not that property exists,

was more than 50% of the fair market value of all of its properties,

(viii) a capital interest in a trust (other than a unit trust) resident in Canada,

(ix) a unit of a unit trust (other than a mutual fund trust) resident in Canada,

(x) a unit of a mutual fund trust if, at any particular time during the 5-year period that ends at that time, not less than 25% of the issued units of the trust belonged to the non-resident person, to persons with whom the non-resident person did not deal at arm's length, or to the non-resident person and persons with whom the non-resident person did not deal at arm's length,

(xi) an interest in a non-resident trust where, at any particular time during the 12-month period that ends at that time,

(A) the fair market value of all of the properties of the trust each of which was

(I) a taxable Canadian property,

(II) a Canadian resource property,

(III) a timber resource property,

(IV) an income interest in a trust resident in Canada, or

(V) an interest in or option in respect of a property described in subclauses (II) to (IV), whether or not the property exists,

was more than 50% of the fair market value of all of its properties, and

(B) more than 50% of the fair market value of the interest is derived directly or indirectly from one or any combination of

(I) real property situated in Canada,

(II) Canadian resource properties, and

(III) timber resource properties, or

(xii) a property deemed by any provision of this Act to be taxable Canadian property,

but does not include a share of the capital stock of a non-resident-owned investment corporation if, on the first day of the year, the corporation did not own taxable Canadian property, Canadian resource property, timber resource property nor an income interest in a trust resident in Canada,

### Proposed Amendment — 115(1)(b)

(b) the only taxable capital gains and allowable capital losses referred to in paragraph 3(b) were taxable capital gains and allowable capital losses from dispositions of taxable Canadian properties (other than treaty-protected properties), and

**Application**: Bill C-43 (First Reading September 20, 2000), subsec. 60(2), will amend para. 115(1)(b) to read as above, applicable after October 1, 1996, except that, in its application to dispositions that occurred before the 1998 taxation year, para. 115(1)(b) shall be read as follows:

(b) the only taxable capital gains and allowable capital losses referred to in paragraph 3(b) were taxable capital gains and allowable capital losses from dispositions of taxable Canadian properties, and

**Technical Notes**: Paragraph 115(1)(b) lists the types of property (called "taxable Canadian property" or TCP) in respect of which taxable gains and allowable capital losses are considered in the calculation of a non-resident's taxable income earned in Canada. As a result of the relocation of the general TCP definition to subsection 248(1) of the Act, paragraph 115(1)(b) can be greatly simplified. In its new form, the paragraph simply refers to taxable capital gains and allowable capital losses on TCP that is not "treaty-protected property" (as defined in subsection 248(1) of the Act).

Amended paragraph 115(1)(b) generally applies after October 1, 1996. Since the definition (and the concept) of "treaty-protected property" was introduced only with the 1998 Budget [see 115(1)(b.1) — ed.], and applies for the 1998 and later taxation years, a transitional version of amended paragraph 115(1)(b) omits the reference to treaty-protected property for dispositions that occur before the 1998 taxation year.

**Notice of Ways and Means Motion (re taxpayer emigration), October 2, 1996**: [See under 248(1) "taxable Canadian property" — ed.]

(b.1) notwithstanding paragraph (b), the taxable capital gains and allowable capital losses referred to in paragraph 3(b) did not include taxable capital gains and allowable capital losses from dispositions at any time in the year of taxable Canadian property that was treaty-protected property of the non-resident at that time, and

### Proposed Repeal — 115(1)(b.1)

**Application**: Bill C-43 (First Reading September 20, 2000), subsec. 60(2), will repeal para. (b.1), applicable after October 1, 1996.

**Technical Notes**: Paragraph 115(1)(b.1) excludes from the computation of a non-resident's taxable income earned in Canada any taxable capital gain or allowable capital loss from the disposition of a taxable Canadian property that was treaty-protected property of the non-resident. Since this exclusion now forms part of amended paragraph 115(1)(b), paragraph 115(1)(b.1) can be repealed.

(c) the only losses for the year referred to in paragraph 3(d) were losses from duties of an office or employment performed by the person in Canada and businesses (other than treaty-protected businesses) carried on by the person in Canada and allowable business investment losses in respect of property any gain from the disposition of which would, because of this subsection, be included in computing the person's taxable income earned in Canada,

exceeds the total of

(d) the deductions permitted by subsection 111(1) and, to the extent that they relate to amounts included in computing the amount determined under any of paragraphs (a) to (c), the deductions permitted by any of paragraphs 110(1)(d), (d.1), (d.2) and (f) and subsection 110.1(1),

### Proposed Amendment — 115(1)(d)

(d) the deductions permitted by subsection 111(1) and, to the extent that they relate to amounts included in computing the amount determined under any of paragraphs (a) to (c), the deductions permitted by any of paragraphs 110(1)(d) to (d.2) and (f) and subsection 110.1(1),

**Application**: The December 21, 2000 draft legislation, subsec. 56(1), will amend para. 115(1)(d) to read as above, applicable to 2000 et seq.

**Technical Notes**: Section 115 determines the amount of a non-resident person's income that is subject to tax under Part I. This amount is referred to as the non-resident's "taxable income earned in Canada". Subsection 115(1) provides the general rules for the calculation of this amount, including deductions provided under paragraphs 115(1)(d) to (f).

Subsection 115(1) sets out the general rules for determining the amount of a non-resident person's income that is subject to tax under Part I. Paragraph 115(1)(d) allows certain deductions under subsections 110(1), 110.1(1) and 111(1) to be taken into account in determining this amount.

Paragraph 115(1)(d) is amended to allow a deduction under new paragraph 110(1)(d.01) to be taken into account. Paragraph 110(1)(d.01) allows a deduction where certain employee option securities (or proceeds from the disposition of such securities) are donated to a qualifying charity. The deduction may be taken into account to the extent that the securities option benefit to which the deduction relates is included in computing the amount of the non-resident person's income that is subject to tax under Part I.

(e) the deductions permitted by any of subsections 112(1) and (2) and 138(6) in respect of a dividend received by the non-resident person, to the extent that the dividend is included in computing the non-resident person's taxable income earned in Canada for the year, and

### Proposed Addition — 115(1)(e.1)

(e.1) the deduction permitted by subsection (4.1), and

**Application**: The December 21, 2000 draft legislation, subsec. 56(2), will add para. 115(1)(e.1), applicable to taxation years that begin after February 27, 2000.

**Technical Notes**: Paragraph 115(1)(e.1) is introduced to allow the deduction provided under subsection 115(4.1) in computing a non-resident's taxable income earned in Canada.

Notwithstanding that a non-resident taxpayer is precluded under subsections 66(4) and 66.21(4) from claiming deductions for foreign exploration and development expenses (FEDE) and foreign resource expenses (FRE) in computing income, new subsection 115(4.1) permits a non-resident taxpayer (who ceased to be resident in Canada after February 27, 2000) to claim a deduction in computing taxable income earned in Canada with reference to the rules in those subsections. The amount so claimed by a taxpayer is based on the taxpayer's unused FEDE and FRE balances immediately after ceasing to reside in Canada. The claim for the first taxation year of non-residence cannot exceed 10% of that balance, and does not depend on the level of related foreign resource income. The 10% limit also applies to subsequent taxation years, but is determined with reference to those balances (computed net of relevant deductions previously claimed under subsection 115(4.1)).

(f) where all or substantially all of the non-resident person's income for the year is included in computing the non-resident person's taxable income earned in Canada for the year, such of the other deductions permitted for the purpose of computing taxable income as may reasonably be considered wholly applicable.

**Related Provisions**: 2(3) — Tax on non-resident's taxable income earned in Canada; 4(3) — Whether deductions are applicable to a particular source; 13(4.1)(c) — Replacement of depreciable TCP with new TCP; 33.1 — International banking centres; 40(9) — Prorating for gains not taxed before April 27, 1995; 44(5)(c) — replacement of capital TCP with new TCP; 52(8) — Cost to non-resident of share of corporation that becomes resident in Canada; 85(1)(i), 85.1(1)(a) — Shares received on rollover of TCP deemed to be TCP; 87(10) — New share issued on amalgamation of public corporation deemed to be listed on prescribed stock exchange; 94(3)(a) [proposed] — Application to trust deemed resident in Canada; 107.3(1)(b) — Income of non-resident beneficiary of mining reclamation trust/qualifying environmental trust; 111(8)"non-capital loss"B — Carryforward of 115(1)(b)(vii) amount; 111(9) — Carryover of losses where taxpayer not resident in Canada; 112(3)(b)(i) — Reduction in loss under 115(1)(d.1) on subsequent disposition of share; 112(5.2)B(b)(i), (ii) — Adjustment for dividends received on mark-to-market property; 114 — Individual resident in Canada during part only of year; 115(3) [to be repealed] — Interest in or option in respect of TCP; 115.1 — Competent authority agreements under tax treaties; 115.2 — Non-resident investment or pension fund deemed not to be carrying on business in Canada; 116 — Certificate required where non-resident disposes of TCP; 118.94 — Tax payable by non-resident individual; 128.1(4)(b)(i) [to be repealed] — TCP excluded from deemed disposition on becoming resident in Canada; 133 — Non-resident-owned investment corporations; 141(5) — Demutualized life insurance corporation or holding corporation deemed not to be TCP; 217 — Election respecting certain payments; 219(1) — Branch tax on non-resident corporations; 248(1) — Definition of "taxable Canadian property"; 248(1)"taxable income earned in Canada" — Definition applies to entire Act but cannot be less than nil; 250.1(a) — Taxation year of non-resident person; Canada-U.S. Tax Convention, Art. VII — Business profits of U.S. resident; Art. XIII — Taxation of capital gains.

**Notes**: The tax imposed under 2(3) and 115(1) is relieved in certain cases by Canada's bilateral tax treaties. The Canada-U.S. and Canada-U.K. treaties are reproduced at the end of this book. Note, for example, that the tax on gains under 115(1)(b) is often relieved by treaty for gains on personal property (but not real property).

The amendments effective April 26, 1995 increased the scope of taxation of capital gains of non-residents, to include, for example, non-resident corporations whose value is "primarily" (greater than 50%) attributable to real property in Canada, provided the specific share being acquired also meets this test (see 115(1)(b)(v)(B)). However, a transitional rule in 40(9) prorates this gain to reduce it by months before May 1995. In addition, the fourth protocol to the Canada-U.S. tax treaty, ratified in December 1997, prevents this tax from applying to U.S. residents in respect of non-resident corporations. See Art. XVIII of the treaty.

Note that for purposes of ss. 2, 128.1 and 150, "taxable Canadian property" is given an extended definition by 248(1); but this will change when the June 5, 2000 draft legislation is enacted.

Shares that temporarily replace listed shares as part of a corporate amalgamation will be considered as listed on a prescribed exchange for purposes of the amendment to 115(1)(b)(iii). See 87(10).

See also Notes to 2(3) re carrying on business in Canada.

Opening words of 115(1) amended by 1998 Budget, effective for 1998 and later taxation years. For earlier years, read:

> (1) For the purposes of this Act, the taxable income earned in Canada for a taxation year of a person who at no time in the year is resident in Canada is the amount of the non-resident person's income for the year that would be determined under section 3 if

115(1)(a)(iii.21) added by 1994 tax amendments bill (Part I), effective for taxation years that end after February 21, 1994.

115(1)(b) amended by 1995-97 technical bill, effective April 27, 1995, except in respect of the disposition of a property before 1996

(a) to a person who was obliged on April 26, 1995 to acquire the property pursuant to the terms of an agreement in writing made by that day (and, for the purpose of this rule, a person shall be considered not to be obliged to acquire property where the person can be excused from the obligation if there is a change to the Act or if there is an adverse assessment under the Act); or

(b) pursuant to a prospectus or similar document filed with the relevant securities authority before April 27, 1995.

Before April 27, 1995, or for grandfathered dispositions as above, read:

(b) the only taxable capital gains and allowable capital losses referred to in paragraph 3(b) were taxable capital gains and allowable capital losses from dispositions of property each of which was a disposition of property or an interest therein (in this Act referred to as a "taxable Canadian property") that was

(i) real property situated in Canada,

(ii) any capital property used by the non-resident person in carrying on a business (other than an insurance business) in Canada,

(ii.1) where the non-resident person is an insurer, any capital property that is its designated insurance property for the year,

(iii) a share of the capital stock of a corporation resident in Canada (other than a public corporation),

(iv) a share of the capital stock of a public corporation if at any time during such part of the period of 5 years immediately preceding the disposition thereof as is after 1971, not less than 25% of the issued shares of any class of the capital stock of the corporation belonged to the non-resident person, to persons with whom the non-resident person did not deal at arm's length, or to the non-resident person and persons with whom the non-resident person did not deal at arm's length,

(v) an interest in a partnership, if, at any time during the 12 months immediately preceding the disposition thereof, the fair market value of such of the partnership property as was, at that time,

(A) a Canadian resource property,

(B) a timber resource property,

(C) an income interest in a trust resident in Canada, or

(D) any other property described in this paragraph

was not less than 50% of the total of

(E) the fair market value at that time of all of the partnership property, and

(F) the amount of any money of the partnership on hand at that time,

(vi) a capital interest in a trust (other than a unit trust) resident in Canada,

(vii) a unit of a unit trust (other than a mutual fund trust) resident in Canada,

(viii) a unit of a mutual fund trust, if at any time during such part of the period of 5 years immediately preceding the disposition thereof as is after 1971, not less than 25% of the issued units of the trust belonged to the non-resident person, to persons with whom the non-resident person did not deal at arm's length, or to the non-resident person and persons with whom the non-resident person did not deal at arm's length, or

(ix) any other property deemed by any provision of this Act to be taxable Canadian property,

but not including a share of the capital stock of a non-resident-owned investment corporation, if, on the first day of the taxation year of the corporation in which the disposition was made, the corporation did not own any property that was property referred to in clauses (v)(A) to (D), and

115(1)(b)(ii.1) (which later became 115(1)(b)(iii)) amended by 1996 Budget, effective for dispositions that occur in an insurer's 1997 or later taxation year (changed from 1996 at Second Reading of the Budget bill), to use the term "designated insurance property" in place of an older term. For earlier years since 1982, read:

(ii.1) where the non-resident person is an insurer, any capital property that is property used by it in the year in, or held by it in the year in the course of, carrying on an insurance business in Canada,

115(1)(b.1) added and (c)–(e) replaced (with former (d.1) becoming new (e)) by 1998 Budget, effective for 1998 and later taxation years. For earlier years, read:

(c) the only losses for the year referred to in paragraph 3(d) were losses from duties of an office or employment performed by the person in Canada and businesses carried on by the person in Canada and allowable business investment losses in respect of property any gain from the disposition of which would, because of this subsection, be included in computing the person's taxable income earned in Canada,

minus the total of

(d) the deductions permitted by paragraphs 110(1)(d), (d.1), (d.2) and (f) and subsection 110.1(1),

(d.1) the deductions permitted by subsections 112(1) and (2) and 138(6), to the extent that a dividend or portion thereof has been included in computing the non-resident person's taxable income earned in Canada,

(e) such of the deductions from income permitted by section 111 as may reasonably be considered to be applicable to the duties of an office or employment performed by the non-resident person in Canada, a business carried on by the non-resident person in Canada or a disposition of property, any profit or gain on which would have been required by this subsection to be included in computing the non-resident person's taxable income earned in Canada, and

115(1)(c) amended by 1992 technical bill, effective 1991. For earlier taxation years, read "the only losses referred to in paragraph 3(d) were losses from businesses carried on by him in Canada".

115(1)(d.1) added by 1991 technical bill, effective 1983.

The CCRA takes the position that "all or substantially all", used in 115(1)(f), means 90% or more.

**Regulations**: 3200, 3201 (prescribed stock exchanges); will be amended to apply to 115(1)(b)(iii)–(v), but see also ITA 87(10)).

**I.T. Application Rules**: 26(30) (taxable Canadian property under new rules effective April 26, 1995).

**Interpretation Bulletins**: IT-113R4: Benefits to employees — stock options; IT-150R2: Acquisition from a non-resident of certain property by death or mortgage foreclosure or by virtue of a deemed disposition; IT-176R2: Taxable Canadian property — Interests in and options on real property and shares; IT-242R: Retired partners; IT-262R2: Losses of non-residents and part-year residents; IT-379R: Employees profit sharing plans — allocations to beneficiaries; IT-393R2: Election re tax on rents and timber royalties — non-residents; IT-421R: Benefits to individuals, corporations and shareholders from loans or debt; IT-434R: Rental of real property by individual; IT-451R: Deemed disposition and acquisition on ceasing to be or becoming resident in Canada; IT-465R: Non-resident beneficiaries of trusts See also list at end of s. 115.

**Information Circulars**: 72-17R4: Procedures concerning the disposition of taxable Canadian property by non-residents of Canada — section 116; 88-2 Supplement, para. 7: General anti-avoidance rule — section 245 of the *Income Tax Act*.

Division D — Taxable Income Earned in Canada by Non-Residents  S. 115(2)(e)(i)(B)

**Advance Tax Rulings:** ATR-70: Distribution of taxable Canadian property by a trust to a non-resident.

**Forms:** T2 SCH 91: Information concerning claims for treaty-based exemptions; T2061: Election by an emigrant to defer deemed disposition of property and capital gains thereon; T2061A: Election by an emigrant to report deemed dispositions of taxable Canadian property and capital gains and/or losses thereon.

**(2) Idem [persons deemed employed in Canada]** — Where, in a taxation year, a non-resident person was

(a) a student in full-time attendance at an educational institution in Canada that is a university, college or other educational institution providing courses at a post-secondary school level in Canada,

(b) a student attending, or a teacher teaching at, an educational institution outside Canada that is a university, college or other educational institution providing courses at a post-secondary school level, who had, in any previous year, ceased to be resident in Canada in the course of or subsequent to moving to attend or to teach at, as the case may be, that institution,

(b.1) an individual who had, in any previous year, ceased to be resident in Canada in the course of or subsequent to moving to carry on research or any similar work under a grant received by the individual to enable the individual to carry on that research or work,

**Proposed Amendment — 115(2)(b), (b.1)**

(b) a student attending, or a teacher teaching at, an educational institution outside Canada that is a university, college or other educational institution providing courses at a post-secondary school level, who in any preceding taxation year ceased to be resident in Canada in the course of or subsequent to moving to attend or to teach at the institution,

(b.1) an individual who in any preceding taxation year ceased to be resident in Canada in the course of or subsequent to moving to carry on research or any similar work under a grant received by the individual to enable the individual to carry on the research or work,

**Application:** Bill C-43 (First Reading September 20, 2000), subsec. 60(3), will amend paras. 115(2)(b) and (b.1) to read as above, applicable to 1998 et seq.

**Technical Notes:** Subsection 115(2) applies, in certain special circumstances, to tax remuneration and specified other amounts received by a non-resident. Because of paragraphs 115(2)(b) and (b.1), subsection 115(2) applies to post-secondary students at Canadian institutions and former Canadian residents who have moved abroad to carry out research or similar work under a grant. The paragraphs are amended, with application to the 1998 and subsequent taxation years, to update their language to reflect current drafting styles. The amendments make no substantive change to the paragraphs.

(c) an individual

(i) who had, in any previous year, ceased to be resident in Canada,

(ii) who received, in the taxation year, salary or wages or other remuneration in respect of an office or employment that was paid to the individual directly or indirectly by a person resident in Canada, and

(iii) who was, under an agreement or a convention with one or more countries that has the force of law in Canada, entitled to an exemption from an income tax otherwise payable in any of those countries in respect of the salary or wages or other remuneration, or

(c.1) a person who received in the year an amount, under a contract, that was or will be deductible in computing the income of a taxpayer subject to tax under this Part and the amount can, irrespective of when the contract was entered into or the form or legal effect of the contract, reasonably be regarded as having been received, in whole or in part,

(i) as consideration or partial consideration for entering into a contract of service or an agreement to perform a service where any such service is to be performed in Canada, or for undertaking not to enter into such a contract or agreement with another party, or

(ii) as remuneration or partial remuneration from the duties of an office or employment or as compensation or partial compensation for services to be performed in Canada,

the following rules apply:

(d) for the purposes of subsection 2(3) the non-resident person shall be deemed to have been employed in Canada in the year,

(e) for the purposes of subparagraph (1)(a)(v), the total determined under this paragraph in respect of the non-resident person is the total of

(i) any remuneration in respect of an office or employment that was paid to the non-resident person directly or indirectly by a person resident in Canada and was received by the non-resident person in the year, except to the extent that such remuneration is attributable to the duties of an office or employment performed by the non-resident person anywhere outside Canada and

(A) is subject to an income or profits tax imposed by the government of a country other than Canada, or

(B) is paid in connection with the selling of property, the negotiating of contracts or the rendering of services for the non-resident person's employer, or a foreign affiliate of the employer, or any other person with whom the employer does not deal at arm's length, in the ordinary course of a business carried on by the employer, that foreign affiliate or that person,

(ii) amounts that would be required by paragraph 56(1)(n) or (o) to be included in computing the non-resident person's income for the year if the non-resident person were resident in Canada throughout the year and the reference in the applicable paragraph to "received by the taxpayer in the year" were read as a reference to "received by the taxpayer in the year from a source in Canada",

(iii) [Repealed]

(iv) amounts that would be required by paragraph 56(1)(q) to be included in computing the non-resident person's income for the year if the non-resident person were resident in Canada throughout the year, and

(v) amounts described in paragraph (c.1) received by the non-resident person in the year, except to the extent that they are otherwise required to be included in computing the non-resident person's taxable income earned in Canada for the year, and

(f) there may be deducted in computing the taxable income of the non-resident person for the year the amount that would be deductible in computing the non-resident person's income for the year by virtue of section 62 if

(i) the definition "eligible relocation" in subsection 248(1) were read without reference to subparagraph (a)(i) of that definition, and

(ii) the amounts described in subparagraph 62(1)(c)(ii) were the amounts described in subparagraph (e)(ii) of this subsection.

**Related Provisions**: 4(3) — Deductions applicable; 33.1 — International banking centres; 52(8) — Reduction in cost base of share of corporation that becomes resident in Canada; 94(3)(a) [proposed] — Application to trust deemed resident in Canada; 114.1 — Application of subsec. 115(2); 146(1)"earned income"(d) — RRSPs — "earned income"; 153(1)(o) — Withholding of tax on amount described in 115(2)(c.1); 250(1) — Individuals deemed resident in Canada.

**Notes**: 115(2)(c) amended by 1998 Budget, effective for 1998 and later taxation years. The new rule effectively allows Canada to tax foreign employment income of an expatriate only if the other country has agreed in a tax treaty with Canada to refrain from doing so. For earlier years, read:

(c) an individual who had, in any previous year, ceased to be resident in Canada and who was, in the taxation year, in receipt of remuneration in respect of an office or employment that was paid to the individual directly or indirectly by a person resident in Canada, or

115(2)(e)(iii) repealed by 1992 Child Benefit bill, effective 1993. For 1990 to 1992, read:

(iii) amounts that would be required by subsection 56(5) to be included in computing the non-resident person's income for the year if the non-resident person were resident in Canada throughout the year;

115(2)(f)(i)–(iii) replaced with (i) and (ii) by 1998 Budget, effective 1998. For earlier years, read:

(i) that section were read without reference to paragraph 62(1)(a),

(ii) that section were applicable in computing the taxable income of non-resident persons, and

(iii) the amounts described in subparagraph 62(1)(f)(ii) were the amounts described in subparagraph (e)(ii) of this subsection.

**Interpretation Bulletins**: IT-75R3: Scholarships, fellowships, bursaries, prizes, and research grants; IT-161R3: Non-residents — exemption from tax deductions at source on employment income; IT-178R3: Moving expenses. See also list at end of s. 115.

**(3) Property deemed to include interests and options** — For the purpose of this section, a property described in subparagraphs (1)(b)(i) to (xii) is deemed to include any interest therein or option in respect thereof, whether or not such property is in existence.

**Proposed Repeal — 115(3)**

**Application**: Bill C-43 (First Reading September 20, 2000), subsec. 60(4), will repeal subsec. 115(3), applicable after October 1, 1996.

**Technical Notes**: Subsection 115(3) of the Act provides that, for the purposes of section 115 of the Act, taxable Canadian property includes an interest in, or an option in respect of, a property, regardless of whether or not the property is in existence. Because the definition "taxable Canadian property" has been moved from subsection 115(1) to subsection 248(1) of the Act, and the new definition contains in paragraph (l) a similar rule for interests and options, subsection 115(3) is no longer needed and is repealed, effective after October 1, 1996.

**Related Provisions**: 248(4) — Interest in real property.

**Notes**: 115(3) amended by 1995-97 technical bill, effective on the same basis as the amendments to 115(1)(b), to change "(ix)" to "(xii)" (in consequence of the amendments to 115(1)(b)).

115(3) amended by 1991 technical bill, effective July 14, 1990, to add the reference to "any interest therein".

**Interpretation Bulletins**: IT-116R3: Rights to buy additional shares; IT-176R2: Taxable Canadian property — Interests in and options on real property and shares. See also list at end of s. 115.

**(4) Non-resident's income from Canadian resource property** — Where a non-resident person ceases at any particular time in a taxation year to carry on such of the businesses described in any of paragraphs (a) to (g) of the definition "principal business corporation" in subsection 66(15) as were carried on by the non-resident person immediately before that time at one or more fixed places of business in Canada and either does not commence after that time and during the year to carry on any business so described at a fixed place of business in Canada or disposes of Canadian resource property at any time in the year during which the non-resident person was not carrying on any business so described at a fixed place of business in Canada, the following rules apply:

(a) the taxation year of the non-resident person that would otherwise have included the particular time shall be deemed to have ended at such time

## Division D — Taxable Income Earned in Canada by Non-Residents — S. 115

and a new taxation year shall be deemed to have commenced immediately thereafter;

(b) the non-resident person or any partnership of which the non-resident person was a member immediately after the particular time shall be deemed, for the purpose only of computing the non-resident person's income earned in Canada for the taxation year that is deemed to have ended, to have disposed immediately before the particular time of each Canadian resource property that was owned by the non-resident person or by the partnership immediately after the particular time and to have received therefor immediately before the particular time proceeds of disposition equal to the fair market value thereof at the particular time; and

(c) the non-resident person or any partnership of which the non-resident person was a member immediately after the particular time shall be deemed, for the purpose only of computing the non-resident person's income earned in Canada for a taxation year commencing after the particular time, to have reacquired immediately after the particular time, at a cost equal to the amount deemed by paragraph (b) to have been received by the non-resident person or the partnership as the proceeds of disposition therefor, each property deemed by that paragraph to have been disposed of.

**Related Provisions**: 4(3) — Deductions applicable; 66.2(7) — Exception — Canadian development expense; 66.4(7) — Share of partner; 115(5) — Partnership excludes prescribed partnership; 115.1 — Competent authority agreements under tax treaties.

**Interpretation Bulletins**: IT-125R4: Dispositions of resource properties.

### Proposed Addition — 115(4.1)

**(4.1) Foreign resource pool expenses** — Where a taxpayer ceases at any time after February 27, 2000 to be resident in Canada, a particular taxation year of the taxpayer ends after that time and the taxpayer was non-resident throughout the period (in this subsection referred to as the "non-resident period") that begins at that time and ends at the end of the particular year,

(a) in computing the taxpayer's taxable income earned in Canada for the particular year, there may be deducted each amount that would be permitted to be deducted in computing the taxpayer's income for the particular year under subsection 66(4) or 66.21(4) if

(i) subsection 66(4) were read without reference to the words "who is resident throughout a taxation year in Canada" and as if the amount determined under subparagraph 66(4)(b)(ii) were nil, and

(ii) subsection 66.21(4) were read without reference to the words "throughout which the taxpayer is resident in Canada" and as if the amounts determined under subparagraph 66.21(4)(a)(ii) and paragraph 66.21(4)(b) were nil; and

(b) an amount deducted under this subsection in computing the taxpayer's taxable income earned in Canada for the particular year is deemed, for the purpose of applying subsection 66(4) or 66.21(4), as the case may be, to a subsequent taxation year, to have been deducted in computing the taxpayer's income for the particular year.

**Application**: The December 21, 2000 draft legislation, subsec. 56(3), will add subsec. 115(4.1), applicable to taxation years that begin after February 27, 2000.

**Technical Notes**: See under 115(1)(e.1).

**(5) Interpretation of "partnership"** — For the purposes of subsection (4), "partnership" does not include a prescribed partnership.

**Regulations**: No prescribed partnerships to date.

**(6) Application of subsec. 138(12)** — The definitions in subsection 138(12) apply to this section.

**Notes**: 115(6) added in the R.S.C. 1988 (5th Supp.) consolidation, effective for taxation years ending after November 1991. This rule was formerly in the opening words of 138(12). It is now superfluous, since "designated insurance policy" and "life insurance policy in Canada" are both defined in 248(1).

**Definitions [s. 115]**: "allowable business investment loss" — 38(c), 248(1); "allowable capital loss" — 38(b), 248(1); "amount", "authorized foreign bank", "business" — 248(1); "Canada" — 255; "Canadian resource property" — 66(15), 248(1); "capital interest" — in a trust 108(1), 248(1); "capital property" — 54, 248(1); "class of shares" — 248(6); "corporation" — 248(1), Interpretation Act 35(1); "designated insurance property" — 138(12), 248(1); "dividend", "employed", "employment" — 248(1); "foreign affiliate" — 95(1), 248(1); "foreign resource pool expense" — 248(1); "income interest" — 108(1), 248(1); "individual" — 248(1); "interest" — in real property 248(4); "international traffic" — 248(1); "life insurance policy in Canada" — 138(12), 248(1); "listed" — 87(10); "mutual fund corporation" — 131(8), 248(1); "mutual fund trust" — 132(6)-(7), 132.2(1)(q), 248(1); "non-resident", "office" — 248(1); "partnership" — 115(5) (and see Notes to 96(1)); "person", "prescribed" — 248(1); "prescribed stock exchange" — Reg. 3200, 3201; "property" — 248(1); "property used by it in the year in, or held by it in the year in the course of carrying on an insurance business" — 115(6), 138(12); "public corporation" — 89(1), 248(1); "resident in Canada" — 250; "salary or wages", "share" — 248(1); "taxable Canadian property" — 248(1); "taxable capital gain" — 38(a), 248(1); "taxable income" — 2(2), 248(1); "taxable income earned in Canada" — 115(1), 248(1); "taxation year" — 249, 250.1(a); "taxpayer" — 248(1); "timber resource property" — 13(21), 248(1); "treaty-protected business", "treaty-protected property" — 248(1); "trust" — 104(1), 248(1), (3); "unit trust" — 108(2), 248(1)..

**Interpretation Bulletins [s. 115]**: IT-81R: Partnerships — income of non-resident partners; IT-163R2: Election by non-resident individuals on certain Canadian source income; IT-168R3: Athletes and players employed by football, hockey and similar clubs; IT-171R2: Non-resident individuals — computation of taxable income earned in Canada and non-refundable tax credits; IT-193 SR: Taxable income of individuals resident in Canada during part of a year (Special Release); IT-328R3: Losses on shares on which dividends have been received; IT-393R2: Election re tax on rents and timber royalties — non-residents; IT-420R3: Non-residents — income earned in Canada.

## 115.1 (1) Competent authority agreements —
Notwithstanding any other provision of this Act, where the Minister and another person have, under a provision contained in a tax convention or agreement with another country that has the force of law in Canada, entered into an agreement with respect to the taxation of the other person, all determinations made in accordance with the terms and conditions of the agreement shall be deemed to be in accordance with this Act.

## (2) Transfer of rights and obligations —
Where rights and obligations under an agreement described in subsection (1) have been transferred to another person with the concurrence of the Minister, that other person shall be deemed, for the purpose of subsection (1), to have entered into the agreement with the Minister.

**Related Provisions [s. 115.1]**: 115(1) — Non-resident's taxable income earned in Canada; 116(1) — Disposition by non-resident of certain property; Canada-U.S. tax treaty, Art. XXVI — Mutual agreement procedure; Canada-U.K. tax treaty, Art. 23 — Mutual agreement procedure.

**Notes**: 115.1 rewritten by 1992 technical bill, retroactive to 1985, to extend its application. The former version applied only to the disposition of property by a non-resident where the Minister agreed to defer taxation pursuant to a prescribed tax treaty provision; para. XIII(8) of the Canada-U.S. treaty and para. 13(6) of the Canada-Netherlands treaty were prescribed in Reg. 7400 for this purpose. The new provision is much more general.

As of June 2000, Canada's designated "competent authority" for purposes of its tax treaties is Gary Zed, Deputy Director General, International Tax Directorate, (613) 952-8738.

Some of Canada's recent tax treaties include an arbitration provision which may apply if the competent authorities cannot agree on a disputed issue. However, these provisions will not operate in practice until Canada has seen the results of the experience of other countries that have added this provision to their treaties.

**Definitions [s. 115.1]**: "Canada" — 255; "Minister", "person" — 248(1).

**Interpretation Bulletins [s. 115.1]**: IT-173R2: Capital gains derived in Canada by residents of the United States; IT-270R2: Foreign tax credit; IT-420R3: Non-residents — income earned in Canada.

**Information Circulars [s. 115.1]**: 71-17R4: Requests for competent authority consideration under mutual agreement procedures in income tax conventions.

**Forms [s. 115.1]**: T2029: Waiver in respect of the normal reassessment period.

## 115.2 Non-Residents with Canadian Investment Service Providers — (1) Definitions — The definitions in this subsection apply in this section.

**"Canadian service provider"** means a corporation resident in Canada, a trust resident in Canada or a Canadian partnership.

**Notes**: See Notes at end of 115.2.

**"designated investment services"** provided to a qualified non-resident means any one or more of the services described in the following paragraphs:

(a) investment management and advice with respect to qualified investments, regardless of whether the manager has discretionary authority to buy or sell;

(b) purchasing and selling qualified investments, exercising rights incidental to the ownership of qualified investments such as voting, conversion and exchange, and entering into and executing agreements with respect to such purchasing and selling and the exercising of such rights;

(c) investment administration services, such as receiving, delivering and having custody of investments, calculating and reporting investment values, receiving subscription amounts from, and paying distributions and proceeds of disposition to, investors in and beneficiaries of the qualified non-resident, record keeping, accounting and reporting to the qualified non-resident and its investors and beneficiaries; and

(d) if the qualified non-resident is a corporation, trust or partnership the only undertaking of which is the investing of its funds in qualified investments, marketing investments in the qualified non-resident to non-resident investors.

**"promoter"** of a qualified non-resident that is a corporation, trust or partnership means a person or partnership that initiates or directs the founding, organization or substantial reorganization of the non-resident, or a person or partnership affiliated with such a person or partnership.

**"qualified investment"** of a qualified non-resident means

(a) a share of the capital stock of a corporation, or an interest in a partnership, trust, entity, fund or organization, other than a share or an interest

(i) that is either

(A) not listed on a prescribed stock exchange, or

(B) listed on a prescribed stock exchange, if the qualified non-resident, together with all persons with whom the non-resident does not deal at arm's length, owns 25% or more of the issued shares of any class of the capital stock of the corporation or of the total value of interests in the partnership, entity, trust, fund or organization, as the case may be, and

(ii) of which more than 50% of the fair market value is derived from one or more of

(A) real property situated in Canada,

(B) Canadian resource property, and

(C) timber resource property;

Division D — Taxable Income Earned in Canada by Non-Residents    S. 116(1)

(b) indebtedness;

(c) annuities;

(d) commodities or commodities futures purchased or sold, directly or indirectly in any manner whatever, on a commodities or commodities futures exchange;

(e) currency; and

(f) options, interests, rights and forward and futures agreements in respect of property described in any of paragraphs (a) to (e) or this paragraph, and agreements under which obligations are derived from interest rates, from the price of property described in any of those paragraphs, from payments made in respect of such a property by its issuer to holders of the property, or from an index reflecting a composite measure of such rates, prices or payments, whether or not the agreement creates any rights in or obligations regarding the referenced property itself.

**Regulations**: 3200, 3201 (prescribed stock exchanges for cls. (a)(i)(A) and (B); not yet prescribed).

**"qualified non-resident"** means a non-resident person or a partnership no member of which is resident in Canada.

**(2) Not carrying on business in Canada** — For the purposes of subsection 115(1) and Part XIV, a qualified non-resident is not considered to be carrying on business in Canada at any particular time solely because of the provision to the non-resident at the particular time of designated investment services by a Canadian service provider if

(a) in the case of a non-resident who is an individual other than a trust, the non-resident is not affiliated at the particular time with the Canadian service provider; and

(b) in the case of a non-resident that is a corporation, trust or partnership,

(i) the non-resident has not, before the particular time, directly or through its agents, directed any promotion of investments in itself principally at, or sold such investments to, persons that the non-resident knew or ought to have known after reasonable enquiry were resident in Canada or partnerships that the non-resident knew or ought to have known after reasonable enquiry had members that were resident in Canada,

(ii) the non-resident has not, before the particular time, directly or through its agents, filed any document with a public authority in Canada in accordance with the securities legislation of Canada or of any province in order to permit the distribution of interests in the non-resident to persons resident in Canada, and

(iii) when the particular time is more than one year after the time at which the non-resident was created, the total of the fair market value, at the particular time, of investments in the non-resident that are beneficially owned by persons and partnerships (other than a designated entity in respect of the Canadian service provider) that are affiliated with the Canadian service provider does not exceed 25% of the fair market value, at the particular time, of all investments in the non-resident.

**(3) Interpretation** — For the purposes of subparagraph (2)(b)(iii) and this subsection,

(a) the fair market value of an investment in a corporation, trust or partnership shall be determined without regard to any voting rights attaching to that investment; and

(b) a person or partnership is, at a particular time, a designated entity in respect of a Canadian service provider if the total of the fair market value at the particular time, of investments in the entity that are beneficially owned by persons and partnerships (other than another designated entity in respect of the Canadian service provider) that are affiliated with the Canadian service provider does not exceed 25% of the fair market value, at the particular time, of all investments in the entity.

**(4) Transfer pricing** — For the purpose of section 247, where subsection (2) applies to a qualified non-resident, if the Canadian service provider referred to in that subsection does not deal at arm's length with the promoter of the qualified non-resident, the service provider is deemed not to deal at arm's length with the non-resident.

**Notes**: 115.2 added by 1999 Budget, effective for taxation years that end after 1998. It ensures that a non-resident investment or pension fund is not considered to be carrying on business in Canada (see s. 253) solely by engaging a Canadian firm to provide certain investment management and administration services, provided certain conditions are met.

**Definitions [s. 115.2]**: "affiliated" — 251.1; "amount", "annuity" — 248(1); "arm's length" — 251(1); "business" — 248(1); "Canada" — 255, *Interpretation Act* 35(1); "Canadian partnership" — 102, 248(1); "Canadian resource property" — 66(15), 248(1); "Canadian service provider" — 115.2(1); "corporation" — 248(1), *Interpretation Act* 35(1); "designated entity" — 115.2(3)(b); "designated investment services" — 115.2(1); "disposition" — 248(1); "fair market value" — 115.2(3)(a); ; "individual", "non-resident" — 248(1); "partnership" — see Notes to 96(1); "person", "prescribed" — 248(1); "prescribed stock exchange" — Reg. 3200, 3201; "promoter" — 115.2(1); "property" — 248(1); "province" — *Interpretation Act* 35(1); "qualified investment", "qualified non-resident" — 115.2(1); "record" — 248(1); "resident in Canada" — 250; "share" — 248(1); "taxation year" — 249; "timber resource property" — 13(21), 248(1); "trust" — 104(1), 248(1), (3).

**116. (1) Disposition by non-resident person of certain property** — Where a non-resident person proposes to dispose of any property that would, if the non-resident person disposed of it, be taxable Canadian property of that person (other than property described in subsection (5.2) and excluded property) the non-resident person may, at any time before the disposition, send to the Minister a notice setting out

## S. 116(1) — Income Tax Act, Part I

### Proposed Amendment — 116(1) opening words

**116. (1) Disposition by non-resident person of certain property** — If a non-resident person proposes to dispose of any taxable Canadian property (other than property described in subsection (5.2) and excluded property) the non-resident person may, at any time before the disposition, send to the Minister a notice setting out

**Application**: Bill C-43 (First Reading September 20, 2000), subsec. 61(1), will amend the opening words of subsec. 116(1) to read as above, applicable after October 1, 1996.

**Technical Notes**: Section 116 of the Act establishes procedures for collecting tax from non-residents on the disposition of taxable Canadian property, Canadian resource properties, and certain other properties.

Where a non-resident plans to dispose of property the proceeds from the disposition of which are subject to Canadian tax, the non-resident can obtain a "clearance certificate" from the Minister of National Revenue. The certificate, which is provided as well to the prospective purchaser, verifies that the non-resident vendor has made arrangements for the payment of any resulting tax. Without such a certificate, the purchaser may be required to remit a portion of the purchase price to the Receiver General.

Subsections 116(1), (5.1) and (5.2) set out some of the rules and procedures for this process. These subsections are amended, with application after October 1, 1996, to reflect the amended definition "taxable Canadian property" in subsection 248(1) of the Act. In particular, that amended definition clarifies that a property's status as taxable Canadian property does not depend on its being disposed of; this allows the references in these subsections to be simplified.

(a) the name and address of the person to whom proposes to dispose of the property (in this section referred to as the "proposed purchaser");

(b) a description of the property sufficient to identify it;

(c) the estimated amount of the proceeds of disposition to be received by the non-resident person for the property; and

(d) the amount of the adjusted cost base to him [the non-resident person] of the property at the time of the sending of the notice.

**Related Provisions**: 115.1 — Competent authority agreements under tax treaties; 116(2) — Certificate in respect of proposed disposition; 116(3) — Notice to Minister; 116(6) — Excluded property.

**Notes**: 116(1) is optional in that a non-resident is not technically *required* to apply for a certificate in respect of a proposed disposition. However, if no certificate is obtained under 116(2) or (4), the purchaser is liable for $1/4$ of the amount of the purchase price, and can withhold that amount on closing. 116 protects the Canadian government's ability to collect tax on the sale of real estate in Canada, private corporation shares, etc., even though it has no direct jurisdiction over the non-resident selling the property. See Notes to 223(3) re collection of tax from non-residents.

A parallel certificate may be required from Revenu Québec if the property is in Quebec, failing which the purchaser can be liable for up to 18% (likely to be reduced) of the purchase price: *Taxation Act* s. 1101.

No s. 116 certificate is required for a transfer as a result of death: see Interpretation Bulletin IT-150R2. (A Quebec certificate may be required: Revenu Québec Interpretation Bulletin IMP.1097-1/R1.)

When a s. 116 certificate is requested, the CCRA's practice is to ask for information about past rentals of the property, and to request payment of back taxes under 212(1)(d) on all rents if tax was not withheld and remitted. Legally, however, once tax on the gain has been paid, the CCRA is required by 116(2) or (4) to issue the certificate even if tax on the rents is not paid.

Note that even the sale of shares in non-resident corporations and interests in non-resident trusts and partnerships may require a s. 116 certificate. See 115(1)(b)(v), (vii) and (ix), and proposed 248(1)"taxable Canadian property"(e), (g) and (k).

Opening words of 116(1) amended by 1995-97 technical bill, effective April 27, 1995, to change "depreciable property" to "property described in subsection (5.2)".

**Interpretation Bulletins**: See Interpretation Bulletins and Information Circulars at end of s. 116.

**Forms**: T2062: Request by a non-resident of Canada for a certificate of compliance related to the disposition of taxable Canadian property; T2062A: Request by a non-resident of Canada for a certificate of compliance related to the disposition of Canadian resource property, Canadian real property (other than capital property), Canadian timber resource property and/or depreciable taxable Canadian property.

**(2) Certificate in respect of proposed disposition** — Where a non-resident person who has sent to the Minister a notice under subsection (1) in respect of a proposed disposition of any property has

(a) paid to the Receiver General, as or on account of tax under this Part payable by the non-resident person for the year, $33^{1}/_{3}\%$ of the amount, if any, by which the estimated amount set out in the notice in accordance with paragraph (1)(c) exceeds the amount set out in the notice in accordance with paragraph (1)(d), or

(b) furnished the Minister with security acceptable to the Minister in respect of the proposed disposition of the property,

the Minister shall forthwith issue to the non-resident person and the proposed purchaser a certificate in prescribed form in respect of the proposed disposition, fixing therein an amount (in this section referred to as the "certificate limit") equal to the estimated amount set out in the notice in accordance with paragraph (1)(c).

### Proposed Amendment — 116(2)

**Application**: The December 21, 2000 draft legislation, s. 57, will amend subsec. 116(2) to replace the reference to "33 1/3%" with "25%", applicable to taxation years that end after February 27, 2000, except that, for a taxation year that ended after February 27, 2000 and before October 18, 2000, it shall be read as a reference to "30%".

**Technical Notes**: Section 116 provides for the issuance of a certificate for non-residents disposing of taxable Canadian property. In order to receive the certificate, an amount equal to 33 1/3% of the anticipated gain must be paid by the non-resident on account of income taxes that may become payable as a result of the disposition. This amount is based on the tax rate and the capital gains inclusion rate.

These subsections are amended to replace the reference to the percentage "33 1/3%" with a reference to the percent-

Division D — Taxable Income Earned in Canada by Non-Residents     S. 116(5)(d)

age "25%", consequential on the reduction of the inclusion rate for capital gains from 3/4 to 1/2 [see 38(a) — ed.]. These amendments apply to taxation years that end after February 27, 2000 except that for a taxation year that ends after February 27, 2000 and before October 18, 2000, the reference to the percentage "25%" is to be read as reference to the percentage "30%". These modifications are required in order to reflect the capital gains/losses rate for the year.

**Related Provisions**: 116(5) — Non-residents — Liability of purchaser; 164(1.6) — Security not to be released while appeal pending.

**Interpretation Bulletins**: See Interpretation Bulletins and Information Circulars at end of s. 116.

**Forms**: T2064: Certificate with respect to the proposed disposition of property by a non-resident of Canada.

**(3) Notice to Minister** — Every non-resident person who in a taxation year disposes of any taxable Canadian property of that person (other than property described in subsection (5.2) and excluded property) shall, not later than 10 days after the disposition, send to the Minister, by registered mail, a notice setting out

(a) the name and address of the person to whom the non-resident person disposed of the property (in this section referred to as the "purchaser"),

(b) a description of the property sufficient to identify it, and

(c) a statement of the proceeds of disposition of the property and the amount of its adjusted cost base to the non-resident person immediately before the disposition,

unless the non-resident person has, at any time before the disposition, sent to the Minister a notice under subsection (1) in respect of any proposed disposition of that property and

(d) the purchaser was the proposed purchaser referred to in that notice,

(e) the estimated amount set out in that notice in accordance with paragraph (1)(c) is equal to or greater than the proceeds of disposition of the property, and

(f) the amount set out in that notice in accordance with paragraph (1)(d) does not exceed the adjusted cost base to the non-resident person of the property immediately before the disposition.

**Related Provisions**: 116(6) — Excluded property; 238(1) — Offences; 248(7) — Mail deemed received on day mailed.

**Notes**: See Notes to 116(1).

Opening words of 116(3) amended by 1995-97 technical bill, effective April 27, 1995, to change "depreciable property" to "property described in subsection (5.2)".

**Interpretation Bulletins**: See Interpretation Bulletins and Information Circulars at end of s. 116.

**Forms**: T2062: Request by a non-resident of Canada for a certificate of compliance related to the disposition of taxable Canadian property; T2062A: Request by a non-resident of Canada for a certificate of compliance related to the disposition of Canadian resource property, Canadian real property (other than capital property), Canadian timber resource property and/or depreciable taxable Canadian property.

**(4) Certificate in respect of property disposed of** — Where a non-resident person who has sent to the Minister a notice under subsection (3) in respect of a disposition of any property has

(a) paid to the Receiver General, as or on account of tax under this Part payable by the non-resident person for the year, $33^1/_3\%$ of the amount, if any, by which the proceeds of disposition of the property exceed the adjusted cost base to the non-resident person of the property immediately before the disposition, or

(b) furnished the Minister with security acceptable to the Minister in respect of the disposition of the property,

the Minister shall forthwith issue to the non-resident person and the purchaser a certificate in prescribed form in respect of the disposition.

**Proposed Amendment — 116(4)**

**Application**: The December 21, 2000 draft legislation, s. 57, will amend subsec. 116(4) to replace the reference to "33 1/3%" with "25%", applicable to taxation years that end after February 27, 2000, except that, for a taxation year that ended after February 27, 2000 and before October 18, 2000, it shall be read as a reference to "30%".

**Technical Notes**: See under 116(2).

**Related Provisions**: 116(5) — Non-residents — liability of purchaser; 164(1.6) — Security not to be released while appeal pending.

**Notes**: See Notes to 116(1).

**Interpretation Bulletins**: See Interpretation Bulletins and Information Circulars at end of s. 116.

**Forms**: T2068: Certificate with respect to the disposition of property by a non-resident of Canada.

**(5) Liability of purchaser** — Where in a taxation year a purchaser has acquired from a non-resident person any taxable Canadian property (other than depreciable property or excluded property) of the non-resident person, the purchaser, unless

(a) after reasonable inquiry the purchaser had no reason to believe that the non-resident person was not resident in Canada, or

(b) a certificate under subsection (4) has been issued to the purchaser by the Minister in respect of the property,

is liable to pay, and shall remit to the Receiver General within 30 days after the end of the month in which the purchaser acquired the property, as tax under this Part for the year on behalf of the non-resident person, $33^1/_3\%$ of the amount, if any, by which

(c) the cost to the purchaser of the property so acquired

exceeds

(d) the certificate limit fixed by the certificate, if any, issued under subsection (2) in respect of the disposition of the property by the non-resident person to the purchaser,

987

and is entitled to deduct or withhold from any amount paid or credited by the purchaser to the non-resident person or otherwise recover from the non-resident person any amount paid by the purchaser as such a tax.

> **Proposed Amendment — 116(5)**
>
> **Application**: The December 21, 2000 draft legislation, s. 57, will amend subsec. 116(5) to replace the reference to "33 1/3%" with "25%", applicable to taxation years that end after February 27, 2000, except that, for a taxation year that ended after February 27, 2000 and before October 18, 2000, it shall be read as a reference to "30%".
>
> **Technical Notes**: See under 116(2).

**Related Provisions**: 116(2) — Certificate in respect of proposed disposition; 116(4) — Certificate in respect of property disposed of; 116(6) — Excluded property; 227(9) — Failure to remit tax — penalty; 227(9.3) — Interest on tax not paid; 227(10.1) — Assessment; 248(7) — Mail deemed received on day mailed.

**Notes**: 116(5) amended by 1989 Budget, effective April 28, 1989; for acquisitions until the end of 1989, read "30%" in place of "33 1/3%". See also Notes to 116(1).

**Interpretation Bulletins**: See Interpretation Bulletins and Information Circulars at end of s. 116.

**(5.1) Idem** — Where a non-resident person has disposed of or proposes to dispose of a life insurance policy in Canada, a Canadian resource property or any property that is or would, if the non-resident person disposed of it, be taxable Canadian property of the non-resident person other than

> **Proposed Amendment — 116(5.1) opening words**
>
> **(5.1) Gifts, etc.** — If a non-resident person has disposed of or proposes to dispose of a life insurance policy in Canada, a Canadian resource property or a taxable Canadian property other than
>
> **Application**: Bill C-43 (First Reading September 20, 2000), subsec. 61(2), will amend the opening words of subsec. 116(5.1) to read as above, applicable after October 1, 1996.
>
> **Technical Notes**: See under 116(1).

(a) excluded property, or

(b) property that has been transferred or distributed on or after the non-resident person's death and as a consequence thereof

to any person by way of gift *inter vivos* or to a person with whom the non-resident person was not dealing at arm's length for no proceeds of disposition or for proceeds of disposition less than the fair market value of the property at the time the non-resident person so disposed of it or proposes to dispose of it, as the case may be, the following rules apply:

(c) the reference in paragraph (1)(c) to "the proceeds of disposition to be received by the non-resident person for the property" shall be read as a reference to "the fair market value of the property at the time the non-resident person proposes to dispose of it",

(d) the references in subsections (3) and (4) to "the proceeds of disposition of the property" shall be read as references to "the fair market value of the property immediately before the disposition",

(e) the references in subsection (5) to "the cost to the purchaser of the property so acquired" shall be read as references to "the fair market value of the property at the time it was so acquired", and

(f) the reference in subsection (5.3) to "the amount payable by the taxpayer for the property so acquired" shall be read as a reference to "the fair market value of the property at the time it was so acquired".

**Related Provisions**: 110.4(4) — Death of a taxpayer; 116(6) — Excluded property.

**Interpretation Bulletins**: IT-150R2: Taxable Canadian property — acquisition from a non-resident of certain property on death or mortgage foreclosure or by virtue of a deemed disposition. See also Interpretation Bulletins and Information Circulars at end of s. 116.

**Forms**: T2062B: Notice of dispositions of life insurance policies in Canada by a non-resident; T2062B — Sched. 1: Certification and remittance notice.

**(5.2) Certificates for dispositions** — Where a non-resident person has, in respect of a disposition or proposed disposition to a taxpayer in a taxation year of property (other than excluded property) that is a life insurance policy in Canada, a Canadian resource property, a property (other than capital property) that is real property situated in Canada, a timber resource property, depreciable property that is or would, if the non-resident person disposed of it, be a taxable Canadian property of the non-resident person or any interest in, or option in respect of, a property to which this subsection applies (whether or not the property exists),

> **Proposed Amendment — 116(5.2) opening words**
>
> **(5.2) Certificates for dispositions** — If a non-resident person has, in respect of a disposition or proposed disposition to a taxpayer in a taxation year of property (other than excluded property) that is a life insurance policy in Canada, a Canadian resource property, a property (other than capital property) that is real property situated in Canada, a timber resource property, depreciable property that is a taxable Canadian property or any interest in or option in respect of a property to which this subsection applies (whether or not that property exists),
>
> **Application**: Bill C-43 (First Reading September 20, 2000), subsec. 61(3), will amend the opening words of subsec. 116(5.2) to read as above, applicable after October 1, 1996.
>
> **Technical Notes**: See under 116(1).

(a) paid to the Receiver General, as or on account of tax under this Part payable by the non-resident person for the year, such amount as is acceptable to the Minister in respect of the disposition or proposed disposition of the property, or

Division D — Taxable Income Earned in Canada by Non-Residents   S. 116(6)(a)

(b) furnished the Minister with security acceptable to the Minister in respect of the disposition or proposed disposition of the property,

the Minister shall forthwith issue to the non-resident person and to the taxpayer a certificate in prescribed form in respect of the disposition or proposed disposition fixing therein an amount equal to the proceeds of disposition, proposed proceeds of disposition or such other amount as is reasonable in the circumstances.

**Related Provisions**: 116(5.1), (5.3) — Liability of purchaser; 164(1.6) — Security not to be released while appeal pending; 248(4) — Interest in real property.

**Notes**: Opening words of 116(5.2) amended by 1995-97 technical bill, effective for dispositions after 1996. The substantive changes were the new references to excluded property (see 116(6)) and to interests or options. For earlier dispositions, read:

(5.2) **Certificates for dispositions** — Where a non-resident person has, in respect of a disposition or proposed disposition to a taxpayer in a taxation year of a life insurance policy in Canada of the non-resident person, a Canadian resource property of the non-resident person, a property (other than capital property) that is real property situated in Canada of the non-resident person (including any interest therein or option in respect thereof, whether or not the property is in existence), a timber resource property of the non-resident person or any interest therein or option in respect thereof, or depreciable property that is or would, if the non-resident person disposed of it, be a taxable Canadian property of the non-resident person,

116(5.2) amended by 1990 Budget, effective for dispositions after February 20, 1990 (other than dispositions pursuant to agreements in writing entered into before February 21, 1990), to extend to real estate inventory and timber resource properties, as well as any interest in or option in respect of such property.

**Interpretation Bulletins**: See Interpretation Bulletins and Information Circulars at end of s. 116.

(5.3) **Liability of purchaser in certain cases** — Where in a taxation year a taxpayer has acquired from a non-resident person property referred to in subsection (5.2),

(a) the taxpayer, unless after reasonable inquiry the taxpayer had no reason to believe that the non-resident person was not resident in Canada, is liable to pay, as tax under this Part for the year on behalf of the non-resident person, 50% of the amount, if any, by which

(i) the amount payable by the taxpayer for the property so acquired

exceeds

(ii) the amount fixed in the certificate, if any, issued under subsection (5.2) in respect of the disposition of the property by the non-resident person to the taxpayer

and is entitled to deduct or withhold from any amount paid or credited by the taxpayer to the non-resident person or to otherwise recover from the non-resident person any amount paid by the taxpayer as such a tax; and

(b) the taxpayer shall, within 30 days after the end of the month in which the taxpayer acquired the property, remit to the Receiver General the tax for which the taxpayer is liable under paragraph (a).

**Related Provisions**: 227(9) — Failure to remit tax — penalty; 227(9.3) — Interest on tax not paid; 227(10.1) — Assessment; 248(7) — Mail deemed received on day mailed.

**Interpretation Bulletins**: See Interpretation Bulletins and Information Circulars at end of s. 116.

**Forms**: T2064: Certificate with respect to the proposed disposition of property by a non-resident of Canada.

(5.4) **Presumption** — Where there has been a disposition by a non-resident of a life insurance policy in Canada by virtue of subsection 148(2) or any of paragraphs (a) to (c) and (e) of the definition "disposition" in subsection 148(9), the insurer under the policy shall, for the purposes of subsections (5.2) and (5.3) be deemed to be the taxpayer who acquired the property for an amount equal to the proceeds of disposition as determined under section 148.

**Interpretation Bulletins**: See Interpretation Bulletins and Information Circulars at end of s. 116.

(6) **Definition of "excluded property"** — For the purposes of this section, "excluded property" of a non-resident person means

(a) property described in subparagraph 115(1)(b)(xii);

**Proposed Amendment — 116(6)(a), (a.1)**

(a) a property that is a taxable Canadian property solely because a provision of this Act deems it to be a taxable Canadian property;

(a.1) a property (other than real property situated in Canada, a Canadian resource property or a timber resource property) that is described in an inventory of a business carried on in Canada by the person;

**Application**: Bill C-43 (First Reading September 20, 2000), subsec. 61(4), will amend para. 116(6)(a) to read as above, and add para. (a.1), applicable after October 1, 1996.

**Technical Notes**: The various rules in section 116 of the Act, which provides a withholding procedure for purchasers of certain properties, do not apply where the property is excluded property. "Excluded property" is defined in subsection 116(6).

Paragraph 116(6)(a) provides that any property referred to in subparagraph 115(1)(b)(xii) of the Act (property that is deemed by a provision of the Act to be taxable Canadian property) is excluded property. Due to the amended definition "taxable Canadian property" in subsection 248(1) of the Act, paragraph 116(6)(a) is amended, effective after October 1, 1996, to remove the reference to subparagraph 115(1)(b)(xii), and to provide that a property is excluded property if it is a taxable Canadian property solely because it is deemed to be so by a provision of the Act.

New paragraph 116(6)(a.1) provides that property described in an inventory of a business carried on in Canada is excluded property for the purposes of section 116 of the Act. This new provision is a result of the change to paragraph (b) of the definition "taxable Canadian property" in subsection 248(1), which now includes as taxable Canadian

S. 116(6)(a)                                Income Tax Act, Part I

property the inventory of a business carried on in Canada. Effective after October 1, 1996, new paragraph 116(6)(a.1) excludes such inventory from the requirements of section 116. However, the exclusion does not apply to inventory that is real property situated in Canada, a Canadian resource property or a timber resource property.

(b) a share of a class of the capital stock of a corporation that is listed on a prescribed stock exchange, or an interest in the share;

(c) a unit of a mutual fund trust;

(d) a bond, debenture, bill, note, mortgage or similar obligation; or

(e) any other property that is prescribed to be excluded property.

**Related Provisions**: 87(10) — New share issued on amalgamation of public corporation deemed to be listed on prescribed stock exchange.

**Notes**: The term "bond, debenture, bill, note, mortgage or similar obligation" may not include bankers' acceptances. See *Federated Cooperatives Ltd.*, [2000] 2 C.T.C. 2382 (TCC).

116(6)(a) and (b) amended by 1995-97 technical bill, effective on the same basis as the amendments to 115(1)(b). Para. (a) was amended to change reference from 115(1)(b)(ix) to (xii) (no substantive change; consequential on amendments to 115(1). Para (b) was amended to change "public corporation" to "corporation listed on a prescribed stock exchange".

**Regulations**: 810 (property prescribed to be excluded property); 3200, 3201 (prescribed stock exchanges; will be amended to cover 116(6), but see also ITA 87(10)).

**(7) Application of subsec. 138(12)** — The definitions in subsection 138(12) apply to this section.

**Notes**: 116(7) added in the R.S.C. 1985 (5th Supp.) consolidation, effective for taxation years ending after November 1991. This rule was formerly in the opening words of 138(12).

**Definitions [s. 116]**: "adjusted cost base" — 54, 248(1); "amount" — 248(1); "Canada" — 255; "Canadian resource property" — 66(15), 248(1); "class of shares" — 248(6); "consequence thereof" — 248(8); "depreciable property" — 13(21), 248(1); "excluded property" — 116(6); "interest" in real property — 248(4); "life insurance policy in Canada" — 138(12), 248(1); "listed" — 87(10) "Minister" — 248(1); "mutual fund trust" — 132(6)–(7), 132.2(1)(q), 248(1); "non-resident", "person", "prescribed" — 248(1); "prescribed stock exchange" — Reg. 3200, 3201; "property" — 248(1); "public corporation" — 89(1), 248(1); "resident in Canada" — 250; "taxable Canadian property" — 248(1); "taxation year" — 249, 250.1(a); "taxpayer", "timber resource property" — 248(1). See also 116(7).

**Interpretation Bulletins [s. 116]**: IT-150R2: Acquisition from non-resident of certain property on death or mortgage foreclosure or by virtue of a deemed disposition; IT-474R: Amalgamations of Canadian corporations.

**Information Circulars [s. 116]**: 72-17R4: Procedures concerning the disposition of taxable Canadian property by non-residents of Canada — section 116.

## DIVISION E — COMPUTATION OF TAX

### Subdivision a — Rules Applicable to Individuals

**117. (1) Tax payable under this Part** — For the purposes of this Division, except section 120 (other than subparagraph (a)(ii) of the definition "tax otherwise payable under this Part" in subsection 120(4)), tax payable under this Part, tax otherwise payable under this Part and tax under this Part shall be computed as if this Part were read without reference to Division E.1.

**Related Provisions**: 248(2) — Rates of tax.

**Notes**: Division E.1 is sections 127.5 to 127.55, the Alternative Minimum Tax.

117(1) amended by 1999 Budget, this version effective for 2000 and later taxation years. For 1998-99, read "subparagraph (a)(ii)" as "paragraph (b)". For 1987-1998, read:

> (1) Tax payable under this Part — For the purposes of this Division, except section 120 (other than paragraph (b) of the definition "tax otherwise payable under this Part" in subsection 120(4)) and section 120.1 (other than subsection 120.1(2)), tax payable under this Part, tax otherwise payable under this Part and tax under this Part shall be computed as if this Part were read without reference to Division E.1.

**(2) 1988 and subsequent taxation years rates** — The tax payable under this Part by an individual on the individual's taxable income or taxable income earned in Canada, as the case may be, (in this subdivision referred to as the "amount taxable") for the 1988 and subsequent taxation years is

(a) 17% of the amount taxable if the amount taxable does not exceed $27,500;[10]

(b) $4,675[10] plus 26% of the amount by which the amount taxable exceeds $27,500[10] if the amount taxable exceeds $27,500[10] and does not exceed $55,000[10]; and

(c) $11,825[10] plus 29% of the amount by which the amount taxable exceeds $55,000.[10]

**Proposed Amendment — Tax bracket changes**

**(2) Rate for 2000** — The tax payable under this Part by an individual on the individual's taxable income or taxable income earned in Canada, as the case may be, (in this subdivision referred to as the "amount taxable") for the 2000 taxation year is

(a) 17% of the amount taxable, if the amount taxable does not exceed $30,004;

(b) $5,101 plus 25% of the amount by which the amount taxable exceeds $30,004, if the amount taxable exceeds $30,004 and does not exceed $60,009; and

---

[10] Indexed by s. 117.1 after 1988 — ed.

(c) $12,602 plus 29% of the amount by which the amount taxable exceeds $60,009, if the amount taxable exceeds $60,009.

**Application**: The December 21, 2000 draft legislation, subsec. 58(1), will amend subsec. 117(2) to read as above, applicable to the 2000 taxation year.

**Technical Notes**: See under 117(2), (3) below.

**Notice of Ways and Means Motion, Economic Statement, October 18, 2000**: (1) That, for the 2001 and subsequent taxation years, the tax payable by an individual (other than an inter vivos trust) under Part I of the Act be determined in accordance with the following rate structure:

(a) 16% of taxable income up to $30,004 (indexed after 2000),

(b) 22% of taxable income between $30,004 and $60,009 (both amounts indexed after 2000),

(c) 26% of taxable income between $60,009 (indexed after 2000) and $100,000 (indexed after 2001), and

(d) 29% of taxable income that exceeds $100,000 (indexed after 2001),

and that, as a result, the "appropriate percentage" used in computing the individual's non-refundable personal tax credits and alternative minimum tax reflect the rate referred to in subparagraph (a).

**Notice of Ways and Means Motion, federal budget, February 28, 2000**: *Tax Payable by Individuals*

(4) That the calculation of an individual's tax otherwise payable under Part I of the Act be modified to reduce the 26% tax rate applicable to the portion of the individual's taxable income in excess of $29,590 and less than $59,180 (those two threshold amounts being indexed) to

(a) 25% for the 2000 taxation year, and

(b) 24% for the 2001 and subsequent taxation years,

such that the tax rate structure for the 2000 taxation year be

(c) 17% of taxable income up to $30,004,

(d) 25% of taxable income between $30,004 and $60,009, and

(e) 29% of taxable income that exceeds $60,009.

**Federal budget, supplementary information, February 28, 2000**: *Reducing the Middle Tax Rate*

The budget proposes to reduce the middle tax rate from 26% to 24% effective July 1, 2000. Tax forms for the year 2000 would show a rate of 25%.

The middle tax rate will drop further to 23% within the next five years.

### Proposed Amendment — Tax bracket changes in 2004

**(2) Rates for years after 2000** — The tax payable under this Part by an individual on the individual's taxable income or taxable income earned in Canada, as the case may be, (in this subdivision referred to as the "amount taxable") for a taxation year is

(a) 16% of the amount taxable, if the amount taxable does not exceed $30,754[11];

(b) $4,921[11] plus 22% of the amount by which the amount taxable exceeds $30,754[11], if the amount taxable exceeds $30,754[11] and does not exceed $61,509[11]

(b.1) $11,687[11] plus 26% of the amount by which the amount taxable exceeds $61,509[11], if the amount taxable exceeds $61,509[11] and does not exceed $100,000; and

(c) $21,695 plus 29% of the amount by which the amount taxable exceeds $100,000[11], if the amount taxable exceeds $100,000.

**Related Provisions**: 117(3) — Minimum thresholds for 2004.

**Notes**: See 117.1 for indexing from 2002 on, and 117(3) for minimum amounts for 2004.

**(3) Minimum thresholds for 2004** — Each of the amounts of $30,754, $61,509 and $100,000 referred to in subsection (2) is deemed, for the purposes of applying subsection (2) to the 2004 taxation year, to be the greater of

(a) the amount that would be used for the 2004 taxation year if this section were read without reference to this subsection; and

(b) in the case of

(i) the amount of $30,754, $35,000,

(ii) the amount of $61,509, $70,000, and

(iii) the amount of $100,000, $113,804.

**Application**: The December 21, 2000 draft legislation, subsec. 58(2), will amend subsec. 117(2) to read as above and add subsec. 117(3), applicable to 2001 *et seq.*

**Technical Notes**: Subsection 117(2) provides the marginal tax rates of federal tax. These amendments provide two tax rate structures: one for 2000 and the other for the 2001 and subsequent taxation years.

The 2000 tax structure is as follows:

- 17% of taxable income up to $30,004
- 25% of taxable income between $30,004 and $60,009
- 29% of taxable income that exceeds $60,009.

The tax structure for 2001 and subsequent years is as follows:

- 16% of taxable income up to $30,754
- 22% of taxable income between $30,754 and $61,509
- 26% of taxable income between $61,509 and $100,000
- 29% of taxable income that exceeds $100,000.

New subsection 117(3) provides that the income thresholds of $30,754, $61,509 and $100,000 used in computing an individual's tax for the 2004 taxation year will not be less than $35,000, $70,000 and $113,804, respectively, regardless of the annual increase provided under the indexing provisions of the Act.

---

[11] Indexed by 117.1 after 2001, but see also 117(3) — ed.

**S. 117(3)**      Income Tax Act, Part I, Division E

This amendment applies to the 2004 taxation year.

**Notice of Ways and Means Motion, Economic Statement, October 18, 2000**: *Guaranteed Minimum Relief in 2004*

(9) That (a) for the 2004 and subsequent taxation years,

    (i) [reproduced under 118(1)B(a) — ed.]

    (ii) the amounts of $30,004, $60,009 and $100,000 referred to in paragraph (1) be no less than $35,000, $70,000 and $113,804, respectively, and (b) [reproduced under 122.61(1)B — ed.]

**Notice of Ways and Means Motion, federal budget, February 28, 2000**: *Tax Payable by Individuals*

(4) That the calculation of an individual's tax otherwise payable under Part I of the Act be modified to reduce the 26% tax rate applicable to the portion of the individual's taxable income in excess of $29,590 and less than $59,180 (those two threshold amounts being indexed) to

    (a) 25% for the 2000 taxation year, and

    (b) 24% for the 2001 and subsequent taxation years,

such that the tax rate structure for the 2000 taxation year be

    (c) 17% of taxable income up to $30,004,

    (d) 25% of taxable income between $30,004 and $60,009, and

    (e) 29% of taxable income that exceeds $60,009.

**Federal budget, supplementary information, February 28, 2000**: *Reducing the Middle Tax Rate*

The budget proposes to reduce the middle tax rate from 26% to 24% effective July 1, 2000. Tax forms for the year 2000 would show a rate of 25%.

The middle tax rate will drop further to 23% within the next five years.

### Proposed Amendment — Allowing Provinces to Impose Tax on Income

**Department of Finance/CCRA news release, January 25, 2000**: *Government Outlines Measures to Make Tax Systems More Flexible for Provinces and Territories*

Finance Minister Paul Martin and National Revenue Minister Martin Cauchon today released the document *Federal Administration of Provincial Taxes: New Directions*, which outlines recent measures that will give provinces and territories greater tax policy flexibility.

"The federal government has taken the initiative of offering provinces and territories the option to levy their personal income taxes on either taxable income or basic federal tax," said Mr. Martin. "This is the biggest change in federal-provincial-territorial tax collection arrangements in over 30 years. It will allow the provinces and territories to pursue their own policy objectives while insulating their revenue bases from ongoing federal initiatives to reduce taxes."

A tax-on-income system eliminates the impact of changes to federal tax rates and credits on provincial-territorial revenues. At the same time, maintaining a common federal-provincial-territorial taxable income base will preserve the following benefits associated with the federal-provincial-territorial Tax Collection Agreements (TCAs):

- uniformity across provinces and territories with respect to what income should be taxed by both levels of government;
- a single form for taxpayers;
- a single tax collection agency; and
- substantial cost savings for the provinces and territories as a result of the federal government collecting their taxes generally free of charge — over the past five years the provinces and territories have saved some $1.5 billion as a result of the federal government administering their taxes.

"New guidelines have also been developed to allow for federal collection of a much broader range of provincial and territorial taxes," said Minister Cauchon. "The tax collection guidelines establish a simpler system, now in place, that is objective and transparent." Under the guidelines, the costs charged to provinces and territories are graduated to reflect the degree to which their taxes are harmonized with their federal counterparts.

The Organisation for Economic Co-operation and Development (OECD) asserts that the TCAs have worked well. In its 1997 Canada Review the OECD said, "The benefits of decentralized taxing authority can be achieved without sacrificing a harmonized and administratively simple tax system by federal tax collection agreements. This has been a success story in the case of income taxes in Canada."

Backgrounders providing additional details on the tax-on-income model and the new guidelines are attached [not reproduced here — ed].

Copies of the *Federal Administration of Provincial Taxes: New Directions* document may be obtained free of charge from the Department of Finance Distribution Centre at (613) 943-8665 or on the Department's Internet site at www.fin.gc.ca.

For further information: Munir A. Sheikh, Tax Policy Branch, Department of Finance, (613) 992-1630; Bill McCloskey, Policy and Legislation, Canada Customs and Revenue Agency, (613) 957-2041; Jean-Michel Catta, Public Affairs and Operations Division, Department of Finance, (613) 996-8080.

**Notes**: All provinces have switched to "tax on income" effective 2001. Several provinces switched for 2000.

**Related Provisions**: 117(1) — Minimum tax to be ignored for purposes of 117(2); 117.1(1) — Indexing for inflation; 120(2) — Rate reduction for residents of Quebec; 122 — Top rate of tax payable by *inter vivos* trust; 127.5 — Minimum tax; 180.1 — Individual surtax; 180.2 — "Clawback" tax on old age security.

**Notes**: Since 1992 annual inflation has been below 3%, so the brackets above have remained at $29,590 and $59,180, which is where indexing under 117.1 took them from 1988 to 1992 as a result of inflation.

In addition to the tax under 117, surtax under Part I.1 and "clawback" tax under Part I.2, an individual is also subject to provincial or territorial income tax. Except for Quebec, which collects its own tax on separate income tax returns, each province imposes a personal income tax that is collected for the province by the federal government on a joint tax return. (For the Ontario *Income Tax Act*, see David M. Sherman, *The Practitioner's Ontario Taxes, Annotated* (Carswell). Or see *Provincial TaxPartner* (CD-ROM) for all provinces.) Income of an individual is generally taxed by the province in which the individual is resident on December 31. For rates and surtaxes see introductory pages. For income not earned in a province, the federal government imposes an additional tax under 120(1).

The federal rates for residents of Quebec are actually 83.5% of the rates shown here. See 120(2) and Notes thereto.

**Interpretation Bulletins**: IT-513R: Personal tax credits; IT-515R2: Education tax credit; IT-516R2: Tuition tax credit; IT-519R2: Medical expense and disability tax credits and attendant care expense deduction.

### (3)–(5.2) [Repealed under former Act]

**Notes**: 117(3)–(5.2), repealed by 1988 tax reform, set out the personal tax rates for years before 1988.

### (6) [Repealed]

**Notes**: 117(6) repealed by 1999 Budget, effective for 1998 and later taxation years. It allowed Revenue Canada to publish tax tables that could be used in place of the detailed calculations. Since the 1995 return, these Tables A and B provided with the T1 General Tax Return Guide were eliminated, to save printing costs. (Revenue Canada news release, November 22, 1995.)

### (7) [Repealed]

**Notes**: 117(7) repealed by 1992 Child Benefit Bill, effective 1993. It provided the so-called "notch provision", allowing a reduction for a dependant's medical expenses. The reduction for medical expenses of a dependant who has some income is now found in formula element D of the medical expense credit calculation of 118.2(1).

**Definitions [s. 117]**: "amount", "individual", "person", "prescribed" — 248(1); "tax payable" — 117(1), 248(2); "taxable income" — 2(2), 248(1); "taxable income earned in Canada" — 115(1), 248(1); "taxation year" — 249; "taxpayer" — 248(1).

**Interpretation Bulletins [s. 117]**: IT-406R2: Tax payable by an *inter vivos* trust.

## Annual Adjustment of Deductions and Other Amounts

### 117.1 (1) Annual adjustment [indexing] —
Each of the amounts expressed in dollars in subsection 117(2), the description of B in subsection 118(1), subsections 118(2), 118.2(1), 118.3(1), 122.5(3) and 122.51(1) and (2) and Part I.2 in relation to tax payable under this Part or Part I.2 for a taxation year shall be adjusted so that the amount to be used under those provisions for the year is the total of

(a) the amount that would, but for subsection (3), be the amount to be used under those provisions for the preceding taxation year, and

(b) the product obtained by multiplying

(i) the amount referred to in paragraph (a)

by

(ii) the amount, adjusted in such manner as may be prescribed and rounded to the nearest one-thousandth, or, where the result obtained is equidistant from two consecutive one-thousandths, to the higher thereof, that is determined by the formula

$$\frac{A}{B} - 1$$

where

A is the Consumer Price Index for the 12 month period that ended on September 30 next before that year, and

B is the Consumer Price Index for the 12 month period immediately preceding the period mentioned in the description of A.

**Related Provisions**: 117(1.1) — Indexing of specific amounts; 122.5(3.1) — Indexing of GST Credit amounts; 122.61(5) — Indexing of Child Tax Benefit; 257 — Formula cannot calculate to less than zero.

**Notes**: 117.1(1) amended by 2000 first budget bill (C-32), effective for 2000 and later taxation years, to change "1.03" in the formula to "1". The effect is to restore full indexing (inflation adjustment) to the Consumer Price Index, as announced in the February 28, 2000 federal Budget. From 1988 to 1999, the figure "1.03" meant that tax brackets (s. 117) and personal credits (118–118.3) were only indexed to the extent inflation to the previous September exceeded 3%. Since inflation was under 3% from 1991–1998, the brackets and credits remained the same from 1992–99. See 117.1(1.1) for the credit amounts that apply for 2000.

For the Consumer Price Index indexing amount for each year since 1988, see the first line of the table at the end of 117.1.

117.1(1)(a) through (d)(i) replaced with 117.1(1)(a) to (b)(i) by 1999 Budget, effective for 2001 and later taxation years. For earlier years read:

117.1 (1) Each of

(a) the amount of $6,456 referred to in clause (a)(ii)(B) of the definition "preferred beneficiary" in subsection 108(1) in relation to a beneficiary's income (computed without reference to subsection 104(14)) for a taxation year,

(b) the amounts expressed in dollars in subsection 117(2), paragraphs (b.1) to (d) of the description of B in subsection 118(1), subsections 118(2), 118.2(1) and 118.3(1) and Part I.2 in relation to tax payable under this Part or Part I.2 for a taxation year,

(b.1) the amounts of $5,000 and $6,000 referred to in subsection (2) and paragraphs (a) and (b) of the description of B in subsection 118(1) in relation to tax payable under this Part for a taxation year, and

(b.2) the amounts expressed in dollars in subsections 122.5(3) and 122.51(1) and (2) in relation to tax payable under this Part for a taxation year

shall be adjusted so that the amount to be used under those provisions for the year is the total of

(c) the amount that would, but for subsection (3), be the amount to be used under those provisions for the immediately preceding taxation year, and

(d) the product obtained by multiplying

(i) the amount referred to in paragraph (c)

by

117.1(1)(b) amended by 1998 Budget to change "(c) and (d)" to "(b.1) to (d)", effective

(a) for 2000 and later taxation years for amounts referred to in 118(1)B(b.1), and

(b) for 1999 and later taxation years for amounts referred to in 118(1)B(c.1).

Everything before 117.1(1)(c) amended by 1997 Budget, this version effective 1998. For 1997, delete the references to 122.51(1) and (2).

The amending legislation provides that for the purpose of 117.1(1)(c), the amount to be used under 108(1)"preferred beneficiary"(a)(ii)(B) in relation to income for the 1996 taxation year is deemed to be $6,456.

## S. 117.1(1) — Income Tax Act, Part I, Division E

For 1996, read:

**117.1 (1) Each of**

(a) the amounts of $5,000 and $6,000 referred to in subsection (2) and paragraphs (a) and (b) of the description of B in subsection 118(1),

(a.1) the amounts expressed in dollars in subsection 122.5(3), and

(b) the amounts expressed in dollars in subsection 117(2), paragraphs (c) and (d) of the description of B in subsection 118(1), subsections 118(2), 118.2(1) and 118.3(1) and Part I.2

shall be adjusted, for each taxation year after 1996 for amounts referred to in paragraph (d) of the description of B in subsection 118(1), for each taxation year after 1990 for amounts referred to in subsection 122.5(3) and for each taxation year after 1988 in any other case, so that the amount to be used under those provisions for the year is an amount equal to the total of

Earlier changes:

Reference to Part I.2 in 117.1(1)(b) added by 1995 Budget, effective 1996. For 1990-95, read "180.2(1)" instead, as added by 1989 Budget.

In 117.1(1), two references to 122.5(3) added by 1990 GST, effective 1991.

The text between paras. (b) and (c) amended by 1996 Budget, effective 1996, to add the rule indexing the numbers in 118(1)B(d) after 1996.

**Interpretation Bulletins**: IT-406R2: Tax payable by an *inter vivos* trust.

**(1.1) Adjustment of certain amounts** — Notwithstanding any other provision of this section, for the purpose of making the adjustment provided under subsection (1) for the 2000 taxation year, the amounts used for the 1999 taxation year

(a) in respect of the amounts of $6,000, $5,000 and $500 referred to in paragraphs (a), (b) and (c) of the description of B in subsection 118(1) and the amount of $625 referred to in subparagraph 180.2(4)(a)(ii) are deemed to be $7,131, $6,055, $606 and $665, respectively; and

(b) in respect of the amounts of $6,456 and $4,103 referred to in paragraph (d) of the description of B in subsection 118(1) are deemed to be $7,131 and $4,778, respectively.

**Related Provisions**: 122.5(3.1) — Indexing of GST Credit amounts.

**Notes**: 117.1(1.1) added by 2000 first budget bill (C-32), effective for 2000 and later taxation years. It sets the base for which to calculate indexing under 117.1(1) to determine the figures for 2000 (using indexing of 1.4%). The figures listed for 1999 of $7,131, $6,055, $606, $665 and $4,778 are, for 2000, $7,231, $6,140, $614, $674 and $4,845 respectively.

**(2) Idem** — [Repealed]

**Notes**: 117.1(2) repealed by 1999 Budget, effective for 1999 and later taxation years. For earlier years read:

(2) **Idem** — The amount of $500 referred to in subparagraphs (a)(ii) and (b)(iv) of the description of B in subsection 118(1) shall be adjusted for each taxation year after 1988 so that the amount to be used under those subparagraphs for the year is the amount determined by the formula

$$\frac{1}{2} \times (\$6,000^{10} - \$5,000^{10})$$

**(3) Rounding** — Where an amount referred to in this section, when adjusted as provided in this section, is not a multiple of one dollar, it shall be rounded to the nearest multiple of one dollar or, where it is equidistant from two such consecutive multiples, to the higher thereof.

**(4) Consumer Price Index** — In this section, the Consumer Price Index for any 12 month period is the result arrived at by

(a) aggregating the Consumer Price Index for Canada, as published by Statistics Canada under the authority of the *Statistics Act*, adjusted in such manner as is prescribed, for each month in that period;

(b) dividing the aggregate obtained under paragraph (a) by twelve; and

(c) rounding the result obtained under paragraph (b) to the nearest one-thousandth or, where the result obtained is equidistant from two consecutive one-thousandths, to the higher thereof.

**Notes**: 117.1(4)(a) amended by 2000 first budget bill (C-32), effective for 2000 and later taxation years, to change "Consumer Price Index" to "Consumer Price Index for Canada", and to change "as may be prescribed" to "as is prescribed".

**(5)–(8)** [Repealed under former Act]

**Notes**: 117.1(5), repealed in 1986, provided indexing for the notch provision in former 117(7). 117.1(6), repealed by 1988 tax reform, provided for rounding of amounts (now covered by 117(1)(d)). 117.1(7), repealed by 1988 tax reform, provided the definition now in 117.1(4). 117.1(7.1) and (8), repealed in 1985 and 1986, provided rules relating to indexing before 1986.

**INDEXED PERSONAL TAX CREDITS** (see introductory pages for more details)

| | 1988 | 1989 | 1990 | 1991 | 1992-95 | 1996-98 | 1999 | 2000 | 2001 |
|---|---|---|---|---|---|---|---|---|---|
| Indexing factor from previous year | n/a | 1.011 | 1.017 | 1.018 | 1.028 | 1.000 | 1.000 | 1.014 | 1.025 |
| 118(1)B(c): basic personal credit | $1,020 | $1,031 | $1,049 | $1,068 | $1,098 | $1,098 | $1,155 | $1,229 | $1,186 |
| 118(1)B(a), (b): married/equivalent-to-married | 850 | 859 | 874 | 890 | 915 | 915 | 972 | 1,044 | 1,007 |
| — income limit | 500 | 506 | 514 | 524 | 538 | 538 | 572 | 614 | 629 |
| 118(1)B(d): dependent child under 18, each of first two (pre-1993) | 66 | 67 | 68 | 69 | 71 (1992) | | | | |

[10] Indexed by s. 117.1 after 1988 — ed.

Subdivision a — Computation of Tax: Individuals    S. 118(1)

**INDEXED PERSONAL TAX CREDITS** (see introductory pages for more details)

| | 1988 | 1989 | 1990 | 1991 | 1992-95 | 1996-98 | 1999 | 2000 | 2001 |
|---|---|---|---|---|---|---|---|---|---|
| — for each additional such dependant (pre-1993) | 132 | 133 | 136 | 138 | 142 (1992) | | | | |
| infirm under age 18 | | | | | | | | 500 | 560 |
| 118(1)B(d): infirm age 18 or over | 250 | 253 | 257 | 262 | 269 | 400 | 400 | 406 | 560 |
| — income limit | 2,500 | 2,528 | 2,570 | 2,617 | 2,690 | 4,103 | 4,103 | 4,845 | 4,966 |
| 118(2): age 65 or older (low-income only, since 1994) | 550 | 556 | 566 | 576 | 592 | 592 | 592 | 600 | 579 |
| 118(3): maximum pension credit | 170 | 170 | 170 | 170 | 170 | 170 | 170 | 170 | 160 |
| 118.3(1): disability credit | 550 | 556 | 566 | 700 | 720 | 720 | 720 | 730 | 960 |
| 118(1)B(c.1): caregiver | | | | | | | 400 | 406 | 560 |
| 118.2(1): medical expense credit — income threshold | 1,500 | 1,517 | 1,542 | 1,570 | 1,614 | 1,614 | 1,614 | 1,637 | 1,678 |
| 117(7): notch provision (after 1992, see 118.2(1)D) | 6,000 | 6,066 | 6,169 | 6,280 | 6,456 | 6,456 | 6,794 | 7,231 | 7,412 |
| 180.2(1): OAS/family allowance clawback — income threshold | | 50,000 | 50,850 | 51,765 | 53,215 | 53,215 | 53,215 | 53,960 | 55,309 |
| 180.2(4): OAS monthly grind-down | | | | | 665 | 665 | 665 | 675 | 691 |

### INDEXED FEDERAL TAX RATES FOR INDIVIDUALS

**1988 Income Tax Rate Schedule**

| Taxable Income | Tax |
|---|---|
| $27,500 or less | 17% |
| In excess of: | |
| $27,500 | $ 4,675 + 26% on next $27,500 |
| 55,000 | $11,825 + 29% on remainder |

**1989 Income Tax Rate Schedule**

| Taxable Income | Tax |
|---|---|
| $27,803 or less | 17% |
| In excess of: | |
| $27,803 | $ 4,726 + 26% on next $27,802 |
| 55,605 | $11,955 + 29% on remainder |

**1990 Income Tax Rate Schedule**

| Taxable Income | Tax |
|---|---|
| $28,275 or less | 17% |
| In excess of: | |
| $28,275 | $ 4,807 + 26% on next $28,275 |
| 56,550 | $12,158 + 29% on remainder |

**1991 Income Tax Rate Schedule**

| Taxable Income | Tax |
|---|---|
| $28,784 or less | 17% |
| In excess of: | |
| $28,784 | $ 4,893 + 26% on next $28,784 |
| 57,568 | $12,377 + 29% on remainder |

**1992–1999 Income Tax Rate Schedule**

| Taxable Income | Tax |
|---|---|
| (inflation less than 3% per year) | |
| $29,590 or less | 17% |
| In excess of: | |
| $29,590 | $ 5,030 + 26% on next $29,590 |
| 59,180 | $12,724 + 29% on remainder |

**2000 Income Tax Rate Schedule**

| Taxable Income | Tax on Lower Limit | Tax Rate on Excess | Surtax Rate | Threshold |
|---|---|---|---|---|
| $0 — 30,004 | $ — | 17% | 5% | $15,500 |
| 30,005 — 60,009 | 5,101 | 25% | | |
| 60,010 and over | 12,602 | 29% | | |

**2001 Income Tax Rate Schedule**

| Taxable Income | Tax on Lower Limit | Tax Rate on Excess |
|---|---|---|
| $0 — 30,754 | $ — | 16% |
| 30,755 — 61,509 | 4,921 | 22% |
| 61,510 — 100,000 | 11,687 | 26% |
| 100,001 and over | 21,694 | 29% |

**Notes:**

See s. 180.1 regarding surtax and 127.5–127.55 regarding minimum tax. See also more detailed tables in introductory pages of the book.

**Definitions [s. 117.1]**: "amount" — 248(1); "Consumer Price Index" — 117.1(4); "individual", "prescribed", "regulation" — 248(1); "taxation year" — 249.

**118. (1) Personal credits** — For the purpose of computing the tax payable under this Part by an individual for a taxation year, there may be deducted an amount determined by the formula

$$A \times B$$

where

A is the appropriate percentage for the year, and

B is the total of,

**Notes**: "The appropriate percentage" is 16%, the same as the lowest bracket rate under 117(2)(a). The effect of a credit at 16% is the same as a deduction from the "bottom" rather than the "top" of income. For a taxpayer with taxable income under $30,000, the credit is worth the same as a deduction.

(a) **married status** — in the case of an individual who at any time in the year is a married person or a person who is in a common-law partnership who supports the individual's

## S. 118(1) — Income Tax Act, Part I, Division E

spouse or common-law partner and is not living separate and apart from the spouse or common-law partner by reason of a breakdown of their marriage or common-law partnership, an amount equal to the total of

(i) $7,131[12], and

(ii) the amount determined by the formula

$$\$6,055^{12} - (C - \$606^{12})$$

where

C is the greater of $606[12] and the income of the individual's spouse or common-law partner for the year or, where the individual and the individual's spouse or common-law partner are living separate and apart at the end of the year because of a breakdown of their marriage or common-law partnership, the spouse or common-law partner's income for the year while married or in a common-law partnership and not so separated,

---

**Proposed Amendment — Basic personal amount and spousal amount**

**Notice of Ways and Means Motion, federal budget, February 28, 2000**: (2) That, for the purpose of indexing amounts for 2000,

(a) the basic personal amount for 1999 be considered to be $7,131 (indexed to $7,231 for 2000),

(b) the spouse and equivalent-to-spouse amounts for 1999 be considered to be $6,055 (indexed to $6,140 for 2000), and

(c) the income threshold for 1999 used in computing the spouse and equivalent-to-spouse tax credits be considered to be $606 (indexed to $614 for 2000).

---

**Proposed Amendment — Basic personal amount and spousal amount by 2004**

**Oct. 2000 Economic Statement NWMM**: *Guaranteed Minimum Relief in 2004*

(9) That

(a) for the 2004 and subsequent taxation years,

(i) the amounts on which the basic personal amount and the spouse or common-law partner tax credit (including the equivalent tax credit for a wholly dependent relative) are calculated be no less than $8,000 and $6,800, respectively, and

(ii) [reproduced under 117(2) — ed.]

(b) [reproduced under 122.61(1)B — ed.]

---

**Related Provisions**: 82(3) — Optional inclusion into income of dividends received by spouse; 117.1(1) — Indexing for inflation; 118(3.1) — Minimum amounts for 2004 and later; 118(4) — Limitations; 118(5) — No deduction where claim made for support; 118.91 — Individual resident in Canada for part of the year; 118.95(b) — Application in year individual becomes bankrupt.

---

[12]Indexed by 117.1(1) after 2000 — ed.

---

**Notes**: The "appropriate percentage" is 16% as of 2001. See the table preceding s. 118 and the tables in the introductory pages of the book. Note that the spousal credit can be claimed for a common-law spouse or same-sex partner; see 248(1)"common-law partner".

118(1)B(a) amended by 2000 same-sex partners bill to add reference to "common-law partner" and "common-law partnership", effective for the 2001 and later taxation years, or earlier by election (see Notes to 248(1)"common-law partner").

118(1)B(a)(i), (ii) amended by 1999 Budget, this version effective for 2000 and later taxation years. For 1999, read "$7,131", "$6,055" and "$606" as "$6,794", "$5,718" and "$572", respectively. For 1988-98, read "$6,000", "$5,000" and "$500", but note that these amounts were indexed by 117.1 after 1988.

118(1)B(a) amended by 1996 Budget, effective 1997, to add the words "and is not living separate and apart from the spouse by reason of a breakdown of their marriage". See 118(5).

**Interpretation Bulletins**: IT-295R4: Taxable dividends received after 1987 by a spouse; IT-513R: Personal tax credits.

**Forms**: T1 Sched. 6: Amounts for infirm dependants age 18 or older.

(b) **wholly dependent person ["equivalent to spouse" credit]** — in the case of an individual who does not claim a deduction for the year because of paragraph (a) and who, at any time in the year,

(i) is

(A) a person who is unmarried and who does not live in a common-law partnership, or

(B) a person who is married or in a common-law partnership, who neither supported nor lived with their spouse or common-law partner and who is not supported by that spouse or common-law partner, and

(ii) whether alone or jointly with one or more other persons, maintains a self-contained domestic establishment (in which the individual lives) and actually supports in that establishment a person who, at that time, is

(A) except in the case of a child of the individual, resident in Canada,

(B) wholly dependent for support on the individual, or the individual and the other person or persons, as the case may be,

(C) related to the individual, and

(D) except in the case of a parent or grandparent of the individual, either under 18 years of age or so dependent by reason of mental or physical infirmity,

an amount equal to the total of

(iii) $7,131[12], and

(iv) the amount determined by the formula

$$\$6,055^{12} - (D - \$606^{12})$$

where

D is the greater of $\$606^{12}$ and the dependent person's income for the year,

> **Proposed Amendment — Equivalent-to-spouse amount**
> **Notice of Ways and Means Motion, federal budget, February 28, 2000**: [Dollar amounts to be $7,231, $6,140 and $614 for 2000. See under 118(1)B(a).]

> **Proposed Amendment — Basic personal amount and spousal amount by 2004**
> **Oct. 2000 Economic Statement NWMM**: [See under 118(1)B(a) — ed.]

**Related Provisions**: 117.1(1) — Indexing for inflation; 118(3.1) — Minimum amounts for 2004 and later; 118(4) — Limitations; 118(5) — No deduction where claim made for support; 118.3(2) — Dependant having impairment; 118.91 — Individual resident in Canada for part of the year; 118.95(b) — Application in year individual becomes bankrupt.

**Notes**: Including the indexing factor and reduced provincial tax, the $1,157 (for 2001) "equivalent to spouse" credit is worth approximately $1,600. See the table preceding s. 118 and the tables in the introductory pages of the book.

118(1)B(b)(i) amended by 2000 same-sex partners bill, effective for the 2001 and later taxation years, or earlier by election (see Notes to 248(1)"common-law partner"). It formerly read:

> (i) is an unmarried person or a married person who neither supported nor lived with the married person's spouse and is not supported by the spouse, and

118(1)B(b)(iii), (iv) amended by 1999 Budget, this version effective for 2000 and later taxation years. For 1999, read "$7,131", "$6,055" and "$606" as "$6,794", "$5,718" and "$572" respectively. For 1988-98, read "$6,000", "$5,000" and "$500", but note that these amounts were indexed after 1988.

Opening words of 118(1)B(b) amended by 1996 Budget, effective 1997. For taxation years 1988 through 1996, read:

> (b) in the case of an individual not entitled to a deduction by reason of paragraph (a) who, at any time in the year,

**Interpretation Bulletins**: IT-513R: Personal tax credits.

**Forms**: T1 Sched. 5: Details of dependant.

(b.1) **supplementary amount [low-income individuals]** — [Repealed]

**Notes**: 118(1)B(b.1) repealed by 1999 Budget, effective for 2000 and later taxation years. For 1999, read:

> (b.1) **supplementary amount** — for each individual (other than a trust), 1/2 of the amount, if any, by which the total of
> (i) $500, and
> (ii) if an amount is deducted under paragraph (a) or (b) by the individual for the year in respect of another individual (or would be so deducted if the other individual had no income for the year), the lesser of
>   (A) $500, and
>   (B) the amount, if any, by which
>     (I) the total of $500 and the amount used under paragraph (c) for the year

exceeds

    (II) the other individual's income for the year or, where the other individual is the individual's spouse and both persons are living separate and apart at the end of the year by reason of a breakdown of their marriage, the other individual's income for the year while married and not so separated

exceeds

(iii) 4% of the amount, if any, by which

  (A) the individual's income for the year

exceeds

  (B) the total of $500, the amount used under paragraph (c) for the year and, if subparagraph (ii) applies for the year to the individual, the amount determined under clause (ii)(B) for the year,

For 1998, read as for 1999, but without the words "1/2 of" in the opening words. 118(1)B(b.1) was added by 1998 Budget effective 1998. It implemented a supplementary personal tax credit for low-income taxpayers through a $500 addition to the basic personal and spousal amounts, phased out at 4¢ per dollar of net income over $6,956. This was later extended to all taxpayers via an increase in the basic personal amount under 118(1)B(a) and (c).

(c) **single status** — except in the case of an individual entitled to a deduction because of paragraph (a) or (b), $7,131$^{12}$,

> **Proposed Amendment — Basic personal amount**
> **Notice of Ways and Means Motion, federal budget, February 28, 2000**: [$7,131 to be $7,231 for 2000. See under 118(1)B(a).]

> **Proposed Amendment — Basic personal amount by 2004**
> **Oct. 2000 Economic Statement NWMM**: [See under 118(1)B(a) — ed.]

**Related Provisions**: 117.1(1) — Indexing for inflation; 118(3.1) — Minimum amounts for 2004 and later; 118.91 — Individual resident in Canada for part of the year; 118.95(b) — Application in year individual becomes bankrupt; 122(1.1) — Credits not permitted to trust.

**Notes**: Including the indexing factor and provincial tax, the basic personal credit of $1,157 (for 2001) is worth about $1,600. See the table preceding s. 118 and the tables in the introductory pages of the book.

118(1)B(c) amended by 1999 Budget, this version effective for 2000 and later taxation years. For 1999, read "$7,131" as "$6,794". For 1988-98, read "$6,000", but note that this was indexed after 1988.

**Interpretation Bulletins**: IT-500R: RRSPs — death of an annuitant; IT-513R: Personal tax credits.

(c.1) **in-home care of relative [caregiver credit]** — in the case of an individual who, at any time in the year alone or jointly with one or more persons, maintains a self-contained domestic establishment which is the ordinary

---

[12] Indexed by 117.1(1) after 2000 — ed.

**S. 118(1)**        Income Tax Act, Part I, Division E

place of residence of the individual and of a particular person

(i) who has attained the age of 18 years before that time,

(ii) who is

(A) the individual's child or grandchild, or

(B) resident in Canada and is the individual's parent, grandparent, brother, sister, aunt, uncle, nephew or niece, and

### Proposed Amendment — 118(1)B(c.1)(ii)(B)

(B) resident in Canada and is the parent, grandparent, brother, sister, aunt, uncle, nephew or niece of the individual or of the individual's spouse or common-law partner, and

**Application**: Bill C-43 (First Reading September 20, 2000), s. 62, will amend cl. (c.1)(ii)(B) of the description of B in subsec. 118(1) to read as above, applicable to 1998 et seq. except that the cl. shall be read without reference to "or common-law partner" for any taxation year that ends before 2001 unless a valid election is made by the taxpayer under s. 144 of the *Modernization of Benefits and Obligations Act*, S.C. 2000, c. 12 that that Act apply to the taxpayer in respect of one or more taxation years that includes the year.

This amendment also reflects changes proposed under Bill C-23, the *Modernization of Benefits and Obligations Act* [see Notes to 248(1)"common-law partner"].

**Technical Notes**: Paragraph (c.1) of the description of B in section 118(1) of the Act provides a tax credit to an individual who provides in-home care for an adult relative. The relative in respect of whom the credit may be claimed has to be the individual's child, grandchild, parent, grandparent, brother, sister, aunt, uncle, nephew or niece. The paragraph is amended to also allow a taxpayer to claim the caregiver tax credit in respect of such relatives of the taxpayer's spouse.

(iii) who is

(A) the individual's parent or grandparent and has attained the age of 65 years before that time, or

(B) dependent on the individual because of the particular person's mental or physical infirmity,

the amount determined by the formula

$$\$13,853^{13} - D.1$$

where

D.1 is the greater of $11,500[13] and the particular person's income for the year,

### Proposed Amendment — 118(1)B(c.1)

the amount determined by the formula

$$\$15,453^{14} - D.1$$

where

D.1 is the greater of $11,953[14] and the particular person's income for the year,

**Application**: The December 21, 2000 draft legislation, subsec. 59(1), will amend the portion of para. (c.1) of the description of B in subsec. 118(1) after cl. (iii)(B) to read as above, applicable to 2001 et seq.

**Technical Notes**: Section 118 provides for the calculation of various personal tax credits.

Paragraph (c.1) of the description of B in subsection 118(1) provides a tax credit to an individual who provides in-home care for an adult relative, while paragraph (d) of that description provides a tax credit to an individual who supports an infirm dependent relative. These amendments increase the amounts on which each credit is computed to $3,500 from $2,446.

These amendments apply to the 2001 and subsequent taxation years.

**Notice of Ways and Means Motion, Economic Statement, October 18, 2000**: (7) That the amount on which the caregiver tax credit and the infirm dependant tax credit [118(1)B(d) — ed.] are calculated be increased from $2,386 for 2000 to $3,500 for 2001 (indexed after 2001).

**Minister's Speech, Economic Statement, October 18, 2000**: Mr. Speaker, in 1998, to recognize the increasing burden that many families bear as a result of an aging population, we introduced the Caregiver Credit. Today, effective January 1, we will increase the amount for that credit from $2,386 to $3,500.

**Related Provisions**: 117.1(1) — Indexing for inflation; 118(1)B(e) — Credit for infirm dependant; 118(4) — Limitations; 118(5) — No deduction where claim made for support; 118.2(2)(l.8) — Medical expense credit for caregiver training; 118.3(2) — Dependant having impairment; 118.91 — Individual resident in Canada for part of the year; 118.95(b) — Application in year individual becomes bankrupt.

**Notes**: 118(1)B(c.1) added by 1998 Budget, effective for 1998 and later taxation years. It provides a "caregiver" federal credit of up to $406 for 2000 (worth about $600 in most provinces) for individuals residing with and providing in-home care for a parent or grandparent (including in-laws) 65 or over or an infirm dependent relative. The federal credit is reduced by 16¢ for each dollar of the dependant's net income over $11,661 (for 2000).

(d) **dependants** — for each dependant of the individual for the year who

(i) attained the age of 18 years before the end of the year, and

(ii) was dependent on the individual because of mental or physical infirmity,

the amount determined by the formula

$$\$7,131^{12} - E$$

where

---

[12] Indexed by 117.1(1) after 2000 — ed.

[13] Indexed by s. 117.1 after 1998 — ed.

[14] Indexed by s. 117.1 after 2001 — ed.

Subdivision a — Computation of Tax: Individuals    S. 118(2)

E is the greater of $4,778[12] and the dependant's income for the year, and

> **Proposed Amendment — 118(1)B(d)**
>
> the amount determined by the formula
>
> $$\$8,466^{14} - E$$
>
> where
>
> E is the greater of $4,966[14] and the dependant's income for the year, and
>
> **Application**: The December 21, 2000 draft legislation, subsec. 59(2), will amend the portion of para. (d) of the description of B in subsec. 118(1) after subpara. (ii) to read as above, applicable to 2001 et seq.
>
> **Technical Notes**: See under 118(1)B(c.1) above.
>
> **Notice of Ways and Means Motion, Economic Statement, October 18, 2000**: (7) That the amount on which the caregiver tax credit [118(1)B(c.1) — ed.] and the infirm dependant tax credit are calculated be increased from $2,386 for 2000 to $3,500 for 2001 (indexed after 2001).
>
> **Minister's Speech, Economic Statement, October 18, 2000**: Mr. Speaker, this Government has always understood that there are certain priorities that cannot be deferred. Assisting Canadians with disabilities is one of these. Indeed, even when we were in deficit, we took action. We have enriched the tax credit for infirm dependants, enhanced the medical expense credit, increased the child care expense deduction for children with disabilities and expanded eligibility for the disability tax credit.
>
> Today we will do more. We will further enrich the amount for the infirm dependent tax credit [118(1)B(d) — ed.] from $2,386 to $3,500; we will similarly increase the supplement amount for the disability tax credit for children with severe disabilities [118.3(2) — ed.] from $2,941 to $3,500; and we will increase the amount for the disability tax credit [118.3(1) — ed.] from $4,293 to $6,000.
>
> **Budget Supplementary Information, February 28, 2000**: [Dollar amounts to be $7,231 and $4,845 for 2000.]

**Related Provisions**: 108(1)"preferred beneficiary"(a)(ii)(A) — infirm dependant can be a preferred beneficiary of trust; 117.1(1) — Indexing for inflation; 118(1)B(e) — Credit for infirm dependant who also qualifies for equivalent-to-spouse credit; 118(4) — Limitations; 118(6) — Definition of dependant; 118.3(2) — Dependant having impairment; 118.91 — Individual resident in Canada for part of the year; 118.92 — Ordering of credits; 118.95(b) — Application in year individual becomes bankrupt.

**Notes**: Where the dependant has no income, the calculation works out to $3,500 (for 2001), 16% of which = $560. Including the parallel provincial tax credit, the $560 credit for a dependent adult disabled child is worth approximately $800. See the table preceding s. 118 and the tables in the introductory pages of the book.

118(1)B(d) amended by 1999 Budget, this version effective for 2000 and later taxation years. For 1999 read "$7,131" and "$4,778"

as "$6,794" and "$4,441" respectively. For 1997-98, read "$6,456" and "$4,103".

118(1)B(d) amended by 1996 Budget, effective 1996, to change the formula from "$1,471 − (E − $2,500)" to "$6,456 − E", and to change the dollar figure in E from $2,500 to $4,103. The former numbers were intended to be indexed from 1988, while the new numbers are current, since they are indexed only after 1996; see 117.1(1) between (b) and (c).

118(1)B(d) amended by 1992 Child Benefit Bill, effective 1993, to eliminate the credit for dependent children under 18 (federal credit with $71 for each of first two children, $142 each subsequent child). A single Child Tax Benefit credit, under 122.61, has replaced this credit as well as family allowances and the Child Tax Credit (former 122.2).

**(e) additional amount [re dependant]** — in the case of an individual entitled to a deduction in respect of a person because of paragraph (b) and who would also be entitled, but for paragraph (4)(c), to a deduction because of paragraph (c.1) or (d) in respect of the person, the amount by which the amount that would be determined under paragraph (c.1) or (d), as the case may be, exceeds the amount determined under paragraph (b) in respect of the person.

**Related Provisions**: 118(6) — Definition of dependant; 118.91 — Individual resident in Canada for part of the year; 118.92 — Ordering of credits; 118.95(b) — Application in year individual becomes bankrupt.

**Notes**: 118(1)B(e) added by 1996 Budget, effective 1996. It was added because of the changes to 118(1)B(d). A taxpayer with an infirm dependant over 17 may qualify for both 118(1)B(b) and 118(1)B(d). Where this happens, 118(4)(c) restricts the taxpayer to claiming under 118(1)B(b). As a result of the increase to the income level at which the credit in 118(1)B(d) is reduced, it is possible that the credit under 118(1)B(d) will exceed the credit under 118(1)B(b). This will occur when the income of the dependant exceeds $3,565. To ensure the taxpayer is not penalized by having to claim a lower credit under 118(1)B(b), 118(1)B(e) provides that the amount under 118(1)B(b) will be increased up to the level of 118(1)B(d).

118(1)B(e) amended by 1998 Budget to add references to (c.1), effective for 1998 and later taxation years.

**Interpretation Bulletins**: IT-394R2: Preferred beneficiary election; IT-513R: Personal tax credits.

**Information Circulars**: 92-3: Guidelines for refunds beyond the normal three year period.

**Forms**: RC4064: Information concerning people with disabilities [guide].

**(2) Age credit** — For the purpose of computing the tax payable under this Part for a taxation year by an individual who, before the end of the year, has attained the age of 65 years, there may be deducted the amount determined by the formula

$$A \times (\$3,236^{15} - B)$$

where

A is the appropriate percentage for the year; and

---

[12]Indexed by 117.1(1) after 2000 — ed.

[14]Indexed by s. 117.1 after 2001 — ed.

[15]Indexed by s. 117.1 after 1988. See Notes to 117.1(1).

**S. 118(2)**      Income Tax Act, Part I, Division E

B is 15% of the amount, if any, by which the individual's income for the year would exceed $25,921[16] if no amount were included in respect of a gain from a disposition of property to which section 79 applies in computing that income.

### Proposed Amendment — 118(2)
**Budget Supplementary Information, February 28, 2000**: [Dollar amounts to be $3,531 and $26,284 for 2000. See under 117.1(1) — ed.]

**Related Provisions**: 117.1(1) — Indexing for inflation; 118.8 — Transfer of unused credits to spouse; 118.91 — Individual resident in Canada for part of the year; 118.92 — Ordering of credits; 118.95(b) — Application in year individual becomes bankrupt; 180.2 — "Clawback" tax and withholding of old age security benefits.

**Notes**: Including the indexing factor and parallel provincial credit, the $565 (for 2001: $3,236 × 16%) credit for low-income senior citizens is worth about $800. See the table preceding s. 118, the tables in the introductory pages of the book, and the Notes at the beginning of 118(1).

118(2) amended by 1994 Budget (and retroactively by 1995-97 technical bill to add exclusion for amounts to which s. 79 applies), the above version effective 1995, to add formula element B. The effect is to phase out the old age credit as net income (taxpayer only, ignoring spouse) exceeds $26,284 (for 2000). Once net income reaches $49,824 (in 2000), the credit disappears entirely. For 1994 only, the phase-out was at 7.5% of the excess over $25,921 rather than 15%, and B could not exceed $1,741, so ½ the credit was available even to very high-income seniors. For 1988 to 1993, ignore formula element B.

The form of 118(2) is somewhat bizarre. It is clear from the 1994 Budget documents and the Technical Notes to the implementing legislation that the $3,236 figure is to be indexed from 1988, while the $25,921 figure is to be indexed from 1994. How this could be divined simply by reading the legislation defies belief. See Notes to 117.1(1) and 118.3(1).

For purposes of 118(2), income that is untaxed due to a tax treaty is not considered to be income that reduces the available credit: *Peter*, [1997] 2 C.T.C. 2504 (TCC). This is in contrast to the *Swantje* rule, which applies to the old age security clawback; see Notes to 180.2.

**Interpretation Bulletins**: IT-513R: Personal tax credits.

**Information Circulars**: 92-3: Guidelines for refunds beyond the normal three year period.

**(3) Pension credit** — For the purpose of computing the tax payable under this Part by an individual for a taxation year, there may be deducted an amount determined by the formula

$$A \times B$$

where

A is the appropriate percentage for the year; and

B is the lesser of $1,000[17] and

    (a) where the individual has attained the age of 65 years before the end of the year, the pension income received by the individual in the year, and

    (b) where the individual has not attained the age of 65 years before the end of the year, the qualified pension income received by the individual in the year.

### Proposed Amendment — Abandonment of 1996 Proposal re Seniors' Benefit
**Department of Finance news release, July 28, 1998**: *Finance Minister's Statement on the Seniors Benefit*

[The March 6, 1996 Budget Papers had proposed a non-taxable Seniors Benefit, to be introduced in 2001 and linked to income. The age credit in 118(2) and pension income credit in 118(3) would have been eliminated with the introduction of the Seniors Benefit — ed.]

Finance Minister Paul Martin today issued the following statement regarding Canada's retirement income system: ....

"Second, we proposed the restructuring of the OAS/GIS [Old Age Security/Guaranteed Income Supplement] into a new integrated Seniors Benefit. It is this proposal that I wish to discuss this morning....

"Therefore, in light of the structural enhancements to the public pension system, the turnaround in the country's economic prospects, and because of our commitment to sound fiscal management, the government is today announcing that the proposed Seniors Benefit will not proceed. The existing OAS/GIS system will be fully maintained...."

For further information: Scott Reid, Office of the Minister of Finance, (613) 996-7861; Dale Eisler, Consultations and Communications, (613) 995-5683.

**Related Provisions**: 60(j.2) — Rollover of pension income to spouse's RRSP before 1995; 104(27) — Deemed income of beneficiary; 118(7), (8) — Meaning of "pension income" and "qualified pension income"; 118.8 — Transfer of unused credits to spouse; 118.91 — Individual resident in Canada for part of the year; 118.92 — Ordering of credits; 118.93 — Separate returns; 118.95(a) — Application in year individual becomes bankrupt; 122(1.1) — Credits not permitted to trust.

**Notes**: Including the parallel provincial credit, the maximum value of the $160 pension credit is approximately $220. The effect is to exempt $1,000 of pension income off the "bottom" of income rather than off the "top". See Notes at the beginning of 118(1).

118(3) amended by 1992 technical bill, effective 1992.

**Interpretation Bulletins**: IT-500R: RRSPs — death of an annuitant; IT-517R: Pension tax credit.

**Information Circulars**: 92-3: Guidelines for refunds beyond the normal three year period.

### Proposed Addition — 118(3.1)
**(3.1) Minimum amounts for 2004** — Each of the amounts of $7,131, $6,055 and $606 referred to in paragraphs (a) to (c) of the description of B in subsection (1) is deemed, for the 2004 taxation year, to be the greater of

    (a) the amount in respect thereof that would be used for that year if this section were read without reference to this subsection; and

    (b) in the case of

        (i) the amounts of $7,131, $8,000,

        (ii) the amounts of $6,055, $6,800, and

---

[16]Indexed by s. 117.1 after 1995. See Notes to 117.1(1).

[17]Not indexed for inflation.

(iii) the amounts of $606, $680.

**Application**: The December 21, 2000 draft legislation, subsec. 59(3), will add subsec. 118(3.1), in force on Royal Assent.

**Technical Notes**: New subsection 118(3.1) provides that the amounts of $7,131, $6,055 and $606, which are used in computing an individual's basic tax credit and the tax credit that may be claimed by the individual, in respect of a spouse, a common-law partner or, in some circumstances, a wholly dependent person will not, for the 2004 taxation year, be less than $8,000, $6,800 and $680, respectively, regardless of the annual increase provided under the indexing provisions of the Act.

This amendment applies to the 2004 taxation year.

**(4) Limitations re subsec. (1)** — For the purposes of subsection (1), the following rules apply:

(a) no amount may be deducted under subsection (1) because of paragraphs (a) and (b) of the description of B in subsection (1) by an individual in a taxation year for more than one other person;

(a.1) no amount may be deducted under subsection (1) because of paragraph (b) of the description of B in subsection (1) by an individual for a taxation year for a person in respect of whom an amount is deducted because of paragraph (a) of that description by another individual for the year if, throughout the year, the person and that other individual are married to each other or in a common-law partnership with each other and are not living separate and apart because of a breakdown of their marriage or the common-law partnership, as the case may be;

(b) not more than one individual is entitled to a deduction under subsection (1) because of paragraph (b) of the description of B in subsection (1) for a taxation year in respect of the same person or the same domestic establishment and where two or more individuals otherwise entitled to such a deduction fail to agree as to the individual by whom the deduction may be made, no such deduction for the year shall be allowed to either or any of them;

(c) where an individual is entitled to a deduction under subsection (1) because of paragraph (b) of the description of B in subsection (1) for a taxation year in respect of any person, no amount may be deducted because of paragraph (c.1) or (d) of that description by any individual for the year in respect of the person;

(d) where an individual is entitled to a deduction under subsection (1) because of paragraph (c.1) of the description of B in subsection (1) for a taxation year in respect of any person, the person is deemed not to be a dependant of any individual for the year for the purpose of paragraph (d) of that description; and

(e) where more than one individual is entitled to a deduction under subsection (1) because of paragraph (c.1) or (d) of the description of B in subsection (1) for a taxation year in respect of the same person,

(i) the total of all amounts so deductible for the year shall not exceed the maximum amount that would be so deductible for the year by any one of those individuals for that person if that individual were the only individual entitled to deduct an amount for the year because of that paragraph for that person, and

(ii) if the individuals cannot agree as to what portion of the amount each can so deduct, the Minister may fix the portions.

**Related Provisions**: 118(6) — Definition of "dependant".

**Notes**: 118(4)(a.1) amended by 2000 same-sex partners bill, effective for the 2001 and later taxation years, or earlier by election (see Notes to 248(1)"common-law partner"). It formerly read:

(a.1) no amount may be deducted under subsection (1) because of paragraph (b) of the description of B in subsection (1) by an individual for a taxation year for a person in respect of whom an amount is deducted because of paragraph (a) of that description by another individual for the year if, throughout the year, the person and that other individual are married to each other and are not living separate and apart because of a breakdown of their marriage;

118(4) amended by 1998 Budget to add para. (a.1), and to replace para. (c) and (e) with (c)-(e), effective for 1998 and later taxation years. For earlier years, read:

(c) where an individual is entitled to a deduction under subsection 118 (1) because of paragraph (b) of the description of B in subsection 118 (1) for any person described therein, the person shall be deemed not to be a dependant for the year for the purposes of paragraph (1)(d); and

(e) where more than one individual is, in respect of a taxation year, entitled to deduct an amount under subsection 118 (1) because of paragraph (d) of the description of B in subsection 118 (1) for the same dependant, the total of all amounts so deductible for the year shall not exceed the maximum amount that would be deductible by reason of that paragraph for the year by any one of those individuals for that dependant if that individual were the only individual entitled to deduct an amount for the year by reason of that paragraph for that dependant and, where the individuals cannot agree as to what portion of the amount each can so deduct, the Minister may fix the portions.

Former 118(4)(d) repealed by 1992 Child Benefit bill, effective 1993, in conjunction with the elimination of family allowances in favour of Child Tax Benefit payments under 122.61. For 1988 through 1992, it restricted the credit for dependent children to the parent who reported the family allowance income.

**Interpretation Bulletins**: IT-513R: Personal tax credits; IT-530: Support payments.

**(5) Support** — No amount may be deducted under subsection (1) in computing an individual's tax payable under this Part for a taxation year in respect of a person where the individual is required to pay a support amount (as defined in subsection 56.1(4)) to the individual's spouse or former spouse in respect of the person and the individual

(a) lives separate and apart from the spouse or common-law partner or former spouse or common-law partner throughout the year because of the breakdown of their marriage or common-law partnership; or

(b) claims a deduction for the year because of section 60 in respect of a support amount paid to the spouse or common-law partner or former spouse or common-law partner.

**Notes**: 118(5)(a) and (b) amended by 2000 same-sex partners bill to add reference to "common-law partner" and "common-law partnership", effective for the 2001 and later taxation years, or earlier by election (see Notes to 248(1)"common-law partner").

118(5) amended by 1996 Budget, effective 1997. For 1988 through 1996, read:

(5) Alimony and maintenance — Where an individual in computing the individual's income for a taxation year is entitled to a deduction under paragraph 60(b), (c) or (c.1) in respect of a payment for the maintenance of a spouse or child, the spouse or child shall, for the purposes of this section (other than the definition "qualified pension income" in subsection (7)) be deemed not to be the spouse or child of the individual.

The "equivalent-to-spouse" credit under 118(1)B(b) is available to a single parent with a child under 18. The old 118(5) prohibited the credit to a single parent who was required to pay deductible child support with respect to that child. The new 118(5) reflects the 1996 Budget change eliminating the deduction for child support under agreements or court orders signed after April 1997 (see 60(b) and 56.1(4)"child support amount"). Despite the changes to the inclusion/deduction system, a single parent continues to be precluded from claiming the credit for a child in respect of whom the parent is required to make child support payments during the year. This treatment is consistent with the new child support guidelines, which assume that the equivalent-to-spouse credit will be claimed by the custodial spouse.

**Interpretation Bulletins**: IT-118R3: Alimony and maintenance; IT-513R: Personal tax credits; IT-530: Support payments.

**Information Circulars**: 92-3: Guidelines for refunds beyond the normal three year period.

**(6) Definition of "dependant"** — For the purposes of paragraphs (d) and (e) of the description of B in subsection (1) and paragraph (4)(e), "dependant" of an individual for a taxation year means a person who at any time in the year is dependent on the individual for support and is

(a) the child or grandchild of the individual or of the individual's spouse or common-law partner; or

(b) the parent, grandparent, brother, sister, uncle, aunt, niece or nephew, if resident in Canada at any time in the year, of the individual or of the individual's spouse or common-law partner.

**Related Provisions**: 118(5) — Meaning of "spouse" and "child" where alimony or maintenance being paid.

**Notes**: 118(6) amended by 2000 same-sex partners bill to add reference to "common-law partner", effective for the 2001 and later taxation years, or earlier by election (see Notes to 248(1)"common-law partner").

Opening words of 118(6) amended by 1996 Budget, effective 1996, to add reference to 118(1)B(e).

**Interpretation Bulletins**: IT-394R2: Preferred beneficiary election; IT-513R: Personal tax credits.

**(7) Definitions** — Subject to subsection (8), for the purposes of subsection (3),

**"pension income"** received by an individual in a taxation year means the total of

(a) the total of all amounts each of which is an amount included in computing the individual's income for the year that is

(i) a payment in respect of a life annuity out of or under a superannuation or pension plan,

(ii) an annuity payment under a registered retirement savings plan, under an "amended plan" as referred to in subsection 146(12) or under an annuity in respect of which an amount is included in computing the individual's income by reason of paragraph 56(1)(d.2),

(iii) a payment out of or under a registered retirement income fund or under an "amended fund" as referred to in subsection 146.3(11),

(iv) an annuity payment under a deferred profit sharing plan or under a "revoked plan" as referred to in subsection 147(15),

(v) a payment described in subparagraph 147(2)(k)(v), or

(vi) the amount by which an annuity payment included in computing the individual's income for the year by reason of paragraph 56(1)(d) exceeds the capital element of that payment as determined or established under paragraph 60(a), and

(b) the total of all amounts each of which is an amount included in computing the individual's income for the year by reason of section 12.2 of this Act or paragraph 56(1)(d.1) of the *Income Tax Act*, chapter 148 of the Revised Statutes of Canada, 1952;

**Related Provisions**: 104(27) — Flow-out of pension benefits by trust; 118(8) — Limitations; 118.7 — Credit for UI/EI premium and CPP contribution.

**Notes**: The reference to 56(1)(d.1) is to a provision repealed in 1990 but which still applies in respect of annuity contracts acquired before 1990. See Notes to 56(1)(d.1).

**I.T. Application Rules**: 69 (meaning of "*Income Tax Act*, chapter 148 of the Revised Statutes of Canada, 1952").

**"qualified pension income"** received by an individual in a taxation year means the total of all amounts each of which is an amount included in computing the individual's income for the year and described in

(a) subparagraph (a)(i) of the definition "pension income" in this subsection, or

(b) any of subparagraphs (a)(ii) to (vi) or paragraph (b) of the definition "pension income" in this subsection received by the individual as a consequence of the death of a spouse or common-law partner of the individual.

**Related Provisions**: 104(27) — Fow-out of pension benefits by trust; 118(5) — Alimony and maintenance; 118(8) — Limitations; 118.7 — Credit for UI/EI premium and CPP contribution; 248(8) — Occurrences as a consequence of death.

**Notes**: 118(7)"qualified pension income"(b) amended by 2000 same-sex partners bill to add reference to "common-law partner", effective for the 2001 and later taxation years, or earlier by election (see Notes to 248(1)"common-law partner").

Para (b) amended by 1992 technical bill, effective 1993, due to the extension of the definition of "spouse" to common-law spouses under 252(4). For 1988 to 1992, "spouse" was given an extended meaning under former 146(1.1).

**Interpretation Bulletins**: IT-500R: RRSPS — death of an annuitant; IT-517R: Pension tax credit.

**(8) Interpretation** — For the purposes of subsection (3), "pension income" and "qualified pension income" received by an individual do not include any amount that is

(a) the amount of a pension or supplement under the *Old Age Security Act* or of any similar payment under a law of a province;

(b) the amount of a benefit under the *Canada Pension Plan* or under a provincial pension plan as defined in section 3 of that Act;

(c) a death benefit;

(d) the amount, if any, by which

  (i) an amount required to be included in computing the individual's income for the year

exceeds

  (ii) the amount, if any, by which the amount referred to in subparagraph (i) exceeds the total of all amounts deducted by the individual for the year in respect of that amount; or

(e) a payment received out of or under a salary deferral arrangement, a retirement compensation arrangement, an employee benefit plan, an employee trust or a prescribed provincial pension plan.

**Regulations**: 7800(1) (prescribed provincial pension plan).

**Related Provisions**: 118.91 — Individual resident in Canada for part of the year; 118.92 — Ordering of credits; 118.93 — Credits in separate returns; 118.94 — Tax payable by non-resident individual.

**Interpretation Bulletins**: IT-517R: Pension tax credit.

**Definitions [s. 118]**: "amount", "annuity", "appropriate percentage" — 248(1); "aunt" — 252(2)(e); "brother" — 252(2); "Canada" — 255; "child" — 118(5), 252(1); "common-law partner", "common-law partnership" — 248(1); "consequence of the death" — 248(8); "death benefit" — 248(1); "deferred profit sharing plan" — 147(1), 248(1); "dependant" — 118(5), (6); "employee benefit plan" — 248(1); "grandparent" — 252(2); "individual" — 248(1); "Minister" — 248(1); "nephew", "niece" — 252(2)(g); "parent" — 252(2); "pension income" — 118(7), (8); "person", "prescribed" — 248(1); "province" — *Interpretation Act* 35(1); "qualified pension income" — 118(7), (8); "received" — 248(7); "registered retirement income fund" — 146.3(1), 248(1); "registered retirement savings plan" — 146(1), 248(1); "related" — 251(2); "resident in Canada" — 250; "salary deferral arrangement", "self-contained domestic establishment" — 248(1); "sister" — 252(2); "spouse" — 118(5); "tax payable" — 248(2); "taxation year" — 249; "uncle" — 252(2)(e).

**Interpretation Bulletins [s. 118]**: IT-83R3: Non-profit organizations — Taxation of income from property; IT-171R2: Non-resident individuals — computation of taxable income earned in Canada and non-refundable tax credits; IT-326R3: Returns of deceased persons as "another person"; IT-393R2: Election re tax on rents and timber royalties — non-residents; IT-495R2: Child care expenses; IT-516R2: Tuition tax credit; IT-519R2: Medical expense and disability tax credits and attendant care expense deduction.

**Information Circulars [s. 118]**: 92-3: Guidelines for refunds beyond the normal three year period.

**118.1 (1) Definitions** — In this section

**"total charitable gifts"** of an individual for a taxation year means the total of all amounts each of which is the fair market value of a gift (other than a gift the fair market value of which is included in the total Crown gifts, the total cultural gifts or the total ecological gifts of the individual for the year) made by the individual in the year or in any of the 5 immediately preceding taxation years (other than in a year for which a deduction under subsection 110(2) was claimed in computing the individual's taxable income) to

(a) a registered charity,

(b) a registered Canadian amateur athletic association,

(c) a housing corporation resident in Canada and exempt from tax under this Part because of paragraph 149(1)(i),

(d) a Canadian municipality,

(e) the United Nations or an agency thereof,

(f) a university outside Canada that is prescribed to be a university the student body of which ordinarily includes students from Canada,

(g) a charitable organization outside Canada to which Her Majesty in right of Canada has made a gift during the individual's taxation year or the 12 months immediately preceding that taxation year, or

(g.1) Her Majesty in right of Canada or a province,

to the extent that those amounts were

(h) not deducted in computing the individual's taxable income for a taxation year ending before 1988, and

(i) not included in determining an amount that was deducted under this section in computing the individual's tax payable under this Part for a preceding taxation year;

**Proposed Amendment — Recapture on donation of depreciable property to charity**

**Letter from Department of Finance, February 15, 2000**: See under 216.

**Related Provisions**: 43.1(1) — Charitable gifts excluded from rules re life interests in real property; 46(1), (5) — Capital gain on certain donations of art and other property; 110.1(1)(a) — Parallel deduction for corporations; 110(1)(d.01) — Deduction on donating employee stock-option shares to charity; 118.1(1)"total gifts"(a)(ii) — Charitable gifts limited to 20% of net income; 118.1(2.1) — Ordering of claims; 118.1(5.1), (5.2) — Designation of charity as beneficiary of insurance policy; 118.1(5.3) — Designation of charity as beneficiary of RRSP or RRIF; 118.1(6) — Gift of capital property; 118.1(10.1) — Determination of value by Cana-

S. 118.1(1) tot — Income Tax Act, Part I, Division E

dian Cultural Property Export Review Board; 118.1(13) — Donation of non-qualifying securities; 118.1(16) — Loanback arrangements; 143(3.1) — Hutterite colonies — election in respect of gifts; 149.1(6.4) — Donations to registered national arts service organization; Canada–U.S. tax treaty, Art. XXI:6 — Donations to U.S. charities qualify as gifts for taxpayer with U.S.-source income; Art. XXIX B:1 — Property left to U.S. charity on death.

**Notes**: See Notes to 118.1(1)"total gifts".

The CCRA administratively permits a claim for donations made in the name of one's spouse: T1 General Income Tax Guide, line 349. Thus, receipts in both spouses' names can be pooled and claimed on one return. However, this administrative practice is not enforceable in the Courts: *Douziech*, 2000 CarswellNat 1000 (TCC).

The CCRA considers an Indian band to be a municipality for purposes of para. (d) if it qualifies under 149(1)(c), and will consider other bands on a case-by-case basis: VIEWS doc. 2000-0012547 (June 29, 2000).

A donation of Air Miles or similar points qualifies as a gift if its value can be reasonably estimated: VIEWS doc. 9921267 (Jan. 12, 2000). A gift certificate may also qualify: VIEWS doc. 2000-0030237 (July 25, 2000).

For Quebec provincial tax purposes, a gift of art to a charity cannot be claimed until the charity sells the art, which must be within 5 years of the gift. The credit is limited by the sale price the charity obtains. (This rule does not apply to donations to museums, galleries, recognized artistic organizations, governments or municipalities.) This restriction, introduced in May 1995, was designed to curb abuses where individuals would obtain appraisals entitling them to value donations at higher prices than can be obtained by the charity to whom the art is donated. (Typically, the charity in such cases sells the art at an auction, and the entire valuation, donation and auction process is organized for the charity by an art dealer or tax shelter promoter.) This rule could be copied by the federal government in an upcoming budget. In the meantime, the CCRA is vigorously attacking such "art flip" tax shelters on various grounds including valuation; the proposed amendment to 46(1) and the civil penalties under 163.2 are directly aimed at these shelters. See also Notes to "total cultural gifts" below. See also *Whent*, [2000] 1 C.T.C. 329 (FCA), leave to appeal to SCC denied (Sept. 21, 2000, File 27748), where a purchase for donation purposes was held not to be an adventure in the nature of trade.

For a list of the foreign charities that qualify under para. (g) because Canada has donated to them recently, contact the CCRA's Charities Division, 613-954-0410 or 1-800-267-2384 (fax 613-952-6020), or from www.ccra-adrc.gc.ca/charities (Information Circular 84-3R5 and recent attachments). This list also applies for purposes of 94(1)"exempt foreign trust"(c)(iii).

Note that in addition to the above and the universities listed in Reg. Schedule VIII (as prescribed by Reg. 3503 for purposes of para. (f)), U.S. charities qualify for donations where the taxpayer has U.S.-source income. See Article XXI(6) of the Canada-U.S. tax treaty.

For the rule extending the deadline for most 1997 donations to January 31, 1998, see Notes to "total gifts" below.

Reference to "total ecological gifts" added to opening words by 1995 Budget, effective for gifts made after February 27, 1995.

Para. (g.1) added by 1997 Budget, effective for taxation years that begin after 1996. Gifts to the Crown, including to Crown foundations, are now treated as charitable donations rather than subject to a special rule as "total Crown gifts".

**Regulations**: 3503, Sch. VIII (prescribed universities).

**Forms**: RC4142: Tax advantages of donating to a charity [guide].

**Interpretation Bulletins**: See lists at end of 118.1(1) and at end of 118.1.

**Information Circulars**: 75-23: Tuition fees and charitable donations paid to privately supported secular and religious schools; 84-3R5: Gifts to certain charitable organizations outside Canada. See also list at end of 118.1.

**I.T. Technical News**: No. 17 (loan of property as a gift).

**Registered Charities Newsletters**: 1 (Donation of services); 2 (Issuing official donation receipts where there are prizes); 3 (Gifts of property other than cash); 4 (Issuing receipts for gifts of art); 6 (Can registered charities issue donation tax receipts for tuition fees?; The "art" of issuing official donation receipts); 7 (Fundraising golf tournaments; Fundraising auctions); 8 (Further questions on golf tournaments; Directed donations; Issuing receipts for gifts of art; Gifts of units in a hedge fund; Membership fees; Official donation receipts — Quebec donors); 9 (How do you establish the value of gifts-in-kind?).

"**total Crown gifts**" of an individual for a taxation year means the total of all amounts each of which is the fair market value of a gift (other than a gift the fair market value of which is included in the total cultural gifts or the total ecological gifts of the individual for the year) made by the individual in the year or in any of the 5 immediately preceding taxation years to Her Majesty in right of Canada or a province, to the extent that those amounts were

(a) not deducted in computing the individual's taxable income for a taxation year ending before 1988,

(b) not included in determining an amount that was deducted under this section in computing the individual's tax payable under this Part for a preceding taxation year, and

(c) in respect of gifts made before February 19, 1997 or under agreements in writing made before that day;

**Related Provisions**: 43.1(1) — Crown gifts excluded from rules re life interests in real property; 110.1(1)(b) — Parallel deduction for corporations; 118.1(1)"total gifts"(b — Crown gifts not limited to 20% of net income; 118.1(2.1) — Ordering of claims; 118.1(6) — Gift of capital property; 143(3.1) — Election in respect of gifts.

**Notes**: Reference to "total ecological gifts" added to opening words of definition by 1995 Budget, effective for gifts made after February 27, 1995.

Para. (c) added by 1997 Budget, effective for taxation years that begin after 1996. It effectively repeals the definition by making it inapplicable in the future. Gifts to the Crown are now subject to the same 75% limit as charitable donations; see 118.1(1)"total charitable gifts"(g.1). The change was made in response to universities and other institutions setting up Crown foundations (created by the province but with funds redirected to the institution), which had an unfair advantage over other regular charities in competing for major gifts.

**Advance Tax Rulings**: ATR-63: Donations to agents of the Crown.

**I.T. Technical News**: No. 17 (loan of property as a gift).

"**total cultural gifts**" of an individual for a taxation year means the total of all amounts each of which is the fair market value of a gift

(a) of an object that the Canadian Cultural Property Export Review Board has determined meets the criteria set out in paragraphs 29(3)(b) and (c) of the *Cultural Property Export and Import Act*, and

(b) that was made by the individual in the year or in any of the 5 immediately preceding taxation years to an institution or a public authority in Canada that was, at the time the gift was made, designated under subsection 32(2) of the *Cultural Property Export and Import Act* either generally or for a specified purpose related to that object,

to the extent that those amounts were

(c) not deducted in computing the individual's taxable income for a taxation year ending before 1988, and

(d) not included in determining an amount that was deducted under this section in computing the individual's tax payable under this Part for a preceding taxation year;

**Related Provisions**: 39(1)(a)(i.1) — Meaning of capital gain and capital loss; 110.1(1)(c) — Parallel deduction for corporations; 118.1(1)"total gifts"(c) — Cultural gifts not limited to 20% of net income; 118.1(2.1) — Ordering of claims; 118.1(7.1) — Gifts of cultural property — deemed proceeds; 118.1(10) — Determination of fair market value; 118.1(10.1) — Determination of value by Canadian Cultural Property Export Review Board; 143(3.1) — Election in respect of gifts; 207.3 — Tax on institution that disposes of cultural property.

**Notes**: The Canadian Cultural Property Export Review Board has indicated that, where donated art has not been held for at least two years, the Board will normally not value the art at higher than the price at which the donor purchased it. See also 118.1(10.1).

**Interpretation Bulletins**: IT-407R4: Dispositions of cultural property to designated Canadian institutions. See also list at end of 118.1.

**I.T. Technical News**: No. 17 (loan of property as a gift).

"**total ecological gifts**" of an individual for a taxation year means the total of all amounts each of which is the fair market value of a gift (other than a gift the fair market value of which is included in the total cultural gifts of the individual for the year) of land, including a servitude for the use and benefit of a dominant land, a covenant or an easement, that is certified by the Minister of the Environment, or a person designated by that Minister, to be ecologically sensitive land, the conservation and protection of which is, in the opinion of that Minister, or that person, important to the preservation of Canada's environmental heritage, which gift was made by the individual in the year or in any of the 5 immediately preceding taxation years to

**Proposed Amendment — 118.1(1)"total ecological gifts" opening words**

"**total ecological gifts**" of an individual for a taxation year means the total of all amounts each of which is the fair market value of a gift (other than a gift the fair market value of which is included in the total cultural gifts of the individual for the year) of land, including a servitude for the use and benefit of a dominant land, a covenant or an easement, the fair market value of which is certified by the Minister of the Environment and that is certified by that Minister, or a person designated by that Minister, to be ecologically sensitive land, the conservation and protection of which is, in the opinion of that Minister, or that person, important to the preservation of Canada's environmental heritage, which gift was made by the individual in the year or in any of the five immediately preceding taxation years to

**Application**: The December 21, 2000 draft legislation, subsec. 60(1), will amend the opening words of the definition "total ecological gifts" in subsec. 118.1(1) to read as above, applicable in respect of gifts made, or proposed to be made, after February 27, 2000.

**Technical Notes**: Subsection 118.1(3) provides for a tax credit in respect of gifts made by individuals to registered charities and certain other entities. Unlike most charitable gifts, the eligible value of qualified ecological gifts is not subject to an annual 75% income limit. An ecological gift is defined in subsection 118.1(1) as a gift of land (including a covenant, an easement or a servitude) that is certified by the Minister of the Environment to be ecologically sensitive land, the conservation and protection of which is, in the opinion of that Minister, important to the preservation of Canada's environmental heritage. The beneficiary must be the federal government, a provincial or territorial government, a municipality or a registered charity approved by the Minister of the Environment.

The definition "total ecological gifts" in subsection 118.1(1) is amended to require that the fair market value of the gift [not just the existence of the gift — ed.] be certified by the Minister of the Environment. The fair market value is relevant to the calculation of the tax credit available to the individual under paragraph 110.1(1)(d) and of the taxable capital gain under section 38.

(a) Her Majesty in right of Canada or a province or a municipality in Canada, or

(b) a registered charity one of the main purposes of which is, in the opinion of the Minister of the Environment, the conservation and protection of Canada's environmental heritage, and that is approved by that Minister, or that person, in respect of that gift,

to the extent that those amounts were not included in determining an amount that was deducted under this section in computing the individual's tax payable under this Part for a preceding taxation year;

**Related Provisions**: 38(a.2) — Reduced capital gain inclusion on ecological gift; 110.1(1)(d) — Parallel deduction for corporations; 118.1(1)"total gifts"(d) — Ecological gifts not limited to 20% of net income; 118.1(2.1) — Ordering of claims; 118.1(10.1)–(10.5) — Determination of fair market value by Minister of the Environment; 118.1(12) — Fair market value of ecological servitude, covenant or easement; 207.31 — Tax if donee disposes of the property.

**Notes**: Note that if the donee ever disposes of the land without authorization from the Minister of the Environment, a special 50% tax applies under 207.31.

For the administrative definition of "ecologically sensitive land" and further discussion of this credit, see Environment Canada's publication, *Ecological Gifts* (October 18, 2000), which supersedes Environment Canada's Information Circulars Nos. 1, 2 and 3. To obtain it, contact Manjit Kess-Upal, Environment Canada, Canadian Wildlife Service, Ecological Gifts Program Secretariat, Ottawa K1A 0H3, tel. 819-994-6687, fax 819-953-3575, email manjit.kess-upal@ec.gc.ca. An updated version is available electronically at www.cws-scf.ec.gc.ca/ecogifts.

Definition "total ecological gifts" added by 1995 Budget, effective for gifts made after February 27, 1995. Para. (a) amended by 1997 Budget, effective for gifts made after February 18, 1997, to add reference to Her Majesty in right of Canada or a province. Crown gifts are no longer given a special preference of up to 100% of net income (see Notes to "total Crown gifts"). Therefore ecological gifts to the Crown are now included in this definition so that they continue to benefit from the 100% rate.

**I.T. Technical News**: No. 17 (loan of property as a gift).

**"total gifts"** of an individual for a taxation year means the total of

(a) the least of

(i) the individual's total charitable gifts for the year,

(ii) the individual's income for the year where the individual dies in the year or in the following taxation year, and

(iii) in any other case, the lesser of the individual's income for the year and the amount determined by the formula

$$0.75A + 0.25(B + C + D - E)$$

where

A is the individual's income for the year,

B is the total of all amounts each of which is a taxable capital gain of the individual for the year from a disposition that is the making of a gift made by the individual in the year, which gift is included in the individual's total charitable gifts for the year,

C is the total of all amounts each of which is a taxable capital gain of the individual for the year, because of subsection 40(1.01), from a disposition of a property in a preceding taxation year,

D is the total of all amounts each of which is determined in respect of the individual's depreciable property of a prescribed class and equal to the lesser of

(A) the amount included under subsection 13(1) in respect of the class in computing the individual's income for the year, and

(B) the total of all amounts each of which is determined in respect of a disposition that is the making of a gift of property of the class made by the individual in the year that is included in the individual's total charitable gifts for the year and equal to the lesser of

(I) the proceeds of disposition of the property minus any outlays and expenses to the extent that they were made or incurred by the individual for the purpose of making the disposition, and

(II) the capital cost to the individual of the property, and

E is the total of all amounts each of which is the portion of an amount deducted under section 110.6 in computing the individual's taxable income for the year that can reasonably be considered to be in respect of a gift referred to in the description of B or C,

(b) the individual's total Crown gifts for the year,

(c) the individual's total cultural gifts for the year, and

(d) the individual's total ecological gifts for the year.

**Related Provisions**: 257 — Formula cannot calculate to less than zero.

**Notes**: Charitable donations are limited to 75% of net income (50% for 1996, 20% before 1996) plus ¼ of the additional amounts in B to E (i.e., 100% of those components of income). Any unclaimed amount can be claimed in any of the next 5 years (see opening words of 118.1(1)"total charitable gifts"). Unclaimed amounts can also be used for minimum tax purposes; see Notes to 127.531. Cultural gifts and ecological gifts are not subject to the percentage limitation. Crown gifts were not subject to any limitation before 1997, but are now subject to the 75% limit: see Notes to 118.1(1)"total Crown gifts".

The deadline for most 1997 donations was extended to January 31, 1998 due to the postal strike of Nov. 19–Dec. 4/97. S. 33 of the 1998 Budget bill provides:

33. For the purposes of the Act, if

(a) a taxpayer made a gift at any particular time before February 1998, and after the end of a taxation year that ended after November 15, 1997 and before 1998, that would be deductible under section 110.1 or 118.1 of the Act in computing the taxpayer's taxable income or tax payable under Part I of the Act for the year if it were made immediately before the end of the year,

(b) the gift was a gift of tangible property (other than real property) or a gift by cash, cheque, credit card or money order,

(c) the gift was not made (i) through a payroll deduction, or (ii) where the taxpayer died after 1997, by the taxpayer's will, and

(d) the taxpayer so elects in the taxpayer's return of income under the Act for the year or by notifying the Minister of National Revenue in writing before 1999,

the taxpayer is deemed to have made the gift and, in the case of a gift of tangible property, to have disposed of the property immediately before the end of the taxpayer's taxation year that ended before 1998 and not to have done so at the particular time.

Donations subject to the 20% limit before 1996 can be carried forward and included in the claim of 50% of net income in 1996 or a later year. The increased limit is not restricted to donations made after 1995. The same applies for the increase to 75% for 1997.

Subpara. (a)(iii) amended by 1997 Budget, effective for taxation years that begin after 1996. Previously read:

(iii) in any other case, the amount determined by the formula

$$0.5(A + B - C)$$

where

A is the individual's income for the year,

B is the total of all amounts each of which is the amount of a taxable capital gain from a gift of property made by the individual in the year to a donee described in the definition "total charitable gifts", and

C  is the total of all amounts each of which is the portion of an amount deducted under section 110.6 in computing the individual's taxable income for the year that can reasonably be considered to be in respect of a gift of capital property made by the individual in the year to a donee described in the definition "total charitable gifts",

Para. (a) amended by 1996 Budget, effective for 1996 and later taxation years, effectively to change the limit from 20% to 50%, to add subpara. (ii) for the year of death, and to add elements B and C. Note that the formula will change further as a result of the 1997 federal budget. For 1988 through 1995 read:

(a) the lesser of

(i) the individual's total charitable gifts for the year, and

(ii) 1/5 of the individual's income for the year,

Para. (d) added by 1995 Budget, effective for gifts made after February 27, 1995. See Notes to 118.1(1)"total ecological gifts".

**I.T. Technical News**: No. 17 (loan of property as a gift).

**Notes [subsec. 118.1(1)]**: 118.1(1) amended by 1991 technical bill, effective December 11, 1988, to update references to the *Cultural Property Export and Import Act*, to make the wording more consistent, and to ensure that a gift that falls into more than one category will be considered first a cultural gift, then a Crown gift, and finally a charitable gift. (Ecological gifts, added in 1995, come after "cultural" and before "Crown".)

**Interpretation Bulletins [subsec. 118.1(1)]**: IT-110R3: Gifts and official donation receipts; IT-226R: Gift to a charity of a residual interest in real property or an equitable interest in a trust; IT-288R2: Gifts of capital properties to a charity and others; IT-297R2: Gifts in kind to charity and others; IT-407R3: Disposition after 1987 of Canadian cultural property; IT-504R2: Visual artists and writers. See also list at end of s. 118.1.

**Information Circulars**: See list at end of s. 118.1.

**(2) Proof of gift** — A gift shall not be included in the total charitable gifts, total Crown gifts, total cultural gifts or total ecological gifts of an individual unless the making of the gift is proven by filing with the Minister a receipt therefor that contains prescribed information.

### Proposed Amendment — 118.1(2)

**(2) Proof of gift** — A gift shall not be included in the total charitable gifts, total Crown gifts, total cultural gifts or total ecological gifts of an individual unless the making of the gift is proven by filing with the Minister

(a) a receipt for the gift that contains prescribed information;

(b) in the case of a gift described in the definition "total cultural gifts" in subsection (1), the certificate issued under subsection 33(1) of the *Cultural Property Export and Import Act*; and

(c) in the case of a gift described in the definition "total ecological gifts" in subsection (1), both certificates referred to in that definition.

**Application**: The December 21, 2000 draft legislation, subsec. 60(2), will amend subsec. 118.1(2) to read as above, applicable in respect of gifts made, or proposed to be made, after February 27, 2000, except that the subsec., as amended, shall be read without reference to para. 118.1(2)(b) in respect of gifts made before December 21, 2000.

**Technical Notes**: Subsection 118.1(2) provides that no deduction may be made in respect of a charitable donation or a gift to the Crown unless the gift is evidenced by a receipt containing prescribed information. The subsection is amended to clarify that, in the case of a gift of cultural property or an ecological gift, certificates issued by the Cultural Property Export Review Board or the Minister of the Environment must also be submitted.

This amendment applies to gifts made after February 27, 2000, except that the amendment in respect of cultural property does not apply to gifts made before December 21, 2000.

**Related Provisions**: 149.1(1)"disbursement quota"A — Charity must disburse 80% of receipted gifts; 188(1) — Revocation tax where registration of charity is revoked; 230(2) — Books and records to be kept by charity.

**Notes**: See Notes to 110.1 and 149.1(1)"disbursement quota" re taking a business deduction instead of a donation receipt.

Reference to "total ecological gifts" added to definition by 1995 Budget, effective for gifts made after February 27, 1995.

**Regulations**: 3501 (prescribed information).

**Interpretation Bulletins**: IT-407R4: Dispositions of cultural property to designated Canadian institutions. See also list at end of s. 118.1.

**Information Circulars**: 80-10R: Registered charities: operating a registered charity. See also list at end of s. 118.1.

**Advance Tax Rulings**: ATR-63: Donations to agents of the Crown.

**Registered Charities Newsletters**: See under 118.1(1)"total charitable gifts".

**(2.1) Ordering** — For the purposes of determining the total charitable gifts, total Crown gifts, total cultural gifts and total ecological gifts of an individual for a taxation year, no amount in respect of a gift described in any of the definitions of those expressions and made in a particular taxation year shall be considered to have been included in determining an amount that was deducted under this section in computing the individual's tax payable under this Part for a taxation year until amounts in respect of such gifts made in taxation years preceding the particular year that can be so considered are so considered.

**Related Provisions**: 110.1(1.1)(b) — Parallel ordering rule for corporations.

**Notes**: 118.1(2.1) added by 1997 Budget, effective for taxation years that begin after 1996.

**(3) Deduction by individuals for gifts** — For the purpose of computing the tax payable under this Part by an individual for a taxation year, there may be deducted such amount as the individual claims not exceeding the amount determined by the formula

$$(A \times B) + [C \times (D - B)]$$

where

A  is the appropriate percentage for the year;

B  is the lesser of $200 and the individual's total gifts for the year;

C  is the highest percentage referred to in subsection 117(2) that applies in determining tax that might be payable under this Part for the year; and

**S. 118.1(3)**          Income Tax Act, Part I, Division E

D is the individual's total gifts for the year.

**Related Provisions**: 37(5) — Scientific research and experimental development expenditures; 110(2) — Deduction for member of religious order who has taken vow of perpetual poverty; 110.1 — Deduction for gifts by corporations; 117(1) — Tax payable under this Part; 118.1(13)–(20) — No credit for gift of non-qualifying securities; 118.91 — Individual resident in Canada for part of the year; 118.95(a), 128(2)(e)(iii)(B), 128(2)(f)(iv), 128(2)(g)(ii)(B) — Application to bankrupt individual; 152(6) — Reassessment; 164(5), (5.1) — Effect of carryback of loss.

**Notes**: The formula works out to 16% (see 248(1) "appropriate percentage") on the first $200 and 29% on gifts over $200. (The value of the credit is then enhanced to approximately 22% and 40–50% respectively by the parallel provincial tax credit.) The theory is that small gifts are equivalent to a deduction by a person in the lowest (16%) bracket, while gifts over the threshold are equivalent to a deduction at the top bracket (whether or not the taxpayer is actually in the top bracket), which now kicks in only at $100,000.

118.1(3)B amended by 1994 Budget, effective 1994, to reduce the threshold at which the high credit cuts in from $250 to $200.

**Interpretation Bulletins**: IT-111R2: Annuities purchased from charitable organizations; IT-226R: Gift to a charity of a residual interest in real property or an equitable interest in a trust; IT-297R2: Gifts in kind to charity and others; IT-407R4: Dispositions of cultural property to designated Canadian institutions. See also list at end of s. 118.1.

**Information Circulars**: 75-23: Tuition fees and charitable donations paid to privately supported secular and religious schools.

**Registered Charities Newsletters**: See under 118.1(1) "total charitable gifts".

**(4) Gift in year of death** — Subject to subsection (13), a gift made by an individual in the particular taxation year in which the individual dies (including, for greater certainty, a gift otherwise deemed by subsection (5), (13) or (15) to have been so made) is deemed, for the purpose of this section other than this subsection, to have been made by the individual in the immediately preceding taxation year, and not in the particular year, to the extent that an amount in respect of the gift is not deducted in computing the individual's tax payable under this Part for the particular year.

### Proposed Amendment — 118.1(4) [temporary]

**(4) Gift in year of death** — Subject to subsection (13), a gift made by an individual in the particular taxation year in which the individual dies (including, for greater certainty, a gift otherwise deemed by subsection (5), (7), (7.1), (13) or (15) to have been so made) is deemed, for the purpose of this section other than this subsection, to have been made by the individual in the preceding taxation year, and not in the particular year, to the extent that an amount in respect of the gift is not deducted in computing the individual's tax payable under this Part for the particular year.

**Application**: Bill C-43 (First Reading September 20, 2000), subsec. 63(1), will amend subsec. 118.1(4) to read as above, applicable to 2000 et seq., and where a taxpayer or a taxpayer's legal representative so notifies the Minister of National Revenue in writing before 2002 of the intention of the taxpayer or the taxpayer's legal representative that this amendment apply in respect of a gift made after 1996 and before 2000, this amendment applies to the taxation year in which the gift was made.

**Technical Notes**: Section 118.1 of the Act provides the tax credit that may be claimed by individuals who make charitable donations, gifts to the Crown and certain gifts of cultural property and ecologically sensitive land. Donors may carry forward unused claims for up to five years.

Subsection 118.1(4) of the Act treats a gift made in the year of an individual's death as having been made in the preceding year to the extent that it was not deducted in the year of death. The subsection is amended consequential to the amendment of subsections 118.1(7) and (7.1) of the Act, to clarify that it applies for the purposes of those subsections. For further information, see the commentary to those subsections.

### Proposed Amendment — 118.1(4)

**(4) Gift in year of death** — Subject to subsection (13), a gift made by an individual in the particular taxation year in which the individual dies (including, for greater certainty, a gift otherwise deemed by subsection (5), (5.2), (5.3), (7), (7.1), (13) or (15) to have been so made) is deemed, for the purpose of this section other than this subsection, to have been made by the individual in the preceding taxation year, and not in the particular year, to the extent that an amount in respect of the gift is not deducted in computing the individual's tax payable under this Part for the particular year.

**Application**: The December 21, 2000 draft legislation, subsec. 60(3), will amend subsec. 118.1(4) to read as above, applicable in respect of deaths that occur after 1998.

For taxation years before 2000, subsec. 118.1(4) shall be read without reference to subsecs. 118.1(7) and (7.1) except that, where a taxpayer or a taxpayer's legal representative notifies the Minister of National Revenue in writing before July 2001 of the intention of the taxpayer or the taxpayer's legal representative that this subsection apply in respect of a gift made after 1996 and before 2000,

    (a) subsec. 118.1(4), as amended, applies to the taxation year in which the gift was made and, where para. 118.1(7)(d) applies, the amount designated in the notice in respect of the gift is deemed to have been validly designated for the purposes of that paragraph in the taxpayer's return of income for the year in which the gift was made; and

    (b) subsec. 118.1(4), as amended, shall be read, in respect of the 1996 to 1998 taxation years, without reference to subsecs. 118.1(5.2) and (5.3).

**Technical Notes**: Subsection 118.1(4) provides a special rule in the case of gifts that are made by an individual in the taxation year in which the individual dies. Under that subsection, a gift made by the individual in that year is generally considered to have been made in the individual's preceding taxation year, to the extent that the charitable donations tax credit in respect of the amount of the gift is not deducted in computing the individual's tax for the year of death. The gifts of a deceased individual to which subsection 118.1(4) applies include those otherwise deemed by specified provisions in section 118.1 to be gifts made immediately before the individual died.

Subsection 118.1(4) is amended so that new subsections 118.1(5.2) and (5.3) are included among the specified provisions. These subsections deal with cases where a charity is a beneficiary under a life insurance policy or under a trust governed by a registered retirement savings plan or registered retirement income fund. As a consequence of the amendment to subsection 118.1(4), gifts deemed by subsection 118.1(5.2) or (5.3) to have been made by an individual immediately before the individual's death can result in a reduction in the individual's tax for the taxation year preceding the taxation year of the individual's death.

**Related Provisions**: 70(5) — Deemed disposition of property immediately before death; 118.1(5) — Gift made by will deemed made in year of death.

**Notes**: 118.1(4) amended by 1997 Budget, effective for gifts made after July 1997. From 1988 until the amendment, read:

> (4) Time of gift — For the purposes of this section, a gift made by an individual in the taxation year in which the individual dies shall be deemed to have been made by the individual in the immediately preceding taxation year to the extent that an amount in respect thereof is not deducted in computing the individual's tax payable under this Part for the taxation year in which the individual dies.

**Interpretation Bulletins**: IT-288R2: Gifts of capital properties to a charity and others; IT-407R4: Dispositions of cultural property to designated Canadian institutions. See also list at end of s. 118.1.

**(5) Gift by will** — Subject to subsection (13), where an individual by the individual's will makes a gift, the gift is, for the purpose of this section, deemed to have been made by the individual immediately before the individual died.

**Related Provisions**: 38(a.1)(ii) — Gift of publicly-traded securities made on death; 38(a.2) — Reduced capital gain inclusion on ecological gift; 39(1)(a)(i.1) — Gain on disposition not capital gain; 70(5) — Deemed disposition of property immediately before death; 118.1(4) — Carryback of gift made in year of death; 118.1(5.1), (5.2) — Gift of life insurance on death. See additional Related Provisions and Definitions at end of s. 118.1.

**Notes**: For detailed discussion see D. Bruce Ball & Brenda Dietrich, "Bequests and Estate Planning", 47(4) *Canadian Tax Journal* 995–1018 (1999).

118.1(5) amended by 1997 Budget, effective for gifts made after July 1997. From 1988 until the amendment, read:

> (5) Where an individual by the individual's will makes a gift to a donee described in subsection (1), the gift shall, for the purposes of this section, be deemed to have been made by the individual in the taxation year in which the individual dies.

**Interpretation Bulletins**: IT-226R: Gift to a charity of a residual interest in real property or an equitable interest in a trust; IT-407R4: Dispositions of cultural property to designated Canadian institutions. See also list at end of s. 118.1.

### Proposed Addition — 118.1(5.1)–(5.3)

**(5.1) Direct designation — insurance proceeds** — Subsection (5.2) applies to an individual in respect of a life insurance policy where

(a) the policy is a life insurance policy in Canada under which, immediately before the individual's death, the individual's life was insured;

(b) a transfer of money, or a transfer by means of a negotiable instrument, is made as a consequence of the individual's death and solely because of the obligations under the policy, from an insurer to a qualified donee;

(c) immediately before the individual's death,

(i) the individual's consent would have been required to change the recipient of the transfer described in paragraph (b), and

(ii) the donee was neither a policyholder under the policy, nor an assignee of the individual's interest under the policy; and

(d) the transfer occurs within the 36 month period that begins at the time of the death (or, where written application to extend the period has been made to the Minister by the individual's legal representative, within such longer period as the Minister considers reasonable in the circumstances).

**Technical Notes**: See under 118.1(5.2).

**(5.2) Rules applicable re: subsection (5.1)** — Where subsection (5.1) applies to an individual in respect of a life insurance policy under which an insurer is obligated to make a transfer,

(a) for the purpose of this section (other than subsection (5.1) and this subsection) and paragraph (b), the transfer described in subsection (5.1) is deemed to be a gift made, immediately before the individual's death, by the individual to the qualified donee referred to in subsection (5.1); and

(b) the fair market value of the gift is deemed to be the fair market value, at the time of the individual's death, of the right to that transfer (determined without reference to any risk of default with regard to obligations of the insurer).

**Technical Notes**: New subsection 118.1(5.2), in conjunction with new subsection 118.1(5.1), extends the charitable donations tax credit to transfers under a life insurance policy that are made as a consequence of designations under the policy. As a result, the charitable donations tax credit can be claimed on an individual's death as a consequence of qualifying transfers to qualified donees under life insurance policies that insure the individual's life. Each of the conditions set out in paragraphs 118.1(5.1)(a) to (d) must be satisfied for this result to apply.

Paragraph 118.1(5.1)(a) requires the policy to be a life insurance policy in Canada (as defined by subsection 138(12)) under which, immediately before the individual's death, the individual's life was insured. The policy could include a group life insurance policy, an annuity or a segregated fund policy.

Paragraph 118.1(5.1)(b) requires that, as a consequence of the individual's death, a transfer of money (or a transfer by means of a negotiable instrument) to a qualified donee (which is being defined in subsection 248(1) with reference to the existing definition in subsection 149.1(1)) be made from an insurer, solely because of the insurer's obligations under the policy. The transfer might be provided for in the individual's will or in a non-testamentary written designation made by the individual.

Paragraph 118.1(5.1)(c) requires that, immediately before the individual's death, the donee was neither a policyholder under the policy nor an assignee of the individual's interest under the policy. The conditions in paragraph 118.1(5.1)(c) are not satisfied, for example, where an individual takes out a life insurance policy and makes an absolute assignment of the policy to a qualified donee. In the latter case, the CCRA has interpreted this provision to the effect that the individual would generally be considered to have made a gift because of, and at the time of, the assignment. (See Interpretation Bulletin IT-244R3.)

Paragraph 118.1(5.1)(c) also requires that, immediately before the individual's death, the individual was a person whose consent was required to change the recipient of the transfer. Normally, this would mean that the individual must, immediately before death, have been the policyholder. However, in the context of group policies, the individual might instead have rights (immediately before death) in respect of the policy that could be enforced against the policyholder (e.g., the individual's employer or former employer).

Paragraph 118.1(5.1)(d) requires that the transfer occur not more than 36 months after the individual's death, or within such longer period as the Minister of National Revenue considers reasonable.

Where the conditions set out in paragraphs 118.1(5.1)(a) to (d) are satisfied in connection with a transfer under an insurance policy as a consequence of the death of an individual:

- the transfer is deemed to be a gift made by the individual immediately
- before the individual's death (paragraph 118.1(5.2)(a)); and the fair market value of that gift is deemed to be the fair market value, at the time of the individual's death, of the right to the transfer (paragraph 118.1(5.2))(b)). This fair market value is determined without reference to any risk of default with regard to the insurer's obligations. In nearly all cases, this is expected to be the fair market value, at the time of the individual's death, of the money (or of the proceeds of the negotiable instrument) ultimately transferred.

**Related Provisions**: 118.1(4) — Carryback of gift made in year of death.

**(5.3) Direct designation — RRSPs and RRIFs** — Where as a consequence of an individual's death, a transfer of money, or a transfer by means of a negotiable instrument, is made, from a particular trust governed by a registered retirement savings plan or registered retirement income fund to a qualified donee, solely because of the donee's interest as a beneficiary under the particular trust, the individual was the annuitant (within the meaning assigned by subsection 146(1) or 146.3(1)) under the plan or fund immediately before the individual's death and the transfer occurs within the 36 month period that begins at the time of the death (or, where written application to extend the period has been made to the Minister by the individual's legal representative, within such longer period as the Minister considers reasonable in the circumstances),

(a) for the purposes of this section (other than this subsection) and paragraph (b), the transfer is deemed to be a gift made, immediately before the individual's death, by the individual to the donee; and

(b) the fair market value of the gift is deemed to be the fair market value, at the time of the individual's death, of the right to the transfer (determined without reference to any risk of default with regard to the obligations of the trustee of the plan or fund).

**Technical Notes**: New subsection 118.1(5.3) extends the charitable donations tax credit to a transfer of money (or a transfer by means of a negotiable instrument) from a trust governed by a registered retirement savings plan (RRSP) or registered retirement income fund (RRIF), where the transfer is made as a consequence of a qualified donee being named a beneficiary under the trust. As a result, the charitable donations tax credit can be claimed on an individual's death as a consequence of transfers to qualified donees from such a trust if the individual was the annuitant under the plan or fund that governed the trust. For this result to apply, the transfer must be made not more than 36 months after the individual's death, or within such longer period as the Minister of National Revenue considers reasonable.

Refer to the commentary on subsection 248(1) for a discussion of the definition "qualified donee"

Where subsection 118.1(5.3) applies in connection with a transfer from an RRSP or RRIF trust under which an individual was the annuitant:

- the transfer of the property is deemed to be a gift made by the individual immediately before the individual's death (paragraph 118.1(5.3)(a)); and
- the fair market value of that gift is deemed to be the fair market value, at the time of the individual's death, of the right to the transfer, which fair market value is determined without reference to any risk of default with regard to the trust's obligations, (paragraph 118.1(5.3)(b)).

**Application**: The December 21, 2000 draft legislation, subsec. 60(4), will add subsecs. 118.1(5.1) to (5.3), applicable in respect of deaths that occur after 1998.

**Notice of Ways and Means Motion, federal budget, February 28, 2000**: *Charitable Donations Tax Credit*

(21) That the charitable donations tax credit be extended to apply in respect of amounts that are paid directly to a qualified donee as a beneficiary, as a consequence of an individual's death that occurs after 1998, under

(a) a life insurance policy under which the individual was the policyholder and the individual's life was insured,

(b) the individual's coverage under a group life insurance policy under which the individual's life was insured, or

(c) a registered retirement savings plan or registered retirement income fund under which the individual was the annuitant.

**Federal budget, supplementary information, February 28, 2000**: *Charitable Donations: Designations in Favour of Charity*

An individual who is an annuitant under a registered retirement savings plan (RRSP) or registered retirement income fund (RRIF) or the owner of a life insurance policy may wish to have the proceeds in respect thereof donated to a charity on the individual's death. There are two common ways of achieving this goal:

- the individual's will can provide for a cash bequest of the proceeds to the charity; or
- without making any provision in the individual's will, the individual can designate that the proceeds be paid directly to the charity under the terms of the RRSP, RRIF or insurance policy.

In either case, the individual's estate is responsible for satisfying the individual's income tax liabilities on the individual's death.

Under current income tax rules, donations that are made by way of a donor's will qualify for the charitable donations tax credit on death. [See 118.1(5) — ed.] However, donations made as a consequence of a direct designation do not qualify for the credit. In such circumstances, the charitable donations tax credit would not be available to offset income tax arising because of the taxation of an RRSP or RRIF on death. This can lead to liquidity problems for an estate.

In order to provide consistency in the income tax rules in this regard, the budget proposes to extend the charitable donations tax credit to donations of RRSP, RRIF and insurance proceeds that are made as a consequence of direct beneficiary designations. This measure will apply in respect of an individual's death that occurs after 1998.

**Related Provisions**: 118.1(4) — Carryback of gift made in year of death.

**(6) Gift of capital property** — Where, at any time, whether by the individual's will or otherwise, an individual makes a gift of

(a) capital property to a donee described in the definition "total charitable gifts", "total Crown gifts" or "total ecological gifts" in subsection (1), or

(b) in the case of an individual who is a non-resident person, real property situated in Canada to a prescribed donee who provides an undertaking, in a form satisfactory to the Minister, to the effect that such property will be held for use in the public interest,

and the fair market value of the property at that time exceeds its adjusted cost base to the individual, such amount, not greater than the fair market value and not less than the adjusted cost base to the individual of the property at that time, as the individual or the individual's legal representative designates in the individual's return of income under section 150 for the year in which the gift is made shall, if the making of the gift is proven by filing with the Minister a receipt containing prescribed information, be deemed to be the individual's proceeds of disposition of the property and, for the purposes of subsection (1), the fair market value of the gift made by the individual.

**Proposed Amendment — 118.1(6) closing words**

and the fair market value of the property otherwise determined at that time exceeds its adjusted cost base to the individual, such amount, not greater than the fair market value and not less than the adjusted cost base to the individual of the property at that time, as the individual or the individual's legal representative designates in the individual's return of income under section 150 for the year in which the gift is made is, if the making of the gift is proven by filing with the Minister a receipt containing prescribed information, deemed to be the individual's proceeds of disposition of the property and, for the purposes of subsection (1), the fair market value of the gift made by the individual.

**Application**: Bill C-43 (First Reading September 20, 2000), subsec. 63(2), will amend the closing words of subsec. 118.1(6) to read as above, applicable in respect of gifts made after February 27, 1995.

**Technical Notes**: Subsection 118.1(6) of the Act provides that, if an individual donates capital property to a charity, the individual may elect a value between the adjusted cost base and the fair market value of the donated property to be treated both as the proceeds of disposition for the purpose of calculating the individual's capital gain and the amount of the gift for the purpose of calculating the tax credit allowed for charitable donations under subsection 118.1(3) of the Act.

The amendment to subsection 118.1(6) of the Act is complementary to the amendment of subsection 118.1(12) of the Act, which provides that the fair market value of a gift of a covenant, easement or servitude in respect of ecologically sensitive land will not be considered to be less than the decrease in value of the subject land that resulted from the making of the gift. The amendments clarify that an individual donor may nevertheless report a reduced amount of proceeds of disposition of such a gift, where the value of the gift for the purpose of calculating the charitable donations tax credit is reduced accordingly. This amendment applies in respect of gifts made after February 27, 1995.

**Department of Finance news release, June 3, 1999**: [See under 118.11(12).]

**Notes**: Reference to "total ecological gifts" added to 118.1(6)(a) by 1995 Budget, effective for gifts made after February 27, 1995. See Notes to 118.1(1)"total ecological gifts".

As a result of the 1996 Budget changes that increased the amounts of charitable donations that can be claimed for credit, an election under 118.1(6) appears no longer to be useful. However, Department of Finance officials have indicated that 118.1(6) will not be repealed, so as not to raise concerns about eliminating what is perceived to be a beneficial provision (Drache, 4(4) *Canadian Not-For-Profit News* 28-29 (April 1996).

Closing words of 118.1(6) amended by 1992 technical bill, effective for gifts made after December 11, 1988, to deem the proceeds of disposition of the property to be the "fair market value" of the gift for purposes of 110.1(1) rather than the "amount" of the gift, so as to fit with amendments made to 118.1(1) by 1991 technical bill.

**Regulations**: 3500–3502 (prescribed information); 3504 (prescribed donee).

**Interpretation Bulletins**: IT-226R: Gift to a charity of a residual interest in real property or an equitable interest in a trust; IT-288R2: Gifts of capital properties to a charity and others; IT-504R2: Visual artists and writers.

**Forms**: T3 Sched. 1A, T1170: Capital gains on gifts of certain capital property.

**(7) Gifts of art** — Except where subsection (7.1) applies, where at any time, whether by the individual's will or otherwise, an individual makes a gift of a work of art that was created by the individual and that is property in the individual's inventory to a donee described in the definition "total charitable gifts" or "total Crown gifts" in subsection (1) and at that time the fair market value of the work of art exceeds its cost amount to the individual, such amount, not greater than that fair market value and not less than that cost amount, as is designated in the individual's return of income under section 150 for the year in which the gift is made shall, if the making of the gift is proven by filing with the Minister a receipt containing prescribed information, be deemed to be the individual's proceeds of disposition of the work of art and, for the purposes of subsection (1), the fair market value of the gift made by the individual.

### Proposed Amendment — 118.1(7)

**(7) Gifts of art [by artist]** — Except where subsection (7.1) applies, where at any time, whether by the individual's will or otherwise, an individual makes a gift described in the definition "total charitable gifts" or "total Crown gifts" in subsection (1) of a work of art that was

(a) created by the individual and that is property in the individual's inventory, or

(b) acquired under circumstances where subsection 70(3) applied,

and at that time the fair market value of the work of art exceeds its cost amount to the individual, the following rules apply:

(c) where the gift is made as a consequence of the death of the individual, the gift is deemed to have been made immediately before the death, and

(d) the amount, not greater than that fair market value at the time the gift is made and not less than the cost amount of the property to the individual, that is designated in the individual's return of income under section 150 for the year in which the gift is made is, if the making of the gift is proven by filing with the Minister a receipt containing prescribed information, deemed to be the individual's proceeds of disposition of the work of art and, for the purposes of subsection (1), the fair market value of the gift made by the individual.

**Application**: Bill C-43 (First Reading September 20, 2000), subsec. 63(3), will amend subsec. 118.1(7) to read as above, applicable to 2000 *et seq.*, and where a taxpayer or a taxpayer's legal representative so notifies the Minister of National Revenue in writing before 2002 of the intention of the taxpayer or the taxpayer's legal representative that this amendment apply in respect of a gift made after 1996 and before 2000, this amendment applies to the taxation year in which the gift was made and, where para. 118.1(7)(d) applies, the amount designated in the notice in respect of the gift is deemed to have been validly designated for the purposes of that paragraph in the taxpayer's return of income for the year in which the gift was made.

**Technical Notes**: Subsection 118.1(7) of the Act provides that, if an artist donates artwork created by the artist and held in inventory, the artist may designate a value between the cost amount and the fair market value of the artwork to be treated both as the proceeds of disposition for the purpose of calculating the individual's income and the amount of the gift for the purpose of calculating the tax credit allowed for charitable donations under subsection 118.1(3). Such an amount may also be designated by the legal representative of a deceased artist, where the artwork is donated according to the late individual's will.

If the artwork is cultural property, as described in subsection 118.1(1) of the Act, subsection 118.1(7.1) of the Act applies instead of subsection (7) of the Act. Under subsection 118.1(7.1), the individual is also treated as having received proceeds of disposition equal to the cost amount to the individual of the work of art for the purpose of calculating the individual's income, but the fair market value of the artwork is not affected. This means that the artist is entitled to a credit based on the value of the donation, but that the deceased artist recognizes neither a profit nor a loss on the disposition of the work of art in computing income from the artist's business for income tax purposes.

Subsections (7) and (7.1) of the Act are amended to provide that, where artwork is donated as a result of the death of the individual, the gift is deemed to have been made by the individual immediately before the individual's death. These amendments clarify that the proceeds of disposition calculated under these subsections are relevant for the purpose of calculating the income of the late individual in the year of death.

Subsections 118.1(7) and (7.1) of the Act are also amended to apply to artwork that has been donated by an individual who acquired the artwork in circumstances where subsection 70(3) of the Act applied (i.e. as a "right or thing").

Upon the death of an individual, subsections 69(1.1) and 70(3) of the Act provide (if applicable) a rollover of "rights or things" of the late individual to beneficiaries or other persons beneficially interested in the estate or trust of the late individual. That is, if artwork of a late individual is a "right or thing," income from the ultimate disposition of the artwork will be attributed to the beneficiary. (Note, however, that subsection 70(3) of the Act does not apply where the late individual's legal representative has validly filed a "rights or things" return or where the time for filing such a return has expired before the transfer of the artwork to the beneficiary).

New subsections 118.1(7) and (7.1) of the Act apply to such an individual beneficiary if that beneficiary donates the artwork to the same effect as if the artwork had been donated by the deceased person.

### Letter from Department of Finance, April 17, 1998:

Dear [xxx]

Thank you for your letter dated February 2, 1998 concerning the income tax treatment of donations to museums by artists' heirs.

I will be recommending the inclusion of the necessary amendments to the *Income Tax Act* to cause donations of art by artists' heirs to be treated the same way for tax purposes as donations made by artists and collectors. This amendment should be contained in the next technical bill relating to income tax matters. As per my previous correspondence, I will recommend that the amendment apply to the 1997 and subsequent taxation years.

Should you have any concerns please contact Alexandra Maclean of this Department at 992-5636.

> Sincerely,
>
> The Honourable Paul Martin, P.C., M.P.
> Minister of Finance
> c.c.: The Honourable Herb Dhaliwal, P.C., M.P.
> Minister of National Revenue

**Notes**: This amendment resulted from lobbying by the Canadian Museums Association. See Drache, "Artists' Heirs to Get Tax Break on Gifts", 8(1) *Canadian Not-For-Profit News* (Carswell) 5-6 (Jan. 2000).

**Notes**: 118.1(7) amended by 1991 technical bill, effective for gifts made in 1991 or later, to be subject to 118.1(7.1).

**Interpretation Bulletins**: IT-288R2: Gifts of capital properties to a charity and others; IT-504R2: Visual artists and writers.

**(7.1) Gifts of cultural property** — Where at any time, whether by the individual's will or otherwise, an individual makes a gift described in the definition "total cultural gifts" in subsection (1) of a work of art that was created by the individual and that is property in the individual's inventory, the individual shall, if the making of the gift is proven by filing with the Minister a receipt containing prescribed information, be deemed to have received proceeds of disposition in respect of the gift at that time equal to its cost amount to the individual at that time.

### Proposed Amendment — 118.1(7.1)

**(7.1) Gifts of cultural property** — Where at any particular time, whether by the individual's will or otherwise, an individual makes a gift described in the definition "total cultural gifts" in subsection (1) of a work of art that was

(a) created by the individual and that is property in the individual's inventory, or

(b) acquired under circumstances where subsection 70(3) applied,

and at that time the fair market value of the work of art exceeds its cost amount to the individual, the following rules apply:

(c) where the gift is made as a consequence of the death of the individual, the individual is deemed to have made the gift immediately before the death, and

(d) the individual is deemed to have received at the particular time proceeds of disposition in respect of the gift equal to its cost amount to the individual at that time.

**Application**: Bill C-43 (First Reading September 20, 2000), subsec. 63(3), will amend subsec. 118.1(7.1) to read as above, applicable to 2000 *et seq.*, and where a taxpayer or a taxpayer's legal representative so notifies the Minister of National Revenue in writing before 2002 of the intention of the taxpayer or the taxpayer's legal representative that this amendment apply in respect of a gift made after 1996 and before 2000, this amendment applies to the taxation year in which the gift was made.

**Technical Notes and Letter from Dept. of Finance**: See under 118.1(7).

**Related Provisions**: 39(1)(a)(i.1) — Meaning of capital gain and capital loss; 207.3 — Tax on institution that disposes of cultural property.

**Notes**: 118.1(7.1) added by 1991 technical bill, effective for gifts made in 1991 or later. For discussion of this incentive, see Notes to 207.3.

**Interpretation Bulletins**: IT-407R4: Dispositions of cultural property to designated Canadian institutions; IT-504R2: Visual artists and writers. See also list at end of s. 118.1.

**(8) Gifts made by partnership** — Where an individual is, at the end of a fiscal period of a partnership, a member of the partnership, the individual's share of any amount that would, if the partnership were a person, be a gift made by the partnership to any donee shall, for the purposes of this section, be deemed to be a gift made by the individual to that donee in the individual's taxation year in which the fiscal period of the partnership ends.

**Related Provisions**: 53(2)(c)(iii) — Deduction from ACB of partnership interest.

**(9) Commuter's charitable donations** — Where throughout a taxation year an individual resided in Canada near the boundary between Canada and the United States, if

(a) the individual commuted to the individual's principal place of employment or business in the United States, and

(b) the individual's chief source of income for the year was that employment or business,

a gift made by the individual in the year to a religious, charitable, scientific, literary or educational organization created or organized in or under the laws of the United States that would be allowed as a deduction under the *United States Internal Revenue Code* shall, for the purpose of the definition "total charitable gifts" in subsection (1), be deemed to have been made to a registered charity.

**Related Provisions**: Canada-U.S. tax treaty, Art. XXI:6 — Cross-border donations.

**Notes**: Article XXI(6) of the Canada-U.S. tax treaty allows donations to U.S. charities to be treated as donations to Canadian charities, up to a limit of 75% of U.S.-source income. The taxpayer need not be a commuter.

**(10) Determination of fair market value** — For the purposes of paragraph 110.1(1)(c) and the definition "total cultural gifts" in subsection (1), the fair market value of an object is deemed to be the fair market value determined by the Canadian Cultural Property Export Review Board.

**Related Provisions**: 118.1(10.1) — Determination by Board applies for 2 years; 118.1(11) — Assessment consequential on determination of value by Board; 241(4)(d)(xii) — Disclosure of information to Department of Canadian Heritage or the Board.

**Notes**: 118.1(10) amended by 1995 cultural property bill (Bill C-93), in force July 12, 1996 (per Order in Council SI/96-73, *Canada Gazette*, Part II, Vol 130, No. 15, p. 2573).

Under s. 33.1 of the *Cultural Property Export and Import Act*, as introduced by the 1995 cultural property bill and proclaimed in force July 12, 1996, decisions of the Board as to the fair market value of cultural property are appealable to the Tax Court of Canada. This change was first announced in a Communications Canada

**S. 118.1(10)**      Income Tax Act, Part I, Division E

press release of June 10, 1993, and a Department of Canadian Heritage press release of November 4, 1994. An appeal of any decision made by the Board between January 1, 1992 and July 12, 1996 could be launched until January 12, 1997.

118.1(10) added by 1991 Budget, effective for gifts made after February 20, 1990.

**Interpretation Bulletins**: IT-407R4: Dispositions of cultural property to designated Canadian institutions; IT-504R2: Visual artists and writers.

**(10.1) Determination of fair market value [cultural property]** — For the purposes of subparagraph 69(1)(b)(ii), subsection 70(5), section 110.1 and this section, where at any time the Canadian Cultural Property Export Review Board determines or redetermines an amount to be the fair market value of a property that is the subject of a gift described in paragraph 110.1(1)(a) or in the definition "total charitable gifts" in subsection (1) made by a taxpayer within the two-year period that begins at that time, the last amount so determined or redetermined within the period is deemed to be the fair market value of the property at the time the gift was made and, subject to subsection 110.1(3) and subsections (6) and (7), to be the taxpayer's proceeds of disposition of the property.

---

**Proposed Amendment —
118.1(10.1)–(10.5)**

**(10.1) Determination of fair market value [cultural or ecological property]** — For the purposes of subparagraph 69(1)(b)(ii), subsection 70(5) and sections 110.1, 207.31 and this section, where at any time the Canadian Cultural Property Export Review Board or the Minister of the Environment determines or redetermines an amount to be the fair market value of a property that is the subject of a gift described in paragraph 110.1(1)(a), or in the definition "total charitable gifts" in subsection (1), made by a taxpayer within the two-year period that begins at that time, an amount equal to the last amount so determined or redetermined within the period is deemed to be the fair market value of the gift at the time the gift was made and, subject to subsections (6), (7), (7.1) and 110.1(3), to be the taxpayer's proceeds of disposition of the gift.

**Technical Notes**: Subsection 118.1(10.1) applies, for the purposes of section 118.1 (donations and gifts by individuals) and section 110.1 (donations and gifts by corporations), where the Cultural Property Export Review Board has determined or redetermined the fair market value of a property. If the property is the subject of a gift that is made within two years after the Board's valuation, and is claimed as a charitable donation that is not a gift of cultural property, the Board's valuation is deemed to be determinative of the fair market value of the property for the purposes of sections 110.1 and 118.1. An amount equal to that value is also deemed to be the proceeds of disposition of the property, subject to elective provisions in subsections 110.1(3), 118.1(6) and (7).

Subsection 118.1(10.1) is amended to extend its application to determinations and redeterminations of value made by the Minister of the Environment under new subsections 118.1(10.3) and (10.4).

**(10.2) Request for determination by the Minister of the Environment** — Where a person disposes or proposes to dispose of a property that would, if the disposition were made and the certificates described in paragraph 110.1(1)(d) or in the definition "total ecological gifts" in subsection (1) were issued by the Minister of the Environment, be a gift described in those provisions, the person may request, by notice in writing to that Minister, a determination of the fair market value of the property.

**Technical Notes**: See under 118.1(10.5).

**Related Provisions**: 118.1(10.3) — Duty of Minister on receipt of request.

**(10.3) Duty of Minister of the Environment** — In response to a request made under subsection (10.2), the Minister of the Environment shall with all due dispatch make a determination in accordance with subsection (12) or 110.1(5), as the case may be, of the fair market value of the property referred to in that request and give notice of the determination in writing to the person who has disposed of, or who proposes to dispose of, the property, except that no such determination shall be made if the request is received by that Minister after three years after the end of the person's taxation year in which the disposition occurred.

**Technical Notes**: See under 118.1(10.5).

**Related Provisions**: 118.1(10.4) — Redetermination by Minister; 118.1(10.5) — Certificate of fair market value.

**(10.4) Ecological gifts — redetermination** — Where the Minister of the Environment has, under subsection 118.1(10.3), notified a person of the amount determined by that Minister to be the fair market value of a property in respect of its disposition or proposed disposition,

(a) that Minister shall, on receipt of a written request made by the person on or before the day that is 90 days after the day that the person was so notified of the first such determination, with all due dispatch confirm or redetermine the fair market value;

(b) that Minister may, on that Minister's own initiative, at any time redetermine the fair market value;

(c) that Minister shall in either case notify the person in writing of that Minister's confirmation or redetermination; and

(d) any such redetermination is deemed to replace all preceding determinations and redeterminations of the fair market value of that property from the time at which the first such determination was made.

**Technical Notes**: See under 118.1(10.5).

**Related Provisions**: 118.1(10.5) — Certificate of fair market value; 169(1.1) — Appeal of valuation to Tax Court of Canada.

**(10.5) Certificate of fair market value** — Where the Minister of the Environment determines under subsection (10.3) the fair market value of a property, or redetermines that value under subsection (10.4), and the property has been disposed of to a qualified donee described in paragraph 110.1(1)(d) or in the definition "total ecological gifts" in subsection 118.1(1), that Minister shall issue to the person who made the disposition a certificate that states the fair market value of the property so determined or redetermined and, where more than one certificate has been so issued, the last certificate is deemed to replace all preceding certificates from the time at which the first certificate was issued.

**Technical Notes**: New subsections 118.1(10.2) to (10.5) are added to provide administrative procedures regarding the request for a determination of fair market value from the Minister of the Environment, including notification, determination and redetermination. (Appeals to the Tax Court of Canada are provided for in new subsection 169(1.1).) These amendments are concurrent with the amendment of paragraph 110.1(1)(d), "ecological gifts", and the definition "total ecological gifts" in subsection 118.1(1), which require that the fair market value of ecologically sensitive land (including a covenant, an easement or a servitude) be certified by the Minister of the Environment.

New subsection 118.1(10.2) provides that, where a person disposes of, or proposes to dispose of, a property that, with the appropriate certification by the Minister of the Environment, would qualify as an ecological gift, the person may request in writing that Minister make a determination of the fair market value of the property. New subsection 118.1(10.3) provides that, where a person makes such a request before the end of the third taxation year of the person following the year in which the property was disposed of, the Minister of the Environment will notify the person of the determination made.

New subsection 118.1(10.4) provides for the opportunity to request, within 90 days of notification of the determination of fair market value of a property by the Minister of the Environment, a redetermination of that fair market value. That Minister may also take the initiative to redetermine the fair market value at any time, even where no request has been made. In either case, that Minister will issue a notice of redetermination, and the redetermined fair market value is deemed to replace any previous amount determined or redetermined.

It is not necessary for a gift to have been made in order for a determination or redetermination to be made in respect of a person's property, so long as the person has proposed to make a gift of the property. However, no tax credit will be available until the gift is made.

Where a person has made the gift, the fair market value of which has been determined or redetermined by the Minister of the Environment, to the federal government, a provincial or territorial government, a municipality or a registered charity approved by that Minister, the Minister of the Environment will issue a certificate that states the fair market value determined or redetermined by that Minister. Where more than one certificate has been issued (because of a redetermination of fair market value), the last such certificate is deemed to replace any preceding certificate.

**Application**: The December 21, 2000 draft legislation, subsec. 60(5), will amend subsec. 118.1(10.1) to read as above and add subsecs. (10.2) to (10.5), applicable in respect of gifts made, or proposed to be made, after February 27, 2000.

**Notice of Ways and Means Motion, federal budget, February 28, 2000**: *Donations of Ecological Gifts*

(22) That the provisions of the Act relating to ecological gifts be modified to

(a) halve the income inclusion rate for capital gains from such gifts (other than gifts made to a private foundation) made after February 27, 2000, [see 38(a.2) — ed.]

(b) require the donor to file with the return of income for the taxation year in which the gift was made a document obtained from the Minister of the Environment certifying, for the purposes of the Act relating to charitable gifts, the fair market value of the gift as determined by that Minister,

(c) provide a donor with a right to appeal to the Tax Court of Canada a redetermination by that Minister of the fair market value of a gift that has been made, and

(d) provide that such a valuation apply for all purposes of the Act relating to charitable gifts for the two-year period following the time of the last determination or redetermination of the value.

**Federal budget, supplementary information, February 28, 2000**: *Ecologically Sensitive Lands*

The protection of Canada's natural heritage, and especially its species at risk, is a critical objective of the Government. The 1995 budget announced incentives for ecological gifts to the Government of Canada, provincial governments, Canadian municipalities or approved registered charities established for the purpose of protecting Canada's environmental heritage. To be eligible for the special provisions, a gift must be a property certified as ecologically sensitive by the Minister of the Environment. The preservation of these properties is critical to the Government's strategy for the protection of species at risk and the promotion of Canada's system of national and provincial parks and other environmental objectives. This strategy emphasizes providing assistance to encourage Canadians to take voluntary action to protect species and to make responsible stewardship an easy choice.

Donations of ecologically sensitive land from individuals are eligible for the charitable donations tax credit, while those from corporations are eligible for a charitable donation deduction. These provisions apply to transfers of title as well as to covenants, easements and servitudes established under common law, the Civil Code in Quebec, or provincial or territorial legislation allowing for their establishment. Further, ecological gifts are exempt from the rules which would otherwise limit the amount of charitable donations eligible for tax assistance in a year to 75 per cent of net income.

Normally, the value of a donated property is determined to be the price that a purchaser would pay for the property on the open market. As there is no established market for covenants, easements and servitudes, the fair market value of such restrictions on land use is difficult to determine. To provide greater certainty in making these valuations, the 1997 budget introduced a measure to deem the value of these gifts to be not less than the resulting decrease in the value of the land.

The budget proposes a further enhancement of the incentives for the protection of ecologically sensitive lands, including areas containing habitat for species at risk. Specifically, it is proposed that the income inclusion be reduced by one-half in respect of capital gains arising from gifts of ecologically sensitive land and related easements, covenants and servitudes to qualified donees other than private foundations.

Because of the amount of tax assistance offered and the difficulty of valuing such donations, it is proposed that the value of all ecological gifts be determined by a special process to be established by the Minister of the Environment. The value determined by the Minister of the Environment may be appealed to the Tax Court of Canada after an irrevocable gift has been made. This valuation process, together with the certification of the ecological importance of the property, will help to ensure that such donations are effectively and efficiently directed toward the protection of Canada's natural heritage.

The measures with respect to ecologically sensitive land are examples of how the tax system can be used to support the Government's overall environmental policy. Other examples include accelerated depreciation for energy conservation equipment and tax relief for ethanol and methanol used in gasoline-blended fuels.

**Related Provisions**: 118.1(12) — Reassessment beyond limitation period to give effect to certificate; 169(1.1) — Appeal of certificate value to Tax Court of Canada.

**Notes**: 118.1(10.1) added by 1998 Budget, effective for determinations and redeterminations made after February 23, 1998. If the fair market value of a property is determined by the CCPERB, that value will apply to the property for all income tax purposes related to charitable gifts for 2 years from the determination.

**(11) Assessments** — Notwithstanding subsections 152(4) to (5), such assessments or reassessments of a taxpayer's tax, interest or penalties payable under this Act for any taxation year shall be made as are necessary to give effect to a certificate issued under subsection 33(1) of the *Cultural Property Export and Import Act* or to a decision of a court resulting from an appeal made pursuant to section 33.1 of that Act.

### Proposed Amendment — 118.1(11)

**(11) Assessments** — Notwithstanding subsections 152(4) to (5), such assessments or reassessments of a taxpayer's tax, interest or penalties payable under this Act for any taxation year shall be made as are necessary to give effect

(a) to a certificate issued under subsection 33(1) of the *Cultural Property Export and Import Act* or to a decision of a court resulting from an appeal made pursuant to section 33.1 of that Act; or

(b) to a certificate issued under subsection (10.5) or to a decision of a court resulting from an appeal made pursuant to subsection 169(1.1) of this Act.

**Application**: The December 21, 2000 draft legislation, subsec. 60(6), will amend subsec. 118.1(11) to read as above, applicable in respect of gifts made, or proposed to be made, after February 27, 2000.

**Technical Notes**: Subsection 118.1(11) provides that an assessment of tax can be made at any time in order to give effect to a certificate issued by the Cultural Property Export Review Board or to a court decision which varies a determination of the Board. Subsection 165(1.2) provides that no objection may be made to an assessment made under subsection 118.1(11).

Subsection 118.1(11) is amended to extend its application, in respect of ecologically sensitive land, to an assessment of tax resulting from a certificate of fair market value issued by the Minister of the Environment or a decision of a court in respect of an appeal of a redetermination of that Minister under new subsection 169(1.1). Subsection 165(1.2) continues to apply to deny the right to object to an assessment made under subsection 118.1(11). A person's right of review of a determination of fair market value by the Minister of the Environment is provided instead by new subsections 118.1(10.4) and 169(1.1).

**Related Provisions**: 165(1.2) — No objection allowed to assessment under 118.1(11).

**Notes**: 118.1(11) added by 1995 cultural property bill (Bill C-93), in force July 12, 1996 (per Order in Council SI/96-73, *Canada Gazette*, Part II, Vol. 130, No. 15, p. 2573).

**(12) Ecological gifts [fair market value]** — For the purposes of section 207.31 and the definition "total ecological gifts" in subsection (1), the fair market value of a gift of a servitude, a covenant or an easement to which land is subject is deemed to be the greater of its fair market value otherwise determined and the amount by which the fair market value of the land is reduced as a result of the making of the gift.

### Proposed Amendment — 118.1(12)

**(12) Ecological gifts [fair market value]** — For the purpose of applying subparagraph 69(1)(b)(ii), subsection 70(5), section 207.31 and this section in respect of a gift described in the definition "total ecological gifts" in subsection (1) that is made by a taxpayer and that is a servitude, covenant or easement to which land is subject, the greater of

(a) the fair market value otherwise determined of the gift, and

(b) the amount by which the fair market value of the land is reduced as a result of the making of the gift

is deemed to be the fair market value (or, for the purpose of subsection (6), the fair market value otherwise determined) of the gift at the time the gift was made and, subject to subsection (6), to be the taxpayer's proceeds of disposition of the gift.

**Application**: Bill C-43 (First Reading September 20, 2000), subsec. 63(4), will amend subsec. 118.1(12) to read as above, applicable in respect of gifts made after February 27, 1995.

**Technical Notes**: Subsection 118.1(12) provides that the fair market value of a gift of a covenant, easement or servitude in respect of ecologically sensitive land will not be considered to be less than the decrease in value of the subject land that resulted from the making of the gift.

Subsection 118.1(12) is amended to clarify that such amount will also be, subject to the designation of an amount under subsection 118.1(6), the donor's proceeds of disposition for the purposes of calculating income and capital gains.

### Department of Finance news release, June 3, 1999:
*Clarifying Changes to Tax Rules Announced for Donations of Ecologically Sensitive Land*

Finance Minister Paul Martin today announced technical changes to the income tax rules applying to the donation of a servitude, covenant or easement in respect of ecologically sensitive land. The changes clarify the manner in which capital gains and losses on the disposition of the property that is the subject of a charitable gift are to be calculated.

The tax credit or deduction allowed to a donor upon making such a gift should be based on the gift's fair market value. However, the fair market value is often difficult to determine since there is no established market for easements, covenants or servitudes. Accordingly, a 1997 budget measure provided that the fair market value of such a gift be considered to be no less than the decrease in the fair market value of the related land as a result of the gift. The 1997 amendment did not, however, explicitly set out how to determine the cost of the related land that is allocable to the gift for the purpose of calculating any gain or loss that may arise on its disposition. The amendments announced today clarify how this allocation is to be made.

These amendments also clarify that the rules that apply in determining the value of an ecological gift would also apply in determining the donor's proceeds of disposition for calculating a capital gain or loss. Further, where there would be a capital gain, these amendments allow the donor to report a lesser gain and claim a correspondingly lesser charitable donations tax credit or deduction.

"Protection of Canada's environmental heritage is a responsibility for all Canadians," Minister Martin said. "Through the provision of tax incentives, the Government of Canada is encouraging private landowners to preserve this heritage on a voluntary basis."

Attached are the draft amendments to the *Income Tax Act* and a background note providing more details about how the rules apply. These amendments are proposed to apply to gifts made after February 27, 1995, the date on which these measures first became effective.

For further information: Ed Short, Tax Policy Branch, (613) 996-0599; Karl Littler, Executive Assistant to the Secretary of State, (613) 996-7861; Jean-Michel Catta, Public Affairs and Operations Division, (613) 996-8080.

*BACKGROUNDER*

The 1995 budget announced enhanced incentives for the donation of ecologically sensitive land to the Government of Canada, a provincial government, a Canadian municipality or an approved registered charity established for the purpose of protecting Canada's environmental heritage. Donations from individuals are eligible for the charitable donations tax credit, while those from corporations are eligible for a deduction from income. Besides transfers of title, landowners are able to donate covenants, easements and servitudes established under common law, the Civil Code in Quebec, or particular provincial or territorial legislation allowing for their establishment.

Normally, the value of a donated property is determined to be the price that a purchaser would pay for the property on the open market. As there is no established market for covenants, easements and servitudes, the fair market value of such restrictions on land use is difficult to determine. To provide greater certainty in making these valuations, the 1997 budget introduced a measure to deem the value of these gifts to be not less than the resulting decrease in the value of the land. That measure was implemented with application to gifts made after February 27, 1995.

Like other capital property, the value of a covenant, easement or servitude is also relevant in calculating the capital gain or loss that may arise on disposition. To provide taxpayers greater certainty in making this calculation, the amendments announced today will ensure that:

- a reasonable portion of the adjusted cost base of the land is to be allocated to the donated covenant, easement or servitude; and
- the proceeds of disposition for capital gains purposes are equal to the amount deemed for the purpose of the claim of a charitable donation deduction or credit.

For this purpose, an allocation of the adjusted cost base of the land to the gift, in proportion to the percentage decrease in the value of the land as a result of the donation, will be accepted as a reasonable allocation.

A provision is also added to provide a donor with the option of reporting a reduced amount of capital gain, provided that the value of the gift for the purposes of the charitable donations tax credit or deduction is reduced accordingly.

### Proposed Amendment — 118.1(12)

**(12) Ecological gifts [fair market value]** — For the purposes of applying subparagraph 69(1)(b)(ii), subsection 70(5), this section and section 207.31 in respect of a gift described in the definition "total ecological gifts" in subsection (1) that is made by an individual, the amount that is the fair market value (or, for the purpose of subsection (6), the fair market value otherwise determined) of the gift at the time the gift was made and, subject to subsection (6), the individual's proceeds of disposition of the gift, is deemed to be the amount determined by the Minister of the Environment to be

(a) where the gift is land, the fair market value of the gift or;

(b) where the gift is a servitude, covenant or easement to which land is subject, the greater of

(i) the fair market value otherwise determined of the gift, and

(ii) the amount by which the fair market value of the land is reduced as a result of the making of the gift.

**Application**: The December 21, 2000 draft legislation, subsec. 60(6), will amend subsec. 118.1(12) to read as above, applicable in respect of gifts made, or proposed to be made, after February 27, 2000.

**Technical Notes**: Subsection 118.1(12) provides that the fair market value of a gift by an individual of a covenant, easement or servitude in respect of ecologically sensitive land will not be considered to be less than the decrease in value of the subject land that resulted from the making of the gift. That amount is also, subject to the designation of an amount under subsection 118.1(6), the individual's proceeds of disposition for the purposes of calculating income and capital gains.

Subsection 118.1(12) is amended concurrently with the definition of "total ecological gifts" in subsection 118.1(1), to provide that the fair market value of ecologically sensitive land (including a covenant, an easement or a servitude) and, consequentially, the individual's proceeds of disposition, is deemed to be the amount determined by the Minister of the Environment to be its fair market value.

**Related Provisions**: 43(2) — Calculation for 118.1(12) also applies for determining capital gain or loss on disposition; 110.1(5) — Parallel rule for donation deduction for corporations; 118.1(10.1)–(10.5) — Determination of fair market value by Minister of the Environment.

**Notes**: 118.1(12) added by 1997 Budget, effective for gifts made after February 27, 1995 (i.e., retroactive to the introduction of the definition "total ecological gifts").

**(13) Non-qualifying securities** — For the purpose of this section (other than this subsection), where at any particular time an individual makes a gift (including a gift that, but for this subsection and subsection (4), would be deemed by subsection (5) to be made at the particular time) of a non-qualifying security of the individual and the gift is not an excepted gift,

   (a) except for the purpose of applying subsection (6) to determine the individual's proceeds of disposition of the security, the gift is deemed not to have been made;

   (b) if the security ceases to be a non-qualifying security of the individual at a subsequent time that is within 60 months after the particular time and the donee has not disposed of the security at or before the subsequent time, the individual is deemed to have made a gift to the donee of property at the subsequent time and the fair market value of that gift is deemed to be the lesser of the fair market value of the security at the subsequent time and the amount of the gift made at the particular time that would, but for this subsection, have been included in the individual's total charitable gifts or total Crown gifts for a taxation year;

   (c) if the security is disposed of by the donee within 60 months after the particular time and paragraph (b) does not apply to the security, the individual is deemed to have made a gift to the donee of property at the time of the disposition and the fair market value of that gift is deemed to be the lesser of the fair market value of any consideration (other than a non-qualifying security of the individual or a property that would be a non-qualifying security of the individual if the individual were alive at that time) received by the donee for the disposition and the amount of the gift made at the particular time that would, but for this subsection, have been included in the individual's total charitable gifts or total Crown gifts for a taxation year; and

   (d) a designation under subsection (6) or 110.1(3) in respect of the gift made at the particular time may be made in the individual's return of income for the year that includes the subsequent time referred to in paragraph (b) or the time of the disposition referred to in paragraph (c).

**Related Provisions**: 40(1.01) — Capital gains reserve on disposition of non-qualifying security; 88(1)(e.61) — Winding-up of subsidiary — gift deemed made by parent corporation; 110.1(6), (7) — Application to corporation; 118.1(14) — When security exchanged for another non-qualifying security; 118.1(15) — Death of donor; 118.1(18) — Definition of non-qualifying security; 118.1(19) — Excepted gift.

**Notes**: 118.1(13) provides that if an individual makes a gift of a "non-qualifying security" (see 118.1(18)), that gift will be ignored for the purpose of the donation credit. However, if the donee disposes of the security within 5 years or the security ceases to be a non-qualifying security of the individual within 5 years, the individual will be treated as having made a gift at that later time. The value of the later gift will be considered to be the lesser of two amounts. The first amount is the consideration received by the donee for the disposition (except to the extent the consideration is another non-qualifying security of the individual) or in the case of the security ceasing to be a non-qualifying security, its fair market value at that later time. The second amount is the value of the original gift as modified by 118.1(6).

118.1(13) does not apply to an "excepted gift", defined in 118.1(19) as a gift of a share to an arm's length donee that is not a private foundation, provided that if the donee is a charitable organization or a public foundation the donor deals at arm's length with all of the foundation's directors and officers.

The "denial of credit" in 118.1(13) replaces resolution (21) of the February 1997 Budget, which would have imposed a tax on the charity on the receipt of donations of non-qualifying securities.

118.1(13) added by 1997 Budget, effective for gifts made after July 1997.

**Forms**: RC4108: Registered charities and the Income Tax Act [guide].

**(14) Exchanged security** — Where a share (in this subsection referred to as the "new share") that is a non-qualifying security of an individual has been acquired by a donee referred to in subsection (13) in exchange for another share (in this subsection referred to as the "original share") that is a non-qualifying security of the individual by means of a transaction to which section 51, subparagraphs 85.1(1)(a)(i) and (ii) or section 86 or 87 applies, the new share is deemed for the purposes of this subsection and subsection (13) to be the same share as the original share.

**Related Provisions**: 110.1(6) — Application to corporation; 118.1(18) — Definition of non-qualifying security.

**Notes**: 118.1(14) added by 1997 Budget, effective for gifts made after July 1997.

**(15) Death of donor** — If, but for this subsection, an individual would be deemed by subsection (13) to have made a gift after the individual's death, for the purpose of this section the individual is deemed to have made the gift in the taxation year in which the individual died, except that the amount of interest payable under any provision of this Act is the amount that it would be if this subsection did not apply to the gift.

## Subdivision a — Computation of Tax: Individuals — S. 118.1

**Related Provisions**: 118.1(4) — Carryback of gift made in year of death; 152(4)(b)(vi) — Three-year extension to reassessment period; 161(1) — Imposition of interest on late payments of tax.

**Notes**: 118.1(15) added by 1997 Budget, effective for gifts made after July 1997.

**(16) Loanbacks** — For the purpose of this section, where

(a) at any particular time an individual makes a gift of property,

(b) if the property is a non-qualifying security of the individual, the gift is an excepted gift, and

(c) within 60 months after the particular time

(i) the donee holds a non-qualifying security of the individual that was acquired by the donee after the time that is 60 months before the particular time, or

(ii) where the individual and the donee do not deal at arm's length with each other,

(A) the individual or any person or partnership with which the individual does not deal at arm's length uses property of the donee under an agreement that was made or modified after the time that is 60 months before the particular time, and

(B) the property was not used in the carrying on of the donee's charitable activities,

the fair market value of the gift is deemed to be that value otherwise determined minus the total of all amounts each of which is the fair market value of the consideration given by the donee to acquire a non-qualifying security so held or the fair market value of such a property so used, as the case may be.

**Related Provisions**: 110.1(6) — Application to corporation; 118.1(17) — Ordering rule; 118.1(18) — Definition of non-qualifying security; 152(4)(b)(vi) — Three-year extension to reassessment period.

**Notes**: 118.1(16) added by 1997 Budget, effective where

(a) a non-qualifying security referred to in 118.1(16)(c)(i) is acquired after July 1997; or

(b) property referred to in 118.1(16)(c)(ii) has begun to be used after July 1997.

**Forms**: RC4108: Registered charities and the Income Tax Act [guide].

**(17) Ordering rule** — For the purpose of applying subsection (16) to determine the fair market value of a gift made at any time by a taxpayer, the fair market value of consideration given to acquire property described in subparagraph (16)(c)(i) or of property described in subparagraph (16)(c)(ii) is deemed to be that value otherwise determined minus any portion of it that has been applied under that subsection to reduce the fair market value of another gift made before that time by the taxpayer.

**Related Provisions**: 110.1(6) — Application to corporation.

**Notes**: 118.1(17) added by 1997 Budget, effective August 1997. References to (16)(b)(i) and (ii) corrected to (16)(c)(i) and (ii) by *Miscellaneous Statute Law Amendment Act, 1999*.

**(18) Non-qualifying security defined** — For the purposes of this section, "non-qualifying security" of an individual at any time means

(a) an obligation (other than an obligation of a financial institution to repay an amount deposited with the institution or an obligation listed on a prescribed stock exchange) of the individual or the individual's estate or of any person or partnership with which the individual or the estate does not deal at arm's length immediately after that time;

(b) a share (other than a share listed on a prescribed stock exchange) of the capital stock of a corporation with which the individual or the estate does not deal at arm's length immediately after that time; or

(c) any other security (other than a security listed on a prescribed stock exchange) issued by the individual or the estate or by any person or partnership with which the individual or the estate does not deal at arm's length immediately after that time.

**Related Provisions**: 110.1(6) — Application to corporation; 118.1(29) — Meaning of "financial institution".

**Notes**: 118.1(18) added by 1997 Budget, effective August 1997.

**(19) Excepted gift** — For the purposes of this section, a gift made by a taxpayer is an excepted gift if

(a) the security is a share;

(b) the donee is not a private foundation;

(c) the taxpayer deals at arm's length with the donee; and

(d) where the donee is a charitable organization or a public foundation, the taxpayer deals at arm's length with each director, trustee, officer and like official of the donee.

**Related Provisions**: 110.1(6) — Application to corporation; 251(1) — Meaning of arm's length.

**Notes**: 118.1(19) added by 1997 Budget, effective for gifts made after July 1997.

**(20) Financial institution defined** — For the purpose of subsection (18), "financial institution" means a corporation that is

(a) a member of the Canadian Payments Association; or

(b) a credit union that is a shareholder or member of a body corporate or organization that is a central for the purposes of the *Canadian Payments Association Act*.

**Related Provisions**: 110.1(6) — Application to corporation.

**Notes**: 118.1(20) added by 1997 Budget, effective August 1997.

**Definitions [s. 118.1]**: "adjusted cost base" — 54, 248(1); "amount", "appropriate percentage" — 248(1); "arm's length" — 251(1); "assessment", "business" — 248(1); "Canada" — 255; "capital property" — 54, 248(1); "charitable organization" — 149.1(1) [technically does not apply to 118.1]; "cost amount" — 248(1); "credit union" — 137(6), 248(1); "depreciable property" — 13(21), 248(1); "disposition", "employment" — 248(1); "excepted gift" — 118.1(19); "fair market value" — 118.1(13); "financial in-

## S. 118.1 — Income Tax Act, Part I, Division E

stitution" — 118.1(20); "fiscal period" — 249(2), 249.1; "individual", "insurer", "inventory", "legal representative" — 248(1); "life insurance policy", "life insurance policy in Canada" — 138(12), 248(1); "Minister" — 248(1); "month" — *Interpretation Act* 35(1); "non-qualifying security" — 118.1(18); "non-resident" — 248(1); "officer" — 248(1) [under "office"]; "person", "prescribed" — 248(1); "prescribed stock exchange" — Reg. 3200, 3201; "private foundation" — 149.1(1), 248(1); "property" — 248(1); "province" — *Interpretation Act* 35(1); "public foundation", "qualified donee" — 149.1(1), 248(1); "qualified pension income" — 118(7); "registered Canadian amateur athletic association", "registered charity" — 248(1); "registered retirement income fund" — 146.3(1), 248(1); "registered retirement savings plan" — 146(1), 248(1); "resident in Canada" — 250; "share", "shareholder" — 248(1); "tax payable" — 248(2); "taxable capital gain" — 38(a), 248(1); "taxable income" — 2(2), 248(1); "taxation year" — 249; "taxpayer" — 248(1); "that Minister" — 118.1(10.2); "total charitable gifts", "total Crown gifts", "total cultural gifts", "total ecological gifts", "total gifts" — 118.1(1); "trust" — 104(1), 248(1), (3); "writing" — *Interpretation Act* 35(1); "written" — *Interpretation Act* 35(1)"writing".

**Interpretation Bulletins [s. 118.1]**: IT-86R: Vow of perpetual poverty; IT-110R2: Deductible gifts and official donation receipts; IT-111R2: Annuities purchased from charitable organizations; IT-151R5: Scientific research and experimental development expenditures; IT-171R2: Non-resident individuals — computation of taxable income earned in Canada and non-refundable tax credits; IT-226R: Gift to a charity of a residual interest in real property or an equitable interest in a trust; IT-244R3: Gifts by individuals of life insurance policies as charitable donations; IT-326R3: Returns of deceased persons as "another person"; IT-393R2: Election re tax on rents and timber royalties — non-residents.

**Information Circulars [s. 118.1]**: 75-23: Tuition fees and charitable donations paid to privately supported schools; 80-10R: Operating a registered charity; 92-3: Guidelines for refunds beyond the normal three year period.

**118.2 (1) Medical expense credit** — For the purpose of computing the tax payable under this Part by an individual for a taxation year, there may be deducted an amount determined by the formula

$$A(B - C) - D$$

where

A is the appropriate percentage for the year;

B is the total of the individual's medical expenses that are proven by filing receipts therefor with the Minister, that were not included in determining an amount under this subsection or subsection 122.51(2) for a preceding taxation year and that were paid by either the individual or the individual's legal representative,

   (a) where the individual died in the year, within any period of 24 months that includes the day of death, and

   (b) in any other case, within any period of 12 months ending in the year;

C is the lesser of $1,500[10] and 3% of the individual's income for the year; and

---

[10]Indexed by s. 117.1 after 1988 — ed.

---

**Proposed Amendment — 118.2(1)C**
**Budget Supplementary Information, February 28, 2000**: [Dollar amount to be $1,637 for 2000. See under 117.1(1) — ed.]

D is 68% of the total of all amounts each of which is the amount, if any, by which

   (a) the income for the year of a person (other than the individual and the individual's spouse or common-law partner) in respect of whom an amount is included in computing the individual's deduction under this section for the year

exceeds

   (b) the amount used under paragraph (c) of the description of B in subsection 118(1) for the year.

**Related Provisions**: 110.7(1) — Residing in prescribed zone; 117(1) — Tax payable under this Part; 117.1(1) — Indexing for inflation; 118.3 — Mental or physical impairment; 118.4(1) — Severe and prolonged impairment; 118.4(2) — Reference to medical practitioner; 118.91 — Individual resident in Canada for part of the year; 118.92 — Ordering of credits; 118.93 — Credits in separate returns; 118.94 — Computing tax payable by a non-resident individual; 118.95(a) — Application in year individual becomes bankrupt; 122.51 — Refundable credit of up to $500; 257 — Formula cannot calculate to less than zero.

**Notes**: The effect of the credit, including a parallel provincial credit, is that medical expenses over the $1,678 (for 2001) (or "3% of net income") threshold entitle the taxpayer to a credit worth about 23% — equivalent to a deduction for a taxpayer in the lowest bracket. For detailed discussion see David M. Sherman, *Taxes, Health & Disabilities* (Carswell, 1995). Quebec provides a 20% credit but has abandoned the dollar limit to the 3% threshold, so that very high-income taxpayers are effectively precluded from claiming medical expenses for Quebec provincial tax purposes.

An additional credit for low-income earners is available in 122.51.

118.2(1)D(a) amended by 2000 same-sex partners bill to add reference to "common-law partner", effective for the 2001 and later taxation years, or earlier by election (see Notes to 248(1)"common-law partner").

118.2(1)D(b) amended by 1999 Budget, this version effective for 2000 and later taxation years. For 1999, read (b) as "$7,044". For 1998, read:

   (b) the total of $500 and the amount used under paragraph (c) of the description of B in subsection 118(1) for the year.

118.2(1)D(b) amended to add "the total of $500 and" by 1998 Budget, effective for 1998 and later taxation years. This was consequential on new 118(1)B(b.1), which effectively increased from $6,456 to $6,956 the amount that could be earned tax-free for 1998.

Opening words of 118.2(1)B amended by 1997 Budget bill (as amended before Third Reading) to add "or subsection 122.51(2)", effective for 1997 and later taxation years.

118.2(1) amended by 1992 Child Benefit bill, effective 1993, to add D to the calculation (replacing the notch provision formerly in 117(7)). For 1988 through 1992, read the calculation without " – D".

In 118.2(1)D(b), the reference to paragraph "(c)" is missing; the legislation as enacted reads "the amount used under paragraph of the description...". It is clearly intended to be para. (c), however, as indicated in the Department of Finance technical notes and in Revenue Canada's administration of this provision (T1 General income tax guide, line 331, and Interpretation Bulletin IT-519R, para. 18).

**Interpretation Bulletins**: IT-171R2: Non-resident individuals — computation of taxable income earned in Canada and non-refundable tax credits; IT-393R2: Election re tax on rents and timber royalties — non-residents; IT-519R2: Medical expense and disability tax credits and attendant care expense deduction.

**Information Circulars**: 92-3: Guidelines for refunds beyond the normal three year period.

**Forms**: RC4064: Information concerning people with disabilities [guide].

**(2) Medical expenses** — For the purposes of subsection (1), a medical expense of an individual is an amount paid

(a) **[medical and dental services]** — to a medical practitioner, dentist or nurse or a public or licensed private hospital in respect of medical or dental services provided to a person (in this subsection referred to as the "patient") who is the individual, the individual's spouse or common-law partner or a dependant of the individual (within the meaning assigned by subsection 118(6)) in the taxation year in which the expense was incurred;

(b) **[attendant or nursing home care]** — as remuneration for one full-time attendant (other than a person who, at the time the remuneration is paid, is the individual's spouse or common-law partner or is under 18 years of age) on, or for the full-time care in a nursing home of, the patient in respect of whom an amount would, but for paragraph 118.3(1)(c), be deductible under section 118.3 in computing a taxpayer's tax payable under this Part for the taxation year in which the expense was incurred;

(b.1) **[attendant]** — as remuneration for attendant care provided in Canada to the patient if

(i) the patient is a person in respect of whom an amount may be deducted under section 118.3 in computing a taxpayer's tax payable under this Part for the taxation year in which the expense was incurred,

(ii) no part of the remuneration is included in computing a deduction claimed in respect of the patient under section 63 or 64 or paragraph (b), (b.2), (c), (d) or (e) for any taxation year,

(iii) at the time the remuneration is paid, the attendant is neither the individual's spouse or common-law partner nor under 18 years of age, and

(iv) each receipt filed with the Minister to prove payment of the remuneration was issued by the payee and contains, where the payee is an individual, that individual's Social Insurance Number,

to the extent that the total of amounts so paid does not exceed $10,000 (or $20,000 if the individual dies in the year);

(b.2) **[group home care]** — as remuneration for the patient's care or supervision provided in a group home in Canada maintained and operated exclusively for the benefit of individuals who have a severe and prolonged impairment if

(i) because of the patient's impairment, the patient is a person in respect of whom an amount may be deducted under section 118.3 in computing a taxpayer's tax payable under this Part for the taxation year in which the expense is incurred,

(ii) no part of the remuneration is included in computing a deduction claimed in respect of the patient under section 63 or 64 or paragraph (b), (b.1), (c), (d) or (e) for any taxation year, and

(iii) each receipt filed with the Minister to prove payment of the remuneration was issued by the payee and contains, where the payee is an individual, that individual's Social Insurance Number;

(c) **[full-time attendant at home]** — as remuneration for one full-time attendant upon the patient in a self-contained domestic establishment in which the patient lives, if

(i) the patient is, and has been certified by a medical practitioner to be, a person who, by reason of mental or physical infirmity, is and is likely to be for a long-continued period of indefinite duration dependent on others for the patient's personal needs and care and who, as a result thereof, requires a full-time attendant,

(ii) at the time the remuneration is paid, the attendant is neither the individual's spouse or common-law partner nor under 18 years of age, and

(iii) each receipt filed with the Minister to prove payment of the remuneration was issued by the payee and contains, where the payee is an individual, that individual's Social Insurance Number;

(d) **[nursing home care]** — for the full-time care in a nursing home of the patient, who has been certified by a medical practitioner to be a person who, by reason of lack of normal mental capacity, is and in the foreseeable future will continue to be dependent on others for the patient's personal needs and care;

(e) **[school, institution, etc.]** — for the care, or the care and training, at a school, institution or other place of the patient, who has been certified by an appropriately qualified person to be a person who, by reason of a physical or mental handicap, requires the equipment, facilities or personnel specially provided by that school, institution or other place for the care, or the care and training, of individuals suffering from the handicap suffered by the patient;

(f) **[ambulance fees]** — for transportation by ambulance to or from a public or licensed private hospital for the patient;

(g) **[transportation]** — to a person engaged in the business of providing transportation services, to the extent that the payment is made for the transportation of

(i) the patient, and

(ii) one individual who accompanied the patient, where the patient was, and has been certified by a medical practitioner to be, incapable of travelling without the assistance of an attendant

from the locality where the patient dwells to a place, not less than 40 kilometres from that locality, where medical services are normally provided, or from that place to that locality, if

(iii) substantially equivalent medical services are not available in that locality,

(iv) the route travelled by the patient is, having regard to the circumstances, a reasonably direct route, and

(v) the patient travels to that place to obtain medical services for himself or herself and it is reasonable, having regard to the circumstances, for the patient to travel to that place to obtain those services;

(h) **[travel expenses]** — for reasonable travel expenses (other than expenses described in paragraph (g)) incurred in respect of the patient and, where the patient was, and has been certified by a medical practitioner to be, incapable of travelling without the assistance of an attendant, in respect of one individual who accompanied the patient, to obtain medical services in a place that is not less than 80 kilometres from the locality where the patient dwells if the circumstances described in subparagraphs (g)(iii), (iv) and (v) apply;

(i) **[devices]** — for or in respect of an artificial limb, iron lung, rocking bed for poliomyelitis victims, wheel chair, crutches, spinal brace, brace for a limb, iliostomy or colostomy pad, truss for hernia, artificial eye, laryngeal speaking aid, aid to hearing or artificial kidney machine, for the patient;

(i.1) **[devices for incontinence]** — for or in respect of diapers, disposable briefs, catheters, catheter trays, tubing or other products required by the patient by reason of incontinence caused by illness, injury or affliction;

(j) **[eyeglasses]** — for eye glasses or other devices for the treatment or correction of a defect of vision of the patient as prescribed by a medical practitioner or optometrist;

(k) **[various]** — for an oxygen tent or other equipment necessary to administer oxygen or for insulin, oxygen, liver extract injectible for pernicious anaemia or vitamin B12 for pernicious anaemia, for use by the patient as prescribed by a medical practitioner;

(l) **[guide dogs, etc.]** — on behalf of the patient who is blind or profoundly deaf or has a severe and prolonged impairment that markedly restricts the use of the patient's arms or legs,

(i) for an animal specially trained to assist the patient in coping with the impairment and provided by a person or organization one of whose main purposes is such training of animals,

(ii) for the care and maintenance of such an animal, including food and veterinary care,

(iii) for reasonable travel expenses of the patient incurred for the purpose of attending a school, institution or other facility that trains, in the handling of such animals, individuals who are so impaired, and

(iv) for reasonable board and lodging expenses of the patient incurred for the purpose of the patient's full-time attendance at a school, institution or other facility referred to in subparagraph (iii);

(l.1) **[transplant costs]** — on behalf of the patient who requires a bone marrow or organ transplant,

(i) for reasonable expenses (other than expenses described in subparagraph (ii)), including legal fees and insurance premiums, to locate a compatible donor and to arrange for the transplant, and

(ii) for reasonable travel, board and lodging expenses (other than expenses described in paragraphs (g) and (h)) of the donor (and one other person who accompanies the donor) and the patient (and one other person who accompanies the patient) incurred in respect of the transplant;

(l.2) **[alterations to home]** — for reasonable expenses relating to renovations or alterations to a dwelling of the patient who lacks normal physical development or has a severe and prolonged mobility impairment, to enable the patient to gain access to, or to be mobile or functional within, the dwelling;

**Proposed Addition — 118.2(2)(l.21)**

(l.21) **[home construction costs]** — for reasonable expenses, relating to the construction of the principal place of residence of the patient who lacks normal physical development or has a severe and prolonged mobility impairment, that can reasonably be considered to be incremental costs incurred to enable the patient to gain access to, or to be mobile or functional within, the patient's principal place of residence;

**Application**: The December 21, 2000 draft legislation, s. 61, will add para. 118.2(2)(l.21), applicable to 2000 *et seq.*

**Technical Notes**: Subsection 118.2(2) contains a list of expenditures which qualify as medical expenses. New paragraph 118.2(2)(l.21) adds to this list reasonable expenses, relating to the construction of the principal place of residence of an individual who lacks normal physical development or has a severe and prolonged mobility impairment, that can reasonably be considered to be incremental costs incurred to enable the individual to gain access to, or to be mobile or functional within, the individual's principal place of residence. As for all medical expenses, the portion of the expenses which is reimbursed (through special financial assistance, sales tax rebate or otherwise) does not qualify for the medical expenses tax credit, except to the extent that the reimbursement is required to be included in income and is not otherwise deductible in computing taxable income.

**Notes**: See also 146.01(1) "supplemental eligible amount" re using the Home Buyers' Plan for such costs.

This change may have already been allowed by the Courts. See Notes at end of 118.2(2) re the *Hillier* case.

**Notice of Ways and Means Motion, federal budget, February 28, 2000**: *Medical Expense Tax Credit*

(17) That, for the 2000 and subsequent taxation years, there be added to the list of expenses eligible for the medical expense tax credit the portion of reasonable expenses, relating to the construction of the principal place of residence of an individual who lacks normal physical development or has a severe and prolonged mobility impairment, that can reasonably be considered to be incremental costs incurred to enable the individual to gain access to, or to be mobile or functional within, the individual's principal place of residence.

**Federal budget, supplementary information, February 28, 2000**: *The Medical Expense Tax Credit and New Homes*

The medical expense tax credit (METC) provides tax recognition for above-average medical expenses incurred by individuals. For 2000, the METC reduces the federal tax of a claimant by 17 per cent of qualifying unreimbursed medical expenses in excess of the lesser of $1,637 and 3 per cent of net income.

Currently, an individual who lacks normal physical development or has a severe and prolonged mobility impairment may be eligible for the METC in respect of renovation costs incurred to enable the individual to gain access to or to be mobile or functional within the home. The budget proposes to extend tax assistance to such individuals who incur reasonable expenses relating to the construction of a principal place of residence where the expenses can reasonably be considered to be incremental costs incurred to enable the individual to gain access to or to be mobile or functional within the home.

(l.3) **[lip reading and sign language training]** — for reasonable expenses relating to rehabilitative therapy, including training in lip reading and sign language, incurred to adjust for the patient's hearing or speech loss;

(l.4) **[sign language services]** — on behalf of the patient who has a speech or hearing impairment, for sign language interpretation services, to the extent that the payment is made to a person engaged in the business of providing such services;

(l.5) **[moving expenses]** — for reasonable moving expenses (within the meaning of subsection 62(3), but not including any expense deducted under section 62 for any taxation year) of the patient, who lacks normal physical development or has a severe and prolonged mobility impairment, incurred for the purpose of the patient's move to a dwelling that is more accessible by the patient or in which the patient is more mobile or functional, if the total of the expenses claimed under this paragraph by all persons in respect of the move does not exceed $2,000;

(l.6) **[driveway alterations]** — for reasonable expenses relating to alterations to the driveway of the principal place of residence of the patient who has a severe and prolonged mobility impairment, to facilitate the patient's access to a bus;

(l.7) **[van for wheelchair]** — for a van that, at the time of its acquisition or within 6 months after that time, has been adapted for the transportation of the patient who requires the use of a wheelchair, to the extent of the lesser of $5,000 and 20% of the amount by which

(i) the amount paid for the acquisition of the van

exceeds

(ii) the portion, if any, of the amount referred to in subparagraph (i) that is included because of paragraph (m) in computing the individual's deduction under this section for any taxation year;

(l.8) **[caregiver training]** — for reasonable expenses (other than amounts paid to a person who was at the time of the payment the individual's spouse or common-law partner or a person under 18 years of age) to train the individual, or a person related to the individual, if the training relates to the mental or physical infirmity of a person who

(i) is related to the individual, and

(ii) is a member of the individual's household or is dependent on the individual for support;

(l.9) **[therapy]** — as remuneration for therapy provided to the patient because of the patient's severe and prolonged impairment, if

(i) because of the patient's impairment, an amount may be deducted under section 118.3 in computing a taxpayer's tax payable under this Part for the taxation year in which the remuneration is paid,

(ii) the therapy is prescribed by, and administered under the general supervision of,

(A) a medical doctor or a psychologist, in the case of mental impairment, and

(B) a medical doctor or an occupational therapist, in the case of a physical impairment,

(iii) at the time the remuneration is paid, the payee is neither the individual's spouse nor an individual who is under 18 years of age, and

(iv) each receipt filed with the Minister to prove payment of the remuneration was issued by the payee and contains, where the payee is an individual, that individual's Social Insurance Number;

(l.91) **[tutoring services]** — as remuneration for tutoring services that are rendered to, and are supplementary to the primary education of, the patient who

(i) has a learning disability or a mental impairment, and

(ii) has been certified in writing by a medical practitioner to be a person who, because of that disability or impairment, requires those services,

if the payment is made to a person ordinarily engaged in the business of providing such services to individuals who are not related to the payee.

(m) **[prescribed devices]** — for any device or equipment for use by the patient that

(i) is of a prescribed kind,

(ii) is prescribed by a medical practitioner,

(iii) is not described in any other paragraph of this subsection, and

(iv) meets such conditions as may be prescribed as to its use or the reason for its acquisition,

to the extent that the amount so paid does not exceed the amount, if any, prescribed in respect of the device or equipment;

(n) **[drugs]** — for drugs, medicaments or other preparations or substances (other than those described in paragraph (k)) manufactured, sold or represented for use in the diagnosis, treatment or prevention of a disease, disorder, abnormal physical state, or the symptoms thereof or in restoring, correcting or modifying an organic function, purchased for use by the patient as prescribed by a medical practitioner or dentist and as recorded by a pharmacist;

(o) **[lab tests]** — for laboratory, radiological or other diagnostic procedures or services together with necessary interpretations, for maintaining health, preventing disease or assisting in the diagnosis or treatment of any injury, illness or disability, for the patient as prescribed by a medical practitioner or dentist;

(p) **[dentures]** — to a person authorized under the laws of a province to carry on the business of a dental mechanic, for the making or repairing of an upper or lower denture, or for the taking of impressions, bite registrations and insertions in respect of the making, producing, constructing and furnishing of an upper or lower denture, for the patient; or

(q) **[health plan premiums]** — as a premium, contribution or other consideration under a private health services plan in respect of one or more of the individual, the individual's spouse or common-law partner and any member of the individual's household with whom the individual is connected by blood relationship, marriage or adoption, except to the extent that the premium, contribution or consideration is deducted under subsection 20.01(1) in computing an individual's income from a business for any taxation year.

**Related Provisions**: 20(1)(qq), (rr) — Business deduction for disability-related modifications to buildings and disability-related equipment; 20.01 — Deduction from business income for private health plan premiums; 63(3)"child care expense"(d) — Medical expenses are not child care expenses; 64 — Deduction for part-time attendant care; 110.7(3) — Northern Canadian residents — trips to obtain medical services; 118.2(3) — Deemed medical expense; 118.2(4) — Use of own vehicle for transportation under (2)(g); 118.3(2) — Dependant having impairment; 251(6) — Meaning of "connected by blood relationship, marriage or adoption".

**Notes**: The term "nursing home" in 118.2(2)(b) does not include a retirement residence that provides 24-hour nursing care: *Miles*, [2000] 2 C.T.C. 2165 (TCC). This recognizes that the Courts have allowed much more than the previous administrative policy of 5¢/km: see *Enns*, [1996] 2 C.T.C. 2630 (TCC), and *Watt*, [1997] 2 C.T.C. 2651 (TCC).

118.2(2)(l.2) can apply to construction of a new home rather than just renovations to an existing home: *Hillier*, [2000] 3 C.T.C. 2367 (TCC); *Rosen*, [2000] 3 C.T.C. 2640 (TCC).

Per a December 1999 CCRA Fact Sheet, travel expenses under 118.2(2)(h) can optionally be calculated using a simplified calculation without receipts: $11/meal (up to $33/day); and vehicle expenses per qualifying km driven (to cover both ownership and operating expenses), using the table in the Notes to 62(3).

For a detailed discussion of the eligible expenses, see David M. Sherman, *Taxes, Health & Disabilities* (Carswell, 1995).

118.2(2)(a) amended by 1992 Child Benefit bill, effective 1993, to allow medical expenses for dependent children to continue to be claimed despite the elimination of the personal credit for dependent children.

118.2(2)(b), (b.1), (c), (l.8) and (q) amended by 2000 same-sex partners bill to add reference to "common-law partner", effective for the 2001 and later taxation years, or earlier by election (see Notes to 248(1)"common-law partner").

118.2(2)(b) amended and (b.1) added by 1991 Budget/technical bill, effective for expenses incurred after 1990.

118.2(2)(b.1)(ii) amended by 1999 Budget, effective for 1999 and later taxation years. For 1997-98, read:

(ii) no amount is included under section 63 or 64 or paragraph (b), (c), (d) or (e) in computing a deduction claimed in respect of the patient for the taxation year in which the remuneration was paid,

118.2(2)(b.1) amended by 1997 Budget, effective for 1997 and later taxation years, to change $5,000 and $10,000 in the closing words to $10,000 and $20,000 respectively.

118.2(2)(b.2) added by 1999 Budget, effective for 1999 and later taxation years.

118.2(2)(c)(ii), (iii) amended by 1991 Budget/technical bill, effective for expenses incurred after 1990.

118.2(2)(h) corrected by 1991 Budget/technical bill, retroactive to 1988, to ensure that an amount can be claimed when the patient travels alone.

118.2(2)(i) amended and (i.1) added by 1991 Budget/technical bill, effective for expenses incurred after 1990.

118.2(2)(l) amended by 1991 Budget/technical bill, effective for expenses incurred after 1990.

118.2(2)(l.1) added by 1989 Budget, effective 1988. For other instances of deductible legal expenses, see Notes to 60(o).

118.2(2)(l.2) added by 1989 Budget, effective 1988, and amended by 1991 Budget/technical bill, effective for expenses incurred after 1990.

118.2(2)(l.3) added by 1992 Budget/technical bill, effective 1992.

118.2(2)(l.4), (l.5), (l.6) and (l.7) added by 1997 Budget, effective for 1997 and later taxation years.

118.2(2)(l.8) added by 1998 Budget, effective for 1998 and later taxation years. See also 118(1)B(c.1) for a credit for caring for elderly relatives.

118.2(2)(l.9), (l.91) added by 1999 Budget, effective for 1999 and later taxation years.

Closing words of 118.2(2)(m) added by 1997 Budget, effective for 1997 and later taxation years.

118.2(2)(m) amended by 1991 Budget/technical bill, effective December 17, 1991.

118.2(2)(q) amended by 1998 Budget to add everything from "except to the extent that...", effective for 1998 and later taxation years. A deduction under 20.01 will often be preferable to a credit under 118.2(2)(q), either because the taxpayer is not otherwise over the 3%/$1,678 (2001) threshold in 118.2(1)C, or because the taxpayer is in a higher bracket than the 16% (federal) rate at which the credit applies.

See also Notes to Reg. 5700.

**Regulations**: 5700 (prescribed device or equipment, for 118.2(2)(m)).

**Interpretation Bulletins**: IT-339R2: Meaning of "private health services plan"; IT-393R2: Election re tax on rents and timber royalties — non-residents; IT-519R2: Medical expense and disability tax credits and attendant care expense deduction.

**Information Circulars**: 82-2R2: SIN legislation that relates to the preparation of information slips (re 118.2(2)(b.1)(iv), (c)(iii)).

**Forms**: RC4064: Information concerning people with disabilities [guide].

**(3) Deemed medical expense** — For the purposes of subsection (1),

(a) any amount included in computing an individual's income for a taxation year from an office or employment in respect of a medical expense described in subsection (2) paid or provided by an employer at a particular time shall be deemed to be a medical expense paid by the individual at that time; and

(b) there shall not be included as a medical expense of an individual any expense to the extent that

(i) the individual,

(ii) the person referred to in subsection (2) as the patient,

(iii) any person related to a person referred to in subparagraph (i) or (ii), or

(iv) the legal representative of any person referred to in any of subparagraphs (i) to (iii)

is entitled to be reimbursed for the expense, except to the extent that the amount of the reimbursement is required to be included in computing income and is not deductible in computing taxable income.

**Related Provisions**: 251(2) — Related persons.

**Notes**: The reference to a person related to the patient in 118.2(3)(b)(iii) covers a reimbursement that is provided under a health care plan that covers family members. For example, a father might be claiming expenses for a child, while the mother is entitled to reimbursement through her employer-paid drug plan.

118.2(3)(b) amended by 1997 Budget, effective for 1997 and later taxation years. For 1992 to 1996, read:

> (b) there shall not be included as a medical expense of an individual any expense for which the individual, the person referred to in subsection (2) as the patient or the legal representative of either of them has been or is entitled to be reimbursed, except to the extent that the amount thereof is required to be included in computing income under this Part and cannot be deducted in computing taxable income.

118.2(3)(b) amended by 1992 technical bill, effective 1992, to add "the person referred to in subsection (3) as the patient" and "is not deductible in computing taxable income". The changes prevent certain double-counting that might otherwise be available.

**Interpretation Bulletins**: IT-339R2: Meaning of "private health services plan"; IT-393R2: Election re tax on rents and timber royalties — non-residents; IT-519R2: Medical expense and disability tax credits and attendant care expense deduction.

**(4) Deemed payment of medical expenses** — Where, in circumstances in which a person engaged in the business of providing transportation services is not readily available, an individual makes use of a vehicle for a purpose described in paragraph (2)(g), the individual or the individual's legal representative shall be deemed to have paid to a person engaged in the business of providing transportation services, in respect of the operation of the vehicle, such amount as is reasonable in the circumstances.

**Definitions [s. 118.2]**: "amount", "appropriate percentage", "business" — 248(1); "carrying on business" — 253; "common-law partner" — 248(1); "connected" — 251(6); "dentist" — 118.4(2); "employment", "individual", "legal representative" — 248(1); "medical practitioner" — 118.4(2); "Minister" — 248(1); "nurse" — 118.4(2); "office" — 248(1); "optometrist" — 118.4(2); "patient" — 118.2(2)(a); "person", "prescribed", "private health services plan" — 248(1); "province" — *Interpretation Act* 35(1); "related" — 251(2); "resident in Canada" — 250; "self-contained domestic establishment" — 248(1); "tax payable" — 248(2); "taxation year" — 249; "taxpayer" — 248(1).

**Interpretation Bulletins**: IT-326R3: Returns of deceased persons as "another person"; IT-518R: Food, beverages and entertainment expenses.

**118.3 (1) Credit for mental or physical impairment** — Where

(a) an individual has a severe and prolonged mental or physical impairment,

(a.1) the effects of the impairment are such that the individual's ability to perform a basic activity of daily living is markedly restricted,

## S. 118.3(1)(a.1) — Income Tax Act, Part I, Division E

### Proposed Amendment — 118.3(1)(a.1)

(a.1) the effects of the impairment are such that the individual's ability to perform a basic activity of daily living is markedly restricted or would be markedly restricted but for therapy that

(i) is essential to sustain a vital function of the individual,

(ii) is required to be administered at least three times each week for a total duration averaging not less than 14 hours a week, and

(iii) cannot reasonably be expected to be of significant benefit to persons who are not so impaired.

**Application**: The December 21, 2000 draft legislation, subsec. 62(2), will amend para. 118.3(1)(a.1) to read as above, applicable to 2000 et seq.

**Technical Notes**: To be eligible for the disability tax credit (DTC) provided under section 118.3, an individual must be markedly restricted in the activities of daily living. Even with the use of appropriate devices, medication or therapy, an individual must be either blind or generally unable to perform certain fundamental functions to qualify for the credit.

Paragraphs 118.3(1)(a.1) and (a.2) are amended to extend eligibility for the DTC to individuals who would be so markedly restricted but for therapy administered to them at least three times each week for a total duration averaging not less than 14 hours a week in order to sustain one of their vital functions. Examples of taxpayers who will benefit from this extension include individuals with severe kidney disease requiring dialysis and persons with severe cystic fibrosis requiring clapping therapy in order to properly breathe.

**Notice of Ways and Means Motion, federal budget, February 28, 2000**: *Disability Tax Credit*

(14) That, for the 2000 and subsequent taxation years, the disability tax credit be extended to an individual

(a) who has, and has been certified to have, a severe and prolonged mental or physical impairment, and

(b) who has been certified by a medical doctor to be a person whose ability to perform a basic activity of daily living would all or substantially all of the time be markedly restricted but for therapy (other than therapy that can reasonably be expected to be of benefit to persons who are not so impaired) that is

(i) essential to sustain a vital function of the individual, and

(ii) required to be administered at least three times each week for a total period averaging not less than 14 hours a week.

**Federal budget, supplementary information, February 28, 2000**: *Enhancing the Disability Tax Credit*

The disability tax credit (DTC) recognizes the effect of a severe and prolonged disability on an individual's ability to pay tax. It provides tax relief to over 500,000 claimants at an annual cost of $280 million.

To be eligible for the DTC, an individual must have a severe and prolonged disability that markedly restricts the ability to perform a basic activity of daily living.

The basic activities of daily living include perceiving, thinking and remembering, feeding and dressing oneself, speaking, hearing, eliminating and walking. An individual's ability to perform these activities is markedly restricted only where, even with the use of appropriate devices, medication and therapy, the individual is blind, or unable to perform the activity.

Consistent with representations made by organizations representing persons with disabilities, the budget proposes extending eligibility for the DTC to individuals who must undergo therapy several times each week totalling at least 14 hours per week in order to sustain their vital functions. In such cases, the severity of the disability is evident in the requirement for extensive therapy that is essential to the individual's survival. Examples of persons who may be eligible for the DTC under the proposed change include individuals with severe kidney disease requiring dialysis in order to prevent renal failure, and individuals with severe cystic fibrosis requiring clapping therapy in order to breathe. It is estimated that this change will increase the number of persons eligible for the DTC by about 18,000, at a cost of $13 million annually.

**Notes**: This copies a change that took effect in Quebec as of 1999 for Quebec provincial tax purposes, under amendments to *Taxation Act* s. 752.0.17(b) first announced in the March 1999 Quebec budget (Bill 97, Dec. 16, 1999).

(a.2) in the case of

(i) a sight impairment, a medical doctor or an optometrist,

### Proposed Addition — 118.3(1)(a.2)(i.1)

(i.1) a speech impairment, a medical doctor or a speech-language pathologist,

**Application**: The December 21, 2000 draft legislation, subsec. 62(3), will add subpara. 118.3(1)(a.2)(i.1), applicable to certifications made after October 17, 2000.

**Technical Notes**: Paragraph 118.3(1)(a.2) is further amended to authorize speech-language pathologists to certify a severe and prolonged speech impairment.

**Notice of Ways and Means Motion, Economic Statement, October 18, 2000**: (6) That

(c) after October 17, 2000, a person authorized to practice as a speech-language pathologist be allowed to certify the existence of a severe and prolonged speech impairment for the purpose of the disability tax credit.

(ii) a hearing impairment, a medical doctor or an audiologist,

(iii) an impairment with respect to an individual's ability in feeding and dressing themself, or in walking, a medical doctor or an occupational therapist,

(iv) an impairment with respect to an individual's ability in perceiving, thinking and remembering, a medical doctor or a psychologist, and

(v) an impairment not referred to in any of subparagraphs (i) to (iv), a medical doctor

has certified in prescribed form that the impairment is a severe and prolonged mental or physical impairment the effects of which are such that the individual's ability to perform a basic activity of daily living is markedly restricted,

> **Proposed Amendment — 118.3(1)(a.2) closing words**
>
> has certified in prescribed form that the impairment is a severe and prolonged mental or physical impairment the effects of which are such that the individual's ability to perform a basic activity of daily living is markedly restricted or would be markedly restricted but for therapy referred to in paragraph (a.1),
>
> **Application**: The December 21, 2000 draft legislation, subsec. 62(4), will amend the closing words of para. 118.3(1)(a.2) to read as above, applicable to 2000 *et seq.*
>
> **Technical Notes**: See under 118.3(1)(a.1).

(b) the individual has filed for a taxation year with the Minister the certificate described in paragraph (a.2), and

(c) no amount in respect of remuneration for an attendant or care in a nursing home, in respect of the individual, is included in calculating a deduction under section 118.2 (otherwise than because of paragraph 118.2(2)(b.1)) for the year by the individual or by any other person,

for the purposes of computing the tax payable under this Part by the individual for the year, there may be deducted an amount determined by the formula

$$A \times \$4,118^{18}$$

where

A is the appropriate percentage for the year.

> **Proposed Amendment — 118.3(1) after (c)**
>
> there may be deducted in computing the individual's tax payable under this Part for the year the amount determined by the formula
>
> $$A \times (B + C)$$
>
> where
>
> A is the appropriate percentage for the year,
>
> B is $6,000, and
>
> C is
>
> (a) where the individual has not attained the age of 18 years before the end of the year, the amount, if any, by which
>
> (i) $3,500
>
> exceeds
>
> (ii) the amount, if any, by which
>
> (A) the total of all amounts each of which is an amount paid in the year for the care or supervision of the individual and included in computing a deduction under section 63, 64 or 118.2 for a taxation year
>
> exceeds
>
> (B) $2,050, and
>
> (b) in any other case, zero.
>
> **Application**: The December 21, 2000 draft legislation, subsec. 62(5), will amend the portion of subsec. 118.3(1) after para. (c) to read as above, applicable to 2000 *et seq.*, except that, in its application to 2000, the references to "$6,000", "$3,500" and "$2050" in the descriptions of B and C in the formula, as amended, shall be read as references to "$4,293", "$2,941" and "$2,000", respectively.
>
> **Technical Notes**: Subsection 118.3(1) also provides the formula for calculating the DTC. Currently, under the formula, the amount of the credit is equal to 17% of $4,293. The amendment adds another component ("C") to the formula to provide, starting in 2000, a supplement amount of $2,941 for each disabled child under the age of 18 years at the end of the year. The supplement amount is reduced by the excess, over $2,000, of the total of child care and attendant care expenses paid in the year and claimed for income tax purposes in respect of the child. In 2001, the disability basic and supplement amounts are, after indexing, increased to $6,000 and $3,500, respectively. The $2,000 care expense threshold for 2001 is increased, through indexing, to $2,050.
>
> **Notice of Ways and Means Motion, Economic Statement, October 18, 2000**: (6) That
>
> (a) the amount on which the basic disability tax credit is calculated be increased from $4,293 for 2000 to $6,000 for 2001 (indexed after 2001),
>
> (b) in respect of the supplement to the disability tax credit described in subparagraph (15)(a) of the Notice of Ways and Means Motion to amend the *Income Tax Act* tabled by the Minister of Finance in the House of Commons on February 28, 2000 (in this Notice referred to as the "2000 Budget Notice"), the amount on which the supplement is calculated be increased from $2,941 for 2000 to $3,500 for 2001 (indexed after 2001), and
>
> **Minister's Speech, Economic Statement, October 18, 2000**: Mr. Speaker, this Government has always understood that there are certain priorities that cannot be deferred. Assisting Canadians with disabilities is one of these. Indeed, even when we were in deficit, we took action. We have enriched the tax credit for infirm dependants, enhanced the medical expense credit, increased the child care expense deduction for children with disabilities and expanded eligibility for the disability tax credit.
>
> Today we will do more. We will further enrich the amount for the infirm dependent tax credit [118(1)B(d) — ed.] from $2,386 to $3,500; we will similarly increase the supplement amount for the disability tax credit for children with severe disabilities [118.3(2) — ed.] from $2,941 to $3,500; and we will increase the amount for the disability tax credit [118.3(1) — ed.] from $4,293 to $6,000.

---

[18] Indexed by s. 117.1 after 1991 — ed.

S. 118.3(1)                Income Tax Act, Part I, Division E

**Notice of Ways and Means Motion, federal budget, February 28, 2000**: (15) That, for the 2000 and subsequent taxation years,

(a) a $2,941 supplement (indexed after 2000) be added in computing the disability amount that may be claimed in respect of a child who has not attained 18 years of age before the end of the year, and

(b) the amount of the supplement be reduced by the amount by which the total of child care and attendant care expenses claimed for the year in respect of the child exceeds $2,000 (indexed after 2000).

**Federal budget, supplementary information, February 28, 2000**: *Assistance for Caregivers of Children with Severe Disabilities*

The infirm dependant credit and caregiver credit provide tax assistance for the care of infirm dependent adult relatives and seniors. This budget provides additional tax assistance for families caring for children with severe disabilities through a supplement for children eligible for the DTC. The supplement amount will be $2,941 and will reduce federal taxes payable by up to $500. The $500 supplement credit will be in addition to the $730 federal tax value of the disability tax credit as of January 1, 2000. The $2,941 supplement amount will be reduced by the amount of child care expenses and attendant care expenses claimed, in respect of the child, exceeding $2,000. This reduction will target tax assistance to families providing unpaid care for children with severe disabilities. The supplement is reduced to zero when child care and attendant care expenses reach $4,941. It is estimated that this supplement will benefit about 40,000 children eligible for the DTC at a cost of $20 million annually.

**Related Provisions**: 6(16) — Non-taxable disability-related employment benefits; 108(1) — Preferred beneficiary election available after 1995 only to beneficiary with severe and prolonged impairment; 117.1(1) — Indexing for inflation; 118.2 — Credit for medical expenses; 118.3(4) — Additional information requested by CCRA; 118.4(1) — Meaning of severe and prolonged impairment; 118.4(2) — Reference to medical practitioner; 118.6(3) — Education credit for disabled individuals; 118.8 — Transfer of unused credits to spouse; 118.91 — Individual resident in Canada for part of the year; 118.92 — Ordering of credits; 118.93 — Credits in separate returns; 118.94 — Computing tax payable by a non-resident individual; 118.95(b) — Application in year individual becomes bankrupt.

**Notes**: For a detailed review of the case law to mid-1995 on the eligibility for the disability credit, see David M. Sherman, *Taxes, Health & Disabilities* (Carswell, 1995). Cases on this issue under the Tax Court's Informal Procedure continue to be released almost every week. A few such cases have reached the Federal Court of Appeal, which ruled in *Johnston*, [1998] 2 C.T.C. 262, that this section should be given a "humane and compassionate" interpretation.

Dollar figure changed from $3,236 to $4,118 by 1991 technical bill, effective 1991. The 1991 Budget, the Department of Finance's technical notes, and Revenue Canada's T1 General Return (line 316) all indicate an intention that the $4,118 figure apply for 1991 (and, thus, $4,233 for 1992–1999). Technically, however, subsection 117.1(1) provides for the figure to be indexed from 1988. See Notes to 117.1(1).

Including the indexing factor and reduced provincial tax for all provinces other than Quebec, the value of the $730 (for 2000) disability credit is approximately $1,100. See the table preceding s. 118, the tables in the introductory pages of the book, and the Notes at the beginning of 118(1).

118.3(1)(a.2)(iii) renumbered as (v), and (iii) and (iv) added, by 1998 Budget, effective for certifications made after February 24, 1998.

118.3(1)(a.2) amended, effectively to add subpara. (ii) (certification by an audiologist), by 1997 Budget, effective for certifications made after February 18, 1997.

118.3 amended in 1991. See Notes at end of s. 118.3.

**Interpretation Bulletins**: IT-394R2: Preferred beneficiary election. See also list at end of s. 118.3.

**Information Circulars**: 92-3: Guidelines for refunds beyond the normal three year period.

**Forms**: T2201: Disability tax credit information; RC4064: Information concerning people with disabilities [guide].

**(2) Dependant having impairment** — Where

(a) an individual has, in respect of a person (other than a person in respect of whom the person's spouse or common-law partner deducts for a taxation year an amount under section 118 or 118.8) who is resident in Canada at any time in the year and who is entitled to deduct an amount under subsection (1) for the year,

(i) claimed for the year a deduction under subsection 118(1) because of

(A) paragraph (b) of the description of B in that subsection, or

(B) paragraph (c.1) or (d) of that description where the person is the individual's parent, grandparent, child or grandchild, or

**Proposed Amendment — 118.3(2)(a)(i)(B)**

(B) paragraph (c.1) or (d) of that description where the person is a parent, grandparent, child, grandchild, brother, sister, aunt, uncle, nephew or niece of the individual, or of the individual's spouse or common-law partner, or

**Application**: The December 21, 2000 draft legislation, subsec. 62(6), will amend cl. 118.3(2)(a)(i)(B) to read as above, applicable to 2000 *et seq.*

**Technical Notes**: Subsection 118.3(2) provides criteria for determining the entitlement of a supporting individual of a disabled person to claim that person's unused disability tax credit. Currently, a supporting individual who is a parent, grandparent, child or grandchild of a disabled person may claim that person's unused disability tax credit (DTC) where a caregiver credit or an infirm dependant credit may be claimed by the individual in respect of the disabled person. The amendment extends the DTC transferability to other relatives of the disabled person who may claim the caregiver credit or the infirm dependant credit in respect of the disabled person. These include a supporting individual who is a brother, sister, aunt, uncle, nephew or niece of the disabled person, or of the spouse or common-law partner of the disabled person.

**Notice of Ways and Means Motion, federal budget, February 28, 2000**: (16) That, for the 2000 and subsequent taxation years, the list of relatives to whom the unused portion of an individual's disability tax credit may be transferred in certain circumstances for use against Canadian tax payable be expanded to include a

Subdivision a — Computation of Tax: Individuals S. 118.3(4)(a)

person who is a brother, sister, aunt, uncle, nephew or niece of the individual or of the individual's spouse.

**Federal budget, supplementary information, February 28, 2000**: *Enhancing the Disability Tax Credit*

. . . .

The budget also proposes to expand the list of relatives to whom the DTC can be transferred, making it consistent with the medical expense tax credit rules. As a consequence, unused amounts of the DTC may be transferred to individuals supporting a brother, sister, aunt, uncle, niece or nephew, as well as to individuals supporting a spouse, child, grandchild, parent or grandparent.

(ii) could have claimed for the year a deduction referred to in subparagraph (i) in respect of the person if

(A) the person had no income for the year and had attained the age of 18 years before the end of the year, and

(B) in the case of a deduction referred to in clause (i)(A), the individual were not married or not in a common-law partnership, and

(b) no amount in respect of remuneration for an attendant, or care in a nursing home, because of that person's mental or physical impairment, is included in calculating a deduction under section 118.2 (otherwise than under paragraph 118.2(2)(b.1)) for the year by the individual or by any other person,

there may be deducted, for the purpose of computing the tax payable under this Part by the individual for the year, the amount, if any, by which

(c) the amount deductible under subsection (1) in computing that person's tax payable under this Part for the year

exceeds

(d) the amount of that person's tax payable under this Part for the year computed before any deductions under this Division (other than sections 118 and 118.7).

**Related Provisions**: 63(1)(e)(ii)(A)(II), 63(2)(b)(i)(B), 63(3)"child care expense"(c)(i)(B) — Higher child care expenses deduction for disabled child over 7; 118.3(4) — Additional information requested by CCRA; 118.8 — Transfer of disability credit to spouse; 118.91 — Individual resident in Canada for part of the year; 118.92 — Ordering of credits; 118.93 — Credits in separate returns; 118.94 — Computing tax payable by a non-resident individual; 118.95(b) — Application in year individual becomes bankrupt.

**Notes**: 118.3(2)(a) amended by 2000 same-sex partners bill to add references to "common-law partner" and "common-law partnership", effective for the 2001 and later taxation years, or earlier by election (see Notes to 248(1)"common-law partner").

118.3(2)(a) amended by 1998 Budget, effective for 1998 and later taxation years. The substantive change was to add reference to 118(1)B(c.1). For earlier years, read:

(a) an individual has, in respect of a person (other than a person in respect of whom the person's spouse deducts for the year an amount under section 118 or 118.8) who is resident in Canada at any time in a taxation year and who is entitled to deduct an amount under subsection 118.3 (1) for the year,

claimed for the year a deduction under subsection 118(1) because of

(i) paragraph (b) of the description of B in subsection 118(1), or

(ii) paragraph (d) of the description of B in subsection 118(1) where that person is the individual's child or grandchild,

or, where that person is the individual's parent, grandparent, child or grandchild, could have claimed such a deduction if the individual were not married and that person had no income for the year and had attained the age of 18 years before the end of the year, and

Closing words of 118.3(2)(a) amended by 1993 technical bill, effective for 1993 and later taxation years, to add the words "and had attained the age of 18 years before the end of the year".

118.3(2)(b) amended by 1992 technical bill, retroactive to the introduction of 118.2(2)(b.1) for 1991, to enable the supporting individual to claim the disabled person's unused disability tax credit where amounts have been paid to a part-time attendant. For 1988 to 1991, instead of "under section 118.2 (otherwise than under paragraph (2)(b.1) thereof)", read "under subsection 118.2(1)".

**Interpretation Bulletins**: See list at end of 118.3.

**Information Circulars**: 92-3: Guidelines for refunds beyond the normal three year period.

**Forms**: RC4064: Information concerning people with disabilities [guide].

**(3) Partial dependency** — Where more than one individual is entitled to deduct an amount under subsection (2) for a taxation year in respect of the same person, the total of all amounts so deductible for the year shall not exceed the maximum amount that would be deductible under that subsection for the year by an individual in respect of that person if that individual were the only individual entitled to deduct an amount under that subsection in respect of that person, and where the individuals cannot agree as to what portion of the amount each can deduct, the Minister may fix the portions.

**(4) Department of Human Resources Development** — The Minister may obtain the advice of the Department of Human Resources Development as to whether an individual in respect of whom an amount has been claimed under subsection (1) or (2) has a severe and prolonged impairment, the effects of which are such that the individual's ability to perform a basic activity of daily living is markedly restricted, and any person referred to in subsection (1) or (2) shall, on request in writing by that Department for information with respect to an individual's impairment and its effects on the individual, provide the information so requested.

**Proposed Amendment — 118.3(4)**

**(4) Additional Information** — Where a claim under this section or under section 118.8 is made in respect of an individual's impairment

(a) if the Minister requests in writing information with respect to the individual's impairment, its effects on the individual and, where applicable, the therapy referred to in paragraph (1)(a.1) that is required to be administered, from any person referred to in subsection (1) or (2) or section 118.8 in connection with such a claim, that person shall provide the information so requested to the Minister in writing; and

(b) if the information referred to in paragraph (a) is provided by a person referred to in paragraph (1)(a.2), the information so provided is deemed to be included in a certificate in prescribed form.

**Application**: The December 21, 2000 draft legislation, subsec. 62(7), will amend subsec. 118.3(4) to read as above, applicable to 2000 et seq.

**Technical Notes**: Subsection 118.3(4) gives to the Department of Human Resources Development (DHRD) the authority to request, from the disabled person, the supporting individual who claims (in whole or in part) the DTC in respect of the disabled person, or the certifying health professional, additional information to determine the disabled person's entitlement to the DTC. In recent years, the Canada Customs and Revenue Agency has developed its own "in-house" medical staff and, as a result, the advice of DHRD is no longer sought with respect to DTC claims. Accordingly, subsection 118.3(4) is amended to delete references to DHRD. The subsection is also modified as a consequence of the amendment to paragraph 118.3(1)(a.1) which extends the eligibility to the DTC to certain individuals who must undergo extensive therapy subsection 118.3(1). For additional information about the amendment to that paragraph, see the commentary on subsection 118.3(1).

**Related Provisions**: 162(7) — Penalty for failure to comply with request for information.

**Notes [s. 118.3]**: "National Health and Welfare" changed to "Human Resources Development" by S.C. 1996, c. 11, effective July 12, 1996.

118.3 amended by 1991 Budget/technical bill, effective 1991, to reflect the new definition of impairment in 118.4. For 1988 through 1990, ignore 118.3(4) and read 118.3(1) as follows:

118.3 (1) Where

(a) an individual has a severe and prolonged mental or physical impairment that has been certified as such in prescribed form by a medical doctor or, where the impairment is an impairment of sight, by a medical doctor or an optometrist,

(b) the individual has filed for a taxation year with the Minister the certificate described in paragraph (a), and

(c) no amount in respect of remuneration for an attendant, or care in a nursing home, by reason of the mental or physical impairment of the individual is included in calculating a deduction under subsection 118.2(1) for the year by the individual or by any other person,

for the purposes of computing the tax payable under this Part by the individual for the year, there may be deducted an amount determined by the formula

$$A \times \$3,236^{10}$$

where

A is the appropriate percentage for the year.

**Definitions [s. 118.3]**: "amount" — 248(1); "appropriate percentage" — 248(1); "audiologist" — 118.4(2); "aunt" — 252(2)(e); "basic activity of daily living" — 118.4(1)(c); "brother" — 252(2)(b); "Canada" — 255; "child" — 252(1); "common-law partner", "common-law partnership" — 248(1); "grandparent" — 252(2)(d); "individual" — 248(1); "markedly restricted" — 118.4(1)(b); "medical doctor" — 118.4(2); "Minister" — 248(1); "nephew", "niece" — 252(2)(g); "occupational therapist" — 118.4(2); "optometrist" — 118.4(2); "parent" — 252(2)(a); "person", "prescribed" — 248(1); "prolonged" — 118.4(1)(a); "psychologist" — 118.4(2); "resident in Canada" — 250; "sister" — 252(2)(c); "speech-language pathologist" — 118.4(2); "taxation year" — 249; "uncle" — 252(2)(e); "writing" — Interpretation Act 35(1).

**Interpretation Bulletins [s. 118.3]**: IT-171R2: Non-resident individuals — computation of taxable income earned in Canada and non-refundable tax credits; IT-326R3: Returns of deceased persons as "another person"; IT-393R2: Election re tax on rents and timber royalties — non-residents; IT-495R2: Child care expenses; IT-516R2: Tuition tax credit; IT-519R2: Medical expense and disability tax credits and attendant care expense deduction.

**Forms [s. 118.3]**: T929: Attendant care expenses; T2201: Disability tax credit certificate; T2201A: Disability tax credit questionnaire.

**118.4 (1) Nature of impairment** — For the purposes of subsection 6(16), sections 118.2 and 118.3 and this subsection,

(a) an impairment is prolonged where it has lasted, or can reasonably be expected to last, for a continuous period of at least 12 months;

(b) an individual's ability to perform a basic activity of daily living is markedly restricted only where all or substantially all of the time, even with therapy and the use of appropriate devices and medication, the individual is blind or is unable (or requires an inordinate amount of time) to perform a basic activity of daily living;

(c) a basic activity of daily living in relation to an individual means

(i) perceiving, thinking and remembering,

(ii) feeding and dressing oneself,

(iii) speaking so as to be understood, in a quiet setting, by another person familiar with the individual,

(iv) hearing so as to understand, in a quiet setting, another person familiar with the individual,

(v) eliminating (bowel or bladder functions), or

(vi) walking; and

(d) for greater certainty, no other activity, including working, housekeeping or a social or recreational activity, shall be considered as a basic activity of daily living.

**Notes**: See Notes to 118.3(1).

The Tax Court has held repeatedly that "feeding and dressing" in 118.4(1)(c)(ii) means feeding *or* dressing, so that a problem with either one is sufficient to qualify: *Lawlor*, [1996] 2 C.T.C. 2005D; *Dippel*, [1996] 3 C.T.C. 2202; *Mercier*, [1998] 2 C.T.C. 2610; *Tanguay*, [1998] 2 C.T.C. 2963.

---

[10] Indexed by s. 117.1 after 1988 — ed.

Subdivision a — Computation of Tax: Individuals    S. 118.5(1)(a)(iv)

The CCRA takes the position that "all or substantially all", used in 118.4(1)(b), means 90% or more.

118.4(1) amended by 1991 Budget/technical bill, effective 1991, to provide a new definition of impairment.

**Interpretation Bulletins**: IT-326R3: Returns of deceased persons as "another person"; IT-519R2: Medical expense and disability tax credits and attendant care expense deduction.

**(2) Reference to medical practitioners, etc.** — For the purposes of sections 63, 118.2, 118.3 and 118.6, a reference to an audiologist, dentist, medical doctor, medical practitioner, nurse, occupational therapist, optometrist, pharmacist or psychologist is a reference to a person authorized to practise as such,

> **Proposed Amendment — 118.4(2) opening words**
>
> **(2) Reference to medical practitioners, etc.** — For the purposes of sections 63, 118.2, 118.3 and 118.6, a reference to an audiologist, dentist, medical doctor, medical practitioner, nurse, occupational therapist, optometrist, pharmacist, psychologist or speech-language pathologist is a reference to a person authorized to practise as such,
>
> **Application**: The December 21, 2000 draft legislation, s. 63, will amend the opening words of subsec. 118.4(2) to read as above, applicable to certifications made after October 17, 2000.
>
> **Technical Notes**: Subsection 118.4(2) provides a definition of the group of health professionals to whom various references in section 63 (relating to child care expenses), section 118.2 (relating to medical expenses), section 118.3 (relating to the disability tax credit) and section 118.6 (relating to the education tax credit) apply. This amendment is consequential on the amendment to paragraph 118.3(1)(a.2) (see commentary on subsection 118.3(1)), which makes speech-language pathologists eligible to certify, after October 17, 2000, severe and prolonged speech impairments for the purpose of the disability tax credit.

(a) where the reference is used in respect of a service rendered to a taxpayer, pursuant to the laws of the jurisdiction in which the service is rendered;

(b) where the reference is used in respect of a certificate issued by the person in respect of a taxpayer, pursuant to the laws of the jurisdiction in which the taxpayer resides or of a province; and

(c) where the reference is used in respect of a prescription issued by the person for property to be provided to or for the use of a taxpayer, pursuant to the laws of the jurisdiction in which the taxpayer resides, of a province or of the jurisdiction in which the property is provided.

**Notes**: Opening words of 118.4(2) amended by 1998 Budget, effective February 25, 1998, to add references to 118.6 and occupational therapist.

118.4(2) amended by 1997 Budget to add reference to an audiologist, effective February 19, 1997, and to restore a reference to "medical doctor" that was mistakenly deleted in the R.S.C. 1985 Fifth Supplement consolidation, effective for taxation years that end after November 1991 (i.e., retroactive to the consolidation).

**Definitions [s. 118.4]**: "basic activity of daily living" — 118.4(1)(c); "Minister", "person", "property" — 248(1); "province" — *Interpretation Act* 35(1); "taxpayer" — 248(1).

**Forms [s. 118.4]**: T2201: Disability tax credit information.

**118.5 (1) Tuition credit** — For the purpose of computing the tax payable under this Part by an individual for a taxation year, there may be deducted,

(a) **[institution in Canada]** — where the individual was during the year a student enrolled at an educational institution in Canada that is

(i) a university, college or other educational institution providing courses at a post-secondary school level, or

(ii) certified by the Minister of Human Resources Development to be an educational institution providing courses, other than courses designed for university credit, that furnish a person with skills for, or improve a person's skills in, an occupation,

an amount equal to the product obtained when the appropriate percentage for the year is multiplied by the amount of any fees for the individual's tuition paid in respect of the year to the educational institution if the total of those fees exceeds $100,[17] except to the extent that those fees

(ii.1) are paid to an educational institution described in subparagraph (i) in respect of courses that are not at the post-secondary school level,

(ii.2) are paid to an educational institution described in subparagraph (ii) if

(A) the individual had not attained the age of 16 years before the end of the year, or

(B) the purpose of the individual's enrolment at the institution cannot reasonably be regarded as being to provide the individual with skills, or to improve the individual's skills, in an occupation,

(iii) are paid on the individual's behalf by the individual's employer and are not included in computing the individual's income,

(iii.1) are fees in respect of which the individual is or was entitled to receive a reimbursement or any form of assistance under a program of Her Majesty in right of Canada or a province designed to facilitate the entry or re-entry of workers into the labour force, where the amount of the reimbursement or assistance is not included in computing the individual's income,

(iv) were included as part of an allowance received by the individual's parent on the individual's behalf from an employer and are not

---

[17] Not indexed for inflation.

## S. 118.5(1)(a)(iv) — Income Tax Act, Part I, Division E

included in computing the income of the parent by reason of subparagraph 6(1)(b)(ix), or

(v) are paid on the individual's behalf, or are fees in respect of which the individual is or was entitled to receive a reimbursement, under a program of Her Majesty in right of Canada designed to assist athletes, where the payment or reimbursement is not included in computing the individual's income;

**Related Provisions**: See Related Provisions and Definitions at end of s. 118.5.

**Notes**: Including the resulting reduction in provincial tax for all provinces other than Quebec, the tuition credit is worth approximately 25% of the tuition paid.

In *Jacejko*, [1999] 4 C.T.C. 2032 (TCC), $2,000 of the $5,000 cost of an instructional Holy Land tour offered by a theological college as a non-credit course was considered to qualify for the tuition credit for a student enrolled at the college.

"Minister of National Health and Welfare" changed to "Minister of Human Resources Development" in 118.5(1)(a)(ii) by S.C. 1996, c. 11, effective July 12, 1996.

118.5(1)(a) amended by 1992 technical bill, effective 1992.

118.5(1)(a)(iii) added by 1991 technical bill, retroactive to the introduction of 118.5 in 1988.

118.1(1)(a)(v) added by 1995-97 technical bill, effective for 1994 and later taxation years.

**Interpretation Bulletins**: IT-171R2: Non-resident individuals — computation of taxable income earned in Canada and non-refundable tax credits; IT-393R2: Election re tax on rents and timber royalties — non-residents; IT-470R: Employees' fringe benefits; IT-516R2: Tuition tax credit.

**Information Circulars**: 75-23: Tuition fees and charitable donations paid to privately supported secular and religious schools; 92-3: Guidelines for refunds beyond the normal three year period.

**Forms**: T2202A: Tuition and education amount certificate; TL11B: Tuition fees certificate — Flying school.

(b) **[university outside Canada]** — where the individual was during the year a student in full-time attendance at a university outside Canada in a course leading to a degree, an amount equal to the product obtained when the appropriate percentage for the year is multiplied by the amount of any fees for the individual's tuition paid in respect of the year to the university, except any such fees

(i) paid in respect of a course of less than 13 consecutive weeks duration,

(ii) paid on the individual's behalf by the individual's employer to the extent that the amount of the fees is not included in computing the individual's income, or

(iii) paid on the individual's behalf by the employer of the individual's parent, to the extent that the amount of the fees is not included in computing the income of the parent by reason of subparagraph 6(1)(b)(ix); and

**Related Provisions**: See Related Provisions and Definitions at end of 118.5.

**Notes**: The institutions listed in Schedule VIII to the Regulations (among others) are accepted by the CCRA for purposes of 118.5(1)(b). See IT-516R2, paras. 5, 6. In *Drouin*, [1999] 2 C.T.C. 2413 (TCC), the Institut ÉCO-Conseil de Strasbourg (France) was found to qualify as a "university" for this purpose.

**Interpretation Bulletins**: IT-516R2: Tuition tax credit.

**Forms**: T2202A: Tuition and education amount certificate; TL11A: Tuition fees certificate — University outside Canada.

(c) **[cross-border commuter]** — where the individual resided throughout the year in Canada near the boundary between Canada and the United States if the individual

(i) was at any time in the year a student enrolled at an educational institution in the United States that is a university, college or other educational institution providing courses at a post-secondary school level, and

(ii) commuted to that educational institution in the United States,

an amount equal to the product obtained when the appropriate percentage for the year is multiplied by the amount of any fees for the individual's tuition paid in respect of the year to the educational institution if those fees exceed $100, except to the extent that those fees

(iii) are paid on the individual's behalf by the individual's employer and are not included in computing the individual's income, or

(iv) were included as part of an allowance received by the individual's parent on the individual's behalf from an employer and are not included in computing the income of the parent by reason of subparagraph 6(1)(b)(ix).

**Related Provisions**: See Related Provisions and Definitions at end of 118.5.

**Interpretation Bulletins**: IT-516R2: Tuition tax credit.

**I.T. Technical News**: No. 13 (employer-paid educational costs).

**Forms**: T2202A: Tuition and education amount certificate; TL11C: Tuition fees certificate — Commuter to United States.

**(2) Application to deemed residents** — Where an individual is deemed by section 250 to be resident in Canada throughout all or part of a taxation year, in applying subsection (1) in respect of the individual for the period when the individual is so deemed to be resident in Canada, paragraph (1)(a) shall be read without reference to the words "in Canada".

**Forms**: TL11D: Tuition fees certificate — educational institutions outside Canada — deemed resident of Canada.

**(3) Inclusion of ancillary fees and charges** — For the purpose of this section, "fees for an individual's tuition" includes ancillary fees and charges that are paid

(a) to an educational institution referred to in subparagraph (1)(a)(i), and

(b) in respect of the individual's enrolment at the institution in a program at a post-secondary school level,

but does not include

(c) any fee or charge to the extent that it is levied in respect of

(i) a student association,

(ii) property to be acquired by students,

(iii) services not ordinarily provided at educational institutions in Canada that offer courses at a post-secondary school level,

(iv) the provision of financial assistance to students, except to the extent that, if the reference in paragraph 56(1)(n) to "$500" were read as a reference to "nil", the amount of the assistance would be required to be included in computing the income, and not be deductible in computing the taxable income, of the students to whom the assistance is provided, or

(v) the construction, renovation or maintenance of any building or facility, except to the extent that the building or facility is owned by the institution and used to provide

(A) courses at the post-secondary school level, or

(B) services for which, if fees or charges in respect of the services were required to be paid by all students of the institution, the fees or charges would be included because of this subsection in the fees for an individual's tuition, and

(d) any fee or charge for a taxation year that, but for this paragraph, would be included because of this subsection in the fees for the individual's tuition and that is not required to be paid by

(i) all of the institution's full-time students, where the individual is a full-time student at the institution, and

(ii) all of the institution's part-time students, where the individual is a part-time student at the institution,

to the extent that the total for the year of all such fees and charges paid in respect of the individual's enrolment at the institution exceeds $250.

**Notes**: 118.5(3) added by 1997 Budget, effective for 1997 and later taxation years.

**Related Provisions [s. 118.5]**: 117(1) — Tax payable under this Part; 118.5(3) — Ancillary fees included; 118.61(2) — Carryforward of unused credits 118.8 — Transfer of unused credits to spouse; 118.9 — Transfers to supporting person; 118.91 — Individual resident in Canada for part of the year; 118.92 — Ordering of credits; 118.93 — Credits in separate returns; 118.94 — Computing tax payable by a non-resident individual; 118.95(a) — Application in year individual becomes bankrupt; Reg. 5700(w) — Medical expense credit for talking textbooks for disabled students.

**Definitions [s. 118.5]**: "amount", "appropriate percentage" — 248(1); "Canada" — 255; "employer" — 248(1); "fees for tuition" — 118.5(3); "individual" — 248(1); "parent" — 252(2); "property" — 248(1); "province" — *Interpretation Act* 35(1); "resident in Canada" — 250; "tax payable" — 248(2); "taxation year" — 249.

**Interpretation Bulletins**: IT-326R3: Returns of deceased persons as "another person"; IT-516R2: Tuition tax credit.

### 118.6 (1) [Education credit — ] Definitions —

For the purposes of section 63 and this subdivision,

**Proposed Amendment — 118.6(1) opening words**

**118.6 (1) Definitions** — For the purposes of sections 63 and 64 and this subdivision,

**Application**: The December 21, 2000 draft legislation, subsec. 64(1), will amend the opening words of subsec. 118.6(1) to read as above, applicable to 2000 *et seq.*

**Technical Notes**: Section 118.6 provides rules for determining the eligibility for the education tax credit.

Subsection 118.6(1) provides the definition "designated educational institution" which is relevant for the purposes of the child care expense deduction and the tuition fee and education tax credits. Generally speaking, a designated educational institution is an institution providing post-secondary education, an educational institution certified by the Minister of Human Resources Development that furnishes or improves or improve skills in an occupation or a foreign university. The amendment to the preamble of that subsection is strictly consequential on the amendment to section 64 (see commentary on that section), which broadens the scope of the deduction of attendant care expenses to include such expenses incurred to attend a designated educational institution.

**Notes**: Opening words of 118.6(1) amended by 1998 Budget to add reference to s. 63, effective for 1998 and later taxation years.

Opening words of 118.6(1) amended by 1991 technical bill, effective July 1990, to read "subdivision" instead of "section".

**"designated educational institution"** means

(a) an educational institution in Canada that is

(i) a university, college or other educational institution designated by the Lieutenant Governor in Council of a province as a specified educational institution under the *Canada Student Loans Act*, designated by an appropriate authority under the *Canada Student Financial Assistance Act*, or designated by the Minister of Higher Education and Science of the Province of Quebec for the purposes of *An Act respecting financial assistance for students* of the Province of Quebec, or

(ii) certified by the Minister of Human Resources Development to be an educational institution providing courses, other than courses designed for university credit, that furnish a person with skills for, or improve a person's skills in, an occupation,

(b) a university outside Canada at which the individual referred to in subsection (2) was enrolled in a course, of not less than 13 consecutive weeks duration, leading to a degree, or

(c) if the individual referred to in subsection (2) resided, throughout the year referred to in that subsection, in Canada near the boundary between

Canada and the United States, an educational institution in the United States to which the individual commuted that is a university, college or other educational institution providing courses at a post-secondary school level;

**Related Provisions**: 146.1(1)"post-secondary educational institution"(a) — designated education institution qualifies for RESP purposes. See additional Related Provisions and Definitions at end of s. 118.6.

**Notes**: "Minister of National Health and Welfare" changed to "Minister of Human Resources Development" in subpara. (a)(ii) by S.C. 1996, c. 11, effective July 12, 1996.

Subpara. (a)(i) amended by 1994 student financial assistance bill (S.C. 1994, c. 28) to add the words "designated by an appropriate authority under the *Canada Student Financial Assistance Act*" and change "authorized" to "designated" re the Quebec legislation, effective August 1, 1995.

**"qualifying educational program"** means a program of not less than 3 consecutive weeks duration that provides that each student taking the program spend not less than 10 hours per week on courses or work in the program and, in respect of a program at an institution described in the definition "designated educational institution" (other than an institution described in subparagraph (a)(ii) thereof), that is a program at a post-secondary school level but, in relation to any particular student, does not include any such program

(a) if the student receives, from a person with whom the student is dealing at arm's length, any allowance, benefit, grant or reimbursement for expenses in respect of the program other than

(i) an amount received by the student as or on account of a scholarship, fellowship or bursary, or a prize for achievement in a field of endeavour ordinarily carried on by the student, or

(ii) a benefit, if any, received by the student by reason of a loan made to the student in accordance with the requirements of the *Canada Student Loans Act* or *An Act respecting financial assistance for students* of the Province of Quebec, or by reason of financial assistance given to the student in accordance with the requirements of the *Canada Student Financial Assistance Act*, or

(b) if the program is taken by the student

(i) during a period in respect of which the student receives income from an office or employment, and

(ii) in connection with, or as part of the duties of, that office or employment.

**Related Provisions**: 146.1(1)"qualifying educational program" — Only para. (b) of definition applies to RESPs; 146.02(1)"qualifying educational program" — Definition for purposes of LLP (borrowing from RRSP).

**Notes**: Definition "qualifying educational program" amended by 1991 technical bill, effective 1991.

Subpara. (a)(ii) amended by 1994 student financial assistance bill to add reference to the *Canada Student Financial Assistance Act*, effective August 1, 1995.

**"specified educational program"** means a program that would be a qualifying educational program if the definition "qualifying educational program" were read without reference to the words "that provides that each student taking the program spend not less than 10 hours per week on courses or work in the program".

**Notes**: Definition "specified educational program" added by 1998 Budget, effective for 1998 and later taxation years. Effectively, it identifies educational programs that qualify for the education tax credit with respect to part-time education.

**(2) Education credit** — There may be deducted in computing an individual's tax payable under this Part for a taxation year the amount determined by the formula

$$A \times B$$

where

A is the appropriate percentage for the year; and

B is the total of the products obtained when

(a) $200 is multiplied by the number of months in the year during which the individual is enrolled in a qualifying educational program as a full-time student at a designated educational institution, and

(b) $60 is multiplied by the number of months in the year (other than months described in paragraph (a)), each of which is a month during which the individual is enrolled at a designated educational institution in a specified educational program that provides that each student in the program spend not less than 12 hours in the month on courses in the program,

**Proposed Amendment — 118.6(2)B(a), (b)**

(a) $400 is multiplied by the number of months in the year during which the individual is enrolled in a qualifying educational program as a full-time student at a designated educational institution, and

(b) $120 is multiplied by the number of months in the year (other than months described in paragraph (a)), each of which is a month during which the individual is enrolled at a designated educational institution in a specified educational program that provides that each student in the program spend not less than 12 hours in the month on courses in the program,

**Application**: The December 21, 2000 draft legislation, subsec. 64(2), will amend paras. (a) and (b) of the description of B in subsec. 118.6(2) to read as above, applicable to 2001 et seq.

**Technical Notes**: Subsection 118.6(2) provides the formula for the calculation of the education tax credit. For 2000, this tax credit is determined by multiplying the "appropriate percentage" (17 per cent) by $200 ($60 in the case of part-time students) by the number of months in the year during which an individual is enroled in a qualifying program at a designated educational institution. This amendment doubles the monthly amounts for the 2001 and subsequent taxation years such that they will be set at $400 for full-time students and $120 for part-time students. Thus, for those years, the education tax credit will be computed by reference to those increased monthly amounts and the new lowest tax rate (16 per cent) applicable to individual [see 117(2) — ed.].

This amendment applies to the 2001 and subsequent taxation years.

**Notice of Ways and Means Motion, Economic Statement, October 18, 2000**: (5) That, for the 2001 and subsequent taxation years, the $200 and $60 monthly amounts on which the education tax credit is calculated be increased to $400 and $120, respectively.

**Minister's Speech, Economic Statement, October 18, 2000**: Mr. Speaker, ensuring that Canadians enjoy the best learning and research opportunities here in Canada has been a priority in each of our last four budgets. Today, we will do more.

Canadian students rely on the education tax credit to offset the cost of books, lodging and other expenses. As recently as 1995, the amount on which the credit was based was $80 per month. Over the past number of years, we have raised it to $200.

Today we will go further. Over the next five years, we will put an additional $1 billion into the hands of one million students by doubling that amount — to $400 per month, effective January 1, 2001.

if the enrolment is proved by filing with the Minister a certificate in prescribed form issued by the designated educational institution and containing prescribed information and, in respect of a designated educational institution described in subparagraph (a)(ii) of the definition "designated educational institution" in subsection (1), the individual is enrolled in the program to obtain skills for, or improve the individual's skills in, an occupation.

**Proposed Amendment — 118.6(2)B**

if the enrolment is proven by filing with the Minister a certificate in prescribed form issued by the designated educational institution and containing prescribed information and, in respect of a designated educational institution described in subparagraph (a)(ii) of the definition "designated educational institution" in subsection (1), the individual has attained the age of 16 years before the end of the year and is enrolled in the program to obtain skills for, or improve the individual's skills in, an occupation.

**Application**: Bill C-43 (First Reading September 20, 2000), s. 64, will amend the closing words in subsec. 118.6(2) to read as above, applicable to 1999 et seq.

**Technical Notes**: Section 118.6 of the Act provides a tax credit computed by reference to the number of months in a calendar year in which a student is enrolled in a qualified educational program at a designated educational institution. The expressions "qualified educational program" and "designated educational institution" are defined in subsection 118.6(1). Essentially, the education tax credit is granted to students enrolled in post-secondary and vocational job-training courses which qualify for the purposes of the tuition fee tax credit. In the case of vocational schools, fees paid on behalf of students who are under 16 years of age do not qualify for the tuition fee tax credit. The amendment clarifies that a similar restriction applies for the purposes of the education tax credit.

**Related Provisions**: 118.6(3) — Disabled individuals may be enrolled part-time; 118.61(2) — Carryforward of unused credits; 118.8 — Transfer of unused credits to spouse; 118.9 — Transfers to supporting person; 118.91 — Individual resident in Canada for part of the year; 118.92 — Ordering of credits; 118.93 — Credits in separate returns; 118.94 — Computing tax payable by a non-resident individual; 118.95(a) — Application in year individual becomes bankrupt; 146.02 — LLP (loan from RRSP to fund education).

**Notes**: The "appropriate percentage" is 16% as of 2001 (see 248(1)). Note that the credit applies to months "during" which the student is enrolled, and that "month" is defined in s. 35(1) of the *Interpretation Act* to mean a calendar month. If a student is enrolled from August 31 to December 2, that would count as 5 months. "Enrolment" can presumably be effective before classes start.

118.6(2) amended by 1998 Budget, effective for 1998 and later taxation years. For earlier years, read:

(2) For the purpose of computing the tax payable under this Part by an individual for a taxation year, there may be deducted an amount determined by the formula

$$A \times \$200 \times B$$

where

A   is the appropriate percentage for the year, and

B   is the number of months in the year during which the individual is enrolled in a qualifying educational program as a full-time student at a designated educational institution,

if the enrolment is proven by filing with the Minister a certificate in prescribed form issued by the designated educational institution and containing prescribed information and, in respect of a designated educational institution described in subparagraph (a)(ii) of the definition "designated educational institution" in subsection 118.6 (1), the student is enrolled in the program to obtain skills for, or improve the student's skills in, an occupation.

118.6(2) amended by 1992 Budget/technical bill to raise the amount in the formula from $60 to $80 effective 1992; by 1996 Budget to raise it to $100 effective 1996; and by 1997 Budget to raise it to $150 for 1997 and $200 effective 1998.

118.6(2)B amended by 1991 technical bill, effective 1991, to delete a requirement that the student be in full-time *attendance* at the institution. This permits full-time post-secondary students enrolled in distance education programs or correspondence courses to claim the education credit.

**I.T. Technical News**: No. 13 (employer-paid educational costs).

**Forms**: T2202: Education amount certificate; T2202A: Tuition and education amounts certificate.

**(3) Disabled students** — In calculating the amount deductible under subsection (2) in computing an individual's tax payable under this Part for a taxation year, the reference in that subsection to "full-time student" shall be read as "student" if either

(a) an amount may be deducted under section 118.3 in respect of the individual for the year; or

(b) the individual has in the year a mental or physical impairment the effects of which on the individual have been certified in writing, to be

## S. 118.6(3)(b) — Income Tax Act, Part I, Division E

such that the individual cannot reasonably be expected to be enrolled as a full-time student while so impaired, by a medical doctor or, where the impairment is

(i) an impairment of sight, by a medical doctor or an optometrist,

(ii) a hearing impairment, by a medical doctor or an audiologist,

(iii) an impairment with respect to the individual's ability in feeding and dressing themself, or in walking, by a medical doctor or an occupational therapist, or

(iv) an impairment with respect to the individual's ability in perceiving, thinking and remembering, by a medical doctor or a psychologist.

**Related Provisions**: 146.02(1)"full-time student" — Student eligible under 118.6(3) qualifies as full-time student for LLP (loan from RRSP to fund education); 146.1(2)(g.1)(i)(B) — Disabled student may receive RESP funds when enrolled part-time; Reg. 5700(w) — Medical expense credit for talking textbooks.

**Notes**: 118.6(3) amended by 1998 Budget, effective for certifications made

(a) after February 18, 1997, in the case of a hearing impairment referred to in 118.6(3)(b)(ii), and

(b) after February 24, 1998, in any other case. (See 118.3(1).)

For earlier certifications, read:

(3) **Application of subsec. (2) to disabled individuals** — In calculating the amount deductible under subsection 118.6 (2) in computing the tax payable under this Part for a taxation year by an individual

(a) in respect of whom an amount may be deducted under section 118.3 for the year, or

(b) who has in the year a mental or physical impairment, if a medical doctor or, where the impairment is an impairment of sight, a medical doctor or an optometrist, has certified in writing that the effects of the impairment on the individual are such that the individual cannot reasonably be expected to be enrolled as a full-time student while so impaired,

the reference in that subsection to "full-time student" shall be read as "student".

118.6(3) added by 1992 Budget/technical bill, effective 1992. It allows disabled students the education credit even if they are not enrolled on a full-time basis.

**Definitions [s. 118.6]**: "amount", "appropriate percentage" — 248(1); "arm's length" — 251(1); "audiologist" — 118.4(2); "Canada" — 255; "designated educational institution" — 118.6(1); "employment", "individual" — 248(1); "Lieutenant Governor in Council" — *Interpretation Act* 35(1); "medical doctor" — 118.4(2); "Minister" — 248(1); "month" — *Interpretation Act* 35(1); "occupational therapist" — 118.4(2); "office", "person", "prescribed" — 248(1); "province" — *Interpretation Act* 35(1); "psychologist" — 118.4(2); "qualifying educational program", "specified educational program" — 118.6(1); "tax payable" — 248(2); "taxation year" — 249; "writing" — *Interpretation Act* 35(1).

**Interpretation Bulletins [s. 118.6]**: IT-171R2: Non-resident individuals — computation of taxable income earned in Canada and non-refundable tax credits; IT-326R3: Returns of deceased persons as "another person"; IT-393R2: Election re tax on rents and timber royalties — non-residents; IT-515R2: Education tax credit.

**Information Circulars [s. 118.6]**: 92-3: Guidelines for refunds beyond the normal three year period.

**118.61 (1) Unused tuition and education tax credits** — In this section, an individual's unused tuition and education tax credits at the end of a taxation year is the amount determined by the formula

$$A + (B - C) - (D + E)$$

where

A is the individual's unused tuition and education tax credits at the end of the preceding taxation year;

B is the total of all amounts each of which may be deducted under section 118.5 or 118.6 in computing the individual's tax payable under this Part for the year;

C is the lesser of the value of B and the amount that would be the individual's tax payable under this Part for the year if no amount were deductible under section 118.5 or 118.6;

**Proposed Amendment — 118.61(1)C**

C is the lesser of the value of B and the amount that would be the individual's tax payable under this Part for the year if no amount were deductible under any of sections 118.1, 118.2, 118.5, 118.6, 118.62, 118.8, 118.9 and 121;

**Application**: Bill C-43 (First Reading September 20, 2000), subsec. 65(1), will amend the description of C in subsec. 118.61(1) to read as above, applicable to 1999 *et seq.*

**Technical Notes**: Section 118.61 of the Act provides for the deduction of a student's carryforward of unused tuition and education tax credits, as calculated at the end of the previous year. The amendments to the description of C in subsection 118.6(1) and to paragraph 118.61(2)(b) make the calculation of the student's unused tuition and education tax credits compatible with the ordering provided under section 118.92 for the claiming of non-refundable credits. As provided under that section, the tuition fee and education tax credits, as well as the carryforward of the unused portion of those credits, must be claimed before any part of those credits can be transferred to a spouse or supporting individual and before claiming any donation or dividend tax credit.

D is the amount that the individual may deduct under subsection (2) for the year; and

E is the tuition and education tax credits transferred for the year by the individual to the individual's spouse, common-law partner, parent or grandparent.

**Related Provisions**: 118.81 — Tuition and education credits transferred; 257 — Formula cannot calculate to less than zero; 128(2)(g)(ii) — Effect of bankruptcy on unused credits.

**Notes**: 118.61(1) amended by 2000 same-sex partners bill to add reference to "common-law partner", effective for the 2001 and later taxation years, or earlier by election (see Notes to 248(1)"common-law partner").

See also Notes at end of 118.61.

(2) **Deduction of carryforward** — For the purpose of computing an individual's tax payable under

Subdivision a — Computation of Tax: Individuals     S. 118.7

this Part for a taxation year, there may be deducted the lesser of

(a) the individual's unused tuition and education tax credits at the end of the preceding taxation year, and

(b) the amount that would be the individual's tax payable under this Part for the year if no amount were deductible under section 118.5 or 118.6 or this section.

---

**Proposed Amendment — 118.61(2)(b)**

(b) the amount that would be the individual's tax payable under this Part for the year if no amount were deductible under any of sections 118.1, 118.2, 118.5, 118.6, 118.62, 118.8, 118.9 and 121.

**Application**: Bill C-43 (First Reading September 20, 2000), subsec. 65(2), will amend para. 118.61(2)(b) to read as above, applicable to 1999 et seq.

**Technical Notes**: See under 118.61(1)C.

---

**Related Provisions**: 118.91 — Individual resident in Canada for part of the year; 118.92 — Ordering of credits; 128(2)(e), 128(2)(f)(iv) — On bankruptcy, only trustee can claim carryforward.

**Notes [s. 118.61]**: 118.61 added by 1997 Budget, effective for 1997 and later taxation years.

**Definitions [s. 118.61]**: "amount", "common-law partner" — 248(1); "grandparent" — 252(2)(d); "individual" — 248(1); "parent" — 252(2)(a); "taxation year" — 249; "tuition and education tax credits transferred" — 118.81; "unused tuition and education tax credits" — 118.61(1).

## 118.62 Credit for interest on student loan —

For the purpose of computing an individual's tax payable under this Part for a taxation year, there may be deducted the amount determined by the formula

$$A \times B$$

where

A   is the appropriate percentage for the year; and

B   is the total of all amounts (other than any amount paid on account of or in satisfaction of a judgement) each of which is an amount of interest paid in the year (or in any of the five preceding taxation years that are after 1997, to the extent that it was not included in computing a deduction under this section for any other taxation year) by the individual or a person related to the individual on a loan made to, or other amount owing by, the individual under the *Canada Student Loans Act*, the *Canada Student Financial Assistance Act* or a law of a province governing the granting of financial assistance to students at the post-secondary school level.

**Related Provisions**: 20(1)(c) — Interest deductible when money borrowed to earn income; 118.91 — Individual resident in Canada for part of the year; 118.92 — Ordering of credits; 118.93 — Credits in separate returns; 118.94 — Computing tax payable by a non-resident individual; 118.95(a) — Application in year individual becomes bankrupt.

**Notes**: 118.62 added by 1998 Budget, effective for 1998 and later taxation years. It provides a credit for interest paid on a student loan. The federal credit is 16% (17% before 2001) of the interest paid in the year or in any of the 5 preceding years since 1998, to the extent the interest was not counted for another year. (Including reduced provincial tax, the effect of the credit in provinces other than Quebec is about 25%.) The interest must have been paid under one of the indicated federal or provincial student-loan programs, and not under a judgment (for default in payment). Forgiven interest and interest accrued but not paid do not qualify for the credit.

**Definitions [s. 118.62]**: "amount", "appropriate percentage" — 248(1); "individual", "person" — 248(1); "province" — *Interpretation Act* 35(1); "related" — 251(2)–(6); "taxation year" — 249.

## 118.7 Credit for UI [EI] premium and CPP contribution —

For the purpose of computing the tax payable under this Part by an individual for a taxation year, there may be deducted an amount determined by the formula

$$A \times B$$

where

A   is the appropriate percentage for the year; and

B   is the total of

(a) the total of all amounts each of which is an amount payable by the individual as an employee's premium for the year under the *Employment Insurance Act*, not exceeding the maximum amount of such premiums payable by the individual for the year under that Act,

(b) the total of all amounts each of which is an amount payable by the individual for the year as an employee's contribution under the *Canada Pension Plan* or under a provincial pension plan defined in section 3 of that Act, not exceeding the maximum amount of such contributions payable by the individual for the year under the plan, and

(c) the total of all amounts each of which is an amount payable by the individual in respect of self-employed earnings for the year as a contribution under the *Canada Pension Plan* or under a provincial pension plan as defined in section 3 of that Act, not exceeding the maximum amount of such contributions payable by the individual for the year under the plan.

---

**Proposed Amendment — 118.7B(c)**

(c) the amount by which

(i) the total of all amounts each of which is an amount payable by the individual in respect of self-employed earnings for the year as a contribution under the *Canada Pension Plan* or under a provincial pension plan within the meaning assigned by section 3 of that Act (not exceeding the maximum amount of such contributions payable by the individual for the year under the plan)

---

1037

(ii) the amount deductible under paragraph 60(e) in computing the individual's income for the year.

**Application**: The December 21, 2000 draft legislation, s. 65, will amend para. (c) of the description of B in s. 118.7 to read as above, applicable to 2001 et seq.

**Technical Notes**: Section 118.7 provides the formula for calculating an individual's tax credit in respect of CPP/QPP contributions and employment insurance premiums. The amendment to paragraph (c) of the description of B of that formula is consequential on the introduction of paragraph 60(e) (see commentary on that paragraph). New paragraph 60(e) provides for the deduction, in computing an individual's income, of one-half of the CPP/QPP contributions payable on the individual's self-employed earnings, subject to one-half of the maximum of such contributions payable by the individual under the plan. The amendment ensures that the tax credit granted to the individual under section 118.7 in respect of CPP/QPP contributions of the individual's self-employed earnings is computed by reference to the other half of such contributions.

**Notice of Ways and Means Motion and Minister's Speech, Economic Statement, October 18, 2000**: See under 60(e).

**Related Provisions**: 56(1)(a)(iv) — Pension benefits, UI/EI benefits, etc.; 60(e) — Deduction for other half of contributions; 117(1) — Tax payable under this Part; 118.91 — Individual resident in Canada for part of the year; 118.92 — Ordering of credits; 118.93 — Credits in separate returns; 118.94 — Tax payable by non-resident individual; 118.95(a) — Application in year individual becomes bankrupt; 126.1 — Employer's UI premium tax credit for 1993.

**Notes**: The "appropriate percentage" is 16% as of 2001, leading to a credit worth about 23% including the parallel provincial credit. See Notes at beginning of 118(1).

**Definitions [s. 118.7]**: "amount", "appropriate percentage", "employee", "individual" — 248(1); "tax payable" — 248(2); "taxation year" — 249.

**Interpretation Bulletins**: IT-171R2: Non-resident individuals — computation of taxable income earned in Canada and non-refundable tax credits; IT-326R3: Returns of deceased persons as "another person"; IT-393R2: Election re tax on rents and timber royalties — non-residents; IT-516R2: Tuition tax credit; IT-519R2: Medical expense and disability tax credits and attendant care expense deduction.

**Information Circulars**: 92-3: Guidelines for refunds beyond the normal three year period.

**Forms**: T1 Sched. 8: QPP contributions on self-employment and other earnings.

## 118.8 Transfer of unused credits to spouse [or common-law partner]

— For the purpose of computing the tax payable under this Part for a taxation year by an individual who, at any time in the year, is a married person or a person who is in a common-law partnership (other than an individual who, by reason of a breakdown of their marriage or common-law partnership, is living separate and apart from the individual's spouse or common-law partner at the end of the year and for a period of 90 days commencing in the year), there may be deducted an amount determined by the formula

$$A + B - C$$

where

A is the tuition and education tax credits transferred for the year by the spouse or common-law partner to the individual;

B is the total of all amounts each of which is deductible under subsection 118(2) or (3) or 118.3(1) in computing the spouse's or common-law partner's tax payable under this Part for the year; and

C is the amount, if any, by which

(a) the amount that would be the spouse's or common-law partner's tax payable under this Part for the year if no amount were deductible under this Division (other than an amount deductible under subsection 118(1) because of paragraph (c) of the description of B in that subsection or under section 118.61 or 118.7)

exceeds

(b) the lesser of

(i) the total of all amounts that may be deducted under section 118.5 or 118.6 in computing the spouse's or common-law partner's tax payable under this Part for the year, and

(ii) the amount that would be the spouse's or common-law partner's tax payable under this Part for the year if no amount were deductible under this Division (other than an amount deductible under section 118, 118.3, 118.61 or 118.7).

**Related Provisions**: 117(1) — Tax payable under this Part; 118.3(2) — Disability credit claim for disabled dependant; 118.3(4) — Additional information requested by CCRA; 118.61(2) — Carryforward of unused credits; 118.91 — Individual resident in Canada for part of the year; 118.92 — Ordering of credits; 118.93 — Credits in separate returns; 118.94 — Computing tax payable by a non-resident individual; 118.95(b) — Application in year individual becomes bankrupt; 257 — Formula cannot calculate to less than zero.

**Notes**: 118.8 amended by 2000 same-sex partners bill to add references to "common-law partner" and "common-law partnership", effective for the 2001 and later taxation years, or earlier by election (see Notes to 248(1)"common-law partner").

118.8C(a) amended by 1999 Budget, effective for 2000 and later taxation years, to delete a reference in the parentheses to 118(1)B(b.1).

118.8C(a) amended by 1998 Budget to add reference to 118(1)B(b.1), effective for 1998 and later taxation years.

Formula elements A and C amended by 1997 Budget, effective for 1997 and later taxation years. Previously read:

A is the lesser of $850[17] and the total of all amounts each of which is deductible under section 118.5 or 118.6 in

---

[17]Not indexed for inflation.

## Subdivision a — Computation of Tax: Individuals — S. 118.9

computing the spouse's tax payable under this Part for the year;

C is the spouse's tax payable under this Part for the year computed before any deductions under this Division (other than a deduction under subsection 118(1) because of paragraph (c) of the description of B in that subsection or under section 118.7).

118.8 amended by 1992 Budget/technical bill, effective 1992, to raise the amount for A from $600 to $680, and by 1996 Budget, effective 1996, to change $680 to $850. The 1996 Budget also reworded the descriptions of A, B and C to be more consistent with the language used elsewhere. For 1992–95, read:

A is the lesser of $680[17] and the total of all amounts that the individual's spouse may deduct under section 118.5 or 118.6 for the year;

B is the total of all amounts each of which is an amount that the individual's spouse may deduct for the year under subsection 118(2) or (3) or 118.3(1); and

C is the amount of the individual's spouse's tax payable under this Part for the year computed before any deductions under this Division (other than a deduction under subsection 118(1) by reason of paragraph 118(1)(c) or under section 118.7).

**Definitions [s. 118.8]:** "amount", "common-law partner", "common-law partnership""individual" — 248(1); "tax payable" — 248(2); "taxation year" — 249; "tuition and education tax credits transferred" — 118.81.

**Interpretation Bulletins:** IT-171R2: Non-resident individuals — computation of taxable income earned in Canada and non-refundable tax credits; IT-326R3: Returns of deceased persons as "another person"; IT-393R2: Election re tax on rents and timber royalties — non-residents; IT-470R: Employees' fringe benefits; IT-513R: Personal tax credits; IT-515R2: Education tax credit; IT-516R2: Tuition tax credit; IT-517R: Pension tax credit; IT-519R2: Medical expense and disability tax credits and attendant care expense deduction.

**Forms:** T1 Sched. 2: Amounts transferred from spouse.

### 118.81 Tuition and education tax credits transferred
— In this subdivision, the tuition and education tax credits transferred for a taxation year by a person to an individual is the lesser of

(a) the amount determined by the formula

$$A - B$$

where

A is the lesser of

(i) the total of all amounts that may be deducted under section 118.5 or 118.6 in computing the person's tax payable under this Part for the year, and

(ii) $850[17], and

B is the amount that would be the person's tax payable under this Part for the year if no amount were deductible under this Division (other than an amount deductible under section 118, 118.3, 118.61 or 118.7), and

(b) the amount for the year that the person designates in writing for the purpose of section 118.8 or 118.9.

**Related Provisions:** 118.61(2) — Carryforward of unused credits; 257 — Formula cannot calculate to less than zero.

**Notes:** 118.81 added by 1997 Budget, effective for 1997 and later taxation years. The $850 figure in 118.81(a)A(ii) limits the education and tuition amounts transferred to a spouse, parent or grandparent to $5,000 per year ($850 is 17% of $5,000).

**Definitions [s. 118.81]:** "amount", "individual", "person" — 248(1); "tax payable" — 248(2); "taxation year" — 249; "writing" — *Interpretation Act* 35(1).

### 118.9 Transfer to parent or grandparent
— Where for a taxation year a parent or grandparent of an individual (other than an individual in respect of whom the individual's spouse or common-law partner deducts an amount under section 118 or 118.8 for the year) is the only person designated in writing by the individual for the year for the purpose of this section, there may be deducted in computing the tax payable under this Part for the year by the parent or grandparent, as the case may be, the tuition and education tax credits transferred for the year by the individual to the parent or grandparent, as the case may be.

**Notes [s. 118.9]:** 118.9 amended by 2000 same-sex partners bill to add reference to "common-law partner", effective for the 2001 and later taxation years, or earlier by election (see Notes to 248(1)"common-law partner").

118.9 amended by 1997 Budget, effective for 1997 and later taxation years. For 1996, read:

118.9 (1) Transfers to supporting person — Where the parent or grandparent of an individual (other than an individual in respect of whom the individual's spouse deducts an amount under section 118 or 118.8 for the year) files with the Minister for a taxation year a prescribed form containing prescribed information, there may be deducted in computing the tax payable by the parent or grandparent, as the case may be, under this Part for the year an amount determined by the formula

$$A - B$$

where

A is the lesser of $850[17] and the total of all amounts each of which is deductible under section 118.5 or 118.6 in computing the individual's tax payable under this Part for the year; and

B is the amount of the individual's tax payable under this Part for the year computed before any deductions under this Division (other than sections 118, 118.3 and 118.7).

(2) Only one claim per student — Where in computing his or her tax payable under this Part for a taxation year a parent or grandparent of an individual has deducted an amount under section 118 in respect of the individual, that parent or grandparent, as the case may be, is the only person entitled to deduct an amount for the year under subsection (1) in respect of the individual and in any other case only such one of the parents and grandparents of the individual as is designated for the year in writing by the individual is entitled to make such a deduction for the year.

---

[17]Not indexed for inflation.

## S. 118.9 — Income Tax Act, Part I, Division E

The description of A in 118.9(1) amended by 1996 Budget, effective 1996, to change $680 to $850, and to reword slightly. For 1992-95, read:

> A is the lesser of $680[17] and the total of all amounts that the individual may deduct under section 118.5 or 118.6 for the year; and

118.9(1) amended by 1992 Budget/technical bill, effective 1992, to raise the amount for A from $600 to $680 and to ensure that, where an individual is entitled to a tuition fee credit in respect of fees paid for one or more courses, the transferability of the unused portion of the credit to the individual's parent or grandparent will not depend on the nature or level of those courses. This reversed a change made by 1991 technical bill effective July 1990.

**Definitions [s. 118.9]**: "amount", "common-law partner" — 248(1); "grandparent" — 252(2)(d); "individual", "Minister" — 248(1); "parent" — 252(2)(a); "prescribed" — 248(1); "tax payable" — 248(2); "taxation year" — 249; "tuition and education tax credits transferred" — 118.81; "writing" — *Interpretation Act* 35(1).

**Interpretation Bulletins [s. 118.9]**: IT-171R2: Non-resident individuals — computation of taxable income earned in Canada and non-refundable tax credits; IT-326R3: Returns of deceased persons as "another person"; IT-393R2: Election re tax on rents and timber royalties — non-residents; IT-470R: Employees' fringe benefits; IT-515R2: Education tax credit; IT-516R2: Tuition tax credit.

### 118.91 Part-year residents
— Notwithstanding sections 118 to 118.9, where an individual is resident in Canada throughout part of a taxation year and throughout another part of the year is non-resident, for the purpose of computing the individual's tax payable under this Part for the year,

(a) the amount deductible for the year under each such provision in respect of the part of the year that is not included in the period or periods referred to in paragraph (b) shall be computed as though such part were the whole taxation year; and

(b) the individual shall be allowed only

(i) such of the deductions permitted under subsection 118(3) and sections 118.1, 118.2, 118.5, 118.6, 118.62 and 118.7 as can reasonably be considered wholly applicable, and

(ii) such part of the deductions permitted under sections 118 (other than subsection 118(3)), 118.3, 118.8 and 118.9 as can reasonably be considered applicable

to the period or periods in the year throughout which the individual is resident in Canada, computed as though that period or those periods were the whole taxation year,

except that the amount deductible for the year by the individual under each such provision shall not exceed the amount that would have been deductible under that provision had the individual been resident in Canada throughout the year.

**Related Provisions**: 114 — Individual resident in Canada during only part of year; 117(1) — Tax payable under this Part; 217(c) — Election respecting certain payments.

**Notes**: 118.91(b)(i) amended by 1998 Budget to add reference to 118.62, effective for 1998 and later taxation years.

Opening words of 118.91 and closing words of 118.91(b) amended by 1993 technical bill, effective for 1992 and later taxation years. However, it does not apply to the 1992 taxation year if the taxpayer elected by notifying Revenue Canada in writing by December 31, 1994 for the old version of 114 to apply. (See Notes to 114.) Where the old version applies, read:

> 118.91 **Part-year residents** — Notwithstanding the provisions of sections 118 to 118.9, where an individual is resident in Canada throughout part of a taxation year and throughout some other part of the year is not resident in Canada, is not employed in Canada and is not carrying on business in Canada, for the purpose of computing the individual's tax payable under this Part for the year,
>
> .....
>
> to the period or periods in the year throughout which the individual is resident in Canada, is employed in Canada or is carrying on business in Canada, computed as though the period or periods were the whole taxation year,

The amendment corrects the treatment of periods during which the part-year resident was not resident in Canada but was carrying on business in Canada or was employed in Canada.

118.91 amended by 1991 technical bill, retroactive to its introduction in 1988, to provide that an individual resident in Canada for part of a year is entitled to credits not lower than for an individual who is non-resident throughout the year, and not greater than for an individual resident in Canada throughout the year.

**Definitions [s. 118.91]**: "amount" — 248(1); "Canada" — 255; "carrying on business" — 253; "employed", "individual", "non-resident" — 248(1); "resident in Canada" — 250; "tax payable" — 248(2); "taxation year" — 249; "taxpayer" — 248(1).

### 118.92 Ordering of credits
— In computing an individual's tax payable under this Part, the following provisions shall be applied in the following order: subsections 118(1) and (2), section 118.7, subsection 118(3) and sections 118.3, 118.61, 118.5, 118.6, 118.9, 118.8, 118.2, 118.1, 118.62 and 121.

**Related Provisions**: 117(1) — Tax payable under this Part.

**Notes**: 118.92 amended by 1998 Budget to add reference to 118.62, effective for 1998 and later taxation years. Amended by 1997 Budget to add reference to 118.61, effective for 1997 and later taxation years.

**Definitions [s. 118.92]**: "individual" — 248(1); "tax payable" — 248(2).

**Interpretation Bulletins**: IT-523: Order of provisions applicable in computing an individual's taxable income and tax payable.

### 118.93 Credits in separate returns
— Where a separate return of income with respect to a taxpayer is filed under subsection 70(2), 104(23) or 150(4) for a particular period and another return of income under this Part with respect to the taxpayer is filed for a period ending in the calendar year in which the particular period ends, for the purpose of computing the tax payable under this Part by the taxpayer in those returns, the total of all deductions claimed in all those returns under any of subsection 118(3) and sections 118.1 to 118.7 and 118.9 shall not exceed the total that could be deducted under those provi-

---

[17] Not indexed for inflation.

sions for the year with respect to the taxpayer if no separate returns were filed under subsections 70(2), 104(23) and 150(4).

**Related Provisions**: 114.2 — Deductions in separate returns; 117(1) — Tax payable under this Part.

**Definitions [s. 118.93]**: "calendar year" — *Interpretation Act* 37(1)(a); "taxpayer" — 248(1).

**Interpretation Bulletins**: IT-326R3: Returns of deceased persons as "another person"; IT-513R: Personal tax credits; IT-517R: Pension tax credit.

**118.94 Tax payable by non-resident** — Sections 118 and 118.2, subsections 118.3(2) and (3) and sections 118.6, 118.8 and 118.9 do not apply for the purpose of computing the tax payable under this Part for a taxation year by an individual who at no time in the year is resident in Canada unless all or substantially all of the individual's income for the year is included in computing the individual's taxable income earned in Canada for the year.

**Related Provisions**: 117(1) — Tax payable under this Part; 217 — Election respecting certain payments.

**Notes**: The CCRA takes the position that "all or substantially all" means 90% or more.

118.94 amended by 1991 technical bill, retroactive to 1988, to remove the "all or substantially all" requirement for the tuition fee, Canada Pension Plan contribution, and unemployment insurance premium credits (under 118.5 and 118.7).

**Definitions [s. 118.94]**: "amount" — 248(1); "individual" — 248(1); "resident in Canada" — 250; "tax payable" — 248(2); "taxable income" — 2(2), 248(1); "taxable income earned in Canada" — 115(1), 248(1); "taxation year" — 249.

**Interpretation Bulletins**: IT-171R2: Non-resident individuals — computation of taxable income earned in Canada and non-refundable tax credits; IT-513R: Personal tax credits.

**118.95 Credits in year of bankruptcy** — Notwithstanding sections 118 to 118.9, for the purpose of computing an individual's tax payable under this Part for a taxation year that ends in a calendar year in which the individual becomes bankrupt, the individual shall be allowed only

(a) such of the deductions as the individual is entitled to under subsection 118(3) and sections 118.1, 118.2, 118.5, 118.6, 118.62 and 118.7 as can reasonably be considered wholly applicable to the taxation year, and

(b) such part of the deductions as the individual is entitled to under sections 118 (other than subsection 118(3)), 118.3, 118.8 and 118.9 as can reasonably be considered applicable to the taxation year,

except that the total of the amounts so deductible for all taxation years of the individual in the calendar year under any of those provisions shall not exceed the amount that would have been deductible under that provision in respect of the calendar year if the individual had not become bankrupt.

**Related Provisions [s. 118.95]**: 122.5(7) — Parallel rule for GST credit; 122.61(3.1) — Parallel rule for Child Tax Benefit; 128(2)(e)(iii) — Credits allowed on return by trustee.

**Notes**: 118.95(a) amended by 1998 Budget to add reference to 118.62, effective for 1998 and later taxation years.

118.95 added by 1995-97 technical bill, effective for bankruptcies that occur after April 26, 1995. Before this amendment, an individual who went bankrupt could claim full credits on both the pre- and post-bankruptcy returns for the same year (see 128(2)). Now the credits must be prorated (or allocated to one return or the other, for credits based on expenditures or the receipt of certain types of income), so that they cannot be double-claimed.

**Definitions [s. 118.95]**: "bankrupt" — 248(1); "calendar year" — *Interpretation Act* 37(1)(a); "individual" — 248(1); "taxation year" — 249.

**Interpretation Bulletins [s. 118.95]**: IT-513R: Personal tax credits.

**119. (1)–(10)** [Obsolete]

**Notes**: Block averaging under 119(1) was eliminated by 1988 tax reform, effective for any five-year block beginning after 1987 (per 119(4)). The last block for which averaging could be used was 1987–91. For taxpayers with fluctuating incomes, some income averaging may be possible with RRSPs. See 146(5) and (8) and Notes to 146(10). See also Notes to 15(2), and the Proposed Amendment under 56(8). See also the net income stabilization account (NISA) provisions for farmers.

### Proposed Addition — New 119

**119. Former resident — credit for tax paid** — If at any particular time an individual was deemed by subsection 128.1(4) to have disposed of a capital property that was a taxable Canadian property of the individual throughout the period that began at the particular time and that ends at the first time, after the particular time, at which the individual disposes of the property, there may be deducted in computing the individual's tax payable under this Part for the taxation year that includes the particular time the lesser of

(a) that proportion of the individual's tax for the year otherwise payable under this Part (within the meaning assigned by paragraph (a) of the definition "tax for the year otherwise payable under this Part" in subsection 126(7)) that

(i) the individual's taxable capital gain from the disposition of the property at the particular time

is of

(ii) the amount determined under paragraph 114(a) in respect of the individual for the year, and

(b) that proportion of the individual's tax payable under Part XIII in respect of dividends received during the period by the individual in respect of the property and amounts deemed under Part XIII to have been paid during the period to the individual as dividends from corporations resident in Canada, to the extent that the amounts can reasonably be considered to relate to the property, that

(i) the amount by which the individual's loss from the disposition of the property at the end of the period is reduced by subsection 40(3.7)

is of

(ii) the total amount of those dividends.

**Application**: Bill C-43 (First Reading September 20, 2000), s. 66, will repeal s. 119 applicable to 1995 *et seq.*, and add the above s. 119, applicable to dispositions after December 23, 1998 by individuals who cease to be resident in Canada after October 1, 1996.

**Technical Notes**: Existing section 119 of the Act provides for a five-year block averaging for farmers and fishermen. Since the section is no longer active, it is repealed effective for the 1995 and subsequent taxation years.

New section 119 of the Act, which is unrelated to repealed section 119, provides a special tax credit in certain cases where the "stop-loss" rule in new subsection 40(3.7) of the Act applies to an individual who ceased to be resident in Canada.

Under amended subsection 128.1(4) of the Act, individuals who emigrate from Canada are treated as having disposed of most properties, for proceeds equal to the fair market value of the properties. Such an individual may therefore be treated as having realized an accrued gain immediately before leaving Canada, and will be subject to tax on the gain. If the individual subsequently receives dividends in respect of the same property, a loss realized on a later disposition of the property may be reduced by new subsection 40(3.7) of the Act, and thus may not be available to offset the gain that resulted from the subsection 128.1(4) deemed disposition. Part or all of the tax liability arising from the gain would thus remain payable. However, the individual may also have paid tax on those post-departure dividends, under Part XIII of the Act.

New section 119 addresses this possible overlap between the tax resulting from the subsection 128.1(4) deemed disposition of a capital property and the Part XIII tax on dividends that reduce the taxpayer's loss on the property. In general terms, the rule allows a tax credit equal to the tax on those dividends, up to the amount of the tax on the capital gain that arose on emigration from Canada.

More specifically, section 119 allows the individual to deduct, in computing tax otherwise payable under Part I of the Act for the taxation year in which subsection 128.1(4) treated the individual as having disposed of the property, the lesser of two amounts. The first amount, described in paragraph 119(a), is in effect the amount of tax attributable to the gain on the property. This amount is computed as the proportion of the individual's Part I tax for that year that the taxable capital gain on the particular property is of the individual's total income for the year, as determined under new paragraph 114(a) of the Act.

The second amount, set out in paragraph 119(b), is the Part XIII withholding tax paid (or deemed to have been paid) by the individual on dividends that, under new subsection 40(3.7), have reduced the individual's loss from the disposition of the property. This amount is computed as the proportion of the individual's Part XIII tax in respect of dividends in respect of the property that the subsection 40(3.7) loss reduction is of the total amount of those dividends.

A consequential amendment to subsection 152(6) of the Act ensures that any necessary assessments of tax will be made in order to take account of the effect of new section 119.

**Related Provisions**: 126(2.21) — Foreign tax credit for former resident; 128.1(6)(b)(iii) — Effect of election by returning former resident; 128.3 — Shares acquired on rollover deemed to be same shares for s. 119; 152(6)(c.1) — Minister required to reassess past year to allow additional deduction; 161(7)(a)(i), 164(5)(a.1) — Effect of carryback of loss; 180.1(1.4) — Deduction against individual surtax.

**Definitions [s. 119]**: "amount" — 248(1); "capital property" — 54, 248(1); "corporation" — 248(1), *Interpretation Act* 35(1); "dividend", "individual", "property" — 248(1); "resident in Canada" — 250; "taxable Canadian property" — 248(1); "taxable capital gain" — 38(a), 248(1); "taxation year" — 249; "trust" — 104(1), 248(1), (3).

**120. (1) Income not earned in a province** — There shall be added to the tax otherwise payable under this Part by an individual for a taxation year an amount that bears the same relation to 52% of the tax otherwise payable under this Part by the individual for the year that

### Proposed Amendment — 120(1) opening words

**120. (1) Income not earned in a province** — There shall be added to the tax otherwise payable under this Part by an individual for a taxation year the amount that bears the same relation to 48% of the tax otherwise payable under this Part by the individual for the year that

**Application**: The December 21, 2000 draft legislation, s. 66, will amend the opening words of subsec. 120(1) to read as above, applicable to 2000 *et seq.*

**Technical Notes**: Subsection 120(1) provides for the payment by an individual of an additional tax of 52% of the federal tax otherwise payable in respect of the portion of the individual's income for the year that is not earned in a province. The additional tax has the effect of setting the individual's tax on income earned outside Canada at a level approximating that which would apply if provincial income tax were exigible (i.e., combined federal plus provincial tax).

The subsection is amended to reduce the rate of the additional tax to 48%, from 52%, for the 2000 and subsequent taxation years, in recognition of reductions to tax rates in the provinces.

**Notice of Ways and Means Motion, federal budget, February 28, 2000**: *Income Not Earned in a Province*

(12) That, for the 2000 and subsequent taxation years, the surtax applicable to an individual's income not earned in a province be reduced to 48% from 52%.

**Federal budget, supplementary information, February 28, 2000**: *Reduction in Federal Surtax for Non-Residents*

Individuals who have income which is considered to have been earned in Canada, but which is not considered to be earned in a province, pay a special federal surtax in addition to their regular federal tax. Individuals with such income include

- deemed residents, such as members of the Armed Forces who reside outside of Canada and therefore have no province of residence;

- Canadian residents with income from a permanent establishment in a foreign country; and
- non-residents who have business or employment income taxable in Canada.

The federal surtax for non-residents, which is currently 52% of basic federal tax, ensures that deemed residents and others with income not earned in a province face a total income tax burden roughly comparable to that of Canadian residents. The surtax, which was introduced in 1972, is calculated to approximate provincial taxes. The surtax percentage has been adjusted on several occasions since 1972 to reflect changes in average provincial tax rates.

In light of recent changes in provincial tax rates, the budget proposes to reduce the federal surtax on income not earned in a province from 52% of basic federal tax to 48%.

(a) the individual's income for the year, other than the individual's income earned in the year in a province,

bears to

(b) the individual's income for the year.

**Related Provisions**: 117(1) — Tax payable under this Part; 120(3) — "Income for the year" defined; 120(4) — Income earned in the year in a province.

**Notes**: 120(1) replaces the provincial tax that is imposed on income earned in a province (see tables in introductory pages and Notes to 117(2)).

120(1) amended by 1989 Budget, effective 1990. For 1989, read "49.5%" in place of "52%". For 1982 through 1988, read "47%".

**Interpretation Bulletins**: IT-393R2: Election re tax on rents and timber royalties — non-residents; IT-434R: Rental of real property by individual.

**(2) Amount deemed paid in prescribed manner [Quebec abatement]** — Each individual is deemed to have paid, in prescribed manner and on prescribed dates, on account of the individual's tax under this Part for a taxation year an amount that bears the same relation to 3% of the tax otherwise payable under this Part by the individual for the year that

(a) the individual's income earned in the year in a province that, on January 1, 1973, was a province providing schooling allowances within the meaning of the *Youth Allowances Act*, chapter Y-1 of the Revised Statutes of Canada, 1970,

bears to

(b) the individual's income for the year.

**Related Provisions**: 117(1) — Tax payable under this Part; 120(3) — "Income for the year" defined; 152(1)(b) — Determination of amount on assessment; 152(4.2)(d) — Redetermination at taxpayer's request; 160.1 — Where excess refunded.

**Notes**: 120(2)(a) refers to Quebec; 120(2) effectively provides a 3% refundable credit against federal tax for residents of Quebec. A further 13.5% credit is allowed under s. 27 of the *Federal-Provincial Fiscal Arrangements and Federal Post-Secondary Education and Health Contributions Act*, R.S.C. 1985, c. F-8. The combined 16.5% credit is calculated on *tax*, not income. Thus, federal tax is multiplied by 0.835 to apply the credit. The 16%, 24% (for 2000) and 29% federal tax brackets are thus 13.36%, 20.04% and 24.215% respectively for residents of Quebec.

**Regulations**: 6401 (prescribed date is December 31 of each year).

**Remission Orders**: *Income Earned in Quebec Income Tax Remission Order*, P.C. 1989-1204 (reduction in withholdings for certain income related to Quebec).

**(2.1) Idem** — Where section 119 is applicable to the computation of an individual's tax for a taxation year (referred to in that section as the "year of averaging"), notwithstanding subsection (2), the amount deemed by that subsection to have been paid on account of the individual's tax under this Part for the year shall be equal to the amount that would be determined under that subsection if the reference therein to "the tax otherwise payable under this Part by the individual for the year" were read as a reference to "the amount that would be the tax otherwise payable under this Part by the individual if the individual's taxable income for the year were the individual's average net income (within the meaning of paragraph 119(1)(c)) for the year".

**Proposed Repeal — 120(2.1)**

**Application**: Bill C-43 (First Reading September 20, 2000), subsec. 67(1), will repeal subsec. 120(2.1), applicable to 1996 *et seq.*

**Technical Notes**: Subsection 120(2.1) of the Act provides a special rule for computing the amount that is considered, under subsection 120(2), to have been paid on behalf of an individual's tax for a taxation year. This special rule applies where existing section 119 of the Act applies to the individual for the year. Existing section 119 is no longer active, and is replaced with a new, unrelated rule. Subsection 120(2.1) is therefore repealed, for the 1996 and subsequent taxation years.

**(2.2) Amount deemed paid [First Nations tax]** — An individual is deemed to have paid on the last day of a taxation year, on account of the individual's tax under this Part for the year, an amount equal to the individual's income tax payable for the year to an Aboriginal government pursuant to a law of that government made in accordance with a tax sharing agreement between that government and the Government of Canada.

**Related Provisions**: 81(1)(a) — Deduction for amounts exempted under *Indian Act*; 152(1)(b) — Determination of amount on assessment; 152(4.2)(d) — Redetermination at taxpayer's request; 156.1(1)"net tax owing"(b)B, E, F, 156.1(1.3) — First Nations tax counted for instalment purposes.

**Notes**: 120(2.2) added by 1999 Budget, effective for 1999 and later taxation years. It ensures that any amounts payable to a First Nations (aboriginal) government is fully credited against income tax payable for the year, as though it had been paid as an income tax instalment.

**(3) Definition of "the individual's income for the year"** — For the purpose of this section, "the individual's income for the year" means

(a) in the case of an individual to whom section 114 applies who was resident in Canada during part of the year and during some other part of the year was not resident in Canada, the amount that would be determined under that section to be the individual's taxable income for the year if that section were read without reference to the words following paragraph 114(b);

(b) in the case of an individual to whom section 115 applies who was not resident in Canada at any time in the taxation year, the amount that would be determined under Division D to be the individual's taxable income for the year if subsection 115(1) were read without reference to the words following paragraph 115(1)(c); and

**Proposed Amendment — 120(3)(a), (b)**

**(3) Definition of "individual's income for the year"** — In subsections (1) and (2), an "individual's income for the year" means

(a) if section 114 applies to the individual in respect of the year, the amount determined under paragraph 114(a) in respect of the individual for the year; and

(b) if the individual was non-resident throughout the year, the individual's taxable income earned in Canada for the year determined without reference to paragraphs 115(1)(d) to (f).

**Notes**: Finance officials have confirmed that the "and" at the end of para. (a) in the Proposed Amendment will move to the end of para. (b), since para. (c), added by the 1999 Budget, is in force for 2000 and later.

**Application**: Bill C-43 (First Reading September 20, 2000), subsec. 67(2), will amend subsec. 120(3) to read as above, applicable to 1998 et seq.

**Technical Notes**: Section 120 of the Act sets out rules that integrate the federal and provincial income tax systems for individuals. Subsection 120(1) imposes an additional amount of federal tax on income that is not subject to provincial or territorial tax, while subsection 120(2) provides part of the tax abatement for income earned in Quebec (the rest is found in legislation concerning federal-provincial fiscal arrangements).

For the purposes of subsections 120(1) and (2) of the Act, subsection 120(3) defines the phrase "the individual's income for the year" where sections 114 or 115 of the Act — dealing with part-year residents and non-residents, respectively — apply in respect of the individual for the year. Subsection 120(3) is amended, with application to the 1998 and subsequent taxation years, as a consequence of changes to section 114 of the Act. The amendment makes no substantive change, but keeps the reference in step with the changes to section 114. For additional information, see the commentary on section 114.

(c) in the case of an individual who is a specified individual in relation to the year, the individual's income for the year computed without reference to paragraph 20(1)(ww).

**Notes**: 120(3) opening words amended by 1999 Budget, effective for 2000 and later taxation years, to change "In subsections (1) and (2)" to "For the purpose of this section".

120(3)(c) added by 1999 Budget, effective for 2000 and later taxation years.

**(3.1)** [Repealed under former Act]

**Notes**: 120(3.1), repealed by 1985 Budget, provided a federal tax reduction, which varied over the years from $50 to $200 per person.

**(4) Definitions** — In this section,

**"income earned in the year in a province"** means amounts determined under rules prescribed for the purpose by regulations made on the recommendation of the Minister of Finance;

**Notes**: 120(4)"income earned in the year in a province" was para. 120(4)(a) before consolidation in R.S.C. 1985 (5th Supp.), effective for taxation years ending after November 1991.

**Regulations**: 2600–2607 (rules determining income earned in the year in a province).

**Interpretation Bulletins**: IT-434R: Rental of real property by individual.

**"province [para. 120(4)(b)]"** — [Repealed under former Act]

**Notes**: Para. 120(4)(b), which defined "province", was repealed in 1980. See the definition of "province" in subsec. 35(1) of the *Interpretation Act*.

**"tax otherwise payable under this Part"** by an individual for a taxation year means the total of

(a) the greater of

(i) the individual's minimum amount for the year determined under section 127.51, and

(ii) the amount that, but for this section, would be the individual's tax payable under this Part for the year if this Part were read without reference to

(A) subsection 120.4(2) and sections 126, 127, 127.4 and 127.41, and

**Proposed Amendment — 120(4)"tax otherwise payable under this Part"(a)(ii)(A)**

(A) section 119, subsection 120.4(2) and sections 126, 127, 127.4 and 127.41, and

**Application**: Bill C-43 (First Reading September 20, 2000), subsec. 67(3), will amend cl. (a)(ii)(A) of the definition "tax otherwise payable under this Part" in subsec. 120(4) to read as above, applicable to 1996 et seq. except that, in its application to taxation years that end before 2000 [see Notes below], subsec. (3) of the amending legislation shall be read as follows:

(3) Paragraph (b) of the definition "tax otherwise payable under this Part" in subsection 120(4) of the Act is replaced by the following:

(b) the amount that, but for this section and subsection 117(6), would be the tax payable under this Part by the individual for the year if this Part were read without reference to any of sections 119, 126, 127 and 127.4.

**Technical Notes**: Subsection 120(4) includes a definition of "tax otherwise payable under this Part". The amendment to this subsection, which applies to the 1996 and subsequent taxation years, excludes from the definition any deduction from tax in respect of the new credit, under section 119 of the Act, for certain taxes paid by a former resident of Canada. In order to take into account an amendment to the definition of "tax otherwise payable under this Part" in the 1999 budget bill (Bill C-25), a special transitional rule is provided for taxation years that end before 2000.

(B) where the individual is a specified individual in relation to the year, section 121 in its application to dividends included in

Subdivision a — Computation of Tax: Individuals    S. 120.1

computing the individual's split income for the year, and

(b) where the individual is a specified individual in relation to the year, the amount, if any, by which

(i) 29% of the individual's split income for the year

exceeds

(ii) the total of all amounts each of which is an amount that may be deducted under section 121 and that can reasonably be considered to be in respect of a dividend included in computing the individual's split income for the year.

**Related Provisions**: 117(1) — Tax payable under this Part; 127(17) — "Tax otherwise payable".

**Notes**: 120(4)"tax otherwise payable under this Part" amended by 1999 Budget, effective for 2000 and later taxation years. For 1998 and 1999, read:

"tax otherwise payable under this Part" by an individual for a taxation year means the greater of

(a) the amount, if any, by which the total of

(i) the individual's minimum amount for the year determined under section 127.51, and

(ii) any amount required under subsection 120.1(2) to be added to the tax payable by the individual for the year under this Part,

exceeds any amount that may be deducted under subsection 120.1(1) from the tax payable by the individual for the year under this Part, and

(b) the amount that, but for this section and subsection 117(6), would be the tax payable under this Part by the individual for the year if this Part were read without reference to any of sections 126, 127 and 127.4.

Para. (b) amended by 1998 Budget, effective for 1998 and later taxation years, to change "were not entitled to any deduction under" to "were read without reference to"; and to delete an obsolete reference to 127.2. The first change was needed because 127(27)-(35) provide for income inclusions as well as deductions.

120(4)"tax otherwise payable under this Part" was para. 120(4)(c) before consolidation in R.S.C. 1985 (5th Supp.), effective for taxation years ending after November 1991. See Table of Concordance.

**Definitions [s. 120]**: "amount" — 248(1); "Canada" — 255; "income earned in the year in a province" — 120(4); "income for the year" — 120(3); "individual"; "prescribed" — 248(1); "province" — *Interpretation Act* 35(1); "regulation" — 248(1); "resident in Canada" — 250; "specified individual", "split income" — 120.4(1), 248(1); "tax otherwise payable" — 120(4); "tax payable" — 248(2); "taxable income" — 2(2), 248(1); "taxation year" — 249; "taxpayer" — 248(1).

**I.T. Application Rules [s. 120]**: 40(1), (2); 49(3).

## 120.1 [Repealed]

**Notes**: 120.1 repealed by 1999 Budget, effective for 1998 and later taxation years. It provided a credit for amounts forward-averaged before 1988. See Notes to repealed 110.4. For 1990-97, read:

120.1 (1) Forward averaging credit — There may be deducted from the amount that would, but for this section, be the tax otherwise payable under this Part (other than the tax payable with respect to a return of income referred to in subsection 110.4(5)) by an individual for a taxation year an amount equal to the product obtained when

(a) the amount specified in the individual's election for the year under subsection 110.4(2) and, where the individual's legal representative has filed on the individual's behalf an election under subsection (2) for the year, the individual's accumulated averaging amount at the end of the year

is multiplied by

(b) the percentage referred to in paragraph 117(2)(c).

(2) **Year of death** — Where an individual dies in a taxation year before 1998 (and is resident in Canada at the time of death) and the individual's legal representative files with the individual's return of income (other than a return of income referred to in subsection 110.4(5)) for the year an election in prescribed form on or before the day on or before which the return is required to be filed, there shall be added to the amount that would, but for this section, be the individual's tax payable for the year under this Part with respect to the return of income an amount equal to the amount, if any, by which

(a) the total of the taxes that would have been payable by the individual under this Part for the three immediately preceding taxation years if the individual's taxable income otherwise determined for each of those years were increased by ⅓ of the individual's accumulated averaging amount at the end of the year in which the individual died and if this Part were read without reference to sections 119 to 127.3

exceeds

(b) the total of the taxes that would have been payable by the individual under this Part for the three immediately preceding taxation years if this Part were read without reference to sections 119 to 127.3.

(3) **Deduction and additions** — Each amount deducted or added under subsection (1) or (2) in computing the tax payable under this Part by an individual for a taxation year shall, notwithstanding those subsections, be equal to the total of

(a) the amount that would, but for this subsection, be determined for the year under subsection (1) or (2), as the case may be, and

(b) an amount equal to that proportion of 52% of the amount referred to in paragraph (a) that

(i) the individual's income for the year, other than the individual's income earned in the year in a province,

is of

(ii) the individual's income for the year.

(4) **Presumption** — Where the amount deductible by an individual under subsection (1) exceeds the amount that would, but for that subsection, be the individual's tax otherwise payable under this Part for the year, the excess shall be deemed to be an amount paid by the individual, on the day the individual was required to file the election under subsection 110.4(2), on account of the individual's tax for the year under this Part.

(5) **Reduction** — Notwithstanding subsection (4), the amount of the excess referred to in that subsection shall be reduced by an amount equal to that proportion of 16.5% of the amount of the excess that

(a) the individual's income earned in the year in a province that, on January 1, 1973, was a province providing schooling allowances (within the meaning of the *Youth Allowances Act*, chapter Y-1 of the Revised Statutes of Canada, 1970)

S. 120.1      Income Tax Act, Part I, Division E

is of

    (b) the individual's income for the year.

**(6) Individual not resident** — Where an individual was not resident in Canada throughout the taxation years referred to in paragraph (2)(b), the amount determined under that paragraph shall be equal to the amount that would have been so determined if the individual had been resident in Canada throughout those years and the individual's incomes for those years had been from sources in Canada.

**(7) Application** — This section does not apply to an individual described in subsection (6) unless the individual's legal representatives have, on or before the day on or before which they were required to file the individual's return of income under this Part for the taxation year in which the individual died (or would have been required to file such a return had tax been payable by the individual under this Part for the year), filed a return of the individual's income for each of the three taxation years referred to in paragraph (2)(b) in the same form and containing the same information as the return that the individual, or legal representatives, would have been required to file under this Part if the individual had been resident in Canada throughout each of those three years and if tax had been payable by the individual under this Part for each of those three years.

**(8) Amount required to be included** — Where an amount is required by virtue of this section to be included in computing the individual's tax otherwise payable under this Part for a taxation year, the references in subsection 120(1) and section 121 of this Act and subsection 120(3.1) of the *Income Tax Act*, chapter 148 of the Revised Statutes of Canada, 1952, to "the tax otherwise payable under this Part" shall be read as references to "the amount that would, but for section 120.1, be the tax otherwise payable under this Part".

120.1(3) amended by 1991 technical bill, to correspond to 1989 Budget changes made to 120(1). For 1989, read "49.5%" in place of "52%". For 1988, read "47%".

120.1(5)(a) referred to Quebec (see Notes to 120(2)).

**120.2 (1) Minimum tax carry-over** — There may be deducted from the amount that, but for this section, section 120 and subsection 120.4(2), would be an individual's tax payable under this Part for a particular taxation year such amount as the individual claims not exceeding the lesser of

    (a) the portion of the total of the individual's additional taxes determined under subsection (3) for the 7 taxation years immediately preceding the particular year that was not deducted in computing the individual's tax payable under this Part for a taxation year preceding the particular year, and

    (b) the amount, if any, by which

        (i) the amount that, but for this section, section 120 and subsection 120.4(2), would be the individual's tax payable under this Part for the particular year if the individual were not entitled to any deduction under any of sections 126, 127 and 127.4

exceeds

        (ii) the individual's minimum amount for the particular year determined under section 127.51.

**Notes**: See Notes to 127.5 for an overview of the Alternative Minimum Tax (AMT) in 127.5–127.55.

120.2(1) opening words amended by 1999 Budget, effective for 2000 and later taxation years, to change "section 120.1" to "subsection 120.4(2).

120.2(1)(b)(i) amended by 1999 Budget, effective for 2000 and later taxation years. For 1986–99, read:

    (i) the amount that, but for this section, subsection 117(6), sections 120 and 120.1, would be the individual's tax payable under this Part for the particular year if the individual were not entitled to any deduction under any of sections 126, 127 and 127.2 to 127.4

**(2) [Repealed under former Act]**

**Notes**: 120.2(2), repealed by 1988 tax reform, provided a carryback of minimum tax credit from the year of death. Minimum tax no longer applies to the year of death: see 127.55(c).

**(3) Additional tax determined** — For the purposes of subsection (1), additional tax of an individual for a taxation year is the amount, if any, by which

    (a) the individual's minimum amount for the year determined under section 127.51

exceeds the total of

    (b) the amount that, but for section 120 and subsection 120.4(2), would be the individual's tax payable under this Part for the year if the individual were not entitled to any deduction under any of sections 126, 127 and 127.4, and

    (c) that proportion of the amount, if any, by which

        (i) the individual's special foreign tax credit for the year determined under section 127.54

exceeds

        (ii) the total of all amounts deductible under section 126 from the individual's tax for the year

that

        (iii) the amount of the individual's foreign taxes for the year within the meaning assigned by subsection 127.54(1)

is of

        (iv) the amount that would be the individual's foreign taxes for the year within the meaning assigned by subsection 127.54(1) if the definition "foreign taxes" in that subsection were read without reference to "$2/3$ of".

**Related Provisions**: 117(1) — Tax payable under this Part.

**Notes**: 120.2(3)(b) amended by 1999 Budget, effective for 2000 and later taxation years. For 1986-99, read:

    (b) the amount that, but for subsection 117(6) and sections 120 and 120.1, would be the tax payable by the individual under this Part for the year if the individual were not entitled to any deduction under any of sections 126, 127 and 127.2 to 127.4, and

Subdivision a — Computation of Tax: Individuals    S. 120.31

**(4) Where subsec. (1) does not apply** — Subsection (1) does not apply in respect of

(a) an individual's return of income filed under subsection 70(2), paragraph 104(23)(d) or 128(2)(f) or subsection 150(4); or

(b) a taxation year of an individual in respect of which the individual has made an election under section 119.

> **Proposed Amendment — 120.2(4)**
>
> **(4) Where subsection (1) does not apply** — Subsection (1) does not apply in respect of an individual's return of income filed under subsection 70(2), paragraph 104(23)(d) or 128(2)(f) or subsection 150(4).
>
> **Application:** Bill C-43 (First Reading September 20, 2000), s. 68, will amend subsec. 120.2(4) to read as above, applicable to 1996 *et seq.*
>
> **Technical Notes:** Section 120.2 of the Act allows an individual to apply additional taxes, imposed for a given year under the section 127.5 minimum tax, against the individual's ordinary Part I tax liabilities for following years. Paragraph 120.2(4)(b) prevents such a carryforward in respect of any taxation year in which the taxpayer has elected under existing section 119 of the Act. Existing section 119 no longer applies, and is replaced with an unrelated new rule. Subsection 120.2(4) is therefore restructured to remove its reference to section 119. This amendment applies to the 1996 and subsequent taxation years.

**Notes:** 120.2(4)(a) amended by 1995-97 technical bill, effective for taxation years that begin after April 26, 1995, to change reference from 128(2)(e) to 128(2)(f).

**Definitions [s. 120.2]:** "amount", "individual" — 248(1); "tax payable" — 248(2); "taxation year" — 249.

**120.3 CPP/QPP disability [or other] benefits for previous years** — There shall be added in computing an individual's tax payable under this Part for a particular taxation year the total of all amounts each of which is the amount, if any, by which

(a) the amount that would have been the tax payable under this Part by the individual for a preceding taxation year if that portion of any amount not included in computing the individual's income for the particular year because of subsection 56(8) and that relates to the preceding year had been included in computing the individual's income for the preceding year

exceeds

(b) the tax payable under this Part by the individual for the preceding year.

**Notes:** 120.3 added by 1991 Budget, effective 1990. See Notes to 56(8).

**Definitions [s. 120.3]:** "amount", "individual" — 248(1); "tax payable" — 248(2); "taxation year" — 249.

**120.31 Lump-sum payments — (1) Definitions** — The definitions in subsection 110.2(1) apply in this section.

**Notes:** See Notes at end of 120.31.

**(2) Addition to tax payable** — There shall be added in computing an individual's tax payable under this Part for a particular taxation year the total of all amounts each of which is the amount, if any, by which

(a) the individual's notional tax payable for an eligible taxation year to which a specified portion of a qualifying amount received by the individual relates and in respect of which an amount is deducted under section 110.2 in computing the individual's taxable income for the particular year

exceeds

(b) the individual's tax payable under this Part for the eligible taxation year.

**Forms:** T1198: Statement of qualifying retroactive lump-sum payment.

**(3) Notional tax payable** — For the purpose of subsection (2), an individual's notional tax payable for an eligible taxation year, calculated for the purpose of computing the individual's tax payable under this Part for a taxation year (in this subsection referred to as "the year of receipt") in which the individual received a qualifying amount, is the total of

(a) the amount, if any, by which

(i) the amount that would be the individual's tax payable under this Part for the eligible taxation year if the total of all amounts, each of which is the specified portion, in relation to the eligible taxation year, of a qualifying amount received by the individual before the end of the year of receipt, were added in computing the individual's taxable income for the eligible taxation year

exceeds

(ii) the total of all amounts each of which is an amount, in respect of a qualifying amount received by the individual before the year of receipt, that was included because of this paragraph in computing the individual's notional tax payable under this Part for the eligible taxation year, and

(b) where the eligible taxation year ended before the taxation year preceding the year of receipt, an amount equal to the amount that would be calculated as interest payable on the amount determined under paragraph (a) if it were so calculated

(i) for the period that began on May 1 of the year following the eligible taxation year and that ended immediately before the year of receipt, and

(ii) at the prescribed rate that is applicable for the purpose of subsection 164(3) with respect to the period.

**Regulations:** 4301(b) (prescribed rate of interest).

**Notes [s. 120.31]:** 120.31, combined with 110.2, provides retroactive averaging of certain kinds of lump-sum income payments. See Notes to 110.2. It was added by 1999 Budget, effective for 1995 and

1047

later taxation years, and notwithstanding 152(4) to (5), any assessment of an individual's tax payable for any taxation year that ended before 1999 shall be made as necessary to take into account the application of 120.31.

**Definitions [s. 120.31]**: "amount" — 248(1); "eligible taxation year" — 110.2(1), 120.31(1); "individual" — 248(1); "notional tax payable" — 120.31(3); "prescribed" — 248(1); "qualifying amount", "specified portion" — 110.2(1), 120.31(1); "taxable income" — 248(1); "taxation year" — 249; "year of receipt" — 120.31(3).

## 120.4 Tax on split income [Kiddie tax] — (1) Definitions — The definitions in this subsection apply in this section.

**"excluded amount"**, in respect of an individual for a taxation year, means an amount that is the income from a property acquired by or for the benefit of the individual as a consequence of the death of

(a) a parent of the individual; or

(b) any person, if the individual is

(i) enrolled as a full-time student during the year at a post-secondary educational institution (as defined in subsection 146.1(1)), or

(ii) an individual in respect of whom an amount may be deducted under section 118.3 in computing a taxpayer's tax payable under this Part for the year.

**Related Provisions**: 248(8) — Occurrences as a consequence of death.

**Notes**: See Notes at end of 120.4.

**"specified individual"**, in relation to a taxation year, means an individual who

(a) had not attained the age of 17 years before the year;

(b) at no time in the year was non-resident; and

(c) has a parent who is resident in Canada at any time in the year.

**Related Provisions**: 248(1)"specified individual" — Definition applies to entire Act.

**"split income"**, of a specified individual for a taxation year, means the total of all amounts (other than excluded amounts) each of which is

(a) an amount required to be included in computing the individual's income for the year

(i) in respect of taxable dividends received by the individual in respect of shares of the capital stock of a corporation (other than shares of a class listed on a prescribed stock exchange or shares of the capital stock of a mutual fund corporation), or

(ii) because of the application of section 15 in respect of the ownership by any person of shares of the capital stock of a corporation (other than shares of a class listed on a prescribed stock exchange),

(b) a portion of an amount included because of the application of paragraph 96(1)(f) in computing the individual's income for the year, to the extent that the portion

(i) is not included in an amount described in paragraph (a), and

(ii) can reasonably be considered to be income derived from the provision of goods or services by a partnership or trust to or in support of a business carried on by

(A) a person who is related to the individual at any time in the year,

(B) a corporation of which a person who is related to the individual is a specified shareholder at any time in the year, or

(C) a professional corporation of which a person related to the individual is a shareholder at any time in the year, or

(c) a portion of an amount included because of the application of subsection 104(13) or 105(2) in respect of a trust (other than a mutual fund trust) in computing the individual's income for the year, to the extent that the portion

(i) is not included in an amount described in paragraph (a), and

(ii) can reasonably be considered

(A) to be in respect of taxable dividends received in respect of shares of the capital stock of a corporation (other than shares of a class listed on a prescribed stock exchange or shares of the capital stock of a mutual fund corporation),

(B) to arise because of the application of section 15 in respect of the ownership by any person of shares of the capital stock of a corporation (other than shares of a class listed on a prescribed stock exchange), or

(C) to be income derived from the provision of goods or services by a partnership or trust to or in support of a business carried on by

(I) a person who is related to the individual at any time in the year,

(II) a corporation of which a person who is related to the individual is a specified shareholder at any time in the year, or

(III) a professional corporation of which a person related to the individual is a shareholder at any time in the year.

**Related Provisions**: 20(1)(ww) — Split income deducted from income for regular tax purposes; 56(5), 74.4(2)(g), 74.5(13) — Attribution rules do not apply to split income; 108(5) — Split income paid out by trust to beneficiary retains its characteristics; 120.4(2) — Tax on split income; 248(1)"split income" — Definition applies to entire Act.

**Notes**: See Notes at end of 120.4.

The mere rental or lease of property by a partnership or trust is not considered by the CCRA to be the "provision of goods or services" under (c)(i)(C) if no services are provided with the lease: VIEWS doc 2000-0012635.

**(2) Tax on split income** — There shall be added to a specified individual's tax payable under this Part for a taxation year 29% of the individual's split income for the year.

**Related Provisions**: 20(1)(ww) — Split income deducted from income for regular tax purposes; 120.2(1), 120.2(1)(b)(i) — No AMT carryover allowed against split-income tax; 120.4(3) — Minimum amount of income-splitting tax; 127.5 — Alternative minimum tax cannot be less than split-income tax; 160(1.2) — Parent jointly liable with child for tax.

**Notes**: The 29% rate is the same as the top personal rate in 117(2)(c). The effect is to tax children's "split income", such as dividends from private corporations, at the top rate that applies to high-income taxpayers (but without the high-income federal and provincial surtaxes unless the tax reaches the levels that trigger such surtaxes).

**(3) Tax payable by a specified individual** — Notwithstanding any other provision of this Act, where an individual is a specified individual in relation to a taxation year, the individual's tax payable under this Part for the year shall not be less than the amount by which

(a) the amount added under subsection (2) to the individual's tax payable under this Part for the year

exceeds

(b) the total of all amounts each of which is an amount that

(i) may be deducted under section 121 or 126 in computing the individual's tax payable under this Part for the year, and

(ii) can reasonably be considered to be in respect of an amount included in computing the individual's split income for the year.

**Notes [s. 120.4]**: 120.4 added by 1999 Budget, effective for 2000 and later taxation years. It implements the "kiddie tax" on split income at the top marginal rate, but without the high-income surtaxes (see Notes to 120.4(2)). It applies generally to income of a child under 18 attributable to dividends or shareholder appropriations from private corporations, or to income earned through a trust or partnership that is derived from goods or services provided to (or in support of) a related person's business (see 120.4(1)"split income"). It thus effectively overrides *Ferrel*, [1999] 2 C.T.C. 101 (FCA), and catches income of a parent that is diverted, through a trust or otherwise, to a child's tax return. Since federal and provincial surtaxes will not apply to lower amounts of income, there is still some benefit to having income taxed in the child's hands in this way.

For a detailed discussion of 120.4 and some planning ideas, see Donnelly, Magee & Young, "Income Splitting and the New Kiddie Tax: Major Changes for Minor Children", 48(4) *Canadian Tax Journal* 979-1018 (2000).

**Defintions [s. 120.4]**: "amount", "business" — 248(1); "consequence of the death" — 248(8); "corporation" — 248(1), *Interpretation Act* 35(1); "excluded amount" — 120.4(1); "individual" — 248(1); "mutual fund corporation" — 131(8), 248(1); "mutual fund trust" — 132(6)–(7), 132.2(1)(q), 248(1); "non-resident" — 248(1); "parent" — 252(2)(a); "partnership" — see Notes to 96(1); "person" — 248(1); "prescribed" — 248(1); "prescribed stock exchange" — Reg. 3200, 3201; "professional corporation", "property" — 248(1); "related" — 251(2)–(6); "resident in Canada" — 250; "share", "shareholder" — 248(1); "specified individual" — 120.4(1), 248(1);

"specified shareholder" — 248(1); "split income" — 120.4(1), 248(1); "taxable dividend" — 89(1), 248(1); "taxation year" — 249; "taxpayer" — 248(1); "trust" — 104(1), 248(1), (3).

**121. Deduction for taxable dividends** — There may be deducted from the tax otherwise payable under this Part by an individual for a taxation year ⅔ of any amount that is required by paragraph 82(1)(b) to be included in computing the individual's income for the year.

**Related Provisions**: 82(2) — Dividends deemed received by taxpayer; 117(1) — Tax payable under this Part; 118.92 — Ordering of credits.

**Notes**: The ¼ gross-up under 82(1)(b) increases the amount on which personal tax is paid to the theoretical pre-tax corporate income (assuming a corporate federal/provincial tax rate of 20%). The dividend tax credit under 121 then refunds an amount equal to the tax paid, in theory, by the corporation, in order to achieve "integration". The ⅔ figure is to leave room for a parallel provincial tax reduction. The effect of the parallel provincial credit in each province means that the effective dividend tax credit is not exactly the same as the gross-up under 82(1)(b).

**Definitions [s. 121]**: "amount", "individual" — 248(1); "taxation year" — 249.

**I.T. Application Rules**: 40(1), (2).

**Interpretation Bulletins**: IT-67R3: Taxable dividends from corporations resident in Canada; IT-295R4: Taxable dividends received after 1987 by spouse; IT-379R: Employees profit sharing plans — allocations to beneficiaries; IT-524: Trusts — flow-through of taxable dividends to a beneficiary after 1987.

**122. (1) Tax payable by *inter vivos* trust** — Notwithstanding section 117, the tax payable under this Part by an *inter vivos* trust on its amount taxable for a taxation year shall be 29% of its amount taxable for the year.

**Related Provisions**: 104(2) — Multiple trusts can be considered as one, to prevent multiplication of low rate of tax for testamentary trusts; 122(2) — Exception.

**Notes**: This provision sets the tax rate for *inter vivos* trusts (as defined in 108(1)) at a flat rate equal to the highest marginal rate that applies to individuals (see 117(2)(c)). Provincial tax and surtaxes still apply on top of the 29%; see Notes to 117(2) and 180.1.

**Interpretation Bulletins**: IT-83R3: Non-profit organizations — taxation of income from property.

**(1.1) Deductions [personal credits] not permitted [to trust]** — No deduction may be made under section 118 in computing the tax payable by a trust for a taxation year.

**Interpretation Bulletins**: IT-83R3: Non-profit organizations — taxation of income from property; IT-406R2: Tax payable by an *inter vivos* trust.

**(2) Where subsec. (1) does not apply** — Subsection (1) is not applicable for a taxation year of an *inter vivos* trust other than a mutual fund trust if the trust

(a) was established before June 18, 1971;

(b) was resident in Canada on June 18, 1971 and without interruption thereafter until the end of the year;

**S. 122(2)(c)**      Income Tax Act, Part I, Division E

(c) did not carry on any active business in the year;

(d) has not received any property by way of gift since June 18, 1971; and

### Proposed Addition — 122(2)(d.1)

(d.1) was not a trust to which a contribution, within the meaning assigned by section 94, was made after June 22, 2000; and

**Application**: The June 22, 2000 draft legislation, s. 18, will add para. 122(2)(d.1), applicable to taxation years that begin after 2000.

**Technical Notes**: Subsection 122(1) of the Act provides that, instead of graduated income tax rates, *inter vivos* trusts are generally subject to top marginal rates of income tax on their undistributed income. Subsection 122(2) permits graduated income tax rates for certain *inter vivos* trusts established before June 18, 1971. One of the conditions for an *inter vivos* trust continuing to qualify for graduated income tax rates is that it not receive any gifts after June 18, 1971.

Paragraph 122(2)(d.1) is introduced so that the graduated income tax rates cease to apply to a trust in the event that, after June 22, 2000, a "contribution" is made to the trust. The expression "contribution" is defined in new section 94.

This amendment applies to taxation years that begin after 2000.

(e) has not, after June 18, 1971, incurred

    (i) any debt, or

    (ii) any other obligation to pay an amount,

to, or guaranteed by, any person with whom any beneficiary of the trust was not dealing at arm's length.

### Proposed Addition — 122(2)(f)

(f) has not received any property after December 17, 1999, where

    (i) the property was received as a result of a transfer from another trust,

    (ii) subsection (1) applied to a taxation year of the other trust that began before the property was so received, and

    (iii) no change in the beneficial ownership of the property resulted from the transfer.

**Application**: Bill C-43 (First Reading September 20, 2000), s. 69, will add para. 122(2)(f), applicable to 1999 *et seq.*

**Technical Notes**: Subsection 122(1) provides that *inter vivos* trusts are generally subject to income tax at top marginal income tax rates. Subsection 122(2) of the Act permits certain pre-1972 *inter vivos* trusts access to graduated income tax rates.

Subsection 122(2) is amended to ensure that this special treatment does not apply to a trust in the event that property has been transferred after December 17, 1999 to the trust from another trust to which subsection 122(1) applies, if there was no change in the beneficial ownership of the property on its transfer.

**Interpretation Bulletins**: IT-381R3: Trusts — capital gains and losses and the flow-through of taxable capital gains to beneficiaries; IT-406R2: Tax payable by an *inter vivos* trust.

**(3)** [Repealed under former Act]

**Notes**: 122(3), repealed by 1985 technical bill, set out the tax rate for a mutual fund trust, now covered under 122(1).

**Definitions [s. 122]**: "allowable capital loss" — 38(b), 248(1); "amount", "business" — 248(1); "Canada" — 255; "*inter vivos* trust" — 108(1), 248(1); "mutual fund trust" — 132(6)–(7), 132.2(1)(q), 248(1); "person", "property" — 248(1); "resident in Canada" — 250; "tax payable" — 248(2); "taxable capital gain" — 38(a), 248(1); "taxable income" — 2(2), 248(1); "taxation year" — 249; "trust" — 104(1), 248(1), (3).

**Information Circulars [s. 122]**: 78-5R3: Communal organizations.

**122.1** [Repealed under former Act]

**Notes [s. 122.1]**: 122.1, repealed by 1985 technical bill, provided a special reduction from federal tax, for 1978 only, for residents of provinces that agreed to a temporary reduction in their retail sales tax rates, and for 1977 for residents of Quebec.

**122.2** [Child Tax Credit — Repealed]

**Notes**: 122.2 repealed by 1992 Child Benefit bill, effective 1993. For indexed amounts of Child Tax Credit for 1989-92, see table after 117.1.

The refundable Child Tax Credit was replaced, effective January 1993, with a monthly non-taxable Child Tax Benefit payment for lower-income families. See 122.6–122.64.

**122.3 (1) Deduction from tax payable where employment out of Canada [Overseas employment tax credit]** — Where an individual is resident in Canada in a taxation year and, throughout any period of more than 6 consecutive months that commenced before the end of the year and included any part of the year (in this subsection referred to as the "qualifying period")

(a) was employed by a person who was a specified employer, other than for the performance of services under a prescribed international development assistance program of the Government of Canada, and

(b) performed all or substantially all the duties of the individual's employment outside Canada

    (i) in connection with a contract under which the specified employer carried on business outside Canada with respect to

        (A) the exploration for or exploitation of petroleum, natural gas, minerals or other similar resources,

        (B) any construction, installation, agricultural or engineering activity, or

        (C) any prescribed activity, or

    (ii) for the purpose of obtaining, on behalf of the specified employer, a contract to undertake any of the activities referred to in clause (i)(A), (B) or (C),

there may be deducted, from the amount that would, but for this section, be the individual's tax payable

Subdivision a — Computation of Tax: Individuals S. 122.3(1)

under this Part for the year, an amount equal to that proportion of the tax otherwise payable under this Part for the year by the individual that the lesser of

(c) an amount equal to that proportion of $80,000 that the number of days

(i) in that portion of the qualifying period that is in the year, and

(ii) on which the individual was resident in Canada

is of 365, and

(d) 80% of the individual's income for the year from that employment that is reasonably attributable to duties performed on the days referred to in paragraph (c)

is of

(e) the amount, if any, by which

(i) where section 114 does not apply to the individual in respect of the year, the individual's income for the year, and

(ii) where section 114 applies to the individual in respect of the year, the total of

(A) the individual's income for the period or periods in the year referred to in paragraph 114(a), and

(B) the amount that would be determined under paragraph 114(b) in respect of the individual for the year if subsection 115(1) were read without reference to paragraphs 115(1)(d) to (f)

exceeds

(iii) the total of all amounts each of which is an amount deducted by the individual under section 110.6 or paragraph 111(1)(b) or deductible by the individual under paragraph 110(1)(d.2), (d.3), (f) or (j) for the year or in respect of the period or periods referred to in subparagraph (ii), as the case may be.

### Proposed Amendment — 122.3(1)(e)

(e) the amount, if any, by which

(i) if the individual is resident in Canada throughout the year, the individual's income for the year, and

(ii) if the individual is non-resident at any time in the year, the amount determined under paragraph 114(a) in respect of the taxpayer for the year

exceeds

(iii) the total of all amounts each of which is an amount deducted under section 110.6 or paragraph 111(1)(b) or deductible under paragraph 110(1)(d.2), (d.3), (f) or (j) in computing the individual's taxable income for the year.

**Application**: Bill C-43 (First Reading September 20, 2000), s. 70, will amend para. 122.3(1)(e) to read as above, applicable to 1998 et seq.

**Technical Notes**: Section 122.3 of the Act provides a tax credit to Canadian residents who are employed outside Canada by a specified employer for at least six months in connection with resource, construction, installation, agricultural or engineering contracts or for the purpose of obtaining those contracts. This credit — commonly known as the Overseas Employment Tax Credit (OETC) — effectively eliminates 80% of the Canadian tax arising on the first $100,000 of salary or wages earned from such foreign employment.

The OETC is determined by multiplying an employee's Part I tax otherwise payable for a taxation year by a fraction: the numerator of that fraction, determined under paragraphs 122.3(c) and (d) of the Act, generally consists of the lesser of $80,000 and 80% of the individual's overseas employment income for the year; the denominator, determined under paragraph 122.3(1)(e), is the individual's income for the year (or, where section 114 of the Act applies, for the period or periods in the year throughout which the individual is resident in Canada) reduced by certain deductions listed in subparagraph 122.3(1)(e)(iii).

Paragraph 122.3(1)(e) is amended, with application to the 1998 and subsequent taxation years, as a consequence of changes to section 114 of the Act. The amendment makes no substantive change, but keeps the reference in step with the changes to section 114. For additional information, see the commentary on section 114.

**Related Provisions**: 117(1) — Tax payable under this Part; 122.3(1.1) — No credit for incorporated employee. 126(1)(b)(i)(E)(II) — Foreign tax credit.

**Notes**: The overseas employment tax credit effectively allows a qualifying individual to eliminate 80% of the Canadian tax on income earned on an overseas project that lasts at least 6 months. ("Overseas" is a misnomer; it can include the U.S.)

Note the "engineering" can include software engineering, and need not be performed by a professional engineer; *Gabie*, [1999] 1 C.T.C. 2352 (TCC).

The CCRA takes the position that "all or substantially all", used in 122.3(1)(b), means 90% or more.

122.3(1)(b) amended by 1991 technical bill, retroactive to 1986, to refer to "outside Canada" rather than "in a country other than Canada", so that the credit is available for an individual working on a project in international waters.

122.3(1)(c)(ii) amended by 1993 technical bill, effective for 1992 and later taxation years, to delete the words "or carrying on business in Canada" at its end. However, the amendment does not apply to the 1992 taxation year if the taxpayer elected by notifying Revenue Canada in writing by December 31, 1994 for the old version of 114 to apply. (See Notes to 114.)

122.3(1)(e)(i) amended by 1999 Budget, effective for 1998 and later taxation years. From 1984-97, read:

(i) where section 114 is not applicable to the individual in respect of the year, the total of the individual's income for the year and the amount, if any, included pursuant to subsection 110.4(2) in computing the individual's taxable income for the year, and

122.3(1)(e)(ii)(B) added by 1993 technical bill, effective for 1993 and later taxation years.

**Regulations**: 3400 (prescribed international development assistance program for 122.3(1)(a)); 6000 (prescribed activity for 122.3(1)(b)(i)(C) is activity under contract with UN).

**Interpretation Bulletins**: IT-497R3: Overseas employment tax credit.

**Information Circulars**: 92-3: Guidelines for refunds beyond the normal three year period.

**Forms**: T626: Overseas employment tax credit.

**(1.1) Excluded income** — No amount may be included under paragraph (1)(d) in respect of an individual's income for a taxation year from the individual's employment by an employer where

(a) the employer carries on a business of providing services and does not employ in the business throughout the year more than 5 full-time employees;

(b) the individual

(i) does not deal at arm's length with the employer, or is a specified shareholder of the employer, or

(ii) where the employer is a partnership, does not deal at arm's length with a member of the partnership, or is a specified shareholder of a member of the partnership; and

(c) but for the existence of the employer, the individual would reasonably be regarded as an employee of a person or partnership that is not a specified employer.

**Notes**: The test for disallowance of the credit is essentially one of "incorporated employee", similar to that for a personal services business as defined in 125(7). See 18(1)(p). Note that para. (c) requires that the relationship with the non-resident entity that is paying would be an employment relationship were it not for the corporation. An individual whose work can qualify as a consultant or independent contractor (i.e., carrying on business rather than employed) can still incorporate that business and claim the credit for salary paid to the individual by the individual's own corporation, since the relationship between the individual and the non-resident was not an employment relationship in the first place.

The words "more than 5 full-time employees" in 122.3(1.1)(a) mean 6 or more, not 5 plus a part-time employee. See *Hughes & Co. Holdings Ltd.*, [1994] 2 C.T.C. 170 (FCTD). However, in appropriate cases even 4 hours per day could be "full-time": *Ben Raedarc Holdings Ltd.*, [1998] 1 C.T.C. 2774 (TCC).

122.3(1.1) added by 1996 Budget, effective 1997.

**(2) Definitions** — In subsection (1),

**"specified employer"** means

(a) a person resident in Canada,

(b) a partnership in which interests that exceed in total value 10% of the fair market value of all interests in the partnership are owned by persons resident in Canada or corporations controlled by persons resident in Canada, or

(c) a corporation that is a foreign affiliate of a person resident in Canada;

**Related Provisions**: 256(6), (6.1) — Meaning of "controlled".

**"tax otherwise payable under this Part for the year"** means the amount that, but for this section, sections 120 and 120.2, subsection 120.4(2) and sections 121, 126, 127 and 127.4, would be the tax payable under this Part for the year.

**Notes**: 122.3(2)"tax otherwise payable under this Part for the year" amended by 1999 Budget, effective for 2000 and later taxation years, to delete references to 120.1, 127.2 and 127.3 and add reference to 120.4(2).

**Notes**: 122.3(2)"specified employer" was 122.3(2)(a) and "tax otherwise payable under this Part for the year" was 122.3(2)(b) before consolidation in R.S.C. 1985 (5th Supp.), effective for taxation years ending after November 1991. See Table of Concordance.

**Definitions [s. 122.3]**: "amount" — 248(1); "arm's length" — 251(1); "business" — 248(1); "controlled" — 256(6), (6.1); "corporation" — 248(1), *Interpretation Act* 35(1); "employed", "employer", "employment" — 248(1); "foreign affiliate" — 95(1), 248(1); "individual" — 248(1); "partnership" — See Notes to 96(1); "person" — 248(1); "qualifying period" — 122.3(1); "resident in Canada" — 250; "specified employer" — 122.3(2); "specified shareholder" — 248(1); "tax otherwise payable" — 122.3(2); "tax payable" — 248(2); "taxable income" — 2(2), 248(1); "taxation year" — 249.

**122.4 [Repealed under former Act]**

**Notes**: 122.4, repealed by 1990 GST effective 1991, enacted the federal sales tax credit, designed to offset the federal sales tax paid indirectly by low-income taxpayers. It has been replaced by the GST credit in 122.5.

**122.5 (1) [GST credit] Definitions** — In this section,

**"adjusted income"** of an individual for a taxation year means the total of all amounts each of which would be the income for the year of

(a) the individual, or

(b) the individual's qualified relation for the year

if no amount were included in respect of a gain from a disposition of property to which section 79 applies in computing that income;

**Notes**: Para. (c) of "adjusted income" repealed by 1992 technical bill, effective 1992, due to the elimination of the dependent child deduction in section 118 (by the 1992 Child Benefit bill).

Closing words of the definition added by 1995-97 technical bill, retroactive to 1992.

See also Notes at end of 122.5.

**"eligible individual"** for a taxation year means an individual (other than a trust) who, at the end of December 31 of that year, is resident in Canada and is

(a) married or in a common-law partnership,

(b) a parent of a child, or

(c) 19 years of age or over;

**Related Provisions**: 122.5(2) — Persons deemed not to be eligible individuals.

**Notes**: 122.5(1)"eligible individual"(a) amended by 2000 same-sex partners bill to add reference to "common-law partnership", effective for the 2001 and later taxation years, or earlier by election (see Notes to 248(1)"common-law partner").

Opening words amended to change "December" to "December 31" by 1995-97 technical bill, effective April 27, 1995.

**"qualified dependant"** of an individual for a taxation year means a person who is

(a) a person in respect of whom the individual or the individual's qualified relation for the year is the only person who deducts an amount under section 118 for the year, or

(b) a child of the individual residing with the individual at the end of the year, and who is not

(c) an eligible individual for the year,

(d) the qualified relation of an individual for the year, or

(e) a person in respect of whom an amount is deemed under this section to be paid by any other individual for the year;

**Related Provisions**: 122.5(2) — Persons deemed not to be qualified dependants.

**"qualified relation"** of an individual for a taxation year means the person who, at the end of the year, is the individual's cohabiting spouse or common-law partner (within the meaning assigned by section 122.6).

**Notes**: 122.5(1)"qualified relation" amended by 2000 same-sex partners bill to add reference to "common-law partner", effective for the 2001 and later taxation years, or earlier by election (see Notes to 248(1)"common-law partner").

**Related Provisions**: 122.5(2) — Persons deemed not to be qualified relations; 163(2)(c.1) — False statements or omissions.

**Notes**: Definition "qualified relation" amended by 1992 technical bill, effective 1993, to harmonize the GST credit with the Child Tax Benefit in 122.6. For 1992, instead of "at the end of the year", read "at the beginning of the 1993 calendar year" (since the Child Tax Benefit provisions were not yet in force).

See also Notes at end of 122.5.

**(2) Persons not eligible individuals, qualified relations or qualified dependants** — Notwithstanding subsection (1), a person shall be deemed not to be an eligible individual for a taxation year or a qualified relation or qualified dependant of an individual for a taxation year where the person

(a) dies before the end of the year;

(b) is, at the end of the year, a person described in paragraph 149(1)(a) or (b); or

(c) is, at the end of the year, confined to a prison or similar institution and has been so confined for a period of, or periods the total of which in the year was more than, 6 months.

**(3) Deemed payment on account** — Where a return of income (other than a return of income filed under subsection 70(2), paragraph 104(23)(d) or 128(2)(e) or subsection 150(4)) is filed under this Part for a taxation year in respect of an eligible individual and the individual applies therefor in writing, ¼ of the amount, if any, by which the total of

(a) $190[19],

(b) $190[19] for a person who is the qualified relation of the individual for the year,

(c) $190[19], where the individual has no qualified relation for the year and is entitled to deduct an amount for the year under subsection 118(1) because of paragraph (b) of the description of B in subsection 118(1) in respect of a qualified dependant of the individual for the year,

(d) the product obtained when $100[19] is multiplied by the number of qualified dependants of the individual for the year, other than a qualified dependant in respect of whom an amount is included by reason of paragraph (c) in computing an amount deemed to be paid under this subsection for the year, and

(e) where the individual has no qualified relation for the year,

(i) if the individual has one or more qualified dependants for the year, $105, and

(ii) if the individual has no qualified dependant for the year, the lesser of

(A) $105[20], and

(B) 2% of the amount, if any, by which

(I) the individual's income for the year exceeds

(II) $6,546[20],

exceeds

(f) 5% of the amount, if any, by which

(i) the individual's adjusted income for the year

exceeds

(ii) $26,284[21],

shall be deemed to be an amount paid by the individual on account of the individual's tax payable under this Part for the year during each of the months specified for that year under subsection (4).

**Related Provisions**: 117.1(1) — Annual adjustment; 122.5(5) — Exceptions; 152(1)(b) — Assessment; 160.1(1)(b) — Where excess refunded; 160.1(1.1) — Liability for refunds by reason of section 122.5; 163(2)(c.1) — False statements or omissions — penalty; 164(2.1) — Application respecting refunds under section 122.5.

**Notes**: See Notes at end of 122.5.

Opening words of 122.5(3) amended by 1993 technical bill, effective for 1992 and later taxation years, to delete a requirement that a prescribed form be filed for the GST credit. The credit is now applied for on the income tax return itself.

122.5(3)(e)(ii)(B)(II) and 122.5(3)(f)(ii) amended by 2000 first budget bill (C-32), effective for 1999 and later taxation years, to change $6,456 to $6,546 and $29,921 to $26,284. See also Notes to 122.5(3.1).

122.5(3)(e) amended by 1999 first budget bill, effective for amounts deemed to be paid in specified months that are after June 1999. This eliminates the phase-in of the GST Credit supplement for single parents, and provides them with the full value of the supplement as part of the core GST Credit. For amounts deemed paid earlier, read:

(e) where the individual has no qualified relation for the year, the lesser of

(i) $100 [indexed by 117.1 after 1990], and

---

[19] Indexed by s. 117.1 after 1990 — ed.

[20] Indexed by s. 117.1 after 1999 — ed.

[21] Indexed by s. 117.1 after 1992. See Notes to 117.1(1).

(ii) 2% of the amount, if any, by which

(A) the individual's income for the year exceeds

(B) the amount determined for the year for the purposes of paragraph (c) of the description of B in subsection 118(1),

122.5(3)(f)(ii) amended by 1992 Child Benefit bill, effective 1992, consequential upon the repeal of the Child Tax Credit. See Notes to 117.1(1) regarding indexing of the $25,921 figure.

**Information Circulars**: 92-3: Guidelines for refunds beyond the normal three year period.

### (3.1) Adjustment of certain amounts [annual indexing]
— For the purpose of subsection (3) and notwithstanding subsection 117.1(1), the amounts, in respect of the amounts of $190, $100 and $105 referred to in subsection (3), used for the purpose of determining amounts deemed to be paid during months specified under subsection (4)

(a) for the 1999 taxation year are deemed to be $205, $107 and $107, respectively;

(b) for the 2000 taxation year shall be equal to the greater of the amounts referred to in paragraph (a) and the amounts that would otherwise be determined to be paid during those months if this Act were read without reference to this subsection; and

(c) for the 2001 and subsequent taxation years shall be computed without reference to paragraphs (a) and (b).

**Related Provisions**: 117.1(1), (1.1) — Indexing generally.

**Notes**: 122.5(3.1) added by 2000 first budget bill (C-32), effective for 1999 and later taxation years. It implements a February 2000 budget proposal

(a) after June 2000 and before July 2001,

(i) to increase the income thresholds of $6,456 and $25,921 to $6,546 and $26,284, and

(ii) to index to inflation (see Notes to 117.1(1)) the amounts on which the $199 and $105 are based, to $202 and $106 (as rounded), and to provide a one-time supplement to those rounded amounts, such that the amounts used in computing the credit for those months are $205 and $107, and

(b) after June 2001 and before July 2002, to provide, in addition to the indexing adjustment that would otherwise be made to the amounts on which the rounded amounts of $202 and $106 used for the previous 12-month period are based, a one-time supplement equal to the amount by which $205 and $107 exceed the amounts obtained by indexing the amounts on which the rounded amounts of $202 and $106 are based.

### (4) Months specified
— For the purposes of this section, the months specified for a taxation year are July and October of the immediately following taxation year and January and April of the second immediately following taxation year.

**Notes**: The April 1993 federal budget proposed to pay the GST credit twice a year, in April and October, rather than four times a year, in January, April, July and October. This would have taken effect in 1994, and was designed by the Conservative government to give the appearance of reducing the federal deficit for the year ended March 31, 1994 (by not paying the credit in January). It was included in Bill C-136, tabled on June 14, 1993. With the election of a Liberal government in November 1993, it became politically desirable to maximize the 1993-94 deficit (attributable to the Tories). The proposed amendment was thus dropped, as announced in a Dept. of Finance news release on December 20, 1993.

### (5) Exceptions
— Notwithstanding subsection (3),

(a) where an individual is a qualified relation of another individual for a taxation year, only one of them may apply under that subsection for the year;

(b) where the total of all amounts, deemed under that subsection to be paid by an individual for a taxation year during months specified for the year, is less than $100[22], the total shall be deemed to be paid by the individual during the first month specified for the year, and no other amount shall be deemed to be paid under that subsection by the individual for the year; and

(c) no amount shall be deemed to be paid under that subsection by an individual for a taxation year during a month specified for that year where the individual died before that month or was not resident in Canada at the beginning of that month.

**Related Provisions**: 122.5(6) — Qualified relation of a deceased eligible individual.

**Notes**: 122.5(5)(a) amended by 1993 technical bill, effective for 1992 and later taxation years, to change "file a prescribed form" to "apply". (See Notes to 122.5(3).)

122.5(5)(b) amended by 1992 technical bill, effective May 5, 1993, to delete a provision that if the total amount was less than $1 it would be deemed to be nil. According to the Department of Finance, the provision for non-payment of small amounts is "included in the broader administrative policy of Revenue Canada dealing with the levy and refund of small amounts".

122.5(5)(c) amended by 1992 technical bill, retroactive to its introduction in 1989.

122.5(4) and (5)(a) subject to transitional rules for 1990 and 1989, as introduced by 1990 GST bill.

### (6) Qualified relation of deceased eligible individual
— Notwithstanding paragraph (5)(c), on written application made, on or before the day on or before which a return of income (other than a return of income filed under subsection 70(2), paragraph 104(23)(d) or 128(2)(e) or subsection 150(4)) of a deceased person is required to be filed under this Part for the taxation year in which the person died (or would have been so required if the person were liable to pay tax under this Part for that year), by an individual who

(a) is the deceased person's qualified relation for the taxation year in respect of which a payment under this section would, but for that paragraph, be made, and

(b) is not an individual to whom that paragraph applies,

each amount that, but for that paragraph, would be deemed to be paid under subsection (3) by the de-

---

[22]Not indexed.

ceased person during a month specified for a taxation year shall be deemed to be paid during the month on account of the individual's tax payable under this Part for that year.

**Notes**: Opening words of 122.5(6) amended by 1993 technical bill, effective for 1992 and later taxation years, to reflect the change that a prescribed form is no longer filed for the GST credit. (See Notes to 122.5(3).)

122.5(6) amended by 1992 technical bill, retroactive to its introduction in 1989, to change a reference to 122.5(5).

**(7) Effect of bankruptcy** — For the purpose of this section, where in a taxation year an individual becomes bankrupt,

(a) the individual's income for the year shall include the individual's income for the taxation year that begins on January 1 of the calendar year that includes the date of bankruptcy; and

(b) the amount determined for the year under clause (3)(e)(ii)(B) shall include the amount determined for the purpose of paragraph (c) of the description of B in subsection 118(1) for the individual's taxation year that begins on January 1 of the calendar year that includes the date of bankruptcy.

**Related Provisions**: 118.95 — Parallel rule for other credits; 122.61(3.1) — Parallel rule for Child Tax Benefit.

**Notes**: 122.5(7) added by 1995-97 technical bill, effective for bankruptcies that occur after April 26, 1995. It allows the GST credit to be based on income from both the pre- and post-bankruptcy period. See also 128(2), 118.95 and 122.61(3.1).

### Proposed Amendment — Additional credit (heating expenses) to persons eligible for GST Credit

**Notice of Ways and Means Motion, Economic Statement, October 18, 2000**: *Relief for Heating Expenses*

(4) That every individual eligible to receive a goods and services tax credit (GSTC) amount for January 2001 (including individuals who were eligible to receive a GSTC amount in July 2000 in respect of a GSTC amount for January 2001) receive, in addition to that amount, a one-time payment in respect of heating expenses equal to

(a) $250 if, for the 1999 taxation year, the individual had

(i) a qualified relation, or

(ii) a qualified dependant in respect of whom the individual was entitled to claim the tax credit equivalent to the spouse or common-law partner tax credit, and

(b) $125, in any other case.

**Minister's Speech, Economic Statement, October 18, 2000**: Third, Mr. Speaker, as the colder months approach, Canadians are concerned about the impact of rising energy prices on their home heating bills. This concern is particularly acute for those on low incomes.

Three weeks ago, Government members of Parliament proposed an amendment to an Opposition motion in order to ensure that relief is targeted to those who need it most. We agree. We are, therefore, announcing, at a cost of $1.3 billion, a one-time relief of $125 per individual or $250 per family to assist low- and modest-income Canadians in dealing with their home heating expenses.

**Notes**: This amendment had to be implemented immediately so that it could be paid in January 2001, while the new Parliament had not yet reassembled. Unlike tax-reduction measures, this one requires explicit legislative authorization before cheques can be written. As a result, it was passed by Order in Council (i.e. by Cabinet). P.C. 2000-1760, December 12, 2000, provides:

Whereas the Minister of Finance has, on October 18, 2000, announced that a one-time relief for heating expenses would be provided to help low and modest-income Canadians;

Therefore, Her Excellency the Governor General in Council, on the recommendation of the Minister of Finance, hereby makes the annexed *Order Authorizing Ex Gratia Payments for Increased Heating Expenses*.

### Order Authorizing *Ex Gratia* Payments for Increased Heating Expenses

1. Interpretation — (1) In this Order, "eligible individual" means an individual

(a) who, on January 1, 2001, is resident in Canada or deemed under section 250 of the *Income Tax Act* to be resident in Canada; and

(b) in respect of whom an amount is deemed under that Act, or would be deemed if that Act were read without paragraph 122.5(5)(b), to be paid during January 2001 on account of the individual's tax payable under Part I of that Act for the 1999 taxation year because of subsection 122.5(3) of that Act.

(2) In this Order, the expressions "qualified dependant" and "qualified relation" have the meanings assigned by section 122.5 of the *Income Tax Act*.

2. Payment — The Minister of National Revenue is authorized to make an *ex gratia* payment to an eligible individual in an amount equal to the total of the following amounts:

(a) $125, and

(b) $125, if, for the 1999 taxation year, the eligible individual

(i) has a qualified relation, or

(ii) is entitled to deduct in respect of a qualified dependant of the eligible individual an amount under subsection 118(1) of the *Income Tax Act* because of paragraph (b) of the description of B in that subsection.

**CCRA news release, January 29, 2001**: *The Canada Customs and Revenue Agency releases the Relief for Heating Expenses payments*

The Canada Customs and Revenue Agency (CCRA) has announced today that the issuance of the Relief for heating expenses cheques is starting January 31, 2001. The CCRA expects to issue almost $1.4 billion in Relief for Heating Expenses payments to more than 8.6 million recipients across Canada.

Individuals and families who are eligible for the January 2001 goods and services tax/harmonized sales tax (GST/HST) credit will get a Relief for Heating Expenses cheque if they have filed their 1999 income tax returns and applied for the GST/HST credit.

Under this relief measure:

• married and common-law couples will receive $250;

• single-parent families will receive $250; and

- single individuals without children will receive $125.

The Relief for Heating Expenses payments will be exclusively delivered by cheque. Canadians are reminded to make sure that the CCRA has their current mailing address so they can get their cheques as quickly as possible.

Canadians expecting the Relief for Heating Expenses payment can contact the CCRA after February 15, 2001 if they have not received their cheque.

To find more information on the Relief for Heating Expenses, you can call 1-800-959-1953 toll free for service in English and 1-800-959-1954 for service in French. You can also visit the CCRA's Internet site at: www.ccra-adrc.gc.ca

For further information please contact: Michel Proulx, CCRA, (613) 946-3461.

**Notes [s. 122.5]**: 122.5 added by 1990 GST, effective 1989. It enacts the GST credit, designed to offset the goods and services tax paid by low-income taxpayers. It replaces the "federal sales tax credit" in former 122.4. Because the amount is deemed paid by the taxpayer, it, like source deductions or instalments paid, reduces the taxpayer's federal (but not provincial) tax liability and gives rise to a refund under 164 if the total exceeds tax owing for the year. In practice the credit is prepaid by Revenue Canada four times a year, in the "months specified" in 122.5(4).

**Definitions [s. 122.5]**: "adjusted income" — 122.5(1); "amount", "bankrupt" — 248(1); "calendar year" — *Interpretation Act* 37(1)(a); "Canada" — 255; "child" — 252(1); "common-law partner", "common-law partnership" — 248(1); "eligible individual" — 122.5(1); "individual" — 248(1); "parent" — 252(2); "person", "prescribed" — 248(1); "qualified dependant", "qualified relation" — 122.5(1); "resident in Canada" — 250; "taxation year" — 249; "writing" — *Interpretation Act* 35(1).

**122.51 (1) [Refundable medical expense supplement — ] Definitions** — The definitions in this subsection apply in this section.

**"adjusted income"** of an individual for a taxation year has the meaning assigned by section 122.6.

**Notes**: See Notes at end of 122.51.

**"eligible individual"** for a taxation year means an individual (other than a trust)

(a) who is resident in Canada throughout the year (or, if the individual dies in the year, throughout the portion of the year before the individual's death);

(b) who, before the end of the year, has attained the age of 18 years; and

(c) whose incomes for the year from all

(i) offices and employments (computed without reference to paragraph 6(1)(f)), and

(ii) businesses each of which is a business carried on by the individual either alone or as a partner actively engaged in the business

total $2,500 or more.

**Notes**: See Notes at end of 122.51.

**Related Provisions**: 117.1(1)(b.1) — Annual indexing for inflation.

**(2) Deemed payment on account of tax —** Where a return of income (other than a return of income filed under subsection 70(2), paragraph 104(23)(d) or 128(2)(e) or subsection 150(4)) is filed in respect of an eligible individual for a particular taxation year that ends at the end of a calendar year, there is deemed to be paid at the end of the particular year on account of the individual's tax payable under this Part for the particular year the amount determined by the formula

$$A - B$$

where

A is the lesser of

(a) $500, and

(b) 25/17 of the total of all amounts each of which is the amount determined by the formula in subsection 118.2(1) for the purpose of computing the individual's tax payable under this Part for a taxation year that ends in the calendar year; and

**Proposed Amendment — 122.51(2)A(b)**

**Application**: The December 21, 2000 draft legislation, s. 67, will amend para. (b) of the description of A in subsec. 122.51(2) to replace the reference to "25/17" with a reference to "25/16", applicable to 2001 et seq.

**Technical Notes**: Section 122.51 provides a refundable medical expense supplement. The supplement is equal to the lesser of $500 and 25/17 of the medical expense tax credit claimed by an eligible individual for the year. The supplement is reduced by 5% of the individual's "adjusted income" in excess of an indexed threshold ($17,664 for 2000).

Paragraph (b) of the description of A in subsection 122.51(2) is amended to replace the reference to "25/17" with a reference to "25/16", consequential on the reduction, from 17% to 16%, of the lowest tax rate applicable to individuals [see 117(2) — ed.].

B is 5% of the amount, if any, by which

(a) the total of all amounts each of which is the individual's adjusted income for a taxation year that ends in the calendar year

exceeds

(b) the sum of

(i) the greatest total that may be determined in respect of an individual for the year under paragraph (a) of the description of B in subsection 118(1), and

(ii) the dollar amount used for the year in computing the amount that may be claimed under subsection 118.3(1) in respect of an individual who has attained the age of 18 years before the end of the year.

**Related Provisions**: 117.1(1)(b.1) — Annual indexing for inflation; 152(1)(b) — Assessment; 163(2)(c.2) — False statements or omissions — penalty; 257 — Formula cannot calculate to less than zero.

**Notes**: 122.51 provides a refundable medical expense supplement of up to $500 for low-income workers with medical expenses. Because the amount is deemed paid on account of the individual's tax payable, it, like source deductions or instalments paid, reduces the taxpayer's federal (but not provincial) tax liability and gives rise to a refund under 164 if the total exceeds tax owing for the year.

The 25/16 fraction in 122.51(2)A(b) reflects the fact that each province has a parallel provincial credit of somewhere around 6–9%). See Notes to 118.2(1). See the introductory pages for the rates of provincial personal income tax.

Since $500 is 5% of $10,000, the credit under this section disappears entirely once the individual's adjusted income (see 122.51(1)) reaches $27,664 (in 2000).

122.51 was added by 1997 Budget, effective for 1997 and later taxation years. 122.51(2)B amended by 1999 Budget, this version effective for 2000 and later taxation years. For 1999, read para. (b) as "$16,745". For 1997-98 read:

B   is 5% of the amount, if any, by which

(a) the individual's adjusted income for the particular year

exceeds

(b) $16,069

122.51(2)B(b) amended by 2000 first budget bill (C-32), effective for 2000 and later taxation years. For 1997–99, read simply "(b) $17,419". The new calculation for 2000 is (i) $7,231 + $6,140 = $13,371 (under 118(1)B(a)), plus (ii) $4,293 (under 118.3(1)), total $17,664. See Notes to 117.1(1) re inflation indexing.

**Definitions [s. 122.51]**: "adjusted income" — 122.51(1); "business" — 248(1); "calendar year" — *Interpretation Act* 37(1)(a); "eligible individual" — 122.51(1); "employment", "individual", "office" — 248(1); "partner" — see Notes to 96(1); "resident in Canada" — 250; "tax payable" — 248(2); "taxation year" — 249.

## Subdivision a.1 — Canada Child Tax Benefit

**122.6 Definitions** — In this subdivision,

**"adjusted earned income"** — [Repealed]

**Related Provisions**: 122.62(5) — Death of cohabiting spouse; 122.62(6) — Separation from cohabiting spouse.

**Notes**: Definition "adjusted earned income" repealed by 1998 first budget bill, effective July 1998. From 1993 until its repeal, read:

"adjusted earned income" of an individual for a taxation year means the total of all amounts each of which is the earned income for the year of the individual or of the person who was the individual's cohabiting spouse at the end of the year;

**"adjusted income"** of an individual for a taxation year means the total of all amounts each of which would be the income for the year of the individual or of the person who was the individual's cohabiting spouse or common-law partner at the end of the year if no amount were included in respect of a gain from a disposition of property to which section 79 applies in computing that income;

**Related Provisions**: 122.51(1)"adjusted income" — Definition applies for purposes of refundable medical expense supplement; 122.62(5) — Death of cohabiting spouse; 122.62(6) — Separation from cohabiting spouse.

**Notes**: 122.6"adjusted income" amended by 2000 same-sex partners bill to add reference to "common-law partner", effective for the 2001 and later taxation years, or earlier by election (see Notes to 248(1)"common-law partner").

Last portion of the definition (exclusion of amounts under s. 79) added by 1995-97 technical bill, retroactive to 1992.

**"base taxation year"**, in relation to a month, means

(a) where the month is any of the first 6 months of a calendar year, the taxation year that ended on December 31 of the second preceding calendar year, and

(b) where the month is any of the last 6 months of a calendar year, the taxation year that ended on December 31 of the preceding calendar year;

**"cohabiting spouse or common-law partner"** of an individual at any time means the person who at that time is the individual's spouse or common-law partner and who is not at that time living separate and apart from the individual and, for the purpose of this definition, a person shall not be considered to be living separate and apart from an individual at any time unless they were living separate and apart at that time, because of a breakdown of their marriage or common-law partnership, for a period of at least 90 days that includes that time;

**Notes**: 122.6"cohabiting spouse" amended by 2000 same-sex partners bill to add reference to "common-law partner" and "common-law partnership", effective for the 2001 and later taxation years, or earlier by election (see Notes to 248(1)"common-law partner").

**"earned income"** — [Repealed]

**Notes**: Definition "earned income" repealed by 1998 first budget bill, effective July 1998. It read:

"earned income" of an individual for a taxation year has the meaning assigned by subsection 63(3);

See (b) in Notes at end of 122.61 re transitional application for 1992.

**"eligible individual"** in respect of a qualified dependant at any time means a person who at that time

(a) resides with the qualified dependant,

(b) is the parent of the qualified dependant who primarily fulfils the responsibility for the care and upbringing of the qualified dependant,

(c) is resident in Canada or, where the person is the cohabiting spouse or common-law partner of a person who is deemed under subsection 250(1) to be resident in Canada throughout the taxation year that includes that time, was resident in Canada in any preceding taxation year,

(d) is not described in paragraph 149(1)(a) or (b), and

(e) is, or whose cohabiting spouse or common-law partner is, a Canadian citizen or a person who

(i) is a permanent resident (within the meaning assigned by the *Immigration Act*),

(ii) is a visitor in Canada or the holder of a permit in Canada (within the meanings assigned by the *Immigration Act*) who was resident in Canada throughout the 18 month period preceding that time, or

(iii) was determined before that time under the *Immigration Act*, or regulations made under that Act, to be a Convention refugee,

S. 122.6 eli  Income Tax Act, Part I, Division E

and, for the purposes of this definition,

(f) where a qualified dependant resides with the dependant's female parent, the parent who primarily fulfils the responsibility for the care and upbringing of the qualified dependant is presumed to be the female parent,

(g) the presumption referred to in paragraph (f) does not apply in prescribed circumstances, and

(h) prescribed factors shall be considered in determining what constitutes care and upbringing;

**Related Provisions**: 122.62(1) — Eligible individuals.

**Notes**: 122.6"eligible individual" amended by 2000 same-sex partners bill to add reference to "common-law partner", effective for the 2001 and later taxation years, or earlier by election (see Notes to 248(1)"common-law partner").

Para. (c) amended by 1998 Budget effective February 24, 1998. Before that date, read simply "is resident in Canada".

Subpara. (e)(iii) amended by 1995-97 technical bill, effective 1993. Previously read:

(iii) was determined before that time by the Convention Refugee Determination Division of the Immigration and Refugee Board to be a Convention refugee,

Paras. (g) and (h) amended by 1995-97 technical bill, effective August 28, 1995, to reflect the shift in responsibility from Health and Welfare to Revenue Canada. Previously read:

(g) the presumption referred to in paragraph (f) does not apply in circumstances set out in regulations made by the Governor in Council on the recommendation of the Minister of Human Resources Development, and

(h) factors to be considered in determining what constitutes care and upbringing may be set out in regulations made by the Governor in Council on the recommendation of the Minister of Human Resources Development;

"Minister of National Health and Welfare" changed to "Minister of Human Resources Development" in paras. (g) and (h) by S.C. 1996, c. 11, effective July 12, 1996.

**Regulations**: 6301 (for para. (g) — circumstances where the presumption in para. (f) does not apply); 6302 (for para. (h) — factors to be considered).

**"qualified dependant"** at any time means a person who at that time

(a) has not attained the age of 18 years,

(b) is not a person in respect of whom an amount was deducted under paragraph (a) of the description of B in subsection 118(1) in computing the tax payable under this Part by the person's spouse or common-law partner for the base taxation year in relation to the month that includes that time, and

(c) is not a person in respect of whom a special allowance under the *Children's Special Allowances Act* is payable for the month that includes that time;

**Notes**: 122.6"qualified dependant"(b) amended by 2000 same-sex partners bill to add reference to "common-law partner", effective for the 2001 and later taxation years, or earlier by election (see Notes to 248(1)"common-law partner").

---

[23]Indexed by 122.61(5) after base taxation year 1996.

**"return of income"** filed by an individual for a taxation year means

(a) where the individual was resident in Canada throughout the year, the individual's return of income (other than a return of income filed under subsection 70(2) or 104(23), paragraph 128(2)(e) or subsection 150(4)) that is filed or required to be filed under this Part for the year, and

(b) in any other case, a prescribed form containing prescribed information, that is filed with the Minister.

**Related Provisions**: 164(2.3) — Form deemed to be a return of income.

**Notes [s. 122.6]**: 122.6 added by 1992 Child Benefit bill, effective for overpayments deemed to arise in 1993 or later.

**Definitions [s. 122.6]**: "amount" — 248(1); "base taxation year" — 122.6; "calendar year" — *Interpretation Act* 37(1)(a); "Canada" — 255; "cohabiting spouse" — 122.6; "common-law partner", "common-law partnership" — 248(1); "earned income" — 63(3), 122.6; "individual" — 248(1); "Minister" — 248(1); "parent" — 252(2); "prescribed" — 248(1); "qualified dependant" — 122.6; "resident" — 250; "taxation year" — 249.

**Forms [s. 122.6]**: RC64: Children's special allowances; RC66: Child tax benefit application; RC68: Children's special allowances information sheet; CTB9: Child tax benefit — statement of income.

## 122.61 (1) Deemed overpayment [Child Tax Benefit] —
Where a person and, where the Minister so demands, the person's cohabiting spouse or common-law partner at the end of a taxation year have filed a return of income for the year, an overpayment on account of the person's liability under this Part for the year is deemed to have arisen during a month in relation to which the year is the base taxation year, equal to the amount determined by the formula

$$1/12[(A - B) + C]$$

where

A is the total of

(a) the product obtained by multiplying $1,090[23] by the number of qualified dependants in respect of whom the person was an eligible individual at the beginning of the month,

(b) the product obtained by multiplying $75[23] by the number of qualified dependants, in excess of 2, in respect of whom the person was an eligible individual at the beginning of the month, and

(c) the amount determined by the formula

$$D - E$$

where

D is the product obtained by multiplying $213[23] by the number of qualified dependants who have not attained the age of 7 years before the month and in respect

## Subdivision a.1 — Computation of Tax: Canada Child Tax Benefit  S. 122.61(1)

of whom the person is an eligible individual at the beginning of the month, and

E is 25% of the total of all amounts deducted under section 63 in respect of qualified dependants in computing the income for the year of the person or the person's cohabiting spouse or common-law partner;

B is 5% (or where the person is an eligible individual in respect of only one qualified dependant at the beginning of the month, 2 1/2%) of the amount, if any, by which

### Proposed Amendment — 122.61(1)B opening words

B is 4% (or where the person is an eligible individual in respect of only one qualified dependant at the beginning of the month, 2%) of the amount, if any, by which

**Application**: The December 21, 2000 draft legislation, subsec. 68(1), will amend the opening words of the description of B in subsec. 122.61(1) to read as above, applicable with respect to overpayments deemed to arise during months that are after June 2004.

**Technical Notes**: Subsection 122.61(1) contains the calculation of the Canada Child Tax Benefit (CCTB). The CCTB is made up of two parts: a basic amount and a National Child Benefit (NCB) supplement. Unlike the basic amount, the amount of the NCB supplement payable to a family in respect of each qualified dependant varies depending on the number of qualified dependants in the family. Currently, the NCB supplement is $1,155 for the first qualified dependant, $955 for the second qualified dependant and $880 for each of the third and subsequent qualified dependants. Subsection 122.61(1) is amended to increase each of those three amounts by $100.

Currently, the CCTB is reduced by 5 per cent of family net income in excess of the lower income threshold for the second income tax bracket ($30,754 for 2001). These amendments increase this threshold to the greater of $32,000 and the indexed $30,754 income threshold.

These two amendments apply with respect to CCTB paid during months that are after June 2001.

As indicated above, the phase-out rate of the CCTB is currently set at 5 per cent (2 1/2 per cent for families with only one qualified dependant). These amendments reduce this rate to 4 per cent (2 per cent for families with only one qualified dependant) with respect to CCTB paid during months that are after June 2004.

**Notice of Ways and Means Motion, Economic Statement, October 18, 2000**: *Guaranteed Minimum Relief in 2004*

(9) That

(a) [reproduced under 118(1)B(a) and 117(2) — ed.]

(b) after June 2004, the phase-out rate of the base benefit of the Canada Child Tax Benefit be reduced from 5% to 4% (from 2.5% 2% for families with only one eligible child).

(a) the person's adjusted income for the year exceeds

(b) the dollar amount, as adjusted annually and referred to in paragraph 117(2)(a), that is used for the calendar year following the base taxation year; and

### Proposed Amendment — 122.61(1)B(b)

(b) the greater of $32,000 and the dollar amount, as adjusted annually and referred to in paragraph 117(2)(a), that is used for the calendar year following the base taxation year; and

**Application**: The December 21, 2000 draft legislation, subsec. 68(2), will amend para. (b) of the description of B in subsec. 122.61(1) to read as above, applicable with respect to overpayments deemed to arise during months that are after June 2001.

**Technical Notes**: See under 122.61(1)B opening words.

**Supplementary Information, Economic Statement, October 18, 2000**: [See below — ed.]

C is the amount determined by the formula

$$F - (G \times H)$$

where

F is, where the person is, at the beginning of the month, an eligible individual in respect of

(a) only one qualified dependant, $1,155[23], and

(b) two or more qualified dependants, the total of

(i) $1,155[23] for the first qualified dependant,

(ii) $955[23] for the second qualified dependant, and

(iii) $880[23] for each of the third and subsequent qualified dependants,

### Proposed Amendment — 122.61(1)F(a), (b)

(a) only one qualified dependant, $1,255, and

(b) two or more qualified dependants, the total of

(i) $1,255 for the first qualified dependant,

(ii) $1055 for the second qualified dependant, and

(iii) $980 for each of the third and subsequent qualified dependants,

**Application**: The December 21, 2000 draft legislation, subsec. 68(3), will amend paras. (a) and (b) of the description of F in subsec. 122.61(1) to read as above, applicable with respect to overpayments deemed to arise during months that are after June 2001.

---

[23]Indexed by 122.61(5) after base taxation year 1996.

**S. 122.61(1)**     Income Tax Act, Part I, Division E

**Technical Notes**: See under 122.61(1)B opening words.

**Notice of Ways and Means Motion, Economic Statement, October 18, 2000**: (3) That the provisions of the Act relating to the Canada Child Tax Benefit be modified in accordance with proposals described in the documents tabled by the Minister of Finance in the House of Commons on October 18, 2000. [These override the proposals of the February 28, 2000 federal budget — ed.]

**Supplementary Information, Economic Statement, October 18, 2000**

**Canada Child Tax Benefit**

The Canada Child Tax Benefit (CCTB) provides federal assistance through two components: the CCTB base benefit for low- and middle-income families and the National Child Benefit (NCB) supplement, which provides additional assistance for low-income families.

As part of the CCTB enrichments in the 2000 budget, the NCB supplement was scheduled to increase in July 2001 by $200 per child, including indexation. This Statement proposes to increase the NCB supplement by an additional $100 per child in July 2001. Together, the increases in the 2000 budget and this Statement will bring the maximum CCTB benefit in July 2001 to $2,372 for the first child, with corresponding increases for additional children.

**Table A2.13 — Changes to the Components of the Canada Child Tax Benefit**

|  | Maximum Benefit |  |  |  |
|---|---|---|---|---|
|  | As of July 1996 | As of July 2001[2] per Budget 2000 | As of July 2001[2] per Statement | As of July 2004[5] |
|  | (dollars, unless otherwise indicated) | | | |
| Base benefit | | | | |
| Basic amount | 1,020 | 1,117 | 1,117 | 1,187 |
| Additional benefit for third child | 75 | 78 | 78 | 83 |
| Additional benefit for children under 7 years | 213 | 221 | 221 | 235 |
| Phase-out rates | 2.5%/5% | 2.5%/5% | 2.5%/5% | 2%/4% |
| NCB supplement | | | | |
| First child | 500[1] | 1,155[3] | 1,255[4] | 1,333 |
| Second child |  | 955[3] | 1,055[4] | 1,121 |
| Third child |  | 880[3] | 980[4] | 1,041 |
| Total benefit | | | | |
| First child | 1,520 | 2,272 | 2,372 | 2,520 |
| Second child | 1,020 | 2,072 | 2,172 | 2,308 |
| Third child | 1,095 | 2,075 | 2,175 | 2,311 |

**Notes:**

1. In 1996, there was no NCB supplement but there was a Working Income Supplement (WIS) of up to $500 available to low-income families. Prior to 1997, the WIS was provided on a family basis and not on a per-child basis.
2. For 2001, an indexation factor of 2.5% is assumed. Indexation is calculated based on the benefits excluding the extra amount to compensate for the value of indexation for January to June 2000.
3. Increase of $200 per child, including indexation, from the scheduled July 2000 levels in the 1999 budget.
4. Increase of $100 per child, including indexation, from the scheduled July 2001 levels in the 2000 budget.
5. An average annual indexation factor of 2.1% is assumed over five years.

Furthermore, it is proposed that the net family income threshold at which the NCB supplement is fully phased out, and CCTB base benefits begin to be phased out, be increased to $32,000 in 2001. This amount will be indexed thereafter and increased with the second bracket threshold by 2004 to $35,000. It is also proposed that the reduction rate for the CCTB base benefit be cut from 5% (2.5% for one-child families) to 4% (2% for one-child families) by 2004.

**Table A2.14 — Changes to the Income Thresholds of the Canada Child Tax Benefit**

|  | Maximum Benefit |  |  |  |
|---|---|---|---|---|
|  | As of July 1996 | As of July 2001[2] per Budget 2000 | As of July 2001[2] per Statement | As of July 2004[5] |
|  | (dollars) | | | |
| Base benefit | 25,921 | 30,754 | 32,000 | 35,000 |
| NCB supplement | | | | |
| Start phase-out | 20,921 | 21,744 | 21,744 | 23,098[3] |
| End phase-out | 25,921 | 30,754 | 32,000 | 35,000 |

**Notes:**

1. In 1996, there was no NCB supplement but there was a Working Income Supplement of up to $500 per family available to low-income families.
2. For 2001, an indexation factor of 2.5% is assumed.
3. An average indexation factor rate of 2.1% is assumed.

**G** is the amount, if any, by which the person's adjusted income for the year exceeds $21,214[23], and

**H** is the proportion (expressed as a percentage rounded to the nearest one-tenth of one per cent) that

    (a) the total that would be determined under the description of F in respect of the eligible individual if that description were applied without reference to the fourth and subsequent qualified dependants in respect of whom the person is an eligible individual

---

[23] Indexed by 122.61(5) after base taxation year 1996.

## Subdivision a.1 — Computation of Tax: Canada Child Tax Benefit     S. 122.61(1)

is of

(b) the amount by which

(i) the amount referred to in paragraph (b) of the description of B

exceeds

(ii) $21,214.

**Related Provisions**: 74.1(2) — No attribution of income from Child Tax Benefit; 122.63 — Agreement with province to vary calculation; 152(1.2) — Provisions applicable to determination of overpayment; 152(3.2), (3.3) — Determination of deemed overpayment; 160.1(1)(b) — No interest on repayment of Child Tax Benefit overpayment; 160.1(2.1) — Liability for refunds by reason of section 122.61; 164(1) — Refunds; 164(2.2) — Application respecting refunds re section 122.61; 164(2.3) — Form deemed to be a return of income; 164(3) — No interest on late payment of Child Tax Benefit; 257 — Formula amounts cannot calculate to less than zero.

**Notes**: 122.61(1) amended by 2000 same-sex partners bill to add reference to "common-law partner", effective for the 2001 and later taxation years, or earlier by election (see Notes to 248(1)"common-law partner").

122.61(1) amended by 2000 first budget bill (C-32), effective for overpayments deemed to arise during months that are after June 2000 (2001 for amounts in C:F). (See end of these Notes.) For earlier deemed overpayments:

- in 122.61(1)A(a), read "$1,020" for "$1,090".
- read 122.61(1)B(b) as simply "$29,590" (the formula description was then not broken into paras. (a) and (b)).
- in 122.61(1)C:F, in place of $1,155, $955 and $880, read $955, $755 and $680 respectively. For July 2000 through June 2001, read $977, $771 and $694.
- in 122.61(1)C:G, read "$20,921" for "$21,214".
- read 122.61(1)C:H as:

    H is, where the person is an eligible individual in respect of

    (a) only one qualified dependant, 11.0%,

    (b) two qualified dependants, 19.7%, and

    (c) three or more qualified dependants, 27.6%.

122.61(1)C:F amended by 1999 Budget, effective June 18, 1998, to add "at the beginning of the month".

122.61(1)B amended by 1999 first budget bill, effective for overpayments deemed to arise during months that are after June 2000, to change $25,921 to $29,590.

122.61(1)F amended by 1999 first budget bill, effective for overpayments deemed to arise during months that are after June 2000, to change $605 to $955 ($785 for 1999–2000), $405 to $755 ($585 for 1999–2000) and $330 to $680 ($510 for 1999–2000). The $955 figure in F(a) is also subject to this adjustment for 1999-2000; an error omitting this amendment (in para. 36(7)(a) of the 1999 first Budget bill) was corrected in s. 73 of the (main) 1999 Budget bill.

122.61(1)H amended by 1999 first budget bill, effective for overpayments deemed to arise during months that are after June 2000, to change 12.1% to 11.0% (11.5% for 1999–2000), 20.2% to 19.7% (20.1% for 1999–2000), and 26.8% to 27.6% (27.5% for 1999–2000).

In *Debra Ford*, [1999] 1 C.T.C. 2540 (TCC), the Court found that an overpaid Child Tax Benefit, to which the taxpayer was not entitled because of her husband's level of income, could not be recovered by the government since there was no legislation authorizing assessment of such amount.

122.61(1) amended by 1998 first budget bill, effective for overpayments deemed to arise during months that are after June 1998. ("Overpayments" deemed under 122.61 are what creates the refundable credit.) Before July 1998, read:

(1) Where a person and, where the Minister so demands, the person's cohabiting spouse at the end of a taxation year have filed a return of income for the year, an overpayment on account of the person's liability under this Part for the year shall be deemed to have arisen during a month in relation to which the year is the base taxation year, equal to the amount determined by the formula

$$\frac{1}{12}(A - B)$$

where

A is the total of

(a) the product obtained by multiplying $1,020[23] by the number of qualified dependants in respect of whom the person was an eligible individual at the beginning of the month,

(b) the product obtained by multiplying $75[23] by the number of qualified dependants, in excess of 2, in respect of whom the person was an eligible individual at the beginning of the month,

(c) where the person is, at the beginning of the month, an eligible individual in respect of one or more qualified dependants, the amount determined by the formula

$$\left[ C \times \left( \frac{D - \$3,750^{23}}{\$6,250^{24}} \right) \right] - (G \times H)$$

where

C is, where the person is an eligible individual in respect of

(i) only one qualified dependant, $605[23], and

(ii) two or more qualified dependants, the total of

(A) $605[23] for the first qualified dependant,

(B) $405[23] for the second qualified dependant, and

(C) $330[23] for each, if any, of the third and subsequent qualified dependants,

D is the lesser of $10,000[23] and the person's adjusted earned income for the year,

G is the amount, if any, by which the person's adjusted income for the year exceeds $20,921,[25] and

H is, where the person is an eligible individual in respect of

(i) only one qualified dependant, 12.1%,

(ii) two qualified dependants, 20.2%, and

(iii) three or more qualified dependants, 26.8%, and

(d) the amount determined by the formula

---

[23]Indexed by 122.61(5) after base taxation year 1996.

[24]Indexed by 122.61(5.1) after base taxation year 1996.

[25]Indexed by 122.61(6) after base taxation year 1991.

## S. 122.61(1) — Income Tax Act, Part I, Division E

$$E - F$$

where

E  is the product obtained by multiplying $213[23] by the number of qualified dependants who have not attained the age of 7 years before the month and in respect of whom the person is an eligible individual at the beginning of the month, and

F  is 25% of the total of all amounts deducted under section 63 in respect of qualified dependants in computing the income for the year of the person or the person's cohabiting spouse; and

B  is 5% (or where the person is an eligible individual in respect of only one qualified dependant at the beginning of the month, 2½%) of the amount, if any, by which the person's adjusted income for the year exceeds $25,921[23].

122.61(1)A(c) amended by 1997 Budget (first bill), effective for overpayments deemed to arise during months that are after June 1997. This implements the 1997 budget proposals for the Working Income Supplement, which override the 1996 budget proposals. (The 1996 budget proposals, which would have taken effect in July 1997, were not included in the 1996 Budget bill because of this change.)

The 1997 budget changes restructured the Working Income Supplement (WIS) from a family basis to a per-child basis. Maximum levels became $605 for one child, $405 for the second child, and $330 for each subsequent child. The WIS was phased in at annual family earnings of $3,750, reaching the maximum at an earnings level of $10,000. It was reduced based on family net income over $20,921. The reduction rate was 12.1% for a one-child family, 20.2% for a two-child family and 26.8% for families with three or more children.

The 1998 budget changes, which took effect July 1998, replace the Child Tax Benefit and WIS by an "enriched and simplified" program, the Canada Child Tax Benefit (CCTB). The CCTB provides benefits of $1,625 for the first child and $1,425 for each additional child for all families with net income up to $20,921. The CCTB has two major components: the CCTB basic benefit and the CCTB National Child Benefit Supplement. The basic benefit has the same level and structure as the previous basic benefit and includes a supplement of $75 for the third and each subsequent child, and an additional supplement of $213 for each child under age 7 when no child care expenses are claimed. The CCTB National Child Benefit Supplement provides $605 for the first child, $405 for the second child and $330 for each additional child for all families with net income up to $20,921. The supplement is phased out based on family net income above $20,921.

The 1999 budget changes enhanced the credit yet further. (From Revenue Canada Fact Sheet, July 21, 1999): The Canada Child Tax Benefit (CCTB) combines a basic benefit of $85 a month per child with the National Child Benefit Supplement (NCBS) for low income families. Families whose net income is under $20,921 receive the maximum NCBS. Families with income between $20,921 and $27,750 receive a partial NCBS. The maximum monthly CCTB amounts (including NCBS) for families with net income under $20,921 for July 1999 are:

| Family Size | Basic Monthly CCTB Amount | Monthly NCBS | Total Monthly CCTB |
|---|---|---|---|
| 1 child | $ 85.00 | $ 65.41 | $150.41 |
| 2 children | $170.00 | $114.16 | $284.16 |
| 3 children | $261.25 | $156.66 | $417.91 |
| each additional child | $ 91.25 | $ 42.50 | $133.75 |

The February 2000 budget changes (see also 122.61(5), (6) and (6.1)) were described in the budget papers as follows:

- Effective January 2000, Canada Child Tax Benefit (CCTB) parameters will be fully indexed to the change in the Consumer Price Index (CPI) over the 12-month period ending on September 30 of the previous year. As the CCTB program year begins in July, benefits will be adjusted in July 2000 and indexation benefits for January–June 2000 will be paid in the second half of 2000. The higher level of benefits from July–December 2000 will be maintained until future indexation raises benefits further.

- In July 2000, the CCTB base benefit will increase by $70 per child, including indexation. The income thresholds at which the CCTB base benefit begins to be reduced and the National Child Benefit (NCB) supplement is fully phased out will be set equal to the second tax bracket threshold. Consequently, these CCTB thresholds will be fully indexed, as the tax bracket threshold is (under 117.1), and will also follow any increases in the tax bracket threshold beyond indexation. The income threshold at which the NCB supplement begins to be reduced will also be indexed.

- By July 2001, the NCB supplement will be increased by $200 per child, including indexation, from the currently scheduled July 2000 levels of $955 for the first child, $755 for the second child and $680 for each subsequent child. The $200 benefit increase per child will enrich the NCB supplement by $500 million annually as of July 2001.

- These changes bring the maximum CCTB benefit for the first child to $2,056 in July 2000 and $2,265 in July 2001, moving towards a five-year goal of $2,400. For the second child, the goal is to raise the maximum CCTB benefit to $2,200 in 2004. There are also additional benefits for children under age 7 for whom no child care expense is claimed and for larger families. Maximum benefits for a two-child family with one child under 7 will reach $4,550 in July 2001 and $4,832 in July 2004.

CCRA phone number for inquiries about Child Tax Benefit cheques: 1-800-387-1193.

See also Notes at end of 122.61.

**Interpretation Bulletins**: IT-495R2: Child care expenses.

**Forms**: CTB1: Child tax benefit notice.

**(2) Exceptions** — Notwithstanding subsection (1), where a particular month is the first month during which an overpayment that is less than $10 (or such other amount as is prescribed) is deemed under that subsection to have arisen on account of a person's liability under this Part for the base taxation year in relation to the particular month, any such overpayment that would, but for this subsection, reasonably be expected at the end of the particular month to arise during another month in relation to which the year is the base taxation year shall be deemed to arise under that subsection during the particular month and not during the other month.

**(3) Non-residents and part-year residents** — For the purposes of this section, unless a person was resident in Canada throughout a taxation year,

(a) for greater certainty, the person's income for the year shall be deemed to be equal to the amount that would have been the person's in-

---

[23]Indexed by 122.61(5) after base taxation year 1996.

come for the year had the person been resident in Canada throughout the year; and

(b) the person's earned income for the year shall not exceed that portion of the amount that would, but for this paragraph, be the person's earned income that is included because of section 114 or subsection 115(1) in computing the person's taxable income or taxable income earned in Canada, as the case may be, for the year.

**(3.1) Effect of bankruptcy** — For the purposes of this subdivision, where in a taxation year an individual becomes bankrupt,

(a) the individual's income for the year shall include the individual's income for the taxation year that begins on January 1 of the calendar year that includes the date of bankruptcy; and

(b) the total of all amounts deducted under section 63 in computing the individual's income for the year shall include the amount deducted under that section for the individual's taxation year that begins on January 1 of the calendar year that includes the date of bankruptcy.

(c) [Repealed]

**Related Provisions**: 118.95, 122.5(7) — Parallel rule for personal credits and GST credit.

**Notes**: 122.61(3.1)(a)-(b) substituted for (a)-(c) by 1998 first budget bill, effective June 18, 1998. Before then, effective for bankruptcies that occurred after April 26, 1995, read:

(a) the individual's earned income for the year shall include the individual's earned income for the taxation year that begins on January 1 of the calendar year that includes the date of bankruptcy;

(b) the individual's income for the year shall include the individual's income for the taxation year that begins on January 1 of the calendar year that includes the date of bankruptcy; and

(c) the total of all amounts deducted under section 63 in computing the individual's income for the year shall include the amount deducted under that section for the individual's taxation year that begins on January 1 of the calendar year that includes the date of bankruptcy.

122.61(3.1) added by 1995-97 technical bill, effective for bankruptcies that occur after April 26, 1995. See Notes to 122.5(7).

**(4) Amount not to be charged, etc.** — A refund of an amount deemed by this section to be an overpayment on account of a person's liability under this Part for a taxation year

(a) shall not be subject to the operation of any law relating to bankruptcy or insolvency;

(b) cannot be assigned, charged, attached or given as security;

(c) does not qualify as a refund of tax for the purposes of the *Tax Rebate Discounting Act*;

(d) cannot be retained by way of deduction or set-off under the *Financial Administration Act*; and

(e) is not garnishable moneys for the purposes of the *Family Orders and Agreements Enforcement Assistance Act*.

**Notes**: Although the Child Tax Benefit cannot be set off under the *Financial Administration Act*, it presumably can be subject to set-off under 224.1.

**(5) Annual adjustment [indexing]** — Each amount expressed in dollars in subsection (1) shall be adjusted so that, where the base taxation year in relation to a particular month is after 1998, the amount to be used under that subsection for the month is the total of

(a) the amount that would, but for subsection (7), be the relevant amount used under subsection (1) for the month that is one year before the particular month, and

(b) the product obtained by multiplying

(i) the amount referred to in paragraph (a)

by

(ii) the amount, adjusted in such manner as is prescribed and rounded to the nearest one-thousandth or, where the result obtained is equidistant from 2 such consecutive one thousandths, to the higher thereof, that is determined by the formula

$$\frac{A}{B} - 1$$

where

A is the Consumer Price Index (within the meaning assigned by subsection 117.1(4)) for the 12-month period that ended on September 30 of the base taxation year, and

B is the Consumer Price Index for the 12 month period preceding the period referred to in the description of A.

**Related Provisions**: 117.1(1) — Indexing of other amounts; 122.61(6) — Adjustment to amounts of $1,090, $213 and $75; 122.61(6.1) — Exception; 122.61(7) — Rounding of adjusted amounts; 257 — Formula cannot calculate to less than zero.

**Notes**: 122.61(5) amended by 2000 first budget bill (C-32), effective for overpayments deemed to arise during months that are after June 2000, as follows (see end of Notes to 122.61(1)):

- Opening words: change "after 1996" to "after 1998".

- Formula in (b)(ii): change "1.03" to "1". The effect is to introduce full indexing for inflation. See Notes to 117.1(1).

- Formula element A: change "that ended on March 31 in the calendar year following the base taxation year" to "that ended on September 30 of the base taxation year".

Opening words of 122.61(5) amended by 1999 first budget bill, effective in respect of months that are after June 1997, to change "Each amount (other than the amounts of $6,250 and $20,921)" to "Each amount". The excluded amounts were formerly indexed by 122.61(6), which was repealed by the same bill.

122.61(5) amended by 1997 Budget (first bill), effective for overpayments deemed to arise during months that are after June 1997, to add exclusion for $6,250 (covered by subsec. (5.1) below). See also Notes at end of 122.61.

**(5.1) [Repealed]**

**Notes**: 122.61(5.1) repealed by 1998 first budget bill, effective for overpayments deemed to arise during months that are after June 1998. It provided:

(5.1) **Annual adjustment** — The amount of $6,250 referred to in subsection (1) shall be adjusted so that the amount to be used under that subsection for a month in relation to a base taxation year that is after 1996 is equal to the amount by which

(a) the amount of $10,000 referred to in that subsection, as adjusted and rounded under this section for the year,

exceeds

(b) the amount of $3,750 referred to in that subsection, as adjusted and rounded under this section for the year.

122.61(5.1) added by 1997 Budget (first bill), effective for overpayments deemed to arise during months that are after June 1997.

(6) **Adjustment to certain amounts** — For the purpose of subsection (5), the amount of $1,090, and the amounts in respect of the amounts of $213 and $75, referred to in subsection (1), that are used for the purpose of determining the amount deemed to be an overpayment arising during particular months that are

(a) after June 2000 and before July 2001, are deemed to be $1,104, $219 and $77, respectively;

(b) after June 2001 and before July 2002, shall be equal to the greater of the amounts deemed under paragraph (a) to be an overpayment arising during the months referred to in that paragraph and the amounts that would otherwise be determined for those particular months if this Act were read without reference to this subsection; and

(c) after June 2002, shall be computed without reference to paragraphs (a) and (b).

**Notes**: 122.61(6) added by 2000 first budget bill (C-32), effective for overpayments deemed to arise during months that are after June 2000. See end of Notes to 122.61(1).

Former 122.61(6) repealed by 1999 first budget bill, effective in respect of months that are after June 1997. See Notes to 122.61(5).

(6.1) **Exception** — Where section 122.63 applies for the purpose of calculating an overpayment deemed under subsection (1) to arise during a month referred to in paragraph (6)(a) or (b) on account of a person's tax liability, the amount determined under subparagraph (5)(b)(ii) in respect of the person for the month is deemed to be

(a) zero, where the month is referred to

(i) in paragraph (6)(a), or

(ii) in paragraph (6)(b) and the amount otherwise determined under subparagraph (5)(b)(ii) is less than 0.014; and

(b) 1090/1104 of the amount otherwise determined under that subparagraph, in any other case.

**Notes**: 122.61(6.1) added by 2000 first budget bill (C-32), effective for overpayments deemed to arise during months that are after June 2000. See end of Notes to 122.61(1).

(7) **Rounding** — Where an amount referred to in subsection (1), when adjusted as provided in subsection (5), is not a multiple of one dollar, it shall be rounded to the nearest multiple of one dollar or, where it is equidistant from 2 such consecutive multiples, to the higher thereof.

**Notes [s. 122.61]**: 122.61 added by 1992 Child Benefit bill, effective for overpayments deemed to arise in 1993 or later. (By deeming amounts to be overpayments, those amounts, like instalments or source deductions withheld, become payable or refundable under 164 to the taxpayer, but do not reduce provincial tax.) However, with respect to

(a) any amount deemed by 122.61(1) to be an overpayment on account of an individual's liability under Part I

(i) during any month before July 1992, the individual's cohabiting spouse at the end of 1991 includes a person who

(A) is of the opposite sex to the individual,

(B) is at the beginning of the month a parent of a child of whom the individual is a parent, and

(C) is not living separate and apart from the individual for a period of at least 90 days that includes December 31, 1991, and

(ii) during any month after June 1993 and before July 1994, the cohabiting spouse of an individual at the end of 1992 includes the person of the opposite sex who, at the end of 1992, was cohabiting with the individual in a conjugal relationship and

(A) had so cohabited with the individual throughout a 12-month period ending before the end of 1992, or

(B) is a parent of a child of whom the individual is a parent,

and, for the purposes of this subparagraph, where before the end of 1992 the individual and the person cohabited in a conjugal relationship, they shall be deemed to be cohabiting in a conjugal relationship at the end of 1992, unless they were not cohabiting at that time for a period of at least 90 days that includes that time because of a breakdown of their conjugal relationship; and

(b) any amount deemed by 122.61(1) to be an overpayment on account of a person's liability under Part I arising in any month in relation to which the 1992 taxation year is the base taxation year, the expression "earned income" as defined in 122.6 shall be deemed to have the meaning assigned by 63(3) as it reads in respect of 1993.

The implementing legislation (1992 Child Benefit bill) also provided a transitional rule for payment of the credit in 1992-93.

**Definitions [s. 122.61]**: "adjusted earned income", "adjusted income" — 122.6; "amount" — 248(1); "base taxation year" — 122.6; "calendar year" — *Interpretation Act* 37(1)(a); "Canada" — 255; "cohabiting spouse" — 122.6; "common-law partner" — 248(1); "earned income", "eligible individual" — 122.6; "Minister", "person" — 248(1); "qualified dependant" — 122.6; "resident" — 250; "return of income" — 122.6; "taxable income" — 2(2), 248(1); "taxable income earned in Canada" — 115(1), 248(1); "taxation year" — 249.

**122.62 (1) Eligible individuals** — For the purposes of this subdivision, a person may be considered to be an eligible individual in respect of a particular qualified dependant at the beginning of a month only if the person has, no later than 11 months after the end of the month, filed with the Minister a notice in prescribed form containing prescribed information.

**Related Provisions**: 220(2.1) — Waiver of requirement under 122.62(1) to file notice; 241(4)(b) — Disclosure of taxpayer information for purposes of administering the Act.

**Notes**: 122.62(1) amended by 1995-97 technical bill, effective August 28, 1995, to change "filed with the Minister of Human Resources Development a notice in a form authorized, and containing information required, by that Minister" to "filed with the Minister a notice in prescribed form containing prescribed information". This reflects the transfer of authority over Child Tax Benefits from HRD to Revenue Canada.

"National Health and Welfare" changed to "Human Resources Development" by S.C. 1996, c. 11, effective July 12, 1996.

See also Notes at end of 122.62.

Forms: CTB1: Child tax benefit notice.

**(2) Extension for notices** — The Minister may at any time extend the time for filing a notice under subsection (1).

Notes: 122.62(2) amended by 1995-97 technical bill, effective August 28, 1995, to change "Minister of Human Resources Development" to "Minister" [meaning Minister of National Revenue].

"National Health and Welfare" changed to "Human Resources Development" by S.C. 1996, c. 11, effective July 12, 1996.

**(3) Exception** — Where at the beginning of 1993 a person is an eligible individual in respect of a qualified dependant, subsection (1) does not apply to the person in respect of the qualified dependant if the qualified dependant was an eligible child (within the meaning assigned by subsection 122.2(2) because of subparagraph (a)(i) in the definition "eligible child" in that subsection) of the individual for the 1992 taxation year.

**(4) Person ceasing to be an eligible individual** — Where during a particular month a person ceases to be an eligible individual in respect of a particular qualified dependant (otherwise than because of the qualified dependant attaining the age of 18 years), the person shall notify the Minister of that fact before the end of the first month following the particular month.

Notes: A notification under 122.62(4) or election under 122.62(5)–(7) is also deemed to be a notification or election under 8.5(15) of the Ontario *Income Tax Act*, for purposes of the Ontario child care supplement. (That Act is reproduced in David M. Sherman, *The Practitioner's Ontario Taxes Annotated*.)

122.62(2) amended by 1995-97 technical bill, effective August 28, 1995, to change "shall inform the Minister of Human Resources Development of that fact, in such form as that minister may require" to "shall notify the Minister [i.e., of National Revenue] of that fact".

Forms: RC65: Child tax benefit — election to change marital status.

**(5) Death of cohabiting spouse [or common-law partner]** — Where

(a) before the end of a particular month the cohabiting spouse or common-law partner of an eligible individual in respect of a qualified dependant dies, and

(b) the individual so elects, before the end of the eleventh month after the particular month, in a form that is acceptable to the Minister,

for the purpose of determining the amount deemed under subsection 122.61(1) to be an overpayment arising in any month after the particular month on account of the individual's liability under this Part for the base taxation year in relation to the particular month, subject to any subsequent election under subsection (6) or (7), the individual's adjusted income for the year is deemed to be equal to the individual's income for the year.

Notes: 122.62(5)(a) amended by 2000 same-sex partners bill to add reference to "common-law partner", effective for the 2001 and later taxation years, or earlier by election (see Notes to 248(1)"common-law partner").

Former 122.62(5) repealed by 1995-97 technical bill, effective August 28, 1995. It authorized the Minister of Human Resources Development to waive filing requirements under 122.62(1) and (4). It is no longer needed because the CCRA, which now has jurisdiction, has a general power under 220(2.1) to waive filing requirements.

Former 122.62(6) renumbered as 122.62(5) by 1995-97 technical bill, effective August 28, 1995, and amended to change "Minister of Human Resources Development" to "Minister" [meaning Minister of National Revenue], and to update cross-references to subsecs. (7) and (8) to be (6) and (7).

Closing words of 122.62(5) added by 1996 first budget bill, effective June 18, 1998.

Forms: RC65: Child tax benefit — election to change marital status.

**(6) Separation from cohabiting spouse [or common-law partner]** — Where

(a) before the end of a particular month an eligible individual in respect of a qualified dependant begins to live separate and apart from the individual's cohabiting spouse or common-law partner, because of a breakdown of their marriage or common-law partnership, for a period of at least 90 days that includes a day in the particular month, and

(b) the individual so elects, before the end of the eleventh month after the particular month, in a form that is acceptable to the Minister,

for the purpose of determining the amount deemed under subsection 122.61(1) to be an overpayment arising in any month after the particular month on account of the individual's liability under this Part for the base taxation year in relation to the particular month, subject to any subsequent election under subsection (5) or (7), the individual's adjusted income for the year is deemed to be equal to the individual's income for the year.

Notes: 122.62(6)(a) amended by 2000 same-sex partners bill to add reference to "common-law partner" and "common-law partnership", effective for the 2001 and later taxation years, or earlier by election (see Notes to 248(1)"common-law partner").

Former 122.62(7) renumbered as 122.62(6) by 1995-97 technical bill, effective August 28, 1995, and amended to change "Minister of Human Resources Development" to "Minister" [meaning Minister of National Revenue], and to update cross-references to subsecs. (6) and (8) to be (5) and (7).

Forms: RC65: Child tax benefit — election to change marital status.

**(7) Person becoming a cohabiting spouse [or common-law partner]** — Where

(a) at any particular time before the end of a particular month a taxpayer has become the cohabiting spouse or common-law partner of an eligible individual, and

(b) the taxpayer and the eligible individual jointly so elect in prescribed form filed with the Minister before the end of the eleventh month after the particular month,

for the purpose of determining the amount deemed by subsection 122.61(1) to be an overpayment arising in any month after the particular month on account of the eligible individual's liability under this Part for the year, the taxpayer is deemed to have been the eligible individual's cohabiting spouse or common-law partner throughout the period that began immediately before the end of the base taxation year in relation to the particular month and ended at the particular time.

**Notes**: 122.62(7) amended by 2000 same-sex partners bill to add reference to "common-law partner", effective for the 2001 and later taxation years, or earlier by election (see Notes to 248(1)"common-law partner").

Former 122.62(8) renumbered as 122.62(7) by 1995-97 technical bill, effective August 28, 1995, and amended to change "Minister of Human Resources Development" to "Minister" [meaning Minister of National Revenue]. Other changes and rewording were cosmetic and non-substantive.

**Forms**: RC65: Child tax benefit — election to change marital status.

**(8), (9)** [Repealed]

**Notes**: 122.62(8) was renumbered as (7); see Notes above. 122.62(9) repealed by 1995-97 technical bill, effective August 28, 1995. It provided:

(9) Advice of Department of Human Resources Development — The Minister may obtain the advice of the Department of Human Resources Development as to whether

(a) a taxpayer is an eligible individual in respect of a qualified dependant;

(b) a person is a qualified dependant; or

(c) a person is a taxpayer's cohabiting spouse.

**Notes [s. 122.62]**: 122.62 added by 1992 Child Benefit bill, effective for overpayments deemed to arise in 1993 or later.

**Definitions [s. 122.62]**: "adjusted earned income", "adjusted income", "cohabiting spouse or common-law partner" — 122.6; "common-law partner", "common-law partnership" — 248(1); "eligible individual" — 122.6; "individual" — 248(1); "Minister", "person", "prescribed" — 248(1); "qualified dependant" — 122.6; "taxpayer" — 248(1).

**122.63 (1) Agreement** — The Minister of Finance may enter into an agreement with the government of a province whereby the amounts determined under paragraph (a) of the description of A in subsection 122.61(1) with respect to persons resident in the province shall, for the purpose of calculating overpayments deemed to arise under that subsection, be replaced by amounts determined in accordance with the agreement.

**Notes**: 122.63(1) amended by 1995-97 technical bill, effective August 28, 1995, to change "The Minister of Finance and the Minister of Human Resources Development may enter jointly" to "The Minister of Finance may enter". See Notes to 122.62(1).

**(2) Idem** — The amounts determined under paragraph (a) of the description of A in subsection 122.61(1) for a base taxation year because of any agreement entered into with a province and referred to in subsection (1) shall be based on the age of qualified dependants of eligible individuals, or on the number of such qualified dependants, or both, and shall result in an amount in respect of a qualified dependant that is not less, in respect of that qualified dependant, than 85% of the amount that would otherwise be determined under that paragraph in respect of that qualified dependant for that year.

**(3) Idem** — Any agreement entered into with a province and referred to in subsection (1) shall provide that, where the operation of the agreement results in a total of all amounts, each of which is an amount deemed under subsection 122.61(1) to be an overpayment on account of the liability under this Part for a taxation year of a person subject to the agreement, that exceeds 101% of the total of such overpayments that would have otherwise been deemed to have arisen under subsection 122.61(1), the excess shall be reimbursed by the government of the province to the Government of Canada.

**Notes [s. 122.63]**: 122.63 added by 1992 Child Benefit bill, effective for overpayments deemed to arise in 1993 or later.

**Definitions [s. 122.63]**: "amount" — 248(1); "base taxation year", "eligible individual" — 122.6; "person" — 248(1); "province" — *Interpretation Act* 35(1); "qualified dependant" — 122.6; "resident" — 250.

**122.64 (1) Confidentiality of information** — Information obtained under this Act or the *Family Allowances Act* by or on behalf of the Minister of Human Resources Development is deemed to be obtained on behalf of the Minister of National Revenue for the purposes of this Act.

**Related Provisions**: 241 — Rules applicable to taxpayer information; 122.64(2), (3) — Intergovernmental disclosure.

**Notes**: "National Health and Welfare" changed to "Human Resources Development" by S.C. 1996, c. 11, effective July 12, 1996.

**(2) Communication of information** — Notwithstanding subsection 241(1), an official (as defined in subsection 241(10)) may provide information obtained under subsection 122.62(1), (4), (5), (6) or (7) or the *Family Allowances Act*

(a) to an official of the government of a province, solely for the purposes of the administration or enforcement of a prescribed law of the province; or

(b) to an official of the Department of Human Resources Development for the purposes of the administration of the *Family Allowances Act*, the *Canada Pension Plan* or the *Old Age Security Act*.

**Related Provisions**: 122.64(4) — Offence.

**Notes**: 122.64(2) amended by 1995-97 technical bill, this version effective July 12, 1996. From August 28, 1995 to July 12, 1996, read "National Health and Welfare" in place of "Human Resources Development". From January 1, 1993 to August 27, 1995, read:

(2) Communication of information — Notwithstanding subsection 241(1), an official or authorized person may provide

information obtained under subsection 122.62(1), (4), (6), (7) or (8) or the *Family Allowances Act*

(a) to an official of the government of a province, solely for the purposes of the administration or enforcement of a prescribed law of the province; or

(b) to an official of the Department of National Health and Welfare, for the purposes of the administration of the *Children's Special Allowances Act*, the *Canada Pension Plan* and the *Old Age Security Act*.

"National Health and Welfare" changed to "Human Resources Development" by S.C. 1996, c. 11, effective July 12, 1996.

**Regulations**: 3003 (prescribed law of a province).

**(3) Taxpayer's address** — Notwithstanding subsection 241(1), an official or authorized person may provide a taxpayer's name and address that has been obtained by or on behalf of the Minister of National Revenue for the purposes of this subdivision, for the purposes of the administration or enforcement of Part I of the *Family Orders and Agreements Enforcement Assistance Act*.

**Related Provisions**: 122.61(4)(e) — Child Tax Benefit not garnishable under the *Family Orders and Agreements Enforcement Assistance Act*; 122.64(4) — Offence.

**(4) Offence** — Every person to whom information has been provided under subsection (2) or (3) and who knowingly uses, communicates or allows to be communicated that information for any purpose other than that for which it was provided is guilty of an offence and is liable on summary conviction to a fine not exceeding $5,000 or to imprisonment for a term not exceeding 12 months or to both that fine and imprisonment.

**Related Provisions**: 239(2.2), (2.21) — Offence with respect to confidential information.

**(5)** [Repealed]

**Notes**: 122.64(5) repealed by 1995-97 technical bill, effective August 28, 1995. It defined "official" and "authorized person" (used in 122.64(2)) by reference to 241(10).

**Notes [s. 122.64]**: 122.64 added by 1992 Child Benefit bill, effective January 1, 1993.

**Definitions [s. 122.64]**: "authorized person", "official" — 241(10); "person", "prescribed" — 248(1); "province" — *Interpretation Act* 35(1); "taxpayer" — 248(1).

**Notes**: Proposed 122.7 in the draft legislation of December 23, 1997, which provided for a $50 payment to U.S. social security recipients in lieu of interest resulting from Canada-U.S. tax treaty changes, was incorporated into the 1998 Budget bill as Part 2 of the bill rather than in the *Income Tax Act*. It is reproduced under Art. XVIII(5) of the treaty.

## Subdivision b — Rules Applicable to Corporations

**123. (1) Rate for corporations** — The tax payable under this Part for a taxation year by a corporation on its taxable income or taxable income earned in Canada, as the case may be, (in this section referred to as its "amount taxable") for the year is, except where otherwise provided,

(a) 38% of its amount taxable for the year.

**(b)–(d)** [Repealed under former Act]

**Related Provisions**: 117(1) — Tax payable under this Part; 123.2 — Corporate surtax; 123.4(2) — General reduction in tax rate; 124 — Provincial tax abatement for corporations; 125 — Small business deduction; 125.1 — Manufacturing and processing credit; 133(3) — Tax rate for non-resident-owned investment corporation; 137.1(9) — Tax rate for deposit insurance corporation; 157(1) — Monthly instalment requirements; 161(4.1) — Interest on unpaid taxes; 182 — Surtax on tobacco manufacturers; 219(1) — Additional tax on foreign corporations.

**Notes**: See Notes to 123.4(2).

The 38% rate is reduced to 28% by 124(1), to allow room for the provinces to levy tax. Income not earned in a province is not eligible for the abatement (but see 124(4)"province"). For provincial corporate tax rates, see the introductory pages.

**Forms**: T2B-CORPAC: Recalculation and update of corporation income and/or tax; T2 SCH 7: Calculation of aggregate investment income and active business income.

**(2)** [Repealed under former Act]

**Notes**: 123(2) repealed by 1988 Canada–Nova Scotia Offshore Petroleum Resources Accord. For taxation years beginning before December 23, 1989, it dealt with the Nova Scotia offshore area. See 124(4)"province" now.

**Definitions [s. 123]**: "amount taxable" — 123(1); "corporation" — 248(1), *Interpretation Act* 35(1); "taxable income" — 2(2), 248(1); "taxable income earned in Canada" — 115(1), 248(1).

**123.1** [No longer relevant.]

**Notes**: 123.1 sets out the corporate surtax for 1985-86. It has not been formally repealed.

**123.2 Corporation surtax** — There shall be added to the tax otherwise payable under this Part for each taxation year by a corporation (other than a corporation that was throughout the year a non-resident-owned investment corporation) an amount equal to 4% of the amount, if any, by which

(a) the tax payable under this Part by the corporation for the year determined without reference to this section, sections 123.3 and 125 to 126 and subsections 127(3), (5), (27) to (31), (34) and (35) and 137(3) and as if subsection 124(1) did not contain the words "in a province"

### Proposed Amendment — 123.2(a)

(a) the tax payable under this Part by the corporation for the year determined without reference to this section, sections 123.3, 123.4 and 125 to 126 and subsections 127(3), (5), (27) to (31), (34) and (35) and 137(3) and as if subsection 124(1) did not contain the words "in a province"

**Application**: The December 21, 2000 draft legislation, s. 69, will amend para. 123.2(a) to read as above, applicable to 2001 *et seq*.

**Technical Notes**: Section 123.2 levies a 4% surtax on the tax payable under Part I by a corporation, other than a non-resident-owned investment corporation.

The surtax is calculated by reference to federal corporate tax payable after the 10-per-cent provincial abatement, but before tax credits such as the small business deduction and the manufacturing and processing deduction.

## S. 123.2(a) — Income Tax Act, Part I, Division E

> Paragraph 123.2(a) is amended to provide that the corporate surtax is to be based on the amount of federal income tax payable before taking into account any deduction under new section 123.4 as well. New section 123.4 provides a tax reduction to all corporations and an additional tax reduction to Canadian controlled private corporations.

exceeds

(b) in the case of a corporation that was throughout the year an investment corporation or a mutual fund corporation, the amount determined for A in the definition "refundable capital gains tax on hand" in subsection 131(6) in respect of the corporation for the year, and

(c) in any other case, nil.

**Related Provisions**: 141.1 — Insurance corporation deemed not to be private corporation; 157(1) — Tax instalment requirements; 161(4.1) — Interest on unpaid taxes; 182 — Surtax on tobacco manufacturers; Reg. 8602 — Prescribed portion of amount determined under 123.2.

**Notes**: The 4% corporate surtax applies to the 28% federal tax, before the general corporated tax reduction (123.4) small business deduction (125), manufacturing and processing credit (125.1), film production credit (125.4, 125.5), foreign tax credit (126), investment tax credit (127(5)–(35)) or political tax credit (127(3)). However, it does not apply to the refundable 6$\frac{2}{3}$% tax on investment income (123.3), and it applies after the 10-point abatement in 124(1). It is thus generally 1.12% of taxable income (4% of 28%). On income eligible for the small business deduction, for example, the tax is reduced from 28% to 12% by s. 125, but the surtax is still 1.12% for a total rate of 13.12%.

For the surtax on tobacco manufacturing income, see 182 and 183.

Rate of surtax in 123.2 changed from 3% to 4% by 1995 Budget, effective for taxation years that end after February 27, 1995, but prorated for taxation years straddling that date.

123.2(a) amended by 1998 Budget to add reference to 127(27)-(31) and (34)-(35), effective for 1998 and later taxation years.

Reference to 123.3 added to 123.2(a) by 1995 Budget, on the same basis as the increase in the surtax rate.

123.2(a) amended by 1992 technical bill to add reference to 137(3), effective 1992 but prorated for the number of days in the corporation's taxation year straddling January 1, 1992.

123.2 amended by 1989 Budget, effective July 1989, to provide that the surtax is calculated on federal tax before claiming deductions under ss. 125, 125.1 or 129.

**Definitions [s. 123.2]**: "amount" — 248(1); "Canadian-controlled private corporation" — 125(7), 248(1); "corporation" — 248(1), Interpretation Act 35(1); "investment corporation" — 130(3), 248(1); "mutual fund corporation" — 131(8), 248(1); "non-resident-owned investment corporation" — 133(8), 248(1); "tax payable" — 248(2).

**Interpretation Bulletins [s. 123.2]**: IT-243R4: Dividend refund to private corporations.

**Forms [s. 123.2]**: T2 SCH 37: Calculation of unused Part I.3 tax credit and unused surtax credit; T2215: Corporate surtax — 1988 et seq.

### 123.3 Refundable tax on CCPC's investment income
— There shall be added to the tax otherwise payable under this Part for each taxation year by a corporation that is throughout the year a Canadian-controlled private corporation an amount equal to 6$\frac{2}{3}$% of the lesser of

(a) the corporation's aggregate investment income for the year (within the meaning assigned by subsection 129(4)), and

(b) the amount, if any, by which its taxable income for the year exceeds the least of the amounts determined in respect of it for the year under paragraphs 125(1)(a) to (c).

**Related Provisions**: 123.2(a) — Corporate surtax applies to total tax before adding this refundable tax; 125(1)(b)(i), 126(7)"tax for the year otherwise payable under this Part"(b), (c) — Refundable tax ignored for foreign tax credit purposes; 129(3)(a)(i)A — Refund of tax (plus 20 points of regular tax on the same income).

**Notes [s. 123.3]**: The 6 $\frac{2}{3}$% tax under 123.3 is refundable (see 129(3)(a)) once sufficient dividends are paid out; it combines with the former 20% dividend refund for a total refund of 26 $\frac{2}{3}$% of investment income. See Notes to 129(1). The purpose of 123.3 is to ensure that corporations pay about 50% total tax (including provincial tax) up-front on investment income, rather than about 43%; thus, there is no incentive to earn interest income in a corporation rather than personally. However, once sufficient dividends are paid out, the dividend refund under 129(1) combined with the gross-up (82(1)(b)) and dividend tax credit (s. 121) will ensure that the total tax paid on investment income earned through a corporation and paid out as dividends is approximately the same as that on investment income earned directly by an individual.

123.3 added by 1995 Budget, effective for taxation years that end after June 1995 except that, in its application to such taxation years that begin before July 1995, read the reference to "6 $\frac{2}{3}$%" as "that proportion of 6 $\frac{2}{3}$% that the number of days in the year that are after June 1995 is of the number of days in the year". In other words, the 6 $\frac{2}{3}$% rate is prorated according to the number of days in the year that are after June 1995.

Former 123.3 repealed by 1985 technical bill, set out the corporate surtaxes for 1981, 1982 and 1983.

**Definitions [s. 123.3]**: "Canadian-controlled private corporation" — 125(7), 248(1); "corporation" — 248(1), Interpretation Act 35(1); "taxable income" — 2(2), 248(1); "taxation year" — 249.

### 123.4, 123.5 [Repealed under former Act]
**Notes [s. 123.4, 123.5]**: Former 123.4 and 123.5 repealed by 1985 technical bill, set out the corporate surtax for 1982 and 1983 respectively.

> **Proposed Addition — 123.4**
>
> **Technical Notes**: New section 123.4 contains rules that allow a corporation to reduce its tax otherwise payable under Part I by a percentage of the corporation's "full rate taxable income" — a term that is separately defined in the section for Canadian-controlled private corporations (CCPCs) and for other corporations. The applicable percentage will increase in stages from 1% for 2001 to 7% after 2003. Investment corporations, mortgage investment corporations, mutual fund corporations and non-resident owned investment corporations are not eligible for this rate reduction.
>
> New section 123.4 also contains an additional rate reduction specific to CCPC's. This additional rate reduction is, in broad terms, equal to 7% of up to $100,000 of the CCPC's active business income in excess of the amount that benefits from the special rate for small-business income provided under section 125.

Both the corporate rate reduction and the additional CCPC reduction apply to the 2001 and subsequent taxation years, and are prorated to reflect the number of days in a corporation's taxation year that fall in a given calendar year.

New subsection 123.4(1) sets out three definitions for the purposes of new section 123.4.

### 123.4 Corporation Tax Reductions — (1) Definitions — The definitions in this subsection apply in this section.

**"CCPC rate reduction percentage"** of a Canadian-controlled private corporation for a taxation year is that proportion of 7% that the number of days in the year that are after 2000 is of the number of days in the year.

**Technical Notes**: A Canadian-controlled private corporation's "CCPC rate reduction percentage" for a taxation year is that proportion of 7% that the number of days in the corporation's taxation year that are after 2000 is of the total number of days in the year.

**"full rate taxable income"** of a corporation for a taxation year is

(a) if the corporation is not a corporation described in paragraph (b) or (c) for the year, the amount by which the corporation's taxable income for the year exceeds the total of,

(i) if an amount is deducted under subsection 125.1(1) from the corporation's tax otherwise payable under this Part for the year, $100/7$ of the amount deducted,

(ii) if an amount is deducted under subsection 125.1(2) from the corporation's tax otherwise payable under this Part for the year, the amount determined, in respect of the deduction, by the formula in that subsection,

(iii) three times the total of all amounts each of which is deducted under paragraph 20(1)(v.1) in computing the corporation's income from a business or property for the year, and

(iv) if the corporation is a credit union throughout the year, 100/16 of the amount, if any, deducted under subsection 137(3) from the corporation's tax otherwise payable under this Part for the year;

(b) if the corporation is a Canadian-controlled private corporation throughout the year, the amount by which the corporation's taxable income for the year exceeds the total of

(i) the amounts that would, if paragraph (a) applied to the corporation, be determined under subparagraphs (a)(i) to (iv) in respect of the corporation for the year,

(ii) $100/16$ of the amount, if any, deducted under subsection 125(1) from the corporation's tax otherwise payable under this Part for the year,

(iii) the corporation's aggregate investment income for the year, within the meaning assigned by subsection 129(4), and

(iv) $100/7$ of the amount, if any, deducted under subsection (3) from the corporation's tax otherwise payable under this Part for the year; and

(c) if the corporation is throughout the year an investment corporation, a mortgage investment corporation, a mutual fund corporation, or a non-resident-owned investment corporation, nil.

**Technical Notes**: The "full rate taxable income" of a corporation for a taxation year is, in general terms, that part of the corporation's taxable income for the year that has not benefited from any of the various special effective tax rates provided under the Act. This amount is determined differently depending on the nature of the corporation. Paragraph (a) of the definition applies to corporations other than CCPCs and various "specialty corporations" such as investment corporations and mutual fund corporations. Paragraph (b) applies to CCPCs. Investment corporations, mortgage investment corporations, mutual fund corporations and non-resident-owned investment corporations are dealt with in paragraph (c); their full rate taxable income is nil.

Under paragraph (a), the full rate taxable income of a corporation is the amount by which the corporation's taxable income for the year exceeds the total of the following four amounts:

(i) 100/7 of any amount deducted by the corporation from its tax for the year as a manufacturing and processing profits deduction under subsection 125.1(1);

(ii) if the corporation deducted from its tax, under subsection 125.1(2), an amount relating to the creation of electrical energy for sale or steam used to create electrical energy, the amount determined by the formula in that subsection;

(iii) three times the total of all amounts claimed by the corporation under paragraph 20(1)(v.1) as resource allowances for the taxation year; and

(iv) if the corporation is a credit union and claimed the special deduction for credit unions under subsection 137(3), 100/16 of amount claimed.

A corporation that is a CCPC throughout a taxation year must use paragraph (b) to calculate its full rate taxable income for the year. The full rate taxable income of such a CCPC is the amount by which the CCPC's taxable income for the year exceeds the total of the following items:

(i) The amounts that would be determined under subparagraphs (a)(i) to (iv) if paragraph (a) applied to the corporation;

(ii) 100/16 of the amount of the small business deduction claimed by the corporation for the year, under subsection 125(1);

(iii) The corporation's aggregate investment income for the year, as defined in subsection 129(1); and

(iv) 100/7 of any amount deducted under subsection 123.4(3) from the corporation's tax for the year (CCPC rate reduction — see below).

Paragraph (c) applies to corporations that throughout the year are investment corporations, mortgage investment corporations, mutual fund corporations or non-resident owned investment corporations. As noted above, these corporations have no full rate taxable income, and thus are not eligible for the rate reductions.

**"general rate reduction percentage"** of a corporation for a taxation year is the total of

(a) that proportion of 1% that the number of days in the year that are in 2001 is of the number of days in the year;

(b) that proportion of 3% that the number of days in the year that are in 2002 is of the number of days in the year;

(c) that proportion of 5% that the number of days in the year that are in 2003 is of the number of days in the year; and

(d) that proportion of 7% that the number of days in the year that are after 2003 is of the number of days in the year.

**Technical Notes**: A corporation's "general rate reduction percentage" for a taxation year is a percentage that is computed by reference to the calendar year or years in which the taxation year falls. The percentage is the total of 1% for any portion of the taxation year that falls in 2001, 3% for any portion in 2002, 5% for 2003, and 7% for 2004 and later calendar years.

For example, if a corporation's taxation year begins on July 1, 2002 and ends on June 30, 2003, the corporation's general rate reduction percentage for the taxation year is approximately 3.99%, computed as follows:

$$
\begin{array}{rl}
184/365 \times 3\% = & 1.51\% \\
+\ 181/365 \times 5\% = & 2.48\% \\ \hline
& 3.99\%
\end{array}
$$

**(2) General deduction from tax** — There may be deducted from a corporation's tax otherwise payable under this Part for a taxation year the product obtained by multiplying the corporation's general rate reduction percentage for the year by the corporation's full-rate taxable income for the year.

**Technical Notes**: New subsection 123.4(2) allows a corporation a deduction from its tax otherwise payable under Part I for a taxation year. The amount of the deduction is determined by multiplying the corporation's general rate reduction percentage for the year by the corporation's full-rate taxable income for the year.

**Notice of Ways and Means Motion, Economic Statement, October 18, 2000**: *Corporate Income Tax Reduction*

(10) That, for the 2002 and subsequent taxation years, in addition to the deductions described in paragraphs (7) and (8) of the 2000 Budget Notice,

(a) a deduction be provided from the tax otherwise payable under Part I of the Act for the year by a corporation (other than a corporation that is throughout the year a Canadian-controlled private corporation, an investment corporation, a mortgage investment corporation, a mutual fund corporation or a non-resident-owned investment corporation), equal to the designated percentage of the amount by which the corporation's taxable income for the year exceeds the total of

(i) the total of the amounts in respect of which the corporation applied the deductions from tax provided by subsection 125.1(1) or (2) of the Act,

(ii) 3 times the resource allowance deducted under paragraph 20(1)(v.1) of the Act in computing the corporation's income for the year, and

(iii) if the corporation is a credit union, the amount in respect of which the corporation applied the deduction from tax provided by subsection 137(3) of the Act, and

(b) a deduction be provided from the tax otherwise payable under Part I of the Act for the year by a Canadian-controlled private corporation, equal to the designated percentage of the amount by which the corporation's taxable income for the year exceeds the total of

(i) the amounts that would, if subparagraph (a) applied to the corporation, be determined under clauses (a)(i) to (iii) in respect of the corporation for the year,

(ii) the least of the amounts determined under paragraphs 125(1)(a) to (c) of the Act in respect of the corporation's small business deduction for the year,

(iii) the corporation's aggregate investment income determined under subsection 129(4) of the Act for the year, and

(iv) 100/7 times the amount deducted from the corporation's tax for the year in accordance with the rules described in paragraph (8) of the 2000 Budget Notice,

where the designated percentage is 2 per cent for 2002, 4 per cent for 2003, and 6 per cent after 2003, pro-rated for taxation years that include days in more than one calendar year.

**Minister's Speech, Economic Statement, October 18, 2000**: Mr. Speaker, an internationally competitive corporate tax system is essential to sustaining economic growth. At the present time, we have a small business tax rate of 12%. For larger companies, there are a number of Canadian industries that enjoy a competitive tax rate of 21%. However, there are other sectors, like high tech where much of the new job creation is occurring, that face a tax rate of 28%.

In Budget 2000, we set out a five-year plan to lower that rate from 28% to 21%. The plan called for a one-point drop next year with the remaining reduction taking place by the end of five years. Today, to ensure that these companies remain internationally competitive, we are accelerating that plan. In addition to the one-point reduction in the general corporate tax rate scheduled for this coming year, we will now legislate a two-point cut in each of the following three years. By accelerating — and legislating — this timetable, companies can invest with certainty, knowing precisely when, and by how much, their taxes will fall.

**Notice of Ways and Means Motion, federal budget, February 28, 2000**: *Tax Reduction for Corporations*

(7) That, for taxation years that end after December 31, 2000 (pro-rated for years that straddle that date),

(a) a deduction be provided from the tax otherwise payable under Part I of the Act for the year by a corporation (other than a corporation that is throughout the year a Canadian-controlled private corporation, an investment corporation, a mortgage investment corporation, a mutual fund corporation, or a non-resident-owned investment corporation), equal to 1 per cent of the amount by which the corporation's taxable income for the year exceeds the total of

(i) the total of the amounts in respect of which the corporation applied the deductions from tax provided by subsection 125.1(1) or (2) of the Act,

(ii) 3 times the resource allowance deducted under paragraph 20(1)(v.1) of the Act in computing the corporation's income for the year, and

(iii) if the corporation is a credit union, the amount in respect of which the corporation applied the deduction from tax provided by subsection 137(3) of the Act, and

(b) a deduction be provided from the tax otherwise payable under Part I of the Act for the year by a Canadian-controlled private corporation, equal to 1 per cent of the amount by which the corporation's taxable income for the year exceeds the total of

(i) the amounts that would, if subparagraph (a) applied to the corporation, be determined under clauses (a)(i) to (iii) in respect of the corporation for the year,

(ii) the least of the amounts determined under paragraphs 125(1)(a) to (c) of the Act in respect of the corporation's small business deduction for the year,

(iii) the corporation's aggregate investment income determined under subsection 129(4) of the Act for the year, and

(iv) 100/7 times the amount deducted from the corporation's tax for the year in accordance with the rules described in paragraph (8).

[See under 125(1) for the accelerated reduction for Canadian-controlled private corporations — ed.]

**Federal budget, supplementary information, February 28, 2000**: *Corporate Tax Rate Reduction*

Canada must ensure that its business income tax system is internationally competitive. This is important because business income tax rates have a significant impact on the level of business investment, employment, productivity, wages and incomes.

Canada's tax rates for small businesses and the manufacturing and processing (M&P) sector are already competitive. Also, the resource sector (crude oil, natural gas and mining) benefits from special deductions, such as the resource allowance when it exceeds provincial royalties, accelerated exploration and development expenses and fast write-offs for certain capital assets, all of which serve to reduce its effective tax rate.

However, higher overall corporate tax rates apply to other sectors of the economy. These sectors include the fast-growing service and knowledge-based firms that are likely to influence the pace of Canada's future economic and social development.

In addition, Canada imposes a capital tax on large corporations that is higher than in most G-7 countries.

Therefore, the Government intends to reduce, within five years, the federal corporate income tax rate from 28 to 21 per cent on business income not currently eligible for special tax treatment.

As an initial step in achieving this tax rate reduction, the budget proposes that, effective January 1, 2001, the federal corporate income tax rate on such income be reduced by 1 percentage point from 28 to 27 per cent. This rate change will be prorated for taxation years that include January 1, 2001.

The tax rate reduction will not apply to income that benefits from preferential corporate tax treatment such as small business and Canadian M&P income, investment income that benefits from refundable tax provisions or income from non-renewable natural resource activities. The reduction will also not apply to mutual fund corporations, mortgage investment corporations, and investment corporations (as defined in the Income Tax Act), which qualify for special tax provisions.

**Related Provisions**: 123.2(a) — Corporate surtax applies to total tax before applying this reduction.

**Notes**: The above means that the general corporate tax rate (for non-manufacturing, large businesses) will be reduced as follows:

| | |
|---|---|
| 2000 | 28% |
| 2001 | 27% |
| 2002 | 25% |
| 2003 | 23% |
| 2004 | 21% |

It is further reduced to 21% as of 2001, for most corporations, by 123.4(3).

**(3) CCPC deduction** — There may be deducted from the tax otherwise payable under this Part for a taxation year by a Canadian-controlled private corporation the product obtained by multiplying the corporation's CCPC rate reduction percentage for the year by the amount by which the least of

(a) $\frac{7}{2}$ of the corporation's business limit for the year, as determined under section 125 for the purpose of paragraph 125(1)(c),

(b) the amount that would be determined under paragraph 125(1)(a) in respect of the corporation for the year if the references in the description of M in the definition "specified partnership income" in subsection 125(7) to "$200,000" and "$548" were read as references to "$300,000" and "$822", respectively, and

(c) the amount by which the amount determined under paragraph 125(1)(b) in respect of the corporation for the year exceeds the corporation's aggregate investment income determined under subsection 129(4) for the year

exceeds the total of

(d) the amounts that would, if paragraph (a) of the definition "full-rate taxable income" in subsection (1) applied to the corporation for the year, be determined under subparagraphs (a)(i) to (iv) of that definition in respect of the corporation for the year, and

(e) $^{100}/_{16}$ of the amount, if any, deducted under subsection 125(1) from the corporation's tax otherwise payable under this Part for the year.

**Technical Notes**: New subsection 123.4(3) allows a Canadian-controlled private corporation to deduct an amount from its tax otherwise payable for a taxation year under Part I. In general terms, as a result of this deduction the corporate tax rate on income between $200,000 and $300,000 earned by a CCPC from an active business carried on in Canada will be reduced to 21 per cent from 28 per cent, effective January 1, 2001. Associated corporations must share this deduction in proportion to their small business limit. Income eligible for this deduction is reduced to the extent that the corporation has income that has already benefited from a reduced effective tax rate. More particularly, the deduction is computed in a three-step process.

First, the corporation determines the least of the following three amounts:

(i) 3/2 of the corporation's business limit for the year as determined under section 125 for the purpose of paragraph 125(1)(c). This reference to all of section 125 ensures that the section's various modifications of the corporation's business limit apply for this purpose.

(ii) The amount that would have been the corporation's net active business income for the year, under paragraph 125(1)(a), if the amounts contained in the description of M in the definition "specified partnership income" in subsection 125(7) were read as $300,000 and $822, instead of $200,000 and $548, respectively. This adjustment — multiplying those amounts by 3/2 — ensures appropriate results in cases where the corporation has specified partnership income for the year.

(iii) Any excess of the amount determined under paragraph 125(1)(b), in respect of the corporation's taxable income for the year, over the corporation's aggregate investment income for the year as calculated under subsection 129(4).

Second, the corporation subtracts from the least of the above amounts the total of the following:

(i) The total of the amounts that would have been determined under subparagraphs (a)(i) to (iv) of the definition "full-rate taxable income" had paragraph (a) of that definition applied to the corporation; and

(ii) 100/16 times the amount of the small business deduction claimed by the corporation under subsection 125(1).

Third, any remainder is multiplied by the corporation's CCPC rate reduction percentage for the year. The product is the amount of the deduction for the year.

**Related Provisions**: 123.2(a) — Corporate surtax applies to total tax before applying this reduction.

**Application**: The December 21, 2000 draft legislation, s. 70, will add s. 123.4, applicable to 2001 *et seq*.

### Notice of Ways and Means Motion, federal budget, February 28, 2000: *Accelerated Tax Reduction for Small Business Corporations*

(8) That, for taxation years that end after December 31, 2000 (pro-rated for years that straddle that date), a deduction be provided from the tax otherwise payable under Part I of the Act for the year by a corporation that is throughout the year a Canadian-controlled private corporation, equal to 7 per cent of the amount by which

(a) the least of

(i) 150 per cent of the corporation's business limit for the year under paragraph 125(1)(c) of the Act,

(ii) the amount that would be the corporation's net active business income under paragraph 125(1)(a) of the Act for the year if the references in the definition "specified partnership income" in subsection 125(7) of the Act to $200,000 and $548 were read as references to $300,000 and $822, respectively, and

(iii) the taxable income amount determined under paragraph 125(1)(b) of the Act in respect of the corporation for the year, less the corporation's aggregate investment income determined under subsection 129(4) of the Act for the year,

exceeds

(b) the total of

(i) the least of the amounts determined under paragraphs 125(1)(a) to (c) of the Act in respect of the corporation's small business deduction for the year,

(ii) the total of the amounts in respect of which the corporation applied the deductions from tax provided by subsection 125.1(1) or (2) of the Act,

(iii) 3 times the resource allowance deducted under paragraph 20(1)(v.1) of the Act in computing the corporation's income for the year, and

(iv) if the corporation is a credit union, the amount in respect of which the corporation applied the deduction from tax provided by subsection 137(3) of the Act.

### Federal budget, supplementary information, February 28, 2000: *Faster Corporate Tax Rate Reduction for Small Business*

[See under 123(1) for the general rate reduction from 28% to 21% — ed.]

Canada provides very favourable tax treatment for small business; this has a direct impact on their cost of doing business. For example, the lower tax rate on the first $200,000 of active business income alone provides the small business sector with more than $2.5 billion of tax assistance annually, allowing the retention of earnings for expansion. However, income earned by small businesses in excess of the $200,000 threshold is currently subject to the general corporate tax rate of 28 per cent or, for M&P income, to the 21-per-cent M&P rate.

Small businesses that are currently taxed at the 28-per-cent tax rate on their active business income in excess of the $200,000 small business limit will benefit from the proposed 1 percentage point reduction in the general tax rate next year and from the further reductions planned for the future. However, in order to provide additional and more immediate support for this sector, the budget proposes to advance the planned 7-percentage-point rate reduction for small business.

Specifically, the corporate tax rate on income between $200,000 and $300,000 earned by a Canadian-controlled private corporation (CCPC) from an active business carried on in Canada will be reduced to 21 per cent from 28 per cent, effective January 1, 2001 (prorated for taxation years that include that date).

Subdivision b — Computation of Tax: Corporations  S. 124(3)

Associated corporations will share the additional $100,000 of income eligible for the faster rate reduction in proportion to their share of the $200,000 small business limit. Income eligible for this lower rate will be reduced to the extent that a corporation has M&P income subject to the reduced M&P tax rate or income from resource activities.

Table A7.20 illustrates the impact of this faster access to the reduced 21-per-cent rate for a small business.

*Table A7.20*

|  | Part 1 tax based on Existing rates | Proposed rates |
|---|---|---|
| Business income | $ 375,000 | $ 375,000 |
| Income eligible for: |  |  |
|   Existing small business rate | $ 200,000 | $ 200,000 |
|   Faster access to reduced rate {1} | n/a | $ 100,000 |
|   General corporate rate | $ 175,000 | $ 75,000 |
| Applicable federal tax rates on: {2} |  |  |
|   Small business income | 12% | 12% |
|   Income eligible for faster access to the reduced rate | n/a | 21% |
|   Remaining income {3} | 28% | 27% |
| Applicable surtax on all income {4} | 1.12% | 1.12% |
| Part 1 tax on: | $ 24,000 | $ 24,000 |
|   Small business income |  |  |
|   Income eligible for faster access to the reduced rate | n/a | $ 21,000 |
|   Remaining income | $ 49,000 | $ 20,250 |
| Surtax $4,200 |  | $ 4,200 |
| Total Part 1 tax | $ 77,200 | $ 69,450 |

**Notes:**

1. Reduced to the extent that the firm has M&P income subject to the reduced M& tax rate or income from resource activities.
2. Taking into account the 10-per-cent provincial tax abatement.
3. Excluding resource income (such income will continue to be taxed at 28 per cent) and investment income.
4. The surtax remains at 4 per cent of the 28-per-cent corporate tax rate.

*Federal Corporate Tax Rates*

Table A7.21 presents the federal corporate tax rates on various types of income, before and after the proposed rate reduction.

*Table A7.21*

|  | Current rates | Proposed rates January 1, 2001 | Target rates |
|---|---|---|---|
|  | (per cent, after provincial) |  |  |
| On first $200,000 of CCPC's active business income {1} | 12 | 12 | 12 |
| On CCPC's active business income between $200,000 and $300,000 {2} | 28 | 21 | 21 |
| On M & P income | 21 | 21 | 21 |
| On resource income {3} | 21 | 21 | 21 |
| On other income | 28 | 27 | 21 |

**Notes:**

1 The $200,000 limit is reduced where taxable capital exceeds $10 million. Investment income earned by a CCPC will continue to be taxed at 28 per cent, plus the 6 2/3 per cent refundable tax on investment income tax. A portion of these taxes is refundable on the payment of dividends in order to provide integration of corporate and personal tax systems.

2 Reduced to the extent of M&P income subject to a rate reduction or income from resource activities.

3 After taking into account the 25-per-cent resource allowance deduction.

**Definitions [s. 123.4]:** "amount", "business", "business limit" — 248(1); "CCPC rate reduction percentage" — 123.4(1); "Canadian-controlled private corporation" — 125(7), 248(1); "corporation" — 248(1), *Interpretation Act* 35(1); "credit union" — 248(1); "full rate taxable income", "general rate reduction percentage" — 123.4(1); "investment corporation" — 130(3), 248(1); "mortgage investment corporation" — 130.1(6), 248(1); "mutual fund corporation" — 131(8), 248(1); "non-resident-owned investment corporation" — 133(8), 248(1); "property", "taxable income" — 248(1); "taxation year" — 249.

**124. (1) Deduction from corporation tax** — There may be deducted from the tax otherwise payable by a corporation under this Part for a taxation year an amount equal to 10% of the corporation's taxable income earned in the year in a province.

**Related Provisions:** 117(1) — Tax payable under this Part; 123.2(a) — 10% reduction applies for corporate surtax even if income not earned in a province; 123.4(2) — Further 7% rate reduction; 133(4) — No deduction for non-resident-owned investment corporation.

**Notes:** The 10% abatement in 124(1), from 38% to 28%, gives the provinces (and the territories) "room" to levy provincial corporate taxes, which are imposed at various rates on income attributable to a permanent establishment in the province. See the table in the introductory pages. To the extent that corporate income is not allocated to a province (see 124(4) "taxable income ..." and Reg. 400–413), it remains taxable at the full 38% under s. 123.

A further 7% reduction for most corporations, to 21%, is provided by 123.4(2).

**Interpretation Bulletins:** IT-177R2: Permanent establishment of a corporation in a province and of a foreign enterprise in Canada; IT-347R2: Crown corporations; IT-393R2: Election re tax on rents and timber royalties — non-residents.

**(2)–(2.2) [Repealed under former Act]**

**Notes:** 124(2) to (2.2), repealed in 1974, provided for a deduction from corporate tax for production profits from mineral resources.

**(3) Crown agents** — Notwithstanding subsection (1), no deduction may be made under this section from the tax otherwise payable under this Part for a taxation year by a corporation in respect of any taxable income of the corporation for the year that is not, because of an Act of Parliament, subject to tax under this Part or by a prescribed federal Crown corporation that is an agent of Her Majesty.

**Related Provisions:** 27 — Prescribed federal Crown corporations are subject to Part I tax; 149(6) — Apportionment rule.

**Notes:** 124(3) amended by 1992 technical bill, effective for 1992 and later taxation years, to add "by a corporation in respect of any taxable income of the corporation for the year that is not, because of an Act of Parliament, subject to tax under this Part". The change ensures that a corporation that is exempt (under s. 149 or otherwise) cannot have the portion of its income that is taxable reduced by an abatement under 124(1) in respect of the exempt income.

124(3) ensures that the objective of s. 27 is met. 27(2) requires certain federal Crown corporations that operate in the commercial sector to pay tax, in order not to give them an unfair advantage over private-sector businesses. Since such Crown corporations are not subject to provincial corporate income tax for constitutional reasons (relating to the division of powers between the federal and provincial governments), 124(3) provides that they receive no abatement under 124(1). The abatement is designed to allow room for the provinces to levy a tax of about 10%.

**Regulations**: 7100 (prescribed federal Crown corporation).

**Interpretation Bulletins**: IT-347R2: Crown corporations.

**(4) Definitions** — In this section,

**"province"** includes the Newfoundland offshore area and the Nova Scotia offshore area;

**Notes**: Under subsec. 35(1) of the *Interpretation Act*, "province" also includes the Yukon Territory, the Northwest Territories and Nunavut.

124(4)"province" was 124(4)(b) before consolidation in R.S.C. 1985 (5th Supp.), effective for taxation years ending after November 1991.

**Regulations**: 400–413 (taxable income earned in the year in a province).

**"taxable income earned in the year in a province"** means the amount determined under rules prescribed for the purpose by regulations made on the recommendation of the Minister of Finance.

**Notes**: 124(4)"taxable income earned in the year in a province" was 124(4)(a) before consolidation in R.S.C. 1985 (5th Supp.), effective for taxation years ending after November 1991.

**Regulations**: 400–413 (taxable income earned in the year in a province).

**Definitions [s. 124]**: "amount" — 248(1); "corporation" — 248(1), *Interpretation Act* 35(1); "mineral resource", "Newfoundland offshore area", "Nova Scotia offshore area" — 248(1); "province" — 124(4), *Interpretation Act* 35(1); "taxable income" — 2(2), 248(1); "taxable income earned in the year in a province" — 124(4); "taxation year" — 249.

**124.1, 124.2** [Repealed under former Act]

**Notes**: 124.1 and 124.2, repealed in 1976, defined "taxable production profits from a mineral resource in Canada" and "taxable production profits from oil or gas wells in Canada", concepts no longer used.

**125. (1) Small business deduction** — There may be deducted from the tax otherwise payable under this Part for a taxation year by a corporation that was, throughout the year, a Canadian-controlled private corporation, an amount equal to 16% of the least of

(a) the amount, if any, by which the total of

(i) the total of all amounts each of which is the income of the corporation for the year from an active business carried on in Canada (other than the income of the corporation for the year from a business carried on by it as a member of a partnership), and

(ii) the specified partnership income of the corporation for the year

exceeds the total of

(iii) the total of all amounts each of which is a loss of the corporation for the year from an active business carried on in Canada (other than a loss of the corporation for the year from a business carried on by it as a member of a partnership), and

(iv) the specified partnership loss of the corporation for the year,

(b) the amount, if any, by which the corporation's taxable income for the year exceeds the total of

(i) $^{10}/_3$ of the total of the amounts that would be deductible under subsection 126(1) from the tax for the year otherwise payable under this Part by it if those amounts were determined without reference to section 123.3,

(ii) $^{10}/_4$ of the total of amounts deducted under subsection 126(2) from the tax for the year otherwise payable by it under this Part, and

(iii) the amount, if any, of the corporation's taxable income for the year that is not, because of an Act of Parliament, subject to tax under this Part, and

(c) the corporation's business limit for the year.

**Related Provisions**: 123.2(a) — Corporate surtax applies to total tax before claiming small business deduction; 123.4(3) — Reduction in tax rate for CCPC's income over $200,000; 125(2)–(5) — Restriction of deduction to $200,000 of active business income; 125(5.1) — Elimination of small business deduction for large corporations; 137(3), (4) — Credit unions — small business deduction.

**Notes**: 125(1) provides a deduction from tax — that is, a credit against tax otherwise owing. It reduces from 28% to 12% the federal tax on the first $200,000 of a Canadian-controlled private corporation's income from active business in Canada. However, large corporations subject to the Large Corporations (capital) Tax lose part or all of the deduction. See 125(5.1).

Each of the provinces also has a parallel small business deduction to reduce provincial corporate tax (except Quebec, which recently eliminated it). See the table of corporate tax rates in the introductory pages.

Where income is ineligible for the small business deduction because it is investment income rather than active business income, it is subject to an additional 6.67% tax (see 123.3). Both this 6.67% and 20 points of tax on such income (total 26.67%) are refunded to the corporation under 129(1) on payment of sufficient dividends (see 129(3)(a)(i)A). See Notes to 129(1).

Opening words of 125(1) amended by 1995-97 technical bill, retroactive to taxation years that end after June 1988, to correct "throughout a taxation year" to "throughout the year". The amendment ensures that the deduction is only available when the corporation is a CCPC throughout the same year as that for which the deduction is being claimed.

125(1)(b)(i) amended by 1995 Budget, effective for taxation years that end after June 1995, to add "if those amounts were determined without reference to section 123.3". This was done to preserve the effect of 125(1)(b)(i) while avoiding a potential circularity among 123.3, 125(1) and 126.

125(1)(b)(iii) added by 1992 technical bill, effective for 1992 and later taxation years. It ensures that a corporation that is exempt (e.g., under s. 149, s. 81, the *Indian Act* or a tax treaty) cannot have the

Subdivision b — Computation of Tax: Corporations    S. 125(5.1)

portion of its income that is taxable reduced by the small business deduction in respect of the exempt income.

**Interpretation Bulletins**: IT-362R: Patronage dividends; IT-458R2: Canadian-controlled private corporation. See also list at end of s. 125.

**Information Circulars**: 88-2, para. 11: General anti-avoidance rule — section 245 of the *Income Tax Act*.

**I.T. Technical News**: No. 16 (Parthenon Investments case).

**Forms**: T2 SCH 7: Calculation of aggregate investment income and active business income; T2 SCH 341: Nova Scotia corporate tax reduction for new small businesses; T700: Saskatchewan new small business corporate tax reduction; T708: Prince Edward Island small business deduction; T745 — Newfoundland new small business deduction; T1001: Northwest Territories small business deduction.

**(1.1)** [Repealed under former Act]

**Notes**: 125(1.1), repealed in 1984, provided a reduced small business deduction for Canadian-controlled private corporations carrying on a "non-qualifying business" (e.g., certain professionals). Such corporations are now eligible for the regular deduction under 125(1).

**(2) Interpretation of "business limit"** — For the purposes of this section, a corporation's "business limit" for a taxation year is $200,000 unless the corporation is associated in the year with one or more other Canadian-controlled private corporations in which case, except as otherwise provided in this section, its business limit for the year is nil.

**Related Provisions**: 125(3)–(5) — Business limit to be shared among associated corporations; 125(5.1) — Elimination of small business deduction for large corporations; 248(1)"business limit" — Definition applies to entire Act.

**Interpretation Bulletins**: See list at end of s. 125.

**Information Circulars**: 88-2, para. 18: General anti-avoidance rule — section 245 of the *Income Tax Act*.

**(3) Associated corporations** — Notwithstanding subsection (2), if all of the Canadian-controlled private corporations that are associated with each other in a taxation year have filed with the Minister in prescribed form an agreement whereby, for the purposes of this section, they allocate an amount to one or more of them for the taxation year and the amount so allocated or the total of the amounts so allocated, as the case may be, is $200,000, the business limit for the year of each of the corporations is the amount so allocated to it.

**Related Provisions**: 125(4) — Failure to file agreement; 125(5) — Special rules for business limit; 256(1) — Associated corporations.

**Notes**: In *Deneschuk Building Supplies Ltd.*, [1996] 3 C.T.C. 2039 (TCC), the Court ruled that the agreement under 125(3) can be filed at any time, where no notice was issued by the Minister under 125(4).

**Forms**: T2 SCH 23: Agreement among associated Canadian-controlled private corporations to allocate the business limit; T2 SCH 49: Agreement among associated Canadian-controlled private corporations to allocate the expenditure limit.

**(4) Failure to file agreement** — If any of the Canadian-controlled private corporations that are associated with each other in a taxation year has failed to file with the Minister an agreement as contemplated by subsection (3) within 30 days after notice in writing by the Minister has been forwarded to any of them that such an agreement is required for the purpose of any assessment of tax under this Part, the Minister shall, for the purpose of this section, allocate an amount to one or more of them for the taxation year, which amount or the total of which amounts, as the case may be, shall equal $200,000, and in any such case, notwithstanding subsection (2), the business limit for the year of each of the corporations is the amount so allocated to it.

**Related Provisions**: 256(1) — Associated corporations.

**(5) Special rules for business limit** — Notwithstanding subsections (2) to (4),

(a) where a Canadian-controlled private corporation (in this paragraph referred to as the "first corporation") has more than one taxation year ending in the same calendar year and it is associated in 2 or more of those taxation years with another Canadian-controlled private corporation that has a taxation year ending in that calendar year, the business limit of the first corporation for each taxation year ending in the calendar year in which it is associated with the other corporation that ends after the first such taxation year ending in that calendar year is, subject to the application of paragraph (b), an amount equal to the lesser of

(i) its business limit determined under subsection (3) or (4) for the first such taxation year ending in the calendar year, and

(ii) its business limit determined under subsection (3) or (4) for the particular taxation year ending in the calendar year; and

(b) where a Canadian-controlled private corporation has a taxation year that is less than 51 weeks, its business limit for the year is that proportion of its business limit for the year determined without reference to this paragraph that the number of days in the year is of 365.

**Notes**: Opening words of 125(5) changed from "Notwithstanding any other provision of this section" to "Notwithstanding subsections (2) to (4)" by 1994 Budget, effective for taxation years that end after June 1994. 125(5) is now subject to 125(5.1).

125(5)(a) amended by 1992 technical bill, effective for taxation years that end after December 20, 1991, to prevent a group of corporations that has more than one taxation year ending in a calendar year from allocating $200,000 of extra business limit to a corporation that becomes a new member of the group in a second taxation year ending in the same calendar year.

**(5.1) Business limit reduction** — Notwithstanding subsections (2) to (5), a Canadian-controlled private corporation's business limit for a particular taxation year ending in a calendar year is the amount, if any, by which its business limit otherwise determined for the particular year exceeds the amount determined by the formula

$$A \times \frac{B}{\$11,250}$$

where

A is the amount that would, but for this subsection, be the corporation's business limit for the particular year; and

B is

(a) where the corporation is not associated with any other corporation in the particular year, the amount that would, but for subsections 181.1(2) and (4), be the corporation's tax payable under Part I.3 for its preceding taxation year, and

(b) where the corporation is associated with one or more other corporations in the particular year, the total of all amounts each of which would, but for subsections 181.1(2) and (4), be the tax payable under Part I.3 by the corporation or any such other corporation for its last taxation year ending in the preceding calendar year.

**Related Provisions**: 87(2)(j.92) — Amalgamations — continuing corporation; 127(10.2) — Reduction in SR&ED investment tax credits for large corporations.

**Notes**: 125(5.1) eliminates the small business deduction for large corporations, by reducing the deduction for corporations with taxable capital employed in Canada (as calculated for the Large Corporations Tax) exceeding $10 million (see 181.5(1)), and eliminating it entirely once taxable capital employed in Canada exceeds $15 million. This rule took effect July 1, 1994, with a transitional rule (below) for years that straddle July 1, 1994.

The denominator in the formula changed from $10,000 to $12,500 by 1995 Budget, effective

(a) where a corporation is not associated with any other corporation in a particular taxation year and the corporation's preceding taxation year began after February 27, 1995, for the corporation's particular year and subsequent taxation years; and

(b) where a particular corporation is associated with one or more other corporations in a particular taxation year that ends in a calendar year and the last taxation year of the particular corporation and of each of the other corporations that ended in the preceding calendar year began after February 27, 1995, for the particular year and subsequent taxation years of the particular corporation.

The change reflects the increase in the Part I.3 tax rate under 181.1(3) from 0.2% to 0.225%.

The 1995 Budget bill also provides:

47. (3) For the purpose of applying subsection 125(5.1) of the Act, the amount that would, but for subsections 181.1(2) and (4) of the Act, be a corporation's tax payable under Part I.3 of the Act for a taxation year that began before February 28, 1995 shall be determined without reference to the amendment made by subsection (1) [the increase in the tax rate under 181.1(1) to 0.225% — ed.].

125(5.1) added by 1994 Budget, effective for taxation years that end after June 1994. However, for such years that begin before July 1994, read:

(5.1) Notwithstanding subsections (2) to (5), a Canadian-controlled private corporation's business limit for a particular taxation year ending in a calendar year is the amount, if any, by which its business limit otherwise determined for the particular year exceeds the amount determined by the formula

$$A \times \frac{B}{\$10,000} \times \frac{C}{D}$$

where

A is the amount that would, but for this subsection, be the corporation's business limit for the particular year;

B is

(a) where the corporation is not associated with any other corporation in the particular year, the lesser of $10,000 and the amount that would, but for subsections 181.1(2) and (4), be the corporation's tax payable under Part I.3 for its preceding taxation year, and

(b) where the corporation is associated with one or more other corporations in the particular year, the lesser of $10,000 and the total of all amounts each of which would, but for subsections 181.1(2) and (4), be the tax payable under Part I.3 by the corporation or any such other corporation for its last taxation year ending in the preceding calendar year;

C is the number of days in the particular year that are after June 1994; and

D is the number of days in the particular year.

The amending legislation (S.C. 1995, c. 3, s. 35(4)) also provides:

(4) Notwithstanding any other provision of the *Income Tax Act* or of this Act, nothing in this section [the section enacting the 1994 Budget changes to s. 125 — ed.] shall affect the amount of interest payable under the *Income Tax Act* in respect of a corporation for any period or part thereof that is before July 1994.

**(6) Corporate partnerships** — Where in a taxation year a corporation is a member of a particular partnership and in the year the corporation or a corporation with which it is associated in the year is a member of one or more other partnerships and it may reasonably be considered that one of the main reasons for the separate existence of the partnerships is to increase the amount of a deduction of any corporation under subsection (1), the specified partnership income of the corporation for the year shall, for the purposes of this section, be computed in respect of those partnerships as if all amounts each of which is the income of one of the partnerships for a fiscal period ending in the year from an active business carried on in Canada were nil except for the greatest of those amounts.

**Related Provisions**: 125(6.1) — Corporation deemed member of partnership; 125(6.2) — Specified partnership income deemed nil.

**(6.1) Corporation deemed member of partnership** — For the purposes of this section, a corporation that is a member, or is deemed by this subsection to be a member, of a partnership that is a member of another partnership shall be deemed to be a member of the other partnership and the corporation's share of the income of the other partnership for a fiscal period shall be deemed to be equal to the amount of that income to which the corporation was directly or indirectly entitled.

**(6.2) Specified partnership income deemed nil** — Notwithstanding any other provision of this section, where a corporation is a member of a partnership that was controlled, directly or indirectly in any manner whatever, by one or more non-resident persons, by one or more public corporations (other than a prescribed venture capital corporation) or by any combination thereof at any time in its fiscal pe-

Subdivision b — Computation of Tax: Corporations          S. 125(7) Can

riod ending in a taxation year of the corporation, the income of the partnership for that fiscal period from an active business carried on in Canada shall, for the purposes of computing the specified partnership income of a corporation for the year, be deemed to be nil.

**Related Provisions**: 125(6.3) — Partnership deemed to be controlled; 256(5.1), (6.2) — Controlled directly or indirectly.

**Regulations**: 6700 (prescribed venture capital corporation).

**(6.3) Partnership deemed to be controlled** — For the purposes of subsection (6.2), a partnership shall be deemed to be controlled by one or more persons at any time if the total of the shares of that person or those persons of the income of the partnership from any source for the fiscal period of the partnership that includes that time exceeds ½ of the income of the partnership from that source for that period.

**(7) Definitions** — In this section,

**"active business carried on by a corporation"** means any business carried on by the corporation other than a specified investment business or a personal services business and includes an adventure or concern in the nature of trade;

**Related Provisions**: 129(6) — Investment income from associated corporation deemed to be active business income; 248(1) — Definition of "active business" for purposes other than s. 125.

**Notes**: See Notes to 125(7)"specified investment business".

125(7)"active business" was 125(7)(a) before consolidation in R.S.C. 1985 (5th Supp.), effective for taxation years ending after November 1991.

**Interpretation Bulletins**: See list at end of s. 125.

**"Canadian-controlled private corporation"** means a private corporation that is a Canadian corporation other than a corporation

> (a) controlled, directly or indirectly in any manner whatever, by one or more non-resident persons, by one or more public corporations (other than a prescribed venture capital corporation), or by any combination thereof;
>
> (b) that would, if each share of the capital stock of a corporation that is owned by a non-resident person or a public corporation (other than a prescribed venture capital corporation) were owned by a particular person, be controlled by the particular person, or
>
> (c) a class of the shares of the capital stock of which is listed on a prescribed stock exchange;

---

**Proposed Amendment —
125(7)"Canadian-controlled private
corporation"**

**"Canadian-controlled private corporation"** means a private corporation that is a Canadian corporation other than

> (a) a corporation controlled, directly or indirectly in any manner whatever, by one or more non-resident persons, by one or more public corporations (other than a prescribed venture capital corporation), by one or more corporations described in paragraph (c), or by any combination of them,
>
> (b) a corporation that would, if each share of the capital stock of a corporation that is owned by a non-resident person, by a public corporation (other than a prescribed venture capital corporation), or by a corporation described in paragraph (c) were owned by a particular person, be controlled by the particular person, or
>
> (c) a corporation a class of the shares of the capital stock of which is listed on a prescribed stock exchange;

**Application**: Bill C-43 (First Reading September 20, 2000), s. 71, will amend the definition "Canadian-controlled private corporation" in subsec. 125(7) to read as above, applicable to taxation years that begin after 1999.

**Technical Notes**: Section 125 of the Act provides for a corporate tax reduction (called the "small business deduction") in respect of income of a Canadian-controlled private corporation (CCPC) from an active business carried on by it in Canada.

Subsection 125(7) of the Act defines "Canadian-controlled private corporation", among other terms. This definition applies not only to the small business deduction under section 125 of the Act but also, through its incorporation by reference into subsection 248(1) of the Act, to the Act as a whole.

Currently, a corporation is a CCPC if it is a private corporation and a Canadian corporation (both of which terms are defined in subsection 89(1) of the Act), and it is not controlled, directly or indirectly in any manner whatever by one or any combination of public corporations (other than prescribed venture capital corporations) or non-resident persons. A corporation controlled by a group of non-residents or public corporations is not considered a CCPC if each share held by non-residents or public corporations, when attributed to a notional person, results in the notional person having control of the underlying corporation. Nor is a corporation a CCPC if it lists its stock on a prescribed stock exchange in Canada (Regulation 3200) or outside of Canada (Regulation 3201).

This amendment ensures that a corporation controlled by a Canadian resident corporation that lists its shares on a prescribed stock exchange outside of Canada is not a CCPC. This mirrors the treatment of corporations controlled by a Canadian resident corporation that lists its shares on a prescribed stock exchange in Canada (public corporation). Under the current definition these corporations are not CCPCs.

This amendment applies to taxation years beginning after 1999.

---

**Related Provisions**: 136 — Co-operative corporation may be private corporation for purposes of s. 125; 137(7) — Credit union may be private corporation for purposes of s. 125; 248(1)"Canadian-controlled private corporation" — Definition applies to entire Act; 251(5) — Control by related groups, options, etc.; 256(5.1), (6.2) — Controlled directly or indirectly.

**Notes**: The definition of a CCPC does not require Canadian control so much as the *lack* of control by non-residents. 50% Canadian resident voting power is normally sufficient. Note, however, that 256(5.1) provides a *de facto* control test.

In *Parthenon Investments Ltd.*, [1997] 3 C.T.C. 152 (FCA) it was held that "control" means only ultimate control, on the theory that "control cannot allow for two masters simultaneously". Thus, on a chain of corporations with Canadian control at the top and a U.S. corporation in the middle, the lowest tier was not "controlled" by a non-resident. The CCRA does not accept this concept for all purposes (Canadian Tax Foundation 1998 annual conference report, p. 52:24); it can cause problems for taxpayers in other areas, such as 55(3.1)(a) and 88(1)(d). (See Income Tax Technical News No. 16.) Proposed 256(6.1) and (6.2) will reverse this rule effective December 1999, and will provide that the top and middle levels have simultaneous control.

Revenue Canada indicated at the 1994 Canadian Tax Foundation annual conference (Conference Report, p. 47:6; Income Tax Technical News No. 3) that group control is irrelevant for purposes of this definition. If the total control by non-residents and public corporations exceeds 50% of the votes, the CCRA takes the position that the corporation is not a CCPC even if no non-resident (or public corporation) controlling group can be identified. This administrative position has been confirmed with the enactment of para. (b).

Paras. (b) and (c) added by 1995-97 technical bill, effective 1996. (What is now para. (a) was in the body of the definition with no paragraphs.)

125(7)"Canadian-controlled private corporation" was 125(7)(b) before consolidation in R.S.C. 1985 (5th Supp.), effective for taxation years ending after November 1991.

**Regulations**: 3200, 3201 (prescribed stock exchanges); 6700 (prescribed venture capital corporation).

**Interpretation Bulletins**: IT-113R4: Benefits to employees — stock options; IT-243R4: Dividend refund to private corporations; IT-458R2: Canadian-controlled private corporation; IT-484R2: Business investment losses. See also list at end of s. 125.

**I.T. Technical News**: No. 3 (Canadian-controlled private corporation); No. 16 (*Parthenon Investments* case).

**"income of the corporation for the year from an active business"** means the total of

(a) the corporation's income for the year from an active business carried on by it including any income for the year pertaining to or incident to that business, other than income for the year from a source in Canada that is a property (within the meaning assigned by subsection 129(4)), and

(b) the amount, if any, included under subsection 12(10.2) in computing the corporation's income for the year;

**Notes**: Interest on overpaid income taxes will likely be considered income from property rather than pertaining to or incident to the taxpayer's business: see *Munich Reinsurance Co.*, [2000] 2 C.T.C. 2785 (TCC).

125(7)"income of the corporation..." was 125(7)(c) before consolidation in R.S.C. 1985 (5th Supp.), effective for taxation years ending after November 1991. See Table of Concordance.

Para. (b) (formerly 125(7)(c)(ii)) added by 1992 technical bill, effective for 1991 and later taxation years.

**"personal services business"** carried on by a corporation in a taxation year means a business of providing services where

(a) an individual who performs services on behalf of the corporation (in this definition and paragraph 18(1)(p) referred to as an "incorporated employee"), or

(b) any person related to the incorporated employee

is a specified shareholder of the corporation and the incorporated employee would reasonably be regarded as an officer or employee of the person or partnership to whom or to which the services were provided but for the existence of the corporation, unless

(c) the corporation employs in the business throughout the year more than five full-time employees, or

(d) the amount paid or payable to the corporation in the year for the services is received or receivable by it from a corporation with which it was associated in the year;

**Related Provisions**: 18(1)(p) — Limitation on deductions from personal services business income; 122.3(1.1) — Restriction on overseas employment tax credit for incorporated employee; 207.6(3) — Retirement compensation arrangement for incorporated employee; 248(1)"personal services business" — Definition applies to entire Act.

**Notes**: See Notes to 18(1)(p). 125(7)"personal services business" was 125(7)(d) before consolidation in R.S.C. 1985 (5th Supp.), effective for taxation years ending after November 1991. See Table of Concordance.

The words "more than five full-time employees" in para. (c) mean 6 or more, not 5 plus a part-time employee. See *Hughes & Co. Holdings Ltd.*, [1994] 2 C.T.C. 170 (FCTD). However, in appropriate cases even 4 hours per day could be "full-time": *Ben Raedarc Holdings Ltd.*, [1998] 1 C.T.C. 2774 (TCC).

**Interpretation Bulletins**: IT-168R3: Athletes and players employed by football, hockey and similar clubs; IT-406R2: Tax payable by an *inter vivos* trust; IT-421R2: Benefits to individuals, corporations and shareholders from loans or debt. See also list at end of s. 125.

**Forms**: CPT-1: Request for a ruling as to the status of a worker under the *Canada Pension Plan* or *Unemployment Insurance Act*.

**"specified investment business"** carried on by a corporation in a taxation year means a business (other than a business carried on by a credit union or a business of leasing property other than real property) the principal purpose of which is to derive income (including interest, dividends, rents and royalties) from property but, except where the corporation was a prescribed labour-sponsored venture capital corporation at any time in the year, does not include a business carried on by the corporation in the year where

(a) the corporation employs in the business throughout the year more than 5 full-time employees, or

(b) any other corporation associated with the corporation provides, in the course of carrying on an active business, managerial, administrative, financial, maintenance or other similar services to the corporation in the year and the corporation could reasonably be expected to require more than 5 full-time employees if those services had not been provided;

**Related Provisions**: 95(1) — Analogous definition of "investment business" for FAPI purposes; 125(7)"active business" — No small business deduction for specified investment business; 129(4)"income" — Dividend refund available for income from specified investment business; 129(6) — Income from associated corporation deemed to be active business income; 248(1)"specified investment business" — Definition applies to entire Act.

**Notes**: Although it is a "business", the income of a specified investment business is taxed as investment income, and not eligible for the small business deduction under 125(1), since it is excluded from 125(7)"active business". It is eligible for the dividend refund: see 129(4)"income" or "loss". (Note that investment income from an associated corporation may be deemed by 129(6) to be active business income, and thus excluded from specified investment business income.)

The words "more than 5 full-time employees" mean 6 or more, not 5 plus a part-time employee. See *Hughes & Co. Holdings Ltd.*, [1994] 2 C.T.C. 170 (FCTD). However, in appropriate cases even 4 hours per day could be "full-time": *Ben Raedarc Holdings Ltd.*, [1998] 1 C.T.C. 2774 (TCC).

Definition amended by 1995-97 technical bill, effective for 1995 and later taxation years. The only substantive change was at the end of the opening words, changing "unless" to "but, except where the corporation was a prescribed labour-sponsored venture capital corporation at any time in the year, does not include a business carried on by the corporation in the year where".

125(7)"specified investment business" was 125(7)(e) before consolidation in R.S.C. 1985 (5th Supp.), effective for taxation years ending after November 1991. See Table of Concordance.

**Regulations**: 6701 (prescribed labour-sponsored venture capital corporation).

**Interpretation Bulletins**: IT-243R4: Dividend refund to private corporations; IT-406R2: Tax payable by an *inter vivos* trust. See also list at end of s. 125.

**"specified partnership income"** of a corporation for a taxation year means the amount determined by the formula

$$A + B$$

where

A is the total of all amounts each of which is an amount in respect of a partnership of which the corporation was a member in the year equal to the lesser of

(a) the total of all amounts each of which is an amount in respect of an active business carried on in Canada by the corporation as a member of the partnership determined by the formula

$$G - H$$

where

G is the total of all amounts each of which is the corporation's share of the income (determined in accordance with subdivision j of Division B) of the partnership for a fiscal period of the business that ends in the year or an amount included in the corporation's income for the year from the business because of subsection 34.2(5), and

H is the total of all amounts deducted in computing the corporation's income for the year from the business (other than amounts that were deducted in computing the income of the partnership from the business), and

(b) the amount determined by the formula

$$\frac{K}{L} \times M$$

where

K is the total of all amounts each of which is the corporation's share of the income (determined in accordance with subdivision j of Division B) of the partnership for a fiscal period ending in the year from an active business carried on in Canada,

L is the total of all amounts each of which is the income of the partnership for a fiscal period referred to in paragraph (a) from an active business carried on in Canada, and

M is the lesser of

(i) $200,000 and

(ii) the product obtained when $548 is multiplied by the total of all amounts each of which is the number of days contained in a fiscal period of the partnership ending in the year, and

B is the lesser of

(a) the total of the amounts determined in respect of the corporation for the year under subparagraphs (1)(a)(iii) and (iv), and

(b) the total of all amounts each of which is an amount in respect of a partnership of which the corporation was a member in the year equal to the amount determined by the formula

$$N - O$$

where

N is the amount determined in respect of the partnership for the year under paragraph (a) of the description of A, and

O is the amount determined in respect of the partnership for the year under paragraph (b) of the description of A;

**Related Provisions**: 125(6) — Corporate partnerships; 125(6.2) — Specified partnership income deemed nil; 257 — Formula amounts cannot calculate to less than zero. See additional Related Provisions and Definitions at end of s. 125.

**Notes**: Formula element G amended by 1995 Budget, effective for 1995 and later taxation years, to add the reference to income included because of 34.2(5). 34.2(5) includes in income for a taxation year any reserve deducted under 34.2(4) for the preceding taxation year. 34.2(4) establishes a deductible reserve for a taxpayer's 1995 stub-period business income (see Notes to 34.2(4)). Such a reserve for a preceding taxation year is, therefore, to be included in formula element G for a corporation's specified partnership income for the next taxation year, with any new reserve for that following year included in formula element H.

125(7)"specified partnership income" was 125(7)(f) before consolidation in R.S.C. 1985 (5th Supp.), effective for taxation years ending after November 1991. See Table of Concordance in introductory pages.

Formula element H (formerly 125(7)(f)(i)(A)(II)) added by 1991 technical bill, retroactive to 1986, to clarify that amounts deducted by a corporate partner will be taken into account in determining specified partnership income if they were deducted in computing the corporation's income from the business carried on in Canada by the corporation as a member of the partnership.

**"specified partnership loss"** of a corporation for a taxation year means the total of all amounts each of which is an amount in respect of a partnership of which the corporation was a member in the year determined by the formula

$$A + B$$

where

A is the total of all amounts each of which is the corporation's share of the loss (determined in accordance with subdivision j of Division B) of the partnership for a fiscal period ending in the year from an active business carried on in Canada by the corporation as a member of the partnership, and

B is the total of all amounts each of which is an amount determined by the formula

$$G - H$$

where

G is the amount determined for H in the definition "specified partnership income" in this subsection for the year in respect of the corporation's income from an active business carried on in Canada by the corporation as a member of the partnership, and

H is the amount determined for G in the definition "specified partnership income" in this subsection for the year in respect of the corporation's share of the income from the business.

**Related Provisions**: 257 — Formula amount cannot calculate to less than zero.

**Notes**: Formula element B (formerly 125(7)(g)(ii)) added by 1991 technical bill, retroactive to 1986, to clarify that amounts deducted by a corporate partner will be included in specified partnership loss if they were deducted in computing the corporation's income from the business carried on in Canada by the corporation as a member of the partnership.

125(7)"specified partnership loss" was 125(7)(g) before consolidation in R.S.C. 1985 (5th Supp.), effective for taxation years ending after November 1991.

**Related Provisions [subsec. 125(7)]**: 48.1 — Election to trigger capital gains exemption on ceasing to be CCPC.

### (8)–(15) [Repealed under former Act]

**Notes**: 125(8)–(15) repealed in 1984 as part of the simplification of the small business deduction.

**Definitions [s. 125]**: "active business" — 125(7) (see also "income from ..."), 248(1); "amount", "assessment" — 248(1); "associated" — 256; "business" — 248(1); "business limit" — 125(2)–(5); "calendar year" — *Interpretation Act* 37(1)(a); "Canada" — 255; "Canadian-controlled private corporation" — 125(7), 248(1); "carrying on business" — 253; "controlled directly or indirectly" — 256(5.1), (6.2); "corporation" — 248(1), *Interpretation Act* 35(1); "credit union" — 137(6), 248(1); "dividend", "employee" — 248(1); "fiscal period" — 249(2)(b), 249.1; "in Canada" — 255; "income from active business" — 125(7); "incorporated employee" — 248(1); "Minister", "non-resident", "person" — 248(1); "personal services business" — 125(7), 248(1); "pre-scribed" — 248(1); "prescribed labour-sponsored venture capital corporation" — Reg. 6701; "prescribed stock exchange" — Reg. 3200, 3201; "prescribed venture capital corporation" — Reg. 6700; "private corporation" — 89(1), 136, 248(1); "property" — 248(1); "public corporation" — 89(1), 248(1); "share" — 248(1); "specified investment business" — 125(7), 248(1); "specified partnership income" — 125(7); "specified partnership loss" — 125(7); "taxable dividend" — 89(1), 248(1); "taxable income" — 2(2), 248(1); "taxation year" — 249; "writing" — *Interpretation Act* 35(1).

**Interpretation Bulletins [s. 125]**: IT-64R3: Corporations: association and control — after 1988; IT-73R5: The small business deduction; IT-151R5: Scientific research and experimental development expenditures; IT-189R2: Corporations used by practising members of professions; IT-243R4: Dividend refund to private corporations.

### 125.1 (1) Manufacturing and processing profits deductions [M&P credit] 

— There may be deducted from the tax otherwise payable under this Part by a corporation for a taxation year an amount equal to 7% of the lesser of

(a) the amount, if any, by which the corporation's Canadian manufacturing and processing profits for the year exceed, where the corporation was a Canadian-controlled private corporation throughout the year, the least of the amounts determined under paragraphs 125(1)(a) to (c) in respect of the corporation for the year, and

(b) the amount, if any, by which the corporation's taxable income for the year exceeds the total of

(i) where the corporation was a Canadian-controlled private corporation throughout the year, the least of the amounts determined under paragraphs 125(1)(a) to (c) in respect of the corporation for the year,

(ii) $^{10}/_4$ of the total of amounts deducted under subsection 126(2) from the tax for the year otherwise payable under this Part by the corporation, and

(iii) where the corporation was a Canadian-controlled private corporation throughout the year, its aggregate investment income for the year (within the meaning assigned by subsection 129(4)).

**Related Provisions**: 123.2(a) — Corporate surtax applies to total tax before claiming M&P deduction; 125.1(2) — Credit for generating electrical energy; 182 — Manufacturing of tobacco — surtax.

**Notes**: Since 1994, the manufacturing and processing credit is 7% (i.e. an effective reduction of 7 percentage points of federal tax on M&P income, from 28% to 21%). Some provinces also have a reduced rate on M&P income; see tax tables in introductory pages.

See also Notes at end of 125.1.

125.1(1)(b)(iii) amended by 1995 Budget, effective for taxation years that end after June 1995, in consequence of amendments to s. 129. See Notes to 129(3). For earlier taxation years that begin after June 1991, read "the amount determined under clause 129(3)(a)(i)(B) in respect of the corporation for the year" in place of "its aggregate investment income for the year (within the meaning assigned by subsection 129(4))".

125.1(1) amended by 1992 technical bill, effective for taxation years that begin in 1994 or later. The credit was 6% for days in calendar year 1993, and 5% for days before 1993.

125.1(1) amended by 1988 tax reform, effective for taxation years ending after June 1988, but with prorating for such taxation years beginning before July 1991.

**Interpretation Bulletins**: IT-145R: Canadian manufacturing and processing profits — reduced rate of corporate tax.

**Forms**: T2 SCH 27: Calculation of Canadian manufacturing and processing profits; T2 SCH 300: Newfoundland manufacturing and processing profits tax credit; T2 SCH 320: PEI manufacturing and processing profits tax credit; T2 SCH 321: PEI corporate investment tax credit; T2 SCH 344: Nova Scotia manufacturing and processing investment tax credit; T2 SCH 381: Manitoba manufacturing and processing tax credit; T2 SCH 401: Saskatchewan manufacturing and processing tax credit; T2 SCH 402: Saskatchewan manufacturing and processing investment tax credit; T2 SCH 404: Saskatchewan manufacturing and processing profits tax credit; T2 SCH 440: Yukon manufacturing and processing profits tax credit; T2 SCH 460: Northwest Territories investment tax credit; T2 SCH 480: Nunavut investment tax credit; T86: Manitoba manufacturing investment tax credit.

**(2) Generating electrical energy for sale** — A corporation that generates electrical energy for sale, or produces steam for use in the generation of electrical energy for sale, in a taxation year may deduct from its tax otherwise payable under this Part for the year 7% of the amount determined by the formula

### Proposed Amendment — 125.1(2) opening words

**(2) Electrical energy and steam** — A corporation that generates electrical energy for sale, or produces steam for sale, in a taxation year may deduct from its tax otherwise payable under this Part for the year 7% of the amount determined by the formula

**Application**: The December 21, 2000 draft legislation, subsec. 71(1), will amend the opening words of subsec. 125.1(2) to read as above, applicable to taxation years that end after 1999 except that, in its application to such a taxation year that begins before 2002, the reference to "7%" shall be read as a reference to the total of

(a) 0% multiplied by the number of days in the year that are before 1999,

(b) in the case of a corporation that in 1999 generated electrical energy for sale, or produced steam for use in the generation of electrical energy for sale, that proportion of 1% that the number of days in the taxation year that are in the 1999 calendar year is of the number of days in the taxation year,

(c) in the case of a corporation to which para. (b) does not apply, 0% multiplied by the number of days in the taxation year that are in the 1999 calendar year,

(d) that proportion of 3% that the number of days in the taxation year that are in the 2000 calendar year is of the number of days in the taxation year,

(e) that proportion of 5% that the number of days in the taxation year that are in the 2001 calendar year is of the number of days in the taxation year,

(f) that proportion of 7% that the number of days in the taxation year that are in the 2002 calendar year is of the number of days in the taxation year, and

(g) that proportion of 7% that the number of days in the taxation year that are in the 2003 calendar year is of the number of days in the taxation year.

**Technical Notes**: Section 125.1 provides a reduced rate of corporate tax on Canadian manufacturing and processing profits. Generally, the rate reduction takes the form of the deduction, from Part I tax otherwise payable, of an amount equal to a specified percentage — currently 7% — of a corporation's "Canadian manufacturing and processing profits" (other than profits eligible for the small business deduction under section 125).

The definition "Canadian manufacturing and processing profits" in subsection 125.1(3) provides, among other things, that such profits are to be determined under rules prescribed by regulation to be applicable to the "manufacturing or processing in Canada of goods for sale or lease". The definition "manufacturing or processing" in subsection 125.1(3) precludes certain activities from being "manufacturing or processing" activities to which the 7% corporate tax rate reduction in subsection 125.1(1) applies. The list of excluded activities includes producing or processing electrical energy or steam, for sale.

However, subsection 125.1(2) extends the 7% corporate tax rate reduction to a corporation that generates electrical energy for sale, or produces steam for use in the generation of electrical energy for sale. Subsection 125.1(2) is amended to also apply to the production of "steam for sale", regardless of the end use of the steam.

Subsection 125.1(5) provides rules of interpretation for the purpose of applying subsection 125.1(2) and related *Income Tax Regulations* (other than section 5201 of the Regulations). Paragraph 125.1(5)(a) provides that electrical energy is deemed to be a good for the purpose of computing the value of the description of A in subsection 125.1(2). Also, paragraph 125.1(5)(b) deems the generation of electrical energy for sale, or the production steam for use in the generation of electrical energy for sale, to be manufacturing or processing, subject to the 10% gross revenue rule in paragraph (l) of the definition "manufacturing or processing". Unless the 10% gross revenue rule is met by a corporation, the corporation's activity is deemed to be excluded from the meaning of "manufacturing or processing".

For the purposes for which subsection 125.1(5) applies, paragraph 125.1(5)(a) is amended to deem steam to be a good and paragraph 125.1(5)(b) is amended to deem the production of "steam for sale" to be manufacturing or processing (other than for the purpose of applying the 10% gross revenue test in paragraph (l) of the definition "manufacturing or processing" in subsection 125.1(3)).

The tax rate reduction available under these changes is phased in beginning January 1, 2000, with a three percentage point tax rate reduction for the calendar year 2000. The phase in to a full seven-percentage point tax rate reduction will be completed in 2002. The coming-into-force provision provides for a pro-ration of the tax rate reductions for taxation years that straddle calendar years. A taxation year could begin in 2001 and end in 2003 because of the 53-week taxation year rule, and because of this paragraphs (f) and (g) of the coming-into-force rule both refer to the 7% rate applicable to the calendar years 2002 and 2003, respectively.

**Notice of Ways and Means Motion, federal budget, February 28, 2000**: *M&P Rate for Producing Steam for Sale*

(42) That, for the purpose only of applying the manufacturing and processing profits tax rate reduction in subsection 125.1(2) of the Act for the 2000 and subsequent taxation years, the production of steam for sale be considered manufacturing or processing.

**S. 125.1(2)**  Income Tax Act, Part I, Division E

> **Federal budget, supplementary information, February 28, 2000**: *Manufacturing and Processing Tax Rate Reduction Extended to Income from Sale of Steam*
>
> Since 1973, the Government has provided a tax credit to reduce the rate of corporate tax applicable to Canadian manufacturing and processing profits. Before the February 16, 1999, budget, the definition of manufacturing and processing (M&P) had specifically excluded the production or processing of electrical energy or steam for sale. That budget proposed the extension of the M&P tax credit to corporations that produce, for sale, electrical energy or steam used in the generation of electricity.
>
> This budget proposes to extend the M&P tax credit to corporations that produce, for sale, steam for uses other than the generation of electricity. This change will ensure that all producers of steam for sale will face the same income tax rate. Access to the credit will be phased in beginning January 1, 2000, with a three-percentage-point reduction. In each of the two subsequent years, there will be additional two-percentage-point reductions. The phase-in to M&P treatment will be completed in 2002. These proposed rate reductions will be prorated for taxation years that straddle calendar years.

$$A - B$$

where

A is the amount, if any, that would, if the definition "manufacturing or processing" in subsection (3), and in subsection 1104(9) of the *Income Tax Regulations*, were read without reference to paragraph (h) of those definitions (other than for the purpose of applying section 5201 of the *Income Tax Regulations*) and if subsection (5) applied for the purpose of subsection (1), be the lesser of

   (a) the amount determined under paragraph (1)(a) in respect of the corporation for the year, and

   (b) the amount determined under paragraph (1)(b) in respect of the corporation for the year; and

B is the amount, if any, that is the lesser of

   (a) the amount determined under paragraph (1)(a) in respect of the corporation for the year, and

   (b) the amount determined under paragraph (1)(b) in respect of the corporation for the year.

**Related Provisions**: 125.1(5) — Interpretation; 257 — Formula cannot calculate to less than zero.

**Notes**: 125.1(2) added by 1999 Budget, effective for taxation years that end after 1998, except that for a taxation year that begins before 2002, read "7%" as the total of:

   (a) 0% multiplied by the number of days in the year that are before 1999,

   (b) that proportion of "1%" that the number of days in the taxation year that are in the year is of the number of days in the taxation year,

   (c) that proportion of "3%" that the number of days in the taxation year that are in the 2000 calendar year is of the number of days in the taxation year,

   (d) that proportion of "5%" that the number of days in the taxation year that are in the 2001 calendar year is of the number of days in the taxation year,

   (e) that proportion of "7%" that the number of days in the taxation year that are in the 2002 calendar year is of the number of days in the taxation year, and

   (f) that proportion of "7%" that the number of days in the taxation year that are in the 2003 calendar year is of the number of days in the taxation year.

This implements a Budget proposal that the producing or processing of electrical energy or steam for sale be considered as manufacturing or processing for purposes of the M & P credit, except that, in its application to profits from such activity, the 7% credit is 1% for 1999, 3% for 2000, and 5% for 2001, pro-rated for taxation years that straddle a calendar year end.

A former 125.1(2), repealed by 1988 tax reform, provided transitional rules for 1973 through 1976.

**(3) Definitions** — In this section,

**"Canadian manufacturing and processing profits"** of a corporation for a taxation year means such portion of the total of all amounts each of which is the income of the corporation for the year from an active business carried on in Canada as is determined under rules prescribed for that purpose by regulation made on the recommendation of the Minister of Finance to be applicable to the manufacturing or processing in Canada of goods for sale or lease; and

**Notes**: 125.1(3)"Canadian manufacturing and processing profits" was 125.1(3)(a) before consolidation in R.S.C. 1985 (5th Supp.), effective for taxation years ending after November 1991.

**Regulations**: 5200–5204 (Canadian manufacturing and processing profits).

**Interpretation Bulletins**: IT-145R: Canadian manufacturing and processing profits — reduced rate of corporate tax.

**"manufacturing or processing"** does not include

   (a) farming or fishing,

   (b) logging,

   (c) construction,

   (d) operating an oil or gas well or extracting petroleum or natural gas from a natural accumulation of petroleum or natural gas,

   (e) extracting minerals from a mineral resource,

   (f) processing

      (i) ore (other than iron ore or tar sands ore) from a mineral resource located in Canada to any stage that is not beyond the prime metal stage or its equivalent,

      (ii) iron ore from a mineral resource located in Canada to any stage that is not beyond the pellet stage or its equivalent, or

      (iii) tar sands ore from a mineral resource located in Canada to any stage that is not beyond the crude oil stage or its equivalent,

   (g) producing industrial minerals,

   (h) producing or processing electrical energy or steam, for sale,

(i) processing natural gas as part of the business of selling or distributing gas in the course of operating a public utility,

(j) processing heavy crude oil recovered from a natural reservoir in Canada to a stage that is not beyond the crude oil stage or its equivalent,

(k) Canadian field processing, or

(l) any manufacturing or processing of goods for sale or lease, if, for any taxation year of a corporation in respect of which the expression is being applied, less than 10% of its gross revenue from all active businesses carried on in Canada was from

(i) the selling or leasing of goods manufactured or processed in Canada by it, and

(ii) the manufacturing or processing in Canada of goods for sale or lease, other than goods for sale or lease by it.

**Related Provisions**: 127(11)(a) — Meaning of "manufacturing or processing" for investment tax credit purposes; Reg. 1104(9) — Definition of manufacturing or processing for Class 29 purposes.

**Notes**: "Industrial minerals", used in para. (g), are considered by the CCRA to be non-metallic minerals, such as gravel, clay, stone, limestone, sand and feldspar (IT-145R, para. 11).

125.1(3)"manufacturing or processing" was 125.1(3)(b) before consolidation in R.S.C. 1985 (5th Supp.), effective for taxation years ending after November 1991. See Table of Concordance.

Paras. (d) to (k) amended by 1996 Budget, effective for taxation years that begin after 1996. For earlier years since 1990, read:

(d) operating an oil or gas well, extracting petroleum or natural gas from a natural accumulation thereof or processing heavy crude oil recovered from a natural reservoir in Canada to a stage that is not beyond the crude oil stage or its equivalent,

(e) extracting minerals from a mineral resource,

(f) processing ore (other than iron ore or tar sands) from a mineral resource located in Canada to any stage that is not beyond the prime metal stage or its equivalent,

(g) processing iron ore from a mineral resource located in Canada to any stage that is not beyond the pellet stage or its equivalent,

(h) processing tar sands from a mineral resource located in Canada to any stage that is not beyond the crude oil stage or its equivalent,

(i) producing industrial minerals other than sulphur produced by processing natural gas,

(j) producing or processing electrical energy or steam, for sale,

(k) processing gas, if such gas is processed as part of the business of selling or distributing gas in the course of operating a public utility, or

Paras. (f)–(h) (formerly 125.1(3)(b)(vi) to (vi.2)) amended by 1991 technical bill, effective 1990, to add "located in Canada" (paras. (f), (g)) and "from a mineral resource located in Canada" (para. (h)). The amendment allows processing of foreign ore to be eligible for the credit. This change is consequential on the phase-out of earned depletion. Processing of Canadian ore entitles the taxpayer to the resource allowance in 20(1)(v.1).

**Interpretation Bulletins**: IT-92R2: Income of contractors; IT-145R: Canadian manufacturing and processing profits — reduced rate of corporate tax; IT-411R: Meaning of "construction".

**I.T. Technical News**: No. 8 (pre-delivery service of new vehicles); No. 19 (Canadian manufacturing and processing profits — change to Interpretation Bulletin IT-145R).

**(4) Determination of gross revenue** — For the purposes of paragraph (l) of the definition "manufacturing or processing" in subsection (3), where a corporation was a member of a partnership at any time in a taxation year,

(a) there shall be included in the gross revenue of the corporation for the year from all active businesses carried on in Canada, that proportion of the gross revenue from each such business carried on in Canada by means of the partnership, for the fiscal period of the partnership coinciding with or ending in that year, that the corporation's share of the income of the partnership from that business for that fiscal period is of the income of the partnership from that business for that fiscal period; and

(b) there shall be included in the gross revenue of the corporation for the year from all activities described in subparagraphs (l)(i) and (ii) of the definition "manufacturing or processing" in subsection (3), that proportion of the gross revenue from each such activity engaged in in the course of a business carried on by means of the partnership, for the fiscal period of the partnership coinciding with or ending in that year, that the corporation's share of the income of the partnership from that business for that fiscal period is of the income of the partnership from that business for that fiscal period.

**(5) Interpretation** — For the purpose of the description of A in subsection 125.1(2) and for the purpose of applying the *Income Tax Regulations* (other than section 5201 of the Regulations) to that subsection other than the description of B,

(a) electrical energy is deemed to be a good; and

(b) the generation of electrical energy for sale, or the production of steam for use in the generation of electrical energy for sale, is deemed to be, subject to paragraph (l) of the definition "manufacturing or processing" in subsection (3), manufacturing or processing.

---

**Proposed Amendment — 125.1(5)(a), (b)**

(a) electrical energy, and steam, are deemed to be goods; and

(b) the generation of electrical energy for sale, and the production of steam for sale, are deemed to be, subject to paragraph (l) of the definition "manufacturing or processing" in subsection (3), manufacturing or processing.

**Application**: The December 21, 2000 draft legislation, subsec. 71(2), will amend paras. 125.1(5)(a) and (b) to read as above, applicable to taxation years that end after 1999.

**Technical Notes**: See under 125.1(2) opening words.

**Notes [s. 125.1(5)]**: 125.1(5) added by 1999 Budget, effective for taxation years that end after 1998.

**Notes [s. 125.1]**: A mechanism exists for an opposition party to initiate consideration of a reduction or removal of the manufacturing and processing credit. 1973-74, c. 29, subsecs. 1(3) and (4) provide:

(3) **Procedure where motion filed with speaker** — Where, at any time after March 31, 1974, a motion for the consideration of the House of Commons, signed by not less than sixty members of the House, is filed with the Speaker to the effect that section 125.1 of the *Income Tax Act*, as enacted by subsection (1), be amended, or to the effect that subsection (2) be amended, so as to

(a) discontinue the deduction that would otherwise be permitted by the said section 125.1,

(b) reduce the amount of the deduction that would otherwise be permitted by that section, or

(c) in any other manner, restrict the application of the provisions of that section,

for any period commencing after the motion is filed, the House of Commons shall, within the first fifteen days next after the motion is filed that the House is sitting, in accordance with the Rules of the House, take up and consider the motion, and if the motion, with or without amendments, is approved by the House, the Minister of Finance shall forthwith take such steps as are necessary in order that a measure in his name giving effect to the motion may be placed before the House without delay.

(4) **Time for deciding questions** — All questions in connection with any motion taken up and considered by the House of Commons pursuant to subsection (3) shall be debated without interruption and decided not later than the end of the third sitting day next after the day the motion is first so taken up and considered, and any measure required to be placed before the House pursuant to that subsection giving effect to any such motion shall be placed before the House not later than the end of the fifteenth sitting day next after the day the motion, with or without amendments, is approved by the House, and all questions in connection with any such measure shall be debated without interruption and decided not later than the end of the seventh sitting day next after the day the measure is first so placed before the House.

This rule was not included in the reconsolidation of s. 125.1 in R.S.C. 1985 (5th Supp.), which took effect March 1, 1994. However, it should still be considered to be in force; see ITAR 75.

**Definitions [s. 125.1]**: "amount", "business" — 248(1); "Canadian-controlled private corporation" — 125(7), 248(1); "Canadian field processing" — 248(1); "Canadian manufacturing and processing profits" — 125.1(3); "corporation" — 248(1), *Interpretation Act* 35(1); "gross revenue" — 125.1(4), 248(1); "manufacturing or processing" — 125.1(3); "mineral resource", "oil or gas well", "tar sands" — 248(1); "taxable income" — 2(2), 248(1); "taxation year" — 249.

**125.2 (1) Deduction of [pre-1992] Part VI tax** — There may be deducted in computing the tax payable under this Part for a taxation year by a corporation that was throughout the year a financial institution (within the meaning assigned by section 190) an amount equal to such part as the corporation claims of its unused Part VI tax credits for any of its 7 immediately preceding taxation years ending before 1992, to the extent that that amount does not exceed the amount, if any, by which

(a) its tax payable under this Part (determined without reference to this section) for the year

exceeds the total of

(b) the amount that would, but for subsection 190.1(3), be its tax payable under Part VI for the year, and

(c) the lesser of its Canadian surtax payable (within the meaning assigned by subsection 125.3(4)) for the year and the amount that would, but for subsection 181.1(4), be its tax payable under Part I.3 for the year.

**Related Provisions**: 123.2(a) — Corporate surtax applies to total tax before claiming this credit; 181.1(4)–(7) — Credit of surtax against Part VI tax after 1991. See also Related Provisions and Definitions at end of 125.2.

**Notes**: 125.2(1) amended by 1992 technical bill, effective for 1992 and later taxation years. However, if a corporation elected under s. 111 of the amending legislation (see Notes to 190.1(3)) to have that section apply to its taxation years ending in 1991, the amended 125.2(1) applies to the corporation for those years, but without reference to 125.2(1)(c).

Before 1992, surtax was reduced by (credited against) large corporations tax (Part I.3 tax) and financial institutions capital tax (Part VI tax). Conceptually, if a corporation is paying enough income tax to have a high surtax, those capital taxes do not apply (thus they operate as kind of minimum tax). However, foreign corporations were unable to claim foreign tax credits in respect of capital tax paid to Canada, since it was not income tax. Effective 1992, therefore, the crediting of the surtax was reversed: Part I.3 and Part VI taxes are reduced by (credited against) the surtax. The effect on total Canadian tax is intended to be nil, but the surtax payable is eligible for foreign tax credit treatment in foreign jurisdictions.

125.2(1) previously allowed the pre-1992 reduction in surtax for Part VI tax payable. It has been preserved to allow carryforwards (7 years) and carrybacks (3 years). The new credit of Part VI tax against surtax is in 190.1(3). See also Notes at end of 125.2.

**Forms**: T2 SCH 42: Calculation of unused Part VI tax credit and unused Part I tax credit.

**(2) Idem** — For the purposes of this section,

(a) an amount may not be claimed under subsection (1) in computing a corporation's tax payable under this Part for a particular taxation year in respect of its unused Part VI tax credit for another taxation year until its unused Part VI tax credits for taxation years preceding the other year that may be claimed for the particular year have been claimed; and

(b) an amount in respect of a corporation's unused Part VI tax credit for a taxation year may be claimed under subsection (1) in computing its tax payable under this Part for another taxation year only to the extent that it exceeds the total of all amounts each of which is the amount claimed in respect of that unused Part VI tax credit in computing its tax payable under this Part for a taxation year preceding that other year.

**(3) Definition of "unused Part VI tax credit"** — For the purposes of this section, "unused Part VI tax credit" of a corporation for a taxation year is the lesser of

(a) its tax payable under Part VI (determined without reference to subsections 190.1(1.1) and (3)) for the year, and

(b) the amount determined by the formula

$$A - B$$

where

A   is its tax payable under Part VI for the year (determined without reference to subsection 190.1(3)), and

B   is the amount, if any, by which

(i) the amount that would, but for this section, be its tax payable under this Part for the year

exceeds

(ii) the lesser of its Canadian surtax payable (within the meaning assigned by subsection 125.3(4)) and the amount that would, but for subsection 181.1(4), be its tax payable under Part I.3 for the year.

**Notes**: 125.2(3) amended by 1992 technical bill, and 125.2(3)(a) and "lesser of" limitation in opening words added by 1993 technical bill, effective for purposes of computing the amount that may be deducted by a corporation under 125.2(1):

(A) subject to (B) and (C) below, for taxation years that end before 1992 in respect of unused Part VI tax credits for taxation years that end after 1991;

(B) where the corporation has elected under s. 111 of the 1992 technical bill (see Notes to 190.1(3)) to have amended 190.1(3)–(6) apply to its taxation years that end in 1991, the amended 125.2(3) applies for taxation years that end after 1990 in respect of unused Part VI tax credits for taxation years that end after 1990, except that for the purposes of computing its unused Part VI tax credits for taxation years that end in 1991, ignore 125.2(3)(b)B(ii); and

(C) where (B) above does not apply, and the corporation elects under para. 88(2)(b) of the 1993 technical bill (see Notes to 190.11) for amended 190.11(b)(i) to apply to its 1991 and later taxation years, the amended 125.2(3) applies for taxation years that end before 1992 in respect of unused Part VI tax credits for taxation years that end after 1990, except that

(I) for purposes of computing its unused Part VI tax credits for taxation years that end in 1991, ignore 125.2(3)(b)B(ii); and

(II) for purposes of computing the amount the corporation may deduct under 125.2(1) for taxation years that end in 1991, read 125.2(3)(a) as:

(a) its tax payable under Part VI (determined without reference to subsection 190.1(3)) for the year, and

The amendments by the 1992 technical bill ensure that the definition applies without reference to the Part I credit provided under Part VI — that is, that a corporation's Part VI liability, for the purpose of calculating the amount of any excess of that liability over Part I tax payable, is to be determined before accounting for the reduction of Part VI tax by the new Part I credit in 190.1(3). They also provide that the difference between Part VI and Part I tax is to be calculated without reference to any surtax that was creditable against the corporation's liability under Part I.3 — that is, that Part I tax which was already credited under Part I.3 will not also reduce the amount of Part VI tax that may be eligible for carryover to other years.

The amendment by the 1993 technical bill (introducing 125.2(3)(a), and see (C) above) is consequential on the introduction of an additional tax payable by life insurance corporations under 190.1(1.1), and ensures that this additional Part VI tax liability cannot be carried back to reduce Part I tax for taxation years to which the additional tax does not apply.

See also Notes to 125.2(1) and at end of 125.2.

**Related Provisions [s. 125.2]**: 87(2)(j.9) — Amalgamation; 88(1)(e.2) — Windings-up; 152(6) — Reassessment; 161(7)(a)(vi) — Interest — Effect of carryback of loss, etc.; 164(5.1)(g) — Refund of taxes — Interest payable in respect of repayment of amount in controversy; 257 — Formula cannot calculate to less than zero.

**Notes [s. 125.2]**: 125.2 added by 1988 tax reform, effective 1988. The unused Part VI tax credit for taxation years ending before 1987 is deemed to be nil. The 1991 technical bill provides transitional rules for application to corporations described in 190(1)"financial institution"(d) or (e), for taxation years that begin before February 21, 1990.

**Definitions [s. 125.2]**: "amount" — 248(1); "corporation" — 248(1), *Interpretation Act* 35(1); "tax payable" — 248(2); "taxation year" — 249; "unused Part VI tax credit" — 125.2(3).

**Forms**: T2 SCH 42: Calculation of unused Part VI tax credit and unused Part I tax credit.

## 125.3 (1) Deduction of [pre-1992] Part I.3 tax
— There may be deducted in computing the tax payable under this Part for a taxation year by a corporation (other than a corporation that was throughout the year a financial institution, within the meaning assigned by section 190) an amount equal to such part as the corporation claims of its unused Part I.3 tax credits for any of its 7 immediately preceding taxation years ending before 1992, to the extent that that amount does not exceed the amount, if any, by which

(a) its Canadian surtax payable for the year

exceeds

(b) the amount that would, but for subsection 181.1(4), be its tax payable under Part I.3 for the year.

**Related Provisions**: 87(2)(j.9) — Amalgamations — continuing corporation; 88(1)(e.2) — Winding-up; 123.2(a) — Corporate surtax applies to total tax before claiming this credit.

**Notes**: 125.3(1) amended by 1992 technical bill, effective for 1992 and later taxation years.

Before 1992, surtax was reduced by (credited against) large corporations tax (Part I.3 tax) and financial institutions capital tax (Part VI tax). Conceptually, if a corporation is paying enough income tax to have a high surtax, those capital taxes do not apply (thus they operate as a kind of minimum tax). However, foreign corporations were unable to claim foreign tax credits in respect of capital tax paid to Canada, since it was not income tax. Effective 1992, therefore, the crediting of the surtax was reversed: Part I.3 and Part VI taxes are reduced by (credited against) the surtax. The effect on total Canadian tax was intended to be nil, but the surtax payable is eligible for foreign tax credit treatment in foreign jurisdictions.

125.3(1) allowed the pre-1992 reduction in surtax for Part I.3 tax payable. It has been preserved, and 125.3(1.1) enacted, to allow carryforwards (7 years) and carrybacks (3 years). The new credit of Part I.3 tax against surtax is in 181.1(4).

See also Notes at end of 125.3.

**Forms**: T2 SCH 37: Calculation of unused Part I.3 tax credit and unused surtax credit.

**(1.1) Idem** — There may be deducted in computing the tax payable under this Part for a taxation year by a corporation that was a financial institution (within the meaning assigned by section 190) throughout the year an amount equal to such part as the corporation claims of its unused Part I.3 tax credits for any of its 7 immediately preceding taxation years ending before 1992, to the extent that that amount does not exceed the lesser of

(a) the amount, if any, by which its Canadian surtax payable for the year exceeds the amount that would, but for subsection 181.1(4), be its tax payable under Part I.3 for the year, and

(b) the amount, if any, by which its tax payable under this Part (determined without reference to this section and section 125.2) for the year exceeds the amount that would, but for subsections 181.1(4) and 190.1(3), be the total of its taxes payable under Parts I.3 and VI for the year.

**Related Provisions**: 152(6)(f) — Assessments; 161(7)(a)(vii) — Interest — effect of carryback of loss, etc.; 164(5.1)(h) — Refund of taxes — effect of carryback of loss, etc.; 181.1(4)–(7) — Credit of surtax against Part I.3 tax after 1991.

**Notes**: 125.3(1.1) added by 1992 technical bill, effective for 1992 and later taxation years. See Notes to 125.3(1).

**(2) Special rules** — For the purposes of this section,

(a) no amount may be claimed under subsection (1) in computing a corporation's tax payable under this Part for a particular taxation year in respect of its unused Part I.3 tax credit for another taxation year until its unused Part I.3 tax credits for taxation years preceding the other year that may be claimed for the particular year have been claimed; and

(b) an amount in respect of a corporation's unused Part I.3 tax credit for a taxation year may be claimed under subsection (1) in computing its tax payable under this Part for another taxation year only to the extent that it exceeds the total of all amounts each of which is the amount claimed in respect of that unused Part I.3 tax credit in computing its tax payable under this Part for a taxation year preceding that other year.

**(3) Acquisition of control** — Where, at any time, control of a corporation has been acquired by a person or group of persons, no amount in respect of its unused Part I.3 tax credit for a taxation year ending before that time is deductible by the corporation for a taxation year ending after that time and no amount in respect of its unused Part I.3 tax credit for a taxation year ending after that time is deductible by the corporation for a taxation year ending before that time, except that

(a) where a business was carried on by the corporation in a taxation year ending before that time, its unused Part I.3 tax credit for that year is deductible by the corporation for a particular taxation year ending after that time only if that business was carried on by the corporation for profit or with a reasonable expectation of profit throughout the particular year and only to the extent of that proportion of the corporation's Canadian surtax payable for the particular year that

(i) the amount, if any, by which

(A) the total of its income for the particular year from that business and, where properties were sold, leased, rented or developed or services rendered in the course of carrying on that business before that time, its income for the particular year from any other business substantially all the income of which was derived from the sale, leasing, rental or development, as the case may be, of similar properties or the rendering of similar services

exceeds

(B) the total of all amounts each of which is an amount deducted under paragraph 111(1)(a) or (d) for the particular year by the corporation in respect of a non-capital loss or a farm loss, as the case may be, for a taxation year in respect of that business or the other business,

is of the greater of

(ii) the amount determined under subparagraph (i), and

(iii) the corporation's taxable income for the particular year; and

(b) where a business was carried on by the corporation throughout a taxation year ending after that time, its unused Part I.3 tax credit for that year is deductible by the corporation for a particular taxation year ending before that time only if that business was carried on by the corporation for profit or with a reasonable expectation of profit in the particular year and only to the extent of that proportion of the corporation's Canadian surtax payable for the particular year that

(i) the amount, if any, by which

(A) the total of its income for the particular year from that business and, where properties were sold, leased, rented or developed or services rendered in the course of carrying on that business before that time, its income for the particular year from any other business substantially all the income of which was derived from the sale, leasing, rental or development, as the case may be, of similar properties or the rendering of similar services

exceeds

(B) the total of all amounts each of which is an amount deducted under paragraph 111(1)(a) or (d) for the particular year by the corporation in respect of a non-capital loss or a farm loss, as the case may be, for a taxation year in respect of that business or the other business, is of the greater of

   (ii) the amount determined under subparagraph (i), and

   (iii) the corporation's taxable income for the particular year.

**Related Provisions**: 256(6)–(9) — Whether control acquired; 256(9) — Date of acquisition of control.

**Notes**: The CCRA takes the position that "substantially all", used in 125.3(3)(a)(i)(A) and (b)(i)(A), means 90% or more.

**I.T. Technical News**: No. 7 (control by a group — 50/50 arrangement).

**(4) Definitions** — For the purposes of this section,

**"Canadian surtax payable"** of a corporation for a taxation year means

   (a) in the case of a corporation that is non-resident throughout the year, the lesser of

   (i) the amount determined under section 123.2 in respect of the corporation for the year, and

   (ii) its tax payable under this Part for the year, and

   (b) in any other case, the lesser of

   (i) the prescribed proportion of the amount determined under section 123.2 in respect of the corporation for the year, and

   (ii) its tax payable under this Part for the year;

**Notes**: Definition "Canadian surtax payable" amended by 1993 technical bill, effective for 1994 and later taxation years. For taxation years that end from July 1989 through the end of 1993, ignore subparas. (a)(ii) and (b)(ii). The amendment clarifies that Canadian surtax payable may not exceed the corporation's Part I tax liability, after the deduction of all relevant tax credits, for the year.

**Regulations**: 8602 (prescribed proportion).

**"unused Part I.3 tax credit"** of a corporation for a taxation year means

   (a) where the year ended before 1992, the amount, if any, by which its tax payable under Part I.3 for the year exceeds the amount deductible under subsection (1) in computing its tax payable under this Part for the year, and

   (b) where the year ends after 1991, the amount, if any, by which the corporation's tax payable under Part I.3 for the year (determined without reference to subsection 181.1(4)) exceeds its Canadian surtax payable under this Part for the year.

**Related Provisions**: 87(2)(j.9) — Amalgamations; 88(1)(e.2) — Winding-up.

**Notes**: Definition "unused Part I.3 tax credit" retroactively amended by 1992 technical bill, effective for computing the amount deductible under 125.3(1) for taxation years that end after June 1989. The amendment ensures that the definition applies without reference to the new surtax credit provided under Part I.3 (see 181.1(4)). In other words, Part I.3 liability, for purposes of calculating the amount of any excess of that liability over Canadian surtax payable, is determined before accounting for the reduction of Part I.3 tax by the new surtax credit.

**Forms**: T2 SCH 37: Calculation of unused Part I.3 tax credit and unused surtax credit.

**Notes [s. 125.3]**: 125.3 added by 1989 Budget, effective for taxation years ending after June 1989, and prorated for years straddling July 1, 1989. See Notes to 125.3(1).

**Definitions [s. 125.3]**: "amount", "business" — 248(1); "Canada" — 255; "Canadian surtax payable" — 125.3(4); "corporation" — 248(1), *Interpretation Act* 35(1); "farm loss" — 111(8), 248(1); "financial institution" — 190(1); "non-capital loss" — 111(8), 248(1); "prescribed" — 248(1); "resident" — 250; "taxable income" — 2(2), 248(1); "taxation year" — 249; "unused Part I.3 tax credit" — 125.3(4).

## Canadian Film or Video Production Tax Credit

### Proposed Consultations — Changes to Film/Video Production Credit

**Federal budget, supplementary information, February 28, 2000**: *Simplified Film Tax Incentives*

The Canadian film and television production industry has achieved considerable expansion in recent years with the support of the federal and provincial governments. Federal support for Canada's film industry includes two tax credits in respect of qualifying labour expenditures:

- the Canadian Film or Video Production Tax Credit (CFVPTC, generally equal to 25% of eligible labour expenses), for film or video productions certified by the Minister of Canadian Heritage as meeting specific Canadian ownership and artistic criteria [section 125.4 — ed.]; and

- the Film or Video Production Services Tax Credit (FVPSTC, generally equal to 11% of eligible Canadian labour expenses), for other film or video productions produced in Canada [section 125.5 — ed.].

In some cases, the CFVPTC may be difficult for Canadian film producers to access, particularly where financing arrangements are complex. The Government therefore intends to review the rules respecting the CFVPTC, in consultation with industry associations, to develop criteria for a streamlined mechanism for delivering the CFVPTC incentive. The objective of these discussions is to design criteria that

- result in a simplified calculation for the CFVPTC, based more closely on Canadian labour content;

- reflect the original objectives of the existing eligibility requirements for film and video productions that were announced in the 1995 budget; and

- are revenue-neutral in terms of the level of support to be given by the Government.

**125.4 (1) Definitions** — The definitions in this subsection apply in this section.

**"assistance"** means an amount, other than a prescribed amount or an amount deemed under subsection (3) to have been paid, that would be included under paragraph 12(1)(x) in computing a taxpayer's income for any taxation year if that paragraph were read without reference to subparagraphs (v) to (vii).

**Related Provisions**: 87(2)(j.94) — Amalgamations — continuing corporation; 125.4(5) — Credit is deemed to be assistance for all purposes under the Act.

**Notes**: 125.4(1)"assistance" amended by 1998 Budget to add reference to a prescribed amount, effective for amounts received after

## S. 125.4(1) ass — Income Tax Act, Part I, Division E

February 23, 1998. Prescribed amounts (Reg. 1106(8)) will include amounts received from the Canada Television and Cable Production Fund (CTCPF) under its Licence Fee Program.

See also Notes at end of 125.4.

**Regulations**: 1106(8) (prescribed amount).

**"Canadian film or video production"** has the meaning assigned by regulation.

**Regulations**: 1101(5k.1) (separate class for Canadian film or video production); 1106(3) (definition of "Canadian film or video production"); Sch. II:Cl. 10(x) (CCA class for Canadian film or video production).

**"Canadian film or video production certificate"** means a certificate issued in respect of a production by the Minister of Canadian Heritage

(a) certifying that the production is a Canadian film or video production, and

(b) estimating amounts relevant for the purpose of determining the amount deemed under subsection (3) to have been paid in respect of the production.

**Related Provisions**: 125.4(3) — Tax credit where certificate issued; 125.4(6) — Revocation of certificate.

**"investor"** means a person, other than a prescribed person, who is not actively engaged on a regular, continuous and substantial basis in a business carried on through a permanent establishment (as defined by regulation) in Canada that is a Canadian film or video production business.

**Related Provisions**: 125.4(4) — No credit where investor can deduct any amount.

**Regulations**: 1106(7) (prescribed person); 8201 (permanent establishment).

**"labour expenditure"** of a corporation for a taxation year in respect of a property of the corporation that is a Canadian film or video production means, in the case of a corporation that is not a qualified corporation for the year, nil, and in the case of a corporation that is a qualified corporation for the year, subject to subsection (2), the total of the following amounts to the extent that they are reasonable in the circumstances and included in the cost or, in the case of depreciable property, the capital cost to the corporation of the property:

(a) the salary or wages directly attributable to the production that are incurred after 1994 and in the year, or the preceding taxation year, by the corporation for the stages of production of the property, from the final script stage to the end of the post-production stage, and paid by it in the year or within 60 days after the end of the year (other than amounts incurred in that preceding year that were paid within 60 days after the end of that preceding year),

(b) that portion of the remuneration (other than salary or wages and other than remuneration that relates to services rendered in the preceding taxation year and that was paid within 60 days after the end of that preceding year) that is directly attributable to the production of property, that relates to services rendered after 1994 and in the year, or that preceding year, to the corporation for the stages of production, from the final script stage to the end of the post-production stage, and that is paid by it in the year or within 60 days after the end of the year to

(i) an individual who is not an employee of the corporation, to the extent that the amount paid

(A) is attributable to services personally rendered by the individual for the production of the property, or

(B) is attributable to and does not exceed the salary or wages of the individual's employees for personally rendering services for the production of the property,

(ii) another taxable Canadian corporation, to the extent that the amount paid is attributable to and does not exceed the salary or wages of the other corporation's employees for personally rendering services for the production of the property,

(iii) another taxable Canadian corporation all the issued and outstanding shares of the capital stock of which (except directors' qualifying shares) belong to an individual and the activities of which consist principally of the provision of the individual's services, to the extent that the amount paid is attributable to services rendered personally by the individual for the production of the property, or

(iv) a partnership that is carrying on business in Canada, to the extent that the amount paid

(A) is attributable to services personally rendered by an individual who is a member of the partnership for the production of the property, or

(B) is attributable to and does not exceed the salary or wages of the partnership's employees for personally rendering services for the production of the property, and

(c) where

(i) the corporation is a subsidiary wholly-owned corporation of another taxable Canadian corporation (in this section referred to as the "parent"), and

(ii) the corporation and the parent have agreed that this paragraph apply in respect of the production,

the reimbursement made by the corporation in the year, or within 60 days after the end of the year, of an expenditure that was incurred by the parent in a particular taxation year of the parent in respect of that production and that would be included in the labour expenditure of the corporation in respect of the property for the particular taxation year because of paragraph (a) or (b) if

(iii) the corporation had had such a particular taxation year, and

(iv) the expenditure were incurred by the corporation for the same purpose as it was by the parent and were paid at the same time and to the same person or partnership as it was by the parent.

**Related Provisions**: 13(7)–(7.4) — Capital cost of depreciable property; 125.4(1), 248(1) — Extended meaning of salary or wages; 125.4(2) — Rules governing labour expenditure.

**"qualified corporation"** for a taxation year means a corporation that is throughout the year a prescribed taxable Canadian corporation the activities of which in the year are primarily the carrying on through a permanent establishment (as defined by regulation) in Canada of a business that is a Canadian film or video production business.

**Regulations**: 8201 (permanent establishment).

**"qualified labour expenditure"** of a corporation for a taxation year in respect of a property of the corporation that is a Canadian film or video production means the lesser of

(a) the amount, if any, by which

(i) the total of

(A) the labour expenditure of the corporation for the year in respect of the production, and

(B) the amount by which the total of all amounts each of which is the labour expenditure of the corporation for a preceding taxation year in respect of the production exceeds the total of all amounts each of which is a qualified labour expenditure of the corporation in respect of the production for a preceding taxation year before the end of which the principal filming or taping of the production began

exceeds

(ii) where the corporation is a parent, the total of all amounts each of which is an amount that is the subject of an agreement in respect of the production referred to in paragraph (c) of the definition "labour expenditure" between the corporation and its wholly-owned corporation, and

(b) the amount determined by the formula

$$A - B$$

where

A is 48% of the amount by which

(i) the cost or, in the case of depreciable property, the capital cost to the corporation of the production at the end of the year,

exceeds

(ii) the total of all amounts each of which is an amount of assistance in respect of that cost that, at the time of the filing of its return of income for the year, the corporation or any other person or partnership has received, is entitled to receive or can reasonably be expected to receive, that has not been repaid before that time pursuant to a legal obligation to do so (and that does not otherwise reduce that cost), and

B is the total of all amounts each of which is the qualified labour expenditure of the corporation in respect of the production for a preceding taxation year before the end of which the principal filming or taping of the production began.

**Related Provisions**: 257 — Formula cannot calculate to less than zero.

**"salary or wages"** does not include an amount described in section 7 or any amount determined by reference to profits or revenues.

**Related Provisions**: 125.4(2)(a) — Meaning of "remuneration"; 248(1)"salary or wages" — Definition extended to include all income from employment.

**Notes**: "Salary or wages", as defined in 248(1), includes taxable employment benefits, but due to this definition does not include stock option benefits or profit-sharing or sales-based bonuses.

**(2) Rules governing labour expenditure of a corporation** — For the purpose of the definition "labour expenditure" in subsection (1),

(a) remuneration does not include remuneration determined by reference to profits or revenues; and

(b) services referred to in paragraph (b) of that definition that relate to the post-production stage of the production include only the services that are rendered at that stage by a person who performs the duties of animation cameraman, assistant colourist, assistant mixer, assistant sound-effects technician, boom operator, colourist, computer graphics designer, cutter, developing technician, director of post production, dubbing technician, encoding technician, inspection technician — clean up, mixer, optical effects technician, picture editor, printing technician, projectionist, recording technician, senior editor, sound editor, sound-effects technician, special effects editor, subtitle technician, timer, video-film recorder operator, videotape operator or by a person who performs a prescribed duty.

**Proposed Addition — 125.4(2)(c)**

(c) that definition does not apply to an amount to which section 37 applies.

**Application**: Bill C-43 (First Reading September 20, 2000), s. 72, will add para. 125.4(2)(c), applicable after November 1999.

**Technical Notes**: Section 125.4 of the Act generally provides for a tax credit in respect of qualified labour expendi-

**S. 125.4(2)**      Income Tax Act, Part I, Division E

tures incurred after 1994 by a qualified corporation for the production of a Canadian film or video production certified by the Minister of Canadian Heritage.

Paragraph 125.4(2)(a) of the Act is amended to clarify that qualified labour expenditures do not include an amount claimed as an expenditure in respect of Scientific Research and Experimental Development under section 37 of the Act.

This amendment applies after November 30, 1999.

**Notes**: See Notes at end of 125.4.

**(3) Tax credit** — Where

    (a) a qualified corporation for a taxation year files with its return of income for the year

        (i) a Canadian film or video production certificate issued in respect of a Canadian film or video production of the corporation,

        (ii) a prescribed form containing prescribed information, and

        (iii) each other document prescribed in respect of the production, and

    (b) the principal filming or taping of the production began before the end of the year,

the corporation is deemed to have paid on its balance-due day for the year an amount on account of its tax payable under this Part for the year equal to 25% of its qualified labour expenditure for the year in respect of the production.

**Related Provisions**: 87(2)(j.94) — Amalgamations — continuing corporation; 123.2(a) — Corporate surtax applies to total tax before claiming film/video credit; 125.4(4) — No credit where investor can claim deduction; 125.4(5) — Credit constitutes assistance for purposes of the Act generally; 125.4(6) — Credit lost retroactively if certificate revoked; 125.5(4) — No film/video production services credit if Canadian film/video credit is available under 125.4; 152(1)(b) — Assessment of credit; 157(3)(e) — Reduction in monthly instalment to reflect credit; 163(2)(f) — Penalty for false statement or omission; 164(1)(a)(ii) — Refund of credit before assessment; 220(6) — Assignment of refund permitted.

**Notes**: Because the credit is deemed paid on account of tax, it is refunded to the corporation under 164(1) even if the corporation has no tax to pay for the year. Thus, it operates as a grant to a corporation that is not yet making profits and paying tax.

Closing words of 125.4(3) amended by 1996 Budget, effective for 1996 and later taxation years, to use the expression "its balance-due day" (extended in 248(1) to corporations) in place of "the day referred to in paragraph 157(1)(b) on or before which the corporation would be required to pay the remainder of its tax payable under this Part for the year if such a remainder were payable". The change is non-substantive.

See also Notes at end of 125.4, and Notes to 125.5(3).

**Regulations**: 1101(5k.1)(a) (separate class for CCA purposes).

**Forms**: RC4164: Claiming a Canadian film or video production tax credit — guide to Form T1131; T2 SCH 302: Additional certificate numbers for the Newfoundland film and video industry tax credit; T2 SCH 345: Additional certificate numbers for the Nova Scotia film industry tax credit; T2 SCH 365: Additional certificate numbers for the New Brunswick film tax credit; T2 SCH 382: Additional certificate numbers for the Manitoba film and video production tax credit; T2 SCH 410: Additional certificate numbers for the Saskatchewan film employment tax credit; T1131: Claiming a Canadian film or video production tax credit; T1196: B.C. film and television tax credit; T1197: B.C. production services tax credit.

**(4) Exception** — This section does not apply to a Canadian film or video production where an investor, or a partnership in which an investor has an interest, directly or indirectly, may deduct an amount in respect of the production in computing its income for any taxation year.

**Notes**: See Notes at end of 125.4.

**(5) When assistance received** — For the purposes of this Act other than this section, and for greater certainty, the amount that a corporation is deemed under subsection (3) to have paid for a taxation year is assistance received by the corporation from a government immediately before the end of the year.

**Related Provisions**: 12(1)(x) — Inclusion of assistance in income; 13(7.4) — Reduction in capital cost of depreciable property to reflect assistance; 53(2)(k) — Reduction in ACB of capital property to reflect assistance.

**Notes**: Because the amount of the credit is deemed to be government assistance received *before* the end of the year, it reduces the capital cost of production for purposes of claiming capital cost allowance.

See also Notes at end of 125.4. See Notes to 12(1)(x) re treatment of assistance.

**(6) Revocation of a certificate** — A Canadian film or video production certificate in respect of a production may be revoked by the Minister of Canadian Heritage where

    (a) an omission or incorrect statement was made for the purpose of obtaining the certificate, or

    (b) the production is not a Canadian film or video production,

and, for the purpose of subparagraph (3)(a)(i), a certificate that has been revoked is deemed never to have been issued.

**Notes**: 125.4 added by 1995 Budget, effective for 1995 and later taxation years. It provides the Canadian film or video production tax credit, which has replaced an exemption from the at-risk rules in 96(2.2)(d)(ii), now repealed. Generally, this credit (under 125.4(3)) is 25% of qualified labour expenditures incurred after 1994 by a qualified corporation for the production of a Canadian film or video production, except where the financing of the film is eligible for transitional relief from the termination of the capital cost allowance shelter mechanism.

For a detailed discussion of 125.4 and the film shelter rules that preceded it, see Norman Bacal, Mark Jadd & Manon Thivierge, "Raise the Curtain for Act II: Tax Shelter Reform and the New Film Tax Credit Regime", 43(6) *Canadian Tax Journal* 1965–2007 (1995).

Revenue Canada published the following on May 28, 1999:

*Questions and Answers About Film Tax Credit Programs*

Q1 *What tax credit programs are available to help the Canadian film industry?*

A1 The federal government offers two programs to help the film industry in Canada. They are the Canadian Film or Video Production Tax Credit (FTC) and the Film or Video Production Services Tax Credit (PSTC) programs. Many provincial governments also offer similar tax credit programs.

Q2 *What is the purpose of the FTC program?*

A2 The primary objective of the tax credit is to encourage Canadian programming and to stimulate the development of an active domestic production sector. The FTC program gives a tax credit to all qualified producers of eligible productions, and eliminates the need for complex tax shelter schemes that reduce financial help for producers. Canadian control requirements ensure that the incentive is available only to Canadian controlled companies.

The FTC program gives a refundable tax credit of 25% of qualified labour expenditures incurred, after 1994, by a qualified corporation for the production of a Canadian film or video production. The maximum credit available is limited to 12% of production costs net of assistance. The qualified labour expenditures cannot be more than 48% of production costs, net of any governmental or non-governmental assistance. You cannot claim the FTC for a production that gets a benefit under the PSTC program.

Q3 *What is the purpose of the PSTC?*

A3 The PSTC program was announced by the Minister of National Revenue and the Minister of Finance in a news release dated July 30, 1997. The legislation received royal assent in June 1998. The purpose of the PSTC is to give help to film and video productions produced in Canada where Canadian labour is used. This program complements the FTC program, since it is open to both Canadian and foreign-owned companies. The intention of this program is to make Canada a more attractive place for film production and stimulate job growth in the Canadian film industry.

The PSTC gives a refundable tax credit of 11% of qualified Canadian labour expenditures incurred for an accredited production after October 1997. You cannot claim the PSTC for a production that also gets a benefit under the FTC program.

Q4 *Who administers these programs?*

A4 The film tax credit programs are co-administered by Canadian Heritage through the Canadian Audio-Visual Certification Office (CAVCO) and Revenue Canada.

For the FTC program, CAVCO is responsible for issuing a Canadian film or video production certificate, which gives a claimant an estimate of the qualified labour expenditures for the FTC. For the PSTC program, CAVCO is responsible for issuing the accredited film or video production certificate for an accredited production.

Revenue Canada is responsible for reviewing film tax credit claims, assessing corporate income tax returns, and issuing timely refund cheques for the tax credit programs.

CAVCO and Revenue Canada jointly promote the tax-based incentives and help claimants as necessary.

Q5 *How does a corporation claim an FTC or a PSTC?*

A5 The first step to get a tax credit under either program is to get the appropriate certificate from CAVCO. For the FTC program, you have to get a Canadian film or video production certificate. For the PSTC program, you have to get an accreditation certificate for a film or video production.

The next step is to attach the appropriate certificate, or a copy, and Form T1131, Claiming a Canadian Film or Video Production Tax Credit, or Form T1177, Claiming a Film or Video Production Services Tax Credit, to the front of a completed T2 Corporation Income Tax Return. This will help Revenue Canada to quickly identify your claim.

Send your return and attachments to your tax centre. On receipt, the tax centre will send your claim to your tax services office. The tax services office will determine if a full review of your claim is necessary. Revenue Canada has specially trained staff familiar with the film industry to review claims.

Q6 *How long does it take to get a refund?*

A6 The Department tries to issue any applicable refund cheque within 60 days for a complete claim that does not need a review, and to process a claim that needs a review in 120 days.

Q7 *Did the February 16, 1999 federal budget propose income tax changes to either the FTC or the PSTC?*

A7 The February 1999 budget did not have any impact on either of the tax credits. However, the film industry and Revenue Canada are consulting on ways to streamline and improve the film tax credit programs. The goal is to ensure a more collaborative approach to the administration of these incentives in support of the Canadian film industry.

**Definitions [s. 125.4]**: "amount" — 248(1); "assistance" — 125.4(1), (5); "balance-due day" — 248(1); "business" — 248(1); "Canada" — 255; "Canadian film or video production", "Canadian film or video production certificate" — 125.4(1); "capital cost" — of depreciable property 13(7)–(7.4), (10), 70(12), 128.1(1)(c), 128.1(4)(c); "carrying on business in Canada" — 253; "corporation" — 248(1), *Interpretation Act* 35(1); "depreciable property" — 13(21), 248(1); "employee", "individual" — 248(1); "investor" — 125.4(1); "labour expenditure" — 125.4(1), (2); "parent" — 125.4(1)"labour expenditure"(c)(i); "partnership" — see Notes to 96(1); "permanent establishment" — Reg. 8201; "person", "prescribed" — 248(1); "qualified corporation", "qualified labour expenditure" — 125.4(1); "qualifying share" — 192(6), 248(1) *[not intended to apply to s. 125.4]*; "regulation" — 248(1); "remuneration" — 125.4(2)(a); "salary or wages" — 125.4(1), 248(1); "share", "subsidiary wholly-owned corporation" — 248(1); "taxable Canadian corporation" — 89(1), 248(1); "taxation year" — 249.

## Film or Video Production Services Tax Credit

**125.5 (1) Definitions** — The definitions in this subsection apply in this section.

**"accredited film or video production certificate"**, in respect of a film or video production, means a certificate issued by the Minister of Canadian Heritage certifying that the production is an accredited production.

**Related Provisions**: 125.5(3) — Tax credit where certificate issued; 125.5(6) — Revocation of certificate.

**Notes**: See Notes at end of 125.5.

**"accredited production"** has the meaning assigned by regulation.

**Notes**: See Notes at end of 125.5.

**Regulations**: 9300 (meaning of accredited production).

**"assistance"** means an amount, other than an amount deemed under subsection (3) to have been paid, that would be included under paragraph 12(1)(x) in computing the income of a taxpayer for any taxation year if that paragraph were read without reference to subparagraphs (v) to (vii).

**Notes**: See Notes at end of 125.5.

**"Canadian labour expenditure"** of a corporation for a taxation year in respect of an accredited production means, in the case of a corporation that is not an eligible production corporation in respect of the production for the year, nil, and in any other case, subject to subsection (2), the total of the following amounts in respect of the production to the extent that they are reasonable in the circumstances:

(a) the salary or wages directly attributable to the production that are incurred by the corporation after October 1997, and in the year or the preceding taxation year, and that relate to services rendered in Canada for the stages of production of the production, from the final script stage to the end of the post-production stage, and paid by it in the year or within 60 days after the end of the year to employees of the corporation who were resident in Canada at the time the payments were made (other than amounts incurred in that preceding year that were paid within 60 days after the end of that preceding year),

(b) that portion of the remuneration (other than salary or wages and other than remuneration that relates to services rendered in the preceding taxation year and that was paid within 60 days after the end of that preceding year) that is directly attributable to the production, that relates to services rendered in Canada after October 1997 and in the year, or that preceding year, to the corporation for the stages of production of the production, from the final script stage to the end of the post-production stage, and that is paid by it in the year or within 60 days after the end of the year to a person or a partnership, that carries on a business in Canada through a permanent establishment (as defined by regulation), and that is

(i) an individual resident in Canada at the time the amount is paid and who is not an employee of the corporation, to the extent that the amount paid

(A) is attributable to services personally rendered by the individual in Canada in respect of the accredited production, or

(B) is attributable to and does not exceed the salary or wages paid by the individual to the individual's employees at a time when they were resident in Canada for personally rendering services in Canada in respect of the accredited production,

(ii) another corporation that is a taxable Canadian corporation, to the extent that the amount paid is attributable to and does not exceed the salary or wages paid to the other corporation's employees at a time when they were resident in Canada for personally rendering services in Canada in respect of the accredited production,

(iii) another corporation that is a taxable Canadian corporation, all the issued and outstanding shares of the capital stock of which (except directors' qualifying shares) belong to an individual who was resident in Canada and the activities of which consist principally of the provision of the individual's services, to the extent that the amount paid is attributable to services rendered personally in Canada by the individual in respect of the accredited production, or

(iv) a partnership, to the extent that the amount paid

(A) is attributable to services personally rendered in respect of the accredited production by an individual who is resident in Canada and who is a member of the partnership, or

(B) is attributable to and does not exceed the salary or wages paid by the partnership to its employees at a time when they were resident in Canada for personally rendering services in Canada in respect of the accredited production, and

(c) where

(i) the corporation is a subsidiary wholly-owned corporation of another corporation that is a taxable Canadian corporation (in this section referred to as the "parent"), and

(ii) the corporation and the parent have filed with the Minister an agreement that this paragraph apply in respect of the production,

the reimbursement made by the corporation in the year, or within 60 days after the end of the year, of an expenditure that was incurred by the parent in a particular taxation year of the parent in respect of the production and that would be included in the Canadian labour expenditure of the corporation in respect of the production for the particular taxation year because of paragraph (a) or (b) if

(iii) the corporation had had such a particular taxation year, and

(iv) the expenditure were incurred by the corporation for the same purpose as it was incurred by the parent and were paid at the same time and to the same person or partnership as it was paid by the parent.

**Related Provisions**: 13(7)–(7.4) — Capital cost of depreciable property; 87(2)(j.94) — Amalgamations — continuing corporation; 125.5(1), 248(1) — Extended meaning of salary or wages; 125.5(2) — Rules governing labour expenditure.

**Notes**: See Notes at end of 125.5.

**Regulations**: 8201 (permanent establishment).

**"eligible production corporation"**, in respect of an accredited production for a taxation year, means a corporation, the activities of which in the year in Canada are primarily the carrying on through a permanent establishment (as defined by regulation) in Canada of a film or video production business or a film or video production services business and that

(a) owns the copyright in the accredited production throughout the period during which the production is produced in Canada, or

(b) has contracted directly with the owner of the copyright in the accredited production to provide production services in respect of the production, where the owner of the copyright is not an eligible production corporation in respect of the production,

except a corporation that is

> **Proposed Amendment — 125.5(1)"eligible production corporation"**
>
> except a corporation that is, at any time in the year,
>
> **Application**: Bill C-43 (First Reading September 20, 2000), s. 73, will amend the portion of the definition "eligible production corporation" in subsec. 125.5(1) between paras. (b) and (c) to read as above, applicable after November 1999.
>
> **Technical Notes**: The film or video production services tax credit is generally available in respect of qualifying Canadian labour expenditures of an "eligible production corporation" (as defined in subsection 125.5(1) of the Act) that carries on a business in Canada that is primarily a film or video production business or a production services business. An eligible production corporation does not include a corporation which is a tax-exempt entity, a corporation controlled by one or more tax-exempt entities or a prescribed labour-sponsored venture capital corporation.
>
> The definition of "eligible production corporation" is amended to clarify that such corporations will not qualify as eligible production corporations if they are at any time in their taxation year such a corporation.

(c) a person all or part of whose taxable income is exempt from tax under this Part,

(d) controlled directly or indirectly in any manner whatever by one or more persons all or part of whose taxable income is exempt from tax under this Part, or

(e) prescribed to be a labour-sponsored venture capital corporation for the purpose of section 127.4.

**Related Provisions**: 256(5.1), (6.2) — Controlled directly or indirectly.

**Notes**: See Notes at end of 125.5.

**Regulations**: 6701 (prescribed labour-sponsored venture capital corporation); 8201 (permanent establishment).

**"qualified Canadian labour expenditure"** of an eligible production corporation for a taxation year in respect of an accredited production means the amount, if any, by which

(a) the total of all amounts each of which is the corporation's Canadian labour expenditure for the year or a preceding taxation year

exceeds the aggregate of

(b) the total of all amounts, each of which is an amount of assistance that can reasonably be considered to be in respect of amounts included in the total determined under paragraph (a) in respect of the corporation for the year that, at the time of filing its return of income for the year, the corporation or any other person or partnership has received, is entitled to receive or can reasonably be expected to receive, that has not been repaid before that time pursuant to a legal obligation to do so (and that does not otherwise reduce that expenditure),

(c) the total of all amounts, each of which is the qualified Canadian labour expenditure of the corporation in respect of the accredited production for a preceding taxation year before the end of which the principal filming or taping of the production began, and

(d) where the corporation is a parent, the total of all amounts each of which is included in the total determined under paragraph (a) in respect of the corporation for the year and is the subject of an agreement in respect of the accredited production referred to in paragraph (c) of the definition "Canadian labour expenditure" between the corporation and its subsidiary wholly-owned corporation.

**Notes**: See Notes at end of 125.5.

**"salary or wages"** does not include an amount described in section 7 or an amount determined by reference to profits or revenues.

**Related Provisions**: 125.5(2)(a) — Meaning of "remuneration"; 248(1)"salary or wages" — Definition extended to include all income from employment.

**Notes**: "Salary or wages", as defined in 248(1), includes taxable employment benefits, but due to this definition does not include stock option benefits or profit-sharing or sales-based bonuses.

See also Notes at end of 125.5.

**(2) Rules governing Canadian labour expenditure of a corporation** — For the purpose of the definition "Canadian labour expenditure" in subsection (1),

(a) remuneration does not include remuneration determined by reference to profits or revenues;

(b) services referred to in paragraph (b) of that definition that relate to the post-production stage of the accredited production include only the services that are rendered at that stage by a person who performs the duties of animation cameraman, assistant colourist, assistant mixer, assistant sound-effects technician, boom operator, colourist, computer graphics designer, cutter, developing technician, director of post production, dubbing technician, encoding technician, inspection technician — clean up, mixer, optical effects technician, picture editor, printing technician, projectionist, recording technician, senior editor, sound editor, sound-effects technician, special effects editor, subtitle technician, timer, video-film recorder operator, videotape operator or by a person who performs a prescribed duty;

(c) that definition does not apply to an amount to which section 37 applies; and

(d) for greater certainty, that definition does not apply to an amount that is not a production cost including an amount in respect of advertising, marketing, promotion, market research or an amount related in any way to another film or video production.

**S. 125.5(2)**      Income Tax Act, Part I, Division E

**Notes**: See Notes at end of 125.5.

**(3) Tax credit** — Subject to subsection (4), where

(a) an eligible production corporation in respect of an accredited production for a taxation year files with its return of income for the year

(i) a prescribed form containing prescribed information in respect of the production,

(ii) an accredited film or video production certificate in respect of the production, and

(iii) each other document prescribed in respect of the production, and

(b) the principal filming or taping of the production began before the end of the year,

the corporation is deemed to have paid on its balance-due day for the year an amount on account of its tax payable under this Part for the year equal to 11% of its qualified Canadian labour expenditure for the year in respect of the production.

**Related Provisions**: 87(2)(j.94) — Amalgamations — continuing corporation; 123.2(a) — Corporate surtax applies to total tax before claiming film/video credit; 125.5(4) — No credit where Canadian film/video credit allowed under 125.4; 125.5(5) — Credit constitutes assistance for purposes of the Act generally; 125.5(6) — Credit lost retroactively if certificate revoked; 152(1)(b) — Assessment of credit; 157(3)(e) — Reduction in monthly instalments to reflect credit; 163(2)(g) — Penalty for false statement or omission; 164(1)(a)(ii) — Refund of credit before assessment.

**Notes**: Because the credit is deemed paid on account of tax, it is refunded to the corporation even if the corporation has no tax to pay for the year.

This credit is for *foreign* films and videos that are produced in Canada. The credit under 125.4, which takes precedence over this one (see 125.5(4)), is for *Canadian* productions.

See also Notes at end of 125.5 and at end of 125.4.

**Forms**: T1177: Claiming a film or video production services tax credit.

**(4) Canadian film or video production** — Subsection (3) does not apply in respect of a production in respect of which an amount is deemed to have been paid under subsection 125.4(3).

**(5) When assistance received** — For the purposes of this Act other than this section, and for greater certainty, the amount that a corporation is deemed under subsection (3) to have paid for a taxation year is assistance received by the corporation from a government immediately before the end of the year.

**Related Provisions**: 12(1)(x) — Inclusion of assistance into income; 13(7.4) — Reduction in capital cost of depreciable property to reflect assistance; 53(2)(k) — Reduction in ACB of capital property to reflect assistance.

**Notes**: See Notes to 12(1)(x) re treatment of assistance, and Notes at end of 125.5 re enactment.

**(6) Revocation of certificate** — An accredited film or video production certificate in respect of an accredited production may be revoked by the Minister of Canadian Heritage where

(a) an omission or incorrect statement was made for the purpose of obtaining the certificate, or

(b) the production is not an accredited production,

and, for the purpose of subparagraph (3)(a)(ii), a certificate that has been revoked is deemed never to have been issued.

**Notes [125.5]**: 125.5 added by 1995-97 technical bill, effective for taxation years that end after October 1997. It implements a refundable (see 125.5(3)) credit paid for film production services, in order to stimulate the production of foreign films in Canada. For a parallel credit for Canadian film productions, see 125.4.

**Definitions [s. 125.5]**: "accredited film or video production certificate", "accredited production" — 125.5(1); "amount" — 248(1); "assistance" — 125.5(1), (5); "business" — 248(1); "Canada" — 255; "Canadian labour expenditure" — 125.5(1); "carries on business in Canada" — 253; "controlled directly or indirectly" — 256(5.1), (6.2); "corporation" — 248(1), *Interpretation Act* 35(1); eligible production corporation" — 248(1); "employee", "individual" — 248(1); "parent" — 125.5(1)"Canadian labour expenditure"(c)(i); "partnership" — see Notes to 96(1); "permanent establishment" — Reg. 8201; "person", "prescribed" — 248(1); "qualified Canadian labour expenditure" — 125.5(1); "qualifying share" — 192(6), 248(1) *[not intended to apply to s. 125.5]*; "regulation" — 248(1); "remuneration" — 125.5(2)(a); "resident in Canada" — 250; "salary or wages" — 125.5(1), 248(1); "share" — 248(1); "subsidiary wholly-owned corporation" — 248(1); "taxable Canadian corporation" — 89(1), 248(1); "taxation year" — 249.

## Subdivision c — Rules Applicable to All Taxpayers

**126. (1) Foreign tax deduction [foreign tax credit]** — A taxpayer who was resident in Canada at any time in a taxation year may deduct from the tax for the year otherwise payable under this Part by the taxpayer an amount equal to

(a) such part of any non-business-income tax paid by the taxpayer for the year to the government of a country other than Canada (except, where the taxpayer is a corporation, any such tax or part thereof that may reasonably be regarded as having been paid by the taxpayer in respect of income from a share of the capital stock of a foreign affiliate of the taxpayer) as the taxpayer may claim,

not exceeding, however,

(b) that proportion of the tax for the year otherwise payable under this Part by the taxpayer that

(i) the amount, if any, by which the total of the taxpayer's qualifying incomes exceeds the total of the taxpayer's qualifying losses

(A) for the year, if the taxpayer is resident in Canada throughout the year, and

(B) for the part of the year throughout which the taxpayer is resident in Canada, if the taxpayer is non-resident at any time in the year,

from sources in that country, on the assumption that

(C) no businesses were carried on by the taxpayer in that country,

## Subdivision c — Computation of Tax: All Taxpayers     S. 126(1)(b)(ii)(A)

(D) where the taxpayer is a corporation, it had no income from shares of the capital stock of a foreign affiliate of the taxpayer, and

(E) where the taxpayer is an individual,

(I) no amount was deducted under subsection 91(5) in computing the taxpayer's income for the year, and

(II) if the taxpayer deducted an amount under subsection 122.3(1) from the taxpayer's tax otherwise payable under this Part for the year, the taxpayer's income from employment in that country was not from a source in that country to the extent of the lesser of the amounts determined in respect thereof under paragraphs 122.3(1)(c) and (d) for the year,

is of

(ii) the total of

(A) the amount, if any, by which,

(I) where section 114 does not apply to the taxpayer in respect of the year, the taxpayer's income for the year computed without reference to paragraph 20(1)(ww), and

(II) where section 114 applies to the taxpayer in respect of the year, the total of the taxpayer's income for the period or periods in the year referred to in paragraph 114(a) and the amount that would be determined under paragraph 114(b) in respect of the taxpayer for the year if subsection 115(1) were read without reference to paragraphs 115(1)(d) to (f)

exceeds

(III) the total of all amounts each of which is an amount deducted by the taxpayer under section 110.6 or paragraph 111(1)(b), or deductible by the taxpayer under paragraph 110(1)(d), (d.1), (d.2), (d.3), (f) or (j) or section 112 or 113, for the year or in respect of the period or periods referred to in subclause (II), as the case may be, and

### Proposed Amendment — 126(1)(b)(ii)(A)

(A) the amount, if any, by which,

(I) if the taxpayer was resident in Canada throughout the year, the taxpayer's income for the year computed without reference to paragraph 20(1)(ww), and

(II) if the taxpayer was non-resident at any time in the year, the amount determined under paragraph 114(a) in respect of the taxpayer for the year

exceeds

(III) the total of all amounts each of which is an amount deducted under section 110.6 or paragraph 111(1)(b), or deductible under paragraph 110(1)(d), (d.1), (d.2), (d.3), (f) or (j) or section 112 or 113, in computing the taxpayer's taxable income for the year, and

**Application**: Bill C-43 (First Reading September 20, 2000), subsec. 74(1), will amend cl. 126(1)(b)(ii)(A) to read as above, applicable to 1998 et seq. except that, in its application to the 1998 and 1999 taxation years, subcl. (A)(I) shall be read without reference to the expression "computed without reference to paragraph 20(1)(ww)".

**Technical Notes**: Section 126 of the Act provides rules under which taxpayers may deduct, from tax otherwise payable, amounts they have paid in respect of foreign taxes. The present amendments introduce three sorts of changes to these "foreign tax credit" rules. Most importantly, a new foreign tax credit is introduced for non-resident individuals who were formerly resident in Canada. This new credit, along with a comparable credit for non-resident beneficiaries of trusts that are resident in Canada, is found in new subsections 126(2.21) and (2.22).

Second, the existing foreign tax credit for non-residents of Canada, in subsection 126(2.2), is modified to reflect changes to the rules that apply to emigrant taxpayers under subsection 128.1(4) of the Act.

Third, several of the provisions in section 126 are modified to take account of changes to section 114 of the Act.

All of these changes are described in detail in the following notes.

Subsection 126(1) of the Act provides a tax credit in respect of foreign non-business income tax — that is, foreign taxes levied on investment and other non-business income. The credit is determined by multiplying the taxpayer's Part I tax otherwise payable for a taxation year by a fraction: the numerator of that fraction, determined under 126(1)(b)(i), consists of the taxpayer's income for the year (or, where section 114 applies, for the period or periods in the year throughout which the taxpayer is resident in Canada) from sources in the particular country calculated on certain assumptions; the denominator of that fraction, determined under paragraph 126(1)(b)(ii), consists generally of the amount by which the taxpayer's income for the year (or, where section 114 applies, for the period or periods in the year throughout which the taxpayer is resident in Canada) exceeds the deductions listed in subclause 126(1)(b)(ii)(A)(III).

Clause 126(1)(b)(ii)(A) is amended, with application to the 1998 and subsequent taxation years, as a consequence of changes to section 114 of the Act. The amendment removes a reference in subclause 126(1)(b)(ii)(A)(I) to section 114, updates the reference to that section in the following subclause, and simplifies subclause 126(1)(b)(ii)(A)(III)'s reference to the taxpayer's taxable income for the year. These changes keep the provision in step with the changes to section 114. For additional information, see the commentary on section 114.

**S. 126(1)(b)(ii)(B)**  Income Tax Act, Part I, Division E

(B) the amount, if any, added under section 110.5 in computing the taxpayer's taxable income for the year.

**Related Provisions**: 20(11), 20(12) — Deduction instead of credit for foreign taxes paid; 20(12) — Foreign non-business income tax; 94(3)(b) [proposed] — Application to trust deemed resident in Canada; 104(22.1) — Foreign tax credit allocated to beneficiary of trust; 110.5 — Addition to corporation's taxable income to increase foreign tax credit; 123.2(a) — Corporate surtax applies to total tax before claiming foreign tax credit; 126(1.1) — Application to authorized foreign bank; 126(6) — Separate deduction in respect of each country; 126(7)"tax for the year otherwise payable under this Part" — Tax for the year otherwise payable; 126(8) — Incomes deemed from separate sources; 129(3) — Refundable dividend tax on hand; 133(4) — No foreign tax deduction for non-resident-owned investment corporations; 138(8) — No deduction for tax paid on life insurance business income; 144(8.1) — Employees profit sharing plan — foreign tax deduction; 161(6.1) — Delay in interest on foreign tax credit adjustment; 180.1(1.1) — Individual surtax — foreign tax deduction; Canada-U.S. tax treaty, Art. XXIX B:6, 7 — Credit for U.S. estate taxes. See additional Related Provisions and Definitions at end of s. 126.

**Notes**: In very general terms, the foreign tax credit allows a credit to a Canadian resident for foreign income tax paid on foreign-source income, up to a limit of the Canadian tax on that income determined on a proportional basis. The effect is that the taxpayer pays total tax equal to the higher of the two rates of tax (Canadian and foreign) on the foreign-source income. The actual implementation of the credit is highly complex. 126(1) deals with non-business income such as dividends on which foreign tax has been withheld, while 126(2) deals with income from carrying on business in a foreign country. In certain circumstances a deduction may be claimed instead, under 20(11) or (12).

As an alternative (or in addition) to the foreign tax credit, relief may be available under Canada's bilateral tax treaties. See the Canada-U.S. and Canada-U.K. treaties reproduced at the end of this book. Many foreign countries, like Canada, also offer a foreign tax credit in respect of income not arising in those countries.

126(1)(b)(ii)(A)(I) amended by 1999 Budget, effective for 1998 and later taxation years, except that for the 1998 and 1999 taxation years, ignore the words "computed without reference to paragraph 20(1)(ww)". For earlier years, read:

(I) where section 114 is not applicable to the taxpayer in respect of the year, the total of the taxpayer's income for the year and the amount, if any, added under subsection 110.4(2) in computing the taxpayer's taxable income for the year, and

The portion of 126(1)(b)(i) before cl. (C) amended by 1998 Budget, effective for taxation years beginning after February 24, 1998. For earlier years, read:

(i) the total of the taxpayer's incomes from sources in that country, excluding any portion thereof that was deductible by the taxpayer under subparagraph 110(1)(f)(i) or in respect of which an amount was deducted by the taxpayer under section 110.6,

(A) for the year, if section 114 is not applicable, or

(B) if section 114 is applicable, for the period or periods in the year referred to in paragraph 114(a),

on the assumption that

126(1)(b)(ii)(A)(II) amended by 1993 technical bill, effective for 1993 and later taxation years. For 1985 through 1992, read:

(II) where section 114 is applicable to the taxpayer in respect of the year, the taxpayer's income for the period or periods in the year referred to in paragraph 114(a).

**Interpretation Bulletins**: IT-167R6: Registered pension plans — employee's contributions; IT-273R2: Government assistance — general comments; IT-243R4: Dividend refund to private corporations; IT-379R: Employees profit sharing plans — allocations to beneficiaries; IT-393R2: Election re tax on rents and timber royalties — non-residents; IT-395R: Foreign tax credit — foreign-source capital gains and losses; IT-506: Foreign income taxes as a deduction from income; IT-520: Unused foreign tax credits — carryforward and carryback. See also list at end of s. 126.

**Forms**: T2 SCH 5: Tax calculation supplementary — corporations; T2 SCH 21: Federal foreign income tax credits and federal logging tax credit; T2036: Provincial foreign tax credits; T2209: Federal foreign tax credits.

### Proposed Addition — 126(1.1)

**(1.1) Authorized foreign bank** — In applying subsections 20(12) and (12.1) and this subsection in respect of an authorized foreign bank,

(a) the bank is deemed, for the purposes of subsections (1), (4) to (5), (6) and (7), to be resident in Canada in respect of its Canadian banking business;

(b) the references in subsection 20(12) and paragraph (1)(a) to "country other than Canada" shall be read as a reference to "country that is neither Canada nor a country in which the taxpayer is resident at any time in the taxation year";

(c) the reference in subparagraph (1)(b)(i) to "from sources in that country" shall be read as a reference to "in respect of its Canadian banking business from sources in that country";

(d) subparagraph (1)(b)(ii) shall be read as follows:

"(ii) the lesser of

(A) the taxpayer's taxable income earned in Canada for the year, and

(B) the total of the taxpayer's income for the year from its Canadian banking business and the amount determined in respect of the taxpayer under subparagraph 115(1)(a)(vii) for the year;"

(e) in computing the non-business income tax paid by the bank for a taxation year to the government of a country other than Canada, there shall be included only taxes that relate to amounts that are included in computing the bank's taxable income earned in Canada from its Canadian banking business; and

(f) the definition "tax-exempt income" in subsection (7) shall be read as follows:

""tax-exempt income" means income of a taxpayer from a source in a particular country in respect of which

(a) the taxpayer is, because of a comprehensive agreement or convention for the elimination of double taxation on income, which has the force of law in the particular country and to which a country in which the taxpayer is resident is a party, entitled to an exemption from all income or profits taxes, imposed in the particular country, to which the agreement or convention applies, and

(b) no income or profits tax to which the agreement or convention does not apply is imposed in the particular country;"

**Application**: The August 8, 2000 draft legislation, subsec. 9(1), will add subsec. 126(1.1), applicable after June 27, 1999.

**Technical Notes**: Section 126 of the Act provides rules under which taxpayers may deduct, from tax otherwise payable under Part I of the Act, amounts they have paid in respect of foreign taxes. These "foreign tax credits," which are differently calculated and differently applied in respect of foreign business- and non-business-income taxes paid by the taxpayer, are generally available only to persons resident in Canada. These amendments give an authorized foreign bank access to credits for foreign non-business-income tax paid in respect of its Canadian banking business.

The amendments consist principally of a series of directions to read the existing foreign tax credit rules (and certain related provisions) in special ways. These directions are set out in new subsection 126(1.1) of the Act as follows:

- An authorized foreign bank is deemed to be resident in Canada, in respect of its Canadian banking business, for the purposes of the foreign non-business-income tax credit in subsection 126(1) of the Act, the limitations on that credit in subsections 126(4) to (5), the interpretive and related rules in subsection 126(6), and the definitions in subsection 126(7).

- The references in subsection 20(12) of the Act (deduction for foreign tax) and paragraph 126(1)(a) to a country other than Canada are to be read as references to a country that is neither Canada nor a country in which the authorized foreign bank is resident at any time in the year. This ensures, in keeping with standard international practice, that Canada — and not the bank's home country — retains the first right to tax the bank's Canadian business income (subject to credit for third-country taxes).

- The limit on the foreign non-business-income tax credit, in paragraph 126(1)(b), is computed by reference to the lesser of the authorized foreign bank's taxable income earned in Canada and its income for the year from its Canadian banking business (together with any addition under new subparagraph 115(1)(a)(vii)), rather than by reference to its income. Without this special reading, the bank's foreign tax credits would be inappropriately constrained if, for example, the bank had a large amount of income outside its Canadian business.

- The non-business-income tax paid by an authorized foreign bank to the government of another country is restricted to taxes that relate to amounts included in computing the bank's taxable income earned in Canada from its Canadian banking business.

- The definition "tax-exempt income" in subsection 126(7) is modified to describe tax agreements or conventions between an authorized foreign bank's home country and another country rather than using the defined term "tax treaty," which encompasses only a treaty between Canada and another country.

New subsection 126(1.1) applies after June 27, 1999.

**Notice of Ways and Means Motion (authorized foreign banks), February 11, 1999**: (7) That, subject to the general limits imposed under section 126 of the Act, an authorized foreign bank be entitled to deduct, in computing its tax payable under Part I of the Act for a taxation year, an amount in respect of withholding taxes imposed by the government of a foreign country or of a political subdivision of that country, provided that

(a) the bank was not, at any time in the year, resident in that country, and

(b) the taxes were withheld in respect of income for the year from a business carried on by the bank in Canada,

to the extent that the amount does not exceed the tax that would otherwise be payable on that income under Part I of the Act.

**Department of Finance news release, February 11, 1999**: *Foreign Tax Credit*

Canadian banks may claim, in computing their Canadian income tax payable, a credit in respect of taxes paid to a foreign government on income subject to tax in Canada. It is not considered appropriate to give identical treatment to foreign banks, because taxes payable to Canada in respect of a business carried on in Canada should have priority over taxes that are paid to a government in a foreign bank's home jurisdiction.

However, a foreign bank may also pay withholding tax to the government of a third country in respect of income that is subject to tax in Canada. In these circumstances, it is appropriate to allow the foreign bank a tax credit in computing its tax payable in Canada on that income.

It is proposed that a new foreign tax credit be added to the *Income Tax Act* in respect of withholding taxes paid by a foreign bank to governments of countries other than its country of residence on business income subject to tax in Canada.

[For other proposals see under 248(1)"authorized foreign bank" — ed.]

**(2) Idem** — Where a taxpayer who was resident in Canada at any time in a taxation year carried on business in the year in a country other than Canada, the taxpayer may deduct from the tax for the year otherwise payable under this Part by the taxpayer an amount not exceeding the least of

(a) such part of the total of the business-income tax paid by the taxpayer for the year in respect of businesses carried on by the taxpayer in that country and the taxpayer's unused foreign tax credits in respect of that country for the seven taxation years immediately preceding and the three taxation years immediately following the year as the taxpayer may claim,

(b) the amount determined under subsection (2.1) for the year in respect of businesses carried on by the taxpayer in that country, and

(c) the amount by which

(i) the tax for the year otherwise payable under this Part by the taxpayer

exceeds

(ii) the amount or the total of amounts, as the case may be, deducted under subsection (1) by the taxpayer from the tax for the year otherwise payable under this Part.

**Related Provisions**: 87(2)(z) — Amalgamation; 88(1)(e.7) — Winding-up; 94(3)(b) [proposed] — Application to trust deemed resident in Canada; 104(22.1) — Foreign tax credit allocated to beneficiary of trust; 110.5 — Additions for foreign tax deductions; 125 — Small business deduction; 126(2.1) — Amount determined for purposes of para. (2)(b); 126(2.3) — Rules relating to unused foreign tax credit; 126(6) — Separate deduction in respect of each country; 129(3) — Refundable dividend tax on hand; 133(4) — No foreign tax credit for non-resident-owned investment corporation; 138(8) — No foreign credit for life insurance business; 152(6) — Reassessment; 152(6)(f.1) — Minister required to reassess past year to allow unused foreign tax credit; 161(6.1) — Delay in interest on foreign tax credit adjustment; 161(7)(a)(iv.1), 164(5)(e), 164(5.1) — Effect of carryback of loss. See additional Related Provisions and Definitions at end of s. 126.

**Notes**: See Notes to 126(1).

**Interpretation Bulletins**: IT-243R4: Dividend refund to private corporations; IT-273R2: Government assistance — general comments; IT-520: Unused foreign tax credits — carryforward and carryback. See also list at end of s. 126.

**I.T. Technical News**: No. 8 (treatment of United States unitary state taxes).

**Forms**: T2 SCH 5: Tax calculation supplementary — corporations; T2 SCH 21: Federal foreign income tax credits and federal logging tax credit; T2036: Provincial foreign tax credits; T2209: Federal foreign tax credits.

**(2.1) Amount determined for purposes of para. (2)(b)** — For the purposes of paragraph (2)(b), the amount determined under this subsection for a year in respect of businesses carried on by a taxpayer in a country other than Canada is the total of

(a) that proportion of the tax for the year otherwise payable under this Part by the taxpayer that

(i) the amount, if any, by which the total of the taxpayer's qualifying incomes exceeds the total of the taxpayer's qualifying losses

(A) for the year, if the taxpayer is resident in Canada throughout the year, and

(B) for the part of the year throughout which the taxpayer is resident in Canada, if the taxpayer is non-resident at any time in the year,

is of

(ii) the total of

(A) the amount, if any, by which

(I) where section 114 does not apply to the taxpayer in respect of the year, the taxpayer's income for the year computed without reference to paragraph 20(1)(ww), and

(II) where section 114 applies to the taxpayer in respect of the year, the total of the taxpayer's income for the period or periods referred to in paragraph 114(a) and the amount that would be determined under paragraph 114(b) in respect of the taxpayer for the year if subsection 115(1) were read without reference to paragraphs 115(1)(d) to (f)

exceeds

(III) the total of all amounts each of which is an amount deducted by the taxpayer under section 110.6 or paragraph 111(1)(b), or deductible by the taxpayer under paragraph 110(1)(d), (d.1), (d.2), (d.3), (f) or (j) or section 112 or 113, for the year or in respect of the period or periods referred to in subclause (II), as the case may be, and

**Proposed Amendment — 126(2.1)(a)(ii)(A)**

(A) the amount, if any, by which

(I) if the taxpayer is resident in Canada throughout the year, the taxpayer's income for the year computed without reference to paragraph 20(1)(ww), and

(II) if the taxpayer is non-resident at any time in the year, the amount determined under paragraph 114(a) in respect of the taxpayer for the year

exceeds

(III) the total of all amounts each of which is an amount deducted under section 110.6 or paragraph 111(1)(b), or deductible under paragraph 110(1)(d), (d.1), (d.2), (d.3), (f) or (j) or section 112 or 113, in computing the taxpayer's taxable income for the year, and

**Application**: Bill C-43 (First Reading September 20, 2000), subsec 74(2), will amend cl. 126(2.1)(a)(ii)(A) to read as above, applicable to 1998 et seq. except that, in its application to the 1998 and 1999 taxation years, subcl. (A)(I) shall be read without reference to the expression "computed without reference to paragraph 20(1)(ww)".

**Technical Notes**: Subsection 126(2.1) of the Act sets out a limit for the amount of a taxpayer's deduction under subsection 126(2) in respect of businesses carried on by the taxpayer in a country other than Canada.

The limit is the total of amounts computed under paragraphs 126(2.1)(a) and (b). The paragraph (a) amount is computed by multiplying the taxpayer's Part I tax otherwise payable for a taxation year by a fraction. The numerator of that fraction, determined under subparagraph 126(2.1)(a)(i), generally consists of a taxpayer's income for the year (or, where section 114 applies, for the period or periods in the year throughout which the taxpayer is resident in Canada) from businesses carried on by the taxpayer in the particular country. The denominator of this fraction, determined under subparagraph 126(2.1)(a)(ii), consists generally of the amount by which the taxpayer's income for the year (or, where section 114 applies, for the period or periods in the year throughout which the taxpayer is resident in Canada) exceeds the deductions listed in subclause 126(2.1)(a)(i)(A)(III).

Clause 126(2.1)(a)(ii)(A) is amended, with application to the 1998 and subsequent taxation years, as a consequence of changes to section 114. The changes update the references in the clause to section 114. For additional information, see the commentary on section 114.

(B) the amount, if any, added under section 110.5 in computing the taxpayer's taxable income for the year, and

(b) that proportion of the amount, if any, added under subsection 120(1) to the tax for the year otherwise payable under this Part by the taxpayer that

(i) the amount determined under subparagraph (a)(i) in respect of the country

is of

(ii) the amount, if any, by which,

(A) where section 114 does not apply to the taxpayer in respect of the year, the taxpayer's income for the year, and

(B) where section 114 applies to the taxpayer in respect of the year, the total of the taxpayer's income for the period or periods referred to in paragraph 114(a) and the amount that would be determined under paragraph 114(b) in respect of the taxpayer for the year if subsection 115(1) were read without reference to paragraphs 115(1)(d) to (f)

exceeds

(C) the taxpayer's income earned in the year in a province (within the meaning assigned by subsection 120(4)).

**Related Provisions**: 126(8) — Incomes deemed from separate sources. See also Related Provisions and Definitions at end of s. 126.

**Notes**: 126(2.1)(a)(i) amended by 1998 Budget, effective for taxation years beginning after February 24, 1998. For earlier years, read:

(i) the total of the taxpayer's incomes

(A) for the year, if section 114 is not applicable, or

(B) if section 114 is applicable, for the period or periods in the year referred to in paragraph 114(a),

from businesses carried on by the taxpayer in that country, other than any portion of that income that was deductible under subparagraph 110(1)(f)(i) in computing the taxpayer's taxable income for the year

126(2.1)(a)(i) amended by 1991 technical bill, effective for taxation years ending after July 13, 1990, to add the exclusion in the closing words for amounts deductible under 110(1)(f)(i). The amendment prevents a foreign tax credit from being claimed for income which is exempt from Canadian tax due to a treaty provision.

126(2.1)(a)(ii)(A)(I) amended by 1999 Budget, effective for 1998 and later taxation years, except that for the 1998 and 1999 taxation years, ignore the words "computed without reference to paragraph 20(1)(ww)". For earlier years, read:

(I) where section 114 is not applicable to the taxpayer in respect of the year, the total of the taxpayer's income for the year and the amount, if any, included under subsection 110.4(2) in computing the taxpayer's taxable income for the year, and

126(2.1)(a)(ii)(A)(II) amended by 1993 technical bill, effective for 1993 and later taxation years. For 1985 through 1992, read:

(II) where section 114 is applicable to the taxpayer in respect of the year, the taxpayer's income for the period or periods in the year referred to in paragraph 114(a).

126(2.1)(b)(i) amended by 1998 Budget, effective for taxation years beginning after February 24, 1998. For earlier years, read:

(i) the total of the taxpayer's incomes described in subparagraph 126(2.1)(a)(i)

126(2.1)(b)(ii) amended by 1993 technical bill, effective for 1993 and later taxation years. For 1978 through 1992, read:

(ii) the taxpayer's income, other than the taxpayer's income earned in the year in a province (within the meaning assigned by subsection 120(4)),

(A) for the year, if section 114 is not applicable, or

(B) if section 114 is applicable, for the period or periods in the year referred to in paragraph 114(a).

**Interpretation Bulletins**: See list at end of s. 126.

**Forms**: T2036: Provincial foreign tax credits.

**(2.2) Non-residents' foreign tax deduction** — Where at any time in a taxation year a taxpayer who is not at that time resident in Canada disposes of property that was deemed by subsection 48(2), as it read in its application before 1993, or paragraph 128.1(4)(e) to be taxable Canadian property of the taxpayer, the taxpayer may deduct from the tax for the year otherwise payable under this Part by the taxpayer an amount equal to

(a) the amount of any non-business-income tax paid by the taxpayer for the year to the government of a country other than Canada that may reasonably be regarded as having been paid by the taxpayer in respect of any gain or profit from the disposition of that property

not exceeding, however,

**Proposed Amendment — 126(2.2)**

**(2.2) Non-resident's foreign tax deduction** — If at any time in a taxation year a taxpayer who is not at that time resident in Canada disposes of a property that was deemed by subsection 48(2), as it read in its application before 1993, or by paragraph 128.1(4)(e), as it read in its application before October 2, 1996, to be taxable Canadian property of the taxpayer, the taxpayer may deduct from the tax for the year otherwise payable under this Part by the taxpayer an amount equal to the lesser of

(a) the amount of any non-business-income tax paid by the taxpayer for the year to the government of a country other than Canada that can reasonably be regarded as having been paid by the taxpayer in respect of any gain or profit from the disposition of the property, and

**Application**: Bill C-43 (First Reading September 20, 2000), subsec. 74(3), will amend the portion of subsec. 126(2.2) before para. (b) to read as above, applicable to 1996 et seq.

**Technical Notes**: Canada generally makes foreign tax credits available only to persons who are resident in Canada. The only current exception to this principle is subsection 126(2.2), which provides a foreign tax credit to a non-resident individual who, as an emigrant from Canada, made the election provided under existing subparagraph 128.1(4)(b)(iv) of the Act in respect of one or more properties that were not taxable Canadian property.

With this election and the provision of security, the individual emigrant could choose to treat the properties as taxable Canadian property. That meant, on the one hand, that the individual was not treated as having disposed of those properties on emigration; but on the other hand, that any post-departure gain on the properties remained subject to Canadian tax (assuming no tax treaty applied). On the ultimate disposition of the deemed taxable Canadian property, subsection 126(2.2) allowed the former Canadian resident a credit for foreign tax on the gain.

Under the new rules for emigrants from Canada, the election in subparagraph 128.1(4)(b)(iv) is no longer available. Subsection 126(2.2) is therefore amended to apply only to properties that were deemed to be taxable Canadian properties under the election as it read before October 2, 1996. This amendment applies to the 1996 and subsequent taxation years.

Subsection 126(2.2) is also amended, with application to the 1998 and subsequent taxation years, to reflect the changes to section 114 of the Act. For additional information, see the commentary on section 114.

(b) that proportion of the tax for the year otherwise payable under this Part by the taxpayer that

(i) the taxable capital gain from the disposition of that property

is of

(ii) the amount that would be the taxpayer's taxable income earned in Canada

(A) for the year, if section 114 is not applicable, or

(B) if section 114 is applicable, for the portion of the year referred to in paragraph 114(b)

if subsection 115(1) were read without reference to that portion thereof following paragraph 115(1)(c).

**Proposed Amendment — 126(2.2)(b)(ii), (iii)**

(ii) if the taxpayer is non-resident throughout the year, the taxpayer's taxable income earned in Canada for the year determined without reference to paragraphs 115(1)(d) to (f), and

(iii) if the taxpayer is resident in Canada at any time in the year, the amount that would have been the taxpayer's taxable income earned in Canada for the year if the part of the year throughout which the taxpayer was non-resident were the whole taxation year.

**Application**: Bill C-43 (First Reading September 20, 2000), subsec. 74(4), will amend subpara. 126(2.2)(b)(ii) to read as above, and add subpara. (iii), applicable to 1998 et seq.

**Technical Notes**: See at the beginning of 126(2.2) above.

**Related Provisions**: 114 — Residence in Canada for part of year; 126(2.21)–(2.23) — Credit for former resident;; 115(1) — Non-resident's taxable income; 126(7) — "tax for the year otherwise payable under this Part". See additional Related Provisions and Definitions at end of s. 126.

**Notes**: Reference to 128.1(4)(e) in opening words of 126(2.2) added by 1993 technical bill, effective 1993.

**Interpretation Bulletins**: IT-273R2: Government assistance — general comments; IT-395R: Foreign tax credit — foreign-source capital gains and losses; IT-451R: Deemed disposition and acquisition on ceasing to be or becoming resident. See also list at end of s. 126.

**Proposed Addition — 126(2.21)–(2.23)**

**(2.21) Former resident — deduction** — If at any particular time in a particular taxation year a non-resident individual disposes of a property that the individual last acquired because of the application, at any time (in this subsection referred to as the "acquisition time") after October 1, 1996, of paragraph 128.1(4)(c), there may be deducted from the individual's tax otherwise payable under this Part for the year (in this subsection referred to as the "emigration year") that includes the time immediately before the acquisition time an amount not exceeding the lesser of

(a) the total of all amounts each of which is the amount of any business-income tax or non-business-income tax paid by the individual for the particular year

(i) where the property is real property situated in a country other than Canada,

(A) to the government of that country, or

(B) to the government of a country with which Canada has a tax treaty at the particular time and in which the individual is resident at the particular time, or

(ii) where the property is not real property, to the government of a country with which Canada has a tax treaty at the particular time and in which the individual is resident at the particular time,

that can reasonably be regarded as having been paid in respect of that portion of any gain or profit from the disposition of the property that accrued while the individual was resident in Canada and before the time the individual last ceased to be resident in Canada, and

(b) the amount, if any, by which

(i) the amount of tax under this Part that was, after taking into account the application of this subsection in respect of dispositions that occurred before the particular time, otherwise payable by the individual for the emigration year

exceeds

(ii) the amount of such tax that would have been payable if the particular property had not been deemed by subsection 128.1(4) to have been disposed of in the emigration year.

**Related Provisions**: 119 — Former resident — credit for tax paid; 126(2.22) — Parallel credit to trust after distribution to non-resident beneficiary; 126(2.23) — Reduction where foreign tax credit available under foreign system; 128.3 — Shares acquired on rollover deemed to be same shares for 126(2.21); 152(6)(f.1) — Minister required to reassess past year to allow credit; 161(7)(a)(iv.1), 164(5)(e), 164(5.1) — Effect of carryback of loss; Canada-U.S. Tax Convention Art. XIII:1 — Gain on real property taxable by country in which property is situated.

**(2.22) Former resident — trust beneficiary** — If at any particular time in a particular taxation year a non-resident individual disposes of a property that the individual last acquired at any time (in this subsection referred to as the "acquisition time") on a distribution after October 1, 1996 to which paragraphs 107(2)(a) to (c) do not apply only because of subsection 107(5), the trust may deduct from its tax otherwise payable under this Part for the year (in this subsection referred to as the "distribution year") that includes the acquisition time an amount not exceeding the lesser of

(a) the total of all amounts each of which is the amount of any business-income tax or non-business-income tax paid by the individual for the particular year

    (i) where the property is real property situated in a country other than Canada,

        (A) to the government of that country, or

        (B) to the government of a country with which Canada has a tax treaty at the particular time and in which the individual is resident at the particular time, or

    (ii) where the property is not real property, to the government of a country with which Canada has a tax treaty at the particular time and in which the individual is resident at the particular time,

that can reasonably be regarded as having been paid in respect of that portion of any gain or profit from the disposition of the property that accrued before the distribution and after the latest of the times, before the distribution, at which

    (iii) the trust became resident in Canada,

    (iv) the individual became a beneficiary under the trust, or

    (v) the trust acquired the property, and

(b) the amount, if any, by which

    (i) the amount of tax under this Part that was, after taking into account the application of this subsection in respect of dispositions that occurred before the particular time, otherwise payable by the trust for the distribution year

exceeds

    (ii) the amount of such tax that would have been payable by the trust for the distribution year if the particular property had not been distributed to the individual.

**Related Provisions**: 104(22.1) — Foreign tax credit to beneficiary of trust; 126(2.23) — Reduction where foreign tax credit available under foreign system; 128.3 — Shares acquired on rollover deemed to be same shares for 126(2.22); 152(6)(f.1) — Minister required to reassess past year to allow credit; 161(7)(a)(iv.1), 164(5)(e), 164(5.1) — Effect of carryback of loss; 220(4.6)–(4.63) — Security for tax on distribution of taxable Canadian property by trust to non-resident beneficiary; Canada-U.S. Tax Convention Art. XIII:1 — Gain on real property taxable by country in which property is situated.

**(2.23) Where foreign credit available** — For the purposes of subsections (2.21) and (2.22), in computing, in respect of the disposition of a property by an individual in a taxation year, the total amount of taxes paid by the individual for the year to one or more governments of countries other than Canada, there shall be deducted any tax credit (or other reduction in the amount of a tax) to which the individual was entitled for the year, under the law of any of those countries or under a tax treaty between Canada and any of those countries, because of taxes paid or payable by the individual under this Act in respect of the disposition or a previous disposition of the property.

**Related Provisions**: 128.3 — Shares acquired on rollover deemed to be same shares for 126(2.23).

**Application**: Bill C-43 (First Reading September 20, 2000), subsec. 74(5), will add subsecs. 126(2.21) to (2.23), applicable to 1996 et seq.

**Technical Notes**: In some circumstances, an individual who is a former resident of Canada may be subject to tax in another country on a gain that accrued while the individual was resident in Canada, and that has already been subject to Canadian tax on emigration. Similarly, the non-resident beneficiary of a Canadian trust who receives trust property on a distribution may be taxed abroad on a gain that accrued while the property was held by the trust, and that has been taxed in Canada on the distribution.

*EXAMPLE — double taxation of pre-departure gain*

Lee emigrates from Canada to Treatyland at a time when he owns a house in Treatyland. Lee bought the house while resident in Canada; at the time of emigration, the house has an adjusted cost base of $60,000 and a fair market value of $100,000. The resulting $40,000 latent capital gain will produce a taxable capital gain of $30,000 immediately before departure, and that taxable capital gain will be subject to Canadian tax.

Assume that the house increases in value to $120,000 after Lee leaves Canada, and that Lee sells the property in 2005 for that amount.

In principle, the gain that has been subject to Canadian tax ought not to be taxed a second time. However, Treatyland may not yet recognize the tax effect of changes in residence and may simply tax Lee, when the property is disposed of, on the full amount of his gain since first acquiring the property. In that case, Treatyland will tax not only the $20,000 gain realized since Lee left Canada, but also the $40,000 gain that accrued while Lee was resident in Canada. In the end, Lee is taxed twice on the same gain.

The best way to alleviate such results is to modify Canada's tax treaties to ensure appropriate recognition for the Canadian tax that arises on departure. However, treaty changes can take considerable time. As an interim measure, new subsection 126(2.21) provides limited credits against an individual's Canadian tax that arises in the year of the individual's departure from Canada, for post-departure foreign taxes. These foreign taxes can comprise both business-income and non-business-income taxes (defined in subsection 126(7)). New subsection 126(2.22) provides similar limited credits against a trust's Canadian tax that arose in the year of a distribution by the trust to a non-resident beneficiary, for the beneficiary's subsequent foreign taxes. It is intended that these interim foreign tax credits will be reviewed by the Government of Canada as appropriate treaty changes are put in place.

Subsections 126(2.21) and (2.22) will apply, in most cases, only for taxes paid to countries with which Canada has a tax treaty. Exceptions are provided for taxes imposed by a foreign country on gains on real property situated in that country. In keeping with the general international principle that the country in which real property is located has the first right to tax gains on that real property, Canada will always provide credit for such taxes. Similarly, credit for those taxes will be available regardless whether Canada has a tax treaty with the particular country.

More specifically, subject to the conditions described above, the credit provided to an individual under new subsection 126(2.21) is computed on a property-by-property basis, as the lesser of two amounts.

The first amount, described in paragraph 126(2.21)(a), is the total of those portions of the foreign taxes paid in respect of the disposition of the property that can reasonably be considered to relate to the portion of the gain or profit in question that arose before the individual's emigration from Canada. Where the property in question is real property situated outside Canada, the creditable taxes are those paid to the government of the country where the property is located or, to the government of another country in which the individual is resident and with which Canada has a tax treaty. [Note that a tax paid to the government of a political subdivision of a country is included for this purpose in the taxes paid to the government of the country. See the definitions "business-income tax" and "non-business-income tax" in subsection 126(7) of the Act.]

The second amount, described in paragraph 126(2.21)(b), is in effect the amount of the individual's tax under Part I of the Act for the year of emigration that is attributable to the deemed disposition of the particular property under paragraph 128.1(4)(b) of the Act. In determining this amount, previous applications of subsection 126(2.21) are taken into account.

*EXAMPLE — operation of new credit*

In the example above, Lee will be able to claim a credit for the lesser of 2/3 ($40,000/$60,000) of the Treatyland tax on the total amount of the gain, and the Canadian tax that arose because of the deemed disposition on emigration. The credit will be applied against Lee's Canadian tax for the emigration year, with amended subsection 152(6) allowing any necessary reassessment.

Note that since the property in question (a house) is real property, Lee could also claim a credit for tax paid to another treaty country in respect of his pre-emigration gain, if he lived in that other country. For example, if the house were located not in Treatyland but in Nontreatyland, Lee could — as a resident of Treatyland — claim a credit in respect of both Treatyland tax and Nontreatyland tax.

New subsection 126(2.22) sets out a comparable rule in respect of distributions after October 1, 1996 by Canadian-resident trusts to non-resident individuals. While the general operation of this rule is very similar to that of new subsection 126(2.21), it should be noted that in this case the credit involves two taxpayers: foreign taxes paid by the beneficiary are creditable against Canadian taxes paid by the trust.

A consequential amendment to subsection 152(6) of the Act ensures that any necessary assessments of tax will be made in order to take account of the effect of new subsections 126(2.21) and (2.22).

New subsections 126(2.21) and (2.22) apply to the 1996 and subsequent taxation years.

New subsection 126(2.23) of the Act limits the availability of the new foreign tax credits under subsections 126(2.21) and (2.22). This rule requires that in computing, for the purposes of these new credits, the foreign tax an individual has paid in respect of the disposition of a property, the individual must first take into account any relevant tax credit (or other reduction in tax) that the individual is entitled to in respect of the property under the law of a foreign country or under a tax treaty between Canada and a foreign country. This is intended to ensure that the credits under new subsections 126(2.21) and (2.22) are only available to the extent that another country is not required to give credit for Canadian tax in respect of the disposition or a prior disposition of the property.

Subsection 126(2.23) applies to the 1996 and subsequent taxation years.

**Department of Finance news release, June 5, 2000**: *Detailed Notice of Ways and Means Motion Tabled*

Secretary of State (International Financial Institutions) Jim Peterson, on behalf of Finance Minister Paul Martin, today tabled a detailed Notice of Ways and Means Motion in the House of Commons to provide for the implementation of previously announced amendments to the *Income Tax Act*.

These amendments include the following:

- amendments relating to taxpayer migration, which were released in draft form on December 17, 1999. The main purpose of these proposals is to enhance Canada's ability to tax capital gains accrued by emigrants while resident in Canada. Under the Motion tabled today, the seven-year expiry date for the provision of relief against double taxation is proposed to be deferred pending the renegotiation of tax treaties with Canada's treaty partners. The Government will monitor the need for a definitive expiry date as additional countries implement protection against double taxation in respect of capital gains in renegotiated treaties;

.....

**Department of Finance news release, September 10, 1999**: *Taxpayer Migration and Trusts: Technical Backgrounder*

Comments received on the December 1998 detailed proposals regarding taxpayer migration and trusts identified two major concerns: the need for flexibility in accepting security for the later payment of any tax arising from the deemed disposition on departure; and possible overlap between Canadian and foreign taxes. This backgrounder describes the government's proposed response to each of these two concerns. These changes, together with modifications to address more technical issues raised in connection with the December 1998 proposals, will be included in the proposals when they are put into bill form with the 1999 budget legislation.

[For the first proposal, "Security for later payment", see under 220(4.5)–(4.71) — ed.]

*2. Interaction of Canadian and foreign taxes*

The second major concern raised by submissions is the possibility of overlap between Canada's taxation of an emigrating individual's pre-departure capital gains and the later taxation of the same economic value — whether as a capital gain or in another form — by the individual's new country of residence. It was observed that this overlap, if it is not relieved by one country or the other, may result in a total effective tax rate that is well above the prevailing Canadian rate.

In many cases, changes to Canada's tax treaties will resolve issues of overlapping Canadian and foreign tax. To allow an opportunity for treaties to be revised, the December proposals included a time-limited credit for certain foreign taxes paid on pre-departure gains on property other than foreign real estate. A credit would also be available, with no time limit, for certain taxes paid on gains on foreign real estate.

It is reasonable to expect, however, that other situations will arise where Canada's rules and the rules of another country conflict, and where resolution through a tax treaty is not possible in the short term. Provided that Canadian and/or foreign tax is paid at full Canadian rates (in other words, that there is no net avoidance of tax), it may be appropriate in certain of these cases for Canada to recognize and accommodate the foreign tax. Therefore, while the government will continue its efforts to find treaty solutions, it will also consider other options where the scale and the frequency of a problem make that appropriate.

**(2.3) Rules relating to unused foreign tax credit** — For the purposes of this section,

(a) the amount claimed under paragraph (2)(a) by a taxpayer for a taxation year in respect of a country shall be deemed to be in respect of the business-income tax paid by the taxpayer for the year in respect of businesses carried on by the taxpayer in that country to the extent of the amount of that tax, and the remainder, if any, of the amount so claimed shall be deemed to be in respect of the taxpayer's unused foreign tax credits in respect of that country that may be claimed for the taxation year;

(b) no amount may be claimed under paragraph (2)(a) in computing a taxpayer's tax payable under this Part or Part I.1 for a particular taxation year in respect of the taxpayer's unused foreign tax credit in respect of a country for a taxation year until the taxpayer's unused foreign tax credits in respect of that country for taxation years preceding the taxation year that may be claimed for the particular taxation year have been claimed; and

(c) an amount in respect of a taxpayer's unused foreign tax credit in respect of a country for a taxation year may be claimed under paragraph (2)(a) in computing the taxpayer's tax payable under this Part or Part I.1 for a particular taxation year only to the extent that it exceeds the total of all amounts each of which is the amount that may reasonably be considered to have been claimed in respect of that unused foreign tax credit in computing the taxpayer's tax payable under this Part or Part I.1 for a taxation year preceding the particular taxation year.

**Proposed Amendment — 126(2.3)(b), (c)**

(b) no amount may be claimed under paragraph (2)(a) in computing a taxpayer's tax payable under this Part for a particular taxation year in respect of the taxpayer's unused foreign tax credit in respect of a country for a taxation year until the taxpayer's unused foreign tax credits in respect of that country for taxation years preceding the taxation year that may be claimed for the particular taxation year have been claimed; and

(c) an amount in respect of a taxpayer's unused foreign tax credit in respect of a country for a taxation year may be claimed under paragraph (2)(a) in computing the taxpayer's tax payable under this Part for a particular taxation year only to the extent that it exceeds the aggregate of all amounts each of which is the amount that may reasonably be considered to have been claimed in respect of that unused foreign tax credit in computing the taxpayer's tax payable under this Part for a taxation year preceding the particular taxation year.

**Application**: The December 21, 2000 draft legislation, subsec. 72(1), will amend paras. 126(2.3)(b) and (c) to read as above, applicable to 2001 *et seq.*

**Technical Notes**: Subsection 126(2.3) provides rules used to determine the unused foreign tax credit available for carryover to other taxation years. Consequential on the repeal of Part I.1, paragraphs 126(2.3)(a) and (b) are amended to remove the references to that Part, applicable to the 2001 and subsequent taxation years.

**Related Provisions**: 87(2)(z) — Amalgamations; 88(1)(e.7) — Winding-up.

**Interpretation Bulletins**: IT-520: Unused foreign tax credits — carryforward and carryback. See also list at end of s. 126.

**(3) Employees of international organizations** — Where an individual is resident in Canada at any time in a taxation year, there may be deducted from the individual's tax for the year otherwise payable under this Part an amount equal to that proportion of the tax for the year otherwise payable under this Part by the individual that

(a) the individual's income

(i) for the year, where section 114 is not applicable to the individual in respect of the year, and

(ii) for the period or periods in the year referred to in paragraph 114(a), where section 114 is applicable to the individual in respect of the year,

### Proposed Amendment — 126(3)(a)(i), (ii)

(i) for the year, if the individual is resident in Canada throughout the year, and

(ii) for the part of the year throughout which the individual was resident in Canada, if the individual is non-resident at any time in the year,

**Application**: Bill C-43 (First Reading September 20, 2000), subsec. 74(6), will amend subparas. 126(3)(a)(i) and (ii) to read as above, applicable to 1998 *et seq.*

**Technical Notes**: Subsection 126(3) of the Act provides a tax credit to Canadian-resident employees of international governmental organizations other than prescribed international governmental organizations. The amount of the credit is limited to the amount of any levy in lieu of taxes charged to the employee by the organization on the employee's remuneration.

The credit that may be claimed under subsection 126(3) is determined by multiplying the employee's Part I tax otherwise payable for a taxation year by a fraction. The numerator of that fraction, determined under paragraph 126(3)(a), consists of the employee's income for the year (or, where section 114 applies, for the period or periods in the year throughout which the employee is resident in Canada) from employment with the organization; the denominator of the fraction, determined under paragraph 126(3)(b), consists generally of the amount by which the employee's income for the year (or, where section 114 applies, for the period or periods in the year throughout which the employee is resident in Canada) exceeds the deductions listed in subparagraph 126(3)(b)(iii).

Subsection 126(3) is amended, with application to the 1998 and subsequent taxation years, to revise its references to section 114 of the Act to reflect changes to that section. For additional information, see the commentary on section 114.

from employment with an international organization (other than a prescribed international organization), as defined for the purposes of section 2 of the *Foreign Missions and International Organizations Act*

is of

(b) the amount, if any, by which

(i) where section 114 does not apply to the individual in respect of the year, the individual's income for the year computed without reference to paragraph 20(1)(ww), and

(ii) where section 114 applies to the individual in respect of the year, the total of the individual's income for the period or periods in the year referred to in paragraph 114(a) and the amount that would be determined under paragraph 114(b) in respect of the individual for the year if subsection 115(1) were read without reference to paragraphs 115(1)(d) to (f)

exceeds

(iii) the total of all amounts each of which is an amount deducted under section 110.6 or paragraph 111(1)(b), or deductible under paragraph 110(1)(d), (d.1), (d.2), (d.3), (f) or (j), in computing the individual's taxable income for the year or in respect of the period or periods referred to in subparagraph (ii), as the case may be,

### Proposed Amendment — 126(3)(b)

(b) the amount, if any, by which

(i) if the taxpayer is resident in Canada throughout the year, the taxpayer's income for the year computed without reference to paragraph 20(1)(ww), and

(ii) if the taxpayer is non-resident at any time in the year, the amount determined under paragraph 114(a) in respect of the taxpayer for the year

exceeds

(iii) the total of all amounts each of which is an amount deducted under section 110.6 or paragraph 111(1)(b), or deductible under paragraph 110(1)(d), (d.1), (d.2), (d.3), (f) or (j), in computing the taxpayer's taxable income for the year, and

**Application**: Bill C-43 (First Reading September 20, 2000), subsec. 74(7), will amend para. 126(3)(b) to read as above, applicable to 1998 *et seq.* except that, in its application to the 1998 and 1999 taxation years, subpara. (b)(i) shall be read without reference to the expression "computed without reference to paragraph 20(1)(ww)".

**Technical Notes**: See under 126(3)(a)(i), (ii).

except that the amount deductible under this subsection in computing the individual's tax payable under this Part for the year may not exceed that proportion of the total of all amounts each of which is an amount paid by the individual to the organization as a levy (the proceeds of which are used to defray expenses of the organization), computed by reference to the remuneration received by the individual in the year from the organization in a manner similar to the manner in which income tax is computed, that

(c) the individual's income for the year from employment with the organization

is of

(d) the amount that would be the individual's income for the year from employment with the organization if this Act were read without reference to paragraph 81(1)(a).

**Related Provisions**: 110(1)(f)(iii), (iv) — Deductions for income from certain international organizations; 126(7) "tax for the year otherwise payable under this Part" — Tax for year otherwise payable defined. See additional Related Provisions and Definitions at end of s. 126.

**Notes**: 126(3)(b)(ii) amended by 1999 Budget, effective for 1998 and later taxation years, except that for the 1998 and 1999 taxation years, ignore the words "computed without reference to paragraph 20(1)(ww)". For earlier years, read:

(i) where section 114 does not apply to the individual in respect of the year, the total of the individual's income for the year and the amount, if any, included under subsection 110.4(2) in computing the individual's taxable income for the year, and

126(3)(b)(i) and (ii) amended by 1993 technical bill, effective for 1993 and later taxation years. For 1985 through 1992, read:

(i) the total of the individual's income for the year and the amount, if any, included pursuant to subsection 110.4(2) in computing the individual's taxable income for the year, where section 114 is not applicable to the individual in respect of the year, or

(ii) the individual's income for the period or periods in the year referred to in paragraph 114(a), where section 114 is applicable to the individual in respect of the year,

126(3)(a), (b)(iii) and the words between paras. (b) and (c) amended by 1992 technical bill, effective for 1991 and later taxation years.

S. 2 of the *Foreign Missions and International Organizations Act*, S.C. 1991, c. 41, defines "international organization" as follows:

"international organization" means any intergovernmental organization of which two or more states are members.

There is no longer a tax credit for income from prescribed international organizations because there is now a deduction from taxable income under 110(1)(f)(iii). See also 110(1)(f)(iv).

**Interpretation Bulletins**: See list at end of s. 126.

**(4) Portion of foreign tax not included** — For the purposes of this Act, an income or profits tax paid by a person resident in Canada to the government of a country other than Canada or to the government of a state, province or other political subdivision of such a country does not include a tax, or that portion of a tax, imposed by that country or by that state, province or other political subdivision, as the case may be, that would not be imposed if the person were not entitled under this section or under section 113 to a deduction in respect thereof.

### Proposed Amendment — 126(4)

**(4) Portion of foreign tax not included** — For the purposes of this Act, an income or profits tax paid by a person resident in Canada to the government of a country other than Canada does not include a tax, or that portion of a tax, imposed by that government that would not be imposed if the person were not entitled under section 113 or this section to a deduction in respect of the tax or that portion of the tax.

**Application**: The August 8, 2000 draft legislation, subsec. 9(2), will amend subsec. 126(4) to read as above, applicable after June 27, 1999.

**Technical Notes**: Subsection 126(4) of the Act excludes from a taxpayer's creditable foreign taxes amounts that would not be imposed if the taxpayer were not entitled to a deduction under section 113 or section 126 of the Act. The subsection is amended to use the new defined term "government of a country other than Canada." (See the notes to amended subsection 126(6).)

**Related Provisions**: See Related Provisions and Definitions at end of s. 126.

**Interpretation Bulletins**: See list at end of s. 126.

**(4.1) No economic profit** — If a taxpayer acquires a property, other than a capital property, at any time after February 23, 1998 and it is reasonable to expect at that time that the taxpayer will not realize an economic profit in respect of the property for the period that begins at that time and ends when the taxpayer next disposes of the property, the total amount of all income or profits taxes (referred to as the "foreign tax" for the purpose of subsection 20(12.1)) in respect of the property for the period, and in respect of related transactions, paid by the taxpayer for any year to the government of any country other than Canada or to the government of a state, province or other political subdivision of such a country, is not included in computing [the] taxpayer's business-income tax or non-business-income tax for any taxation year.

### Proposed Amendment — 126(4.1)

**(4.1) No economic profit** — If a taxpayer acquires a property, other than a capital property, at any time after February 23, 1998 and it is reasonable to expect at that time that the taxpayer will not realize an economic profit in respect of the property for the period that begins at that time and ends when the taxpayer next disposes of the property, the total amount of all income or profits taxes (referred to as the "foreign tax" for the purpose of subsection 20(12.1)) in respect of the property for the period, and in respect of related transactions, paid by the taxpayer for any year to the government of any country other than Canada, is not included in computing the taxpayer's business-income tax or non-business-income tax for any taxation year.

**Application**: The August 8, 2000 draft legislation, subsec. 9(2), will amend subsec. 126(4.1) to read as above, applicable after June 27, 1999.

**Technical Notes**: Subsection 126(4.1), which limits a taxpayer's foreign tax credits in certain cases where there is no reasonable expectation of profit, is amended to use the newly defined term "government of a country other than Canada", and to correct a minor drafting error in the English version.

**Related Provisions**: 20(12.1) — Deduction from income for amount disallowed as credit by 126(4.1); 126(4.4) — Certain dispositions ignored for 126(4.1).

**Notes**: 126(4.1) added by 1998 Budget, effective for 1998 and later taxation years. See 126(7)"economic profit". The foreign tax credit operates on a country-by-country pooling basis, so income from a source that is taxed in a foreign country at a higher rate than in Canada creates excess credits that may be used to reduce Canadian tax on income from other sources in the country that are taxed at rates lower than the Canadian rate. This cross-crediting can make an otherwise uneconomic transaction attractive, and can amount to a subsidy by the Canadian tax system for such transactions. To limit this effect, 126(4.1) denies the credit in situations where, without the credit, there is no expected economic profit.

**(4.2) Short-term securities acquisitions** — If at any particular time a taxpayer disposes of a property that is a share or debt obligation and the period that began at the time the taxpayer last acquired the property and ended at the particular time is one year or less, the amount included in business-income tax or non-business-income tax paid by the taxpayer for a particular taxation year on account of all taxes (referred to in this subsection and subsections (4.3) and 161(6.1) as the "foreign tax") that are

(a) paid by the taxpayer in respect of dividends or interest in respect of the period that are included in computing the taxpayer's income from the property for any taxation year,

(b) otherwise included in business-income tax or non-business-income tax for any taxation year, and

(c) similar to the tax levied under Part XIII

shall, subject to subsection (4.3), not exceed the amount determined by the formula

$$A \times (B - C) \times D / E$$

where

A is 40%, if the foreign tax would otherwise be included in business-income tax, and 30%, if the foreign tax would otherwise be included in non-business-income tax,

B is the total of the taxpayer's proceeds from the disposition of the property at the particular time and the amount of all dividends or interest from the property in respect of the period included in computing the taxpayer's income for any taxation year,

C is the total of the cost at which the taxpayer last acquired the property and any outlays or expenses made or incurred by the taxpayer for the purpose of disposing of the property at the particular time,

D is the amount of foreign tax that would otherwise be included in computing the taxpayer's business-income tax or non-business-income tax for the particular year, and

E is the total amount of foreign tax that would otherwise be included in computing the taxpayer's business-income tax or non-business-income tax for all taxation years.

**Related Provisions**: 112(2.3) — No domestic deduction on dividend rental arrangement; 126(4.3) — Exceptions; 126(4.4) — Certain dispositions ignored for 126(4.2); 161(6.1) — Delay in interest on foreign tax credit adjustment; 257 — Formula cannot calculate to less than zero.

**Notes**: 126(4.2) added by 1998 Budget, effective for 1998 and later taxation years. It limits the foreign tax credit in respect of dividends or interest on a share or debt obligation that is held by the taxpayer for one year or less. The credit is limited to the Canadian tax that would be payable at a notional rate on the gross income from the security for the hold period. The effect is generally to prevent an excess credit that could be used to shelter other income from the foreign country in respect of which the tax was paid. See the limitations on this rule in 126(4.3) and (4.4).

The rule applies to foreign taxes on dividends or interest that are similar to the Part XIII withholding tax. It limits the foreign tax included in business-income tax or non-business-income tax to 40% or 30% respectively of gross profit from the share or debt. The difference in rates is because non-business foreign income of a corporation resident in Canada is typically taxable by a province, entitling the corporation to a 10% abatement under 124(1). Foreign business income earned through a permanent establishment outside Canada is not taxable by a province.

Gross profit is not defined as such but is in effect measured by a formula as the total of proceeds from disposing of the property and interest or dividends received during the ownership period, less the cost of acquiring the property and expenses of disposition. No deduction is made for carrying charges.

If the ownership period falls into more than one taxation year, the allowable foreign tax is allocated between those years, through D and E in the formula, in the same proportion as that in which it would be allocated without the limit. In this case, if tax payable for the first year increases due to 126(4.2) after disposition of the property in the second year, 161(6.1) provides some relief from payment of interest. The resulting reduction in foreign tax credit is also a "specified future tax consequence" as defined in 248(1).

**(4.3) Exceptions** — Subsection (4.2) does not apply to a property of a taxpayer

(a) that is a capital property;

(b) that is a debt obligation issued to the taxpayer that has a term of one year or less and that is held by no one other than the taxpayer at any time;

(c) that was last acquired by the taxpayer before February 24, 1998; or

(d) in respect of which any foreign tax is, because of subsection (4.1), not included in computing the taxpayer's business-income tax or non-business-income tax.

**Notes**: 126(4.3) added by 1998 Budget, effective for 1998 and later taxation years.

**(4.4) Dispositions ignored** — For the purposes of subsections (4.1) and (4.2) and the definition "economic profit" in subsection (7),

(a) a disposition or acquisition of property deemed to be made by subsection 45(1), section 70 or 128.1, paragraph 132.2(1)(f), subsection 138(11.3) or 142.5(2), paragraph 142.6(1)(b) or subsection 149(10) is not a disposition or acquisition, as the case may be; and

---

**Proposed Amendment — 126(4.4)(a)**

(a) a disposition or acquisition of property deemed to be made by subsection 10(12) or (13), 14(14) or (15) or 45(1), section 70 or 128.1, paragraph 132.2(1)(f), subsection 138(11.3), 142.5(2) or 142.6(1.1) or (1.2), paragraph 142.6(1)(b) or subsection 149(10) is not a disposition or acquisition, as the case may be; and

**Application**: The August 8, 2000 draft legislation, subsec. 9(3), will amend para. 126(4.4)(a) to read as above, applicable after June 27, 1999.

**Technical Notes**: Subsection 126(4.4) of the Act directs that certain dispositions and acquisitions of property be ignored for the purposes of the foreign tax credit limitations in subsections 126(4.1) and (4.2) of the Act. Paragraph 126(4.4)(a) is amended to add to this list dispositions and acquisitions under new subsections 14(14) and (15) and 142.6(1.1) and (1.2) of the Act, as well as proposed subsections 10(12) and (13) of the Act, which are set out in the Notice of Ways and Means Motion tabled in the House of Commons on June 5, 2000.

These amendments apply after June 27, 1999.

    (b) a disposition

        (i) to which section 51.1 applies, of a convertible obligation in exchange for a new obligation,

        (ii) to which subsection 86(1) applies, of old shares in exchange for new shares, or

        (iii) to which subsections 87(4) and (8) apply, of old shares in exchange for new shares,

is not a disposition, and the convertible obligation and the new obligation, or the old shares and the new shares, as the case may be, are deemed to be the same property.

**Notes**: 126(4.4) added by 1998 Budget, effective for 1998 and later taxation years.

**(5) Foreign tax** — A tax paid to the government of a country other than Canada or to the government of a state, province or other political subdivision of such a country may, subject to prescribed conditions, be deemed, for the purposes of this Act, to be an income or profits tax paid to the government of that country.

### Proposed Repeal — 126(5)

**Application**: The August 8, 2000 draft legislation, subsec. 9(4), will repeal subsec. 126(5), applicable after June 27, 1999.

**Technical Notes**: Ordinarily, the only foreign taxes that may be credited against tax under Part I of the Act are income or profits taxes. Subsection 126(5) of the Act provides that a foreign tax may, subject to prescribed conditions, be deemed to be an income or profits tax. No such conditions are in place, and the subsection has no practical effect other than as a source of potential confusion. It is therefore repealed, with effect after June 27, 1999.

### Proposed Addition — New 126(5)

**(5) Foreign oil and gas levies** — A taxpayer who is resident in Canada throughout a taxation year and carries on a foreign oil and gas business in a taxing country in the year is deemed for the purposes of this section to have paid in the year as an income or profits tax to the government of the taxing country an amount equal to the lesser of

    (a) the amount, if any, by which

        (i) 40% of the taxpayer's income from the business in the taxing country for the year

    exceeds

        (ii) the total of all amounts that would, but for this subsection, be income or profits taxes paid in the year in respect of the business to the government of the taxing country, and

    (b) the taxpayer's production tax amount for the business in the taxing country for the year.

**Application**: The December 21, 2000 draft legislation, subsec. 72(2), will amend subsec. 126(5) to read as above, applicable to taxation years of a taxpayer that begin after the earlier of

    (a) December 31, 1999; and

    (b) where, for the purposes of this subsec., a date is designated in writing by the taxpayer and the designation is filed with the Minister of National Revenue on or before the taxpayer's filing-due date for the taxpayer's taxation year that includes the day on which the amending legislation receives Royal Assent, the later of

        (i) the date so designated, and

        (ii) December 31, 1994.

**Technical Notes**: New subsection 126(5), together with several new definitions added to subsection 126(7), treats certain levies imposed by a foreign government in connection with oil and gas businesses as income or profits taxes paid to the government.

These notes describe new subsection 126(5) and the new definitions in the order in which they will appear in the Act. However, because subsection 126(5) relies heavily on the new definitions, and because those definitions are themselves inter-related, readers may find that the best way to understand the provisions is to start by reviewing the definitions in the following order: "taxing country", "foreign oil and gas business", "commercial obligation", and "production tax amount", and only then to review new subsection 126(5).

These amendments (with the exception of the amendment to the definition "unused foreign tax credit" in subsection 126(7)) apply to taxation years that begin after December 31, 1999. However, if a taxpayer makes a written election to have these amendments apply to taxation years that begin after a designated date (which is earlier than December 31, 1999) and the election is filed with the Minister of National Revenue on or before the taxpayer's filing-due date for the taxpayer's taxation year that includes the day on which these amendments receive royal assent, these amendments apply to taxation years that begin on the later of:

    (i) the date so designated by the taxpayer in the election; and

    (ii) December 31, 1994.

The general effect of new subsection 126(5) is to treat a taxpayer's "production tax amount" as a foreign income or profits tax, subject to a maximum of 40 per cent of the taxpayer's income from the business in question. Specifically, where a taxpayer is resident in Canada throughout a taxation year and carries on a "foreign oil and gas business" in a "taxing country" in the year, new subsection 126(5) treats the taxpayer as having paid in the year to the government of the country, as an income or profits tax, the lesser of two amounts. The first amount, described in new paragraph 126(5)(a), is the amount by which 40 per cent of the taxpayer's income from the business in the country in the year exceeds the actual income and profits taxes (that is, those taxes determined without reference to this rule itself) paid in the year in respect of the business to the government of the country. The second amount, in new paragraph 126(5)(b), is the taxpayer's "production tax amount" for the business in the country in the year.

**Notice of Ways and Means Motion, federal budget, February 28, 2000**: *Foreign Tax Credits — Oil and Gas Production Sharing*

(32) That, in applying the foreign tax credit rules in section 126 of the Act in respect of an oil or gas business carried on in a taxation year by a resident of Canada in a country, other than Canada, that imposes an income or profits tax on other business income, there be treated as foreign taxes paid by the taxpayer for the year amounts that

(a) become receivable in the year by a government of that country (or its agent) because of an obligation of the taxpayer in respect of the business,

(b) are computed by reference to the amount or value of oil or gas produced or extracted, net of operating and capital costs,

(c) are not royalties under the foreign country's law, payments made in a purely commercial capacity or otherwise creditable foreign taxes, and

(d) do not exceed, in total, 40 per cent of the taxpayer's income from the business for the year, less amounts otherwise creditable as foreign taxes,

and that this provision apply to those taxation years of a taxpayer that begin after the earlier of December 31, 1999 and a date selected by the taxpayer (which date may in no case be earlier than December 31, 1994).

[See also Resolution (39) under 66(4) — ed.]

**Federal budget, supplementary information, February 28, 2000**: *Foreign Tax Credit and Oil and Gas Production Sharing Agreements*

To limit the impact of the application of Canadian and foreign taxes on the same income, Canada provides its residents with "foreign tax credits" for income or profits taxes they have paid to another country. In most cases, it is clear whether a foreign tax is sufficiently similar to Canada's income tax to qualify for these credits. However, the characterization of a levy as an income tax is less clear with respect to certain levies imposed in some oil- and gas-producing countries.

The levies in question are imposed under "production sharing agreements" between the governments of the countries concerned (or their agents) and Canadian-resident companies. Under a typical production sharing agreement, the company undertakes to conduct exploration activities within a defined territory and, where the exploration efforts are successful, to develop the resource property and exploit it commercially. At the commercial exploitation stage, the resource production is divided between the company and the foreign government, often through a state-owned corporation, according to a sharing formula agreed to in the contract. Such formulas, which vary from contract to contract, typically grant the company enough of the resource production to cover its costs and to generate a profit. Production sharing agreements generally set out in detail how costs are to be recovered over time, what proportion of the production must be allocated to the state in any given year, and other key terms.

Most of the countries that enter into such agreements with Canadian companies also impose a corporate income tax. Rather than applying the tax separately, however, these countries integrate their income tax into the production sharing agreements themselves. In effect, part of the foreign government's share of the production under the agreement is characterized as a payment in satisfaction of the Canadian company's income tax liability to that government.

Because a production sharing agreement both allocates oil and gas production and incorporates the foreign country's income tax, it can be difficult to determine which portion of the foreign government's share is on account of an income tax. Indeed, the *Income Tax Act*'s current foreign tax credit rules may deny credit for any and all payments made pursuant to such agreements. The uncertainty Canadian companies face as a result can put them at a disadvantage relative to those foreign competitors whose domestic taxation rules [most notably the United States and the United Kingdom — ed.] provide foreign tax credits in similar circumstances.

The budget proposes to introduce amendments to the *Income Tax Act* that will clarify the eligibility for a business foreign tax credit of certain payments made by Canadian resident taxpayers to foreign governments on account of levies imposed in connection with production sharing agreements. The proposed amendments will set out those circumstances in which a levy will be considered to be, in substance, an income tax paid by a taxpayer.

More specifically, the proposed amendments will require that, for a foreign levy to qualify, it must be computed by reference to net income, after recognition of relevant expenses, and must not be, under the agreement, either a royalty or any other consideration paid for the exploitation of the resource. Because the amendments are intended to accommodate situations where the foreign income tax is calculated pursuant to a production sharing agreement, as opposed to being assessed separately, the proposed rules will apply only where the foreign country otherwise imposes what can be regarded as an income tax.

The amount eligible for a foreign tax credit cannot, under the proposal, exceed 40 per cent of the taxpayer's income from the business for the year and will be subject to the existing rules of the Act governing the claiming of business foreign tax credits and the carry-overs of unused credits. The 40 per cent rate is an approximation of the Canadian corporate rate and is the same proxy rate currently used for other foreign tax credit purposes.

The amendments to the business foreign tax credit provisions of the Act will also include specific rules for the recognition of a taxpayer's foreign exploration and development expenses (FEDE), discussed in the next section. [See Resolution (33) reproduced under 126(7)"qualifying incomes" — ed.] While there already exists a general requirement in the Act for taxpayers to recognize FEDE in computing the amount of foreign tax credit that can be claimed in respect of foreign source income, these rules will specify how FEDE will be allocated to a particular foreign country for purposes of claiming a foreign tax credit.

The new rules will apply for foreign income taxes paid by any given taxpayer, pursuant to production sharing agreements, in taxation years that begin after the earlier of December 31, 1999, and a date chosen by the taxpayer (which date cannot in any case be earlier than December 31, 1994).

**Related Provisions**: See Related Provisions and Definitions at end of s. 126.

**Regulations**: No prescribed conditions at present. Regulations prescribing conditions were revoked effective 1972.

Interpretation Bulletins: See list at end of s. 126.

**(5.1) Deductions for specified capital gains** — Where in a taxation year an individual has claimed a deduction under section 110.6 in computing the individual's taxable income for the year, for the purposes of this section the individual shall be deemed to have claimed the deduction under section 110.6 in respect of such taxable capital gains or portion thereof as the individual may specify in the individual's return of income required to be filed pursuant to section 150 for the year or, where the individual has failed to so specify, in respect of such taxable capital gains as the Minister may specify in respect of the taxpayer for the year.

Related Provisions: See Related Provisions and Definitions at end of s. 126.

Interpretation Bulletins: IT-395R: Foreign tax credit — foreign-source capital gains and losses. See also list at end of s. 126.

**(6) Construction of subsecs. (1) and (2)** — For greater certainty, where a taxpayer's income for a taxation year is in whole or in part from sources in more than one country other than Canada, subsections (1) and (2) shall be read as providing for separate deductions in respect of each of the countries other than Canada.

### Proposed Amendment — 126(6)

**(6) Rules of construction** — For the purposes of this section,

(a) the government of a country other than Canada includes the government of a state, province or other political subdivision of that country;

(b) where a taxpayer's income for a taxation year is in whole or in part from sources in more than one country other than Canada, subsections (1) and (2) shall be read as providing for separate deductions in respect of each of the countries other than Canada; and

(c) if any income from a source in a particular country would be tax-exempt income but for the fact that a portion of the income is subject to an income or profits tax imposed by the government of a country other than Canada, the portion is deemed to be income from a separate source in the particular country.

Application: The August 8, 2000 draft legislation, subsec. 9(5), will amend subsec. 126(6) to read as above, applicable after June 27, 1999.

Technical Notes: Subsection 126(6) of the Act confirms that foreign tax credits are computed on a country-by-country basis. This confirmation is preserved in new paragraph 126(6)(b), and the provision is expanded to include two other rules that apply for the purposes of section 126. First, new paragraph 126(6)(a) provides that the government of a country other than Canada includes the government of a state, province or other political subdivision of such a country. This new meaning allows several of the foreign tax credit rules to be simplified. Second, new paragraph 126(6)(c) provides that if income from a source in a country would be "tax-exempt income," but is not so only because part of the income is subject to tax, that part is deemed to be income from a separate source in the country. This rule, already found in subsection 126(8) of the Act, is simplified by the use of the new term set out in paragraph (a), and subsection 126(8) is consequently repealed.

Related Provisions: See Related Provisions and Definitions at end of s. 126.

Interpretation Bulletins: See list at end of s. 126.

**(7) Definitions** — In this section,

**"business-income tax"** paid by a taxpayer for a taxation year in respect of businesses carried on by the taxpayer in a country other than Canada (in this definition referred to as the "business country") means, subject to subsections (4.1) and (4.2), the portion of any income or profits tax paid by the taxpayer for the year to the government of any country other than Canada or to the government of a state, province or other political subdivision of any such country that can reasonably be regarded as tax in respect of the income of the taxpayer from any business carried on by the taxpayer in the business country, but does not include a tax, or the portion of a tax, that can reasonably be regarded as relating to an amount that

### Proposed Amendment — 126(7) "business-income tax" opening words

**"business-income tax"** paid by a taxpayer for a taxation year in respect of businesses carried on by the taxpayer in a country other than Canada (in this definition referred to as the "business country") means, subject to subsections (4.1) and (4.2), the portion of any income or profits tax paid by the taxpayer for the year to the government of a country other than Canada that can reasonably be regarded as tax in respect of the income of the taxpayer from a business carried on by the taxpayer in the business country, but does not include a tax, or the portion of a tax, that can reasonably be regarded as relating to an amount that

Application: The August 8, 2000 draft legislation, subsec. 9(6), will amend the opening words of the definition "business-income tax" in subsec. 126(7) to read as above, applicable after June 27, 1999.

Technical Notes: The definitions "business-income tax," "economic profit," and "non-business-income tax" in subsection 126(7) of the Act are simplified through the use of the new term "government of a country other than Canada." In addition, the language of the definition "business-income tax" is improved by replacing the term "any business" with the term "a business."

(a) any other person or partnership has received or is entitled to receive from that government, or

(b) was deductible under subparagraph 110(1)(f)(i) in computing the taxpayer's taxable income for the year;

Related Provisions: 104(22.3) — Deduction in computing non-business-income tax of trust; 126(4) — Portion of foreign tax not included; 126(5) — Foreign tax. See additional Related Provisions and Definitions at end of s. 126.

**Notes**: Opening words amended by 1998 Budget to add "subject to subsections (4.1) and (4.2)", effective for 1998 and later taxation years.

126(7)"business-income tax" was 126(7)(a) before consolidation in R.S.C. 1985 (5th Supp.), effective for taxation years ending after November 1991. See Table of Concordance.

Para. (b) of "business-income tax" (formerly 126(7)(a)(ii)) added by 1991 technical bill, effective for taxation years ending after July 13, 1990, to ensure that no credit can be claimed for income that was exempt from Canadian tax due to a treaty provision.

**Interpretation Bulletins**: IT-201R2: Foreign tax credit — trust and beneficiaries; IT-506: Foreign income taxes as a deduction from income; IT-520: Unused foreign tax credits — carryforward and carryback.

**I.T. Technical News**: No. 8 (treatment of United States unitary state taxes).

### Proposed Addition — 126(7)"commercial obligation"

"**commercial obligation**" in respect of a taxpayer's foreign oil and gas business in a country means an obligation of the taxpayer to a particular person, undertaken in the course of carrying on the business or in contemplation of the business, if the law of the country would have allowed the taxpayer to undertake an obligation, on substantially the same terms, to a person other than the particular person;

**Application**: The December 21, 2000 draft legislation, subsec. 72(6), will add the definition "commercial obligation" to subsec. 126(7), applicable on the same basis as proposed 126(5).

**Technical Notes**: A taxpayer who carries on a foreign oil and gas business in a country may simultaneously have more than one type of obligation to the government of the country or to an agent or instrumentality of that government. In the context of new subsection 126(5), which treats as foreign taxes certain amounts receivable by a foreign government, it is important to distinguish those obligations that can appropriately be treated as entailing income or profits taxes from those that are more in the nature of an ordinary commercial contract. The new definition "commercial obligation" describes the latter. A commercial obligation is one that the taxpayer has undertaken to a particular person, and that the law of the country would have allowed the taxpayer to undertake, on substantially the same terms, to a different person. (An obligation is not necessarily a commercial obligation, however, merely because it arises out of a contract.)

"**economic profit**" of a taxpayer in respect of a property for a period means the part of the taxpayer's profit, from the business in which the property is used, that is attributable to the property in respect of the period or to related transactions, determined as if the only amounts deducted in computing that part of the profit were

  (a) interest and financing expenses incurred by the taxpayer and attributable to the acquisition or holding of the property in respect of the period or to a related transaction,

  (b) income or profits taxes payable by the taxpayer for any year to the government of any country other than Canada or to the government of any state, province or other political subdivision of such a country, in respect of the property for the period or in respect of a related transaction, or

### Proposed Amendment — 126(7)"economic profit"(b)

  (b) income or profits taxes payable by the taxpayer for any year to the government of a country other than Canada, in respect of the property for the period or in respect of a related transaction, or

**Application**: The August 8, 2000 draft legislation, subsec. 9(7), will amend para. (b) of the definition "economic profit" in subsec. 126(7) to read as above, applicable after June 27, 1999.

**Technical Notes**: See under 126(7)"business-income tax".

  (c) other outlays and expenses that are directly attributable to the acquisition, holding or disposition of the property in respect of the period or to a related transaction;

**Related Provisions**: 126(4.4) — Certain dispositions ignored for purposes of this definition.

**Notes**: Definition added by 1998 Budget, effective for 1998 and later taxation years. See Notes to 126(4.1).

### Proposed Addition — 126(7)"foreign oil and gas business"

"**foreign oil and gas business**" of a taxpayer means a business, carried on by the taxpayer in a taxing country, the principal activity of which is the extraction from natural accumulations, or from oil or gas wells, of petroleum, natural gas or related hydrocarbons;

**Application**: The December 21, 2000 draft legislation, subsec. 72(6), will add the definition "foreign oil and gas business" to subsec. 126(7), applicable on the same basis as proposed 126(5).

**Technical Notes**: A taxpayer's foreign oil and gas business is a business the taxpayer carries on in a taxing country, the principal activity of which business is extracting petroleum, natural gas or related hydrocarbons from natural accumulations or from oil or gas wells.

"**foreign-tax carryover [para. 126(7)(b)]**" — [Repealed under former Act]

**Notes**: 126(7)(b), repealed in 1984, defined "foreign-tax carryover", a term no longer used. For the carryover of unused foreign tax credits, see 126(2)(a), 126(2.3) and 126(7)"unused foreign tax credit".

"**non-business-income tax**" paid by a taxpayer for a taxation year to the government of a country other than Canada means, subject to subsections (4.1) and (4.2), the portion of any income or profits tax paid by the taxpayer for the year to the government of that country, or to the government of a state, province or other political subdivision of that country, that

(a) was not included in computing the taxpayer's business-income tax for the year in respect of any business carried on by the taxpayer in any country other than Canada,

(b) was not deductible by virtue of subsection 20(11) in computing the taxpayer's income for the year, and

(c) was not deducted by virtue of subsection 20(12) in computing the taxpayer's income for the year,

but does not include a tax, or the portion of a tax,

(c.1) that is in respect of an amount deducted because of subsection 104(22.3) in computing the taxpayer's business-income tax,

(d) that would not have been payable had the taxpayer not been a citizen of that country and that cannot reasonably be regarded as attributable to income from a source outside Canada,

(e) that may reasonably be regarded as relating to an amount that any other person or partnership has received or is entitled to receive from that government,

(f) that, where the taxpayer deducted an amount under subsection 122.3(1) from the taxpayer's tax otherwise payable under this Part for the year, may reasonably be regarded as attributable to the taxpayer's income from employment to the extent of the lesser of the amounts determined in respect thereof under paragraphs 122.3(1)(c) and (d) for the year,

(g) that can reasonably be attributed to a taxable capital gain or a portion thereof in respect of which the taxpayer or a spouse or common-law partner of the taxpayer has claimed a deduction under section 110.6,

(h) that may reasonably be regarded as attributable to any amount received or receivable by the taxpayer in respect of a loan for the period in the year during which it was an eligible loan (within the meaning assigned by subsection 33.1(1)), or

(i) that can reasonably be regarded as relating to an amount that was deductible under subparagraph 110(1)(f)(i) in computing the taxpayer's taxable income for the year;

### Proposed Amendment — 126(7)"non-business-income tax"

"**non-business-income tax**" paid by a taxpayer for a taxation year to the government of a country other than Canada means, subject to subsections (4.1) and (4.2), the portion of any income or profits tax paid by the taxpayer for the year to the government of that country that

**Application**: The August 8, 2000 draft legislation, subsec. 9(8), will amend the opening words of the definition "non-business-in-come tax" in subsec. 126(7) to read as above, applicable after June 27, 1999.

**Technical Notes**: See under 126(7)"business-income tax".

**Related Provisions**: 4(1) — Income or loss from a source; 104(22.3) — Deduction in computing non-business-income tax of trust; Canada-U.S. Tax Treaty Art. XXIX B:6 — U.S. estate tax allowed for foreign tax credit purposes. See additional Related Provisions and Definitions at end of s. 126.

**Notes**: 126(7)"non-business-income tax"(g) amended by 2000 same-sex partners bill to add reference to "common-law partner", effective for the 2001 and later taxation years, or earlier by election (see Notes to 248(1)"common-law partner").

126(7)"non-business-income tax" was 126(7)(c) before consolidation in R.S.C. 1985 (5th Supp.), effective for taxation years ending after November 1991. See Table of Concordance.

Opening words amended by 1998 Budget to add "subject to subsections (4.1) and (4.2)", effective for 1998 and later taxation years.

Para. (c.1) added by 1993 technical bill, retroactive to taxation years that end after November 12, 1981.

Para. (g) amended by 1994 Budget, effective 1994, to add reference to a taxpayer's spouse and delete requirement that the deduction under 110.6 be for the same year. For 1985-1993, read:

> (g) that may reasonably be attributed to a taxable capital gain or a portion thereof in respect of which the taxpayer has claimed a deduction for the year under section 110.6;

Para. (i) (formerly 126(7)(c)(ix)) added by 1991 technical bill, effective for taxation years ending after July 13, 1990, to ensure that no credit can be claimed for income that was exempt from Canadian tax due to a treaty provision.

**Interpretation Bulletins**: IT-201R2: Foreign tax credit — trust and beneficiaries; IT-395R: Foreign tax credit — foreign-source capital gains and losses; IT-506: Foreign income taxes as a deduction from income. See also list at end of s. 126.

### Proposed Addition — 126(7)"production tax amount"

"**production tax amount**" of a taxpayer for a foreign oil and gas business carried on by the taxpayer in a taxing country for a taxation year means the total of all amounts each of which

(a) became receivable in the year by the government of the country because of an obligation (other than a commercial obligation) of the taxpayer, in respect of the business, to the government or an agent or instrumentality of the government,

(b) is computed by reference to the amount by which

(i) the amount or value of petroleum, natural gas or related hydrocarbons produced or extracted by the taxpayer in the course of carrying on the business in the year

exceeds

(ii) an allowance or other deduction that

(A) is deductible, under the agreement or law that creates the obligation described in paragraph (a), in computing the amount receivable by the government of the country, and

(B) is intended to take into account the taxpayer's operating and capital costs of that production or extraction, and can reasonably be considered to have that effect,

(c) would not, if this Act were read without reference to subsection (5), be an income or profits tax, and

(d) is not identified as a royalty under the agreement that creates the obligation or under any law of the country;

**Application**: The December 21, 2000 draft legislation, subsec. 72(6), will add the definition "production tax amount" to subsec. 126(7), applicable on the same basis as proposed 126(5).

**Technical Notes**: The production tax amount of a taxpayer for a foreign oil and gas business carried on in a taxing country for a taxation year is the total of all amounts that meet the following four conditions.

First, the amounts must have become receivable in the year by the foreign country's government, because of the taxpayer's obligation (other than a commercial obligation) either to that government itself or to an agent or instrumentality of it.

Second, the amounts must be computed on a basis that takes into account the taxpayer's operating and capital costs. This does not mean that the computation must recognize all costs that would be deductible in computing the taxpayer's income for Canadian accounting or tax purposes. It means, rather, that the agreement or law that creates the obligation referred to above must allow for the deduction of some amount that is intended to account for the taxpayer's costs and that can reasonably be considered to have that effect.

Third, the amounts must not be income or profits taxes within the meaning of the Act read without reference to new subsection 126(5). Such taxes are already dealt with under the ordinary foreign tax credit rules, and need not be included in the taxpayer's production tax amount.

Finally, the amounts must not be identified as royalties, either in an agreement that creates the obligation or under the foreign country's law. Royalties are inherently not income or profits taxes, and it is not appropriate that any amount that is explicitly described as a royalty be indirectly characterized as an income tax by being included in the production tax amount.

**Related Provisions**: 12(1)(o.1) — Production tax amount included in income.

"**qualifying incomes**" of a taxpayer from sources in a country means incomes from sources in the country, determined without reference to

(a) any portion of income that was deductible under subparagraph 110(1)(f)(i) in computing the taxpayer's taxable income,

(b) for the purpose of subparagraph 126(1)(b)(i), any portion of income in respect of which an amount was deducted under section 110.6 by the taxpayer, and

(c) any income from a source in the country if any income of the taxpayer from the source would be tax-exempt income;

**Notes**: Definition added by 1998 Budget, effective for taxation years that begin after February 24, 1998.

"**qualifying losses**" of a taxpayer from sources in a country means losses from sources in the country, determined without reference to

(a) any portion of income that was deductible under subparagraph 110(1)(f)(i) in computing the taxpayer's taxable income,

(b) for the purpose of subparagraph 126(1)(b)(i), any portion of income in respect of which an amount was deducted by the taxpayer under section 110.6, and

(c) any loss from a source in the country if any income of the taxpayer from the source would be tax-exempt income;

**Proposed Amendment —
126(7)"qualifying incomes", "qualifying losses"**

"**qualifying incomes**" of a taxpayer from sources in a country means incomes from sources in the country, determined in accordance with subsection (9);

"**qualifying losses**" of a taxpayer from sources in a country means losses from sources in the country, determined in accordance with subsection (9);

**Application**: The December 21, 2000 draft legislation, subsecs. 72(3) and (4), will amend the definitions "qualifying incomes" and "qualifying losses" in subsec. 126(7) to read as above, on the same basis as proposed 126(5).

**Technical Notes**: For commentary on the amendments to these two definitions, see the commentary on new subsection 126(9).

**Notes**: Definition added by 1998 Budget, effective for taxation years that begin after February 24, 1998.

"**related transactions**", in respect of a taxpayer's ownership of a property for a period, means transactions entered into by the taxpayer as part of the arrangement under which the property was owned;

**Notes**: Definition added by 1998 Budget, effective for 1998 and later taxation years.

"**tax for the year otherwise payable under this Part**" means

(a) in paragraph (1)(b) and subsection (3), the amount determined by the formula

$$A - B$$

where

A is the amount that would be the tax payable under this Part for the year if that tax were determined without reference to section 120.3 and before making any deduction under any of sections 121, 122.3 and 125 to 127.41, and

B is the amounts deemed by subsections 120(2) and (2.2) to have been paid on account of tax payable under this Part,

(b) in subparagraph (2)(c)(i) and paragraph (2.2)(b), the tax for the year payable under this Part (determined without reference to sections 120.3 and 123.3 and before making any deduction under any of sections 121, 122.3 and 124 to 127.41), and

(c) in subsection (2.1), the tax for the year payable under this Part (determined without reference to subsection 120(1) and sections 120.3 and 123.3 and before making any deduction under any of sections 121, 122.3 and 124 to 127.41);

**Related Provisions**: 257 — Formula cannot calculate to less than zero. See additional Related Provisions and Definitions at end of s. 126.

**Notes**: 126(7)"tax otherwise payable under this Part for the year"(a)A amended by 1999 Budget, effective for 1998 and later taxation years, to delete reference to 120.1 and effectively to add a reference to 127.1.

Para. (a)B amended by 1999 Budget, effective for 1999 and later taxation years, to change "is the amount, if any" to "is the amounts" and to add reference to 120(2.2).

Paras. (b), (c) amended by 1999 Budget, effective for 1998 and later taxation years, to delete reference to 120.1 and effectively to add a reference to 127.1. For earlier years, read:

(b) in subparagraph (2)(c)(i) and paragraph (2.2)(b), the tax for the year payable under this Part (determined without reference to sections 120.1, 120.3 and 123.3 and before making any deduction under any of sections 121, 122.3, 124 to 127 and 127.2 to 127.41), and

(c) in subsection (2.1), the tax for the year payable under this Part (determined without reference to subsection 120(1) and sections 120.1, 120.3 and 123.3 and before making any deduction under any of sections 121, 122.3, 124 to 127 and 127.2 to 127.41);

Reference to 123.3 added to paras. (b) and (c) by 1995 Budget, effective for taxation years that end after June 1995.

References to 127.41 added to (a)A, (b) and (c) (all changed from "127.2 to 127.4"), and obsolete references to 123(1)(b) deleted from the same three places, by 1994 Budget, effective for taxation years that end after February 22, 1994.

126(7)"tax for the year ..." was para. 126(7)(d) before consolidation in R.S.C. 1985 (5th Supp.), effective for taxation years ending after November 1991. The previous version, identical in meaning, read:

(d) "tax for the year otherwise payable under this Part" means

(i) in paragraph (1)(b) and subsection (3), the amount, if any, by which

(A) the amount that would be the tax payable under this Part for the year if that tax were determined without reference to section 120.1 and paragraph 123(1)(b) and before making any deduction under any of sections 121, 122.3, 125 to 127 and 127.2 to 127.4

exceeds

(B) the amount, if any, deemed by subsection 120(2) to have been paid on account of tax payable under this Part for the year,

(ii) in subparagraph (2)(c)(i) and paragraph (2.2)(b), the tax for the year payable under this Part (determined without reference to section 120.1 and paragraph 123(1)(b) and before making any deduction under any of sections 121, 122.3, 124 to 127 and 127.2 to 127.4), and

(iii) in subsection (2.1), the tax for the year payable under this Part (determined without reference to subsection 120(1), section 120.1 and paragraph 123(1)(b) and before

making any deduction under any of sections 121, 122.3, 124 to 127 and 127.2 to 127.4); and

References to 120.3 added by 1991 technical bill, effective 1990.

**I.T. Application Rules**: 69 (meaning of "*Income Tax Act*, chapter 148 of the Revised Statutes of Canada, 1952").

**"tax-exempt income"** means income of a taxpayer from a source in a country in respect of which

(a) the taxpayer is, because of a tax treaty with that country, entitled to an exemption from all income or profits taxes, imposed in that country, to which the treaty applies, and

(b) no income or profits tax to which the treaty does not apply is imposed in any country other than Canada;

**Notes**: Definition added by 1998 Budget, effective for taxation years that begin after February 24, 1998.

> **Proposed Addition — 126(7)"taxing country"**
>
> **"taxing country"** means a country (other than Canada) the government of which regularly imposes, in respect of income from businesses carried on in the country, a levy or charge of general application that would, if this Act were read without reference to subsection (5), be an income or profits tax.
>
> **Application**: The December 21, 2000 draft legislation, subsec. 72(6), will add the definition "taxing country" to subsec. 126(7), applicable on the same basis as proposed 126(5).
>
> **Technical Notes**: New subsection 126(5) in effect treats as income taxes certain levies imposed on a Canadian resident who carries on an oil or gas business in a foreign country. In order for the subsection to apply, the country in question must be one that regularly imposes an income tax on other business income. The definition "taxing country" incorporates this principle: a taxing country is one whose government regularly imposes, in respect of business income, a levy or charge of general application that is (without reference to subsection 126(5)) an income or profits tax.
>
> These amendments to subsection 126(7) apply to taxation years that begin after December 31, 1999. However, if a taxpayer makes a written election to have these amendments apply to taxation years that begin after a designated date (which is earlier than December 31, 1999) and the election is filed with the Minister of National Revenue on or before the taxpayer's filing-due date for the taxpayer's taxation year that includes the day on which these amendments receive royal assent, these amendments apply to taxation years that begin on the later of:
>
> (i) the date so designated by the taxpayer in the election; and
>
> (ii) December 31, 1994.

**"unused foreign tax credit"** of a taxpayer in respect of a country for a taxation year means the amount determined by the formula

$$A - (B + C)$$

where

A is the business-income tax paid by the taxpayer for the year in respect of businesses carried on by the taxpayer in that country,

B is the amount, if any, deductible under subsection (2) in respect of that country in computing the taxpayer's tax payable under this Part for the year, and

C is that portion of business income tax paid by the taxpayer for the year in respect of businesses carried on by the taxpayer in that country that may reasonably be considered to have been deducted in computing the taxpayer's tax payable under Part I.1 for the year.

### Proposed Amendment — 126(7) "unused foreign tax credit"

"unused foreign tax credit" of a taxpayer in respect of a country for a taxation year means the amount, if any, by which

(a) the business-income tax paid by the taxpayer for the year in respect of businesses carried on by the taxpayer in that country

exceeds

(b) the amount, if any, deductible under subsection (2) in respect of that country in computing the taxpayer's tax payable under this Part for the year.

**Technical Notes:** Consequential on the repeal of Part I.1, this definition is amended to remove the references to that Part, applicable to the 2001 and subsequent taxation years.

**Application:** The December 21, 2000 draft legislation, subsec. 72(5), will amend the definition "unused foreign tax credit" in subsec. 126(7) to read as above, applicable to 2001 et seq.

**Related Provisions:** 152(6)(f.1) — Minister required to reassess past year to allow unused foreign tax credit; 257 — Formula cannot calculate to less than zero. See additional Related Provisions and Definitions at end of s. 126.

**Notes:** 126(7) "unused foreign tax credit" was 126(7)(e) before consolidation in R.S.C. 1985 (5th Supp.), effective for taxation years ending after November 1991. Formula elements A–C were subparas. (i)–(iii).

**Interpretation Bulletins:** IT-488R2: Winding-up of 90%-owned taxable Canadian corporations.

**(8) Deemed separate source** — For the purpose of this section, if any income from a source in a particular country would be tax-exempt income but for the fact that a portion of the income is subject to an income or profits tax imposed by the government of a country other than Canada or of a state, province or other political subdivision of such a country, the portion is deemed to be income from a separate source in the particular country.

### Proposed Repeal — 126(8)

**Application:** The August 8, 2000 draft legislation, subsec. 9(9), will repeal subsec. 126(8), applicable after June 27, 1999.

**Technical Notes:** See under 126(7) "business-income tax".

**Notes:** 126(8) added by 1998 Budget, effective for taxation years that begin after February 24, 1998.

### Proposed Addition — 126(9)

**(9) Computation of qualifying incomes and losses** — The qualifying incomes and qualifying losses for a taxation year of a taxpayer from sources in a country shall be determined

(a) without reference to

(i) any portion of income that was deductible under subparagraph 110(1)(f)(i) in computing the taxpayer's taxable income,

(ii) for the purpose of subparagraph 126(1)(b)(i), any portion of income in respect of which an amount was deducted under section 110.6 in computing the taxpayer's income,

(iii) any income or loss from a source in the country if any income of the taxpayer from the source would be tax-exempt income; and

(b) as if the total of all amounts each of which is that portion of an amount deducted under subsection 66(4), 66.21(4), 66.7(2) or 66.7(2.3) in computing those qualifying incomes and qualifying losses for the year that applies to those sources were the greater of

(i) the total of all amounts each of which is that portion of an amount deducted under subsection 66(4), 66.21(4), 66.7(2) or 66.7(2.3) in computing the taxpayer's income for the year that applies to those sources, and

(ii) the total of

(A) the portion of the maximum amount that would be deductible under subsection 66(4) in computing the taxpayer's income for the year that applies to those sources if the amount determined under subparagraph 66(4)(b)(ii) for the taxpayer in respect of the year were equal to the amount, if any, by which the total of

(I) the taxpayer's foreign resource income (within the meaning assigned by subsection 66.21(1)) for the year in respect of the country, determined as if the taxpayer had claimed the maximum amounts deductible for the year under subsections 66.7(2) and (2.3), and

(II) all amounts each of which would have been an amount included in computing the taxpayer's income for the year under subsection 59(1) in respect of a disposition of a foreign resource property in respect of the country, determined as if each amount determined under subparagraph 59(1)(b)(ii) were nil,

exceeds

(III) the total of all amounts each of which is a portion of an amount (other than a portion that results in a reduction of the amount otherwise determined under subclause (I)) that applies to those sources and that would be deducted under subsection 66.7(2) in computing the taxpayer's income for the year if the maximum amounts deductible for the year under that subsection were deducted,

(B) the maximum amount that would be deductible under subsection 66.21(4) in respect of those sources in computing the taxpayer's income for the year if

(I) the amount deducted under subsection 66(4) in respect of those sources in computing the taxpayer's income for the year were the amount determined under clause (A),

(II) the amounts deducted under subsections 66.7(2) and (2.3) in respect of those sources in computing the taxpayer's income for the year were the maximum amounts deductible under those subsections,

(III) for the purposes of the definition "cumulative foreign resource expense" in subsection 66.21(1), the total of the amounts designated under subparagraph 59(1)(b)(ii) for the year in respect of dispositions by the taxpayer of foreign resource properties in respect of the country in the year were the maximum total that could be so designated without any reduction in the maximum amount that would be determined under clause (A) in respect of the taxpayer for the year in respect of the country if no assumption had been made under subclause (A)(II) in respect of designations made under subparagraph 59(1)(b)(ii), and

(IV) the amount determined under paragraph 66.21(4)(b) were nil, and

(C) the total of all amounts each of which is the maximum amount, applicable to one of those sources, that is deductible under subsection 66.7(2) or (2.3) in computing the taxpayer's income for the year.

**Application**: The December 21, 2000 draft legislation, subsec. 72(7), will add subsec. 126(9), applicable on the same basis as proposed 126(5).

**Technical Notes**: Subsection 126(1) sets out the rules for claiming a credit in respect of foreign taxes on non-business income (that is, the foreign taxes imposed on investment income and other categories of foreign source non-business income). A credit in respect of foreign taxes on business income is provided under subsection 126(2). Neither credit may exceed the Canadian tax otherwise payable in respect of the foreign source income. Canadian tax otherwise payable on foreign source income is generally determined by reference to the ratio of the net income from sources in a foreign country to total income. The net foreign source income is the amount, if any, by which "qualifying incomes" (as defined in subsection 126(7)) from those sources exceeds "qualifying losses" (as defined in the same subsection) from those sources.

The definitions "qualifying income" and "qualifying losses" are amended such that all the rules for determining those amounts are included in new subsection 126(9) — rather than in the body of the definitions — and that the definitions contain references to that subsection.

New subsection 126(9) sets out the amended rules for determining "qualifying incomes" and "qualifying losses". These amended rules consist of the existing rules (that is, those rules that are found in the body of the existing definitions) as well as certain new additional rules. These additional rules relate to deductions under certain provisions of the Act (in these notes referred to as the "particular resource deduction provisions"), namely subsections 66(4) and 66.7(2) and new subsections 66.21(4) and 66.7(2.3). Under these additional rules, the qualifying incomes and qualifying losses for a taxation year of a taxpayer from sources in a country are determined as if such portion of the total amount deducted under the particular resource deduction provisions as applies to those sources were the greater of:

- the total amount actually deducted in respect of those sources under the particular resource deduction provisions; and
- the maximum amount that would be deductible in respect of those sources under the particular resource deduction provisions if specified assumptions were made. These assumptions, in general terms, ignore the taxpayer's income from other sources.

**Notice of Ways and Means Motion, federal budget, February 28, 2000**: *Foreign Tax Credit*

(33) That, in computing a taxpayer's income for a year from sources in a foreign country for the purposes of the foreign tax credit rules in section 126 of the Act, there be deducted an amount equal to the total of

(a) the greater of

(i) the maximum amount that

(A) would, if the taxpayer's only foreign resource income for the year (determined under subparagraph 66(4)(b)(ii) of the Act) were from those sources, be deductible under subsection 66(4) of the Act in computing the taxpayer's income for the year, and

(B) can reasonably be considered to relate to those sources, and to be in respect of foreign exploration and development expenses incurred in a taxation year that begins before 2001, and

(ii) the amount deducted under subsection 66(4) of the Act in computing the taxpayer's income for the year that can reasonably be considered to relate to those sources and to be in respect of foreign exploration and development expenses incurred in a taxation year that begins before 2001, and

(b) the greater of

(i) the maximum amount that would be deductible in computing the taxpayer's income for the year in respect of those sources in connection with a balance described in paragraph (35) [reproduced under 66(15)"foreign exploration and development expenses" — ed.] if the amount determined under paragraph (37) [reproduced under 66(4) — ed.] were nil, and

(ii) the amount deducted in computing the taxpayer's income for the year in respect of those sources in connection with a balance described in paragraph (35),

and that this paragraph apply to taxation years of a taxpayer that begin after the earlier of December 31, 1999 and the date selected by the taxpayer for the application of the rule described in paragraph (32).

**Federal budget, supplementary information, February 28, 2000**: The amendments to the business foreign tax credit provisions of the Act will also include specific rules for the recognition of a taxpayer's foreign exploration and development expenses (FEDE), discussed in the next section. [See Resolution (33) reproduced under 126(7)"qualifying incomes" — ed.] While there already exists a general requirement in the Act for taxpayers to recognize FEDE in computing the amount of foreign tax credit that can be claimed in respect of foreign source income, these rules will specify how FEDE will be allocated to a particular foreign country for purposes of claiming a foreign tax credit.

The new rules will apply for foreign income taxes paid by any given taxpayer, pursuant to production sharing agreements, in taxation years that begin after the earlier of December 31, 1999, and a date chosen by the taxpayer (which date cannot in any case be earlier than December 31, 1994).

**Related Provisions**: 248(1)"foreign resource property" — Meaning of foreign resource property in respect of a country.

**Related Provisions [s. 126]**: 4(3) — Whether deductions are applicable to a particular source; 60(o)(iii) — Deduction for legal expenses in appealing assessment of tax deducted under s. 126; 80.1(2) — Election re interest for expropriation assets required; 87(2.11) — Vertical amalgamations; 104(22)–(22.4) — Trusts — allocation of foreign-source income to beneficiaries; 127.54(2) — Minimum tax — foreign tax credit; 180.1(1.1) — Foreign tax credit on individual surtax; 258(3) — Certain dividends on preferred shares deemed to be interest; 258(5) — Deemed interest on certain shares; Canada–U.S. tax treaty, Art. XXIV — Elimination of double taxation.

**Definitions [s. 126]**: "amount", "authorized foreign bank", "business" — 248(1); "business-income tax" — 126(7); "Canada" — 255; "Canadian banking business" — 248(1); "capital property" — 54, 248(1); "commercial obligation" — 126(7); "common-law partner" — 248(1); "corporation" — 248(1), *Interpretation Act* 35(1); "distribution year" — 126(2.22); "disposition", "dividend" — 248(1); "economic profit" — 126(7); "emigration year" — 126(2.21); "employment" — 248(1); "foreign affiliate" — 95(1), 248(1); "foreign oil and gas business" — 126(7); "foreign resource property" — 66(15), 248(1); "foreign resource property in respect of" — 248(1); "foreign tax" — 126(4.2); "individual" — 248(1); "non-business-income tax" — 126(7); "non-resident" — 126(1.1)(a), 248(1); "office", "oil or gas well", "person", "prescribed" — 248(1); "production tax amount" — 126(7); "property" — 248(1); "province" — *Interpretation Act* 35(1); "qualifying incomes", "qualifying losses" — 126(7), (9); "related transactions" — 126(7); "resident", "resident in Canada" — 126(1.1)(a), 250; "share" — 248(1); "source" — 126(8); "tax for the year otherwise payable" — 126(7); "tax-exempt income" — 126(7); "tax payable" — 248(2); "tax treaty", "taxable Canadian property" — 248(1); "taxable capital gain" — 38(a), 248(1); "taxable income" — 2(2), 248(1); "taxable income earned in Canada" — 248(1); "taxation year" — 249; "taxing country" — 126(7); "taxpayer" — 248(1); "time of disposition" — 128.1(4)(b); "trust" — 104(1), 248(1), (3); "unused foreign tax credit" — 126(7).

**I.T. Application Rules [s. 126]**: 40(1), (2).

**Interpretation Bulletins [s. 126]**: IT-183: Foreign tax credit — member of a partnership; IT-193 SR: Taxable income of individuals resident in Canada during part of a year (Special Release); IT-194: Foreign tax credit — part-time residents; IT-201R2: Foreign tax credit — trust and beneficiaries; IT-270R2: Foreign tax credit and deduction; IT-273R2: Government assistance — general comments; IT-497R3: Overseas employment tax credit.

**Forms**: T2209: Federal foreign tax credits.

**126.1 (1) [1993 UI premium tax credit] Definitions** — In this section,

**"1992 cumulative premium base"** of an employer on any particular day means the total of all qualifying employer premiums of the employer for the period beginning on January 1, 1992 and ending on the day that is 365 days earlier than the particular day that became payable on or before the last day of that period;

**"1992 premium base"** of an employer means the total of all qualifying employer premiums for 1992 of the employer;

**"1993 cumulative premium base"** of an employer on any particular day means the total of all qualifying employer premiums of the employer for the period beginning on January 1, 1993 and ending on the particular day that became payable on or before the last day of that period;

**"1993 premium base"** of an employer means the total of all qualifying employer premiums for 1993 of the employer;

**"employer"** at any time means any person or partnership (other than a person who at that time is exempt because of any of paragraphs 149(1)(a) to (d), (h.1), (o) to (o.2), (o.4) to (s) and (u) to (y) from tax under this Part on all or part of the person's taxable income) that has a qualifying employee in 1992 or 1993;

**"qualifying employee"** of an employer means,

(a) where the employer is not exempt because of subsection 149(1) from tax under this Part on all or part of the employer's taxable income,

(i) any employee of the employer, other than any employee whose remuneration is not deductible in computing income from a business or property, and

(ii) any person in respect of whom the employer is deemed under any regulation under the *Unemployment Insurance Act* to be an employer for the purpose of determining an employer's UI premium, and

(b) in any other case, any employee of the employer;

**"qualifying employer premium"** for a period of an employer means that portion of the employer's UI premium that can reasonably be attributed to the remuneration paid in the period to qualifying employees of the employer;

**"remittance date"** for 1993 of an employer means the day prescribed under the *Unemployment Insurance Act* on or before which the employer is required to remit a UI premium in respect of remuneration paid in 1993;

**"UI premium"** of an employer means a premium under subsection 51(2) of the *Unemployment Insurance Act* payable,

(a) where the employer is a partnership, by the members of the partnership in respect of remuneration paid by the partnership to employees of the partnership, and

(b) in any other case, by the employer.

**(2) Associated employers** — For the purposes of this section,

(a) employers that are corporations that are associated with each other at any time shall be deemed to be employers that are associated with each other at that time; and

(b) where 2 employers

(i) would, but for this paragraph, not be associated with each other at any time, and

(ii) are associated, or are deemed by this subsection to be associated, with another corporation at that time,

they shall be deemed to be associated with each other at that time.

**(3) Idem** — In determining for the purpose of this section whether 2 or more employers are associated with each other at any time, and in determining whether an employer is at any time a specified employer in relation to another employer,

(a) where an employer at any time is an individual, the employer shall be deemed at that time to be a corporation all the issued shares of the capital stock of which, having full voting rights under all circumstances, are owned by the individual; and

(b) where an employer at any time is a partnership,

(i) the employer shall be deemed at that time to be a corporation having one class of issued shares, which shares have full voting rights under all circumstances, and

(ii) each member of the partnership shall be deemed to own at that time the greatest proportion of the number of issued shares of the capital stock of the corporation that

(A) the member's share of the income or loss of the partnership from any source for the fiscal period of the partnership that includes that time

is of

(B) the income or loss of the partnership from that source for that period

and for the purpose of this paragraph, where the income and loss of the partnership from any source for that period are nil, that proportion shall be computed as if the partnership had income from that source for that period in the amount of $1,000,000.

**(4) Business carried on by another employer** — Where at any time before 1994 an employer (referred to in this subsection and subsection (5) as the "successor") carries on, as a separate business or as part of another business, a business or part of a business that was carried on at any earlier time after 1991 by a specified employer in relation to the successor (which business or part of a business is referred to in this subsection as the "specified business"), in determining

(a) the UI premium tax credit of the specified employer and the successor, and

(b) each amount that is or would, but for subsection (13), be deemed by subsection (12) to be paid to the specified employer or the successor at any time after the successor began to carry on the specified business,

that portion of the qualifying employer premiums for any period of the specified employer that can reasonably be considered to relate to the specified business shall be deemed not to be qualifying employer premiums for the period of the specified employer and to be qualifying employer premiums for the period of the successor.

**(5) Definition of "specified employer"** — For the purposes of subsection (4), "specified employer" at any time in relation to a successor means any particular employer with whom the successor at that time is not or would not be dealing at arm's length if,

(a) where the particular employer ceased to exist before that time, the particular employer were in existence at that time, and

(b) the particular employer were controlled at that time by each person or group of persons who at any time in 1992 or 1993 controlled the particular employer,

except that a particular employer is not a specified employer in relation to a successor where the successor is, for the purposes of this section, deemed by paragraph 87(2)(mm) or 88(1)(e.2) to be a continuation of, and the same corporation as, the particular employer.

**(6) UI premium tax credit** — Where an employer (other than a partnership) files with the Minister a prescribed form containing prescribed information, an overpayment on account of the employer's liability under this Part for the employer's last taxation year beginning before 1994 equal to the employer's UI premium tax credit shall be deemed to have arisen on the later of March 1, 1994 and the day on which the form is so filed.

**Related Provisions**: 87(2)(mm) — Amalgamations — continuing corporation; 126.1(11) — UI premium tax credit — associated employers; 152(1.2) — Provisions applicable to determination of overpayment; 152(3.4), (3.5) — Determination of credit by Minister; 164(1.6) — Refund of credit by Minister.

**Notes**: See Notes at end of 126.1.

**(7) Idem** — Where a member of a partnership, acting on behalf of all of the members of the partnership, files with the Minister a prescribed form containing prescribed information, an overpayment on account of each taxpayer's liability under this Part for the taxpayer's last taxation year beginning before 1994 equal to that portion of the partnership's UI premium tax credit that can reasonably be considered to be the taxpayer's share thereof shall be deemed to have arisen on the later of March 1, 1994 and the day on which the form is so filed.

**Related Provisions**: 152(3.4), (3.5) — Determination of credit by Minister; 164(1.6) — Refund of credit by Minister.

**(8) Definition of "UI premium tax credit"** — For the purposes of this section, an employer's "UI premium tax credit" is the lesser of

(a) the amount, if any, by which $30,000 exceeds the amount, if any, by which the employer's 1992 premium base exceeds $30,000, and

(b) the amount, if any, by which the employer's 1993 premium base exceeds the employer's 1992 premium base,

unless the employer is associated at the end of 1993 with any other employer, in which case, subject to subsection (11), the employer's UI premium tax credit is nil.

**(9) Allocation by associated employers** — An employer that is a member of a group of employers that are associated with each other at the end of 1993 (referred to in this subsection and in subsections (10) and (11) as "associated employers") may file with the Minister an agreement in prescribed form on behalf of the associated employers allocating among them an amount not exceeding the lesser of

(a) the amount, if any, by which $30,000 exceeds the amount, if any, by which the total of the 1992 premium bases of all of the associated employers exceeds $30,000, and

(b) the amount, if any, by which

(i) the total of the 1993 premium bases of all of the associated employers

exceeds

(ii) the total of the 1992 premium bases of all of the associated employers.

**(10) Allocation by the Minister** — The Minister may request any of the associated employers to file with the Minister an agreement referred to in subsection (9) and, where the employer does not file the agreement within 30 days after receiving the request, the Minister may allocate among them an amount not exceeding the lesser of the amounts determined under paragraphs (9)(a) and (b).

**(11) UI premium tax credit — associated employers** — For the purposes of this section, the least amount allocated to an associated employer under an agreement described in subsection (9) or the amount allocated to the employer by the Minister under subsection (10), as the case may be, is the UI premium tax credit of the employer.

**(12) Prepayment of UI premium tax credit** — Where before March 1994 an employer or, where the employer is a partnership, any member of the partnership acting on behalf of all of the members of the partnership, files with the Minister a prescribed form containing prescribed information, the Minister shall, subject to subsection (13), be deemed to have paid to the employer on account of the overpayment determined under subsection (6) in respect of the employer, and the employer shall be deemed, for the purpose of paragraph 12(1)(x), to have received and, for the purposes of the *Unemployment Insurance Act* and regulations made under it, to have remitted to the Receiver General on account of the employer's UI premium, on each remittance date for 1993, an amount that is equal to,

(a) where the employer was not associated with any other employer on the remittance date, the lesser of

(i) the amount, if any, by which the lesser of

(A) the amount, if any, by which $30,000 exceeds the amount, if any, by which the 1992 premium base of the employer exceeds $30,000, and

(B) the amount, if any, by which

(I) the 1993 cumulative premium base of the employer on the remittance date

exceeds

(II) the 1992 cumulative premium base of the employer on the remittance date

exceeds the total of all amounts deemed or that would, but for subsection (13), be deemed by this subsection to have been paid to the employer before the remittance date, and

(ii) the amount determined by the formula

$$A - (B + C)$$

where

## Subdivision c — Computation of Tax: All Taxpayers    S. 127(1)

A is the total of all UI premiums of the employer payable on or before the remittance date that can reasonably be attributed to remuneration paid in the period beginning on January 1, 1993 and ending on the remittance date,

B is the total of all amounts (determined without reference to this subsection) remitted by the employer to the Receiver General on or before the remittance date on account of the UI premiums referred to in the description of A, and

C is the total of all amounts deemed or that would, but for subsection (13), be deemed by this subsection to have been paid to the employer before the remittance date; and

(b) where the employer (in this paragraph referred to as the "particular employer") was associated on the remittance date with any other employer (in this paragraph referred to as an "associated employer"), the lesser of

(i) the amount that would be determined under paragraph (a) in respect of the particular employer on the remittance date if the particular employer were not associated on the remittance date with any other employer, and

(ii) the amount, if any, by which the lesser of

(A) the amount, if any, by which $30,000 exceeds the amount, if any, by which the total of the 1992 premium bases of the particular employer and all associated employers exceeds $30,000, and

(B) the amount, if any, by which

(I) the total of all amounts each of which is the 1993 cumulative premium base of the particular employer or an associated employer on the remittance date

exceeds

(II) the total of all amounts each of which is the 1992 cumulative premium base of the particular employer or an associated employer on the remittance date

exceeds the total of

(C) all amounts each of which is an amount deemed or that would, but for subsection (13), be deemed by this subsection to have been paid to the particular employer or an associated employer before the remittance date, and

(D) all amounts each of which is an amount that would be determined under subparagraph (a)(ii) in respect of an associated employer on the remittance date if the associated employer were not associated on that date with any other employer.

**Related Provisions**: 126.1(13) — Amount deemed paid to a partnership; 126.1(14), (15) — Excess prepayments; 257 — Formula cannot calculate to less than zero.

**(13) Idem** — Where an amount would, but for this subsection, be deemed by subsection (12) to be paid at any time to a partnership, that portion of the amount that can reasonably be considered to be a taxpayer's share of it shall be deemed not to have been paid to the partnership and to have been paid at that time by the Minister to the taxpayer on account of the overpayment determined under subsection (7) in respect of the taxpayer.

**(14) Excess prepayment** — Where the total of all amounts paid under subsection (12) to a taxpayer exceeds the taxpayer's UI premium tax credit, the excess shall be deemed to have been refunded to the taxpayer, on the taxpayer's last remittance date for 1993, on account of the taxpayer's liability under this Part for the taxpayer's last taxation year beginning before 1994.

**(15) Idem** — Where the total of all amounts paid under subsection (13) to a taxpayer in respect of a partnership exceeds that portion of the partnership's UI premium tax credit that can reasonably be considered to be the taxpayer's share of it, the excess shall be deemed to have been refunded to the taxpayer, on the partnership's last remittance date for 1993, on account of the taxpayer's liability under this Part for the taxpayer's last taxation year beginning before 1994.

**Notes**: 126.1 added by 1992 Economic Statement, effective 1993. It provided a credit, for 1993 only, to offset increases in UI premiums payable by employers. It was designed to encourage employers to hire additional staff. An earlier 126.1, repealed in 1974, dealt with political contributions, which are now covered under 127(3).

**Definitions [s. 126.1]**: "1992 cumulative premium base", "1992 premium base", "1993 cumulative premium base", "1993 premium base" — 126.1(1); "arm's length" — 251; "associated" — 126.1(2), (3), 256; "business" — 248(1); "corporation" — 248(1), Interpretation Act 35(1); "employee" — 248(1); "employer" — 126.1(1); "fiscal period" — 249.1; "individual", "Minister" — 248(1); "partnership" — see Notes to 96(1);; "prescribed", "property" — 248(1); "qualifying employee" — 126.1(1); "qualifying employer" — 126.1(1), (4); "remittance date" — 126.1(1); "share" — 248(1); "specified employer" — 126.1(5); "successor" — 126.1(4); "taxation year" — 249; "UI premium" — 126.1(1); "UI premium tax credit" — 126.1(8), (11).

**127. (1) Logging tax deduction [credit]** — There may be deducted from the tax otherwise payable by a taxpayer under this Part for a taxation year an amount equal to the lesser of

(a) ²/₃ of any logging tax paid by the taxpayer to the government of a province in respect of income for the year from logging operations in the province, and

(b) 6²/₃% of the taxpayer's income for the year from logging operations in the province referred to in paragraph (a),

except that in no case shall the total of amounts in respect of all provinces that would otherwise be de-

**S. 127(1)**      Income Tax Act, Part I, Division E

ductible under this subsection from the tax otherwise payable under this Part for the year by the taxpayer exceed 6⅔% of the amount that would be the taxpayer's taxable income for the year or taxable income earned in Canada for the year, as the case may be, if this Part were read without reference to paragraphs 60(b), (c) to (c.2), (i) and (v) and sections 62, 63 and 64.

**Related Provisions**: 117(1) — "Tax otherwise payable".

**Notes**: 127(1) amended by 1992 technical bill, effective for the 1991 and later taxation years, to add the words from "if this Part were read" to the end. The amendment effectively increases the base for determining the logging tax credit.

**Interpretation Bulletins**: IT-121R3: Election to capitalize cost of borrowed money.

**Forms**: T2 SCH 5: Tax calculation supplementary — corporations.

**(2) Definitions** — In subsection (1),

"**income for the year from logging operations in the province**" has the meaning assigned by regulation;

**Notes**: 127(2)"income for the year from logging ..." was para. 127(2)(a) before consolidation in R.S.C. 1985 (5th Suppl.), effective for taxation years ending after November 1991.

**Regulations**: 700(1), (2) (meaning of "income for the year from logging operations in a province").

"**logging tax**" means a tax imposed by the legislature of a province that is declared by regulation to be a tax of general application on income from logging operations.

**Notes**: The relevant provinces are British Columbia and Quebec.

127(2)"logging tax" was para. 127(2)(b) before consolidation in R.S.C. 1985 (5th Suppl.), effective for taxation years ending after November 1991.

**Regulations**: 700(3) (provinces are B.C. and Quebec).

**(3) Contributions to registered parties and candidates [political contribution credit]** — There may be deducted from the tax otherwise payable by a taxpayer under this Part for a taxation year in respect of the total of all amounts each of which is a monetary contribution made by the taxpayer in the year to a registered party or to a candidate whose nomination has been confirmed in an election of a member or members to serve in the House of Commons of Canada (in this section referred to as "the total"),

(a) 75% of the total, if the total does not exceed $200,

(b) $150 plus 50% of the amount by which the total exceeds $200, if the total exceeds $200 and does not exceed $550, or

(c) the lesser of

(i) $325 plus 33⅓% of the amount by which the total exceeds $550, and

(ii) $500,

if payment of each monetary contribution that is included in the total is proven by filing a receipt with the Minister, signed by a registered agent of the registered party or by the official agent of the candidate whose nomination has been confirmed, as the case may be, that contains prescribed information.

**Related Provisions**: 18(1)(n) — No deduction from income for political contributions; 120(4) — "Tax otherwise payable under this Part"; 123.2(a) — Corporate surtax applies to total tax before claiming political tax credit; 127(3.1) — Issue of receipts; 127(3.2) — Deposit of amounts contributed; 127(4) — Interpretation; 127(4.1) — Definition of "amount contributed"; 127(4.2) — Allocation of amount contributed among partners; 230.1 — Books and records relating to political contributions.

**Notes**: The sliding scale of credits for political contributions encourages small contributions, with no credit at all for contributions over $1,075 per year, whereas the credit for charitable donations under 118.1 encourages large contributions over the course of a year.

127(3) amended by *Canada Elections Act* (CEA), S.C. 2000, c. 9, effective for 2000 and later taxation years, except that, in its application to contributions made after 1999 and before the coming into force of the CEA (see below), read "a monetary contribution made", "monetary contribution" and "candidate whose nomination has been confirmed" as "an amount contributed", "amount contributed" and "an officially nominated candidate" respectively. The effect of the amendment was to increase the 75% credit threshold so it applies on the first $200 rather than the first $100. The change from $300 to $325 in 127(3)(c) decreased the maximum contribution that generates a credit from $1,150 to $1,075. The maximum credit remains at $500. From 1977 to 1999, read:

> (3) Contributions to registered parties and candidates — There may be deducted from the tax otherwise payable by a taxpayer under this Part for a taxation year in respect of the total of all amounts each of which is an amount contributed by the taxpayer in the year to a registered party or to an officially nominated candidate at an election of a member or members to serve in the House of Commons of Canada (in this section referred to as "the total"),
>
> (a) 75% of the total if the total does not exceed $100,
>
> (b) $75 plus 50% of the amount by which the total exceeds $100 if the total exceeds $100 and does not exceed $550, or
>
> (c) the lesser of
>
> (i) $300 plus 33⅓% of the amount by which the total exceeds $550 if the total exceeds $550, and
>
> (ii) $500,
>
> if payment of each amount contributed that is included in the total is proven by filing a receipt with the Minister, signed by a registered agent of the registered party or by the official agent of the officially nominated candidate, as the case may be, that contains prescribed information.

The CEA comes into force, per s. 577 thereof, on November 30, 2000 (six months after Royal Assent), unless, before that time, the Chief Electoral Officer has published a notice in the *Canada Gazette* that the necessary preparations for the bringing into operation of the CEA have been made and that the CEA may come into force accordingly.

**Regulations**: 2000 (prescribed information).

**Interpretation Bulletins**: IT-143R2: Meaning of "eligible capital expenditure".

**Information Circulars**: 75-2R4: Contributions to a registered political party or to a candidate at a federal election.

**Forms**: T2092: Contributions to a registered party — information return; T2093: Contributions to a candidate at an election — information return.

**(3.1) Issue of receipts** — A receipt referred to in subsection (3) shall not be issued

(a) by a registered agent of a registered party, or

(b) by an official agent of a candidate whose nomination has been confirmed

otherwise than in respect of a monetary contribution and to the contributor who made it.

**Related Provisions**: 238(1) — Offences.

**Notes**: 127(3.1) amended by *Canada Elections Act* (CEA), effective on the coming into force of the CEA (see Notes to 127(3)). Before that date, read:

> (3.1) **Issue of receipts** — A receipt referred to in subsection (3) shall not be issued
>
> (a) by a registered agent of a registered party, or
>
> (b) by an official agent of an officially nominated candidate
>
> otherwise than in respect of an amount contributed and to the contributor of such an amount.

**(3.2) Deposit of amounts contributed** — An official agent of a candidate whose nomination has been confirmed — other than in an electoral district referred to in Schedule 3 to the *Canada Elections Act* — who receives a monetary contribution, shall without delay deposit it in an account in the name of the official agent, in his or her capacity as such, in a branch or other office in Canada of a Canadian financial institution as defined in section 2 of the *Bank Act*, or in an authorized foreign bank, as defined in that section, that is not subject to the restrictions and requirements referred to in subsection 524(2) of that Act.

**Related Provisions**: 238(1) — Offences.

**Notes**: 127(3.2) amended by *Canada Elections Act* (CEA), effective on the coming into force of the CEA (see Notes to 127(3)). Before that date, read:

> (3.2) **Deposit of amounts contributed** — Where an amount contributed has been received by an official agent of an officially nominated candidate other than an officially nominated candidate in any of the electoral districts referred to in Schedule III to the *Canada Elections Act*, the official agent shall forthwith deposit that amount contributed in an account standing to the credit of the official agent in the agent's capacity as such in the records of a branch or other office in Canada of
>
> (a) a bank;
>
> (b) a corporation that is licensed or otherwise authorized under the laws of Canada or a province to carry on in Canada the business of offering to the public its services as trustee; or
>
> (c) a credit union.

**Information Circulars**: 75-2R4: Contributions to a registered political party or to a candidate at a federal election.

**(4) Definitions** — In subsections (3), (3.1), (3.2) and (4.1), the terms "official agent", "registered agent" and "registered party" have the meanings assigned to them by subsection 2(1) of the *Canada Elections Act* and the expression "candidate whose nomination has been confirmed" means a person whom the Chief Electoral Officer has, under subsection 71(1) of the *Canada Elections Act*, confirmed as a candidate in an election.

**Notes**: These terms are defined as follows in the *Canada Elections Act*, S.C. 2000, c. 9:

> 2. (1) "official agent"means the official agent appointed by a candidate as required by subsection 83(1).
>
> 83. (1) A candidate shall appoint an official agent before accepting a contribution or incurring an electoral campaign expense.
>
> [Section 84 lists the persons not eligible to be an official agent.]
>
> 2. (1) "registered agent", in relation to a registered party, means a person referred to in section 375 and includes the chief agent of the registered party.
>
> 375. (1) A registered party may, subject to any terms and conditions that it specifies, appoint persons to act as its registered agents.
>
> 2. (1) "registered party" means a political party that is entered in the registry of parties referred to in section 374 as a registered party.
>
> 374. The Chief Electoral Officer shall maintain a registry of parties that contains the information referred to in paragraphs 366(2)(a) to (h) and in subsections 375(3) and 390(3).

127(4) amended in 2000 by *Canada Elections Act* (CEA), effective on the coming into force of the CEA (see Notes to 127(3)). Before that date, read:

> (4) **Definitions** — In subsections (3), (3.1), (3.2) and (4.1), the terms "official agent", "registered agent" and "registered party" have the meanings assigned to them by section 2 of the *Canada Elections Act* and the term "officially nominated candidate" means a person in respect of whom a nomination paper and deposit have been filed as referred to in the definition "official nomination" in that section of that Act.

**(4.1) Definition of ["money contribution"] "amount contributed"** — In subsections (3), (3.1), (3.2) and (4.2), "monetary contribution" made by a taxpayer means a contribution made by the taxpayer to a registered party or to a candidate whose nomination has been confirmed in the form of cash or in the form of a negotiable instrument issued by the taxpayer, but does not include

(a) a monetary contribution made by an official agent of a candidate whose nomination has been confirmed or a registered agent of a registered party (in the agent's capacity as official agent or registered agent, as the case may be) to another such official agent or registered agent, as the case may be; or

(b) a monetary contribution in respect of which the taxpayer has received or is entitled to receive a financial benefit of any kind (other than a prescribed financial benefit or a deduction under subsection (3)) from a government, municipality or other public authority, whether as a grant, subsidy, forgivable loan or deduction from tax or an allowance or otherwise.

**S. 127(4.1)**      Income Tax Act, Part I, Division E

**Notes**: 127(4.1) amended by *Canada Elections Act* (CEA), effective on the coming into force of the CEA (see Notes to 127(3)). Before that date, read:

> **(4.1) Definition of "amount contributed" ["monetary contribution"]** — In subsections (3), (3.1) and (3.2), "amount contributed" by a taxpayer means a contribution by the taxpayer to a registered party or an officially nominated candidate in the form of cash or in the form of a negotiable instrument issued by the taxpayer, but does not include
>
>> (a) a contribution made by an official agent of an officially nominated candidate or a registered agent of a registered party (in the agent's capacity as such official agent or registered agent, as the case may be) to another such official agent or registered agent, as the case may be; or
>>
>> (b) a contribution in respect of which the taxpayer has received or is entitled to receive a financial benefit of any kind (other than a prescribed financial benefit or a deduction pursuant to subsection (3)) from a government, municipality or other public authority, whether as a grant, subsidy, forgivable loan or deduction from tax or an allowance or otherwise.

Before consolidation in the R.S.C. 1985 (5th Supp.), the opening words of 127(4.1) applied to s. 230.1 as well. That rule of application is now in 230.1(7).

**(4.2) Allocation of amount contributed among partners** — Where a taxpayer was, at the end of a taxation year of a partnership, a member of the partnership, the taxpayer's share of any monetary contribution made by the partnership in that taxation year that would, if the partnership were a person, be a monetary contribution referred to in subsection (3), is, for the purposes of that subsection, deemed to be a monetary contribution made by the taxpayer in the taxpayer's taxation year in which the taxation year of the partnership ended.

**Related Provisions**: 53(2)(c)(iii) — Reduction in ACB of partnership interest.

**Notes**: 127(4.2) amended by *Canada Elections Act* (CEA), effective on the coming into force of the CEA (see Notes to 127(3)), to change "amount contributed" to "monetary contribution" (twice). See 127(4.1).

**(5) Investment tax credit** — There may be deducted from the tax otherwise payable by a taxpayer under this Part for a taxation year an amount not exceeding the lesser of

  (a) the total of

    (i) the taxpayer's investment tax credit at the end of the year in respect of property acquired before the end of the year or of the taxpayer's SR&ED qualified expenditure pool at the end of the year or of a preceding taxation year, and

> **Proposed Amendment — 127(5)(a)(i)**
>
> (i) the taxpayer's investment tax credit at the end of the year in respect of property acquired before the end of the year, of the taxpayer's flow-through mining expenditure for the year or a preceding taxation year or of the taxpayer's SR&ED qualified expenditure pool at the end of the year or of a preceding taxation year, and
>
> **Application**: The December 21, 2000 draft legislation, subsec. 73(1), will amend subpara. 127(5)(a)(i) to read as above, applicable to 2000 *et seq*.
>
> **Technical Notes**: Subsection 127(5) provides for the deduction of investment tax credits from a taxpayer's Part I (and, for taxation years before 2001, Part I.1) tax otherwise payable for a taxation year. The term "investment tax credit" is defined in subsection 127(9).
>
> Subparagraph 127(5)(a)(i) provides that the taxpayer's investment tax credit at the end of the year in respect of property acquired before the end of the year or of the taxpayer's SR&ED qualified expenditure pool at the end of the year or of a preceding taxation year may be deducted in computing the taxpayer's tax payable for the year under Part I. For the 2000 and subsequent taxation years, subparagraph 127(5)(a)(i) is amended to ensure that the taxpayer's investment tax credit at the end of the year in respect of the taxpayer's flow-through mining expenditure for the year or a preceding taxation year may also be deducted in computing the taxpayer's tax payable for the year. The new term "flow-through mining expenditure" is added to the definitions in subsection 127(9).

    (ii) the lesser of

      (A) the taxpayer's investment tax credit at the end of the year in respect of property acquired in a subsequent taxation year or of the taxpayer's SR&ED qualified expenditure pool at the end of a subsequent taxation year to the extent that an investment tax credit was not deductible under this subsection or subsection 180.1(1.2) for the subsequent year, and

> **Proposed Amendment — 127(5)(a)(ii)(A)**
>
> (A) the taxpayer's investment tax credit at the end of the year in respect of property acquired in a subsequent taxation year, of the taxpayer's flow-through mining expenditure for a subsequent taxation year or of the taxpayer's SR&ED qualified expenditure pool at the end of a subsequent taxation year to the extent that an investment tax credit was not deductible under this subsection for the subsequent year, and
>
> **Application**: The December 21, 2000 draft legislation, subsec. 73(2), will amend cl. 127(5)(a)(ii)(A) to read as above, applicable to 2000 *et seq*, except that, for the 2000 taxation year, it shall be read as follows:
>
>> "(A) the taxpayer's investment tax credit at the end of the year in respect of property acquired in a subsequent taxation year, of the taxpayer's flow-through mining expenditure for a subsequent taxation year or of the taxpayer's SR&ED qualified expenditure pool at the end of a subsequent taxation year to the extent that an investment tax credit was not deductible under this subsection or subsection 180.1(1.2) for the subsequent year, and"
>
> **Technical Notes**: Clause 127(5)(a)(ii)(A) provides that the taxpayer's investment tax credit at the end of the year in respect of property acquired in a subsequent taxation

## Subdivision c — Computation of Tax: All Taxpayers     S. 127(6)(a)

year or of the taxpayer's SR&ED qualified expenditure pool at the end of a subsequent taxation year may be deducted in computing the taxpayer's tax payable for the year. For the 2000 and subsequent taxation years, clause 127(5)(a)(ii)(A) is amended to ensure that the investment tax credit in respect of the taxpayer's flow-through mining expenditure for a subsequent year may also be deducted in computing the taxpayer's tax payable under Part I. The new term "flow-through mining expenditure" is added to the definitions in subsection 127(9).

Consequential on the repeal of Part I.1 (i.e., the provisions relating to the individual surtax) for the 2001 and subsequent taxation years, the reference, in clause 127(5)(a)(ii)(A), to subsection 180.1(1.2) is removed for the 2001 and subsequent taxation years. For details concerning the repeal of Part I.1, refer to the commentary on Part I.1.

> (B) the amount, if any, by which the taxpayer's tax otherwise payable under this Part for the year exceeds the amount, if any, determined under subparagraph (i), and
> 
> (b) where Division E.1 applies to the taxpayer for the year, the amount, if any, by which the total of
> 
> (i) the taxpayer's tax otherwise payable under this Part for the year, and
> 
> (ii) the taxpayer's tax payable under Part I.1 for the year before deducting any amount under subsection 180.1(1.2)
> 
> exceeds the taxpayer's minimum amount for the year determined under section 127.51.

### Proposed Amendment — 127(5)(b)

(b) where Division E.1 applies to the taxpayer for the year, the amount, if any, by which

(i) the taxpayer's tax otherwise payable under this Part for the year

exceeds

(ii) the taxpayer's minimum amount for the year determined under section 127.51.

**Application**: The December 21, 2000 draft legislation, subsec. 73(3), will amend para. 127(5)(b) to read as above, applicable to 2001 et seq.

**Technical Notes**: Paragraph 127(5)(b) describes an amount that may be deducted for a taxation year by a taxpayer where the taxpayer is subject to the minimum tax for the year. Consequential on the repeal of Part I.1 (i.e., the provisions relating to the individual surtax) for the 2001 and subsequent taxation years, paragraph 127(5)(b) is amended to remove the reference to subsection 180.1(1.2) for those years. For details concerning the repeal of Part I.1, refer to the commentary on Part I.1.

**Related Provisions**: 12(1)(t) — Income inclusion for ITCs; 13(7.1) — Deemed capital cost; 13(21)"undepreciated capital cost"I — Reduction in u.c.c. of property to reflect ITCs; 37(1)(e) — Deduction for scientific research and experimental development; 53(2)(k)(ii) — Deduction from ACB of property to reflect ITCs; 66.1(6)"cumulative Canadian exploration expense"L — Reduction in CCEE; 87(2.11) — Vertical amalgamations; 117(1), 120(4) — "Tax otherwise payable under this Part"; 123.2(a) — Corporate surtax applies to total tax before claiming ITC; 127(8) — ITC of partnership; 127(11.2) — Time of expenditure and acquisition; 127(26) — Expenditure unpaid within 180 days of end of year; 127.1(3) — Refundable ITC deemed claimed under 127(5); 128(2)(e)(iii)(C) — No credit on return filed by trustee following individual's discharge from bankruptcy; 149(10)(c) — Where corporation becomes or ceases to be exempt; 152(6) — Reassessment; 164(5), (5.1) — Effect of carryback of loss; 180.1(1.2) — Individual surtax — deductions from tax; 192(10) — SPTC claim deemed to be deducted as ITC; 220(6), (7) — Assignment of ITC refund by corporation.

**Notes**: See 127(9)"specified percentage" and 127(9)"investment tax credit" for the calculation of the credit.

127(5)(a)(i) amended by 1995 Budget, effective for taxation years that begin after 1995. For earlier taxation years that begin after 1993, read:

> (i) the taxpayer's investment tax credit at the end of the year in respect of property acquired, or an expenditure made, before the end of the year,

127(5)(a)(ii)(A) amended by 1995 Budget, effective for taxation years that begin after 1995. For earlier taxation years that begin after 1993, read:

> (A) the taxpayer's investment tax credit at the end of the year in respect of property acquired, or an expenditure made, in a subsequent taxation year, to the extent that the investment tax credit was not deductible under this subsection or subsection 180.1(1.2) for the taxation year in which the property was acquired, or the expenditure was made, as the case may be,

127(5) amended by 1993 Budget, effective for taxation years that begin in 1994 or later. For earlier years, the limit was the least of (a), (b) and (c), where (b) and (c) were the post-1993 paras. (a) and (b), and (a) was "the taxpayer's annual investment tax credit limit for the year". See 127(9)"annual investment tax credit limit", also repealed at the same time.

**Regulations**: 4600–4609.

**Interpretation Bulletins**: IT-92R2: Income of contractors; IT-151R5: Scientific research and experimental development expenditures; IT-411R: Meaning of "construction".

**Information Circulars**: 78-4R3: Investment tax credit rates.

**Advance Tax Rulings**: ATR-44: Utilization of deductions and credits within a related corporate group.

**Application Policies**: SR&ED 96-03: Claimants' entitlements and responsibilities; SR&ED 96-05: Penalties under subsec. 163(2).

**Forms**: T2 SCH 31: Investment tax credit — corporations; T661 — Claim for SR&ED carried on in Canada; T665: Simplified claim for expenditures incurred in carrying on SR&ED in Canada; T2038 (Ind.): Investment tax credit (individuals); T4088: Claiming scientific research and experimental development expenditures — guide to form T661.

### (6) Investment tax credit of cooperative corporation

— Where at any particular time in a taxation year a taxpayer that is a cooperative corporation within the meaning assigned by subsection 136(2) has, as required by subsection 135(3), deducted or withheld an amount from a payment made by it to any person pursuant to an allocation in proportion to patronage, the taxpayer may deduct from the amount otherwise required by that subsection to be remitted to the Receiver General, an amount, not exceeding the amount, if any, by which

(a) its investment tax credit at the end of the immediately preceding taxation year in respect of property acquired and expenditures made before the end of that preceding taxation year

exceeds the total of

(b) the amount deducted under subsection (5) from its tax otherwise payable under this Part for the immediately preceding taxation year in respect of property acquired and expenditures made before the end of that preceding taxation year, and

(c) the total of all amounts each of which is the amount deducted by virtue of this subsection from any amount otherwise required to be remitted by subsection 135(3) in respect of payments made by it before the particular time and in the taxation year,

and the amount, if any, so deducted from the amount otherwise required to be remitted by subsection 135(3)

(d) shall be deducted in computing the taxpayer's investment tax credit at the end of the taxation year, and

(e) shall be deemed to have been remitted by the taxpayer to the Receiver General on account of tax under this Part of the person to whom that payment was made.

**Related Provisions**: 12(1)(t) — Inclusion in income of ITCs; 13(7.1) — Deemed capital cost; 13(21) "undepreciated capital cost" I — Reduction in u.c.c. to reflect ITCs; 53(2)(k)(ii) — Deduction from ACB of property to reflect ITCs; 66.1(6) "cumulative Canadian exploration expense" L — Reduction in CCEE.

**Interpretation Bulletins**: IT-362R: Patronage dividends.

**Forms**: T2 SCH 31: Investment tax credit — corporations; T2038A: Business investment tax credit (prior to November 17, 1978).

**(7) Investment tax credit of testamentary trust [or communal organization]** — Where, in a particular taxation year of a taxpayer who is a beneficiary under a testamentary trust or under an *inter vivos* trust that is deemed to be in existence by section 143, an amount is determined in respect of the trust under paragraph (a), (a.1), (b) or (e.1) of the definition "investment tax credit" in subsection (9) for its taxation year that ends in that particular taxation year, the trust may, in its return of income for its taxation year that ends in that particular taxation year, designate the portion of that amount that can, having regard to all the circumstances including the terms and conditions of the trust, reasonably be considered to be attributable to the taxpayer and was not designated by the trust in respect of any other beneficiary of the trust, and that portion shall be added in computing the investment tax credit of the taxpayer at the end of that particular taxation year and shall be deducted in computing the investment tax credit of the trust at the end of its taxation year that ends in that particular taxation year.

**Related Provisions**: 53(2)(h)(ii) — Reduction in ACB of interest in trust; 127(11.2) — Time of expenditure and acquisition.

**Notes**: 127(7) amended by 1995 Budget, effective for taxation years that begin after 1995, to add reference to "investment tax credit"(a.1).

**Application Policies**: SR&ED 2000-01: Cost of materials.

**Forms**: T2038 (Ind): Investment tax credit (individuals) for 1984 *et seq.*; T2 SCH 31: Investment tax credit — corporations.

**(8) Investment tax credit of partnership** — Subject to subsection (28), where, in a particular taxation year of a taxpayer who is a member of a partnership, an amount would be determined in respect of the partnership, for its taxation year that ends in the particular year, under paragraph (a), (a.1), (b) or (e.1) of the definition "investment tax credit" in subsection (9), if

(a) except for the purpose of subsection (13), the partnership were a person and its fiscal period were its taxation year, and

(b) in the case of a taxpayer who is a specified member of the partnership in the taxation year of the partnership, that definition were read without reference to paragraph (a.1) thereof, and paragraph (e.1) of that definition were read without reference to subparagraphs (ii) to (iv) thereof,

the portion of that amount that can reasonably be considered to be the taxpayer's share thereof shall be added in computing the investment tax credit of the taxpayer at the end of the particular year.

**Related Provisions**: 53(2)(c)(vi) — Reduction in ACB of partnership interest; 96(2.1)–(2.4) — Limited partnerships; 127(8.1) — ITC of limited partner; 127(8.3) — ITC not allocated to limited partners; 127(8.4) — Election — renunciation of allocated credits; 127(11.2) — Time of expenditure and acquisition; 127(23) — Taxation year of partnership for rules governing allocation of assistance; 127(28) — Recapture of ITC where partnership property converted to commercial use.

**Notes**: For discussion of ITCs and partnerships, see Peter Lee, "Flow-Through of Partnership R&D Tax Credits to Partners", III (4) *Business Vehicles* (Federated Press), 150–153 (1997).

Opening words of 127(8) amended by 1998 Budget to add "Subject to subsection (28)," effective for dispositions and conversions of property that occur after February 23, 1998.

127(8) amended by 1995 Budget, effective for taxation years that begin after 1995. For earlier taxation years that end after December 2, 1992, read:

(8) Where, in a particular taxation year of a taxpayer who is a member of a partnership, an amount would, if the partnership were a person and its fiscal period were its taxation year, be determined in respect of the partnership, for its taxation year ending in that particular taxation year, under paragraph (a), (b) or (e.1) of the definition "investment tax credit" in subsection (9), if

(a) paragraph (a) of that definition were read without reference to subparagraph (a)(iii) thereof, and

(b) in the case of a taxpayer who is a specified member of the partnership in the taxation year of the partnership,

(i) paragraph (a) of that definition were read without reference to subparagraph (a)(ii) thereof, and

(ii) paragraph (e.1) of that definition were read without reference to the words "the amount of an expenditure made by the taxpayer under paragraph (11.1)(c)",

the portion of that amount that may reasonably be considered to be the taxpayer's share thereof shall be added in computing the investment tax credit of the taxpayer at the end of that particular taxation year.

For taxation years that end before December 3, 1992, in respect of expenditures made after December 15, 1987, read as above but, in

127(8)(b)(ii), the words to be ignored in "investment tax credit"(e.1) are "or that reduced the amount of...".

**Forms**: T2038 (Ind): Investment tax credit (individuals) for 1984 *et seq.*; T2 SCH 31: Investment tax credit — corporations.

### (8.1) Investment tax credit of limited partner
— Where a taxpayer is a limited partner of a partnership at the end of the partnership's taxation year, the amount referred to under subsection (8) as the amount which can reasonably be considered to be the taxpayer's share of the amounts that would be determined under paragraph (a), (a.1), (b) or (e.1) of the definition "investment tax credit" in subsection (9) in respect of the partnership for the year shall not exceed the lesser of

(a) such portion of the amount thereof so determined without reference to this subsection, as is considered to have arisen by virtue of the expenditure by the partnership of an amount equal to the taxpayer's expenditure base (as determined under subsection (8.2)) in respect of the partnership at the end of the year, and

(b) the taxpayer's at-risk amount in respect of the partnership at the end of the year.

**Related Provisions**: 96(2.2) — At-risk amount; 96(2.4) — Limited partner; 127(8.2) — Expenditure base; 127(8.3) — ITC not allocated to limited partners; 127(8.5) — "At-risk amount", "limited partner".

**Notes**: 127(8.1) amended by 1995 Budget, effective for taxation years that begin after 1995, to add reference to "investment tax credit"(a.1).

### (8.2) Expenditure base
— For the purposes of subsection (8.1), a taxpayer's expenditure base in respect of a partnership at the end of a taxation year of the partnership is the lesser of

(a) the amount, if any, by which the total of

(i) the taxpayer's at-risk amount in respect of the partnership at the time the taxpayer last became a limited partner of the partnership,

(ii) all amounts described in subparagraph 53(1)(e)(iv) contributed by the taxpayer after the time the taxpayer last became a limited partner of the partnership and before the end of the taxation year that may reasonably be considered to have increased the taxpayer's at-risk amount in respect of the partnership at the end of the taxation year in which the contribution was made, and

(iii) the amount, if any, by which

(A) the total of all amounts each of which is the taxpayer's share of any income of the partnership as determined under paragraph 96(1)(f) for the year, or a preceding year ending after the time the taxpayer last became a limited partner of the partnership,

exceeds

(B) the total of all amounts each of which is the taxpayer's share of any loss of the partnership as determined under paragraph 96(1)(g) for one of those years

exceeds the total of

(iv) all amounts received by the taxpayer after the time the taxpayer last became a limited partner of the partnership and before the end of the year as, on account or in lieu of payment of, or in satisfaction of, a distribution of the taxpayer's share of partnership profits or partnership capital, and

(v) the total of all amounts each of which is the amount of an expenditure of the partnership referred to in paragraph (8.1)(a) in respect of the taxpayer for a preceding year, and

(b) that proportion of the lesser of

(i) the total of all amounts each of which is, if the partnership were a person and its fiscal period were its taxation year,

(A) an amount a specified percentage of which would be determined in respect of the partnership under paragraph (a), (b) or (e.1) of the definition "investment tax credit" in subsection (9) for the year, or

(B) the amount that would be the SR&ED qualified expenditure pool of the partnership at the end of the year, and

(ii) the total of all amounts each of which is the amount determined under paragraph (a) in respect of each of the limited partners of the partnership at the end of the year

that

(iii) the amount determined in respect of the taxpayer under paragraph (a) for the year

is of

(iv) the amount determined under subparagraph (ii).

**Related Provisions**: 96(2.2) — At-risk amount; 96(2.4) — Limited partner; 127(8.5) — "At-risk amount", "limited partner".

**Notes**: 127(8.2)(b)(i) amended by 1995 Budget, effective for taxation years that begin after 1995. For earlier taxation years, since February 26, 1986, read:

(i) the total of all amounts each of which is an amount a specified percentage of which would, if the partnership were a person and its fiscal period were its taxation year, be determined in respect of the partnership under paragraph (a), (b) or (e.1) of the definition "investment tax credit" in subsection (9), if paragraph (a) of that definition were read without reference to subparagraph (a)(iii) thereof, for the taxation year, and

### (8.3) Investment tax credit not allocated to limited partners
— Where

(a) the amount that would, if the partnership were a person and its fiscal period were its taxation year, be determined in respect of the partnership under paragraph (a), (a.1), (b) or (e.1) of the definition "investment tax credit" in subsection (9) for a taxation year

**S. 127(8.3)**      Income Tax Act, Part I, Division E

exceeds

    (b) the total of all amounts each of which is the amount determined, under subsections (8) and (8.1), to be the share thereof of a limited partner of the partnership,

such portion of the excess as is reasonable in the circumstances (having regard to the investment in the partnership, including debt obligations of the partnership, of each of those members of the partnership who was a member of the partnership throughout the fiscal period of the partnership and who was not a limited partner of the partnership during the fiscal period of the partnership) shall, for the purposes of subsection (8), be considered to be the amount that may reasonably be considered to be that member's share of the amount described in paragraph (a).

**Related Provisions**: 96(2.2) — At-risk amount; 96(2.4) — Limited partner; 127(8) — Election — renunciation of allocated credits; 127(8.4) — Election; 127(8.5) — "At-risk amount", "limited partner".

**Notes**: 127(8.3)(a) amended by 1995 Budget, effective for taxation years that begin after 1995, to add reference to para. (a.1) of the definition of "investment tax credit".

**(8.4) Idem** — Notwithstanding subsection (8), where, pursuant to subsections (8) and (8.3) an amount would, but for this subsection, be required to be added in computing the investment tax credit of a taxpayer for a taxation year, where the taxpayer so elects in prescribed form and manner in the taxpayer's return of income (other than a return of income filed under subsection 70(2) or 104(23), paragraph 128(2)(e) or subsection 150(4)) under this Part for the year, such portion of the amount as is elected by the taxpayer shall, for the purposes of this section, be deemed not to have been required by subsection (8) to have been added in computing the taxpayer's investment tax credit at the end of the year.

**Related Provisions**: 96(2.2) — At-risk amount; 96(2.4) — Limited partner; 127(8.5) — "At-risk amount", "limited partner".

**Forms**: T932: Election by a member of a partnership to renounce investment tax credits pursuant to subsection 127(8.4).

**(8.5) Definitions** — In subsections (8.1) to (8.4), the words "at-risk amount" of a taxpayer and "limited partner" of a partnership have the meanings assigned to those words by subsections 96(2.2) and (2.4), respectively.

**(9) Idem** — In this section,

**Notes**: The opening words of 127(9) applied to s. 127.1 as well before R.S.C. 1985 (5th Supp.) consolidation, effective for taxation years ending after November 1991. That rule of application is now in 127.1(2.1).

**"annual investment tax credit limit"** — [Repealed]

**Notes**: Definition "annual investment tax credit limit" repealed by 1993 Budget, effective for taxation years that begin in 1994 or later.

There is now no limit on the extent to which ITCs can soak up tax payable. See Notes to 127(5). For earlier years, read:

"annual investment tax credit limit" of a taxpayer for a taxation year means

    (a) in the case of a corporation, the total of

        (i) $3/4$ of the corporation's tax otherwise payable under this Part for the year, and

        (ii) where the corporation is a Canadian-controlled private corporation throughout the year, 3% of the least of the amounts determined under paragraphs 125(1)(a) to (c) in respect of the corporation for the year, and

    (b) in any other case, the total of

        (i) $24,000, and

        (ii) $3/4$ of the amount, if any, by which the taxpayer's tax otherwise payable under this Part for the year exceeds $24,000;

**"approved project"** means a project with a total capital cost of depreciable property, determined without reference to subsection 13(7.1) or (7.4), of not less than $25,000 that has, on application in writing before July, 1988, been approved by such member of the Queen's Privy Council for Canada as is designated by the Governor in Council for the purposes of this definition in relation to projects in the appropriate province or region of a province;

**Notes**: 127(9)"approved project" amended in 1990, effective February 23, 1990, to replace "the Minister of Regional Industrial Expansion" with "such member of the Queen's Privy Council for Canada as is designated by the Governor in Council for the purposes of this definition in relation to projects in the appropriate province or region of a province".

**"approved project property"** — [Repealed]

**Notes**: Definition "approved project property" repealed by 1995 Budget, effective for taxation years that begin after 1995, since it is no longer relevant. For earlier years since February 23, 1990, read:

"approved project property" of a taxpayer means property that is certified by the member of the Queen's Privy Council for Canada appointed to be the Minister for the purposes of the *Atlantic Canada Opportunities Agency Act* to be property that has not been used, or acquired for use or lease, for any purpose whatever before it was acquired by the taxpayer, and to be

    (a) a prescribed building, to the extent that it is acquired by the taxpayer after May 23, 1985 and before 1993, or

    (b) prescribed machinery and equipment acquired by the taxpayer after May 23, 1985 and before 1993,

that has been acquired pursuant to a plan by the taxpayer to use the property in Cape Breton primarily for an approved purpose in an approved project or, in the case of a prescribed building, to be leased by the taxpayer to a lessee (other than a person exempt from tax under this Part by virtue of section 149) who can reasonably be expected to use the building pursuant to a plan to use it in Cape Breton primarily for an approved purpose in an approved project, or

    (c) part of a prescribed building to the extent that the part is acquired by the taxpayer after May 23, 1985 and before 1993 to be

        (i) used by the taxpayer, or

        (ii) leased by the taxpayer to a lessee (other than a person exempt from tax under this Part by virtue of section 149) who can reasonably be expected to use that part pursuant to a plan to use that part in Cape Breton primarily for an approved purpose in an approved project, or

(d) where the taxpayer is a leasing corporation, prescribed machinery and equipment acquired by the taxpayer after May 23, 1985 and before 1993, to be leased by the taxpayer in the ordinary course of carrying on a business in Canada to a lessee (other than a person exempt from tax under this Part by virtue of section 149) who can reasonably be expected to use the property in Cape Breton primarily for an approved purpose in an approved project, but this paragraph only applies if the first lessee of the property commenced use of the property after May 23, 1985,

and for the purposes of this definition,

(e) "for an approved purpose" means for the purpose of

(i) any of the activities described in subparagraphs (c)(i) to (ix), (xi) and (xii) of the definition "qualified property" in this subsection,

(ii) farming, or

(iii) a prescribed activity, and

(f) "leasing corporation" means a corporation the principal business of which is leasing property, manufacturing property that it sells or leases, the lending of money, the purchasing of conditional sales contracts, accounts receivable, bills of sale, chattel mortgages, bills of exchange or other obligations representing part or all of the sale price of merchandise or services, or selling or servicing a type of property that it also leases, or any combination thereof;

**Regulations**: 4604(1) (prescribed building); 4604(2) (prescribed machinery and equipment); 4605 (prescribed activity).

**"Cape Breton"** means Cape Breton Island and that portion of the Province of Nova Scotia within the following described boundary:

beginning at a point on the southwesterly shore of Chedabucto Bay near Red Head, said point being S 70 degrees E (Nova Scotia grid meridian) from Geodetic Station Sand, thence in a southwesterly direction to a point on the northwesterly boundary of highway 344, said point being southwesterly 240' from the intersection of King Brook with said highway boundary, thence northwesterly to Crown post 6678, thence continuing northwesterly to Crown post 6679, thence continuing northwesterly to Crown post 6680, thence continuing northwesterly to Crown post 6681, thence continuing northwesterly to Crown post 6632, thence continuing northwesterly to Crown post 6602, thence northerly to Crown post 8575; thence northerly to Crown post 6599, thence continuing northerly to Crown post 6600, thence northwesterly to the southwest angle of the Town of Mulgrave, thence along the westerly boundary of the Town of Mulgrave and a prolongation thereof northerly to the Antigonish-Guysborough county line, thence along said county line northeasterly to the southwesterly shore of the Strait of Canso, thence following the southwesterly shore of the Strait of Canso and the northwesterly shore of Chedabucto Bay southeasterly to the place of beginning;

**"certified property"** of a taxpayer means any property (other than an approved project property) described in paragraph (a) or (b) of the definition "qualified property" in this subsection

(a) that was acquired by the taxpayer

(i) after October 28, 1980 and

(A) before 1987, or

(B) before 1988 where the property is

(I) a building under construction before 1987, or

(II) machinery and equipment ordered in writing by the taxpayer before 1987,

(ii) after 1986 and before 1989, other than a property included in subparagraph (i),

(iii) after 1988 and before 1995,

(iv) after 1994 and before 1996 where

(A) the property is acquired by the taxpayer for use in a project that was substantially advanced by or on behalf of the taxpayer, as evidenced in writing, before February 22, 1994, and

(B) construction of the project by or on behalf of the taxpayer begins before 1995, or

(v) after 1994 where the property

(A) is acquired by the taxpayer under a written agreement of purchase and sale entered into by the taxpayer before February 22, 1994,

(B) was under construction by or on behalf of the taxpayer on February 22, 1994, or

(C) is machinery or equipment that will be a fixed and integral part of property under construction by or on behalf of the taxpayer on February 22, 1994,

and that has not been used, or acquired for use or lease, for any purpose whatever before it was acquired by the taxpayer, and

(b) that is part of a facility as defined for the purposes of the *Regional Development Incentives Act*, chapter R-3 of the Revised Statutes of Canada, 1970, and was acquired primarily for use by the taxpayer in a prescribed area;

**Notes**: Subpara. (a)(iii) amended to add "and before 1995", and subparas. (a)(iv) and (v) added, by 1994 Budget, effective for property acquired and expenditures incurred after 1994.

**Regulations**: 4602 (prescribed area).

**"contract payment"** means

(a) an amount paid or payable to a taxpayer, by a taxable supplier in respect of the amount, for scientific research and experimental development to the extent that it is performed

(i) for or on behalf of a person or partnership entitled to a deduction in respect of the amount because of subparagraph 37(1)(a)(i) or (i.1), and

(ii) at a time when the taxpayer is dealing at arm's length with the person or partnership, or

(b) an amount, other than a prescribed amount, payable by a Canadian government or municipality or other Canadian public authority or by a person exempt, because of section 149, from tax under this Part on all or part of the person's taxable income for scientific research and experimental development to be performed for it or on its behalf;

**Related Provisions**: 127(18)–(22) — Reduction of qualified expenditures to reflect contract payment; 127(25) — Anti-avoidance — deemed contract payment.

**Notes**: Para. (a) of "contract payment" amended by 1995 Budget, effective for taxation years that begin after 1995 (subject to rule reproduced in Notes to 127(9)"qualified expenditure"). For earlier taxation years for amounts that became payable after December 20, 1991, read:

(a) an amount payable for scientific research and experimental development to the extent that it can reasonably be considered to have been performed for, or on behalf of, a person entitled to a deduction in respect of the amount because of subparagraph 37(1)(a)(i) or clause 37(1)(a)(ii)(D), or

Para. (a) of "contract payment" amended and para. (c) repealed by 1992 technical bill, effective for amounts that became payable after December 20, 1991. For earlier amounts, read:

(a) an amount payable by a person resident in Canada for scientific research and experimental development related to the business of that person,

. . . . .

(c) an amount payable by a person not resident in Canada if that person is entitled to a deduction under clause 37(1)(a)(ii)(D) in respect of the amount;

**Regulations**: 4606 (prescribed amount).

**Interpretation Bulletins**: IT-151R5: Scientific research and experimental development expenditures.

**Application Policies**: SR&ED 94-04: Definition of "contract payment" in subsec. 127(9).

**"designated region"** — [Repealed under former Act]

**Notes**: See prescribed designated region in the definition of "specified percentage" in this subsection and in Reg. 4607.

**"eligible taxpayer"** means

(a) a corporation other than a non-qualifying corporation,

(b) an individual other than a trust,

(c) a trust all the beneficiaries of which are eligible taxpayers, and

(d) a partnership all the members of which are eligible taxpayers,

and, for the purpose of this definition, a beneficiary of a trust is a person or partnership that is beneficially interested in the trust;

**Related Provisions**: 248(25) — Meaning of "beneficially interested".

**Notes**: Definition "eligible taxpayer" added by 1992 Economic Statement, effective for property acquired after December 2, 1992. It describes the entities eligible to earn the 10% small business investment tax credit from December 3, 1992 through the end of 1993 (see 127(9)"qualified small-business property").

**"first term shared-use-equipment"** of a taxpayer means depreciable property of the taxpayer (other than prescribed depreciable property of a taxpayer) that is used by the taxpayer, during its operating time in the period (in this subsection and subsection (11.1) referred to as the "first period") beginning at the time the property was acquired by the taxpayer and ending at the end of the taxpayer's first taxation year ending at least 12 months after that time, primarily for the prosecution of scientific research and experimental development in Canada, but does not include general purpose office equipment or furniture;

**Related Provisions**: 88(1)(e.3) closing words — Winding-up — parent deemed continuation of subsidiary; 127(11.5)(b) — Adjustments to qualified expenditures.

**Notes**: Definition "first term shared-use-equipment" added by 1992 Economic Statement, effective for property acquired after December 2, 1992. See 127(11.1)(e).

**Regulations**: 2900(9) (prescribed depreciable property).

### Proposed Addition — 127(9) "flow-through mining expenditure"

**"flow-through mining expenditure"** of a taxpayer for a taxation year means an expense deemed by subsection 66(12.61) (or by subsection 66(18) as a consequence of the application of subsection 66(12.61) to the partnership, referred to in paragraph (c) of this definition, of which the taxpayer is a member) to be incurred by the taxpayer in the year

(a) that is a Canadian exploration expense incurred after October 17, 2000 and before 2004 by a corporation in conducting mining exploration activity from or above the surface of the earth for the purpose of determining the existence or location of a mineral resource described in paragraph (a) or (d) of the definition "mineral resource" in subsection 248(1),

(b) that would be described in paragraph (f) of the definition "Canadian exploration expense" in subsection 66.1(6) if that paragraph were read to exclude expenses in respect of digging test pits and preliminary sampling,

(c) an amount in respect of which is renounced in accordance with subsection 66(12.6) by the corporation to the taxpayer or a partnership of which the taxpayer is a member) under an agreement described in that subsection and made after October 17, 2000,

(d) that is not an expense that was renounced under subsection 66(12.6) to the corporation (or a partnership of which the corporation is a member), unless that renunciation was under an agreement described in that subsection and made after October 17, 2000, and

(e) that is an expense that would be incurred by the corporation before 2004 if this Act were read without reference to subsection 66(12.66);

## Subdivision c — Computation of Tax: All Taxpayers          S. 127(9)

**Application**: The December 21, 2000 draft legislation, subsec. 73(6), will add the definition "flow-through mining expenditure" to subsec. 127(9), applicable after October 17, 2000.

**Technical Notes**: The term "flow-through mining expenditure" is added to subsection 127(9) to define an expenditure that qualifies for the 15% investment tax credit, available to a taxpayer who is an individual (other than a trust), as provided for in new paragraph (a.2) of the definition "investment tax credit" in subsection 127(9). See the commentary on the definition "investment tax credit" for further details.

A flow-through mining expenditure of a taxpayer for a taxation year generally means an expense that is considered by the Act to have been incurred by the taxpayer in the year as a result of a renunciation by a corporation under an agreement for the issue of a flow-through share (this expense being referred to in this commentary as an "investor mining expense") and that meets certain additional conditions set out in paragraphs (a) to (e) of the definition "flow-through mining expenditure".

The term "flow-through share" is defined in subsection 66(15). A flow-through share is generally a share of the capital stock of a principal-business corporation that is issued to a person pursuant to an agreement in writing under which the corporation agrees to incur resource expenses and to renounce those expenses to that person. The term "principal-business corporation" is also defined for these purposes in subsection 66(15). A principal-business corporation for these purposes is generally a corporation the principal business of which is exploration and development of minerals or other resources. Subsection 66(12.6) permits such a principal-business corporation to renounce its Canadian exploration expenses (CEE) to its flow-through shareholders. In general, where a corporation renounces CEE to a shareholder under subsection 66(12.6), the shareholder is deemed by subsection 66(12.61) to have incurred CEE on the effective date of the renunciation.

In some cases, the agreement for the issue of the flow-through share is between the renouncing corporation and a partnership. Paragraph (h) of the definition "Canadian exploration expense" in subsection 66.1(6) provides, in general, that the taxpayer's share of any CEE actually incurred (or deemed incurred) in a fiscal period by a partnership is considered to be CEE of the taxpayer, if at the end of that fiscal period the taxpayer is a member of the partnership. Under subsection 66(18), the taxpayer's CEE is deemed to have been incurred at the end of that fiscal period.

An investor mining expense incurred by a taxpayer in a taxation year is an expense deemed incurred by a taxpayer in the year because of

- subsection 66(12.61)

  (i.e., the case where the agreement for the issue of the flow-through share is between the renouncing corporation and the taxpayer)

or

- subsection 66(18) as a consequence of the application of subsection 66(12.61) to the partnership of which the taxpayer is a member

  (i.e., the case where the agreement for the issue of the flow-through share is between the renouncing corporation and a partnership of which the taxpayer is a member).

An investor mining expense incurred by a taxpayer in a taxation year is a "flow-through mining expenditure" of a taxpayer for the year if the expense meets the requirements set out in paragraphs (a) to (e) of the definition "flow-through mining expenditure" and discussed below.

Paragraph (a) of the definition "flow-through mining expenditure" requires that the expense be a CEE incurred after October 17, 2000 and before 2004 by a corporation in conducting mining exploration activity from or above the surface of the earth for the purpose of determining the existence or location of a mineral resource described in paragraph (a) or (d) of the definition "mineral resource" in subsection 248(1).

Paragraph (b) of the definition "flow-through mining expenditure" requires that the expense be an expense that would be described in paragraph (f) of the definition "Canadian exploration expense" in subsection 66.1(6) if that paragraph were read to exclude expenses in respect of digging test pits and preliminary sampling.

Paragraph (c) of the definition "flow-through mining expenditure" requires that the agreement described in subsection 66(12.6) between the renouncing corporation and the flow-through shareholder be made after October 17, 2000.

Paragraph (d) of the definition "flow-through mining expenditure" contemplates the possibility that expenses renounced by the corporation to the taxpayer (or to a partnership of which the taxpayer is a member) were not actually incurred by the corporation. This is possible where expenses are deemed to have been incurred by the corporation as a result of a renunciation by another corporation under subsection 66(12.6) (referred to in this commentary as the "prior renunciation") to the corporation. Paragraph (d) requires that in these cases the prior renunciation be made under an agreement that is described in subsection 66(12.6) and is made between the corporations after October 17, 2000.

Paragraph (e) of the definition "flow-through mining expenditure" contemplates the effect of subsection 66(12.66) on the timing of expenses. As described above, paragraph (a) requires that the expense be incurred by the corporation before 2004. Subsection 66(12.66) deals with certain types of resource expenses and generally allows a corporation to renounce, effective on the last day of the preceding calendar year, resource expenses that the corporation intends to incur in the current calendar year. In the absence of paragraph (e), expenses incurred by the corporation in 2004 and deemed by subsection 66(12.66) to have been incurred by the corporation in 2003 might otherwise meet the pre-2004 test in paragraph (a). Accordingly, paragraph (e) requires that the expense be an expense that would be incurred by the corporation before 2004 if the Act were read without reference to subsection 66(12.66).

**Related Provisions**: 127(9)"investment tax credit"(a.2) — 15% credit for expenditure; 127(11.1)(c.2) — Reduction for assistance received.

### Proposed Further Amendment — "flow-through mining expenditure"

**Department of Finance news release Backgrounder, December 21, 2000**: *Flow-Through Share Investment Tax Credit*

The Department of Finance has received submissions from the public relating to the category of expenses eligible for the 15% flow-through share investment tax credit announced in the October 2000 Economic Statement and Budget Update.

In response to submissions received, the Government intends to broaden the category of expenses falling within the definition "flow-through mining expenditure" in the following two ways:

- allow, in addition to expenses incurred in determining the "existence" or "location" of a mineral resource, expenses incurred in determining the "extent" or "quality" of the mineral resource; and
- include, in addition to expenses that are described in subparagraph 16(d) of the Notice of Ways and Means Motion in the October Economic Statement and Budget Update, expenses that are described in paragraph (f) of the definition "Canadian exploration expense" in subsection 66.1(6) of the *Income Tax Act* and that are in respect of specified sampling (or in respect of digging test pits for the purpose of carrying out specified sampling).

For this purpose, it is proposed that "specified sampling" be the collecting and testing of samples in respect of a mineral resource to the extent that

- the weight of each sample collected does not exceed 15 tonnes; and
- the total weight of all samples (other than samples that are less than one tonne in weight) collected in respect of any one mineral resource in a calendar year by any person or partnership or any combination of persons and partnerships does not exceed 1,000 tonnes.

The Government intends to include these changes in the Bill that is to be introduced in the House of Commons in early 2001 [expected in March — ed.].

**Notice of Ways and Means Motion, Economic Statement, October 18, 2000**: *Flow-Through Shares*

(16) That the definition "investment tax credit" in subsection 127(9) of the Act be amended to provide a 15% non-refundable investment tax credit to an individual (other than a trust) for expenses

(a) incurred by a corporation after October 17, 2000 and before 2004,

(b) renounced in favour of the individual (directly, or indirectly through a partnership of which the individual is a member) pursuant to a flow-through share agreement made after October 17, 2000,

(c) incurred in conducting mining exploration activity from or above the surface of the earth for the purpose of determining the existence or location of a mineral resource described in paragraph (a) or (d) of the definition "mineral resource" in subsection 248(1) of the Act, and

(d) that would be described in paragraph (f) of the definition "Canadian exploration expense" in subsection 66.1(6) of the Act, if that paragraph were read without the words "digging test pits and preliminary sampling" in subparagraph (iv) thereof,

and that the individual's cumulative Canadian exploration expense at any time in a taxation year be reduced by the amount of this credit claimed for a preceding taxation year.

**Supplementary Information, Economic Statement, October 18, 2000**: *Federal Tax Credit for Flow-Through Share Investors*

Mineral exploration activity in Canada has been low in recent years and the modest recovery in mineral prices has yet to make any significant impact. Rural communities across Canada that depend on mining have been hard hit. To promote mineral exploration activity, several rural communities along with some provincial governments and industry associations have requested that a temporary additional tax incentive be provided for certain flow-through share investments. This incentive would be focused on those exploration activities most likely to find new deposits in Canada. The recent Federal-Provincial Mines Ministers Conference also encouraged the federal government to increase the existing tax assistance for flow-through share investments. As a result, the federal government proposes to introduce a new temporary investment tax credit for mineral exploration. Provincial governments are encouraged to build on this federal initiative by offering similar provincial tax credits.

This federal tax credit will be available to individuals (other than trusts) at the rate of 15% of specified surface "grass roots" mineral exploration expenses incurred in Canada pursuant to a flow-through share agreement. This new credit will apply to specified expenses incurred by an individual pursuant to a flow-through share agreement made after October 17, 2000, in respect of expenses incurred by the corporation after that day and before 2004. This non-refundable credit will reduce the cumulative Canadian exploration expense pool for years following the year in which it is claimed.

The Government will continue to review the definition of eligible expenses and other technical issues related to flow-through shares. In addition, discussions have already begun with the industry in response to concerns identified by the House of Commons Standing Committee on Industry.

"**Gaspé Peninsula**" means that portion of the Gaspé region of the Province of Quebec that extends to the western border of Kamouraska County and includes the Magdalen Islands;

"**government assistance**" means assistance from a government, municipality or other public authority whether as a grant, subsidy, forgivable loan, deduction from tax, investment allowance or as any other form of assistance other than as a deduction under subsection (5) or (6);

**Related Provisions**: 248(16)–(18) — GST input tax credits deemed to be government assistance.

"**investment tax credit**" of a taxpayer at the end of a taxation year means the amount, if any, by which the total of

(a) the total of all amounts each of which is the specified percentage of the capital cost to the taxpayer of certified property or qualified property acquired by the taxpayer in the year,

(a.1) 20% of the taxpayer's SR&ED qualified expenditure pool at the end of the year,

**Proposed Amendment — 127(9)"investment tax credit"(a.1), (a.2)**

(a.1) 20% of the amount by which the taxpayer's SR&ED qualified expenditure pool at the end of the year exceeds the total of all amounts each of which is the super-allowance benefit amount for the year in respect of the taxpayer in respect of a province,

(a.2) where the taxpayer is an individual (other than a trust), 15% of the taxpayer's flow-through mining expenditures for the year,

**Application**: The December 21, 2000 draft legislation, subsec. 73(4), will amend para. (a.1) to read as above and add para. (a.2) to the definition "investment tax credit" in subsec. 127(9). Para. (a.1) is applicable to taxation years that begin after February 2000 except that, if a corporation's first taxation year that begins after February 2000 ends before 2001, it is applicable to the corporation's taxation years that begin after 2000. Para. (a.2) is applicable after October 17, 2000.

**Technical Notes**: Paragraph (a.1) of the definition "investment tax credit" in subsection 127(9) is amended to require taxpayers to reduce the base on which the investment tax credit (ITC) is computed. Existing paragraph (a.1) of the definition requires the inclusion of 20% of the taxpayer's scientific research and experimental development (SR&ED) qualified expenditure pool for a year in the taxpayer's ITC. New paragraph (a.1) of the definition requires the inclusion of 20% of the amount by which a corporation's SR&ED qualified expenditure pool for a year exceeds the corporation's super-allowance benefit amount for each province to which it applies. See the commentary below on the new definition "super-allowance benefit amount" [in 127(9) — ed.].

The amendment to paragraph (a.1) of the definition "investment tax credit" applies to taxation years that begin after February 2000 except that, for corporations whose first taxation year that begins after February 2000 ends before 2001, the amendment applies to taxation years that begin after 2000.

New paragraph (a.2) of the definition provides that, where the taxpayer is an individual (other than a trust), 15% of the taxpayer's flow-through mining expenditures at the end of a taxation year is added to the taxpayer's ITC at the end of the year. (The new expression "flow-through mining expenditure" is added to the definitions in subsection 127(9). See the commentary on subsection 127(9) for further details.)

Paragraph (c) of the definition of "investment tax credit" provides for a three-year carryback and ten-year carryforward of unused ITCs in respect of which an amount is determined under paragraph (a), (a.1) or (b) of that definition. Paragraph (c) of the definition is amended to add a reference to new paragraph (a.2) to ensure that amounts determined in respect of paragraph (a.2) have the same carryover period.

(b) the total of amounts required by subsection (7) or (8) to be added in computing the taxpayer's investment tax credit at the end of the year,

(c) the total of all amounts each of which is an amount determined under paragraph (a), (a.1) or (b) in respect of the taxpayer for any of the 10 taxation years immediately preceding or the 3 taxation years immediately following the year,

> **Proposed Amendment — 127(9)"investment tax credit"(c)**
>
> (c) the total of all amounts each of which is an amount determined under paragraph (a), (a.1), (a.2) or (b) in respect of the taxpayer for any of the 10 taxation years immediately preceding or the 3 taxation years immediately following the year,
>
> **Application**: The December 21, 2000 draft legislation, subsec. 73(5), will amend para. (c) of the definition "investment tax credit" in subsec. 127(9), applicable after October 17, 2000.
>
> **Technical Notes**: See under 127(9)"investment tax credit"(a.1), (a.2) above.

(d) the total of all amounts each of which is an amount required by subsection 119(9) to be added in computing the taxpayer's investment tax credit at the end of the year or at the end of any of the 10 taxation years immediately preceding the year,

(e) the total of all amounts each of which is an amount required by subsection (10.1) to be added in computing the taxpayer's investment tax credit at the end of the year or at the end of any of the 10 taxation years immediately preceding or the 3 taxation years immediately following the year,

(e.1) the total of all amounts each of which is the specified percentage of that part of a repayment made by the taxpayer in the year or in any of the 10 taxation years immediately preceding or the 3 taxation years immediately following the year that can reasonably be considered to be a repayment of government assistance, non-government assistance or a contract payment that reduced

(i) the capital cost to the taxpayer of a property under paragraph (11.1)(b),

(ii) the amount of a qualified expenditure incurred by the taxpayer under paragraph (11.1)(c) for taxation years that began before 1996,

(iii) the prescribed proxy amount of the taxpayer under paragraph (11.1)(f) for taxation years that began before 1996, or

(iv) a qualified expenditure incurred by the taxpayer under any of subsections (18) to (20), and

(e.2) the total of all amounts each of which is the specified percentage of ¼ of that part of a repayment made by the taxpayer in the year or in any of the 10 taxation years immediately preceding or the 3 taxation years immediately following the year that can reasonably be considered to be a repayment of government assistance, non-government assistance or a contract payment that reduced

(i) the amount of a qualified expenditure incurred by the taxpayer under paragraph (11.1)(e) for taxation years that began before 1996, or

(ii) a qualified expenditure incurred by the taxpayer under any of subsections (18) to (20),

in respect of first term shared-use-equipment or second term shared-use-equipment, and, for that purpose, a repayment made by the taxpayer in any taxation year preceding the first taxation year that ends coincidentally with the first period or the second period in respect of first term shared-use-equipment or second term shared-use-equipment, respectively, is deemed to have been incurred by the taxpayer in that first taxation year,

exceeds the total of

(f) the total of all amounts each of which is an amount deducted under subsection (5) from the tax otherwise payable under this Part by the taxpayer for a preceding taxation year in respect of property acquired, or an expenditure incurred, in the year or in any of the 10 taxation years immediately preceding or the 2 taxation years immediately following the year, or in respect of the taxpayer's SR&ED qualified expenditure pool at the end of such a year,

(g) the total of all amounts each of which is an amount required by subsection (6) to be deducted in computing the taxpayer's investment tax credit

(i) at the end of the year, or

(ii) [Repealed]

(iii) at the end of any of the 9 taxation years immediately preceding or the 3 taxation years immediately following the year,

(h) the total of all amounts each of which is an amount required by subsection (7) to be deducted in computing the taxpayer's investment tax credit

(i) at the end of the year, or

(ii) [Repealed]

(iii) at the end of any of the 10 taxation years immediately preceding or the 3 taxation years immediately following the year,

(i) the total of all amounts each of which is an amount claimed under subparagraph 192(2)(a)(ii) by the taxpayer for the year or a preceding taxation year in respect of property acquired, or an expenditure made, in the year or the 10 taxation years immediately preceding the year,

(j) where the taxpayer is a corporation control of which has been acquired by a person or group of persons at any time before the end of the year, the amount determined under subsection (9.1) in respect of the taxpayer, and

(k) where the taxpayer is a corporation control of which has been acquired by a person or group of persons at any time after the end of the year, the amount determined under subsection (9.2) in respect of the taxpayer,

except that no amount shall be included in the total determined under any of paragraphs (a) to (e.2) in respect of an outlay, expense or expenditure that would, if this Act were read without reference to subsections (26) and 78(4), be made or incurred by the taxpayer in the course of earning income in a particular taxation year, and no amount shall be added under paragraph (b) in computing the taxpayer's investment tax credit at the end of a particular taxation year in respect of an outlay, expense or expenditure made or incurred by a trust or a partnership in the course of earning income, if

(l) any of the income is exempt income, or

**Proposed Amendment — 127(9) "investment tax credit" (l)**

(l) any of the income is exempt income or is exempt from tax under this Part,

**Application**: Bill C-43 (First Reading September 20, 2000), s. 75, will amend para. (l) of the definition "investment tax credit" in subsec. 127(9) to read as above, applicable to all taxation years.

**Technical Notes**: Subsection 127(9) of the Act provides definitions that are used in the provisions relating to the investment tax credit ("ITC").

The definition "investment tax credit" was amended by S.C. 1998, c. 19, ss. 33(1) [formerly Bill C-28] to exclude expenditures in respect of which a taxpayer has not filed a prescribed form with Revenue Canada within one year after the taxpayer's filing-due date for the taxation year in which the expenditure was incurred. That amendment, which applied to all taxation years, incorrectly replaced the reference to "income exempt from tax under this Part" in the former "post-amble" to the definition "investment tax credit" with the concept "exempt income". The phrase "income exempt from tax under this Part" excluded from the definition of "investment tax credit" amounts incurred by a person whose taxable income is exempt from tax, as well as income that is exempt income for the purpose of calculating income under section 3 of the Act. Paragraph (l) of the definition "investment tax credit" is amended to correct this oversight, applicable to all taxation years.

(m) the taxpayer does not file with the Minister a prescribed form containing prescribed information in respect of the amount on or before the day that is one year after the taxpayer's filing-due date for the particular year;

**Related Provisions**: 37(11) — Filing deadline for R&D claims; 66(10.1)(b) — Joint exploration corporation; 87(2)(qq) — Amalgamations — continuation of corporation; 87(2.11) — Vertical amalgamations; 88(1)(e.3) — Flow-through of ITC to parent on wind-up of corporation; 127(7) — ITC of testamentary trust; 127(8) — ITC of partnership; 127(9.1) — Where control acquired before end of year; 127(9.2) — Where control acquired after beginning of year; 127(10.1) — Addition to ITC for SR&ED done by CCPC; 127(10.8) — Regeneration of ITCs where entitlement to assistance expires; 127(11.1), (11.2) — ITC calculation rules; 127(26) — Expenditure unpaid within 180 days of end of year; 127(27), (29) — Reduction of ITC where property converted to commercial use; 127(28) — Recapture of negative ITC; 127.1(2), (2.01) — Refundable investment tax credit; 139.1(18) — Holding corporation deemed not to acquire control of insurer on demutualization; 149(10)(c) — Where corporation becomes or ceases to be exempt; 248(1) "investment tax credit" — Definition applies to entire Act; 256(6)–(9) — Whether control acquired (for paras. (j), (k)).

## Subdivision c — Computation of Tax: All Taxpayers — S. 127(9) inv

**Notes**: See Notes to "specified percentage" below.

Ignoring the special cases, the ITC is (a) the specified percentage of the cost of qualified property, plus (a.1) 20% of R&D expenditures (but see also 127(10.1)), plus (a.2) 15% of flow-through mining expenditures, plus ITCs of other years (10 before, 3 after), minus (f) those ITCs of other years that were claimed in those other years.

Former closing words of "investment tax credit" replaced with new words and new paras. (l) and (m) by 1997 Budget, effective for all taxation years except that, where the taxpayer's filing-due date (as defined in 248(1) but applicable to all years) is before June 1996, the taxpayer could file the prescribed form under para. (m) until May 31, 1997. The closing words previously read:

> except that no amount shall be included in the total determined under any of paragraphs (a) to (e.2) in respect of any qualified expenditure incurred by the taxpayer in the course of earning income from a business, or in respect of any certified property or qualified property acquired by the taxpayer for use in the course of earning income from a business, if any of the income from that business is exempt from tax under this Part;

Definition "investment tax credit" amended by 1995 Budget, effective for taxation years that begin after 1995. For earlier years, read:

"investment tax credit" of a taxpayer at the end of a taxation year means the amount, if any, by which the total of

(a) the total of all amounts each of which is the specified percentage of

(i) the capital cost to the taxpayer of approved project property, certified property, qualified construction equipment, qualified property, qualified small-business property or qualified transportation equipment acquired by the taxpayer in the year,

(ii) a qualified expenditure made by the taxpayer in the year, or

(iii) the taxpayer's qualified Canadian exploration expenditure for the year,

(b) the total of amounts required by subsection (7) or (8) to be added in computing the taxpayer's investment tax credit at the end of the year,

(c) the total of all amounts each of which is

(i) an amount determined under paragraph (a) or (b) in respect of the taxpayer for any of the 5 taxation years immediately preceding the year, where the property was acquired, or the qualified expenditure was made, before April 20, 1983, or

(ii) an amount determined under paragraph (a) or (b) in respect of the taxpayer for any of the 10 taxation years immediately preceding or the 3 taxation years immediately following the year, where the property was acquired, or the qualified expenditure was made, after April 19, 1983 or the qualified Canadian exploration expenditure was for a taxation year ending after November 30, 1985,

(d) the total of all amounts each of which is an amount required by subsection 119(9) to be added in computing the taxpayer's investment tax credit at the end of the year or at the end of any of the 10 taxation years immediately preceding the year,

(e) the total of all amounts each of which is an amount required by subsection (10.1) to be added in computing the taxpayer's investment tax credit at the end of the year or at the end of any of the 10 taxation years immediately preceding or the 3 taxation years immediately following the year,

(e.1) the total of all amounts each of which is the specified percentage of that part of a repayment made by the taxpayer in the year or in any of the 10 taxation years immediately preceding or the 3 taxation years immediately following the year that can reasonably be considered to be a repayment of government assistance, non-government assistance or a contract payment that reduced the capital cost to the taxpayer of a property under paragraph (11.1)(b), the amount of an expenditure made by the taxpayer under paragraph (11.1)(c) or the prescribed proxy amount of the taxpayer under paragraph (11.1)(f), and

(e.2) the total of all amounts each of which is the specified percentage of $1/4$ of that part of a repayment made by the taxpayer in the year or in any of the 10 taxation years immediately preceding or the 3 taxation years immediately following the year that can reasonably be considered to be a repayment of government assistance, non-government assistance or a contract payment that reduced the amount of an expenditure made by the taxpayer under paragraph (11.1)(e) in respect of first term shared-use-equipment or second term shared-use-equipment, and, for that purpose, a repayment made by the taxpayer in any taxation year preceding the first taxation year ending co-incidentally with the first period or the second period in respect of first term shared-use-equipment or second term shared-use-equipment, respectively, shall be deemed to have been made by the taxpayer in that first taxation year,

exceeds the total of

(f) the total of all amounts each of which is an amount deducted under subsection (5) from the tax otherwise payable under this Part by the taxpayer for a preceding taxation year in respect of

(i) property acquired, or an expenditure made, in any of the 5 taxation years immediately preceding the year, where the property was acquired, or the expenditure was made, before April 20, 1983, or

(ii) property acquired, or an expenditure made, in the year or in any of the 10 taxation years immediately preceding or the 2 taxation years immediately following the year, where the property was acquired, or the expenditure was made, after April 19, 1983,

(g) the total of all amounts each of which is an amount required by subsection (6) to be deducted in computing the taxpayer's investment tax credit

(i) at the end of the year,

(ii) in respect of property acquired, or an expenditure made, before April 20, 1983, at the end of any of the 4 taxation years immediately preceding the year, or

(iii) in respect of property acquired, or an expenditure made, after April 19, 1983, at the end of any of the 9 taxation years immediately preceding or the 3 taxation years immediately following the year,

(h) the total of all amounts each of which is an amount required by subsection (7) to be deducted in computing the taxpayer's investment tax credit

(i) at the end of the year,

(ii) in respect of property acquired, or an expenditure made, before April 20, 1983, at the end of any of the 5 taxation years immediately preceding the year, or

(iii) in respect of property acquired, or an expenditure made, after April 19, 1983, at the end of any of the 10 taxation years immediately preceding or the 3 taxation years immediately following the year,

(i) the total of all amounts each of which is an amount claimed under subparagraph 192(2)(a)(ii) by the taxpayer for the year or a preceding taxation year in respect of property acquired, or an expenditure made, in the year or the 10 taxation years immediately preceding the year,

1133

(j) where the taxpayer is a corporation control of which has been acquired by a person or group of persons at any time before the end of the year, the amount determined under subsection (9.1) in respect of the taxpayer, and

(k) where the taxpayer is a corporation control of which has been acquired by a person or group of persons at any time after the end of the year, the amount determined under subsection (9.2) in respect of the taxpayer,

except that no amount shall be included in the total determined under any of paragraphs (a) to (e.2) in respect of any qualified expenditure incurred by the taxpayer in the course of earning income from a business, or in respect of any certified property or qualified property acquired by the taxpayer for use in the course of earning income from a business, if any of the income from that business is exempt from tax under this Part;

The changes made by 1995 Budget can be outlined as follows:

The amendments to para. *(a)* removed references to obsolete provisions.

Para. *(a.1)* was added. It provides the credit with respect to SR&ED. This credit was formerly available through subpara. (a)(ii), which referred to a "qualified expenditure", and "specified percentage"(e)(v), which set the percentage at 20%. See now 127(9)"SR&ED qualified expenditure pool".

The changes to para. *(c)* removed references to obsolete provisions and added reference to para. (a.1). The former version applied since 1988.

The changes to para *(e.1)* limited subparas. (ii) and (iii) to taxation years that began before 1996, and added subpara. (iv).

The changes to para. *(e.2)* limited subpara. (i) to taxation years that began before 1996, and added subpara. (ii).

The changes to para. *(f)* eliminated reference to obsolete provisions, and ensure that any ITC deducted under 127(5) in respect of a taxpayer's SR&ED qualified expenditure pool reduces the taxpayer's ITC pool.

The changes to para. *(g)* eliminated subpara. (ii) and some obsolete words in subpara. (iii). The former version applied since 1985.

The changes to para. *(h)* eliminated subpara. (ii) and some obsolete words in subpara. (iii). The former version applied since 1985.

Paras. *(i)*, *(j)* and *(k)* were unchanged by 1995 Budget.

The *closing words* of the definition were amended to remove reference to obsolete terms.

Earlier changes:

Reference to qualified small-business property added to subpara. *(a)*(i) by 1992 Economic Statement, effective for property acquired after December 2, 1992.

Para. *(e.1)* amended by 1992 Economic Statement, effective for taxation years ending after December 2, 1992, to add reference to prescribed proxy amount under 127(11.1)(f).

Para. *(e.2)* added by 1992 Economic Statement, effective for taxation years ending after December 2, 1992.

References to para. (e.2) and qualified small-business property added to para. *(k)* by 1992 Economic Statement, effective for property acquired after December 2, 1992.

*Closing words* of the definition (beginning "except that") added by 1991 technical bill, effective for property acquired and expenditures made by a taxpayer after July 13, 1990, other than property acquired and expenditures made after that day and before 1992

(a) pursuant to an agreement in writing entered into by the taxpayer on or before July 13, 1990; or

(b) for the purpose of completing the construction of property that was under construction by or on behalf of the taxpayer on or before July 13, 1990.

The closing words ensure that an ITC will only be available where the income from the business to which the expenditure or property relates is subject to tax.

**Interpretation Bulletins**: IT-121R3: Election to capitalize cost of borrowed money; IT-151R5: Scientific research and experimental development expenditures; IT-273R: Government assistance — general comments.

**Information Circulars**: 78-4R3: Investment tax credit rates.

**Forms**: T2 SCH 38: Investment tax credit (ITC) — corporations; T661 — Claim for SR&ED carried on in Canada; T665: Simplified claim for expenditures incurred in carrying on SR&ED in Canada; T2038 (Ind): Investment tax credit (ITC) — individuals; T4088: Claiming scientific research and experimental development expenditures — guide to form T661.

**"non-government assistance"** means an amount that would be included in income by virtue of paragraph 12(1)(x) if that paragraph were read without reference to subparagraphs 12(1)(x)(vi) and (vii);

**"non-qualifying corporation"** at any time means

(a) a corporation that is, at that time, not a Canadian-controlled private corporation,

(b) a corporation that would be liable to pay tax under Part I.3 for the taxation year of the corporation that includes that time if that Part were read without reference to subsection 181.1(4) and if the amount determined under subsection 181.2(3) in respect of the corporation for the year were determined without reference to amounts described in any of paragraphs 181.2(3)(a), (b), (d) and (f) to the extent that the amounts so described were used to acquire property that would be qualified small-business property if the corporation were not a non-qualifying corporation, or

(c) a corporation that at that time is related for the purposes of section 181.5 to a corporation described in paragraph (b);

**Notes**: Definition "non-qualifying corporation" added by 1992 Economic Statement, effective for property acquired after December 2, 1992. It describes a corporation ineligible for the temporary 10% small business investment tax credit for "qualified small-business property". See 127(9)"eligible taxpayer"(a).

**"qualified Canadian exploration expenditure"** — [Repealed]

**Notes**: Definition "qualified Canadian exploration expenditure" repealed by 1995 Budget, effective for taxation years that begin after 1995, since it is no longer relevant. It applied to expenditures before 1991.

**Regulations**: 4608 (prescribed expenditure).

**"qualified construction equipment"** — [Repealed]

**Notes**: Definition "qualified construction equipment" repealed by 1995 Budget, effective for taxation years that begin after 1995, since it is no longer relevant. It applied to property acquired before 1989.

**Regulations**: 4603 (prescribed equipment).

**"qualified expenditure"** incurred by a taxpayer in a taxation year means

(a) an amount that is an expenditure incurred in the year by the taxpayer in respect of scientific research and experimental development that is an expenditure

    (i) for first term shared-use-equipment or second term shared-use-equipment,

    (ii) described in paragraph 37(1)(a), or

    (iii) described in subparagraph 37(1)(b)(i), or

(b) a prescribed proxy amount of the taxpayer for the year (which, for the purpose of paragraph (e), is deemed to be an amount incurred in the year),

but does not include

(c) a prescribed expenditure incurred in the year by the taxpayer,

(d) where the taxpayer is a corporation, an expenditure specified by the taxpayer for the year for the purpose of clause 194(2)(a)(ii)(A),

(e) [Repealed]

(f) an expenditure (other than an expenditure that is salary or wages of an employee of the taxpayer) incurred by the taxpayer in respect of scientific research and experimental development to the extent that it is performed by another person or partnership at a time when the taxpayer and the person or partnership to which the expenditure is paid or payable do not deal with each other at arm's length,

(g) an expenditure described in paragraph 37(1)(a) that is paid or payable by the taxpayer to or for the benefit of a person or partnership that is not a taxable supplier in respect of the expenditure, other than an expenditure in respect of scientific research and experimental development directly undertaken by the taxpayer, and

(h) an amount that would otherwise be a qualified expenditure incurred by the taxpayer in the year to the extent of any reduction in respect of the amount that is required under any of subsections (18) to (20) to be applied;

**Related Provisions**: 18(9)(e) — Prepaid expenses deemed incurred in later taxation year; 127(11.5) — Adjustments to qualified expenditures; 127(13)–(16) — Agreement to transfer expenditures to non-arm's length person who performs research; 127(18)–(21) — Reduction to reflect government assistance; 127(24) — Anti-avoidance rule — exclusion from qualified expenditure; 127(26) — Amounts not paid within 180 days of end of year.

**Notes**: A qualified expenditure is not only fully deductible under 37(1), but also entitles the taxpayer to a 20% or 35% investment tax credit. See 127(9)"SR&ED qualified expenditure pool"A, 127(9)"investment tax credit"(a.1) and 127(5) for the first 20%; and 127(10.1) for the additional 15%.

Where para. (f) applies to exclude an expenditure because it was performed be a person not dealing at arm's length with the taxpayer, an election under 127(13) may be available to allow the expenditure to qualify for a credit.

Para. (e) repealed, (f) amended to change "performed for or on behalf of the taxpayer" to "performed by another person or partnership", and (g) amended to move the "other than" clause from the middle to the end of the para. to remove ambiguity; all by 1997 Budget, effective for taxation years that begin after 1995. For earlier years, read para. (e) as:

    (e) subject to subsection (11.4), an amount in respect of which the taxpayer does not file with the Minister a prescribed form containing prescribed information on or before the day that is 12 months after the taxpayer's filing-due date for the particular taxation year in which the amount would have been incurred if this Act were read without reference to subsections (26) and 78(4) where the particular year begins after 1995,

Definition "qualified expenditure" amended by 1995 Budget, effective for taxation years that begin after 1995. However, subsec. 30(26.1) of the 1995 Budget bill, as amended by 1995-97 technical bill (s. 306) provides that where, because of the amendment, an amount paid or payable by a person or partnership to a taxpayer with whom the person or partnership does not deal at arm's length otherwise

    (a) would be a qualified expenditure of the person or partnership but would not be a contract payment received or receivable by the taxpayer, or

    (b) would not be a qualified expenditure of the person or partnership but would be a contract payment received or receivable by the taxpayer,

the amount is deemed not to be a qualified expenditure of the person or partnership and not to be a contract payment received or receivable by the taxpayer.

For earlier years, read:

"qualified expenditure" means an expenditure in respect of scientific research and experimental development incurred by a taxpayer that is an expenditure in respect of first term shared-use-equipment or second term shared-use-equipment or an expenditure described in paragraph 37(1)(a) or subparagraph 37(1)(b)(i) and includes an amount that is a prescribed proxy amount of a taxpayer, but does not include

    (a) a prescribed expenditure,

    (b) in the case of a taxpayer that is a corporation, an expenditure specified by the taxpayer for the purposes of clause 194(2)(a)(ii)(A), or

    (c) subject to subsection (11.4), an expenditure in respect of which the taxpayer does not, by the day on or before which the taxpayer's return of income under this Part for the taxpayer's taxation year after that in which the expenditure was incurred is required to be filed, or would be required to be filed if tax under this Part were payable by the taxpayer for that following year, file with the Minister a prescribed form containing prescribed information;

Para. (c) added by 1993 technical bill, effective February 22, 1994 for expenditures incurred at any time. However, for an expenditure incurred in a taxation year ending before February 22, 1994, the taxpayer could file the prescribed form up to September 13, 1994. All R&D claims — even if not yet being claimed for tax purposes — must now be identified on Form T661, filed within 1 year after the due date for the return for the year in which the expenditure was incurred. This rule is now in 127(9)"investment tax credit"(m).

Opening words of 127(9)"qualified expenditure" amended by 1992 Economic Statement, effective for taxation years ending after December 2, 1992, to add references to first term shared-use-equipment, second-term shared-use-equipment and prescribed proxy amount.

**Regulations**: 2900(4) (prescribed proxy amount); 2902 (prescribed expenditure).

**Interpretation Bulletins**: IT-104R2: Deductibility of fines or penalties; IT-151R5: Scientific research and experimental development expenditures.

**Information Circulars**: 97-1: SR&ED — Administrative guidelines for software development.

**Application Policies**: SR&ED 96-01: Reclassification of SR&ED expenditures per subsec. 127(11.4)..

**Forms**: T2 SCH 301: Newfoundland scientific research and experimental development tax credit; T2 SCH 340: Nova Scotia research and development tax credit; T2 SCH 360: New Brunswick research and development tax credit; T2 SCH 380: Manitoba research and development tax credit; T2 SCH 403: Saskatchewan research and development tax credit; T661 — Claim for SR&ED carried on in Canada; T1129: Newfoundland research and development tax credit (individuals); T4088: Claiming scientific research and experimental development expenditures — guide to form T661.

**"qualified property"** of a taxpayer means property (other than an approved project property or a certified property) that is

(a) a prescribed building to the extent that it is acquired by the taxpayer after June 23, 1975, or

(b) prescribed machinery and equipment acquired by the taxpayer after June 23, 1975,

that has not been used, or acquired for use or lease, for any purpose whatever before it was acquired by the taxpayer and that is

(c) to be used by the taxpayer in Canada primarily for the purpose of

(i) manufacturing or processing goods for sale or lease,

(ii) farming or fishing,

(iii) logging,

(iv) operating an oil or gas well or extracting petroleum or natural gas from a natural accumulation of petroleum or natural gas,

(v) extracting minerals from a mineral resource,

(vi) processing

(A) ore (other than iron ore or tar sands ore) from a mineral resource to any stage that is not beyond the prime metal stage or its equivalent,

(B) iron ore from a mineral resource to any stage that is not beyond the pellet stage or its equivalent, or

(C) tar sands ore from a mineral resource to any stage that is not beyond the crude oil stage or its equivalent,

(vii) producing industrial minerals,

(viii) processing heavy crude oil recovered from a natural reservoir in Canada to a stage that is not beyond the crude oil stage or its equivalent,

(ix) Canadian field processing,

(x) exploring or drilling for petroleum or natural gas,

(xi) prospecting or exploring for or developing a mineral resource,

(xii) storing grain, or

(xiii) harvesting peat,

(c.1) to be used by the taxpayer in Canada primarily for the purpose of producing or processing electrical energy or steam in a prescribed area, where

(i) all or substantially all of the energy or steam

(A) is used by the taxpayer for the purpose of gaining or producing income from a business (other than the business of selling the product of the particular property), or

(B) is sold directly (or indirectly by way of sale to a provincially regulated power utility operating in the prescribed area) to a person related to the taxpayer, and

(ii) the energy or steam is used by the taxpayer or the person related to the taxpayer primarily for the purpose of manufacturing or processing goods in the prescribed area for sale or lease, or

(d) to be leased by the taxpayer to a lessee (other than a person exempt from tax under this Part because of section 149) who can reasonably be expected to use the property in Canada primarily for any of the purposes referred to in subparagraphs (c)(i) to (xiii), but this paragraph does not apply to property that is prescribed for the purpose of paragraph (b) unless use of the property by the first person to whom it was leased began after June 23, 1975 and

(i) the property is leased in the ordinary course of carrying on a business in Canada by a corporation whose principal business is leasing property, lending money, purchasing conditional sales contracts, accounts receivable, bills of sale, chattel mortgages, bills of exchange or other obligations representing all or part of the sale price of merchandise or services, or any combination thereof,

(ii) the property is manufactured and leased in the ordinary course of carrying on business in Canada by a corporation whose principal business is manufacturing property that it sells or leases,

(iii) the property is leased in the ordinary course of carrying on business in Canada by a corporation whose principal business is selling or servicing property of that type, or

(iv) the property is a fishing vessel, including the furniture, fittings and equipment attached to it, leased by an individual (other than a trust) to a corporation, controlled by the individual, that carries on a fishing business in connection with one or more commercial fishing licences issued by the Government of Canada to the individual,

and, for the purpose of this definition, "Canada" includes the offshore region prescribed for the purpose of the definition "specified percentage";

**Related Provisions**: 127(11) — Interpretation.

**Notes**: "Industrial minerals", used in (c)(vii), are considered by the CCRA to be non-metallic minerals, such as gravel, clay, stone, limestone, sand and feldspar (IT-145R, para. 11).

Subparas. (c)(ii) to (xii) amended by 1996 Budget, effective for taxation years that begin after 1996. For earlier years since 1986, read:

> (ii) operating an oil or gas well, extracting petroleum or natural gas from a natural accumulation thereof or processing heavy crude oil recovered from a natural reservoir in Canada to a stage that is not beyond the crude oil stage or its equivalent,
>
> (iii) extracting minerals from a mineral resource,
>
> (iv) processing ore (other than iron ore or tar sands) from a mineral resource to a stage that is not beyond the prime metal stage or its equivalent,
>
> (v) processing iron ore from a mineral resource to a stage that is not beyond the pellet stage or its equivalent,
>
> (vi) processing tar sands to a stage that is not beyond the crude oil stage or its equivalent,
>
> (vii) exploring or drilling for petroleum or natural gas,
>
> (viii) prospecting or exploring for or developing a mineral resource,
>
> (ix) logging,
>
> (x) farming or fishing,
>
> (xi) storing grain,
>
> (xii) producing industrial minerals,

Subpara. (c)(xiii) of definition "qualified property" added by 1991 technical bill, retroactive to 1985.

Para. (c.1) of the definition added by 1993 technical bill, effective for property acquired after 1991. The areas prescribed are the four Atlantic provinces and the Gaspé Peninsula.

Subpara. (d)(iv) added by 1993 technical bill, retroactive to 1980 and later taxation years.

Para. (d) of the definition amended by 1991 technical bill, effective for property acquired after July 13, 1990, to add additional restrictions. For property acquired before July 14, 1990, read:

> (d) to be leased by the taxpayer to a lessee (other than a person exempt from tax under section 149) who can reasonably be expected to use the property in Canada primarily for any of the purposes referred to in subparagraphs (c)(i) to (xii), but this paragraph does not apply in respect of property that is a prescribed property for the purposes of paragraph (b) unless
>
> > (i) the property is leased by the taxpayer in the ordinary course of carrying on a business in Canada and the taxpayer is a corporation whose principal business is leasing property, manufacturing property that it sells or leases, the lending of money, the purchasing of conditional sales contracts, accounts receivable, bills of sale, chattel mortgages, bills of exchange or other obligations representing part or all of the sale price of merchandise or services, or selling or servicing a type of property that it also leases, or any combination thereof, and
>
> > (ii) use of the property by the first lessee commenced after June 23, 1975;

Closing words of paragraph (d), defining "Canada", added by 1991 technical bill, effective February 26, 1986.

**Regulations**: 4600 (prescribed building, machinery); 4610 (prescribed area for para. (c.1)).

**Forms**: T2 SCH 321: PEI corporate investment tax credit.

### "qualified small-business property" — [Repealed]

**Notes**: Definition "qualified small-business property" repealed by 1995 Budget, effective for taxation years that begin after 1995, since it is no longer relevant.

Definition added by 1992 Economic Statement, effective for property acquired after December 2, 1992. It described property that qualified for the 10% small business investment tax credit from December 3, 1992 through the end of 1993.

### "qualified transportation equipment" — [Repealed]

**Notes**: Definition "qualified transportation equipment" repealed by 1995 Budget, effective for taxation years that begin after 1995, since it is no longer relevant. It applied to property acquired before 1989.

**Regulations**: 4601 (prescribed equipment).

### "SR&ED qualified expenditure pool" of a taxpayer at the end of a taxation year means the amount determined by the formula

$$A + B - C$$

where

A is the total of all amounts each of which is a qualified expenditure incurred by the taxpayer in the year,

B is the total of all amounts each of which is an amount determined under paragraph (13)(e) for the year in respect of the taxpayer, and in respect of which the taxpayer files with the Minister a prescribed form containing prescribed information by the day that is 12 months after the taxpayer's filing-due date for the year, and

C is the total of all amounts each of which is an amount determined under paragraph (13)(d) for the year in respect of the taxpayer;

### Proposed Amendment — Administration of R&D credits

**Federal budget, supplementary information, February 28, 2000**: *Scientific Research and Experimental Development*

Canada provides one of the most generous tax incentive regimes among industrialized countries for scientific research and experimental development (SR&ED). It is important that this support only benefits those activities to which the program was intended to apply.

In claiming credits for SR&ED (including information technology), three basic criteria must be met:

- scientific or technological uncertainty,
- scientific or technological advancement, and
- scientific or technological content.

Technological advancement is a key element of the program. Technological advancement does not include the application of technology that is merely new to a particular taxpayer or industry. In particular, development work that is routine in nature does not qualify as SR&ED. While the definition of SR&ED was amended in 1985 to include experimental development, consistent with international usage, experimental development does not include projects involving only routine engineering or routine development.

This is reflected in the Canada Customs and Revenue Agency's administrative guidelines for software development, which were developed in consultation with industry. Nevertheless, the administration of the SR&ED program has come under increasing pressure, particularly in regard

## S. 127(9) SR&    Income Tax Act, Part I, Division E

to its application to information technology. A disproportionate number of disputes between taxpayers and the Government continue to be in the area of information technology. The Canada Customs and Revenue Agency has been faced with a number of very large and complex claims, many of which are not consistent with its administrative guidelines. These claims are in respect of internal use software, such as management information systems and automated services.

Many of the large claims have been made by corporations whose core business is not software development. CCRA has determined that substantially all of these claims reflect the application of available technology, which result in business improvements but do not embody technological advancement that the SR&ED program is intended to benefit. The Government is committed to rigorously applying the existing well established three basic criteria to address the backlog of SR&ED claims related to information technology.

In addition, the Government will consult with industry representatives to ensure that the guidelines on software development, in particular internal use software, both reflect government policy and provide clarity and certainty of application for compliance purposes as well as administration. Once consultations are completed, the Government will determine whether amendments to the *Income Tax Act* are required.

**Related Provisions**: 127(5)(a)(i), 127(5)(a)(ii)(A) — Investment tax credit; 127(9)"investment tax credit"(a.1) — 20% of pool claimable; 127(10.1)(b) — Additional ITC for CCPC; 127(13) — Transfer of pool to other taxpayer; 127(14) — Identification of amounts transferred as current or capital; 257 — Formula cannot calculate to less than zero.

**Notes**: The Auditor General strongly criticized the CCRA for inconsistent (and overly lenient) administration of R&D credit claims in his April 2000 report (Chapter 6), available from www.oag-bvg.gc.ca.

Definition "SR&ED qualified expenditure pool" added by 1995 Budget, effective for taxation years that begin after 1995. 20% of the pool is allowed as an ITC under 127(9)"investment tax credit"(a.1). (This was previously in 127(9)"specified percentage"(e)(v).) A further 15% is allowed to certain Canadian-controlled private corporations by 127(10.1).

**Application Policies**: SR&ED 94-01: Retroactive claims for scientific research (TPRs); SR&ED 95-04R: Conflict of interest with regard to outside consultants; SR&ED 96-05: Penalties under subsec. 163(2); SR&ED 96-07: Prototypes, custom products/commercial assets, pilot plants and experimental production..

**Forms**: T661 — Claim for SR&ED carried on in Canada; T665: Simplified claim for expenditures incurred in carrying on SR&ED in Canada; T4088: Claiming scientific research and experimental development expenditures — guide to form T661.

**"second term shared-use-equipment"** of a taxpayer means property of the taxpayer that was first term shared-use-equipment of the taxpayer and that is used by the taxpayer, during its operating time in the period (in this subsection and subsection (11.1) referred to as the "second period") beginning at the time the property was acquired by the taxpayer and ending at the end of the taxpayer's first taxation year ending at least 24 months after that time, primarily for the prosecution of scientific research and experimental development in Canada;

**Related Provisions**: 88(1)(e.3) closing words — Winding-up — parent deemed continuation of subsidiary; 127(11.5)(b) — Adjustments to qualified expenditures.

**Notes**: Definition "second term shared-use-equipment" added by 1992 Economic Statement, effective for property acquired after December 2, 1992. See 127(11.1)(e).

**"specified percentage"** means

(a) in respect of a qualified property

(i) acquired before April, 1977, 5%,

(ii) acquired after March 31, 1977 and before November 17, 1978 primarily for use in

(A) the Province of Nova Scotia, New Brunswick, Prince Edward Island or Newfoundland or the Gaspé Peninsula, 10%,

(B) a prescribed designated region, $7^{1}/_{2}$%, and

(C) any other area in Canada, 5%,

(iii) acquired primarily for use in the Province of Nova Scotia, New Brunswick, Prince Edward Island or Newfoundland or the Gaspé Peninsula,

(A) after November 16, 1978 and before 1989, 20%,

(B) after 1988 and before 1995, 15%,

(C) after 1994, 15% where the property

(I) is acquired by the taxpayer under a written agreement of purchase and sale entered into by the taxpayer before February 22, 1994,

(II) was under construction by or on behalf of the taxpayer on February 22, 1994, or

(III) is machinery or equipment that will be a fixed and integral part of property under construction by or on behalf of the taxpayer on February 22, 1994, and

(D) after 1994, 10% where the property is not property to which clause (C) applies,

(iv) acquired after November 16, 1978 and before February 26, 1986 primarily for use in a prescribed offshore region, 7%,

(v) acquired primarily for use in a prescribed offshore region and

(A) after February 25, 1986 and before 1989, 20%,

(B) after 1988 and before 1995, 15%,

(C) after 1994, 15% where the property

(I) is acquired by the taxpayer under a written agreement of purchase and sale entered into by the taxpayer before February 22, 1994,

(II) was under construction by or on behalf of the taxpayer on February 22, 1994, or

(III) is machinery or equipment that will be a fixed and integral part of property under construction by or on behalf of the taxpayer on February 22, 1994, and

(D) after 1994, 10% where the property is not property to which clause (C) applies,

(vi) acquired primarily for use in a prescribed designated region and

(A) after November 16, 1978 and before 1987, 10%,

(B) in 1987, 7%,

(C) in 1988, 3%, and

(D) after 1988, 0%, and

(vii) acquired primarily for use in Canada (other than a property described in subparagraph (iii), (iv), (v) or (vi)), and

(A) after November 16, 1978 and before 1987, 7%,

(B) in 1987, 5%,

(C) in 1988, 3%, and

(D) after 1988, 0%,

(b) in respect of qualified transportation equipment acquired

(i) before 1987, 7%

(ii) in 1987, 5%, and

(iii) in 1988, 3%,

(c) in respect of qualified construction equipment acquired

(i) before 1987, 7%,

(ii) in 1987, 5%, and

(iii) in 1988, 3%,

(d) in respect of certified property

(i) included in subparagraph (a)(i) of the definition "certified property" in this subsection, 50%,

(ii) included in subparagraph (a)(ii) of that definition, 40%, and

(iii) in any other case, 30%,

(e) in respect of a qualified expenditure

(i) made after March 31, 1977 and before November 17, 1978 in respect of scientific research and experimental development to be carried out in

(A) the Province of Nova Scotia, New Brunswick, Prince Edward Island or Newfoundland or the Gaspé Peninsula, 10%,

(B) a prescribed designated region, 7½%, and

(C) any other area in Canada, 5%,

(ii) made by a taxpayer after November 16, 1978 and before the taxpayer's taxation year that includes November 1, 1983 or made by the taxpayer in the taxpayer's taxation year that includes November 1, 1983 or a subsequent taxation year if the taxpayer deducted an amount under section 37.1 in computing the taxpayer's income for the year,

(A) where the expenditure was made by a Canadian-controlled private corporation in a taxation year of the corporation in which it is or would, if it had sufficient taxable income for the year, be entitled to a deduction under section 125 in computing its tax payable under this Part for the year, 25%, and

(B) where clause (A) is not applicable and the qualified expenditure was in respect of scientific research and experimental development to be carried out in

(I) the Province of Nova Scotia, New Brunswick, Prince Edward Island or Newfoundland or the Gaspé Peninsula, 20%, and

(II) any other area in Canada, 10%,

(iii) made by a taxpayer in the taxpayer's taxation year that ends after October 31, 1983 and before January 1, 1985, other than a qualified expenditure in respect of which subparagraph (ii) is applicable,

(A) where the expenditure was made by a Canadian-controlled private corporation in a taxation year of the corporation in which it is or would, if it had sufficient taxable income for the year, be entitled to a deduction under section 125 in computing its tax payable under this Part for the year, 35%, and

(B) where clause (A) is not applicable and the qualified expenditure was in respect of scientific research and experimental development to be carried out in

(I) the Province of Nova Scotia, New Brunswick, Prince Edward Island or Newfoundland or the Gaspé Peninsula, 30%, and

(II) any other area in Canada, 20%,

(iv) made by a taxpayer

(A) after the taxpayer's 1984 taxation year and before 1995, or

(B) after 1994 under a written agreement entered into by the taxpayer before February 22, 1994,

(other than a qualified expenditure in respect of which subparagraph (ii) applies) in respect of scientific research and experimental development to be carried out in

(C) the Province of Newfoundland, Prince Edward Island, Nova Scotia or New

Brunswick or the Gaspé Peninsula, 30%, and

(D) in any other area in Canada, 20%, and

(v) made by a taxpayer after 1994, 20% where the amount is not an amount to which clause (iv)(B) applies,

(f) in respect of the repayment of government assistance, non-government assistance or a contract payment that reduced

(i) the capital cost to the taxpayer of a property under paragraph (11.1)(b),

(ii) the amount of a qualified expenditure incurred by the taxpayer under paragraph (11.1)(c) or (e) for taxation years that began before 1996, or

(iii) the prescribed proxy amount of the taxpayer under paragraph (11.1)(f) for taxation years that began before 1996,

the specified percentage that applied in respect of the property, the expenditure or the prescribed proxy amount, as the case may be,

(f.1) in respect of the repayment of government assistance, non-government assistance or a contract payment that reduced a qualified expenditure incurred by the taxpayer under any of subsections (18) to (20), 20%,

(g) in respect of an approved project property acquired

(i) before 1989, 60%, and

(ii) after 1988, 45%,

(h) in respect of the qualified Canadian exploration expenditure of a taxpayer for a taxation year, 25%, and

(i) in respect of qualified small-business property, 10%.

**Related Provisions**: 13(27)(f) — Interpretation — available for use; 127(10.1) — Additional amount for R&D; 127(10.8) — Regeneration of ITCs where entitlement to assistance expires.

**Notes**: For the current operative percentages for the credit, see (a)(iii)(D), (a)(v)(D), (f), (f.1), "investment tax credit"(a.1) and 127(10.1). The rest of the definition deals with expenditures incurred or committed to in the past. The 20% R&D credit has been moved from "specified percentage"(e)(v) to "investment tax credit"(a.1). A further 15% may be provided by 127(10.1).

Cls. (a)(iii)(B) and (a)(v)(B) amended to add "and before 1995", and (a)(iii)(C) and (D) and (a)(v)(C) and (D) added, by 1994 Budget, effective for property acquired and expenditures incurred after 1994.

Subpara. (e)(iv) amended (effectively adding (e)(iv)(B)), and (e)(v) added, by 1994 Budget, effective for property acquired and expenditures incurred after 1994. For earlier expenditures, read (e)(iv) as:

(iv) made by a taxpayer in [the taxpayer's] 1985 taxation year or a subsequent taxation year, other than a qualified expenditure in respect of which subparagraph (ii) is applicable, in respect of scientific research and experimental development to be carried out in

(A) the Province of Nova Scotia, New Brunswick, Prince Edward Island or Newfoundland or the Gaspé Peninsula, 30%, and

(B) any other area in Canada, 20%,

Para. (f) amended by 1995-97 technical bill, effective for taxation years that begin after 1995, to add "for taxation years that began before 1996" to subparas. (ii) and (iii). (The para. was not divided into subparas. before the amendment.) Para. (f.1) added by 1995-97 technical bill, effective on the same basis.

Para. (f) amended by 1992 Economic Statement, effective for taxation years ending after December 2, 1992, to add references to 127(11.1)(e) and to prescribed proxy amount under 127(11.1)(f).

**Regulations**: 4607 (prescribed designated region); 4609 (prescribed offshore region).

**Interpretation Bulletins**: IT-151R5: Scientific research and experimental development expenditures.

**Information Circulars**: 78-4R3: Investment tax credit rates; 87-5: Capital cost of property where trade-in is involved.

### Proposed Addition — 127(9) "super-allowance benefit amount"

**"super-allowance benefit amount"** for a particular taxation year in respect of a corporation in respect of a province means the amount determined by the formula

$$(A - B) \times C$$

where

A is the total of all amounts each of which is an amount that is or may become deductible by the corporation, in computing income or taxable income relevant in calculating an income tax payable by the corporation under a law of the province for any taxation year, in respect of an expenditure on scientific research and experimental development incurred in the particular year,

B is the amount by which the amount of the expenditure exceeds the total of all amounts that would be required by subsections (18) to (20) to reduce the corporation's qualified expenditures otherwise determined under this section if the definitions "government assistance" and "non-government assistance" did not apply to assistance provided under that law,

C is,

(a) where the corporation's expenditure limit for the particular year is nil, the maximum rate of the province's income tax that applies for that year to active business income earned in the province by a corporation, and

(b) in any other case, the rate of the province's income tax for that year that would apply to the corporation if

(i) it were not associated with any other corporation in the year,

(ii) its taxable income for the year were less than $200,000, and

(iii) its taxable income for the year were earned in the province in respect of an active business carried on in the province;

Subdivision c — Computation of Tax: All Taxpayers   S. 127(9.1)(d)(i)(B)

**Application:** The December 21, 2000 draft legislation, subsec. 73(6), will add the definition "super-allowance benefit amount" to subsec. 127(9), applicable to taxation years that begin after February 2000 except that, if a corporation's first taxation year that begins after February 2000 ends before 2001, it is applicable to the corporation's taxation years that begin after 2000.

**Technical Notes:** The "super-allowance benefit amount" of a corporation for a taxation year is calculated by reference to the formula $(A - B) \times C$. The factor $(A - B)$ describes the amount by which a provincial income tax deduction exceeds the SR&ED expenditure otherwise determined (without reference to provincial income tax credits). Variable C is the provincial rate of tax to be applied to convert the excess deduction into a tax-credit equivalent. For corporations with an expenditure limit for the year for SR&ED purposes (as determined under subsection 127(10.2)) that is greater than nil, the applicable tax rate for variable C is the rate that the province applies to small business income earned in the year. Where the taxpayer's expenditure limit is nil, the applicable rate is the general corporate income tax rate for the year in the province for active business income.

The new definition "super-allowance benefit amount" applies to taxation years that begin after February 2000 except that, for corporations whose first taxation year that begins after February 2000 ends before 2001, the amendment applies to taxation years that begin after 2000.

**Notice of Ways and Means Motion, federal budget, February 28, 2000:** [See under 37(1)(d.1) — ed.]

**Related Provisions:** 37(1)(d.1) — Amount reduces R & D deduction pool; 127(9)"investment tax credit"(a.1) — No direct ITC for amount; 127(10.1)(b) — Addition to ITC for amount; 257 — Formula cannot calculate to less than zero.

"taxable supplier" in respect of an amount means

   (a) a person resident in Canada or a Canadian partnership, or

   (b) a non-resident person, or a partnership that is not a Canadian partnership,

     (i) by which the amount was payable, or

     (ii) by or for whom the amount was receivable

in the course of carrying on a business through a permanent establishment (as defined by regulation) in Canada.

**Notes:** Definition "taxable supplier" added by 1995 Budget, effective for taxation years that begin after 1995, and amended retroactive to its introduction by 1997 Budget bill to correct a formatting error by moving the closing words out of subpara. (b)(ii).

**Regulations:** 8201 (permanent establishment).

**(9.1) Control acquired before the end of the year** — Where a taxpayer is a corporation the control of which has been acquired by a person or group of persons (each of whom is in this subsection referred to as the "purchaser") at any time (in this subsection referred to as "that time") before the end of a taxation year of the corporation, the amount determined for the purposes of paragraph (j) of the definition "investment tax credit" in subsection (9) is the amount, if any, by which

   (a) the amount, if any, by which

     (i) the total of all amounts added in computing its investment tax credit at the end of the year in respect of a property acquired, or an expenditure made, before that time

exceeds

     (ii) the total of all amounts each of which is an amount

        (A) deducted in computing its investment tax credit at the end of the year under paragraph (f) or (g) of the definition "investment tax credit" in subsection (9), or

        (B) deducted in computing its investment tax credit at the end of the taxation year immediately preceding the year under paragraph (i) of that definition,

to the extent that the amount may reasonably be considered to have been so deducted in respect of a property or expenditure in respect of which an amount is included in subparagraph (i)

exceeds the total of

   (b) [Repealed under former Act]

   (c) the amount, if any, by which its refundable Part VII tax on hand at the end of the year exceeds the total of all amounts each of which is an amount designated under subsection 192(4) in respect of a share issued by it

     (i) in the period commencing one month before that time and ending at that time, or

     (ii) after that time,

and before the end of the year, and

   (d) that proportion of the amount that, but for subsections (3) and (5) and sections 126, 127.2 and 127.3, would be its tax payable under this Part for the year that,

     (i) where throughout the year the corporation carried on a particular business in the course of which a property was acquired, or an expenditure was made, before that time in respect of which an amount is included in computing its investment tax credit at the end of the year, the amount, if any, by which the total of all amounts each of which is

        (A) its income for the year from the particular business, or

        (B) its income for the year from any other business substantially all the income of which was derived from the sale, leasing, rental or development of properties or the rendering of services similar to the properties sold, leased, rented or developed, or the services rendered, as the case may be, by the corporation in carrying on the particular business before that time

exceeds

    (C) the total of all amounts each of which is an amount deducted under paragraph 111(1)(a) or (d) for the year by the corporation in respect of a non-capital loss or a farm loss, as the case may be, for a taxation year in respect of the particular business or the other business,

is of the greater of

  (ii) the amount determined under subparagraph (i), and

  (iii) its taxable income for the year.

**Related Provisions**: 139.1(18) — Holding corporation deemed not to acquire control of insurer on demutualization; 249(4) — Deemed year-end on change of control; 256(6)–(9) — Whether control acquired.

**Notes**: See Notes to 111(5), which has the same purpose.

127(9.1) amended in 1987, effective for acquisitions of control after January 15, 1987, other than acquisitions of control before 1988 where the persons acquiring the control were obliged on January 15, 1987 to acquire the control pursuant to the terms of agreements in writing entered into on or before that date. For this purpose, the amending legislation provides that "a person shall be considered not to be obliged ... to dispose of ... property ... if the person may be excused from performing the obligation as a result of changes to the *Income Tax Act* affecting acquisitions or dispositions of property or acquisitions of control of corporations".

The CCRA takes the position that "substantially all", used in 127(9.1)(d)(i)(B), means 90% or more.

**Interpretation Bulletins**: IT-151R5: Scientific research and experimental development expenditures.

**I.T. Technical News**: No. 7 (control by a group — 50/50 arrangement).

**Forms**: T2 SCH 31: Investment tax credit — corporations.

**(9.2) Control acquired after the end of the year** — Where a taxpayer is a corporation the control of which has been acquired by a person or group of persons at any time (in this subsection referred to as "that time") after the end of a taxation year of the corporation, the amount determined for the purposes of paragraph (k) of the definition "investment tax credit" in subsection (9) is the amount, if any, by which

  (a) the total of all amounts each of which is an amount included in computing its investment tax credit at the end of the year in respect of a property acquired, or an expenditure made, after that time

exceeds the total of

  (b) [Repealed under former Act]

  (c) its refundable Part VII tax on hand at the end of the year, and

  (d) that proportion of the amount that, but for subsections (3) and (5) and sections 126, 127.2 and 127.3, would be its tax payable under this Part for the year that,

    (i) where the corporation acquired a property or made an expenditure, in the course of carrying on a particular business throughout the portion of a taxation year that is after that time, in respect of which an amount is included in computing its investment tax credit at the end of the year, the amount, if any, by which the total of all amounts each of which is

    (A) its income for the year from the particular business, or

    (B) where the corporation carried on a particular business in the year, its income for the year from any other business substantially all the income of which was derived from the sale, leasing, rental or development of properties or the rendering of services similar to the properties sold, leased, rented or developed, or the services rendered, as the case may be, by the corporation in carrying on the particular business before that time

exceeds

    (C) the total of all amounts each of which is an amount deducted under paragraph 111(1)(a) or (d) for the year by the corporation in respect of a non-capital loss or a farm loss, as the case may be, for a taxation year in respect of the particular business or the other business

is of the greater of

  (ii) the amount determined under subparagraph (i), and

  (iii) its taxable income for the year.

**Related Provisions**: 139.1(18) — Holding corporation deemed not to acquire control of insurer on demutualization; 249(4) — Deemed year-end on change of control; 256(6)–(9) — Whether control acquired.

**Notes**: 127(9.2) amended in 1987, effective for acquisitions of control after January 15, 1987, other than acquisitions of control before 1988 where the persons acquiring the control were obliged on January 15, 1987 to acquire the control pursuant to the terms of agreements in writing entered into on or before that date. For this purpose, the amending legislation provides that "a person shall be considered not to be obliged ... to dispose of ... property ... if the person may be excused from performing the obligation as a result of changes to the *Income Tax Act* affecting acquisitions or dispositions of property or acquisitions of control of corporations".

The CCRA takes the position that "substantially all", used in 127(9.2)(d)(i)(B), means 90% or more.

**Interpretation Bulletins**: IT-151R5: Scientific research and experimental development expenditures.

**I.T. Technical News**: No. 7 (control by a group — 50/50 arrangement).

**Forms**: T2 SCH 31: Investment tax credit — corporations.

**(10) Ascertainment of certain property** — The Minister may

  (a) obtain the advice of the appropriate minister for the purposes of the *Regional Development Incentives Act*, chapter R-3 of the Revised Statutes of Canada, 1970, as to whether any property is property as described in paragraph (b) of the definition "certified property" in subsection (9);

(b) obtain a certificate from the appropriate minister for the purposes of the *Regional Development Incentives Act* certifying that any property specified therein is property as described in paragraph (b) of that definition; or

(c) provide advice to the member of the Queen's Privy Council for Canada appointed to be the Minister for the purposes of the *Atlantic Canada Opportunities Agency Act* as to whether any property qualifies for certification under the definition "approved project property" in subsection (9).

**Notes**: 127(10) amended in 1990, effective February 23, 1990, to refer to various untitled Ministers in place of the Minister of Regional Industrial Expansion.

**(10.1) Additions to investment tax credit** — For the purpose of paragraph (e) of the definition "investment tax credit" in subsection (9), where a corporation was throughout a taxation year a Canadian-controlled private corporation, there shall be added in computing the corporation's investment tax credit at the end of the year the amount that is 15% of the least of

(a) such amount as the corporation claims;

(b) the SR&ED qualified expenditure pool of the corporation at the end of the year; and

**Proposed Amendment — 127(10.1)(b)**

(b) the amount by which the corporation's SR&ED qualified expenditure pool at the end of the year exceeds the total of all amounts each of which is the super-allowance benefit amount for the year in respect of the corporation in respect of a province; and

**Application**: The December 21, 2000 draft legislation, subsec. 73(7), will amend para. 127(10.1)(b) to read as above, applicable to taxation years that begin after February 2000 except that, if a corporation's first taxation year that begins after February 2000 ends before 2001, it is applicable to the corporation's taxation years that begin after 2000.

**Technical Notes**: Subsection 127(10.1) provides an additional 15% ITC to Canadian-controlled private corporations, based on the least of the amount that the corporation claims (paragraph 127(10.1)(a)), the corporation's SR&ED qualified expenditure pool for the year (paragraph 127(10.1)(b)) and the corporation's expenditure limit for the year (paragraph 127(10.1)(c)). Subsection 127(10.1) is amended to reduce the amount determined under paragraph 127(10.1)(b) by the taxpayer's super-allowance benefit amount for the year for each province to which it applies.

(c) the corporation's expenditure limit for the year.

**Related Provisions**: 88(1)(e.8) — Winding-up; 127(10.2)–(10.4) — Expenditure limit and associated corporations; 127(10.7) — Further additions to ITCs; 127.1(2)"refundable investment tax credit"(f)(i) — Addition to refundable ITC; 127.1(2.01) — Addition to refundable investment tax credit; 136 — Cooperative can be private corporation for purposes of 127(10.1).

**Notes**: 127(10.1) provides an additional ITC (i.e., total 35% instead of 20%) for qualifying R&D expenditures incurred by certain Canadian-controlled private corporations (CCPCs). Large corporations cannot claim this additional credit; see Notes to 127(10.2).

127(10.1) amended by 1995 Budget, effective for taxation years that begin after 1995. The amended version is much simpler but accomplishes the same effect of providing a 15% additional credit, to raise the total ITC to 35% (see 127(9)"investment tax credit"(a.1)). An earlier amendment by 1994 Budget (removing reference to taxable income because of the introduction of 127(10.2)), which would have been effective for taxation years that begin after 1995, has been superseded by this amendment. For taxation years that begin in 1994 or 1995, read:

(10.1) For the purpose of paragraph (e) of the definition "investment tax credit" in subsection (9), where a corporation was throughout a particular taxation year a Canadian-controlled private corporation, there shall be added in computing the corporation's investment tax credit at the end of the particular year the amount determined by the formula

$$\left(\frac{35}{100} \times A\right) - B$$

where

A is the lesser of

(a) the total of all expenditures described in any of subparagraphs (e)(iv) and (v) of the definition "specified percentage" in subsection (9) made by the corporation in the particular year and that were designated by it in its return of income under this Part for the particular year, and

(b) the corporation's expenditure limit for the particular year; and

B is the total of all amounts determined under paragraph (a) of the definition "investment tax credit" in subsection (9) in respect of an expenditure referred to in paragraph (a) of the description of A.

Opening words of 127(10.1) amended by 1993 Budget, effective for taxation years that begin in 1994 or 1995, to add the word "twice" before "the total of the business limits". The purpose of the change was to phase out the 35% R&D rate for CCPCs with taxable income over $200,000 as their taxable income approached $400,000, rather than cutting it off at $200,000. See 127(10.2). However, this has now been replaced with a new regime that eliminates the higher rate for large businesses by referring to their taxable capital; see the amendments to 125(5.1).

**Forms**: T2 SCH 31: Investment tax credit — corporations.

**(10.2) Expenditure limit determined** — For the purpose of subsection (10.1), a corporation's expenditure limit for a particular taxation year is the amount determined by the formula

$$(\$4,000,000 - 10A) \times \frac{B}{\$200,000}$$

where

A is the greater of $200,000 and either

(a) where the corporation is associated with one or more other corporations in the particular year and the particular year ends in a calendar year, the total of all amounts each of which is the taxable income of the corporation or such an associated corporation for its last taxation year that ended in the preceding calendar year (determined before taking into consideration the specified future tax consequences for that last year), or

**S. 127(10.2)** — Income Tax Act, Part I, Division E

(b) where paragraph (a) does not apply, the corporation's taxable income for its immediately preceding taxation year (determined before taking into consideration the specified future tax consequences for that preceding year), and

B is the total of the business limits under section 125 for the particular year of the corporation and any such other corporations for the particular year,

unless the corporation is associated in the particular year with one or more other Canadian-controlled private corporations, in which case, except as otherwise provided in this section, its expenditure limit for the particular year is nil.

**Related Provisions**: 87(2)(oo) — Effect of amalgamation; 88(1)(e.8) — Winding-up; 125(5.1) — Elimination of business limit (and therefore the expenditure limit) for large corporations; 127(10.3)–(10.6) — Expenditure limit to be shared among associated corporations; 127(10.6)(c) — Short taxation year; 257 — Formula cannot calculate to less than zero.

**Notes**: 127(10.2) amended by 1994 Budget and retroactively by 1996 Budget, both effective for taxation years that begin after 1995. The expenditure limit is reduced proportionately when the business limit in s. 125 is reduced. For large corporations, 125(5.1) effectively wipes out the business limit, so the expenditure limit under 127(10.2)B is zero, and no credit is provided under 127(10.1). For taxation years that began in 1994 or 1995, read:

(10.2) For the purpose of subsection (10.1), a corporation's expenditure limit for a particular taxation year is the amount determined by the formula

$$\$4,000,000 - 10A$$

where

A is the greater of

(a) $200,000, and

(b) the total of the taxable income of the corporation for the taxation year preceding the particular year and the taxable incomes of all corporations with which it was associated in the particular year for their taxation years ending in the calendar year preceding the calendar year in which the taxpayer's particular year ended,

unless the corporation is associated in the particular year with one or more other Canadian-controlled private corporations in which case, except as otherwise provided in this section, its expenditure limit for the particular year is nil.

The 1996 Budget amendment introduced the reference to "specified future tax consequences" (see definition in 248(1)). "Specified future tax consequences" refers to adjustments from the carryback of losses or similar amounts or because of corrections of certain amounts renounced in connection with the issuance of flow-through shares. Note that there are no "specified future tax consequences" for previous taxation years referred to above unless they end after 1995.

127(10.2) amended by 1993 Budget, effective for taxation years that begin in 1994 or later, to allow the additional ITC (which raises the rate on R&D expenditures from 20% to 35%) to be phased out after taxable income exceeds $200,000 rather than cut off entirely. For taxation years since 1985 and that begin before 1994, read:

(10.2) **Expenditure limit determined** — For the purposes of subsection (10.1), a corporation's expenditure limit for a taxation year is $2,000,000 unless the corporation is associated in the year with one or more other Canadian-controlled private corporations in which case, except as otherwise provided in this section, its expenditure limit for the year is nil.

**Interpretation Bulletins**: IT-151R5: Scientific research and experimental development expenditures.

**(10.3) Associated corporations** — If all of the Canadian-controlled private corporations that are associated with each other in a taxation year file with the Minister in prescribed form an agreement whereby, for the purpose of subsection (10.1), they allocate an amount to one or more of them for the year and the amount so allocated or the total of the amounts so allocated, as the case may be, does not exceed the amount determined for the year by the formula in subsection (10.2), the expenditure limit for the year of each of the corporations is the amount so allocated to it.

**Notes**: 127(10.3) amended by 1993 Budget, effective for taxation years that begin in 1994 or later, to change "is $2,000,000" to "does not exceed the amount determined for the year by the formula in subsection (10.2)".

**Interpretation Bulletins**: IT-151R5: Scientific research and experimental development expenditures.

**Forms**: T2 SCH 23: Agreement among associated Canadian-controlled private corporations to allocate the business limit; T2 SCH 49: Agreement among associated Canadian-controlled private corporations to allocate the expenditure limit.

**(10.4) Failure to file agreement** — If any of the Canadian-controlled private corporations that are associated with each other in a taxation year fails to file with the Minister an agreement as contemplated by subsection (10.3) within 30 days after notice in writing by the Minister is forwarded to any of them that such an agreement is required for the purposes of this Part, the Minister shall, for the purpose of subsection (10.1), allocate an amount to one or more of them for the year, which amount or the total of which amounts, as the case may be, shall equal the amount determined for the year by the formula in subsection (10.2), and in any such case the expenditure limit for the year of each of the corporations is the amount so allocated to it.

**Notes**: 127(10.4) amended by 1993 Budget, effective for taxation years that begin in 1994 or later, to change "shall equal $2,000,000" to "shall equal the amount determined for the year by the formula in subsection (10.2)".

**(10.5)** [Repealed under former Act]

**Notes**: 127(10.5) repealed in 1985, retroactive to its introduction.

**(10.6) Expenditure limit determination in certain cases** — Notwithstanding any other provision of this section,

(a) where a Canadian-controlled private corporation (in this paragraph referred to as the "first corporation") has more than one taxation year ending in the same calendar year and it is associated in two or more of those taxation years with another Canadian-controlled private corporation that has a taxation year ending in that calendar year, the expenditure limit of the first corporation for each taxation year in which it is associated with the other corporation ending in that calendar year is, subject to the application of paragraph (b), an amount equal to its expenditure limit for the first such taxation year determined without reference to paragraph (b);

(b) where a Canadian-controlled private corporation has a taxation year that is less than 51 weeks, its expenditure limit for the year is that proportion of its expenditure limit for the year determined without reference to this paragraph that the number of days in the year is of 365; and

(c) [effective for taxation years that begin in 1996 or later] for the purpose of subsection (10.2), where a Canadian-controlled private corporation has a taxation year that is less than 51 weeks, the taxable income and business limit of the corporation for the year shall be determined by multiplying those amounts by the ratio that 365 is of the number of days in that year.

**Notes**: 127(10.6)(c) added by 1994 Budget, effective for taxation years that begin after 1995.

**Interpretation Bulletins**: IT-151R5: Scientific research and experimental development expenditures.

**(10.7) Further additions to investment tax credit [repaid assistance]** — Where a taxpayer has in a particular taxation year repaid an amount of government assistance, non-government assistance or a contract payment that was applied to reduce

(a) the amount of a qualified expenditure incurred by the taxpayer under paragraph (11.1)(c) for a preceding taxation year that began before 1996,

(b) the prescribed proxy amount of the taxpayer under paragraph (11.1)(f) for a preceding taxation year that began before 1996, or

(c) a qualified expenditure incurred by the taxpayer under any of subsections (18) to (20) for a preceding taxation year,

there shall be added to the amount otherwise determined under subsection (10.1) in respect of the taxpayer for the particular year the amount, if any, by which

(d) the amount that would have been determined under subsection (10.1) in respect of the taxpayer for that preceding year if subsections (11.1) and (18) to (20) had not applied in respect of the government assistance, non-government assistance or contract payment, as the case may be, to the extent of the amount so repaid,

exceeds

(e) the amount determined under subsection (10.1) in respect of the taxpayer for that preceding year.

**Related Provisions**: 127(10.8) — Further additions to investment tax credits.

**Notes**: 127(10.7) amended by 1995 Budget, effective for taxation years that begin after 1995. For earlier years, read:

(10.7) Where a taxpayer has in a particular taxation year repaid an amount of government assistance, non-government assistance or a contract payment that had, because of subsection (11.1), resulted in a reduction of the amount of a qualified expenditure for a preceding taxation year, there shall be added to the amount otherwise determined under subsection (10.1) in respect of the taxpayer for the particular year the amount, if any, by which

(a) the amount that would have been determined under subsection (10.1) in respect of the taxpayer for that preceding year if subsection (11.1) had not applied in respect of the government assistance, non-government assistance or contract payment, as the case may be, to the extent of the amount so repaid,

exceeds

(b) the amount determined under subsection (10.1) in respect of the taxpayer for that preceding year.

127(10.7) added by 1991 technical bill, effective for amounts repaid after May 23, 1985.

**(10.8) Further additions to investment tax credit [expired assistance]** — For the purposes of paragraph (e.1) of the definition "investment tax credit" in subsection (9), subsection (10.7) and paragraph 37(1)(c), an amount of government assistance, non-government assistance or a contract payment that

(a) was applied to reduce

(i) the capital cost to a taxpayer of a property under paragraph (11.1)(b),

(ii) the amount of a qualified expenditure incurred by a taxpayer under paragraph (11.1)(c) for taxation years that began before 1996,

(iii) the prescribed proxy amount of a taxpayer under paragraph (11.1)(f) for taxation years that began before 1996, or

(iv) a qualified expenditure incurred by a taxpayer under any of subsections (18) to (20),

(b) was not received by the taxpayer, and

(c) ceased in a taxation year to be an amount that the taxpayer can reasonably be expected to receive,

is deemed to be the amount of a repayment by the taxpayer in the year of the government assistance, non-government assistance or contract payment, as the case may be.

**Related Provisions**: 127(9)"investment tax credit"(e.1), (e.2) — Repayment of assistance; 127(9)"specified percentage"(f) — Repayment of assistance.

**Notes**: 127(10.8) allows a taxpayer to regenerate an ITC where entitlement to assistance expires without the assistance being received.

127(10.8) amended by 1995 Budget, effective for taxation years that begin after 1995. For earlier taxation years since 1991, read:

(10.8) For the purposes of paragraph (e.1) of the definition "investment tax credit" in subsection (9), subsection (10.7) and paragraph 37(1)(c), where an amount of assistance that

(a) was applied in reduction of

(i) the capital cost to a taxpayer of a property, because of paragraph (11.1)(b), or

(ii) the amount of a qualified expenditure made by a taxpayer, because of paragraph (11.1)(c),

(b) was not received by the taxpayer, and

**S. 127(10.8)**           Income Tax Act, Part I, Division E

(c) ceased in a taxation year to be an amount that the taxpayer can reasonably be expected to receive,

that amount shall be deemed to be an amount of assistance repaid by the taxpayer in the year.

127(10.8) added by 1992 technical bill, effective for 1991 and later taxation years.

**(11) Interpretation** — For the purposes of the definition "qualified property" in subsection (9),

  (a) "manufacturing or processing" does not include any of the activities

    (i) referred to in any of paragraphs (a) to (e) and (g) to (i) of the definition "manufacturing or processing" in subsection 125.1(3),

    (ii) that would be referred to in paragraph (f) of that definition if that paragraph were read without reference to the expression "located in Canada",

    (iii) that would be referred to in paragraph (j) of that definition if that paragraph were read without reference to the expression "in Canada", or

    (iv) that would be referred to in paragraph (k) of that definition if the definition "Canadian field processing" in subsection 248(1) were read without reference to the expression "in Canada"; and

  (b) for greater certainty, the purposes referred to in paragraph (c) of the definition "qualified property" in subsection (9) do not include

    (i) storing (other than the storing of grain), shipping, selling or leasing finished goods,

    (ii) purchasing raw materials,

    (iii) administration, including clerical and personnel activities,

    (iv) purchase and resale operations,

    (v) data processing, or

    (vi) providing facilities for employees, including cafeterias, clinics and recreational facilities.

**Notes**: 127(11)(a) amended by 1996 Budget, effective for taxation years that begin after 1996. For earlier years since 1990, read:

(a) "manufacturing or processing" does not include any of the activities

  (i) referred to in any of paragraphs (a) to (e) and (i) to (k) of the definition "manufacturing or processing" in subsection 125.1(3), or

  (ii) that would be referred to in any of paragraphs (f) to (h) of that definition if those paragraphs were read without reference to the expression "located in Canada"; and

127(11)(a) amended by 1991 technical bill, effective 1990, as a result of amendments to 125.1(3)"manufacturing or processing" (formerly 125.1(3)(b)). For 1985 to 1989, read as simply:

(a) "manufacturing or processing" does not include any of the activities referred to in paragraphs (a) to (k) of the definition "manufacturing or processing" in subsection 125.1(3); and

**Interpretation Bulletins**: IT-411R: Meaning of "construction".

**(11.1) Investment tax credit** — For the purposes of the definition "investment tax credit" in subsection (9),

  (a) the capital cost to a taxpayer of a property shall be computed as if no amount were added thereto by virtue of section 21;

  (b) the capital cost to a taxpayer of a property shall be deemed to be the capital cost to the taxpayer of the property, determined without reference to subsections 13(7.1) and (7.4), less the amount of any government assistance or non-government assistance that can reasonably be considered to be in respect of, or for the acquisition of, the property and that, at the time of the filing of the taxpayer's return of income under this Part for the taxation year in which the property was acquired, the taxpayer has received, is entitled to receive or can reasonably be expected to receive;

  (c) [Repealed]

  (c.1) the amount of a taxpayer's qualified Canadian exploration expenditure for a taxation year shall be deemed to be the amount of the taxpayer's qualified Canadian exploration expenditure for the year as otherwise determined less the amount of any government assistance, non-government assistance or contract payment (other than assistance under the *Petroleum Incentives Program Act* or the *Petroleum Incentives Program Act*, Chapter P-4.1 of the Statutes of Alberta, 1981) in respect of expenditures included in determining the taxpayer's qualified Canadian exploration expenditure for the year that, at the time of the filing of the taxpayer's return of income for the year, the taxpayer has received, is entitled to receive or can reasonably be expected to receive; and

**Proposed Addition — 127(11.1)(c.2)**

(c.2) the amount of a taxpayer's flow-through mining expenditure for a taxation year is deemed to be the amount of the taxpayer's flow-through mining expenditure for the year as otherwise determined less the amount of any government assistance or non-government assistance in respect of expenses included in determining the taxpayer's flow-through mining expenditure for the year that, at the time of the filing of the taxpayer's return of income for the year, the taxpayer has received, is entitled to receive or can reasonably be expected to receive; and

**Application**: The December 21, 2000 draft legislation, subsec. 73(8), will add para. 127(11.1)(c.2), applicable to 2000 *et seq.*

**Technical Notes**: Subsection 127(11.1) sets out various rules for determining amounts to be included for the purpose of the definition "investment tax credit" in subsection 127(9). These rules provide for the reduction of capital cost and qualified expenditures by certain amounts that qualify as assistance or contract payments.

Subdivision c — Computation of Tax: All Taxpayers          S. 127(11.2)

New paragraph 127(11.1) (c.2) reduces a taxpayer's "flow-through mining expenditure" (as newly defined in subsection 127(9)) by the amount of assistance that the taxpayer has received, is entitled to receive or can reasonably be expected to receive relating to expenses included in determining the taxpayer's flow-through mining expenditure.

(d) where at a particular time a taxpayer who is a beneficiary of a trust or a member of a partnership has received, is entitled to receive or can reasonably be expected to receive government assistance, non-government assistance or a contract payment, the amount thereof that may reasonably be considered to be in respect of, or for the acquisition of, depreciable property of the trust or partnership or in respect of an expenditure by the trust or partnership shall be deemed to have been received at that time by the trust or partnership, as the case may be, as government assistance, non-government assistance or as a contract payment in respect of the property or the expenditure, as the case may be.

(e), (f) [Repealed]

**Related Provisions**: 12(1)(x) — Payments as inducement or reimbursement etc.; 127(9)"investment tax credit"(e.1), (e.2) — Inclusion in ITC; 127(10.7), (10.8) — Further additions to ITCs; 248(16) — GST — input tax credit and rebate; 248(18) — GST repayment of input tax credit.

**Notes**: 127(11.1)(c), (e) and (f) repealed by 1995 Budget, effective for taxation years that begin after 1995. These provisions, which reduced the amount of qualified expenditures that were taken into account in the calculation of ITC, are replaced by 127(11.5) and (18) to (21). For earlier taxation years, read:

(c) the amount of a qualified expenditure (other than a prescribed proxy amount or an amount determined under paragraph (e)) made by a taxpayer shall be deemed to be the amount of the qualified expenditure, determined without reference to subsections 13(7.1) and (7.4), less the amount of any government assistance, non-government assistance or contract payment that can reasonably be considered to be in respect of the expenditure and that, at the time of the filing of the taxpayer's return of income under this Part for the taxation year in which the expenditure was made, the taxpayer has received, is entitled to receive or can reasonably be expected to receive;

. . . . .

(e) the amount of a qualified expenditure made by a taxpayer in the taxation year ending coincidentally with the end of the first period (within the meaning assigned in the definition "first term shared-use-equipment" in subsection (9)) or the second period (within the meaning assigned in the definition "second term shared-use-equipment" in subsection (9)) in respect of first term shared-use-equipment or second term shared-use-equipment, respectively, of the taxpayer shall be deemed to be ¼ of the capital cost of the equipment that would be determined in accordance with paragraphs (a) and (b) if paragraph (b) were read as

"(b) the capital cost to a taxpayer of a property shall be deemed to be the capital cost to the taxpayer of the property, determined without reference to subsections 13(7.1) and (7.4), less the amount of any government assistance, non-government assistance or contract payment that can reasonably be considered to be in respect of, or for the acquisition of, the property and that, at the time of the filing of the return of income under this

Part for the taxation year ending coincidentally with the first period, the taxpayer has received, is entitled to receive or can reasonably be expected to receive;"; and

(f) the prescribed proxy amount of a taxpayer for a taxation year shall be deemed to be the prescribed proxy amount of the taxpayer for the taxation year less the amount of any government assistance, non-government assistance or contract payment that can reasonably be considered to be in respect of an expenditure described in subparagraph 37(8)(a)(ii), other than an expenditure described in clause (B) of that subparagraph, and that, at the time of the filing of the taxpayer's return of income under this Part for the taxation year in which the expenditure was made, the taxpayer has received, is entitled to receive or can reasonably be expected to receive.

127(11.1) amended by 1992 Economic Statement, effective for taxation years that end after December 2, 1992. For earlier years, ignore the phrase "can reasonably be considered to be" in paras. (b) and (c); ignore the exclusion for "a prescribed proxy amount or an amount determined under (e)" in para. (c); and ignore paras. (e) and (f).

127(11.1) amended by 1985 Budget, effective for property acquired and expenditures made after May 23, 1985, other than property acquired and expenditures made after that date under the terms of an agreement in writing entered into on or before that date.

**Interpretation Bulletins [subsec. 127(11.1)]**: IT-151R5: Scientific research and experimental development expenditures.

**(11.2) Time of expenditure and acquisition** — In applying subsections (5), (7) and (8), paragraphs (a) and (a.1) of the definition "investment tax credit" in subsection (9) and section 127.1,

(a) certified property, qualified property and first term shared-use-equipment are deemed not to have been acquired, and

(b) expenditures incurred to acquire property described in subparagraph 37(1)(b)(i) are deemed not to have been incurred

by a taxpayer before the property is considered to have become available for use by the taxpayer, determined without reference to paragraphs 13(27)(c) and (28)(d).

**Related Provisions**: 13(26) — No CCA until property available for use; 37(1.2) — No R&D deduction for capital expenditure until property available for use; 248(19) — When property available for use.

**Notes**: 127(11.2) amended by 1995 Budget, effective for taxation years that begin after 1995. The changes are generally non-substantive and relate to the changes in wording in 127(9)"investment tax credit". For earlier taxation years, read:

(11.2) In applying subsections (5), (7) and (8), paragraph (a) of the definition "investment tax credit" in subsection (9) and section 127.1,

(a) property described in subparagraph (a)(i) of the definition "investment tax credit" in subsection (9) shall be deemed not to have been acquired,

(b) property that is first term shared-use-equipment the expenditure for which is a qualified expenditure included in subparagraph (a)(ii) of the definition "investment tax credit" in subsection (9) shall be deemed not to have been acquired, and

(c) expenditures incurred to acquire property described in subparagraph 37(1)(b)(i) shall be deemed not to have been incurred,

1147

## S. 127(11.2) — Income Tax Act, Part I, Division E

by the taxpayer before the property is considered to have become available for use by the taxpayer, determined without reference to paragraphs 13(27)(c) and (28)(d).

127(11.2) amended by 1994 Budget, essentially to add para. (b), effective for property acquired and expenditures incurred after February 21, 1994. For earlier acquisitions and expenditures, read:

> (11.2) For the purposes of this section and section 127.1, property described in subparagraph (a)(i) of the definition "investment tax credit" in subsection (9) shall be deemed not to have been acquired, and expenditures made to acquire property described in subparagraph 37(1)(b)(i) shall be deemed not to have been made, by a taxpayer before the property is considered to have become available for use by the taxpayer, determined without reference to paragraphs 13(27)(c) and (28)(d).

127(11.2) added by 1991 technical bill, effective for property acquired and expenditures made in 1990 or later.

**Interpretation Bulletins**: IT-151R5: Scientific research and experimental development expenditures.

**Advance Tax Rulings**: ATR-44: Utilization of deductions and credits within a related corporate group.

**(11.3) Decertification of approved project property** — For the purposes of the definition "approved project property" in subsection (9), a property that has been certified by the Minister of Regional Industrial Expansion, the Minister of Industry, Science and Technology or the member of the Queen's Privy Council for Canada appointed to be the Minister for the purposes of the *Atlantic Canada Opportunities Agency Act* may have its certification revoked by the latter Minister where

(a) an incorrect statement was made in the furnishing of information for the purpose of obtaining the certificate, or

(b) the taxpayer does not conform to the plan described in that definition,

and a certificate that has been so revoked shall be void from the time of its issue.

**Related Provisions**: 241(4) — Communication of information — exception.

**(11.4) [Repealed]**

**Notes**: 127(11.4) repealed by 1997 Budget, effective for 1997 and later taxation years. See now 37(12). For the 1996 taxation year (per the 1997 Budget bill, which changed the reference at the beginning from "qualified expenditure"(e) to "investment tax credit"(m)), read:

> (11.4) Reclassified expenditures — Paragraph (m) of the definition "investment tax credit" in subsection (9) does not apply to an expenditure incurred in a taxation year by a taxpayer if the expenditure is reclassified by the Minister on an assessment of the taxpayer's tax payable under this Part for the year, or on a determination that no tax under this Part is payable for the year by the taxpayer, as an expenditure in respect of scientific research and experimental development.

127(11.4) amended by 1995 Budget, effective for taxation years that begin after 1995, to change the first two words from "Paragraph (c)" to "Paragraph (e)", as a result of amendments to 127(9)"qualified expenditure".

127(11.4) added by 1993 technical bill, effective February 22, 1994 for expenditures incurred at any time.

**Application Policies**: SR&ED 96-03: Claimants' entitlements and responsibilities.

**(11.5) Adjustments to qualified expenditures** — For the purpose of the definition "qualified expenditure" in subsection (9),

(a) the amount of an expenditure (other than a prescribed proxy amount or an amount described in paragraph (b)) incurred by a taxpayer in a taxation year is deemed to be the amount of the expenditure, determined without reference to subsections 13(7.1) and (7.4) and after the application of subsection (11.6); and

(b) the amount of an expenditure incurred by a taxpayer in the taxation year that ends coincidentally with the end of the first period (within the meaning assigned in the definition "first term shared-use-equipment" in subsection (9)) or the second period (within the meaning assigned in the definition "second term shared-use-equipment" in subsection (9)) in respect of first term shared-use-equipment or second term shared-use-equipment, respectively, of the taxpayer is deemed to be $\frac{1}{4}$ of the capital cost of the equipment determined after the application of subsection (11.6) in accordance with the following rules:

(i) the capital cost to the taxpayer shall be computed as if no amount were added thereto because of section 21, and

(ii) the capital cost to the taxpayer is determined without reference to subsections 13(7.1) and (7.4).

**Related Provisions**: 12(1)(x)(vi) — Income inclusion from reimbursement or assistance; 127(11.6) — Non-arm's length costs; 127(18) — Reduction of qualified expenditures.

**Notes**: 127(11.5) added by 1995 Budget, effective for taxation years that begin after 1995. It is similar to former 127(11.1)(c) and (e), and reduces the qualified expenditures incurred by a taxpayer in a taxation year. For interpretation rules, see 127(11.6)–(11.8). See also 127(18).

**(11.6) Non-arm's length costs** — For the purpose of subsection (11.5), where

(a) a taxpayer would, if this Act were read without reference to subsection (26), incur at any time an expenditure as consideration for a person or partnership (referred to in this subsection as the "supplier") rendering a service (other than a service rendered by a person as an employee of the taxpayer) or providing a property to the taxpayer, and

(b) at that time the taxpayer does not deal at arm's length with the supplier,

the amount of the expenditure incurred by the taxpayer for the service or property and the capital cost to the taxpayer of the property are deemed to be

(c) in the case of a service rendered to the taxpayer, the lesser of

(i) the amount of the expenditure otherwise incurred by the taxpayer for the service, and

Subdivision c — Computation of Tax: All Taxpayers   S. 127(11.7) adj

(ii) the adjusted service cost to the supplier of rendering the service, and

(d) in the case of a property sold to the taxpayer, the lesser of

(i) the capital cost to the taxpayer of the property otherwise determined, and

(ii) the adjusted selling cost to the supplier of the property.

**Related Provisions**: 12(1)(x)(vi) — Income inclusion from reimbursement or assistance; 127(11.7) — Meaning of adjusted selling cost and adjusted service cost; 127(11.8) — Interpretation; 127(24) — Exclusion from qualified expenditure.

**Notes**: 127(11.6) added by 1995 Budget, effective for taxation years that begin after 1995. It provides rules for determining the expenditures in respect of purchases of goods and services from non-arm's length parties.

**(11.7) Definitions** — The definitions in this subsection apply in this subsection and subsection (11.6).

**"adjusted selling cost"** to a person or partnership (referred to in this definition as the "supplier") of a property is the amount determined by the formula

$$A - B$$

where

A is

(a) where the property is purchased from another person or partnership with which the supplier does not deal at arm's length, the lesser of

(i) the cost to the supplier of the property, and

(ii) the adjusted selling cost to the other person or partnership of the property, and

(b) in any other case, the cost to the supplier of the property,

and for the purpose of paragraph (b),

(c) where part of the cost to a supplier of a particular property is attributable to another property acquired by the supplier from a person or partnership with which the supplier does not deal at arm's length, that part of the cost is deemed to be the lesser of

(i) the amount of that part of the cost otherwise determined, and

(ii) the adjusted selling cost to the person or the partnership of the other property,

(d) where part of the cost to a supplier of a property is attributable to a service (other than a service rendered by a person as an employee of the supplier) rendered to the supplier by a person or partnership with which the supplier does not deal at arm's length, that part of the cost is deemed to be the lesser of

(i) the amount of that part of the cost otherwise determined, and

(ii) the adjusted service cost to the person or partnership of rendering the service, and

(e) no part of the cost to a supplier of a property that is attributable to remuneration based on profits or a bonus paid or payable to an employee of the supplier shall be included, and

B is the total of all amounts each of which is the amount of government assistance or non-government assistance that can reasonably be considered to be in respect of the property and that the supplier has received, is entitled to receive or can reasonably be expected to receive.

**Related Provisions**: 127(11.8) — Interpretation; 257 — Formula cannot calculate to less than zero.

**Notes**: Definition "adjusted selling cost" added by 1995 Budget, effective for taxation years that begin after 1995. It traces the costs incurred by non-arm's length parties in providing a service or a property, for purposes of 127(11.6).

**"adjusted service cost"** to a person or partnership (referred to in this definition as the "supplier") of rendering a particular service is the amount determined by the formula:

$$A - B - C - D - E$$

where

A is the cost to the supplier of rendering the particular service,

B is the total of all amounts each of which is the amount, if any, by which

(a) the cost to the supplier for a service (other than a service rendered by a person as an employee of the supplier) rendered by a person or partnership that does not deal at arm's length with the supplier to the extent that the cost is incurred for the purpose of rendering the particular service

exceeds

(b) the adjusted service cost to the person or partnership referred to in paragraph (a) of rendering the service referred to in that paragraph to the supplier,

C is the total of all amounts each of which is the amount, if any, by which

(a) the cost to the supplier of a property acquired by the supplier from a person or partnership that does not deal at arm's length with the supplier

exceeds

(b) the adjusted selling cost to the person or partnership referred to in paragraph (a) of the property,

to the extent that the excess relates to the cost of rendering the particular service,

D is the total of all amounts each of which is remuneration based on profits or a bonus paid or payable to an employee of the supplier to the extent

1149

that it is included in the cost to the supplier of rendering the particular service, and

E is the total of all amounts each of which is government assistance or non-government assistance that can reasonably be considered to be in respect of rendering the particular service and that the supplier has received, is entitled to receive or can reasonably be expected to receive;

**Related Provisions**: 257 — Formula cannot calculate to less than zero.

**Notes**: Definition "adjusted service cost" added by 1995 Budget, effective for taxation years that begin after 1995. It traces the costs incurred by non-arm's length parties in providing a service or a property, for purposes of 127(11.7).

**(11.8) Interpretation for non-arm's length costs** — For the purposes of this subsection and subsections (11.6) and (11.7),

(a) the cost to a person or partnership (referred to in this paragraph as the "supplier") of rendering a service or providing a property to another person or partnership (referred to in this paragraph as the "recipient") with which the supplier does not deal at arm's length does not include,

(i) where the cost to the recipient of the service rendered or property provided by the supplier would, but for this paragraph, be a cost to the recipient incurred in rendering a particular service or providing a particular property to a person or partnership with which the recipient does not deal at arm's length, any expenditure of the supplier to the extent that it would, if it were incurred by the recipient in rendering the particular service or providing the particular property, be excluded from a cost to the recipient because of this paragraph, and

(ii) in any other case, any expenditure of the supplier to the extent that it would, if it were incurred by the recipient, not be a qualified expenditure of the recipient;

(b) paragraph 69(1)(c) does not apply in determining the cost of a property; and

(c) the leasing of a property is deemed to be the rendering of a service.

**Notes**: 127(11.8) added by 1995 Budget, effective for taxation years that begin after 1995. It provides additional rules relating to non-arm's length purchases of goods and services.

**(12) Interpretation** — For the purposes of subsection 13(7.1), where, pursuant to a designation or an allocation from a trust or partnership, an amount is required by subsection (7) or (8) to be added in computing the investment tax credit of a taxpayer at the end of the taxpayer's taxation year, the portion thereof that can reasonably be considered to relate to depreciable property shall be deemed to have been received by the partnership or trust, as the case may be, at the end of its fiscal period in respect of which the designation or allocation was made as assistance from a government for the acquisition of depreciable property.

**(12.1) Idem** — For the purposes of section 37, where, pursuant to a designation or an allocation from a trust or partnership, an amount is required by subsection (7) or (8) to be added in computing the investment tax credit of a taxpayer at the end of the taxpayer's taxation year, the portion thereof that may reasonably be regarded as relating to expenditures of a current nature in respect of scientific research and experimental development that are qualified expenditures shall, at the end of the fiscal period of the trust or partnership, as the case may be, in respect of which the designation or allocation was made, reduce the total of such expenditures of a current nature as may be claimed by the trust or partnership in respect of scientific research and experimental development.

**(12.2) Idem** — For the purposes of paragraphs 53(2)(c), (h) and (k), where in a taxation year a taxpayer has deducted under subsection (5) an amount that may reasonably be regarded as attributable to amounts included in computing the investment tax credit of the taxpayer at the end of the year in respect of property acquired, or an expenditure made, in a subsequent taxation year, the taxpayer shall be deemed to have made the deduction under that subsection in that subsequent taxation year.

**(12.3) Idem** — For the purposes of the determination of J in the definition "cumulative Canadian exploration expense" in subsection 66.1(6), where, pursuant to a designation by a trust, an amount is required by subsection (7) to be added in computing the investment tax credit of a taxpayer at the end of the taxpayer's taxation year, the portion thereof that can reasonably be considered to relate to a qualified Canadian exploration expenditure of the trust for a taxation year shall be deemed to have been received by the trust at the end of its taxation year in respect of which the designation was made as assistance from a government in respect of that expenditure.

**Related Provisions**: 248(16) — GST — input tax credit and rebate deemed to be assistance; 248(18) — GST — repayment of input tax credit.

**(13) Agreement to transfer qualified expenditures** — Where a taxpayer (referred to in this subsection and subsections (15) and (16) as the "transferor") and another taxpayer (referred to in this subsection and subsection (15) as the "transferee") file with the Minister an agreement or an amended agreement in respect of a particular taxation year of the transferor, the least of

(a) the amount specified in the agreement for the purpose of this subsection,

(b) the amount that but for the agreement would be the transferor's SR&ED qualified expenditure pool at the end of the particular year, and

(c) the total of all amounts each of which is an amount that, if the transferor were dealing at arm's length with the transferee, would be a contract payment

(i) for the performance of scientific research and experimental development for, or on behalf of, the transferee,

(ii) that is paid by the transferee to the transferor on or before the day that is 180 days after the end of the particular year, and

(iii) that would be in respect of

(A) a qualified expenditure that

(I) would be incurred by the transferor in the particular year (if this Act were read without reference to subsections (26) and 78(4)) in respect of that portion of the scientific research and experimental development that was performed at a time when the transferor did not deal at arm's length with the transferee, and

(II) is paid by the transferor on or before the day that is 180 days after the end of the particular year, or

(B) an amount added because of this subsection to the transferor's SR&ED qualified expenditure pool at the end of the particular year where the amount is attributable to an expenditure in respect of the scientific research and experimental development

is deemed to be

(d) an amount determined in respect of the transferor for the particular year for the purpose of determining the value of C in the definition "SR&ED qualified expenditure pool" in subsection (9), and

(e) an amount determined in respect of the transferee for the transferee's first taxation year that ends at or after the end of the particular year for the purpose of determining the value of B in the definition "SR&ED qualified expenditure pool" in subsection (9),

and where the total of all amounts each of which is an amount specified in an agreement filed with the Minister under this subsection in respect of a particular taxation year of a transferor exceeds the amount that would be the transferor's SR&ED qualified expenditure pool at the end of the particular year if no agreement were filed with the Minister in respect of the particular year, the least of the amounts determined under paragraphs (a) to (c) in respect of each such agreement is deemed to be nil.

**Related Provisions**: 37(1)(e)(iii) — Reduced SR&ED deduction; 127(8)(a) — Partnership not a person for purposes of this subsection; 127(14) — Identification of amounts transferred as current or capital; 127(15) — Filing requirements; 127(16) — Anti-avoidance; 127(17) — Assessment of other years to take agreement into account; 127(29) — Recapture of ITC of allocating taxpayer.

**Notes**: 127(13) added by 1995 Budget, effective for taxation years that begin after 1995. It provides for the transfer of qualified expenditures between non-arm's length taxpayers. Otherwise, the payer's expenditures in respect of the contract would not be qualified expenditures for ITC purposes: 127(9)"qualified expenditure"(f). In addition, the amount received or receivable by the performer would not be considered to be a contract payment. Qualified expenditures of the performer may be transferred to the payer up to a maximum of the contract amount.

Former 127(13)–(16), repealed by 1988 tax reform effective 1989, enacted the employment tax credit, which no longer exists.

**Forms**: T1146: Agreement to transfer qualified expenditures incurred re SR&ED contracts.

**(14) Identification of amounts transferred** — Where

(a) a transferor and a transferee have filed an agreement under subsection (13) in respect of a taxation year of the transferor,

(b) the agreement includes a statement identifying the amount specified in the agreement for the purpose of subsection (13), or a part of that amount, as being related to

(i) a particular qualified expenditure included in the value of A in the formula in the definition "SR&ED qualified expenditure pool" in subsection (9) for the purpose of determining the transferor's SR&ED qualified expenditure pool at the end of the year, or

(ii) a particular amount included in the value of B in the formula in that definition for the purpose of determining the transferor's SR&ED qualified expenditure pool at the end of the year that is deemed by paragraph (d) to be a qualified expenditure, and

(c) the total of all amounts so identified in agreements filed by the transferor under subsection (13) as being related to the particular expenditure or the particular amount does not exceed the particular expenditure or the particular amount, as the case may be,

for the purposes of this section (other than the description of A in the definition "SR&ED qualified expenditure pool" in subsection (9)) and section 127.1,

(d) the amount so identified that is included in the value of B in the formula in that definition for the purpose of determining the transferee's SR&ED qualified expenditure pool at the end of the taxation year of the transferee is deemed to be a qualified expenditure either of a current nature or of a capital nature, incurred by the transferee in that year, where the particular expenditure or the particular amount was an expenditure of a current nature or of a capital nature, as the case may be, and

(e) except for the purpose of paragraph (b), the amount of the transferor's qualified expenditures of a current nature incurred in the taxation year of the transferor in respect of which the agreement is made is deemed not to exceed the amount by which the amount of such expenditures otherwise determined exceeds the total of all amounts identified under paragraph (b) by the transferor in agreements filed under subsection (13) in respect of the year as being related to expenditures of a current nature.

Notes: 127(14) added by 1995 Budget, effective for taxation years that begin after 1995. It was not included in the draft legislation of July 19, 1995, but was added in the draft of December 12, 1995.

**(15) Invalid agreements** — An agreement or amended agreement referred to in subsection (13) between a transferor and a transferee is deemed not to have been filed with the Minister for the purpose of that subsection where

(a) it is not in prescribed form;

(b) it is not filed

(i) on or before the transferor's filing-due date for the particular taxation year to which the agreement relates,

(ii) in the period within which the transferor may serve a notice of objection to an assessment of tax payable under this Part for the particular year, or

(iii) in the period within which the transferee may serve a notice of objection to an assessment of tax payable under this Part for its first taxation year that ends at or after the end of the transferor's particular year;

(c) it is not accompanied by,

(i) where the transferor is a corporation and its directors are legally entitled to administer its affairs, a certified copy of their resolution authorizing the agreement to be made,

(ii) where the transferor is a corporation and its directors are not legally entitled to administer its affairs, a certified copy of the document by which the person legally entitled to administer its affairs authorized the agreement to be made,

(iii) where the transferee is a corporation and its directors are legally entitled to administer its affairs, a certified copy of their resolution authorizing the agreement to be made, and

(iv) where the transferee is a corporation and its directors are not legally entitled to administer its affairs, a certified copy of the document by which the person legally entitled to administer its affairs authorized the agreement to be made; or

(d) an agreement amending the agreement has been filed in accordance with subsection (13) and this subsection, except where subsection (16) applies to the original agreement.

Notes: 127(15) added by 1995 Budget, effective for taxation years that begin after 1995. It was 127(14) in the draft legislation of July 19, 1995.

**(16) Non-arm's length parties** — Where a taxpayer does not deal at arm's length with another taxpayer as a result of a transaction, event or arrangement, or a series of transactions or events, the principal purpose of which can reasonably be considered to have been to enable the taxpayers to enter into an agreement referred to in subsection (13), for the purpose of paragraph (13)(e) the least of the amounts determined under paragraphs (13)(a) to (c) in respect of the agreement is deemed to be nil.

Related Provisions: 248(10) — Series of transactions.

Notes: 127(16) added by 1995 Budget, effective for taxation years that begin after 1995. It was 127(15) in the draft legislation of July 19, 1995. See also Notes to 127(13).

**(17) Assessment** — Notwithstanding subsections 152(4) and (5), such assessment of the tax, interest and penalties payable by any taxpayer in respect of any taxation year that began before the day an agreement or amended agreement is filed under subsection (13) or (20) shall be made as is necessary to take into account the agreement or the amended agreement.

Notes: 127(17) added by 1995 Budget, effective for taxation years that begin after 1995. It was 127(16) in the draft legislation of July 19, 1995.

**(18) Reduction of qualified expenditures** — Where on or before the filing-due date for a taxation year of a person or partnership (referred to in this subsection as the "taxpayer") the taxpayer has received, is entitled to receive or can reasonably be expected to receive a particular amount that is government assistance, non-government assistance or a contract payment that can reasonably be considered to be in respect of scientific research and experimental development, the amount by which the particular amount exceeds all amounts applied for preceding taxation years under this subsection or subsection (19) or (20) in respect of the particular amount shall be applied to reduce the taxpayer's qualified expenditures otherwise incurred in the year that can reasonably be considered to be in respect of the scientific research and experimental development.

Related Provisions: 127(9)"investment tax credit"(e.1)(iv); 127(9)"investment tax credit"(e.2)(ii) — Inclusion in ITC; 127(9)"qualified expenditure"(h) — Exclusion from qualified expenditure; 127(10.7)(c), (d) — Further addition to ITC; 127(11.5) — Adjustments to qualified expenditures; 127(21) — Failure to allocate; 127(23) — Partnership's taxation year and filing-due date.

Notes: 127(18) added by 1995 Budget, effective for taxation years that begin after 1995. It was 127(17) in the draft legislation of July 19, 1995.

**(19) Reduction of qualified expenditures** — Where on or before the filing-due date for a taxation year of a person or partnership (referred to in this subsection as the "recipient") the recipient has received, is entitled to receive or can reasonably be expected to receive a particular amount that is government assistance, non-government assistance or a contract payment that can reasonably be considered to be in respect of scientific research and experimental development and the particular amount exceeds the total of

(a) all amounts applied for preceding taxation years under this subsection or subsection (18) or (20) in respect of the particular amount,

(b) the total of all amounts each of which would be a qualified expenditure that is incurred in the year by the recipient and that can reasonably be considered to be in respect of the scientific research and experimental development if subsection (18) did not apply to the particular amount, and

(c) the total of all amounts each of which would, but for the application of this subsection to the particular amount, be a qualified expenditure

(i) that was incurred by a person or partnership in a taxation year of the person or partnership that ended in the recipient's taxation year, and

(ii) that can reasonably be considered to be in respect of the scientific research and experimental development to the extent that it was performed by the person or partnership at a time when the person or partnership was not dealing at arm's length with the recipient,

the particular amount shall be applied to reduce each qualified expenditure otherwise determined that is referred to in paragraph (c).

**Related Provisions**: 127(9)"investment tax credit"(e.1)(iv), 127(9)"investment tax credit"(e.2)(ii) — Inclusion in ITC; 127(9)"qualified expenditure"(h) — Exclusion from qualified expenditure; 127(21) — Failure to allocate; 127(23) — Partnership's taxation year and filing-due date.

**Notes**: 127(19) added by 1995 Budget, effective for taxation years that begin after 1995. It was 127(18) in the draft legislation of July 19, 1995.

**(20) Agreement to allocate** — Where

(a) on or before the filing-due date for a taxation year of a person or partnership (referred to in this subsection and subsection (22) as the "taxpayer") the taxpayer has received, is entitled to receive or can reasonably be expected to receive a particular amount that is government assistance, non-government assistance or a contract payment that can reasonably be considered to be in respect of scientific research and experimental development,

(b) subsection (19) does not apply to the particular amount in respect of the year, and

(c) the taxpayer and a person or partnership (referred to in this subsection and subsection (22) as the "transferee") with which the taxpayer does not deal at arm's length file an agreement or amended agreement with the Minister,

the lesser of

(d) the amount specified in the agreement, and

(e) the total of all amounts each of which would, but for the agreement, be a qualified expenditure

(i) that was incurred by the transferee in a particular taxation year of the transferee that ended in the taxpayer's taxation year, and

(ii) that can reasonably be considered to be in respect of the scientific research and experimental development to the extent that it was performed by the transferee at a time when the transferee was not dealing at arm's length with the taxpayer

shall be applied to reduce the qualified expenditures otherwise determined that are described in paragraph (e).

**Related Provisions**: 127(9)"investment tax credit"(e.1)(iv), (e.2)(ii) — Inclusion in ITC; 127(9)"qualified expenditure"(h) — Exclusion from qualified expenditure; 127(17) — Assessment of other years to take agreement into account; 127(21) — Failure to allocate; 127(22) — Filing requirements; 127(23) — Partnership's taxation year and filing-due date.

**Notes**: 127(20) added by 1995 Budget, effective for taxation years that begin after 1995. It was 127(19) in the draft legislation of July 19, 1995.

**Forms**: T1145: Agreement to allocate assistance for SR&ED expenditures between persons not dealing at arm's length.

**(21) Failure to allocate** — Where on or before the filing-due date for a taxation year of a person or partnership (referred to in this subsection as the "recipient") the recipient has received, is entitled to receive or can reasonably be expected to receive a particular amount that is government assistance, non-government assistance or a contract payment that can reasonably be considered to be in respect of scientific research and experimental development and subsection (19) does not apply to the particular amount in respect of the year, the lesser of

(a) the total of all amounts each of which is a qualified expenditure

(i) that was incurred by a particular person or partnership in a taxation year of the particular person or partnership that ended in the recipient's taxation year, and

(ii) that can reasonably be considered to be in respect of the scientific research and experimental development to the extent that it was performed by the particular person or partnership at a time when the particular person or partnership was not dealing at arm's length with the recipient, and

(b) the amount, if any, by which the particular amount exceeds the total of amounts applied for the year and preceding taxation years under subsection (18), (19) or (20) in respect of the particular amount

is deemed for the purposes of this section to be an amount of government assistance received at the end of the particular year by the particular person or partnership in respect of the scientific research and experimental development.

**Related Provisions**: 127(23) — Partnership's taxation year and filing-due date.

**Notes**: 127(21) added by 1995 Budget, effective for taxation years that begin after 1995. It was 127(20) in the draft legislation of July 19, 1995.

**(22) Invalid agreements** — An agreement or amended agreement referred to in subsection (20) between a taxpayer and a transferee is deemed not to have been filed with the Minister where

(a) it is not in prescribed form;

(b) it is not filed

(i) on or before the taxpayer's filing-due date for the particular taxation year to which the agreement relates,

(ii) in the period within which the taxpayer may serve a notice of objection to an assessment of tax payable under this Part for the particular year, or

(iii) in the period within which the transferee may serve a notice of objection to an assessment of tax payable under this Part for its first taxation year that ends at or after the end of the taxpayer's particular year;

(c) it is not accompanied by,

(i) where the taxpayer is a corporation and its directors are legally entitled to administer its affairs, a certified copy of their resolution authorizing the agreement to be made,

(ii) where the taxpayer is a corporation and its directors are not legally entitled to administer its affairs, a certified copy of the document by which the person legally entitled to administer its affairs authorized the agreement to be made,

(iii) where the transferee is a corporation and its directors are legally entitled to administer its affairs, a certified copy of their resolution authorizing the agreement to be made, and

(iv) where the transferee is a corporation and its directors are not legally entitled to administer its affairs, a certified copy of the document by which the person legally entitled to administer its affairs authorized the agreement to be made; or

(d) an agreement amending the agreement has been filed in accordance with subsection (20) and this subsection.

**Related Provisions**: 127(23) — Partnership's taxation year and filing-due date.

**Notes**: 127(22) added by 1995 Budget, effective for taxation years that begin after 1995. It was 127(21) in the draft legislation of July 19, 1995.

**(23) Partnership's taxation year** — For the purposes of subsections (18) to (22), the taxation year of a partnership is deemed to be its fiscal period and its filing-due date for a taxation year is deemed to be the day that would be its filing-due date for the year if it were a corporation.

**Notes**: 127(23) added by 1995 Budget, effective for taxation years that begin after 1995. It was 127(22) in the draft legislation of July 19, 1995.

**(24) Exclusion from qualified expenditure** — Where

(a) a person or partnership (referred to in this subsection as the "first person") does not deal at arm's length with another person or partnership (referred to in this subsection as the "second person"),

(b) there is an arrangement under which an amount is paid or payable by the first person to a person or partnership with which the first person deals at arm's length and an amount is received or receivable by the second person from a person or partnership with which the second person deals at arm's length, and

(c) one of the main purposes of the arrangement can reasonably be considered to be to cause the amount paid or payable by the first person to be a qualified expenditure,

the amount paid or payable by the first person is deemed not to be a qualified expenditure.

**Related Provisions**: 127(11.6) — Non-arm's length costs.

**Notes**: 127(24) added by 1995 Budget, effective for taxation years that begin after 1995. It was 127(23) in the draft legislation of July 19, 1995.

**(25) Deemed contract payment** — Where

(a) a person or partnership (referred to in this subsection as the "first person") deals at arm's length with another person or partnership (referred to in this subsection as the "second person"),

(b) there is an arrangement under which an amount is paid or payable by the first person to a person or partnership (other than the second person) and a particular amount is received or receivable in respect of scientific research and experimental development by the second person from a person or partnership that is not a taxable supplier in respect of the particular amount, and

(c) one of the main purposes of the arrangement can reasonably be considered to be to cause the amount received or receivable by the second person not to be a contract payment,

the amount received or receivable by the second person is deemed to be a contract payment in respect of scientific research and experimental development.

**Notes**: 127(25) added by 1995 Budget, effective for taxation years that begin after 1995. It was 127(24) in the draft legislation of July 19, 1995.

**(26) Unpaid amounts** — For the purposes of subsections (5) to (25) and section 127.1, a taxpayer's expenditure described in paragraph 37(1)(a) that is unpaid on the day that is 180 days after the end of the taxation year in which the expenditure is otherwise incurred is deemed

(a) not to have been incurred in the year; and

(b) to be incurred at the time it is paid.

**Related Provisions**: 127(11.6) — Non-arm's length costs.

**Notes**: 127(26) added by 1995 Budget, effective for amounts that are incurred at any time, except that it does not apply to amounts paid before September 19, 1996. It was 127(25) in the draft legislation of July 19, 1995.

**(27) Recapture of investment tax credit** — Where

(a) a taxpayer acquired a particular property from a person or partnership in a taxation year of the taxpayer or in any of the 10 preceding taxation years,

(b) the cost of the particular property was a qualified expenditure to the taxpayer,

(c) the cost of the particular property is included in an amount, a percentage of which can reasonably be considered to be included in computing the taxpayer's investment tax credit at the end of the taxation year, and

(d) in the year and after February 23, 1998, the taxpayer converts to commercial use, or disposes of without having previously converted to commercial use, the particular property or another property that incorporates the particular property,

there shall be added to the taxpayer's tax otherwise payable under this Part for the year the lesser of the amount that can reasonably be considered to be included in computing the taxpayer's investment tax credit in respect of the particular property and the amount that is the percentage (described in paragraph (c)) of

(e) if the particular property or the other property is disposed of to a person who deals at arm's length with the taxpayer, the proceeds of disposition of that property, and

(f) in any other case, the fair market value of the particular property or the other property at the time of the conversion or disposition.

**Related Provisions**: 37(1)(c.2) — Deduction allowed in subsequent year; 127(28) — Recapture of ITC of partnership; 127(29) — Recapture of ITC of allocating taxpayer; 127(32) — Meaning of "cost of the particular property"; 127(33) — No application to certain non-arm's length transfers.

**Notes**: 127(27) added by 1998 Budget, effective for dispositions and conversions of property that occur after February 23, 1998. It provides for recapture (i.e., repayment to the government) of ITCs claimed on the cost of property that is converted to commercial use or sold within 10 years. It thus overrules *Consoltex Inc.*, [1997] 2 C.T.C. 2846 (TCC).

Amounts added to tax payable under 127(27) will increase the SR&ED pool for the following year: 37(1)(c.2).

**(28) Recapture of investment tax credit of partnership** — For the purpose of computing the amount determined under subsection (8) in respect of a partnership at the end of a particular fiscal period, where

(a) a particular property, the cost of which is a qualified expenditure, is acquired by the partnership from a person or partnership in the particular fiscal period or in any of the 10 preceding fiscal periods of the partnership,

(b) the cost of the particular property is included in an amount, a percentage of which can reasonably be considered to have been included in computing the amount determined under subsection (8) in respect of the partnership at the end of a fiscal period, and

(c) in the particular fiscal period and after February 23, 1998, the partnership converts to commercial use, or disposes of without having previously converted to commercial use, the particular property or another property that incorporates the particular property,

there shall be deducted in computing the amount determined under subsection (8) in respect of the partnership at the end of the particular fiscal period the lesser of

(d) the amount that can reasonably be considered to have been included in respect of the particular property in computing the amount determined under subsection (8) in respect of the partnership, and

(e) the percentage (described in paragraph (b)) of

(i) where the particular property or the other property is disposed of to a person who deals at arm's length with the partnership, the proceeds of disposition of that property, and

(ii) in any other case, the fair market value of the particular property or the other property at the time of the conversion or disposition.

**Related Provisions**: 127(30) — Addition to tax where ITC goes negative; 127(32) — Meaning of "cost of the particular property"; 127(33) — No application to certain non-arm's length transfers.

**Notes**: 127(28) added by 1998 Budget, effective for dispositions and conversions of property that occur after February 23, 1998. It implements the same rule as 127(27), but for a partnership.

**(29) Recapture of investment tax credit of allocating taxpayer** — Where

(a) a taxpayer acquired a particular property from a person or partnership in a taxation year or in any of the 10 preceding taxation years,

(b) the cost of the particular property was a qualified expenditure to the taxpayer,

(c) all or part of the qualified expenditure can reasonably be considered to have been the subject of an agreement made under subsection (13) by the taxpayer and another taxpayer (in this subsection referred to as the "transferee"), and

(d) in the year and after February 23, 1998, the taxpayer converts to commercial use, or disposes of without having previously converted to commercial use, the particular property or another property that incorporates the particular property, there shall be added to the taxpayer's tax otherwise payable under this Part for the year the lesser of

(e) the amount that can reasonably be considered to have been included in computing the transferee's investment tax credit in respect of the qualified expenditure that was the subject of the agreement, and

(f) the amount determined by the formula

$$A \times B - C$$

where

A is the percentage applied by the transferee in determining its investment tax credit in respect of the qualified expenditure that was the subject of the agreement,

B is

(i) where the particular property or the other property is disposed of to a person who deals at arm's length with the taxpayer, the proceeds of disposition of that property, and

(ii) in any other case, the fair market value of the particular property or the other property at the time of the conversion or disposition, and

C is the amount, if any, added to the taxpayer's tax payable under subsection (27) in respect of the particular property.

**Related Provisions**: 37(1)(c.2) — Deduction allowed in subsequent year; 127(32) — Meaning of "cost of the particular property"; 127(33) — No application to certain non-arm's length transfers; 257 — Formula cannot calculate to less than zero.

**Notes**: 127(29) added by 1998 Budget, effective for dispositions and conversions of property that occur after February 23, 1998. It implements the same rule as 127(27) does, but where the original ITC was transferred by agreement under 127(13).

**(30) Addition to tax** — Where a taxpayer is a member of a partnership and the total of

(a) the total of all amounts each of which is the lesser of the amounts described in paragraphs (28)(d) and (e) in respect of a property of the partnership, and

(b) the total of all amounts each of which is the lesser of the amounts described in paragraphs (35)(c) and (d) in respect of a property of the partnership,

exceeds the amount that would be determined in respect of the partnership under subsection (8) if that subsection were read without reference to subsections (28) and (35), the portion of the excess that can reasonably be considered to be the taxpayer's share of the excess shall be added to the taxpayer's tax otherwise payable under this Part for the year.

**Related Provisions**: 37(1)(c.3) — Deduction allowed in subsequent year; 53(1)(e)(xiii) — Addition to adjusted cost base of partnership interest; 127(31) — Tiered partnership.

**Notes**: 127(30) added by 1998 Budget, effective for dispositions and conversions of property that occur after February 23, 1998. It applies where, at the end of a taxation year, a taxpayer is a member of a partnership that does not have enough ITC otherwise available for allocation under 127(8) to offset the ITC recapture required by 127(28) or (35). In such a case, the amounts added in calculating the partnership ITC for 127(8) would be less than the amounts that reduce the partnership ITC. The excess "negative" partnership ITC that can reasonably be considered to be the taxpayer's share is added to the *taxpayer's* tax payable. Amounts payable under 127(30) by members of the partnership will increase the partnership's SR&ED pool for the next year: 37(1)(c.3). As well, the ACB of the partnership interest will be increased: 53(1)(e)(xiii).

**(31) Tiered partnership** — Where a taxpayer is a member of a particular partnership that is a member of another partnership and an amount would be added to the particular partnership's tax payable under this Part for the year pursuant to subsection (30) if the particular partnership were a person and its fiscal period were its taxation year, that amount is deemed to be an amount that is the lesser of the amounts described in paragraphs (28)(d) and (e), in respect of a property of the particular partnership, that is required by subsection (28) to be deducted in computing the amount under subsection (8) in respect of the particular partnership at the end of the fiscal period.

**Notes**: 127(31) added by 1998 Budget, effective for dispositions and conversions of property that occur after February 23, 1998. It is a "look-through" rule to deal with tiers of partnerships. It directs partnerships and their members to continue allocating these amounts down through their members until a level is reached at which the members are taxpayers and not partnerships. This is accomplished by deeming the amount that would be the member partnership's addition to tax under 127(30) if the member were a taxpayer, to be the amount of an ITC recapture under 127(28) in respect of the member partnership. 127(28) will then apply to reduce the ITC available for allocation by the lower-tier partnership under 127(8). If the amount is, in turn, "negative", 127(30) will cause the lower-tier partnership to allocate the addition to tax to its members. If necessary, 127(31) will apply again to allocate the addition to tax down a further level, if the members of the partnership at the next level are partnerships as well.

**(32) Meaning of cost** — For the purposes of subsections (27), (28) and (29), "cost of the particular property" to a taxpayer shall not exceed the amount paid by the taxpayer to acquire the particular property from a transferor of the particular property and, for greater certainty, does not include amounts paid by the taxpayer to maintain, modify or transform the particular property.

**Notes**: 127(32) added by 1998 Budget, effective for dispositions and conversions of property that occur after February 23, 1998. It defines "cost" for purposes of the recapture rules in 127(27)-(29) as the laid-out cost for initial acquisition of the property, not including inputs (such as overhead) which might otherwise be imputed to the cost.

**(33) Certain non-arm's length transfers** — Subsections (27) to (29), (34) and (35) do not apply to a taxpayer or partnership (in this subsection referred to as the "transferor") that disposes of a property to a person or partnership (in this subsection and subsections (34) and (35) referred to as the "purchaser"), that does not deal at arm's length with the transferor, if the purchaser acquired the property in circumstances where the cost of the property to the purchaser would have been an expenditure of the purchaser described in subclause 37(8)(a)(ii)(A)(III) or (B)(III) but for subparagraph 2902(b)(iii) of the *Income Tax Regulations*.

**Related Provisions**: 127(34), (35) — Recapture on disposition or conversion to commercial use.

**Notes**: 127(33) added by 1998 Budget, effective for dispositions and conversions of property that occur after February 23, 1998. It provides that the ITC recapture provisions (see Notes to 127(27)) do not apply to a taxpayer who disposes of SR&ED property to a non-arm's length purchaser if the purchaser continues to use the property all or substantially all for SR&ED (i.e., the property can be moved around within a corporate group). However, on a later disposition or conversion to commercial use, recapture will apply under 127(34) or (35).

**(34) Recapture of investment tax credit** — Where, at any particular time in a taxation year and after February 23, 1998, a purchaser (other than a partnership) converts to commercial use, or disposes of without having previously converted to commercial use, a property

(a) that was acquired by the purchaser in circumstances described in subsection (33) or that is another property that incorporates a property acquired in such circumstances; and

(b) that was first acquired, or that incorporates a property that was first acquired, by a person or partnership (in this subsection referred to as the "original user") with which the purchaser did not deal at arm's length at the time at which the purchaser acquired the property, in the original user's taxation year or fiscal period that includes the particular time (on the assumption that the original user had such a taxation year or fiscal period) or in any of the original user's 10 preceding taxation years or fiscal periods,

there shall be added to the purchaser's tax otherwise payable under this Part for the year the lesser of

(c) the amount

(i) included, in respect of the property, in the investment tax credit of the original user, or

(ii) where the original user is a partnership, that can reasonably be considered to have been included in respect of the property in computing the amount determined under subsection (8) in respect of the original user, and

(d) the amount determined by applying the percentage that was applied by the original user in determining the amount referred to in paragraph (c) to

(i) if the property or the other property is disposed of to a person who deals at arm's length with the purchaser, the proceeds of disposition of that property, and

(ii) in any other case, the fair market value of the property or the other property at the time of the conversion or disposition.

**Related Provisions**: 37(1)(c.2) — Deduction allowed in subsequent year; 127(33) — No application to certain non-arm's length transfers.

**Notes**: 127(34) added by 1998 Budget, effective for dispositions and conversions of property that occur after February 23, 1998. See Notes to 127(33).

**(35) Recapture of investment tax credit** — Where, at any particular time in a fiscal period and after February 23, 1998, a purchaser is a partnership that converts to commercial use, or disposes of without having previously converted to commercial use, a property

(a) that was acquired by the purchaser in circumstances described in subsection (33) or that is another property that incorporates a property acquired in such circumstances, and

(b) that was first acquired, or that incorporates a property that was first acquired, by a person or partnership (in this subsection referred to as the "original user") with which the purchaser did not deal at arm's length at the time at which the purchaser acquired the property, in the original user's taxation year or fiscal period that includes the particular time (on the assumption that the original user had such a taxation year or fiscal period) or in any of the original user's 10 preceding taxation years or fiscal periods,

there shall be deducted in computing the amount determined under subsection (8) in respect of the purchaser at the end of the fiscal period the lesser of

(c) the amount

(i) included, in respect of the property, in the investment tax credit of the original user, or

(ii) where the original user is a partnership, that can reasonably be considered to have been included in respect of the property in computing the amount determined under subsection (8) in respect of the original user, and

(d) the amount determined by applying the percentage that was applied by the original user in determining the amount referred to in paragraph (c) to

(i) if the property or the other property is disposed of to a person who deals at arm's length with the purchaser, the proceeds of disposition of that property, and

(ii) in any other case, the fair market value of the property or the other property at the time of the conversion or disposition.

**Related Provisions**: 127(30) — Addition to tax where ITC goes negative; 127(33) — No application to certain non-arm's length transfers.

**Notes**: 127(35) added by 1998 Budget, effective for dispositions and conversions of property that occur after February 23, 1998. See Notes to 127(33).

**Definitions [s. 127]**: "acquired" — 256(7)–(9); "active business" — 248(1); "adjusted selling cost", "adjusted service cost" — 127(11.7); "allowable capital loss" — 38(b), 248(1); "amount" — 127(11.6), 248(1); "annual investment tax credit limit", "approved project", "approved project property" — 127(9); "arm's length" — 251(1); "assessment" — 248(1); "assistance" — 79(4), 125.4(5), 248(16), (18); "associated" — 256; "at-risk amount" — 96(2.2), 127(8.5); "available for use" — 13(27)–(32), 248(19); "bank" —

248(1), *Interpretation Act* 35(1); "beneficially interested" — 248(25); "business" — 248(1); "calendar year" — *Interpretation Act* 37(1)(a); "Canada" — 127(9)"qualified property"(d), 255; "Canadian-controlled private corporation" — 125(7), 136(1), 248(1); "Canadian field processing" — 248(1); "Canadian exploration expense" — 66.1(6), 248(1); "Canadian partnership" — 102(1), 248(1); "Cape Breton" — 127(9); "capital cost" — 13(7.1)–(7.4), 127(11.1)(a), (b); "capital gain" — 39(1)(a), 248(1); "capital property" — 54, 248(1); "carrying on business" — 253; "certified property" — 127(9); "contract payment" — 127(9), (25); "control" — 256(6)–(9); "controlled" — 256(6), (6.1); "corporation" — 248(1), *Interpretation Act* 35(1); "cost" — 127(11.8)(a); "cost of the particular property" — 127(32); "credit union" — 137(6), 248(1); "depreciable property" — 13(21), 248(1); "disposition" — 248(1); "eligible taxpayer" — 127(9); "employee", "exempt income" — 248(1); "expenditure" — 127(11.6), (26); "farm loss" — 111(8), 248(1); "filing-due date" — 127(23), 248(1); "first-term shared-use-equipment" — 127(9); "fiscal period" — 249(2)(b), 249.1; "flow-through mining expenditure" — 127(9), (11.1)(c.2); "Gaspé Peninsula", "government assistance" — 127(9); "incurred" — 127(26); "individual" — 248(1); *inter vivos* trust" — 108(1), 248(1); "investment tax credit" — 127(9), 248(1); "legislature" — *Interpretation Act* 35(1); "limited partner" — 96(2.4), 127(8.5); "manufacturing or processing" — 127(11)(a); "mineral resource", "Minister" — 248(1); "monetary contribution" — 127(4.1); "non-capital loss" — 111(8), 248(1); "non-government assistance", "non-qualifying corporation" — 127(9); "non-resident" — 248(1); "official agent" — 127(4); "oil or gas well" — 248(1); "partnership" — see Notes to 96(1); "permanent establishment" — Reg. 8201; "person", "prescribed", "property" — 248(1); "province" — *Interpretation Act* 35(1); "purchaser" — 127(33); "purposes" — 127(11)(b); "qualified Canadian exploration expenditure" — 127(9), (11.1)(c.1); "qualified construction equipment" — 127(9); "qualified expenditure" — 127(9), (14), (24); "qualified property", "qualified small-business property", "qualified transportation equipment" — 127(9); "record" — 248(1); "refundable Part VII tax on hand" — 192(3), 248(1); "registered agent", "registered party" — 127(4); "regulation" — 248(1); "resident in Canada" — 250; "SR&ED qualified expenditure pool" — 127(9), (14); "scientific research and experimental development" — 37(13), 248(1); "second-term shared-use-equipment" — 127(9); "series of transactions" — 248(10); "service" — 127(11.8)(c); "share", "specified future tax consequence", "specified member" — 248(1); "specified percentage", "super-allowance benefit amount" — 127(9); "tar sands" — 248(1); "tax otherwise payable" — 117(1), 120(4), 127(17); "tax payable" — 248(2); "taxable capital gain" — 38(a), 248(1); "taxable income" — 2(2), 248(1); "taxable income earned in Canada" — 115(1), 248(1); "taxable supplier" — 127(9); "taxation year" — 127(23), 249; "taxpayer" — 248(1); "testamentary trust" — 108(1), 248(1); "transferor" — 127(13); "trust" — 104(1), 248(1), (3); "undepreciated capital cost" — 13(21), 248(1); "writing" — *Interpretation Act* 35(1).

## 127.1 (1) Refundable investment tax credit —
Where a taxpayer (other than a person exempt from tax under section 149) files

(a) with the taxpayer's return of income (other than a return of income filed under subsection 70(2) or 104(23), paragraph 128(2)(f) or subsection 150(4)) for a taxation year, or

(b) with a prescribed form amending a return referred to in paragraph (a)

a prescribed form containing prescribed information, the taxpayer is deemed to have paid on the taxpayer's balance-due day for the year an amount on account of the taxpayer's tax payable under this Part for the year equal to the lesser of

(c) the taxpayer's refundable investment tax credit for the year, and

(d) the amount designated by the taxpayer in the prescribed form.

**Related Provisions**: 13(24) — Acquisition of control — limitation re calculation of refundable investment tax credit; 127(14) — Identification of amounts transferred as current or capital; 127.1(3) — Refundable ITC deemed claimed under 127(5); 136 — Cooperative not private corporation — exception; 152(1) — Assessment; 157(3)(e) — Reduction in monthly corporate instalments to reflect credit; 160.1 — Where excess refunded; 164(1)(a) — Refunds; 220(6) — Assignment of refund by corporation permitted; 256(2.1) — Anti-avoidance.

**Notes**: Because the taxpayer is "deemed to have paid" the amount in question, it, like instalments or source deductions, is treated as a credit to the account that is fully refundable even if no tax is payable for the year.

127.1(1)(a) amended by 1995-97 technical bill, effective for taxation years that begin after April 26, 1995, to change reference from 128(2)(e) to 128(2)(f).

Words between (b) and (c) amended by 1996 Budget, effective for taxation years that end after February 22, 1994, to use the term "balance-due day" (see 248(1)) in place of "the day on which the return referred to in paragraph (a) or the form referred to in paragraph (b), as the case may be, is filed". The change is non-substantive.

**Application Policies**: SR&ED 96-03: Claimants' entitlements and responsibilities; SR&ED 96-05: Penalties under subsec. 163(2).

## (2) Definitions — In this section,

**"excluded corporation"** for a taxation year means a corporation that is, at any time in the year,

(a) controlled directly or indirectly, in any manner whatever, by

(i) one or more persons exempt from tax under this Part by virtue of section 149,

(ii) Her Majesty in right of a province, a Canadian municipality or any other public authority, or

(iii) any combination of persons each of whom is a person referred to in subparagraph (i) or (ii), or

(b) related to any person referred to in paragraph (a);

**Related Provisions**: 256(5.1), (6.2) — Controlled directly or indirectly — control in fact.

**"qualifying corporation"** for a particular taxation year that ends in a calendar year means

(a) a corporation that is a Canadian-controlled private corporation throughout the particular year (other than a corporation associated with another corporation in the particular year) the taxable income of which for its immediately preceding taxation year (determined before taking into consideration the specified future tax consequences for that preceding year) does not exceed its business limit for that preceding year, or

(b) a corporation that is a Canadian-controlled private corporation throughout the particular year and associated with another corporation in the particular year, where the total of all amounts each of which is the taxable income of the corporation or such an associated corporation for its last taxation year that ended in the preceding calendar year (determined before taking into consideration the specified future tax consequences for that last year) does not exceed the total of all amounts each of which is the business limit of the corporation or such an associated corporation for that last year;

**Related Provisions:** 87(2)(oo), (oo.1) — Effect of amalgamation; 88(1)(e.9) — Winding-up; 127.1(2.01) — Additional refundable amount for corporation that is not a qualifying corporation.

**Notes:** Definition "qualifying corporation" amended by 1996 Budget, effective for taxation years that begin after 1995. For earlier years that end after June 1994, read:

"qualifying corporation" for a particular taxation year means a corporation that is, throughout the particular year, a Canadian-controlled private corporation the taxable income of which for its preceding taxation year or, if it is associated with one or more other corporations in the particular year, the taxable income of the corporation for its last taxation year ending in the preceding calendar year plus the taxable incomes of all such other corporations for their last taxation years ending in the preceding calendar year, does not exceed the total of the business limits (as determined under section 125) of the corporation and the other corporations for those preceding years, except that for a particular taxation year that begins before 1996 the total of the business limits shall be determined under section 125 as that section read in its application to taxation years ending before July 1994;

See also Notes to 248(1)"specified future tax consequences".

Definition amended by 1994 Budget, effective for taxation years that end after June 1994. For earlier years, read:

"qualifying corporation" for a particular taxation year means a corporation that is, throughout the particular year, a Canadian-controlled private corporation whose taxable income for the immediately preceding taxation year together with the taxable incomes of all corporations with which it was associated in the particular year for their taxation years ending in the calendar year immediately preceding the calendar year in which the particular year of the corporation ended does not exceed the total of the business limits (as determined under section 125) of the corporation and the associated corporations for those preceding years;

The 1994 amendment was consequential on the restriction on the small business deduction in 125(5.1). The amendment ensures that the business limits of the corporation and its associated corporations, as determined under new 125, apply only to taxation years that begin after 1995. For taxation years that begin before 1996, the business limits under section 125 continue to be determined in the same way as for taxation years ending before July 1994. This 2-year postponement, of the consequential effect of the small business deduction changes on the refundability of ITCs, matches the effective date of the changes to 127(10.1) and (10.2).

**"refundable investment tax credit"** of a taxpayer for a taxation year means, in the case of a taxpayer who is

(a) a qualifying corporation for the year,

(b) an individual other than a trust, or

(c) a trust each beneficiary of which is a person referred to in paragraph (a) or (b),

an amount equal to 40% of the amount, if any, by which

(d) the total of all amounts included in computing the taxpayer's investment tax credit at the end of the year

(i) in respect of property (other than qualified small-business property) acquired, or a qualified expenditure (other than an expenditure in respect of which an amount is included under paragraph (f) in computing the taxpayer's refundable investment tax credit for the year) incurred, by the taxpayer in the year, or

(ii) because of paragraph (b) of the definition "investment tax credit" in subsection 127(9) in respect of a property (other than qualified small-business property) acquired or a qualified expenditure (other than an expenditure in respect of which an amount is included under paragraph (f) in computing the taxpayer's refundable investment tax credit for the year) incurred

exceeds

(e) the total of

(i) the portion of the total of all amounts deducted under subsection 127(5) for the year or a preceding taxation year (other than an amount deemed by subsection (3) to be so deducted for the year) that can reasonably be considered to be in respect of the total determined under paragraph (d), and

(ii) the portion of the total of all amounts required by subsection 127(6) or (7) to be deducted in computing the taxpayer's investment tax credit at the end of the year that can reasonably be considered to be in respect of the total determined under paragraph (d),

plus, where the taxpayer is a qualifying corporation (other than an excluded corporation) for the year, the amount, if any, by which

(f) the total of

(i) the portion of the amount required by subsection 127(10.1) to be added in computing the taxpayer's investment tax credit at the end of the year that is in respect of qualified expenditures (other than expenditures of a capital nature) incurred by the taxpayer in the year, and

(ii) all amounts determined under paragraph (a.1) of the definition "investment tax credit" in subsection 127(9) in respect of expenditures for which an amount is included in subparagraph (i)

exceeds

(g) the total of

(i) the portion of the total of all amounts deducted by the taxpayer under subsection 127(5) for the year or a preceding taxation year (other than an amount deemed by subsection (3) to be so deducted for the year) that can reasonably be considered to be in respect of the total determined under paragraph (f), and

(ii) the portion of the total of all amounts required by subsection 127(6) to be deducted in computing the taxpayer's investment tax credit at the end of the year that can reasonably be considered to be in respect of the total determined under paragraph (f).

**Related Provisions**: 88(1)(e.8) — Winding-up; 127(14) — Identification of amounts transferred as current or capital; 127.1(2.01) — Addition to refundable investment tax credit; 256(2.1) — Anti-avoidance; 256(5.1), (6.2) — Controlled directly or indirectly — control in fact.

**Notes**: Subpara. (f)(ii) of definition amended to refer to "investment tax credit"(a.1) instead of (a), and subpara. (f)(i) amended to add the words "by the taxpayer", by 1995 Budget, both effective for taxation years that begin after 1995.

Definition "refundable investment tax credit" amended by 1992 Economic Statement, effective for taxation years that end after December 2, 1992. The substantive changes were to add exclusions for qualified small-business property in para. (d), for the 10% temporary small business investment tax credit; and to add references to qualified expenditures in para. (f), so as to extend refundability to credits earned in respect of a prescribed proxy amount (see Reg. 2900(4)).

**(2.01) Addition to refundable investment tax credit** — In the case of a taxpayer that is a Canadian-controlled private corporation other than a qualifying corporation or an excluded corporation, the refundable investment tax credit of the taxpayer for a taxation year is 40% of the amount, if any, by which

(a) the total of

(i) the portion of the amount required by subsection 127(10.1) to be added in computing the taxpayer's investment tax credit at the end of the year that is in respect of qualified expenditures (other than expenditures of a current nature) incurred by the taxpayer in the year, and

(ii) all amounts determined under paragraph (a.1) of the definition "investment tax credit" in subsection 127(9) in respect of expenditures for which an amount is included in subparagraph (i)

exceeds

(b) the total of

(i) the portion of the total of all amounts deducted by the taxpayer under subsection 127(5) for the year or a preceding taxation year (other than an amount deemed by subsection (3) to have been so deducted for the year) that can reasonably be considered to be in respect of the total determined under paragraph (a), and

(ii) the portion of the total of all amounts required by subsection 127(6) to be deducted in computing the taxpayer's investment tax credit at the end of the year that can reasonably be considered to be in respect of the total determined under paragraph (a)

plus the amount, if any, by which

(c) the total of

(i) the portion of the amount required by subsection 127(10.1) to be added in computing the taxpayer's investment tax credit at the end of the year that is in respect of qualified expenditures (other than expenditures of a capital nature) incurred by the taxpayer in the year, and

(ii) all amounts determined under paragraph (a.1) of the definition "investment tax credit" in subsection 127(9) in respect of expenditures for which an amount is included in subparagraph (i)

exceeds

(d) the total of

(i) the portion of the total of all amounts deducted by the taxpayer under subsection 127(5) for the year or a preceding taxation year (other than an amount deemed by subsection (3) to have been so deducted for the year) that can reasonably be considered to be in respect of the total determined under paragraph (c), and

(ii) the portion of the total of all amounts required by subsection 127(6) to be deducted in computing the taxpayer's investment tax credit at the end of the year that can reasonably be considered to be in respect of the total determined under paragraph (c).

**Notes**: 127.1(2.01) permits a corporation with taxable income over $200,000 (i.e., not a "qualifying corporation" under 127.1(2)) to obtain partial refundability of the 35% ITC for R&D expenditures, phased out as taxable income approaches $400,000.

127(2.01)(a)(ii) and (c)(ii) amended to refer to "investment tax credit"(a.1) instead of (a), and 127(2.01)(a)(i) and (c)(i) amended to add the words "by the taxpayer", by 1995 Budget, both effective for taxation years that begin after 1995.

127.1(2.01) added by 1993 Budget, effective for taxation years that begin in 1994 or later. (It was earlier proposed as 127.1(2.1), but the reconsolidation of the Act as R.S.C. 1985 (5th Supp.) on March 1, 1994 introduced a new 127.1(2.1), below.)

**(2.1) Application of subsec. 127(9)** — The definitions in subsection 127(9) apply to this section.

**Notes**: 127.1(2.1) added in the R.S.C. 1985 (5th Supp.) consolidation, effective for taxation years ending after November 1991. This rule was formerly in the opening words of 127(9).

**(3) Deemed deduction** — For the purposes of this Act, the amount deemed under subsection (1) to have been paid by a taxpayer for a taxation year shall be deemed to have been deducted by the taxpayer under subsection 127(5) for the year.

**Definitions [s. 127.1]**: "active business" — 125(7), 248(1); "amount" — 248(1); "approved project property" — 127(9), 127.1(2.1); "associated" — 256(1); "balance-due day" — 248(1); "business limit" — 125(2)–(5.1), 248(1); "calendar year" — *Inter-*

*pretation Act* 37(1)(a); "Canadian-controlled private corporation" — 125(7), 248(1); "Canadian exploration expense" — 66.1(6), 248(1); "controlled directly or indirectly" — 256(5.1), (6.2); "corporation" — 248(1), *Interpretation Act* 35(1); "excluded corporation" — 127.1(2); "individual" — 248(1); "investment tax credit" — 127(9), 248(1); "person", "prescribed", "property" — 248(1); "province" — *Interpretation Act* 35(1); "qualified Canadian exploration expenditure", "qualified expenditure", "qualified small-business property" — 127(9), 127.1(2.1); "qualifying corporation", "refundable investment tax credit" — 127.1(2); "related" — 251(2); "scientific research and experimental development" — 37(13), 248(1); "specified employee", "specified future tax consequence" — 248(1); "taxable income" — 2(2), 248(1); "taxation year" — 249; "taxpayer" — 248(1); "trust" — 104(1), 248(1), (3).

**Interpretation Bulletins [s. 127.1]:** IT-151R5: Scientific research and experimental development expenditures.

**127.2 (1) [Pre-1987] Share-purchase tax credit** — There may be deducted from the tax otherwise payable under this Part by a taxpayer for a taxation year an amount not exceeding the total of

(a) the taxpayer's share-purchase tax credit for the year, and

(b) the taxpayer's unused share-purchase tax credit for the taxation year immediately following the year.

**Notes**: Share-purchase tax credits have not formally been repealed, but they are no longer available. Under 192(4), no designation of a share-purchase tax credit can be made after 1986. Section 127.2 is therefore generally irrelevant, except for 127.2(8), which determines the cost of a share designated for purposes of the credit. See also 192(4.1), which deals with the paid-up capital of such a share.

**(2) Persons exempt from tax** — Where a taxpayer who was throughout a taxation year a person described in any of paragraphs 149(1)(e) to (y) files with the taxpayer's return of income under this Part for the year a prescribed form containing prescribed information, the taxpayer shall be deemed to have paid, on the day on which the return is filed, an amount, on account of the taxpayer's tax under this Part for the year, equal to the taxpayer's share-purchase tax credit for the year.

**(3) Trust** — Where, in a particular taxation year of a taxpayer who is a beneficiary under a trust, an amount is included in computing the share-purchase tax credit of the trust for its taxation year ending in that particular taxation year, the trust may, in its return of income for its taxation year ending in that particular taxation year, designate as attributable to the taxpayer such portion of that amount

(a) as may, having regard to all the circumstances (including the terms and conditions of the trust arrangement), reasonably be considered to be attributable to the taxpayer, and

(b) as was not designated by the trust in respect of any other beneficiary of that trust,

and, where the trust so designates such a portion, an amount equal to that portion shall be

(c) added in computing the share-purchase tax credit of the taxpayer for the particular taxation year, and

(d) deducted in computing the share-purchase tax credit of the trust for its taxation year ending in the particular taxation year.

**Related Provisions**: 53(2)(h)(iii) — Deduction from cost base of beneficiary's capital interest in a trust.

**(3.1) Exclusion of certain trusts** — For the purposes of subsection (3), a trust does not include a trust that is

(a) governed by an employee benefit plan or a revoked deferred profit sharing plan; or

(b) exempt from tax under section 149.

**(4) Partnership** — Where, in a taxation year of a taxpayer who is a member of a partnership, an amount is included in computing the share-purchase tax credit of the partnership for its fiscal period ending in that year, such portion of that amount as may reasonably be considered to be the taxpayer's share thereof shall be

(a) added in computing the share-purchase tax credit of the taxpayer for that year; and

(b) deducted in computing the share-purchase tax credit of the partnership for that fiscal period.

**Related Provisions**: 53(2)(c)(vii) — Deductions from cost base of partnership interest.

**(5) Cooperative corporation** — Where at any particular time in a taxation year a taxpayer that is a cooperative corporation (within the meaning assigned by subsection 136(2)) has, as required by subsection 135(3), deducted or withheld an amount from a payment made by it to any person pursuant to an allocation in proportion to patronage, the taxpayer may deduct from the amount otherwise required by subsection 135(3) to be remitted to the Receiver General, an amount not exceeding the amount, if any, by which

(a) the amount that would, but for this subsection, be its share-purchase tax credit for the taxation year in which it made the payment if that year had ended immediately before the particular time

exceeds

(b) the total of all amounts each of which is the amount deducted by virtue of this subsection from any amount otherwise required to be remitted by subsection 135(3) in respect of payments made by it before the particular time and in the taxation year,

and the amount, if any, so deducted from the amount otherwise required to be remitted by subsection 135(3) shall be

(c) deducted in computing the share-purchase tax credit of the taxpayer for the taxation year, and

(d) deemed to have been remitted by the taxpayer to the Receiver General on account of tax under this Part of the person to whom that payment was made.

**(6) Definitions** — In this section,

"share-purchase tax credit" of a taxpayer for a taxation year means the amount determined by the formula

$$(A + B) - C$$

where

A  is the total of all amounts each of which is an amount designated by a corporation under subsection 192(4) in respect of a share acquired by the taxpayer in the year where the taxpayer is the first person, other than a broker or dealer in securities, to be a registered holder,

B  is the total of all amounts each of which is an amount required by subsection (3) or (4) to be added in computing the taxpayer's share-purchase tax credit for the year, and

C  the total of all amounts each of which is an amount required by subsection (3), (4) or (5) to be deducted in computing the taxpayer's share-purchase tax credit for the year;

**Related Provisions**: 257 — Formula cannot calculate to less than zero.

**Notes**: 127.2(6)"share-purchase tax credit" was 127.2(6)(a) before consolidation in R.S.C. 1985 (5th Supp.), effective for taxation years ending after November 1991, and was in descriptive form rather than a formula. See Table of Concordance.

"unused share-purchase tax credit" of a taxpayer for a taxation year means the amount determined by the formula

$$A - (B + C)$$

where

A  is the taxpayer's share-purchase tax credit for the year,

B  the taxpayer's tax otherwise payable under this Part for the year, the amount deemed by subsection (2) to have been paid on account of the taxpayer's tax payable under this Part for the year or, where Division E.1 is applicable to the taxpayer for the year, the amount, if any, by which the taxpayer's tax otherwise payable under this Part for the year exceeds the taxpayer's minimum amount for the year determined under section 127.51, as the case may be, and

C  is the taxpayer's refundable Part VII tax on hand at the end of the year.

**Related Provisions**: 248(1)"unused share-purchase tax credit" — Definition applies to entire Act; 257 — Formula cannot calculate to less than zero.

**Notes**: 127.2(6)"unused share-purchase tax credit" was 127.2(6)(b) before consolidation in R.S.C. 1985 (5th Supp.), effective for taxation years ending after November 1991, and was in descriptive form rather than a formula. See Table of Concordance.

**(7) Definition of "tax otherwise payable"** — In this section, "tax otherwise payable" under this Part by a taxpayer means the amount that would, but for this section and section 120.1, be the tax payable under this Part by the taxpayer.

**(8) Deemed cost of acquisition** — For the purposes of this Act, where, at any time in a taxation year, a taxpayer has acquired a share and is the first registered holder of the share, other than a broker or dealer in securities, and an amount is, at any time, designated by a corporation under subsection 192(4) in respect of the share, the following rules apply:

(a) the taxpayer shall be deemed to have acquired the share at a cost to the taxpayer equal to the amount by which

(i) its cost to the taxpayer as otherwise determined

exceeds

(ii) the amount so designated in respect of the share; and

(b) where the amount determined under subparagraph (a)(ii) exceeds the amount determined under subparagraph (a)(i), the excess shall

(i) where the share is a capital property to the taxpayer, be deemed to be a capital gain of the taxpayer for the year from the disposition of that property, and

(ii) in any other case, be included in computing the income of the taxpayer for the year,

and the cost to the taxpayer of the share shall be deemed to be nil.

**Related Provisions**: 192(4.1) — Paid-up capital of designated share.

**(9) Partnership** — For the purposes of this section and subsection 193(5), a partnership shall be deemed to be a person and its taxation year shall be deemed to be its fiscal period.

**(10) Election re first holder** — Where a share of a public corporation has been lawfully distributed to the public in accordance with a prospectus, registration statement or similar document filed with a public authority in Canada pursuant to and in accordance with the law of Canada or of any province, and, where required by law, accepted for filing by such a public authority, the corporation, if it has designated an amount under subsection 192(4) in respect of the share, may, in the prescribed form required to be filed under that subsection, elect that, for the purposes of this section, the first person, other than a broker or dealer in securities, to have acquired the share (and no other person) shall be considered to be the first person to be a registered holder of the share.

**(11) Calculation of consideration** — For greater certainty,

(a) for the purposes of this section and Part VII, the amount of consideration for which a share is acquired and issued includes the amount of any consideration for the designation under subsection 192(4) in respect of the share; and

(b) the amount received by a corporation as consideration for a designation under subsection

192(4) in respect of a share issued by it shall not be included in computing its income.

**Notes**: See Notes to 127.2(1).

**Definitions [s. 127.2]**: "amount" — 248(1); "Canada" — 255; "capital gain" — 39(1)(a), 248(1); "capital property" — 54, 248(1); "corporation" — 248(1), *Interpretation Act* 35(1); "deferred profit sharing plan", "employee benefit plan" — 248(1); "partnership" — see Notes to 96(1);; "person" — 127.2(9), 248(1); "prescribed" — 248(1); "province" — *Interpretation Act* 35(1); "public corporation" — 248(1); "refundable Part VII tax on hand" — 192(3), 248(1); "share" — 248(1); "tax payable" — 248(2); "taxation year" — 249; "taxpayer" — 248(1); "trust" — 104(1), 248(1), (3).

## 127.3 (1) [Pre-1986] Scientific research and experimental development tax credit — There may be deducted from the tax otherwise payable under this Part by a taxpayer for a taxation year an amount not exceeding the total of the taxpayer's

(a) scientific research and experimental development tax credit for the year, and

(b) unused scientific research and experimental development tax credit for the taxation year immediately following the year.

**Related Provisions**: 117(1) — Tax payable under this Part; 194(4.2) — Where amount may not be designated; 195(5) — Evasion of tax; 195(6) — Undue deferral of refundable tax.

**Notes**: Scientific research tax credits (SRTCs) have not formally been repealed, but they are no longer available. Under 194(4.2), no designation of an SRTC can be made after 1985. Section 127.3 is therefore generally irrelevant, except for 127.3(6), which determines the cost of a share, debt obligation or right designated for purposes of the SRTC. See Notes to 195. (See also 194(4.1), which deals with the paid-up capital of a designated share.) Credits for scientific research are available under 127 (investment tax credits), and deductions are available under 37.

**(2) Definitions** — In this section,

**"scientific research and experimental development tax credit"** of a taxpayer for a taxation year means the amount determined by the formula

$$A - B$$

where

A is the total of all amounts each of which is an amount equal to

(a) where the taxpayer is a corporation, 50%, or

(b) where the taxpayer is an individual other than a trust, 34%

of an amount designated by a corporation under subsection 194(4) in respect of

(c) a share acquired by the taxpayer in the year where the taxpayer is the first person, other than a broker or dealer in securities, to be a registered holder thereof,

(d) a bond, debenture, bill, note, mortgage or similar obligation (in this section referred to as a "debt obligation") acquired by the taxpayer in the year where the taxpayer is the first person, other than a broker or dealer in securities, to be a registered holder of that debt obligation, or

(e) a right acquired by the taxpayer in the year where the taxpayer is the first person, other than a broker or dealer in securities, to have acquired that right, and

B is the total of all amounts required by subsection (5) to be deducted in computing the taxpayer's scientific research and experimental development tax credit for the year;

**Related Provisions**: 248(1) "scientific research and experimental development tax credit" — Definition applies to entire Act; 257 — Formula cannot calculate to less than zero.

**Notes**: 127.3(2) "scientific research and experimental development tax credit" was 127.3(2)(a) before consolidation in R.S.C. 1985 (5th Supp.), effective for taxation years ending after November 1991, and was in descriptive form rather than a formula. See Table of Concordance.

**"unused scientific research and experimental development tax credit"** of a taxpayer for a taxation year means the amount determined by the formula

$$A - (B + C)$$

where

A is the taxpayer's scientific research and experimental development tax credit for the year,

B is the taxpayer's tax otherwise payable under this Part for the year or, where Division E.1 is applicable to the taxpayer for the year, the amount, if any, by which the taxpayer's tax otherwise payable under this Part for the year exceeds the taxpayer's minimum amount for the year determined under section 127.51, as the case may be, and

C is the taxpayer's refundable Part VIII tax on hand at the end of the year.

**Related Provisions**: 248(1) "unused scientific research and experimental development tax credit" — Definition applies to entire Act; 257 — Formula cannot calculate to less than zero.

**Notes**: 127.3(2) "unused scientific ... tax credit" was 127.3(2)(b) before consolidation in R.S.C. 1985 (5th Supp.), effective for taxation years ending after November 1991, and was in descriptive form rather than a formula. See Table of Concordance.

**(3) Trust** — For the purposes of this section and section 53, where a taxpayer, other than a broker or dealer in securities, is a beneficiary under a trust and an amount is designated by a corporation under subsection 194(4) in respect of a share, debt obligation or right acquired by the trust in a taxation year of the trust where the trust is the first person, other than a broker or dealer in securities, to be a registered holder of the share or debt obligation or to have acquired the right, as the case may be,

(a) the trust may, in its return of income for that year, specify such portion of that amount as may, having regard to all the circumstances (including the terms and conditions of the trust arrangement), reasonably be considered to be attributable to the taxpayer and as was not specified by the trust in respect of any other beneficiary under that trust; and

(b) the portion specified pursuant to paragraph (a) shall be deemed to be an amount designated on the last day of that year by the corporation under subsection 194(4) in respect of a share, debt obligation or right, as the case may be, acquired by the taxpayer on that day where the taxpayer is the first person, other than a broker or dealer in securities, to be a registered holder of the share or debt obligation or to have acquired the right, as the case may be.

**Related Provisions**: 53(2)(h)(iv) — Deductions from cost base of beneficiary's capital interest in a trust.

**(3.1) Exclusion of certain trusts** — For the purposes of subsection (3), a trust does not include a trust that is

(a) governed by an employee benefit plan or a revoked deferred profit sharing plan; or

(b) exempt from tax under section 149.

**(4) Partnership** — For the purposes of this section and section 53, where a taxpayer, other than a broker or dealer in securities, is a member of a partnership and an amount is designated by a corporation under subsection 194(4) in respect of a share, debt obligation or right acquired by the partnership in a taxation year of the partnership where the partnership is the first person, other than a broker or dealer in securities, to be a registered holder of the share or debt obligation or to have acquired the right, as the case may be, such portion of that amount as may reasonably be considered to be the taxpayer's share thereof shall be deemed to be an amount designated on the last day of that year by the corporation under subsection 194(4) in respect of a share, debt obligation or right, as the case may be, acquired by the taxpayer on that day where the taxpayer is the first person, other than a broker or dealer in securities, to be a registered holder of the share or debt obligation or to have acquired the right, as the case may be.

**Related Provisions**: 53(2)(c)(viii) — Deductions from cost base of partnership interest re scientific research and experimental development tax credit.

**(5) Cooperative corporation** — Where at any particular time in a taxation year a taxpayer that is a cooperative corporation (within the meaning assigned by subsection 136(2)) has, as required by subsection 135(3), deducted or withheld an amount from a payment made by it to any person pursuant to an allocation in proportion to patronage, the taxpayer may deduct from the amount otherwise required by subsection 135(3) to be remitted to the Receiver General, an amount not exceeding the amount, if any, by which

(a) the amount that would, but for this subsection, be its scientific research and experimental development tax credit for the taxation year in which it made the payment if that year had ended immediately before the particular time

exceeds

(b) the total of all amounts each of which is the amount deducted by virtue of this subsection from any amount otherwise required to be remitted by subsection 135(3) in respect of payments made by it before the particular time and in the taxation year,

and the amount, if any, so deducted from the amount otherwise required to be remitted by subsection 135(3) shall be

(c) deducted in computing the scientific research and experimental development tax credit of the taxpayer for the taxation year, and

(d) deemed to have been remitted by the taxpayer to the Receiver General on account of tax under this Part of the person to whom that payment was made.

**(6) Deduction from cost** — For the purposes of this Act, where at any time in a taxation year a taxpayer has acquired a share, debt obligation or right and is the first registered holder of the share or debt obligation or the first person to have acquired the right, as the case may be, other than a broker or dealer in securities, and an amount is, at any time, designated by a corporation under subsection 194(4), in respect of the share, debt obligation or right, the following rules apply:

(a) the taxpayer shall be deemed to have acquired the share, debt obligation or right at a cost to the taxpayer equal to the amount by which

(i) its cost to the taxpayer as otherwise determined

exceeds

(ii) 50% of the amount so designated in respect thereof; and

(b) where the amount determined under subparagraph (a)(ii) exceeds the amount determined under subparagraph (a)(i), the excess shall

(i) where the share, debt obligation or right, as the case may be, is a capital property to the taxpayer, be deemed to be a capital gain of the taxpayer for the year from the disposition of that property, and

(ii) in any other case, be included in computing the income of the taxpayer for the year,

and the cost to the taxpayer of the share, debt obligation or right, as the case may be, shall be deemed to be nil.

**Related Provisions**: 194(4.1) — Computation of paid-up capital of designated share.

**(7) Partnership** — For the purposes of this section and Part VIII, a partnership shall be deemed to be a person and its taxation year shall be deemed to be its fiscal period.

**(8) Definition of "tax otherwise payable"** — In this section, "tax otherwise payable" under this Part by a taxpayer means the amount that would, but for this section and section 120.1, be the tax payable under this Part by the taxpayer.

**(9) Election re first holder** — Where a share or debt obligation of a public corporation has been lawfully distributed to the public in accordance with a prospectus, registration statement or similar document filed with a public authority in Canada pursuant to and in accordance with the law of Canada or of any province, and, where required by law, accepted for filing by that public authority, the corporation, if it has designated an amount under subsection 194(4) in respect of the share or debt obligation, may, in the prescribed form required to be filed under that subsection, elect that, for the purposes of this section, the first person, other than a broker or dealer in securities, to have acquired the share or debt obligation, as the case may be, (and no other person) shall be considered to be the first person to be a registered holder thereof.

**(10) Calculation of consideration** — For greater certainty,

(a) for the purposes of this section and Part VIII, the amount of consideration for which a share, debt obligation or right was acquired and issued or granted includes the amount of any consideration for the designation under subsection 194(4) in respect of the share, debt obligation or right; and

(b) the amount received by a corporation as consideration for a designation under subsection 194(4) in respect of a share, debt obligation or right issued or granted by it shall not be included in computing its income.

**Notes [s. 127.3]**: See Notes to 127.3(1) and 195.

**Definitions [s. 127.3]**: "amount" — 248(1); "Canada" — 255; "capital gain" — 39(1)(a), 248(1); "capital property" — 54, 248(1); "corporation" — 248(1), *Interpretation Act* 35(1); "deferred profit sharing plan", "employee benefit plan", "individual", "Minister" — 248(1); "partnership" — see Notes to 96(1); "person" — 127.3(7), 248(1); "prescribed" — 248(1); "province" — *Interpretation Act* 35(1); "public corporation" — 89(1), 248(1); "refundable Part VIII tax on hand" — 194(3), 248(1); "share" — 248(1); "taxation year" — 249; "taxpayer" — 248(1); "trust" — 104(1), 248(1), (3).

## 127.4 (1) [Labour-sponsored funds tax credit] Definitions — In this section,

**"approved share"** means a share of the capital stock of a prescribed labour-sponsored venture capital corporation, but does not include

(a) a share issued by a registered labour-sponsored venture capital corporation the venture capital business of which was discontinued before the time of the issue, and

(b) a share issued by a prescribed labour-sponsored venture capital corporation (other than a registered labour-sponsored venture capital corporation) if, at the time of the issue, every province under the laws of which the corporation is a prescribed labour-sponsored venture capital corporation has suspended or terminated its assistance in respect of the acquisition of shares of the capital stock of the corporation;

**Related Provisions**: 131(8) — Prescribed LSVCC is a mutual fund corporation; 204.8(2) — Determining when an RLSVCC discontinues its business; 211.7(1)"approved share" — Definition applies to Part XII.5.

**Notes**: 127.4(1)"approved share" amended by 1999 Budget, effective for 1999 and later taxation years, to add everything from "but does not include ...".

Definition "approved share" amended by 1996 Budget, effective for 1996 and later taxation years. For earlier taxation years since 1989, read:

> "approved share" means a share of the capital stock of a prescribed labour-sponsored venture capital corporation acquired or irrevocably subscribed and paid for by an individual where the individual is or will be the first person, other than a broker or dealer in securities, to be a registered holder thereof;

Definition extended by 1991 technical bill, effective 1989, to a share "irrevocably subscribed and paid for" rather than just "acquired".

**Regulations**: 100(5) (reduction in withholding where share purchased from payroll); 6701 (prescribed labour-sponsored venture capital corporation).

**"labour-sponsored funds tax credit"** — [Repealed]

**Notes**: Definition "labour-sponsored funds tax credit" repealed by 1996 Budget, effective for 1996 and later taxation years. (See now 127.4(5) and (6).) For earlier taxation years for shares acquired since May 23, 1985, read:

> "labour-sponsored funds tax credit" of an individual for a taxation year means the amount computed under subsection (3) in respect of the individual for that year;

**"net cost"** to an individual of an approved share means the amount, if any, by which

(a) the amount of consideration paid by the individual to acquire or subscribe for the share

exceeds

(b) the amount of any assistance (other than an amount included in computing a tax credit of the individual in respect of that share) provided or to be provided by a government, municipality or any public authority in respect of, or for the acquisition of, the share;

**Related Provisions**: 211.7(1)"net cost" — Definition applies to Part XII.5.

**Notes**: Definition "net cost" amended by 1991 technical bill, effective 1989, to correspond to the changes to the definition of "approved share".

**"original acquisition"** of a share means the first acquisition of the share, except that

(a) where the share is irrevocably subscribed and paid for before its first acquisition, subject to paragraphs (b) and (c), the original acquisition of the share is the first transaction whereby the share is irrevocably subscribed and paid for,

(b) a share is deemed never to have been acquired and never to have been irrevocably subscribed and paid for unless the first registered holder of the share is, subject to paragraph (c), the first person to either acquire or irrevocably subscribe and pay for the share, and

**S. 127.4(1) ori**  Income Tax Act, Part I, Division E

(c) for the purpose of this definition, a broker or dealer in securities acting in that capacity is deemed never to acquire or subscribe and pay for the share and never to be the registered holder of the share;

**Related Provisions**: 127.4(5.1) — Direction for original acquisition to be deemed to occur at beginning of year; 204.8(1)"original acquisition" — Definition applies to Part X.3; 211.7(1)"original acquisition" — Definition applies to Part XII.5.

**Notes**: Definition "original acquisition" added by 1996 Budget, effective 1996.

**"qualifying trust"** for an individual in respect of a share means

(a) a trust governed by a registered retirement savings plan, under which the individual is the annuitant, that is not a spousal plan (in this definition having the meaning assigned by subsection 146(1)) in relation to another individual, or

(b) a trust governed by a registered retirement savings plan, under which the individual or the individual's spouse or common-law partner is the annuitant, that is a spousal plan in relation to the individual or the individual's spouse or common-law partner, if the individual and no other person claims a deduction under subsection 127.4(2) in respect of the share;

**Related Provisions**: 127.4(6)(a) — Credit to individual for investment by qualifying trust; 211.7(1)"qualifying trust" — Definition applies to Part XII.5.

**Notes**: 127.4(1)"qualifying trust"(b) amended by 2000 same-sex partners bill to add reference to "common-law partner", effective for the 2001 and later taxation years, or earlier by election (see Notes to 248(1)"common-law partner").

Definition amended by 1998 Budget, effective for 1998 and later taxation years. For earlier years, read:

"qualifying trust" for an individual in respect of a share means a trust governed by a registered retirement savings plan where

(a) the individual makes contributions to the trust and those contributions (and no other funds) can reasonably be considered to have been used by the trust to acquire or subscribe for the share, and

(b) the annuitant under the plan is the individual or a spouse of the individual;

The change allows the acquisition by an RRSP trust to always be taken into account in claiming the LSVCC credit for the RRSP annuitant (or, for a spousal RRSP, for the contributor spouse or the annuitant spouse who claims the LSVCC credit). This amendment is linked to the repeal of the "3-year cooling-off period" in 127.4(3) and (4); the previous definition prevented reinvestment in shares issued by LSVCCs in some cases.

Definition "qualifying trust" added by 1992 Economic Statement, effective for 1992 and later taxation years. See 127.4(6)(a).

**"tax otherwise payable"** by an individual means the amount that, but for this section, would be the individual's tax payable under this Part.

**Notes**: 127.4(1)"tax otherwise payable" amended by 1999 Budget, effective for 1998 and later taxation years, to change "but for this section and section 120.1" to "but for this section".

**(1.1) Amalgamations or mergers** — Subsections 204.8(2) and 204.85(3) apply for the purpose of this section.

**Notes**: 127.4(1.1) added by 1999 Budget, effective February 17, 1999.

**(2) Deduction of labour-sponsored funds tax credit** — There may be deducted from the tax otherwise payable by an individual (other than a trust) for a taxation year such amount as the individual claims not exceeding the individual's labour-sponsored funds tax credit limit for the year.

**Related Provisions**: 127.4(5) — Determination of labour-sponsored funds tax credit limit; 211.8 — Repayment of credit on early disposition of share.

**Notes**: Most provinces provide a credit for investment of up to $5,000 in a labour-sponsored venture capital corporation, to parallel the 15% federal credit (20% before March 6, 1996). Some provinces have restrictions on which fund may be invested in for the credit, however.

See Notes to 248(1)"registered labour-sponsored venture capital corporation".

127.4(2) amended by 1998 Budget to delete "Subject to subsections (3) and (4)" at the beginning, effective for 1998 and later taxation years.

127.4(2) amended by 1996 Budget, this version effective for 1996 and later taxation years. For 1992 to 1995, read:

(2) There may be deducted from the tax otherwise payable by an individual (other than a trust) for a taxation year the lesser of $1,000 and the individual's labour-sponsored funds tax credit (determined as if an approved share in respect of which an individual receives a payment under section 211.9 had never been either acquired nor irrevocably subscribed and paid for).

127.4(2) amended by 1992 technical bill, effective 1992. For 1985 to 1991, the dollar limit was $700.

**Regulations**: 100(5) (reduction in withholding where share purchased from payroll).

**(3) [Repealed]**

**Notes**: 127.4(3) repealed by 1998 Budget, effective for 1998 and later taxation years. For earlier years, read:

(3) **3-year cooling-off period** — Subject to subsection 127.4 (4), no amount may be deducted under subsection 127.4 (2) from an individual's tax otherwise payable for a taxation year that ends after 1996 where

(a) an approved share of the capital stock of a corporation is redeemed, acquired or cancelled by the corporation

(i) after March 5, 1996 (otherwise than pursuant to a request in writing made to the corporation before March 6, 1996), and

(ii) in the year or in either of the 2 preceding taxation years; and

(b) the original acquisition of the share was by the individual or by a qualifying trust for the individual in respect of the share.

127.4(3) replaced by 1996 Budget, effective for 1996 and later taxation years, to contain the "cooling-off period" rule, which prevented someone from redeeming an LSVCC share and buying new shares shortly thereafter for an additional credit. For 1992 to 1995, read:

(3) **Computation of tax credit** — The labour-sponsored funds tax credit of an individual for a taxation year is the total of all amounts, in respect of an approved share acquired or irrevocably subscribed and paid for by the individual (or by a qualifying trust for the individual in respect of the share) in

the year or within 60 days after the end of the year (to the extent that it was not deducted in computing the individual's tax payable under this Part for the preceding taxation year), each of which is

(a) where a tax credit is provided under the law of a province in respect of the acquisition of, or subscription for, the share by the individual or the trust, and the share is not a share of a registered labour-sponsored venture capital corporation (within the meaning assigned by section 204.8), the amount, if any, by which

(i) 40% of the net cost to the individual or the trust of the share

exceeds

(ii) the amount of the tax credit so provided; and

(b) in any other case, where the information return described in paragraph 204.81(6)(c) in respect of the share was filed with the individual's return of income under this Part for the year (other than a return of income filed under subsection 70(2), paragraph 104(23)(d) or 128(2)(e) or subsection 150(4)), 20% of the net cost to the individual or the trust of the share.

Former 127.4(3) amended by 1992 Economic Statement, effective for 1992 and later taxation years, to add references to a qualifying trust. The amendment allowed an individual's RRSP to subscribe for LSVCC shares directly with new money provided for that purpose, with the credit going to the individual. See 127.4(1)"qualifying trust", and see now 127.4(6)(a). Previously the individual had to purchase the shares on personal account and then transfer them to the RRSP.

Former 127.4(3) amended by 1991 technical bill, effective 1989.

**(4) [Repealed]**

**Notes**: 127.4(4) repealed by 1998 Budget, effective for 1998 and later taxation years. For earlier years, read:

(4) **Exceptions to cooling-off period** — Subsection 127.4 (3) does not apply to an individual for a taxation year as a consequence of the redemption, acquisition or cancellation of a share where

(a) the individual dies in the year and before the redemption, acquisition or cancellation;

(b) the individual's labour-sponsored funds tax credit in respect of the original acquisition of the share is nil;

(c) tax becomes payable under Part XII.5 because of the redemption, acquisition or cancellation;

(d) an amount determined under regulations made for the purpose of clause 204.81(1)(c)(v)(F) is directed to be remitted to the Receiver General in order to permit the redemption, acquisition or cancellation; or

(e) the individual becomes either disabled and permanently unfit for work or terminally ill in the year

(i) after the last original acquisition in the year of any approved share by the individual or by a qualifying trust for the individual in respect of that share, and

(ii) before the redemption, acquisition or cancellation.

127.4(4) replaced by 1996 Budget, effective for 1996 and later taxation years. For 1992-95, read:

(4) **Idem** — Notwithstanding subsection (3), where paragraph (3)(a) applies in computing an individual's labour-sponsored funds tax credit for a taxation year in respect of an approved share and the amount of the tax credit referred to in that paragraph is less than 20% of the consideration for which the share was issued, the amount determined under that paragraph for the year in respect of the share shall be deemed to be nil.

Former 127.4(4) amended by 1992 Economic Statement, effective for 1992 and later taxation years, to change "approved share acquired by the individual" to "approved share", in recognition of the amendment to 127.4(3) allowing the share to be purchased by a qualifying trust (RRSP).

**(5) Labour-sponsored funds tax credit limit** — For the purpose of subsection (2), an individual's labour-sponsored funds tax credit limit for a taxation year is the lesser of

(a) $750, and

(b) the amount, if any, by which

(i) the total of all amounts each of which is the individual's labour-sponsored funds tax credit in respect of an original acquisition in the year or in the first 60 days of the following taxation year of an approved share

exceeds

(ii) the portion of the total described in subparagraph (i) that was deducted under subsection (2) in computing the individual's tax payable under this Part for the preceding taxation year.

**Related Provisions**: 127.4(5.1) — Extension of investment deadline by CCRA so that acquisition deemed made at beginning of year; 127.4(6) — Determination of labour-sponsored funds tax credit.

**Notes**: 127.4(5)(a) amended by 1998 Budget to change $525 to $750, effective for 1998 and later taxation years. The $750 credit reaches its maximum on an investment of $5,000, since the credit under 127.4(6)(a) is 15%.

The provincial LSVCC legislation generally parallels the 1998 federal changes, increasing the maximum annual eligible investment from $3,500 to $5,000, eliminating the cooling-off period, and modifying the calculation of the business investment requirement.

127.4(5) added by 1996 Budget, this version effective for 1997 and later taxation years. For 1996, read:

(5) For the purpose of subsection (2), an individual's labour-sponsored funds tax credit limit for a taxation year is the lesser of

(a) the total of

(i) the lesser of $1,000 and the amount, if any, by which

(A) the total of all amounts each of which is the individual's labour-sponsored funds tax credit in respect of an original acquisition after 1995 and before March 6, 1996 of an approved share

exceeds

(B) such portion of the amount deducted under subsection (2) in computing the individual's tax payable under this Part for the 1995 taxation year as is attributable to the original acquisition after 1995 of an approved share, and

(ii) the amount, if any, by which $525 exceeds the amount determined under subparagraph (i) in respect of the individual for the year, and

(b) the amount, if any, by which

(i) the total of all amounts each of which is the individual's labour-sponsored funds tax credit in respect of an original acquisition in the year or in the first 60 days of the following taxation year of an approved share

exceeds

(ii) the portion of the total described in subparagraph (i) that was deducted under subsection (2) in computing the individual's tax payable under this Part for the preceding taxation year.

**(5.1) Deemed original acquisition** — If the Minister so directs, an original acquisition of an approved share that occurs in an individual's taxation year (other than in the first 60 days of the year) is deemed for the purpose of this section to have occurred at the beginning of the year and not at the time it actually occurred.

Notes: 127.4(5.1) added by 1998 Budget, effective for acquisitions made after 1997.

This specific extension provides a general authorization, in 127.4(5.1) (and 146(22) for RRSPs), allowing the CCRA to direct that a late contribution was made at the beginning of the year — and thus within the first 60 days, qualifying it for a credit for the previous year.

**(6) Labour-sponsored funds tax credit** — For the purpose of subsection (5), an individual's labour-sponsored funds tax credit in respect of an original acquisition of an approved share is equal to the least of

(a) 15% of the net cost to the individual (or to a qualifying trust for the individual in respect of the share) for the original acquisition of the share by the individual or by the trust,

(b) nil, where the share was issued by a registered labour-sponsored venture capital corporation unless the information return described in paragraph 204.81(6)(c) is filed with the individual's return of income for the taxation year for which a claim is made under subsection (2) in respect of the original acquisition of the share (other than a return of income filed under subsection 70(2), paragraph 104(23)(d) or 128(2)(e) or subsection 150(4)),

(c) nil, where the individual dies after December 5, 1996 and before the original acquisition of the share, and

(d) nil, where a payment in respect of the disposition of the share has been made under section 211.9.

Related Provisions: 211.7(1) "labour-sponsored funds tax credit" — Determination of credit for purposes of Part XII.5 where share redeemed early.

Notes: 127.4(6) opening words amended by 1998 Budget to change "subsections (4) and (5)" to "subsection (5)", effective for 1998 and later taxation years.

127.4(6) added by 1996 Budget, effective for 1996 and later taxation years, except that for original acquisitions that occurred before March 6, 1996, read "20%" instead of "15%" in 127.4(6)(a).

Definitions [s. 127.4]: "amount" — 248(1); "annuitant" — 146(1); "approved share" — 127.4(1); "business", "common-law partner" — 248(1); "corporation" — 248(1), *Interpretation Act* 35(1); "discontinued" — 204.8(2); "individual" — 248(1); "labour-sponsored funds tax credit" — 127.4(1), (6); "labour-sponsored funds tax credit limit" — 127.4(5); "Minister" — 248(1); "net cost" — 127.4(1); "original acquisition" — 248(1); "prescribed" — 248(1); "prescribed labour-sponsored venture capital corporation" — Reg. 6701; "province" — *Interpretation Act* 35(1); "qualifying trust" — 127.4(1); "registered labour-sponsored venture capital corporation" — 248(1); "registered retirement savings plan" — 146(1), 248(1); "share" — 248(1); "tax otherwise payable" — 127.4(1); "tax payable" — 248(2); "taxation year" — 249; "trust" — 104(1), 248(1), (3).

Forms [s. 127.4]: T5006 Supp: Statement of registered LSVCC class A shares.

**127.41 (1) Part XII.4 tax credit [qualifying environmental trust beneficiary]** — In this section, the Part XII.4 tax credit of a taxpayer for a particular taxation year means the total of

(a) all amounts each of which is an amount determined by the formula

$$A \times \frac{B}{C}$$

where

A is the tax payable under Part XII.4 by a qualifying environmental trust for a taxation year (in this paragraph referred to as the "trust's year") that ends in the particular year,

B is the amount, if any, by which the total of all amounts in respect of the trust that were included (otherwise than because of being a member of a partnership) because of the application of subsection 107.3(1) in computing the taxpayer's income for the particular year exceeds the total of all amounts in respect of the trust that were deducted (otherwise than because of being a member of a partnership) because of the application of subsection 107.3(1) in computing that income, and

C is the trust's income for the trust's year, computed without reference to subsections 104(4) to (31) and sections 105 to 107, and

(b) in respect of each partnership of which the taxpayer was a member, the total of all amounts each of which is the amount that can reasonably be considered to be the taxpayer's share of the relevant credit in respect of the partnership and, for this purpose, the relevant credit in respect of a partnership is the amount that would, if a partnership were a person and its fiscal period were its taxation year, be the Part XII.4 tax credit of the partnership for its taxation year that ends in the particular year.

Related Provisions: 87(2)(j.93) — Amalgamations — continuing corporation; 126(7) "tax for the year otherwise payable under this Part" — Credit under 127.41 ignored for foreign tax credit purposes.

Notes: Description of A amended by 1997 Budget, effective for taxation years that end after February 18, 1997, to change "mining reclamation trust" to "qualifying environmental trust". (The same change was made throughout the Act.)

Description of B amended by 1995-97 technical bill, retroactive to its introduction (see Notes at end of 127.41), to add "(otherwise than because of being a member of a partnership)".

**(2) Reduction of Part I tax** — There may be deducted from a taxpayer's tax otherwise payable under this Part for a taxation year such amount as the taxpayer claims not exceeding the taxpayer's Part XII.4 tax credit for the year.

**Notes:** See Notes at end of 127.41.

**(3) Deemed payment of Part I tax** — There is deemed to have been paid on account of the tax payable under this Part by a taxpayer (other than a tax-payer exempt from such tax) for a taxation year on the taxpayer's balance-due day for the year, such amount as the taxpayer claims not exceeding the amount, if any, by which

(a) the taxpayer's Part XII.4 tax credit for the year

exceeds

(b) the amount deducted under subsection (2) in computing the taxpayer's tax payable under this Part for the year.

**Related Provisions:** 152(1)(b) — Assessment of amount deemed paid; 157(3)(e) — Reduction in monthly corporate instalments to reflect credit; 163(2)(e) — Penalty for false statement or omission.

**Notes:** Since an amount elected under 127.41(3) is deemed paid on account of tax, the amount, like an instalment or an amount withheld at source, will create a refund under 164(1) even if the taxpayer pays no tax for the year, but will not reduce provincial tax. The credit is thus a "refundable credit".

127.41(3) amended by 1996 Budget, effective for 1996 and later taxation years, to use the expression "the taxpayer's balance-due day for the year" (see 248(1)"balance-due day") in place of "the individual's balance-due day for the year and, where the taxpayer is a corporation, on the day referred to in paragraph 157(1)(b) on or before which the remainder of the taxes payable under this Part for the year by the taxpayer would be required to be paid if such a remainder were payable". The change is non-substantive.

**Notes [s. 127.41]:** 127.41 added by 1994 Budget, effective for taxation years that end after February 22, 1994. It provides a refundable tax credit to beneficiaries of a qualifying environmental trust (formerly a mining reclamation trust), since income subject to the special tax at the trust level under 211.6 is also included in computing a beneficiary's income under 107.3(1). The refundable credit avoids the double taxation of the same income in the hands of a QET and its beneficiaries.

**Definitions [s. 127.41]:** "amount", "balance-due day" — 248(1); "fiscal period" — 249(2)(b), 249.1; "Part XII.4 tax credit" — 127.41(1); "partnership" — see Notes to 96(1); "qualifying environmental trust" — 248(1); "taxation year" — 11(2), 249; "taxpayer" — 248(1); "trust's year" — 107.3(1).

# DIVISION E.1 — MINIMUM TAX

**127.5 Obligation to pay minimum tax** — Notwithstanding any other provision of this Act but subject to subsection 120.4(3) and section 127.55, where the amount that, but for section 120, would be determined under Division E to be an individual's tax payable for a taxation year is less than the amount determined under paragraph (a) in respect of the individual for the year, the individual's tax payable under this Part for the year is the total of

(a) the amount, if any, by which

(i) the individual's minimum amount for the year determined under section 127.51

exceeds

(ii) the individual's special foreign tax credit determined under section 127.54 for the year, and

(b) the amount, if any, required by section 120 to be added to the individual's tax otherwise payable under this Part for the year.

**Related Provisions:** 117(1) — "Tax payable" to be calculated without reference to minimum tax; 120.2 — Minimum tax carryover; 127.54(2) — Foreign tax credit; 127.55 — Where minimum tax not applicable.

**Notes:** Alternative Minimum Tax (AMT) is calculated under 127.5–127.55. The taxpayer must pay the higher of AMT and regular federal tax; provincial tax (before 2001) and all surtaxes are then based on this higher amount. Any excess (i.e., AMT minus regular basic federal tax) is available for carryforward under 120.2(1) for 7 years, and can be claimed to the extent regular federal tax exceeds AMT in those years, to reduce regular federal tax.

Since October 18, 2000, the AMT can bite deeper for taxpayers who claim the capital gains exemption, because 30% (formerly the untaxed 1/4) of the capital gain is considered a preference for AMT purposes. See 127.52(1)(d)(i).

For a thorough overview of the extent to which the AMT really works, see Department of Finance, *Tax Expenditures and Evaluations 2000* (Sept. 1, 2000), pp. 59-84 (available at www.fin.gc.ca). For 1997 there were 25,000 taxpayers paying AMT of $105 million, 31,000 claiming carryover credits of $81 million, for net $24 million in federal revenues.

127.5 amended by 1999 Budget, effective for 1998 and later taxation years, except that for 1998 and 1999, ignore the words "subsection 120.4(3) and". For 1992-97, read:

> 127.5 Notwithstanding any other provision of this Act but subject to section 127.55, where the amount that, but for sections 120 and 120.1, would be determined under Division E to be the tax payable by an individual for a taxation year is less than the amount determined under subparagraph (a)(i) in respect of the individual, the tax payable under this Part for the year by the individual is the amount, if any, by which
>
> (a) the total of
>
> (i) the amount, if any, by which the minimum amount for the year of the individual determined under section 127.51 exceeds the individual's special foreign tax credit determined under section 127.54 for the year, and
>
> (ii) the total of all amounts required under sections 120 and 120.1 to be added to the tax otherwise payable under this Part by the individual for the year
>
> exceeds
>
> (b) the amount, if any, that may be deducted under subsection 120.1(1) from the tax otherwise payable under this Part by the individual for the year.

Opening words of 127.5 amended by 1995-97 technical bill, effective 1992, to remove exclusions for related segregated fund trusts and mutual fund trusts from being subject to the section. These are now exempted in 127.55(f) instead.

**Definitions [s. 127.5]:** "amount", "individual" — 248(1); "mutual fund trust" — 132(6)–(7), 132.2(1)(q), 248(1); "taxation year" — 249.

**Interpretation Bulletins:** IT-270R2: Foreign tax credit.

**Forms:** T3 Sched. 12: Minimum tax; T7B-2: Calculation of instalments on minimum tax; T7B-3: Calculation of instalments on minimum tax (farmers and fishermen); T691: Alternative minimum tax; T691A: Minimum tax supplement — multiple jurisdictions.

**127.51 Minimum amount determined** — An individual's minimum amount for a taxation year is the amount determined by the formula

$$A(B - C) - D$$

where

A is the appropriate percentage for the year;

B is the individual's adjusted taxable income for the year determined under section 127.52;

C is the individual's basic exemption for the year determined under section 127.53; and

D is the individual's basic minimum tax credit for the year determined under section 127.531.

**Related Provisions:** 127(5) — Investment tax credit; 257 — Formula cannot calculate to less than zero.

**Definitions [s. 127.51]:** "appropriate percentage", "individual" — 248(1); "taxable income" — 2(2), 248(1); "taxation year" — 249.

**Forms:** T3 Sched. 12: Minimum tax; T7B-2: Calculation of instalments on minimum tax; T7B-3: Calculation of instalments on minimum tax (farmers and fishermen); T691: Alternative minimum tax; T691A: Minimum tax supplement — multiple jurisdictions.

**127.52 (1) Adjusted taxable income determined** — Subject to subsection (2), an individual's adjusted taxable income for a taxation year is the amount that would be the individual's taxable income for the year or the individual's taxable income earned in Canada for the year, as the case may be, if it were computed on the assumption that

(a) [Repealed]

(b) the total of all amounts each of which is an amount deductible under paragraph 20(1)(a) or any of paragraphs 20(1)(c) to (f) in computing the individual's income for the year in respect of a rental or leasing property (other than an amount included in the individual's share of a loss referred to in paragraph (c.1)) were the lesser of the total of all amounts otherwise so deductible and the amount, if any, by which the total of

(i) the total of all amounts each of which is the individual's income for the year from the renting or leasing of a rental or leasing property owned by the individual or by a partnership, computed without reference to paragraphs 20(1)(a) and (c) to (f), and

(ii) the amount, if any, by which

(A) the total of all amounts each of which is the individual's taxable capital gain for the year from the disposition of a rental or leasing property owned by the individual or by a partnership

exceeds

(B) the total of all amounts each of which is the individual's allowable capital loss for the year from the disposition of a rental or leasing property owned by the individual or by a partnership

exceeds the total of all amounts each of which is the individual's loss for the year from the renting or leasing of a rental or leasing property owned by the individual or by a partnership (other than an amount included in the individual's share of a loss referred to in paragraph (c.1)), computed without reference to paragraphs 20(1)(a) and (c) to (f);

(c) the total of all amounts each of which is an amount deductible under paragraph 20(1)(a) or any of paragraphs 20(1)(c) to (f) in computing the individual's income for the year in respect of a film property referred to in paragraph (w) of Class 10 of Schedule II to the *Income Tax Regulations* (other than an amount included in the individual's share of a loss referred to in paragraph (c.1)) were the lesser of the total of all amounts otherwise so deductible by the individual for the year and the amount, if any, by which the total of

(i) the total of all amounts each of which is the individual's income for the year from the renting or leasing of a film property owned by the individual or by a partnership, computed without reference to paragraphs 20(1)(a) and (c) to (f), and

(ii) the amount, if any, by which

(A) the total of all amounts each of which is the individual's taxable capital gain for the year from the disposition of such a film property owned by the individual or by a partnership

exceeds

(B) the total of all amounts each of which is the individual's allowable capital loss for the year from the disposition of such a film property owned by the individual or by a partnership

exceeds the total of all amounts each of which is the individual's loss for the year from such a film property owned by the individual or by a partnership (other than amounts included in the individual's share of a loss referred to in paragraph (c.1)), computed without reference to paragraphs 20(1)(a) and (c) to (f);

(c.1) where, during a partnership's fiscal period that ends in the year (other than a fiscal period that ends because of the application of subsection 99(1)), the individual is a limited partner of the partnership or a member of the partnership who was a specified member of the partnership at all times since becoming a member of the partnership, or the individual's interest in the partnership is an interest for which an identification number is required to be, or has been, obtained under section 237.1,

(i) the individual's share of allowable capital losses of the partnership for the fiscal period were the lesser of

(A) the total of all amounts each of which is the individual's

(I) share of a taxable capital gain for the fiscal period from the disposition of property (other than property acquired by the partnership in a transaction to which subsection 97(2) applied), or

(II) taxable capital gain for the year from the disposition of the individual's interest in the partnership if the individual, or a person who does not deal at arm's length with the individual, does not have an interest in the partnership (otherwise than because of the application of paragraph 98(1)(a) or 98.1(1)(a)) throughout the following taxation year, and

(B) the individual's share of allowable capital losses of the partnership for the fiscal period,

(ii) the individual's share of each loss from a business of the partnership for the fiscal period were the lesser of

(A) the individual's share of the loss, and

(B) the amount, if any, by which

(I) the total of all amounts each of which is the individual's

1. share of a taxable capital gain for the fiscal period from the disposition of property used by the partnership in the business (other than property acquired by the partnership in a transaction to which subsection 97(2) applied), or

2. taxable capital gain for the year from the disposition of the individual's interest in the partnership if the individual, or a person who does not deal at arm's length with the individual, does not have an interest in the partnership (otherwise than because of the application of paragraph 98(1)(a) or 98.1(1)(a)) throughout the following taxation year

exceeds

(II) the total of all amounts each of which is the individual's share of an allowable capital loss for the fiscal period, and

(iii) the individual's share of losses from property of the partnership for the fiscal period were the lesser of

(A) the total of

(I) the individual's share of incomes for the fiscal period from properties of the partnership, and

(II) the amount, if any, by which the total of all amounts each of which is the individual's

1. share of a taxable capital gain for the fiscal period from the disposition of property held by the partnership for the purpose of earning income from property (other than property acquired by the partnership in a transaction to which subsection 97(2) applied), or

2. taxable capital gain for the year from the disposition of the individual's interest in the partnership if the individual, or a person who does not deal at arm's length with the individual, does not have an interest in the partnership (otherwise than because of the application of paragraph 98(1)(a) or 98.1(1)(a)) throughout the following taxation year,

exceeds the total of all amounts each of which is the individual's share of an allowable capital loss for the fiscal period, and

(B) the individual's share of losses from property of the partnership for the fiscal period;

(c.2) where, during a fiscal period of a partnership that ends in the year (other than a fiscal period that ends because of the application of subsection 99(1)),

(i) the individual is a limited partner of the partnership, or is a member of the partnership who was a specified member of the partnership at all times since becoming a member of the partnership, or

(ii) the partnership owns a rental or leasing property or a film property and the individual is a member of the partnership,

the total of all amounts each of which is an amount deductible under any of paragraphs 20(1)(c) to (f) in computing the individual's income for the year in respect of the individual's acquisition of the partnership interest were the lesser of

(iii) the total of all amounts otherwise so deductible, and

(iv) the total of all amounts each of which is the individual's share of any income of the

S. 127.52(1)(c.2)(iv)  Income Tax Act, Part I

partnership for the fiscal period, determined in accordance with subsection 96(1);

(c.3) the total of all amounts each of which is an amount deductible in computing the individual's income for the year in respect of a property for which an identification number is required to be, or has been, obtained under section 237.1 (other than an amount to which any of paragraphs (b) to (c.2) applies) were nil;

(d) except in respect of dispositions of property occurring before 1986 or to which section 79 applies,

(i) sections 38 and 41 were read without the references therein to "³⁄₄ of", other than in the case of a capital gain from a disposition that is the making of a gift of property to a qualified donee (as defined in subsection 149.1(1)), and

### Proposed Amendment — 127.52(1)(d)(i)

**Application**: The December 21, 2000 draft legislation, subsec. 74(1), will amend subpara. 127.52(1)(d)(i) by replacing the reference to "3/4" with "1/2", applicable to taxation years that end after February 27, 2000 except that, for a taxpayer's taxation year that includes either February 28, 2000 or October 17, 2000, the reference to "1/2" shall be read as reference to the fraction in para. 38(a), as amended [by the December 21, 2000 draft legislation], that applies to the taxpayer for the year.

**Technical Notes**: Section 127.52 defines the "adjusted taxable income" of an individual for a taxation year for the purpose of determining the individual's minimum tax liability under Part I.

Subsection 127.52(1) defines an individual's adjusted taxable income for a taxation year for the purpose of determining the individual's minimum tax liability under Part I, and generally requires that the portion of capital gains that is not included in income, because of the inclusion rate, be added in computing adjusted taxable income.

The amendments replace the reference to the fraction "3/4" with a reference to the fraction "1/2" in subparagraph 127.52(1)(d)(i) (realized capital gains), replace the reference to the expression "4/3 of" with a reference to the word "twice" in subparagraph 127.52(1)(d)(ii) (gains allocated from a trust) and replace the reference to the fraction "1/3" with a reference to the fraction "1/2" in subparagraph 127.52(1)(g)(ii) (gains allocated by a trust).

The amendments are consequential on the reduction of the inclusion rate from 3/4 to 1/2 [see 38(a) — ed.].

### Proposed Amendment — AMT rate on capital gains

**Department of Finance news release Backgrounder, December 21, 2000**: *Alternative Minimum Tax (AMT) and Capital Gains*

The February 2000 budget and the October 2000 Economic Statement and Budget Update proposed a staged reduction, to 50% from 75%, of the capital gains inclusion rate. As a consequence of the manner in which these amendments interact with the AMT, it is also proposed that the *inclusion rate for capital gains for AMT purposes be reduced to 80%*, and that 40% of the stock option deduction claimed in calculating regular income tax in respect of taxable stock option benefits be deductible in calculating taxable income for AMT purposes.

[This apparently means that the add-back for AMT will be 30%, taking the AMT inclusion from 50% to 80%, where before 2000 it was 1/4, taking the AMT inclusion from 3/4 to full inclusion — ed.]

Draft legislation to implement these changes will be developed for inclusion in the Bill when it is introduced in Parliament, effective for the 2000 and subsequent taxation years.

(ii) each amount deemed by subsection 104(21) to be a taxable capital gain for the year of the individual were equal to ⁴⁄₃ of that amount;

### Proposed Amendment — 127.52(1)(d)(ii)

**Application**: The December 21, 2000 draft legislation, subsec. 74(2), will amend subpara. 127.52(1)(d)(ii) by replacing the expression "4/3 of" with "twice", applicable to taxation years that end after February 27, 2000 except that, for a taxpayer's taxation year that includes either February 28, 2000 or October 17, 2000, the reference to "twice" shall be read as a reference to "the fraction that is the reciprocal of the fraction in para. 38(a), as amended [by the December 21, 2000 draft legislation], that applies to the taxpayer for the year, multiplied by".

**Technical Notes**: See under 127.52(1)(d)(i).

(e) the total of all amounts deductible under section 65, 66, 66.1, 66.2 or 66.4 or under subsection 29(10) or (12) of the *Income Tax Application Rules* in computing the individual's income for the year were the lesser of the amounts otherwise so deductible by the individual for the year and the total of

### Proposed Amendment — 127.52(1)(e) opening words

(e) the total of all amounts deductible under section 65, 66, 66.1, 66.2, 66.21 or 66.4 or under subsection 29(10) or (12) of the *Income Tax Application Rules* in computing the individual's income for the year were the lesser of the amounts otherwise so deductible by the individual for the year and the total of

**Application**: The December 21, 2000 draft legislation, subsec. 74(3), will amend the opening words of para. 127.52(1)(e) to read as above, applicable to taxation years that begin after 2000.

**Technical Notes**: "Adjusted taxable income" is calculated on the basis of the various assumptions set out in paragraphs 127.52(1)(a) to (j). Paragraph 127.52(1)(e) provides that "adjusted taxable income" is computed on the assumption that the total of specified resource-related deductions does not exceed specified resource income. Paragraph 127.52(1)(e.1) provides that "adjusted taxable income" is computed on the assumption that financing expenses deductible under paragraphs 20(1)(c) to (f) in respect of the acquisition of flow-through shares, Canadian resource properties or foreign resource properties do not exceed the amount by which the same specified resource income exceeds the same specified resource-related deductions.

Paragraphs 127.52(1)(e) and (e.1) are amended so that the resource-related deductions so specified include the deduction under new subsection 66.21(4).

    (i) the individual's income for the year from royalties in respect of, and such part of the individual's income, other than royalties, for the year as may reasonably be considered as attributable to, the production of petroleum, natural gas and minerals, determined before deducting those amounts, and

    (ii) all amounts included in computing the individual's income for the year under section 59;

(e.1) the total of all amounts each of which is an amount deductible under any of paragraphs 20(1)(c) to (f) in computing the individual's income for the year in respect of a property that is a flow-through share (if the individual is the person to whom the share was issued under an agreement referred to in the definition "flow-through share" in subsection 66(15)), a Canadian resource property or a foreign resource property were the lesser of the total of the amounts otherwise so determined for the year and the amount, if any, by which

    (i) the total of all amounts each of which is an amount described in subparagraph (e)(i) or (ii), determined without reference to paragraphs 20(1)(c) to (f),

exceeds

    (ii) the total of all amounts each of which is an amount deductible under section 65, 66, 66.1, 66.2 or 66.4 or under subsection 29(10) or (12) of the *Income Tax Application Rules* in computing the individual's income for the year;

### Proposed Amendment — 127.52(1)(e.1)(ii)

(ii) the total of all amounts each of which is an amount deductible under section 65, 66, 66.1, 66.2, 66.21 or 66.4 or under subsection 29(10) or (12) of the *Income Tax Application Rules* in computing the individual's income for the year;

**Application**: The December 21, 2000 draft legislation, subsec. 74(4), will amend subpara. 127.52(1)(e.i)(ii) to read as above, applicable to taxation years that begin after 2000.

**Technical Notes**: See under 127.52(1)(e) opening words.

(f) subsection 82(1) were read without reference to that portion following paragraph 82(1)(a);

(g) the total of all amounts deductible under section 104 in computing the income of a trust for the year were equal to the total of

    (i) the total of all amounts otherwise deductible under that section, and

    (ii) the total of all amounts each of which is $1/3$ of

        (A) amounts designated by the trust under subsection 104(21) for the year, or

        (B) that portion of a net taxable capital gain of the trust that may reasonably be considered to

            (I) be part of an amount included, by virtue of subsection 104(13) or section 105, in computing the income for the year of a non-resident beneficiary of the trust, or

            (II) have been paid in the year by a trust governed by an employee benefit plan to a beneficiary thereunder;

### Proposed Amendment — 127.52(1)(g)(ii)

**Application**: The December 21, 2000 draft legislation, subsec. 74(5), will amend subpara. 127.52(1)(g)(ii) by replacing the reference to "1/3" with "1/2", applicable to taxation years that end after February 27, 2000 except that, for a taxation year of a trust that includes either February 28, 2000 or October 17, 2000, the reference to "1/2 of" shall be read as a reference to "the fraction that is equal to the amount obtained when 1 is subtracted from the reciprocal of the fraction in para. 38(a), as amended [by the December 21, 2000 draft legislation], that applies to the trust for that year, multiplied by".

**Technical Notes**: See under 127.52(1)(d)(i).

(h) the only amounts deductible under sections 110 to 110.7 in computing the individual's taxable income for the year or taxable income earned in Canada for the year, as the case may be, were the amounts deducted under any of subsections 110(2), 110.6(2), (2.1), (3) and (12) and 110.7(1) and the amount that would be deductible under paragraph 110(1)(f) if paragraph (d) were applicable in computing the individual's income for the year;

(h.1) the formula in paragraph 110.6(21)(a) were read as

$$A - B$$

(i) in computing the individual's taxable income for the year or the individual's taxable income earned in Canada for the year, as the case may be, the only amounts deductible under

    (i) paragraphs 111(1)(a), (c), (d) and (e) were the lesser of

        (A) the amount deducted under those paragraphs for the year, and

        (B) the total of all amounts that would be deductible under those paragraphs for the year if

            (I) paragraphs (b), (c) and (e) of this subsection, as they read in respect of taxation years that began after 1985 and before 1995, applied in computing the individual's non-capital loss, restricted farm loss, farm loss and limited partnership loss for any of those years, and

(II) paragraphs (b) to (c.3), (e) and (e.1) of this subsection applied in computing the individual's non-capital loss, restricted farm loss, farm loss and limited partnership loss for any taxation year that begins after 1994, and

(ii) paragraph 111(1)(b) were the lesser of

(A) the total of all amounts each of which is an amount that can reasonably be considered to be the amount that the individual would have deducted under paragraph 111(1)(b) had paragraph (d) of this subsection been applicable in computing the amount deductible under paragraph 111(1)(b), and

(B) the total of all amounts that would be deductible under that paragraph for the year if

(I) paragraph (d) of this subsection applied in computing the individual's net capital loss for any taxation year that began before 1995, and

(II) paragraphs (c.1) and (d) of this subsection applied in computing the individual's net capital loss for any taxation year that begins after 1994; and

(j) the *Income Tax Application Rules* were read without reference to section 40 of that Act.

**Related Provisions**: 127.52(2) — Certain CCA claims by partnership deemed claimed by partner; 127.52(2.1) — Specified member of partnership — anti-avoidance rule; 127.52(3) — Rental or leasing property; 248(8) — Occurrences as a consequence of death.

**Notes**: 127.52(1)(a) repealed by 1998 Budget, effective for 1998 and later taxation years. RRSP contributions (under 146(5) and (5.1)) and retiring-allowance rollovers (under 60(j.1)) are no longer considered a tax preference, and thus are deductible for AMT purposes. For earlier years, read:

(a) the total of all amounts deductible under any of paragraphs 8(1)(m) and 60(i) to (j.2) in computing the individual's income for the year were the lesser of

(i) the total of the amounts otherwise so deductible, and

(ii) the total of

(A) the amount otherwise so deductible under paragraph 60(i) by reason of subsection 146(6.1), and

(B) all amounts each of which was included in computing the individual's income for the year and is a single payment out of or under a deferred profit sharing plan, a superannuation or pension fund or plan or a foreign retirement arrangement

(I) as a consequence of the death, withdrawal from the fund, plan or arrangement or termination of employment of a person,

(II) on the winding-up of the fund, plan or arrangement in full satisfaction of all rights of the payee in or under the fund, plan or arrangement, or

(III) to which the individual is entitled because of an amendment to the fund, plan or arrangement;

Subsec. 50(1) of the 1998 Budget bill provides the following transitional rule:

(1) Where an individual's tax payable under Part I of the Act for a particular taxation year that began after 1993 and before 1998 is greater than the tax that would have been so payable if the Act were read without reference to paragraph 127.52(1)(a) and the individual was resident in Canada throughout, and was not a bankrupt at any time in, the period that began immediately after the end of the particular year and that ended at the end of 1997, the individual's minimum amount for the particular year under section 127.51 of the Act is deemed to be equal to the amount, if any, by which

(a) the amount that would be the individual's minimum amount for the particular year determined without reference to this subsection

exceeds

(b) the part of the individual's additional tax for the particular year determined under subsection 120.2(3) of the Act that can reasonably be considered to be attributable to the application of paragraph 127.52(1)(a) of the Act and not deductible in computing the individual's tax payable under Part I of the Act for any of the taxation years that began after the end of the particular year and before 1998.

Subsec. 50(1) of the 1998 Budget bill is effective for the 1994 and later taxation years, and, notwithstanding 152(4) to (5), such assessment of an individual's tax payable under the Act for any taxation year shall be made as is necessary to take its application into account. In effect, the transitional rule applies the amendment to individuals who had to pay AMT in any of 1994-97 due to 127.52(1)(a). However, this retroactive relief applies only to the extent they were unable to recover the extra tax during that period, and only if they were resident in Canada throughout, and were not bankrupt at any time in, the period that began at the end of the year for which they had to pay minimum tax and that ended at the end of 1997. This relief is not available for individuals who died before 1998.

127.52(1)(a)(ii)(B) amended by 1991 technical bill, effective 1990 (but see 1990 pension bill change below), to add reference to a foreign retirement arrangement.

127.52(1)(a) amended by 1990 pension bill, effective 1991, as a result of the repeal of 8(1)(m.1) and related changes.

127.52(1)(b) and (c) amended, and (c.1), (c.2) and (c.3) added, by 1995-97 technical bill, effective for taxation years of an individual that begin after 1994. For earlier years, read:

(b) the total of all amounts deductible by the individual under paragraph 20(1)(a) for the year in respect of residential properties were the lesser of the total of all amounts otherwise so deductible by the individual for the year and the amount, if any, by which

(i) the total of the individual's incomes for the year from the renting or leasing of residential properties owned by the individual or by a partnership, computed without reference to paragraph 20(1)(a),

exceeds

(ii) the total of the individual's losses for the year from the renting or leasing of residential properties owned by the individual or by a partnership, computed without reference to paragraph 20(1)(a);

(c) the total of all amounts deductible by the individual under paragraph 20(1)(a) for the year in respect of film properties were the lesser of the total of all amounts otherwise so deductible by the individual for the year and the amount, if any, by which

(i) the total of the individual's incomes for the year from the renting or leasing of film properties owned by the individual or by a partnership, computed without reference to paragraph 20(1)(a),

exceeds

    (ii) the total of the individual's losses for the year from the renting or leasing of film properties owned by the individual or by a partnership, computed without reference to paragraph 20(1)(a);

127.52(1)(d)(i) amended by 1997 Budget, effective for taxation years of an individual that begin after 1996, to add everything from "other than...".

127.52(1)(d)(ii) added by 1992 technical bill, effective 1991.

127.52(1)(e.1) added by 1995-97 technical bill, effective for taxation years of an individual that begin after 1994.

127.52(1)(h) amended by 1991 technical bill, retroactive to 1988, to ensure that the deduction allowed under 110(1)(f) for minimum tax purposes reflects any increase in adjusted taxable income resulting from a capital gain for which a deduction was available under 110(1)(f).

127.52(1)(h.1) added by 1995-97 technical bill, effective only for the 1994 and 1995 taxation years.

127.52(1)(i)(i)(B) and (ii)(B) amended by 1995-97 technical bill, effective for all taxation years, effectively to add subcl. (B)(II) in both cases.

127.52(1)(i) amended by 1991 technical bill, retroactive to 1986, to account for limited partnership losses under 111(1)(e).

**Advance Tax Rulings**: ATR-28: Redemption of capital stock of family farm corporation.

**(2) Partnerships** — For the purposes of subsection (1) and this subsection, any amount deductible under a provision of this Act in computing the income or loss of a partnership for a fiscal period is, to the extent of a member's share of the partnership's income or loss, deemed to be deductible by the member under that provision in computing the member's income for the taxation year in which the fiscal period ends.

**Notes**: 127.52(2) amended by 1995-97 technical bill, effective for taxation years of an individual that begin after 1994. It was previously a special rule applying to CCA claims by a member of a partnership that owned a residential building or certified Canadian film production. It now applies to any amount deductible in computing the income or loss of a partnership. For earlier taxation years since 1986, read:

> (2) **Partnerships** — For the purposes of paragraphs (1)(b) and (c), where an individual was a member of that partnership at the end of its fiscal period, any amount deducted by that partnership as a deduction under paragraph 20(1)(a) in respect of a residential property or a film property in computing its income shall, to the extent of the individual's share thereof, be deemed to have been deducted by the individual under that paragraph in computing the individual's income in respect of the property for the taxation year in which the fiscal period ended.

**(2.1) Specified member of a partnership** — Where it can reasonably be considered that one of the main reasons that a member of a partnership was not a specified member of the partnership at all times since becoming a member of the partnership is to avoid the application of this section to the member's interest in the partnership, the member is deemed for the purpose of this section to have been a specified member of the partnership at all times since becoming a member of the partnership.

**Related Provisions**: 40(3.131) — Parallel rule for negative adjusted cost base of partnership interest.

**Notes**: 127.52(2.1) added by 1995-97 technical bill, effective April 27, 1995.

**(3) Definitions** — For the purposes of this section,

**"film property"** means a property described in paragraph (n) of Class 12, or paragraph (w) of Class 10, of Schedule II to the *Income Tax Regulations*;

**"limited partner"** has the meaning that would be assigned by subsection 96(2.4) if that subsection were read without reference to "if the member's partnership interest is not an exempt interest (within the meaning assigned by subsection (2.5)) at that time and";

**Notes**: Definition "limited partner" added by 1995-97 technical bill, effective for taxation years of an individual that begin after 1994.

**"rental or leasing property"** means a property that is a rental property or a leasing property for the purpose of section 1100 of the *Income Tax Regulations*.

**Related Provisions**: 127.52(1)(b), (c.2)(ii) — Application of minimum tax.

**Notes**: Definition "rental or leasing property" added by 1995-97 technical bill, effective for taxation years of an individual that begin after 1994.

**Regulations**: 1100(14)–(14.2) (definition of rental property); 1100(17)–(20) (definition of leasing property).

**"residential property"** — [Repealed]

**Notes**: Definition "residential property" repealed by 1995-97 technical bill, effective for taxation years of an individual that begin after 1994. For earlier taxation years since 1986, read:

> "residential property" means a property described in Class 31 or 32 of Schedule II to the *Income Tax Regulations* and furniture, fixtures and equipment, if any, located in, and ancillary to, that property.

**Definitions [s. 127.52]**: "allowable capital loss" — 38(a), 248(1); "amount" — 248(1); "arm's length" — 251(1); "business" — 248(1); "Canada" — 255; "capital gain" — 54, 248(1); "deferred profit sharing plan" — 147(1), 248(1); "disposition"; of capital property — 54; "employment" — 248(1); "farm loss" — 111(8), 248(1); "film property" — 127.52(3); "fiscal period" — 248(1), 249(2)(b), 249.1; "flow-through share" — 66(15), 248(1); "foreign retirement arrangement" — 248(1); "identical" — 40(3.5), 248(12); "individual" — 248(1); "limited partner" — 127.52(3); "limited partnership loss" — 96(2.1)(e), 248(1); "mineral" — 248(1); "non-capital loss" — 111(8), 248(1); "partnership" — see Notes to 96(1); "person", "property", "regulation" — 248(1); "rental or leasing property", "residential property" — 127.52(3); "restricted farm loss" — 31, 248(1); "specified member" — 127.52(2.1), 248(1); "taxable capital gain" — 38(a), 248(1); "taxable income" — 2(2), 248(1); "taxable income earned in Canada" — 115(1), 248(1); "taxation year" — 249; "trust" — 104(1), 248(1), (3).

**Forms [s. 127.52]**: T3 Sched. 12: Minimum tax; T7B-2: Calculation of instalments on minimum tax; T7B-3: Calculation of instalments on minimum tax (farmers and fishermen); T691: Alternative minimum tax; T691A: Minimum tax supplement — multiple jurisdictions.

**127.53 (1) Basic exemption** — An individual's basic exemption for a taxation year is

    (a) $40,000, in the case of an individual other than a trust;

(b) $40,000, in the case of a testamentary trust or an *inter vivos* trust described in subsection 122(2); and

(c) in any other case, nil.

**(2) Multiple trusts** — Notwithstanding paragraph (1)(b), where more than one trust described in that paragraph arose as a consequence of contributions to the trusts by an individual and those trusts have filed with the Minister in prescribed form an agreement whereby, for the purpose of this Division, they allocate an amount to one or more of them for a taxation year and the total of the amounts so allocated does not exceed $40,000, the basic exemption for the year of each of the trusts is the amount so allocated to it.

**Related Provisions**: 104(2) — Grouping of multiple trusts for regular tax purposes.

**Forms**: T3 Sched. 6: Trusts' agreement to allocate the basic exemption from minimum tax.

**(3) Failure to file agreement** — Notwithstanding paragraph (1)(b), where more than one trust described in that paragraph arose as a consequence of contributions to the trusts by an individual and no agreement as contemplated by subsection (2) has been filed with the Minister before the expiry of 30 days after notice in writing has been forwarded by the Minister to any of the trusts that such an agreement is required for the purpose of an assessment of tax under this Part, the Minister may, for the purpose of this Division, allocate an amount to one or more of the trusts for a taxation year, the total of all of which amounts does not exceed $40,000, and the basic exemption for the year of each of the trusts is the amount so allocated to it.

**Definitions [s. 127.53]**: "amount", "assessment", "individual" — 248(1); "*inter vivos* trust" — 108(1), 248(1); "Minister", "prescribed" — 248(1); "taxation year" — 249; "testamentary trust" — 108(1), 248(1); "trust" — 104(1), 248(1), (3); "writing" — *Interpretation Act* 35(1).

**Interpretation Bulletins [s. 127.53]**: IT-406R2: Tax payable by an *inter vivos* trust.

**Forms [s. 127.53]**: T3 Sched. 12: Minimum tax; T691: Alternative minimum tax; T691A: Minimum tax supplement — multiple jurisdictions.

**127.531 Basic minimum tax credit determined** — An individual's basic minimum tax credit for a taxation year is the total of amounts that may be deducted in computing the individual's tax payable for the year under this Part under any of subsections 118(1) and (2), sections 118.1 and 118.2, subsection 118.3(1) and sections 118.5 to 118.7.

**Notes**: The basic minimum tax credit is the total of amounts that *may be* deducted under the indicated provisions, whether or not they *are* deducted. Thus, for example, charitable donations that are available for credit under 118.1, but are not claimed in the year and are being saved for carryforward, can be claimed under 127.531. The CCRA's Form T691 is wrong in this respect, as it refers to the amounts claimed on page 3 of the T1 General income tax return as the basis for calculating the basic minimum tax credit.

The CCRA's computer system will automatically reject a claim for credits under 127.531 that does not match the actual credits claimed for regular tax purposes. The Tax Court of Canada confirmed that the CCRA is wrong, and that all amounts that "may be" deducted for regular tax purposes can be deducted for AMT purposes, in *David M. Sherman*, [2000] 1 C.T.C. 2696 (TCC). The CCRA has since accepted this argument at the Notice of Objection level in subsequent cases.

**Definitions [s. 127.531]**: "amount", "individual" — 248(1); "tax payable" — 248(2); "taxation year" — 249.

**127.54 (1) Definitions** — In this section,

**"foreign income"** of an individual for a taxation year means the total of

(a) the individual's incomes for the year from businesses carried on by the individual in countries other than Canada, and

(b) the individual's incomes for the year from sources in countries other than Canada in respect of which the individual has paid non-business-income taxes, within the meaning assigned by subsection 126(7), to governments of countries other than Canada;

**"foreign taxes"** of an individual for a taxation year means the total of the business-income taxes, within the meaning assigned by subsection 126(7), paid by the individual for the year in respect of businesses carried on by the individual in countries other than Canada and ⅔ of the non-business-income taxes, within the meaning assigned by that subsection, paid by the individual for the year to the governments of countries other than Canada.

**(2) Foreign tax credit** — For the purposes of section 127.5, an individual's special foreign tax credit for a taxation year is the greater of

(a) the total of all amounts deductible under section 126 from the individual's tax for the year, and

(b) the lesser of

(i) the individual's foreign taxes for the year, and

(ii) 17% of the individual's foreign income for the year.

**Definitions [s. 127.54]**: "amount", "business" — 248(1); "Canada" — 255; "foreign income", "foreign taxes" — 127.54(1); "individual" — 248(1); "taxation year" — 249.

**127.55 Application of section 127.5** — Section 127.5 does not apply in respect of

(a) a return of income of an individual filed under subsection 70(2), paragraph 104(23)(d) or 128(2)(e) or subsection 150(4);

(b) a taxation year of an individual in respect of which the individual has made an election under section 119;

**Proposed Repeal — 127.55(b)**

**Application**: Bill C-43 (First Reading September 20, 2000), s. 76, will repeal para. 127.55(b), applicable to 1996 *et seq.*

> **Technical Notes**: Section 127.55 of the Act limits the application of the alternative minimum tax set out in section 127.5 of the Act. Paragraph 127.55(b) refers to existing section 119. Existing section 119 is no longer active, and is replaced with a new, unrelated rule. Paragraph 127.55(b) is therefore repealed, for the 1996 and subsequent taxation years.

(c) an individual for the taxation year in which the individual dies;

(d) an individual for the 1986 taxation year if the individual dies in 1987;

(e) a trust described in paragraph 104(4)(a) or (a.1) for its taxation year that includes the day determined in respect of the trust under that paragraph; and

(f) a taxation year of a trust throughout which the trust is

(i) a related segregated fund trust (within the meaning assigned by paragraph 138.1(1)(a)),

(ii) a mutual fund trust, or

(iii) a trust prescribed to be a master trust.

**Notes**: 127.55(e) added by 1991 technical bill, retroactive to 1986, and amended by 1992 technical bill, effective 1993, to add reference to 104(4)(a.1). For 1986 to 1992, read:

(e) a trust described in paragraph 104(4)(a) for its taxation year in which the spouse referred to in that paragraph dies.

127.55(f) added by 1995-97 technical bill, effective for 1992 and later taxation years. Subparas. (i) and (ii) were formerly covered in the opening words to 127.5(1); subpara. (iii) is new.

**Definitions [s. 127.55]**: "individual" — 248(1); "mutual fund trust" — 132(6); "prescribed" — 248(1); "taxation year" — 249; "trust" — 104(1), 248(1), (3).

**Interpretation Bulletins [s. 127.55]**: IT-326R2: Returns of deceased persons as "another person".

## DIVISION F — SPECIAL RULES APPLICABLE IN CERTAIN CIRCUMSTANCES

### Bankruptcies

**128. (1) Where corporation bankrupt** — Where a corporation has become a bankrupt, the following rules are applicable:

(a) the trustee in bankruptcy shall be deemed to be the agent of the bankrupt for all purposes of this Act;

(b) the estate of the bankrupt shall be deemed not to be a trust or an estate for the purposes of this Act;

(c) the income and the taxable income of the corporation for any taxation year of the corporation during which it was a bankrupt and for any subsequent year shall be calculated as if

(i) the property of the bankrupt did not pass to and vest in the trustee in bankruptcy on the receiving order being made or the assignment filed but remained vested in the bankrupt, and

(ii) any dealing in the estate of the bankrupt or any act performed in the carrying on of the business of the bankrupt estate by the trustee was done as agent on behalf of the bankrupt and any income of the trustee from such dealing or carrying on is income of the bankrupt and not of the trustee;

(d) a taxation year of the corporation shall be deemed to have commenced on the day the corporation became a bankrupt and a taxation year of the corporation that would otherwise have ended after the corporation became a bankrupt shall be deemed to have ended on the day immediately before the day on which the corporation became a bankrupt;

(e) where, in the case of any taxation year of the corporation ending during the period the corporation is a bankrupt, the corporation fails to pay any tax payable by the corporation under this Act for any such year, the corporation and the trustee in bankruptcy are jointly and severally liable to pay the tax, except that

(i) the trustee is only liable to the extent of the property of the bankrupt in the trustee's possession, and

(ii) payment by either of them shall discharge the joint obligation;

(f) in the case of any taxation year of the corporation ending during the period the corporation is a bankrupt, the corporation shall be deemed not to be associated with any other corporation in the year; and

(g) where an absolute order of discharge is granted in respect of the corporation, for the purposes of section 111 any loss of the corporation for any taxation year preceding the year in which the order of discharge was granted is not deductible by the corporation in computing its taxable income for the taxation year of the corporation in which the order was granted or any subsequent year.

**Related Provisions**: 39(1)(c)(iv)(B) — Business investment loss on debt of bankrupt corporation; 50(1) — Capital loss on debts and shares of bankrupt corporation; 56.3 — No debt forgiveness reserve inclusion while corporation bankrupt; 80(1)"forgiven amount"B(i) — Debt forgiveness rules do not apply; 129(1.1) — No dividend refund on dividend paid to bankrupt controlling corporation; 181.1(3)(b) — Where tax not payable; 227(5) — Amount in trust not part of estate.

**Regulations**: 206(2) (information return).

**Interpretation Bulletins**: IT-64R3: Corporations: association and control — after 1988; IT-179R: Change of fiscal period (to be revised re bankrupt corporations — see I.T. Technical News No. 8); IT-206R: Separate businesses.

**I.T. Technical News**: No. 8 (bankrupt corporation — change of fiscal period).

## S. 128(2) — Income Tax Act, Part I

**(2) Where individual bankrupt** — Where an individual has become a bankrupt, the following rules are applicable:

(a) the trustee in bankruptcy shall be deemed to be the agent of the bankrupt for all purposes of this Act;

(b) the estate of the bankrupt shall be deemed not to be a trust or an estate for the purposes of this Act;

(c) the income and the taxable income of the individual for any taxation year during which the individual was a bankrupt and for any subsequent year shall be calculated as if

(i) the property of the bankrupt did not pass to and vest in the trustee in bankruptcy on the receiving order being made or the assignment filed but remained vested in the bankrupt, and

(ii) any dealing in the estate of the bankrupt or any act performed in the carrying on of the business of the bankrupt estate by the trustee was done as agent on behalf of the bankrupt and any income of the trustee from such dealing or carrying on is income of the bankrupt and not of the trustee;

(d) except for the purposes of subsections 146(1), 146.01(4) and 146.02(4) and Part X.1,

(i) a taxation year of the individual is deemed to have begun at the beginning of the day on which the individual became a bankrupt, and

(ii) the individual's last taxation year that began before that day is deemed to have ended immediately before that day;

(d.1) where, by reason of paragraph (d), a taxation year of the individual is not a calendar year,

(i) paragraph 146(5)(b) shall, for the purpose of the application of subsection 146(5) to the taxation year, be read as follows:

"(b) the amount, if any, by which

(i) the taxpayer's RRSP deduction limit for the particular calendar year in which the taxation year ends

exceeds

(ii) the total of the amounts deducted under this subsection and subsection (5.1) in computing the taxpayer's income for any preceding taxation year that ends in the particular calendar year.",

and

(ii) paragraph 146(5.1)(b) shall, for the purpose of the application of subsection 146(5.1) to the taxation year, be read as follows:

"(b) the amount, if any, by which

(i) the taxpayer's RRSP deduction limit for the particular calendar year in which the taxation year ends

exceeds

(ii) the total of the amount deducted under subsection (5) in computing the taxpayer's income for the year and the amounts deducted under this subsection and subsection (5) in computing the taxpayer's income for any preceding taxation year that ends in the particular calendar year.";

(d.2) where, by reason of paragraph (d), the individual has two taxation years ending in a calendar year, each amount deducted in computing the individual's income for either of the taxation years shall be deemed, for the purposes of the definition "unused RRSP deduction room" in subsection 146(1) and Part X.1, to have been deducted in computing the individual's income for the calendar year;

(e) where the individual was a bankrupt at any time in a calendar year the trustee shall, within 90 days from the end of the year, file a return with the Minister, in prescribed form, on behalf of the individual of the individual's income for any taxation year occurring in the calendar year computed as if

(i) the only income of the individual for that taxation year was the income for the year, if any, arising from dealings in the estate of the bankrupt or acts performed in the carrying on of the business of the bankrupt by the trustee,

(ii) in computing the individual's taxable income for that taxation year, no deduction were permitted by Division C, other than

(A) an amount under paragraph 110(1)(d), (d.1), (d.2) or (d.3) or section 110.6 to the extent that the amount is in respect of an amount included in income under subparagraph (i) for that taxation year, and

**Proposed Amendment — 128(2)(e)(ii)(A)**

(A) an amount under any of paragraphs 110(1)(d) to (d.3) and section 110.6 to the extent that the amount is in respect of an amount included in income under subparagraph (i) for that taxation year, and

**Application**: The December 21, 2000 draft legislation, subsec. 75(1), will amend cl. 128(2)(e)(ii)(A) to read as above, applicable to 2000 et seq.

**Technical Notes**: Paragraph 128(2)(e) requires a trustee in bankruptcy to file, for each taxation year in the calendar year in which an individual becomes bankrupt, an income tax return with respect to certain income of the estate and businesses of the individual. For this purpose, the individual's income is to be determined as if no deductions other than those specifically listed were available to the individual.

Paragraph 128(2)(e) is amended to include in the list of allowable deductions a deduction under new paragraph 110(1)(d.01). Paragraph 110(1)(d.01) allows a deduction

1178

where certain employee option securities (or proceeds from the disposition of such securities) are donated to a qualifying charity. This deduction is available to the extent that the securities option benefit to which the deduction relates is included in computing the individual's taxable income for the taxation year for which the return is being filed.

Paragraph 128(2)(f) requires an individual who is bankrupt at any time in a taxation year to file an income tax return for the year, in addition to the return required under paragraph 128(2)(e) to be filed by the trustee in bankruptcy. For this purpose, the individual's income is to be determined as if certain listed deductions were not available.

Paragraph 128(2)(f) is amended to include in the list of deductions that are not available a deduction under new paragraph 110(1)(d.01).

(B) an amount under section 111 to the extent that the amount was in respect of a loss of the individual for any taxation year that ended before the individual was discharged absolutely from bankruptcy, and

(iii) in computing the individual's tax payable under this Part for that taxation year, no deduction were allowed

(A) under section 118, 118.2, 118.3, 118.5, 118.6, 118.8 or 118.9,

(B) under section 118.1 with respect to a gift made by the individual on or after the day the individual became bankrupt,

(B.1) under section 118.62 with respect to interest paid on or after the day on which the individual became bankrupt, and

(C) under subsection 127(5) with respect to an expenditure incurred or property acquired by the individual in any taxation year that ends after the individual was discharged absolutely from bankruptcy,

and the trustee is liable to pay any tax so determined for that taxation year;

(f) notwithstanding paragraph (e), the individual shall file a separate return of the individual's income for any taxation year during which the individual was a bankrupt, computed as if

(i) the income required to be reported in respect of the year by the trustee under paragraph (e) was not the income of the individual,

(ii) in computing income, the individual was not entitled to deduct any loss sustained by the trustee in the year in dealing with the estate of the bankrupt or in carrying on the business of the bankrupt,

(iii) in computing the individual's taxable income for the year, no amount were deductible under paragraph 110(1)(d), (d.1), (d.2) or (d.3) or section 110.6 in respect of an amount included in income under subparagraph (e)(i),

and no amount were deductible under section 111, and

> **Proposed Amendment — 128(2)(f)(iii)**
>
> (iii) in computing the individual's taxable income for the year, no amount were deductible under any of paragraphs 110(1)(d) to (d.3) and section 110.6 in respect of an amount included in income under subparagraph (e)(i), and no amount were deductible under section 111, and
>
> **Application**: The December 21, 2000 draft legislation, subsec. 75(2), will amend subpara. 128(2)(f)(iii) to read as above, applicable to 2000 *et seq.*
>
> **Technical Notes**: See under 128(2)(e)(ii)(A).

(iv) in computing the individual's tax payable under this Part for the year, no amount were deductible under

(A) section 118.1 in respect of a gift made before the day on which the individual became bankrupt,

(B) section 118.62 in respect of interest paid before the day on which the individual became bankrupt, or

(C) section 118.61 or 120.2 or subsection 127(5),

and the individual is liable to pay any tax so determined for that taxation year;

(g) notwithstanding subparagraphs (e)(ii) and (iii) and (f)(iii) and (iv), where at any time an individual was discharged absolutely from bankruptcy,

(i) in computing the individual's taxable income for any taxation year that ends after that time, no amount shall be deducted under section 111 in respect of losses for taxation years that ended before that time,

(ii) in computing the individual's tax payable under this Part for any taxation year that ends after that time,

(A) no amount shall be deducted under section 118.61 or 120.2 in respect of an amount for any taxation year that ended before that time,

(B) no amount shall be deducted under section 118.1 in respect of a gift made before the individual became bankrupt,

(B.1) no amount shall be deducted under section 118.62 in respect of interest paid before the day on which the individual became bankrupt, and

(C) no amount shall be deducted under subsection 127(5) in respect of an expenditure incurred or a property acquired by the individual in any taxation year that ended before that time, and

(iii) the individual's unused tuition and education tax credits at the end of the last taxation year that ended before that time is deemed to be nil;

(h) where, in a taxation year commencing after an order of discharge has been granted in respect of the individual, the trustee deals in the estate of the individual who was a bankrupt or performs any act in the carrying on of the business of the individual, paragraphs (e), (f) and (g) shall apply as if the individual were a bankrupt in the year; and

(i) the portion of the individual's non-capital loss for a particular taxation year in which paragraph (e) applied in respect of the individual and any preceding taxation year that does not exceed the lesser of

(i) the amount of the individual's allowable business investment losses for the particular taxation year, and

(ii) any portion of the individual's non-capital loss for that particular year that was not deducted in computing the individual's taxable income for any taxation year in which paragraph (e) applied in respect of the individual or any preceding taxation year,

shall, for the purpose of determining the individual's cumulative gains limit under section 110.6 for taxation years following the taxation year in which paragraph (e) was last applicable in respect of the individual, be deemed not to have been an allowable business investment loss.

**Related Provisions**: 56.2, 56.3 — No debt forgiveness reserve inclusion while individual bankrupt; 80(1)"forgiven amount"B(i) — Debt forgiveness rules do not apply; 118.95 — Credits allowed on return filed by bankrupt individual; 120.2(4)(a) — No minimum tax carryover on individual's return under 128(2)(f); 122.5(7) — GST credit for year of bankruptcy; 122.61(3,1) — Child Tax Benefit for year of bankruptcy; 127.1(1)(a) — No refundable investment tax credit on individual's return under 128(2)(f); 127.55 — Minimum tax not applicable; 150(3) — Trustee in bankruptcy required to file return; 227(5) — Amount in trust not part of estate; Reg. 2701(2) — Calculation of group term life insurance benefit where individual bankrupt.

**Notes**: 128(2)(d) amended by 1998 Budget, effective for 1999 and later taxation years. For earlier years, read:

(d) except for the purposes of subsections 146(1) and 146.01(4), (9) and (10) and Part X.1, a taxation year of the individual shall be deemed to have begun on the day in the calendar year on which the individual became a bankrupt and the individual's taxation year that would otherwise have ended on the last day of that calendar year shall be deemed to have ended on the day immediately before the day the individual became a bankrupt;

128(2)(e)(iii)(B.1) and (g)(ii)(B.1) added, and (f)(iv) amended, by 1998 Budget, effective for bankruptcies that occur after 1997. For earlier bankruptcies, read (f)(iv) as:

(iv) in computing the individual's tax payable under this Part for the year, no amount were deductible under section 118.1 in respect of a gift made before the day the individual became bankrupt or under section 118.61 or 120.2 or subsection 127(5),

128(2)(e), (f) and (g) amended by 1995-97 technical bill, this version effective for taxation years that end in 1997 or later. For earlier taxation years, for bankruptcies that occur after April 26, 1995, ignore references to 118.61 in 128(2)(e)(iii)(A), 128(2)(f)(iv) and 128(2)(g)(ii)(A), and ignore 128(2)(g)(iii).

For bankruptcies since 1988 but before April 27, 1995, read:

(e) where the individual was a bankrupt at any time in a calendar year the trustee shall, within 90 days from the end of the year, file a return with the Minister, in prescribed form, on behalf of the individual of the individual's income for any taxation year occurring in the calendar year computed as if

(i) the only income of the individual for that taxation year was the income for the year, if any, arising from dealings in the estate of the bankrupt or acts performed in the carrying on of the business of the bankrupt by the trustee,

(ii) in computing taxable income, the individual was not entitled to any deduction permitted by Division C for that taxation year except any deduction permitted by section 111, and

(iii) in computing the tax payable under this Part by the individual, the individual was not entitled to deduct any amount under any of sections 118 to 118.3, 118.5, 118.6, 118.8 and 118.9,

and the trustee is liable to pay any tax payable under this Part by the individual in respect of that taxable income for that taxation year;

(f) notwithstanding paragraph (e), the individual shall file a separate return of the individual's income for any taxation year during which the individual was a bankrupt, computed as if

(i) the income required to be reported in respect of the year by the trustee under paragraph (e) was not the income of the individual,

(ii) in computing income, the individual was not entitled to deduct any loss sustained by the trustee in the year in dealing with the estate of the bankrupt or in carrying on the business of the bankrupt,

(iii) in computing taxable income, the individual was not entitled to any deduction under section 111 with respect to any losses for a previous taxation year,

and the individual is liable to pay any tax payable under this Part by the individual in respect of that taxable income for the taxation year;

(g) where an absolute order of discharge is granted in respect of the individual, for the purpose of section 111 any loss of the individual for a taxation year preceding the year in which the order of discharge was granted is not deductible by the individual in computing the individual's taxable income for the taxation year in which the order was granted or any subsequent year;

128(2)(d) amended by 1992 technical bill to add references to 146.01(4) and (9), effective 1992, and by 1992 Economic Statement to add references to 146.01(10), effective 1993.

128(2) amended by 1990 pension bill, effective 1991. For 1990 and 1989, delete paras. (d.1) and (d.2), and delete the opening words of para. (d): "except for the purposes of subsection 146(1) and Part X.1".

**Regulations**: 206(2) (information return).

**Interpretation Bulletins**: IT-124R6: Contributions to registered retirement savings plans; IT-179R: Change of fiscal period; IT-206R: Separate businesses; IT-415R2: Deregistration of registered retirement savings plans; IT-513R: Personal tax credits.

## (3) [Repealed]

**Notes**: 128(3) repealed by 1995-97 technical bill, effective for bankruptcies that occur after April 26, 1995. It defined "bankrupt"

Division F — Special Rules in Certain Circumstances    S. 128.1(1)(b)(iv)

and "estate of the bankrupt" with reference to the *Bankruptcy and Insolvency Act*. These are now in 248(1).

**Definitions [s. 128]**: "allowable business investment loss" — 38(c), 248(1); "amount" — 248(1); "associated" — 128(1)(f), 256; "bankrupt" — 248(1); "business" — 248(1); "calendar year" — *Interpretation Act* 37(1)(a); "capital gain", "capital loss" — 39(1), 248(1); "corporation" — 248(1), *Interpretation Act* 35(1); "estate of the bankrupt" — 248(1); "individual", "Minister" — 248(1); "non-capital loss" — 111(8), 248(1); "prescribed", "property" — 248(1); "RRSP deduction limit" — 146(1), 248(1); "tax payable" — 248(2); "taxable income" — 2(2), 248(1); "taxation year" — 128(2)(d), 249; "taxpayer" — 248(1); "trust" — 104(1), 248(1), (3); "unused tuition and education tax credits" — 118.61(1) [technically does not apply to s. 128].

## Changes in Residence

### Proposed Amendments — 128.1

**Technical Notes [Bill C-43]**: Section 128.1 sets out the income tax effects of becoming or ceasing to be resident in Canada. The present amendments make several important additions to section 128.1, including:

- a more comprehensive deemed disposition of property by individual emigrants;
- greater clarity as to the exclusion of certain pension and other rights from the deemed dispositions on emigration and immigration;
- special accommodation of individuals (other than trusts) who, having emigrated from Canada, re-establish residence in Canada;
- the ability for post-emigration losses in effect to reduce gains realized as a result of the deemed disposition on emigration;
- information reporting requirements for individuals who emigrate from Canada; and
- in certain circumstances, a deemed end to the fiscal period of a business carried on by an individual emigrant.

In addition, these amendments make a number of clarifying and updating changes to section 128.1. They also revise the section as necessary to reflect other amendments such as the restructured definition "taxable Canadian property" and the changes to section 114 of the Act.

**128.1 (1) Immigration** — For the purposes of this Act, where at a particular time a taxpayer becomes resident in Canada,

(a) **year-end, fiscal period** — where the taxpayer is a corporation or a trust,

(i) the taxpayer's taxation year that would otherwise include the particular time shall be deemed to have ended immediately before the particular time and a new taxation year of the taxpayer shall be deemed to have begun at the particular time, and

(ii) for the purpose of determining the taxpayer's fiscal period after the particular time, the taxpayer shall be deemed not to have established a fiscal period before the particular time;

(b) **deemed disposition** — the taxpayer is deemed to have disposed, at the time (in this subsection referred to as the "time of disposition") that is immediately before the time that is immediately before the particular time, of each property owned by the taxpayer, other than, if the taxpayer is an individual,

(i) property that would be taxable Canadian property if the taxpayer had been resident in Canada at no time in the taxpayer's last taxation year that began before the particular time,

### Proposed Amendment — 128.1(1)(b)(i)

(i) property that is a taxable Canadian property,

**Application**: Bill C-43 (First Reading September 20, 2000), subsec. 77(1), will amend subpara. 128.1(1)(b)(i) to read as above, applicable to changes in residence that occur after October 1, 1996.

**Technical Notes**: Subsection 128.1(1) of the Act sets out rules that apply where a taxpayer becomes resident in Canada. Paragraph 128.1(1)(b) treats a taxpayer who becomes resident in Canada as having disposed of the taxpayer's property, with certain exceptions, for proceeds equal to the property's fair market value. This disposition is deemed to have taken place immediately before the time that is immediately before the time at which the taxpayer becomes resident.

The properties excluded from the deemed disposition on immigration under paragraph 128.1(1)(b) are essentially those properties that were, ignoring any relevant tax treaty, already subject to tax in Canada. Subparagraph 128.1(1)(b)(i) sets out one type of excluded property, being taxable Canadian property. Subparagraph 128.1(1)(b)(i) is amended, with application after October 1, 1996, to simplify its description of taxable Canadian property. This change is a consequence of the relocation of the main definition of taxable Canadian property to subsection 248(1) of the Act.

(ii) property that is described in the inventory of a business carried on by the taxpayer in Canada at the time of disposition,

(iii) eligible capital property in respect of a business carried on by the taxpayer in Canada at the time of disposition,

(iv) property in respect of which the taxpayer elected under paragraph 48(1)(c), as it read in its application before 1993, or subparagraph (4)(b)(iv) in respect of the last preceding time the taxpayer ceased to be resident in Canada, and

(v) a right to acquire shares of the capital stock of a corporation where section 7 would apply if the taxpayer disposed of the right to a person with whom the taxpayer was dealing at arm's length,

### Proposed Amendment — 128.1(1)(b)(iv), (v)

(iv) an excluded right or interest of the taxpayer (other than an interest in a non-resident testamentary trust that was never acquired for consideration),

**Application**: Bill C-43 (First Reading September 20, 2000), subsec. 77(2), will amend subpara. 128.1(1)(b)(iv) to read as above, and repeal subpara. (v), applicable to changes in residence that occur after October 1, 1996.

**Technical Notes**: As described above, paragraph 128.1(1)(b) of the Act provides for a deemed disposition of most properties owned by a taxpayer who becomes resident in Canada. Subparagraph 128.1(1)(b)(iv) excludes from this deemed disposition property that was the subject of an election under existing subparagraph 128.1(4)(b)(iv) of the Act — an election not to be treated as having disposed of the property on an earlier emigration from Canada. One of the effects of having made the election is that the property is deemed to be taxable Canadian property, which in any case is (as a result of subparagraph 128.1(1)(b)(i)) excluded from the deemed disposition on immigration. The current version of subparagraph 128.1(1)(b)(iv) is thus not necessary, and can be replaced with a different rule.

New subparagraph 128.1(1)(b)(iv) excludes from the deemed disposition on immigration any property (other than an interest acquired for no consideration in a non-resident testamentary trust) that is an "excluded right or interest" of the taxpayer. As defined in new subsection 128.1(10) of the Act, the term "excluded right or interest" includes many kinds of income rights and other properties. Since the term also encompasses rights under agreements referred to in subsections 7(1) and 7(1.1) of the Act (options of employees to acquire shares of a corporation or units of a mutual fund trust), existing subparagraph 128.1(1)(b)(v), which refers only to employee stock options, is unnecessary and is repealed.

for proceeds equal to its fair market value at the time of disposition;

(c) **deemed acquisition** — the taxpayer shall be deemed to have acquired at the particular time each property deemed by paragraph (b) to have been disposed of by the taxpayer, at a cost equal to the proceeds of disposition of the property;

(c.1) **deemed dividend to immigrating corporation** — if the taxpayer is a particular corporation that immediately before the time of disposition owned a share of the capital stock of another corporation resident in Canada, a dividend is deemed to have been paid by the other corporation, and received by the particular corporation, immediately before the time of disposition, equal to the amount, if any, by which the fair market value of the share immediately before the time of disposition exceeds the total of

(i) the paid-up capital in respect of the share immediately before the time of disposition, and

(ii) if the share immediately before the time of disposition was taxable Canadian property that is not treaty-protected property, the amount by which, at the time of disposition, the fair market value of the share exceeds its cost amount;

(c.2) **deemed dividend to shareholder of immigrating corporation** — if the taxpayer is a corporation and an amount has been added to the paid-up capital in respect of a class of shares of the corporation's capital stock because of paragraph (2)(b),

(i) the corporation is deemed to have paid, immediately before the time of disposition, a dividend on the issued shares of the class equal to the amount of the paid-up capital adjustment in respect of the class, and

(ii) a dividend is deemed to have been received, immediately before the time of disposition, by each person (other than a person in respect of whom the corporation is a foreign affiliate) who held any of the issued shares of the class equal to that proportion of the dividend so deemed to have been paid that the number of shares of the class held by the person immediately before the time of disposition is of the number of issued shares of the class outstanding immediately before the time of disposition; and

(d) **foreign affiliate** — where the taxpayer was, immediately before the particular time, a foreign affiliate of another taxpayer that is resident in Canada,

(i) the affiliate shall be deemed to have been a controlled foreign affiliate (within the meaning assigned by subsection 95(1)) of the other taxpayer immediately before the particular time, and

(ii) such amount as is prescribed shall be included in the foreign accrual property income (within the meaning assigned by subsection 95(1)) of the affiliate for its taxation year ending immediately before the particular time.

**Related Provisions**: 44(2)(d) — Exchanges of property; 52(8) — Cost of corporation's shares on its becoming resident in Canada; 53(1)(b.1) — Addition to ACB for deemed dividend under 128.1(1)(c.2); 53(4) — Effect on ACB of share, partnership interest or trust interest; 54"superficial loss"(c) — Superficial loss rule does not apply; 66(4.3) — Foreign exploration and development expenses on becoming resident; 66.21(5) — Foreign resource expenses on becoming resident; 70(5.3) — Value of shares of corporation holding life insurance policy; 84(7) — When deemed dividend payable; 94(3)(c) [proposed] — Application to trust deemed resident in Canada; 96(8) — Cost of properties of partnership when partner becomes resident in Canada; 106(1.1)(b) — Deemed cost of income interest in trust; 107(1.1)(b)(ii) — Deemed cost of income interest in trust; 114 — Individual resident during only part of year; 139.1(5) — Value of ownership rights in insurer during demutualization; 215(1.1) — Limitation on requirement to withhold tax on deemed dividend under 128.1(1)(c.1); Reg. 808(1.1) — Investment allowance for branch tax deemed nil before immigration.

**Notes**: 128.1(1)(b) and (c) bump up the cost of most property to its fair market value for tax purposes on immigration. See Notes at end of 128.1 and the Proposed Amendment above.

128.1(1)(c.1) provides that if an immigrating corporation (Forco) at the time of immigration holds a share of a corporation resident in Canada (Canco), Canco is deemed to have paid a dividend to Forco immediately before Forco is deemed to dispose of its Canco shares. Generally, the deemed dividend is equal to the fair market value of the share minus its paid-up capital. However, if the Canco share is taxable Canadian property and Canada's right to tax any gain on the share realized by Forco is not removed by a tax treaty, the deemed dividend is in effect reduced by the amount of any capital gain realized by Forco on the deemed disposition of the Canco share.

The effect of 128.1(1)(c.1) is to treat Canco as if it had distributed to Forco the portion of Canco's surplus allocable to the shares held by Forco, except to the extent that surplus has been realized as a capital gain taxable in Canada. Since the dividend is deemed to be paid to Forco before immigration, it is subject to withholding tax under 212(2). If Canco and Forco deal at arm's length, 215(1.1) relieves Canco of the requirement to withhold tax.

Where a corporation immigrates to Canada, unremitted profits of a Canadian branch will be treated similarly to the undistributed surplus of a Canadian corporation in which it holds shares. Reg. 808(1.1) will provide that when a corporation becomes resident in Canada, its allowance in respect of its investment in property in Canada will be nil for the year that is deemed to end before immigration. Since the corporation will be unable to claim an investment allowance, it will pay branch tax under s. 219 on any unremitted profits of a Canadian branch arising in the year or deferred from previous years.

128.1(1)(c.2) provides that if a corporation becomes resident in Canada and elects to increase PUC under 128.1(2)(b), it is deemed to have paid a dividend (equal to the increase in PUC) on the shares of that class before immigrating. (PUC generally can be returned to shareholders tax-free.) The dividend primarily affects shareholders resident in Canada, for whom a dividend from a foreign corporation is generally taxable. No dividend is deemed received, however, by a shareholder for whom the immigrating corporation is a foreign affiliate (FA). Taxation of the accrued surplus of a FA that becomes resident in Canada is dealt with under 128.1(1)(d).

Where a resident shareholder is deemed to receive a dividend from an immigrating corporation by 128.1(1)(c.2), the amount of the deemed dividend is added to the ACB of the share under 53(1)(b.1).

128.1(1)(b) opening words amended by 1998 Budget to add "if the taxpayer is an individual," effective for corporations that become resident in Canada after February 23, 1998.

128.1(1)(c.1) and (c.2) added by 1998 Budget, effective for corporations that become resident in Canada after February 23, 1998.

See also Notes at end of 128.1.

**Regulations**: 5907(13) (prescribed amount of FAPI; expected to be amended to apply to 128.1(1)(d)(ii)).

**I.T. Application Rules**: 26(10) (ITAR 26 does not apply to property owned since before 1972).

**Interpretation Bulletins**: IT-259R3: Exchanges of property.

**(2) Paid-up capital adjustment** — If a corporation becomes resident in Canada at a particular time,

(a) for the purposes of subsection (1) and this subsection, the "paid-up capital adjustment" in respect of a particular class of shares of the corporation's capital stock in respect of that acquisition of residence is the positive or negative amount determined by the formula

$$(A \times B/C) - D$$

where

A is the amount, if any, by which

(i) the total of all amounts each of which is an amount deemed by paragraph (1)(c) to be the cost to the corporation of property deemed under that paragraph to have been acquired by the corporation at the particular time

exceeds

(ii) the total of all amounts each of which is the amount of a debt owing by the corporation, or any other obligation of the corporation to pay an amount, that is outstanding at the particular time,

B is the fair market value at the particular time of all of the shares of the particular class,

C is the total of all amounts each of which is the fair market value at the particular time of all of the shares of a class of shares of the corporation's capital stock, and

D is the paid-up capital at the particular time, determined without reference to this subsection, in respect of the particular class; and

(b) for the purposes of this Act, in computing the paid-up capital in respect of a class of shares of the corporation's capital stock at any time after the particular time and before the time, if any, at which the corporation next becomes resident in Canada, there shall be

(i) added the amount of the paid-up capital adjustment in respect of the particular class, if that amount is positive and the corporation so elects for all such classes in respect of that acquisition of residence by notifying the Minister in writing within 90 days after the particular time, and

(ii) deducted, if the amount of the paid-up capital adjustment in respect of the particular class is negative, the absolute value of that amount.

**Related Provisions**: 128.1(1)(c.2) — Deemed dividend to shareholder of immigrating corporation; 257 — Formula cannot calculate to less than zero.

**Notes**: Note that the general anti-avoidance rule in s. 245 may apply to schemes that extract paid-up capital, even where 128.1(2) does not apply (or did not apply before its amendment). See *RMM Canadian Enterprises (Equilease)*, [1998] 1 C.T.C. 2300 (TCC).

128.1(2) amended by 1998 Budget, effective for corporations that become resident in Canada after February 23, 1998, except that an election made under 128.1(2)(b)(i) is deemed to have been made on time if it is made by the corporation, with the consent of all who were shareholders of the corporation immediately before the "time of disposition" (as defined in 128.1(1)(b)), by March 31, 1999. Before the amendment, read:

(2) Idem — paid-up capital — For the purposes of this Act, where at a particular time a corporation becomes resident in Canada, in computing the paid-up capital at any time after the particular time in respect of a particular class of shares of the capital stock of the corporation, there shall be deducted the amount determined by the formula

$$\frac{A}{B} \times (C - D)$$

where

A is the paid-up capital, determined without reference to this subsection, of the particular class of shares at the particular time;

B is the paid-up capital, determined without reference to this subsection, in respect of all of the shares of the corporation at the particular time;

C is the total of

(a) the paid-up capital, determined without reference to this subsection, in respect of all of the shares of the corporation at the particular time,

(b) all amounts each of which is the amount of any debt owing by the corporation, or any other obligation of the corporation to pay an amount, that is outstanding at the particular time, and

(c) any amount claimed under paragraph 219(1)(j) by the corporation for its last taxation year that began before the particular time; and

D is the total of

(a) all amounts each of which is deemed by paragraph 128.1(1)(c) to be the cost to the corporation of property (other than property described in paragraph 128.1(2)D (d)) deemed under paragraph 128.1(1)(c) to have been acquired by the corporation at the particular time,

(b) all amounts each of which is the cost amount to the corporation, immediately after the particular time, of property (other than a Canadian resource property or property described in paragraph 128.1(2)D (a) or (d)),

(c) the total of

(i) all Canadian exploration and development expenses incurred by the corporation before the particular time, except to the extent that those expenses were deducted in computing a taxpayer's income for a taxation year that ended before the particular time,

(ii) the corporation's cumulative Canadian exploration expense at the particular time (within the meaning assigned by subsection 66.1(6)),

(iii) the corporation's cumulative Canadian development expense at the particular time (within the meaning assigned by subsection 66.2(5)), and

(iv) the corporation's cumulative Canadian oil and gas property expense at the particular time (within the meaning assigned by subsection 66.4(5)), and

(d) the total of all amounts each of which is the paid-up capital in respect of a share of the capital stock of another corporation resident in Canada and connected with the corporation (within the meaning that would be assigned by subsection 186(4) if the references therein to "payer corporation" and "particular corporation" were read as references to the other corporation and the corporation, respectively) immediately after the particular time, owned by the corporation at the particular time.

128.1(2)C(c) amended by 1995-97 technical bill to change reference to 219(1)(h) to 219(1)(j), effective for taxation years that begin in 1997 or later. For taxation years that begin in 1996, read "paragraph 219(1)(h) as it read in its application to the 1995 taxation year or paragraph 219(1)(j)".

See also Notes at end of 128.1.

**(3) Paid-up capital adjustment** — In computing the paid-up capital at any time in respect of a class of shares of the corporation's capital stock, there shall be deducted an amount equal to the lesser of A and B, and added an amount equal to the lesser of A and C, where

A is the absolute value of the difference between

(a) the total of all amounts deemed by subsection 84(3), (4) or (4.1) to be a dividend on shares of the class paid before that time by the corporation, and

(b) the total that would be determined under paragraph (a) if this Act were read without reference to subsection (2),

B is the total of all amounts required by subsection (2) to be added in computing the paid-up capital in respect of the class before that time, and

C is the total of all amounts required by subsection (2) to be subtracted in computing the paid-up capital in respect of the class before that time.

**Related Provisions**: 66(4.3) — Foreign exploration and development expenses on ceasing to be resident; 66.21(5) — Foreign resource expenses on ceasing to be resident.

**Notes**: 128.1(3) amended by 1998 Budget, effective for corporations that become resident in Canada after February 23, 1998. Before the amendment, read:

(3) **Idem** — In computing the paid-up capital at any time in respect of a class of shares of the capital stock of a corporation, there shall be added an amount equal to the lesser of

(a) the amount, if any, by which

(i) the total of all amounts deemed by subsection 84(3), (4) or (4.1) to be a dividend on shares of the class paid before that time by the corporation

exceeds

(ii) the total that would be determined under subparagraph 128.1(3)(a)(i) if this Act were read without reference to subsection 128.1(2), and

(b) the total of all amounts required by subsection 128.1(2) to be deducted in computing the paid-up capital in respect of that class of shares before that time.

See also Notes at end of 128.1.

**(4) Emigration** — For the purposes of this Act, where at any particular time a taxpayer ceases to be resident in Canada,

(a) **year-end, fiscal period** — where the taxpayer is a corporation or a trust,

(i) the taxpayer's taxation year that would otherwise include the particular time shall be deemed to have ended immediately before the particular time and a new taxation year of the taxpayer shall be deemed to have begun at the particular time, and

(ii) for the purpose of determining the taxpayer's fiscal period after the particular time, the taxpayer shall be deemed not to have established a fiscal period before the particular time;

**Proposed Addition — 128.1(4)(a.1)**

(a.1) **fiscal period** — if the taxpayer is an individual (other than a trust) and carries on a business at the particular time, otherwise than through a permanent establishment (as defined by regulation) in Canada,

   (i) the fiscal period of the business is deemed to have ended immediately before the particular time and a new fiscal period of the business is deemed to have begun at the particular time, and

   (ii) for the purpose of determining the fiscal period of the business after the particular time, the taxpayer is deemed not to have established a fiscal period of the business before the particular time;

**Application**: Bill C-43 (First Reading September 20, 2000), subsec. 77(3), will add para. 128.1(4)(a.1), applicable to changes in residence that occur after October 1, 1996.

**Technical Notes**: Subsection 128.1(4) sets out rules that apply where a taxpayer ceases to be resident in Canada. New paragraph 128.1(4)(a.1) provides that the fiscal period of any business carried on by an individual emigrant (other than a trust), otherwise than through a permanent establishment in Canada, is deemed to have ended immediately before the emigration time and a new fiscal period of the business is deemed to have begun at the emigration time. This ensures the appropriate measurement of the individual's pre-departure income or loss from the business. The paragraph, which applies to changes in residence after October 1, 1996, also allows the emigrant to choose a new fiscal period of the business.

(b) **deemed disposition** — the taxpayer shall be deemed to have disposed, at the time (in this paragraph and paragraph (d) referred to as the "time of disposition") that is immediately before the time that is immediately before the particular time, of each property owned by the taxpayer, other than

   (i) where the taxpayer is an individual, property that would be taxable Canadian property if the taxpayer had been resident in Canada at no time in the taxpayer's last taxation year that began before the particular time,

   (ii) where the taxpayer is an individual, property that is described in the inventory of a business carried on by the taxpayer in Canada at the particular time,

   (iii) where the taxpayer is an individual, a right to receive a payment described in any of paragraphs 212(1)(h) and (j) to (q), a right under a registered education savings plan or a right to receive any payment of a benefit under the *Canada Pension Plan* or a provincial pension plan as defined in section 3 of that Act,

   (iv) where the taxpayer is an individual other than a trust, each capital property not described in any of subparagraphs (i) to (iii) in respect of which, on or before the taxpayer's balance-due day for the taxation year in which the taxpayer ceased to be resident in Canada, the taxpayer elects in prescribed manner and furnishes to the Minister security acceptable to the Minister for the payment of the additional tax that would have been payable by the taxpayer under this Part for the year had the taxpayer not so elected,

   (v) where the taxpayer is an individual other than a trust and was, during the 10 years immediately preceding the particular time, resident in Canada for a period or periods totalling 60 months or less, property that was

      (A) owned by the taxpayer at the time the taxpayer last became resident in Canada, or

      (B) acquired by the taxpayer by inheritance or bequest after the taxpayer last became resident in Canada, and

   (vi) a right to acquire shares of the capital stock of a corporation where section 7 would apply if the taxpayer disposed of the right to a person with whom the taxpayer was dealing at arm's length,

for proceeds equal to its fair market value at the time of disposition, which proceeds shall be deemed to have become receivable and to have been received by the taxpayer at the time of disposition;

**Proposed Amendment — 128.1(4)(b)**

(b) **deemed disposition** — the taxpayer is deemed to have disposed, at the time (in this paragraph and paragraph (d) referred to as the "time of disposition") that is immediately before the time that is immediately before the particular time, of each property owned by the taxpayer other than, if the taxpayer is an individual,

   (i) real property situated in Canada, a Canadian resource property or a timber resource property,

   (ii) capital property used in, eligible capital property in respect of or property described in the inventory of, a business carried on by the taxpayer through a permanent establishment (as defined by regulation) in Canada at the particular time,

   (iii) an excluded right or interest of the taxpayer,

   (iv) if the taxpayer is not a trust and was not, during the 120-month period that ends at the particular time, resident in Canada for more than 60 months, property that was owned by the taxpayer at the time the taxpayer last became resident in Canada or that was acquired by the taxpayer by inheritance or bequest after the taxpayer last became resident in Canada, and

   (v) any property in respect of which the taxpayer elects under paragraph (6)(a) for the taxation year that includes the first time, af-

**S. 128.1(4)(b)(v)**      Income Tax Act, Part I

ter the particular time, at which the taxpayer becomes resident in Canada,

for proceeds equal to its fair market value at the time of disposition, which proceeds are deemed to have become receivable and to have been received by the taxpayer at the time of disposition;

**Application**: Bill C-43 (First Reading September 20, 2000), subsec. 77(3), will amend para. 128.1(4)(b) to read as above, applicable to changes in residence that occur after October 1, 1996.

S. 78 of the amending legislation provides:

> 78. (1) If an individual ceased at any time after 1992 and before October 2, 1996 to be resident in Canada and so elects in writing and files the election with the Minister of National Revenue before the end of the sixth month following the month in which this Act is assented to, subparagraph 128.1(4)(b)(iii) of the Act as it read at that time shall, in respect of the cessation of residence, be read as enacted by this Act and as though subsection 128.1(10) of the Act, as enacted by this Act, applied.
>
> (2) Where an individual makes an election under subsection (1), notwithstanding subsections 152(4) to (5) of the Act, any reassessment of the individual's tax, interest or penalties for any year shall be made that is necessary to take the election into account.

**Technical Notes**: Paragraph 128.1(4)(b) treats a taxpayer who ceases to be resident in Canada as having disposed of the taxpayer's property, for proceeds equal to fair market value. This disposition is deemed to have taken place at a "time of disposition" that is immediately before the time that is immediately before the time the taxpayer ceases to be resident. The time of cessation of residence is referred to in the provision as the "particular time" and in these notes as the "emigration time."

Where the taxpayer is an individual, certain types of property are exempted from the deemed disposition. These properties, generally, are those that would be subject to Canadian taxation in the hands of a non-resident.

Paragraph 128.1(4)(b) is amended to ensure that this policy is better reflected in the legislation. Under amended paragraph 128.1(4)(b), an individual emigrant from Canada is treated as having disposed of all property other than:

(i) real property situated in Canada, Canadian resource properties and timber resource properties;

(ii) property of a business carried on by the individual, at the emigration time, through a permanent establishment in Canada – including capital property, eligible capital property and property described in the inventory of the business;

(iii) property that is an "excluded right or interest" of the individual. As defined in new subsection 128.1(10) of the Act, the term "excluded right or interest" includes many kinds of income rights and other properties. See the commentary on new subsection 128.1(10) for more details;

(iv) certain property of short-term residents (see below); and

(v) certain property of a short-term non-resident (see the commentary on new subsection 128.1(6) of the Act).

Since the definition "excluded right or interest" in new subsection 128.1(10) encompasses rights under agreements referred to in subsections 7(1) and 7(1.1) of the Act (options of employees to acquire shares of a corporation or units of a mutual fund trust), existing subparagraph 128.1(4)(b)(vi), which refers only to employee stock options, is unnecessary and is repealed.

Under new subparagraph 128.1(4)(b)(iv), an individual (other than a trust) who has been resident in Canada for 60 months or less during the 10-year period preceding the cessation of residence is not deemed to dispose of any property that the individual owned on becoming resident in Canada, or that the individual inherited after becoming resident here. (This exception was formerly provided under subparagraph 128.1(4)(b)(v) of the Act.)

Where an individual (other than a trust) ceases to be resident in Canada after October 1, 1996 and re-establishes Canadian residence at a later time, a special rule, set out in new subsection 128.1(6), enables the individual to exclude all property from the deemed disposition in respect of the cessation of residence. For additional information, see the commentary on subsection 128.1(6).

Two additional points should be noted. First, where an emigrating individual owns shares of a corporation which owns a life insurance policy under which the individual's life is insured, upon the deemed disposition at departure of the individual's shares in the corporation, a special rule contained in amended subsection 70(5.3) of the Act will be used in the valuation of the corporation's shares — the cash surrender value of the life insurance policy owned by the corporation will be treated as the fair market value of that policy. Second, the Regulations will be amended after these amendments receive Royal Assent, so that the definition "permanent establishment" in section 8201 of the Regulations will apply for the purpose of subparagraph 128.1(4)(b)(ii) of the Act.

Amended paragraph 128.1(4)(b) generally applies after October 1, 1996. In addition, an individual who ceased to be a Canadian resident after 1992 and before October 2, 1996 may also elect to exclude from the deemed disposition at emigration property described in the definition "excluded right or interest" in new subsection 128.1(10) of the Act. This election must be made in writing filed with the Minister of National Revenue within six months of these amendments receiving Royal Assent. It should also be noted that this election will cause amended subparagraph 115(1)(a)(i) of the Act to apply. For additional information, see the commentary on subsection 115(1).

Transition

Paragraph 128.1(4)(b) of the Act treats a person who ceases to be resident in Canada as having disposed of most of the person's properties. The changes these amendments introduce to that deemed disposition apply, as a general matter, after October 1, 1996. However, certain of the changes are relieving clarifications of the scope of the deemed disposition. This provision allows a taxpayer who ceased to be resident in Canada after 1992 and before October 2, 1996 to elect that those relieving changes apply to that cessation of residence. In particular, an election under this provision will allow an individual who ceased to be resident in Canada after 1992 and before October 2, 1996 to rely on the new definition "excluded right or interest" in new subsection 128.1(10) of the Act in respect of that cessation of residence, for the purpose of the deemed disposition rules under subsection 128.1(4) of the Act.

It should be noted that such an election, which must be made in writing filed with the Minister of National Revenue before the end of the sixth month following Royal Assent to these amendments, will also cause certain changes

Division F — Special Rules in Certain Circumstances    S. 128.1(4)

to section 115 of the Act to apply. For additional information, see the commentary on section 115 and 128.1(4)(d)–(f).

**Notice of Ways and Means Motion (re taxpayer migration), June 5, 2000**: See under 128.1(4)(d)–(f).

(c) **reacquisition** — the taxpayer shall be deemed to have reacquired, at the particular time, each property deemed by paragraph (b) to have been disposed of by the taxpayer, at a cost equal to the proceeds of disposition of the property;

(d) **individual** — notwithstanding paragraphs (b) and (c), where a taxpayer who is an individual other than a trust so elects in prescribed manner, on or before the taxpayer's balance-due day for the taxation year that includes the particular time, in respect of any property described in subparagraph (b)(i) or (ii), the taxpayer shall be deemed to have disposed of the property at the time of disposition for proceeds equal to its fair market value at that time, and to have reacquired the property at the particular time at a cost equal to those proceeds;

(e) **deemed [taxable Canadian] property** — capital property in respect of which a taxpayer elects under subparagraph (b)(iv) shall be deemed to be taxable Canadian property of the taxpayer from the particular time until the earlier of

(i) the time when the taxpayer disposes of the property, and

(ii) the time when the taxpayer next becomes resident in Canada; and

(f) **losses on election** — where a taxpayer elects under subparagraph (b)(iv) or paragraph (d),

(i) the taxpayer's income for the taxation year that includes the particular time shall be deemed to be the greater of

(A) that income otherwise determined, and

(B) the lesser of

(I) that income determined without reference to this subsection, and

(II) that income determined without reference to subparagraph (b)(iv) and paragraph (d), and

(ii) the amount of each of the taxpayer's non-capital loss, net capital loss, restricted farm loss, farm loss and limited partnership loss for the taxation year that includes the particular time shall be deemed to be the lesser of

(A) that amount otherwise determined, and

(B) the greater of

(I) that amount determined without reference to this subsection, and

(II) that amount determined without reference to subparagraph (b)(iv) and paragraph (d).

**Proposed Amendment — 128.1(4)(d)–(f)**

(d) **individual — elective disposition** — notwithstanding paragraphs (b) to (c), if the taxpayer is an individual (other than a trust) and so elects in prescribed form and manner in respect of a property described in subparagraph (b)(i) or (ii),

(i) the taxpayer is deemed to have disposed of the property at the time of disposition for proceeds equal to its fair market value at that time and to have reacquired the property at the particular time at a cost equal to those proceeds,

(ii) the taxpayer's income for the taxation year that includes the particular time is deemed to be the greater of

(A) that income determined without reference to this subparagraph, and

(B) the lesser of

(I) that income determined without reference to this subsection, and

(II) that income determined without reference to subparagraph (i), and

(iii) each of the taxpayer's non-capital loss, net capital loss, restricted farm loss, farm loss and limited partnership loss for the taxation year that includes the particular time is deemed to be the lesser of

(A) that amount determined without reference to this subparagraph, and

(B) the greater of

(I) that amount determined without reference to this subsection, and

(II) that amount determined without reference to subparagraph (i); and

(d.1) **employee CCPC stock option shares** — if the taxpayer is deemed by paragraph (b) to have disposed of a share which was acquired under circumstances to which subsection 7(1.1) applied, there shall be deducted from the taxpayer's proceeds of disposition the amount that would, if section 7 were read without reference to subsection 7(1.6), be added under paragraph 53(1)(j) in computing the adjusted cost base to the taxpayer of the share as a consequence of the deemed disposition.

**Application**: Bill C-43 (First Reading September 20, 2000), subsec. 77(4), will amend para. 128.1(4)(d) to read as above, add para. (d.1) and repeal paras. (e) and (f), applicable to changes in residence that occur after October 1, 1996 except for para. (d.1) which is applicable to changes in residence that occur after 1992.

**Technical Notes**: Paragraph 128.1(4)(b) treats taxpayers that cease to be resident in Canada as having disposed of their property, subject to certain exceptions, for proceeds equal to the property's fair market value. Paragraph 128.1(4)(d) allows an individual (other than a trust) to choose to treat certain of the properties that would otherwise be exempt from that deemed disposition as having been disposed of. An emigrant might make this choice if, for example, the emigrant wanted to realize a latent loss on such a property in order to offset a gain resulting from the deemed disposition.

This optional deemed disposition is retained in amended paragraph (d). In addition, the paragraph reproduces the effect of existing paragraph 128.1(4)(f), which ensures that losses realized as a result of a paragraph (d) election may only offset the increase, if any, in the taxpayer's income as a result of the deemed disposition on emigration. With this effect now provided in paragraph (d) itself, paragraph (f) is no longer necessary and is repealed.

New paragraph 128.1(4)(d.1) is introduced to ensure appropriate tax consequences where an individual (other than a trust) emigrates from Canada holding shares acquired under a employee stock option granted by a Canadian-controlled private corporation (CCPC). Under section 7 of the Act, an individual who acquires shares under an employee stock option agreement is deemed to have received an employment benefit equal to the fair market value of the shares at the time of acquisition less the price paid by the individual to acquire the shares. In the case of CCPC options, subsection 7(1.1) defers the income inclusion to the year in which the individual disposes of the shares. When this occurs, the amount of the benefit is added (by virtue of paragraph 53(1)(j)) to the adjusted cost base (ACB) of the shares, thus affecting the capital gain (or loss) determined in connection with the disposition of the shares.

New subsection 7(1.6) provides that the deemed disposition rules in subsection 128.1(4) do not apply for the purposes of section 7. Thus, in the case of shares acquired by an individual under a CCPC option, there is no income inclusion under section 7 triggered by the individual's emigration and similarly no adjustment to the ACB of the shares under paragraph 53(1)(j). However, for capital gains purposes, new paragraph 128.1(4)(d.1) applies to reduce the individual's proceeds of disposition in respect of the shares by the amount that would have been added to the ACB of the shares (by virtue of paragraph 53(1)(j)) had there been a deemed disposition for the purposes of section 7. This ensures that the individual's capital gain (or loss) determined in connection with the deemed disposition on emigration takes into account the amount that will eventually be taxed under section 7.

*EXAMPLE — CCPC shares acquired under employee stock option*

From 1993 to 1998, Katharine was employed by a Canadian-controlled private corporation (CCPC). Part of Katharine's compensation for 1995 was an option to buy 100 shares of the corporation at a price of $1 a share. In 1996, when the shares were worth $2 each, Katharine exercised the option. In 1999, when the shares are worth $6 each, Katharine emigrates from Canada.

Under amended paragraph 128.1(4)(b), Katharine will be treated as having disposed of the shares for proceeds of $600 (= 100 × $6 fair market value). Ordinarily, the disposition would trigger an income inclusion of $100 under section 7 (= 100 × ($2 - $1)), a corresponding addition of $100 to the ACB of the shares under paragraph 53(1)(j) (resulting in a total ACB of $200), a deduction of $25 (= .25 × $100) under paragraph 110(1)(d.1) in computing taxable income, and a taxable capital gain of $300 (= .75 × ($600 - $200)).

However, as a result of new subsection 7(1.6), Katharine will not be subject to any income inclusion under section 7 in respect of the deemed disposition and, thus, there will be no addition to the ACB of the shares under paragraph 53(1)(j). Were it not for new paragraph 128.1(4)(d.1), this would result in Katharine having a taxable capital gain of $375 (= .75 ($600 - $100)) on the deemed disposition of the shares under paragraph 128.1(4)(b), and an additional income inclusion of $100 minus $25 on the actual disposition of the shares.

Paragraph 128.1(4)(d.1) addresses this by deducting from the proceeds of disposition, for capital gains purposes, the $100 that paragraph 53(1)(j) would have added to the ACB of the shares if there had been an income inclusion under section 7 on emigration. As a result, Katharine will realize a taxable capital gain of $300 on the deemed disposition of the shares (and an additional income inclusion of $100 less $25 when she actually disposes of the shares).

Existing paragraph 128.1(4)(e) relates to the election, under existing subparagraph (b)(iv), to exclude from the deemed disposition on emigration a property that is not taxable Canadian property. If an emigrant uses this optional exclusion, paragraph (e) treats the property as taxable Canadian property of the taxpayer until the property is disposed of or the taxpayer returns to Canada. Since the subparagraph (b)(iv) election is no longer available, paragraph (e) is repealed.

New paragraph 128.1(4)(d.1) applies to changes in residence after 1992. The other amendments described above apply to changes in residence after October 1, 1996.

**Notice of Ways and Means Motion (re taxpayer emigration), October 2, 1996:** *Property used in carrying on business in Canada*

(3) That any capital property used by a non-resident person at any time after October 1, 1996 in carrying on a business (other than an insurance business) in Canada, and that ceases at any subsequent time to be so used by that person (otherwise than by reason of the property's disposition) be deemed to have been disposed of by the person for proceeds equal to the property's fair market value at that subsequent time.

*Information reporting*

(4) That all individuals who cease at any time after 1995 to be Canadian residents and who own at that time property the total fair market value of which is greater than $25,000 be required to provide a report in prescribed form listing each property that they owned at that time (other than a personal-use property that has a fair market value of less than $10,000).

*Deemed disposition on emigration*

(5) That the deemed disposition on emigration under subsection 128.1(4) of the Act be revised, in respect of an individual who at any time after October 1, 1996 ceases to be resident in Canada, to:

(a) provide for the mandatory deemed disposition and reacquisition at fair market value of all the individual's property other than

(i) real property situated in Canada,

(ii) capital property used in, or property described in an inventory of, a business carried on by the individual through a permanent establishment in Canada immediately before that time, and

(iii) property described in subparagraph 128.1(4)(b)(iii), (v) or (vi) of the Act, and

(b) permit the individual to provide security acceptable to the Minister of National Revenue for the payment of any tax liability arising as a result of the deemed disposition described in subparagraph (a).

*Trust distributions*

(6) That

(a) any property (other than property described in any of clauses (5)(a)(i) to (iii)) distributed by a trust at any time after October 1, 1996 to a non-resident beneficiary be deemed to have been disposed of by the trust at its fair market value at that time, and that the trust or the beneficiary be allowed to provide security acceptable to the Minister of National Revenue for the payment of any tax arising as a result of the deemed disposition of any property that was taxable Canadian property, and

(b) any property that was taxable Canadian property of a trust and that was distributed by the trust to a beneficiary on or before October 1, 1996 be deemed, for greater certainty, to be taxable Canadian property of the beneficiary after that date.

[For resolutions (1) and (2) in the same Notice of Ways and Means Motion, see under 115(1)(b) — ed.]

## Technical Background
### Taxpayer Migration
#### 1. Overview

This Notice of Ways and Means Motion expresses the Government's intention to recommend certain changes to the income tax rules that apply to taxpayers who enter or leave Canada. Most of these changes are rather technical in nature. The most far-reaching proposals will require a more comprehensive deemed disposition and reacquisition of an emigrant's property, and will impose new reporting requirements on individual emigrants.

The Government recognizes the significance of these proposed changes, and invites Canadians to comment on them as they proceed toward implementation.

#### 2. The current rules

Canada is among the very few countries that impose any special tax rules on individuals who become or cease to be residents. The main purpose of these rules, which have applied since 1972, is to ensure that immigrants and emigrants are taxed in Canada on all their gains on Canadian property, and on other gains that accrued while they were resident in Canada.

*Immigration*

A taxpayer who becomes a resident of Canada is generally treated as having disposed of and reacquired all of the taxpayer's property at its fair market value. This ensures that Canada will tax only that part of any gain on the property that accrued after the person became resident here. Property in respect of which any gain was already subject to tax in Canada ("taxable Canadian property", or TCP) is not subject to this deemed disposition. That is because Canada's *Income Tax Act* subjects the full amount of such gains to tax when the property is actually disposed of.

*Example*

N. moved to Canada from Country A in 1985. At the time of the move, N. owned an apartment building situated in Country A, and one in Canada. Each property cost N. $75,000 (or the equivalent), and each had a fair market value in 1985 of $100,000. N. sold both buildings in 1995, for $125,000 each.

For Canadian tax purposes N. was treated as having disposed of and reacquired the building in Country A for $100,000 before becoming a resident of Canada. N.'s tax cost of the building is now $100,000. Canada will thus tax only the $18,750 taxable capital gain ($25,000 capital gain X 75%) on the building in Country A that accrued while N. was a resident of Canada. Since the Canadian building is taxable Canadian property, N. was not treated as having disposed of it in 1985. Canada will tax, in 1995, the full $37,500 taxable capital gain ($50,000 capital gain X 75%) on that building.

*Emigration*

A taxpayer who ceases to be resident in Canada is generally treated as having disposed of and reacquired, at fair market value, all the taxpayer's property other than taxable Canadian property, stock options, and certain pension and similar rights. Individuals (other than trusts, which are individuals for tax purposes) can also choose not to be treated as having disposed of any non-TCP, provided they give security for any tax they would otherwise have had to pay.

*Example*

X. moved to Country B from Canada in 1990. At the time of the move, X. owned an apartment building situated in Country B, and one in Canada. Each property cost X. $75,000 (or the equivalent), and each had a fair market value in 1990 of $100,000. X. sold both buildings in 1995, for $125,000 each.

For Canadian tax purposes X. was treated as having disposed of and reacquired the building in Country B for $100,000 before ceasing to be a resident of Canada. Canada thus taxed the $18,750 taxable capital gain ($25,000 capital gain X 75%) on the Country B building that accrued while X. was a resident of Canada. But Canada will not tax X.'s post-departure gain on that building. Since the Canadian building is taxable Canadian property, X. was not treated as having disposed of it in 1990. Canada will tax the full $37,500 taxable capital gain ($50,000 capital gain X 75%) on that building.

*Special rules*

Several special rules apply to particular kinds of taxpayer. A Canadian trust, for example, may distribute property to a non-resident beneficiary: the rules treat that distribution as a fair market value disposition, except where the property is taxable Canadian property. Other rules treat property that is acquired on a tax-deferred ("rollover") basis in exchange for TCP as being itself TCP.

#### 3. What will change

The most important changes proposed in this Notice of Ways and Means Motion relate to individuals (including trusts) who emigrate from Canada. First, the class of properties treated as having been sold on emigration will be expanded. Anyone who ceases to be a resident of Canada after October 1, 1996 will be treated as having disposed of and reacquired all property (including taxable Canadian property) other than Canadian real estate, Canadian business property and the properties described in current *Income Tax Act* subparagraphs 128.1(4)(b)(iii) (pension and other rights), (v) (certain property of short-term residents) and (vi) (stock options). This will have the effect of determining the emigrant's tax liability in respect of any accrued capital gains. The emigrant can either pay the tax immediately, or give Revenue Canada security for paying it later (without interest charges), when the property is actually sold.

Second, all individual emigrants who own property with a total value of more than $25,000 will be required to report their property holdings to Revenue Canada. An exception will be made for any personal-use property (a defined term that includes clothing, household goods, cars, etc.) with a value of less than $10,000. This reporting requirement will apply to all individuals who have left Canada after 1995, and will take the form of a schedule or similar document to be included with those persons' income tax returns for the year they left Canada.

Other changes include:

- Extending to 5 years the period for determining whether certain shares and partnership and trusts interests are taxable Canadian property. This will make it more difficult for non-resident taxpayers to manipulate the status of a share or interest by changing the investment mix of the corporation, partnership or trust.
- Deeming a disposition and reacquisition at fair market value of any capital property (such as shares or bonds held on capital account) that ceases to be used by a non-resident person in carrying on a business in Canada. This will reduce the opportunity for non-residents to avoid Canadian tax by changing the use of a property to benefit from tax-treaty protection.
- Deeming a disposition at fair market value of all property (other than Canadian real estate) distributed by a trust to a non-resident beneficiary (with the trust and beneficiary being provided the right to provide security for the tax otherwise payable), and clarifying that taxable Canadian property distributed by a trust remains taxable Canadian property to the beneficiary.
- Clarifying that property may be taxable Canadian property not only to non-residents, but also to residents of Canada. This will ensure that a number of aspects of the migration rules work as intended.

## 4. Next steps

The Government invites comment on these proposals. Comments may be directed to the Minister of Finance.

**Notes**: For an overview of the proposed amendments, see Douglas Powrie, "Taxpayer Migration: The December 1998 Proposals", *International Tax Planning* (Federated Press), Vol. VIII No. 2 (1999), pp. 556-564.

## Questions and Answers on Proposed Changes

### Background

*Q. What events led up to the changes being announced today?*

A. The Auditor-General raised certain concerns about a 1991 tax ruling [see ATR-70 — ed.] that allowed a taxpayer to transfer property out of Canada without being subject to immediate capital gains tax in Canada. The Finance Committee examined the issue and found that Revenue Canada's interpretation of the law as it stood in 1991 was legally correct in the context of a system that taxed emigrating Canadians on their property gains only when they ultimately sold the property.

The Committee noted, however, that Canada's right to impose tax on former Canadian residents was sometimes limited under the terms of its tax treaties with other countries. It thus recommended that the system be changed to ensure that Canadian tax be assessed at the point when property is transferred to persons living outside of Canada, or when the individual or trust owning the property leaves the country. These changes implement this recommendation.

### Structure of previous system

*Q. How did the system work that was in effect before today?*

A. The previous system provided that gains on property owned by individuals or trusts when they moved from Canada were either taxable in Canada or, if a tax treaty applied, in their new country of residence, when the property was ultimately sold. Similar rules applied to trust distributions to foreign beneficiaries: either the trust would pay tax when the property was distributed, or the beneficiaries would be liable to tax in Canada or in their country of residence.

### Effect on trusts

*Q. Will the proposed changes affect transactions like that highlighted in the Auditor General's report?*

A. Yes. These changes will ensure that gains on property held in a trust are subject to Canadian tax when the trust moves, or the property is distributed to people who live outside Canada.

The transaction described in the Auditor General's report involved the distribution of Canadian property by a trust to a beneficiary that lived in another country. If that transaction were to take place today, any gains accruing on the property while it was owned by the trust would be subject to Canadian tax — with the tax being payable either on distribution or, where security is provided, when the property is sold by the beneficiary.

### Family trusts

*Q. Does this eliminate the tax advantages associated with family trusts?*

A. This issue is not specifically about family trusts. Any remaining tax advantages that family trusts may have had were eliminated by the changes announced in the 1995 budget.

The changes being made today concern all taxpayers who move out of Canada or who, in the case of trusts, distribute property to persons living outside of Canada. In effect, the changes ensure that gains arising while living in Canada will ultimately be subject to Canadian tax, and they apply equally to individuals and trusts. (Corporations are already taxable on such gains when they leave Canada, and this rule is to be maintained.)

### Timing of announcement

*Q. Should these changes have been announced before today?*

A. The government has acted as soon as it was reasonable to do so. In May of this year the Auditor-General identified a concern with the tax system. The government immediately referred the issue to the Finance Committee, which examined the issue and issued its report two weeks ago. The government is now proposing to implement the Committee's recommendations, with effect as of today.

### Retroactivity

*Q. Why isn't the government giving these changes retroactive effect?*

A. It would be inappropriate and unfair to tell taxpayers that their past actions will now be retroactively taxed under a set of rules that they couldn't have known about before today. The changes announced today reflect a new policy — one that taxpayers will have to take into account in their future affairs.

## Consultation

*Q. Will there be an opportunity for taxpayers to comment on the proposed changes before they are implemented?*

A. The changes are reasonable and responsive to the concerns that the Auditor-General and the Finance Committee raised but, as is the case with all income tax proposals, taxpayers' comments on the effect of these changes are invited and will be taken into account in developing the implementing legislation.

## Effect of proposed changes

*Q. What do these changes do?*

A. Most significantly, the changes will treat individuals and trusts who leave Canada as having realized any gains accrued on their property up to that point in time. They will have the option of paying the tax on those gains when they file their tax return for the year they leave Canada or, by providing security to Revenue Canada, can defer their payment until the property is sold.

In other words, the proposed changes ensure that all emigrants from Canada — including trusts — will pay Canadian tax on any capital gains that have accrued in Canada up to the time of departure. They also apply to ensure that trust distributions to foreign beneficiaries will be subject to Canadian tax. In both cases, the Canadian tax can be paid immediately, or security can be provided to Revenue Canada to pay the tax, without interest charges, when the property is actually sold.

The proposals also include several technical changes:

- to tighten the rules for taxing non-residents of Canada on gains they realize from the sale of interests in partnerships and trusts which have significant interests in Canadian property;
- to ensure that Canadian tax is payable with respect to gains from property used by non-residents in carrying on business in Canada;
- to confirm that the term "taxable Canadian property" applies to Canadian residents as well as non-residents, thus ensuring that a resident planning to leave Canada can't limit the gains which are taxable in Canada by exchanging TCP for non-TCP before he leaves;
- to clarify that Canadian tax with respect to gains on trust property distributed to non-resident beneficiaries before today will (subject to Canada's tax treaties) be taxed in the beneficiaries' hands if the trust wasn't liable to tax itself; and
- to require all individuals and trusts leaving Canada to file an information return reporting all of the significant assets they hold at the point of departure.

## Compliance concerns

*Q. What new obligations will this place on taxpayers?*

A. To minimize any immediate tax burden that these changes might otherwise create, the emigrant will be able to pay the tax when the property is actually sold, provided the emigrant gives Revenue Canada security for that later payment. No interest will be charged on the tax liability during this period.

The changes will also require departing Canadians to file an information return listing all of their significant assets. This return, which in the case of individuals is required to be filed by April 30 of the year following the year of departure, will not be required for taxpayers having property with a total value of less than $25,000.

## Department of Finance press release, October 2, 1996: Taxpayer Migration Rules to be Tightened

Finance Minister Paul Martin today announced major changes to the income tax rules for people who leave Canada. These changes will ensure that taxpayers who move or transfer property from Canada will remain subject to Canadian tax on their gains from such property.

"Canada already has one of the strictest systems in the world when it comes to taxpayer migration," the Minister said. "This will make our system even better."

The Minister noted that the Auditor General had raised the issue of Canada's taxpayer migration rules in his report earlier this year, and that the House of Commons Finance Committee recently made several recommendations for improving Canada's tax system in this regard. Today's changes follow the recommendations of the Committee majority.

"From now on, all emigrants — including trusts — will be subject to Canadian tax on any gains that have accrued up to the time of departure, other than on Canadian real estate and a limited group of other assets — which Canada always retains the right to tax," Mr. Martin explained. "The only people this will not apply to are people who have been in Canada only temporarily."

Until now, emigrants have not been taxed on gains on certain Canadian property at the time they leave. Instead, either Canada or (where a tax treaty applies) their new country taxes those gains when they actually dispose of the property.

People who leave Canada under the new rules will calculate their tax as though they had disposed of all their property other than Canadian real estate and certain other assets. They can either pay the tax immediately or give Revenue Canada security for paying it at a later date.

In addition, today's changes implement the technical recommendations put forward by the Committee, including those regarding trusts that distribute property to non-residents.

A copy of the Notice of Ways and Means Motion tabled by the Minister today, accompanied by the Minister's remarks on tabling, is attached. A technical background note and a series of questions and answers relating to the changes are also attached.

For further information: Brian Ernewein, Tax Legislation Division, (613) 992-3045.

**Related Provisions**: 7(1.6) — Deemed disposition does not apply to stock option rules; 10(12) — Non-resident ceasing to use inventory — deemed disposition; 28(4), (4.1) — Farmer or fisherman emigrating; 44(2)(d) — Exchanges of property; 53(4) — Effect on ACB of share, partnership interest or trust interest; 54"superficial loss"(c) — Superficial loss rule does not apply; 66(4)(b) — Foreign exploration and development expenses — deduction after emigration; 70(5.3) — Value of shares of corporation that owns life insurance policy; 74.2(3) — Application of spousal attribution rule to disposition on emigration; 104(4)(a.3) — Deemed disposition of property by trust on emigration of transferor; 106(1.1)(b) — Deemed cost of income interest in trust; 107(1.1)(b)(ii) — Deemed cost of income interest in trust; 114 — Individual resident during only part of year; 119 — Credit where stop-loss rule in 40(3.7) applies; 126(2.2) — Foreign tax credit on property deemed to be taxable Canadian property; 126(2.21), (2.22) — Foreign tax credit after emigration; 128.1(1)(b) — Deemed disposition on immigration; 128.1(5) — Deemed disposition does not increase instalment requirements; 128.1(6) — Returning former resident; 128.1(8) — Post-emigration loss; 128.1(9) — Information reporting;

## S. 128.1(4) — Income Tax Act, Part I

139.1(5) — Value of ownership rights in insurer during demutualization; 159(4), (4.1) — Election where subsec. 128.1(4) applies; 219.1 — Tax on corporate emigration; 220(3.2) — Late filing of elections under 128.1(4)(b)(iv) and 128.1(4)(d); 220(4.5)–(4.54) — Deferral of payment of departure tax; 226 — Demand for payment of taxes owing when taxpayer leaving Canada, and seizure of goods; Canada-U.S. Tax Convention Art. XIII:6, 7 — effect of emigration to U.S. on future capital gains; Canada-U.K. Tax Convention Art. 13:9 — effect of emigration to U.K. on future capital gains.

**Notes**: See at end of 128.1.

**Regulations**: 600(c), (c.1) (late filing of elections under (4)(b)(iv) and (4)(d)); 1300 (election under 128.1(4)(b)(iv)); 1302 (election under 128.1(4)(d)); 8201 (permanent establishment; to be prescribed for (4)(b)(ii)).

**Interpretation Bulletins**: IT-113R4: Benefits to employees — stock options; IT-137R3: Additional tax on certain corporations carrying on business in Canada; IT-259R3: Exchanges of property; IT-451R: Deemed disposition and acquisition on ceasing to be or becoming resident in Canada.

**Information Circulars**: 92-1: Guidelines for accepting late, amended or revoked elections.

**Advance Tax Rulings**: ATR-70: Distribution of taxable Canadian property by a trust to a non-resident. [This was the 1991 ruling criticized by the Auditor General in 1996 that led to the October 2, 1996 proposals — ed.].

**Forms**: T2061: Election by emigrant to defer deemed disposition of property and capital gains thereon; T2061A: Election by emigrant to report deemed dispositions of taxable Canadian property and capital gains and/or losses thereon.

### Proposed Addition — 128.1(5)–(10)

**(5) Instalment interest** — If an individual is deemed by subsection (4) to have disposed of a property in a taxation year, in applying sections 155 and 156 and subsections 156.1(1) to (3) and 161(2), (4) and (4.01) and any regulations made for the purposes of those provisions, the individual's total taxes payable under this Part and Part I.1 for the year are deemed to be the lesser of

(a) the individual's total taxes payable under this Part and Part I.1 for the year, determined before taking into consideration the specified future tax consequences for the year, and

(b) the amount that would be determined under paragraph (a) if subsection (4) did not apply to the individual for the year.

**Technical Notes**: Sections 155 and 156 of the Act set out rules for computing the instalment obligations of individuals for a taxation year. Subsections 161(2), (4) and (4.01) of the Act set out rules for computing the interest payable by taxpayers on any deficiency in instalments made during a taxation year.

New subsection 128.1(5) of the Act provides a special rule for computing the instalment and instalment interest obligation of an individual for a taxation year in which the individual ceases to be a resident of Canada. This subsection applies to exclude, in computing an individual's liability for instalments for the year, the tax attributable to any deemed disposition under paragraph 128.1(4)(b), where that paragraph has the effect of increasing the individual's total tax payable under Parts I and I.1 of the Act for the year.

New subsection 128.1(5) applies to changes in residence that occur after October 1, 1996.

**(6) Returning former resident** — If an individual (other than a trust) becomes resident in Canada at a particular time in a taxation year and the last time (in this subsection referred to as the "emigration time"), before the particular time, at which the individual ceased to be resident in Canada was after October 1, 1996,

(a) subject to paragraph (b), if the individual so elects in writing and files the election with the Minister on or before the individual's filing-due date for the year, paragraphs (4)(b) and (c) do not apply to the individual's cessation of residence at the emigration time in respect of all properties that were taxable Canadian properties of the individual throughout the period that began at the emigration time and that ends at the particular time;

(b) where, if a property in respect of which an election under paragraph (a) is made had been acquired by the individual at the emigration time at a cost equal to its fair market value at the emigration time and had been disposed of by the individual immediately before the particular time for proceeds of disposition equal to its fair market value immediately before the particular time, the application of subsection 40(3.7) would reduce the amount that would, but for subsection 40(3.7) and this subsection, be the individual's loss from the disposition,

(i) the individual is deemed to have disposed of the property at the time of disposition (within the meaning assigned by paragraph (4)(b)) in respect of the emigration time for proceeds of disposition equal to the total of

(A) the adjusted cost base to the individual of the property immediately before the time of disposition, and

(B) the amount, if any, by which that reduction exceeds the lesser of

(I) the adjusted cost base to the individual of the property immediately before the time of disposition, and

(II) the amount, if any, which the individual specifies for the purposes of this paragraph in the election under paragraph (a) in respect of the property,

(ii) the individual is deemed to have reacquired the property at the emigration time at a cost equal to the amount, if any, by which the amount determined under clause (i)(A) exceeds the lesser of that reduction and the amount specified by the individual under subclause (i)(B)(II), and

(iii) for the purposes of section 119, the individual is deemed to have disposed of the property immediately before the particular time;

(c) if the individual so elects in writing and files the election with the Minister on or before the individual's filing-due date for the year, in respect of each property that the individual owned throughout the period that began at the emigration time and that ends at the particular time and that is deemed by paragraph (1)(b) to have been disposed of because the individual became resident in Canada, notwithstanding paragraphs (1)(c) and (4)(b) the individual's proceeds of disposition at the time of disposition (within the meaning assigned by paragraph (4)(b)), and the individual's cost of acquiring the property at the particular time, are deemed to be those proceeds and that cost, determined without reference to this paragraph, minus the least of

(i) the amount that would, but for this paragraph, have been the individual's gain from the disposition of the property deemed by paragraph (4)(b) to have occurred,

(ii) the fair market value of the property at the particular time, and

(iii) the amount that the individual specifies for the purposes of this paragraph in the election; and

(d) notwithstanding subsections 152(4) to (5), any assessment of tax that is payable under this Act by the individual for any taxation year that is before the year that includes the particular time and that is not before the year that includes the emigration time shall be made that is necessary to take an election under this subsection into account, except that no such assessment shall affect the computation of

(i) interest payable under this Act to or by a taxpayer in respect of any period that is before the day on which the taxpayer's return of income for the taxation year that includes the particular time is filed, or

(ii) any penalty payable under this Act.

**Technical Notes**: New subsection 128.1(6) of the Act provides special rules that apply to an individual (other than a trust) who ceases to be resident in Canada at any time after October 1, 1996 (the "emigration time") and re-establishes Canadian residence at any particular time after that time. These rules allow the individual in effect to unwind the application of paragraphs 128.1(4)(b) and (c) to properties that were owned by the individual throughout the period beginning at the emigration time and ending at the particular time.

In broad terms, new subsection 128.1(6) means that an emigrant who returns to Canada at any time after emigration will no longer be treated as having realized accrued gains on departure. Four points should be noted about these rules. First, because there is no certain way of knowing which emigrants will return to Canada, this rule does not directly affect the obligations that arise on emigration. Rather, the rule does allow the returning individual retrospectively to modify the obligations. As a practical matter, it is expected that most individuals who plan to return to Canada will use the security provisions of subsection 220(4.5) to defer payment of any tax arising as a result of emigration. In that case, the main effect of new subsection 128.1(6) will be to allow the security to be given back intact to the returning emigrant.

Second, these rules do not affect any interest or penalties owing by an individual, including interest and penalties levied on taxes in respect of the individual's emigration, calculated without reference to the rule.

Third, these rules include features designed to prevent surplus-stripping. Without these features, a resident of Canada could use a temporary period of non-residence to extract, as dividends subject only to low-rate withholding tax, value that represents accrued gains.

Fourth, the rules require separate elections in respect of taxable Canadian property (paragraph (a)) and other property (paragraph (c)). The effects of the elections differ: the paragraph (a) election removes taxable Canadian properties from the deemed disposition and reacquisition on emigration, subject to special rules in paragraph (b); while the paragraph (c) election adjusts the emigration proceeds of disposition and the returning adjusted cost base of the other properties. Each election covers all property of the given sort, but the returning individual may choose to make one election and not the other.

Paragraph 128.1(6)(a) allows the individual to make an election in respect of property that was taxable Canadian property at the emigration time and throughout the period that the individual was non-resident. The effect of making this election is that paragraphs 128.1(4)(b) and (c) do not apply in respect of all such properties of the individual for the taxation year that includes the emigration time.

Where an individual has made an election under paragraph 128.1(6)(a), paragraph 128.1(6)(b) provides special surplus-stripping rules in respect of the property covered by the election. The basic purpose of paragraph (b) is to ensure that gains that accrued before emigration from Canada, and that have been extracted in the form of dividends during the individual's residence abroad, are subject to Canadian tax as gains.

Paragraph 128.1(6)(b) applies, in respect of a paragraph (a) taxable Canadian property, where two conditions are met:

— a loss has accrued on the property during the individual's period of non-residence — that is, the property's fair market value immediately before the individual becomes resident is less than its fair market value when the individual left Canada; and

— if the individual had acquired the property for its fair market value on emigration, and disposed of the property immediately before becoming resident, new subsection 40(3.7) (which applies to current and former non-resident individuals a version of the stop-loss rules in section 112 of the Act) would reduce the loss.

Where these conditions are met, paragraph (b) has four related effects. First, it treats the individual as having disposed of the property immediately before emigration, notwithstanding the paragraph (a) election. Second, it establishes the individual's proceeds of disposition of the property at that time, as the total of:

(A) the adjusted cost base of the property on emigration; and

(B) the amount, if any, by which the notional loss reduction under subsection 40(3.7) exceeds the lesser of (I) the adjusted cost base on emigration, and (II) an amount chosen by the individual.

Third, paragraph 128.1(6)(b) treats the individual as having reacquired the property on emigration, at a cost equal to the excess, if any, of the property's adjusted cost base on emigration (the (A) and (B)(I) amount above) over the lesser of the notional loss reduction under subsection 40(3.7) and the amount chosen by the individual in (B)(II) above.

The practical result of the second and third effects is that the income (in this case, dividends) that gives rise to the notional subsection 40(3.7) loss reduction is recharacterized as gains. Those gains are, subject to election, distributed between the post-return period and the deemed disposition on emigration.

Fourth, paragraph 128.1(6)(b) treats the individual, for the purposes of new section 119 of the Act, as having disposed of the property immediately before returning to Canada. This ensures that appropriate credit is given for any tax withheld under Part XIII of the Act on the income that triggered the application of paragraph 128.1(6)(b).

*EXAMPLE — 128.1(6)(b)*

Marie emigrates from Canada in 1999. Marie is the majority shareholder of a Canadian-controlled private corporation (CCPC) when she leaves Canada. The shares, which are taxable Canadian property to Marie, have a fair market value (FMV) at that time of $50,000 and an adjusted cost base (ACB) of $15,000, for a latent gain of $35,000. Marie receives $35,000 of dividends from the CCPC in 2000. In 2001, Marie returns to Canada. At that time, the shares have a FMV of $15,000. Marie uses the election in subsection 128.1(6) to minimize the tax consequences of her earlier emigration from Canada.

If Marie actually disposed of the shares immediately before re-establishing Canadian residence, subsection 40(3.7) of the Act would reduce her loss. Therefore, paragraph 128.1(6)(b) applies in respect of the shares.

Under paragraph 128.1(6)(b), Marie is treated as having disposed of and reacquired the shares on emigration. Assuming she elects $10,000, Marie's emigration proceeds of disposition are deemed to be $40,000, being the emigration ACB ($15,000) plus the difference between the subsection 40(3.7) reduction ($35,000) and the ACB/specified amount ($10,000). Marie thus realizes a $25,000 capital gain in the emigration year.

Marie's reacquisition cost is deemed to be $5,000, being the original ACB ($15,000) minus the lesser of the subsection 40(3.7) reduction ($35,000) and the specified amount ($10,000). Since the shares have a FMV of $15,000, Marie will eventually realize a gain of $10,000 (subject to other adjustments to ACB and FMV).

The result is that Marie's $25,000 gain on departure and remaining $10,000 latent gain equal the $35,000 she extracted in the form of dividends. The full $35,000 will thus be realized as capital gains, and section 119 will give Marie credit for any withholding tax she paid on the dividends.

Marie could have altered the timing of her capital gains on the shares. For example, if she had elected an amount of $5,000 under paragraph (a) in respect of the property, Marie's emigration proceeds of disposition would have been $45,000 ($15,000 ACB + ($35,000 40(3.7) reduction - $5,000 elected amount)), giving an emigration gain of $30,000. This would have been balanced by an increase in Marie's reacquisition cost from $5,000 to $10,000, which in turn would reduce the eventual gain Marie will realize on the shares.

New paragraph 128.1(6)(c) allows the returning individual to make an election, in respect of each property the individual owned at the emigration time and throughout the non-resident period that is subject to a deemed acquisition on immigration, under paragraph 128.1(1)(c) of the Act. In general, this describes property other than taxable Canadian property. The election adjusts, on a property-by-property basis, both the proceeds of disposition that were deemed to arise as a consequence of the deemed disposition in paragraph 128.1(4)(b) on the individual's earlier emigration, and the deemed acquisition cost under paragraph 128.1(1)(c).

Specifically, each of these amounts is adjusted by subtracting the least of:

- the amount that would otherwise be the individual's gain on the property as a result of the deemed disposition in paragraph 128.1(4)(b),
- the fair market value of the property immediately before the individual becomes resident in Canada, and
- any other amount specified by the individual.

As a result of these adjustments, the returning individual can generally defer Canadian tax on gains that had accrued before emigration, while still protecting from Canadian tax gains that accrued during periods of non-residence.

*EXAMPLE — 128.1(6)(c)*

Noah emigrates from Canada in 1999. Noah owns shares of a foreign corporation. When Noah leaves, the shares have a fair market value of $25,000 and an adjusted cost base of $15,000, for an accrued gain of $10,000. In 2012, Noah returns to Canada. At that time the shares have a fair market value of $80,000. Noah chooses to take advantage of the election in paragraph 128.1(6)(c) to control the tax consequences of ceasing to be a Canadian resident. Because he had a capital loss in 1999 of $7,000 from another source, Noah is content to realize a $7,000 capital gain on emigration, but he does not want to realize the other $3,000 accrued gain. Noah therefore chooses an elected amount of $3,000.

Noah's proceeds of disposition under paragraph 128.1(4)(b) are deemed to be $22,000, being the proceeds of disposition that would otherwise be determined under paragraph 128.1(4)(b) ($25,000) minus the least of:

- the amount that would have been Noah's gain on the shares under 128.1(4)(b) had this paragraph not applied ($10,000);
- the fair market value of the property at the particular time ($80,000); and
- the elected amount specified ($3,000).

Noah thus reduces his emigration-year gain to $7,000. The same $3,000 that reduces Noah's emigration proceeds is also subtracted from his reacquisition cost under paragraph 128.1(1)(c) ($80,000), leaving his new adjusted cost base in respect of the property $77,000. The property thus has a latent gain of $3,000 at the time Noah re-establishes Canadian residence in 2012.

Noah could have deferred tax on the full $10,000 gain that accrued before emigration, by increasing his elected amount in respect of the shares to $10,000.

New subsection 128.1(6) applies to changes in residence that occur after October 1, 1996. The subsection provides that, notwithstanding the Act's ordinary rules governing assessments, any necessary assessments of tax will be made in order to take account of the effect of this new subsection.

A special transitional rule accommodates individuals who cease to be resident in Canada after October 1, 1996 and before these amendments receive Royal Assent, and who wish to make elections under new subsection 128.1(6). The elections for these transition period emigrants will be considered to have been made in a timely manner if they are made on or before the individual's filing-due date for the taxation year that includes the day on which Royal Assent is received.

In addition, the Regulations will be amended to ensure that the Minister of National Revenue has discretion under the "fairness package" to allow elections under new subsection 128.1(6) to be late-filed. For additional information, see the commentary in the Appendix.

**Related Provisions:** 40(3.7) — Stop-loss rule applicable while non-resident; 128.1(7) — Returning trust beneficiary; 128.3 — Shares acquired on rollover deemed to be same shares for 128.1(6); 161(7)(a)(xi), 164(5)(h.02), 164(5.1) — Effect of carryback of loss; 220(3.2) — Late filing of elections under (6)(a) and (c); 220(4.5)–(4.54) — Deferral of payment of tax on emigration.

**Regulations:** 600(c) (late filing of elections under (6)(a) and (c)).

## (7) Returning trust beneficiary — If an individual (other than a trust)

(a) becomes resident in Canada at a particular time in a taxation year,

(b) owns at the particular time a property that the individual last acquired on a trust distribution to which subsection 107(2) would, but for subsection 107(5), have applied and at a time (in this subsection referred to as the "distribution time") that was after October 1, 1996 and before the particular time, and

(c) was a beneficiary of the trust at the last time, after October 1, 1996 and before the particular time, at which the individual ceased to be resident in Canada,

the following rules apply:

(d) subject to paragraphs (e) and (f), if the individual and the trust jointly so elect in writing and file the election with the Minister on or before the earlier of their filing-due dates for their taxation years that include the particular time, subsection 107(2.1) does not apply to the distribution in respect of all properties acquired by the individual on the distribution that were taxable Canadian properties of the individual throughout the period that began at the distribution time and that ends at the particular time;

(e) paragraph (f) applies in respect of the individual, the trust and a property in respect of which an election under paragraph (d) is made where, if the individual

(i) had been resident in Canada at the distribution time,

(ii) had acquired the property at the distribution time at a cost equal to its fair market value at that time,

(iii) had ceased to be resident in Canada immediately after the distribution time, and

(iv) had, immediately before the particular time, disposed of the property for proceeds of disposition equal to its fair market value immediately before the particular time,

the application of subsection 40(3.7) would reduce the amount that would, but for that subsection and this subsection, have been the individual's loss from the disposition;

(f) where this paragraph applies in respect of an individual, a trust and a property,

(i) notwithstanding paragraph 107(2.1)(a), the trust is deemed to have disposed of the property at the distribution time for proceeds of disposition equal to the total of

(A) the cost amount to the trust of the property immediately before the distribution time, and

(B) the amount, if any, by which the reduction under subsection 40(3.7) described in paragraph (e) exceeds the lesser of

(I) the cost amount to the trust of the property immediately before the distribution time, and

(II) the amount, if any, which the individual and the trust jointly specify for the purposes of this paragraph in the election under paragraph (d) in respect of the property, and

(ii) notwithstanding paragraph 107(2.1)(b), the individual is deemed to have acquired the property at the distribution time at a cost equal to the amount, if any, by which the amount otherwise determined under paragraph 107(2)(b) exceeds the lesser of the reduction under subsection 40(3.7) described in paragraph (e) and the amount specified under subclause (i)(B)(II);

(g) if the individual and the trust jointly so elect in writing and file the election with the Minister on or before the later of their filing-due dates for their taxation years that include the particular time, in respect of each property that the individual owned throughout the period that began at the distribution time and that ends at the particular time and that is deemed by paragraph (1)(b) to have been disposed of because the individual became resident in Canada, notwithstanding paragraphs 107(2.1)(a) and (b), the trust's proceeds of disposition under paragraph 107(2.1)(a) at the distribution time, and the individual's cost of acquiring the property at the particular time, are deemed to be those proceeds and that cost determined without reference to this paragraph, minus the least of

    (i) the amount that would, but for this paragraph, have been the trust's gain from the disposition of the property deemed by paragraph 107(2.1)(a) to have occurred,

    (ii) the fair market value of the property at the particular time, and

    (iii) the amount that the individual and the trust jointly specify for the purposes of this paragraph in the election;

(h) if the trust ceases to exist before the individual's filing-due date for the individual's taxation year that includes the particular time,

    (i) an election or specification described in this subsection may be made by the individual alone in writing if the election is filed with the Minister on or before that filing-due date, and

    (ii) if the individual alone makes such an election or specification, the individual and the trust are jointly and severally liable for any amount payable under this Act by the trust as a result of the election or specification; and

(i) notwithstanding subsections 152(4) to (5), such assessment of tax payable under the Act by the trust or the individual for any year that is before the year that includes the particular time and that is not before the year that includes the distribution time shall be made as is necessary to take an election under this subsection into account, except that no such assessment shall affect the computation of

    (i) interest payable under this Act to or by the trust or the individual in respect of any period that is before the individual's filing-due date for the taxation year that includes the particular time, or

    (ii) any penalty payable under this Act.

**Technical Notes**: New subsection 128.1(7) of the Act provides special rules, which parallel new subsection 128.1(6) of the Act, applicable to an individual trust beneficiary (other than one that is itself a trust) who emigrates from Canada, receives distributions of trust property as a non-resident, and then re-establishes residence in Canada while still owning the property. In general terms, these rules allow the beneficiary and the trust to jointly elect, upon the beneficiary's return to Canada, to unwind the tax consequences to the trust that occurred when it distributed the property to the non-resident beneficiary.

A number of conditions must be met for the application of these rules: the individual must have been a resident of Canada and then ceased to be resident in Canada after October 1, 1996; the individual must have been a beneficiary of the trust at the time he or she ceased to be resident in Canada; the distribution must occur after October 1, 1996 and before the individual re-establishes residence in Canada; the distribution must be such that subsection 107(2) of the Act would have applied but for subsection 107(5); and the individual must re-establish residence in Canada after October 1, 1996 while still owning the property distributed by the trust.

Where these conditions are met, paragraph (d) provides an election for taxable Canadian property similar to the election provided in paragraph 128.1(6)(a). Paragraphs (e) and (f) provide anti-stripping rules similar to those provided by paragraph 128.1(6)(b). Paragraph (g) provides an election for property other than taxable Canadian property, similar to the election provided in paragraph 128.1(6)(c).

Paragraph (h) provides a special rule applicable if the trust ceases to exist before the individual's filing-due date for his or her taxation year during which he or she re-establishes residence in Canada. In such cases, the elections or specifications provided in new subsection 128.1(7) can be made by the individual alone. However, the individual and the trust will then be jointly and severally liable for any amount payable under the Act by the trust as a result of the election or specification.

Paragraph (i) allows any assessment of tax to be made that is necessary for the elections under new subsection 128.1(7) to be taken into account, but provides that no such assessment shall affect the computation of interest or penalties payable.

New subsection 128.1(7) applies to changes in residence that occur after October 1, 1996. A special transitional rule accommodates individuals who cease to be resident in Canada after October 1, 1996 and before these amendments receive Royal Assent, and who wish to make elections under new subsection 128.1(7). The elections for these transition period emigrants will be considered to have been made in a timely manner if they are made on or before the individual's filing-due date for the taxation year that includes the day on which Royal Assent is received.

In addition, it is proposed that the Regulations be amended to ensure that the Minister of National Revenue has discretion under the "fairness package" to allow elections under new subsection 128.1(7) to be late-filed.

**Related Provisions**: 40(3.7) — Stop-loss rule applicable while non-resident; 128.1(6) — Returning former resident; 128.3 — Shares acquired on rollover deemed to be same shares for 128.1(7); 161(7)(a)(xi), 164(5)(h.02), 164(5.1) — Effect of carryback of loss; 220(3.2) — Late filing of elections under (7)(d) and (g); 220(4.5)–(4.54) — Deferral of payment of tax on emigration.

**Notes**: This subsection was not in the draft legislation of December 17, 1999. It is modelled on 128.1(6).

**Regulations**: 600(c) (late filed elections under (7)(d), (g)).

**(8) Post-emigration loss** — If an individual (other than a trust)

(a) was deemed by paragraph (4)(b) to have disposed of a capital property at any particular time after October 1, 1996,

(b) has disposed of the property at a later time at which the property was a taxable Canadian property of the individual, and

(c) so elects in writing in the individual's return of income for the taxation year that includes the later time,

there shall, except for the purpose of paragraph (4)(c), be deducted from the individual's proceeds of disposition of the property at the particular time, and added to the individual's proceeds of disposition of the property at the later time, an amount equal to the least of

(d) the amount specified in respect of the property in the election,

(e) the amount that would, but for the election, be the individual's gain from the disposition of the property at the particular time, and

(f) the amount that would be the individual's loss from the disposition of the property at the later time, if the loss were determined having reference to every other provision of this Act including, for greater certainty, subsection 40(3.7) and section 112, but without reference to the election.

**Technical Notes**: New subsection 128.1(8) of the Act provides relief to an individual (other than a trust) who disposes of a taxable Canadian property, after having emigrated from Canada, for proceeds that are less than the deemed proceeds that arose under paragraph 128.1(4)(b) in respect of the property when the individual emigrated.

Under subsection 128.1(8) the individual may elect to reduce the proceeds of disposition that were deemed to arise under paragraph 128.1(4)(b) in respect of a property by the least of:

- an amount specified by the individual;
- the amount that would be the individual's gain from the deemed disposition of the property under paragraph 128.1(4)(b), but for this subsection; and
- the amount that would be the individual's loss from the disposition of the property at the time the property is actually disposed of, if the loss were determined with reference to every other provision in the Act (including the stop-loss rules in subsection 40(3.7) and section 112 of the Act) but this subsection.

The same amount is added to the individual's proceeds of disposition realized at the time of actual disposition.

*EXAMPLE — 128.1(8)*

Odile emigrates from Canada in 1999, owning a capital interest in a trust resident in Canada that she purchased in 1997. The interest has a fair market value at the emigration time of $150,000 and an adjusted cost base of $40,000, for a latent gain of $110,000 on departure. Odile's tax is assessed on that basis, and she posts security for the tax.

In 2001, Odile sells her trust interest for $60,000. Since Odile has realized a smaller gain than assumed in her tax assessment on emigration, she elects under subsection 128.1(8) to reduce the gain she was deemed to have realized when she emigrated.

To obtain the maximum benefit from the subsection, Odile specifies an amount of $90,000 in respect of the election. Her proceeds of disposition at the emigration time are deemed to be $60,000, being the proceeds of disposition that would otherwise be determined under paragraph 128.1(4)(b) ($150,000) minus the least of:

- the amount specified ($90,000);
- the amount that would have been her taxable gain in respect of the trust interest under 128.1(4)(b) had this paragraph not applied ($110,000); and
- the amount that would have been her loss on actual disposition of the trust interest had this paragraph not applied ($150,000 - $60,000 = $90,000).

The same $90,000 amount is added to Odile's proceeds of the actual disposition of the trust interest. The result is that, in respect of the trust interest, Odile is treated as having realized a $20,000 gain in 1999, and no gain or loss on the actual disposition of the property in 2001.

It should be noted that the election in subsection 128.1(8) does not affect any interest or penalties owing by the individual at the time of making the election, including interest and penalties levied on taxes in respect of the property, calculated without reference to the subsection.

A consequential amendment to subsection 152(6) of the Act ensures that any necessary assessments of tax will be made in order to take account of the effect of new subsection 128.1(8).

New subsection 128.1(8) applies to changes in residence that occur after October 1, 1996. A special transitional rule accommodates individuals who cease to be resident in Canada after October 1, 1996 and before these amendments receive Royal Assent, and who wish to make the election under new subsection 128.1(8). The election for these transition period emigrants will be considered to have been made in a timely manner if it is made on or before the individual's filing-due date for the taxation year that includes the day on which Royal Assent is received.

In addition, the Regulations will be amended to ensure that the Minister of National Revenue has discretion under the "fairness package" to allow an election under new subsection 128.1(8) to be late-filed.

**Related Provisions**: 128.3 — Shares acquired on rollover deemed to be same shares for 128.1(7); 152(6)(f.2) — Minister required to reassess past year to allow unused foreign tax credit; 161(7)(a)(xi), 164(5)(h.02), 164(5.1) — Effect of carryback of loss; 220(3.2) — Late filing of election under (8)(c).

**Notes**: This was 128.1(7) in the draft legislation of December 17, 1999.

**Regulations**: 600(c) (late filed elections under (8)(c)).

**(9) Information reporting** — An individual who ceases at a particular time in a taxation year to be resident in Canada, and who owns immediately after the particular time one or more reportable properties the total fair market value of which at the particular time is greater than $25,000, shall file with the Minister in prescribed form, on or before the individual's filing-due date for the year, a list of all the reportable properties that the individual owned immediately after the particular time.

**Technical Notes**: New subsection 128.1(9) of the Act requires an individual who ceases to be resident in Canada after 1995 to file with the Minister of National Revenue, in prescribed form, a list of all the reportable properties that the individual owned at emigration time. This reporting requirement does not apply where the total fair market value of the individual's reportable properties at emigration time is $25,000 or less. However, where an individual owns reportable properties at emigration time with a total fair market value greater than $25,000, the individual must disclose all reportable properties on the information reporting form.

The term "reportable property" is defined in new subsection 128.1(10). For additional information, see the commentary on that subsection.

New subsection 128.1(9) applies to changes in residence that occur after 1995. The information reporting form must be filed on or before the individual's filing-due date for the year of emigration from Canada. However, a special transitional rule accommodates individuals who cease to be resident in Canada after 1995 and before these amendments receive Royal Assent – a form filed by these transition period emigrants will be considered to have been filed in a timely manner if it is filed on or before the individual's filing-due date for the taxation year that includes the day on which Royal Assent for these amendments is received.

**Related Provisions**: 128.1(10)"reportable property" — Exclusions.

**Notes**: This was 128.1(8) in the draft legislation of December 17, 1999.

**(10) Definitions** — The definitions in this subsection apply in this section.

**"excluded right or interest"** of a taxpayer that is an individual means

(a) a right of the individual under, or an interest of the individual in a trust governed by,

(i) a registered retirement savings plan or a plan referred to in subsection 146(12) as an "amended plan",

(ii) a registered retirement income fund,

(iii) a registered education savings plan,

(iv) a deferred profit sharing plan or a plan referred to in subsection 147(15) as a "revoked plan",

(v) an employees profit sharing plan,

(vi) an employee benefit plan (other than an employee benefit plan described in subparagraph (b)(i) or (ii)),

(vii) a plan or arrangement (other than an employee benefit plan) under which the individual has a right to receive in a year remuneration in respect of services rendered by the individual in the year or a prior year,

(viii) a superannuation or pension fund or plan (other than an employee benefit plan),

(ix) a retirement compensation arrangement,

(x) a foreign retirement arrangement, or

(xi) a registered supplementary unemployment benefit plan;

(b) a right of the individual to a benefit under an employee benefit plan that is

(i) a plan or arrangement described in paragraph (j) of the definition "salary deferral arrangement" in subsection 248(1) that would, but for paragraphs (j) and (k) of that definition, be a salary deferral arrangement, or

(ii) a plan or arrangement that would, but for paragraph 6801(c) of the *Income Tax Regulations*, be a salary deferral arrangement,

to the extent that the benefit can reasonably be considered to be attributable to services rendered by the individual in Canada;

(c) a right of the individual under an agreement referred to in subsection 7(1) or (1.1);

(d) a right of the individual to a retiring allowance,

(e) a right of the individual under, or an interest of the individual in, a trust that is

(i) an employee trust,

(ii) an amateur athlete trust,

(iii) a cemetery care trust, or

(iv) a trust governed by an eligible funeral arrangement;

(f) a right of the individual to receive a payment under

(i) an annuity contract, or

(ii) an income-averaging annuity contract;

(g) a right of the individual to a benefit under

(i) the *Canada Pension Plan* or a provincial plan described in section 3 of that Act,

(ii) the *Old Age Security Act*,

(iii) a provincial pension plan prescribed for the purpose of paragraph 60(v), or

(iv) a plan or arrangement instituted by the social security legislation of a country other than Canada or of a state, province or other political subdivision of such a country;

(h) a right of the individual to a benefit described in any of subparagraphs 56(1)(a)(iii) to (vi);

(i) a right of the individual to a payment out of a NISA Fund No. 2;

(j) an interest of the individual in a personal trust resident in Canada if the interest was never acquired for consideration and did not arise as a consequence of a qualifying disposition by the individual (within the meaning that would be assigned by subsection 107.4(1) if that subsection were read without reference to paragraphs 107.4(1)(h) and (i));

(k) an interest of the individual in a non-resident testamentary trust if the interest was never acquired for consideration; or

(l) an interest of the individual in a life insurance policy in Canada, except for that part of the policy in respect of which the individual is deemed by paragraph 138.1(1)(e) to have an interest in a related segregated fund trust.

**Technical Notes**: New subsection 128.1(10) of the Act contains two new definitions that are used in section 128.1: "excluded right or interest" and "reportable property".

In general terms, an individual's excluded rights or interests include rights of the individual to future benefits or other payments under certain plans or arrangements, many of which are employer-sponsored or legislated in nature. It also includes interests of the individual in certain trusts and insurance contracts. The definition "excluded right or interest" is relevant for three main purposes.

First, the definition is relevant for paragraphs 128.1(1)(b) and (4)(b) of the Act, which treat individuals as having disposed of (and to have immediately reacquired) most of their property on immigrating to or emigrating from Canada. With one exception that applies with regard to individuals immigrating to Canada (see subparagraph 128.1(1)(b)(iv) for more details), excluded rights or interests are exempted from these deemed disposition rules.

Second, the definition is relevant for subclause 78(1) of the amending Notice of Ways and Means Motion, which allows individuals who emigrated from Canada after 1992 but before October 2, 1996 to elect to have their excluded rights or interests exempted from the deemed disposition rules at departure. For additional information, see the commentary on clause 78.

Third, the definition is relevant for the purpose of the information reporting requirement under new subsection 128.1(9) of the Act, which exempts from the reporting requirement certain properties that fall within the definition "excluded right or interest".

Paragraph (a) of the definition "excluded right or interest" refers to rights of the individual under, or an interest of the individual in a trust governed by, certain plans. The plans referred to in this paragraph include pension plans (including registered pension plans), retirement compensation arrangements, registered retirement savings plans, registered retirement income funds and foreign retirement arrangements (defined in section 6803 of the Regulations to mean certain Individual Retirement Accounts established under the United States Internal Revenue Code). Also included are deferred profit sharing plans, employee profit sharing plans, employee benefit plans (EBPs) (other than those described in paragraph (b) of this definition) and plans under which the individual has a right to receive remuneration for services rendered in the year or a previous year (including, for example, salary deferral arrangements (SDAs), unfunded bonus deferrals, self-funded leaves of absence and phantom stock plans). Registered supplementary unemployment benefit plans and registered education savings plans are also included in this paragraph.

Paragraph (b) of the definition refers to rights of the individual to a benefit under an EBP that would be an SDA if it were not specifically exempted from being an SDA by virtue of paragraphs (j) and (k) of the definition of "salary deferral arrangement" in subsection 248(1) of the Act or by virtue of paragraph 6801(c) of the Regulations. (The former exemption is for deferred salary arrangements for professional athletes, the latter for deferred salary arrangements for National Hockey League on-ice officials.) Only the right that relates to the portion of the benefit that is attributable to services rendered by the individual in Canada is included in "excluded right or interest".

Paragraph (c) of the definition refers to rights of the individual under an agreement referred to in subsection 7(1) or (1.1) of the Act. Those subsections refer to agreements under which employees of a corporation or of a mutual fund trust are granted certain rights to acquire shares of the corporation (or a related corporation) or units of the trust.

Paragraph (d) of the definition refers to rights of the individual to a retiring allowance.

Paragraph (e) of the definition refers to rights of the individual under, or an interest of the individual in, an employee trust, an amateur athlete trust, a cemetery care trust or a trust governed by an eligible funeral arrangement.

Paragraph (f) of the definition refers to rights of the individual to receive payments under an annuity contract or an income-averaging annuity contract.

Paragraph (g) of the definition refers to rights of the individual to benefits under the *Canada Pension Plan*, the Québec Pension Plan, the Old Age Security Act and the Saskatchewan Pension Plan. It also refers to rights of the individual to benefits under foreign social security arrangements.

Paragraph (h) of the definition refers to rights of the individual to benefits referred to in subparagraphs 56(1)(a)(iii) to (vi) of the Act. Those subparagraphs refer to death benefits, certain employment insurance benefits, certain benefits provided in connection with the Canada-United States Agreement on Automotive Products and prescribed benefits received under government assistance programs.

Paragraph (i) of the definition refers to a right of the individual to a payment out of a NISA ("net income stabilization account") Fund No. 2 under the Farm Income Protection Act.

Paragraph (j) of the definition refers to an interest of the individual in a personal trust resident in Canada, provided the interest was never acquired (by any person) for consideration and did not arise as a consequence of a transfer by the individual that would be a "qualifying disposition" under subsection 107.4(1) if that subsection were read without reference to paragraphs 107.4(1)(h) and (i). See further in this regard, the commentary on new subsections 107.4(1), 108(6) and 108(7) and new paragraph 107.4(3)(h). Each of these provisions is relevant for the purposes of determining the scope of paragraph (j).

Paragraph (k) of the definition refers to an interest of the individual in a non-resident testamentary trust, provided the interest was never acquired (by any person) for consideration.

Paragraph (l) of the definition refers to an interest of the individual in a life insurance policy in Canada (except for

**S. 128.1(10) exc**      Income Tax Act, Part I

that part of the policy in respect of which the individual is deemed by paragraph 138.1(1)(e) of the Act to have an interest in a related segregated fund trust).

**Related Provisions**: 108(6) — Where terms of trust are varied; 108(7) — Meaning of "acquired for consideration"; 128.1(1)(b)(iv) — No deemed disposition on immigration; 128.1(4)(b)(iii) — No deemed disposition on emigration; 128.1(4)(d.1) — Where share acquired under stock option before emigration; 128.1(10) "reportable property" — No requirement to report most excluded personal property.

**Notes**: This was 128.1(9) "excluded personal property" in the draft legislation of December 17, 1999.

**"reportable property"** of an individual at a particular time means any property other than

(a) money that is legal tender in Canada and deposits of such money;

(b) property that would be an excluded right or interest of the individual if the definition "excluded right or interest" in this subsection were read without reference to paragraphs (c), (j) and (l) of that definition;

(c) if the individual is not a trust and was not, during the 120-month period that ends at the particular time, resident in Canada for more than 60 months, property described in subparagraph (4)(b)(iv) that is not taxable Canadian property; and

(d) any item of personal-use property the fair market value of which, at the particular time, is less than $10,000.

**Technical Notes**: The definition "reportable property" is relevant for the purpose of the information reporting requirement, for individuals who emigrate from Canada, under new subsection 128.1(9) of the Act.

"Reportable property" means any property of the individual other than the following:

(a) money that is legal tender in Canada and deposits of such money;

(b) property falling within the definition "excluded right or interest" in new subsection 128.1(10) of the Act, except for employee options in shares of corporations or in units of mutual fund trusts, certain interests in personal trusts resident in Canada, and interests in a life insurance policy in Canada;

(c) for individuals (other than trusts) who were resident in Canada for 60 months or less in the 120-month period that precedes the time of emigration, property, other than taxable Canadian property, that was owned by the individual before the individual became resident in Canada or that was acquired by the individual by inheritance or bequest after becoming resident in Canada; and

(d) any item of personal-use property the fair market value of which at emigration time is less than $10,000.

**Notes**: This definition was in 128.1(9) in the draft legislation of December 17, 1999.

**Application**: Bill C-43 (First Reading September 20, 2000), subsec. 77(5), will add subsecs. 128.1(5) to (10), applicable (other than subsec. 128.1(9) and the definition "reportable property" in subsec. 128.1(10)) to changes in residence that occur after October 1, 1996, and

(a) an election made under any of paras. 128.1(6)(a) and (c), 128.1(7)(d) and (g) and 128.1(8)(c) by an individual who ceased to be resident in Canada before the day on which this Act is assented to, is deemed to have been made in a timely manner if it is made on or before the individual's filing-due date for the taxation year that includes that day; and

(b) a form described in subsec. 128.1(9), filed by an individual who ceased to be resident in Canada before the day on which this Act is assented to, is deemed to have been filed in a timely manner if it is filed on or before the individual's filing-due date for the taxation year that includes that day.

Subsec. 128.1(9) and the definition "reportable property" in subsec. 128.1(10) apply to changes in residence that occur after 1995.

**Notes [s. 128.1]**: 128.1(4)(b) creates what is informally called a "departure tax" or "emigration tax". It triggers a deemed disposition of most property at its fair market value when a person becomes non-resident. The resulting capital gain is then taxed under the normal rules for capital gains (see 38-40).

In its tax treaty negotiations, Canada is seeking to have other countries allow a parallel increase in the cost base of property to fair market value on immigration (as we have under 128.1(1)(c)), to prevent double taxation when the property is eventually sold. See also the foreign tax credit for former residents in 126(2.21), which deals with the same issue; and proposed s. 119.

For tax planning for emigrants to the U.S. based on the December 1998 (now Bill C-43) proposals, see Roanne Bratz, "Canadians Moving to the United States", 46(6) *Canadian Tax Journal* 1322-1348 (1998). For comments about the new rules generally see Cindy Rajan, "Are You Sure You Want to Leave Canada? The New Taxpayer Migration Rules", 47(5) *Canadian Tax Journal* 1342-1366 (1999).

Note that "taxable Canadian property" has an extended meaning for purposes of s. 128.1. See 248(1).

128.1 added by 1993 technical bill, effective January 1, 1993, replacing s. 48. However, where a corporation continued before 1993 elects for new 250(5.1) to apply earlier (see Notes to 250(5.1)), 128.1 applies from the corporation's "time of continuation".

128.1(4)(b)(iii) amended by 1997 Budget, effective for changes of residence after October 1, 1996, to add reference to rights under a RESP.

**Definitions [s. 128.1]**: "adjusted cost base" — 54, 248(1); "amateur athlete trust" — 143.1(1), 248(1); "amount" — 248(1); "annuity" — 248(1); "arm's length" — 251(1); "assessment" — 248(1); "balance-due day", "business" — 248(1); "Canada" — 255, *Interpretation Act* 35(1); "Canadian exploration and development expenses", "Canadian resource property" — 66(15), 248(1); "capital property" — 54, 248(1); "cemetery care trust" — 148.1(1), 248(1); "class of shares" — 248(6); "consideration" — 108(7); "controlled foreign affiliate" — 95(1), 248(1); "corporation" — 248(1), *Interpretation Act* 35(1); "cost amount", "dividend" — 248(1); "deferred profit sharing plan" — 147(1), 248(1); "disposition", "eligible capital property" — 54, 248(1); "distribution time" — 128.1(7)(b); "eligible funeral arrangement" — 148.1(1), 248(1); "emigration time" — 128.1(6); "employee benefit plan" — 248(1); "employee trust" — 248(1); "employees profit sharing plan" — 144(1), 248(1); "excluded right or interest" — 128.1(10); "farm loss" — 111(8), 248(1); "filing-due date" — 248(1); "fiscal period" — 249.1; "foreign accrual property income" — 95(1), (2), 248(1); "foreign affiliate" — 95(1), 248(1); "foreign retirement arrangement" — 248(1), Reg 6803; "income-averaging annuity contract", "individual", "inventory" — 248(1); "limited partnership loss" — 96(2.1), 248(1); "life insurance policy in Canada" — 138(12), 248(1); "Minister" — 248(1); "month" — *Interpretation Act* 35(1); "net capital loss", "non-capital loss" — 111(8), 248(1); "non-resident" — 248(1); "paid-up capital" — 89(1), 248(1); "paid-up capital adjustment" — 128.1(2)(a); "permanent establishment" — Reg. 8201; "person", "personal trust" — 248(1); "personal-use property" — 54, 248(1); "prescribed" — 248(1); "proceeds of disposition" — 54; "property" — 248(1); "province" — *Interpretation Act* 35(1); "registered education savings plan" — 146.1(1), 248(1); "registered retirement income fund" — 146.3(1), 248(1); "registered retirement savings plan" — 146(1), 248(1); "registered supplementary unemployment benefit plan" — 145(1), 248(1); "regulation" — 248(1); "reportable property" — 128.1(10); "resident", "resident in Canada" — 250; "restricted farm loss" — 31(1.1), 248(1); "retirement compensation arrangement", "retiring allowance" — 248(1); "salary deferral arrangement"; "share", "shareholder" — 248(1); "specified future tax consequence" — 248(1); "taxable Canadian property" — 248(1); "taxation year" — 249, 250.1(a); "taxpayer" — 248; "testamentary trust" — 108(1), 248(1); "timber resource property" — 13(21), 248(1); "time of disposition" — 128.1(1)(b), 128.1(4)(b); "treaty-protected property" — 248(1); "trust" — 104(1), 248(1), (3); "writing" — *Interpretation Act* 35(1).

**128.2 (1) Cross-border mergers** — Where a corporation formed at a particular time by the amalgamation or merger of, or by a plan of arrangement or other corporate reorganization in respect of, 2 or more corporations (each of which is referred to in this section as a "predecessor") is at the particular time resident in Canada, a predecessor that was not immediately before the particular time resident in Canada shall be deemed to have become resident in Canada immediately before the particular time.

**(2) Idem** — Where a corporation formed at a particular time by the amalgamation or merger of, or by a plan of arrangement or other corporate reorganization in respect of, 2 or more corporations is at the particular time not resident in Canada, a predecessor that was immediately before the particular time resident in Canada shall be deemed to have ceased to be resident in Canada immediately before the particular time.

**(3) Windings-up excluded** — For greater certainty, subsections (1) and (2) do not apply to reorganizations occurring solely because of the acquisition of property of one corporation by another corporation, pursuant to the purchase of the property by the other corporation or because of the distribution of the property to the other corporation on the winding-up of the corporation.

**Notes [s. 128.2]**: 128.2 added by 1993 technical bill, effective January 1, 1993. However, where a corporation continued before 1993 elects for new 250(5.1) to apply earlier (see Notes to 250(5.1)), 128.2 applies from the corporation's "time of continuation".

**Definitions [s. 128.2]**: "corporation" — 248(1), *Interpretation Act* 35(1); "predecessor" — 128.2(1); "property" — 248(1); "resident in Canada" — 250.

### Proposed Addition — 128.3

**128.3 Former resident — replaced shares** — If, in a transaction to which section 51, subparagraphs 85.1(1)(a)(i) and (ii) or section 86 or 87 apply, a person acquires a share (in this section referred to as the "new share") in exchange for another share (in this section referred to as the "old share"), for the purposes of section 119, subsections 126(2.21) to (2.23), 128.1(6) to (8), 180.1(1.4) and 220(4.5) and (4.6), the person is deemed not to have disposed of the old share, and the new share is deemed to be the same share as the old share.

**Application**: Bill C-43 (First Reading September 20, 2000), s. 79, will add s. 128.3, applicable after October 1, 1996.

**Technical Notes**: New section 128.3 of the Act applies to shares ("old shares") that were received in exchange for other shares ("new shares") on a tax-deferred basis pursuant to section 51 (convertible property), subparagraphs 85.1(1)(a)(i) or (ii) (transfer of property to a corporation by shareholders), section 86 (exchange of shares by a shareholder in the course of a reorganization of a company's capital) or section 87 (amalgamation) of the Act. For the purposes of section 119 and subsections 126(2.21) to (2.23), 128.1(6) to (8), 180.1(1.4) and 220(4.5) and (4.6) of the Act, the individual is deemed not to have disposed of the old shares, and the new shares are deemed to be the old shares. This ensures that the relief available under those provisions is not lost as a result of such a share-for-share exchange.

New section 128.3 applies after October 1, 1996.

**Definitions [s. 128.3]**: "new share", "old share" — 128.3; "person", "share" — 248(1).

## Private Corporations

**129. (1) Dividend refund to private corporation** — Where a return of a corporation's income under this Part for a taxation year is made within 3 years after the end of the year, the Minister

(a) may, on mailing the notice of assessment for the year, refund without application therefor an amount (in this Act referred to as its "dividend refund" for the year) equal to the lesser of

(i) ⅓ of all taxable dividends paid by the corporation on shares of its capital stock in the year and at a time when it was a private corporation, and

(ii) its refundable dividend tax on hand at the end of the year; and

(b) shall, with all due dispatch, make the dividend refund after mailing the notice of assessment if an application for it has been made in writing by the corporation within the period within which the Minister would be allowed under subsection 152(4) to assess tax payable under this Part by the corporation for the year if that subsection were read without reference to paragraph 152(4)(a).

**Related Provisions**: 15.1(2)(b) — Amount paid on small business development bond not a dividend for 129(1); 129(2) — Application to other liability; 131(5) — Mutual fund corporation deemed to be a private corporation; 141.1 — Insurance corporation deemed not to be private corporation; 152(1)(a) — Determination of refund by Minister; 157(3) — Reduction in instalment obligations to reflect dividend refund; 160.1 — Where excess refunded; 186(5) — Deemed private corporation; 260(7) — Securities lending arrangement — amount deemed paid as a taxable dividend. See additional Related Provisions and Definitions at end of s. 129.

**Notes**: The refund rate is ⅓ so that, of $100 of corporate income, the dividend refund of $26.67 (see 129(3)(a)(i)A) will be refunded once $80 in dividends is paid ($26.67 × 3). The $80 is what remains after 20% corporate tax, reflecting the expected refund. The upfront corporate tax is $40 (presumed federal/provincial rate of 40%) plus $6.67 under s. 123.3, or $46.67. That leaves the corporation (up front) with $53.33 which, added to the $26.67 dividend refund, gives the corporation $80 to pay out as a dividend. Once the corporation receives the dividend refund of $26.67, its total tax is reduced to $20 — the rate at which the dividend gross-up under 82(1)(b) and the dividend tax credit under 121 lead to full integration.

129(1)(a)(i) amended to change "¼" to "⅓" by 1995 Budget, effective for taxation years that end after June 1995 except that, for such years that began before July 1995, the amount determined under 129(1)(a)(i) was the total of ¼ of the dividends paid before July 1995 and ⅓ of the dividends paid after June 1995. The change from ¼ to ⅓ was co-ordinated with the extra 6.67% tax under 123.3; see explanatory paragraph above.

Opening words of 129(1) amended by 1992 technical bill, effective for 1993 and later taxation years, to delete a requirement that the corporation be a private corporation at the end of the taxation year. 129(1)(a)(i) amended at the same time to add the words "at a time when it was a private corporation". For taxation years that begin before 1993 and end after 1992, read 129(1)(a)(i) as:

(i) the total of

(A) ¼ of all taxable dividends paid by the corporation on shares of its capital stock in the year and before 1993, where the corporation was a private corporation at the end of the year, and

(B) ¼ of all taxable dividends paid by the corporation on shares of its capital stock in the year and at a time after 1992 when it was a private corporation, and

129(1)(b) amended by 1989 Budget, effective April 28, 1989, to refer to "the period determined under paragraph 152(4)(b) or (c)" rather than to a 6-year or 3-year period; and amended by 1995-97 technical bill, also effective April 28, 1989, to make non-substantive wording changes and to update references to 152(4) as amended.

See Notes to 186(1).

**Interpretation Bulletins**: IT-243R4: Dividend refund to private corporations; IT-432R2: Benefits conferred on shareholders.

### (1.1) Dividends paid to bankrupt controlling corporation
— In determining the dividend refund for a taxation year ending after 1977 of a particular corporation, no amount may be included by virtue of subparagraph (1)(a)(i) in respect of a taxable dividend paid to a shareholder that

(a) was a corporation that controlled (within the meaning assigned by subsection 186(2)) the particular corporation at the time the dividend was paid; and

(b) was a bankrupt (within the meaning assigned by subsection 128(3)) at any time during that taxation year of the particular corporation.

**Interpretation Bulletins**: IT-243R4: Dividend refund to private corporations.

### (1.2) Dividends deemed not to be taxable dividends
— Where a dividend is paid on a share of the capital stock of a corporation and the share (or another share for which the share was substituted) was acquired by its holder in a transaction or as part of a series of transactions one of the main purposes of which was to enable the corporation to obtain a dividend refund, the dividend shall, for the purpose of subsection (1), be deemed not to be a taxable dividend.

**Related Provisions**: 87(2)(aa), (ii) — Amalgamations; 88(1)(e.5) — Winding-up; 129(7) — Capital gains dividend excluded; 248(10) — Series of transactions. See additional Related Provisions and Definitions at end of s. 129.

**Interpretation Bulletins**: IT-243R4: Dividend refund to private corporations.

### (2) Application to other liability
— Instead of making a refund that might otherwise be made under subsection (1), the Minister may, where the corporation is liable or about to become liable to make any payment under this Act, apply the amount that would otherwise be refundable to that other liability and notify the corporation of that action.

**Interpretation Bulletins**: IT-243R4: Dividend refund to private corporations.

### (2.1) Interest on dividend refund
— Where a dividend refund for a taxation year is paid to, or applied to a liability of, a corporation, the Minister shall pay or apply interest on the refund at the prescribed rate for the period beginning on the day that is the later of

(a) the day that is 120 days after the end of the year, and

(b) the day on which the corporation's return of income under this Part for the year was filed under section 150, unless the return was filed on or before the day on or before which it was required to be filed,

and ending on the day on which the refund is paid or applied.

**Related Provisions**: 161.1 — Offset of refund interest against arrears interest.

**Notes**: 129(2.1) added by 1992 technical bill, effective for dividend refunds paid or applied in respect of taxation years that begin after 1991.

**Regulations**: 4301(b) (prescribed rate of interest).

### (2.2) Excess interest on dividend refund
— Where, at any particular time, interest has been paid to, or applied to a liability of, a corporation under subsection (2.1) in respect of a dividend refund and it is determined at a subsequent time that the dividend refund was less than that in respect of which interest was so paid or applied,

(a) the amount by which the interest that was so paid or applied exceeds the interest, if any, computed in respect of the amount that is determined at the subsequent time to be the dividend refund shall be deemed to be an amount (in this subsection referred to as the "amount payable") that became payable under this Part by the corporation at the particular time;

(b) the corporation shall pay to the Receiver General interest at the prescribed rate on the amount payable, computed from the particular time to the day of payment; and

Division F — Special Rules in Certain Circumstances     S. 129(3)

(c) the Minister may at any time assess the corporation in respect of the amount payable and, where the Minister makes such an assessment, the provisions of Divisions I and J apply, with such modifications as the circumstances require, in respect of the assessment as though it had been made under section 152.

**Related Provisions**: 20(1)(ll) — Deduction on repayment of interest; 161.1 — Offset of refund interest against arrears interest; 221.1 — Application of interest where legislation retroactive; 248(11) — Interest compounded daily.

**Notes**: 129(2.2) added by 1992 technical bill, effective for dividend refunds paid or applied in respect of taxation years that begin after 1991.

**Regulations**: 4301(a) (prescribed rate of interest).

**(3) Definition of "refundable dividend tax on hand"** — In this section, "refundable dividend tax on hand" of a corporation at the end of a taxation year means the amount, if any, by which the total of

(a) where the corporation was a Canadian-controlled private corporation throughout the year, the least of

(i) the amount determined by the formula

$$A - B$$

where

A is $26^2/_3\%$ of the corporation's aggregate investment income for the year, and

B is the amount, if any, by which

(I) the amount deducted under subsection 126(1) from the tax for the year otherwise payable by it under this Part

exceeds

(II) $9^1/_3\%$ of its foreign investment income for the year,

(ii) $26^2/_3\%$ of the amount, if any, by which the corporation's taxable income for the year exceeds the total of

(A) the least of the amounts determined under paragraphs 125(1)(a) to (c) in respect of the corporation for the year,

(B) $^{25}/_9$ of the total of amounts deducted under subsection 126(1) from its tax for the year otherwise payable under this Part, and

(C) $^{10}/_4$ of the total of amounts deducted under subsection 126(2) from its tax for the year otherwise payable under this Part, and

(iii) the corporation's tax for the year payable under this Part determined without reference to section 123.2,

(b) the total of the taxes under Part IV payable by the corporation for the year, and

(c) where the corporation was a private corporation at the end of its preceding taxation year, the corporation's refundable dividend tax on hand at the end of that preceding year

exceeds

(d) the corporation's dividend refund for its preceding taxation year.

**Related Provisions**: 129(3.1) — Grandfathering for property disposed of before November 13, 1981; 141.1 — Insurance corporation deemed not to be private corporation; 257 — Formula cannot calculate to less than zero.

**Notes**: See Notes to 129(1) for a general explanation of the calculation of the dividend refund. The calculation of B factors in the effect of the foreign tax credit.

129(3) completely rewritten by 1995 Budget, effective for taxation years that end after June 1995 except that, for such years that began before July 1995, in computing the amount determined under each of 129(3)(a)(i) and (ii), there shall be deducted an amount equal to that proportion of $^1/_4$ of the amount otherwise determined under the subparagraph that the number of days in the year that are before July 1995 is of the number of days in the year. (The $^1/_4$ has the effect of reducing the inclusion rate from 26.6667% to the former rate of 20%, since $^1/_4$ of 26.6667% is 6.6667%.)

For earlier taxation years, read:

(3) Definition of "refundable dividend tax on hand" — In this section, "refundable dividend tax on hand" of a corporation at the end of any particular taxation year means the amount, if any, by which the total of

(a) the total of all amounts each of which is an amount in respect of a taxation year commencing after it last became a private corporation and ending not later than the end of the particular taxation year and, where the taxation year commences after November 12, 1981, throughout which the corporation was a Canadian-controlled private corporation, equal to, in respect of taxation years ending before 1978, the least of, in respect of taxation years ending after 1977 and commencing before 1987, $^2/_3$ of the least of, in respect of taxation years commencing after 1986 and before 1988, the least of, and in respect of taxation years commencing after 1987, $^4/_5$ of the least of

(i) 25% of the total of all amounts each of which is

(A) in respect of a taxation year ending before November 13, 1981, the amount, if any, by which the total of its Canadian investment income for the year and its foreign investment income for the year exceeds the amount deductible under paragraph 111(1)(b) from the corporation's income for the year, or

(B) in respect of a taxation year ending after November 12, 1981, the amount, if any, by which the total of the amounts that would, if subsection (4) were read without reference to C in the definition "Canadian investment income" in that subsection, be its Canadian investment income for the year and its foreign investment income for the year, exceeds the total of

(I) the amount, if any, deducted under paragraph 111(1)(b) from the corporation's income for the year, and

(II) the total of all amounts each of which is the amount of the corporation's loss for the year from a source that is property,

(ii) the amount, if any, by which the total of

(A) 25% of the corporation's Canadian investment income for the year, and

(B) the amount, if any, by which 30% of the corporation's foreign investment income for the

1203

year exceeds the total of amounts deducted under subsection 126(1) from the tax for the year otherwise payable by it under this Part,

exceeds 25% of the amount, if any, deducted under paragraph 111(1)(b) from the corporation's income for the year,

(iii) 25% of the amount, if any, by which the corporation's taxable income for the year exceeds the total of

(A) the least of the amounts determined under paragraphs 125(1)(a) to (c) in respect of the corporation for the year,

(B) $10/3$ of the total of amounts deducted under subsection 126(1) from its tax for the year otherwise payable under this Part, and

(C) $10/4$ of the total of amounts deducted under subsection 126(2) from its tax for the year otherwise payable under this Part, and

(iv) $5/4$ of the amount of the corporation's tax for the year payable under this Part determined without reference to section 123.2,

(b) the total of the taxes under Part IV payable by the corporation for the particular taxation year and any previous taxation years ending after it last became a private corporation, and

(b.1) the amount, if any, of the corporation's addition at December 31, 1986 of refundable dividend tax on hand

exceeds the total of

(c) the total of the corporation's dividend refunds for taxation years ending after it last became a private corporation and before the particular taxation year,

(d) the amount, if any, of the corporation's reduction at December 31, 1977 of refundable dividend tax on hand, and

(e) the amount, if any, of the corporation's reduction at December 31, 1987 of refundable dividend tax on hand.

**Interpretation Bulletins**: IT-243R4: Dividend refund to private corporations; IT-269R3: Part IV tax on taxable dividends received by a private corporation or a subject corporation.

**Forms**: T713: Addition at December 31, 1986 of RDTOH.

**(3.1)–(3.5) [Repealed]**

**Notes**: 129(3.1)–(3.5) repealed by 1995 Budget, effective for taxation years that end after June 1995. For earlier taxation years since 1988, read:

(3.1) Definition of "reduction at December 31, 1977 of refundable dividend tax on hand" — In subsection (3), "reduction at December 31, 1977 of refundable dividend tax on hand" of a corporation means the amount that is $1/3$ of the amount, if any, by which the total of

(a) the amount, if any, of the corporation's refundable dividend tax on hand at the end of its 1977 taxation year, and

(b) the amount, if any, of the tax under Part IV payable by the corporation for its 1978 taxation year in respect of taxable dividends received by it in that year and before 1978,

exceeds the total of

(c) the corporation's dividend refund, if any, for its 1977 taxation year, and

(d) $1/3$ of the taxable dividends, if any, paid by the corporation in its 1978 taxation year and before 1978.

(3.2) Application — Where, in a taxation year commencing after November 12, 1981, a corporation that last became a private corporation on or before that date and that was throughout the year a private corporation, other than a Canadian-controlled private corporation, has included in its income for the year an amount in respect of property that the corporation

(a) disposed of before November 13, 1981,

(b) was obligated to dispose of under the terms of an agreement in writing entered into before November 13, 1981, or

(c) is deemed by subsection 44(2) to have disposed of at any time after November 12, 1981 by virtue of an event referred to in paragraph (b), (c) or (d) of the definition "proceeds of disposition" in section 54 in respect of the disposition that occurred before November 13, 1981,

paragraph (3)(a) shall apply as if the corporation were a Canadian-controlled private corporation throughout the year, except that the total of the amounts determined under that paragraph in respect of the year shall not exceed the amount that would be so determined if the only income of the corporation for the year were the amount included in respect of the disposition of such property.

(3.3) Definition of "addition at December 31, 1986 of refundable dividend tax on hand" — In subsection (3), "addition at December 31, 1986 of refundable dividend tax on hand" of a corporation means the amount that is $1/2$ of the amount, if any, by which

(a) the amount, if any, of the corporation's refundable dividend tax on hand at the end of its last taxation year commencing before 1987, determined without reference to paragraph (3)(b.1),

exceeds the total of

(b) the amount, if any, of the tax payable under Part IV by the corporation for its last taxation year commencing before 1987 in respect of taxable dividends received by it in that year and after 1986,

(c) $1/4$ of the taxable dividends, if any, paid by the corporation before 1987 in its last taxation year commencing before 1987, and

(d) any amount added under paragraph 88(1)(e.5) in computing the corporation's refundable dividend tax on hand at the end of its last taxation year commencing before 1987 in respect of the refundable dividend tax on hand of a subsidiary (within the meaning assigned by subsection 88(1)) for its 1987 or 1988 taxation year.

(3.4) Reduction under para. (3.3)(a) — Where a corporation has received a taxable dividend after February 25, 1986 and before 1987 as part of a transaction effected after February 25, 1986 or series of transactions each of which was effected after that day and it may be reasonably considered that one of the main purposes thereof was to increase the corporation's refundable dividend tax on hand at the end of a taxation year by virtue of the application of subsection (3.3), the amount otherwise determined under paragraph (3.3)(a) in respect of the corporation shall be reduced by the tax payable under Part IV by the corporation in respect of the dividend.

(3.5) Definition of "reduction at December 31, 1987 of refundable dividend tax on hand" — In subsection (3), "reduction at December 31, 1987 of refundable dividend tax on hand" of a corporation means the amount that is $1/4$ of the amount, if any, by which

(a) the amount, if any, of the corporation's refundable dividend tax on hand at the end of its last taxation year commencing before 1988, determined without reference to paragraph (3)(e),

exceeds the total of

(b) the amount, if any, of the tax payable under Part IV by the corporation for its last taxation year commencing before 1988 in respect of taxable dividends received by it in that year and after 1987,

(c) ⅓ of the taxable dividends, if any, paid by the corporation before 1988 in its last taxation year commencing before 1988,

(d) any amount added, under paragraph 88(1)(e.5) in computing the corporation's refundable dividend tax on hand at the end of its last taxation year beginning before 1988, in respect of the refundable dividend tax on hand of a subsidiary (within the meaning assigned by subsection 88(1)) for a taxation year ending after 1987, and

(e) an amount equal to that proportion of ⅓ of the least of the amounts determined under subparagraphs (3)(a)(i) to (iv) in respect of its last taxation year commencing before 1988 that the number of days in the year that are after 1987 is of the number of days in the year.

### Proposed Addition — 129(3.1)

**(3.1) Application** — Where, in a taxation year that begins after November 12, 1981, a corporation that last became a private corporation on or before that date and that was throughout the year a private corporation, other than a Canadian-controlled private corporation, has included in its income for the year an amount in respect of property that the corporation

(a) disposed of before November 13, 1981,

(b) was obligated to dispose of under the terms of an agreement in writing entered into before November 13, 1981, or

(c) is deemed by subsection 44(2) to have disposed of at any time after November 12, 1981 because of an event referred to in paragraph (b), (c) or (d) of the definition "proceeds of disposition" in section 54 in respect of the disposition that occurred before November 13, 1981,

paragraph 3(a) shall apply as if the corporation were a Canadian-controlled private corporation throughout the year, except that the total of the amounts determined under that paragraph in respect of the corporation for the year shall not exceed the amount that would be so determined if the only income of the corporation for the year were the amount included in respect of the disposition of such property.

**Notes**: In the closing words, "paragraph 3(a) shall apply" should read "paragraph (3)(a) shall apply", in order to refer correctly to 129(3)(a).

**Application**: Bill C-43 (First Reading September 20, 2000), s. 80, will add subsec. 129(3.1), applicable to taxation years that end after June 1995 and before 2003.

**Technical Notes**: New subsection 129(3.1) revives a transitional rule previously contained in subsection 129(3.2). That transitional rule allowed a private corporation, other than a Canadian-controlled private corporation (CCPC), to include in its refundable dividend tax on hand (RDTOH) for taxation years commencing after November 12, 1981 certain income in respect of property disposed of by it before November 13, 1981. The rule was intended to allow certain private corporations that were not CCPCs to benefit for a transitional period from some aspects of the RDTOH scheme that became, after 1981, limited only to CCPCs.

The RDTOH computation rules were subsequently simplified for taxation years ending after June 1995. As part of this simplification process, subsection 129(3.2) was repealed on the assumption that it had fulfilled its transitional function. It has since been determined that, despite the passage of almost 14 years since the transitional provision was enacted, at least one taxpayer was still using subsection 129(3.2) in 1995. The rule is therefore being revived for taxation years ending after June 1995 and before 2003, in order to give adequate opportunity for this and any other taxpayers who may be relying on the rule to adjust to the 1981 RDTOH provisions.

**Letter from Department of Finance, May 18, 1999**:

Dear [xxx]

SUBJECT: *Repeal of subsection 129(3.2) of the Income Tax Act*

This is in response to your letters dated March 30, 1999 and April 21, 1999 regarding the repeal of subsection 129(3.2) of the *Income Tax Act*, and the effect of that repeal on [xxx]. As you know, subsection 129(3.2) was a transitional provision that allowed a private corporation, other than a Canadian-controlled private corporation, to include in its refundable dividend tax on hand for taxation years commencing after November 12, 1981 certain income in respect of property disposed of by it before November 13, 1981.

According to the information you have provided, [xxx] has relied on subsection 129(3.2) for calculating income taxes on property income which it has continued to earn under an agreement entered into on February 20, 1974. You have provided a letter showing that Revenue Canada has, until recently, accepted the applicability of subsection 129(3.2) with respect to this income. However, you state that the repeal of the subsection effective for taxation years ending after June 1995 has led Revenue Canada to review [xxx]'s corporate income tax returns for the 1996, 1997 and 1998 taxation years. Your concern is that your client will lose the benefit of the grandfathering that was available to it under subsection 129(3.2) unless the repeal is reversed.

We have reviewed this matter and agree with you that the repeal of subsection 129(3.2) was not intended to effect any substantive change to the law. Rather, it was our understanding at the time that taxpayers were no longer relying on this transitional provision, and hence that the grandfathering was no longer necessary. From our policy point of view, the effect on your client is therefore an unintended result.

I can confirm therefore that we will recommend an amendment to the *Income Tax Act* to revive subsection 129(3.2), so as to continue the grandfathering that was previously available under that subsection, effective for taxation years ending after June 1995. However, since the subsection was intended only as a transitional rule, it is our view that it should not apply for an indefinite period of time. Accordingly, we believe that it would be appropriate to terminate the effect of the revived subsection for taxation years ending after November 12, 2001, thus allowing corporations such as your client a 20-year transition period to rely on subsection 129(3.2). We shall therefore recommend, for inclusion in the next package of income tax technical amendments, the restoration of the subsection for the period from 1995 to November 12, 2001.

I trust that this addresses the concerns you have raised in your letters. I am forwarding a copy of this letter to Revenue Canada to let them know of our intention to recommend this change.

Thank you for bringing this matter to our attention.

Yours sincerely,

Brian Ernewein
Director
Tax Legislation Division, Tax Policy Branch
c.c.: Mr. Jim Gauvreau, Revenue Canada

**(4) Definitions** — The definitions in this subsection apply in this section.

**"aggregate investment income"** of a corporation for a taxation year means the amount, if any, by which the total of all amounts, each of which is

(a) the amount, if any, by which

(i) the eligible portion of the corporation's taxable capital gains for the year

exceeds the total of

(ii) the eligible portion of its allowable capital losses for the year, and

(iii) the amount, if any, deducted under paragraph 111(1)(b) in computing its taxable income for the year, or

(b) the corporation's income for the year from a source that is a property, other than

(i) exempt income,

(ii) an amount included under subsection 12(10.2) in computing the corporation's income for the year,

(iii) the portion of any dividend that was deductible in computing the corporation's taxable income for the year, and

(iv) income that, but for paragraph 108(5)(a), would not be income from a property,

exceeds the total of all amounts, each of which is the corporation's loss for the year from a source that is a property;

**Related Provisions:** 123.3 — Refundable tax on CCPC's investment income; 129(3)(a)(i)A — Refund of 26²⁄₃% of aggregate investment income; 129(4)"income" or "loss" — Specified investment business income and income relating to an active business; 131(11)(b) — Application of definition to labour-sponsored venture capital corporation.

**Notes:** Definition "aggregate investment income" added by 1995 Budget, effective for taxation years that end after June 1995. (For earlier years, see "Canadian investment income" below.)

**Interpretation Bulletins:** IT-484R2: Business investment losses.

**"Canadian investment income"** — [Repealed]

**Notes:** Definition "Canadian investment income" repealed by 1995 Budget, effective for taxation years that end after June 1995. For earlier taxation years since 1991, read:

"Canadian investment income" of a corporation for a taxation year means the amount determined by the formula

$$(A + B) - C$$

where

A is the amount determined by the formula

$$(K - L) - (M - N)$$

where

K is the total of such of the corporation's taxable capital gains for the year from dispositions of property as may reasonably be considered to be income from sources in Canada,

L is the total of all amounts each of which is the portion of a taxable capital gain referred to in the description of K in this definition from the disposition by it of a property, other than a designated property, that may reasonably be regarded as having accrued while the property, or a property for which it was substituted, was property of a corporation other than a Canadian-controlled private corporation, an investment corporation, a mortgage investment corporation or a mutual fund corporation,

M is the total of such of the corporation's allowable capital losses for the year from dispositions of property as may reasonably be considered to be losses from sources in Canada, and

N is the total of all amounts each of which is the portion of an allowable capital loss referred to in the description of M in this definition from the disposition by it of a property, other than a designated property, that may reasonably be regarded as having accrued while the property, or a property for which it was substituted, was property of a corporation other than a Canadian-controlled private corporation, an investment corporation, a mortgage investment corporation or a mutual fund corporation,

B is the total of all amounts each of which is the corporation's income for the year from a source in Canada that is property (other than exempt income, an amount included under subsection 12(10.2) in the corporation's income for the year, any dividend the amount of which was deductible in computing its taxable income for the year or income that, but for paragraph 108(5)(a), would not be income from a property), determined after deducting all outlays and expenses deductible in computing the corporation's income for the year to the extent that they can reasonably be regarded as having been made or incurred for the purpose of earning income from that property[, and]

C is the total of all amounts each of which is the corporation's loss for the year from a source in Canada that is a property;

See now "aggregate investment income" above.

Description of "B" (formerly 129(4)(a)(ii)) amended by 1992 technical bill, effective for 1991 and later taxation years, to exclude payments received under a net income stabilization account from "Canadian investment income". For earlier years, ignore the words "an amount included under subsection 12(10.2) in the corporation's income for the year".

129(4)"Canadian investment income" was 129(4)(a) before consolidation in R.S.C. 1985 (5th Supp.), effective for taxation years ending after November 1991. The previous version, identical in meaning, was in descriptive rather than formula form.

**"eligible portion"** of a corporation's taxable capital gains or allowable capital losses for a taxation year is the total of all amounts each of which is the portion of a taxable capital gain or an allowable capital loss, as the case may be, of the corporation for the year from a disposition of a property that, except where the property was a designated property (within the meaning assigned by subsection 89(1)), cannot reasonably be regarded as having accrued while the property, or a property for which it was substituted, was property of a corporation other than a Canadian-controlled private corporation, an investment corporation, a mortgage investment corporation or a mutual fund corporation;

**Related Provisions**: 248(5) — Substituted property.

**Notes**: Definition "eligible portion" added by 1995 Budget, effective for taxation years that end after June 1995.

**"foreign investment income"** of a corporation for a taxation year is the amount that would be its aggregate investment income for the year if

(a) every amount of its income, loss, capital gain or capital loss for the year that can reasonably be regarded as being from a source in Canada were nil,

(b) no amount were deducted under paragraph 111(1)(b) in computing its taxable income for the year, and

(c) this Act were read without reference to paragraph (a) of the definition "income" or "loss" in this subsection;

**Notes**: Definition "foreign investment income" amended by 1995 Budget, effective for taxation years that end after June 1995. For earlier taxation years since 1980, read:

> "foreign investment income" of a corporation for a taxation year means the amount that would be determined under the definition "Canadian investment income" in this subsection in respect of the corporation for the year if the references in that definition to "in Canada" were read as references to "outside Canada" and this Act were read without reference to subsection (4.1).

129(4)"foreign investment income" was 129(4)(b) before consolidation in R.S.C. 1985 (5th Supp.), effective for taxation years ending after November 1991.

**"income" or "loss"** of a corporation for a taxation year from a source that is a property

(a) includes the income or loss from a specified investment business carried on by it in Canada other than income or loss from a source outside Canada, but

(b) does not include the income or loss from any property

(i) that is incident to or pertains to an active business carried on by it, or

(ii) that is used or held principally for the purpose of gaining or producing income from an active business carried on by it.

**Related Provisions**: 129(4)"foreign investment income"(c) — Para. (a) ignored for purposes of determining foreign investment income.

**Notes**: Definition "income or loss" added by 1995 Budget, effective for taxation years that end after June 1995. This was formerly 129(4.1) and (4.2).

**(4.1), (4.2), (4.3), (5) [Repealed]**

**Notes**: 129(4.1) and (4.2) repealed by 1995 Budget, effective for taxation years that end after June 1995. See now 129(4)"income" or "loss". For earlier taxation years since 1985, read:

> (4.1) **Interpretation of "income" or "loss"** — For the purposes of the definition "Canadian investment income" in subsection (4) and subsection (6), "income" or "loss" of a corporation for a year from a source in Canada that is a property includes the income or loss from a specified investment business carried on by it in Canada other than income or loss from a source outside Canada but does not include income or loss
>
> (a) from any other business;
>
> (b) from any property that is incident to or pertains to an active business carried on by it; or
>
> (c) from any property used or held principally for the purpose of gaining or producing income from an active business carried on by it.
>
> (4.2) **Idem** — For the purposes of the definition "foreign investment income" in subsection (4), "income" or "loss" of a corporation for a year from a source outside Canada that is a property does not include the income or loss from any property
>
> (a) that is incident to or pertains to an active business carried on by it; or
>
> (b) that is used or held principally for the purpose of gaining or producing income from an active business carried on by it.

129(4.3) repealed by 1995 Budget, effective for taxation years that end after June 1995. For earlier taxation years since November 13, 1981, read:

> (4.3) **Definition of "designated property"** — In this section, "designated property" has the meaning assigned by subsection 89(1).

129(5) repealed by 1995 Budget, effective for taxation years that end after June 1995. For earlier taxation years since 1978, read:

> (5) **Reduction of refundable dividend tax on hand** — Notwithstanding any other provision of this section, the least of the amounts determined under subparagraphs (3)(a)(i) to (iv) in respect of the 1972 or 1973 taxation year of a corporation is,
>
> (a) in respect of its 1972 taxation year, 93% of the least of the amounts so determined; and
>
> (b) in respect of its 1973 taxation year, the total of
>
> (i) 93% of that proportion of the least of the amounts so determined that the number of days in that portion of the year that is before 1973 is of the number of days in the whole year, and
>
> (ii) 100% of that proportion of the least of the amounts so determined that the number of days in that portion of the year that is after 1972 is of the number of days in the whole year.

**(6) Investment income from associated corporation deemed to be active business income** — Where any particular amount paid or payable to a corporation (in this subsection referred to as the "recipient corporation") by another corporation (in this subsection referred to as the "associated corporation") with which the recipient corporation was associated in any particular taxation year commencing after 1972, would otherwise be included in computing the income of the recipient corporation

**S. 129(6)**        Income Tax Act, Part I

for the particular year from a source in Canada that is a property, the following rules apply:

  (a) for the purposes of subsection (4), in computing the recipient corporation's income for the year from a source in Canada that is a property,

    (i) there shall not be included any portion (in this subsection referred to as the "deductible portion") of the particular amount that was or may be deductible in computing the income of the associated corporation for any taxation year from an active business carried on by it in Canada, and

    (ii) no deduction shall be made in respect of any outlay or expense, to the extent that that outlay or expense may reasonably be regarded as having been made or incurred by the recipient corporation for the purpose of gaining or producing the deductible portion; and

  (b) for the purposes of this subsection and section 125,

    (i) the deductible portion shall be deemed to be income of the recipient corporation for the particular year from an active business carried on by it in Canada, and

    (ii) any outlay or expense, to the extent described in subparagraph (a)(ii), shall be deemed to have been made or incurred by the recipient corporation for the purpose of gaining or producing that income.

**Related Provisions**: 125(3) — Allocation of active business income among associated corporations; 256(1) — Associated corporations.

**Notes**: 129(6) allows the character of active business income to be preserved when it is paid as income from property (e.g. interest or rent) to an associated corporation. Thus, it can remain eligible for the small business deduction (s. 125), and will not be investment income that creates refundable dividend tax on hand for purposes of s. 129.

**Interpretation Bulletins**: IT-73R5: The small business deduction; IT-243R4: Dividend refund to private corporations.

**(7) Meaning of "taxable dividend"** — For the purposes of this section, "taxable dividend" does not include a capital gains dividend within the meaning assigned by subsection 131(1).

**Related Provisions**: 129(1.2) — Dividends deemed not to be taxable dividends; 157(3) — Private, mutual fund and non-resident owned investment corporations.

**(8) Application of section 125** — Expressions used in this section and not otherwise defined for the purposes of this section have the same meanings as in section 125.

**Definitions [s. 129]**: "active business" — 125(7), 129(8), 248(1); "aggregate investment income" — 129(4); "allowable capital loss" — 38(b), 248(1); "amount", "assessment" — 248(1); "associated corporation" — 256(1); "business" — 248(1); "Canada" — 255; "Canadian-controlled private corporation" — 125(7), 248(1); "Canadian investment income" — 129(4), (8); "carrying on business" — 253; "corporation" — 248(1), *Interpretation Act* 35(1); "designated property" — 89(1), 129(4.3); "dividend" — 248(1); "dividend refund" — 129(1); "eligible portion" — 129(4); "exempt income" — 248(1); "foreign investment income", "foreign investment loss" — 129(4); "income" — from property 129(4.1), (4.2); "income of the corporation for the year from an active business" — 125(7), 129(6), 129(8); "investment corporation" — 130(3), 248(1); "investment tax credit" — 127(9), 248(1); "loss" — from property 129(4.1), (4.2); "Minister" — 248(1); "prescribed rate" — Reg. 4301; "private corporation" — 89(1), 131(5), 186(5), 248(1); "property" — 129(4.1), (4.2), 248(1); "refundable dividend tax on hand" — 129(3); "series of transactions or events" — 248(10); "share" — 248(1); "specified investment business" — 125(7), 248(1); "substituted property" — 248(5); "tax payable" — 248(2); "taxable capital gain" — 38(a), 248(1); "taxable dividend" — 89(1), 129(1.2), 129(7), 248(1); "taxable income" — 2(2), 248(1); "taxation year" — 249; "writing" — *Interpretation Act* 35(1).

## Investment Corporations

**130. (1) Deduction from tax** — A corporation that was, throughout a taxation year, an investment corporation may deduct from the tax otherwise payable by it under this Part for the year an amount equal to 20% of the amount, if any, by which its taxable income for the year exceeds its taxed capital gains for the year.

**Related Provisions**: 131(10) — Investment corporation can elect not to be restricted financial institution; 142.2(1)"financial institution"(c)(i) — Investment corporation not subject to mark-to-market rules.

**Interpretation Bulletins**: IT-98R2: Investment corporations.

**(2) Application of subsecs. 131(1) to (3.2) and (6)** — Where a corporation was an investment corporation throughout a taxation year (other than a corporation that was a mutual fund corporation throughout the year), subsections 131(1) to (3.2) and (6) apply in respect of the corporation for the year

  (a) as if the corporation had been a mutual fund corporation throughout that and all previous taxation years ending after 1971 throughout which it was an investment corporation; and

  (b) as if its capital gains redemptions for that and all previous taxation years ending after 1971, throughout which it would, but for the assumption made by paragraph (a), not have been a mutual fund corporation, were nil.

**Notes**: 130(2) amended by 1992 technical bill, effective for capital gains refunds paid or applied in respect of taxation years that begin after 1991, to add references to 131(3.1) and (3.2); and by 1995-97 technical bill, effective for 1993 and later taxation years, to add reference to 131(6).

**Interpretation Bulletins**: IT-98R2: Investment corporations.

**Forms**: T5 Segment; T5 Summary: Return of investment income; T5 Supplementary: Statement of investment income.

**(3) Meaning of expressions "investment corporation" and "taxed capital gains"** — For the purposes of this section,

  (a) a corporation is an "investment corporation" throughout any taxation year in respect of which the expression is being applied if it complied with the following conditions:

    (i) it was throughout the year a Canadian corporation that was a public corporation,

(ii) at least 80% of its property throughout the year consisted of shares, bonds, marketable securities or cash,

(iii) not less than 95% of its income (determined without reference to subsection 49(2)) for the year was derived from, or from dispositions of, investments described in subparagraph (ii),

(iv) not less than 85% of its gross revenue for the year was from sources in Canada,

(v) not more than 25% of its gross revenue for the year was from interest,

(vi) at no time in the year did more than 10% of its property consist of shares, bonds or securities of any one corporation or debtor other than Her Majesty in right of Canada or of a province or a Canadian municipality,

(vii) no person would have been a specified shareholder of the corporation in the year if

(A) the portion of the definition "specified shareholder" in subsection 248(1) before paragraph (a) were read as follows:

""specified shareholder" of a corporation in a taxation year means a taxpayer who owns, directly or indirectly, at any time in the year, more than 25% of the issued shares of any class of the capital stock of the corporation and, for the purposes of this definition,"

(B) paragraph (a) of that definition were read as follows:

"(a) a taxpayer is deemed to own each share of the capital stock of a corporation owned at that time by a person related to the taxpayer,"

(C) that definition were read without reference to paragraph (d) of that definition, and

(D) paragraph 251(2)(a) were read as follows:

"(a) an individual and

(i) the individual's child (as defined in subsection 70(10)) who is under 19 years of age, or

(ii) the individual's spouse or common-law partner;"

(viii) an amount not less than 85% of the total of

(A) ⅔ of the amount, if any, by which its taxable income for the year exceeds its taxed capital gains for the year, and

(B) the amount, if any, by which all taxable dividends received by it in the year to the extent of the amount thereof deductible under section 112 or 113 from its income for the year exceeds the amount that the corporation's non-capital loss for the year would be if the amount determined in respect of the corporation for the year under paragraph 3(b) was nil,

(less any dividends or interest received by it in the form of shares, bonds or other securities that had not been sold before the end of the year) was distributed, otherwise than by way of capital gains dividends, to its shareholders before the end of the year; and

(b) the amount of the "taxed capital gains" of a taxpayer for a taxation year is the amount, if any, by which

(i) its taxable capital gains for the year from dispositions of property

exceeds

(ii) the total of its allowable capital losses for the year from dispositions of property and the amount, if any, deducted under paragraph 111(1)(b) for the purpose of computing its taxable income for the year.

**Related Provisions**: 4(1) — Income or loss from a source; 112 — Deduction of dividends received; 113 — Deduction for dividends from foreign affiliate; 130(2) — Application of mutual fund corporation rules; 130(4) — Wholly owned subsidiaries; 132(5) — Taxed capital gains definition applies to mutual fund trusts; 184(2) — Tax on excess dividend paid by corporation; 248(1)"investment corporation" — Definition applies to entire Act.

**Notes**: 130(3)(a)(iii) amended by 1991 technical bill, effective 1990, to add the parenthetical instruction to ignore 49(2).

130(3)(a)(vii)(D) amended by 2000 same-sex partners bill to add reference to "common-law partner", effective for the 2001 and later taxation years, or earlier by election (see Notes to 248(1)"common-law partner").

130(3)(a)(vii) amended by 1995-97 technical bill (subsec. 155(2) of the bill), as itself amended by 1998 Budget bill (s. 92), effective for corporations' taxation years that begin after June 20, 1996. However, subsecs. 155(4)–(11) (originally 155(4)–(9)) of the 1995-97 technical bill, as itself amended by 1998 Budget bill (s. 92), provide the following extensive grandfathering for existing shareholders who would otherwise violate the new 25% test:

(4) [The amendment to 130(3)(a)(vii)] applies to corporations for taxation years that begin after June 20, 1996 except that, where

(a) a corporation was an investment corporation on June 20, 1996,

(b) a particular person is a specified shareholder of the corporation in the year, and

(c) the particular person

(i) was a specified shareholder of the corporation on June 20, 1996, or

(ii) both

(A) was a specified shareholder of the corporation at any time after June 20, 1996 and before August 14, 1998, and

(B) would have been a specified shareholder of the corporation on June 20, 1996 if subparagraph 130(3)(a)(vii), [as amended,] were read without reference to clauses (B) and (D),

subparagraph 130(3)(a)(vii), [as amended,] does not apply to the corporation, with respect to the particular person and persons related to the particular person, except as provided in subsections 155(5) to (11).

(5) [The amendment to 130(3)(a)(vii)] applies to a corporation that was an investment corporation on June 20, 1996 for a taxation year that begins after that day if, at any time after that day and before the end of the year, a particular person described in paragraph [155(4)(b) of the 1995-97 technical bill (above)] in respect of the corporation for the year contributes capital to the corporation or acquires a share of the capital stock of the corporation other than by a permitted acquisition.

(6) [The amendment to 130(3)(a)(vii)] applies to a corporation that was an investment corporation on June 20, 1996 for a taxation year that begins after that day where, at any time after that day and before the end of the year, a newly related person in respect of the corporation

(a) contributed capital to the corporation; or

(b) held at any particular time property (in this paragraph referred to as an "ineligible investment") that is

(i) a share of the capital stock of the corporation, or

(ii) a share of the capital stock of a corporation, or an interest in a partnership or trust, that held an ineligible investment at the particular time.

(7) For the purpose of subsection (6), a newly related person in respect of a corporation at any time means a person who, at any other time that is before that time and after June 20, 1996, became related to a particular person described in paragraph [155(4)(b) of the 1995-97 technical bill (above)] in respect of the corporation, but does not include a person who would, if the taxation year of the corporation that includes that other time had ended immediately before that other time, have been a particular person described in paragraph [155(4)(b) of the 1995-97 technical bill (above)] in respect of the corporation for the year.

(8) [Repealed by 1998 Budget bill]

(9) For the purposes of subsections (5) to (8),

(a) where at a particular time

(i) a trust that existed on June 20, 1996 distributes a share of the capital stock of a corporation to a person who was a beneficiary under the trust throughout the period from June 20, 1996 to the particular time in satisfaction of all or any part of the beneficiary's capital interest in the trust, or

(ii) a partnership that existed on June 20, 1996 distributes, on ceasing to exist, a share of the capital stock of a corporation or an interest in a share to a person who was a member of the partnership throughout the period from June 20, 1996 to the particular time,

the share is deemed to have been owned by the beneficiary or member from the later of June 20, 1996 and the time the share was last acquired by the trust or partnership until the particular time; and

(b) where a person who is a beneficiary of a trust or a member of a partnership is deemed by paragraph (b), (c) or (e) of the definition "specified shareholder" in subsection 248(1) of the Act to own a share owned by the partnership or trust, the person is deemed to have acquired the share at the later of the time the share was last acquired by the trust or partnership and the time the person last became a beneficiary of the trust or a member of the partnership.

(10) At any time on or after the day of the death of a person described in paragraph [155(4)(c) of the 1995-97 technical bill (above)] in respect of a corporation and before the third anniversary of that day,

(a) the estate of the deceased person is deemed to be a person described in paragraphs (4)(b) and (c) [of the said 1995-97 technical bill (above)] who is related to each person who, throughout the period that begins at the end of June 20, 1996 and ends at the time of death, was related to the deceased person;

(b) notwithstanding subsection (7), the estate is deemed not to be a newly related person in respect of the corporation;

(c) notwithstanding subsection (11), the acquisition of shares of the corporation's capital stock by the estate from the deceased person is deemed to be a permitted acquisition; and

(d) the estate is deemed not to be a trust for the purposes of subparagraph (9)(a)(i) of this Act and paragraphs (b) and (e) of the definition "specified shareholder" in subsection 248(1) of the *Income Tax Act*.

(11) The definitions in this subsection apply in subsections (4) to (10) [of the said 1995-97 technical bill (above)] and this subsection.

"permitted acquisition" means an acquisition by a particular person of a share of a class of the capital stock of a corporation that was

(a) held, at each particular time after June 20, 1996 and before the time at which the particular person acquired it, or

(b) issued after June 20, 1996 by the corporation as a stock dividend and held, at each particular time after the time the share was issued and before the time at which the particular person acquired it,

by the particular person or by a person who was related to the particular person throughout the period that begins at the end of June 20, 1996 and ends at the particular time if, immediately after the time at which the particular person acquires the share, the total percentage of the issued shares of that class held by the particular person and persons related to the particular person (or in the case of acquisitions before August 14, 1998, by the particular person and persons with whom the particular person did not deal at arm's length immediately after the acquisition) does not exceed the permitted percentage for the particular person in respect of that class of shares.

"permitted percentage" for a particular person in respect of any class of shares of the capital stock of a corporation means

(a) in respect of acquisitions of shares before August 14, 1998, the greatest percentage that is the total percentage of the issued shares of a class of the capital stock of the corporation held at the end of June 20, 1996 by the particular person and persons with whom the particular person did not at that time deal at arm's length; and

(b) in any other case, the greater of

(i) the greatest percentage that is the total percentage of the issued shares of a class of the capital stock of the corporation held at the end of June 20, 1996 by the particular person and persons related to the particular person, and

(ii) the greatest percentage that is the total percentage of the issued shares of a class of the capital stock of the corporation held at the beginning of August 14, 1998 by the particular person and persons related to the particular person.

"related persons" and persons related to each other have, for purposes other than applying the definitions "permitted acquisition" and "permitted percentage" in respect of acquisitions of shares before August 14, 1998, the meaning that would be assigned by section 251 of the Act if paragraph 251(2)(a) of the Act were read as follows:

(a) an individual and

(i) the individual's child (as defined in subsection 70(10)) who is under 19 years of age, or

(ii) the individual's spouse;

"specified shareholder" has the meaning assigned by subparagraph 130(3)(a)(vii) of the Act, as enacted by subsection (2).

These changes were first announced in a Dept. of Finance news release, August 14, 1998. Before the amendment by 1995-97 technical bill (as itself amended by 1998 Budget bill), read:

(vii) none of its shareholders at any time in the year held more than 25% of the issued shares of the capital stock of the corporation, and

**Interpretation Bulletins**: IT-98R2: Investment corporations.

**(4) Wholly owned subsidiaries** — Where a corporation so elects in its return of income under this Part for a taxation year, each of the corporation's properties that is a share or indebtedness of another Canadian corporation that is at any time in the year a subsidiary wholly owned corporation of the corporation shall, for the purposes of subparagraphs (3)(a)(ii) and (vi), be deemed not to be owned by the corporation at any such time in the year, and each property owned by the other corporation at that time shall, for the purposes of those subparagraphs, be deemed to be owned by the corporation at that time.

**Notes**: 130(4) added by 1991 technical bill, effective 1987. For a year for which the corporation's Part I return was filed before December 18, 1991, the election under 130(4) may be filed with Revenue Canada until March 16, 1992.

**Interpretation Bulletins**: IT-98R2: Investment corporations.

**Definitions [s. 130]**: "allowable capital loss" — 38(b), 248(1); "amount" — 248(1); "Canada" — 255; "Canadian corporation" — 89(1), 248(1); "capital gain" — 39(1)(a), 248(1); "common-law partner" — 248(1); "corporation" — 248(1), *Interpretation Act* 35(1); "dividend", "gross revenue" — 248(1); "investment corporation" — 130(3)(a), 248(1); "mutual fund corporation" — 131(8), 248(1); "property" — 248(1); "public corporation" — 89(1), 248(1); "share", "shareholder", "subsidiary wholly owned corporation" — 248(1); "taxable capital gain" — 38(a), 248(1); "taxable dividend" — 89(1), 248(1); "taxable income" — 2(2), 248(1); "taxation year" — 249; "taxed capital gains" — 130(3)(b).

**Information Circulars [s. 130]**: 78-14R2: Guidelines for trust companies and other persons responsible for filing T3-IND, T3R-G, T3RIF-IND, T3RIF-G, T3H-IND, T3H-G, T3D, T3P, T3S, T3RI, T3F.

## Mortgage Investment Corporations

**130.1 (1) Deduction from tax** — In computing the income for a taxation year of a corporation that was, throughout the year, a mortgage investment corporation,

(a) there may be deducted the total of

(i) all taxable dividends, other than capital gains dividends, paid by the corporation during the year or within 90 days after the end of the year to the extent that those dividends were not deductible by the corporation in computing its income for the preceding year, and

(ii) ¾ of all capital gains dividends paid by the corporation during the period commencing 91 days after the commencement of the year and ending 90 days after the end of the year; and

### Proposed Amendment — 130.1(1)(a)(ii)

**Application**: The December 21, 2000 draft legislation, subsec. 76(1), will amend subpara. 130.1(1)(a)(ii) by replacing the reference to "3/4" with "1/2", applicable to taxation years that end after February 27, 2000 except that, for a corporation's taxation year that includes either February 28, 2000 or October 17, 2000, the reference to "1/2" shall be read as a reference to the fraction in para. 38(a), as amended [by the December 21, 2000 draft legislation], that applies to the corporation for the year.

**Technical Notes**: Section 130.1 sets out rules that apply to mortgage investment corporations and their shareholders. A mortgage investment corporation is essentially treated as a conduit in that its income may be flowed through to its shareholders and taxed in their hands rather than in the corporation.

Subsection 130.1(1) provides rules for calculating the income of a mortgage investment corporation for a taxation year. The amendment to subparagraph 130.1(1)(a)(ii) replaces the reference to the fraction "3/4" with a reference to the fraction "1/2", consequential on the reduction of the inclusion rate for capital gains from 3/4 to 1/2 [see 38(a) — ed.].

The amendment applies to taxation years that end after February 27, 2000 except that, for a taxation year of a mortgage investment corporation that includes either February 28, 2000 or October 17, 2000, the reference to the fraction "1/2" is to be read as reference to the fraction in amended paragraph 38(a) that applies to the corporation for the year. These modifications are required in order to reflect the capital gains/losses rate for the year.

(b) no deduction may be made under section 112 in respect of taxable dividends received by it from other corporations.

**Related Provisions**: 142.2(1)"financial institution"(c)(ii) — Mortgage investment corporation not subject to mark-to-market rules; 181.3(3)(a) — Capital of financial institution.

**(2) Dividend equated to bond interest** — For the purposes of this Act, any amount received from a mortgage investment corporation by a shareholder of the corporation as or on account of a taxable dividend, other than a capital gains dividend, shall be deemed to have been received by the shareholder as interest payable on a bond issued by the corporation after 1971.

**Related Provisions**: 130.1(3) — Application; 214(3)(e) — Non-resident withholding tax.

**(3) Application of subsec. (2)** — Subsection (2) applies where the taxable dividend (other than a capital gains dividend) described in that subsection was paid during a taxation year throughout which the paying corporation was a mortgage investment corporation or within 90 days thereafter.

**(4) Election re capital gains dividend** — Where at any particular time during the period that begins

**S. 130.1(4)**  Income Tax Act, Part I

91 days after the beginning of a taxation year of a corporation that was, throughout the year, a mortgage investment corporation and ends 90 days after the end of the year, a dividend is paid by the corporation to shareholders of the corporation, if the corporation so elects in respect of the full amount of the dividend in prescribed manner and at or before the earlier of the particular time and the first day on which any part of the dividend was paid,

(a) the dividend shall be deemed to be a capital gains dividend to the extent that it does not exceed the amount, if any, by which

(i) $4/3$ of the taxed capital gains of the corporation for the year

### Proposed Amendment — 130.1(4)(a)(i)

**Application**: The December 21, 2000 draft legislation, subsec. 76(2), will amend subpara. 130.1(4)(a)(i) by replacing the expression "4/3 of" with the word "twice", applicable to taxation years that end after February 27, 2000 except that, for a corporation's taxation year that includes either February 28, 2000 or October 17, 2000, the word "twice" shall be read as "the fraction that is the reciprocal of the fraction in para. 38(a), as amended [by the December 21, 2000 draft legislation], that applies to the corporation for the year, multiplied by".

**Technical Notes**: Where a mortgage investment corporation elects in respect of the full amount of a dividend, subsection 130.1(4) deems the dividend to be capital gains dividend to the extent that it does not exceed 4/3 of the undistributed taxed capital gains of the corporation for the year, and the dividend is deemed to be a capital gain of the dividend recipient from the disposition of property in the year in which the dividend was received.

The amendment to subparagraph 130.1(4)(a)(i) replaces the reference to the expression "4/3 of" with a reference to the word "twice". The amendment is consequential on the reduction of the inclusion rate for capital gains from 3/4 to 1/2 [see 38(a) — ed.].

The amendment applies to taxation years that end after February 27, 2000 except that, for a taxation year of a mortgage investment corporation that includes either February 28, 2000 or October 17, 2000, the reference the word "twice" in subparagraph 130.1(4)(a)(i) is to be read as reference to the expression "the fraction that is the reciprocal of the fraction in paragraph 38(a) that applies to the corporation for the year, multiplied by". These modifications are required in order to reflect the capital gains/losses rate for the year.

exceeds

(ii) the total of all dividends, and parts of dividends, paid by the corporation during the period and before the particular time that are deemed by this paragraph to be capital gains dividends; and

(b) notwithstanding any other provision of this Act, any amount received by a taxpayer in a taxation year as, on account of, in lieu of payment of or in satisfaction of, the dividend shall not be included in computing the taxpayer's income for the year as income from a share of the capital stock of the corporation, but shall be deemed to be a capital gain of the taxpayer for the year from a disposition, in the year and after February 22, 1994, by the taxpayer of capital property.

**Related Provisions**: 39.1(1)"exempt capital gains balance"C(c), 39.1(6) — Reduction in gain to reflect capital gains exemption election; 130.1(4.2) — Reporting to shareholder of capital gains tax rate; 130.1(4.3) — Allocation of capital gains tax rate for 2000; 184(2) — Tax on excessive elections; 184(3) — Election to treat excess as separate dividend; 185(4) — Joint and several liability from excessive elections.

**Notes**: 130.1(4) amended by 1994 Budget, effective for dividends paid after February 22, 1994. The change results from the elimination of the general $100,000 capital gains exemption in 110.6(3). Since it is no longer necessary to treat capital gains of a MIC that are flowed out to shareholders as either eligible or ineligible for the exemption, a capital gains dividend is now simply treated as a capital gain in the shareholder's hands.

130.1(4) amended by 1992 technical bill, effective for 1992 and later taxation years, to reflect the capital gains exemption restrictions on real estate exemptions.

**Regulations**: 2104.1 (prescribed manner, prescribed form).

**Forms**: T5 Segment; T5 Summary: Return of investment income; T5 Supplementary: Statement of investment income; T2012: Election in respect of a capital gains dividend.

**(4.1) Application of subsecs. 131(1.1) to (1.4)** — Where at any particular time a mortgage investment corporation paid a dividend to its shareholders and subsection (4) would have applied to the dividend except that the corporation did not make an election under subsection (4) on or before the day on or before which it was required by that subsection to be made, subsections 131(1.1) to (1.4) apply with such modifications as the circumstances require.

### Proposed Addition — 130.1(4.2), (4.3)

**(4.2) Reporting** — Where subparagraph (4)(a)(i) or (ii) applies to a dividend paid by a mortgage investment corporation to a shareholder of any class of shares of its capital stock, the corporation shall disclose to the shareholder in prescribed form the amount of the dividend that is in respect of capital gains realized on dispositions of property that occurred

(a) before February 28, 2000,

(b) after February 27, 2000 and before October 18, 2000, and

(c) after October 17, 2000

and, if it does not do so, the dividend is deemed to be in respect of capital gains realized on dispositions of property that occurred before February 28, 2000.

**Technical Notes**: Subsection 130.1(4) applies where a dividend is payable by a mortgage investment corporation and the corporation elects to have the dividend deemed to be a capital gains dividend. Where that subsection applies in respect of a dividend paid in a taxation year by a mortgage investment corporation to a shareholder of any class of shares of its capital stock, new subsection 130.1(4.2) requires the corporation to disclose to the shareholder in prescribed form the amount of the dividend that can reasonably be considered to have been paid out of its capital gains realized on dispositions by the corporation of property in each of the following three periods in the year:

- before February 28, 2000;
- after February 27, 2000 and before October 18, 2000; and
- after October 17, 2000.

If it does not do so, the dividend is deemed to be in respect of capital gains realized on dispositions of property that occurred before February 27, 2000.

**(4.3) Allocation [for 2000]** — Where subsection (4) applies in respect of a dividend paid by a mortgage investment corporation in the period commencing 90 days after the beginning of the corporation's taxation year that includes either February 28, 2000 or October 17, 2000 and ending 90 days after the end of that year, and the corporation so elects under this subsection in its return of income for the year, the following rules apply:

(a) the portion of the dividend that is in respect of capital gains realized on dispositions of property that occurred in the year and before February 28, 2000 is deemed to equal that proportion of the dividend that the number of days that are in that year and before February 28, 2000 is of the number of days that are in that year;

(b) the portion of the dividend that is in respect of capital gains realized on dispositions of property that occurred in the year and in the period that began at the beginning of February 28, 2000 and ended at the end of October 17, 2000 is deemed to equal that proportion of the dividend that the number of days that are in the year and in that period is of the number of days that are in the year; and

(c) the portion of the dividend that is in respect of capital gains realized on dispositions of property that occurred in the year and in the period that begins at the beginning of October 18, 2000 and ends at the end of the year, is deemed to equal that proportion of the dividend that the number of days that are in the year and in that period is of the number of days that are in the year.

**Technical Notes**: New subsection 130.1(4.3) provides that a mortgage investment corporation can elect, for its taxation year that includes either February 28, 2000 or October 17, 2000, to apportion its capital gains dividends for the year amongst the three periods in the year described above.

The portion for each period is determined to be that proportion of the dividend that the number of days that are in the year and in that period is of the number of days in the year.

**Application**: The December 21, 2000 draft legislation, subsec. 76(3), will add subsecs. 130.1(4.2) and (4.3), applicable to taxation years that end after February 27, 2000.

**(5) Public corporation** — Notwithstanding any other provision of this Act, a mortgage investment corporation shall be deemed to be a public corporation.

**(6) Meaning of "mortgage investment corporation"** — For the purposes of this section, a corporation is a "mortgage investment corporation" throughout a taxation year if, throughout the year,

(a) it was a Canadian corporation;

(b) its only undertaking was the investing of funds of the corporation and it did not manage or develop any real property;

(c) none of the property of the corporation consisted of

(i) debts owing to the corporation that were secured on real property situated outside Canada,

(ii) debts owing to the corporation by non-resident persons, except any such debts that were secured on real property situated in Canada,

(iii) shares of the capital stock of corporations not resident in Canada, or

(iv) real property situated outside Canada, or any leasehold interest in such property;

(d) there were 20 or more shareholders of the corporation and no person would have been a specified shareholder of the corporation at any time in the year if

(i) the portion of the definition "specified shareholder" in subsection 248(1) before paragraph (a) were read as follows:

" "specified shareholder" of a corporation at any time means a taxpayer who owns, directly or indirectly, at that time, more than 25% of the issued shares of any class of the capital stock of the corporation and, for the purposes of this definition,"

(ii) paragraph (a) of that definition were read as follows:

"(a) a taxpayer is deemed to own each share of the capital stock of a corporation owned at that time by a person related to the taxpayer,"

(iii) that definition were read without reference to paragraph (d) of that definition, and

(iv) paragraph 251(2)(a) were read as follows:

"(a) an individual and

(i) the individual's child (as defined in subsection 70(10)) who is under 18 years of age, or

(ii) the individual's spouse or common-law partner;"

(e) any holders of preferred shares of the corporation had a right, after payment to them of their preferred dividends, and payment of dividends in a like amount per share to the holders of the common shares of the corporation, to participate *pari passu* with the holders of the common shares in any further payment of dividends;

(f) the cost amount to the corporation of such of its property as consisted of

(i) debts owing to the corporation that were secured, whether by mortgages or in any other manner, on houses (as defined in section 2 of the *National Housing Act*) or on property included within a housing project (as defined in that section), and

(ii) amounts of any deposits standing to the corporation's credit in the records of

(A) a bank or other corporation any of whose deposits are insured by the Canada Deposit Insurance Corporation or the Régie de l'assurance-dépôts du Québec, or

(B) a credit union,

plus the amount of any money of the corporation was at least 50% of the cost amount to it of all of its property;

(g) the cost amount to the corporation of all real property of the corporation, including leasehold interests in such property, (except real property acquired by the corporation by foreclosure or otherwise after default made on a mortgage or agreement of sale of real property) did not exceed 25% of the cost amount to it of all of its property;

(h) its liabilities did not exceed 3 times the amount by which the cost amount to it of all of its property exceeded its liabilities, where at any time in the year the cost amount to it of such of its property as consisted of property described in subparagraphs (f)(i) and (ii) plus the amount of any money of the corporation was less than $2/3$ of the cost amount to it of all of its property; and

(i) its liabilities did not exceed 5 times the amount by which the cost amount to it of all its property exceeded its liabilities, where paragraph (h) is not applicable.

**Related Provisions**: 130.1(7) — How shareholders counted; 130.1(8) — First taxation year; 142.2(1)"financial institution"(c)(ii) — Mortgage investment corporation not subject to mark-to-market rules; 248(1)"mortgage investment corporation" — Definition applies to entire Act; 253.1 — Deeming rule re investments in limited partnerships.

**Notes**: 130.1(6)(d)(iv) amended by 2000 same-sex partners bill to add reference to "common-law partner", effective for the 2001 and later taxation years, or earlier by election (see Notes to 248(1)"common-law partner").

130.1(6)(d) amended by 1998 Budget bill, subsec. 53(1), effective as set out in subsecs 53(3)–(10) of the 1998 Budget bill, which provides:

(3) [The amendments] apply in determining whether a corporation is a mortgage investment corporation for a taxation year that begins after January 14, 1998, except that [the amendments] apply to the corporation, with respect to a particular person and persons related to the particular person, only as provided in subsections (4) to (10) [of the amending legislation — see below] if

(a) the corporation was a mortgage investment corporation at the end of January 14, 1998,

(b) the particular person is a specified shareholder of the corporation at any time in the year, and

(c) the particular person

(i) was a specified shareholder of the corporation at the end of January 14, 1998, or

(ii) both

(A) was a specified shareholder of the corporation at any time after January 14, 1998 and before August 14, 1998, and

(B) would have been a specified shareholder of the corporation at the end of January 14, 1998 if paragraph 130.1(6)(d), [as amended,] were read without reference to subparagraphs (ii) and (iv).

(4) [The amendments] apply to a corporation that was a mortgage investment corporation at the end of January 14, 1998 for a taxation year that begins after that day if a person who at any time in the year is a specified shareholder of the corporation contributes capital to the corporation, or acquires a share of the corporation's capital stock other than by a permitted acquisition, at any time after January 14, 1998 and before the end of the year.

(5) [The amendments] apply to a corporation that was a mortgage investment corporation at the end of January 14, 1998 for a taxation year that begins after that day if a newly related person in respect of a person who at any time in the year is a specified shareholder of the corporation

(a) contributes capital to the corporation, or

(b) holds property (in this paragraph referred to as an "ineligible investment") that is

(i) a share of the capital stock of the corporation, or

(ii) a share of the capital stock of a corporation that holds an ineligible investment

at any time after January 14, 1998 and before the end of the year.

(6) [The amendments] apply to a corporation that was a mortgage investment corporation at the end of January 14, 1998 for a taxation year that ends after that day if

(a) at any particular time after January 14, 1998 and before the end of the year, a mortgage lender is a specified shareholder of the corporation; and

(b) at any time that is in the taxation year that includes the particular time and that is after January 14, 1998, any person contributes capital to the corporation or acquires from the corporation a share of the corporation's capital stock, other than a share that was issued to the person as a stock dividend.

(7) [The amendments] apply to a corporation that was a mortgage investment corporation at the end of January 14, 1998 for a taxation year that ends after 2007 if a mortgage lender is a specified shareholder of the corporation at any time in the year or in a taxation year that ends before the year and after 2007.

(8) For the purposes of subsections (4) to (7),

(a) if at a particular time

(i) a trust distributes a share of the capital stock of a corporation to a person who was a beneficiary under the trust throughout the period from the end of January 14, 1998 to the particular time in satisfaction of all or any part of the beneficiary's capital interest in the trust, or

(ii) a partnership distributes, to a person who was a member of the partnership throughout the period from the end of January 14, 1998 to the particular time, on the partnership ceasing to exist or on the ceasing of the person to be a member of the partnership, a share of the capital stock of a corporation or an interest in such a share,

the share is deemed to have been owned by the beneficiary or member throughout the period that begins at the later of the end of January 14, 1998 and the time the share was last acquired by the trust or partnership and that ends at the particular time; and

(b) if a person who is a beneficiary under a trust or who is a member of a partnership is deemed by paragraph (b), (c) or (e) of the definition "specified shareholder" in subsection 248(1) of the Act to own a share owned by the trust or partnership, the person is deemed to own the share and to have acquired the share at the later of the time the share was acquired by the trust or partnership and the time the person last became a beneficiary under the trust or a member of the partnership.

(9) At any time on or after the day of the death of a person described in paragraph (3)(c) in respect of a corporation and before the third anniversary of that day,

(a) the estate of the deceased person is deemed to be a person described in paragraphs (3)(b) and (c) who is related to each person who, throughout the period that begins at the beginning of January 15, 1998 and ends at the time of death, was related to the deceased person;

(b) notwithstanding subsection (10),

(i) the estate is deemed not to be a newly related person in respect of the corporation, and

(ii) the acquisition of shares of the corporation's capital stock by the estate from the deceased person is deemed to be a permitted acquisition; and

(c) the estate is deemed not to be a trust for the purposes of subparagraph (8)(a)(i) and paragraphs (b) and (e) of the definition "specified shareholder" in subsection 248(1) of the Act.

(10) The definitions in this subsection apply in subsections (3) to (9) and this subsection.

"mortgage lender" means a particular corporation where the ordinary business of

(a) the particular corporation, or

(b) a corporation (other than a mortgage investment corporation) or partnership affiliated with the particular corporation

includes the holding of debts that are secured, whether by mortgage or in any other manner, on houses (as defined in section 2 of the *National Housing Act*) or on property included within a housing project (as defined in that section).

"newly related persons" means persons who are related to each other and who became so related after January 14, 1998.

"permitted acquisition" means an acquisition by a particular person of a share of a class of the capital stock of a corporation that was

(a) held, at each particular time after January 14, 1998 and before the time at which the particular person acquired it, or

(b) issued after January 14, 1998 by the corporation as a stock dividend and held, at each particular time after the time the share was issued and before the time at which the particular person acquired it,

by the particular person or by a person who was related to the particular person throughout the period that began at the beginning of January 15, 1998 and that ends at the particular time if, immediately after the time at which the particular person acquires the share, the percentage of the issued shares of that class held by the particular person and persons related to the particular person (or in the case of acquisitions before August 14, 1998, by the particular person and persons with whom the particular person did not deal at arm's length immediately after the acquisition) does not exceed the permitted percentage for the particular person in respect of that class of shares.

"permitted percentage" for a particular person in respect of a class of shares of the capital stock of a corporation means

(a) in respect of acquisitions of shares before August 14, 1998, the percentage of the issued shares of that class held at the end of January 14, 1998 by the particular person and persons with whom the particular person did not at that time deal at arm's length; and

(b) in any other case, the greater of

(i) the percentage of the issued shares of that class held at the end of January 14, 1998 by the particular person and persons related at that time to the particular person, and

(ii) the percentage of the issued shares of that class held at the beginning of August 14, 1998 by the particular person and persons related at that time to the particular person.

"related persons" and persons related to each other have, for purposes other than applying the definitions "permitted acquisition" and "permitted percentage" in respect of acquisitions of shares before August 14, 1998, the meaning that would be assigned by section 251 of the Act if paragraph 251(2)(a) of the Act were read as follows:

(a) an individual and

(i) the individual's child (as defined in subsection 70(10)) who is under 19 years of age, or

(ii) the individual's spouse;

"specified shareholder" has the meaning assigned by paragraph 130.1(6)(d) of the Act, as enacted by subsection (1).

Before the amendment, read:

(d) subject to subsections 130.1 (7) and (8), the number of shareholders of the corporation was not less than twenty and no one shareholder held more than 25% of the issued shares of the capital stock of the corporation;

130.1(6)(f)(i) amended by 1995-97 technical bill, effective June 23, 1993, the date of repeal of the *Residential Mortgage Financing Act*, to change a reference to "residential property" under that Act to "houses" under the *National Housing Act*. S. 2 of the latter Act provides:

"house" means a building or movable structure intended for human habitation containing not more than two family housing units, together with the land, if any, on which the building or movable structure is situated;

"housing project" means a project consisting of one or more houses, one or more multiple-family dwellings, housing accommodation of the hostel or dormitory type, one or more condominium units or any combination thereof, together with any public space, recreational facilities, commercial space and other buildings appropriate to the project, but does not include a hotel.

## (7) How shareholders counted — In paragraph (6)(d), a trust governed by a registered pension plan or deferred profit sharing plan by which shares of the capital stock of a corporation are held shall be counted as four shareholders of the corporation for the purpose of determining the number of shareholders of the corporation, but as one shareholder for the

purpose of determining whether any person is a specified shareholder (as defined for the purpose of that paragraph).

Notes: 130.1(7) amended by 1998 Budget, effective on the same basis as the amendment to 130.1(6)(d). Before the amendment, read:

> (7) For the purposes of paragraph 130.1(6)(d), a trust governed by a registered pension plan or deferred profit sharing plan by which shares of the capital stock of a corporation are held shall be counted as four shareholders of the corporation, and a trust governed by a registered retirement savings plan by which shares of the capital stock of a corporation are held shall be counted as one shareholder of the corporation, but, for the purpose of calculating the limitation on the holding of shares of the capital stock of a mortgage investment corporation by a trust governed by a registered pension plan or deferred profit sharing plan, the trust shall be counted as one shareholder.

**(8) First taxation year** — For the purposes of subsection (6), a corporation that was incorporated after 1971 shall be deemed to have complied with paragraph (6)(d) throughout the first taxation year of the corporation in which it carried on business if it complied with that paragraph on the last day of that taxation year.

**(9) Definitions** — In this section,

**"liabilities"** of a corporation at any particular time means the total of all debts owing by the corporation, and all other obligations of the corporation to pay an amount, that were outstanding at that time;

Notes: 130.1(9)"liabilities" was 130.1(9)(a) before consolidation in R.S.C. 1985 (5th Supp.), effective for taxation years ending after November 1991.

**"non-qualifying real property"** — [Repealed]

Notes: Definition "non-qualifying real property" repealed by 1994 Budget, effective February 23, 1994, as a result of the repeal of the general capital gains exemption in 110.6(3). From 1992 to February 22, 1994, the term was defined by reference to the definition in 131(6). It was added by 1992 technical bill, effective for 1992 and later taxation years. Before redrafting to fit the R.S.C. 1985 (5th Supp.), it was para. 130.1(9)(d).

**"non-qualifying taxed capital gains"** — [Repealed]

Notes: Definition "non-qualifying taxed capital gains" repealed by 1994 Budget, effective February 23, 1994, as a result of the repeal of the general capital gains exemption in 110.6(3)

130.1(9)"non-qualifying taxed capital gains" (formerly 130.1(9)(b) before redrafting to fit the R.S.C. 1985 (5th Supp.)) added by 1992 technical bill, effective for 1992 and later taxation years. For earlier years, 130.1(9)(b) defined "taxed capital gains" by reference to 130(3)(b).

**"qualifying taxed capital gains"** — [Repealed]

Notes: Definition "qualifying taxed capital gains" repealed by 1994 Budget, effective February 23, 1994, as a result of the repeal of the general capital gains exemption in 110.6(3).

See now "taxed capital gains" below.

130.1(9)"qualifying taxed capital gains" (formerly 130.1(9)(c) before redrafting to fit the R.S.C. 1985 (5th Supp.)) added by 1992 technical bill, effective for 1992 and later taxation years.

**"taxed capital gains"** has the meaning assigned by paragraph 130(3)(b).

Notes: Definition "taxed capital gains" added by 1994 Budget, effective February 23, 1994. (The same definition was in force before 1992.) It replaces the definitions "non-qualifying taxed capital gains" and "qualifying taxed capital gains". As a result of the repeal of the general capital gains exemption in 110.6(3), no distinction between such gains is needed any more. See Notes to 130.1(4).

Former 130.1(9)"taxed capital gains" repealed by 1992 technical bill.

**Definitions [s. 130.1]**: "allowable capital loss" — 38(b), 248(1); "amount" — 248(1); "bank" — 248(1), Interpretation Act 35(1); "capital gain" — 39(1)(a), 248(1); "capital gains dividend" — 130.1(4); "capital loss" — 39(1)(b), 248(1); "capital property" — 54, 248(1); "class of shares" — 248(6); "common share", "common-law partner" — 248(1); "corporation" — 248(1), Interpretation Act 35(1); "deferred profit sharing plan" — 147(1), 248(1); "disposition", "dividend" — 248(1); "eligible real property gain" — 110.6(1); "liabilities" — 130.1(9); "mortgage investment corporation" — 130.1(6), 248(1); "non-qualifying taxed capital gains" — 130.1(9); "preferred share", "prescribed", "property" — 248(1); "province" — Interpretation Act 35(1); "public corporation" — 89(1), 130.1(5), 248(1); "qualifying taxed capital gains" — 130.1(9); "received" — 248(1); "record", "registered pension plan" — 248(1); "resident in Canada" — 250; "share", "shareholder", "specified shareholder" — 248(1); "taxable capital gain" — 38(a), 248(1); "taxation year" — 249; "taxed capital gains" — 130(3)(b), 130.1(9); "taxpayer" — 248(1);"trust" — 104(1), 248(1), (3); "undertaking" — 253.1(a).

## Mutual Fund Corporations

**131. (1) Election re capital gains dividend** — Where at any particular time a dividend became payable by a corporation, that was throughout the taxation year in which the dividend became payable a mutual fund corporation, to shareholders of any class of its capital stock, if the corporation so elects in respect of the full amount of the dividend in prescribed manner and at or before the earlier of the particular time and the first day on which any part of the dividend was paid,

(a) the dividend shall be deemed to be a capital gains dividend payable out of the corporation's capital gains dividend account to the extent that it does not exceed the corporation's capital gains dividend account at the particular time; and

(b) notwithstanding any other provision of this Act, any amount received by a taxpayer in a taxation year as, on account of, in lieu of payment of or in satisfaction of, the dividend shall not be included in computing the taxpayer's income for the year as income from a share of the capital stock of the corporation, but shall be deemed to be a capital gain of the taxpayer for the year from a disposition, in the year and after February 22, 1994, by the taxpayer of capital property.

**Proposed Amendment — 131(1)(b)**

(b) notwithstanding any other provision of this Act, any amount received by a taxpayer in a taxation year as, on account of, in lieu of payment of or in satisfaction of, the dividend shall

Division F — Special Rules in Certain Circumstances    S. 131(1)

not be included in computing the taxpayer's income for the year as income from a share of the capital stock of the corporation, and

(i) where the dividend was in respect of capital gains of the corporation from dispositions of property that occurred before February 28, 2000, and the taxation year of the taxpayer began after February 27, 2000 and ended before October 18, 2000, 9/8 of the dividend is deemed to be a capital gain of the taxpayer from the disposition by the taxpayer of a capital property in the year,

(ii) where the dividend was in respect of capital gains of the corporation from dispositions of property that occurred before February 28, 2000, and the taxation year of the taxpayer includes February 27, 2000, the dividend is deemed to be a capital gain of the taxpayer from the disposition by the taxpayer of a capital property in the year and before February 28, 2000,

(iii) where the dividend was in respect of capital gains of the corporation from dispositions of property that occurred after February 27, 2000 and before October 18, 2000, and the taxation year of the taxpayer began after October 17, 2000, 4/3 of the dividend is deemed to be a capital gain of the taxpayer from the disposition by the taxpayer of a capital property in the year,

(iv) where the dividend was in respect of capital gains of the corporation from dispositions of property that occurred after February 27, 2000 and before October 18, 2000, and the taxation year of the taxpayer includes October 17, 2000, the dividend is deemed to be a capital gain of the taxpayer from the disposition by the taxpayer of a capital property in the year and before October 18, 2000, and

(v) in any other case, the dividend is deemed to be a capital gain of the taxpayer from the disposition of capital property after October 17, 2000 and in the year.

**Application**: The December 21, 2000 draft legislation, subsec. 77(1), will amend para. 131(1)(b) to read as above, applicable to taxation years that end after February 27, 2000.

**Technical Notes**: Where a mutual fund corporation elects in respect of the full amount of a dividend, the dividend, to the extent that it does not exceed the corporation's capital gains dividend account, is deemed to be a capital gains dividend and the dividend recipient is deemed to have a capital gain for the taxation year in which the dividend is received from the disposition of property in the year.

The amendment to paragraph 131(1)(b), which is applicable for taxation years that end after February 27, 2000, is consequential on the change to the inclusion rate for capital gains [see 38(a) — ed.]. The amendment ensures that the inclusion rate for capital gains realised on property disposed of prior to February 27, 2000 is 3/4.

Where the taxation year of the dividend recipient began after February 27, 2000 and ended before October 18, 2000 and the capital gains dividend was paid out of capital gains from property disposed of before February 27, 2000, under subparagraph 131(1)(b)(i) 9/8 of the dividend is deemed to be a capital gain from the disposition of property.

Where the taxation year of the dividend recipient began before and ended after February 27, 2000 and the capital gains dividend was paid out of capital gains from property disposed of before February 27, 2000, under subparagraph 131(1)(b)(ii) the dividend is deemed to be a capital gain of the recipient from property disposed of before February 27, 2000.

Where the taxation year of the dividend recipient began after October 17, 2000 and the capital gains dividend was paid out of capital gains from property disposed of after February 27, 2000 and before October 18, 2000, under subparagraph 131(1)(b)(iii) 4/3 of the dividend is deemed to be a capital gain of the recipient from property disposed in the year.

Where the taxation year of the dividend recipient includes October 17, 2000 and the capital gains dividend was paid out of capital gains from property disposed of after February 27, 2000 and before October 18, 2000, under subparagraph 131(1)(b)(iv) the dividend is deemed to be a capital gain of the recipient from property disposed in the year and before October 18, 2000. In any other case, under subparagraph 131(1)(b)(v) the dividend is deemed to be a capital gain of the taxpayer from property disposed of after October 17, 2000 and in the year the dividend was received.

**Related Provisions**: 39.1(1)"exempt capital gains balance"C(c), 39.1(6) — Reduction in gain to reflect capital gains exemption election; 84(7) — When deemed dividend deemed payable; 112(4)(d), 112(4.1)(d), 112(4.2)(d) — Capital gains dividend excluded from stop-loss and share inventory valuation rules; 112(6) — No deduction for capital gains dividend; 129(7) — No dividend refund for capital gains dividend; 130(2) — Application to investment corporation; 130(3) — Meaning of investment corporation and taxed capital gains; 131(1.1) — Deemed date of election; 131(1.5) — Reporting to shareholder of capital gains tax rate; 131(1.6) — Allocation of capital gains tax rate for 2000; 131(4) — Application of s. 84; 132.2 — Mutual fund reorganizations; 152(1) — Assessment; 142.2(1)"financial institution"(c)(iii) — Mutual fund corporation not subject to mark-to-market rules; 184(2) — Tax on excessive elections; 184(3) — Election to treat excess as separate dividend; 212(2) — No withholding tax on capital gains dividend.

**Notes**: 131(1) amended by 1994 Budget, effective for dividends paid after February 22, 1994. The change results from the elimination of the capital gains exemption in 110.6(3). Since it is no longer necessary to treat capital gains of a mutual fund corporation that are flowed out to shareholders as either eligible or ineligible for the exemption, a capital gains dividend is now simply treated as a capital gain in the shareholder's hands.

131(1) amended by 1992 technical bill, effective for 1992 and later taxation years, to reflect the capital gains exemption restrictions on real estate investments. For earlier years, ignore subpara. (a)(iii) and para. (b).

**Regulations**: 2104 (prescribed manner of making election).

**Interpretation Bulletins**: IT-98R2: Investment corporations; IT-243R4: Dividend refund to private corporations; IT-328R3: Losses on shares on which dividends have been received.

**Forms**: T5 Segment; T5 Summ: Return of investment income; T5 Supp: Statement of investment income; T2055: Election in respect

**S. 131(1)**      Income Tax Act, Part I

of a capital gains dividend under subsection 131(1); RC4169: Tax treatment of mutual funds for individuals.

**(1.1) Deemed date of election** — Where at any particular time a dividend has become payable by a mutual fund corporation to shareholders of any class of shares of its capital stock and subsection (1) would have applied to the dividend except that the election referred to in that subsection was not made on or before the day on or before which the election was required by that subsection to be made, the election shall be deemed to have been made at the particular time or on the first day on which any part of the dividend was paid, whichever is the earlier, if

(a) the election is thereafter made in prescribed manner and prescribed form;

(b) an estimate of the penalty in respect of the election is paid by the corporation when the election is made; and

(c) the directors or other person or persons legally entitled to administer the affairs of the corporation have, before the time the election is made, authorized the election to be made.

**Related Provisions**: 130(2) — Application to investment corporation; 131(1.2) — Request to make election; 131(1.3), (1.4) — Penalty; 152(1) — Assessment.

**Regulations**: 2104(f) (prescribed manner).

**(1.2) Request to make election** — The Minister may at any time, by written request served personally or by registered mail, request that an election referred to in paragraph (1.1)(a) be made by a mutual fund corporation and where the mutual fund corporation on which such a request is served does not comply therewith within 90 days after service of the request, subsection (1.1) does not apply to such an election made thereafter by it.

**Related Provisions**: 248(7)(a) — Mail deemed received on day mailed.

**(1.3) Penalty** — For the purposes of this section, the penalty in respect of an election referred to in paragraph (1.1)(b) is an amount equal to the lesser of

(a) 1% per annum of the amount of the dividend referred to in the election for each month or part of a month during the period commencing with the time that the dividend became payable, or the first day on which any part of the dividend was paid if that day is earlier, and ending with the day on which the election was made, and

(b) the product obtained when $500 is multiplied by the proportion that the number of months or parts of months during the period referred to in paragraph (a) bears to 12.

**(1.4) Assessment and payment of penalty** — The Minister shall, with all due dispatch, examine each election referred to in paragraph (1.1)(a), assess the penalty payable and send a notice of assessment to the mutual fund corporation and the corporation shall pay forthwith to the Receiver General, the amount, if any, by which the penalty so assessed exceeds the total of all amounts previously paid on account of that penalty.

**Related Provisions**: 152(1) — Assessment.

**Proposed Addition — 131(1.5), (1.6)**

**(1.5) Reporting** — Where subparagraph (1)(b)(i) to (iv) applies to a dividend paid by a mutual fund corporation to a shareholder of any class of shares of its capital stock, the corporation shall disclose to the shareholder in prescribed form the amount of the dividend that is in respect of capital gains realized on dispositions of property that occurred before February 28, 2000, after February 27, 2000 and before October 18, 2000, and after October 17, 2000, and, if it does not do so, the dividend is deemed to be in respect of capital gains realized on dispositions of property that occurred before February 28, 2000.

**(1.6) Allocation [for 2000]** — Where subsection (1) applies in respect of a dividend paid by a mutual fund corporation in the period commencing 60 days after the beginning of the corporation's taxation year that includes either February 28, 2000 or October 17, 2000 and ending 60 days after the end of that year, and the corporation so elects under this paragraph in its return of income

(a) the portion of the dividend that is in respect of capital gains realized on dispositions of property that occurred in the year and before February 28, 2000 is deemed to equal that proportion of the dividend that the number of days that are in that year and before February 28, 2000 is of the number of days that are in that year;

(b) the portion of the dividend that is in respect of capital gains realized on dispositions of property that occurred in the year and in the period that began at the beginning of February 28, 2000 and ended at the end of October 17, 2000 is deemed to equal that proportion of the dividend that the number of days that are in the year and in that period is of the number of days that are in the year; and

(c) the portion of the dividend that is in respect of capital gains realized on dispositions of property that occurred in the year and in the period that begins at the beginning of October 18, 2000 and ends at the end of the year, is deemed to equal that proportion of the dividend that the number of days that are in the year and in that period is of the number of days that are in the year.

**Application**: The December 21, 2000 draft legislation, subsec. 77(2), will add subsecs. 131(1.5) and (1.6), applicable to taxation years that end after February 27, 2000.

**Technical Notes**: Section 131 applies where a dividend is payable by a mutual fund corporation and the corporation elects the dividend to be a capital gains dividend.

Section 131 is amended to add new subsections 131(1.5) and (1.6), applicable for taxation years that end after February 27, 2000.

Where a capital gains dividend is paid by a mutual fund corporation to a shareholder of any class of shares of its capital stock, new subsection 131(1.5) provides that the corporation must disclose to the shareholder in prescribed form the amount of the dividend that can reasonably be considered to have been paid out of its capital gains realized on dispositions by the corporation of property before February 28, 2000, after February 27, 2000 and before October 18, 2000, and after October 17, 2000. If it does not do so, the dividend is deemed to be in respect of capital gains realized on dispositions of property that occurred before February 28, 2000.

New subsection 131(1.6) provides that a mutual fund corporation can elect, for its taxation year that includes either February 28, 2000 or October 17, 2000, to treat a portion of its capital gains dividends for the year to be in respect of capital gains realized on dispositions of property

- before February 28, 2000,
- in the period that begins at the beginning of February 28, 2000 and ends at the end of October 17, 2000, and
- in the period that begins at the beginning of October 18, 2000 and ends at the end of the year.

The portion is determined as that proportion of the dividend that the number of days that are in the year and in that period is of the number of days in the year.

**(2) Capital gains refund to mutual fund corporation** — Where a corporation was, throughout a taxation year, a mutual fund corporation and a return of its income for the year has been made within 3 years from the end of the year, the Minister

(a) may, on mailing the notice of assessment for the year, refund without application therefor an amount (in this section referred to as its "capital gains refund" for the year) equal to the lesser of

(i) 21% of the total of

(A) all capital gains dividends paid by the corporation in the period commencing 60 days after the commencement of the year and ending 60 days after the end of the year, and

(B) its capital gains redemptions for the year, and

(ii) the corporation's refundable capital gains tax on hand at the end of the year; and

### Proposed Amendment — 131(2)(a)

(a) may, on sending the notice of assessment for the year, refund an amount (in this subsection referred to as its "capital gains refund" for the year) equal to the lesser of

(i) the total of

(A) 14% of the total of

(I) all capital gains dividends paid by the corporation in the period commencing 60 days after the beginning of the year and ending 60 days after the end of the year, and

(II) its capital gains redemptions for the year, and

(B) the amount, if any, that the Minister determines to be reasonable in the circumstances, after giving consideration to the percentages applicable in determining the corporation's capital gains refund for the year and preceding taxation years and the percentages applicable in determining the corporation's refundable capital gains tax on hand at the end of the year, and

(ii) the corporation's refundable capital gains tax on hand at the end of the year; and

**Application**: The December 21, 2000 draft legislation, subsec. 77(3), will amend para. 131(2)(a) to read as above, applicable to taxation years that end after February 27, 2000 except that, for a taxation year of a mutual fund corporation that includes either February 28, 2000 or October 17, 2000, the reference to "14%" in cl. 131(2)(a)(i)(A) shall be read as a reference to the percentage determined when 28% is multiplied by the fraction in para. 38(a), as amended [by the December 21, 2000 draft legislation], that applies to the corporation for the year.

**Technical Notes**: A mutual fund corporation is entitled to a capital gains refund for a taxation year equal to the lesser of 21% of the total of its capital gains dividends paid for the year, its capital gains redemptions for the year and the amount of its refundable capital gains tax on hand at the end of the year.

Generally, the refundable capital gains tax on hand of a mutual fund corporation is 28% of its taxed capital gains (or 21% of its capital gains for the year where the relevant inclusion rate for capital gains is 3/4). The refundable capital gains tax on hand could be less then 21% of capital gains where taxable income of the mutual fund corporation is less than its taxed capital gains.

The amendments to paragraph 131(2)(a) replace the reference to "21%" with the reference to "14%", and add that the Minister can determine another amount after giving consideration to the percentages applicable in determining the corporation's capital gains refund and refundable capital gains tax on hand for the year and preceding taxation years. These amendments are consequential on the reduction of the inclusion rate for capital gains from 3/4 to 1/2 [see 38(a) — ed.].

The amendments apply to taxation years that end after February 27, 2000 except that, for the taxation year of a mutual fund corporation that includes either February 28, 2000 or October 17, 2000, the reference to the percentage "14%" in subparagraph 131(2)(a)(i) is to be read as reference to the percentage determined when 28% is multiplied by the fraction in amended paragraph 38(a) that applies to the corporation for the year. These modifications are required in order to reflect the capital gains/losses rate for the year.

(b) shall, with all due dispatch, make that capital gains refund after mailing the notice of assessment if an application for it has been made in writing by the corporation within the period within which the Minister would be allowed under subsection 152(4) to assess tax payable under this Part by the corporation for the year if that subsection were read without reference to paragraph 152(4)(a).

**S. 131(2)** — Income Tax Act, Part I

**Related Provisions**: 130(2) — Application; 131(3) — Application to other liability; 131(3.1), (3.2) — Interest; 152(1) — Assessment; 157(3)(c) — Reduction in instalment obligations to reflect capital gains refund; 160.1 — Where excess refunded.

**Notes**: 131(2)(b) amended by 1989 Budget, effective April 28, 1989, to refer to "the period determined under paragraph 152(4)(b) or (c)" rather than to a 6-year or 3-year period; and amended by 1995-97 technical bill, also effective April 28, 1989, to make non-substantive wording changes and to update references to 152(4) as amended.

**Interpretation Bulletins**: IT-98R2: Investment corporations.

**(3) Application to other liability** — Instead of making a refund that might otherwise be made under subsection (2), the Minister may, where the corporation is liable or about to become liable to make any payment under this Act, apply the amount that would otherwise be refunded to that other liability and notify the corporation of that action.

**Related Provisions**: 130(2) — Application to investment corporation; 152(1) — Assessment.

**(3.1) Interest on capital gains refund** — Where a capital gains refund for a taxation year is paid to, or applied to a liability of, a corporation, the Minister shall pay or apply interest on the refund at the prescribed rate for the period beginning on the day that is the later of

(a) the day that is 120 days after the end of the year, and

(b) the day on which the corporation's return of income under this Part for the year was filed under section 150, unless the return was filed on or before the day on or before which it was required to be filed,

and ending on the day the refund is paid or applied.

**Related Provisions**: 130(2) — Application to investment corporation; 131(3.2) — Excess interest on capital gains refund; 161.1 — Offset of refund interest against arrears interest; 221.1 — Application of interest where legislation retroactive; 248(11) — Interest compounded daily.

**Notes**: 131(3.1) added by 1992 technical bill, effective for capital gains refunds paid or applied in respect of taxation years that begin after 1991.

**Regulations**: 4301(b) (prescribed rate of interest).

**(3.2) Excess interest on capital gains refund** — Where at any particular time interest has been paid to, or applied to a liability of, a corporation under subsection (3.1) in respect of a capital gains refund and it is determined at a subsequent time that the capital gains refund was less than that in respect of which interest was so paid or applied,

(a) the amount by which the interest that was so paid or applied exceeds the interest, if any, computed in respect of the amount that is determined at the subsequent time to be the capital gains refund shall be deemed to be an amount (in this subsection referred to as the "amount payable") that became payable under this Part by the corporation at the particular time; and

(b) the corporation shall pay to the Receiver General interest at the prescribed rate on the amount payable, computed from the particular time to the day of payment; and

(c) the Minister may at any time assess the corporation in respect of the amount payable and, where the Minister makes such an assessment, the provisions of Divisions I and J apply, with such modifications as the circumstances require, in respect of the assessment as though it had been made under section 152.

**Related Provisions**: 20(1)(ll) — Deduction on repayment of interest; 130(2) — Application to investment corporation; 161.1 — Offset of refund interest against arrears interest; 221.1 — Application of interest where legislation retroactive; 248(11) — Interest compounded daily.

**Notes**: 131(3.2) added by 1992 technical bill, effective for capital gains refunds paid or applied in respect of taxation years that begin after 1991.

**Regulations**: 4301(a) (prescribed rate of interest).

**(4) Application of section 84** — Section 84 does not apply to deem a dividend to have been paid by a corporation to any of its shareholders, or to deem any of the shareholders of a corporation to have received a dividend on any shares of the capital stock of the corporation, if at the time the dividend would, but for this subsection, be deemed by that section to have been so paid or received, as the case may be, the corporation was a mutual fund corporation.

**Related Provisions**: 131(11)(c) — Rules re prescribed labour-sponsored venture capital corporations; 132.2(1)(o)(i) — Mutual fund reorganization.

**(5) Dividend refund to mutual fund corporation** — A corporation that was a mutual fund corporation throughout a taxation year

(a) is deemed for the purposes of paragraph 87(2)(aa) and section 129 to have been a private corporation throughout the year, except that its refundable dividend tax on hand at the end of the year (within the meaning assigned by subsection 129(3)) shall be determined without reference to paragraph 129(3)(a); and

(b) where it was not an investment corporation throughout the year, is deemed for the purposes of Part IV to have been a private corporation throughout the year except that, in applying subsection 186(1) to the corporation in respect of the year, that subsection shall be read without reference to paragraph 186(1)(b).

**Related Provisions**: 112 — Deduction of dividends received by resident corporation; 113 — Deduction of dividend from foreign affiliate; 131(1) — Election re capital gains dividend; 131(2) — Capital gains refund; 131(4) — Application of s. 84; 131(11)(c) — Rules re prescribed labour-sponsored venture capital corporations; 152(1) — Assessment; 157(3) — Private, mutual fund, non-resident-owned investment corporations.

**Notes**: 131(5) amended by 1995-97 technical bill, effective for 1993 and later taxation years. This retroactively overrides amendments made to 131(5)(a) by 1995 Budget bill, in consequence of amendments to s. 129, which had been effective for taxation years that end after June 1995. For 1988-92, read:

(5) A corporation that was, throughout a taxation year, a mutual fund corporation other than an investment corporation

shall, for the purposes of paragraph 87(2)(aa), section 129 and Part IV, be deemed to have been a private corporation throughout the year, except that

(a) for the purposes of section 129, its refundable dividend tax on hand at the end of the year shall be deemed to be the amount, if any, by which the total of

(i) the total of amounts each of which is an amount in respect of the year or any preceding taxation year throughout which it is deemed by this subsection to have been a private corporation, equal to the tax under Part IV payable by it for that year, and

(i.1) the amount, if any, of the corporation's addition at December 31, 1986 of refundable dividend tax on hand (within the meaning assigned by subsection 129(3.3)),

exceeds the total of

(ii) the total of amounts each of which is the corporation's dividend refund for any previous taxation year described in subparagraph (i),

(iii) the amount, if any, of the corporation's reduction at December 31, 1977 of refundable dividend tax on hand (within the meaning assigned by subsection 129(3.1)), and

(iv) the amount, if any, of the corporation's reduction at December 31, 1987 of refundable dividend tax on hand (within the meaning assigned by subsection 129(3.5)); and

(b) in its application to the corporation in respect of the year, subsection 186(1) shall be read without reference to paragraph 186(1)(b).

**(6) Definitions** — In this section,

**"capital gains dividend account"** of a mutual fund corporation at any time means the amount, if any, by which

(a) its capital gains, for all taxation years that began more than 60 days before that time, from dispositions of property after 1971 and before that time while it was a mutual fund corporation

exceeds

(b) the total of

(i) its capital losses, for all taxation years that began more than 60 days before that time, from dispositions of property after 1971 and before that time while it was a mutual fund corporation,

(ii) all capital gains dividends that became payable by the corporation before that time and more than 60 days after the end of the last taxation year that ended more than 60 days before that time, and

(iii) all amounts each of which is an amount in respect of any taxation year that ended more than 60 days before that time throughout which it was a mutual fund corporation, equal to $100/21$ of its capital gains refund for that year;

---

**Proposed Amendment — 131(6)"capital gains dividend account"(b)(iii)**

(iii) the total of all amounts each of which is

(A) an amount equal to $100/21$ of its capital gains refund for any taxation year throughout which it was a mutual fund corporation where the year ended

(I) more than 60 days before that time, and

(II) before February 28, 2000,

(B) an amount equal to of its capital gains refund for any taxation year throughout which it was a mutual fund corporation where the year ended

(I) more than 60 days before that time, and

(II) after February 27, 2000 and before October 18, 2000, or

(C) an amount equal to $100/14$ of its capital gain refund for any taxation year throughout which it was a mutual fund corporation where the year ended

(I) more than 60 days before that time, and

(II) after October 17, 2000;

**Application**: The December 21, 2000 draft legislation, subsec. 77(4), will amend subpara. (b)(iii) of the definition "capital gains dividend account" in subsec. 131(6) to read as above, applicable to taxation years that end after February 27, 2000 except that, for a taxation year of a mutual fund corporation that includes either February 28, 2000 or October 17, 2000, the reference to "100/18.7" in cl. (b)(iii)(B) shall be read as "100/28X", where "X" is the fraction in para. 38(a), as amended [by the December 21, 2000 draft legislation], that applies to the corporation for the year.

**Technical Notes**: The "capital gains dividend account" of a mutual fund corporation represents the cumulative net undistributed capital gains of the corporation on which it paid refundable capital gains tax.

In determining its capital gains dividend account balance, a mutual fund corporation must deduct 100/21 of its capital gains refunds for the year, representing capital gains distributions in respect of which the corporation received capital gains refunds.

The amendment to subparagraph (b)(iii) of the definition "capital gains dividend account" is consequential on the reduction of the inclusion rate for capital gains from 3/4 to 1/2 for taxation years that end after February 27, 2000 [see 38(a) — ed.]. With the inclusion rate reduction to 1/2 and using a 28% corporate tax rate, refundable tax and refunds approximate 14% of capital gains. For taxation years that ended before February 28, 2000, the rate remains unchanged at 21%.

The amendment applies to taxation years that end after February 27, 2000 except that, for the taxation year of a mutual fund corporation that includes either February 28, 2000 or October 17, 2000, the reference to the percentage "14%" in subsection 131(6)(b)(iii)(B) is to be read as reference to the fraction "100/28X", where "X" is the fraction in amended paragraph 38(a) that applies to the corpo-

## S. 131(6) cap

ration for the year. These modifications are required in order to reflect the capital gains/losses rate for the year.

**Related Provisions:** 88(2)(a)(i.1) — Winding-up; 87(2)(bb) — Amalgamation — addition to amounts determined under 131(6)"capital gains dividend account"(a) and (b).

**Notes:** Definition "capital gains dividend account" amended by 1994 Budget, effective February 23, 1994, as a result of the repeal of the general capital gains exemption in 110.6(3). From 1992 to February 22, 1994, read:

"capital gains dividend account" of a mutual fund corporation at any time means the amount, if any, by which the total of

(a) its capital gains, for all taxation years beginning more than 60 days before that time, from dispositions of property (other than its non-qualifying real property) after 1971 and before that time while it was a mutual fund corporation, and

(b) all amounts each of which is an amount determined by the formula

$$A \times \frac{B}{C}$$

where

A is its capital gain, for a taxation year beginning more than 60 days before that time, from the disposition of a non-qualifying real property of the corporation before that time while it was a mutual fund corporation,

B is the number of calendar months in the period that begins with the later of the calendar month in which the property was last acquired by it and January 1972 and ends with February 1992, and

C is the number of calendar months in the period that begins with the later of the calendar month in which the property was last acquired by it and January 1972 and ends with the calendar month in which the property was disposed of by it

exceeds the total of

(c) its capital losses, for all taxation years beginning more than 60 days before that time, from dispositions of property (other than its non-qualifying real property) after 1971 and before that time while it was a mutual fund corporation,

(d) all amounts each of which is an amount determined by the formula

$$D \times \frac{E}{F}$$

where

D is its capital loss, for a taxation year beginning more than 60 days before that time, from the disposition of a non-qualifying real property of the corporation before that time while it was a mutual fund corporation,

E is the number of calendar months in the period that begins with the later of the calendar month in which the property was last acquired by it and January 1972 and ends with February 1992, and

F is the number of calendar months in the period that begins with the later of the calendar month in which the property was last acquired by it and January 1972 and ends with the calendar month in which the property was disposed of by it,

(e) all capital gains dividends that became payable by the corporation before that time and more than 60 days after the end of the last taxation year ending more than 60 days

before that time, other than any such dividends that became payable out of the corporation's non-qualifying real property capital gains dividend account,

(f) all amounts each of which is an amount in respect of any taxation year ending more than 60 days before that time throughout which it was a mutual fund corporation, equal to 100/21 of its capital gains refund for that year, and

(g) the amount, if any, by which the total of the amounts determined under paragraphs (b) and (c) of the definition "non-qualifying real property capital gains dividend account" in respect of the corporation at that time exceeds the amount determined under paragraph (a) of that definition in respect of the corporation at that time;

Amended by 1992 Budget/technical bill, effective for 1992 and later taxation years, to reflect the restrictions on non-qualifying real property. For earlier years, read only paras. (a), (c) (without the reference to non-qualifying real property), (e) (without the words beginning "other than such dividends"), and (f).

131(6)"capital gains dividend account" was 131(6)(b) before consolidation in R.S.C. 1985 (5th Supp.), effective for taxation years ending after November 1991. See Table of Concordance.

**"capital gains redemptions"** of a mutual fund corporation for a taxation year means the amount determined by the formula

$$\frac{A}{B} \times (C + D)$$

where

A is the total of all amounts paid by the corporation in the year on the redemption of shares of its capital stock,

B is the total of the fair market value at the end of the year of all the issued shares of its capital stock and the amount determined for A in respect of the corporation for the year,

C is 100/21 of the corporation's refundable capital gains tax on hand at the end of the year, and

### Proposed Amendment — 131(6)"capital gains redemptions"C

**Application:** The December 21, 2000 draft legislation, subsec. 77(5), will amend the description of C in the definition "capital gains redemptions" in subsec. 131(6) to replace the reference to "100/21" with "100/14", applicable to taxation years that end after February 27, 2000 except that, for a taxation year of a mutual fund corporation that includes either February 28, 2000 or October 17, 2000, "100/14" shall be read as "100/28X", where "X" is the fraction in para. 38(a), as amended [by the December 21, 2000 draft legislation], that applies to the corporation for the year.

**Technical Notes:** The "capital gains redemptions" of a mutual fund corporation for a year are used in determining the mutual fund corporation's capital gains refund for the year. In calculating the capital gains redemptions, the corporation must allocate accrued capital gains and undistributed realized net capital gains across all payments on the redemptions of shares in the year.

The amendment to the description of C in the definition "capital gains redemptions" replaces the fraction "100/21" with the fraction "100/14", and is consequential on the reduction of the inclusion rate for capital gains from 3/4 to 1/2.

The amendment applies to taxation years that end after February 27, 2000 except that, for the taxation year of a

> mutual fund corporation that includes either February 28, 2000 or October 17, 2000, the reference to the fraction "100/14" in the description of C in the definition "capital gains redemptions" in subsection 131(6) is to be read as reference to fraction "100/28X", where "X" is the fraction in amended paragraph 38(a) that applies to the corporation for the year. These modifications are required in order to reflect the capital gains/losses rate for the year.

D is the amount determined by the formula

$$(K + L) - (M + N)$$

where

K is the amount of the fair market value at the end of the year of all the issued shares of the corporation's capital stock,

L is the total of all amounts each of which is the amount of any debt owing by the corporation, or of any other obligation of the corporation to pay an amount, that was outstanding at that time,

M is the total of the cost amounts to the corporation at that time of all its properties, and

N is the amount of any money of the corporation on hand at that time;

**Related Provisions**: 130(2) — Application to investment corporation; 132.2(1)(p) — Mutual fund reorganizations; 257 — Formula amount cannot calculate to less than zero.

**Notes**: 131(6)"capital gains redemptions" was 131(6)(a) before consolidation in R.S.C. 1985 (5th Supp.), effective for taxation years ending after November 1991. See Table of Concordance in introductory pages.

### "dividend refund [para. 131(6)(c)]" — [Repealed under former Act]

**Notes**: 131(6)(c), which defined "dividend refund", repealed in 1985. It referred to the definition in 129(1), which applies for the entire Act.

### "non-qualifying real property" — [Repealed]

**Notes**: Definition "non-qualifying real property" repealed by 1994 Budget, effective February 23, 1994, as a result of the repeal of the general capital gains exemption in 110.6(3). From 1992 to February 22, 1994, read:

> "non-qualifying real property" of a corporation or trust (other than a personal trust) means property disposed of by the corporation or trust after February 1992 that at the time of its disposition is
>
> (a) real property,
>
> (b) a share of the capital stock of a corporation, the fair market value of which is derived principally from real property, other than real property that was used
>
>  (i) throughout that part of the 24-month period immediately preceding that time while it was owned by the corporation or a corporation related to the corporation, or
>
>  (ii) throughout all or substantially all of the time in the period preceding that time during which it was owned by the corporation or a corporation related to the corporation,
>
> principally in an active business carried on by the corporation or a corporation related to it, but not including a share of the capital stock of a corporation the fair market value of which is derived principally from real property owned by another corporation the shares of which would, if owned by the corporation or the trust, not be non-qualifying real property of the corporation or the trust,
>
> (c) an interest in a partnership or trust, the fair market value of which is derived principally from real property, other than real property that was used
>
>  (i) throughout that part of the 24-month period immediately preceding that time while it was property of the partnership or trust, or
>
>  (ii) throughout all or substantially all of the time in the period preceding that time during which it was property of the partnership or trust,
>
> principally in an active business carried on by one or more persons as members of the partnership or by the trust, or
>
> (d) an interest or an option in respect of property described in any of paragraphs (a) to (c),
>
> and, for the purposes of this definition, an "active business" carried on by a person at any time means a business carried on by the person at that time other than a business (other than a business carried on by a credit union or a business of leasing property that is not real property) the principal purpose of which is to derive income from property (including interest, dividends, rents or royalties), unless the person or, where the person carries on the business as a member of a partnership, the partnership
>
> (e) employs in the business at that time more than 5 individuals on a full-time basis, or
>
> (f) in the course of carrying on the business has managerial, administrative, financial, maintenance or other similar services provided to it at that time and the person or partnership could reasonably be expected to require more than 5 full-time employees if those services had not been so provided;

131(6)"non-qualifying real property" added by 1992 Budget/technical bill, effective for 1992 and later taxation years. Before redrafting to fit the R.S.C. 1985 (5th Supp.), it was para. 131(6)(c.1).

Closing words of para. (b) amended by 1993 technical bill, retroactive to 1992 and later taxation years, to add "but not including..." through to the end of the para.

The CCRA takes the position that "all or substantially all", used in (b)(ii) and (c)(ii) of "non-qualifying real property", means 90% or more, and that "principally" means more than 50%.

### "non-qualifying real property capital gains dividend account" — [Repealed]

**Notes**: Definition "non-qualifying real property capital gains dividend account" repealed by 1994 Budget, effective February 23, 1994, as a result of the repeal of the general capital gains exemption in 110.6(3). From 1992 to February 22, 1994, read:

> "non-qualifying real property capital gains dividend account" of a mutual fund corporation at any time means the amount, if any, by which
>
> (a) the total of all amounts each of which is the amount by which its capital gain, for a taxation year beginning more than 60 days before that time, from the disposition of a non-qualifying real property of the corporation before that time while it was a mutual fund corporation exceeds the amount determined under paragraph (b) of the definition "capital gains dividend account" in respect of that disposition
>
> exceeds the total of
>
> (b) all amounts each of which is the amount by which its capital loss, for a taxation year beginning more than 60 days before that time, from the disposition of a non-qual-

ifying real property of the corporation before that time while it was a mutual fund corporation exceeds the amount determined under paragraph (d) of the definition "capital gains dividend account" in respect of that disposition;

(c) all capital gains dividends that became payable by the corporation before that time and more than 60 days after the end of the last taxation year ending more than 60 days before that time, other than any such dividends that became payable out of the corporation's capital gains dividend account, and

(d) the amount, if any, by which the total of all amounts determined under paragraphs (c) to (f) of the definition "capital gains dividend account" in respect of the corporation at that time exceeds the total of all amounts determined under paragraphs (a) and (b) of that definition in respect of the corporation at that time;

131(6)"non-qualifying real property capital gains dividend account" added by 1992 Budget/technical bill, effective for 1992 and later taxation years. Before redrafting to fit the R.S.C. 1985 (5th Supp.), it was para. 131(6)(c.1).

**"refundable capital gains tax on hand"** of a mutual fund corporation at the end of a taxation year means the amount determined by the formula

$$A - B$$

where

A is the total of all amounts each of which is an amount in respect of that or any previous taxation year throughout which the corporation was a mutual fund corporation, equal to the least of

(a) 28% of its taxable income for the year,

(b) 28% of its taxed capital gains for the year, and

(c) the tax payable by it under this Part for the year determined without reference to section 123.2, and

B is the total of all amounts each of which is an amount in respect of any previous taxation year throughout which the corporation was a mutual fund corporation, equal to its capital gains refund for the year.

**Related Provisions**: 87(2)(bb) — Amalgamation — addition to amounts determined under 131(6)"refundable capital gains tax on hand" A and B; 130(2) — Application to investment corporation; 131(7) — Taxed capital gains defined; 132.2(1)(l) — RCGTOH minus capital gains refund added to RCGTOH of transferee on qualifying exchange of property between mutual funds; 257 — Formula cannot calculate to less than zero.

**Notes**: 131(6)"refundable capital gains tax on hand" was 131(6)(d) before consolidation in R.S.C. 1985 (5th Supp.), effective for taxation years ending after November 1991. The previous version, identical in meaning, read:

(d) "refundable capital gains tax on hand" of a mutual fund corporation at the end of a taxation year means the amount, if any, by which

(i) the aggregate of amounts each of which is an amount in respect of that or any previous taxation year throughout which it was a mutual fund corporation, equal to the least of

(A) 28% of its taxable income for the year,

(B) 28% of its taxed capital gains for the year, and

(C) the tax payable by it under this Part for the year determined without reference to section 123.2,

exceeds

(ii) the aggregate of amounts each of which is an amount in respect of any previous taxation year throughout which it was a mutual fund corporation, equal to its capital gains refund for the year.

**(7) Definition of "taxed capital gains"** — In subsection (6), "taxed capital gains" of a taxpayer for a taxation year has the meaning assigned by subsection 130(3).

**(8) Meaning of "mutual fund corporation"** — Subject to subsection (8.1), a corporation is, for the purposes of this section, a mutual fund corporation at any time in a taxation year if, at that time, it was a prescribed labour-sponsored venture capital corporation or

(a) it was a Canadian corporation that was a public corporation;

(b) its only undertaking was

(i) the investing of its funds in property (other than real property or an interest in real property),

(ii) the acquiring, holding, maintaining, improving, leasing or managing of any real property (or interest in real property) that is capital property of the corporation, or

(iii) any combination of the activities described in subparagraphs (i) and (ii), and

(c) the issued shares of the capital stock of the corporation included shares

(i) having conditions attached thereto that included conditions requiring the corporation to accept, at the demand of the holder thereof and at prices determined and payable in accordance with the conditions, the surrender of the shares, or fractions or parts thereof, that are fully paid, or

(ii) qualified in accordance with prescribed conditions relating to the redemption of the shares,

and the fair market value of such of the issued shares of its capital stock as had conditions attached thereto that included such conditions or as were so qualified, as the case may be, was not less than 95% of the fair market value of all of the issued shares of the capital stock of the corporation (such fair market values being determined without regard to any voting rights attaching to shares of the capital stock of the corporation).

**Related Provisions**: 131(8.1) — Corporation deemed not to be mutual fund corporation; 132.2(1)(q) — Corporation deemed not to be mutual fund corporation after rollover of property to mutual fund trust; 142.2(1)"financial institution"(c)(iii) — Mutual fund corporation not subject to mark-to-market rules; 248(1)"mutual fund corporation" — Definition applies to entire Act; 253.1 — Deeming rule re investments in limited partnerships.

**Notes**: For an overview of the taxation of mutual fund corporations, and the way in which the corporate reorganization rules can be used to allow tax-deferred switches between funds, see Hugh Chasmar, "Mutual Fund 'Switch Funds' ", 46(1) *Canadian Tax Journal* 172-194 (1998).

Opening words of 131(8) amended by 1991 technical bill, effective 1990, to make it subject to 131(8.1) and to include a prescribed labour-sponsored venture capital corporation.

131(8)(b) amended by 1994 tax amendments bill (Part V), and by 1995-97 technical bill to add references to an interest in real property, both effective for 1994 and later taxation years. For 1972-93, read:

> (b) its only undertaking was the investing of funds of the corporation; and

**Regulations**: 6701 (prescribed labour-sponsored venture capital corporation).

**I.T. Technical News**: No. 6 (mutual funds trading — meaning of "investing its funds in property" in 131(8)(b)(i)); No. 14 (reporting of derivative income by mutual funds).

**Advance Tax Rulings**: ATR-62: Mutual fund distribution limited partnership — amortization of selling commissions.

**(8.1) Idem** — Where, at any time, it can reasonably be considered that a corporation, having regard to all the circumstances, including the terms and conditions of the shares of its capital stock, was established or is maintained primarily for the benefit of non-resident persons, the corporation shall be deemed not to be a mutual fund corporation after that time unless

(a) throughout the period beginning on the later of February 21, 1990 and the day of its incorporation and ending at that time, all or substantially all of its property consisted of property other than

(i) real property situated in Canada (including any interest therein or option in respect thereof, whether or not the property is in existence), and

(ii) property that would, if

(A) the corporation were non-resident,

(B) paragraph 115(1)(b) were read without reference to subparagraphs 115(1)(b)(i) and (ii), and

(C) the property were disposed of,

be taxable Canadian property of the corporation; or

**Proposed Amendment — 131(8.1)(a)**

(a) throughout the period that begins on the later of February 21, 1990 and the day of its incorporation and ends at that time, all or substantially all of its property consisted of property other than property that would be taxable Canadian property if the definition "taxable Canadian property" in subsection 248(1) were read without reference to paragraph (b) of that definition; or

**Application**: Bill C-43 (First Reading September 20, 2000), s. 81, will amend para. 131(8.1)(a) to read as above, applicable after October 1, 1996.

**Technical Notes**: Section 131 of the Act sets out rules relating to the taxation of mutual fund corporations and their shareholders.

Subsection 131(8.1) of the Act provides that a corporation is not a mutual fund corporation after a particular time if, at that time, it is reasonable to conclude that the corporation was established or maintained primarily for the benefit of non-resident persons. Two conditions provide exceptions to this rule. The first of these conditions, which is set out in paragraph 131(8.1)(a), is met if, throughout the period that started on February 21, 1990 (or if later, the date of incorporation) and that ends at the particular time, all or substantially all of the corporation's property consisted of property other than Canadian real property, options therein and other taxable Canadian property.

Paragraph 131(8.1)(a) is replaced, with effect after October 1, 1996, with new wording that incorporates changes in the definition of "taxable Canadian property" and the relocation of that definition from paragraph 115(1)(b) of the Act to subsection 248(1) of the Act.

(b) it has not issued a share (other than a share issued as a stock dividend) of its capital stock after February 20, 1990 and before that time to a person who, after reasonable inquiry, it had reason to believe was non-resident, except where the share was issued to that person under an agreement in writing entered into before February 21, 1990.

**Related Provisions**: 248(4) — Interest in real property.

**Notes**: 131(8.1) added by 1991 Budget, effective February 21, 1990.

The CCRA takes the position that "all or substantially all", used in 131(8.1)(a), means 90% or more.

**(9) Reduction of refundable capital gains tax on hand** — Notwithstanding any other provision of this section, the amount determined for A in the definition "refundable capital gains tax on hand" in subsection (6) in respect of the 1972 or 1973 taxation year of a corporation is,

(a) in respect of its 1972 taxation year, 91.25% of the amount so determined; and

(b) in respect of its 1973 taxation year, the total of

(i) 91.25% of that proportion of the amount so determined that the number of days in that portion of the year that is before 1973 is of the number of days in the whole year, and

(ii) 100% of that proportion of the amount so determined that the number of days in that portion of the year that is after 1972 is of the number of days in the whole year.

**Related Provisions**: 131(1) — Election re capital gains dividend; 131(6) — Definitions.

**(10) Restricted financial institution** — Notwithstanding any other provision of this Act, a mutual fund corporation or an investment corporation that at any time would, but for this subsection, be a restricted financial institution shall, if it has so elected in prescribed manner and prescribed form before that time, be deemed not to be a restricted financial institution at that time.

**Related Provisions**: 112(2.1) — Where no deduction of dividend permitted.

**Forms**: T2143: Election not to be a restricted financial institution.

**(11) Rules respecting prescribed labour-sponsored venture capital corporations** — Notwithstanding any other provision of this Act, in applying this Act to a corporation that was at any time a prescribed labour-sponsored venture capital corporation,

(a) for the purposes of subparagraphs 129(3)(a)(i) and (ii), the amount deducted under paragraph 111(1)(b) from the corporation's income for each taxation year ending after that time shall be deemed to be nil;

(b) the definition "aggregate investment income" in subsection 129(4) shall be read without reference to paragraph (a) of that definition in its application to taxation years that end after that time;

(c) notwithstanding subsection (4), if it so elects in its return of income under this Part for a taxation year ending after that time, subsection 84(1) applies for that year and all subsequent taxation years;

(d) subsection (5) does not apply for taxation years ending after that time; and

(e) the amount of the corporation's capital dividend account at any time after that time shall be deemed to be nil.

**Related Provisions**: 186.1 — Exempt corporations.

**Notes**: See Notes to 248(1)"registered labour-sponsored venture capital corporation".

131(11)(b) amended by 1995 Budget, effective for taxation years that end after June 1995, as a result of amendments to s. 129. For earlier taxation years since 1990, read:

(b) the value of A in the definition "Canadian investment income" in subsection 129(4) shall be deemed to be zero for taxation years ending after that time;

131(11) added by 1991 technical bill, effective 1990.

**Definitions [s. 131]**: "active business" — 248(1); "amount", "assessment", "business" — 248(1); "Canada" — 255; "Canadian corporation" — 89(1), 248(1); "capital dividend account" — 89(1) [technically not applicable to s. 131]; "capital gain" — 39(1)(a), 248(1); "capital gains dividend account", "capital gains redemptions" — 131(6); "capital gains refund" — 131(2); "capital loss" — 39(1)(b), 248(1); "capital property" — 54, 248(1); "class of shares" — 248(6); "corporation" — 248(1), Interpretation Act 35(1); "cost amount" — 248(1); "credit union" — 137(6), 248(1); "disposition", "dividend" — 248(1); "interest — in real property 248(4); "investment corporation" — 130(3), 248(1); "Minister" — 248(1); "mutual fund corporation" — 131(8), (8.1), 132.2(1)(o)(i), 132.2(1)(q), 248(1); "payable" — 84(7); "person", "prescribed" — 248(1); "prescribed labour-sponsored venture capital corporation" — Reg. 6701; "prescribed rate" — Reg. 4301; "private corporation" — 89(1), 248(1); "property" — 248(1); "public corporation" — 89(1), 248(1); "received" — 248(7); "refundable capital gains tax on hand" — 131(6); "resident in Canada" — 250; "restricted financial institution", "share", "shareholder", "stock dividend" — 248(1); "tax payable" — 248(2); "taxable Canadian property" — 248(1); "taxable capital gain" — 38(a), 248(1); "taxable income" — 2(2), 248(1); "taxation year" — 249; "taxed capital gains" — 130(3)(b), 131(7); "taxpayer" — 248(1); "trust" — 104(1), 248(1), (3); "undertaking" — 253.1(a); "writing" — Interpretation Act 35(1).

**Regulations [s. 131]**: 6701 (prescribed labour-sponsored venture capital corporation).

## Mutual Fund Trusts

**132. (1) Capital gains refund to mutual fund trust** — Where a trust was, throughout a taxation year, a mutual fund trust and a return of its income for the year has been made within 3 years from the end of the year, the Minister

(a) may, on mailing the notice of assessment for the year, refund without application therefor an amount (in this section referred to as its "capital gains refund" for the year) equal to the lesser of

(i) 21.75% of the trust's capital gains redemptions for the year, and

(ii) the trust's refundable capital gains tax on hand at the end of the year; and

### Proposed Amendment — 132(1)(a)

(a) may, on sending the notice of assessment for the year, refund an amount (in this subsection referred to as its "capital gains refund" for the year) equal to the lesser of

(i) the total of

(A) 14.5% of the total of the trust's capital gains redemptions for the year,

(B) the amount, if any, that the Minister determines to be reasonable in the circumstances, after giving consideration to the percentages applicable in determining the trust's capital gains refunds for the year and preceding taxation years and the percentages applicable in determining the trust's refundable capital gains tax on hand at the end of the year, and

(ii) the trust's refundable capital gains tax on hand at the end of the year; and

**Application**: The December 21, 2000 draft legislation, subsec. 78(1), will amend subpara. 132(1)(a) to read as above, applicable to taxation years that end after February 27, 2000 except that, for a taxation year of a mutual fund trust that includes either February 28, 2000 or October 17, 2000, the reference to "14.5%" shall be read as a reference to the percentage determined when 29% is multiplied by the fraction in para. 38(a), as amended [by the December 21, 2000 draft legislation], that applies to the trust for the year.

**Technical Notes**: Section 132 provides for a refund to a mutual fund trust in respect of the tax which the fund has paid on its capital gains distributed to its beneficiaries through a redemption of units. This mechanism is to avoid double taxation.

A mutual fund trust is entitled to capital gains refund for a year equal to the lesser of 21.75% of its capital gains redemptions for the year and its refundable capital gains tax on hand at the end of the year.

The 21.75% rate is based a trust tax rate of 29% and a 3/4 inclusion rate for capital gains. The rate is changed to 14.5%, applicable to taxation years that end after February 27, 2000 and the Minister will be able to determine another amount after giving consideration to the percentages applicable in determining the trust's capital gains refund for the year and preceding taxation years. Those changes are consequential on the decrease of the inclu-

Division F — Special Rules in Certain Circumstances    S. 132(4) cap

sion rate for capital gains from 3/4 to 1/2 [see 38(a) — ed.].

The amendments apply to taxation years that end after February 27, 2000 except that, for the taxation year of a mutual fund trust that includes either February 28, 2000 or October 17, 2000, the reference to the percentage "14.5%" in subparagraph 132(1)(a)(i) is to be read as reference to the percentage determined when 29% is multiplied by the fraction in amended paragraph 38(a) that applies to the trust for the year. These modifications are required in order to reflect the capital gains/losses rate for the year.

**Letter from Department of Finance, September 29, 2000**: See under 38(a).

(b) shall, with all due dispatch, make that capital gains refund after mailing the notice of assessment if an application for it has been made in writing by the trust within the period within which the Minister would be allowed under subsection 152(4) to assess tax payable under this Part by the trust for the year if that subsection were read without reference to paragraph 152(4)(a).

**Related Provisions**: 104(21) — Allocation of capital gains and losses to beneficiaries; 127.55(f)(ii) — No minimum tax on mutual fund trust; 132(2) — Application to other liability; 132(2.1), (2.2) — Interest; 132.1 — Deduction for certain amounts designated by mutual fund trust; 132.2 — Mutual fund reorganizations; 142.2(1)"financial institution"(d) — Mutual fund trust not subject to mark-to-market rules; 152(1) — Assessment; 160.1 — Where excess refunded.

**Notes**: For an overview of mutual fund trusts, see Peter Botz, "Mutual Fund Trusts and Unit Trusts: Selected Tax and Legal Issues", 42(4) *Canadian Tax Journal* 1037-1058 (1994). See also Notes to 132(6).

132(1)(b) amended by 1989 Budget, effective April 28, 1989, to refer to "the period determined under paragraph 152(4)(b) or (c)" rather than to a 6-year or 3-year period; and amended by 1995-97 technical bill, also effective April 28, 1989, to make non-substantive wording changes and to update references to 152(4) as amended.

**Forms**: T184: Capital gains refund for a mutual fund trust.

**(2) Application to other liability** — Instead of making a refund that might otherwise be made under subsection (1) the Minister may, where the trust is liable or about to become liable to make any payment under this Act, apply the amount that would otherwise be refunded to that other liability and notify the trust of that action.

**Related Provisions**: 132(4) — Definitions; 132(6) — Meaning of mutual fund corporation; 152(1) — Assessment.

**(2.1) Interest on capital gains refund** — Where a capital gains refund for a taxation year is paid to, or applied to a liability of, a mutual fund trust, the Minister shall pay or apply interest on the refund at the prescribed rate for the period beginning on the day that is 45 days after the later of

(a) the day that is 90 days after the end of the year, and

(b) the day on which the trust's return of income under this Part for the year was filed under section 150

and ending on the day on which the refund is paid or applied.

**Related Provisions**: 132(2.2) — Excess interest on capital gains refund; 161.1 — Offset of refund interest against arrears interest; 221.1 — Application of interest where legislation retroactive; 248(11) — Interest compounded daily.

**Notes**: 132(2.1) added by 1992 technical bill, effective for capital gains refunds paid or applied with respect to taxation years that begin after 1991.

**Regulations**: 4301(b) (prescribed rate of interest).

**(2.2) Excess interest on capital gains refund** — Where at any particular time interest has been paid to, or applied to a liability of, a trust under subsection (2.1) in respect of a capital gains refund and it is determined at a subsequent time that the capital gains refund was less than that in respect of which interest was so paid or applied,

(a) the amount by which the interest that was so paid or applied exceeds the interest, if any, computed in respect of the amount that is determined at the subsequent time to be the capital gains refund shall be deemed to be an amount (in this subsection referred to as the "amount payable") that became payable under this Part by the trust at the particular time;

(b) the trust shall pay to the Receiver General interest at the prescribed rate on the amount payable, computed from the particular time to the day of payment; and

(c) the Minister may at any time assess the trust in respect of the amount payable and, where the Minister makes such an assessment, the provisions of Divisions I and J apply, with such modifications as the circumstances require, in respect of the assessment as though it had been made under section 152.

**Related Provisions**: 20(1)(ll) — Deduction on repayment of interest; 161.1 — Offset of refund interest against arrears interest; 221.1 — Application of interest where legislation retroactive; 248(11) — Interest compounded daily.

**Notes**: 132(2.2) added by 1992 technical bill, effective for capital gains refunds paid or applied with respect to taxation years that begin after 1991.

**Regulations**: 4301(a) (prescribed rate of interest).

**(3) Application of subsec. 104(20)** — In its application in respect of a mutual fund trust, subsection 104(20) shall be read as if the reference therein to "a dividend (other than a taxable dividend)" were read as a reference to "a capital dividend".

**(4) Definitions** — In this section,

**"capital gains redemptions"** of a mutual fund trust for a taxation year means the amount determined by the formula

$$\frac{A}{B} \times (C + D)$$

1227

## Proposed Amendment — 132(4) "capital gains redemptions" formula

$$(A/B \times (C + D)) - E$$

**Application**: The December 21, 2000 draft legislation, subsec. 78(2), will amend the first formula in the definition "capital gains redemptions" in subsec. 132(4) to read as above, applicable to taxation years that end after February 27, 2000.

**Technical Notes**: Subsection 132(4) defines two expressions for the purpose of the section 132.

The capital gains redemptions of a mutual fund trust for a year are used in determining the mutual fund trust's capital gains refund for the year. In calculating the capital gains redemptions, the trust must allocate accrued capital gains and undistributed realized net capital gains across all payments on the redemptions of units in the year. The first amendment replaces the first formula in the definition "capital gains redemptions" in subsection 132(4). The new formula provides for the deduction of an amount "E" in the calculation of the amount of the trust's capital gains redemptions. The amendment applies to taxation years that end after February 27, 2000.

where

A is the total of all amounts paid by the trust in the year on the redemption of units of the trust,

### Proposed Amendment — 132(4) "capital gains redemptions" A

A is the total of all amounts each of which is a portion of an amount paid by the trust in the year on the redemption of a unit in the trust that is included in the proceeds of disposition in respect of that redemption,

**Application**: The December 21, 2000 draft legislation, subsec. 78(3), will amend the description of A in the definition "capital gains redemptions" in subsec. 132(4) to read as above, applicable to taxation years that end after February 27, 2000.

**Technical Notes**: The second amendment replaces the description of A in the definition. The amended description refers to the portion of payments on the redemption of units that are included in the proceeds of disposition in respect of the redeemed units. The amendment applies to taxation years that end after February 27, 2000.

B is the total of the fair market value at the end of the year of all the issued units of the trust and the amount determined for A in respect of the trust for the year,

C is 100/21.75 of the trust's refundable capital gains tax on hand at the end of the year, and

### Proposed Amendment — 132(4) "capital gains redemptions" C

**Application**: The December 21, 2000 draft legislation, subsec. 78(4), will amend the description of C in the definition "capital gains redemptions" in subsec. 132(4) to replace the reference to the fraction "100/21.75" with a reference to the fraction "100/14.5", applicable to taxation years that end after February 27, 2000 except that, for a taxation year of a mutual fund trust that includes either February 28, 2000 or October 17, 2000, the reference to the fraction "100/14.5" shall be read as a reference to the fraction "100/29X", where "X" is the fraction in para. 38(a), as amended [by the December 21, 2000 draft legislation], that applies to the trust for the year.

**Technical Notes**: The third amendment replaces the fraction "100/21.75" with the fraction "100/14.5" in the description of C in the definition, and is consequential on the reduction of the inclusion rate for capital gains from 3/4 to 1/2 [see 38(a) — ed.]. The amendment applies to taxation years that end after February 27, 2000 except that, for a taxation year of a mutual fund trust that includes either February 28, 2000 or October 17, 2000 the references to the fraction "100/14.5" in the description of C in the definition "capital gains redemptions" in subsection 132(4) is to be read as a reference to the fraction "100/29X", where "X" is the fraction in amended paragraph 38(a) that applies to the trust for the year.

D is the amount determined by the formula

$$(K + L) - (M + N)$$

where

K is the amount of the fair market value at the end of the year of all the issued units of the trust,

L is the total of all amounts each of which is the amount of any debt owing by the trust, or of any other obligation of the trust to pay an amount, that was outstanding at that time,

M is the total of the cost amounts to the trust at that time of all its properties, and

N is the amount of any money of the trust on hand at that time;

### Proposed Addition — 132(4) "capital gains redemptions" E

E is twice the total of all amounts each of which is an amount designated under subsection 104(21) for the year by the trust in respect of a unit of the trust redeemed by the trust at any time in the year and after December 21, 2000;

**Application**: The December 21, 2000 draft legislation, subsec. 78(5), will add the description of E to the definition "capital gains redemptions" in subsec. 132(4), applicable to taxation years that end after February 27, 2000 except that, for a taxation year of a mutual fund trust that includes either February 28, 2000 or October 17, 2000, the word "twice" shall be read as "the fraction that is the reciprocal of the fraction in para. 38(a), as amended [by the December 21, 2000 draft legislation], that applies to the taxpayer for the year, multiplied by".

**Technical Notes**: The last amendment adds the description of E. This refers to twice the total of all amounts each of which is an amount designated by the trust under subsection 104(21) in respect of units redeemed by the trust in the year and after December 21, 2000. The amendment applies to taxation years that end after February 27, 2000 except that, for a taxation year of a mutual fund trust that includes either February 28, 2000 or October 17, 2000, the reference to the word "twice" is to be read as a reference to the expression "the fraction that is the reciprocal of the fraction in paragraph 38(a) that applies to the taxpayer for the year, multiplied by". These modifications are required in order to reflect the capital gains/losses rate for the year.

**Related Provisions**: 132.2(1)(p) — Mutual fund reorganizations; 257 — Formula amounts cannot calculate to less than zero.

**Notes**: 132(4) "capital gains redemptions" was 132(4)(a) before consolidation in R.S.C. 1985 (5th Supp.), effective for taxation years ending after November 1991. See Table of Concordance in the introductory pages.

**"refundable capital gains tax on hand"** of a mutual fund trust at the end of a taxation year means the amount determined by the formula

$$A - B$$

where

A is the total of all amounts each of which is an amount in respect of that or any previous taxation year throughout which the trust was a mutual fund trust, equal to the least of

    (a) 29% of its taxable income for the year,

    (b) 29% of its taxed capital gains for the year, and

    (c) where the taxation year ended after May 6, 1974, the tax payable under this Part by it for the year, and

B is the total of all amounts each of which is an amount in respect of any previous taxation year throughout which the trust was a mutual fund trust, equal to its capital gains refund for the year.

**Related Provisions**: 132(5) — Taxed capital gains defined; 132.2(1)(l) — Addition to RCGTOH on qualifying exchange of property between mutual funds; 257 — Formula cannot calculate to less than zero.

**Notes**: 132(4)"refundable capital gains tax on hand" was 132(4)(b) before consolidation in R.S.C. 1985 (5th Supp.), effective for taxation years ending after November 1991. See Table of Concordance in the introductory pages.

**(5) Definition of "taxed capital gains"** — In subsection (4), "taxed capital gains" of a taxpayer for a taxation year has the meaning assigned by subsection 130(3).

**(6) Meaning of "mutual fund trust"** — Subject to subsection (7), for the purposes of this section, a trust is a mutual fund trust at any time if at that time

    (a) it was a unit trust resident in Canada,

    (b) its only undertaking was

        (i) the investing of its funds in property (other than real property or an interest in real property),

        (ii) the acquiring, holding, maintaining, improving, leasing or managing of any real property (or interest in real property) that is capital property of the trust, or

        (iii) any combination of the activities described in subparagraphs (i) and (ii), and

    (c) it complied with prescribed conditions relating to the number of its unit holders, dispersal of ownership of its units and public trading of its units.

**Proposed Amendment — Trusts with no prospectus filed to be qualified investment**

**Letter from Department of Finance, December 10, 1998**: See under Reg. 4900(1)(d).

**Related Provisions**: 104(21) — Allocation of capital gains and losses to beneficiaries; 132(6.1) — Election to be MFT from beginning of first year; 132(6.2) — Retention of MFT status to end of year; 132.11 — Optional December 15 year-end; 132.1(1)(q) — Trust deemed not to be MFT after rollover of property to another trust; 142.2(1)"financial institution"(d) — MFT not subject to mark-to-market rules; 156(2) — Payment of tax by MFT; 210.1(b) — MFT not subject to Part XII.2 tax; 212(9)(c) — Interest received by MFT and paid to non-residents — withholding tax exemption; 248(1)"mutual fund trust" — Definition applies to entire Act; 253.1 — Deeming rule re investments in limited partnerships.

**Notes**: Opening words of 132(6) amended by 1991 Budget/technical bill, effective February 21, 1990, to be subject to 132(7).

132(6)(b) amended by 1994 tax amendments bill (Part V), and by 1995-97 technical bill to add references to an interest in real property, both effective for 1994 and later taxation years. For 1972-93, read:

> (b) its only undertaking was the investing of funds of the trust, and

The amendment allows for real estate investment trusts to be mutual fund trusts. For discussion of REITs see Denise Dunn McMullen, "Canadian Real Estate Investment Trusts: The Latest in the Series", *Business Vehicles* (Federated Press), Vol. III, No. 2 (1997), pp. 125-127.

Closing words of 132(6) repealed by 1995-97 technical bill, effective for 1994 and later taxation years. This rule has been changed and moved to 132(6.1). For 1972-93, read:

> except that where a trust's first taxation year ended after 1971 and the trust has, after 1971 and on or before the day on or before which it was required by section 150 to file its return of income for that year, become a mutual fund trust, it shall, if it so elected in that return, be deemed to have been a mutual fund trust from the commencement of that year until the day on which it so became a mutual fund trust.

See also Notes to 132(1).

**Regulations**: 4801 (prescribed conditions).

**I.T. Technical News**: No. 6 (mutual funds trading — meaning of "investing its funds in property" in 132(6)(b)(i)); No. 14 (reporting of derivative income by mutual funds).

**Advance Tax Rulings**: ATR-62: Mutual fund distribution limited partnership — amortization of selling commissions.

**Forms**: RC4169: Tax treatment of mutual funds for individuals.

**(6.1) Election to be mutual fund** — Where a trust becomes a mutual fund trust at any particular time before the 91st day after the end of its first taxation year, and the trust so elects in its return of income for that year, the trust is deemed to have been a mutual fund trust from the beginning of that year until the particular time.

**Notes**: 132(6.1) amended by 1998 Budget to change "the calendar year in which its first taxation year began" to "its first taxation year", effective for 1998 and later taxation years. The amendment is consequential on the introduction of 132.11, which allows qualifying trusts to elect to have a December 15 year-end. A related amendment was also made to 142.6(1).

132(6.1) added by 1995-97 technical bill, effective for 1994 and later taxation years. This replaces a rule formerly in the closing words of 132(6).

## Proposed Addition — 132(6.2)

**(6.2) Retention of status as mutual fund trust** — A trust is deemed to be a mutual fund trust throughout a calendar year where

    (a) at any time in the year, the trust would, if this section were read without reference to this subsection, have ceased to be a mutual fund trust

        (i) because the condition described in paragraph 108(2)(a) ceased to be satisfied, or

        (ii) because of the application of paragraph (6)(c);

    (b) the trust was a mutual fund trust at the beginning of the year; and

    (c) the trust would, throughout the portion of the year throughout which it was in existence, have been a mutual fund trust if

        (i) in the case where the condition described in paragraph 108(2)(a) was satisfied at any time in the year, that condition were satisfied throughout the year,

        (ii) subsection (6) were read without reference to paragraph (c) of that subsection, and

        (iii) this section were read without reference to this subsection.

**Related Provisions**: 250(6.1) — Similar rule for trust's residence in Canada.

**Application**: Bill C-43 (First Reading September 20, 2000), subsec. 82(1), will add subsec. 132(6.2), applicable to 1990 et seq.

**Technical Notes**: New subsection 132(6.2) of the Act is a rule that applies where a mutual fund trust ceases to exist. The taxation year of the mutual fund trust (determined with reference to paragraph 249(1)(b)) is not affected by its termination, unless paragraph 132.2(1)(b) applies. Consequently, the last taxation year of a mutual fund trust under the existing income tax rules is generally the calendar year in which it terminates. This leads to unintended consequences under a number of provisions of the Act (including the capital gains refund measure in subsection 132(1), the exemption from the alternative minimum tax in subparagraph 127.55(f)(ii) and the exemption from Part XII.2 tax in section 210.1) that require that a trust be a mutual fund trust throughout a taxation year.

New subsection 132(6.2) is intended to address these unintended consequences. A trust is deemed to be a mutual fund trust throughout a calendar year where:

- but for new subsection 132(6.2), at any time in the year the trust would have ceased to be a mutual fund trust because of the non-application of paragraph 108(2)(a) (i.e., units cease to be redeemable) or the application of 132(6)(c) (i.e., 150 unitholder requirement no longer satisfied);

- the trust was a mutual fund trust at the beginning of the year; and

- the trust would, throughout the portion of the year throughout which it was in existence, have been a mutual fund trust if

    — where the condition in paragraph 108(2)(a) was satisfied at the beginning of the year, that condition were satisfied throughout the year, and

    — paragraph 132(6)(c) and subsection 132(6.2) were not taken into account.

This amendment, which is similar to new subsection 250(6.1), applies to the 1990 and subsequent taxation years.

**Letter from Department of Finance, May 12, 1999**:

Dear [xxx]

This is in reply to your letter of May 3, 1999 to Simon Thompson.

We note that Part XII.2 tax does not apply to a trust for a taxation year if the trust has been a mutual fund trust throughout the year. In policy terms, we think that it is not appropriate that a trust's exemption from Part XII.2 tax for a taxation year is lost merely because the trust ceases in the year to be a mutual fund trust because of the application of paragraph 132(6)(c) of the *Income Tax Act*.

Consequently, we are prepared to recommend a relieving amendment in these circumstances that would apply to a trust for a taxation year if the trust was a mutual fund trust at the beginning of the year. The amendment would apply to the trust only if the trust would, but for that paragraph, have been a mutual fund trust throughout the portion of the year during which it is in existence. In these circumstances, the trust will be treated for the purposes of the Act as having been a mutual fund trust throughout the relevant taxation year. We are prepared to recommend that this amendment applies to the 1999 and subsequent taxation years.

Thank you for writing.

    Yours sincerely,

    Brian Ernewein
    Director, Tax Legislation Division, Tax Policy Branch

**Letter from Department of Finance, January 21, 2000**:

Dear [xxx]

This is in reply to your letter of January 18, 2000 concerning the proposed addition of subsection 132(6.2) of the *Income Tax Act* that was part of Legislative Proposals on Trusts released by the Department of Finance on December 17, 1999.

We have examined the application of this amendment as it applies in the circumstances raised in your letter. From a tax policy perspective, our view is that the relief provided by the proposed amendment may be too narrow. Consequently, we will recommend that the application of this amendment be extended to a trust that ceases to be a mutual fund trust because of the application of paragraph 108(2)(a) of the Act. We will further recommend that this refinement apply as of the same time that the present version of the amendment applies.

Thank you for writing on this matter.

    Yours sincerely,

    Brian Ernewein
    Director, Tax Legislation Division, Tax Policy Branch

**(7) Idem** — Where, at any time, it can reasonably be considered that a trust, having regard to all the cir-

Division F — Special Rules in Certain Circumstances    S. 132.1(1)(a)(ii)

cumstances, including the terms and conditions of the units of the trust, was established or is maintained primarily for the benefit of non-resident persons, the trust shall be deemed not to be a mutual fund trust after that time unless

(a) throughout the period beginning on the later of February 21, 1990 and the day of its creation and ending at that time, all or substantially all of its property consisted of property other than

   (i) real property situated in Canada (including any interest therein or option in respect thereof, whether or not the property is in existence), and

   (ii) property that would, if

      (A) the trust were non-resident,

      (B) paragraph 115(1)(b) were read without reference to subparagraphs 115(1)(b)(i) and (ii), and

      (C) the property were disposed of,

   be taxable Canadian property of the trust; or

(b) it has not issued a unit (other than a unit issued to a person in satisfaction of the person's right under the trust to an amount referred to in paragraph 104(13)(c)) of the trust after February 20, 1990 and before that time to a person who, after reasonable inquiry, it had reason to believe was non-resident, except where the unit was issued to that person under an agreement in writing entered into before February 21, 1990.

**Proposed Amendment — 132(7)(a), (b)**

(a) throughout the period that began on the later of February 21, 1990 and the day of its creation and ended at that time, all or substantially all of its property consisted of property other than property that would be taxable Canadian property if the definition "taxable Canadian property" in subsection 248(1) were read without reference to paragraph (b) of that definition; or

(b) it has not issued any unit (other than a unit issued to a person as a payment, or in satisfaction of the person's right to enforce payment, of an amount out of the trust's income, determined before the application of subsection 104(6) or out of the trust's capital gains) of the trust after February 20, 1990 and before that time to a person who, after reasonable inquiry, it had reason to believe was non-resident, except where the unit was issued to that person under an agreement in writing entered into before February 21, 1990.

**Application:** Bill C-43 (First Reading September 20, 2000), subsec. 82(2), will amend paras. 132(7)(a) and (b) to read as above, para. (a) applicable after October 1, 1996, and para. (b) applicable after February 20, 1990.

**Technical Notes:** Under subsection 132(7) of the Act, a trust does not qualify as a mutual fund trust in certain cases where it is reasonable to conclude that the trust was established primarily for the benefit of non-resident persons. The provision's purpose was to discourage the use of mutual fund trusts as intermediaries through which non-residents could invest in Canadian real estate and other taxable Canadian property without recognizing any gains on the disposition of units in trust. However, transitional relief was intended to be provided in the case of a trust which did not issue units after February 20, 1990 otherwise than as a capitalization of an income distribution.

Subsection 132(7) is amended to change references to Canadian real estate, and to specified other taxable Canadian property in section 115, to references to the same types of property in the new definition "taxable Canadian property" in subsection 248(1).

Subsection 132(7) is also amended to ensure that the transitional relief operates as described above. The amendment also ensures that this transitional relief is not interrupted by reason only of an issue of units in satisfaction of payments made out of a trust's capital gains.

**Related Provisions:** 248(4) — Interest in real property.

**Notes:** 132(7) added by 1991 technical bill, effective February 20, 1990.

The CCRA takes the position that "all or substantially all", used in 132(7)(a), means 90% or more.

**Definitions [s. 132]:** "amount", "assessment" — 248(1); "calendar year" — *Interpretation Act* 37(1)(a); "Canada" — 255; "capital dividend" — 83(2), 248(1); "capital gain" — 39(1)(a), 248(1); "capital gains redemptions" — 132(4); "capital gains refund" — 132(1); "capital property" — 54, 248(1); "cost amount", "dividend" — 248(1); "interest" — in real property 248(4); "Minister" — 248(1); "mutual fund trust" — 132(6)–(7), 132.2(1)(q), 248(1); "non-resident", "person" — 248(1); "prescribed rate" — Reg. 4301; "property" — 248(1); "refundable capital gains tax on hand" — 132(4); "resident in Canada" — 250; "taxable Canadian property" — 248(1); "taxable capital gain" — 38(a), 248(1); "taxable dividend" — 89(1), 248(1); "taxable income" — 2(2), 248(1); "taxation year" — 249; "taxed capital gains" — 130(3), 132(5); "trust" — 104(1), 248(1), (3); "undertaking" — 253.1(a); "unit trust" — 108(2), 248(1); "writing" — *Interpretation Act* 35(1).

**Information Circulars [s. 132]:** 78-14R2: Guidelines for trust companies and other persons responsible for filing T3R-IND, T3R-G, T3RIF-IND, T3RIF-G, T3H-IND, T3H-G, T3D, T3P, T3S, T3RI, T3F.

### 132.1 (1) Amounts designated by mutual fund trust

— Where a trust in its return of income under this Part for a taxation year throughout which it was a mutual fund trust designates an amount in respect of a particular unit of the trust owned by a taxpayer at any time in the year equal to the total of

(a) such amount as the trust may determine in respect of the particular unit for the year not exceeding the amount, if any, by which

   (i) the total of all amounts that were determined by the trust under subsection 104(16) of the *Income Tax Act*, chapter 148 of the Revised Statutes of Canada, 1952, for taxation years of the trust commencing before 1988

exceeds

   (ii) the total of all amounts determined by the trust under this paragraph for the year or a preceding taxation year in respect of all units of the trust, other than amounts determined in respect of the particular unit for the year under this paragraph, and

(b) such amount as the trust may determine in respect of the particular unit for the year not exceeding the amount, if any, by which

(i) the total of all amounts described in subparagraph 53(2)(h)(i.1) that became payable by the trust after 1987 and before the year

exceeds

(ii) the total of all amounts determined by the trust under this paragraph for the year or a preceding taxation year in respect of all units of the trust, other than amounts determined in respect of the particular unit for the year under this paragraph,

the amount so designated shall

(c) subject to subsection (3), be deductible in computing the income of the trust for the year, and

(d) be included in computing the income of the taxpayer for the taxpayer's taxation year in which the year of the trust ends, except that where the particular unit was owned by two or more taxpayers during the year, such part of the amount so designated as the trust may determine shall be included in computing the income of each such taxpayer for the taxpayer's taxation year in which the year of the trust ends if the total of the parts so determined is equal to the amount so designated.

**Related Provisions**: 12(1)(m) — Income inclusion — benefits from trust; 132.2(1)(n) — Mutual fund reorganization — continuation of trust; 214(3)(f.1) — Non-resident withholding tax.

**Notes**: See Notes to 12(1)(m).

**I.T. Application Rules**: 69 (meaning of *Income Tax Act*, chapter 148 of the Revised Statutes of Canada, 1952").

**Forms**: RC4169: Tax treatment of mutual funds for individuals.

**(2) Adjusted cost base of unit where designation made** — In computing, at any time in a taxation year of a taxpayer, the adjusted cost base to the taxpayer of a unit in a mutual fund trust, there shall be added that part of the amount included under subsection (1) in computing the taxpayer's income that is reasonably attributable to the amount determined under paragraph (1)(b) by the trust for its taxation year ending in the year in respect of the unit owned by the taxpayer.

**Related Provisions**: 12(1)(m) — Amounts to be included from business or property — benefits from trusts; 53(1)(d.2) — Addition to adjusted cost base of share.

**(3) Limitation on current year deduction** — The total of amounts deductible by reason of paragraph (1)(c) in computing the income of a trust for a taxation year shall not exceed the amount that would be the income of the trust for the year if no deductions were made under this section and subsection 104(6).

**Related Provisions**: 132.2(1)(n) — Mutual fund reorganization — continuation of trust.

**(4) Carryover of excess** — The amount, if any, by which the total of all amounts each of which is an amount designated for the year under subsection (1) exceeds the amount deductible under this section in computing the income of the trust for the year, shall, for the purposes of paragraph (1)(c) and subsection (3), be deemed designated under subsection (1) by the trust for its immediately following taxation year.

**Related Provisions**: 132.2(1)(n) — Mutual fund reorganization — continuation of trust.

**(5) Where designation has no effect** — Where it is reasonable to conclude that an amount determined by a mutual fund trust

(a) under paragraph (1)(a) or (b) for a taxation year of the trust in respect of a unit owned at any time in the year by a taxpayer who was a person exempt from tax under this Part by reason of subsection 149(1), or

(b) under paragraph (1)(d) for the year in respect of the amount designated under subsection (1) for the year in respect of the unit

differs from the amount that would have been so determined for the year in respect of the taxpayer had the taxpayer not been a person exempt from tax under this Part by reason of subsection 149(1), the amount designated for the year in respect of the unit under subsection (1) shall have no effect for the purposes of paragraph (1)(c).

**Related Provisions**: 132.2(1)(n) — Mutual fund reorganization — continuation of trust.

**Definitions [s. 132.1]**: "adjusted cost base" — 54, 248(1); "amount" — 248(1); "Canadian property" — 133(8); "mutual fund trust" — 132(6)–(7), 132.2(1)(q), 248(1); "person" — 248(1); "taxation year" — 249; "taxpayer" — 248(1); "trust" — 104(1), 248(1), (3).

**132.11 (1) Taxation year of mutual fund trust** — Notwithstanding any other provision of this Act, where a trust (other than a prescribed trust) that was a mutual fund trust on the 74th day after the end of a particular calendar year so elects in writing filed with the Minister with the trust's return of income for the trust's taxation year that includes December 15 of the particular year,

(a) the trust's taxation year that began before December 16 of the particular year and, but for this paragraph, would end at the end of the particular year (or, where the first taxation year of the trust began after December 15 of the preceding calendar year and no return of income was filed for a taxation year of the trust that ended at the end of the preceding calendar year, at the end of the preceding calendar year) is deemed to end at the end of December 15 of the particular year;

(b) where the trust's taxation year ends on December 15 because of paragraph (a), each subsequent taxation year of the trust is deemed to be the period that begins at the beginning of December 16 of a calendar year and ends at the end of December 15 of the following calendar year or at such earlier time as is determined under paragraph 132.2(1)(b) or subsection 142.6(1); and

(c) each fiscal period of the trust that begins in a taxation year of the trust that ends on December 15 because of paragraph (a) or that ends in a subsequent taxation year of the trust shall end no later than the end of the year or the subsequent year, as the case may be.

### Proposed Amendment — Reverting to December 31 Year-End

**Letter from Department of Finance, August 16, 2000:**

Dear [xxx]

Thank you for your letter of June 29, 2000, concerning the *Income Tax Act* (Act) provisions permitting certain mutual fund trusts to elect for a December 15th year-end.

You are requesting an amendment to these provisions so that a trust that has a December 15th year-end because of an election under subsection 132.11(1) of the Act may elect to return to a December 31st year-end. You note that in certain circumstances (e.g., a qualifying exchange under section 132.2 of the Act, or a joining of the management of two different families of mutual fund trusts), it may be more practicable for a trust that has elected for a December 15th year-end to be able to return to a December 31st year-end. You advise that the Canada Customs and Revenue Agency (CCRA) concurs with your view that the present provisions do not provide relief in these circumstances.

The objective of section 132.11 is to provide mutual fund trusts with an administratively workable basis for calculating income and distributions for a taxation year and for reporting on a timely basis. We agree that, from a tax policy perspective, it would not be inconsistent with this objective to permit a trust to return to a December 31st year-end. However, to guard against the possible use of that section for inappropriate tax planning purposes, the "revocation" of an election under section 132.11 would be available only to a trust that was, in its immediately preceding taxation year, subject to a "qualifying exchange" under section 132.2 of the Act. Accordingly, we will recommend that the income tax provisions be amended to permit such a trust to apply to the CCRA to change from a December 15th year-end to a December 31st year-end.

We will further recommend that this amendment apply to taxation years that end after 1999.

Thank you for writing,

Yours sincerely,

Len Farber
General Director, Tax Legislation Division, Tax Policy Branch

**Related Provisions:** 132.11(2) — Where trust is member of partnership; 132.11(3) — Where trust is beneficiary of another trust; 132.11(6) — Additional income.

**Notes:** See Notes at end of 132.11.

**(2) Electing trust's share of partnership income and losses** — Where a trust is a member of a partnership a fiscal period of which ends in a calendar year after December 15 of the year and a particular taxation year of the trust ends on December 15 of the year because of subsection (1), each amount otherwise determined under paragraph 96(1)(f) or (g) to be the trust's income or loss for a subsequent taxation year of the trust is deemed to be the trust's income or loss determined under paragraph 96(1)(f) or (g) for the particular year and not for the subsequent year.

**Notes:** See Notes at end of 132.11.

**(3) Electing trust's income from other trusts** — Where a particular trust is a beneficiary under another trust a taxation year of which (in this subsection referred to as the "other year") ends in a calendar year after December 15 of the year and a particular taxation year of the trust ends on December 15 of the year because of subsection (1), each amount determined or designated under subsection 104(13), (19), (21), (22) or (29) for the other year that would otherwise be included, or taken into account, in computing the income of the particular trust for a subsequent taxation year of the trust shall

(a) be included, or taken into account, in computing the particular trust's income for the particular year; and

(b) not be included, or taken into account, in computing the particular trust's income for the subsequent year.

**Notes:** See Notes at end of 132.11.

**(4) Amounts paid or payable to beneficiaries** — For the purposes of subsections 52(6) and 104(6) and (13) and subsections (5) and (6) and notwithstanding subsection 104(24), each amount that is paid, or that becomes payable, by a trust to a beneficiary after the end of a particular taxation year of the trust that ends on December 15 of a calendar year because of subsection (1) and before the end of that calendar year is deemed to have been paid or to have become payable, as the case may be, to the beneficiary at the end of the particular taxation year and not at any other time.

### Proposed Amendment — 132.11(4)

**(4) Amounts paid or payable to beneficiaries** — For the purposes of subsections (5) and (6) and subsections 104(6) and (13), notwithstanding subsection 104(24), each amount that is paid, or that becomes payable, by a trust to a beneficiary after the end of a particular taxation year of the trust that ends on December 15 of a calendar year because of subsection (1) and before the end of that calendar year, is deemed to have been paid or to have become payable, as the case may be, to the beneficiary at the end of the particular year and not at any other time.

**Application:** Bill C-43 (First Reading September 20, 2000), subsec. 83(1), will amend subsec. 132.11(4) to read as above, applicable to 2000 *et seq.*

**S. 132.11(4)**      Income Tax Act, Part I

**Technical Notes**: Section 132.11 of the Act generally allows mutual fund trusts to elect to have taxation years that end on December 15, rather than on December 31.

Subsection 132.11(4) is designed to permit distributions made in the last 16 days of a calendar year in respect of a trust's taxation year ending on December 15 of the calendar year to be treated as if they were made at the end of that taxation year. Subsection 132.11(6) generally permits a trust that has a December 15 taxation year end to distribute additional income to its unitholders, to the extent that this income is reflected by amounts made payable to these unitholders. Both of these subsections are worded so that rights to these distributions are treated as rights to which subsection 52(6) applies, with the result that there is no capital gain on the satisfaction of these rights.

Subsections 132.11(4) and (6) are amended to reflect the repeal of subsection 52(6) and the introduction of paragraphs (g) and (h) of the definition "disposition" in subsection 248(1). As a consequence of these paragraphs, there is no disposition (and, as a consequence no capital gain or loss) that arises on the mere satisfaction of the right to enforce payment from a mutual fund trust.

**Notes**: See Notes at end of 132.11.

**(5) Special rules where change in status of beneficiary** — Where an amount is deemed by subsection (4) to have been paid or to have become payable at the end of December 15 of a calendar year by a trust to a beneficiary who was not a beneficiary under the trust at that time,

(a) notwithstanding any other provision of this Act, where the beneficiary did not exist at that time, except for the purpose of this paragraph, the first taxation year of the beneficiary is deemed to include the period that begins at that time and ends immediately before the beginning of the first taxation year of the beneficiary;

(b) the beneficiary is deemed to exist throughout the period described in paragraph (a); and

(c) where the beneficiary was not a beneficiary under the trust at that time, the beneficiary is deemed to have been a beneficiary under the trust at that time.

**Related Provisions**: 132.11(4) — Amounts paid to beneficiary from December 16-31.

**Notes**: See Notes at end of 132.11.

**(6) Additional income of electing trust** — Where a particular amount is designated under this subsection by a trust in its return of income for a particular taxation year that ends on December 15 because of subsection (1) or throughout which the trust was a mutual fund trust and the trust does not designate an amount under subsection 104(13.1) or (13.2) for the particular year,

(a) the particular amount shall be added in computing its income for the particular year;

(b) for the purposes of subsections 104(6) and (13), each portion of the particular amount that is allocated under this paragraph to a beneficiary under the trust in the trust's return of income for the particular year in respect of an amount paid or payable to the beneficiary in the particular year shall be considered to be additional income of the trust for the particular year (determined without reference to subsection 104(6)) that was paid or payable, as the case may be, to the beneficiary at the end of the particular year; and

(c) for the purpose of subsection 52(6), where a portion of the particular amount is allocated to a beneficiary under paragraph (b) in respect of an amount that became payable to the beneficiary in the particular year, the right to the amount so payable shall be considered to be a right to enforce payment by the trust to the beneficiary out of the trust's income (determined without reference to the provisions of this Act) for the particular year.

**Proposed Repeal — 132.11(6)(c)**

**Application**: Bill C-43 (First Reading September 20, 2000), subsec. 83(2), will repeal para. 132.11(6)(c), applicable to 2000 et seq.

**Technical Notes**: See under 132.11(4).

**Related Provisions**: 132.11(4) — Amounts paid to beneficiary from December 16-31; 220(3.21)(b) — Late filing, amendment or revocation of designation or allocation.

**Notes**: See Notes at end of 132.11.

**(7) Deduction** — Subject to subsection (8), the lesser of the amount designated under subsection (6) by a trust for a taxation year and the total of all amounts each of which is allocated by the trust under paragraph (6)(b) in respect of the year shall be deducted in computing the trust's income for the following taxation year.

**Related Provisions**: 132.11(8) — Anti-avoidance rule.

**Notes**: See Notes at end of 132.11.

**(8) Anti-avoidance** — Subsection (7) does not apply in computing the income of a trust for a taxation year where it is reasonable to consider that the designation under subsection (6) for the preceding taxation year was part of a series of transactions or events that includes a change in the composition of beneficiaries under the trust.

**Notes [s. 132.11]**: 132.11 added by 1998 Budget, effective for 1998 and later taxation years. It generally allows mutual fund trusts (MFTs) to elect to have taxation years that end on December 15 rather than December 31. The purpose is to allow MFTs to calculate income and distributions for a taxation year on a more administratively workable basis, to allow for more accurate and timely reporting, and to minimize the risk of errors which can have adverse financial consequences for MFTs and their unitholders.

Where the election is made, the trust's income must be adjusted to take into account investments in partnership interests and units of other trusts. Special provision is also made to allow for the allocation to unitholders of income paid or payable during December 16–31. In addition, "overdistributions" by the trust to unitholders may be treated as income for those unitholders. The trust is generally allowed to deduct the amount of those overdistributions for the next taxation year. The mechanism for overdistributions ensures that MFTs can maximize their capital gain refunds and provides for more straightforward tax consequences for unitholders.

The optional December 15 year-end in 132.11 is a change from the original proposal in the February 1998 budget, which would have allowed distributions within a month after year-end. For discussion see Judith Harris, "Recent Legislative Proposals: Taxation Year End Election", V(1) *Business Vehicles* (Federated Press) 222–224 (1999).

**Definitions [s. 132.11]:** "amount" — 248(1); "fiscal period" — 249.1; "Minister" — 248(1); "mutual fund trust" — 132(6)–(7), 132.2(1)(q), 248(1); "partnership" — see Notes to 96(1); "prescribed" — 248(1) "share" — 248(1); "taxation year" — 249; "trust" — 104(1), 248(1), (3); "writing" — *Interpretation Act* 35(1).

## 132.2 (1) Mutual funds — qualifying exchange [rollover] 

— Where a mutual fund corporation or a mutual fund trust has at any time disposed of a property to a mutual fund trust in a qualifying exchange,

(a) the transferee shall be deemed to have acquired the property at the time (in this subsection referred to as the "acquisition time") that is immediately after the time that is immediately after the transfer time, and not to have acquired the property at the transfer time;

(b) subject to paragraph (o), the last taxation years of the funds that began before the transfer time shall be deemed to have ended at the acquisition time, and their next taxation years shall be deemed to have begun immediately after those last taxation years ended;

(c) the transferor's proceeds of disposition of the property and the transferee's cost of the property shall be deemed to be the lesser of

(i) the fair market value of the property at the transfer time, and

(ii) the greatest of

(A) the cost amount to the transferor of the property at the transfer time or, where the property is depreciable property, the lesser of its capital cost and its cost amount to the transferor immediately before the transfer time,

(B) the amount that the funds have agreed upon in respect of the property in their election in respect of the qualifying exchange, and

(C) the fair market value at the transfer time of the consideration (other than units of the transferee) received by the transferor for the disposition of the property;

(d) where the property is depreciable property and its capital cost to the transferor exceeds the transferor's proceeds of disposition of the property under paragraph (c), for the purposes of sections 13 and 20 and any regulations made for the purposes of paragraph 20(1)(a),

(i) the property's capital cost to the transferee shall be deemed to be the amount that was its capital cost to the transferor, and

(ii) the excess shall be deemed to have been allowed to the transferee in respect of the property under regulations made for the purposes of paragraph 20(1)(a) in computing income for taxation years ending before the transfer time;

(e) where two or more depreciable properties of a prescribed class are disposed of by the transferor to the transferee in the same qualifying exchange, paragraph (c) applies as if each property so disposed of had been separately disposed of in the order designated by the transferor at the time of making the election in respect of the qualifying exchange or, if the transferor does not so designate any such order, in the order designated by the Minister;

(f) each property of a fund, other than

(i) depreciable property of a prescribed class to which paragraph (g) would, but for this paragraph, apply, and

(ii) property disposed of by the transferor to the transferee at the transfer time

shall be deemed to have been disposed of, and to have been reacquired by the fund, immediately before the acquisition time for an amount equal to the lesser of

(iii) the fair market value of the property at the transfer time, and

(iv) the greater of

(A) its cost amount or, where the property is depreciable property, the lesser of its capital cost and its cost amount to the disposing fund at the transfer time, and

(B) the amount that the fund designates in respect of the property in a notification to the Minister accompanying the election in respect of the qualifying exchange;

(g) where the undepreciated capital cost to a fund of depreciable property of a prescribed class immediately before the acquisition time exceeds the total of

(i) the fair market value of all the property of that class immediately before the acquisition time, and

(ii) the amount in respect of property of that class otherwise allowed under regulations made for the purposes of paragraph 20(1)(a) or deductible under subsection 20(16) in computing the fund's income for the taxation year that includes the transfer time,

the excess shall be deducted in computing the fund's income for the taxation year that includes the transfer time and shall be deemed to have been allowed in respect of property of that class under regulations made for the purposes of paragraph 20(1)(a);

(h) except as provided in paragraph (p), the transferor's cost of any particular property received by the transferor from the transferee as consideration for the disposition of the property is deemed to be

(i) nil, where the particular property is a unit of the transferee, and

(ii) the particular property's fair market value at the transfer time, in any other case;

(i) the transferor's proceeds of disposition of any units of the transferee received as consideration for the disposition of the property that were disposed of by the transferor within 60 days after the transfer time in exchange for shares of the transferor shall be deemed to be nil;

(j) where shares of the transferor have been disposed of by a taxpayer to the transferor in exchange for units of the transferee within 60 days after the transfer time,

(i) the taxpayer's proceeds of disposition of the shares and the cost to the taxpayer of the units shall be deemed to be equal to the cost amount to the taxpayer of the shares immediately before the transfer time, and

(ii) where all of the taxpayer's shares of the transferor have been so disposed of, for the purposes of applying section 39.1 in respect of the taxpayer after that disposition, the transferee shall be deemed to be the same entity as the transferor;

(k) where a share to which paragraph (j) applies would, but for this paragraph, cease to be a qualified investment (within the meaning assigned by subsection 146(1), 146.1(1) or 146.3(1) or section 204) as a consequence of the qualifying exchange, the share is deemed to be a qualified investment until the earlier of the day that is 60 days after the transfer time and the time at which it is disposed of in accordance with paragraph (j);

(l) there shall be added to the amount determined under the description of A in the definition "refundable capital gains tax on hand" in subsection 132(4) in respect of the transferee for its taxation years that begin after the transfer time the amount, if any, by which

(i) the transferor's refundable capital gains tax on hand (within the meaning assigned by subsection 131(6) or 132(4), as the case may be) at the end of its taxation year that includes the transfer time

exceeds

(ii) the transferor's capital gains refund (within the meaning assigned by paragraph 131(2)(a) or 132(1)(a), as the case may be) for that year;

(m) no amount in respect of a non-capital loss, net capital loss, restricted farm loss, farm loss or limited partnership loss of a fund for a taxation year that began before the transfer time is deductible in computing its taxable income for a taxation year that begins after the transfer time;

(n) where the transferor is a mutual fund trust, for the purposes of subsections 132.1(1) and (3) to (5), the transferee shall be deemed after the transfer time to be the same mutual fund trust as, and a continuation of, the transferor;

(o) where the transferor is a mutual fund corporation,

(i) for the purposes of subsection 131(4), the transferor is deemed in respect of any share disposed of in accordance with paragraph (j) to be a mutual fund corporation at the time of the disposition, and

(ii) for the purposes of Part I.3, the transferor's taxation year that, but for this paragraph, would have included the transfer time is deemed to have ended immediately before the transfer time (except that, for greater certainty, nothing in this paragraph shall affect the computation of any amount determined under this Part);

(p) for the purpose of determining the funds' capital gains redemptions (as defined in subsection 131(6) or 132(4)), for their taxation years that include the transfer time,

(i) the total of the cost amounts to the transferor of all its properties at the end of the year is deemed to be the total of all amounts each of which is

(A) the transferor's proceeds of disposition of a property that was transferred to a transferee on the qualifying exchange, or

(B) the cost amount to the transferor at the end of the year of a property that was not transferred on the qualifying exchange, and

(ii) the transferee is deemed not to have acquired any property that was transferred to it on the qualifying exchange; and

(q) except as provided in subparagraph (o)(i), the transferor is, notwithstanding subsections 131(8) and 132(6), deemed to be neither a mutual fund corporation nor a mutual fund trust for taxation years that begin after the transfer time.

**Related Provisions**: 7(1.4) — Exchange of options giving mutual fund trust employee right to acquire units; 54"superficial loss"(c) — No superficial loss on deemed disposition and reacquisition.

**Notes**: 132.2(1)(k) amended by 1998 Budget to add reference to 146.1(1), effective 1998.

132.2(1) added by 1994 tax amendments bill (Part VI), effective July 1994; 132.2(1)(p) amended, (h) amended to be subject to (p), and (o)(i) and (q) added, all by 1995-97 technical bill, also effective July 1994 (i.e., retroactive to the introduction of 132.2). However, amended 132.2(1)(p) does not apply to a qualifying exchange between funds that occurred before November 1996, if the funds jointly elect in writing filed with Revenue Canada by September 30, 1998; in which case read (p) as:

(p) the transferor shall, notwithstanding subsections 131(8) and 132(6), be deemed to be neither a mutual fund corpora-

Division F — Special Rules in Certain Circumstances    S. 133(1)(d)

tion nor a mutual fund trust for taxation years beginning after the transfer time.

See Notes at end of 132.2 for initial enactment.

**Regulations**: 1105 (prescribed classes of depreciable property).

**(2) Definitions** — In this section,

**"qualifying exchange"** means a transfer at any time (in this section referred to as the "transfer time") of all or substantially all of the property of a mutual fund corporation or mutual fund trust to a mutual fund trust (in this section referred to as the "transferor" and "transferee", respectively, and as the "funds") where

(a) all or substantially all of the shares issued by the transferor and outstanding immediately before the transfer time are within 60 days after the transfer time disposed of to the transferor,

(b) no person disposing of shares of the transferor to the transferor within that 60-day period (otherwise than pursuant to the exercise of a statutory right of dissent) receives any consideration for the shares other than units of the transferee, and

(c) the funds jointly elect, by filing a prescribed form with the Minister within 6 months after the transfer time, to have this section apply with respect to the transfer;

**Notes**: Definition "qualifying exchange" added with the enactment of 132.2 by 1994 tax amendments bill (Part VI), effective July 1994; and para. (b) amended retroactive to its introduction by 1995-97 technical bill to add the parenthesized exception for the exercise of a right of dissent.

An election under para. (c) was valid if made by end of 1995.

**Forms**: T1169: Election on disposition of property by a mutual fund corporation (or a mutual fund trust) to a mutual fund trust.

**"share"** means a share of the capital stock of a mutual fund corporation and a unit of a mutual fund trust.

**Notes**: 132.2 added by 1994 tax amendments bill (Part VI), effective July 1994.

**Definitions [s. 132.2]**: "acquisition time" — 132.2(1)(a); "cost amount" — 248(1); "depreciable property" — 13(21), 248(1); "farm loss" — 111(8), 248(1); "limited partnership loss" — 96(2.1)(e), 248(1); "Minister" — 248(1); "mutual fund corporation" — 131(8), 248(1); "mutual fund trust" — 132(6)–(7), 132.2(1)(q), 248(1); "net capital loss", "non-capital loss" — 111(8), 248(1); "proceeds of disposition" — 54; "prescribed", "property" — 248(1); "qualifying exchange" — 132.2(2); "regulation" — 248(1); "restricted farm loss" — 31, 248(1); "share" — 132.2(2); "taxable income" — 2(2), 248(1); "taxation year" — 132.2(1)(b), 249; "transfer time" — 132.2(2)"qualifying exchange"; "undepreciated capital cost" — 13(21), 248(1).

## Non-Resident-Owned Investment Corporations

### Proposed Amendment — Elimination of NROs

**Technical Notes [December 21, 2000]**: Section 133 provides rules for the taxation of non-resident-owned investment corporations (NROs) on a basis that attempts to approximate the tax treatment that would apply if their non-resident shareholders held investments directly. Pursuant to changes announced in the 2000 Budget, NROs are to be phased out over a three-year period, effective after February 27, 2000.

The 2000 Budget also announced that existing NROs will not be permitted to increase their overall assets or debt during the three-year phase-out period.

The phase out of NROs is given effect through the amended definition "non-resident-owned investment corporation" and the new definition "increase in capital" in subsection 133(8). See the commentary on those definitions for further details.

**133. (1) Computation of income** — In computing the income of a non-resident-owned investment corporation for a taxation year,

(a) no deduction may be made in respect of interest on its bonds, debentures, securities or other indebtedness, and

(b) no deduction may be made under subsection 65(1),

and its income and taxable income shall be computed as if

(c) the only taxable capital gains and allowable capital losses referred to in paragraph 3(c) were taxable capital gains and allowable capital losses from dispositions of taxable Canadian property or property that would be taxable Canadian property if at no time in the year the corporation had been resident in Canada,

### Proposed Amendment — 133(1)(c)

(c) the only taxable capital gains and allowable capital losses referred to in paragraph 3(b) were from dispositions of taxable Canadian property,

**Application**: Bill C-43 (First Reading September 20, 2000), subsec. 84(1), will amend para. 133(1)(c) to read as above, applicable after October 1, 1996.

**Technical Notes**: Section 133 provides rules for the taxation of non-resident-owned investment corporations on a basis that approximates the treatment that would apply if its non-resident shareholders had invested directly in Canada.

Subsection 133(1) provides rules for computing the income and taxable income of a non-resident-owned investment corporation. Paragraph 133(1)(c) provides that the only taxable capital gains and allowable capital losses that are included in computing such a corporation's income are those from dispositions of taxable Canadian property.

Paragraph 133(1)(c) is amended, with application after October 1, 1996, to reflect the changes in the definition of "taxable Canadian property" and that definition's relocation from subsection 115(1) to subsection 248(1).

(d) any taxable capital gain or allowable capital loss of the corporation were an amount equal to $4/3$ of the amount thereof otherwise determined, and

### Proposed Amendment — 133(1)(d)

**Application**: The December 21, 2000 draft legislation, subsec. 79(1), will amend para. 133(1)(d) to read as above, applicable to taxation years that end after February 27, 2000 except that, for a taxation year of a corporation that includes either February 28, 2000

S. 133(1)(d)   Income Tax Act, Part I

or October 17, 2000, the word "twice" shall be read "the fraction that is the reciprocal of the fraction in para. 38(a), as amended [by the December 21, 2000 draft legislation], that applies to the taxpayer for the year, multiplied by".

**Technical Notes**: Subsection 133(1) provides rules for the purposes of determining the income and the taxable income of a non-resident owned investment corporation.

The amendment to paragraph 133(1)(d) replaces the reference to the expression "4/3 of" with a reference to the word "twice". It is consequential on the reduction of the inclusion rate for capital gains from 3/4 to 1/2 [see 38(a) — ed.].

This amendment applies to taxation years that end after February 27, 2000 except that, for a taxation year that includes either February 28, 2000 or October 17, 2000, the reference to the word "twice" is to be read as reference to the expression "the fraction that is the reciprocal fraction in paragraph 38(a) that applies to the corporation for the year multiplied by". These modifications are required in order to reflect the capital gains/losses rate for the year.

(e) subsection 83(2) were read without reference to paragraph 83(2)(b).

**Related Provisions**: 104(10) — Where dividends and interest paid to trust for non-residents; 104(11) — Dividend received from NRO; 134 — NRO not a Canadian corporation etc.; 186.1(b) — NRO not subject to Part IV tax; 212(9)(a) — Dividends received by trust from NRO — no withholding tax; Canada–U.S. tax treaty, Art. XXIX:6(b) — Treaty provisions inapplicable to NRO.

**Regulations**: 502 (annual certificate of changes of ownership of shares and debt).

**(2) Non-resident-owned investment corporations** — In computing the taxable income of a non-resident-owned investment corporation for a taxation year, no deduction may be made from its income for the year, except

(a) interest received in the year from other non-resident-owned investment corporations;

(b) taxes paid to the government of a country other than Canada in respect of any part of the income of the corporation for the year derived from sources therein; and

(c) net capital losses as provided for by section 111.

**Related Provisions**: 88(2)(a) — Winding-up of Canadian corporation.

**(3) Special tax rate** — The tax payable under this Part by a corporation for a taxation year when it was a non-resident-owned investment corporation is an amount equal to 25% of its taxable income for the year.

**Related Provisions**: 88(2)(a) — Winding-up of Canadian corporation; 157(3)(d) — Instalments payable by NRO.

**Advance Tax Rulings**: ATR-43: Utilization of a non-resident-owned investment corporation as a holding corporation.

**(4) No deduction for foreign taxes** — No deduction from the tax payable under this Part by a non-resident-owned investment corporation may be made under section 124 or in respect of taxes paid to the government of a country other than Canada.

**Related Provisions**: 88(2)(a)(iv) — Winding-up of Canadian corporation; 111 — Losses deductible; 115 — Non-residents' taxable income; 133(8) — Non-resident-owned investment corporation.

**(5) [Repealed under former Act]**

**Notes**: 133(5), repealed in 1978, dealt with 1971 undistributed income and capital surplus on hand, concepts now long gone from the Act.

**(6) Allowable refund to non-resident-owned investment corporations** — If the return of a non-resident-owned investment corporation's income for a taxation year has been made within 3 years from the end of the year, the Minister

(a) may, on mailing the notice of assessment for the year, refund without application therefor its allowable refund for the year; and

(b) shall, with all due dispatch, make that allowable refund after mailing the notice of assessment if an application for it has been made in writing by the corporation within the period within which the Minister would be allowed under subsection 152(4) to assess tax payable by the corporation for the year if that subsection were read without reference to paragraph 152(4)(a).

**Related Provisions**: 88(2)(a) — Winding-up of Canadian corporation; 133(7) — Application to other liability; 133(7.01), (7.02) — Interest; 134.1 — Transitional rule re elimination of NROs; 152(1) — Assessment of refund; 157(3) — Reduction in instalment obligations to reflect allowable refund; 160.1 — Where excess refunded.

**Notes**: 133(6)(b) amended by 1989 Budget, effective April 28, 1989, to refer to "the period determined under paragraph 152(4)(b) or (c)" rather than to a 6-year or 3-year period; and amended by 1995-97 technical bill, also effective April 28, 1989, to make non-substantive wording changes and to update references to 152(4) as amended.

**(7) Application to other liability** — Instead of making a refund that might otherwise be made under subsection (6), the Minister may, where the taxpayer is liable or about to become liable to make any payment under this Act, apply the amount that would otherwise be refunded to that other liability and notify the taxpayer of that action.

**Related Provisions**: 88(2)(a) — Winding-up of Canadian corporation; 134.1 — Transitional rule re elimination of NROs.

**(7.01) Interest on allowable refund** — Where an allowable refund for a taxation year is paid to, or applied to a liability of, a non-resident-owned investment corporation, the Minister shall pay or apply interest on the refund at the prescribed rate for the period beginning on the day that is the later of

(a) the day that is 120 days after the end of the year, and

(b) the day on which the corporation's return of income under this Part for the year was filed under section 150, unless the return was filed on or before the day on or before which it was required to be filed,

and ending on the day the refund is paid or applied.

**Related Provisions**: 133(7.02) — Where excess interest paid; 134.1 — Transitional rule re elimination of NROs; 161.1 — Offset of refund interest against arrears interest.

**Notes**: 133(7.01) added by 1992 technical bill, effective for allowable refunds paid or applied in respect of taxation years that begin after 1991.

**Regulations**: 4301(b) (prescribed rate of interest).

### (7.02) Excess interest on allowable refund —
Where at any particular time interest has been paid to, or applied to a liability of, a corporation under subsection (7.01) in respect of an allowable refund and it is determined at a subsequent time that the allowable refund was less than that in respect of which interest was so paid or applied,

(a) the amount by which the interest that was so paid or applied exceeds the interest, if any, computed in respect of the amount that is determined at the subsequent time to be the allowable refund shall be deemed to be an amount (in this subsection referred to as the "amount payable") that became payable under this Part by the corporation at the particular time;

(b) the corporation shall pay to the Receiver General interest at the prescribed rate on the amount payable, computed from the particular time to the day of payment; and

(c) the Minister may at any time assess the corporation in respect of the amount payable and, where the Minister makes such an assessment, the provisions of Divisions I and J apply, with such modifications as the circumstances require, in respect of the assessment as though it had been made under section 152.

**Related Provisions**: 20(1)(ll) — Deduction on repayment of interest; 161.1 — Offset of refund interest against arrears interest; 221.1 — Application of interest where legislation retroactive; 248(11) — Interest compounded daily.

**Notes**: 133(7.02) added by 1992 technical bill, effective for allowable refunds paid or applied in respect of taxation years that begin after 1991.

**Regulations**: 4301(a) (prescribed rate of interest).

### (7.1) Election re capital gains dividend —
Where at any particular time after 1971 a dividend has become payable by a non-resident-owned investment corporation to shareholders of any class of shares of its capital stock, if the corporation so elects in respect of the full amount of the dividend, in prescribed manner and prescribed form and at or before the particular time or the first day on which any part of the dividend was paid if that day is earlier than the particular time, the following rules apply:

(a) the dividend shall be deemed to be a capital gains dividend to the extent that it does not exceed the corporation's capital gains dividend account immediately before the particular time; and

(b) any amount received by another non-resident-owned investment corporation in a taxation year as, on account or in lieu of payment of, or in satisfaction of the capital gains dividend shall not be included in computing its income for the year.

**Related Provisions**: 83(2) — Capital dividends; 84(7) — When dividend payable; 88(2)(b)(i) — Winding-up of Canadian corporation; 133(7.2) — Simultaneous dividends; 133(7.3) — Application of subsecs. 131(1.1)–(1.4); 133(8) — Canadian property; 133(8) — Capital gains dividend account; 133(8) — Taxable dividend; 134.1 — Transitional rule re elimination of NROs; 212(2) — No withholding tax on capital gains dividends paid to non-residents.

**Regulations**: 2105 (prescribed manner of making election).

**Interpretation Bulletins**: IT-149R4: Winding-up dividend.

**Forms**: T5 Segment; T5 Summ: Return of investment income; T5 Supp: Statement of investment income; T2063: Election in respect of a capital gains dividend under subsection 133(7.1).

### (7.2) Simultaneous dividends —
Where a dividend becomes payable at the same time on more than one class of shares of the capital stock of a non-resident-owned investment corporation, for the purposes of subsection (7.1), the dividend on any such class of shares shall be deemed to become payable at a different time than the dividend on the other class or classes of shares and to become payable in the order designated

(a) by the corporation on or before the day on or before which the election described in subsection (7.1) is required to be filed; or

(b) in any other case, by the Minister.

**Related Provisions**: 88(2)(a) — Winding-up of Canadian corporation; 89(3) — Simultaneous dividends.

### (7.3) Application of subsecs. 131(1.1) to (1.4) —
Where at any particular time a non-resident-owned investment corporation paid a dividend to its shareholders and subsection (7.1) would have applied to the dividend except that the corporation did not make an election under that subsection on or before the day on or before which it was required by that subsection to be made, subsections 131(1.1) to (1.4) apply with such modifications as the circumstances require.

### (8) Definitions — In this section,

"allowable refund" of a non-resident-owned investment corporation for a taxation year means the total of amounts each of which is an amount in respect of a taxable dividend paid by the corporation in the year on a share of its capital stock, determined by the formula

$$\frac{A}{B} \times C$$

where

A is the corporation's allowable refundable tax on hand immediately before the dividend was paid,

B is the greater of the amount of the dividend so paid and the corporation's cumulative taxable income immediately before the dividend was paid, and

C is the amount of the dividend so paid;

**Notes**: 133(8)"allowable refund" was 133(8)(a) before consolidation in R.S.C. 1985 (5th Supp.), effective for taxation years ending after November 1991. The previous version, identical in meaning, read:

(a) "allowable refund" of a non-resident-owned investment corporation for a taxation year means the aggregate of amounts each of which is an amount in respect of a taxable dividend paid by the corporation in the year on a share of its capital stock, equal to that proportion of the dividend that

(i) the corporation's allowable refundable tax on hand immediately before the dividend was paid

is of

(ii) the greater of the amount of the dividend so paid and the corporation's cumulative taxable income immediately before the dividend was paid;

**"Canadian property"** means

(a) property of a corporation that would be taxable Canadian property if at no time in the year the corporation had been resident in Canada, and

> **Proposed Amendment —
> 133(8)"Canadian property"(a)**
>
> (a) taxable Canadian property, and
>
> **Application**: Bill C-43 (First Reading September 20, 2000), subsec. 84(2), will amend para. (a) of the definition "Canadian property" in subsec. 133(8) to read as above, applicable after October 1, 1996.
>
> **Technical Notes**: Subsection 133(8) of the Act sets out certain definitions that apply for the purposes of section 133.
>
> Paragraph (a) of the definition of "Canadian property" in subsection 133(8) is amended, with application after October 1, 1996, to reflect the changes in the definition of "taxable Canadian property" and that definition's relocation from subsection 115(1) to subsection 248(1) of the Act.

(b) any other property not being foreign property within the meaning assigned by section 206;

**Notes**: 133(8)"Canadian property" was 133(8)(b) before consolidation in R.S.C. 1985 (5th Supp.), effective for taxation years ending after November 1991. See Table of Concordance.

**"capital gains dividend account"** of a non-resident-owned investment corporation at any particular time means the amount determined by the formula

$$A - B$$

where

A is the total of the following amounts in respect of the period commencing January 1, 1972 and ending immediately after the corporation's last taxation year ending before the particular time:

(a) the corporation's capital gains for taxation years ending in the period from dispositions in the period of Canadian property or shares of another non-resident-owned investment corporation, and

(b) amounts received by the corporation in the period as, on account or in lieu of payment of, or in satisfaction of capital gains dividends from other non-resident-owned investment corporations, and

B is the total of the following amounts in respect of the period referred to in the description of A:

(a) the corporation's capital losses for taxation years ending in the period from dispositions in the period of Canadian property or shares of another non-resident-owned investment corporation,

(b) all capital gains dividends that became payable by the corporation before the particular time, and

(c) the amount determined by the formula

$$0.25 \times (M - N)$$

where

M is the total of the corporation's capital gains for taxation years ending in the period from dispositions in the period of taxable Canadian property or property that would be taxable Canadian property if at no time in the period the corporation had been resident in Canada, and

> **Proposed Amendment —
> 133(8)"capital gains dividend
> account"B(c)M**
>
> M is the total of the corporation's capital gains for taxation years ending in the period from dispositions in the period of taxable Canadian property, and
>
> **Application**: Bill C-43 (First Reading September 20, 2000), subsec. 84(3), will amend the description of M in para. (c) of the description of B in the definition "capital gains dividend account" in subsec. 133(8) to read as above, applicable after October 1, 1996.
>
> **Technical Notes**: The description of M in paragraph (c) of the definition of "capital gains dividend account" in subsection 133(8) is amended, with application after October 1, 1996, to reflect the changes in the definition of "taxable Canadian property" and that definition's relocation from subsection 115(1) to subsection 248(1) of the Act.

N is the total of the corporation's capital losses for the taxation years ending in the period from dispositions in the period of property of the kinds referred to in the description of M;

**Related Provisions**: 88(2)(a) — Winding-up of Canadian corporation; 134.1 — Transitional rule re elimination of NROs; 257 — Formula amounts cannot calculate to less than zero.

**Notes**: 133(8)"capital gains dividend account" was 133(8)(c) before consolidation in R.S.C. 1985 (5th Supp.), effective for taxation years ending after November 1991. The previous version, identical in meaning, read:

(c) "capital gains dividend account" of a non-resident-owned investment corporation at any particular time means the amount, if any, by which the aggregate of the following amounts in respect of the period commencing January 1, 1972 and ending immediately after its last taxation year ending before the particular time, namely:

(i) the corporation's capital gains for taxation years ending in the period from dispositions in the period of Canadian property or shares of another non-resident-owned investment corporation, and

(ii) amounts received by the corporation in the period as, on account or in lieu of payment of, or in satisfaction of capital gains dividends from other non-resident-owned investment corporations,

exceeds the aggregate of

(iii) the corporation's capital losses for taxation years ending in the period from dispositions in the period of Canadian property or shares of another non-resident-owned investment corporation,

(iv) 25% of the amount, if any, by which the aggregate of the corporation's capital gains for taxation years ending in the period from dispositions in the period of taxable Canadian property or property that would be taxable Canadian property if at no time in the period the corporation had been resident in Canada, exceeds the aggregate of its capital losses for those years from dispositions in the period of such property, and

(v) all capital gains dividends that became payable by the corporation before the particular time;

### Proposed Addition — 133(8) "Increase in capital"

**"increase in capital"** in respect of a corporation means a transaction (other than a transaction carried out pursuant to an agreement in writing made before February 28, 2000, referred to in this definition as a "specified transaction") in the course of which the corporation issues additional shares of its capital stock or incurs indebtedness, if the transaction has the effect of increasing the total of

(a) the corporation's liabilities, and

(b) the fair market value of all the shares of its capital stock

to an amount that is substantially greater than that total would have been on February 27, 2000 if all specified transactions had been carried out immediately before that day;

**Application**: The December 21, 2000 draft legislation, subsec. 79(3), will add the definition "increase in capital" to subsec. 133(8), applicable after February 27, 2000.

**Technical Notes**: The new definition "increase in capital" in subsection 133(8) defines an increase in capital to be a transaction in the course of which a corporation issues additional shares or incurs indebtedness, where the transaction has the effect of increasing the total of the corporation's liabilities and the fair market value of all of its shares to an amount that is substantially greater than that total was on February 27, 2000. Transactions carried out pursuant to an agreement in writing made before February 28, 2000 are exempted from this rule.

A number of consequences that follow from this definition should be noted. First, since the "total" referred to is of both the liabilities of the corporation and the fair market value of all of its shares, an increase in either will increase this "total". For example, if a corporation incurs debt to acquire a new asset, the total fair market value of its shares may remain the same, but its liabilities will increase, thus increasing the "total". Second, an increase in the fair market value of a corporation's shares that results from market appreciation of the value of its assets will not by itself be an "increase in capital", because the definition requires that there be a transaction involving the issuance of shares or the incurring of indebtedness. Finally, since the issuance of additional shares through the payment of stock dividends does not ordinarily increase the fair market value of a corporation's shares or increase its liabilities, such a payment of stock dividends will not be an "increase in capital."

**"non-resident-owned investment corporation"** means a corporation incorporated in Canada that, throughout the whole of the period commencing on the later of June 18, 1971 and the day on which it was incorporated and ending on the last day of the taxation year in respect of which the expression is being applied, complied with the following conditions:

(a) all of its issued shares and all of its bonds, debentures and other funded indebtedness were

(i) beneficially owned by non-resident persons (other than any foreign affiliate of a taxpayer resident in Canada),

(ii) owned by trustees for the benefit of non-resident persons or their unborn issue, or

(iii) owned by a non-resident-owned investment corporation, all of the issued shares of which and all of the bonds, debentures and other funded indebtedness of which were beneficially owned by non-resident persons or owned by trustees for the benefit of non-resident persons or their unborn issue, or by two or more such corporations,

(b) its income for each taxation year ending in the period was derived from

(i) ownership of or trading or dealing in bonds, shares, debentures, mortgages, bills, notes or other similar property or any interest therein,

(ii) lending money with or without security,

(iii) rents, hire of chattels, charterparty fees or remunerations, annuities, royalties, interest or dividends,

(iv) estates or trusts, or

(v) disposition of capital property,

(c) not more than 10% of its gross revenue for each taxation year ending in the period was derived from rents, hire of chattels, charterparty fees or charterparty remunerations,

(d) its principal business in each taxation year ending in the period was not

(i) the making of loans, or

(ii) trading or dealing in bonds, shares, debentures, mortgages, bills, notes or other similar property or any interest therein,

(e) it has, not later than 90 days after the commencement of its first taxation year commencing after 1971, elected in prescribed manner to be taxed under this section, and

(f) it has not, before the end of the last taxation year in the period, revoked in prescribed manner the election so made by it,

except that in no case shall a new corporation (within the meaning assigned by section 87) formed as a result of an amalgamation after June 18, 1971 of two or more predecessor corporations be regarded as a non-resident-owned investment corporation unless each of the predecessor corporations was, immediately before the amalgamation, a non-resident-owned investment corporation;

**Proposed Amendment — 133(8)"non-resident-owned investment corporation"(e)–(i)**

(e) it has, on or before the earlier of February 27, 2000 and the day that is 90 days after the beginning of its first taxation year that begins after 1971, elected in prescribed manner to be taxed under this section, and

(f) it has not, before the end of the last taxation year in the period, revoked in prescribed manner its election,

except that

(g) a new corporation (within the meaning assigned by section 87) formed as a result of an amalgamation after June 18, 1971 of two or more predecessor corporations is not a non-resident-owned investment corporation unless each of the predecessor corporations was, immediately before the amalgamation, a non-resident-owned investment corporation,

(h) where a corporation is a new corporation described in paragraph (g), and each of the predecessor corporations elected in a timely manner under paragraph (e), paragraph (e) shall be read, in its application to the new corporation, without reference to the words "the earlier of February 27, 2000 and", and

(i) subject to section 134.1, a corporation is not a non-resident-owned investment corporation in any taxation year that ends after the earlier of,

(i) the first time, if any, after February 27, 2000 at which the corporation effects an increase in capital, and

(ii) the corporation's last taxation year that begins before 2003;

**Application**: The December 21, 2000 draft legislation, subsec. 79(2), will amend the portion of the definition "non-resident-owned investment corporation" in subsec. 133(8) after para. (d) to read as above, applicable after February 27, 2000.

**Technical Notes**: Paragraph (e) of the definition "non-resident-owned investment corporation" in subsection 133(8) provides that a corporation that wishes to be treated as an NRO must have elected to be taxed as an NRO on or before the day that is 90 days after the beginning of its first taxation year that begins after 1971. This paragraph is amended to require the election to have been made on or before the earlier of that day and February 27, 2000. New paragraph (h) provides that a corporation created through the amalgamation of two or more corporations, each of which elected in a timely manner under amended paragraph (e) to be taxed as an NRO, will be able to elect after February 27, 2000 to be taxed as an NRO. New paragraph (i) gives effect to the three-year phase-out period for all NROs, including those created through amalgamations referred to in new paragraph (h), by providing that no corporation is an NRO in any taxation year that ends after its last taxation year that begins before 2003. New paragraph (i) provides that, if at any time during the three-year phase-out period, a corporation effects an "increase in capital" (as defined in subsection 133(8)), it will lose its status as an NRO for any taxation year that ends after that time.

**Notice of Ways and Means Motion, federal budget, February 28, 2000**: *Non-Resident-Owned Investment Corporations*

(27) That,

(a) a corporation that elected before February 28, 2000 to be taxed as a non-resident-owned investment corporation cease to be such a corporation no later than the end of its last taxation year that begins before 2003, and

(b) no election to be taxed as a non-resident-owned investment corporation be permitted after February 27, 2000.

**Federal budget, supplementary information, February 28, 2000**: *Non-Resident-Owned Investment Corporations*

Section 133 of the *Income Tax Act* allows a foreign-owned Canadian corporation to elect to be a "non-resident-owned investment corporation" (NRO). By so doing, income received by the corporation is taxed at the same 25-per-cent rate that would apply to income paid to a non-resident from a Canadian source that is subject to the maximum rate of Part XIII withholding tax. The tax is then refunded when the NRO pays dividends to its foreign parent, at which time withholding tax applies on the dividends. The intended effect of the provision is to place the non-resident shareholder of the NRO in a position similar to that of non-resident investors who hold investments directly.

However, NROs are increasingly being used in ways that erode the Canadian tax base. For example, an NRO may be used to lend money indirectly to an affiliated Canadian corporation. This transaction results in an interest deduction at full rates for the Canadian corporation, while the interest income is subject only to a refundable 25-per-cent tax in the NRO's hands. In addition, this tax planning strategy can allow a double interest deduction for non-resident shareholders, if these shareholders borrow money in order to invest in the NRO.

The budget proposes to repeal the NRO provisions for elections made after February 27, 2000. To allow for an orderly restructuring of their operations, existing NROs will be entitled to retain their status until the end of their last taxation year that begins before 2003. However, existing NROs will not be allowed to issue new shares, other than by way of reorganization, or increase debt levels to finance new investments, subject to grandfathering of arrangements in writing entered into before February 28, 2000.

**Notes**: "At a recent meeting of the Montreal Senior Tax Practitioners' group, the Department of Finance indicated, informally,

Division F — Special Rules in Certain Circumstances     S. 133(9) cum

that NROs set up to hold investment portfolios *may* not lose their status, while NROs created for financing reasons (double-dips) *will* lose their status. It remains to be seen what is mean by this distinction and whether the denial of NRO status will be narrowly circumscribed or will result in the proverbial baby being thrown out with the bath water." — Monica Biringer, "NROs: Here Today, Gone Tomorrow?", VIII(1) *Corporate Finance* (Federated Press) 711, 712 (2000).

**Related Provisions**: 108(1) — "excluded property"; 134.1 — Election to remain NRO for one more year for certain purposes; 248(1)"non-resident-owned investment corporation" — Definition applies to entire Act.

**Notes**: 133(8)"non-resident-owned investment corporation" was 133(8)(d) before consolidation in R.S.C. 1985 (5th Supp.), effective for taxation years ending after November 1991. See Table of Concordance.

**Regulations**: 500, 501 (prescribed manner of making and revoking election).

**I.T. Application Rules**: 59(2) (application of conditions in para. (a) during 1972-75).

**Interpretation Bulletins**: IT-290: NRO investment corporations — meaning of principal business; IT-465R: Non-resident beneficiaries of trusts.

**Advance Tax Rulings**: ATR-43: Utilization of a non-resident-owned investment corporation as a holding corporation.

**"taxable dividend"** does not include a capital gains dividend.

**Notes**: 133(8)"taxable dividend" was 133(8)(e) before consolidation in R.S.C. 1985 (5th Supp.), effective for taxation years ending after November 1991.

**(9) Definitions** — In the definition "allowable refund" in subsection (8),

**"allowable refundable tax on hand"** of a corporation at any particular time means the amount determined by the formula

$$(A + B + C) - (D + E + F)$$

where

A is the total of all amounts each of which is an amount in respect of any taxation year commencing after 1971 and ending before the particular time, equal to the tax under this Part payable by the corporation for the year,

B is an amount equal to 15% of the amount determined for B in the definition "cumulative taxable income" in this subsection in respect of the corporation,

C where the corporation's 1972 taxation year commenced before 1972, is an amount equal to 10% of the amount that would be determined for C in the definition "cumulative taxable income" in this subsection if the reference in the description of C in that definition to "the 1972 taxation year or any taxation year commencing after 1971 and ending before the particular time" were read as a reference to "the 1972 taxation year",

D is the total of all amounts each of which is an amount, in respect of the 1972 taxation year or any taxation year commencing after 1971 and ending before the particular time, determined by the formula

$$0.25 \times [L - (M + N)]$$

where

L is the total of the corporation's taxable capital gains for the year from dispositions after 1971 of property described in paragraph (1)(c), computed in accordance with the assumption set out in paragraph (1)(d),

M is the total of the corporation's allowable capital losses for the year from dispositions after 1971 of property described in paragraph (1)(c), computed in accordance with the same assumption, and

N is the amount deductible from the corporation's income for the year by virtue of paragraph (2)(c),

E is the total of all amounts each of which is an amount equal to $1/3$ of any amount paid or credited by the corporation after the commencement of its 1972 taxation year and before the particular time, as, on account or in lieu of payment of, or in satisfaction of interest, and

F is the total of all amounts each of which is an amount in respect of any taxable dividend paid by the corporation on a share of its capital stock before the particular time and after the commencement of its first taxation year commencing after 1971, equal to the amount in respect of the dividend determined under the definition "allowable refund" in subsection (8);

**Related Provisions**: 88(2)(a) — Winding-up of Canadian corporation; 87(2)(cc) — Amalgamation — non-resident-owned investment corporation; 134.1 — Transitional rule re elimination of NROs; 257 — Formula amounts cannot calculate to less than zero.

**Notes**: 133(9)"allowable refundable tax on hand" was 133(9)(a) before consolidation in R.S.C. 1985 (5th Supp.), effective for taxation years ending after November 1991. See Table of Concordance in introductory pages.

**"cumulative taxable income"** of a corporation at any particular time means the amount determined by the formula

$$(A + B) - (C + D + E)$$

where

A is the total of the corporation's taxable incomes for taxation years commencing after 1971 and ending before the particular time,

B where the corporation's 1972 taxation year commenced before 1972, is the amount determined by the formula

$$L - (M + N)$$

where

L is the corporation's taxable income for its 1972 taxation year,

1243

M is the total of all amounts received by the corporation as described in paragraph 196(4)(b), and

N is the lesser of the amount determined under paragraph 196(4)(e) in respect of the corporation and the amount, if any, by which the total of amounts determined under paragraphs 196(4)(d) to (f) in respect of the corporation exceeds the total of amounts determined under paragraphs 196(4)(a) to (c) in respect of the corporation,

C is the total of all amounts each of which is an amount, in respect of the 1972 taxation year or any taxation year commencing after 1971 and ending before the particular time, determined by the formula

$$P - (Q + R)$$

where

P is the total of the corporation's taxable capital gains for the year from dispositions after 1971 of property described in paragraph (1)(c), computed in accordance with the assumption set out in paragraph (1)(d),

Q is the total of the corporation's allowable capital losses for the year from dispositions after 1971 of property described in paragraph (1)(c), computed in accordance with the same assumption, and

R is the amount deductible from the corporation's income for the year by virtue of paragraph (2)(c),

D is the total of all amounts each of which is an amount equal to $4/3$ of any amount paid or credited by the corporation, after the commencement of its 1972 taxation year and before the particular time, as, on account or in lieu of payment of, or in satisfaction of interest, and

E is the total of all amounts each of which is the amount of any taxable dividend paid by the corporation on a share of its capital stock before the particular time and after the commencement of its first taxation year commencing after 1971.

**Related Provisions**: 88(2)(a) — Winding-up of Canadian corporation; 157(3) — Private, mutual and non-resident-owned investment corporation; 134.1 — Transitional rule re elimination of NROs; 257 — Formula amounts cannot calculate to less than zero.

**Notes**: 133(9)"cumulative taxable income" was 133(9)(b) before consolidation in R.S.C. 1985 (5th Supp.), effective for taxation years ending after November 1991. See Table of Concordance in introductory pages.

**Definitions [s. 133]**: "allowable capital loss" — 38(b), 248(1); "allowable refund" — 133(8); "allowable refundable tax on hand" — 133(9); "amount", "annuity", "assessment" — 248(1); "Canada" — 255; "Canadian property" — 133(8); "capital gain" — 39(1)(a), 248(1); "capital gains dividend" — 133(7.1); "capital gains dividend account" — 133(8); "capital loss" — 39(1)(b), 248(1); "capital property" — 54, 248(1); "class of shares" — 248(6); "corporation" — 248(1), *Interpretation Act* 35(1); "cumulative taxable income" — 133(9); "dividend" — 248(1); "estate" — 104(1), 248(1); "foreign affiliate" — 95(1), 248(1); "gross revenue" — 248(1); "incorporated in Canada" — 248(1)"corporation incorporated in Canada"; "increase in capital" — 133(8); "Minister" — 248(1); "net capital loss" — 111(8), 248(1); "non-resident" — 248(1); "non-resident-owned investment corporation" — 133(8), 248(1); "payable" — 84(7); "person", "prescribed" — 248(1); "prescribed rate" — Reg. 4301; "resident in Canada" — 250; "share", "shareholder" — 248(1); "taxable Canadian property" — 248(1); "taxable capital gain" — 38(a), 248(1); "taxable dividend" — 133(8), 89(1), 248(1); "taxable income" — 2(2), 248(1); "taxation year" — 249; "taxpayer" — 248(1); "trust" — 104(1), 248(1), (3); "writing" — *Interpretation Act* 35(1).

**Regulations [s. 133]**: 500–502 (prescribed manner of making and revoking elections; certified statement required with annual return).

## 134. Non-resident-owned corporation not a Canadian corporation, etc.

— Notwithstanding any other provision of this Act, a non-resident-owned investment corporation that would, but for this section, be a Canadian corporation, taxable Canadian corporation or private corporation shall be deemed not to be a Canadian corporation, taxable Canadian corporation or private corporation, as the case may be, except for the purposes of section 87, subsection 88(2) and sections 212.1 and 219.

**Definitions [s. 134]**: "Canadian corporation" — 89(1), 248(1); "non-resident-owned investment corporation" — 133(8), 248(1); "private corporation", "taxable Canadian corporation" — 89(1), 248(1).

### Proposed Addition — 134.1

**134.1 (1) NRO — transition** — This section applies to a corporation that

(a) was a non-resident-owned investment corporation in a taxation year;

(b) is not a non-resident-owned investment corporation in the following taxation year (in this section referred to as the corporation's "first non-NRO year"); and

(c) elects in writing filed with the Minister on or before the corporation's filing-due day for its first non-NRO year to have this section apply.

**(2) Application** — A corporation to which this section applies is deemed to be a non-resident-owned investment corporation in its first non-NRO year for the purposes of applying, in respect of dividends paid on shares of its capital stock in its first non-NRO year, subsections 133(6) to (9) (other than the definition "non-resident-owned investment corporation" in subsection 133(8)) and section 212 and any tax treaty.

**Application**: The December 21, 2000 draft legislation, s. 80, will add s. 134.1, applicable to taxation years that end after 1996. An election under para. 134.1(1)(c) is deemed to have been made in a timely manner if it is made on or before the electing corporation's filing-due date for its first taxation year that ends after the amending legislation receives Royal Assent.

**Technical Notes**: New section 134.1 provides special transitional rules to accommodate the phase out of non-resident-owned investment corporations (NROs). The present NRO rules allow an NRO to claim a refund of its 25% refundable tax when it pays dividends to its non-resident shareholders (at which time the dividend withholding tax in Part XIII applies). However, to access the pool of refundable tax for a given taxation year, the refund mechanism requires dividends to be paid in a subsequent taxation year. Since the amended definition "non-resident-owned investment corporation" in subsection 133(8) calls for the phase-out of NROs over a three-year period, a corporation that ceases to be an NRO would not be able to claim a refund of the 25% refundable tax that it would pay in respect of its last taxation year as an NRO. To accommodate the refund of this tax, new paragraph 134.1(1)(c) provides an election through which a corporation that ceases to be an NRO can elect to have its status as an NRO extended for this specific purpose for its first non-NRO year.

**Definitions [s. 134.1]**: "corporation" — 248(1), *Interpretation Act* 35(1); "dividend" — 248(1); "first non-NRO year" — 134.1(1)(b); "Minister" — 248(1); "non-resident-owned investment corporation" — 133(8), 248(1); "share", "tax treaty" — 248(1); "taxation year" — 249; "writing" — *Interpretation Act* 35(1).

## Patronage Dividends

**135. (1) Deduction in computing income** — Notwithstanding anything in this Part, there may be deducted, in computing the income of a taxpayer for a taxation year, the total of the payments made, pursuant to allocations in proportion to patronage, by the taxpayer

(a) within the year or within 12 months thereafter to the taxpayer's customers of the year; and

(b) within the year or within 12 months thereafter to the taxpayer's customers of a previous year, the deduction of which from income of a previous taxation year was not permitted.

**Related Provisions**: 20(1)(u) — Deduction from income for amount allowed under 135(1); 135(2) — Limitation — non-member customers; 135(4) — Definitions; 136 — Cooperative deemed not to be private corporation; 157(2) — Exemption from instalment obligations where taxable income not over $10,000; 181.2(3)(j) — Large corporations tax — deduction from capital; 212(1)(g) — Non-resident withholding tax.

**Regulations**: 218 (information return).

**Interpretation Bulletins**: See list at end of s. 135.

**Forms**: T2 SCH 16: Patronage dividend deduction.

**(2) Limitation where non-member customer** — Notwithstanding subsection (1), if the taxpayer has not made allocations in proportion to patronage in respect of all the taxpayer's customers of the year at the same rate, with appropriate differences for different types or classes of goods, products or services, or classes, grades or qualities thereof, the amount that may be deducted under subsection (1) is an amount equal to the lesser of

(a) the total of the payments mentioned in that subsection, and

(b) the total of

(i) the part of the income of the taxpayer for the year attributable to business done with members, and

(ii) the allocations in proportion to patronage made to non-member customers of the year.

**Related Provisions**: 135(2.1) — Carryforward.

**Interpretation Bulletins**: See list at end of s. 135.

**(2.1) Deduction carried over** — Where, in a taxation year ending after 1985, all or a portion of a payment made by a taxpayer pursuant to an allocation in proportion to patronage to the taxpayer's customers who are members is not deductible in computing the taxpayer's income for the year because of the application of subsection (2) (in this subsection referred to as the "undeducted amount"), there may be deducted in computing the taxpayer's income for a subsequent taxation year, an amount equal to the lesser of

(a) the undeducted amount, except to the extent that that amount was deducted in computing the taxpayer's income for any preceding taxation year, and

(b) the amount, if any, by which

(i) the taxpayer's income for the subsequent taxation year (computed without reference to this subsection) attributable to business done with the taxpayer's customers of that year who are members

exceeds

(ii) the amount deducted in computing the taxpayer's income for the subsequent taxation year by virtue of subsection (1) in respect of payments made by the taxpayer pursuant to allocations in proportion to patronage to the taxpayer's customers of that year who are members.

**Interpretation Bulletins**: See list at end of s. 135.

**(3) Amount to be deducted or withheld from payment to customer** — Where at any particular time in a calendar year and after 1971 a payment pursuant to an allocation in proportion to patronage is made by a taxpayer to a person who is resident in Canada and is not exempt from tax under section 149, the taxpayer shall, notwithstanding any agreement or any law to the contrary, deduct or withhold therefrom an amount equal to 15% of the lesser of the amount of the payment and the amount, if any, by which

(a) the total of the amount of the payment and the amounts of all other payments pursuant to allocations in proportion to patronage made by the taxpayer to that person in the calendar year and before the particular time

exceeds

(b) $100,

and forthwith remit that amount to the Receiver General on behalf of that person on account of that person's tax under this Part.

**Related Provisions**: 127(6) — Investment tax credit of cooperative corporation; 135(2) — Limitation — non-member customers;

**S. 135(3)**  Income Tax Act, Part I

135(6) — Amount of payment to customers; 227(1), (4), (5), (8.3), (8.4), (9), (9.2), (9.4), (11), (12), (13) — Withholding taxes — administration and enforcement; 227.1 — Liability of directors.

**Notes**: Under s. 227, withholdings under 135(3) are generally subject to the same stringent rules as employee source withholdings (s. 153) and non-resident withholding taxes (s. 212).

**Interpretation Bulletins**: See list at end of s. 135.

**Forms**: T2 SCH 16: Patronage dividend deduction; T4A Supp: Statement of pension, retirement, annuity, and other income; RC4157(E): Employers' Guide: Filing the T4A Slip and Summary Form.

**(4) Definitions** — For the purposes of this section,

**"allocation in proportion to patronage"** for a taxation year means an amount credited by a taxpayer to a customer of that year on terms that the customer is entitled to or will receive payment thereof, computed at a rate in relation to the quantity, quality or value of the goods or products acquired, marketed, handled, dealt in or sold, or services rendered by the taxpayer from, on behalf of or to the customer, whether as principal or as agent of the customer or otherwise, with appropriate differences in the rate for different classes, grades or qualities thereof, if

(a) the amount was credited

(i) within the year or within 12 months thereafter, and

(ii) at the same rate in relation to quantity, quality or value aforesaid as the rate at which amounts were similarly credited to all other customers of that year who were members or to all other customers of that year, as the case may be, with appropriate differences aforesaid for different classes, grades or qualities, and

(b) the prospect that amounts would be so credited was held out by the taxpayer to the taxpayer's customers of that year who were members or non-member customers of that year, as the case may be;

**Related Provisions**: 135(1) — Deduction for allocations; 212(1)(g) — Withholding tax on allocations to non-residents.

**Notes**: 135(4)"allocation in proportion to patronage" was 135(4)(a) before consolidation in R.S.C. 1985 (5th Supp.), effective for taxation years ending after November 1991. See Table of Concordance.

**"consumer goods or services"** means goods or services the cost of which was not deductible by the taxpayer in computing the income from a business or property;

**Notes**: 135(4)"consumer goods or services" was 135(4)(b) before consolidation in R.S.C. 1985 (5th Supp.), effective for taxation years ending after November 1991.

**"customer"** means a customer of a taxpayer and includes a person who sells or delivers goods or products to the taxpayer, or for whom the taxpayer renders services;

**Notes**: 135(4)"customer" was 135(4)(c) before consolidation in R.S.C. 1985 (5th Supp.), effective for taxation years ending after November 1991.

**"income of the taxpayer attributable to business done with members"** of any taxation year means that proportion of the income of the taxpayer for the year (before making any deduction under this section) that the value of the goods or products acquired, marketed, handled, dealt in or sold or services rendered by the taxpayer from, on behalf of, or for members, is of the total value of goods or products acquired, marketed, handled, dealt in or sold or services rendered by the taxpayer from, on behalf of, or for all customers during the year;

**Notes**: 135(4)"income of the taxpayer attributable ... members" was 135(4)(d) before consolidation in R.S.C. 1985 (5th Supp.), effective for taxation years ending after November 1991.

**"member"** means a person who is entitled as a member or shareholder to full voting rights in the conduct of the affairs of the taxpayer (being a corporation) or of a corporation of which the taxpayer is a subsidiary wholly-owned corporation;

**Notes**: 135(4)"member" was 135(4)(e) before consolidation in R.S.C. 1985 (5th Supp.), effective for taxation years ending after November 1991.

**"non-member customer"** means a customer who is not a member;

**Notes**: 135(4)"non-member customer" was 135(4)(f) before consolidation in R.S.C. 1985 (5th Supp.), effective for taxation years ending after November 1991.

**"payment"** includes

(a) the issue of a certificate of indebtedness or shares of the taxpayer or of a corporation of which the taxpayer is a subsidiary wholly-owned corporation if the taxpayer or that corporation has in the year or within 12 months thereafter disbursed an amount of money equal to the total face value of all certificates or shares so issued in the course of redeeming or purchasing certificates of indebtedness or shares of the taxpayer or that corporation previously issued,

(b) the application by the taxpayer of an amount to a member's liability to the taxpayer (including, without restricting the generality of the foregoing, an amount applied in fulfilment of an obligation of the member to make a loan to the taxpayer and an amount applied on account of payment for shares issued to a member) pursuant to a by-law of the taxpayer, pursuant to statutory authority or at the request of the member, or

(c) the amount of a payment or transfer by the taxpayer that, under subsection 56(2), is required to be included in computing the income of a member.

**Notes**: 135(4)"payment" was 135(4)(g) before consolidation in R.S.C. 1985 (5th Supp.), effective for taxation years ending after November 1991. See Table of Concordance.

**Interpretation Bulletins**: See list at end of s. 135.

**(5) Holding out prospect of allocations** — For the purpose of this section a taxpayer shall be deemed to have held out the prospect that amounts would be credited to a customer of a taxation year by way of allocation in proportion to patronage, if

(a) throughout the year the statute under which the taxpayer was incorporated or registered, its charter, articles of association or by-laws or its contract with the customer held out the prospect that amounts would be so credited to customers who are members or non-member customers, as the case may be; or

(b) prior to the commencement of the year or prior to such other day as may be prescribed for the class of business in which the taxpayer is engaged, the taxpayer has published an advertisement in prescribed form in a newspaper or newspapers of general circulation throughout the greater part of the area in which the taxpayer carried on business holding out that prospect to customers who are members or non-member customers, as the case may be, and has filed copies of the newspapers with the Minister before the end of the 30th day of the taxation year or within 30 days from the prescribed day, as the case may be.

**Related Provisions**: 20(1)(u) — Patronage dividends.

**Interpretation Bulletins**: See list at end of s. 135.

**(6) Amount of payment to customer** — For greater certainty, the amount of any payment pursuant to an allocation in proportion to patronage is the amount thereof determined before deducting any amount required by subsection (3) to be deducted or withheld from that payment.

**Related Provisions**: 20(1)(u) — Deduction — patronage dividends; 135(3) — Amount to be deducted or withheld from payment to customer; 157(2) — Exemption from instalment obligations where taxable income not over $10,000.

**Interpretation Bulletins**: See list at end of s. 135.

**(7) Payment to customer to be included in income** — Where a payment pursuant to an allocation in proportion to patronage (other than an allocation in respect of consumer goods or services) has been received by the taxpayer, the amount of the payment shall be included in computing the recipient's income for the taxation year in which the payment was received and, without restricting the generality of the foregoing, where a certificate of indebtedness or a share was issued to a person pursuant to an allocation in proportion to patronage, the amount of the payment by virtue of the issue thereof shall be included in computing the recipient's income for the taxation year in which the certificate or share was received and not in computing the recipient's income for the year in which the indebtedness was subsequently discharged or the share was redeemed.

**Related Provisions**: 20(1)(u) — Patronage dividend deduction; 212(1)(g) — Non-resident withholding tax.

**Interpretation Bulletins**: See list at end of s. 135.

**Forms**: RC4157(E): Employers' Guide: Filing the T4A Slip and Summary Form; T2 SCH 16: Patronage dividend deduction; T4A Supp: Statement of pension, retirement, annuity, and other income.

**(8) Patronage dividends** — For the purposes of this section, where

(a) a person has sold or delivered a quantity of goods or products to a marketing board established by or pursuant to a law of Canada or a province,

(b) the marketing board has sold or delivered the same quantity of goods or products of the same class, grade or quality to a taxpayer of which the person is a member, and

(c) the taxpayer has credited that person with an amount based on the quantity of goods or products of that class, grade or quality sold or delivered to it by the marketing board,

the quantity of goods or products referred to in paragraph (c) shall be deemed to have been sold or delivered by that person to the taxpayer and to have been acquired by the taxpayer from that person.

**Definitions [s. 135]**: "amount", "business" — 248(1); "calendar year" — *Interpretation Act* 37(1)(a); "Canada" — 255; "corporation" — 248(1), *Interpretation Act* 35(1); "Minister", "person", "prescribed", "property" — 248(1); "province" — *Interpretation Act* 35(1); "resident in Canada" — 250; "share", "subsidiary wholly-owned corporation" — 248(1); "taxation year" — 249; "taxpayer" — 248(1). See also 135(4).

**Regulations [s. 135]**: 218 (information return).

**Interpretation Bulletins [s. 135]**: IT-362R: Patronage dividends; IT-493: Agency cooperative corporations.

## Cooperative Corporations

**136. (1) Cooperative not private corporation** — Notwithstanding any other provision of this Act, a cooperative corporation that would, but for this section, be a private corporation is deemed not to be a private corporation except for the purposes of sections 15.1, 125, 125.1, 127, 127.1, 152 and 157, the definition "mark-to-market property" in subsection 142.2(1) and the definition "small business corporation" in subsection 248(1) as it applies for the purpose of paragraph 39(1)(c).

**Notes**: In 136(1), reference to 152 added by 1989 Budget, effective April 28, 1989; reference to 125.1 added by 1991 technical bill, effective July 1988; and reference to 142.2(1)"mark-to-market property" added by 1995-97 technical bill, effective for taxation years that end after February 22, 1994.

**(2) Definition of "cooperative corporation"** — In this section, "cooperative corporation" means a corporation that was incorporated by or under a law of Canada or a province providing for the establishment of the corporation or respecting the establishment of cooperative corporations for the purpose of marketing (including processing incident to or connected therewith) natural products belonging to or acquired from its members or customers, of purchasing supplies, equipment or household necessaries for or to be sold to its members or customers or of performing services for its members or customers, if

(a) the statute by or under which it was incorporated, its charter, articles of association or by-laws or its contracts with its members or its members and customers held out the prospect that payments would be made to them in proportion to patronage;

(b) none of its members (except other cooperative corporations) have more than one vote in the conduct of the affairs of the corporation; and

(c) at least 90% of its members are individuals, other cooperative corporations, or corporations or partnerships that carry on the business of farming, and at least 90% of its shares, if any, are held by those persons or partnerships.

---

**Proposed Amendment — 136(2)(c)**

**Letter from Department of Finance, June 11, 1999:**

Dear [xxx]

This is in response to your letter dated June 4, 1999 to Len Farber respecting paragraph 136(2)(c) of the *Income Tax Act* and subsection 4900(12) of the *Income Tax Regulations*. Paragraph 136(2)(c) of the Act provides, as part of the definition of "cooperative corporation" in section 136, that at least 90% of a cooperative's shares must be held by members who are individuals, other cooperative corporations or corporations or partnerships that carry on the business of farming. Subsection 4900(12) of the Regulations provides that shares of specified cooperative corporations are qualified investments that may be held in an RRSP. You are concerned that the ability of a cooperative's members to hold their shares in RRSPs could, because the RRSPs may not be "members", cause the corporation to lose its cooperative status under section 136.

You have been advised by officials of the Tax Legislation Division that an amendment to paragraph 136(2)(c) is anticipated which would ensure that a cooperative does not lose its status as a consequence of its members contributing their shares to their RRSPs. You are seeking confirmation in writing of this information.

I can confirm that we intend to recommend that paragraph 136(2)(c) of the Act be amended to enable individual members of a cooperative to contribute their shares to their own RRSPs without any adverse consequences to the cooperative under the Act. The details of the amendment to be recommended remain to be developed. In general terms, however, I would foresee it being structured either as a rule which attributed the shares held by an RRSP to the annuitant, or which reformed paragraph 136(2)(c) to provide that shares contributed to an RRSP by a cooperative member would be treated as shares held by individuals who are members of a cooperative. We will recommend that this amendment apply to the 1998 and subsequent taxation years.

Yours sincerely,

Brian Ernewein

Director, Tax Legislation Division, Tax Policy Branch

---

**Related Provisions [s. 136]:** 15.1(3) — Eligible small business corporation; 89(1)"paid-up capital"(b) — Paid-up capital of cooperative corporation; 125 — Small business deduction; 127(6) — Investment tax credit of cooperative corporation; 135 — Patronage dividend; 137 — Deductions in computing income; 181.1(3)(f) — Certain cooperative corporations exempt from Part I.3 tax; 248(1) — "share" includes a share of a cooperative corporation.

**Definitions [s. 136]:** "carrying on business" — 253; "corporation" — 248(1), *Interpretation Act* 35(1); "farming", "individual", "person" — 248(1); "private corporation" — 89(1), 248(1); "province" — *Interpretation Act* 35(1); "share", "small business corporation" — 248(1).

**Interpretation Bulletins [s. 136]:** IT-493: Agency cooperative corporations.

## Credit Unions, Savings and Credit Unions, and Deposit Insurance Corporations

**137. (1)** [Repealed under former Act]

**Notes:** 137(1), repealed by 1988 tax reform, dealt with a credit union's reserve for doubtful debts. The normal reserve in 20(1)(l) now applies to credit unions.

**(2) Payments pursuant to allocations in proportion to borrowing** — Notwithstanding anything in this Part, there may be deducted, in computing the income for a taxation year of a credit union, the total of bonus interest payments and payments pursuant to allocations in proportion to borrowing made by the credit union within the year or within 12 months thereafter to members of the credit union, to the extent that those payments were not deductible under this subsection in computing the income of the credit union for the immediately preceding taxation year.

**Related Provisions:** 110.1(1)(a) — 137(2) ignored for purposes of charitable donations limit; 135 — Patronage dividends; 137(6) — Maximum cumulative reserve; 157(2) — Instalment obligations — special case; 181.3(3)(a) — Capital of financial institution.

**Interpretation Bulletins:** IT-483: Credit unions.

**(3) Additional deduction** — There may be deducted from the tax otherwise payable under this Part for a taxation year by a corporation that was, throughout the year, a credit union, an amount equal to 16% of the amount, if any, by which the lesser of

(a) the corporation's taxable income for the year, and

(b) the amount, if any, by which $4/3$ of the corporation's maximum cumulative reserve at the end of the year exceeds the corporation's preferred-rate amount at the end of the immediately preceding taxation year

exceeds

(c) the least of the amounts determined under paragraphs 125(1)(a) to (c) in respect of the corporation for the year.

**Related Provisions:** 123.2 — Corporation surtax calculated before deducting credit under 137(3).

**Interpretation Bulletins:** IT-483: Credit unions.

**(4) Amount deemed deductible under section 125** — For the purposes of this Act, any amount deductible or any deduction under subsection (3) from the tax otherwise payable by a credit union under this Part for a taxation year shall be deemed to be an amount deductible or a deduction, as the case may be, under section 125 from that tax.

**Related Provisions:** 125 — Small business deduction; 137(6) — Maximum cumulative reserve.

**Interpretation Bulletins**: IT-483: Credit unions.

**(4.1) Payments in respect of shares** — Notwithstanding any other provision of this Act, an amount paid or payable by a credit union to a member thereof in respect of a share of a class of the capital stock of the credit union (other than any such amount paid or payable as or on account of a reduction of the paid-up capital, redemption, acquisition or cancellation of the share by the credit union to the extent of the paid-up capital of the share) shall, where the share is not listed on a prescribed stock exchange, be deemed to have been paid or payable, as the case may be, by the credit union as interest and to have been received or to have been receivable, as the case may be, by the member as interest.

**Related Provisions**: 12(1)(c) — Interest included in income; 84(4) — Deemed dividend on reduction of paid-up capital where share is listed on prescribed stock exchange; 137(4.2) — Deemed interest not a dividend.

**Notes**: 137(4.1) amended by 1993 technical bill, effective for transactions occurring after December 21, 1992.

**Regulations**: 3200 (prescribed stock exchange; needs to be amended to apply to 137(4.1)).

**Interpretation Bulletins**: IT-483: Credit unions.

**(4.2) Deemed interest not a dividend** — Notwithstanding any other provision of this Act, an amount that is deemed by subsection (4.1) to be interest shall be deemed not to be a dividend.

**Related Provisions**: 84(2) — Deemed dividend on winding-up; 84(3) — Deemed dividend on redemption of shares; 84(4) — Deemed dividend — reduction of paid-up capital.

**Notes**: 137(4.2) amended by 1993 technical bill, effective for transactions occurring after December 21, 1992.

**Interpretation Bulletins**: IT-483: Credit unions.

**(4.3) Determination of preferred-rate amount of a corporation** — For the purposes of subsection (3),

(a) the preferred-rate amount of a corporation at the end of a taxation year is an amount equal to the total of its preferred-rate amount at the end of its immediately preceding taxation year and $^{25}/_4$ of the amount deductible under section 125 from the tax for the year otherwise payable by it under this Part;

(b) where at any time a new corporation has been formed as a result of an amalgamation of two or more predecessor corporations, within the meaning of subsection 87(1), it shall be deemed to have had a taxation year ending immediately before that time and to have had, at the end of that year, a preferred-rate amount equal to the total of the preferred-rate amounts of each of the predecessor corporations at the end of their last taxation years; and

(c) where there has been a winding-up as described in subsection 88(1), the preferred-rate amount of the parent (referred to in that subsection) at the end of its taxation year immediately preceding its taxation year in which it received the assets of the subsidiary (referred to in that subsection) on the winding-up shall be deemed to be the total of the amount that would otherwise be its preferred-rate amount at the end of that year and the preferred-rate amount of the subsidiary at the end of its taxation year in which its assets were distributed to the parent on the winding-up.

**Interpretation Bulletins**: IT-483: Credit unions.

**(5) Member's income** — Where a payment has been received by a taxpayer from a credit union in a taxation year in respect of an allocation in proportion to borrowing, the amount thereof shall, if the money so borrowed was used by the taxpayer for the purpose of earning income from a business or property (otherwise than to acquire property the income from which would be exempt or to acquire a life insurance policy), be included in computing the taxpayer's income for the year.

**(5.1) Allocations of taxable dividends and capital gains** — A credit union (referred to in this subsection and in subsection (5.2) as the "payer") may, at any time within 120 days after the end of its taxation year, elect in prescribed form to allocate in respect of the year to a member that is a credit union such portion of each of the following amounts as may reasonably be regarded as attributable to the member:

(a) the total of all amounts each of which is the amount of a taxable dividend received by the payer from a taxable Canadian corporation in the year;

(b) the amount if any, by which

(i) the total of all amounts each of which is the amount by which the payer's capital gain from the disposition of a property in the year exceeds the payer's taxable capital gain from the disposition

exceeds

(ii) the total of all amounts each of which is the amount by which the payer's capital loss from the disposition of a property in the year exceeds the payer's allowable capital loss from the disposition; and

(c) each amount deductible under paragraph (5.2)(c) in computing the payer's taxable income for the year.

**Related Provisions**: 137(5.2) — Allocations of taxable dividends and capital gains.

**Notes**: 137(5.1)(b) amended to correct a technical deficiency and 137(5.1)(c) added by 1991 technical bill, effective 1988.

**Interpretation Bulletins**: IT-483: Credit unions.

**(5.2) Idem** — Notwithstanding any other provision of this Act,

(a) there shall be deducted from the amount that would, but for this subsection, be deductible under section 112 in computing a payer's taxable

**S. 137(5.2)(a)**     Income Tax Act, Part I

income for a taxation year such portion of the total referred to in paragraph (5.1)(a) as the payer allocated to its members under subsection (5.1) in respect of the year;

(b) there shall be included in computing the income of a payer for a taxation year an amount equal to that portion of the amount referred to in paragraphs (5.1)(b) and (c) that the payer allocated under subsection (5.1) in respect of the year to its members; and

(c) each amount allocated under subsection (5.1) to a member may be deducted by that member in computing the member's taxable income for its taxation year that includes the last day of the payer's taxation year in respect of which the amount was so allocated.

**Notes**: 137(5.2)(b) amended by 1991 technical bill, effective 1988, to add reference to 137(5.1)(c).

137(5.2)(c) amended by 1992 technical bill, effective for 1991 and later taxation years, to correct a technical deficiency where the taxation year during which the member credit union receives amounts has ended before the date on which the allocation by the central credit union was made. For earlier years, in place of "that includes the last day of the payer's taxation years in respect of which", read "during which".

**Interpretation Bulletins**: IT-483: Credit unions.

**(6) Definitions** — In this section,

**"allocation in proportion to borrowing"** for a taxation year means an amount credited by a credit union to a person who was a member of the credit union in the year on terms that the member is entitled to or will receive payment thereof, computed at a rate in relation to

(a) the amount of interest payable by the member on money borrowed from the credit union, or

(b) the amount of money borrowed by the member from the credit union,

if the amount was credited at the same rate in relation to the amount of interest or money, as the case may be, as the rate at which amounts were similarly credited for the year to all other members of the credit union of the same class;

**Notes**: 137(6)"allocation in proportion to borrowing" was 137(6)(a) before consolidation in R.S.C. 1985 (5th Supp.), effective for taxation years ending after November 1991. See Table of Concordance.

**"bonus interest payment"** for a taxation year means an amount credited by a credit union to a person who was a member of the credit union in the year on terms that the member is entitled to or will receive payment thereof, computed at a rate in relation to

(a) the amount of interest payable in respect of the year by the credit union to the member on money standing to the member's credit from time to time in the records or books of account of the credit union, or

(b) the amount of money standing to the member's credit from time to time in the year in the records or books of account of the credit union,

if the amount was credited at the same rate in relation to the amount of interest or money, as the case may be, as the rate at which amounts were similarly credited in the year to all other members of the credit union of the same class;

**Notes**: 137(6)"bonus interest payment" was 137(6)(a.1) before consolidation in R.S.C. 1985 (5th Supp.), effective for taxation years ending after November 1991. See Table of Concordance.

**"credit union"** means a corporation, association or federation incorporated or organized as a credit union or cooperative credit society if

(a) it derived all or substantially all of its revenues from

(i) loans made to, or cashing cheques for, members,

(ii) debt obligations or securities of, or guaranteed by, the Government of Canada or a province, a Canadian municipality, or an agency thereof, or debt obligations or securities of a municipal or public body performing a function of government in Canada or an agency thereof,

(iii) debt obligations of or deposits with, or guaranteed by, a corporation, commission or association not less than 90% of the shares or capital of which was owned by the Government of Canada or a province or by a municipality in Canada,

(iv) debt obligations of or deposits with, or guaranteed by, a bank, or debt obligations of or deposits with a corporation licensed or otherwise authorized under a law of Canada or a province to carry on in Canada the business of offering to the public its services as trustee,

(v) charges, fees and dues levied against members or members of members,

(vi) loans made to or deposits with a credit union or cooperative credit society of which it is a member, or

(vii) a prescribed revenue source,

(b) all or substantially all the members thereof having full voting rights therein were corporations, associations or federations

(i) incorporated as credit unions or cooperative credit societies, all of which derived all or substantially all of their revenues from the sources described in paragraph (a), or all or substantially all of the members of which were credit unions, cooperatives or a combination thereof,

(ii) incorporated, organized or registered under, or governed by a law of Canada or a province with respect to cooperatives, or

(iii) incorporated or organized for charitable purposes,

or were corporations, associations or federations no part of the income of which was payable to, or otherwise available for the personal benefit of, any shareholder or member thereof, or

(c) the corporation, association or federation would be a credit union by virtue of paragraph (b) if all the members (other than individuals) having full voting rights in each member thereof that is a credit union were members having full voting rights in the corporation, association or federation;

**Related Provisions**: 89(1)"paid-up capital"(b) — PUC of credit union; 137.1(7) — Deposit insurance corporation deemed not credit union; 157(2) — Exemption from instalment obligations where taxable income not over $10,000; 248(1)"credit union" — Definition applies to entire Act; 248(1)"share" — Share of a credit union is a share; Reg. 9002(3) — Mark-to-market rules — property held by credit union.

**Notes**: 137(6)"credit union" was 137(6)(b) before consolidation in R.S.C. 1985 (5th Supp.), effective for taxation years ending after November 1991. See Table of Concordance.

The CCRA takes the position that "all or substantially all" means 90% or more.

**Interpretation Bulletins**: IT-320R2: RRSP — qualified investments; IT-483: Credit unions.

**"maximum cumulative reserve"** of a credit union at the end of any particular taxation year means an amount determined by the formula

$$0.05 \times (A + B)$$

where

A is the total of all amounts each of which is the amount of any debt owing by the credit union to a member thereof or of any other obligation of the credit union to pay an amount to a member thereof, that was outstanding at the end of the year, including, for greater certainty, the amount of any deposit standing to the credit of a member of the credit union in the records of the credit union, but excluding, for greater certainty, any share in the credit union of any member thereof, and

B is the total of all amounts each of which is the amount, as of the end of the year, of any share in the credit union of any member thereof;

**Notes**: 137(6)"maximum cumulative reserve" was 137(6)(c) before consolidation in R.S.C. 1985 (5th Supp.), effective for taxation years ending after November 1991. See Table of Concordance.

**I.T. Application Rules**: 58(3.2) (reduction in maximum cumulative reserve to reflect level at end of 1971).

**"member"** of a credit union means a person who is recorded as a member on the records of the credit union and is entitled to participate in and use the services of the credit union.

**Related Provisions**: Reg. 1404(2)"acquisition costs"(a)(iii.1) — Insurer established to provide insurance to credit union members — policy reserves.

**Notes**: 137(6)"member" was 137(6)(d) before consolidation in R.S.C. 1985 (5th Supp.), effective for taxation years ending after November 1991.

**(7) Credit union not private corporation** — Notwithstanding any other provision of this Act, a credit union that would, but for this section, be a private corporation shall be deemed not to be a private corporation except for the purposes of sections 123.1, 125, 127, 127.1, 152 and 157 and the definition "small business corporation" in subsection 248(1) as it applies for the purposes of paragraph 39(1)(c).

**Notes**: In 137(7), reference to 152 added by 1989 Budget, effective April 28, 1989.

**Definitions [s. 137]**: "allocation in proportion to borrowing" — 137(6); "allowable capital loss" — 38(b), 248(1); "amount" — 248(1); "bank" — 248(1), Interpretation Act 35(1); "bonus interest payment" — 137(6); "business" — 248(1); "class" — of shares 248(6); "corporation" — 248(1), Interpretation Act 35(1); "credit union" — 137(6), 248(1); "disposition" — 248(1); "dividend" — 137(4.1), (4.2), 248(1); "interest" — 137(4.1), (4.2); "life insurance policy" — 138(12), 248(1); "maximum cumulative reserve", "member" — 137(6); "payer" — 137(5.1); "person" — 248(1); "preferred-rate amount" — 137(4.3); "prescribed" — 248(1); "prescribed stock exchange" — Reg. 3200, 3201; "private corporation" — 89(1), 137(7), 248(1); "property" — 248(1); "province" — Interpretation Act 35(1); "record", "share", "shareholder", "small business corporation" — 248(1); "taxable Canadian corporation" — 89(1), 248(1); "taxable capital gain" — 38(a), 248(1); "taxable income" — 2(2), 248(1); "taxation year" — 249; "taxpayer" — 248(1).

**I.T. Application Rules [s. 137]**: 58 (property of credit union acquired before 1972).

**Interpretation Bulletins [s. 137]**: IT-483: Credit unions.

**137.1 (1) Amounts included in income of deposit insurance corporation** — For the purpose of computing the income for a taxation year of a taxpayer that is a deposit insurance corporation, the following rules apply:

(a) the corporation's income shall, except as otherwise provided in this section, be computed in accordance with the rules applicable in computing income for the purposes of this Part; and

(b) there shall be included in computing the corporation's income such of the following amounts as are applicable:

(i) the total of profits or gains made in the year by the corporation in respect of bonds, debentures, mortgages, notes or other similar obligations owned by it that were disposed of by it in the year, and

(ii) the total of each such portion of each amount, if any, by which the principal amount, at the time it was acquired by the corporation, of a bond, debenture, mortgage, note or other similar obligation owned by the corporation at the end of the year exceeds the cost to the corporation of acquiring it as was included by the corporation in computing its profit for the year.

S. 137.1(1)  Income Tax Act, Part I

**Related Provisions**: 137.1(3) — Deductions from income of deposit insurance corporation; 137.1(5) — Deposit insurance corporation defined; 137.1(10) — Amounts paid by a deposit insurance corporation; 137.2 — Valuation of property owned since before 1975; 142.2(1)"financial institution"(c)(iv) — Deposit insurance corporation not subject to mark-to-market rules.

**Notes**: The term "bond, debenture, mortgage, note or other similar obligation" may not include bankers' acceptances. See *Federated Cooperatives Ltd.*, [2000] 2 C.T.C. 2382 (TCC).

**(2) Amounts not included in income** — The amount of any premiums or assessments received or receivable by a taxpayer that is a deposit insurance corporation from its member institutions in a taxation year shall not be included in computing its income.

**Related Provisions**: 137.1(4) — Limitation on deduction; 137.1(11) — Deductions for payments by member institution.

**(3) Amounts deductible in computing income of deposit insurance corporation** — There may be deducted in computing the income for a taxation year of a taxpayer that is a deposit insurance corporation such of the following amounts as are applicable:

(a) the total of losses sustained in the year by the corporation in respect of bonds, debentures, mortgages, notes or other similar obligations owned by it and issued by a person other than a member institution that were disposed of by it in the year;

(b) the total of each such portion of each amount, if any, by which the cost to the corporation of acquiring a bond, debenture, mortgage, note or other similar obligation owned by the corporation at the end of the year exceeds the principal amount of the bond, debenture, mortgage, note or other similar obligation, as the case may be, at the time it was so acquired as was deducted by the corporation in computing its profit for the year;

(c) [Repealed under former Act]

(d) the total of all expenses incurred by the taxpayer in collecting premiums or assessments from member institutions;

(e) the total of all expenses incurred by the taxpayer

(i) in the performance of its duties as curator of a bank, or as liquidator or receiver of a member institution when duly appointed as such a curator, liquidator or receiver,

(ii) in the course of making or causing to be made such inspections as may reasonably be considered to be appropriate for the purposes of assessing the solvency or financial stability of a member institution, and

(iii) in supervising or administering a member institution in financial difficulty; and

(f) the total of all amounts each of which is an amount that is not otherwise deductible by the taxpayer for the year or any other taxation year and that is

(i) an amount paid by the taxpayer in the year pursuant to a legal obligation to pay interest on borrowed money used

(A) to lend money to, or otherwise provide assistance to, a member institution in financial difficulty,

(B) to assist in the payment of any losses suffered by members or depositors of a member institution in financial difficulty,

(C) to lend money to a subsidiary wholly-owned corporation of the taxpayer where the subsidiary is deemed by subsection (5.1) to be a deposit insurance corporation,

(D) to acquire property from a member institution in financial difficulty, or

(E) to acquire shares of the capital stock of a member institution in financial difficulty, or

(ii) an amount paid by the taxpayer in the year pursuant to a legal obligation to pay interest on an amount that would be deductible under subparagraph (i) if it were paid in the year.

**Related Provisions**: 137.2 — Valuation of property owned since before 1975.

**Notes**: See Notes to 137.1(1).

**(4) Limitation on deduction** — No deduction shall be made in computing the income for a taxation year of a taxpayer that is a deposit insurance corporation in respect of

(a) any grant, subsidy or other assistance to member institutions provided by it;

(b) an amount equal to the amount, if any, by which the amount paid or payable by it to acquire property exceeds the fair market value of the property at the time it was so acquired;

(c) any amounts paid to its member institutions as allocations in proportion to any amounts described in subsection (2); or

(d) [Repealed under former Act]

(e) any amount that may otherwise be deductible under paragraph 20(1)(p) in respect of debts owing to it by any of its member institutions that has not been included in computing its income for the year or a preceding taxation year.

**Related Provisions**: 20(1)(p) — Bad debts; 137.1(2) — Amounts not included in income.

**(5) Definitions** — In this section,

**"amortized cost [para. 137.1(5)(d)]"** — [Repealed under former Act]

**Notes**: 137.1(5)(d), repealed by 1988 tax reform, defined "amortized cost", a term now defined in 248(1) and no longer used in this section.

**"deposit insurance corporation"** means

(a) a corporation that was incorporated by or under a law of Canada or a province respecting the establishment of a stabilization fund or board if

(i) it was incorporated primarily

(A) to provide or administer a stabilization, liquidity or mutual aid fund for credit unions, and

(B) to assist in the payment of any losses suffered by members of credit unions in liquidation, and

(ii) throughout any taxation year in respect of which the expression is being applied,

(A) it was a Canadian corporation, and

(B) the cost amount to the corporation of its investment property was at least 50% of the cost amount to it of all its property (other than a debt obligation of, or a share of the capital stock of, a member institution issued by the member institution at a time when it was in financial difficulty), or

(b) a corporation incorporated by the *Canada Deposit Insurance Corporation Act*;

**Related Provisions**: 137.1(5.1) — Deeming provision; 137.1(8) — Deemed compliance with Act; 181.1(3)(e) — Large Corporations Tax not payable by deposit insurance corporation.

**Notes**: 137.1(5)"deposit insurance corporation" was 137.1(5)(a) before consolidation in R.S.C. 1985 (5th Supp.), effective for taxation years ending after November 1991. See Table of Concordance.

**"investment property"** means

(a) bonds, debentures, mortgages, notes or other similar obligations

(i) of or guaranteed by the Government of Canada,

(ii) of the government of a province or an agent thereof,

(iii) of a municipality in Canada or a municipal or public body performing a function of government in Canada,

(iv) of a corporation, commission or association not less than 90% of the shares or capital of which is owned by Her Majesty in right of a province or by a Canadian municipality, or of a subsidiary wholly-owned corporation that is subsidiary to such a corporation, commission or association, or

(v) of an educational institution or a hospital if repayment of the principal amount thereof and payment of the interest thereon is to be made, or is guaranteed, assured or otherwise specifically provided for or secured by the government of a province,

(b) any deposits, deposit certificates or guaranteed investment certificates with

(i) a bank,

(ii) a corporation licensed or otherwise authorized under the laws of Canada or a province to carry on in Canada the business of offering to the public its services as trustee, or

(iii) a credit union or central that is a member of the Canadian Payments Association or a credit union that is a shareholder or member of a central that is a member of the Canadian Payments Association,

(c) any money of the corporation, and

(d) in relation to a particular deposit insurance corporation, debt obligations of, and shares of the capital stock of, a subsidiary wholly-owned corporation of the particular corporation where the subsidiary is deemed by subsection (5.1) to be a deposit insurance corporation;

**Notes**: 137.1(5)"investment property" was 137.1(5)(c) before consolidation in R.S.C. 1985 (5th Supp.), effective for taxation years ending after November 1991. See Table of Concordance.

**"member institution"**, in relation to a particular deposit insurance corporation, means

(a) a corporation whose liabilities in respect of deposits are insured by, or

(b) a credit union that is qualified for assistance from

that deposit insurance corporation.

**Related Provisions**: 142.2(1)"financial institution"(c)(iv) — Deposit insurance corporation not subject to mark-to-market rules.

**Notes**: 137.1(5)"member institution" was 137.1(5)(b) before consolidation in R.S.C. 1985 (5th Supp.), effective for taxation years ending after November 1991. See Table of Concordance.

**(5.1) Deeming provision** — For the purposes of this section, other than subsection (2), paragraph (3)(d), subparagraph (3)(e)(i), subsection (9) and paragraph (11)(a), a subsidiary wholly-owned corporation of a particular corporation described in the definition "deposit insurance corporation" in subsection (5) shall be deemed to be a deposit insurance corporation, and any member institution of the particular corporation shall be deemed to be a member institution of the subsidiary, where all or substantially all of the property of the subsidiary has at all times since the subsidiary was incorporated consisted of

(a) investment property;

(b) shares of the capital stock of a member institution of the particular corporation obtained by the subsidiary at a time when the member institution was in financial difficulty;

(c) debt obligations issued by a member institution of the particular corporation at a time when the member institution was in financial difficulty;

(d) property acquired from a member institution of the particular corporation at a time when the member institution was in financial difficulty; or

(e) any combination of property described in paragraphs (a) to (d).

**Notes**: Opening words of 137.1(5.1) amended by 1993 technical bill, effective for 1992 and later taxation years, to change reference to subsection (11) to be a reference to paragraph (11)(a). This ensures that the deduction under 137.1(11)(b) is available where assistance is repaid by a member institution to a subsidiary wholly-owned corporation of a deposit insurance corporation.

The CCRA takes the position that "all or substantially all", used in the opening words of 137.1(5.1), means 90% or more.

**(6) Deemed not to be a private corporation** — Notwithstanding any other provision of this Act, a deposit insurance corporation that would, but for this subsection, be a private corporation shall be deemed not to be a private corporation.

**(7) Deposit insurance corporation deemed not a credit union** — Notwithstanding any other provision of this Act, a deposit insurance corporation that would, but for this subsection, be a credit union shall be deemed not to be a credit union.

**Related Provisions**: 137 — Credit unions.

**(8) Deemed compliance** — For the purposes of subsection (5), a corporation shall be deemed to have complied with clause (a)(ii)(B) of the definition "deposit insurance corporation" in subsection (5) throughout the 1975 taxation year if it complied with that clause on the last day of that taxation year.

**(9) Special tax rate** — The tax payable under this Part by a corporation for a taxation year throughout which it was a deposit insurance corporation (other than a corporation incorporated under the *Canada Deposit Insurance Corporation Act*) is an amount equal to 22% of its taxable income for the year.

**Related Provisions**: 220(4.3), (4.4) — Security furnished by member institution of a deposit insurance corporation.

**(10) Amounts paid by a deposit insurance corporation** — Where in a taxation year a taxpayer is a member institution, there shall be included in computing its income for the year the total of all amounts each of which is

(a) an amount received by the taxpayer in the year from a deposit insurance corporation that is an amount described in any of paragraphs (4)(a) to (c), to the extent that the taxpayer has not repaid the amount to the deposit insurance corporation in the year,

(b) an amount received from a deposit insurance corporation in the year by a depositor or member of the taxpayer as, on account of, in lieu of payment of, or in satisfaction of, deposits with, or share capital of, the taxpayer, to the extent that the taxpayer has not repaid the amount to the deposit insurance corporation in the year, or

(c) the amount by which

(i) the principal amount of any obligation of the taxpayer to pay an amount to a deposit insurance corporation that is settled or extinguished in the year without any payment by the taxpayer or by the payment by the taxpayer of an amount less than the principal amount

exceeds

(ii) the amount, if any, paid by the taxpayer on the settlement or extinguishment of the obligation

to the extent that the excess is not otherwise required to be included in computing the taxpayer's income for the year or a preceding taxation year.

**Related Provisions**: 80(1)"forgiven amount" — Debt forgiveness; 137.1(10.1) — Principal amount of an obligation to pay interest; 137.1(12) — Repayment excluded; 220(4.3), (4.4) — Security furnished by a member institution of a deposit insurance corporation.

**(10.1) Principal amount of an obligation to pay interest** — For the purposes of paragraph (10)(c), an amount of interest payable by a member institution to a deposit insurance corporation on an obligation shall be deemed to have a principal amount equal to that amount.

**Related Provisions**: 137.1(11) — Deduction for payments by member institution.

**(11) Deduction by member institutions** — There may be deducted in computing the income for a taxation year of a taxpayer that is a member institution such of the following amounts as are applicable:

(a) any amount paid or payable by the taxpayer in the year that is described in subsection (2) to the extent that it was not deducted in computing the taxpayer's income for a preceding taxation year; and

(b) any amount repaid by the taxpayer in the year to a deposit insurance corporation on account of an amount described in paragraph (10)(a) or (b) that was received in a preceding taxation year to the extent that it was not, by reason of subsection (12), excluded from the taxpayer's income for the preceding year.

**Notes**: See Notes to 137.1(5.1).

**(12) Repayment excluded** — Where

(a) a member institution has in a taxation year repaid an amount to a deposit insurance corporation on account of an amount that was included by virtue of paragraph (10)(a) or (b) in computing its income for a preceding taxation year,

(b) the member institution has filed its return of income required by section 150 for the preceding year, and

(c) on or before the day on or before which the member institution is required by section 150 to file a return of income for the taxation year, it has filed an amended return for the preceding year excluding from its income for that year the amount repaid,

the amount repaid shall be excluded from the amount otherwise included by virtue of paragraph (10)(a) or (b) in computing the member institution's income

Division F — Special Rules in Certain Circumstances    S. 138(2)

for the preceding year and the Minister shall make such reassessment of the tax, interest and penalties payable by the member institution for preceding taxation years as is necessary to give effect to the exclusion.

**Definitions [s. 137.1]**: "amount" — 248(1); "Canadian corporation" — 89(1), 248(1); "corporation" — 248(1), *Interpretation Act* 35(1); "credit union" — 137(6), 137.1(7), 248(1); "deposit insurance corporation" — 137.1(5), (5.1); "insurance corporation" — 248(1); "investment property" — 137.1(5); "member institution" — 137.1(5); "Minister" — 248(1); "private corporation" — 89(1), 248(1); "property" — 248(1); "province" — *Interpretation Act* 35(1); "share", "shareholder", "subsidiary wholly-owned corporation" — 248(1); "tax payable" — 248(2); "taxable income" — 2(2), 248(1); "taxation year" — 249; "taxpayer" — 248(1).

**Interpretation Bulletins [s. 137.1]**: IT-483: Credit unions.

## 137.2 Computation of income for 1975 and subsequent years
— For the purpose of computing the income of a deposit insurance corporation for the 1975 and subsequent taxation years,

(a) property of the corporation that is a bond, debenture, mortgage, note or other similar obligation owned by it at the commencement of the corporation's 1975 taxation year shall be valued at its cost to the corporation less the total of all amounts that, before that time, the corporation was entitled to receive as, on account or in lieu of payment of, or in satisfaction of, the principal amount of the bond, debenture, mortgage, note or other similar obligation,

(i) plus a reasonable amount in respect of the amortization of the amount by which the principal amount of the property at the time it was acquired by the corporation exceeded its actual cost to the corporation, or

(ii) minus a reasonable amount in respect of the amortization of the amount by which its actual cost to the corporation exceeded the principal amount of the property at the time it was acquired by the corporation;

(b) property of the corporation that is a debt owing to the corporation (other than property described in paragraph (a) or a debt that became a bad debt before its 1975 taxation year) acquired by it before the commencement of its 1975 taxation year shall be valued at any time at the amount thereof outstanding at that time;

(c) property of the corporation (other than property in respect of which any amount for the year has been included under paragraph (a)) that was acquired, by foreclosure or otherwise, after default made under a mortgage shall be valued at its cost amount to the corporation; and

(d) any other property shall be valued at its cost amount to the corporation.

**Notes**: 137.2 added in the R.S.C. 1985 (5th Supp.) consolidation, effective for taxation years ending after November 1991. This was formerly a rule of application in 1974-75-76, c. 26, s. 94.

**Definitions [s. 137.2]**: "amount", "cost amount" — 248(1); "deposit insurance corporation" — 137.1(5), (5.1) [does not explicitly apply to 137.2]; "income" — 3; "principal amount", "property" — 248(1); "taxation year" — 249.

## Insurance Corporations

**138. (1) Insurance corporations** — It is hereby declared that a corporation, whether or not it is a mutual corporation, that has, in a taxation year, been a party to insurance contracts or other arrangements or relationships of a particular class whereby it can reasonably be regarded as undertaking

(a) to insure other persons against loss, damage or expense of any kind, or

(b) to pay insurance moneys to other persons

(i) on the death of any person,

(ii) on the happening of an event or contingency dependent on human life,

(iii) for a term dependent on human life, or

(iv) at a fixed or determinable future time,

whether or not such persons are members or shareholders of the corporation, shall, regardless of the form or legal effect of those contracts, arrangements or relationships, be deemed, for the purposes of this Act, to have been carrying on an insurance business of that class in the year for profit, and in any such case, for the purpose of computing the income of the corporation, the following rules apply:

(c) every amount received by the corporation under, in consideration of, in respect of or on account of such a contract, arrangement or relationship shall be deemed to have been received by it in the course of that business,

(d) the income shall, except as otherwise provided in this section, be computed in accordance with the rules applicable in computing income for the purposes of this Part,

(e) all income from property vested in the corporation shall be deemed to be income of the corporation, and

(f) all taxable capital gains and allowable capital losses from dispositions of property vested in the corporation shall be deemed to be taxable capital gains or allowable capital losses, as the case may be, of the corporation.

**Related Provisions**: 87(2.2) — Amalgamation of insurance corporations; 94.2(10)(a)(ii) — No application to foreign insurance policy of foreign investment entity; 138(6) — Deductions for dividends from taxable corporations; 138(9) — Computation of income; 139, 139.1 — Mutualization and demutualization of insurer; 142 — Taxable capital gains where insurer carries on business in Canada and outside Canada; 148(1) — Amount included in life insurance policyholder's income; 149(1)(m), (t) — Exemptions — insurers; 190.1 — Financial institutions capital tax.

**Notes**: See Notes at end of s. 138.

**(2) Insurer's income or loss** — Notwithstanding any other provision of this Act, where a life insurer resident in Canada carries on an insurance business

**S. 138(2)** — Income Tax Act, Part I

in Canada and in a country other than Canada in a taxation year

(a) its income or loss for the year from carrying on an insurance business is the amount of its income or loss for the year, computed in accordance with this Act, from the business in Canada; and

(b) no amount shall be included in computing its income for the year in respect of its taxable capital gains and allowable capital losses from dispositions of property (other than property disposed of in a taxation year in which it was designated insurance property) of the insurer used or held by it in the course of carrying on an insurance business.

**Related Provisions**: 20(7)(c) — No deduction for certain reserves; 20(26) — Deduction for unpaid claims reserve adjustment; 94.2(10)(a)(ii) — No application to foreign insurance policy of foreign investment entity; 138(1) — Insurance corporations; 138(6) — Deduction for dividends; 138(9) — Computation of income; 140(1), (2) — Deductions and inclusions in income of insurer; 142 — Application of rule in 138(2)(b) before 1996; 211.1 — Tax on investment income of life insurer.

**Notes**: 138(2) amended by 1996 Budget, effective for 1997 and later taxation years (changed from 1996 at Second Reading of the Budget bill). For 1990 through 1995, read:

(2) Notwithstanding any other provision of this Act, where a life insurer is resident in Canada,

(a) its income for a taxation year from carrying on an insurance business is the amount of its income for the year from carrying on that insurance business in Canada; and

(b) its loss sustained in a taxation year in carrying on an insurance business is the amount of its loss, if any, sustained in the year in carrying on that insurance business in Canada, computed by applying, with such modifications as the circumstances require, the provisions of this Act respecting the computation of income from an insurance business of the class carried on by it.

The rule now in 138(2)(b) was formerly in s. 142.

Opening words of 138(2) amended by 1991 technical bill, effective 1990, to apply only to an insurer that is resident in Canada. (Non-residents are not subject to Canadian tax on their foreign income anyway, so the application of 138(2) to non-residents was unnecessary.) See also Notes at end of s. 138.

**(3) Deductions allowed in computing income [of life insurer]** — In computing a life insurer's income for a taxation year from carrying on its life insurance business in Canada, there may be deducted

(a) such of the following amounts as are applicable:

(i) any amount that the insurer claims as a policy reserve for the year in respect of its life insurance policies, not exceeding the total of amounts that the insurer is allowed by regulation to deduct in respect of the policies,

(ii) any amount that the insurer claims as a reserve in respect of claims that were received by the insurer before the end of the year under its life insurance policies and that are unpaid at the end of the year, not exceeding the total of amounts that the insurer is allowed by regulation to deduct in respect of the policies,

(ii.1) the amount included under paragraph (4)(b) in computing the insurer's income for the taxation year preceding the year,

(iii) an amount equal to the lesser of

(A) the amount, if any, by which the total of policy dividends (except the portion thereof paid out of segregated funds) that became payable by the insurer after its 1968 taxation year and before the end of the year under its participating life insurance policies exceeds the total of amounts deductible under this subparagraph in computing its incomes for taxation years before the year, and

(B) the amount, if any, by which the total of all amounts, each of which is the insurer's income, determined in accordance with prescribed rules, for the year or a preceding taxation year ending after 1968 from its participating life insurance business carried on in Canada exceeds the total of all amounts each of which is an amount deductible under this subparagraph or subparagraph (iv) in computing its incomes for taxation years ending before the year,

(iv) an amount as a reserve for policy dividends that will become payable by the insurer in the immediately following taxation year equal to the least of

(A) that portion of policy dividends that has accrued in the year or a preceding taxation year to or for the benefit of participating life insurance policyholders of the insurer, to the extent that an amount in respect thereof has not been included, either explicitly or implicitly, in the calculation of the amount deductible by the insurer for the year under subparagraph (i) and, for the purpose of this clause, a policy dividend in respect of a life insurance policy shall be deemed to accrue in equal daily amounts between anniversary dates of the policy,

(B) 110% of the amount paid or unconditionally credited in the taxation year immediately following the year in respect of the portion referred to in clause (A) of policy dividends that has accrued in the year or a preceding taxation year, and

(C) the amount, if any, by which the amount described in clause (iii)(B) for the year exceeds the amount described in clause (iii)(A) for the year, and

(v) each amount (other than an amount credited under a participating life insurance policy) that would be deductible under section 140 in computing the insurer's income for the

1256

Division F — Special Rules in Certain Circumstances    S. 138(4)

year if the reference in that section to "an insurance business other than a life insurance business" were read as a reference to "a life insurance business in Canada";

(b) [Repealed]

(c) [Repealed under former Act]

(d) [Repealed]

(e) the total of amounts each of which is a policy loan made by the insurer in the year and after 1977;

(f) where the taxation year is the first taxation year of the insurer ending after November 12, 1981, the total of all amounts each of which is the amount, if any, in respect of interest on a policy loan that was included in computing the insurer's income for a taxation year ending before November 13, 1981

(i) to the extent that the interest had accrued to it before the commencement of its 1969 taxation year, or

(ii) to the extent that the interest had been included in computing its income for a preceding taxation year; and

(g) the amount of tax under Part XII.3 payable by the insurer in respect of its taxable Canadian life investment income for the year.

**Related Provisions**: 4(1) — Income or loss from a source; 18(1)(e.1) — No deduction for unpaid claims; 20(1)(l) — Deductions — reserve for doubtful debts; 20(7)(c) — Policy reserves for non-life insurance business; 20(26) — Deduction for unpaid claims reserve adjustment; 39.1(1)"exempt capital gains balance"C(c), 39.1(6) — Reduction in gain to reflect capital gains exemption election; 138(3.1) — Excess policy dividend deduction deemed deductible; 138(4) — Amounts included in computing income; 138(4.01) — Life insurance policy includes group life benefit or annuity contract; 138(9) — Computation of income; 138(11.91)(d.1) — Computation of income for non-resident insurer; 138(12) — "Maximum tax actuarial reserve"; 139.1(8)(b) — No deduction for policy dividend paid on demutualization; 140 — Adjustments to income of insurance corporation; 148(1) — Amounts included in computing policyholder's income; 148(2) — Policy dividends deemed to be proceeds of disposition; 149(10)(a.1) — Exempt corporations.

**Notes**: 138(3)(a)(i) and (ii) amended, and (iii) added, by 1996 Budget, effective for 1996 and later taxation years. For earlier years since 1988 (beginning after June 17, 1987), read:

(i) such amount in respect of a policy reserve for the year for life insurance policies of a particular class as is allowed by regulation,

(ii) such amount as is allowed by regulation as a reserve in respect of claims that were received by the insurer before the end of the year under life insurance policies and that are unpaid at the end of the year,

138(3)(b) repealed by 1994 tax amendments bill (Part III), effective for taxation years that begin after February 22, 1994. (The new rules in 142.2–142.6 now apply to shares and debt held by financial institutions.) For the taxation year that includes February 22, 1994, read:

(b) the total of losses sustained in the year by the insurer in respect of Canada securities owned by it that were disposed of by it in the year and before February 23, 1994;

For earlier taxation years since 1972, ignore the words "and before February 23, 1994".

138(3)(c), repealed by 1988 tax reform, provided a deduction for an investment reserve. A reserve can now be claimed under 20(1)(l)(ii).

138(3)(d) repealed by 1994 tax amendments bill (Part III), effective for taxation years that end after February 22, 1994. For earlier taxation years since 1969, read:

(d) the total of each such portion of each amount, if any, by which the cost to the insurer of acquiring a Canada security owned by it at the end of the year exceeds the principal amount of the security at the time it was so acquired as was deducted by the insurer in computing its profit for the year;

See also Notes at end of s. 138.

**Regulations**: 1102(1)(j) (no CCA on property used in life insurance business outside Canada); 1401(1) (policy reserves for pre-1996 policies); 1401(4) (unpaid claims reserve for pre-1996 policies); 1404(1) (policy reserves for post-1995 policies); 1405 (unpaid claims reserve for post-1995 policies); 2402 (amounts to be included in income).

**(3.1) Excess policy dividend deduction deemed deductible** — For the purposes of clause (3)(a)(iii)(A),

(a) an insurer's 1975-76 excess policy dividend deduction shall be deemed to be an amount that was deductible under subparagraph (3)(a)(iii) in computing its incomes for taxation years before its 1977 taxation year; and

(b) the amount prescribed to be an insurer's 1977 excess policy dividend deduction shall be deemed to be an amount that was deductible under subparagraph (3)(a)(iii) in computing its incomes for taxation years before its 1978 taxation year.

**Regulations**: 2407 (insurer's 1977 excess policy dividend deduction).

**(4) Amounts included in computing income** — In computing a life insurer's income for a taxation year from carrying on its life insurance business in Canada, there shall be included

(a) each amount deducted under subparagraph (3)(a)(i), (ii) or (iv) in computing the insurer's income for the preceding taxation year;

(b) the amount prescribed in respect of the insurer for the year in respect of its life insurance policies; and

(c) the total of all amounts received by the insurer in the year in respect of the repayment of policy loans or in respect of interest on policy loans.

**Related Provisions**: 94.2(10)(a)(ii) — No application to foreign insurance policy of foreign investment entity; 138(1) — Insurance corporations; 138(3) — Deductions allowed in computing income; 138(4.01) — Life insurance policy includes group life benefit or annuity contract; 138(4.1)–(4.4) — Amounts included in computing income; 138(9) — Computation of income; 138(11.5)(j.1) — Transfer of business by non-resident insurer; 138(11.91)(d) — Computation of income of non-resident insurer.

**Notes**: 138(4) amended by 1996 Budget, effective for 1996 and later taxation years. The substantive change was to add para. (b). For earlier years, read:

> (4) In computing a life insurer's income for a taxation year from carrying on its life insurance business in Canada, there shall be included
>
> (a) each amount deducted by the insurer under subparagraph (3)(a)(i), (ii) or (iv) in computing its income for the immediately preceding taxation year; and
>
> (b), (c) [Repealed]
>
> (d) the total of amounts each of which is an amount received by the insurer in the year in respect of the repayment of a policy loan or in respect of interest on a policy loan.

138(4)(b) repealed by 1994 tax amendments bill (Part III), effective for taxation years that begin after February 22, 1994. For the taxation year that includes February 22, 1994, read (b) as:

> (b) the total of profits or gains made in the year by the insurer in respect of Canada securities owned by it that were disposed of by it in the year and before February 23, 1994;

For earlier taxation years since 1972, ignore the words "and before February 23, 1994".

138(4)(c) repealed by 1994 tax amendments bill (Part III), effective for taxation years that end after February 22, 1994. For taxation years that end before February 23, 1994 (and since 1969), read (c) as:

> (c) the total of each such portion of each amount, if any, by which the principal amount, at the time it was acquired by the insurer, of a Canada security owned by it at the end of the year exceeds the cost to the insurer of so acquiring it as was included by the insurer in computing its profit for the year; and

**Regulations**: 1404(2) (amount prescribed for 138(4)(b)); 8103 (prescribed amount).

**(4.01) Life insurance policy** — For the purposes of subsections (3) and (4), a life insurance policy includes a benefit under a group life insurance policy or a group annuity contract.

**Related Provisions**: Reg. 1408(1)"life insurance policy in Canada" — Same definition for purposes of policy reserve regulations.

**Notes**: 138(4.01) added by 1996 Budget, effective for 1996 and later taxation years.

**(4.1) Idem** — For the purposes of paragraph (4)(a), an insurer shall be deemed to have deducted in computing its income for its 1976 taxation year,

(a) under subparagraph (3)(a)(i), the total of

(i) the amount deducted under that subparagraph in computing its income from its life insurance business in Canada for its 1976 taxation year, and

(ii) the lesser of

(A) the amount, if any, of its 1975-76 excess policy reserves, and

(B) the amount, if any, by which its 1975 branch accounting election deficiency exceeds the total of

(I) the amount determined under subparagraph (d)(ii),

(II) the total of amounts each of which is an amount determined under paragraph 13(22)(b) with respect to depreciable property of a prescribed class of the insurer,

(III) the amount determined under subparagraph (b)(ii), and

(IV) the total of amounts each of which is a portion of a non-capital loss that is deemed by subsection 111(7.1) to have been deductible in computing the insurer's income for a taxation year ending before 1977;

(b) under subparagraph (3)(a)(ii), the total of

(i) the amount deducted under that subparagraph in computing its income from its life insurance business in Canada for its 1976 taxation year, and

(ii) the lesser of

(A) the amount, if any, of its 1975-76 excess additional group term reserves, and

(B) the amount, if any, by which its 1975 branch accounting election deficiency exceeds the total of

(I) the amount determined under subparagraph (d)(ii),

(II) the total of amounts each of which is an amount determined under paragraph 13(22)(b) with respect to depreciable property of a prescribed class of the insurer, and

(III) the total described in subclause (a)(ii)(B)(IV);

(c) under subparagraph (3)(a)(iv), the total of

(i) the amount deducted under that subparagraph in computing its income from its life insurance business in Canada for its 1976 taxation year, and

(ii) the amount, if any, of its 1975-76 excess policy dividend reserve; and

(d) under paragraph 138(3)(c) of the *Income Tax Act*, chapter 148 of the Revised Statutes of Canada, 1952, the total of

(i) the amount deducted under that paragraph in computing its income from its life insurance business in Canada for its 1976 taxation year, and

(ii) the lesser of

(A) the amount, if any, of its 1975-76 excess investment reserve, and

(B) the amount, if any, of its 1975 branch accounting election deficiency.

**I.T. Application Rules**: 69 (meaning of "*Income Tax Act*, chapter 148 of the Revised Statutes of Canada, 1952").

**(4.2) Idem** — For the purposes of paragraph (4)(a), a life insurer shall be deemed to have deducted the

Division F — Special Rules in Certain Circumstances          S. 138(4.4)(d)

following amounts in computing its income for its 1977 taxation year

(a) under subparagraph (3)(a)(i), the amount if any, by which the total of

(i) the insurer's maximum tax actuarial reserve for its 1977 taxation year, if that reserve had been determined on the basis of the rules applicable to its 1978 taxation year,

(ii) where the insurer has deducted the amount of any policy loan made by it in the year in computing its income from its life insurance business in Canada for any taxation year before its 1978 taxation year or not included in respect of any such loan in computing its gross investment revenue for any taxation year before its 1978 taxation year, the total of amounts that were outstanding at the end of the insurer's 1977 taxation year each of which is an amount payable to it in respect of a policy loan, and

(iii) that portion of the amount deducted by the insurer under subparagraph (3)(a)(i) in computing its income for its 1977 taxation year that is in respect of segregated fund policies

exceeds

(iv) the amount prescribed to be its 1977 carryforward deduction;

(b) under subparagraph (3)(a)(iv), the total of

(i) the amount deducted under that subparagraph in computing its income from its life insurance business in Canada for its 1977 taxation year, and

(ii) the amount, if any, by which

(A) the amount that would have been deductible under that subparagraph for its 1977 taxation year if that subparagraph were read without reference to clause (3)(a)(iv)(C),

exceeds

(B) the amount determined under subparagraph (i) for that taxation year; and

(c) under paragraph 138(3)(c) of the *Income Tax Act*, chapter 148 of the Revised Statutes of Canada, 1952, the total of

(i) the amount deducted under that paragraph in computing its income from its life insurance business in Canada for its 1977 taxation year, and

(ii) the amount, if any, by which,

(A) where the insurer has made an election under subsection (9) in respect of its 1975 taxation year, the amount that would have been deductible under paragraph 138(3)(c) of that Act in computing its income for its 1977 taxation year if the insurer had claimed the maximum allowable amount in its 1977 taxation year, or

(B) where the insurer has not made an election under subsection (9) in respect of its 1975 taxation year, the amount that would have been deductible under paragraph 138(3)(c) of that Act in computing its income for its 1977 taxation year if the insurer had claimed the maximum allowable amount in each of its taxation years ending before 1978 and after 1974

exceeds

(C) the amount determined under subparagraph (i).

**Related Provisions:** 111(7.2) — Non-capital loss of life insurer.

**Regulations:** 2408 (1977 carryforward deduction).

**I.T. Application Rules:** 69 (meaning of "*Income Tax Act*, chapter 148 of the Revised Statutes of Canada, 1952").

**(4.3) Idem** — For the purposes of paragraph (4)(a), in computing a life insurer's income from carrying on its life insurance business in Canada for its first taxation year ending after 1984, the amount, if any, by which

(a) the total of all amounts each of which is an amount deducted by the insurer in computing its income for a taxation year ending after 1968 and before 1985 in respect of a claim under a life insurance policy that was likely to arise after the end of the particular taxation year in respect of a death that occurred in the particular taxation year

exceeds

(b) the total of all amounts each of which is an amount paid by the insurer or included in computing its income before the commencement of its first taxation year ending after 1984 in respect of amounts described in paragraph (a)

shall be deemed to be an amount that was deducted by the insurer under subparagraph (3)(a)(i) in computing its income from that business for its last taxation year ending before 1985.

**(4.4) Idem** — Where, for a period of time in a taxation year, a life insurer

(a) owned land (other than land referred to in paragraph (c) or (d)) or an interest therein that was not held primarily for the purpose of gaining or producing income from the land for the period,

(b) had an interest in a building that was being constructed, renovated or altered,

(c) owned land subjacent to the building referred to in paragraph (b) or an interest therein, or

(d) owned land immediately contiguous to the land referred to in paragraph (c) or an interest therein that was used or was intended to be used for a parking area, driveway, yard, garden or other use necessary for the use or intended use of the building referred to in paragraph (b),

1259

there shall be included in computing the insurer's income for the year, where the land, building or interest was designated insurance property of the insurer for the year, or property used or held by it in the year in the course of carrying on an insurance business in Canada, the total of all amounts each of which is the amount prescribed in respect of the insurer's cost or capital cost, as the case may be, of the land, building or interest for the period, and the amount prescribed shall, at the end of the period, be included in computing

(e) where the land or interest therein is property described in paragraph (a), the cost to the insurer of the land or the interest therein, and

(f) where the land, building or interest therein is property described in paragraphs (b) to (d), the capital cost to the insurer of the interest in the building described in paragraph (b).

**Related Provisions**: 138(4.5) — Anti-avoidance rule; 138(4.6) — Meaning of "completed"; 248(4) — Interest in real property.

**Notes**: Text between paras. (d) and (e) amended by 1996 Budget, effective for 1997 and later taxation years (changed from 1996 at Second Reading of the Budget bill). For earlier years since 1988 (beginning after June 17, 1987), read:

the life insurer shall, where that land or building was property used by it in the year in, or held by it in the year in the course of, carrying on an insurance business in Canada, include a prescribed amount in computing its income for the year in respect of the cost or capital cost, as the case may be, of the land, building or interest therein to the insurer for the period, and the amount so included shall, at the end of the period, be included in computing

**Regulations**: 2410 (prescribed amount).

**(4.5) Application** — Where a life insurer transfers or lends property, directly or indirectly in any manner whatever, to a person or partnership (in this subsection referred to as the "transferee") that is affiliated with the insurer or a person or partnership that does not deal at arm's length with the insurer and

(a) that property,

(b) property substituted for that property, or

(c) property the acquisition of which was assisted by the transfer or loan of that property

was property described in paragraph (4.4)(a), (b), (c) or (d) of the transferee for a period of time in a taxation year of the insurer, the following rules apply:

(d) subsection (4.4) shall apply to include an amount in the insurer's income for the year on the assumption that the property was owned by the insurer for the period, was property described in paragraph (4.4)(a), (b), (c) or (d) of the insurer and was used or held by it in the year in the course of carrying on an insurance business in Canada, and

(e) an amount included in the insurer's income for the year under subsection (4.4) by reason of the application of this subsection shall

(i) where subparagraph (ii) does not apply, be added by the insurer in computing the cost to it of shares of the capital stock of or an interest in the transferee at the end of the year, or

(ii) where the insurer and the transferee have jointly elected in prescribed form on or before the day that is the earliest of the days on or before which any taxpayer making the election is required to file a return pursuant to section 150 for the taxation year that includes the period, be added in computing

(A) where the property is land or an interest therein of the transferee described in paragraph (4.4)(a), the cost to the transferee of the land or the interest therein, and

(B) where the property is land, a building or an interest therein described in paragraphs (4.4)(b) to (d), the capital cost to the transferee of the interest in the building described in paragraph (4.4)(b).

**Related Provisions**: 248(4) — Interest in real property; 248(5) — Substituted property; 251.1 — Affiliated persons.

**Notes**: Opening words of 138(4.5) and 138(4.5)(d) amended by 1996 Budget, effective for 1997 and later taxation years (changed from 1996 at Second Reading of the Budget bill). For earlier years since 1988 (beginning after June 17, 1987), read:

(4.5) Where, after 1987, a life insurer has transferred or lent property, directly or indirectly in any manner whatever, to a transferee that was a designated corporation of the insurer (within the meaning assigned by subsection 2405(3) of the *Income Tax Regulations*) or a person or partnership that does not deal at arm's length with the insurer and

. . . .

(d) subsection (4.4) shall apply to include an amount in the insurer's income for the year on the assumption that the property was owned by the insurer for the period, was property described in paragraph (4.4)(a), (b), (c) or (d) of the insurer and was used by it in the year in, or held by it in the year in the course of, carrying on an insurance business in Canada, and

**(4.6) Completion** — For the purposes of subsection (4.4), the construction, renovation or alteration of a building is completed at the earlier of the day on which the construction, renovation or alteration is actually completed and the day on which all or substantially all of the building is used for the purpose for which it was constructed, renovated or altered.

**Notes**: The CCRA takes the position that "all or substantially all" means 90% or more.

**(5) Deductions not allowed** — Notwithstanding any other provision of this Act,

(a) in the case of an insurer, no deduction may be made under paragraph 20(1)(l) in computing its income for a taxation year from an insurance business in Canada in respect of a premium or other consideration for a life insurance policy in Canada or an interest therein; and

(b) in the case of a non-resident insurer or a life insurer resident in Canada that carries on any of its insurance business in a country other than Canada, no deduction may be made under paragraph 20(1)(c) or (d) in computing its income for a taxation year from carrying on an insurance business in Canada, except in respect of

(i) interest on borrowed money used to acquire designated insurance property for the year in respect of the business,

### Proposed Amendment — 138(5)(b)(i)

(i) interest on borrowed money used to acquire designated insurance property for the year, or to acquire property for which designated insurance property for the year was substituted property, for the period in the year during which the designated insurance property was held by the insurer in respect of the business,

**Application:** Bill C-43 (First Reading September 20, 2000), subsec. 85(1), will amend subpara. 138(5)(b)(i) to read as above, applicable to 1997 et seq.

**Technical Notes:** Section 138 of the Act sets out detailed rules relating to the taxation of insurance corporations.

Currently, interest on borrowed money used to acquire designated insurance property for a year may be deducted by an insurer in respect of its insurance business. Interest on borrowed money used to acquire property other than designated insurance property is not deductible. Subparagraph 138(5)(b)(i) is amended to allow interest on borrowed money used to acquire property for which designated insurance property is substituted property to be deducted. As well, the deduction is limited to the interest that relates to the period in the year during which the designated insurance property was held by the insurer.

(ii) interest on amounts payable for designated insurance property for the year in respect of the business,

(iii) interest on deposits received or other amounts held by the insurer that arose in connection with life insurance policies in Canada or with policies insuring Canadian risks, or

(iv) other interest that does not exceed a prescribed amount.

### Proposed Repeal — 138(5)(b)(iv)

**Application:** Bill C-43 (First Reading September 20, 2000), subsec. 85(2), will repeal subpara. 138(5)(b)(iv), applicable to 1997 et seq.

**Technical Notes:** Paragraph 138(5)(b) of the Act limits the deductibility of interest by resident multinational life insurers and non-resident insurers to those amounts set forth in subparagraphs 138(5)(b)(i) to (iv). Subparagraph 138(5)(b)(iv) was added to the Act to permit a deduction up to a prescribed amount that was to have been set out in regulation 2404 proposed as part of the draft Regulations for insurance companies that were published in September 1997. Changes made to the draft Regulations since their release have eliminated the need for subparagraph 138(5)(b)(iv). Subparagraph 138(5)(b)(iv) is, therefore, repealed.

**Related Provisions:** 248(4) — Interest in real property; 248(5) — Substituted property.

**Notes:** 138(5)(b) amended by 1996 Budget, effective for 1997 and later taxation years (changed from 1996 at Second Reading of the Budget bill). The substance of the amendment was to add subpara. (iv) and to use the new term "designated insurance property" in place of the former wording. For earlier years since 1982, read:

(b) in the case of a non-resident insurer or a life insurer resident in Canada that carries on any of its insurance business in a country other than Canada, no deduction may be made under paragraph 20(1)(c) or (d) in computing its income for a taxation year from carrying on an insurance business in Canada, except in respect of interest on

(i) borrowed money used to acquire property used by it in the year in, or held by it in the year in the course of, carrying on that insurance business in Canada, to the extent that the interest is paid or payable in respect of that portion of the year during which the property was so used or held,

(ii) amounts payable for its property used by it in the year in, or held by it in the year in the course of, carrying on that insurance business in Canada to the extent that the interest is paid or payable in respect of that portion of the year during which the property was so used or held, or

(iii) deposits received or other amounts held by the insurer that arose in connection with life insurance policies in Canada or with policies insuring Canadian risks.

**Regulations:** 2404 (prescribed amount for 138(5)(b)(iv)).

**(5.1) No deduction** — No deduction shall be made under subsection 20(12) in computing the income of a life insurer resident in Canada in respect of foreign taxes attributable to its insurance business.

**Interpretation Bulletins:** IT-506: Foreign income taxes as a deduction from income.

**(5.2) [Repealed]**

**Notes:** 138(5.2) repealed by 1994 tax amendments bill (Part III), effective for dispositions occurring after October 30, 1994, except the disposition of a debt obligation before July 1995 where

(a) the disposition is part of a series of transactions or events that began before October 31, 1994;

(b) as part of the series of transactions or events, the taxpayer who acquired the debt obligation disposed of property before October 31, 1994; and

(c) it is reasonable to consider that one of the main reasons for the acquisition of the debt obligation by the taxpayer was to obtain a deduction because, as a consequence of the disposition referred to in paragraph (b),

(i) an amount was included in the taxpayer's income for any taxation year, or

(ii) an amount was subtracted from a balance of undeducted outlays, expenses or other amounts of the taxpayer and the subtracted amount exceeded the portion, if any, of the balance that could reasonably be considered to be in respect of the property.

(The same application rule applies to new 142.6(7).) Where 138(5.2) applies (last amended in 1987), read:

(5.2) **Idem** — Notwithstanding paragraph (3)(b) and subsection (11.4), in computing an insurer's income for a taxation year from carrying on an insurance business, no amount shall be deducted in respect of a loss sustained by the insurer on a disposition (other than a disposition occurring as a result of the application of subsection (11.3)) of property that is a share, bond, debenture, mortgage, note, agreement of sale or any other form of indebtedness that was not a capital property of the insurer and was used by it in the year in, or held by it in the year in the course of, carrying on an insurance business in any case where

(a) during the period commencing 30 days before and ending 30 days after the disposition, the insurer or a person or partnership that does not deal at arm's length with the insurer acquired or agreed to acquire the same or an identical property (in this subsection referred to as the "substituted property"), and

(b) at the end of the period referred to in paragraph (a), the insurer or the person or partnership, as the case may be, owned or had a right to acquire the substituted property,

and any such loss shall be added in computing the cost to the insurer or the person or partnership, as the case may be, of the substituted property.

**(6) Deduction for dividends from taxable corporations** — In computing the taxable income of a life insurer for a taxation year, no deduction from the income of the insurer for the year may be made under section 112 but, except as otherwise provided by that section, there may be deducted from that income the total of taxable dividends (other than dividends on term preferred shares that are acquired in the ordinary course of the business carried on by the life insurer) included in computing the insurer's income for the year and received by the insurer in the year from taxable Canadian corporations.

**Related Provisions**: 18(1)(c) — Limitation re exempt income; 55(2) — Deemed proceeds or capital gain; 87(2)(x) — Amalgamations; 111(7.2) — "Non-capital loss" of life insurer; 111(8)"non-capital loss"A:E — Amount included in non-capital loss; 112(2.2), (2.4) — Where no deduction permitted; 112(3)(b)(i) — Reduction in loss on subsequent disposition of share; 112(4)(d) — Loss on share held as inventory; 112(5.2)B(b)(i), (ii) — Adjustment for dividends received on mark-to-market property; 115(1)(d.1) — Deduction from income of non-resident; 141(2) — Life insurance corporation deemed to be public corporation; 148(4) — Income from disposition; 187.2 — Tax on dividends on taxable preferred shares; 187.3 — Tax on dividends on taxable RFI shares; 191(4) — Subsec. 138(6) deemed not to apply; 248(14) — Corporations deemed related; 258 — Deemed dividend on term preferred share.

**Interpretation Bulletins**: IT-52R4: Income bonds and income debentures; IT-328R3: Losses on shares on which dividends have been received; IT-385R2: Disposition of an income interest in a trust.

**(7) [Repealed]**

**Notes**: 138(7) repealed by 1996 Budget, effective for 1996 and later taxation years. It required a stock life insurer to include additional amounts in income in respect of dividends paid to its shareholders, and was designed to tax profits accumulated before 1969, and certain foreign branch profits, when these profits were distributed to shareholders. For 1979 through 1995, read:

(7) Amounts paid to shareholders included in taxable income — The taxable income for a taxation year of a life insurer resident in Canada is its taxable income for the year otherwise computed under this Part, plus 2 times the amount, if any, by which the total of amounts each of which is an amount paid by it after the end of its 1968 taxation year and before the end of the year as, on account or in lieu of payment of, or in satisfaction of dividends or stock dividends or any other amounts that, but for paragraph 84(1)(c.1), would have been dividends, exceeds the total of

(a) the insurer's undistributed income on hand at the end of its 1968 taxation year in respect of which tax under this Part has been paid by it,

(b) the surplus funds derived from operations of the insurer as of the end of the year,

(c) the total of amounts of surplus contributed to the insurer before the end of the year,

(d) ½ the total of amounts that, by virtue of this subsection, have been added to the taxable income of the insurer otherwise computed under this Part in computing its taxable income for taxation years before the year,

(e) where in the taxation year the insurer carried on an insurance business in a country other than Canada, the lesser of

(i) the total of dividends and stock dividends in respect of shares of the capital stock of the insurer paid by it in the year out of property other than property used by the insurer in the year in, or held by it in the year in the course of, carrying on an insurance business in Canada, and

(ii) the amount of tax for the year paid by the insurer to the government of a country other than Canada under the income tax laws of that country out of property other than property used by the insurer in the year in, or held by it in the year in the course of, carrying on an insurance business in Canada,

(f) where in the taxation year the insurer did not carry on an insurance business in a country other than Canada, the lesser of

(i) the total of dividends and stock dividends in respect of shares of the capital stock of the insurer paid by it in the year, and

(ii) the amount of tax for the year paid by the insurer to the government of a country other than Canada under the income tax laws of that country,

(g) the total of all amounts determined under paragraphs (e) and (f) in respect of the insurer for taxation years before the year, and

(h) the amount, if any, by which the lesser of

(i) the total of amounts paid after the end of the insurer's 1968 taxation year and before 1978 as, on account or in lieu of payment of, in satisfaction of, dividends or stock dividends in respect of shares of the capital stock of the insurer, and

(ii) the amount, if any, determined in respect of the insurer under paragraph 138(7)(c) of the *Income Tax Act*, chapter 148 of the Revised Statutes of Canada, 1952, as it read in its application to the 1976 taxation year

exceeds

(iii) the total of amounts of surplus contributed to the insurer before 1978.

**(8) No deduction for foreign tax** — No deduction shall be made under section 126 from the tax payable under this Part for a taxation year by a life insurer resident in Canada in respect of such part of an income or profits tax as can reasonably be attributable to income from its insurance business.

**(9) Computation of income** — Where in a taxation year an insurer (other than an insurer resident in Canada that does not carry on a life insurance business) carries on an insurance business in Canada and in a country other than Canada, there shall be included in computing its income for the year from carrying on its insurance businesses in Canada the total of

(a) its gross investment revenue for the year from its designated insurance property for the year, and

(b) the amount prescribed in respect of the insurer for the year.

**Related Provisions**: 88(1)(g) — Winding up — gross investment revenue; 111(7.1) — Effect of election by insurer under ss. 138(9) re 1975 taxation year; 138(3) — Deductions allowed in computing income; 138(7) — Amounts paid to shareholders included in taxable income; 138(11.5)(i) — Transfer of insurance business by non-resident insurer; 138(11.91)(d) — Computation of income for non-resident insurer; 138(11.92)(c) — Computation of income where insurance business transferred; 142 — Taxable capital gains, etc.; 148(1) — Amounts included in computing policyholder's income; 219(4) — Non-resident insurers.

**Notes**: 138(9) amended by 1996 Budget, effective for 1997 and later taxation years (changed from 1996 at Second Reading of the Budget bill). The substance of the amendment was to use the new term "designated insurance property"; the other changes are cosmetic. For earlier years since 1988 (beginning after June 17, 1987), read:

(9) Where in a taxation year an insurer (other than a resident of Canada that does not carry on a life insurance business) carried on an insurance business in Canada and in a country other than Canada, there shall be included in computing its income for the year from carrying on its insurance businesses in Canada the total of

(a) that part of its gross investment revenue for the year that is gross investment revenue from property used by it in the year in, or held by it in the year in the course of, carrying on those insurance businesses in Canada, and

(b) such additional amount as is prescribed in respect of the insurer for the year by regulation.

**Regulations**: 2411 (prescribed amount).

**Forms**: T2S(1)(L): Tax calculations for life insurance companies (plus schedules L.1 to L.9); T2016: Part XIII tax return — tax on income from Canada of registered non-resident insurers.

**(9.1) [Repealed under former Act]**

**Notes**: 138(9.1) provided rules where an insurer had elected under the pre-1978 version of 138(9).

**(10) Application of financial institution rules** — Notwithstanding sections 142.3, 142.4 and 142.5, where in a taxation year an insurer (other than an insurer resident in Canada that does not carry on a life insurance business) carries on an insurance business in Canada and in a country other than Canada, in computing its income for the year from carrying on an insurance business in Canada,

(a) sections 142.3 and 142.5 apply only in respect of property that is designated insurance property for the year in respect of the business; and

(b) section 142.4 applies only in respect of the disposition of property that, for the taxation year in which the insurer disposed of it, was designated insurance property in respect of the business.

**Related Provisions**: 94.2(10)(a)(ii) — No application to foreign insurance policy of foreign investment entity.

**Notes**: 138(10) amended by 1996 Budget, effective for 1997 and later taxation years (changed from 1996 at Second Reading of the Budget bill). For earlier years, read:

(10) Where in a taxation year an insurer (other than an insurer resident in Canada that does not carry on a life insurance business) carried on an insurance business in Canada and in a country other than Canada, in computing the income of the insurer for the year from carrying on an insurance business in Canada,

(a) sections 142.3 and 142.5 apply with respect to property used by it in the year in, or held by it in the year in the course of, carrying on that business; and

(b) section 142.4 applies with respect to the disposition of property that, in the taxation year in which the insurer disposed of it, was property used by it in the year in, or held by it in the year in the course of, carrying on that business.

138(10) added by 1994 tax amendments bill (Part III), effective for taxation years that end after February 22, 1994.

Former 138(10) provided rules where an insurer had elected under the pre-1978 version of 138(9).

**(11) [Repealed]**

**Notes**: 138(11) repealed by 1994 tax amendments bill (Part III), effective for taxation years that begin after February 22, 1994. The repeal is consequential on the repeal of 138(3)(b) and (4)(b). For earlier taxation years since 1969, read:

(11) Profit or loss in respect of Canada security — For the purposes of paragraphs (3)(b) and (4)(b),

(a) the profit or gain made by an insurer in a taxation year in respect of a Canada security owned by it that was disposed of by it in the year is the amount by which the proceeds of disposition to which the insurer thereby became entitled exceeds the amortized cost of the security to the insurer at the time of the disposition; and

(b) the loss sustained by an insurer in a taxation year in respect of a Canada security owned by it that was disposed of by it in the year is the amount by which the amortized cost of the security to the insurer at the time of the disposition exceeds the proceeds of the disposition to which the insurer thereby became entitled.

**(11.1) Identical properties** — For the purpose of section 47, any property of a life insurance corporation that would, but for this subsection, be identical to any other property of the corporation is deemed not to be identical to the other property unless both properties are

(a) designated insurance property of the insurer in respect of a life insurance business carried on in Canada; or

(b) designated insurance property of the insurer in respect of an insurance business in Canada other than a life insurance business.

**Related Provisions**: 248(12) — Identical properties.

**Notes**: 138(11.1) amended by 1996 Budget, effective for 1997 and later taxation years (changed from 1996 at Second Reading of the Budget bill). The substance of the amendment was to use the new term "designated insurance property"; the other changes are cosmetic. For earlier years, read:

(11.1) For the purposes of section 47, any property of a life insurance corporation that would, but for this subsection, be identical to any other property of the corporation shall be

## S. 138(11.1) — Income Tax Act, Part I

deemed not to be identical to that other property unless both properties are

   (a) non-segregated property used by it in the year in, or held by it in the year in the course of, carrying on a life insurance business in Canada; or

   (b) non-segregated property used by it in the year in, or held by it in the year in the course of, carrying on an insurance business in Canada other than a life insurance business.

**I.T. Application Rules**: 26(8.1) (property owned since before 1972).

**Interpretation Bulletins**: IT-387R2: Meaning of "identical properties".

**(11.2) Computation of capital gain on pre-1969 depreciable property** — For the purposes of computing the amount of a capital gain from the disposition of any depreciable property acquired by a life insurer before 1969, the capital cost of the property to the insurer shall be its capital cost determined without reference to paragraph 32(1)(a) of *An Act to amend the Income Tax Act*, chapter 44 of the Statutes of Canada 1968-69, as it read in its application to the 1971 taxation year.

**(11.3) Deemed disposition** — Subject to subsection (11.31), where a property of a life insurer resident in Canada that carries on an insurance business in Canada and in a country other than Canada or of a non-resident insurer is

   (a) designated insurance property of the insurer for a taxation year, was owned by the insurer at the end of the preceding taxation year and was not designated insurance property of the insurer for that preceding year, or

   (b) not designated insurance property for a taxation year, was owned by the insurer at the end of the preceding taxation year and was designated insurance property of the insurer for that preceding year,

the insurer is deemed to have disposed of the property at the beginning of the year for proceeds of disposition equal to its fair market value at that time and to have immediately thereafter reacquired the property at a cost equal to that fair market value.

### Proposed Amendment — 138(11.3)

the following rules apply:

   (c) the insurer is deemed to have disposed of the property at the beginning of the year for proceeds of disposition equal to its fair market value at that time and to have reacquired the property immediately after that time at a cost equal to that fair market value,

   (d) where paragraph (a) applies, any gain or loss arising from the disposition is deemed not to be a gain or loss from designated insurance property of the insurer in the year, and

   (e) where paragraph (b) applies, any gain or loss arising from the disposition is deemed to be a gain or loss from designated insurance property of the insurer in the year.

**Application**: Bill C-43 (First Reading September 20, 2000), subsec. 85(3), will amend the portion of subsec. 138(11.3) after para. (b) to read as above, applicable to 1997 *et seq*.

**Technical Notes**: Subsection 138(11.3) of the Act provides for a deemed disposition and reacquisition of property owned by a resident multinational life insurer or a non-resident insurer where property either becomes designated insurance property or ceases to be designated insurance property of the insurer. The purpose of the subsection is to ensure that gains and losses from property accruing while property is designated insurance property are included in computing the insurer's income from carrying on an insurance business in Canada.

New paragraphs 138(11.3)(d) and (e) ensure that only gains and losses accruing while property is designated insurance property are included in computing an insurer's income.

**Related Provisions**: 54"superficial loss"(c) — Superficial loss rule does not apply; 138(11.31) — Exception where mark-to-market deemed disposition has applied; 138(11.4) — Loss deductible only in year property disposed of.

**Notes**: Except for certain limited purposes, 138(11.3) provides for a deemed disposition and reacquisition of property owned by a resident multinational life insurer or a non-resident insurer where there is a change in use of the property.

138(11.3) amended by 1996 Budget, effective for 1997 and later taxation years (changed from 1996 at Second Reading of the Budget bill). For earlier years, read:

   (11.3) Subject to subsection (11.31), and except for the purposes of paragraph 20(1)(l), the description of A in the definition "undepreciated capital cost" in subsection 13(21) and paragraph (b) of the description of F in that definition and any regulations made for the purpose of the definition "property used by it in the year in, or held by it in the year in the course of" in subsection (12), where a life insurer resident in Canada, or a non-resident insurer, that carries on an insurance business in Canada and in a country other than Canada, at any time,

   (a) acquires property for some other purpose and at a later time commences to use that property as property used by it in the year in, or held by it in the year in the course of, carrying on an insurance business in Canada, or

   (b) acquires property for use as property used by it in the year in, or held by it in the year in the course of, carrying on an insurance business in Canada and at a later time commences to use the property for some other purpose,

   (c), (d) [Repealed]

the insurer shall be deemed to have disposed of the property at that later time for proceeds of disposition equal to its fair market value at that time and to have immediately thereafter reacquired the property at a cost equal to that fair market value.

The 1996 Budget bill changes reflect the new definition of "designated insurance property", and provide that any deemed disposition or reacquisition is considered to have occurred at the beginning of the year. This reflects the fact that property either is, or is not, designated insurance property for the *entire* year.

Opening words of 138(11.3) amended by 1994 tax amendments bill (Part III), to change "Except for the purposes of paragraphs [138](3)(d), (4)(c) and 20(1)(l)" to "Subject to subsection (11.31) and except for the purposes of paragraph 20(1)(l)", effective for changes in use of property occurring in taxation years that begin after October 1994.

Division F — Special Rules in Certain Circumstances    S. 138(11.5)(b)

138(11.3)(c) and (d) repealed by 1994 tax amendments bill (Part III), effective for changes in use of property occurring after February 22, 1994. For earlier changes in use, read:

> (c) acquires property that is a bond, debenture, mortgage, agreement of sale or any other form of indebtedness for use as property used by it in the year in, or held by it in the year in the course of, carrying on a life insurance business in Canada and at a later time commences to use the property in, or hold it in the course of, carrying on a business other than a life insurance business in Canada, or
>
> (d) acquires property that is a bond, debenture, mortgage, agreement of sale or any other form of indebtedness for use in, or to be held in the course of, carrying on a business other than a life insurance business in Canada and at a later time commences to use the property as property used by it in the year in, or held by it in the year in the course of, carrying on a life insurance business in Canada,

138(11.3) amended by 1988 tax reform and (retroactively) by 1991 technical bill. For taxation years ending before 1988, or beginning before June 18, 1987, for changes in use of property for taxation years beginning after November 12, 1981, delete paras. (c) and (d) and read the opening words as follows:

> (11.3) Except for the purposes of paragraph (12)(b) as it applies to paragraph (3)(c), subparagraph 13(21)(f)(i), clause 13(21)(f)(iv)(B), paragraphs (3)(d) and (4)(c) and any regulation made under paragraph (12)(l), where a life insurer resident in Canada, or a non-resident insurer, that carries on an insurance business in Canada and in a country other than Canada, at any time,

138(11.3) did not apply for taxation years beginning before November 13, 1981.

**I.T. Application Rules:** 26(17.1) (ITAR 26 does not apply to property owned since before 1972 where 138(11.3) applies).

### (11.31) Exclusion from deemed disposition —
Subsection (11.3) does not apply

(a) to deem a disposition in a taxation year of a property of an insurer where subsection 142.5(2) deemed the insurer to have disposed of the property in its preceding taxation year; nor

(b) for the purposes of paragraph 20(1)(l), the description of A and paragraph (b) of the description of F in the definition "undepreciated capital cost" in subsection 13(21) and the definition "designated insurance property" in subsection (12).

**Notes:** 138(11.31) amended by 1996 Budget, effective for 1997 and later taxation years (changed from 1996 at Second Reading of the Budget bill). The substance of the change was to add para. (b). For earlier years, read:

> (11.31) Subsection (11.3) does not apply in respect of a change in use of a property of an insurer where subsection 142.5(2) deemed the insurer to have disposed of the property in the taxation year that ended immediately before the change in use.

138(11.31) added by 1994 tax amendments bill (Part III), effective for changes in use of property occurring in taxation years that begin after October 1994.

### (11.4) Deduction of loss —
Notwithstanding any other provision of this Act, where an insurer has a loss for a taxation year from the disposition, because of subsection (11.3), of a property other than a specified debt obligation (as defined in subsection 142.2(1)), and the loss would, but for this subsection, have been deductible in the year, the loss shall be deductible only in the taxation year in which the taxpayer disposes of the property otherwise than because of subsection (11.3).

**Notes:** 138(11.4) amended by 1994 tax amendments bill (Part III), effective for property deemed by 138(11.3) to be disposed of after 1994. For taxation years that begin after November 12, 1981, read:

> (11.4) Rules on deemed disposition and reacquisition — Where, but for this subsection, an insurer in a taxation year would, by virtue of subsection (11.3), have realized an otherwise deductible loss for the year in respect of any property, notwithstanding any other provision of this Act, that loss shall be deductible only in the taxation year in which the insurer disposes of the property otherwise than by virtue of subsection (11.3).

### (11.41) [Repealed]

**Notes:** 138(11.41) repealed by 1994 tax amendments bill (Part III), effective for changes in use of property occurring after February 22, 1994. For earlier changes in use, read:

> (11.41) Inclusion of gain — Where, by reason of a change in use referred to in paragraph (11.3)(c) or (d) of a property that is a bond, debenture, mortgage, agreement of sale or any other form of indebtedness, an insurer would, by reason of subsection (11.3), have realized an otherwise taxable gain at any time in respect of such property, that gain shall be included in computing the income of the insurer only in the taxation year in which the insurer disposes of or is deemed to have disposed of the property otherwise than by reason of a change in use of the property referred to in paragraph (11.3)(c) or (d).

### (11.5) Transfer of insurance business by non-resident insurer — Where

(a) a non-resident insurer (in this subsection referred to as the "transferor") has, at any time in a taxation year, ceased to carry on all or substantially all of an insurance business carried on by it in Canada in that year,

(b) the transferor has, at that time or within 60 days thereafter, transferred all or substantially all of the property owned by it at that time and used by it in the year in, or held by it in the year in the course of, carrying on that insurance business in Canada in that year (in this subsection referred to as the "transferred property") to a corporation (in this subsection referred to as the "transferee") that is a qualified related corporation (within the meaning assigned by subsection 219(8)) of the transferor that, immediately after that time, began to carry on that insurance business in Canada and the consideration for the transfer includes shares of the capital stock of the transferee,

**Proposed Amendment — 138(11.5)(b)**

(b) the transferor has, at that time or within 60 days after that time, transferred all or substantially all of the property (in this subsection referred to as the "transferred property") that is owned by it at that time and that was designated insurance property in respect of the business for

## S. 138(11.5)(b)

the taxation year that, because of paragraph (h), ended immediately before that time

(i) to a corporation (in this subsection referred to as the "transferee") that is a qualified related corporation (within the meaning assigned by subsection 219(8)) of the transferor that began immediately after that time to carry on that insurance business in Canada, and

(ii) for consideration that includes shares of the capital stock of the transferee,

**Application:** Bill C-43 (First Reading September 20, 2000), subsec. 85(4), will amend para. 138(11.5)(b) to read as above, applicable to 1999 et seq. except that, where a taxpayer or a taxpayer's legal representative so elects in writing, filed with the Minister of National Revenue before 2002, the amended para. applies to the taxpayer's 1997 and subsequent taxation years.

**Technical Notes:** Subsection 138(11.5) of the Act sets out the rules that allow a non-resident insurer to transfer, on a tax-deferred basis, an insurance business carried on in Canada to a qualified related corporation. This provision is elective and, in order to be entitled to elect the rollover treatment, the conditions set out in paragraphs 138(11.5)(a) to (d) must be met. Paragraph 138(11.5)(b) requires that the transferor transfer all or substantially all of the property owned by it that was used or held by it in its insurance business in Canada to a qualified related corporation that commences to carry on that insurance business in Canada. The amendment to paragraph 138(11.5)(b) is consequential on the definition "designated insurance property" being added to subsection 138(12) and requires that the transferor transfer all or substantially all of its designated insurance property for the year to a corporation that is a qualified related corporation that commences to carry on that insurance business in Canada.

(c) the transferee has, at that time or within 60 days thereafter, assumed or reinsured all or substantially all of the obligations of the transferor that arose in the course of carrying on that insurance business in Canada, and

(d) the transferor and the transferee have jointly elected in prescribed form and in accordance with subsection (11.6),

the following rules apply:

(e) subject to paragraph (k.1), where the fair market value, at that time, of the consideration (other than shares of the capital stock of the transferee or a right to receive any such shares) received or receivable by the transferor for the transferred property does not exceed the total of the cost amounts to the transferor, at that time, of the transferred property, the proceeds of disposition of the transferor and the cost to the transferee of the transferred property shall be deemed to be the cost amount, at that time, to the transferor of the transferred property, and in any other case, the provisions of subsection 85(1) shall be applied in respect of the transfer,

(f) where the provisions of subsection 85(1) are not required to be applied in respect of the transfer, the cost to the transferor of any particular property (other than shares of the capital stock of the transferee or a right to receive any such shares) received or receivable by it as consideration for the transferred property shall be deemed to be the fair market value, at that time, of the particular property,

(g) where the provisions of subsection 85(1) are not required to be applied in respect of the transfer, the cost to the transferor of any shares of the capital stock of the transferee received or receivable by the transferor as consideration for the transferred property shall be deemed to be

(i) where the shares are preferred shares of any class of the capital stock of the transferee, the lesser of

(A) the fair market value of those shares immediately after the transfer of the transferred property, and

(B) the amount determined by the formula

$$A \times \frac{B}{C}$$

where

A is the amount, if any, by which the proceeds of disposition of the transferor of the transferred property determined under paragraph (e) exceed the fair market value, at that time, of the consideration (other than shares of the capital stock of the transferee or a right to receive any such shares) received or receivable by the transferor for the transferred property,

B is the fair market value, immediately after the transfer of the transferred property, of those preferred shares of that class, and

C is the fair market value, immediately after the transfer of the transferred property, of all preferred shares of the capital stock of the transferee receivable by the transferor as consideration for the transferred property, and

(ii) where the shares are common shares of any class of the capital stock of the transferee, the amount determined by the formula

$$A \times \frac{B}{C}$$

where

A is the amount, if any, by which the proceeds of disposition of the transferor of the transferred property determined under paragraph (e) exceed the total of the fair market value, at that time, of the consideration (other than shares of the capital stock of the transferee or a right to receive any such shares) received or receivable by the transferor for the transferred property and the cost to the transferor of all preferred shares of the capital stock of the transferee receivable by the transferor as consideration for the transferred property,

B is the fair market value, immediately after the transfer of the transferred property, of those shares of that class, and

C is the fair market value, immediately after the transfer of the transferred property, of all common shares of the capital stock of the transferee receivable by the transferor as consideration for the transferred property,

(h) for the purposes of this Act, the transferor and the transferee shall be deemed to have had taxation years ending immediately before that time and, for the purposes of determining the fiscal periods of the transferor and transferee after that time, they shall be deemed not to have established fiscal periods before that time,

(i) for the purpose of determining the amount of gross investment revenue required by subsection (9) to be included in computing the transferor's income for the particular taxation year referred to in paragraph (h) and its gains and losses from its designated insurance property for its subsequent taxation years, the transferor is deemed to have transferred the business referred to in paragraph (a), the property referred to in paragraph (b) and the obligations referred to in paragraph (c) to the transferee on the last day of the particular year,

(j) for the purpose of determining the income of the transferor and the transferee for their taxation years following their taxation years referred to in paragraph (h), amounts deducted by the transferor as reserves under subparagraphs (3)(a)(i), (ii) and (iv), paragraphs 20(1)(l) and (l.1) and 20(7)(c) of this Act and section 33 and paragraph 138(3)(c) of the *Income Tax Act*, chapter 148 of the Revised Statutes of Canada, 1952, in its taxation year referred to in paragraph (h) in respect of the transferred property referred to in paragraph (b) or the obligations referred to in paragraph (c) shall be deemed to have been deducted by the transferee, and not the transferor, for its taxation year referred to in paragraph (h),

(j.1) for the purpose of determining the income of the transferor and the transferee for their taxation years following their taxation years referred to in paragraph (h), amounts included under paragraphs (4)(b) and 12(1)(e.1) in computing the transferor's income for its taxation year referred to in paragraph (h) in respect of the insurance policies of the business referred to in paragraph (a) are deemed to have been included in computing the income of the transferee, and not of the transferor, for their taxation years referred to in paragraph (h),

(k) for the purposes of this section, sections 12, 12.3, 12.4, 20, 138.1, 140 and 142, subsections 142.5(5) and (7), paragraphs 142.4(4)(c) and (d), section 148 and Part XII.3, the transferee shall, in its taxation years following its taxation year referred to in paragraph (h), be deemed to be the same person as, and a continuation of, the transferor in respect of the business referred to in paragraph (a), the transferred property referred to in paragraph (b) and the obligations referred to in paragraph (c),

(k.1) except for the purpose of this subsection, where the provisions of subsection 85(1) are not required to be applied in respect of the transfer,

(i) the transferor shall be deemed not to have disposed of a transferred property that is a specified debt obligation (other than a mark-to-market property), and

(ii) the transferee shall be deemed, in respect of a transferred property that is a specified debt obligation (other than a mark-to-market property), to be the same person as, and a continuation of, the transferor,

and for the purpose of this paragraph, "mark-to-market property" and "specified debt obligation" have the meanings assigned by subsection 142.2(1),

(k.2) for the purposes of subsections 112(5) to (5.2) and (5.4) and the definition "mark-to-market property" in subsection 142.2(1), the transferee shall be deemed, in respect of the transferred property, to be the same person as, and a continuation of, the transferor,

(l) for the purposes of this subsection and subsections (11.7) and (11.9), the fair market value of consideration received by the transferor from the transferee in respect of the assumption or reinsurance of a particular obligation referred to in paragraph (c) shall be deemed to be the total of the amounts deducted by the transferor as a reserve under subparagraphs (3)(a)(i), (ii) and (iv) and paragraph 20(7)(c) in its taxation year referred to in paragraph (h) in respect of the particular obligation, and

(m) for the purpose of computing the income of the transferor or the transferee for their taxation years following their taxation years referred to in paragraph (h),

(i) an amount in respect of a reinsurance premium paid or payable by the transferor to the transferee in respect of the obligations referred to in paragraph (c), or

(ii) an amount in respect of a reinsurance commission paid or payable by the transferee to the transferor in respect of the amount referred to in subparagraph (i)

under a reinsurance arrangement undertaken to effect the transfer of the insurance business to

## S. 138(11.5)(m) — Income Tax Act, Part I

which this subsection applied shall be included or deducted, as the case may be, only to the extent that may be reasonably regarded as necessary to determine the appropriate amount of income of both the transferor and the transferee.

**Related Provisions**: 138(11.6) — Time of election; 138(11.7) — Computation of paid-up capital; 138(11.94) — Transfer of business by resident insurer; 142.6(5), (6) — Acquisition of specified debt obligation by financial institution in rollover transaction; 181.3(3)(d)(i)(A)(III), 190.13(c)(i)(A)(III) — Effect on capital tax; 219(5.2) — Branch tax — election by non-resident insurer who has transferred business; Reg. 8101(4) — Inclusion in income of transferee re unpaid claims reserve; Reg. 8103(4) — Mark-to-market — transition inclusion; Reg. 9204(3) — Residual portion of specified debt obligation.

**Notes**: 138(11.5) allows the "domestication" of a non-resident insurer's branch insurance operation by transferring it to a Canadian resident corporation. 138(11.94) provides a parallel rollover for a Canadian insurer. See Jillian Welch, "Rare Rollovers: The Reorganization of a Life Insurance Business — Part I", Taxation of Corporate Reorganizations, 46(4) *Canadian Tax Journal* 908-918 (1998).

The CCRA takes the position that "all or substantially all" means 90% or more.

138(11.5)(i) amended by 1996 Budget, effective for the transfer by an insurer of an insurance business in its 1997 or a subsequent taxation year (changed from 1996 at Second Reading of the Budget bill). The substance of the amendment was to use the new term "designated insurance property"; the other changes were cosmetic. For taxation years to 1996, read:

(i) for the purpose of determining the amount of gross investment revenue required to be included in computing the transferor's income for the year under subsection (9) and its gains and losses from property used by it in the year in, or held by it in the year in the course of, carrying on an insurance business in Canada for its taxation years following its year referred to in paragraph (h), the transferor shall be deemed to have transferred the business referred to in paragraph (a), the property referred to in paragraph (b) and the obligations referred to in paragraph (c) to the transferee on the last day of its taxation year referred to in paragraph (h),

138(11.5)(j.1) added by 1996 Budget, effective for 1996 and later taxation years. It provides that negative policy reserves included in the transferor's income under 12(1)(e.1) and 138(4)(b) for the taxation year deemed to have ended before the transfer are deemed to have been included in the transferee's income for that year. This enables the transferee to claim a deduction for such amounts in the following year under 20(22) or 138(3)(a)(ii.1).

References in 138(11.5)(k) to 142.4 and 142.5 added by 1994 tax amendments bill (Part III), effective for transfers of insurance businesses occurring after October 1994.

138(11.5)(k.1), and reference to it in 138(11.5)(e), added by 1994 tax amendments bill (Part III), effective for transfers of insurance businesses occurring after February 22, 1994.

138(11.5)(k.2) added by 1994 tax amendments bill (Part III), effective for transfers of insurance businesses occurring at any time (including before Royal Assent to the amendments bill).

138(11.5) added by 1981 Budget and amended by 1988 tax reform and 1991 technical bill, effective for transfers of an insurance business after December 15, 1987. However, where the transferor has, before December 16, 1987 and with the approval of the Minister of Finance, entered into an agreement to transfer, after December 15, 1987 and before 1988, an insurance business to the transferee and the transferor and the transferee subsequently amend the agreement or enter into another agreement in 1988 in respect of the transfer of the insurance business and the transfer of the insurance business is made before 1989, then, if the amended or subsequent agreement so provides the transferor and the transferee jointly so elect in accordance with subsec. 138(11.6), the transfer shall be deemed to have occurred on January 1, 1988.

For transfers of property from April 1, 1983 through December 15, 1987, read:

(11.5) Where a non-resident insurer

(a) has ceased to carry on an insurance business in Canada in a taxation year or is entitled to make an election under subsection 219(4) in respect of a taxation year,

(b) has transferred all property used by it in the year in, or held by it in the year in the course of, carrying on an insurance business in Canada to a qualified related corporation of the insurer (within the meaning assigned by subsection 219(8)) or to a corporation resident in Canada that carries on an insurance business in Canada and is a subsidiary wholly-owned corporation of a qualified related corporation of the insurer, and

(c) has jointly so elected, in prescribed form and within the time determined under subsection (11.6), with the corporation to which the property was transferred,

subsection (11.3) shall not apply in respect of the transferred property and, where no election was made under subsection 85(1) in respect of the transferred property, the proceeds of disposition thereof to the non-resident insurer and the cost thereof to the corporation to which it was transferred shall be deemed to be the cost amount to the non-resident insurer of the transferred property.

For transfers of property before April 1983, read as for 1983 to 1987, but read "any property" instead of "all property" in para. (b).

138(11.5) applies only to taxation years commencing after November 12, 1981.

**I.T. Application Rules**: 69 (meaning of "*Income Tax Act*, chapter 148 of the Revised Statutes of Canada, 1952").

**Forms**: T2100: Joint election in respect of an insurance business transferred by a non-resident insurer.

**(11.6) Time of election** — Any election under subsection (11.5) shall be made on or before the day that is the earliest of the days on or before which any taxpayer making the election is required to file a return of income pursuant to section 150 for the taxation year in which the transactions to which the election relates occurred.

**(11.7) Computation of paid-up capital** — Where, after December 15, 1987, subsection (11.5) is applicable in respect of a transfer of property by a non-resident insurer to a qualified related corporation of the insurer and the provisions of subsection 85(1) were not required to be applied in respect of the transfer, the following rules apply:

(a) in computing the paid-up capital, at any time after the transfer, in respect of any particular class of shares of the capital stock of the qualified related corporation, there shall be deducted an amount determined by the formula

$$(A - B) \times \frac{C}{A}$$

where

A is the increase, if any, determined without reference to this subsection as it applies to the transfer, in the paid-up capital in respect of all the shares of the capital stock of the corporation as a result of the transfer,

B is the amount, if any, by which the cost of the transferred property to the corporation, immediately after the transfer, exceeds the fair market value, immediately after the transfer, of any consideration (other than shares of the capital stock of the corporation) received or receivable by the insurer from the corporation for the property, and

C is the increase, if any, determined without reference to this subsection as it applies to the transfer, in the paid-up capital in respect of the particular class of shares as a result of the acquisition by the corporation of the transferred property; and

(b) in computing the paid-up capital, at any time after December 15, 1987, in respect of any particular class of shares of the capital stock of the qualified related corporation, there shall be added an amount equal to the lesser of

(i) the amount, if any, by which

(A) the total of all amounts each of which is an amount deemed by subsection 84(3), (4) or (4.1) to be a dividend on shares of that class paid after December 15, 1987 and before that time by the corporation

exceeds

(B) the total of such dividends that would have been determined under clause (A) if this Act were read without reference to paragraph (a), and

(ii) the total of all amounts each of which is an amount required by paragraph (a) to be deducted in computing the paid-up capital in respect of that class of shares after December 15, 1987 and before that time.

**Related Provisions**: 138(11.5)(l) — Transfer of insurance business by non-resident insurer; 257 — Formula cannot calculate to less than zero.

**(11.8) Rules on transfers of depreciable property** — Where

(a) subsection (11.5) is applicable in respect of a transfer of depreciable property by a non-resident insurer to a qualified related corporation,

(b) the provisions of subsection 85(1) were not required to be applied in respect of the transfer, and

(c) the capital cost to the insurer of the depreciable property exceeds its proceeds of disposition therefor,

for the purposes of sections 13 and 20 and any regulations made under paragraph 20(1)(a), the following rules apply:

(d) the capital cost of the depreciable property to the corporation shall be deemed to be the amount that was the capital cost thereof to the insurer, and

(e) the excess shall be deemed to have been allowed to the corporation in respect of the property under regulations made under paragraph 20(1)(a) in computing its income for taxation years ending before the transfer.

**Notes**: 138(11.8) added by 1988 tax reform, effective for transfers of property occurring after December 15, 1987.

**(11.9) Computation of contributed surplus** — Where, after December 15, 1987, subsection (11.5) or 85(1) is applicable in respect of a transfer of property by a person or partnership to an insurance corporation resident in Canada and

(a) the total of

(i) the fair market value, immediately after the transfer, of any consideration (other than shares of the capital stock of the corporation) received or receivable by the person or partnership from the corporation for the transferred property,

(ii) the increase, if any, in the paid-up capital of all the shares of the capital stock of the corporation (determined without reference to subsection (11.7) or 85(2.1) as it applies in respect of the transfer) arising on the transfer, and

(iii) the increase, if any, in the contributed surplus of the corporation (determined without reference to this subsection as it applies in respect of the transfer) arising on the transfer

exceeds

(b) the total of

(i) the total of all amounts each of which is an amount required to be deducted in computing the paid-up capital of a class of shares of the capital stock of the corporation under subsection (11.7) or 85(2.1), as the case may be, as it applies in respect of the transfer, and

(ii) the cost to the corporation of the transferred property,

for the purposes of paragraph 84(1)(c.1) and subsections 219(5.2) and (5.3), the contributed surplus of the corporation arising on the transfer shall be deemed to be the amount, if any, by which the amount of the contributed surplus otherwise determined exceeds the amount, if any, by which the total determined under paragraph (a) exceeds the total determined under paragraph (b).

**Related Provisions**: 138(11.5)(l) — Transfer of insurance business by non-resident insurer.

**(11.91) Computation of income of non-resident insurer** — Where, at any time in a particular taxation year,

(a) a non-resident insurer carries on an insurance business in Canada, and

(b) immediately before that time, the insurer was not carrying on an insurance business in Canada or ceased to be exempt from tax under this Part

## S. 138(11.91)(b) — Income Tax Act, Part I

on any income from such business by reason of any Act of Parliament or anything approved, made or declared to have the force of law thereunder,

for the purpose of computing the income of the insurer for the particular taxation year,

(c) the insurer shall be deemed to have had a taxation year ending immediately before the commencement of the particular taxation year,

(d) for the purposes of paragraphs 12(1)(d) and (e), paragraph (4)(a), subsection (9) and the definition "designated insurance property" in subsection (12), the insurer is deemed to have carried on the business in Canada in that preceding year and to have claimed the maximum amounts to which it would have been entitled under paragraphs 20(1)(l) and (l.1) and 20(7)(c) and subparagraphs (3)(a)(i), (ii) and (iv) for that year,

(d.1) for the purposes of subsection 20(22) and subparagraph (3)(a)(ii.1),

(i) the insurer is deemed to have carried on the business referred to in paragraph (a) in Canada in the preceding taxation year referred to in paragraph (c), and

(ii) the amounts, if any, that would have been prescribed in respect of the insurer for the purposes of paragraphs (4)(b) and 12(1)(e.1) for that preceding year in respect of the insurance policies of that business are deemed to have been included in computing its income for that year,

(e) the insurer shall, immediately before the commencement of the particular taxation year, be deemed to have disposed of each property that was owned by it at that time and used by it in the year in, or held by it in the year in the course of, carrying on the business referred to in paragraph (a) for proceeds of disposition equal to the fair market value of the property at that time and to have reacquired the property at that time at a cost equal to that fair market value, and

### Proposed Amendment — 138(11.91)(e)

(e) the insurer is deemed to have disposed, immediately before the beginning of the particular taxation year, of each property owned by it at that time that is designated insurance property in respect of the business referred to in paragraph (a) for the particular taxation year, for proceeds of disposition equal to the fair market value at that time and to have reacquired, at the beginning of the particular taxation year, the property at a cost equal to that fair market value, and

**Application**: Bill C-43 (First Reading September 20, 2000), subsec. 85(5), will amend para. 138(11.91)(e) to read as above, applicable to 1999 *et seq.* except that, where a taxpayer or a taxpayer's legal representative so elects in writing, filed with the Minister of National Revenue before 2002, the amended para. applies to the taxpayer's 1997 and subsequent taxation years.

**Technical Notes**: Subsection 138(11.91) provides rules for the purpose of computing the income of a non-resident insurer that commences to carry on an insurance business in Canada at any time in a particular taxation year or that ceases to be exempt from tax under Part I of the Act in a particular taxation year. Paragraph 138(11.91)(e) deems an insurer to have disposed, immediately before the beginning of the particular taxation year, of each property owned by the insurer that was used or held by it in the course of carrying on an insurance business in Canada in the year, at its fair market value and to have reacquired it at that time at that fair market value. Paragraph 138(11.91)(e) ensures that non-resident insurers will report the appropriate amount of gain or loss from the disposition of property used in carrying on an insurance business in Canada. Paragraph 138(11.91)(e) is amended to make reference to property that is designated insurance property. This amendment is consequential to the addition in subsection 138(12) of the definition "designated insurance property", applicable to the 1997 and subsequent taxation years.

(f) where paragraph (e) applies in respect of depreciable property of the insurer and the cost thereof to the insurer immediately before the commencement of the particular taxation year exceeds the fair market value thereof at that time, for the purposes of sections 13 and 20 and any regulations made under paragraph 20(1)(a),

(i) the capital cost of the property to the insurer at that time shall be deemed to be the cost thereof to the insurer at that time, and

(ii) the excess shall be deemed to have been allowed to the insurer in respect of the property under regulations made under paragraph 20(1)(a) in computing its income for taxation years ending before the commencement of the particular taxation year.

**Related Provisions**: 95(2)(k)(v) — Application to start-up of business of foreign affiliate.

**Notes**: 138(11.91)(d) amended by 1996 Budget, effective for 1997 and later taxation years (changed from 1996 at Second Reading of the Budget bill), due to the introduction of the new term "designated insurance property". For earlier years since 1988 (beginning after June 17, 1987), read:

(d) for the purposes of paragraphs 12(1)(d) and (e), paragraph (4)(a) and subsection (9) and any regulations made under the definition "property used by it in the year in, or held by it in the year in the course of" in subsection (12), the insurer shall be deemed to have carried on the business referred to in paragraph (a) in the immediately preceding taxation year referred to in paragraph (c) and to have claimed the maximum amounts to which it would have been entitled under subparagraphs (3)(a)(i), (ii) and (iv), paragraphs 20(1)(l) and (l.1) and 20(7)(c) of this Act and section 33 and paragraph 138(3)(c) of the *Income Tax Act*, chapter 148 of the Revised Statutes of Canada, 1952, for that year,

138(11.91)(d.1) added by 1996 Budget, effective for 1996 and later taxation years. It deems the non-resident insurer to have carried on business in Canada in the prior year and to have included in income the negative policy reserves that would have been prescribed under 12(1)(e.1) and 138(4)(b). This enables the non-resident insurer to deduct these amounts under 20(22) or 138(3)(a)(ii.1).

**I.T. Application Rules**: 69 (meaning of "*Income Tax Act*, chapter 148 of the Revised Statutes of Canada, 1952").

**(11.92) Computation of income where insurance business is transferred** — Where, at any time in a taxation year, an insurer (in this subsection referred to as the "vendor") has disposed of

(a) all or substantially all of an insurance business carried on by it in Canada, or

(b) all or substantially all of a line of business of an insurance business carried on by it in Canada

to a person (in this subsection referred to as the "purchaser") and obligations in respect of the business or line of business, as the case may be, in respect of which a reserve may be claimed under subparagraph (3)(a)(i) or (ii) or paragraph 20(7)(c) (in this subsection referred to as the "obligations") were assumed by the purchaser, the following rules apply:

(c) for the purpose of determining the amount of the gross investment revenue required to be included in computing the income of the vendor and the purchaser under subsection (9) and the amount of the gains and losses of the vendor and the purchaser from designated insurance property for the year

(i) the vendor and the purchaser shall, in addition to their normal taxation years, be deemed to have had a taxation year ending immediately before that time, and

(ii) for the taxation years of the vendor and the purchaser following that time, the business or line of business, as the case may be, disposed of to, and the obligations assumed by, the purchaser shall be deemed to have been disposed of or assumed, as the case may be, on the last day of the taxation year referred to in subparagraph (i),

(d) for the purpose of computing the income of the vendor and the purchaser for taxation years ending after that time,

(i) an amount paid or payable by the vendor to the purchaser in respect of the obligations, or

(ii) an amount in respect of a commission paid or payable by the purchaser to the vendor in respect of the amount referred to in subparagraph (i)

shall be deemed to have been paid or payable or received or receivable, as the case may be, by the vendor or the purchaser, as the case may be, in the course of carrying on the business or line of business, as the case may be, and

(e) where the vendor has disposed of all or substantially all of an insurance business referred to in paragraph (a), the vendor shall, for the purposes of section 219, be deemed to have ceased to carry on that business at that time.

**Related Provisions**: 181.3(3)(d)(i)(A)(III), 190.13(c)(i)(A)(III) — Effect on capital tax.

**Notes**: Opening words of 138(11.92)(c) amended by 1996 Budget to reflect the new term "designated insurance property", effective for the disposition by an insurer of an insurance business or a line of business of an insurance business in its 1997 or a later taxation year (changed from 1996 at Second Reading of the Budget bill). For earlier dispositions, read:

(c) for the purpose of determining the amount of the gross investment revenue required to be included in the income of the vendor and the purchaser under subsection (9) and the amount of the gains and losses of the vendor and the purchaser from property used by it in the year in or held by it in the year in the course of carrying on an insurance business in Canada

138(11.92) added by 1988 tax reform, effective for dispositions of an insurance business, or a line of business of an insurance business, after December 15, 1987.

The CCRA takes the position that "all or substantially all" means 90% or more.

**(11.93) Property acquired on default in payment** — Where, at any time in a taxation year of an insurer, the beneficial ownership of property is acquired or reacquired by the insurer in consequence of the failure to pay all or any part of an amount (in this subsection referred to as the "insurer's claim") owing to the insurer at that time in respect of a bond, debenture, mortgage, agreement of sale or any other form of indebtedness owned by the insurer, the following rules apply to the insurer:

(a) section 79.1 does not apply in respect of the acquisition or reacquisition;

(b) the insurer shall be deemed to have acquired or reacquired, as the case may be, the property at an amount equal to the fair market value of the property, immediately before that time;

(c) the insurer shall be deemed to have disposed at that time of the portion of the indebtedness represented by the insurer's claim for proceeds of disposition equal to that fair market value and, immediately after that time, to have reacquired that portion of the indebtedness at a cost of nil;

(d) the acquisition or reacquisition shall be deemed to have no effect on the form of the indebtedness; and

(e) in computing the insurer's income for the year or a subsequent taxation year, no amount is deductible under paragraph 20(1)(l) in respect of the insurer's claim.

**Notes**: 138(11.93) amended by 1994 tax amendments bill (Part I), effective for property acquired or reacquired after February 21, 1994, other than pursuant to a court order made by that date. For earlier acquisitions or reacquisitions, read:

(11.93) Notwithstanding section 79, where, at any time in a taxation year, an insurer has acquired or reacquired the beneficial ownership of property in consequence of another person's failure to pay all or any part of an amount (in this subsection referred to as the "insurer's claim") owing by the other person to the insurer in respect of a bond, debenture, mortgage, agreement of sale or any other form of indebtedness owned by the insurer, the following rules apply:

(a) in computing the other person's proceeds of disposition of the property, there shall be included the amount of the insurer's claim;

(b) any amount paid by the other person after the acquisition or reacquisition, as the case may be, of the property on account of or in satisfaction of the insurer's claim shall be deemed to be a loss of that person from the disposition of the property for that person's taxation year in which payment of that amount was made;

(c) the insurer shall be deemed to have acquired or reacquired, as the case may be, the property at an amount equal to the fair market value of the property, immediately before that time, and to have disposed of the bond, debenture, mortgage, agreement of sale or other form of indebtedness, as the case may be, for proceeds of disposition equal to that fair market value;

(d) the cost amount to the insurer of the insurer's claim shall be deemed to be nil and the insurer's claim shall be deemed to be a bond, debenture, mortgage, agreement of sale or other form of indebtedness, as the case may be; and

(e) in computing the insurer's income for the year or a subsequent year, no amount is deductible in respect of the insurer's claim by reason of paragraph 20(1)(l).

138(11.93) added by 1988 tax reform, effective for taxation years beginning after June 17, 1987 that end after 1987.

### (11.94) Transfer of insurance business by resident insurer — Where

(a) an insurer resident in Canada (in this subsection referred to as the "transferor") has, at any time in a taxation year, ceased to carry on all or substantially all of an insurance business carried on by it in Canada in that year,

(b) the transferor has, at that time or within 60 days thereafter, in the year transferred all or substantially all of the property used or held by it in the year in the course of carrying on that insurance business in Canada to a corporation resident in Canada (in this subsection referred to as the "transferee") that is a subsidiary wholly-owned corporation of the transferor which, immediately after that time, began to carry on that insurance business in Canada and the consideration for the transfer includes shares of the capital stock of the transferee,

#### Proposed Amendment — 138(11.94)(b)

(b) the transferor has, at that time or within 60 days after that time,

(i) in the case of a transferor that is a life insurer and that carries on an insurance business in Canada and in a country other than Canada in the year, transferred all or substantially all of the property (in subsection (11.5) referred to as the "transferred property") that is owned by it at that time and that was designated insurance property in respect of the business for the taxation year that, because of paragraph (11.5)(h), ended immediately before that time, or

(ii) in any other case, transferred all or substantially all of the property owned by it at that time and used by it in the year in, or held by it in the year in the course of, carrying on that insurance business in Canada in that year (in subsection (11.5) referred to as the "transferred property"),

to a corporation resident in Canada (in this subsection referred to as the "transferee") that is a subsidiary wholly-owned corporation of the transferor that, immediately after that time, began to carry on that insurance business in Canada for consideration that includes shares of the capital stock of the transferee,

**Application**: Bill C-43 (First Reading September 20, 2000), subsec. 85(6), will amend para. 138(11.94)(b) to read as above, applicable to 1999 et seq. except that, where a taxpayer or a taxpayer's legal representative so elects in writing, filed with the Minister of National Revenue before 2002, the amended para. applies to the taxpayer's 1997 and subsequent taxation years.

**Technical Notes**: Subsection 138(11.94) of the Act provides rules that apply to the transfer of an insurance business carried on in Canada by an insurer resident in Canada to a corporation resident in Canada that is a subsidiary wholly-owned corporation of the insurer on a tax-deferred or rollover basis. This provision can apply if the conditions set out in paragraphs 138(11.94)(a) to (d) are met. Paragraph 138(11.94)(b) requires that the transferor transfer all or substantially all of the property owned by it that was used or held by it in its insurance business in Canada to a subsidiary wholly-owned corporation that commences to carry on that insurance business in Canada. Paragraph 138(11.94)(b) is amended to distinguish a multinational life insurer resident in Canada from other resident insurers. In regards to the former, the defined term "designated insurance property" has been substituted for "property used or held by it in the year in the course of carrying on that insurance business in Canada". In respect of other resident insurers, the rollover provisions continue to apply in respect of "property used or held by it in the year in the course of carrying on that insurance business in Canada".

**Letter from Department of Finance, February 28, 2000**:

Dear [xxx]

I am replying to your letter of January 10, 2000 and to the concerns you have expressed regarding the proposed amendment to paragraph 138(11.94)(b) of the *Income Tax Act* (the "Act") as released by the Department of Finance on November 30, 1999.

Subsection 138(11.94) of the Act is a rollover rule that applies with respect to certain transfers of insurance businesses carried on in Canada by a resident insurer to certain taxable Canadian corporations. The amendments to the subsection which are proposed to apply to the 1997 and subsequent taxation years, were meant to clarify that the property required to be transferred with the business was designated insurance property under the *Income Tax Regulations* in respect of the business. Gains on designated insurance property not transferred under the rollover rule will have to be realized under subsection 138(11.3) of the Act.

You are of the view that the existing subsection permitted a transfer of property other than designated insurance property.

Based on your representations, we are prepared to recommend to the Minister of Finance that the amendments to paragraph 138(11.94)(b) of the Act apply to 1999 and subsequent taxation years unless a taxpayer elects to have them apply to 1997 and subsequent years.

I trust that such a change would address the concerns of all taxpayers.

Yours sincerely,

Brian Ernewein
Director, Tax Legislation Division, Tax Policy Branch

(c) the transferee has, at that time or within 60 days thereafter, assumed or reinsured all or substantially all of the obligations of the transferor that arose in the course of carrying on that insurance business in Canada, and

(d) the transferor and the transferee have jointly elected in prescribed form and in accordance with subsection (11.6),

paragraphs (11.5)(e) to (m) and subsections (11.7) to (11.9) apply in respect of the transfer.

**Related Provisions**: 142.6(5), (6) — Acquisition of specified debt obligation by financial institution in rollover transaction; Reg. 8101(4) — Inclusion in income of transferee re unpaid claims reserve; Reg. 8103(4) — Mark-to-market — transition inclusion; Reg. 9204(3) — Residual portion of specified debt obligation.

**Notes**: See Notes to 138(11.5).

138(11.94)(b) amended by 1996 Budget to reflect the new term "designated insurance property", effective for 1997 and later taxation years (changed from 1996 at Second Reading of the Budget bill). For earlier years, read:

(b) the transferor has, at that time or within 60 days thereafter, transferred all or substantially all of the property used by it in the year in, or held by it in the year in the course of, carrying on that insurance business in Canada in that year to a corporation resident in Canada (in this subsection referred to as the "transferee") that is a subsidiary wholly-owned corporation of the transferor which, immediately after that time, commenced to carry on that insurance business in Canada and the consideration for the transfer includes shares of the capital stock of the transferee,

138(11.94) added by 1988 tax reform, effective for transfers of an insurance business after December 15, 1987.

The CCRA takes the position that "all or substantially all" means 90% or more.

**(12) Definitions** — In this section,

**"accumulated 1968 deficit"** — [Repealed]

**Notes**: Definition "accumulated 1968 deficit" repealed by 1996 Budget, effective for 1997 and later taxation years (changed from 1996 at Second Reading of the Budget bill). The definition has been moved to 219(7), since it is no longer used in 138 but is still used for purposes of the branch tax in Part XIV. For earlier years, read:

"accumulated 1968 deficit" of a life insurer means such amount as can be established by the insurer to be its deficit as of the end of its 1968 taxation year from carrying on its life insurance business in Canada on the assumption that the amounts of its assets and liabilities (including reserves of any kind)

(a) as of the end of any taxation year before its 1968 taxation year, were the amounts thereof determined for the purposes of the relevant authority, and

(b) as of the end of its 1968 taxation year, were

(i) in respect of depreciable property, the capital cost thereof as of the first day of its 1969 taxation year,

(ii) in respect of policy reserves, the insurer's maximum tax actuarial reserves for its 1968 taxation year for life insurance policies issued by it in the course of carrying on its life insurance business in Canada, and

(iii) in respect of other assets and liabilities, the amounts thereof determined as of the end of that year for the purpose of computing its income for its 1969 taxation year;

138(12)"accumulated 1968 deficit" was 138(12)(a) before consolidation in R.S.C. 1985 (5th Supp.), effective for taxation years ending after November 1991. See Table of Concordance.

**"amortized cost [para. 138(12)(b)]"** — [Repealed under former Act]

**Notes**: 138(12)(b), repealed by 1988 tax reform, defined "amortized cost", a term that now appears in 248(1).

**"amount payable"**, in respect of a policy loan at a particular time, means the amount of the policy loan and the interest thereon that is outstanding at that time;

**Related Provisions**: 148(9) — "amount payable".

**Notes**: 138(12)"amount payable" was 138(12)(b.1) before consolidation in R.S.C. 1985 (5th Supp.), effective for taxation years ending after November 1991.

**"Canada security"** — [Repealed]

**Notes**: Definition "Canada security" repealed by 1994 tax amendments bill (Part III), effective for taxation years that begin after February 22, 1994. The definition was used by 138(3)(b) and (4)(b), which were repealed due to the introduction of 142.2–142.6, and by 138(11) and (11.3)(c), (d). For earlier taxation years, read:

"Canada security" in respect of a life insurer that carried on a business in Canada in a taxation year, means a bond, debenture, mortgage, agreement of sale or any other indebtedness that was property used by it in the year in, or held by it in the year in the course of, carrying on its life insurance business in Canada, other than property included in a segregated fund;

138(12)"Canada security" was 138(12)(c) before consolidation in R.S.C. 1985 (5th Supp.), effective for taxation years ending after November 1991.

**"cost"** — [Repealed]

**Notes**: Definition "cost" repealed by 1994 tax amendments bill (Part III), effective for taxation years that begin after February 22, 1994. For earlier taxation years, read:

"cost" to an insurer of acquiring a mortgage includes any amount advanced by the insurer to the borrower by way of loan under the terms of the mortgage;

138(12)"cost" was 138(12)(d) before consolidation in R.S.C. 1985 (5th Supp.), effective for taxation years ending after November 1991.

**"designated insurance property"** for a taxation year of an insurer (other than an insurer resident in Canada that at no time in the year carried on a life insurance business) that, at any time in the year, carried on an insurance business in Canada and in a country other than Canada, means property determined in accordance with prescribed rules except that, in its application to any taxation year, "designated insurance property" for the 1996 or a preceding taxation year means property that was, under this subsection as it read in its application to that year, property used by it in the year in, or held by it in the year in the course of carrying on an insurance business in Canada;

S. 138(12) des	Income Tax Act, Part I

### Proposed Amendment — 138(12) "designated insurance property"

"designated insurance property" for a taxation year of an insurer (other than an insurer resident in Canada that at no time in the year carried on a life insurance business) that, at any time in the year, carried on an insurance business in Canada and in a country other than Canada, means property determined in accordance with prescribed rules except that, in its application to any taxation year, "designated insurance property" for the 1998 or a preceding taxation year means property that was, under this subsection as it read in its application to taxation years that ended in 1996, property used by it in the year in, or held by it in the year in the course of, carrying on an insurance business in Canada;

**Application**: Bill C-43 (First Reading September 20, 2000), subsec. 85(7), will amend the definition "designated insurance property" in subsec. 138(12) to read as above, applicable to 1997 et seq.

**Technical Notes**: The definition of the expression "designated insurance property" in subsection 138(12) of the Act currently directs insurers (other than resident non-life insurers) to use prescribed rules for the 1997 and subsequent taxation years to determine the property falling within its meaning. For earlier years, the expression is to take its meaning from the meaning, in those years, that the expression "property used by it in the year in, or held by it in the year in the course of carrying on an insurance business in Canada" had. The direction to use the prescribed rules is predicated on the proposed regulations dealing with the taxation of resident multinational life insurers and non-resident insurers that carry on an insurance business in Canada starting to apply in 1997.

The definition is amended to provide that insurers must use the prescribed rules to determine its meaning only for the 1999 and subsequent taxation years. For earlier years, it is to take its meaning from the meaning that the expression "property used by it in the year in, or held by it in the year in the course of carrying on an insurance business in Canada" had for the 1996 taxation year. This amendment is consequential on the application of the proposed regulations being delayed to the 1999 and subsequent taxation years.

**Related Provisions**: 138(11.31)(b) — Change in use rule for insurance properties does not apply for purposes of this definition; 248(1) "designated insurance property" — Definition applies to entire Act.

**Notes**: Definition "designated insurance property" added by 1996 Budget, effective for 1997 and later taxation years (changed from 1996 at Second Reading of the Budget bill). It replaces the term "property used by it in the year in, or held by it in the year in the course of".

**Regulations**: 2401, 2405 (prescribed rules).

"gross investment revenue" of an insurer for a taxation year means the amount determined by the formula

$$A + B + C + D + E + F - G$$

where

A  is the total of the following amounts included in its gross revenue for the year:

(a) taxable dividends, and

(b) amounts received or receivable as, on account of, in lieu of or in satisfaction of, interest, rentals or royalties, other than amounts in respect of debt obligations to which subsection 142.3(1) applies for the year,

B  is its income for the year from each trust of which it is a beneficiary,

C  is its income for the year from each partnership of which it is a member,

D  is the total of all amounts required by subsection 16(1) to be included in computing its income for the year,

E  is the total of

(a) all amounts required by paragraph 142.3(1)(a) to be included in computing its income for the year, and

(b) all amounts required by subsection 12(3) or 20(14) to be included in computing its income for the year except to the extent that those amounts are included in the computation of A,

F  is the amount determined by the formula

$$V - W$$

where

V  is the total of all amounts included under paragraph 56(1)(d) in computing its income for the year, and

W  is the total of all amounts deducted under paragraph 60(a) in computing its income for the year, and

G  is the total of all amounts each of which is

(a) an amount deemed by subparagraph 16(6)(a)(ii) to be paid by it in respect of the year as interest, or

(b) an amount deductible under paragraph 142.3(1)(b) in computing its income for the year;

**Related Provisions**: 148(9) — "interest"; 257 — Formula amounts cannot calculate to less than zero.

**Notes**: Description of A amended by 1994 tax amendments bill (Part III), effective for taxation years that end after February 22, 1994, to add "other than amounts in respect of debt obligations to which subsection 142.3(1) applies for the year".

Para. E(a) added by 1994 tax amendments bill (Part III), effective for taxation years that end after February 22, 1994.

Formula element G added by 1994 tax amendments bill (Part III), this version effective for taxation years that end after February 22, 1994. For taxation years that end from October 17, 1991 through February 22, 1994, read:

G  is the total of all amounts deemed by subparagraph 16(6)(a)(ii) to be paid by it in respect of the year as interest

138(12) "gross investment revenue" was 138(12)(e) before consolidation in R.S.C. 1985 (5th Supp.), effective for taxation years end-

Division F — Special Rules in Certain Circumstances    S. 138(12) pro

ing after November 1991. The previous version, identical in meaning, read:

(e) "gross investment revenue" of an insurer for a taxation year means the aggregate of

(i) all taxable dividends, interest, rentals and royalties included in its gross revenue for the year,

(ii) its income for the year from each trust of which it is a beneficiary,

(iii) its income for the year from each partnership of which it is a member,

(iv) all amounts required by subsection 16(1) to be included in computing its income for the year, and

(v) all amounts required by subsection 12(3) or 20(14) to be included in computing its income for the year except to the extent that such amounts are amounts included in computing its gross investment revenue by virtue of subparagraph (i);

138(12)(e)(i) amended and (e)(vi) (now "gross investment revenue" A and F) added by 1991 technical bill, effective 1990. For 1978 through 1989, read (e)(i) as follows:

(i) all taxable dividends, interest, rentals and royalties included in its gross revenue for the year.

"group term insurance policy [para. 138(12)(p)]" — [Repealed under former Act]

**Notes**: This definition was moved from 138(12)(p) to 138(15) in the R.S.C. 1985 (5th Supp.) consolidation, effective for taxation years ending after November 1991. See Notes to 138(15).

"interest", in relation to a policy loan, means the amount in respect of the policy loan that is required to be paid under the terms and conditions of the policy in order to maintain the policyholder's interest in the policy;

**Notes**: 138(12)"interest" was 138(12)(e.1) before consolidation in R.S.C. 1985 (5th Supp.), effective for taxation years ending after November 1991.

"life insurance policy" includes an annuity contract and a contract all or any part of the insurer's reserves for which vary in amount depending on the fair market value of a specified group of assets;

**Related Provisions**: 12.2(10) — Riders; 211(1) — "Life insurance policy" for purposes of Part XII.3 tax; 248(1)"life insurance policy" — Definition applies to entire Act.

**Notes**: 138(4.01)"life insurance policy" includes group life benefit or annuity contract for certain purposes.

138(12)"life insurance policy" was 138(12)(f) before consolidation in R.S.C. 1985 (5th Supp.), effective for taxation years ending after November 1991.

**Interpretation Bulletins**: IT-87R2: Policyholders' income from life insurance policies; IT-355R2: Interest on loans to buy life insurance policies and annuity contracts, and interest on policy loans.

"life insurance policy in Canada" means a life insurance policy issued or effected by an insurer on the life of a person resident in Canada at the time the policy was issued or effected;

**Related Provisions**: 128.1(10)"excluded right or interest"(l) — Life insurance policy in Canada excluded from deemed disposition on emigration; 248(1)"life insurance policy in Canada" — Definition applies to entire Act.

**Notes**: 138(12)"life insurance policy in Canada" was 138(12)(g) before consolidation in R.S.C. 1985 (5th Supp.), effective for taxation years ending after November 1991.

**Interpretation Bulletins**: IT-355R2: Interest on loans to buy life insurance policies and annuity contracts, and interest on policy loans.

"maximum tax actuarial reserve" for a particular class of life insurance policy for a taxation year of a life insurer means, except as otherwise expressly prescribed, the maximum amount allowable under subparagraph (3)(a)(i) as a policy reserve for the year in respect of policies of that class;

**Notes**: 138(12)"maximum tax actuarial reserve" was 138(12)(h) before consolidation in R.S.C. 1985 (5th Supp.), effective for taxation years ending after November 1991.

"net Canadian life investment income [para. 138(12)(i)]" — [Repealed under former Act]

**Notes**: 138(12)(i), repealed in 1978, defined "net Canadian life investment income", a term no longer used.

"non-segregated property" of an insurer means its property other than property included in a segregated fund;

**Related Provisions**: 181.3(1)(a) — Taxable capital employed in Canada of financial institution.

**Notes**: 138(12)"non-segregated property" was 138(12)(j) before consolidation in R.S.C. 1985 (5th Supp.), effective for taxation years ending after November 1991.

"participating life insurance policy" means a life insurance policy under which the policyholder is entitled to share (other than by way of an experience rating refund) in the profits of the insurer other than profits in respect of property in a segregated fund;

**Notes**: 138(12)"participating life insurance policy" was 138(12)(k) before consolidation in R.S.C. 1985 (5th Supp.), effective for taxation years ending after November 1991.

"policy loan" means an amount advanced at a particular time by an insurer to a policyholder in accordance with the terms and conditions of a life insurance policy in Canada;

**Notes**: 138(12)"policy loan" was 138(12)(k.1) before consolidation in R.S.C. 1985 (5th Supp.), effective for taxation years ending after November 1991.

**Interpretation Bulletins**: IT-355R2: Interest on loans to buy life insurance policies and annuity contracts, and interest on policy loans.

"property used by it in the year in, or held by it in the year in the course of" — [Repealed]

**Related Provisions**: 18(5) — Meaning of certain expressions; 138(11.91)(d) — Computation of income of non-resident insurer.

**Notes**: Definition "property used by it in the year in, or held by it in the year in the course of" repealed by 1996 Budget, effective for 1997 and later taxation years (changed from 1996 at Second Reading of the Budget bill). It has been replaced by "designated insurance property", above.

138(12)"property used by it ..." was 138(12)(l) before consolidation in R.S.C. 1985 (5th Supp.), effective for taxation years ending after November 1991.

**Regulations**: 2400 (prescribed rules).

**Interpretation Bulletins**: IT-291R2: Transfer of property to a corporation under subsection 85(1).

"**qualified related corporation**" of a non-resident insurer has the meaning assigned by subsection 219(8);

**Notes**: 138(12)"qualified related corporation" was 138(12)(l.1) before consolidation in R.S.C. 1985 (5th Supp.), effective for taxation years ending after November 1991.

"**relevant authority**" — [Repealed]

**Notes**: Definition "relevant authority" repealed by 1996 Budget, effective for 1997 and later taxation years (changed from 1996 at Second Reading of the Budget bill). The term is no longer used. For earlier years, read:

"relevant authority", in relation to a life insurer, means

(a) the Superintendent of Financial Institutions, if the insurer is required by law to report to the Superintendent of Financial Institutions, or

(b) in any other case, the superintendent of insurance or other similar officer or authority of the province under the laws of which the insurer is incorporated;

138(12)"relevant authority" was 138(12)(m) before consolidation in R.S.C. 1985 (5th Supp.), effective for taxation years ending after November 1991. See Table of Concordance.

"**segregated fund**" has the meaning given that expression in subsection 138.1(1);

**Notes**: 138(12)"segregated fund" was 138(12)(n) before consolidation in R.S.C. 1985 (5th Supp.), effective for taxation years ending after November 1991.

"**surplus funds derived from operations**" of an insurer as of the end of a particular taxation year means the amount determined by the formula

$$(A + B + C) - (D + E + F + G + H)$$

where

A  is the total of the insurer's income for each taxation year in the period beginning with its 1969 taxation year and ending with the particular year from all insurance businesses carried on by it,

B  is the total described in subclause (4.1)(a)(ii)(B)(IV), and

C  is the total of all profits or gains made by the insurer in the period in respect of non-segregated property of the insurer disposed of by it that was used by it in, or held by it in the course of, carrying on an insurance business in Canada, except to the extent that those profits or gains have been or are included in computing the insurer's income or loss, if any, for any taxation year in the period from carrying on an insurance business,

D  is the total of its loss, if any, for each taxation year in the period from all insurance businesses carried on by it,

E  is the total of all losses sustained by the insurer in the period in respect of non-segregated property disposed of by it that was used by it in, or held by it in the course of, carrying on an insurance business in Canada, except to the extent that those losses have been or are included in computing the insurer's income or loss, if any, for any taxation year in the period from carrying on an insurance business,

F  is the total of

(a) all taxes payable under this Part by the insurer, and all income taxes payable by it under the laws of each province, for each taxation year in the period, except such portion thereof as would not have been payable by it if subsection (7) had not been enacted, and

(b) all taxes payable under Parts I.3 and VI by the insurer for each taxation year in the period,

G  is the total of all gifts made in the period by the insurer to a person or organization described in paragraph 110.1(1)(a) or (b), and

H  is the amount determined by the formula

$$M - N$$

where

M  is the amount determined in respect of the insurer for the particular taxation year under clause (3)(a)(iii)(A), and

N  is the amount so determined under clause (3)(a)(iii)(B);

**Related Provisions**: 257 — Formula amounts cannot calculate to less than zero.

**Notes**: Para. F(b) added by 1993 technical bill, effective for 1992 and later taxation years, to permit the special taxes under Parts I.3 and VI to be deducted in computing surplus funds derived from operations. See Notes to 125.2(1) and 125.3(1).

138(12)"surplus funds derived from operations" was 138(12)(o) before consolidation in R.S.C. 1985 (5th Supp.), effective for taxation years ending after November 1991. The previous version, identical in meaning, read:

(o) "surplus funds derived from operations" of an insurer as of the end of a particular taxation year means the aggregate of

(i) its income for each taxation year in the period beginning with its 1969 taxation year and ending with the particular year from all insurance businesses carried on by it,

(i.1) the aggregate described in subclause (4.1)(a)(ii)(B)(IV), and

(ii) all profits or gains made by the insurer in the period in respect of non-segregated property of the insurer disposed of by it that was used by it in, or held by it in the course of, carrying on an insurance business in Canada, except to the extent that such profits or gains have been or are included in computing the insurer's income or loss, if any, for any taxation year in the period from carrying on an insurance business,

minus the aggregate of

(iii) its loss, if any, for each taxation year in the period from all insurance businesses carried on by it,

(iv) all losses sustained by the insurer in the period in respect of non-segregated property disposed of by it that was used by it in, or held by it in the course of, carrying on an insurance business in Canada, except to the extent that such losses have been or are included in computing the insurer's income or loss, if any, for any taxation year in the period from carrying on an insurance business,

(v) the aggregate of any taxes payable by the insurer under this Part and any income tax payable by it under the laws of any province for each taxation year in the period, except such portion thereof as would not have been payable by it if subsection (7) had not been enacted,

Division F — Special Rules in Certain Circumstances   S. 138(12) 1975–76 exc

(vi) all gifts made in the period by the insurer to a person or organization described in paragraph 110.1(1)(a) or (b), and

(vii) the amount, if any, by which the amount determined in respect of the insurer for the particular taxation year under clause (3)(a)(iii)(A) exceeds the amount so determined under clause (3)(a)(iii)(B);

**I.T. Application Rules**: 60.1 (reference to "this Part" in description of F includes Part IA of pre-1972 Act).

**"1975 branch accounting election deficiency"** of an insurer that has made an election under subsection 138(9) of the *Income Tax Act*, chapter 148 of the Revised Statutes of Canada, 1952, as it read in its application to the 1977 taxation year, in respect of its 1975 taxation year means the amount determined by the formula

$$(A + B) - (C + D + E + F + G)$$

where

A is such portion of the total of the insurer's gross investment revenue and all amounts determined under paragraphs (4)(b) and (c) as would have been required to be included in computing its income for its 1975 taxation year if

(a) it had not made the election under subsection 138(9) of that Act in respect of that year, and

(b) where it had made the election under subsection 138(9) of that Act in respect of its 1974 taxation year, it had adopted for its 1975 taxation year, with the concurrence of the Minister, the method required by subsection 138(9) of that Act if it had not elected under that subsection and the Minister had specified no terms and conditions under subsection 138(10) of that Act,

B is the total of the amounts deducted in computing the insurer's income for its 1975 taxation year under paragraphs (3)(b) and (d),

C is the total of the insurer's gross investment revenue included in computing its income for its 1975 taxation year and the amounts included in computing its income for that year under paragraphs (4)(b) and (c),

D is such portion of the total of all amounts determined under paragraphs (3)(b) and (d) as would have been deductible in computing the insurer's income for its 1975 taxation year if

(a) it had not made the election under subsection 138(9) of that Act in respect of that year, and

(b) where it had made the election under subsection 138(9) of that Act in respect of its 1974 taxation year, it had adopted for its 1975 taxation year, with the concurrence of the Minister, the method required by subsection 138(9) of that Act if it had not elected under that subsection and the Minister had specified no terms and conditions under subsection 138(10) of that Act,

E is the amount determined by the formula

$$P - Q$$

where

P is the total of the insurer's outlays or expenses that would have been deductible in computing its income from its insurance businesses for its 1975 taxation year (other than amounts deductible under subsection (3), section 140 and regulations made under paragraph 20(1)(a) and 20(7)(c)), if

(a) it had not made the election under subsection 138(9) of that Act in respect of that year, and

(b) where it had made the election under subsection 138(9) of that Act in respect of its 1974 taxation year, it had adopted for its 1975 taxation year, with the concurrence of the Minister, the method required by subsection 138(9) of that Act if it had not elected under that subsection and the Minister had specified no terms and conditions under subsection 138(10) of that Act,

Q is the total of the insurer's outlays or expenses deducted in computing its income from its insurance businesses for its 1975 taxation year (other than amounts deducted under subsection (3), section 140 and regulations made under paragraphs 20(1)(a) and 20(7)(c)),

F is the amount of the insurer's 1975-76 excess policy dividend deduction, and

G is the amount of the insurer's 1975-76 excess policy dividend reserve;

**Related Provisions**: 257 — Formula amounts cannot calculate to less than zero.

**Notes**: 138(12)"1975 branch accounting election deficiency" was 138(12)(q) before consolidation in R.S.C. 1985 (5th Supp.), effective for taxation years ending after November 1991, and was in descriptive form rather than a formula. See Table of Concordance.

**I.T. Application Rules**: 69 (meaning of "*Income Tax Act*, chapter 148 of the Revised Statutes of Canada, 1952").

**"1975–76 excess additional group term reserve"** of an insurer that has made an election under subsection 138(9) of the *Income Tax Act*, chapter 148 of the Revised Statutes of Canada, 1952, as it read in its application to the 1977 taxation year, in respect of its 1975 taxation year means the amount determined by the formula

$$A - B$$

where

A is the amount that would have been deductible under subparagraph (3)(a)(ii) in computing the insurer's income for its 1976 taxation year if it had claimed the maximum allowable amount under that subparagraph for that year, and

B is the amount deducted under that subparagraph in computing its income for its 1976 taxation year;

**Related Provisions:** 257 — Formula cannot calculate to less than zero.

**Notes:** 138(12)"1975-76 excess additional group term reserve" was 138(12)(w) before consolidation in R.S.C. 1985 (5th Supp.), effective for taxation years ending after November 1991, and was in descriptive form rather than a formula. See Table of Concordance.

**I.T. Application Rules:** 69 (meaning of "*Income Tax Act*, chapter 148 of the Revised Statutes of Canada, 1952").

**"1975–76 excess capital cost allowance"** of depreciable property of a prescribed class of an insurer that has made an election under subsection 138(9) of the *Income Tax Act*, chapter 148 of the Revised Statutes of Canada, 1952, as it read in its application to the 1977 taxation year, in respect of its 1975 taxation year means the amount determined by the formula

$$(A + B) - C$$

where

A is the amount determined by the formula

$$P - Q$$

where

P is the amount that would have been deductible under paragraph 20(1)(a) by the insurer in computing its income for its 1975 taxation year with respect to that class, if it had claimed the maximum allowable amount under that paragraph in that year with respect to that class and if

(a) it had not made the election under subsection 138(9) of that Act in respect of its 1975 taxation year, and

(b) where it made the election under subsection 138(9) of that Act in respect of its 1974 taxation year, it had adopted for its 1975 taxation year, with the concurrence of the Minister, the method required by subsection 138(9) of that Act if it had not elected under that subsection and the Minister had specified no terms and conditions under subsection 138(10) of that Act, and

Q is the amount deducted under paragraph 20(1)(a) by the insurer in computing its income for its 1975 taxation year with respect to that class,

B is the amount determined by the formula

$$R - S$$

where

R is the amount that would have been deductible under paragraph 20(1)(a) by the insurer in computing its income for its 1976 taxation year with respect to that class if it had claimed the maximum allowable amount under that paragraph in that year and in its 1975 taxation year with respect to that class on the basis of the assumptions made in paragraphs (a) to (d) of the description of A in the definition "1975-76 excess policy dividend reserve" in this subsection, and

S is the amount deducted under paragraph 20(1)(a) by the insurer in computing its income for its 1976 taxation year with respect to that class, and

C is the amount determined by the formula

$$T - U$$

where

T is the amount determined for S, and

U is the amount determined for R;

**Related Provisions:** 257 — Formula amounts cannot calculate to less than zero.

**Notes:** 138(12)"1975-76 excess capital cost allowance" was 138(12)(u) before consolidation in R.S.C. 1985 (5th Supp.), effective for taxation years ending after November 1991, and was in descriptive form rather than a formula. See Table of Concordance.

**I.T. Application Rules:** 69 (meaning of "*Income Tax Act*, chapter 148 of the Revised Statutes of Canada, 1952").

**"1975–76 excess investment reserve"** of an insurer that has made an election under subsection 138(9) of the *Income Tax Act*, chapter 148 of the Revised Statutes of Canada, 1952, as it read in its application to the 1977 taxation year, in respect of its 1975 taxation year means the amount determined by the formula

$$A - B$$

where

A is the amount that would have been deductible under paragraph 138(3)(c) of the *Income Tax Act*, chapter 148 of the Revised Statutes of Canada, 1952, by the insurer in computing its income for its 1976 taxation year if it had claimed the maximum allowable amount under that paragraph in that year and that amount was determined without reference to subparagraph 138(3)(c)(ii) of that Act, and

B is the amount deducted by the insurer under paragraph 138(3)(c) of the *Income Tax Act*, chapter 148 of the Revised Statutes of Canada, 1952, in computing its income for its 1976 taxation year;

**Related Provisions:** 257 — Formula cannot calculate to less than zero.

**Notes:** 138(12)"1975-76 excess investment reserve" was 138(12)(t) before consolidation in R.S.C. 1985 (5th Supp.), effective for taxation years ending after November 1991, and was in descriptive form rather than a formula. See Table of Concordance.

**I.T. Application Rules:** 69 (meaning of "*Income Tax Act*, chapter 148 of the Revised Statutes of Canada, 1952").

**"1975–76 excess policy dividend deduction"** of an insurer that has made an election under subsection 138(9) of the *Income Tax Act*, chapter 148 of the Revised Statutes of Canada, 1952, as it read in its application to the 1977 taxation year, in respect of its 1975 taxation year means the amount determined by the formula

$$(A + B) - C$$

where

A is the amount determined by the formula

$$P - Q$$

where

P is the amount that would have been deductible under subparagraph (3)(a)(iii) by the insurer in computing its income for its 1975 taxation year if that amount had been determined on the assumptions made in paragraphs (a) to (d) of the description of A in the definition "1975-76 excess policy dividend reserve" in this subsection, and

Q is the amount deducted under subparagraph (3)(a)(iii) by the insurer in computing its income for its 1975 taxation year,

B is the amount determined by the formula

$$R - S$$

where

R is the amount that would have been deductible under subparagraph (3)(a)(iii) by the insurer in computing its income for its 1976 taxation year if that amount had been determined on the basis that the amount of its income for that year from its participating life insurance business carried on in Canada was computed in accordance with prescribed rules on the assumptions made in paragraph (e) of the description of A in the definition "1975-76 excess policy dividend reserve" in this subsection, and

S is the amount deducted by the insurer under subparagraph (3)(a)(iii) in computing its income for its 1976 taxation year, and

C is the amount determined by the formula

$$T - U$$

where

T is the amount determined for S, and

U is the amount determined for R;

**Related Provisions**: 257 — Formula amounts cannot calculate to less than zero.

**Notes**: 138(12)"1975-76 excess policy dividend deduction" was 138(12)(r) before consolidation in R.S.C. 1985 (5th Supp.), effective for taxation years ending after November 1991, and was in descriptive form rather than a formula. See Table of Concordance.

**I.T. Application Rules**: 69 (meaning of "*Income Tax Act*, chapter 148 of the Revised Statutes of Canada, 1952").

**"1975–76 excess policy dividend reserve"** of an insurer that has made an election under subsection 138(9) of the *Income Tax Act*, chapter 148 of the Revised Statutes of Canada, 1952, as it read in its application to the 1977 taxation year, in respect of its 1975 taxation year means the amount determined by the formula

$$A - B$$

where

A is the amount that would have been deductible under subparagraph (3)(a)(iv) by the insurer in computing its income for its 1976 taxation year if

(a) it had not made the election under subsection 138(9) of that Act in respect of its 1975 taxation year,

(b) where it made an election under subsection 138(9) of that Act in respect of its 1974 taxation year, it had adopted for its 1975 taxation year, with the concurrence of the Minister, the method required by subsection 138(9) of that Act if it had not elected under that subsection and the Minister had specified no terms and conditions under subsection 138(10) of that Act,

(c) it had claimed the maximum allowable amount under paragraph 138(3)(c) of the *Income Tax Act*, chapter 148 of the Revised Statutes of Canada, 1952, in computing its income for its 1975 taxation year,

(d) it had claimed the maximum allowable amount that would have been deductible under regulations made under paragraph 20(1)(a) in computing its income for its 1975 taxation year with respect to property of each of its prescribed classes, and

(e) the amount of its income for its 1976 taxation year from its participating life insurance business carried on in Canada was computed in accordance with prescribed rules and as if the amount deducted under subparagraph (3)(a)(iv) by it in computing its income for its 1975 taxation year was the amount that would have been deductible under that subparagraph on the basis of the assumptions made in paragraphs (a) to (d) of this description, and

B is the amount deducted by the insurer under subparagraph (3)(a)(iv) in computing its income for its 1976 taxation year;

**Related Provisions**: 257 — Formula cannot calculate to less than zero.

**Notes**: 138(12)"1975-76 excess policy dividend reserve" was 138(12)(s) before consolidation in R.S.C. 1985 (5th Supp.), effective for taxation years ending after November 1991, and was in descriptive form rather than a formula. See Table of Concordance.

**I.T. Application Rules**: 69 (meaning of "*Income Tax Act*, chapter 148 of the Revised Statutes of Canada, 1952").

**"1975–76 excess policy reserves"** of an insurer that has made an election under subsection 138(9) of the *Income Tax Act*, chapter 148 of the Revised Statutes of Canada, 1952, as it read in its application to the 1977 taxation year, in respect of its 1975 taxation year means the amount determined by the formula

$$A - B$$

where

A is the amount that would have been deductible under subparagraph (3)(a)(i) in computing the insurer's income for its 1976 taxation year if it had claimed the maximum allowable amount under that subparagraph for that year, and

B is the amount deducted under that subparagraph in computing its income for its 1976 taxation year.

**Related Provisions**: 257 — Formula cannot calculate to less than zero.

**Notes**: 138(12)"1975-76 excess policy reserves" was 138(12)(v) before consolidation in R.S.C. 1985 (5th Supp.), effective for taxation years ending after November 1991, and was in descriptive form rather than a formula. See Table of Concordance.

**I.T. Application Rules**: 69 (meaning of *Income Tax Act*, chapter 148 of the Revised Statutes of Canada, 1952").

**Related Provisions [subsec. 138(12)]**: 211(1) — Definitions.

**Notes**: The opening words of 138(12) redrafted in R.S.C. 1985 (5th Supp.) consolidation, effective for taxation years ending after November 1991; formerly applied explicitly for purposes of numerous other provisions. These rules of application are now in 12.2(12), 13(23.1), 20(27.1), 70(11), 89(1.01), 111(7.11), 115(6), 116(7) and 142.1. See also 211(1).

### (13) Variation in "tax basis" and "amortized cost" — Where

(a) in a taxation year that ended after 1968 and before 1978 an insurer carried on a life insurance business in Canada and an insurance business in a country other than Canada,

(b) the insurer did not make an election in respect of the year under subsection 138(9) of the *Income Tax Act*, chapter 148 of the Revised Statutes of Canada, 1952, as it applied to that year, and

(c) the ratio of the value for the year of the insurer's specified Canadian assets to its Canadian investment fund for the year exceeded one,

each of the amounts included or deducted as follows in respect of the year shall be multiplied by the ratio referred to in paragraph (c):

(d) under paragraph (c), (d), (k) or (l) of the definition "tax basis" in subsection 142.4(1) in determining the tax basis of a debt obligation to the insurer, or

(e) under paragraph (c), (d), (f) or (h) of the definition "amortized cost" in subsection 248(1) in determining the amortized cost of a debt obligation to the insurer.

**Related Provisions**: 138(14) — Meaning of certain expressions; 142.4(1)"tax basis"(c), (d), (k), (l) — Disposition of specified debt obligation by financial institution.

**Notes**: 138(13) amended by 1994 tax amendments bill (Part III), effective for taxation years that end after February 22, 1994. For earlier years (last amended in 1987), read:

(13) Where meaning of "amortized cost" varied — For the purposes of the definition "amortized cost" in subsection 248(1), where in a taxation year ending after 1968 and before the particular time referred to in that definition an insurer carried on a life insurance business in Canada and an insurance business in a country other than Canada and has not made an election under subsection 138(9) of the *Income Tax Act*, chapter 148 of the Revised Statutes of Canada, 1952, as it

read in its application to the 1977 taxation year, in respect of that year, each of the amounts referred to in paragraph (c), (d), (f) or (h) in that definition shall, in respect of that year, be deemed to be the greater of

(a) each such amount, and

(b) that proportion of the amount referred to in paragraph (a) that the value for the taxation year of the insurer's specified Canadian assets is of its Canadian investment fund for the taxation year.

**I.T. Application Rules**: 69 (meaning of *Income Tax Act*, chapter 148 of the Revised Statutes of Canada, 1952").

### (14) Meaning of certain expressions — For the purposes of subsection (13), the expressions "Canadian investment fund for a taxation year", "specified Canadian assets" and "value for the taxation year" have the meanings prescribed therefor.

**Regulations**: 2400(4)(a) (draft), 2405(2) (to be repealed) (prescribed meanings).

### (15) Definition not to apply — In this section, in construing the meaning of the expression "group term insurance policy", the definition "group term life insurance policy" in subsection 248(1) does not apply.

**Notes**: 138(15) was 138(12)(p) before consolidation in R.S.C. 1985 (5th Supp.), effective for taxation years ending after November 1991.

138(15) appears to be meaningless. The term "group term insurance policy" is not used anywhere in the Act or the Regulations. The term "group term life insurance policy" is defined in 248(1), but is not used anywhere in the Act other than s. 6. It is also used in Regs. 304, 1401 and 1900. See Reg. 1408(2).

### (16) [Repealed under former Act]

**Notes**: Former 138(15) and (16), repealed in 1978, allowed the Minister to designate property of an insurer as used in the course of carrying on an insurance business in Canada.

**Notes [s. 138]**: For additional taxes on life insurance corporations, see Part VI (financial institutions tax) and Part XII.3 (tax on investment income). See s. 148 for the treatment of life insurance policyholders.

For an overview of s. 138 and its history, see William J. Strain, "Taxation of Life Insurance", 45(5) *Canadian Tax Journal* 1506–1546 (1995).

**Definitions [s. 138]**: "accumulated 1968 deficit" — 138(12); "affiliated" — 251.1; "allowable capital loss" — 38(b), 248(1); "amortized cost" — 138(13), 248(1); "amount" — 248(1); "amount payable" — (in respect of a policy loan) 138(12); "arm's length" — 251(1); "borrowed money", "business" — 248(1); "Canada" — 255; "Canada security" — 138(12); "Canadian investment fund" — 138(14); "capital gain" — 39(1)(a), 248(1); "capital property" — 54, 248(1); "carrying on business" — 253; "class of shares" — 248(6); "common share" — 248(1); "completed" — 138(4.6); "corporation" — 248(1), *Interpretation Act* 35(1); "cost" — (to an insurer of acquiring a mortgage or hypothec) 138(12); "cost amount" — 248(1); "depreciable property" — 13(21), 248(1); "designated insurance property" — 138(12), 248(1); "dividend" — 248(1); "fiscal period" — 249(2)(b), 249.1; "gross investment revenue" — 138(12); "identical" — 138(11.1), 248(12); "insurer" — 248(1); "interest in real property" — 248(4); "interest" — in relation to a policy loan 138(12); "life insurance business" — 248(1); "life insurance policy" — 138(4.01), (12), 248(1); "life insurance policy in Canada" — 138(12), 248(1); "life insurer" — 248(1); "maximum tax actuarial reserve" — 138(12); "Minister" — 248(1); "net Canadian life investment income" — 209(2); "1975 branch accounting election deficiency" — 138(12); "1975-76 excess policy dividend deduction" — 138(3.1), 138(12); "1975-76 excess policy dividend reserve", "1975-76 excess additional group term reserves", "1975-76 excess policy reserves" — 138(12); "non-resident" — 248(1); "non-segregated property" — 138(12); "paid-up capital" — 89(1), 138(11.7), 248(1); "participating life insurance policy" — 138(12); "partnership" — see Notes to 96(1); "person" — 248(1); "policy dividend" — 139.1(8)(a); "policy loan" — 138(12); "preferred share", "prescribed", "principal amount", "property" — 248(1); "property used by it in the year in, or held by it in the year in the course of" — carrying on an insurance business 138(12); "province" — *Interpretation Act* 35(1); "qualified related corporation" — 138(12), 219(8); "received" — 248(7); "registered pension plan" — 248(1); "registered retirement savings plan" — 146(1), 248(1); "regulation" — 248(1); "relevant authority" — 138(12); "resident in Canada" — 250; "segregated fund" — 138(12); "share", "shareholder" — 248(1); "specified Canadian assets" — 138(14); "subsidiary wholly-owned corporation" — 248(1); "substituted property" — 248(5); "surplus funds derived from operations" — 138(12); "taxable Canadian corporation" — 89(1), 248(1); "taxable capital gain" — 38(a), 248(1); "taxable dividend" — 89(1), 248(1); "taxable income" — 2(2), 248(1); "taxation year" — 249; "taxpayer", "term preferred share" — 248(1); "transferred property" — 138(11.94)(b)(i); "used" — 138(12)"property used by it in the year in, or held by it in the year in the course of"; "value for the taxation year" — 138(14).

**138.1 (1) Rules relating to segregated funds** — In respect of life insurance policies for which all or any portion of an insurer's reserves vary in amount depending on the fair market value of a specified group of properties (in this section referred to as a "segregated fund"), for the purposes of this Part, the following rules apply:

(a) an *inter vivos* trust (in this section referred to as the "related segregated fund trust") is deemed to be created at the time that is the later of

(i) the day that the segregated fund is created, and

(ii) the day on which the insurer's 1978 taxation year commences,

and to continue in existence throughout the period during which the fund determines any portion of the benefits under those policies that vary in amount depending on the fair market value of the property in the segregated fund (in this section referred to as "segregated fund policies");

(b) property that has been allocated to and that remains a part of the segregated fund, and any income that has accrued on that property is deemed to be the property and income of the related segregated fund trust and not to be the property and income of the insurer;

(c) the insurer is deemed to be

(i) the trustee who has ownership or control of the related segregated fund trust property,

(ii) a resident of Canada in respect of the related segregated fund trust property used or held by it in the course of carrying on the insurer's life insurance business in Canada, and

(iii) a non-resident of Canada in respect of the related segregated fund trust property not used or held by it in the course of carrying on the insurer's life insurance business in Canada;

(d) where at a particular time there is property in the segregated fund that was not funded with premiums paid under a segregated fund policy,

(i) the insurer is deemed to have an interest in the related segregated fund trust that is not in respect of any particular property or source of income, and

(ii) the cost at any time of that interest to the insurer is deemed to be the total of

(A) for property of the trust at that time allocated by the insurer to the segregated fund prior to 1978, the amount that would be its adjusted cost base to the insurer if the interest had been a capital property at all relevant times prior to 1978 and if the rules in this section had been applicable for the taxation years after 1971 and before 1978, and

(B) for property of the trust at that time allocated by the insurer to the segregated fund after 1977, the fair market value of the property at the time it was last allocated to the segregated fund by the insurer;

(e) where at any particular time there is property in the segregated fund that was funded with a portion of the premiums paid before that time under a segregated fund policy,

(i) the respective segregated fund policyholder is deemed to have an interest in the related segregated fund trust that is not in respect of any particular property or source of income,

(ii) the cost of that interest is deemed to be the amount that is the total of

(A) the amount that would be its adjusted cost base to the insurer at December 31, 1977 if the interest had been a capital property at all relevant times prior to 1978 and if the rules in this section (if subsection (3) were read without reference to the expressions "or capital loss" and "or loss") had been applicable for taxation years after 1971 and before 1978, and

(B) the total of amounts each of which is that portion of a premium paid before that time and after the day referred to in subparagraph (a)(ii) under a segregated fund policy that was or is to be used by the insurer to fund property allocated to the segregated fund (other than the portion of the premium that is an acquisition fee), and

(iii) the portion of a premium included in a segregated fund is deemed not to be an amount paid in respect of a premium under the policy;

(f) the income of the related segregated fund trust is deemed for the purposes of subsections 104(6),

(13) and (24) to be an amount that has become payable in the year to the beneficiaries under the segregated fund trust and the amount therefor in respect of any particular beneficiary is equal to the amount determined by reference to the terms and conditions of the segregated fund policy;

(g) where at a particular time the fair market value of property transferred by the insurer to the segregated fund results in an increase at that time in the portion of the insurer's reserves for a segregated fund policy held by a policyholder that vary with the fair market value of the segregated fund and a decrease in the portion of its reserves for the policy that do not so vary, the amount of that increase shall,

(i) for the purpose of the determination of H in the definition "adjusted cost basis" in subsection 148(9), be deemed to be proceeds of disposition that the policyholder became entitled to receive at that time,

(ii) for the purpose of computing the adjusted cost base to the policyholder of the policyholder's interest in the related segregated fund trust, be added at that time to the cost to the policyholder of that interest, and

(iii) for the purpose of computing the insurer's income, be deemed to be a payment under the terms and conditions of the policy at that time;

(h) where at a particular time the fair market value of property transferred by the insurer from the segregated fund results in an increase at that time in the portion of the insurer's reserves for a segregated fund policy that do not vary with the fair market value of the segregated fund and a decrease in the portion of its reserves for the policy that so vary, the amount of that increase shall, for the purpose of calculating the insurer's income, be deemed to be a premium received by the insurer at that time;

(i) where at a particular time the policyholder of a segregated fund policy disposes of all or a portion of the policyholder's interest in the related segregated fund trust, that proportion of the amount, if any, by which the acquisition fee with respect to the particular policy exceeds the total of amounts each of which is an amount determined under this paragraph with respect to the particular policy before that time, that

(i) the fair market value of the interest disposed of at that time

is of

(ii) the fair market value of the policyholder's interest in the particular segregated fund trust immediately before that time,

is deemed to be a capital loss of the related segregated fund trust that reduces the policyholder's benefits under the particular policy by that amount for the purposes of subsection (3);

(j) the obligations of an insurer in respect of a benefit that is payable under a segregated fund policy, the amount of which benefit varies with the fair market value of the segregated fund at the time the benefit becomes payable, are deemed to be obligations of the trustee under the related segregated fund trust and not of the insurer and any amount received by the policyholder or that the policyholder became entitled to receive at any particular time in a year in respect of those obligations is deemed to be proceeds from the disposition of an interest in the related segregated fund trust;

(k) a reference to "the terms and conditions of the trust arrangement" in section 104 or subsection 127.2(3) is deemed to include a reference to the terms and conditions of the related segregated fund policy and the trustee is deemed to have designated the amounts referred to in that section in accordance with those terms and conditions; and

(l) where at any time an insurer acquires a share as a first registered holder thereof and allocates the share to a related segregated fund trust, the trust shall be deemed to have acquired the share at that time as the first registered holder thereof for the purpose of computing its share-purchase tax credit and the insurer shall be deemed not to have acquired the share for the purpose of computing its share-purchase tax credit.

**Related Provisions:** 39(1)(a)(iii) — Meaning of capital gain; 53(1)(l), 53(2)(q) — Adjustments to cost base; 87(2.2) — Amalgamation of insurance corporations; 88(1)(g) — Winding-up of subsidiary insurance corporations; 94.2(10)(a)(ii) — No application to foreign insurance policy of foreign investment entity; 107.4(3)(g) — Application of 138.1(1)(i) on qualifying disposition to trust; 127.55(f)(i) — No minimum tax on related segregated fund trust; 138(11.5)(k) — Transfer of business by non-resident insurer; 138.1(7) — Where subsections (1) to (6) not to apply; 218.1 — Application to non-resident withholding tax; 248(1)"disposition"(f)(vi) — Rollover from one trust to another; Reg. 9000 — Certain segregated funds excluded from definition of "financial institution".

**Notes:** The opening words of 138.1(1) redrafted in R.S.C. 1985 (5th Supp.) consolidation, effective for taxation years ending after November 1991, to change "for the purposes of this Part and Part XIII" to "for the purposes of this Part". The application to Part XIII is now in 218.1.

**(2) Rules relating to property in segregated funds at end of 1977 taxation year** — Where an insurer holds property at the end of its 1977 taxation year in connection with a segregated fund, the following rules apply:

(a) the property is deemed to have been acquired by the related segregated fund trust on the day determined under paragraph (1)(a) at a cost equal to the adjusted cost base of the property to the insurer on that day and that transaction is deemed to be a transaction between persons not dealing at arm's length;

(b) the property is deemed to have been disposed of by the insurer on the day referred to in paragraph (a) for proceeds equal to the adjusted cost base of the property to the insurer on that day; and

(c) for the purpose of computing the insurer's income for its 1978 taxation year it shall be deemed to have made a payment to its policyholders in satisfaction of their rights under their segregated fund policies in that year equal to that portion of the amount deducted under subparagraph 138(3)(a)(i) in computing its income for its 1977 taxation year that is in respect of segregated fund policies.

**Related Provisions**: 39.1(2)B(c), 39.1(5) — Reduction in gain to reflect capital gains exemption election; 138.1(7) — Where subsections (1) to (6) not to apply.

### (3) Capital gains and capital losses of related segregated fund trusts
— A capital gain or capital loss of a related segregated fund trust from the disposition of any property shall, to the extent that a policyholder's benefits under a policy or the interest in the trust of any other beneficiary is affected by that gain or loss, be deemed to be a capital gain or capital loss, as the case may be, of the policyholder or other beneficiary and not that of the trust.

**Related Provisions**: 39.1(2)B(c), 39.1(5) — Reduction in gain to reflect 1994 capital gains exemption election; 53(1)(l)(iv), 53(2)(q)(ii) — Adjustments to cost base; 138.1(7) — Where subsections (1) to (6) not to apply.

### (4) Election and allocation
— Where at any particular time after 1977, a policyholder withdraws all or part of the policyholder's interest in a segregated fund policy, the trustee of a related segregated fund trust may elect in prescribed manner and prescribed form to treat any capital property of the trust as having been disposed of, whereupon the property shall be deemed to have been disposed of on any day designated by the trustee for proceeds of disposition equal to

(a) the fair market value of the property on that day,

(b) the adjusted cost base to the trust of the property on that day, or

(c) an amount that is neither greater than the greater of nor less than the lesser of the amounts determined under paragraphs (a) and (b),

whichever is designated by the trustee, and to have been reacquired by the trust immediately thereafter at a cost equal to those proceeds, and where the trustee of a related segregated fund trust has made such an election, the following rules apply:

(d) the amount of any capital gain or capital loss resulting from the deemed disposition shall be allocated by the trustee to any policyholder withdrawing all or part of the policyholder's interest in the policyholder's policy at that time to the extent that the amount of the policyholder's benefits under the policy at that time is affected by the capital gain or capital loss in respect of property held by the related segregated fund trust at that time,

(e) the allocation referred to in paragraph (d) is deemed to have been made immediately before the withdrawal,

(f) any capital gain not so allocated is deemed to be allocated in accordance with the terms and conditions of the policy, and

(g) any capital loss not so allocated is deemed to be a superficial loss of each policyholder to the extent that the policyholder's benefits under the policy would be affected by the loss.

**Related Provisions**: 39.1(1)"exempt capital gains balance"C(c), 39.1(6) — Reduction in gain to reflect capital gains exemption election; 53(1)(l)(iii), 53(2)(q)(i) — Adjustments to cost base; 138.1(7) — Where subsections (1) to (6) not to apply.

**Regulations**: 6100 (prescribed manner and time).

**Forms**: T3018: Election for deemed disposition and reacquisition of capital property of a life insurance segregated fund under subsection 138.1(4).

### (5) Adjusted cost base of property in related segregated fund trust
— At any particular time, the adjusted cost base of each capital property of a related segregated fund trust shall be deemed to be the amount, if any, by which

(a) the adjusted cost base of the property to the trust immediately before that time

exceeds

(b) the total of amounts each of which is an amount in respect of the disposition by a policyholder of all or part of the policyholder's interest in the related segregated fund trust at that time equal to that proportion of the amount, if any, by which

(i) the adjusted cost base to the policyholder of that interest at that time

exceeds

(ii) the policyholder's proceeds of the disposition of that interest in the trust

that

(iii) the fair market value of the capital property at that time

is of

(iv) the total of amounts each of which is the fair market value of a capital property of the related segregated fund trust at that time.

**Related Provisions**: 53(1)(l), 53(2)(q) — ACB of interest in related segregated fund trust; 138(11.5)(k) — Transfer of business by non-resident insurer; 138.1(7) — Where subsections (1) to (6) not to apply.

### (6) Definition of "acquisition fee"
— In this section, "acquisition fee" means the amount, if any, by which the total of amounts each of which is

(a) that portion of a premium charged by the insurer under a segregated fund policy that is not included in the related segregated fund or cannot reasonably be regarded as an amount required to fund a mortality or maturity benefit,

(b) a transfer from the segregated fund that cannot reasonably be regarded as an amount required to fund a mortality or maturity benefit other than an annual administration fee or charge, or,

(c) any amount by which the proceeds payable to the policyholder under a particular segregated fund policy is reduced on the surrender or partial surrender of the policy that may reasonably be regarded as a surrender fee,

exceeds

(d) the total of amounts each of which is that portion of an amount described in paragraph (a), (b) or (c) that may reasonably be considered to be in respect of an interest in the segregated fund that was disposed of before 1978.

**(7) Where subsecs. (1) to (6) do not apply** — Subsections (1) to (6) do not apply to the holder of a segregated fund policy with respect to such a policy that is issued or effected as a registered retirement savings plan or a registered retirement income fund or that is issued under a registered pension plan.

**Related Provisions**: 148(1) — Amounts included in computing policyholder's income.

**Notes**: 138.1(7) amended by 1992 technical bill, effective for 1991 and later taxation years, to clarify its intent and extend its application to segregated fund policies that are issued as RRIFs. For 1986 to 1990, read:

> (7) Where policyholder deemed to be trust, etc. — For the purposes of this section, where a segregated fund policy is issued or effected as a registered retirement savings plan or is issued pursuant to a registered pension plan, the policyholder of the policy shall be deemed to be a trust or a trust or corporation described by paragraph 149(1)(r) or (o), respectively.

**Definitions [s. 138.1]**: "acquisition fee" — 138.1(6); "adjusted cost base" — 54, 248(1); "amount" — 248(1); "arm's length" — 251(1); "capital gain", "capital loss" — 39(1), 248(1); "corporation" — 248(1), *Interpretation Act* 35(1); "insurer" — 248(1); "inter vivos trust" — 108(1), 248(1); "life insurance business", "prescribed", "property", "registered pension plan" — 248(1); "registered retirement income fund" — 146.3(1), 248(1); "registered retirement savings plan" — 146(1), 248(1); "related segregated fund trust" — 138.1(1)(a); "segregated fund" — 138.1(1); "segregated fund policy" — 138.1(1)(a); "taxation year" — 249; "trust" — 104(1), 248(1), (3).

## 139. Conversion of insurance corporations into mutual corporations

— Where an insurance corporation that is a Canadian corporation applies an amount in payment for shares of the corporation purchased or otherwise acquired by it under a mutualization proposal under Division III of Part VI of the *Insurance Companies Act* or under a law of the province under the laws of which the corporation is incorporated that provides for the conversion of the corporation into a mutual corporation by the purchase of its shares in accordance with that law,

(a) section 15 does not apply to require the inclusion, in computing the income of a shareholder of the corporation, of any part of that amount; and

(b) no part of that amount shall be deemed, for the purpose of subsection 138(7), to have been paid to shareholders or, for the purpose of section 84, to have been received as a dividend.

**Notes**: Opening words of 139 referring to a mutualization proposal under the *Insurance Companies Act* added by 1991 financial institutions bill (S.C. 1994, c. 7, Sch. I (1991, c. 47), s. 734), effective June 1, 1992.

**Definitions [s. 139]**: "amount" — 248(1); "Canadian corporation" — 89(1), 248(1); "dividend", "insurance corporation" — 248(1); "; "province" — *Interpretation Act* 35(1); "share", "shareholder" — 248(1).

## Demutualization of Insurance Corporations

**139.1 (1) Definitions** — The definitions in this subsection apply in this section and sections 139.2 and 147.4.

**"conversion benefit"** means a benefit received in connection with the demutualization of an insurance corporation because of an interest, before the demutualization, of any person in an insurance policy to which the insurance corporation has been a party.

**Related Provisions**: 139.1(2), (3) — Determining when benefit received; 139.1(11) — Conversion benefit is not a shareholder benefit. See also Related Provisions under "taxable conversion benefit".

**Notes**: See Notes at end of 139.1.

**"deadline"** for a payment in respect of a demutualization of an insurance corporation means the latest of

(a) the end of the day that is 13 months after the time of the demutualization,

(b) where the entire amount of the payment depends on the outcome of an initial public offering of shares of the corporation or a holding corporation in respect of the insurance corporation, the end of the day that is 60 days after the day on which the offering is completed,

(c) where the payment is made after the initial deadline for the payment and it is reasonable to conclude that the payment was postponed beyond that initial deadline because there was not sufficient information available 60 days before that initial deadline with regard to the location of a person, the end of the day that is six months after such information becomes available, and

(d) the end of any other day that is acceptable to the Minister.

**Related Provisions**: 139.1(1)"initial deadline" — Definition.

**"demutualization"** means the conversion of an insurance corporation from a mutual company into a corporation that is not a mutual company.

**Related Provisions**: 139.1(4) — Effect of demutualization; 237(4) — Authority to communicate SIN to agent of shareholder.

**Notes**: Demutualizations have been undertaken by Mutual Life, Manufacturers Life, Sun Life, Canada Life and Industrial-Alliance Life.

"**holding corporation**" means a corporation that

(a) in connection with the demutualization of an insurance corporation, has issued shares of its capital stock to stakeholders; and

(b) owns shares of the capital stock of the insurance corporation acquired in connection with the demutualization that entitle it to 90% or more of the votes that could be cast in respect of shares under all circumstances at an annual meeting of

(i) shareholders of the insurance corporation, or

(ii) shareholders of the insurance corporation and holders of insurance policies to which the insurance corporation is a party.

**Related Provisions**: 139.1(4)(e) — Cost to holding corporation of shares acquired on demutualization; 141(3) — Holding corporation deemed to be public corporation.

"**initial deadline**" for a payment is the time that would, if the definition "deadline" were read without reference to paragraph (c) of that definition, be the deadline for the payment.

"**mutual holding corporation**" in respect of an insurance corporation, means a mutual company established to hold shares of the capital stock of the insurance corporation, where the only persons entitled to vote at an annual meeting of the mutual company are policyholders of the insurance corporation.

**Related Provisions**: 139.1(4)(d) — Receipt of ownership rights in MHC on demutualization; 139.2 — Deemed dividend on distribution of property by MHC.

"**ownership rights**" means

(a) in a particular mutual holding corporation, the following rights and interests held by a person in respect of the particular corporation because of an interest or former interest of any person in an insurance policy to which an insurance corporation, in respect of which the particular corporation is the mutual holding corporation, has been a party:

(i) rights that are similar to rights attached to shares of the capital stock of a corporation, and

(ii) all other rights with respect to, and interests in, the particular corporation as a mutual company; and

(b) in a mutual insurance corporation, the following rights and interests held by a person in respect of the mutual insurance corporation because of an interest or former interest of any person in an insurance policy to which that corporation has been a party:

(i) rights that are similar to rights attached to shares of the capital stock of a corporation,

(ii) all other rights with respect to, and interests in, the mutual insurance corporation as a mutual company, and

(iii) any contingent or absolute right to receive a benefit in connection with the demutualization of the mutual insurance corporation.

**Related Provisions**: 139.1(4)(a), (d) — Rollover where shares acquired in exchange for ownership rights.

"**person**" includes a partnership.

"**share**" of the capital stock of a corporation includes a right granted by the corporation to acquire a share of its capital stock.

"**specified insurance benefit**" means a taxable conversion benefit that is

(a) an enhancement of benefits under an insurance policy;

(b) an issuance of an insurance policy;

(c) an undertaking by an insurance corporation of an obligation to pay a policy dividend; or

(d) a reduction in the amount of premiums that would otherwise be payable under an insurance policy.

**Related Provisions**: 139.1(8) — Effect of stakeholder receiving specified insurance benefit.

"**stakeholder**" means a person who is entitled to receive or who has received a conversion benefit but, in respect of the demutualization of an insurance corporation, does not include a holding corporation in connection with the demutualization or a mutual holding corporation in respect of the insurance corporation.

**Related Provisions**: 139.1(4) — Effect of demutualization on stakeholder.

"**taxable conversion benefit**" means a conversion benefit received by a stakeholder in connection with the demutualization of an insurance corporation, other than a conversion benefit that is

(a) a share of a class of the capital stock of the corporation;

(b) a share of a class of the capital stock of a corporation that is or becomes a holding corporation in connection with the demutualization; or

(c) an ownership right in a mutual holding corporation in respect of the insurance corporation.

**Related Provisions**: 139.1(2), (3) — Determining when benefit received; 139.1(4)(f) — TCB deemed to be a dividend; 139.1(8)(a) — Policy dividend that is TCB deemed not to be policy dividend; 139.1(10) — Cost of TCB.

**(2) Rules of general application** — For the purposes of this section,

(a) subject to paragraphs (b) to (g), if in providing a benefit in respect of a demutualization, a corporation becomes obligated, either absolutely or contingently, to make or arrange a payment, the person to whom the undertaking to make or arrange the payment was given is considered to have received a benefit

(i) as a consequence of the undertaking of the obligation, and

(ii) not as a consequence of the making of the payment;

(b) where, in providing a benefit in respect of a demutualization, a corporation makes a payment (other than a payment, made pursuant to the terms of an insurance policy, that is not a policy dividend) at any time on or before the deadline for the payment,

(i) subject to paragraphs (f) and (g), the recipient of the payment is considered to have received a benefit as a consequence of the making of the payment, and

(ii) no benefit is considered to have been received as a consequence of the undertaking of an obligation, that is either contingent or absolute, to make or arrange the payment;

(c) no benefit is considered to have been received as a consequence of the undertaking of an absolute or contingent obligation of a corporation to make or arrange a payment (other than a payment, made pursuant to the terms of an insurance policy, that is not a policy dividend) unless it is reasonable to conclude that there is sufficient information with regard to the location of a person to make or arrange the payment;

(d) where a corporation's obligation to make or arrange a payment in connection with a demutualization ceases on or before the initial deadline for the payment and without the payment being made in whole or in part, no benefit is considered to have been received as a consequence of the undertaking of the obligation unless the payment was to be a payment (other than a policy dividend) pursuant to the terms of an insurance policy;

(e) no benefit is considered to have been received as a consequence of the undertaking of an absolute or contingent obligation of a corporation to make or arrange a payment where

(i) paragraph (a) would, but for this paragraph, apply with respect to the obligation,

(ii) paragraph (d) would, if that paragraph were read without reference to the words "on or before the initial deadline for the payment", apply in respect of the obligation,

(iii) it is reasonable to conclude that there was not, before the initial deadline for the payment, sufficient information with regard to the location of a person to make or arrange the payment, and

(iv) such information becomes available on a particular day after the initial deadline and the obligation ceases not more than six months after the particular day;

(f) no benefit is considered to have been received as a consequence of

(i) an undertaking of an absolute or contingent obligation of a corporation to make or arrange an annuity payment through the issuance of an annuity contract, or

(ii) a receipt of an annuity payment under the contract so issued

where it is reasonable to conclude that the purpose of the undertaking or the making of the annuity payment is to supplement benefits provided under either an annuity contract to which subsection 147.4(1) or paragraph 254(a) applied or a group annuity contract that had been issued under, or pursuant to, a registered pension plan that has wound up;

(g) no benefit is considered to have been received as a consequence of

(i) an amendment to which subsection 147.4(2) would, but for subparagraph 147.4(2)(a)(ii), apply, or

(ii) a substitution to which paragraph 147.4(3)(a) applies;

(h) the time at which a stakeholder is considered to receive a benefit in connection with the demutualization of an insurance corporation is,

(i) where the benefit is a payment made at or before the time of demutualization or is a payment to which paragraph (b) applies, the time at which the payment is made, and

(ii) in any other case, the latest of

(A) the time of the demutualization,

(B) where the extent of the benefit or the stakeholder's entitlement to it depends on the outcome of an initial public offering of shares of the corporation or a holding corporation in respect of the insurance corporation and the offering is completed before the day that is 13 months after the time of the demutualization, the time at which the offering is completed,

(C) where the entire amount of the benefit depends on the outcome of an initial public offering of shares of the corporation or a holding corporation in respect of the insurance corporation, the time at which the offering is completed,

(D) where it is reasonable to conclude that the person conferring the benefit does not have sufficient information with regard to the location of the stakeholder before the later of the times determined under clauses (A) to (C), to advise the stakeholder of the benefit, the time at which sufficient information with regard to the location of the stakeholder to so advise the stakeholder was received by that person, and

(E) the end of any other day that is acceptable to the Minister;

(i) the time at which an insurance corporation is considered to demutualize is the time at which it first issues a share of its capital stock (other than shares of its capital stock issued by it when it was a mutual company if the corporation did not cease to be a mutual company because of the issuance of those shares); and

(j) subject to paragraph (3)(b), the value of a benefit received by a stakeholder is the fair market value of the benefit at the time the stakeholder receives the benefit.

**Related Provisions**: 49.1 — Acquisition in satisfaction of obligation deemed not to be a disposition.

**Notes**: In the December 15, 1998 draft, paras. (d), (h), (i) and (j) were (c)–(f) respectively. Current paras. (c) and (e)–(g) were not included in that draft.

**(3) Special cases** — For the purposes of this section,

(a) where benefits under an insurance policy are enhanced (otherwise than by way of an amendment to which subsection 147.4(2) would, but for subparagraph 147.4(2)(a)(ii), apply) in connection with a demutualization, the value of the enhancement is deemed to be a benefit received by the policyholder and not by any other person;

(b) where premiums payable under an insurance policy to an insurance corporation are reduced in connection with a demutualization, the policyholder is deemed, as a consequence of the undertaking to reduce the premiums, to have received a benefit equal to the present value at the time of the demutualization of the additional premiums that would have been payable if the premiums had not been reduced in connection with the demutualization;

(c) the payment of a policy dividend by an insurance corporation or an undertaking of an obligation by the corporation to pay a policy dividend is considered to be in connection with the demutualization of the corporation only to the extent that

(i) the policy dividend is referred to in the demutualization proposal sent by the corporation to stakeholders,

(ii) the obligation to make the payment is contingent on stakeholder approval for the demutualization, and

(iii) the payment or undertaking cannot reasonably be considered to have been made or given, as the case may be, to ensure that policy dividends are not adversely affected by the demutualization;

(d) except for the purposes of paragraphs (c), (e) and (f), where part of a policy dividend is a conversion benefit in respect of the demutualization of an insurance corporation and part of it is not, each part of the dividend is deemed to be a policy dividend that is separate from the other part;

(e) a policy dividend includes an amount that is in lieu of payment of, or in satisfaction of, a policy dividend;

(f) the payment of a policy dividend includes the application of the policy dividend to pay a premium under an insurance policy or to repay a policy loan;

(g) where the demutualization of an insurance corporation is effected by the merger of the corporation with one or more other corporations to form one corporate entity, that entity is deemed to be the same corporation as, and a continuation of, the insurance corporation;

(h) an insurance corporation shall be considered to have become a party to an insurance policy at the time that the insurance corporation becomes liable in respect of obligations of an insurer under the policy; and

(i) notwithstanding paragraph 248(7)(a), where a cheque or other means of payment sent to an address is returned to the sender without being received by the addressee, it is deemed not to have been sent.

**Related Provisions**: 139.1(2)(i) — Determining time of demutualization; 87(2.2) — Amalgamation of insurers.

**(4) Consequences of demutualization** — Where a particular insurance corporation demutualizes,

(a) each of the income, loss, capital gain and capital loss of a taxpayer, from the disposition, alteration or dilution of the taxpayer's ownership rights in the particular corporation as a result of the demutualization, is deemed to be nil;

(b) no amount paid or payable to a stakeholder in connection with the disposition, alteration or dilution of the stakeholder's ownership rights in the particular corporation is an eligible capital expenditure;

(c) no election may be made under subsection 85(1) or (2) in respect of ownership rights in the particular corporation;

(d) where the consideration given by a person for a share of the capital stock of the particular corporation or a holding corporation in connection with the demutualization (or for particular ownership rights in a mutual holding corporation in respect of the particular corporation) includes the transfer, surrender, alteration or dilution of ownership rights in the particular corporation, the cost of the share (or the particular ownership rights) to the person is deemed to be nil;

(e) where a holding corporation in connection with the demutualization acquires, in connection with the demutualization, a share of the capital stock of the particular corporation from the particular corporation and issues a share of its own capital stock to a stakeholder as consideration for the share of the capital stock of the particular corporation, the cost to the holding corporation of the share of the capital stock of the particular corporation is deemed to be nil;

(f) where at any time a stakeholder receives a taxable conversion benefit and subsection (14) does not apply to the benefit,

(i) the corporation that conferred the benefit is deemed to have paid a dividend at that time on shares of its capital stock equal to the value of the benefit, and

(ii) subject to subsection (16), the benefit received by the stakeholder is deemed to be a dividend received by the stakeholder at that time;

(g) for the purposes of this Part, where a dividend is deemed by paragraph (f) or by paragraph (16)(i) to have been paid by a non-resident corporation, that corporation is deemed in respect of the payment of the dividend to be a corporation resident in Canada that is a taxable Canadian corporation unless any amount is claimed under section 126 in respect of tax on the dividend;

(h) for the purposes of section 70, subsection 104(4) and section 128.1, the fair market value of rights to benefits that are to be received in connection with the demutualization is, before the time of the receipt, deemed to be nil; and

(i) where a person acquires an annuity contract in respect of which, because of the application of paragraph (2)(f), no benefit is considered to have been received for the purpose of this section,

(i) the cost of the annuity contract to the person is deemed to be nil, and

(ii) section 12.2 does not apply to the annuity contract.

**Related Provisions**: 12(1)(j), 82(1), 90 — Inclusion in income of deemed dividend; 87(2)(j.6) — Amalgamations — continuing corporation; 139 — Mutualization proposal; 139.1(2)(j) — Value of benefit; 212(2) — Non-resident withholding tax on deemed dividend.

**Notes**: See Notes at end of 139.1.

**(5) Fair market value of ownership rights** — For the purposes of section 70, subsection 104(4) and section 128.1, where an insurance corporation makes, at any time, a public announcement that it intends to seek approval for its demutualization, the fair market value of ownership rights in the corporation is deemed to be nil throughout the period that

(a) begins at that time; and

(b) ends either at the time of the demutualization or, in the event that the corporation makes at any subsequent time a public announcement that it no longer intends to demutualize, at the subsequent time.

**Related Provisions**: 87(2)(j.6) — Amalgamations — continuing corporation.

**Notes**: This subsection was not included in the draft legislation of December 15, 1998.

**(6) Paid-up capital — insurance corporation** — Where an insurance corporation resident in Canada has demutualized, in computing the paid-up capital at any particular time in respect of a class of shares of the capital stock of the corporation,

(a) there shall be deducted the total of all amounts each of which would, but for this subsection, have been deemed by subsection 84(1) to have been paid at or before the particular time by the corporation as a dividend on a share of that class because of an increase in paid-up capital (determined without reference to this subsection) in connection with the demutualization; and

(b) there shall be added the amount, if any, by which

(i) the total of all amounts each of which is deemed by subsection 84(3), (4) or (4.1) to be a dividend on shares of that class paid by the corporation before the particular time

exceeds

(ii) the total of all amounts each of which would be deemed by subsection 84(3), (4) or (4.1) to be a dividend on shares of that class paid by the corporation before the particular time, if this Act were read without reference to this subsection.

**Related Provisions**: 87(2)(j.6) — Amalgamations — continuing corporation.

**Notes**: This was subsection (5) in the draft legislation of December 15, 1998.

**(7) Paid-up capital — holding corporation** — Where a particular corporation resident in Canada was at any time a holding corporation in connection with the demutualization of an insurance corporation, in computing the paid-up capital at any particular time in respect of a class of shares of the capital stock of the particular corporation,

(a) there shall be deducted the total of all amounts each of which is an amount by which the paid-up capital would, but for this subsection, have increased at or before the particular time as a result of the acquisition of shares of a class of the capital stock of the insurance corporation from the corporation on its demutualization; and

(b) there shall be added the amount, if any, by which

(i) the total of all amounts each of which is deemed by subsection 84(3), (4) or (4.1) to be a dividend on shares of that class paid by the particular corporation before the particular time

exceeds

(ii) the total of all amounts each of which would be deemed by subsection 84(3), (4) or (4.1) to be a dividend on shares of that class paid by the particular corporation before the particular time, if this Act were read without reference to this subsection.

**Related Provisions**: 87(2)(j.6) — Amalgamations — continuing corporation.

**Notes**: This was subsection (6) in the draft legislation of December 15, 1998.

**(8) Policy dividends** — Where the payment of a policy dividend by an insurance corporation is a taxable conversion benefit,

(a) for the purposes of this Act other than this section, the policy dividend is deemed not to be a policy dividend; and

(b) no amount in respect of the policy dividend may be included, either explicitly or implicitly, in the calculation of an amount deductible by the insurer for any taxation year under paragraph 20(7)(c) or subsection 138(3).

**Related Provisions**: 87(2)(j.6) — Amalgamations — continuing corporation.

**Notes**: This was subsection (7) in the draft legislation of December 15, 1998.

**(9) Payment and receipt of premium** — Where, in connection with the demutualization of an insurance corporation, a person would, if subsection (2) were read without reference to paragraphs (f) and (g) and paragraph (3)(a) were read without reference to the application of subsection 147.4(2), receive a particular benefit that is a specified insurance benefit,

(a) the insurance corporation that is obligated to pay benefits under the policy to which the particular benefit relates is deemed to have received a premium at the time of the demutualization in respect of that policy equal to the value of the particular benefit;

(b) for the purpose of paragraph (a), to the extent that the obligations of a particular insurance corporation under the policy were assumed by another insurance corporation before the time of the demutualization, the particular corporation is deemed not to be obligated to pay benefits under the policy; and

(c) subject to paragraph (15)(e), where the person receives the particular benefit, the person is deemed to have paid, at the time of demutualization, a premium in respect of the policy to which the benefit relates equal to the value of the particular benefit.

**Related Provisions**: 139.1(2)(i) — Determining time of demutualization; 139.1(2)(j) — Value of benefit.

**Notes**: This was subsection (8) in the draft legislation of December 15, 1998.

**(10) Cost of taxable conversion benefit** — Where, in connection with the demutualization of an insurance corporation, a stakeholder receives a taxable conversion benefit (other than a specified insurance benefit), the stakeholder is deemed to have acquired the benefit at a cost equal to the value of the benefit.

**Related Provisions**: 139.1(2)(j) — Value of benefit.

**Notes**: This was subsection (9) in the draft legislation of December 15, 1998.

**(11) No shareholder benefit** — Subsection 15(1) does not apply to a conversion benefit.

**Notes**: This was subsection (10) in the draft legislation of December 15, 1998.

**(12) Exclusion of benefit from RRSP and other rules** — Subject to subsection (14), for the purposes of the provisions of this Act (other than paragraph (9)(c)) that relate to registered retirement savings plans, registered retirement income funds, retirement compensation arrangements, deferred profit sharing plans and superannuation or pension funds or plans, the receipt of a conversion benefit shall be considered to be neither a contribution to, nor a distribution from, such a plan, fund or arrangement.

**Notes**: This was subsection (11) in the draft legislation of December 15, 1998.

**(13) RRSP registration rules, etc.** — For the purposes of this Act, paragraphs 146(2)(c.4) and 146.3(2)(g) and subsection 198(6) shall be applied without reference to any conversion benefit.

**Notes**: This subsection was not included in the draft legislation of December 15, 1998.

**(14) Retirement benefit** — A conversion benefit received because of an interest in a life insurance policy held by a trust governed by a registered retirement savings plan, registered retirement income fund, deferred profit sharing plan or superannuation or pension fund or plan is deemed to be received under the plan or fund, as the case may be, if it is received by any person (other than the trust).

**Related Provisions**: 139.1(4)(j) — Deemed dividend where 139.1(12) does not apply.

**Notes**: This was subsection (12) in the draft legislation of December 15, 1998.

**(15) Employee-paid insurance** — Where

(a) a stakeholder receives a conversion benefit because of the stakeholder's interest in a group insurance policy under which individuals have been insured in the course of or because of their employment,

(b) at all times before the payment of a premium described in paragraph (c), the full cost of a particular insurance coverage under the policy was borne by the individuals who were insured under the particular coverage,

(c) the stakeholder pays a premium under the policy in respect of the particular coverage or under another group insurance policy in respect of coverage that has replaced the particular coverage, and

(d) either

(i) the premium is deemed by paragraph (9)(c) to have been paid, or

(ii) it is reasonable to conclude that the purpose of the premium is to apply, for the benefit of the individuals who are insured under the particular coverage or the replacement coverage, all or part of the value of the portion of the conversion benefit that can reasonably be considered to be in respect of the particular coverage,

the following rules apply:

(e) for the purposes of paragraph 6(1)(f) and regulations made for the purposes of subsection 6(4), the premium is deemed to be an amount paid by the individuals who are insured under the particular coverage or the replacement coverage, as the case may be, and not to be an amount paid by the stakeholder, and

(f) no amount may be deducted in respect of the premium in computing the stakeholder's income.

**Related Provisions**: 87(2)(j.6) — Amalgamations — continuing corporation.

**Notes**: This was subsection (13) in the draft legislation of December 15, 1998.

## (16) Flow-through of conversion benefits to employees and others — Where

(a) a stakeholder receives a conversion benefit (in this subsection referred to as the "relevant conversion benefit") because of the interest of any person in an insurance policy,

(b) the stakeholder makes a payment of an amount (otherwise than by way of a transfer of a share that was received by the stakeholder as all or part of the relevant conversion benefit and that was not so received as a taxable conversion benefit) to a particular individual

(i) who has received benefits under the policy,

(ii) who has, or had at any time, an absolute or contingent right to receive benefits under the policy,

(iii) for whose benefit insurance coverage was provided under the policy, or

(iv) who received the amount because an individual satisfied the condition in subparagraph (i), (ii) or (iii),

(c) it is reasonable to conclude that the purpose of the payment is to distribute an amount in respect of the relevant conversion benefit to the particular individual,

(d) either

(i) the main purpose of the policy was to provide retirement benefits or insurance coverage to individuals in respect of their employment with an employer, or

(ii) all or part of the cost of insurance coverage under the policy had been borne by individuals (other than the stakeholder),

(e) subsection (14) does not apply to the relevant conversion benefit, and

(f) one of the following applies, namely,

(i) the particular individual is resident in Canada at the time of the payment, the stakeholder is a person the taxable income of which is exempt from tax under this Part and the payment would, if this section were read without reference to this subsection, be included in computing the income of the particular individual,

(ii) the payment is received before December 7, 1999 and the stakeholder elects in writing filed with the Minister, on a day that is not more than six months after the end of the taxation year in which the stakeholder receives the relevant conversion benefit (or a later day acceptable to the Minister), that this subsection applies in respect of the payment,

(iii) the payment is received after December 6, 1999, the payment would, if this section were read without reference to this subsection, be included in computing the income of the particular individual and the stakeholder elects in writing filed with the Minister, on a day that is not more than six months after the end of the taxation year in which the stakeholder receives the relevant conversion benefit (or a later day acceptable to the Minister), that this subsection applies in respect of the payment, or

(iv) the payment is received after December 6, 1999 and the payment would, if this section were read without reference to this subsection, not be included in computing the income of the particular individual,

the following rules apply:

(g) subject to paragraph (l), no amount is, because of the making of the payment, deductible in computing the stakeholder's income,

(h) except for the purpose of this subsection and without affecting the consequences to the particular individual of any transaction or event that occurs after the time that the payment was made, the payment is deemed not to have been received by, or made payable to, the particular individual,

(i) the corporation that conferred the relevant conversion benefit is deemed to have paid to the particular individual at the time the payment was made, and the particular individual is deemed to have received at that time, a dividend on shares of the capital stock of the corporation equal to the amount of the payment,

(j) all obligations that would, but for this subsection, be imposed by this Act or the Regulations on the corporation because of the payment of the dividend apply to the stakeholder as if the stakeholder were the corporation, and do not apply to the corporation,

(k) where the relevant conversion benefit is a taxable conversion benefit, except for the purpose of this subsection and the purposes of determining the obligations imposed by this Act or the Regulations on the corporation because of the conferral of the relevant conversion benefit, the stakeholder is deemed, to the extent of the fair market value of the payment, not to have received the relevant conversion benefit, and

(l) where the relevant conversion benefit was a share received by the stakeholder (otherwise than as a taxable conversion benefit),

(i) where the share is, at the time of the payment, capital property held by the stakeholder, the amount of the payment shall, after that time, be added in computing the adjusted cost base to the stakeholder of the share,

(ii) where subparagraph (i) does not apply and the share was capital property disposed of by the stakeholder before that time, the amount of the payment is deemed to be a capital loss of the stakeholder from the disposition of a property for the taxation year of the stakeholder in which the payment is made, and

(iii) in any other case, paragraph (g) shall not apply to the payment.

**Related Provisions**: 53(1)(d.01) — Addition to ACB for amount under 139.1(16)(l); 87(2)(j.6) — Amalgamations — continuing corporation; 96(3) — Election by members of partnership; 139.1(17) — Flow-through of share benefits.

**Notes**: Under subsec. 38(2) of the 1999 Budget bill which enacted 139.1, an election is deemed filed on a timely basis if it is filed by the end of 2000. See Notes at end of 139.1.

This subsection was not included in the draft legislation of December 15, 1998.

**(17) Flow-through of share benefits to employees and others** — Where

(a) because of the interest of any person in an insurance policy, a stakeholder receives a conversion benefit (other than a taxable conversion benefit) that consists of shares of the capital stock of a corporation,

(b) the stakeholder transfers some or all of the shares at any time to a particular individual

(i) who has received benefits under the policy,

(ii) who has, or had at any time, an absolute or contingent right to receive benefits under the policy,

(iii) for whose benefit insurance coverage was provided under the policy, or

(iv) who received the shares because an individual satisfied the condition in subparagraph (i), (ii) or (iii),

(c) it is reasonable to conclude that the purpose of the transfer is to distribute all or any portion of the conversion benefit to the particular individual,

(d) either

(i) the main purpose of the policy was to provide retirement benefits or insurance coverage to individuals in respect of their employment with an employer, or

(ii) all or part of the cost of insurance coverage under the policy had been borne by individuals (other than the stakeholder),

(e) subsection (14) does not apply to the conversion benefit, and

(f) one of the following applies, namely,

(i) the particular individual is resident in Canada at the time of the transfer, the stakeholder is a person the taxable income of which is exempt from tax under this Part and the amount of the transfer would, if this section were read without reference to this subsection, be included in computing the income of the particular individual,

(ii) the transfer is made before December 7, 1999 and the stakeholder elects in writing filed with the Minister, on a day that is not more than six months after the end of the taxation year in which the stakeholder receives the conversion benefit (or a later day acceptable to the Minister), that this subsection applies in respect of the transfer,

(iii) the transfer is made after December 6, 1999, the amount of the transfer would, if this section were read without reference to this subsection, be included in computing the income of the particular individual and the stakeholder elects in writing filed with the Minister, on a day that is not more than six months after the end of the taxation year in which the stakeholder receives the conversion benefit (or a later day acceptable to the Minister), that this subsection applies in respect of the transfer, or

(iv) the transfer is made after December 6, 1999 and the amount of the transfer would, if this section were read without reference to this subsection, not be included in computing the income of the particular individual,

the following rules apply:

(g) no amount is, because of the transfer, deductible in computing the stakeholder's income,

(h) except for the purpose of this subsection and without affecting the consequences to the particular individual of any transaction or event that occurs after the time that the transfer was made, the transfer is deemed not to have been made to the particular individual nor to represent an amount payable to the particular individual, and

(i) the cost of the shares to the particular individual is deemed to be nil.

**Related Provisions**: 87(2)(j.6) — Amalgamations — continuing corporation; 139.1(16) — Flow-through of conversion benefits.

**Notes**: Under subsec. 38(2) of the 1999 Budget bill which enacted 139.1, an election is deemed filed on a timely basis if it is filed by the end of 2000. See Notes at end of 139.1.

This subsection was not included in the draft legislation of December 15, 1998.

**(18) Acquisition of control** — For the purposes of subsections 10(10), 13(21.2) and (24), 14(12) and 18(15), sections 18.1 and 37, subsection 40(3.4), the definition "superficial loss" in section 54, section 55, subsections 66(11), (11.4) and (11.5), 66.5(3) and 66.7(10) and (11), section 80, paragraph 80.04(4)(h), subsections 85(1.2) and 88(1.1) and (1.2), sections 111 and 127 and subsections 249(4) and 256(7), control of an insurance corporation (and each corporation controlled by it) is deemed not to be acquired solely because of the acquisition of shares of the capital stock of the insurance corporation, in connection with the demutualization of the insurance corporation, by a particular corporation that at a particular time becomes a holding corporation in connection with the demutualization where, immediately after the particular time,

(a) the particular corporation is not controlled by any person or group of persons; and

(b) 95% of the fair market value of all the assets of the particular corporation is less than the total of all amounts each of which is

(i) the amount of the particular corporation's money,

(ii) the amount of a deposit, with a financial institution, of such money standing to the credit of the particular corporation,

(iii) the fair market value of a bond, debenture, note or similar obligation that is owned by the particular corporation that had, at the time of its acquisition, a maturity date of not more than 24 months after that time, or

(iv) the fair market value of a share of the capital stock of the insurance corporation held by the particular corporation.

**Related Provisions**: 87(2)(j.6) — Amalgamations — continuing corporation; 256(6), (6.1) — Meaning of "controlled".

**Notes**: This was subsection (14) in the draft legislation of December 15, 1998.

**Notes [s. 139.1]**: 139.1 provides rules for "demutualization" of insurance companies, whereby Canada's large life insurers, formerly owned by their policyholders as mutual insurance companies, converted themselves to share corporations and issued tradeable shares to their policyholders. This was done by Canada Life, Industrial-Alliance Life, Manufacturer's Life, Mutual Life and Sun Life. The thrust of 139.1 is to provide that there is no tax consequence to the policyholder on receiving the shares (139.1(4)(a)), but that the shares have a cost base of zero (139.1(4)(d)) so that all cash received on the sale of the shares will be taxed as a capital gain under 38(a).

For planning ideas, see Susan Nickerson & David Wentzell, "Insurance Company Demutualization: Tax Planning Issues", 11(6) *Taxation of Executive Compensation and Retirement* (Federated Press) 235-239 (Feb. 2000).

139.1 added by 1999 Budget bill, effective for transactions that occur after December 15, 1998 (the date on which the demutualization proposals were first announced by the Department of Finance). See also Notes to 139.1(16) and (17) re deadlines for elections.

**Definitions [s. 139.1]**: "adjusted cost base" — 54, 248(1); "amount", "annuity" — 248(1); "capital gain" — 39(1), 248(1); "capital loss" — 39(1)(b), 248(1); "capital property" — 54, 248(1); "controlled" — 256(6), (6.1); "conversion benefit" — 139.1(1); "corporation" — 248(1), *Interpretation Act* 35(1); "deadline" — 139.1(1); "deferred profit sharing plan" — 147(1), 248(1); "demutualization" — 139.1(1); "disposition", "dividend" — 248(1); "eligible capital expenditure" — 14(5), 248(1); "employee", "employer", "employment" — 248(1); "holding corporation" — 139.1(1); "individual" — 248(1); "initial deadline" — 139.1(1); "insurance corporation", "insurance policy", "insurer" — 248(1); "life insurance policy" — 138(12), 248(1); "Minister" — 248(1); "month" — *Interpretation Act* 35(1); "mutual holding corporation" — 139.1(1); "non-resident" — 248(1); "ownership rights" — 139.1(1); "paid-up capital" — 89(1), 248(1); "partnership" — see Notes to 96(1); "person" — 139.1(1), 248(1); "property", "registered pension plan" — 248(1); "registered retirement income fund" — 146.3(1), 248(1); "registered retirement savings plan" — 146(1), 248(1); "relevant conversion benefit" — 139.1(16)(a); "resident in Canada" — 250; "retirement compensation arrangement" — 248(1); "share" — 139.1(1), 248(1); "shareholder" — 248(1); "specified insurance benefit", "stakeholder" — 139.1(1); "taxable Canadian corporation" — 89(1), 248(1); "taxable conversion benefit" — 139.1(1); "taxable income" — 248(1); "taxation year" — 249; "taxpayer" — 248(1); "trust" — 104(1), 248(1), (3); "writing" — *Interpretation Act* 35(1).

## 139.2 Mutual holding corporations
— Where at any time a mutual holding corporation (as defined in subsection 139.1(1)) in respect of an insurance corporation distributes property to a policyholder of the insurance corporation, the mutual holding corporation is deemed to have paid, and the policyholder is deemed to have received from the mutual holding corporation, at that time a dividend on shares of the capital stock of the mutual holding corporation, equal to the fair market value of the property.

**Related Provisions**: 139.1 — Demutualization.

**Notes**: 139.2 added by 1999 Budget, effective for transactions that occur after December 15, 1998. Its most common application is with respect to the distribution by a mutual holding corporation of dividends received on shares of the insurance corporation.

**Definitions [s. 139.2]**: "corporation" — 248(1), *Interpretation Act* 35(1); "dividend", "insurance corporation" — 248(1); "mutual holding corporation" — 139.1(1); "property", "share" — 248(1).

## 140. (1) [Insurance corporation] Deductions in computing income
— In computing the income for a taxation year of an insurance corporation, whether a mutual corporation or a joint stock company, from carrying on an insurance business other than a life insurance business, there may be deducted every amount credited in respect of that business for the year or a preceding taxation year to a policyholder of the corporation by way of a policy dividend, refund of premiums or refund of premium deposits if the amount was, during the year or within 12 months thereafter,

(a) paid or unconditionally credited to the policyholder; or

Division F — Special Rules in Certain Circumstances   S. 141(5)

(b) applied in discharge, in whole or in part, of a liability of the policyholder to pay premiums to the corporation.

**Related Provisions:** 87(2.2) — Amalgamation of insurance corporations; 88(1)(g) — Winding-up of subsidiary insurance corporations; 138(11.5)(k) — Transfer of business by non-resident insurer; 149(10)(a.1) — Exempt corporations; Reg. 1401(3)J — Policy reserves — non-life insurance business.

**Notes:** 140(1) amended by 1999 Budget, effective December 16, 1998, to change "dividend" to "policy dividend".

**(2) Inclusion in computing income** — There shall be included in computing the income of an insurance corporation, whether a mutual corporation or a joint stock company, from carrying on an insurance business for its first taxation year that commences after June 17, 1987 and ends after 1987 (in this subsection referred to as its "1988 taxation year") the amount, if any, by which

(a) the total of all amounts each of which is an amount deducted by the corporation in computing its income for a taxation year ending before its 1988 taxation year pursuant to paragraph 140(c) of the *Income Tax Act*, chapter 148 of the Revised Statutes of Canada, 1952, or pursuant to that paragraph by reason of subparagraph 138(3)(a)(v) of that Act as it read in respect of those taxation years in respect of amounts credited to the account of the policyholder on terms that the policyholder is entitled to payment thereof on or before the expiration or termination of the policy

exceeds

(b) the total of all amounts each of which is an amount paid or unconditionally credited to a policyholder or applied in discharge, in whole or in part, of a liability of the policyholder to pay premiums to the corporation before the corporation's 1988 taxation year in respect of the amounts credited to the account of the policyholder referred to in paragraph (a).

**Related Provisions [subsec. 140(2)]:** 87(2.2) — Amalgamation of insurance corporations; 88(1)(g) — Winding-up of insurance corporations; 138(3) — Deductions allowed in computing income; 138(11.5)(k) — Transfer of business by non-resident insurer.

**I.T. Application Rules:** 69 (meaning of "*Income Tax Act*, chapter 148 of the Revised Statutes of Canada, 1952").

**Definitions [s. 140]:** "amount", "business" — 248(1); "carrying on business" — 253; "corporation" — 248(1), *Interpretation Act* 35(1); "dividend", "insurance corporation", "life insurance business", "policy dividend" — 139.1(8)(a), 248(1); "taxation year" — 249.

**141. (1) Definitions** — In this section, "demutualization" and "holding corporation" have the same meaning as in subsection 139.1(1).

**Notes:** See Notes at end of s. 141.

**(2) Life insurance corporation deemed to be public corporation** — Notwithstanding any other provision of this Act, a life insurance corporation that is resident in Canada is deemed to be a public corporation.

**(3) Holding corporation deemed to be public corporation** — A corporation resident in Canada that is a holding corporation because of its acquisition of shares in connection with the demutualization of a life insurance corporation resident in Canada is deemed to be a public corporation at each time in the specified period of the holding corporation at which the holding corporation would have satisfied conditions prescribed under subparagraph (b)(i) of the definition "public corporation" in subsection 89(1) if the words "shareholders, the dispersal of ownership of its shares and the public trading of its shares" in that subparagraph were read as "shareholders and the dispersal of ownership of its shares".

**Related Provisions:** 141(4) — Meaning of "specified period"; 141(5) — Shares of holding corporation deemed not to be taxable Canadian property.

**(4) Specified period** — For the purpose of subsection (3), the specified period of a corporation

(a) begins at the time the corporation becomes a holding corporation; and

(b) ends at the first time the corporation is a public corporation because of any provision of this Act other than subsection (3).

**(5) Exclusion from taxable Canadian property** — For the purpose of subparagraph 115(1)(b)(iv), a share of the capital stock of a corporation is deemed to be listed at any time on a stock exchange prescribed for the purpose of that subparagraph where

---

**Proposed Amendment — 141(5) opening words**

**(5) Exclusion from taxable Canadian property** — For the purpose of paragraph (d) of the definition "taxable Canadian property" in subsection 248(1), a share of the capital stock of a corporation is deemed to be listed at any time on a stock exchange prescribed for the purpose of that definition where

**Application:** Bill C-43 (First Reading September 20, 2000), s. 86, will amend the opening words of subsec. 141(5) to read as above, applicable after December 15, 1998.

**Technical Notes:** Under amendments contained in the 1999 budget bill (Bill C-25), new subsection 141(5) of the Act provides for shares issued by a life insurance corporation (or a holding corporation in respect of the life insurance corporation) to be considered, for the purposes of subparagraph 115(1)(b)(iv) of the Act, as listed on a stock exchange for up to six months after the demutualization of the life insurance corporation. As a consequence, such a share is not treated as taxable Canadian property during that period. This treatment accommodates non-resident shareholders wishing to dispose of such shares without Canadian income tax consequences before the shares become listed on a prescribed stock exchange.

Because of the relocation of the definition "taxable Canadian property" from subsection 115(1) to subsection 248(1)

of the Act, existing subparagraph 115(1)(b)(iv) is effectively being replaced by paragraph (d) of the definition "taxable Canadian property" in subsection 248(1).

This additional amendment to subsection 141(5) would simply change the reference to subparagraph 115(1)(b)(iv) to a reference to paragraph (d) of the definition "taxable Canadian property" in subsection 248(1). This amendment is intended to apply after December 15, 1998, in order to be consistent with the 1999 budget bill.

(a) the corporation is

(i) a life insurance corporation resident in Canada that has demutualized and that, at that time, would have satisfied conditions prescribed under subparagraph (b)(i) of the definition "public corporation" in subsection 89(1) if the words "shareholders, the dispersal of ownership of its shares and the public trading of its shares" in that subparagraph were read as "shareholders and the dispersal of ownership of its shares", or

(ii) a holding corporation that is deemed by subsection (3) to be a public corporation at that time;

(b) no share of the capital stock of the corporation is listed on any stock exchange at that time; and

(c) that time is not later than six months after the time of demutualization of

(i) the corporation, where the corporation is a life insurance corporation, and

(ii) in any other case, the life insurance corporation in respect of which the corporation is a holding corporation.

**Related Provisions**: 138(1) — Insurance corporations; 141.1 — Insurance corporation deemed not to be private corporation; 142 — Taxable capital gains of life insurer.

**Notes [s. 141]**: 141 renumbered as 141(2) and the rest of 141 added by 1999 Budget, effective December 16, 1998. 141 had not previously changed since 1972.

**Definitions [s. 141]**: "Canada" — 255; "corporation" — 248(1), *Interpretation Act* 35(1); "demutualization" — 139.1(1), 141(1); "dividend" — 248(1); "holding corporation" — 139.1(1), 141(1); "insurance corporation", "life insurance corporation" — 248(1); "month" — *Interpretation Act* 35(1); "prescribed" — 248(1); "public corporation" — 89(1), 248(1); "resident in Canada" — 250; "share" — 248(1); "specified period" — 141(4); "taxable Canadian property" — 248(1).

### 141.1 [Insurance corporation] deemed not to be a private corporation — Notwithstanding any other provision of this Act, an insurance corporation (other than a life insurance corporation) that would, but for this section, be a private corporation is deemed not to be a private corporation for the purposes of subsection 55(5), the definition "capital dividend account" in subsection 89(1) and sections 123.3 and 129.

**Related Provisions**: 141(2) — Life insurance corporation deemed to be public corporation.

**Notes**: Reference to 123.3 added, and an obsolete reference to former 89(1)(b.2) deleted, by 1995-97 technical bill, effective for taxation years that end after June 1995.

**Definitions [s. 141.1]**: "insurance corporation", "life insurance corporation" — 248(1); "private corporation" — 89(1), 248(1).

**I.T. Application Rules**: 69 (meaning of "*Income Tax Act*, chapter 148 of the Revised Statutes of Canada, 1952").

### 142. [Repealed]

**Notes**: 142 repealed by 1996 Budget, effective for 1997 and later taxation years (changed from 1996 at Second Reading of the Budget bill). This rule has been incorporated into 138(2)(b). For 1990–96, read:

142. Taxable capital gains etc. [of life insurer] — Notwithstanding any other provision of this Act, where in a taxation year a life insurer resident in Canada carries on an insurance business in Canada and in a country other than Canada, such of its taxable capital gains for the year and allowable capital losses for the year

(a) as were from dispositions of property used by it in the year in, or held by it in the year in the course of, carrying on an insurance business, and

(b) as were not from dispositions of property used by it in the year in, or held by it in the year in the course of, carrying on an insurance business in Canada,

shall not be included in computing its income for the year.

Opening words of 142 amended by 1991 technical bill, effective 1990, to be restricted to a resident of Canada. The same rule already applied to non-resident insurers under 115(1)(b)(ii.1).

### 142.1 [Repealed]

**Notes**: 142.1 repealed by 1996 Budget, effective for 1997 and later taxation years (changed from 1996 at Second Reading of the Budget bill). It provided that the definitions in subsection 138(12) applied to section 142. It was added in the R.S.C. 1985 (5th Supp.) consolidation, effective for taxation years ending after November 1991. This rule was formerly in the opening words of 138(12).

## Financial Institutions

### Interpretation

**142.2 (1) Definitions** — In this section and sections 142.3 to 142.6,

#### Proposed Amendment — 142.2(1) opening words

**142.2 (1) Definitions** — In this section and sections 142.3 to 142.7,

**Application**: The August 8, 2000 draft legislation, s. 10, will amend the opening words of subsec. 142.2(1) to read as above, applicable after June 27, 1999.

**Technical Notes**: Subsection 142.2(1) of the Act defines several terms for the purposes of the rules in sections 142.2 to 142.6 relating to securities held by financial institutions. These terms include "financial institution", "mark-to-market property" and "specified debt obligation". The subsection is amended to specify that the definitions also apply for the purposes of the new rules in section 142.7 of the Act relating to the conversion of foreign bank affiliates to branch operations.

This amendment applies after June 27, 1999.

**"financial institution"** at any time means

(a) a corporation that is, at that time,

(i) a corporation referred to in any of paragraphs (a) to (e.1) of the definition "restricted financial institution" in subsection 248(1),

(ii) an investment dealer, or

(iii) a corporation controlled by one or more persons or partnerships each of which is a financial institution at that time, other than a corporation the control of which was acquired by reason of the default of a debtor where it is reasonable to consider that control is being retained solely for the purpose of minimizing any losses in respect of the debtor's default, and

(b) a trust or partnership more than 50% of the fair market value of all interests in which are held at that time by one or more financial institutions,

but does not include

(c) a corporation that is, at that time,

(i) an investment corporation,

(ii) a mortgage investment corporation,

(iii) a mutual fund corporation, or

(iv) a deposit insurance corporation (as defined in subsection 137.1(5)),

(d) a trust that is a mutual fund trust at that time, nor

(e) a prescribed person or partnership;

**Related Provisions**: 20(1)(l)(ii) — Reserve for doubtful debts; 20(1)(p)(ii) — Deduction for bad debts; 85(1.4), 87(1.5) — Definition applies to other provisions; 87(2)(e.3), (e.4) — Amalgamations — continuing corporation; 94.1 — Foreign investment entities — accrual rules; 94.2 — Foreign investment entities — mark-to-market; 112(6)(c) — Definition applies to other provisions; 142.5 — Mark-to-market rules applicable to financial institution; 142.6(1) — Becoming or ceasing to be a financial institution; 248(1)"cost amount" — Definition applies to other provisions; 256(6)–(9) — Whether control acquired; Reg. 8103(4) — Mark-to-market — transition inclusion on ceasing to be a financial institution; Reg. 9204(2) — Residual portion of specified debt obligation on ceasing to be a financial institution.

**Notes**: 142.2(1)"financial institution"(a)(i) amended by 1998 Budget to change "(a) to (e)" to "(a) to (e.1)", effective for taxation years that begin after 1998.

See also Notes at end of 142.2.

**Regulations**: 8604 (prescribed financial institutions); 9000 (prescribed person for para. (e) — segregated fund).

**I.T. Technical News**: No. 14 (reporting of derivative income by mutual funds).

**"investment dealer"** at any time means a corporation that is, at that time, a registered securities dealer;

**Related Provisions**: 142.2(1)"financial institution" — Investment dealer is a financial institution; 142.2(1)"mark-to-market property"(c) — debt held by investment dealer subject to mark-to-market rules.

**"mark-to-market property"** of a taxpayer for a taxation year means property held by the taxpayer in the year that is

(a) a share,

(b) where the taxpayer is not an investment dealer, a specified debt obligation that

(i) was carried at fair market value in the taxpayer's financial statements

(A) for the year, where the taxpayer held the obligation at the end of the year, and

(B) for each preceding taxation year that ended after the taxpayer acquired the obligation, or

(ii) was acquired and disposed of in the year, where it is reasonable to expect that the obligation would have been carried in the taxpayer's financial statements for the year at fair market value if the taxpayer had not disposed of the obligation,

other than a specified debt obligation of the taxpayer that was (or would have been) carried at fair market value

(iii) solely because its fair market value was less than its cost to the taxpayer, or

(iv) because of a default of the debtor, and

(c) where the taxpayer is an investment dealer, a specified debt obligation,

but does not include

(d) a share of a corporation in which the taxpayer has a significant interest at any time in the year, nor

(e) a prescribed property;

**Related Provisions**: 85(1.4), 87(1.5) — Definition applies to other provisions; 87(2)(e.4), (e.5) — Amalgamations — continuing corporation; 88(1)(h) — Windup — continuing corporation; 94.1(1)"exempt interest"(c) — Mark-to-market property excluded from foreign investment entity accrual rules; 112(6)(c) — Definition applies to other provisions; 136(1) — Cooperative not private corporation — exception; 138(11.5)(k.2) — Transfer of business by non-resident insurer; 142.2(2), (3), (5) — Significant interest; 142.3(3) — Mark-to-market property not subject to rules re income from specified debt obligations; 142.5 — Mark-to-market rules; 248(1)"cost amount" — Definition applies to other provisions; 248(1)"cost amount"(c.1) — Cost amount of mark-to-market property; Reg. 6209(b)(i) — Prescribed securities for lending assets.

**Regulations**: 9001(2), 9002 (prescribed property for para. (e)).

**"specified debt obligation"** of a taxpayer means the interest held by the taxpayer in

(a) a loan, bond, debenture, mortgage, note, agreement of sale or any other similar indebtedness, or

(b) a debt obligation, where the taxpayer purchased the interest,

other than an interest in

(c) an income bond, an income debenture, a small business development bond, a small business bond or a prescribed property, or

**S. 142.2(1) spe**  Income Tax Act, Part I

(d) an instrument issued by or made with a person to whom the taxpayer is related or with whom the taxpayer does not otherwise deal at arm's length, or in which the taxpayer has a significant interest.

**Related Provisions**: 85(1.4), 87(1.5) — Definition applies to other provisions; 87(2)(e.3) — Amalgamation of holder of obligation; 138(11.5)(k.1) — Definition applies to other provisions; 142.2(1)"mark-to-market property"(b), (c) — Mark-to-market rules for financial institutions; 142.2(2), (3) — Meaning of "significant interest"; 142.3(1) — Income from specified debt obligations; 142.4 — Disposition of specified debt obligation; 142.5 — Mark-to-market rules for financial institutions; 248(1)"cost amount" — Definition applies to other provisions; 248(1)"cost amount"(d.2) — Cost amount of specified debt obligation; 248(1) — Definition of "lending asset"; Reg. 6209(b)(ii) — Prescribed securities for lending assets.

**Regulations**: 9004 (prescribed property).

**(2) Significant interest** — For the purpose of subsection (5) and the definition "mark-to-market property" in subsection (1), a taxpayer has a significant interest in a corporation at any time if

(a) the taxpayer is related (otherwise than because of a right referred to in paragraph 251(5)(b)) to the corporation at that time; or

(b) the taxpayer holds, at that time,

(i) shares of the corporation that give the taxpayer 10% or more of the votes that could be cast under all circumstances at an annual meeting of shareholders of the corporation, and

(ii) shares of the corporation having a fair market value of 10% or more of the fair market value of all the issued shares of the corporation.

**Related Provisions**: 142.2(3) — Rules for determining significant interest; 142.2(4) — Extended meaning of "related".

**Notes**: See at end of 142.2.

**(3) Rules re significant interest** — For the purpose of determining under subsection (2) whether a taxpayer has a significant interest in a corporation at any time,

(a) the taxpayer shall be deemed to hold each share that is held at that time by a person or partnership to whom the taxpayer is related (otherwise than because of a right referred to in paragraph 251(5)(b));

(b) a share of the corporation acquired by the taxpayer by reason of the default of a debtor shall be disregarded where it is reasonable to consider that the share is being retained for the purpose of minimizing any losses in respect of the debtor's default; and

(c) a share of the corporation that is prescribed in respect of the taxpayer shall be disregarded.

**Related Provisions**: 142.2(4) — Extended meaning of "related".

**Regulations**: 9003 (prescribed share for 142.2(3)(c)).

**(4) Extension of meaning of "related"** — For the purposes of this subsection and subsections (2) and (3), a person or partnership shall be deemed to be related to a person or partnership where they would be related if, for the purpose of section 251,

(a) every partnership and trust were considered to be a corporation;

(b) subject to paragraph (c), all decisions relating to the conduct of a trust were made by majority vote of the beneficiaries of the trust, with each beneficiary having, at any time, a number of votes equal to the number determined by the formula

$$100 \times \frac{A}{B}$$

where

A  is the fair market value at that time of the beneficiary's beneficial interest in the trust, and

B  is the total of all amounts each of which is the fair market value at that time of a beneficial interest in the trust; and

(c) where the amount that would be determined for B in paragraph (b) in respect of a trust is nil, the trust were considered not to be controlled by any person, partnership or group each member of which is a person or partnership.

**(5) Significant interest — transition** — For the purpose of the definition "mark-to-market property" in subsection (1), where

(a) on October 31, 1994, a taxpayer whose 1994 taxation year ends after October 30, 1994 held a share of a corporation in which the taxpayer did not have a significant interest at any time in the year, and

(b) at any time after the end of the year and before May 1995, the taxpayer has a significant interest in the corporation,

the taxpayer has a significant interest in the corporation in the year and in any subsequent taxation year ending before the earliest time referred to in paragraph (b).

**Related Provisions**: 142.2(2), (3) — Significant interest.

**Notes**: 142.2 added by 1994 tax amendments bill (Part III), effective for taxation years that end after February 22, 1994.

**Definitions [s. 142.2]**: "acquired" — 256(7)–(9); "control" — 256(6)–(9); "controlled" — 256(6), (6.1); "corporation" — 248(1), Interpretation Act 35(1); "financial institution" — 142.2(1); "fiscal period" — 249(2)(b), 249.1; "income bond", "income debenture", "indexed", "investment corporation" — 130(3)(a), 248(1); "investment dealer" — 142.2(1); "mortgage investment corporation" — 130.1(6), 248(1); "mutual fund corporation" — 131(8), 248(1); "mutual fund trust" — 132(6)–(7), 132.2(1)(q), 248(1); "partnership" — see Notes to 96(1); "person", "prescribed", "property", "registered securities dealer" — 248(1); "related" — 142.2(4), 251(2); "share", "shareholder" — 248(1); "significant interest" — 142.2(2), (3); "small business bond" — 15.2(3), 248(1); "small business development bond" — 15.1(3), 248(1); "specified debt obligation" — 142.2(1); "taxation year" — 249; "taxpayer" — 248(1); "trust" — 104(1), 248(1).

## Income from Specified Debt Obligations

**142.3 (1) Amounts to be included and deducted** — Subject to subsections (3) and (4), where a taxpayer that is, in a taxation year, a financial institution holds a specified debt obligation at any time in the year,

(a) there shall be included in computing the income of the taxpayer for the year the amount, if any, prescribed in respect of the obligation;

(b) there shall be deducted in computing the income of the taxpayer for the year the amount, if any, prescribed in respect of the obligation; and

(c) except as provided by this section, paragraphs 12(1)(d) and (i) and 20(1)(l) and (p) and section 142.4, no amount shall be included or deducted in respect of payments under the obligation (other than fees and similar amounts) in computing the income of the taxpayer for the year.

**Related Provisions**: 87(2)(e.3) — Amalgamations — continuing corporation; 138(10)(a) — Application to insurance corporation; 138(12)"gross investment revenue"E(a), 138(12)"gross investment revenue"G(b) — Gross investment revenue of insurer; 142.3(3) — Exception for certain obligations; 142.3(4) — Impaired specified debt obligations; 142.4(1)"tax basis"(b), (i) — Disposition of specified debt obligation by financial institution; 142.4(9) — Disposition of part of obligation.

**Notes**: Opening words of 142.3(1) amended to change reference from subsec. (2) to subsec. (3) retroactive to its introduction, and to add reference to subsec. (4) effective on the same basis as the addition of 142.3(4), by 1995-97 technical bill.

142.3(1)(c) amended retroactive to its introduction by 1995-97 technical bill, to change "this subsection" to "this section". The effect is to allow new 142.3(2) to apply with respect to the determination of amounts to be included or deducted in respect of specified debt obligations.

For initial enactment of 142.3(1) see Notes at end of 142.3.

**Regulations**: 9101 (prescribed amounts).

**(2) Failure to report accrued amounts** — Subject to subsection (3), where

(a) a taxpayer holds a specified debt obligation at any time in a particular taxation year in which the taxpayer is a financial institution, and

(b) all or part of an amount required by paragraph (1)(a) or subsection 12(3) to be included in respect of the obligation in computing the taxpayer's income for a preceding taxation year was not so included,

that part of the amount shall be included in computing the taxpayer's income for the particular year, to the extent that it was not included in computing the taxpayer's income for a preceding taxation year.

**Related Provisions**: 142.3(3) — Exception for certain obligations; 142.4(1)"tax basis"(b) — Disposition of specified debt obligation by financial institution.

**Notes**: 142.3(2) added by 1995-97 technical bill, effective retroactive to the introduction of 142.3 (see Notes at end of 142.3). Former 142.3(2) was moved to 142.3(3).

**(3) Exception for certain obligations** — Subsections (1) and (2) do not apply for a taxation year in respect of a taxpayer's specified debt obligation that is

(a) a mark-to-market property for the year; or

(b) an indexed debt obligation, other than a prescribed obligation.

**Notes**: 142.3(3) renumbered from 142.3(2) and amended to refer to new subsec. (2) by 1995-97 technical bill, effective retroactive to the introduction of 142.3 (see Notes at end of 142.3).

**(4) Impaired specified debt obligations** — Subsection (1) does not apply to a taxpayer in respect of a specified debt obligation for the part of a taxation year throughout which the obligation is impaired where an amount in respect of the obligation is deductible because of subparagraph 20(1)(l)(ii) in computing the taxpayer's income for the year.

**Notes**: 142.3(4) added by 1995-97 technical bill, effective

(a) for taxation years that end after September 1997; and

(b) for taxation years that end after 1995 and before October 1997, if the taxpayer files an election for amended 20(1)(l) to apply to such years (see Notes to 20(1)(l)).

**Notes [s. 142.3]**: 142.3 added by 1994 tax amendments bill (Part III), effective for taxation years that end after February 22, 1994, except that it does not apply to debt obligations disposed of before February 23, 1994.

**Definitions [s. 142.3]**: "amount" — 248(1); "financial institution", "investment dealer", "mark-to-market property" — 142.2(1); "prescribed" — 248(1); "specified debt obligation" — 142.2(1); "taxation year" — 249; "taxpayer" — 248(1).

## Disposition of Specified Debt Obligations

**142.4 (1) Definitions** — In this section,

**"tax basis"** of a specified debt obligation at any time to a taxpayer means the amount, if any, by which the total of all amounts each of which is

(a) the cost of the obligation to the taxpayer,

(b) an amount included under subsection 12(3) or 16(2) or (3), paragraph 142.3(1)(a) or subsection 142.3(2) in respect of the obligation in computing the taxpayer's income for a taxation year that began before that time,

(c) subject to subsection 138(13), where the taxpayer acquired the obligation in a taxation year ending before February 23, 1994, the part of the amount, if any, by which

(i) the principal amount of the obligation at the time it was acquired

exceeds

(ii) the cost to the taxpayer of the obligation

that was included in computing the taxpayer's income for a taxation year ending before February 23, 1994,

(d) subject to subsection 138(13), where the taxpayer is a life insurer, an amount in respect of the obligation that was deemed by paragraph

142(3)(a) of the *Income Tax Act*, chapter 148 of the Revised Statutes of Canada, 1952, as it read in its application to the 1977 taxation year, to be a gain for a taxation year ending before 1978,

(e) where the obligation is an indexed debt obligation, an amount determined under subparagraph 16(6)(a)(i) in respect of the obligation and included in computing the income of the taxpayer for a taxation year beginning before that time,

(f) an amount in respect of the obligation that was included in computing the taxpayer's income for a taxation year ending at or before that time in respect of changes in the value of the obligation attributable to the fluctuation in the value of a currency of a country other than Canada relative to Canadian currency, other than an amount included under paragraph 142.3(1)(a),

(g) an amount in respect of the obligation that was included under paragraph 12(1)(i) in computing the taxpayer's income for a taxation year beginning before that time, or

(h) where the obligation was a capital property of the taxpayer on February 22, 1994, an amount required by paragraph 53(1)(f) or (f.1) to be added in computing the adjusted cost base of the obligation to the taxpayer on that day

exceeds the total of all amounts each of which is

(i) an amount deducted under paragraph 142.3(1)(b) in respect of the obligation in computing the taxpayer's income for a taxation year beginning before that time,

(j) the amount of a payment received by the taxpayer under the obligation at or before that time, other than

(i) a fee or similar payment, and

(ii) proceeds of disposition of the obligation,

(k) subject to subsection 138(13), where the taxpayer acquired the obligation in a taxation year ending before February 23, 1994, the part of the amount, if any, by which

(i) the cost to the taxpayer of the obligation

exceeds

(ii) the principal amount of the obligation at the time it was acquired

that was deducted in computing the taxpayer's income for a taxation year ending before February 23, 1994,

(l) subject to subsection 138(13), where the taxpayer is a life insurer, an amount in respect of the obligation that was deemed by paragraph 142(3)(b) of the *Income Tax Act*, chapter 148 of the Revised Statutes of Canada, 1952, as it read in its application to the 1977 taxation year, to be a loss for a taxation year ending before 1978,

(m) an amount that was deducted under subsection 20(14) in respect of the obligation in computing the taxpayer's income for a taxation year beginning before that time,

(n) where the obligation is an indexed debt obligation, an amount determined under subparagraph 16(6)(a)(ii) in respect of the obligation and deducted in computing the income of the taxpayer for a taxation year beginning before that time,

(o) an amount in respect of the obligation that was deducted in computing the taxpayer's income for a taxation year ending at or before that time in respect of changes in the value of the obligation attributable to the fluctuation in the value of a currency of a country other than Canada relative to Canadian currency, other than an amount deducted under paragraph 142.3(1)(b),

(p) an amount in respect of the obligation that was deducted under paragraph 20(1)(p) in computing the taxpayer's income for a taxation year ending at or before that time, or

(q) where the obligation was a capital property of the taxpayer on February 22, 1994, an amount required by paragraph 53(2)(b.2) or (g) to be deducted in computing the adjusted cost base of the obligation to the taxpayer on that day;

**Related Provisions**: 138(13) — Variation in tax basis of certain insurers; 248(1)"cost amount"(d.2) — Cost amount of specified debt obligation is tax basis.

**Notes**: Definition "tax basis" added with the enactment of 142.4 by 1994 tax amendments bill (Part III), effective for taxation years that end after February 22, 1994; and amended retroactive to its introduction by 1995-97 technical bill. The amendments added a reference to 142.3(2) in para. (b); and amended para. (j) to add subpara. (j)(i) and to have the para. apply to all payments rather than only those included under paras. (a)-(f).

**"transition amount"** of a taxpayer in respect of the disposition of a specified debt obligation has the meaning assigned by regulation.

**Related Provisions**: 142.4(7)A — Current amount based on transition amount.

**Regulations**: 9201 (transition amount).

**(2) Scope of section** — This section applies to the disposition of a specified debt obligation by a taxpayer that is a financial institution, except that this section does not apply to the disposition of a specified debt obligation that is a mark-to-market property for the taxation year in which the disposition occurs.

**Related Provisions**: 87(2)(e.3) — Amalgamations — continuing corporation; 138(10)(b) — Application to insurance corporation; 142.3(1)(c) — Amount deductible in respect of specified debt obligation; 142.4(9) — Disposition of part of obligation.

**Notes**: See at end of 142.4.

**(3) Rules applicable to disposition** — Where a taxpayer has disposed of a specified debt obligation after February 22, 1994,

(a) except as provided by paragraph 79.1(7)(d) or this section, no amount shall be included or de-

Division F — Special Rules in Certain Circumstances  S. 142.4(6)(b)

ducted in respect of the disposition in computing the taxpayer's income; and

(b) except where the obligation is an indexed debt obligation (other than a prescribed obligation), paragraph 20(14)(a) shall not apply in respect of the disposition.

**Related Provisions**: 142.4(2) — Scope of section.

**Notes**: 142.4(3) added with the enactment of 142.4 by 1994 tax amendments bill (Part III), effective for taxation years that end after February 22, 1994; and amended retroactive to its introduction by 1995-97 technical bill to add reference to 79.1(7)(d).

**(4) Inclusions and deductions re disposition** — Subject to subsection (5), where after 1994 a taxpayer disposes of a specified debt obligation in a taxation year,

(a) where the transition amount in respect of the disposition of the obligation is positive, it shall be included in computing the income of the taxpayer for the year;

(b) where the transition amount in respect of the disposition of the obligation is negative, the absolute value of the transition amount shall be deducted in computing the income of the taxpayer for the year;

(c) where the taxpayer has a gain from the disposition of the obligation,

(i) the current amount of the gain shall be included in computing the income of the taxpayer for the year, and

(ii) there shall be included in computing the taxpayer's income for taxation years that end on or after the day of disposition the amount allocated, in accordance with prescribed rules, to the year in respect of the residual portion of the gain; and

(d) where the taxpayer has a loss from the disposition of the obligation,

(i) the current amount of the loss shall be deducted in computing the taxpayer's income for the year, and

(ii) there shall be deducted in computing the taxpayer's income for taxation years that end on or after the day of disposition the amount allocated, in accordance with prescribed rules, to the year in respect of the residual portion of the loss.

**Related Provisions**: 39(1)(a)(ii.2) — No capital gain on disposition; 87(2)(g.2) — Amalgamations — continuing corporation; 142.4(2) — Scope of section; 142.4(5) — Where subsec. (4) does not apply; 142.4(7) — Current amount; 142.4(8) — Residual portion; 142.4(9) — Disposition of part of obligation; 142.4(11) — Payments received on or after disposition; Reg. 2405(3)"gross Canadian life investment income"(d.1), (i.1) — Inclusion in/deduction from life insurer's income; Reg. 2411(4.1) — Inclusion in insurer's net investment revenue.

**Notes**: 142.4(4) added with the enactment of 142.4 by 1994 tax amendments bill (Part III), effective for taxation years that end after February 22, 1994; and amended retroactive to its introduction by 1995-97 technical bill to change "current amount" to "transition amount" and to add subparas. (c)(i) and (d)(i). (Other changes were cosmetic.)

**Regulations**: 9203, 9204 (prescribed rules — residual portion).

**(5) Gain or loss not amortized** — Where after February 22, 1994 a taxpayer disposes of a specified debt obligation in a taxation year, and

(a) the obligation is

(i) an indexed debt obligation (other than a prescribed obligation), or

(ii) a debt obligation prescribed in respect of the taxpayer,

(b) the disposition occurred

(i) before 1995,

(ii) after 1994 in connection with the transfer of all or part of a business of the taxpayer to a person or partnership, or

(iii) because of paragraph 142.6(1)(c), or

(c) in the case of a taxpayer other than a life insurance corporation,

(i) the disposition occurred before 1996, and

(ii) the taxpayer elects in writing, filed with the Minister before July 1997, to have this paragraph apply,

the following rules apply:

(d) subsection (4) does not apply to the disposition,

(e) there shall be included in computing the taxpayer's income for the year the amount, if any, by which the taxpayer's proceeds of disposition exceed the tax basis of the obligation to the taxpayer immediately before the disposition, and

(f) there shall be deducted in computing the taxpayer's income for the year the amount, if any, by which the tax basis of the obligation to the taxpayer immediately before the disposition exceeds the taxpayer's proceeds of disposition.

**Related Provisions**: 39(1)(a)(ii.2) — No capital gain on disposition; 142.4(2) — Scope of section; Reg. 2411(4)A(c.1), 2411(4)B(a.1) — Inclusion in insurer's net investment revenue.

**Notes**: 142.4(5) added with the enactment of 142.4 by 1994 tax amendments bill (Part III), effective for taxation years that end after February 22, 1994; and amended retroactive to its introduction by 1995-97 technical bill to add para. (c) [thus renumbering (c)–(e) as (d)–(f)] and to provide explicit calculations in (e) and (f) rather than simply referring to the "gain" or "loss".

**Regulations**: 9202(2), (4), (5) (debt obligations prescribed for 142.2(5)(a)(ii)).

**(6) Gain or loss from disposition of obligation** — For the purposes of this section,

(a) where the amount determined under paragraph (c) in respect of the disposition of a specified debt obligation by a taxpayer is positive, that amount is the taxpayer's gain from the disposition of the obligation;

(b) where the amount determined under paragraph (c) in respect of the disposition of a specified debt obligation by a taxpayer is negative, the absolute value of that amount is the taxpayer's loss from the disposition of the obligation; and

(c) the amount determined under this paragraph in respect of the disposition of a specified debt obligation by a taxpayer is the positive or negative amount determined by the formula

$$A - (B + C)$$

where

A  is the taxpayer's proceeds of disposition,

B  is the tax basis of the obligation to the taxpayer immediately before the time of disposition, and

C  is the taxpayer's transition amount in respect of the disposition.

**Related Provisions**: 257 — Formula cannot calculate to less than zero.

**Notes**: 142.4(6) added with the enactment of 142.4 by 1994 tax amendments bill (Part III), effective for taxation years that end after February 22, 1994; and amended retroactive to its introduction by 1995-97 technical bill to add "the absolute value of" in 142.4(6)(b), and to have formula element C always be the transition amount, rather than only being the transition amount if 142.4(4) applied and nil otherwise. (Thus, the transition amount is always taken into account in determining the gain or loss.)

**(7) Current amount** — For the purposes of subsections (4) and (8), the current amount of a taxpayer's gain or loss from the disposition of a specified debt obligation is

(a) where the taxpayer has a gain from the disposition of the obligation, the part, if any, of the gain that is reasonably attributable to a material increase in the probability, or perceived probability, that the debtor will make all payments as required by the obligation; and

(b) where the taxpayer has a loss from the disposition of the obligation, the amount that the taxpayer claims not exceeding the part, if any, of the loss that is reasonably attributable to a default by the debtor or a material decrease in the probability, or perceived probability, that the debtor will make all payments as required by the obligation.

**Notes**: 142.4(7) added with the enactment of 142.4 by 1994 tax amendments bill (Part III), effective for taxation years that end after February 22, 1994; and amended retroactive to its introduction by 1995-97 technical bill to add reference to subsec. (8) and to remove a formula element A which added the transition amount to the total (formerly B, now the body of paras. (a) and (b)).

**(8) Residual portion of gain or loss** — For the purpose of subsection (4), the residual portion of a taxpayer's gain or loss from the disposition of a specified debt obligation is the amount, if any, by which the gain or loss exceeds the current amount of the gain or loss.

**Related Provisions**: 142.4(7) — Current amount.

**Notes**: 142.4(8) added with the enactment of 142.4 by 1994 tax amendments bill (Part III), effective for taxation years that end after February 22, 1994; and amended retroactive to its introduction by 1995-97 technical bill in consequence of the amendments to 142.4(7).

**(9) Disposition of part of obligation** — Where a taxpayer disposes of part of a specified debt obligation, section 142.3 and this section apply as if the part disposed of and the part retained were separate specified debt obligations.

**Related Provisions**: 248(27) — Partial forgiveness of debt obligation — effect on debtor.

**Notes**: 142.4(9) added with the enactment of 142.4 by 1994 tax amendments bill (Part III), effective for taxation years that end after February 22, 1994; and amended retroactive to its introduction by 1995-97 technical bill to add reference to 142.3.

**(10) Penalties and bonuses** — Notwithstanding subsection 18(9.1), where a taxpayer that holds a specified debt obligation receives a penalty or bonus because of the repayment before maturity of all or part of the principal amount of the debt obligation, the payment is deemed to be received by the taxpayer as proceeds of disposition of the specified debt obligation.

**Notes**: 142.4(10) added by 1995-97 technical bill, effective for taxation years that end after February 22, 1994 (i.e., retroactive to the introduction of 142.4).

**(11) Payments received on or after disposition** — For the purposes of this section, where at any time a taxpayer receives a payment (other than proceeds of disposition) under a specified debt obligation on or after the disposition of the obligation, the payment is deemed not to have been so received at that time but to have been so received immediately before the disposition.

**Notes [subsec. 142.4(11)]**: 142.4(11) added by 1995-97 technical bill, effective for taxation years that end after February 22, 1994 (i.e., retroactive to the introduction of 142.4).

**Notes [s. 142.4]**: 142.4 added by 1994 tax amendments bill (Part III), effective for taxation years that end after February 22, 1994.

**Definitions [s. 142.4]**: "adjusted cost base" — 54, 248(1); "amount" — 248(1); "capital property" — 54, 248(1); "current amount" — 142.4(7); "financial institution" — 142.2(1); "indexed debt obligation" — 248(1); "investment dealer" — 142.2(1); "life insurance corporation", "life insurer" — 248(1); "mark-to-market property" — 142.2(1); "Minister" — 248(1); "partnership" — see Notes to 96(1); "person", "prescribed", "principal amount", "regulation" — 248(1); "residual portion" — 142.4(8); "specified debt obligation" — 142.2(1); "tax basis" — 142.4(1); "taxation year" — 249; "taxpayer" — 248(1); "transition amount" — 142.4(1); "writing" — *Interpretation Act* 35(1).

## *Mark-to-Market Properties*

**142.5 (1) Income treatment for profits and losses** — Where, in a taxation year that begins after October 1994, a taxpayer that is a financial institution in the year disposes of a property that is a mark-to-market property for the year,

(a) there shall be included in computing the taxpayer's income for the year the profit, if any, from the disposition; and

Division F — Special Rules in Certain Circumstances  S. 142.5(7)

(b) there shall be deducted in computing the taxpayer's income for the year the loss, if any, from the disposition.

**Related Provisions**: 39(1)(a)(ii.2) — No capital gain on disposition; 138(10)(a) — Application to insurance corporation; 142.5(2) — Deemed disposition at year-end.

**Notes**: See at end of 142.5.

**(2) Mark-to-market requirement** — Where a taxpayer that is a financial institution in a taxation year holds, at the end of the year, a mark-to-market property for the year, the taxpayer shall be deemed

(a) to have disposed of the property immediately before the end of the year for proceeds equal to its fair market value at the time of disposition, and

(b) to have reacquired the property at the end of the year at a cost equal to those proceeds.

**Related Provisions**: 54"superficial loss"(c) — Superficial loss rule does not apply; 88(1)(i) — Windup of subsidiary into parent; 112(5.6)(a)(i) — Stop-loss rules inapplicable; 138(10)(a) — Application to insurance corporation; 138(11.31)(a) — Change in use rules for insurer do not apply; 142.5(4)–(9) — Transitional rules; 142.6(2) — Acquisition date under 142.5(2) to be ignored; 142.6(8)–(10) — Transitional election re year that includes February 22, 1994; Reg. 2405(5) — 142.5(2) to be ignored for definitions in Reg. 2405(3).

**Notes**: See at end of 142.5.

**I.T. Technical News**: No. 14 (reporting of derivative income by mutual funds).

**(3) Mark-to-market debt obligation** — Where a taxpayer is a financial institution in a particular taxation year that begins after October 1994, the following rules apply with respect to a specified debt obligation that is a mark-to-market property of the taxpayer for the particular year:

(a) paragraph 12(1)(c) and subsections 12(3) and 20(14) and (21) do not apply to the obligation in computing the taxpayer's income for the particular year;

(b) there shall be included in computing the taxpayer's income for the particular year an amount received by the taxpayer in the particular year as, on account of, in lieu of payment of, or in satisfaction of, interest on the obligation, to the extent that the interest was not included in computing the taxpayer's income for a preceding taxation year; and

(c) for the purpose of paragraph (b), where the taxpayer was deemed by subsection (2) or paragraph 142.6(1)(b) to have disposed of the obligation in a preceding taxation year, no part of an amount included in computing the income of the taxpayer for that preceding year because of the disposition shall be considered to be in respect of interest on the obligation.

**Related Provisions**: 138(10)(a) — Application to insurance corporation.

**(4) Transition — deduction re non-capital amounts** — There may be deducted in computing the income of a taxpayer for the taxpayer's taxation year that includes October 31, 1994 such amount as the taxpayer claims not exceeding a prescribed amount in respect of properties (other than capital properties) disposed of by the taxpayer because of subsection (2).

**Related Provisions**: 138(11.5)(k) — Transfer of business by non-resident insurer; 142.5(5) — Inclusion re non-capital amounts.

**Regulations**: 8102(2) (prescribed amount).

**(5) Transition — inclusion re non-capital amounts** — Where an amount is deducted under subsection (4) in computing a taxpayer's income, there shall be included, in computing the taxpayer's income for each taxation year that begins before 1999 and ends after October 30, 1994, the total of all amounts prescribed for the year.

**Related Provisions**: 87(2)(g.2) — Amalgamations — continuing corporation; 138(11.5)(k) — Transfer of business by non-resident insurer; Reg. 2402(a.1)A — Inclusion in income from participating life insurance business.

**Notes**: 142.5(5) added with the enactment of 142.5 by 1994 tax amendments bill (Part III), effective for taxation years that end after October 30, 1994; and amended retroactive to its introduction by 1995-97 technical bill to change "the prescribed portion for the year of the amount so deducted" to "the total of all amounts prescribed for the year". This merely modifies the way 142.5(5) confers regulation-making authority.

**Regulations**: 8103 (prescribed amount).

**(6) Transition — deduction re net capital gains** — Such amount as a taxpayer elects, not exceeding a prescribed amount in respect of capital properties disposed of by the taxpayer because of subsection (2), is deemed to be an allowable capital loss of the taxpayer for its taxation year that includes October 31, 1994 from the disposition of property (or, where the taxpayer is non-resident throughout the year, from the disposition of taxable Canadian property).

**Related Provisions**: 138(11.5)(k) — Transfer of business by non-resident insurer; 142.5(7) — Inclusion re net capital gains.

**Notes**: 142.5(6) added with the enactment of 142.5 by 1994 tax amendments bill (Part III), effective for taxation years that end after October 30, 1994; and amended retroactive to its introduction by 1995-97 technical bill to add the parenthesized words.

**Regulations**: 8104(2) (prescribed amount).

**(7) Transition — inclusion re net capital gains** — A taxpayer that elects an amount under subsection (6) is deemed, for each taxation year that begins before 1999 and ends after October 30, 1994, to have a taxable capital gain for the year from the disposition of property (or, where the taxpayer is non-resident throughout the year, from the disposition of taxable Canadian property) equal to the total of all amounts prescribed for the year.

**Related Provisions**: 87(2)(g.2) — Amalgamations — continuing corporation; 138(11.5)(k) — Transfer of business by non-resident insurer; Reg. 2402(a.1)B — Inclusion in income from participating life insurance business.

**Notes**: 142.5(7) added with the enactment of 142.5 by 1994 tax amendments bill (Part III), effective for taxation years that end after October 30, 1994; and amended retroactive to its introduction by

S. 142.5(7) Income Tax Act, Part I

1995-97 technical bill to add the parenthesized words, and to change "the prescribed portion for the year of the amount so deducted" to "the total of all amounts prescribed for the year".

**Regulations**: 8105(2) (prescribed amount).

**(8) First deemed disposition of debt obligation** — Where

(a) in a particular taxation year that ends after October 30, 1994, a taxpayer disposed of a specified debt obligation that is a mark-to-market property of the taxpayer for the following taxation year, and

(b) either

(i) the disposition occurred because of subsection (2) and the particular year includes October 31, 1994, or

(ii) the disposition occurred because of paragraph 142.6(1)(b),

the following rules apply:

(c) subsection 20(21) does not apply to the disposition, and

(d) where

(i) an amount has been deducted under paragraph 20(1)(p) in respect of the obligation in computing the taxpayer's income for the particular year or a preceding taxation year, and

(ii) section 12.4 does not apply to the disposition,

there shall be included in computing the taxpayer's income for the particular year the amount, if any, by which

(iii) the total of all amounts referred to in subparagraph (i)

exceeds

(iv) the total of all amounts included under paragraph 12(1)(i) in respect of the obligation in computing the taxpayer's income for the particular year or a preceding taxation year.

**(9) Transition — property acquired on rollover** — Where

(a) a taxpayer acquired a property before October 31, 1994 at a cost less than the fair market value of the property at the time of acquisition,

(b) the property was transferred, directly or indirectly, to the taxpayer by a person that would never have been a financial institution before the transfer if the definition "financial institution" in subsection 142.2(1) had always applied,

(c) the cost is less than the fair market value because subsection 85(1) applied in respect of the disposition of the property by the person, and

(d) subsection (2) deemed the taxpayer to have disposed of the property in its particular taxation year that includes October 31, 1994,

the following rules apply:

(e) where the taxpayer would, but for this paragraph, have a taxable capital gain for the particular year from the disposition of the property, the part of the taxable capital gain that can reasonably be considered to have arisen while the property was held by a person described in paragraph (b) shall be deemed to be a taxable capital gain of the taxpayer from the disposition of the property for the taxation year in which the taxpayer disposes of the property otherwise than because of subsection (2), and not to be a taxable capital gain for the particular year, and

(f) where the taxpayer has a profit (other than a capital gain) from the disposition of the property, the part of the profit that can reasonably be considered to have arisen while the property was held by a person described in paragraph (b) shall be included in computing the taxpayer's income for the taxation year in which the taxpayer disposes of the property otherwise than because of subsection (2), and shall not be included in computing the taxpayer's income for the particular year.

**Notes**: 142.5 added by 1994 tax amendments bill (Part III), effective for taxation years that end after October 30, 1994.

**Definitions [s. 142.5]**: "allowable capital loss" — 38(b), 248(1); "amount" — 248(1); "capital gain" — 39(1)(a), 248(1); "capital property" — 54, 248(1); "financial institution", "mark-to-market property" — 142.2(1); "non-resident", "prescribed", "property" — 248(1); "specified debt obligation" — 142.2(1); "taxable Canadian property" — 248(1); "taxable capital gain" — 38(a), 248(1); "taxation year" — 249; "taxpayer" — 248(1).

## Additional Rules

**142.6 (1) Becoming or ceasing to be a financial institution** — Where, at a particular time after February 22, 1994, a taxpayer becomes or ceases to be a financial institution,

(a) where a taxation year of the taxpayer would not, but for this paragraph, end immediately before the particular time,

(i) except for the purpose of subsection 132(6.1), the taxpayer's taxation year that would otherwise have included the particular time is deemed to have ended immediately before that time and a new taxation year of the taxpayer is deemed to have begun at that time, and

(ii) for the purpose of determining the taxpayer's fiscal period after the particular time, the taxpayer shall be deemed not to have established a fiscal period before that time;

(b) where the taxpayer becomes a financial institution, the taxpayer shall be deemed to have disposed, immediately before the end of its taxation year that ends immediately before the particular time, of each property held by the taxpayer that is

(i) a specified debt obligation (other than a mark-to-market property for the year), or

(ii) where the year ends after October 30, 1994, a mark-to-market property for the year

for proceeds equal to its fair market value at the time of disposition;

(c) where the taxpayer ceases to be a financial institution, the taxpayer shall be deemed to have disposed, immediately before the end of its taxation year that ends immediately before the particular time, of each property held by the taxpayer that is a specified debt obligation (other than a mark-to-market property of the taxpayer for the year), for proceeds equal to its fair market value at the time of disposition; and

(d) the taxpayer shall be deemed to have reacquired, at the end of the taxation year referred to in paragraph (b) or (c), each property deemed by that paragraph to have been disposed of by the taxpayer, at a cost equal to the proceeds of disposition of the property.

**Related Provisions**: 54"superficial loss"(c) — Superficial loss rule does not apply to disposition under 142.6(1)(b); 87(2)(g.2) — Application of rule to predecessors corporation on amalgamation; 112(5.6)(a)(ii) — Stop-loss rules inapplicable; 142.4(5)(b)(iii) — Gain or loss not amortized; 142.5(8)(b)(ii) — First deemed disposition of debt obligation; 142.6(2) — Acquisition date under 142.6(1) to be ignored.

**Notes**: 142.6(1)(a)(i) amended by 1998 Budget to add "except for the purpose of subsection 132(6.1)," effective 1998.

142.6(1) added by 1994 tax amendments bill (Part III), effective February 23, 1994.

### Proposed Addition — 142.6(1.1)–(1.3)

**Technical Notes**: Section 142.6 contains rules dealing with special situations involving securities held by financial institutions. This section is amended by adding new subsections 142.6(1.1) and (1.2), which deal with securities that a non-resident financial institution (other than a life insurer — dealt with in subsection 138(11.3) of the Act) begins or ceases to use in a Canadian business. These rules complement existing or proposed provisions in subsections 10(12) and (13), 13(9), new 14(14) and (15), paragraph 45(1)(d) and new section 76.1 of the Act. An application rule is set out in new subsection 142.6(1.3) and subsection 142.6(2) is modified to take into account the deemed dispositions and acquisitions in new subsections (1.1) and (1.2).

**(1.1) Ceasing to use property in Canadian business** — If at a particular time in a taxation year a taxpayer that is a non-resident financial institution (other than a life insurance corporation) ceases to use, in connection with a business or part of a business carried on by the taxpayer in Canada immediately before the particular time, a property that is a mark-to-market property of the taxpayer for the year or a specified debt obligation, but that is not a property that was disposed of by the taxpayer at the particular time,

(a) the taxpayer is deemed

(i) to have disposed of the property immediately before the time that was immediately before the particular time for proceeds equal to its fair market value at the time of disposition and to have received those proceeds at the time of disposition in the course of carrying on the business or the part of the business, as the case may be, and

(ii) to have reacquired the property at the particular time at a cost equal to those proceeds; and

(b) in determining the consequences of the disposition in subparagraph (a)(i), subsection 142.4(11) does not apply to any payment received by the taxpayer after the particular time.

**Technical Notes**: New subsection 142.6(1.1) of the Act provides that a non-resident financial institution (other than a life insurer) that at a particular time ceases to use a mark-to-market property or a specified debt obligation in a business in Canada — otherwise than by actually disposing of the property — will be treated as having disposed of the property two moments before the particular time. The provision applies, for example, if a taxpayer removes such property from a business carried on in Canada and begins to use it in a business carried on outside Canada. The taxpayer is deemed to receive, in the course of carrying on the business, proceeds of disposition equal to the property's fair market value and to re-acquire the property at the particular time at a cost equal to those proceeds. Paragraph 142.6(1.1)(b) indicates that the rule in subsection 142.4(11) relating to payments received after a disposition is not applicable with respect to this deemed disposition.

**Related Provisions**: 10(12) — Parallel rule for inventory; 14(14) — Parallel rule for eligible capital property; 142.6(1.3) — Specified debt obligation market to market; 142.6(2) — No effect on determination of when share acquired.

**(1.2) Beginning to use property in a Canadian business** — If at a particular time a taxpayer that is a non-resident financial institution (other than a life insurance corporation) begins to use, in connection with a business or part of a business carried on by the taxpayer in Canada, a property that is a mark-to-market property of the taxpayer for the year that includes the particular time or a specified debt obligation, but that is not a property that was acquired by the taxpayer at the particular time, the taxpayer is deemed

(a) to have disposed of the property immediately before the time that was immediately before the particular time for proceeds equal to its fair market value at the time of disposition; and

(b) to have reacquired the property at the particular time at a cost equal to those proceeds.

**Technical Notes**: New subsection 142.6(1.2) of the Act provides that a non-resident financial institution (other than a life insurer) that begins to use a mark-to-market property or a specified debt obligation in a business in Canada — other than a property that the taxpayer acquired at that time — is deemed to dispose of the property two moments before the particular time, and to reacquire it at the particular time, for an amount equal to its fair market value.

**Related Provisions**: 10(14) — Parallel rule for inventory; 14(15) — Parallel rule for eligible capital property; 142.6(2) — No effect on determination of when share acquired.

**(1.3) Specified debt obligation marked to market** — In applying subsection (1.1) to a taxpayer in respect of a property in a taxation year,

(a) the definition "mark-to-market property" in subsection 142.2(1) shall be applied as if the year ended immediately before the particular time referred to in subsection (1.1); and

(b) if the taxpayer does not have financial statements for the period ending immediately before the particular time referred to in subsection (1.1), references in the definition to financial statements for the year shall be read as references to the financial statements that it is reasonable to expect would have been prepared if the year had ended immediately before the particular time.

**Technical Notes**: New subsection 142.6(1.3) of the Act is an interpretive rule regarding the application of paragraph (b) of the definition "mark-to-market property" in subsection 142.2(1) — dealing with specified debt obligations that are marked to market — in the context of new subsection 142.6(1.1). The rule indicates that in determining whether a specified debt obligation is a mark-to-market property, the taxation year in which the property ceases to be used in the Canadian business is deemed to have ended immediately before the time of that cessation. (If financial statements are not prepared for the period thus ending, the reference in the definition to financial statements is to be read as a reference to the statements that it is reasonable to expect would have been prepared if the year ended at that time.) This ensures that a specified debt obligation that is marked to market in the Canadian business will be considered for the purposes of subsection 142.5(1) to have been disposed of when it ceases to be used in the Canadian business, even if it does not continue to be marked to market for financial statement purposes after it is transferred out of the Canadian business.

**Application**: The August 8, 2000 draft legislation (authorized foreign banks), s. 11, will add subsecs. (1.1) to (1.3) to read as above, applicable after June 27, 1999 in respect of an authorized foreign bank, and after August 8, 2000 in any other case.

**(2) Deemed disposition not applicable** — For the purposes of this Act, the determination of when a taxpayer acquired a share shall be made without regard to a disposition or acquisition that occurred because of subsection (1) or 142.5(2).

### Proposed Amendment — 142.6(2)

**(2) Deemed disposition not applicable** — For the purposes of this Act, the determination of when a taxpayer acquired a share shall be made without regard to a disposition or acquisition that occurred because of subsection 142.5(2) or subsection (1), (1.1) or (1.2).

**Technical Notes**: Subsection 142.6(2) provides that for the purposes of the Act a deemed disposition and reacquisition of a share under certain rules relating to securities held by financial institutions does not affect the time at which a taxpayer is considered to have acquired the share. This provision is amended to add a reference to new subsections 142.6(1.1) and (1.2).

These amendments to section 142.6 apply after June 27, 1999 in respect of an authorized bank and after August 8, 2000 in any other case.

**Application**: The August 8, 2000 draft legislation, s. 11, will amend subsec. 142.6(2) to read as above, applicable after June 27, 1999 in respect of an authorized foreign bank, and after August 8, 2000 in any other case.

**Notes**: 142.6(2) added by 1994 tax amendments bill (Part III), effective for taxation years that end after February 22, 1994.

**(3) Property not inventory** — Where a taxpayer is a financial institution in a taxation year, inventory of the taxpayer in the year does not include property that is

(a) a specified debt obligation (other than a mark-to-market property for the year); or

(b) where the year begins after October 1994, a mark-to-market property for the year.

**Related Provisions**: 66.3(1)(a)(ii) — Rule in 142.6(3) overrides rule for certain exploration and development shares; 142.6(4) — Property that was inventory before introduction of new rules.

**Notes**: 142.6(3) added by 1994 tax amendments bill (Part III), effective for taxation years that end after February 22, 1994.

**(4) Property that ceases to be inventory** — Where a taxpayer that was a financial institution in its particular taxation year that includes February 23, 1994 held, on that day, a specified debt obligation (other than a mark-to-market property for the year) that was inventory of the taxpayer at the end of its preceding taxation year,

(a) the taxpayer shall be deemed to have disposed of the property at the beginning of the particular year for proceeds equal to

(i) where subparagraph (ii) does not apply, the amount at which the property was valued at the end of the preceding taxation year for the purpose of computing the taxpayer's income for the year, and

(ii) where the taxpayer is a bank and the property is prescribed property for the particular year, the cost of the property to the taxpayer (determined without reference to paragraph (b));

(b) for the purpose of determining the taxpayer's profit or loss from the disposition, the cost of the property to the taxpayer shall be deemed to be the amount referred to in subparagraph (a)(i); and

(c) the taxpayer shall be deemed to have reacquired the property, immediately after the beginning of the particular year, at a cost equal to the proceeds of disposition of the property.

Division F — Special Rules in Certain Circumstances  S. 142.6(8)(b)

**Notes**: 142.6(4) added by 1994 tax amendments bill (Part III), effective for taxation years that end after February 22, 1994.

**(5) Debt obligations acquired in rollover transactions** — Where,

(a) on February 23, 1994, a financial institution that is a corporation held a specified debt obligation (other than a mark-to-market property for the taxation year that includes that day) that was at any particular time before that day held by another corporation, and

(b) between the particular time and February 23, 1994, the only transactions affecting the ownership of the property were rollover transactions,

the financial institution shall be deemed, in respect of that obligation, to be the same corporation as, and a continuation of, the other corporation.

**Related Provisions**: 87(2)(e), (e.2) — Rule overrides normal rules on amalgamation; 87(2)(e.3) — Continuity of corporation on amalgamation; 138(11.5)(k.1) — Continuity of corporation on rollover of insurance business by non-resident; 142.6(6) — Rollover transaction.

**Notes**: 142.6(5) added by 1994 tax amendments bill (Part III), effective for taxation years that end after February 22, 1994.

**(6) Definition of "rollover transaction"** — For the purpose of subsection (5), "rollover transaction" means a transaction to which subsection 87(2), 88(1) or 138(11.5) or (11.94) applies, other than a transaction to which paragraph 138(11.5)(e) requires the provisions of subsection 85(1) to be applied.

**Notes**: 142.6(6) added by 1994 tax amendments bill (Part III), effective for taxation years that end after February 22, 1994.

**(7) Superficial loss rule not applicable** — Subsection 18(13) does not apply to the disposition of a property by a taxpayer after October 30, 1994 where

(a) the taxpayer is a financial institution when the disposition occurs and the property is a specified debt obligation or a mark-to-market property for the taxation year in which the disposition occurs; or

(b) the disposition occurs because of paragraph (1)(b).

**Notes**: 142.6(7) added by 1994 tax amendments bill (Part III), effective for dispositions occurring after October 30, 1994, except the disposition of a debt obligation before July 1995 where

(a) the disposition is part of a series of transactions or events that began before October 31, 1994;

(b) as part of the series of transactions or events, the taxpayer who acquired the debt obligation disposed of property before October 31, 1994; and

(c) it is reasonable to consider that one of the main reasons for the acquisition of the debt obligation by the taxpayer was to obtain a deduction because, as a consequence of the disposition referred to in (b) above,

(i) an amount was included in the taxpayer's income for any taxation year, or

(ii) an amount was subtracted from a balance of undeducted outlays, expenses or other amounts of the taxpayer and the subtracted amount exceeded the portion, if any, of the balance that could reasonably be considered to be in respect of the property.

(The same application rule applies to the repeal of 138(5.2).)

**(8) Accrued capital gains and losses election** — Where a taxpayer that is a financial institution in its first taxation year that ends after February 22, 1994 so elects by notifying the Minister in writing before July 1998 or within 90 days after the day on which a notice of assessment of tax payable under this Part for the year, notification that no tax is payable under this Part for the year or notification that an election made by the taxpayer under this subsection is deemed by subsection (9) or (10) not to have been made is mailed to the taxpayer,

(a) each property of the taxpayer

(i) that was a capital property (other than a depreciable property) of the taxpayer at the end of the taxpayer's last taxation year that ended before February 23, 1994,

(ii) that was a mark-to-market property for, or a specified debt obligation in, the taxpayer's first taxation year that begins after that time,

(iii) that had a fair market value at that time greater than its adjusted cost base to the taxpayer at that time, and

(iv) that is designated by the taxpayer in the election

is deemed to have been disposed of by the taxpayer at that time for proceeds of disposition equal to, and to have been reacquired by the taxpayer immediately after that time at a cost equal to, the lesser of

(v) the fair market value of the property at that time, and

(vi) the greater of the adjusted cost base to the taxpayer of the property immediately before that time and the amount designated by the taxpayer in the election in respect of the property;

(b) each property of the taxpayer

(i) that was a capital property (other than a depreciable property) of the taxpayer at the end of the taxpayer's last taxation year that ended before February 23, 1994,

(ii) that was not a mark-to-market property for, or a specified debt obligation in, the taxpayer's first taxation year that begins after that time,

(iii) that had an adjusted cost base to the taxpayer at that time greater than its fair market value at that time, and

(iv) that is designated by the taxpayer in the election

is deemed to have been disposed of by the taxpayer at that time for proceeds of disposition equal to, and to have been reacquired by the tax-

## S. 142.6(8)(b) — Income Tax Act, Part I

payer immediately after that time at a cost equal to, the greater of

(v) the fair market value of the property at that time, and

(vi) the lesser of the adjusted cost base to the taxpayer of the property immediately before that time and the amount designated by the taxpayer in the election in respect of the property; and

(c) notwithstanding subsections 152(4) to (5), such assessment of the taxpayer's tax payable under this Act for the taxpayer's last taxation year that ended before February 23, 1994 shall be made as is necessary to take the election into account.

**Related Provisions**: 142.6(9) — Accrued capital gains election limit; 142.6(10) — Accrued capital losses election limit.

**Notes**: 142.6(8) added by 1995-97 technical bill, effective for 1993 and later taxation years.

**(9) Accrued capital gains election limit** — Where a taxpayer has made an election under subsection (8) in which a property was designated under subparagraph (8)(a)(iv), the election is deemed not to have been made where

(a) the amount that would be the taxpayer's taxable capital gains from dispositions of property for the taxpayer's last taxation year that ended before February 23, 1994 if this subsection and subsection (10) did not apply

exceeds the total of

(b) the amount that would be the taxpayer's allowable capital losses for the year from dispositions of property if this subsection and subsection (10) did not apply,

(c) the maximum amount that would have been deductible in computing the taxpayer's taxable income for the year in respect of the taxpayer's net capital losses for preceding taxation years if there were sufficient taxable capital gains for the year from dispositions of property, and

(d) the amount, if any, by which

(i) the amount that would be the taxpayer's taxable capital gains for the taxpayer's last taxation year that ended before February 23, 1994 from dispositions of property if no election were made under subsection (8)

exceeds the total of

(ii) the amount that would be the taxpayer's allowable capital losses for the year from dispositions of property if no election were made under subsection (8), and

(iii) the maximum amount that would have been deductible in computing the taxpayer's taxable income for the year in respect of the taxpayer's net capital losses for preceding taxation years if no election were made under subsection (8).

**(10) Accrued capital losses election limit** — Where a taxpayer has made an election under subsection (8) in which a property was designated under subparagraph (8)(b)(iv), the election is deemed not to have been made where

(a) the total of the amounts determined under paragraphs (9)(b) and (c) in respect of the taxpayer exceeds the amount determined under paragraph (9)(a) in respect of the taxpayer; or

(b) the total of all amounts each of which would, if this subsection did not apply, be the taxpayer's allowable capital loss for the taxpayer's last taxation year that ended before February 23, 1994 from the disposition of a property deemed to have been disposed of under paragraph (8)(b) exceeds the total of all amounts each of which is the taxpayer's taxable capital gain for the year from the disposition of a property deemed to have been disposed of under paragraph (8)(a).

**Notes**: 142.6(10) added by 1995-97 technical bill, effective for 1993 and later taxation years.

**Definitions [s. 142.6]**: "adjusted cost base" — 54, 248(1); "allowable capital loss" — 38(b), 248(1); "amount", "assessment", "authorized foreign bank" — 248(1); "bank" — 248(1), *Interpretation Act* 35(1); "business" — 248(1); "Canada" — 255, *Interpretation Act* 35(1); "capital property" — 54, 248(1); "corporation" — 248(1), *Interpretation Act* 35(1); "disposition" — 54; "financial institution" — 142.2(1); "fiscal period" — 249.1; "inventory" — 248(1); "life insurance corporation" — 248(1); "mark-to-market property" — 142.2(1); "Minister" — 248(1); "net capital loss" — 111(8), 248(1); "non-resident", "prescribed", "property" — 248(1); "rollover transaction" — 142.6(6); "share" — 248(1); "specified debt obligation" — 142.2(1); "taxable capital gain" — 38(a), 248(1); "taxation year" — 249; "taxpayer" — 248(1); "writing" — *Interpretation Act* 35(1).

### Proposed Addition — 142.7

**Technical Notes**: New section 142.7 of the Act, which applies after June 27, 1999, provides special, time-limited rules to facilitate foreign banks' transformation of certain Canadian operations, currently carried out through subsidiaries, into Canadian branches of the foreign banks themselves. The section includes three main forms of relief:

- The "branch-establishment rollover" rules allow a tax-deferred transfer of certain eligible property from an eligible subsidiary — a "Canadian affiliate" — to a foreign bank that is starting branch operations in Canada — an "entrant bank." Specific rules deal with particular kinds of property such as specified debt obligations, mark-to-market properties, and properties in respect of which certain reserves would be taken, as well as the consequences of assuming debt obligations.

- The "branch-establishment dividend" rules allow property to flow from a Canadian affiliate to an entrant bank (or to an affiliate resident in the same country as the bank) as a tax-free dividend, provided the entrant bank redeploys the dividend proceeds in its Canadian banking business.

- Where the Canadian affiliate is wound up as part of the entrant bank's move into Canada, special loss rules allow the entrant bank to inherit the affiliate's non-capital and net capital losses, on much the same terms as a Canadian corporation inherits the losses of its wound-up Canadian subsidiary. A special rule ensures continuity of amortization schedules in respect of specified debt obligations in these circumstances.

All of these provisions are subject to timing constraints and other conditions described in detail in the following notes.

New subsection 142.7(1) of the Act sets out definitions that apply in the section.

## Conversion of Foreign Bank Affiliate to Branch

**142.7 (1) Definitions** — The definitions in this subsection apply in this section.

**"Canadian affiliate"** of an entrant bank at any time means a Canadian corporation that was, throughout the period that began on February 11, 1999 and ends at that time,

(a) affiliated with the entrant bank; and

(b) either

(i) a bank,

(ii) a corporation authorized under the *Trust and Loan Companies Act* to carry on the business of offering to the public its services as trustee, or

(iii) a corporation of which the principal activity in Canada consists of any of the activities referred to in subparagraphs 518(3)(a)(i) to (v) of the *Bank Act* and in which the entrant bank or a non-resident person affiliated with the entrant bank holds shares under the authority, directly or indirectly, of an order issued by the Minister of Finance or the Governor in Council under subsection 521(1) of that Act.

**Technical Notes**: A Canadian corporation is a "Canadian affiliate" of an "entrant bank" (see below) at a particular time if the corporation is a bank, a trust company or a non-bank subsidiary in which the entrant bank is authorized to invest under certain provisions of the *Bank Act*, and it has been affiliated with the entrant bank continuously from February 11, 1999 to the particular time.

**"eligible property"** of a Canadian affiliate at any time means a property described in any of paragraphs 85(1.1)(a) to (g.1) that is, immediately before that time, used or held by it in carrying on its business in Canada.

**Technical Notes**: The definition of a Canadian affiliate's "eligible property" for purposes of new section 142.7 incorporates by reference paragraphs (a) to (g.1) of the definition, in subsection 85(1.1) of the Act, that applies for transfers under subsection 85(1) of the Act. Provided they are used or held by the Canadian affiliate immediately before the relevant time in carrying on its business in Canada, eligible properties thus generally include:

- capital property;
- Canadian and foreign resource property;
- eligible capital property;
- inventory (other than real property);
- securities and debt obligations that are neither capital, inventory nor mark-to-market properties and that are used or held by the affiliate in the course of an insurance or money-lending business; and
- specified debt obligations (other than mark-to-market properties).

**"entrant bank"** means a non-resident corporation that is, or has applied to the Superintendent of Financial Institutions to become, an authorized foreign bank.

**Technical Notes**: An "entrant bank" is a non-resident corporation that is an "authorized foreign bank" (see the notes to subsection 248(1) of the Act, below), or that has applied to the Superintendent of Financial Institutions to become an authorized foreign bank.

**(2) Amalgamation and merger** — For the purpose of the definition "Canadian affiliate" in subsection (1), if an entrant bank was formed as the result of an amalgamation or merger, after February 11, 1999, of two or more non-resident corporations (referred to in this subsection as "predecessors"), and at the time immediately before the amalgamation or merger, there were one or more Canadian corporations (referred to in this subsection as "predecessor affiliates"), each of which at that time would have been a Canadian affiliate of a predecessor if the predecessor were an entrant bank at that time,

(a) each predecessor affiliate is deemed to have been affiliated with the entrant bank throughout the period that began on February 11, 1999 and ended at the time of the amalgamation or merger;

(b) the expression "entrant bank" in subparagraph (b)(iii) of the definition is deemed to include a predecessor; and

(c) if two or more of the predecessor affiliates are amalgamated or merged at any time after February 11, 1999 to form a new corporation, the new corporation is deemed to have been affiliated with the entrant bank throughout the period that began on February 11, 1999 and ended at the time of the amalgamation or merger of the predecessor affiliates.

**Technical Notes**: In general, the rules in new section 142.7 of the Act apply only where a foreign bank has operated a Canadian subsidiary since at least February 11, 1999. In some cases, however, two or more foreign banks may have amalgamated or otherwise merged after that date to form a new entrant bank. New subsection 142.7(2) ensures that the merged bank and its Canadian subsidiary or subsidiaries are not disqualified from the benefits of the section.

Specifically, the subsection provides that a corporation that would, immediately before the merger, have been a Canadian affiliate of one of the merging banks if the bank were an entrant bank at that time, is deemed to have been affiliated with the merged entrant from February 11, 1999 to the time of the merger. As well, if two or more Canadian subsidiaries of merging entrant banks themselves amalgamate or merge after February 11, 1999, the new merged subsidiary is treated as having been affiliated with the merged entrant bank since that date.

**(3) Branch-establishment rollover** — If a Canadian affiliate of an entrant bank transfers an eligible property to the entrant bank, the entrant bank begins immediately after the transfer to use or hold the transferred property in its Canadian banking business and the Canadian affiliate and the entrant bank jointly elect, in accordance with subsection (11), to have this subsection apply in respect of the transfer, subsections 85(1) (other than paragraph (e.2)), (1.1), (1.4) and (5) apply, with any modifications that the circumstances require, in respect of the transfer, except that the portion of subsection 85(1) before paragraph (a) shall be read as follows:

> "85. (1) Where a taxpayer that is a Canadian affiliate of an entrant bank (within the meanings assigned by subsection 142.7(1)) has, in a taxation year, disposed of any of the taxpayer's property to the entrant bank (referred to in this subsection as the "corporation"), if the taxpayer and the corporation have jointly elected under subsection 142.7(3), the following rules apply:"

**Technical Notes**: New subsection 142.7(3) of the Act allows an entrant bank's Canadian affiliate to transfer eligible property to the entrant bank on a tax-deferred basis. The model for this "branch-establishment rollover" is the tax-deferred transfer of property by a shareholder to a corporation under existing subsection 85(1) of the Act, and subsection 142.7(3) is structured in large part as a modification of subsection 85(1). The most notable difference between the two types of transaction is that the branch-establishment rollover, unlike the subsection 85(1) transfer, does not require that the transferor (the Canadian affiliate) take back a share of the transferee corporation (the entrant bank) as consideration.

In order to carry out a branch-establishment rollover, the entrant bank and its Canadian affiliate must meet two special conditions. First, immediately after the transfer the entrant bank must use or hold the eligible property in question in its "Canadian banking business" (see the notes to subsection 248(1) of the Act, below). Second, the entrant bank and the Canadian affiliate must jointly elect in accordance with subsection 142.7(11), described below.

Where these conditions are met, subsections 85(1) (except for paragraph (e.2)), (1.1), (1.4) and (5) of the Act apply to the transfer, except that the opening words of subsection 85(1) are modified to refer to the Canadian affiliate and the entrant bank, to remove the requirement that the consideration for the transfer include a share, and to refer to subsection 142.7(11).

It is proposed that a reference to new subsection 142.7(3) be added to subsection 5301(7) of the *Income Tax Regulations*, to ensure carry-over a Canadian affiliate's instalment base to the entrant bank if all or substantially all of the affiliate's property is transferred to the bank.

**Related Provisions**: 142.7(4) — No shareholder benefit or adjustment of terms; 142.7(5) — Transfers of specified debt obligations; 142.7(11) — Requirements for election; Reg. 5301(8) — Effect of transfer on instalment base of transferee.

**(4) No shareholder benefit or adjustment of terms** — If a Canadian affiliate of an entrant bank and the entrant bank make an election under subsection (3) in respect of a transfer of property by the Canadian affiliate to the entrant bank, receipt by the Canadian affiliate of consideration having a value which is less than the fair market value of the property but not less than the amount agreed to by the Canadian affiliate and the entrant bank in their election shall not in itself be a basis for the application of subsection 15(1), 69(1), (4) or (5) or 247(2) in respect of the transfer.

**Technical Notes**: A number of provisions of the Act, including subsections 15(1), 69(1), (4) and (5) and 247(2), may apply where a transaction between a corporation and its non-resident shareholder takes place on terms that do not reflect arm's length or fair market value standards. New subsection 142.7(4) of the Act limits the application of these rules where an entrant bank and its Canadian affiliate elect to have new subsection 142.7(3) of the Act apply to the affiliate's transfer of a property to the bank.

Provided the affiliate has at least received consideration that is equal to the elected amount in respect of the property, new subsection 142.7(4) provides that the rules listed above will not apply to the transfer just because the affiliate has received less than fair market value proceeds in consideration for the property. (This does not exclude the possibility that those rules might apply for other reasons.)

**(5) Specified debt obligations** — If a Canadian affiliate of an entrant bank transfers a specified debt obligation to the entrant bank in a transaction in respect of which an election is made under subsection (3), the Canadian affiliate is a financial institution in its taxation year in which the transfer is made, and the amount that the Canadian affiliate and the entrant bank agree on in their election in respect of the obligation is equal to the tax basis of the obligation within the meaning assigned by subsection 142.4(1), the entrant bank is deemed, in respect of the obligation, for the purposes of sections 142.2 to 142.4 and 142.6, to be the same corporation as, and a continuation of, the Canadian affiliate.

**Technical Notes**: New subsection 142.7(5) of the Act applies where a Canadian affiliate that is a financial institution (as defined in subsection 142.2(1)) transfers a specified debt obligation (that is not a mark-to-market property) to the affiliate's entrant bank, and the affiliate and the bank elect to transfer the obligation at its tax cost under the new branch-establishment rollover provisions. New subsection 142.7(5) is a continuity rule that deems the entrant bank to be the same corporation as, and a continuation of, the Canadian affiliate in respect of the obligation. This ensures that the tax treatment of the obligation is the same to the entrant bank as it would have been to the Canadian affiliate. Existing subsection 142.6(5) of the Act contains a similar continuity rule for other "rollover" transactions listed in subsection 142.6(6) of the Act.

**(6) Mark-to-market property** — If a Canadian affiliate of an entrant bank described in paragraph (11)(a) transfers at any time within the period described in paragraph (11)(c) to the entrant bank a property that is, for the Canadian affiliate's taxation year in which the property is transferred, a mark-to-market property of the Canadian affiliate,

(a) for the purposes of subsections 112(5) to (5.21) and (5.4), the definition "mark-to-market property" in subsection 142.2(1) and subsection 142.5(9), the entrant bank is deemed, in respect of the property, to be the same corporation as and a continuation of, the Canadian affiliate; and

(b) for the purpose of applying subsection 142.5(2) in respect of the property, the Canadian affiliate's taxation year in which the property is transferred is deemed to have ended immediately before the time the property was transferred.

**Technical Notes**: New subsection 142.7(6) of the Act applies where a Canadian affiliate of the entrant bank transfers a mark-to-market property to the entrant bank within the period during which branch-establishment rollovers may be made. Paragraph 142.7(6)(a) provides that for the purpose of applying certain of the dividend stop-loss rules in section 112 relating to mark-to-market properties and determining whether certain specified debt obligations constitute "mark-to-market property" within the meaning of the definition in subsection 142.2(1), the entrant bank is deemed to be the same corporation as, and a continuation of, the Canadian affiliate. This provision may be compared to paragraph 87(2)(e.5) of the Act, which contains a similar rule.

Paragraph 142.7(6)(b) provides that for the purposes of the rule requiring marking-to-market at year-end, the Canadian affiliate's taxation year in which the property was transferred is deemed to have ended immediately before the time of transfer. This ensures that the property is marked-to-market for tax purposes at the time of transfer in spite of the continuity imposed by paragraph (a).

**Related Provisions**: 87(2)(e.5) — Parallel rule on amalgamations.

**(7) Reserves** — If, at a particular time, a Canadian affiliate of an entrant bank is a financial institution and transfers to the entrant bank an obligation or property that is an instrument or commitment described in paragraph 20(1)(l.1), or a loan or lending asset, for an amount equal to its fair market value, the entrant bank begins immediately after the transfer to owe, use or hold the obligation or property in its Canadian banking business and the Canadian affiliate and the entrant bank jointly elect, in accordance with subsection (11), to have this subsection apply in respect of the transfer,

(a) for the purposes of the application of paragraphs 20(1)(l), (l.1) and (p), the taxation year of the affiliate that includes the particular time is deemed to have ended immediately before the particular time; and

(b) any amount deducted by the Canadian affiliate in respect of the obligation or property under paragraph 20(1)(l) or (l.1) in the year that includes the particular time, or under paragraph 20(1)(p) in that year or a preceding year (to the extent that the amount has not been included in the affiliate's income under paragraph 12(1)(i)), is deemed to have been so deducted by the entrant bank in the last taxation year of the entrant bank that ended before the particular time.

**Technical Notes**: New subsection 142.7(7) of the Act provides an election that ensures continuity of reserve treatment upon transfer from a Canadian affiliate that is a financial institution to an entrant bank of certain assets and obligations in respect of which reserves have been claimed.

Subsection 142.7(7) applies to a transfer at fair market value of an instrument or commitment described in paragraph 20(1)(l.1), a loan or a lending asset that, immediately after the transfer, is owed, used or held by the entrant bank in its Canadian banking business. If the election is made, the taxation year of the Canadian affiliate in which the transfer is made is deemed to have ended immediately before the transfer for the purposes of the application of the deductions under paragraphs 20(1)(l) (reserve for doubtful or impaired debts), 20(1)(l.1) (reserve for credit risks under guarantees and other commitments) and 20(1)(p) (bad debts) of the Act. The deemed year-end allows the Canadian affiliate to claim a reserve for the year in which the obligation or property is transferred.

An amount deducted by the Canadian affiliate under any of those provisions in that year (and, with respect to subsection 20(1)(p), in previous years) is deemed to have been deducted by the entrant bank in its last taxation year that ended before the time of the transfer. This ensures that the reserve amounts will subsequently be included in the entrant bank's income and that the bank will be subject to an income inclusion if there is a subsequent recovery of a bad debt amount. Subsection 20(27) of the Act will typically ensure the entrant's bank's ability to claim a reserve in respect of the transferred obligations and properties.

**Related Provisions**: 142.7(11) — Requirements for election.

**(8) Assumption of debt obligation** — If a Canadian affiliate of an entrant bank described in paragraph (11)(a) transfers at any time within the period described in paragraph (11)(c) property to the entrant bank, and any part of the consideration for the transfer is the assumption by the entrant bank in respect of its Canadian banking business of a debt obligation of the Canadian affiliate,

(a) where the Canadian affiliate and the entrant bank jointly elect in accordance with subsection (11) to have this paragraph apply,

(i) both

(A) the value of that part of the consideration for the transfer of the property, and

(B) for the purpose of determining the consequences of the assumption of the obligation and any subsequent settlement or extinguishment of it, the value of the consideration given to the entrant bank for the assumption of the obligation,

are deemed to be an amount (in this paragraph referred to as the "assumption amount") equal to the amount outstanding on account of the principal amount of the obligation at that time, and

(ii) the assumption amount shall not be considered a term of the transaction that differs from that which would have been made between persons dealing at arm's length solely because it is not equal to the fair market value of the obligation at that time; and

(b) where the obligation is denominated in a foreign currency, and the Canadian affiliate and the entrant bank jointly elect in accordance with subsection (11) to have this paragraph apply,

(i) the amount of any income, loss, capital gain or capital loss in respect of the obligation due to the fluctuation in the value of the foreign currency relative to Canadian currency realized by

(A) the Canadian affiliate on the assumption of the obligation is deemed to be nil, and

(B) the entrant bank on the settlement or extinguishment of the obligation shall be determined based on the amount of the obligation in Canadian currency at the time it became an obligation of the Canadian affiliate, and

(ii) for the purpose of an election made in respect of the obligation under paragraph (a), the amount outstanding on account of the principal amount of the obligation at that time is the total of all amounts each of which is an amount that was advanced to the Canadian affiliate on account of principal, that remains outstanding at that time, and that is determined using the exchange rate that applied between the foreign currency and Canadian currency at the time of the advance.

**Technical Notes**: In many cases, an entrant bank will assume some or all of its Canadian affiliate's debt obligations. Such an assumption may serve as consideration for the transfer of property by the affiliate to the entrant bank, either on a branch-establishment rollover or otherwise. Where this is the case, new subsection 142.7(8) of the Act applies to govern the tax consequences of the assumption.

New paragraph 142.7(8)(a) of the Act provides an election to assume a debt obligation at face value and so can ensure that changes in the value of the obligation that result from, for example, interest rate changes since the affiliate issued or acquired the obligation, do not produce an immediate tax consequence Under subparagraph (a)(i), where a joint election is made in accordance with subsection (11), for the purpose of determining the consequences of the disposition of the property, the consideration for its transfer is deemed to be the outstanding principal amount of the obligation — referred to as the "settlement amount". The settlement amount is also considered to be the amount of consideration given to the bank for the assumption of the obligation. This is relevant to determining whether or not the assumption gives rise to debt forgiveness consequences or a loss to the affiliate, as well as the consequences to the entrant bank of eventual settlement of the obligation. Subparagraph (a)(ii) provides that assumption of the obligation at the settlement amount (even if that differs from the fair market value of the obligation) is not considered a non-arm's length term. This is relevant for such purposes as the transfer pricing rules in section 247 of the Act.

New paragraph 142.7(8)(b) of the Act provides an election to ensure that the assumption of a foreign currency debt obligation does not give rise to immediate tax consequences on account of foreign exchange fluctuations. Subsection (b)(i) provides for deferral of any foreign exchange gains or losses until the obligation is settled by the entrant bank. Subparagraph (b)(ii) ensures that the election in paragraph (a) operates net of foreign exchange effects.

**Related Provisions**: 142.7(11) — Requirements for election.

**(9) Branch-establishment dividend** — Despite any other provision of this Act, the rules in subsection (10) apply if

(a) a dividend is paid by a Canadian affiliate of an entrant bank to the entrant bank or to a person that is affiliated with the Canadian affiliate and that is resident in the country in which the entrant bank is resident, or

(b) a dividend is deemed to be paid for the purposes of this Part or Part XIII as a result of a transfer of property from the Canadian affiliate to such a person,

and the Canadian affiliate and the entrant bank jointly elect in accordance with subsection (11) to have subsection (10) apply in respect of the dividend.

**Technical Notes**: New subsections 142.7(9) and (10) of the Act allow an entrant bank to receive (directly or indirectly) a non-taxable dividend from its Canadian affiliate, provided certain conditions are met and provided the proceeds are immediately redeployed in the bank's Canadian branch operation.

New subsection 142.7(9) sets out the conditions for the payment of this "branch-establishment dividend." First, the Canadian affiliate must pay (or must be deemed to pay, as a result of transferring property) a dividend either to the entrant bank or to another person that is affiliated with the entrant bank and that is resident in the same country as the entrant bank. If, for example, an entrant bank does not hold the shares of its Canadian affiliate directly, but rather holds them through a holding company resident in its home country, the Canadian affiliate may pay a branch-establishment dividend to the holding company. Second, the Canadian affiliate and the entrant bank itself — whether or not the dividend is paid directly to the entrant bank — must jointly elect as set out in new subsection 142.7(11) of the Act to have these rules apply to the dividend.

Where these conditions are met, new paragraph 142.7(10)(a) of the Act provides that the dividend is deemed not to be a taxable dividend, except for the purposes of the dividend stop-loss rules in subsections 112(3) to (7) of the Act. The recipient of the dividend will thus not be subject to Canadian tax on the dividend, and a subsequent loss to the recipient on the shares of the Canadian affiliate may be adjusted to reflect that exemption.

The purpose of the tax exemption for branch-establishment dividends is to allow entrant banks to redeploy to their new Canadian branch operations the property (particularly retained earnings) that their Canadian affiliates hold in Canada. It is expected that normally the proceeds of any dividend to which these rules apply will immediately be used or held by the entrant bank in its Canadian banking business. Should this not be the case, it is appropriate that the dividend be subject to tax. New paragraph 142.7(10)(b) ensures this result by treating the dividend as having formed part of the entrant bank's prior-year "investment allowance" under paragraph 219(1)(g) of the Act, and thus including it in the bank's Part XIV branch tax base for the current year. To the extent the dividend proceeds have been redeployed to the entrant bank's Canadian banking business, they will figure in the bank's current-year investment allowance, and will be deducted from the branch tax base for the current year; to the extent they have not been so redeployed, they will be subject to the branch tax (which is comparable to withholding tax on a dividend).

In determining the addition to the paragraph 219(1)(g) amount, it should be noted that where a branch-establishment dividend is paid by, or arises from, a branch-establishment rollover of eligible property, the amount of the addition is reduced by any latent gain on the property. Since the amount of the dividend is the value of the property transferred, this rule ensures that the gain is deferred as long as long as the property remains deployed in the entrant bank's Canadian banking business.

**(10) Treatment of dividend** — If the conditions in subsection (9) are met,

(a) the dividend is deemed (except for the purposes of subsections 112(3) to (7)) not to be a taxable dividend; and

(b) there is added to the amount otherwise determined under paragraph 219(1)(g) in respect of the entrant bank for its first taxation year that ends after the time at which the dividend is paid, the amount of the dividend less, where the dividend is paid by means of, or arises as a result of, a transfer of eligible property in respect of which the Canadian affiliate and the entrant bank have jointly elected under subsection (3), the amount by which the fair market value of the property transferred exceeds the amount the Canadian affiliate and the entrant bank have agreed on in their election.

**Technical Notes**: See under 142.7(9).

**Related Provisions**: 142.7(11) — Requirements for election.

**(11) Elections** — An election under subsection (3) or (7), paragraph (8)(a) or (b) or subsection (10) is valid only if

(a) the entrant bank by which the election is made has, on or before March 31, 2001, complied with paragraphs 1.0(1.1)(b) and (c) of the "Guide to Foreign Bank Branching" in respect of the establishment and commencement of business of a foreign bank branch in Canada issued by the Office of the Superintendent of Financial Institutions, as it read on December 31, 1999;

(b) the election is made in prescribed form on or before the earlier of the filing-due date of the Canadian affiliate and the filing-due date of the entrant bank, for the taxation year that includes the time at which the dividend or the transfer to which the election relates is paid or made, as the case may be; and

(c) the dividend or the transfer to which the election relates is paid or made, as the case may be,

(i) after the day on which the Superintendent makes an order in respect of the entrant bank under subsection 534(1) of the *Bank Act*, and

(ii) on or before the earlier of

(A) the day that is 6 months after that day, and

(B) December 31, 2002.

**Technical Notes**: New subsection 142.7(11) of the Act sets out the procedural requirements for the various elections provided in the section. In general terms, an election is valid only if: (a) the entrant bank has, on or before March 31, 2001, formally applied for regulatory approval to operate in branch form in Canada; (b) the election is duly made on or before the earlier of the entrant bank's and the Canadian affiliate's filing-due date for the year in which the dividend or transfer was paid or made, as the case may be; and (c) the dividend or transfer is effected both (i) after a regulatory order has been made allowing the entrant bank to start operations in Canada in branch form, and (ii) before the earlier of December 31, 2002 and the day 6 months after the date of that order.

**Related Provisions**: 142.7(6) — Transfer of mark-to-market property; 142.7(8) — Assumption of debt obligation.

**(12) Winding-up of Canadian affiliate: losses** — If

(a) a Canadian affiliate of an entrant bank has been dissolved pursuant to section 342 or 346 of the *Bank Act* or section 347 or 351 of the *Trust and Loan Companies Act*, or otherwise wound up under the terms of the corporate law that governs the affiliate,

(b) before the earlier of the dates described in subparagraph (11)(c)(ii) in respect of the entrant bank,

(i) the Minister of Finance has issued letters patent under section 342 of the *Bank Act* or section 347 of the *Trust and Loan Companies Act* dissolving the Canadian affiliate or an order under section 345 of the *Bank Act* or section 350 of the *Trust and Loan Companies Act* approving the Canadian affiliate's application for dissolution (such letters patent or order being referred to in this subsection as the "dissolution order"), or

(ii) the affiliate has been wound up under the terms of the corporate law that governs it, and

(c) the entrant bank carries on all or part of the business in Canada that was formerly carried on by the Canadian affiliate,

in applying section 111 for the purpose of computing the taxable income earned in Canada of the entrant bank for any taxation year that begins after the date of the dissolution order or the commencement of the winding up, as the case may be,

(d) subject to paragraphs (e) and (h), the portion of a non-capital loss of the Canadian affiliate for a taxation year (in this paragraph referred to as the "Canadian affiliate's loss year") that can reasonably be regarded as being its loss from carrying on a business in Canada (in this paragraph referred to as the "loss business") or being in respect of a claim made under section 110.5, to the extent that it

(i) was not deducted in computing the taxable income of the Canadian affiliate for any taxation year, and

(ii) would have been deductible in computing the taxable income of the Canadian affiliate for any taxation year that begins after the date of the dissolution order or the commencement of the winding up, as the case may be, on the assumption that it had such a taxation year and that it had sufficient income for that year,

is deemed, for the taxation year of the entrant bank in which the Canadian affiliate's loss year ended, to be a non-capital loss of the entrant bank from carrying on the loss business (or, in respect of a claim made under section 110.5, to be a non-capital loss of the entrant bank in respect of a claim under subparagraph 115(1)(a)(vii)) that was not deductible by the entrant bank in computing its taxable income earned in Canada for any taxation year that began before the date of the dissolution order or the commencement of the winding up, as the case may be,

(e) if at any time control of the Canadian affiliate or entrant bank has been acquired by a person or group of persons, no amount in respect of the Canadian affiliate's non-capital loss for a taxation year that ends before that time is deductible in computing the taxable income earned in Canada of the entrant bank for a particular taxation year that ends after that time, except that the portion of the loss that can reasonably be regarded as the Canadian affiliate's loss from carrying on a business in Canada and, where a business was carried on by the Canadian affiliate in Canada in the earlier year, the portion of the loss that can reasonably be regarded as being in respect of an amount deductible under paragraph 110(1)(k) in computing its taxable income for the year are deductible only

(i) if that business is carried on by the Canadian affiliate or the entrant bank for profit or with a reasonable expectation of profit throughout the particular year, and

(ii) to the extent of the total of the entrant bank's income for the particular year from that business, and where properties were sold, leased, rented or developed or services rendered in the course of carrying on that business before that time, from any other business substantially all of the income of which was derived from the sale, leasing, rental or development, as the case may be, of similar properties or the rendering of similar services,

and, for the purpose of this paragraph, where subsection 88(1.1) applied to the dissolution of another corporation in respect of which the Canadian affiliate was the parent and paragraph 88(1.1)(e) applied in respect of losses of that other corporation, the Canadian affiliate is deemed to be the same corporation as, and a continuation of, that other corporation with respect to those losses,

(f) subject to paragraphs (g) and (h), a net capital loss of the Canadian affiliate for a taxation year (in this paragraph referred to as the "Canadian affiliate's loss year") is deemed to be a net capital loss of the entrant bank for its taxation year in which the Canadian affiliate's loss year ended to the extent that the loss

(i) was not deducted in computing the taxable income of the Canadian affiliate for any taxation year, and

(ii) would have been deductible in computing the taxable income of the Canadian affiliate for any taxation year beginning after the date of the dissolution order or the commencement of the winding-up, as the case may be, on the assumption that the Canadian affiliate had such a taxation year and that it had sufficient income and taxable capital gains for that year,

(g) if at any time control of the Canadian affiliate or the entrant bank has been acquired by a person or group of persons, no amount in respect of the Canadian affiliate's net capital loss for a taxation year that ends before that time is deductible in computing the entrant bank's taxable income earned in Canada for a taxation year that ends after that time, and

(h) any loss of the Canadian affiliate that would otherwise be deemed by paragraph (d) or (f) to be a loss of the entrant bank for a particular taxation year that begins after the date of the dissolution order or the commencement of the winding-up, as the case may be, is deemed, for the purpose of computing the entrant bank's taxable income earned in Canada for taxation years that begin after that date, to be such a loss of the entrant bank for its immediately preceding taxation year and not for the particular year, if the entrant bank so elects in its return of income for the particular year.

**Technical Notes**: New subsection 142.7(12) of the Act sets out rules that give an entrant bank access to losses of its Canadian affiliate, where the affiliate is wound up as part of the entrant bank's commencement of Canadian operations.

Paragraphs 142.7(12)(a) through (c) set out the conditions that must be met for subsection (8) to apply. First, the Canadian affiliate must have been dissolved or wound up under the applicable corporate regulatory legislation: section 342 or 346 of the *Bank Act*, section 347 or 351 of the *Trust and Loan Companies Act*, or whatever other statutory provisions govern the winding-up of the affiliate. Second, the winding-up order or dissolution order must have been issued, or the wind-up accomplished, before the earlier of December 31, 2002 and the day six months after the Superintendent of Financial Institutions makes the order allowing the entrant bank to commence operations in Canada. Third, the entrant bank must carry on all or part of the Canadian business that the Canadian affiliate formerly carried on.

Where these conditions are met, new subsection 142.7(12) allows the entrant bank to treat the Canadian affiliate's unused non-capital losses and net capital losses as its own, in a similar manner as existing subsections 88(1.1) and (1.2) of the Act give a taxable Canadian corporation access to the losses of its wound-up Canadian subsidiary. The main features of these new rules are as follows:

- The Canadian affiliate's unused non-capital loss for a taxation year (the "loss year") from carrying on a business (the "loss business") in Canada is treated as a loss of the entrant bank from the loss business for its taxation year in which the Canadian affiliate's loss year ended. Losses in respect of a claim by the Canadian affiliate under section 110.5 (taxable income addition for foreign tax credit purposes) are also accommodated. (Paragraph (d))

- Similarly, the Canadian affiliate's unused net capital loss for a taxation year is treated as a net capital loss of the entrant bank for its taxation year in which the Canadian affiliate's loss year ended. (Paragraph (f))

- If control of the Canadian affiliate or of the entrant bank is acquired at any time, the affiliate's non-capital losses are streamed, and its net capital losses are blocked.

- Pre-acquisition non-capital losses of the affiliate are usable by the entrant bank in a given post-acquisition year only if it or the affiliate carries on the loss business throughout the year, and only to the extent of the income from that or a similar business (defined in a manner identical to that set out for Canadian corporations in existing paragraph 88(1.1)(e)). (Paragraph (e))

- The entrant bank may not use pre-acquisition net capital losses of the affiliate in any post-acquisition year. (Paragraph (g))

- Where a loss of the Canadian affiliate would be treated as a loss of the entrant bank for a year that begins after the date of the affiliate's dissolution order (or after its winding-up commences), the entrant bank can choose to treat the loss as having arisen in its immediately preceding year. This may enable the entrant bank to use the affiliate's final-year loss in its own first taxation year that begins after the dissolution of the affiliate. (Paragraph (h))

**(13) Winding-up of Canadian affiliate: SDOs** — If a Canadian affiliate of an entrant bank and the entrant bank meet the conditions set out in paragraphs (12)(a) to (c), the entrant bank is deemed to be the same corporation as, and a continuation of, the Canadian affiliate for the purposes of paragraphs 142.4(4)(c) and (d) in respect of any specified debt obligation disposed of by the Canadian affiliate.

**Regulations**: 9204(2.1) (winding-up into authorized foreign bank).

**Technical Notes**: New subsection 142.7(13) of the Act is a continuity rule that applies where a Canadian affiliate of an entrant bank is wound-up and all or part of its business is transferred to the entrant bank in accordance with the conditions in paragraphs 142.7(12)(a) to (c). In those circumstances, for the purpose of the amortization rules relating to specified debt obligations in paragraphs 142.4(c) and (d) of the Act, the entrant bank is deemed to be the same corporation as, and a continuation of, the Canadian affiliate. This ensures that, where a specified debt obligation was previously disposed of by the Canadian affiliate and the residual portion of the resulting gain or loss has been amortized over the remaining term to maturity of the obligation, the amortization schedule is not disrupted by the transfer of the affiliate's business to the entrant bank.

To implement this rule, it is proposed that section 9204 of the *Income Tax Regulations* be amended to extend the winding-up rule in subsection 9204(2) to the situation described in new subsection 142.7(13) of the Act and to exclude that situation from the rule in subsection 9204(5) of the Regulations dealing with cessation of business. On the other hand, it is proposed that this latter rule be extended to apply whenever a non-resident ceases to carry on all or substantially all of the part of its business that was carried on in Canada.

**Application**: The August 8, 2000 draft legislation, s. 12(1), will add s. 142.7, applicable after June 27, 1999.

**Definitions [s. 142.7]**: "affiliated" — 251.1; "amount" — 248(1); "arm's length" — 251(1); "authorized foreign bank", "bank", "business" — 248(1); "Canada" — 255, *Interpretation Act* 35(1); "Canadian affiliate" — 142.7(1); "Canadian banking business" — 248(1); "Canadian corporation" — 89(1), 248(1); "capital gain" — 39(1)(a), 248(1); "capital loss" — 39(1)(b), 248(1); "commencement" — *Interpretation Act* 35(1); "corporation" — 248(1), *Interpretation Act* 35(1); "dividend" — 248(1);

"eligible property", "entrant bank" — 142.7(1); "filing-due date" — 248(1); "financial institution" — 142.2(1); "foreign currency" — 248(1); "Governor" — *Interpretation Act* 35(1); "lending asset" — 248(1); "mark-to-market property" — 142.2(1); "Minister" — 248(1); "month" — *Interpretation Act* 35(1); "net capital loss", "non-capital loss" — 111(8), 248(1); "non-resident" — 248(1); "parent" — 88(1.1); "person", "prescribed", "principal amount", "property" — 248(1); "resident" — 250; "share", "shareholder" — 248(1); "specified debt obligation" — 142.2(1); "taxable capital gain" — 38(a), 248(1); "taxable dividend" — 89(1), 248(1); "taxable income", "taxable income earned in Canada" — 248(1); "taxation year" — 249; "taxpayer" — 248(1).

## Communal Organizations

**143. (1) Communal organizations** — Where a congregation, or one or more business agencies of the congregation, carries on one or more businesses for purposes that include supporting or sustaining the congregation's members or the members of any other congregation, the following rules apply:

(a) an *inter vivos* trust is deemed to be created on the day that is the later of

(i) December 31, 1976, and

(ii) the day the congregation came into existence;

(b) the trust is deemed to have been continuously in existence from the day determined under paragraph (a);

(c) the property of the congregation is deemed to be the property of the trust;

(d) the property of each business agency of the congregation in a calendar year is deemed to be property of the trust throughout the portion of the year throughout which the trust exists;

(e) where the congregation is a corporation, the corporation is deemed to be the trustee having control of the trust property;

(f) where the congregation is not a corporation, its council, committee of leaders, executive committee, administrative committee, officers or other group charged with its management are deemed to be the trustees having control of the trust property;

(g) the congregation is deemed to act and to have always acted as agent for the trust in all matters relating to its businesses and other activities;

(h) each business agency of the congregation in a calendar year is deemed to have acted as agent for the trust in all matters in the year relating to its businesses and other activities;

(i) the members of the congregation are deemed to be the beneficiaries under the trust;

(j) tax under this Part is payable by the trust on its taxable income for each taxation year;

(k) in computing the income of the trust for any taxation year,

(i) subject to paragraph (l), no deduction may be made in respect of salaries, wages or benefits of any kind provided to the members of the congregation, and

(ii) no deduction may be made under subsection 104(6), except to the extent that any portion of the trust's income (determined without reference to that subsection) is allocated to the members of the congregation in accordance with subsection (2);

(l) for the purpose of applying section 20.01 to the trust,

(i) each member of the congregation is deemed to be a member of the trust's household, and

(ii) section 20.01 shall be read without reference to paragraphs 20.01(2)(b) and (c) and subsection 20.01(3); and

(m) where the congregation or one of the business agencies is a corporation, section 15.1 shall, except for the purposes of paragraphs 15.1(2)(a) and (c) (other than subparagraphs 15.1(2)(c)(i) and (ii)), apply as if this subsection were read without reference to paragraphs (c), (d), (g) and (h).

**Related Provisions**: 108(1)"trust"(c) — S. 143 trust deemed not a trust for certain purposes; 127(7) — Investment tax credit of trust; 143(2) — Election in respect of income.

**Notes**: S.143 was enacted to deal with Hutterite colonies, and to overrule *Wipf*, [1975] C.T.C. 79 (FCA), [1976] C.T.C. 57 (SCC). See also subsec. 191(6.1) of the *Excise Tax Act*, which excludes such organizations from the GST self-supply rules for residential property.

143(1) amended by 1999 Budget, effective for 1998 and later taxation years. For 1992-97, read:

143. (1) Where a congregation

(a) the members of which live and work together,

(b) that does not permit any of its members to own any property in the member's own right, and

(c) that requires that its members devote their working lives to the activities of the congregation

carries on one or more businesses or has the effective management or control of one or more corporations, trusts or other persons (which corporations, trusts and other persons are in this section collectively referred to as "business agencies") that carry on one or more businesses for purposes that include supporting or sustaining its members or the members of any other congregation, an *inter vivos* trust shall be deemed to have been in existence on December 31, 1976 and continuously thereafter and the following rules apply:

(d) the property of the congregation and the property of all business agencies of the congregation shall be deemed to be the property of the *inter vivos* trust,

(e) where the congregation is a corporation, the corporation shall be deemed to be the trustee having control of the trust property,

(f) where the congregation is not a corporation, its council, committee of leaders, executive committee, administrative committee, officers or other group charged with the management of the congregation shall be deemed to be the trustees having control of the trust property,

(g) the congregation and all business agencies of the congregation shall be deemed to act and have always acted as agents for the *inter vivos* trust in all matters relating to their business and other activities,

(h) the members of the congregation shall be deemed to be the beneficiaries under the trust,

(i) tax under this Part is payable by the trust on its taxable income for each taxation year,

(j) in computing the income of the trust for any taxation year, no deduction may be made in respect of salaries, wages or benefits of any kind whatever, paid to the members of the congregation, and

(k) where the congregation or one of the business agencies is a corporation, section 15.1 shall, except for the purposes of paragraphs 15.1(2)(a) and (c) (other than subparagraphs 15.1(2)(c)(i) and (ii)), apply as if this subsection were read without reference to paragraphs (d) and (g).

143(1)(k) added by 1993 technical bill, effective 1992, to permit a communal organization to issue small business development bonds.

**Information Circulars**: 78-5R3: Communal organizations.

**(2) Election in respect of income** — Where the *inter vivos* trust referred to in subsection (1) in respect of a congregation so elects in respect of a taxation year in writing filed with the Minister on or before the trust's filing-due date for the year and all the congregation's participating members are specified in the election in accordance with subsection (5), the following rules apply:

(a) for the purposes of subsections 104(6) and (13), the amount payable in the year to a particular participating member of the congregation out of the income of the trust (determined without reference to subsection 104(6)) is the amount determined by the formula

$$0.8 \, (A \times B/C) + D + (0.2A - E)/F$$

where

A is the taxable income of the trust for the year (determined without reference to subsection 104(6) and specified future tax consequences for the year),

B is

(i) where the particular member is identified in the election as a person to whom this subparagraph applies (in this subsection referred to as a "designated member"), 1, and

(ii) in any other case, 0.5,

C is the total of

(i) the number of designated members of the congregation, and

(ii) ½ of the number of other participating members of the congregation in respect of the year,

D is the amount, if any, that is specified in the election as an additional allocation under this subsection to the particular member,

E is the total of all amounts each of which is an amount specified in the election as an additional allocation under this subsection to a participating member of the congregation in respect of the year, and

F is the number of participating members of the congregation in respect of the year;

(b) the designated member of each family at the end of the year is deemed to have supported the other members of the family during the year and the other members of the family are deemed to have been wholly dependent on the designated member for support during the year; and

(c) the taxable income for the year of each member of the congregation shall be computed without reference to subsection 110(2).

**Related Provisions**: 143(3) — Election not binding unless taxes paid; 143(5) — Specification of family members; 257 — Formula cannot calculate to less than zero.

**Notes**: 143(2) amended by 1999 Budget, effective for 1998 and later taxation years. For 1988-97, read:

(2) Election in respect of taxable income — Where the *inter vivos* trust referred to in subsection (1) in respect of a congregation so elects in respect of a taxation year, the amount determined under paragraph (a) for that taxation year shall be deemed to have been payable by the trust in the year to the beneficiaries thereunder in accordance with the following rules:

(a) determine the amount that would be the taxable income of the trust for the year if no deductions were made in respect of expenses incurred for the support, maintenance and satisfaction or personal needs of its members,

(b) determine the amount that is the quotient obtained when the amount so determined is divided by 1¼ times the number of adults who are members of the congregation at the end of the year,

(c) allocate to each family in the congregation at the end of the year the amount equal to the product obtained when the amount determined under paragraph (b) is multiplied by the number of adults in the family at the end of the year, and

(d) allocate among the families in the congregation at the end of the year in such manner as the congregation determines the amount by which the amount determined under paragraph (a) exceeds the total of amounts allocated under paragraph (c) or, if such an allocation is not made and specified in the election under this subsection in respect of the year, allocate to each of the families in the congregation at the end of the year the amount equal to the proportion of the excess that the number of adults in the family at that time is of the number of adults in all of the families in the congregation at that time,

and the total of amounts so allocated to a family shall be deemed to be payable in the year to, and to be received in the year by, the adult member of the family who is specified in the election under this subsection in respect of the year and that member of the family shall be deemed to have supported each of the other members of the family during that taxation year and the other members of the family shall be deemed to have been wholly dependent on that member for support during that taxation year.

**Information Circulars**: 78-5R3: Communal organizations.

**(3) Refusal to accept election** — An election under subsection (2) in respect of a congregation for a particular taxation year is not binding on the Minister unless all taxes, interest and penalties payable under this Part, as a consequence of the application of subsection (2) to the congregation for preceding taxation years, are paid at or before the end of the particular year.

**Notes**: 143(3) amended by 1999 Budget, effective for 1998 and later taxation years. For 1977-97, read:

(3) **Idem** — An election under subsection (2) in respect of a taxation year is not binding on the Minister unless

(a) the election is made on or before the day on or before which the *inter vivos* trust is required by section 150 to file a return of income for the year;

(b) all tax, interest and penalties, if any, payable under this Part by adult members designated in accordance with subsection (2) have been paid within the time required by this Act; and

(c) no amounts are, by virtue of subsection 110(2), deducted in computing the taxable income for the year of the members designated in accordance with subsection (2).

**Information Circulars**: 78-5R3: Communal organizations.

**(3.1) Election in respect of gifts** — For the purposes of section 118.1, where the fair market value of a gift made in a taxation year by an *inter vivos* trust referred to in subsection (1) in respect of a congregation would, but for this subsection, be included in the total charitable gifts, total Crown gifts, total cultural gifts or total ecological gifts of the trust for the year and the trust so elects in its return of income under this Part for the year,

(a) the trust is deemed not to have made the gift; and

(b) each participating member of the congregation is deemed to have made, in the year, such a gift the fair market value of which is the amount determined by the formula

$$A \times B/C$$

where

A is the fair market value of the gift made by the trust,

B is the amount determined for the year in respect of the member under paragraph (2)(a) as a consequence of an election under subsection (2) by the trust, and

C is the total of all amounts each of which is an amount determined for the year in respect of a participating member of the congregation under paragraph (2)(a) as a consequence of an election under subsection (2) by the trust.

**Notes**: 143(3.1) amended by 1999 Budget, effective for 1998 and later taxation years; however, the amendment to the opening words is effective for 1995 and later taxation years. For earlier years, read:

(3.1) For the purposes of section 118.1, where the fair market value of a gift made in a taxation year by an *inter vivos* trust referred to in subsection (1) would, but for this subsection, be included in the total charitable gifts, total Crown gifts or total cultural gifts of the trust for the year and the trust so elects in its return of income under this Part for the year,

(a) the trust shall be deemed not to have made the gift; and

(b) each adult member of a family to whom an amount is deemed under subsection (2) to be payable in the year shall be deemed to have made, in the year, such a gift the fair market value of which is the amount determined by the formula

$$A \times \frac{B}{C}$$

where

A is the fair market value of the gift made by the trust,

B is the amount deemed under subsection (2) to be payable in the year in respect of the trust to the adult member, and

C is the total of all amounts deemed under subsection (2) to be payable in the year in respect of the trust to an adult member of a family.

143(3.1) added by 1991 technical bill, effective 1990.

**Information Circulars**: 78-5R3: Communal organizations.

**(4) Definitions** — For the purposes of this section,

**"adult"** means an individual who, before the time at which the term is applied, has attained the age of eighteen years or is married or in a common-law partnership;

**Notes**: 143(4)"adult" amended by 2000 same-sex partners bill to add reference to "common-law partnership", effective for the 2001 and later taxation years, or earlier by election (see Notes to 248(1)"common-law partner").

**"business agency"**, of a congregation at any time in a particular calendar year, means a corporation, trust or other person, where the congregation owned all the shares of the capital stock of the corporation (except directors' qualifying shares) or every interest in the trust or other person, as the case may be, throughout the portion of the particular calendar year throughout which both the congregation and the corporation, trust or other person, as the case may be, were in existence;

**Notes**: 143(4)"business agency" added by 1999 Budget, effective for 1998 and later taxation years, except that for taxation years that end before 2001, read:

"business agency", of a congregation at any time in a particular calendar year, means

(a) a corporation, trust or other person, where the congregation owned all the shares of the capital stock of the corporation (except directors' qualifying shares) or ever interest in the trust or other person, as the case may be, throughout the portion of the particular year throughout which both the congregation and the corporation trust or other person, as the case may be, existed, or

(b) a corporation, trust or other person of which the congregation

(i) has effective management or control throughout the portion of the particular year throughout which both the congregation and the corporation, trust or other person, as the case may be, were in existence, and

(ii) had effective management or control during a taxation year of the corporation, trust or other person that began before March 1999 and ended in the particular year;

**"congregation"** means a community, society or body of individuals, whether or not incorporated,

(a) the members of which live and work together,

(b) that adheres to the practices and beliefs of, and operates according to the principles of, the religious organization of which it is a constituent part,

(c) that does not permit any of its members to own any property in their own right, and

(d) that requires its members to devote their working lives to the activities of the congregation;

**Notes**: 143(4)"congregation" amended by 1999 Budget, effective for 1998 and later taxation years, to add paras. (a), (c) and (d) ((b) was formerly in the body of the definition).

**"family"** means,

(a) in the case of an adult who is unmarried and who is not in a common-law partnership, that person and the person's children who are not adults, not married and not in a common-law partnership, and

(b) in the case of an adult who is married or in a common-law partnership, that person and the person's spouse or common-law partner and the children of either or both of them who are not adults, not married and not in a common-law partnership

but does not include an individual who is included in any other family or who is not a member of the congregation in which the family is included;

**Notes**: 143(4)"family" amended by 2000 same-sex partners bill, effective for the 2001 and later taxation years, or earlier by election (see Notes to 248(1)"common-law partner"). It formerly read:

"family" means,

(a) in the case of an unmarried adult, that person and the person's unmarried children who are not adults, and

(b) in the case of a married adult, that person and the person's spouse and the unmarried children of either or both of them who are not adults

but does not include an individual who is included in any other family or who is not a member of the congregation in which the family is included;

**"member of a congregation"** means

(a) an adult, living with the members of the congregation, who conforms to the practices of the religious organization of which the congregation is a constituent part whether or not that person has been formally accepted into the organization, and

(b) a child who is unmarried and not in a common-law partnership, other than an adult, of an adult referred to in paragraph (a), if the child lives with the members of the congregation;

**Notes**: Para. (b) amended to add reference to common-law partnership by 2000 same-sex partners bill, effective for the 2001 and later taxation years, or earlier by election (see Notes to 248(1)"common-law partner").

**"participating member"**, of a congregation in respect of a taxation year, means an individual who, at the end of the year, is an adult who is a member of the congregation;

**Notes**: 143(4)"participating member" added by 1999 Budget, effective for 1998 and later taxation years.

**"religious organization"** means an organization, other than a registered charity, of which a congregation is a constituent part, that adheres to beliefs, evidenced by the religious and philosophical tenets of the organization, that include a belief in the existence of a supreme being;

**"total charitable gifts"** has the meaning assigned by subsection 118.1(1);

**"total Crown gifts"** has the meaning assigned by subsection 118.1(1);

**"total cultural gifts"** has the meaning assigned by subsection 118.1(1).

**"total ecological gifts"** has the same meaning as in subsection 118.1(1).

**Notes**: 143(4)"total ecological gifts" added by 1999 Budget, effective for gifts made after February 27, 1995.

**Notes**: 143(4)"adult" was 143(4)(a); "congregation", 143(4)(b); "family", 143(4)(c); "member of a congregation", 143(4)(d); "religious organization", 143(4)(e); "total charitable gifts", "total Crown gifts" and "total cultural gifts", 143(4)(f) before consolidation in R.S.C. 1985 (5th Supp.), effective for taxation years ending after November 1991.

**(5) Specification of family members** — For the purpose of applying subsection (2) to a particular election by the *inter vivos* trust referred to in subsection (1) in respect of a congregation for a particular taxation year,

(a) subject to paragraph (b), a participating member of the congregation is considered to have been specified in the particular election in accordance with this subsection only if the member is identified in the particular election and

(i) where the member's family includes only one adult at the end of the particular year, the member is identified in the particular election as a person to whom subparagraph (i) of the description of B in subsection (2) (in this subsection referred to as the "relevant subparagraph") applies, and

(ii) in any other case, only one of the adults in the member's family is identified in the particular election as a person to whom the relevant subparagraph applies; and

(b) an individual is considered not to have been specified in the particular election in accordance with this subsection if

(i) the individual is one of two individuals who were married to each other at the end of a preceding taxation year of the trust and at the end of the particular year,

(ii) one of those individuals was

(A) where the preceding year ended before 1998, specified in an election under subsection (2) by the trust for the preceding year, and

(B) in any other case, identified in an election under subsection (2) by the trust for the preceding year as a person to whom the relevant subparagraph applied, and

(iii) the other individual is identified in the particular election as a person to whom the relevant subparagraph applies.

**Notes**: 143(5) amended by 1999 Budget, effective for 1998 and later taxation years. For earlier years, read:

(5) Effect of specification of member of family — Where an adult member (in this subsection referred to as a "specified person") of a family is specified in an election under subsection (2) in respect of a taxation year, no other member of that family may be specified in an election in respect of any subsequent taxation year at the end of which the specified person was a member of that family.

**Definitions [s. 143]**: "adult" — 143(4); "amount", "business" — 248(1); "business agency" — 143(4); "child" — 252(1); "congregation" — 143(4); "corporation" — 248(1), *Interpretation Act* 35(1); "family" — 143(4); "filing-due date", "individual" — 248(1); "inter vivos trust" — 108(1), 248(1); "member of a congregation" — 143(4); "Minister", "officer" — 248(1); "participating member" — 143(4); "person", "property" — 248(1); "qualifying share" — 192(6), 248(1); "registered charity" — 248(1); "religious organization" — 143(4); "share", "specified future tax consequence" — 248(1); "taxable income" — 248(1); "taxation year" — 249; "total charitable gifts", "total Crown gifts", "total cultural gifts", "total ecological gifts" — 143(4); "trust" — 104(1), 248(1), (3); "writing" — *Interpretation Act* 35(1).

## 143.1 (1) Amateur athletes' reserve funds —

Where a national sport organization that is a registered Canadian amateur athletic association receives an amount for the benefit of an individual under an arrangement made under rules of an international sport federation that require amounts to be held, controlled and administered by the organization in order to preserve the eligibility of the individual to compete in a sporting event sanctioned by the federation,

(a) an *inter vivos* trust (in this section referred to as an "amateur athlete trust") shall be deemed to be created on the day that is the later of

(i) the day on which the first such amount is received by the organization, and

(ii) January 1, 1992,

and to exist continuously thereafter until subsection (3) or (4) applies in respect of the trust;

(b) all property required to be held after 1991 under the arrangement shall be deemed to be property of the trust and not property of any other person;

(c) any amount received at any time under the arrangement by the organization shall, to the extent that it would, but for this subsection, be included in computing the individual's income for the taxation year that includes that time, be deemed to be income of the trust for the taxation year and not to be income of the individual;

(d) all amounts paid at any time by the organization under the arrangement to or for the benefit of the individual shall be deemed to be amounts distributed at that time to the individual by the trust;

(e) the individual shall be deemed to be the beneficiary under the trust;

(f) the organization shall be deemed to be the trustee of the trust; and

(g) no tax is payable under this Part by the trust on its taxable income for any taxation year.

**Related Provisions**: 128.1(10)"excluded right or interest"(e)(ii) — No deemed disposition on emigration of athlete; 149(1)(v) — Exemptions — amateur athlete trust; 210.2(1.1) — Part XII.2 tax payable by amateur athlete trust; 248(1)"amateur athlete trust" — Definition applies to entire Act; 248(1)"disposition"(f)(vi) — Rollover from one trust to another.

**Notes**: See at end of 143.1.

**Forms**: T3ATH-IND: Amateur athlete trust income tax return; T1061: Canadian amateur athlete trust group information return.

**(2) Amounts included in beneficiary's income** — In computing the income for a taxation year of the beneficiary under an amateur athlete trust, there shall be included the total of all amounts distributed in the year to the beneficiary by the trust.

**Related Provisions**: 12(1)(z) — Inclusion in income of amateur athlete trust payments; 210.2(1.1) — Application of Part XII.2 tax to amateur athlete trusts; 212(1)(u) — Non-resident withholding tax — amateur athlete trust payments; 214(3)(k) — Non-resident withholding tax.

**(3) Termination of amateur athlete trust** — Where an amateur athlete trust holds property on behalf of a beneficiary who has not competed in an international sporting event as a Canadian national team member for a period of 8 years that ends in a particular taxation year and begins in the year that is the later of

(a) where the beneficiary has competed in such an event, the year in which the beneficiary last so competed, and

(b) the year in which the trust was created,

the trust shall be deemed to have distributed, at the end of the particular taxation year to the beneficiary, an amount equal to

(c) where the trust is liable to pay tax under Part XII.2 in respect of the particular year, 64% of the fair market value of all property held by it at that time, and

(d) in any other case, the fair market value of all property held by it at that time.

**Related Provisions**: 210.2(1.1) — Application of Part XII.2 tax to amateur athlete trusts.

**(4) Death of beneficiary** — Where an amateur athlete trust holds property on behalf of a beneficiary who dies in a year, the trust shall be deemed to have distributed, immediately before the death, to the beneficiary, an amount equal to

(a) where the trust is liable to pay tax under Part XII.2 in respect of the year, 64% of the fair market value of all property held by it at that time; and

(b) in any other case, the fair market value of all property held by it at that time.

**Related Provisions**: 210.2(1.1) — Application of Part XII.2 tax to amateur athlete trusts.

**Notes [s. 143.1]**: 143.1 added by 1992 technical bill, effective for 1992 and later taxation years. It also applies to the 1988 to 1991 taxation years, if an individual and a national sport organization that has received an amount for the benefit of that individual jointly elect by notifying Revenue Canada in writing. In such a case, read "1992" in 143.1(1)(a) as the taxation year for which the election is made; and read "1991" in 143.1(1)(b) as the preceding taxation year.

**Definitions [s. 143.1]**: "amateur athlete trust" — 143.1(1)(a), 248(1); "amount" — 248(1); "beneficiary" — 108(1); "individual" — 248(1); *inter vivos* trust" — 108(1), 248(1); "property", "registered Canadian amateur athletic association" — 248(1); "taxation year" — 11(2), 249.

## Cost of Tax Shelter Investments

**143.2 (1) Definitions** — The definitions in this subsection apply in this section.

**"expenditure"** means an outlay or expense or the cost or capital cost of a property.

**Related Provisions**: 143.2(2) — At-risk adjustment in respect of expenditures; 143.2(6) — Expenditures reduced by at-risk adjustment.

**Notes**: See Notes at end of 143.2.

**"limited partner"** has the meaning that would be assigned by subsection 96(2.4) if that subsection were read without reference to "if the member's partnership interest is not an exempt interest (within the meaning assigned by subsection (2.5)) at that time and".

**"limited-recourse amount"** means the unpaid principal amount of any indebtedness for which recourse is limited, either immediately or in the future and either absolutely or contingently.

**Related Provisions**: 143.2(7), (8), (13) — Whether unpaid principal deemed to be limited-recourse amount; 248(1) — Definition of "principal amount"; Reg. 231(6.1) — Limited-recourse amount may be prescribed benefit for purposes of definition of tax shelter.

**"taxpayer"** includes a partnership.

**Notes**: The effect of this definition is that the restrictions on tax shelter investments in 143.2 are calculated at the partnership level.

See also Notes at end of 143.2.

**"tax shelter investment"** means

(a) a property that is a tax shelter for the purpose of subsection 237.1(1); or

(b) a taxpayer's interest in a partnership where

(i) an interest in the taxpayer

(A) is a tax shelter investment, and

(B) the taxpayer's partnership interest would be a tax shelter investment if

(I) this Act were read without reference to this paragraph and to the words "having regard to statements or representations made or proposed to be made in connection with the property" in the definition "tax shelter" in subsection 237.1(1),

(II) the references in that definition to "represented" were read as references to "that can reasonably be expected", and

(III) the reference in that definition to "is represented" were read as a reference to "can reasonably be expected",

(ii) another interest in the partnership is a tax shelter investment, or

(iii) the taxpayer's interest in the partnership entitles the taxpayer, directly or indirectly, to a share of the income or loss of a particular partnership where

(A) another taxpayer holding a partnership interest is entitled, directly or indirectly, to a share of the income or loss of the particular partnership, and

(B) that other taxpayer's partnership interest is a tax shelter investment.

**Related Provisions**: 18.1(13) — Matchable expenditure deemed to be a tax shelter investment; 53(2)(c)(i.3) — Tax shelter investment excluded from certain ACB reductions; 143.2(6) — Limitation on cost of tax shelter investment; 150(1)(d)(ii)(A) — Tax shelter investment does not entitle individual to June 15 filing deadline; 249.1(5) — Election for non-calendar year-end not permitted for tax shelters; Reg. 1100(20.1) — limitation on CCA claim for computer software tax shelter property.

**Notes**: For discussion of tax shelters see Donald Watkins, "The Tax-Shelter Rules: An Update", 1998 Canadian Tax Foundation annual conference proceedings, pp. 5:1-5:32.

See Notes at end of 143.2 re in-force application.

**(2) At-risk adjustment** — For the purpose of this section, an at-risk adjustment in respect of an expenditure of a particular taxpayer, other than the cost of a partnership interest to which subsection 96(2.2) applies, means any amount or benefit that the particular taxpayer, or another taxpayer not dealing at arm's length with the particular taxpayer, is entitled, either immediately or in the future and either absolutely or contingently, to receive or to obtain, whether by way of reimbursement, compensation, revenue guarantee, proceeds of disposition, loan or any other form of indebtedness, or in any other form or manner whatever, granted or to be granted for the purpose of reducing the impact, in whole or in part, of any loss that the particular taxpayer may sustain in respect of the expenditure or, where the expenditure is the cost or capital cost of a property, any loss from the holding or disposition of the property.

**Related Provisions**: 96(2.2) — At-risk amount for limited partnership; 143.2(3) — Exclusions from at-risk adjustment;

143.2(4) — Determination of amount or benefit; 143.2(6) — Expenditures reduced by at-risk adjustment; 143.2(9) — Timing.

**Notes**: See Notes at end of 143.2.

**(3) Amount or benefit not included** — For the purpose of subsection (2), an at-risk adjustment in respect of a taxpayer's expenditure does not include an amount or benefit

(a) to the extent that it is included in determining the value of J in the definition "cumulative Canadian exploration expense" in subsection 66.1(6), of M in the definition "cumulative Canadian development expense" in subsection 66.2(5) or of I in the definition "cumulative Canadian oil and gas property expense" in subsection 66.4(5) in respect of the taxpayer; or

(b) the entitlement to which arises

(i) because of a contract of insurance with an insurance corporation dealing at arm's length with the taxpayer (and, where the expenditure is the cost of an interest in a partnership, with each member of the partnership) under which the taxpayer is insured against any claim arising as a result of a liability incurred in the ordinary course of carrying on the business of the taxpayer or the partnership,

(ii) as a consequence of the death of the taxpayer,

(iii) in respect of an amount not included in the expenditure, determined without reference to subparagraph (6)(b)(ii), or

(iv) because of an excluded obligation (as defined in subsection 6202.1(5) of the *Income Tax Regulations*) in relation to a share issued to the taxpayer or, where the expenditure is the cost of an interest in a partnership, to the partnership.

**Notes**: See Notes at end of 143.2.

**(4) Amount or benefit** — For the purposes of subsections (2) and (3), where the amount or benefit to which a taxpayer is entitled at any time is provided by way of an agreement or other arrangement under which the taxpayer has a right, either immediately or in the future and either absolutely or contingently (otherwise than as a consequence of the death of the taxpayer), to acquire property, for greater certainty the amount or benefit to which the taxpayer is entitled under the agreement or arrangement is considered to be not less than the fair market value of the property at that time.

**(5) Amount or benefit** — For the purposes of subsections (2) and (3), where the amount or benefit to which a taxpayer is entitled at any time is provided by way of a guarantee, security or similar indemnity or covenant in respect of any loan or other obligation of the taxpayer, for greater certainty the amount or benefit to which the taxpayer is entitled under the guarantee or indemnity at any particular time is considered to be not less than the total of the unpaid amount of the loan or obligation at that time and all other amounts outstanding in respect of the loan or obligation at that time.

**(6) Amount of expenditure** — Notwithstanding any other provision of this Act, the amount of any expenditure that is, or is the cost or capital cost of, a taxpayer's tax shelter investment, and the amount of any expenditure of a taxpayer an interest in which is a tax shelter investment, shall be reduced to the amount, if any, by which

(a) the amount of the taxpayer's expenditure otherwise determined

exceeds

(b) the total of

(i) the limited-recourse amounts of

(A) the taxpayer, and

(B) all other taxpayers not dealing at arm's length with the taxpayer

that can reasonably be considered to relate to the expenditure,

(ii) the taxpayer's at-risk adjustment in respect of the expenditure, and

(iii) each limited-recourse amount and at-risk adjustment, determined under this section when this section is applied to each other taxpayer who deals at arm's length with and holds, directly or indirectly, an interest in the taxpayer, that can reasonably be considered to relate to the expenditure.

**Related Provisions**: 18.1(13) — Subpara. (6)(b)(ii) inapplicable for matchable expenditures; Reg. 1100(20.1) — limitation on CCA claim for computer software tax shelter property.

**Notes**: See Notes at end of 143.2.

**(7) Repayment of indebtedness** — For the purpose of this section, the unpaid principal of an indebtedness is deemed to be a limited-recourse amount unless

(a) *bona fide* arrangements, evidenced in writing, were made, at the time the indebtedness arose, for repayment by the debtor of the indebtedness and all interest on the indebtedness within a reasonable period not exceeding 10 years; and

(b) interest is payable at least annually, at a rate equal to or greater than the lesser of

(i) the prescribed rate of interest in effect at the time the indebtedness arose, and

(ii) the prescribed rate of interest applicable from time to time during the term of the indebtedness,

and is paid in respect of the indebtedness by the debtor no later than 60 days after the end of each taxation year of the debtor that ends in the period.

**Related Provisions**: 143.2(12) — Series of loans or repayments; Reg. 4301(c) (prescribed rate of interest).

**(8) Limited-recourse amount** — For the purpose of this section, the unpaid principal of an indebtedness is deemed to be a limited-recourse amount of a taxpayer where the taxpayer is a partnership and recourse against any member of the partnership in respect of the indebtedness is limited, either immediately or in the future and either absolutely or contingently.

**(9) Timing** — Where at any time a taxpayer has paid an amount (in this subsection referred to as the "repaid amount") on account of the principal amount of an indebtedness that was, before that time, the unpaid principal amount of a loan or any other form of indebtedness to which subsection (2) applies (in this subsection referred to as the "former amount or benefit") relating to an expenditure of the taxpayer,

(a) the former amount or benefit is considered to have been an amount or benefit under subsection (2) in respect of the taxpayer at all times before that time; and

(b) the expenditure is, subject to subsection (6), deemed to have been made or incurred at that time to the extent of, and by the payment of, the repaid amount.

**Notes**: This was 143.2(5.1) in the draft legislation of December 14, 1995. See Notes at end of 143.2.

**(10) Timing** — Where at any time a taxpayer has paid an amount (in this subsection referred to as the "repaid amount") on account of the principal amount of an indebtedness which was, before that time, an unpaid principal amount that was a limited-recourse amount (in this subsection referred to as the "former limited-recourse indebtedness") relating to an expenditure of the taxpayer,

(a) the former limited-recourse indebtedness is considered to have been a limited-recourse amount at all times before that time; and

(b) the expenditure is, subject to subsection (6), deemed to have been made or incurred at that time to the extent of, and by the amount of, the repaid amount.

**Related Provisions**: 231.6 — Foreign-based information.

**Notes**: This was 143.2(9) in the draft legislation of December 14, 1995. See Notes at end of 143.2.

**(11) Short-term debt** — Where a taxpayer pays all of the principal of an indebtedness no later than 60 days after that indebtedness arose and the indebtedness would otherwise be considered to be a limited-recourse amount solely because of the application of subsection (7) or (8), that subsection does not apply to the indebtedness unless

(a) any portion of the repayment is made with a limited-recourse amount; or

(b) the repayment can reasonably be considered to be part of a series of loans or other indebtedness and repayments that ends more than 60 days after the indebtedness arose.

**Related Provisions**: 231.6 — Foreign-based information; 251(1) — Arm's length.

**Notes**: This subsection was not included in the draft legislation of December 14, 1995. See Notes at end of 143.2.

**(12) Series of loans or repayments** — For the purpose of paragraph (7)(a), a debtor is considered not to have made arrangements to repay an indebtedness within 10 years where the debtor's arrangement to repay can reasonably be considered to be part of a series of loans or other indebtedness and repayments that ends more than 10 years after it begins.

**Notes**: This was 143.2(7.1) in the draft legislation of December 14, 1995. See Notes at end of 143.2.

**(13) Information located outside Canada** — For the purpose of this section, where it can reasonably be considered that information relating to indebtedness that relates to a taxpayer's expenditure is available outside Canada and the Minister is not satisfied that the unpaid principal of the indebtedness is not a limited-recourse amount, the unpaid principal of the indebtedness relating to the taxpayer's expenditure is deemed to be a limited-recourse amount relating to the expenditure unless

(a) the information is provided to the Minister; or

(b) the information is located in a country with which the Government of Canada has entered into a tax convention or agreement that has the force of law in Canada and includes a provision under which the Minister can obtain the information.

**Notes**: This was 143.2(10) in the draft legislation of December 14, 1995. See Notes at end of 143.2.

**(14) Information located outside Canada** — For the purpose of this section, where it can reasonably be considered that information relating to whether a taxpayer is not dealing at arm's length with another taxpayer is available outside Canada and the Minister is not satisfied that the taxpayer is dealing at arm's length with the other taxpayer, the taxpayer and the other taxpayer are deemed not to be dealing with each other at arm's length unless

(a) the information is provided to the Minister; or

(b) the information is located in a country with which the Government of Canada has entered into a tax convention or agreement that has the force of law in Canada and includes a provision under which the Minister can obtain the information.

**Notes**: This was 143.2(11) in the draft legislation of December 14, 1995. See Notes at end of 143.2.

**(15) Assessments** — Notwithstanding subsections 152(4) to (5), such assessments, determinations and redeterminations may be made as are necessary to give effect to this section.

**Related Provisions**: 237(6.1) — Late assessment to deny deduction when penalty unpaid.

**Notes**: This was 143.2(12) in the draft legislation of December 14, 1995. See Notes below.

## S. 143.2

**Notes [s. 143.2]:** 143.2 added by 1995-97 technical bill, effective for property acquired and outlays and expenses made or incurred by a taxpayer after November 1994, except that

(a) it does not apply where

(i) the property was acquired, or the outlay or expense was made or incurred, before 1995 pursuant to an agreement in writing made by the taxpayer before December 1994, or

(ii) the property is

(A) a film production prescribed for the purpose of 96(2.2)(d)(ii) where

(I) the principal photography of the production began before 1995, or, in the case of a production that is a television series, one episode of the series began before 1995, and

(II) the principal photography of the production was completed before March 2, 1995, or

(B) an interest in a partnership (all or substantially all of the property of which is a film production referred to in clause (A)) acquired before 1995 by a taxpayer that is a partnership

and the following conditions are met:

(iii) in the case of an interest that is a tax shelter for which s. 237.1 requires an identification number to be obtained, an identification number was obtained before December 1994, and

(iv) there is no agreement or other arrangement under which the taxpayer's obligations with respect to the interest can be changed, reduced or waived if there is a change to the Act or if there is an adverse assessment under the Act;

(b) it does not apply to revenue guarantees prescribed for the purpose of subpara. 96(2.2)(d)(ii) that were granted before 1996;

(c) 143.2(6)(b)(ii) does not apply

(i) to property acquired, or outlays or expenses made or incurred, by a taxpayer before April 27, 1995, or

(ii) to property acquired, or outlays or expenses made or incurred, by a taxpayer before 1996 pursuant to a particular agreement in writing made by the taxpayer before April 27, 1995 where the following conditions are met:

(A) in the case of a property that is a tax shelter for which s. 237.1 requires an identification number, an identification number was obtained before April 27, 1995, and

(B) there is no agreement or other arrangement under which the taxpayer's obligations under the particular agreement can be changed, reduced or waived if there is a change to the Act or if there is an adverse assessment under the Act;

(d) 143.2(7)(a) shall be read without reference to "not exceeding 10 years" where

(i) the indebtedness arises

(A) pursuant to the terms of an agreement in writing made by the taxpayer before April 27, 1995,

(B) before 1996, in respect of the acquisition of a film production prescribed for the purpose of 96(2.2)(d)(ii) or an interest in a partnership all or substantially all of the property of which is either a film production prescribed for the purpose of that subparagraph or an interest in one or more partnerships all or substantially all of the property of each of which is such a film production, where

(I) the principal photography of the production began before 1996, or, in the case of a production that is a television series, the principal photography of one episode of the series began before 1996, and

(II) the principal photography of the production was completed before March 1996, or

(C) before July 1995

(I) pursuant to the terms of a document that is a prospectus, preliminary prospectus or registration statement filed before April 27, 1995 with a public authority in Canada pursuant to and in accordance with the securities legislation of Canada or of any province and, where required by law, accepted for filing by the public authority, and the funds so raised were expended before 1996 on expenditures contemplated by the document, or

(II) pursuant to the terms of an offering memorandum distributed as part of an offering of securities where

1. the memorandum contained a complete or substantially complete description of the securities contemplated in the offering as well as the terms and conditions of the offering,

2. the memorandum was distributed before April 27, 1995,

3. solicitations in respect of the sale of the securities contemplated by the memorandum were made before April 27, 1995,

4. the sale of the securities was substantially in accordance with the memorandum, and

5. the funds were expended before 1996 in accordance with the memorandum, and

(ii) the following conditions are met:

(A) in the case of an interest to which clause (i)(A) or (C) applies that is a tax shelter for which s. 237.1 requires an identification number to be obtained, an identification number was obtained before April 27, 1995, and

(B) there is no agreement or other arrangement under which the taxpayer's obligations with respect to the interest can be changed, reduced or waived if there is a change to the Act or if there is an adverse assessment under the Act; and

(e) 143.2(8) does not apply to a taxpayer in respect of an indebtedness

(i) where the indebtedness

(A) arose, and

(B) is related to property acquired, or outlays or expenses made or incurred, by the taxpayer

before April 27, 1995, nor

(ii) where the indebtedness

(A) arose, and

(B) is related to property acquired, or outlays or expenses made or incurred, by the taxpayer,

before 1996 pursuant to a particular agreement in writing made by the taxpayer before April 27, 1995 and there is no agreement or other arrangement under which the taxpayer's obligations under the particular agreement can be changed, reduced or waived if there is a change to the Act or if there is an adverse assessment under the Act.

**Definitions [s. 143.2]:** "amount" — 143.2(4), (5.1), (6), 248(1); "arm's length" — 143.2(11), 251(1); "at-risk adjustment" — 143.2(2), (3); "benefit" — 143.2(4), (5.1); "business" — 248(1); "Canada" — 255; "consequence of the death" — 248(8); "expenditure" — 143.2(1), (6); "former limited-recourse indebtedness" — 143.2(9); "insurance corporation" — 248(1); "limited partner" —

143.2(1); "limited-recourse amount" — 143.2(1), (7), (8); "Minister" — 248(1); "partnership" — see Notes to 96(1); "prescribed" — 248(1); "prescribed rate" — Reg. 4301; "principal amount", "property" — 248(1); "repaid amount" — 143.2(9); "regulation" — 248(1); "specified member" — 248(1), (28); "tax shelter investment" — 143.2(1); "taxpayer" — 143.2(1), 248(1); "taxation year" — 249.

## DIVISION G — DEFERRED AND OTHER SPECIAL INCOME ARRANGEMENTS

### Employees Profit Sharing Plans

**144. (1) Definitions** — The definitions in this subsection apply in this section.

**"employees profit sharing plan"** at a particular time means an arrangement

(a) under which payments computed by reference to

(i) an employer's profits from the employer's business,

(ii) the profits from the business of a corporation with which the employer does not deal at arm's length, or

(iii) any combination of the amounts described in subparagraphs (i) and (ii)

are required to be made by the employer to a trustee under the arrangement for the benefit of employees of the employer or of a corporation with which the employer does not deal at arm's length; and

(b) in respect of which the trustee has, since the later of the beginning of the arrangement and the end of 1949, allocated, either contingently or absolutely, to those employees

(i) in each year that ended at or before the particular time, all amounts received in the year by the trustee from the employer or from a corporation with which the employer does not deal at arm's length,

(ii) in each year that ended at or before the particular time, all profits for the year from the property of the trust (determined without regard to any capital gain made by the trust or capital loss sustained by it at any time after 1955),

(iii) in each year that ended after 1971 and at or before the particular time, all capital gains and capital losses of the trust for the year,

(iv) in each year that ended after 1971, before 1993 and at or before the particular time, 100/15 of the total of all amounts each of which is deemed by subsection (9) to be paid on account of tax under this Part in respect of an employee because the employee ceased to be a beneficiary under the plan in the year, and

(v) in each year that ended after 1991 and at or before the particular time, the total of all amounts each of which is an amount that may be deducted under subsection (9) in computing the employee's income because the employee ceased to be a beneficiary under the plan in the year.

**Related Provisions**: 94(1)"exempt foreign trust"(g) — Non-resident EPSP excluded from non-resident trust rules; 128.1(10)"excluded right or interest"(a)(v) — No deemed disposition on emigration; 144(9) — Refunds; 144(10) — Payments out of profits; 144(11) — Year-end on becoming DPSP; 147(6) — DPSP deemed not to be EPSP; 233.2(1)"exempt trust"(b)(iv)(B) — foreign EPSP exempt from foreign trust reporting rules; 248(1)"disposition"(f)(vi) — Rollover from one trust to another; 248(1)"employees profit sharing plan" — Definition applies to entire Act; 251(1) — Arm's length.

**Notes**: Definition amended by 1993 technical bill, effective for 1992 and later taxation years; and where an amount was paid to a person before 1993 without first have been allocated to that person, it shall be deemed for purposes of the amended definition to have been allocated to that person.

**Regulations**: 204(3)(b) (no requirement to file regular trust return); 212 (information return).

**Interpretation Bulletins**: IT-280R: Employees profit sharing plans — payments computed by reference to profits; IT-379R: Employees profit sharing plans — allocations to beneficiaries.

**"unused portion of a beneficiary's exempt capital gains balance"** in respect of a trust governed by an employees profit sharing plan, at any particular time in a taxation year of the beneficiary, means

(a) where the year ends before 2005, the amount, if any, by which the beneficiary's exempt capital gains balance (in this paragraph having the same meaning as in subsection 39.1(1)) in respect of the trust for the year exceeds the total of all amounts each of which is an amount by which a capital gain is reduced under section 39.1 in the year because of the beneficiary's exempt capital gains balance in respect of the trust; or

(b) where the year ends after 2004, the amount, if any, by which

(i) the amount, if any, that would, if the definition "exempt capital gains balance" in subsection 39.1(1) were read without reference to "that ends before 2005", be the beneficiary's exempt capital gains balance in respect of the trust for the year

exceeds

(ii) where there has been a disposition of an interest or a part of an interest of the beneficiary in the trust after the beneficiary's 2004 taxation year (other than a disposition that is a part of a transaction described in paragraph (7.1)(c) in which property is received in satisfaction of all or a portion of the beneficiary's interests in the trust), the total of all amounts each of which is an amount by which the adjusted cost base of an interest or a part of an interest disposed of by the beneficiary (other than an interest or a part of an interest that is

**S. 144(1) unu**　　Income Tax Act, Part I

all or a portion of the beneficiary's interests referred to in paragraph (7.1)(c)) was increased because of paragraph 53(1)(p), and

(iii) in any other case, nil.

**Notes**: Definition "unused portion of a beneficiary's exempt capital gains balance" added by 1995-97 technical bill, effective for 1994 and later taxation years.

**(2) No tax while trust governed by a plan** — No tax is payable under this Part by a trust on the taxable income of the trust for a taxation year throughout which the trust is governed by an employees profit sharing plan.

**Related Provisions**: 149(1)(p) — Exemption from tax.

**Notes**: 144(2) amended by 1993 technical bill, effective for 1993 and later taxation years, to require that the EPSP be in place "throughout" the year.

**(3) Allocation contingent or absolute taxable** — There shall be included in computing the income for a taxation year of an employee who is a beneficiary under an employees profit sharing plan each amount that is allocated to the employee contingently or absolutely by the trustee under the plan at any time in the year otherwise than in respect of

(a) a payment made by the employee to the trustee;

(b) a capital gain made by the trust before 1972;

(c) a capital gain of the trust for a taxation year ending after 1971;

(d) a gain made by the trust after 1971 from the disposition of a capital property except to the extent that the gain is a capital gain described in paragraph (c); or

(e) a dividend received by the trust from a taxable Canadian corporation.

(f) [Repealed]

**Related Provisions**: 6(1)(d) — Inclusion in income from employment; 144(8) — Allocation of credit for dividends; 147(11) — Portion of receipts deductible where EPSP later becomes a DPSP.

**Notes**: 144(3)(f) repealed by 1993 technical bill, effective for 1992 and later taxation years. However, a taxpayer could elect to have 144(3)(f) continue to apply to the 1992 taxation year by notifying Revenue Canada in writing by December 31, 1994. For 1988 to 1991 (or 1992 with the above election), read:

(f) interest received by the trust.

**Regulations**: 212 (information return).

**Interpretation Bulletins**: IT-379R: Employees' profit sharing plans — allocations to beneficiaries.

**Forms**: T4PS Segment; T4PS Summary: Return of allocations and payments under employees profit sharing plan; T4PS Supplementary: Statement of employees profit sharing plan allocations and payments.

**(4) Allocated capital gains and losses** — Each capital gain and capital loss of a trust governed by an employees profit sharing plan from the disposition of any property shall, to the extent that it is allocated by the trust to an employee who is a beneficiary under the plan, be deemed to be a capital gain or capital loss, as the case may be, of the employee from the disposition of that property for the taxation year of the employee in which the allocation was made and, for the purposes of section 110.6, the property shall be deemed to have been disposed of by the employee on the day on which it was disposed of by the trust.

**Related Provisions**: 6(1)(d) — Allocations etc. under profit sharing plan; 39.1(1) "exempt capital gains balance" "C(c), 39.1(6) — Reduction in gain to reflect capital gains exemption election.

**Notes**: 144(4) amended by 1994 Budget, effective 1994, to ensure that allocated gains are eligible for the capital gains exemption in 110.6(3) where they arose before February 23, 1994. From 1972 to February 22, 1994, read:

(4) Any capital gain of a trust governed by an employees profit sharing plan or any capital loss of the trust for a taxation year ending after 1971 from the disposition of any property shall, to the extent that it has been allocated by the trust to an employee who is a beneficiary under the plan, be deemed to be a capital gain or capital loss, as the case may be, of the employee from the disposition of that property, for the taxation year of the employee in which the allocation was made.

**Interpretation Bulletins**: IT-379R: Employees profit sharing plans — allocations to beneficiaries.

**(4.1) Idem** — Notwithstanding subsection 26(6) of the *Income Tax Application Rules*, where at any time before 1976 the trustee of a trust governed by an employees profit sharing plan so elects in prescribed manner, the trust shall be deemed

(a) to have, on December 31, 1971, disposed of each property owned by the trust on that day for proceeds of disposition equal to the fair market value of the property on that day, and

(b) to have, on January 1, 1972, reacquired each property described in paragraph (a) for the amount referred to in that paragraph,

if the trustee under the plan has, before 1976, allocated the total of all capital gains and capital losses resulting from the deemed dispositions among the employees or other beneficiaries under the plan to the extent that the trustee under the plan has not previously so allocated them.

**Related Provisions**: 54 "superficial loss"(c) — Superficial loss rule does not apply.

**Regulations**: 1500(1) (prescribed manner).

**Interpretation Bulletins**: IT-379R: Employees profit sharing plans — allocations to beneficiaries.

**(4.2) Idem** — Where a trust governed by an employees profit sharing plan

(a) was governed by an employees profit sharing plan on December 31, 1971, and the trustee of the trust has made an election under subsection (4.1), or

(b) was not governed by an employees profit sharing plan on December 31, 1971,

the trustee of the trust may, in any taxation year after 1973, elect in prescribed manner and prescribed form to treat any capital property of the trust as having been disposed of, in which event the property shall be deemed to have been disposed of on any day designated by the trustee for proceeds of disposition equal to

(c) the fair market value of the property on that day,

(d) the adjusted cost base to the trust of the property on that day, or

(e) an amount that is neither greater than the greater of the amounts determined under paragraphs (c) and (d) nor less than the lesser of the amounts determined under those paragraphs

whichever is designated by the trustee and to have been reacquired by the trust immediately thereafter at a cost equal to those proceeds.

**Related Provisions**: 54"superficial loss"(c) — Superficial loss rule does not apply.

**Regulations**: 1500(2) (prescribed manner).

**Interpretation Bulletins**: IT-379R: Employees profit sharing plans — allocations to beneficiaries.

**Forms**: T3009: Election for deemed disposition and reacquisition of any capital property of an employees profit sharing plan under subsection 144(4.2).

**(5) Employer's contribution to trust deductible** — An amount paid by an employer to a trustee under an employees profit sharing plan during a taxation year or within 120 days thereafter may be deducted in computing the employer's income for the taxation year to the extent that it was not deductible in computing income for a previous taxation year.

**Related Provisions**: 12(1)(n) — Benefits from employees profit sharing plan — income to employer; 18(1)(k) — Limitation re employer's contribution under profit sharing plan; 20(1)(w) — Employer's contribution under profit sharing plan.

**(6) Beneficiary's receipts deductible** — An amount received in a taxation year by a beneficiary from a trustee under an employees profit sharing plan shall not be included in computing the beneficiary's income for the year.

**Related Provisions**: 12(1)(n) — Benefits from employees profit sharing plan — income to employer; 18(1)(k)(i), 20(1)(w) — Deduction for employer's contribution.

**(7) Beneficiary's receipts that are not deductible** — Notwithstanding subsection (6), such portion of an amount received in a taxation year by a beneficiary from the trustee under an employees profit sharing plan as cannot be established to be attributable to

(a) payments made by the employee to the trustee,

(b) amounts required to be included in computing the income of the employee for that or a previous taxation year,

(c) a capital gain made by the trust before 1972,

(d) a capital gain made by the trust for a taxation year ending after 1971, to the extent allocated by the trust to the beneficiary,

(e) a gain made by the trust after 1971 from the disposition of a capital property, except to the extent that the gain is a capital gain made by the trust for a taxation year ending after 1971,

(f) the portion, if any, of the increase in the value of property transferred to the beneficiary by the trustee that would have been considered to be a capital gain made by the trust in 1971 if the trustee had sold the property on December 31, 1971 for its fair market value at that time, or

(g) a dividend received by the trust from a taxable Canadian corporation other than a dividend described in subsection 83(1), to the extent allocated by the trust to the beneficiary,

shall be included in computing the beneficiary's income for the year in which the amount was received, except that in determining the amount of any payments or other things described in any paragraph of this subsection, the amount thereof otherwise determined shall be reduced by such portion of the total of all capital losses of the trust for taxation years ending after 1971 as has been allocated by the trust to the beneficiary and has not been applied to reduce the amount of any payments or other things described in any other paragraph of this subsection.

**Related Provisions**: 6(1)(d) — Allocations etc. under profit sharing plan; 212 — Tax on Canadian income of non-resident persons.

**Interpretation Bulletins**: IT-379R: Employees profit sharing plan — allocations to beneficiaries.

**Forms**: T4PS Segment; T4PS Summary: Return of allocations and payments under employees profit sharing plan; T4PS Supplementary: Statement of employees profit sharing plan allocations and payments.

**(7.1) Where property other than money received by beneficiary** — Where, at any particular time in a taxation year of a trust governed by an employees profit sharing plan, an amount was received by a beneficiary from the trustee under the plan and the amount so received was property other than money, the following rules apply in respect of each such property so received by the beneficiary at the particular time:

(a) the amount that was the cost amount to the trust of the property immediately before the particular time shall be deemed to be the trust's proceeds of disposition of the property; and

(b) that proportion of

(i) such portion of the amount received by the beneficiary as can be established to be attributable to the payments or other things described in paragraphs (7)(a) to (g) (on the assumption that the amount of any payments or other things described in any such paragraph is the amount thereof determined as provided in subsection (7))

that

(ii) the cost amount to the trust of the property immediately before the particular time

is of

(iii) the cost amounts to the trust of all properties, other than money, so received by the beneficiary at the particular time,

is, subject to paragraph (c), deemed to be

(iv) the cost to the beneficiary of the property, and

(v) for the purposes of subsection (7) but not for the purposes of this subsection, the amount so received by the beneficiary by virtue of the receipt by the beneficiary of the property.

(c) where a particular property received is all or a portion of property received in satisfaction of all or a portion of the beneficiary's interests in the trust and the beneficiary files with the Minister on or before the beneficiary's filing-due date for the taxation year that includes the particular time an election in respect of the particular property in prescribed form, there shall be included in the cost to the beneficiary of the particular property determined under paragraph (b) the least of

(i) the amount, if any, by which the unused portion of the beneficiary's exempt capital gains balance in respect of the trust at the particular time exceeds the total of all amounts each of which is an amount included because of this paragraph in the cost to the beneficiary of another property received by the beneficiary at or before the particular time in the year,

(ii) the amount, if any, by which the fair market value of the particular property at the particular time exceeds the amount deemed by subparagraph (b)(iv) to be the cost to the beneficiary of the particular property, and

(iii) the amount designated in the election in respect of the particular property.

**Related Provisions**: 39.1(1)"exempt capital gains balance"F(a) — Exempt capital gains balance of flow-through entity.

**Notes**: 144(7.1)(c) (and reference to it in (b)) added by 1995-97 technical bill, effective for 1994 and later taxation years; and a prescribed form filed under 144(7.1)(c) by the end of 1998 is deemed filed on time.

**Interpretation Bulletins**: IT-379R: Employees profit sharing plan — allocations to beneficiaries.

**Forms**: T4PS Segment; T4PS Summary: Return of allocations and payments under employees profit sharing plan; T4PS Supplementary: Statement of employees profit sharing plan allocations and payments.

**(8) Allocation of credit for dividends** — Where there has been included in computing the income of a trust for a taxation year during which the trust was governed by an employees profit sharing plan taxable dividends from taxable Canadian corporations and there has been allocated by the trustee under the plan for the purposes of this subsection an amount for the year to one or more of the employees who are beneficiaries under the plan, which amount or the total of which amounts does not exceed the amount of the taxable dividends so included, each of the employees who are beneficiaries under the plan shall be deemed to have received a taxable dividend from a taxable Canadian corporation equal to the lesser of

(a) the amount, if any, that would be included in computing the employee's income for the year by virtue of this section, if this section were read without reference to paragraph (3)(e), and

(b) the amount, if any, so allocated for the purposes of this subsection to the employee.

**Interpretation Bulletins**: IT-379R: Employees profit sharing plans — allocations to beneficiaries.

**(8.1) Foreign tax deduction [foreign tax credit]** — For the purpose of subsection 126(1), the following rules apply:

(a) such portion of the income for a taxation year of a trust governed by an employees profit sharing plan from sources (other than businesses carried on by it) in a foreign country as

(i) may reasonably be considered (having regard to all the circumstances including the terms and conditions of the plan) to be part of

(A) the income that, by virtue of subsection (3), was included in computing the income for a taxation year of a particular employee who was a beneficiary under the plan, or

(B) the amount, if any, by which

(I) the total of amounts each of which is a capital gain of the trust that, by virtue of subsection (4), was deemed to be a capital gain of the particular employee for a taxation year

exceeds

(II) the total of amounts each of which is a capital loss of the trust that, by virtue of subsection (4), was deemed to be a capital loss of the particular employee for the taxation year, and

(ii) was not designated by the trust in respect of any other employee who was a beneficiary under the plan,

shall, if so designated by the trust in respect of the particular employee in its return of income for the year under this Part, be deemed to be income of the particular employee for the taxation year from sources in that country; and

(b) an employee who is a beneficiary under an employees profit sharing plan shall be deemed to have paid as non-business-income tax for a taxation year, on the income that the employee is deemed by paragraph (a) to have for the year from sources in a foreign country, to the government of that country an amount equal to that proportion of the non-business-income tax paid by the trust governed by the plan for the year to the government of that country, or to the government of a state, province or other political subdivision of that country (except such portion of that tax as was deductible under subsection 20(11) in computing its income for the year) that

(i) the income that the employee is deemed by paragraph (a) to have for the year from sources in that country

is of

(ii) the income of the trust for the year from sources (other than businesses carried on by it) in that country.

**(8.2)** [Repealed]

**Notes**: 144(8.2) repealed by 1993 technical bill, effective for 1992 and later taxation years. However, a taxpayer could elect to have it continue to apply to the 1992 taxation year by notifying Revenue Canada in writing by December 31, 1994.

**(9) Deduction for forfeited amounts** — Where a person ceases at any time in a taxation year to be a beneficiary under an employees profit sharing plan and does not become a beneficiary under the plan after that time and in the year, there may be deducted in computing the person's income for the year the amount determined by the formula

$$A - B - \frac{C}{4} - D$$

where

A is the total of all amounts each of which is an amount included in computing the person's income for the year or a preceding taxation year (other than an amount received before that time under the plan or an amount under the plan that the person is entitled at that time to receive) because of an allocation (other than an allocation to which subsection (4) applies) to the person made contingently under the plan before that time;

B is the portion, if any, of the value of A that is included in the value of A because of paragraph 82(1)(b);

C is the total of all taxable dividends deemed to be received by the person because of allocations under subsection (8) in respect of the plan; and

D is the total of all amounts deductible under this subsection in computing the person's income for a preceding taxation year because the person ceased to be a beneficiary under the plan in a preceding taxation year.

**Related Provisions**: 8(1)(o.1) — Deduction from employment income; 144(3) — Allocation contingent or absolute taxable; 144(10) — Payments out of profits; 152(1) — Assessment; 160.1 — Where excess refunded; 257 — Formula cannot calculate to less than zero.

**Notes**: 144(9) amended by 1993 technical bill, effective for 1992 and later taxation years. However, a taxpayer could elect to have the former version apply to the 1992 taxation year by notifying Revenue Canada in writing by December 31, 1994.

**(10) Payments out of profits** — Where the terms of an arrangement under which an employer makes payments to a trustee specifically provide that the payments shall be made "out of profits", the arrangement shall, if the employer so elects in prescribed manner, be deemed, for the purpose of subsection (1), to be an arrangement under which payments computed by reference to the employer's profits are required.

**Notes**: 144(10) amended by 1993 technical bill, effective for 1992 and later taxation years, to have the wording correspond to amendments to 144(9).

**Regulations**: 1500(3) (prescribed manner).

**Interpretation Bulletins**: IT-280R: Employees' profit sharing plans — payments computed by reference to profits.

**(11) Taxation year of trust** — Where an employees profit sharing plan is accepted for registration by the Minister as a deferred profit sharing plan, the taxation year of the trust governed by the employees profit sharing plan shall be deemed to have ended immediately before the plan is deemed to have become registered as a deferred profit sharing plan pursuant to subsection 147(5).

**Definitions [s. 144]**: "adjusted cost base" — 54, 248(1); "amount", "business" — 248(1); "Canadian corporation" — 89(1), 248(1); "capital gain", "capital loss" — 39(1), 248(1); "capital property" — 54, 248(1); "corporation" — 248(1), Interpretation Act 35(1); "dividend", "employee" — 248(1); "employees profit sharing plan" — 144(1), 248(1); "employer", "Minister", "officer", "prescribed", "property" — 248(1); "province" — Interpretation Act 35(1); "taxable Canadian corporation" — 89(1), 248(1); "taxable capital gain" — 38(a), 248(1); "taxable dividend" — 89(1), 248(1); "taxable income" — 2(2), 248(1); "taxation year" — 144(11), 249; "trust" — 104(1), 248(1); "unused portion of a beneficiary's exempt capital gains balance" — 144(1).

**Information Circulars [s. 144]**: 77-1R4: Deferred profit sharing plans; 79-8R3: Forms to use to directly transfer funds to or between plans, or to purchase an annuity.

## Registered Supplementary Unemployment Benefit Plans

**145. (1) Definitions** — In this section,

**"registered supplementary unemployment benefit plan"** means a supplementary unemployment benefit plan accepted by the Minister for registration for the purposes of this Act in respect of its constitution and operations for the taxation year under consideration;

**Related Provisions**: 128.1(10)"excluded right or interest"(a)(xi) — No deemed disposition on emigration; 248(1)"disposition"(f)(vi) — Rollover from one trust to another; 248(1)"registered supplementary unemployment benefit plan" — Definition applies to entire Act.

**Notes**: 145(1)"registered supplementary unemployment benefit plan" was 145(1)(a) before consolidation in R.S.C. 1985 (5th Supp.), effective for taxation years ending after November 1991.

**Forms**: T3S: Supplementary unemployment benefit plan — income tax return.

**"supplementary unemployment benefit plan"** means an arrangement, other than an arrangement in the nature of a superannuation or pension fund or plan or an employees profit sharing plan, under which payments are made by an employer to a trustee in trust exclusively for the payment of periodic amounts to employees or former employees of the

## S. 145(1) sup — Income Tax Act, Part I

employer who are or may be laid off for any temporary or indefinite period.

**Notes:** 145(1)"supplementary unemployment benefit plan" was 145(1)(b) before consolidation in R.S.C. 1985 (5th Supp.), effective for taxation years ending after November 1991.

**Information Circulars:** 72-5R: Registration of supplementary unemployment benefit plans; 78-14R2: Guidelines for trust companies and other persons responsible for filing.

**(2) No tax while trust governed by plan** — No tax is payable under this Part by a trust on the taxable income of the trust for a period during which the trust was governed by a registered supplementary unemployment benefit plan.

**Related Provisions:** 149(1)(q) — Exemption — trust under a registered supplementary unemployment benefit plan.

**Forms:** T3S: Supplementary unemployment benefit plan — income tax return.

**(3) Amounts received taxable** — There shall be included in computing the income of a taxpayer for a taxation year each amount received by the taxpayer under a supplementary unemployment benefit plan from the trustee under the plan at any time in the year.

**Related Provisions:** 56(1)(g) — Income inclusion; 153(1)(e) — Withholding; 212(1)(k) — Withholding tax on payment to non-resident.

**(4) Amounts received on amendment or winding-up of plan** — There shall be included in computing the income for a taxation year of a taxpayer who, as an employer, has made any payment to a trustee under a supplementary unemployment benefit plan, any amount received by the taxpayer in the year as a result of an amendment to or modification of the plan or as a result of the termination or winding-up of the plan.

**Related Provisions:** 56(1)(g) — Income inclusion; 153(1)(e) — Withholding; 212(1)(k) — Withholding tax on payment to non-resident.

**(5) Payments by employer deductible** — An amount paid by an employer to a trustee under a registered supplementary unemployment benefit plan during a taxation year or within 30 days thereafter may be deducted in computing the employer's income for the taxation year to the extent that it was not deductible in computing income for a previous taxation year.

**Related Provisions:** 6(1)(a)(i) — Employer's contribution is not a taxable benefit; 18(1)(i) — Limitation re employer's contribution under supplementary unemployment benefit plan; 20(1)(x) — Deduction for employer's contribution.

**Definitions [s. 145]:** "amount", "employee" — 248(1); "employees profit sharing plan" — 144(1), 248(1); "employer", "Minister" — 248(1); "taxable income" — 2(2), 248(1); "taxation year" — 249; "taxpayer" — 248(1); "trust" — 104(1), 248(1).

## Registered Retirement Savings Plans

**146. (1) Definitions** — In this section,

**"annuitant"** means

(a) until such time after maturity of the plan as an individual's spouse or common-law partner becomes entitled, as a consequence of the individual's death, to receive benefits to be paid out of or under the plan, the individual referred to in paragraph (a) or (b) of the definition "retirement savings plan" in this subsection for whom, under a retirement savings plan, a retirement income is to be provided, and

(b) thereafter, the spouse or common-law partner referred to in paragraph (a);

**Related Provisions:** 60(l) — Transfer of RRSP premium refunds; 128.1(10)"excluded right or interest"(a)(i), (a)(ii) — No deemed disposition on emigration of annuitant; 146(16) — RRSP — deduction on transfer of funds; 160.2(1) — Joint and several liability in respect of amounts received out of or under RRSP; 248(8) — Occurrences as a consequence of death.

**Notes:** 146(1)"annuitant" amended by 2000 same-sex partners bill to add reference to "common-law partner", effective for the 2001 and later taxation years, or earlier by election (see Notes to 248(1)"common-law partner").

146(1)"annuitant" was 146(1)(a) before consolidation in R.S.C. 1985 (5th Supp.), effective for taxation years ending after November 1991. (It was also amended by 1995-97 technical bill, retroactive to the 5th Supp. change, to correct "the spouse's death" to "the individual's death".) See Table of Concordance.

**Information Circulars:** 72-22R9: Registered retirement savings plans.

**Forms:** RC4177: Death of an RRSP annuitant [guide].

**"benefit"** includes any amount received out of or under a retirement savings plan other than

(a) the portion thereof received by a person other than the annuitant that can reasonably be regarded as part of the amount included in computing the income of an annuitant by virtue of subsections (8.8) and (8.9),

(b) an amount received by the person with whom the annuitant has the contract or arrangement described in the definition "retirement savings plan" in this subsection as a premium under the plan,

(c) an amount, or part thereof, received in respect of the income of the trust under the plan for a taxation year for which the trust was not exempt from tax by virtue of paragraph (4)(c), and

(c.1) a tax-paid amount described in paragraph (b) of the definition "tax-paid amount" in this subsection that relates to interest or another amount included in computing income otherwise than because of this section

and without restricting the generality of the foregoing includes any amount paid to an annuitant under the plan

(d) in accordance with the terms of the plan,

(e) resulting from an amendment to or modification of the plan, or

(f) resulting from the termination of the plan;

**Related Provisions:** 160.2(1) — Joint and several liability in respect of amounts received out of or under RRSP.

**Notes**: Para. (c.1) added by 1995-97 technical bill, effective for deaths after 1992.

146(1)"benefit" was 146(1)(b) before consolidation in R.S.C. 1985 (5th Supp.), effective for taxation years ending after November 1991. See Table of Concordance.

**Advance Tax Rulings**: ATR-37: Refund of premiums transferred to spouse.

"**earned income**" of a taxpayer for a taxation year means the amount, if any, by which the total of all amounts each of which is

(a) the taxpayer's income for a period in the year throughout which the taxpayer was resident in Canada from

  (i) an office or employment, determined without reference to paragraphs 8(1)(c), (m) and (m.2),

  (ii) a business carried on by the taxpayer either alone or as a partner actively engaged in the business, or

  (iii) property, where the income is derived from the rental of real property or from royalties in respect of a work or invention of which the taxpayer was the author or inventor,

(b) an amount included under paragraph 56(1)(b), (c), (c.1), (c.2), (g) or (o) in computing the taxpayer's income for a period in the year throughout which the taxpayer was resident in Canada,

(b.1) an amount received by the taxpayer in the year and at a time when the taxpayer is resident in Canada as, on account of, in lieu of payment of or in satisfaction of, a disability pension under the *Canada Pension Plan* or a provincial pension plan as defined in section 3 of that Act,

(c) the taxpayer's income for a period in the year throughout which the taxpayer was not resident in Canada from

  (i) the duties of an office or employment performed by the taxpayer in Canada, determined without reference to paragraphs 8(1)(c), (m) and (m.2), or

  (ii) a business carried on by the taxpayer in Canada, either alone or as a partner actively engaged in the business

except to the extent that the income is exempt from income tax in Canada by reason of a provision contained in a tax convention or agreement with another country that has the force of law in Canada, or

(d) in the case of a taxpayer described in subsection 115(2), the total that would be determined under paragraph 115(2)(e) in respect of the taxpayer for the year if

  (i) that paragraph were read without reference to subparagraphs 115(2)(e)(iii) and (iv), and

  (ii) subparagraph 115(2)(e)(ii) were read without any reference therein to paragraph 56(1)(n),

except any part thereof included in the total determined under this definition by reason of paragraph (c) or exempt from income tax in Canada by reason of a provision contained in a tax convention or agreement with another country that has the force of law in Canada,

exceeds the total of all amounts each of which is

(e) the taxpayer's loss for a period in the year throughout which the taxpayer was resident in Canada from

  (i) a business carried on by the taxpayer, either alone or as a partner actively engaged in the business, or

  (ii) property, where the loss is sustained from the rental of real property,

(f) an amount deductible under paragraph 60(b), (c) or (c.1), or deducted under paragraph 60(c.2), in computing the taxpayer's income for the year,

(g) the taxpayer's loss for a period in the year throughout which the taxpayer was not resident in Canada from a business carried on by the taxpayer in Canada, either alone or as a partner actively engaged in the business, or

(h) the portion of an amount included under subparagraph (a)(ii) or (c)(ii) in determining the taxpayer's earned income for the year because of subparagraph 14(1)(a)(v)

and, for the purposes of this definition, the income or loss of a taxpayer for any period in a taxation year is the taxpayer's income or loss computed as though that period were the whole taxation year;

**Notes**: "Earned income" is used as the basis for determining RRSP contribution eligibility. In general, 18% of earned income in a given year, subject to a $13,500 limit and minus the pension adjustment, is the contribution limit for the following year. See Notes to 146(1)"RRSP deduction limit" and 146(5).

Note that income from "office or employment" under (a)(i) includes all taxable benefits and stock option benefits under ss. 6 and 7, in addition to salary or wages taxable under s. 5. Business income and real property rental income under (a)(ii) and (iii) refer to *net* income from the business or property (i.e., after deductible expenses), as determined for purposes of 9(1).

146(1)"earned income" was 146(1)(c) before consolidation in R.S.C. 1985 (5th Supp.), effective for taxation years ending after November 1991. See Table of Concordance.

Para. (b.1) amended by 1997 Budget, effective for amounts received after 1994, to change from referring to amounts described in 56(8)(a) to refer to CPP disability benefits. The change was non-substantive; since 56(8) was extended to apply to all CPP benefits rather than just disability benefits, para. (b.1) was amended so that it continues to apply only to disability benefits.

Para. (h) added by 1995-97 technical bill, effective for 1995 and later taxation years.

Paras. (b) and (f) (formerly 146(1)(c)(ii) and (vi)) amended, and (b.1) (formerly 146(1)(c)(ii.1)) added, by 1992 technical bill, effective 1991. For 1990, read subpara. (ii) (now para. (b)) without the reference to 56(1)(c.2), and read subpara. (vi) (now para. (f)) without the reference to 60(c.2). Para. (b.1) implements the 1992 Budget announcement that CPP disability pensions are to be "earned income" for RRSP purposes.

146(1)(c) (now 146(1)"earned income") amended by 1990 pension bill, effective 1990, with an alternate version effective 1989.

**Interpretation Bulletins**: IT-377R: Director's, executor's or juror's fees; IT-434R: Rental of real property by individual.

**I.T. Technical News**: No. 11 (reporting of amounts paid out of an employee benefit plan).

**Forms**: T1023: RRSP deduction limit — calculation of earned income.

**"issuer"** means the person referred to in the definition "retirement savings plan" in this subsection with whom an annuitant has a contract or arrangement that is a retirement savings plan;

**Notes**: 146(1)"issuer" was 146(1)(c.1) before consolidation in R.S.C. 1985 (5th Supp.), effective for taxation years ending after November 1991.

**"maturity"** means the date fixed under a retirement savings plan for the commencement of any retirement income the payment of which is provided for by the plan;

**Notes**: 146(1)"maturity" was 146(1)(d) before consolidation in R.S.C. 1985 (5th Supp.), effective for taxation years ending after November 1991.

**"net past service pension adjustment"** of a taxpayer for a taxation year means the positive or negative amount determined by the formula

$$P + Q - G$$

where

P is the total of all amounts each of which is the taxpayer's past service pension adjustment for the year in respect of an employer,

Q is the total of all amounts each of which is a prescribed amount in respect of the taxpayer for the year, and

G is the amount of the taxpayer's PSPA withdrawals for the year, determined as of the end of the year in accordance with prescribed rules;

**Related Provisions**: 204.2(1.3) — Net past service pension adjustment for purposes of Part X.1 tax; 257 — Formula cannot calculate to less than zero.

**Notes**: Q added by 1993 technical bill, effective for 1993 and later taxation years.

146(1)"net past service pension adjustment" was 146(1)(d.1) before consolidation in R.S.C. 1985 (5th Supp.), effective for taxation years ending after November 1991. 146(1)(d.1) added by 1990 pension bill and amended retroactively by 1992 technical bill (to eliminate a deduction for PSPA transfers), effective 1989.

**Regulations**: 8307(5) (prescribed rules); 8308.4(2) (prescribed amount for formula element Q).

**"non-qualified investment"**, in relation to a trust governed by a registered retirement savings plan, means property acquired by the trust after 1971 that is not a qualified investment for the trust;

**Notes**: 146(1)"non-qualified investment" was 146(1)(e) before consolidation in R.S.C. 1985 (5th Supp.), effective for taxation years ending after November 1991. See also Notes to 146(10.1).

**"premium"** means any periodic or other amount paid or payable under a retirement savings plan

(a) as consideration for any contract referred to in paragraph (a) of the definition "retirement savings plan" to pay a retirement income, or

(b) as a contribution or deposit referred to in paragraph (b) of that definition for the purpose stated in that paragraph

but, except for the purposes of paragraph (b) of the definition "benefit" in this subsection, paragraph (2)(b.3), subsection (22) and the definition "excluded premium" in subsection 146.02(1), does not include a repayment to which paragraph (b) of the definition "excluded withdrawal" in either subsection 146.01(1) or 146.02(1) applies or an amount that is designated under subsection 146.01(3) or 146.02(3);

**Related Provisions**: 60(j) — Transfer of superannuation benefits; 60(j.01) — Transfer of surplus; 60(j.2) — Transfer to spousal RRSP; 60(l) — Transfer of RRSP premium refunds.

**Notes**: Closing words of the definition amended by 1998 Budget, effective for 1997 and later taxation years. For earlier years, read:

but, except for the purposes of paragraph (b) of the definition "benefit" in this subsection and paragraph 146 (2)(b.3), does not include a repayment described in subparagraph (b)(ii) of the definition "excluded withdrawal" in subsection 146.01(1) or an amount designated under subsection 146.01(3).

Closing words added by 1992 technical bill, effective 1992; and amended by 1994 Budget bill, effective 1995, to add the words "in this subsection" and "an amount" for clarification.

146(1)"premium" was 146(1)(f) before consolidation in R.S.C. 1985 (5th Supp.), effective for taxation years ending after November 1991. See Table of Concordance.

**Regulations**: Reg. 100(3)(c) (no source withholding where premium is paid by employer directly to RRSP).

**Interpretation Bulletins**: IT-528: Transfers of funds between registered plans.

**"qualified investment"** for a trust governed by a registered retirement savings plan means

(a) an investment that would be described in any of paragraphs (a), (b), (d) and (f) to (h) of the definition "qualified investment" in section 204 if the references in that definition to a trust were read as references to the trust governed by the registered retirement savings plan,

(b) a bond, debenture, note or similar obligation of a corporation the shares of which are listed on a prescribed stock exchange in Canada,

(c) an annuity described in the definition "retirement income" in respect of the annuitant under the plan, if purchased from a licensed annuities provider,

(c.1) a contract for an annuity issued by a licensed annuities provider where

(i) the trust is the only person who, disregarding any subsequent transfer of the contract by the trust, is or may become entitled to any annuity payments under the contract, and

(ii) the holder of the contract has a right to surrender the contract at any time for an amount that would, if reasonable sales and administration charges were ignored, approximate the value of funds that could otherwise be applied to fund future periodic payments under the contract,

(c.2) a contract for an annuity issued by a licensed annuities provider where

(i) annual or more frequent periodic payments are or may be made under the contract to the holder of the contract,

(ii) the trust is the only person who, disregarding any subsequent transfer of the contract by the trust, is or may become entitled to any annuity payments under the contract,

(iii) neither the time nor the amount of any payment under the contract may vary because of the length of any life, other than the life of the annuitant under the plan (in this definition referred to as the "RRSP annuitant"),

(iv) the day on which the periodic payments began or are to begin (in this paragraph referred to as the "start date") is not later than the end of the year in which the RRSP annuitant attains 70 years of age,

(v) either

(A) the periodic payments are payable for the life of the RRSP annuitant and either there is no guaranteed period under the contract or there is a guaranteed period that begins at the start date and does not exceed a term equal to 90 years minus the lesser of

(I) the age in whole years at the start date of the RRSP annuitant (determined on the assumption that the RRSP annuitant is alive at the start date), and

(II) the age in whole years at the start date of a spouse or common-law partner of the RRSP annuitant (determined on the assumption that a spouse or common-law partner of the RRSP annuitant at the time the contract was acquired is a spouse or common-law partner of the RRSP annuitant at the start date), or

(B) the periodic payments are payable for a term equal to

(I) 90 years minus the age described in subclause (A)(I), or

(II) 90 years minus the age described in subclause (A)(II), and

(vi) the periodic payments

(A) are equal, or

(B) are not equal solely because of one or more adjustments that would, if the contract were an annuity under a retirement savings plan, be in accordance with sub-paragraphs (3)(b)(iii) to (v) or that arise because of a uniform reduction in the entitlement to the periodic payments as a consequence of a partial surrender of rights to the periodic payments, and

(d) such other investments as may be prescribed by regulations of the Governor in Council made on the recommendation of the Minister of Finance;

**Related Provisions**: 87(10) — New share issued on amalgamation of public corporation deemed to be listed on prescribed stock exchange; 132.2(1)(k) — Where share ceases to be qualified investment due to mutual fund reorganization; 146(10.1) — Tax payable on income from non-qualified investments; 207.1(1) — Tax payable by RRSP.

**Notes**: For the most common prescribed qualified investments, see Reg. 4900(1).

146(1)"qualified investment"(c.2)(v)(A)(II) amended by 2000 same-sex partners bill to add reference to "common-law partner", effective for the 2001 and later taxation years, or earlier by election (see Notes to 248(1)"common-law partner").

Para. (c) amended, and (c.1) and (c.2) added, by 1995-97 technical bill, effective 1997. Para. (c) previously referred to "person licensed or otherwise authorized under the laws of Canada or a province to carry on in Canada an annuities business" instead of "licensed annuities provider", which is now defined in 248(1).

Paras. (c.1) and (c.2) (and 146.3(1)"qualified investment"(b.1), (b.2)) were originally proposed as amendments to Reg. 4900(1) in a Dept. of Finance news release of December 16, 1996.

146(1)"qualified investment" was 146(1)(g) before consolidation in R.S.C. 1985 (5th Supp.), effective for taxation years ending after November 1991. See Table of Concordance.

See also Notes to 146(10.1) and to Reg. 4900(1).

**Regulations**: 221 (information return by issuer of qualified investment); 3200, 3201 (prescribed stock exchanges; but see also ITA 87(10)); 4900, 4901, 5100–5104 (prescribed investments).

**I.T. Application Rules**: 65(1), (3).

**Remission Orders**: *Lionaird Capital Corporation Notes Remission Order*, P.C. 1999-737 (tax under 146(10) waived because taxpayers thought they were qualified investments).

**Interpretation Bulletins**: IT-320R2: Registered retirement savings plans — qualified investments.

**Forms**: T3F: Investments prescribed to be qualified or not to be foreign property information return.

**"RRSP deduction limit"** of a taxpayer for a taxation year means the amount determined by the formula

$$A + B + R - C$$

where

A is the taxpayer's unused RRSP deduction room at the end of the preceding taxation year,

B is the amount, if any, by which

(a) the lesser of the RRSP dollar limit for the year and 18% of the taxpayer's earned income for the preceding taxation year

exceeds the total of all amounts each of which is

(b) the taxpayer's pension adjustment for the preceding taxation year in respect of an employer, or

## S. 146(1) RRS — Income Tax Act, Part I

(c) a prescribed amount in respect of the taxpayer for the year,

C is the taxpayer's net past service pension adjustment for the year, and

R is the taxpayer's total pension adjustment reversal for the year;

**Related Provisions**: 128(2)(d) — Where individual bankrupt; 146(5) — Amount of RRSP premiums deductible; 146(5.1) — Amount of spousal RRSP premiums deductible; 146(5.21) — Anti-avoidance; 204.1(2.1) — Tax payable by individuals — contributions after 1990; 248(1)"RRSP deduction limit" — Definition applies to entire Act; 257 — Formula cannot calculate to less than zero; Reg. 8307(2) — Prescribed condition for registered pension plan.

**Notes**: The RRSP deduction limit for 1996 through 2003 is the lesser of $13,500 and 18% of the taxpayer's previous year's earned income, minus the pension adjustment. The $13,500 figure comes from 146(1)"RRSP dollar limit" and 147.1(1)"money purchase limit"(e). For 2004, the dollar limit is $14,500, and for 2005, $15,500. Most taxpayers receive a statement from the CCRA on their annual Notice of Assessment (T451) showing the calculation of their RRSP contribution limit.

Formula element R added by 1997 Budget, effective 1998 (technically it was added retroactive to 1988 along with some corrective restructuring of the language of the definition, but deemed to be nil for taxation years before 1998). The "pension adjustment reversal" (PAR) was to be part of the new RRSP system introduced by the 1989 Budget, but was removed before enactment in 1990 to make the system simpler. It has now been reintroduced. There will generally be PAR (see Reg. 8304.1) when the individual ceases, after 1996 and before retirement, to be entitled to benefits under the RPP or DPSP (usually by terminating employment). In general terms, PAR under a defined benefit RPP is the total of the individual's pension credits and PSPAs since 1990, minus any lump sum amounts paid out or transferred to an RRSP or other money purchase plan, in respect of the individual's post-1989 benefits under the RPP. An individual's PAR under a DPSP or money purchase RPP is the pension credits included under the plan or provision since 1990 but not vested in the individual.

Reporting of PAR to the CCRA is required by Reg. 8402.01.

146(1)"RRSP deduction limit" was 146(1)(g.1) before consolidation in R.S.C. 1985 (5th Supp.), effective for taxation years ending after November 1991. See Table of Concordance.

146(1)(g.1) (now 146(1)"RRSP deduction limit") added by 1990 pension bill.

**Regulations**: 8304.1 (pension adjustment reversal); 8308(2), 8308.2, 8308.4(2), 8309 (prescribed amount).

**Forms**: T1 General Sched. 7; RRSP contributions, transfers and designations of repayments under the home buyers' plan; T452: Notice of Assessment with calculation of RRSP contribution limit; T1023: RRSP deduction limit — calculation of earned income.

### "RRSP dollar limit" for a calendar year means

(a) for years other than 1996, the money purchase limit for the preceding year, and

(b) for 1996, $13,500;

**Related Provisions**: 204.2(1.1) — Cumulative excess amount in respect of RRSPs; 248(1)"RRSP dollar limit" — Definition applies to entire Act.

**Notes**: See Notes to 146(1)"RRSP deduction limit" and under 147.1(1)"money purchase limit" for the dollar limits.

Definition "RRSP dollar limit" amended by 1995 Budget, effective 1996, to add the special case for 1996. Formerly read: "...means the money purchase limit for the immediately preceding calendar year."

146(1)"RRSP dollar limit" was 146(1)(g.2) before consolidation in R.S.C. 1985 (5th Supp.), effective for taxation years ending after November 1991. 146(1)(g.2) added by 1990 pension bill, effective 1989.

### "refund of premiums" means

(a) any amount paid to a spouse or common-law partner of the annuitant out of or under a registered retirement savings plan of the annuitant (other than any part of the amount that is a tax-paid amount in respect of the plan), where the annuitant died before the maturity of the plan and the amount was paid as a consequence of the death, or

(b) any amount paid out of or under a registered retirement savings plan of the annuitant (other than any part of the amount that is a tax-paid amount in respect of the plan) after the death to a child or grandchild (in this definition referred to as a "dependant") of the annuitant, who was, at the time of the death, financially dependent on the annuitant for support,

and for the purpose of paragraph (b), it is assumed, unless the contrary is established, that a dependant was not financially dependent on the annuitant for support at the time of the annuitant's death if the dependant's income for the year preceding the taxation year in which the annuitant died exceeded the amount used under paragraph (c) of the description of B in subsection 118(1) for that preceding year;

**Related Provisions**: 146(8.1) — Deemed receipt of refund of premiums; 146(8.9) — Effect of death where person other than spouse becomes entitled; 146.3(1)"designated benefit" — Application of definition to RRIFs; 248(8) — Occurrences as a consequence of death.

**Notes**: See Notes to 146(8.8).

146(1)"refund of premiums"(a) amended by 2000 same-sex partners bill to add reference to "common-law partner", effective for the 2001 and later taxation years, or earlier by election (see Notes to 248(1)"common-law partner").

Para. (b) amended by 1999 Budget to delete the initial words "if the annuitant had no spouse at the time of the annuitant's death", effective for deaths that occur after 1995.

However, subsec. 42(4) of the 1999 Budget bill provides that, in respect of a death in 1996–98, ignore the amendment in connection with an amount paid out of an RRSP or RRIF, unless the following persons jointly elect otherwise in writing filed with the Minister of National Revenue before May 2000 (or before such later day as is acceptable to the Minister):

(a) the legal representative of the deceased individual; and

(b) the individual in whose income an amount would be required to be included as a result of the election, or would be so required to be included if Part I of the Act applied.

Notwithstanding 152(4) to (5), the Minister shall make such assessments, reassessments and additional assessments of tax, interest and penalties and such determinations and redeterminations as are necessary to give effect to the above election.

For earlier years, read:

(b) if the annuitant had no spouse at the time of the annuitant's death, any amount paid out of or under a registered retirement savings plan of the annuitant (other than any part of the amount that is a tax-paid amount in respect of the plan) after the death to a child or grandchild (in this definition referred to as a "dependant") of the annuitant, who was, at the time of the death, financially dependent on the annuitant for support,

Closing words amended by 1999 Budget, effective for 2000 and later taxation years, to delete "the total of $500 and" before "the amount used under". However, for the 2000 taxation year, in place of "the amount used under paragraph (c) of the description of B in subsection 118(1) for that preceding taxation year", read "$7,044". (This is expected to change as a result of the February 2000 budget.)

Closing words amended to add "the total of $500 and" by 1998 Budget, effective for 1999 and later taxation years. This reflects the $500 supplementary credit in 118(1)B(b.1), which effectively increased the income that can be earned tax-free from $6,456 to $6,956 for 1998.

Paras. (a) and (b) amended by 1995-97 technical bill, effective for deaths after 1992, to add the exclusions for tax-paid amounts (see 146(1)"tax-paid amount").

Paras. (a) and (b) amended by 1993 technical bill, effective for deaths in 1993 or later. Previously read:

> (a) any amount paid to a spouse of the annuitant, as a consequence of the annuitant's death, out of or under a registered retirement savings plan of the annuitant prior to its maturity, or
>
> (b) if the annuitant had no spouse at the time of the annuitant's death, any amount paid out of or under a registered retirement savings plan of the annuitant to a child or grandchild (in this definition referred to as a "dependant") of the annuitant, who was, at the time the annuitant died, financially dependent on the annuitant for support,

146(1)"refund of premiums" (formerly 146(1)(h)) amended by 1992 Child Benefit bill, effective 1993, as a result of the elimination of the credit for dependent children under 18, in 118(1)B(d).

146(1)(h)(ii) (now 146(1)"refund of premiums") amended by 1990 pension bill, effective 1989.

146(1)"refund of premiums" was 146(1)(h) before consolidation in R.S.C. 1985 (5th Supp.), effective for taxation years ending after November 1991. Subparas. (i), (ii) became paras. (a), (b).

**Interpretation Bulletins**: IT-500R: RRSPs — death of an annuitant.

**Information Circulars**: 79-8R3: Forms to use to directly transfer funds to or between plans, or to purchase an annuity.

**Advance Tax Rulings**: ATR-37: Refund of premiums transferred to spouse.

**Forms**: RC4177: Death of an RRSP annuitant [guide].

**"registered retirement savings plan"** means a retirement savings plan accepted by the Minister for registration for the purposes of this Act as complying with the requirements of this section;

**Related Provisions**: 128.1(10)"excluded right or interest"(a)(i) — No deemed disposition of RRSP on emigration; 206(2), 206.1 — Tax payable by a trust governed by RRSP; 207.1(1) — Tax payable by RRSP; 207.2 — Return and payment of tax by RRSP; 248(1)"disposition"(g) — Transfer between RRSPs/RRIFs not a disposition; 248(1)"foreign retirement arrangement" — U.S. Individual Retirement Account; 248(1)"registered retirement savings plan" — Definition applies to entire Act.

**Notes**: 146(1)"registered retirement savings plan" was 146(1)(i) before consolidation in R.S.C. 1985 (5th Supp.), effective for taxation years ending after November 1991.

**Interpretation Bulletins**: IT-415R2: Deregistration of RRSPs; IT-528: Transfers of funds between registered plans.

**"retirement income"** means

(a) an annuity commencing at maturity, and with or without a guaranteed term commencing at maturity, not exceeding the term referred to in paragraph (b), or, in the case of a plan entered into before March 14, 1957, not exceeding 20 years, payable to

(i) the annuitant for the annuitant's life, or

(ii) the annuitant for the lives, jointly, of the annuitant and the annuitant's spouse or common-law partner and to the survivor of them for the survivor's life, or

(b) an annuity commencing at maturity, payable to the annuitant, or to the annuitant for the annuitant's life and to the spouse or common-law partner after the annuitant's death, for a term of years equal to 90 minus either

(i) the age in whole years of the annuitant at the maturity of the plan, or

(ii) where the annuitant's spouse or common-law partner is younger than the annuitant and the annuitant so elects, the age in whole years of the spouse or common-law partner at the maturity of the plan,

issued by a person described in the definition "retirement savings plan" in this subsection with whom an individual may have a contract or arrangement that is a retirement savings plan,

or any combination thereof;

**Notes**: 146(1)"retirement income"(b) amended by 2000 same-sex partners bill to add reference to "common-law partner", effective for the 2001 and later taxation years, or earlier by election (see Notes to 248(1)"common-law partner").

146(1)"retirement income" was 146(1)(i.1) before consolidation in R.S.C. 1985 (5th Supp.), effective for taxation years ending after November 1991. See Table of Concordance.

**Information Circulars**: 72-22R9: Registered retirement savings plans; 74-1R5: Form T2037, Notice of purchase of annuity with "plan" funds; 79-8R3: Forms to use to directly transfer funds to or between plans, or to purchase an annuity.

**Forms**: T2037: Notice of purchase of annuity with "plan" funds.

**"retirement savings plan"** means

(a) a contract between an individual and a person licensed or otherwise authorized under the laws of Canada or a province to carry on in Canada an annuities business, under which, in consideration of payment by the individual or the individual's spouse or common-law partner of any periodic or other amount as consideration under the contract, a retirement income commencing at maturity is to be provided for the individual, or

(b) an arrangement under which payment is made by an individual or the individual's spouse or common-law partner

(i) in trust to a corporation licensed or otherwise authorized under the laws of Canada or a province to carry on in Canada the business of offering to the public its services as trustee, of any periodic or other amount as a contribution under the trust,

(ii) to a corporation approved by the Governor in Council for the purposes of this section that is licensed or otherwise authorized under the laws of Canada or a province to issue investment contracts providing for the payment to or to the credit of the holder thereof of a fixed or determinable amount at maturity, of any periodic or other amount as a contribution under such a contract between the individual and that corporation, or

(iii) as a deposit with a branch or office, in Canada, of

(A) a person who is, or is eligible to become, a member of the Canadian Payments Association, or

(B) a credit union that is a shareholder or member of a body corporate referred to as a "central" for the purposes of the *Canadian Payments Association Act*,

(in this section referred to as a "depositary") to be used, invested or otherwise applied by that corporation or that depositary, as the case may be, for the purpose of providing for the individual, commencing at maturity, a retirement income;

**Related Provisions**: 248(1)"foreign retirement arrangement" — U.S. Individual Retirement Account; 248(1)"retirement savings plan" — Definition applies to entire Act.

**Notes**: 146(1)"retirement savings plan" amended by 2000 same-sex partners bill to add reference to "common-law partner", effective for the 2001 and later taxation years, or earlier by election (see Notes to 248(1)"common-law partner").

146(1)"retirement savings plan" was 146(1)(j) before consolidation in R.S.C. 1985 (5th Supp.), effective for taxation years ending after November 1991. See Table of Concordance.

**Information Circulars**: 72-22R9: Registered retirement savings plans; 74-1R5 — Form T2037: Notice of purchase of annuity with "plan" funds; 78-14R2 — Guidelines for trust companies and others; 79-8R3: Forms to use to directly transfer funds to or between plans, or to purchase an annuity.

**Forms**: T3G: Certification of no tax liability by a group of RRSPs, RRIFs, or RESPs; T3IND: T3IND income tax return for RRSP, RRIF, or RESP; T4RSP Segment; T4RSP Summ: Return of RRSP income; T4RSP Supp: Statement of RRSP income; T4079: T4RSP and T4RIF guide.

**"spousal plan"**, in relation to a taxpayer, means

(a) a registered retirement savings plan

(i) to which the taxpayer has, at a time when the taxpayer's spouse or common-law partner was the annuitant under the plan, paid a premium, or

(ii) that has received a payment out of or a transfer from a registered retirement savings plan or a registered retirement income fund that was a spousal plan in relation to the taxpayer, or

(b) a registered retirement income fund that has received a payment out of or a transfer from a spousal plan in relation to the taxpayer;

**Related Provisions**: 74.5(12) — Application; 146(5.1) — Deduction for contribution to spousal RRSP; 146(8.3) — Attribution on withdrawal from spousal RRSP; 146.3(5.1) — Amount included in income.

**Notes**: See 146(5.1) and Notes to 146(8.3).

146(1)"spousal plan"(a)(i) amended by 2000 same-sex partners bill to add reference to "common-law partner", effective for the 2001 and later taxation years, or earlier by election (see Notes to 248(1)"common-law partner").

146(1)"spousal plan" was 146(1)(k) before consolidation in R.S.C. 1985 (5th Supp.), effective for taxation years ending after November 1991. See Table of Concordance. 146(1)(k) added by 1990 pension bill, effective 1989.

**"tax-paid amount"** paid to a person in respect of a registered retirement saving plan means

(a) an amount paid to the person in respect of the amount that would, if this Act were read without reference to subsection 104(6), be income of a trust governed by the plan for a taxation year for which the trust was subject to tax because of paragraph (4)(c), or

(b) where

(i) the plan is a deposit with a depositary referred to in clause (b)(iii)(B) of the definition "retirement savings plan" in this subsection, and

(ii) an amount is received at any time out of or under the plan by the person,

the portion of the amount that can reasonably be considered to relate to interest or another amount in respect of the deposit that was required to be included in computing the income of any person (other than the annuitant) otherwise than because of this section;

**Related Provisions**: 146(1)"benefit"(c.1) — Whether tax-paid amount is a "benefit"; 146(1)"refund of premiums" — Exclusion of tax-paid amount; 146(8.9) — RRSP income inclusion on death; 146.3(5)(c) — Tax-paid amount from RRIF excluded from income; 146.3(6.2) — RRIF income inclusion on death.

**Notes**: "Tax-paid amount" added by 1995-97 technical bill, effective for deaths after 1992. The first "tax-paid amounts" could be received beginning in 1995 in respect of post-1994 income, since 104(6)(c) applies for deaths in 1993 or later and allows one further calendar year of exemption. See also 146(1)"refund of premiums"(a) and (b), which exclude a tax-paid amount; and 146(8.9) and 146.3(6.2), under which the RRSP and RRIF income inclusions on death are determined.

**"unused RRSP deduction room"** of a taxpayer at the end of a taxation year means,

(a) for taxation years ending before 1991, nil, and

(b) for taxation years that end after 1990, the amount, which can be positive or negative, determined by the formula

$$A + B + R - (C + D)$$

where

Division G — Deferred & Special Income Arrangements S. 146(2)(c.2)

A is the taxpayer's unused RRSP deduction room at the end of the preceding taxation year,

B is the amount, if any, by which

(i) the lesser of the RRSP dollar limit for the year and 18% of the taxpayer's earned income for the preceding taxation year

exceeds the total of all amounts each of which is

(ii) the taxpayer's pension adjustment for the preceding taxation year in respect of an employer, or

(iii) a prescribed amount in respect of the taxpayer for the year,

C is the taxpayer's net past service pension adjustment for the year,

D is the total of the amounts deducted by the taxpayer under subsections (5) and (5.1) and paragraph 60(v) in computing the taxpayer's income for the year, and

R is the taxpayer's total pension adjustment reversal for the year.

**Related Provisions**: 128(2)(d), (d.2) — Where individual bankrupt; 146(1) — RRSP deduction limit; 146(5.21) — Anti-avoidance; 204.2(1.1) — Cumulative excess amount re RRSPs; 248(1)"unused RRSP deduction room" — Definition applies to entire Act; 257 — Formula cannot calculate to less than zero.

**Notes**: Formula element R added by 1997 Budget, effective 1998 (technically it was added retroactive to 1989 along with some corrective restructuring of the language of the definition, but deemed to be nil for taxation years before 1998). For discussion of the pension adjustment reversal (PAR), see Notes to 146(1)"RRSP deduction limit".

Para. (b) amended by 1996 Budget, effective April 25, 1997, to delete subpara. (ii) and to delete the words "the lesser of" from the opening words. Subpara. (b)(ii) imposed a cap based on earned income for the previous 7 years. This cap would have first had an effect in determining unused room carried forward from 1998 to 1999. By being eliminated, it effectively never comes into operation, and taxpayers can now carry forward unused RRSP room indefinitely. Subpara. (b)(ii) was worded:

(ii) the greater of

(A) the total of all amounts each of which is the amount, determined in respect of a particular taxation year that is the year or such of the six taxation years immediately preceding the year as end after 1990, that is the lesser of 18% of the taxpayer's earned income for the taxation year immediately preceding the particular taxation year and the RRSP dollar limit for the particular taxation year, and

(B) ⁷/₂ of the RRSP dollar limit for the year.

146(1)"unused RRSP deduction room" was 146(1)(l) before consolidation in R.S.C. 1985 (5th Supp.), effective for taxation years ending after November 1991. See Table of Concordance. 146(1)(l) added by 1990 pension bill, effective 1989.

**Regulations**: 8304.1 (pension adjustment reversal); 8308(2), 8308.2, 8308.4(2) (prescribed amount).

**Forms**: T1 General Sched. 7: RRSP contributions, transfers and designations of repayments under the home buyers' plan.

**Interpretation Bulletins**: IT-124R6: Contributions to registered retirement savings plans; IT-307R3: Spousal registered retirement savings plans; IT-415R2: Deregistration of RRSPs.

**(1.1)** [Repealed]

**Notes**: 146(1.1) added by 1990 pension bill, effective 1988, and repealed by 1992 technical bill, effective 1993. It defined "spouse" to include a common-law spouse for purposes of 146(1)(a), (h), (i.1), (3)(b), (8.8), (8.91) and (16). For 1993–2000, see repealed 252(4). Effective 2001, all references in the Act to "spouse" have been amended to add "or common-law partner", which is defined to include same-sex partners.

**(2) Acceptance of plan for registration [ — conditions]** — The Minister shall not accept for registration for the purposes of this Act any retirement savings plan unless, in the Minister's opinion, it complies with the following conditions:

(a) the plan does not provide for the payment of any benefit before maturity except

(i) a refund of premiums, and

(ii) a payment to the annuitant;

(b) the plan does not provide for the payment of any benefit after maturity except

(i) by way of retirement income to the annuitant,

(ii) to the annuitant in full or partial commutation of retirement income under the plan, and

(iii) in respect of a commutation referred to in paragraph (c.2);

(b.1) the plan does not provide for a payment to the annuitant of a retirement income except by way of equal annual or more frequent periodic payments until such time as there is a payment in full or partial commutation of the retirement income and, where that commutation is partial, equal annual or more frequent periodic payments thereafter;

(b.2) the plan does not provide for periodic payments in a year under an annuity after the death of the first annuitant, the total of which exceeds the total of the payments under the annuity in a year before that death;

(b.3) the plan does not provide for the payment of any premium after maturity;

(b.4) the plan does not provide for maturity after the end of the year in which the annuitant attains 69 years of age;

(c) the plan provides that retirement income under the plan may not be assigned in whole or in part;

(c.1) notwithstanding paragraph (a), the plan permits the payment of an amount to a taxpayer where the amount is paid to reduce the amount of tax otherwise payable under Part X.1 by the taxpayer;

(c.2) the plan requires the commutation of each annuity payable thereunder that would otherwise become payable to a person other than an annuitant under the plan;

1335

(c.3) the plan, where it involves a depositary, includes provisions stipulating that

   (i) the depositary has no right of offset as regards the property held under the plan in connection with any debt or obligation owing to the depositary, and

   (ii) the property held under the plan cannot be pledged, assigned or in any way alienated as security for a loan or for any purpose other than that of providing for the annuitant, commencing at maturity, a retirement income;

(c.4) the plan requires that no advantage, other than

   (i) a benefit,

   (i.1) an amount described in paragraph (a) or (c) of the definition "benefit" in subsection (1),

   (ii) the payment or allocation of any amount to the plan by the issuer,

   (iii) an advantage from life insurance in effect on December 31, 1981, or

   (iv) an advantage derived from the provision of administrative or investment services in respect of the plan,

that is conditional in any way on the existence of the plan may be extended to the annuitant or to a person with whom the annuitant was not dealing at arm's length; and

(d) the plan in all other respects complies with regulations of the Governor in Council made on the recommendation of the Minister of Finance.

**Related Provisions:** 139.1(13) — Para. 146(2)(c.4) inapplicable to conversion benefit on demutualization of insurer; 146(3) — Minister may accept plan despite certain other conditions; 146(12) — Change in plan after registration; 146(13.1) — Effect of extending an advantage; 146(13.2) — Where pre-1997 plan does not mature by age 69; 204.2(1.2) — Undeducted RRSP premiums; 248(1)"disposition"(g) — Transfer with same annuitant not a disposition.

**Notes:** 146(2)(b.4) amended by 1996 Budget to change "71 years" to "69 years", effective 1996, except that

   (a) the amendment does not apply to an RSP accepted for registration before 1997;

   (b) the amendment does not apply to an RSP whose annuitant turned 70 before 1997; and

   (c) for an RSP whose annuitant turned 69 in 1996, read "70 years".

The non-applicability to pre-1997 plans does not mean that the plan does not need to mature by age 69. It merely means that the plan need not be amended to provide for the maturity in its terms. If it does not mature by the year the annuitant turns 69, 146(13.2) will cause it to be deregistered. See Notes to 146(13.2) re grandfathering for those who turned 70 or 71 in 1997.

146(2)(c.1) amended by 1990 pension bill, effective 1991.

146(2)(c.3) applies only to depositary plans. Where assets in a self-directed plan are pledged, see 146(10); where this condition is violated, see 146(12). If a depositary RRSP is pledged in violation of the condition required by 146(2)(c.3), the pledge is valid and can be enforced: *Re Whaling*, [1999] 4 C.T.C. 221 (Ont. CA). Where a bank seizes an RRSP to satisfy another debt, in breach of the requirement in 146(2)(c.3)(i), the bank will be liable for damages: *Belliveau v. Royal Bank* (2000), 14 C.B.R. (4th) 17 (NBCA).

146(2)(c.4) amended by 1989 Budget, effective for advantages extended after 1988.

**Interpretation Bulletins:** IT-124R6: Contributions to registered retirement savings plans; IT-307R3: Spousal registered retirement savings plans; IT-415R2: Deregistration of RRSPs.

**Information Circulars:** 72-22R9: Registered retirement savings plans; 79-8R3: Forms to use to directly transfer funds to or between plans, or to purchase an annuity.

**Forms:** T550: Application for registration.

**(3) Idem** — The Minister may accept for registration for the purposes of this Act any retirement savings plan notwithstanding that the plan

(a) provides for the payment of a benefit after maturity by way of dividend;

(b) provides for any annual or more frequent periodic amount payable

   (i) to the annuitant referred to in subparagraph (a)(ii) of the definition "retirement income" in subsection (1) by way of an annuity described in paragraph (a) of that definition to be reduced, in the event of the death of the annuitant's spouse or common-law partner during the lifetime of the annuitant, in such manner as to provide for the payment of equal annual or more frequent periodic amounts throughout the lifetime of the annuitant thereafter,

   (ii) to any person by way of an annuity, to be reduced if a pension becomes payable to that person under the *Old Age Security Act*, by an annual or other periodic amount not exceeding the amount payable to that person in that period under that Act,

   (iii) to any person by way of an annuity, to be increased or reduced depending on the increase or reduction in the value of a specified group of assets constituting the assets of a separate and distinct account or fund maintained in respect of a variable annuities business by a person licensed or otherwise authorized under the laws of Canada or a province to carry on in Canada that business,

   (iii.1) to any person by way of an annuity under a contract that provides for the increase or reduction of the annuity in accordance only with a change in the interest rate on which the annuity is based, if the interest rate, as increased or reduced, equals or approximates a generally available Canadian market interest rate,

   (iv) that may be adjusted annually to reflect

      (A) in whole or in part increases in the Consumer Price Index, as published by Statistics Canada under the authority of the *Statistics Act*, or

      (B) increases at a rate specified in the annuity contract, not exceeding 4% per annum, or

(v) to the annuitant by way of an annuity to be increased annually to the extent the amount or rate of return that would have been earned on a pool of investment assets (available for purchase by the public and specified in the annuity contract) exceeds an amount or rate specified in the plan and provides that no other increase may be made in the amount payable;

(c) [Repealed under former Act]

(d) provides for the payment of any amount after the death of an annuitant thereunder;

(e) is adjoined to a contract or other arrangement that is not a retirement savings plan; or

(f) contains such other terms and provisions, not inconsistent with this section, as are authorized or permitted by regulations of the Governor in Council made on the recommendation of the Minister of Finance.

**Related Provisions**: 60(l)(ii) — Transfer of RRSP premium refunds; 172(3) — Appeal from refusal to register.

**Notes**: 146(3)(b)(i) amended by 2000 same-sex partners bill to add reference to "common-law partner", effective for the 2001 and later taxation years, or earlier by election (see Notes to 248(1)"common-law partner").

**Interpretation Bulletins**: IT-124R6: Contributions to registered retirement savings plans; IT-307R3: Spousal registered retirement savings plans; IT-320R2: RRSPs — qualified investments; IT-415R2: Deregistration of RRSPs.

**Information Circulars**: 72-22R9: Registered retirement savings plans.

### (4) No tax while trust governed by plan — 
Except as provided in subsection (10.1), no tax is payable under this Part by a trust on the taxable income of the trust for a taxation year if, throughout the period in the year during which the trust was in existence, the trust was governed by a registered retirement savings plan, except that

(a) if the trust has borrowed money (other than money used in carrying on a business) in the year or has, after June 18, 1971, borrowed money (other than money used in carrying on a business) that it has not repaid before the commencement of the year, tax is payable under this Part by the trust on its taxable income for the year;

(b) in any case not described in paragraph (a), if the trust has carried on any business or businesses in the year, tax is payable under this Part by the trust on the amount, if any, by which

(i) the amount that its taxable income for the year would be if it had no incomes or losses from sources other than from that business or those businesses, as the case may be,

exceeds

(ii) such portion of the amount determined under subparagraph (i) in respect of the trust for the year as can reasonably be considered to be income from, or from the disposition of, qualified investments for the trust; and

(c) if the last annuitant under the plan has died, tax is payable under this Part by the trust on its taxable income for each year after the year following the year in which the last annuitant died.

**Related Provisions**: 104(6)(a.2) — Deduction for amounts paid out to beneficiaries; 146(8.9)A(b), (c) — No income inclusion for tax-paid amounts on death; 146(10.1) — Tax on income from non-qualified investment; 146(20) — Amount credited to deposit RRSP deemed not received by annuitant or any other person; 149(1)(r) — No tax on RRSP; 204.6 — Tax in respect of registered investments; 206(2) — Part XI tax on excess holdings of foreign property; 207.1(1) — Tax on non-qualified investments; Canada-U.S. tax treaty, Art. XIX:7 — Election to defer U.S. tax on income accruing in RRSP; Art. XXI:2(a) — RRSP exempt from U.S. tax.

**Notes**: An RRSP or RRIF is exempt from U.S. withholding tax on dividends and interest: Canada-U.S. tax treaty Art. XXI:2. Where the plan holds U.S. stocks, the trustee should advise the U.S. payor not to withhold tax on dividends.

146(4)(b) and (c) amended by 1993 technical bill, effective for 1993 and later taxation years. For 1986 through 1992, ignore 146(4)(b)(ii), and read the last few words of 146(4)(c) as "for each year after the year of the annuitant's death". Tax is now payable by the trust only from the second year following death. (The same applies to RRIFs, under 146.3(3.1).)

**Interpretation Bulletins**: IT-415R2: Deregistration of RRSPs.

**Information Circulars**: 72-22R9: Registered retirement savings plans.

**Advance Tax Rulings**: ATR-37: Refund of premiums transferred to spouse.

### (5) Amount of RRSP premiums deductible — 
There may be deducted in computing a taxpayer's income for a taxation year such amount as the taxpayer claims not exceeding the lesser of

(a) the amount, if any, by which the total of all amounts each of which is a premium paid by the taxpayer after 1990 and on or before the day that is 60 days after the end of the year under a registered retirement savings plan under which the taxpayer was the annuitant at the time the premium was paid, other than the portion, if any, of the premium

(i) that was deducted in computing the taxpayer's income for a preceding taxation year,

(ii) that was designated for any taxation year for the purposes of paragraph 60(j), (j.1) or (l),

(iii) in respect of which the taxpayer received a payment that was deducted under subsection (8.2) in computing the taxpayer's income for a preceding taxation year,

(iv) that was deductible under subsection (6.1) in computing the taxpayer's income for any taxation year, or

(iv.1) that would be considered to be withdrawn by the taxpayer as an eligible amount (as defined in subsection 146.01(1) or 146.02(1)) less than 90 days after it was paid, if earnings in respect of a registered retirement savings plan were considered to be withdrawn before premiums paid under that plan and premiums were considered to be withdrawn in the order in which they were paid

exceeds

(v) the amount, if any, by which

(A) the total of all amounts deducted under subsection 147.3(13.1) in computing the taxpayer's income for the year or a preceding taxation year

exceeds

(B) the total of all amounts, in respect of transfers occurring before 1991 from registered pension plans, deemed by paragraph 147.3(10)(b) or (c) to be a premium paid by the taxpayer to a registered retirement savings plan, and

(b) the taxpayer's RRSP deduction limit for the year.

**Related Provisions**: 18(1)(u) — Investment counselling and administration fees for RRSP are non-deductible; 18(11)(b) — No deduction for interest on money borrowed to make RRSP contribution; 60(i) — Deduction for RRSP premium paid; 60(j) — Transfer of superannuation benefits; 60(j.1) — Transfer of retiring allowances; 60(l) — Transfer of RRSP premium refunds; 60(v) — Contribution to a provincial pension plan; 146(5.1) — Deduction for contribution to spousal RRSP; 146(5.21) — Anti-avoidance; 146(8.2) — Deduction where non-deducted overcontribution withdrawn from plan; 146(8.21) — Premium deemed not paid; 146(16) — Deduction on transfer of funds; 146(22) — Deadline extension for ice storm and for 1998 PAR; 147.3(13.1) — Withdrawal of excessive transfers to RRSPs and RRIFs; 204.1(2.1) — Tax payable by individuals — contributions after 1990; 204.2(1.2)I(a)(vi) — Amount non-deductible due to 146(5)(a)(iv.1) not included for Part X.1 penalty tax purposes; Canada-U.S. tax treaty, Art. XIX:7 — Election to defer U.S. tax on income accruing in RRIF; Art. XXI:2(a) — RRIF exempt from U.S. tax.

**Notes**: The "RRSP deduction limit" for 1996 through 2003, as defined in 146(1), is the lesser of $13,500 and 18% of the taxpayer's previous year's earned income, minus the pension adjustment. The $13,500 figure comes from 146(1)"RRSP dollar limit" and 147.1(1)"money purchase limit"(e). See Notes to the definitions of "RRSP deduction limit" and "RRSP dollar limit" in 146(1).

The contribution deadline is 60 days after the end of the year, which is normally March 1. In a leap year such as 2000, however, the deadline is February 29. It is also extended by 146(22) in certain situations, such as for the January 1998 ice storm and for taxpayers with 1998 pension adjustment reversals.

RRSP contributions are no longer subject to minimum tax. See the 1998 Budget repeal of 127.52(1)(a).

146(5)(a)(iv.1) amended by 1998 Budget to add reference to 146.02(1), effective for 1998 and later taxation years.

146(5)(a)(iv.1) added by 1994 Budget, effective for the withdrawal of amounts paid after March 1, 1994.

146(5)(a) amended by 1992 technical bill (as itself amended by 1993 technical bill, s. 136) and by 1993 technical bill, effective for 1992 and later taxation years. For 1991, ignore 146(5)(a)(v). (A subpara. 146(5)(a)(vi), introduced by the 1992 technical bill, is now deemed never to have been in force, as it was superseded by the 1993 technical bill amendment.)

146(5) amended by 1990 pension bill, effective 1991. For 1989 and 1990, the rule read very differently, with a limit of 20% of current year's earned income, capped at $3,500 minus deductible RPP contributions for members of registered pension plans and $7,500 otherwise.

**Regulations**: 100(3)(c) (no source withholding where premium is paid by employer directly to RRSP).

**Remission Orders**: *Certain Taxpayers Remission Order, 1998-2*, P.C. 1998-2092, s. (judges in Quebec who made contributions in 1989 or 1990); *Certain Taxpayers Remission Order, 1999-2*, P.C. 1999-1855, s. 2 (remission to Quebec judges for excess contributions in 1989-90).

**Interpretation Bulletins**: IT-124R6: Contributions to registered retirement savings plans; IT-307R3: Spousal registered retirement savings plans; IT-320R2: RRSPs — qualified investments; IT-500R: RRSPs — death of an annuitant.

**Advance Tax Rulings**: ATR-2: Contribution to pension plan for past service; ATR-17: Employee benefit plan — purchase of company shares; ATR-37: Refund of premiums transferred to spouse.

**Forms**: T1 General Sched. 7: RRSP contributions, transfers and designations of repayments under the home buyers' plan; T1023: RRSP deduction limit — calculation of earned income; T4040: RRSPs and other registered plans for retirement [guide].

**(5.1) Amount of spousal RRSP premiums deductible** — There may be deducted in computing a taxpayer's income for a taxation year such amount as the taxpayer claims not exceeding the lesser of

(a) the total of all amounts each of which is a premium paid by the taxpayer after 1990 and on or before the day that is 60 days after the end of the year under a registered retirement savings plan under which the taxpayer's spouse (or, where the taxpayer died in the year or within 60 days after the end of the year, an individual who was the taxpayer's spouse immediately before the death) was the annuitant at the time the premium was paid, other than the portion, if any, of the premium

(i) that was deducted in computing the taxpayer's income for a preceding taxation year,

(ii) that was designated for any taxation year for the purposes of paragraph 60(j.2),

(iii) in respect of which the taxpayer or the taxpayer's spouse or common-law partner has received a payment that has been deducted under subsection (8.2) in computing the taxpayer's income for a preceding taxation year, or

(iv) that would be considered to be withdrawn by the taxpayer's spouse or common-law partner as an eligible amount (as defined in subsection 146.01(1) or 146.02(1)) less than 90 days after it was paid, if earnings in respect of a registered retirement savings plan were considered to be withdrawn before premiums paid under that plan and premiums were considered to be withdrawn in the order in which they were paid, and

(b) the amount, if any, by which the taxpayer's RRSP deduction limit for the year exceeds the amount deducted under subsection (5) in computing the taxpayer's income for the year.

**Related Provisions**: 60(i) — Deduction for RRSP premiums paid; 60(l) — Transfer of RRSP premium refunds; 60(v) — Contribution to provincial pension plan; 74.5(12)(a) — Attribution rules do not apply to spousal contribution; 146(5) — Deduction for contribution to own plan; 146(8.21) — Premium deemed not paid; 146(8.3) — Attribution of income when amount withdrawn from RRSP; 146(16) — Deduction on transfer of funds; 146(22) — Deadline extension for ice storm; 146.3(5.1) — Attribution on withdrawal from RRIF; 146.3(5.4) — RRIF — Spouse's income; 204.1(2.1) — Tax payable by individuals — contributions after 1990; 204.2(1.2)I(a)(vi) — Amount non-deductible due to 146(5.1)(a)(iv) not included for Part X.1 penalty tax purposes; 252(3) — Extended meaning of "spouse".

**Notes**: See Notes to 146(8.3) re attribution on withdrawals.

146(5.1)(a)(iii), (iv) amended by 2000 same-sex partners bill to add reference to "common-law partner", effective for the 2001 and later taxation years, or earlier by election (see Notes to 248(1)"common-law partner").

Opening words of 146(5.1)(a) amended by 1993 technical bill, effective for 1992 and later taxation years, to add the parenthesized words dealing with death.

146(5.1)(a)(iv) added by 1994 Budget, effective for the withdrawal of amounts paid after March 1, 1994, and amended by 1998 Budget to add reference to 146.02(1), effective for 1998 and later taxation years.

146(5.1) amended by 1990 pension bill, effective 1991. Before then, it related to the pre-1991 version of 146(5).

**Regulations**: 100(3)(c) (deduction of RRSP contribution from payroll reduces source withholding).

**Interpretation Bulletins**: IT-124R6: Contributions to registered retirement savings plans; IT-307R3: Spousal registered retirement savings plans; IT-500R: RRSPs — death of an annuitant.

**Information Circulars**: 72-22R9: Registered retirement savings plans.

**Forms**: T4040: RRSPs and other registered plans for retirement [guide].

**(5.2)** [Repealed under former Act]

**Notes**: 146(5.2) repealed by 1990 pension bill, effective 1991. It defined "pension fund or plan" to exclude the CPP and similar plans.

**(5.21) Anti-avoidance** — Notwithstanding any other provision of this section, where

(a) a registered pension plan is amended or administered in such a manner as to terminate, suspend or delay

 (i) the membership of an individual in the plan for the individual's 1990 taxation year,

 (ii) contributions under the plan by or for the benefit of the individual in respect of the year, or

 (iii) the accrual of retirement benefits under the plan for the individual in respect of the year, or

(b) a deferred profit sharing plan is amended or administered in such a manner as to terminate, suspend or delay contributions under the plan for the year in respect of an individual,

and one of the main reasons for the termination, suspension or delay may reasonably be considered to be to reduce the pension adjustment of the individual for the year in respect of an employer, the only amount that may be deducted in computing the income for the year of the individual, in respect of premiums paid to registered retirement savings plans, is the amount that would have been deductible had that termination, suspension or delay not occurred.

**Notes**: 146(5.21) added by 1990 pension bill, effective for 1990 only.

**(5.3)–(5.5)** [Repealed under former Act]

**Notes**: 146(5.3)–(5.5), repealed by 1985 Budget, dealt with a special rollover of farm property into an RRSP. It was abolished due to the introduction of the capital gains exemption in 110.6. See 110.6(2).

**(6) Disposition of non-qualified investment** — Where in a taxation year a trust governed by a registered retirement savings plan disposes of a property that, when acquired, was a non-qualified investment, there may be deducted, in computing the income for the taxation year of the taxpayer who is the annuitant under the plan, an amount equal to the lesser of

(a) the amount that, by virtue of subsection (10), was included in computing the income of that taxpayer in respect of the acquisition of that property, and

(b) the proceeds of disposition of the property.

**Related Provisions**: 146(10) — Tax on acquisition of non-qualified investment; 146(11) — Life insurance policy; 259(1) — Election for proportional holdings in trust property.

**Notes**: See Notes to 146(10.1).

**Regulations**: 214(2) (information return).

**Interpretation Bulletins**: IT-320R2: RRSPs — qualified investments; IT-415R2: Deregistration of registered retirement savings plans.

**Forms**: T3G: Certification of no tax liability by a group of RRSPs, RRIFs, or RESPs; T3IND: T3IND income tax return for RRSP, RRIF, or RESP.

**(6.1) Recontribution of certain withdrawals** — There may be deducted in computing a taxpayer's income for a particular taxation year the total of all amounts each of which is such portion of a prescribed premium for the particular year as was not designated for any taxation year for the purposes of paragraph 60(j), (j.1) or (l).

**Related Provisions**: 60(i) — Deduction for RRSP premiums paid; 127.52(1)(a)(ii)(A) — Addition to adjusted taxable income for minimum tax purposes; 146(5) — Amount of RRSP premiums deductible; 146.01(1)"excluded premium"(c) — Premium deducted under 146(6.1) not eligible for Home Buyers' Plan; 146.02(1)"excluded premium"(d) — Premium deducted under 146(6.1) not eligible for LLP; 152(6) — Reassessment.

**Regulations**: 8307(7) (prescribed premium).

**Interpretation Bulletins**: IT-124R6: Contributions to registered retirement savings plans.

**(7) Recovery of property used as security** — Where in a taxation year a loan, for which a trust governed by a registered retirement savings plan has used or permitted to be used trust property as security, ceases to be extant, and the fair market value of the property so used was included by virtue of subsection (10) in computing the income of the taxpayer who is the annuitant under the plan, there may be deducted, in computing the income of the taxpayer for the taxation year, an amount equal to the amount, if any, remaining when

(a) the net loss (exclusive of payments by the trust as or on account of interest) sustained by the trust in consequence of its using the property, or permitting it to be used, as security for the loan and not as a result of a change in the fair market value of the property

is deducted from

(b) the amount so included in computing the income of the taxpayer in consequence of the trust's using the property, or permitting it to be used, as security for the loan.

**Related Provisions**: 60(i) — Deduction in computing income; 146(10) — Where acquisition of non-qualified investment by trust.

**Notes**: See Notes to 146(10).

**Regulations**: 214(2) (information return).

**Forms**: T3G: Certification of no tax liability by a group of RRSPs, RRIFs, or RESPs; T3IND: T3IND income tax return for RRSP, RRIF, or RESP.

**(8) Benefits taxable** — There shall be included in computing a taxpayer's income for a taxation year the total of all amounts received by the taxpayer in the year as benefits out of or under registered retirement savings plans, other than excluded withdrawals (as defined in subsection 146.01(1) or 146.02(1)) of the taxpayer and amounts that are included under paragraph (12)(b) in computing the taxpayer's income.

**Proposed Amendment — Income inclusion on conversion to Roth IRA**
**Department of Finance press release, December 18, 1998**: [See under 248(1)"foreign retirement arrangement" — ed.]

**Related Provisions**: 56(1)(h) — Income from RRSP; 60(l) — Transfer of RRSP premium refunds; 139.1(12) — Conversion benefit on demutualization of insurance corporation not taxable; 146(8.01) — Benefits from RRSP re Home Buyers' Plan; 146(8.3) — Attribution from spousal RRSP; 146(12) — Change in plan after registration; 146(16) — Deduction on transfer of funds; 146(20) — Amount credited to deposit RRSP deemed not received by annuitant; 146.01(4) — Home Buyers' Plan — portion of eligible amount not repaid; 146.01(5), (6) — Home Buyers' Plan — other income inclusions; 146.02(4) — LLP — portion of eligible amount not repaid; 146.02(5), (6) — LLP — other income inclusions; 147.3(13.1) — Withdrawal of excessive transfers to RRSPs and RRIFs; 153(1)(j) — Withholding of tax at source; 160.2(1) — Joint and several liability in respect of amounts received out of or under RRSP; 212(1)(l) — Withholding tax on payments to non-residents.

**Notes**: Management fees and investment counsel fees paid from inside the plan are not a benefit conferred on the annuitant. See Notes to 18(1)(u).

146(8) amended by 1998 Budget to add reference to 146.02(1), effective for 1999 and later taxation years.

146(8) amended by 1992 Budget/technical bill, effective 1992, to add the exception for excluded withdrawals. In other words, withdrawals under the Home Buyers' Plan in 146.01 are not brought into income. Reg. 104(3) permits the RRSP administrator to pay such funds to the annuitant without withholding tax at source.

**Regulations**: 100(1)"remuneration"(i) (payment from RRSP subject to source withholding); 103(4), (6) (withholding requirements on withdrawal from RRSP); 104(3) (no withholding on Home Buyers' Plan withdrawal); 104.1 (no withholding on Lifelong Learning Plan withdrawal); 214(1), (4) (information return).

**I.T. Application Rules**: 61(2) (where annuitant died before 1972).

**Interpretation Bulletins**: IT-307R3: Spousal registered retirement savings plans; IT-500R: RRSPs — death of an annuitant.

**Information Circulars**: 72-22R9: Registered retirement savings plans.

**Advance Tax Rulings**: ATR-37: Refund of premiums transferred to spouse.

**Forms**: T4RSP Segment; T4RSP Summ: Return of RRSP income; T4RSP Supp: Statement of RRSP income; T4040: RRSPs and other registered plans for retirement [guide]; T4079: T4RSP and T4RIF guide.

**(8.01) Subsequent re-calculation** — If a designated withdrawal (as defined in subsection 146.01(1)) or an amount referred to in paragraph (a) of the definition "eligible amount" in subsection 146.02(1) is received by a taxpayer in a taxation year and, at any time after that year, it is determined that the amount is not an excluded withdrawal (as defined in subsection 146.01(1) or 146.02(1)), notwithstanding subsections 152(4) to (5), such assessments of tax, interest and penalties shall be made as are necessary to give effect to the determination.

**Notes**: 146(8.01) provides that if an amount is withdrawn under the Home Buyers' Plan (146.01) or Lifelong Learning Plan (146.02) and it is later determined that it should have been taxable, the correcting assessment can be made outside the normal (3-year) time limit.

146(8.01) amended by 1998 Budget, effective for 1999 and later taxation years. For 1992-98, read:

(8.01) **Idem — subsequent re-calculation** — Where an amount referred to in paragraph (a) of the definition "eligible amount" in subsection 146.01(1) is received by a taxpayer in a taxation year and, at any time after that year, it is determined that the amount is not an excluded withdrawal (within the meaning assigned by that subsection), notwithstanding subsections 152(4) to (5), such assessments of tax, interest and penalties shall be made as are necessary to give effect to the determination.

146(8.01) added by 1992 technical bill, effective 1992.

**Interpretation Bulletins**: IT-415R2: Deregistration of RRSPs.

**(8.1) Deemed receipt of refund of premiums** — Where a portion of an amount paid out of or under a registered retirement savings plan of a deceased annuitant to the annuitant's legal representative would have been a refund of premiums if it had been paid under the plan to a beneficiary of the deceased's estate, it is, to the extent it is so designated jointly by the legal representative and the beneficiary in prescribed form filed with the Minister, deemed to be received by the beneficiary (and not by the legal representative) at the time it was so paid as a benefit that is a refund of premiums.

**Related Provisions**: 60(l) — Transfer of RRSP premium refunds; 60(l)(v)(B.1) — Rollover of designated benefits to child or grandchild on death; 146(8.9) — Effect of death where person other than spouse becomes entitled; 146.3(6.1) — Parallel rule for RRIFs; 160.2(1) — Joint and several liability in respect of amounts re-

Division G — Deferred & Special Income Arrangements    S. 146(8.21)(a)

ceived out of or under RRSP; 214(3)(c) — Non-resident withholding tax.

**Notes**: 146(8.1) amended by 1999 Budget, effective for 1999 and later taxation years. The amendment clarifies that the refund of premiums is deemed to be received by the beneficiary (and not by the legal representative) at the same time as the corresponding RRSP amount was paid to the legal representative. This is consistent with a similar rule for RRIFs in 146.3(6.1). For earlier years, read:

(8.1) Such portion of an amount paid in a taxation year out of or under a registered retirement savings plan of a deceased annuitant to the annuitant's legal representative as, had that portion been paid under the plan to a beneficiary of the deceased's estate, would have been a refund of premiums shall, to the extent it is so designated jointly by the legal representative and the beneficiary in prescribed form filed with the Minister, be deemed to be received by the beneficiary in the year as a benefit that is a refund of premiums.

**Information Circulars**: 79-8R3: Forms to use to directly transfer funds to or between plans, or to purchase an annuity.

**Advance Tax Rulings**: ATR-37: Refund of premiums transferred to spouse.

**Forms**: T2019: Death of an RRSP annuitant — refund of premiums.

**(8.2) Amount deductible** — Where

(a) all or any portion of the premiums paid in a taxation year by a taxpayer to one or more registered retirement savings plans under which the taxpayer or the taxpayer's spouse or common-law partner was the annuitant was not deducted in computing the taxpayer's income for any taxation year,

(b) the taxpayer or the taxpayer's spouse or common-law partner can reasonably be regarded as having received a payment from a registered retirement savings plan or a registered retirement income fund in respect of such portion of the undeducted premiums as

(i) was not paid by way of a transfer of an amount from a registered pension plan to a registered retirement savings plan,

(ii) was not paid by way of a transfer of an amount from a deferred profit sharing plan to a registered retirement savings plan in accordance with subsection 147(19), and

(iii) was not paid by way of a transfer of an amount from a provincial pension plan prescribed for the purpose of paragraph 60(v) to a registered retirement savings plan in circumstances to which subsection (21) applied,

(c) the payment is received by the taxpayer or the taxpayer's spouse or common-law partner in a particular taxation year that is

(i) the year in which the premiums were paid by the taxpayer,

(ii) the year in which a notice of assessment for the taxation year referred to in subparagraph (i) was sent to the taxpayer, or

(iii) the year immediately following the year referred to in subparagraph (i) or (ii), and

(d) the payment is included in computing the taxpayer's income for the particular year,

the payment (except to the extent that it is a prescribed withdrawal) may be deducted in computing the taxpayer's income for the particular year unless it is reasonable to consider that

(e) the taxpayer did not reasonably expect that the full amount of the premiums would be deductible in the taxation year in which the premiums were paid or in the immediately preceding taxation year, and

(f) the taxpayer paid all or any portion of the premiums with the intent of receiving a payment that, but for this paragraph and paragraph (e), would be deductible under this subsection.

**Related Provisions**: 60(i) — Deduction for RRSP premiums paid; 146(5) — Deduction for contribution to own RRSP; 146(5.1) — Deduction for contribution to spousal RRSP; 146(8.21) — Excess premium deemed not paid; 146(16) — Deduction on transfer of funds; 147.3(13.1) — Withdrawal of excessive transfers to RRSPs and RRIFs; Reg. 8307(4) — Eligibility of withdrawn amount for designation.

**Notes**: 146(8.2) allows non-deducted RRSP premiums (typically RRSP overcontributions, but also amounts contributed for a year when the Home Buyers' Plan or Lifelong Learning Plan was used) to be withdrawn on a tax-free basis within a specified timeframe. Technically the withdrawal is not tax-free, but 146(8.2) provides a deduction to offset the income inclusion.

146(8.2) amended by 2000 same-sex partners bill to add reference to "common-law partner", effective for the 2001 and later taxation years, or earlier by election (see Notes to 248(1) "common-law partner").

146(8.2)(b)(iii) added by 1993 technical bill, effective for 1992 and later taxation years. It refers to the Saskatchewan Pension Plan.

146(8.2)(b) amended by 1992 technical bill, effective for 1992 and later taxation years. For the 1991 taxation year, read subpara. (i) as:

(i) was not paid by way of a transfer of an amount from a registered pension plan to a registered retirement savings plan in accordance with any of subsections 147.3(1) and (4) to (7), and

146(8.2) amended by 1990 pension bill, effective for premiums paid after 1990. For premiums paid before 1991, and taxation years beginning in 1986 it read differently.

**Regulations**: 8307(6) (prescribed withdrawal).

**Interpretation Bulletins**: IT-307R3: Spousal registered retirement savings plans; IT-124R6: Contributions to registered retirement savings plans.

**Forms**: T746: Calculating your deduction for refund of unused RRSP contributions; T3012A: Tax deduction waiver on the refund of your undeducted RRSP contributions.

**(8.21) Premium deemed not paid** — Where a taxpayer or the taxpayer's spouse or common-law partner has, at any time in a taxation year, received a payment from a registered retirement savings plan or a registered retirement income fund in respect of all or any portion of a premium paid by the taxpayer to a registered retirement savings plan and the payment has been deducted under subsection (8.2) in computing the taxpayer's income for the year, the premium or portion thereof, as the case may be, shall,

(a) for the purposes of determining, after that time, the amount that may be deducted under subsection (5) or (5.1) in computing the taxpayer's income for the year or a preceding taxation year, and

(b) for the purposes of subsections (8.3) and 146.3(5.1) after that time, in the case of a payment received by the taxpayer,

be deemed not to have been a premium paid by the taxpayer to a registered retirement savings plan.

**Related Provisions**: 146(8.6) — Spouse's income.

**Notes**: 146(8.21) amended by 2000 same-sex partners bill to add reference to "common-law partner", effective for the 2001 and later taxation years, or earlier by election (see Notes to 248(1)"common-law partner").

146(8.21) added by 1990 pension bill, effective for premiums paid after 1990.

**Interpretation Bulletins**: IT-124R6: Contributions to registered retirement savings plans.

**(8.3) Spousal RRSP payments [attribution rule]** — Where at any time in a taxation year a particular amount in respect of a registered retirement savings plan that is a spousal plan in relation to a taxpayer is required by reason of subsection (8) or paragraph (12)(b) to be included in computing the income of the taxpayer's spouse before the plan matures or as a payment in full or partial commutation of a retirement income under the plan and the taxpayer is not living separate and apart from the taxpayer's spouse at that time by reason of the breakdown of their marriage or common-law partnership, there shall be included at that time in computing the taxpayer's income for the year an amount equal to the lesser of

(a) the total of all amounts each of which is a premium paid by the taxpayer in the year or in one of the two immediately preceding taxation years to a registered retirement savings plan under which the taxpayer's spouse or common-law partner was the annuitant at the time the premium was paid, and

(b) the particular amount.

**Related Provisions**: 56(1)(h) — Income from RRSP; 60(j.2) — Transfer to spousal RRSP; 74.5(12) — Regular attribution rule does not apply; 146(8.21) — Premium deemed not paid; 146(8.5) — Ordering; 146(8.6) — Spouse's income; 146(8.7) — Where subsec. (8.3) does not apply; 146.3(5.1) — Parallel rule for RRIFs; 146.3(5.4) — Spouse's income; 147.3(13.1) — Withdrawal of excessive transfers to RRSPs and RRIFs; 153(1)(j) — Withholding of tax at source.

**Notes**: Premiums to one's spouse's plan can be deducted (within total RRSP contribution room allowed) under 146(5.1). If contributions to *any* spousal plan are withdrawn in the calendar year a contribution was made or in the next two calendar years, they are attributed back to the contributor to the extent of that contribution (subject to the exclusions in 146(8.7)). It does not matter whether the withdrawal is from the same plan as was most recently contributed to.

Note that if A and B are spouses, a gift or loan from A to B that enables B to contribute to B's plan could result in attribution back to A under 74.1 when the RRSP proceeds are taxed many years later. This can be avoided by A giving funds to B that B contributes to A's plan while A makes a spousal contribution to B's plan and

waits for the period under 146(8.3) to expire! (There is no attribution on a spousal contribution except under 146(8.3); see 74.5(12).)

146(8.3)(a) amended by 2000 same-sex partners bill to add reference to "common-law partner" and "common-law partnership", effective for the 2001 and later taxation years, or earlier by election (see Notes to 248(1)"common-law partner").

146(8.3) amended by 1990 pension bill, effective 1991. Before 1991, it read differently.

**Interpretation Bulletins**: IT-124R6: Contributions to registered retirement savings plans; IT-307R3: Spousal registered retirement savings plans; IT-415R2: Deregistration of RRSPs.

**Forms**: T2205: Calculation of amounts from a spousal RRSP or RRIF to be included in income.

**(8.4)** [Repealed under former Act]

**Notes**: 146(8.4) repealed by 1990 pension bill, effective 1991.

**(8.5) Ordering** — Where a taxpayer has paid more than one premium described in subsection (8.3), such a premium or part thereof paid by the taxpayer at any time shall be deemed to have been included in computing the taxpayer's income by virtue of that subsection before premiums or parts thereof paid by the taxpayer after that time.

**Interpretation Bulletins**: IT-307R3: Spousal registered retirement savings plans.

**(8.6) Spouse's [or common-law partner's] income** — Where, in respect of an amount required at any time in a taxation year to be included in computing the income of a taxpayer's spouse or common-law partner, all or part of a premium has by reason of subsection (8.3) been included in computing the taxpayer's income for the year, the following rules apply:

(a) the premium or part thereof, as the case may be, shall, for the purposes of subsections (8.3) and 146.3(5.1) after that time, be deemed not to have been a premium paid to a registered retirement savings plan under which the taxpayer's spouse or common-law partner was the annuitant; and

(b) an amount equal to the premium or part thereof, as the case may be, may be deducted in computing the income of the spouse or common-law partner for the year.

**Related Provisions**: 146(8.21) — Premium deemed not paid; 146.3(5.4) — Spouse's income.

**Notes**: 146(8.6) amended by 2000 same-sex partners bill to add reference to "common-law partner", effective for the 2001 and later taxation years, or earlier by election (see Notes to 248(1)"common-law partner").

146(8.6) amended by 1990 pension bill, this version effective 1991.

**Interpretation Bulletins**: IT-307R3: Spousal registered retirement savings plans; IT-415R2: Deregistration of RRSPs.

**(8.7) Where subsec. (8.3) does not apply** — Subsection (8.3) does not apply

(a) in respect of a taxpayer at any time during the year in which the taxpayer died;

(b) in respect of a taxpayer where either the taxpayer or the taxpayer's spouse or common-law partner is a non-resident at the particular time referred to in that subsection;

(c) in respect of amounts paid out of or under a plan referred to in subsection (12) as an "amended plan" to which paragraph (12)(a) applied before May 26, 1976;

(d) to any payment that is received in full or partial commutation of a registered retirement income fund or a registered retirement savings plan and in respect of which a deduction was made under paragraph 60(l) if, where the deduction was in respect of the acquisition of an annuity, the terms of the annuity provide that it cannot be commuted, and it is not commuted, in whole or in part within 3 years after the acquisition; or

(e) in respect of an amount that is deemed by subsection (8.8) to have been received by an annuitant under a registered retirement savings plan immediately before the annuitant's death.

**Notes**: 146(8.7)(b) amended by 2000 same-sex partners bill to add reference to "common-law partner", effective for the 2001 and later taxation years, or earlier by election (see Notes to 248(1)"common-law partner").

146(8.7)(e) added by 1990 pension bill, effective 1988.

**Interpretation Bulletins**: IT-307R3: Spousal registered retirement savings plans; IT-415R2: Deregistration of RRSPs.

**(8.8) Effect of death where person other than spouse [or common-law partner] becomes entitled** — Where the annuitant under a registered retirement savings plan (other than a plan that had matured before June 30, 1978) dies after June 29, 1978, the annuitant shall be deemed to have received, immediately before the annuitant's death, an amount as a benefit out of or under a registered retirement savings plan equal to the amount, if any, by which

(a) the fair market value of all the property of the plan at the time of death

exceeds

(b) where the annuitant died after the maturity of the plan, the fair market value at the time of the death of the portion of the property described in paragraph (a) that, as a consequence of the death, becomes receivable by a person who was the annuitant's spouse or common-law partner immediately before the death, or would become so receivable should that person survive throughout all guaranteed terms contained in the plan.

**Related Provisions**: 60(l)(v)(B.1) — Transfer of RRSP premium refunds; 118.1(5.3) — Designation of charity as beneficiary of RRSP; 146(8.7) — Where subsec. (8.3) does not apply; 146(8.9) — Effect of death where person other than spouse becomes entitled; 146.3(6) — Parallel rule for RRIFs; 160.2(1) — Joint and several liability in respect of amounts received out of or under RRSP; 214(3)(c) — Non-resident withholding tax.

**Notes**: Where the deceased leaves the RRSP to a financially dependent child or grandchild, there is no income inclusion to the estate: see 146(1)"refund of premiums". The child or grandchild can then roll the amounts into their own RRSP to avoid tax: see 60(l)(v)(B.1). Where the deceased leaves the RRSP to a spouse, see also 146(8.91).

For discussion of 146(8.8) and (8.9), see William Crawford, "Tax-Free Transfers and Rollovers of RRSPs and RRIFs After Death", IV(2) *RRSP Planning* (Federated Press) 244-248 (1997).

146(8.8)(b) amended by 2000 same-sex partners bill to add reference to "common-law partner", effective for the 2001 and later taxation years, or earlier by election (see Notes to 248(1)"common-law partner").

146(8.8)(b) amended by 1993 technical bill, effective for deaths in 1993 or later. For deaths from 1979 through 1992, read:

(b) the portion thereof that, as a consequence of the annuitant's death, becomes receivable by the annuitant's spouse, or would become so receivable should that spouse survive throughout all guaranteed terms contained in the plan.

**Regulations**: 214(4) (information return).

**Interpretation Bulletins**: IT-307R3: Spousal registered retirement savings plans; IT-500R: RRSPs — death of an annuitant.

**Advance Tax Rulings**: ATR-37: Refund of premiums transferred to spouse.

**Forms**: RC4177: Death of an RRSP annuitant [guide].

**(8.9) Idem** — There may be deducted from the amount deemed by subsection (8.8) to have been received by an annuitant as a benefit out of or under a registered retirement savings plan an amount not exceeding the amount determined by the formula

$$A \times \left[1 - \frac{(B + C - D)}{(B + C)}\right]$$

where

A is the total of

(a) all refunds of premiums in respect of the plan,

(b) all tax-paid amounts in respect of the plan paid to individuals who, otherwise than because of subsection (8.1), received refunds of premiums in respect of the plan, and

(c) all amounts each of which is a tax-paid amount in respect of the plan paid to the legal representative of the annuitant under the plan, to the extent that the legal representative would have been entitled to designate that tax-paid amount under subsection (8.1) if tax-paid amounts were not excluded in determining refunds of premiums;

B is the fair market value of the property of the plan at the particular time that is the later of

(a) the end of the first calendar year that begins after the death of the annuitant, and

(b) the time immediately after the last time that any refund of premiums in respect of the plan is paid out of or under the plan;

C is the total of all amounts paid out of or under the plan after the death of the annuitant and before the particular time; and

D is the lesser of

(a) the fair market value of the property of the plan at the time of the annuitant's death, and

**S. 146(8.9)** — Income Tax Act, Part I

(b) the sum of the values of B and C in respect of the plan.

**Related Provisions**: 60(l) — Transfer of RRSP premium refunds; 146.3(6.2) — Parallel rule for RRIFs; 160.2(1) — Joint and several liability in respect of amounts received out of or under RRSP.

**Notes**: See Notes to 146(8.8).

146(8.9) amended by 1993 technical bill and by 1995-97 technical bill (to add paras. (b) and (c) — see Notes to 146(1)"tax-paid amount"), both effective for deaths in 1993 or later. For deaths from 1979 through 1992, read:

> (8.9) There may be deducted from the amount deemed by subsection (8.8) to have been received by an annuitant as a benefit out of or under a registered retirement savings plan the total of all amounts each of which is
>
> (a) that portion of an amount paid out of or under the plan that is deemed to be received by a beneficiary as a benefit that is a refund of premiums pursuant to subsection (8.1); or
>
> (b) an amount received under the plan by a child or grandchild of the annuitant as a refund of premiums.

**Interpretation Bulletins**: IT-500R: RRSPs — death of an annuitant.

**Advance Tax Rulings**: ATR-37: Refund of premiums transferred to spouse.

**Forms**: RC4177: Death of an RRSP annuitant [guide].

**(8.91) Amounts deemed receivable by spouse [or common-law partner]** — Where, as a consequence of the death of an annuitant after the maturity of the annuitant's registered retirement savings plan, the annuitant's legal representative has become entitled to receive amounts out of or under the plan for the benefit of the spouse or common-law partner of the deceased and the legal representative and the spouse or common-law partner file with the Minister a joint election in prescribed form,

(a) the spouse or common-law partner shall be deemed to have become the annuitant under the plan as a consequence of the annuitant's death; and

(b) such amounts shall be deemed to be receivable by the spouse or common-law partner and, when paid, to be received by the spouse or common-law partner as a benefit under the plan, and not to be received by any other person.

**Related Provisions**: 60(l) — Transfer of RRSP premium refunds; 160.2(1) — Joint and several liability in respect of amounts received out of or under RRSP; 214(3)(c) — Non-resident withholding tax; 248(8) — Occurrences as a consequence of death.

**Notes**: 146(8.91) amended by 2000 same-sex partners bill to add reference to "common-law partner", effective for the 2001 and later taxation years, or earlier by election (see Notes to 248(1)"common-law partner").

**Interpretation Bulletins**: IT-307R3: Spousal registered retirement savings plans; IT-500R: RRSPs — death of an annuitant.

**Forms**: RC4177: Death of an RRSP annuitant [guide].

**(9) Where disposition of property by trust** — Where in a taxation year a trust governed by a registered retirement savings plan

(a) disposes of property for a consideration less than the fair market value of the property at the time of the disposition, or for no consideration, or

(b) acquires property for a consideration greater than the fair market value of the property at the time of the acquisition,

the difference between the fair market value and the consideration, if any, shall be included in computing the income for the taxation year of the annuitant under the plan.

**Related Provisions**: 146(11) — Life insurance policies; 146(12) — Change in plan after registration; 214(3)(c) — Non-resident withholding tax.

**Regulations**: 214(2) (information return).

**Forms**: T3G: Certification of no tax liability by a group of RRSPs, RRIFs, or RESPs; T3IND: T3IND income tax return for RRSP, RRIF, or RESP.

**(10) Where acquisition of non-qualified investment by trust** — Where at any time in a taxation year a trust governed by a registered retirement savings plan

(a) acquires a non-qualified investment, or

(b) uses or permits to be used any property of the trust as security for a loan,

the fair market value of

(c) the non-qualified investment at the time it was acquired by the trust, or

(d) the property used as security at the time it commenced to be so used,

as the case may be, shall be included in computing the income for the year of the taxpayer who is the annuitant under the plan at that time.

**Related Provisions**: 146(6) — Disposition of non-qualified investment; 146(7) — Recovery of property used as security; 146(10.1) — Tax payable by trust; 146(11) — Life insurance policies; 207.1(1) — Tax payable by RRSP; 214(3)(c) — Non-resident withholding tax; 259(1) — Election for proportional holdings in trust property.

**Notes**: See Notes to 146(10.1).

146(10) can be used, together with 146(7), as a bizarre form of advance income averaging by pledging self-directed RRSP assets as security or acquiring a non-qualified investment. (A depositary RRSP cannot be pledged; see 146(2)(c.3)(ii), but see also Notes to 146(12).) This can bring income into a low-tax year and allow a deduction in a later high-tax year under 146(6) or (7), for a person who has funds in an RRSP and anticipates increases in income in future years. (See also Notes to 15(2) for another method.) The general anti-avoidance rule in s. 245 might apply to this scheme, however, and tax would be payable under 146(10.1) and 207.1(1) on non-qualified investments. See also *Foreman (Chambers)*, [1996] 1 C.T.C. 265 (FCTD), where a similar scheme that involved repaying the RRSP before year-end was found not to artificially reduce income.

**Regulations**: 214(2) (information return).

**Remission Orders**: *Lionaird Capital Corporation Notes Remission Order*, P.C. 1999-737 (tax under 146(10) waived because taxpayers thought they were qualified investments).

**Interpretation Bulletins**: IT-320R2: RRSP — qualified investments; IT-415R2: Deregistration of RRSPs.

**Forms**: T3G: Certification of no tax liability by a group of RRSPs, RRIFs, or RESPs; T3IND: T3IND income tax return for RRSP, RRIF, or RESP.

**(10.1) Where tax payable [income from non-qualified investment]** — Where in a taxation year a trust governed by a registered retirement savings plan holds a property that is a non-qualified investment,

(a) tax is payable under this Part by the trust on the amount that its taxable income for the year would be if it had no incomes or losses from sources other than non-qualified investments and no capital gains or losses other than from dispositions of non-qualified investments; and

(b) for the purposes of paragraph (a),

(i) "income" includes dividends described in section 83, and

(ii) paragraphs 38(a) and (b) shall be read without reference to the fractions set out in those paragraphs.

**Related Provisions**: 146(4) — Tax not otherwise payable by trust; 259(1) — Election for proportional holdings in trust property.

**Notes**: 146(10.1) imposes tax on the *income* from non-qualified investments. 207.1(1) imposes a penalty tax on the *holding* of the non-qualified investments. 146(10) taxes the beneficiary on the *acquisition* of the non-qualified investment, with an offsetting deduction under 146(6) when it is disposed of.

**Interpretation Bulletins**: IT-320R2: RRSPs — qualified investments.

**(11) Life insurance policies** — Subsections 198(6) and (8) are applicable, with such modifications as the circumstances require, to subsections (6), (9) and (10), except that in the application of subsection 198(8) to the latter subsections paragraph 198(8)(a) shall be read as follows:

(a) "the trust shall be deemed, for the purposes of subsection 146(6), to have disposed of each non-qualified investment that, by virtue of payments under the policy, it was deemed by subsection 146(10) to have acquired, and"

**Related Provisions**: 139.1(12) — Effect of conversion benefit on demutualization of insurance corporation; 146(1)"qualified investment"(c)–(c.2) — Annuity contracts as qualified investments; 146(11.1) — Subsec. (11) does not apply to contracts issued after 1997.

**Interpretation Bulletins**: IT-408R: Life insurance policies as investments of RRSPs and DPSPs.

**(11.1) Exception** — Subsection (11) does not apply to annuity contracts issued after 1997.

**Notes**: 146(11.1) added by 1995-97 technical bill, effective 1998. In place of 146(11), 146(1)"qualified investment"(c)–(c.2) expressly provide the types of annuity contracts which are qualified investments for trusteed RRSPs.

**(12) Change in plan after registration** — Where, on any day after a retirement savings plan has been accepted by the Minister for registration for the purposes of this Act, the plan is revised or amended or a new plan is substituted for it, and the plan as revised or amended or the new plan, as the case may be (in this subsection referred to as the "amended plan"), does not comply with the requirements of this section for its acceptance by the Minister for registration for the purposes of this Act, subject to subsection (13.1), the following rules apply:

(a) the amended plan shall be deemed, for the purposes of this Act, not to be a registered retirement savings plan; and

(b) the taxpayer who was the annuitant under the plan before it became an amended plan shall, in computing the taxpayer's income for the taxation year that includes that day, include as income received at that time an amount equal to the fair market value of all the property of the plan immediately before that time.

**Related Provisions**: 146(2) — Requirements for registration; 146(8.3) — Spousal RRSP payments; 146(8.7) — Where ss. (8.3) does not apply; 146(13) — Change in plan after registration; 147.3(13.1) — Withdrawal of excessive transfers to RRSPs and RRIFs; 146(13.2), (13.3) — Pre-1997 plan that does not mature by age 69 is deemed deregistered; 204.1 — Tax in respect of over-contribution to deferred income plans; 204.2(1.4) — Deemed receipt where RRSP or RRIF amended; 214(3)(c) — Non-resident withholding tax.

**Notes**: Where the prohibition against a depositary RRSP being pledged as security is violated, the RRSP is revocable, but the pledge is not void and the bank to which the RRSP is pledged can use it to set off a loan: *Re Whaling*, [1999] 4 C.T.C. 221 (Ont. CA). See also Notes to 146(2).

146(12) reworded and made subject to 146(13.1) by 1989 Budget, effective 1989.

**Regulations**: 214(3) (information return).

**Interpretation Bulletins**: IT-307R3: Spousal registered retirement savings plans; IT-415R2: Deregistration of RRSPs.

**Forms**: T3G: Certification of no tax liability by a group of RRSPs, RRIFs, or RESPs; T3IND: T3IND income tax return for RRSP, RRIF, or RESP; T4RSP Segment; T4RSP Summary: Return of RRSP income; T4RSP Supplementary: Statement of RRSP income; T2205: Calculation of amounts to be included in income out of spousal RRSP or RRIF; T4079: T4RSP and T4RIF guide.

**(13) Idem** — For the purposes of subsection (12), an arrangement under which a right or obligation under a retirement savings plan is released or extinguished either wholly or in part and either in exchange or substitution for any right or obligation, or otherwise (other than an arrangement the sole object and legal effect of which is to revise or amend the plan) or under which payment of any amount by way of loan or otherwise is made on the security of a right under a retirement savings plan, shall be deemed to be a new plan substituted for that retirement savings plan.

**Related Provisions**: 146(2), (3) — Acceptance of plan registration; 146(16) — Deduction on transfer of funds.

**Interpretation Bulletins**: IT-415R2: Deregistration of RRSPs.

**(13.1) RRSP advantages** — Where an issuer of a registered retirement savings plan or any person not dealing at arm's length with the issuer has extended an advantage to the annuitant of the plan (or to a person not dealing at arm's length with the annuitant) and that advantage would have been prohibited if the plan had met the requirement for registration contained in paragraph (2)(c.4),

(a) paragraphs (12)(a) and (b) do not apply by reason only of the extension of that advantage; and

(b) the issuer is liable to a penalty equal to the greater of $100 and the amount or value of that advantage.

**Related Provisions**: 18(1)(t) — Penalty is non-deductible; 146(2)(c.4) — Prohibition against extending advantage; 146(5)(a) — Amount of RRSP premiums deductible.

**Notes**: See Notes to 238(1).

146(13.1) amended by 1989 Budget, effective 1989.

**Interpretation Bulletins**: IT-415R2: Deregistration of RRSPs.

**Information Circulars**: 72-22R9: Registered retirement saving plans.

**(13.2) Maturity after age 69** — For the purpose of subsection (12), where a retirement savings plan accepted for registration before 1997 does not mature by the end of the particular year in which the annuitant under the plan attains 69 years of age,

(a) the plan is deemed to have been amended immediately after the particular year; and

(b) the plan as amended is deemed not to comply with the requirements of this section for its acceptance by the Minister for registration for the purposes of this Act.

**Related Provisions**: 146(12)(b) — Deregistration and income inclusion as a result of deemed amendments to plan; 146(13.3) — Notification required that plan will be deregistered; 147(10.6) — Parallel rules for DPSPs.

**Notes**: 146(13.2) added by 1996 Budget, effective 1997, but subject to the following grandfathering rules:

(a) it does not apply to an RSP whose annuitant turned 70 before 1997;

(b) in applying it to an RSP whose annuitant turned 69 in 1996, read "70 years" instead of "69 years";

(c) it does not apply to an RSP where an annuity contract was issued before March 6, 1996 under, pursuant to or as the plan to provide the retirement income under the plan and, under the terms and conditions of the contract as they read immediately before that day,

(i) the day on which annuity payments are to begin under the plan is fixed and determined and is after the year in which the annuitant turns

(A) 69, where the annuitant had not turned 69 before 1997, or

(B) 70, where the annuitant turned 69 in 1996, and

(ii) the amount and timing of each annuity payment are fixed and determined; and

(d) it does not apply to an RSP that is part of a life insurance policy that was issued before March 6, 1996 and that has a life insurance component that is not an RSP where, under the terms and conditions of the policy as they read immediately before that day,

(i) the amount of each premium, if any, subsequently payable in respect of the life insurance component of the policy, and a date by which each such premium is to be paid, are fixed and determined,

(ii) the amount payable under the policy because of the death of the annuitant (determined without reference to any amount payable as, on account of, in lieu of payment of or in satisfaction of, a policy dividend or related interest) is fixed and determined, and

(iii) insurance on the life of the annuitant is provided under the policy for a period of time after the year in which the annuitant turns

(A) 69, where the annuitant had not turned 69 before 1997, or

(B) 70, where the annuitant turned 69 in 1996.

Where, because of (d) above, 146(13.2) does not apply to an RSP that is part of a life insurance policy, any part of a premium paid under the policy after March 5, 1996 that was not fixed and determined under the terms and conditions of the policy as they read at the end of that day is deemed, for the purposes of 146(5), (5.1) and (8.2), not to have been paid under the policy.

Effectively, the grandfathering under (a) and (b) above means that anyone born in 1926, 1927 or 1928 (age 71, 70 or 69 by the end of 1997) had his/her RRSP terminate at the end of 1997, and had to convert it to a life annuity or a RRIF (see 146.3) to avoid full income inclusion under 146(12)(b) of the amount in the RRSP as of December 31, 1997.

**(13.3) Notice** — Where a retirement savings plan accepted for registration before 1997 does not prevent maturity after the particular year in which the annuitant under the plan attains 69 years of age, the issuer of the plan shall, before July of the particular year, notify the annuitant in writing that, pursuant to subsections (12) and (13.2), the plan will cease to be a registered retirement savings plan if it does not mature by the end of the particular year, except that no such notification is required where, before that month,

(a) the plan has matured; or

(b) arrangements have been made for the plan to mature, or for the property under the plan to be transferred or otherwise paid out of the plan, by the end of the particular year.

**Related Provisions**: 162(7) — Penalty for failure to comply.

**Notes**: 146(13.3) added by 1996 Budget, effective on the same basis as 146(13.2). See Notes to 146(13.2).

**(14) Premiums paid in taxation year** — Where any amount has been paid in a taxation year as a premium under a retirement savings plan that was, at the end of that taxation year, a registered retirement savings plan, the amount so paid shall be deemed, for the purposes of this Act, to have been paid in that year as a premium under a registered retirement savings plan.

**Related Provisions**: 146(1) — "Retirement savings plan".

**(15) Plan not registered at end of year entered into** — Notwithstanding anything in this section, where an amount is received in a taxation year as a benefit under a registered retirement savings plan that was not, at the end of the year in which the plan was entered into, a registered retirement savings plan, such part, if any, of the amount so received as may be prescribed shall be deemed, for the purposes of this Act, to have been received in the taxation year otherwise than as a benefit or other payment under a registered retirement savings plan.

**Regulations**: Part I.

**(16) Transfer of funds** — Notwithstanding any other provision in this section, a registered retirement savings plan may at any time be revised or amended to provide for the payment or transfer before the maturity of the plan, on behalf of the annuitant under the plan (in this subsection referred to as the "transferor"), of any property thereunder by the issuer thereof

(a) to a registered pension plan for the benefit of the transferor or to a registered retirement savings plan or registered retirement income fund under which the transferor is the annuitant, or

(b) to a registered retirement savings plan or registered retirement income fund under which the spouse or common-law partner or former spouse or common-law partner of the transferor is the annuitant, where the transferor and the transferor's spouse or common-law partner or former spouse or common-law partner are living separate and apart and the payment or transfer is made under a decree, order or judgment of a competent tribunal, or under a written separation agreement, relating to a division of property between the transferor and the transferor's spouse or common-law partner or former spouse or common-law partner in settlement of rights arising out of, or on the breakdown of, their marriage or common-law partnership,

and, where there has been such a payment or transfer of such property on behalf of the transferor before the maturity of the plan,

(c) the amount of the payment or transfer shall not, solely because of the payment or transfer, be included in computing the income of the transferor or the transferor's spouse or common-law partner or former spouse or common-law partner,

(d) no deduction may be made under subsection (5), (5.1) or (8.2) or section 8 or 60 in respect of the payment or transfer in computing the income of any taxpayer, and

(e) where the payment or transfer was made to a registered retirement savings plan, for the purposes of subsection (8.2), the amount of the payment or transfer shall be deemed not to be a premium paid to that plan by the taxpayer.

**Related Provisions**: 60(l) — Transfer of RRSP premium refunds; 146.3(14) — Transfer of RRIF on marriage breakdown; 160.2(1) — Joint and several liability in respect of amounts received out of or under RRSP; 204.2(1) — Excess amount for a year for RRSP; 204.2(2) — Where terminated plan deemed to continue to exist; 252(3) — Extended meaning of "spouse" and "former spouse".

**Notes**: 146(16)(b), (c) amended by 2000 same-sex partners bill to add reference to "common-law partner" and "common-law partnership", effective for the 2001 and later taxation years, or earlier by election (see Notes to 248(1)"common-law partner").

146(16)(b) amended by 1992 technical bill, effective 1993, due to the introduction of an extended definition of "marriage" in 252(4)(b), which applied from 1993 to 2000. Before 1993, in place of "in settlement of rights arising out of, or on the breakdown of, their marriage", read "in settlement of rights arising out of their marriage or other conjugal relationship, on or after the breakdown of the marriage or other relationship".

146(16) amended by 1992 technical bill, effective 1991, to clarify that, where a taxpayer has made overcontributions to a transferor RRSP, the taxpayer will not be prevented from withdrawing the overcontributions on a tax-free basis under 146(8.2) from another RRSP to which amounts have been transferred from the transferor RRSP under 146(16).

146(16) amended by 1990 pension bill, effective for revisions or amendments made to RRSPs after 1989. The amended version is also effective for a payment or transfer of property made after 1989 on behalf of the annuitant (in this paragraph referred to as the "transferor") under an RRSP, other than a payment or transfer pursuant to a revision or amendment made to the plan before 1990 where the payment or transfer is to an RRSP or an RRIF under which the transferor's spouse or former spouse (within the meaning then assigned by 146(1.1) and 252(3)) is the annuitant.

**Regulations**: 214(5), (6) (information return).

**Remission Orders**: *Certain Taxpayers Remission Order, 1999-2*, 1999-1855, s. 2 (remission to Quebec judges for excess contributions in 1989-90 transferred under 146(16)).

**Interpretation Bulletins**: IT-307R3: Spousal registered retirement savings plans; IT-415R2: Deregistration of RRSPs; IT-528: Transfers of funds between registered plans.

**Information Circulars**: 72-22R9: Registered retirement savings plans; 74-1R5: Form T2037, Notice of purchase of annuity with "plan" funds; 79-8R3: Forms to use to directly transfer funds to or between plans, or to purchase an annuity.

**Advance Tax Rulings**: ATR-31: Funding of divorce settlement amount from DPSP.

**Registered Plans Division Newsletters**: 91-4R (Registration rules for money purchase provisions).

**Forms**: T2033: Direct transfer under para. 146(16)(a) or 146.3(2)(e); T2220: Transfer between retirement savings plans or retirement income funds on marriage breakdown.

**(17)–(19) [Repealed under former Act]**

**Notes**: 146(17) repealed by 1991 pension bill, effective for premiums paid after 1990. It applied where a payment was made under the pre-1991 version of 146(2)(c.1). 146(18) and (19), repealed in 1986, provided rules that no longer apply.

**(20) Credited or added amount deemed not received** — Where

(a) an amount is credited or added to a deposit with a depositary referred to in subparagraph (b)(iii) of the definition "retirement savings plan" in subsection (1) as interest or income in respect of the deposit,

(b) the deposit is a registered retirement savings plan at the time the amount is credited or added to the deposit, and

(c) during the calendar year in which the amount is credited or added or during the preceding calendar year, the annuitant under the plan was alive,

the amount shall be deemed not to be received by the annuitant or any other person solely because of the crediting or adding.

**Related Provisions**: 81(1)(r) — No income inclusion where amount credited or added to foreign retirement arrangement; 146(8) — Tax on withdrawals from plan.

**Notes**: 146(20) amended by 1993 technical bill, effective for deaths in 1993 or later. For deaths from 1981 through 1992, read:

> (20) **Where amount credited or added deemed not received** — Where an amount is credited or added to a deposit with a depositary referred to in subparagraph (b)(iii) of the definition "retirement savings plan" in subsection (1) as interest or income in respect of the deposit, and where
>
> > (a) the deposit is a registered retirement savings plan at the time the amount is credited or added to the deposit, and
> >
> > (b) the annuitant under the plan is alive during the year in which the amount is credited or added,
>
> the amount shall be deemed not to be received by the annuitant by reason only of the crediting or adding.

**Interpretation Bulletins**: IT-415R2: Deregistration of RRSPs.

**Information Circulars**: 72-22R9: Registered retirement savings plans.

**(21) Prescribed provincial pension plans** — Where

(a) an amount (other than an amount that is part of a series of periodic payments) is transferred directly from an individual's account under a provincial pension plan prescribed for the purpose of paragraph 60(v)

> (i) to a registered retirement savings plan or registered retirement income fund under which the individual, or a spouse or common-law partner or former spouse or common-law partner of the individual, is the annuitant,
>
> (ii) to acquire from a licensed annuities provider an annuity that would be described in subparagraph 60(l)(ii) if the individual, or a spouse or common-law partner or former spouse or common-law partner of the individual, were the taxpayer referred to in that subparagraph and if that subparagraph were read without reference to clause 60(l)(ii)(B), or
>
> (iii) to an account under the plan of a spouse or common-law partner or former spouse or common-law partner of the individual, and

(b) if the transfer is in respect of a spouse or common-law partner or former spouse or common-law partner of the individual,

> (i) the individual and the spouse or common-law partner or former spouse or common-law partner are living separate and apart and the transfer is made under a decree, order or judgment of a competent tribunal, or under a written separation agreement, relating to a division of property in settlement of rights arising out of, or on the breakdown of, their marriage or common-law partnership, or
>
> (ii) the amount is transferred as a consequence of the individual's death,

the following rules apply:

(c) the amount shall not, solely because of the transfer, be included because of subparagraph 56(1)(a)(i) in computing the income of a taxpayer, and

(d) no deduction may be made under any provision of this Act in respect of the transfer in computing the income of a taxpayer.

**Related Provisions**: 56(1)(d.2) — Income inclusion; 70(3.1) — Rights or things; 146.3(2)(f)(vii) — Conditions for RRIF — transfer of funds under 146(21); 148(1)(e) — Amounts included in computing policyholder's income; 204.2(1.2)I(a)(iii) — Transfer under 146(21) excluded from cumulative excess RRSP amount; 212(1)(h)(iii.1)(A), 212(1)(h)(iv.1) — Transfers under 146(21) excluded from withholding tax on pension benefits.

**Notes**: 146(21) allows transfer of a lump sum from the Saskatchewan Pension Plan to an RRSP or RRIF.

146(21) amended by 2000 same-sex partners bill to add reference to "common-law partner" and "common-law partnership", effective for the 2001 and later taxation years, or earlier by election (see Notes to 248(1)"common-law partner").

146(21) amended by 1998 Budget, effective for transfers made after 1994. For earlier transfers, read:

> (21) Where an amount (other than an amount that is part of a series of periodic payments) is transferred on behalf of a particular individual directly from a provincial pension plan prescribed for the purpose of paragraph 60(v)
>
> > (a) to a registered retirement savings plan or a registered retirement income fund under which the particular individual is the annuitant,
> >
> > (b) to a registered retirement savings plan or registered retirement income fund under which the spouse or former spouse of the particular individual is the annuitant, where the particular individual and the spouse or former spouse are living separate and apart and the transfer is made under a decree, order or judgment of a competent tribunal, or under a written separation agreement, relating to a division of property between the particular individual and the spouse or former spouse in settlement of rights arising out of, or on the breakdown of, their marriage,
> >
> > (c) to acquire, from a person licensed or otherwise authorized under the laws of Canada or a province to carry on in Canada an annuities business, an annuity that would be described in subparagraph 60(l)(ii) if the particular individual were the taxpayer referred to therein and if that subparagraph were read without reference to clause (B) thereof, or
> >
> > (d) to acquire, from a person licensed or otherwise authorized under the laws of Canada or a province to carry on in Canada an annuities business, an annuity that would be described in subparagraph 60(l)(ii) if the particular individual's spouse or former spouse were the taxpayer referred to therein and if that subparagraph were read without reference to clause (B) thereof, where the particular individual and the spouse or former spouse are living separate and apart and the transfer is made under a decree, order or judgment of a competent tribunal, or under a written separation agreement, relating to a division of property between the individual and the spouse or former spouse in settlement of rights arising out of, or on the breakdown of, their marriage,

except where the amount arose as a consequence of the death of an individual (other than the particular individual or a spouse or former spouse of the particular individual),

(e) the amount shall not, solely because of that transfer, be included because of subparagraph 56(1)(a)(i) in computing the income of a taxpayer, and

(f) no deduction may be made under any provision of this Act in respect of the transfer in computing the income of a taxpayer.

146(21) added by 1993 technical bill, effective for transfers occurring after 1991. However:

(a) if the taxpayer elected for 60(1)(v)(B.2) to apply to the 1992 taxation year (see Notes to 60(l)), 146(21) does not apply to transfers made on behalf of the taxpayer in 1992; and

(b) with respect to transfers made in 1992, read "spouse" in 146(21) as having the meaning assigned by 146(1.1) as it applied for 1992, and read "marriage" in 146(21)(b) and (d) as "marriage or other conjugal relationship". (For 1993–2000, these terms were defined in 252(4) to include certain common-law relationships.)

**Regulations**: 7800(1) (prescribed provincial pension plan is the Saskatchewan Pension Plan).

**Interpretation Bulletins**: IT-528: Transfers of funds between registered plans.

### (22) Deemed payment of RRSP premiums and provincial pension plan contributions [extension of contribution deadline] — If the Minister so directs,

(a) except for the purposes of subparagraphs (5)(a)(iv.1) and (5.1)(a)(iv), an amount paid by an individual in a taxation year (other than an amount paid in the first 60 days of the year) as a contribution to an account under a prescribed provincial pension plan or as a premium is deemed to have been paid at the beginning of the year and not at the time it was actually paid;

(b) all or part of the amount may be designated in writing by the individual for the purpose of paragraph 60(j), (j.1) or (l) or subsection 146.01(3) or 146.02(3); and

(c) the designation is deemed to have been made in the individual's return of income for the preceding taxation year or in a prescribed form filed with that return, as the case may be.

**Notes**: 146(22) added by 1998 Budget, effective for amounts paid after 1997. It allows the CCRA to treat RRSP contributions made after March 1 as made on January 1, and thus deductible for the previous year. It was introduced to implement the RRSP contribution deadline extension announced by Revenue Canada on February 5 and 16, 1998 for taxpayers affected by the January 1998 ice storm.

The extension is implemented in the legislation as a general authorization, in 146(22) (and 127.4(5.1) for LSVCCs), allowing the CCRA to direct that a late contribution was made at the beginning of the year — and thus within the first 60 days, qualifying it for a deduction for the previous year.

This provision was also used as the authority for the extension of the 1998 contribution deadline to April 30, 1999 for individuals with a 1998 pension adjustment reversal (see Dept. of Finance news release, Oct. 2, 1998)).

**Definitions [s. 146]**: "amount" — 248(1); "annuitant" — 146(1); "annuity" — 248(1); "arm's length" — 251(1); "assessment" — 248(1); "benefit" — 146(1); "business" — 248(1); "calendar year" — Interpretation Act 37(1)(a); "Canada" — 255; "carrying on business" — 253; "child" — 252(1); "common-law partner", "common-law partnership" — 248(1); "consequence of the death", "consequence of the annuitant's death", "consequence of the individual's death" — 248(8); "corporation" — 248(1), Interpretation Act 35(1); "credit union" — 137(6), 248(1); "death benefit" — 248(1); "deferred profit sharing plan" — 147(1), 248(1); "depositary" — 146(1)"retirement savings plan"(b)(iii); "designated withdrawal" — 146.01(1); "earned income" — 146(1); "employer", "employment" — 248(1); "estate" — 104(1), 248(1); "farm loss" — 111(8), 248(1); "farming" — 248(1); "former spouse" — 252(3); "individual" — 248(1); "interest in a family farm partnership" — 70(10); "issuer" — 146(1); "legal representative" — 248(1); "licensed annuities provider" — 147(1), 248(1); "life insurance policy" — 138(12), 248(1); "listed" — 87(10); "listed personal property" — 54, 248(1); "maturity" — 146(1); "Minister" — 248(1); "money purchase limit" — 147.1(1), 248(1); "net past service pension adjustment", "non-qualified investment" — 146(1); "office" — 248(1); "PSPA withdrawals" — Reg. 8307(5); "parent" — 252(2); "past service pension adjustment" — 248(1), Reg. 8303; "pension adjustment" — 248(1), Reg. 8301(1); "person" — 248(1); "premium" — 146(1); "prescribed" — 248(1); "prescribed stock exchange in Canada" — Reg. 3200; "prescribed withdrawal" — Reg. 8306(6); "property" — 248(1); "province" — Interpretation Act 35(1); "qualified investment" — 146(1); "RRSP deduction limit", "RRSP dollar limit" — 146(1), 248(1); "received" — 146(20); "refund of premiums" — 146(1); "registered pension plan" — 248(1); "registered retirement income fund" — 146.3(1), 248(1); "registered retirement savings plan" — 146(1), 248(1); "regulation" — 248(1); "resident" — 250; "retirement income" — 146(1); "retirement savings plan" — 146(1), 248(1); "retiring allowance", "salary or wages", "separation agreement", "share" — 248(1); "spousal plan" — 146(1); "spouse" — 252(3); "superannuation or pension benefit" — 248(1); "tax-paid amount" — 146(1); "tax payable" — 248(2); "taxable capital gain" — 38, 248(1); "taxable income" — 2(2), 248(1); "taxation year" — 249; "taxpayer" — 248(1); "testamentary trust" — 108(1), 248(1); "total pension adjustment reversal" — 248(1); "trust" — 104(1), 248(1), (3); "unused RRSP deduction room" — 146(1), 248(1); "writing" — Interpretation Act 35(1).

## Home Buyers' Plan

### 146.01 (1) Definitions — In this section,

**"annuitant"** has the meaning assigned by subsection 146(1);

**"benefit"** has the meaning assigned by subsection 146(1);

**"completion date"**, in respect of an amount received by an individual, is

(a) where the amount was received before March 2, 1993, October 1, 1993,

(b) where the amount was received after March 1, 1993 and before March 2, 1994, October 1, 1994, and

(c) in any other case, October 1 of the calendar year following the calendar year in which the amount was received;

**Notes**: The completion date is generally the date by which a qualifying home must be acquired in order for an RRSP withdrawal to be an eligible amount under the Home Buyers' Plan. See 146.01(1)"eligible amount"(c).

Definition added by 1992 Economic Statement, retroactive to 1992 (see Notes at end of 146.01). Para. (b) amended (formerly read "in any other case, October 1, 1994") and para. (c) added by 1994 Budget, effective 1994.

**"designated withdrawal"** of an individual is an amount received by the individual, as a benefit out of or under a registered retirement savings plan, pursuant to the individual's written request in the prescribed form referred to in paragraph (a) of the definition "eligible amount" (as that definition read in its application to amounts received before 1999), paragraph (a) of the definition "regular eligible amount" or paragraph (a) of the definition "supplemental eligible amount";

**Notes**: Definition added by 1998 Budget, effective 1999.

**"eligible amount"** of an individual is a regular eligible amount or supplemental eligible amount of the individual;

**Related Provisions**: 146(5)(a)(iv.1), 146(5.1)(a)(iv) — Amount withdrawn within 90 days under Home Buyers' Plan ineligible for RRSP contribution; 146.01(2) — Interpretation; 146.01(3), (4) — Repayment of eligible amounts to RRSP.

**Notes**: The CCRA considers that the amount paid out to the individual is whatever is left over after costs incurred by the RRSP in cashing in its investments (such as mutual fund redemption fees): VIEWS doc 2000-0018235.

Definition amended by 1998 Budget, effective for amounts received after 1998. Before the amendment, read:

"eligible amount" in respect of an individual means an amount received at a particular time by the individual as a benefit out of or under a registered retirement savings plan where

(a) the amount is received after February 25, 1992 pursuant to the written request of the individual in prescribed form in which the individual sets out the location of a qualifying home that the individual has begun, or intends not later than one year after its acquisition by the individual to begin, using as a principal place of residence,

(b) the individual is resident in Canada at the particular time and entered into an agreement in writing before the particular time for the acquisition of the qualifying home or with respect to its construction,

(c) the individual acquires the qualifying home (or replacement property for the qualifying home) after February 25, 1992 and before the completion date in respect of the amount,

(d) neither the individual nor the individual's spouse acquired the qualifying home more than 30 days before the particular time,

(d.1) if the particular time is after March 1, 1994,

(i) the individual did not have an owner-occupied home in the period that began at the beginning of the fourth preceding calendar year that ended before the particular time and ended on the 31st day before the particular time, and

(ii) the individual's spouse did not have an owner-occupied home in the period referred to in subparagraph (i)

(A) that is inhabited by the individual during the spouse's marriage to the individual, or

(B) that is a share of the capital stock of a cooperative housing corporation that relates to a housing unit that is inhabited by the individual during the spouse's marriage to the individual,

(e) unless the individual acquired the qualifying home before the particular time, the individual is resident in Canada throughout the period beginning immediately after the particular time and ending at the earliest of any time at which the individual acquired the qualifying home or any replacement property for the qualifying home,

(f) the total of the amount and all eligible amounts received by the individual at or before the particular time does not exceed $20,000,

(g) if the particular time is after March 1, 1993 and before March 2, 1994, neither the individual, nor another individual who was, at any time after February 25, 1992 and before the particular time, a spouse of the individual, received an eligible amount before March 2, 1993,

(h) if the particular time is after March 1, 1994 and before 1995, the individual did not receive an eligible amount before March 2, 1994, and

(i) if the particular time is after 1994, the individual did not receive an eligible amount before the calendar year that includes the particular time;

Para. (a) amended to delete the words "and before March 2, 1994" (after "after February 25, 1992"); by 1994 Budget, effective 1994.

Paras. (d.1), (h) and (i) added by 1994 Budget, effective 1994.

Para. (g) amended by 1994 Budget, retroactive to 1992 (see Notes at end of 146.01).

Definition "eligible amount" amended by 1992 Economic Statement, retroactive to 1992, to change "1993" to "1994" in para. (a); to change "before October 1, 1993" to "before the completion date in respect of the amount" in para. (c); and to add para. (g). For initial enactment of the definition and explanation of the HBP, see Notes at end of 146.01.

**Forms**: T1036: Home buyers' plan — request to withdraw funds from an RRSP; RC4135: Home Buyers' Plan [guide].

**"excluded premium"** in respect of an individual means a premium under a registered retirement savings plan where the premium

(a) was designated by the individual for the purposes of paragraph 60(j), (j.1), (j.2) or (l),

(b) was an amount transferred directly from a registered retirement savings plan, registered pension plan, registered retirement income fund, deferred profit sharing plan or a provincial pension plan prescribed for the purpose of paragraph 60(v),

(c) was deductible under subsection 146(6.1) in computing the individual's income for any taxation year, or

(d) was deducted in computing the individual's income for the 1991 taxation year;

**Notes**: Para. (b) of "excluded premium" amended by 1993 technical bill, effective for 1992 and later taxation years, to add reference to a provincial pension plan prescribed for purposes of 60(v) (i.e., the Saskatchewan Pension Plan). See also Notes at end of 146.01.

**"excluded withdrawal"** of an individual means

(a) an eligible amount received by the individual,

(b) a particular amount (other than an eligible amount) received while the individual was resident in Canada and in a calendar year if

(i) the particular amount would be an eligible amount of the individual if the definition "regular eligible amount" were read without reference to paragraphs (c) and (g) of that definition and the definition "supplemental eligible amount" were read without reference to paragraphs (d) and (f) of that definition,

(ii) a payment (other than an excluded premium) equal to the particular amount is made by the individual under a retirement saving plan that is, at the end of the taxation year of the payment, a registered retirement savings plan under which the individual is the annuitant,

(iii) the payment is made before the particular time that is

(A) if the individual was not resident in Canada at the time the individual filed a return of income for the taxation year in which the particular amount was received, the earlier of

(I) the end of the following calendar year, and

(II) the time at which the individual filed the return,

(B) where clause (A) does not apply and the particular amount would, but for subclause (2)(c)(ii)(A)(II), be an eligible amount, the end of the second following calendar year, and

(C) in any other case, the end of the following calendar year, and

(iv) either

(A) if the particular time is before 2000, the payment is made, as a repayment of the particular amount, to the issuer of the registered retirement savings plan from which the particular amount was received, no other payment is made as a repayment of the particular amount and that issuer is notified of the payment in prescribed form submitted to the issuer at the time the payment is made, or

(B) the payment is made after 1999 and before the particular time and the payment (and no other payment) is designated under this clause as a repayment of the particular amount in prescribed form filed with the Minister on or before the particular time (or before such later time as is acceptable to the Minister), or

(c) an amount (other than an eligible amount) that is received in a calendar year before 1999 and that would be an eligible amount of the individual if the definition "eligible amount", as it applied to amounts received before 1999, were read without reference to paragraphs (c) and (e) of that definition, where the individual

(i) died before the end of the following calendar year, and

(ii) was resident in Canada throughout the period that began immediately after the amount was received and ended at the time of the death;

**Related Provisions**: 146(1)"premium" — Definition excludes repayment described in para. (b); 146(8) — Home Buyers' Plan withdrawal not to be included in income; 146.01(2)(c) — Special rules.

**Notes**: Definition amended by 1998 Budget, this version effective for amounts received after 1998. For amounts received in 1997 and 1998, read para. (b) opening words and (b)(i) as:

(b) a particular amount (other than an eligible amount), received in a calendar year, that would be an eligible amount of the individual if

(i) the definition "eligible amount" were read without reference to paras. (c) and (e) of that definition.

For amounts received from 1992 to 1996, read:

"excluded withdrawal" in respect of an individual means

(a) an eligible amount received by the individual, or

(b) an amount (other than an eligible amount) that would, if the definition "eligible amount" were read without reference to paragraphs (c) and (e) thereof, be an eligible amount received by the individual out of or under a registered retirement savings plan in respect of which a person is the issuer, where either

(i) the individual

(A) died before the end of the calendar year that includes the completion date in respect of the amount, and

(B) was resident in Canada throughout the period beginning immediately after the amount was received and ending at the time of the death, or

(ii) the amount is repaid before the end of the calendar year described in clause (i)(A) to a registered retirement savings plan in respect of which the person is the issuer (or, where the individual was not resident in Canada at the time the individual filed a return of income under this Part for the taxation year in which the amount was received by the individual, before the earlier of the end of the calendar year described in clause (i)(A) and the time at which the individual filed that return) and the issuer is notified of the repayment in prescribed form submitted to the issuer at the time the repayment is made,

except that where an amount would, but for subclause 146.01 (2)(c)(ii)(A)(II), be an eligible amount, subparagraph (b)(ii) applies in respect of the amount as if the first reference therein to "described in clause (i)(A)" were read as "following the calendar year described in clause (i)(A)";

Para. (b) and closing words of "excluded withdrawal" amended by 1992 Economic Statement, retroactive to 1992. (For initial enactment of the definition, see Notes at end of 146.01.)

**Regulations**: 104(3) — No tax withheld at source on excluded withdrawal.

**Forms**: T1037: Designating your RRSP contributions as your 1995 repayment under the Home buyers' plan.

**"HBP balance"** of an individual at any time means the amount, if any, by which the total of all eligible amounts received by the individual at or before that time exceeds the total of

(a) all amounts designated under subsection (3) by the individual for taxation years that ended before that time, and

(b) all amounts each of which is included under subsection (4) or (5) in computing the individual's income for a taxation year that ended before that time;

**Related Provisions**: 150(1.1)(b)(iv) — Individual with HBP balance must file tax return.

**Notes**: Definition added by 1998 Budget, effective 1999.

**"issuer"** has the meaning assigned by subsection 146(1);

**"participation period"** of an individual means each period

(a) that begins at the beginning of a calendar year in which the individual receives an eligible amount, and

(b) that ends immediately before the beginning of the first subsequent calendar year at the beginning of which the individual's HBP balance is nil;

**Notes**: Definition added by 1998 Budget, effective 1999.

**"premium"** has the meaning assigned by subsection 146(1);

**"qualifying home"** means

(a) a housing unit located in Canada, or

(b) a share of the capital stock of a cooperative housing corporation, the holder of which is entitled to possession of a housing unit located in Canada,

except that, where the context so requires, a reference to a qualifying home that is a share described in paragraph (b) means the housing unit to which the share described in that paragraph relates;

**"quarter"** means any of the following periods in a calendar year:

(a) the period beginning on January 1 and ending on March 31,

(b) the period beginning on April 1 and ending on June 30,

(c) the period beginning on July 1 and ending on September 30, and

(d) the period beginning on October 1 and ending on December 31;

**"regular eligible amount"** of an individual means an amount received at a particular time by the individual as a benefit out of or under a registered retirement savings plan if

(a) the amount is received pursuant to the individual's written request in a prescribed form in which the individual sets out the location of a qualifying home that the individual has begun, or intends not later than one year after its acquisition by the individual to begin, using as a principal place of residence,

(b) the individual entered into an agreement in writing before the particular time for the acquisition of it or with respect to its construction,

(c) the individual

(i) acquires the qualifying home (or a replacement property for the qualifying home) before the completion date in respect of the amount, or

(ii) dies before the end of the calendar year that includes the completion date in respect of the amount,

(d) neither the individual nor the individual's spouse or common-law partner acquired the qualifying home more than 30 days before the particular time,

(e) the individual did not have an owner-occupied home in the period

(i) that began at the beginning of the fourth preceding calendar year that ended before the particular time, and

(ii) that ended on the 31st day before the particular time,

(f) the individual's spouse or common-law partner did not, in the period referred to in paragraph (e), have an owner-occupied home

(i) that was inhabited by the individual during the spouse's or common-law partner's marriage or common-law partnership to the individual, or

(ii) that was a share of the capital stock of a cooperative housing corporation that relates to a housing unit inhabited by the individual during the spouse's or common-law partner's marriage or common-law partnership to the individual,

(g) the individual

(i) acquired the qualifying home before the particular time and is resident in Canada at the particular time, or

(ii) is resident in Canada throughout the period that begins at the particular time and ends at the earlier of the time of the individual's death and the earliest time at which the individual acquires the qualifying home or a replacement property for it,

(h) the total of the amount and all other eligible amounts received by the individual in the calendar year that includes the particular time does not exceed $20,000, and

(i) the individual's HBP balance at the beginning of the calendar year that includes the particular time is nil;

**Notes**: 146.01(1)"regular eligible amount"(d), (f) amended by 2000 same-sex partners bill to add reference to "common-law partner" and "common-law partnership", effective for the 2001 and later taxation years, or earlier by election (see Notes to 248(1)"common-law partner").

Definition added by 1998 Budget, effective for amounts received after 1998. (For 1992-98, see "eligible amount".)

1352

**"replacement property"** for a particular qualifying home in respect of an individual, or of a specified disabled person in respect of the individual, means another qualifying home that

(a) the individual or the specified disabled person agrees to acquire, or begins the construction of, at a particular time that is after the latest time that the individual made a request described in the definition "designated withdrawal" in respect of the particular qualifying home,

(b) at the particular time, the individual intends to be used by the individual or the specified disabled person as a principal place of residence not later than one year after its acquisition, and

(c) none of the individual, the individual's spouse or common-law partner, the specified disabled person or that person's spouse or common-law partner had acquired before the particular time;

**Notes**: 146.01(1)"replacement property"(c) amended by 2000 same-sex partners bill to add reference to "common-law partner", effective for the 2001 and later taxation years, or earlier by election (see Notes to 248(1)"common-law partner").

Definition amended by 1998 Budget, effective 1999. For 1992–98, read:

> "replacement property" for a particular qualifying home in respect of an individual means another qualifying home where
> 
> (a) the individual
> 
> (i) agreed to acquire, or
> 
> (ii) began the construction of
> 
> the other qualifying home at a particular time that is after the latest time that the individual requested a withdrawal in respect of the particular qualifying home under paragraph (a) of the definition "eligible amount",
> 
> (b) the individual intended, at the particular time, that the other qualifying home be used by the individual as a principal place of residence not later than one year after its acquisition, and
> 
> (c) neither the individual nor the individual's spouse had acquired the other qualifying home before the particular time.

**"specified disabled person"**, in respect of an individual at any time, means a person who

(a) is the individual or is related at that time to the individual, and

(b) would be entitled to a deduction under subsection 118.3(1) in computing tax payable under this Part for the person's taxation year that includes that time if that subsection were read without reference to paragraph (c) of that subsection;

**Related Provisions**: 146.01(1)"supplemental eligible amount" — Withdrawal to acquire accessible home for specified disabled person.

**Notes**: Definition added by 1998 Budget, effective 1999.

**"spouse"** — [Repealed]

**Notes**: Definition of "spouse" added by 1992 technical bill for 1992 only (for 1993–2000 the extension of the term "spouse" to include a common-law spouse applied for all purposes under 252(4)). For 1992, it applied the meaning under 146(1.1).

**"supplemental eligible amount"** of an individual means an amount received at a particular time by the individual as a benefit out of or under a registered retirement savings plan if

(a) the amount is received pursuant to the individual's written request in a prescribed form identifying a specified disabled person in respect of the individual and setting out the location of a qualifying home

(i) that has begun to be used by that person as a principal place of residence, or

(ii) that the individual intends to be used by that person as a principal place of residence not later than one year after its first acquisition after the particular time,

(b) the purpose of receiving the amount is to enable the specified disabled person to live

(i) in a dwelling that is more accessible by that person or in which that person is more mobile or functional, or

(ii) in an environment better suited to the personal needs and care of that person,

(c) the individual or the specified disabled person entered into an agreement in writing before the particular time for the acquisition of the qualifying home or with respect to its construction,

(d) either

(i) the individual or the specified disabled person acquires the qualifying home (or a replacement property for it) after 1998 and before the completion date in respect of the amount, or

(ii) the individual dies before the end of the calendar year that includes the completion date in respect of the amount,

(e) none of the individual, the spouse or common-law partner of the individual, the specified disabled person or the spouse or common-law partner of that person acquired the qualifying home more than 30 days before the particular time,

(f) either

(i) the individual or the specified disabled person acquired the qualifying home before the particular time and the individual is resident in Canada at the particular time, or

(ii) the individual is resident in Canada throughout the period that begins at the particular time and ends at the earlier of the time of the individual's death and the earliest time at which

(A) the individual acquires the qualifying home or a replacement property for it, or

(B) the specified disabled person acquires the qualifying home or a replacement property for it,

(g) the total of the amount and all other eligible amounts received by the individual in the calendar year that includes the particular time does not exceed $20,000, and

(h) the individual's HBP balance at the beginning of the calendar year that includes the particular time is nil.

**Related Provisions**: 118.2(2)(l.2), (l.21) — Medical expense credit for disability-related renovations and construction costs.

**Notes**: 146.01(1)"supplemental eligible amount"(e) amended by 2000 same-sex partners bill to add reference to "common-law partner", effective for the 2001 and later taxation years, or earlier by election (see Notes to 248(1)"common-law partner").

Definition added by 1998 Budget, effective for amounts received after 1998. It allows greater access to the Home Buyers' Plan for persons with disabilities.

**(2) Special rules** — For the purposes of this section,

(a) an individual shall be considered to have acquired a qualifying home if the individual acquired it jointly with one or more other persons;

(a.1) an individual shall be considered to have an owner-occupied home at any time where, at that time, the individual owns, whether jointly with another person or otherwise, a housing unit or a share of the capital stock of a cooperative housing corporation and

(i) the housing unit is inhabited by the individual as the individual's principal place of residence at that time, or

(ii) the share was acquired for the purpose of acquiring a right to possess a housing unit owned by the corporation and that unit is inhabited by the individual as the individual's principal place of residence at that time;

(b) where an individual agrees to acquire a condominium unit, the individual shall be deemed to have acquired it on the day the individual is entitled to immediate vacant possession of it;

(c) except for the purposes of subparagraph (g)(ii) of the definition "regular eligible amount" and subparagraph (f)(ii) of the definition "supplemental eligible amount", an individual or a specified disabled person in respect of the individual is deemed to have acquired, before the completion date in respect of a designated withdrawal received by the individual, the qualifying home in respect of which the designated withdrawal was received if

(i) neither the qualifying home nor a replacement property for it was acquired by the individual or the specified disabled person before that completion date, and

(ii) either

(A) the individual or the specified disabled person

(I) is obliged under the terms of a written agreement in effect on that completion date to acquire the qualifying home (or a replacement property for it) on or after that date, and

(II) acquires the qualifying home or a replacement property for it before the day that is one year after that completion date, or

(B) the individual or the specified disabled person made payments, the total of which equalled or exceeded the total of all designated withdrawals that were received by the individual in respect of the qualifying home,

(I) to persons with whom the individual was dealing at arm's length,

(II) in respect of the construction of the qualifying home or a replacement property for it, and

(III) in the period that begins at the time the individual first received a designated withdrawal in respect of the qualifying home and that ends before that completion date; and

(d) an amount received by an individual in a particular calendar year is deemed to have been received by the individual at the end of the preceding calendar year and not at any other time if

(i) the amount is received in January of the particular year (or at such later time as is acceptable to the Minister),

(ii) the amount would not be an eligible amount if this section were read without reference to this paragraph, and

(iii) the amount would be an eligible amount if the definition "regular eligible amount" in subsection (1) were read without reference to paragraph (i) of that definition and the definition "supplemental eligible amount" were read without reference to paragraph (h) of that definition.

**Related Provisions**: 146(5)(a)(iv.1), 146(5.1)(a)(iv) — Amount withdrawn within 90 days under Home Buyers' Plan ineligible for RRSP contribution.

**Notes**: 146.01(2)(a.1) added by 1994 Budget, effective 1994. 146.01(2)(d)(ii) and (iii) and 146.01(2)(e) amended by 1994 Budget, retroactive to 1992. 146.01(2)(f) added by 1994 Budget, effective 1995.

146.01(2)(c)–(f) replaced with (c)–(d) by 1998 Budget, effective for amounts received after 1998. Before the amendment, read:

(c) where

(i) neither a qualifying home in respect of which an individual withdrew an amount described in paragraph (a) of the definition "eligible amount" in subsection 146.01 (1) nor a replacement property for the qualifying home has been acquired by the individual before the completion date in respect of the amount, and

(ii) either

(A) the individual

(I) is obliged under the terms of a written agreement in effect on that completion date to acquire the qualifying home (or a replacement property for the qualifying home) on or after that date,

(II) acquires the qualifying home or a replacement property for the qualifying home before the day that is one year after that completion date, and

(III) is resident in Canada throughout the period beginning on that completion date and ending on the earlier of October 1 in the first calendar year beginning after that date and the earliest of any day on which the individual acquires the qualifying home or a replacement property for the qualifying home, or

(B) the individual made payments

(I) to persons with whom the individual was dealing at arm's length,

(II) in respect of the construction of the qualifying home or a replacement property for the qualifying home, and

(III) in the period beginning at the time the individual first withdrew an amount described in paragraph (a) of that definition in respect of the qualifying home and ending before that completion date,

and the total of all payments so made was not less than the total of all amounts described in that paragraph in respect of the qualifying home that were withdrawn by the individual,

except for the purpose of this paragraph, the individual shall be deemed to have acquired the qualifying home before that completion date;

(d) where

(i) an individual or a spouse of the individual receives an eligible amount before March 2, 1993,

(ii) at a particular time after March 1, 1993 and before April 1993 (or at such later time in 1993 as is acceptable to the Minister), the individual receives another amount that would, if the definition "eligible amount" in subsection 146.01 (1) were read without reference to paragraph (g) thereof, be an eligible amount, and

(iii) the request described in paragraph (a) of the definition "eligible amount" in subsection 146.01 (1) pursuant to which the other amount was received was made before March 2, 1993 or at such later time as is acceptable to the Minister,

except for the purposes of paragraphs (a) to (f) of the definition "eligible amount" in subsection 146.01 (1) and the purposes of this paragraph, the other amount shall be deemed to have been received by the individual on March 1, 1993 and not at the particular time and any premium paid by the individual or the individual's spouse after March 1, 1993 and before the particular time under a registered retirement savings plan shall be deemed to have been paid on March 1, 1993;

(e) where

(i) at a particular time after March 1, 1994 and before April 1994 (or at such later time in 1994 as is acceptable to the Minister), an individual receives an amount that would, if paragraph (g) of the definition "eligible amount" in subsection 146.01 (1) were read without reference to the words "and before March 2, 1994" and that definition were read without reference to paragraphs (d.1) and (h) thereof, be an eligible amount,

(ii) the request described in paragraph (a) of the definition "eligible amount" in subsection 146.01 (1) pursuant to which the amount was received was made before March 2, 1994 or, where the individual received an eligible amount before March 2, 1994, at such later time as is acceptable to the Minister, and

(iii) the individual does not elect by notifying the Minister in writing before the end of 1995 that this paragraph not apply

except for the purposes of this paragraph and paragraphs (a) to (f) of the definition "eligible amount" in subsection 146.01 (1), that amount shall be deemed to have been received by the individual on March 1, 1994 and not at the particular time and any premium paid under a registered retirement savings plan by the individual or the individual's spouse after March 1, 1994 and before the particular time shall be deemed to have been paid on March 1, 1994; and

(f) where

(i) an individual receives an eligible amount in a particular calendar year,

(ii) at a particular time in January of the following calendar year (or at such later time in that following year as is acceptable to the Minister), an individual receives another amount that would, if the definition "eligible amount" in subsection 146.01 (1) were read without reference to paragraph 146.01(2)(f) (i) thereof, be an eligible amount, and

(iii) the request described in paragraph (a) of the definition "eligible amount" in subsection 146.01 (1) pursuant to which the other amount was received was made before the end of the particular calendar year

except for the purposes of this paragraph and paragraphs (a) to (h) of the definition "eligible amount" in subsection 146.01 (1), the other amount shall be deemed to have been received by the individual at the end of the particular calendar year and not at the particular time.

146.01(2)(c) amended to change references to October 1, 1993 to the "completion date", and 146.01(2)(d) and (e) added, by 1992 Economic Statement, retroactive to 1992. (For initial enactment, see Notes at end of 146.01.)

**Forms**: RC4135: Home Buyers' Plan [guide].

**(3) Repayment of eligible amount** — An individual may designate a single amount for a taxation year in a prescribed form filed with the individual's return of income for the year if the amount does not exceed the lesser of

(a) the total of all amounts (other than excluded premiums, repayments to which paragraph (b) of the definition "excluded withdrawal" in subsection (1) applies and amounts paid by the individual in the first 60 days of the year that can reasonably be considered to have been deducted in computing the individual's income, or designated under this subsection, for the preceding taxation year) paid by the individual in the year or within 60 days after the end of the year under a retirement savings plan that is at the end of the year or the following taxation year a registered retirement savings plan under which the individual is the annuitant, and

(b) the amount, if any, by which

(i) the total of all eligible amounts received by the individual before the end of the year

exceeds the total of

(ii) all amounts designated by the individual under this subsection for preceding taxation years, and

(iii) all amounts each of which is an amount included in computing the income of the individual under subsection (4) or (5) for a preceding taxation year.

**Related Provisions**: 146.02(1)"excluded premium"(a) — Amount claimed under Home Buyers' Plan ineligible for LLP.

**Notes**: See also Notes at end of 146.01.

Opening words of 146.01(3) amended by 1998 Budget, effective for 1999 and later taxation years. For earlier years, read:

(3) An individual may designate a single amount for a taxation year in prescribed form filed with the individual's return of income required to be filed for the year or, if a return of income for the year is not required to be filed, filed with the Minister on or before the individual's filing-due date for the year, where the amount does not exceed the lesser of

146.01(3)(a) amended by 1998 Budget to add "repayments to which paragraph (b) of the definition "excluded withdrawal" in subsection (1) applies", effective for 1996 and later taxation years.

146.01(3) amended by 1995 Budget, effective 1995. The minor change to the opening words results from the filing deadline for individuals carrying on business (and their spouses) having been extended from April 30 to June 15 (see 150(1)(d)). This change incorporates and supersedes amendments made by 1994 Budget, also effective 1995. For 1992 to 1994, read:

(3) An amount (other than an excluded premium) paid by an individual at a particular time in a taxation year under a retirement savings plan that was at the end of the year a registered retirement savings plan under which the individual is the annuitant may be designated by the individual under this subsection (in prescribed form submitted to the issuer of the plan at the time of the payment or at such later time as is acceptable to the Minister) to the extent that the amount so paid does not exceed the amount, if any, by which

(a) the total of all eligible amounts received by the individual before the particular time

exceeds the total of

(b) all amounts designated under this subsection in respect of amounts paid before the particular time to registered retirement savings plans under which the individual is the annuitant, and

(c) all amounts each of which is an amount included in computing the income of the individual under subsection (4) or (5) for a taxation year ending before the particular time.

**Forms**: T1 General Sched. 7: RRSP contributions, transfers and designations of repayments under the home buyers' plan; T1037: Designating your RRSP contributions as your 1995 repayment under the Home buyers' plan; RC4135: Home Buyers' Plan [guide].

**(4) Portion of eligible amount not repaid** — There shall be included in computing an individual's income for a particular taxation year included in a particular participation period of the individual the amount determined by the formula

$$\frac{(A - B - C)}{(15 - D)} - E$$

where

A is

(a) where

(i) the individual died or ceased to be resident in Canada in the particular year, or

(ii) the completion date in respect of an eligible amount received by the individual was in the particular year

nil, and

(b) in any other case, the total of all eligible amounts received by the individual in preceding taxation years included in the particular period,

B is

(a) nil, if the completion date in respect of an eligible amount received by the individual was in the preceding taxation year, and

(b) in any other case, the total of all amounts each of which is designated under subsection (3) by the individual for a preceding taxation year included in the particular period;

C is the total of all amounts each of which is included under this subsection or subsection (5) in computing the individual's income for a preceding taxation year included in the particular period;

D is the lesser of 14 and the number of taxation years of the individual ending in the period beginning

(a) where the completion date in respect of an eligible amount received by the individual was before 1995, January 1, 1995, and

(b) in any other case, January 1 of the first calendar year beginning after the completion date in respect of an eligible amount received by the individual

and ending at the beginning of the particular year, and

E is

(a) if the completion date in respect of an eligible amount received by the individual was in the preceding taxation year, the total of all amounts each of which is designated under subsection (3) by the individual for the particular year or any preceding taxation year included in the particular period, and

(b) in any other case, the amount designated under subsection (3) by the individual for the particular year.

**Related Provisions**: 257 — Formula cannot calculate to less than zero.

**Notes**: Opening words of 146.01(4) amended by 1998 Budget to change "ending after 1994" to "included in a particular participation period of the individual", effective for 1999 and later taxation years.

146.01(4)A(b) amended by 1998 Budget to add "included in the particular period", effective for 1999 and later taxation years.

146.01(4)B amended by 1998 Budget, effective for 1999 and later taxation years. For 1992-98, read:

B is

(a) where the particular year is the 1995 taxation year, nil, and

(b) in any other case, the total of all amounts designated by the individual under subsection 146.01 (3) for preceding taxation years;

146.01(4)C amended by 1998 Budget to add "included in the particular period", effective for 1999 and later taxation years.

146.01(4)E(a) and (c) replaced with (a)–(b) by 1998 Budget, effective for 1999 and later taxation years. For 1994-98, read:

E is

(a) where the particular year is the 1995 taxation year, the total of all amounts each of which is an amount designated under subsection 146.01 (3) by the individual for the particular year or a preceding taxation year,

(b) where the particular year begins after 1995 and the completion date in respect of an eligible amount received by the individual was in the preceding taxation year, the total of all amounts each of which is designated under subsection 146.01 (3) by the individual for the particular year or a preceding taxation year, and

(c) in any other case, the total of all amounts designated under subsection (3) by the individual for the particular year.

146.01(4)A(a)(ii) added by 1994 Budget, effective 1994.

146.01(4)D, E amended by 1994 Budget, effective 1994. For 1992 and 1993, read:

D is the lesser of 14 and the number of taxation years of the individual ending in the period beginning on January 1, 1995 and ending at the beginning of the particular year; and

E is

(a) where the particular year is the 1995 taxation year, the total of all amounts each of which is an amount designated by the individual under subsection (3) for the particular year or any of the 3 preceding taxation years, and

(b) in any other case, the total of all amounts designated under subsection (3) by the individual for the particular year.

146.01(4) amended to change "1994" to "1995", "1993" to "1994", and "either of the 2 preceding years" to "any of the 3 preceding years", by 1992 Economic Statement, retroactive to 1992. (For initial enactment, see Notes at end of 146.01.)

**Forms**: RC4135: Home Buyers' Plan [guide].

**(5) Where individual becomes a non-resident** — Where at any time in a taxation year an individual ceases to be resident in Canada, there shall be included in computing the income of the individual for the period in the year during which the individual was resident in Canada the amount, if any, by which

(a) the total of all amounts each of which is an eligible amount received by the individual in the year or a preceding taxation year

exceeds the total of

(b) all amounts designated under subsection (3) by the individual in respect of amounts paid not later than 60 days after that time and before the individual files a return of income for the year, and

(c) all amounts included under subsection (4) or this subsection in computing the individual's income for preceding taxation years.

**Related Provisions**: 56(1)(h.1) — Home buyers' plan — income inclusion.

**Notes**: 146.01(5)(b) amended by 1994 Budget, effective 1995. For 1992-94, read:

(b) all amounts designated by the individual under subsection (3) that are paid not later than 90 days after that time and before the individual files a return of income under this Part for the year, and

146.01(5)(c) amended to add "or this subsection" by 1998 Budget, effective for 1999 and later taxation years.

**(6) Death of individual** — If an individual dies at any time in a taxation year, there shall be included in computing the individual's income for the year the amount, if any, by which

(a) the individual's HBP balance immediately before that time

exceeds

(b) the amount designated under subsection (3) by the individual for the year.

**Related Provisions**: 56(1)(h.1) — Home buyers' plan — income inclusion; 146.01(7) — Optional transfer of repayment obligation to spouse.

**Notes**: 146.01(6) amended by 1998 Budget, this version effective for 2000 and later years. For 1997-99, read:

(6) Where individual dies — Where an individual dies at any time in a taxation year, there shall be included in computing the income of the individual for the year the amount, if any, by which

(a) the total of all excluded withdrawals in respect of the individual received before that time (other than excluded withdrawals in respect of the individual that were repaid as described in the definition "excluded withdrawal" in subsection (1)).

exceeds the total of

(b) all amounts designated by the individual under subsection (3) that were paid before that time, and

(c) all amounts each of which is an amount included under subsection (4) or (5) in computing the income of the individual for a preceding taxation year.

For 1992-96, read "subpara. (b)(ii) of the definition" in place of "the definition".

**(7) Exception** — If a spouse or common-law partner of an individual was resident in Canada immediately before the individual's death at a particular time in a taxation year and the spouse or common-law partner and the individual's legal representatives jointly so elect in writing in the individual's return of income for the year,

(a) subsection (6) does not apply to the individual;

(b) the spouse or common-law partner is deemed to have received a particular eligible amount at the particular time equal to the amount that, but for this subsection, would be determined under subsection (6) in respect of the individual;

(c) for the purposes of subsection (4) and paragraph (d), the completion date in respect of the particular amount is deemed to be

(i) if the spouse or common-law partner received an eligible amount before the death (other than an eligible amount received in a participation period of the spouse or common-law partner that ended before the beginning of the year), the completion date in respect of that amount, and

(ii) in any other case, the completion date in respect of the last eligible amount received by the individual; and

(d) for the purpose of subsection (4), the completion date in respect of each eligible amount received by the spouse or common-law partner, after the death and before the end of the spouse or common-law partner's participation period that includes the time of the death, is deemed to be the completion date in respect of the particular amount.

**Related Provisions**: 220(3.2), Reg. 600(b) — Late filing of election or revocation.

**Notes**: 146.01(7) amended by 2000 same-sex partners bill to add reference to "common-law partner", effective for the 2001 and later taxation years, or earlier by election (see Notes to 248(1)"common-law partner").

146.01(7) amended by 1998 Budget, this version effective for deaths after 1999. For deaths in 1999, read 146.01(7)(c)(ii) as:

(ii) in any other case,

(A) the completion date in respect of an eligible amount, if any, received by the individual in a participation period of the individual that includes the time of the death, or

(B) if clause (A) does not apply, October 1, 2000; and

For deaths before 1999, read:

(7) Where subsec. (6) does not apply — Where

(a) an individual's spouse was resident in Canada immediately before the death of the individual in a taxation year,

(b) the spouse and the individual's legal representatives jointly so elect in writing in the individual's return of income under this Part for the year, and

(c) either

(i) the spouse or the individual did not receive any eligible amount before the death, or

(ii) the spouse and the individual both received eligible amounts before the death and all the completion dates in respect of those amounts were the same or occurred before 1995,

the following rules apply:

(d) subsection 146.01 (6) does not apply to the individual;

(e) the spouse shall be deemed to have received an eligible amount at the time of the death equal to the amount that would, but for this subsection, be determined under subsection 146.01 (6) in respect of the individual;

(f) for the purpose only of determining whether an amount received after the death is an eligible amount in respect of the spouse, the spouse shall be deemed to have received all eligible amounts in respect of the individual at the times that those amounts were received by the individual; and

(g) the completion date in respect of the eligible amount deemed by paragraph 146.01(7) (e) to have been received by the spouse shall be deemed to be

(i) where the spouse received an eligible amount before the death, the completion date in respect of that amount,

(ii) where subparagraph 146.01(7)(g) (i) does not apply and the individual received an eligible amount before the death, the completion date in respect of that amount, and

(iii) in any other case, October 1 of the year.

146.01(7) amended by 1994 Budget, effective 1994. For 1992 and 1993, read:

(7) **Idem** — Where an individual's spouse was resident in Canada immediately before the death of the individual in a taxation year and the spouse and the individual's legal representative jointly so elect in writing in the individual's return of income under this Part for the year,

(a) subsection (6) does not apply in respect of the individual; and

(b) except for the purposes of subsections (9) and (10), the spouse shall be deemed to have received an eligible amount at the time of the individual's death equal to the amount that would, but for this subsection, be determined under subsection (6) in respect of the individual.

146.01(7)(b) amended to add reference to 146.01(10) by 1992 Economic Statement, retroactive to 1992. (For initial enactment, see Notes at end of 146.01.)

**(8) Filing of prescribed form** — A prescribed form referred to in this section that is submitted to an issuer shall be filed with the Minister by the issuer not later than 15 days after the quarter in which it was submitted to the issuer.

**Forms**: T1 Sched. 7: RRSP unused contributions, transfers, and HBP or LLP activities; T1036: Home buyers' plan — request to withdraw funds from an RRSP; T1037: Designating your RRSP contributions as your 1995 repayment under the Home buyers' plan; T1048: Home buyers' plan — 1993 income inclusion for certain RRSP contributions.

**(9)–(13) [Repealed]**

**Notes**: 146.01(9)–(13) repealed by 1994 Budget, effective 1994. They provided income inclusions for 1992 and 1993 where recent RRSP contributions were withdrawn under the HBP. The rules in 146(5)(a)(iv.1) and 146(5.1)(a)(iv) now prevent certain RRSP contributions from being deducted, if those contributions are withdrawn under the Home Buyers' Plan within 90 days of being contributed.

**Notes [s. 146.01]**: 146.01 provides the Home Buyers' Plan, which (simplified) allows up to $20,000 per person to be withdrawn from RRSPs for purchasing or building a qualifying home, provided the person and spouse have not owned a home within the past 5 years. See 146.01(1)"eligible amount" and 146(8). No withholding applies to the withdrawal: see Reg. 104(3). The amount withdrawn should be repaid to the RRSP over a 15-year period beginning the year after the withdrawal. To the extent the repayments are not made, the amounts will be included in income under 146.01(4).

For investment in the home mortgage by the RRSP as an alternative to the Home Buyers' Plan, see Reg. 4900(1)(j).

146.01 added by 1992 Budget/technical bill, effective for 1992 and later taxation years.

**Definitions [s. 146.01]**: "amount" — 248(1); "annuitant" — 146(1), 146.01(1); "arm's length" — 251(1); "benefit" — 146(1),

146.01(1); "calendar year" — *Interpretation Act* 37(1)(a); "Canada" — 255; "common-law partner", "common-law partnership" — 248(1); "completion date" — 146.01(1); "corporation" — 248(1), *Interpretation Act* 35(1); "deferred profit sharing plan" — 147(1), 248(1); "designated withdrawal" — 146.01(1); "eligible amount", "excluded premium", "excluded withdrawal" — 146.01(1); "filing-due date" — 150(1), 248(1); "HBP balance" — 146.01(1); "have an owner-occupied home" — 146.01(2)(a.1); "individual" — 248(1); "issuer" — 146(1), 146.01(1); "legal representative", "Minister" — 248(1); "net premium balance" — 146.01(11), (12); "owner-occupied home" — 146.01(2)(a.1); "participation period" — 146.01(1); "person" — 248(1); "premium" — 146(1), 146.01(1); "prescribed", "property" — 248(1); "qualifying home", "quarter" — 146.01(1); "registered pension plan" — 248(1); "registered retirement income fund" — 146.3(1), 248(1); "registered retirement savings plan" — 146(1), 248(1); "regular eligible amount" — 146.01(1); "related" — 251(2)–(6); "resident", "resident in Canada" — 250; "retirement savings plan" — 146(1), 248(1); "share" — 248(1); "specified disabled person" — 146.01(1); "spouse" — 252(3); "supplemental eligible amount" — 146.01(1); "taxation year" — 128(2)(d), 249; "writing" — *Interpretation Act* 35(1); "written" — *Interpretation Act* 35(1)"writing".

## Lifelong Learning Plan

**146.02 (1) Definitions** — The definitions in this subsection apply in this section.

**"annuitant"** has the meaning assigned by subsection 146(1).

**Notes:** See Notes at end of 146.02.

**"benefit"** has the meaning assigned by subsection 146(1).

**"eligible amount"** of an individual means a particular amount received at a particular time in a calendar year by the individual as a benefit out of or under a registered retirement savings plan if

(a) the particular amount is received after 1998 pursuant to the individual's written request in a prescribed form;

(b) in respect of the particular amount, the individual designates in the form a person (in this definition referred to as the "designated person") who is the individual or the individual's spouse or common-law partner;

(c) the total of the particular amount and all other eligible amounts received by the individual at or before the particular time and in the year does not exceed $10,000;

(d) the total of the particular amount and all other eligible amounts received by the individual at or before the particular time (other than amounts received in participation periods of the individual that ended before the year) does not exceed $20,000;

(e) the individual did not receive an eligible amount at or before the particular time in respect of which someone other than the designated person was designated (other than an amount received in a participation period of the individual that ended before the year);

(f) the designated person

(i) is enrolled at the particular time as a full-time student in a qualifying educational program, or

(ii) has received written notification before the particular time that the designated person is absolutely or contingently entitled to enrol before March of the following year as a full-time student in a qualifying educational program;

(g) the individual is resident in Canada throughout the period that begins at the particular time and ends immediately before the earlier of

(i) the beginning of the following year, and

(ii) the time of the individual's death;

(h) except where the individual dies after the particular time and before April of the following year, the designated person is enrolled as a full-time student in a qualifying educational program after the particular time and before March of the following year and

(i) the designated person completes the program before April of the following year,

(ii) the designated person does not withdraw from the program before April of the following year, or

(iii) less than 75% of the tuition paid, after the beginning of the year and before April of the following year, in respect of the designated person and the program is refundable; and

(i) if an eligible amount was received by the individual before the year, the particular time is neither

(i) in the individual's repayment period for the individual's participation period that includes the particular time, nor

(ii) after January (or a later month where the Minister so permits) of the fifth calendar year of that participation period.

**Related Provisions:** 146(5)(a)(iv.1), 146(5.1)(a)(iv) — Amount withdrawn within 90 days under LLP ineligible for RRSP contribution; 146.01(2) — Interpretation; 146.02(3), (4) — Repayment of eligible amounts to RRSP.

**Notes:** The CCRA considers that the amount paid out to the individual for purposes of the LLP is whatever is left over after costs incurred by the RRSP in cashing in its investments (such as mutual fund redemption fees): VIEWS doc 2000-0018235.

146.02(1)"eligible amount"(b) amended by 2000 same-sex partners bill to add reference to "common-law partner", effective for the 2001 and later taxation years, or earlier by election (see Notes to 248(1)"common-law partner").

**Forms:** RC96: LLP — request to withdraw funds from an RRSP; RC4112: Lifelong learning plan [guide].

**"excluded premium"** of an individual means a premium that

(a) was designated by the individual for the purpose of paragraph 60(j), (j.1) or (l) or subsection 146.01(3);

(b) was a repayment to which paragraph (b) of the definition "excluded withdrawal" in subsection 146.01(1) applies;

(c) was an amount transferred directly from a registered retirement savings plan, registered pension plan, registered retirement income fund, deferred profit sharing plan or a provincial pension plan prescribed for the purpose of paragraph 60(v); or

(d) was deductible under subsection 146(6.1) in computing the individual's income for any taxation year.

"**excluded withdrawal**" of an individual means

(a) an eligible amount received by the individual; or

(b) a particular amount (other than an eligible amount) received while the individual was resident in Canada and in a calendar year if

(i) the particular amount would be an eligible amount of the individual if the definition "eligible amount" were read without reference to paragraphs (g) and (h) of that definition,

(ii) a payment (other than an excluded premium) equal to the particular amount is paid by the individual under a retirement savings plan that is, at the end of the taxation year of payment, a registered retirement savings plan under which the individual is the annuitant,

(iii) the payment is made before the particular time that is,

(A) if the individual was not resident in Canada at the time the individual filed a return of income for the taxation year in which the particular amount was received, the earlier of

(I) the end of the following calendar year, and

(II) the time at which the individual filed the return, and

(B) in any other case, the end of the following calendar year, and

(iv) the payment (and no other payment) is designated under this subparagraph as a repayment of the particular amount in prescribed form filed with the Minister on or before the particular time (or before such later time as is acceptable to the Minister).

**Related Provisions:** 146(1)"premium" — Definition excludes repayment described in para. (b); 146(8) — LLP withdrawal not to be included in income.

"**full-time student**" in a taxation year includes an individual to whom subsection 118.6(3) applies for the purpose of computing tax payable under this Part for the year or the following taxation year.

"**LLP balance**" of an individual at any time means the amount, if any, by which the total of all eligible amounts received by the individual at or before that time exceeds the total of

(a) all amounts designated under subsection (3) by the individual for taxation years that ended before that time, and

(b) all amounts each of which is included under subsection (4) or (5) in computing the individual's income for a taxation year that ended before that time.

**Related Provisions:** 150(1.1)(b)(iv) — Individual with LLP balance must file tax return.

"**participation period**" of an individual means each period

(a) that begins at the beginning of a calendar year

(i) in which the individual receives an eligible amount, and

(ii) at the beginning of which the individual's LLP balance is nil; and

(b) that ends immediately before the beginning of the first subsequent calendar year at the beginning of which the individual's LLP balance is nil.

"**premium**" has the meaning assigned by subsection 146(1).

"**qualifying educational program**" means a qualifying educational program (as defined in subsection 118.6(1)) at a designated educational institution (as defined in subsection 118.6(1)), except that the definition "qualifying educational program" in subsection 118.6(1) shall be read

(a) without reference to paragraphs (a) and (b) of that definition; and

(b) as if the expression "3 consecutive weeks" were "3 consecutive months".

"**repayment period**" of an individual for a participation period of the individual in respect of a person designated under paragraph (b) of the definition "eligible amount" means the period, if any, within the participation period

(a) that begins

(i) at the beginning of the third calendar year within the participation period, if the person would not be entitled to claim an amount under subsection 118.6(2) in respect of at least three months in each of the second and third calendar years within the participation period, if that subsection were read without reference to paragraph (b) of the description of B in that subsection,

(ii) at the beginning of the fourth calendar year within the participation period, if subparagraph (i) does not apply and the person would not be entitled to claim an amount under subsection 118.6(2) in respect of at least three months in each of the third and fourth calendar years within the participation period, if that subsection were read without reference to paragraph (b) of the description of B in that subsection,

(iii) at the beginning of the fifth calendar year within the participation period, if subparagraphs (i) and (ii) do not apply and the person would not be entitled to claim an amount under subsection 118.6(2) in respect of at least three months in each of the fourth and fifth calendar years within that period, if that subsection were read without reference to paragraph (b) of the description of B in that subsection, and

(iv) in any other case, at the beginning of the sixth calendar year within the participation period; and

(b) that ends at the end of the participation period.

**Notes**: See Notes at end of 146.02.

**Forms**: RC96: LLP — request to withdraw funds from an RRSP; RC4112: Lifelong learning plan [guide].

**(2) Rule of application** — For the purpose of the definition "eligible amount" in subsection (1), a particular person is deemed to be the only person in respect of whom a particular amount was designated under paragraph (b) of that definition if

(a) an individual received the particular amount;

(b) the individual files a prescribed form with the Minister in which the particular person is specified in connection with the receipt of the particular amount;

(c) the particular amount would be an eligible amount of the individual if

(i) that definition were read without reference to paragraphs (b) and (e) of that definition, and

(ii) each reference in the portion of that definition after paragraph (d) to "designated person" were read as "individual" or "individual's spouse or common-law partner"; and

(d) the Minister so permits.

**Related Provisions**: 146(5)(a)(iv.1), 146(5.1)(a)(iv) — Amount withdrawn within 90 days under LLP ineligible for RRSP contribution.

**Notes**: 146.02(2)(c)(ii) amended by 2000 same-sex partners bill to add reference to "common-law partner", effective for the 2001 and later taxation years, or earlier by election (see Notes to 248(1)"common-law partner").

See also Notes at end of 146.02.

**Forms**: RC96: LLP — request to withdraw funds from an RRSP.

**(3) Repayment of eligible amount** — An individual may designate a single amount for a taxation year in prescribed form filed with the individual's return of income for the year if the amount does not exceed the lesser of

(a) the total of all amounts (other than excluded premiums, repayments to which paragraph (b) of the definition "excluded withdrawal" in subsection (1) applies and amounts paid by the individual in the first 60 days of the year that can reasonably be considered to have been deducted in computing the individual's income, or designated under this subsection, for the preceding taxation year) paid by the individual in the year or within 60 days after the end of the year under a retirement savings plan that is at the end of the year or the following taxation year a registered retirement savings plan under which the individual is the annuitant, and

(b) the individual's LLP balance at the end of the year.

**Notes**: See Notes at end of 146.02.

**Forms**: RC96: LLP — request to withdraw funds from an RRSP.

**(4) If portion of eligible amount not repaid** — There shall be included in computing an individual's income for a particular taxation year that begins after 2000 the amount determined by the formula

$$[(A - B - C)/(10 - D)] - E$$

where

A is

(a) nil, if

(i) the individual died or ceased to be resident in Canada in the particular year, or

(ii) the beginning of the particular year is not included in a repayment period of the individual, and

(b) in any other case, the total of all eligible amounts received by the individual in preceding taxation years (other than taxation years in participation periods of the individual that ended before the particular year);

B is

(a) nil, if the particular year is the first taxation year in a repayment period of the individual, and

(b) in any other case, the total of all amounts designated under subsection (3) by the individual for preceding taxation years (other than taxation years in participation periods of the individual that ended before the particular year);

C is the total of all amounts each of which is included under this subsection or subsection (5) in computing the individual's income for a preceding taxation year (other than a taxation year included in a participation period of the individual that ended before the particular year);

D is the lesser of nine and the number of taxation years of the individual that end in the period that

(a) begins at the beginning of the individual's last repayment period that began at or before the beginning of the particular year, and

(b) ends at the beginning of the particular year; and

E is

(a) if the particular year is the first taxation year within a repayment period of the individual, the total of the amount designated under subsection (3) by the individual for the particular year and all amounts so designated for preceding taxation years (other than taxation years in participation periods of the individual that ended before the particular year), and

(b) in any other case, the amount designated under subsection (3) by the individual for the particular year.

**Related Provisions**: 56(1)(h.1) — Inclusion in income; 257 — Formula cannot calculate to less than zero.

**Notes**: See Notes at end of 146.02.

**Forms**: RC4112: Lifelong learning plan [guide].

**(5) Ceasing residence in Canada** — If at any time in a taxation year an individual ceases to be resident in Canada, there shall be included in computing the individual's income for the period in the year during which the individual was resident in Canada the amount, if any, by which

(a) the total of all amounts each of which is an eligible amount received by the individual in the year or a preceding taxation year

exceeds the total of

(b) all amounts designated under subsection (3) by the individual in respect of amounts paid not later than 60 days after that time and before the individual files a return of income for the year, and

(c) all amounts included under subsection (4) or this subsection in computing the individual's income for preceding taxation years.

**Related Provisions**: 56(1)(h.2) — LLP — income inclusion; 128.1(4) — Ceasing residence in Canada.

**Notes**: See Notes at end of 146.02.

**(6) Death of individual** — If an individual dies at any time in a taxation year, there shall be included in computing the individual's income for the year the amount, if any, by which

(a) the individual's LLP balance immediately before that time

exceeds

(b) the amount designated under subsection (3) by the individual for the year.

**Related Provisions**: 56(1)(h.2) — LLP — income inclusion; 70(5) — Effect of death; 146.01(7) — Optional transfer of repayment obligation to spouse.

**Notes**: See Notes at end of 146.02.

**(7) Exception** — If a spouse or common-law partner of an individual was resident in Canada immediately before the individual's death at a particular time in a taxation year and the spouse or common-law partner and the individual's legal representatives jointly so elect in writing in the individual's return of income for the year,

(a) subsection (6) does not apply to the individual;

(b) the spouse or common-law partner is deemed to have received a particular eligible amount at the particular time equal to the amount that, but for this subsection, would be determined under subsection (6) in respect of the individual;

(c) subject to paragraph (d), for the purpose of applying this section after the particular time, the spouse or common-law partner is deemed to be the person designated under paragraph (b) of the definition "eligible amount" in subsection (1) in respect of the particular amount; and

(d) where the spouse or common-law partner received an eligible amount before the particular time in the spouse's or common-law partner's participation period that included the particular time and the particular individual designated under paragraph (b) of the definition "eligible amount" in subsection (1) in respect of that eligible amount was not the spouse or common-law partner, for the purpose of applying this section after the particular time the particular individual is deemed to be the person designated under that paragraph in respect of the particular amount.

**Related Provisions**: 220(3.2), Reg. 600(b) — Late filing of election or revocation.

**Notes [subsec. 146.02(7)]**: 146.02(7) amended by 2000 same-sex partners bill to add reference to "common-law partner", effective for the 2001 and later taxation years, or earlier by election (see Notes to 248(1)"common-law partner").

See also Notes at end of 146.02.

**Notes [s. 146.02]**: 146.02 added by 1998 Budget, effective 1999. The Lifelong Learning Plan (LLP) allows withdrawal of funds from an RRSP to fund education. As with the Home Buyers' Plan in 146.01, the amounts borrowed must be repaid over a period of time, failing which they are included into income under 146.02(4).

**Definitions [s. 146.02]**: "amount" — 248(1); "annuitant", "benefit" — 146(1), 146.01(1); "Canada" — 255, *Interpretation Act* 35(1); "common-law partner" — 248(1); "deferred profit sharing plan" — 147(1), 248(1); "eligible amount", "excluded premium", "excluded withdrawal", "full-time student" — 146.02(1); "individual", "legal representative", "Minister" — 248(1); "LLP balance" — 146.02(1); "month" — *Interpretation Act* 35(1); "participation period" — 146.02(1); "person" — 248(1); "premium" — 146(1), 146.02(1); "prescribed", "registered pension plan" — 248(1); "qualifying educational program" — 146.02(1); "registered retirement income fund" — 146.3(1), 248(1); "registered retirement savings plan" — 146(1), 248(1); "repayment period" — 146.02(1); "resident in Canada" — 250; "retirement savings plan" — 146(1), 248(1); "revocable" — 146.1(2.1); "taxation year" — 249; "written" — *Interpretation Act* 35(1)"writing".

**Forms**: RC96: LLP — request to withdraw funds from an RRSP; RC4112: Lifelong learning plan [guide].

# Registered Education Savings Plans

**146.1 (1) Definitions** — In this section,

**Related Provisions**: 204.9(1.1) — Application of subsec. 146.1(1).

Division G — Deferred & Special Income Arrangements    S. 146.1(1) pos

**Notes**: The opening words of 146.1(1) redrafted in R.S.C. 1985 (5th Supp.) consolidation, effective for taxation years ending after November 1991. The former version made reference to Part X.4. That rule is now in 204.9(1.1).

**"accumulated income payment"** under an education savings plan means any amount paid out of the plan, other than a payment described in any of paragraphs (a) and (c) to (e) of the definition "trust", to the extent that the amount so paid exceeds the fair market value of any consideration given to the plan for the payment of the amount;

**Related Provisions**: 146.1(2)(d.1) — Limitations on accumulated income payments; 146.1(7.1) — Accumulated income payments included in recipient's income; 153(1)(t) — Withholding of tax at source from payments; 204.94 — Tax on accumulated income payments not transferred to RRSP.

**Notes**: "Accumulated income payment" added by 1997 Budget, effective 1998. These payments are included in the recipient's income under 146.1(7.1) and are relevant for the special 20% tax in 204.94. The circumstances in which they can be made are limited by 146.1(2)(d.1).

Definition amended by 1998 Budget to change "(c), (d) and (e)" to "(c) to (e)" (i.e., effectively adding reference to (c.1)), effective 1998.

**Regulations**: 103(4), 103(6)(g), 103(8) (withholding at source); 200(2)(j) (information return).

**"beneficiary"**, in respect of an education savings plan, means a person, designated by a subscriber, to whom or on whose behalf an educational assistance payment under the plan is agreed to be paid if the person qualifies under the plan;

**Related Provisions**: 146.1(2)(j) — Restrictions on who can be beneficiaries.

**Notes**: 146.1(1)"beneficiary" was 146.1(1)(a) before consolidation in R.S.C. 1985 (5th Supp.), effective for taxation years ending after November 1991.

**"contribution"** into an education savings plan does not include an amount paid into the plan by the Minister of Human Resources Development under Part III.1 of the *Department of Human Resources Development Act*;

**Notes**: Definition added by 1998 Budget, effective 1998.

**"education savings plan"** means a contract made at any time between

    (a) either

        (i) one individual (other than a trust), or

        (ii) an individual (other than a trust) and the spouse or common-law partner of the individual, and

    (b) a person or organization (in this section referred to as a "promoter")

under which the promoter agrees to pay or to cause to be paid educational assistance payments to or for one or more beneficiaries;

---

**Proposed Amendment — RESPs as trusts**

**Department of Finance news release, July 20, 1999**: *Technical Change Announced for Registered Education Savings Plans*

Finance Minister Paul Martin today announced that he will propose changes to the *Income Tax Act* to accommodate a common industry practice concerning registered education savings plans (RESPs).

Under the current legislative framework, an RESP must be structured as a contractual arrangement. However, over the years many RESPs have been structured as trust arrangements.

The proposed changes will allow Canadian trust companies to issue RESPs structured as trust arrangements. This will accommodate a long-standing industry practice and recognize that a trust arrangement is an appropriate vehicle in which to allow Canadians to save for their children's education.

The Minister indicated that draft legislation to implement this proposal will be released at the earliest opportunity.

For further information: Dave Wurtele, Tax Legislation Division, (613) 992-4390; Jean-Michel Catta, Public Affairs and Operations Division, (613) 996-8080

---

**Notes**: 146.1(1)"education savings plan" amended by 2000 same-sex partners bill to add reference to "common-law partner", effective for the 2001 and later taxation years, or earlier by election (see Notes to 248(1)"common-law partner").

"Education savings plan" amended by 1997 Budget, effective for contracts made in 1998 or later. For contracts made from 1972-97, read:

> "education savings plan" means a contract entered into at any time between an individual (in this section referred to as a "subscriber") and a person or organization (in this section referred to as a "promoter") under which, in consideration of payment by the subscriber of any periodic or other amount as consideration under the contract, the promoter agrees to pay or to cause to be paid to or for a beneficiary educational assistance payments;

146.1(1)"education savings plan" was 146.1(1)(c) before consolidation in R.S.C. 1985 (5th Supp.), effective for taxation years ending after November 1991.

**"educational assistance payment"** means any amount, other than a refund of payments, paid out of an education savings plan to or for an individual to assist the individual to further the individual's education at a post-secondary school level;

**Related Provisions**: 146.1(2)(g), (g.1) — Limitations on educational assistance payments; 146.1(7) — Educational assistance payments included in income; 153(1)(t) — Withholding of tax at source from payments; 212(1)(r) — Tax on educational assistance payments.

**Notes**: "Educational assistance payment" amended by 1997 Budget, effective 1998. For 1972-97, read:

> "educational assistance payment" means any amount, other than a refund of payments, paid or payable under an education savings plan to or for a beneficiary to assist the beneficiary to further the beneficiary's education at the post-secondary school level;

146.1(1)"educational assistance payment" was 146.1(1)(b) before consolidation in R.S.C. 1985 (5th Supp.), effective for taxation years ending after November 1991.

**Regulations**: 200(2)(j) (information return).

**"post-secondary educational institution"** means

    (a) an educational institution in Canada that is described in paragraph (a) of the definition "designated educational institution" in subsection 118.6(1), or

(b) an educational institution outside Canada that is a university, college or other educational institution that provides courses at a post-secondary school level at which a beneficiary was enrolled in a course of not less than 13 consecutive weeks;

**Notes**: 146.1(1)"post-secondary education institution" (formerly para. 146.1(1)(c.1) before consolidation in R.S.C. 1985 (5th Supp.)) added to subsec. 146.1(1) by 1990 Budget, effective February 21, 1990.

**"pre-1972 income"** — [Repealed]

**Notes**: "Pre-1972 income" repealed by 1997 Budget, effective 1998, in conjunction with the repeal of 146.1(8)–(10). It read:

"pre-1972 income" means the total of all amounts each of which is the income (within the meaning of the *Income Tax Act*, chapter 148 of the Revised Statutes of Canada, 1952, as it read in its application to the particular taxation year) for a taxation year ending before 1972 of a trust governed by an education savings plan;

146.1(1)"pre-1972 income" was 146.1(1)(d) before consolidation in R.S.C. 1985 (5th Supp.), effective for taxation years ending after November 1991.

**"qualified investment"** for a trust governed by a registered education savings plan means

(a) an investment that would be described in any of paragraphs (a), (b), (d) and (f) to (h) of the definition "qualified investment" in section 204 if the reference in that definition to "a trust governed by a deferred profit sharing plan or revoked plan" were read as a reference to "a trust governed by a registered education savings plan",

(b) a bond, debenture, note or similar obligation of a corporation the shares of which are listed on a prescribed stock exchange in Canada,

(c) a contract for an annuity issued by a licensed annuities provider where

(i) the trust is the only person who, disregarding any subsequent transfer of the contract by the trust, is or may become entitled to any annuity payments under the contract, and

(ii) the holder of the contract has a right to surrender the contract at any time for an amount that would, if reasonable sales and administration charges were ignored, approximate the value of funds that could otherwise be applied to fund future periodic payments under the contract,

(d) an investment that was acquired by the trust before October 28, 1998, and

(e) a prescribed investment;

**Related Provisions**: 87(10) — New share issued on amalgamation of public corporation deemed listed on prescribed stock exchange; 132.2(1)(k) — Where share ceases to be qualified investment due to mutual fund reorganization; 146.1(2.1)(a) — Acquisition of non-qualified investment makes plan revocable; 207.1(3) — Tax payable by RESP on holding non-qualified investments.

**Notes**: Definition added by 1998 Budget, effective 1998.
**Regulations**: 3200 (prescribed stock exchange in Canada); 4900 (prescribed investment).

**"qualifying educational program"** has the meaning that would be assigned by the definition of that expression in subsection 118.6(1) if that definition were read without reference to paragraph (a);

**Notes**: Definition amended by 1996 Budget, effective for 1996 and later taxation years, to add the exclusion of para. (a) of the definition in 118.6(1). Thus, the condition that a student not receive certain benefits, allowances, grants or reimbursements does not apply. As a result, payments may be made out of a RESP to a student even where the student is in receipt of other benefits.

146.1(1)"qualifying educational program" (formerly 146.1(1)(d.1) before consolidation in R.S.C. 1985 (5th Supp.)) added by 1990 Budget, effective February 21, 1990.

**"RESP annual limit"** for a year means,

(a) for 1990 to 1995, $1,500,

(b) for 1996, $2,000, and

(c) for 1997 and subsequent years, $4,000;

**Related Provisions**: 146.1(2)(k) — Contributions not to exceed RESP annual limit; 204.9"excess amount"(a) — Penalty tax on exceeding RESP annual limit.

**Notes**: "RESP annual limit" added by 1997 Budget, effective 1990. It represents the maximum amount that can be contributed to a RESP in a year for a beneficiary (see 146.1(2)(k) and 204.91(2)"excess amount"(a)). Only $2,000 is needed to generate the maximum Canada Education Savings Grant each year; see Notes to 60(x).

**"refund of payments"** at any time under a particular registered education savings plan means

(a) a refund at that time of a contribution that had been made at a previous time, if the contribution was made

(i) otherwise than by way of a transfer from another registered education savings plan, and

(ii) into the particular plan by or on behalf of a subscriber under the particular plan, or

(b) a refund at that time of an amount that was paid at a previous time into the particular plan by way of a transfer from another registered education savings plan, where the amount would have been a refund of payments under the other plan if it had been paid at the previous time directly to a subscriber under the other plan;

**Notes**: "Refund of payments" amended by 1997 Budget, effective for 1997 and later taxation years. For 1972-96, read:

"refund of payments" means any amount (not in excess of the total of amounts paid by or on behalf of a subscriber under an education savings plan) paid or payable to the subscriber, the subscriber's heirs, executors or assigns as or on account of a refund of amounts paid to the plan by or on behalf of the subscriber under the plan;

146.1(1)"refund of payments" was 146.1(1)(e) before consolidation in R.S.C. 1985 (5th Supp.), effective for taxation years ending after November 1991.

**"registered education savings plan"** means

(a) an education savings plan registered for the purposes of this Act, or

(b) a registered education savings plan as it is amended from time to time

but, except for the purposes of subsections (7) and (7.1) and Part X.4, a plan ceases to be a registered education savings plan immediately after the day as of which its registration is revoked under subsection (13);

**Related Provisions**: 128.1(10)"excluded right or interest"(a)(iii) — No deemed disposition of RESP on emigration; 248(1)"disposition"(f)(vi) — Rollover from one trust to another; 248(1)"registered education savings plan" — Definition applies to entire Act.

**Notes**: "Registered education savings plan" amended by 1997 Budget, effective 1998. For 1972-97, read:

> "registered education savings plan" means an education savings plan accepted by the Minister for registration for the purposes of this Act as complying with the requirements of this section;

146.1(1)"registered education savings plan" was 146.1(1)(f) before consolidation in R.S.C. 1985 (5th Supp.), effective for taxation years ending after November 1991.

**Information Circulars**: 93-3: Registered education savings plans.

**"subscriber"** under an education savings plan at any time means

(a) each individual with whom the promoter of the plan entered into the plan,

(b) an individual who has before that time acquired a subscriber's rights under the plan pursuant to a decree, order or judgment of a competent tribunal, or under a written agreement, relating to a division of property between the individual and a subscriber under the plan in settlement of rights arising out of, or on the breakdown of, their marriage or common-law partnership, or

(c) after the death of a subscriber under the plan, any other person (including the estate of the subscriber) who makes contributions into the plan in respect of a beneficiary

but does not include an individual who, before that time, disposed of the individual's rights as a subscriber under the plan in the circumstances described in paragraph (b);

**Notes**: 146.1(1)"subscriber"(b) amended by 2000 same-sex partners bill to add reference to "common-law partnership", effective for the 2001 and later taxation years, or earlier by election (see Notes to 248(1)"common-law partner").

"Subscriber" added by 1997 Budget, effective for contracts made in 1998 or later.

**"tax-paid-income"** — [Repealed]

**Notes**: "Tax-paid income" repealed by 1997 Budget, effective 1998, in conjunction with the repeal of 146.1(8)–(10). It read:

> "tax-paid-income" means the amount determined by the formula
>
> $$A - (B - C)$$
>
> where
>
> A    is the fair market value on December 31, 1971 of all the property of a trust governed by an education savings plan,

B    is the total of all amounts paid to the plan on or before December 31, 1971 by or on behalf of the subscriber under the plan, and

C    is the total amount of all refunds of payments made under the plan on or before December 31, 1971; and

146.1(1)"tax-paid income" was 146.1(1)(g) before consolidation in R.S.C. 1985 (5th Supp.), effective for taxation years ending after November 1991. See Table of Concordance.

**"trust"**, except in this definition and the definition "education savings plan", means any person who irrevocably holds property under an education savings plan for any of, or any combination of, the following purposes:

(a) the payment of educational assistance payments,

(b) the payment after 1997 of accumulated income payments,

(c) the refund of payments,

(c.1) the repayment of amounts under Part III.1 of the *Department of Human Resources Development Act*,

(d) the payment to, or to a trust in favour of, designated educational institutions in Canada referred to in subparagraph (a)(i) of the definition of that expression in subsection 118.6(1), or

(e) the payment to a trust that irrevocably holds property pursuant to a registered education savings plan for any of the purposes set out in paragraphs (a) to (d).

**Related Provisions**: 104(1) — Reference to trust or estate; 108(1)"trust"(a) — "trust" does not include a RESP for certain purposes.

**Notes**: Opening words and paras. (a) and (b) amended by 1997 Budget, effective 1998. Before 1998, read:

> "trust", except in this definition, means any person who irrevocably holds property pursuant to an education savings plan for
>
> (a) the payment of educational assistance payments,
>
> (b) the payment of scholarships or other amounts to persons, other than a beneficiary, to assist them to further their education at the post-secondary school level,

Para. (c.1) added by 1998 Budget, effective 1998.

146.1(1)"trust" was 146.1(1)(h) before consolidation in R.S.C. 1985 (5th Supp.), effective for taxation years ending after November 1991. See Table of Concordance.

146.1(1)(h) (now 146.1(1)"trust") amended by 1991 technical bill, effective July 14, 1990, to change "holds property or money" to "holds property" (no change in meaning), and to add the requirement now in para. (e), which permits transfers between plans, that the transferee trust be set up pursuant to a RESP.

**(2) Conditions for registration** — The Minister shall not accept for registration for the purposes of this Act any education savings plan of a promoter unless, in the Minister's opinion, the following conditions are complied with:

(a) the plan provides that the property of any trust governed by the plan (after the payment of trustee and administration charges) is irrevocably held for any of the purposes described in the definition "trust" in subsection (1) by a corporation licensed or otherwise authorized under the laws of Canada or a province to carry on in Canada the business of offering to the public its services as a trustee;

(b) at the time of the application by the promoter for registration of the plan, there are not fewer than 150 plans entered into with the promoter each of which complied, at the time it was entered into, with all the other conditions set out in this subsection, as it read at that time;

(b.1) application for registration of the plan is made by the promoter in prescribed form containing prescribed information;

(c) the promoter and all trusts governed by the plan are resident in Canada;

(d) the plan does not allow for any payment before 1998 to a subscriber, other than a refund of payments, unless the subscriber is also the beneficiary under the plan;

(d.1) subject to subsection (2.2), the plan does not allow accumulated income payments under the plan, or the plan allows an accumulated income payment at a particular time only if

(i) the payment is made to, or on behalf of, a person and not jointly to, or on behalf of, more than one person,

(ii) the particular time is after 1997,

(iii) the person is resident in Canada at the particular time,

(iv) either

(A) the person is a subscriber under the plan at the particular time, or

(B) an individual died at any previous time and was a subscriber under the plan immediately before death,

(v) each individual in respect of whom a subscriber has made a contribution into the plan

(A) has before the particular time attained 21 years of age and is not, at the particular time, eligible under the plan to receive an educational assistance payment, or

(B) has died before the particular time, and

(vi) either

(A) the particular time is after the 9th year that follows the year in which the plan was entered into, or

(B) each individual in respect of whom a subscriber has made a contribution into the plan has died before the particular time and was, or was related to, a subscriber under the plan (or was the nephew, niece, great nephew or great niece of a subscriber under the plan);

(e) the plan is substantially similar to the type of plan described in or annexed to a prospectus filed by the promoter with a securities commission in Canada or a body performing a similar function in a province;

(f) in the event that a trust governed by the plan is terminated, the property held by the trust is required to be used for any of the purposes described in the definition "trust" in subsection (1);

(g) the plan does not allow for the payment of educational assistance payments before 1997 to an individual unless the individual is, at the time the payment is made, a student in full-time attendance at a post-secondary educational institution and enrolled in a qualifying educational program at the institution;

(g.1) the plan does not allow for the payment of an educational assistance payment to or for an individual at any time after 1996 unless

(i) either

(A) the individual is at that time enrolled as a full-time student in a qualifying educational program at a post-secondary educational institution, or

(B) the individual is at that time enrolled as a student in a qualifying educational program at a post-secondary educational institution and has at that time a mental or physical impairment the effects of which on the individual have been certified in writing, by a person described in paragraph 118.3(1)(a.2) in relation to the individual's impairment, to be such that the individual cannot reasonably be expected to be enrolled as a full-time student, and

(ii) either

(A) the individual has satisfied the condition set out in subparagraph (i) throughout at least 13 consecutive weeks in the 12-month period that ends at that time, or

(B) the total of the payment and all other educational assistance payments made under a registered educational savings plan of the promoter to or for the individual in the 12-month period that ends at that time does not exceed $5,000 or such greater amount as the Minister of Human Resources Development approves in writing with respect to the individual;

(g.2) the plan does not allow for any contribution into the plan, other than a contribution made by or on behalf of a subscriber under the plan in respect of a beneficiary under the plan or a contribution made by way of transfer from another registered education savings plan;

(h) the plan provides that no payments may be made into the plan by or on behalf of a subscriber after the 21st year following the year in which the plan is entered into;

(i) the plan provides that it must be terminated on or before the last day of the 25th year following the year in which the plan is entered into;

(i.1) if the plan allows accumulated income payments in accordance with paragraph (d.1), the plan provides that it must be terminated before March of the year following the year in which the first such payment is made out of the plan;

(i.2) the plan does not allow for the receipt of property by way of direct transfer from another registered education savings plan after the other plan has made any accumulated income payment;

(j) if the plan allows more than one beneficiary under the plan at any one time, the plan provides

(i) that each of the beneficiaries under the plan is required to be connected to each living subscriber under the plan, or to have been connected to a deceased original subscriber under the plan, by blood relationship or adoption,

(ii) that a contribution into the plan in respect of a beneficiary is permitted to be made only if

(A) the beneficiary had not attained 21 years of age before the time of the contribution, or

(B) the contribution is made by way of transfer from another registered education savings plan that allows more than one beneficiary at any one time, and

(iii) that an individual is permitted to become a beneficiary under the plan at any particular time only if

(A) the individual had not attained 21 years of age before the particular time, or

(B) the individual was, immediately before the particular time, a beneficiary under another registered education savings plan that allows more than one beneficiary at any one time;

(k) the plan does not allow the total of all contributions made into the plan in respect of a beneficiary for a year (other than contributions made by way of transfer from registered education savings plans) to exceed the RESP annual limit for the year;

(l) the plan provides that the promoter shall, within 90 days after an individual becomes a beneficiary under the plan, notify the individual (or, where the individual is under 19 years of age at that time and ordinarily resides with a parent of the individual, that parent) in writing of the existence of the plan and the name and address of the subscriber in respect of the plan;

(m) the Minister has no reasonable basis to believe that the promoter will not take all reasonable measures to ensure that the plan will continue to comply with the conditions set out in paragraphs (a), (c) to (d.1) and (f) to (l) for its registration for the purposes of this Act; and

(n) the Minister has no reasonable basis to believe that the plan will become revocable.

### Proposed Amendment — RESPs as Trusts

**Department of Finance news release, July 20, 1999**: See under 146.1(1)"education savings plan".

**Related Provisions**: 146.1(2.1) — RESP becoming revocable; 146.1(2.2) — Waiver of conditions for disabled beneficiary; 146.1(3) — Deemed registration; 146.1(4) — Registration of plans without prospectus; 146.1(4.1) — Amendments must be filed with CCRA; 146.1(13) — Revocation where plan ceases to comply with requirements; 172(3) — Appeal from refusal to register; 204.9(1)"excess amount" — Limit on RESP contributions; 204.91 — Tax payable by subscribers.

**Notes**: 146.1(2) amended by 1998 Budget as follows:

- Para. (b.1) added, effective for plans entered into after 1998.
- Para. (d.1) amended to add "subject to subsection (2.2)," effective 1998.
- Para.(g.1) amended, effective for plans entered into after February 20, 1990, except that

   (a) for plans entered into before 1998, read "individual" as "beneficiary"; and

   (b) subpara. (g.1)(ii) does not apply to plans entered into before 1999.

The substance of this amendment was to add everything after (g.1)(i)(A). Before the amendment, read simply:

(g.1) the plan does not allow for the payment of educational assistance payments after 1996 to an individual unless the individual is, at the time the payment is made, enrolled in a qualifying educational program as a full-time student at a post-secondary educational institution;

- Subpara. (j)(ii) amended and (j)(iii) added, effective for plans entered into after 1998. For earlier years, read:

(ii) that a contribution into the plan in respect of a beneficiary is permitted to be made only if

(A) the beneficiary had not attained 21 years of age at the time the plan was entered into,

(B) the contribution is made by way of transfer from another registered education savings plan into which a contribution had been made before the transfer in respect of the beneficiary, or

(C) the contribution is made (after a contribution to which clause 146.1(2)(j)(ii) (B) applied was made) into the plan in respect of the beneficiary;

- Para. (n) added effective 1998.

146.1(2) extensively amended by 1997 Budget, generally effective for applications made after 1997. The changes increase the annual limit from $2,000 to $4,000, allow accumulated income to be returned to the subscriber and transferred to an RRSP, introduce a 20% penalty tax in 204.94 where it is returned but not so transferred, allow a sibling to replace a beneficiary, permit transfers between RESPs, allow distance education program to qualify as full-time instruction, and repeal the provisions relating to pre-1972 income. The specific changes were as follows:

- Opening words: for applications before 1998, read "it complied with the following conditions" in place of "the following conditions are complied with". The amendment ensures that the requirements do not only relate to the terms of the plan.
- Para. (b): for applications before 1998, read "150 subscribers who have entered into education savings plans with the promoter" in place of "150 plans entered into with the promoter".

(A redundant reference to the previous version of 146.1(2) was also deleted.)

- Para. (d): the words "before 1998" were added effective 1998. Income can now be returned to the subscriber under (d.1), although there will be an income inclusion and possibly a penalty tax (see 146.1(7.1) and 204.94).

  Para. (d.1) was added effective 1998. (See under (d) above.)

- Para. (g): the words "before 1997" were added, effective for plans entered into after February 20, 1990. (See (g.1) instead.)

- Para. (g.1) was added, effective for plans entered into after February 20, 1990 except that, for plans entered into before 1998, read "beneficiary" in place of "individual". Because it refers to enrolment rather than attendance, it allows educational assistance payments to be made from a RESP to students who are taking distance education courses, such as correspondence courses.

- Para. (g.2) was added, effective for 1997 and later taxation years.

- Para. (i.1) was added, effective for 1998 and later taxation years.

- Para. (i.2) was added, effective for 1998 and later taxation years. It ensures that transfers between plans cannot be used to extend the life of a plan beyond the term provided under (i.1).

- Para. (j): the amendment applies to 1998 and later taxation years, but the amendment does not apply to plans entered into before July 14, 1990, and subpara. (j)(ii) does not apply to plans entered into before 1998. The earlier version read:

    (j) where the plan provides that a subscriber may name more than one beneficiary under the plan at any one time, the plan provides that each of the beneficiaries under the plan is required to be connected to the subscriber by blood relationship or adoption;

  (See 251(6) re connection by blood relationship or adoption.) Note that 146.1(2)(j)(ii)(B) permits transfers between plans.

- Para. (k): amended for plans entered into after February 20, 1990 to increase the limit to $4,000 and allow transfers from other plans (previously limited all payments into the plan in respect of a beneficiary for a year to $2,000).

- Para. (m): for applications made before 1998, read: "the plan complies with prescribed conditions". (No conditions were prescribed for this purpose.)

146.1(2) extensively amended by 1990 Budget/1991 technical bill.

146.1(2)(a), (b) apply to plans entered into after February 20, 1990. For earlier plans, read:

  (a) the plan provides that the property of any trust established under the plan (after payment of trustee and administration charges) is irrevocably held for any of the purposes described in the definition "trust" in subsection (1);

  (b) at the time of the application by the promoter for registration of the plan, there are not less than 150 subscribers who have entered into education savings plans with the promoter that comply with the conditions set out in paragraphs (a) and (c) to (g);

146.1(2)(c) amended effective July 14, 1990. Before that date, read "established under the plan" in place of "governed by the plan".

146.1(2)(f) amended effective July 14, 1990. Before that date, read:

  (f) in the event that a trust established under the plan is terminated, the property or money held by the trust is required to be used for any of the purposes described in paragraph (1)(h); and

146.1(2)(g) to (i), (k) and (m) apply to plans entered into after February 20, 1990. For earlier plans, read as follows in place of (g) through (m):

  (g) the plan in all other respects complies with any regulations of the Governor in Council made on the recommendation of the Minister of Finance.

146.1(2)(j) applies to plans entered into after July 13, 1990.

146.1(2)(k) amended by 1996 Budget to change "$1,500" to "$2,000", effective for 1996 and later taxation years, except in respect of plans entered into before February 21, 1990. See also Notes to 204.9(1)"excess amount".

146.1(2)(l) applies to plans entered into after March 1991.

**Regulations**: No prescribed conditions for 146.1(2)(m).

**I.T. Application Rules**: 69 (meaning of *Income Tax Act*, chapter 148 of the Revised Statutes of Canada, 1952").

**Information Circulars**: 93-3: Registered education savings plans.

**Forms**: T3G: Certification of no tax liability by a group of RRSPs, RRIFs, or RESPs; T3IND: T3IND income tax return for RRSP, RRIF, or RESP; T550: Application for registration; T1171: Tax withholding waiver on accumulated income payments from RESPs; T1172: Additional tax on accumulated income payments from RESPs.

**(2.1) RESP is revocable** — For the purposes of paragraphs (2)(n) and (12.1)(d), a registered education savings plan is revocable at any time after October 27, 1998 at which

  (a) a trust governed by the plan acquires property that is not a qualified investment for the trust;

  (b) property held by a trust governed by the plan ceases to be a qualified investment for the trust and the property is not disposed of by the trust within 60 days after that time;

  (c) a trust governed by the plan begins carrying on a business; or

  (d) a trustee that holds property in connection with the plan borrows money for the purposes of the plan, except where

   (i) the money is borrowed for a term not exceeding 90 days,

   (ii) the money is not borrowed as part of a series of loans or other transactions and repayments, and

   (iii) none of the property of the trust is used as security for the borrowed money.

**Related Provisions**: 146.1(12.1) — Notice of intent to revoke registration; 146.1(12.2), (13) — Revocation of registration.

**Notes**: 146.1(2.1) added by 1998 Budget, effective 1998.

**(2.2) Waiver of conditions for accumulated income payments** — The Minister may, on written application of the promoter of a registered education savings plan, waive the application of the conditions in subparagraphs (2)(d.1)(v) and (vi) in respect of the plan where a beneficiary under the plan suffers from a severe and prolonged mental impairment that prevents, or can reasonably be expected to prevent, the beneficiary from enrolling in a qualifying educational program at a post-secondary educational institution.

**Notes**: 146.1(2.2) added by 1998 Budget, effective 1998.

**(3) Deemed registration** — Where in any year an education savings plan cannot be accepted for registration solely because the condition set out in paragraph (2)(b) has not been complied with, if the plan is subsequently registered, it shall be deemed to have been registered on the first day of January of

(a) the year in which all of the conditions set out in subsection (2) (except in paragraph (2)(b)) were complied with, or

(b) the year preceding the year in which the plan was subsequently registered,

whichever is the later.

**Related Provisions**: 146.1(12) — Deemed date of registration; 212(1)(r) — Non-residents — registered education savings plan.

**Information Circulars**: 93-3: Registered education savings plans.

**(4) Registration of plans without prospectus** — Notwithstanding paragraph (2)(e), where a promoter has not filed a prospectus in respect of an education savings plan referred to in that paragraph, the Minister may register the plan if the promoter is not otherwise required by the laws of Canada or a province to file such a prospectus with a securities commission in Canada or a body performing a similar function in a province and the plan complies with the other conditions set out in subsection (2).

**Notes**: 146.1(4) amended by 1990 Budget, effective for plans registered after February 20, 1990. For earlier plans, read:

> (4) Registration of plans in existence on October 15, 1973 — Notwithstanding paragraph (2)(e), where a promoter has not filed a prospectus referred to in that paragraph, the Minister may register an education savings plan if the plan was in existence on October 15, 1973 and as of that date the other conditions set out in subsection (2) had been complied with.

**(4.1) Obligation to file amendment** — When a registered education savings plan is amended, the promoter shall file the text of the amendment with the Minister not later than 60 days after the day on which the plan is amended.

**Related Provisions**: 162(7) — Penalty for failure to comply.

**Notes**: 146.1(4.1) added by 1997 Budget, effective June 18, 1998.

**(5) Trust not taxable** — No tax is payable under this Part by a trust on the taxable income of the trust for a taxation year if, throughout the period in the year during which the trust was in existence, the trust was governed by a registered education savings plan.

**Related Provisions**: 18(11)(h) — No deduction for interest paid on money borrowed to make RESP contribution; 149(1)(u) — Exemption from tax.

**Information Circulars**: 93-3: Registered education savings plans.

**Forms**: T3G: Certification of no tax liability by a group of RRSPs, RRIFs, or RESPs; T3IND: T3IND income tax return for RRSP, RRIF, or RESP.

**(6) Subscriber not taxable** — No tax is payable by a subscriber on the income of a trust for a taxation year after 1971 throughout which the trust was governed by a registered education savings plan.

**Related Provisions**: 146.1(5) — Trust not taxable; 204.91 — Tax payable by subscribers; 212(1)(r) — Non-residents — registered education savings plan.

**(6.1) Transfers between plans** — Where property irrevocably held by a trust governed by a registered education savings plan (in this subsection referred to as the "transferor plan") is transferred to a trust governed by another registered education savings plan (in this subsection referred to as the "transferee plan"),

(a) [Repealed]

(b) for the purposes of this paragraph, subparagraph (2)(d.1)(vi) and paragraphs (2)(h) and (i), the transferee plan is deemed to have been entered into on the day that is the earlier of

(i) the day on which the transferee plan was entered into, and

(ii) the day on which the transferor plan was entered into; and

(c) notwithstanding subsections (7) and (7.1), no amount shall be included in computing the income of any person because of the transfer.

**Related Provisions**: 146.1(2)(g.2), (i.2) — Restrictions on transfers between RESPs; 209.4(5) — Transfers between RESPs.

**Notes**: 146.1(6.1) amended by 1997 Budget as follows:

- Para. (a) repealed, effective for transfers made after 1996. See now 204.9(5).
- Para. (b) amended to add reference to 146.1(2)(d.1)(vi), effective 1998.
- Para. (c) added, effective for transfers made after 1997. It exempts transferred amounts from being included in anyone's income.

146.1(6.1) added by 1990 Budget/1991 technical bill, effective February 21, 1990.

**Information Circulars**: 93-3: Registered education savings plans.

**(7) Educational assistance payments** — There shall be included in computing an individual's income for a taxation year the total of all educational assistance payments paid out of registered education savings plans to or for the individual in the year.

**Related Provisions**: 56(1)(q) — Income inclusion from RESP; 60(x) — Deduction for repayment of Canada Education Savings Grant; 153(1)(t) — Withholding of tax at source; 212(1)(r) — Withholding tax on RESP payments to non-residents.

**Notes**: 146.1(7) amended by 1997 Budget, effective for 1998 and later taxation years. For 1979-97, read:

> (7) Amounts to be included in beneficiary's income — There shall be included in computing the income for a taxation year of a taxpayer who is or was a beneficiary under a registered education savings plan, the amount, if any, by which the total of
>
> (a) educational assistance payments paid to the taxpayer or on the taxpayer's behalf in the year under the plan, and
>
> (b) amounts paid to the taxpayer or on the taxpayer's behalf to the extent that those amounts may reasonably be regarded as a distribution of property that had been transferred from a trust established under a registered education savings plan, of property substituted therefor or of income from any such property

exceeds

(c) the taxpayer's portion of the tax-paid-income in the year under the plan.

**Regulations**: 200(2)(j) (information return).

**Information Circulars**: 93-3: Registered education savings plans.

**(7.1) Other income inclusions** — There shall be included in computing a taxpayer's income for a taxation year

(a) each accumulated income payment received in the year by the taxpayer under a registered education savings plan; and

(b) each amount received in the year by the taxpayer in full or partial satisfaction of a subscriber's interest under a registered education savings plan (other than any excluded amount in respect of the plan).

**Related Provisions**: 146.1(7.2) — Excluded amount; 153(1)(t) — Withholding of tax at source.

**Notes**: 146.1(7.1) added by 1997 Budget, effective for 1998 and later taxation years. It requires accumulated income payments received from an RESP to be included in income for the year. In order to discourage trading of RESP interests, it also requires inclusion of any amounts received from the disposition of a subscriber's interest under an RESP, other than amounts excluded by 146.1(7.2).

**Regulations**: 103(4), 103(6)(g), 103(8) (withholding of 20% at source); 200(2)(j) (information return).

**(7.2) Excluded amount** — For the purpose of paragraph (7.1)(b), an excluded amount in respect of a registered education savings plan is

(a) any amount received under the plan;

(b) any amount received in satisfaction of a right to a refund of payments under the plan; or

(c) any amount received by a taxpayer under a decree, order or judgment of a competent tribunal, or under a written agreement, relating to a division of property between the taxpayer and the taxpayer's spouse or common-law partner or former spouse or common-law partner in settlement of rights arising out of, or on the breakdown of, their marriage or common-law partnership.

**Notes**: 146.1(7.2)(c) amended by 2000 same-sex partners bill to add reference to "common-law partner" and "common-law partnership", effective for the 2001 and later taxation years, or earlier by election (see Notes to 248(1)"common-law partner").

146.1(7.2) added by 1997 Budget, effective for 1998 and later taxation years.

**(8)–(10)** [Repealed]

**Notes**: 146.1(8), (9) and (10) repealed by 1997 Budget, effective for 1998 and later taxation years. They contained income exclusion rules for the distribution of property relating to pre-1972 income of a RESP. To the extent trust income earned before 1972 had been included in the subscriber's income, the rules provided a deduction for the portion of "tax-paid-income" included in payments to a beneficiary. These rules are no longer relevant, since pre-1972 plans should have been wound up by now. For 1972-97, read:

(8) Definition of "beneficiary's portion of the tax-paid-income" — For the purposes of subsection (7), a "beneficiary's portion of the tax-paid-income" for a taxation year under a registered education savings plan means the greater of

(a) the lesser of

(i) one-third of the pre-1972 income reported on or before April 30, 1972 by the trust governed by the plan to the subscriber as having been earned in respect of amounts paid to the plan by or on behalf of the subscriber, and

(ii) the amount, if any, by which

(A) the pre-1972 income reported on or before April 30, 1972 by the trust governed by the plan to the subscriber as having been earned in respect of amounts paid to the plan by or on behalf of the subscriber

exceeds

(B) the total of all amounts, if any, referred to in paragraph (7)(c) in respect of preceding taxation years, and

(b) the amount of the tax-paid-income actually allocated under the trust governed by the plan to the beneficiary in the year.

(9) Limitation on allocation of tax-paid-income — For the purposes of paragraph (8)(b), no amount of the tax-paid-income shall be allocated in a particular taxation year if an allocation has been made in respect of the same amount in a previous taxation year.

(10) Allocation of tax-paid-income — For the purposes of this subsection and subsections (8) and (9), in any taxation year there shall be allocated by the trust governed by a registered education savings plan an amount of the tax-paid-income to a beneficiary that is not less than the amount determined under paragraph (8)(a) for the year.

**(11) Trust deemed to be *inter vivos* trust** — For any taxation year during which an education savings plan is not registered, a trust governed by the plan shall be deemed, for the purposes of section 122, to be a trust referred to in subsection 122(1) established after June 17, 1971.

**(12) Deemed date of registration** — Subject to subsection (3), an education savings plan that is registered

(a) before 1976 shall be deemed to have been registered since the later of

(i) January 1, 1972, and

(ii) the first day of January of the year in which the plan was created; and

(b) after 1975 shall be deemed to have been registered on the first day of January in the year of registration.

**(12.1) Notice of intent to revoke registration** — When a particular day is

(a) a day on which a registered education savings plan ceases to comply with the conditions of subsection (2) for the plan's registration,

(b) a day on which a registered education savings plan ceases to comply with any provision of the plan,

(c) the last day of a month in respect of which tax is payable under Part X.4 by an individual because of contributions made, or deemed for the purpose of Part X.4 to have been made, by or on behalf of the individual into a registered education savings plan,

(d) a day on which a registered education savings plan is revocable, or

(e) a day on which a person fails to comply with a condition or obligation imposed under Part III.1 of the *Department of Human Resources Development Act* that applies with respect to a registered education savings plan,

the Minister may send written notice (referred to in this subsection and subsection (12.2) as a "notice of intent") to the promoter of the plan that the Minister proposes to revoke the registration of the plan as of the day specified in the notice of intent, which day shall not be earlier than the particular day.

**Related Provisions**: 146.1(2.1) — RESP becoming revocable; 146.1(12.2) — Notice of revocation; 172(3)(e.1) — Appeal to Federal Court of Appeal from giving of notice of intent; 180(1)(c.1) — Deadline for filing appeal to Federal Court of Appeal; 248(7) — Notice deemed received on day mailed.

**Notes**: 146.1(12.1)(d) and (e) added by 1998 Budget, effective 1998.

146.1(12.1) added by 1997 Budget, effective 1998.

**(12.2) Notice of revocation** — When the Minister sends a notice of intent to revoke the registration of a registered education savings plan to the promoter of the plan, the Minister may, after 30 days after the receipt by the promoter of the notice, send written notice (referred to in this subsection and subsection (13) as a "notice of revocation") to the promoter that the registration of the plan is revoked as of the day specified in the notice of revocation, which day shall not be earlier than the day specified in the notice of intent.

**Related Provisions**: 146.1(13) — Revocation; 248(7) — Notice deemed received on day mailed.

**Notes**: 146.1(12.2) added by 1997 Budget, effective 1998.

**(13) Revocation of registration** — When the Minister sends a notice of revocation of the registration of a registered education savings plan under subsection (12.2) to the promoter of the plan, the registration of the plan is revoked as of the day specified in the notice of revocation, unless the Federal Court of Appeal or a judge thereof, on application made at any time before the determination of an appeal under subsection 172(3), orders otherwise.

**Related Provisions**: 146.1(2) — Requirements for registration; 146.1(5) — Trust becomes taxable after revocation; 244(5) — Proof of service by mail; 248(7)(a) — Mail deemed received on day mailed.

**Notes**: 146.1(13) amended by 1997 Budget, effective 1998 (in conjunction with the introduction of (12.1) and (12.2). For 1972-97, read:

> (13) Where at any time an education savings plan that has been accepted by the Minister for registration for the purposes of this Act ceases to comply with the requirements of this section for its registration as such, the Minister may revoke its registration as of any date after that time and shall give notice of the revocation by registered mail to the subscriber and to the promoter.

**(13.1) RESP information** — Every trustee under a registered education savings plan shall, in prescribed form and manner, file with the Minister information returns in respect of the plan.

**Related Provisions**: 146.1(15) — Information returns by promoters.

**Notes**: 146.1(13.1) added by 1998 first budget bill, effective June 18, 1998.

**(14)** [Repealed]

**Notes**: 146.1(14) repealed by 1997 Budget, effective 1998. It is no longer necessary in light of other consequences of revocation of a RESP: inclusion in income under 146.1(7) and (7.1), and penalty tax under 204.94. For 1972-97, read:

> (14) Rules applicable to revoked plan — Where at any time in a taxation year the Minister revokes the registration of an education savings plan that had previously been accepted for registration, there shall be included in computing the income of the subscriber under the plan for that year the amount, if any, by which
>
> (a) the fair market value at that time of all of the property of the trust governed by the plan
>
> exceeds
>
> (b) the amount by which
>
> (i) the total of all amounts each of which is
>
> (A) an amount paid to the plan by or on behalf of the subscriber, or
>
> (B) the amount of the pre-1972 income reported on or before April 30, 1972 by the trust governed by the plan to the subscriber as having been earned in respect of amounts paid to the plan by or on behalf of the subscriber
>
> exceeds
>
> (ii) the total of all refunds of payments paid or payable under the plan to the subscriber.

**(15) Regulations** — The Governor in Council may make regulations requiring promoters of education savings plans to file information returns in respect of the plans.

**Related Provisions**: 146.1(13.1) — Information returns by trustees.

**Notes**: 146.1(15) added by 1997 Budget, effective June 18, 1998.

**Notes [s. 146.1]**: For detailed reviews of RESPs and recent changes, see Joanne Magee, "Tax Planning for Post-Secondary Education", 46(5) *Canadian Tax Journal* 1079-1115 (1998); and Maureen Donnelly *et al.*, "Registered Education Savings Plans: A Tax Incentive Response to Higher Education Access", 47(1) *CTJ* 81-109 (1999).

**Definitions [s. 146.1]**: "accumulated income payment" — 146.1(1); "adoption" — 251(6)(c); "amount", "annuity" — 248(1); "beneficiary" — 146.1(1); "blood relationship" — 251(6)(a); "borrowed money", "business" — 248(1); "Canada" — 255; "common-law partner", "common-law partnership" — 248(1); "connected" — 251(6); "contribution" — 146.1(1); "corporation" — 248(1), *Interpretation Act* 35(1); "educational assistance payment"; "education savings plan" — 146.1(1); "excluded amount" — 146.1(7.2); "Governor in Council" — *Interpretation Act* 35(1); "individual" — 248(1); "licensed annuities provider" — 147(1), 248(1); "Minister" — 248(1); "nephew", "niece" — 252(2)(g); "notice of intent" — 146.1(12.1); "notice of revocation" — 146.1(12.2); "parent" — 252(2); "person" — 248(1); "portion" — 146.1(8); "prescribed" — 248(1); "prescribed stock exchange in Canada" — Reg. 3200; "promoter" — 146.1(1)"education savings plan"(b); "property" — 248(1); "province" — *Interpretation Act* 35(1);

## S. 146.1 — Income Tax Act, Part I

"qualified investment" — 146.1(1); "RESP annual limit", "refund of payments" — 146.1(1); "registered education savings plan" — 146.1(1), 248(1); "regulation" — 248(1); "resident in Canada" — 250; "security" — *Interpretation Act* 35(1); "share" — 248(1); "subscriber" — 146.1(1); "substituted property" — 248(5); "taxable income" — 2(2), 248(1); "taxation year" — 249; "tax-paid income" — 146.1(1); "trust" — 104(1), 108(1), 146.1(1), 248(1), (3); "writing" — *Interpretation Act* 35(1); "written" — *Interpretation Act* 35(1) "writing".

## Registered Home Ownership Savings Plans

### 146.2 [Repealed under former Act or irrelevant]

**Notes [s. 146.2]:** 146.2 dealt with registered home ownership savings plans (RHOSPs).

146.2(1) to (21) repealed by 1985 Budget. 146.2(22) was not repealed (and was reenacted in R.S.C. 1985 (5th Supp.) with an interpretation provision in 146.2(23)), but it applied only to the 1985 taxation year.

Although RHOSP funds can be withdrawn for any purpose without federal tax consequences, Quebec still required that the funds be used for a home or certain furniture or appliances if no provincial tax was to be imposed on the withdrawal. Some Quebec residents therefore still maintained RHOSPs, but these were revoked effective December 31, 1999 and the beneficiary deemed to receive the value of the property (Quebec *Taxation Act*, s. 946.1). For federal income tax purposes, all properties in an RHOSP are deemed to have been acquired at their fair market value on January 1, 1986: see 50(3).

Payments out of an RHOSP to a non-resident are partially subject to a 25% withholding tax: see 212(1)(p). The death of the non-resident beneficiary will trigger this tax: see 214(3)(g).

## Registered Retirement Income Funds

### 146.3 (1) Definitions — In this section,

**"annuitant"** under a retirement income fund at any time means

(a) the first individual to whom the carrier has undertaken to make payments described in the definition "retirement income fund" out of or under the fund, where the first individual is alive at that time;

(b) after the death of the first individual, a spouse or common-law partner (in this definition referred to as the "survivor") of the first individual to whom the carrier has undertaken to make payments described in the definition "retirement income fund" out of or under the fund after the death of the first individual, where the survivor is alive at that time and the undertaking was made pursuant to an election described in that definition of the first individual with the consent of the legal representative of the first individual, and

(c) after the death of the survivor, another spouse or common-law partner of the survivor to whom the carrier has undertaken, with the consent of the legal representative of the survivor, to make payments described in the definition "retirement income fund" out of or under the fund after the death of the survivor, where that other spouse or common-law partner is alive at that time;

**Notes:** 146.3(1) "annuitant" (b) and (c) amended by 2000 same-sex partners bill, effective for the 2001 and later taxation years, or earlier by election (see Notes to 248(1) "common-law partner"). The paras. formerly read:

(b) after the death of the first individual, a spouse (in this paragraph[26] referred to as the "surviving spouse") of the first individual to whom the carrier has undertaken to make payments described in the definition "retirement income fund" out of or under the fund after the death of the first individual, where the surviving spouse is alive at that time and the undertaking was made pursuant to an election described in that definition of the first individual or with the consent of the legal representative of the first individual, and

(c) after the death of the surviving spouse, another spouse of the surviving spouse to whom the carrier has undertaken, with the consent of the legal representative of the surviving spouse, to make payments described in the definition "retirement income fund" out of or under the fund after the death of the surviving spouse, where that other spouse is alive at that time;

146.3(1) "annuitant" was 146.3(1)(a) before consolidation in R.S.C. 1985 (5th Supp.), effective for taxation years ending after November 1991. See Table of Concordance.

146.3(1) "annuitant" (formerly 146.3(1)(a)) amended by 1992 technical bill, effective for deaths after 1990. For other cases, read:

(a) "annuitant" under a retirement income fund at any particular time means the individual to whom the carrier has undertaken to make the payments described in the definition "retirement income fund" in this subsection out of or under the fund;

**Forms:** RC4178: Death of a RRIF annuitant [guide].

**"carrier"** of a retirement income fund means

(a) a person licensed or otherwise authorized under the laws of Canada or a province to carry on in Canada an annuities business,

(b) a corporation licensed or otherwise authorized under the laws of Canada or a province to carry on in Canada the business of offering to the public its services as trustee,

(c) a corporation approved by the Governor in Council for the purposes of section 146 that is licensed or otherwise authorized under the laws of Canada or a province to issue investment contracts, or

(d) a person referred to as a depositary in section 146,

that has agreed to make payments under a retirement income fund to the individual who is the annuitant under the fund;

**Notes:** 146.3(1) "carrier" was para. 146.3(1)(b) before consolidation in R.S.C. 1985 (5th Supp.), effective for taxation years ending after November 1991. See Table of Concordance.

**Forms:** T3G: Certification of no tax liability by a group of RRSPs, RRIFs, or RESPs; T3IND: T3IND income tax return for RRSP, RRIF, or RESP.

---

[26] *Sic.* This should read "in this definition".

**"designated benefit"** of an individual in respect of a registered retirement income fund means the total of

(a) such amounts paid out of or under the fund after the death of the last annuitant thereunder to the legal representative of that annuitant

(i) as would, had they been paid under the fund to the individual, have been refunds of premiums (in this paragraph having the meaning assigned by subsection 146(1)) if the fund were a registered retirement savings plan that had not matured before the death, and

(ii) as are designated jointly by the legal representative and the individual in prescribed form filed with the Minister, and

(b) amounts paid out of or under the fund after the death of the last annuitant thereunder to the individual that would be refunds of premiums had the fund been a registered retirement savings plan that had not matured before the death;

**Related Provisions**: 146.3(6.1) — Designated benefit deemed received; 146.3(6.11) — Transfer of designated benefit.

**Notes**: Definition "designated benefit" added by 1993 technical bill, effective for deaths after 1992. See 146.3(6.1) and (6.11).

**Forms**: T1090: Death of a RRIF annuitant — designated benefit.

**"minimum amount"** under a retirement income fund for a year is the amount determined by the formula

$$(A \times B) + C$$

where

A is the total fair market value of all properties held in connection with the fund at the beginning of the year (other than annuity contracts held by a trust governed by the fund that, at the beginning of the year, are not described in paragraph (b.1) of the definition "qualified investment");

B is

(a) where the first annuitant under the fund elected in respect of the fund under paragraph (b) of the definition "minimum amount" in this subsection, as it read before 1992, or under subparagraph 146.3(1)(f)(i) of the *Income Tax Act*, chapter 148 of the Revised Statutes of Canada, 1952, to use the age of another individual, the prescribed factor for the year in respect of the other individual,

(b) where paragraph (a) does not apply and the first annuitant under the fund so elects before any payment has been made under the fund by the carrier, the prescribed factor for the year in respect of an individual who was the spouse or common-law partner of the first annuitant at the time of the election, and

(c) in any other case, the prescribed factor for the year in respect of the first annuitant under the fund, and

C is, where the fund governs a trust, the total of all amounts each of which is

(a) a periodic payment under an annuity contract held by the trust at the beginning of the year (other than an annuity contract described at the beginning of the year in paragraph (b.1) of the definition "qualified investment") that is paid to the trust in the year, or

(b) if the periodic payment under such an annuity contract is not made to the trust because the trust disposed of the right to that payment in the year, a reasonable estimate of that payment on the assumption that the annuity contract had been held throughout the year and no rights under the contract were disposed of in the year;

**Related Provisions**: 146.3(1)"retirement income fund" — Requirement to withdraw minimum amount annually; 146.3(2)(e.1), (e.2) — Requirement for carrier to retain enough property to pay out minimum amount; 146.3(5.1) — Amount included in income; Reg. 100(1)"remuneration"(j.1), 103(6)(d.1) — Withholding tax on payments; *Income Tax Conventions Interpretation Act* 5"periodic pension payment"(c) — Withdrawal of more than twice the minimum amount per year is not "periodic".

**Notes**: 146.3(1)"minimum amount"B(b) amended by 2000 same-sex partners bill to add reference to "common-law partner", effective for the 2001 and later taxation years, or earlier by election (see Notes to 248(1)"common-law partner").

146.3(1)"minimum amount" amended by 1995-97 technical bill, effective:

(a) for 1998 and later taxation years, with respect to

(i) RIFs entered into after February 1986, and

(ii) RIFs entered into before March 1986 and revised or amended after February 1986 and before 1998;

(b) for the year in which a RIF is first revised or amended after 1997, and for later years, if the RIF was entered into before March 1986 and was not revised or amended after February 1986 and before 1998; and

(c) with respect to a RIF that governs a trust that, after July 1997, holds a contract for an annuity, for all years that begin after the first day

(i) that is after July 1997, and

(ii) on which the trust holds such a contract.

Before the amendment, the definition read:

"minimum amount" under a retirement income fund for the year in which the fund is entered into is nil and for each subsequent year is the product obtained when the fair market value of the property held in connection with the fund at the beginning of that subsequent year is multiplied by

(a) where the first annuitant under the fund elected in respect of the fund under paragraph (b), as it read before 1992, or under subparagraph 146.3(1)(f)(i) of the *Income Tax Act*, chapter 148 of the Revised Statutes of Canada, 1952, as it read before 1986, to use the age of another individual, the prescribed amount for that subsequent year in respect of the other individual,

(b) where paragraph (a) does not apply and the first annuitant under the fund so elects before any payment has been made under the fund by the carrier, the prescribed amount for that subsequent year in respect of an individual who was the spouse of the first annuitant at the time of the election, or

## S. 146.3(1) min — Income Tax Act, Part I

(c) in any other case, the prescribed amount for that subsequent year in respect of the first annuitant under the fund;

(The amendments are largely consequential on new 146.3(1)"qualified investment"(b.1) and (b.2), which permit a trusteed RRIF to hold certain types of annuity contracts. These amendments avoid the difficulty of determining the value of a locked-in annuity each year, and make it practical for a minimum amount to be calculated and distributed where a locked-in annuity is held by an RRIF. If an RRIF holds only locked-in annuities at the beginning of a year, the minimum amount for the year will never exceed the annuity payments received by the trust in that year.)

146.3(1)"minimum amount" was 146.3(1)(b.1) before consolidation in R.S.C. 1985 (5th Supp.), effective for taxation years ending after November 1991. See Table of Concordance.

146.3(1)"minimum amount" (formerly 146.3(1)(b.1)) amended by 1992 Budget/technical bill, applicable

(a) to the 1992 and later taxation years with respect to

(i) retirement income funds entered into after February 1986, and

(ii) retirement income funds entered into before March 1986 and revised or amended after February 1986 and before 1992; and

(b) to the taxation year in which a retirement income fund is first revised or amended after February 1986 and to later taxation years, where the fund was entered into before March 1986 and was not revised or amended after February 1986 and before 1992.

However, for the purposes of determining withholding taxes (regulations made under 153(1)), for the application of the spousal attribution rule for RRIFs in 146.3(5.1), and for section 5 of the *Income Tax Conventions Interpretation Act*, the new definition is effective only for payments made in 1993 or later.

The change allows RRIF funds (for RRIFs entered into or amended after February 1986) to be withdrawn at a slower rate after age 78. Under the old rules, the minimum amount each year was 1/N, where N was the number of years left until the taxpayer turned 90. The new table was constructed from a complicated formula that caps out at 20% per year of the remaining balance once the taxpayer reaches 94. Thus, a taxpayer over 90 can continue to have funds in a RRIF after age 90, for any number of years until death. Under Reg. 7308, a RRIF entered into before 1993, with no contribution of property to it after 1992, is a "qualifying retirement income fund" and the minimum withdrawal for years up to age 78 is the lower amount in the table for each year.

| OLD RULES AGE | NEW RULES General | Qualifying RIFs |
|---|---|---|
| 71 | .0526 | .0738 | .0526 |
| 72 | .0556 | .0748 | .0556 |
| 73 | .0588 | .0759 | .0588 |
| 74 | .0625 | .0771 | .0625 |
| 75 | .0667 | .0785 | .0667 |
| 76 | .0714 | .0799 | .0714 |
| 77 | .0769 | .0815 | .0769 |
| 78 | .0833 | .0833 | .0833 |
| 79 | .0909 | .0853 | .0853 |
| 80 | .1000 | .0875 | .0875 |
| 81 | .1111 | .0899 | .0899 |
| 82 | .1250 | .0927 | .0927 |
| 83 | .1429 | .0958 | .0958 |
| 84 | .1667 | .0993 | .0993 |
| 85 | .2000 | .1033 | .1033 |
| 86 | .2500 | .1079 | .1079 |
| 87 | .3333 | .1133 | .1133 |
| 88 | .5000 | .1196 | .1196 |
| 89 | 1.0000 | .1271 | .1271 |
| 90 | N/A | .1362 | .1362 |
| 91 | N/A | .1473 | .1473 |
| 92 | N/A | .1612 | .1612 |
| 93 | N/A | .1792 | .1792 |
| 94 + | N/A | .2000 | .2000 |

For ages below 71, the formula $1/(90 - N)$ is used (e.g., for age 70, $1/20$, or 5%). See Reg. 7308. This will not be changed as a result of the 1996 budget change that forces an RRSP to be closed out (or converted to an RRIF) by the end of the year that the taxpayer turns 69 (see 146(2)(b.4)).

**Regulations**: 7308 (prescribed factor).

**I.T. Application Rules**: 69 (meaning of "*Income Tax Act*, chapter 148 of the Revised Statutes of Canada, 1952").

**Interpretation Bulletins**: IT-528: Transfers of funds between registered plans.

**Information Circulars**: 78-18R5: Registered retirement income funds.

**"property held"** in connection with a retirement income fund means property held by the carrier of the fund, whether held by the carrier as trustee or beneficial owner thereof, the value of which, or the income or loss from which, is relevant in determining the amount for a year payable to the annuitant under the fund;

**Notes**: 146.3(1)"property held" was 146.3(1)(c) before consolidation in R.S.C. 1985 (5th Supp.), effective for taxation years ending after November 1991.

146.3(1)(c) (now 146.3(1)"property held") amended in 1986, effective for RRIFs entered into after February 1986. Where an earlier RRIF is revised or amended after February 1986, effective as of the taxation year in which it is revised or amended. For earlier RRIFs that are not revised or amended, read:

(c) "property held in connection with the arrangement" means property held by a carrier of a retirement income fund, whether held by the carrier as trustee or beneficial owner thereof,

(i) the value of which, or

(ii) the income or loss from which

is relevant in determining the amount payable in a year to the annuitant under the fund;

**"qualified investment"** for a trust governed by a registered retirement income fund means

(a) an investment that would be described in any of paragraphs (a), (b), (d) and (f) to (h) of the definition "qualified investment" in section 204 if the references in that definition to "a trust governed by a deferred profit sharing plan or revoked plan" were read as references to "a trust governed by a registered retirement income fund",

(b) a bond, debenture, note or similar obligation of a corporation the shares of which are listed on a prescribed stock exchange in Canada, (b.1) a contract for an annuity issued by a licensed annuities provider where

(i) the trust is the only person who, disregarding any subsequent transfer of the contract by the trust, is or may become entitled to any annuity payments under the contract, and

(ii) the holder of the contract has a right to surrender the contract at any time for an amount that would, if reasonable sales and administration charges were ignored, approximate the value of funds that could otherwise be applied to fund future periodic payments under the contract,

(b.2) a contract for an annuity issued by a licensed annuities provider where

(i) annual or more frequent periodic payments are or may be made under the contract to the holder of the contract,

(ii) the trust is the only person who, disregarding any subsequent transfer of the contract by the trust, is or may become entitled to any annuity payments under the contract,

(iii) neither the time nor the amount of any payment under the contract may vary because of the length of any life, other than

(A) if the annuitant under the fund (in this paragraph referred to as the "RRIF annuitant") has made the election referred to in the definition "retirement income fund" in respect of the fund and a spouse or common-law partner, the life of the RRIF annuitant or the life of the spouse or common-law partner, and

(B) in any other case, the life of the RRIF annuitant,

(iv) the day on which the periodic payments began or are to begin (in this paragraph referred to as the "start date") is not later than the end of the year following the year in which the contract was acquired by the trust,

(v) either

(A) the periodic payments are payable for the life of the RRIF annuitant or the joint lives of the RRIF annuitant and the RRIF annuitant's spouse or common-law partner and either there is no guaranteed period under the contract or there is a guaranteed period that begins at the start date and does not exceed a term equal to 90 years minus the lesser of

(I) the age in whole years at the start date of the RRIF annuitant (determined on the assumption that the RRIF annuitant is alive at the start date), and

(II) the age in whole years at the start date of a spouse or common-law partner of the RRIF annuitant (determined on the assumption that a spouse or common-law partner of the RRIF annuitant at the time the contract was acquired is a spouse or common-law partner of the RRIF annuitant at the start date), or

(B) the periodic payments are payable for a term equal to

(I) 90 years minus the age described in subclause (A)(I), or

(II) 90 years minus the age described in subclause (A)(II), and

(vi) the periodic payments

(A) are equal, or

(B) are not equal solely because of one or more adjustments that would, if the contract were an annuity under a retirement savings plan, be in accordance with subparagraphs 146(3)(b)(iii) to (v) or that arise because of a uniform reduction in the entitlement to the periodic payments as a consequence of a partial surrender of rights to the periodic payments, and

(c) such other investments as may be prescribed by regulations of the Governor in Council made on the recommendation of the Minister of Finance;

**Related Provisions**: 87(10) — New share issued on amalgamation of public corporation deemed to be listed on prescribed stock exchange; 132.2(1)(k) — Where share ceases to be qualified investment due to mutual fund reorganization; 146.3(7) — Tax on acquisition of non-qualified investment; 146.3(9) — Tax on income from non-qualified investment; 207.1(4) — Tax on holding of non-qualified investment.

**Notes**: 146.3(1)"qualified investment" amended by 2000 same-sex partners bill to add reference to "common-law partner", effective for the 2001 and later taxation years, or earlier by election (see Notes to 248(1)"common-law partner").

Paras. (b.1) and (b.2) added by 1995-97 technical bill, effective 1997. Annuities in (b.2) are generally referred to as "locked-in annuities". See also 146(1)"qualified investment"(c.1) and (c.2), which provide parallel rules for RRSPs, and amendments made to 146.3(1)"minimum amount" to accommodate these annuities.

146.3(1)"qualified investment" was 146.3(1)(d) before consolidation in R.S.C. 1985 (5th Supp.), effective for taxation years ending after November 1991. See Table of Concordance. See also Notes to 146.3(9).

Note that many of the most common qualified investments are listed in Reg. 4900(1).

See Notes to 146.3(9) re acquisition of non-qualified investment.

**Regulations**: 221 (information return by issuer of qualified investment); 3200, 3201 (prescribed stock exchanges; but see also ITA 87(10)); 4900, 4901, 5100–5104 (prescribed investments).

**Remission Orders**: *Lionaird Capital Corporation Notes Remission Order*, P.C. 1999-737 (tax under 146.3(7) waived because taxpayers thought they were qualified investments).

**Information Circulars**: 78-18R5: Registered retirement income funds.

**Forms**: T3F: Investments prescribed to be qualified or not to be foreign property information return.

**"registered retirement income fund"** means a retirement income fund accepted by the Minister for registration for the purposes of this Act and registered under the Social Insurance Number of the first annuitant under the fund;

**Related Provisions**: 18(1)(u) — Investment counselling fees for RRSP are non-deductible; 128.1(10)"excluded right or interest"(a)(ii) — No deemed disposition of RRIF on emigration; 248(1)"disposition"(g) — Transfer between RRSPs/RRIFs not a disposition; 248(1)"registered retirement income fund" — Definition applies to entire Act.

**Notes**: 146.3(1)"registered retirement income fund" was 146.3(1)(e) before consolidation in R.S.C. 1985 (5th Supp.), effective for taxation years ending after November 1991.

See also Notes at end of 146.3.

**Interpretation Bulletins**: IT-415R2: Deregistration of RRSPs; IT-528: Transfers of funds between registered plans.

**Forms**: T2033: Direct transfer of RRSP property.

**"retirement income fund"** means an arrangement between a carrier and an annuitant under which, in consideration for the transfer to the carrier of property, the carrier undertakes to pay to the annuitant and, where the annuitant so elects, to the annuitant's spouse or common-law partner after the annuitant's death, in each year that begins not later than the first calendar year after the year in which the arrangement was entered into one or more amounts the total of which is not less than the minimum amount under the arrangement for the year, but the amount of any such payment shall not exceed the value of the property held in connection with the arrangement immediately before the time of the payment.

**Related Provisions**: 146.3(1)"minimum amount" — determination of minimum amount to be paid out; 248(1)"retirement income fund" — Definition applies to entire Act.

**Notes**: 146.3(1)"retirement income fund" amended by 2000 same-sex partners bill to add reference to "common-law partner", effective for the 2001 and later taxation years, or earlier by election (see Notes to 248(1)"common-law partner").

Definition "retirement income fund" amended by 1993 technical bill, effective as follows:

- For a RIF entered into before March 1986 and not revised or amended, the new definition does not apply.

- For a RIF entered into before March 1986 and revised or amended from March 1986 through the end of 1991, the new definition is effective for 1992 and later taxation years.

- For a RIF entered into before March 1986 and first revised or amended in 1992 or later, the new definition is effective for the taxation year in which the RIF is first revised or amended and for all later taxation years.

- For a RIF entered into after February 1986, the new definition is effective for 1992 and later taxation years.

The amendment removes the requirement that the full value of the RIF be paid out at the end of the year in which the last payment is made. Under 146.3(1)"minimum amount", payments from a RRIF can now continue through the annuitant's lifetime. The old definition (now deemed never to have been in force since the amendment was retroactive to the in-force date of the previous amendments, below) read:

"retirement income fund" means an arrangement between a carrier and an annuitant under which, in consideration for the transfer to the carrier of property (including money), the carrier undertakes to pay to the annuitant and, where the annuitant so elects, to the annuitant's spouse after the annuitant's death,

(a) in each year, commencing not later than the first calendar year after the year in which the arrangement is entered into, one or more amounts the total of which is not less than the minimum amount under the arrangement for a year, but the amount of any such payment shall not exceed the value of the property held in connection with the arrangement immediately before the time of the payment, and

(b) at the end of the year in which the last payment under the arrangement is, in accordance with the terms and conditions of the arrangement, required to be made, an amount equal to the value of the property, if any, held in connection with the arrangement at that time.

146.3(1)"retirement income fund" was 146.3(1)(f) before consolidation in R.S.C. 1985 (5th Supp.), effective for taxation years ending after November 1991. See Table of Concordance.

146.3(1)(f) (now 146.3(1)"retirement income fund") amended in 1986, effective for RRIFs entered into after February 1986. Where an earlier RRIF is revised or amended after February 1986, the new version is effective as of the taxation year in which it is revised or amended. For earlier RRIFs that are not revised or amended, read:

(f) "retirement income fund" means an arrangement between a carrier and an individual under which, in consideration for the transfer to the carrier of property (including money), the carrier undertakes to pay to the individual and, where the individual so elects, to his spouse after his death should he die before the arrangement ceases,

(i) in each year, commencing with the first complete calendar year after the arrangement is entered into, one or more amounts, the aggregate of which is equal to the amount that would be payable in the year under a single premium annuity contract purchased at a cost equal to the fair market value of the property held in connection with the arrangement at the beginning of the year if

(A) the annuity provided for equal annual payments throughout its term,

(B) the interest rate, if any, used in computing the annuity payment were such rate as the annuitant designates in respect of the year, not exceeding 6% per annum, and

(C) the term of the annuity in years were equal to the number that is

(I) the difference between 90 and the number that is, or would be, the age in whole years of the individual at the beginning of the year, or

(II) if the individual's spouse is younger than the individual and he so elects before the beginning of the first complete calendar year after the arrangement is entered into, the difference between 90 and the number that is, or would be, the age in whole years of his spouse at the beginning of the year,

but the amount of any such payment shall not exceed the value of the property held in connection with the arrangement immediately before the time of the payment, and

(ii) at the end of the year in which the last payment under the arrangement is, in accordance with the terms and conditions of the arrangement, required to be made, an amount equal to the value of the property, if any, held in connection with the arrangement at that time.

See also Notes at end of 146.3.

**Interpretation Bulletins**: IT-415R2: Deregistration of RRSPs.

Division G — Deferred & Special Income Arrangements    S. 146.3(2)(f)(iv)

**Information Circulars**: 78-18R5: Registered retirement income funds.

**(1.1)** [Repealed]

**Notes**: 146.3(1.1) added by 1990 pension bill, effective 1988, and repealed by 1992 technical bill, effective 1993. It defined "spouse" to include a common-law spouse for purposes of 146.3(1)"minimum amount", "retirement income fund", (2)(d), (2)(f)(iv), (6) and (14)(b). A similar rule, extending the meaning of "spouse" to include common-law spouses, applied from 1993 to 2000 for all purposes of the Act, in 252(4).

**(2) Acceptance of fund for registration** — The Minister shall not accept for registration for the purposes of this Act any retirement income fund of an individual unless, in the Minister's opinion, the following conditions are complied with:

(a) the fund provides that the carrier shall make only those payments described in any of paragraphs (d) and (e), the definition "retirement income fund" in subsection (1) and paragraph (14)(b);

(b) the fund provides that payments thereunder may not be assigned in whole or in part;

(c) where the carrier is a person referred to as a depository in section 146, the fund provides that

   (i) the carrier has no right of offset as regards the property held in connection with the fund in respect of any debt or obligation owing to the carrier, and

   (ii) the property held in connection with the fund cannot be pledged, assigned or in any way alienated as security for a loan or for any purpose other than that of the making by the carrier to the annuitant those payments described in paragraph (a);

(d) the fund provides that, except where the annuitant's spouse or common-law partner becomes the annuitant under the fund, the carrier shall, as a consequence of the death of the annuitant, distribute the property held in connection with the fund at the time of the annuitant's death or an amount equal to the value of such property at that time;

(e) the fund provides that, at the direction of the annuitant, the carrier shall transfer all or part of the property held in connection with the fund, or an amount equal to its value at the time of the direction (other than property required to be retained in accordance with the provision described in paragraph (e.1) or (e.2)), together with all information necessary for the continuance of the fund, to a person who has agreed to be a carrier of another registered retirement income fund of the annuitant;

(e.1) where the fund does not govern a trust or the fund governs a trust created before 1998 that does not hold an annuity contract as a qualified investment for the trust, the fund provides that if an annuitant, at any time, directs that the carrier transfer all or part of the property held in connection with the fund, or an amount equal to its value at that time, to a person who has agreed to be a carrier of another registered retirement income fund of the annuitant, the transferor shall retain an amount equal to the lesser of

   (i) the fair market value of such portion of the property as would, if the fair market value thereof does not decline after the transfer, be sufficient to ensure that the minimum amount under the fund for the year in which the transfer is made may be paid to the annuitant in the year, and

   (ii) the fair market value of all the property;

(e.2) where paragraph (e.1) does not apply, the fund provides that if an annuitant, at any time, directs that the carrier transfer all or part of the property held in connection with the fund, or an amount equal to its value at that time, to a person who has agreed to be a carrier of another registered retirement income fund of the annuitant, the transferor shall retain property in the fund sufficient to ensure that the total of

   (i) all amounts each of which is the fair market value, immediately after the transfer, of a property held in connection with the fund that is

      (A) property other than an annuity contract, or

      (B) an annuity contract described, immediately after the transfer, in paragraph (b.1) of the definition "qualified investment" in subsection (1), and

   (ii) all amounts each of which is a reasonable estimate, as of the time of the transfer, of the amount of an annual or more frequent periodic payment under an annuity contract (other than an annuity contract described in clause (i)(B)) that the trust may receive after the transfer and in the year of the transfer

is not less than the amount, if any, by which the minimum amount under the fund for that year exceeds the total of all amounts received out of or under the fund before the transfer that are included in computing the income of the annuitant under the fund for that year;

(f) the fund provides that the carrier shall not accept property as consideration thereunder other than property transferred from

   (i) a registered retirement savings plan under which the individual is the annuitant,

   (ii) another registered retirement income fund under which the individual is the annuitant,

   (iii) the individual to the extent only that the amount of the consideration was an amount described in subparagraph 60(l)(v),

   (iv) a registered retirement income fund or registered retirement savings plan of the individual's spouse or common-law partner or

1377

former spouse or common-law partner under a decree, order or judgment of a competent tribunal, or under a written separation agreement, relating to a division of property between the individual and the individual's spouse or common-law partner or former spouse or common-law partner in settlement of rights arising out of, or on the breakdown of, their marriage or common-law partnership,

(v) a registered pension plan of which the individual is a member (within the meaning assigned by subsection 147.1(1)),

(vi) a registered pension plan in accordance with subsection 147.3(5) or (7), or

(vii) a provincial pension plan in circumstances to which subsection 146(21) applies;

(g) the fund requires that no benefit or loan, other than

(i) a benefit the amount of which is required to be included in computing the annuitant's income,

(ii) an amount referred to in paragraph (5)(a) or (b), or

(iii) the benefit derived from the provision of administrative or investment services in respect of the fund,

that is conditional in any way on the existence of the fund may be extended to the annuitant or to a person with whom the annuitant was not dealing at arm's length; and

(h) the fund in all other respects complies with regulations of the Governor in Council made on the recommendation of the Minister of Finance.

**Related Provisions**: 139.1(13) — Para. 146(2)(c.4) inapplicable to conversion benefit on demutualization of insurer; 146.3(11) — Change in fund after registration; 146.3(14) — Transfers; 172(5) — Appeal from refusal to register; 248(1)"disposition"(g) — Transfer with same annuitant not a disposition; 248(8) — Occurrences as a consequence of death; 252(3) — Extended meaning of "spouse" and "former spouse".

**Notes**: 146.3(2)(d) and (f)(iv) amended by 2000 same-sex partners bill to add reference to "common-law partner" and "common-law partnership", effective for the 2001 and later taxation years, or earlier by election (see Notes to 248(1)"common-law partner").

146.3(2) amended by 1995-97 technical bill as follows:

- Para. (a) amended to add the missing word "fund", accidentally left out in the R.S.C. 1985 (5th Supp.) consolidation, retroactive to taxation years that end after November 1991.
- Para. (e) amended effective for RIFs entered into after July 13, 1990, to add reference to para. (e.2) and to delete a requirement that the transfer by the carrier be "in prescribed form an manner" for all RIFs (including those entered into earlier).
- Para. (e.1) amended, effective for RIFs entered into after July 13, 1990, so that it applies to a RRIF that governs a trust only if the trust was created before 1998 and the trust does not hold an annuity contract as a qualified investment. In any other case where a RRIF governs a trust, see (e.2) instead.
- Para. (e.2) added, effective for RIFs entered into after July 13, 1990. Like 146.3(2)(e.1), it essentially requires the carrier to retain sufficient property to enable it to pay the "minimum

amount" for the year to the annuitant after the transfer. However, it provides special rules dealing with the holding of annuity contracts as qualified investments. While annuities that can be surrendered for cash are treated in the same manner as other RRIF property, for other annuities, the "fair market value" of the retained annuity is ignored. Instead, only the annuity payments estimated to be made after the transfer and in the year of the transfer will effectively be considered to have been retained by the RRIF trust for the purposes of para. (e.2).

146.3(2)(d) amended by 1992 technical bill, effective 1991, as a result of the expanded definition of "annuitant" in 146.3(1). Before 1991, after the words "becomes the annuitant under the fund", read "pursuant to the terms of the fund or the provisions of the will of the deceased annuitant".

146.3(2)(e) amended and (e.1) added by 1991 technical bill, effective for RIFs entered into after July 13, 1990. For earlier RIFs, ignore (e.1) and the parenthetical exclusion in (e) that refers to (e.1).

146.3(2)(f)(iv) amended by 1990 pension bill, effective 1988, and by 1992 technical bill, effective 1993, due to the introduction of an extended definition of "marriage" in 252(4)(b). From 1988 to 1992, in place of "in settlement of rights arising out of, or on the breakdown of, their marriage", read "in settlement of rights arising out of their marriage or other conjugal relationship, on or after the breakdown of the marriage or other relationship".

146.3(2)(f)(v) and (vi) added by 1992 technical bill, effective August 30, 1990, so that a RRIF may receive certain property transferred from a registered pension plan. See 147.3.

146.3(2)(f)(vii) added by 1993 technical bill, effective 1992, to permit a RRIF to receive a lump sum transfer from the Saskatchewan Pension Plan.

**Interpretation Bulletins**: IT-307R3: Spousal registered retirement savings plans.

**Information Circulars**: 78-18R5: Registered retirement income funds; 79-8R3: Forms to use to directly transfer funds to or between plans, or to purchase an annuity.

**Forms**: T550: Application for registration; T2033: Direct transfer under para. 146(16)(a) or 146.3(2)(e).

**(3) No tax while trust governed by fund** — Except as provided in subsection (9), no tax is payable under this Part by a trust on the taxable income of the trust for a taxation year if, throughout the period in the year during which the trust was in existence, the trust was governed by a registered retirement income fund of an individual, except that if the trust has

(a) borrowed money in the year or has borrowed money that it has not repaid before the commencement of the year,

(b) received a gift of property (other than a transfer from a registered retirement savings plan under which the individual is the annuitant (within the meaning of subsection 146(1)) or a transfer from a registered retirement income fund under which the individual is the annuitant)

(i) in the year, or

(ii) in a preceding year and has not divested itself of the property or any property substituted therefor before the commencement of the year, or

(c) carried on any business or businesses in the year,

Division G — Deferred & Special Income Arrangements     S. 146.3(5.1)

tax is payable under this Part by the trust,

(d) where paragraph (a) or (b) applies, on its taxable income for the year, and

(e) where neither paragraph (a) nor (b) applies and where paragraph (c) applies, on the amount, if any, by which

(i) the amount that its taxable income for the year would be if it had no incomes or losses from sources other than from the business or businesses, as the case may be,

exceeds

(ii) such portion of the amount determined under subparagraph (i) in respect of the trust for the year as can reasonably be considered to be income from, or from the disposition of, qualified investments for the trust.

**Related Provisions**: 146.3(3.1) — Exception; 146.3(9) — Tax on income from non-qualified investments; 146.3(15) — Amount earned on RRIF deposit account not taxable to annuitant; 149(1)(x) — RRIF exempt from tax; 206(2) — Part XI tax on excess holdings of foreign property; 207.1(4) — Tax on holding non-qualified investments; 248(5) — Substituted property; Canada-U.S. tax treaty, Art. XVIII:5 — Deferral of income accruing in retirement plan.

**Notes**: See Notes to 146(4) re exemption from U.S. withholding taxes.

146.3(3)(e)(ii) added by 1993 technical bill, effective for 1993 and later taxation years. The amendment recognizes that business income may be allocated to units in limited partnerships that are held by RRIFs, and that the disposition of qualified investments can, in some cases, result in business income (rather than capital gains).

**Information Circulars**: 78-18R5: Registered retirement income funds.

**(3.1) Exception** — Notwithstanding subsection (3), if the last annuitant under a registered retirement income fund has died, tax is payable under this Part by the trust governed by the fund on its taxable income for each year after the year following the year in which the last annuitant under the fund died.

**Related Provisions**: 104(6)(a.2) — Deduction for amounts paid out to beneficiaries.

**Notes**: 146(3.1) amended by 1993 technical bill, effective for 1993 and later taxation years. For 1986 through 1992, read the last few words as "for each year after the year of the annuitant's death". Tax is now payable by the trust only from the second year following death. (The same applies to RRSPs, under 146(4)(c).)

**(4) Disposition or acquisition of property by trust** — Where at any time in a taxation year a trust governed by a registered retirement income fund

(a) disposes of property for a consideration less than the fair market value of the property at the time of the disposition, or for no consideration, or

(b) acquires property for a consideration greater than the fair market value of the property at the time of the acquisition,

2 times the difference between that fair market value and the consideration, if any, shall be included in computing the income for the taxation year of the taxpayer who is the annuitant under the fund at that time.

**Related Provisions**: 212(1)(q), 214(3)(i) — Non-resident withholding tax.

**Regulations**: 215(3) (information return).

**Information Circulars**: 78-18R5: Registered retirement income funds.

**(5) Benefits taxable** — There shall be included in computing the income of a taxpayer for a taxation year all amounts received by the taxpayer in the year out of or under a registered retirement income fund other than the portion thereof that can reasonably be regarded as

(a) part of the amount included in computing the income of another taxpayer by virtue of subsections (6) and (6.2); or

(b) an amount received in respect of the income of the trust under the fund for a taxation year for which the trust was not exempt from tax by virtue of subsection (3.1).

(c) an amount that relates to interest, or to another amount included in computing income otherwise than because of this section, and that would, if the fund were a registered retirement savings plan, be a tax-paid amount (within the meaning assigned by paragraph (b) of the definition "tax-paid amount" in subsection 146(1)).

**Related Provisions**: 56(1)(t) — Income from RRIF; 60(l) — Transfer of refund of premium under RRSP; 139.1(12) — Conversion benefit on demutualization of insurance corporation not taxable; 146.3(1)"retirement income fund" — Requirement to withdraw minimum amount annually; 146.3(15) — Amount earned in RRIF deposit account not taxable; 147.3(13.1) — Withdrawal of excessive transfers to RRSPs and RRIFs; 153(1)(l) — Withholding of tax on RRIF payments; 160.2(2) — Joint and several liability where non-annuitant receives amount from RRIF; 212(1)(q) — Withholding tax on RRIF payment to non-resident; Canada-U.S. tax treaty, Art. XXI:2(a) — RRSP exempt from U.S. tax.

**Notes**: 146.3(5)(c) added by 1995-97 technical bill, effective for deaths after 1992.

See also Notes at end of 146.3.

**Regulations**: 215(2) (information return).

**Information Circulars**: 78-18R5: Registered retirement income funds.

**Forms**: T4RIF: Statement of income from a registered retirement income fund; T4RIF Segment; T4RIF Summ: Return of income out of a registered retirement income fund; T4040: RRSPs and other registered plans for retirement [guide].

**(5.1) Amount included in income** — Where at any time in a taxation year a particular amount in respect of a registered retirement income fund that is a spousal plan (within the meaning assigned by subsection 146(1)) in relation to a taxpayer is required to be included in the income of the taxpayer's spouse or common-law partner and the taxpayer is not living separate and apart from the taxpayer's spouse or common-law partner at that time by reason of the breakdown of their marriage or common-law partnership, there shall be included at that time in computing the taxpayer's income for the year an amount equal to the least of

(a) the total of all amounts each of which is a premium (within the meaning assigned by subsection 146(1)) paid by the taxpayer in the year or in one of the two immediately preceding taxation years to a registered retirement savings plan under which the taxpayer's spouse or common-law partner was the annuitant (within the meaning assigned by subsection 146(1)) at the time the premium was paid,

(b) the particular amount, and

(c) the amount, if any, by which

(i) the total of all amounts each of which is an amount in respect of the fund that is required, in the year and at or before that time, to be included in the income of the taxpayer's spouse or common-law partner

exceeds

(ii) the minimum amount under the fund for the year.

**Related Provisions**: 60(l) — Transfer of refund of premiums under RRSP; 60(j.2) — Transfer to spousal RRSP; 146(8.21) — Premium deemed not paid; 146(8.3) — Spousal RRSP payments; 146(8.6) — RRSP — Spouse's income; 146.3(5.4) — Spouse's income; 146.3(5.5) — Application of subsec. (5.1); 147.3(13.1) — Withdrawal of excessive transfers to RRSPs and RRIFs.

**Notes**: 146.3(5.1) amended by 2000 same-sex partners bill to add reference to "common-law partner" and "common-law partnership", effective for the 2001 and later taxation years, or earlier by election (see Notes to 248(1)"common-law partner").

146.3(5.1) amended by 1990 pension bill, effective 1991. For 1989 and 1990, read:

(5.1) Where at any time in a taxation year a particular amount, in respect of a registered retirement income fund that received property from a registered retirement savings plan to which a premium deductible under paragraph 60(j.2) or subsection 146(5.1) has been paid, is required to be included in the income of the taxpayer's spouse, except where the taxpayer is living separate and apart from the taxpayer's spouse at that time by reason of the breakdown of their marriage, all premiums paid by the taxpayer in the year or in one of the two immediately preceding taxation years to the extent that they were deductible under paragraph 60(j.2) or subsection 146(5.1) in computing the taxpayer's income for a year shall be included at that time in computing the taxpayer's income for the year to the extent that the aggregate of the particular amounts paid in the year exceeds the minimum amount under the fund for the year.

1992 technical bill, subsec. 84(10), provides that amended 146.3(1)"minimum amount" does not apply for the purposes of subsec. 146.3(5.1) to payments made before 1993.

**Interpretation Bulletins**: IT-307R3: Spousal registered retirement savings plans; IT-124R6: Contributions to registered retirement savings plans.

**Forms**: T4RIF: Statement of income from a registered retirement income fund; T4RIF Segment; T4RIF Summ: Return of income out of a registered retirement income fund; T2205: Calculation of amounts from a spousal RRSP or RRIF to be included in income.

**(5.2)** [Repealed under former Act]

**Notes**: 146.3(5.2) repealed by 1990 pension bill, effective 1991. It provided a rule of interpretation that is now superfluous.

**(5.3) Ordering** — Where a taxpayer has paid more than one premium described in subsection (5.1), such a premium or part thereof paid by the taxpayer at any time shall be deemed to have been included in computing the taxpayer's income by virtue of that subsection before premiums or parts thereof paid by the taxpayer after that time.

**(5.4) Spouse's income** — Where, in respect of an amount required at any time in a taxation year to be included in computing the income of a taxpayer's spouse or common-law partner, all or part of a premium has, by reason of subsection (5.1), been included in computing the taxpayer's income for the year, the following rules apply:

(a) the premium or part thereof, as the case may be, shall, for the purposes of subsections (5.1) and 146(8.3) after that time, be deemed not to have been a premium paid to a registered retirement savings plan under which the taxpayer's spouse or common-law partner was the annuitant (within the meaning assigned by subsection 146(1)); and

(b) an amount equal to the premium or part thereof, as the case may be, deducted in computing the income of the spouse or common-law partner for the year.

**Related Provisions**: 146(8.6) — Spouse's income.

**Notes**: 146.3(5.4) amended by 2000 same-sex partners bill to add reference to "common-law partner", effective for the 2001 and later taxation years, or earlier by election (see Notes to 248(1)"common-law partner").

146.3(5.4) amended by 1990 pension bill, effective 1991.

**(5.5) Where subsec. (5.1) does not apply** — Subsection (5.1) does not apply

(a) in respect of a taxpayer at any time during the year in which the taxpayer dies;

(b) in respect of a taxpayer where either the taxpayer or the annuitant is a non-resident at the particular time referred to in that subsection;

(c) to any payment that is received in full or partial commutation of a registered retirement savings plan or a registered retirement income fund and in respect of which a deduction was made under paragraph 60(l) if, where the deduction was in respect of the acquisition of an annuity, the terms of the annuity provide that it cannot be commuted, and it is not commuted, in whole or in part within 3 years after the acquisition; or

(d) in respect of an amount that is deemed by subsection (6) to have been received by an annuitant under a registered retirement income fund immediately before the annuitant's death.

**Notes**: 146.3(5.5)(d) added by 1990 pension bill, effective 1988.

**(6) Where last annuitant dies** — Where the last annuitant under a registered retirement income fund dies, that annuitant shall be deemed to have received, immediately before death, an amount out of or under a registered retirement income fund equal to the fair market value of the property of the fund at the time of the death.

**Related Provisions**: 56(1)(t) — Income from RRIF; 146(8.8) — Parallel rule for RRSPs; 146.3(5.5) — Application of subsec. (5.1); 146.3(6.2) — Amount deductible; 160.2(2) — Joint and several liability for tax owing on payment from RRIF; 212(1)(q), 214(3)(i) — Non-resident withholding tax; 257 — Formula cannot calculate to less than zero.

**Notes**: 146.3(6) amended by 1993 technical bill, effective for deaths in 1993 or later. For deaths from 1979 through 1992, read:

> (6) **Effect of death where person other than spouse becomes entitled** — Where the last annuitant under a registered retirement income fund dies, the annuitant shall be deemed to have received, immediately before the annuitant's death, an amount out of or under a registered retirement income fund equal to the amount, if any, by which
>
> > (a) the fair market [value] of all the property of the fund at the time of death
>
> exceeds
>
> > (b) the portion thereof that, as a consequence of the death, becomes receivable by the annuitant's spouse.

**Regulations**: 215(4) (information return).

**Forms**: RC4178: Death of a RRIF annuitant [guide].

**(6.1) Designated benefit deemed received** — A designated benefit of an individual in respect of a registered retirement income fund that is received by the legal representative of the last annuitant under the fund shall be deemed

(a) to be received by the individual out of or under the fund at the time it is received by the legal representative; and

(b) except for the purpose of the definition "designated benefit" in subsection (1), not to be received out of or under the fund by any other person.

**Related Provisions**: 60(l)(v)(B.1) — Rollover of designated benefits to child or grandchild on death; 146(8.1) — Parallel rule for RRSPs; 212(1)(q), 214(3)(i) — Non-resident withholding tax.

**Notes**: 146.3(6.1) amended by 1993 technical bill, effective for deaths in 1993 or later. For deaths from 1979 through 1992, read:

> (6.1) **Amount deemed received by child or grandchild as a result of death** — Such portion of an amount paid in a taxation year out of or under a registered retirement income fund after the death of the last annuitant thereunder to the annuitant's legal representative as, had that portion been paid under the fund to a beneficiary of the deceased's estate, would have been a refund of premiums (within the meaning assigned by subsection 146(1)) if the fund were a registered retirement savings plan shall, to the extent it is so designated jointly by the legal representative and the beneficiary in prescribed form filed with the Minister, be deemed
>
> > (a) to be received by the beneficiary in the year as a benefit that is a refund of premiums under a registered retirement savings plan (within the meanings assigned by subsection 146(1)); and
> >
> > (b) not to be received out of or under a registered retirement income fund.

**Forms**: RC4178: Death of a RRIF annuitant [guide].

**(6.11) Transfer of designated benefit** — For the purpose of subparagraph 60(l)(v), the eligible amount of a particular individual for a taxation year in respect of a registered retirement income fund is nil unless the particular individual was

(a) a spouse or common-law partner of the last annuitant under the fund, or

(b) a child or grandchild of that annuitant who was dependent because of physical or mental infirmity on that annuitant,

in which case the eligible amount shall be determined by the formula

$$A \times \left[ 1 - \frac{(B-C)}{D} \right]$$

where

A is the portion of the designated benefit of the particular individual in respect of the fund that is included because of subsection (5) in computing the particular individual's income for the year,

B is the minimum amount under the fund for the year,

C is the lesser of

(a) the total amounts included because of subsection (5) in computing the income of an annuitant under the fund for the year in respect of amounts received by the annuitant out of or under the fund, and

(b) the minimum amount under the fund for the year, and

D is the total of all amounts each of which is the portion of a designated benefit of an individual in respect of the fund that is included because of subsection (5) in computing the individual's income for the year.

**Related Provisions**: 257 — Formula cannot calculate to less than zero.

**Notes**: 146.3(6.11)(a) amended by 2000 same-sex partners bill to add reference to "common-law partner", effective for the 2001 and later taxation years, or earlier by election (see Notes to 248(1)"common-law partner").

146.3(6.11) added by 1993 technical bill, effective for deaths in 1993 or later.

**Forms**: RC4178: Death of a RRIF annuitant [guide].

**(6.2) Amount deductible** — There may be deducted from the amount deemed by subsection (6) to be received by an annuitant out of or under a registered retirement income fund an amount not exceeding the amount determined by the formula

$$A \times \left[ 1 - \frac{(B + C - D)}{(B + C)} \right]$$

where

A is the total of

(a) all designated benefits of individuals in respect of the fund,

(b) all amounts that would, if the fund were a registered retirement savings plan, be tax-paid amounts (in this subsection having the meaning assigned by subsection 146(1)) in respect of the fund received by individuals who received, otherwise than because of subsection (6.1), designated benefits in respect of the fund, and

(c) all amounts each of which is an amount that would, if the fund were a registered retirement savings plan, be a tax-paid amount in respect of the fund received by the legal representative of the last annuitant under the fund, to the extent that the legal representative would have been entitled to designate that tax-paid amount under paragraph (a) of the definition "designated benefit" in subsection (1) if tax-paid amounts were not excluded in determining refunds of premiums (as defined in subsection 146(1));

B is the fair market value of the property of the fund at the particular time that is the later of

(a) the end of the first calendar year that begins after the death of the annuitant, and

(b) the time immediately after the last time that any designated benefit in respect of the fund is received by an individual;

C is the total of all amounts paid out of or under the fund after the death of the last annuitant thereunder and before the particular time; and

D is the lesser of

(a) the fair market value of the property of the fund at the time of the death of the last annuitant thereunder, and

(b) the sum of the values of B and C in respect of the fund.

**Related Provisions**: 118.1(5.3) — Designation of charity as beneficiary of RRIF; 146(8.9) — Parallel rule for RRSPs.

**Notes**: 146.3(6.2) amended by 1993 technical bill and by 1995-97 technical bill (to add paras. A(b) and (c)), both effective for deaths in 1993 or later. For deaths from 1979 through 1992, read:

(6.2) There may be deducted from the amount deemed by subsection (6) to have been received by an annuitant under a registered retirement income fund the total of all amounts each of which is

(a) that portion of an amount paid out of or under the fund that is deemed to be received by a beneficiary as a benefit that is a refund of premiums pursuant to subsection (6.1), or

(b) an amount paid under the fund to a child or grandchild of the annuitant that would be a refund of premiums (within the meaning assigned by subsection 146(1)) had the fund been a registered retirement savings plan

and each amount described in paragraph (b) that is paid to a child or grandchild of the deceased shall be deemed to be received by the child or grandchild, as the case may be, as a benefit that is a refund of premiums under a registered retirement savings plan (within the meanings assigned by subsection 146(1)) and not to be received out of or under a registered retirement income fund.

**Forms**: RC4178: Death of a RRIF annuitant [guide].

**(7) Acquisition of non-qualified investment by trust** — Where at any time in a taxation year a trust governed by a registered retirement income fund

(a) acquires an investment that is not a qualified investment, or

(b) uses or permits to be used a property of the trust as security for a loan,

the fair market value of

(c) the investment at the time it was acquired by the trust, or

(d) the property used as security at the time it commenced to be so used

as the case may be, shall be included in computing the income for the year of the taxpayer who is the annuitant under the fund at that time.

**Related Provisions**: 146.3(9) — Tax payable where non-qualified investment acquired; 146.3(10) — Recovery of property used as security; 212(1)(q), 214(3)(i) — Non-resident withholding tax; 259(1) — Election for proportional holdings in trust property.

**Notes**: See Notes to 146.3(9) and 146(10).

**Regulations**: 215(3) (information return).

**Remission Orders**: *Lionaird Capital Corporation Notes Remission Order*, P.C. 1999-737 (tax under 146(10) waived because taxpayers thought they were qualified investments).

**(8) Disposition of non-qualified investment** — Where at any time in a taxation year a trust governed by a registered retirement income fund disposes of a property that, when acquired, was not a qualified investment, there may be deducted in computing the income for the taxation year of the taxpayer who is the annuitant under the fund at that time, an amount equal to the lesser of

(a) the amount that, by virtue of subsection (7), was included in computing the income of a taxpayer in respect of the acquisition of that property, and

(b) the proceeds of disposition of the property.

**Related Provisions**: 259(1) — Election for proportional holdings in trust property.

**Regulations**: 215(3) (information return).

**(9) Tax payable where non-qualified investment acquired** — Where a trust governed by a registered retirement income fund has acquired a property that is not a qualified investment,

(a) tax is payable under this Part by the trust on the amount that its taxable income for the year would be if it had no incomes or losses from sources other than the property that is not a qualified investment or no capital gains or capital losses other than from the disposition of that property, as the case may be; and

(b) for the purposes of paragraph (a),

(i) "income" includes dividends described in section 83, and

(ii) paragraphs 38(a) and (b) shall be read without reference to the fractions set out therein.

**Related Provisions**: 146.3(3) — No tax while trust governed by fund; 146.3(7) — Acquisition of non-qualified investment by trust; 149(1)(x) — RRIF exemption. 201.7(4) — Tax payable by RRIF on non-qualified investments; 259(1) — Election for proportional holdings in trust property.

**Notes**: 146.3(9) imposes tax on the *income* from non-qualified investments. 207.1(4) imposes a penalty tax on the *holding* of the non-qualified investments. 146.3(7) taxes the beneficiary on the *acquisition* of the non-qualified investment, with an offsetting deduction under 146.3(8) when it is disposed of. See Notes to 146(10.1).

**Information Circulars**: 78-18R5: Registered retirement income funds.

### (10) Recovery of property used as security —

Where at any time in a taxation year a loan for which a trust governed by a registered retirement income fund has used or permitted to be used trust property as security ceases to be extant, and the fair market value of the property so used was included by virtue of subsection (7) in computing the income of a taxpayer who was the annuitant under the fund, there may be deducted in computing the income for a taxation year of the taxpayer who is at that time the annuitant, an amount equal to the amount, if any, remaining when

(a) the net loss (exclusive of payments by the trust as or on account of interest) sustained by the trust in consequence of its using or permitting to be used the property as security for the loan and not as a result of a change in the fair market value of the property

is deducted from

(b) the amount so included in computing the income of a taxpayer in consequence of the trust's using or permitting to be used the property as security for the loan.

**Regulations**: 215(3) (information return).

### (11) Change in fund after registration —

Where, on any day after a retirement income fund has been accepted by the Minister for registration for the purposes of this Act, the fund is revised or amended or a new fund is substituted therefor, and the fund as revised or amended or the new fund substituted therefor, as the case may be, (in this subsection referred to as the "amended fund") does not comply with the requirements of this section for its acceptance by the Minister for registration for the purposes of this Act, the following rules apply:

(a) the amended fund shall be deemed, for the purposes of this Act, not to be a registered retirement income fund; and

(b) the taxpayer who was the annuitant under the fund before it became an amended fund shall, in computing the taxpayer's income for the taxation year that includes that day, include as income received out of the fund at that time an amount equal to the fair market value of all the property held in connection with the fund immediately before that time.

**Related Provisions**: 146.3(2) — Requirements for acceptance for registration; 146.3(12) — Where arrangement deemed to be new fund substituted for RRIF; 146.3(13) — Where fund deemed revised or amended; 147.3(13.1) — Withdrawal of excessive transfers to RRSPs and RRIFs; 153(1)(l) — Withholdings; 204.2(1.4) — Deemed receipt where RRSP or RRIF amended; 212(1)(q), 214(3)(i) — Non-resident withholding tax.

**Information Circulars**: 78-18R5: Registered retirement income funds.

**Forms**: T2205: Calculation of amounts from a spousal RRSP or RRIF to be included in income.

### (12) Idem —

For the purposes of subsection (11), an arrangement under which a right or obligation under a retirement income fund is released or extinguished either wholly or in part and either in exchange or substitution for any right or obligation, or otherwise (other than an arrangement the sole object and legal effect of which is to revise or amend the fund) or under which payment of any amount by way of loan or otherwise is made on the security of a right under a retirement income fund, shall be deemed to be a new fund substituted for the retirement income fund.

**Regulations**: 215(4) (information return).

### (13) Idem —

Where at any time a benefit or loan is extended or continues to be extended as a consequence of the existence of a registered retirement income fund and that benefit or loan would be prohibited if the fund met the requirement for registration contained in paragraph (2)(g), for the purposes of subsection (11), the fund shall be deemed to have been revised or amended at that time so that it fails to meet the requirement for registration contained in paragraph (2)(g).

### (14) Transfers —

Notwithstanding anything in this section, an amount

(a) transferred as described in paragraph (2)(e), or

(b) transferred from a registered retirement income fund of an annuitant to a registered retirement income fund or registered retirement savings plan of the annuitant's spouse or common-law partner or former spouse or common-law partner under a decree, order or judgment of a competent tribunal, or under a written separation agreement, relating to a division of property between the annuitant and the annuitant's spouse or common-law partner or former spouse or common-law partner in settlement of rights arising out of, or on the breakdown of, their marriage or common-law partnership,

shall be deemed not to be an amount received by the annuitant out of or under a registered retirement income fund.

**Related Provisions**: 146(16)(b) — Transfer of RRSP on marriage breakdown; 146.3(2)(c) — Acceptance of fund for registration; 252(3) — Extended meaning of "spouse" and "former spouse".

**Notes**: 146.3(14) amended by 2000 same-sex partners bill to add reference to "common-law partner" and "common-law partnership", effective for the 2001 and later taxation years, or earlier by election (see Notes to 248(1)"common-law partner").

146.3(14)(b) amended by 1990 pension bill, effective 1988, and amended by 1992 technical bill, effective 1993, due to the introduc-

**S. 146.3(14)** — Income Tax Act, Part I

tion of an extended definition of "marriage" in 252(4)(b). Before 1993, in place of "arising out of, or on the breakdown of, their marriage", read "arising out of their marriage or other conjugal relationship, on or after the breakdown of the marriage or other relationship".

**Interpretation Bulletins**: IT-307R3: Spousal registered retirement savings plans; IT-528: Transfers of funds between registered plans.

**Remission Orders**: *Certain Taxpayers Remission Order, 1999-2*, 1999-1855, s. 2 (remission to Quebec judges for excess contributions in 1989-90 transferred under 146.3(14)).

**Information Circulars**: 78-18R5: Registered retirement income funds; 79-8R3: Forms to use to directly transfer funds to or between plans, or to purchase an annuity.

**Forms**: T2033: Direct transfer under para. 146(16)(a) or 146.3(2)(e); T2220: Transfer between RRSPs or RRIFs on marriage breakdown.

**(15) Credited or added amount deemed not received** — Where

(a) an amount is credited or added to a deposit with a depositary referred to in paragraph (d) of the definition "carrier" in subsection (1) as interest or income in respect of the deposit,

(b) the deposit is a registered retirement income fund at the time the amount is credited or added to the deposit, and

(c) during the calendar year in which the amount is credited or added or during the preceding calendar year, the annuitant under the fund was alive,

the amount shall be deemed not to be received by the annuitant or any other person solely because of the crediting or adding.

**Notes**: 146.3(15) amended by 1993 technical bill, effective for deaths in 1993 or later. (The same change with respect to RRSPs was made in 146(20).) For deaths from 1981 through 1992, read:

(15) Where amount credited or added deemed not received — Where an amount is credited or added to a deposit with a depositary referred to in paragraph (d) of the definition "carrier" in subsection (1) as interest or income in respect of the deposit, and where

(a) the deposit is a registered retirement income fund at the time the amount is credited or added to the deposit, and

(b) the annuitant under the fund is alive during the year in which the amount is credited or added,

the amount shall be deemed not to be received by the annuitant by reason only of the crediting or adding.

**Notes [s. 146.3]**: For a recent review of RRIFs, see Mark Kaplan, "Registered Retirement Income Funds: An Update", 47(1) *Canadian Tax Journal* 134-147 (1999).

**Definitions [s. 146.3]**: "amount" — 248(1); "annuitant" — 146.3(1); "annuity" — 248(1); "arm's length" — 251(1); "beneficial owner" — 248(3); "calendar year" — *Interpretation Act* 37(1)(a); "capital gain", "capital loss" — 39(1), 248(1); "carrier" — 146.3(1); "common-law partner", "common-law partnership" — 248(1); "consequence of the death" — 248(8); "corporation" — 248(1), *Interpretation Act*; "depositary" — 146(1)"retirement savings plan"(b)(iii), 146.3(1)"carrier"(d); "former spouse" — 252(3); "held" — 146.3(1); "individual", "legal representative" — 248(1); "licensed annuities provider" — 147(1), 248(1); "listed" — 87(10); "minimum amount" — 146.3(1); "Minister", "non-resident", "person", "prescribed" — 248(1); "prescribed stock exchange in Canada" — Reg. 3200; "property" — 248(1); "property held" — 146.3(1); "province" — *Interpretation Act* 35(1); "qualified investment" — 146.3(1); "received" — 146.3(15); "registered retirement income fund" — 146.3(1), 248(1); "registered retirement savings plan" — 146(1), 248(1); "retirement income fund" — 146.3(1), 248(1); "separation agreement" — 248(1); "spouse" — 252(3); "substituted property" — 248(5); "surviving spouse" — 146.3(1)"annuitant"(b); "taxable income" — 2(2), 248(1); "taxation year" — 249; "taxpayer" — 248(1); "trust" — 104(1), 248(1), (3).

## Deferred Profit Sharing Plans

**147. (1) Definitions** — In this section,

**"deferred profit sharing plan"** means a profit sharing plan accepted by the Minister for registration for the purposes of this Act, on application therefor in prescribed manner by a trustee under the plan and an employer of employees who are beneficiaries under the plan, as complying with the requirements of this section;

**Related Provisions**: 128.1(10)"excluded right or interest"(a)(iv) — No deemed disposition of DPSP on emigration.

**Interpretation Bulletins**: IT-528: Transfers of funds between registered plans.

**"forfeited amount"**, under a deferred profit sharing plan or a plan the registration of which has been revoked pursuant to subsection (14) or (14.1), means an amount to which a beneficiary under the plan has ceased to have any rights, other than the portion thereof, if any, that is payable as a consequence of the death of the beneficiary to a person who is entitled thereto by virtue of the participation of the beneficiary in the plan;

**"licensed annuities provider"** means a person licensed or otherwise authorized under the laws of Canada or a province to carry on in Canada an annuities business;

**Related Provisions**: 248(1)"licensed annuities provider" — Definition applies to entire Act.

**Notes**: Definition "licensed annuities provided" added by 1996 Budget, retroactive to 1992.

**"profit sharing plan"** means an arrangement under which payments computed by reference to an employer's profits from the employer's business, or by reference to those profits and the profits, if any, from the business of a corporation with which the employer does not deal at arm's length, are or have been made by the employer to a trustee in trust for the benefit of employees or former employees of that employer.

**Related Provisions**: 147(16) — Payments out of profits; 248(1)"deferred profit sharing plan", "profit sharing plan" — Definitions apply to entire Act; 248(8) — Occurrences as a consequence of death.

**Notes**: 147(1) amended by 1990 pension bill, effective 1991. For 1972 through 1990, 147(1)(a) defined "deferred profit sharing plan" and 147(1)(b), "profit sharing plan".

**Regulations**: 1501 (prescribed manner).

**Interpretation Bulletins**: IT-280R: Employees profit sharing plans — payments computed by reference to profits.

1384

**Information Circulars**: 77-1R4: Deferred profit sharing plans; 79-8R3: Forms to use to directly transfer funds to or between plans, or to purchase an annuity. See also list at end of s. 147.

**Forms**: T3D: Income tax return for DPSP or revoked DPSP.

**(1.1) Participating employer** — An employer is considered to participate in a profit sharing plan where the employer makes or has made payments under the plan to a trustee in trust for the benefit of employees or former employees of the employer.

**Notes**: 147(1.1) added by 1996 Budget, retroactive to 1989. The Department of Finance indicates that it was "added for clarity and does not represent a change in policy."

**(2) Acceptance of plan for registration** — The Minister shall not accept for registration for the purposes of this Act any profit sharing plan unless, in the Minister's opinion, it complies with the following conditions:

(a) the plan provides that each payment made under the plan to a trustee in trust for the benefit of beneficiaries thereunder is the total of amounts each of which is required to be allocated by the trustee in the year in which it is received by the trustee, to the individual beneficiary in respect of whom the amount was so paid;

(a.1) the plan includes a stipulation that no contribution may be made to the plan other than

(i) a contribution made in accordance with the terms of the plan by an employer for the benefit of the employer's employees who are beneficiaries under the plan, or

(ii) an amount transferred to the plan in accordance with subsection (19);

(b) the plan does not provide for the payment of any amount to an employee or other beneficiary thereunder by way of loan;

(c) the plan provides that no part of the funds of the trust governed by the plan may be invested in notes, bonds, debentures, bankers' acceptances or similar obligations of

(i) an employer by whom payments are made in trust to a trustee under the plan for the benefit of beneficiaries thereunder, or

(ii) a corporation with whom that employer does not deal at arm's length;

(d) the plan provides that no part of the funds of the trust governed by the plan may be invested in shares of a corporation at least 50% of the property of which consists of notes, bonds, debentures, bankers' acceptances or similar obligations of an employer or a corporation described in paragraph (c);

(e) the plan includes a provision stipulating that no right or interest under the plan of an employee who is a beneficiary thereunder is capable, either in whole or in part, of surrender or assignment;

(f) the plan includes a provision stipulating that each of the trustees under the plan shall be resident in Canada;

(g) the plan provides that, if a corporation licensed or otherwise authorized under the laws of Canada or a province to carry on in Canada the business of offering to the public its services as trustee is not a trustee under the plan, there shall be at least 3 trustees under the plan who shall be individuals;

(h) the plan provides that all income received, capital gains made and capital losses sustained by the trust governed by the plan must be allocated to beneficiaries under the plan on or before a day 90 days after the end of the year in which they were received, made or sustained, as the case may be, to the extent that they have not been allocated in years preceding that year;

(i) the plan provides that each amount allocated or reallocated by a trustee under the plan to a beneficiary under the plan vest irrevocably in that beneficiary,

(i) in the case of an amount allocated or reallocated before 1991, at a time that is not later than 5 years after the end of the year in which it was allocated or reallocated, unless the beneficiary becomes, before that time, an individual who is not an employee of any employer who participates in the plan, and

(ii) in the case of any other amount, not later than the later of the time of allocation or reallocation and the day on which the beneficiary completes a period of 24 consecutive months as a beneficiary under the plan or under any other deferred profit sharing plan for which the plan can reasonably be considered to have been substituted;

(i.1) the plan requires that each forfeited amount under the plan and all earnings of the plan reasonably attributable thereto be paid to employers who participate in the plan, or be reallocated to beneficiaries under the plan, on or before the later of December 31, 1991 and December 31 of the year immediately following the calendar year in which the amount is forfeited, or such later time as is permitted in writing by the Minister under subsection (2.2);

(j) the plan provides that a trustee under the plan inform, in writing, all new beneficiaries under the plan of their rights under the plan;

(k) the plan provides that, in respect of each beneficiary under the plan who has been employed by an employer who participates in the plan, all amounts vested under the plan in the beneficiary become payable

(i) to the beneficiary, or

(ii) in the event of the beneficiary's death, to another person designated by the beneficiary or to the beneficiary's estate, not later than the earlier of

(iii) the end of the year in which the beneficiary attains 69 years of age, and

(iv) 90 days after the earliest of

(A) the death of the beneficiary,

(B) the day on which the beneficiary ceases to be employed by an employer who participates in the plan where, at the time of ceasing to be so employed, the beneficiary is not employed by another employer who participates in the plan, and

(C) the termination or winding-up of the plan,

except that the plan may provide that, on election by the beneficiary, all or any part of the amounts payable to the beneficiary may be paid

(v) in equal instalments payable not less frequently than annually over a period not exceeding 10 years from the day on which the amount became payable, or

(vi) by a trustee under the plan to a licensed annuities provider to purchase for the beneficiary an annuity where

(A) payment of the annuity is to begin not later than the end of the year in which the beneficiary attains 69 years of age, and

(B) the guaranteed term, if any, of the annuity does not exceed 15 years;

(k.1) the plan requires that no benefit or loan, other than

(i) a benefit the amount of which is required to be included in computing the beneficiary's income,

(ii) an amount referred to in paragraph (10)(b),

(ii.1) an amount paid pursuant to or under the plan by a trustee under the plan to a licensed annuities provider to purchase for a beneficiary under the plan an annuity to which subparagraph (k)(vi) applies,

(iii) a benefit derived from an allocation or reallocation referred to in subsection (2), or

(iv) the benefit derived from the provision of administrative or investment services in respect of the plan,

that is conditional in any way on the existence of the plan may be extended to a beneficiary thereunder or to a person with whom the beneficiary was not dealing at arm's length;

(k.2) the plan provides that no individual who is

(i) a person related to the employer,

(ii) a person who is, or is related to, a specified shareholder of the employer or of a corporation related to the employer,

(iii) where the employer is a partnership, a person related to a member of the partnership, or

(iv) where the employer is a trust, a person who is, or is related to, a beneficiary under the trust

may become a beneficiary under the plan; and

(l) the plan, in all other respects, complies with regulations of the Governor in Council made on the recommendation of the Minister of Finance.

**Related Provisions**: 56(1)(d.2)(iii) — Income from annuity purchased with plan funds is taxable; 146(5.21)(b) — Anti-avoidance re pension adjustment; 147(1.1) — Meaning of "participates" in a profit sharing plan; 147(2.1) — Terms limiting contributions; 147(2.2) — Reallocation of forfeitures; 147(10)(a) — Amount used to purchase annuity under 147(2)(k)(vi) is not taxable; 147(10.3) — Amount contributed to or forfeited under a plan; 147(10.6) — Where pre-1997 annuity has not begun by age 69; 147(14) — Revocation of registration where plan ceases to comply with requirements; 147(17) — Meaning of "other beneficiary"; 147(21) — Restrictions re transfers from DPSPs; 172(3) — Appeal from refusal to register, revocation of registration, etc.; 198–204 — Taxes on DPSPs and revoked plans; 204.1(3) — Tax payable by DPSP on excess contributions; 204.2(4) — Definition of "excess amount" for a DPSP.

**Notes**: 147(2)(a.1) and (i.1) added and para. (i) amended by 1990 pension bill, effective 1991. Subpara. (i)(ii) does not apply for years before 1991.

147(2)(c) and (d) amended by 1993 technical bill to add reference to bankers' acceptances, effective for 1993 and later taxation years.

147(2)(k) amended by 1996 Budget, effective 1997, except that

(a) where a beneficiary under a profit sharing plan turned 70 before 1997,

(i) in applying 147(2)(k)(iii), read it as:

(iii) 90 days after the day on which the beneficiary attains 71 years of age, and

(ii) in applying 147(2)(k)(vi)(A), read "the end of the year in which the beneficiary attains 69 years of age" as "the day on which the beneficiary attains 71 years of age", and

(b) where the beneficiary under a profit sharing plan turned 69 in 1996, in applying 147(2)(k)(iii) and (vi)(A), read "70 years" instead of "69 years".

The above amendment requires a DPSP to provide for vested amounts to become payable no later than the end of the year in which the employee turns 69 (rather than 90 days after the employee turns 71). This is consistent with the RRSP changes in 146(2)(b.4). The amendment also requires any annuity whose purchase is provided for by the terms of a DPSP to commence by the end of the year in which the employee turns 69. Finally, it requires a DPSP to provide for amounts to become payable on termination of employment with a participating employer only if, at that time, the employee is not employed by any other employer participating in the plan.

Since these amendments apply after 1996, any existing DPSPs that did not comply as of January 1, 1997 became revocable due to 147(14)(c.2) and (h). (See also 147(10.6) re DPSP annuities purchased before 1997.)

Before the amendments, since 1972, read:

(k) the plan provides that, in respect of each employee who is a beneficiary under the plan, all amounts vested in the employee become payable to the employee or, in the event of the employee's death, to a beneficiary designated by the employee or to the employee's estate, not later than 90 days after the earliest of

    (i) the death of the employee,

    (ii) the day on which the employee ceases to be employed by an employer who makes or has made payments under the plan to a trustee under the plan,

    (iii) the day on which the employee becomes 71 years of age, and

    (iv) the termination or winding up of the plan, except that the plan may provide that, on election by the employee, all or any part of the amounts payable to the employee may be paid

    (v) in equal instalments payable not less frequently than annually over a period not exceeding 10 years from the day on which the amount became payable, or

    (vi) by a trustee under the plan to a person licensed or otherwise authorized under the laws of Canada or a province to carry on in Canada an annuities business, to purchase for the employee an annuity commencing not later than a day 71 years after the day of the employee's birth, the guaranteed term of which, if any, does not exceed 15 years;

147(2)(k.1) amended by 1996 Budget, retroactive to 1992, to delete reference to 147(10)(a) from subpara. (ii) and to add subpara. (ii.1).

**Regulations**: 4900(2) (obligations described in 147(2)(c) are not qualified investments).

**Interpretation Bulletins**: IT-280R: Employees profit sharing plans — payments computed by reference to profits; IT-281R2: Elections on single payments from a deferred profit-sharing plan; IT-363R2: Deferred profit sharing plans — deductibility of employer contributions and taxation of amounts received by a beneficiary; IT-517R: Pension tax credit.

**Information Circulars**: 74-1R5: Form T2037 — Notice of purchase of annuity with "plan" funds; 78-14R2: Guidelines for trust companies and other persons responsible for filing. See also list at end of s. 147.

**Forms**: T2037: Notice of purchase of annuity with "plan" funds; T2214: Application for registration as a deferred profit sharing plan.

**(2.1) Terms limiting contributions** — The Minister shall not accept for registration for the purposes of this Act a profit sharing plan unless it includes terms that are adequate to ensure that the requirements of subsection (5.1) in respect of the plan will be satisfied for each calendar year.

**Notes**: 147(2.1) added by 1990 pension bill, effective 1991.

**(2.2) Reallocation of forfeitures** — The Minister may, on written application, extend the time for satisfying the requirements of paragraph (2)(i.1) where

    (a) the total of the forfeited amounts arising in a calendar year is greater than normal because of unusual circumstances; and

    (b) the forfeited amounts are to be reallocated on a reasonable basis to a majority of beneficiaries under the plan.

**Notes**: 147(2.2) added by 1990 pension bill, effective 1991.

**(3) Acceptance of employees profit sharing plan for registration** — The Minister shall not accept for registration for the purposes of this Act any employees profit sharing plan unless all the capital gains of or made by the trust governed by the plan before the date of application for registration of the plan and all the capital losses of or sustained by the trust before that date have been allocated by the trustee under the plan to employees and other beneficiaries thereunder.

**(4) Capital gains determined** — For the purposes of subsections (3) and (11), such amount as may be determined by the Minister, on request in prescribed manner by the trustee of a trust governed by an employees profit sharing plan, shall be deemed to be the amount of

    (a) the capital gains of or made by the trust governed by the plan before the date of application for registration of the plan, or

    (b) the capital losses of or sustained by the trust before that date,

as the case may be.

**(5) Registration date** — Where a profit sharing plan is accepted by the Minister for registration as a deferred profit sharing plan, the plan shall be deemed to have become registered as a deferred profit sharing plan

    (a) on the date the application for registration of the plan was made; or

    (b) where in the application for registration a later date is specified as the date on which the plan is to commence as a deferred profit sharing plan, on that date.

**Related Provisions**: 144(11) — Taxation year of trust accepted as DPSP.

**(5.1) Contribution limits** — For the purposes of subsections (2.1) and (9) and paragraph (14)(c.4), the requirements of this subsection in respect of a deferred profit sharing plan are satisfied for a calendar year if, in the case of each beneficiary under the plan and each employer in respect of whom the beneficiary's pension credit (as prescribed by regulation) for the year under the plan is greater than nil,

    (a) the total of all amounts each of which is the beneficiary's pension credit (as prescribed by regulation) for the year in respect of the employer under a deferred profit sharing plan does not exceed the lesser of

        (i) $1/2$ of the money purchase limit for the year, and

        (ii) 18% of the amount that would be the beneficiary's compensation (within the meaning assigned by subsection 147.1(1)) from the employer for the year if the definition "compensation" in subsection 147.1(1) were read without reference to paragraph (b) of that definition;

    (b) the total of all amounts each of which is the beneficiary's pension credit (as prescribed by regulation) for the year under a deferred profit sharing plan in respect of

        (i) the employer, or

(ii) any other employer who, at any time in the year, does not deal at arm's length with the employer

does not exceed ½ of the money purchase limit for the year; and

(c) the total of

(i) the beneficiary's pension adjustment for the year in respect of the employer, and

(ii) the total of all amounts each of which is the beneficiary's pension adjustment for the year in respect of any other employer who, at any time in the year, does not deal at arm's length with the employer

does not exceed the lesser of

(iii) the money purchase limit for the year, and

(iv) 18% of the total of all amounts each of which is the beneficiary's compensation (within the meaning assigned by subsection 147.1(1)) for the year from the employer or any other employer referred to in subparagraph (ii).

**Related Provisions**: 147(2.1) — Terms limiting contributions; 147(5.11) — Compensation; 147(9) — Limitation on deduction; 147(14) — Revocation of registration; 147(22) — Excess transfer; 147.1(8) — Pension adjustment limits; Reg. 8301(11) — Timing of contributions.

**Notes**: 147(5.1) added by 1990 pension bill, effective 1991. The deduction limit is ½ of the "money purchase limit" for the year as defined in 147.1(1). Thus, the DPSP deduction limits since 1991 are:

| | | |
|---|---|---|
| | 1991–92 | $6,250 |
| | 1993 | $6,750 |
| | 1994 | $7,250 |
| | 1995 | $7,750 |
| | 1996–2002 | $6,750 |
| | 2003 | $7,250 |
| | 2004 | $7,750 |

**Regulations**: 8301(2), (3) (pension credit under DPSP).

**Interpretation Bulletins**: IT-528: Transfers of funds between registered plans.

**Information Circulars**: See list at end of s. 147.

**Registered Plans Division Newsletters**: 96-1 (Changes to retirement savings limits).

**(5.11) Compensation** — Where at any time in a calendar year an individual ceases to be employed by an employer,

(a) for the purposes of paragraph (5.1)(a), the amount that would be the individual's compensation (in this subsection having the meaning assigned by subsection 147.1(1)) from the employer for the year if the definition "compensation" in subsection 147.1(1) were read without reference to paragraph (b) of that definition shall be deemed to be the greater of

(i) that amount determined without reference to this paragraph, and

(ii) the amount that would be the individual's compensation from the employer for the immediately preceding year if the definition "compensation" in subsection 147.1(1) were read without reference to paragraph (b) of that definition; and

(b) for the purposes of paragraph (5.1)(c), the individual's compensation from the employer for the year shall be deemed to be the greater of

(i) that compensation determined without reference to this paragraph, and

(ii) the individual's compensation from the employer for the immediately preceding year.

**Notes**: 147(5.11) added by 1990 pension bill, effective 1991.

**(6) Deferred plan not employees profit sharing plan** — For a period during which a plan is a deferred profit sharing plan, the plan shall be deemed, for the purposes of this Act, not to be an employees profit sharing plan.

**Related Provisions**: 144(11) — Year-end of EPSP on becoming DPSP.

**(7) No tax while trust governed by plan** — No tax is payable under this Part by a trust on the taxable income of the trust for a period during which the trust was governed by a deferred profit sharing plan.

**Related Provisions**: 149(1)(s) — Exemption for DPSP; 198 — Tax on acquisition of non-qualified investments and use of assets as security; 206(2) — Part XI tax on excess holdings of foreign property; 207.1(2) — Tax payable by DPSP on holding non-qualified investments.

**(8) Amount of employer's contribution deductible** — Subject to subsection (9), there may be deducted in computing the income of an employer for a taxation year the total of all amounts each of which is an amount paid by the employer in the year or within 120 days after the end of the year to a trustee under a deferred profit sharing plan for the benefit of the employer's employees who are beneficiaries under the plan, to the extent that the amount was paid in accordance with the terms of the plan and was not deducted in computing the employer's income for a preceding taxation year.

**Related Provisions**: 6(1)(a)(i) — Employer's contribution to DPSP not a taxable benefit; 20(1)(y) — Employer's contribution to DPSP deductible; 147(5.1) — Contribution limits; 147(9), (9.1) — Limitations on deduction; 147(20) — Taxation of amount transferred; 204.1(3) — Tax payable by DPSP on excess amount.

**Notes**: 147(8) amended by 1990 pension bill, effective 1991 for amounts paid to DPSPs after 1990. Before 1991, the deduction was based on 20% of current year's earned income, and capped at $3,500 minus any deductible employee RPP contributions for the year.

**Interpretation Bulletins**: IT-280R: Employees profit sharing plans — payments computed by reference to profits; IT-363R2: Deferred profit sharing plans — deductibility of employer contributions and taxation of amounts received by a beneficiary.

**(9) Limitation on deduction** — Where the requirements of subsection (5.1) in respect of a deferred profit sharing plan are not satisfied for a calendar year by reason that the pension credits of a

Division G — Deferred & Special Income Arrangements    S. 147(10.2)(b)

beneficiary under the plan in respect of a particular employer do not comply with paragraph (5.1)(a) or the beneficiary's pension credits or pension adjustments in respect of a particular employer and other employers who do not deal at arm's length with the particular employer do not comply with paragraph (5.1)(b) or (c), the particular employer is not entitled to a deduction under subsection (8) in computing the particular employer's income for any taxation year in respect of an amount paid to a trustee under the plan in the calendar year except to the extent expressly permitted in writing by the Minister, and, for the purposes of this subsection, an amount paid to a trustee of a deferred profit sharing plan in the first two months of a calendar year shall be deemed to have been paid in the immediately preceding year and not to have been paid in the year to the extent that the amount can reasonably be considered to be in respect of the immediately preceding year.

**Notes**: 147(9) amended by 1990 pension bill, effective 1990 for amounts paid to DPSPs after 1990. Before 1991, it related to the pre-1991 version of 147(8).

**(9.1) No deduction** — Notwithstanding subsection (8), no deduction shall be made in computing the income of an employer for a taxation year in respect of an amount paid by the employer for the year to a trustee under a deferred profit sharing plan in respect of a beneficiary who is described in paragraph (2)(k.2) in respect of the plan.

**Interpretation Bulletins**: IT-280R: Employees profit sharing plans — payments computed by reference to profits; IT-363R2: Deferred profit sharing plans — deductibility of employer contributions and taxation of amounts received by a beneficiary.

**(10) Amounts received taxable** — There shall be included in computing the income of a beneficiary under a deferred profit sharing plan for a taxation year the amount, if any, by which

   (a) the total of all amounts received by the beneficiary in the year from a trustee under the plan (other than as a result of acquiring an annuity described in subparagraph (2)(k)(vi) under which the beneficiary is the annuitant)

exceeds

   (b) the total of all amounts each of which is an amount determined for the year under subsection (10.1), (11) or (12) in relation to the plan and in respect of the beneficiary.

**Related Provisions**: 56(1)(d.2)(iii) — Income from annuity purchased with plan funds is taxable; 56(1)(i) — Deferred profit sharing plan; 60(j) — Transfer of superannuation benefits; 104(27.1) — DPSP benefits; 128.1(10)"excluded right or interest"(a)(iv) — No deemed disposition of DPSP on emigration; 139.1(12) — Conversion benefit on demutualization of insurance corporation not taxable; 147(10.1) — Single payment on retirement etc.; 147(10.4) — Income on disposal of shares; 147(11) — Portion of receipts deductible; 147(18) — Inadequate consideration on purchase from or sale to trust; 147(20) — Taxation of amount transferred; 153(1)(h) — Withholdings; 212(1)(m), 214(3)(d) — Withholding tax on payments to non-residents.

**Notes**: 147(10)(b) added by 1996 Budget, retroactive to 1992. It was added so that an amount paid to purchase an annuity does not reduce the amount included in the beneficiary's income under 147(10). Since the amount is not received by the beneficiary, the purchase of the annuity is meant to be entirely disregarded for the purpose of computing the beneficiary's income.

**Interpretation Bulletins**: IT-280R: Employees profit sharing plans — payments computed by reference to profits; IT-281R2: Elections on single payments from a deferred profit-sharing plan; IT-363R2: Deferred profit sharing plans — deductibility of employer contributions and taxation of amounts received by a beneficiary; IT-528: Transfers of funds between registered plans.

**Information Circulars**: See list at end of s. 147.

**Advance Tax Rulings**: ATR-31: Funding of divorce settlement amount from DPSP.

**(10.1) Single payment on retirement, etc.** — For the purposes of subsections (10) and (10.2), where a beneficiary under a deferred profit sharing plan has received, in a taxation year and when the beneficiary was resident in Canada, from a trustee under the plan a single payment that included shares of the capital stock of a corporation that was an employer who contributed to the plan or of a corporation with which the employer did not deal at arm's length on the beneficiary's withdrawal from the plan or retirement from employment or on the death of an employee or former employee and has made an election in respect thereof in prescribed manner and prescribed form, the amount determined for the year under this subsection in relation to the plan and in respect of the beneficiary is the amount, if any, by which the fair market value of those shares, immediately before the single payment was made, exceeds the cost amount to the plan of those shares at that time.

**Related Provisions**: 47(3)(a) — No averaging of cost on disposition of securities; 147(10) — Amounts received taxable; 147(10.2) — Single payment on retirement etc.; 147(11) — Portion of receipts deductible.

**Notes**: 147(10.1) amended by 1985 Budget, effective for terminations of interests in DPSPs after May 23, 1985.

**Regulations**: 1503 (prescribed manner, prescribed form).

**Interpretation Bulletins**: IT-281R2: Election on single payments from a deferred profit-sharing plan; IT-528: Transfers of funds between registered plans.

**Forms**: T2078: Election under subsection 147(10.1) in respect of a single payment received from a deferred profit sharing plan.

**(10.2) Idem** — Where a trustee under a deferred profit sharing plan has at any time in a taxation year made under the plan a single payment that included shares referred to in subsection (10.1) to a beneficiary who was resident in Canada at the time and the beneficiary has made an election under that subsection in respect of that payment,

   (a) the trustee shall be deemed to have disposed of those shares for proceeds of disposition equal to the cost amount to the trust of those shares immediately before the single payment was made;

   (b) the cost to the beneficiary of those shares shall be deemed to be their cost amount to the trust immediately before the single payment was made;

## S. 147(10.2)(c) — Income Tax Act, Part I

(c) the cost to the beneficiary of each of those shares shall be deemed to be the amount determined by the formula

$$A \times \frac{B}{C}$$

where

A is the amount determined under paragraph (a) in respect of all of those shares,

B is the fair market value of that share at the time the single payment was made, and

C is the fair market value of all those shares at the time the single payment was made; and

(d) for the purposes of paragraph 60(j), the cost to the beneficiary of those shares is an eligible amount in respect of the beneficiary for the year.

**Notes:** 147(10.2)(d) added by 1990 pension bill, effective 1989.

147(10.2) amended by 1985 Budget, effective for terminations of interests in DPSPs after May 23, 1985. For terminations of interests from 1972 through May 23, 1985, read:

(10.2) Where in a taxation year a trustee under a deferred profit sharing plan has made a single payment to a beneficiary under the plan and the beneficiary has made an election under subsection (10.1) in respect of that payment

(a) the trustee shall be deemed to have disposed of each property that was included in the single payment and that was neither money nor an amount described in paragraph (10)(b) for proceeds of disposition equal to the cost amount to the trust of the property immediately before the single payment was made;

(b) the cost to the beneficiary of all such property shall be deemed to be the fair market value, at the time the single payment was made, of such property minus the amount determined for the year under subsection (10.1) [as it read before May 24, 1985] in relation to the plan and in respect of the beneficiary; and

(c) the cost to the beneficiary of each such property shall be deemed to be the proportion of the amount determined under paragraph (b) that the fair market value, at the time the single payment was made, of that property is of the fair market value at that time of all such property.

**Interpretation Bulletins:** IT-281R2: Elections on single payments from a deferred profit-sharing plan; IT-528: Transfers of funds between registered plans.

**Forms:** TD2: Tax deduction waiver for a direct transfer of an eligible retiring allowance.

### (10.3) Amount contributed to or forfeited under a plan

There shall be included in computing the income for a taxation year of a beneficiary described in paragraph (2)(k.2) the total of amounts allocated or reallocated to the beneficiary in the year in respect of

(a) any amount contributed after December 1, 1982 by an employer to, or

(b) any forfeited amount under

a deferred profit sharing plan or a plan the registration of which has been revoked pursuant to subsection (14) or (14.1).

**Notes:** 147(10.3) amended by 1990 pension bill, effective 1991. For years before 1991, 147(10.3)(b) referred to an amount forfeited under (former) 201(3) rather than a "forfeited amount".

**Interpretation Bulletins:** IT-363R2: Deferred profit sharing plans — deductibility of employer contributions and taxation of amounts received by a beneficiary.

### (10.4) Income on disposal of shares

Where a taxpayer has a share in respect of which the taxpayer has made an election under subsection (10.1), there shall be included in computing the taxpayer's income for the taxation year in which the taxpayer disposed of or exchanged the share or ceased to be a resident of Canada, whichever is the earlier, the amount, if any, by which the fair market value of the share at the time the taxpayer acquired it exceeds the cost to the taxpayer, determined under paragraph (10.2)(c), of the share at the time the taxpayer acquired it.

**Related Provisions:** 7(1.3) — Order of disposition of securities acquired under stock option agreement; 110(1)(d.3) — Employer's shares — deduction from taxable income; 147(10.5) [to be repealed] — Order of disposal of shares.

**Interpretation Bulletins:** IT-281R2: Elections on single payments from a deferred profit-sharing plan.

### (10.5) Order of disposal of shares

For the purposes of subsection (10.4), a taxpayer shall be deemed to have disposed of or exchanged shares that are identical properties in the order in which the taxpayer acquired them.

> **Proposed Repeal — 147(10.5)**
>
> **Application:** The December 21, 2000 draft legislation, s. 81, will repeal subsec. 147(10.5), applicable to shares acquired, but not disposed of, before February 28, 2000 and to shares acquired after February 27, 2000.
>
> **Technical Notes:** Subsection 147(10.5) contains a special ordering rule which provides that, for the purposes of subsection 147(10.4), identical shares are considered to have been disposed of in the order in which they were acquired. Subsection 147(10.4) provides that, in certain circumstances, an employee who receives employer shares on withdrawing from a DPSP must include in income in the year the shares are disposed of the excess of the fair market value of the shares at the time of the withdrawal over the cost amount of the shares to the DPSP.
>
> Subsection 147(10.5) is repealed. This is consequential on subsection 7(1.3) being amended to have that subsection apply for the purposes of subsection 147(10.5) with respect to shares acquired after February 27, 2000, and to shares acquired before February 28, 2000 but not disposed of before that date. (See the commentary on subsection 7(1.3) for further details.)

**Interpretation Bulletins:** IT-281R2: Elections on single payments from a deferred profit-sharing plan.

### (10.6) Commencement of annuity after age 69

Where an amount is paid before 1997 pursuant to or under a deferred profit sharing plan to purchase for a beneficiary under the plan an annuity to which subparagraph (2)(k)(vi) applies, and payment of the annuity has not begun by the end of the particular year in which the beneficiary attains 69 years of age,

(a) the beneficiary is deemed to have disposed of the annuity immediately after the particular year and to have received as proceeds of the disposition an amount equal to the fair market value of the annuity at the end of the particular year;

(b) the beneficiary is deemed to have acquired immediately after the particular year an interest in the annuity as a separate and newly issued annuity contract at a cost equal to the amount referred to in paragraph (a); and

(c) the issue and acquisition of the contract referred to in paragraph (b) are deemed not to be pursuant to or under a deferred profit sharing plan.

**Related Provisions**: 56(1)(d.2)(iii) — Beneficiary required to include fair market value of annuity in income; 146(13.2) — Parallel rules for RRSPs; 198(6)(d) — Life insurance policy purchased with DPSP maturing by age 69.

**Notes**: 147(10.6) contains rules relating to annuities purchased for a DPSP beneficiary before 1997, which apply if payment of the annuity does not begin by the end of the year in which the beneficiary turns 69. The beneficiary is deemed to have disposed of the annuity immediately after the year for an amount equal to the fair market value of the annuity determined at the end of the year. Under 56(1)(d.2), the beneficiary must include this amount in income. This parallels the treatment of RRSPs under 146(13.2).

147(10.6) also deems the beneficiary to have acquired the annuity as a separate and newly-issued contract immediately after the year at a cost equal to its fair market value at the end of the year and it deems the contract not to have been issued pursuant to or under a deferred profit sharing plan. As a result, the contract ceases to be a prescribed annuity contract under Reg. 304(1) and becomes subject to the accrual rules in 12.2.

147(10.6) added by 1996 Budget, effective 1997 except that

(a) where a beneficiary under a profit sharing plan turned 70 before 1997, 147(10.6) does not apply to an annuity purchased for the beneficiary;

(b) where a beneficiary turned 69 in 1996, in applying 147(10.6) to an annuity purchased for the beneficiary, read "70 years" instead of "69 years"; and

(c) 147(10.6) does not apply to an annuity purchased before March 6, 1996 for a beneficiary under a DPSP where, under the terms and conditions of the annuity contract as they read immediately before that day,

(i) the day on which annuity payments are to begin under the contract is fixed and determined and is after the year in which the beneficiary turns

(A) 69, where the beneficiary had not turned 69 before 1997, or

(B) 70, where the beneficiary turned 69 in 1996, and

(ii) the amount and timing of each annuity payment are fixed and determined.

**(11) Portion of receipts deductible** — For the purposes of subsections (10), (10.1) and (12), where an amount was received in a taxation year from a trustee under a deferred profit sharing plan by an employee or other beneficiary thereunder, and the employee was a beneficiary under the plan at a time when the plan was an employees profit sharing plan, the amount determined for the year under this subsection in relation to the plan and in respect of the beneficiary is such portion of the total of the amounts so received in the year as does not exceed

(a) the total of

(i) each amount included in respect of the plan in computing the income of the employee for the year or for a previous taxation year by virtue of section 144,

(ii) each amount paid by the employee to a trustee under the plan at a time when it was an employees profit sharing plan, and

(iii) each amount that was allocated to the employee or other beneficiary by a trustee under the plan, at a time when it was an employees profit sharing plan, in respect of a capital gain made by the trust before 1972,

minus

(b) the total of

(i) each amount received by the employee or other beneficiary in a previous taxation year from a trustee under the plan at a time when it was an employees profit sharing plan,

(ii) each amount received by the employee or other beneficiary in a previous taxation year from a trustee under the plan at a time when it was a deferred profit sharing plan, and

(iii) each amount allocated to the employee or other beneficiary by a trustee under the plan, at a time when it was an employees profit sharing plan, in respect of a capital loss sustained by the trust before 1972.

**Related Provisions**: 147(10) — Amounts received taxable; 147(17) — Meaning of "other beneficiary".

**Interpretation Bulletins**: IT-281R2: Elections on single payments from a deferred profit-sharing plan; IT-363R2: Deferred profit sharing plans — deductibility of employer contributions and taxation of amounts received by a beneficiary.

**(12) Idem** — For the purposes of subsections (10) and (10.1), where an amount was received in a taxation year from a trustee under a deferred profit sharing plan by an employee or other beneficiary thereunder, and the employee has made a payment in the year or a previous year to a trustee under the plan at a time when the plan was a deferred profit sharing plan, the amount determined for the year under this subsection in relation to the plan and in respect of the beneficiary is such portion of the total of the amounts so received in the year (minus any amount determined for the year under subsection (11) in relation to the plan and in respect of the beneficiary) as does not exceed

(a) the total of all amounts each of which was so paid by the employee in the year or a previous year to the extent that the payment was not deductible in computing the employee's income,

minus

(b) the total of all amounts each of which was received by the employee or other beneficiary from a trustee under the plan, at a time when it was a deferred profit sharing plan, to the extent that it was included in the computation of an amount determined for a previous year under this subsection in relation to the plan and in respect of the employee or other beneficiary.

**Related Provisions**: 60(j) — Transfer of superannuation benefits; 147(10) — Amounts received taxable; 147(11) — Portion of receipts deductible; 147(17) — Meaning of "other beneficiary".

**Interpretation Bulletins**: IT-281R2: Elections on single payments from a deferred profit-sharing plan; IT-363R2: Deferred profit sharing plans — deductibility of employer contributions and taxation of amounts received by a beneficiary.

**(13) Appropriation of trust property by employer** — Where funds or property of a trust governed by a deferred profit sharing plan have been appropriated in any manner whatever to or for the benefit of a taxpayer who is

(a) an employer by whom payments are made in trust to a trustee under the plan, or

(b) a corporation with which that employer does not deal at arm's length,

otherwise than in payment of or on account of shares of the capital stock of the taxpayer purchased by the trust, the amount or value of the funds or property so appropriated shall be included in computing the income of the taxpayer for the taxation year of the taxpayer in which the funds or property were so appropriated, unless the funds or property or an amount in lieu thereof equal to the amount or value of the funds or property was repaid to the trust within one year from the end of the taxation year, and it is established by subsequent events or otherwise that the repayment was not made as part of a series of appropriations and repayments.

**Related Provisions**: 201 — Tax on forfeitures; 214(3)(d) — Non-resident withholding tax; 248(10) — Series of transactions.

**(14) Revocation of registration** — Where, at any time after a profit sharing plan has been accepted by the Minister for registration for the purposes of this Act,

(a) the plan has been revised or amended or a new plan has been substituted therefor, and the plan as revised or amended or the new plan substituted therefor, as the case may be, ceased to comply with the requirements of this section for its acceptance by the Minister for registration for the purposes of this Act,

(b) any provision of the plan has not been complied with,

(c) the plan is a plan that did not, as of January 1, 1968,

(i) comply with the requirements of paragraphs (2)(a), (b) to (h), (j) and (k), and paragraph 147(2)(i) of the *Income Tax Act*, chapter 148 of the Revised Statutes of Canada, 1952, as it read on January 1, 1972, and

(ii) provide that the amounts held by the trust for the benefit of beneficiaries thereunder that remain unallocated on December 31, 1967 must be allocated or reallocated, as the case may be, before 1969,

(c.1) the plan becomes a revocable plan pursuant to subsection (21),

(c.2) the plan does not comply with the requirements of paragraphs (2)(a) to (k) and (l),

(c.3) in the case of a plan that became registered after March, 1983, the plan does not comply with the requirements of paragraphs (2)(k.1) and (k.2),

(c.4) the requirements of subsection (5.1) in respect of the plan are not satisfied for a calendar year, or

(c.5) an employer who participates in the plan fails to file an information return reporting a pension adjustment of a beneficiary under the plan as and when required by regulation,

the Minister may revoke the registration of the plan,

(d) where paragraph (a) applies, as of the date that the plan ceased so to comply, or any subsequent date,

(e) where paragraph (b) applies, as of the date that any provision of the plan was not so complied with, or any subsequent date,

(f) where paragraph (c) applies, as of any date following January 1, 1968,

(g) where paragraph (c.1) applies, as of the date on which the plan became a revocable plan, or any subsequent date,

(h) where paragraph (c.2) or (c.3) applies, as of the date on which the plan did not so comply, or any subsequent date, but not before January 1, 1991,

(i) where paragraph (c.4) applies, as of the end of the year for which the requirements of subsection (5.1) in respect of the plan are not satisfied, or any subsequent date, and

(j) where paragraph (c.5) applies, as of any date after the date by which the information return was required to be filed,

and the Minister shall thereafter give notice of the revocation by registered mail to a trustee under the plan and to an employer of employees who are beneficiaries under the plan.

**Related Provisions**: 147(2) — Requirements for registration; 147(10.3) — Amount contributed to or forfeited under a plan; 147(15) — Rules applicable to revoked plan; 172(3)(c) — Appeal from refusal to register, revocation of registration, etc.; 198 — Tax on non-qualified investments and use of assets as security; 204 — "Revoked plan"; 244(5) — Proof of service by mail; 248(7)(a) — Mail deemed received on day mailed.

**Notes**: 147(14)(c)(i) amended by 1990 pension bill, effective 1991.

147(14)(c.1), (c.2)–(c.5), (g), and (h)–(j) added by 1990 pension bill, effective 1989, 1991, 1988 and 1991 respectively.

**I.T. Application Rules**: 69 (meaning of "*Income Tax Act*, chapter 148 of the Revised Statutes of Canada, 1952").

**(14.1) Idem** — Where on any day after June 30, 1982 a benefit or loan is extended or continues to be extended as a consequence of the existence of a deferred profit sharing plan and that benefit or loan would be prohibited if the plan met the requirement for registration contained in paragraph (2)(k.1), the Minister may revoke the registration of the plan as of that or any subsequent day that is specified by the Minister in a notice given by registered mail to a trustee under the plan and to an employer of employees who are beneficiaries under the plan.

**Related Provisions**: 147(15) — Rules applicable to revoked plan; 198 — Tax on non-qualified investments and use of assets as security; 204 — "Revoked plan"; 244(5) — Proof of service by mail; 248(7)(a) — Mail deemed received on day mailed.

**(15) Rules applicable to revoked plan** — Where the Minister revokes the registration of a deferred profit sharing plan, the plan (in this section referred to as the "revoked plan") shall be deemed, for the purposes of this Act, not to be a deferred profit sharing plan, and notwithstanding any other provision of this Act, the following rules shall apply:

(a) the revoked plan shall not be accepted for registration for the purposes of this Act or be deemed to have become registered as a deferred profit sharing plan at any time within a period of one year commencing on the date the plan became a revoked plan;

(b) subsection (7) does not apply to exempt the trust governed by the plan from tax under this Part on the taxable income of the trust for a taxation year in which, at any time therein, the trust was governed by the revoked plan;

(c) no deduction shall be made by an employer in computing the employer's income for a taxation year in respect of an amount paid by the employer to a trustee under the plan at a time when it was a revoked plan;

(d) there shall be included in computing the income of a taxpayer for a taxation year

(i) all amounts received by the taxpayer in the year from a trustee under the revoked plan that, by virtue of subsection (10), would have been so included if the revoked plan had been a deferred profit sharing plan at the time the taxpayer received those amounts, and

(ii) the amount or value of any funds or property appropriated to or for the benefit of the taxpayer in the year that, by virtue of subsection (13), would have been so included if the revoked plan had been a deferred profit sharing plan at the time of the appropriation of the funds or property; and

(e) the revoked plan shall be deemed, for the purposes of this Act, not to be an employees profit sharing plan or a retirement compensation arrangement.

**Related Provisions**: 128.1(10)"excluded right or interest"(a)(iv) — Emigration — no deemed disposition of interest in revoked plan; 147(14), (14.1) — Revocation of DPSP; 147(18) — Inadequate consideration on purchase from or sale to trust; 214(3)(d) — Non-resident withholding tax.

**Notes**: The words "or a retirement compensation arrangement" added to 147(15)(e) by 1990 pension bill, effective October 9, 1986.

**(16) Payments out of profits** — Where the terms of an arrangement under which an employer makes payments to a trustee specifically provide that the payments shall be made "out of profits", the arrangement shall be deemed, for the purpose of subsection (1), to be an arrangement for payments "computed by reference to an employer's profits from the employer's business".

**Interpretation Bulletins**: IT-280R: Employees profit sharing plans — payments computed by reference to profits.

**(17) Interpretation of "other beneficiary"** — Where the expression "employee or other beneficiary" under a profit sharing plan occurs in this section, the words "other beneficiary" shall be construed as meaning any person, other than the employee, to whom any amount is or may become payable by a trustee under the plan as a result of payments made to the trustee under the plan in trust for the benefit of employees, including the employee.

**Related Provisions**: 202(1) — Returns and payment of estimated tax.

**(18) Inadequate consideration on purchase from or sale to trust** — Where a trust governed by a deferred profit sharing plan or revoked plan

(a) disposes of property to a taxpayer for a consideration less than the fair market value of the property at the time of the transaction, or for no consideration, or

(b) acquires property from a taxpayer for a consideration greater than the fair market value of the property at the time of the transaction,

the difference between that fair market value and the consideration, if any

(c) shall, for the purposes of subsections (10) and (15), be deemed to be an amount received by the taxpayer at the time of the disposal or acquisition, as the case may be, from a trustee under the plan as if the taxpayer were a beneficiary under the plan, and

(d) is an amount taxable under section 201 for the calendar year in which the trust disposes of or acquires the property, as the case may be.

**Related Provisions**: 201 — 50% tax payable on amount taxable.

**Notes**: 147(18) amended by 1990 pension bill, effective 1991. For years through 1990, read the portion following para. (b) as follows:

the difference between such fair market value and the consideration, if any, shall be deemed to be,

(c) for the purposes of subsections (10) and (15), an amount received by the taxpayer from a trustee under the plan as if the taxpayer were a beneficiary under the plan, and

(d) for the purposes of section 201, an amount forfeited in the trust and reallocated to the taxpayer, as if the taxpayer were an employee who was a beneficiary under the plan,

at the time of the disposal or acquisition, as the case may be.

**Information Circulars**: 77-1R4 — Deferred profit sharing plans.

**(19) Transfer to RPP, RRSP or DPSP** — An amount is transferred from a deferred profit sharing plan in accordance with this subsection if the amount

(a) is not part of a series of periodic payments;

(b) is transferred on behalf of an individual

(i) who is an employee or former employee of an employer who participated in the plan on the employee's behalf, or

(ii) who is entitled to the amount as a consequence of the death of an employee or former employee referred to in subparagraph (i) and who was, at the date of the employee's death, a spouse or common-law partner of the employee,

in full or partial satisfaction of the individual's entitlement to benefits under the plan;

(c) would, if it were paid directly to the individual, be included under subsection (10) in computing the individual's income for a taxation year; and

(d) is transferred for the benefit of the individual directly to

(i) a registered pension plan,

(ii) a registered retirement savings plan under which the individual is the annuitant (within the meaning assigned by subsection 146(1)), or

(iii) a deferred profit sharing plan that can reasonably be expected to have at least 5 beneficiaries at all times throughout the calendar year in which the transfer is made.

**Related Provisions**: 60(j) — Transfer of superannuation benefits; 60(j.2) — Transfer to spousal RRSP; 60(k) — re 1989 — Transfers to DPSPs; 104(27.1) — DPSP benefits; 146(8.2) — Amount deductible where withdrawn after mistaken contribution; 147(2)(a.1) — Acceptance of plan for registration; 147(10.2) — Single payment on retirement etc.; 147(20) — Taxation of amount transferred; 147(22) — Excess transfer; 248(8) — Occurrences as a consequence of death; 248(10) — Series of transactions.

**Notes**: 147(19)(b)(ii) amended by 2000 same-sex partners bill to add reference to "common-law partner", effective for the 2001 and later taxation years, or earlier by election (see Notes to 248(1)"common-law partner").

147(19) added by 1990 pension bill, effective for amounts transferred in 1989 or later. Amended by 1995-97 technical bill, effective 1993, to change "spouse (within the meaning assigned by subsection 146(1.1))" to "spouse". The extended definition of "spouse" was provided from 1993 to 2000 in 252(4)(a).

**Interpretation Bulletins**: IT-528: Transfers of funds between registered plans.

**Information Circulars**: See list at end of s. 147.

**Registered Plans Division Newsletters**: 91-4R (Registration rules for money purchase provisions).

**Forms**: T2151: Record of direct transfer of a "single amount".

**(20) Taxation of amount transferred** — Where an amount is transferred on behalf of an individual in accordance with subsection (19),

(a) the amount shall not, by reason only of that transfer, be included by virtue of this section in computing the income of any taxpayer; and

(b) no deduction may be made under any provision of this Act in respect of the amount in computing the income of any taxpayer.

**Related Provisions**: 56(1)(i) — Amount received taxable; 212(1)(m)(i) — Transferred amount not subject to non-resident withholding tax.

**Notes**: 147(20) added by 1990 pension bill, effective for amounts transferred in 1989 or later.

**Interpretation Bulletins**: IT-528: Transfers of funds between registered plans.

**(21) Restriction re transfers** — A deferred profit sharing plan becomes a revocable plan at any time that an amount is transferred from the plan to a registered pension plan, a registered retirement savings plan or another deferred profit sharing plan unless

(a) the transfer is in accordance with subsection (19); or

(b) the amount is deductible under paragraph 60(j) or (j.2) of this Act or paragraph 60(k) of the *Income Tax Act*, chapter 148 of the Revised Statutes of Canada, 1952, by the individual on whose behalf the transfer is made.

**Related Provisions**: 147(14)(c.1) — Revocation of registration.

**Notes**: 147(21) added by 1990 pension bill, effective for amounts transferred in 1989 or later.

**I.T. Application Rules**: 69 (meaning of "*Income Tax Act*, chapter 148 of the Revised Statutes of Canada, 1952").

**Interpretation Bulletins**: IT-528: Transfers of funds between registered plans.

**(22) Excess transfer** — Where

(a) the transfer of an amount from a deferred profit sharing plan in a calendar year on behalf of a beneficiary under the plan would, but for this subsection, be in accordance with subsection (19), and

(b) the requirements of subsection (5.1) in respect of the plan are not satisfied for the year by reason that the beneficiary's pension credits or pension adjustments do not comply with any of paragraphs (5.1)(a) to (c),

such portion of the amount transferred as may reasonably be considered to derive from amounts allocated or reallocated to the beneficiary in the year or from earnings reasonably attributable to those amounts shall, except to the extent otherwise expressly provided in writing by the Minister, be deemed to be an amount that was not transferred in accordance with subsection (19).

**Notes**: 147(22) added by 1990 pension bill, effective for amounts transferred in 1989 or later.

**Interpretation Bulletins**: IT-528: Transfers of funds between registered plans.

**Registered Plans Division Newsletters:** 91-4R (Registration rules for money purchase provisions).

**Definitions [s. 147]:** "amount", "annuity", "business" — 248(1); "calendar year" — *Interpretation Act* 37(1)(a); "Canada" — 255; "capital gain", "capital loss" — 39(1), 248(1); "common-law partner" — 248(1); "consequence of the death" — 248(8); "corporation" — 248(1), *Interpretation Act* 35(1); "deferred profit sharing plan" — 147(1), 248(1); "employed", "employee" — 248(1); "employees profit sharing plan" — 144(1), 248(1); "employer", "employment" — 248(1); "estate" — 104(1), 248(1); "forfeited amount" — 147(1); "identical" — 248(12); "individual" — 248(1); "licensed annuities provider" — 147(1); "Minister" — 248(1); "money purchase limit" — 147.1(1), 248(1); "other beneficiary" — 147(17); "participate" — 147(1.1); "pension adjustment" — 248(1), Reg. 8301(1); "person", "prescribed" — 248(1); "profit sharing plan" — 147(1), 248(1); "property" — 248(1); "province" — *Interpretation Act* 35(1); "registered pension plan" — 248(1); "registered retirement savings plan" — 146(1), 248(1); "regulation" — 248(1); "related" — 251(2); "resident in Canada" — 250; "retirement compensation arrangement" — 248(1); "revoked plan" — 147(15); "series of transactions" — 248(10); "share", "specified shareholder" — 248(1); "taxable income" — 2(2), 248(1); "taxation year" — 249; "taxpayer" — 248(1); "trust" — 104(1), 248(1), (3); "writing" — *Interpretation Act* 35(1).

**Information Circulars [s. 147]:** 74-1R5; Form T2037 — Notice of purchase of annuity with "plan" funds; 77-1R4: Deferred profit sharing plans; 79-8R3: Forms to use to directly transfer funds to or between plans, or to purchase an annuity.

## Registered Pension Plans

**147.1 (1) Definitions** — In this section and sections 147.2 and 147.3,

**"actuary"** means a Fellow of the Canadian Institute of Actuaries;

**"administrator"** of a pension plan means the person or body of persons that has ultimate responsibility for the administration of the plan;

**Related Provisions:** 147.1(6) — Administrator; 147.1(7) — Obligations of administrator.

**"average wage"** for a calendar year means the amount that is obtained by dividing by 12 the total of all amounts each of which is the wage measure for a month in the 12 month period ending on June 30 of the immediately preceding calendar year;

**Notes:** See Notes to 147.1(1)"wage measure".

**"compensation"** of an individual from an employer for a calendar year means the total of all amounts each of which is

(a) an amount in respect of

(i) the individual's employment with the employer, or

(ii) an office in respect of which the individual is remunerated by the employer

that is required (or that would be required but for paragraph 81(1)(a) as it applies with respect to the *Indian Act*) by section 5 or 6 to be included in computing the individual's income for the year, except such portion of the amount as

(iii) may reasonably be considered to relate to a period throughout which the individual was not resident in Canada, and

(iv) is not attributable to the performance of the duties of the office or employment in Canada or is exempt from income tax in Canada by reason of a provision contained in a tax convention or agreement with another country that has the force of law in Canada,

(b) a prescribed amount, or

(c) an amount acceptable to the Minister in respect of remuneration received by the individual from any employer for a period in the year throughout which the individual was not resident in Canada, to the extent that the amount is not otherwise included in the total;

**Related Provisions:** 147(5.1) — DPSP Contribution limits; 147(5.11) — Compensation; 147.1(8) — Pension adjustment limits; 147.1(9) — Pension adjustment limits — multi-employer plans.

**Regulations:** 8507 (prescribed amount).

**Information Circulars:** 98-2: Prescribed compensation for registered pension plans.

**"defined benefit provision"** of a pension plan means terms of the plan under which benefits in respect of each member are determined in any way other than that described in the definition "money purchase provision" in this subsection;

**Related Provisions:** 60(j.01) — Transfer of surplus.

**Interpretation Bulletins:** IT-167R6: Registered pension plans — employee's contributions; IT-528: Transfers of funds between registered plans.

**"member"** of a pension plan means an individual who has a right, either immediate or in the future and either absolute or contingent, to receive benefits under the plan, other than an individual who has such a right only by reason of the participation of another individual in the plan;

**Related Provisions:** 128.1(10)"excluded right or interest"(a)(viii) — No deemed disposition on emigration of member.

**"money purchase limit"** for a calendar year means

(a) for years before 1990, nil,

(b) for 1990, $11,500,

(c) for 1991 and 1992, $12,500,

(d) for 1993, $13,500,

(e) for 1994, $14,500,

(f) for 1995, $15,500, and

(g) for years after 1995 and before 2003, $13,500,

(h) for 2003, $14,500,

(i) for 2004, $15,500, and

(j) for each year after 2004, the greater of

(i) the product of

(A) $15,500, and

## S. 147.1(1) mon — Income Tax Act, Part I

(B) the quotient obtained when the average wage for the year is divided by the average wage for 2004,

rounded to the nearest multiple of $10, or, if that product is equidistant from 2 such consecutive multiples, to the higher thereof, and

(ii) the money purchase limit for the preceding year;

**Related Provisions**: 146(1) — RRSP dollar limit; 147.1(8) — Pension adjustment limits; 147.1(9) — Pension adjustment limits — multi-employer plans; 248(1)"money purchase limit" — Definition applies to entire Act.

**Notes**: The dollar amounts shown limit RRSP contributions for the following taxation year (except for 1996). See Notes to 146(1)"RRSP deduction limit" and "RRSP dollar limit". For the effect on DPSP limits, see Notes to 147(5.1).

Paras. (g) to (j) amended by 1996 Budget, effective 1997. Before these changes, the amounts were scheduled to be $13,500 for 1996, $14,500 for 1997, $15,500 for 1998, and indexed after 1998. Each increase has been postponed for six years.

Para. (g) amended, and (h)–(j) added, by 1995 Budget, effective 1996. The current (j) was the former (g), applying "for each year thereafter". A previously scheduled increase in the limits was delayed as announced in the February 1995 federal budget.

147.1(1) amended by 1992 Budget/technical bill, to delay the $1,000 increase that would have taken effect in 1992 (thus affecting 1993 RRSP contribution limits).

**Registered Plans Division Newsletters**: 96-1 (Changes to retirement savings limits).

**"money purchase provision"** of a pension plan means terms of the plan

(a) which provide for a separate account to be maintained in respect of each member, to which are credited contributions made to the plan by, or in respect of, the member and any other amounts allocated to the member, and to which are charged payments made in respect of the member, and

(b) under which the only benefits in respect of a member are benefits determined solely with reference to, and provided by, the amount in the member's account;

**Notes**: A "money purchase" RPP, also known as a "defined contribution" RPP, is one where an amount is invested on behalf of an individual member, and the benefits will be based on whatever those funds have earned over time (like an RRSP/RRIF). The more common form is a "defined benefit" RPP, where the benefits on retirement are predetermined.

**Interpretation Bulletins**: IT-167R6: Registered pension plans — employee's contributions; IT-528: Transfers of funds between registered plans.

**Registered Plans Division Newsletters**: 91-4R (Registration rules for money purchase provisions).

**"multi-employer plan"** in a calendar year has the meaning assigned by regulation;

**Related Provisions**: 147.1(9) — Pension adjustment limits — multi-employer plans; 252.1 — Where union is employer; Reg. 8510(5) — Special rules — multi-employer plan.

**Regulations**: 8500(1), 8510(1) (meaning of "multi-employer plan").

**"participating employer"**, in relation to a pension plan, means an employer who has made, or is required to make, contributions to the plan in respect of the employer's employees or former employees, or payments under the plan to the employer's employees or former employees, and includes a prescribed employer;

**Regulations**: 8308(7)(c) (prescribed employer).

**Interpretation Bulletins**: IT-363R2: Deferred profit sharing plans — deductibility of employer contributions and taxation of amounts received by a beneficiary.

**"past service event"** has the meaning assigned by regulation;

**Related Provisions**: 147.1(10) — Past service benefits.

**Regulations**: 8300(1), (2) (past service event).

**"single amount"** means an amount that is not part of a series of periodic payments;

**Interpretation Bulletins**: IT-528: Transfers of funds between registered plans.

**"specified multi-employer plan"** in a calendar year has the meaning assigned by regulation;

**Related Provisions**: 252.1 — Where union is employer.

**Regulations**: 8510(2), (3) (meaning of "specified multi-employer plan").

**"spouse"** — [Repealed]

**Notes**: Definition "spouse" repealed by 1992 technical bill, effective 1993. A similar rule, extending the meaning of "spouse" to include common-law spouses, applied from 1993 to 2000 for all purposes of the Act, in 252(4). For periods before 1993, "spouse" was defined here to have the meaning it had under 146(1.1).

**"wage measure"** for a month means the average weekly wages and salaries of

(a) the Industrial Aggregate in Canada for the month as published by Statistics Canada under the *Statistics Act*, or

(b) in the event that the Industrial Aggregate ceases to be published, such other measure for the month as is prescribed by regulation under the *Canada Pension Plan* for the purposes of paragraph 18(5)(b) of that Act.

**Notes**: The average weekly earnings (including overtime, not seasonally adjusted) of the Industrial Aggregate for Canada are:

1993

| | | | |
|---|---|---|---|
| Jan. | $554.61 | July | $559.95 |
| Feb. | $553.34 | Aug. | $558.80 |
| March | $556.11 | Sept. | $562.03 |
| April | $558.20 | Oct. | $560.49 |
| May | $553.79 | Nov. | $560.01 |
| June | $558.75 | Dec. | $558.90 |

1994

| | | | |
|---|---|---|---|
| Jan. | $561.80 | July | $572.18 |
| Feb. | $560.59 | Aug. | $568.27 |
| March | $565.71 | Sept. | $572.80 |
| April | $567.95 | Oct. | $570.86 |
| May | $564.32 | Nov. | $571.63 |
| June | $571.82 | Dec. | $570.34 |

1995

Division G — Deferred & Special Income Arrangements       S. 147.1(3)(b)(i)

| | | | |
|---|---|---|---|
| Jan. | $571.05 | July | $572.12 |
| Feb. | $571.61 | Aug. | $575.01 |
| March | $574.27 | Sept. | $578.40 |
| April | $570.15 | Oct. | $575.56 |
| May | $567.44 | Nov. | $576.61 |
| June | $575.34 | Dec. | $576.99 |

1996

| | | | |
|---|---|---|---|
| Jan. | $571.55 | July | $589.65 |
| Feb. | $575.80 | Aug. | $590.01 |
| March | $579.50 | Sept. | $589.87 |
| April | $575.79 | Oct. | $595.26 |
| May | $583.74 | Nov. | $592.96 |
| June | $592.67 | Dec. | $594.85 |

1997

| | | | |
|---|---|---|---|
| Jan. | $594.54 | July | $600.78 |
| Feb. | $594.43 | Aug. | $598.71 |
| March | $595.51 | Sept. | $598.48 |
| April | $597.26 | Oct. | $597.18 |
| May | $600.90 | Nov. | $600.09 |
| June | $600.78 | Dec. | $599.93 |

1998

| | | | |
|---|---|---|---|
| Jan. | $605.13 | July | $606.76 |
| Feb. | $606.14 | Aug. | $605.77 |
| March | $605.99 | Sept. | $602.89 |
| April | $608.06 | Oct. | $608.11 |
| May | $603.94 | Nov. | $606.04 |
| June | $608.04 | Dec. | $608.90 |

1999

| | | | |
|---|---|---|---|
| Jan. | $605.95 | July | $612.94 |
| Feb. | $604.68 | Aug. | $611.45 |
| March | $605.68 | Sept. | $611.51 |
| April | $608.15 | Oct. | $613.72 |
| May | $608.11 | Nov. | 612.73 |
| June | $611.80 | Dec. | $617.47 |

2000

| | | | |
|---|---|---|---|
| Jan. | $620.06 | July | $627.51 |
| Feb. | $621.60 | Aug. | $629.04 |
| Mar. | $622.70 | Sept. | $629.02 |
| Apr. | $624.11 | Oct. | $628.46 |
| May | $624.95 | Nov. | $630.46 |
| June | $627.26 | | |

Current figures are available from Statistics Canada, Employment Earnings and Hours Division, Ottawa (613) 951-4090. See also www.statcan.ca, database L57711.

**Interpretation Bulletins**: IT-124R6: Contributions to registered retirement savings plans.

**(2) Registration of plan** — The following rules apply with respect to the registration of pension plans:

(a) the Minister shall not register a pension plan unless

(i) application for registration is made in prescribed manner by the plan administrator,

(ii) the plan complies with prescribed conditions for registration, and

(iii) where the plan is required to be registered under the *Pension Benefits Standards Act*, *1985* or a similar law of a province, application for such registration has been made;

(b) where a pension plan that was submitted for registration before 1992 is registered by the Minister, the registration is effective from the day specified in writing by the Minister; and

(c) where a pension plan that is submitted for registration after 1991 is registered by the Minister, the registration is effective from the later of

(i) January 1 of the calendar year in which application for registration is made in prescribed manner by the plan administrator, and

(ii) the day the plan began.

**Related Provisions**: 149(1)(o) — Exemption — pension trust; 172(5) — Deemed refusal to register; 241(4)(j) — Communication of information — exception.

**Notes**: In addition to registration under the *Income Tax Act*, a registered pension plan must be registered under the provincial *Pension Benefits Act* or similar legislation, or, for industries under federal jurisdiction, the *Pension Benefits Standards Act* (see 147.1(2)(a)(iii)).

147.1(2)(b) and (c) amended by 1992 technical bill to provide a one-year delay. In the earlier version, "before 1992" and "after 1991" were "before 1991" and "after 1990".

**Regulations**: Part LXXXV; 8501(1) (prescribed conditions); 8512(1), (2) (prescribed conditions, prescribed manner).

**Information Circulars**: 72-13R8: Employees' pension plans [partly superseded by new Regulations].

**Registered Plans Division Newsletters**: 95-1 (New approach to plan registration); 95-2 (Registered plan division services); 95-6 (Specimen pension plans — speeding up the process); 95-7 (Quebec simplified pension plans); 98-1 (Simplified pension plans).

**Forms**: T510: Application for registration of a pension plan.

**(3) Deemed registration** — Where application is made to the Minister for registration of a pension plan for the purposes of this Act and, where the manner for making the application has been prescribed, the application is made in that manner by the administrator,

(a) subject to paragraph (b), the plan is, for the purposes of this Act other than paragraphs 60(j) and (j.2) and sections 147.3 and 147.4, deemed to be a registered pension plan throughout the period that begins on the latest of

(i) January 1 of the calendar year in which the application is made,

(ii) the day of commencement of the plan, and

(iii) January 1, 1989

and ending on the day on which a final determination is made with respect to the application; and

(b) where the final determination made with respect to the application is a refusal to register the plan, this Act shall, after the day of the final determination, apply as if the plan had never been deemed, under paragraph (a), to be a registered pension plan, except that

(i) any information return otherwise required to be filed under subsection 207.7(3) before

**S. 147.1(3)(b)(i)**      Income Tax Act, Part I

the particular day that is 90 days after the day of the final determination is not required to be filed until the particular day, and

(ii) subsections 227(8) and (8.2) are not applicable with respect to contributions made to the plan on or before the day of the final determination.

**Related Provisions**: 172(3) — Appeal from refusal to register, revocation of registration, etc.; 172(5) — Deemed refusal to register.

**Notes**: Reference to 147.4 added to opening words of 147.1(3)(a) by 1995-97 technical bill, effective 1997.

**Registered Plans Division Newsletters**: 95-1 (New approach to plan registration); 95-2 (Registered plan division services); 95-6 (Specimen pension plans — speeding up the process); 95-7 (Quebec simplified pension plans); 98-1 (Simplified pension plans).

**(4) Acceptance of amendments** — The Minister shall not accept an amendment to a registered pension plan unless

(a) application for the acceptance is made in prescribed manner by the plan administrator;

(b) the plan as amended complies with prescribed conditions for registration; and

(c) the amendment complies with prescribed conditions.

**Related Provisions**: 147.1(15) — Plan as registered.

**Regulations**: 8501(1), 8511 (prescribed conditions); 8512 (prescribed manner).

**Registered Plans Division Newsletters**: 95-6 (Specimen pension plans — speeding up the process); 95-7 (Quebec simplified pension plans); 98-1 (Simplified pension plans).

**Forms**: T920: Application for acceptance of an amendment to an RPP.

**(5) Additional conditions** — The Minister may, at any time, impose reasonable conditions applicable with respect to registered pension plans, a class of such plans or a particular registered pension plan.

**Notes**: For discussion of the conditions imposed on individual pension plans, see Jayne Casanova, "Portability and Proportionality of Individual Pension Plans", 11(1) *Taxation of Executive Compensation & Retirement* (Federated Press) 174–176 (July-Aug. 1999).

**Registered Plans Division Newsletters**: 96-3 (Flexible pension plans); 98-1 (Simplified pension plans).

**(6) Administrator** — There shall, for each registered pension plan, be a person or a body of persons that has ultimate responsibility for the administration of the plan and, except as otherwise permitted in writing by the Minister, the person or a majority of the persons who constitute the body shall be a person or persons resident in Canada.

**Related Provisions**: 147.1(7) — Obligations of administrator; 147.1(11) — Revocation of registration — notice of intention; 250 — Residents.

**(7) Obligations of administrator** — The administrator of a registered pension plan shall

(a) administer the plan in accordance with the terms of the plan as registered except that, where the plan fails to comply with the prescribed conditions for registration or any other requirement of this Act or the regulations, the administrator may administer the plan as if it were amended to so comply;

(b) before July, 1990, in the case of a person or body that is the administrator on January 1, 1989 or becomes the administrator before June, 1990, and, in any other case, within 30 days after becoming the administrator, inform the Minister in writing

(i) of the name and address of the person who is the administrator, or

(ii) of the names and addresses of the persons who constitute the body that is the administrator; and

(c) where there is any change in the information provided to the Minister in accordance with this paragraph or paragraph (b), inform the Minister in writing, within 60 days after the change, of the new information.

**Related Provisions**: 147.1(11) — Revocation of registration; 147.1(15) — Plan as registered; 147.1(18) — Regulations; 238(1) — Offences; 248(7)(a) — Mail deemed received on day mailed.

**Regulations**: Part LXXXV (prescribed conditions).

**Forms**: T3P: Employees' pension plan information and income tax return.

**(8) Pension adjustment limits** — Except as otherwise provided by regulation, a registered pension plan (other than a multi-employer plan) becomes, at the end of a calendar year after 1990, a revocable plan where

(a) the pension adjustment for the year of a member of the plan in respect of a participating employer exceeds the lesser of

(i) the money purchase limit for the year, and

(ii) 18% of the member's compensation from the employer for the year; or

(b) the total of

(i) the pension adjustment for the year of a member of the plan in respect of a participating employer, and

(ii) the total of all amounts each of which is the member's pension adjustment for the year in respect of an employer who, at any time in the year, does not deal at arm's length with the employer referred to in subparagraph (i)

exceeds the money purchase limit for the year.

**Related Provisions**: 147(5.1)(c) — Contribution limits; 147.1(11) — Revocation of registration — notice of intention; 147.3(13) — Excess transfer; 252.1 — Multi-employer plan — union as employer.

**Regulations**: 8509(12) (limitation on application of 147.1(8)); 8518 (where subsec. 147.1(8) not to apply).

**Interpretation Bulletins**: IT-528: Transfers of funds between registered plans.

**Information Circulars**: 98-2: Prescribed compensation for registered pension plans.

**Registered Plans Division Newsletters**: 91-4R (Registration rules for money purchase provisions); 96-1 (Changes to retirement savings limits).

**Forms**: T10: Summary of PARs.

**(9) Idem — multi-employer plans** — Except as otherwise provided by regulation, a registered pension plan that is a multi-employer plan (other than a specified multi-employer plan) in a calendar year after 1990 becomes, at the end of the year, a revocable plan where

(a) for a member and an employer, the total of all amounts each of which is the member's pension credit (as prescribed by regulation) for the year in respect of the employer under a defined benefit or money purchase provision of the plan exceeds the lesser of

(i) the money purchase limit for the year, and

(ii) 18% of the member's compensation from the employer for the year; or

(b) for a member, the total of all amounts each of which is the member's pension credit (as prescribed by regulation) for the year in respect of an employer under a defined benefit or money purchase provision of the plan exceeds the money purchase limit for the year.

**Related Provisions**: 147.1(11) — Revocation of registration — notice of intention; 147.1(14) — Anti-avoidance — multi-employer plans; 147.3(13) — Excess transfer; Reg. 8301 — Pension adjustment.

**Regulations**: 8301(4)–(6), (8) (pension credit); 8509(12) (limitation on application of 147.1(9)).

**Interpretation Bulletins**: IT-528: Transfers of funds between registered plans.

**Information Circulars**: 98-2: Prescribed compensation for registered pension plans.

**Registered Plans Division Newsletters**: 91-4R (Registration rules for money purchase provisions); 95-7 (Quebec simplified pension plans); 96-1 (Changes to retirement savings limits); 98-1 (Simplified pension plans).

**(10) Past service benefits** — With respect to each past service event that is relevant to the determination of benefits in respect of a member under a defined benefit provision of a registered pension plan, such benefits as are in respect of periods after 1989 and before the calendar year in which the event occurred shall be determined, for the purpose of a payment to be made from the plan or a contribution to be made to the plan at a particular time, with regard to the event only if

(a) where the member is alive at the particular time and except as otherwise provided by regulation, the Minister has certified in writing, before the particular time, that prescribed conditions are satisfied,

(b) where the member died before the particular time and the event occurred before the death of the member,

(i) this subsection did not require that the event be disregarded in determining benefits that were payable to the member immediately before the member's death (or that would have been so payable had the member been entitled to receive benefits under the provision immediately before the member's death), or

(ii) the event, as it affects the benefits provided to each individual who is entitled to benefits as a consequence of the death of the member, is acceptable to the Minister,

(c) where the member died before the particular time and the event occurred after the death of the member, the event, as it affects the benefits provided to each individual who is entitled to benefits as a consequence of the death of the member, is acceptable to the Minister, and

(d) no past service event that occurred before the event is required by reason of the application of this subsection to be disregarded at the particular time in determining benefits in respect of the member,

and, for the purposes of this subsection as it applies with respect to contributions that may be made to a registered pension plan, where application has been made for a certification referred to in paragraph (a) and the Minister has not refused to issue the certification, the Minister shall be deemed to have issued the certification.

**Related Provisions**: 147.1(11) — Revocation of registration — notice of intention; 147.1(18) — Regulations; 147.2(1) — Pension contributions deductible — employer contributions; 241(4)(c) — Communication of information — exception; 248(8) — Occurrences as a consequence of death.

**Regulations**: 8300(6) (prescribed rules); 8306 (certification not required); 8307(2) (prescribed conditions); 8308(1) (benefits provided before registration); 8519 (prescribed manner).

**Interpretation Bulletins**: IT-167R6: Registered pension plans — employee's contributions.

**Forms**: T1004: Application for certification of a provisional past service pension adjustment.

**(11) Revocation of registration — notice of intention** — Where, at any time after a pension plan has been registered by the Minister,

(a) the plan does not comply with the prescribed conditions for registration,

(b) the plan is not administered in accordance with the terms of the plan as registered,

(c) the plan becomes a revocable plan,

(d) a condition imposed by the Minister in writing and applicable with respect to the plan (including a condition applicable generally to registered pension plans or a class of such plans and a condition first imposed before 1989) is not complied with,

(e) a requirement under subsection (6) or (7) is not complied with,

(f) a benefit is paid by the plan, or a contribution is made to the plan, contrary to subsection (10),

(g) the administrator of the plan fails to file an information return or actuarial report relating to the plan or to a member of the plan as and when required by regulation,

(h) a participating employer fails to file an information return relating to the plan or to a member of the plan as and when required by regulation, or

(i) registration of the plan under the *Pension Benefits Standards Act, 1985* or a similar law of a province is refused or revoked,

the Minister may give notice (in this subsection and subsection (12) referred to as a "notice of intent") by registered mail to the plan administrator that the Minister proposes to revoke the registration of the plan as of a date specified in the notice of intent, which date shall not be earlier than the date as of which,

(j) where paragraph (a) applies, the plan failed to so comply,

(k) where paragraph (b) applies, the plan was not administered in accordance with its terms as registered,

(l) where paragraph (c) applies, the plan became a revocable plan,

(m) where paragraph (d) or (e) applies, the condition or requirement was not complied with,

(n) where paragraph (f) applies, the benefit was paid or the contribution was made,

(o) where paragraph (g) or (h) applies, the information return or actuarial report was required to be filed, and

(p) where paragraph (i) applies, the registration referred to in that paragraph was refused or revoked.

**Related Provisions**: 147.1(8) — Pension adjustment limits; 147.1(9) — Pension adjustment limits — multi-employer plans; 147.1(12) — Notice of revocation; 147.1(13) — Revocation of registration; 147.1(15) — Meaning of "plan" as registered; 147.1(18)(b) — Regulations; 147.3(12) — Restriction re transfers; 147.4(1)(d) — RPP annuity contract; 172(3) — Appeal from refusal to register, revocation of registration, etc.; 180(1) — Appeals to Federal Court of Appeal; 244(5) — Proof of service by mail; 248(7)(a) — Mail deemed received on day mailed.

**Regulations**: 8501(2); 8503(15).

**(12) Notice of revocation** — Where the Minister gives a notice of intent to the administrator of a registered pension plan, or the plan administrator applies to the Minister in writing for the revocation of the plan's registration, the Minister may,

(a) where the plan administrator has applied to the Minister in writing for the revocation of the plan's registration, at any time after receiving the administrator's application, and

(b) in any other case, after 30 days after the day of mailing of the notice of intent,

give notice (in this subsection and in subsection (13) referred to as a "notice of revocation") by registered mail to the plan administrator that the registration of the plan is revoked as of the date specified in the notice of revocation, which date may not be earlier than the date specified in the notice of intent or the administrator's application, as the case may be.

**(13) Revocation of registration** — Where the Minister gives a notice of revocation to the administrator of a registered pension plan, the registration of the plan is revoked as of the date specified in the notice of revocation, unless the Federal Court of Appeal or a judge thereof, on application made at any time before the determination of an appeal pursuant to subsection 172(3), orders otherwise.

**Related Provisions**: 147.1(12) — Notice of revocation; 244(5) — Proof of service by mail; 248(7)(a) — Mail deemed received on day mailed.

**(14) Anti-avoidance — multi-employer-plans** — Where at any time the Minister gives written notice to the administrators of two or more registered pension plans, each of which is a multi-employer plan, that this subsection is applicable in relation to those plans with respect to a calendar year,

(a) each of those plans that is a specified multi-employer plan in the year shall, for the purposes of subsection (9) (other than for the purpose of determining the pension credits referred to in paragraphs (9)(a) and (b)), be deemed to be a multi-employer plan that is not a specified multi-employer plan; and

(b) the totals determined for the year under paragraphs (9)(a) and (b) shall be the amounts that would be determined if all the plans were a single plan.

**Registered Plans Division Newsletters**: 95-7 (Quebec simplified pension plans); 98-1 (Simplified pension plans).

**(15) Plan as registered** — Any reference in this Act and the regulations to a pension plan as registered means the terms of the plan on the basis of which the Minister has registered the plan for the purposes of this Act and as amended by

(a) each amendment that has been accepted by the Minister, and

(b) each amendment that has been submitted to the Minister for acceptance and that the Minister has neither accepted nor refused to accept, if it is reasonable to expect the Minister to accept the amendment,

and includes all terms that are not contained in the documents constituting the plan but that are terms of the plan by reason of the *Pension Benefits Standards Act, 1985* or a similar law of a province.

**(16) Separate liability for obligations** — Every person who is a member of a body that is the administrator of a registered pension plan is subject to all obligations imposed on administrators by this Act or a regulation as if the person were the administrator of the plan.

**Related Provisions**: 238(1) — Offences.

**(17) Superintendent of Financial Institutions** — The Minister may, for the purposes of this Act, obtain the advice of the Superintendent of Financial Institutions with respect to any matter relating to pension plans.

**(18) Regulations** — The Governor in Council may make regulations

(a) prescribing conditions for the registration of pension plans and enabling the Minister to impose additional conditions or waive any conditions that are prescribed;

(b) prescribing circumstances under which a registered pension plan becomes a revocable plan;

(c) specifying the manner of determining, or enabling the Minister to determine, the portion of a member's benefits under a registered pension plan that is in respect of any period;

(d) requiring administrators of registered pension plans to make determinations in connection with the computation of pension adjustments, past service pension adjustments, total pension adjustment reversals or any other related amounts (all such amounts referred to in this subsection as "specified amounts");

(e) requiring that the method used to determine a specified amount be acceptable to the Minister, where more than one method would otherwise comply with the regulations;

(f) enabling the Minister to permit or require a specified amount to be determined in a manner different from that set out in the regulations;

(g) requiring that any person who has information required by another person in order to determine a specified amount provide the other person with that information;

(h) enabling the Minister to require any person to provide the Minister with information relating to the method used to determine a specified amount;

(i) enabling the Minister to require any person to provide the Minister with information relevant to a claim that paragraph (10)(a) is not applicable by reason of an exemption provided by regulation;

(j) respecting applications for certifications for the purposes of subsection (10);

(k) enabling the Minister to waive the requirement for a certification for the purposes of subsection (10);

(l) prescribing rules for the purposes of subsection (10), so that that subsection applies or does not apply with respect to benefits provided as a consequence of particular transactions, events or circumstances;

(m) requiring any person to provide the Minister or the administrator of a registered pension plan with information in connection with an application for certification for the purposes of subsection (10);

(n) requiring any person who obtains a certification for the purposes of subsection (10) to provide the individual in respect of whom the certification was obtained with an information return;

(o) requiring administrators of registered pension plans to file information with respect to amendments to such plans and to the arrangements for funding benefits thereunder;

(p) requiring administrators of registered pension plans to file information returns respecting such plans;

(q) enabling the Minister to require any person to provide the Minister with information for the purpose of determining whether the registration of a pension plan may be revoked;

(r) requiring administrators of registered pension plans to submit reports to the Minister, prescribing the class of persons by whom the reports shall be prepared and prescribing information to be contained in those reports;

(s) enabling the Minister to impose any requirement that may be imposed by regulation made under paragraph (r);

(t) defining, for the purposes of this Act, the expressions "multi-employer plan", "past service event", "past service pension adjustment", "pension adjustment", "specified multi-employer plan" and "total pension adjustment reversal"; and

(u) generally to carry out the purposes and provisions of this Act relating to registered pension plans and the determination and reporting of specified amounts.

**Related Provisions**: 221 — Regulations generally; 238(1) — Offences.

**Notes**: 147.1(18)(d) and (t) amended by 1997 Budget, effective 1997, to add reference to total pension adjustment reversals.

**Regulations**: 8300–8520.

**Forms**: T3P: Employees' pension plan income tax return; T10: Pension adjustment reversal; T10 Summ: Summary of PARs; T10 Segment.

**Related Provisions [s. 147.1]**: 87(2)(q) — Amalgamations — registered plans.

**Notes [s. 147.1]**: 147.1 added by 1990 pension bill. Subsecs. (1) to (15) are effective 1989; however, the definition "money purchase provision" in subsec. (1) is effective 1985, and the definitions "defined benefit provision" and "single amount" are effective 1988.

**Definitions [s. 147.1]**: "actuary", "administrator" — 147.1(1); "amount" — 248(1); "as registered" — 147.1(15); "average wage" — 147.1(1); "calendar year" — *Interpretation Act* 37(1)(a); "Canada" — 255; "compensation" — 147.1(1); "consequence of the death" — 248(8); "defined benefit provision" — 147.1(1); "employer", "employment" — 248(1); "Governor in Council" — *Interpretation Act* 35(1); "individual" — 248(1); "member" — 147.1(1); "Minister" — 248(1); "money purchase limit" — 147.1(1), 248(1); "money purchase provision" — 147.1(1); "multi-employer plan" — 147.1(1), Reg. 8500(1), 8510(1); "office" — 248(1); "participating employer" — 147.1(1); "past service event" — 147.1(1), Reg. 8300(1), (2); "past service pension adjustment" — 248(1), Reg. 8303; "pension adjustment" — 248(1), Reg. 8301(1); "pension credit" — Reg. 8301(2)–(8), (10), (16); "person", "prescribed" —

248(1); "province" — *Interpretation Act* 35(1); "registered pension plan", "regulation" — 248(1); "resident in Canada" — 250; "single amount" — 147.1(1); "specified amount" — 147.1(18)(d); "specified multi-employer plan" — 147.1(1), Reg. 8510(2), (3); "spouse" — 146(1.1), 147.1(1); "total pension adjustment reversal" — 248(1); "wage measure" — 147.1(1); "writing" — *Interpretation Act* 35(1).

**147.2 (1) Pension contributions deductible — employer contributions** — For a taxation year ending after 1990, there may be deducted in computing the income of a taxpayer who is an employer the total of all amounts each of which is a contribution made by the employer after 1990 and either in the taxation year or within 120 days after the end of the taxation year to a registered pension plan in respect of the employer's employees or former employees, to the extent that

(a) in the case of a contribution in respect of a money purchase provision of a plan, the contribution was made in accordance with the plan as registered and in respect of periods before the end of the taxation year;

(b) in the case of a contribution in respect of the defined benefit provisions of a plan (other than a specified multi-employer plan), the contribution

(i) is an eligible contribution,

(ii) was made to fund benefits provided to employees and former employees of the employer in respect of periods before the end of the taxation year, and

(iii) complies with subsection 147.1(10);

(c) in the case of a contribution made to a plan that is a specified multi-employer plan, the contribution was made in accordance with the plan as registered and in respect of periods before the end of the taxation year; and

(d) the contribution was not deducted in computing the income of the employer for a preceding taxation year.

**Related Provisions**: 6(1)(a)(i) — Employer's contribution not a taxable benefit; 20(1)(q) — Employer's contributions deductible; 147.1(8), (9) — Pension adjustment limits; 147.2(2) — Employer contributions — defined benefit provisions.

**Registered Plans Division Newsletters**: 91-4R (Registration rules for money purchase provisions).

**(2) Employer contributions — defined benefit provisions** — For the purposes of subsection (1), a contribution made by an employer to a registered pension plan in respect of the defined benefit provisions of the plan is an eligible contribution if it is a prescribed contribution or if it complies with prescribed conditions and is made pursuant to a recommendation by an actuary in whose opinion the contribution is required to be made so that the plan will have sufficient assets to pay benefits under the defined benefit provisions of the plan, as registered, in respect of the employees and former employees of the employer, where

(a) the recommendation is based on an actuarial valuation that complies with the following conditions, except the conditions in subparagraphs (iii) and (iv) to the extent that they are inconsistent with any other conditions that apply for the purpose of determining whether the contribution is an eligible contribution:

(i) the effective date of the valuation is not more than 4 years before the day on which the contribution is made,

(ii) actuarial liabilities and current service costs are determined in accordance with an actuarial funding method that produces a reasonable matching of contributions with accruing benefits,

(iii) all assumptions made for the purposes of the valuation are reasonable at the time the valuation is prepared and at the time the contribution is made,

(iv) the valuation is prepared in accordance with generally accepted actuarial principles,

(v) the valuation complies with prescribed conditions, which conditions may include conditions regarding the benefits that may be taken into account for the purposes of the valuation, and

(vi) where more than one employer participates in the plan, assets and actuarial liabilities are apportioned in a reasonable manner among participating employers in respect of their employees and former employees, and

(b) the recommendation is approved by the Minister in writing,

and, for the purposes of this subsection and except as otherwise provided by regulation,

(c) the benefits taken into account for the purposes of a recommendation may include anticipated cost-of-living and similar adjustments where the terms of a pension plan do not require that those adjustments be made but it is reasonable to expect that they will be made, and

(d) a recommendation with respect to the contributions required to be made by an employer in respect of the defined benefit provisions of a pension plan may be prepared without regard to such portion of the assets of the plan apportioned to the employer in respect of the employer's employees and former employees as does not exceed the least of

(i) the amount of actuarial surplus in respect of the employer,

(ii) 20% of the amount of actuarial liabilities apportioned to the employer in respect of the employer's employees and former employees, and

(iii) the greater of

(A) 2 times the estimated amount of current service contributions that would, if there were no actuarial surplus, be required to be made by the employer and the employer's employees for the 12 months immediately following the effective date of the actuarial valuation on which the recommendation is based, and

(B) the amount that would be determined under subparagraph (ii) if the reference therein to "20%" were read as a reference to "10%".

**Related Provisions**: 147.2(3) — Filing of actuarial report.

**Notes**: 147.2(2)(b) amended by 1995-97 technical bill, effective April 1996, to delete the words "on the advice of the Superintendent of Financial Institutions". The Pension Advice Section of the Office of the Superintendent of Financial Institutions has been transferred to Revenue Canada.

**Regulations**: 8515(5) (prescribed conditions); 8516(1) (prescribed contribution).

**Information Circulars**: 72-13R8: Employees' pension plans.

**Registered Plans Division Newsletters**: 95-3 (Actuarial report content); 96-1 (Changes to retirement savings limits).

**(3) Filing of actuarial report** — Where, for the purposes of subsection (2), a person seeks the Minister's approval of a recommendation made by an actuary in connection with the contributions to be made by an employer to a registered pension plan in respect of the defined benefit provisions of the plan, the person shall file with the Minister a report prepared by the actuary that contains the recommendation and any other information required by the Minister.

**Related Provisions**: Reg. 8410 — Actuarial report required on demand.

**Registered Plans Division Newsletters**: 95-3 (Actuarial report content).

**(4) Amount of employee's pension contributions deductible** — There may be deducted in computing the income of an individual for a taxation year ending after 1990 an amount equal to the total of

(a) **service after 1989** — the total of all amounts each of which is a contribution (other than a prescribed contribution) made by the individual in the year to a registered pension plan in respect of a period after 1989, to the extent that the contribution was made in accordance with the plan as registered,

### Proposed Amendment — 147.2(4)(a)

(a) **service after 1989** — the total of all amounts each of which is a contribution (other than a prescribed contribution) made by the individual in the year to a registered pension plan that is in respect of a period after 1989 or that is a prescribed eligible contribution, to the extent that the contribution was made in accordance with the plan as registered,

**Application**: Bill C-43 (First Reading September 20, 2000), s. 87, will amend para. 147.2(4)(a) to read as above, applicable to contributions made after 1990.

**Technical Notes**: Subsection 147.2(4) of the Act provides rules that govern the deductibility of employee contributions to registered pension plans (RPPs). Paragraph 147.2(4)(a) allows an individual to deduct contributions made after 1990 to an RPP in respect of years after 1989, to the extent that the contributions are made in accordance with the terms of the plan as registered. This rule applies whether a contribution is made under a money purchase provision or a defined benefit provision, and whether a contribution is a current service contribution or a past service contribution.

Paragraph 147.2(4)(a) is amended to allow an individual to deduct, in addition to the contributions described above, prescribed eligible contributions. Draft subsection 8501(6.2) of the Regulations prescribes, for this purpose, certain employee contributions that are made under a defined benefit provision of an RPP pursuant to an arrangement under which members of the plan make contributions towards an unfunded liability under the plan. For further details, refer to the commentary on draft subsections 8501(6.1) and (6.2) of the Regulations in Appendix D.

(b) **service before 1990 while not a contributor** — the least of

(i) the amount, if any, by which

(A) the total of all amounts each of which is a contribution (other than an additional voluntary contribution or a prescribed contribution) made by the individual in the year or a preceding taxation year and after 1945 to a registered pension plan in respect of a particular year before 1990, if all or any part of the particular year is included in the individual's eligible service under the plan and if

(I) in the case of a contribution that the individual made before March 28, 1988 or was obliged to make under the terms of an agreement in writing entered into before March 28, 1988, the individual was not a contributor to the plan in the particular year, or

(II) in any other case, the individual was not a contributor to any registered pension plan in the particular year

exceeds

(B) the total of all amounts each of which is an amount deducted, in computing the individual's income for a preceding taxation year, in respect of contributions included in the total determined in respect of the individual for the year under clause (A),

(ii) $3,500, and

(iii) the amount determined by the formula

$$(\$3,500 \times Y) - Z$$

where

Y is the number of calendar years before 1990 each of which is a year

(A) all or any part of which is included in the individual's eligible service under a registered pension plan to which the individual has made a contribution that is included in the total determined under clause (i)(A) and in which the individual was not a contributor to any registered pension plan, or

(B) all or any part of which is included in the individual's eligible service under a registered pension plan to which the individual has made a contribution

(I) that is included in the total determined under clause (i)(A), and

(II) that the individual made before March 28, 1988 or was obliged to make under the terms of an agreement in writing entered into before March 28, 1988, and in which the individual was not a contributor to the plan, and

Z is the total of all amounts each of which is an amount deducted, in computing the individual's income for a preceding taxation year,

(A) in respect of contributions included in the total determined in respect of the individual for the year under clause (i)(A), or

(B) where the preceding year was before 1987, under subparagraph 8(1)(m)(ii) (as it read in its application to that preceding year) in respect of additional voluntary contributions made in respect of a year that satisfies the conditions in the description of Y, and

(c) **service before 1990 while a contributor** — the lesser of

(i) the amount, if any, by which

(A) the total of all amounts each of which is a contribution (other than an additional voluntary contribution, a prescribed contribution or a contribution included in the total determined in respect of the individual for the year under clause (b)(i)(A)) made by the individual in the year or a preceding taxation year and after 1962 to a registered pension plan in respect of a particular year before 1990 that is included, in whole or in part, in the individual's eligible service under the plan

exceeds

(B) the total of all amounts each of which is an amount deducted, in computing the individual's income for a preceding taxa-

tion year, in respect of contributions included in the total determined in respect of the individual for the year under clause (A), and

(ii) the amount, if any, by which $3,500 exceeds the total of the amounts deducted by reason of paragraphs (a) and (b) in computing the individual's income for the year.

**Related Provisions**: 8(1)(m) — Employee's RPP contributions deductible; 56(1)(a)(i) — Pension benefits taxable when received; 147.1(8), (9) — Pension adjustment limits; 147.2(5) — Teachers; 147.2(6) — Additional deduction for year taxpayer dies; 152(6)(f) — Minister required to reassess past year to allow additional deduction following death; 257 — Formula cannot calculate to less than zero.

**Notes**: 147.2(4)(b)(iii)Z(B) amended by 1995-97 technical bill, retroactive to 1991, to refer to past service AVCs that were deducted in computing income for years before 1987, and to refer to 8(1)(m)(ii) as it read in the year in which the deductions were claimed rather than as it read for 1990. This amendment was made because 8(1)(m)(ii) did not permit the deduction of past service AVCs after 1986.

**Regulations**: 100(3)(a) (deduction of pension contribution from payroll reduces source withholding); 8501(6.2) (prescribed eligible contribution); 8502(b)(i), 8503(4)(a), (b) (RPP contributions permitted by employee).

**Interpretation Bulletins**: IT-167R6: Registered pension plans — employee's contributions.

**Forms**: T4040: RRSPs and other registered plans for retirement [guide].

**(5) Teachers** — For the purpose of determining whether a teacher may deduct an amount contributed by the teacher to a registered pension plan in computing the teacher's income for a taxation year ending after 1990 and before 1995 during which the teacher was employed by Her Majesty or a person exempt from tax for the year under section 149,

(a) clause (4)(b)(i)(A) shall be read without reference to subclauses (4)(b)(i)(A)(I) and (II); and

(b) the description of Y in subparagraph (4)(b)(iii) shall be read as follows:

"Y is the number of calendar years before 1990 each of which is a year all or any part of which is included in the individual's eligible service under a registered pension plan to which the individual has made a contribution that is included in the total determined under clause (i)(A), and"

**Related Provisions**: 8(7) (applicable before 1991).

**Interpretation Bulletins**: IT-167R6: Registered pension plans — employee's contributions.

**(6) Deductible contributions when taxpayer dies** — Where a taxpayer dies in a taxation year, for the purpose of computing the taxpayer's income for the year and the preceding taxation year,

(a) paragraph (4)(b) shall be read without reference to subparagraph (ii) and as if the reference to "the least of" were a reference to "the lesser of"; and

(b) paragraph (4)(c) shall be read without reference to subparagraph (ii) and the words "the lesser of".

**Related Provisions [subsec. 147.2(6)]**: 152(6)(f) — Minister required to reassess past year to allow additional deduction; 163(4)(b.1) — Additional deduction ignored when calculating penalties; 164(5)(h.01), 164(5.1)(h.01) — No back interest on refund where past year reassessed.

**Notes**: 147.2(6) added by 1995-97 technical bill, effective for deaths after 1992. It provides that for the year of death and the preceding year, the $3,500 annual limits in 147.2(4)(b) and (c) do not apply.

**Related Provisions [s. 147.2]**: 87(2)(q) — Amalgamations — registered plans.

**Notes [147.2]**: 147.2 added by 1990 pension bill, effective 1989. Employee RPP deductions were governed before 1991 by 8(1)(m), (m.1) and 8(6)–8(8).

**Definitions [s. 147.2]**: "actuary" — 147.1(1); "additional voluntary contribution", "amount" — 248(1); "as registered" — 147.1(15); "defined benefit provision" — 147.1(1); "eligible contribution" — 147.2(2); "employee", "employer", "individual", "Minister" — 248(1); "money purchase provision", "participating employer" — 147.1(1); "person", "prescribed", "registered pension plan", "regulation" — 248(1); "specified multi-employer plan" — 147.1(1), Reg. 8510(2), (3); "taxation year" — 249; "taxpayer" — 248(1); "writing" — *Interpretation Act* 35(1).

## 147.3 (1) Transfer — money purchase to money purchase, RRSP or RRIF — An amount is transferred from a registered pension plan in accordance with this subsection if the amount

(a) is a single amount;

(b) is transferred on behalf of a member in full or partial satisfaction of the member's entitlement to benefits under a money purchase provision of the plan as registered; and

(c) is transferred directly to

   (i) another registered pension plan to provide benefits in respect of the member under a money purchase provision of that plan,

   (ii) a registered retirement savings plan under which the member is the annuitant (within the meaning assigned by subsection 146(1)), or

   (iii) a registered retirement income fund under which the member is the annuitant (within the meaning assigned by subsection 146.3(1)).

**Related Provisions**: 146(8.2) — Amount deductible where withdrawn after mistaken contribution; 147.3(9) — Taxation of amount transferred; 147.3(13) — Excess transfer. See additional Related provisions at end of s. 147.3.

**Notes**: Although 147.3(1) and 147.3(4) permit transfers from an RPP to an RRSP or RRIF, provincial pensions legislation will generally require that any such transfers be to a locked-in RRSP or a life income fund (LIF, essentially a locked-in RRIF). Since 1996, LIFs can also be used for former federal employees, as well as those in federally-regulated industries such as banking and telecommunications.

147.3(1)(c)(iii) added by 1992 technical bill, effective August 30, 1990, to permit transfers to RRIFs.

**Interpretation Bulletins**: IT-528: Transfers of funds between registered plans.

**Information Circulars**: 79-8R3: Forms to use to directly transfer funds to or between plans, or to purchase an annuity.

**Registered Plans Division Newsletters**: 91-4R (Registration rules for money purchase provisions).

**Forms**: T2151: Record of direct transfer of a "single amount".

## (2) Transfer — money purchase to defined benefit — An amount is transferred from a registered pension plan in accordance with this subsection if the amount

(a) is a single amount;

(b) is transferred on behalf of a member in full or partial satisfaction of the member's entitlement to benefits under a money purchase provision of the plan as registered; and

(c) is transferred directly to another registered pension plan to fund benefits provided in respect of the member under a defined benefit provision of that plan.

**Related Provisions**: 147.1(10) — Past service benefits; 147.3(9) — Taxation of amount transferred; 147.3(13) — Excess transfer. See additional Related provisions at end of s. 147.3.

**Interpretation Bulletins**: IT-528: Transfers of funds between registered plans.

**Information Circulars**: 79-8R3: Forms to use to directly transfer funds to or between plans, or to purchase an annuity.

**Registered Plans Division Newsletters**: 91-4R (Registration rules for money purchase provisions).

**Forms**: T2151: Record of direct transfer of a "single amount".

## (3) Transfer — defined benefit to defined benefit — An amount is transferred from a registered pension plan (in this subsection referred to as the "transferor plan") in accordance with this subsection if the amount

(a) is a single amount;

(b) consists of all or any part of the property held in connection with a defined benefit provision of the transferor plan;

(c) is transferred directly to another registered pension plan to be held in connection with a defined benefit provision of the other plan; and

(d) is transferred as a consequence of benefits becoming provided under the defined benefit provision of the other plan to one or more individuals who were members of the transferor plan.

**Related Provisions**: 147.3(9) — Taxation of amount transferred. See additional Related Provisions at end of s. 147.3.

**Regulations**: 8517 (prescribed amount).

**Interpretation Bulletins**: IT-528: Transfers of funds between registered plans.

**Information Circulars**: 79-8R3: Forms to use to directly transfer funds to or between plans, or to purchase an annuity.

**Forms**: T2151: Record of direct transfer of a "single amount".

## (4) Transfer — defined benefit to money purchase, RRSP or RRIF — An amount is trans-

## S. 147.3(4) — Income Tax Act, Part I

ferred from a registered pension plan in accordance with this subsection if the amount

(a) is a single amount no portion of which relates to an actuarial surplus;

(b) is transferred on behalf of a member in full or partial satisfaction of benefits to which the member is entitled, either absolutely or contingently, under a defined benefit provision of the plan as registered;

(c) does not exceed a prescribed amount; and

(d) is transferred directly to

(i) another registered pension plan and allocated to the member under a money purchase provision of that plan,

(ii) a registered retirement savings plan under which the member is the annuitant (within the meaning assigned by subsection 146(1)), or

(iii) a registered retirement income fund under which the member is the annuitant (within the meaning assigned by subsection 146.3(1)).

**Related Provisions**: 146(8.2) — Amount deductible where withdrawn after mistaken contribution; 147.3(9) — Taxation of amount transferred. See additional Related Provisions at end of s. 147.3.

**Notes**: See Notes to 147.3(1).

147.3(4)(d)(iii) added by 1992 technical bill, effective August 30, 1990, to permit transfers to RRIFs. (Other amendments, made at the same time, were retroactive to 1989. For the rules for 1988, see Notes at end of 147.3.)

**Regulations**: 8517 (prescribed amount).

**Interpretation Bulletins**: IT-528: Transfers of funds between registered plans.

**Information Circulars**: 79-8R3: Forms to use to directly transfer funds to or between plans, or to purchase an annuity.

**Registered Plans Division Newsletters**: 91-4R (Registration rules for money purchase provisions).

**Forms**: T2151: Record of direct transfer of a "single amount".

**(4.1) Transfer of surplus — defined benefit to money purchase** — An amount is transferred from a registered pension plan in accordance with this subsection if the amount

(a) is transferred in respect of the actuarial surplus under a defined benefit provision of the plan; and

(b) is transferred directly to another registered pension plan and allocated under a money purchase provision of that plan to one or more members of that plan.

**Related Provisions**: 60(j.01) — Transfer of surplus.

**Notes**: 147.3(4.1) added by 1992 technical bill, effective 1991.

**Interpretation Bulletins**: IT-528: Transfers of funds between registered plans.

**Information Circulars**: 79-8R3: Forms to use to directly transfer funds to or between plans, or to purchase an annuity.

**Registered Plans Division Newsletters**: 91-4R (Registration rules for money purchase provisions); 95-5 (Conversion of a defined benefit provision to a money purchase provision).

**Forms**: T2151: Record of direct transfer of a "single amount".

**(5) Transfer to RPP, RRSP or RRIF for spouse [or common-law partner] on marriage [or partnership] breakdown** — An amount is transferred from a registered pension plan in accordance with this subsection if the amount

(a) is a single amount;

### Proposed Amendment — 147.3(5)(a)

(a) is a single amount no portion of which relates to an actuarial surplus;

**Application**: Bill C-43 (First Reading September 20, 2000), subsec. 88(1), will amend para. 147.3(5)(a) to read as above, applicable to transfers that occur after November 1999.

**Technical Notes**: Section 147.3 of the Act provides rules governing the transfer of funds from registered pension plans (RPPs) to registered retirement savings plans (RRSPs), registered retirement income funds (RRIFs) and other RPPs.

Subsection 147.3(5) of the Act permits the direct transfer of a lump sum amount from an RPP to another RPP, an RRSP or a RRIF for the benefit of the spouse or former spouse of a plan member, where the spouse or former spouse is entitled to the amount pursuant to a court order or written agreement relating to a division of property on marriage breakdown.

Paragraph 147.3(5)(a) is amended to deny the transfer of an amount relating to actuarial surplus. This change is consistent with the transfer rules set out in subsections 147.3(4) and (7), which do not permit a plan member's share of an actuarial surplus to be transferred tax-free to another registered plan.

(b) is transferred on behalf of an individual who is a spouse or common-law partner or former spouse or common-law partner of a member of the plan and who is entitled to the amount under a decree, order or judgment of a competent tribunal, or under a written agreement, relating to a division of property between the member and the individual in settlement of rights arising out of, or on a breakdown of, their marriage or common-law partnership; and

(c) is transferred directly to

(i) another registered pension plan for the benefit of the individual,

(ii) a registered retirement savings plan under which the individual is the annuitant (within the meaning assigned by subsection 146(1)), or

(iii) a registered retirement income fund under which the individual is the annuitant (within the meaning assigned by subsection 146.3(1)).

**Related Provisions**: 146.3(2)(f)(vi) — Conditions for RRIF; 147.3(9) — Taxation of amount transferred; 252(3) — Extended meaning of "spouse" and "former spouse". See additional Related Provisions at end of s. 147.3.

**Notes**: 147.3(5)(b) amended by 2000 same-sex partners bill to add reference to "common-law partner" and "common-law partnership", effective for the 2001 and later taxation years, or earlier by election (see Notes to 248(1)"common-law partner").

147.3(5)(b) amended by 1992 technical bill, effective 1993, due to the introduction of an extended definition of "marriage" in

252(4)(b). From 1989 to 1992, in place of "arising out of, or on the breakdown of, their marriage", read "arising out of their marriage or other conjugal relationship, on or after the breakdown of the marriage or other relationship".

147.3(5)(c)(iii) added by 1992 technical bill, effective August 30, 1990, to permit transfers to RRIFs.

**Interpretation Bulletins**: IT-440R2: Transfer of rights to income; IT-528: Transfers of funds between registered plans.

**Information Circulars**: 79-8R3: Forms to use to directly transfer funds to or between plans, or to purchase an annuity.

**Registered Plans Division Newsletters**: 91-4R (Registration rules for money purchase provisions).

**Forms**: T2151: Record of direct transfer of a "single amount".

**(6) Transfer — pre-1991 contributions** — An amount is transferred from a registered pension plan in accordance with this subsection if the amount

(a) is a single amount;

(b) is transferred on behalf of a member who is entitled to the amount as a return of contributions made by the member under a defined benefit provision of the plan before 1991, or as interest (computed at a rate not exceeding a reasonable rate) in respect of those contributions; and

(c) is transferred directly to

(i) another registered pension plan for the benefit of the member,

(ii) a registered retirement savings plan under which the member is the annuitant (within the meaning assigned by subsection 146(1)), or

(iii) a registered retirement income fund under which the member is the annuitant (within the meaning assigned by subsection 146.3(1)).

**Related Provisions**: 147.3(9) — Taxation of amount transferred. See additional Related Provisions at end of s. 147.3.

**Notes**: 147.3(6)(c)(iii) added by 1992 technical bill, effective August 30, 1990, to permit transfers to RRIFs.

**Interpretation Bulletins**: IT-528: Transfers of funds between registered plans.

**Information Circulars**: 79-8R3: Forms to use to directly transfer funds to or between plans, or to purchase an annuity.

**Registered Plans Division Newsletters**: 91-4R (Registration rules for money purchase provisions); 98-2 (Treating excess member contributions under a registered pension plan).

**Forms**: T2151: Record of direct transfer of a "single amount".

**(7) Transfer — lump sum benefits on death** — An amount is transferred from a registered pension plan in accordance with this subsection if the amount

(a) is a single amount no portion of which relates to an actuarial surplus;

(b) is transferred on behalf of an individual who is entitled to the amount as a consequence of the death of a member of the plan and who was a spouse or common-law partner or former spouse or common-law partner of the member at the date of the member's death; and

(c) is transferred directly to

(i) another registered pension plan for the benefit of the individual,

(ii) a registered retirement savings plan under which the individual is the annuitant (within the meaning assigned by subsection 146(1)), or

(iii) a registered retirement income fund under which the individual is the annuitant (within the meaning assigned by subsection 146.3(1)).

**Related Provisions**: 104(27) — Pension benefits; 146.3(2)(f)(vi) — Conditions for RRIF; 147.3(9) — Taxation of amount transferred; 248(8) — Occurrences as a consequence of death; 252(3) — Extended definition of "spouse" and "former spouse". See additional Related Provisions at end of s. 147.3.

**Notes**: 147.3(7)(b) amended by 2000 same-sex partners bill to add reference to "common-law partner", effective for the 2001 and later taxation years, or earlier by election (see Notes to 248(1)"common-law partner").

147.3(7)(c)(iii) added by 1992 technical bill, effective August 30, 1990, to permit transfers to RRIFs.

**Interpretation Bulletins**: IT-528: Transfers of funds between registered plans.

**Information Circulars**: 79-8R3: Forms to use to directly transfer funds to or between plans, or to purchase an annuity.

**Registered Plans Division Newsletters**: 91-4R (Registration rules for money purchase provisions).

**Forms**: T2151: Record of direct transfer of a "single amount".

---

**Proposed Addition — 147.3(7.1)**

**(7.1) Transfer where money purchase plan replaces money purchase plan** — An amount is transferred from a registered pension plan (in this subsection referred to as the "transferor plan") in accordance with this subsection if

(a) the amount is a single amount;

(b) the amount is transferred in respect of the surplus (as defined by regulation) under a money purchase provision (in this subsection referred to as the "former provision") of the transferor plan;

(c) the amount is transferred directly to another registered pension plan to be held in connection with a money purchase provision (in this subsection referred to as the "current provision") of the other plan;

(d) the amount is transferred in conjunction with the transfer of amounts from the former provision to the current provision on behalf of all or a significant number of members of the transferor plan whose benefits under the former provision are replaced by benefits under the current provision; and

(e) the transfer is acceptable to the Minister and the Minister has so notified the administrator of the transferor plan in writing.

**Application**: Bill C-43 (First Reading September 20, 2000), subsec. 88(2), will add subsec. 147.3(7.1), applicable to transfers that occur after 1998.

**Technical Notes**: New subsection 147.3(7.1) of the Act is introduced to permit surplus to be transferred directly from a money purchase provision of an RPP to a money purchase provision of another RPP, where the second

## S. 147.3(7.1)

plan replaces all or part of the first plan. Subsection 147.3(7.1) is intended to apply to situations involving the reorganization of a money purchase RPP, such as the splitting of one plan into two or more plans or the transfer of one group of employees from one plan to another. The subsection ensures that money purchase surplus can be transferred directly to a replacement money purchase plan. This will enable an employer to use the surplus, for example, to satisfy its obligations to make contributions under the money purchase provision, to make additional allocations to plan members or to pay plan expenses.

Subsection 147.3(7.1) provides that the term "surplus" has the meaning assigned by the Regulations. Subsection 8500(1) of the Regulations, in conjunction with draft subsection 8500(1.1), defines "surplus" for this purpose. "Surplus" under a money purchase provision of an RPP is the portion of the unallocated amount held under the provision that is not attributable to forfeited amounts, employer contributions that will be allocated to members as part of the regular allocation of contributions, or to certain earnings of the plan. Generally, a money purchase surplus would exist only if actuarial surplus was originally transferred from a defined benefit provision of an RPP and if the actuarial surplus was not credited to the members' accounts under the money purchase provision at the time of the transfer.

The following conditions must be met in order for the subsection to apply with respect to the transfer of money purchase surplus:

- the surplus must be transferred in conjunction with the transfer of amounts on behalf of all or a significant number of members of the transferor plan whose money purchase benefits are being replaced by money purchase benefits under the recipient plan; and
- the transfer must be approved in writing by the Minister of National Revenue.

Appendix D contains consequential amendments to Parts LXXXIII and LXXXV of the Regulations to reflect the introduction of subsection 147.3(7.1).

**Regulations**: 8500(1)"surplus", 8500(1.1) (meaning of "surplus").

**(8) Transfer where money purchase plan replaces defined benefit plan** — An amount is transferred from a registered pension plan (in this subsection referred to as the "transferor plan") in accordance with this subsection if

(a) the amount is a single amount;

(b) the amount consists of all or any portion of the property held in connection with a defined benefit provision of the transferor plan;

(c) the amount is transferred directly to another registered pension plan to be held in connection with a money purchase provision of the other plan and used to satisfy employer obligations to make contributions under the money purchase provision;

**Proposed Amendment — 147.3(8)(b), (c)**

(b) the amount is transferred in respect of the actuarial surplus under a defined benefit provision of the transferor plan;

(c) the amount is transferred directly to another registered pension plan to be held in connection with a money purchase provision of the other plan;

**Application**: Bill C-43 (First Reading September 20, 2000), subsec. 88(3), will amend paras. 147.3(8)(b) and (c) to read as above, applicable to transfers that occur after 1990.

**Technical Notes**: Subsection 147.3(8) of the Act permits, in certain circumstances, the direct transfer of property from a defined benefit provision of an RPP to a money purchase provision of another RPP. Subsection 147.3(8) is intended to accommodate the transfer of actuarial surplus where a defined benefit RPP is replaced by a money purchase RPP. One of the conditions that must be met in order for the subsection to apply is that the recipient plan must provide that the surplus be used to satisfy the obligation of employers to make contributions under the recipient plan.

Subsection 147.3(8) is amended to eliminate the condition that the surplus be used to satisfy employer contribution obligations. This will permit the surplus to be used for other purposes relating to the operation of the plan, such as to pay plan expenses or to make additional allocations to plan members. In addition, subsection 147.3(8) is amended to clarify that the provision is intended to apply only to accommodate the transfer of actuarial surplus. It should be noted that paragraph 8506(2)(c) of the Regulations prohibits employer contributions to a money purchase provision where there is a surplus under the provision.

(d) the amount is transferred in conjunction with the transfer of amounts from the defined benefit provision to the money purchase provision on behalf of all or a significant number of members of the transferor plan whose benefits under the defined benefit provision are replaced by benefits under the money purchase provision; and

(e) the transfer is acceptable to the Minister and the Minister has so notified the administrator of the transferor plan in writing.

**Related Provisions**: 147.3(9) — Taxation of amount transferred; 147.3(10) — Division of transferred amount, See additional Related Provisions at end of s. 147.3.

**Interpretation Bulletins**: IT-528: Transfers of funds between registered plans.

**Information Circulars**: 79-8R3: Forms to use to directly transfer funds to or between plans, or to purchase an annuity.

**Registered Plans Division Newsletters**: 91-4R (Registration rules for money purchase provisions); 95-5 (Conversion of a defined benefit provision to a money purchase provision); 98-1 (Simplified pension plans).

**Forms**: T2151: Record of direct transfer of a "single amount".

**(9) Taxation of amount transferred** — Where an amount is transferred in accordance with any of subsections (1) to (8),

(a) the amount shall not, by reason only of that transfer, be included by reason of subparagraph 56(1)(a)(i) in computing the income of any taxpayer; and

(b) no deduction may be made under any provision of this Act in respect of the amount in computing the income of any taxpayer.

**Related Provisions**: 147.3(11) — Division of transferred amount; 147.3(14.1) — Transfer of property between benefit provisions of the same plan; 212(1)(h)(iii.1)(A) — Amount transferred under 147.3 excluded from withholding tax on pension benefits. See additional Related provisions at end of s. 147.3.

**Interpretation Bulletins**: IT-528: Transfers of funds between registered plans.

**(10) Idem** — Where, on behalf of an individual, an amount is transferred from a registered pension plan (in this subsection referred to as the "transferor plan") to another plan or fund (in this subsection referred to as the "transferee plan") that is a registered pension plan, a registered retirement savings plan or a registered retirement income fund and the transfer is not in accordance with any of subsections (1) to (7),

(a) the amount is deemed to have been paid from the transferor plan to the individual;

(b) subject to paragraph (c), the individual shall be deemed to have paid the amount as a contribution or premium to the transferee plan; and

(c) where the transferee plan is a registered retirement income fund, for the purposes of subsection 146(5) and Part X.1, the individual shall be deemed to have paid the amount at the time of the transfer as a premium under a registered retirement savings plan under which the individual was the annuitant (within the meaning assigned by subsection 146(1)).

**Related Provisions**: 146(5)(a)(v)(B) — Amount of RRSP premiums deductible; 147.3(11) — Division of transferred amount; 147.3(12) — Restriction re transfers; 147.3(13.1) — Withdrawal of excessive transfers to RRSPs and RRIFs; 147.3(14.1) — Transfer of property between benefit provisions of the same plan. See additional Related Provisions at end of s. 147.3.

**Notes**: 147.3(10)(a) amended to delete the initial words "Notwithstanding section 254" by 1995-97 technical bill, effective for transfers after July 30, 1997. (See now 147.4.)

147.3(10)(c) and the reference to RRIFs in the opening words of 147.3(10) added by 1992 technical bill, effective August 30, 1990. See Notes to 147.3(1), (4), (5), (6) and (7).

**Interpretation Bulletins**: IT-528: Transfers of funds between registered plans.

**(11) Division of transferred amount** — Where an amount is transferred from a registered pension plan to another registered pension plan, to a registered retirement savings plan or to a registered retirement income fund and a portion, but not all, of the amount is transferred in accordance with any of subsections (1) to (8),

(a) subsection (9) applies with respect to the portion of the amount that is transferred in accordance with any of subsections (1) to (8); and

(b) subsection (10) applies with respect to the remainder of the amount.

**Related Provisions**: 147.3(14.1) — Transfer of property between benefit provisions of the same plan.

**Notes**: 147.3(11) amended by 1992 technical bill, effective August 30, 1990, to add reference to RRIFs.

**(12) Restriction re transfers** — A registered pension plan becomes a revocable plan at any time that an amount is transferred from the plan to another registered pension plan, to a registered retirement savings plan or to a registered retirement income fund unless

(a) the amount is transferred in accordance with any of subsections (1) to (8); or

(b) where the amount is transferred on behalf of an individual,

(i) the amount is deductible by the individual under paragraph 60(j) or (j.2), or

(ii) the *Pension Benefits Standards Act, 1985* or a similar law of a province prohibits the payment of the amount to the individual.

**Related Provisions**: 147.1(11) — Revocation of registration — notice of intention. See additional Related Provisions at end of s. 147.3.

**Notes**: Opening words 147.3(12) amended by 1992 technical bill, effective August 30, 1990, to add reference to RRIFs.

**Interpretation Bulletins**: IT-528: Transfers of funds between registered plans.

**Registered Plans Division Newsletters**: 91-4R (Registration rules for money purchase provisions).

**(13) Excess transfer** — Where

(a) the transfer in a calendar year of an amount from a registered pension plan on behalf of a member of the plan would, but for this subsection, be in accordance with subsection (1) or (2), and

(b) the plan becomes, at the end of the year, a revocable plan as a consequence of an excess determined under any of paragraphs 147.1(8)(a) and (b) and (9)(a) and (b) with respect to the member (whether or not such an excess is also determined with respect to any other member),

such portion of the amount transferred as may reasonably be considered to derive from amounts allocated or reallocated to the member in the year or from earnings reasonably attributable to those amounts shall, except to the extent otherwise expressly provided in writing by the Minister, be deemed to be an amount that was not transferred in accordance with subsection (1) or (2), as the case may be.

**Interpretation Bulletins**: IT-528: Transfers of funds between registered plans.

**(13.1) Withdrawal of excessive transfers to RRSPs and RRIFs** — There may be deducted in computing the income of an individual for a taxation year the lesser of

(a) the amount, if any, by which

(i) the total of all amounts each of which is an amount included under subsection 146(8), (8.3) or (12) or 146.3(5), (5.1) or (11) in computing the individual's income for the year, to the extent that the amount is not a prescribed withdrawal,

exceeds

  (ii) the total of all amounts each of which is an amount deductible under paragraph 60(l) or subsection 146(8.2) in computing the income of the individual for the year, and

(b) the amount, if any, by which

  (i) the total of all amounts each of which is an amount that was

  (A) transferred to a registered retirement savings plan or registered retirement income fund under which the individual was the annuitant (within the meaning assigned by subsection 146(1) or 146.3(1), as the case may be),

  (B) included in computing the income of the individual for the year or a preceding taxation year, and

  (C) deemed by paragraph (10)(b) or (c) to have been paid by the individual as a premium to a registered retirement savings plan,

exceeds

  (ii) the total of all amounts each of which is an amount

  (A) deductible under this subsection in computing the individual's income for a preceding taxation year, or

  (B) deducted under subsection 146(5) in computing the individual's income for a preceding taxation year, to the extent that the amount can reasonably be considered to be in respect of an amount referred to in subparagraph (i).

**Related Provisions**: 60(i) — Premium or payment under RRSP or RRIF; 146(5) — Amount of RRSP premiums deductible; 146(8.2) — Amount deductible where withdrawn after mistaken contribution; Reg. Reg. 8307(4) — Eligibility of withdrawal amount for designation.

**Notes**: 147.3(13.1) added by 1992 technical bill, effective 1992. However, for the 1992 taxation year, there is an additional deduction equal to the total of the deductions that would have been allowed for 1989 to 1991. Thus, for 1992, ignore clause (ii)(A), and, in subparas. (a)(i) and (a)(ii), instead of "for the year", read "for a taxation year ending after 1988 and before 1993".

**Regulations**: 8307(6) (prescribed withdrawal).

**Interpretation Bulletins**: IT-124R6: Contributions to registered retirement savings plans; IT-528: Transfers of funds between registered plans.

**Forms**: T1043: Calculating your deduction to offset RRSP or RRIF income if an excess amount from an RPP has been transferred to an RRSP or a RRIF.

**(14) Deemed transfer** — For the purposes of this section and the regulations, where property held in connection with a particular pension plan is made available to pay benefits under another pension plan, the property shall be deemed to have been transferred from the particular plan to the other plan.

**(14.1) Transfer of property between provisions** — Where property held in connection with a benefit provision of a registered pension plan is made available to pay benefits under another benefit provision of the plan, subsections (9) to (11) apply in respect of the transaction by which the property is made so available in the same manner as they would apply if the other benefit provision were in another registered pension plan.

**Notes**: 147.3(14.1) added by 1997 Budget, effective for transfers after July 30, 1997.

**(15)** [Repealed]

**Notes**: 147.3(15), "Annuity contract commencing after age 69", added by 1996 Budget and repealed by 1995-97 technical bill, retroactive to its introduction (which was generally effective 1997). It has been re-enacted as 147.4(4).

**Related Provisions [s. 147.3]**: 60(j) — Transfer of superannuation benefits; 60(j.01) — transfer of surplus; 60(j.1) — Transfer of retiring allowances; 60(l) — Transfer of refund of RRSP premium; 147(19)–(22) — Transfer to RPP, RRSP or DPSP; 147.1(3)(a) — Deemed registration; Reg. 8502(k).

**Notes [s. 147.3]**: 147.3 added by 1990 pension bill, this version effective for amounts transferred in 1989 or later. For amounts transferred in 1988, 147.3 read differently.

**Definitions [s. 147.3]**: "administrator" — 147.1(1); "amount" — 248(1); "as registered" — 147.1(15); "calendar year" — *Interpretation Act* 37(1)(a); "common-law partner", "common-law partnership" — 248(1); "consequence of the death" — 248(8); "defined benefit provision" — 147.1(1); "employer", "forfeited amount" — 147(1); "former spouse" — 252(3); "individual" — 248(1); "member" — 147.1(1); "Minister" — 248(1); "money purchase provision" — 147.1(1); "prescribed withdrawal" — Reg. 8306(6); "property" — 248(1); "province" — *Interpretation Act* 35(1); "registered pension plan" — 248(1); "registered retirement savings plan" — 146(1), 248(1); "regulation" — 248(1); "single amount" — 147.1(1); "spouse" — 252(3); "surplus" — Reg. 8500(1), (1.1); "taxpayer" — 248(1); "transfer", "transferred" — 147.3(14); "writing" — *Interpretation Act* 35(1).

**Forms [s. 147.3]**: T4040: RRSPs and other registered plans for retirement [guide].

**147.4 (1) RPP annuity contract** — Where

(a) at any time an individual acquires, in full or partial satisfaction of the individual's entitlement to benefits under a registered pension plan, an interest in an annuity contract purchased from a licensed annuities provider,

(b) the rights provided for under the contract are not materially different from those provided for under the plan as registered,

(c) the contract does not permit premiums to be paid at or after that time, other than a premium paid at that time out of or under the plan to purchase the contract,

(d) either the plan is not a plan in respect of which the Minister may, under subsection 147.1(11), give a notice of intent to revoke the registration of the plan or the Minister waives the application of this paragraph with respect to the contract and so notifies the administrator of the plan in writing, and

(e) the individual does not acquire the interest as a consequence of a transfer of property from the plan to a registered retirement savings plan or a registered retirement income fund,

the following rules apply for the purposes of this Act:

(f) the individual is deemed not to have received an amount out of or under the registered pension plan as a consequence of acquiring the interest, and

(g) other than for the purposes of sections 147.1 and 147.3, any amount received at or after that time by any individual under the contract is deemed to have been received under the registered pension plan.

**Related Provisions**: 147.4(2) — Amendment to RPP annuity contract.

**Notes**: 147.4(1) added by 1995-97 technical bill, effective for annuity contract acquisitions, amendments and substitutions that occur after July 30, 1997.

**(2) Amended contract** — Where

(a) an amendment is made at any time to an annuity contract to which subsection (1) or paragraph 254(a) applies, other than an amendment the sole effect of which is to

(i) provide for an earlier annuity commencement that avoids the application of paragraph (4)(b), or

(ii) enhance benefits under the annuity contract in connection with the demutualization (as defined by subsection 139.1(1)) of an insurance corporation that is considered for the purpose of section 139.1 to have been a party to the annuity contract, and

(b) the rights provided for under the contract are materially altered as a consequence of the amendment,

the following rules apply for the purposes of this Act:

(c) each individual who has an interest in the contract immediately before that time is deemed to have received at that time the payment of an amount under a pension plan equal to the fair market value of the interest immediately before that time,

(d) the contract as amended is deemed to be a separate annuity contract issued at that time otherwise than pursuant to or under a superannuation or pension fund or plan, and

(e) each individual who has an interest in the separate annuity contract immediately after that time is deemed to have acquired the interest at that time at a cost equal to the fair market value of the interest immediately after that time.

**Related Provisions**: 139.1(2)(g) — No demutualization benefit.

**Notes**: 147.4(2)(a)(ii) added by 1999 Budget, effective for amendments and substitutions that occur after December 15, 1998.

147.4(2) added by 1995-97 technical bill, effective for annuity contract acquisitions, amendments and substitutions that occur after July 30, 1997.

**(3) New contract** — For the purposes of this Act, where an annuity contract (in this subsection referred to as the "original contract") to which subsection (1) or paragraph 254(a) applies is, at any time, substituted by another contract,

(a) if the rights provided for under the other contract

(i) are not materially different from those provided for under the original contract, or

(ii) are materially different from those provided for under the original contract only because of an enhancement of benefits that can reasonably be considered to have been provided solely in connection with the demutualization (as defined by subsection 139.1(1)) of an insurance corporation that is considered for the purposes of section 139.1 to have been a party to the original contract,

the other contract is deemed to be the same contract as, and a continuation of, the original contract; and

(b) in any other case, each individual who has an interest in the original contract immediately before that time is deemed to have received at that time the payment of an amount under a pension plan equal to the fair market value of the interest immediately before that time.

**Related Provisions**: 139.1(2)(g) — No demutualization benefit due to substitution under 147.4(3)(a).

**Notes**: 147.4(3)(a)(ii) added by 1999 Budget, effective for amendments and substitutions that occur after December 15, 1998.

147.4(3) added by 1995-97 technical bill, effective for annuity contract acquisitions, amendments and substitutions that occur after July 30, 1997.

**(4) RPP annuity contract beginning after age 69** — For the purposes of this Act, where, under circumstances to which paragraph 254(a) applied, an individual acquired before 1997 an interest in an annuity contract in full or partial satisfaction of the individual's entitlement to benefits under a registered pension plan, and payment of the annuity has not begun by the end of the particular year in which the individual attains 69 years of age,

(a) the interest is deemed not to exist after the particular year;

(b) the individual is deemed to have received immediately after the particular year the payment of an amount from the plan equal to the fair market value of the interest at the end of the particular year;

(c) the individual is deemed to have acquired immediately after the particular year an interest in the contract as a separate annuity contract issued immediately after the particular year at a cost equal to the amount referred to in paragraph (b); and

## S. 147.4(4)(d)      Income Tax Act, Part I

(d) the issue and acquisition of the separate annuity contract are deemed not to be pursuant to or under a registered pension plan.

**Notes**: 147.4(4) added by 1995-97 technical bill, effective 1997, except that

   (a) it does not apply to an individual who turned 70 before 1997;

   (b) in applying it to an individual who turned 69 in 1996, read "70" instead of "69"; and

   (c) it does not apply to an annuity contract if an individual received an interest in the contract before March 6, 1996 and, under the terms and conditions of the contract as they read immediately before that day,

     (i) the day on which the annuity payments are to begin under the contract is fixed and determined and is after the year in which the individual turns

       (A) 69, if the individual had not turned 69 before 1997, or

       (B) 70, if the individual turned 69 in 1996, and

     (ii) the amount and timing of each annuity payment are fixed and determined.

**Definitions [147.4]**: "annuity" — 248(1); demutualization — 139.1(1); "individual", "licensed annuities provider", "Minister", "registered pension plan" — 248(1); "registered retirement income fund" — 146.3(1), 248(1); "registered retirement savings plan" — 146(1), 248(1); "writing" — *Interpretation Act* 35(1).

## Life Insurance Policies

**148. (1) Amounts included in computing policyholder's income** — There shall be included in computing the income for a taxation year of a policyholder in respect of the disposition of an interest in a life insurance policy, other than a policy that is or is issued pursuant to

(a) a registered pension plan,

(b) a registered retirement savings plan,

(b.1) a registered retirement income fund,

(c) an income-averaging annuity contract,

(d) a deferred profit sharing plan, or

(e) an annuity contract where

   (i) the payment for the annuity contract was deductible under paragraph 60(l) in computing the policyholder's income, or

   (ii) the policyholder acquired the annuity contract in circumstances to which subsection 146(21) applied,

the amount, if any, by which the proceeds of the disposition of the policyholder's interest in the policy that the policyholder, beneficiary or assignee, as the case may be, became entitled to receive in the year exceeds the adjusted cost basis to the policyholder of that interest immediately before the disposition.

**Related Provisions**: 20(1)(e.2) — Deduction for premiums on life insurance used as collateral; 56(1)(j) — Income inclusion — life insurance policy proceeds; 60(s) — Deduction of policy loan repayment; 138(3) — Deductions allowed in computing income; 138.1(7) — Where segregated fund policyholder deemed to be trust, etc.; 148(2) — Deemed proceeds of disposition; 148(9)"adjusted cost basis"C — disposition amount included in adjusted cost basis. See additional Related Provisions and Definitions at end of s. 148.

**Notes**: Where a life insurance policyholder surrenders a policy and receives the cash surrender value, this is a "disposition" under 148(9). If the "proceeds of the disposition" (148(9)) exceed the "adjusted cost basis" (148(9)), the excess is included in income under 148(1).

Where a terminally ill person "sells" his existing life insurance policy for cash by designating another person as his beneficiary, the CCRA considers that this is a disposition of the interest in the insurance policy, so 148(1) will apply to include the proceeds of the disposition received into income. This is an exception to the normal administrative rule that a change of beneficiary is not a disposition of the policy. See Views doc. 9828187F (in French) on *TaxPartner*.

Where, as an alternative to cash in the policy, the policyholder effectively donates it to a charity by designating the charity as beneficiary, see 118.1(5.1) and (5.2).

148(1)(b.1) added by 1992 technical bill, effective 1991.

148(1)(e)(ii) added by 1993 technical bill, effective for dispositions after August 1992. It permits a transfer of an amount from the Saskatchewan Pension Plan to acquire an annuity.

See also Notes at end of s. 138.

**Regulations**: 217(2) (information return).

**Interpretation Bulletins**: IT-87R2: Policyholders' income from life insurance policies; IT-244R3: Gifts by individuals of life insurance policies as charitable donations; IT-379R: Employees profit sharing plans — allocations to beneficiaries.

**(1.1) Amount included in computing taxpayer's income** — There shall be included in computing the income for a taxation year of a taxpayer in respect of a disposition of an interest in a life insurance policy described in paragraph (e) of the definition "disposition" in subsection (9) the amount, if any, by which the amount of a payment described in paragraph (e) of that definition that the taxpayer became entitled to receive in the year exceeds the amount that would be the taxpayer's adjusted cost basis of the taxpayer's interest in the policy immediately before the disposition if, for the purposes of the definition "adjusted cost basis" in subsection (9), the taxpayer were, in respect of that interest in the policy, the policyholder.

**Related Provisions**: 56(1)(j) — Life insurance policy proceeds included in income. See additional Related Provisions and Definitions at end of s. 148.

**Regulations**: 217(2) (information return).

**(2) Deemed proceeds of disposition** — For the purposes of subsections (1) and 20(20) and the definition "adjusted cost basis" in subsection (9),

   (a) where at any time a policyholder becomes entitled to receive under a life insurance policy a particular amount as, on account of, in lieu of payment of or in satisfaction of, a policy dividend, the policyholder shall be deemed

     (i) to have disposed of an interest in the policy at that time, and

     (ii) to have become entitled to receive proceeds of the disposition equal to the amount, if any, by which

       (A) the particular amount

exceeds

(B) the part of the particular amount applied immediately after that time to pay a premium under the policy or to repay a policy loan under the policy, as provided for under the terms and conditions of the policy;

(b) where in a taxation year a holder of an interest in, or a person whose life is insured or who is the annuitant under, a life insurance policy (other than an annuity contract or an exempt policy) last acquired after December 1, 1982 or an annuity contract (other than a life annuity contract, as defined by regulation, entered into before November 13, 1981 or a prescribed annuity contract) dies, the policyholder shall be deemed to have disposed of the policyholder's interest in the policy or the contract, as the case may be, immediately before the death;

(c) where, as a consequence of a death, a disposition of an interest in a life insurance policy is deemed to have occurred under paragraph (b), the policyholder immediately after the death shall be deemed to have acquired the interest at a cost equal to the accumulating fund in respect thereof, as determined in prescribed manner, immediately after the death; and

(d) where at any time a life insurance policy last acquired after December 1, 1982, or a life insurance policy to which subsection 12.2(9) of the *Income Tax Act*, chapter 148 of the Revised Statutes of Canada, 1952, applies by virtue of paragraph 12.2(9)(b) of that Act, ceases to be an exempt policy (otherwise than as a consequence of the death of an individual whose life is insured under the policy or at a time when that individual is totally and permanently disabled), the policyholder shall be deemed to have disposed of the policyholder's interest in the policy at that time for proceeds of disposition equal to the accumulating fund with respect to the interest, as determined in prescribed manner, at that time and to have reacquired the interest immediately after that time at a cost equal to those proceeds.

**Related Provisions**: See Related Provisions and Definitions at end of s. 148.

**Notes**: 148(2)(a)(ii) amended by 1992 technical bill, effective for policy dividends received or receivable in taxation years that begin after December 20, 1991, to deal with the case where part of the policy dividend is automatically applied to pay a premium or repay a policy loan, as provided under the terms of the policy. For earlier dividends, read simply "that amount shall be deemed to be proceeds of disposition that he became entitled to receive at that time".

**Regulations**: 301 (life annuity contract); 304 (prescribed annuity contract); 307 (accumulating fund).

**I.T. Application Rules**: 69 (meaning of "*Income Tax Act*, chapter 148 of the Revised Statutes of Canada, 1952").

**Interpretation Bulletins**: IT-87R2: Policyholders' income from life insurance policies; IT-210R2: Income of deceased persons — periodic payments and investment tax credit; IT-430R3: Life insurance proceeds received by a private corporation or a partnership as a consequence of death.

**(3) Special rules for certain policies** — For the purposes of this section, where all or any part of an insurer's reserves for a life insurance policy vary in amount depending on the fair market value of a specified group of properties (in this subsection referred to as a "segregated fund"),

(a) in computing the adjusted cost basis of the policy,

(i) an amount paid by the policyholder or on the policyholder's behalf as or on account of premiums under the policy or to acquire an interest in the policy shall, to the extent that the amount was used by the insurer to acquire property for the purposes of the segregated fund, be deemed not to have been so paid, and

(ii) any transfer of property by the insurer from the segregated fund that resulted in an increase in the portion of its reserves for the policy that do not vary with the fair market value of the segregated fund shall be deemed to have been a premium paid under the policy by the policyholder; and

(b) the proceeds of the disposition of an interest in the policy shall be deemed not to include the portion thereof, if any, payable out of the segregated fund.

**(4) Income from disposition** — For the purpose of computing a taxpayer's income from the disposition (other than a disposition deemed to have occurred under paragraph (2)(a) or a disposition described in paragraph (b) of the definition "disposition" in subsection (9)) of a part of the taxpayer's interest in a life insurance policy (other than an annuity contract) last acquired after December 1, 1982 or an annuity contract, the adjusted cost basis to the taxpayer, immediately before the disposition, of the part is the proportion of the adjusted cost basis to the taxpayer of the taxpayer's interest immediately before the disposition that

(a) the proceeds of the disposition

are of

(b) the accumulating fund with respect to the taxpayer's interest, as determined in prescribed manner, immediately before the disposition.

**Regulations**: 307 (accumulating fund).

**Interpretation Bulletins**: IT-87R2: Policyholders' income from life insurance policies.

**(4.1), (5)** [Repealed under former Act]

**Notes**: 148(4.1) and (5) repealed as of 1978.

**(6) Proceeds receivable as annuity** — Where, under the terms of a life insurance policy (other than an annuity contract) last acquired before December 2, 1982, a policyholder became entitled to receive from the insurer at any time before the death of the person whose life was insured thereunder, all the proceeds (other than policy dividends) payable at that time under the policy in the form of an annuity contract or annuity payments,

(a) the payments shall be regarded as annuity payments made under an annuity contract;

(b) the purchase price of the annuity contract shall be deemed to be the adjusted cost basis of the policy to the policyholder immediately before the first payment under that contract became payable; and

(c) the annuity contract or annuity payments shall be deemed not to be proceeds of the disposition of an interest in the policy.

**Related Provisions**: 148(10)(b) — References to "person whose life was insured". See also Related Provisions and Definitions at end of s. 148.

**(7) Disposition at non-arm's length and similar cases** — Where, otherwise than by virtue of a deemed disposition under paragraph (2)(b), an interest of a policyholder in a life insurance policy is disposed of by way of a gift (whether during the policyholder's lifetime or by the policyholder's will), by distribution from a corporation or by operation of law only to any person, or in any manner whatever to any person with whom the policyholder was not dealing at arm's length, the policyholder shall be deemed thereupon to become entitled to receive proceeds of the disposition equal to the value of the interest at the time of the disposition, and the person who acquires the interest by virtue of the disposition shall be deemed to acquire it at a cost equal to that value.

**Related Provisions**: See Related Provisions and Definitions at end of s. 148.

**Notes**: 148(7) amended by 1981 Budget, effective for dispositions after November 12, 1981. For dispositions from January 1, 1978 through November 12, 1981, read:

(7) Where an interest of a policyholder in a life insurance policy other than an annuity contract that is not a life annuity contract as defined by regulation, is disposed of by way of gift (whether during his lifetime or by his will), by distribution from a corporation or by operation of law only to any person, or in any manner whatever to any person with whom the policyholder was not dealing at arm's length, the policyholder shall be deemed thereupon to become entitled to receive proceeds of the disposition equal to the value of the interest at the time of the disposition, and the person who acquires the interest by virtue of the disposition shall be deemed to acquire it at a cost equal to such value.

For dispositions from 1972 through 1977, read as for 1978 through 1981, but delete the words "that is not a life annuity contract as defined by regulation,".

**(8) Idem** — Notwithstanding any other provision in this section, where

(a) an interest of a policyholder in a life insurance policy (other than an annuity contract) has been transferred to the policyholder's child for no consideration, and

(b) a child of the policyholder or a child of the transferee is the person whose life is insured under the policy,

the interest shall be deemed to have been disposed of by the policyholder for proceeds of the disposition equal to the adjusted cost basis to the policyholder of the interest immediately before the transfer, and to have been acquired by the person who acquired the interest at a cost equal to those proceeds.

**Related Provisions**: 148(8.1) — *Inter vivos* transfer to spouse; 148(8.2) — Transfer to spouse at death. See additional Related Provisions and Definitions at end of s. 148.

**Notes**: 148(8) extended by 1991 technical bill, effective for transfers and distributions in 1990 or later, to a spouse and former spouse. For transfers and distributions from 1983 to 1989, read 148(8)(a) and (b) as follows:

(a) an interest of a policyholder in a life insurance policy (other than an annuity contract) has been transferred to

(i) the policyholder's spouse or child, for no consideration,

(ii) the spouse or a former spouse of the policyholder, in settlement of rights arising out of their marriage, or

(iii) an individual, pursuant to a decree, order or judgment of a competent tribunal made in accordance with prescribed provisions of the law of a province if that individual is a person within a prescribed class of persons referred to in such provisions, and

(b) the transferee or a child of the policyholder or transferee is the person whose life is insured under the policy,

**Regulations**: 6500(1) (prescribed provisions and prescribed class of persons, for former 148(8)(a)(iii)).

**Interpretation Bulletins**: IT-87R2: Policyholders' income from life insurance policies.

**(8.1) *Inter vivos* transfer to spouse [or common-law partner]** — Notwithstanding any other provision of this section, where

(a) an interest of a policyholder in a life insurance policy (other than a policy that is, or is issued under, a plan or contract referred to in any of paragraphs (1)(a) to (e)) is transferred to

(i) the policyholder's spouse or common-law partner, or

(ii) a former spouse or common-law partner of the policyholder in settlement of rights arising out of their marriage or common-law partnership, and

(iii) [Repealed]

(b) both the policyholder and the transferee are resident in Canada at the time of the transfer,

unless an election is made in the policyholder's return of income under this Part for the taxation year in which the interest was transferred to have this subsection not apply, the interest shall be deemed to have been disposed of by the policyholder for proceeds of the disposition equal to the adjusted cost basis to the policyholder of the interest immediately before the transfer and to have been acquired by the transferee at a cost equal to those proceeds.

**Related Provisions**: 73(1) — *Inter vivos* transfer of property of spouse, etc., or trust; 148(8.2) — Transfer to spouse at death; 252(3) — Extended meaning of "spouse" and "former spouse". See additional Related Provisions and Definitions at end of s. 148.

Division G — Deferred & Special Income Arrangements   S. 148(9) adj

**Notes**: 148(8.1)(a) amended by 2000 same-sex partners bill to add reference to "common-law partner" and "common-law partnership", effective for the 2001 and later taxation years, or earlier by election (see Notes to 248(1)"common-law partner").

148(8.1)(a)(iii) repealed by 1992 technical bill, effective 1993, as a result of new 252(4), which extended, for 1993 to 2000, the definitions of "spouse" and "marriage" for the entire Act. For 1990 to 1992, read:

> (iii) an individual of the opposite sex under an order for the support or maintenance of the individual made by a competent tribunal in accordance with the laws of a province, where the individual and the taxpayer cohabited in a conjugal relationship before the date of the order, and

148(8.1) added by 1991 technical bill, effective for transfers and dispositions after 1989. For transfers and distributions in 1990, the election could be made by notifying Revenue Canada in writing by November 5, 1993 (deadline extended by 1992 technical bill, s. 159).

**Interpretation Bulletins**: IT-87R2: Policyholders' income from life insurance policies.

**(8.2) Transfer to spouse [or common-law partner] at death** — Notwithstanding any other provision of this section, where, as a consequence of the death of a policyholder who was resident in Canada immediately before the policyholder's death, an interest of the policyholder in a life insurance policy (other than a policy that is or is issued under a plan or contract referred to in any of paragraphs (1)(a) to (e)) is transferred or distributed to the policyholder's spouse or common-law partner who was resident in Canada immediately before the death, unless an election is made in the policyholder's return of income under this Part for the taxation year in which the policyholder died to have this subsection not apply, the interest shall be deemed to have been disposed of by the policyholder immediately before the death for proceeds of the disposition equal to the adjusted cost basis to the policyholder of the interest immediately before the transfer and to have been acquired by the spouse or common-law partner at a cost equal to those proceeds.

**Related Provisions**: 70(6) — Where transfer or distribution to spouse or trust; 148(9)"adjusted cost basis"G.1 — "adjusted cost basis"; 248(8) — Occurrences as a consequence of death; 252(3) — Extended meaning of "spouse". See additional Related Provisions and Definitions at end of s. 148.

**Notes**: 148(8.2) amended by 2000 same-sex partners bill to add reference to "common-law partner", effective for the 2001 and later taxation years, or earlier by election (see Notes to 248(1)"common-law partner").

148(8.2) added by 1991 technical bill, effective for transfers and dispositions after 1989. For transfers and distributions in 1990, the election could be made by notifying Revenue Canada in writing by November 5, 1993 (deadline extended by 1992 technical bill, s. 159).

**Interpretation Bulletins**: IT-87R2: Policyholders' income from life insurance policies.

**(9) Definitions** — In this section and paragraph 56(1)(d.1) of the *Income Tax Act*, chapter 148 of the Revised Statutes of Canada, 1952,

**Related Provisions**: 12.2(12) — Application of subsecs. 138(12) and 148(9). See additional Related Provisions and Definitions at end of s. 148.

**Notes**: The opening words of 148(9) redrafted in the R.S.C. 1985 (5th Supp.) consolidation, effective for taxation years ending after November 1991. The former version made reference to section 12.2; that rule of application is now in 12.2(12).

**I.T. Application Rules**: 69 (meaning of "*Income Tax Act*, chapter 148 of the Revised Statutes of Canada, 1952").

**Interpretation Bulletins**: IT-379R: Employees profit sharing plans — allocations to beneficiaries.

**"adjusted cost basis"** to a policyholder as at a particular time of the policyholder's interest in a life insurance policy means the amount determined by the formula

$$(A + B + C + D + E + F + G + G.1) - (H + I + J + K + L)$$

where

A  is the total of all amounts each of which is the cost of an interest in the policy acquired by the policyholder before that time but not including an amount referred to in the description of B or E,

B  is the total of all amounts each of which is an amount paid before that time by or on behalf of the policyholder in respect of a premium under the policy, other than amounts referred to in clause (2)(a)(ii)(B), in subparagraph (iii) of the description of C in paragraph (a) of the definition "proceeds of the disposition" or in subparagraph (b)(i) of that definition,

C  is the total of all amounts each of which is an amount in respect of the disposition of an interest in the policy before that time that was required to be included in computing the policyholder's income or taxable income earned in Canada for a taxation year,

D  is the total of all amounts each of which is an amount in respect of the policyholder's interest in the policy that was included by virtue of subsection 12(3) or section 12.2 or of paragraph 56(1)(d.1) of the *Income Tax Act*, chapter 148 of the Revised Statutes of Canada, 1952, in computing the policyholder's income for any taxation year ending before that time or the portion of an amount paid to the policyholder in respect of the policyholder's interest in the policy on which tax was imposed by virtue of paragraph 212(1)(o) before that time,

E  is the total of all amounts each of which is an amount in respect of the repayment before that time and after March 31, 1978 of a policy loan not exceeding the total of the proceeds of the disposition, if any, in respect of that loan and the amount, if any, described in the description of J but not including any payment of interest thereon, any loan repayment that was deductible under paragraph 60(s) of this Act or paragraph 20(1)(hh) of the *Income Tax Act*, chapter 148 of the Revised Statutes of Canada, 1952 (as it applied in taxation years before 1985) or any loan repayment referred to in clause (2)(a)(ii)(B),

F is the amount, if any, by which the cash surrender value of the policy as at its first anniversary date after March 31, 1977 exceeds the adjusted cost basis (determined under the *Income Tax Act*, chapter 148 of the Revised Statutes of Canada, 1952, as it would have read on that date if subsection 148(8) of that Act, as it read in its application to the period ending immediately before April 1, 1978, had not been applicable) of the policyholder's interest in the policy on that date,

G is, in the case of an interest in a life annuity contract, as defined by regulation, to which subsection 12.2(1) applies for the taxation year that includes that time (or would apply if the contract had an anniversary day in the year at a time when the taxpayer held the interest), the total of all amounts each of which is a mortality gain, as defined by regulation and determined by the issuer of the contract in accordance with the regulations, in respect of the interest immediately before the end of the calendar year ending in a taxation year commencing before that time,

G.1 [is,] in the case of an interest in a life insurance policy (other than an annuity contract) to which subsection (8.2) applied before that time, the total of all amounts each of which is a mortality gain, as defined by regulation and determined by the issuer of the policy in accordance with the regulations, in respect of the interest immediately before the end of the calendar year ending in a taxation year beginning before that time,

H is the total of all amounts each of which is the proceeds of the disposition of the policyholder's interest in the policy that the policyholder became entitled to receive before that time,

I is the total of all amounts each of which is an amount in respect of the policyholder's interest in the policy that was deducted by virtue of subsection 20(19) in computing the policyholder's income for any taxation year commencing before that time,

J is the amount payable on March 31, 1978 in respect of a policy loan in respect of the policy,

K is the total of all amounts each of which is an amount received before that time in respect of the policy that the policyholder was entitled to deduct under paragraph 60(a) in computing the policyholder's income for a taxation year, and

L is

(a) in the case of an interest in a life insurance policy (other than an annuity contract) that was last acquired after December 1, 1982 by the policyholder, the total of all amounts each of which is the net cost of pure insurance, as defined by regulation and determined by the issuer of the policy in accordance with the regulations, in respect of the interest immediately before the end of the calendar year ending in a taxation year commencing after May 31, 1985 and before that time,

(b) in the case of an interest in an annuity contract to which subsection 12.2(1) applies for the taxation year that includes that time (or would apply if the contract had an anniversary day in the year and while the taxpayer held the interest), the total of all annuity payments paid in respect of the interest before that time and while the policyholder held the interest, or

(c) in the case of an interest in a contract referred to in the description of G, the total of all amounts each of which is a mortality loss, as defined by regulation and determined by the issuer of the contract in accordance with the regulations, in respect of the interest before that time;

**Related Provisions**: 12.2(5) — Amounts included in income — taxpayer's interest in an annuity contract; 148(2) — Deemed proceeds of disposition; 257 — Formula cannot calculate to less than zero. See additional Related Provisions and Definitions at end of s. 148.

**Notes**: See Notes to 148(1). The adjusted cost basis (not to be confused with "adjusted cost base" of capital property under s. 54) is, in simplest terms, any amount paid to acquire the policy (A), plus premiums paid (B), plus various amounts included in income in respect of the policy (C, D). It is reduced by the proceeds of disposition of an interest in the policy (H) and various other amounts.

148(9)"adjusted cost basis" was 148(9)(a) before consolidation in R.S.C. 1985 (5th Supp.), effective for taxation years ending after November 1991. The previous version, identical in meaning, read:

(a) "adjusted cost basis" to a policyholder as at a particular time of his interest in a life insurance policy means the amount, if any, by which the aggregate of

(i) the cost of each interest in the policy acquired by him before that time but not including an amount referred to in subparagraph (ii) or (iv),

(ii) all amounts each of which is an amount paid before that time, by him or on his behalf, in respect of a premium under the policy,

(iii) the aggregate of all amounts, each of which is an amount in respect of the disposition of an interest in the policy before that time that was required to be included in computing his income or taxable income earned in Canada for a taxation year,

(iii.1) the aggregate of all amounts each of which is an amount in respect of his interest in the policy that was included by virtue of subsection 12(3), section 12.2 or paragraph 56(1)(d.1) in computing his income for any taxation year ending before that time or the portion of an amount paid to him in respect of his interest in the policy on which tax was imposed by virtue of paragraph 212(1)(o) before that time,

(iv) all amounts, each of which is an amount in respect of the repayment before that time and after March 31, 1978 of a policy loan not exceeding the aggregate of the proceeds of the disposition, if any, in respect of that loan and the amount, if any, described in subparagraph (vii) but not including any payment of interest thereon or any repayment of the loan that was deductible pursuant to paragraph 20(1)(hh) or 60(s),

(v) the amount, if any, by which the cash surrender value of the policy as at its first anniversary date after March 31, 1977 exceeds the adjusted cost basis (determined under this Act as it would have read on that date if subsection (8) had not been applicable) of his interest in the policy on that date, and

(v.1) in the case of an interest in a life annuity contract, as defined by regulation, to which subsection 12.2(1) or (3) applies for the taxation year that includes that time, the aggregate of all amounts each of which is a mortality gain, as defined by regulation and determined by the issuer of the contract in accordance with the regulations, in respect of the interest immediately before the end of the calendar year ending in a taxation year commencing before that time

exceeds the aggregate of

(vi) the aggregate of amounts each of which is proceeds of the disposition of his interest in the policy that he became entitled to receive before that time,

(vi.1) the aggregate of all amounts each of which is an amount in respect of his interest in the policy that was deducted by virtue of subsection 20(19) in computing his income for any taxation year commencing before that time,

(vii) the amount payable on March 31, 1978 in respect of a policy loan in respect of the policy,

(viii) the aggregate of all amounts each of which is an amount received before that time in respect of the policy that he was entitled to deduct under paragraph 60(a) in computing his income for a taxation year;

(ix) in the case of an interest in a life insurance policy (other than an annuity contract) that was last acquired after December 1, 1982 by the policyholder, the aggregate of all amounts each of which is the net cost of pure insurance, as defined by regulation and determined by the issuer of the policy in accordance with the regulations, in respect of the interest immediately before the end of the calendar year ending in a taxation year commencing after May 31, 1985 and before that time,

(x) in the case of an interest in an annuity contract to which subsection 12.2(1) or (3) applies, the aggregate of all amounts each of which is an annuity payment paid in respect of the interest before that time and while the policyholder held the interest, and

(xi) in the case of an interest in a contract described in subparagraph (v.1), the aggregate of all amounts each of which is a mortality loss, as defined by regulation and determined by the issuer of the contract in accordance with the regulations, in respect of the interest before that time;

Description of B (formerly 148(9)(a)(ii)) amended by 1992 technical bill, effective for amounts paid in taxation years that begin after December 20, 1991, to add the exclusion beginning "other than amounts".

Description of E (formerly 148(9)(a)(iv)) amended by 1992 technical bill, effective for amounts paid in taxation years that begin after December 20, 1991, to add "(as it applied in taxation years before 1985)" and "or any loan repayment referred to in clause (2)(a)(ii)(B)".

Formula element G.1 (formerly 148(9)(a)(v.2)) added by 1992 technical bill, effective 1990, to deal with the case where an interest in a life insurance policy has been transferred on a rollover basis to a surviving spouse on the death of the policyholder.

Description of G, and para. L(b) (formerly 148(9)(a)(v.1) and (x)), amended by 1989 Budget and 1991 technical bill, effective for policies last acquired in 1990 or later. For earlier policies, read:

G is, in the case of an interest in a life annuity contract, as defined by regulation, to which subsection 12.2(1) or (3) applies for the taxation year that includes that time, the total of all amounts each of which is a mortality gain, as defined by regulation and determined by the issuer of the contract in accordance with the regulations, in respect of the interest immediately before the end of the calendar year ending in a taxation year commencing before that time.

(b) in the case of an interest in an annuity contract to which subsection 12.2(1) or (3) applies, the total of all amounts each of which is an annuity payment paid in respect of the interest before that time and while the policyholder held the interest, or

**Regulations**: 301 (life annuity contract — for 148(9)"adjusted cost basis"G); 308 (net cost of pure insurance — for 148(9)"adjusted cost basis"L(a)).

**I.T. Application Rules**: 69 (meaning of "*Income Tax Act*, chapter 148 of the Revised Statutes of Canada, 1952").

**Interpretation Bulletins**: IT-87R2: Policyholders' income from life insurance policies; IT-149R4: Winding-up dividend; IT-355R2: Interest on loans to buy life insurance policies and annuity contracts, and interest on policy loans; IT-430R3: Life insurance proceeds received by a private corporation or a partnership as a consequence of death. See additional Related Provisions and Definitions at end of s. 148.

**"amount payable"**, in respect of a policy loan, has the meaning assigned by subsection 138(12);

Notes: 148(9)"amount payable" was 148(9)(a.1) before consolidation in R.S.C. 1985 (5th Supp.), effective for taxation years ending after November 1991.

**"cash surrender value"** at a particular time of a life insurance policy means its cash surrender value at that time computed without regard to any policy loans made under the policy, any policy dividends (other than paid-up additions) payable under the policy or any interest payable on those dividends;

**Related Provisions**: Reg. 1408(1)"cash surrender value" — Definition applies for policy reserve calculation.

Notes: 148(9)"cash surrender value" was 148(9)(b) before consolidation in R.S.C. 1985 (5th Supp.), effective for taxation years ending after November 1991.

**"child"** of a policyholder includes a child as defined in subsection 70(10);

**Related Provisions**: 252(1) — Extended meaning of "child".

Notes: 148(9)"child" was 148(9)(b.1) before consolidation in R.S.C. 1985 (5th Supp.), effective for taxation years ending after November 1991.

**"disposition"**, in relation to an interest in a life insurance policy, includes

(a) a surrender thereof,

(b) a policy loan made after March 31, 1978,

(c) the dissolution of that interest by virtue of the maturity of the policy,

(d) a disposition of that interest by operation of law only, and

(e) the payment by an insurer of an amount (other than an annuity payment, a policy loan or a policy dividend) in respect of a policy (other than a policy described in paragraph (1)(a), (b), (c), (d) or (e)) that is a life annuity contract, as defined by regulation, entered into after November 16, 1978, and before November 13, 1981,

but does not include

(f) an assignment of all or any part of an interest in the policy for the purpose of securing a debt or a loan other than a policy loan,

(g) a lapse of the policy in consequence of the premiums under the policy remaining unpaid, if the policy was reinstated not later than 60 days after the end of the calendar year in which the lapse occurred,

(h) a payment under a policy as a disability benefit or as an accidental death benefit,

(i) an annuity payment,

(j) a payment under a life insurance policy (other than an annuity contract) that

(i) was last acquired before December 2, 1982, or

(ii) is an exempt policy

in consequence of the death of any person whose life was insured under the policy, or

(k) any transaction or event by which an individual becomes entitled to receive, under the terms of an exempt policy, all of the proceeds (including or excluding policy dividends) payable under the policy in the form of an annuity contract or annuity payments, if, at the time of the transaction or event, the individual whose life is insured under the policy was totally and permanently disabled;

**Related Provisions**: 60(s) — Deduction of policy loan repayment; 148(10)(b) — References to "person whose life was insured"; 248(8) — Occurrences as a consequence of death. See additional Related Provisions and Definitions at end of s. 148.

**Notes**: 148(9)"disposition" was 148(9)(c) before consolidation in R.S.C. 1985 (5th Supp.), effective for taxation years ending after November 1991. See Table of Concordance.

**Regulations**: 301 (life annuity contract — for 148(9)"disposition"(e)).

**Interpretation Bulletins**: IT-85R2: Health and welfare trusts for employees; IT-87R2: Policyholders' income from life insurance policies.

**"interest"**, in relation to a policy loan, has the meaning assigned by subsection 138(12);

**Notes**: 148(9)"interest" was 148(9)(c.1) before consolidation in R.S.C. 1985 (5th Supp.), effective for taxation years ending after November 1991.

**"life insurance policy"** — [Repealed under former Act]

**Notes**: 148(9)(d), repealed in 1985, defined "life insurance policy" and "relevant authority". These definitions are now found in 248(1) and 148(9)"relevant authority" respectively.

**"policy loan"** means an amount advanced by an insurer to a policyholder in accordance with the terms and conditions of the life insurance policy;

**Notes**: 148(9)"policy loan" was 148(9)(e) before consolidation in R.S.C. 1985 (5th Supp.), effective for taxation years ending after November 1991.

**"premium"** under a policy includes

(a) interest paid after 1977 to a life insurer in respect of a policy loan, other than interest deductible in the 1978 or any subsequent taxation year pursuant to paragraph 20(1)(c) or (d), and

(b) a prepaid premium under the policy to the extent that it cannot be refunded otherwise than on termination or cancellation of the policy,

but does not include

(c) where the interest in the policy was last acquired after December 1, 1982, that portion of any amount paid after May 31, 1985 under the policy with respect to

(i) an accidental death benefit,

(ii) a disability benefit,

(iii) an additional risk as a result of insuring a substandard life,

(iv) an additional risk in respect of the conversion of a term policy into another policy after the end of the year,

(v) an additional risk under a settlement option,

(vi) an additional risk under a guaranteed insurability benefit, or

(vii) any other prescribed benefit that is ancillary to the policy;

**Related Provisions**: 60(s) — Repayment of policy loan. See additional Related provisions and Definitions at end of s. 148.

**Notes**: 148(9)"premium" was 148(9)(e.1) before consolidation in R.S.C. 1985 (5th Supp.), effective for taxation years ending after November 1991. See Table of Concordance.

**"proceeds of the disposition"** of an interest in a life insurance policy means the amount of the proceeds that the policyholder, beneficiary or assignee, as the case may be, is entitled to receive on a disposition of an interest in the policy and for greater certainty,

(a) in respect of a surrender or maturity thereof, means the amount determined by the formula

$$(A - B) - C$$

where

A is the cash surrender value of that interest in the policy at the time of surrender or maturity,

B is that portion of the cash surrender value represented by A that is applicable to the policyholder's interest in the related segregated fund trust as referred to in paragraph 138.1(1)(e), and

C is the total of amounts each of which is

(i) an amount payable at that time by the policyholder in respect of a policy loan in respect of the policy,

(ii) a premium under the policy that is due but unpaid at that time, or

(iii) an amount applied, immediately after the time of the surrender, to pay a premium under the policy, as provided for under the terms and conditions of the policy,

(b) in respect of a policy loan made after March 31, 1978 means the lesser of

(i) the amount of the loan, other than the part thereof applied, immediately after the loan, to pay a premium under the policy, as provided for under the terms and conditions of the policy, and

(ii) the amount, if any, by which the cash surrender value of the policy immediately before the loan was made exceeds the total of the balances outstanding at that time of any policy loans in respect of the policy,

(c) in respect of a payment described in paragraph (e) of the definition "disposition" in this subsection, means the amount of that payment, and

(d) in respect of a disposition deemed to have occurred under paragraph (2)(b), means the accumulating fund in respect of the interest, as determined in prescribed manner,

(i) immediately before the time of death in respect of a life insurance policy (other than an annuity contract) last acquired after December 1, 1982, or

(ii) immediately after the time of death in respect of an annuity contract;

**Related Provisions**: 257 — Formula cannot calculate to less than zero. See additional Related Provisions and Definitions at end of s. 148.

**Notes**: 148(9)"proceeds of the disposition" was 148(9)(e.2) before consolidation in R.S.C. 1985 (5th Supp.), effective for taxation years ending after November 1991. See Table of Concordance in introductory pages.

Subpara. "proceeds of the disposition"(a)C(iii) (formerly 148(9)(e.2)(i)(B)(III)) added by 1992 technical bill, effective for surrenders in taxation years that begin after December 20, 1991.

Subpara. "proceeds of the disposition"(b)(i) (formerly 148(9)(e.2)(ii)(A)) amended by 1992 technical bill, effective for policy loans made in taxation years that begin after December 20, 1991. For earlier loans, read simply "the amount of the loan".

**"relevant authority"** — [Repealed]

**Notes**: Definition "relevant authority" repealed by 1996 Budget, effective April 25, 1997 (Royal Assent). It was defined with reference to the definition in 138(12), now also repealed. The only place it was used was in 148(5), a rule for computing a foreign tax credit in respect of allocations from a segregated fund, which was repealed long ago. The term is also defined in Reg. 1408(1).

148(9)"relevant authority" was 148(9)(e.3) before consolidation in R.S.C. 1985 (5th Supp.), effective for taxation years ending after November 1991.

**"tax anniversary date"**, in relation to a life insurance policy, means the second anniversary date of the policy to occur after October 22, 1968;

**Notes**: 148(9)"tax anniversary date" was 148(9)(f) before consolidation in R.S.C. 1985 (5th Supp.), effective for taxation years ending after November 1991.

**"value"** at a particular time of an interest in a life insurance policy means

(a) where the interest includes an interest in the cash surrender value of the policy, the amount in respect thereof that the holder of the interest would be entitled to receive if the policy were surrendered at that time, and

(b) in any other case, nil.

**Notes**: 148(9)"value" was 148(9)(g) before consolidation in R.S.C. 1985 (5th Supp.), effective for taxation years ending after November 1991. See Table of Concordance.

**(9.1) Application of subsec. 12.2(11)** — The definitions in subsection 12.2(11) apply to this section.

**Notes**: 148(9.1) added in the R.S.C. 1985 (5th Supp.) consolidation, effective for taxation years ending after November 1991. This rule was formerly in the opening words of 12.2(11).

**(10) Life annuity contracts** — For the purposes of this section,

(a) a reference to "insurer" or "life insurer" shall be deemed to include a reference to a person who is licensed or otherwise authorized under a law of Canada or a province to issue contracts that are annuity contracts;

(b) a reference to a "person whose life was insured" shall be deemed to include a reference to an annuitant under a life annuity contract, as defined by regulation, entered into before November 17, 1978;

(c) where a policyholder is a person who has held an interest in a life insurance policy continuously since its issue date, the interest shall be deemed to have been acquired on the later of the date on which

(i) the policy came into force, and

(ii) the application in respect of the policy signed by the policyholder was filed with the insurer;

(d) except as otherwise provided, a policyholder shall be deemed not to have disposed of or acquired an interest in a life insurance policy (other than an annuity contract) as a result only of the exercise of any provision (other than a conversion into an annuity contract) of the policy; and

(e) where an interest in a life insurance policy (other than an annuity contract) last acquired before December 2, 1982 to which subsection 12.2(9) of the *Income Tax Act*, chapter 148 of the Revised Statutes of Canada, 1952, does not apply has been acquired by a taxpayer from a person with whom the taxpayer was not dealing at arm's length, the interest shall be deemed to have been last acquired by the taxpayer before December 2, 1982.

**Related Provisions**: 12.2(13) — Application of subsec. 148(10); 56(1)(j) — Life insurance policy proceeds. See also below.

**Notes**: The opening words of 148(10) redrafted in the R.S.C. 1985 (5th Supp.) consolidation, effective for taxation years ending after

## S. 148(10)
### Income Tax Act, Part I

November 1991, to delete reference to 12.2. This rule of application is now in 12.2(13).

**Regulations**: 301 (meaning of "life annuity contract").

**I.T. Application Rules**: 69 (meaning of *Income Tax Act*, chapter 148 of the Revised Statutes of Canada, 1952").

**Related Provisions [s. 148]**: 12.2 — Accrual of income on certain life insurance policies including annuity contracts; 20(1)(c), 20(2.2) — Deductibility of interest and compound interest on money borrowed to acquire a life insurance policy; 20(2.1) — Deductibility of interest paid or incurred in respect of a policy loan; 20(19) — Deduction from payment under an annuity contract for amounts previously included in income; 20(20) — Deduction re disposition of life insurance policy for accrued income previously included in income; 56(1)(d), (d.1) — Inclusion in income of annuity payments in respect of annuities not subject to accrual rules under subsec. 12.2; 60(a) — Deduction of capital element of annuity payments; 70(3.1) — "Rights or things" not to include interest in a life insurance policy; 70(5.3) — Valuation of shares of a corporation where it is beneficiary of life insurance policy on deceased; 87(2.2) — Amalgamation of insurance corporations; 88(1)(g) — Winding-up of subsidiary insurance corporations; 89(1)"capital dividend account"(d) — When gains on life insurance policy issued on or before June 28, 1982 included in capital dividend account; 89(2)(a) — When gain on life insurance policy issued on or before June 28, 1982, excluded from capital dividend account; 115(1)(a)(vi), 116(5.1), (5.2) — Proceeds of disposition by non-resident of life insurance policy in Canada; 138 — Insurance corporations; 138.1 — Rules relating to segregated funds.

**Definitions [s. 148]**: "accumulating fund" — Reg. 307; "adjusted cost basis" — 148(9); "amount" — 248(1); "amount payable" — (in respect of a policy loan) 148(9); "anniversary day" — 12.2(11), 148(9.1); "annuity" — 248(1); "arm's length" — 251(1); "calendar year" — *Interpretation Act* 37(1)(a); "Canada" — 255; "cash surrender value" — 148(9); "child" — 70(10), 148(9), 252(1); "common-law partner", "common-law partnership" — 248(1); "consequence of a death", "consequence of the death" — 248(8); "corporation" — 248(1), *Interpretation Act* 35(1); "disposition" — (in relation to an interest in a life insurance policy) 148(9); "dividend" — 248(1); "exempt policy" — 12.2(11), 148(9.1); "former spouse" — 252(3); "gross revenue", "income-averaging annuity contract", "individual" — 248(1); "insurer" — 148(10)(a), 248(1); "interest" — (in relation to a policy loan) 148(9); "life annuity contract" — Reg. 301; "life insurance policy" — 138(12), 248(1); "life insurer" — 148(10)(a), 248(1); "non-resident" — 248(1); "paid-up addition" — 12.2(10); "person" — 248(1); "person whose life was insured" — 148(10)(b); "policy dividend" — 139.1(8)(a); "policy loan", "premium" — 148(9); "prescribed" — 248(1); "prescribed annuity contract" — Reg. 304; "proceeds of the disposition" (of an interest in a life insurance policy) — 148(9); "property" — 248(1); "province" — *Interpretation Act* 35(1); "registered pension plan" — 248(1); "registered retirement savings plan" — 146(1), 248(1); "resident in Canada" — 250; "segregated fund" — 138.1(1); "segregated fund policy" — 138.1(1)(a); "share" — 248(1); "spouse" — 252(3); "taxable Canadian corporation" — 89(1), 248(1); "taxable capital gain" — 38(a), 248(1); "taxable dividend" — 89(1), 248(1); "taxable income" — 2(2), 248(1); "taxable income earned in Canada" — 115(1), 248(1); "taxation year" — 249; "taxpayer" — 248(1); "third anniversary" — 12.2(11), 148(9.1); "value" (of an interest in a life insurance policy) — 148(9).

**Regulations [s. 148]**: 300–310.

## Eligible Funeral Arrangements

**148.1 (1) Definitions** — In this section,

**"cemetery care trust"** means a trust established pursuant to an Act of a province for the care and maintenance of a cemetery;

**Related Provisions**: 128.1(10)"excluded right or interest"(e)(iii) — No deemed disposition on emigration of individual; 149(1)(s.2) — No tax on cemetery care trust; 248(1)"cemetery care trust" — Definition applies to entire Act.

**Notes**: "Cemetery care trust" added by 1995-97 technical bill, effective for 1993 and later taxation years.

**Regulations**: 204(3)(d.1) (cemetery care trust need not file T3 return).

**Interpretation Bulletins**: IT-531: Eligible funeral arrangements.

**"cemetery services"** with respect to an individual means property (including interment vaults, markers, flowers, liners, urns, shrubs and wreaths) and services that relate directly to cemetery arrangements in Canada in consequence of the death of the individual including, for greater certainty, property and services to be funded out of a cemetery care trust;

**Notes**: "Cemetery services" added by 1995-97 technical bill, effective for 1993 and later taxation years.

**Interpretation Bulletins**: IT-531: Eligible funeral arrangements.

**"custodian"** of an arrangement means

(a) where a trust is governed by the arrangement, a trustee of the trust, and

(b) in any other case, a qualifying person who receives a contribution under the arrangement as a deposit for the provision by the person of funeral or cemetery services;

**Related Provisions**: 212(1)(v) — Withholding tax on payment by custodian to non-resident person.

**Notes**: See Notes at end of 148.1. Para. (b) amended by 1995-97 technical bill, retroactive to its introduction, to add reference to cemetery services.

**Interpretation Bulletins**: IT-87R2: Policyholders' income from life insurance policies; IT-531: Eligible funeral arrangements.

**"eligible funeral arrangement"** at a particular time means an arrangement established and maintained by a qualifying person solely for the purpose of funding funeral or cemetery services with respect to one or more individuals and of which there is one or more custodians each of whom was resident in Canada at the time the arrangement was established, where

(a) each contribution made before the particular time under the arrangement was made for the purpose of funding funeral or cemetery services to be provided by the qualifying person with respect to an individual, and

(b) for each such individual, the total of all relevant contributions made before the particular time in respect of the individual does not exceed

(i) $15,000, where the arrangement solely covers funeral services with respect to the individual,

(ii) $20,000, where the arrangement solely covers cemetery services with respect to the individual, and

(iii) $35,000, in any other case,

and, for the purpose of this definition, any payment (other than the portion of the payment to be applied as a contribution to a cemetery care trust) that is made in consideration for the immediate acquisition of a right to burial in or on property that is set apart or used as a place for the burial of human remains or of any interest in a building or structure for the permanent placement of human remains, shall be considered to have been made pursuant to a separate arrangement that is not an eligible funeral arrangement;

**Related Provisions**: 128.1(10)"excluded right or interest"(e)(iv) — No deemed disposition on emigration of individual; 149(1)(s.1) — No tax on eligible funeral arrangement; 212(1)(v) — Withholding tax on payment from eligible funeral arrangement to non-resident; 248(1)"eligible funeral arrangement" — Definition applies to entire Act.

**Notes**: See Notes at end of 148.1. Definition amended by 1995-97 technical bill, retroactive to its introduction (effective 1993), to add references to cemetery services, the additional $20,000 for them (previously it was limited to $15,000 for funeral services only), and the closing words.

**Regulations**: 201(1)(f) (information return on return of funds); 202(2)(m) (information return on payment to non-resident).

**Interpretation Bulletins**: IT-531: Eligible funeral arrangements.

**"funeral or cemetery services"** with respect to an individual means funeral services with respect to the individual, cemetery services with respect to the individual or any combination of such services;

**Notes**: "Funeral or cemetery services" added by 1995-97 technical bill, effective for 1993 and later taxation years.

**Interpretation Bulletins**: IT-531: Eligible funeral arrangements.

**"funeral services"** with respect to an individual means property and services (other than cemetery services with respect to the individual) that relate directly to funeral arrangements in Canada in consequence of the death of the individual;

**Related Provisions**: 255 — "Canada" includes coastal waters.

**Notes**: See Notes at end of 148.1. Definition "funeral services" amended by 1995-97 technical bill, retroactive to its introduction, to add exclusion of cemetery services and to limit the definition to funeral arrangements.

**Interpretation Bulletins**: IT-531: Eligible funeral arrangements.

**"qualifying person"** means a person licensed or otherwise authorized under the laws of a province to provide funeral or cemetery services with respect to individuals;

**Notes**: See Notes at end of 148.1. Definition "qualifying person" amended by 1995-97 technical bill, retroactive to its introduction, to add reference to cemetery services.

**Interpretation Bulletins**: IT-531: Eligible funeral arrangements.

**"relevant contribution"** in respect of an individual under a particular arrangement means

(a) a contribution under the particular arrangement (other than a contribution made by way of a transfer from an eligible funeral arrangement) for the purpose of funding funeral or cemetery services with respect to the individual, or

(b) such portion of a contribution to another arrangement that was an eligible funeral arrangement (other than any such contribution made by way of a transfer from any eligible funeral arrangement) as can reasonably be considered to have subsequently been used to make a contribution under the particular arrangement by way of a transfer from an eligible funeral arrangement for the purpose of funding funeral or cemetery services with respect to the individual.

**Related Provisions**: 148.1(1)"eligible funeral arrangement"(b) — Dollar limits on relevant contributions.

**Notes**: Paras. (a) and (b) amended by 1995-97 technical bill, retroactive to their introduction, to add references to cemetery services.

**Interpretation Bulletins**: IT-531: Eligible funeral arrangements.

**(2) Exemption for eligible funeral arrangements** — Notwithstanding any other provision of this Act,

(a) no amount that has accrued, is credited or is added to an eligible funeral arrangement shall be included in computing the income of any person solely because of such accrual, crediting or adding;

(b) subject to paragraph (c) and subsection (3), no amount shall be

(i) included in computing a person's income solely because of the provision by another person of funeral or cemetery services under an eligible funeral arrangement, or

(ii) included in computing a person's income because of the disposition of an interest under an eligible funeral arrangement or an interest in a trust governed by an eligible funeral arrangement; and

(c) subparagraph (b)(ii) shall not affect the consequences under this Act of the disposition of any right under an eligible funeral arrangement to payment for the provision of funeral or cemetery services.

**Related Provisions**: 149(1)(s.1) — No tax on trust governing an eligible funeral arrangement; 149(1)(s.2) — No tax on cemetery care trust.

**Notes**: See Notes at end of 148.1. 148.1(2)(b) and (c) amended by 1995-97 technical bill, retroactive to their introduction, to add references to cemetery services.

**Interpretation Bulletins**: IT-531: Eligible funeral arrangements.

**(3) Income inclusion on return of funds** — Where at any particular time in a taxation year a particular amount is distributed (otherwise than as payment for the provision of funeral or cemetery services with respect to an individual) to a taxpayer from an arrangement that was, at the time it was established, an eligible funeral arrangement and the particular amount is paid from the balance in respect of the individual under the arrangement, there shall be added in computing the taxpayer's income for the year from property the lesser of the particular amount and the amount determined by the formula

## S. 148.1(3) — Income Tax Act, Part I

$$A + B - C$$

where

A is the balance in respect of the individual under the arrangement immediately before the particular time (determined without regard to the value of property in a cemetery care trust);

B is the total of all payments made from the arrangement before the particular time for the provision of funeral or cemetery services with respect to the individual (other than cemetery services funded by property in a cemetery care trust); and

C is the total of all relevant contributions made before the particular time in respect of the individual under the particular arrangement (other than contributions in respect of the individual that were in a cemetery care trust).

**Related Provisions [subsec. 148.1(3)]:** 12(1)(z.4) — Inclusion into income from property; 212(1)(v) — Withholding tax on payment to non-resident; 257 — Formula cannot calculate to less than zero.

**Notes:** 148.1(3) amended by 1995-97 technical bill, retroactive to its introduction, to add references to cemetery services and to add the exclusions relating to cemetery care trusts in each of the descriptions of A, B and C.

**Regulations [subsec. 148.1(3)]:** 201(1)(f) (information return).

**Interpretation Bulletins [subsec. 148.1(3)]:** IT-531: Eligible funeral arrangements.

**Notes [s. 148.1]:** 148.1 added by 1994 tax amendments bill (Part IV), effective 1993, and amended by 1995-97 technical bill retroactive to its introduction. In simple terms, it permits every individual to place up to $35,000 in an eligible funeral arrangement, as defined in 148.1(1), to cover both funeral services ($15,000) and cemetery services ($20,000). The interest earned on the funds is not taxable to the trust (see 149(1)(s.1), (s.2)). Revenue Canada had allowed these arrangements on an administrative basis for many years (see Interpretation Bulletin IT-246, "Funeral directors — prepaid funeral costs" (August 25, 1975)) but had proposed to cancel its administrative policy effective after 1992. See now Interpretation Bulletin IT-531.

For a detailed discussion see Thomas Kingissepp, "Eligible Funeral Arrangements", 43(4) *Canadian Tax Journal* 983–995 (1995).

**Definitions [s. 148.1]:** "amount" — 248(1); "Canada" — 255; "custodian" — 148.1(1); "eligible funeral arrangement" — 148.1(1), 248(1); "funeral services" — 148.1(1); "individual", "property" — 248(1); "province" — *Interpretation Act* 35(1); "qualifying person", "relevant contribution" — 148.1(1); "resident in Canada" — 250; "taxation year" — 249; "taxpayer" — 248(1); "trust" — 104(1), 248(1), (3).

## DIVISION H — EXEMPTIONS

### Miscellaneous Exemptions

**149. (1) Miscellaneous exemptions** — No tax is payable under this Part on the taxable income of a person for a period when that person was

**(a) employees of a country other than Canada** — an officer or servant of the government of a country other than Canada whose duties require that person to reside in Canada

(i) if, immediately before assuming those duties, the person resided outside Canada,

(ii) if that country grants a similar privilege to an officer or servant of Canada of the same class,

(iii) if the person was not, at any time in the period, engaged in a business or performing the duties of an office or employment in Canada other than the person's position with that government, and

(iv) if the person was not during the period a Canadian citizen;

**Related Provisions:** 94.1(1)"exempt taxpayer"(b) — Exclusion from foreign investment entity accrual rules; 149(1)(b) — Family members and servants; 212(14)(c)(i) — Certificate of exemption; Canada-U.S. tax treaty, Art. XIX — Government service; Canada-U.S. tax treaty, Art. XXVIII — Diplomatic agents and consular officers; Canada-UK Tax Convention, Art. 25 — Diplomatic and consular officials.

**Notes:** Members of armed forces of other countries in Canada may effectively be exempt on non-Canadian-source income by being deemed non-resident by the *Visiting Forces Act*. See Notes to 250(1).

**(b) members of the family and servants of employees of a country other than Canada** — a member of the family of a person described in paragraph (a) who resides with that person, or a servant employed by a person described in that paragraph,

(i) if the country of which the person described in paragraph (a) is an officer or servant grants a similar privilege to members of the family residing with and servants employed by an officer or servant of Canada of the same class,

(ii) in the case of a member of the family, if that member was not at any time lawfully admitted to Canada for permanent residence, or at any time in the period engaged in a business or performing the duties of an office or employment in Canada,

(iii) in the case of a servant, if, immediately before assuming his or her duties as a servant of a person described in paragraph (a), the servant resided outside Canada and, since first assuming those duties in Canada, has not at any time engaged in a business in Canada or been employed in Canada other than by a person described in that paragraph, and

(iv) if the member of the family or servant was not during the period a Canadian citizen;

**Related Provisions:** 94.1(1)"exempt taxpayer"(b) — Exclusion from foreign investment entity accrual rules.

**(c) municipal authorities** — a municipality in Canada, or a municipal or public body performing a function of government in Canada;

**Related Provisions:** 94.1(1)"exempt taxpayer"(b) — Exclusion from foreign investment entity accrual rules; 149(1)(d)–(d.5) — Municipal or provincial corporations.

**Notes:** The provinces cannot be taxed by the federal government: *Constitution Act, 1867*, s. 125. 149(1)(c) to (d.6) extend this rule to federal Crown corporations (subject to 27(2)) and various other

Division H — Exemptions  S. 149(1)(d.2)

public bodies and creations of the provinces and municipalities, which have no constitutional protection from federal taxation.

The CCRA treats Indian bands as municipalities for purposes of 149(1)(c). See Revenue Canada Round Table, Q.36, Canadian Tax Foundation 1992 annual conference report, pp. 54:23–24. A corporation owned by an Indian band can be exempt under 149(1)(d.5), but only if at least 90% of its income is based on the reserve.

(d) **corporations owned by the Crown** — a corporation, commission or association all of the shares (except directors' qualifying shares) or of the capital of which was owned by Her Majesty in right of Canada or a province;

> **Proposed Amendment — 149(1)(d)**
>
> (d) **corporations owned by the Crown** — a corporation, commission or association all of the shares (except directors' qualifying shares) or of the capital of which was owned by one or more persons each of which is Her Majesty in right of Canada or Her Majesty in right of a province;
>
> **Application**: Bill C-43 (First Reading September 20, 2000), subsec. 89(1), will amend para. 149(1)(d) to read as above, applicable to taxation years and fiscal periods that begin after 1998.
>
> **Technical Notes**: Paragraphs 149(1)(d) to (d.6) of the Act exempt from tax the taxable income of any corporation, commission or association 100% (or in some instances 90%) of the shares or capital of which is owned by the federal government, a provincial government or a municipality in Canada. The exemption also applies to a wholly-owned subsidiary of such a corporation, commission or association. Paragraphs 149(1)(d) to (d.4) and (d.6) are amended strictly to clarify that the ownership test referred to in those paragraphs can be met through combined ownership. For example, where the federal government and a provincial government each owns 50% of the shares of a corporation, the taxable income of the corporation will be exempt by virtue of paragraph 149(1)(d).

**Related Provisions**: 27(2) — Prescribed federal Crown corporations are taxable; 94.1(1)"exempt taxpayer"(b) — Exclusion from foreign investment entity accrual rules; 149(1.1) — No exemption where other person has a right to acquire shares; 181.1(3)(c) — Exemption from Part I.3 tax; 212(1)(b)(ii)(C)(IV) — No withholding tax on bond interest paid to non-residents; 227(14) — Exemption from tax under other Parts; 227(16) — Corporation deemed not private corporation for Part IV tax; Reg. 1216 — Exemption from Part XII tax.

**Notes**: 149(1)(d) amended by 1995-97 technical bill, effective for taxation years and fiscal periods that begin after 1998 (changed from 1997 before Third Reading of the amending bill). The former para. has been expanded and split up into (d)-(d.5). See Notes to 149(1)(c). For 1972 to 1997, read:

> (d) a corporation, commission or association not less than 90% of the shares or capital of which was owned by Her Majesty in right of Canada or a province or by a Canadian municipality, or a wholly-owned corporation subsidiary to such a corporation, commission or association, but this paragraph does not apply
>
> (i) to such a corporation, commission or association if a person other than Her Majesty in right of Canada or a province or a Canadian municipality had, during the period, a right under a contract, in equity or otherwise either immediately or in the future and either absolutely or contingently, to, or to acquire, shares or capital of that corporation, commission or association, and
>
> (ii) to such a wholly-owned subsidiary corporation if a person other than Her Majesty in right of Canada or a province or a Canadian municipality had, during the period, a right under a contract, in equity or otherwise either immediately or in the future and either absolutely or contingently, to, or to acquire, shares or capital of that wholly-owned subsidiary corporation or of the corporation, commission or association of which it is a wholly-owned subsidiary corporation;

**Interpretation Bulletins**: IT-347R2: Crown corporations.

(d.1) **corporations 90% owned by the Crown** — a corporation, commission or association not less than 90% of the shares (except directors' qualifying shares) or of the capital of which was owned by Her Majesty in right of Canada or a province;

> **Proposed Amendment — 149(1)(d.1)**
>
> (d.1) **corporations 90% owned by the Crown** — a corporation, commission or association not less than 90% of the shares (except directors' qualifying shares) or of the capital of which was owned by one or more persons each of which is Her Majesty in right of Canada or Her Majesty in right of a province;
>
> **Application**: Bill C-43 (First Reading September 20, 2000), subsec. 89(1), will amend para. 149(1)(d.1) to read as above, applicable to taxation years and fiscal periods that begin after 1998.
>
> **Technical Notes**: See under 149(1)(d).

**Related Provisions**: 27(2) — Prescribed federal Crown corporations are taxable; 94.1(1)"exempt taxpayer"(b) — Exclusion from foreign investment entity accrual rules; 149(1.1) — No exemption where other person has a right to acquire shares; 181.1(3)(c) — Exemption from Part I.3 tax; 212(1)(b)(ii)(C)(IV) — No withholding tax on bond interest paid to non-residents; 227(14) — Exemption from tax under other Parts; 227(16) — Corporation deemed not private corporation for Part IV tax; Reg. 1216 — Exemption from Part XII tax.

**Notes**: 149(1)(d.1) added by 1995-97 technical bill, effective for taxation years and fiscal periods that begin after 1998 (changed from 1997 before Third Reading of the amending bill). See Notes to 149(1)(c) and (d).

(d.2) **wholly-owned corporations** — a corporation all of the shares (except directors' qualifying shares) or of the capital of which was owned by a corporation, commission or association to which this paragraph or paragraph (d) applies for the period;

> **Proposed Amendment — 149(1)(d.2)**
>
> (d.2) **wholly-owned corporations** — a corporation all of the shares (except directors' qualifying shares) or of the capital of which was owned by one or more persons each of which is a corporation, commission or association to which this paragraph or paragraph (d) applies for the period;
>
> **Application**: Bill C-43 (First Reading September 20, 2000), subsec. 89(1), will amend para. 149(1)(d.2) to read as above, applicable to taxation years and fiscal periods that begin after 1998.
>
> **Technical Notes**: See under 149(1)(d).

**Related Provisions**: 27(2) — Prescribed federal Crown corporations are taxable; 94.1(1)"exempt taxpayer"(b) — Exclusion from

## S. 149(1)(d.2) — Income Tax Act, Part I

foreign investment entity accrual rules; 149(1.1) — No exemption where other person has a right to acquire shares; 149(1.11) — Election for corporation that was taxable before 1999 to remain taxable; 181.1(3)(c) — Exemption from Part I.3 tax; 212(1)(b)(ii)(C)(IV) — No withholding tax on bond interest paid to non-residents; 227(14) — Exemption from tax under other Parts; 227(16) — Corporation deemed not private corporation for Part IV tax; Reg. 1216 — Exemption from Part XII tax.

**Notes**: 149(1)(d.2) added by 1995-97 technical bill, effective for taxation years and fiscal periods that begin after 1998 (changed from 1997 before Third Reading of the amending bill). See Notes to 149(1)(c) and (d).

(d.3) **90% owned corporations** — a corporation, commission or association not less than 90% of the shares (except directors' qualifying shares) or of the capital of which was owned by

(i) Her Majesty in right of Canada or a province or a person to which paragraph (d) or (d.2) applies for the period, or

**Proposed Amendment — 149(1)(d.3)(i)**

(i) one or more persons each of which is Her Majesty in right of Canada or a province or a person to which paragraph (d) or (d.2) applies for the period, or

**Application**: Bill C-43 (First Reading September 20, 2000), subsec. 89(2), will amend subpara. 149(1)(d.3)(i) to read as above, applicable to taxation years and fiscal periods that begin after 1998.

**Technical Notes**: See under 149(1)(d).

(ii) one or more municipalities in Canada in combination with one or more persons each of which is Her Majesty in right of Canada or a province or a person to which paragraph (d) or (d.2) applies for the period;

**Related Provisions**: 27(2) — Prescribed federal Crown corporations are taxable; 94.1(1)"exempt taxpayer"(b) — Exclusion from foreign investment entity accrual rules; 149(1.1) — No exemption where other person has a right to acquire shares; 149(1.11) — Election for corporation that was taxable before 1999 to remain taxable; 181.1(3)(c) — Exemption from Part I.3 tax; 212(1)(b)(ii)(C)(IV) — No withholding tax on bond interest paid to non-residents; 227(14) — Exemption from tax under other Parts; 227(16) — Corporation deemed not private corporation for Part IV tax; Reg. 1216 — Exemption from Part XII tax.

**Notes**: 149(1)(d.3) added by 1995-97 technical bill, effective for taxation years and fiscal periods that begin after 1998 (changed from 1997 before Third Reading of the amending bill). See Notes to 149(1)(c) and (d).

(d.4) **combined [Crown] ownership** — a corporation all of the shares (except directors' qualifying shares) or of the capital of which was owned by a corporation, commission or association to which this paragraph or any of paragraphs (d) to (d.3) applies for the period;

**Proposed Amendment — 149(1)(d.4)**

(d.4) **combined [Crown] ownership** — a corporation all of the shares (except directors' qualifying shares) or of the capital of which was owned by one or more persons each of which is a corporation, commission or association to which this paragraph or any of paragraphs (d) to (d.3) applies for the period;

**Application**: Bill C-43 (First Reading September 20, 2000), subsec. 89(3), will amend para. 149(1)(d.4) to read as above, applicable to taxation years and fiscal periods that begin after 1998.

**Technical Notes**: See under 149(1)(d).

**Related Provisions**: 27(2) — Prescribed federal Crown corporations are taxable; 94.1(1)"exempt taxpayer"(b) — Exclusion from foreign investment entity accrual rules; 149(1.1) — No exemption where other person has a right to acquire shares; 149(1.11) — Election for corporation that was taxable before 1999 to remain taxable; 181.1(3)(c) — Exemption from Part I.3 tax; 212(1)(b)(ii)(C)(IV) — No withholding tax on bond interest paid to non-residents; 227(14) — Exemption from tax under other Parts; 227(16) — Corporation deemed not private corporation for Part IV tax; Reg. 1216 — Exemption from Part XII tax.

**Notes**: 149(1)(d.4) added by 1995-97 technical bill, effective for taxation years and fiscal periods that begin after 1998 (changed from 1997 before Third Reading of the amending bill). See Notes to 149(1)(c) and (d).

(d.5) **municipal corporations** — subject to subsections (1.2) and (1.3), a corporation, commission or association not less than 90% of the capital of which was owned by one or more municipalities in Canada, if the income for the period of the corporation, commission or association from activities carried on outside the geographical boundaries of the municipalities does not exceed 10% of its income for the period;

**Related Provisions**: 94.1(1)"exempt taxpayer"(b) — Exclusion from foreign investment entity accrual rules; 149(1.1) — No exemption where other person has a right to acquire shares; 149(1.2) — Meaning of "outside the geographical boundaries"; 149(1.3) — Meaning of capital ownership; 181.1(3)(c) — Exemption from Part I.3 tax; 212(1)(b)(ii)(C)(IV) — No withholding tax on bond interest paid to non-residents; 227(14) — Exemption from tax under other Parts; 227(16) — Corporation deemed not private corporation for Part IV tax; Reg. 1216 — Exemption from Part XII tax.

**Notes**: 149(1)(d.5) added by 1995-97 technical bill, effective for taxation years and fiscal periods that begin after 1998 (changed from 1997 before Third Reading of the amending bill). See Notes to 149(1)(c) and (d).

(d.6) **[subsidiaries of municipal corporations]** — subject to subsections (1.2) and (1.3), a particular corporation all the shares (except directors' qualifying shares) or of the capital of which was owned by another corporation, commission or association to which paragraph (d.5) or this paragraph applies for the period if the income for the period of the particular corporation from activities carried on outside

**Proposed Amendment — 149(1)(d.6) opening words**

(d.6) **subsidiaries of municipal corporations** — subject to subsections (1.2) and (1.3), a particular corporation all of the shares (except directors' qualifying shares) or of the capital of which was owned by one or more persons each of which is a corporation, commission or association to which paragraph (d.5) or this paragraph applies for the period if the income for the period of the particular corporation from activities carried on outside

**Application**: Bill C-43 (First Reading September 20, 2000), subsec. 89(4), will amend the opening words of para. 149(1)(d.6) to read as above, applicable to taxation years and fiscal periods that begin after 1998.

**Technical Notes**: See under 149(1)(d).

(i) if paragraph (d.5) applies to the other corporation, commission or association, the geographical boundaries of the municipalities referred to in that paragraph in its application to that other corporation, commission or association, or

(ii) if this paragraph applies to the other corporation, commission or association, the geographical boundaries of the municipalities referred to in subparagraph (i) in its application to that other corporation, commission or association, does not exceed 10% of its income for the period;

**Related Provisions**: 94.1(1)"exempt taxpayer"(b) — Exclusion from foreign investment entity accrual rules; 149(1.1) — No exemption where other person has a right to acquire shares; 149(1.2) — Meaning of "outside the geographical boundaries"; 181.1(3)(c) — Exemption from Part I.3 tax; 212(1)(b)(ii)(C)(IV) — No withholding tax on bond interest paid to non-residents; 227(14) — Exemption from tax under other Parts; 227(16) — Corporation deemed not private corporation for Part IV tax; Reg. 1216 — Exemption from Part XII tax.

**Notes**: 149(1)(d.6) added by 1995-97 technical bill, effective for taxation years and fiscal periods that begin after 1998 (changed from 1997 before Third Reading of the amending bill). See Notes to 149(1)(c) and (d).

(e) **certain organizations** — an agricultural organization, a board of trade or a chamber of commerce, no part of the income of which was payable to, or was otherwise available for the personal benefit of, any proprietor, member or shareholder thereof;

**Related Provisions**: 94.1(1)"exempt taxpayer"(b) — Exclusion from foreign investment entity accrual rules; 149(2) — Income not to include taxable capital gains; 149(12) — Information returns; 181.1(3)(c) — Exemption from Part I.3 tax; 227(14) — Exemption from tax under other Parts.

(f) **registered charities** — a registered charity;

**Related Provisions**: 94.1(1)"exempt taxpayer"(b) — Exclusion from foreign investment entity accrual rules; 149.1 — Charities; 181.1(3)(c), 227(14) — Exemption from tax under other Parts; 248(1)"registered charity" — Registration provisions; Canada-U.S. tax treaty, Art. XXI:1 — Religious, literary, scientific, educational or charitable organization — exemption from tax.

(g), (h) [Repealed under former Act]

**Notes**: 149(1)(g) and (h), repealed in 1977, provided exemptions for non-profit corporations and charitable trusts. See 149(1)(l) now.

(h.1) **Association of Universities and Colleges of Canada** — the Association of Universities and Colleges of Canada, incorporated by the *Act to incorporate Association of Universities and Colleges of Canada*, chapter 75 of the Statutes of Canada, 1964-65;

**Related Provisions**: 94.1(1)"exempt taxpayer"(b) — Exclusion from foreign investment entity accrual rules; 181.1(3)(c), 227(14) — Exemption from tax under other Parts.

(i) **certain housing corporations** — a corporation that was constituted exclusively for the purpose of providing low-cost housing accommodation for the aged, no part of the income of which was payable to, or was otherwise available for the personal benefit of, any proprietor, member or shareholder thereof;

**Related Provisions**: 94.1(1)"exempt taxpayer"(b) — Exclusion from foreign investment entity accrual rules; 149(2) — Income not to include taxable capital gains; 181.1(3)(c), 227(14) — Exemption from tax under other Parts.

(j) **non-profit corporations for scientific research and experimental development** — a corporation that was constituted exclusively for the purpose of carrying on or promoting scientific research and experimental development, no part of whose income was payable to, or was otherwise available for the personal benefit of, any proprietor, member or shareholder thereof, that has not acquired control of any other corporation and that, during the period,

(i) did not carry on any business, and

(ii) expended amounts in Canada each of which is

(A) an expenditure on scientific research and experimental development (within the meaning that would be assigned by paragraph 37(8)(a) if subsection 37(8) were read without reference to paragraph 37(8)(d)) directly undertaken by or on behalf of the corporation, or

(B) a payment to an association, university, college or research institute or other similar institution, described in clause 37(1)(a)(ii)(A) or (B) to be used for scientific research and experimental development, and

the total of which is not less than 90% of the amount, if any, by which the corporation's gross revenue for the period exceeds the total of all amounts paid in the period by the corporation because of subsection (7.1);

**Related Provisions**: 37(1)(a)(ii)(C), 37(1)(a)(iii) — Deduction for R&D payments to corporation described in 149(1)(j); 94.1(1)"exempt taxpayer"(b) — Exclusion from foreign investment entity accrual rules; 149(2) — Income not to include taxable capital gains; 149(7) — Prescribed form to be filed; 149(8), (9) — Interpretation rules; 149(9) — Rules; 181.1(3)(c) — Exemption from Part I.3 tax; 227(14) — Exemption from tax under other Parts; 256(6)–(9) — Whether control acquired.

**Notes**: 149(1)(j)(ii)(A) amended by 1995 Budget, retroactive to taxation years ending after November 1991, to correct reference to 37(7) to be 37(8)(a).

Closing words of 149(1)(j)(ii) amended by 1995 Budget, effective for taxation years that begin after June 1995. Formerly read: "the total of which is not less than 90% of the corporation's income for the period".

S. 149(1)(j) — Income Tax Act, Part I

**Regulations**: 2900(1) (definition of SR&ED, except where work performed pursuant to agreement in writing entered into before February 28, 1995).

**Interpretation Bulletins**: IT-151R5: Scientific research and experimental development expenditures.

**Information Circulars**: 86-4R3: Scientific research and experimental development.

**Application Policies**: SR&ED 96-10: Third party payments — approval process.

(k) **labour organizations** — a labour organization or society or a benevolent or fraternal benefit society or order;

**Related Provisions**: 94.1(1)"exempt taxpayer"(b) — Exclusion from foreign investment entity accrual rules.

**Interpretation Bulletins**: IT-389R: Vacation pay trusts established under collective agreements.

(l) **non-profit organizations** — a club, society or association that, in the opinion of the Minister, was not a charity within the meaning assigned by subsection 149.1(1) and that was organized and operated exclusively for social welfare, civic improvement, pleasure or recreation or for any other purpose except profit, no part of the income of which was payable to, or was otherwise available for the personal benefit of, any proprietor, member or shareholder thereof unless the proprietor, member or shareholder was a club, society or association the primary purpose and function of which was the promotion of amateur athletics in Canada;

**Related Provisions**: 94.1(1)"exempt taxpayer"(b) — Exclusion from foreign investment entity accrual rules; 149(2) — Income not to include taxable capital gains; 149(3) — Application of subsec. (1); 149(5) — Exception re investment income of certain clubs; 149(12) — Information returns; 181.1(3)(c) — Exemption from Part I.3 tax; 227(14) — Exemption from tax under other Parts; 248(1) — "person"; 248(1) — "registered Canadian amateur athletic association"; Reg. 4900(1)(r) — Debt of non-profit corporation as qualified investment for RRSP, etc.

**Interpretation Bulletins**: IT-83R3: Non-profit organizations — Taxation of income from property; IT-304R2: Condominiums; IT-409: Winding-up of a non-profit organization; IT-496: Non-profit organizations.

**I.T. Technical News**: No. 4 (condominium corporations).

**Advance Tax Rulings**: ATR-29: Amalgamation of social clubs.

(m) **mutual insurance corporations** — a mutual insurance corporation that received its premiums wholly from the insurance of churches, schools or other charitable organizations;

**Related Provisions**: 94.1(1)"exempt taxpayer"(b) — Exclusion from foreign investment entity accrual rules; 181.1(3)(c) — Exemption from Part I.3 tax; 227(14) — Exemption from tax under other Parts.

(n) **housing companies** — a limited-dividend housing company (within the meaning of that expression as defined in section 2 of the *National Housing Act*), all or substantially all of the business of which is the construction, holding or management of low-rental housing projects;

**Related Provisions**: 94.1(1)"exempt taxpayer"(b) — Exclusion from foreign investment entity accrual rules; 149.1(1) — Definitions — "non-qualified investment"; 181.1(3)(c) — Exemption from Part I.3 tax; 227(14) — Exemption from tax under other Parts.

**Notes**: *National Housing Act*, R.S.C. 1985, c. N-11, s. 2 provides:

"limited-dividend housing company" means a company incorporated to construct, hold and manage a low-rental housing project, the dividends payable by which are limited by the terms of its charter or instrument of incorporation to five per cent per annum or less;

The CCRA takes the position that "all or substantially all" means 90% or more.

(o) **pension trusts** — a trust governed by a registered pension plan;

**Related Provisions**: 94.1(1)"exempt taxpayer"(b) — Exclusion from foreign investment entity accrual rules; 138.1(7) — Where policyholder deemed to be trust, etc.; 205 — Application of Part XI to pension trust; 210.1(c) — Pension trust not subject to Part XII.2 tax; Canada-U.S. tax treaty, Art. XXI:2 — Exemption from tax.

(o.1) **pension corporations** — a corporation

(i) incorporated and operated throughout the period either

(A) solely for the administration of a registered pension plan, or

(B) for the administration of a registered pension plan and for no other purpose other than acting as trustee of, or administering, a trust governed by a retirement compensation arrangement, where the terms of the arrangement provide for benefits only in respect of individuals who are provided with benefits under the registered pension plan, and

(ii) accepted by the Minister as a funding medium for the purpose of the registration of the pension plan;

**Related Provisions**: 94.1(1)"exempt taxpayer"(b) — Exclusion from foreign investment entity accrual rules; 149(1)(q.1) — No tax on RCA trust; 181.1(3)(c) — Exemption from Part I.3 tax; 205 — Application of Part XI to pension corporation; 227(14) — Exemption from tax under other Parts; Canada-U.S. tax treaty, Art. XXI:2 — Exemption from tax.

**Notes**: 149(1)(o.1)(i)(B) added by 1995-97 technical bill, effective for 1994 and later taxation years.

(o.2) **idem** — a corporation

(i) incorporated before November 17, 1978 solely in connection with, or for the administration of, a registered pension plan,

(ii) that has at all times since the later of November 16, 1978 and the date on which it was incorporated

(A) limited its activities to acquiring, holding, maintaining, improving, leasing or managing capital property that is real property or an interest therein owned by the corporation, another corporation described by this subparagraph and subparagraph (iv) or a registered pension plan,

(B) made no investments other than in real property or an interest therein or investments that a pension plan is permitted to make under the *Pension Benefits Stan-*

Division H — Exemptions    S. 149(1)(q)

*dards Act, 1985* or a similar law of a province, and

(C) borrowed money solely for the purpose of earning income from real property or an interest therein,

(ii.1) that throughout the period

(A) limited its activities to

(I) acquiring Canadian resource properties by purchase or by incurring Canadian exploration expense or Canadian development expense, or

(II) holding, exploring, developing, maintaining, improving, managing, operating or disposing of its Canadian resource properties,

(B) made no investments other than in

(I) Canadian resource properties,

(II) property to be used in connection with Canadian resource properties described in clause (A),

(III) loans secured by Canadian resource properties for the purpose of carrying out any activity described in clause (A) with respect to Canadian resource properties, or

(IV) investments that a pension fund or plan is permitted to make under the *Pension Benefits Standards Act, 1985* or a similar law of a province, and

(C) borrowed money solely for the purpose of earning income from Canadian resource properties, or

(iii) that made no investments other than investments that a pension fund or plan was permitted to make under the *Pension Benefits Standards Act, 1985* or a similar law of a province, and

(A) the assets of which were at least 98% cash and investments,

(B) that had not issued debt obligations or accepted deposits, and

(C) that had derived at least 98% of its income for the period that is a taxation year of the corporation from, or from the disposition of, investments

if, at all times since the later of November 16, 1978 and the date on which it was incorporated,

(iv) all of the shares, and rights to acquire shares, of the capital stock of the corporation are owned by

(A) one or more registered pension plans,

(B) one or more trusts all the beneficiaries of which are registered pension plans,

(C) one or more related segregated fund trusts (within the meaning assigned by paragraph 138.1(1)(a)) all the beneficiaries of which are registered pension plans, or

(D) one or more prescribed persons, or

(v) in the case of a corporation without share capital, all the property of the corporation has been held exclusively for the benefit of one or more registered pension plans,

and for the purposes of subparagraph (iv), where a corporation has been formed as a result of the merger of two or more other corporations, it shall be deemed to be the same corporation as, and a continuation of, each such other corporation and the shares of the merged corporations shall be deemed to have been altered, in form only, by virtue of the merger and to have continued in existence in the form of shares of the corporation formed as a result of the merger;

**Related Provisions**: 94.1(1)"exempt taxpayer"(b) — Exclusion from foreign investment entity accrual rules; 181.1(3)(c) — Exemption from Part I.3 tax; 205 — Application of Part XI; 206(2.1) — Exemption from Part XI tax when proportional holdings election made; 212(14)(c)(i) — Certificate of exemption; 227(14) — Exemption from tax under other Parts; 248(4) — Interest in real property; 259(5)"qualified corporation" — proportional holdings in trust property.

**Regulations**: 4802 (prescribed persons).

**I.T. Technical News**: No. 1 (permissible activities of pension fund realty corporations).

(o.3) **prescribed small business investment corporations** — a corporation that is prescribed to be a small business investment corporation;

**Related Provisions**: 94.1(1)"exempt taxpayer"(b) — Exclusion from foreign investment entity accrual rules; 181.1(3)(c) — Exemption from Part I.3 tax; 227(14) — Exemption from tax under other Parts.

**Regulations**: 5101.

(o.4) **master trusts** — a trust that is prescribed to be a master trust and that elects to be such a trust under this paragraph in its return of income for its first taxation year ending in the period;

**Related Provisions**: 94.1(1)"exempt taxpayer"(b) — Exclusion from foreign investment entity accrual rules; 127.55(f)(iii) — Trust not subject to minimum tax; 205 — Application of Part XI; 206(2.1) — Exemption from Part XI tax when proportional holdings election made; 210.1(c) — Trust not subject to Part XII.2 tax; 248(1)"disposition"(f)(vi) — Rollover from one trust to another; 259(1) — Election for proportional holdings in trust property; 259(3) — Qualified trusts.

**Regulations**: 5001 (master trust).

(p) **trusts under profit sharing plan** — a trust under an employees profit sharing plan to the extent provided by section 144;

**Related Provisions**: 94.1(1)"exempt taxpayer"(b) — Exclusion from foreign investment entity accrual rules; 144(2) — No tax while trust governed by plan; 210.1(c) — Trust not subject to Part XII.2 tax; 212(14)(c)(i) — Certificate of exemption.

(q) **trusts under a registered supplementary unemployment benefit plan** — a trust under a registered supplementary

**S. 149(1)(q)**          Income Tax Act, Part I

unemployment benefit plan to the extent provided by section 145;

**Related Provisions**: 94.1(1)"exempt taxpayer"(b) — Exclusion from foreign investment entity accrual rules; 145(2) — No tax while trust governed by plan; 210.1(c) — Trust not subject to Part XII.2 tax; 212(14)(c)(i) — Certificate of exemption.

(q.1) **RCA trusts** — an RCA trust (within the meaning assigned by subsection 207.5(1));

**Related Provisions**: 149(1)(o.1)(i)(B) — No tax on corporation administering RCA trust; 207.7(1) — Part XI.3 tax on RCA trust; 210.1(c) — RCA trust not subject to Part XII.2 tax.

(r) **trusts under registered retirement savings plan** — a trust under a registered retirement savings plan to the extent provided by section 146;

**Related Provisions**: 94.1(1)"exempt taxpayer"(b) — Exclusion from foreign investment entity accrual rules; 138.1(7) — Where policyholder deemed to be trust, etc.; 146(4) — No tax while trust governed by plan; 146(10) — Tax on beneficiary when RRSP acquires non-qualified investment; 146(10.1) — Tax on income from non-qualified investments; 207.1(1) — Tax on holding non-qualified investment; 210.1(c) — RRSP not subject to Part XII.2 tax; 212(14)(c)(i) — Certificate of exemption.

**Interpretation Bulletins**: IT-415R2: Deregistration of RRSPs.

**Information Circulars**: 72-22R9: Registered retirement savings plans.

(s) **trusts under deferred profit sharing plan** — a trust under a deferred profit sharing plan to the extent provided by section 147;

**Related Provisions**: 94.1(1)"exempt taxpayer"(b) — Exclusion from foreign investment entity accrual rules; 147(7) — No tax while trust governed by plan; 198 — Tax on acquisition of non-qualified investment or use of assets as security; 207.1(2) — Tax on holding non-qualified investment; 210.1(c) — DPSP not subject to Part XII.2 tax; 212(14)(c)(i) — Certificate of exemption.

(s.1) **trust governed by eligible funeral arrangement** — a trust governed by an eligible funeral arrangement;

**Related Provisions**: 94.1(1)"exempt taxpayer"(b) — Exclusion from foreign investment entity accrual rules; 148.1(2) — No tax on income accruing in funeral arrangement or on provision of funeral or cemetary services.

**Notes**: 149(1)(s.1) added by 1994 tax amendments bill (Part IV), effective 1993. See Notes to 148.1.

**Interpretation Bulletins**: IT-531: Eligible funeral arrangements.

(s.2) **cemetery care trust** — a cemetery care trust;

**Related Provisions**: 94.1(1)"exempt taxpayer"(b) — Exclusion from foreign investment entity accrual rules.

**Notes**: 149(1)(s.2) added by 1995-97 technical bill, effective for 1993 and later taxation years.

**Interpretation Bulletins**: IT-531: Eligible funeral arrangements.

(t) **farmers' and fishermen's insurer** — an insurer that, throughout the period, is not engaged in any business other than insurance if, in the opinion of the Minister, on the advice of the Superintendent of Financial Institutions or of the superintendent of insurance of the province under the laws of which the insurer is incorporated, not less than 20% of the total of the gross premium income (net of reinsurance ceded) earned in the

period by the insurer and, where the insurer is not a prescribed insurer, by all other insurers that

(i) are specified shareholders of the insurer,

(ii) are related to the insurer, or

(iii) where the insurer is a mutual corporation, are part of a group that controls, directly or indirectly in any manner whatever, or are controlled, directly or indirectly in any manner whatever by, the insurer,

is in respect of insurance of property used in farming or fishing or residences of farmers or fishermen;

> **Proposed Amendment —
> Amalgamation of Farmers' and
> Fishermen's Insurers**
> **Letter from Department of Finance, February 21, 2000**: [See under 87(1) — ed.]

**Related Provisions**: 138 — Insurance corporations; 149(4.1) — Extent of exemption; 149(4.2) — Application of subsection (1); 149(4.3) — Computation of taxable income of insurer; 181.1(3)(c) — Exemption from Part I.3 tax; 212(14)(c)(i) — Certificate of exemption; 227(14) — Exemption from tax under other Parts; 256(5.1), (6.2) — Controlled directly or indirectly.

**Notes**: 149(1)(t) amended by 1996 Budget, effective for 1996 and later taxation years. The substantive amendment was to change 25% to 20%; the other changes are cosmetic. For 1989–95, read:

(t) an insurer who, during the period, was not engaged in any business other than insurance if, in the opinion of the Minister, on the advice of the Superintendent of Financial Institutions or of the superintendent of insurance of the province under the laws of which the insurer is incorporated, not less than 25% of the total of the gross premium income (net of reinsurance ceded) earned in the period by the insurer and, where the insurer is not a prescribed insurer, of all other insurers that

(i) were specified shareholders of the insurer,

(ii) were related to the insurer, or

(iii) where the insurer is a mutual corporation, were part of a group that controlled, directly or indirectly in any manner whatever, or were controlled, directly or indirectly in any manner whatever, by the insurer,

was in respect of the insurance of farm property, property used in fishing or residences of farmers or fishermen;

Other substantive changes made by the 1996 Budget are in 149(4.1), which limits the exemption under 149(1)(t).

149(1)(t) amended by 1991 technical bill, effective 1989, to provide that, for prescribed insurers, eligibility for the exemption is determined without reference to the gross premium income (net of reinsurance ceded) of other insurers.

**Regulations**: 4802(2) (prescribed insurers).

(u) **registered education savings plans** — a trust governed by a registered education savings plan to the extent provided by section 146.1;

**Related Provisions**: 94.1(1)"exempt taxpayer"(b) — Exclusion from foreign investment entity accrual rules; 146.1(5) — Trust not taxable; 212(14)(c)(i) — Certificate of exemption.

(v) **amateur athlete trust** — an amateur athlete trust;

**Related Provisions**: 94.1(1)"exempt taxpayer"(b) — Exclusion from foreign investment entity accrual rules; 143.1 — Rules for am-

Division H — Exemptions S. 149(1.1)

ateur athletic trusts; 210.1(c) — Amateur athlete trust not subject to Part XII.2 tax; 210.2(1.1) — Tax payable by amateur athlete trust.

**Notes:** 149(1)(v) added by 1992 technical bill, effective 1988. See 143.1.

Former 149(1)(v), repealed by 1985 Budget, exempted a registered home ownership savings plan (RHOSP) from tax. See Notes to 146.2.

**(w) trusts to provide compensation** — a trust established as required under a law of Canada or of a province in order to provide funds out of which to compensate persons for claims against an owner of a business identified in the relevant law where that owner is unwilling or unable to compensate a customer or client, if no part of the property of the trust, after payment of its proper trust expenses, is available to any person other than as a consequence of that person being a customer or client of a business so identified;

**Related Provisions:** 94.1(1)"exempt taxpayer"(b) — Exclusion from foreign investment entity accrual rules; 210.1(c) — Trust not subject to Part XII.2 tax; 212(14)(c)(i) — Certificate of exemption.

**(x) registered retirement income funds** — a trust governed by a registered retirement income fund to the extent provided by section 146.3;

**Related Provisions:** 94.1(1)"exempt taxpayer"(b) — Exclusion from foreign investment entity accrual rules; 146.3(3) — No tax while trust governed by fund; 146.3(7) — Tax on beneficiary when RRIF acquires non-qualified investment; 146.3(9) — Tax on income from non-qualified investments; 207.1(4) — Tax on holding non-qualified investments; 210.1(c) — RRIF not subject to Part XII.2 tax; 212(14)(c)(i) — Certificate of exemption.

**(y) trusts to provide vacation pay** — a trust established pursuant to the terms of a collective agreement between an employer or an association of employers and employees or their labour organization for the sole purpose of providing for the payment of vacation or holiday pay, if no part of the property of the trust, after payment of its reasonable expenses, is

　　(i) available at any time after 1980, or

　　(ii) paid after December 11, 1979

to any person (other than a person described in paragraph (k)) otherwise than as a consequence of that person being an employee or an heir or legal representative thereof; or

**Related Provisions:** 16(2) — Obligation issued at discount; 94.1(1)"exempt taxpayer"(b) — Exclusion from foreign investment entity accrual rules; 210.1(c) — Trust not subject to Part XII.2 tax; 212(14)(c)(i) — Certificate of exemption.

**Interpretation Bulletins:** IT-389R: Vacation pay trusts established under collective agreements.

**(z) qualifying environmental trust** — a qualifying environmental trust.

**Related Provisions:** 12(1)(z.1), 107.3(1) — Tax on beneficiary; 211.6 — Part XII.4 tax on trust.

**Notes:** 149(1)(z) amended by 1997 Budget, effective for 1997 and later taxation years, to change "mining reclamation trust" to "qualifying environmental trust". (The same change was made throughout the Act.)

149(1)(z) added by 1994 Budget, effective 1994.

**Interpretation Bulletins [subsec. 149(1)]:** IT-465R: Non-resident beneficiaries of trusts.

**(1.1) Exception** — Paragraphs (1)(d) to (d.6) do not apply to a corporation, commission or association during a period in which a person other than Her Majesty in right of Canada or a province or a municipality in Canada had a right under a contract, in equity or otherwise, either immediately or in the future and either absolutely or contingently to, or to acquire, shares or capital of the corporation, commission or association.

**Proposed Amendment — 149(1.1)**

**(1.1) Exception** — Where at any time a person other than Her Majesty in right of Canada or a province or a municipality in Canada has a right under a contract, in equity or otherwise, either immediately or in the future and either absolutely or contingently, to, or to acquire, shares or capital of a corporation, commission or association, paragraphs (1)(d) to (d.6) apply as if the right had been exercised and the shares or capital had been so acquired immediately before that time and held at that time by the person.

**Application:** Bill C-43 (First Reading September 20, 2000), subsec. 89(5), will amend subsec. 149(1.1) to read as above, applicable to taxation years and fiscal periods that begin after 1998 except that, where a corporation, commission or association so elects in writing and files the election with the Minister of National Revenue on or before the day that is six months after the end of the month in which this Act receives royal assent, the reference to "at any time" in the subsec. shall be read as a reference to "at any time after November 1999".

**Technical Notes:** Subsection 149(1.1) stipulates that, in order for a corporation, commission or association to benefit from the exemption provided under any of paragraphs 149(1)(d) to (d.6), only the federal government, a province or a municipality in Canada can have the right to acquire shares or capital of the corporation, commission or association. The amendment to subsection 149(1.1) ensures that entities that need only to meet a 90% (rather than a 100%) ownership test would still qualify for the exemption under paragraph 149(1)(d.2), (d.3) or (d.5), as the case may be, provided that non-governmental entities do not, collectively, own shares or capital (or rights to such shares or capital) in excess of 10%.

**Letter from Department of Finance, December 29, 1999:** [Editorial Summary: Takes into account the possible negative impact of the retroactive effect of new 149(1.1) by allowing an election to not have it apply to Jan. to Nov. 1999.]

Maître,

La présente fait suite à votre lettre du 8 décembre 1999 adressée à monsieur Robert Dubrule de ma division au sujet de la modification proposée au paragraphe 149(1.1) de la *Loi de l'impot sur le revenu*, qui a été rendue publique le 30 novembre derier.

Comme vous l'avez indiqué dans votre lettre, l'objectif de la modification proposée est de faire en sorte que les entités assujetties à un critère de propriété de 90 p. cent (au lieu de 100 p. cent) puissent être exonérées aux termes du paragraphe 149(1) de la Loi, à condition que la proportion d'actions ou de capital (ou de droits d'acquérir des actions ou du capital) que détiennent ensemble des entités non gouvernementales ne dépasse pas 10, p. cent. Comme il s'agit d'un allégement, nous avons cru opportun de prévoir pour cette modification une entrée en vigueur qui correspond à celle prévue pour les changements apportés récemment au paragraphe 149(1) de la Loi, à savoir les exercices et années d'imposition commençant après 1998.

Toutefois, comme vous l'avez souligné, la modification proposée peut, compte tenu de son libellé et de son entrée en vigueur, causer un préjudice à une société qui est imposable (et qui veut le demeurer) et qui, au cours de 1999, a effectué des transactions qui, à la lumière du libellé actuel du paragraphe 149(1) de la Loi, confirment le statut imposable de la société. La modification proposée pourrait ainsi faire en sorte que la société devienne, contre son gré, une société exonérée, et ce, rétroactivement au début de 1999. Ce résultat peut ne pas être avantageux pour la société qui se retrouverait assujettie au paragraphe 149(10) de la Loi qui prévoit, entre autres, la reconnaissance des gains en capital accumulés jusqu'à la date de changement de statut. Ce résultat, en plus de ne pas avoir été prévu, n'est pas voulu.

Compte tenu de ce qui précède, j'aimerais confirmer notre intention de recommander que soit apporté, à la première occasion, un changement aux propositions législatives du 30 novembre dernier, qui tiendra compte de vos préoccupations relativement au caractère rétroactif de la modification proposée au paragraphe 149(1.1) de la Loi.

Veuillez agréer, Maître, l'expression de mes meilleurs sentiments.

Le Directeur de la Division de la législation,
Brian Ernewein

**Notes**: 149(1.1) added by 1995-97 technical bill, effective (as amended before Third Reading of the bill) for taxation years and fiscal periods that begin after 1998.

**Forms [subsec. 149(1.1)]**: RC4107E, Registered charities: education, advocacy and political activities (draft) [guide].

### Proposed Addition — 149(1.11)

**(1.11) Election** — Subsection (1) does not apply in respect of a person's taxable income for a taxation year that begins after 1998 where

(a) paragraph (1)(d) did not apply in respect of the person's taxable income for the person's last taxation year that began before 1999;

(b) paragraph (1)(d.2), (d.3) or (d.4) would, but for this subsection, have applied in respect of the person's taxable income for the person's first taxation year that began after 1998;

(c) there has been no change in the ownership of the shares or capital of the person (other than a change with respect to directors' qualifying shares) since the beginning of the person's first taxation year that began after 1998;

(d) the person has elected in writing in its return of income for its first taxation year that began after 1998 that this subsection apply; and

(e) the person has not notified the Minister in writing before the year that the election has been revoked.

**Application**: Bill C-43 (First Reading September 20, 2000), subsec. 89(5), will add subsec. (1.11), applicable to taxation years and fiscal periods that begin after 1998 except that, where a corporation, commission or association so elects in writing and files the election with the Minister of National Revenue on or before the day that is six months after the end of the month in which this Act receives royal assent, the reference to "at any time" in subsec. (1.11) shall be read as a reference to "at any time after November 1999".

**Technical Notes**: A number of entities which were taxable before 1999 became, as a result of the amendment to paragraph 149(1)(d) of the Act and the addition of paragraphs 149(1)(d.2) to (d.4), exempt under those paragraphs with respect to their post-1998 fiscal periods. This result, which is appropriate from a tax policy standpoint, may not be beneficial for a limited number of entities since it would trigger the application of subsection 149(10) which provides, among other things, that any gain or loss that accrued before the entities become tax-exempt are to be recognized before the change of status. Accordingly, this amendment allows an entity, which has become exempt because of any of paragraphs 149(1)(d.2) to (d.4) but which was taxable for its last taxation year that began before 1999, to elect to retain its taxable status provided there has been no change in the share or capital ownership of the entity since the beginning of the entity's first taxation year that began after 1998.

**(1.2) Income test [for municipal corporation]** — For the purposes of paragraphs (1)(d.5) and (d.6), income of a corporation, commission or association from activities carried on outside the geographical boundaries of a municipality does not include income from activities carried on under an agreement in writing between

(a) the corporation, commission or association, and

(b) a person who is Her Majesty in right of Canada or a province or a municipality or corporation to which any of paragraphs (1)(d) to (d.6) applies and that is controlled by Her Majesty in right of Canada or a province or by a municipality in Canada

within the geographical boundaries of,

(c) where the person is Her Majesty in right of Canada or a corporation controlled by Her Majesty in right of Canada, Canada,

(d) where the person is Her Majesty in right of a province or a corporation controlled by Her Majesty in right of a province, the province, and

(e) where the person is a municipality in Canada or a corporation controlled by a municipality in Canada, the municipality.

### Proposed Amendment — 149(1.2)

**(1.2) Income test [for municipal corporation]** — For the purposes of paragraphs (1)(d.5) and (d.6), income of a corporation, commission or association from activities carried on outside the geographical boundaries of a municipality does not include income from activities carried on

(a) under an agreement in writing between

(i) the corporation, commission or association, and

(ii) a person who is Her Majesty in right of Canada or a province or a municipality or corporation to which any of paragraphs (1)(d) to (d.6) applies and that is controlled by Her Majesty in right of Canada or a province or by a municipality in Canada

within the geographical boundaries of,

(iii) where the person is Her Majesty in right of Canada or a corporation controlled by Her Majesty in right of Canada, Canada,

(iv) where the person is Her Majesty in right of a province or a corporation controlled by Her Majesty in right of a province, the province, and

(v) where the person is a municipality in Canada or a corporation controlled by a municipality in Canada, the municipality; or

(b) in a province as

(i) a producer of electrical energy or natural gas, or

(ii) a distributor of electrical energy, heat, natural gas or water,

where the activities are regulated under the laws of the province.

**Application**: Bill C-43 (First Reading September 20, 2000), subsec. 89(6), will amend subsec. 149(1.2) to read as above, applicable to taxation years and fiscal periods that begin after 1998.

**Technical Notes**: Subsection 149(1.2) of the Act excludes, for the purposes of paragraphs 149(1)(d.5) and (d.6), certain income from the determination of whether more than 10% of the income of an entity to which one of those two paragraphs applies is derived from activities carried on outside the geographical boundaries of the municipality or municipalities that own the entity. The amendment ensures that income from activities carried on in a province by an entity, as a producer of electrical energy or natural gas or as a distribution of electrical energy, heat, natural gas or water, is not included in the determination where those activities are regulated under the laws of the province.

**Related Provisions**: 149(1.3) — Determination of capital ownership; 256(6), (6.1) — Meaning of "controlled".

**Notes**: 149(1.2) added by 1995-97 technical bill, effective (as amended before Third Reading of the bill) for taxation years and fiscal periods that begin after 1998.

**(1.3) Capital ownership [by municipality]** — For the purposes of paragraph (1)(d.5) and subsection (1.2), 90% of the capital of a corporation that has issued share capital is owned by one or more municipalities only when the municipalities own shares of the capital stock of the corporation that give the municipalities 90% or more of the votes that could be cast under all circumstances at an annual meeting of shareholders of the corporation.

**Notes**: 149(1.3) added by 1995-97 technical bill, effective (as amended before Third Reading of the bill) for taxation years and fiscal periods that begin after 1998.

**(2) Determination of income** — For the purposes of paragraphs (1)(e), (i), (j) and (l), in computing the part, if any, of any income that was payable to or otherwise available for the personal benefit of any person or the total of any amounts that is not less than a percentage specified in any of those paragraphs of any income for a period, the amount of such income shall be deemed to be the amount thereof determined on the assumption that the amount of any taxable capital gain or allowable capital loss is nil.

**Notes**: 149(2) amended by 1992 technical bill, effective for 1992 and later taxation years, so that allowable capital losses (as well as taxable capital gains) are ignored in determining "income" for the stated purposes. For 1977 to 1991, in place of "determined on the assumption that the amount of any taxable capital gain or allowable capital loss is nil", read "determined less the amount of any taxable capital gains included therein".

**Interpretation Bulletins**: IT-409: Winding-up of a non-profit organization.

**(3) Application of subsec. (1)** — Subsection (1) does not apply in respect of the taxable income of a benevolent or fraternal society or order from carrying on a life insurance business or, for greater certainty, from the sale of property used by it in the year in, or held by it in the year in the course of, carrying on a life insurance business.

**Related Provisions**: 16(2) — Obligation issued at discount; 149(4) — Computation of taxable income; 212(14)(c)(i) — Certificate of exemption.

**(4) Idem** — For the purposes of subsection (3), the taxable income of a benevolent or fraternal benefit society or order from carrying on a life insurance business shall be computed on the assumption that it had no income or loss from any other sources.

**(4.1) Income exempt under 149(1)(t)** — Subject to subsection (4.2), subsection (1) applies to an insurer described in paragraph (1)(t) only in respect of the part of its taxable income for a taxation year determined by the formula

$$\frac{A \times B \times C}{D}$$

where

A is its taxable income for the year;

B is

(a) ½, where less than 25% of the total of the gross premium income (net of reinsurance ceded) earned in the year by it and, where it is not a prescribed insurer for the purpose of paragraph (1)(t), by all other insurers that

(i) are specified shareholders of the insurer,

(ii) are related to the insurer, or

(iii) where the insurer is a mutual corporation, are part of a group that controls, di-

**S. 149(4.1)**        Income Tax Act, Part I

rectly or indirectly in any manner whatever, or are controlled, directly or indirectly in any manner whatever by, the insurer,

is in respect of insurance of property used in farming or fishing or residences of farmers or fishermen; and

(b) 1 in any other case;

C is the part of the gross premium income (net of reinsurance ceded) earned by it in the year that, in the opinion of the Minister, on the advice of the Superintendent of Financial Institutions or of the superintendent of insurance of the province under the laws of which it is incorporated, is in respect of insurance of property used in farming or fishing or residences of farmers or fishermen; and

D is the gross premium income (net of reinsurance ceded) earned by it in the year.

**Related Provisions**: 149(4.2) — Application of subsection (1): computation of taxable income of insurer; 256(5.1), (6.2) — Controlled directly or indirectly.

**Notes**: 149(4.1) limits the exemption provided under 149(1)(t). The exemption is limited to that portion of the insurer's taxable income that the insurer's gross premium income (net of reinsurance ceded) earned for the year from the insurance of residences of farmers and fishermen, farm property and property used in fishing is of its total gross premium income (net of reinsurance ceded) for the year. This applies for insurers who reach the 25% threshold of total gross premium income (net of reinsurance ceded) of the insurer and certain other insurers that are grouped for this purpose being from the insurance of farm risks. For those between 20% and 25%, only half of the insurer's taxable income attributable to premium income arising from such risks is eligible for the exemption. (The 20% threshold is found in 149(1)(t).)

149(4.1) amended by 1996 Budget, effective for 1996 and later taxation years. For 1989–95, read:

(4.1) **Idem** — Subject to subsection (4.2), subsection (1) applies in respect of an insurer described in paragraph (1)(t) only in respect of that proportion of the insurer's taxable income for a taxation year that

(a) the part of the gross premium income (net of reinsurance ceded) earned in the year by the insurer that, in the opinion of the Minister, on the advice of the Superintendent of Financial Institutions or of the superintendent of insurance of the province under the laws of which the insurer is incorporated, was in respect of insurance of farm property, property used in fishing or residences of farmers or fishermen

is of

(b) the gross premium income (net of reinsurance ceded) earned in the year by the insurer.

149(4.1) amended by 1991 technical bill, retroactive to the introduction of the subsection in 1989.

**(4.2) Idem** — Subsection (4.1) does not apply to an insurer described in paragraph (1)(t) in respect of the taxable income of the insurer for a taxation year where more than 90% of the total of the gross premium income (net of reinsurance ceded) earned in the year by the insurer and, where the insurer is not a prescribed insurer, all other insurers that

(a) are specified shareholders of the insurer,

(b) are related to the insurer, or

(c) where the insurer is a mutual corporation, are part of a group that controls, directly or indirectly in any manner whatever, or are controlled, directly or indirectly in any manner whatever, by the insurer,

is in respect of insurance of property used in farming or fishing or residences of farmers or fishermen.

**Related Provisions**: 256(5.1), (6.2) — Controlled directly or indirectly.

**Notes**: Closing words of 149(4.2) amended by 1996 Budget, effective for 1996 and later taxation years. For 1989–95, read:

is in respect of insurance of farm property, property used in fishing or residences of farmers or fishermen.

149(4.2) amended by 1991 technical bill, retroactive to the introduction of the subsection in 1989.

**(4.3) Computation of taxable income of insurer** — For the purposes of this Part, in computing the taxable income of an insurer for a particular taxation year, the insurer shall be deemed to have deducted under paragraphs 20(1)(a), 20(7)(c) and 138(3)(a) and section 140 in each taxation year preceding the particular year and in respect of which paragraph (1)(t) applied to the insurer, the greater of

(a) the amount it claimed or deducted under those provisions for that preceding year, and

(b) the greatest amount that could have been claimed or deducted under those provisions to the extent that the total thereof does not exceed the amount that would be its taxable income for that preceding year if no amount had been claimed or deducted under those provisions.

**Notes**: 149(4.3) added by 1991 technical bill, this version effective 1991.

**(5) Exception re investment income of certain clubs** — Notwithstanding subsections (1) and (2), where a club, society or association was for any period, a club, society or association described in paragraph (1)(l) the main purpose of which was to provide dining, recreational or sporting facilities for its members (in this subsection referred to as the "club"), an *inter vivos* trust shall be deemed to have been created on the later of the commencement of the period and the end of 1971 and to have continued in existence throughout the period, and, throughout that period, the following rules apply:

(a) the property of the club shall be deemed to be the property of the trust;

(b) where the club is a corporation, the corporation shall be deemed to be the trustee having control of the trust property;

(c) where the club is not a corporation, the officers of the club shall be deemed to be the trustees having control of the trust property;

(d) tax under this Part is payable by the trust on its taxable income for each taxation year;

(e) the income and taxable income of the trust for each taxation year shall be computed on the as-

1432

sumption that it had no incomes or losses other than

(i) incomes and losses from property, and

(ii) taxable capital gains and allowable capital losses from dispositions of property, other than property used exclusively for and directly in the course of providing the dining, recreational or sporting facilities provided by it for its members;

(f) in computing the taxable income of the trust for each taxation year

(i) there may be deducted, in addition to any other deductions permitted by this Part, $2,000, and

(ii) no deduction shall be made under section 112 or 113; and

(g) the provisions of subdivision k of Division B (except subsections 104(1) and (2)) do not apply in respect of the trust.

**Related Provisions**: 16(2) — Obligation issued at discount; 212(14)(c)(i) — Certificate of exemption.

**Interpretation Bulletins**: IT-83R3: Non-profit organizations — Taxation of income from property; IT-406R2: Tax payable by an *inter vivos* trust; IT-409: Winding-up of a non-profit organization.

**Advance Tax Rulings**: ATR-29: Amalgamation of social clubs.

**(6) Apportionment rule** — Where it is necessary for the purpose of this section to ascertain the taxable income of a taxpayer for a period that is a part of a taxation year, the taxable income for the period shall be deemed to be the proportion of the taxable income for the taxation year that the number of days in the period is of the number of days in the taxation year.

**Related Provisions**: 124(3) — Crown agents; 149(10) — Corporation becoming or ceasing to be exempt; 212(14)(c)(i) — Certificate of exemption; 249.1(1)(b)(i) — Exempt individuals not subject to forced calendar year-end.

**Interpretation Bulletins**: IT-347R2: Crown corporations; IT-409: Winding-up of a non-profit organization.

**(7) [Prescribed form for R&D corporation — ] Time for filing** — A corporation the taxable income of which for a taxation year is exempt from tax under this Part because of paragraph (1)(j) shall file with the Minister a prescribed form containing prescribed information on or before its filing-due date for the year.

**Related Provisions**: 149(7.1) — Penalty for late filing.

**Notes**: 149(7) added by 1995 Budget, effective for taxation years that end after February 27, 1995. A form filed with Revenue Canada by September 18, 1996 (90 days after Royal Assent) is deemed to have been filed on time.

Former 149(7), repealed in 1977, provided rules dealing with control of a corporation, for purposes of 149(1)(g) and (h), now repealed.

**Forms**: T661: Claim for scientific research and experimental development expenditures carried on in Canada; T4088: Claiming scientific research and experimental development expenditures — guide to form T661.

**(7.1) Penalty for failure to file on time** — Where a corporation fails to file the prescribed form as required by subsection (7) for a taxation year, it is liable to a penalty equal to the amount determined by the formula

$$A \times B$$

where

A is the greater of

(a) $500, and

(b) 2% of its taxable income for the year; and

B is the lesser of

(a) 12, and

(b) the number of months in whole or in part that are in the period that begins on the day on or before which the prescribed form is required to be filed and ends on the day it is filed.

**Notes**: 149(7.1) added by 1995 Budget, effective for taxation years that end after February 27, 1995. See Notes to 149(7) re extension of filing deadline to September 18, 1996.

See Notes to 238(1).

**(8) Interpretation of para. (1)(j)** — For the purpose of paragraph (1)(j),

(a) a corporation is controlled by another corporation if more than 50% of its issued share capital (having full voting rights under all circumstances) belongs to

(i) the other corporation, or

(ii) the other corporation and persons with whom the other corporation does not deal at arm's length,

but a corporation shall be deemed not to have acquired control of a corporation if it has not purchased (or otherwise acquired for a consideration) any of the shares in the capital stock of that corporation; and

(b) there shall be included in computing a corporation's income and in determining its gross revenue the amount of all gifts received by the corporation and all amounts contributed to the corporation to be used for scientific research and experimental development.

**Related Provisions**: 212(14)(c)(i) — Certificate of exemption; 256(6), (6.1) — Extended meaning of "control".

**Notes**: 149(8)(b) amended by 1995 Budget, effective for taxation years that begin after June 1995, to add "and in determining its gross revenue". (See the amendment to 149(1)(j)(ii) closing words.)

**Regulations**: 2900(1) (definition of SR&ED, except where work performed pursuant to agreement in writing entered into before February 28, 1995; but see also ITA 248(1)"scientific research and experimental development").

**(9) Rules for determining gross revenue** — In determining the gross revenue of a corporation for

**S. 149(9)**            Income Tax Act, Part I

the purpose of determining whether it is described by paragraph (1)(j) for a taxation year,

(a) there may be deducted an amount not exceeding its gross revenue for the year computed without including or deducting any amount under this subsection; and

(b) there shall be included any amount that has been deducted under this subsection for the preceding taxation year.

**Related Provisions:** 212(14)(c)(i) — Certificate of exemption; 248(1) — Definition of "gross revenue".

**Notes:** 149(9) amended by 1995 Budget, effective for taxation years that begin after June 1995, to change "income" to "gross revenue" in both the opening words and para. (a). (See the amendment to 149(1)(j)(ii) closing words.)

**(10) Exempt corporations [becoming or ceasing to be exempt]** — Where, at any time (in this subsection referred to as "that time"), a corporation becomes or ceases to be exempt from tax under this Part on its taxable income otherwise than by reason of paragraph (1)(t), the following rules apply:

(a) the taxation year of the corporation that would otherwise have included that time is deemed to have ended immediately before that time, a new taxation year of the corporation is deemed to have begun at that time and, for the purpose of determining the taxpayer's fiscal period after that time, the taxpayer is deemed not to have established a fiscal period before that time;

(a.1) for the purpose of computing the corporation's income for its first taxation year ending after that time, the corporation shall be deemed to have deducted under sections 20, 138 and 140 in computing its income for its taxation year ending immediately before that time, the greatest amount that could have been claimed or deducted for that year as a reserve under those sections;

(b) the corporation is deemed to have disposed, at the time (in this subsection referred to as the "disposition time") that is immediately before the time that is immediately before that time, of each property that was owned by it immediately before that time for an amount equal to its fair market value at that time and to have reacquired the property at that time at a cost equal to that fair market value;

(c) for the purposes of applying sections 37, 65 to 66.4, 66.7, 111 and 126, subsections 127(5) to (26) and section 127.3 to the corporation, the corporation is deemed to be a new corporation the first taxation year of which began at that time; and

**Proposed Amendment — 149(10)(c)**

(c) for the purposes of applying sections 37, 65 to 66.4, 66.7, 94.1 to 94.3, 111 and 126, subsections 127(5) to (35) and section 127.3 to the corporation, the corporation is deemed to be a new corporation the first taxation year of which began at that time; and

**Application:** The June 22, 2000 draft legislation, s. 19, will amend para. 149(10)(c) to read as above, applicable to each corporation that, after 2000, becomes or ceases to be exempt from tax on its taxable income under Part I of the Act.

**Technical Notes:** Subsection 149(10) of the Act applies where, at a particular time, a corporation becomes or ceases to be exempt from tax under Part I on its taxable income (otherwise than by reason of the exemption for certain insurers in paragraph 149(1)(t)). A new taxation year is considered to start at the particular time and the corporation's properties are deemed to have been disposed of at fair market value and reacquired at the particular time for the same amount. Paragraph 149(10)(c) provides that the corporation is, for specified purposes in the Act, treated as a new corporation. One of the specified purposes is with regard to the investment tax credit regime set out in subsections 127(5) to (26).

Paragraph 149(10)(c) is amended to make a reference to additional rules for the investment tax credit that are set out in subsections 127(27) to (35). This amendment is strictly consequential on the earlier enactment of these subsections.

Paragraph 149(10)(c) is also amended so that it also applies for the purposes of sections 94.1 to 94.3 (foreign investment entities). For example, a corporation's "deferral amount" (as defined in new subsection 94.2(1)) in respect of any interest it holds in a foreign investment entity is determined without reference to taxation years that occurred before the corporation's change of status. This will typically result in a nil deferral amount for the corporation.

These amendments apply to corporations that, after 2000, become or cease to be exempt from tax on their taxable income under Part I of the Act.

(d) where, immediately before the disposition time, the corporation's cumulative eligible capital in respect of a business exceeds the total of

(i) $\frac{3}{4}$ of the fair market value of the eligible capital property in respect of the business, and

(ii) the amount otherwise deducted under paragraph 20(1)(b) in computing the corporation's income from the business for the taxation year that ended immediately before that time,

the excess shall be deducted under paragraph 20(1)(b) in computing the corporation's income from the business for the taxation year that ended immediately before that time.

**Related Provisions:** 16(2), (3) — Obligation issued at discount; 54"superficial loss"(c), (g) — Superficial loss rule does not apply; 87(2.1)(b) — Losses of predecessor corporation; 89(1.2) — Capital dividend account of corporation ceasing to be tax-exempt; 100 — Disposition of an interest in a partnership; 124(3) — Crown agents; 149(6) — Apportionment rule; 212(14) — Certificate of exemption; 216(1) — Alternative re rents and timber royalties; 219(2) — Exempt corporations; 227(14) — Application of Parts III, IV and VI to certain public corporations.

**Notes:** 149(10)(a) and (b)-(d) amended by 1995-97 technical bill, effective for a corporation that becomes or ceases to be exempt from tax on its taxable income under Part I after April 26, 1995. Before then (since January 15, 1987), ignore the rule in para. (a)

1434

that deems the taxpayer not to have established a fiscal period (see 249.1(7)); and read paras. (b)-(d) as:

(b) the corporation shall be deemed to have disposed, immediately before the time that is immediately before that time, of each property (other than, where, at that time, the corporation ceases to be exempt from tax under this Part on its taxable income, a Canadian resource property or a foreign resource property) that was owned by it immediately before that time for an amount equal to its fair market value at that time and to have reacquired the property at that time at a cost equal to that fair market value;

(c) where paragraph (b) applies in respect of depreciable property of the corporation and the capital cost thereof to the corporation immediately before the disposition exceeds the fair market value thereof at that time, for the purposes of sections 13 and 20 and any regulations made under paragraph 20(1)(a),

(i) the capital cost of the property to the corporation at that time shall be deemed to be the amount that was its capital cost thereof immediately before the disposition, and

(ii) the excess shall be deemed to have been allowed to the corporation in respect of the property under regulations made under paragraph 20(1)(a) in computing its income for taxation years ending before that time; and

(d) notwithstanding section 111, no amount is deductible in computing the corporation's taxable income for a taxation year ending after that time in respect of a non-capital loss, net capital loss, restricted farm loss, farm loss or limited partnership loss for a taxation year ending before that time to the extent that the loss could have been applied to reduce the corporation's taxable income for taxation years ending before that time.

149(10)(a.1) added by 1992 technical bill, effective for 1992 and later taxation years.

149(10) amended by 1987 press releases and by 1988 tax reform. The phrase "other than by reason of paragraph (1)(t)" was added effective 1989. Paras. (a), (b) and (c) are effective where a corporation

(a) stopped being exempt after January 15, 1987; or

(b) became exempt after June 5, 1987, other than where a corporation became exempt after that day as a result of an acquisition of shares pursuant to

(i) an agreement entered into on or before that day, or

(ii) a take-over bid made in accordance with the applicable securities legislation in Canada and a take-over bid circular or similar document to give notice to the public of the take-over bid was filed with a public authority of stock exchange in Canada on or before that day.

149(10)(d) is effective where a corporation became or stopped being exempt after June 5, 1987.

For corporations that became or stopped being exempt after November 12, 1981 and before the dates given above, read:

(10) Where at any time after November 12, 1981 a corporation ceases to be exempt from tax under this Part on its taxable income, the following rules apply:

(a) the taxation year of the corporation that would otherwise have included that time shall be deemed to have ended at that time and a new taxation year shall be deemed to have commenced immediately thereafter;

(b) the corporation shall be deemed to have disposed, immediately before that time, of each property, other than a Canadian resource property or foreign resource property, that was owned by it immediately before that time for an amount equal to its fair market value at that time and to have reacquired the property immediately after that time at a cost equal to that fair market value; and

(c) where paragraph (b) applies in respect of depreciable property of the corporation and the capital cost thereof to the corporation immediately before that time exceeds the fair market value thereof at that time, for the purposes of sections 13 and 20 and any regulations made under paragraph 20(1)(a),

(i) the capital cost of the property to the corporation immediately after that time shall be deemed to be the amount that was its capital cost thereof immediately before that time, and

(ii) the excess shall be deemed to have been allowed to the corporation in respect of the property under regulations made under paragraph 20(1)(a) in computing its income for taxation years ending before that time;

149(10) became effective November 12, 1981.

**Interpretation Bulletins**: IT-302R3: Losses of a corporation — the effect that acquisitions of control, amalgamations, and windings-up have on their deductibility — after January 15, 1987.

**(11)** [Repealed]

**Notes**: 149(11) repealed by 1995-97 technical bill, effective June 18, 1998. It was considered redundant due to the passage of time (although technically it could still have applied, such as where there is an agreement that will come into effect on the death of an individual). It read:

(11) **Exception** — Subsection (10) does not apply to a corporation that ceases to be exempt from tax under this Part after November 12, 1981 by reason of control of the corporation being acquired by a person or persons pursuant to an agreement in writing entered into on or before that date.

**(12) Information returns** — Every person who, because of paragraph (1)(e) or (l), is exempt from tax under this Part on all or part of the person's taxable income shall, within 6 months after the end of each fiscal period of the person and without notice or demand therefor, file with the Minister an information return for the period in prescribed form and containing prescribed information, if

(a) the total of all amounts each of which is a taxable dividend or an amount received or receivable by the person as, on account of, in lieu of or in satisfaction of, interest, rentals or royalties in the period exceeds $10,000;

(b) at the end of the person's preceding fiscal period the total assets of the person (determined in accordance with generally accepted accounting principles) exceeded $200,000; or

(c) an information return was required to be filed under this subsection by the person for a preceding fiscal period.

**Related Provisions**: 162(7)(a) — Penalty for failure to file; 233 — Demand for information return.

**Notes**: 149(12) added by 1992 technical bill, effective for fiscal periods that end in 1993 or later. It imposes a filing requirement on large non-profit organizations, so that the CCRA can find out who they are and how large they are. The CCRA is fairly lenient about late filing penalties: see letter from Wayne Amundson in 6(11) *Canadian Not-For-Profit News* (Carswell) 86 (Nov. 1998).

**S. 149(12)**     Income Tax Act, Part I

**Forms**: T1044: Non-profit organization (NPO) information return; T4117: Income tax guide to the Non-Profit Organization (NPO) information return [guide].

**Definitions [s. 149]**: "allowable capital loss" — 38(b), 248(1); "amateur athlete trust" — 143.1(1)(a), 248(1); "amount", "business" — 248(1); "Canada" — 255; "Canadian resource property" — 66(15), 248(1); "cemetery care trust" — 148.1(1), 248(1); "control" — 149(8); "controlled" — 256(6), (6.1); "controlled directly or indirectly" — 256(5.1), (6.2); "corporation" — 248(1), *Interpretation Act* 35(1); "deferred profit sharing plan" — 147(1), 248(1); "depreciable property" — 13(21), 248(1); "dividend", "employed" — 248(1); "eligible funeral arrangement" — 148.1(1), 248(1); "employees profit sharing plan" — 144(1), 248(1); "employment" — 248(1); "farm loss" — 111(8), 248(1); "farming" — 248(1); "filing-due date" — 150(1); "fishing" — 248(1); "foreign resource property" — 66(15), 248(1); "gross revenue" — 149(8)(b), 149(9), 248(1); "Her Majesty" — *Interpretation Act* 35(1); "income" — 149(1.2); "insurer" — 248(1); "*inter vivos* trust*" — 108(1), 248(1); "interest" in real property — 248(4); "life insurance business" — 248(1); "limited partnership loss" — 96(2.1)(e), 248(1); "Minister" — 248(1); "net capital loss", "non-capital loss" — 111(8), 248(1); "office" — 248(1); "outside the geographical boundaries" — 149(1.2); "owned" — 149(1.3); "person", "prescribed", "property" — 248(1); "province" — *Interpretation Act* 35(1); "qualifying environmental trust" — 248(1); "qualifying share" — 192(6), 248(1) [not intended to apply to s. 149]; "registered pension plan" — 248(1); "registered retirement income fund" — 146.3(1), 248(1); "registered retirement savings plan" — 146(1), 248(1); "registered supplementary unemployment benefit plan" — 145(1), 248(1); "regulation" — 248(1); "related" — 251(2); "restricted farm loss" — 31, 248(1); "retirement compensation arrangement", "scientific research and experimental development" — 248(1), Reg. 2900(1); "servant" — 248(1)"employment"; "share", "shareholder", "specified shareholder", "subsidiary wholly-owned corporation" — 248(1); "taxable capital gain" — 38(a), 248(1); "taxable income" — 2(2), 248(1); "taxation year" — 249; "taxpayer" — 248(1); "trust" — 104(1), 248(1), (3); "writing" — *Interpretation Act* 35(1).

**Interpretation Bulletins [s. 149]**: IT-151R5: Scientific research and experimental development expenditures; IT-167R6: Registered pension plans — employee's contributions; IT-269R3: Part IV tax on dividends received by a private corporation or a subject corporation; IT-362R: Patronage dividends.

## Charities

**149.1 (1) Definitions** — In this section,

**Related Provisions**: 172(6), 187.7 — Application of subsec. 149.1(1).

**Notes**: Opening words of 149.1(1) redrafted in R.S.C. 1985 (5th Supp.) consolidation, effective for taxation years ending after November 1991, to delete reference to s. 172 and Part V. These rules of application are now in 172(6) and 187.7.

**"charitable foundation"** means a corporation or trust that is constituted and operated exclusively for charitable purposes, no part of the income of which is payable to, or is otherwise available for, the personal benefit of any proprietor, member, shareholder, trustee or settlor thereof, and that is not a charitable organization;

**Related Provisions**: 149 — Exemptions; 149.1(6.1) — Charitable purposes; 149.1(12)(b) — Rules — income.

**Notes**: 149.1(1)"charitable foundation" was 149.1(1)(a) before consolidation in R.S.C. 1985 (5th Supp.), effective for taxation years ending after November 1991.

For the registration of charities, see 248(1)"registered charity".

**Interpretation Bulletins**: IT-83R3: Non-profit organizations — Taxation of income from property; IT-111R2: Annuities purchased from charitable organizations. See also list at end of s. 149.1.

**Forms**: RC4108: Registered charities and the Income Tax Act [guide]; T4063: Registering a charity for income tax purposes [guide].

**"charitable organization"** means an organization, whether or not incorporated,

(a) all the resources of which are devoted to charitable activities carried on by the organization itself,

(b) no part of the income of which is payable to, or is otherwise available for, the personal benefit of any proprietor, member, shareholder, trustee or settlor thereof,

(c) more than 50% of the directors, trustees, officers or like officials of which deal with each other and with each of the other directors, trustees, officers or officials at arm's length, and

(d) where it has been designated as a private foundation or public foundation pursuant to subsection (6.3) of this section or subsection 110(8.1) or (8.2) of the *Income Tax Act*, chapter 148 of the Revised Statutes of Canada, 1952, or has applied after February 15, 1984 for registration under paragraph 110(8)(c) of that Act or under the definition "registered charity" in subsection 248(1), not more than 50% of the capital of which has been contributed or otherwise paid into the organization by one person or members of a group of persons who do not deal with each other at arm's length and, for the purpose of this paragraph, a reference to any person or to members of a group does not include a reference to Her Majesty in right of Canada or a province, a municipality, another registered charity that is not a private foundation, or any club, society or association described in paragraph 149(1)(l);

**Related Provisions**: 149 — Exemptions; 149.1(6), (6.2) — Whether resources devoted to charitable activities; 149.1(6.3) — Designation as public foundation, etc.; 149.1(6.4) — Registered national arts service organization deemed to be charitable organization; 149.1(12)(b) — Rules — income; 188(1) — Revocation tax.

**Notes**: The 1976 legislation that introduced 149.1 provides that an organization that was a registered Canadian charitable organization (as then defined) at the end of 1976 is deemed to be a registered charity until such time as its registration is revoked.

For the registration of charities, see 248(1)"registered charity".

For the leading case on what constitutes "charitable activities", see *Vancouver Society of Immigrant & Visible Minority Women*, [1999] 2 C.T.C. 1 (SCC).

149.1(1)"charitable organization" was para. 149.1(1)(b) before consolidation in R.S.C. 1985 (5th Supp.), effective for taxation years ending after November 1991. See Table of Concordance.

**I.T. Application Rules**: 69 (meaning of "*Income Tax Act*, chapter 148 of the Revised Statutes of Canada, 1952").

**Interpretation Bulletins**: IT-83R3: Non-profit organizations — Taxation of income from property; IT-111R2: Annuities purchased from charitable organizations. See also list at end of s. 149.1.

**Information Circulars**: 80-10R: Registered charities: operating a registered charity.

Division H — Exemptions  S. 149.1(1) dis

**Forms**: RC4108: Registered charities and the Income Tax Act [guide]; T2095: Registered charities — application for re-designation; T4063: Registering a charity for income tax purposes [guide].

**"charitable purposes"** includes the disbursement of funds to qualified donees;

**Notes**: 149.1(1)"charitable purposes" was 149.1(1)(c) before consolidation in R.S.C. 1985 (5th Supp.), effective for taxation years ending after November 1991.

**"charity"** means a charitable organization or charitable foundation;

**Related Provisions**: 149(1)(f) — Exemptions for registered charity;  149(1)(l) — Non-profit organizations;  188(1) — Revocation tax; 248(1) — "registered charity".

**Notes**: 149.1(1)"charity" was 149.1(1)(d) before consolidation in R.S.C. 1985 (5th Supp.), effective for taxation years ending after November 1991.

**Forms**: RC4108: Registered charities and the Income Tax Act [guide]; T2050: Application to register a charity under the ITA; T2095: Registered charities — application for re-designation.

**"disbursement quota"** for a taxation year of a charitable foundation means the amount determined by the formula

$$A + A.1 + B + \frac{C \times 0.045 \, [D - (E + F)]}{365} + G$$

where

A is 80% of the total of all amounts each of which is the amount of a gift for which the foundation issued a receipt described in subsection 110.1(2) or 118.1(2) in its immediately preceding taxation year, other than

  (a) a gift of capital received by way of bequest or inheritance,

  (b) a gift received subject to a trust or direction to the effect that the property given, or property substituted therefor, is to be held by the foundation for a period of not less than 10 years, or

  (c) a gift received from a registered charity,

A.1 is 80% of the total of all amounts each of which is the amount of a gift received in a preceding taxation year, to the extent that the amount of the gift

  (a) is expended in the year, and

  (b) was excluded from the disbursement quota of the foundation

    (i) because of paragraph (a) of the description of A for a taxation year that begins after 1993, or

    (ii) because of paragraph (b) of the description of A,

B is

  (a) in the case of a private foundation, the total of all amounts each of which is an amount received by it in its immediately preceding taxation year from a registered charity, other than an amount that is a specified gift, or

  (b) in the case of a public foundation, 80% of the total of all amounts each of which is an amount received by it in its immediately preceding taxation year from a registered charity, other than an amount that is a specified gift,

C is the number of days in the taxation year,

D is the prescribed amount for the year in respect of property (other than a prescribed property) or a portion thereof owned by the foundation at any time in the immediately preceding 24 months that was not used directly in charitable activities or administration,

E is 5/4 of the total of the amounts determined for A and A.1 for the year in respect of the foundation,

F is the amount equal to

  (a) in the case of a private foundation, the amount determined as the value of B for the year in accordance with paragraph (a) of the description of B, or

  (b) in the case of a public foundation, 5/4 of the amount determined as the value of B for the year in accordance with paragraph (b) of the description of B, and

G is, for each of the first 10 taxation years of the foundation commencing after 1983, a portion of the amount, if any, by which

  (a) 90% of the amount, if any, by which the amount deducted by the foundation, for its last taxation year that commenced before 1984, pursuant to paragraph 149.1(18)(a) of the *Income Tax Act*, chapter 148 of the Revised Statutes of Canada, 1952, as it read for that year, exceeds the total of the amounts determined in respect of the foundation under clauses 149.1(1)(e)(iv)(B) to (D) of that Act for its first taxation year commencing after 1983

exceeds

  (b) the total of all amounts each of which is an amount that, for a preceding taxation year, has been determined as the value of G or included under subparagraph 149.1(1)(e)(v) of the above-mentioned Act in determining the disbursement quota of the foundation,

that is not less than the amount obtained when such excess is divided by the difference between 10 and the number of preceding taxation years of the foundation that commenced after 1983 and before the year.

**Related Provisions**: 149.1(1.2) — Authority of Minister — calculation of prescribed amount; 149.1(4.1) — Anti-avoidance rule re disbursement quota; 149.1(8) — Accumulated property deemed expended on charitable activities; 149.1(12) — Rules; 149.1(21)(c) — Disbursement excess of registered charity; 248(5) — Substituted property; 257 — Formula cannot calculate to less than zero.

**Notes**: This definition effectively applies to charitable organizations as well (formula elements A and A.1 only). See 149.1(21).

The disbursement quota (essentially 80% of receipted donations) must be disbursed on charitable activities, which do not include

1437

fund-raising. Where fund-raising and other non-charitable expenses are high, there may be options for obtaining funds that do not enter the disbursement quota, such as government support, gifts from foreign donors, donations by businesses that can deduct the expense as advertising without a charitable receipt, or asking a donor to forgo a receipt. See Drache, "Funding Fundraising", 8(5) *Canadian Not-For-Profit News* 35-36 (May 2000).

Definition "disbursement quota" amended by 1995-97 technical bill, effective for taxation years that end after November 1991 (i.e., retroactive to the R.S.C. 1985 (5th Supp.) consolidation), to change "0.8A" to "A" in the formula and to move the 80% calculation to the description of A. (It is not entirely clear why this correction was needed; the Technical Notes indicate that it was needed to "properly account for the mathematical relationship between gifts received by a charitable foundation and the amount that such a foundation is required to disburse".)

Formula element A.1 added, and description of E amended to refer to it, by 1993 technical bill, effective for taxation years that begin after 1992. Element A.1 requires that gifts previously excluded from the disbursement quota (such as gifts of capital received through bequests and inheritances, and gifts subject to binding instructions that they not be spent for at least 10 years) be added back into the calculation when they are actually spent by the charity.

149.1(1) "disbursement quota" was 149.1(1)(e) before consolidation in R.S.C. 1985 (5th Supp.), effective for taxation years ending after November 1991. The previous version, identical in meaning, read:

(e) "disbursement quota" for a taxation year of a charitable foundation means an amount equal to the aggregate of

(i) 80% of the aggregate of all amounts each of which is the amount of a gift for which the foundation issued a receipt described in paragraph 110.1(1)(a) or 118.1(1)(a) in its immediately preceding taxation year, other than

(A) a gift of capital received by way of bequest or inheritance,

(B) a gift received subject to a trust or direction to the effect that the property given, or property substituted therefor, is to be held by the foundation for a period of not less than 10 years, or

(C) a gift received from a registered charity,

(ii) in the case of a private foundation, the aggregate of all amounts each of which is an amount received by it in its immediately preceding taxation year from a registered charity, other than an amount that is a specified gift,

(iii) in the case of a public foundation, 80% of the aggregate of all amounts each of which is an amount received by it in its immediately preceding taxation year from a registered charity, other than an amount that is a specified gift,

(iv) the proportion that the number of days in the year is of 365 of 4½% of the amount, if any, by which

(A) the prescribed amount for the year in respect of property (other than a prescribed property) or a portion thereof owned by the foundation at any time in the immediately preceding 24 months that was not used directly in charitable activities or administration

exceeds the aggregate of

(B) ⅝ of the amount determined in respect of the foundation under subparagraph (i) for the year,

(C) the amount determined in respect of the foundation under subparagraph (ii) for the year, and

(D) ⅝ of the amount determined in respect of the foundation under subparagraph (iii) for the year, and

(v) in each of its first 10 taxation years commencing after 1983, a portion of the amount, if any, by which

(A) 90% of the amount, if any, by which the amount deducted by the foundation, for its last taxation year

that commenced before 1984, pursuant to paragraph (18)(a), as it read for that year, exceeds the aggregate of the amounts determined in respect of the foundation under clauses (iv)(B) to (D) for its first taxation year commencing after 1983

exceeds

(B) the aggregate of all amounts each of which is an amount included under this subparagraph in determining the disbursement quota of the foundation for a preceding taxation year,

that is not less than the amount obtained when such excess is divided by the difference between 10 and the number of preceding taxation years of the foundation that commenced after 1983 and before the year.

**Regulations**: 3701 (prescribed amount).

**I.T. Application Rules**: 69 (meaning of "*Income Tax Act*, chapter 148 of the Revised Statutes of Canada, 1952").

**Interpretation Bulletins**: IT-244R3: Gifts by individuals of life insurance policies as charitable donations. See also list at end of s. 149.1.

**Information Circulars**: 80-10R: Registered charities: operating a registered charity.

**Forms**: RC4108: Registered charities and the Income Tax Act [guide]; T3010: Registered charity information return and public information return (Schedules 2, 4: disbursement quota calculation); T4033: Completing the registered charity information return [guide].

**Registered Charities Newsletters**: 4 (Issuing receipts for gifts of art); 9 (Once a charity has met its disbursement quota...).

**"non-qualified investment"** of a private foundation means

(a) a debt (other than a pledge or undertaking to make a gift) owing to the foundation by

(i) a person (other than an excluded corporation)

(A) who is a member, shareholder, trustee, settlor, officer, official or director of the foundation,

(B) who has, or is a member of a group of persons who do not deal with each other at arm's length who have, contributed more than 50% of the capital of the foundation, or

(C) who does not deal at arm's length with any person described in clause (A) or (B), or

(ii) a corporation (other than an excluded corporation) controlled by the foundation, by any person or group of persons referred to in subparagraph (i), by the foundation and any other private foundation with which it does not deal at arm's length or by any combination thereof,

(b) a share of a class of the capital stock of a corporation (other than an excluded corporation) referred to in paragraph (a) held by the foundation (other than a share listed on a prescribed stock exchange or a share that would be a qualifying share within the meaning assigned by subsection 192(6) if that subsection were read without refer-

Division H — Exemptions    S. 149.1(1) qua

ence to the expression "issued after May 22, 1985 and before 1987"), and

(c) a right held by the foundation to acquire a share referred to in paragraph (b),

and, for the purpose of this definition, an "excluded corporation" is

(d) a limited-dividend housing company to which paragraph 149(1)(n) applies,

(e) a corporation all of the property of which is used by a registered charity in its administration or in carrying on its charitable activities, or

(f) a corporation all of the issued shares of which are held by the foundation;

**Related Provisions**: 149.1(21)(c) — Disbursement excess of registered charity; 189 — Tax regarding non-qualified investment; 256(6), (6.1) — Meaning of "controlled".

**Notes**: 149.1(1)"non-qualified investment" was 149.1(1)(e.1) before consolidation in R.S.C. 1985 (5th Supp.), effective for taxation years ending after November 1991. See Table of Concordance.

"Non-qualified investment"(b) (formerly 149.1(1)(e.1)(ii)) amended by 1991 technical bill. For shares issued before 1986 to which 192(6), as it read on May 22, 1985, applied, read "after June 30, 1983" in place of "after May 22, 1985". (This change applied in the original version of the Act as amended in 1986 and by S.C. 1991, c. 49 (Bill C-18). The new reference to May 22, 1985 was, however, included in the base version of the Act as R.S.C. 1985 (5th Supp.), without a rule preserving the former version for shares issued before 1986 as above. Nevertheless, the old rule should be considered as still in force, since the *Revised Statutes of Canada, 1985 Act*, S.C. 1987, c. 48, makes it clear that the consolidation of legislation into R.S.C. 1985 is not intended to change the law. See also ITAR 75. Officials at the Department of Finance have confirmed informally that this interpretation is correct; however, in the absence of complaint by affected charities, no steps will be taken to remedy the error.)

Para. (f) (formerly 149.1(1)(e.1)(vi)) added by 1991 technical bill, effective 1984, to make Part V tax not apply where a private foundation owns all the shares of a corporation.

**Regulations**: 3200 (prescribed stock exchange).

**"private foundation"** means a charitable foundation that is not a public foundation;

**Related Provisions**: 149.1(6.3) — Designation as public foundation, etc.; 149.1(13) — Designation of private foundation as public; 189 — Tax on private foundation with non-qualified investments; 248(1)"private foundation" — Definition applies to entire Act.

**Notes**: Donations of private company shares to a charity (including a private foundation) are generally non-creditable; see 118.1(13)–(20).

149.1(1)"private foundation" was 149.1(1)(f) before consolidation in R.S.C. 1985 (5th Supp.), effective for taxation years ending after November 1991.

**Interpretation Bulletins**: IT-83R3: Non-profit organizations — Taxation of income from property. See also list at end of s. 149.1.

**Information Circulars**: 80-10R: Registered charities: operating a registered charity.

**Forms**: T2095: Registered charities — application for redesignation.

**"public foundation"** means a charitable foundation of which,

(a) where the foundation has been registered after February 15, 1984 or designated as a charitable organization or private foundation pursuant to subsection (6.3) or to subsection 110(8.1) or (8.2) of the *Income Tax Act*, chapter 148 of the Revised Statutes of Canada, 1952,

(i) more than 50% of the directors, trustees, officers or like officials deal with each other and with each of the other directors, trustees, officers or officials at arm's length, and

(ii) not more than 50% of the capital contributed or otherwise paid in to the foundation has been so contributed or otherwise paid in by one person or members of a group of such persons who do not deal with each other at arm's length, or

(b) in any other case,

(i) more than 50% of the directors or trustees deal with each other and with each of the other directors or trustees at arm's length, and

(ii) not more than 75% of the capital contributed or otherwise paid in to the foundation has been so contributed or otherwise paid in by one person or by a group of persons who do not deal with each other at arm's length

and, for the purpose of subparagraph (a)(ii), a reference to any person or to members of a group does not include a reference to Her Majesty in right of Canada or a province, a municipality, another registered charity that is not a private foundation, or any club, society or association described in paragraph 149(1)(l);

**Related Provisions**: 149.1(6.3) — Designation as public foundation, etc.; 149.1(13) — Designation of private foundation as public; 248(1)"private foundation" — Definition applies to entire Act.

**Notes**: 149.1(1)"public foundation" was 149.1(1)(g) before consolidation in R.S.C. 1985 (5th Supp.), effective for taxation years ending after November 1991. See Table of Concordance.

**I.T. Application Rules**: 69 (meaning of "*Income Tax Act*, chapter 148 of the Revised Statutes of Canada, 1952").

**Interpretation Bulletins**: IT-83R3: Non-profit organizations — Taxation of income from property. See also list at end of s. 149.1.

**Information Circulars**: 80-10R: Registered charities: operating a registered charity.

**Forms**: T2095: Registered charities — application for redesignation.

**"qualified donee"** means a donee described in any of paragraphs 110.1(1)(a) and (b) and the definitions "total charitable gifts" and "total Crown gifts" in subsection 118.1(1);

**Related Provisions**: 248(1)"qualified donee" — Definition applies to entire Act.

**Notes**: 149.1(1)"qualified donee" was 149.1(1)(h) before consolidation in R.S.C. 1985 (5th Supp.), effective for taxation years ending after November 1991.

**Registered Charities Newsletters**: 3 (Registered national arts service organizations).

**"qualified investment [para. 149.1(1)(i)]"** — [Repealed under former Act]

**Notes**: 149.1(1)(i), repealed in 1984, defined "qualified investment". It was replaced by the definition of "non-qualified investment".

**"related business"**, in relation to a charity, includes a business that is unrelated to the objects of the charity if substantially all persons employed by the charity in the carrying on of that business are not remunerated for that employment;

**Notes**: This definition and 149.1(2)(a) provide, in effect, permission for charities to operate an unrelated business that is substantially all operated by volunteers. Another option, effective with the increased donation limits in 110.1 since 1997, is for a taxable corporation to be created that donates 75% of its profits to the charity and pays tax on the balance. (Note that certain provinces have restrictions on charities owning shares in corporations.) See Arthur Drache, "Charities, Non-Profits and Business Activities" in the 1997 Canadian Tax Foundation annual conference proceedings, at p. 30:4.

149.1(1)"related business" was 149.1(1)(j) before consolidation in R.S.C. 1985 (5th Supp.), effective for taxation years ending after November 1991.

The CCRA takes the position that "substantially all" means 90% or more.

**"specified gift"** means that portion of a gift, made in a taxation year by a registered charity, that is designated as a specified gift in its information return for the year;

**Notes**: 149.1(1)"specified gift" was 149.1(1)(k) before consolidation in R.S.C. 1985 (5th Supp.), effective for taxation years ending after November 1991.

**Information Circulars**: 80-10R: Registered charities: operating a registered charity.

**"taxation year"** means, in the case of a registered charity, a fiscal period.

**Notes**: 149.1(1)"taxation year" was 149.1(1)(l) before consolidation in R.S.C. 1985 (5th Supp.), effective for taxation years ending after November 1991.

**(1.1) Exclusions** — For the purposes of paragraphs (2)(b), (3)(b), (4)(b) and (21)(a), the following shall be deemed to be neither an amount expended in a taxation year on charitable activities nor a gift made to a qualified donee:

(a) a specified gift; and

(b) an expenditure on political activities made by a charitable organization or a charitable foundation.

**Related Provisions**: 149.1(6.1), (6.2) — Political activities that are ancillary and incidental to charitable activities.

**Notes**: In February 2000, the CCRA's Charities Division released a draft of RC4107, "Registered Charities: Education, Advocacy and Political Activities". Comments were requested by May 31, 2000 to charities@ccra-adrc.gc.ca or by fax to (613) 946-2423.

**Information Circulars**: 80-10R: Registered charities: operating a registered charity; 87-1: Registered charities — ancillary and incidental political activities.

**Registered Charities Newsletters**: 1 (Partisan political activities); 2 (Is participation on a municipal advisory committee a partisan political activity?); 6 (Can registered charities average political expenses over time?).

**(1.2) Authority of Minister** — For the purposes of the determination of D in the definition "disbursement quota" in subsection (1), the Minister may

(a) authorize a change in the number of periods chosen by a charitable foundation in determining the prescribed amount; and

(b) accept any method for the determination of the fair market value of property or a portion thereof that may be required in determining the prescribed amount.

**(2) Revocation of registration of charitable organization** — The Minister may, in the manner described in section 168, revoke the registration of a charitable organization for any reason described in subsection 168(1) or where the organization

(a) carries on a business that is not a related business of that charity; or

(b) fails to expend in any taxation year, on charitable activities carried on by it and by way of gifts made by it to qualified donees, amounts the total of which is at least equal to the total of

(i) the amount that would be the value of A for the year, and

(ii) the amount that would be the value of A.1 for the year,

in the definition "disbursement quota" in subsection (1) in respect of the organization if it were a charitable foundation.

**Related Provisions**: 149.1(1.1) — Exclusions; 172(3)(a) — Appeal from refusal to register, revocation of registration, etc.; 180(1) — Appeals to Federal Court of Appeal; 188 — Revocation tax; 230(2) — Charity must keep books and records to allow Minister to determine if there are grounds for revocation of registration; 248(1)"registered charity" — Application for registration.

**Notes**: 149.1(2)(b)(i) and (ii) amended by 1995-97 technical bill (as amended before Third Reading), effective for taxation years that end after November 1991 (i.e., retroactive to the R.S.C. 1985 (5th Supp.) consolidation). They had read:

(i) 80% of the amount that would be determined for the year for A, and

(ii) the amount that would be determined for the year for A.1,

See Notes to 149.1(1)"disbursement quota".

149.1(2)(b)(ii) added by 1993 technical bill, effective for taxation years that begin after 1992. See Notes to 149.1(1)"disbursement quota".

**Interpretation Bulletins**: IT-244R3: Gifts by individuals of life insurance policies as charitable donations. See also list at end of s. 149.1.

**Information Circulars**: 80-10R: Registered charities: operating a registered charity.

**(3) Revocation of registration of public foundation** — The Minister may, in the manner described in section 168, revoke the registration of a public foundation for any reason described in subsection 168(1) or where the foundation

(a) carries on a business that is not a related business of that charity;

(b) fails to expend in any taxation year, on charitable activities carried on by it and by way of

Division H — Exemptions      S. 149.1(6.1)(c)

gifts made by it to qualified donees, amounts the total of which is at least equal to the foundation's disbursement quota for that year;

(c) since June 1, 1950, acquired control of any corporation;

(d) since June 1, 1950, incurred debts, other than debts for current operating expenses, debts incurred in connection with the purchase and sale of investments and debts incurred in the course of administering charitable activities; or

(e) at any time within the 24 month period preceding the day on which notice is given to the foundation by the Minister pursuant to subsection 168(1) and at a time when the foundation was a private foundation, took any action or failed to expend amounts such that the Minister was entitled, pursuant to subsection (4), to revoke its registration as a private foundation.

**Related Provisions**: 149.1(1.1) — Exclusions; 149.1(12) — Rules; 149.1(18) — Rules relating to computation of income; 149.1(20) — Rule regarding disbursement excess; 172(3)(a) — Appeal from refusal to register, revocation of registration, etc.; 180(1) — Appeals to Federal Court of Appeal; 188(1) — Revocation tax; 230(2) — Charity must keep books and records to allow Minister to determine if there are grounds for revocation of registration; 248(1)"registered charity" — Application for registration; 256(6)–(9) — Whether control acquired.

**Information Circulars**: 80-10R: Registered charities: operating a registered charity.

**(4) Revocation of registration of private foundation** — The Minister may, in the manner described in section 168, revoke the registration of a private foundation for any reason described in subsection 168(1) or where the foundation

(a) carries on any business;

(b) fails to expend in any taxation year, on charitable activities carried on by it and by way of gifts made by it to qualified donees, amounts the total of which is at least equal to the foundation's disbursement quota for that year;

(c) since June 1, 1950, acquired control of any corporation; or

(d) since June 1, 1950, incurred debts, other than debts for current operating expenses, debts incurred in connection with the purchase and sale of investments and debts incurred in the course of administering charitable activities.

**Related Provisions**: 149.1(1.1) — Exclusions; 149.1(12) — Rules; 172(3)(a) — Appeal from refusal to register, revocation of registration, etc.; 180(1) — Appeals to Federal Court of Appeal; 188(1) — Revocation tax; 230(2) — Charity must keep books and records to allow Minister to determine if there are grounds for revocation of registration; 248(1)"registered charity" — Application for registration; 256(6)–(9) — Whether control acquired.

**Information Circulars**: 80-10R: Registered charities: operating a registered charity.

**(4.1) Revocation of registration of registered charity** — Where a registered charity has made a gift to another registered charity and it may reasonably be considered that one of the main purposes of making the gift was to unduly delay the expenditure of amounts on charitable activities, the Minister may, in the manner described in section 168, revoke the registration of the charity that made the gift and, where it may reasonably be considered that the charities acted in concert, of the other charity.

**Related Provisions**: 172(3)(a) — Appeal from refusal to register, revocation of registration, etc.; 180(1) — Appeals to Federal Court of Appeal; 188(1) — Revocation tax; 230(2) — Charity must keep books and records to allow Minister to determine if there are grounds for revocation of registration.

**Notes**: 149.1(4.1) is an anti-avoidance rule designed to prevent avoidance of the annual disbursement requirement in 149.1(1)"disbursement quota" and 149.1(21).

**Information Circulars**: 80-10R: Registered charities: operating a registered charity.

**(5) Reduction** — The Minister may, on application made to the Minister in prescribed form by a registered charity, specify an amount in respect of the charity for a taxation year and, for the purpose of paragraph (2)(b), (3)(b) or (4)(b), as the case may be, that amount shall be deemed to be an amount expended by the charity in the year on charitable activities carried on by it.

**Information Circulars**: 80-10R: Registered charities: operating a registered charity.

**Forms**: T2094: Registered charities — Application to reduce disbursement quota.

**(6) Devoting resources to charitable activity** — A charitable organization shall be considered to be devoting its resources to charitable activities carried on by it to the extent that

(a) it carries on a related business;

(b) in any taxation year, it disburses not more than 50% of its income for that year to qualified donees; or

(c) it disburses income to a registered charity that the Minister has designated in writing as a charity associated with it.

**Related Provisions**: 149.1(7) — Designation of associated charities; 149.1(12)(b) — Rules — income.

**Information Circulars**: 77-6: Registered charities: designation as associated charities; 80-10R: Registered charities: operating a registered charity.

**Forms**: RC4108: Registered charities and the Income Tax Act [guide].

**(6.1) Charitable purposes** — For the purposes of the definition "charitable foundation" in subsection (1), where a corporation or trust devotes substantially all of its resources to charitable purposes and

(a) it devotes part of its resources to political activities,

(b) those political activities are ancillary and incidental to its charitable purposes, and

(c) those political activities do not include the direct or indirect support of, or opposition to, any political party or candidate for public office, the corporation or trust shall be considered to be constituted and operated for charitable purposes to the extent of that part of its resources so devoted.

**Notes**: The CCRA takes the position that "substantially all" means 90% or more.

See also Notes to 149.1(1.1).

**Information Circulars**: 87-1: Registered charities — ancillary and incidental political activities.

**Registered Charities Newsletters**: 1 (Partisan political activities); 2 (Is participation on a municipal advisory committee a partisan political activity?); 6 (Can registered charities average political expenses over time?).

**(6.2) Charitable activities** — For the purposes of the definition "charitable organization" in subsection (1), where an organization devotes substantially all of its resources to charitable activities carried on by it and

(a) it devotes part of its resources to political activities,

(b) those political activities are ancillary and incidental to its charitable activities, and

(c) those political activities do not include the direct or indirect support of, or opposition to, any political party or candidate for public office,

the organization shall be considered to be devoting that part of its resources to charitable activities carried on by it.

**Related Provisions**: 149.1(1.1)(b) — Expenditures on political activities.

**Notes**: The CCRA takes the position that "substantially all" means 90% or more.

See also Notes to 149.1(1) "charitable organization" and 149.1(1.1).

**Information Circulars**: 87-1: Registered charities — ancillary and incidental political activities.

**Registered Charities Newsletters**: 1 (Partisan political activities); 2 (Is participation on a municipal advisory committee a partisan political activity?); 6 (Can registered charities average political expenses over time?).

**(6.3) Designation as public foundation, etc.** — The Minister may, by notice sent by registered mail to a registered charity, on the Minister's own initiative or on application made to the Minister in prescribed form, designate the charity to be a charitable organization, private foundation or public foundation and the charity shall be deemed to be registered as a charitable organization, private foundation or public foundation, as the case may be, for taxation years commencing after the day of mailing of the notice unless and until it is otherwise designated under this subsection or its registration is revoked under subsection (2), (3), (4), (4.1) or 168(2).

**Related Provisions**: 149.1(13) — Designation of private foundation as public; 172(3) — Appeal from refusal to designate; 244(5) — Proof of service by mail; 244(14) — Notice presumed mailed on date of notice; 248(7)(a) — Mail deemed received on day mailed.

**Forms**: T2095: Registered charities — application for re-designation.

**(6.4) National arts service organizations** — Where an organization that

(a) has, on written application to the Minister of Communications describing all of its objects and activities, been designated by that Minister on approval of those objects and activities to be a national arts service organization,

(b) has, as its exclusive purpose and its exclusive function, the promotion of arts in Canada on a nation-wide basis,

(c) is resident in Canada and was formed or created in Canada, and

(d) complies with prescribed conditions

applies in prescribed form to the Minister of National Revenue for registration, that Minister may register the organization for the purposes of this Act and, where the organization so applies or is so registered, this section, paragraph 38(a.1), sections 110.1, 118.1, 168, 172, 180 and 230 and Part V apply, with such modifications as the circumstances require, to the organization as if it were an applicant for registration as a charitable organization or as if it were a registered charity that is designated as a charitable organization, as the case may be.

**Proposed Amendment — 149.1(6.4) closing words**

applies in prescribed form to the Minister of National Revenue for registration, that Minister may register the organization for the purposes of this Act and, where the organization so applies or is so registered, this section, paragraph 38(a.1), sections 110.1, 118.1, 168, 172, 180 and 230, subsection 241(3.2) and Part V apply, with such modifications as the circumstances require, to the organization as if it were an applicant for registration as a charitable organization or as if it were a registered charity that is designated as a charitable organization, as the case may be.

**Application**: Bill C-43 (First Reading September 20, 2000), s. 90, will amend the closing words of subsec. 149.1(6.4) to read as above, in force on Royal Assent.

**Technical Notes**: Subsection 149.1(6.4) provides that a national arts service organization that is designated by the Minister of Canadian Heritage and registered by the Minister of National Revenue as meeting prescribed criteria shall be treated, for income tax purposes, as if it were a registered charity that is designated as a charitable organization. To this end, that subsection includes references to various provisions of the Act that apply to a charitable organization. The amendment corrects an oversight by adding a reference to subsection 241(3.2) which deals with the communication of information relating to a registered charity.

**Related Provisions**: 149.1(6.2) — Charitable activities; 149.1(6.5) — Revocation of designation.

**Notes**: The *Department of Canadian Heritage Act* (S.C. 1995, c. 11), in force July 12, 1996, provides:

46. **Other references** — Every reference made to the Minister of Communications, the Minister of Multiculturalism and Citizenship and the Secretary of State of Canada in relation to any matter to which the powers, duties and functions of the

Minister of Canadian Heritage extend by virtue of this Act, in any other Act of Parliament or in any order, regulation or other instrument made under any Act of Parliament shall, unless the context otherwise requires, be read as a reference to the Minister of Canadian Heritage.

Closing words of 149.1(6.4) amended to add reference to 38(a.1) by 1997 Budget, effective February 19, 1997.

149.1(6.4) added by 1991 technical bill, effective July 14, 1990. Where an organization applied to Revenue Canada for registration before December 17, 1991 and Revenue Canada has accepted the application as meeting the requirements, the organization is deemed to have become registered on the day the application was made (or, where in the application a later day was specified as the day on which the organization is to become registered, on that later day).

**Regulations**: 8700 (prescribed conditions for 149.1(6.4)(d)).

**Registered Charities Newsletters**: 2 (Registered national arts service organizations can issue tax receipts); 3 (Registered national arts service organizations).

**(6.5) Revocation of designation** — The Minister of Communications may, at any time, revoke the designation of an organization made for the purpose of subsection (6.4) where

(a) an incorrect statement was made in the furnishing of information for the purpose of obtaining the designation, or

(b) the organization has amended its objects after its last designation was made,

and, where the designation is so revoked, the organization shall be deemed for the purpose of section 168 to have ceased to comply with the requirements of this Act for its registration under this Act.

**Notes**: See Notes to 149.1(6.4) re *Department of Canadian Heritage Act*.

149.1(6.5) added by 1991 technical bill, effective July 14, 1990.

**(7) Designation of associated charities** — On application made to the Minister in prescribed form, the Minister may, in writing, designate a registered charity as a charity associated with one or more specified registered charities where the Minister is satisfied that the charitable aim or activity of each of the registered charities is substantially the same, and on and after a date specified in such a designation, the charities to which it relates shall, until such time, if any, as the Minister revokes the designation, be deemed to be associated.

**Related Provisions**: 149.1(6)(c) — Disbursement to associated charity.

**Information Circulars**: 77-6: Registered charities: designation as associated charities; 80-10R: Registered charities: operating a registered charity.

**Forms**: RC4108: Registered charities and the Income Tax Act [guide]; T2050: Application to register a charity under the ITA; T3011: Registered charities — Application for designation as associated charities.

**(8) Accumulation of property** — A registered charity may, with the approval in writing of the Minister, accumulate property for a particular purpose, on terms and conditions, and over such period of time, as the Minister specifies in the approval, and any property accumulated after receipt of such an approval and in accordance therewith, including any income earned in respect of the property so accumulated, shall be deemed

(a) to have been expended on charitable activities carried on by the charity in the taxation year in which it was so accumulated; and

(b) not to have been expended in any other year.

**Notes**: 149.1(8)(b) added by 1993 technical bill, effective for taxation years that begin after 1992. Since accumulated property is deemed to be expended in the year it is accumulated, it is not appropriate to provide a subsequent counting of the same property in a charity's disbursement quota calculation for the year in which the accumulated property is actually expended.

**Information Circulars**: 80-10R: Registered charities: operating a registered charity.

**(9) Idem** — Property accumulated by a registered charity as provided in subsection (8), including any income earned in respect of that property, that is not used for the particular purpose for which it was accumulated either

(a) before the expiration of any period of time specified by the Minister in the Minister's approval of the accumulation, or

(b) at an earlier time at which the registered charity decides not to use the property for that purpose

shall, notwithstanding subsection (8), be deemed to be income of the charity for, and the amount of a gift for which it issued a receipt described in subsection 110.1(2) or 118.1(2) in, its taxation year in which the period referred to in paragraph (a) expires or the time referred to in paragraph (b) occurs, as the case may be.

**(10) Deemed charitable activity** — An amount paid by a charitable organization to a qualified donee that is not paid out of the income of the charitable organization shall be deemed to be a devotion of a resource of the charitable organization to a charitable activity carried on by it.

**Related Provisions**: 149.1(12)(b) — Rules — income.

**(11)** [Repealed under former Act]

**Notes**: 149.1(11), repealed in 1984, excluded capital gains from the calculation of income of a charitable foundation for its disbursement requirements. Such income calculation is no longer required.

**(12) Rules** — For the purposes of this section,

(a) a corporation is controlled by a charitable foundation if more than 50% of the corporation's issued share capital, having full voting rights under all circumstances, belongs to

(i) the foundation, or

(ii) the foundation and persons with whom the foundation does not deal at arm's length,

but, for the purpose of paragraph (3)(c) or (4)(c), as the case may be, a charitable foundation shall be deemed not to have acquired control of a corporation if it has not purchased or otherwise acquired for consideration more than 5% of the issued shares of any class of the capital stock of that corporation;

(b) there shall be included in computing the income of a charity for a taxation year all gifts received by it in the year including gifts from any other charity but not including

(i) a specified gift or a gift referred to in paragraph (a) or (b) of the description of A in the definition "disbursement quota" in subsection (1),

(ii) any gift or portion of a gift in respect of which it is established that the donor is not a charity and

(A) has not been allowed a deduction under paragraph 110.1(1)(a) in computing the donor's taxable income or under subsection 118.1(3) in computing the donor's tax payable under this Part, or

(B) was not taxable under section 2 for the taxation year in which the gift was made, or

(iii) any gift or portion of a gift in respect of which it is established that the donor is a charity and that the gift was not made out of the income of the donor; and

(c) subsections 104(6) and (12) are not applicable in computing the income of a charitable foundation that is a trust.

**Related Provisions**: 256(6), (6.1) — Control.

**Interpretation Bulletins**: IT-244R3: Gifts by individuals of life insurance policies as charitable donations. See also list at end of s. 149.1.

**Information Circulars**: 80-10R: Registered charities: operating a registered charity.

**(13) Designation of private foundation as public** — On application made to the Minister by a private foundation, the Minister may, on such terms and conditions as the Minister considers appropriate, designate the foundation to be a public foundation, and on and after the date specified in such a designation, the foundation to which it relates shall, until such time, if any, as the Minister revokes the designation, be deemed to be a public foundation.

**Related Provisions**: 149.1(6.3) — Designation as public foundation, etc.

**Forms**: T2095: Registered charities — application for re-designation.

**(14) Information returns** — Every registered charity shall, within 6 months from the end of each taxation year of the charity, file with the Minister both an information return and a public information return for the year, each in prescribed form and containing prescribed information, without notice or demand therefor.

**Related Provisions**: 149.1(15) — Public information return may be disclosed to the public; 150(1.1)(a) — Charity not required to file corporate tax return; Reg. 204(3)(c) — Annual T3 return not required.

**Information Circulars**: 80-10R: Registered charities: operating a registered charity.

**Forms**: RC4108: Registered charities and the Income Tax Act [guide]; T3010: Registered charities information return; T4033: Completing the registered charity information return [guide].

**Registered Charities Newsletters**: 1 (Annual due date); 2 (Revised annual information return); 5 (When does your charity have to file its T3010 return?); 6 (How have we revised the T3010 return that each registered charity has to file annually?); 7 (Annual charity information return (T3010) — frequently asked questions); 8 (Increased transparency; Changes in departmental policy on applications for re-registration).

**(15) Information may be communicated** — Notwithstanding section 241,

(a) the information contained in a public information return referred to in subsection (14) shall be communicated or otherwise made available to the public by the Minister in such manner as the Minister deems appropriate; and

(b) the Minister may make available to the public in such manner as the Minister deems appropriate an annual listing of all registered or previously registered charities indicating for each the name, location, registration number, date of registration and, in the case of a charity the registration of which has been revoked, annulled or terminated, the effective date of the revocation, annulment or termination.

**Related Provisions**: 241(3.2) — Additional disclosure permitted of charity information.

**Information Circulars**: 80-10R: Registered charities: operating a registered charity.

**(16)–(19)** [Repealed under former Act]

**Notes**: 149.1(16) and (17), repealed in 1984, enacted penalty taxes that now appear in 188(1) and (2).

149.1(18) repealed effective 1984. The pre-1984 version, still required by 149.1(1)"disbursement quota"G(a) (former 149.1(1)(e)(v)(A)), reads:

(18) **Rules relating to computation of income** — In computing the income of a charitable foundation for a taxation year for the purpose of subparagraphs (1)(e)(ii) or (3)(b)(ii)

(a) there may be deducted an amount not exceeding its income for the year computed without including or deducting any amount under this subsection; and

(b) there shall be included any amount that has been deducted under this subsection for the immediately preceding taxation year.

149.1(19), repealed effective 1981, provided an election to allocate disbursements in a charitable foundation's second taxation year to its first year.

**(20) Rule regarding disbursement excess** — Where a registered charity has expended a disbursement excess for a taxation year, the charity may, for the purpose of determining whether it complies with the requirements of paragraph (2)(b), (3)(b) or (4)(b), as the case may be, for the immediately preceding taxation year of the charity and 5 or less of its immediately subsequent taxation years, include in the computation of the amounts expended on charitable activities carried on by it and by way of gifts made by it to qualified donees, such portion of that disbursement excess as was not so included under this subsection for any preceding taxation year.

**Related Provisions**: 149.1(21) — "Disbursement excess" defined.

**Information Circulars**: 80-10R: Registered charities: operating a registered charity.

### (21) Definition of "disbursement excess" —
For the purpose of subsection (20), "disbursement excess" for a taxation year of a charity means the amount, if any, by which

(a) the total of amounts expended in the year by the charity on charitable activities carried on by it or by way of gifts made by it to qualified donees

exceeds

(b) in the case of a charitable foundation, its disbursement quota for the year, and

(c) in the case of a charitable organization, the total of

(i) the amount that would be the value of A for the year, and

(ii) the amount that would be the value of A.1 for the year,

in the definition "disbursement quota" in subsection (1) in respect of the organization if it were a charitable foundation.

**Related Provisions**: 149.1(1.1) — Exclusions.

**Notes**: 149.1(21)(c)(i) and (ii) amended by 1995-97 technical bill (as amended before Third Reading), effective for taxation years that end after November 1991 (i.e., retroactive to the R.S.C. 1985 (5th Supp.) consolidation). They had read:

(i) 80% of the amount that would be determined for the year for A, and

(ii) the amount that would be determined for the year for A.1,

See Notes to 149.1(1)"disbursement quota".

149.1(21)(c)(ii) added by 1993 technical bill, effective for taxation years that begin after 1992. See Notes to 149.1(1)"disbursement quota".

**Forms**: RC4108: Registered charities and the Income Tax Act [guide]; T3010: Registered charity information return and public information return (Schedule 2, line 19: net disbursement excess); T4033: Completing the registered charity information return [guide].

**Registered Charities Newsletters**: See under 149.1(1)"disbursement quota".

**Definitions [s. 149.1]**: "acquired" — 149.1(12)(a), 256(7)–(9); "amount" — 248(1); "arm's length" — 251(1); "associated" — 149.1(7); "charitable activities" — 149.1(6), (6.1), (6.2); "charitable foundation", "charitable organization", "charitable purposes", "charity" — 149.1(1); "class" — of shares 248(6); "control" — 149.1(12)(a), 256(6)–(9); "controlled" — 149.1(12)(a), 256(6), (6.1); "corporation" — 248(1), *Interpretation Act* 35(1); "deferred profit sharing plan" — 147(1), 248(1); "disbursement excess" — 149.1(21); "disbursement quota" — 149.1(1); "income" — of charity 149.1(12)(b); "Minister" — 248(1); "mutual fund corporation" — 131(8), 248(1); "mutual fund trust" — 132(6)–(7), 132.2(1)(q), 248(1); "non-qualified investment" — 149.1(1); "person", "prescribed" — 248(1); "prescribed stock exchange" — Reg. 3200, 3201; "private foundation" — 149.1(1), 248(1); "property" — 248(1); "province" — *Interpretation Act* 35(1); "public foundation" — 149.1(1), 248(1); "qualified donee" — 149.1(1); "qualifying share" — 192(6), 248(1); "registered charity" — 149.1(6.4), 248(1); "related business" — 149.1(1); "resident in Canada" — 250; "share" — 248(1); "specified gift" — 149.1(1); "substituted property" — 248(5); "tax payable" — 248(2); "taxable income" — 2(2), 248(1); "taxation year" — 149.1(1), 249; "trust" — 104(1), 248(1), (3); "writing" — *Interpretation Act* 35(1).

**Interpretation Bulletins [s. 149.1]**: IT-496: Non-profit organizations.

## DIVISION I — RETURNS, ASSESSMENTS, PAYMENT AND APPEALS

### Returns

### 150. (1) Filing returns of income — general rule — 
Subject to subsection (1.1), a return of income that is in prescribed form and that contains prescribed information shall be filed with the Minister, without notice or demand for the return, for each taxation year of a taxpayer,

**Notes**: Where the deadline for filing a return expires on a weekend or holiday, it is extended administratively by the CCRA to 11:59 p.m. of the next business day. See also Notes to 165(1) re statutory extension.

The taxpayer is responsible for errors in the return, even if they were made by an accountant or bookkeeper. However, this liability may or may not extend to penalties for the accountant's gross negligence: *Udell*, [1969] C.T.C. 704 (Exch. Ct.); *Columbia Enterprises Ltd.*, [1983] C.T.C. 204 (FCA).

Opening words of 150(1) amended by 1998 Budget, effective for taxation years that begin after 1998. For earlier years, read:

(1) Returns — A return of income for each taxation year in the case of a corporation (other than a corporation that was a registered charity throughout the year) and in the case of an individual, for each taxation year for which tax is payable by the individual or in which the individual has a taxable capital gain or has disposed of a capital property, shall, without notice or demand therefor, be filed with the Minister in prescribed form and containing prescribed information,

Opening words of 150(1) amended by 1992 Child Benefit bill, effective for the 1993 taxation year (returns due in 1994).

See also Related Provisions and Information Circulars annotations at end of 150(1).

(a) **corporations** — in the case of a corporation, by or on behalf of the corporation within six months after the end of the year if

(i) at any time in the year the corporation

(A) is resident in Canada,

(B) carries on business in Canada,

(C) has a taxable capital gain, or

(D) disposes of a taxable Canadian property, or

(ii) tax under this Part is, or but for a tax treaty would be, payable by the corporation for the year;

**Related Provisions**: 115(1)(b) — Dispositions of taxable Canadian property; 162(2.1) — Minimum non-filing penalty for non-resident corporation; 183(1) — Return deadline for tobacco manufacturers' surtax; 235 — Penalty on large corporations for failure to file return even where no balance owing; 236 — Execution of documents by corporations; 250(1) — Meaning of resident of Canada;

S. 150(1)(a)      Income Tax Act, Part I

253 — Extended meaning of carrying on business in Canada. See additional Related Provisions and Definitions at end of 150(1) and at end of s. 150.

**Notes**: See Notes to 150.1 re electronic filing of corporate tax returns.

Business income must now be reported using the GIFI (General Index of Financial Information), which will allow financial details, such as specific types of income and expenses, to be stored on the CCRA's computers in a way that is easily accessible for audit and sampling purposes.

For more detail see the CCRA's T2 Web page at www.ccra-adrc.gc.ca/t2return.

Non-resident T2 returns should be sent to the International Tax Services Office, 2204 Walkley Rd., Ottawa K1A 1A8. Inquiries: 613-954-9681 (collect calls accepted) or 1-800-267-5177. See CCRA news release, July 7, 2000. Non-resident corporations claiming tax treaty exemption must file Schedule 91, failing which a penalty of $100 per day, maximum $2,500, may apply under 162(2.1) or (7).

150(1)(a) amended by 1998 Budget to add "if" and subparas. (i) and (ii), effective for taxation years that begin after 1998. This implements a budget proposal that non-residents claiming tax treaty protection be required to file an information return with Revenue Canada. The U.S. has had a similar requirement in s. 6114 of the Internal Revenue Code since 1989.

**Interpretation Bulletins**: IT-243R4: Dividend refund to private corporations; IT-304R2: Condominiums.

**Information Circulars**: See list at end of subsec. 150(1).

**Forms**: RC1: Request for a business number; RC6: Request to convert to the business number; RC57: Request for a business number — Quebec; T2: Corporation income tax return; T2 Short: A simpler return for eligible corporations; T2 SCH 46: Part II — tobacco manufacturers' surtax; T2 SCH 91: Information concerning claims for treaty-based exemptions; T2 SCH 100: Balance sheet information; T2 SCH 101: Opening balance sheet information; T2 SCH 125: Opening statement information; T2 SCH 141: Notes checklist; T2 SCH 341: Nova Scotia tax deduction for new small businesses; T2 SCH 400: Saskatchewan royalty tax rebate calculation (corporations); T2 SCH 424: B.C. two-year tax holiday for new small businesses; T2-FTC: Sched 1 — 1987 *et seq.*; T2S(1)(L): Tax calculations for life insurance companies (plus schedules L.1 to L.9); T9R-C: Remittance form — corporations; T700: Saskatchewan new small business corporate tax reduction; T708: Prince Edward Island small business deduction; T745: Newfoundland new small business deduction; T800: Manitoba corporate tax reduction for new small businesses; T1001: Northwest Territories small business deduction; T2131: Supplementary information schedule; T2203: Provincial and territorial taxes — multiple jurisdictions; T4012: T2 corporation income tax guide [guide].

(b) **deceased individuals** — in the case of an individual who dies after October of the year and before the day that would be the individual's filing due date for the year if the individual had not died, by the individual's legal representatives on or before the day that is the later of the day on or before which the return would otherwise be required to be filed and the day that is 6 months after the day of death;

**Related Provisions**: 70(2) — Return for rights or things; 70(7)(a) — Special rules applicable re trust for benefit of spouse; 127.55 — Minimum tax not applicable; 150(1)(d)(iii) — Deadline for deceased's cohabiting spouse; 150(4) — Death of partner or proprietor of business; 159(1) — Payments on behalf of others. See additional Related Provisions and Definitions at end of 150(1) and at end of s. 150.

**Notes**: 150(1)(b) amended by 1995 Budget, effective for 1995 and later taxation years. For earlier years, read:

    (b) in the case of an individual who dies after October in the year and before May in the immediately following taxation year, by the individual's legal representatives within 6 months after the day of death;

150(1)(b) amended by 1991 technical bill, effective for deaths after October 1990, to conform to Revenue Canada administrative practice. Where an individual dies in the first 10 months of the year, the deadline for the terminal return is April 30 or June 15, under 150(1)(d), rather than (the earlier date of) 6 months from death.

**Regulations**: 206 (information return).

**Information Circulars**: See list at end of subsec. 150(1).

**Forms**: T4011: Preparing returns for deceased persons [guide]. See also under 150(1)(d).

(c) **trusts or estates** — in the case of an estate or trust, within 90 days from the end of the year;

**Related Provisions**: 104(23) — Testamentary trusts; 159(1) — Payments on behalf of others. See additional Related Provisions and Definitions at end of 150(1) and at end of s. 150.

**Notes**: The CCRA's *T3 Guide* (T4013), chapter 1, indicates that a return is required only if the trust has any of: tax payable; a taxable capital gain [see 150(1.1)(b)(ii)]; total income of more than $500; a benefit of more than $100 to any beneficiary; or any income allocated to a non-resident beneficiary.

The filing deadline for a trust whose taxation year is the calendar year is normally March 31. However, in a leap year such as 2000, the deadline for the previous year's return is March 30.

The deadline for certain testamentary trusts and partnerships (Reg. 229 information return) for the 1994 return for off-calendar year-ends was extended administratively to March 31, 1995 by Revenue Canada (news release, June 24, 1994). The extension applied where they had property eligible for the capital gains exemption under 110.6(19), a beneficiary or partner who qualified for the exemption, and a 1994 taxation year or fiscal period ending after February 21, 1994.

**Regulations**: 204 (information return).

**Information Circulars**: 78-14R2: Guidelines for trust companies and other persons responsible for filing T3R-IND, T3R-G, T3RIF-IND, T3RIF-G, T3H-IND, T3H-G, T3D, T3P, T3S, T3RI and T3F returns. See also list at end of subsec. 150(1).

**Forms**: T3: Trust income tax and information return, with schedules; T3 Summ: Summary of trust income allocations and designations; T3 Supp: Statement of trust income; T3ATH-IND: Amateur athlete trust income tax return; T3D: Income tax return for DPSP or revoked DPSP; T3G: Certification of no tax liability by a group of RRSPs, RRIFs, or RESPs; T3IND: T3IND income tax return for RRSP, RRIF, or RESP; T3P: Employees' pension plan income tax return; T3S: Supplementary unemployment benefit plan — income tax return; T1013: Consent form; T1061: Canadian amateur athlete trust group information return; T1139: Reconciliation of business income for tax purposes.

(d) **individuals** — in the case of any other person, on or before

    (i) the following April 30 by that person or, if the person is unable for any reason to file the return, by the person's guardian, committee or other legal representative (in this paragraph referred to as the person's "guardian"),

    (ii) the following June 15 by that person or, if the person is unable for any reason to file the

1446

Division I — Returns, Assessments, Payment and Appeals          S. 150(2)

return, by the person's guardian where the person is

(A) an individual who carried on a business in the year, unless the expenditures made in the course of carrying on the business were primarily the cost or capital cost of tax shelter investments (as defined in subsection 143.2(1)), or

(B) at any time in the year a cohabiting spouse or common-law partner (within the meaning assigned by section 122.6) of an individual to whom clause (A) applies, or

(iii) where at any time in the year the person is a cohabiting spouse or common-law partner (within the meaning assigned by section 122.6) of an individual to whom paragraph (b) applies for the year, on or before the day that is the later of the day on or before which the person's return would otherwise be required to be filed and the day that is 6 months after the day of the individual's death; or

**Related Provisions**: 70(7)(a) — Special rules applicable re trust for benefit of spouse; 96(1.6) — Members of partnership deemed to carry on business of partnership for purposes of s. 150; 180.2(5) — Return required by residents and non-residents for OAS clawback calculation; 237(1) — Application for Social Insurance Number. See additional Related Provisions and Definitions at end of 150(1) and at end of s. 150.

**Notes**: 150(1)(d)(iii) amended by 2000 same-sex partners bill to add reference to "common-law partner", effective for the 2001 and later taxation years, or earlier by election (see Notes to 248(1)"common-law partner").

150(1)(d) amended by 1995 Budget, effective for 1995 and later taxation years, and 150(1)(d)(ii)(A) amended by 1995-97 technical bill, effective on the same basis, to change a reference from 237.1(1)"tax shelter" to 143.2(1)"tax shelter investment". For earlier years, read:

(d) in the case of any other person, on or before April 30 in the next year by that person or, if the person is unable for any reason to file the return, by the person's guardian, committee or other legal representative; or

The change was made because of the removal of off-calendar year reporting for most individual taxpayers carrying on business (except where they choose to make an election under 249.1(4)). Since such taxpayers have less time to prepare their financial statements because their business year-end is now December 31, the filing deadline was extended from April 30 to June 15. However, interest still runs on any balance owing after April 30; see 156.1(4), 161(1) and 248(1)"balance-due day". The deadline under 150(1)(d) is defined in 248(1) as the "filing-due date".

Until the 1996 taxation year, GST and income tax returns could be filed together by individuals who are annual filers under the GST, and any balance owing on one account could be credited with a refund from the other on Form T1124. This return had to be mailed to the Winnipeg Taxation Centre. Effective for the 1997 taxation year (returns filed in spring 1998), this "combined annual business return" has been eliminated, as it was not widely used.

**Forms**: T1 General: Individual income tax return; T1-Adj: Adjustment request; T1C: Provincial tax credits; T1-CP Summ: Return in respect of certified productions; T1-CP Supp: Statement of certified productions; T1-MTR: Manitoba tax reduction; T1-KS: T1 keying schedule; T2 SCH 301: Newfoundland scientific research and experimental development tax credit; T2 SCH 340: Nova Scotia research and development tax credit; T2 SCH 420: B.C. royalty and deemed income rebate calculation and application; T2 SCH 421: B.C. mining exploration tax credit; T2 SCH 441: Yukon mineral exploration tax credit; T78: Manitoba mineral tax rebate application (individuals); T79: Alberta royalty tax rebate calculation and application (individuals); T81 (IND): B.C. royalty and deemed income rebate calculation and application; T82: Saskatchewan royalty tax rebate calculation (individuals); T87: British Columbia refundable tax credits; T89: Alberta stock savings plan tax credit; T1159: Income tax return: electing under s. 216; T1199: Yukon mineral exploration tax credit.

(e) **designated persons** — in a case where no person described by paragraph (a), (b) or (d) has filed the return, by such person as is required by notice in writing from the Minister to file the return, within such reasonable time as the notice specifies.

**Related Provisions [subsec. 150(1)]**: 149(12) — Non-profit organizations — information return; 149.1(14) — Charity information returns; 150.1 — Electronic filing; 162(1) — Penalty for late filing; 220(3) — Extension of time for filing return; 233.1 — Return of transactions with related non-residents; 248(1) — Definition of "filing-due date"; Reg. 229 — Partnership information returns; Reg. 8409 — Registered pension plan information return; *Interpretation Act* 26 — Extension of deadline where it falls on Sunday or holiday. See also Related Provisions and Definitions at end of s. 150.

**Notes**: See at beginning of 150(1), before para. (a).

**Information Circulars [subsec. 150(1)]**: 78-5R3: Communal organizations; 94-3: List of forms and publications available for use by the public; 97-2: Customized forms — returns and information slips; 00-1: Voluntary disclosures program.

**Forms**: T2203: Provincial and territorial taxes — multiple jurisdictions.

**(1.1) Exception** — Subsection (1) does not apply to a taxation year of a taxpayer if

(a) the taxpayer is a corporation that was a registered charity throughout the year; or

(b) the taxpayer is an individual unless

(i) tax is payable under this Part by the individual for the year,

(ii) where the individual is resident in Canada at any time in the year, the individual has a taxable capital gain or disposes of capital property in the year,

(iii) where the individual is non-resident throughout the year, the individual has a taxable capital gain or disposes of a taxable Canadian property in the year, or

(iv) at the end of the year the individual's HBP balance or LLP balance (as defined in subsection 146.01(1) or 146.02(1)) is a positive amount.

**Related Provisions**: 149.1(14) — Charity must file information return.

**Notes**: 150(1.1) added by 1998 Budget, effective for taxation years that begin after 1998.

**(2) Demands for returns** — Every person, whether or not the person is liable to pay tax under this Part for a taxation year and whether or not a return has been filed under subsection (1) or (3), shall, on demand from the Minister, served personally or by registered letter, file, within such reasonable time as may be stipulated in the demand, with the Minister in prescribed form and containing prescribed information a return of the income for the taxation year designated in the demand.

**Related Provisions**: 162(2) — Repeated penalties; 233 — Demand for information return; 238(1) — Fine or imprisonment for failure to file; 248(7)(a) — Mail deemed received on day mailed. See additional Related Provisions and Definitions at end of s. 150.

**(3) Trustees, etc.** — Every trustee in bankruptcy, assignee, liquidator, curator, receiver, trustee or committee and every agent or other person administering, managing, winding up, controlling or otherwise dealing with the property, business, estate or income of a person who has not filed a return for a taxation year as required by this section shall file a return in prescribed form of that person's income for that year.

**Related Provisions**: 159 — Payments on behalf of others; 162(3) — Penalties; 163(1) — Repeated failures. See additional Related provisions and Definitions at end of s. 150.

**Regulations**: 204 (information returns).

**(4) Death of partner or proprietor** — Where

(a) subsection 34.1(9) or 34.2(8) applies in computing an individual's income for a taxation year from a business, or

(b) an individual who carries on a business in a taxation year dies in the year and after the end of a fiscal period of the business that ends in the year, another fiscal period of the business (in this subsection referred to as the "short period") ends in the year because of the individual's death, and the individual's legal representative elects that this subsection apply,

the individual's income from businesses for short periods, if any, shall not be included in computing the individual's income for the year and the individual's legal representative shall file an additional return of income for the year in respect of the individual as if the return were filed in respect of another person and shall pay the tax payable under this Part by that other person for the year computed as if

(c) the other person's only income for the year were the amount determined by the formula

$$A + B - C$$

where

A is the total of all amounts each of which is the individual's income from a business for a short fiscal period,

B is the total of all amounts each of which is an amount deducted under subsection 34.2(8) in computing the individual's income for the taxation year in which the individual dies, and

C is the total of all amounts each of which is an amount included under subsection 34.1(9) in computing the individual's income for the taxation year in which the individual dies, and

(d) subject to sections 114.2 and 118.93, that other person were entitled to the deductions to which the individual is entitled under sections 110, 118 to 118.7 and 118.9 for the year in computing the individual's taxable income or tax payable under this Part, as the case may be, for the year.

**Related Provisions**: 34.1(9)(d)(ii) — Additional income inclusion for off-calendar business year; 34.2(8)(d)(ii) — Deduction for 1995 stub period reserve; 70 — Rules for year of death; 114.2 — Deductions in separate returns; 118.93 — Credits in separate returns; 120.2(4)(a) — No minimum tax carryover; 127.1(1)(a) — No refundable investment tax credit; 127.55 — Minimum tax not applicable to year of death; 150(1)(b) — Deadline for deceased's return; 162(5) — Penalties — failure to provide information return; 163(1) — Repeated failures; 257 — Formula cannot calculate to less than zero. See additional Related Provisions and Definitions at end of s. 150.

**Notes**: 150(4) amended by 1995-97 technical bill, effective for 1996 and later taxation years. For 1988-95, read:

> (4) Where a taxpayer who is a partner or an individual who is a proprietor of a business died after the end of a fiscal period but before the end of the calendar year in which the fiscal period ended, the taxpayer's income as such partner or proprietor for the period commencing immediately after the end of the fiscal period and ending at the time of death shall be included in computing the taxpayer's income for the taxation year in which the taxpayer died unless the taxpayer's legal representative has elected otherwise, in which case the legal representative shall file a separate return of income for the period under this Part and pay the tax for the period under this Part as if
>
> (a) the taxpayer were another person;
>
> (b) the period were a taxation year;
>
> (c) that other person's only income for the period were that person's income as such partner or proprietor for that period; and
>
> (d) subject to sections 114.2 and 118.93, that other person were entitled to the deductions to which the taxpayer was entitled under sections 110, 118 to 118.7 and 118.9 for the period in computing the taxpayer's taxable income or tax payable under this Part, as the case may be, for the period.

**Interpretation Bulletins [subsec. 150(4)]**: IT-278R2: Death of a partner or of a retired partner; IT-326R3: Returns of deceased persons as "another person".

**Forms**: T4011: Preparing returns for deceased persons [guide].

**Related Provisions [s. 150]**: 1i — Proprietor of business; 149.1(14) — Registered charity information returns; 151 — Estimate of tax; 152(6) — Reassessment; 162 — Penalties; 163 — Failure to file return; 180.1(3) — Individual surtax — return; 220(3) — Extension for filing return; 238 — Offences.

**Definitions [s. 150]**: "amount", "business" — 248(1); "calendar year" — *Interpretation Act* 37(1)(a); "capital property" — 54, 248(1); "carries on business in Canada" — 253; "common-law partner" — 248(1); "corporation" — 248(1), *Interpretation Act* 35(1); "estate" — 104(1), 248(1); "filing-due date" — 248(1); "fiscal period" — 249.1; "HBP balance" — 146.01(1); "individual" — 248(1); "LLP balance" — 146.02(1); "legal representative", "Minister" — 248(1); "month" — *Interpretation Act* 35(1); "non-resident", "person", "prescribed", "property", "registered charity" — 248(1); "resident in Canada" — 250; "tax payable" — 248(2); "tax treaty", "taxable Canadian property" — 248(1); "taxable capital gain" — 38(a), 248(1); "taxable income" — 2(2), 248(1); "taxation year" — 249; "taxpayer" — 248(1); "trust" — 104(1), 248(1), (3); "writing" — *Interpretation Act* 35(1).

Division I — Returns, Assessments, Payment and Appeals   S. 150.1

**Interpretation Bulletins [s. 150]**: IT-109R2: Unpaid amounts.

**150.1 (1) Definition of "electronic filing"** — For the purposes of this section, "electronic filing" means using electronic media in a manner specified in writing by the Minister.

**(2) Filing of return by electronic transmission** — A person who meets the criteria specified in writing by the Minister may file a return of income for a taxation year by way of electronic filing.

> **Proposed Amendment — Internet Filing**
>
> **CCRA news release, March 2, 2000**: *Introducing NETFILE!*
>
> The Canada Customs and Revenue Agency is launching a new pilot project for the 1999 tax filing period: NETFILE, a system that will enable more than 3.8 million Canadians to send in their individual tax returns over the Internet. If you used tax preparation software last year, we sent you an invitation, including an access code for the website at http://www.netfile.gc.ca.
>
> However, you will need to equip yourself with certified software... and some restrictions apply.
>
> Just think! No hard copy return to print and mail!
>
> A faster refund - in about two weeks!
>
> Safety and confidentiality assured!
>
> Available 7 days a week!
>
> And, we still offer the following programs and services:
>
> TELEFILE: A telephone-based system for filing individual tax returns.
>
> T.I.P.S.: Tax Information Phone Service.
>
> EFILE: Electronic filing of tax returns.
>
> DIRECT DEPOSIT: Instead of getting a cheque, have your refund deposited directly in your bank account.
>
> Whether for NETFILE or any of the other electronic services, consult your tax return kit or visit our website at http://www.ccra-adrc.gc.ca and go to the Electronic Services page.
>
> FOR FURTHER INFORMATION PLEASE CONTACT: Canada Customs and Revenue Agency, Lynda-Joan Fortin, Communications Manager, (418) 649-3127; or Louise Moissan, EFILE Co-ordinator, (418) 649-4022.

**Related Provisions**: 244(21) — Proof of electronic filing; 244(22) — Electronic filing of information return.

**Notes**: See Notes at end of 150.1.

**Forms**: RC4018: Electronic Filers Manual [guide]; T183: Information return for electronic filing of an individual's income tax and benefit return; T200: Electronic filing application for returns of individuals; T200 corp: Corporate EFILE application; T4077(E): EFILE: Electronic filing for individuals [guide].

**(3) Deemed date of filing** — For the purposes of section 150, where a return of income of a taxpayer for a taxation year is filed by way of electronic filing, it shall be deemed to be a return of income filed with the Minister in prescribed form on the day the Minister acknowledges acceptance of it.

**(4) Declaration** — Where a return of income of a taxpayer for a taxation year is filed by way of electronic filing by a particular person (in this subsection referred to as the "filer") other than the person who is required to file the return, the person who is required to file the return shall make an information return in prescribed form containing prescribed information, sign it, retain a copy of it and provide the filer with the information return, and that return and the copy shall be deemed to be a record referred to in section 230 in respect of the filer and the other person.

**Forms**: RC4018: Electronic Filers Manual [guide]; T183: Information return for electronic filing of an individual's income tax and benefit return; T183 corp: Information return for corporations filing electronically.

**(5) Application to other Parts** — This section also applies to Parts I.1 to XIII, with such modifications as the circumstances require.

> **Proposed Amendment — 150.1(5)**
>
> **(5) Application to other Parts** — This section also applies to Parts I.2 to XIII, with such modifications as the circumstances require.
>
> **Application**: The December 21, 2000 draft legislation, s. 82, will amend subsec. 150.1(5) to read as above, applicable to 2001 *et seq.*
>
> **Technical Notes**: Section 150.1 provides for the use of electronic media for filing tax returns. The amendment to subsection 150.1(5) is strictly consequential on the repeal of the surtax imposed on individuals under Part I.1 (see commentary on that Part).

**Notes [s. 150.1]**: 150.1 added by 1992 technical bill (and 150.1(4) amended retroactively by 1993 technical bill), effective for 1992 and later taxation years. 150.1(5), in its application to Parts X, X.1, X.2, X.4, XI, XI.1 and XI.2 is effective January 1, 1992 as if subsecs. (1) to (4) were effective January 1, 1992.

Electronic filing of corporate income tax returns is now available. The corporate tax return has been redesigned so that it is inherently electronic, although paper filing will still be permitted. Returns will be processed electronically, and corporate financial information will be gathered and stored using the *General Index of Financial Information* (GIFI), which includes specific codes for each line of financial information (e.g., each kind of expense). See www.ccra-adrc.gc.ca/t2return.

E-Filing of personal income tax returns has been phased in since beginning as a pilot project in 1990. Since 1995, taxpayers throughout Canada can use EFILE; Quebec taxpayers can also file their provincial returns electronically.

In 1995, Revenue Canada began experimenting with TELEFILE, a process by which selected taxpayers with simple returns can transmit their income tax information via touch-tone phone.

Internet filing began in the spring of 2000 and expanded in 2001.

Being an E-File transmitter has been held to be a privilege, not a right, and the Courts will generally not interfere with the CCRA's discretion to cut off E-File access to a tax preparer: *Pan-Tax Inc.*, [1997] 2 C.T.C. 315 (FCTD).

**Definitions [s. 150.1]**: "electronic filing" — 150.1(1); "filer" — 150.1(4); "Minister", "person", "prescribed", "regulation" — 248(1); "taxation year" — 249; "writing" — *Interpretation Act* 35(1).

**Forms**: T4077(E): EFILE: Electronic filing for individuals [guide].

## Estimate of Tax

**151. Estimate of tax** — Every person required by section 150 to file a return of income shall in the return estimate the amount of tax payable.

**Related Provisions**: 104(23) — Testamentary trusts; 150 — Returns; 155 — Farmers and fishermen; 156.1(4) — Payment of balance owing — individuals; 157(1), (2) — Corporations; 162(3) — Penalty — failure to complete return; 180.1 — Individual surtax — Estimate of tax; 183(3) — Provision applicable to Part II; 187(3) — Provision applicable to Part IV; 193(8) — Provision applicable to Part VII; 195(8) — Provision applicable to Part VIII; 219(3) — Provision applicable to Part XIV.

**Definitions [s. 151]**: "amount", "person" — 248(1).

## Assessment

**152. (1) Assessment** — The Minister shall, with all due dispatch, examine a taxpayer's return of income for a taxation year, assess the tax for the year, the interest and penalties, if any, payable and determine

(a) the amount of refund, if any, to which the taxpayer may be entitled by virtue of section 129, 131, 132 or 133 for the year; or

(b) the amount of tax, if any, deemed by subsection 120(2) or (2.2), 122.5(3), 122.51(2), 125.4(3), 125.5(3), 127.1(1), 127.41(3) or 210.2(3) or (4) to be paid on account of the taxpayer's tax payable under this Part for the year.

**Related Provisions**: 152(1.4) — Determination of income of partnership; 152(2) — Notice of assessment; 152(4), (5) — Reassessment; 158 — Remainder payable forthwith upon assessment; 160.2(3) — Minister may assess recipient under RRSP or RRIF; 166 — Irregularity or error in assessment; 244(15) — Date when assessment made.

**Notes**: Although the Minister is supposed to issue an assessment "with all due dispatch", the assessment is still valid even if it is not issued for a long time: *Ginsberg*, [1996] 3 C.T.C. 63 (FCA). The only remedy would be to bring action in the Federal Court–Trial Division for an order of *mandamus* forcing the Minister to issue an assessment.

Reference in 152(1)(b) to 120(2.2) added by 1999 Budget, effective for 1999 and later taxation years.

The reference in 152(1)(b) to 122.5(3) (the GST credit) was added by 1990 GST, effective 1989. For 1989 and 1990, read in a reference to 122.4(3) (federal sales tax credit).

Reference to 127.41(3) added by 1994 Budget, effective for taxation years that end after February 22, 1994.

Reference to 125.4(3) added by 1995 Budget, effective for 1995 and later taxation years.

References to 122.51(2) and 125.5(3) added, and reference to 119(2) deleted, by 1997 Budget, effective for the 1997 and later taxation years. Reference to 120.1(4) deleted by 1997 Budget effective for the 1998 and later taxation years.

152(1)(b) amended by 1992 Child Benefit bill, effective for 1993 and later taxation years, to delete reference to the Child Tax Credit and other repealed provisions. Also amended by 1993 technical bill, effective for 1993 and later taxation years, to delete reference to 144(9). For 1991 and 1992, read:

(b) the amount of tax, if any, deemed by subsection 119(2), 120(2), 120.1(4), 122.2(1), 127.1(1), 127.2(2), 144(9),

210.2(3) or (4) to have been paid on account of his tax under this Part for the year.

To find out whether a personal tax return has been assessed, call TIPS at 1-800-267-6999 (see Notes to 164(1)).

**Forms**: T452: Notice of assessment.

**(1.1) Determination of losses** — Where the Minister ascertains the amount of a taxpayer's non-capital loss, net capital loss, restricted farm loss, farm loss or limited partnership loss for a taxation year and the taxpayer has not reported that amount as such a loss in the taxpayer's return of income for that year, the Minister shall, at the request of the taxpayer, determine, with all due dispatch, the amount of the loss and shall send a notice of determination to the person by whom the return was filed.

**Related Provisions**: 111 — Losses deductible; 152(1.4) — Determination of loss of partnership; 160.2(3) — Minister may assess recipient under RRSP or RRIF; 244(14) — Presumption re date of mailing of notice of determination; 244(15) — Determination deemed made on date mailed; 248(7)(a) — Mail deemed received on day mailed.

**Notes**: If the taxpayer's tax payable for the year is nil, a determination of loss must be issued to start the 3- or 4-year clock running under 152(4). Otherwise the CCRA can effectively deny a loss carryforward in a future year by changing an earlier year's loss. Such a change is not otherwise statute-barred because the assessment for the earlier year remains at nil. No appeal can be taken from a nil assessment: *Okalta Oil Ltd.*, [1955] C.T.C. 271 (SCC); *Wilson*, [1996] 3 C.T.C. 203 (FCTD).

It is therefore prudent, after receiving the initial assessment for any year where tax is nil and a loss carryover is created, to request a determination of loss under 152(1.1). Once it is issued, 152(1.2) will cause the clock to start running. If the CCRA refuses to issue the determination, it can be compelled to do so by an order of *mandamus* from the Federal Court: see *Burnet*, [1999] 3 C.T.C. 60 (FCA).

Note also that even where there is a nil assessment, but no determination of loss, for year X, one can appeal a denied loss of year X by appealing the assessment of another year in which the loss carryover from year X is denied.

**Interpretation Bulletins**: IT-488R2: Winding-up of 90%-owned taxable Canadian corporations; IT-512: Determination and redetermination of losses.

**Information Circulars**: 84-1: Revision of capital cost allowance claims and other permissive deductions.

**(1.11) Determination pursuant to subsec. 245(2)** — Where at any time the Minister ascertains the tax consequences to a taxpayer by reason of subsection 245(2) with respect to a transaction, the Minister

(a) shall, in the case of a determination pursuant to subsection 245(8), or

(b) may, in any other case,

determine any amount that is relevant for the purposes of computing the income, taxable income or taxable income earned in Canada of, tax or other amount payable by, or amount refundable to, the taxpayer under this Act and, where such a determination is made, the Minister shall send to the taxpayer, with all due dispatch, a notice of determination stating the amount so determined.

Division I — Returns, Assessments, Payment and Appeals    S. 152(1.5)

**Related Provisions**: 152(1.111) — Definitions in subsec. 245(1) apply; 152(1.12) — Limitation; 152(1.3) — Determination binding; 244(14) — Presumption re date of mailing of notice of determination; 244(15) — Determination deemed made on date mailed; 248(7)(a) — Mail deemed received on day mailed.

**(1.111) Application of subsec. 245(1)** — The definitions in subsection 245(1) apply to subsection (1.11).

**Notes**: 152(1.111) added in the R.S.C. 1985 (5th Supp.) consolidation, effective for taxation years ending after November 1991. This rule was formerly contained in the opening words of subsec. 245(1).

**(1.12) When determination not to be made** — A determination of an amount shall not be made with respect to a taxpayer under subsection (1.11) at a time where that amount is relevant only for the purposes of computing the income, taxable income or taxable income earned in Canada of, tax or other amount payable by, or amount refundable to, the taxpayer under this Act for a taxation year ending before that time.

**(1.2) Provisions applicable** — Paragraphs 56(1)(l) and 60(o), this Division and Division J, as they relate to an assessment or a reassessment and to assessing or reassessing tax, apply, with such modifications as the circumstances require, to a determination or redetermination of an amount under this Division or an amount deemed under section 122.61 or 126.1 to be an overpayment on account of a taxpayer's liability under this Part, except that

(a) subsections (1) and (2) do not apply to determinations made under subsections (1.1) and (1.11);

(b) an original determination of a taxpayer's non-capital loss, net capital loss, restricted farm loss, farm loss or limited partnership loss for a taxation year may be made by the Minister only at the request of the taxpayer; and

(c) subsection 164(4.1) does not apply to a determination made under subsection (1.4).

**Related Provisions**: 96(2.1) — Limited partnership losses; 111 — Losses deductible; 160.2(3) — Minister may assess recipient under RRSP or RRIF.

**Notes**: 152(1.2)(c) added by 1995-97 technical bill, effective for determinations made after June 18, 1998.

See Notes to 152(1.1).

152(1.2) amended by 1992 Economic Statement, effective 1993, to add references to 122.61 (child tax benefit) and 126.1 (UI premium credit).

**Interpretation Bulletins**: IT-488R2: Winding-up of 90%-owned taxable Canadian corporations; IT-512: Determination and redetermination of losses.

**(1.3) Determination binding** — For greater certainty, where the Minister makes a determination of the amount of a taxpayer's non-capital loss, net capital loss, restricted farm loss, farm loss or limited partnership loss for a taxation year or makes a determination under subsection (1.11) with respect to a taxpayer, the determination is (subject to the taxpayer's rights of objection and appeal in respect of the determination and to any redetermination by the Minister) binding on both the Minister and the taxpayer for the purpose of calculating the income, taxable income or taxable income earned in Canada of, tax or other amount payable by, or amount refundable to, the taxpayer, as the case may be, for any taxation year.

**Related Provisions**: 96(2.1) — Limited partnership loss; 111 — Losses deductible; 160.2(3) — Minister may assess recipient under RRSP or RRIF.

**Interpretation Bulletins**: IT-488R2: Winding-up of 90%-owned taxable Canadian corporations; IT-512: Determination and redetermination of losses.

**(1.4) Determination in respect of a partnership** — The Minister may, within 3 years after the day that is the later of

(a) the day on or before which a member of a partnership is, or but for subsection 220(2.1) would be, required under section 229 of the *Income Tax Regulations* to make an information return for a fiscal period of the partnership, and

(b) the day the return is filed,

determine any income or loss of the partnership for the fiscal period and any deduction or other amount, or any other matter, in respect of the partnership for the fiscal period that is relevant in determining the income, taxable income or taxable income earned in Canada of, tax or other amount payable by, or any amount refundable to or deemed to have been paid or to have been an overpayment by, any member of the partnership for any taxation year under this Part.

**Related Provisions**: 152(1.2)(c) — Subsec. 164(4.1) does not apply to determination under 152(1.4); 152(1.5), (1.6) — Notice of determination; 152(1.7) — Determination binding; 152(1.8) — Assessment where partnership found not to exist; 165(1.15) — Objection to determination; 244(15) — Determination deemed made on date mailed.

**Notes**: Before 152(1.4), Revenue Canada had to assess each partner separately, and assessments could be objected to and appealed separately by one or more partners. Now a determination of the partnership's income or loss is binding on all of the partners, and can only be objected to by one partner on behalf of all of them (see 165(1.15)).

To start time running under 152(1.4)(b), a partnership return should be filed even if no return is required by Reg. 229(1), such as for a partnership with fewer than 6 partners. The CCRA considers that 152(1.4) allows assessment of partnership income beyond the normal reassessment period if no partnership return has been filed: VIEWS docs 9726115 and 2000-0010935. See 152(1.7)(b).

152(1.4) added by 1995-97 technical bill, effective for determinations made after June 18, 1998.

**(1.5) Notice of determination** — Where a determination is made under subsection (1.4) in respect of a partnership for a fiscal period, the Minister shall send a notice of the determination to the partnership and to each person who was a member of the partnership during the fiscal period.

**Related Provisions**: 152(1.6) — Determination valid even if notice not received by partners; 244(14) — Presumption re date of mailing of determination; 248(7)(a) — Mail deemed received on day mailed.

**Notes:** 152(1.5) added by 1995-97 technical bill, effective for determinations made after June 18, 1998.

**(1.6) Absence of notification** — No determination made under subsection (1.4) in respect of a partnership for a fiscal period is invalid solely because one or more persons who were members of the partnership during the period did not receive a notice of the determination.

**Notes:** This applies only where one or more *partners* have not received the notice. If the *partnership* does not receive the notice, 152(1.6) does not apply, and it can be argued that the determination is invalid because it was never mailed. See *Aztec Industries Inc.*, [1995] 1 C.T.C. 327 (FCA) (but see also *Schafer*, [2000] G.S.T.C. 82 (FCA), where the notice is mailed but not received). In such a case, 152(1.7) would not apply, and the partner would have the right to object to a reassessment that was based on the CCRA's determination of the partnership's income.

152(1.6) added by 1995-97 technical bill, effective for determinations made after June 18, 1998.

**(1.7) Binding effect of determination** — Where the Minister makes a determination under subsection (1.4) or a redetermination in respect of a partnership,

(a) subject to the rights of objection and appeal of the member of the partnership referred to in subsection 165(1.15) in respect of the determination or redetermination, the determination or redetermination is binding on the Minister and each member of the partnership for the purposes of calculating the income, taxable income or taxable income earned in Canada of, tax or other amount payable by, or any amount refundable to or deemed to have been paid or to have been an overpayment by, the members for any taxation year under this Part; and

(b) notwithstanding subsections (4), (4.01), (4.1) and (5), the Minister may, before the end of the day that is one year after the day on which all rights of objection and appeal expire or are determined in respect of the determination or redetermination, assess the tax, interest, penalties or other amounts payable and determine an amount deemed to have been paid or to have been an overpayment under this Part in respect of any member of the partnership and any other taxpayer for any taxation year as may be necessary to give effect to the determination or redetermination or a decision of the Tax Court of Canada, the Federal Court of Canada or the Supreme Court of Canada.

**Notes:** 152(1.7) added by 1995-97 technical bill, effective for determinations made after June 18, 1998.

**(1.8) Time to assess** — Where, as a result of representations made to the Minister that a person was a member of a partnership in respect of a fiscal period, a determination is made under subsection (1.4) for the period and the Minister, the Tax Court of Canada, the Federal Court of Canada or the Supreme Court of Canada concludes at a subsequent time that the partnership did not exist for the period or that, throughout the period, the person was not a member of the partnership, the Minister may, notwithstanding subsections (4), (4.1) and (5), within one year after that subsequent time, assess the tax, interest, penalties or other amounts payable, or determine an amount deemed to have been paid or to have been an overpayment under this Part, by any taxpayer for any taxation year, but only to the extent that the assessment or determination can reasonably be regarded

(a) as relating to any matter that was relevant in the making of the determination made under subsection (1.4);

(b) as resulting from the conclusion that the partnership did not exist for the period; or

(c) as resulting from the conclusion that the person was, throughout the period, not a member of the partnership.

**Related Provisions [subsec. 152(1.8)]:** 165(1.1)(a), (d) — Limitation of right to object; 169(2)(a), (d) — Limitation of right to appeal.

**Notes:** 152(1.8) added by 1995-97 technical bill, effective for determinations made after June 18, 1998.

**(2) Notice of assessment** — After examination of a return, the Minister shall send a notice of assessment to the person by whom the return was filed.

**Related Provisions:** 158 — Remainder payable forthwith after assessment mailed; 244(14), (15) — Mailing date of assessment.

**Forms:** T67A, T67AC, T67AN, T452, T453, T456, T457, T492: Notices of assessment.

**(3) Liability not dependent on assessment** — Liability for the tax under this Part is not affected by an incorrect or incomplete assessment or by the fact that no assessment has been made.

**Related Provisions:** 152(4), (6), (8) — Assessment and reassessment; 160.2(3) — Minister may assess recipient; 165 — Objections to assessments; 166 — Assessment not to be vacated by reason of improper procedures; 169 — Appeal.

**(3.1) Definition of "normal reassessment period"** — For the purposes of subsections (4), (4.01), (4.2), (4.3), (5) and (9), the normal reassessment period for a taxpayer in respect of a taxation year is

(a) where at the end of the year the taxpayer is a mutual fund trust or a corporation other than a Canadian-controlled private corporation, the period that ends 4 years after the earlier of the day of mailing of a notice of an original assessment under this Part in respect of the taxpayer for the year and the day of mailing of an original notification that no tax is payable by the taxpayer for the year; and

(b) in any other case, the period that ends 3 years after the earlier of the day of mailing of a notice of an original assessment under this Part in respect of the taxpayer for the year and the day of mailing of an original notification that no tax is payable by the taxpayer for the year.

**Related Provisions:** 136(1) — Cooperative corporation may be private corporation for purposes of s. 152; 137(7) — Credit union may be private corporation; 152(4), (6), (8) — Assessment and reassessment; 160.2(3) — Minister may assess recipient; 165 — Objections to assessments; 166 — Irregularities; 169, 172 — Appeal; 244(14) — Notice presumed mailed on date of notice; 244(15) — Date when assessment made.

**Notes**: Opening words amended by 1998 Budget bill to add reference to 152(9), effective for appeals disposed of after June 17, 1999.

152(3.1) amended by 1995-97 technical bill, retroactive to its introduction effective April 28, 1989, to add reference to 152(4.01) in the opening words and to add "the earlier of" in paras. (a) and (b).

Opening words of 152(3.1) amended by 1992 technical bill to refer to 152(4.3), effective on the same basis as 152(4.3).

Opening words of 152(3.1) amended by 1991 technical bill, effective for assessments and redeterminations in respect of 1985 and later years, to add reference to 152(4.2).

152(3.1) added by 1989 Budget, effective April 28, 1989, other than for a taxation year for which an original notice of assessment (or notification that no tax is payable) was mailed by April 27, 1986.

See also Notes to 152(4).

In *Brunette*, 2000 D.T.C. 1783 (Fr.) (TCC), the Court held that the day of the initial assessment is excluded from the calculation, as per *Interpretation Act* s. 27(4).

### (3.2) Determination of deemed overpayment [Child Tax Benefit]
— A taxpayer may, during any month, request in writing that the Minister determine the amount deemed by subsection 122.61(1) to be an overpayment on account of the taxpayer's liability under this Part for a taxation year that arose during the month or any of the 11 preceding months.

**Related Provisions**: 152(3.3) — Notice of determination.

**Notes**: 152(3.2) added by 1992 Child Benefit bill, effective 1993.

### (3.3) Notice of determination [Child Tax Benefit]
— On receipt of the request referred to in subsection (3.2), the Minister shall, with all due dispatch, determine the amounts deemed by subsection 122.61(1) to be overpayments on account of the taxpayer's liability under this Part that arose during the months in respect of which the request was made or determine that there is no such amount, and shall send a notice of the determination to the taxpayer.

**Notes**: 152(3.3) added by 1992 Child Benefit bill, effective 1993.

### (3.4) Determination of UI premium tax credit
— A taxpayer may request in writing that the Minister determine the amount deemed by subsection 126.1(6) or (7) to be an overpayment on account of the taxpayer's liability under this Part for a taxation year.

**Related Provisions**: 152(3.5) — Notice of determination.

**Notes**: 152(3.4) added by 1992 Economic Statement, effective 1993.

### (3.5) Notice of determination [UI premium tax credit]
— On receipt of the request referred to in subsection (3.4), the Minister shall, with all due dispatch, determine the amount deemed by subsection 126.1(6) or (7), as the case may be, to be an overpayment on account of the taxpayer's liability under this Part for a taxation year, or determine that there is no such amount, and shall send a notice of the determination to the taxpayer.

**Notes**: 152(3.5) added by 1992 Economic Statement, effective 1993.

### (4) Assessment and reassessment [limitation period]
— The Minister may at any time make an assessment, reassessment or additional assessment of tax for a taxation year, interest or penalties, if any, payable under this Part by a taxpayer or notify in writing any person by whom a return of income for a taxation year has been filed that no tax is payable for the year, except that an assessment, reassessment or additional assessment may be made after the taxpayer's normal reassessment period in respect of the year only if

(a) the taxpayer or person filing the return

(i) has made any misrepresentation that is attributable to neglect, carelessness or wilful default or has committed any fraud in filing the return or in supplying any information under this Act, or

(ii) has filed with the Minister a waiver in prescribed form within the normal reassessment period for the taxpayer in respect of the year; or

(b) the assessment, reassessment or additional assessment is made before the day that is 3 years after the end of the normal reassessment period for the taxpayer in respect of the year and

(i) is required pursuant to subsection (6) or would be so required if the taxpayer had claimed an amount by filing the prescribed form referred to in that subsection on or before the day referred to therein,

(ii) is made as a consequence of the assessment or reassessment pursuant to this paragraph or subsection (6) of tax payable by another taxpayer,

(iii) is made as a consequence of a transaction involving the taxpayer and a non-resident person with whom the taxpayer was not dealing at arm's length,

**Proposed Addition — 152(4)(b)(iii.1)**

(iii.1) is made, if the taxpayer is non-resident and carries on a business in Canada, as a consequence of

(A) an allocation by the taxpayer of revenues or expenses as amounts in respect of the Canadian business (other than revenues and expenses that relate solely to the Canadian business, that are recorded in the books of account of the Canadian business, and the documentation in support of which is kept in Canada), or

(B) a notional transaction between the taxpayer and its Canadian business, where the transaction is recognized for the purposes of the computation of an amount under this Act or an applicable tax treaty.

S. 152(4)(b)(iii.1)    Income Tax Act, Part I

**Application**: The August 8, 2000 draft legislation, s. 13(1), will add subpara. 152(4)(b)(iii.1), applicable to 2000 et seq.

**Technical Notes**: Subsection 152(4) of the Act provides the time limits within which assessments, reassessments and additional assessments may be made. Paragraph (b) describes the circumstances in which the Minister of National Revenue may, after a taxpayer's normal reassessment period for a taxation year, assess or reassess tax payable under Part I of the Act for the year. The subsection is amended by adding new subparagraph 152(4)(b)(iii.1), to allow the Minister under certain circumstances to assess or reassess, within three years after the end of the normal assessment period, the tax of a non-resident that carries on business in Canada. Such a (re)assessment may be made if it results from the taxpayer's allocation of revenue or expenses in respect of the Canadian business (unless the revenue or expenses relate solely to the Canadian business and are fully documented in Canada), or from a notional transaction between the taxpayer and its Canadian business, which transaction is recognized under the Act or a tax treaty. An example of such a notional transaction is a "branch advance" contemplated by new section 20.2 of the Act, which applies to a foreign bank that operates a branch in Canada. New subparagraph 152(4)(b)(iii.1) will treat such allocations and notional transactions in the same manner as transactions between a taxpayer and a non-resident person with whom the taxpayer does not deal at arm's length, which are covered by subparagraph (iii).

New subparagraph 152(4)(b)(iii.1) of the Act applies to the 2000 and subsequent taxation years.

(iv) is made as a consequence of a payment or reimbursement of any income or profits tax to or by the government of a country other than Canada or a government of a state, province or other political subdivision of any such country,

(v) is made as a consequence of a reduction under subsection 66(12.73) of an amount purported to be renounced under section 66, or

(vi) is made in order to give effect to the application of subsection 118.1(15) or (16).

**Related Provisions**: 12(2.2) — Late assessment where amount elected re 12(1)(x) inclusion; 13(6) — Misclassified property; 21(5) — Late assessment to permit capitalization of interest; 67.5(2) — Late assessment re illegal payments; 69(12) — Late assessment on disposition of property below market value; 80.04(9) — Late assessment re transfer of forgiven amount of debt to related person; 104(5.31) — Revocation beyond the deadline of trust's election to defer 21-year deemed disposition; 118.1(11) — Late assessment on determination of value of cultural property; 127(17) — Assessment re ITC SR&ED pool beyond the deadline; 128.1(6)(d) — Late assessment to eliminate departure tax paid by taxpayer who returns to Canada; 143.2(15) — Limitation period inapplicable to reassessment of tax shelter investment; 146(8.01) — Home Buyer's Plan & LLP — late assessment of tax on withdrawal; 152(1.7) — Limitation period re determination of partnership income or loss; 152(3.1) — Normal reassessment period; 152(4.01) — Limitation on extended assessments; 152(4.1) — Where waiver revoked; 152(4.2) — Reassessment with taxpayer's consent; 152(4.3) — Consequential assessment; 152(5) — Limitation on assessments; 158 — Payment of balance on assessment; 160.2(3) — Minister may assess recipient under RRSP or RRIF; 161.1(7) — Late assessment to allow interest offset allocation; 164(1)(b) — Refunds; 165(1.1) — Limitation of right to object; 165(5) — Effect of filing of notice of objection; 169(2) — Limitation of right to appeal; 173(2) — Time during consideration not to count; 174(5) — Time during consideration of question not counted; 184(4) — Late assessment after election re excess capital dividend; 231.6 — Foreign-based information; 237.1(6.2) — Late assessment denying tax shelter deduction while penalty unpaid; 244(15) — Date when assessment made.

**Notes**: The normal rule is in the opening words of 152(4): 3 or 4 years from the original assessment date (i.e., the "normal reassessment period" — see 152(3.1)). It is extended by a further 3 years for any of the reasons in 152(4)(b). If a waiver is filed or there is fraud or a misrepresentation attributable due to "neglect, carelessness or wilful default", there is no time limit on a reassessment (152(4)(a)) relating to the misrepresentation, fraud or waiver (152(4.01)(a)). A waiver is not valid unless filed before the limitation period expires, but the CCRA will normally accept one filed by fax. A waiver can be revoked on 6 months' notice; see 152(4.1).

152(4) does not prevent the CCRA from examining a return beyond the reassessment period to determine the cost of an asset for later CCA claims: *Lussier*, [1998] 2 C.T.C. 2794 (TCC).

See Notes to 152(1.1) re starting the clock running for a determination of a loss.

Note that for Ontario corporate tax purposes, the normal reassessment period is one year longer than for federal purposes, even though the basis for the reassessment may be identical to the federal. (See s. 80(10) of the *Corporations Tax Act*, reproduced in the *Practitioner's Ontario Taxes Annotated*.)

Many provisions throughout the Act and its amending bills provide that assessments can be made "notwithstanding subsections 152(4) and (5)", thus overriding this subsection.

152(4) amended by 1995-97 technical bill to read as it does now, retroactive to April 28, 1989, except that 152(4)(b)(v) applies as of the 1996 taxation year, and 152(4)(b)(vi) applies as of August 1997.

152(4) amended by 1989 Budget, effective April 28, 1989, other than for a taxation year for which an original notice of assessment (or notification that no tax is payable) was mailed by April 27, 1986. The "normal reassessment period", now 3 or 4 years under 152(3.1), was 3 years before the amendment.

**I.T. Application Rules**: 62(1) (152(4) applies to assessments since December 23, 1971).

**Interpretation Bulletins**: IT-64R3: Corporations: Association and control — after 1988; IT-109R2: Unpaid amounts; IT-121R3: Election to capitalize cost of borrowed money; IT-185R: Losses from theft, defalcation or embezzlement; IT-384R: Reassessment where option exercised in subsequent year.

**Information Circulars**: 75-7R3: Reassessment of a return of income; 77-11: Sales tax reassessments — deductibility in computing income; 84-1: Revision of capital cost allowance claims and other permissive deductions; 92-3: Guidelines for refunds beyond the normal three year period.

**Forms**: T2029: Waiver in respect of the normal reassessment period.

**(4.01) Assessment to which para. 152(4)(a) or (b) applies** — Notwithstanding subsections (4) and (5), an assessment, reassessment or additional assessment to which paragraph (4)(a) or (4)(b) applies in respect of a taxpayer for a taxation year may be made after the taxpayer's normal reassessment period in respect of the year to the extent that, but only to the extent that, it can reasonably be regarded as relating to,

    (a) where paragraph (4)(a) applies to the assessment, reassessment or additional assessment,

        (i) any misrepresentation made by the taxpayer or a person who filed the taxpayer's return of income for the year that is attributable to neglect, carelessness or wilful default or any fraud committed by the taxpayer or that person in filing the return or supplying any information under this Act, or

        (ii) a matter specified in a waiver filed with the Minister in respect of the year; and

    (b) where paragraph (4)(b) applies to the assessment, reassessment or additional assessment,

        (i) the assessment, reassessment or additional assessment to which subparagraph (4)(b)(i) applies,

        (ii) the assessment or reassessment referred to in subparagraph (4)(b)(ii),

        (iii) the transaction referred to in subparagraph (4)(b)(iii),

        (iv) the payment or reimbursement referred to in subparagraph (4)(b)(iv),

        (v) the reduction referred to in subparagraph (4)(b)(v), or

        (vi) the application referred to in subparagraph (4)(b)(vi).

**Related Provisions**: 152(1.7) — Limitation period re determination of partnership income or loss; 152(3.1) — Normal reassessment period.

**Notes**: 152(4.01) added by 1995-97 technical bill to read as it does now, retroactive to April 27, 1989, except that 152(4.01)(b)(v) applies as of the 1996 taxation year, and 152(4.01)(b)(vi) applies as of August 1997.

152(4.01)(a) was formerly covered in 152(5)(b) and (c). See Notes to 152(4) and (5).

**(4.1) Where waiver revoked** — Where the Minister would, but for this subsection, be entitled to reassess, make an additional assessment or assess tax, interest or penalties by virtue only of the filing of a waiver under subparagraph (4)(a)(ii), the Minister may not make such reassessment, additional assessment or assessment after the day that is six months after the date on which a notice of revocation of the waiver in prescribed form is filed.

**Related Provisions**: 152(1.7) — Limitation period re determination of partnership income or loss; 152(4.2) — Reassessment with taxpayer's consent; 165(1.2) — No objection permitted where right to object waived; 169(2.2) — No appeal where right to object or appeal waived.

**Notes**: This is a convoluted way of saying that a waiver can be revoked on 6 months' notice. (The 6 months gives the CCRA time to issue a reassessment if it wishes.) Note that nothing in 152(4.1) requires the revocation of a waiver to be filed in prescribed *manner* (e.g., at the same Tax Services Office as the waiver is filed), even though Form T652 purports to require this.

Although a waiver filed federally applies automatically for Ontario corporate tax purposes (*Corporations Tax Act* 80(11)(a)(v)), a federal revocation is not valid for Ontario purposes unless a copy is filed with the Ontario Ministry of Finance (CTA 80(12)(b)).

**Forms**: T652: Notice of revocation of waiver.

**(4.2) [Reassessment with taxpayer's consent]** — Notwithstanding subsections (4), (4.1) and (5), for the purpose of determining, at any time after the expiration of the normal reassessment period for a taxpayer who is an individual (other than a trust) or a testamentary trust in respect of a taxation year,

    (a) the amount of any refund to which the taxpayer is entitled at that time for that year, or

    (b) a reduction of an amount payable under this Part by the taxpayer for that year,

the Minister may, if application therefor has been made by the taxpayer,

    (c) reassess tax, interest or penalties payable under this Part by the taxpayer in respect of that year, and

    (d) redetermine the amount, if any, deemed by subsection 120(2) or (2.2), 122.5(3), 122.51(2), 127.1(1), 127.41(3) or 210.2(3) or (4) to be paid on account of the taxpayer's tax payable under this Part for the year or deemed by subsection 122.61(1) to be an overpayment on account of the taxpayer's liability under this Part for the year.

**Related Provisions**: 152(3.1) — Normal reassessment period; 152(4.3) — Consequential assessment; 164(1.5) — Refunds; 164(3.2) — Interest on refunds and repayments; 165(1.2) — Limitation of right to object; 225.1(1) — No collection restrictions following assessment.

**Notes**: Reference to 120(2.2) in 152(4.2)(d) added by 1999 Budget, effective for 1999 and later taxation years.

152(4.2) added by 1991 technical bill (as part of the "Fairness Package"), effective for assessments and redeterminations in respect of 1985 and later years. It permits the CCRA to reassess any year from 1985 on, at the taxpayer's request (for example, to allow a deduction or credit the taxpayer neglected to claim). Without this provision (and as still is the case for corporations), the CCRA has no jurisdiction to open up a return that is statute-barred under 152(4) even with the taxpayer's consent: *Canadian Marconi*, [1991] 2 C.T.C. 352 (FCA).

152(4.2)(d) amended by 1992 Child Benefit bill, effective for redeterminations made in respect of 1993 and later taxation years, to delete a reference to former 122.2(1), and by 1992 Economic Statement, effective 1993, to add references to 126.1. For redeterminations in respect of 1991 and 1992, read as follows:

    (d) redetermine the amount, if any, deemed by subsection 120(2), 120.1(4), 122.2(1), 122.5(3), 127.1(1), 144(9) or 210.2(3) or (4) to be paid on account of the taxpayer's tax under this Part for the year or deemed by subsection 119(2) or 122.61(1) to be an overpayment on account of the taxpayer's liability under this Part for the year.

Reference in 152(4.2)(d) to 127.41(3) added, and reference to 144(9) deleted, by 1994 Budget, effective for taxation years that end after February 22, 1994.

Reference to 122.51(2) added, and references to 119(2) and 126.1(6) and (7) deleted, by 1997 Budget, effective for the 1997 and later taxation years. Reference to 120.1(4) deleted by 1997 Budget effective for the 1998 and later taxation years.

**Information Circulars**: 75-7R3: Reassessment of a return of income; 92-3: Guidelines for refunds beyond the normal three year period.

**Application Policies**: SR&ED 94-01: Retroactive claims for scientific research (TPRs).

**(4.3) Consequential assessment** — Notwithstanding subsections (4), (4.1) and (5), where the result of an assessment or a decision on an appeal is to change a particular balance of a taxpayer for a particular taxation year, the Minister may, or where the taxpayer so requests in writing, shall, before the later of the expiration of the normal reassessment period in respect of a subsequent taxation year and the end of the day that is one year after the day on which all rights of objection and appeal expire or are determined in respect of the particular year, reassess the tax, interest or penalties payable, or redetermine an amount deemed to have been paid or to have been an overpayment, under this Part by the taxpayer in respect of the subsequent taxation year, but only to the extent that the reassessment or redetermination can reasonably be considered to relate to the change in the particular balance of the taxpayer for the particular year.

**Related Provisions**: 152(3.1) — Normal reassessment period; 152(4.4) — Definition of "balance"; 165(1.1) — Limitation of right to object to assessments or determinations; 169(2) — Limitation of right to appeal.

**Notes**: 152(4.3) added by 1992 technical bill, effective for reassessments and redeterminations made after June 10, 1993, where they relate to changes in balances for other taxation years that were made as a result of assessments made, or decisions on appeals rendered, after December 20, 1991. However, where the day referred to in the subsec. as "the day on which all rights of objection and appeal have expired or been determined in respect of the particular year" is before June 10, 1993, read that reference as a reference to June 10, 1993. (In other words, where all rights of objection and appeal with respect to the other year have expired or been determined before June 10, 1993, which was the date of Royal Assent to the 1992 technical bill, the one-year period for consequential reassessments or redeterminations with respect to preceding or subsequent taxation years did not start to run until that date.)

152(4.3) amended by 1993 technical bill, retroactive to its introduction (as described above), to limit its application to reassessments of taxation years that follow the year of adjustment, so that it cannot be used for reassessing preceding taxation years; and to allow the Minister to redetermine an amount deemed to have been an overpayment.

**(4.4) Definition of "balance"** — For the purpose of subsection (4.3), a "balance" of a taxpayer for a taxation year is the income, taxable income, taxable income earned in Canada or any loss of the taxpayer for the year, or the tax or other amount payable by, any amount refundable to, or any amount deemed to have been paid or to have been an overpayment by, the taxpayer for the year.

**Related Provisions**: 152(4.3) — Consequential assessment; 165(1.11)(b) — Balance adjustment to be requested specifically on large corporation's notice of objection.

**Notes**: 152(4.4) added by 1992 technical bill, effective on the same basis as 152(4.3). Amended by 1993 technical bill, retroactive to its introduction, to include reference to an overpayment.

**(5) Limitation on assessments** — There shall not be included in computing the income of a taxpayer for a taxation year, for the purpose of an assessment, reassessment or additional assessment made under this Part after the taxpayer's normal reassessment period in respect of the year, any amount that was not included in computing the taxpayer's income for the purpose of an assessment, reassessment or additional assessment made under this Part before the end of the period.

**Related Provisions**: 12(2.2) — Deemed outlay or expense; 67.5(2) — Reassessments; 110.4(6) — Forward averaging — death of a taxpayer; 127(17) — Assessment re ITC SR&ED pool beyond the deadline; 152(1.7) — Limitation period re determination of partnership income or loss; 152(3.1) — Normal reassessment period; 152(4.01) — Limitation on extended assessments; 152(4.2) — Assessment; 152(4.3) — Consequential assessment; 152(9) — Minister allowed to raise alternative ground of assessment; 160.2(3) — Minister may assess recipient under RRSP or RRIF; 161.1(7) — Late assessment to allow interest offset allocation.

**Notes**: Many provisions throughout the Act and its amending bills provide that assessments can be made "notwithstanding subsections 152(4) and (5)", thus overriding this rule.

152(5) amended by 1995-97 technical bill, retroactive to April 28, 1989, to delete paras. (b) and (c) and fold what was para. (a) into the body of the subsection. Paras. (b) and (c) are now covered in 152(4.01)(a)(i) and (ii). Paras. (b) and (c) had read:

(b) in respect of which the taxpayer establishes that the failure so to include it did not result from any misrepresentation that is attributable to negligence, carelessness or wilful default or from any fraud in filing a return of the taxpayer's income or supplying any information under this Act; and

(c) where any waiver has been filed by the taxpayer with the Minister, in the form and within the time referred to in subsection (4), with respect to a taxation year to which the reassessment, additional assessment or assessment of tax, interest or penalties, as the case may be, relates, that the taxpayer establishes cannot reasonably be regarded as relating to a matter specified in the waiver.

152(5) amended by 1989 Budget, effective April 28, 1989, other than for a taxation year for which an original notice of assessment (or notification that no tax is payable) was mailed by April 27, 1986. The normal reassessment period was 3 years before the amendment.

**I.T. Application Rules**: 62(1) (where waiver filed before December 23, 1971).

**Interpretation Bulletins**: IT-241: Reassessments made after the four-year limit.

**(6) Reassessment where certain deductions claimed [carrybacks]** — Where a taxpayer has filed for a particular taxation year the return of income required by section 150 and an amount is subsequently claimed by the taxpayer or on the taxpayer's behalf for the year as

(a) a deduction under paragraph 3(e) of the *Income Tax Act*, chapter 148 of the Revised Statutes of Canada, 1952, by virtue of the taxpayer's death in a subsequent taxation year and the consequent application of section 71 of that Act in respect of an allowable capital loss for the year,

(b) a deduction under section 41 in respect of the taxpayer's listed-personal-property loss for a subsequent taxation year,

(b.1) a deduction under paragraph 60(i) in respect of a premium (within the meaning assigned by subsection 146(1)) paid in a subsequent taxation year under a registered retirement savings plan where the premium is deductible by reason of subsection 146(6.1),

(c) a deduction under section 118.1 in respect of a gift made in a subsequent taxation year or under section 111 in respect of a loss for a subsequent taxation year,

(c.1) a deduction under subsection 126(2) in respect of an unused foreign tax credit (within the meaning assigned by subsection 126(7)) for a subsequent taxation year,

### Proposed Amendment — 152(6)(c.1)

(c.1) a deduction under section 119 in respect of a disposition in a subsequent taxation year,

**Application**: Bill C-43 (First Reading September 20, 2000), subsec. 91(1), will amend para. 152(6)(c.1) to read as above, applicable to taxation years that end after October 1, 1996. (The text of existing (c.1) is moved to (f.1) below.)

**Technical Notes**: A number of provisions of the Act allow a taxpayer to carry back amounts from one taxation year to reduce the taxpayer's income, taxable income or tax for a prior year. Where an amount is carried back under one of these provisions, subsection 152(6) of the Act directs the Minister of National Revenue to reassess the taxpayer's tax for the relevant year or years to take the carry-back into account.

Subsection 152(6) is amended to include in its list of carry-back provisions new section 119 and new subsections 126(2.21) and (2.22) and 128.1(8) of the Act. [See 152(6)(f.1), (f.2) below — ed.] These additions apply to taxation years that end after October 1, 1996. As well, a taxpayer who wishes to use the newly-added provisions will be deemed to have filed the prescribed form required under subsection 152(6) in a timely manner if the form is filed on or before the later of the normal deadline for filing the form and the taxpayer's filing-due date for the taxation year that includes the day on which Royal Assent for these amendments is received.

(d) a deduction under subsection 127(5) in respect of property acquired or an expenditure made in a subsequent taxation year,

(e) a deduction under subsection 125.2 in respect of an unused Part VI tax credit (within the meaning assigned by subsection 125.2(3)) for a subsequent taxation year,

(f) a deduction under section 125.3 in respect of an unused Part I.3 tax credit (within the meaning assigned by subsection 125.3(3)) for a subsequent taxation year,

### Proposed Addition — 152(6)(f.1), (f.2)

(f.1) a deduction under subsection 126(2) in respect of an unused foreign tax credit (within the meaning assigned by subsection 126(7)), or under subsection 126(2.21) or (2.22) in respect of foreign taxes paid, for a subsequent taxation year,

(f.2) a deduction under subsection 128.1(8) as a result of a disposition in a subsequent taxation year,

**Application**: Bill C-43 (First Reading September 20, 2000), subsec. 91(2), will add paras. 152(6)(f.1) and (f.2), applicable to taxation years that end after October 1, 1996.

In respect of

(a) a deduction under s. 119, or an adjustment under subsec. 128.1(8), in respect of a disposition by a taxpayer, or

(b) a deduction under subsec. 126(2.21) or (2.22) in respect of foreign taxes paid by a taxpayer,

the taxpayer is deemed to have filed a prescribed form described in subsec. 152(6) in a timely manner if the taxpayer files the form with the Minister on or before the later of the day on or before which the taxpayer would, but for this application, be required to file the form and the taxpayer's filing-due date for the taxation year that includes the day on which the amending legislation is assented to.

**Technical Notes**: See under 152(6)(c.1).

(g) a deduction under subsection 147.2(4) because of the application of subsection 147.2(6) as a result of the taxpayer's death in the subsequent taxation year, or

(h) a deduction by virtue of an election for a subsequent taxation year under paragraph 164(6)(c) or (d) by the taxpayer's legal representative,

by filing with the Minister, on or before the day on or before which the taxpayer is, or would be if a tax under this Part were payable by the taxpayer for that subsequent taxation year, required by section 150 to file a return of income for that subsequent taxation year, a prescribed form amending the return, the Minister shall reassess the taxpayer's tax for any relevant taxation year (other than a taxation year preceding the particular taxation year) in order to take into account the deduction claimed.

**Related Provisions**: 111 — Losses deductible; 150 — Returns; 160.2(3) — Minister may assess recipient under RRSP or RRIF; 161(7)(b)(iii) — Effect of carryback of loss, etc.; 164(5), (5.1) — No back interest on refund where past year reassessed; 165(1.1) — Limitation of right to object to assessments or determinations; 169(2)(a) — Limitation of right to appeal.

**Notes**: 152(6)(b.1) added by 1990 pension bill, effective 1991.

152(6)(f) added by 1989 Budget, effective for taxation years ending after June 1989.

152(6)(g) added by 1995-97 technical bill, effective for deaths after 1992.

**I.T. Application Rules**: 69 (meaning of "*Income Tax Act*, chapter 148 of the Revised Statutes of Canada, 1952").

**Interpretation Bulletins**: IT-124R6: Contributions to registered retirement savings plans; IT-232R3: Losses — their deductibility in the loss year or in other years; IT-520: Unused foreign tax credits — carryforward and carryback.

**Information Circulars**: 75-7R3: Reassessment of a return of income.

**Forms**: T1ADJ: Adjustment request; T2 SCH 4: Corporation loss continuity and application; T67B, T67BCD, T67BD, T458, T459, T493: Notices of reassessment.

S. 152(6.1) — Income Tax Act, Part I

## Proposed Addition — 152(6.1)

**(6.1) Reassessment where amount included in income under subsec. 91(1) is reduced** — Where

(a) a taxpayer has filed for a particular taxation year the return of income required by section 150,

(b) the amount included in computing the taxpayer's income for the particular year under subsection 91(1) is subsequently reduced because of a reduction in the foreign accrual property income of a foreign affiliate of the taxpayer for a taxation year of the affiliate that ends in the particular year and is

(i) attributable to the amount prescribed to be the deductible loss of the affiliate for the year that arose in a subsequent year of the affiliate that ends in a subsequent taxation year of the taxpayer, and

(ii) included in the description of F of the definition "foreign accrual property income" in subsection 95(1) in respect of the affiliate for the year, and

(c) the taxpayer has filed with the Minister, on or before the filing-due-date for the taxpayer's subsequent taxation year, a prescribed form amending the return,

the Minister shall reassess the taxpayer's tax for any relevant taxation year (other than a taxation year preceding the particular taxation year) in order to take into account the reduction in the amount included under subsection 91(1) in computing the income of the taxpayer for the year.

**Application**: Bill C-43 (First Reading September 20, 2000), subsec. 91(3), will add subsec. 152(6.1) to read as above, applicable to taxation years of foreign affiliates that begin after November 1999.

**Technical Notes**: New subsection 152(6.1) of the Act is consequential to the extension of the deductible loss carryover period for foreign accrual property losses in the description of F in the definition "foreign accrual property income" in subsection 95(1) and section 5903 of the Regulations. Subsection 152(6.1) provides for the reassessment of all relevant taxation years (other than taxation years preceding the particular taxation year) where the taxpayer has filed a prescribed form carrying back a deductible loss from a subsequent taxation year that reduces the taxpayer's income for the particular year under subsection 91(1).

**Related Provisions**: Reg. 5903(1) — Loss carryback.

**(7) Assessment not dependent on return or information** — The Minister is not bound by a return or information supplied by or on behalf of a taxpayer and, in making an assessment, may, notwithstanding a return or information so supplied or if no return has been filed, assess the tax payable under this Part.

**Related Provisions**: 152(4) — Reassessment; 160.2(3) — Minister may assess recipient under RRSP or RRIF; 165 — Objections to assessments; 169 — Appeal to Tax Court of Canada.

**Notes**: The CCRA will make what it calls a "net worth" assessment of a taxpayer who is found to have significant assets without a satisfactory explanation as to the source of income. 152(7) confirms that this can be done with cheerful disregard for whatever the taxpayer reported on his or her return. See, for example, *Biron*, [1985] 1 C.T.C. 2014 (TCC). The onus remains on the taxpayer to disprove the assessment, as clearly established by the case law (e.g., *Johnston (R.W.S.)*, [1948] C.T.C. 195 (SCC)). Nevertheless, the Minister may be required to prove that the audit work was done properly: *Huyen*, [1997] G.S.T.C. 42 (TCC).

**(8) Assessment deemed valid and binding** — An assessment shall, subject to being varied or vacated on an objection or appeal under this Part and subject to a reassessment, be deemed to be valid and binding notwithstanding any error, defect or omission in the assessment or in any proceeding under this Act relating thereto.

**Related Provisions**: 152(3) — Liability for tax not affected by incorrect or incomplete assessment; 152(4) — Reassessment; 158 — Assessed amount payable forthwith; 160(2) — Minister may assess transferee; 160.2(3) — Minister may assess recipient; 165 — Objections to assessments; 166 — Assessment not to be vacated by reason of improper procedures; 172 — Appeal; 225.1 — Collection restrictions while assessment under objection or appeal.

**(9) Alternative basis for assessment** — The Minister may advance an alternative argument in support of an assessment at any time after the normal reassessment period unless, on an appeal under this Act

(a) there is relevant evidence that the taxpayer is no longer able to adduce without the leave of the court; and

(b) it is not appropriate in the circumstances for the court to order that the evidence be adduced.

**Related Provisions**: 152(5) — Limitation on income inclusion after normal reassessment period.

**Notes**: 152(9) added by 1998 Budget bill, effective for appeals disposed of after June 17, 1999. It overturns the Supreme Court of Canada's ruling in *Continental Bank of Canada*, [1997] 4 C.T.C. 77, that the Crown is not permitted to advance a new basis for assessment after the limitation period has expired. For further discussion see Patrick Bendin, "Challenging and Defending Assessments before the Tax Court of Canada and Appellate Courts: A Postscript to the *Continental Bank* Case", 48(1) *Canadian Tax Journal* 35-59 (2000).

Note that 152(9) is subject to 152(5), which generally prevents the inclusion of amounts in income that were not included before the expiration of the normal reassessment period.

**I.T. Technical News**: No. 16 (*Continental Bank* case).

## Proposed Addition — 152(10)

**(10) Where tax deemed not to be assessed** — Notwithstanding any other provision of this section, an amount of tax for which adequate security is accepted by the Minister under subsection 220(4.5) or (4.6) is, until the end of the period during which the security is accepted by the Minister, deemed for the purpose of any agreement entered into by or on behalf of the Government of Canada under section 7 of the *Federal-Provincial*

*Fiscal Arrangements Act* not to have been assessed under this Act.

**Application**: Bill C-43 (First Reading September 20, 2000), subsec. 91(4), will add subsec. 152(10), applicable to taxation years that end after October 1, 1996.

**Technical Notes**: New subsection 152(10) provides that an amount of tax for which adequate security is accepted by the Minister of National Revenue under subsection 220(4.5) or (4.6) of the Act shall not be treated as an amount assessed under the Act, for the period during which such security is accepted, for the purpose of any agreement entered into by the federal government under section 7 of the *Federal-Provincial Fiscal Arrangements Act*.

**Definitions [s. 152]**: "allowable capital loss" — 38(b), 248(1); "amount", "assessment" — 248(1); "balance" — 152(4.4); "Canadian-controlled private corporation" — 125(7), 248(1); "farm loss" — 111(8), 248(1); "foreign accrual property income" — 95(1), (2), 248(1); "foreign affiliate" — 95(1), 248(1); "limited partnership loss" — 96(2.1)(e), 248(1); "listed personal property" — 54, 248(1); "Minister" — 248(1); "net capital loss", "non-capital loss" — 111(8), 248(1); "non-resident" — 248(1); "normal reassessment period" — 152(3.1); "person", "prescribed", "property" — 248(1); "province" — *Interpretation Act* 35(1); "registered retirement savings plan" — 146(1), 248(1); "restricted farm loss" — 31, 248(1); "tax consequences" — 152(1.111), 245(1); "taxable income" — 2(2), 248(1); "taxable income earned in Canada" — 115(1), 248(1); "taxation year" — 249; "taxpayer" — 248(1); "testamentary trust" — 248(1); "transaction" — 152(1.111), 245(1); "trust" — 104(1), 108(1), 248(1), (3); "writing" — *Interpretation Act* 35(1).

## Payment of Tax

**153. (1) Withholding** — Every person paying at any time in a taxation year

(a) salary or wages or other remuneration,

(b) a superannuation or pension benefit,

(c) a retiring allowance,

(d) a death benefit,

(d.1) an amount described in subparagraph 56(1)(a)(iv),

(e) an amount as a benefit under a supplementary unemployment benefit plan,

(f) an annuity payment or a payment in full or partial commutation of an annuity,

(g) fees, commissions or other amounts for services,

(h) a payment under a deferred profit sharing plan or a plan referred to in section 147 as a revoked plan,

(i) [Repealed]

(j) a payment out of or under a registered retirement savings plan or a plan referred to in subsection 146(12) as an "amended plan",

(k) an amount as, on account or in lieu of payment of, or in satisfaction of, proceeds of the surrender, cancellation or redemption of an income-averaging annuity contract,

(l) a payment out of or under a registered retirement income fund or a fund referred to in subsection 146.3(11) as an "amended fund",

(m) a prescribed benefit under a government assistance program;

(m.1) [Repealed]

(n) one or more amounts to an individual who has elected for the year in prescribed form in respect of all such amounts,

(o) an amount described in paragraph 115(2)(c.1),

(p) a contribution under a retirement compensation arrangement,

(q) an amount as a distribution to one or more persons out of or under a retirement compensation arrangement,

(r) an amount on account of the purchase price of an interest in a retirement compensation arrangement,

(s) an amount described in paragraph 56(1)(r), or

(t) a payment made under a plan that was a registered education savings plan

shall deduct or withhold therefrom such amount as is determined in accordance with prescribed rules and shall, at such time as is prescribed, remit that amount to the Receiver General on account of the payee's tax for the year under this Part or Part XI.3, as the case may be, and, where at that prescribed time the person is a prescribed person, the remittance shall be made to the account of the Receiver General at a financial institution (within the meaning that would be assigned by the definition "financial institution" in subsection 190(1) if that definition were read without reference to paragraphs (1)'financial institution'(d) and (1)'financial institution'(e) thereof).

**Proposed Amendment — 153(1) closing words**

shall deduct or withhold from the payment the amount determined in accordance with prescribed rules and shall, at the prescribed time, remit that amount to the Receiver General on account of the payee's tax for the year under this Part or Part XI.3, as the case may be, and, where at that prescribed time the person is a prescribed person, the remittance shall be made to the account of the Receiver General at a designated financial institution.

**Application**: The August 8, 2000 draft legislation, subsec. 14(1), will amend the closing words of subsec. 153(1) to read as above, applicable after June 27, 1999.

**Technical Notes**: Section 153 of the Act authorizes the withholding of tax from certain payments, described in paragraphs 153(1)(a) to (t). The person making such a payment is required to remit the amount withheld to the Receiver General on behalf of the payee. Certain prescribed persons can make that remittance by depositing the withheld amount to the Receiver General's account at certain financial institutions, defined by reference to subsection 190(1).

## S. 153(1) — Income Tax Act, Part I

Section 153 is amended to change the special purpose definition of financial institution with a reference to the new term "designated financial institution", which is defined in new subsection 153(6) of the Act. The language of the subsection is also updated, without changing its effect.

This amendment applies after June 27, 1999.

**Related Provisions**: 7(15) — No withholding required on inclusion of deferred stock option benefit; 78(1)(b) — Withholding of tax on unpaid amounts; 153(1.1) — Undue hardship — reduction in withholding; 153(1.2) — Election to increase withholding; 153(1.3) — Payments of tax by trustee; 153(3) — Amount withheld deemed received by payee; 153(6) — Meaning of "designated financial institution"; 154 — Tax transfer payments to provinces; 221.2 — Transfers of balances from one account to other; 227 — Withholding taxes — administration and enforcement; 227.1 — Corporation's directors liable for unremitted source deductions; 238(1) — Offences; 248(7)(b)(i) — Remittance deemed made when received; 252.1(d) — Where union is employer; Canada-U.S. tax treaty, Art. XVII — Withholding of taxes in respect of personal services.

**Notes**: Once an amount is withheld and a net salary paid, the amount is credited to the employee's account for T1 filing purposes even if the employer never remits it: *Manke*, [1999] 1 C.T.C. 2186 (TCC). However, if there was no obligation to remit because the taxpayer was an independent contractor, the taxpayer will receive no credit for such unremitted amounts: *Liu*, [1995] 2 C.T.C. 2971D (TCC).

Due to the extended definition of "salary and wages" in 248(1), which covers all employment income, 153(1)(a) applies to all taxable employment benefits (e.g., employee benefit plan benefits under 6(1)(g), or stock option benefits taxable under s. 7, except where deferred under 7(15)).

See Reg. 105 re withholding on fees and commissions paid to non-residents who are not employees.

See 227 for the rules that apply to source withholdings, including their being held in trust for the Crown.

153(1)(d.1) amended by 1995-97 technical bill effective June 30, 1996, to change a reference to the *Employment Insurance Act* to refer to 56(1)(a)(iv) instead. This effectively re-applies the rule to the *Unemployment Insurance Act*, which is still in force in respect of past periods.

153(1)(f) amended by 1991 technical bill, effective July 14, 1990, to add "a payment in full or partial commutation of an annuity".

153(1)(l) amended by 1991 technical bill, effective July 14, 1990, to add reference to an amended fund.

153(1)(m) amended by 1993 technical bill, effective for payments made after October 1991, replacing 153(1)(m) and (m.1), which formerly read:

(m) an amount as a benefit under the *Labour Adjustment Benefits Act*,

(m.1) an income assistance payment made pursuant to an agreement under section 5 of the *Department of Labour Act*,

153(1)(m.1) added by 1991 technical bill, effective September 15, 1989, to deal with income assistance for eligible workers under the Program for Older Worker Adjustment. It was repealed because it is now covered under 153(1)(m) as a "prescribed benefit". See 56(1)(a)(vi).

153(1)(s) added by 1997 Budget, effective for payments made after 1992.

153(1)(t) added by 1997 Budget, effective for payments made after 1997. See Reg. 100(1)"remuneration"(n), 103(6)(g) and 103(8).

Closing words of 153(1) amended by 1992 technical bill, effective 1993, to add the portion beginning "and, where at that prescribed time". The change forces large employers (see Reg. 110) to remit source withholdings through a financial institution. This prevents them from bringing a cheque to a CCRA office late on the due date (and too late for the funds to get to the bank that day), which would give them an extra day's (or weekend's) interest on the funds.

**Regulations**: 100–108 (withholding and remittance requirements); 110 (prescribed persons for the closing words of 153(1)); 200 (information returns); 5502 (prescribed benefits for 153(1)(m)).

**Interpretation Bulletins**: IT-337R3: Retiring allowances; IT-379R: Employees profit sharing plans — allocations to beneficiaries.

**Information Circulars**: 75-6R: Required withholding from amounts paid to non-resident persons performing services in Canada; 72-22R9: Registered retirement savings plans; 92-3: Guidelines for refunds beyond the normal three year period. See also "Employers' Guide to Payroll Deductions".

**I.T. Technical News**: No. 11 (reporting of amounts paid out of an employee benefit plan).

**Forms**: PD20: Employer registration; RC4157(E): Employers' guide: — filing the T4A slip and summary form; RC4163: Employers' guide — remitting payroll deductions; TD3F: Fisherman's election for tax deductions at source; T4A Supp: Statement of pension, retirement, annuity and other income; T4A: Segment; T4A Summ: Summary of remuneration paid (pension, retirement, annuity, and other income); T4 Segment; T4A-RCA Summ: Return of distributions from an RCA; T4A-RCA Supp: Statement of amounts paid from an RCA; T619: Magnetic media transmittal; T695: T4A/T4A-NR data tape transmittal; T735: Application for a remittance number for tax withheld from an RCA; T1213: Request to reduce tax deductions at source; T4001: Employer's guide to payroll deductions — Basic information [guide]; T4032: Payroll deductions tables [guide]; T4127: Payroll deductions formulas for computer programs [guide]; T4130: Employer's guide to payroll deductions — taxable benefits [guide]; T5 filing transmittal; TD1: personal tax credits return.

### (1.1) Undue hardship

Where the Minister is satisfied that the deducting or withholding of the amount otherwise required to be deducted or withheld under subsection (1) from a payment would cause undue hardship, the Minister may determine a lesser amount and that amount shall be deemed to be the amount determined under that subsection as the amount to be deducted or withheld from that payment.

**Related Provisions**: 180.2(6) — Reduced withholding available on old age security benefits; 227(8) — Withholding taxes; 227.1 — Liability of directors.

**Notes**: An application for reduction of withholding is made to the local Tax Services Office and will be considered on a case-by-case basis. The request may be accepted for a variety of reasons, including that the income will be exempt under 110(1)(f)(i) due to a tax treaty, or that the individual receiving the income will have substantially reduced tax due to medical expenses, RRSP contributions or charitable donations. The CCRA does not, in practice, require a demonstration of any actual "hardship" beyond the fact that the taxpayer will be owed a refund after filing a return. (This practice was strongly criticized in the Auditor General's May 1996 report, at paras. 11.71–11.76.) Form T1213, introduced in July 2000, should be used.

Reduction or waiver of withholding will be allowed to federal government pay equity settlement recipients for up to $10,000 that is contributed to an RRSP for the year in which it is received. See "Reduction of tax withholding on lump-sum employment income payments — Information Notice", on the Treasury Board web site at www.tbs-sct.gc.ca/wnew/PayEquity/info_tax_e.html.

**Forms**: T1213: Request to reduce tax deductions at source for year(s) ___.

**(1.2) Election to increase withholding** — Where a taxpayer so elects in prescribed manner and prescribed form, the amount required to be deducted or withheld under subsection (1) from any payment to the taxpayer shall be deemed to be the total of

(a) the amount, if any, otherwise required to be deducted or withheld under that subsection from that payment, and

(b) the amount specified by the taxpayer in that election with respect to that payment or with respect to a class of payments that includes that payment.

**Related Provisions**: 227.1 — Liability of directors.

**Notes**: The CCRA issued a notice in January 2000 suggesting that taxpayers receiving Canada Pension Plan benefits may wish to use this provision to have tax withheld from the benefits.

**Regulations**: 109 (prescribed manner for making election, and effect).

**Forms**: TD3: Request for income tax deductions on non-employment income.

**(1.3), (1.4) [Repealed]**

**Notes**: 153(1.3) and (1.4) repealed by 1995 Budget, effective for payments made after June 20, 1996. They have been replaced by more general rules in 227(5)–(5.2). Section 227 consolidates all the administrative rules relating to withholding taxes. 153(1.3) and (1.4) formerly read:

(1.3) Payments by trustee, etc. — For the purposes of subsection (1), where a trustee who is administering, managing, distributing, winding up, controlling or otherwise dealing with the property, business, estate or income of another person authorizes or otherwise causes a payment referred to in that subsection to be made on behalf of that other person, the trustee shall be deemed to be a person making the payment and the trustee and that other person shall be jointly and severally liable in respect of the amount required under that subsection to be deducted or withheld and to be remitted on account of the payment.

(1.4) Definition of "trustee" — In subsection (1.3), "trustee" includes a liquidator, receiver, receiver-manager, trustee in bankruptcy, assignee, executor, administrator, sequestrator or any other person performing a function similar to that performed by any such person.

**(2) [Repealed]**

**Notes**: 153(2) repealed by 1993 Budget, effective 1995. The new determination of the threshold for instalments being required is in amended 156.1. For the 1994 taxation year, read:

(2) Payment of remainder — Subject to sections 155, 156 and 156.1, where amounts have been deducted or withheld under this section from the remuneration or other payments received by an individual in a taxation year, if the total of the remuneration and other payments from which such amounts have been deducted or withheld and which the individual had received in the year is equal to or greater than ¾ of the individual's income for the year, the individual shall, on or before the individual's balance-due day for the year, pay to the Receiver General the remainder of the individual's tax for the year as estimated under section 151.

For 1990 through 1993 taxation years, read:

(2) Where amounts were deducted or withheld under this section from the remuneration or other payments received by an individual in a taxation year, if the total of the remuneration and other payments from which the amounts were deducted or withheld and which the individual received in the year is equal to or greater than ¾ of the individual's income for the year, the individual shall, on or before the individual's balance-due day for the year, pay to the Receiver General the remainder of the individual's tax for the year as estimated under section 151.

153(2) amended by 1991 technical bill, effective 1990, to refer to the "balance-due day" rather than April 30. The balance-due day (defined in 248(1)) corresponded before 1995 to the return deadline under 150(1).

**Forms**: T7DR: Remittance form.

**(3) Deemed effect of deduction** — When an amount has been deducted or withheld under subsection (1), it shall, for all the purposes of this Act, be deemed to have been received at that time by the person to whom the remuneration, benefit, payment, fees, commissions or other amounts were paid.

**Related Provisions**: 78(1)(b) — Unpaid amounts; 227 — Withholding taxes — rules; 227.1 — Liability of directors.

**Notes**: Draft 153(3.1), "Amounts withheld under Part I.2", was included in the drafts of the 1995 Budget legislation released on July 19 and December 12, 1995. It was deleted from the revised draft of March 28, 1996 which was enacted as 1996, c. 21. It has been replaced with amendments to 156.1(1)"net tax owing", which include Part I.2 in the base for instalment calculations.

**(4) Unclaimed dividends, interest and proceeds** — Where at the end of a taxpayer's taxation year the person beneficially entitled to an amount received by the taxpayer after 1984 and before the year as or in respect of dividends, interest or proceeds of disposition of property is unknown to the taxpayer, the taxpayer shall remit to the Receiver General on or before the day that is 60 days after the end of the year on account of the tax payable under this Act by that person an amount equal to

(a) in the case of dividends, $33\frac{1}{3}\%$ of the total amount of the dividends,

(b) in the case of interest, 50% of the total amount of the interest, and

(c) in the case of proceeds of disposition of property, 50% of the total of all amounts each of which is the amount, if any, by which the proceeds of disposition of a property exceed the total of any outlays and expenses made or incurred by the taxpayer for the purpose of disposing of the property (to the extent that those outlays and expenses were not deducted in computing the taxpayer's income for any taxation year or attributable to any other property),

except that no remittance under this subsection shall be required in respect of an amount that was included in computing the taxpayer's income for the year or a preceding taxation year or in respect of an amount on which the tax under this subsection was previously remitted.

**Related Provisions**: 153(5) — Effect of deduction; 227.1 — Liability of directors.

**Regulations**: 108(4) (remittance deadline).

**Interpretation Bulletins**: IT-67R3: Taxable dividends from corporations resident in Canada.

**Information Circulars**: 71-9R: Unclaimed dividends.

**(5) Deemed effect of remittance** — An amount remitted by a taxpayer under subsection (4) in respect of dividends, interest or proceeds of disposition of property shall be deemed

(a) to have been received by the person beneficially entitled thereto; and

(b) to have been deducted or withheld from the amount otherwise payable by the taxpayer to the person entitled thereto.

**Related Provisions**: 227(6), (9) — Withholding taxes; 227(10) — Assessment; 227(13) — Withholding tax; 227.1 — Liability of directors.

### Proposed Addition — 153(6)

**(6) Meaning of "designated financial institution"** — In this section, "designated financial institution" means a corporation that

(a) is a bank, other than an authorized foreign bank that is subject to the restrictions and requirements referred to in subsection 524(2) of the *Bank Act*;

(b) is authorized under the laws of Canada or a province to carry on the business of offering its services as a trustee to the public; or

(c) is authorized under the laws of Canada or a province to accept deposits from the public and carries on the business of lending money on the security of real estate or investing in mortgages on real estate.

**Application**: The August 8, 2000 draft legislation, subsec. 14(2), will add subsec. 153(6), applicable after June 27, 1999.

**Technical Notes**: New subsection 153(6) defines the term "designated financial institution", which is used in subsection 153(1), as a bank (other than an authorized foreign bank subject to the restrictions in subsection 524(2) of the *Bank Act* — i.e. one which operates as a so-called lending branch), a trust company and a deposit-taking mortgage lender. The definition effectively includes only those authorized foreign banks that operate a so-called full-service branch in Canada.

**Notice of Ways and Means Motion (authorized foreign banks), February 11, 1999**: (11) That an authorized foreign bank that is subject to the restrictions and requirements referred to in subsection 524(2) of the *Bank Act* not be permitted to accept remittances made to the account of the Receiver General under section 153 of the Act.

**Department of Finance news release, February 11, 1999**: *Remittance of Withholding Amounts*

Taxpayers may pay taxes owing under the *Income Tax Act* in respect of most types of income by making a remittance to the account of the Receiver General at a bank or other financial institution. This service is permitted to facilitate the payment of income taxes.

It is proposed that the Canadian branch of a foreign bank be permitted to accept tax payments on behalf of the Receiver General of Canada in the same manner as Canadian resident banks unless the foreign bank is subject to the restrictions and requirements (relating primarily to deposit-taking) referred to in subsection 524(2) of the *Bank Act*.

**Related Provisions**: 153(1) closing words — Large remittances to be made through designated financial institution.

**Notes**: Under the closing words of 153(1), large employers (see Reg. 108(1.1)) must make their remittances through a designated financial institution. This prevents them from delivering a cheque to the CCRA just before closing time on the due date, which would effectively give them an extra day's or weekend's interest on the money.

**Definitions [s. 153]**: "amount", "annuity", "authorized foreign bank", "balance-due day", "business" — 248(1); "Canada" — 255, *Interpretation Act* 35(1); "corporation" — 248(1), *Interpretation Act* 35(1); "death benefit" — 248(1); "deferred profit sharing plan" — 147(1), 248(1); "designated financial institution" — 153(6); "dividend", "employee" — 248(1); "estate" — 104(1), 248(1); "income-averaging annuity contract", "individual", "Minister", "person", "prescribed", "property" — 248(1); "province" — *Interpretation Act* 35(1); "registered education savings plan" — 146.1(1), 248(1); "registered retirement income fund" — 146.3(1), 248(1); "registered retirement savings plan" — 146(1), 248(1); "retirement compensation arrangement", "retiring allowance", "salary or wages" — 248(1); "security" — *Interpretation Act* 35(1); "superannuation or pension benefit" — 248(1); "supplementary unemployment benefit plan" — 145(1), 248(1); "tax payable" — 248(2); "tax treaty" — 248(1); "taxation year" — 249; "taxpayer" — 248(1); "trustee" — 153(1.4).

**154. (1) Agreements providing for tax transfer payments** — The Minister may, with the approval of the Governor in Council, enter into an agreement with the government of a province to provide for tax transfer payments and the terms and conditions relating to such payments.

**(2) Tax transfer payment** — Where, on account of the tax for a taxation year payable by an individual under this Part, an amount has been deducted or withheld under subsection 153(1) on the assumption that the individual was resident in a place other than the province in which the individual resided on the last day of the year, and the individual

(a) has filed a return of income for the year with the Minister,

(b) is liable to pay tax under this Part for the year, and

(c) is resident on the last day of the year in a province with which an agreement described in subsection (1) has been entered into,

the Minister may make a tax transfer payment to the government of the province not exceeding an amount equal to the product obtained by multiplying the amount or the total of the amounts so deducted or withheld by a prescribed rate.

**Notes**: 152(4)(a) amended by 1995-97 technical bill, effective for 1996 and later taxation years, to clarify that it is the Part I return that must be filed. For 1972-95, read "has filed a return under this Act".

**Regulations**: 3300 (prescribed rate is 40%).

**(3) Payment deemed received by individual** — Where, pursuant to an agreement entered into under subsection (1), an amount has been transferred by the Minister to the government of a province with respect to an individual, the amount shall, for all purposes of this Act, be deemed to have been received by the individual at the time the amount was transferred.

**(4) Payment deemed received by Receiver General** — Where, pursuant to an agreement entered into under subsection (1), an amount has been transferred by the government of a province to the Minister with respect to an individual, the amount shall, for all purposes of this Act, be deemed to have been received by the Receiver General on account of the individual's tax under this Part for the year in respect of which the amount was transferred.

**(5) Amount not to include refund** — In this section, an amount deducted or withheld does not include any refund made in respect of that amount.

**Related Provisions [s. 154]**: 228 — Applying payments under collection agreements.

**Definitions [s. 154]**: "amount" — 154(5), 248(1); "individual", "Minister", "prescribed" — 248(1); "province" — *Interpretation Act* 35(1); "taxation year" — 249.

**155. (1) [Instalments — ] Farmers and fishermen** — Subject to section 156.1, every individual whose chief source of income for a taxation year is farming or fishing shall, on or before December 31 in the year, pay to the Receiver General in respect of the year, ²/₃ of

(a) the amount estimated by the individual to be the tax payable under this Part by the individual for the year, or

(b) the individual's instalment base for the preceding taxation year.

**Related Provisions**: 31 — Loss from farming where farming not chief source of income; 104(23)(e) — Alternative rule for testamentary trust; 107(5.1) — Trust's gain on distribution to non-resident beneficiary does not increase instalment requirements; 128.1(5) — Deemed disposition on emigration does not increase instalment requirements; 151 — Estimate of tax; 156(1) — Other individuals; 156.1 — No instalment required; 161(2) — Interest on late or insufficient instalments; 161(4) — Limitation on interest — farmers and fishermen; 163.1 — Penalty for late or deficient instalments; 248(7) — Receipt of things mailed.

**Notes**: 155(1) amended by 1993 Budget, effective for 1994 and later taxation years. (See new 156.1.) For 1990 through 1993 taxation years, read:

(1) Subject to section 156.1, every individual whose chief source of income is farming or fishing, other than an individual to whom subsection 153(2) applies, shall pay to the Receiver General in respect of each taxation year

(a) on or before December 31 in the year, ²/₃ of

(i) the amount estimated by the individual to be the tax payable under this Part by the individual for the year, or

(ii) the individual's instalment base for the immediately preceding taxation year; and

(b) on or before the individual's balance-due day for the year, the remainder of the individual's tax as estimated under section 151.

155(1) amended by 1991 technical bill, effective 1990, to refer to the "balance-due day" rather than April 30. The balance-due day (defined in 248(1)) corresponds to the return deadline under 150(1).

**Forms**: T4F Summ: Summary of remuneration; T4F Supp: Statement of fishing income; T7B: Instalment guide for farmers and fishermen; T7B-3: Calculation of instalments on minimum tax (farmers and fishermen); T2042: Statement of farming income and expenses; T2121: Statement of fishing activities.

**(2) Definition of "instalment base"** — In this section, "instalment base" of an individual for a taxation year means the amount determined in prescribed manner to be the individual's instalment base for the year.

**Regulations**: 5300 (instalment base).

**Definitions [s. 155]**: "balance-due day" — 248(1); "farming", "fishing", "individual" — 248(1); "taxable income" — 2(2), 248(1); "taxation year" — 249.

**156. (1) [Instalments — ] Other individuals** — Subject to section 156.1, in respect of each taxation year every individual (other than one to whom section 155 applies for the year) shall pay to the Receiver General

(a) on or before March 15, June 15, September 15 and December 15 in the year, an amount equal to ¼ of

(i) the amount estimated by the individual to be the tax payable under this Part by the individual for the year, or

(ii) the individual's instalment base for the preceding taxation year, or

(b) on or before

(i) March 15 and June 15 in the year, an amount equal to ¼ of the individual's instalment base for the second preceding taxation year, and

(ii) September 15 and December 15 in the year, an amount equal to ½ of the amount, if any, by which

(A) the individual's instalment base for the preceding taxation year

exceeds

(B) ½ of the individual's instalment base for the second preceding taxation year.

**Related Provisions**: 104(23)(e) — Alternative rule for testamentary trust; 107(5.1) — Trust's gain on distribution to non-resident beneficiary does not increase instalment requirements; 128.1(5) — Deemed disposition on emigration does not increase instalment requirements; 156.1(2) — No instalment required; 156.1(4) — Payment of balance by April 30; 161(2) — Interest on instalments; 161(4.01) — Minimum instalment payments to avoid interest charges; 163.1 — Penalty for late or deficient instalments; 248(7) — Receipt of things mailed.

**Notes**: Under s. 33 of the *Canada Pension Plan*, instalments for CPP contributions on self-employed earnings are due on the same basis as those for income tax. In practice, the instalment requirement for CPP contributions is simply added to that for income tax, with a single remittance made to Revenue Canada.

For provinces other than Quebec, instalments of provincial tax are required on the same basis as under section 156. (See, for example, s. 13 of the Ontario *Income Tax Act*, reproduced in *The Practitioner's Ontario Taxes, Annotated*.) Again, in practice the provincial instalment is simply combined with the federal instalment and a single payment made to the CCRA.

## S. 156(1) — Income Tax Act, Part I

Opening words of 156(1) amended by 1993 Budget, effective for amounts that become payable after June 1994. For earlier amounts, read:

> (1) Subject to section 156.1, every individual, other than one to whom subsection 153(2) or section 155 applies, shall pay to the Receiver General in respect of each taxation year

Closing words of 156(1) repealed by 1993 Budget, effective for the 1994 and later taxation years, as 156.1(4) now requires payment of the balance by the balance-due day. For earlier years, read:

> and, on or before the individual's balance-due day for the year, the remainder of the individual's tax estimated under section 151.

156(1)(b) added by 1992 technical bill, effective 1992. It provides a third option for instalment remittances. Instalments may be based on the estimated tax for the year (subpara. (a)(i)), the actual tax for the preceding year (subpara. (a)(ii)), or the method in para. (b), which uses the second-preceding year for the March and June instalments and the preceding year for the September and December instalments (with adjustments to correct for overpayment or underpayment in March and June, so that the total instalments for the year equal the tax for the preceding year). Revenue Canada mails notices of instalment requirements to taxpayers each quarter using the method in para. (b); of course, taxpayers who wish to use one of the other methods need not pay the amounts in the notices. However, interest under 161(4.01) will apply if the taxpayer gets it wrong, and possibly a penalty under 163.1.

156(1) amended by 1991 technical bill, effective 1990, to refer to the "balance-due day" rather than April 30. The balance-due day (defined in 248(1)) corresponded before 1995 to the return deadline under 150(1).

156(1) amended by 1988 tax reform, effective 1990. For earlier years, the deadline was the last day (rather than the 15th) of March, June, September and December.

**Forms:** P110: Paying your income tax by instalments (pamphlet); T7B: Instalment guide for individuals; T7B-2: Calculation of instalments on minimum tax; T1033-WS: Worksheet for calculating instalment payments.

**(2) Payment by mutual fund trusts** — Notwithstanding subsection (1), the amount payable by a mutual fund trust to the Receiver General on or before any day referred to in paragraph (1)(a) in a taxation year shall be deemed to be the amount, if any, by which

(a) the amount so payable otherwise determined under that subsection,

exceeds

(b) ¼ of the trust's capital gains refund (within the meaning assigned by section 132) for the year.

**Related Provisions:** 156.1 — No instalment required.

**(3) Definition of "instalment base"** — In this section, "instalment base" of an individual for a taxation year means the amount determined in prescribed manner to be the individual's instalment base for the year.

**Related Provisions:** 120(2) — Deemed payment of tax; 161(2) — Interest on instalments; 161(4) — Limitation of instalment base.

**Regulations:** 5300 (instalment base).

**Definitions [s. 156]:** "amount", "balance-due day" — 248(1); "individual" — 248(1); "instalment base" — 156(3), Reg. 5300(1); "mutual fund trust" — 132(6); "share" — 248(1); "taxable income" — 2(2), 248(1); "taxation year" — 249.

---

**156.1 (1) [Instalments exemption — ] Definitions** — For the purposes of this section,

**"instalment threshold"** of an individual for a taxation year means

(a) in the case of an individual resident in the Province of Quebec at the end of the year, $1,200, and

(b) in any other case, $2,000;

**Notes:** The $2,000 includes provincial tax collected by Revenue Canada for all provinces other than Quebec; see B in "net tax owing" below, and Notes at end of 156.1.

**"net tax owing"** by an individual for a taxation year means

(a) in the case of an individual resident in the Province of Quebec at the end of the year, the amount determined by the formula

$$A - C - D - F$$

and

(b) in any other case, the amount determined by the formula

$$A + B - C - E - F$$

where

A is the total of the taxes payable under this Part and Parts I.1, I.2 and X.5 by the individual for the year,

> **Proposed Amendment — 156.1(1)"net tax owing"(b)A**
>
> A is the total of the taxes payable under this Part and Parts I.2 and X.5 by the individual for the year,
>
> **Application:** The December 21, 2000 draft legislation, s. 83, will amend the description of A in para. (b) of the definition "net tax owing" in subsec. 156.1(1) to read as above, applicable to 2001 et seq.
>
> **Technical Notes:** Subsection 156(1) sets out definitions that are relevant in determining whether an individual is required to make tax instalments. The amendment to the definition "net tax owing" is strictly consequential on the repeal of the surtax imposed on individuals under Part I.1 (see commentary on that Part).

B is the total of all income taxes payable by the individual for the year under any law of a province or of an Aboriginal government with which the Minister of Finance has entered into an agreement for the collection of income taxes payable by individuals to the province or Aboriginal government under that law,

C is the total of the taxes deducted or withheld under section 153 and Part I.2 on behalf of the individual for the year,

D is the amount determined under subsection 120(2) in respect of the individual for the year,

E is the total of all amounts deducted or withheld on behalf of the individual for the year under a law of a province or of an Aboriginal government with which the Minister of Finance has entered into an agreement for the collection of income taxes payable by individuals to the province or Aboriginal government under that law, and

F is the amount determined under subsection 120(2.2) in respect of the individual for the year.

**Related Provisions**: 156.1(1) — Rules for calculating formula elements A and B; 156.1(1.2) — Rule for calculating D; 156.1(1.3) — Rule for calculating F — First Nations Tax; 257 — Formulas cannot calculate to less than zero.

**Notes**: 156.1(1)"net tax owing"(b) amended by 1999 Budget, effective for 1999 and later taxation years, to add formula element F (see also 156(1.3)) and references to Aboriginal governments (in B and E).

Reference to Part X.5 added to description of A by 1997 Budget, effective for 1998 and later taxation years.

Formula elements A and C in 156.1(1)"net tax owing" amended to add references to Part I.2 by 1995 Budget, effective for 1996 and later taxation years, except that, for the 1996 taxation year, read A as follows:

> A is the total of
> 
> (i) the taxes payable under this Part and Part I.1 by the individual for the year, and
> 
> (ii) half the tax payable under Part I.2 by the individual for the year,

Closing words of definition repealed by 1996 Budget, effective for amounts payable in 1996 or later. These rules were moved to 156.1(1.1) and (1.2). For earlier amounts, read:

> and for the purposes of this definition, income taxes payable for a taxation year by an individual are determined after deducting all tax credits to which the individual is entitled for the year relating to those taxes (other than tax credits that become payable to the individual after the individual's balance-due day for the year and prescribed tax credits) and before taking into consideration amounts referred to in subparagraphs 161(7)(a)(ii) to (v).

See also Notes at end of 156.1.

**Forms**: P110: Paying your income tax by instalments (pamphlet); T7B: Instalment guide for individuals.

**(1.1) Values of A and B in "net tax owing"** — For the purposes of determining the values of A and B in the definition "net tax owing" in subsection (1), income taxes payable by an individual for a taxation year are determined

(a) before taking into consideration the specified future tax consequences for the year; and

(b) after deducting all tax credits to which the individual is entitled for the year relating to those taxes (other than tax credits that become payable to the individual after the individual's balance-due day for the year, prescribed tax credits and amounts deemed to have been paid because of the application of either subsection 120(2) or (2.2)).

**Notes**: 156.1(1.1)(b) amended by 1999 Budget, effective for 1999 and later taxation years, to add reference to 120(2.2).

156(1.1) added by 1996 Budget, effective for amounts payable in 1996 or later. For earlier years, see the closing words of 156.1(1)"net tax owing".

**(1.2) Value of D in "net tax owing"** — For the purpose of determining the value of D in the definition "net tax owing" in subsection (1), the amount deemed by subsection 120(2) to have been paid on account of an individual's tax under this Part for a taxation year is determined before taking into consideration the specified future tax consequences for the year.

**Notes**: 156(1.2) added by 1996 Budget, effective for amounts payable in 1996 or later. For earlier years, see the closing words of 156.1(1)"net tax owing".

**(1.3) Value of F in "net tax owing"** — For the purpose of determining the value of F in the definition "net tax owing" in subsection (1), the amount deemed by subsection 120(2.2) to have been paid on account of an individual's tax under this Part for a taxation year is determined before taking into consideration the specified future tax consequences for the year.

**Notes**: 156.1(1.3) added by 1999 Budget, effective for 1999 and later taxation years.

**(2) No instalment required** — Sections 155 and 156 do not apply to an individual for a particular taxation year where

(a) the individual's chief source of income for the particular year is farming or fishing and the individual's net tax owing for the particular year, or either of the 2 preceding taxation years, does not exceed the individual's instalment threshold for that year; or

(b) the individual's net tax owing for the particular year, or for each of the 2 preceding taxation years, does not exceed the individual's instalment threshold for that year.

**Related Provisions**: 107(5.1) — Trust's gain on distribution to non-resident beneficiary does not increase instalment requirements; 128.1(5) — Deemed disposition on emigration does not increase instalment requirements; 157(2.1) — Threshold of $1,000 for corporations; 161(2) — Interest on late or insufficient instalments.

**Notes**: See Notes at end of 156.1.

**Forms**: T7B: Instalment guide for individuals.

**(3) Idem** — Sections 155 and 156 do not require the payment of any amount in respect of an individual that would otherwise become due under either of those sections on or after the day on which the individual dies.

**Notes**: See Notes at end of 156.1 for pre-1995 amendments.

**(4) Payment of remainder** — Every individual shall, on or before the individual's balance-due day for each taxation year, pay to the Receiver General in respect of the year the amount, if any, by which the individual's tax payable under this Part for the year exceeds the total of

(a) all amounts deducted or withheld under section 153 from remuneration or other payments received by the individual in the year, and

(b) all other amounts paid to the Receiver General on or before that day on account of the individual's tax payable under this Part for the year.

**Related Provisions**: 104(23)(e) — Alternative rule for testamentary trust; 161(1) — Interest payable if balance not paid on time.

## S. 156.1(4)      Income Tax Act, Part I

**Notes**: See Notes to 107(5.2) and 128.1(5).

**Notes [s. 156.1]**: In simple terms, if the total payable on filing (i.e., total tax minus source deductions) exceeds $2,000 for both the current year and either of the previous two years, instalments are required. The $2,000 includes provincial tax for all provinces whose personal income taxes are collected by the CCRA; for residents of Quebec, the threshold is $1,200 and applies to federal tax only. (A parallel $1,200 threshold applies to Quebec residents in respect of provincial tax: *Taxation Act* s. 1026.0.2.)

156.1 amended by 1993 Budget, subsecs. (1)–(3) effective for amounts payable after June 1994 and subsec. (4) effective for the 1994 and later taxation years.

For amounts payable before July 1994 (i.e., for instalments up to and including the one due on June 15, 1994), read:

> 156.1 (1) **No instalment required** — Where the total of the taxes payable (before taking into consideration any amount referred to in any of subparagraphs 161(7)(a)(ii) to (v) or (viii) that was excluded or deducted, as the case may be) under this Part and Part I.1 by an individual for a particular taxation year or for the taxation year preceding that year is not more than the total of $1,000 and the amount, if any, determined in respect of the individual for that year under subsection 120(2),
>
>> (a) sections 155 and 156 do not apply to that individual for the particular year; and
>>
>> (b) the individual shall pay to the Receiver General, on or before the individual's balance-due day for the particular year, the individual's tax as estimated under section 151 for the particular year.
>
> (2) **Idem** — Paragraphs 155(1)(a) and 156(1)(a) and (b) do not require the payment of any amount in respect of an individual that would otherwise become due under any of those paragraphs on or after the day on which the individual died.

In opening words of former 156.1, the reference to Part I.1 (individual surtax) added by 1989 Budget, effective 1989.

Former 156.1(1) amended by 1991 technical bill, effective 1990, to refer to the "balance-due day" rather than April 30. The balance-due day (defined in 248(1)) corresponded before 1995 to the return deadline under 150(1).

Former 156.1(1) amended by 1991 technical bill, effective 1990 (but see below), to add the parenthetical exclusion of amounts referred to in 161(7)(a)(ii) to (v), so that instalment interest cannot be eliminated by the carryback of a loss that reduces tax payable to $1,000 or less. The change is effective 1990, and applies also to amounts in respect of subsequent taxation years ending after 1989.

Former 156.1(1) amended by 1992 transportation industry assistance bill to add reference to 161(7)(a)(viii), effective 1992.

Former 156.1(2) added by 1991 technical bill, effective as of the 1990 taxation year, so that the legal representative is not required to remit instalments that would otherwise be due after death. This conforms to Revenue Canada's established administrative practice.

Former 156.1(2) amended by 1992 technical bill, effective 1992, to add the reference to 156(1)(b).

**Definitions [s. 156.1]**: "amount", "balance-due day", "farming", "fishing", "individual" — 248(1); "instalment threshold", "net tax owing" — 156.1(1); "prescribed" — 248(1); "province" — *Interpretation Act* 35(1); "specified future tax consequence" — 248(1); "taxpayer" — 248(1); "taxation year" — 249.

**157. (1) Payment by corporations** — Every corporation shall, in respect of each of its taxation years, pay to the Receiver General

(a) either

(i) on or before the last day of each month in the year, an amount equal to $1/12$ of the total of the amounts estimated by it to be the taxes payable by it under this Part and Parts I.3, VI and VI.1 for the year,

---

**Proposed Amendment — 157(1)(a)(i)**

(i) on or before the last day of each month in the year, an amount equal to $1/12$ of the total of the amounts estimated by it to be the taxes payable by it under this Part and Parts I.3, VI, VI.1 and XIII.1 for the year,

**Application**: The August 8, 2000 draft legislation, subsec. 15(1), will amend subpara. 157(1)(a)(i) to read as above, applicable to 2001 *et seq.*

**Technical Notes**: Section 157 of the Act sets out the required payment dates for corporate income tax instalments and for any balance of corporate income tax payable. The list, in subparagraph 157(1)(a)(i), of Parts in respect of which monthly instalments are required is amended by adding a reference to new Part XIII.1 (the "additional tax on authorized foreign banks," or "branch interest tax"). The same reference is also added to the rules in paragraph 157(1)(b) that relate to the payment of the remainder of tax owing. As a result, a foreign bank's payments of Part XIII.1 tax will follow the same schedule as its payments of Part I tax.

Subsection 157(2.1) of the Act exempts a corporation from the requirement to pay its tax for a taxation year by instalments, where either the total of its taxes payable for the year or its "first instalment base" (defined by regulation) is $1,000 or less. The subsection is amended to include tax under new Part XIII.1 among the taxes covered by this rule.

These amendments apply to the 2001 and subsequent taxation years. More information on new Part XIII.1 itself is set out in the notes to new section 218.2 of the Act.

---

(ii) on or before the last day of each month in the year, an amount equal to $1/12$ of its first instalment base for the year, or

(iii) on or before the last day of each of the first two months in the year, an amount equal to $1/12$ of its second instalment base for the year, and on or before the last day of each of the following months in the year, an amount equal to $1/10$ of the amount remaining after deducting the amount computed pursuant to this subparagraph in respect of the first two months from its first instalment base for the year; and

(b) the remainder of the taxes payable by it under this Part and Parts I.3, VI and VI.1 for the year

---

**Proposed Amendment — 157(1)(b) opening words**

(b) the remainder of the taxes payable by it under this Part and Parts I.3, VI, VI.1 and XIII.1 for the year

**Application**: The August 8, 2000 draft legislation, subsec. 15(2), will amend the opening words of para. 157(1)(b) to read as above, applicable to 2001 *et seq.*

**Technical Notes**: See under 157(1)(a)(i).

Division I — Returns, Assessments, Payment and Appeals   S. 157(2)

(i) on or before the end of the third month following the end of the year, where

(A) an amount was deducted by virtue of section 125 in computing the tax payable under this Part by the corporation for the year or its immediately preceding taxation year,

(B) the corporation is, throughout the year, a Canadian-controlled private corporation,

(C) a particular calendar year immediately preceded the calendar year in which the year ends, and

(D) either

(I) the corporation is not associated with another corporation in the taxation year and its taxable income for its immediately preceding taxation year (determined before taking into consideration the specified future tax consequences for that preceding year) does not exceed its business limit for that preceding year, or

(II) where the corporation is associated with another corporation in the taxation year, the total of all amounts each of which is the taxable income of the corporation or such an associated corporation for its last taxation year that ended in the particular calendar year (determined before taking into consideration the specified future tax consequences for that last year) does not exceed the total of all amounts each of which is the business limit of the corporation or such an associated corporation for that last year, or

(ii) on or before the end of the second month following the end of the year, in any other case.

**Related Provisions**: 87(2)(oo.1) — Effect of amalgamation; 88(1)(e.8), (e.9) — Winding-up; 151 — Estimate of tax; 157(2), (2.1), (3) — Special cases; 161(1) — Interest on taxes due; 161(2) — Interest on unpaid tax instalments; 161(2.2) — Interest on instalments; 161(4.1) — Minimum instalment payments to avoid interest charges; 163.1 — Penalty for late or deficient instalments; 221.2 — Transfers of instalments to other years' accounts; 248(1)"balance-due day"(d) — Deadline under 157(1)(b) is the balance-due day of corporation; 248(7) — Receipt of things mailed; 256 — Associated corporations.

**Notes**: Corporate instalments are due monthly, in contrast to an individual's instalments, which under 156(1) are due quarterly. Under 157(1)(b)(ii), the balance is normally due 2 months after year-end, even though the return under 150(1)(c) is not due until 6 months after year-end. 157(1)(b)(i) extends the balance-due date by one month for Canadian-controlled private corporations that claim the small business deduction and that have taxable income (together with associated corporations) not exceeding $200,000.

Instalments paid earlier than required will generate "contra interest" under 161(2.2) to offset interest on late instalments. This can effectively allow a corporation to delay its instalment payments until fairly late in the year, to reduce the economic risk of overpaying instalments that may not be needed. See Glenn Feltham & Alan Macnaughton, "Optimal Payment Strategy for Corporate Income Tax Instalments", 48(1) *Canadian Tax Journal* 60-89 (2000).

157(1)(b)(i)(B) amended, and (C) and (D) added, by 1996 Budget bill; the version in the text applies for taxation years that end in 1998 or later. For amounts payable in 1996 or later in respect of taxation years that end before 1998, read (D)(II) as:

(II) where the corporation is associated with another corporation in the year,

1. the total of the taxable income of the corporation for its immediately preceding taxation year (determined before taking into consideration the specified future tax consequences for that preceding year) and the total of the taxable incomes of all such associated corporations for their taxation years that ended in the particular calendar year (determined before taking into consideration the specified future tax consequences for those years)

does not exceed

2. the total of the business limit of the corporation for its immediately preceding taxation year and the total of the business limits of all such associated corporations for their taxation years that ended in the particular calendar year, or

"Specified future tax consequences" in 157(1)(b)(i)(D) (see definition in 248(1)) refers to adjustments from the carryback of losses or similar amounts or because of corrections of certain amounts renounced in connection with the issuance of flow-through shares. The purpose of the 1996 Budget amendment is to ensure that subsequent events do not affect the obligation to pay tax instalments and remainders of tax payable.

157(1)(a)(i) and 157(1)(b) amended by 1992 technical bill, effective for 1992 and later taxation years, to add references to Parts I.3 and VI. This integrates the instalment requirements for Part I and VI.1 with those for Parts I.3 and VI, thus allowing offset interest for an overpayment of tax under one Part to credit against interest for late payment under another Part.

**Forms**: T7B CORP: Corporation instalment guide.

**(2) Special case [co-op or credit union]** — Where in a taxation year a corporation

(a) has held out the prospect that it will make allocations in proportion to patronage as described in section 135, or

(b) is a credit union,

and for the year or the preceding taxation year

(c) its taxable income (determined before taking into consideration the specified future tax consequences for the year or that preceding year, as the case may be) was not more than $10,000, and

(d) no tax was payable by it under any of Parts I.3, VI and VI.1 (determined before taking into consideration the specified future tax consequences for the year or that preceding year, as the case may be),

it may, instead of paying the instalments required by subsection (1), pay to the Receiver General at the end of the third month following the end of the year the total of the taxes payable by it under this Part and Parts I.3, VI and VI.1 for the year.

**Related Provisions**: 135 — Patronage dividend deduction; 151 — Estimate of tax; 161(3) — Special 3% interest charge repealed.

**Notes**: 157(2) amended by 1995-97 technical bill, effective for taxation years that end after February 22, 1994, to add "in a taxation

S. 157(2) — Income Tax Act, Part I

year" in the opening words and delete the unnecessary words "to its customers of a taxation year" after "patronage". The amendment to the opening words ensures that the conditions apply to credit unions on a year-by-year basis.

157(2)(c) and (d) amended by 1996 Budget, effective for amounts that become payable in 1996 or later, to add the parenthesized exclusion of specified future tax consequences. "Specified future tax consequences" (see definition in 248(1)) refers to adjustments from the carryback of losses or similar amounts or because of corrections of certain amounts renounced in connection with the issuance of flow-through shares.

157(2)(d) and closing words of 157(2) amended by 1992 technical bill, effective for 1992 and later taxation years, to add references to Parts I.3 and VI. See Notes to 157(1).

**(2.1) Idem [$1,000 threshold]** — Where

(a) the total of the taxes payable under this Part and Parts I.3, VI and VI.1 by a corporation for a taxation year (determined before taking into consideration the specified future tax consequences for the year), or

(b) the corporation's first instalment base for the year

is not more than $1,000, the corporation may, instead of paying the instalments required for the year by paragraph (1)(a), pay to the Receiver General, under paragraph (1)(b), the total of the taxes payable by it under this Part and Parts I.3, VI and VI.1 for the year.

**Proposed Amendment — 157(2.1)**

**(2.1) $1,000 threshold** — Where

(a) the total of the taxes payable under this Part and Parts I.3, VI, VI.1 and XIII.1 by a corporation for a taxation year (determined before taking into consideration the specified future tax consequences for the year), or

(b) the corporation's first instalment base for the year,

is not more than $1,000, the corporation may, instead of paying the instalments required for the year by paragraph (1)(a), pay to the Receiver General, under paragraph (1)(b), the total of the taxes payable by it under this Part and Parts I.3, VI, VI.1 and XIII.1 for the year.

**Application**: The August 8, 2000 draft legislation, subsec. 15(3), will amend subsec. 157(2.1) to read as above, applicable to 2001 et seq.

**Technical Notes**: See under 157(1)(a)(i).

**Related Provisions**: 156.1(1) — No instalment required.

**Notes**: 157(2.1)(a) amended by 1996 Budget, effective for amounts that become payable in 1996 or later, to add the parenthesized exclusion of specified future tax consequences in place of the existing exclusion. ("Specified future tax consequences" (see definition in 248(1)) refers to adjustments from the carryback of losses or similar amounts or because of corrections of certain amounts renounced in connection with the issuance of flow-through shares.) For earlier amounts payable, read:

(a) the total of the taxes payable (before taking into consideration any amount referred to in any of subparagraphs 161(7)(a)(ii) to (x) that was excluded or deducted, as the case

may be) under this Part and Parts I.3, VI and VI.1 by a corporation for a taxation year, or

157(2.1)(a) and closing words of 157(2.1) amended by 1992 technical bill, effective for 1992 and later taxation years, to add references to subparas. 161(7)(a)(ix) and (x), and Parts I.3 and VI. See Notes to 157(1).

157(2.1) amended by 1992 transportation industry assistance bill to add reference to 161(7)(a)(viii), effective 1992.

157(2.1)(a) amended by 1991 technical bill, effective for subsequent taxation years ending after 1989, to add the parenthetical exclusion of amounts referred to in 161(7)(a)(ii) to (vii), so that instalment interest cannot be eliminated by the carryback of a loss that reduces tax payable to $1,000 or less.

In 157(2.1)(a), a reference to Part I.3 (large corporations tax) was added by 1989 Budget, effective 1989, and deleted by 1991 technical bill, effective 1990.

**(3) Private, mutual fund and non-resident-owned investment corporations** — Notwithstanding subsection (1), the amount payable for a taxation year by a corporation to the Receiver General on or before the last day of any month in the year shall be deemed to be the amount, if any, by which

(a) the amount so payable as determined under that subsection for the month

exceeds

(b) where the corporation is neither a mutual fund corporation nor a non-resident-owned investment corporation, $1/12$ of the corporation's dividend refund (within the meaning assigned by subsection 129(1)) for the year,

(c) where the corporation is a mutual fund corporation, $1/12$ of the total of

(i) the corporation's capital gains refund (within the meaning assigned by section 131) for the year, and

(ii) the amount that, by virtue of subsection 131(5), is the corporation's dividend refund (within the meaning assigned by section 129) for the year,

(d) where the corporation is a non-resident-owned investment corporation, $1/12$ of the corporation's allowable refund (within the meaning assigned by section 133) for the year, and

(e) $1/12$ of the total of the amounts each of which is deemed by subsection 125.4(3), 125.5(3), 127.1(1) or 127.41(3) to have been paid on account of the corporation's tax payable under this Part for the year.

**Related Provisions**: 131(5) — Dividend refund to mutual fund corporation; 136 — Cooperative not private corporation — exception.

**Notes**: 157(3)(b) amended by 1992 technical bill, effective for 1993 and later taxation years. For earlier years, para. (b) applies only to private corporations. See Notes to 129(1).

157(3)(e) added by 1994 Budget (referring only to 127.41(3)), effective for taxation years that end after February 22, 1994. Amended by 1995 Budget, effective for 1995 and later taxation years, to add reference to 125.4(3). Amended by 1995-97 technical bill to add reference to 127.1(1) effective for taxation years that end

1468

after February 22, 1994, and to add reference to 125.5(3) effective for taxation years that end after October 1997.

**Interpretation Bulletins**: IT-243R4: Dividend refund to private corporations.

**(4) Definitions** — In this section, "first instalment base" and "second instalment base" of a corporation for a taxation year have the meanings prescribed by regulation.

**Regulations**: 5301 (meaning of "first instalment base", "second instalment base").

**Definitions [s. 157]**: "amount" — 248(1); "associated" — 256; "business limit" — 125(2)–(5.1), 248(1); "calendar year" — *Interpretation Act* 37(1)(a); "corporation" — 248(1), *Interpretation Act* 35(1); "credit union" — 137(6), 248(1); "first instalment base" — 157(4), Reg. 5301(1); "mutual fund corporation" — 131(8); "non-resident-owned investment corporation" — 133(8), 248(1); "prescribed" — 248(1); "resident in Canada" — 250; "second instalment base" — 157(4), Reg. 5301(2); "share" — 248(1); "specified future tax consequence" — 248(1); "tax payable" — 248(2); "taxable income" — 2(2), 248(1); "taxation year" — 249.

**158. Payment of remainder** — Where the Minister mails a notice of assessment of any amount payable by a taxpayer, that part of the amount assessed then remaining unpaid is payable forthwith by the taxpayer to the Receiver General.

**Related Provisions**: 156.1(4) — Obligation of individual to pay balance by balance-due date; 157(1)(b) — Obligation of corporation to pay balance; 164(3) — Interest on overpayments; 220(4) — Security for taxes; 222–225 — Collection of taxes; 225.1 — Collection restrictions; 248(7)(a) — Mail deemed received on day mailed.

**Notes**: Although the amount assessed is technically payable "forthwith", it is effectively stopped (for all taxpayers except large corporations, which must pay half) by filing a notice of objection or notice of appeal, since the CCRA is then precluded from taking collection action. See 225.1(1). However, non-deductible (see 18(1)(t)) interest on the balance will continue to run under 161(1), compounded daily at the high rate prescribed in Reg. 4301(a), so payment of an amount in dispute is usually a good idea and will have no bearing on the resolution of the dispute. If the taxpayer succeeds, any refund will bear taxable (see 12(1)(c)) interest at the prescribed rate under 164(3) and Reg 4301(b), which is 2 percentage points lower.

Where there is a question as to which taxation year a payment should be allocated to, see Notes to 221.2.

**Definitions [s. 158]**: "assessment", "Minister", "taxpayer" — 248(1).

**Forms [s. 158]**: T7D: Statement of account.

**159. (1) Person acting for another** — For the purposes of this Act, where a person is a legal representative of a taxpayer at any time,

(a) the legal representative is jointly and severally liable with the taxpayer

(i) to pay each amount payable under this Act by the taxpayer at or before that time and that remains unpaid, to the extent that the legal representative is at that time in possession or control, in the capacity of legal representative, of property that belongs or belonged to, or that is or was held for the benefit of, the taxpayer or the taxpayer's estate, and

(ii) to perform any obligation or duty imposed under this Act on the taxpayer at or before that time and that remains outstanding, to the extent that the obligation or duty can reasonably be considered to relate to the responsibilities of the legal representative acting in that capacity; and

(b) any action or proceeding in respect of the taxpayer taken under this Act at or after that time by the Minister may be so taken in the name of the legal representative acting in that capacity and, when so taken, has the same effect as if it had been taken directly against the taxpayer and, if the taxpayer no longer exists, as if the taxpayer continued to exist.

**Related Provisions**: 150(3) — Obligation to file taxpayer's return; 227.1 — Liability of corporate directors; 248(7)(a) — Mail deemed received on day mailed.

**Notes**: 159(1) amended by 1995-97 technical bill, effective June 18, 1998. See the new definition of "legal representative" in 248(1). From October 30, 1985 to June 17, 1998, read:

(1) Payment on behalf of others — Where the Minister mails to a person required by section 150 to file a return of the income of a taxpayer for a taxation year a notice of assessment of any amount payable for the year by or in respect of the taxpayer, that part of the amount assessed then remaining unpaid is payable forthwith by the person to the Receiver General to the extent that the person has or had, at any time after the end of the taxation year, in his or her possession or control property belonging to the taxpayer or the taxpayer's estate and on payment thereof the person shall be deemed to have made the payment on behalf of the taxpayer.

**(2) Certificate before distribution** — Every legal representative (other than a trustee in bankruptcy) of a taxpayer shall, before distributing to one or more persons any property in the possession or control of the legal representative acting in that capacity, obtain a certificate from the Minister, by applying for one in prescribed form, certifying that all amounts

(a) for which the taxpayer is or can reasonably be expected to become liable under this Act at or before the time the distribution is made, and

(b) for the payment of which the legal representative is or can reasonably be expected to become liable in that capacity

have been paid or that security for the payment thereof has been accepted by the Minister.

**Related Provisions**: 159(3) — Liability where property distributed with no certificate; 159(3.1) — Appropriation of property; 220(4) — Security for taxes; 227.1 — Liability of directors for withholding taxes.

**Notes**: The certificate described in 159(2) is commonly referred to as a "clearance certificate".

159(2) amended by 1995-97 technical bill, effective June 18, 1998. See the new definition of "legal representative" in 248(1). From December 18, 1991 to June 17, 1998, read:

(2) Every person (other than a trustee in bankruptcy) who is an assignee, liquidator, receiver, receiver-manager, administrator, executor or any other like person (in this section referred to as the "responsible representative") administering, winding up, controlling or otherwise dealing with a property,

**S. 159(2)**          Income Tax Act, Part I

business or estate of another person shall, before distributing to one or more persons any property over which the responsible representative has control in the capacity of the responsible representative, obtain a certificate from the Minister, by applying therefor in prescribed form, certifying that all amounts

    (a) for which any taxpayer is liable under this Act in respect of the taxation year in which the distribution is made, or any preceding taxation year, and

    (b) for the payment of which the responsible representative is or can reasonably be expected to become liable in that capacity

have been paid or that security for the payment thereof has been accepted by the Minister.

Opening words of 159(2) amended by 1991 technical bill, effective December 18, 1991, to require applications to be in prescribed form.

**Interpretation Bulletins**: IT-488R2: Winding-up of 90%-owned taxable Canadian corporations; CPP-2: Canada pension plan — status of employer where trustee in bankruptcy, receiver or receiver and manager is appointed; UI-3: *Unemployment Insurance Act* — status of employer where trustee in bankruptcy, receiver or receiver and manager is appointed.

**Information Circulars**: 82-6R2: Clearance certificate; 98-1R: Collections policies.

**Forms**: TX19: Asking for clearance certificate.

**(3) Personal liability** — Where a legal representative (other than a trustee in bankruptcy) of a taxpayer distributes to one or more persons property in the possession or control of the legal representative, acting in that capacity, without obtaining a certificate under subsection (2) in respect of the amounts referred to in that subsection, the legal representative is personally liable for the payment of those amounts to the extent of the value of the property distributed, and the Minister may at any time assess the legal representative in respect of any amount payable because of this subsection, and the provisions of this Division apply, with any modifications that the circumstances require, to an assessment made under this subsection as though it had been made under section 152.

**Related Provisions**: 159(3.1) — Appropriation of property.

**Notes**: 159(3) amended by 1995-97 technical bill, effective June 18, 1998. See the new definition of "legal representative" in 248(1). From October 30, 1985 to June 17, 1998, read:

    (3) Where a responsible representative distributes to one or more persons property over which the responsible representative has control in that capacity without obtaining a certificate under subsection (2) in respect of the amounts referred to in that subsection, the responsible representative is personally liable for the payment of those amounts to the extent of the value of the property distributed and the Minister may assess the responsible representative therefor in the same manner and with the same effect as an assessment made under section 152.

**Interpretation Bulletins**: IT-488R2: Winding-up of 90%-owned taxable Canadian corporations.

**Information Circulars**: 98-1R: Collections policies.

**(3.1) Appropriation of property** — For the purposes of subsections (2) and (3), an appropriation by a legal representative of a taxpayer of property in the possession or control of the legal representative acting in that capacity is deemed to be a distribution of the property to a person.

**Notes**: 159(3.1) added by 1995-97 technical bill, effective June 18, 1998.

**(4) Election on emigration** — Where an individual to whom subsection 128.1(4) applies

    (a) so elects in prescribed manner on or before the individual's balance-due day for the taxation year in which the individual ceased to be resident in Canada, and

    (b) furnishes to the Minister security acceptable to the Minister for payment of any tax under this Act the payment of which is deferred by the election,

all or any portion of such part of that tax as is equal to the amount, if any, by which that tax exceeds the amount that would be that tax if this Act were read without reference to subsection 128.1(4) may, subject to subsection (4.1), be paid in such number of equal annual instalments as is specified in the election by the individual.

> **Proposed Repeal — 159(4), (4.1)**
>
> **Application**: Bill C-43 (First Reading September 20, 2000), subsec. 92(1), will repeal subsecs. 159(4) and (4.1), applicable to individuals who cease to be resident in Canada after October 1, 1996.
>
> **Technical Notes**: Subsections 159(4) and (4.1) allow an individual who has ceased to be resident in Canada to elect to pay any tax resulting from the deemed disposition of property under subsection 128.1(4) in up to six annual instalments, provided the individual gives the Minister of National Revenue adequate security.
>
> The present amendments include, in new subsections 220(4.5) and 220(4.6), more comprehensive and more liberal security rules than these. Subsections 159(4) and (4.1) are therefore repealed, with application to individuals who cease to be resident in Canada after October 1, 1996.

**Related Provisions**: 159(4.1) — Instalment requirements; 159(7) — Form and manner of election, and interest.

**Notes**: 159(4) amended by 1993 technical bill, effective for changes in residence that occur in 1993 or later. From February 16, 1984 through the end of 1992, read:

    (4) Election where subsec. 48(1) applicable — Where subsection 48(1) is applicable in respect of a taxpayer who has ceased to be resident in Canada in a taxation year, and the taxpayer so elects and furnishes the Minister with security acceptable to the Minister for payment of any tax the payment of which is deferred by the election, notwithstanding any provision of this Part respecting the time within which payment shall be made of the tax payable under this Part by the taxpayer for the year, all or any portion of such part of that tax as is equal to the amount, if any, by which that tax exceeds the amount that that tax would be, if this Act were read without reference to subsection 48(1), may be paid in such number (not exceeding 6) of equal consecutive annual instalments as is specified by the taxpayer in the election, the first instalment of which shall be paid on or before the day on or before which payment of that tax would, but for the election, have been required to be made and each subsequent instalment of which shall be paid on or before the next following anniversary of that day.

**Regulations**: 1301 (prescribed manner of making election).

**Interpretation Bulletins**: IT-451R: Deemed disposition and acquisition on ceasing to be or becoming resident in Canada.

**Forms**: T2074: Election, under subsection 159(4) of the ITA, to defer payment of income tax on the deemed disposition of property.

**(4.1) Idem** — Where an individual to whom subsection 128.1(4) applies elects under subsection (4),

(a) the number of equal annual instalments provided in the election shall be deemed to be the lesser of 6 and such other number as is specified in the election by the individual;

(b) the first instalment shall be paid on or before the individual's balance-due day for the taxation year; and

(c) each subsequent instalment shall be paid on or before the next following anniversary of the day described in paragraph (b).

### Proposed Repeal — 159(4.1)

See under 159(4).

**Notes**: 159(4.1) added by 1993 technical bill, effective for changes in residence that occur in 1993 or later.

**(5) Election where certain provisions applicable [on death]** — Where subsection 70(2), (5) or (5.2) of this Act or subsection 70(9.4) of the *Income Tax Act*, chapter 148 of the Revised Statutes of Canada, 1952, is applicable in respect of a taxpayer who has died, and the taxpayer's legal representative so elects and furnishes the Minister with security acceptable to the Minister for payment of any tax the payment of which is deferred by the election, notwithstanding any provision of this Part or the *Income Tax Application Rules* respecting the time within which payment shall be made of the tax payable under this Part by the taxpayer for the taxation year in which the taxpayer died, all or any portion of such part of that tax as is equal to the amount, if any, by which that tax exceeds the amount that that tax would be, if this Act were read without reference to subsections 70(2), (5) and (5.2) and the *Income Tax Act*, chapter 148 of the Revised Statutes of Canada, 1952, were read without reference to subsections 70(2), (5), (5.2) and (9.4) of that Act, may be paid in such number (not exceeding 10) of equal consecutive annual instalments as is specified by the legal representative in the election, the first instalment of which shall be paid on or before the day on or before which payment of that tax would, but for the election, have been required to be made and each subsequent instalment of which shall be paid on or before the next following anniversary of that day.

**Related Provisions**: 159(5.1) — Pre-1972 professional business; 159(6) — Meaning of "tax payable under this Part"; 159(7) — Form and manner of election, and interest.

**Regulations**: 1001 (prescribed manner of making election).

**I.T. Application Rules**: 69 (meaning of "*Income Tax Act*, chapter 148 of the Revised Statutes of Canada, 1952").

**Interpretation Bulletins**: IT-125R4: Dispositions of resource properties; IT-212R3: Income of deceased persons — rights or things; IT-278R2: Death of a partner or of a retired partner.

**Forms**: T2075: Election to defer payment of income tax under subsec. 159(5) by a deceased taxpayer's legal representative or trustee; T4011: Preparing returns for deceased persons [guide].

**(5.1) Idem [pre-1972 professional business]** — Where, in the taxation year in which a taxpayer dies, an amount is included in computing the taxpayer's income by virtue of paragraph 23(3)(c) of the *Income Tax Application Rules*, the provisions of subsection (5) apply, with such modifications as the circumstances require, as though the amount were an amount included in computing the taxpayer's income for the year by virtue of subsection 70(2) or an amount deemed to have been received by the taxpayer by virtue of subsection 70(5).

**Related Provisions**: 70(2) — Deceased taxpayer — amounts receivable; 70(5) — Depreciable and other capital property.

**I.T. Application Rules**: 23(3).

**Interpretation Bulletins**: IT-212R3: Income of deceased persons — rights or things; IT-278R2: Death of a partner or of a retired partner.

**(6) Idem** — For the purposes of subsection (5), the "tax payable under this Part" by a taxpayer for the taxation year in which the taxpayer died includes any tax payable under this Part by virtue of an election in respect of the taxpayer's death made by the taxpayer's legal representative under subsection 70(2) or under the provisions of that subsection as they are required to be read by virtue of the *Income Tax Application Rules*.

**(6.1) Election where subsec. 104(4) applicable** — Where a day determined under paragraph 104(4)(a), (a.1), (b) or (c) in respect of a trust occurs in a taxation year of the trust and the trust so elects and furnishes to the Minister security acceptable to the Minister for payment of any tax the payment of which is deferred by the election, notwithstanding any other provision of this Part respecting the time within which payment shall be made of the tax payable under this Part by the trust for the year, all or any portion of such part of that tax as is equal to the amount, if any, by which that tax exceeds the amount that that tax would be if this Act were read without reference to paragraph 104(4)(a), (a.1), (b) or (c), as the case may be, may be paid in such number (not exceeding 10) of equal consecutive annual instalments as is specified by the trust in the election, the first instalment of which shall be paid on or before the day on or before which payment of that tax would, but for the election, have been required to be made and each subsequent instalment of which shall be paid on or before the next following anniversary of that day.

### Proposed Amendment — 159(6.1)

**(6.1) Election where subsec. 104(4) applicable** — Where a day determined under paragraph 104(4)(a), (a.1), (a.2), (a.3), (b) or (c) in respect of a trust occurs in a taxation year of the trust and the trust so elects and furnishes to the Minister security acceptable to the Minister for payment of any tax

**S. 159(6.1)**     Income Tax Act, Part I

the payment of which is deferred by the election, notwithstanding any other provision of this Part respecting the time within which payment shall be made of the tax payable under this Part by the trust for the year, all or any portion of the part of that tax that is equal to the amount, if any, by which that tax exceeds the amount that that tax would be if this Act were read without reference to paragraph 104(4)(a), (a.1), (a.2), (a.3), (b) or (c), as the case may be, may be paid in the number (not exceeding 10) of equal consecutive annual instalments that is specified by the trust in the election, the first instalment of which shall be paid on or before the day on or before which payment of that tax would, but for the election, have been required to be made and each subsequent instalment of which shall be paid on or before the next following anniversary of that day.

**Application**: Bill C-43 (First Reading September 20, 2000), subsec. 92(2), will amend subsec. 159(6.1) to read as above, applicable to 2000 *et seq.*

**Technical Notes**: Subsection 159(6.1) permits payments of a trust's tax liability resulting from a deemed disposition under paragraph 104(4)(a), (a.1), (b) or (c) to be paid (with interest) over 10 years.

Subsection 159(6.1) is amended so that this rule also applies in regard to a trust's tax liability resulting from a deemed disposition under new paragraphs 104(4)(a.2) and (a.3), described in the notes above.

**Related Provisions**: 104(5.3) — Election to postpone deemed disposition; 159(7) — Form and manner of election, and interest.

**Notes**: 159(6.1) added by 1992 technical bill, effective for 1993 and later taxation years. It allows trusts to pay the tax arising from the 21-year deemed disposition rule in up to 10 annual instalments (with interest: see 159(7)).

**Forms**: T2223: Election under s. 159(6.1) by trust to defer payment of income tax.

**(7) Form and manner of election and interest** — Every election made by a taxpayer under subsection (4) or (6.1) or by the legal representative of a taxpayer under subsection (5) shall be made in prescribed form and on condition that, at the time of payment of any amount payment of which is deferred by the election, the taxpayer shall pay to the Receiver General interest on the amount at the prescribed rate in effect at the time the election was made, computed from the day on or before which the amount would, but for the election, have been required to be paid to the day of payment.

**Related Provisions**: 221.1 — Application of interest where legislation retroactive; 248(11) — Interest compounded daily.

**Notes**: 159(7) amended by 1992 technical bill, effective for 1993 and later taxation years, to add reference to 159(6.1).

**Regulations**: 4301(a) (prescribed rate of interest).

**Forms**: T2074: Election, under subsection 159(4) of the *Income Tax Act*, to defer payment of income tax on deemed disposition of property; T2075: Election to defer payment of income tax under subsec. 159(5) by a deceased taxpayer's legal representative or trustee; T2223: Election under s. 159(6.1) by trust to defer payment of income tax.

**Definitions [s. 159]**: "amount", "assessment", "balance-due day" — 248(1); "Canada" — 255; "individual", "legal representative", "Minister", "person", "prescribed" — 248(1); "prescribed rate" — Reg. 4301; "property" — 248(1); "taxation year" — 249; "tax payable under this Part" — 159(6); "taxpayer" — 248(1).

**160. (1) Tax liability re property transferred not at arm's length** — Where a person has, on or after May 1, 1951, transferred property, either directly or indirectly, by means of a trust or by any other means whatever, to

   (a) the person's spouse or common-law partner or a person who has since become the person's spouse or common-law partner,

   (b) a person who was under 18 years of age, or

   (c) a person with whom the person was not dealing at arm's length,

the following rules apply:

   (d) the transferee and transferor are jointly and severally liable to pay a part of the transferor's tax under this Part for each taxation year equal to the amount by which the tax for the year is greater than it would have been if it were not for the operation of sections 74 to 75.1 of this Act and section 74 of the *Income Tax Act*, chapter 148 of the Revised Statutes of Canada, 1952, in respect of any income from, or gain from the disposition of, the property so transferred or property substituted therefor, and

   (e) the transferee and transferor are jointly and severally liable to pay under this Act an amount equal to the lesser of

     (i) the amount, if any, by which the fair market value of the property at the time it was transferred exceeds the fair market value at that time of the consideration given for the property, and

     (ii) the total of all amounts each of which is an amount that the transferor is liable to pay under this Act in or in respect of the taxation year in which the property was transferred or any preceding taxation year,

but nothing in this subsection shall be deemed to limit the liability of the transferor under any other provision of this Act.

**Related Provisions**: 74–75.1 — Attribution of income on non-arm's length transfers; 160(3.1) — Fair market value of undivided interest in property; 160(4) — Transfer to spouse on breakdown of marriage; 248(5) — Substituted property.

**Notes**: 160(1) makes a non-arm's length transferee liable for money or property transferred by a person who owes tax. It prevents a tax debtor from simply transferring assets to a spouse or other relative and then not having any assets with which to pay. The essence is in 160(1)(e) — the transferee is liable for the value of what was transferred, minus anything given in return, up to a limit (160(1)(e)(ii)) of the transferor's liability under the Act as of the year of the transfer. A typical application is where a husband transfers his interest in the family home to his wife, leaving himself with no assets that the CCRA can attach for his tax debts (see 160(3.1) in such cases).

Note that s. 160 can apply to a payment of dividends by a corporation to a shareholder with which it does not deal at arm's length. See *Algoa Trust*, [1993] 1 C.T.C. 2294 (TCC); but see also *Davis*, [1994] 2 C.T.C. 2033 (TCC), where the taxpayers succeeded. It can apply where the dividend recipient is only a 50% shareholder, since "arm's length" is a question of fact: *Gosselin*, [1997] 2 C.T.C. 2830. It can also apply to a bequest by a deceased non-resident who left Canada with taxes owing many years earlier: *Montreuil*, [1996] 1 C.T.C. 2182 (TCC). It can also apply where the tax debtor makes mortgage payments on the family home: *Medland*, [1999] 4 C.T.C. 293 (FCA). The transferee will be liable even if the transferor went bankrupt before either of them was assessed: *Heavyside*, [1997] 2 C.T.C. 1 (FCA). However, no interest can be assessed on a s. 160 assessment, according to the Tax Court in *Algoa Trust*, [1998] 4 C.T.C. 2001. A class action (*Ho-A-Shoo*) is underway in the Ontario courts to recover interest collected under such assessments: *Canadian Tax Highlights* (Canadian Tax Foundation), Sept. 27/99.

A person assessed under s. 160 may challenge the underlying assessment of the transferor even if the transferor did not: *Gaucher*, 2000 CarswellNat 2656 (FCA).

Liability applies for any transfer from the *beginning* of the taxation year in which the tax liability arose, even if it did not arise until after the transfer: 160(1)(e)(ii). Only if fair value is received in exchange for the transferred property (see 160(1)(e)(i)) will there be no liability.

A parallel rule applies for any GST owing at the time of the transfer; see s. 325 of the *Excise Tax Act*, reproduced in the *Practitioner's Goods and Services Tax, Annotated* and the *Canada GST Service*.

160(1)(a) amended by 2000 same-sex partners bill to add reference to "common-law partner", effective for the 2001 and later taxation years, or earlier by election (see Notes to 248(1)"common-law partner").

**I.T. Application Rules**: 69 (meaning of "*Income Tax Act*, chapter 148 of the Revised Statutes of Canada, 1952").

**Interpretation Bulletins**: IT-258R2: Transfer of property to a spouse; IT-260R: Transfer of property to a minor; IT-369R: Attribution of trust income to settlor; IT-510: Transfers and loans of property made after May 22, 1985 to a related minor; IT-511R: Interspousal and certain other transfers and loans of property.

**Information Circulars**: 98-1R: Collections policies.

**I.T. Technical News**: No. 4 (section 160 — the *Davis* case).

**(1.1) Joint liability where subsec. 69(11) applies** — Where a particular person or partnership is deemed by subsection 69(11) to have disposed of a property at any time, the person referred to in that subsection to whom a benefit described in that subsection was available in respect of a subsequent disposition of the property or property substituted for the property is jointly and severally liable with each other taxpayer to pay a part of the other taxpayer's liabilities under this Act in respect of each taxation year equal to the amount determined by the formula

$$A - B$$

where

A is the total of amounts payable under this Act by the other taxpayer in respect of the year, and

B is the amount that would, if the particular person or partnership were not deemed by subsection 69(11) to have disposed of the property, be determined for A in respect of the other taxpayer in respect of the year,

but nothing under this subsection is deemed to limit the liability of the other taxpayer under any other provision of this Act.

**Related Provisions**: 257 — Formula cannot calculate to less than zero.

**Notes**: 160(1.1) added by 1995-97 technical bill, effective for dispositions deemed by 69(11) to occur after April 26, 1995.

**(1.2) Joint liability — tax on split income** — A parent of a specified individual is jointly and severally liable with the individual for the amount required to be added because of subsection 120.4(2) in computing the specified individual's tax payable under this Part for a taxation year if, during the year, the parent

(a) carried on a business that purchased goods or services from a business the income of which is directly or indirectly included in computing the individual's split income for the year;

(b) was a specified shareholder of a corporation that purchased goods or services from a business the income of which is directly or indirectly included in computing the individual's split income for the year;

(c) was a specified shareholder of a corporation, dividends on the shares of the capital stock of which were directly or indirectly included in computing the individual's split income for the year;

(d) was a shareholder of a professional corporation that purchased goods or services from a business the income of which is directly or indirectly included in computing the individual's split income for the year; or

(e) was a shareholder of a professional corporation, dividends on the shares of the capital stock of which were directly or indirectly included in computing the individual's split income for the year.

**Notes**: 160(1.2) added by 1999 Budget, effective for 2000 and later taxation years. It makes the parent jointly liable for the child's "kiddie tax" (income splitting tax) in certain circumstances.

Another 160(1.2), dealing with the value of an undivided interest in property, was moved to 160(3.1) before being enacted by the 1999-2000 GST technical bill.

**(2) Assessment** — The Minister may at any time assess a taxpayer in respect of any amount payable because of this section and the provisions of this Division apply, with any modifications that the circumstances require, in respect of an assessment made under this section as though it had been made under section 152.

**Related Provisions**: 152 — Assessment.

**Notes**: The words "at any time" mean that the 3-year reassessment period does not start running with either the transfer of property (*Davis*, [1994] 2 C.T.C. 2033 (TCC)), nor with the original assessment of income tax for the year (*Sarraf*, [1994] 1 C.T.C. 2519 (TCC)). However, once an assessment has been issued under 160(2) in respect of a given transfer of property, the reassessment period under 152(4) will begin to run in respect of any subsequent assessments based on the same transfer of property, since "the provisions

**S. 160(2)**      Income Tax Act, Part I

of this Division" apply. The CCRA has conceded this point at the Notice of Objection level.

160(2) amended by 1995-97 technical bill, effective June 18, 1998. The substantive amendment was to change "assess a transferee" to "assess a taxpayer", since 160(2) now extends to assessments under 160(1.1). From taxation years ending after November 1991 to June 17, 1998, read:

> (2) **Minister may assess transferee** — The Minister may at any time assess a transferee in respect of any amount payable by virtue of this section and the provisions of this Division are applicable, with such modifications as the circumstances require, in respect of an assessment made under this section as though it had been made under section 152.

**(3) Discharge of liability** — Where a particular taxpayer has become jointly and severally liable with another taxpayer under this section in respect of part or all of a liability under this Act of the other taxpayer,

(a) a payment by the particular taxpayer on account of that taxpayer's liability shall to the extent of the payment discharge the joint liability; but

(b) a payment by the other taxpayer on account of that taxpayer's liability discharges the particular taxpayer's liability only to the extent that the payment operates to reduce that other taxpayer's liability to an amount less than the amount in respect of which the particular taxpayer is, by this section, made jointly and severally liable.

**Notes**: 160(3) amended by 1995-97 technical bill, effective June 18, 1998. The substantive amendment was for the same reason as 160(2) (to accommodate 160(1.1)). From taxation years ending after November 1991 to June 17, 1998, read:

> (3) **Rules applicable** — Where a transferor and transferee have, by virtue of subsection (1), become jointly and severally liable in respect of part or all of a liability of the transferor under this Act, the following rules apply:
>
> (a) a payment by the transferee on account of the transferee's liability shall to the extent thereof discharge the joint liability; but
>
> (b) a payment by the transferor on account of the transferor's liability only discharges the transferee's liability to the extent that the payment operates to reduce the transferor's liability to an amount less than the amount in respect of which the transferee was, by subsection (1), made jointly and severally liable.

**(3.1) Fair market value of undivided interest** — For the purposes of this section and section 160.4, the fair market value at any time of an undivided interest in a property, expressed as a proportionate interest in that property, is, subject to subsection (4), deemed to be equal to the same proportion of the fair market value of that property at that time.

**Notes**: 160(3.1) added by 2000 GST bill, effective for transfers of property made after June 4, 1999. It ensures that in the typical situation where husband H and wife W share an undivided interest in a property (such as the family home), and H transfers his interest in the property to W, the valuation of what W has received for purposes of 160(1) is 50% of the property's value. (This rule was previously applied administratively by the CCRA anyway.)

This provision was 160(1.2) in Bill C-88, the earlier version of this bill first released on June 4, 1999.

**(4) Special rules re transfer of property to spouse [or common-law partner]** — Notwithstanding subsection (1), where at any time a taxpayer has transferred property to the taxpayer's spouse or common-law partner pursuant to a decree, order or judgment of a competent tribunal or pursuant to a written separation agreement and, at that time, the taxpayer and the spouse or common-law partner were separated and living apart as a result of the breakdown of their marriage or common-law partnership, the following rules apply:

(a) in respect of property so transferred after February 15, 1984,

(i) the spouse or common-law partner shall not be liable under subsection (1) to pay any amount with respect to any income from, or gain from the disposition of, the property so transferred or property substituted therefor, and

(ii) for the purposes of paragraph (1)(e), the fair market value of the property at the time it was transferred shall be deemed to be nil, and

(b) in respect of property so transferred before February 16, 1984, where the spouse or common-law partner would, but for this paragraph, be liable to pay an amount under this Act by virtue of subsection (1), the spouse's or common-law partner's liability in respect of that amount shall be deemed to have been discharged on February 16, 1984,

but nothing in this subsection shall operate to reduce the taxpayer's liability under any other provision of this Act.

**Related Provisions**: 248(5) — Substituted property.

**Notes**: Note the extended definition of "separation agreement" in subsection 248(1).

160(4) amended by 2000 same-sex partners bill to add reference to "common-law partner" and "common-law partnership", effective for the 2001 and later taxation years, or earlier by election (see Notes to 248(1)"common-law partner").

**Information Circulars**: 98-1R: Collections policies.

**Definitions [s. 160]**: "amount", "assessment", "business", "common-law partner", "common-law partnership" — 248(1); "corporation" — 248(1), *Interpretation Act* 35(1); "dividend" — 248(1); "fair market value" — 160(3.1); "individual" — 248(1); "Minister" — 248(1); "parent" — 252(2)(a); "person", "professional corporation", "property", "separation agreement", "share", "shareholder" — 248(1); "specified individual" — 120.4(1), 248(1); "specified shareholder" — 248(1); "split income" — 120.4(1), 248(1); "substituted property" — 248(5); "taxation year" — 249; "taxpayer" — 248(1); "trust" — 104(1), 248(1), (3).

**160.1 (1) Where excess refunded** — Where at any time the Minister determines that an amount has been refunded to a taxpayer for a taxation year in excess of the amount to which the taxpayer was entitled as a refund under this Act, the following rules apply:

(a) the excess shall be deemed to be an amount that became payable by the taxpayer on the day on which the amount was refunded; and

1474

(b) the taxpayer shall pay to the Receiver General interest at the prescribed rate on the excess (other than any portion thereof that can reasonably be considered to arise as a consequence of the operation of section 122.5 or 122.61) from the day it became payable to the date of payment.

**Related Provisions**: 160.1(3) — Assessment; 161.1 — Offset of refund interest against arrears interest; 221.1 — Application of interest where legislation retroactive; 248(11) — Interest compounded daily.

**Notes**: 160.1(1)(b) amended by 1991 technical bill, effective 1989, and by 1992 Child Benefit bill, effective 1993, to add the references to 122.5 and 122.61(1), so that no interest is charged on the portion of a refund that represents a repayment of the GST credit or the Child Tax Benefit.

**Regulations**: 4301(a) (prescribed rate of interest).

**(1.1) Liability for refunds by reason of section 122.5 [GST credit]** — Where a person is a qualified relation of an individual for a taxation year (within the meaning assigned by subsection 122.5(1)), the person and the individual are jointly and severally liable to pay any excess described in subsection (1) that was refunded in respect of the year to, or applied to a liability of, the individual as a consequence of the operation of section 122.5, but nothing in this subsection shall be deemed to limit the liability of any person under any other provision of this Act.

**Related Provisions**: 160.1(3) — Assessment.

**Notes**: 160.1(1.1) added by 1990 GST, effective 1989.

**(2) [Repealed]**

**Notes**: 160.1(2) repealed by 1992 Child Benefit bill, effective as of the 1993 taxation year. It made both parents liable for any overpayment of the former Child Tax Credit in 122.2.

**(2.1) Liability for refunds by reason of section 122.61 [Child Tax Benefit]** — Where a person was a cohabiting spouse or common-law partner (within the meaning assigned by section 122.6) of an individual at the end of a taxation year, the person and the individual are jointly and severally liable to pay any excess described in subsection (1) that was refunded in respect of the year to, or applied to a liability of, the individual as a consequence of the operation of section 122.61 if the person was the individual's cohabiting spouse or common-law partner at the time the excess was refunded, but nothing in this subsection shall be deemed to limit the liability of any person under any other provision of this Act.

**Related Provisions**: 160.1(3) — Assessment.

**Notes**: 160.1(2.1) amended by 2000 same-sex partners bill to add reference to "common-law partner", effective for the 2001 and later taxation years, or earlier by election (see Notes to 248(1)"common-law partner").

160.1(2.1) added by 1992 Child Benefit bill, effective for 1991 and later taxation years. It relates to the Child Tax Credit. Earlier version repealed by 1990 GST effective 1991. For 1986 through 1990, it related to the FST credit in 122.4.

**(2.2) Liability for excess refunds under section 126.1 to partners [UI premium tax credit]** — Every taxpayer who, on the day on which an amount has been refunded to, or applied to the liability of, a member of a partnership as a consequence of the operation of subsection 126.1(7) or (13) in excess of the amount to which the member was so entitled, is a member of that partnership is jointly and severally liable with each other taxpayer who on that day is a member of the partnership to pay the excess and to pay interest on the excess, but nothing in this subsection shall be deemed to limit the liability of any person under any other provision of this Act.

**Notes**: 160.1(2.2) added by 1992 Economic Statement, effective for 1993 and later taxation years.

**(3) Assessment** — The Minister may at any time assess a taxpayer in respect of any amount payable by the taxpayer because of subsection (1) or (1.1) or for which the taxpayer is liable because of subsection (2.1) or (2.2), and this Division applies, with such modifications as the circumstance require, in respect of an assessment made under this section as though it were made under section 152.

**Notes**: 160.1(3) amended by 1992 Child Benefit bill to delete reference to 160.1(2), and by 1992 Economic Statement to add reference to 160.1(2.2), both effective for 1993 and later taxation years.

**(4) Where amount applied to liability** — Where an amount is applied to a liability of a taxpayer to Her Majesty in right of Canada in excess of the amount to which the taxpayer is entitled as a refund under this Act, this section applies as though that amount had been refunded to the taxpayer on the day on which it was so applied.

**Notes [subsec. 160.1(4)]**: 160.1(4) amended by 1991 technical bill, effective 1990.

**Definitions [s. 160.1]**: "amount", "assessment" — 248(1); "child" — 252(1); "cohabiting spouse or common-law partner" — 122.6; "common-law partner", "common-law partnership", "individual", "Minister" — 248(1); "partnership" — see Notes to 96(1); "person", "prescribed" — 248(1); "prescribed rate" — Reg. 4301; "taxation year" — 249; "taxpayer" — 248(1).

**160.2 (1) Joint and several liability in respect of amounts received out of or under RRSP** — Where

(a) an amount is received out of or under a registered retirement savings plan by a taxpayer other than an annuitant (within the meaning assigned by subsection 146(1)) under the plan, and

(b) that amount or part thereof would, but for paragraph (a) of the definition "benefit" in subsection 146(1), be received by the taxpayer as a benefit (within the meaning assigned by that definition),

the taxpayer and the last annuitant under the plan are jointly and severally liable to pay a part of the annuitant's tax under this Part for the year of the annuitant's death equal to that proportion of the amount by which the annuitant's tax for the year is greater than it would have been if it were not for the operation of subsection 146(8.8) that the total of all amounts each of which is an amount determined

**S. 160.2(1)**

under paragraph (b) in respect of the taxpayer is of the amount included in computing the annuitant's income by virtue of that subsection, but nothing in this subsection shall be deemed to limit the liability of the annuitant under any other provision of this Act.

**Interpretation Bulletins:** IT-500R: RRSPs — death of an annuitant.

**(2) Joint and several liability in respect of amounts received out of or under RRIF** — Where

(a) an amount is received out of or under a registered retirement income fund by a taxpayer other than an annuitant (within the meaning assigned by subsection 146.3(1)) under the fund, and

(b) that amount or part thereof would, but for paragraph 146.3(5)(a), be included in computing the taxpayer's income for the year of receipt pursuant to subsection 146.3(5),

the taxpayer and the annuitant are jointly and severally liable to pay a part of the annuitant's tax under this Part for the year of the annuitant's death equal to that proportion of the amount by which the annuitant's tax for the year is greater than it would have been if it were not for the operation of subsection 146.3(6) that the amount determined under paragraph (b) is of the amount included in computing the annuitant's income by virtue of that subsection, but nothing in this subsection shall be deemed to limit the liability of the annuitant under any other provision of this Act.

**(3) Minister may assess recipient** — The Minister may at any time assess a taxpayer in respect of any amount payable by virtue of this section and the provisions of this Division are applicable, with such modifications as the circumstances require, in respect of an assessment made under this section as though it had been made under section 152.

**(4) Rules applicable** — Where a taxpayer and an annuitant have, by virtue of subsection (1) or (2), become jointly and severally liable in respect of part or all of a liability of the annuitant under this Act, the following rules apply:

(a) a payment by the taxpayer on account of the taxpayer's liability shall to the extent thereof discharge the joint liability; but

(b) a payment by the annuitant on account of the annuitant's liability only discharges the taxpayer's liability to the extent that the payment operates to reduce the annuitant's liability to an amount less than the amount in respect of which the taxpayer was, by subsection (1) or (2), as the case may be, made jointly and severally liable.

**Definitions [s. 160.2]:** "amount", "assessment", "Minister" — 248(1); "registered retirement income fund" — 146.3(1), 248(1); "registered retirement savings plan" — 146(1), 248(1); "taxpayer" — 248(1).

**Interpretation Bulletins [s. 160.2]:** IT-500R: RRSPs — death of an annuitant.

**160.3 (1) Liability in respect of amounts received out of or under RCA trust** — Where an amount required to be included in the income of a taxpayer by virtue of paragraph 56(1)(x) is received by a person with whom the taxpayer is not dealing at arm's length, that person is jointly and severally liable with the taxpayer to pay a part of the taxpayer's tax under this Part for the taxation year in which the amount is received equal to the amount by which the taxpayer's tax for the year exceeds the amount that would be the taxpayer's tax for the year if the amount had not been received, but nothing in this subsection shall be deemed to limit the liability of the taxpayer under any other provision of this Act.

**(2) Minister may assess recipient** — The Minister may at any time assess a person in respect of any amount payable by the person by virtue of this section and the provisions of this Division are applicable, with such modifications as the circumstances require, in respect of an assessment made under this section as though it had been made under section 152.

**(3) Rules applicable** — Where a taxpayer and another person have, by virtue of subsection (1), become jointly and severally liable in respect of part or all of a liability of the taxpayer under this Act, the following rules apply:

(a) a payment by the other person on account of the other person's liability shall to the extent thereof discharge the joint liability; but

(b) a payment by the taxpayer on account of the taxpayer's liability only discharges the other person's liability to the extent that the payment operates to reduce the taxpayer's liability to an amount less than the amount in respect of which the other person was, by subsection (1), made jointly and severally liable.

**Related Provisions [s. 160.3]:** Part XI.3 — Tax in respect of retirement compensation arrangements.

**Definitions [s. 160.3]:** "amount" — 248(1); "arm's length" — 251(1); "assessment", "Minister", "person" — 248(1); "taxation year" — 249; "taxpayer" — 248(1).

**160.4 (1) Liability in respect of transfers by insolvent corporations** — Where property is transferred at any time by a corporation to a taxpayer with whom the corporation does not deal at arm's length at that time and the corporation is not entitled because of subsection 61.3(3) to deduct an amount under section 61.3 in computing its income for a taxation year because of the transfer or because of the transfer and one or more other transactions, the taxpayer is jointly and severally liable with the corporation to pay an amount of the corporation's tax under this Part for the year equal to the amount, if any, by which the fair market value of the property at that time exceeds the fair market value at that time of the consideration given for the property, but nothing in this subsection limits the liability of the corporation under any other provision of this Act.

Division I — Returns, Assessments, Payment and Appeals    S. 161(1)

**Related Provisions**: 160(3.1) — Fair market value of undivided interest in property.

**Notes**: See Notes to 61.3(1) and at end of 160.4.

**(2) Indirect transfers** — Where

(a) property is transferred at any time from a taxpayer (in this subsection referred to as the "transferor") to another taxpayer (in this subsection referred to as the "transferee") with whom the transferor does not deal at arm's length,

(b) the transferor is liable because of subsection (1) or this subsection to pay an amount of the tax of another person (in this subsection referred to as the "debtor") under this Part, and

(c) it can reasonably be considered that one of the reasons of the transfer would, but for this subsection, be to prevent the enforcement of this section,

the transferee is jointly and severally liable with the transferor and the debtor to pay an amount of the debtor's tax under this Part equal to the lesser of the amount of such tax that the transferor was liable to pay at that time and the amount, if any, by which the fair market value of the property at that time exceeds the fair market value at that time of the consideration given for the property, but nothing in this subsection limits the liability of the debtor or the transferor under any provision of this Act.

**(3) Minister may assess recipient** — The Minister may at any time assess a person in respect of any amount payable by the person because of this section and the provisions of this Division apply, with such modifications as the circumstances require, in respect of an assessment made under this section, as though it had been made under section 152.

**(4) Rules applicable** — Where a corporation and another person have, because of subsection (1) or (2), become jointly and severally liable in respect of part or all of a liability of the corporation under this Act

(a) a payment by the other person on account of that person's liability shall to the extent thereof discharge the joint liability; and

(b) a payment by the corporation on account of the corporation's liability discharges the other person's liability only to the extent that the payment operates to reduce the corporation's liability to an amount less than the amount in respect of which the other person was, by subsection (1) or (2), as the case may be, made liable.

**Notes [s. 160.4]**: 160.4 added by 1994 tax amendments bill (Part I), effective for transfers that occur after December 20, 1994.

**Definitions [s. 160.4]**: "amount" — 248(1); "arm's length" — 251(1); "corporation" — 248(1), *Interpretation Act* 35(1); "debtor" — 160.4(2)(b); "fair market value" — 160(3.1); "Minister", "person", "property" — 248(1); "taxation year" — 249(1); "taxpayer" — 248(1); "transferee", "transferor" — 160.4(2)(a).

## Interest

**161. (1) General [interest on late balances]** — Where at any time after a taxpayer's balance-due day for a taxation year

(a) the total of the taxpayer's taxes payable under this Part and Parts I.3, VI and VI.1 for the year

exceeds

(b) the total of all amounts each of which is an amount paid at or before that time on account of the taxpayer's tax payable and applied as at that time by the Minister against the taxpayer's liability for an amount payable under this Part or Part I.3, VI or VI.1 for the year,

the taxpayer shall pay to the Receiver General interest at the prescribed rate on the excess, computed for the period during which that excess is outstanding.

**Related Provisions**: 18(1)(t) — Interest is non-deductible; 150 — Filing of returns; 156.1(4) — Due date for payment of balance; 161(5), (6.1), (7) — Special rules; 161.1 — Offset of refund interest against arrears interest; 164(3) — Interest on refunds paid by CCRA; 220(4.5)(b)(i) — No interest on unpaid departure tax where security provided; 220(4.6)(d)(i) — No interest on unpaid tax on distribution of property by trust to non-resident beneficiary where security provided; 221.1 — Application of interest where legislation retroactive; 227(8.3), (9.3) — Interest on certain withholding taxes not paid; 248(11) — Interest compounded daily.

**Notes**: Interest payable to the CCRA is non-deductible (18(1)(t)) and compounds daily (248(11)) at a prescribed rate which changes quarterly (see list of rates in Notes to Reg. 4301).

The CCRA gives individuals, on a statement of account, a due date by which the balance on the statement may be paid without further interest accruing (usually 20 days). See Revenue Canada Fact Sheet, March 24, 1994 (reproduced under 161(1) in David M. Sherman, *Income Tax Act: Department of Finance Technical Notes* (Carswell, annual)).

161(1) amended by 1983 Budget, 1988 tax reform, 1992 technical bill and 1996 Budget. The current version applies to 1996 and later taxation years, but is substantively identical to that which applies to 1992–95. The change was to use the term "balance-due day" (now extended in 248(1) to apply to corporations) in place of "the day on or before which a taxpayer is required to pay the remainder of the taxpayer's tax payable under this Part for a taxation year (or would be so required if a remainder of such tax were payable)".

For tax payable for 1989–91, ignore the references in paras. (a) and (b) to Parts I.3, VI and VI.1, and ignore the words "(or would be so required if a remainder of such tax were payable)" in the opening words. For earlier interest, calculated from April 20, 1983 and on, read the opening words as:

161. (1) Where at any time after the day on or before which a return of a taxpayer's income was required under this Part to be filed for a taxation year,

For interest relating to any period before April 20, 1983, read 161(1) as follows:

161. (1) Where the amount paid on account of tax payable by a taxpayer under this Part for a taxation year before the expiration of the time allowed for filing the return of the taxpayer's income is less than the amount of tax payable for the year under this Part, the person liable to pay the tax shall pay interest at a prescribed rate per annum on the difference between those two amounts from the expiration of the time for filing the return of income to the day of payment.

1477

S. 117 of the 1993 technical bill provides: "Notwithstanding any other provision of the said Act [i.e., the *Income Tax Act*] or of this Act [i.e., the 1993 technical bill], nothing in this Act shall affect the amount of any interest payable under the *Income Tax Act* by a life insurance corporation in respect of any period or part thereof that is before March 15, 1993." (The amendments in question are in sections 138, 181.3, 190.1, 190.11, 190.13, 190.15 and 190.16, which may have altered a corporation's tax liability for the 1992 and, in some cases, 1991 taxation years.)

Note also that the provision in 248(11) for daily compounding of interest applies only since January 1, 1987; interest accrued since before 1987 is compounded from that date only.

**Regulations**: 4301(a) (prescribed rate of interest).

**I.T. Application Rules**: 62(2) (subsec. 161(1) applies to interest payable in respect of any period after December 23, 1971).

**Information Circulars**: 92-2: Guidelines for the cancellation and waiver of interest and penalties.

**(2) Interest on instalments** — In addition to the interest payable under subsection (1), where a taxpayer who is required by this Part to pay a part or instalment of tax has failed to pay all or any part thereof on or before the day on or before which the tax or instalment, as the case may be, was required to be paid, the taxpayer shall pay to the Receiver General interest at the prescribed rate on the amount that the taxpayer failed to pay computed from the day on or before which the amount was required to be paid to the day of payment, or to the beginning of the period in respect of which the taxpayer is required to pay interest thereon under subsection (1), whichever is earlier.

**Related Provisions**: 18(1)(t) — Interest is non-deductible; 107(5.1) — Trust's gain on distribution to non-resident beneficiary does not increase instalment requirements; 128.1(5) — Deemed disposition on emigration does not increase instalment requirements; 155–157 — Times for instalments; 161(4) — Limitation — farmers and fishermen; 161(4.01) — Limitation — other individuals; 161(4.1) — Limitation — corporations; 161(5), (6.1), (7) — Special rules; 161(8) — Deemed instalments; 161(10) — When amount deemed paid; 163.1 — Penalty for late or deficient instalments; 211.5(2) — Interest on instalments of Part XII.3 tax; 221.1 — Application of interest where legislation retroactive; 248(11) — Interest compounded daily.

**Notes**: See Notes to 156(1). By paying the instalments suggested by the CCRA (based on previous years' income), one can prevent interest from being payable under 161(2). A taxpayer who pays lower instalments based on expected tax for the current year runs the risk of interest if tax is unexpectedly higher: *Elkharadly*, [1995] 1 C.T.C. 2273D (TCC).

The 1995 Budget bill provides:

49. (4) No interest is payable under subsection 161(2) of the Act in respect of any amount that became payable before July 1995 because of subsection 190.1(1.2) of the Act, as enacted by subsection (1) [which added 190.1(1.2) — ed.].

**Regulations**: 4301(a) (prescribed rate of interest).

**I.T. Application Rules**: 62(2) (subsec. 161(2) applies to interest payable in respect of any period after December 23, 1971.

**Interpretation Bulletins**: IT-243R4: Dividend refund to private corporations.

**Information Circulars**: 92-2: Guidelines for the cancellation and waiver of interest and penalties.

**(2.1) Exception** — Where the total of all amounts each of which is an amount of interest payable under subsection (2) by a taxpayer, including any interest payable under subsection (2) because of its application under section 36 of the *Canada Pension Plan* to any amount paid or payable under that Act, or under any provision of an Act of a province with which the Minister of Finance has entered into an agreement for the collection of the taxes payable to the province under that Act that is similar to subsection (2) does not exceed $25 for a taxation year, the Minister shall not assess the interest.

**Notes**: 161(2.1) amended by 1991 technical bill, effective December 17, 1991, to add reference to interest payable by reason of s. 36 of the *Canada Pension Plan*.

**(2.2) Contra interest [offset interest]** — Notwithstanding subsections (1) and (2), the total amount of interest payable by a taxpayer (other than a testamentary trust) under those subsections, for the period that begins on the first day of the taxation year for which a part or instalment of tax is payable and ends on the taxpayer's balance-due day for the year, in respect of the taxpayer's tax or instalments of tax payable for the year shall not exceed the amount, if any, by which

(a) the total amount of interest that would be payable for the period by the taxpayer under subsections (1) and (2) in respect of the taxpayer's tax and instalments of tax payable for the year if no amount were paid on account of the tax or instalments

exceeds

(b) the amount of interest that would be payable under subsection 164(3) to the taxpayer in respect of the period on the amount that would be refunded to the taxpayer in respect of the year or applied to another liability if

(i) no tax were payable by the taxpayer for the year,

(ii) no amount had been remitted under section 153 to the Receiver General on account of the taxpayer's tax for the year,

(iii) the rate of interest prescribed for the purpose of subsection (1) were prescribed for the purpose of subsection 164(3), and

(iv) the latest of the days described in paragraphs 164(3)(a), (b) and (c) were the first day of the year.

**Related Provisions**: 161.1 — Offset of refund interest and arrears interest of different years.

**Notes**: 161(2.2) allows "offset" interest (sometimes called "contra" interest), to be earned on early or overpaid instalments, to reduce the interest charge resulting from late or insufficient instalments for the same year. Thus, as long as interest rates remain flat, a single instalment payment at the midpoint of all instalment due dates for the year should result in no instalment interest being assessed. See also proposed 161.1.

161(2.2) amended by 1996 Budget, effective for 1996 and later taxation years. The changes are non-substantive and result from the extension of the definition of "balance-due day" in 248(1) to corporations. 161(2.2) previously read:

> **(2.2) Interest on instalments [offset interest]** — Notwithstanding subsections (1) and (2), the total amount of interest payable by a taxpayer (other than a testamentary trust) under those subsections for the period commencing on the first day of the taxation year for which a part or instalment of tax is payable and ending
>
> > (a) where the taxpayer is a corporation, on the day on or before which the corporation is, pursuant to paragraph 157(1)(b), required to pay the remainder of its tax payable under this Part for the year or would be so required if a remainder of the tax were payable, and
> >
> > (b) in the case of an individual, on the individual's balance-due day for the year,
>
> in respect of the tax or instalments thereof payable for the year shall not exceed the amount, if any, by which
>
> > (c) the total amount of interest that would be payable for the period by the taxpayer under subsections (1) and (2) in respect of the taxpayer's tax and instalments thereof payable for the year if no amount were paid on account of the tax or instalments
>
> exceeds
>
> > (d) the amount of interest that would be payable under subsection 164(3) to the taxpayer in respect of the period on the amount that would be refunded to the taxpayer in respect of the year or applied to another liability if
> >
> > > (i) no tax were payable by the taxpayer for the year,
> > >
> > > (ii) no amount had been remitted under section 153 to the Receiver General on account of the taxpayer's tax for the year,
> > >
> > > (iii) the rate of interest prescribed for the purpose of subsection (1) were prescribed for the purpose of subsection 164(3), and
> > >
> > > (iv) the latest of the days described in paragraphs 164(3)(a), (b) and (c) were the first day of the year.

161(2.2)(b) amended by 1991 technical bill, effective 1990, to refer to the "balance-due day" rather than April 30. The balance-due day (defined in 248(1)) corresponds to the return deadline under 150(1). The change ensures that offset interest under 161(2.2) and refund interest under 164(3) may be determined in respect of successive and non-overlapping periods for deceased individuals and *inter vivos* trusts.

161(2.2)(d)(iii) added by 1995 Budget, for interest that is calculated in respect of periods after June 1995, to ensure that "contra" interest is calculated at the same rate as interest on overdue payments, now that the refund interest rate is 2 points lower than the late-payment rate. (See Reg. 4301.) The former 161(2.2) had the same text as subparas. (i), (ii) and (iv) but without being broken down into subparagraphs.

**Regulations**: Reg. 4301(a) (prescribed rate of interest).

**(3) [Repealed]**

**Notes**: 161(3) repealed by 1991 technical bill, retroactive to 1988. It imposed an extra 3% interest charge on a cooperative corporation or credit union in certain circumstances.

**(4) Limitation — farmers and fishermen** — For the purposes of subsection (2) and section 163.1, where an individual is required to pay a part or instalment of tax for a taxation year computed by reference to a method described in subsection 155(1), the individual shall be deemed to have been liable to pay on or before the day referred to in subsection 155(1) a part or instalment computed by reference to

(a) the amount, if any, by which

> (i) the tax payable under this Part by the individual for the year, determined before taking into consideration the specified future tax consequences for the year,

exceeds

> (ii) the amounts deemed by subsections 120(2) and (2.2) to have been paid on account of the individual's tax under this Part for the year, determined before taking into consideration the specified future tax consequences for the year,

(b) the individual's instalment base for the preceding taxation year, or

(c) the amount stated to be the amount of the instalment payable by the individual for the year in the notice, if any, sent to the individual by the Minister,

whichever method gives rise to the least amount required to be paid by the individual on or before that day.

**Related Provisions**: 107(5.1) — Trust's gain on distribution to non-resident beneficiary does not increase instalment requirements; 128.1(5) — Deemed disposition on emigration does not increase instalment requirements.

**Notes**: 161(4)(a)(ii) amended by 1999 Budget, effective for 1999 and later taxation years, to add reference to 120(2.2).

See Notes to 161(4.01).

**(4.01) Limitation — other individuals** — For the purposes of subsection (2) and section 163.1, where an individual is required to pay a part or instalment of tax for a taxation year computed by reference to a method described in subsection 156(1), the individual shall be deemed to have been liable to pay on or before each day referred to in subsection 156(1) a part or instalment computed by reference to

(a) the amount, if any, by which

> (i) the tax payable under this Part by the individual for the year, determined before taking into consideration the specified future tax consequences for the year,

exceeds

> (ii) the amounts deemed by subsections 120(2) and (2.2) to have been paid on account of the individual's tax under this Part for the year, determined before taking into consideration the specified future tax consequences for the year,

(b) the individual's instalment base for the preceding taxation year,

(c) the amounts determined under paragraph 156(1)(b) in respect of the individual for the year, or

(d) the amounts stated to be the amounts of instalments payable by the individual for the year in the notices, if any, sent to the individual by the Minister,

reduced by the amount, if any, determined under paragraph 156(2)(b) in respect of the individual for the year, whichever method gives rise to the least total amount of such parts or instalments required to be paid by the individual by that day.

**Related Provisions**: 107(5.1) — Trust's gain on distribution to non-resident beneficiary does not increase instalment requirements; 128.1(5) — Deemed disposition on emigration does not increase instalment requirements.

**Notes**: 161(4.01)(a)(ii) amended by 1999 Budget, effective for 1999 and later taxation years, to add reference to 120(2.2).

161(4)(a) and (4.01)(a) both amended by 1996 Budget, effective for 1996 and later taxation years, to add the exclusion of specified future tax consequences in place of the existing exclusion. ("Specified future tax consequences" (see definition in 248(1)) refers to adjustments from the carryback of losses or similar amounts or because of corrections of certain amounts renounced in connection with the issuance of flow-through shares.) For earlier years, read both paras. as simply:

(a) the amount, if any, by which the tax payable under this Part by the individual for the year exceeds the amount deemed by subsection 120(2) to have been paid on account of the individual's tax under this Part for the year,

161(4) amended and (4.01) added by 1992 technical bill, and (4.01) amended retroactively by 1993 technical bill, all effective for 1992 and later taxation years. However, for instalments payable on or before June 10, 1993 (the date of Royal Assent to the 1992 technical bill), ignore the references to 163.1 (so that 161(4) and (4.01) do not apply for purposes of that section). For taxation years before 1992, read:

(4) Limitation respecting individuals — For the purposes of subsection (2), where an individual is required to pay a part or instalment of tax for a taxation year computed by reference to

(a) the amount estimated by him to be the tax payable under this Part by him for the year computed without reference to sections 127.2 and 127.3, or

(b) his instalment base for the immediately preceding taxation year,

he shall be deemed to have been liable to pay a part or instalment computed by reference to the lesser of

(c) the amount, if any, by which the tax payable under this Part by him for the year computed without reference to sections 127.2 and 127.3 exceeds the amount deemed by subsection 120(2) to have been paid on account of his tax under this Part for the year, and

(d) his instalment base for the immediately preceding taxation year.

**(4.1) Limitation — corporations** — For the purposes of subsection (2) and section 163.1, where a corporation is required to pay a part or instalment of tax for a taxation year computed by reference to a method described in subsection 157(1), the corporation shall be deemed to have been liable to pay on or before each day referred to in subparagraphs 157(1)(a)(i) to (iii) a part or instalment computed by reference to

(a) the total of the taxes payable under this Part and Parts I.3, VI and VI.1 by the corporation for the year, determined before taking into consideration the specified future tax consequences for the year,

(b) its first instalment base for the year, or

(c) its second instalment base and its first instalment base for the year,

reduced by the amount, if any, determined under any of paragraphs 157(3)(b) to (d) in respect of the corporation for the year, whichever method gives rise to the least total amount of such parts or instalments of tax for the year.

**Notes**: 161(4.1) amended by 1992 technical bill and 1993 technical bill, both effective for 1992 and later taxation years, but for instalments payable on or before June 10, 1993, ignore the reference to 163.1. For taxation years before 1992, ignore the references to Parts I.3 and VI. See Notes to 157(1).

**Regulations**: 5301(7), (9) (instalment obligations of parent after windup of subsidiary).

**(5) Participation certificates** — Notwithstanding any other provision in this section, no interest is payable in respect of the amount by which the tax payable by a person is increased by a payment made by The Canadian Wheat Board on a participation certificate previously issued to the person until 30 days after the payment is made.

**(6) Income of resident from a foreign country in blocked currency** — Where the income of a taxpayer for a taxation year, or part thereof, is from sources in another country and the taxpayer by reason of monetary or exchange restrictions imposed by the law of that country is unable to transfer it to Canada, the Minister may, if the Minister is satisfied that payment as required by this Part of the whole of the additional tax under this Part for the year reasonably attributable to income from sources in that country would impose extreme hardship on the taxpayer, postpone the time for payment of the whole or a part of that additional tax for a period to be determined by the Minister, but no such postponement may be granted if any of the income for the year from sources in that country has been

(a) transferred to Canada,

(b) used by the taxpayer for any purpose whatever, other than payment of income tax to the government of that other country on income from sources in that country, or

(c) disposed of by the taxpayer,

and no interest is payable under this section in respect of that additional tax, or part thereof, during the period of postponement.

**Interpretation Bulletins**: IT-351: Income from a foreign source — blocked currency.

**(6.1) Foreign tax credit adjustment** — Notwithstanding any other provision in this section, where the tax payable under this Part by a taxpayer for a particular taxation year is increased because of

(a) an adjustment of an income or profits tax payable by the taxpayer to the government of a country other than Canada or to the government of a state, province or other political subdivision of such a country, or

(b) a reduction in the amount of foreign tax deductible under subsection 126(1) or (2) in computing the taxpayer's tax otherwise payable under this Part for the particular year, as a result of the application of subsection 126(4.2) in respect of a share or debt obligation disposed of by the taxpayer in the taxation year following the particular year,

no interest is payable, in respect of the increase in the taxpayer's tax payable, for the period

(c) that ends 90 days after the day on which the taxpayer is first notified of the amount of the adjustment, if paragraph (a) applies, and

(d) before the date of the disposition, if paragraph (b) applies.

**Related Provisions**: 248(1)"specified future tax consequence"(c) — Adjustment under 161(6.1) is a specified future tax consequence.

**Notes**: 161(6.1) amended, effectively to add paras. (b) and (d), by 1998 Budget, effective for 1998 and later taxation years. For earlier years, read:

(6.1) Adjustment of foreign tax payable — Notwithstanding any other provision in this section, where the tax payable under this Part by a taxpayer for a taxation year is increased by virtue of an adjustment of an income or profits tax payable by the taxpayer to the government of a country other than Canada or to the government of a state, province or other political subdivision of any such country, no interest is payable, in respect of the increase in the taxpayer's tax payable, for the period ending 90 days after the day on which the taxpayer is first notified of the amount of the adjustment.

**(6.2) Flow-through share renunciations** — Where the tax payable under this Part by a taxpayer for a taxation year is more than it otherwise would be because of a consequence for the year described in paragraph (b) of the definition "specified future tax consequence" in subsection 248(1) in respect of an amount purported to be renounced in a calendar year, for the purposes of the provisions of this Act (other than this subsection) relating to interest payable under this Act, an amount equal to the additional tax payable is deemed

(a) to have been paid on the taxpayer's balance-due day for the taxation year on account of the taxpayer's tax payable under this Part for the year; and

(b) to have been refunded on April 30 of the following calendar year to the taxpayer on account of the taxpayer's tax payable under this Part for the taxation year.

**Notes**: 161(6.2) added by 1996 Budget, effective for 1996 and later taxation years. It applies where tax payable under Part I is more than it otherwise would be because of 248(1)"specified future tax consequence"(b). That results from reduction under 66(12.73) of an amount purported to be renounced under 66(12.6) or (12.601) because of the application of 66(12.66). Where 161(6.2) applies, the taxpayer's Part I tax account for the year is, on the balance-due day, credited with an amount equal to such additional tax payable. The account is subsequently debited, on April 30 of the calendar year that follows the year of the renunciation, with the same amount.

The main purpose of this rule, in conjunction with amendments to 156.1 and 157 and Reg. 5300–5301 re tax instalments, is to avoid arrears interest being payable by an investor because of adjustments to renunciations made due to the new 1-year look-back rule under 66(12.66). In effect, the taxpayer has a grace period until April 30 of the year following the year in which the renunciation was made. (161(6.2) is also relevant in determining refund interest under 164 because of its effect on a taxpayer's "overpayment" of tax; see 164(7).)

**(7) Effect of carryback of loss, etc.** — For the purpose of computing interest under subsection (1) or (2) on tax or a part of an instalment of tax for a taxation year, and for the purpose of section 163.1,

(a) the tax payable under this Part and Parts I.3, VI and VI.1 by the taxpayer for the year is deemed to be the amount that it would be if the consequences of the deduction or exclusion of the following amounts were not taken into consideration:

(i) [Repealed under former Act]

**Proposed Addition — 161(7)(a)(i)**

(i) any amount deducted under section 119 in respect of a disposition in a subsequent taxation year,

**Application**: Bill C-43 (First Reading September 20, 2000), subsec. 93(1), will add subpara. 161(7)(a)(i), applicable to taxation years that end after October 1, 1996.

**Technical Notes**: Section 161 provides for the payment of interest on outstanding amounts of tax payable under Part I, as well as on late or deficient instalments in respect of such tax.

Subsection 161(7) provides that, where the amount of tax payable for a taxation year is reduced because of certain deductions or exclusions arising from tax credits, the carryback of losses, or events in subsequent years, interest on any unpaid tax for the taxation year is calculated without regard to the reduction until the latest of several dates.

Paragraph 161(7)(a) is amended to include in its list of deductions and exclusions: a deduction under new section 119 in respect of the disposition of a taxable Canadian property of the taxpayer in a subsequent year; a deduction under new subsection 126(2.21) or (2.22) of the Act in respect of a disposition in a subsequent year; and deductions under new subsections 128.1(6) to (8) of the Act in respect of an election in a subsequent year.

(ii) any amount deducted under section 41 in respect of the taxpayer's listed-personal-property loss for a subsequent taxation year,

(iii) any amount excluded from the taxpayer's income for the year by virtue of section 49 in respect of the exercise of an option in a subsequent taxation year,

(iv) any amount deducted under section 118.1 in respect of a gift made in a subsequent taxation year or under section 111 in respect of a loss for a subsequent taxation year,

(iv.1) any amount deducted under subsection 126(2) in respect of an unused foreign tax credit (within the meaning assigned by subsection 126(7)) for a subsequent taxation year,

S. 161(7)(a)(iv.1)      Income Tax Act, Part I

### Proposed Amendment — 161(7)(a)(iv.1)

(iv.1) any amount deducted under subsection 126(2) in respect of an unused foreign tax credit (within the meaning assigned by subsection 126(7)), or under subsection 126(2.21) or (2.22) in respect of foreign taxes paid, for a subsequent taxation year,

**Application**: Bill C-43 (First Reading September 20, 2000), subsec. 93(2), will amend subpara. 161(7)(a)(iv.1) to read as above, applicable to taxation years that end after October 1, 1996.

**Technical Notes**: See under 161(7)(a)(i).

(iv.2) any amount deducted in computing the taxpayer's income for the year by virtue of an election in a subsequent taxation year under paragraph 164(6)(c) or (d) by the taxpayer's legal representative,

(v) any amount deducted under subsection 127(5) in respect of property acquired or an expenditure made in a subsequent taxation year,

(vi) any amount deducted under section 125.2 in respect of an unused Part VI tax credit (within the meaning assigned by subsection 125.2(3)) for a subsequent taxation year,

(vi.1) [Repealed under former Act]

(vii) any amount deducted under section 125.3 in respect of an unused Part I.3 tax credit (within the meaning assigned by subsection 125.3(3)) for a subsequent taxation year,

(viii) any amount deducted, in respect of a repayment under subsection 68.4(7) of the *Excise Tax Act* made in a subsequent taxation year, in computing the amount determined under subparagraph 12(1)(x.1)(ii),

(viii.1) any amount deducted under subsection 147.2(4) in computing the taxpayer's income for the year because of the application of subsection 147.2(6) as a result of the taxpayer's death in the subsequent taxation year,

(ix) any amount deducted under subsection 181.1(4) in respect of any unused surtax credit (within the meaning assigned by subsection 181.1(6)) of the taxpayer for a subsequent taxation year, and

(x) any amount deducted under subsection 190.1(3) in respect of any unused Part I tax credit (within the meaning assigned by subsection 190.1(5)) of the taxpayer for a subsequent taxation year; and

### Proposed Addition — 161(7)(a)(xi)

(xi) any amount deducted under any of subsections 128.1(6) to (8) from the taxpayer's proceeds of disposition of a property because of an election made in a return of income for a subsequent taxation year,

**Application**: Bill C-43 (First Reading September 20, 2000) subsec. 93(3), will add subpara. 161(7)(a)(xi), applicable to taxation years that end after October 1, 1996.

**Technical Notes**: See under 161(7)(a)(i).

(b) the amount by which the tax payable under this Part and Parts I.3, VI and VI.1 by the taxpayer for the year is reduced as a consequence of the deduction or exclusion of amounts described in paragraph (a) is deemed to have been paid on account of the taxpayer's tax payable under this Part for the year on the day that is the latest of

(i) the first day immediately following that subsequent taxation year,

(ii) the day on which the taxpayer's or the taxpayer's legal representative's return of income for that subsequent taxation year was filed,

(iii) where an amended return of the taxpayer's income for the year or a prescribed form amending the taxpayer's return of income for the year was filed in accordance with subsection 49(4) or 152(6) or paragraph 164(6)(e), the day on which the amended return or prescribed form was filed, and

(iv) where, as a consequence of a request in writing, the Minister reassessed the taxpayer's tax for the year to take into account the deduction or exclusion, the day on which the request was made.

**Related Provisions**: 162(11) — Effect of carryback of losses etc.; 248(1)"specified future tax consequence"(a) — Deduction or exclusion of amount referred to in 161(7)(a) is a specified future tax consequence.

**Notes**: Opening words of 161(7) amended by 1992 technical bill, effective for instalments payable after June 10, 1993, to add reference to 163.1.

Opening words of 161(7)(a) amended to incorporate what was the closing words of the para. (for clarity; no substantive change) by 1995-97 technical bill, effective for amounts that become payable after December 1995. Previously read "if none of the following amounts, namely, ... [text of subparas. (i)-(x)] were so excluded or deducted for the year, as the case may be".

Opening words of 161(7)(a) and of 161(7)(b) amended by 1992 technical bill, effective for 1992 and later taxation years, to add references to Parts I.3, VI and VI.1. See Notes to 157(1).

161(7)(a)(vii) added by 1989 Budget, effective for taxation years ending after June 1989.

161(7)(a)(viii), and reference to it in 161(7)(b), added by 1992 transportation industry assistance bill, effective 1992. Amended by 1997 Budget (first bill), effective for 1997 and later taxation years, due to the expansion of the fuel tax rebate program to cover aviation fuel rebates (see Notes to 12(1)(x.1)). For 1992–96, read:

(viii) any amount excluded from the amount determined under clause 12(1)(x.1)(ii)(A) because of subclause 12(1)(x.1)(ii)(A)(II) in respect of a fuel tax rebate repayment made in a subsequent taxation year,

161(7)(a)(viii.1) added by 1995-97 technical bill, effective for deaths after 1992.

161(7)(a)(ix) added by 1992 technical bill and amended retroactively by 1996 Budget, effective for 1992 and later taxation years. The tax resulting from the carryback on an unused surtax credit is thus not taken into account in determining interest charges on unpaid tax until the later of the dates specified in 161(7)(b).

1482

161(7)(a)(x) (and reference to it in 161(7)(b)) added by 1992 technical bill and amended retroactively by 1996 Budget, effective for 1991 and later taxation years. The tax resulting from the carryback of an unused Part I tax credit is thus not taken into account in determining interest charges on unpaid tax until the later of the dates specified in 161(7)(b).

(The 1996 Budget amendment to 161(7)(a)(ix) and (x) corrected the text so that reductions of the tax payable under Parts I.3 and VI for a taxation year as a consequence of a deduction for the year under 181.1(4) or 190.1(3) are linked to unused credits for a subsequent taxation year. The previous version erroneously referred to deductions for the *subsequent* year.)

Closing words of 161(7)(a) repealed and incorporated into the opening words by 1995-97 technical bill, as noted above.

Opening words of 161(7)(b) amended (for clarity; no substantive change) by 1995-97 technical bill, effective for amounts that become payable after December 1995.

**I.T. Application Rules**: 69 (meaning of "*Income Tax Act*, chapter 148 of the Revised Statutes of Canada, 1952").

**(8) Certain amounts deemed to be paid as instalments** — For the purposes of subsection (2), where in a taxation year an amount has been paid by a non-resident person pursuant to subsection 116(2) or (4) or an amount has been paid on that person's behalf by another person in accordance with subsection 116(5), the amount shall be deemed to have been paid by that non-resident person in the year as an instalment of tax on the first day on which the non-resident person was required under this Act to pay an instalment of tax for that year.

**(9) Definitions of "instalment base", etc.** — In this section,

(a) "instalment base" of an individual for a taxation year means the amount determined in prescribed manner to be the individual's instalment base for the year; and

(b) "first instalment base" and "second instalment base" of a corporation for a taxation year have the meanings prescribed by regulation.

**Regulations**: 5300 ("instalment base"); 5301 ("first instalment base", "second instalment base").

**(10) When amount deemed paid** — For the purposes of subsection (2), where an amount has been deducted by virtue of paragraph 127.2(1)(a) or 127.3(1)(a) in computing the tax payable under this Part by a taxpayer for a taxation year, the amount so deducted shall be deemed to have been paid by the taxpayer

(a) in the case of a taxpayer who has filed a return of income under this Part for the year as required by section 150, on the last day of the year; and

(b) in any other case, on the day on which the taxpayer filed the taxpayer's return of income under this Part for the year.

**(11) Interest on penalties** — Where a taxpayer is required to pay a penalty, the taxpayer shall pay the penalty to the Receiver General together with interest thereon at the prescribed rate computed,

(a) in the case of a penalty payable under section 162, 163 or 235, from the day on or before which

(i) the taxpayer's return of income for a taxation year in respect of which the penalty is payable was required to be filed, or would have been required to be filed if tax under this Part were payable by the taxpayer for the year, or

(ii) the information return, return, ownership certificate or other document in respect of which the penalty is payable was required to be made,

as the case may be, to the day of payment;

(b) in the case of a penalty payable for a taxation year because of section 163.1, from the taxpayer's balance-due day for the year to the day of payment of the penalty;

(b.1) in the case of a penalty under subsection 237.1(7.4), from the day on which the taxpayer became liable to the penalty to the day of payment; and

(c) in the case of a penalty payable by reason of any other provision of this Act, from the day of mailing of the notice of original assessment of the penalty to the day of payment.

**Related Provisions**: 18(1)(t) — Interest and penalty are non-deductible; 161.1 — Offset of refund interest against arrears interest; 163(2.9) — Partnership liable to interest on penalty re tax shelters; 221.1 — Application of interest where legislation retroactive; 248(11) — Interest compounded daily.

**Notes**: Reference to 235 in 161(11)(a) added by 1991 technical bill, effective December 17, 1991.

161(11)(b) amended by 1996 Budget, effective for 1996 and later taxation years, to use "the taxpayer's balance-due day" in place of "the day on or before which the taxpayer is required to pay the remainder of the taxpayer's tax payable under this Part". (The term "balance-due day" in 248(1) has been extended to include corporations.)

161(11)(b.1) added by 1995-97 technical bill, effective December 2, 1994.

**Regulations**: 4301(a) (prescribed rate of interest).

**Interpretation Bulletins**: IT-407R4: Dispositions of cultural property to designated Canadian institutions.

**Information Circulars**: 92-2: Guidelines for the cancellation and waiver of interest and penalties.

**(12) [Repealed]**

**Notes**: 161(12) repealed by 1999 Budget, effective June 29, 2000. This rule is now covered by 163(2.9). From December 2, 1994 (as added by 1995-97 technical bill) through June 28, 2000, read:

(12) Partnership liable to interest — Where a partnership is liable to a penalty under subsection 237.1(7.4), sections 152, 158 to 160.1, this section and sections 164 to 167 and Division J apply, with such modifications as the circumstances require, with respect to interest on the penalty as if the partnership were a corporation.

This rule is needed because a partnership is not a "person" as defined in 248(1). See Notes to 96(1).

**Definitions [s. 161]**: "allowable capital loss" — 38(b), 248(1); "amount", "assessment", "balance-due day" — 248(1); "calendar year" — *Interpretation Act* 37(1)(a); "corporation" — 248(1), *Interpretation Act* 35(1); "foreign tax" — 126(4.2); "individual" — 248(1); "instalment base" — 161(9); "Minister" — 123(1); "partnership" — see Notes to 96(1); "person", "prescribed" — 248(1); "prescribed rate" — Reg. 4301; "property" — 248(1); "province" — *Interpretation Act* 35(1); "share", "specified future tax consequence" — 248(1); "tax payable" — 248(2); "taxable income" — 2(2), 248(1); "taxation year" — 249; "taxpayer" — 248(1); "testamentary trust" — 108(1), 248(1); "writing" — *Interpretation Act* 35(1).

## Offset of Refund Interest and Arrears Interest

**161.1 (1) Definitions** — The definitions in this subsection apply in this section.

**"accumulated overpayment amount"**, of a corporation for a period, means the overpayment amount of the corporation for the period together with refund interest (including, for greater certainty, compound interest) that accrued with respect to the overpayment amount before the date specified under paragraph (3)(b) by the corporation in its application for the period.

**Notes**: See Notes at end of 161.1.

**"accumulated underpayment amount"**, of a corporation for a period, means the underpayment amount of the corporation for the period together with arrears interest (including, for greater certainty, compound interest) that accrued with respect to the underpayment amount before the date specified under paragraph (3)(b) by the corporation in its application for the period.

**"arrears interest"** means interest computed under paragraph (5)(b), 129(2.2)(b), 131(3.2)(b), 132(2.2)(b), 133(7.02)(b) or 160.1(1)(b), subsection 161(1) or (11), paragraph 164(3.1)(b) or (4)(b) or subsection 187(2).

**"overpayment amount"**, of a corporation for a period, means the amount referred to in subparagraph (2)(a)(i) that is refunded to the corporation, or the amount referred to in subparagraph (2)(a)(ii) to which the corporation is entitled.

**"refund interest"** means interest computed under subsection 129(2.1), 131(3.1), 132(2.1), 133(7.01) or 164(3) or (3.2).

**"underpayment amount"**, of a corporation for a period, means the amount referred to in paragraph (2)(b) payable by the corporation on which arrears interest is computed.

**(2) Concurrent refund interest and arrears interest** — A corporation may apply in writing to the Minister for the reallocation of an accumulated overpayment amount for a period that begins after 1999 on account of an accumulated underpayment amount for the period if, in respect of tax paid or payable by the corporation under this Part or Part I.3, II, IV, IV.1, VI, VI.1 or XIV,

(a) refund interest for the period

(i) is computed on an amount refunded to the corporation, or

(ii) would be computed on an amount to which the corporation is entitled, if that amount were refunded to the corporation; and

(b) arrears interest for the period is computed on an amount payable by the corporation.

**Related Provisions**: 161.1(3) — Contents of and deadline for application; 161.1(5) — Where refund previously paid.

**Notes**: See Notes at end of 161.1.

**(3) Contents of application** — A corporation's application referred to in subsection (2) for a period is deemed not to have been made unless

(a) it specifies the amount to be reallocated, which shall not exceed the lesser of the corporation's accumulated overpayment amount for the period and its accumulated underpayment amount for the period;

(b) it specifies the effective date for the reallocation, which shall not be earlier than the latest of

(i) the date from which refund interest is computed on the corporation's overpayment amount for the period, or would be so computed if the overpayment amount were refunded to the corporation,

(ii) the date from which arrears interest is computed on the corporation's underpayment amount for the period, and

(iii) January 1, 2000; and

(c) it is made on or before the day that is 90 days after the latest of

(i) the day of mailing of the first notice of assessment giving rise to any portion of the corporation's overpayment amount to which the application relates,

(ii) the day of mailing of the first notice of assessment giving rise to any portion of the corporation's underpayment amount to which the application relates,

(iii) if the corporation has served a notice of objection to an assessment referred to in subparagraph (i) or (ii), the day of mailing of the notification under subsection 165(3) by the Minister in respect of the notice of objection,

(iv) if the corporation has appealed, or applied for leave to appeal, from an assessment referred to in subparagraph (i) or (ii) to a court of competent jurisdiction, the day on which the court dismisses the application, the application or appeal is discontinued or final judgment is pronounced in the appeal, and

(v) the day of mailing of the first notice to the corporation indicating that the Minister has determined any portion of the corporation's overpayment amount to which the application relates, if the overpayment amount has not been determined as a result of a notice of assessment mailed before that day.

**Related Provisions**: 161.1(4) — Amount reallocated is deemed to have been refunded.

**(4) Reallocation** — The amount to be reallocated that is specified under paragraph (3)(a) by a corporation is deemed to have been refunded to the corporation and paid on account of the accumulated underpayment amount on the date specified under paragraph (3)(b) by the corporation.

**Related Provisions**: 161.1(6) — Consequential reallocations.

**(5) Repayment of refund** — If an application in respect of a period is made under subsection (2) by a corporation and a portion of the amount to be reallocated has been refunded to the corporation, the following rules apply:

(a) a particular amount equal to the total of

(i) the portion of the amount to be reallocated that was refunded to the corporation, and

(ii) refund interest paid or credited to the corporation in respect of that portion

is deemed to have become payable by the corporation on the day on which the portion was refunded; and

(b) the corporation shall pay to the Receiver General interest at the prescribed rate on the particular amount from the day referred to in paragraph (a) to the date of payment.

**Related Provisions**: 248(11) — Interest compounded daily.

**(6) Consequential reallocations** — If a particular reallocation of an accumulated overpayment amount under subsection (4) results in a new accumulated overpayment amount of the corporation for a period, the new accumulated overpayment amount shall not be reallocated under this section unless the corporation so applies in its application for the particular reallocation.

**(7) Assessments** — Notwithstanding subsections 152(4), (4.01) and (5), the Minister shall assess or reassess interest and penalties payable by a corporation in respect of any taxation year as necessary in order to take into account a reallocation of amounts under this section.

**Related Provisions**: 165(1.1) — Limitation of right to object to assessment.

### Proposed Amendment — Extension of s. 161.1 to individuals

**Notice of Ways and Means Motion, federal budget, February 28, 2000**: *Offsetting of Interest on Personal Tax Overpayments and Underpayments*

(23) That, for individuals other than trusts, the taxable amount of refund interest accruing over any period after 1999 on overpayments of income tax be reduced by the amount of any arrears interest accruing over the same period on unpaid income tax.

**Federal budget, supplementary information, February 28, 2000**: *Offsetting of Interest on Personal Tax Overpayments and Underpayments*

An individual who has made an overpayment of income tax may be entitled to receive refund interest from the government on the overpayment. Refund interest is included in income for tax purposes, in the same manner as interest from other sources.

If, on the other hand, an individual has failed to pay an amount of income tax when due, the individual is required to pay arrears interest to the government. Arrears interest is not deductible in computing a taxpayer's income for tax purposes.

The taxation of refund interest and non-deductibility of arrears interest can produce inappropriate results in situations where an individual who owes interest on unpaid tax from one taxation year is concurrently owed interest on a tax overpayment from a different taxation year. In this circumstance, the cost of the non-deductible interest payable by the individual exceeds the after-tax value of the taxable interest receivable by the individual. In many instances, this difference results from the non-deductibility of interest paid and the inclusion in income of interest received.

This budget proposes a relieving mechanism for these individuals. Refund interest accruing over a period will be taxable only to the extent that it exceeds any arrears interest that accrued over the same period to which the refund interest relates. As under current practice, the individual's notice of assessment will indicate the full amount of refund interest. In addition, the Canada Customs and Revenue Agency will issue an information slip indicating the amount, if any, of the refund interest that must be included in the individual's income for tax purposes.

This measure will apply to individuals other than trusts in respect of arrears and refund interest amounts that accrue concurrently after 1999, regardless of the taxation year to which the amounts relate.

**Department of Finance news release Backgrounder, December 21, 2000**: *Offset Interest*

The 2000 budget proposed an interest offset mechanism in respect of overpayments and underpayments of tax by individuals. The Department of Finance and the Canada Customs and Revenue Agency are working to develop a mechanism under which this proposal can be given effect, for implementation at the earliest opportunity.

**Notes [s. 161.1]**: 161.1 added by 1999 Budget, effective after 1999. It allows a corporation to net interest payable to the CCRA for one taxation year against interest on refunds for another taxation year, where they accrue over the same period. It is needed because interest on unpaid tax is non-deductible under 18(1)(t) and applies at a high rate under Reg. 4301(a), while refund interest is taxable under 12(1)(c) and applies at two percentage points less under Reg. 4301(b)). This rule is to be extended to individuals as proposed in the February 2000 budget, but as per the December 2000 announcement above, implementation has been postponed while the mechanism is developed.

**Definitions [s. 161.1]**: "accumulated overpayment amount", "accumulated underpayment amount" — 161.1(1); "amount" — 248(1); "arrears interest" — 161.1(1); "assessment" — 248(1); "corporation" — 248(1), *Interpretation Act* 35(1); "Minister" — 248(1); "overpayment amount" — 161.1(1); "prescribed" — 248(1); "refund interest" — 161.1(1); "taxation year" — 249; "underpayment amount" — 161.1(1); "writing" — *Interpretation Act* 35(1).

## Penalties

**162. (1) Failure to file return of income** — Every person who fails to file a return of income for a taxation year as and when required by subsection 150(1) is liable to a penalty equal to the total of

    (a) an amount equal to 5% of the person's tax payable under this Part for the year that was unpaid when the return was required to be filed, and

    (b) the product obtained when 1% of the person's tax payable under this Part for the year that was unpaid when the return was required to be filed is multiplied by the number of complete months, not exceeding 12, from the date on which the return was required to be filed to the date on which the return was filed.

**Related Provisions**: 162(2.1) — Minimum penalty for non-resident corporation; 162(11) — Effect of carryback of losses, etc.; 235 — Additional penalty on large corporation for late filing even where no balance owing. See additional Related Provisions and Definitions at end of s. 162.

**Notes**: The late-filing penalty under 162(1) is based on the tax unpaid as of the return due date (April 15 or June 30 for individuals; 6 months after year-end for corporations). If the return is not ready, it is thus wise to guess at the amount owing and make a payment by the return due date.

The penalty is based on the amount actually owing on the due date, and is not reduced by the carryback of a loss from a later year: *Cloud*, [1995] 1 C.T.C. 2726 (TCC).

See also Notes to 238(1).

**Information Circulars**: 92-2: Guidelines for the cancellation and waiver of interest and penalties; 00-1: Voluntary disclosures program.

**(2) Repeated failure to file** — Every person

    (a) who fails to file a return of income for a taxation year as and when required by subsection 150(1),

    (b) on whom a demand for a return for the year has been served under subsection 150(2), and

    (c) by whom, before the time of failure, a penalty was payable under this subsection or subsection (1) in respect of a return of income for any of the 3 preceding taxation years

is liable to a penalty equal to the total of

    (d) an amount equal to 10% of the person's tax payable under this Part for the year that was unpaid when the return was required to be filed, and

    (e) the product obtained when 2% of the tax payable under this Part for the year that was unpaid when the return was required to be filed is multiplied by the number of complete months, not exceeding 20, from the date on which the return was required to be filed to the date on which the return was filed.

**Related Provisions**: 162(2.1) — Minimum penalty for non-resident corporation; 162(11) — Effect of carryback of losses, etc. See additional Related Provisions and Definitions at end of s. 162.

**Notes**: See Notes to 238(1).

**Information Circulars**: 92-2: Guidelines for the cancellation and waiver of interest and penalties; 00-1: Voluntary disclosures program.

**(2.1) Failure to file — non-resident corporation** — Notwithstanding subsections (1) and (2), if a non-resident corporation is liable to a penalty under subsection (1) or (2) for failure to file a return of income for a taxation year, the amount of the penalty is the greater of

    (a) the amount computed under subsection (1) or (2), as the case may be, and

    (b) an amount equal to the greater of

        (i) $100, and

        (ii) $25 times the number of days, not exceeding 100, from the day on which the return was required to be filed to the day on which the return is filed.

**Related Provisions**: 150(1)(a)(i), (ii) — Obligation on non-resident to file return.

**Notes**: 162(2.1) added by 1998 Budget, effective for taxation years that begin after 1998.

**(3) Failure to file by trustee** — Every person who fails to file a return as required by subsection 150(3) is liable to a penalty of $10 for each day of default but not exceeding $50.

**Related Provisions**: See Related Provisions and Definitions at end of s. 162.

**Notes**: See Notes to 238(1).

**Information Circulars**: 92-2: Guidelines for the cancellation and waiver of interest and penalties; 00-1: Voluntary disclosures program.

**(4) Ownership certificate** — Every person who

    (a) fails to complete an ownership certificate as required by section 234,

    (b) fails to deliver an ownership certificate in the manner prescribed at the time prescribed and at the place prescribed by regulations made under that section, or

    (c) cashes a coupon or warrant for which an ownership certificate has not been completed pursuant to that section,

is liable to a penalty of $50.

**Related Provisions**: See Related Provisions and Definitions at end of s. 162.

**Notes**: See Notes to 238(1).

**Information Circulars**: 92-2: Guidelines for the cancellation and waiver of interest and penalties; 00-1: Voluntary disclosures program.

**(5) Failure to provide information on form** — Every person who fails to provide any information required on a prescribed form made under this Act or a regulation is liable to a penalty of $100 for each such failure, unless

    (a) in the case of information required in respect of another person or partnership, a reasonable effort was made by the person to obtain the information from the other person or partnership; or

(b) in the case of a failure to provide a Social Insurance Number on a return of income, the person had applied for the assignment of the Number and had not received it at the time the return was filed.

**Related Provisions**: 162(8.1) — Where partnership liable to penalty. See also Related provisions and Definitions at end of s. 162.

**Notes**: See Notes to 238(1).

162(5)(a) amended by 1995-97 technical bill to add references to a partnership, effective June 18, 1998.

162(5) amended by 1991 technical bill, effective December 17, 1991, to delete the authority of the Minister to waive the penalty for an individual. A general discretion to waive penalties is now provided in 220(3.1).

**Information Circulars**: 82-2R2: SIN legislation that relates to the preparation of information slips; 00-1: Voluntary disclosures program.

**(6) Failure to provide identification number** — Every person or partnership who fails to provide on request their Social Insurance Number or their business number to a person required under this Act or a regulation to make an information return requiring the number is liable to a penalty of $100 for each such failure, unless

(a) an application for the assignment of the number is made within 15 days after the request was received; and

(b) the number is provided to the person who requested the number within 15 days after the person or partnership received it.

**Related Provisions**: 162(8.1) — Where partnership liable to penalty; 237(1), (1.1), (2) — Obligation to apply for and provide Social Insurance Number on information return. See additional Related provisions and Definitions at end of s. 162.

**Notes**: See Notes to 238(1).

162(6) amended by 1995-97 technical bill to apply to a business number (previously applied only to a Social Insurance Number), effective June 18, 1998.

162(6) amended by 1991 technical bill, effective December 17, 1991, to delete the authority of the Minister to waive the penalty for an individual. A general discretion to waive penalties is now provided in 220(3.1).

**Information Circulars**: 82-2R2: SIN legislation that relates to the preparation of information slips; 00-1: Voluntary disclosures program.

**(7) Failure to comply** — Every person (other than a registered charity) or partnership who fails

(a) to file an information return as and when required by this Act or the regulations, or

(b) to comply with a duty or obligation imposed by this Act or the regulations

is liable in respect of each such failure, except where another provision of this Act (other than subsection (10) or (10.1) or 163(2.22)) sets out a penalty for the failure, to a penalty equal to the greater of $100 and the product obtained when $25 is multiplied by the number of days, not exceeding 100, during which the failure continues.

**Related Provisions**: 149(4.1), 188 — Revocation of registration and penalty tax for registered charity; 162(8.1) — Where partnership liable to penalty. See additional Related Provisions and Definitions at end of s. 162.

**Notes**: Parenthetical exclusion of a registered charity added to opening words of 162(7) by 1993 technical bill, effective June 15, 1994. Since charities may be subject to revocation of their registration (and resulting tax under Part V) for failure to comply with the Act, that is considered sufficient penalty and no penalty under 162(7) can be imposed.

Reference to 162(10.1) and 163(2.22) in closing words added by 1996 Budget, effective for returns required to be filed in 1998 or later, and for duties and obligations first imposed in 1998 or later.

**Information Circulars**: 89-4: Tax shelter reporting; 92-2: Guidelines for the cancellation and waiver of interest and penalties; 00-1: Voluntary disclosures program.

**(7.1) Failure to make partnership information return** — Where a member of a partnership fails to file an information return as a member of the partnership for a fiscal period of the partnership as and when required by this Act or the regulations and subsection (10) does not set out a penalty for the failure, the partnership is liable to a penalty equal to the greater of $100 and the product obtained when $25 is multiplied by the number of days, not exceeding 100, during which the failure continues.

**Related Provisions**: 96(1) — Taxation of partnership; 162(8.1) — Rules where partnership is liable to penalty. See additional Related Provisions and Definitions at end of s. 162.

**Notes**: See Notes to 238(1).

162(7.1) amended by 1996 Budget to add the words "and subsection (10) does not set out a penalty for the failure", effective for returns required to be filed in 1998 or later, and for duties and obligations first imposed in 1998 or later.

162(7.1) added by 1991 technical bill (in the form of an amendment to the 1988 tax reform bill), effective December 17, 1991.

**(8) Repeated failure to file** — Where

(a) a penalty was payable under subsection (7.1) in respect of a failure by a member of a partnership to file an information return as a member of the partnership for a fiscal period of the partnership,

(b) a demand for the return or for information required to be contained in the return has been served under section 233 on the member, and

(c) a penalty was payable under subsection (7.1) in respect of the failure by a member of a partnership to file an information return as a member of the partnership for any of the 3 preceding fiscal periods,

the partnership is liable, in addition to the penalty under subsection (7.1), to a penalty of $100 for each member of the partnership for each month or part of a month, not exceeding 24 months, during which the failure referred to in paragraph (a) continues.

**Related Provisions**: 162(8.1) — Rules where partnership is liable to penalty. See additional Related Provisions and Definitions at end of s. 162.

S. 162(8.1)        Income Tax Act, Part I

**(8.1) Rules where partnership liable to a penalty** — Where a partnership is liable to a penalty under subsection (5), (6), (7), (7.1), (8) or (10), sections 152, 158 to 160.1, 161 and 164 to 167 and Division J apply, with any modifications that the circumstances require, to the penalty as if the partnership were a corporation.

**Notes**: 162(8.1) is needed because a partnership is not a "person" as defined in 248(1) and could not otherwise be assessed a penalty. See 96(1)(a).

162(8.1) amended by 1995-97 technical bill, effective June 18, 1998, to add references to 162(5) and (6) and delete a reference to 162(10.1).

162(8.1) amended by 1996 Budget, effective for returns required to be filed in 1998 or later, and for duties and obligations first imposed in 1998 or later. The substantive effect was to add references to 162(7), (10) and (10.1); the other changes were cosmetic. The previous version read:

(8.1) Rules where partnership is liable to penalty — Where a partnership is liable to a penalty under subsection (7.1) or (8), sections 152, 158 to 160.1, 161 and 164 to 167 and Division J apply, with such modifications as the circumstances require, with respect to the penalty as if the partnership were a corporation.

162(8.1) added by 1991 technical bill (in the form of an amendment to the 1988 tax reform bill), effective December 17, 1991.

**(9) [Repealed]**

**Notes**: 162(9) repealed by 1995-97 technical bill, effective December 2, 1994. It has been replaced by a penalty in 237.1(7.4). From September 1989 to December 1, 1994, read:

(9) **Tax shelter identification number** — Every person who

(a) files false or misleading information with the Minister in an application under subsection 237.1(2) for an identification number for a tax shelter, or

(b) whether as a principal or as an agent, sells, issues or accepts a contribution for the acquisition of an interest in a tax shelter before the Minister has issued an identification number therefor,

is liable to a penalty equal to the greater of

(c) $500, and

(d) 3% of the total of all amounts each of which is the cost to each person who acquired an interest in the tax shelter before the correct information is filed with the Minister or the identification number is issued, as the case may be.

**(10) Failure to furnish foreign-based information** — Every person or partnership who,

(a) knowingly or under circumstances amounting to gross negligence, fails to file an information return as and when required by any of sections 233.1 to 233.4, or

(b) where paragraph (a) does not apply, knowingly or under circumstances amounting to gross negligence, fails to comply with a demand under section 233 to file a return

is liable to a penalty equal to the amount determined by the formula

$$(\$500 \times A \times B) - C$$

where

A is

(c) where paragraph (a) applies, the lesser of 24 and the number of months, beginning with the month in which the return was required to be filed, during any part of which the return has not been filed, and

(d) where paragraph (b) applies, the lesser of 24 and the number of months, beginning with the month in which the demand was served, during any part of which the return has not been filed,

B is

(e) where the person or partnership has failed to comply with a demand under section 233 to file a return, 2, and

(f) in any other case, 1, and

C is the penalty to which the person or partnership is liable under subsection (7) in respect of the return.

**Related Provisions**: 162(7) — Initial calculation of penalty; 162(8.1) — Where partnership liable to penalty; 162(10.1) — Additional penalty; 163(2.4)–(2.91) — Penalty for false statement or omission in return; 233.5 — Due diligence defence; 257 — Formula cannot calculate to less than zero. See also Related Provisions and Definitions at end of s. 162.

**Notes**: 162(10) amended by 1996 Budget, effective for returns required to be filed by April 30, 1998 or later. (See also 162(10.1)–(10.4), added at the same time.) For earlier returns, read:

(10) Every corporation

(a) that fails to file an information return required by section 233.1,

(b) on which a demand under section 233 has been served for the return, and

(c) that does not comply with the demand within 90 days after the day the demand was served on it,

is liable in respect of each such failure, in addition to the penalty under subsection (7), to a penalty of $1,000 for each month or part of a month, not exceeding 24 months, during which the failure continues.

Since the penalty under 162(10)(b) can only be assessed where a demand was served for "the" return, it arguably does not apply (under the pre-amendment wording, i.e., for returns due before April 30, 1998) to a return under 233.1 unless the demand has identified the specific non-resident about whom information is sought.

**(10.1) Additional penalty** — Where

(a) a person or partnership is liable to a penalty under subsection (10) for the failure to file a return (other than an information return required to be filed under section 233.1),

(b) if paragraph (10)(a) applies, the number of months, beginning with the month in which the return was required to be filed, during any part of which the return has not been filed exceeds 24, and

(c) if paragraph (10)(b) applies, the number of months, beginning with the month in which the demand referred to in that paragraph was served, during any part of which the return has not been filed exceeds 24, the person or partnership is liable, in addition to the penalty determined under subsection (10), to a penalty equal to the amount determined by the formula

$$A - B$$

where

A is

(d) where the return is required to be filed under section 233.2, 5% of the total of all amounts each of which is the fair market value of property transferred or loaned (determined as of the time of the transfer or loan) because of which there would, if no other transfer or loan were taken into account, be an obligation to file the return,

### Proposed Amendment — 162(10.1)A(d)

(d) where the return is required to be filed under section 233.2 in respect of a trust, 5% of the total of all amounts each of which is the fair market value, at the time it was made, of a contribution of the person or partnership made to the trust before the end of the last taxation year of the trust in respect of which the return is required,

**Application**: The June 22, 2000 draft legislation, subsec. 20(1), will amend para. (d) of the description of A in subsec 162(10.1) to read as above, applicable to returns in respect of taxation years that begin after 2000.

**Technical Notes**: Subsection 162 and 163 of the Act impose penalties for infractions such as failing to provide certain information on a return, failing to file a return for a taxation year, and making false statements on a return.

Subsection 162(10.1) of the Act imposes a penalty on any person or partnership that is more than 24 months late in filing an information return that the person or partnership was required to file under any of sections 233.1 to 233.4. (This penalty applies in addition to the penalties imposed under subsections 162(7) and (10)).

The penalty imposed under subsection 162(10.1) with respect to a particular information return is equal to a specified amount less the amount of the penalties imposed under subsections 162(7) and (10) with respect to the return. The specified amount with respect to an information return for a trust required to be filed by a person or partnership under section 233.2 is equal to 5% of the total fair market value of any property transferred or loaned to the trust that, if no other loan or transfer were taken into account, would have imposed an obligation on the person or partnership to file the return.

Subsection 162(10.1) is amended as a consequence of amendments made to section 233.2, by changing the manner in which the specified amount is determined. The specified amount is now to be determined with reference to the fair market value of "contributions" made by the person or partnership to the trust.

(e) where the return is required to be filed under section 233.3 for a taxation year or fiscal period, 5% of the greatest of all amounts each of which is the total of the cost amounts to the person or partnership at any time in the year or period of a specified foreign property (as defined by subsection 233.3(1)) of the person or partnership, and

(f) where the return is required to be filed under section 233.4 for a taxation year or fiscal period in respect of a foreign affiliate of the person or partnership, 5% of the greatest of all amounts each of which is the total of the cost amounts to the person or partnership at any time in the year or period of a property of the person or partnership that is a share of the capital stock or indebtedness of the affiliate, and

B is the total of the penalties to which the person or partnership is liable under subsections (7) and (10) in respect of the return.

**Related Provisions**: 162(7) — Initial calculation of penalty; 162(10.11) — Application to trust contributions; 162(10.2) — Shares or debt owned by controlled foreign affiliate; 162(10.3) — Application to partnerships; 162(10.4) — Application to non-resident trusts; 163(2.4)–(2.91) — Penalty for false statement or omission in return; 233.5 — Due diligence defence to penalty; 257 — Formula cannot calculate to less than zero.

**Notes**: 162(10.1) added by 1996 Budget, effective for returns required to be filed by April 30, 1998 or later.

### Proposed Addition — 162(10.11)

**(10.11) Application to trust contributions** — Subsections 94(1) and (2) apply for the purpose of paragraph (d) of the description of A in subsection (10.1), except that for this purpose the definition "arm's length transfer" in subsection 94(1) shall be read without reference to subparagraph (a)(v) of that definition.

**Application**: The June 22, 2000 draft legislation, subsec. 20(2), will add subsec. 162(10.11), applicable to returns in respect of taxation years that begin after 2000.

**Technical Notes**: New subsection 162(10.11) provides that, for the purpose of the calculation in subsection 162(10.1), the definitions and rules in subsections 94(1) and (2) generally apply. Subsection 162(10.11) is similar to amended subsection 233.2(2), described in greater detail in the commentary below.

This amendment applies to returns in respect of taxation years that begin after 2000.

**(10.2) Shares or debt owned by controlled foreign affiliate** — For the purpose of paragraph (f) of the description of A in subsection (10.1),

(a) shares or indebtedness owned by a controlled foreign affiliate of a person or partnership are deemed to be owned by the person or partnership; and

(b) the cost amount at any time of such shares or indebtedness to the person or partnership is deemed to be equal to 20% of the cost amount at that time to the controlled foreign affiliate of the shares or indebtedness.

**Related Provisions**: 162(10.3) — Application to partnerships; 162(10.4) — Application to non-resident trusts.

**S. 162(10.2)**      Income Tax Act, Part I

**Notes:** 162(10.2) added by 1996 Budget, effective for returns required to be filed by April 30, 1998 or later.

**(10.3) Application to partnerships** — For the purposes of paragraph (f) of the description of A in subsection (10.1) and subsection (10.2), in determining whether a non-resident corporation or trust is a foreign affiliate or a controlled foreign affiliate of a partnership,

> **Proposed Amendment — 162(10.3) opening words**
>
> **(10.3) Application to partnerships** — For the purposes of paragraph (f) of the description of A in subsection (10.1) and subsection (10.2), in determining whether a non-resident corporation is a foreign affiliate or a controlled foreign affiliate of a partnership,
>
> **Application:** The June 22, 2000 draft legislation, subsec. 20(3), will amend the opening words of subsec. 162(10.3) to read as above, applicable to returns in respect of taxation years that begin after 2000.
>
> **Technical Notes:** Existing paragraph 94(1)(d) of the Act provides for non-resident trusts to be treated as foreign affiliates, but is being repealed as a consequence of the introduction of new rules for non-resident trusts in section 94. Subsections 162(10.3) and (10.4) are rules affecting the calculation of penalty tax in respect of a person's or partnership's failure to file a return in respect of a foreign affiliate. Subsections 163(2.6) and (2.91) are similar provisions that affect the calculation of penalty tax in respect of false statements and omissions in such a return.
>
> Subsections 162(10.3) and 163(2.6) are amended to reflect the changes to section 94 under which non-resident trusts are no longer treated as foreign affiliates. Subsections 162(10.4) and 163(2.91) are repealed for the same reason.
>
> These amendments apply to returns in respect of taxation years that begin after 2000.

    (a) the definitions "direct equity percentage" and "equity percentage" in subsection 95(4) shall be read as if a partnership were a person; and

    (b) the definitions "controlled foreign affiliate" and "foreign affiliate" in subsection 95(1) shall be read as if a partnership were a taxpayer resident in Canada.

**Notes:** 162(10.3) added by 1996 Budget, effective for returns required to be filed by April 30, 1998 or later.

**(10.4) Application to non-resident trusts** — For the purposes of this subsection, paragraph (f) of the description of A in subsection (10.1) and subsection (10.2),

    (a) a non-resident trust is deemed to be a controlled foreign affiliate of each beneficiary of which the trust is a controlled foreign affiliate for the purpose of section 233.4;

    (b) the trust is deemed to be a non-resident corporation having a capital stock of a single class divided into 100 issued shares;

    (c) each beneficiary under the trust is deemed to own at any time the number of the issued shares of the corporation that is equal to the proportion of 100 that

        (i) the fair market value at that time of the beneficiary's beneficial interest in the trust

is of

        (ii) the fair market value at that time of all beneficial interests in the trust; and

    (d) the cost amount to a beneficiary at any time of a share of the corporation is deemed to be equal to the amount determined by the formula

$$\frac{A}{B}$$

where

A    is the fair market value at that time of the beneficiary's beneficial interest in the trust, and

B    is the number of shares deemed under paragraph (c) to be owned at that time by the beneficiary in respect of the corporation.

> **Proposed Repeal — 162(10.4)**
>
> **Application:** The June 22, 2000 draft legislation, subsec. 20(4), will repeal subsec. 162(10.4), in force on Royal Assent.
>
> **Technical Notes:** See under 162(10.3).

**Notes:** 162(10.4) added by 1996 Budget, effective for returns required to be filed by April 30, 1998 or later.

**(11) Effect of subsequent events** — For the purpose of computing a penalty under subsection (1) or (2) in respect of a person's return of income for a taxation year, the person's tax payable under this Part for the year shall be determined before taking into consideration the specified future tax consequences for the year.

**Notes:** 162(11) amended by 1996 Budget, effective for 1996 and later taxation years, as a result of the new definition "specified future tax consequence" in 248(1). For earlier taxation years ending after July 13, 1990, read:

> (11) Effect of carryback of losses etc. — In determining a person's tax for a taxation year for the purpose of computing a penalty under subsection (1) or (2) in respect of the person's return of income for the year, paragraph 161(7)(a) applies with such modifications as the circumstances require.

162(11) added by 1991 technical bill, effective in respect of carrybacks from taxation years ending after July 13, 1990. The change means that, in computing penalties under 161(1) and (2), tax is determined without reference to deductions that arise from later years' events, such as loss carrybacks or unused foreign tax credits from later years.

A former version of 162(11), enacted in 1988, would have imposed a $10 penalty on any taxpayer issuing a cheque that was dishonoured. It was never proclaimed and was repealed in 1991 without ever becoming effective.

**Related Provisions [s. 162]:** 18(1)(t) — Penalties are non-deductible; 161(11) — Interest on penalty; 180.1(4), 180.2(6), 181.7, 183(3), 183.2(2), 187(3), 187.6, 189(8), 190.21, 191.4(2), 193(8), 195(8), 196(4), 202(3), 204.3(2), 204.7(3), 204.87, 204.93, 204.94(4), 207(3), 207.2(3), 207.4(2), 207.7(4), 208(4), 209(5), 210.2(7), 211.5, 211.6(5), 211.91(3), 218.2(5), 219(3), 247(11) — Provisions of s. 162 apply for purposes of Parts I.1, I.2, I.3, II, II.1, IV, IV.1, V, VI, VI.1, VII, VIII, IX, X, X.1, X.2, X.3, X.4, X.5, XI, XI.1, XI.2, XI.3, XII, XII.1, XII.2, XII.3, XII.4, XII.6, XIII.1, XIV and XVI.1 respectively; 220(3.1) — Waiver of penalty or interest; 227(10.01), (10.1) — Provisions of s. 162 apply to withholding taxes under Parts XII.5 and XIII; 238(1), (3) — Offences; 239(3) — Penalty assessment cannot be issued after charge laid if person convicted.

**Definitions [s. 162]**: "amount", "business number" — 248(1); "controlled foreign affiliate" — 95(1), 162(10.3), (10.4)(a), 248(1); "corporation" — 162(10.4)(b), 248(1), *Interpretation Act* 35(1); "fiscal period" — 249.1; "foreign affiliate" — 95(1), 162(10.3), 248(1); "individual", "Minister", "non-resident" — 248(1); "owned" — 162(10.2); "partnership" — see Notes to 96(1); "person", "prescribed", "property" — 248(1); "received" — 248(7); "registered charity", "regulation" — 248(1); "tax shelter" — 237.1(1), 248(1); "taxation year" — 249; "trust" — 104(1), 248(1), (3).

**Information Circulars [s. 162]**: 00-1: Voluntary disclosures program.

**163. (1) Repeated failures [to report income]** — Every person who

(a) fails to report an amount required to be included in computing the person's income in a return filed under section 150 for a taxation year, and

(b) had failed to report an amount required to be so included in any return filed under section 150 for any of the three preceding taxation years

is liable to a penalty equal to 10% of the amount described in paragraph (a), except where the person is liable to a penalty under subsection (2) in respect of that amount.

**Related Provisions**: 163(3) — Burden of proof. See also Related Provisions and Definitions at end of s. 163.

**Notes**: See Notes to 238(1).

**Information Circulars**: 00-1: Voluntary disclosures program.

**(2) False statements or omissions** — Every person who, knowingly, or under circumstances amounting to gross negligence, has made or has participated in, assented to or acquiesced in the making of, a false statement or omission in a return, form, certificate, statement or answer (in this section referred to as a "return") filed or made in respect of a taxation year for the purposes of this Act, is liable to a penalty of the greater of $100 and 50% of the total of

(a) the amount, if any, by which

(i) the amount, if any, by which

(A) the tax for the year that would be payable by the person under this Act

exceeds

(B) the amounts that would be deemed by subsections 120(2) and (2.2) to have been paid on account of the person's tax for the year

if the person's taxable income for the year were computed by adding to the taxable income reported by the person in the person's return for the year that portion of the person's understatement of income for the year that is reasonably attributable to the false statement or omission and if the person's tax payable for the year were computed by subtracting from the deductions from the tax otherwise payable by the person for the year such portion of any such deduction as may reasonably be attributable to the false statement or omission

exceeds

(ii) the amount, if any, by which

(A) the tax for the year that would have been payable by the person under this Act

exceeds

(B) the amounts that would be deemed by subsections 120(2) and (2.2) to have been paid on account of the person's tax for the year

had the person's tax payable for the year been assessed on the basis of the information provided in the person's return for the year,

(b) [Repealed]

(c) the total of all amounts each of which is the amount, if any, by which

(i) the amount that would be deemed by subsection 122.61(1) to be an overpayment on account of the person's liability under this Part for the year that arose during a particular month or, where that person is a cohabiting spouse or common-law partner (within the meaning assigned by section 122.6) of an individual at the end of the year and at the beginning of the particular month, of that individual's liability under this Part for the year that arose during the particular month, as the case may be, if that total were calculated by reference to the information provided

exceeds

(ii) the amount that is deemed by subsection 122.61(1) to be an overpayment on account of the liability of that person or that individual, as the case may be, under this Part for the year that arose during the particular month,

(c.1) the amount, if any, by which

(i) the total of all amounts each of which is an amount that would be deemed by section 122.5 to be paid by that person during a month specified for the year or, where that person is a qualified relation of an individual for the year (within the meaning assigned by subsection 122.5(1)), by that individual, as the case may be, if that total were calculated by reference to the information provided in the prescribed form filed for the year under section 122.5

exceeds

(ii) the total of all amounts each of which is an amount that is deemed under section 122.5 to be paid by that person or that qualified relation during a month specified for the year,

## S. 163(2)(c.2) — Income Tax Act, Part I

(c.2) the amount, if any, by which

(i) the amount that would be deemed under subsection 122.51(2) to be paid on account of the person's tax payable under this Part for the year if the amount were calculated by reference to the information provided in the return

exceeds

(ii) the amount that is deemed under subsection 122.51(2) to be paid on account of the person's tax payable under this Part for the year,

(d) the amount, if any, by which

(i) the amount that would be deemed by subsection 127.1(1) to be paid for the year by the person if that amount were calculated by reference to the information provided in the return or form filed for the year pursuant to that subsection

exceeds

(ii) the amount that is deemed by that subsection to be paid for the year by the person,

(e) the amount, if any, by which

(i) the amount that would be deemed by subsection 127.41(3) to have been paid for the year by the person if that amount were calculated by reference to the person's claim for the year under that subsection

exceeds

(ii) the maximum amount that the person is entitled to claim for the year under subsection 127.41(3),

(f) the amount, if any, by which

(i) the amount that would be deemed by subsection 125.4(3) to have been paid for the year by the person if that amount were calculated by reference to the information provided in the return filed for the year pursuant to that subsection

exceeds

(ii) the amount that is deemed by that subsection to be paid for the year by the person, and

(g) the amount, if any, by which

(i) the amount that would be deemed by subsection 125.5(3) to have been paid for the year by the person if that amount were calculated by reference to the information provided in the return filed for the year pursuant to that subsection

exceeds

(ii) the amount that is deemed by that subsection to be paid for the year by the person.

**Related Provisions:** 163(2.1) — Interpretation; 163(3) — Burden of proof; 163.2(15)(c) — Deemed liability for certain acts of employee; 239(1) — Offence — false statements. See also Related Provisions and Definitions at end of s. 163.

**Notes:** See Notes to 238(1) with respect to the difference between an administrative penalty and criminal prosecution for an offence.

The penalty under 163(2) relates to the undeclared income, and can apply even if the income could have been offset by additional discretionary deductions such as CCA: *MacDonald*, [1997] 3 C.T.C. 2195 (TCC). See 163(2.1)(a)(ii).

For the meaning of "gross negligence" under 163(2), see *Venne*, [1984] C.T.C. 223 at 234 (FCTD): "Gross negligence must be taken to involve greater neglect than simply a failure to use reasonable care. It must involve a high degree of negligence tantamount to intentional acting, an indifference as to whether the law is complied with or not." The CCRA was excoriated for applying the gross-negligence penalty without evidence, in *897366 Ontario Ltd.*, [2000] G.S.T.C. 13 (TCC): "The imposition of [such] penalties ... requires a serious and deliberate consideration by the taxing authority of the taxpayer's conduct to determine whether it demonstrates a degree of wilfulness or gross negligence justifying the penalty.... penalties may only be imposed in the clearest of cases, and after an assiduous scrutiny of the evidence."

Where the taxpayer's accountant or bookkeeper is grossly negligent, the taxpayer may or may not be subject to the penalty: *Udell*, [1969] C.T.C. 704 (Exch. Ct.); *Columbia Enterprises Ltd.*, [1983] C.T.C. 204 (FCA). The accountant or bookkeeper may now be liable under 163.2.

Because 163(2)(a) refers to tax payable "by the person", the penalty under 163(2) applies only to the taxpayer and not to advisers such as accountants who take part in false statements. However, proposed 163.2 can apply to such third parties.

163(2)(c)(i) amended by 2000 same-sex partners bill to add reference to "common-law partner", effective for the 2001 and later taxation years, or earlier by election (see Notes to 248(1)"common-law partner").

Opening words of 163(2) amended by 1995-97 technical bill, effective June 21, 1996, to delete the words "in the carrying out of any duty or obligation imposed by or under this Act" after "gross negligence". The intention was to ensure that taxpayers who volunteer false information for the purposes of the Act are liable to a penalty.

163(2)(a)(i)(B) and (ii)(B) amended by 1999 Budget, effective for 1999 and later taxation years, to add reference to 120(2.2).

163(2)(b) repealed by 1992 Child Benefit bill, effective as of the 1993 taxation year, due to the elimination of the Child Tax Credit (122.2) and its replacement by the Child Tax Benefit (122.61). From September 13, 1988 through the 1992 taxation year, read:

(b) the amount, if any, by which

(i) the amount that would be deemed by subsection 122.2(1) to be paid for the year by the person or, where the person is a supporting person of an eligible child of an individual for the year (within the meaning assigned by subsection 122.2(2)) and resided with the individual at the end of the year, by that individual, as the case may be, if that amount were calculated by reference to the information provided in the return filed for the year pursuant to that subsection

exceeds

(ii) the amount that is deemed by subsection 122.2(1) to be paid for the year by the person or the individual referred to in subparagraph (i), as the case may be,

163(2)(c) repealed by 1990 GST, re-enacted by 1992 Child Benefit bill, effective 1991. For 1989 and 1990, it referred to the FST credit in 122.4.

163(2)(c.1) added by 1990 GST, effective 1989.

163(2)(c.2) added by 1992 Economic Statement, effective 1993; it applied to amounts deemed under 126.1 to be an overpayment on account of the person's liability. It was amended effective for the 1997 and later taxation years by 1997 Budget to refer to 122.51(2) instead (126.1, the UI tax credit, no longer applies).

163(2)(e) added by 1994 Budget, effective for taxation years that end after February 22, 1994.

163(2)(f) added by 1995 Budget, effective for 1995 and later taxation years.

163(2)(g) added by 1995-97 technical bill, effective November 1997.

**Interpretation Bulletins**: IT-256R: Gains from theft, defalcation or embezzlement.

**Information Circulars**: 73-10R3: Tax evasion; 00-1: Voluntary disclosures program.

**Application Policies**: SR&ED 96-05: Penalties under subsec. 163(2)..

**(2.1) Interpretation** — For the purposes of subsection (2), the taxable income reported by a person in the person's return for a taxation year shall be deemed not to be less than nil and the "understatement of income" for a year of a person means the total of

(a) the amount, if any, by which

(i) the total of all amounts that were not reported by the person in the person's return and that were required to be included in computing the person's income for the year

exceeds

(ii) the total of such of the amounts deductible by the person in computing the person's income for the year under the provisions of this Act as were wholly applicable to the amounts referred to in subparagraph (i) and were not deducted by the person in computing the person's income for the year reported by the person in the person's return,

(b) the amount, if any, by which

(i) the total of all amounts deducted by the person in computing the person's income for the year reported by the person in the person's return

exceeds

(ii) the total of such of the amounts referred to in subparagraph (i) as were deductible by the person in computing the person's income for the year in accordance with the provisions of this Act, and

(c) the amount, if any, by which

(i) the total of all amounts deducted by the person (otherwise than by virtue of section 111) from the person's income for the purpose of computing the person's taxable income for the year reported by the person in the person's return

exceeds

(ii) the total of all amounts deductible by the person (otherwise than by virtue of section 111) from the person's income for the purpose of computing the person's taxable income for the year in accordance with the provisions of this Act.

**Related Provisions**: 163(3) — Burden of proof; 163(4) — Effect of carryback of losses etc.

**(2.2) False statement or omission** — Every person who, knowingly or under circumstances amounting to gross negligence, has made or has participated in, assented to or acquiesced in the making of, a false statement or omission in a renunciation that was to have been effective as of a particular date and that is purported to have been made under any of subsections 66(10) to (10.3), (12.6), (12.601) and (12.62), otherwise than because of the application of subsection 66(12.66), is liable to a penalty of 25% of the amount, if any, by which

(a) the amount set out in the renunciation in respect of Canadian exploration expenses, Canadian development expenses or Canadian oil and gas property expenses

exceeds

(b) the amount in respect of Canadian exploration expenses, Canadian development expenses or Canadian oil and gas property expenses, as the case may be, that the corporation was entitled under the applicable subsection to renounce as of that particular date.

**Related Provisions**: 163(2.21) — Penalty relating to 66(12.66); 163(3) — Burden of proof. See also Related Provisions and Definitions at end of s. 163.

**Notes**: Opening words of 163(2.2) amended by 1996 Budget, effective April 25, 1997 (Royal Assent), to add the words "otherwise than because of the application of subsection 66(12.66)". (A new penalty for renunciations that use the 1-year look-back rule in 66(12.66) is found in 163(2.21) and (2.22) instead.) The opening words were also amended to change "is effective" and "is made" to "was to have been effective" and "is purported to have been made" respectively; these changes are likely non-substantive.

163(2.2) also amended by 1996 Budget, effective for purported renunciations made in 1999 or later, to delete reference to 66(12.64).

Opening words of 163(2.2) amended by 1992 Economic Statement, effective 1993, to add reference to 66(12.601).

**Information Circulars**: 00-1: Voluntary disclosures program.

**(2.21) False statement or omissions with respect to look-back rule** — A person is liable to the penalty determined under subsection (2.22) where the person,

(a) knowingly or under circumstances amounting to gross negligence has made or has participated in, assented to or acquiesced in the making of, a false statement or omission in a document required to be filed under subsection 66(12.73) in respect of a renunciation purported to have been made because of the application of subsection 66(12.66); or

(b) fails to file the document on or before the day that is 24 months after the day on or before which it was required to be filed.

**Notes**: 163(2.21) added by 1996 Budget, effective April 25, 1997 (Royal Assent).

**(2.22) Penalty** — For the purpose of subsection (2.21), the penalty to which a person is liable in respect of a document required to be filed under subsection 66(12.73) is equal to 25% of the amount, if any, by which

(a) the portion of the excess referred to in subsection 66(12.73) in respect of the document that was known or that ought to have been known by the person

exceeds

(b) where paragraph (2.21)(b) does not apply, the portion of the excess identified in the document, and

(c) in any other case, nil.

**Related Provisions**: 162(7) — Additional penalty. See additional Related Provisions and Definitions at end of s. 163.

**Notes**: 163(2.22) added by 1996 Budget, effective April 25, 1997 (Royal Assent).

**(2.3) Idem** — Every person who, knowingly or under circumstances amounting to gross negligence, makes or participates in, assents to or acquiesces in the making of, a false statement or omission in a prescribed form required to be filed under subsection 66(12.691) or (12.701) is liable to a penalty of 25% of the amount, if any, by which

(a) the assistance required to be reported in respect of a person or partnership in the prescribed form

exceeds

(b) the assistance reported in the prescribed form in respect of the person or partnership.

**Related Provisions**: See Related Provisions and Definitions at end of s. 163.

**Notes**: 163(2.3) added by 1991 technical bill, effective December 17, 1991.

**(2.4) False statement or omission [re foreign asset reporting]** — Every person or partnership who, knowingly or under circumstances amounting to gross negligence, makes or participates in, assents to or acquiesces in, the making of a false statement or omission in a return is liable to a penalty of

(a) where the return is required to be filed under section 233.1, $24,000;

(b) where the return is required to be filed under section 233.2, the greater of

(i) $24,000, and

(ii) 5% of the total of all amounts each of which is the fair market value of property transferred or loaned (determined as of the time of the transfer or loan) because of which there would, if no other transfer or loan were taken into account, be an obligation to file the return;

**Proposed Amendment — 163(2.4)(b)**

(b) where the return is required to be filed under section 233.2 in respect of a trust, the greater of

(i) $24,000, and

(ii) 5% of the total of all amounts each of which is the fair market value, at the time it was made, of a contribution of the person or partnership made to the trust before the end of the last taxation year of the trust in respect of which the return is required;

**Application**: The June 22, 2000 draft legislation, subsec. 2 (1), will amend para. 163(2.4)(b) to read as above, applicable to returns in respect of taxation years that begin after 2000.

**Technical Notes**: Subsection 163(2.4) of the Act imposes a penalty on any person or partnership that, knowingly or under circumstances amounting to gross negligence, has made or has participated in, assented to, or acquiesced in, the making of a false statement or omission in a return required to be filed under any of sections 233.1 to 233.6. The penalty under paragraph 163(2.4)(b) relates to a return required to be filed under section 233.2. The existing penalty is the greater of $24,000 and 5% of the total fair market value of the property that the person or partnership loaned or transferred to the trust that gave rise to the obligation to file.

Paragraph 163(2.4)(b) is amended as a consequence of changes made to the non-resident trust rules in section 94 and the annual reporting requirement in respect of non-resident trusts under section 233.2. Under amended section 233.2, a person is subject to the annual reporting requirement where a "contribution" is made to the trust by the person.

Accordingly, amended paragraph 163(2.4)(b) provides for a penalty for a person equal the greater of $24,000 and 5% of a specified amount in respect of the return. The specified amount for a person is essentially equal to 5% of the fair market value of "contributions" made by the person. The specified amount is calculated in the same way as the specified amount under amended subsection 162(10.1) in respect of late-filed returns. Under new subsection 163(2.41), the definitions and rules in subsections 94(1) and (2) generally apply. Subsection 163(2.41) is similar to amended subsection 233.2(2), described in greater detail in the commentary below.

This amendment applies to returns in respect of taxation years that begin after 2000.

(c) where the return is required to be filed under section 233.3 for a taxation year or fiscal period, the greater of

(i) $24,000, and

(ii) 5% of the greatest of all amounts each of which is the total of the cost amounts to the person or partnership at any time in the year or period of a specified foreign property (as defined by subsection 233.3(1)(a)) of the person or partnership in respect of which the false statement or omission is made;

(d) where the return is required to be filed under section 233.4 for a taxation year or fiscal period, the greater of

(i) $24,000, and

(ii) 5% of the greatest of all amounts each of which is the total of the cost amounts to the person or partnership at any time in the year or period of a property of the person or partnership that is a share of the capital stock or indebtedness of the foreign affiliate in respect of which the return is being filed; and

(e) where the return is required to be filed under section 233.6 for a taxation year or fiscal period, the greater of

(i) $2,500, and

(ii) 5% of the total of

(A) all amounts each of which is the fair market value of a property that is distributed to the person or partnership in the year or period by the trust and in respect of which the false statement or omission is made, and

(B) all amounts each of which is the greatest unpaid principal amount of a debt that is owing to the trust by the person or partnership in the year or period and in respect of which the false statement or omission is made.

**Related Provisions**: 162(10), (10.1) — Penalty for failure to file return; 163(2.41) — Application to trust contributions; 163(2.5) — Shares or debt owned by controlled foreign affiliate; 163(2.6), (2.7) — Application to partnerships; 163(2.9) — Where partnership liable to penalty; 163(2.91) — Application to non-resident trusts; 233.5 — Due diligence defence to penalty.

**Notes**: 163(2.4) added by 1996 Budget, effective for returns required to be filed by April 30, 1998 or later. The penalty was originally to be 10%, but was changed to 5% when the legislation was revised before being enacted.

**Information Circulars**: 00-1: Voluntary disclosures program.

### Proposed Addition — 163(2.41)

**(2.41) Application to trust contributions** — Subsections 94(1) and (2) apply for the purpose of subparagraph (b)(ii), except that for this purpose the definition "arm's length transfer" in subsection 94(1) shall be read without reference to subparagraph (a)(v) of that definition.

**Application**: The June 22, 2000 draft legislation, subsec. 21(2), will add subsec. 163(2.41), applicable to returns in respect of taxation years that begin after 2000.

**Technical Notes**: See under 163(2.4)(b).

**(2.5) Shares or debt owned by controlled foreign affiliate** — For the purpose of paragraph (2.4)(d),

(a) shares or indebtedness owned by a controlled foreign affiliate of a person or partnership are deemed to be owned by the person or partnership; and

(b) the cost amount at any time of such shares or indebtedness to the person or partnership is deemed to be equal to 20% of the cost amount at that time to the controlled foreign affiliate of the shares or indebtedness.

**Related Provisions**: 163(2.6) — Application to partnerships; 163(2.91) — Application to non-resident trusts.

**Notes**: 163(2.5) added by 1996 Budget, effective for returns required to be filed by April 30, 1998 or later.

**(2.6) Application to partnerships** — For the purposes of paragraph (2.4)(d) and subsection (2.5), in determining whether a non-resident corporation or trust is a foreign affiliate or a controlled foreign affiliate of a partnership

### Proposed Amendment — 163(2.6) opening words

**(2.6) Application to partnerships** — For the purposes of paragraph (2.4)(d) and subsection (2.5), in determining whether a non-resident corporation is a foreign affiliate or a controlled foreign affiliate of a partnership,

**Application**: The June 22, 2000 draft legislation, subsec. 21(3), will amend the opening words of para. 163(2.6) to read as above, applicable to returns in respect of taxation years that begin after 2000.

**Technical Notes**: See under 162(10.3).

(a) the definitions "direct equity percentage" and "equity percentage" in subsection 95(4) shall be read as if a partnership were a person; and

(b) the definitions "controlled foreign affiliate" and "foreign affiliate" in subsection 95(1) shall be read as if a partnership were a taxpayer resident in Canada.

**Notes**: 163(2.6) added by 1996 Budget, effective for returns required to be filed by April 30, 1998 or later.

**(2.7) Application to partnerships** — For the purpose of subsection (2.4), each act or omission of a member of a partnership in respect of an information return required to be filed by the partnership under section 233.3, 233.4 or 233.6 is deemed to be an act or omission of the partnership in respect of the return.

**Related Provisions**: 163(2.8) — Tiers of partnerships.

**Notes**: 163(2.7) added by 1996 Budget, effective for returns required to be filed by April 30, 1998 or later.

**(2.8) Application to members of partnerships** — For the purposes of this subsection and subsection (2.7), a person who is a member of a partnership that is a member of another partnership is deemed to be a member of the other partnership.

**Notes**: 163(2.8) added by 1996 Budget, effective for returns required to be filed by April 30, 1998 or later. This rule looks through tiers of partnerships.

**(2.9) Where partnership liable to penalty** — Where a partnership is liable to a penalty under subsection (2.4) or section 163.2 or 237.1, sections 152, 158 to 160.1, 161, and 164 to 167 and Division J apply, with any changes that the circumstances require, in respect of the penalty as if the partnership were a corporation.

**Notes**: This rule is needed because a partnership is not a "person" as defined in 248(1). See Notes to 96(1).

163(2.9) amended by 1999 Budget, effective June 29, 2000, to add references to 163.2 and 237.1. This rule previously applied to 237.1(7.4) under 161(12), which has been repealed.

163(2.9) added by 1996 Budget, effective for returns required to be filed by April 30, 1998 or later.

**(2.91) Application to non-resident trusts —** For the purposes of this subsection, paragraph (2.4)(d) and subsection (2.5),

(a) a non-resident trust is deemed to be a controlled foreign affiliate of each beneficiary of which the trust is a controlled foreign affiliate for the purpose of section 233.4;

(b) the trust is deemed to be a non-resident corporation having a capital stock of a single class divided into 100 issued shares;

(c) each beneficiary under the trust is deemed to own at any time the number of the issued shares of the corporation that is equal to the proportion of 100 that

   (i) the fair market value at that time of the beneficiary's beneficial interest in the trust

is of

   (ii) the fair market value at that time of all beneficial interests in the trust; and

(d) the cost amount to a beneficiary at any time of a share of the corporation is deemed to be equal to the amount determined by the formula

$$\frac{A}{B}$$

where

A   is the fair market value at that time of the beneficiary's beneficial interest in the trust, and

B   is the number of shares deemed under paragraph (c) to be owned at that time by the beneficiary in respect of the corporation.

**Proposed Repeal — 163(2.91)**

**Application**: The June 22, 2000 draft legislation, subsec. 21(4), will repeal subsec. 163(2.91), applicable to returns in respect of taxation years that begin after 2000.

**Technical Notes**: See under 162(10.3).

**Notes**: 163(2.91) added by 1996 Budget, effective for returns required to be filed by April 30, 1998 or later. For purposes of the penalty under 163(2.4), it treats non-resident trusts as foreign affiliates or controlled foreign affiliates of their beneficiaries, if they are treated as such for the reporting requirements in 233.4. As well, a cost amount is ascribed to shares deemed to be issued by such trusts to beneficiaries. The cost amount is based on the fair market value of beneficiaries' interests in the trust.

**(3) Burden of proof in respect of penalties —** Where, in an appeal under this Act, a penalty assessed by the Minister under this section or section 163.2 is in issue, the burden of establishing the facts justifying the assessment of the penalty is on the Minister.

**Related Provisions**: 15.1(5) — Small business development bond — penalties; 15.2(5) — Small business bond — penalties; 163.2(10) — Exception where valuation wrong by more than prescribed percentage.

**Notes**: See Notes to 238(1).

163(3) amended by 1999 Budget, effective for 1999 and later taxation years, to add reference to 163.2.

**(4) Effect of carryback of losses etc. —** In determining under subsection (2.1) the understatement of income for a taxation year of a person, the following amounts shall be deemed not to be deductible or excludable in computing the person's income for the year:

(a) any amount that may be deducted under section 41 in respect of the person's listed-personal-property loss for a subsequent taxation year;

(b) any amount that may be excluded from the person's income because of section 49 in respect of the exercise of any option in a subsequent taxation year;

(b.1) any amount that may be deducted under subsection 147.2(4) in computing the person's income for the year because of the application of subsection 147.2(6) as a result of the person's death in the subsequent taxation year; and

(c) any amount that may be deducted in computing the person's income for the year because of an election made under paragraph 164(6)(c) or

(d) in a subsequent taxation year by the person's legal representative.

**Notes**: 163(4)(b.1) added by 1995-97 technical bill, effective for deaths after 1992.

163(4) added by 1991 technical bill, effective where the "subsequent taxation year" referred to ends after July 13, 1990.

**Related Provisions [s. 163]**: 18(1)(t) — Penalty is non-deductible; 161(11) — Interest on penalty; 180.1(4), 180.2(6), 181.7, 183(3), 183.2(2), 187(3), 187.6, 189(8), 190.2(1), 191.4(2), 193(8), 195(8), 196(4), 202(3), 204.3(2), 204.7(3), 204.87, 204.93, 204.94(4), 207(3), 207.2(3), 207.4(2), 207.7(4), 208(4), 209(5), 210.2(7), 211.5, 211.6(5), 211.91(3), 218.2(5), 219(3), 247(11) — Provisions of s. 163 apply for purposes of Parts I.1, I.2, I.3, II, II.1, IV, IV.1, V, VI, VI.1, VII, VIII, IX, X, X.1, X.2, X.3, X.4, X.5, XI, XI.1, XI.2, XI.3, XII, XII.1, XII.2, XII.3, XII.4, XII.6, XIII.1, XIV and XVI.1 respectively; 220(3.1) — Waiver of penalty; 227(10.01), (10.1) — Provisions of s. 163 apply to withholding taxes under Parts XII.5 and XIII; 239(3) — Penalty assessment cannot be issued after charge laid if person convicted.

**Definitions [s. 163]**: "amount", "assessment" — 248(1); "Canadian development expense" — 66.2(5), 248(1); "Canadian exploration expense" — 66.1(6), 248(1); "Canadian oil and gas property expense" — 66.4(5), 248(1); "child" — 252(1); "cohabiting spouse or common-law partner" — 122.6; "common-law partner" — 248(1); "controlled foreign affiliate" — 95(1), 163(2.91)(a), 248(1); "corporation" — 163(2.91)(b), 248(1), *Interpretation Act* 35(1); "fiscal period" — 249.1; "individual", "Minister" — 248(1); "net capital loss", "non-capital loss" — 111(8), 248(1); "owned" — 163(2.5); "partnership" — see Notes to 96(1); "person", "prescribed", "property" — 248(1); "restricted farm loss" — 31, 248(1); "return" — 163(2); "tax payable" — 248(2); "taxable income" — 2(2), 248(1); "taxation year" — 249; "trust" — 104(1), 248(1), (3); "understatement of income" — 163(2.1).

**Information Circulars [s. 163]**: 73-10R3: Tax evasion.

**163.1 Penalty for late or deficient instalments —** Every person who fails to pay all or any part of an instalment of tax for a taxation year on or before the day on or before which the instalment is required by this Part to be paid is liable to a penalty equal to 50% of the amount, if any, by which

(a) the interest payable by the person under section 161 in respect of all instalments for the year

exceeds the greater of

(b) $1,000, and

(c) 25% of the interest that would have been payable by the person under section 161 in respect of all instalments for the year if no instalment had been made for that year.

**Related Provisions**: 18(1)(t) — Penalty is non-deductible; 161(2.2) — Offset interest from prepaying instalments; 161(4) — Interest — limitation — farmers and fishermen; 161(4.01) — Limitation — other individuals; 161(4.1) — Limitation — corporations; 161(7) — Effect of carryback of loss, etc.; 161(11) — Interest on penalties; 211.5(2) — Interest on instalments of Part XII.3 tax. See also Related Provisions at end of s. 163.

**Notes**: See Notes to 238(1).

163.1 added by 1988 tax reform, effective for taxation years beginning after June 1989.

**Definitions [s. 163.1]**: "amount" — 248(1); "instalment" — 155–157; "person" — 248(1); "taxation year" — 249.

**Information Circulars**: 92-2: Guidelines for the cancellation and waiver of interest and penalties; 00-1: Voluntary disclosures program.

## Misrepresentation of a Tax Matter by a Third Party

**163.2 (1) Definitions** — The definitions in this subsection apply in this section.

**"culpable conduct"** means conduct, whether an act or a failure to act, that

(a) is tantamount to intentional conduct;

(b) shows an indifference as to whether this Act is complied with; or

(c) shows a wilful, reckless or wanton disregard of the law.

**Notes**: The "culpable conduct" standard is a legislated version of the judicial definition of "gross negligence" in *Venne* (see Notes to 163(2)). However, the word "or" suggests that each of the three tests is a standalone test, which makes the threshold for culpable conduct merely "indifference", potentially a much lower standard than *Venne*. Arguably, despite the use of "or", the definition should be read as applying the *Venne* standard whereby some elements of all three of (a), (b) and (c) must be present.

See also Notes at end of 163.2.

**"entity"** includes an association, a corporation, a fund, a joint venture, an organization, a partnership, a syndicate and a trust.

**"excluded activity"**, in respect of a false statement, means the activity of

(a) promoting or selling (whether as principal or agent or directly or indirectly) an arrangement, an entity, a plan, a property or a scheme (in this definition referred to as the "arrangement") where it can reasonably be considered that

(i) subsection 66(12.68) applies to the arrangement,

(ii) the definition "tax shelter" in subsection 237.1(1) applies to a person's interest in the arrangement, or

(iii) one of the main purposes for a person's participation in the arrangement is to obtain a tax benefit; or

(b) accepting (whether as principal or agent or directly or indirectly) consideration in respect of the promotion or sale of an arrangement.

**"false statement"** includes a statement that is misleading because of an omission from the statement.

**"gross compensation"** of a particular person at any time, in respect of a false statement that could be used by or on behalf of another person, means all amounts to which the particular person, or any person not dealing at arm's length with the particular person, is entitled, either before or after that time and either absolutely or contingently, to receive or obtain in respect of the statement.

**Related Provisions**: 163.2(12)(c) — Exclusion of penalty assessed to another person under subsec. (5).

**"gross entitlements"** of a person at any time, in respect of a planning activity or a valuation activity of the person, means all amounts to which the person, or another person not dealing at arm's length with the person, is entitled, either before or after that time and either absolutely or contingently, to receive or obtain in respect of the activity.

**Related Provisions**: 163.2(12) — Special rules re gross entitlements.

**"participate"** includes

(a) to cause a subordinate to act or to omit information; and

(b) to know of, and to not make a reasonable attempt to prevent, the participation by a subordinate in an act or an omission of information.

**"person"** includes a partnership.

**"planning activity"** includes

(a) organizing or creating, or assisting in the organization or creation of, an arrangement, an entity, a plan or a scheme; and

(b) participating, directly or indirectly, in the selling of an interest in, or the promotion of, an arrangement, an entity, a plan, a property or a scheme.

**"subordinate"**, in respect of a particular person, includes any other person over whose activities the particular person has direction, supervision or control whether or not the other person is an employee of the particular person or of another person, except that, if the particular person is a member of a partnership, the other person is not a subordinate of the particular person solely because the particular person is a member of the partnership.

**"tax benefit"** means a reduction, avoidance or deferral of tax or other amount payable under this Act or an increase in a refund of tax or other amount under this Act.

**"valuation activity"** of a person means anything done by the person in determining the value of a property or a service.

**(2) Penalty for misrepresentations in tax planning arrangements** — Every person who makes or furnishes, participates in the making of or causes another person to make or furnish a statement that the person knows, or would reasonably be expected to know but for circumstances amounting to culpable conduct, is a false statement that could be used by another person (in subsections (6) and (15) referred to as the "other person") for a purpose of this Act is liable to a penalty in respect of the false statement.

**Related Provisions**: 18(1)(t) — Penalty is non-deductible; 161(11) — Interest on penalty; 163(2.9) — Where partnership is liable to penalty; 163(3) — Burden of proof of penalty is on CCRA; 163.2(3) — Amount of penalty; 163.2(6) — Reliance in good faith on information provided; 163.2(8) — Multiple false statements in respect of one arrangement; 163.2(12) — Special rules re gross entitlements; 163.2(14) — Where penalty applies under both (2) and (4); 163.2(15) — Transfer of liability of certain employees to employer; 220(3.1) — Waiver of penalty; 239(3) — Penalty cannot be assessed after charge laid if person convicted. See also Related Provisions at end of s. 163 re application to other Parts.

**Notes**: See Notes at end of 163.2.

**Information Circulars**: 00-1: Voluntary disclosures program; 01-1: Third party civil penalties.

**(3) Amount of penalty** — The penalty to which a person is liable under subsection (2) in respect of a false statement is

(a) where the statement is made in the course of a planning activity or a valuation activity, the greater of $1,000 and the total of the person's gross entitlements, at the time at which the notice of assessment of the penalty is sent to the person, in respect of the planning activity and the valuation activity; and

(b) in any other case, $1,000.

**(4) Penalty for participating in a misrepresentation** — Every person who makes, or participates in, assents to or acquiesces in the making of, a statement to, or by or on behalf of, another person (in this subsection and subsections (5) and (6), paragraph 12(c) and subsection (15) referred to as the "other person") that the person knows, or would reasonably be expected to know but for circumstances amounting to culpable conduct, is a false statement that could be used by or on behalf of the other person for a purpose of this Act is liable to a penalty in respect of the false statement.

**Related Provisions**: 18(1)(t) — Penalty is non-deductible; 161(11) — Interest on penalty; 163(2.9) — Where partnership is liable to penalty; 163(3) — Burden of proof of penalty is on CCRA; 163.2(5) — Amount of penalty; 163.2(6) — Reliance in good faith on information provided; 163.2(14) — Where penalty applies under both (2) and (4); 163.2(15) — Transfer of liability of certain employees to employer; 220(3.1) — Waiver of penalty; 239(3) — Penalty cannot be assessed after charge laid if person convicted. See also Related Provisions at end of s. 163 re application to other Parts.

**Notes**: See Notes at end of 163.2.

**Information Circulars**: 00-1: Voluntary disclosures program; 01-1: Third party civil penalties.

**(5) Amount of penalty** — The penalty to which a person is liable under subsection (4) in respect of a false statement is the greater of

(a) $1,000, and

(b) the lesser of

(i) the penalty to which the other person would be liable under subsection 163(2) if the other person made the statement in a return filed for the purposes of this Act and knew that the statement was false, and

(ii) the total of $100,000 and the person's gross compensation, at the time at which the notice of assessment of the penalty is sent to the person, in respect of the false statement that could be used by or on behalf of the other person.

**Related Provisions**: 163.2(4) — Meaning of "other person".

**(6) Reliance in good faith** — For the purposes of subsections (2) and (4), a person (in this subsection and in subsection (7) referred to as the "advisor") who acts on behalf of the other person is not considered to have acted in circumstances amounting to culpable conduct in respect of the false statement referred to in subsection (2) or (4) solely because the advisor relied, in good faith, on information provided to the advisor by or on behalf of the other person or, because of such reliance, failed to verify, investigate or correct the information.

**Related Provisions**: 163.2(2), (4) — Meaning of "other person"; 163.2(7) — No application to "excluded activity" such as selling tax shelters.

**(7) Non-application of subsec. (6)** — Subsection (6) does not apply in respect of a statement that an advisor makes (or participates in, assents to or acquiesces in the making of) in the course of an excluded activity.

**(8) False statements in respect of a particular arrangement** — For the purpose of applying this section (other than subsections (4) and (5)),

(a) where a person makes or furnishes, participates in the making of or causes another person to make or furnish, two or more false statements, the false statements are deemed to be one false statement if the statements are made or furnished in the course of

(i) one or more planning activities that are in respect of a particular arrangement, entity, plan, property or scheme, or

(ii) a valuation activity that is in respect of a particular property or service; and

(b) for greater certainty, a particular arrangement, entity, plan, property or scheme includes an arrangement, an entity, a plan, a property or a scheme in respect of which

(i) an interest is required to have, or has, an identification number issued under section 237.1 that is the same number as the number that applies to each other interest in the property,

(ii) a selling instrument in respect of flow-through shares is required to be filed with the Minister because of subsection 66(12.68), or

(iii) one of the main purposes for a person's participation in the arrangement, entity, plan or scheme, or a person's acquisition of the property, is to obtain a tax benefit.

**(9) Clerical services** — For the purposes of this section, a person is not considered to have made or furnished, or participated in, assented to or acquiesced in the making of, a false statement solely because the person provided clerical services (other than bookkeeping services) or secretarial services with respect to the statement.

**(10) Valuations** — Notwithstanding subsections (6) and 163(3), a statement as to the value of a property or a service (which value is in this subsection referred to as the "stated value"), made by the person who opined on the stated value or by a person in the course of an excluded activity is deemed to be a statement that the person would reasonably be expected to know, but for circumstances amounting to culpable conduct, is a false statement if the stated value is

(a) less than the product obtained when the prescribed percentage for the property or service is multiplied by the fair market value of the property or service; or

(b) greater than the product obtained when the prescribed percentage for the property or service is multiplied by the fair market value of the property or service.

### Proposed Amendment — 163.2(10)
**Letter from Department of Finance, July 11, 2000:**

Dear [xxx]:

Thank you for your letter of February 4, 2000 concerning our meeting of November 4, 1999 regarding the 1999 budget proposal to introduce a civil penalty in respect of misrepresentations of tax matters by third parties. As you may know, the legislation implementing this proposal received Royal Assent on June 29, 2000 (i.e., S.C. 2000, c. 19).

Your letter replies to our request for input from the [xxx] on the appropriate prescribed percentages for the purpose of establishing a deviation range under new subsection 163.2(10) of the *Income Tax Act* (the "Act"). In your letter, you have indicated that the Institute has concluded that, if a percentage threshold is to be set by the government, it should be the 200% test adopted by the U.S. under section 6700 of the Internal Revenue Code (the "IRC"). The Institute is also of the view that providing separate prescribed percentages for different industries would be inappropriate because it would be unworkable from a practical perspective — diversifications and business combinations defeat industry classification.

We agree with your observation that it may be impractical to have prescribed percentages that differ for various industries. However, we remain of the view that the deviation range established by prescribed percentages should be narrower than that which would exist under a range that is based upon a 200% standard.

It is our understanding that the U.S. 200% test for gross overstatements results in an automatic application of the penalty under section 6700 of the IRC, subject only to an exception for valuations for which there is a reasonable basis, which were made in good faith and then only if the Secretary of the Treasury waives the penalty under the authority of subsection 6700(b)(2) of the IRC. In contrast, section 163.2 of the Act merely provides a reverse onus. That is to say, in the case of valuations outside of the range, the onus is on the valuator to establish to the Minister of National Revenue or the judiciary that the valuation was reasonable in the circumstances, was made in good faith and was not based on a misleading assumption. The Canadian approach favours Canadian valuators.

The objective of the reverse onus rule in the Canadian provisions is to ensure that valuators and tax shelter promoters justify a substantial deviation from actual value. We would expect that a *bona fide* professional valuator would be prepared to substantiate that a particular valuation is reasonable in the circumstances (regardless of whether it is, on an ex post facto basis, proven to be inaccurate), that the valuation was made in good faith and that it is not based upon misleading assumptions. In this regard, therefore, it would be inappropriate to permit valuators to refuse to justify valuations that are proven to be inaccurate by a wide margin.

We anticipate a deviation range for all valuations that is narrower than 200%. However, consideration will be given within this parameter as to whether the deviation range for valuations used in a non-tax shelter context should differ from valuations used in a tax-shelter context and, if so, the appropriate percentages. If you wish to make further presentations to the Department on this issue, please contact Mr. Kerry Harnish at (613) 992-4385.

Finally, you should be aware that we intend to recommend that the percentages, which are "prescribed" for the purpose of applying new subsection 163.2(10) of the Act, be effective only for statements made after the day on which they are announced.

Thank you again for bringing your concerns to our attention.

Yours sincerely,
Len Farber
General Director, Tax Legislation Division, Tax Policy Branch

**Related Provisions**: 163.2(11) — Exception where valuation was reasonable and made in good faith.

**(11) Exception** — Subsection (10) does not apply to a person in respect of a statement as to the value of a property or a service if the person establishes that the stated value was reasonable in the circumstances and that the statement was made in good faith and, where applicable, was not based on one or more assumptions that the person knew or would reasonably be expected to know, but for circumstances amounting to culpable conduct, were unreasonable or misleading in the circumstances.

**(12) Special rules** — For the purpose of applying this section,

(a) where a person is assessed a penalty that is referred to in subsection (2) the amount of which is based on the person's gross entitlements at any time in respect of a planning activity or a valuation activity and another assessment of the penalty is made at a later time,

   (i) if the person's gross entitlements in respect of the activity are greater at that later time, the assessment of the penalty made at that later time is deemed to be an assessment of a separate penalty, and

   (ii) in any other case, the notice of assessment of the penalty sent before that later time is deemed not to have been sent;

(b) a person's gross entitlements at any time in respect of a planning activity or a valuation activity, in the course of which the person makes or furnishes, participates in the making of or causes another person to make or furnish a false statement, shall exclude the total of all amounts each of which is the amount of a penalty (other than a penalty the assessment of which is void because of subsection (13)) determined under paragraph (3)(a) in respect of the false statement for which notice of the assessment was sent to the person before that time; and

(c) where a person is assessed a penalty that is referred to in subsection (4), the person's gross compensation at any time in respect of the false statement that could be used by or on behalf of the other person shall exclude the total of all amounts each of which is the amount of a penalty (other than a penalty the assessment of which is void because of subsection (13)) determined under subsection (5) to the extent that the false statement was used by or on behalf of that other person and for which notice of the assessment was sent to the person before that time.

**Related Provisions**: 163.2(4) — Meaning of "other person".

**(13) Assessment void** — For the purposes of this Act, if an assessment of a penalty that is referred to in subsection (2) or (4) is vacated, the assessment is deemed to be void.

**(14) Maximum penalty** — A person who is liable at any time to a penalty under both subsections (2) and (4) in respect of the same false statement is liable to pay a penalty that is not more than the greater of

(a) the total amount of the penalties to which the person is liable at that time under subsection (2) in respect of the statement, and

(b) the total amount of the penalties to which the person is liable at that time under subsection (4) in respect of the statement.

**(15) Employees** — Where an employee (other than a specified employee or an employee engaged in an excluded activity) is employed by the other person referred to in subsections (2) and (4),

(a) subsections (2) to (5) do not apply to the employee to the extent that the false statement could be used by or on behalf of the other person for a purpose of this Act; and

(b) the conduct of the employee is deemed to be that of the other person for the purposes of applying subsection 163(2) to the other person.

**Related Provisions**: 163.2(2), (4) — Meaning of "other person".

**Notes [s. 163.2]**: 163.2 added by 1999 Budget, effective for statements made after June 29, 2000. It implements a civil penalty for third parties such as tax preparers, advisors, tax shelter promoters and valuators who cause others to misrepresent their tax owing. There are two separate penalties, in 163.2(2) and (4), with different calculations as set out in 163.2(3) and (5) respectively. See also Notes to 163.2(1)"culpable conduct").

Concerns have been expressed that any assessment of this penalty against lawyers would put them in conflict with their clients. A lawyer might not be able to defend against assessment of the penalty without breaching solicitor-client privilege by revealing client communications.

For a comprehensive review and stinging critique of the penalties on the basis that they are far too broad, see Brian Nichols, "Civil Penalties for Third Parties", 1999 Ontario Tax Conference proceedings (Canadian Tax Foundation), tab 1. Some of the issues raised in this article were solved by subsequent amendments to 163.2, including the House of Commons Finance Committee report amendments of June 2, 2000 which introduced 163.2(15) as protection for many employees.

The CCRA has stated that assessments under 163.2 will only be issued upon prior approval from a Headquarters committee. The CCRA also announced in September 2000 that it was engaging in consultations with the private sector on the form and content of the guidelines for administering the provisions, and that comments should be directed to the Assistant Commissioner, Compliance Programs Branch, fax 613-957-0109, email tpp.comments@ccra-adrc.gc.ca until Feb. 16/01; final guidelines are to be issued by March 31, 2001. For the draft guidelines, see draft Information Circular 01-1, "Third party civil penalties" (January 12, 2001).

See also Brian Nichols, "Third Party Penalties", 2000 Ontario Tax Conference proceedings (Canadian Tax Foundation), tab 3. Nichols suggests in his 2000 paper that 163.2 could be contrary to fundamental principles of law in that tax advisors are required to act in their clients' best interests, per *Hodgkinson v. Simms*, 95 D.T.C. 5135 (SCC); and that it could be contrary to the *Charter of Rights*, given that a very onerous fine can be equivalent to a criminal charge, per *R. v. Wigglesworth*, [1987] 2 S.C.R. 541 (SCC).

**Definitions [s. 163.2]**: advisor" — 163.2(6); "amount" — 248(1); "arm's length" — 251(1); "assessment" — 248(1); "corporation" —

248(1), *Interpretation Act* 35(1); "culpable conduct" — 163.2(1); "employee" — 248(1); "entity", "excluded activity" — 163.2(1); "false statement" — 163.2(1); "flow-through share" — 66(15), 248(1); "gross compensation" — 163.2(1), (12)(c); "gross entitlements" — 163.2(1); "Minister" — 248(1); "other person" — 163.2(2), (4); "participates" — 163.2(1); "partnership" — see Notes to 96(1); "person" — 163.2(1), 248(1); "planning activity" — 163.2(1); "prescribed", "property", "specified employee" — 248(1); "subordinate", "tax benefit" — 163.2(1); "trust" — 104(1), 248(1), (3); "valuation activity" — 163.2(1).

**Information Circulars [s. 163.2]**: 01-1: Third party civil penalties.

## Refunds

**164. (1) Refunds** — If the return of a taxpayer's income for a taxation year has been made within 3 years from the end of the year, the Minister

(a) may,

(i) before mailing the notice of assessment for the year, where the taxpayer is a qualifying corporation (as defined in subsection 127.1(2)) and claims in its return of income under this Part for the year to have paid an amount on account of its tax payable under this Part for the year by reason of subsection 127.1(1) in respect of its refundable investment tax credit (as defined in subsection 127.1(2)), refund without application therefor, all or any part of any amount claimed in the return as an overpayment for the year, not exceeding the amount by which the total determined under paragraph (f) of the definition "refundable investment tax credit" in subsection 127.1(2) in respect of the taxpayer for the year exceeds the total determined under paragraph (g) of that definition in respect of the taxpayer for the year, and

(ii) on or after mailing the notice of assessment for the year, refund without application therefor, any overpayment for the year, to the extent that the overpayment was not refunded pursuant to subparagraph (i); and

(b) shall, with all due dispatch, make the refund referred to in subparagraph (a)(ii) after mailing the notice of assessment if application for it is made in writing by the taxpayer within the period within which the Minister would be allowed under subsection 152(4) to assess tax payable under this Part by the taxpayer for the year if that subsection were read without reference to paragraph 152(4)(a).

### Proposed Amendment — 164(1)(a), (b)

(a) may,

(i) before mailing the notice of assessment for the year, where the taxpayer is a qualifying corporation (as defined in subsection 127.1(2)) and claims in its return of income for the year to have paid an amount on account of its tax payable under this Part for the year because of subsection 127.1(1) in respect of its refundable investment tax credit (as defined in subsection 127.1(2)), refund all or part of any amount claimed in the return as an overpayment for the year, not exceeding the amount by which the total determined under paragraph (f) of the definition "refundable investment tax credit" in subsection 127.1(2) in respect of the taxpayer for the year exceeds the total determined under paragraph (g) of that definition in respect of the taxpayer for the year,

(ii) before mailing the notice of assessment for the year, where the taxpayer is a qualified corporation (as defined in subsection 125.4(1)) or an eligible production corporation (as defined in subsection 125.5(1)) and an amount is deemed under subsection 125.4(3) or 125.5(3) to have been paid on account of its tax payable under this Part for the year, refund all or part of any amount claimed in the return as an overpayment for the year, not exceeding the total of those amounts so deemed to have been paid, and

(iii) on or after mailing the notice of assessment for the year, refund any overpayment for the year, to the extent that the overpayment was not refunded pursuant to subparagraph (i) or (ii); and

(b) shall, with all due dispatch, make the refund referred to in subparagraph (a)(iii) after mailing the notice of assessment if application for it is made in writing by the taxpayer within the period within which the Minister would be allowed under subsection 152(4) to assess tax payable under this Part by the taxpayer for the year if that subsection were read without reference to paragraph 152(4)(a).

**Application**: Bill C-43 (First Reading September 20, 2000), subsec. 94(1), will amend paras. 164(1)(a) and (b) to read as above, applicable to 1999 *et seq.*

**Technical Notes**: Subsection 164(1) provides rules governing refunds of overpayments of tax.

Subparagraph 164(1)(a)(ii) is amended to authorize the Minister of National Revenue to refund all or part of a corporation's claim for a taxation year of a Canadian Film or Video Production Tax Credit under section 125.4 or of a Film or Video Production Services Tax Credit under section 125.5 of the Act, before having issued an assessment in respect of the corporation for the year.

Former subparagraph 164(1)(a)(ii) is re-numbered as subparagraph (iii) and, along with subparagraph (i), is amended to conform to the language in amended subparagraph (ii). Paragraph 164(1)(b) is amended to reflect the renumbering of subparagraph 164(1a)(ii) as subparagraph 164(1)(a)(iii).

**Related Provisions**: 144(9) — Employees profit sharing plans — refunds; 160.1 — Where excess refunded; 164(1.5) — Late refund of overpayment; 164(1.8) — Request to pay refund to prescribed province; 164(2.2) — Child Tax Benefit form deemed to be a return of income; 164(3) — Interest on refunds; 220(6) — Assignment of corporation's tax refund; *Tax Rebate Discounting Act* — Assignment of personal income tax refund to tax return preparer.

**Notes**: For information as to the status of a personal tax refund, call the Tax Information Phone Service (TIPS) at 1-800-267-6999. One must provide (through touch-tones) the taxpayer's social insurance number, month and year of birth, and total income from line 150 of the T1 return.

Where the 3-year limit in the opening words is not met, one can still ask the CCRA to transfer an unrefunded instalment balance to another year under 221.2. That section was enacted more recently than 164(3) and appears to solve what the Tax Court described in *Chalifoux*, [1991] 2 C.T.C. 2243 (TCC) as a "confiscation of the appellant's property" that was "deplorable". CCRA Headquarters has accepted this argument. For an individual or testamentary trust, relief is also available under 164(1.5) at the CCRA's discretion.

164(1)(a)(i) amended by 1995-97 technical bill, effective for taxation years that end after December 2, 1992, to change references from 127.1(2)"refundable investment tax credit"(a)(vi) and (vii) to (f) and (g).

164(1)(b) amended by 1989 Budget, effective April 28, 1989, to refer to 152(4) instead of 6-year and 3-year limits explicitly; and amended by 1995-97 technical bill, also effective April 28, 1989, to make non-substantive wording changes and to update references to 152(4) as amended.

**Information Circulars**: 01-1: Third party civil penalties; 75-7R3: Reassessment of a return of income; 92-3: Guidelines for refunds beyond the normal three-year period.

**Forms**: T1-DD: Direct deposit request — individuals.

**(1.1) Repayment on objections and appeals** — Subject to subsection (1.2), where a taxpayer

(a) has under section 165 served a notice of objection to an assessment and the Minister has not within 120 days after the day of service confirmed or varied the assessment or made a reassessment in respect thereof, or

(b) has appealed from an assessment to the Tax Court of Canada,

and has applied in writing to the Minister for a payment or surrender of security, the Minister shall, where no authorization has been granted under subsection 225.2(2) in respect of the amount assessed, with all due dispatch repay all amounts paid on account of that amount or surrender security accepted therefor to the extent that

(c) the lesser of

(i) the total of the amounts so paid and the value of the security, and

(ii) the amount so assessed

exceeds

(d) the total of

(i) the amount, if any, so assessed that is not in controversy, and

(ii) where the taxpayer is a large corporation (within the meaning assigned by subsection 225.1(8)), ½ of the amount so assessed that is in controversy.

**Related Provisions**: 164(1.6) — 164(1.1) does not apply to security under s. 116; 225.1(7) — Limitation on collection restrictions — large corporations.

**Notes**: 164(1.1) is consistent with 225.1(1), which permits most taxpayers to withhold payment of tax under dispute. See Notes to 158.

164(1.1)(b) amended by 1988 Tax Court bill, effective January 1, 1991, to delete "or to the Federal Court–Trial Division".

164(1.1)(d)(ii) added by 1992 technical bill, effective after June 10, 1993. For (calendar) 1993, with respect to a notice of assessment mailed before 1992, read "¼" instead of "½". Before 1993, the repayment requirement for large corporations did not apply (see 221.1(7)).

**(1.2) Collection in jeopardy** — Notwithstanding subsection (1.1), where, on application by the Minister made within 45 days after the receipt by the Minister of a written request by a taxpayer for repayment of an amount or surrender of a security, a judge is satisfied that there are reasonable grounds to believe that the collection of all or any part of an amount assessed in respect of the taxpayer would be jeopardized by the repayment of the amount or the surrender of the security to the taxpayer under that subsection, the judge shall order that the repayment of the amount or a part thereof not be made or that the security or part thereof not be surrendered or make such other order as the judge considers reasonable in the circumstances.

**Related Provisions**: 225.2(2) — Lifting of collection restrictions where collection of tax in jeopardy.

**(1.3) Notice of application** — The Minister shall give 6 clear days notice of an application under subsection (1.2) to the taxpayer in respect of whom the application is made.

**Related Provisions**: *Interpretation Act* 27(1) — Calculation of "clear days".

**(1.31) Application of subsecs. 225.2(4), (10), (12) and (13)** — Where an application under subsection (1.2) is made by the Minister, subsections 225.2(4), (10), (12) and (13) are applicable in respect of the application with such modifications as the circumstances require.

**(1.4) Provincial refund** — Where, at any time, a taxpayer is entitled to a refund or repayment on account of taxes imposed by a province or as a result of a deduction in computing the taxes imposed by a province and the Government of Canada has agreed to make the refund or repayment on behalf of the province, the amount thereof shall be a liability of the Minister of National Revenue to the taxpayer.

**(1.5) [Late refund of overpayment]** — Notwithstanding subsection (1), the Minister may, on or after mailing a notice of assessment for a taxation year, refund all or any portion of any overpayment of a taxpayer for the year

(a) if the taxpayer is an individual (other than a trust) or a testamentary trust and the taxpayer's return of income under this Part for the year was filed later than 3 years after the end of the year; or

(b) where an assessment or a redetermination was made under subsection 152(4.2) or 220(3.1) or (3.4) in respect of the taxpayer.

**Related Provisions**: 152(4.2) — Reassessment with taxpayer's consent; 164(3.2) — Interest on refunds and repayments.

**Notes**: 164(1.5) added by 1991 technical bill (as part of the "Fairness Package") and amended retroactively by 1992 technical bill, effective for refunds for 1985 and later taxation years. It permits an overpayment to be refunded after the 3-year limit for applying for it expires (but not to a corporation or an *inter vivos* trust). For years before 1985, where application was made before 1993, the *Income Tax Refunds Remission Order*, P.C. 1992-658 (April 2, 1992) provided similar relief.

**Information Circulars**: 75-7R3: Reassessment of a return of income; 92-3: Guidelines for refunds beyond the normal three-year period.

### (1.6) Refund of UI premium tax credit — Notwithstanding subsection (1), where an overpayment on account of a taxpayer's liability under this Part is deemed to have arisen under subsection 126.1(6) or (7), the Minister shall, with all due dispatch, refund the amount of the overpayment without application for it.

**Related Provisions**: 164(3) — No interest on refund.

**Notes**: 164(1.6) added by 1992 Economic Statement, effective 1993. The other proposed version of 164(1.6) was enacted as 164(1.7), below.

### (1.7) Limitation of repayment on objections and appeals — Subsection (1.1) does not apply in respect of an amount paid or security furnished under section 116 by a non-resident person.

**Notes**: 164(1.7) added by 1992 Economic Statement/1993 Budget bill, effective May 12, 1994 (the date of Royal Assent). This amendment was originally proposed as 164(1.6) in the draft technical bill of December 21, 1992, reissued on August 30, 1993, but was moved into the budget bill for quick passage (and because of overlap with the other 164(1.6)) rather than left for inclusion in the 1993 technical bill.

### (1.8) Request to pay refund to province — An individual (other than a trust) may, in the individual's return of income for a taxation year, request the Minister to pay to Her Majesty in right of a prescribed province all or any part of a refund for the year claimed by the individual in the return and, where the individual makes such a request,

(a) the Minister may make the payment to Her Majesty in right of the province in accordance with the request; and

(b) the amount of the payment is deemed to have been refunded under this section to the individual at the time a notice of an original assessment of tax payable under this Part by the individual for the year, or a notification that no tax is payable under this Part by the individual for the year, is sent to the individual.

**Related Provisions**: 241(4)(m) — Disclosure of information by CCRA to prescribed province.

**Notes**: 164(1.8) added by 1995-97 technical bill, effective for requests made in returns for 1997 and later taxation years that are filed after 1997. For the purpose of 164(1.8), Ontario is deemed to be a prescribed province until the Regulations are amended to prescribe any provinces.

**Regulations**: None yet, but subsec. 190(12) of the 1995-97 technical bill (1998, c. 19) deems Ontario to be a prescribed province until Regulations are provided. Ontario is to be prescribed in the Regulations (Department of Finance Technical Notes, December 1997).

### (2) Application to other debts — Instead of making a refund or repayment that might otherwise be made under this section, the Minister may, where the taxpayer is, or is about to become, liable to make any payment to Her Majesty in right of Canada or in right of a province, apply the amount of the refund or repayment to that other liability and notify the taxpayer of that action.

**Related Provisions**: 164(2.1) — Application of GST credit; 164(2.2) — Application to refunds under s. 122.61; 164(3.2) — Interest on refunds and repayments; 164(7) — Overpayment defined; 165 — Objections to assessments; 169 — Appeals; 172 — Appeals; 203 — Set-off of Part X refund; 224.1 — Set-off of tax debt against other amount owing by the Crown to the taxpayer; 227 — Withholding taxes; 241(4)(d)(xiii)(B) — Disclosure of information by CCRA to provincial officials for set-off purposes.

**Notes**: 164(2) amended by 1995-97 technical bill to add the words "or in right of a province", effective June 18, 1998.

164(2) amended by 1991 technical bill, effective December 17, 1991, to apply to debts to Her Majesty generally rather than just amounts owing under this Act.

### (2.1) Application respecting refunds under s. 122.5 [GST credit] — Where an amount deemed under section 122.5 to be paid by an individual during a month specified for a taxation year is applied under subsection (2) to a liability of the individual and the individual's return of income for the year is filed on or before the individual's balance-due day for the year, the amount is deemed to have been so applied on the day on which the amount would have been refunded if the individual were not liable to make a payment to Her Majesty in right of Canada.

**Notes**: 164(2.1) amended by 1995-97 technical bill, effective June 18, 1998. Previously read:

> (2.1) Where an amount deemed under section 122.5 to be paid by an individual during a month specified for a taxation year is, in accordance with subsection (2), applied to a liability of the individual, for the purposes of that subsection, the amount shall, to the extent that it is so applied, be deemed to be paid on the latest of
>
> (a) the last day of the month,
>
> (b) where the month is the first month specified for a taxation year ending after 1989, the day that is the earlier of the day the amount is applied and the last day of the second month specified for the year, and
>
> (c) where the individual's return of income for the year or the individual's prescribed form for the year referred to in subsection 122.5(3) is filed after the day on or before which the return is required to be filed, the day the amount is applied.

164(2.1) added by 1990 GST, effective 1989. It relates to the GST credit.

### (2.2) Application respecting refunds re section 122.61 [Child Tax Benefit] — Subsection (2) does not apply to a refund to be made to a taxpayer and arising because of section 122.61 ex-

**S. 164(2.2)**      Income Tax Act, Part I

cept to the extent that the taxpayer's liability referred to in that subsection arose from the operation of paragraph 160.1(1)(a) with respect to an amount refunded to the taxpayer in excess of the amount to which the taxpayer was entitled because of section 122.61.

**Notes**: 164(2.2) added by 1992 Child Benefit bill, effective for overpayments arising in 1993 or later. It related to the Child Tax Benefit.

**(2.3) [Child Tax Benefit] Form deemed to be a return of income** — For the purpose of subsection (1), where a taxpayer files the form referred to in paragraph (b) of the definition "return of income" in section 122.6 for a taxation year, the form shall be deemed to be a return of the taxpayer's income for that year and a notice of assessment thereof shall be deemed to have been mailed by the Minister.

**Notes**: 164(2.3) added by 1992 Child Benefit bill, effective for overpayments arising in 1993 or later.

**(3) Interest on refunds and repayments** — Where under this section an amount in respect of a taxation year (other than an amount or portion thereof that can reasonably be considered to arise from the operation of section 122.5, 122.61 or 126.1) is refunded or repaid to a taxpayer or applied to another liability of the taxpayer, the Minister shall pay or apply interest on it at the prescribed rate for the period beginning on the day that is the latest of

(a) where the taxpayer is an individual, the day that is 45 days after the individual's balance-due day for the year,

(b) where the taxpayer is a corporation, the day that is 120 days after the end of the year,

(c) where the taxpayer is

    (i) a corporation, the day on which its return of income for the year was filed under section 150, unless the return was filed on or before the corporation's filing-due date for the year, and

    (ii) an individual, the day that is 45 days after the day on which the individual's return of income for the year was filed under section 150,

(d) in the case of a refund of an overpayment, the day the overpayment arose, and

(e) in the case of a repayment of an amount in controversy, the day an overpayment equal to the amount of the repayment would have arisen if the total of all amounts payable on account of the taxpayer's liability under this Part for the year were the amount by which

    (i) the lesser of the total of all amounts paid on account of the taxpayer's liability under this Part for the year and the total of all amounts assessed by the Minister as payable under this Part by the taxpayer for the year

exceeds

    (ii) the amount repaid,

and ending on the day the amount is refunded, repaid or applied, unless the amount of the interest so calculated is less than $1, in which event no interest shall be paid or applied under this subsection.

**Related Provisions**: 12(1)(c) — Interest is taxable; 129(2.1) — Interest on dividend refund; 131(3.1), 132(2.1) — Interest on capital gains refund; 133(7.01) — Interest on allowable refund; 161.1 — Offset of refund interest against arrears interest; 221.1 — Application of interest where legislation retroactive; 248(11) — Interest compounded daily.

**Notes**: Parenthetical exclusion in opening words of 164(3) added by 1990 GST (to refer to 122.5), effective 1989; reference to 122.61 added by 1992 Child Benefit bill, effective for overpayments arising after 1992; reference to 126.1 added by 1992 Economic Statement, effective 1993.

164(3)(a) and (c) amended by 1995 Budget, effective for 1995 and later taxation years. For earlier years, read:

    (a) where the taxpayer is an individual, the day that is 45 days after the day on or before which the taxpayer's return of income under this Part for the year was required to be filed under section 150 or would have been required to be so filed if tax under this Part were payable by the taxpayer for the year,

    .....

    (c) the day or, where the taxpayer is an individual, the day that is 45 days after the day, on which the taxpayer's return of income under this Part for the year was filed under section 150, unless the return was filed on or before the day on or before which it was required to be filed,

164(3)(a) and (c) amended by 1992 Budget/technical bill, effective for returns filed after 1992, to add "that is 45 days after the day". Thus, interest is payable on personal income tax refunds (that were filed on time) only after June 14, rather than April 30.

Except for the above changes, the current version of 164(3) has been in force since January 1, 1987 and applies to refunds payable since that date.

**Regulations**: 4301(b) (prescribed rate of interest).

**I.T. Application Rules**: 62(2) (subsec. 164(3) applies to interest payable in respect of any period after December 23, 1971).

**(3.1) Idem** — Where at a particular time interest has been paid to, or applied to a liability of, a taxpayer under subsection (3) or (3.2) in respect of an overpayment and it is determined at a subsequent time that the actual overpayment was less than the overpayment in respect of which interest was paid or applied,

(a) the amount by which the interest that has been paid or applied exceeds the interest, if any, computed in respect of the amount that is determined at the subsequent time to be the actual overpayment shall be deemed to be an amount (in this subsection referred to as "the amount payable") that became payable under this Part by the taxpayer at the particular time;

(b) the taxpayer shall pay to the Receiver General interest at the prescribed rate on the amount payable computed from that particular time to the day of payment; and

(c) the Minister may at any time assess the taxpayer in respect of the amount payable and, where the Minister makes such an assessment, the provisions of this Division are applicable, with such modifications as the circumstances require, in respect of the assessment as though it had been made under section 152.

**Related Provisions**: 20(1)(ll) — Deduction on repayment of interest; 161.1 — Offset of refund interest against arrears interest; 221.1 — Application of interest where legislation retroactive; 248(11) — Interest compounded daily.

**Notes**: Opening words of 164(3.1) amended by 1991 technical bill, effective for refunds for 1985 and later years, to add reference to 164(3.2).

**Regulations**: 4301(a) (prescribed rate of interest).

**(3.2) Idem** — Notwithstanding subsection (3), where the amount of an overpayment of a taxpayer for a taxation year is determined because of an assessment made under subsection 152(4.2) or 220(3.1) or (3.4) and an amount in respect thereof is refunded to, or applied to another liability of, the taxpayer under subsection (1.5) or (2), the Minister shall pay or apply interest thereon at the prescribed rate for the period beginning on the day the Minister received the application therefor, in a form satisfactory to the Minister, and ending on the day the amount is refunded or applied, unless the amount of the interest so calculated is less than $1, in which case no interest shall be paid or applied under this subsection.

**Related Provisions**: 161.1 — Offset of refund interest against arrears interest; 221.1 — Application of interest where legislation retroactive; 248(11) — Interest compounded daily.

**Notes**: 164(3.2) added by 1991 technical bill (as part of the "Fairness Package"; see 164(1.5)) and amended retroactively by 1992 technical bill, effective for refunds for 1985 and later taxation years.

**Regulations**: 4301(b) (prescribed rate of interest).

**(4) Interest on interest repaid** — Where at any particular time interest has been paid to, or applied to a liability of, a taxpayer pursuant to subsection (3) in respect of the repayment of an amount in controversy made to, or applied to a liability of, the taxpayer and it is determined at a subsequent time that the repayment or a part thereof is payable by the taxpayer under this Part, the following rules apply:

(a) the interest so paid or applied on that part of the repayment that is determined at the subsequent time to be payable by the taxpayer under this Part shall be deemed to be an amount (in this subsection referred to as the "interest excess") that became payable under this Part by the taxpayer at the particular time;

(b) the taxpayer shall pay to the Receiver General interest at the prescribed rate on the interest excess computed from the particular time to the day of payment; and

(c) the Minister may at any time assess the taxpayer in respect of the interest excess and, where the Minister makes such an assessment, the provisions of this Division and Division J are applicable, with such modifications as the circumstances require, in respect of the assessment as though it had been made under section 152.

**Related Provisions**: 12(1)(c) — Interest is taxable; 20(1)(ll) — Deduction for interest repaid; 161.1 — Offset of refund interest against arrears interest; 221.1 — Application of interest where legislation retroactive; 248(11) — Interest compounded daily.

**Regulations**: 4301(a) (prescribed rate of interest).

**I.T. Application Rules**: 62(2) (subsec. 164(4) applies to interest payable in respect of any period after December 23, 1971).

**(4.1) Duty of Minister** — Where the Tax Court of Canada, the Federal Court of Appeal or the Supreme Court of Canada has, on the disposition of an appeal in respect of taxes, interest or a penalty payable under this Act by a taxpayer resident in Canada,

(a) referred an assessment back to the Minister for reconsideration and reassessment, or

(b) varied or vacated an assessment,

the Minister shall with all due dispatch, whether or not an appeal from the decision of the Court has been or may be instituted,

(c) where the assessment has been referred back to the Minister, reconsider the assessment and make a reassessment in accordance with the decision of the Court, unless otherwise directed in writing by the taxpayer, and

(d) refund any overpayment resulting from the variation, vacation or reassessment,

and the Minister may repay any tax, interest or penalties or surrender any security accepted therefor by the Minister to that taxpayer or any other taxpayer who has filed another objection or instituted another appeal if, having regard to the reasons given on the disposition of the appeal, the Minister is satisfied that it would be just and equitable to do so, but for greater certainty, the Minister may, in accordance with the provisions of this Act, the *Tax Court of Canada Act*, the *Federal Court Act* or the *Supreme Court Act* as they relate to appeals from decisions of the Tax Court of Canada or the Federal Court, appeal from the decision of the Court notwithstanding any variation or vacation of any assessment by the Court or any reassessment made by the Minister under paragraph (c).

**Related Provisions**: 152(1.2)(c) — Subsec. 164(4.1) does not apply to determination under 152(1.4); 169(2)(a) — Limitation of right to appeal.

**Notes**: 164(4.1) amended by 1988 Tax Court bill, effective January 1, 1991. The pre-1991 version, in addition to paras. (a) and (b), also dealt with the case where the Court had "ordered the Minister to repay tax, interest or penalties"; as well, the closing portion of the subsec. lacked the words "that taxpayer or" which now precede "any other taxpayer".

**(5) Effect of carryback of loss, etc.** — For the purpose of subsection (3), the portion of any overpayment of the tax payable by a taxpayer for a taxation year that arose as a consequence of

(a) the deduction of an amount, in respect of a repayment under subsection 68.4(7) of the *Excise Tax Act* made in a subsequent taxation year, in computing the amount determined under subparagraph 12(1)(x.1)(ii),

**S. 164(5)(a.1)** — Income Tax Act, Part I

### Proposed Addition — 164(5)(a.1)

(a.1) any amount deducted under section 119 in respect of the disposition of a taxable Canadian property in a subsequent taxation year,

**Application**: Bill C-43 (First Reading September 20, 2000), subsec. 94(2), will add para. 164(5)(a.1), applicable to taxation years that end after October 1, 1996.

**Technical Notes**: Section 164 relates to tax refunds. Subsection 164(5) provides that, where the tax payable for a taxation year is reduced because of listed deductions or exclusions that relate to subsequent years, interest payable to a taxpayer on any resulting overpayment of tax is to be calculated as if the overpayment had arisen on the latest of several dates.

These amendments add to the list of deductions and exclusions: a deduction under new section 119 in respect of a disposition of taxable Canadian property by a taxpayer in a subsequent taxation year; a deduction under new subsection 126(2.21) or (2.22) in respect of foreign taxes paid for a subsequent taxation year; and deductions under new subsections 128.1(6) to (8) in respect of an election in a subsequent taxation year.

(b) the deduction of an amount under section 41 in respect of the taxpayer's listed-personal-property loss for a subsequent taxation year,

(c) the exclusion of an amount from the taxpayer's income for the year by virtue of section 49 in respect of the exercise of an option in a subsequent taxation year,

(d) the deduction of an amount under section 118.1 in respect of a gift made in a subsequent taxation year or under section 111 in respect of a loss for a subsequent taxation year,

(e) the deduction of an amount under subsection 126(2) in respect of an unused foreign tax credit (within the meaning assigned by subsection 126(7)) for a subsequent taxation year,

### Proposed Amendment — 164(5)(e)

(e) the deduction of an amount under subsection 126(2) in respect of an unused foreign tax credit (within the meaning assigned by subsection 126(7)), or under subsection 126(2.21) or (2.22) in respect of foreign taxes paid, for a subsequent taxation year,

**Application**: Bill C-43 (First Reading September 20, 2000), subsec. 94(3), will amend para. 164(5)(e) to read as above, applicable to taxation years that end after October 1, 1996.

**Technical Notes**: See under 164(5)(a.1).

(f) the deduction of an amount under subsection 127(5) in respect of property acquired or an expenditure made in a subsequent taxation year,

(g) the deduction of an amount under section 125.2 in respect of an unused Part VI tax credit (within the meaning assigned by subsection 125.2(3)) for a subsequent taxation year,

(h) the deduction of an amount under section 125.3 in respect of an unused Part I.3 tax credit (within the meaning assigned by subsection 125.3(3)) for a subsequent taxation year,

(h.01) the deduction of an amount under subsection 147.2(4) in computing the taxpayer's income for the year because of the application of subsection 147.2(6) as a result of the taxpayer's death in the following taxation year,

### Proposed Addition — 164(5)(h.02)

(h.02) the deduction under any of subsections 128.1(6) to (8) of an amount from the taxpayer's proceeds of disposition of a property, because of an election made in a return of income for a subsequent taxation year,

**Application**: Bill C-43 (First Reading September 20, 2000), subsec. 94(4), will add para. 164(5)(h.02), applicable to taxation years that end after October 1, 1996.

**Technical Notes**: See under 164(5)(a.1).

(h.1) the deduction of an amount in computing the taxpayer's income for the year by virtue of an election for a subsequent taxation year under paragraph (6)(c) or (d) by the taxpayer's legal representative,

(h.2) the deduction of an amount under subsection 181.1(4) in respect of an unused surtax credit (within the meaning assigned by subsection 181.1(6)) of the taxpayer for a subsequent taxation year, or

(h.3) the deduction of an amount under subsection 190.1(3) in respect of an unused Part I tax credit (within the meaning assigned by subsection 190.1(5)) of the taxpayer for a subsequent taxation year,

shall be deemed to have arisen on the day that is the latest of

(i) the first day immediately following that subsequent taxation year,

(j) the day on which the taxpayer's or the taxpayer's legal representative's return of income for that subsequent taxation year was filed,

(k) where an amended return of the taxpayer's income for the year or a prescribed form amending the taxpayer's return of income for the year was filed under paragraph (6)(e) or subsection 49(4) or 152(6), the day on which the amended return or prescribed form was filed, and

(l) where, as a consequence of a request in writing, the Minister reassessed the taxpayer's tax for the year to take into account the deduction or exclusion, the day on which the request was made.

**Related Provisions**: 161(7) — Effect of loss carryback.

**Notes**: 164(5)(a) added by 1992 transportation industry assistance bill, effective 1992, and amended by 1997 Budget, effective for 1997 and later taxation years. For 1992–96, read:

(a) the deduction of an amount under subclause 12(1)(x.1)(ii)(A)(II) in respect of a fuel tax rebate repayment made in a subsequent taxation year,

164(5)(h) added by 1989 Budget, effective for taxation years ending after June 1989.

164(5)(h.01) added by 1995-97 technical bill, effective for taxpayers who die after 1992.

164(5)(h.2) and (h.3) added by 1992 technical bill. (h.2) effective for 1992 and later taxation years and (h.3) for 1991 and later taxation years. An overpayment of tax resulting from the carryback of an unused surtax credit of Part I tax credit is thus not taken into account in determining interest payable on a refund until the later of the dates specified in 164(5)(i) to (l).

**(5.1) Idem** — Where a repayment made under subsection (1.1) or (4.1) or an amount applied under subsection (2) in respect of a repayment, or a part thereof, may reasonably be regarded as being in respect of a claim made by a taxpayer in an objection to or appeal from an assessment of tax for a taxation year for

(a) the deduction of an amount, in respect of a repayment under subsection 68.4(7) of the *Excise Tax Act* made in a subsequent taxation year, in computing the amount determined under subparagraph 12(1)(x.1)(ii),

(b) the deduction of an amount under section 41 in respect of the taxpayer's listed-personal-property loss for a subsequent taxation year,

(c) the exclusion of an amount from the taxpayer's income for the year by virtue of section 49 in respect of the exercise of an option in a subsequent taxation year,

(d) the deduction of an amount under section 118.1 in respect of a gift made in a subsequent taxation year or under section 111 in respect of a loss for a subsequent taxation year,

(e) the deduction of an amount under subsection 126(2) in respect of an unused foreign tax credit (within the meaning assigned by subsection 126(7)) for a subsequent taxation year,

(f) the deduction of an amount under subsection 127(5) in respect of property acquired or an expenditure made in a subsequent taxation year,

(g) the deduction of an amount under section 125.2 in respect of an unused Part VI tax credit (within the meaning assigned by subsection 125.2(3)) for a subsequent taxation year,

(h) the deduction of an amount under section 125.3 in respect of an unused Part I.3 tax credit (within the meaning assigned by subsection 125.3(3)) for a subsequent taxation year,

(h.01) the deduction of an amount under subsection 147.2(4) in computing the taxpayer's income for the year because of the application of subsection 147.2(6) as a result of the taxpayer's death in the following taxation year,

(h.1) the deduction of an amount in computing the taxpayer's income for the year by virtue of an election for a subsequent taxation year under paragraph (6)(c) or (d) by the taxpayer's legal representative,

(h.2) the deduction of an amount under subsection 181.1(4) in respect of an unused surtax credit (within the meaning assigned by subsection 181.1(6)) of the taxpayer for a subsequent taxation year, or

(h.3) the deduction of an amount under subsection 190.1(3) in respect of an unused Part I tax credit (within the meaning assigned by subsection 190.1(5)) of the taxpayer for a subsequent taxation year,

interest shall not be paid or applied thereon for any part of a period that is before the latest of

(i) the first day immediately following that subsequent taxation year,

(j) the day on which the taxpayer's or the taxpayer's legal representative's return of income for that subsequent taxation year was filed,

(k) where an amended return of the taxpayer's income for the year or a prescribed form amending the taxpayer's return of income for the year was filed under paragraph (6)(e) or subsection 49(4) or 152(6), the day on which the amended return or prescribed form was filed, and

(l) where, as a consequence of a request in writing, the Minister reassessed the taxpayer's tax for the year to take into account the deduction or exclusion, the day on which the request was made.

**Proposed Amendment — 164(5.1)**

**(5.1) Interest — disputed amounts** — Where a portion of a repayment made under subsection (1.1) or (4.1), or an amount applied under subsection (2) in respect of a repayment, can reasonably be regarded as being in respect of a claim made by the taxpayer in an objection to or appeal from an assessment of tax for a taxation year for a deduction or exclusion described in subsection (5) in respect of a subsequent taxation year, interest shall not be paid or applied on the portion for any part of a period that is before the latest of the dates described in paragraphs (5)(i) to (l).

**Application**: Bill C-43 (First Reading September 20, 2000), subsec. 94(5), will amend subsec. 164(5.1) to read as above, applicable to taxation years that end after October 1, 1996.

**Technical Notes**: Subsection 164(5) provides that, where the tax payable for a taxation year is reduced because of certain deductions or exclusions arising from tax credits, the carryback of losses, or events in subsequent years, interest payable to a taxpayer on any resulting overpayment of tax is to be calculated as if the overpayment had arisen on the latest of several dates. Subsection 164(5.1), which deals with the calculation of interest on repayments of amounts in dispute, parallels the rules contained in subsection 164(5).

Subsection 164(5.1) is amended to simplify its structure and to accommodate the new deductions listed in the commentary on subsection 164(5), above.

**Notes**: 164(5.1)(a) added by 1992 transportation industry assistance bill, effective 1992, and amended by 1997 Budget, effective for 1997 and later taxation years. For 1992-96, read:

(a) the deduction of an amount under subclause 12(1)(x.1)(ii)(A)(II) in respect of a fuel tax rebate repayment made in a subsequent taxation year,

164(5.1)(h) added by 1989 Budget, effective for taxation years ending after June 1989.

164(5.1)(h.01) added by 1995-97 technical bill, effective for taxpayers who die after 1992.

164(5.1)(h.2) and (h.3) added by 1992 technical bill, (h.2) effective for 1992 and later taxation years and (h.3) for 1991 and later taxation years. See Notes to 164(5).

**(6) Where disposition of property by legal representative of deceased taxpayer** — Where in the course of administering the estate of a deceased taxpayer, the taxpayer's legal representative has, within the first taxation year of the estate,

(a) disposed of capital property of the estate so that the total of all amounts each of which is a capital loss from the disposition of a property exceeds the total of all amounts each of which is a capital gain from the disposition of a property, or

(b) disposed of all of the depreciable property of a prescribed class of the estate so that the undepreciated capital cost to the estate of property of that class at the end of the first taxation year of the estate is, by virtue of subsection 20(16) or any regulation made under paragraph 20(1)(a), deductible in computing the income of the estate for that year,

notwithstanding any other provision of this Act, the following rules apply:

(c) such parts of one or more capital losses of the estate from the disposition of properties in the year (the total of which is not to exceed the excess referred to in paragraph (a)) as the legal representative so elects, in prescribed manner and within a prescribed time, are deemed (except for the purpose of subsection 112(3) and this paragraph) to be capital losses of the deceased taxpayer from the disposition of the properties by the taxpayer in the taxpayer's last taxation year and not to be capital losses of the estate from the disposition of those properties,

(d) such part of the amount of any deduction described in paragraph (b) (not exceeding the amount that, but for this subsection, would be the total of the non-capital loss and the farm loss of the estate for its first taxation year) as the legal representative so elects, in prescribed manner and within a prescribed time, shall be deductible in computing the income of the taxpayer for the taxpayer's taxation year in which the taxpayer died and shall not be an amount deductible in computing any loss of the estate for its first taxation year,

(e) the legal representative shall, at or before the time prescribed for filing the election referred to in paragraphs (c) and (d), file an amended return of income for the deceased taxpayer for the taxpayer's taxation year in which the taxpayer died to give effect to the rules in those paragraphs, and

(f) in computing the taxable income of the deceased taxpayer for a taxation year preceding the year in which the taxpayer died, no amount may be deducted in respect of an amount referred to in paragraph (c) or (d).

**Related Provisions**: 152(1) — Assessment; 152(6)(h) — Reassessment to give effect to election; 161(7)(b)(iii) — Effect of carryback of loss, etc.; 220(3.2), Reg. 600(b) — Late filing of election or revocation.

**Notes**: For planning ideas involving 164(6), see H. Elise Rees, "Testamentary Planning to Avoid Double Taxation", 48(1) *Canadian Tax Journal* 155-172 (2000).

164(6)(c) amended by 1995-97 technical bill, effective for deaths after 1993. For deaths from 1984 to 1993, read:

(c) such part of one or more capital losses from the disposition of properties referred to in paragraph (a) (the total of which amounts is not to exceed the excess referred to in that paragraph) as the legal representative so elects, in prescribed manner and within a prescribed time, shall be deemed to be capital losses of the deceased taxpayer from the disposition of the properties by the taxpayer in the taxpayer's taxation year in which the taxpayer died and not to be capital losses of the estate from the disposition of those properties for its first taxation year,

Clause 191 of the 1995-97 technical bill provides the following special application rule:

191. Where

(a) the first taxation year of an estate of an individual ended after April 26, 1995 and before 1997,

(b) the estate had a capital loss from the disposition after the year and before 1997 of a share of the capital stock of a corporation that was owned by the individual or the estate on April 26, 1995 and acquired by the estate as a consequence of the individual's death, and

(c) the individual's legal representative so elects in writing filed with the Minister of National Revenue within 6 months after the month in which this Act is assented to,

the following rules apply:

(d) the disposition is deemed to have occurred in the first taxation year of the estate,

(e) an election under paragraph 164(6)(c) of the Act, as enacted by subsection 190(8), for the year is deemed to have been filed on time if it is filed with the Minister of National Revenue within 6 months after the month in which this Act is assented to, and

(f) an amended return of income under Part I of the Act for the individual's last taxation year is deemed for the purpose of paragraph 164(6)(e) of the Act to have been filed on time if it is filed with the Minister of National Revenue within 6 months after the month in which this Act is assented to.

This transitional rule provides a limited opportunity for an estate to transfer a capital loss on the disposition of a share to the taxpayer's last taxation year even though the election was not made within the prescribed time, or the disposition occurred after the end of the estate's first taxation year. (See Finance news release, December 14, 1995.)

**Regulations**: 1000 (prescribed manner, prescribed time).

**Interpretation Bulletins**: IT-140R3: Buy-sell agreements; IT-484R2: Business investment losses.

**Information Circulars**: 92-1: Guidelines for accepting late, amended or revoked elections.

**(6.1) Realization of deceased employees' options** — Notwithstanding any other provision of this Act, if a right to acquire securities (as defined in subsection 7(7)) under an agreement in respect of which a benefit was deemed by paragraph 7(1)(e) to have been received by a taxpayer (in this subsection referred to as "the right") is exercised or disposed of by the taxpayer's legal representative within the first taxation year of the estate of the taxpayer and the representative so elects in prescribed manner and on or before a prescribed day,

(a) the amount, if any, by which

(i) the amount of the benefit deemed by paragraph 7(1)(e) to have been received by the taxpayer in respect of the right

exceeds the total of

(ii) the amount, if any, by which the value of the right immediately before the time it was exercised or disposed of exceeds the amount, if any, paid by the taxpayer to acquire the right, and

(iii) where in computing the taxpayer's taxable income for the taxation year in which the taxpayer died an amount was deducted under paragraph 110(1)(d) in respect of the benefit deemed by paragraph 7(1)(e) to have been received by the taxpayer in that year by reason of paragraph 7(1)(e) in respect of that right, 1/4 of the amount, if any, by which the amount determined under subparagraph (i) exceeds the amount determined under subparagraph (ii),

**Proposed Amendment — 164(6.1)(a)(iii)**

**Application**: The December 21, 2000 draft legislation, s. 84, will amend subpara. 164(6.1)(a)(iii) to replace the reference to the fraction "1/4" with a reference to the fraction "1/2", applicable to deaths that occur after February 27, 2000 except that, for deaths that occurred after February 27, 2000 and before October 18, 2000, the reference to the fraction "1/2" shall be read as a reference to the fraction "1/3".

**Technical Notes**: Subsection 164(6.1) applies to certain employee stock options in respect of which a benefit has been included in a deceased taxpayer's income by reason of subparagraph 7(1)(e). This subsection applies where the employee stock option is exercised or disposed of by the deceased's legal representative in the first taxation year of the deceased's estate.

Subparagraph 164(6.1)(a)(iii) is amended by replacing the reference to the fraction "1/4" with a reference to the fraction "1/2". The change is consequential on the reduction in the capital gains inclusion rate from 3/4 to 1/2 [see 38(a) — ed.].

The amendment applies to deaths that occur after February 27, 2000 except that, for deaths that occur after February 27, 2000 and before October 18, 2000, the reference to the fraction "1/2" in subparagraph 164(6.1)(a)(iii) is to be read as a reference to "1/3". These modifications are required in order to reflect the capital gains/losses rate for the year.

shall be deemed to be a loss of the taxpayer from employment for the year in which the taxpayer died;

(b) there shall be deducted in computing the adjusted cost base to the estate of the right at any time the amount of the loss that would be determined under paragraph (a) if that paragraph were read without reference to subparagraph (a)(iii); and

(c) the legal representative shall, at or before the time prescribed for filing the election under this subsection, file an amended return of income for the taxpayer for the taxation year in which the taxpayer died to give effect to paragraph (a).

**Related Provisions**: 53(2)(t) — Deduction from adjusted cost base of right to acquire shares or units.

**Notes**: Opening words of 164(6.1) amended by 1998 Budget, effective for deaths that occur after February 1998. The effect of the amendment is to extend the rule to mutual fund trust units (see Notes to 7(1)). For deaths from July 14, 1990 to February 28, 1998, read:

(6.1) Exercise or disposition of employee stock option by legal representative of deceased employee — Where, within the first taxation year of the estate of a deceased taxpayer, a right to acquire shares under an agreement in respect of which a benefit was deemed by paragraph 7(1)(e) to have been received by the taxpayer (in this subsection referred to as "the right") is exercised or disposed of by the taxpayer's legal representative, notwithstanding any other provision of this Act, where the taxpayer's legal representative elects in prescribed manner and on or before a prescribed day,

164(6.1) added by 1992 technical bill, effective for deaths after July 13, 1990 (the same application as 7(1)(e)).

**(7) Definition of "overpayment"** — In this section, "overpayment" of a taxpayer for a taxation year means

(a) where the taxpayer is not a corporation, the total of all amounts paid on account of the taxpayer's liability under this Part for the year minus all amounts payable in respect thereof; and

(b) where the taxpayer is a corporation, the total of all amounts paid on account of the corporation's liability under this Part or Parts I.3, VI or VI.1 for the year minus all amounts payable in respect thereof.

**Notes**: 164(7)(b) added by 1992 technical bill, effective for 1992 and later taxation years. For earlier years, the rule for all taxpayers was the same; i.e., ignore the references to Parts I.3, VI and VI.1. See Notes to 157(1).

**Related Provisions [s. 164]**: 144(9) — Refunds — employees profit sharing plans. See also Related Provisions at end of s. 163.

**Definitions [s. 164]**: "allowable capital loss" — 38(b), 248(1); "amount", "assessment", "balance-due day" — 248(1); "Canada" — 255; "capital loss" — 39(1)(b), 248(1); "capital property" — 54, 248(1); "clear days" — *Interpretation Act* 27(1); "corporation" — 248(1), *Interpretation Act* 35(1); "depreciable property" — 13(21), 248(1); "eligible production corporation" — 125.5(1); "estate" — 104(1), 248(1); "farm loss" — 111(8); "Federal Court" — *Interpretation Act* 35(1); "filing-due date", "individual" — 248(1); "investment tax credit" — 127(9), 248(1); "legal representative" — 248(1); "listed personal property" — 54, 248(1); "Minister" — 248(1); "net capital loss", "non-capital loss" — 111(8), 248(1); "overpayment" — 164(7); "prescribed" — 248(1); "prescribed rate" — Reg. 4301; "property" — 248(1); "province" — *Interpretation Act* 35(1); "qualified corporation" — 125.4(1); "regulation" — 248(1); "security" — *Interpretation Act* 35(1); "share" — 248(1); "taxable income" — 2(2), 248(1); "taxation year" — 249; "taxpayer" — 248(1); "testamentary trust" — 248(1); "writing" — *Interpretation Act* 35(1).

## 164.1 [Repealed]

**Notes**: 164.1 repealed by 1992 Child Benefit bill, effective as of the 1993 taxation year. Until 1992, it allowed Revenue Canada to prepay up to ⅔ of the refundable Child Tax Credit provided certain conditions were met. See now 122.61(1) for the Child Tax Benefit.

## Objections to Assessments

**165. (1) Objections to assessment** — A taxpayer who objects to an assessment under this Part may serve on the Minister a notice of objection, in writing, setting out the reasons for the objection and all relevant facts,

(a) where the assessment is in respect of the taxpayer for a taxation year and the taxpayer is an individual (other than a trust) or a testamentary trust, on or before the later of

(i) the day that is one year after the taxpayer's filing-due date for the year, and

(ii) the day that is 90 days after the day of mailing of the notice of assessment; and

(b) in any other case, on or before the day that is 90 days after the day of mailing of the notice of assessment.

**Related Provisions**: 164(4) — Interest on overpayments; 165(1.1), (1.2) — Limitations on right to object; 165(1.11) — Large corporations — detail required on notice of objection; 165(2) — Service of notice of objection; 165(2.1) — Application of 165(1)(a); 165(3) — Duties of Minister on receipt of notice of objection; 166.1, 166.2 — Applications for extension of time to object; 167(1) — Application to Tax Court of Canada for time extension; 173(2), 174(5) — Time during consideration not to count; 225.1(2) — Collection restrictions; 244(10) — Proof that no notice of objection filed; *Interpretation Act* 26 — Deadline on Sunday or holiday extended to next business day.

**Notes**: Section 26 of the *Interpretation Act*, which applies to all federal statutes, provides:

> 26. Time limits and holidays — Where the time limited for the doing of a thing expires or falls on a holiday, the thing may be done on the day next following that is not a holiday.

Subsection 35(1) of that Act defines "holiday" to mean Sunday as well as statutory holidays. The case law suggests that where the deadline expires on a Saturday or other day when CCRA offices are closed, the deadline may be judicially extended. (See the discussion in the *Canada GST Service* at s. 301.)

The 90-day period begins from the date of mailing of the assessment, which is normally presumed to be the date of the assessment; see Notes to 244(15). It is advisable to keep the envelope showing the postmark, especially if it was not mailed until a later date. See also Notes to 244(14) re the CCRA's possible inability to prove the date of mailing of the assessment.

No objection can be brought against a nil assessment (e.g., to change a loss calculation); see Notes to 152(1.1).

165(1)(a)(i) amended to change "balance-due day" to "filing-due date" by 1995 Budget, effective for 1995 and later taxation years. The change was needed because of the extended filing deadline (June 15) for certain taxpayers under 150(1)(d).

165(1) amended by 1991 technical bill (as part of the "Fairness Package"), effective for objections made after December 17, 1991, to add 165(1)(a)(i) and to simplify the filing requirements to not require that the election be in duplicate and in prescribed form.

**Information Circulars**: 98-1R: Collections policies.

**Forms**: T400A: Notice of objection. (The prescribed form does not have to be used, however. See 165(2)).

**(1.1) Limitation of right to object to assessments or determinations** — Notwithstanding subsection (1), where at any time the Minister assesses tax, interest, penalties or other amounts payable under this Part by, or makes a determination in respect of, a taxpayer

(a) under subsection 67.5(2) or 152(1.8), subparagraph 152(4)(b)(i) or subsection 152(4.3) or (6), 161.1(7), 164(4.1), 220(3.4) or 245(8) or in accordance with an order of a court vacating, varying or restoring an assessment or referring the assessment back to the Minister for reconsideration and reassessment,

(b) under subsection (3) where the underlying objection relates to an assessment or a determination made under any of the provisions or circumstances referred to in paragraph (a), or

(c) under a provision of an Act of Parliament requiring an assessment to be made that, but for that provision, would not be made because of subsections 152(4) to (5),

the taxpayer may object to the assessment or determination within 90 days after the day of mailing of the notice of assessment or determination, but only to the extent that the reasons for the objection can reasonably be regarded

(d) where the assessment or determination was made under subsection 152(1.8), as relating to any matter or conclusion specified in paragraph 152(1.8)(a), (b) or (c), and

(e) in any other case, as relating to any matter that gave rise to the assessment or determination

and that was not conclusively determined by the court, and this subsection shall not be read or construed as limiting the right of the taxpayer to object to an assessment or a determination issued or made before that time.

**Related Provisions**: 169(2) — Limitation of right to appeal.

**Notes**: 165(1.1) provides that, where a reassessment is made after the normal deadline under a special provision (such as those allowing for reassessment with the taxpayer's consent), the taxpayer cannot use that as an excuse to open up a return that was otherwise statute-barred (to the taxpayer) and claim additional deductions or credits beyond those that are the subject of the special reassessment. (See 169(2) for the same rule as it applies to appeals.) For more on 165(1.1), see *Chevron Canada Resources Ltd.*, [1999] 3 C.T.C. 140 (FCA), and the commentaries on *Chevron* by Karen Sharlow in *Tax Litigation* (Federated Press), Vol. VI No. 4 (1998) pp. 394-397 and by Jeffrey Galway & David Spiro, pp. 398-400. The rule of *res judicata* may also apply; see *Chevron Canada Resources Ltd.*

Opening words of 165(1.1) amended to add "or other amounts"; reference to 152(1.8) added to 165(1.1)(a); and 165(1.1)(d) added (splitting (e) out of the body of the subsection); all by 1995-97 technical bill, effective for determinations made after June 18, 1998.

165(1.1)(a) amended by 1999 Budget, effective after 1999, to add reference to 161.1(7).

Reference to 152(4.3) added to 165(1.1)(a) by 1992 technical bill, effective June 10, 1993.

165(1.1) added by 1991 technical bill, effective for objections made after December 17, 1991.

**(1.11) Objections by large corporations** — Where a corporation that was a large corporation in a taxation year (within the meaning assigned by subsection 225.1(8)) objects to an assessment under this Part for the year, the notice of objection shall

(a) reasonably describe each issue to be decided;

(b) specify in respect of each issue, the relief sought, expressed as the amount of a change in a balance (within the meaning assigned by subsection 152(4.4)) or a balance of undeducted outlays, expenses or other amounts of the corporation; and

(c) provide facts and reasons relied on by the corporation in respect of each issue.

**Related Provisions**: 165(1.12) — Late compliance with 165(1.11); 165(1.13) — Corporation may only object on grounds raised; 169(2.1)(a) — Appeal only on grounds raised in objection.

**Notes**: 165(1.11) added by 1994 tax amendments bill (Part VII), effective after September 26, 1994 for notices of objection filed at any time, except where an appeal of the assessment has been instituted by June 22, 1995. Where a taxpayer submitted to a Chief of Appeals (see 165(2)) in writing before March 1995 the information required by 165(1.11) to be provided in a notice of objection served by the taxpayer before 1995, the taxpayer is deemed to have complied with 165(1.11).

If there is any uncertainty as to the quantum of the dispute, a corporation should always overestimate the amount under 165(1.11)(b). The amount specified may form a cap on the relief that can be granted by the Tax Court, under the closing words of 169(2.1).

One should also consider putting additional issues into the notice of objection, where the corporation may wish to make elective claims if it loses on the main issue. These might include capital cost allowance claims and using loss carryforwards.

For Revenue Canada's administrative comments on these rules, see Robert Beith, "Draft Legislation on Income Tax Objections and Appeals", 1994 Canadian Tax Foundation annual conference report, 34:1–34.5.

Similar rules are now provided for objections to Ontario tax assessments, even for small corporations (*Corporations Tax Act*, s. 84(1.1); see David M. Sherman, *The Practitioner's Ontario Taxes Annotated* (Carswell, annual)).

**(1.12) Late compliance** — Notwithstanding subsection (1.11), where a notice of objection served by a corporation to which that subsection applies does not include the information required by paragraph (1.11)(b) or (c) in respect of an issue to be decided that is described in the notice, the Minister may in writing request the corporation to provide the information, and those paragraphs shall be deemed to be complied with in respect of the issue if, within 60 days after the request is made, the corporation submits the information in writing to a Chief of Appeals referred to in subsection (2).

**Notes**: 165(1.12) added by 1994 tax amendments bill (Part VII), effective after September 26, 1994 for notices of objection filed at any time, except where an appeal of the assessment has been instituted by June 22, 1995.

**(1.13) Limitation on objections by large corporations** — Notwithstanding subsections (1) and (1.1), where under subsection (3) a particular assessment was made for a taxation year pursuant to a notice of objection served by a corporation that was a large corporation in the year (within the meaning assigned by subsection 225.1(8)), except where the objection was made to an earlier assessment made under any of the provisions or circumstances referred to in paragraph (1.1)(a), the corporation may object to the particular assessment in respect of an issue

(a) only if the corporation complied with subsection (1.11) in the notice with respect to that issue; and

(b) only with respect to the relief sought in respect of that issue as specified by the corporation in the notice.

**Related Provisions**: 165(1.14) — Application.

**Notes**: 165(1.13) added by 1994 tax amendments bill (Part VII), effective after September 26, 1994 for notices of objection filed at any time, except where an appeal of the assessment has been instituted by June 22, 1995.

**(1.14) Application of subsec. (1.13)** — Where a particular assessment is made under subsection (3) pursuant to an objection made by a taxpayer to an earlier assessment, subsection (1.13) does not limit the right of the taxpayer to object to the particular assessment in respect of an issue that was part of the particular assessment and not part of the earlier assessment.

**Notes**: 165(1.14) added by 1994 tax amendments bill (Part VII), effective after September 26, 1994 for notices of objection filed at any time, except where an appeal of the assessment has been instituted by June 22, 1995.

**(1.15) Partnership** — Notwithstanding subsection (1), where the Minister makes a determination under subsection 152(1.4) in respect of a fiscal period of a partnership, an objection in respect of the determination may be made only by one member of the partnership, and that member must be either

(a) designated for that purpose in the information return made under section 229 of the *Income Tax Regulations* for the fiscal period; or

(b) otherwise expressly authorized by the partnership to so act.

**Notes**: 165(1.15) added by 1995-97 technical bill, effective for determinations made after June 18, 1998. See Notes to 152(1.4).

Partnerships will generally wish to determine who is the "tax matters partner" for dealing with Revenue Canada.

**(1.2) Determination of fair market value [Limitation on objections]** — Notwithstanding subsection[s] (1) [and (1.1)], no objection may be

**S. 165(1.2)**      Income Tax Act, Part I

made [by a taxpayer] to an assessment made under subsection 118.1(11), 152(4.2), 169(3) or 220(3.1) [nor, for greater certainty, in respect of an issue for which the right of objection has been waived in writing by the taxpayer].

**Related Provisions**: 169(2.2) — No appeal permitted where right to object or appeal waived.

**Notes**: 165(1.2) amended by 1995 cultural property bill (Bill C-93), in force July 12, 1996. Before July 12, 1996, ignore the reference to 118.1(11) and read in the words in square brackets. These words were deleted unintentionally by Bill C-93 and should be restored. They were added by 1994 tax amendments bill (Part VII), effective after September 26, 1994 for waivers signed at any time. They are parallel to 169(2.2), which applies to appeals.

165(1.2) added by 1991 technical bill, effective 1991. Since an assessment under 152(4.2) is made for the taxpayer's benefit, no objection can be made to it.

**(2) Service** — A notice of objection under this section shall be served by being addressed to the Chief of Appeals in a District Office or a Taxation Centre of the Canada Customs and Revenue Agency and delivered or mailed to that Office or Centre.

**Related Provisions**: 165(6) — Acceptance of notice of objection; 248(7)(a) — Mail deemed received on day mailed.

**Notes**: 165(2) amended by *Canada Customs & Revenue Agency Act*, effective November 1, 1999, to change "Department of National Revenue" to "Canada Customs and Revenue Agency".

"Department of National Revenue, Taxation" changed to "Department of National Revenue" by Department of National Revenue Act amending bill, effective May 12, 1994.

165(2) simplified by 1991 technical bill (as part of the "Fairness Package"), effective for objections made after December 17, 1991. For earlier objections, read:

> (2) A notice of objection under this section shall be served by being sent by registered mail addressed to the Deputy Minister of National Revenue for Taxation at Ottawa.

**Forms**: T400A: Notice of objection. (The prescribed form does not have to be used, however).

**(2.1) Application** — Notwithstanding any other provision of this Act, paragraph (1)(a) shall apply only in respect of assessments, determinations and redeterminations under this Part, Part I.1 and Part I.2.

---

**Proposed Amendment — 165(2.1)**

**(2.1) Application** — Notwithstanding any other provision of this Act, paragraph (1)(a) shall apply only in respect of assessments, determinations and redeterminations under this Part and Part I.2.

**Application**: The December 21, 2000 draft legislation, s. 85, will amend subsec. 165(2.1) to read as above, applicable to 2001 et seq.

**Technical Notes**: Subsection 165(2.1) provides that the extension of time to object to an assessment referred to in subsection 165(1) applies only in respect of assessments and determinations made under Parts I, I.1 and I.2. The amendment to subsection 165(2.1) is strictly consequential on the repeal of the surtax imposed on individuals under Part I.1 (see commentary on that Part).

---

**Notes**: 165(2.1) added by 1991 technical bill, effective for objections made after December 17, 1991. It is needed because section 165 is deemed by numerous other provisions of the Act (e.g., 202(3)) to apply for the purposes of the taxes under various Parts.

**(3) Duties of Minister** — On receipt of a notice of objection under this section, the Minister shall, with all due dispatch, reconsider the assessment and vacate, confirm or vary the assessment or reassess, and shall thereupon notify the taxpayer in writing of the Minister's action.

**Related Provisions**: 152(9) — Minister may raise new basis for assessment during appeal process; 165(5) — Normal reassessment limitations do not apply to reassessment under 165(3); 169 — Appeals; 244(5) — Proof of service by mail; 244(14) — Date of mailing presumed to be date of notification; 248(7)(a) — Mail deemed received on day mailed.

**Notes**: A notice of objection is considered by an Appeals Officer, who is a CCRA employee but is independent of the audit (Verification and Enforcement) branch within the same local Tax Services office. As a result of the Appeals Renewal Initiative announced by Revenue Canada on April 17, 1997, the Appeals Officer will provide the taxpayer or taxpayer's representative with copies of the auditor's report and all supporting documents that the Appeals Officer is considering. As well, any meeting between the Appeals Officer and the auditor must be documented, and the minutes of the meeting made available to the taxpayer or representative. See David M. Sherman, "The Appeals Renewal Initiative: Substantive Improvements or Window Dressing?", *GST & Commodity Tax* (Carswell), Vol XI, No. 6 (July/August 1997), pp. 41–43.

Once the basis for assessment has been determined and the limitation period under 152(4) has otherwise expired, the Crown could not advance a new basis for assessment during the course of an appeal: *Continental Bank of Canada*, [1998] 4 C.T.C. 77 (SCC). However, this rule has been reversed by 152(9), introduced on December 23, 1998 and enacted in 1999.

165(3)(b) amended by 1988 Tax Court bill, effective January 1, 1991, to delete reference to a direct appeal to the Federal Court. (The Tax Court of Canada replaced the role of the Federal Court–Trial Division, as of 1991.) 165(3)(b) repealed (and 165(3) consolidated to read as it does now) by 1992 technical bill, effective June 10, 1993. It provided:

> (b) where the taxpayer indicates in the notice of objection that the taxpayer wishes to appeal immediately to the Tax Court of Canada and that the taxpayer waives reconsideration of the assessment and the Minister consents, file a copy of the notice of objection with the Registrar of that Court,

**I.T. Application Rules**: 62(4).

**Interpretation Bulletins**: IT-241: Reassessments made after the four-year limit.

**Information Circulars**: 98-1R: Collections policies.

**(3.1), (3.2), (4)** [Repealed]

**Notes**: 165(3.1) added by 1992 Child Benefit bill effective 1993, and repealed by 1995-97 technical bill effective August 28, 1995, as a result of the transfer of all responsibility for the Child Tax Benefit to Revenue Canada. From 1993 to August 27, 1995, read:

> **(3.1) Decision by Minister of National Health and Welfare** — Notwithstanding subsection (3), on receipt of a notice of objection to a determination that includes matters relating to whether, for the purposes of subdivision a.1 of Division E,
>
> (a) a taxpayer is an eligible individual in respect of a qualified dependant,
>
> (b) a person is a qualified dependant, or
>
> (c) a person is a taxpayer's cohabiting spouse,
>
> the Minister of National Revenue shall refer those matters to the Minister of National Health and Welfare who shall, with

all due dispatch, decide the matters and notify the Minister of National Revenue of the decision.

165(3.2) added by 1992 Child Benefit bill effective 1993, and repealed by 1995-97 technical bill effective August 28, 1995, as a result of the transfer of all responsibility for the Child Tax Benefit to Revenue Canada. From 1993 to August 27, 1995, read:

(3.2) **Reconsideration of determination** — On receipt of the notification of a decision of the Minister of National Health and Welfare under subsection (3.1), the Minister of National Revenue shall, with all due dispatch, reconsider the determination to which the decision relates and vacate, confirm or vary the determination or redetermine in accordance with the decision, and shall thereupon notify the taxpayer in writing of that action.

165(4) repealed by 1992 technical bill, effective June 10, 1993, in conjunction with the repeal of 165(3)(b). It provided:

(4) **Effect of filing of notice of objection** — Where the Minister files a copy of a notice of objection pursuant to paragraph (3)(b), the Minister shall be deemed, for the purpose of section 169, to have confirmed the assessment to which the notice relates and the taxpayer who served the notice shall be deemed to have thereupon instituted an appeal in accordance with that section.

165(4) amended by 1988 Tax Court bill, effective January 1, 1991, to delete a reference to 172(2) in addition to 169.

(5) **Validity of reassessment** — The limitations imposed under subsections 152(4) and (4.01) do not apply to a reassessment made under subsection (3).

**Notes**: 165(5) amended by 1995-97 technical bill, effective April 28, 1989, in consequence of amendments to 152(4) and the addition of 152(4.01).

**Interpretation Bulletins**: IT-241: Reassessments made after the four-year limit.

(6) **Validity of notice of objection** — The Minister may accept a notice of objection served under this section that was not served in the manner required by subsection (2).

**Notes**: 165(6) amended by 1991 technical bill (as Part of the "Fairness Package"), to substitute "in the manner required" for "in duplicate or in the manner required", effective for objections made after January 16, 1992.

(7) **Notice of objection not required** — Where a taxpayer has served in accordance with this section a notice of objection to an assessment and thereafter the Minister reassesses the tax, interest, penalties or other amount in respect of which the notice of objection was served or makes an additional assessment in respect thereof and sends to the taxpayer a notice of the reassessment or of the additional assessment, as the case may be, the taxpayer may, without serving a notice of objection to the reassessment or additional assessment,

(a) appeal therefrom to the Tax Court of Canada in accordance with section 169; or

(b) amend any appeal to the Tax Court of Canada that has been instituted with respect to the assessment by joining thereto an appeal in respect of the reassessment or the additional assessment in such manner and on such terms, if any, as the Tax Court of Canada directs.

**Related Provisions**: 169(2.1)(b) — Grounds for appeal by large corporation.

**Notes**: 165(7) amended by 1988 Tax Court bill, effective January 1, 1991, to reflect the changes that permit appeals to be launched only to the Tax Court, and not to the Federal Court.

Opening words of 165(7) amended by 1991 technical bill, effective for 1986 and later taxation years, to refer to interest and penalties as well as tax.

**Related Provisions [s. 165]**: See Related Provisions at end of s. 163.

**Definitions [s. 165]**: "amount", "assessment" — 248(1); "Canada Customs and Revenue Agency" — *Canada Customs and Revenue Agency Act* s. 4(1); "filing-due date" — 150(1), 248(1); "individual", "Minister", "prescribed" — 248(1); "large corporation" — 225.1(8); "taxation year" — 249; "taxpayer" — 248(1); "testamentary trust" — 248(1); "trust" — 104(1), 108(1), 248(1), (3); "writing" — *Interpretation Act* 35(1).

## General

**166. Irregularities** — An assessment shall not be vacated or varied on appeal by reason only of any irregularity, informality, omission or error on the part of any person in the observation of any directory provision of this Act.

**Related Provisions**: 152(3) — Liability for tax not affected by incorrect or incomplete assessment; 152(8) — Assessment valid despite error; 158 — Assessment payable forthwith; 165(3) — Objections — Duties of Minister. See also Related Provisions annotation at end of s. 163.

**Definitions [s. 166]**: "assessment", "person" — 248(1).

### 166.1 (1) Extension of time [to object] by Minister — Where no notice of objection to an assessment has been served under section 165, nor any request under subsection 245(6) made, within the time limited by those provisions for doing so, the taxpayer may apply to the Minister to extend the time for serving the notice of objection or making the request.

**Related Provisions**: 244(10) — Proof that no notice of objection filed.

**Notes**: See Notes to 166.2(1), which allows the Court to extend time if the CCRA refuses.

(2) **Contents of application** — An application made under subsection (1) shall set out the reasons why the notice of objection or the request was not served or made, as the case may be, within the time otherwise limited by this Act for doing so.

(3) **How application made** — An application under subsection (1) shall be made by being addressed to the Chief of Appeals in a District Office or a Taxation Centre of the Canada Customs and Revenue Agency and delivered or mailed to that Office or Centre, accompanied by a copy of the notice of objection or a copy of the request, as the case may be.

**Related Provisions**: 248(7)(a) — Mail deemed received on day mailed.

**Notes**: 166.1(3) amended by *Canada Customs & Revenue Agency Act*, effective November 1, 1999, to change "Department of National Revenue" to "Canada Customs and Revenue Agency".

"Department of National Revenue, Taxation" changed to "Department of National Revenue" by Department of National Revenue Act amending bill, effective May 12, 1994.

**(4) Idem** — The Minister may accept an application under this section that was not made in the manner required by subsection (3).

**(5) Duties of Minister** — On receipt of an application made under subsection (1), the Minister shall, with all due dispatch, consider the application and grant or refuse it, and shall thereupon notify the taxpayer in writing of the Minister's decision.

Related Provisions: 166.2(1) — Extension of time by Tax Court; 244(14) — Date of mailing presumed to be date of notification;

Notes: 166.1(5) amended by 1992 technical bill, effective June 10, 1993. Before that date, the Minister was required to notify the taxpayer by registered mail rather than simply "in writing".

**(6) Date of objection or request if application granted** — Where an application made under subsection (1) is granted, the notice of objection or the request, as the case may be, shall be deemed to have been served or made on the day the decision of the Minister is mailed to the taxpayer.

**(7) When order to be made** — No application shall be granted under this section unless

(a) the application is made within one year after the expiration of the time otherwise limited by this Act for serving a notice of objection or making a request, as the case may be; and

(b) the taxpayer demonstrates that

(i) within the time otherwise limited by this Act for serving such a notice or making such a request, as the case may be, the taxpayer

(A) was unable to act or to instruct another to act in the taxpayer's name, or

(B) had a *bona fide* intention to object to the assessment or make the request,

(ii) given the reasons set out in the application and the circumstances of the case, it would be just and equitable to grant the application, and

(iii) the application was made as soon as circumstances permitted.

Related Provisions: 248(7)(a) — Mail deemed received on day mailed.

Notes: 166.1 added by 1991 technical bill, effective for applications filed after January 16, 1992. For earlier times, see 167.

Definitions [s. 166.1]: "assessment", "Minister", "taxpayer" — 248(1); "Canada Customs and Revenue Agency" — *Canada Customs and Revenue Agency Act* s. 4(1); "writing" — *Interpretation Act* 35(1).

**166.2 (1) Extension of time [to object] by Tax Court** — A taxpayer who has made an application under subsection 166.1[(1)] may apply to the Tax Court of Canada to have the application granted after either

(a) the Minister has refused the application, or

(b) 90 days have elapsed after service of the application under subsection 166.1(1) and the Minister has not notified the taxpayer of the Minister's decision,

but no application under this section may be made after the expiration of 90 days after the day on which notification of the decision was mailed to the taxpayer.

Notes: See Notes to 165(1) with respect to time limits and weekends. See also Notes to 244(14) re determining when the assessment was mailed to start the 90-day clock running.

**(2) How application made** — An application under subsection (1) shall be made by filing in the Registry of the Tax Court of Canada, in accordance with the provisions of the *Tax Court of Canada Act*, three copies of the documents referred to in subsection 166.1(3) and three copies of the notification, if any, referred to in subsection 166.1(5).

Related Provisions: 248(7)(a) — Mail deemed received on day mailed.

Notes: 166.2(2) amended by 2000 GST bill, effective October 20, 2000, to change "or by sending by registered mail addressed to an office of the Registry" to "in accordance with the provisions of the *Tax Court of Canada Act*".

**(3) Copy to Commissioner** — The Tax Court of Canada shall send a copy of each application made under this section to the office of the Commissioner of Customs and Revenue.

Notes: 166.2(3) amended by *Canada Customs & Revenue Agency Act*, effective November 1, 1999, to change "Department of National Revenue" to "Canada Customs and Revenue Agency".

**(4) Powers of Court** — The Tax Court of Canada may grant or dismiss an application made under subsection (1) and, in granting an application, may impose such terms as it deems just or order that the notice of objection be deemed to have been served on the date of its order.

**(5) When application to be granted** — No application shall be granted under this section unless

(a) the application was made under subsection 166.1(1) within one year after the expiration of the time otherwise limited by this Act for serving a notice of objection or making a request, as the case may be; and

(b) the taxpayer demonstrates that

(i) within the time otherwise limited by this Act for serving such a notice or making such a request, as the case may be, the taxpayer

(A) was unable to act or to instruct another to act in the taxpayer's name, or

(B) had a *bona fide* intention to object to the assessment or make the request,

(ii) given the reasons set out in the application and the circumstances of the case, it would be just and equitable to grant the application, and

(iii) the application was made under subsection 166.1(1) as soon as circumstances permitted.

**Related Provisions**: 169 — Appeals.

**Notes**: 166.2 added by 1991 technical bill, effective for applications filed after January 16, 1992. For earlier times, see 167.

"Deputy Minister of National Revenue for Taxation" in 166.2(3) changed to "Deputy Minister of National Revenue" by Department of National Revenue Act amending bill, effective May 12, 1994.

**Definitions [s. 166.2]**: "Commissioner of Customs and Revenue" — *Canada Customs and Revenue Agency Act* s. 25; "Minister", "taxpayer" — 248(1).

**167. (1) Extension of time to appeal** — Where an appeal to the Tax Court of Canada has not been instituted by a taxpayer under section 169 within the time limited by that section for doing so, the taxpayer may make an application to the Court for an order extending the time within which the appeal may be instituted and the Court may make an order extending the time for appealing and may impose such terms as it deems just.

**Notes**: See Notes at end of 167.

**(2) Contents of application** — An application made under subsection (1) shall set out the reasons why the appeal was not instituted within the time limited by section 169 for doing so.

**(3) How application made** — An application made under subsection (1) shall be made by filing in the Registry of the Tax Court of Canada, in accordance with the provisions of the *Tax Court of Canada Act*, three copies of the application accompanied by three copies of the notice of appeal.

**Related Provisions**: 165(2) — Service.

**Notes**: 167(3) amended by 2000 GST bill, effective October 20, 2000, to change "or by sending by registered mail addressed to an office of the Registry" to "in accordance with the provisions of the *Tax Court of Canada Act*".

**(4) Copy to Deputy Attorney General** — The Tax Court of Canada shall send a copy of each application made under this section to the office of the Deputy Attorney General of Canada.

**(5) When order to be made** — No order shall be made under this section unless

(a) the application is made within one year after the expiration of the time limited by section 169 for appealing; and

(b) the taxpayer demonstrates that

(i) within the time otherwise limited by section 169 for appealing the taxpayer

(A) was unable to act or to instruct another to act in the taxpayer's name, or

(B) had a *bona fide* intention to appeal,

(ii) given the reasons set out in the application and the circumstances of the case, it would be just and equitable to grant the application,

(iii) the application was made as soon as circumstances permitted, and

(iv) there are reasonable grounds for the appeal.

**Related Provisions**: 169 — Appeal.

**Notes [s. 167]**: 167 rewritten by 1991 technical bill, effective for applications filed after January 16, 1992, and previously amended by 1988 Tax Court bill, effective for appeals filed after 1990.

**Definitions [s. 167]**: "taxpayer" — 248(1).

## Revocation of Registration of Certain Organizations and Associations

**168. (1) Notice of intention to revoke registration** — Where a registered charity or a registered Canadian amateur athletic association

(a) applies to the Minister in writing for revocation of its registration,

(b) ceases to comply with the requirements of this Act for its registration as such,

(c) fails to file an information return as and when required under this Act or a regulation,

(d) issues a receipt for a gift or donation otherwise than in accordance with this Act and the regulations or that contains false information,

(e) fails to comply with or contravenes any of sections 230 to 231.5, or

(f) in the case of a registered Canadian amateur athletic association, accepts a gift or donation the granting of which was expressly or impliedly conditional on the association making a gift or donation to another person, club, society or association,

the Minister may, by registered mail, give notice to the registered charity or registered Canadian amateur athletic association that the Minister proposes to revoke its registration.

**Related Provisions**: 149.1(2) — Revocation of registration of charity; 149.1(3) — Revocation of registration of public foundation; 149.1(6.4), (6.5) — Application of s. 168 to registered national arts service organizations; 172(3)(a) — Appeal from revocation; 180(1) — Appeals to Federal Court of Appeal; 188(1), (2) — Revocation tax; 230(2) — Charity must keep records to allow Minister to determine if there are grounds for revocation of registration; 244(5) — Proof of service by mail; 248(1)"registered Canadian amateur athletic association", "registered charity" — Application for registration; 248(7)(a) — Mail deemed received on day mailed.

**Interpretation Bulletins**: IT-496: Non-profit organizations.

**Information Circulars**: 80-10R: Registered charities: operating a registered charity.

**Forms**: T280: Information — Registered charities and registered Canadian amateur athletic associations; T1189: Application to register a Canadian amateur athletic association under the ITA; T2050: Application to register a charity under the ITA; T2052: Registered Canadian amateur athletic association return of information.

**Registered Charities Newsletters**: 4 (Issuing receipts for gifts of art).

**(2) Revocation of registration** — Where the Minister gives notice under subsection (1) to a regis-

**S. 168(2)**            Income Tax Act, Part I

tered charity or to a registered Canadian amateur athletic association,

(a) if the charity or association has applied to the Minister in writing for the revocation of its registration, the Minister shall, forthwith after the mailing of the notice, publish a copy of the notice in the *Canada Gazette*, and

(b) in any other case, the Minister may, after the expiration of 30 days from the day of mailing of the notice, or after the expiration of such extended period from the day of mailing of the notice as the Federal Court of Appeal or a judge of that Court, on application made at any time before the determination of any appeal pursuant to subsection 172(3) from the giving of the notice, may fix or allow, publish a copy of the notice in the *Canada Gazette*,

and on that publication of a copy of the notice, the registration of the charity or association is revoked.

**Related Provisions**: 149.1(4) — Revocation of registration of private foundation; 172(3) — Appeal from refusal to register or revocation of registration; 180 — Appeals to Federal Court of Appeal; 188(1) — Revocation tax.

**Information Circulars**: 80-10R: Registered charities: operating a registered charity.

**Definitions [s. 168]**: "contravene" — *Interpretation Act* 35(1); "Minister", "person", "registered Canadian amateur athletic association", "registered charity", "regulation" — 248(1); "writing" — *Interpretation Act* 35(1).

## DIVISION J — APPEALS TO THE TAX COURT OF CANADA AND THE FEDERAL COURT

### Proposed Amendment — Division J — Title

**Application**: Bill C-40 (First Reading June 15, 2000), s. 144, will amend the heading before s. 169 by substituting "Federal Court of Appeal" for "Federal Court", in force on a day to be fixed by order of the Governor in Council.

**169. (1) Appeal** — Where a taxpayer has served notice of objection to an assessment under section 165, the taxpayer may appeal to the Tax Court of Canada to have the assessment vacated or varied after either

(a) the Minister has confirmed the assessment or reassessed, or

(b) 90 days have elapsed after service of the notice of objection and the Minister has not notified the taxpayer that the Minister has vacated or confirmed the assessment or reassessed,

but no appeal under this section may be instituted after the expiration of 90 days from the day notice has been mailed to the taxpayer under section 165 that the Minister has confirmed the assessment or reassessed.

**Related Provisions**: 152(9) — Minister may raise new basis for assessment during appeal; 167 — Application for time extension; 170 — Informal procedure appeals; 173(2), 174(5) — Time during consideration not to count; 175 — General procedure appeals;

179.1 — Where no reasonable grounds for appeal; 225.1(3) — Collection restrictions; *Interpretation Act* 26 — Deadline on Sunday or holiday extended to next business day.

**Notes**: Appeals are governed by the *Tax Court of Canada Act*. Under s. 18 of that Act, an appeal of an income tax assessment may use the Court's "informal procedure" if the amount of *federal* tax and penalties (excluding interest) at issue is $12,000 or less ($7,000 for appeals filed before September 1993). Otherwise the Court's "general procedure", which requires a lawyer and follows formal rules of court, is used. See McMechan & Bourgard, *Tax Court Practice* (Carswell, looseleaf).

Since November 1998, Informal Procedure appeals to the Tax Court require a filing fee of $100, and appeals must be *received* by the Court by the 90-day deadline, rather than mailed. See 18.15(3)(b) and 18.15(3.2) of the *Tax Court of Canada Act*, as added by 1995-97 technical bill (1998, c. 19, s. 292).

Section 26 of the *Interpretation Act*, which applies to all federal statutes, provides:

> 26. Time limits and holidays — Where the time limited for the doing of a thing expires or falls on a holiday, the thing may be done on the day next following that is not a holiday.

Subsection 35(1) of that Act defines "holiday" to mean Sunday as well as statutory holidays. The case law suggests that where the deadline expires on a Saturday or other day when the Tax Court offices are closed, the deadline may be judicially extended. See the commentary in the *Canada GST Service* at s. 306.

**Information Circulars**: 98-1R: Collections policies.

**Forms**: T400A: Notice of objection; TLA4: Notification of rejection of notice of objection; TLA7: Filing appeals to the Tax Court of Canada.

### Proposed Addition — 169(1.1)

**(1.1) Ecological gifts** — Where at any particular time a taxpayer has disposed of a property, the fair market value of which has been confirmed or redetermined by the Minister of the Environment under subsection 118.1(10.4), the taxpayer may, within 90 days after the day on which that Minister has issued a certificate under subsection 118.1(10.5), appeal the confirmation or redetermination to the Tax Court of Canada.

**Application**: The December 21, 2000 draft legislation, s. 86, will add subsec. 169(1.1), applicable in respect of gifts made after February 27, 2000.

**Technical Notes**: New subsection 169(1.1) is added to provide a person with a right to appeal, within 90 days of the issue of a certificate by the Minister of the Environment under subsection 118.1(10.5), that Minister's redetermination or confirmation under subsection 118.1(10.4) of the fair market value of donated ecologically sensitive land.

**Related Provisions**: 171(1.1) — Powers of Tax Court on appeal.

**(2) Limitation of right to appeal from assessments or determinations** — Notwithstanding subsection (1), where at any time the Minister assesses tax, interest, penalties or other amounts payable under this Part by, or makes a determination in respect of, a taxpayer

(a) under subsection 67.5(2) or 152(1.8), subparagraph 152(4)(b)(i) or subsection 152(4.3) or (6), 164(4.1), 220(3.4) or 245(8) or in accordance with an order of a court vacating, varying or restoring the assessment or referring the assessment back to the Minister for reconsideration and reassessment,

(b) under subsection 165(3) where the underlying objection relates to an assessment or a determination made under any of the provisions or circumstances referred to in paragraph (a), or

(c) under a provision of an Act of Parliament requiring an assessment to be made that, but for that provision, would not be made because of subsections 152(4) to (5),

the taxpayer may appeal to the Tax Court of Canada within the time limit specified in subsection (1), but only to the extent that the reasons for the appeal can reasonably be regarded

(d) where the assessment or determination was made under subsection 152(1.8), as relating to any matter specified in paragraph 152(1.8)(a), (b) or (c), and

(e) in any other case, as relating to any matter that gave rise to the assessment or determination

and that was not conclusively determined by the Court, and this subsection shall not be read or construed as limiting the right of the taxpayer to appeal from an assessment or a determination issued or made before that time.

**Related Provisions**: 165(1.1) — Limitation of right to object to assessments or determinations.

**Notes**: 169(2) provides that, where a reassessment is made after the normal deadline under a special provision (such as those allowing for reassessment with the taxpayer's consent), the taxpayer cannot use that as an excuse to open up a return that was otherwise statute-barred and claim additional deductions or credits beyond those that are the subject of the special reassessment. (See 165(1.1) for the same rule as it applies to objections.)

Opening words of 169(2) amended to add "or other amounts"; reference to 152(1.8) added to 169(2)(a); and 169(2)(d) added (splitting (e) out of the body of the subsection); all by 1995-97 technical bill, effective for determinations made after June 18, 1998.

169(2)(a) amended by 1992 technical bill, effective June 10, 1993, to add reference to 152(4.3).

169(2) added by 1991 technical bill, effective for appeals from assessments or determinations objected to after December 17, 1991

### (2.1) Limitation on appeals by large corporations

— Notwithstanding subsections (1) and (2), where a corporation that was a large corporation in a taxation year (within the meaning assigned by subsection 225.1(8)) served a notice of objection to an assessment under this Part for the year, the corporation may appeal to the Tax Court of Canada to have the assessment vacated or varied only with respect to

(a) an issue in respect of which the corporation has complied with subsection 165(1.11) in the notice, or

(b) an issue described in subsection 165(1.14) where the corporation did not, because of subsection 165(7), serve a notice of objection to the assessment that gave rise to the issue

and, in the case of an issue described in paragraph (a), the corporation may so appeal only with respect to the relief sought in respect of the issue as specified by the corporation in the notice.

**Related Provisions**: 171(1) — Jurisdiction of Tax Court on appeal.

**Notes**: 169(2.1) added by 1994 tax amendments bill (Part VII), effective for appeals instituted after June 22, 1995.

It is not clear how far the courts will allow their jurisdiction to be fettered by this provision. Some judges may view it as an infringement on a court's inherent jurisdiction to hear cases before it and grant the appropriate relief. See Notes to 171(1), but see also *Chevron Canada Resources Ltd.*, [1999] 3 C.T.C. 140 (FCA). Note also that 169(2.1) does not limit the grounds on which a case can be appealed from the Tax Court to the Federal Court of Appeal; however, if certain grounds of appeal are unavailable at the Tax Court, the taxpayer may be unable to lead evidence to support an appeal to the Federal Court on those grounds.

### (2.2) Waived issues

— Notwithstanding subsections (1) and (2), for greater certainty a taxpayer may not appeal to the Tax Court of Canada to have an assessment under this Part vacated or varied in respect of an issue for which the right of objection or appeal has been waived in writing by the taxpayer.

**Related Provisions**: 165(1.2) — No objection permitted where right to object waived.

**Notes**: 169(2.2) added by 1994 tax amendments bill (Part VII), effective after June 22, 1995 for waivers signed at any time.

The word "or" in the phrase "right of objection or appeal" is ambiguous. If a taxpayer waived the right of objection but not of appeal, does 169(2.2) apply? Arguably, in such a case, the condition that the "right of objection or appeal has been waived" is not met. (In practice the CCRA normally requests a waiver of both rights at the same time.)

Note, however, that 169(2.2) is "for greater certainty" only. The Supreme Court of Canada confirmed the validity of a waiver of appeal rights in *Smerchanski*, [1976] C.T.C. 488.

### (3) Disposition of appeal on consent

— Notwithstanding section 152, for the purpose of disposing of an appeal made under a provision of this Act, the Minister may at any time, with the consent in writing of the taxpayer, reassess tax, interest, penalties or other amounts payable under this Act by the taxpayer.

**Related Provisions**: 165(1.2) — Limitation of right to object; 169(4) — Provisions applicable; 225.1(1) — No collection restrictions following assessment.

**Notes**: Although a case may be settled on consent, there must still be a legal basis for the settlement. See *Galway*, [1974] C.T.C. 313 (FCTD) and *Cohen*, [1980] C.T.C. 318 (FCA). Thus, for example, interest can be waived or a mid-point valuation agreed on as part of a settlement; but where there is a yes/no issue whose outcome is uncertain, the CCRA has no authority to "split the difference" and agree on half the assessment for settlement purposes or to allow for "litigation risk."

169(3) added by 1992 technical bill, effective June 10, 1993.

### (4) Provisions applicable

— Division I applies, with such modifications as the circumstances require, in respect of a reassessment made under subsection (3) as though it had been made under section 152.

S. 169(4)      Income Tax Act, Part I

**Notes**: 169(4) added by 1992 technical bill, effective June 10, 1993.

**Definitions [s. 169]**: "assessment", "Minister", "taxpayer" — 248(1); "writing" — *Interpretation Act* 35(1).

**I.T. Application Rules [ss. 169–180]**: 62(5).

**170. (1) [Informal Procedure appeals — ] Notice to Commissioner** — Where an appeal is made to the Tax Court of Canada under section 18 of the *Tax Court of Canada Act*, the Court shall forthwith send a copy of the notice of the appeal to the office of the Commissioner of Customs and Revenue.

**(2) Notice, etc., to be forwarded to Tax Court of Canada** — Forthwith after receiving notice under subsection (1) of an appeal, the Commissioner of Customs and Revenue shall forward to the Tax Court of Canada copies of all returns, notices of assessment, notices of objection and notification, if any, that are relevant to the appeal.

**Related Provisions [s. 170]**: 169 — Appeal.

**Notes**: 170(1) and (2) amended by *Canada Customs & Revenue Agency Act*, effective November 1, 1999, to change "Deputy Minister of National Revenue" to "Commissioner of Customs and Revenue".

"Deputy Minister of National Revenue for Taxation" in 170(1) and (2) changed to "Deputy Minister of National Revenue" by Department of National Revenue Act amending bill, effective May 12, 1994.

**Definitions [s. 170]**: "assessment" — 248(1); "Commissioner of Customs and Revenue" — *Canada Customs and Revenue Agency Act* s. 25.

**I.T. Application Rules [s. 170]**: 62(5).

**171. (1) Disposal of appeal** — The Tax Court of Canada may dispose of an appeal by

(a) dismissing it; or

(b) allowing it and

  (i) vacating the assessment,

  (ii) varying the assessment, or

  (iii) referring the assessment back to the Minister for reconsideration and reassessment.

**Related Provisions**: 152(1.2) — Assessment — provisions applicable; 152(9) — Minister may raise new basis for assessment during appeal process; 169 — Appeal; 202(3) Returns and payment of estimated tax — provisions applicable; 227(7) — Withholding taxes; 227(10) — Assessment.

**Notes**: For discussion of whether the Tax Court has jurisdiction to entertain Charter arguments as to the constitutionality of tax law, see Alison Scott Butler, "Making Charter Arguments in Civil Tax Cases: Can the Courts Help Taxpayers?", 41(5) *Canadian Tax Journal* 847-880 (1993).

**Proposed Addition — 171(1.1)**

**(1.1) Ecological gifts** — On an appeal under subsection 169(1.1), the Tax Court of Canada may confirm or vary the amount determined to be the fair market value of a property and the value determined by the Court is deemed to be the fair market value of the property determined by the Minister of the Environment.

**Application**: The December 21, 2000 draft legislation, s. 87, will add subsec. 171(1.1), applicable in respect of gifts made after February 27, 2000.

**Technical Notes**: Section 171 provides the rules applicable to income tax appeals disposed of by the Tax Court of Canada. New subsection 171(1.1) adds rules applicable to appeals under new subsection 169(1.1) in respect of determinations of the fair market value of donated ecologically sensitive land.

**(2), (3) [Repealed under former Act]**

**Notes**: 171(2), repealed in 1984, related to appeals from a direction given under 246, a discretionary anti-avoidance rule that was repealed at the same time.

171(3), repealed in 1984, provided that the Tax Court of Canada could not award costs. Section 18 of the *Tax Court of Canada Act* now permits costs to be awarded in certain cases.

**(4) [Repealed]**

**Notes**: 171(4) repealed by 1993 GST bill, effective June 10, 1993 (this rule is now provided in subsec. 18.22(3) of the *Tax Court of Canada Act*). Formerly read:

(4) Copy of decision to Minister and appellant — On the disposition of an appeal referred to in section 18 of the *Tax Court of Canada Act*, the Tax Court of Canada shall forthwith forward, by registered mail, a copy of the decision and written reasons, if any, given therefor to the Minister and the appellant.

**Definitions [s. 171]**: "assessment", "Minister" — 248(1).

**172. (1), (2) [Repealed under former Act]**

**Notes**: 172(1), (2), repealed by 1988 Tax Court bill (effective January 1, 1991), permitted an appeal to the Federal Court of Canada. For appeals launched before 1991, read:

172. (1) Appeal — The Minister or the taxpayer may, within 120 days from the day on which the Registrar of the Tax Court of Canada mails the decision on an appeal under section 169 to the Minister and the taxpayer, appeal to the Federal Court of Canada.

(2) Appeal to Federal Court of Canada — Where a taxpayer has served a notice of objection to an assessment under section 165, he may, in place of appealing to the Tax Court of Canada under section 169, appeal to the Federal Court of Canada at a time when, under section 169, he could have appealed to the Tax Court of Canada.

**(3) Appeal from refusal to register, revocation of registration, etc.** — Where the Minister

(a) refuses to register an applicant for registration as a charitable organization, private foundation, public foundation or Canadian amateur athletic association, or gives notice under subsection 149.1(2), (3), (4) or (4.1) or 168(1) to any such organization, foundation or association that the Minister proposes to revoke its registration,

(a.1) designates or refuses to designate a registered charity pursuant to subsection 149.1(6.3) of this Act or subsection 110(8.1) or (8.2) of the *Income Tax Act*, chapter 148 of the Revised Statutes of Canada, 1952,

## Division J — Appeals to Tax Court and Federal Court — S. 172

(b) refuses to accept for registration for the purposes of this Act any retirement savings plan,

(c) refuses to accept for registration for the purposes of this Act any profit sharing plan or revokes the registration of such a plan,

(d) refuses to issue a certificate of exemption under subsection 212(14),

(e) refuses to accept for registration for the purposes of this Act an education savings plan,

(e.1) sends notice under subsection 146.1(12.1) to a promoter that the Minister proposes to revoke the registration of an education savings plan,

(f) refuses to register for the purposes of this Act any pension plan or gives notice under subsection 147.1(11) to the administrator of a registered pension plan that the Minister proposes to revoke its registration,

(f.1) refuses to accept an amendment to a registered pension plan, or

(g) refuses to accept for registration for the purposes of this Act any retirement income fund,

the applicant or the organization, foundation, association or registered charity, as the case may be, in a case described in paragraph (a) or (a.1), the applicant in a case described in paragraph (b), (d), (e) or (g), a trustee under the plan or an employer of employees who are beneficiaries under the plan, in a case described in paragraph (c), the promoter in a case described in paragraph (e.1), or the administrator of the plan or an employer who participates in the plan, in a case described in paragraph (f) or (f.1), may appeal from the Minister's decision, or from the giving of the notice by the Minister, to the Federal Court of Appeal.

**Related Provisions**: 147.1(13) — Revocation of registration; 149.1(6.4) — Application to registered national arts service organizations; 168(2) — Revocation of registration of certain organizations; 172(4), (5) — Deemed refusal to register; 175 — Institution of appeals; 180(1) — Deadline for filing notice of appeal; 204.81(9) — Right of appeal; 212(14) — Certificate of exemption.

**Notes**: 172(3)(a) amended by 1991 technical bill, effective 1990, to add references to 149.1.

172(3)(e) amended to delete "or revokes the registration of any such plan"; (e.1) added; and the closing words amended to refer to the promoter under (e.1); all by 1997 Budget, effective 1998.

172(3)(f) and (f.1) added and 172(3)(g) amended by 1990 pension bill, effective 1989. Reference in (g) to revocation of an RRIF was deleted, as revocation is no longer an administrative process: see 146.3(11).

**I.T. Application Rules**: 69 (meaning of *"Income Tax Act,* chapter 148 of the Revised Statutes of Canada, 1952").

**Information Circulars**: 80-10R: Registered charities: operating a registered charity.

**Forms**: T285: Information re appeal from Minister's refusal to register as a charity or Canadian amateur athletic association.

**(4) Deemed refusal to register** — For the purposes of subsection (3), the Minister shall be deemed to have refused

(a) to register an applicant for registration as a charitable organization, private foundation, public foundation or Canadian amateur athletic association,

(a.1) to designate a registered charity pursuant to an application under subsection 149.1(6.3) of this Act or subsection 110(8.2) of the *Income Tax Act,* chapter 148 of the Revised Statutes of Canada, 1952,

(b) to accept for registration for the purposes of this Act any retirement savings plan or profit sharing plan,

(c) to issue a certificate of exemption under subsection 212(14),

(d) to accept for registration for the purposes of this Act any education savings plan, or

(e) [Repealed under former Act]

(f) to accept for registration for the purposes of this Act any retirement income fund,

where the Minister has not notified the applicant of the disposition of the application within 180 days after the filing of the application with the Minister, and, in any such case, an appeal from the refusal to the Federal Court of Appeal pursuant to subsection (3) may, notwithstanding anything in subsection 180(1), be instituted under section 180 at any time by filing a notice of appeal in the Court.

**Related Provisions**: 167(4) — Application for time extension; 180 — Appeals to Federal Court of Appeal.

**I.T. Application Rules**: 69 (meaning of *"Income Tax Act,* chapter 148 of the Revised Statutes of Canada, 1952").

**(5) Idem** — For the purposes of subsection (3), the Minister shall be deemed to have refused

(a) to register for the purposes of this Act any pension plan, or

(b) to accept an amendment to a registered pension plan

where the Minister has not notified the applicant of the Minister's disposition of the application within 1 year after the filing of the application with the Minister, and, in any such case, an appeal from the refusal to the Federal Court of Appeal pursuant to subsection (3) may, notwithstanding anything in subsection 180(1), be instituted under section 180 at any time by filing a notice of appeal in the Court.

**Notes**: 172(5) added by 1990 pension bill, effective 1989.

**(6) Application of subsec. 149.1(1)** — The definitions in subsection 149.1(1) apply to this section.

**Notes**: 172(6) added in the R.S.C. 1985 (5th Supp.) consolidation, effective for taxation years ending after November 1991. This rule was formerly included in the opening words of 149.1(1).

**Definitions [s. 172]**: "administrator" — 147.1(1); "Canadian amateur athletic association" — 110(8), 248(1); "charitable foundation", "charitable organization", "charitable purposes", "charity" —

149.1(1); "employee", "employer", "Minister" — 248(1); "private foundation" — 149.1(1), 248(1); "profit sharing plan" — 147(1); "promoter" — 146.1(1); "public foundation" — 149.1(1), 248(1); "registered Canadian amateur athletic association", "registered charity" — 248(1); "registered education savings plan" — 146.1(1), 248(1); "registered pension plan" — 248(1); "retirement income fund" — 146.3(1), 248(1); "retirement savings plan" — 146(1), 248(1); "taxpayer" — 248(1).

**Information Circulars [s. 172]**: 80-10R: Registered charities: operating a registered charity.

## 173. (1) References to Tax Court of Canada —
Where the Minister and a taxpayer agree in writing that a question of law, fact or mixed law and fact arising under this Act, in respect of any assessment, proposed assessment, determination or proposed determination, should be determined by the Tax Court of Canada, that question shall be determined by that Court.

**Related Provisions**: 174 — Reference of common questions to Tax Court; 225.1(4) — Collection by the Minister.

**Notes**: 173(1) amended by 1988 Tax Court bill, effective January 1, 1991, to change "Federal Court" to "Tax Court of Canada".

### (2) Time during consideration not to count —
The time between the day on which proceedings are instituted in the Tax Court of Canada to have a question determined pursuant to subsection (1) and the day on which the question is finally determined shall not be counted in the computation of

(a) the periods determined under subsection 152(4),

(b) the time for service of a notice of objection to an assessment under section 165, or

(c) the time within which an appeal may be instituted under section 169,

for the purpose of making an assessment of the tax payable by the taxpayer who agreed in writing to the determination of the question, for the purpose of serving a notice of objection thereto or for the purpose of instituting an appeal therefrom, as the case may be.

**Notes**: 173(2) amended by 1988 Tax Court bill, effective January 1, 1991, to change "Federal Court" to "Tax Court of Canada".

**Definitions [s. 173]**: "assessment", "Minister", "taxpayer" — 248(1); "writing" — *Interpretation Act* 35(1).

## 174. (1) Reference of common questions to Tax Court of Canada —
Where the Minister is of the opinion that a question of law, fact or mixed law and fact arising out of one and the same transaction or occurrence or series of transactions or occurrences is common to assessments or proposed assessments in respect of two or more taxpayers, the Minister may apply to the Tax Court of Canada for a determination of the question.

**Related Provisions**: 173 — Reference to Tax Court; 225.1(4) — Collection by the Minister; 248(10) — Series of transactions.

### (2) Application to Court — 
An application under subsection (1) shall set out

(a) the question in respect of which the Minister requests a determination,

(b) the names of the taxpayers that the Minister seeks to have bound by the determination of the question, and

(c) the facts and reasons on which the Minister relies and on which the Minister based or intends to base assessments of tax payable by each of the taxpayers named in the application,

and a copy of the application shall be served by the Minister on each of the taxpayers named in the application and on any other persons who, in the opinion of the Tax Court of Canada, are likely to be affected by the determination of the question.

### (3) Where Tax Court of Canada may determine question — 
Where the Tax Court of Canada is satisfied that a determination of the question set out in an application under this section will affect assessments or proposed assessments in respect of two or more taxpayers who have been served with a copy of the application and who are named in an order of the Tax Court of Canada pursuant to this subsection, it may

(a) if none of the taxpayers so named has appealed from such an assessment, proceed to determine the question in such manner as it considers appropriate; or

(b) if one or more of the taxpayers so named has or have appealed, make such order joining a party or parties to that or those appeals as it considers appropriate and proceed to determine the question.

### (4) Determination final and conclusive — 
Subject to subsection (4.1), where a question set out in an application under this section is determined by the Tax Court of Canada, the determination thereof is final and conclusive for the purposes of any assessments of tax payable by the taxpayers named by it pursuant to subsection (3).

### (4.1) Appeal — 
Where a question set out in an application under this section is determined by the Tax Court of Canada, the Minister or any of the taxpayers who have been served with a copy of the application and who are named in an order of the Court pursuant to subsection (3) may, in accordance with the provisions of this Act, the *Tax Court of Canada Act*, or the *Federal Court Act*, as they relate to appeals from decisions of the Tax Court of Canada, appeal from the determination.

### (5) Time during consideration of question not counted — 
The time between the day on which an application under this section is served on a taxpayer pursuant to subsection (2) and

(a) in the case of a taxpayer named in an order of the Tax Court of Canada pursuant to subsection

(3), the day on which the determination becomes final and conclusive and not subject to any appeal, or

(b) in the case of any other taxpayer, the day on which the taxpayer is served with notice that the taxpayer has not been named in an order of the Tax Court of Canada pursuant to subsection (3),

shall not be counted in the computation of

(c) the periods determined under subsection 152(4),

(d) the time for service of a notice of objection to an assessment under section 165, or

(e) the time within which an appeal may be instituted under section 169,

for the purpose of making an assessment of the tax, interest or penalties payable by the taxpayer, serving a notice of objection thereto or instituting an appeal therefrom, as the case may be.

**Notes**: 174 amended by 1988 Tax Court bill, effective January 1, 1991, to change "Federal Court" to "Tax Court of Canada" and to make related amendments.

**Definitions [s. 174]**: "assessment", "Minister", "person", "series of transactions", "taxpayer" — 248(1).

### 175. Institution of appeals — An appeal to the Tax Court of Canada under this Act, other than one referred to in section 18 of the *Tax Court of Canada Act*, shall be instituted in the manner set out in that Act or in any rules made under that Act.

**Related Provisions**: 170(1) — Informal procedure appeals.

**Notes**: This refers to General Procedure appeals. Section 18 of the *Tax Court of Canada Act* provides for the Court's "informal procedure". See Notes to 169(1).

175(1)(b), 175(2) and 175(3) repealed by 1992 technical bill, effective June 10, 1993. From January 1, 1991 to June 9, 1993, read:

> 175. (1) Institution of appeals — An appeal to the Tax Court of Canada under this Act, other than one referred to in section 18 of the *Tax Court of Canada Act*, shall be instituted
> 
> (a) in the manner set forth in the *Tax Court of Canada Act* or any rules made under that Act; or
> 
> (b) by the filing by the Minister in the Registry of the Tax Court of Canada of a copy of a notice of objection pursuant to paragraph 165(3)(b).
> 
> (2) Service of originating document — Where a copy of a notice of objection is filed in the Registry of the Tax Court of Canada by the Minister pursuant to paragraph 165(3)(b) and the Minister files a copy of the notice of objection, together with two additional copies thereof and a certificate as to the latest known address of the taxpayer, an officer of the Registry of the Court shall, after verifying the accuracy of the copies, forthwith on behalf of the Minister serve the copy of the notice of objection on the taxpayer by sending the additional copies thereof by registered mail addressed to the taxpayer at the address set forth in the certificate.
> 
> (3) Certificate — Where copies have been served on a taxpayer under subsection (2), a certificate signed by an officer of the Registry of the Tax Court of Canada as to the date of filing and the date of mailing of the copies shall be transmitted to the office of the Deputy Attorney General of Canada and such certificate is evidence of the date of filing and the date of service of the document referred to therein.

175 amended by 1988 Tax Court bill, effective January 1, 1991, to reflect the change in jurisdiction from the Federal Court to the Tax Court. For appeals launched before 1991, read:

> 175. (1) Institution of appeals — An appeal to the Federal Court under this Act, other than an appeal to which section 180 applies, shall be instituted,
> 
> (a) in the case of an appeal by a taxpayer,
> 
> (i) in the manner set forth in section 48 of the *Federal Court Act*, or
> 
> (ii) by the filing by the Minister in the Registry of the Federal Court of a copy of a notice of objection pursuant to paragraph 165(3)(b); and
> 
> (b) in the case of an appeal by the Minister, in the manner provided by the Federal Court Rules for the commencement of an action.
> 
> (2) Counterclaim or cross-demand — If the respondent to an appeal from a decision of the Tax Court of Canada desires to appeal from that decision, he may do so, whether or not the time fixed by section 172 has expired, by a counterclaim or cross-demand instituted in accordance with the Federal Court Rules.
> 
> (3) Deemed action — An appeal instituted under this section shall be deemed to be an action in the Federal Court to which the *Federal Court Act* and the Federal Court Rules applicable to an ordinary action apply, except as varied by special rules made in respect of such appeals, and except that
> 
> (a) the Rules concerning joinder of parties and causes of action do not apply except to permit the joinder of appeals instituted under this section;
> 
> (b) a copy of a notice of objection filed in the Registry of the Federal Court by the Minister pursuant to paragraph 165(3)(b) shall be deemed to be a statement of claim or declaration that was filed in the Registry of the Federal Court by the taxpayer and served by him on the Minister on the day on which it was so filed by the Minister; and
> 
> (c) an originating document or copy of a notice of objection filed by the Minister in the Registry of the Federal Court shall be served in the manner provided in subsection (4).
> 
> (4) Service of originating document — Where an appeal is instituted by the Minister under this section or a copy of a notice of objection is filed in the Registry of the Federal Court by him pursuant to paragraph 165(3)(b) and the Minister files the originating document or the copy of the notice of objection, together with two copies or additional copies thereof and a certificate as to the latest known address of the taxpayer, an officer of the Registry of the Court shall, after verifying the accuracy of the copies, forthwith on behalf of the Minister serve the originating document or the copy of the notice of objection on the taxpayer by sending the copies or additional copies thereof by registered mail addressed to him at the address set forth in the certificate.
> 
> (5) Certificate — Where copies have been served on a taxpayer under subsection (4), a certificate signed by an officer of the Registry of the Federal Court as to the date of filing and the date of mailing of the copies shall be transmitted to the office of the Deputy Attorney General of Canada and such certificate is evidence of the date of filing and the date of service of the document referred to therein.

**Definitions [s. 175]**: "Minister", "taxpayer" — 248(1).

### 176. (1) Notice, etc., to be forwarded to Tax Court of Canada — As soon as is reasonably practicable after receiving notice of an appeal to the Tax Court of Canada, other than one referred to in section 18 of the *Tax Court of Canada Act*, the Min-

## S. 176(1) — Income Tax Act, Part I

ister shall cause to be transmitted to the Tax Court of Canada and to the appellant, copies of all returns, notices of assessment, notices of objection and notifications, if any, that are relevant to the appeal.

**Notes**: 176(1) was struck down in its entirety by the Federal Court of Appeal in *Gernhart*, [2000] 1 C.T.C. 192 (FCA). The Court ruled that the disclosure of the taxpayer's personal income tax returns under 176(1) was an unreasonable seizure, and thus was in violation of s. 8 of the *Charter of Rights*.

**(2) Documents to be transferred to Federal Court** — As soon as is reasonably practicable after receiving notice of an appeal to the Federal Court of Appeal in respect of which section 180 applies, the Minister shall cause to be transmitted to the Registry of the Federal Court copies of all documents that are relevant to the decision of the Minister appealed from.

> **Proposed Amendment — 176(2)**
>
> **(2) Documents to be transferred to Federal Court of Appeal** — As soon as is reasonably practicable after receiving notice of an appeal to the Federal Court of Appeal in respect of which section 180 applies, the Minister shall cause to be transmitted to the registry of that Court copies of all documents that are relevant to the decision of the Minister appealed from.
>
> **Application**: Bill C-40 (First Reading June 15, 2000), s. 145, will amend subsec. 176(2) to read as above, in force on a day to be fixed by order of the Governor in Council.

**Notes**: 176 amended by 1988 Tax Court bill, effective 1991, to reflect the change in jurisdiction from the Federal Court to the Tax Court. For appeals launched before 1991, it dealt with the transfer of documents to the Federal Court.

**Definitions [s. 176]**: "assessment", "Minister" — 248(1).

### 177. [Repealed under former Act]

**Notes**: 177 repealed by 1988 Tax Court bill, effective 1991, to reflect the change in jurisdiction from the Federal Court to the Tax Court. See now 171(1). For appeals launched before 1991, read:

> 177. **Disposal of appeal** — The Federal Court may dispose of an appeal, other than an appeal to which section 180 applies, by
>
> (a) dismissing it; or
>
> (b) allowing it and
>
> (i) vacating the assessment,
>
> (ii) varying the assessment,
>
> (iii) restoring the assessment, or
>
> (iv) referring the assessment back to the Minister for reconsideration and reassessment.

### 178. [Repealed under former Act]

**Notes**: 178 repealed by 1988 Tax Court bill, effective January 1, 1991, to reflect the change in jurisdiction from the Federal Court to the Tax Court. For earlier appeals disposed of after December 20, 1984, read:

> 178. (1) **Court may order payment of tax, etc.** — The Federal Court may, in delivering judgment disposing of an appeal, order payment or repayment of tax, interest, penalties or, subject to subsection (2), costs by the taxpayer or the Minister.

**(2) Costs payable by Minister in certain cases** — Where, on an appeal by the Minister, other than by way of cross-appeal, from a decision of the Tax Court of Canada, the amount of

(a) tax, refund or amount payable under subsection 196(2) (in the case of an assessment of the tax or determination the refund or the amount payable, as the case may be) that is in controversy does not exceed $10,000, or

(b) loss (in the case of a determination of the loss) that is in controversy does not exceed $20,000,

the Federal Court, in delivering judgment disposing of the appeal, shall order the Minister to pay all reasonable and proper costs of the taxpayer in connection therewith.

### 179. Hearings *in camera* 
Proceedings in the Federal Court under this Division may, on the application of the taxpayer, be held *in camera* if the taxpayer establishes to the satisfaction of the Court that the circumstances of the case justify *in camera* proceedings.

**Notes**: An order under s. 179 will rarely be granted, and can possibly be challenged under para. 2(b) of the *Charter of Rights*. See *Roseland Farms Ltd.*, [1996] 1 C.T.C. 176 (FCA).

**Definitions [s. 179]**: "taxpayer" — 248(1).

### 179.1 No reasonable grounds for appeal
Where the Tax Court of Canada disposes of an appeal by a taxpayer in respect of an amount payable under this Part or where such an appeal has been discontinued or dismissed without trial, the Court may, on the application of the Minister and whether or not it awards costs, order the taxpayer to pay to the Receiver General an amount not exceeding 10% of any part of the amount that was in controversy in respect of which the Court determines that there were no reasonable grounds for the appeal, if in the opinion of the Court one of the main purposes for instituting or maintaining any part of the appeal was to defer the payment of any amount payable under this Part.

**Related Provisions**: 18(1)(t) — No deduction for payments under Act.

**Notes**: 179.1 amended by 1992 technical bill, effective June 11, 1993, with respect to appeals instituted after June 1992, to give the Court the flexibility to order payment of 10% of *any part of* the amount in dispute rather than of the entire amount. From January 1, 1991 to June 10, 1993 (and after June 10, 1993 in respect of appeals instituted before July 1992), read:

> 179.1 Where the Tax Court of Canada disposes of an appeal by a taxpayer in respect of an amount payable under this Part or where such an appeal has been discontinued or dismissed without trial, the Court may, on the application of the Minister and whether or not it awards costs, order the taxpayer to pay to the Receiver General an amount not exceeding 10% of the amount that was in controversy if it determines that there were no reasonable grounds for the appeal and one of the main purposes for instituting or maintaining the appeal was to defer the payment of an amount payable under this Part.

179.1 amended by 1988 Tax Court bill, effective January 1, 1991, to delete reference to the Federal Court–Trial Division.

**Definitions [s. 179.1]**: "amount", "Minister", "taxpayer" — 248(1).

**180. (1) Appeals to Federal Court of Appeal** — An appeal to the Federal Court of Appeal pursuant to subsection 172(3) may be instituted by filing a notice of appeal in the Court within 30 days from

(a) the time the decision of the Minister to refuse the application for registration or for a certificate of exemption, to revoke the registration, to designate or to refuse to designate was mailed, or otherwise communicated in writing, by the Minister to the party instituting the appeal,

(b) the mailing of notice to the registered charity or registered Canadian amateur athletic association under subsection 149.1(2), (3), (4) or (4.1) or 168(1),

(c) the mailing of notice to the administrator of the registered pension plan under subsection 147.1(11),

(c.1) the sending of a notice to a promoter of a registered education savings plan under subsection 146.1(12.1), or

(d) the time the decision of the Minister to refuse the application for acceptance of the amendment to the registered pension plan was mailed, or otherwise communicated in writing, by the Minister to any person,

as the case may be, or within such further time as the Court of Appeal or a judge thereof may, either before or after the expiration of those 30 days, fix or allow.

**Related Provisions**: 172(4) — Deemed refusal to register; 212(14) — Certificate of exemption; 248(7)(a) — Mail deemed received on day mailed.

**Notes**: 180(1)(b) amended by 1991 technical bill, effective 1990, to add references to 149.1.

180(1) amended by 1990 pension bill, effective 1989, to add paras. (c) and (d), and to refer to "mailed or otherwise communicated in writing" instead of just registered mail.

180(1)(c.1) added by 1997 Budget, effective 1998.

**Forms**: T285: Information re appeal from Minister's refusal to register as a charity or Canadian amateur athletic association.

**(2) No jurisdiction in Tax Court of Canada or Federal Court–Trial Division** — Neither the Tax Court of Canada nor the Federal Court–Trial Division has jurisdiction to entertain any proceeding in respect of a decision of the Minister from which an appeal may be instituted under this section.

**(3) Summary disposition of appeal** — An appeal to the Federal Court of Appeal instituted under this section shall be heard and determined in a summary way.

**Related Provisions**: 172(4) — Deemed refusal to register; 176(2) — Transfer of relevant documents to the Federal Court.

**Definitions [s. 180]**: "administrator" — 147.1(1); "Minister" — 248(1); "profit sharing plan" — 147(1); "promoter" — 146.1(1); "registered Canadian amateur athletic association", "registered charity", "registered pension plan" — 248(1); "writing" — *Interpretation Act* 35(1).

**Information Circulars [s. 180]**: 80-10R: Registered charities: operating a registered charity.

# PART I.1 — INDIVIDUAL SURTAX

### Proposed Repeal — Part I.1

**Application**: The December 21, 2000 draft legislation, subsec. 88(2), will repeal Part I.1, applicable to 2001 et seq.

**Technical Notes**: Part I.1 imposes a 5 per-cent surtax on that portion of an individual's Part I tax in excess of $12,500. This surtax is repealed, effective for the 2001 and subsequent taxation years. For 2000, this surtax is equal to 5 per cent of the individual's Part I tax in excess of $15,500.

**Notice of Ways and Means Motion, Economic Statement, October 18, 2000**: (2) That, for the 2001 and subsequent taxation years, the individual surtax imposed under section 180.1 of the Act be eliminated.

**180.1 (1) Individual surtax** — Every individual shall pay a tax under this Part for each taxation year equal to 5% of the amount, if any, by which the tax payable under Part I by the individual for the year exceeds $12,500.

### Proposed Amendment — 180.1(1)

**180.1 (1) Individual surtax** — Every individual shall pay a tax under this Part for each taxation year equal to 5% of the amount, if any, by which the tax payable under Part I by the individual for the year exceeds $15,500.

**Application**: The December 21, 2000 draft legislation, subsec. 88(1), will amend subsec. 180.1(1) to read as above, applicable to the 2000 taxation year.

**Technical Notes**: See under Part I.1 above.

**Notice of Ways and Means Motion, federal budget, February 28, 2000**: *Individual Surtax*

(5) That the 5 per cent surtax required to be paid by an individual

(a) be based on the individual's tax otherwise payable under Part I of the Act in excess of $15,500, for the 2000 taxation year, and

(b) be reduced to 4 per cent of the individual's tax otherwise payable under Part I of the Act in excess of $18,500, for the 2001 and subsequent taxation years. [It was later eliminated completely as of 2001; see Oct. 18, 2000 announcement above — ed.]

**Federal budget, supplementary information, February 28, 2000**: *5% Surtax*

Under the current rules, a 5% surtax applies to basic federal tax in excess of $12,500 (at an income level of about $65,000). The budget proposes to raise this amount to $18,500 (at an income level of about $85,000) effective July 1, 2000. Raising the surtax threshold to $18,500 of basic federal tax as of July 1, 2000, means that, for the 2000 taxation year, the 5% surtax would apply on basic federal tax in excess of $15,500.

The budget also proposes to reduce the surtax rate from 5% to 4% effective January 1, 2001.

The 5% surtax will be eliminated within the next five years [later changed to "effective 2000" — ed.].

**Notes**: 180.1(1) amended by 1989 Budget, by 1991 technical bill, by 1992 technical bill and by 1998 Budget.

**S. 180.1(1)**      Income Tax Act

For 1989, the basic surtax was 4% and the additional surtax was 1.5% of basic federal tax over $15,000.

For 1990, the basic surtax was 5% and the additional surtax was 3% of basic federal tax over $15,000.

For 1991, the basic surtax was 5% and the additional surtax is 5% of basic federal tax over $12,500.

For 1992, the basic surtax was 4.5% and the additional surtax was 5% of basic federal tax over $12,500.

For 1993 to 1997, the basic surtax was 3% and the additional surtax was 5% of basic federal tax over $12,500.

For 1998, the basic surtax was 3% but reduced to 1.5% for many taxpayers, and the additional surtax was 5% of basic federal tax over $12,500. For 1998, read 180.1(1)(a)(ii) opening words and (ii)(A) as:

(ii) 50% of the amount, if any, by which

(A) the lesser of $250 and the amount computed under subpara. (i) for the year exceeds

For 1999, the 3% surtax was cut in half even for high-income taxpayers, and the additional surtax was 5% of basic federal tax over $12,500. For 1999, read (this is the same as for 1998 but with the addition of "½ of" in 180.1(1)(a)):

(1) Every individual shall pay a tax under this Part for each taxation year equal to the total of

(a) ½ of the amount, if any, by which

(i) 3% of the individual's tax payable under Part I for the year

exceeds

(ii) the amount, if any, by which

(A) $250

exceeds

(B) 6% of the amount, if any, by which

(I) the individual's tax payable under Part I for the year

exceeds

(II) $8,333, and

(b) 5% of the amount, if any, by which the tax payable under Part I by the individual for the year exceeds $12,500.

For 2000, the basic surtax is eliminated and (per February 2000 budget proposals) the high-income surtax is 5% of basic federal tax over $15,500.

For 2001 and later years, all surtaxes are eliminated.

**(1.1) Foreign tax deduction** — There may be deducted from the tax otherwise payable under this Part for a taxation year (computed without reference to subsection (1.2)) by an individual the amount, if any, by which

(a) the total of all amounts that would be

(i) deductible by the individual under section 126 for the year, or

(ii) the individual's special foreign tax credit for the year determined under section 127.54,

if the references in section 126 to "the tax for the year otherwise payable under this Part by the taxpayer" were read as "the total of the tax for the year otherwise payable under this Part by the individual and the tax for the year that would be payable by the individual under Part I.1 but for subsections 180.1(1.1) and (1.2)"

exceeds

(b) the total of all amounts deductible by the individual under section 126 for the year and the individual's special foreign tax credit for the year determined under section 127.54.

**Related Provisions:** 180.1(1.4) — Former resident — credit for tax paid on emigration.

**Notes:** 180.1(1.1) amended by 1992 technical bill, retroactive to 1988, to correct a circularity relating to 180.1(1.2).

**Interpretation Bulletins:** IT-270R2: Foreign tax credit.

**(1.2) Deduction from tax [investment tax credit]** — There may be deducted from the tax otherwise payable under this Part for a taxation year by an individual the amount, if any, by which the amount determined under paragraph 127(5)(a) in respect of the individual for the year exceeds the amount, if any, deducted under subsection 127(5) for the year by the individual other than an amount deemed by subsection (1.3) to be so deducted.

**Related Provisions:** 180.1(1.3) — Amount deducted deemed claimed as investment tax credit.

**Notes:** 180.1(1.2) amended by 1993 Budget, effective for taxation years that begin in 1994 or later. (See Notes to 127(5).) For earlier years ending in 1988 or later, read:

(1.2) There may be deducted from the tax otherwise payable under this Part for a taxation year by an individual an amount not exceeding the lesser of

(a) ¾ of the amount that would be the individual's tax otherwise payable under this Part for the year if the individual deducted the amount, if any, allowed to be deducted under subsection (1.1) for the year, and

(b) the amount, if any, by which the amount determined under paragraph 127(5)(b) in respect of the individual for the year exceeds the amount, if any, deducted by the individual under subsection 127(5) for the year.

**(1.3) Idem** — For the purposes of this Act, the amount deducted under subsection (1.2) for a taxation year shall be deemed to be an amount deducted under subsection 127(5) for the year.

**Notes:** 180.1(1.3) amended by 1993 Budget, effective for taxation years that begin in 1994 or later. (See Notes to 127(5).) For earlier years ending in 1988 or later, read:

(1.3) Amount deemed deducted under subsec. (1.2) — For the purposes of this Act, other than for the purpose of determining the amount under paragraph (1.2)(b) for the year, the amount deducted under subsection (1.2) for a taxation year shall be deemed to be an amount deducted under subsection 127(5) for the year.

**Proposed Addition — 180.1(1.4)**

**(1.4) Former resident — credit for tax paid** — There may be deducted from the tax otherwise payable under this Part by an individual for a taxation year (computed without reference to subsections (1.1) and (1.2)) the amount, if any, by which

(a) the amount that would be deductible under section 119 in computing the individual's tax payable under Part I for the year if, in applying for that purpose paragraph (a) of the definition "tax for the year otherwise payable under this

1524

Part" in subsection 126(7), the reference in that paragraph to "tax payable under this Part for the year" were read as a reference to "the total of taxes that, but for subsections 180.1(1.1), (1.2) and (1.4), would be payable under this Part and Part I.1 for the year"

exceeds

(b) the amount deductible under section 119 in computing the individual's tax payable under Part I for the year.

**Application**: Bill C-43 (First Reading September 20, 2000), subsec. 95(1), will add subsec. 180.1(1.4), applicable after October 1, 1996.

**Technical Notes**: Section 180.1 imposes a surtax on individuals at a rate of 3% of the tax payable under Part I. An additional 5% surtax is imposed on that portion of an individual's Part I tax in excess of $12,500.

New subsection 40(3.7) provides a "stop-loss" rule that may apply to reduce the loss of an individual from the disposition of property at a particular time, where the individual was non-resident at any time before the particular time and received dividends in respect of the property while non-resident. New section 119 provides a special tax credit in certain cases where subsection 40(3.7) applies to an individual who ceased to be resident in Canada. If an individual's Part I tax for the year that includes the emigration is less than the amount deductible under section 119, new subsection 180.1(1.4) provides that the individual may deduct the balance from the tax otherwise payable under Part I.1 for that year.

**(2) Meaning of tax payable under Part I** — For the purposes of subsection (1), the tax payable under Part I by an individual for a taxation year is the amount, if any, by which

(a) where section 119 is applicable in computing the individual's tax payable for the year, the amount that would be the individual's average tax for the year of averaging, as determined under paragraph 119(1)(d), if the expression "deductible under subsection 127(5)" in that paragraph were read as "added under subsection 120(1) or deductible under sections 122.3, 126, 127 and 127.2 to 127.4", and

(b) in any other case, the amount that would be the individual's tax payable under that Part for the year if that Part were read without reference to subsection 120(1) and sections 122.3, 126, 127, 127.2 to 127.4 and 127.54

exceeds

(c) where the individual was throughout the year a mutual fund trust, the least of the amounts determined under paragraphs (a), (b) and (c) of the description of A in the definition "refundable capital gains tax on hand" in subsection 132(4) in respect of the trust for the year, and

(d) in any other case, nil.

**Proposed Amendment — 180.1(2)**

**(2) Meaning of tax payable under Part I** — For the purposes of subsection (1), the tax payable under Part I by an individual for a taxation year is the amount, if any, by which

(a) the amount that would be the individual's tax payable under that Part for the year if that Part were read without reference to section 119, subsection 120(1) and sections 122.3, 126, 127, 127.4 and 127.54

exceeds

(b) if the individual was throughout the year a mutual fund trust, the least of the amounts determined under paragraphs (a), (b) and (c) of the description of A in the definition "refundable capital gains tax on hand" in subsection 132(4) in respect of the trust for the year, and

(c) in any other case, nil.

**Application**: Bill C-43 (First Reading September 20, 2000), subsec. 95(2), will amend subsec. 180.1(2) to read as above, applicable after October 1, 1996.

**Technical Notes**: Subsection 180.1(2) provides rules for calculating Part I tax for the purposes of determining the base for tax under Part I.1 ("surtax"). Essentially, the tax base for surtax is the individual's tax payable for the year under Part I, calculated without reference to certain amounts. Paragraphs 180.1(2)(a) and (b) are amended to add to the list of those amounts an amount deductible under new section 119 in respect of a former resident of Canada.

**Related Provisions**: 128.3 — Shares acquired on rollover deemed to be same shares for 180.2(1.4).

**(3) Return** — Every individual liable to pay tax under this Part for a taxation year shall, on or before the day on or before which the individual is required by section 150 to file a return of income for the year under Part I, or would be so required if the individual were liable to pay tax under Part I for the year,

(a) file with the Minister, without notice or demand therefor, a return for the year under this Part in prescribed form and containing prescribed information; and

(b) pay the tax under this Part for the year for which the individual is liable.

**Related Provisions**: 150.1(5) — Electronic filing.

**Notes**: 180.1(3) amended by 1989 Budget, effective 1989.

**Forms**: T1 General income tax return, Schedule 1, line 419.

**(4) Provisions applicable to Part** — Sections 151, 152, 155, 156, 156.1 and 158 to 167 and Division J of Part I are applicable to this Part with such modifications as the circumstances require.

**Notes**: 180.1(4) amended by 1989 Budget, effective 1989, to add reference to 151 and delete reference to 153.

**Definitions [s. 180.1]**: "amount", "individual" — 248(1); "mutual fund trust" — 132(6)–(7), 132.2(1)(q), 248(1); "tax payable" — 248(2); "taxation year" — 249.

# Part I.2 — Tax on Old Age Security Benefits

**180.2 (1) Definitions** — The definitions in this subsection apply in this Part.

**"adjusted income"** of an individual for a taxation year means the amount that would be the individual's income under Part I for the year if no amount were deductible under paragraph 60(w) nor included in respect of a gain from a disposition of property to which section 79 applies.

*Notes*: See Notes at end of 180.2.

**"base taxation year"**, in relation to a month, means

(a) where the month is any of the first 6 months of a calendar year, the taxation year that ended on December 31 of the second preceding calendar year, and

(b) where the month is any of the last 6 months of a calendar year, the taxation year that ended on December 31 of the preceding calendar year.

**"return of income"** in respect of an individual for a taxation year means

(a) where the individual was resident in Canada throughout the year, the individual's return of income (other than a return of income filed under subsection 70(2) or 104(23), paragraph 128(2)(e) or subsection 150(4)) that is filed or required to be filed under Part I for the year, and

(b) in any other case, a prescribed form containing prescribed information.

*Related Provisions*: 60(v.1) — UI benefit repayment; 60(w) — Other deductions — tax under Part I.2.

*Notes*: See Notes at end of 180.2.

**(2) Tax payable** — Every individual shall pay a tax under this Part for each taxation year equal to the amount determined by the formula

$$A(1 - B)$$

where

A is the lesser of

(a) the amount, if any, by which

(i) the total of all amounts each of which is the amount of any pension, supplement or spouse's or common-law partner's allowance under the *Old Age Security Act* included in computing the individual's income under Part I for the year

exceeds

(ii) the amount of any deduction allowed under subparagraph 60(n)(i) in computing the individual's income under Part I for the year, and

(b) 15% of the amount, if any, by which the individual's adjusted income for the year exceeds $50,000[27]; and

B is the rate of tax payable by the individual under Part XIII on amounts described in paragraph (a) of the description of A.

*Related Provisions*: 117.1(1)(b) — Indexing for inflation; 180.2(3) — Withholding of tax from OAS benefits.

*Notes*: This tax is known as the "clawback" of OAS benefits. However, since July 1996, the benefits are simply not paid to high-income couples, rather than clawed back; see 180.2(3).

The $50,000 figure, which was $53,215 for 1999, is $53,960 for 2000 and $55,309 for 2001.

See also Notes at end of 180.2.

180.2(2)(a)(i) amended by 2000 same-sex partners bill to add reference to "common-law partner", effective for the 2001 and later taxation years, or earlier by election (see Notes to 248(1)"common-law partner").

*Forms*: T1 General income tax return, lines 235 and 422; T4155: Old age security return of income guide for non-residents [guide].

**(3) Withholding** — Where at any time Her Majesty pays an amount described in paragraph (a) of the description of A in subsection (2) in respect of a month to an individual, there shall be deducted or withheld from that amount on account of the individual's tax payable under this Part for the year the amount determined under subsection (4) in respect of that amount.

*Related Provisions*: 227 — Rules applicable to withholding.

*Notes*: See Notes at end of 180.2.

**(4) Determination of amount to be withheld** — The amount determined in respect of a particular amount described in subsection (3) is

(a) where the individual has filed a return of income for the base taxation year in relation to the month in which the particular amount is paid, the lesser of

(i) the amount by which the particular amount exceeds the amount of tax payable under Part XIII by the individual on the particular amount, and

(ii) the amount determined by the formula

$$(0.0125A - \$625^{28})(1 - B)$$

> **Proposed Amendment — 180.2(4)(a)(ii)**
>
> $$(0.0125A - \$665)(1-B)$$
>
> *Application*: Bill C-43 (First Reading September 20, 2000), s. 96, will amend the formula in subpara. 180.2(4)(a)(ii) to read as above, applicable to amounts paid after November 1999.
>
> *Technical Notes*: Section 180.2 provides for the recovery of Old Age Security (OAS) benefits paid to an individual to the extent that the individual's income for a year exceeds a partially indexed $50,000 threshold ($53,215 for 1999). In

---

[27] Indexed by s. 117.1 to $53,215 for 1992-2000 — ed.

[28] Indexed by s. 117.1 after 1989 or 1996? See Notes to 117.1(1).

1996, the structure of the recovery of OAS benefits was modified by providing for tax to be withheld on the benefits. Given that the amount of the benefits recovered is computed, in part, by reference to 15% of the individual's income in excess of $50,000 (or effectively 1.25% of the excess on a monthly basis), the formula in subsection 180.2(4) includes an amount of $625, which is equal to 1.25% of $50,000. However, because the recovery of OAS benefits through withholding was introduced in 1996, at the time where the partially indexed threshold was equal to $53,215, the amount used in the formula should have then been set at $665, i.e., 1.25% of $53,215. This amendment corrects this oversight. [The figure for 2000 is $53,960. — ed.]

where

A  is the individual's adjusted income for the base taxation year, and

B  is the rate of tax payable under Part XIII by the individual on the particular amount;

(b) where the individual has not filed a return of income for the base taxation year in relation to the month and

(i) the Minister has demanded under subsection 150(2) that the individual file the return, or

(ii) the individual was non-resident at any time in the base taxation year,

the amount by which the particular amount exceeds the amount of tax payable under Part XIII by the individual on the particular amount; and

(c) in any other case, nil.

**Related Provisions**: 117.1(1)(b) — Indexing for inflation; 180.2(5) — Obligation to file return; 257 — Formula cannot calculate to less than zero.

**Notes**: The $625 figure is ¹/₁₂ of $7,500, which is 15% of $50,000, the figure in 180.2(2). All dollar figures are indexed since 1988, or since their introduction, or since 1989; see Notes to 117.1(1). The effect of 180.2(4)(b)(ii) is that for a non-resident who does not file a return under 180.2(5)(a)(ii) showing total income, no OAS benefits will be paid.

See also Notes at end of 180.2.

**(5) Return** — Every individual liable to pay tax under this Part for a taxation year shall

(a) file with the Minister, without notice or demand therefor,

(i) where the individual is resident in Canada throughout the taxation year, a return for the year under this Part in prescribed form and containing prescribed information on or before the individual's filing-due date for the year, and

(ii) in any other case, a return of income for the year on or before the individual's balance-due day for the year; and

(b) pay the individual's tax payable under this Part for the year on or before the individual's balance-due day for the year.

**Related Provisions**: 180.2(4)(b)(ii) — No OAS benefits paid to non-resident who does not file return.

**Notes**: See Notes at end of 180.2.

**Forms**: T4155: Old age security return of income guide for non-residents [guide].

**(6) Provisions applicable to this Part** — Subsection 150(3), sections 150.1, 151 and 152, subsections 153(1.1), (1.2) and (3), sections 155 to 156.1 and 158 to 167 and Division J of Part I apply to this Part with any modifications that the circumstances require.

**Notes [s. 180.2]**: The tax under 180.2(2) is informally known as the "clawback" of old age security and pre-1993 family allowance benefits. Family allowance benefits were discontinued in 1993 in favour of a new non-taxable Child Tax Benefit payment for lower-income families, under 122.61.

The $50,000 income threshold in 180.2(2)A(b) is indexed by 117.1 to $53,215 for 1992–1997.

In *Swantje*, [1994] 1 C.T.C. 2559 (TCC), the clawback was held to be a tax on German pension income (which was supposed to be exempt by treaty) because it took that income into account. However, the Federal Court of Appeal ([1994] 2 C.T.C. 381) reversed that decision, ruling that the purpose of the clawback was to require repayment of social benefits by taxpayers who, because of their higher incomes, had a lesser need of them. The Supreme Court of Canada upheld this decision, [1996] 1 C.T.C. 355. This position has been confirmed for U.S. residents by new Article XXIV(10) of the Canada-U.S. tax treaty. See also Notes to 118(2).

180.2 completely rewritten by 1995 Budget, effective as follows: 180.2(1) applies after June 1996; 180.2(2), (5) and (6) apply to 1996 and later taxation years; 180.2(3) and (4) apply to amounts paid after June 1996. For the pre-1996 clawback, read:

(1) Tax payable — Every individual (other than a trust) shall pay a tax under this Part for each taxation year that is equal to the lesser of

(a) the total of all amounts each of which is the amount of any pension, supplement or spouse's allowance under the *Old Age Security Act* included in computing the individual's income under Part I for the year, to the extent that no deduction is allowed under paragraph 60(n) for the year or any subsequent taxation year in respect of that amount, and

(b) 15% of the amount, if any, by which

(i) the amount that would be the individual's income under Part I for the year if no amount were

(A) deductible under paragraph 60(w), or

(B) included in respect of a gain from a disposition of property to which section 79 applies

in computing that income

exceeds

(ii) $50,000.[29]

(2) Return — Every individual liable to pay tax under this Part for a taxation year shall, on or before the day on or before which the individual is required by section 150 to file a return of income for the year under Part I, or would be so

---

[29]Indexed by s. 117.1 after 1988. See table after s. 117.1.

required if the individual were liable to pay tax under Part I for the year,

    (a) file with the Minister, without notice or demand therefor, a return for the year under this Part in prescribed form and containing prescribed information; and

    (b) pay the tax under this Part for the year for which the individual is liable.

(3) **Provisions applicable to Part** — Sections 151, 152 and 158 to 167 and Division J of Part I are applicable to this Part with such modifications as the circumstances require.

180.2(1)(b)(i)(B) added by 1991 technical bill, retroactive to 1989, to exclude capital gains realized on mortgage foreclosures from the clawback threshold.

180.2 added by 1989 Budget, this version effective 1991. For 1990, read as for 1991, except read "²/₃ of the lesser of" in place of "the lesser of" in the opening words of 180.2(1). For 1989, read "¹/₃ of the lesser of".

180.2(1)(a) amended by 1992 Child Benefit bill, to eliminate the clawback of family allowances under the *Family Allowances Act* effective 1993.

**Definitions [s. 180.2]**: "adjusted income" — 180.2(1); "amount", "balance-due day" — 248(1); "base taxation year" — 180.2(1); "calendar year" — *Interpretation Act* 37(1)(a); "common-law partner" — 248(1); "filing-due date" — 150(1), 248(1); "individual" — 248(1); "Minister", "non-resident" — 248(1); "resident in Canada" — 250; "return of income" — 180.2(1); "tax payable" — 248(2); "taxation year" — 249.

**Interpretation Bulletins**: IT-326R3: Returns of deceased persons as "another person".

## PART I.3 — TAX ON LARGE CORPORATIONS

**181. (1) Definitions** — For the purposes of this Part,

**"financial institution"**, in respect of a taxation year, means a corporation that at any time in the year is

    (a) a bank or credit union,

    (b) an insurance corporation that carries on business in Canada,

    (c) authorized under the laws of Canada or a province to carry on the business of offering its services as a trustee to the public,

    (d) authorized under the laws of Canada or a province to accept deposits from the public and carries on the business of lending money on the security of real estate or investing in mortgages on real estate,

    (e) a registered securities dealer,

    (f) a mortgage investment corporation, or

    (g) a prescribed corporation;

**Related Provisions**: 142.2(1)"financial institution"(a)(i), 248(1)"restricted financial institution"(e.1), "specified financial institution"(e.1) — Prescribed corporation under this definition deems to be FI, RFI and SFI.

**Notes**: Para. (e) amended by 1994 tax amendments bill (Part VIII), retroactive to taxation years that end after June 1989. Formerly read "registered or licensed under the laws of a province to trade in securities". The term "registered securities dealer" is now defined in 248(1).

Para. (f) amended by 1991 technical bill, effective for taxation years ending after June 1989, to tax mortgage investment corporations and to delete deposit insurance corporations (which are now exempt from Part I.3 tax: see 181.1(3)(e)).

**Regulations**: 8604 (prescribed corporations).

**"long-term debt"** means,

    (a) in the case of a bank, its subordinated indebtedness (within the meaning assigned by section 2 of the *Bank Act*) evidenced by obligations issued for a term of not less than 5 years,

    (b) in the case of an insurance corporation, its subordinated indebtedness (within the meaning assigned by section 2 of the *Insurance Companies Act*) evidenced by obligations issued for a term of not less than 5 years, and

    (c) in the case of any other corporation, its subordinated indebtedness (within the meaning that would be assigned by section 2 of the *Bank Act* if the definition of that expression in that section were applied with such modifications as the circumstances require) evidenced by obligations issued for a term of not less than 5 years,

but does not include, where the corporation is a prescribed federal Crown corporation for the purpose of section 27, any indebtedness evidenced by obligations issued to and held by Her Majesty in right of Canada;

**Notes**: Definition "long-term debt" amended by 1993 technical bill, effective June 1, 1992. Previously read:

    "long-term debt" means

        (a) in the case of a bank, its indebtedness evidenced by bank debentures within the meaning assigned by the *Bank Act*, and

        (b) in the case of a financial institution that is not a bank, its subordinate indebtedness evidenced by obligations issued for a term of not less than 5 years (other than, where the financial institution is a prescribed federal Crown corporation for the purposes of section 27, such indebtedness evidenced by obligations issued to and held by Her Majesty in right of Canada);

Para. (b) of "long-term debt" amended by 1992 technical bill, effective for 1991 and later taxation years, to add the parenthetical exclusion.

**"reserves"**, in respect of a corporation for a taxation year, means the amount at the end of the year of all of the corporation's reserves, provisions and allowances (other than allowances in respect of depreciation or depletion) and, for greater certainty, includes any provision in respect of deferred taxes.

**I.T. Technical News**: No. 18 (*Oerlikon Aérospatiale* case).

**(2) Prescribed expressions** — For the purposes of this Part, the expressions "attributed surplus", "Canadian assets", "Canadian premiums", "Canadian reserve liabilities", "permanent establishment", "total assets", "total premiums" and "total reserve liabilities" have such meanings as may be prescribed.

**Regulations**: 8600 (prescribed meanings of expressions).

**(3) Determining values and amounts** — For the purposes of determining the carrying value of a

Part I.3 — Tax on Large Corporations    S. 181.1(2)

corporation's assets or any other amount under this Part in respect of a corporation's capital, investment allowance, taxable capital or taxable capital employed in Canada for a taxation year or in respect of a partnership in which a corporation has an interest,

(a) the equity and consolidation methods of accounting shall not be used; and

(b) subject to paragraph (a) and except as otherwise provided in this Part, the amounts reflected in the balance sheet

(i) presented to the shareholders of the corporation (in the case of a corporation that is neither an insurance corporation to which subparagraph (ii) applies nor a bank) or the members of the partnership, as the case may be, or, where such a balance sheet was not prepared in accordance with generally accepted accounting principles or no such balance sheet was prepared, the amounts that would be reflected if such a balance sheet had been prepared in accordance with generally accepted accounting principles, or

(ii) accepted by the Superintendent of Financial Institutions, in the case of a bank or an insurance corporation that is required by law to report to the Superintendent, or the superintendent of insurance or other similar officer or authority of the province under whose laws the corporation is incorporated, in the case of an insurance corporation that is required by law to report to that officer or authority,

shall be used.

**Related Provisions**: 190(2) — Rules in 181(3) apply to Part VI also.

**Notes**: The definitions in Part I.3 are generally to be interpreted in accordance with accounting principles rather than legal terminology: *Oerlikon Aérospatiale Inc.*, [1999] 4 C.T.C. 358 (FCA), leave to appeal to SCC denied (May 11, 2000), File 27352.

**I.T. Technical News**: No. 18 (*Oerlikon Aérospatiale* case).

**(4) Limitations respecting inclusions and deductions** — Unless a contrary intention is evident, no provision of this Part shall be read or construed to require the inclusion or to permit the deduction, in computing the amount of a corporation's capital, investment allowance, taxable capital or taxable capital employed in Canada for a taxation year, of any amount to the extent that that amount has been included or deducted, as the case may be, in computing the first-mentioned amount under, in accordance with or by reason of any other provision of this Part.

**Related Provisions**: 190(2) — Rules in 181(4) apply to Part VI also; 248(28) — Similar rule for the Act as a whole.

**Definitions [s. 181]**: "amount" — 248(1); "bank" — 248(1), *Interpretation Act* 35(1); "business" — 248(1); "Canada" — 255; "carrying on business in Canada" — 253; "corporation" — 248(1), *Interpretation Act* 35(1); "credit union" — 137(6), 248(1); "insurance corporation" — 248(1); "mortgage investment corporation" — 130.1(6), 248(1); "province" — *Interpretation Act* 35(1); "registered securities dealer" — 248(1); "taxation year" — 249.

**Interpretation Bulletins [s. 181]**: IT-532: Part I.3 — tax on large corporations.

**181.1 (1) Tax payable** — Every corporation shall pay a tax under this Part for each taxation year equal to 0.225% of the amount, if any, by which

(a) its taxable capital employed in Canada for the year

exceeds

(b) its capital deduction for the year.

**Related Provisions**: 125.3 — Deduction re Part I.3 tax; 132.2(1)(o)(ii) — Deemed taxation year of mutual fund corporation on reorganization; 157(1), (2.1) — Instalments — corporations; 161(1) — Interest; 161(4.1) — Interest — limitation respecting corporations; 181.1(2) — Reduction for short taxation year; 181.6 — Return; 190.1(1) — Financial institutions capital tax; 235 — Penalty on large corporation for late filing.

**Notes**: Where the taxpayer calculates taxable capital employed in Canada as less than the $10 million capital deduction (181.5(1)), so that no LCT is payable, it may still be advisable to file a nil return for Part I.3 tax and obtain an assessment. Otherwise the reassessment deadline under 152(4) never starts running and tax could be assessed any time in the future if the taxpayer's calculation was wrong.

181.1(1) added by 1989 Budget, effective for taxation years ending after June 1989 and prorated so as to apply only effective July 1, 1989.

181.1(1) amended by 1991 technical bill (as per GST modifications announced on December 19, 1989, with the reduction in the GST rate from 9% to 7%), to increase the rate from 0.175% to 0.2%. The change is effective as of the 1991 taxation year, and prorated so that the new rate took effect on January 1, 1991.

Tax rate in 181.1(1) changed from 0.2% to 0.225% by 1995 Budget, effective for taxation years that end after February 27, 1995, except that, in its application to taxation years that began before February 28, 1995, there shall be deducted from the tax otherwise payable under 181.1(1) an amount equal to that proportion of $1/9$ of the tax otherwise payable under that subsection of the Act that the number of days in the year that were before February 28, 1995 is of the number of days in the year (i.e., the increase only applies to the days in the year after February 27, 1995). The "$1/9$" figure is used because a reduction of $1/9$ of 0.225% for any given period will reduce the tax rate from 0.225% to 0.2% for that period.

The 1995 Budget bill also provided:

47. (3) For the purpose of applying subsection 125(5.1) of the Act, the amount that would, but for subsections 181.1(2) and (4) of the Act, be a corporation's tax payable under Part I.3 of the Act for a taxation year that began before February 28, 1995 shall be determined without reference to the amendment made by subsection (1) [which increased the rate from 0.2% to 0.225% — ed.].

**(2) Short taxation years** — Where a taxation year of a corporation is less than 51 weeks, the amount determined under subsection (1) for the year in respect of the corporation shall be reduced to that proportion of that amount that the number of days in the year is of 365.

**Related Provisions**: 132.2(1)(o) — Deemed taxation year of mutual fund corporation on reorganization.

**Notes**: 181.1(2) amended by 1992 technical bill, effective for 1992 and later taxation years, to ensure that the deduction in 181.1(4) for

## S. 181.1(2) — Income Tax Act

surtax attributable to a short taxation year is applied after prorating the Part I.3 tax under 181.1(2). For earlier years, read:

> (2) Where a taxation year of a corporation is less than 51 weeks, the tax payable under this Part for the year by the corporation shall be that proportion of its tax otherwise payable under this Part for the year that the number of days in the year is of 365.

**(3) Where tax not payable** — No tax is payable under this Part for a taxation year by a corporation

(a) that was a non-resident-owned investment corporation throughout the year;

(b) that was a bankrupt (within the meaning assigned by subsection 128(3)) at the end of the year;

(c) that was throughout the year exempt from tax under section 149 on all of its taxable income;

(d) that neither was resident in Canada nor carried on business through a permanent establishment in Canada at any time in the year;

(e) that was throughout the year a deposit insurance corporation (within the meaning assigned by subsection 137.1(5)) or a corporation deemed by subsection 137.1(5.1) to be a deposit insurance corporation; or

(f) that was throughout the year a corporation described in subsection 136(2) the principal business of which was marketing (including processing incidental to or connected therewith) natural products belonging to or acquired from its members or customers.

**Related Provisions**: 125.3(1) — Large corporations tax.

**Notes**: 181.1(3)(e) added by 1991 technical bill and 181.3(3)(f) added by 1992 technical bill, both retroactive to the introduction of the tax (taxation years ending after June 1989).

**Interpretation Bulletins**: IT-347R2: Crown corporations; IT-532: Part I.3 — tax on large corporations.

**(4) Deduction** — There may be deducted from a corporation's tax otherwise payable under this Part for a taxation year an amount equal to the total of

(a) its Canadian surtax payable for the year, and

(b) such part as the corporation claims of its unused surtax credits for its 7 immediately preceding and 3 immediately following taxation years,

to the extent that that total does not exceed the amount by which

(c) the amount that would, but for this subsection, be its tax payable under this Part for the year

exceeds

(d) the total of all amounts each of which is the amount deducted under subsection 125.3(1) in computing the corporation's tax payable under Part I for a taxation year ending before 1992 in respect of its unused Part I.3 tax credit (within the meaning assigned by section 125.3) for the year.

**Related Provisions**: 87(2)(j.91) — Amalgamation; 87(2.11) — Vertical amalgamations; 125.2, 125.3 — Credit of Parts VI and I.3 tax against surtax before 1992; 161(7)(a)(ix), 164(5)(h.1), 164(5.1)(h.2) — Effect of carryback of loss etc.; 181.6 — Return.

**Notes**: 181.1(4) added by 1992 technical bill (and para. (c) corrected retroactively by 1993 technical bill to change "section" to "subsection"), effective for 1992 and later taxation years. For rationale, see Notes to 125.3(1).

**Interpretation Bulletins**: IT-532: Part I.3 — tax on large corporations.

**Forms**: T2 SCH 37: Calculation of unused Part I.3 tax credit and unused surtax credit.

**(5) Idem** — For the purposes of this subsection and subsections (4), (6) and (7),

(a) an amount may not be claimed under subsection (4) in computing a corporation's tax payable under this Part for a particular taxation year in respect of its unused surtax credit for another taxation year until its unused surtax credits, if any, for taxation years preceding the other year that may be claimed under this Part for the particular year have been claimed; and

(b) an amount in respect of a corporation's unused surtax credit for a taxation year may be claimed under subsection (4) in computing its tax payable under this Part for another taxation year only to the extent that it exceeds the total of all amounts each of which is an amount claimed in respect of that unused surtax credit in computing its tax payable under this Part or Part VI for a taxation year preceding that other year.

**Related Provisions**: 87(2.11) — Vertical amalgamations.

**Notes**: 181.1(5) added by 1992 technical bill, effective for 1992 and later taxation years.

**(6) Definitions** — For the purposes of this subsection and subsections (4), (5) and (7),

**"Canadian surtax payable"** of a corporation for a taxation year has the meaning assigned by subsection 125.3(4);

**"unused surtax credit"** for a taxation year ending after 1991

(a) of a corporation (other than a corporation that was throughout the year a financial institution, within the meaning assigned by section 190) means the amount, if any, by which

(i) its Canadian surtax payable for the year

exceeds the total of

(ii) the amount that would, but for subsection (4), be its tax payable under this Part for the year, and

(iii) the amount, if any, deducted under section 125.3 in computing the corporation's tax payable under Part I for the year, and

(b) of a corporation that was throughout the year a financial institution (within the meaning assigned by section 190) means the lesser of

(i) the amount, if any, by which

(A) its Canadian surtax payable for the year

exceeds the total of

(B) the amount that would, but for subsection (4), be its tax payable under this Part for the year, and

(C) the amount, if any, deducted under section 125.3 in computing the corporation's tax payable under Part I for the year, and

(ii) the amount, if any, by which its tax payable under Part I for the year exceeds the amount that would, but for subsection (4) and subsection 190.1(3), be the total of its taxes payable under Parts I.3 and VI for the year.

**Related Provisions**: 87(2.11) — Vertical amalgamations; 256(9) — Date of acquisition of control.

**Notes**: 181.1(6) added by 1992 technical bill, effective for 1992 and later taxation years.

**(7) Acquisition of control** — Where at any time control of a corporation has been acquired by a person or group of persons, no amount in respect of its unused surtax credit for a taxation year ending before that time is deductible by the corporation for a taxation year ending after that time and no amount in respect of its unused surtax credit for a taxation year ending after that time is deductible by the corporation for a taxation year ending before that time, except that

(a) the corporation's unused surtax credit for a particular taxation year that ended before that time is deductible by the corporation for a taxation year that ends after that time (in this paragraph referred to as the "subsequent year") to the extent of that proportion of the corporation's Canadian surtax payable for the particular year that

(i) the amount, if any, by which

(A) the total of all amounts each of which is

(I) its income under Part I for the particular year from a business that was carried on by the corporation throughout the subsequent year for profit or with a reasonable expectation of profit, or

(II) where properties were sold, leased, rented or developed or services were rendered in the course of carrying on that business before that time, its income under Part I for the particular year from any other business all or substantially all of the income of which was derived from the sale, leasing, rental or development, as the case may be, of similar properties or the rendering of similar services

exceeds

(B) the total of all amounts each of which is an amount deducted under paragraph 111(1)(a) or (d) in computing its taxable income for the particular year in respect of a non-capital loss or a farm loss, as the case may be, for a taxation year in respect of any business referred to in clause (A)

is of the greater of

(ii) the amount determined under subparagraph (i), and

(iii) the corporation's taxable income for the particular year; and

(b) the corporation's unused surtax credit for a particular taxation year that ends after that time is deductible by the corporation for a taxation year that ended before that time (in this paragraph referred to as the "preceding year") to the extent of that proportion of the corporation's Canadian surtax payable for the particular year that

(i) the amount, if any, by which

(A) the total of all amounts each of which is

(I) its income under Part I for the particular year from a business that was carried on by the corporation in the preceding year and throughout the particular year for profit or with a reasonable expectation of profit, or

(II) where properties were sold, leased, rented or developed or services were rendered in the course of carrying on that business before that time, the corporation's income under Part I for the particular year from any other business all or substantially all of the income of which was derived from the sale, leasing, rental or development, as the case may be, of similar properties or the rendering of similar services

exceeds

(B) the total of all amounts each of which is an amount deducted under paragraph 111(1)(a) or (d) in computing the corporation's taxable income for the particular year in respect of a non-capital loss or a farm loss, as the case may be, for a taxation year in respect of any business referred to in clause (A)

is of the greater of

(ii) the amount determined under subparagraph (i), and

(iii) the corporation's taxable income for the particular year.

**Related Provisions**: 87(2.11) — Vertical amalgamations; 256(6)–(9) — Anti-avoidance — deemed exercise of right to increase voting power.

## S. 181.1(7) — Income Tax Act

**Notes**: See Notes to 111(5), which has the same general purpose.

181.1(7)(a) and (b) amended by 1995-97 technical bill, effective for acquisitions of control that occur after April 26, 1995. For earlier acquisitions since the 1992 taxation year, read:

(a) where a business was carried on by the corporation in a taxation year ending before that time, its unused surtax credit for that year is deductible by the corporation for a particular taxation year ending after that time only if that business was carried on by the corporation for profit or with a reasonable expectation of profit throughout the particular year and only to the extent of that proportion of the corporation's tax payable under this Part for the particular year that

(i) the amount, if any, by which

(A) the total of its income under Part I for the particular year from that business and, where properties were sold, leased, rented or developed or services were rendered in the course of carrying on that business before that time, its income under Part I for the particular year from any other business substantially all of the income of which was derived from the sale, leasing, rental or development, as the case may be, of similar properties or the rendering of similar services

exceeds

(B) the total of all amounts each of which is an amount deducted under paragraph 111(1)(a) or (d) in computing its taxable income under Part I for the particular year in respect of a non-capital loss or a farm loss, as the case may be, for a taxation year in respect of that business or the other business

is of the greater of

(ii) the amount determined under subparagraph (i), and

(iii) the corporation's taxable income under Part I for the particular year; and

(b) where a business was carried on by the corporation throughout a taxation year ending after that time, its unused surtax credit for that year is deductible by the corporation for a particular taxation year ending before that time only if that business was carried on by the corporation for profit or with a reasonable expectation of profit in the particular year and only to the extent of that proportion of the corporation's tax payable under this Part for the particular year that

(i) the amount, if any, by which

(A) the total of its income under Part I for the particular year from that business and, where properties were sold, leased, rented or developed or services were rendered in the course of carrying on that business before that time, its income under Part I for the particular year from any other business substantially all of the income of which was derived from the sale, leasing, rental or development, as the case may be, of similar properties of the rendering of similar services

exceeds

(B) the total of all amounts each of which is an amount deducted under paragraph 111(1)(a) or (d) in computing its taxable income under Part I for the particular year in respect of a non-capital loss or a farm loss, as the case may be, for a taxation year in respect of that business or the other business

is of the greater of

(ii) the amount determined under subparagraph (i), and

(iii) the corporation's taxable income under Part I for the particular year.

181.1(7) added by 1992 technical bill, effective for 1992 and later taxation years.

**I.T. Technical News**: No. 7 (control by a group — 50/50 arrangement).

**Interpretation Bulletins**: IT-532: Part I.3 — tax on large corporations.

**Definitions [s. 181.1]**: "acquired" — 256(7)–(9); "amount" — 181(3), 248(1); "business" — 248(1); "capital deduction" — 181.5(1); "Canadian surtax payable" — 125.3(4), 181.1(6); "carrying on business in Canada" — 253; "control" — 256(6)–(9); "corporation" — 248(1), *Interpretation Act* 35(1); "farm loss" — 111(8); "financial institution" — 190(1); "non-capital loss" — 111(8), 248(1); "non-resident-owned investment corporation" — 133(8), 248(1); "permanent establishment" — 181(2), Reg. 8602; "property" — 248(1); "resident in Canada" — 250; "taxable capital employed in Canada" — 181.2(1), 181.3(1), 181.4; "taxable income" — 2(2), 248(1); "taxation year" — 249; "unused surtax credit" — 181.1(6).

**181.2 (1) Taxable capital employed in Canada** — The taxable capital employed in Canada of a corporation for a taxation year (other than a financial institution or a corporation that was throughout the year not resident in Canada) is the prescribed proportion of the corporation's taxable capital for the year.

**Related Provisions**: 66(12.6012) — Definition used for limitation on renunciation of Canadian development expenses to flow-through shareholder as Canadian exploration expense; 181(4) — Limitations respecting inclusions and deductions; 181.3(1) — Taxable capital employed in Canada of financial institution.

**Regulations**: 8601 (prescribed proportion).

**(2) Taxable capital** — The taxable capital of a corporation (other than a financial institution) for a taxation year is the amount, if any, by which its capital for the year exceeds its investment allowance for the year.

**Related Provisions**: 181(4) — Limitations respecting inclusions and deductions.

**(3) Capital** — The capital of a corporation (other than a financial institution) for a taxation year is the amount, if any, by which the total of

(a) the amount of its capital stock (or, in the case of a corporation incorporated without share capital, the amount of its members' contributions), retained earnings, contributed surplus and any other surpluses at the end of the year,

(b) the amount of its reserves for the year, except to the extent that they were deducted in computing its income for the year under Part I,

(b.1) the amount of its deferred unrealized foreign exchange gains at the end of the year,

(c) the amount of all loans and advances to the corporation at the end of the year,

(d) the amount of all indebtedness of the corporation at the end of the year represented by bonds, debentures, notes, mortgages, bankers' acceptances or similar obligations,

(e) the amount of any dividends declared but not paid by the corporation before the end of the year,

(f) the amount of all other indebtedness (other than any indebtedness in respect of a lease) of the corporation at the end of the year that has been outstanding for more than 365 days before the end of the year, and

(g) where the corporation was a member of a partnership at the end of the year, that proportion of the amount, if any, by which

(i) the total of all amounts (other than amounts owing to the member or to other corporations that are members of the partnership) that would be determined under this paragraph and paragraphs (b) to (d) and (f) in respect of the partnership at the end of its last fiscal period that ends at or before the end of the year (if paragraphs (b) to (d) and (f) applied to partnerships in the same way that they apply to corporations)

exceeds

(ii) the amount of the partnership's deferred unrealized foreign exchange losses at the end of that period

that the member's share of the partnership's income or loss for that period is of the partnership's income or loss for that period

exceeds the total of

(h) the amount of its deferred tax debit balance at the end of the year,

(i) the amount of any deficit deducted in computing its shareholders' equity at the end of the year, and

(j) any amount deducted under subsection 135(1) in computing its income under Part I for the year, to the extent that the amount can reasonably be regarded as being included in the amount determined under any of paragraphs (a) to (g) in respect of the corporation for the year.

(k) the amount of its deferred unrealized foreign exchange losses at the end of the year.

### Possible Future Amendment — Joint debt

**Letter from Department of Finance, August 6, 1997:**

Dear [xxx]

This is in response to your memorandum dated July 29, 1997 respecting the application of the Large Corporation Tax (LCT) to joint debt. You are concerned that joint debt may be fully taxed in the hands of each co-borrower under the LCT, even though the advance is divided among those borrowers. Using the example provided in your note, a joint debt in the amount of $400 million might be shared so that one party is advanced $100 million and the other, $300 million. You believe that the aggregate addition to capital in respect of the debt should be $400 million for the two borrowers; your concern is that, under the current law, each of them would be required to add $400 million to capital with the result that a total of $800 million would be subject to LCT.

Your concern is based on the current wording of subsection 181(3) of the Act, which provides that, "except as otherwise provided under this Part", the amounts to be used in calculating LCT are those set out on the taxpayer's balance sheet, prepared in accordance with GAAP. You feel that the definition of capital in paragraph 181.2(3) of the Act "provides otherwise" for these purposes, and hence, that the amounts set out on the balance sheet may not be relevant.

As you have described it, GAAP currently provides that only the portion of a jointly-incurred debt that is actually advanced to a borrower is recorded as a liability on the balance sheet. A note to the balance sheet indicates the full value of the joint debt in order to disclose the legal liability of the borrower for that part of the debt that was not received by that borrower. If subsection 181(3) applies, you reason that the taxpayers in your example would be taxed on $100 million and $300 million in capital respectively. If subsection 181(3) does not apply, each taxpayer would be taxed on the full amount of their legal indebtedness, being $400 million.

In our view, the definition of capital in subsection 181.2(3) of the Act does not constitute an exception to the application of subsection 181(3) of the Act. Rather, our intention — which we believe to be reflected in the existing legislation — is that subsection 181(3) apply to use the amounts reflected in a borrower's balance sheet to quantify the amounts included in its capital.

That being said, there may be a risk of double-counting in the application of the LCT to jointly-incurred debt. As notes to the financial statements are an integral part of the balance sheet, there is a possibility that the amount set out in the notes would be assessed as the corporation's capital in respect of a joint debt. If this were to occur, each co-borrower under a joint debt would be taxed for the full amount of the debt, irrespective of the amount actually advanced to that borrower.

In principle, we agree that the amount of a joint debt should only be taxed once, and we hope to discuss this matter further with Revenue Canada officials to determine whether that result can be achieved under the current law. If that proves unsuccessful, we are prepared to consider legislative changes to ensure this outcome. As noted, GAAP currently allocates joint debt based on the amount of cash advanced to each co-borrower — for LCT purposes, other factors may be relevant in making such an allocation. If a change to the law should prove necessary, we would be pleased [to] have your views in this respect.

If you would like to discuss this matter in more detail, please feel free to contact Robin Maley (992-4859) or Brian Ernewein (992-3045) of the Division directly.

Yours sincerely,

Len Farber
Director General, Tax Legislation Division

**Related Provisions**: 132.2(1)(o) — Deemed year-end of mutual fund corporation on reorganization; 181(4) — Limitations respecting inclusions and deductions.

**Notes**: 181.2(3)(b.1) added by 1995-97 technical bill, effective for 1995 and later taxation years.

181.2(3)(d) amended by 1992 technical bill, effective for taxation years that end after December 20, 1991, to add "bankers' acceptances".

181.2(3)(g)(ii) added by 1995-97 technical bill, effective for 1995 and later taxation years.

181.2(3)(j) added by 1991 technical bill, retroactive to the introduction of the tax (taxation years ending after June 1989).

**S. 181.2(3)**

181.2(3)(k) added by 1995-97 technical bill, effective for 1995 and later taxation years.

In *Autobus Thomas Inc.*, [1999] 2 C.T.C. 2001 (TCC), aff'd 2000 CarswellNat 400 (FCA), a bus dealer purchased school buses from manufacturers by way of conditional sales contracts. The debts owing to the bank were held to be part of "capital" for purposes of 181.2(3).

**I.T. Technical News**: No. 18 (*Oerlikon Aérospatiale* case).

**(4) Investment allowance** — The investment allowance of a corporation (other than a financial institution) for a taxation year is the total of all amounts each of which is the carrying value at the end of the year of an asset of the corporation that is

(a) a share of another corporation,

(b) a loan or advance to another corporation (other than a financial institution),

(c) a bond, debenture, note, mortgage or similar obligation of another corporation (other than a financial institution),

(d) long-term debt of a financial institution,

(d.1) a loan or advance to, or a bond, debenture, note, mortgage or similar obligation of, a partnership all of the members of which, throughout the year, were other corporations (other than financial institutions) that were not exempt from tax under this Part (otherwise than because of paragraph 181.1(3)(d)),

(e) an interest in a partnership, or

(f) a dividend payable to the corporation at the end of the year on a share of the capital stock of another corporation,

other than a share of the capital stock of, a dividend payable by, or indebtedness of, a corporation that is exempt from tax under this Part (otherwise than because of paragraph 181.1(3)(d)).

**Related Provisions**: 181(4) — Limitations respecting inclusions and deductions; 181.1(6) — Deemed amount of loan.

**Notes**: 181.2(4)(d.1) added by 1992 technical bill, effective for 1991 and later taxation years.

181.2(4)(f) added by 1991 technical bill, retroactive to the introduction of the tax (taxation years ending after June 1989).

The term "bond, debenture, note, mortgage or similar obligation" in 181.2(4)(c) does not include bankers' acceptances. See *Federated Cooperatives Ltd.*, [2000] 2 C.T.C. 2382 (TCC).

**(5) Value of interest in partnership** — For the purposes of subsection (4), the carrying value, at the end of a taxation year, of an interest of a corporation in a partnership shall be deemed to be an amount equal to that proportion of

(a) the total of all amounts each of which is the carrying value of an asset of the partnership, at the end of its last fiscal period ending at or before the end of the year, described in any of paragraphs (4)(a) to (d) and (f), other than an asset that is a share of the capital stock of, a dividend payable by, or indebtedness of, a corporation that is exempt from tax under this Part

(otherwise than because of paragraph 181.1(3)(d)),

that

(b) the corporation's share of the partnership's income or loss for that period

is of

(c) the partnership's income or loss for that period.

**Notes**: 181.2(5)(a) amended by 1991 technical bill, retroactive to the introduction of the tax (taxation years ending after June 1989).

**(6) Loan** — For the purpose of subsection (4), where a corporation made a particular loan to a trust that neither

(a) made any loans or advances to nor received any loans or advances from, nor

(b) acquired any bond, debenture, note, mortgage or similar obligation of nor issued any bond, debenture, note, mortgage or similar obligation to

a person not related to the corporation, as part of a series of transactions in which the trust made a loan to another corporation (other than a financial institution) to which the corporation is related, the least of

(c) the amount of the particular loan,

(d) the amount of the loan from the trust to the other corporation, and

(e) the amount, if any, by which

(i) the total of all amounts each of which is the amount of a loan from the trust to any corporation

exceeds

(ii) the total of all amounts each of which is the amount of a loan (other than the particular loan) from any corporation to the trust

at any time shall be deemed to be the amount of a loan from the corporation to the other corporation at that time.

**Notes**: 181.2(6) added by 1992 technical bill, retroactive to the introduction of the tax (effective July 1989).

**Definitions [s. 181.2]**: "amount" — 181(3), 181.2(6), 248(1); "carrying value" — 181(2); "corporation" — 248(1), *Interpretation Act* 35(1); "financial institution" — 181(1); "fiscal period" — 249(2)(b), 249.1; "long-term debt" — 181(1); "permanent establishment" — 181(2), Reg. 8602; "reserves" — 181(1); "resident in Canada" — 250; "share" — 248(1); "taxation year" — 249.

**Interpretation Bulletins [s. 181.2]**: IT-532: Part I.3 — tax on large corporations.

**181.3 (1) Taxable capital employed in Canada of financial institution** — The taxable capital employed in Canada of a financial institution for a taxation year is the total of

(a) the total of all amounts each of which is the carrying value at the end of the year of an asset of the financial institution (other than property held by the institution primarily for the purpose of resale that was acquired by the financial institution, in the year or the preceding taxation year, as a consequence of another person's default, or anticipated default, in respect of a debt owed to the institution) that is tangible property used in Canada and, in the case of a financial institution that is an insurance corporation, that is non-segregated property, within the meaning assigned by subsection 138(12),

(b) the total of all amounts each of which is an amount in respect of a partnership in which the financial institution has an interest at the end of the year equal to that proportion of

    (i) the total of all amounts each of which is the carrying value of an asset of the partnership, at the end of its last fiscal period ending at or before the end of the year, that is tangible property used in Canada

that

    (ii) the financial institution's share of the partnership's income or loss for that period

is of

    (iii) the partnership's income or loss for that period, and

(c) an amount that is equal to

    (i) in the case of a financial institution other than an insurance corporation, that proportion of its taxable capital for the year that its Canadian assets at the end of the year is of its total assets at the end of the year,

**Proposed Amendment — 181.3(1)(c)(i)**

(i) in the case of a financial institution, other than an authorized foreign bank or an insurance corporation, that proportion of its taxable capital for the year that its Canadian assets at the end of the year is of its total assets at the end of the year.

**Application**: The August 8, 2000 draft legislation, subsec. 16(1), will amend subpara. 181.3(1)(c)(i) to read as above, applicable after June 27, 1999.

**Technical Notes**: Part I.3 of the Act imposes a tax (generally known as the "large corporations tax" or LCT) on the amount by which a large corporation's taxable capital employed in Canada exceeds a $10 million "capital deduction" (shared among related corporations).

Section 181.3 of the Act provides rules for determining the capital, taxable capital, taxable capital employed in Canada and investment allowance of a financial institution (as defined in subsection 181(1) of the Act) for the purposes of the LCT. The section is amended to include new rules, applicable after June 27, 1999, for determining these amounts in respect of an authorized foreign bank.

Subsection 181.3(1) of the Act provides the rules for determining the amount of a financial institution's "taxable capital" — that is, its capital less its allowance for investments in related financial institutions — that is employed in Canada for purposes of Part I.3.

Subparagraph (c)(i) is amended to exclude authorized foreign banks, while subparagraph (c)(iv) is amended to specify that the relevant amount for an authorized foreign bank is its taxable capital for the year. It is not necessary to pro-rate this amount, since by definition all of the taxable capital of an authorized foreign bank is related to its Canadian banking business. By virtue of paragraphs 181.3(1)(a) and (b), the taxable capital employed in Canada of an authorized foreign bank also includes tangible property used in Canada.

These amendments apply after June 27, 1999.

    (ii) in the case of an insurance corporation that was resident in Canada at any time during the year and carried on a life insurance business at any time in the year, the total of

        (A) that proportion of the amount, if any, by which the total of

            (I) its taxable capital for the year, and

            (II) the amount prescribed for the year in respect of the corporation

exceeds

            (III) the amount prescribed for the year in respect of the corporation

that its Canadian reserve liabilities as at the end of the year is of the total of

            (IV) its total reserve liabilities as at the end of the year, and

            (V) the amount prescribed for the year in respect of the corporation, and

        (B) the amount, if any, by which

            (I) the amount of its reserves for the year (other than its reserves in respect of amounts payable out of segregated funds) that may reasonably be regarded as having been established in respect of its insurance businesses carried on in Canada

exceeds the total of

            (II) the total of all amounts each of which is the amount of a reserve (other than a reserve described in subparagraph 138(3)(a)(i)) to the extent that it was included in the amount determined under subclause (I) and was deducted in computing its income under Part I for the year,

            (III) the total of all amounts each of which is the amount of a reserve described in subparagraph 138(3)(a)(i) to the extent that it was included in the amount determined under subclause (I) and was deductible under subparagraph 138(3)(a)(i) in computing its income under Part I for the year, and

            (IV) the total of all amounts each of which is the amount outstanding (including any interest accrued thereon) as at the end of the year in respect of a policy loan (within the meaning assigned by subsection 138(12)) made by the corporation, to the extent that it was deducted in computing the total determined under subclause (III),

(iii) in the case of an insurance corporation that was resident in Canada at any time in the year and throughout the year did not carry on a life insurance business, that proportion of its taxable capital for the year that the total amount of its Canadian premiums for the year is of its total premiums for the year, and

(iv) in the case of an insurance corporation that was throughout the year not resident in Canada and carried on an insurance business in Canada at any time in the year, its taxable capital for the year.

### Proposed Amendment — 181.3(1)(c)(iv)

(iv) in the case of an insurance corporation that was throughout the year not resident in Canada and carried on an insurance business at any time in the year, or in the case of an authorized foreign bank, its taxable capital for the year.

**Application**: The August 8, 2000 draft legislation, subsec. 16(2), will amend subpara. 181.3(1)(c)(iv) to read as above, applicable after June 27, 1999.

**Technical Notes**: See under 181.3(1)(c)(i).

**Related Provisions**: 181(4) — Limitations respecting inclusions and deductions; 190.11 — Taxable capital employed in Canada for Part VI tax.

**Notes**: 181.3(1)(a) amended by 1992 technical bill, retroactive to the introduction of the tax (taxation years ending after June 1989).

181.3(1)(c)(ii)(A)(II) and (IV) added by 1993 technical bill, effective for taxation years that end after February 25, 1992. As well, where the corporation elects under para. 88(2)(b) of the 1993 technical bill (see Notes to 190.11) for amended 190.11(b)(i) to apply to its 1991 and later taxation years, the amended 181.3(1)(c)(ii)(A) applies to the 1991 and 1992 taxation years; and in that case, notwithstanding 152(4) to (5), such assessments and determinations in respect of any taxation year shall be made as are necessary to give effect to the election.

**Regulations**: 8605 (prescribed amounts for 181.3(1)(c)(ii)(A)(II), (III) and (V)).

**(2) Taxable capital of financial institution** — The taxable capital of a financial institution for a taxation year is the amount, if any, by which its capital for the year exceeds its investment allowance for the year.

**Related Provisions**: 181(4) — Limitations respecting inclusions and deductions; 190.12 — Taxable capital for Part VI tax.

**(3) Capital of financial institution** — The capital of a financial institution for a taxation year is

(a) in the case of a financial institution other than an insurance corporation, the amount, if any, by which the total at the end of the year of

### Proposed Amendment — 181.3(3)(a) opening words

(a) in the case of a financial institution, other than an authorized foreign bank or an insurance corporation, the amount, if any, by which the total at the end of the year of

**Application**: The August 8, 2000 draft legislation, subsec. 16(3), will amend the opening words of para. 181.3(3)(a) to read as above, applicable after June 27, 1999.

**Technical Notes**: Subsection 181.3(3) of the Act sets out the rules for calculating the capital of a financial institution for the purposes of Part I.3. This provision is amended to define a notional amount of capital for an authorized foreign bank.

Paragraph 181.3(3)(a) is amended to exclude authorized foreign banks from the general rule and new paragraph 181.3(3)(e) is added, to define the capital of an authorized foreign bank for a taxation year. This definition is based on the regulatory capital requirements that Canada's Office of the Superintendent of Financial Institutions (OSFI) applies to Canadian banks. Specifically, the capital of an authorized foreign bank for a year is the total of two amounts:

- Under new subparagraph 181.3(3)(e)(i), 10% of the bank's risk-weighted assets and exposures at the end of the year, in respect of its Canadian banking business, as those would be reported under OSFI's risk-weighting guidelines if the guidelines applied and required reporting at that time. For this purpose, the relevant OSFI guidelines are newly defined in subsection 248(1) of the Act to mean the guidelines issued under authority of section 600 of the Bank Act, as those guidelines stood on August 8, 2000.

- Under new subparagraph 181.3(3)(e)(ii), all amounts in respect of the business, at the end of the year, that would be deducted from the bank's capital, under OSFI's risk-based capital adequacy guidelines, in determining the adequacy of the bank's capital if the bank were a bank listed in Schedule II to the *Bank Act*. These amounts, which include goodwill that is recorded on the bank's balance sheet, unconsolidated investments in subsidiaries, and other substantial investments, generally carry a risk-weighting of zero, and so will not figure in the bank's capital for LCT purposes under subparagraph (e)(i). On the other hand, certain securitized assets, loss facilities in connection with which would be deducted from a Schedule II bank's capital, are nonetheless included in a foreign bank's risk-weighted assets pool at ratings greater that zero: to avoid counting these assets twice for LCT purposes, new clause (e)(ii)(B) excludes from the subparagraph (ii) amount any amount in respect of a loss protection facility that OSFI's asset securitization guidelines require to be deducted from capital.

These amendments apply after June 27, 1999.

(i) the amount of its long-term debt,

(ii) the amount of its capital stock (or, in the case of an institution incorporated without share capital, the amount of its members' contributions), retained earnings, contributed surplus and any other surpluses, and

(iii) the amount of its reserves for the year, except to the extent that they were deducted in computing its income under Part I for the year,

exceeds the total of

(iv) the amount of its deferred tax debit balance at the end of the year,

(v) the amount of any deficit deducted in computing its shareholders' equity at the end of the year, and

(vi) any amount deducted under subsection 130.1(1) or 137(2) in computing its income under Part I for the year, to the extent that the amount can reasonably be regarded as being included in the amount determined under subparagraph (i), (ii) or (iii) in respect of the institution for the year;

(b) in the case of an insurance corporation that was resident in Canada at any time in the year and carried on a life insurance business at any time in the year, the amount, if any, by which the total at the end of the year of

(i) the amount of its long-term debt, and

(ii) the amount of its capital stock (or, in the case of an insurance corporation incorporated without share capital, the amount of its members' contributions), retained earnings, contributed surplus and any other surpluses

exceeds the total of

(iii) the amount of its deferred tax debit balance at the end of the year, and

(iv) the amount of any deficit deducted in computing its shareholders' equity at the end of the year;

(c) in the case of an insurance corporation that was resident in Canada at any time in the year and throughout the year did not carry on a life insurance business, the amount, if any, by which the total at the end of the year of

(i) the amount of its long-term debt,

(ii) the amount of its capital stock (or, in the case of an insurance corporation incorporated without share capital, the amount of its members' contributions), retained earnings, contributed surplus and any other surpluses, and

(iii) the amount of its reserves for the year, except to the extent that they were deducted in computing its income under Part I for the year,

exceeds the total of

(iv) the amount of its deferred tax debit balance at the end of the year,

(v) the amount of any deficit deducted in computing its shareholders' equity at the end of the year, and

(vi) the total amount of its deferred acquisition expenses in respect of its property and casualty insurance business in Canada, to the extent that it can reasonably be attributed to an amount included in the amount determined under subparagraph (iii); and

(d) in the case of an insurance corporation that was throughout the year not resident in Canada and carried on an insurance business in Canada at any time in the year, the total at the end of the year of

(i) the amount that is the greater of

(A) the amount, if any, by which

(I) the corporation's surplus funds derived from operations (as defined in subsection 138(12)) as of the end of the year, computed as if no tax were payable under this Part or Part VI for the year

exceeds the total of all amounts each of which is

(II) an amount on which the corporation was required to pay, or would but for subsection 219(5.2) have been required to pay, tax under Part XIV for a preceding taxation year, except the portion, if any, of the amount on which tax was payable, or would have been payable, because of subparagraph 219(4)(a)(i.1), and

(III) an amount on which the corporation was required to pay, or would but for subsection 219(5.2) have been required to pay, tax under subsection 219(5.1) for the year because of the transfer of an insurance business to which subsection 138(11.5) or (11.92) has applied, and

(B) the corporation's attributed surplus for the year,

(ii) any other surpluses relating to its insurance businesses carried on in Canada,

(iii) the amount of its long-term debt that may reasonably be regarded as relating to its insurance businesses carried on in Canada, and

(iv) the amount, if any, by which

(A) the amount of its reserves for the year (other than its reserves in respect of amounts payable out of segregated funds) that may reasonably be regarded as having been established in respect of its insurance businesses carried on in Canada

exceeds the total of

(B) the total of all amounts each of which is the amount of a reserve (other than a reserve described in subparagraph 138(3)(a)(i)) to the extent that it was in-

**S. 181.3(3)(d)(iv)(B)**      Income Tax Act

cluded in the amount determined under clause (A) and was deducted in computing its income under Part I for the year,

(C) the total of all amounts each of which is the amount of a reserve described in subparagraph 138(3)(a)(i) to the extent that it was included in the amount determined under clause (A) and was deductible under subparagraph 138(3)(a)(i) in computing its income under Part I for the year,

(D) the total of all amounts each of which is the amount outstanding (including any interest accrued thereon) as at the end of the year in respect of a policy loan (within the meaning assigned by subsection 138(12)) made by the corporation, to the extent that it was deducted in computing the amount determined under clause (C), and

(E) the total amount of its deferred acquisition expenses in respect of its property and casualty insurance business in Canada, to the extent that it can reasonably be attributed to an amount included in the amount determined under clause (A).

### Proposed Addition — 181.3(3)(e)

(e) in the case of an authorized foreign bank, the total of

(i) 10% of the total of all amounts, each of which is the risk-weighted amount at the end of the year of an on-balance sheet asset or an off-balance sheet exposure of the bank in respect of its Canadian banking business that the bank would be required to report under the OSFI risk-weighting guidelines if those guidelines applied and required a report at that time, and

(ii) the total of all amounts, each of which is an amount at the end of the year in respect of the bank's Canadian banking business that

(A) if the bank were a bank listed in Schedule II to the *Bank Act*, would be required under the risk-based capital adequacy guidelines issued by the Superintendent of Financial Institutions and applicable at that time to be deducted from the bank's capital in determining the amount of capital available to satisfy the Superintendent's requirement that capital equal a particular proportion of risk-weighted assets and exposures, and

(B) is not an amount in respect of a loss protection facility required to be deducted from capital under the Superintendent's guidelines respecting asset securitization applicable at that time.

**Application**: The August 8, 2000 draft legislation, subsec. 16(4), will add para. 181.3(3)(e), applicable after June 27, 1999.

**Technical Notes**: See under 181.3(3)(a).

**Notice of Ways and Means Motion (authorized foreign banks), February 11, 1999**: (5) That, for the purposes of Part I.3 and Part VI of the Act, the capital of an authorized foreign bank be an amount equal to 10% of the bank's risk-weighted assets as determined under prescribed rules based on the risk-weighted asset guidelines of the Superintendent of Financial Institutions.

**Department of Finance news release, February 11, 1999**: *Capital Tax*

Banks are subject to capital tax under Part I.3 and Part VI of the *Income Tax Act*. While the definitions of "capital" for regulatory and tax purposes differ slightly, the components of a Canadian bank's regulatory capital are generally subject to capital tax. Thus, the regulatory capital requirements applicable to Canadian banks guarantee that those entities have a minimum amount of taxable capital employed in Canada.

Because foreign banks having branches in Canada will be subject to the capital adequacy requirements imposed by the banks' home countries, the branches themselves will not be required to comply with Canadian capital requirements applicable to Canadian banks. Given that Canadian capital taxes are based to a large extent on the capital requirements imposed by Canadian regulators, a foreign branch could pay substantially less capital tax than its domestic competitors.

A new capital tax base is proposed to apply to foreign banks. For tax purposes, the capital of a foreign bank that has a Canadian branch will equal 10% of the "risk-weighted assets" of the Canadian branch, which will be defined, for these purposes, with regard to the risk-weighted asset requirements currently used by the Office of the Superintendent of Financial Institutions.

**Related Provisions**: 181(4) — Limitations respecting inclusions and deductions; 190.13 — Capital for Part VI tax.

**Notes**: 181.3(3)(a)(vi) added by 1991 technical bill, retroactive to the introduction of the tax (taxation years ending after June 1989).

181.3(3)(c)(vi), the words "computed as if ... for the year" in 181.3(3)(d)(i), and 181.3(3)(d)(iv)(E) added by 1993 technical bill, effective for 1992 and later taxation years.

181.3(3)(d)(i)(A)(II) and (III) added by 1995-97 technical bill, effective for 1995 and later taxation years. (The previous text was all in the body of subpara. (i), not broken down to the clause level.)

**(4) Investment allowance of financial institution** — The investment allowance of a financial institution for a taxation year is,

(a) in the case of a financial institution that was resident in Canada at any time in the year, the total of all amounts each of which is the carrying value at the end of the year of an asset of the financial institution that is a share of the capital stock or long-term debt of another financial institution (other than an institution that is exempt from tax under this Part) that is related to the institution (and, in the case of a financial institution that is an insurance corporation, that is non-segregated property within the meaning assigned by subsection 138(12)),

(b) in the case of an insurance corporation that was throughout the year not resident in Canada, the total of all amounts each of which is the carrying value at the end of the year of an asset of the financial institution that

    (i) is non-segregated property (within the meaning assigned by subsection 138(12)),

    (ii) is a share of the capital stock or long-term debt of another financial institution (other than an institution that is exempt from tax under this Part) that is related to the institution, and

    (iii) was used by it in the year in, or held by it in the year in the course of, carrying on an insurance business in Canada, and

(c) in any other case, nil,

and, for the purposes of this subsection, a credit union and another credit union of which the credit union is a shareholder or member shall be deemed to be related to each other.

### Proposed Amendment — 181.3(4), (5)

**(4) Investment allowance of financial institution** — The investment allowance for a taxation year of a corporation that is a financial institution is

(a) in the case of a corporation that was resident in Canada at any time in the year, the total of all amounts each of which is the carrying value at the end of the year of an eligible investment of the corporation;

(b) in the case of an insurance corporation that was throughout the year not resident in Canada, the total of all amounts each of which is the carrying value at the end of the year of an eligible investment of the corporation that was used or held by it in the year in the course of carrying on an insurance business in Canada;

(c) in the case of an authorized foreign bank, the total of all amounts each of which is the amount at the end of the year, before the application of risk weights, that the bank would be required to report under the OSFI risk-weighting guidelines if those guidelines applied and required a report at that time, of an eligible investment used or held by the bank in the year in the course of carrying on its Canadian banking business; and

(d) in any other case, nil.

**Technical Notes:** Subsection 181.3(4) of the Act defines the investment allowance of a financial institution for a taxation year for the purposes of Part I.3. Paragraphs (4)(a) and (b) are amended to refer to an "eligible investment", a term defined in new subsection 181.3(5), which incorporates conditions previously contained in the text of these paragraphs, as well as a new residency condition.

New paragraph 181.3(4)(c) defines the investment allowance of an authorized foreign bank. Like other financial institutions, an authorized foreign bank's taxable capital for a taxation year is the amount, if any, by which its capital for the year exceeds its investment allowance for the year. Its investment allowance for a taxation year is essentially the full (i.e. not risk-weighted) year-end amount of its "eligible investments" used or held in its Canada banking business as those would be required to be reported under the OSFI risk-weighting guidelines (defined in subsection 248(1)) if the guidelines were applicable.

This amendment applies after June 27, 1999.

**(5) Interpretation** — For the purpose of subsection (4),

(a) an **eligible investment** of a corporation is a share of the capital stock or long-term debt (and, where the corporation is an insurance corporation, is non-segregated property within the meaning assigned by subsection 138(12)) of a financial institution that at the end of the year

    (i) is related to the corporation,

    (ii) is not exempt from tax under this Part, and

    (iii) is resident in Canada or can reasonably be regarded as using the proceeds of the share or debt in a business carried on by the institution through a permanent establishment (as defined by regulation) in Canada; and

(b) a credit union and another credit union of which the credit union is a shareholder or member are deemed to be related to each other.

**Technical Notes:** Amended subsection 181.3(5) of the Act defines an "eligible investment" of a financial institution for the purpose of determining its investment allowance under subsection 181.3(4) of the Act. The main conditions, previously set out directly in subsection 181.3(4), are that the investment be a share or long-term debt of a related financial institution that is not exempt from tax. A new requirement is introduced that the investee corporation be either resident in Canada or use the proceeds of the share or debt in a business carried on through a permanent establishment in Canada. It is proposed that the definition of permanent establishment for this purpose be that set out in section 8201 of the *Income Tax Regulations*. New paragraph 181.3(5)(b) sets out an interpretive rule relating to credit unions that was previously contained in subsection 181.3(4) of the Act.

New subsection 181.3(5) generally applies after June 27, 1999 except that the coming-into-force of the requirement in subparagraph (5)(a)(iii) is deferred for taxpayers other than authorized foreign banks until the 2002 taxation year.

**Application:** The August 8, 2000 draft legislation, subsec. 16(5), will amend subsec. 181.3(4) to read as above, and add subsec. (5), applicable after June 27, 1999, except that in its application to taxpayers other than authorized foreign banks for taxation years that end before 2002, paragraph 181.3(5)(a) shall be read without reference to subpara. (iii) thereof.

**Regulations:** 8201 (meaning of "permanent establishment" for 181.3(5)(a)(iii)).

**Related Provisions:** 181(4) — Limitations respecting inclusions and deductions; 181.3(5) — Meaning of "eligible investment"; 181.5(6) — Whether corporations related.

**Notes**: 181.3(4)(a) and (b)(ii) amended by 1991 technical bill, retroactive to the introduction of the tax (taxation years ending after June 1989), to include the words in parentheses dealing with a related financial institution that is exempt from Part I.3 tax.

181.3(4)(e), which provided a rule deeming deposit insurance corporations to be related to their member institution, repealed by 1991 technical bill, also retroactive to the introduction of the tax. A deposit insurance corporation is no longer a financial institution or subject to Part I.3 tax.

**Definitions [s. 181.3]**: "amount" — 181(3), 248(1); "attributed surplus" — 181(2), Reg. 2405(3), 8602; "authorized foreign bank", "bank", "business" — 248(1); "Canada" — 255, *Interpretation Act* 35(1); "Canadian assets" — 181(2), Reg. 8602; "Canadian banking business" — 248(1); "Canadian premiums", "Canadian reserve liabilities" — 181(2), Reg. 8602; "carrying on business in Canada" — 253; "carrying value" — 181(2); "corporation" — 248(1), *Interpretation Act* 35(1); "credit union" — 137(6), 248(1); "eligible investment" — 181.3(5); "financial institution" — 181(1); "fiscal period" — 249, 249.1; "insurance corporation", "life insurance business" — 248(1); "long-term debt" — 181(1); "OSFI risk-weighting guidelines" — 248(1); "permanent establishment" — Reg. 8201; "property", "regulation" — 248(1); "related" — 181.3(4), 181.3(5)(b), 181.5(6), (7), 251(2); "reserves" — 181(1); "resident in Canada" — 250; "share", "shareholder", "subsidiary wholly-owned corporation" — 248(1); "taxation year" — 249; "total assets", "total premiums", "total reserve liabilities" — 181(2), Reg. 8602.

**Interpretation Bulletins [s. 181.3]**: IT-532: Part I.3 — tax on large corporations.

## 181.4 Taxable capital employed in Canada of non-resident
— The taxable capital employed in Canada for a taxation year of a corporation (other than a financial institution) that was throughout the year not resident in Canada is the amount, if any, by which

(a) the total of all amounts each of which is the carrying value at the end of the year of an asset of the corporation used by it in the year in, or held by it in the year in the course of, carrying on any business carried on by it during the year through a permanent establishment in Canada

exceeds the total of

(b) the amount of the corporation's indebtedness at the end of the year (other than indebtedness described in any of paragraphs 181.2(3)(c) to (f)) that may reasonably be regarded as relating to a business carried on by it during the year through a permanent establishment in Canada,

(c) the total of all amounts each of which is the carrying value at the end of the year of an asset described in subsection 181.2(4) of the corporation that was used by it in the year in, or held by it in the year in the course of, carrying on any business carried on by it during the year through a permanent establishment in Canada, and

(d) the total of all amounts each of which is the carrying value at the end of the year of an asset of the corporation that

(i) is a ship or aircraft operated by the corporation in international traffic or is personal property used in its business of transporting passengers or goods by ship or aircraft in international traffic, and

(ii) was used by the corporation in the year in, or held by it in the year in the course of, carrying on any business during the year through a permanent establishment in Canada,

if the country in which the corporation is resident imposed neither a capital tax for the year on similar assets nor a tax for the year on the income from the operation of a ship or aircraft in international traffic, of any corporation resident in Canada during the year.

**Notes**: 181.4(d)(i) amended by 1995-97 technical bill, effective for 1995 and later taxation years, to add "by ship or aircraft".

181.4(d) added by 1991 technical bill, retroactive to the introduction of the tax (taxation years ending after June 1989).

**Definitions [s. 181.4]**: "amount" — 181(3), 248(1); "business" — 248(1); "Canada" — 255; "carrying on business in Canada" — 253; "carrying value" — 181(2); "corporation" — 248(1), *Interpretation Act* 35(1); "financial institution" — 181(1); "international traffic" — 248(1); "permanent establishment" — 181(2), Reg. 8602; "resident in Canada" — 250.

**Interpretation Bulletins [s. 181.4]**: IT-532: Part I.3 — tax on large corporations.

## 181.5 (1) Capital deduction
— The capital deduction of a corporation for a taxation year is $10,000,000 unless the corporation was related to another corporation at any time in the year, in which case, subject to subsection (4), its capital deduction for the year is nil.

**(2) Related corporations** — A corporation that is related to any other corporation at any time in a taxation year of the corporation ending in a calendar year may file with the Minister in prescribed form an agreement on behalf of the related group of which the corporation is a member under which an amount that does not exceed $10,000,000 is allocated among all corporations that are members of the related group for each taxation year of each such corporation ending in the calendar year and at a time when it was a member of the related group.

**Related Provisions**: 181.5(4) — Amount allocated; 181.5(6) — Corporations deemed not related.

**Forms**: T2 SCH 36: Agreement among related corporations — Part I.3 tax.

**(3) Idem** — The Minister may request a corporation that is related to any other corporation at the end of a taxation year to file with the Minister an agreement referred to in subsection (2) and, if the corporation does not file such an agreement within 30 days after receiving the request, the Minister may allocate an amount among the members of the related group of which the corporation is a member for the year not exceeding $10,000,000.

**(4) Idem** — The least amount allocated for a taxation year to a member of a related group under an agreement described in subsection (2) or by the Minister pursuant to subsection (3) is the capital deduction of that member for that taxation year.

**(5) Idem** — Where a corporation (in this subsection referred to as the "first corporation") has more than one taxation year ending in the same calendar year and is related in 2 or more of those taxation years to another corporation that has a taxation year ending in that calendar year, the capital deduction of the first corporation for each such taxation year at the end of which it is related to the other corporation is an amount equal to its capital deduction for the first such taxation year.

**(6) Idem** — Two corporations that would, but for this subsection, be related to each other by reason only of

(a) the control of any corporation by Her Majesty in right of Canada or a province, or

(b) a right referred to in paragraph 251(5)(b),

are, for the purposes of this section and subsection 181.3(4), deemed not to be related to each other except that, where at any time a taxpayer has a right referred to in paragraph 251(5)(b) with respect to shares and it can reasonably be considered that one of the main purposes for the acquisition of the right was to avoid any limitation on the amount of a corporation's capital deduction for a taxation year, for the purpose of determining whether a corporation is related to any other corporation, the corporations are, for the purposes of this section, deemed to be in the same position in relation to each other as if the right were immediate and absolute and as if the taxpayer had exercised the right at that time.

**Related Provisions**: 256(6), (6.1) — Meaning of "control".

**Notes**: Closing words of 181.5(6) amended by 1995-97 technical bill, effective April 27, 1995, to add the words "as if the right were immediate and absolute and" near the end.

**(7) Related corporations that are not associated** — For the purposes of subsection 181.3(4) and this section, a Canadian-controlled private corporation and another corporation to which it would, but for this subsection, be related at any time shall be deemed not to be related to each other at that time where the corporations are not associated with each other at that time.

**Notes**: 181.5(7) added by 1991 technical bill, effective 1991. It also applies to a corporation's 1989 and 1990 taxation years, if it so elects by notifying Revenue Canada in writing (and, where applicable, by filing in prescribed form a revised agreement under 181.5(2)) by December 10, 1993 (deadline extended by 1992 technical bill, s. 159).

**Definitions [s. 181.5]**: "amount" — 181(3), 248(1); "calendar year" — *Interpretation Act* 37(1)(a); "control" — 256(6), (6.1); "corporation" — 248(1), *Interpretation Act* 35(1); "Minister" — 248(1); "province" — *Interpretation Act* 35(1); "related" — 181.5(6), (7), 251(2); "related group" — 251(4); "share" — 248(1); "taxation year" — 249.

**Interpretation Bulletins [s. 181.5]**: IT-532: Part I.3 — tax on large corporations.

**181.6 Return** — Every corporation that is or would, but for subsection 181.1(4), be liable to pay tax under this Part for a taxation year shall file with the Minister, not later than the day on or before which the corporation is required by section 150 to file its return of income for the year under Part I, a return of capital for the year in prescribed form containing an estimate of the tax payable under this Part by it for the year.

**Related Provisions**: 150.1(5) — Electronic filing; 235 — Penalty for failure to file return even where no balance owing.

**Notes**: 181.6 amended by 1992 technical bill, effective for 1992 and later taxation years, to add "or would, but for subsection 181.1(4), be". In other words, a return must still be filed even if no Part I.3 tax is payable because it is fully credited against surtax.

**Definitions [s. 181.6]**: "corporation" — 248(1), *Interpretation Act* 35(1); "Minister" — 248(1); "taxation year" — 249.

**Forms**: T2 SCH 33: Part I.3 tax on large corporations; T2 SCH 34: Part I.3 tax on financial institutions; T2 SCH 35: Part I.3 tax on large insurance corporations; T2 SCH 342: Nova Scotia tax on large corporations; T2 SCH 343: Nova Scotia tax on large corporations — agreement among related corporations; T2 SCH 37: Calculation of unused Part I.3 tax credit and unused surtax credit; T2 SCH 361: New Brunswick tax on large corporations; T2 SCH 362: New Brunswick tax on large corporations — agreement among related corporations.

**181.7 Provisions applicable to Part** — Sections 152, 158 and 159, subsection 161(11), sections 162 to 167 and Division J of Part I apply to this Part with such modifications as the circumstances require and, for the purpose of this section, paragraph 152(6)(a) shall be read as follows:

"(a) a deduction under section 181.1(4) in respect of any unused surtax credit (within the meaning assigned by subsection 181.1(6)) for a subsequent taxation year,"

**Related Provisions**: 157(1), (2), (2.1) — Instalment and payment obligations; 161(1), (4.1) — Interest.

**Notes**: 181.7 enacted to replace 181.7, 181.8 and 181.9 by 1992 technical bill, effective for 1992 and later taxation years. The former 181.7 and 181.8 dealt specifically with payment of tax, payment of instalments, and interest; while 181.9 caused various other provisions of the Act to apply, as 181.7 does now.

Former 181.7(1) added by 1989 Budget and amended by 1991 technical bill. An election re when to pay the final balance, in former 181.7(1)(b), could be made by notifying Revenue Canada in writing by December 10, 1993 (deadline extended by 1992 technical bill, s. 159).

For taxation years commencing before 1990, 181.7(1) read differently.

1989 Budget and 1991 technical bill provide a transitional rule, prorating the instalment base around July 1, 1989.

Part I.3 (181 to 181.9) added by 1989 Budget, effective for taxation years that end after June 1989, and 181.8(3) amended by 1991 technical bill, effective for taxation years that begin after 1989.

**Interpretation Bulletins [s. 181.7]**: IT-532: Part I.3 — tax on large corporations.

**181.71 Provisions applicable — Crown corporations** — Section 27 applies to this Part with any modifications that the circumstances require.

S. 181.71　　　　　　　　　　Income Tax Act

**Notes**: 181.71 added by 1995-97 technical bill, effective for taxation years that end after June 1989. It confirms that a prescribed federal Crown corporation is liable to tax under Part I.3. Specifically, it provides that s. 27 applies to Part I.3 with whatever modifications may be necessary. The main effects of s. 27 are to treat income and property of Her Majesty that is administered by a Crown corporation that is an agent of Her Majesty as though they were the corporation's own, and to provide that the exemption in 149(1)(d) does not apply.

**Interpretation Bulletins [s. 181.71]**: IT-532: Part I.3 — tax on large corporations.

## PART II — TOBACCO MANUFACTURERS' SURTAX

**182. (1) Surtax** — Every corporation shall pay a tax under this Part for each taxation year equal to 40% of the corporation's Part I tax on tobacco manufacturing profits for the year.

**Related Provisions**: 183 — Return and payment of tax.

**Notes**: 182(1) amended by 2000 GST bill, effective for taxation years that end after February 8, 2000, to extend the surtax indefinitely beyond that date (as announced by Dept of Finance news release, November 5, 1999). 182(1) previously read:

(1) Surtax — Every corporation shall pay a tax under this Part for each taxation year equal to 40% of that proportion of the corporation's Part I tax on tobacco manufacturing profits for the year that

(a) the number of days in the year that are after February 8, 1994 and before February 9, 2000

is of

(b) the number of days in the year.

182(1)(a) amended by 1997 Budget (first bill) to change "1997" to "2000". This extended the tobacco manufacturers' surtax by 3 years, as announced by the Department of Finance on November 28, 1996. See also Notes at end of 183.

**(2) Definitions** — In this Part,

**"Part I tax on tobacco manufacturing profits"** of a corporation for a taxation year means 21% of the amount determined by the formula

$$\left(\frac{A \times B}{C}\right) - D$$

where

A is the amount that would be the corporation's Canadian manufacturing and processing profits for the year, within the meaning assigned by subsection 125.1(3), if the total of all amounts, each of which is the corporation's loss for the year from an active business, other than tobacco manufacturing, carried on by it in Canada, were equal to the lesser of

(a) that total otherwise determined, and

(b) the total of all amounts, each of which is the amount of the corporation's income for the year from an active business, other than tobacco manufacturing, carried on by it in Canada.

B is the corporation's tobacco manufacturing capital and labour cost for the year,

C is the total of the corporation's cost of manufacturing and processing capital for the year and its cost of manufacturing and processing labour for the year, within the meanings assigned by regulations made for the purposes of section 125.1, and

D is

(a) where the corporation is a Canadian-controlled private corporation throughout the year, the corporation's business limit for the year as determined for the purpose of section 125, and

(b) in any other case, nil;

**Related Provisions**: 257 — Formula cannot calculate to less than zero.

**Regulations**: 5202, 5204 (cost of manufacturing and processing capital, cost of manufacturing and processing labour).

**"tobacco manufacturing"** means any activity (other than farming) relating to the manufacture or processing in Canada of tobacco or tobacco products in or into any form that is, or would after any further activity become, suitable for smoking;

**"tobacco manufacturing capital and labour cost"** of a corporation for a taxation year means the total of the amounts that would be the corporation's cost of manufacturing and processing capital for the year and its cost of manufacturing and processing labour for the year, within the meanings assigned by regulations made for the purpose of section 125.1, if the manufacturing or processing referred to in the definition "qualified activities" in those regulations were tobacco manufacturing.

**Regulations**: 5202, 5204 (cost of manufacturing and processing capital, cost of manufacturing and processing labour).

**Notes [s. 182]**: See at end of 183.

**Definitions [s. 182]**: "active business", "amount" — 248(1); "business limit" — 125(2)–(5); "Canada" — 255; "Canadian-controlled private corporation" — 125(7), 248(1); "carried on in Canada" — 253; "corporation" — 248(1), *Interpretation Act* 35(1); "farming" — 248(1); "Part I tax on tobacco manufacturing profits" — 182(2); "taxation year" — 249; "tobacco manufacturing", "tobacco manufacturing capital and labour cost" — 182(2).

**183. (1) Return** — Every corporation that is liable to pay tax under this Part for a taxation year shall file with the Minister a return for the year in prescribed form not later than the day on or before which the corporation is required by section 150 to file its return of income for the year under Part I.

**Related Provisions**: 150(1)(a) — Deadline for Part I return; 150.1(5) — Electronic filing.

**Forms**: T2 SCH 46: Part II — tobacco manufacturers' surtax.

**(2) Payment** — Every corporation shall pay to the Receiver General on or before its balance-due day for each taxation year its tax payable under this Part for the year.

**Notes**: 182(1) amended by 2000 GST bill, effective for taxation years that end after February 8, 2000. For earlier taxation years read:

> **(2) Payment** — Every corporation shall pay to the Receiver General on or before the later of June 30, 1994 and the last day of the second month after the end of each taxation year its tax payable under this Part for the year.

**(3) Provisions applicable** — Subsections 150(2) and (3), sections 151, 152, 158 and 159, subsections 161(1) and (11), sections 162 to 167 and Division J of Part I apply to this Part with such modifications as the circumstances require.

**Definitions [s. 183]**: "balance-due day" — 248(1); "corporation" — 248(1), *Interpretation Act* 35(1); "Minister", "prescribed" — 248(1); "prescribed rate" — Reg. 4301; "taxation year" — 249.

**Notes [Part II]**: Part II added by 1994 tobacco tax reduction bill, effective for taxation years that end after February 8, 1994.

The surtax is designed to offset a portion of the revenues given up due to drastic reductions in excise taxes and duties on tobacco products. Those reductions came in response to extensive tobacco smuggling.

Former Part II (181, 182) repealed in 1986. From 1982 to 1986, Part II imposed a tax on a corporation that paid dividends out of income subject to the small business deduction, in order to bring the effective tax rate up from 25% to 33.33% (including provincial tax).

Before 1978, a different Part II (181–183) imposed a tax when a corporation redeemed or acquired certain of its shares at a premium.

# PART II.1 — TAX ON CORPORATE DISTRIBUTIONS

**183.1 (1) Application of Part** — This Part applies to a corporation (other than a mutual fund corporation) for a taxation year in which the corporation, at any time in the year,

(a) was a public corporation; or

(b) was resident in Canada and had a class of shares outstanding that were purchased and sold in the manner in which such shares normally are purchased and sold by any member of the public in the open market.

**(2) Tax payable** — Where, as a part of a transaction or series of transactions or events,

(a) a corporation, or any person with whom the corporation was not dealing at arm's length, has, at any time, paid an amount, directly or indirectly, to any person as proceeds of disposition of any property, and

(b) all or any portion of the amount may reasonably be considered, having regard to all the circumstances, to have been paid as a substitute for dividends that would otherwise have been paid in the normal course by the corporation,

the corporation shall, on or before the day on or before which it is required to file its return of income under Part I for its taxation year that includes that time, pay a tax of 45% of that amount or portion thereof, as the case may be.

**Related Provisions**: 248(10) — Series of transactions.

**(3) Stock dividend** — Where, as a part of a transaction or series of transactions or events,

(a) a share was issued by a corporation as a stock dividend and the amount of the stock dividend was less than the fair market value of the share at the time that it was issued, and

(b) the share or any other share of the capital stock of the corporation was purchased, directly or indirectly, by the corporation, or by a person with whom the corporation was not dealing at arm's length, for an amount in excess of its paid-up capital,

that excess shall, for the purposes of subsection (2), be deemed to have been paid as a substitute for dividends that would otherwise have been paid in the normal course by the corporation.

**(4) Purchase of shares** — Where, as a part of a transaction or series of transactions or events,

(a) a share of the capital stock of a corporation was purchased, directly or indirectly, by the corporation, or any person with whom the corporation was not dealing at arm's length, and

(b) any portion of the amount paid for the share may reasonably be considered, having regard to all the circumstances, as consideration for a dividend that had been declared, but not yet paid, on the share,

that portion of the amount shall, for the purposes of subsection (2), be deemed to have been paid as a substitute for dividends that would otherwise have been paid in the normal course by the corporation notwithstanding that the dividend was actually paid thereafter.

**(5) Indirect payment** — Where, as a part of a transaction or series of transactions or events, a person received a payment from a corporation, or from any person with whom the corporation was not dealing at arm's length, in consideration, in whole or in part, for paying an amount to any other person as proceeds of disposition of any property, the corporation shall, for the purposes of subsection (2), be deemed to have paid the amount indirectly to the other person.

**(6) Where subsec. (2) does not apply** — Subsection (2) does not apply if none of the purposes of the transaction or series of transactions or events referred to therein may reasonably be considered, having regard to all the circumstances, to have been to enable shareholders of a corporation who are individuals or non-resident persons to receive an amount, directly or indirectly, as proceeds of disposition of property rather than as a dividend on a share that was of a class that was listed on a stock exchange or that was purchased and sold in the manner in which shares are normally purchased and sold by any member of the public in the open market.

## S. 183.1(7)      Income Tax Act

**(7) Where subsec. 110.6(8) does not apply** — Where this section has been applied in respect of an amount, subsection 110.6(8) does not apply to the capital gain in respect of which the amount formed all or a part of the proceeds of disposition.

**Definitions [s. 183.1]**: "adjusted cost base" — 54, 248(1); "amount" — 248(1); "arm's length" — 251(1); "Canada" — 255; "capital gain" — 39(1)(a), 248(1); "class of shares" — 248(6); "corporation" — 248(1), *Interpretation Act* 35(1); "dividend", "employee", "individual" — 248(1); "mutual fund corporation" — 131(8), 248(1); "non-resident" — 248(1); "paid-up capital" — 89(1), 248(1); "person", "prescribed", "property" — 248(1); "public corporation" — 89(1), 248(1); "resident in Canada" — 250; "series of transactions or events" — 248(10); "share", "shareholder" — 248(1); "substituted property" — 248(5); "taxation year" — 249.

**183.2 (1) Return** — Every corporation liable to pay tax under this Part for a taxation year shall, on or before the day on or before which it is required to file its return of income under Part I for the year, file with the Minister a return for the year under this Part in prescribed form.

**Related Provisions**: 150.1(5) — Electronic filing.

**Forms**: T2141: Part II.1 tax return — tax on corporate distributions.

**(2) Provisions applicable to Part** — Subsections 150(2) and (3), sections 152, 158 and 159, subsections 160.1(1) and 161(1) and (11), sections 162 to 167 and Division J of Part I are applicable to this Part with such modifications as the circumstances require.

**Definitions [s. 183.2]**: "corporation" — 248(1), *Interpretation Act* 35(1); "Minister", "prescribed" — 248(1); "taxation year" — 249.

## PART III — ADDITIONAL TAX ON EXCESSIVE ELECTIONS

**184. (1)** [Repealed under former Act]

**Notes**: 184(1), repealed as of 1979, imposed a tax on excessive elections under former 83(1), which provided an election for a dividend to be deemed paid out of "tax-paid undistributed surplus" or "1971 capital surplus on hand".

**(2) Tax on excessive elections** — Where a corporation has elected in accordance with subsection 83(2), 130.1(4) or 131(1) in respect of the full amount of any dividend payable by it on shares of any class of its capital stock and the full amount of the dividend exceeds the portion thereof deemed by that subsection to be a capital dividend or capital gains dividend, as the case may be, the corporation shall, at the time of the election, pay a tax under this Part equal to $3/4$ of the excess.

**Related Provisions**: 18(1)(t) — Tax is non-deductible; 87(2)(z.2) — Amalgamation — continuing corporation; 184(3) — Election to treat excess as separate dividend.

**Interpretation Bulletins**: IT-66R6: Capital dividends.

**(2.1) Reduction of excess** — Notwithstanding subsection (2), where a corporation has elected in accordance with subsection 83(2) in respect of the full amount of a dividend that became payable by it at a particular time in its 1988 taxation year and before June 18, 1987, the amount of the excess referred to in subsection (2) in respect of the dividend shall be deemed, for the purposes of subsection (2), to be the amount of the excess that would have been determined under subsection (2) in respect of the dividend if the corporation's taxation year had ended on December 31, 1987.

**Interpretation Bulletins**: IT-66R6: Capital dividends.

**(3) Election to treat excess as separate dividend** — Where, in respect of a dividend payable at a particular time after 1971, a corporation would, but for this subsection, be required to pay a tax under this Part equal to all or a portion of an excess referred to in subsection (2) of this section or subsection 184(1) of the *Income Tax Act*, chapter 148 of the Revised Statutes of Canada, 1952, it may elect in prescribed manner on or before a day that is not later than 90 days after the day that is the later of December 15, 1977 and the day of mailing of the notice of assessment in respect of the tax that would otherwise be payable under this Part, and on such an election being made, subject to subsection (4), the following rules apply:

(a) the amount by which the full amount of the dividend exceeds the amount of the excess shall be deemed for the purposes of the election that the corporation made in respect of the dividend under subsection 83(2), 130.1(4) or 131(1) of this Act or subsection 83(1) of the *Income Tax Act*, chapter 148 of the Revised Statutes of Canada, 1952, and for all other purposes of this Act to be the full amount of a separate dividend that became payable at the particular time;

(b) such part of the excess as the corporation may claim shall, for the purposes of any election in respect thereof under subsection 83(2), 130.1(4) or 131(1) of this Act or subsection 83(1) of the *Income Tax Act*, chapter 148 of the Revised Statutes of Canada, 1952, and, where the corporation has so elected, for all purposes of this Act, be deemed to be the full amount of a separate dividend that became payable immediately after the particular time;

(c) the amount by which the excess exceeds any portion deemed by paragraph (b) to be a separate dividend for all purposes of this Act shall be deemed to be a separate dividend that is a taxable dividend that became payable at the particular time; and

(d) each person who held any of the issued shares of the class of shares of the capital stock of the corporation in respect of which the full amount of the dividend was paid shall be deemed

(i) not to have received any portion of the dividend, and

(ii) to have received at the time the dividend was paid the proportion of any separate dividend, determined under paragraph (a), (b) or (c), that the number of shares of that class held by the person at the time the dividend was paid is of the number of shares of that class outstanding at that time except that, for the purpose of Part XIII, a separate dividend that is a taxable dividend, a capital dividend or a life insurance capital dividend shall be deemed to have been paid on the day that the election in respect of this subsection is made.

**Related Provisions**: 184(4) — Concurrence with election; 220(3.2), Reg. 600(b) — Late filing of election or revocation.

**Notes**: A dividend must all qualify (i.e., the "capital dividend account" in 89(1) must be high enough) to be a capital dividend. Where it does not (typically due to a miscalculation of the CDA), 183(3) allows the two parts to be split into separate dividends, provided the requirements of Reg. 2106 are followed.

**Regulations**: 2106 (prescribed manner).

**I.T. Application Rules**: 69 (meaning of "*Income Tax Act*, chapter 148 of the Revised Statutes of Canada, 1952").

**Interpretation Bulletins**: IT-66R6: Capital dividends.

**Information Circulars**: 92-1: Guidelines for accepting late, amended or revoked elections.

**(3.1) Election to treat dividend as loan** — Where a corporation has elected in accordance with subsection 83(1) of the *Income Tax Act*, chapter 148 of the Revised Statutes of Canada, 1952, in respect of the full amount of any dividend that became payable by it at a particular time after March 31, 1977 and before 1979 and the corporation made a reasonable attempt to correctly determine its tax-paid undistributed surplus on hand immediately before the particular time and its 1971 capital surplus on hand immediately before the particular time and all or any portion of the dividend

(a) has given rise to a gain from the disposition of a share of the corporation by virtue of subsection 40(3), or

(b) is an excess referred to in subsection 184(1) of the *Income Tax Act*, chapter 148 of the Revised Statutes of Canada, 1952,

if the corporation so elects under this subsection,

(c) in any case referred to in paragraph (a), not later than December 31, 1982 or such earlier day as is 90 days after the latest of

(i) February 26, 1981,

(ii) the day on which a notice of assessment or reassessment is mailed to a shareholder of the corporation in respect of a gain referred to in paragraph (a), and

(iii) such day as is agreed to by the Minister in writing, or

(d) in any other case, not later than 90 days after the later of

(i) February 26, 1981, and

(ii) the day on which the Minister notifies the corporation by registered letter that it has an excess referred to in subsection 184(1) of the *Income Tax Act*, chapter 148 of the Revised Statutes of Canada, 1952, in respect of the dividend,

and the penalty referred to in subsection (5) in respect of the election is paid by the corporation at the time the election is made, the following rules apply:

(e) the whole dividend or such portion of it as the corporation may claim shall, for the purposes of this Act, be deemed not to be a dividend but to be a loan made at the particular time by the corporation to the persons who received all or any portion of the dividend if the full amount of the loan is repaid to the corporation before such date as is stipulated by the Minister and the corporation satisfies such terms and conditions as are specified by the Minister, and

(f) sections 15 and 80.4 do not apply to such a loan.

**Related Provisions**: 248(7)(a) — Mail deemed received on day mailed.

**I.T. Application Rules**: 69 (meaning of "*Income Tax Act*, chapter 148 of the Revised Statutes of Canada, 1952").

**Interpretation Bulletins**: IT-66R6: Capital dividends.

**(3.2) Idem** — Where a corporation has elected in accordance with subsection 83(2) in respect of the full amount of any dividend that became payable by it at a particular time after December 3, 1985 and before 1986 and the corporation made a reasonable attempt to correctly determine its capital dividend account immediately before the particular time and all or any portion of the dividend is an excess referred to in subsection (2), if

(a) the corporation so elects under this subsection not later than 90 days after the later of

(i) December 19, 1986, and

(ii) the day on which the Minister notifies the corporation by registered letter that it has an excess referred to in subsection (2) in respect of the dividend, and

(b) the penalty referred to in subsection (5) in respect of the election is paid by the corporation at the time the election under this subsection is made,

the following rules apply:

(c) the whole dividend or such portion of it as the corporation may claim shall, for the purposes of this Act, be deemed not to be a dividend but to be a loan made at the particular time by the corporation to the persons who received all or any portion of the dividend if the full amount of the loan is repaid to the corporation before such date as is stipulated by the Minister and the corporation satisfies such terms and conditions as are specified by the Minister, and

(d) sections 15 and 80.4 do not apply to such a loan.

**Related Provisions**: 248(7)(a) — Mail deemed received on day mailed.

**S. 184(3.2)** — Income Tax Act

**Interpretation Bulletins**: IT-66R6: Capital dividends.

**(4) Concurrence with election** — An election under subsection (3) is not valid unless

    (a) it is made with the concurrence of the corporation and all its shareholders

        (i) who received or were entitled to receive all or any portion of the dividend in respect of which a tax would, but for subsection (3), be payable under this Part, and

        (ii) whose addresses were known to the corporation; and

    (b) either

        (i) it is made on or before the day that is 30 months after the day on which the dividend became payable, or

        (ii) each shareholder described in subparagraph (a)(i) concurs with the election, in which case, notwithstanding subsections 152(4) to (5), such assessment of the tax, interest and penalties payable by each such shareholder for any taxation year may be made as is necessary to take the corporation's election into account.

**Related Provisions**: 185 — Assessment of tax.

**Notes**: 184(4)(b) added by 1991 technical bill, effective July 14, 1990.

**(5) Penalty** — The penalty in respect of an election under subsection (3.1) or (3.2) in relation to a particular dividend is an amount equal to the product obtained when $500 is multiplied by the proportion that the number of months or parts of months during the period commencing on the day the dividend became payable and ending on the day on which that election was made is of 12.

**Related Provisions**: 18(1)(t) — Penalty is non-deductible; 220(3.1) — Waiver of penalty by CCRA.

**Definitions [s. 184]**: "amount", "assessment" — 248(1); "capital dividend" — 83(2), 248(1); "class of shares" — 248(6); "corporation" — 248(1), *Interpretation Act* 35(1); "dividend", "life insurance capital dividend", "Minister", "person", "prescribed", "share", "shareholder" — 248(1); "taxable dividend" — 89(1), 248(1); "taxation year" — 249; "writing" — *Interpretation Act* 35(1).

**Interpretation Bulletins**: IT-66R6: Capital dividends.

**185. (1) Assessment of tax** — The Minister shall, with all due dispatch, examine each election made by a corporation in accordance with subsection 83(2), 130.1(4) or 131(1), assess the tax, if any, payable under this Part in respect of the election and send a notice of assessment to the corporation.

**Related Provisions**: 184 — Tax on excessive election; 227(14) — No application to corporation exempt under s. 149.

**(2) Payment of tax and interest** — Where an election has been made by a corporation in accordance with subsection 83(2), 130.1(4) or 131(1) and the Minister mails a notice of assessment under this Part in respect of the election, that part of the amount assessed then remaining unpaid and interest thereon at the prescribed rate computed from the day of the election to the day of payment is payable forthwith by the corporation to the Receiver General.

**Related Provisions**: 221.1 — Application of interest where legislation retroactive; 248(7) — Mail deemed received on day mailed; 248(11) — Interest compounded daily.

**Notes**: See Notes to s. 158.

**Regulations**: 4301(a) (prescribed rate of interest).

**(3) Provisions applicable to Part** — Subsections 152(3), (4), (5), (7) and (8) and 161(11), sections 163 to 167 and Division J of Part I are applicable to this Part with such modifications as the circumstances require.

**(4) Joint and several liability from excessive elections** — Each person who has received a dividend from a corporation in respect of which the corporation elected under subsection 83(2), 130.1(4) or 131(1) is jointly and severally liable with the corporation to pay that proportion of the corporation's tax payable under this Part because of the election that

    (a) the amount of the dividend received by the person

is of

    (b) the full amount of the dividend in respect of which the election was made,

but nothing in this subsection limits the liability of any person under any other provision of this Act.

**Related Provisions**: 185(5) — Assessment; 185(6) — Rules applicable.

**Notes**: 185(4) added by 1991 technical bill, effective for dividends paid after July 13, 1990.

**(5) Assessment** — The Minister may, at any time after the last day on which a corporation may make an election under subsection 184(3) in respect of a dividend, assess a person in respect of any amount payable under subsection (4) in respect of the dividend, and the provisions of Division I of Part I apply, with such modifications as the circumstances require, to an assessment made under this subsection as though it were made under section 152.

**Notes**: 185(5) added by 1991 technical bill, effective for dividends paid after July 13, 1990.

**(6) Rules applicable** — Where under subsection (4) a corporation and another person have become jointly and severally liable to pay part or all of the corporation's tax payable under this Part in respect of a dividend described in subsection (4),

    (a) a payment at any time by the other person on account of the liability shall, to the extent of the payment, discharge the joint liability after that time; and

    (b) a payment at any time by the corporation on account of its liability shall discharge the other person's liability only to the extent of the amount determined by the formula

$$(A - B) \times \frac{C}{D}$$

where

A is the total of

(i) the amount of the corporation's liability, immediately before that time, under this Part in respect of the full amount of the dividend, and

(ii) the amount of the payment,

B is the amount of the corporation's liability, immediately before that time, under this Act,

C is the amount of the dividend received by the other person, and

D is the full amount of the dividend.

**Related Provisions**: 257 — Formula cannot calculate to less than zero.

**Notes**: 185(6) added by 1991 technical bill, effective for dividends paid after July 13, 1990.

**Definitions [s. 185]**: "assessment" — 248(1); "corporation" — 248(1), *Interpretation Act* 35(1); "dividend", "Minister", "person", "prescribed" — 248(1); "prescribed rate" — Reg. 4301.

## PART IV — TAX ON TAXABLE DIVIDENDS RECEIVED BY PRIVATE CORPORATIONS

**186. (1) Tax on assessable dividends** — Every corporation (in this section referred to as the "particular corporation") that is at any time in a taxation year a private corporation or a subject corporation shall, on or before the last day of the third month after the end of the year, pay a tax under this Part for the year equal to the amount, if any, by which the total of

(a) $1/3$ of all assessable dividends received by the particular corporation in the year from corporations other than payer corporations connected with it, and

(b) all amounts, each of which is an amount in respect of an assessable dividend received by the particular corporation in the year from a private corporation or a subject corporation that was a payer corporation connected with the particular corporation, equal to that proportion of the payer corporation's dividend refund (within the meaning assigned by paragraph 129(1)(a)) for its taxation year in which it paid the dividend that

(i) the amount of the dividend received by the particular corporation

is of

(ii) the total of all taxable dividends paid by the payer corporation in its taxation year in which it paid the dividend and at a time when it was a private corporation or a subject corporation

exceeds $1/3$ of the total of

(c) such part of the particular corporation's non-capital loss and farm loss for the year as it claims, and

(d) such part of the particular corporation's

(i) non-capital loss for any of its 7 taxation years immediately preceding or 3 taxation years immediately following the year, and

(ii) farm loss for any of its 10 taxation years immediately preceding or 3 taxation years immediately following the year

as it claims, not exceeding the portion thereof that would have been deductible under section 111 in computing its taxable income for the year if subparagraph 111(3)(a)(ii) were read without reference to the words "the particular taxation year and" and if the corporation had sufficient income for the year.

**Related Provisions**: 15.1(1), 15.2(1) — Interest on small business development bond or small business bond not a dividend for Part IV tax; 18(1)(t) — Part IV tax is non-deductible; 87(2.11) — Losses, etc., on amalgamation with subsidiary wholly-owned corporation; 88(1.1) — Non-capital losses, etc., of subsidiary; 88(1.3) — Computation of income and tax of parent; 129(1) — Part IV tax is refundable; 129(3)(b) — "Refundable dividend tax on hand"; 131(5) — Dividend refund to mutual fund corporation; 186(6) — Partnerships; 186.1 — Exempt corporations; 186.2 — Exempt dividends; 227(14) — No tax on corporation exempt under s. 149; 227(16) — Municipal or provincial corporation excepted.

**Notes**: The Part IV tax is refundable to private corporations under 129(1), once the corporation pays out sufficient dividends. The amount of Part IV tax paid goes into "refundable dividend tax on hand" (RDTOH) under 129(3). Under 129(1)(a), the RDTOH is fully refunded if 3 times the RDTOH is paid out as taxable dividends. (The Part IV tax is 33.33%; if it is $33.33 on $100, then by paying out $100 in dividends — the $66.67 left after Part IV tax and the $33.33 to be refunded — the $33.33 can be recovered, or simply not remitted.)

Part IV tax is imposed on two kinds of dividends: (a) portfolio dividends (that is, dividends from corporations not "connected" with the recipient corporation, as defined in 186(4)); and (b) dividends that entitle the payer corporation to a dividend refund under 129(1). That dividend refund arises if the payer corporation has an RDTOH balance. The RDTOH arises under 129(3) from Part IV tax paid and from $26^{2}/_{3}$% (see Notes to 129(1)) of a corporation's investment income (thus reducing the corporate tax on investment income that is flowed out to a shareholder to a rate that achieves integration; see 82(1) and 121).

186(1) amended by 1995 Budget, effective for taxation years that end after June 1995, except that, in applying it to any such taxation year that begins before July 1995,

(a) in applying 186(1) to amounts described in 186(1)(a) and (b) that were received by the corporation in the year and before July 1995, the references to "$1/3$" shall be read as "$1/4$";

(b) amounts deducted by the corporation for the year under 186(1)(c) and (d)

(i) are deemed to have been deducted in respect of amounts described in 186(1)(a) and (b) that were received by the corporation in the year and after June 1995, and

(ii) to the extent that the amounts so deducted exceed the amounts referred to in subparagraph (i), are deemed to have been deducted in respect of amounts described in 186(1)(a) and (b) that were received by the corporation in the year and before July 1995.

The transitional rule ensures that the former 25% tax rate applies to dividends received from unconnected corporations before July 1995, and that losses applied against the Part IV base are used first to offset post-June 1995 dividends, which are subject to tax at the higher rate.

## S. 186(1)  Income Tax Act

For earlier taxation years, read:

**(1) Tax on certain taxable dividends** — Every corporation (in this section referred to as the "particular corporation") that was, at any time in a taxation year, a private corporation) resident in Canada and controlled, whether by reason of a beneficial interest in one or more trusts or otherwise, by or for the benefit of an individual (other than a trust) or a related group of individuals (other than trusts) (in this Part referred to as a "subject corporation") or a private corporation shall, on or before the last day of the third month after the end of the year, pay a tax under this Part for the year equal to ¼ of the amount, if any, by which the total of

(a) all amounts received by the particular corporation in the year and at a time when it was a subject corporation or a private corporation as, on account of, in lieu of payment of or in satisfaction of, taxable dividends from corporations (other than payer corporations connected with it),

    (i) that are deductible under subsection 112(1) from its income for the year, or

    (ii) to the extent of the amounts in respect of those dividends that are deductible under paragraph 113(1)(a), (b) or (d) or subsection 113(2) from its income for the year, and

(b) all amounts, each of which is an amount in respect of a taxable dividend, in respect of which an amount is deductible under subsection 112(1) in computing its taxable income for the year, received by the particular corporation in the year and at a time when it was a subject corporation or a private corporation from a subject corporation or a private corporation that was a payer corporation connected with the particular corporation equal to that proportion of

    (i) 4 times the dividend refund of the payer corporation for its taxation year in which it paid the dividend

that

    (ii) the amount in respect of the dividend so received by the particular corporation

is of

    (iii) the total of all taxable dividends paid by the payer corporation in its taxation year in which it paid the dividend and at a time when it was a subject corporation or a private corporation,

(b.1) [Repealed under former Act]

exceeds the total of

(c) such part of the particular corporation's non-capital loss and such part of its farm loss for the year as it may claim, and

(d) such part of the particular corporation's

    (i) non-capital loss for a taxation year that is any of the 7 taxation years immediately preceding or the 3 taxation years immediately following the year, and

    (ii) farm loss for a taxation year that is any of the 10 taxation years immediately preceding or the 3 taxation years immediately following the year

as it may claim, not exceeding the portion thereof that would have been deductible under section 111 in computing the corporation's taxable income for the year if subparagraph 111(3)(a)(ii) were read without reference to the words "the particular taxation year and" and if the corporation had sufficient income for the year.

Opening words of 186(1)(a), and 186(1)(b)(iii), amended by 1992 technical bill, effective for dividends received and paid in 1993 or later, to add "at a time when it was a subject corporation or a private corporation". (The dividend refund was formerly built into the opening words of 129(1). See Notes to 129(1).)

Opening words of 186(1)(b) similarly amended by 1992 technical bill. For dividends received before 1993, instead of "and at a time when it was a subject corporation or a private corporation that was a payer corporation", read "from a corporation (in this section referred to as the "payer corporation")".

**Interpretation Bulletins:** IT-232R3: Losses — their deductibility in the loss year or in other years; IT-269R3: Part IV tax on taxable dividends received by a private corporation or a subject corporation; IT-328R3: Losses on shares on which dividends have been received.

**Information Circulars:** 88-2, para. 14: General anti-avoidance rule — section 245 of the *Income Tax Act*.

**Advance Tax Rulings:** ATR-32: Rollover of fixed assets from Opco into Holdco; ATR-35: Partitioning of assets to get specific ownership — "butterfly".

**Forms:** T2 SCH 3: Dividends received, taxable dividends paid, and Part IV tax calculation.

**(1.1) Reduction where Part IV.1 tax payable** — Notwithstanding subsection (1), where an assessable dividend was received by a corporation in a taxation year and was included in an amount in respect of which tax under Part IV.1 was payable by the corporation for the year, the tax otherwise payable under this Part by the corporation for the year shall be reduced

    (a) where the assessable dividend is described in paragraph (1)(a), by 10% of the assessable dividend, and

    (b) where the assessable dividend is described in paragraph (1)(b), by 30% of the amount determined under that paragraph in respect of the assessable dividend.

**Notes:** Part IV.1 (187.1–187.61) levies a 10% tax on certain dividends received by certain corporations. Both Part IV tax and Part IV.1 tax may apply to the same dividend. To relieve this duplication, 186(1.1) in effect, deducts from Part IV tax the Part IV.1 tax payable on any dividend figuring in the Part IV tax base.

186(1.1) amended by 1995 Budget, effective for taxation years that end after June 1995, except that, in applying it to amounts described in 186(1.1)(b) that were received by the corporation in the year and before July 1, 1995, the reference in 186(1.1)(b) to "30%" shall be read as "40%".

The changes are generally simplifying and non-substantive. For earlier taxation years, read:

    **(1.1) Reduction in tax** — Notwithstanding subsection (1), where a taxable dividend referred to in paragraph (1)(a) or (b) was received by a corporation in a taxation year and was included in an amount in respect of which tax under Part IV.1 was payable by the corporation for the year, the tax otherwise payable under this Part by the corporation for the year shall be reduced

        (a) where the dividend is a taxable dividend referred to in paragraph (1)(a), by 10% of the amount determined in respect of that dividend under that paragraph; and

        (b) where the dividend is a taxable dividend referred to in paragraph (1)(b), by 10% of the amount determined in respect of that dividend under that paragraph.

**Interpretation Bulletins:** IT-269R3: Part IV tax on taxable dividends received by a private corporation or a subject corporation.

**(2) When corporation controlled** — For the purposes of this Part, other than for the purpose of determining whether a corporation is a subject corporation, one corporation is controlled by another corporation if more than 50% of its issued share capital (having full voting rights under all circumstances) belongs to the other corporation, to persons with whom the other corporation does not deal at arm's length, or to the other corporation and persons with whom the other corporation does not deal at arm's length.

**Related Provisions**: 88(1)(d.2) — Winding-up — when taxpayer last acquired control; 111(3)(a) — Limitation on deductibility; 112(1) — Deduction of taxable dividends received by corporation resident in Canada; 113(1) — Deduction re dividend received from foreign affiliate; 195(6) — Undue deferral of refundable tax.

**Interpretation Bulletins**: IT-243R4: Dividend refund to private corporations; IT-269R3: Part IV tax on taxable dividends received by a private corporation or a subject corporation; IT-302R3: Losses of a corporation — the effect that acquisitions of control, amalgamations, and windings-up have on their deductibility — after January 15, 1987; IT-489R: Non-arm's length sale of shares to a corporation.

**(3) Definitions** — The definitions in this subsection apply in this Part.

**"assessable dividend"** means an amount received by a corporation at a time when it is a private corporation or a subject corporation as, on account of, in lieu of payment of or in satisfaction of, a taxable dividend from a corporation, to the extent of the amount in respect of the dividend that is deductible under section 112, paragraph 113(1)(a), (b) or (d) or subsection 113(2) in computing the recipient corporation's taxable income for the year.

**Notes**: Definition "assessable dividend" added by 1995 Budget, effective for taxation years that end after June 1995.

**"subject corporation"** means a corporation (other than a private corporation) resident in Canada and controlled, whether because of a beneficial interest in one or more trusts or otherwise, by or for the benefit of an individual (other than a trust) or a related group of individuals (other than trusts).

**Notes**: Definition "subject corporation" added by 1995 Budget, effective for taxation years that end after June 1995.

Former 186(3), repealed by 1985 technical bill, defined "dividend refund", a term defined by 129(1) for purposes of the entire Act.

**(4) Corporations connected with particular corporation** — For the purposes of this Part, a payer corporation is connected with a particular corporation at any time in a taxation year (in this subsection referred to as the "particular year") of the particular corporation if

(a) the payer corporation is controlled (otherwise than by virtue of a right referred to in paragraph 251(5)(b)) by the particular corporation at that time; or

(b) the particular corporation owned, at that time,

(i) more than 10% of the issued share capital (having full voting rights under all circumstances) of the payer corporation, and

(ii) shares of the capital stock of the payer corporation having a fair market value of more than 10% of the fair market value of all of the issued shares of the capital stock of the payer corporation.

**Related Provisions**: 186(2) — Extended meaning of "controlled".

**Notes**: The words defining "particular year" in the opening words of 186(4) are superfluous, as the term "particular year" is not otherwise used in the subsection. They are left over from earlier wording that has been repealed.

**Interpretation Bulletins**: IT-269R3: Part IV tax on taxable dividends received by a private corporation or a subject corporation; IT-302R3: Losses of a corporation — the effect that acquisitions of control, amalgamations, and windings-up have on their deductibility — after January 15, 1987; IT-489R: Non-arm's length sale of shares to a corporation.

**Advance Tax Rulings**: ATR-42: Transfer of shares; ATR-55: Amalgamation followed by sale of shares.

**(5) Deemed private corporation** — A corporation that is at any time in a taxation year a subject corporation shall, for the purposes of paragraph 87(2)(aa) and section 129, be deemed to be a private corporation at that time, except that its refundable dividend tax on hand (within the meaning assigned by subsection 129(3)) at the end of the year shall be determined without reference to paragraph 129(3)(a).

**Notes**: 186(5) provides that a subject corporation (see 186(3)) is treated as a private corporation for the purposes of 129. This ensures that a subject corporation may claim a dividend refund, under 129, of Part IV tax paid on its dividend income and included in its RDTOH under 129(3).

186(5) amended by 1995 Budget, effective for taxation years that end after June 1995. For earlier years ending after 1992, read:

(5) A corporation that is at any time a subject corporation shall, for the purposes of paragraphs 87(2)(aa) and 88(1)(e.5) and section 129, be deemed to be a private corporation at that time, except that its refundable dividend tax on hand at the end of any taxation year shall be deemed to be the amount, if any, by which the total of

(a) the total of the taxes under this Part payable by the corporation for the year and any previous taxation years ending after it last became a subject corporation, and

(a.1) the amount, if any, of the corporation's addition at December 31, 1986 of refundable dividend tax on hand (within the meaning assigned by subsection 129(3.3)),

exceeds the total of

(b) the total of the corporation's dividend refunds for taxation years ending after it last became a subject corporation and before the year, and

(c) the amount, if any, of the corporation's reduction at December 31, 1987 of refundable dividend tax on hand (within the meaning assigned by subsection 129(3.5)).

Opening words of 186(5) amended by 1992 technical bill, effective for 1993 and later taxation years. For earlier taxation years, read:

(5) Presumption — A corporation that was at the end of a taxation year commencing after November 12, 1981 a subject corporation or a private corporation that was at any time in the year a subject corporation shall, for the purposes of paragraphs 87(2)(aa) and 88(1)(e.5) and section 129, be deemed to have been a private corporation at the times in the year that it was a subject corporation, except that its refundable dividend tax on hand at the end of the year shall be deemed to be the amount, if any, by which the aggregate of

## S. 186(5)
## Income Tax Act

**Interpretation Bulletins**: IT-269R3: Part IV tax on taxable dividends received by a private corporation or a subject corporation; IT-302R3: Losses of a corporation — the effect that acquisitions of control, amalgamations, and windings-up have on their deductibility — after January 15, 1987.

**(6) Partnerships** — For the purposes of this Part,

(a) all amounts received in a fiscal period by a partnership as, on account or in lieu of payment of, or in satisfaction of, taxable dividends shall be deemed to have been received by each member of the partnership in the member's fiscal period or taxation year in which the partnership's fiscal period ends, to the extent of that member's share thereof; and

(b) each member of a partnership shall be deemed to own at any time that proportion of the number of the shares of each class of the capital stock of a corporation that are property of the partnership at that time that the member's share of all dividends received on those shares by the partnership in its fiscal period that includes that time is of the total of all those dividends.

**Definitions [s. 186]**: "amount" — 248(1); "assessable dividend" — 186(3); "Canada" — 255; "class of shares" — 248(6); "connected" — 186(4); "controlled" — 186(2); "corporation" — 248(1), *Interpretation Act* 35(1); "dividend" — 248(1); "dividend refund" — 129(1); "farm loss" — 111(8); "fiscal period" — 249(2), 249.1; "individual", "insurance corporation" — 248(1); "non-capital loss" — 111(8), 248(1); "non-resident-owned investment corporation" — 133(8), 248(1); "particular corporation" — 186(1); "partnership" — see Notes to 96(1); "person" — 248(1); "private corporation" — 89(1), 186(5), 227(16), 248(1); "related group" — 251(4); "resident in Canada" — 250; "share" — 248(1); "subject corporation" — 186(3); "taxable dividend" — 89(1), 186.2, 248(1); "taxable income" — 2(2), 248(1); "taxation year" — 249; "trust" — 104(1), 248(1).

**Interpretation Bulletins [s. 186]**: IT-269R3: Part IV tax on taxable dividends received by a private corporation or a subject corporation.

**186.1 Exempt corporations** — No tax is payable under this Part for a taxation year by a corporation

(a) that was, at any time in the year, a bankrupt (within the meaning assigned by subsection 128(3)); or

(b) that was, throughout the year,

(i) a bank,

(ii) a corporation licensed or otherwise authorized under the laws of Canada or a province to carry on in Canada the business of offering to the public its services as a trustee,

(iii) an insurance corporation,

(iv) a prescribed labour-sponsored venture capital corporation,

(v) a prescribed investment contract corporation,

(vi) a non-resident-owned investment corporation, or

(vii) a registered securities dealer that was throughout the year a member of a prescribed stock exchange in Canada.

**Related Provisions**: 131(11)(d) — Rules re prescribed labour-sponsored venture capital corporations; 227(14) — Application to exempt corporations; 227(16) — Application to municipal and provincial corporations.

**Notes**: 186.1(b) amended by 1995-97 technical bill, consequential on amendments to 39(5), this version effective for taxation years that end in 1997 or later. For earlier years, but after February 23, 1994, ignore 186.1(b)(vii). Before February 22, 1994, read:

(b) that was, throughout the year, a prescribed labour-sponsored venture capital corporation, a prescribed investment contract corporation, an insurance corporation, a corporation described in paragraph 39(5)(b) or (c) or a non-resident-owned investment corporation.

**Definitions [s. 186.1]**: "bank" — 248(1), *Interpretation Act* 35(1); "business" — 248(1); "corporation" — 248(1), *Interpretation Act* 35(1); "insurance corporation" — 248(1); "non-resident-owned investment corporation" — 133(8), 248(1); "prescribed" — 248(1); "prescribed labour-sponsored venture capital corporation" — Reg. 6701; "prescribed stock exchange in Canada" — Reg. 3200; "province" — *Interpretation Act* 35(1); "taxation year" — 249.

**Regulations [s. 186.1]**: 6701 (prescribed labour-sponsored venture capital corporation); 6703 (prescribed investment contract corporation).

**Interpretation Bulletins [s. 186.1]**: IT-269R3: Part IV tax on dividends received by a private corporation or a subject corporation.

**186.2 Exempt dividends** — For the purposes of subsection 186(1), dividends received in a taxation year by a corporation that was, throughout the year, a prescribed venture capital corporation from a corporation that was a prescribed qualifying corporation with respect to those dividends shall be deemed not to be taxable dividends.

**Definitions [s. 186.2]**: "corporation" — 248(1), *Interpretation Act* 35(1); "dividend", "prescribed" — 248(1); "prescribed venture capital corporation" — Reg. 6700; "taxable dividend" — 89(1), 248(1); "taxation year" — 249.

**Regulations [s. 186.2]**: 6700 (prescribed venture capital corporation); 6704 (prescribed qualifying corporation).

**Interpretation Bulletins [s. 186.2]**: IT-269R3: Part IV tax on dividends received by a private corporation or a subject corporation; IT-328R3: Losses on shares on which dividends have been received.

**187. (1) Information return** — Every corporation that is liable to pay tax under this Part for a taxation year in respect of a dividend received by it in the year shall, on or before the day on or before which it is required to file its return of income under Part I for the year, file a return for the year under this Part in prescribed form.

**Related Provisions**: 150(1)(a) — Corporations — Part I return; 150.1(5) — Electronic filing; 186 — Tax payable on certain taxable dividends.

**Interpretation Bulletins**: IT-269R3: Part IV tax on dividends received by a private corporation or a subject corporation.

**Forms**: T2 Corporate income tax return, "Part IV Tax on Taxable Dividends Received".

**(2) Interest** — Where a corporation is liable to pay tax under this Part and has failed to pay all or any part thereof on or before the day on or before which the tax was required to be paid, it shall pay to the Receiver General interest at the prescribed rate on the amount that it failed to pay computed from the day on or before which the tax was required to be paid to the day of payment.

**Related Provisions**: 161.1 — Offset of refund interest against arrears interest; 221.1 — Application of interest where legislation retroactive; 248(11) — Interest compounded daily.

**Regulations**: 4301(a) (prescribed rate of interest).

**(3) Provisions applicable to Part** — Sections 151, 152, 158 and 159, subsections 161(7) and (11), sections 162 to 167 and Division J of Part I are applicable to this Part with such modifications as the circumstances require.

**Definitions [s. 187]**: "amount" — 248(1); "corporation" — 248(1), *Interpretation Act* 35(1); "dividend", "prescribed" — 248(1); "prescribed rate" — Reg. 4301; "taxation year" — 249.

## PART IV.1 — TAXES ON DIVIDENDS ON CERTAIN PREFERRED SHARES RECEIVED BY CORPORATIONS

**187.1 Definition of "excepted dividend"** — In this Part, "excepted dividend" means a dividend

(a) received by a corporation on a share of the capital stock of a foreign affiliate of the corporation, other than a dividend received by a specified financial institution on a share acquired in the ordinary course of the business carried on by the institution;

(b) received by a corporation from another corporation (other than a corporation described in any of paragraphs (a) to (f) of the definition "financial intermediary corporation" in subsection 191(1)) in which it has or would have, if the other corporation were a taxable Canadian corporation, a substantial interest (as determined under section 191) at the time the dividend was paid;

(c) received by a corporation that was, at the time the dividend was received, a private corporation or a financial intermediary corporation (within the meaning assigned by subsection 191(1));

(d) received by a corporation on a short-term preferred share of the capital stock of a taxable Canadian corporation other than a dividend described in paragraph (b) or (c) of the definition "excluded dividend" in subsection 191(1); or

(e) received by a corporation on a share (other than a taxable RFI share or a share that would be a taxable preferred share if the definition "taxable preferred share" in subsection 248(1) were read without reference to paragraph (a) of that definition) of the capital stock of a mutual fund corporation.

**Related Provisions**: 191(4)(d) — Deemed excepted dividend.

**Notes**: 187.1(a) amended by 1991 technical bill, retroactive to the introduction of Part IV.1 in 1988, to limit Part IV.1 tax on dividends from foreign affiliate shares (acquired in the ordinary course of business) to specified financial institutions.

**Definitions [s. 187.1]**: "business" — 248(1); "carrying on business" — 253; "corporation" — 248(1), *Interpretation Act* 35(1); "dividend" — 248(1); "foreign affiliate" — 248(1); "mutual fund corporation" — 131(8), 248(1); "private corporation" — 89(1), 248(1); "received" — 248(7); "share", "short-term preferred share" — 248(1); "taxable Canadian corporation" — 89(1), 248(1); "taxable preferred share", "taxable RFI share" — 248(1).

**187.2 Tax on dividends on taxable preferred shares** — Every corporation shall, on or before the last day of the second month after the end of each taxation year, pay a tax under this Part for the year equal to 10% of the total of all amounts each of which is a dividend, other than an excepted dividend, received by the corporation in the year on a taxable preferred share (other than a share of a class in respect of which an election under subsection 191.2(1) has been made) to the extent that an amount in respect of the dividend was deductible under section 112 or 113 or subsection 138(6) in computing its taxable income for the year or under subsection 115(1) in computing its taxable income earned in Canada for the year.

**Related Provisions**: 18(1)(t) — Tax is non-deductible; 87(4.2) — Exchanged shares; 186(1.1) — Reduction in tax; 187.4 — Amounts received by partnerships; 187.5 — Information return; 191(3) — Substantial interest; 191(4)(d) — Deemed dividends; 227(14) — No tax on corporation exempt under s. 149.

**Definitions [s. 187.2]**: "amount" — 248(1); "corporation" — 248(1), *Interpretation Act* 35(1); "dividend" — 248(1); "excepted dividend" — 187.1; "received" — 248(7); "share" — 248(1); "taxable income" — 2(2), 248(1); "taxable income earned in Canada" — 115(1), 248(1); "taxable preferred share" — 248(1); "taxation year" — 249.

**Interpretation Bulletins**: IT-88R2: Stock dividends.

**Advance Tax Rulings**: ATR-46: Financial difficulty.

**Forms**: T2 SCH 43: Calculation of Parts IV.1 and VI.1 taxes.

**187.3 (1) Tax on dividends on taxable RFI shares** — Every restricted financial institution shall, on or before the last day of the second month after the end of each taxation year, pay a tax under this Part for the year equal to 10% of the total of all amounts each of which is a dividend, other than an excepted dividend, received by the institution at any time in the year on a share acquired by any person before that time and after 8:00 p.m. Eastern Daylight Saving Time, June 18, 1987 that was, at the time the dividend was paid, a taxable RFI share to the extent that an amount in respect of the dividend was deductible under section 112 or 113 or subsection 138(6) in computing its taxable income for the year or under subsection 115(1) in computing its taxable income earned in Canada for the year.

**Related Provisions**: 87(4.2) — Exchanged shares; 186(1.1) — Reduction in tax; 187.3(2) — Time of acquisition of share; 187.4 — Partnerships; 187.5 — Information return; 191(3) — Substantial interest.

**Advance Tax Rulings**: ATR-46: Financial difficulty.

**(2) Time of acquisition of share** — For the purposes of subsection (1),

(a) a share of the capital stock of a corporation acquired by a person after 8:00 p.m. Eastern Daylight Saving Time, June 18, 1987 pursuant to an agreement in writing entered into before that time shall be deemed to have been acquired by that person before that time;

(b) a share of the capital stock of a corporation acquired by a person after 8:00 p.m. Eastern Daylight Saving Time, June 18, 1987 and before 1988 as part of a distribution to the public made in accordance with the terms of a prospectus, preliminary prospectus, registration statement, offering memorandum or notice filed before 8:00 p.m. Eastern Daylight Saving Time, June 18, 1987 with a public authority pursuant to and in accordance with the securities legislation of the jurisdiction in which the shares are distributed shall be deemed to have been acquired by that person before that time;

(c) a share (in this paragraph referred to as the "new share") of the capital stock of a corporation that is acquired by a person after 8:00 p.m. Eastern Daylight Saving Time, June 18, 1987 in exchange for

(i) a share of a corporation that was issued before 8:00 p.m. Eastern Daylight Saving Time, June 18, 1987 or is a grandfathered share, or

(ii) a debt obligation of a corporation that was issued before 8:00 p.m. Eastern Daylight Saving Time, June 18, 1987, or issued after that time pursuant to an agreement in writing entered into before that time,

where the right to the exchange for the new share and all or substantially all the terms and conditions of the new share were established in writing before that time shall be deemed to have been acquired by that person before that time;

(d) a share of a class of the capital stock of a Canadian corporation listed on a prescribed stock exchange in Canada that is acquired by a person after 8:00 p.m. Eastern Daylight Saving Time, June 18, 1987 on the exercise of a right

(i) that was issued before that time and listed on a prescribed stock exchange in Canada, and

(ii) the terms of which at that time included the right to acquire the share,

where all or substantially all the terms and conditions of the share were established in writing before that time shall be deemed to have been acquired by that person before that time;

(e) where a share that was owned by a particular restricted financial institution at 8:00 p.m. Eastern Daylight Saving Time, June 18, 1987 has, by one or more transactions between related restricted financial institutions, been transferred to another restricted financial institution, the share shall be deemed to have been acquired by the other restricted financial institution before that time unless at any particular time after 8:00 p.m. Eastern Daylight Saving Time, June 18, 1987 and before the share was transferred to the other restricted financial institution the share was owned by a shareholder who, at that particular time, was a person other than a restricted financial institution related to the other restricted financial institution; and

(f) where, at any particular time, there has been an amalgamation within the meaning assigned by section 87, and

(i) each of the predecessor corporations was a restricted financial institution throughout the period from 8:00 p.m. Eastern Daylight Saving Time, June 18, 1987 to the particular time and the predecessor corporations were related to each other throughout that period, or

(ii) each of the predecessor corporations and the new corporation is a corporation described in any of paragraphs (a) to (d) of the definition "restricted financial institution" in subsection 248(1),

a taxable RFI share acquired by the new corporation from a predecessor corporation on the amalgamation shall be deemed to have been acquired by the new corporation at the time it was acquired by the predecessor corporation.

**Notes**: The CCRA takes the position that "all or substantially all", used in 187.3(2)(c) and (d)(ii), means 90% or more.

**Definitions [s. 187.3]**: "amount" — 248(1); "class of shares" — 248(6); "dividend" — 248(1); "excepted dividend" — 187.1; "grandfathered share", "person" — 248(1); "prescribed stock exchange in Canada" — Reg. 3200; "related" — 251(2); "restricted financial institution", "share" — 248(1); "taxable income" — 2(2), 248(1); "taxable income earned in Canada" — 115(1), 248(1); "taxable RFI share" — 248(1); "taxation year" — 249; "writing" — *Interpretation Act* 35(1).

**Regulations [s. 187.3]**: 3200 (prescribed stock exchange); 6201 (prescribed shares).

**Interpretation Bulletins [s. 187.3]**: IT-88R2: Stock dividends.

**187.4 Partnerships** — For the purposes of this Part,

(a) all amounts received in a fiscal period by a partnership as, on account or in lieu of payment of, or in satisfaction of, dividends shall be deemed to have been received by each member of the partnership in the member's fiscal period or taxation year in which the partnership's fiscal period ends, to the extent of that member's share thereof;

(b) each member of a partnership shall be deemed to own at any time that proportion of the number of the shares of each class of the capital stock of a corporation that are property of the partnership at that time that the member's share of all dividends received on those shares by the partnership in its fiscal period that includes that time is of the total of all those dividends; and

(c) a reference to a person includes a partnership.

**Definitions [s. 187.4]**: "amount" — 248(1); "class of shares" — 248(6); "dividend" — 248(1); "fiscal period" — 249(2), 249.1; "partnership" — see Notes to 96(1); "person" — 187.4(c), 248(1); "share" — 248(1); "taxation year" — 249.

**187.5 Information return** — Every corporation liable to pay tax under this Part for a taxation year shall file with the Minister, not later than the day on or before which it is required by section 150 to file its return of income for the year under Part I, a return for the year under this Part in prescribed form containing an estimate of the taxes payable by it under sections 187.2 and 187.3 for the year.

**Related Provisions**: 150.1(5) — Electronic filing.

**Definitions [s. 187.5]**: "corporation" — 248(1), *Interpretation Act* 35(1); "Minister", "prescribed" — 248(1); "taxation year" — 249.

**Forms**: T2 SCH 43: Calculation of Parts IV.1 and VI.1 taxes.

**187.6 Provisions applicable to Part** — Sections 152, 158 and 159, subsections 161(1), (2) and (11), sections 162 to 167 and Division J of Part I are applicable to this Part with such modifications as the circumstances require.

**187.61 Provisions applicable — Crown corporations** — Section 27 applies to this Part with any modifications that the circumstances require.

**Notes**: 187.61 added by 1995-97 technical bill, retroactive to 1988. It confirms that a prescribed federal Crown corporation is liable to tax under Part IV.1. See Notes to 181.71.

# PART V — TAX IN RESPECT OF REGISTERED CHARITIES

**187.7 Application of subsec. 149.1(1)** — The definitions in subsection 149.1(1) apply to this Part.

**Notes**: 187.7 added in the R.S.C. 1985 (5th Supp.) consolidation, effective for taxation years ending after November 1991. This rule was formerly contained in the opening words of 149.1(1).

**188. (1) Revocation tax** — Where the registration of a charity is revoked, the charity shall, on or before the day (in this subsection referred to as the "payment day") in a taxation year that is one year after the day on which the revocation is effective,

(a) pay a tax under this Part for the year equal to the amount determined by the formula

$$A + B - C - D - E - F$$

where

A is the total of all amounts each of which is the fair market value of an asset of the charity on the day (in this section referred to as the "valuation day") that is 120 days before the day on which notice of the Minister's intention to revoke its registration is mailed,

B is the total of all amounts each of which is the amount of a gift for which it issued a receipt described in subsection 110.1(2) or 118.1(2) in the period (in this section referred to as the "winding-up period") that begins on the valuation day and ends immediately before the payment day, or an amount received by it in the winding-up period from a registered charity,

C is the total of all amounts each of which is the fair market value, at the time of the transfer, of an asset transferred by it in the winding-up period to a qualified donee,

D is the total of all amounts each of which is expended by it in the winding-up period on charitable activities carried on by it,

E is the total of all amounts each of which is paid by it in the winding-up period in respect of its debts that were outstanding on the valuation day and not included in determining the value of D, and

F is the total of all amounts each of which is a reasonable expense incurred by it in the winding-up period and not included in determining the value of D; and

(b) file with the Minister a return in prescribed form and containing prescribed information, without notice or demand therefor.

**Related Provisions**: 149.1(6.4) — Application to registered national arts service organizations; 257 — Formula cannot calculate to less than zero.

**Notes**: 188(1) amended by 1993 technical bill, effective where the registration of a charity is revoked pursuant to a notice of intention to revoke that is mailed in 1993 or later. Where the notice was mailed before 1993, since the 1988 taxation year, read:

(1) Where the registration of a charity is revoked, the charity shall, on or before the day in a taxation year that is one year after the day on which the revocation is effective, pay a tax for the year under this Part equal to the amount, if any, by which the total of

(a) the fair market value, on the day that notice of the Minister's intention to revoke its registration is mailed, of all its assets on that day, and

(b) the total of all gifts for which it issued receipts described in subsection 110.1(2) or 118.1(2) after the day referred to in paragraph (a) and all amounts received after that day from registered charities

exceeds the total of

(c) the fair market value on the day referred to in paragraph (a) of each asset of the charity transferred by it to a qualified donee within the period commencing immediately after that day and expiring at the end of one year from the day on which the revocation is effective,

(d) amounts expended by it within the period described in paragraph (c) on charitable activities carried on by it,

(e) amounts paid by the charity after the day referred to in paragraph (a) in respect of *bona fide* debts of the charity that were outstanding on that day, and

(f) the amount of such reasonable expenses as are incurred by the charity within the period described in paragraph (c).

**Information Circulars**: 80-10R: Registered charities: operating a registered charity.

**Forms**: RC4108: Registered charities and the *Income Tax Act* [guide].

**(2) Idem** — A person (other than a qualified donee) who, after the valuation day of a charity, receives an amount from the charity is jointly and severally liable with the charity for the tax payable under subsection (1) by the charity in an amount not exceeding the amount by which the total of all such amounts so received by the person exceeds the total of all amounts each of which is

(a) a portion of such an amount that is included in determining an amount in the description of C, D, E or F in subsection (1) in respect of the charity, or

(b) the consideration given by the person in respect of such an amount.

**Notes**: 188(2) amended by 1993 technical bill, effective where the registration of a charity is revoked pursuant to a notice of intention to revoke that is mailed in 1993 or later. Where the notice was mailed before 1993, since the 1984 taxation year, read:

(2) A person (other than a qualified donee) who, on or after the day that notice of the Minister's intention to revoke the registration of a charity is mailed, receives any amount from that charity is jointly and severally liable with the charity for the tax imposed on the charity by subsection (1) in an amount not exceeding the amount by which the amount so received by the person from the charity exceeds the total of

(a) the total of amounts so received by the person from the charity each of which is an amount described in paragraph (1)(d), (e) or (f), and

(b) the consideration, if any, given by the person in respect of the amount so received by the person.

**Information Circulars**: 80-10R: Registered charities: operating a registered charity.

**(3) Transfer of property tax** — Where, as a result of a transaction or series of transactions, property owned by a registered charity that is a charitable foundation and having a net value greater than 50% of the net asset amount of the charitable foundation immediately before the transaction or series of transactions, as the case may be, is transferred before the end of a taxation year, directly or indirectly, to one or more charitable organizations and it may reasonably be considered that the main purpose of the transfer is to effect a reduction in the disbursement quota of the foundation, the foundation shall pay a tax under this Part for the year equal to the amount by which 25% of the net value of that property determined as of the day of its transfer exceeds the total of all amounts each of which is its tax payable under this subsection for a preceding taxation year in respect of the transaction or series of transactions.

**Related Provisions**: 149.1(6.4) — Application to registered national arts service organizations.

**Information Circulars**: 80-10R: Registered charities: operating a registered charity.

**(4) Idem** — Where property has been transferred to a charitable organization in circumstances described in subsection (3) and it may reasonably be considered that the organization acted in concert with a charitable foundation for the purpose of reducing the disbursement quota of the foundation, the organization is jointly and severally liable with the foundation for the tax imposed on the foundation by that subsection in an amount not exceeding the net value of the property.

**Information Circulars**: 80-10R: Registered charities: operating a registered charity.

**(5) Definitions** — In this section,

**"net asset amount"** of a charitable foundation at any time means the amount determined by the formula

$$A - B$$

where

A is the fair market value at that time of all the property owned by the foundation at that time, and

B is the total of all amounts each of which is the amount of a debt owing by or any other obligation of the foundation at that time;

**Related Provisions**: 257 — Formula cannot calculate to less than zero.

**Notes**: 188(5)"net asset amount" was 188(5)(a) before consolidation in R.S.C. 1985 (5th Supp.), effective for taxation years ending after November 1991. The previous version was in descriptive rather than formula form.

**"net value"** of property owned by a charitable foundation, as of the day of its transfer, means the amount determined by the formula

$$A - B$$

where

A is the fair market value of the property on that day, and

B is the amount of any consideration given to the foundation for the transfer.

**Related Provisions**: 257 — Formula cannot calculate to less than zero.

**Notes**: 188(5)"net value" was 188(5)(b) before consolidation in R.S.C. 1985 (5th Supp.), effective for taxation years ending after November 1991. The previous version was in descriptive rather than formula form.

**Definitions [s. 188]**: "amount" — 248(1); "charitable foundation", "charitable organization", "charitable purposes", "charity", "disbursement quota" — 149.1(1), 187.7; "Minister" — 248(1); "net asset amount" — 188(5); "net value" — 188(5); "non-qualified investment" — 149.1(1), 187.7; "person", "prescribed" — 248(1); "private foundation" — 149.1(1), 187.7; "property" — 248(1); "public foundation", "qualified donee", "qualified investment" — 149.1(1), 187.7; "registered charity" — 248(1); "related business", "specified gift" — 149.1(1), 187.7; "valuation day" — 188(1)(a)A; "winding-up period" — 188(1)(a)B.

**189. (1) Tax regarding non-qualified investment** — Where at any particular time in a taxation year a debt (other than a debt in respect of which subsection 80.4(1) applies or would apply but for subsection 80.4(3)) is owing by a taxpayer to a registered charity that is a private foundation and at that time the debt was a non-qualified investment of the foundation, the taxpayer shall pay a tax under this Part for the year equal to the amount, if any, by which

(a) the amount that would be payable as interest on that debt for the period in the year during which it was outstanding and was a non-qualified investment of the foundation if the interest were payable at such prescribed rates as are in effect from time to time during the period

exceeds

(b) the amount of interest for the year paid on that debt by the taxpayer not later than 30 days after the end of the year.

**Related Provisions**: 149.1(6.4) — Application to registered national arts service organizations.

**Regulations**: 4301(c) (prescribed rate of interest).

**Information Circulars**: 80-10R: Registered charities: operating a registered charity.

**(2) Computation of interest on debt** — For the purpose of paragraph (1)(a), where a debt in respect of which subsection (1) applies (other than a share or right that is deemed by subsection (3) to be a debt) is owing by a taxpayer to a private foundation, interest on that debt for the period referred to in that paragraph shall be computed at the least of

(a) such prescribed rates as are in effect from time to time during the period,

(b) the rate per annum of interest on that debt that, having regard to all the circumstances (including the terms and conditions of the debt), would have been agreed on, at the time the debt was incurred, had the taxpayer and the foundation been dealing with each other at arm's length and had the ordinary business of the foundation been the lending of money, and

(c) where that debt was incurred before April 22, 1982, a rate per annum equal to 6% plus 2% for each calendar year after 1982 and before the taxation year referred to in subsection (1).

**Regulations**: 4301(c) (prescribed rate of interest).

**(3) Share deemed to be debt** — For the purpose of subsection (1), where a share, or a right to acquire a share, of the capital stock of a corporation held by a private foundation at any particular time during the corporation's taxation year was at that time a non-qualified investment of the foundation, the share or right shall be deemed to be a debt owing at that time by the corporation to the foundation

(a) the amount of which was equal to,

(i) in the case of a share or right last acquired before April 22, 1982, the greater of its fair market value on April 21, 1982 and its cost amount to the foundation at the particular time, or

(ii) in any other case, its cost amount to the foundation at the particular time,

(b) that was outstanding throughout the period for which the share or right was held by the foundation during the year, and

(c) in respect of which the amount of interest paid in the year is equal to the total of all amounts each of which is the amount of a dividend received on the share by the foundation in the year,

and the reference in paragraph (1)(a) to "such prescribed rates as are in effect from time to time during the period" shall be read as a reference to "$2/3$ of such prescribed rates as are in effect from time to time during the period".

**(4) Computation of interest with respect to a share** — For the purposes of subsection (3), where a share or right in respect of which that subsection applies was last acquired before April 22, 1982, the reference therein to "$2/3$ of such prescribed rates as are in effect from time to time during the period" shall be read as a reference to "the lesser of

(a) a rate per annum equal to 4% plus 1% for each 5 calendar years contained in the period commencing after 1982 and ending before the particular time, and

(b) a rate per annum equal to $2/3$ of such prescribed rates as are in effect from time to time during the year".

**(5) Share substitution** — For the purpose of subsection (3), where a share or right is acquired by a charity in exchange for another share or right in a transaction after April 21, 1982 to which section 51, 85, 85.1, 86 or 87 applies, it shall be deemed to be the same share or right as the one for which it was substituted.

**(6) Taxpayer to file return and pay tax** — Every taxpayer who is liable to pay tax under this Part (except a charity that is liable to pay tax under [sub]section 188(1)) for a taxation year shall, on or before the day on or before which the taxpayer is, or would be if tax were payable by the taxpayer under Part I for the year, required to file a return of income or an information return under Part I for the year,

(a) file with the Minister a return for the year in prescribed form and containing prescribed information, without notice or demand therefor;

(b) estimate in the return the amount of tax payable by the taxpayer under this Part for the year; and

(c) pay to the Receiver General the amount of tax payable by the taxpayer under this Part for the year.

**Related Provisions**: 150.1(5) — Electronic filing.

**Notes**: 189(6) amended by 1993 technical bill, effective 1993. From 1984 to 1992, read:

(6) Every taxpayer who is liable to pay tax under this Part for a taxation year shall, on or before the day on or before which the taxpayer is required, or would be required if tax were payable by the taxpayer under Part I or if, in the case of a charity, the registration thereof had not been revoked, to file a return of income or an information return under Part I for the year,

(a) file with the Minister a return for the year in prescribed form and containing prescribed information, without notice or demand therefor;

(b) estimate in the return the amount of tax payable by the taxpayer under this Part for the year; and

(c) except where subsection 188(1) applies with respect to the payment of the tax, pay to the Receiver General the amount of tax payable by the taxpayer under this Part for the year.

**Forms**: T2046: Tax return where registration of a charity is revoked; T2140: Return of tax payable under s. 189 on non-qualified investments issued to a private foundation.

**(7) Interest** — Where a taxpayer is liable to pay tax under this Part and has failed to pay all or any part thereof on or before the day on or before which the tax was required to be paid, the taxpayer shall pay to the Receiver General interest at the prescribed rate on the amount that the taxpayer failed to pay computed from the day on or before which the tax was required to be paid to the day of payment.

**Related Provisions**: 221.1 — Application of interest where legislation retroactive; 248(11) — Interest compounded daily.

**Regulations**: 4301 (prescribed rate of interest).

**(8) Provisions applicable to Part** — Subsections 150(2) and (3), sections 152 and 158, subsection 161(11), sections 162 to 167 and Division J of Part I are applicable to this Part with such modifications as the circumstances require.

**Definitions [s. 189]**: "amount" — 248(1); "arm's length" — 251(1); "business" — 248(1); "calendar year" — *Interpretation Act* 37(1)(a); "charitable foundation", "charitable organization", "charitable purposes", "charity" — 149.1(1), 187.7; "corporation" — 248(1), *Interpretation Act* 35(1); "disbursement quota", "dividend", "Minister" — 248(1); "non-qualified investment" — 149.1(1), 187.7; "prescribed" — 248(1); "prescribed rate" — Reg. 4301; "private foundation" — 149.1(1), 187.7, 248(1); "public foundation", "qualified donee", "qualified investment" — 149.1(1), 187.7; "registered charity" — 248(1); "related business" — 149.1(1), 187.7; "share" — 248(1); "specified gift", "taxation year" — 149.1(1), 187.7; "taxpayer" — 248(1).

# PART VI — TAX ON CAPITAL OF FINANCIAL INSTITUTIONS

**Notes**: Life insurers are also subject to Part XII.3 tax. See 211 to 211.5.

**190. (1) Definitions** — For the purposes of this Part,

**"financial institution"** means a corporation that

(a) is a bank,

(b) is authorized under the laws of Canada or a province to carry on the business of offering its services as a trustee to the public,

(c) is authorized under the laws of Canada or a province to accept deposits from the public and carries on the business of lending money on the security of real estate or investing in mortgages on real estate,

(d) is a life insurance corporation that carries on business in Canada, or

(e) is a corporation all or substantially all of the assets of which are shares or indebtedness of corporations described in any of paragraphs (a) to (d) or this paragraph to which the corporation is related;

**Related Provisions**: 253 — Extended meaning of "carrying on business in Canada".

**Notes**: Paras. (d) and (e) added by 1990 Budget/1991 technical bill, effective February 21, 1990 (prorated for taxation years that began before then). This extends Part VI tax to life insurance corporations (which are also subject to Part XII.3 tax) and to certain holding companies.

The CCRA takes the position that "all or substantially all", in para. (e), means 90% or more.

**"long-term debt"** means

(a) in the case of a bank, its subordinated indebtedness (within the meaning assigned by section 2 of the *Bank Act*) evidenced by obligations issued for a term of not less than 5 years,

(b) in the case of an insurance corporation, its subordinated indebtedness (within the meaning assigned by section 2 of the *Insurance Companies Act*) evidenced by obligations issued for a term of not less than 5 years, and

(c) in the case of any other corporation, its subordinated indebtedness (within the meaning that would be assigned by section 2 of the *Bank Act* if the definition of that expression in that section were applied with such modifications as the circumstances require) evidenced by obligations issued for a term of not less than 5 years;

**Notes**: Definition "long-term debt" amended by 1993 technical bill, effective June 1, 1992. Previously read:

"long-term debt" means

(a) in the case of a bank, its indebtedness evidenced by bank debentures, within the meaning assigned by the *Bank Act*, and

(b) in the case of a corporation that is not a bank, its subordinate indebtedness evidenced by obligations issued for a term of not less than 5 years.

**"reserves"**, in respect of a financial institution for a taxation year, means the amount at the end of the year of all of the institution's reserves, provisions and allowances (other than allowances in respect of depreciation or depletion) and, for greater certainty, includes any provision in respect of deferred taxes.

**Notes**: Definition "reserves" added by 1993 technical bill, effective for 1992 and later taxation years.

**(1.1) Prescribed meanings** — For the purposes of this Part, the expressions "attributed surplus", "Canadian assets", "Canadian reserve liabilities",

Part VI — Financial Institutions Capital Tax     S. 190.1(1.2)

"total assets" and "total reserve liabilities" have the meanings that are prescribed.

**Regulations**: 8603 (prescribed meanings of expressions).

**(2) Application of subsecs. 181(3) and (4)** — Subsections 181(3) and (4) apply to this Part with such modifications as the circumstances require.

**Notes**: 190(2) amended by 1993 technical bill, effective for 1992 and later taxation years. For 1986 to 1991, read:

(2) Accounting method — For the purposes of reporting, calculating or determining an amount under this Part on a non-consolidated basis, the equity method of accounting shall not be used.

This rule is now in 248(24).

**Definitions [s. 190]**: "amount" — 248(1); "bank" — 248(1), *Interpretation Act* 35(1); "business" — 248(1); "Canada" — 255; "carrying on business in Canada" — 253; "corporation" — 248(1), *Interpretation Act* 35(1); "life insurance corporation", "prescribed" — 248(1); "province" — *Interpretation Act* 35(1).

## Calculation of Capital Tax

**190.1 (1) Tax payable** — Every corporation that is a financial institution at any time during a taxation year shall pay a tax under this Part for the year equal to 1.25% of the amount, if any, by which its taxable capital employed in Canada for the year exceeds its capital deduction for the year.

**Related Provisions**: 18(1)(t) — Tax is non-deductible; 125.2 — Deduction of Part VI tax; 157(1) — Instalment and payment obligations; 161(1), (4.1) — Interest; 181.1(1) — Large Corporations Tax; 190.1(1.1) — Additional tax on life insurance corporations; 190.1(1.2) — Additional tax on deposit-taking institutions; 227(14) — No tax on corporation exempt under s. 149.

**Notes**: For the financial institutions to which this tax applies, see 190(1)"financial institution". See also Part I.3, which imposes the Large Corporations Tax.

**(1.1) Additional tax payable by life insurance corporations** — Every life insurance corporation that carries on business in Canada at any time in a taxation year shall pay a tax under this Part for the year, in addition to any tax payable under subsection (1), equal to 1% of the amount determined by the formula

$$(A - B) \times \frac{C}{365}$$

where

A  is its taxable capital employed in Canada for the year;

B  is its capital allowance for the year; and

C  is the number of days in the year that are after February 25, 1992 and before 1999.

**Proposed Amendment — 190.1(1.1)C**

C is the number of days in the year that are after February 25, 1992 and before 2001.

**Application**: Bill C-43 (First Reading September 20, 2000), s. 97, will amend the description of C in subsec. 190.1(1.1) to read as above, applicable to taxation years that end after 1998.

**Technical Notes**: Subsection 190.1(1.1) imposes an additional temporary tax on the capital employed in Canada for a taxation year of a life insurer in excess of its capital allowance. The additional tax, which was first announced in the 1992 budget, was scheduled to expire on December 31, 1998. The description of C in the subsection is amended to extend the application of the additional tax for two further years — until December 31, 2000.

**Dept. of Finance news release, July 29, 1999**: *Update on income tax regulations for multinational insurance corporations*

. . . .

Also, the additional capital tax on life insurers, introduced in 1992, will be extended for two further years, to the 2000 taxation year.

[For the complete text of this news release, see under Reg. 2400–2401 — ed.]

**Related Provisions**: 18(1)(t) — Tax is non-deductible; 125.2(3)(a) — No carryback of additional tax to year where it did not apply; 157(1) — Instalment and payment obligations; 161(1), (4.1) — Interest; 190.11 (Application rule) — Exclusion of deferred realized gains from taxable capital employed in Canada; 211.1 — Tax on investment income of life insurer: 227(14) — No tax on corporation exempt under s. 149; 257 — Formula cannot calculate to less than zero.

**Notes**: 190.1(1.1)C amended by 1996 Budget, effective February 26, 1992, to change "1996" to "1999", thus extending the additional tax on life insurers by 3 years.

190(1.1) added by 1993 technical bill, effective for taxation years that end after February 25, 1992. As well, where the corporation elects under para. 88(2)(b) of the 1993 technical bill (see Notes to 190.11) for amended 190.11(b)(i) to apply to its 1991 and later taxation years, read the reference in 190.1(1.1) to "February 25, 1992" as "the day immediately preceding the first day of the corporation's first taxation year that ends after 1990"; and in that case, notwithstanding 152(4) to (5), such assessments and determinations in respect of taxation years ending before February 25, 1992 shall be made as are necessary to give effect to the election.

**(1.2) Additional tax payable by deposit-taking institutions** — Every corporation (other than a life insurance corporation) that is a financial institution at any time in a taxation year shall pay a tax under this Part for the year, in addition to any tax payable under subsection (1), equal to the amount determined by the formula

$$0.0015 \times (A - B) \times \frac{C}{365}$$

where

A  is the corporation's taxable capital employed in Canada for the year;

B  is its enhanced capital deduction for the year; and

C  is the number of days in the year that are after February 27, 1995 and before November 2000.

**Proposed Amendment — Expiry of Surtax**

**Department of Finance news release Backgrounder, December 21, 2000**: *Federal Temporary Surcharge on Deposit-Taking Institutions*

Budget 2000 indicated that the federal temporary surcharge on deposit-taking institutions was being analyzed as part of

1557

## S. 190.1(1.2) — Income Tax Act

the federal-provincial review of capital taxes on financial institutions originally announced in its 1999 paper *Reforming Canada's Financial Services Sector: A Framework for the Future*.

Both the Task Force on the Future of the Canadian Financial Services Sector and the House of Commons Standing Committee on Finance have recommended that the level of capital taxes should be reduced. The Government has completed its review of capital taxes levied on financial institutions and determined that they reduce the international competitiveness of the Canadian financial services industry. The federal government has encouraged provinces to review their capital tax structures, particularly as they apply to financial institutions. A number of provinces have reduced their capital taxes on financial institutions in recent years. As a consequence of the review, the federal temporary surcharge on deposit-taking institutions *will not be extended beyond its scheduled expiry date of October 31, 2000.* [This overrides an announcement in the February 2000 budget extending the surtax to October 2001 — ed.]

**Related Provisions**: 190.17 — Enhanced capital deduction; 257 — Formula cannot calculate to less than zero.

**Notes**: 190.1(1.2) imposes an additional "temporary" Part VI tax on the taxable capital employed in Canada of financial institutions, other than life insurance corporations. It is 0.15% of a corporation's taxable capital employed in Canada in excess of its "enhanced capital deduction". Under 190.17, a corporation's enhanced capital deduction for a taxation year is $400 million unless the corporation is related to another financial institution at the end of the year, in which case the deduction must be shared by members of the related group in accordance with that section. By virtue of 190.1(3)(c), the additional tax may not be reduced by tax payable under Part I of the Act.

190.1(1.2)C amended by 1996 Budget, retroactive to its introduction, to change "1996" to "1997", thus extending the additional tax on banks and other deposit-taking institutions by a year; amended by 1997 Budget to change "1997" to "1998"; amended by 1998 Budget to change "1998" to "1999"; and amended by 1999 Budget to change "1999" to "2000", each time extending it by yet another year.

190.1(1.2) added by 1995 Budget, effective for taxation years that end after February 27, 1995. It includes a built-in prorating for years that straddle the start date of February 28, 1995 and the end date, which as amended will be October 31, 1998.

The 1995 Budget bill also provided:

> 49. (4) No interest is payable under subsection 161(2) of the Act in respect of any amount that became payable before July 1995 because of subsection 190.1(1.2) of the Act, as enacted by subsection (1) [which added 190.1(1.2) — ed.].

**(2) Short taxation years** — Where a taxation year of a corporation is less than 51 weeks, the amount determined under subsection (1) for the year in respect of the corporation shall be reduced to that proportion of that amount that the number of days in the year is of 365.

**Notes**: 190.1(2) amended by 1992 technical bill, effective for 1992 and later taxation years, to ensure that the deduction in 190.1(3) for Part I tax attributable to a short taxation year is applied after prorating the Part VI tax under 190.1(2). For earlier years, read:

> (2) Where a taxation year of a corporation is less than 51 weeks, the tax payable for the year by the corporation under this Part shall be that proportion of its tax otherwise payable under this Part for the year that the number of days in the year is of 365.

**(3) Deduction** — There may be deducted in computing a corporation's tax payable under this Part for a taxation year an amount equal to the total of

(a) the amount, if any, by which

(i) the corporation's tax payable under Part I for the year

exceeds the lesser of

(ii) the corporation's Canadian surtax payable (within the meaning assigned by section 125.3) for the year, and

(iii) the amount that would, but for subsection 181.1(4), be its tax payable under Part I.3 for the year, and

(b) such part as the corporation claims of its unused Part I tax credits and unused surtax credits for its 7 taxation years immediately before and its 3 taxation years immediately after the year,

to the extent that that amount does not exceed the amount by which

(c) the amount that would, but for subsection (1.2) and this subsection, be its tax payable under this Part for the year

exceeds

(d) the total of all amounts each of which is the amount deducted under subsection 125.2(1) in computing the corporation's tax payable under Part I for a taxation year ending before 1992 in respect of its unused Part VI tax credit (within the meaning assigned by section 125.2) for the year.

**Related Provisions**: 87(2)(j.91) — Amalgamations — continuing corporation; 87(2.11) — Vertical amalgamations; 125.2(3)(a) — Limitation on carryover of Part VI tax; 161(7)(a)(x), 164(5)(h.2), 164(5.1)(h.3) — Effect of carryback of loss etc.; 190.2 — Return.

**Notes [subsec. 190.1(3)–(6)]**: Under 190.1(3), a financial institution can reduce Part VI tax payable by the total of its Part I tax liability for the year, plus such amount as it chooses of its unused Part I tax credits and unused surtax credits for the 7 preceding and 3 following taxation years that end after 1991 (or after 1990, where a special election is made).

190.1(3)(c) amended by 1995 Budget to add reference to 190.1(1.2). The effect is to prevent the additional tax under 190.1(1.2) from being reduced by Part I tax payable, unused Part I tax credits and unused surtax credits.

190.1(3)–(6) added by 1992 technical bill, effective for 1992 and later taxation years. However, a financial institution could elect for 190.1(3)–(6) to apply to its taxation year(s) ending in 1991 as well, by filing an election with Revenue Canada by December 10, 1993 (that is, 6 months after Royal Assent to the 1992 technical bill). If such an election is made,

(a) read 190.1(3)(a) and (b) as follows:

> (a) the corporation's tax payable under Part I for the year, and
>
> (b) such part as the corporation claims of its unused Part I tax credits for its 7 taxation years immediately preceding and 3 taxation years immediately following the year,

(b) read the reference in 190.1(3)(d) to "1992" as a reference to "1991";

(c) ignore 190.1(4)(a)(ii) and (b)(ii);

## Part VI — Financial Institutions Capital Tax    S. 190.1(6)(a)(i)(A)(I)

(d) read 190.1(5) as follows [but see Proposed Amendment below]:

(5) For the purposes of subsections (3) and (4), this subsection and subsection (6), "unused Part I tax credit" of a corporation for a taxation year ending after 1990 means the amount, if any, by which its tax payable under Part I for the year exceeds the amount that would, but for subsection (3), be its tax payable under this Part for the year.

and

(e) read 190.1(6) without reference to the expressions "or unused surtax credit" and "and unused surtax credit".

Para. 87(3)(a) of the 1993 technical bill provides that where a corporation elected under subsec. 111(2) of the 1992 technical bill for 190.1(3) to (6) to apply to its taxation year(s) ending in 1991 (as described above), and does not elect under para. 88(2)(b) of the 1993 technical bill (see Notes to 190.11) for amended 190.11(b)(i) to apply to its 1991 and later taxation years, then for the purposes of determining the corporation's unused Part I tax credit for the 1991 taxation year, 190.1(5) is to be read as follows:

(5) For the purpose of computing the amount that may, because of paragraph (3)(b), be deducted by a corporation in computing its tax payable under this Part for a particular taxation year, in respect of its tax payable under Part I for a taxation year ending in 1991, and for the purposes of subsections (4) and (6), the corporation's "unused Part I tax credit" for the 1991 taxation year is the lesser of

(a) the amount, if any, by which its tax payable under Part I for the 1991 taxation year exceeds the amount that would, but for subsection (3), be its tax payable under this Part for that year, and

(b) its tax payable under this Part (determined without reference to subsections (1.1) and (3)) for the particular year.

For the rationale of 190.1(3) to (6), see Notes to 125.2(1).

**Forms**: T2 SCH 42: Calculation of unused Part VI tax credit and unused Part I tax credit.

**(4) Idem** — For the purposes of this subsection and subsections (3), (5) and (6),

(a) an amount may not be claimed under subsection (3) in computing a corporation's tax payable under this Part for a particular taxation year

(i) in respect of its unused Part I tax credit for another taxation year, until its unused Part I tax credits for taxation years preceding the other year that may be claimed under this Part for the particular year have been claimed, and

(ii) in respect of its unused surtax credit for another taxation year, until its unused surtax credits for taxation years preceding the other year that may be claimed under Part I.3 or this Part for the particular year have been claimed; and

(b) an amount may be claimed under subsection (3) in computing a corporation's tax payable under this Part for a particular taxation year

(i) in respect of its unused Part I tax credit for another taxation year, only to the extent that it exceeds the total of all amounts each of which is the amount claimed in respect of that unused Part I tax credit in computing its tax payable under this Part for a taxation year preceding the particular year, and

(ii) in respect of its unused surtax credit for another taxation year, only to the extent that it exceeds the total of all amounts each of which is the amount claimed in respect of the unused surtax credit

(A) in computing its tax payable under this Part for a taxation year preceding the particular year, or

(B) in computing its tax payable under Part I.3 for the particular year or a taxation year preceding the particular year.

**Related Provisions**: 87(2.11) — Vertical amalgamations.

**Notes**: See Notes to 190.1(3).

**(5) Definitions** — For the purposes of subsections (3), (4) and (6),

**"unused Part I tax credit"** of a corporation for a taxation year ending after 1991 means the amount, if any, by which

(a) the corporation's tax payable under Part I for the year

exceeds the total of

(b) the amount that would, but for subsection (3), be its tax payable under this Part for the year, and

(c) the corporation's Canadian surtax payable (within the meaning assigned by section 125.3) for the year;

**"unused surtax credit"** of a corporation for a taxation year has the meaning assigned by subsection 181.1(6).

**Related Provisions [subsec. 190.1(5)]**: 87(2.11) — Vertical amalgamations.

**Notes**: See Notes to 190.1(3).

**(6) Acquisition of control** — Where at any time control of a corporation was acquired by a person or group of persons, no amount in respect of its unused Part I tax credit or unused surtax credit for a taxation year ending before that time is deductible by the corporation for a taxation year ending after the time and no amount in respect of its unused Part I tax credit or unused surtax credit for a taxation year ending after that time is deductible by the corporation for a taxation year ending before that time, except that

(a) the corporation's unused Part I tax credit and unused surtax credit for a particular taxation year that ended before that time is deductible by the corporation for a taxation year that ends after that time (in this paragraph referred to as the "subsequent year") to the extent of that proportion of the corporation's tax payable under Part I for the particular year that

(i) the amount, if any, by which

(A) the total of all amounts each of which is

(I) its income under Part I for the particular year from a business that was carried on by the corporation for profit

1559

**S. 190.1(6)(a)(i)(A)(I)**      Income Tax Act

or with a reasonable expectation of profit throughout the subsequent year, or

(II) where properties were sold, leased, rented or developed or services were rendered in the course of carrying on that business before that time, its income under Part I for the particular year from any other business all or substantially all of the income of which was derived from the sale, leasing, rental or development, as the case may be, of similar properties or the rendering of similar services

exceeds

(B) the total of all amounts each of which is an amount deducted under paragraph 111(1)(a) or (d) in computing its taxable income for the particular year in respect of a non-capital loss or a farm loss, as the case may be, for a taxation year in respect of any business referred to in clause (A)

is of the greater of

(ii) the amount determined under subparagraph (i), and

(iii) the corporation's taxable income for the particular year; and

(b) the corporation's unused Part I tax credit and unused surtax credit for a particular taxation year that ends after that time is deductible by the corporation for a taxation year (in this paragraph referred to as the "preceding year") that ended before that time to the extent of that proportion of the corporation's tax payable under Part I for the particular year that

(i) the amount, if any, by which

(A) the total of all amounts each of which is

(I) its income under Part I for the particular year from a business that was carried on by the corporation in the preceding year and throughout the particular year for profit or with a reasonable expectation of profit, or

(II) where properties were sold, leased, rented or developed or services were rendered in the course of carrying on that business before that time, its income under Part I for the particular year from any other business all or substantially all of the income of which was derived from the sale, leasing, rental or development, as the case may be, of similar properties or the rendering of similar services

exceeds

(B) the total of all amounts each of which is an amount deducted under paragraph

111(1)(a) or (d) in computing its taxable income for the particular year in respect of a non-capital loss or a farm loss, as the case may be, for a taxation year in respect of any business referred to in clause (A)

is of the greater of

(ii) the amount determined under subparagraph (i), and

(iii) the corporation's taxable income for the particular year.

**Related Provisions**: 87(2.11) — Vertical amalgamations; 256(6)–(9) — Anti-avoidance — deemed exercise of right to increase voting power.

**Notes**: 190.1(6)(a) and (b) amended by 1995-97 technical bill, effective for acquisitions of control that occur after April 26, 1995. For earlier acquisitions since the 1992 taxation year, read:

(a) where a business was carried on by the corporation in a taxation year ending before that time, its unused Part I tax credit and unused surtax credit for that year are deductible by the corporation for a particular taxation year ending after that time only if that business was carried on by the corporation for profit or with a reasonable expectation of profit throughout the particular year and only to the extent of that proportion of the corporation's tax payable under this Part for the particular year that

(i) the amount, if any, by which

(A) the total of its income under Part I for the particular year from that business and, where properties were sold, leased, rented or developed or services were rendered in the course of carrying on that business before that time, its income under Part I for the particular year from any other business substantially all the income of which was derived from the sale, leasing, rental or development, as the case may be, of similar properties or the rendering of similar services

exceeds

(B) the total of all amounts each of which is an amount deducted under paragraph 111(1)(a) or (d) in computing its taxable income under Part I for the particular year in respect of a non-capital loss or a farm loss, as the case may be, for a taxation year in respect of that business or the other business

is of the greater of

(ii) the amount determined under subparagraph (i), and

(iii) the corporation's taxable income under Part I for the particular year; and

(b) where a business was carried on by the corporation throughout a taxation year ending after that time, its unused Part I tax credit and unused surtax credit for that year are deductible by the corporation for a particular taxation year ending before that time only if that business was carried on by the corporation for profit or with a reasonable expectation of profit in the particular year and only to the extent of that proportion of the corporation's tax payable under this Part for the particular year that

(i) the amount, if any, by which

(A) the total of its income under Part I for the particular year from that business and, where properties were sold, leased, rented or developed or services were rendered in the course of carrying on that business before that time, its income under Part I for the particular year from any other business substantially all the income of which was derived from the sale, leasing, rental or development, as the case may be, of similar properties or the rendering of similar services

exceeds

(B) the total of all amounts each of which is an amount deducted under paragraph 111(1)(a) or (d) in computing its taxable income under Part I for the particular year in respect of a non-capital loss or a farm loss, as the case may be, for a taxation year in respect of that business or the other business

is of the greater of

(ii) the amount determined under subparagraph (i), and

(iii) the corporation's taxable income under Part I for the particular year.

See Notes to 190.1(3).

**I.T. Technical News**: No. 7 (control by a group — 50/50 arrangement).

**Definitions [s. 190.1]**: "acquired" — 256(7)–(9); "amount" — 181(3), 190(2), 248(1); "business" — 248(1); "Canadian surtax payable" — 125.3(4); "capital allowance" — 190.16; "capital deduction" — 190.15; "control" — 256(6)–(9); "corporation" — 248(1), *Interpretation Act* 35(1); "enhanced capital deduction" — 190.17; "farm loss" — 111(8), 248(1); "financial institution" — 190(1); "non-capital loss" — 111(8), 248(1); "property" — 248(1); "tax payable" — 248(2); "taxable capital employed in Canada" — 190.11; "taxation year" — 249; "unused Part I credit", "unused surtax credit" — 190.1(5).

### 190.11 Taxable capital employed in Canada —

For the purposes of this Part, the taxable capital employed in Canada of a financial institution for a taxation year is,

(a) in the case of a financial institution other than a life insurance corporation, that proportion of its taxable capital for the year that its Canadian assets at the end of the year is of its total assets at the end of the year;

**Proposed Amendment — 190.11(a)**

(a) in the case of a financial institution, other than an authorized foreign bank or a life insurance corporation, that proportion of its taxable capital for the year that its Canadian assets at the end of the year is of its total assets at the end of the year;

**Application**: The August 8, 2000 draft legislation, subsec. 17(1), will amend para. 190.11(a) to read as above, applicable after June 27, 1999.

**Technical Notes**: Part VI of the Act taxes the amount by which a financial institution's taxable capital employed in Canada exceeds a capital deduction of up to $220 million (which is shared among related institutions). Part VI also applies additional taxes to life insurance corporations and deposit-taking institutions. Part VI is amended, with application after June 27, 1999, to include special rules for the taxation of authorized foreign banks.

Section 190.11 of the Act provides rules for determining the amount of a financial institution's "taxable capital employed in Canada" for the purposes of Part VI. Section 190.11 is amended to exclude authorized foreign banks from the general rule in paragraph (a) and to provide, in amended paragraph (c), that an authorized foreign bank's taxable capital employed in Canada for a taxation year is its taxable capital for the year.

These amendments apply after June 27, 1999.

(b) in the case of a life insurance corporation that was resident in Canada at any time in the year, the total of

(i) that proportion of the amount, if any, by which the total of

(A) its taxable capital for the year, and

(B) the amount prescribed for the year in respect of the corporation

exceeds

(C) the amount prescribed for the year in respect of the corporation

that its Canadian reserve liabilities as at the end of the year is of the total of

(D) its total reserve liabilities as at the end of the year, and

(E) the amount prescribed for the year in respect of the corporation, and

(ii) the amount, if any, by which

(A) the amount of its reserves for the year (other than its reserves in respect of amounts payable out of segregated funds) that can reasonably be regarded as having been established in respect of its insurance businesses carried on in Canada

exceeds the total of

(B) all amounts each of which is the amount of a reserve (other than a reserve described in subparagraph 138(3)(a)(i)), to the extent that it is included in the amount determined under clause (A) and is deducted in computing its income under Part I for the year,

(C) all amounts each of which is the amount of a reserve described in subparagraph 138(3)(a)(i), to the extent that it is included in the amount determined under clause (A) and is deductible under subparagraph 138(3)(a)(i) in computing its income under Part I for the year, and

(D) all amounts each of which is the amount outstanding (including any interest accrued thereon) at the end of the year in respect of a policy loan (within the meaning assigned by subsection 138(12)) made by the corporation, to the extent that it is deducted in computing the total determined under clause (C); and

(c) in the case of a life insurance corporation that was non-resident throughout the year, its taxable capital for the year.

**Proposed Amendment — 190.11(c)**

(c) in the case of a life insurance corporation that was non-resident throughout the year, or in the case of an authorized foreign bank, its taxable capital for the year.

**Application:** The August 8, 2000 draft legislation, subsec. 17(2), will amend para. 190.11(c) to read as above, applicable after June 27, 1999.

**Technical Notes:** See under 190.11(a).

### Proposed Amendment — Application of 1995-97 technical bill amendment to 190.11

**Application:** Bill C-43 (First Reading September 20, 2000), s. 121, will amend the application of the amendment made to s. 190.11 by S.C. 1998, c. 19, s. 206 (1995–97 technical bill) to replace references to "1999" with "2001", applicable to taxation years that end after 1998.

**Technical Notes:** Subsection 190.1(1.1) of the *Income Tax Act* imposes an additional temporary Part VI tax on the taxable capital employed in Canada of life insurance corporations. Section 206 of the *Income Tax Amendments Act, 1997* provided that deferred realized gains and losses of life insurance corporations on investment properties would not be added or deducted in computing the Part VI tax base. Consequential on the extension of the additional tax to December 31, 2000, this amendment extends the exclusion of deferred realized gains and losses in calculating the Part VI tax base to the same date.

**Related Provisions:** 181.3(1) — Taxable capital employed in Canada for Part I.3 tax; 257 — Formula cannot calculate to less than zero [applies to amending legislation by virtue of *Interpretation Act* subsec. 42(3)].

**Notes:** S. 206 of the 1995-97 technical bill provides the following rule of application for 190.11:

> 206. Where an amount in respect of deferred realized gains or losses of a life insurance corporation is added or deducted, as the case may be, in computing its taxable capital employed in Canada or capital under Part VI of the Act for a taxation year that ends after February 25, 1992 and began before 1999, the amount determined by the formula
>
> $$(A - B) \times C/D$$
>
> shall be deducted, or, where the amount is negative, the absolute value of the amount shall be added, in computing the corporation's taxable capital employed in Canada under Part VI of the Act for the year, where
>
> A is the corporation's taxable capital employed in Canada for the year under Part VI of the Act (determined without reference to this section);
>
> B is the amount that would be the value of A if no amount were added or deducted in computing the corporation's taxable capital employed in Canada or capital for the year under Part VI of the Act in respect of its deferred realized gains or losses, as the case may be;
>
> C is the number of days in the year that are after February 25, 1992 and before 1999; and
>
> D is the number of days in the year.

190.11(b)(i) amended by 1993 technical bill, effective for taxation years that end after February 25, 1992. As well, para. 88(2)(b) of the 1993 technical bill provides that where a corporation elects by notifying Revenue Canada in writing by December 31, 1994, the amended 190.11(b)(i) applies to the corporation's 1991 and 1992 taxation years. Where such an election is made, then notwithstanding 152(4) to (5), such assessments and determinations in respect of any taxation year shall be made as are necessary to give effect to the election. Where the old version applies, read:

> (i) that proportion of its taxable capital for the year that its Canadian reserve liabilities at the end of the year is of its total reserve liabilities at the end of the year, and

190.11(b) and (c) added by 1990 Budget/1991 technical bill, effective for taxation years ending after February 20, 1990.

**Definitions [s. 190.11]:** "amount" — 181(3), 190(2), 248(1); "authorized foreign bank" — 248(1); "Canadian assets" — 190(1.1), Reg. 8602, 8603(a); "Canadian reserve liabilities" — 190(1.1), Reg. 2405(3), Reg. 8602, Reg. 8603(b); "capital allowance" — 190.16; "corporation" — 248(1), *Interpretation Act* 35(1); "financial institution" — 190(1); "life insurance corporation" — 248(1); "reserves" — 190(1); "resident in Canada" — 250; "taxable capital" — 190.12; "taxation year" — 249; "total assets" — 190(1.1), Reg. 8602, Reg. 8603(a); "total reserve liabilities" — 190(1.1), Reg. 2405(3), Reg. 8602, Reg. 8603(b).

**Regulations:** 8605 (prescribed amounts for 190.11(b)(i)(B), (C) and (E)).

**190.12 Taxable capital** — For the purposes of this Part, the taxable capital of a corporation for a taxation year is the amount, if any, by which its capital for the year exceeds the total determined under section 190.14 in respect of its investments for the year in financial institutions related to it.

**Related Provisions:** 181.3(2) — Taxable capital for Part I.3 tax.

**Definitions [s. 190.12]:** "amount" — 181(3), 190(2), 248(1); "capital" — 190.13; "corporation" — 248(1), *Interpretation Act* 35(1); "financial institution" — 190(1); "investments in financial institutions" — 190.14; "taxation year" — 249.

**190.13 Capital** — For the purposes of this Part, the capital of a financial institution for a taxation year is,

(a) in the case of a financial institution other than a life insurance corporation, the amount, if any, by which the total at the end of the year of

### Proposed Amendment — 190.13(a) opening words

(a) in the case of a financial institution, other than an authorized foreign bank or a life insurance corporation, the amount, if any, by which the total at the end of the year of

**Application:** The August 8, 2000 draft legislation, subsec. 18(1), will amend the opening words of para. 190.13(a) to read as above, applicable after June 27, 1999.

**Technical Notes:** Section 190.13 of the Act defines the capital of a financial institution for a taxation year for the purposes of Part VI. The section is amended to include, in new paragraph 190.13(d), a special rule for authorized foreign banks. This new rule defines such a bank's capital for purposes of Part VI in the same way as new paragraph 181.3(3)(e) of the Act does for the purposes of the large corporations tax in Part I.3 of the Act. Readers may refer to the notes to that provision for more information.

This amendment applies after June 27, 1999.

(i) the amount of its long-term debt,

(ii) the amount of its capital stock (or, in the case of an institution incorporated without share capital, the amount of its members' contributions), retained earnings, contributed surplus and any other surpluses, and

(iii) the amount of its reserves, except to the extent that they were deducted in computing its income under Part I for the year, exceeds the total at the end of the year of

(iv) the amount of its deferred tax debit balance, and

(v) the amount of any deficit deducted in computing its shareholders' equity;

(b) in the case of a life insurance corporation that was resident in Canada at any time in the year, the amount, if any, by which the total at the end of the year of

(i) the amount of its long-term debt, and

(ii) the amount of its capital stock (or, in the case of an insurance corporation incorporated without share capital, the amount of its members' contributions), retained earnings, contributed surplus and any other surpluses

exceeds the total at the end of the year of

(iii) the amount of its deferred tax debit balance, and

(iv) the amount of any deficit deducted in computing its shareholders' equity; and

(c) in the case of a life insurance corporation that was non-resident throughout the year, the total at the end of the year of

(i) the amount that is the greater of

(A) the amount, if any, by which

(I) its surplus funds derived from operations (as defined in subsection 138(12)) as of the end of the year, computed as if no tax were payable under Part I.3 or this Part for the year

exceeds the total of all amounts each of which is

(II) an amount on which it was required to pay, or would but for subsection 219(5.2) have been required to pay, tax under Part XIV for a preceding taxation year, except the portion, if any, of the amount on which tax was payable, or would have been payable, because of subparagraph 219(4)(a)(i.1), and

(III) an amount on which it was required to pay, or would but for subsection 219(5.2) have been required to pay, tax under subsection 219(5.1) for the year because of the transfer of an insurance business to which subsection 138(11.5) or (11.92) has applied, and

(B) its attributed surplus for the year,

(ii) any other surpluses relating to its insurance businesses carried on in Canada,

(iii) the amount of its long-term debt that can reasonably be regarded as relating to its insurance businesses carried on in Canada, and

(iv) the amount, if any, by which

(A) the amount of its reserves for the year (other than its reserves in respect of

amounts payable out of segregated funds) that can reasonably be regarded as having been established in respect of its insurance businesses carried on in Canada

exceeds the total of

(B) all amounts each of which is the amount of a reserve (other than a reserve described in subparagraph 138(3)(a)(i)), to the extent that it is included in the amount determined under clause (A) and is deducted in computing its income under Part I for the year,

(C) all amounts each of which is the amount of a reserve described in subparagraph 138(3)(a)(i), to the extent that it is included in the amount determined under clause (A) and is deductible under subparagraph 138(3)(a)(i) in computing its income under Part I for the year, and

(D) all amounts each of which is the amount outstanding (including any interest accrued thereon) at the end of the year in respect of a policy loan (within the meaning assigned by subsection 138(12)) made by the corporation, to the extent that it is deducted in computing the amount determined under clause (C).

**Proposed Addition — 190.13(d)**

(d) in the case of an authorized foreign bank, the total of

(i) 10% of the total of all amounts, each of which is the risk-weighted amount at the end of the year of an on-balance sheet asset or an off-balance sheet exposure of the bank in respect of its Canadian banking business that the bank would be required to report under the OSFI risk-weighting guidelines if those guidelines applied and required a report at that time, and

(ii) the total of all amounts, each of which is an amount at the end of the year in respect of the bank's Canadian banking business that

(A) if the bank were a bank listed in Schedule II to the *Bank Act*, would be required under the risk-based capital adequacy guidelines issued by the Superintendent of Financial Institutions to be deducted from the bank's capital in determining the amount of capital available to satisfy the Superintendent's requirement that capital equal a particular proportion of risk-weighted assets and exposures, and

(B) is not an amount in respect of a loss protection facility required to be deducted from capital under the Superin-

**S. 190.13(d)(ii)(B)**     Income Tax Act

> tendent's guidelines respecting asset securitization applicable at that time.
>
> **Application**: The August 8, 2000 draft legislation, subsec. 18(2), will add para. 190.13(d), applicable after June 27, 1999.
>
> **Technical Notes**: See under 190.13(a).
>
> **Notice of Ways and Means Motion (authorized foreign banks), February 11, 1999**: (5) That, for the purposes of Part I.3 and Part VI of the Act, the capital of an authorized foreign bank be an amount equal to 10% of the bank's risk-weighted assets as determined under prescribed rules based on the risk-weighted asset guidelines of the Superintendent of Financial Institutions.
>
> **Department of Finance news release, February 11, 1999**: See under 181.3(3).

**Related Provisions**: 181.3(3) — Capital for Part I.3 tax.

**Notes**: Opening words of each of 190.13(a), (b) and (c) amended by 1993 technical bill, effective for 1992 and later taxation years, to change "total, computed at the end of the year on a non-consolidated basis", to "total". This change is consequential on the amendment to 190(2), since the same requirement is already in 181(2).

190.13(a)(iii) amended by 1993 technical bill, effective for 1992 and later years, to change "provisions or reserves (including, for greater certainty, any provision or reserve in respect of deferred taxes)" to "reserves". The repealed words were included for greater certainty and are now provided in the definition of "reserves" in 190(1). As well, the words "at the end of the year" were added to the phrase between 190.13(a)(iii) and (iv).

190.13(c)(i)(A)(II) and (III) added by 1995-97 technical bill, effective for 1994 and later taxation years. (The previous text was all in the body of subpara. (i), not broken down to the clause level.)

190.13(c)(i) amended by 1993 technical bill, effective for 1992 and later taxation years, to add the words "computed as if no tax were payable by it under Part I.3 of this Part for the year". This avoids a circularity problem, since "surplus funds from operations" as defined in 138(12) depends in part on the corporation's liability under Parts I.3 and VI.

190.13(b) and (c) added by 1990 Budget/1991 technical bill, effective for taxation years ending after February 20, 1990.

**Definitions [s. 190.13]**: "amount" — 181(3), 190(2), 248(1); "attributed surplus" — 190(2), Reg. 2405(3), 8602, 8603(b); "authorized foreign bank", "Canadian banking business" — 248(1); "corporation" — 248(1), *Interpretation Act* 35(1); "financial institution" — 190(1); "insurance corporation", "life insurance corporation" — 248(1); "long-term debt", "reserves" — 190(1); "taxation year" — 249.

**190.14 Investment in related institutions** — A corporation's investments[30] for a taxation year in a financial institution related to it is,

  (a) in the case of a corporation that was resident in Canada at any time in the year, the total of

    (i) all amounts each of which is the carrying value at the end of the year of

      (A) any share of the capital stock of the financial institution, or

      (B) any long-term debt of the financial institution

    that is owned by the corporation at the end of the year (and, where the corporation is a life insurance corporation, that is non-segregated property within the meaning assigned by subsection 138(12)), and

    (ii) the amount of any surplus of the financial institution contributed by the corporation, other than an amount included under subparagraph (i); and

  (b) in the case of a life insurance corporation that was non-resident throughout the year, the total that would, if the corporation were resident in Canada in the year, be determined under paragraph (a) in respect of the corporation for the year in respect of shares and long-term debt of the financial institution that were used by the corporation in, or held by it in the year in the course of, carrying on an insurance business in Canada and in respect of surplus of the financial institution contributed by the corporation.

> **Proposed Amendment — 190.14**
>
> **190.14 (1) Investment in related institutions** — A corporation's investment for a taxation year in a financial institution related to it is
>
> (a) in the case of a corporation that was resident in Canada at any time in the year, the total of all amounts each of which is the carrying value (or in the case of contributed surplus, the amount) at the end of the year of an eligible investment of the corporation in the financial institution;
>
> (b) in the case of a life insurance corporation that was non-resident throughout the year, the total of all amounts each of which is the carrying value (or is, in the case of contributed surplus, the amount) at the end of the year of an eligible investment of the corporation in the financial institution that was used or held by the corporation in the year in the course of carrying on an insurance business in Canada (or that, in the case of contributed surplus, was contributed by the corporation in the course of carrying on that business); and
>
> (c) in the case of a corporation that is an authorized foreign bank, the total of all amounts each of which is the amount at the end of the year, before the application of risk weights, that would be required to be reported under the OSFI risk-weighting guidelines if those guidelines applied and required a report at that time, of an eligible investment of the corporation in the financial institution that was used or held by the corporation in the year in the course of carrying on its Canadian banking business or, in the case of an eligible investment that is contributed surplus of the financial institution at the end of the year, the amount of the surplus contributed by the corporation in the course of carrying on that business.

---

[30]*Sic.* Should be "investment" — ed.

1564

**Technical Notes**: Section 190.14 of the Act applies for the purpose of determining, under Part VI, the amount of a corporation's investment in related financial institutions. This amount is deductible from the corporation's capital, as determined under section 190.13 of the Act, in computing its taxable capital under section 190.12 of the Act.

Section 190.14 is amended by incorporating most of its content into a new subsection (1). Paragraphs (a) and (b) are amended to refer to an "eligible investment", a term defined in new subsection 190.14(2), which incorporates conditions previously contained in the text of these paragraphs, as well as a new residency condition.

New paragraph 190.14(1)(c) defines the investment allowance of an authorized foreign bank. The bank's investment in related institutions is essentially the full (i.e. not risk-weighted) year-end amount of its "eligible investments" used or held in its Canadian banking business as those would be reported under the OSFI risk-weighting guidelines (defined in subsection 248(1)) if the guidelines were applicable. The new provision clarifies that the relevant amount in respect of surplus contributed to an institution is the amount of such surplus contributed by the bank in the course of carrying on its Canadian banking business.

**Related Provisions**: 190.14(2) — Meaning of "eligible investment".

**(2) Interpretation** — For the purpose of subsection (1), an **eligible investment** of a corporation in a financial institution is a share of the capital stock or long-term debt (and, where the corporation is an insurance corporation, is non-segregated property within the meaning assigned by subsection 138(12)) of the financial institution or any surplus of the financial institution contributed by the corporation (other than an amount otherwise included as a share or debt) if the financial institution at the end of the year is

(a) related to the corporation; and

(b) resident in Canada or can reasonably be regarded as using the surplus or the proceeds of the share or debt in a business carried on by the financial institution through a permanent establishment (as defined by regulation) in Canada.

**Regulations [subsec. 190.14(2)]**: 8201 (meaning of "permanent establishment" for 190.14(2)(b)).

**Application**: The August 8, 2000 draft legislation, s. 19, will amend s. 190.14 to read as above, applicable after June 27, 1999 except that, in its application to taxpayers other than authorized foreign banks for taxation years that end before 2002, subsec. 190.14(2) shall be read without reference to para. (b) thereof.

**Technical Notes**: New subsection 190.14(2) of the Act defines an "eligible investment" of a corporation in a financial institution for the purpose of determining its investment allowance under subsection (1). The main conditions, previously set out directly in paragraphs 190.14(a) and (b) are that the investment be a share or long-term debt of, or surplus contributed to, a related financial institution. A new requirement is introduced in new paragraph 190.14(2)(b) that the investee financial institution be either resident in Canada or use the surplus or the proceeds of the share or debt in a business carried on through a permanent establishment in Canada. It is proposed that the definition of permanent establishment for this purpose be that set out in section 8201 of the *Income Tax Regulations*.

These amendments generally apply after June 27, 1999 except that the coming-into-force of the requirement in subsection 190.14(2)(b) is deferred for taxpayers other than authorized foreign banks until the 2002 taxation year.

**Definitions [s. 190.14]**: "amount", "authorized foreign bank", "business" — 248(1); "Canada" — 255, *Interpretation Act* 35(1); "Canadian banking business" — 248(1); "corporation" — 248(1), *Interpretation Act* 35(1); "eligible investment" — 190.14(2); "insurance corporation", "life insurance corporation", "non-resident", "OSFI risk-weighting guidelines", "property", "regulation" — 248(1); "related" — 251(2)–(6); "resident in Canada" — 250; "share" — 248(1); "taxation year" — 249.

**Related Provisions**: 190.15(6) — Related financial institution.

**Notes**: Opening words of 190.14(a)(i) and 190.14(a)(i)(A) amended by 1993 technical bill, effective for 1992 and later taxation years. For the 1990 and 1991 taxation years, read:

> (i) the cost to it, that would be shown on its balance sheet at the end of the year if its balance sheet were prepared on a non-consolidated basis, of
>
> (A) any share of the capital stock of the financial institution, and

190.14 amended by 1990 Budget/1991 technical bill, effective for taxation years ending after February 20, 1990. For earlier taxation years, what is now 190.14(a) applied in all cases.

## 190.15 (1) Capital deduction

— For the purposes of this Part, the capital deduction of a corporation for a taxation year during which it was at any time a financial institution is the total of $200,000,000 and the lesser of

(a) $20,000,000, and

(b) 1/5 of the amount, if any, by which its taxable capital employed in Canada for the year exceeds $200,000,000,

unless the corporation was related to another financial institution at the end of the year, in which case, subject to subsection (4), its capital deduction for the year is nil.

**(2) Related financial institution** — A corporation that is a financial institution at any time during a taxation year and that was related to another financial institution at the end of the year may file with the Minister an agreement in prescribed form on behalf of the related group of which the corporation is a member under which an amount that does not exceed the total of $200,000,000 and the lesser of

(a) $20,000,000, and

(b) 1/5 of the amount, if any, by which the total of all amounts, each of which is the taxable capital employed in Canada of a financial institution for the year that is a member of the related group, exceeds $200,000,000

is allocated among the members of the related group for the taxation year.

**Related Provisions**: 190.15(6) — Where corporations deemed not related.

**Forms**: T2 SCH 39: Agreement among related financial institutions Part VI tax.

**(3) Idem** — The Minister may request a corporation that is a financial institution at any time during a taxation year and that was related to any other financial institution at the end of the year to file with the Minister an agreement referred to in subsection (2) and, if the corporation does not file such an agreement within 30 days after receiving the request, the Minister may allocate an amount among the members of the related group of which the corporation is a member for the year not exceeding the total of $200,000,000 and the lesser of

(a) $20,000,000, and

(b) 1/5 of the amount, if any, by which the total of all amounts, each of which is the taxable capital employed in Canada of a financial institution for the year that is a member of the related group, exceeds $200,000,000.

**Notes**: 190.15(1)(b), (2)(b) and (3)(b) amended by 1991 technical bill, retroactive to 1990, to provide for the capital deduction to be determined by reference to "taxable capital employed in Canada" rather than "taxable capital", and to delete a requirement to calculate a corporation's taxable capital employed in Canada as though its capital deduction were nil.

**(4) Idem** — For the purposes of this Part, the least amount allocated for a taxation year to each member of a related group under an agreement described in subsection (2) or by the Minister pursuant to subsection (3) is the capital deduction for the taxation year of that member, but, if no such allocation is made, the capital deduction of each member of the related group for that year is nil.

**(5) Idem** — Where a corporation (in this subsection referred to as the "first corporation") has more than one taxation year ending in the same calendar year and is related in 2 or more of those taxation years to another corporation that has a taxation year ending in that calendar year, the capital deduction of the first corporation for each such taxation year at the end of which it is related to the other corporation is, for the purposes of this Part, an amount equal to its capital deduction for the first such taxation year.

**Related Provisions**: 190.16(5) — Rule in 190.15(5) applies to allocation of capital allowance; 190.17(5) — Rule in 190.15(5) applies to allocation of enhanced capital deduction.

**(6) Idem** — Two corporations that would, but for this subsection, be related to each other solely because of

(a) the control of any corporation by Her Majesty in right of Canada or a province, or

(b) a right referred to in paragraph 251(5)(b),

are, for the purposes of this section and section 190.14, deemed not to be related to each other except that, where at any time a taxpayer has a right referred to in paragraph 251(5)(b) with respect to shares and it can reasonably be considered that one of the main purposes for the acquisition of the right was to avoid any limitation on the amount of a corporation's capital deduction for a taxation year, for the purpose of determining whether a corporation is related to any other corporation, the corporations are, for the purpose of this section, deemed to be in the same position in relation to each other as if the right were immediate and absolute and as if the taxpayer had exercised the right at that time.

**Related Provisions**: 190.16(5) — Rule in 190.15(6) applies to allocation of capital allowance; 190.17(5) — Rule in 190.15(6) applies to allocation of enhanced capital deduction; 256(6), (6.1) — Meaning of "control".

**Notes**: Closing words of 190.15(6) amended by 1995-97 technical bill, effective April 27, 1995, to add the words "as if the right were immediate and absolute and" near the end.

190.15(6) added by 1992 technical bill, retroactive to 1989 and later taxation years.

**Definitions [s. 190.15]**: "amount" — 181(3), 190(2), 248(1); "calendar year" — *Interpretation Act* 37(1)(a); "control" — 256(6), (6.1); "corporation" — 248(1), *Interpretation Act* 35(1); "financial institution" — 190(1); "Minister" — 248(1); "province" — *Interpretation Act* 35(1); "related" — 190.15(6), 251; "related group" — 251(4); "taxation year" — 249.

**190.16 (1) Capital allowance** — For the purposes of this Part, the capital allowance for a taxation year of a life insurance corporation that carries on business in Canada at any time in the year is the total of

(a) $10,000,000,

(b) 1/2 of the amount, if any, by which the lesser of

(i) $50,000,000, and

(ii) its taxable capital employed in Canada for the year

exceeds $10,000,000,

(c) 1/4 of the amount, if any, by which the lesser of

(i) $100,000,000, and

(ii) its taxable capital employed in Canada for the year

exceeds $50,000,000,

(d) 1/2 of the amount, if any, by which the lesser of

(i) $300,000,000, and

(ii) its taxable capital employed in Canada for the year

exceeds $200,000,000, and

(e) 3/4 of the amount, if any, by which its taxable capital employed in Canada for the year exceeds $300,000,000,

unless the corporation is related at the end of the year to another life insurance corporation that carries on business in Canada, in which case, subject to subsection (4), its capital allowance for the year is nil.

**(2) Related life insurance corporation** — A life insurance corporation that carries on business in Canada at any time in a taxation year and that is related at the end of the year to another life insurance corporation that carries on business in Canada may file with the Minister an agreement, in prescribed form on behalf of the related group of life insurance corporations of which the corporation is a member, under which an amount that does not exceed the total of

(a) $10,000,000,

(b) ½ of the amount, if any, by which the lesser of

(i) $50,000,000, and

(ii) the total of all amounts, each of which is the taxable capital employed in Canada of a life insurance corporation for the year that is a member of the related group,

exceeds $10,000,000,

(c) ¼ of the amount, if any, by which the lesser of

(i) $100,000,000, and

(ii) the total of all amounts, each of which is the taxable capital employed in Canada of a life insurance corporation for the year that is a member of the related group,

exceeds $50,000,000,

(d) ½ of the amount, if any, by which the lesser of

(i) $300,000,000, and

(ii) the total of all amounts, each of which is the taxable capital employed in Canada of a life insurance corporation for the year that is a member of the related group,

exceeds $200,000,000, and

(e) ¾ of the amount, if any, by which the total of all amounts, each of which is the taxable capital employed in Canada of a life insurance corporation for the year that is a member of the related group, exceeds $300,000,000

is allocated among the members of that related group for the year.

**Forms**: T2 SCH 40: Agreement among related life insurance corporations.

**(3) Idem** — The Minister may request a life insurance corporation that carries on business in Canada at any time in a taxation year and that, at the end of the year, is related to any other life insurance corporation that carries on business in Canada to file with the Minister an agreement referred to in subsection (2) and, if the corporation does not file such an agreement within 30 days after receiving the request, the Minister may allocate among the members of the related group of life insurance corporations of which the corporation is a member for the year an amount not exceeding the total of

(a) $10,000,000,

(b) ½ of the amount, if any, by which the lesser of

(i) $50,000,000, and

(ii) the total of all amounts, each of which is the taxable capital employed in Canada of a life insurance corporation for the year that is a member of the related group,

exceeds $10,000,000,

(c) ¼ of the amount, if any, by which the lesser of

(i) $100,000,000, and

(ii) the total of all amounts, each of which is the taxable capital employed in Canada of a life insurance corporation for the year that is a member of the related group,

exceeds $50,000,000,

(d) ½ of the amount, if any, by which the lesser of

(i) $300,000,000, and

(ii) the total of all amounts, each of which is the taxable capital employed in Canada of a life insurance corporation for the year that is a member of the related group,

exceeds $200,000,000, and

(e) ¾ of the amount, if any, by which the total of all amounts, each of which is the taxable capital employed in Canada of a life insurance corporation for the year that is a member of the related group, exceeds $300,000,000.

**(4) Idem** — For the purposes of this Part, the least amount allocated for a taxation year to a member of a related group under an agreement described in subsection (2) or by the Minister under subsection (3) is the capital allowance for that year of the member.

**(5) Provisions applicable to Part** — Subsections 190.15(5) and (6) apply to this section with such modifications as the circumstances require.

**Notes**: 190.16 added by 1993 technical bill, effective for taxation years that end after February 25, 1992. As well, where the corporation elects under para. 88(2)(b) of the 1993 technical bill (see Notes to 190.11) for amended 190.11(b)(i) to apply to its 1991 and later taxation years, 190.16 applies to the 1991 and 1992 taxation years; and in that case, notwithstanding 152(4) to (5), such assessments and determinations in respect of any taxation year shall be made as are consequential on the application of 190.16 to taxation years that end before February 26, 1992.

**Definitions [s. 190.16]**: "amount", "business" — 248(1); "Canada" — 255; "carrying on business in Canada" — 253; "life insurance corporation", "Minister", "prescribed" — 248(1); "related" — 251(2); "related group" — 251(4); "taxable capital employed in Canada" — 190.11; "taxation year" — 249.

**190.17 (1) Enhanced capital deduction** — For the purpose of subsection 190.1(1.2), the enhanced capital deduction of a corporation for a taxation year is $400,000,000, unless the corporation was related to a financial institution (other than a life insurance corporation) at the end of the year, in which case, subject to subsection (4), the corporation's enhanced capital deduction for the year is nil.

S. 190.17(1)          Income Tax Act

**Related Provisions**: 190.1(1.2) — Additional tax payable by deposit-taking institutions; 190.17(2)–(4) — Allocation of deduction among related institutions.

**(2) Related financial institution** — A corporation that is a financial institution at any time in a taxation year and that is related to another financial institution (other than a life insurance corporation) at the end of the year may file with the Minister an agreement in prescribed form on behalf of the related group of which the corporation is a member under which an amount that does not exceed $400,000,000 is allocated among the members of the group for the year.

**(3) Minister's powers** — The Minister may request a corporation that is a financial institution at any time in a taxation year and that is related to any other financial institution (other than a life insurance corporation) at the end of the year to file with the Minister an agreement referred to in subsection (2) and, if the corporation does not file such an agreement within 30 days after receiving the request, the Minister may allocate an amount that does not exceed $400,000,000 among the members of the related group of which the corporation is a member for the year.

**(4) Least amount allocated** — The least amount allocated for a taxation year to a member of a related group under an agreement described in subsection (2) or by the Minister under subsection (3) is the enhanced capital deduction for the taxation year of the member, but, if no such allocation is made, the enhanced capital deduction of the member for the year is nil.

**(5) Provisions applicable to Part** — Subsections 190.15(5) and (6) apply to this section with such modifications as the circumstances require.

**Notes**: 190.17 added by 1995 Budget, effective for taxation years that end after February 27, 1995. It contains the rules for determining the amount of a corporation's enhanced capital deduction for the purposes of the new temporary Part VI capital tax on financial institutions, other than life insurance corporations, in 190.1(1.2). These rules parallel the rules in 190.15 concerning a corporation's capital deduction for purposes of the basic Part VI tax.

190.17 to 190.19 applied to the pre-1990 Part VI tax. Part VI was completely revised by 1989 Budget, effective 1990.

## Administrative Provisions

**190.2 Return** — A corporation that is or would, but for subsection 190.1(3), be liable to pay tax under this Part for a taxation year shall file with the Minister, not later than the day on or before which the corporation is required by section 150 to file its return of income for the year under Part I, a return of capital for the year in prescribed form containing an estimate of the tax payable under this Part by it for the year.

**Related Provisions**: 150.1(5) — Electronic filing; 235 — Penalty for late filing of return even where no balance owing.

**Notes**: 190.2 amended by 1992 technical bill, effective for 1991 and later taxation years, to add "or would, but for subsection 190.1(3), be". In other words, a return must still be filed if no Part VI tax is payable only because it is fully credited against Part I tax.

**Definitions [s. 190.2]**: "corporation" — 248(1), *Interpretation Act* 35(1); "Minister", "prescribed" — 248(1); "tax payable" — 248(2); "taxation year" — 249.

**Forms [s. 190.2]**: T2 SCH 38: Part VI tax on capital of financial institutions; T2 SCH 42: Calculation of unused Part VI tax credit and unused Part I tax credit.

**190.21 Provisions applicable to Part** — Sections 152, 158 and 159, subsection 161(11), sections 162 to 167 and Division J of Part I apply to this Part with such modifications as the circumstances require and, for the purpose of this section, paragraph 152(6)(a) shall be read as follows:

"(a) a deduction under subsection 190.1(3) in respect of any unused surtax credit or unused Part I tax credit (within the meanings assigned by subsection 190.1(5)) for a subsequent taxation year,".

**Notes**: 190.21 enacted to replace 190.21 to 190.24 by 1992 technical bill, effective for 1992 and later taxation years. For the 1991 taxation year, read 190.24 as follows:

190.24 Section 152, subsection 157(2.1), sections 158 and 159, subsections 161(2.1), (2.2), (7) and (11), sections 162 to 167 and Division J of Part I apply to this Part with such modifications as the circumstances require and, for the purpose of this section, paragraph 152(6)(a) shall be read as follows:

(a) a deduction under subsection 190.1(3) in respect of any unused Part I tax credit (within the meaning assigned by subsection 190.1(5)) for a subsequent taxation year,

For years before the above amendments, 190.21 dealt with payment of instalments; 190.22 defined the instalment bases; 190.23 dealt with interest; and 190.24 was similar to the present 190.21.

The definition "financial institution" in 190(1) was amended by 1990 Budget/1991 technical bill to add life insurance corporations and certain holding companies. For taxation years commencing before February 21, 1990 of such corporations, payment of Part VI tax was prorated to begin on February 21, 1990 by reading 190.21 differently.

**190.211 Provisions applicable — Crown corporations** — Section 27 applies to this Part with any modifications that the circumstances require.

**Notes**: 190.211 added by 1995-97 technical bill, retroactive to May 24, 1985. It confirms that a prescribed federal Crown corporation is liable to tax under Part VI. See Notes to 181.71.

# PART VI.1 — TAX ON CORPORATIONS PAYING DIVIDENDS ON TAXABLE PREFERRED SHARES

**191. (1) Definitions** — In this Part,

**"excluded dividend"** means a dividend

(a) paid by a corporation to a shareholder that had a substantial interest in the corporation at the time the dividend was paid,

(b) paid by a corporation that was a financial intermediary corporation or a private holding corporation at the time the dividend was paid,

(c) paid by a particular corporation that would, but for paragraphs (h) and (i) of the definition "financial intermediary corporation" in this subsection, have been a financial intermediary corporation at the time the dividend was paid, except where the dividend was paid to a controlling corporation in respect of the particular corporation or to a specified person (within the meaning assigned by paragraph (h) of the definition "taxable preferred share" in subsection 248(1)) in relation to such a controlling corporation,

(d) paid by a mortgage investment corporation, or

(e) that is a capital gains dividend within the meaning assigned by subsection 131(1);

**Related Provisions**: 191(4)(d) — Deemed excluded dividend.

**"financial intermediary corporation"** means a corporation that is

(a) a corporation described in subparagraph (b)(ii) of the definition "retirement savings plan" in subsection 146(1),

(b) an investment corporation,

(c) a mortgage investment corporation,

(d) a mutual fund corporation,

(e) a prescribed venture capital corporation, or

(f) a prescribed labour-sponsored venture capital corporation,

but does not include

(g) a prescribed corporation,

(h) a corporation that is controlled by or for the benefit of one or more corporations (each of which is referred to in this subsection as a "controlling corporation") other than financial intermediary corporations or private holding corporations unless the controlling corporations and specified persons (within the meaning assigned by paragraph (h) of the definition "taxable preferred share" in subsection 248(1)) in relation to the controlling corporations do not own in the aggregate shares of the capital stock of the corporation having a fair market value of more than 10% of the fair market value of all of the issued and outstanding shares of the capital stock of the corporation (those fair market values being determined without regard to any voting rights attaching to those shares), or

(i) any particular corporation in which another corporation (other than a financial intermediary corporation or a private holding corporation) has a substantial interest unless the other corporation and specified persons (within the meaning assigned by paragraph (h) of the definition "taxable preferred share" in subsection 248(1)) in relation to the other corporation do not own in the aggregate shares of the capital stock of the particular corporation having a fair market value of more than 10% of the fair market value of all of the issued and outstanding shares of the capital stock of the particular corporation (those fair market values being determined without regard to any voting rights attaching to those shares);

**Related Provisions**: 256(6), (6.1) — Meaning of "controlled".

**Regulations**: 6700 (prescribed venture capital corporation); 6701 (prescribed labour-sponsored venture capital corporation).

**"private holding corporation"** means a private corporation the only undertaking of which is the investing of its funds, but does not include

(a) a specified financial institution,

(b) any particular corporation that owns shares of another corporation in which it has a substantial interest, except where the other corporation would, but for that substantial interest, be a financial intermediary corporation or a private holding corporation, or

(c) any particular corporation in which another corporation owns shares and has a substantial interest, except where the other corporation would, but for that substantial interest, be a private holding corporation.

**Notes**: Para. (b) amended by 1991 technical bill, retroactive to 1988, to correct a circularity problem.

**Related Provisions**: 253.1 — Deeming rule re investments in limited partnerships.

**(2) Substantial interest** — For the purposes of this Part, a shareholder has a substantial interest in a corporation at any time if the corporation is a taxable Canadian corporation and

(a) the shareholder is related (otherwise than by reason of a right referred to in paragraph 251(5)(b)) to the corporation at that time; or

(b) the shareholder owned, at that time,

(i) shares of the capital stock of the corporation that would give the shareholder 25% or more of the votes that could be cast under all circumstances at an annual meeting of shareholders of the corporation,

(ii) shares of the capital stock of the corporation having a fair market value of 25% or more of the fair market value of all the issued shares of the capital stock of the corporation,

and either

(iii) shares (other than shares that would be taxable preferred shares if the definition "taxable preferred share" in subsection 248(1) were read without reference to subparagraph (b)(iv) thereof and if they were issued after June 18, 1987 and were not grandfathered shares) of the capital stock of the corporation having a fair market value of 25% or more of the fair market value of all those shares of the capital stock of the corporation, or

(iv) in respect of each class of shares of the capital stock of the corporation, shares of that class having a fair market value of 25% or more of the fair market value of all the issued shares of that class,

and for the purposes of this paragraph, a shareholder shall be deemed to own at any time each share of the capital stock of a corporation that is owned, otherwise than by reason of this paragraph, at that time by a person to whom the shareholder is related (otherwise than by reason of a right referred to in paragraph 251(5)(b)).

**Related Provisions**: 191(3) — Substantial interest.

**(3) Idem** — Notwithstanding subsection (2),

(a) where it can reasonably be considered that the principal purpose for a person acquiring an interest that would, but for this subsection, be a substantial interest in a corporation is to avoid or limit the application of Part I or IV.1 or this Part, the person shall be deemed not to have a substantial interest in the corporation;

(b) where it can reasonably be considered that the principal purpose for an acquisition of a share of the capital stock of a corporation (in this paragraph referred to as the "issuer") by any person (in this paragraph referred to as the "acquirer") who had, immediately after the time of the acquisition, a substantial interest in the issuer from another person who did not, immediately before that time, have a substantial interest in the issuer, was to avoid or limit the application of Part I or IV.1 or this Part with respect to a dividend on the share, the acquirer and specified persons (within the meaning assigned by paragraph (h) of the definition "taxable preferred share" in subsection 248(1)) in relation to the acquirer shall be deemed not to have a substantial interest in the issuer with respect to any dividend paid on the share;

(c) a corporation described in paragraphs (a) to (f) of the definition "financial intermediary corporation" in subsection (1) shall be deemed not to have a substantial interest in another corporation unless it is related (otherwise than by reason of a right referred to in paragraph 251(5)(b)) to the other corporation;

(d) any partnership or trust, other than

(i) a partnership all the members of which are related to each other otherwise than by reason of a right referred to in paragraph 251(5)(b),

(ii) a trust in which each person who is beneficially interested is

(A) related (otherwise than because of a right referred to in paragraph 251(5)(b)) to each other person who is beneficially interested in the trust and who is not a registered charity, or

(B) a registered charity

and, for the purpose of this subparagraph, where a particular person who is beneficially interested in the trust is an aunt, uncle, niece or nephew of another person, the particular person and any person who is a child or descendant of the particular person shall be deemed to be related to the other person and to any person who is the child or descendant of the other person, or

(iii) a trust in which only one person (other than a registered charity) is beneficially interested,

shall be deemed not to have a substantial interest in a corporation; and

(e) where at any time a shareholder holds a share of the capital stock of a corporation to which paragraph (g) of the definition "taxable preferred share" in subsection 248(1) or paragraph (e) of the definition "taxable RFI share" in that subsection applies to deem the share to be a taxable preferred share or a taxable RFI share, the shareholder shall be deemed not to have a substantial interest in the corporation at that time.

**Related Provisions**: 248(25) — Beneficially interested.

**Notes**: 191(3)(a) and (b) amended by 1992 technical bill, effective for dividends paid or received after December 20, 1991. For earlier dividends, ignore the references to "Part I" in each para.

191(3)(d)(ii) and (iii) amended by 1992 technical bill, effective 1991. Before 1991, ignore clause (ii)(B) and read subpara. (iii) without the words "other than a registered charity".

**(4) Deemed dividends** — Where at any particular time

(a) a share of the capital stock of a corporation is issued,

(b) the terms or conditions of a share of the capital stock of a corporation are changed, or

(c) an agreement in respect of a share of the capital stock of a corporation is changed or entered into,

and the terms or conditions of the share or the agreement in respect of the share specify an amount in respect of the share, including an amount for which the share is to be redeemed, acquired or cancelled (together with, where so provided, any accrued and unpaid dividends thereon) and where paragraph (a) applies, the specified amount does not exceed the fair market value of the consideration for which the share was issued, and where paragraph (b) or (c) applies, the specified amount does not exceed the fair market value of the share immediately before the particular time, the amount of any dividend deemed to have been paid on a redemption, acquisition or cancellation of the share to which subsection 84(2) or (3) applies shall

(d) for the purposes of this Part and section 187.2, be deemed to be an excluded dividend and an excepted dividend, respectively, unless

(i) where paragraph (a) applies, the share was issued for consideration that included a taxable preferred share, or

(ii) where paragraph (b) or (c) applies, the share was, immediately before the particular time, a taxable preferred share, and

(e) be deemed not to be a dividend to which subsection 112(2.1) or 138(6) applies to deny a deduction with respect to the dividend in computing the taxable income of a corporation under subsection 112(1) or (2) or 138(6), unless

(i) where paragraph (a) applies, the share was issued for consideration that included a term preferred share or for the purpose of raising capital or as part of a series of transactions or events the purpose of which was to raise capital, and

(ii) where paragraph (b) or (c) applies, the share was, immediately before the particular time, a term preferred share, or the terms or conditions of the share were changed, or the agreement in respect of the share was changed or entered into for the purpose of raising capital or as part of a series of transactions or events the purpose of which was to raise capital.

**Related Provisions**: 87(2)(rr) — Amalgamations — continuing corporation; 87(4.2)(f) — Amalgamations — where amount specified for purposes of 191(4); 248(10) — Series of transactions.

**(5) Where subsec. (4) does not apply** — Subsection (4) does not apply to the extent that the total of

(a) the amount paid on the redemption, acquisition or cancellation of the share, and

(b) all amounts each of which is an amount (other than an amount deemed by subsection 84(4) to be a dividend) paid, after the particular time and before the redemption, acquisition or cancellation of the share, on a reduction of the paid-up capital of the corporation in respect of the share

exceeds the specified amount referred to in subsection (4).

**Definitions [s. 191]**: "aunt" — 252(2)(e); "beneficially interested" — 248(25); "capital gain" — 39(1)(a), 248(1); "child" — 252(1); "class of shares" — 248(6); "control" — 256(6), (6.1); "corporation" — 248(1), *Interpretation Act* 35(1); "dividend" — 248(1); "excluded dividend", "financial intermediary corporation" — 191(1); "grandfathered share" — 248(1); "investment corporation" — 130.1(6), 248(1); "mortgage investment corporation" — 130.1(6), 248(1); "mutual fund corporation" — 131(8), 248(1); "nephew", "niece" — 252(2)(g); "paid-up capital" — 89(1), 248(1); "person", "prescribed" — 248(1); "prescribed labour-sponsored venture capital corporation" — Reg. 6701; "prescribed venture capital corporation" — Reg. 6700; "private corporation" — 89(1), 248(1); "private holding corporation" — 191(1); "registered char-

ity" — 248(1); "related" — 251(2); "series of transactions or events" — 248(10); "share", "shareholder", "specified financial institution" — 248(1); "substantial interest" — 191(2), (3); "taxable Canadian corporation" — 89(1), 248(1); "taxable income" — 2(2), 248(1); "taxable preferred share", "taxable RFI share", "term preferred share" — 248(1); "trust" — 104(1), 248(1), (3); "uncle" — 252(2)(e); "undertaking" — 253.1(a).

**191.1 (1) Tax on taxable dividends** — Every taxable Canadian corporation shall pay a tax under this Part for each taxation year equal to the amount, if any, by which

(a) the total of

(i) 66⅔% of the amount, if any, by which the total of all taxable dividends (other than excluded dividends) paid by the corporation in the year and after 1987 on short-term preferred shares exceeds the corporation's dividend allowance for the year,

(ii) 40% of the amount, if any, by which the total of all taxable dividends (other than excluded dividends) paid by the corporation in the year and after 1987 on taxable preferred shares (other than short-term preferred shares) of all classes in respect of which an election under subsection 191.2(1) has been made exceeds the amount, if any, by which the corporation's dividend allowance for the year exceeds the total of the dividends referred to in subparagraph (i),

(iii) 25% of the amount, if any, by which the total of all taxable dividends (other than excluded dividends) paid by the corporation in the year and after 1987 on taxable preferred shares (other than short-term preferred shares) of all classes in respect of which an election under subsection 191.2(1) has not been made exceeds the amount, if any, by which the corporation's dividend allowance for the year exceeds the total of the dividends referred to in subparagraphs (i) and (ii), and

(iv) the total of all amounts each of which is an amount determined for the year in respect of the corporation under paragraph 191.3(1)(d)

exceeds

(b) the total of all amounts each of which is an amount determined for the year in respect of the corporation under paragraph 191.3(1)(c).

**Related Provisions**: 18(1)(t) — Tax is non-deductible; 87(4.2) — Exchanged shares; 110(1)(k) — Deduction of ¾ of Part VI.1 tax from taxable income; 157(1)–(3) — Payment of Part VI.1 tax; 161(4.1) — Limitation respecting corporations; 191.3(6) — Payment by transferor corporation; 227(14) — No tax on corporation exempt under s. 149.

**Notes**: The legislation enacting Part VI.1 (1988 tax reform) provides that in the application of 191.1(1) to shares issued before December 16, 1987 (other than shares deemed by the Act to have been issued after December 15, 1987) the references to "short-term preferred shares" shall be read as references to "short-term preferred shares issued after December 15, 1987".

**S. 191.1(1)**          Income Tax Act

**Advance Tax Rulings**: ATR-46: Financial difficulty.

**Forms**: T2 SCH 43: Calculation of Parts IV.1 and VI.1 taxes.

**(2) Dividend allowance** — For the purposes of this section, a taxable Canadian corporation's "dividend allowance" for a taxation year is the amount, if any, by which

    (a) $500,000

exceeds

    (b) the amount, if any, by which the total of taxable dividends (other than excluded dividends) paid by it on taxable preferred shares, or shares that would be taxable preferred shares if they were issued after June 18, 1987 and were not grandfathered shares, in the calendar year immediately preceding the calendar year in which the taxation year ended exceeds $1,000,000,

unless the corporation is associated in the taxation year with one or more other taxable Canadian corporations, in which case, except as otherwise provided in this section, its dividend allowance for the year is nil.

**Related Provisions**: 87(2)(rr) — Amalgamations — continuing corporation.

**(3) Associated corporations** — If all of the taxable Canadian corporations that are associated with each other in a taxation year and that have paid taxable dividends (other than excluded dividends) on taxable preferred shares in the year have filed with the Minister in prescribed form an agreement whereby, for the purposes of this section, they allocate an amount to one or more of them for the taxation year, and the amount so allocated or the total of the amounts so allocated, as the case may be, is equal to the total dividend allowance for the year of those corporations and all other taxable Canadian corporations with which each such corporation is associated in the year, the dividend allowance for the year for each of the corporations is the amount so allocated to it.

**Forms**: T1174: Agreement among associated corporations.

**(4) Total dividend allowance** — For the purposes of this section, the "total dividend allowance" of a group of taxable Canadian corporations that are associated with each other in a taxation year is the amount, if any, by which

    (a) $500,000

exceeds

    (b) the amount, if any, by which the total of taxable dividends (other than excluded dividends) paid by those corporations on taxable preferred shares, or shares that would be taxable preferred shares if they were issued after June 18, 1987 and were not grandfathered shares, in the calendar year immediately preceding the calendar year in which the taxation year ended exceeds $1,000,000.

**Related Provisions**: 87(2)(rr) — Amalgamations — continuing corporation.

**(5) Failure to file agreement** — If any of the taxable Canadian corporations that are associated with each other in a taxation year and that have paid taxable dividends (other than excluded dividends) on taxable preferred shares in the year has failed to file with the Minister an agreement as contemplated by subsection (3) within 30 days after notice in writing by the Minister has been forwarded to any of them that such an agreement is required for the purpose of any assessment of tax under this Part, the Minister shall, for the purpose of this section, allocate an amount to one or more of them for the taxation year, which amount or the total of which amounts, as the case may be, shall equal the total dividend allowance for the year for those corporations and all other taxable Canadian corporations with which each such corporation is associated in the year, and the dividend allowance for the year of each of the corporations is the amount so allocated to it.

**(6) Dividend allowance in short years** — Notwithstanding any other provision of this section,

    (a) where a corporation has a taxation year that is less than 51 weeks, its dividend allowance for the year is that proportion of its dividend allowance for the year determined without reference to this paragraph that the number of days in the year is of 365; and

    (b) where a taxable Canadian corporation (in this paragraph referred to as the "first corporation") has more than one taxation year ending in a calendar year and is associated in two or more of those taxation years with another taxable Canadian corporation that has a taxation year ending in that calendar year, the dividend allowance of the first corporation for each taxation year in which it is associated with the other corporation ending in that calendar year is, subject to the application of paragraph (a), an amount equal to the amount that would be its dividend allowance for the first such taxation year if the allowance were determined without reference to paragraph (a).

**Definitions [s. 191.1]**: "amount" — 248(1); "associated" — 256; "calendar year" — *Interpretation Act* 37(1)(a); "corporation" — 248(1), *Interpretation Act* 35(1); "dividend" — 248(1); "dividend allowance" — 191.1(2); "excluded dividend" — 191(1); "grandfathered share", "Minister", "prescribed", "share", "short-term preferred share" — 248(1); "taxable Canadian corporation", "taxable dividend" — 89(1), 248(1); "taxable preferred share" — 248(1); "taxation year" — 249; "total dividend allowance" — 191.1(4); "writing" — *Interpretation Act* 35(1).

**Interpretation Bulletins [s. 191.1]**: IT-88R2: Stock dividends.

**191.2 (1) Election** — For the purposes of determining the tax payable by reason of subparagraphs 191.1(1)(a)(ii) and (iii), a taxable Canadian corporation (other than a financial intermediary corporation or a private holding corporation) may make an election with respect to a class of its taxable preferred shares the terms and conditions of which require an election to be made under this subsection by filing a prescribed form with the Minister

(a) not later than the day on or before which its return of income under Part I is required by section 150 to be filed for the taxation year in which shares of that class are first issued or first become taxable preferred shares; or

(b) within the 6 month period commencing on any of the following days, namely,

(i) the day of mailing of any notice of assessment of tax payable under this Part or Part I by the corporation for that year,

(ii) where the corporation has served a notice of objection to an assessment described in subparagraph (i), the day of mailing of a notice that the Minister has confirmed or varied the assessment,

(iii) where the corporation has instituted an appeal in respect of an assessment described in subparagraph (i) to the Tax Court of Canada, the day of mailing of a copy of the decision of the Court to the taxpayer, and

(iv) where the corporation has instituted an appeal in respect of an assessment described in subparagraph (i) to the Federal Court of Canada or the Supreme Court of Canada, the day on which the judgment of the Court is pronounced or delivered or the day on which the corporation discontinues the appeal.

**Related Provisions**: 87(4.2)(e) — Amalgamation; 187.2 — Tax on dividends on taxable preferred shares.

**Forms**: T769: Election under section 191.2 by an issuer of taxable preferred shares to pay Part VI.1 tax at a rate of 40%.

**(2) Time of election** — An election with respect to a class of taxable preferred shares filed in accordance with subsection (1) shall be deemed to have been filed before any dividend on a share of that class is paid.

**(3) Assessment** — Where an election has been filed under subsection (1), the Minister shall, notwithstanding subsections 152(4) and (5), assess or reassess the tax, interest or penalties payable under this Act by any corporation for any relevant taxation year in order to take into account the election.

**Definitions [s. 191.2]**: "assessment" — 248(1); "corporation" — 248(1), *Interpretation Act* 35(1); "dividend" — 248(1); "financial intermediary corporation" — 191(1); "Minister", "prescribed" — 248(1); "private holding corporation" — 191(1); "share" — 248(1); "tax payable" — 248(2); "taxable Canadian corporation" — 89(1), 248(1); "taxable preferred share" — 248(1); "taxation year" — 249; "taxpayer" — 248(1).

**Interpretation Bulletins [s. 191.2]**: IT-88R2: Stock dividends.

**191.3 (1) Agreement respecting liability for tax** — Where a corporation (in this section referred to as the "transferor corporation") and a taxable Canadian corporation (in this section referred to as the "transferee corporation") that was related (otherwise than because of a right referred to in paragraph 251(5)(b) or because of the control of any corporation by Her Majesty in right of Canada or a province) to the transferor corporation

(a) throughout a particular taxation year of the transferor corporation (or, where the transferee corporation came into existence in that year, throughout the part of that year in which the transferee corporation was in existence), and

(b) throughout the last taxation year of the transferee corporation ending at or before the end of the particular taxation year (or, where the transferor corporation came into existence in that last taxation year of the transferee corporation, throughout that part of that last year in which the transferor corporation was in existence)

file as provided in subsection (2) an agreement or amended agreement with the Minister under which the transferee corporation agrees to pay all or any portion, as is specified in the agreement, of the tax for that taxation year of the transferor corporation that would, but for the agreement, be payable under this Part by the transferor corporation (other than any tax payable by the transferor corporation by reason of another agreement made under this section), the following rules apply, namely,

(c) the amount of tax specified in the agreement is an amount determined for that taxation year of the transferor corporation in respect of the transferor corporation for the purpose of paragraph 191.1(1)(b),

(d) the amount of tax specified in the agreement is an amount determined in respect of the transferee corporation for its last taxation year ending at or before the end of that taxation year of the transferor corporation for the purpose of subparagraph 191.1(1)(a)(iv), and

(e) the transferor corporation and the transferee corporation are jointly and severally liable to pay the amount of tax specified in the agreement and any interest or penalty in respect thereof.

**Related Provisions**: 87(2)(ss) — Amalgamations — continuing corporation; 110(1)(k) — Part VI.1 tax; 191.3(1.1) — Consideration for entering into agreement deemed to be nil; 191.3(6) — Payment by transferor corporation; 256(6), (6.1) — Meaning of "control".

**Notes**: Opening words of 191.3(1) amended by 1995-97 technical bill, effective for taxation years of the transferor corporation that end after April 26, 1995, to add "or because of the control of any corporation by Her Majesty in right of Canada or a province".

191.3(1)(a) and (b) amended by 1995-97 technical bill, effective for taxation years of a transferor corporation that begin after 1994, to add the parenthesized words in both paragraphs.

**Forms**: T2 SCH 45: Agreement respecting liability for Part VI.1 tax.

**(1.1) Consideration for agreement** — For the purposes of Part I of this Act, where property is acquired at any time by a transferee corporation as

**S. 191.3(1.1)**      Income Tax Act

consideration for entering into an agreement with a transferor corporation that is filed under this section,

  (a) where the property was owned by the transferor corporation immediately before that time,

    (i) the transferor corporation shall be deemed to have disposed of the property at that time for proceeds equal to the fair market value of the property at that time, and

    (ii) the transferor corporation shall not be entitled to deduct any amount in computing its income as a consequence of the transfer of the property, except any amount arising as a consequence of subparagraph (i);

  (b) the cost at which the property was acquired by the transferee corporation at that time shall be deemed to be equal to the fair market value of the property at that time;

  (c) the transferee corporation shall not be required to add an amount in computing its income solely because of the acquisition at that time of the property; and

  (d) no benefit shall be deemed to have been conferred on the transferor corporation as a consequence of the transferor corporation entering into an agreement filed under this section.

**Notes**: 191.3(1.1) added by 1994 tax amendments bill (Part I), retroactive to 1988. It is similar to 80.04(5).

**(2) Manner of filing agreement** — An agreement or amended agreement referred to in subsection (1) between a transferor corporation and a transferee corporation shall be deemed not to have been filed with the Minister unless

  (a) it is in prescribed form;

  (b) it is filed on or before the day on or before which the transferor corporation's return for the year in respect of which the agreement is filed is required to be filed under this Part or within the 90 day period commencing on the day of mailing of a notice of assessment of tax payable under this Part or Part I by the transferor corporation for the year or by the transferee corporation for its taxation year ending in the calendar year in which the taxation year of the transferor corporation ends or the mailing of a notification that no tax is payable under this Part or Part I for that taxation year;

  (c) it is accompanied by,

    (i) where the directors of the transferor corporation are legally entitled to administer its affairs, a certified copy of their resolution authorizing the agreement to be made,

    (ii) where the directors of the transferor corporation are not legally entitled to administer its affairs, a certified copy of the document by which the person legally entitled to administer the corporation's affairs authorized the agreement to be made,

    (iii) where the directors of the transferee corporation are legally entitled to administer its affairs, a certified copy of their resolution authorizing the agreement to be made, and

    (iv) where the directors of the transferee corporation are not legally entitled to administer its affairs, a certified copy of the document by which the person legally entitled to administer the corporation's affairs authorized the agreement to be made; and

  (d) where the agreement is not an agreement to which subsection (4) applies, an agreement amending the agreement has not been filed in accordance with this section.

  (e) [Repealed]

**Notes**: 191.3(2)(e), repealed by 1991 technical bill effective 1989, required that the transferor corporation have no Part I tax liability for the year.

**(3) Assessment** — Where an agreement or amended agreement between a transferor corporation and a transferee corporation has been filed under this section with the Minister, the Minister shall, notwithstanding subsections 152(4) and (5), assess or reassess the tax, interest and penalties payable under this Act by the transferor corporation and the transferee corporation for any relevant taxation year in order to take into account the agreement or amended agreement.

**(4) Related corporations** — Where, at any time, a corporation has become related to another corporation and it may reasonably be considered, having regard to all the circumstances, that the main purpose of the corporation becoming related to the other corporation was to transfer, by filing an agreement or an amended agreement under this section, the benefit of a deduction under paragraph 110(1)(k) to a transferee corporation, the amount of the tax specified in the agreement shall, for the purposes of paragraph (1)(c), be deemed to be nil.

**(5) Assessment of transferor corporation** — The Minister may at any time assess a transferor corporation in respect of any amount for which it is jointly and severally liable by reason of paragraph (1)(e) and the provisions of Division I of Part I are applicable in respect of the assessment as though it had been made under section 152.

**(6) Payment by transferor corporation** — Where a transferor corporation and a transferee corporation are by reason of paragraph (1)(e) jointly and severally liable in respect of tax payable by the transferee corporation under subparagraph 191.1(1)(a)(iv) and any interest or penalty in respect thereof, the following rules apply:

  (a) a payment by the transferor corporation on account of the liability shall, to the extent thereof, discharge the joint liability; and

  (b) a payment by the transferee corporation on account of its liability discharges the transferor corporation's liability only to the extent that the payment operates to reduce the transferee corporation's liability under this Act to an amount less than the amount in respect of which the transferor corporation was, by paragraph (1)(e), made jointly and severally liable.

**Definitions [s. 191.3]:** "acquired" — 256(7)–(9); "amount", "assessment" — 248(1); "calendar year" — *Interpretation Act* 37(1)(a); "control" — 256(6)–(9); "corporation" — 248(1), *Interpretation Act* 35(1); "Minister", "prescribed" — 248(1); "province" — *Interpretation Act* 35(1); "related" — 251(2); "tax payable" — 248(2); "taxable Canadian corporation" — 89(1), 248(1); "taxation year" — 249; "transferee corporation", "transferor corporation" — 191.3(1).

**Interpretation Bulletins [s. 191.3]:** IT-88R2: Stock dividends.

**191.4 (1) Information return** — Every corporation that is or would, but for section 191.3, be liable to pay tax under this Part for a taxation year shall, not later than the day on or before which it is required by section 150 to file its return of income for the year under Part I, file with the Minister a return for the year under this Part in prescribed form containing an estimate of the tax payable by it under this Part for the year.

**Related Provisions:** 150.1(5) — Electronic filing; 157(1) — Payment of Part VI.1 tax; 157(2), (2.1) — Special cases; 161(4.1) — Limitation respecting corporations.

**Forms:** T2 SCH 43: Calculation of Parts IV.1 and VI.1 taxes.

**(2) Provisions applicable to Part** — Sections 152, 158 and 159, subsection 161(11), sections 162 to 167 and Division J of Part I apply to this Part with such modifications as the circumstances require.

**Notes:** 191.4(2) amended by 1992 technical bill, effective for 1992 and later taxation years, to delete reference to 161(1) and (2). The change results from the integration of the interest provisions for Parts I, I.3, VI and VI.1 in section 161. See Notes to 157(1).

**(3) Provisions applicable — Crown corporations** — Section 27 applies to this Part with any modifications that the circumstances require.

**Notes:** 191.4(3) added by 1995-97 technical bill, retroactive to 1988. It confirms that a prescribed federal Crown corporation is liable to tax under Part VI.1. See Notes to 181.71.

**Definitions [s. 191.4]:** "corporation" — 248(1), *Interpretation Act* 35(1); "Minister", "prescribed" — 248(1); "tax payable" — 248(2); "taxation year" — 249.

**Interpretation Bulletins [Part VI.1]:** IT-88R2: Stock dividends.

# PART VII — REFUNDABLE TAX ON CORPORATIONS ISSUING QUALIFYING SHARES

**192. (1) Corporation to pay tax** — Every corporation shall pay a tax under this Part for a taxation year equal to the total of all amounts each of which is an amount designated under subsection (4) in respect of a share issued by it in the year.

**Related Provisions:** 227.1(1) — Liability of directors for unpaid Part VII tax.

**Notes:** See Notes at end of s. 193.

**(2) Definition of "Part VII refund"** — In this Part, the "Part VII refund" of a corporation for a taxation year means an amount equal to the lesser of

(a) the total of

(i) the amount, if any, by which the share-purchase tax credit of the corporation for the year exceeds the amount, if any, deducted in respect thereof by it for the year under subsection 127.2(1) from its tax otherwise payable under Part I for the year or the amount deemed by subsection 127.2(2) to have been paid on account of its tax payable under Part I for the year, as the case may be, and

(ii) such amount as the corporation may claim, not exceeding the amount that would, if paragraph (i) of the definition "investment tax credit" in subsection 127(9) were read without reference to the words "the year or", be its investment tax credit at the end of the year in respect of property acquired, or an expenditure made, after April 19, 1983 and on or before the last day of the year, and

(b) the refundable Part VII tax on hand of the corporation at the end of the year.

**Related Provisions:** 248(1)"lawyer" — Definition applies to entire Act.

**(3) Definition of "refundable Part VII tax on hand"** — In this Part, "refundable Part VII tax on hand" of a corporation at the end of a taxation year means the amount, if any, by which

(a) the total of the taxes payable by it under this Part for the year and all preceding taxation years

exceeds the total of

(b) the total of its Part VII refunds for all preceding taxation years, and

(c) the total of all amounts each of which is an amount of tax included in the total described in paragraph (a) in respect of a share that was issued by the corporation and that, at the time it was issued, was not a qualifying share.

**Related Provisions:** 248(1)"refundable Part VII tax on hand" — Definition applies to entire Act.

**(4) Corporation may designate amount** — Every taxable Canadian corporation may, by filing a prescribed form with the Minister at any time on or before the last day of the month immediately following the month in which it issued a qualifying share of its capital stock (other than a share issued before July, 1983 or after 1986, or a share in respect of which the corporation has, on or before that day, designated an amount under subsection 194(4)), designate, for the purposes of this Part and Part I, an amount in respect of that share not exceeding 25% of the amount by which

(a) the amount of the consideration for which the share was issued

exceeds

(b) the amount of any assistance (other than an amount included in computing the share-purchase tax credit of a taxpayer in respect of that share) provided or to be provided by a government, municipality or any other public authority in respect of, or for the acquisition of, the share.

**Related Provisions**: 127.2(10) — Election re first holder; 127.2(11) — Calculation of consideration; 193(2) — Corporation to make payment on account of tax; 193(7) — Avoidance of tax.

**Regulations**: 227 (information returns).

**(4.1) Computing paid-up capital after designation** — Where a corporation has designated an amount under subsection (4) in respect of shares issued at any time after May 23, 1985, in computing, at any particular time after that time, the paid-up capital in respect of the class of shares of the capital stock of the corporation that includes those shares

(a) there shall be deducted the amount, if any, by which

(i) the increase as a result of the issue of those shares in the paid-up capital in respect of all shares of that class, determined without reference to this subsection as it applies to those shares,

exceeds

(ii) the amount, if any, by which the total amount of consideration for which those shares were issued exceeds the total amount designated by the corporation under subsection (4) in respect of those shares; and

(b) there shall be added an amount equal to the lesser of

(i) the amount, if any, by which

(A) the total of all amounts each of which is an amount deemed by subsection 84(3), (4) or (4.1) to be a dividend on shares of that class paid by the corporation after May 23, 1985 and before the particular time

exceeds

(B) the total that would be determined under clause (A) if this Act were read without reference to paragraph (a), and

(ii) the total of all amounts each of which is an amount required by paragraph (a) to be deducted in computing the paid-up capital in respect of that class of shares after May 23, 1985 and before the particular time.

**Related Provisions**: 127.2(8) — Deemed cost of designated share.

**(5) Presumption** — For the purposes of this Act, the Part VII refund of a corporation for a taxation year shall be deemed to be an amount paid on account of its tax under this Part for the year on the last day of the second month following the end of the year.

**(6) Definition of "qualifying share"** — In this Part, "qualifying share", at any time, means a prescribed share of the capital stock of a taxable Canadian corporation issued after May 22, 1985 and before 1987.

**Related Provisions**: 248(1)"qualifying share" — Definition applies to entire Act.

**Regulations**: 6203 (prescribed shares).

**(7) Effect of obligation to acquire shares** — When determining under section 251 whether a corporation and any other person do not deal with each other at arm's length for the purposes of any regulations made for the purposes of subsection (6), a person who has an obligation in equity, under a contract or otherwise, either immediately or in the future and either absolutely or contingently, to acquire shares in a corporation, shall be deemed to be in the same position in relation to the control of the corporation as if that person owned the shares.

**(8) Late designation** — Where a taxable Canadian corporation that issued a share does not designate an amount under subsection (4) in respect of the share on or before the day on or before which the designation was required by that subsection, the corporation shall be deemed to have made the designation on that day if

(a) the corporation has filed with the Minister a prescribed information return relating to the share-purchase tax credit in respect of the share within the time that it would have been so required to file the return had the designation been made on that day, and

(b) within 3 years after that day, the corporation has

(i) designated an amount in respect of the share by filing a prescribed form with the Minister, and

(ii) paid to the Receiver General, at the time the prescribed form referred to in subparagraph (i) is filed, an amount that is a reasonable estimate of the penalty payable by the corporation for the late designation in respect of the share,

except that, where the Minister has mailed a notice to the corporation that a designation has not been made in respect of the share under subsection (4), the designation and payment described in paragraph (b) must be made by the corporation on or before the day that is 90 days after the day of the mailing.

**(9) Penalty for late designation** — Where, pursuant to subsection (8), a corporation made a late designation in respect of a share issued in a month, the corporation shall pay, for each month or part of a month that elapsed during the period beginning on the last day on or before which an amount could have been designated by the corporation under subsection (4) in respect of the share and ending on the day that the late designation is made, a penalty for the late designation in respect of the share in an amount equal to 1% of the amount designated in respect of the share, except that the maximum penalty payable under this subsection by the corporation for a month shall not exceed $500.

**(10) Deemed deduction** — For the purposes of this Act, other than the definition "investment tax credit" in subsection 127(9), the amount, if any, claimed under subparagraph (2)(a)(ii) by a taxpayer for a taxation year shall be deemed to have been deducted by the taxpayer under subsection 127(5) for the year.

**(11) Restriction** — Where at any time a corporation has designated an amount under subsection (4) in respect of a share, no amount may be designated by the corporation at any subsequent time in respect of that share.

**Definitions [s. 192]:** "amount" — 248(1); "arm's length" — 251(1); "class of shares" — 248(6); "corporation" — 248(1), *Interpretation Act* 35(1); "dividend", "Minister" — 248(1); "paid-up capital" — 89(1), 248(1); "person", "property" — 248(1); "qualifying share" — 192(6), 248(1); "share" — 248(1); "taxable Canadian corporation" — 89(1), 248(1); "taxation year" — 249; "taxpayer" — 248(1); "trust" — 104(1), 248(1), (3).

**Interpretation Bulletins [s. 192]:** IT-328R3: Losses on shares on which dividends have been received.

**193. (1) Corporation to file return** — Every corporation that is liable to pay tax under this Part for a taxation year shall, on or before the day on or before which it is required to file its return of income under Part I for the year, file with the Minister a return for the year under this Part in prescribed form.

**Forms:** T2112: Corporation Part VII tax return.

**(2) Corporation to make payment on account of tax** — Where, in a particular month in a taxation year, a corporation issues a share in respect of which it designates an amount under section 192, the corporation shall, on or before the last of the month following the particular month, pay to the Receiver General on account of its tax payable under this Part for the year an amount equal to the total of all amounts so designated.

**(3) Interest** — Where a corporation is liable to pay tax under this Part and has failed to pay all or any part or instalment thereof on or before the day on or before which the tax or instalment, as the case may be, was required to be paid, it shall pay to the Receiver General interest at the prescribed rate on the amount that it failed to pay computed from the day on or before which the amount was required to be paid to the day of payment.

**Related Provisions:** 248(11) — Interest compounded daily.

**Regulations:** 4301(a) (prescribed rate of interest).

**(4) Idem** — For the purposes of computing interest payable by a corporation under subsection (3) for any month or months in the period commencing on the first day of a taxation year and ending two months after the last day of the year in which period the corporation has designated an amount under section 192 in respect of a share issued by it in a particular month in the year, the corporation shall be deemed to have been liable to pay, on or before the last day of the month immediately following the particular month, a part or an instalment of tax for the year equal to that proportion of the amount, if any, by which its tax payable under this Part for the year exceeds its Part VII refund for the year that

(a) the total of all amounts so designated by it under section 192 in respect of shares issued by it in the particular month

is of

(b) the total of all amounts so designated by it under section 192 in respect of shares issued by it in the year.

**(5) Evasion of tax** — Where a corporation that is liable to pay tax under this Part in respect of a share issued by it wilfully, in any manner whatever, evades or attempts to evade payment of the tax and a purchaser of the share or, where the purchaser is a partnership, a member of the partnership knew or ought to have known, at the time the share was acquired, that the corporation would wilfully evade or attempt to evade the tax, for the purposes of section 127.2, the share shall be deemed not to have been acquired.

**(6) Undue deferral** — Where, in a transaction or as part of a series of transactions, a taxpayer acquires a share of a corporation that the taxpayer controls (within the meaning assigned by subsection 186(2)) and it may reasonably be considered that one of the main purposes of the acquisition was to reduce for a period interest on the taxpayer's liability for tax under this Part, the share shall, for the purposes of section 127.2 and this Part (other than this subsection), be deemed not to have been acquired by the taxpayer and not to have been issued by the corporation until the end of that period.

**Related Provisions:** 248(10) — Series of transactions.

**(7) Avoidance of tax** — Where, as part of a series of transactions or events one of the main purposes of which may reasonably be considered to be the avoidance of tax that might otherwise have been or become payable under Part II by any corporation, a particular corporation has issued a share in a taxation year in respect of which it has designated an amount under subsection 192(4), the particular corporation shall, on or before the last day of the second month after the end of the year, pay a tax under this Part for the year equal to 125% of the amount of tax under Part II that is or may be avoided by reason of the series of transactions or events.

**(7.1) Tax on excess** — Where a corporation has in a taxation year made an election under subsection 127.2(10) in respect of any share that was part of a distribution of shares referred to in that subsection and, at the end of that year or any subsequent taxation year,

(a) the total of the amounts designated under subsection 192(4) in respect of those shares as evidenced by the prescribed information returns required by regulation to be filed with the Minister by a taxpayer other than the corporation

exceeds

(b) the total of the amounts designated under subsection 192(4) in respect of those shares acquired by the taxpayer and in respect of which another taxpayer was required by regulation to provide the taxpayer with a prescribed information return relating to the designation under that subsection,

the taxpayer is liable to pay a tax under this Part for the taxation year at the end of which there is such an excess equal to the amount of the excess, which tax is to be paid to the Receiver General within 60 days after the end of the taxation year, and the excess shall be included in determining the total under paragraph (b) for any taxation year of the taxpayer subsequent to that year.

**(8) Provisions applicable to Part** — Sections 151, 152, 158 and 159, subsection 161(11), sections 162 to 167 and Division J of Part I are applicable to this Part with such modifications as the circumstances require.

**Definitions [s. 193]**: "amount" — 248(1); "corporation" — 248(1), *Interpretation Act* 35(1); "Minister" — 248(1); "person" — 127.2(9), 248(1); "prescribed" — 248(1); "series of transactions" — 248(10); "share", "taxpayer" — 248(1); "taxation year" — 249.

**Notes [Part VII]**: Part VII effectively expired at the end of 1986. Some provisions, such as 192(4.1), are still of relevance. See Notes to 127.2(1). See also 227.1(1) regarding liability of corporate directors for unpaid Part VII tax.

An earlier Part VII was repealed in 1977. It imposed a tax on the recipient of a dividend paid out of "designated surplus".

# PART VIII — REFUNDABLE TAX ON CORPORATIONS IN RESPECT OF SCIENTIFIC RESEARCH AND EXPERIMENTAL DEVELOPMENT TAX CREDIT

**194. (1) Corporation to pay tax** — Every corporation shall pay a tax under this Part for a taxation year equal to 50% of the total of all amounts each of which is an amount designated under subsection (4) in respect of a share or debt obligation issued by it in the year or a right granted by it in the year.

**Related Provisions**: 227.1(1) — Liability of directors for unpaid Part VIII tax.

**Notes**: See Notes at end of s. 195.

**(2) Definition of "Part VIII refund"** — In this Act, the "Part VIII refund" of a corporation for a taxation year means an amount equal to the lesser of

(a) the total of

(i) the amount, if any, by which the scientific research and experimental development tax credit of the corporation for the year exceeds the amount, if any, deducted by it under subsection 127.3(1) from its tax otherwise payable under Part I for the year, and

(ii) such amount as the corporation may claim, not exceeding 50% of the amount, if any, by which

(A) the total of all expenditures made by it after April 19, 1983 and in the year or the immediately preceding taxation year each of which is an expenditure (other than an expenditure prescribed for the purposes of the definition "qualified expenditure" in subsection 127(9)) claimed under paragraph 37(1)(a) or (b) to the extent that the expenditure is specified by the corporation in its return of income under Part I for the year

exceeds the total of

(B) the total of all expenditures each of which is an expenditure made by it in the immediately preceding taxation year, to the extent that the expenditure was included in determining the total under clause (A) and resulted in

(I) a refund to it under this Part for the immediately preceding taxation year,

(II) a deduction by it under subsection 37(1) for the immediately preceding taxation year, or

(III) a deduction by it under subsection 127(5) for any taxation year, and

(C) twice the portion of the total of amounts each of which is an amount deducted by it in computing its income for the year or the immediately preceding taxation year under section 37.1 that can reasonably be considered to relate to expenditures that were included in determining the total under clause (A), and

(b) the refundable Part VIII tax on hand of the corporation at the end of the year.

**Related Provisions**: 37(1)(g) — Reduction of amount deductible; 87(2)(l) — Amalgamations — continuation; 248(1)"Part VIII refund" — Definition applies to entire Act.

**(3) Definitions** — In this Part,

**"debt obligation"** has the meaning assigned by paragraph (d) of the description of A in the formula found in the definition "scientific research and experimental development tax credit" in subsection 127.3(2);

**Notes**: 194(3)"debt obligation" added in the R.S.C. 1985 (5th Supp.) consolidation, effective for taxation years ending after November 1991. The application of the definition to Part VIII was formerly included in subpara. 127.3(2)(a)(iv) (now para. 127.3(2)"scientific research and experimental development tax credit"A(d)).

**"refundable Part VIII tax on hand"** of a corporation at the end of a taxation year means the amount, if any, by which

(a) the total of the taxes payable by it under this Part for the year and all preceding taxation years

exceeds

(b) the total of its Part VIII refunds for all preceding taxation years.

**Related Provisions**: 248(1)"refundable Part VIII tax on hand" — Definition applies to entire Act.

**(4) Corporation may designate amount** — Every taxable Canadian corporation may, by filing a prescribed form with the Minister at any time on or before the last day of the month immediately following a month in which it issued a share or debt obligation or granted a right under a scientific research and experimental development financing contract (other than a share or debt obligation issued or a right granted before October, 1983, or a share in respect of which the corporation has, on or before that day, designated an amount under subsection 192(4)) designate, for the purposes of this Part and Part I, an amount in respect of that share, debt obligation or right not exceeding the amount by which

(a) the amount of the consideration for which it was issued or granted, as the case may be,

exceeds

(b) in the case of a share, the amount of any assistance (other than an amount included in computing the scientific research and experimental development tax credit of a taxpayer in respect of that share) provided, or to be provided by a government, municipality or any other public authority in respect of, or for the acquisition of, that share.

**Related Provisions**: 127.3(9) — Election re first holder; 127.3(10) — Calculation of consideration; 195(2) — Corporation to make payment on account of tax; 195(3), (4) — Interest on amount in default; 195(7) — Avoidance of tax.

**Regulations**: 226 (information return).

**(4.1) Computing paid-up capital after designation** — Where a corporation has designated an amount under subsection (4) in respect of shares issued at any time after May 23, 1985, in computing, at any particular time after that time, the paid-up capital in respect of the class of shares of the capital stock of the corporation that includes those shares

(a) there shall be deducted the amount, if any, by which

(i) the increase as a result of the issue of those shares in the paid-up capital in respect of all shares of that class, determined without reference to this subsection as it applies to those shares,

exceeds

(ii) the amount, if any, by which the total amount of consideration for which those shares were issued exceeds 50% of the amount designated by the corporation under subsection (4) in respect of those shares; and

(b) there shall be added an amount equal to the lesser of

(i) the amount, if any, by which

(A) the total of all amounts each of which is an amount deemed by subsection 84(3), (4) or (4.1) to be a dividend on shares of that class paid by the corporation after May 23, 1985 and before the particular time

exceeds

(B) the total that would be determined under clause (A) if this Act were read without reference to paragraph (a), and

(ii) the total of all amounts each of which is an amount required by paragraph (a) to be deducted in computing the paid-up capital in respect of that class of shares after May 23, 1985 and before the particular time.

**Related Provisions**: 127.3(6) — Deemed cost of designated share, debt obligation or right.

**(4.2) Where amount may not be designated** — Notwithstanding subsection (4), no amount may be designated by a corporation in respect of

(a) a share issued by the corporation after October 10, 1984, other than

(i) a qualifying share issued before May 23, 1985, or

(ii) a qualifying share issued after May 22, 1985 and before 1986

(A) under the terms of an agreement in writing entered into by the corporation before May 23, 1985, other than pursuant to an option to acquire the share if the option was not exercised before May 23, 1985, or

(B) as part of a lawful distribution to the public in accordance with a prospectus, preliminary prospectus or registration statement filed before May 24, 1985 with a public authority in Canada pursuant to and in accordance with the securities legislation of Canada or of any province and, where required by law, accepted for filing by that public authority;

(b) a share or debt obligation issued or a right granted by the corporation after October 10,

1984, other than a share or debt obligation issued or a right granted before 1986

(i) under the terms of an agreement in writing entered into by the corporation before October 11, 1984, other than pursuant to an option to acquire the share, debt obligation or right if the option was not exercised before October 11, 1984, or

(ii) where arrangements, evidenced in writing, for the issue of the share or debt obligation or the granting of the right were substantially advanced before October 10, 1984; or

(c) a share or debt obligation issued, or a right granted, at any time after June 15, 1984, by a corporation that was an excluded corporation (within the meaning assigned by subsection 127.1(2)) at that time.

**(5) Presumption** — For the purposes of this Act, the Part VIII refund of a corporation for a taxation year shall be deemed to be an amount paid on account of its tax under this Part for the year on the last day of the second month following the end of the year.

**(6) Definition of "scientific research and experimental development financing contract"** — In this Part, "scientific research and experimental development financing contract" means a contract in writing pursuant to which an amount is paid by a person to a corporation as consideration for the granting by the corporation to that person of any right, either absolute or contingent, to receive income, other than interest or dividends.

**(7) Late designation** — Where a taxable Canadian corporation that issued a share or debt obligation or granted a right under a scientific research and experimental development financing contract does not designate an amount under subsection (4) in respect of the share, debt obligation or right on or before the day on or before which the designation was required by that subsection, the corporation shall be deemed to have made the designation on that day if

(a) the corporation has filed with the Minister a prescribed information return relating to the scientific research and experimental development tax credit in respect of the share, debt obligation or right within the time that it would have been so required to file the return had the designation been filed on that day, and

(b) within 3 years after that day, the corporation has

(i) designated an amount in respect of the share, debt obligation or right by filing a prescribed form with the Minister, and

(ii) paid to the Receiver General, at the time the prescribed form referred to in subparagraph (i) is filed, an amount that is a reasonable estimate of the penalty payable by the corporation for the late designation in respect of the share, debt obligation or right,

except that, where the Minister has mailed a notice to the corporation that a designation has not been made in respect of the share, debt obligation or right under subsection (4), the designation and payment described in paragraph (b) must be made by the corporation on or before the day that is 90 days after the day of the mailing.

**Regulations**: 226(2) (prescribed information return).

**Forms**: T661: Claim for scientific research and experimental development expenditures carried on in Canada; T665: Simplified claim for expenditures incurred in carrying on SR&ED in Canada.

**(8) Penalty for late designation** — Where, pursuant to subsection (7), a corporation made a late designation in respect of a share or debt obligation issued, or a right granted, in a month, the corporation shall pay, for each month or part of a month that elapsed during the period beginning on the last day on or before which an amount could have been designated by the corporation under subsection (4) in respect of the share, debt obligation or right and ending on the day that the late designation is made, a penalty for the late designation in respect of the share, debt obligation or right in an amount equal to 1% of the amount designated in respect of the share, debt obligation or right, except that the maximum penalty payable under this subsection by the corporation for a month shall not exceed $500.

**(9) Restriction** — Where at any time a corporation has designated an amount under subsection (4) in respect of a share, debt obligation or right, no amount may be designated by the corporation at any subsequent time in respect of that share, debt obligation or right.

**Definitions [s. 194]**: "amount" — 248(1); "Canada" — 255; "class of shares" — 248(6); "corporation" — 248(1), *Interpretation Act* 35(1); "debt obligation" — 194(3); "dividend", "Minister" — 248(1); "paid-up capital" — 89(1), 248(1); "person" — 127.3(7), 248(1); "prescribed" — 248(1); "province" — *Interpretation Act* 35(1); "qualifying share" — 192(6), 248(1); "refundable Part VIII tax on hand" — 194(3); "scientific research and experimental development financing contract" — 194(6); "share" — 248(1); "taxable Canadian corporation" — 89(1), 248(1); "taxation year" — 249; "writing" — *Interpretation Act* 35(1).

**Interpretation Bulletins [s. 194]**: IT-151R5: Scientific research and experimental development expenditures.

**195. (1) Corporation to file return** — Every corporation that is liable to pay tax under this Part for a taxation year shall, on or before the day on or before which it is required to file its return of income under Part I for the year, file with the Minister a return for the year under this Part in prescribed form.

**Forms**: T2115: Corporation Part VIII tax return.

**(2) Corporation to make payment on account of tax** — Where, in a particular month in a taxation year, a corporation issues a share or debt obligation, or grants a right, in respect of which it designates an amount under section 194, the corporation shall, on or before the last day of the month following the particular month, pay to the Receiver General on account of its tax payable under this Part for the year an amount equal to 50% of the total of all amounts so designated.

**(3) Interest** — Where a corporation is liable to pay tax under this Part and has failed to pay all or any part or instalment thereof on or before the day on or before which the tax or instalment, as the case may be, was required to be paid, it shall pay to the Receiver General interest at the prescribed rate on the amount that it failed to pay computed from the day on or before which the amount was required to be paid to the day of payment.

Related Provisions: 248(11) — Interest compounded daily.

Regulations: 4301(a) (prescribed rate of interest).

**(4) Idem** — For the purposes of computing interest payable by a corporation under subsection (3) for any month or months in the period commencing on the first day of a taxation year and ending two months after the last day of the year in which period the corporation has designated an amount under section 194 in respect of a share or debt obligation issued, or right granted, by it in a particular month in the year, the corporation shall be deemed to have been liable to pay, on or before the last day of the month immediately following the particular month, a part or an instalment of tax for the year equal to that proportion of the amount, if any, by which its tax payable under this Part for the year exceeds its Part VIII refund for the year that

  (a) the total of all amounts so designated by it under section 194 in respect of shares or debt obligations issued, or rights granted, by it in the particular month

is of

  (b) the total of all amounts so designated by it under section 194 in respect of shares or debt obligations issued, or rights granted, by it in the year.

**(5) Evasion of tax** — Where a corporation that is liable to pay tax under this Part in respect of a share or debt obligation issued or a right granted by it wilfully, in any manner whatever, evades or attempts to evade payment of the tax and a purchaser of the share, debt obligation or right or, where the purchaser is a partnership, a member of the partnership knew or ought to have known, at the time the share, debt obligation or right was acquired, that the corporation would wilfully evade or attempt to evade the tax, for the purposes of section 127.3, the share, debt obligation or right shall be deemed not to have been acquired.

**(6) Undue deferral** — Where, in a transaction or as part of a series of transactions, a taxpayer acquires a share or debt obligation of a corporation or a right granted by a corporation and the corporation is controlled (within the meaning assigned by subsection 186(2)) by the taxpayer and it may reasonably be considered that one of the main purposes of the acquisition was to reduce for a period interest on the taxpayer's liability for tax under this Part, the share, debt obligation or right shall, for the purposes of this Part (other than this subsection) and section 127.3, be deemed not to have been acquired by the taxpayer and not to have been issued or granted, as the case may be, by the corporation until the end of that period.

**(7) Avoidance of tax** — Where, as part of a series of transactions or events one of the main purposes of which may reasonably be considered to be the avoidance of tax that might otherwise have been or become payable under Part II of the *Income Tax Act*, chapter 148 of the Revised Statutes of Canada, 1952, by any corporation, a particular corporation has issued a share or debt obligation or granted a right in a taxation year in respect of which it has designated an amount under subsection 194(4), the particular corporation shall, on or before the last day of the second month after the end of the year, pay a tax under this Part for the year equal to 125% of the amount of tax under Part II of the *Income Tax Act*, chapter 148 of the Revised Statutes of Canada, 1952, that is or may be avoided by reason of the series of transactions or events.

I.T. Application Rules: 69 (meaning of "*Income Tax Act*, chapter 148 of the Revised Statutes of Canada, 1952").

**(7.1) Tax on excess** — Where a corporation has in a taxation year made an election under subsection 127.3(9) in respect of any share or debt obligation that was part of a distribution of shares or debt obligations referred to in that subsection and, at the end of that year or any subsequent taxation year,

  (a) the total of the amounts designated under subsection 194(4) in respect of those shares or debt obligations as evidenced by the prescribed information returns required by regulation to be filed with the Minister by a taxpayer other than the corporation

exceeds

  (b) the total of the amounts designated under subsection 194(4) in respect of those shares or debt obligations acquired by the taxpayer and in respect of which another taxpayer was required by regulation to provide the taxpayer with a prescribed information return relating to the designation under that subsection,

the taxpayer is liable to pay a tax under this Part, for the taxation year at the end of which there is such an excess, equal to 50% of the excess, which tax is to be paid to the Receiver General within 60 days after the end of the taxation year, and the excess shall be included in determining the total under paragraph (b) for any taxation year of the taxpayer subsequent to that year.

**(8) Provisions applicable to Part** — Sections 151, 152, 158 and 159, subsection 161(11), sections 162 to 167 (except subsections 164(1.1) to (1.3)) and Division J of Part I are applicable to this Part with such modifications as the circumstances require and, for greater certainty, the Minister may assess, before the end of a taxation year, an amount payable under this Part for the year.

**Definitions [s. 195]**: "amount" — 248(1); "corporation" — 248(1), *Interpretation Act* 35(1); "Minister" — 248(1); "person" — 127.3(7), 248(1); "prescribed", "series of transactions or events", "share" — 248(1); "taxation year" — 249; "taxpayer" — 248(1).

**Notes [Part VIII]**: Part VIII effectively expired at the end of 1985, following amendments introduced to repeal the scientific research tax credit (SRTC) due to widespread abuse. Some provisions, such as 194(4.1), are still of relevance; and, of course, there are still corporations in existence that never met their Part VIII tax liability. See Notes to 127.3(1). See also 227.1(1) regarding liability of corporate directors for unpaid Part VIII tax.

An earlier Part VIII was repealed in 1977. It imposed a tax on a corporation paying a dividend out of "designated surplus".

## PART IX — TAX ON DEDUCTION UNDER SECTION 66.5

**196. (1) Tax in respect of cumulative offset account** — Every corporation shall pay a tax under this Part for each taxation year equal to 30% of the amount deducted under subsection 66.5(1) in computing its income for the year.

**Related Provisions**: 18(1)(t) — Tax is non-deductible.

**(2) Return** — Every corporation that is liable to pay tax under this Part for a taxation year shall file with the Minister, not later than the day on or before which it is required under section 150 to file a return of its income for the year under Part I, a return for the year under this Part in prescribed form containing an estimate of the amount of tax payable by it under this Part for the year.

**Related Provisions**: 150.1(5) — Electronic filing.

**Forms**: T2099: Part IX tax return in respect of amounts deducted under subsection 66.5(1).

**(3) Instalments** — Where a corporation is liable to pay tax for a taxation year under this Part, the corporation shall pay in respect of the year, to the Receiver General

(a) on or before the last day of each month in the year, an amount equal to $1/12$ of the amount of tax payable by it under this Part for the year; and

(b) the remainder, if any, of the tax payable by it under this Part for the year, on or before the end of the second month following the end of the year.

**(4) Provisions applicable to Part** — Sections 152, 158 and 159, subsections 161(1) and (2), sections 162 to 167 and Division J of Part I are applicable to this Part, with such modifications as the circumstances require.

**Notes [Part IX]**: Part IX was added in 1985.

An earlier Part IX (196, 197), repealed in 1977, imposed a tax on a corporation's "1971 undistributed income on hand" in certain circumstances.

**Definitions [Part IX]**: "amount" — 248(1); "corporation" — 248(1), *Interpretation Act* 35(1); "Minister", "prescribed" — 248(1); "tax payable" — 248(2); "taxation year" — 249.

## PART X — TAXES ON DEFERRED PROFIT SHARING PLANS AND REVOKED PLANS

**198. (1) Tax on non-qualified investments and use of assets as security** — Every trust governed by a deferred profit sharing plan or revoked plan that

(a) acquires a non-qualified investment, or

(b) uses or permits to be used any property of the trust as security for a loan,

shall pay a tax equal to the fair market value of

(c) the non-qualified investment at the time it was acquired by the trust, or

(d) the property used as security at the time it commenced to be so used.

**Related Provisions**: 147(14) — DPSP — revocation of registration; 198(4), (5) — Refund of tax on disposition of investment or release of security; 199–204 — Taxes on deferred profit sharing plans; 207.1(2) — Tax payable while non-qualifying investment held by DPSP; 259(1) — Proportional holdings in trust property.

**(2) Payment of tax** — A trustee of a trust liable to pay tax under subsection (1) shall remit the amount of the tax to the Receiver General within 10 days of the day on which the non-qualified investment is acquired or the property is used as security for a loan, as the case may be.

**(3) Trustee liable for tax** — Where a trustee of a trust liable to pay tax under subsection (1) does not remit to the Receiver General the amount of the tax within the time specified in subsection (2), the trustee is personally liable to pay on behalf of the trust the full amount of the tax and is entitled to recover from the trust any amount paid by the trustee as tax under this section.

**(4) Refund of tax on disposition of non-qualified investment** — Where a trust disposes of a property that, when acquired, was a non-qualified investment, the trust is, on application in accordance with section 202, entitled to a refund of an amount equal to the lesser of

(a) the amount of the tax imposed under this section as a result of the acquisition of the property, and

(b) the proceeds of disposition of the property.

**Related Provisions**: 198(6) — Special rules re life insurance policies; 200 — Distribution deemed disposition; 202(4) — Application to certain provisions of Part I; 203 — Application to other taxes.

Part X — Taxes on DPSPs and Revoked Plans　　　　S. 198(8)(b)(i)

**(5) Refund of tax on recovery of property given as security** — Where a loan, for which a trust has used or permitted to be used trust property as security, ceases to be extant, the trust is, on application in accordance with section 202, entitled to a refund of an amount equal to the amount remaining, if any, when

(a) the net loss (exclusive of payments by the trust as or on account of interest) sustained by the trust in consequence of its using or permitting to be used the property as security for the loan and not as a result of a change in the fair market value of the property

is deducted from

(b) the tax imposed under this section in consequence of the trust's using or permitting to be used the property as security for the loan.

**Related Provisions**: 202(4) — Application of certain provisions of Part I; 203 — Application to other taxes.

**(6) Special rules relating to life insurance policies** — For the purposes of this section,

(a) the acquisition of an interest in or the payment of an amount under a life insurance policy shall be deemed not to be the acquisition of a non-qualified investment, and

(b) the disposition of an interest in a life insurance policy shall be deemed not to be the disposition of a non-qualified investment,

except that where a trust governed by a deferred profit sharing plan or revoked plan makes a payment under or to acquire an interest in a life insurance policy, other than a life insurance policy under which

(c) the trust is, or by virtue of the payment about to become, the only person entitled to any rights or benefits under the policy (other than the rights or benefits of the insurer),

(d) the cash surrender value of the policy (exclusive of accumulated dividends) is or will be, at or before the end of the year in which the insured person attains 69 years of age, if all premiums under the policy are paid, not less than the maximum total amount (exclusive of accumulated dividends) payable by the insurer under the policy, and

(e) the total of the premiums payable in any year under the policy is not greater than the total of the amounts that, if the annual premiums had been payable in monthly instalments, would have been payable as such instalments in the 12 months commencing with the date the policy was issued,

the making of the payment shall be deemed to be the acquisition of a non-qualified investment at a cost equal to the amount of the payment.

**Related Provisions**: 139.1(13) — No application to conversion benefit on demutualization of insurer; 146(11) — RRSP — life insurance policies.

**Notes**: 198(6)(d) amended by 1996 Budget to change "at a time before the 71st anniversary of the birth of the insured person" to "at or before the end of the year in which the insured person attains 69 years of age". The change is effective after 1996, except that

(a) the amendment does not apply to a policy held by a trust where the trust acquired the policy before 1997;

(b) the amendment does not apply to a policy where the insured person turned 70 before 1997; and

(c) in applying it to a policy where the insured person turned 69 in 1996, read "70 years" in place of "69 years".

Similar grandfathering is provided for the RRSP rules in 146(13.2) and for DPSPs in 147(10.6). See also 146(2)(b.4) (RRSPs) and 147(2)(k) (DPSPs).

**Interpretation Bulletins**: IT-408R: Life insurance policies as investments of RRSPs and DPSPs.

**(6.1) Idem** — A life insurance policy giving an option to the policyholder to receive annuity payments that otherwise complies with paragraph (6)(d) shall be deemed,

(a) where the option has not been exercised, to comply with that paragraph; and

(b) where at a particular time the option is exercised, to have been disposed of at that time for an amount equal to the cash surrender value of the policy immediately before that time, and an annuity contract shall be deemed to have been acquired at that time at a cost equal to that amount.

**Interpretation Bulletins**: IT-408R: Life insurance policies as investments of RRSPs and DPSPs.

**(7) Idem** — Notwithstanding subsection (6), where the total of all payments made in a year by a trust governed by a deferred profit sharing plan or revoked plan under or to acquire interests in life insurance policies in respect of which the trust is the only person entitled to any rights or benefits (other than the rights or benefits of the insurer) does not exceed an amount equal to 25% of the total of all amounts paid by employers to the trust in the year under the plan for the benefit of beneficiaries thereunder, the making of the payments under or to acquire interests in such policies shall be deemed, for the purposes of this section, not to be the acquisition of non-qualified investments.

**Interpretation Bulletins**: IT-408R: Life insurance policies as investments of RRSPs and DPSPs.

**(8) Idem** — Where a trust surrenders, cancels, assigns or otherwise disposes of its interest in a life insurance policy,

(a) the trust shall be deemed, for the purposes of subsection (4), to have disposed of each non-qualified investment that, by virtue of payments under the policy, it was deemed by subsection (6) to have acquired; and

(b) the proceeds of the disposition shall be deemed to be the amount, if any, by which

(i) the amount received by the trust in consequence of the surrender, cancellation, assignment or other disposition of its interest in the policy

## S. 198(8)(b)   Income Tax Act

exceeds the total of

(ii) each amount paid by the trust under or to acquire an interest in the policy, the payment of which is deemed by this section not to be the acquisition of a non-qualified investment, and

(iii) the cash surrender value on December 21, 1966 of the interest of the trust in the policy on that date.

**Related Provisions**: 146(11) — RRSP — life insurance policies; 202(5) — Interest; 204 — "Qualified investment".

**Definitions [s. 198]**: "amount", "annuity" — 248(1); "deferred profit sharing plan" — 147(1), 248(1); "disposition" — 198(6)(b), 200; "dividend", "employer", "insurer" — 248(1); "life insurance policy" — 138(12), 248(1); "non-qualified investment" — 204; "person", "property" — 248(1); "revoked plan" — 204; "trust" — 104(1), 248(1), (3).

**Information Circulars [s. 198]**: 77-1R4: Deferred profit sharing plans.

### 199. (1) Tax on initial non-qualified investments not disposed of — Every trust governed by a deferred profit sharing plan or revoked plan shall pay a tax

(a) for 1967, equal to the amount, if any, by which 20% of the initial base of the trust exceeds the proceeds of disposition of its initial non-qualified investments disposed of after December 21, 1966 and before 1968;

(b) for 1968, equal to the amount, if any, by which 40% of the initial base of the trust exceeds the total of

(i) the proceeds of disposition of its initial non-qualified investments disposed of after December 21, 1966 and before 1969, and

(ii) the tax payable by the trust determined under paragraph (a);

(c) for 1969, equal to the amount, if any, by which 60% of the initial base of the trust exceeds the total of

(i) the proceeds of disposition of its initial non-qualified investments disposed of after December 21, 1966 and before 1970, and

(ii) the tax payable by the trust determined under paragraphs (a) and (b); and

(d) for 1970, equal to the amount, if any, by which 100% of the initial base of the trust exceeds the total of

(i) the proceeds of disposition of its initial non-qualified investments disposed of after December 21, 1966 and before 1971, and

(ii) the tax payable by the trust determined under paragraphs (a), (b) and (c).

**Related Provisions**: 201 — Tax on forfeitures.

**(2) Refund** — Where at the end of a year,

(a) the total of all taxes paid by a trust under subsection (1)

exceeds

(b) the total of

(i) all refunds made to the trust under this subsection, and

(ii) the amount, if any, by which the initial base of the trust exceeds the proceeds of disposition of its initial non-qualified investments disposed of after December 21, 1966 and before the end of the year,

the trust is, on application in accordance with section 202, entitled to a refund equal to the amount by which the total described in paragraph (a) exceeds the total described in paragraph (b).

**Related Provisions**: 201 — Tax on forfeitures; 202(2) — Returns and payment of estimated tax; 202(4) — Application of certain provisions of Part I; 203 — Application to other taxes.

**Definitions [s. 199]**: "amount" — 248(1); "deferred profit sharing plan" — 147(1), 248(1); "disposition" — 198(6)(b), 200; "initial base" — 204; "initial non-qualified investment" — 204; "revoked plan" — 204; "trust" — 104(1), 248(1), (3).

**Information Circulars [s. 199]**: 77-1R4: Deferred profit sharing plans.

### 200. Distribution deemed disposition — For the purposes of this Part, a distribution by a trust of a non-qualified investment to a beneficiary of the trust shall be deemed to be a disposition of that non-qualified investment and the proceeds of disposition of that non-qualified investment shall be deemed to be its fair market value at the time of the distribution.

**Definitions [s. 200]**: "non-qualified investment" — 204; "trust" — 104(1), 248(1), (3).

### 201. Tax where inadequate consideration on purchase or sale — Every trust governed by a deferred profit sharing plan or a revoked plan shall, for each calendar year after 1990, pay a tax equal to 50% of the total of all amounts each of which is, by reason of subsection 147(18), an amount taxable under this section for the year.

**Notes**: 201 amended by 1990 pension bill, effective 1991. For years before 1991, it provided detailed rules rather than referring to 147(18).

**Definitions [s. 201]**: "amount" — 248(1); "calendar year" — Interpretation Act 37(1)(a); "deferred profit sharing plan" — 147(1), 248(1); "revoked plan" — 204; "trust" — 104(1), 248(1), (3).

**Information Circulars**: 77-1R4: Deferred profit sharing plans.

### 202. (1) Returns and payment of estimated tax — Within 90 days from the end of each year after 1965, a trustee of every trust governed by a deferred profit sharing plan or revoked plan shall

(a) file with the Minister a return for the year under this Part in prescribed form and containing prescribed information, without notice or demand therefor;

(b) estimate in the return the amount of tax payable by the trust under this Part for the year;

(c) estimate in the return the amount of any refund to which the trust is entitled under this Part for the year; and

(d) pay to the Receiver General the unpaid balance of the trust's tax for the year minus any refund to which it is entitled under this Part, or apply in the return for any amount owing to it.

**Related Provisions**: 150.1(5) — Electronic filing.

**Forms**: T3D: Income tax return for DPSP or revoked DPSP.

**(2) Consideration of application for refund** — Where a trustee of a trust has made application for an amount owing to it pursuant to subsection (1), the Minister shall

(a) consider the application;

(b) determine the amount of any refund; and

(c) send to the trustee a notice of refund and any amount owing to the trust, or a notice that no refund is payable.

**Related Provisions**: 198(4) — Refund of tax on disposition of non-qualified investment; 198(5) — Refund of tax on recovery of property given as security.

**(3) Provisions applicable to Part** — Subsection 150(2), sections 152 and 158, subsections 161(1) and (11), sections 162 to 167 and Division J of Part I are applicable to this Part with such modifications as the circumstances require and, for the purposes of the application of those provisions to this Part, a notice of refund under this section shall be deemed to be a notice of assessment.

**(4) Provisions applicable to refunds** — Subsections 164(3) to (4) are applicable, with such modifications as the circumstances require, to refunds of tax under subsection 198(4) or (5) or 199(2).

**Related Provisions**: 198 — Tax on non-qualified investments and use of assets as security; 199 — Tax on initial non-qualified investments not disposed of.

**(5) Interest** — In addition to the interest payable under subsection 161(1), where a taxpayer is required by section 198 to pay a tax and has failed to pay all or any part thereof on or before the day on or before which the tax was required to be paid, the taxpayer shall pay to the Receiver General interest at the prescribed rate on the amount that the taxpayer failed to pay computed from the day on or before which the amount was required to be paid to the day of payment or to the beginning of the period in respect of which the taxpayer is required by subsection 161(1) to pay interest thereon, whichever is earlier.

**Related Provisions**: 202(6) — Deemed payment of tax; 221.1 — Application of interest where legislation retroactive; 248(11) — Interest compounded daily.

**Regulations**: 4301(a) (prescribed rate of interest).

**I.T. Application Rules**: 62(2) (subsec. 202(5) applies to interest payable in respect of any period after December 23, 1971).

**(6) Deemed payment of tax** — For the purposes of subsections 161(1) and 202(5), where a trust is liable to pay tax under this Part on the acquisition by it of a non-qualified investment or on the use of its property as security for a loan, it shall, except to the extent that the tax has previously been paid, be deemed to have paid tax on the date on which the property is disposed of or on which the loan ceases to be extant, as the case may be, in an amount equal to the refund referred to in subsection 198(4) in respect of that property or subsection 198(5) in respect of the loan, as the case may be.

**Related Provisions**: 161(1) — Interest; 198(4) — Refund of tax on disposition of non-qualified investment; 198(5) — Refund of tax on recovery of property given as security.

**Definitions [s. 202]**: "amount", "assessment" — 248(1); "deferred profit sharing plan" — 147(1), 248(1); "Minister" — 248(1); "non-qualifying investment" — 204; "prescribed" — 248(1); "prescribed rate" — Reg. 4301; "property" — 248(1); "revoked plan" — 204; "taxpayer" — 248(1); "trust" — 104(1), 248(1), (3).

**203. Application to other taxes** — Instead of making a refund to which a trust is entitled under subsection 198(4) or (5) or 199(2), the Minister may, where the trust is liable or about to become liable to make another payment under this Act, apply the amount of the refund or any part thereof to that other liability and notify a trustee of the trust of that action.

**Related Provisions**: 164(2) — Set-off of Part I refund; 224.1 — Recovery by set-off.

**Definitions [s. 203]**: "amount", "Minister" — 248(1); "trust" — 104(1), 248(1), (3).

**204. Definitions** — In this Part,

"equity share" means

(a) a share, other than an excluded share or a non-participating share, the owner of which has, as owner thereof, a right

(i) to a dividend, and

(ii) to a part of the surplus of the corporation after repayment of capital and payment of dividend arrears on the redemption of the share, a reduction of the capital of the corporation or the winding-up of the corporation,

at least as great, in any event, as the right of the owner of any other share, other than a non-participating share, of the corporation, when the magnitude of the right in each case is expressed as a rate based on the paid-up capital value of the share to which the right relates, or

(b) a share, other than an excluded share or a non-participating share, the owner of which has, as owner thereof, a right

(i) to a dividend, after a dividend at a rate not in excess of 12% per annum of the paid-up capital value of each share has been paid to the owners of shares of a class other than the class to which that share belongs, and

(ii) to a part of the surplus of the corporation after repayment of capital and payment of dividend arrears on the redemption of the share, a reduction of the capital of the corporation or the winding-up of the corporation, after a payment of a part of the surplus at a rate not in excess of 10% of the paid-up capital value of each share has been made to the owners of shares of a class other than the class to which that share belongs,

at least as great, in any event, as the right of the owner of any other share, other than a non-participating share, of the corporation, when the magnitude of the right in each case is expressed as a rate based on the paid-up capital value of the share to which the right relates;

**Notes**: 204"equity share" was 204(a) before consolidation in R.S.C. 1985 (5th Supp.), effective for 1991 and later calendar years. See Table of Concordance.

**"excluded share"** means each share of the capital stock of a private corporation where

(a) the paid-up capital of the corporation that is represented by all its issued and outstanding shares that would, but for this definition, be equity shares is less than 50% of the paid-up capital of the corporation that is represented by all its issued and outstanding shares other than non-participating shares, or

(b) a non-participating share of the corporation is issued and outstanding and the owner of which has, as owner thereof, a right to a dividend

(i) at a fixed annual rate in excess of 12%, or

(ii) at an annual rate not in excess of a fixed maximum annual rate, if the fixed maximum annual rate is in excess of 12%,

when the right to the dividend is expressed as a rate based on the paid-up capital value of the share to which the right relates;

**Notes**: 204"excluded share" was 204(a.1) before consolidation in R.S.C. 1985 (5th Supp.), effective for 1991 and later calendar years. See Table of Concordance.

**"initial base"** of a trust means the total of the values of all initial non-qualified investments held by the trust on December 21, 1966 when each such investment is valued at the lower of

(a) its cost to the trust, and

(b) its fair market value on December 21, 1966;

**Notes**: 204"initial base" was 204(b) before consolidation in R.S.C. 1985 (5th Supp.), effective for 1991 and later calendar years. See Table of Concordance.

**"initial non-qualified investment"** of a trust means an investment held by the trust on December 21, 1966 that was, on that date, a non-qualified investment but does not include

(a) any interest in a life insurance policy, or

(b) an equity share that would be a qualified investment if the date of acquisition of the share were December 21, 1966;

**Notes**: 204"initial non-qualified investment" was 204(c) before consolidation in R.S.C. 1985 (5th Supp.), effective for 1991 and later calendar years. See Table of Concordance.

**"non-participating share"** means

(a) in the case of a private corporation, a share the owner of which is not entitled to receive, as owner thereof, any dividend, other than a dividend, whether cumulative or not,

(i) at a fixed annual rate or amount, or

(ii) at an annual rate or amount not in excess of a fixed annual rate or amount, and

(b) in the case of a corporation other than a private corporation, any share other than a common share;

**Notes**: 204"non-participating share" was 204(a.2) before consolidation in R.S.C. 1985 (5th Supp.), effective for 1991 and later calendar years. See Table of Concordance.

**"non-qualified investment"** means property that is not a qualified investment for a trust governed by a deferred profit sharing plan or revoked plan within the meaning of the definition "qualified investment" in this subsection;

**Notes**: 204"non-qualified investment" was 204(d) before consolidation in R.S.C. 1985 (5th Supp.), effective for 1991 and later calendar years.

**Information Circulars**: 77-1R4: Deferred profit sharing plans.

**"paid-up capital value"** of a share means the amount determined by the formula

$$\frac{A}{B}$$

where

A is the paid-up capital of the corporation that is represented by the shares of the class to which that share belongs, and

B is the number of shares of that class that are in fact issued and outstanding;

**Notes**: 204"paid-up capital value" was 204(a.3) before consolidation in R.S.C. 1985 (5th Supp.), effective for 1991 and later calendar years. The previous version was in descriptive rather than formula form.

**"qualified investment"** for a trust governed by a deferred profit sharing plan or revoked plan means

(a) money that is legal tender in Canada, other than money the fair market value of which exceeds its stated value as legal tender, and deposits (within the meaning assigned by the *Canada Deposit Insurance Corporation Act* or with a bank) of such money standing to the credit of the trust,

**Proposed Amendment — 204"qualified investment"(a)**

(a) money (other than money the fair market value of which exceeds its stated value as legal tender in the country of issuance or money that is held for its numismatic value) and deposits (within the meaning assigned by the *Canada Deposit Insurance Corporation Act* or with a

Part X — Taxes on DPSPs and Revoked Plans    S. 204

branch in Canada of a bank) of such money standing to the credit of the trust,

**Application**: The August 8, 2000 draft legislation, s. 20, will amend para. (a) of the definition "qualified investment" in s. 204 to read as above, applicable after June 27, 1999 except that, before 2003, para. (a) shall be read as follows:

(a) money (other than money the fair market value of which exceeds its stated value as legal tender in the country of issuance or money that is held for its numismatic value) and deposits (within the meaning assigned by the *Canada Deposit Insurance Corporation Act* or with a bank listed in Schedule I or II to the *Bank Act* or with a branch in Canada of an authorized foreign bank) of such money standing to the credit of the trust,

**Technical Notes**: The definition "qualified investment" in section 204 of the Act is relevant directly to deferred profit sharing plans (DPSPs), and indirectly to other tax-deferred registered plans such as registered retirement savings plans (RRSPs).

The definition of a qualified investment is amended in three respects. First, the definition is modified (with effect after June 27, 1999) to include money denominated in any currency, whether Canadian or foreign. An exception excludes currency held as a collectible or as a commodity: that is, money whose fair market value exceeds its stated value as legal tender in its country of issue or that is held for its numismatic value.

Second, deposits with a Canadian branch of an authorized foreign bank will, after June 27, 1999, be qualified investments.

Third, after 2002, the only deposits that will be qualified investments will be those that are either deposits within the meaning of the *Canada Deposit Insurance Act*, or deposits with bank branches in Canada. As a result, bank deposits that are excluded from the *Canada Deposit Insurance Act* definition because they are repayable outside Canada will not be qualified investments if they are made with a branch outside Canada.

(b) bonds, debentures, notes, mortgages, or similar obligations described in clause 212(1)(b)(ii)(C), whether issued before, on or after April 15, 1966,

(c) bonds, debentures, notes or similar obligations of a corporation the shares of which are listed on a prescribed stock exchange in Canada, other than those described in paragraph 147(2)(c),

(d) shares listed on a prescribed stock exchange in Canada,

(e) equity shares of a corporation by which, before the date of acquisition by the trust of the shares, payments have been made in trust to a trustee under the plan for the benefit of beneficiaries thereunder, if the shares are of a class in respect of which

(i) there is no restriction on their transferability, and

(ii) in each of 4 taxation years of the corporation in the period of the corporation's 5 consecutive taxation years that ended less than 12 months before the date of acquisition of the shares by the trust, and in the corporation's last taxation year in that period, the corporation

(A) paid a dividend on each share of the class of an amount not less than 4% of the cost per share of the shares to the trust, or

(B) had earnings attributable to the shares of the class of an amount not less than the amount obtained when 4% of the cost per share to the trust of the shares is multiplied by the total number of shares of the class that were outstanding immediately after the acquisition,

(f) guaranteed investment certificates issued by a trust company incorporated under the laws of Canada or of a province,

(g) investment contracts described in subparagraph (b)(ii) of the definition "retirement savings plan" in subsection 146(1) and issued by a corporation approved by the Governor in Council for the purposes of that subparagraph,

(h) shares listed on a prescribed stock exchange in a country other than Canada, and

(i) such other investments as may be prescribed by regulations of the Governor in Council made on the recommendation of the Minister of Finance;

**Related Provisions**: 87(10) — New share issued on amalgamation of public corporation deemed to be listed on prescribed stock exchange; 132.2(1)(k) — Where share ceases to be qualified investment due to mutual fund reorganization; 146(1)"qualified investment"(a) — Certain investments in 204"qualified investment" are qualified investments for RRSPs; 146.3(1)"qualified investment"(a) — Certain investments in 204"qualified investment" are qualified investments for RRIFs; 248(1)"qualifying environmental trust"(e) — Trust must acquire only certain qualified investments.

**Notes**: 204"qualified investment" was 204(e) before consolidation in R.S.C. 1985 (5th Supp.), effective for 1991 and later calendar years. See Table of Concordance. See also Notes to Reg. 4900(1).

**Regulations**: 221 (information return by issuer of qualified investment); 3200, 3201 (prescribed stock exchanges; but see also ITA 87(10)); 4900(1)–(3), (7), (11), 4901(2) (investments prescribed as qualified investments).

**Interpretation Bulletins**: IT-320R2: RRSPs — qualified investments.

**Information Circulars**: 77-1R4: Deferred profit sharing plans.

**Forms**: T3F: Investments prescribed to be qualified or not to be foreign property information return.

**"revoked plan"** means a deferred profit sharing plan the registration of which has been revoked by the Minister pursuant to subsection 147(14) or (14.1).

**Notes**: 204"revoked plan" was 204(f) before consolidation in R.S.C. 1985 (5th Supp.), effective for calendar years ending after November 1991.

**Definitions [s. 204]**: "amount", "authorized foreign bank" — 248(1); "Canada" — 255, *Interpretation Act* 35(1); "common share" — 248(1); "corporation" — 248(1), *Interpretation Act* 35(1); "deferred profit sharing plan" — 147(1), 248(1); "dividend" — 248(1); "equity share", "excluded share", "initial non-qualified investment" — 204; "investment corporation" — 130(3), 248(1); "life insurance policy" — 138(12), 248(1); "listed" — 87(10) "Minister" — 248(1); "non-participating share", "non-qualified investment", "paid-up capital value" — 204; "prescribed" — 248(1); "prescribed stock exchange in a country other than Canada" — Reg. 3201; "prescribed stock exchange in Canada" — Reg. 3200; "private corporation" — 89(1), 248(1); "property" — 248(1); "province" — *Interpretation Act* 35(1); "qualified investment" — 204; "regulation" — 248(1); "revoked plan" — 204; "share" — 248(1); "taxation year" — 249; "trust" — 104(1), 248(1), (3).

# PART X.1 — TAX IN RESPECT OF OVER-CONTRIBUTIONS TO DEFERRED INCOME PLANS

**204.1 (1) Tax payable by individuals [before 1991]** — Where, at the end of any month after May, 1976, an individual has an excess amount for a year in respect of registered retirement savings plans, the individual shall, in respect of that month, pay a tax under this Part equal to 1% of that portion of the total of all those excess amounts that has not been paid by those plans to the individual before the end of that month.

**Related Provisions**: 18(1)(t) — Tax is non-deductible; 146(2)(c.1) — RRSP must permit payment to taxpayer to reduce overcontributions; 204.1(2.1) — Tax payable by individuals — contributions after 1990; 204.3 — Return and payment of tax.

**Notes**: 204.1(1) does not apply after 1990; 204.1(2.1) applies instead. See 204.2(1)(a).

**Remission Orders**: *Certain Taxpayers Remission Order, 1998-2*, P.C. 1998-2092, s. 2 (judges in Quebec who made contributions in 1989 or 1990).

**Advance Tax Rulings**: ATR-24: RRSP damages suit against investment management companies.

**(2) Amount deemed repaid** — For the purposes of subsection (1), where an amount in respect of a plan has been included in computing an individual's income pursuant to paragraph 146(12)(b), that amount shall be deemed to have been paid to the individual by the plan at the time referred to in that paragraph.

**(2.1) Tax payable by individuals — contributions after 1990** — Where, at the end of any month after December, 1990, an individual has a cumulative excess amount in respect of registered retirement savings plans, the individual shall, in respect of that month, pay a tax under this Part equal to 1% of that cumulative excess amount.

**Related Provisions**: 18(1)(t) — Tax is non-deductible; 146(2)(c.1) — RRSP must permit payment to taxpayer to reduce overcontributions; 204.1(4) — Waiver of tax by CCRA; 204.3 — Return and payment of tax.

**Notes**: 204.1(2.1) added by 1990 pension bill. See Notes to 204.2(1.1).

**Advance Tax Rulings**: ATR-24: RRSP damages suit against investment management companies.

**Forms**: T4040: RRSPs and other registered plans for retirement [guide].

**(3) Tax payable by deferred profit sharing plan** — Where, at the end of any month after May, 1976, a trust governed by a deferred profit sharing plan has an excess amount, the trust shall, in respect of that month, pay a tax under this Part equal to 1% of the excess amount.

**Related Provisions**: 204.2(4) — Definition of "excess amount" for a DPSP.

**(4) Waiver of tax** — Where an individual would, but for this subsection, be required to pay a tax under subsection (1) or (2.1) in respect of a month and the individual establishes to the satisfaction of the Minister that

(a) the excess amount or cumulative excess amount on which the tax is based arose as a consequence of reasonable error, and

(b) reasonable steps are being taken to eliminate the excess,

the Minister may waive the tax.

**Notes**: 204.1(4) added by 1990 pension bill, effective June 27, 1990.

**Definitions [s. 204.1]**: "amount" — 248(1); "cumulative excess amount" — 204.2(1.1); "deferred profit sharing plan" — 147(1), 248(1); "excess amount" — 204.2(1), (4); "individual", "Minister" — 248(1); "registered retirement savings plan" — 146(1), 248(1); "trust" — 104(1), 248(1), (3).

**Interpretation Bulletins [s. 204.1]**: IT-124R6: Contributions to registered retirement savings plans.

**204.2 (1) Definition of "excess amount for a year in respect of registered retirement savings plans" [before 1991]** — "Excess amount for a year in respect of registered retirement savings plans" of an individual at a particular time means,

(a) where the excess amount is for a year after 1990, nil; and

(b) where the excess amount is for a year before 1991, the amount, if any, by which the total of

(i) all amounts paid by the individual to such plans under which the individual or the individual's spouse or common-law partner is the annuitant, other than amounts

(A) to which paragraph 60(j), (j.01), (j.1), (j.2) or (l) applies or would, if the individual were resident in Canada throughout the year, apply, or

(B) transferred to the plan in accordance with any of subsections 146(16), 147(19) and 147.3(1) and (4) to (7), and

(ii) all gifts made to such a plan under which the individual is the annuitant, other than gifts made thereto by the individual's spouse or common-law partner,

in the year and before the particular time, exceeds the total of

(iii) all amounts that may be deducted in computing the individual's income for the immediately preceding year in respect of those payments, and

(iv) the greater of $5,500 and the amount that may be deducted in computing the individual's income for the year in respect of those payments.

**Related Provisions**: 128(2)(d), (d.2) — Where individual bankrupt; 204.1(1) — Tax payable by individuals; 204.2(3) — When retirement savings plan deemed to be a registered plan.

**Notes**: 204.2(1) amended by 2000 same-sex partners bill to add reference to "common-law partner", effective for the 2001 and later taxation years, or earlier by election (see Notes to 248(1)"common-law partner"). (Since this subsection only applies before 1991, this amendment is meaningless.)

204.2(1) amended by 1990 pension bill, effective for payments made to RRSPs in 1989 or later. For such payments in 1988, ignore the reference to "(j.2)" in clause (a)(i)(A), and the references to "147(19) and 147.3(1) and (4) to (7)" in clause (a)(i)(B).

**Advance Tax Rulings**: ATR-24: RRSP damages suit against investment management companies.

**Forms**: T1-OVP: Individual income tax return for RRSP excess contributions; T1-OVP Sched.: Calculating the amount of RRSP contributions made before 1991 that are subject to tax.

### (1.1) Cumulative excess amount in respect of RRSPs
— The cumulative excess amount of an individual in respect of registered retirement savings plans at any time in a taxation year is the amount, if any, by which

(a) the amount of the individual's undeducted RRSP premiums at that time

exceeds

(b) the amount determined by the formula

$$A + B + R + C + D + E$$

where

A is the individual's unused RRSP deduction room at the end of the preceding taxation year,

B is the amount, if any, by which

(i) the lesser of the RRSP dollar limit for the year and 18% of the individual's earned income (as defined in subsection 146(1)) for the preceding taxation year

exceeds the total of all amounts each of which is

(ii) the individual's pension adjustment for the preceding taxation year in respect of an employer, or

(iii) a prescribed amount in respect of the individual for the year,

C is, where the individual attained 18 years of age in a preceding taxation year, $2,000, and in any other case, nil,

D is the group RRSP amount in respect of the individual at that time,

E is, where the individual attained 18 years of age before 1995, the individual's transitional amount at that time, and in any other case, nil, and

R is the individual's total pension adjustment reversal for the year.

**Related Provisions**: 204.1(2.1) — Tax payable by individuals — Contributions after 1990; 204.2(1.2) — Undeducted RRSP premiums; 204.2(1.3) — Group RRSP amount; 204.2(1.5) — Transitional amount.

**Notes**: Formula element R added by 1997 Budget, effective for 1998 and later taxation years. For discussion of pension adjustment reversals, see Notes to 146(1)"RRSP deduction limit", and Reg. 8304.1.

204.2(1.1)(b) amended by 1995 Budget, effective for 1996 and later taxation years. The effect is to reduce the "free" (non-deductible but unpenalized) overcontribution room from $8,000 to $2,000. For earlier years, read:

(b) the amount determined by the formula

$$A + B - C + M$$

where

A is the individual's unused RRSP deduction room at the end of the immediately preceding taxation year,

B is the amount, if any, by which the lesser of the RRSP dollar limit for the year and 18% of the individual's earned income (within the meaning assigned by subsection 146(1)) for the immediately preceding taxation year exceeds the total of all amounts each of which is the individual's pension adjustment for the immediately preceding taxation year in respect of an employer or a prescribed amount in respect of the taxpayer for the year,

C is the individual's net past service pension adjustment, at that time, for the year, and

M is, where the individual attained 18 years of age in a preceding taxation year, $8,000, and otherwise, nil.

204.2(1.1) added by 1990 pension bill, effective 1989. "M" in the calculation allows a $2,000 cumulative overcontribution "cushion" for those who may be improperly advised as to their RRSP contribution limits. The overcontribution is not deductible but is not subject to the penalty tax. Some people use the $2,000 for additional non-deductible contributions (eventually deducted in a later year) that can grow tax-free in the RRSP. Note that it is not available for children under 18; see formula element C.

**Regulations**: 8308(2), 8308.2, 8308.4(2), 8309 (prescribed amounts for "B").

**Interpretation Bulletins**: IT-307R3: Spousal registered retirement savings plans.

**Advance Tax Rulings**: ATR-24: RRSP damages suit against investment management companies.

### (1.2) Undeducted RRSP premiums
— For the purposes of subsection (1.1) and the description of K in paragraph (1.3)(a), the amount of undeducted RRSP premiums of an individual at any time in a taxation year is the amount determined by the formula

$$H + I - J$$

where

H is, for taxation years ending before 1992, nil, and for taxation years ending after 1991, the amount, if any, by which

(a) the amount of the individual's undeducted RRSP premiums at the end of the immediately preceding taxation year

exceeds

(b) the total of the amounts deducted under subsections 146(5) and (5.1) in computing the individual's income for the immediately preceding taxation year, to the extent that each amount was deducted in respect of premiums paid under registered retirement savings plans in or before that preceding year,

I   is the total of all amounts each of which is

(a) a premium (within the meaning spouse or common-law partner assigned by subsection 146(1)) paid by the individual in the year and before that time under a registered retirement savings plan under which the individual or the individual's spouse or common-law partner was the annuitant (within the meaning assigned by subsection 146(1)) at the time the premium was paid, other than

(i) an amount paid to the plan in the first 60 days of the year and deducted in computing the individual's income for the immediately preceding taxation year,

(ii) an amount paid to the plan in the year and deducted under paragraph 60(j), (j.1), (j.2) or (l) in computing the individual's income for the year or the immediately preceding taxation year,

(iii) an amount transferred to the plan on behalf of the individual in accordance with any of subsections 146(16), 147(19) and 147.3(1) and (4) to (7) or in circumstances to which subsection 146(21) applies,

(iv) an amount deductible under subsection 146(6.1) in computing the individual's income for the year or a preceding taxation year,

(v) where the individual is a non-resident person, an amount that would, if the individual were resident in Canada throughout the year and the immediately preceding taxation year, be deductible under paragraph 60(j), (j.1), (j.2) or (l) in computing the individual's income for the year or the immediately preceding taxation year, or

(vi) an amount paid to the plan in the year that is not deductible in computing the individual's income for the year because of subparagraph 146(5)(a)(iv.1) or (5.1)(a)(iv), or

(b) a gift made in the year and before that time to a registered retirement savings plan under which the individual is the annuitant (within the meaning assigned by subsection 146(1)), other than a gift made thereto by the individual's spouse or common-law partner, and

J   is the amount, if any, by which

(a) the total of all amounts each of which is an amount (other than the portion thereof that reduces the amount on which tax is payable by the individual under subsection 204.1(1)) received by the individual in the year and before that time out of or under a registered retirement savings plan or a registered retirement income fund and included in computing the individual's income for the year

exceeds

(b) the amount deducted under paragraph 60(l) in computing the individual's income for the year.

**Related Provisions:** 204.2(1.4) — Deemed receipt where RRSP or RRIF amended; 204.2(3) — When retirement savings plan deemed to be registered plan; 257 — Formula cannot calculate to less than zero.

**Notes:** 204.2(1.2)I amended by 2000 same-sex partners bill to add reference to "common-law partner", effective for the 2001 and later taxation years, or earlier by election (see Notes to 248(1)"common-law partner").

Reference to 204.2(1.3)(a)C added to 204.2(1.2) by 1995 Budget, effective for 1996 and later taxation years.

204(1.2)I(a)(vi) added by 1994 Budget, effective 1994.

204.2(1.2) added by 1990 pension bill, effective 1989. 204.2(1.2)I(a)(iii) amended by 1993 technical bill, effective for 1992 and later taxation years, to add reference to 146(21), which allows a transfer to an RRSP from the Saskatchewan Pension Plan.

**(1.3) Group RRSP amount** — For the purposes of this section, the group RRSP amount in respect of an individual at any time in a taxation year is the lesser of

(a) the lesser of the value of F and the amount determined by the formula

$$F - (G - K)$$

where

F   is the lesser of

(i) the total of all amounts each of which is a qualifying group RRSP premium paid by the individual, to the extent that the premium is included in determining the value of I in subsection (1.2) in respect of the individual at that time, and

(ii) the RRSP dollar limit for the following taxation year,

G   is the amount that would be determined under paragraph (1.1)(b) in respect of the individual at that time if the values of C, D and E in that paragraph were nil, and

K   is

(i) where the year is the 1996 taxation year, the amount, if any, by which the amount of the individual's undeducted RRSP premiums at the beginning of the year exceeds the individual's cumulative excess amount in respect of registered retirement savings plans at the end of the 1995 taxation year, and

(ii) in any other case, the group RRSP amount in respect of the individual at the end of the preceding taxation year, and

(b) the amount that would be the individual's cumulative excess amount in respect of registered retirement savings plans at that time if the value of D in paragraph (1.1)(b) were nil.

**Related Provisions**: 146(1) — Meaning of "net past service pension adjustment" for RRSP rules; 204.2(1.2) — Undeducted RRSP premiums; 204.2(1.31) — Qualifying group RRSP premium; 257 — Formula amounts cannot calculate to less than zero.

**Notes**: 204.2(1.3) amended by 1995 Budget, effective for 1996 and later taxation years. For earlier years since 1989, read:

> (1.3) Net past service pension adjustment — For the purposes of subsection (1.1), the net past service pension adjustment of an individual, at any time, for a taxation year is the positive or negative amount determined by the formula
>
> $$P - G$$
>
> where
>
> P is the total of all amounts each of which is the accumulated PSPA of the individual for the year in respect of an employer, determined as of that time in accordance with prescribed rules; and
>
> G is the amount of the individual's PSPA withdrawals for the year, determined as of that time in accordance with prescribed rules.

204.2(1.3) added by 1990 pension bill and amended retroactively by 1992 technical bill (to eliminate a deduction for PSPA transfers), effective 1989.

**Regulations**: 8303(2) (accumulated PSPA before 1996); 8307(5) (individual's PSPA withdrawals before 1996).

**(1.31) Qualifying group RRSP premium** — For the purpose of the description of F in paragraph (1.3)(a), a qualifying group RRSP premium paid by an individual is a premium paid under a registered retirement savings plan where

(a) the plan is part of a qualifying arrangement,

(b) the premium is an amount to which the individual is entitled for services rendered by the individual (whether or not as an employee), and

(c) the premium was remitted to the plan on behalf of the individual by the person or body of persons that is required to remunerate the individual for the services, or by an agent for that person or body,

but does not include the part, if any, of a premium that, by making (or failing to make) an election or exercising (or failing to exercise) any other right under the arrangement after beginning to participate in the arrangement and within 12 months before the time the premium was paid, the individual could have prevented from being paid under the plan and that would not as a consequence have been required to be remitted on behalf of the individual to another registered retirement savings plan or to a registered pension plan in respect of a money purchase provision of the plan.

**Related Provisions**: 204.2(1.32) — Qualifying arrangement.

**Notes**: 204.2(1.31) added by 1995 Budget, effective for 1996 and later taxation years.

**(1.32) Qualifying arrangement** — For the purpose of paragraph (1.31)(a), a qualifying arrangement is an arrangement under which premiums that satisfy the conditions in paragraphs (1.31)(b) and (c) are remitted to registered retirement savings plans on behalf of two or more individuals, but does not include an arrangement where it is reasonable to consider that one of the main purposes of the arrangement is to reduce tax payable under this Part.

**Notes**: 204.2(1.32) added by 1995 Budget, effective for 1996 and later taxation years.

**(1.4) Deemed receipt where RRSP or RRIF amended** — For the purposes of subsection (1.2),

(a) where an amount in respect of a registered retirement savings plan has been included in computing an individual's income pursuant to paragraph 146(12)(b), that amount shall be deemed to have been received by the individual out of the plan at the time referred to in that paragraph; and

(b) where an amount in respect of a registered retirement income fund has been included in computing an individual's income pursuant to paragraph 146.3(11)(b), that amount shall be deemed to have been received by the individual out of the fund at the time referred to in that paragraph.

**Notes**: 204.2(1.4) added by 1990 pension bill, effective 1989.

**(1.5) Transitional amount** — For the purpose of the description of E in paragraph (1.1)(b), an individual's transitional amount at any time in a taxation year is the lesser of

(a) $6,000, and

(b) where the value of L is nil, nil, and in any other case, the amount determined by the formula

$$L - M$$

where

L is the amount, if any, by which

(i) the amount that would be determined under subsection (1.2) to be the amount of the individual's undeducted RRSP premiums at that time if

(A) the value of I in that subsection were determined for the 1995 taxation year without including premiums paid after February 26, 1995,

(B) the value of I in that subsection were nil for the 1996 and subsequent taxation years, and

(C) the value of J in that subsection were determined for the 1995 and subsequent taxation years without including the part, if any, of an amount received by the individual out of or under a registered retirement savings plan or registered retirement income fund that can reasonably be considered to be in respect of premiums paid after February 26, 1995 by the individual under a registered retirement savings plan

exceeds

(ii) the total of all amounts each of which is an amount deducted under subsection 146(5) or (5.1) in computing the individual's income for a preceding taxation year, to the extent that the amount was deducted in respect of premiums paid after that year (other than premiums paid before February 27, 1995), and

M is the amount that would be determined by the formula in paragraph (1.1)(b) in respect of the individual at that time if the values of D and E in that paragraph were nil and section 257 did not apply to that formula.

**Related Provisions**: 257 — Formula cannot calculate to less than zero.

**Notes**: 204.2(1.5) added by 1995 Budget, effective for 1996 and later taxation years. The transitional amount provides an exemption from Part X.1 tax for RRSP contributions made before February 27, 1995 that would otherwise become subject to the tax after 1995 because of the reduction in the overcontribution margin from $8,000 to $2,000 (see 204.2(1.1)(b). The exemption applies until an individual has sufficient RRSP deduction room to deduct the contributions.

In general terms, an individual's transitional amount for a year is the lesser of $6,000 (the amount by which the margin has been reduced) and the amount needed to ensure that there is no penalty tax on the portion of the individual's pre-February 27, 1995 RRSP contributions that have not been deducted before the year. For this purpose, contributions are treated as being deducted in the order in which they are made.

**(2) Where terminated plan deemed to continue to exist** — Notwithstanding paragraph 146(12)(a), for the purposes of this Part, where a registered retirement savings plan ceases to exist and a payment or transfer of funds out of that plan has been made to which subsection 146(16) applied, if an individual's excess amount for a year in respect of registered retirement savings plans would have been greater had that plan not ceased to exist, for the purpose of computing the excess amount for a year in respect of registered retirement savings plans for so long as the individual or the individual's spouse or common-law partner is the annuitant under any registered retirement savings plan under which an annuity has not commenced to be paid to the annuitant, the plan that ceased to exist shall be deemed to remain in existence and the individual or the individual's spouse or common-law partner, as the case may be, shall be deemed to continue to be the annuitant thereunder.

**Notes**: 204.2(2) amended by 2000 same-sex partners bill to add reference to "common-law partner", effective for the 2001 and later taxation years, or earlier by election (see Notes to 248(1)"common-law partner").

**Forms**: T3012: Application for refund of RRSP excess contributions.

**(3) When retirement savings plan deemed to be a registered plan** — Where a retirement savings plan under which an individual or the individual's spouse or common-law partner is the annuitant (within the meaning assigned by subsection 146(1)) is accepted by the Minister for registration, for the purpose of determining

(a) the amount of undeducted RRSP premiums of the individual at any time, and

(b) the excess amount for a year in respect of registered retirement savings plans of the individual at any time,

the retirement savings plan shall be deemed to have become a registered retirement savings plan on the later of the day on which the plan came into existence and May 25, 1976.

**Notes**: 204.2(3) amended by 2000 same-sex partners bill to add reference to "common-law partner", effective for the 2001 and later taxation years, or earlier by election (see Notes to 248(1)"common-law partner").

204.2(3)(a) added by 1990 pension bill, effective 1989.

**(4) Definition of "excess amount" for a DPSP** — "Excess amount" at any time for a trust governed by a deferred profit sharing plan means the total of all amounts each of which is

(a) such portion of the total of all contributions made to the trust before that time and after May 25, 1976 by a beneficiary under the plan, other than

(i) contributions that have been deducted by the beneficiary under paragraph 60(k) of the *Income Tax Act*, chapter 148 of the Revised Statutes of Canada, 1952,

(ii) amounts transferred to the plan on behalf of the beneficiary in accordance with subsection 147(19), or

(iii) the portion of the contributions (other than contributions referred to in subparagraphs (i) and (ii)) made by the beneficiary in each calendar year before 1991 not in excess of $5,500,

as has not been returned to the beneficiary before that time; or

(b) a gift received by the trust before that time and after May 25, 1976.

**Related Provisions**: 147(2)(a.1) — Acceptance of plan for registration.

**Notes**: 204.2(4)(a) amended by 1990 pension bill, effective 1989, to add subpara. (ii) and limit subpara. (iii) to contributions made before 1991.

**I.T. Application Rules**: 69 (meaning of "*Income Tax Act*, chapter 148 of the Revised Statutes of Canada, 1952").

**Definitions [s. 204.2]**: "amount", "annuity" — 248(1); "calendar year" — *Interpretation Act* 37(1)(a); "Canada" — 255; "common-law partner" — 248(1); "cumulative excess amount" — 204.2(1.1); "deferred profit sharing plan" — 147(1), 248(1); "employer" — 248(1); "group RRSP amount" — 204.2(1.3); "individual", "Minister" — 248(1); "net past service pension adjustment" — 204.2(1.3); "past service pension adjustment" — 248(1), Reg. 8303; "pension adjustment" — 248(1), Reg. 8301(1); "prescribed" — 248(1); "qualifying arrangement" — 204.2(1.31); "qualifying group RRSP premium" — 204.2(1.31); "registered retirement income fund" — 146.3(1), 248(1); "registered retirement savings plan" — 146(1), 248(1); "RRSP dollar limit" — 146(1), 248(1); "resident in Canada" — 250; "retirement savings plan" — 146(1), 248(1); "taxation year" — 249; "taxpayer" — 104(1), 248(1); "total pension adjustment reversal" — 248(1); "transitional amount" — 204.2(1.5); "trust" — 104(1), 248(1), (3); "undeducted RRSP premiums" — 204.2(1.2).

**Interpretation Bulletins [s. 204.2]**: IT-124R6: Contributions to registered retirement savings plans.

**204.3 (1) Return and payment of tax** — Within 90 days after the end of each year after 1975, a taxpayer to whom this Part applies shall

(a) file with the Minister a return for the year under this Part in prescribed form and containing prescribed information, without notice or demand therefor;

(b) estimate in the return the amount of tax, if any, payable by the taxpayer under this Part in respect of each month in the year; and

(c) pay to the Receiver General the amount of tax, if any, payable by the taxpayer under this Part in respect of each month in the year.

**Related Provisions**: 150.1(5) — Electronic filing.

**Information Circulars**: 78-14R2: Guidelines for trust companies and other persons responsible for filing.

**Forms**: T1-OVP: Individual income tax return for RRSP excess contributions; T1-OVP Sched.: Calculating the amount of RRSP contributions made before 1991 that are subject to tax; T3D: Income tax return for DPSP or revoked DPSP; T3IND: T3IND income tax return for RRSP, RRIF, or RESP.

**(2) Provisions applicable to Part** — Subsections 150(2) and (3), sections 152 and 158, subsections 161(1) and (11), sections 162 to 167 and Division J of Part I are applicable to this Part with such modifications as the circumstances require.

**Definitions [s. 204.3]**: "amount", "Minister", "prescribed", "taxpayer" — 248(1).

**Interpretation Bulletins [s. 204.3]**: IT-124R6: Contributions to registered retirement savings plans.

## PART X.2 — TAX IN RESPECT OF REGISTERED INVESTMENTS

**204.4 (1) Definition of "registered investment"** — In this Part, "registered investment" means a trust or a corporation that has applied in prescribed form as of a particular date in the year of application and has been accepted by the Minister as of that date as a registered investment for one or more of the following:

(a) registered retirement savings plans,

(b) [Repealed under former Act]

(c) registered retirement income funds, and

(d) deferred profit sharing plans

and that has not been notified by the Minister that it is no longer registered under this Part.

### Proposed Amendment — Segregated fund policies

**Department of Finance news release, December 19, 1996**: Issuers of segregated fund policies will be allowed to elect to have their segregated funds registered under Part X.2 of the Act. The result of this election would be to exclude interests in registered segregated funds from the "foreign property" definition. However, as a consequence of the election in respect of a segregated fund, the issuer of the segregated fund would be required to pay any penalty tax under Part XI of the Act in respect of foreign property holdings of the segregated fund. [For the rest of this proposal, see under 206(1)"foreign property" — ed.]

**Department of Finance news release, October 23, 1997**: 4. Registered Investments

Under the proposed rules, Revenue Canada will be able to accept a segregated fund as a registered investment under subsection 204.4(1) of the *Income Tax Act*. If a segregated fund is accepted, an interest in the fund will not be a foreign property for the purposes of the Act. However, the insurer administering the segregated fund will be subject to tax under Part XI of the Act if the foreign property held by the segregated fund ever exceeds the 20% foreign property limit.

The proposed amendments include a transitional provision. If a segregated fund that was created before 1997 is accepted by Revenue Canada as a registered investment under subsection 204.4(1) of the Act, the foreign property limit under Part XI in respect of the fund will be 60% in 1999 and 40% in 2000. [For the rest of this proposal, see under 206(1)"foreign property" — ed.]

**Related Provisions**: 248(1)"registered investment" — Definition applies to entire Act.

**Notes**: See Notes to 204.5 re published list of registered investments.

204.4(1)(b), repealed after 1985, listed "registered home ownership savings plans". See Notes to 146.2.

**Interpretation Bulletins**: IT-320R2: RRSPs — qualified investments.

**(2) Acceptance of applicant for registration** — The Minister may accept for registration for the purposes of this Part any applicant that is

(a) a trust that has as its sole trustee a corporation licensed or otherwise authorized under the laws of Canada or a province to carry on in Canada the business of offering to the public its services as trustee if, on the particular date referred to in subsection (1),

(i) all the property of the applicant is held in trust for the benefit of not fewer than 20 beneficiaries and

(A) not fewer than 20 beneficiaries are taxpayers described in paragraph 205(a) or (c), or

(B) not fewer than 100 beneficiaries are taxpayers described in paragraph 205(b) or (e),

(ii) the total of

(A) the fair market value at the time of acquisition of its shares, bonds, mortgages, marketable securities and cash, and

> **Proposed Amendment — 204.4(2)(a)(ii)(A)**
>
> **Letter from Department of Finance, July 4, 2000:**
>
> Dear [xxx]
>
> Thank you for your letter of June 14, 2000 concerning eligible investments for deferred income plans and registered investments.
>
> You are seeking an amendment to clause 204.4(2)(a)(ii)(A) of the *Income Tax Act* to include a reference to "debentures, notes and other similar obligations". Such a change would be similar to recent changes to subsection 108(2) of the Act and the definition "pooled fund trust" in subsection 5000(7) of the *Income Tax Regulations*. From a tax policy perspective, we agree that clause 204.4(2)(a)(ii)(A) should be amended to include such a reference. We understand that the Minister of National Revenue would not be in a position to accept for registration as a registered investment under paragraph 204.4(2)(a) a corporation or a trust holding such property, until after such an amendment has received Royal Assent. Consequently, while we will recommend that an amendment to this effect apply to property acquired after the date of the amendment's public announcement, we do not anticipate registration by that Minister of new corporations and trusts on the basis of this amendment until after Royal Assent.
>
> You also request a change to Part 49 of the Regulations to add exchange-traded futures contracts to the list of qualified investments for RRSPs and other deferred income plans. While we will consider your request in the context of our ongoing review of the qualified investment rules, we are not prepared at this time to recommend the changes you seek in this regard.
>
> Thank you for writing.
>
> Yours sincerely,
>
> Len Farber
> General Director, Tax Legislation Division, Tax Policy Branch

(B) the amount by which the fair market value at the time of acquisition of its real property that may reasonably be regarded as being held for the purpose of producing income from property exceeds the total of all amounts each of which is owing by it on account of its acquisition of the real property

is not less than 80% of the amount by which the fair market value at the time of acquisition of all its property exceeds the total of all amounts each of which is owing by it on account of its acquisition of real property,

(iii) the fair market value at the time of acquisition of its shares, bonds, mortgages and other securities of any one corporation or debtor (other than bonds, mortgages and other securities of or guaranteed by Her Majesty in right of Canada or a province or Canadian municipality) is not more than 10% of the amount by which the fair market value at the time of acquisition of all its property exceeds the total of all amounts each of which is an amount owing by it on account of its acquisition of real property,

(iv) the amount by which

(A) the fair market value at the time of acquisition of any one of its real properties

exceeds

(B) the total of all amounts each of which is owing by it on account of its acquisition of the real property

is not more than 10% of the amount by which the fair market value at the time of acquisition of all its property exceeds the total of all amounts each of which is owing by it on account of its acquisition of real property,

(v) not less than 95% of the income of the applicant for its most recently completed fiscal period, or where no such period exists, that part of its current fiscal period before the particular date, was derived from investments described in subparagraph (ii),

(vi) the total value of all interests in the applicant owned by all trusts or corporations described in paragraph 205(a) or (c) to which any one employer, either alone or together with persons with whom the employer was not dealing at arm's length, has made contributions does not exceed 25% of the value of all its property,

(vii) the total value of all interests in the applicant owned by all trusts described in paragraph 205(b) or (e) to which any one taxpayer, either alone or together with persons with whom the taxpayer was not dealing at arm's length, has made contributions does not exceed 25% of the value of all its property, and

(viii) the applicant does not hold property acquired by it after May 26, 1975 that is

(A) a mortgage (other than a mortgage insured under the *National Housing Act*), or an interest therein, in respect of which the mortgagor is the annuitant under a registered retirement savings plan or a registered retirement income fund, or a person with whom the annuitant is not dealing at arm's length, if any of the funds of a trust governed by such a plan or fund have been used to acquire an interest in the applicant, or

(B) a bond, debenture, note or similar obligation issued by a cooperative corporation (within the meaning assigned by subsection 136(2)) or a credit union that has granted any benefit or privilege to any annuitant or beneficiary under a plan or fund referred to in subsection (1) that is dependent on or related to

(I) ownership by a trust governed by any such plan or fund of shares, bonds, debentures, notes or similar obligations of the cooperative corporation or credit union, or

(II) ownership by the applicant of shares, bonds, debentures, notes or similar obligations of the cooperative corporation or credit union if the trust governed by any such plan or fund has used any of its funds to acquire an interest in the applicant;

(b) a trust that

(i) would be a trust described in paragraph (a) if that paragraph were read without reference to subparagraphs (a)(i), (vi) and (vii), and

(ii) holds only prescribed investments for the type of plan or fund in respect of which it has applied for registration;

(c) a mutual fund trust;

(d) a trust that

(i) would be a mutual fund trust if paragraph 132(6)(c) were not applicable, and

(ii) holds only prescribed investments for the type of plan or fund in respect of which it has applied for registration;

(e) a mutual fund corporation or investment corporation; or

(f) a corporation that

(i) would be a mutual fund corporation or investment corporation if it could have elected to be a public corporation under paragraph (b) of the definition "public corporation" in subsection 89(1) had the conditions prescribed therefor required only that a class of shares of its capital stock be qualified for distribution to the public, and

(ii) holds only prescribed investments for the type of plan or fund in respect of which it has applied for registration.

**Related Provisions**: 204.6(1), (2), (3) — Tax payable.

**Regulations**: 4900, 4901 (prescribed investments).

**Forms**: T3RI: Registered investment and income tax return; T2217: Application for registration as a registered investment.

**(3) Revocation of registration** — The Minister shall notify a registered investment that it is no longer registered

(a) on being satisfied that, at a date subsequent to its registration date, it no longer satisfies one or more of the conditions necessary for it to be acceptable for registration under this Part, other than a condition the failure of which to satisfy would make it liable for tax under section 204.6; or

(b) within 30 days after receipt of a request in prescribed form from the registered investment for termination of its registration.

**(4) Suspension of revocation** — Notwithstanding a notification to a taxpayer under subsection (3), for the purposes of sections 204.6 and 204.7 and Part XI, the taxpayer shall be deemed to be a registered investment for each month or part thereof after the notification during which an interest in, or a share of the capital stock of, the taxpayer continues, by virtue of having been a registered investment, to be a qualified investment for a plan or fund referred to in subsection (1).

**(5) Cancellation of revocation** — Where a registered investment has been notified pursuant to paragraph (3)(a) and within 3 months from the date of notification it satisfies the Minister that it is acceptable for registration under this Part, the Minister may declare the notification to be a nullity.

**(6) Successor trust** — Where at any time in a year a particular trust described in paragraph (2)(a) or (b) has substantially the same beneficiaries and can reasonably be regarded as being a continuation of another trust that was a registered investment in the year or the immediately preceding year, for the purposes of this Part, the particular trust shall be deemed to be the same trust as the other trust.

**(7) Deemed registration of registered investment** — Where at the end of any month a registered investment could qualify for acceptance at that time under subsection (2), it shall be deemed for the purposes of section 204.6 to have been registered under the first of the following paragraphs under which it is registrable regardless of the paragraph under which it was accepted for registration by the Minister:

(a) paragraph (2)(c) or (e), as the case may be;

(b) paragraph (2)(a);

(c) paragraph (2)(d) or (f), as the case may be; and

(d) paragraph (2)(b).

**Definitions [s. 204.4]**: "amount" — 248(1); "arm's length" — 251(1); "Canada" — 255; "class of shares" — 248(6); "corporation" — 248(1), *Interpretation Act* 35(1); "credit union" — 137(6), 248(1); "deferred profit sharing plan" — 147(1), 248(1); "fiscal period" — 249(2)(b), 249.1; "investment corporation" — 130(3), 248(1); "Minister" — 248(1); "mutual fund corporation" — 131(8), 248(1); "mutual fund trust" — 132(6)–(7), 132.2(1)(q), 248(1); "prescribed", "property" — 248(1); "province" — *Interpretation Act* 35(1); "public corporation" — 89(1), 248(1); "registered investment" — 204.4(1), 248(1); "registered retirement income fund" — 146.3(1), 248(1); "registered retirement savings plan" — 146(1), 248(1); "share", "taxpayer" — 248(1); "trust" — 104(1), 248(1), (3).

**204.5 Publication of list in *Canada Gazette*** — Each year the Minister shall cause to be published in the *Canada Gazette* a list of all registered investments as of December 31 of the preceding year.

**Notes:** For the list of registered investments to December 31, 1999, as printed in *Canada Gazette* Part I, April 15, 2000, see *TaxPartner* CD-ROM under the "Tables" heading in the Table of Contents.

**Definitions [s. 204.5]:** "Minister" — 248(1); "registered investment" — 204.4(1), 248(1).

**204.6 (1) Tax payable** — Where at the end of any month a taxpayer that is a registered investment described in paragraph 204.4(2)(b), (d) or (f) holds property that is not a prescribed investment for that taxpayer, it shall, in respect of that month, pay a tax under this Part equal to 1% of the fair market value at the time of its acquisition of each such property.

**Related Provisions:** 204.4(3) and (4) — Revocation of registration; 205 — Application of Part XI; 259 — Proportional holdings in trust property.

**Regulations:** 4901 (prescribed investment).

**(2) Idem** — Where at the end of any month a taxpayer that is a registered investment described in paragraph 204.4(2)(a) or (b) holds property that is a share, bond, mortgage or other security of a corporation or debtor (other than bonds, mortgages and other securities of or guaranteed by Her Majesty in right of Canada or a province or Canadian municipality), it shall, in respect of that month, pay a tax under this Part equal to 1% of the amount, if any, by which

(a) the total of all amounts each of which is the fair market value of such a property at the time of its acquisition

exceeds

(b) 10% of the amount by which

(i) the total of all amounts each of which is the fair market value, at the time of acquisition, of one of its properties

exceeds

(ii) the total of all amounts each of which is an amount owing by the trust at the end of the month in respect of the acquisition of real property.

**Related Provisions:** 205 — Application of Part XI; 259 — Proportional holdings in trust property.

**(3) Idem** — Where at the end of any month a taxpayer that is a registered investment described in paragraph 204.4(2)(a) holds real property, it shall, in respect of that month, pay a tax under this Part equal to 1% of the total of all amounts each of which is the amount by which the excess of

(a) the fair market value at the time of its acquisition of any one real property of the taxpayer

over

(b) the total of all amounts each of which was an amount owing by it at the end of the month on account of its acquisition of the real property

was greater than 10% of the amount by which the total of all amounts each of which is the fair market value at the time of its acquisition of a property held by it at the end of the month exceeds the total of all amounts each of which was an amount owing by it at the end of the month on account of its acquisition of real property.

**Related Provisions:** 205 — Application of Part XI.

**Definitions [s. 204.6]:** "amount" — 248(1); "corporation" — 248(1), *Interpretation Act* 35(1); "prescribed", "property" — 248(1); "registered investment" — 204.4(1), 248(1); "share", "taxpayer" — 248(1); "trust" — 104(1), 248(1), (3).

**204.7 (1) Return and payment of tax** — Within 90 days from the end of each taxation year commencing after 1980, a registered investment shall

(a) file with the Minister a return for the year under this Part in prescribed form and containing prescribed information, without notice or demand therefor;

(b) estimate in the return the amount of tax, if any, payable by it under this Part for the year; and

(c) pay to the Receiver General the amount of tax, if any, payable by it under this Part for the year.

**Related Provisions:** 150.1(5) — Electronic filing.

**Forms:** T3RI: Registered investment and income tax return.

**(2) Liability of trustee** — Where the trustee of a registered investment that is liable to pay tax under this Part does not remit to the Receiver General the amount of the tax within the time specified in subsection (1), the trustee is personally liable to pay on behalf of the registered investment the full amount of the tax and is entitled to recover from the registered investment any amount paid by the trustee as tax under this section.

**(3) Provisions applicable to Part** — Subsections 150(2) and (3), sections 152 and 158, subsections 161(1) and (11), sections 162 to 167 and Division J of Part I are applicable to this Part with such modifications as the circumstances require.

**Definitions [s. 204.7]:** "amount", "Minister", "prescribed" — 248(1); "registered investment" — 204.4(1), 248(1); "taxation year" — 249.

# PART X.3 — LABOUR-SPONSORED VENTURE CAPITAL CORPORATIONS

**Proposed Amendment — Part X.3**

**Federal budget, supplementary information, February 16, 1999:** *RRSP withdrawals under the Home Buyers' Plan (HBP) and the Lifelong Learning Plan (LLP)*

The HBP and the LLP allow a qualifying individual to withdraw RRSP funds on a tax-free basis to purchase a home or to pay for education. HBP withdrawals are repayable over a 15-year period, while LLP withdrawals are repayable over a 10-year period. To the extent that a scheduled repayment for a year is not made, it is added in computing the participant's income for the year.

The Quebec government has proposed to allow individuals to withdraw proceeds from the redemption of provincial

LSVCC shares held within an RRSP, without the provincial LSVCC credit being recovered if the withdrawal is made under the HBP or the LLP. Under existing law, the federal credit will not be recovered in these circumstances. Individuals making such withdrawals are expected to acquire replacement shares in annual amounts determined under the existing HBP and LLP repayment schedules. These replacement purchases are not eligible for the Quebec LSVCC credit. Where an individual fails to acquire LSVCC replacement shares, a special Quebec tax of 15 per cent of the shortfall is imposed on the individual to recover the LSVCC credit that Quebec provided on the purchase of the redeemed shares.

The budget proposes that purchases of replacement shares in Quebec LSVCCs likewise not be eligible for the federal LSVCC credit. In addition, where an individual fails to acquire a replacement share, it is proposed to levy a federal penalty tax that matches the special 15 per cent Quebec tax. These proposals will apply from the date the corresponding Quebec proposals apply.

Similar changes are not contemplated for federally-registered LSVCCs or LSVCCs registered in other provinces. Because shares in Quebec LSVCCs are not normally redeemable until retirement, amounts on which an LSVCC credit was paid will be available for small business investment for a considerable period of time even if withdrawn under the HBP or the LLP for part of that time. In contrast, because shares in federally-registered LSVCCs or in LSVCCs registered in other provinces may generally be redeemed without a recovery of the federal credit after eight years, it would be inappropriate to allow the amounts invested in these shares not to be available for small business investment for any length of time in that period.

**Notes**: This measure has not yet appeared as draft legislation, as it was awaiting enactment of the relevant Quebec legislation.

### 204.8 (1) Definitions — In this Part,

**Notes [204.8(1)]**: 204.8 renumbered as 204.8(1) by 1999 Budget, effective for 1999 and later taxation years.

**"annuitant"** has the meaning assigned by subsection 146(1);

**"eligible business entity"**, at any time, means a particular entity that is

(a) a prescribed corporation, or

(b) a Canadian partnership or a taxable Canadian corporation, all or substantially all of the fair market value of the property of which is, at that time, attributable to

(i) property used in a specified active business carried on by the particular entity or by a corporation controlled by the particular entity,+

(ii) shares of the capital stock or debt obligations of one or more entities that, at that time, are eligible business entities related to the particular entity, or

(iii) any combination of properties described in subparagraph (i) or (ii),

**Related Provisions**: 256(6), (6.1) — Meaning of "controlled".

**Notes**: The CCRA takes the position that "all or substantially all" means 90% or more.

"204.8(1)"eligible business entity" amended by 1999 Budget, effective for 1999 and later taxation years, to add para. (a). (Subparas. (b)(i)–(iv) were formerly paras. (a)–(d).)

**"eligible investment"** of a particular corporation means

(a) a share that was issued to the particular corporation and that is a share of the capital stock of a corporation that was an eligible business entity at the time the share was issued,

(b) a particular debt obligation that was issued to the particular corporation by an entity that was an eligible business entity at the time the particular debt obligation was issued where

(i) the entity is not restricted by the terms of the particular debt obligation or by the terms of any agreement related to that obligation from incurring other debts,

(ii) the particular debt obligation, if secured, is secured solely by a floating charge on the assets of the entity or by a guarantee referred to in paragraph (c), and

(iii) the particular debt obligation, by its terms or any agreement relating to that obligation, is subordinate to all other debt obligations of the entity, except that, where the entity is a corporation, the particular debt obligation need not be subordinate to

(A) a debt obligation issued by the entity that is prescribed to be a small business security for the purposes of paragraph (a) of the definition "small business property" in subsection 206(1), or

(B) a debt obligation owing to a shareholder of the entity or to a person related to any such shareholder,

(c) a guarantee provided by the particular corporation in respect of a debt obligation that would, if the debt obligation had been issued to the particular corporation at the time the guarantee was provided, have been at that time an eligible investment because of paragraph (b), or

(d) an option or a right granted by an eligible business entity that is a corporation, in conjunction with the issue of a share or debt obligation that is an eligible investment, to acquire a share of the capital stock of the eligible business entity that would be an eligible investment if that share were issued at the time that the option or right was granted,

if the following conditions are satisfied:

(e) immediately after the time the share or debt obligation was issued, the guarantee was provided or the option or right was granted, as the case may be, the total of the costs to the particular corporation of all shares, options, rights and debt obligations of the eligible business entity and all corporations related to it and 25% of the amount of all guarantees provided by the particular corporation in respect of debt obligations of the eligible business entity and the related corporations does not exceed the lesser of $15,000,000 and 10% of the shareholders' equity in the particular corporation, determined in accordance with generally accepted accounting principles, on a cost basis and without taking into account any unrealized gains or losses on the investments of the particular corporation, and

(f) immediately before the time the share or debt obligation was issued, the guarantee was provided or the option or right was granted, as the case may be,

(i) the carrying value of the total assets of the eligible business entity and all corporations (other than prescribed labour-sponsored venture capital corporations) related to it (determined in accordance with generally accepted accounting principles on a consolidated or combined basis, where applicable) did not exceed $50,000,000, and

(ii) the total of

(A) the number of employees of the eligible business entity and all corporations related to it who normally work at least 20 hours per week for the entity and the related corporations, and

(B) ½ of the number of other employees of the entity and the related corporations,

did not exceed 500;

**Related Provisions**: 204.81(4) — Determination of cost.

**Notes**: Everything after para. (d) to end of the definition amended by 1997 Budget, effective for property acquired after February 18, 1997. From December 3, 1992 to February 17, 1997, read:

if, immediately after the time the share or debt obligation was issued, the guarantee was provided or the option or right was granted, as the case may be,

(e) the total of the costs to the particular corporation of all shares, options, rights and debt obligations of the eligible business entity and all corporations related to it and 25% of the amount of all guarantees provided by the particular corporation in respect of debt obligations of such eligible business entity and all corporations related to it does not exceed the lesser of $10,000,000 and 10% of the shareholders' equity in the particular corporation at that time, determined in accordance with generally accepted accounting principles, on a cost basis and without taking into account any unrealized gains or losses on the investments of the particular corporation,

(f) the carrying value of the total assets of the eligible business entity and all corporations related to it (determined in accordance with generally accepted accounting principles on a consolidated or combined basis, where applicable) does not exceed $50,000,000, and

(g) the number of employees of the eligible business entity and all corporations related to it does not exceed 500;

Para. (a) of "eligible investment" amended by 1992 Economic Statement, effective December 3, 1992, to delete a requirement that the share be prescribed for purposes of 110.6(8) and (9) (i.e., a prescribed share under Reg. 6205). The effect is that preferred shares issued by qualifying small and medium-sized businesses are included in the definition.

Para. (f) of "eligible investment" amended by 1992 Budget/technical bill, effective for 1992 and later taxation years, to raise the limit from $35 million to $50 million.

**Regulations**: 6701 (prescribed labour-sponsored venture capital corporation, for subpara. (f)(i)).

**"eligible labour body"** means a trade union, as defined in the *Canada Labour Code*, that represents employees in more than one province, or an organization that is composed of 2 or more such unions;

**Notes**: Definition "eligible labour body" added by 1992 Budget/technical bill, effective for 1992 and later taxation years. It replaces "national central labour body".

**"labour-sponsored funds tax credit"** — [Repealed]

**Notes**: Definition "labour-sponsored funds tax credit" repealed by 1996 Budget, effective 1996. It simply referred to the definition in 127.4(1), and is no longer needed due to amendments to 204.8"specified individual".

**"national central labour body"** — [Repealed]

**Notes**: Definition "national central labour body" repealed by 1992 Budget/technical bill, effective for 1992 and later taxation years. See "eligible labour body" above.

**"original acquisition"** of a share has the meaning assigned by subsection 127.4(1);

**Notes**: Definition "original acquisition" added by 1996 Budget, effective 1996.

**"original purchaser"** — [Repealed]

**Notes**: Definition "original purchaser" repealed by 1996 Budget, effective 1996. It is no longer needed due to an amendment to 204.81(1)(c)(v)(A)(I). Before 1996, read:

"original purchaser", in relation to a share, means the individual to whom the share was issued;

**"registered labour-sponsored venture capital corporation"** — [Repealed]

**Notes**: Definition "registered labour-sponsored venture capital corporation" repealed by 1996 Budget, effective 1996. It has been moved, in revised form, to 248(1). Before 1996, read:

"registered labour-sponsored venture capital corporation" means a corporation registered under subsection 204.81(1);

**"reserve"** means property described in any of paragraphs (a), (b), (c), (f) and (g) of the definition "qualified investment" in section 204;

**"revoked corporation"** means a corporation the registration of which has been revoked under subsection 204.81(6);

**Related Provisions**: 211.7(1)"revoked corporation" — Definition for Part XII.5.

**"specified active business"**, at any time, means an active business that is carried on in Canada where

(a) at least 50% of the full-time employees employed at that time in respect of the business are employed in Canada, and

(b) at least 50% of the salaries and wages paid to employees employed at that time in respect of the business are reasonably attributable to services rendered in Canada by the employees;

**Notes**: It is not clear whether the definition "salary or wages" in 248(1) is intended to apply to the phrase "salaries and wages" in para. (b).

Definition amended to add the words "at that time" in paras. (a) and (b) and delete them from the end of the closing words, by 1995-97 technical bill, retroactive to 1989.

**"specified individual"**, in respect of a share, means an individual (other than a trust) whose labour-sponsored funds tax credit (as defined by subsection 127.4(6)) in respect of the original acquisition of the share is not nil or would not be nil if this Act were read without reference to paragraphs 127.4(6)(b) and (d).

**Notes**: Definition "specified individual" amended by 1996 Budget, effective 1996. From December 3, 1992 through 1995, read:

> "specified individual", in respect of a share, means an individual (other than a trust) whose labour-sponsored funds tax credit for a taxation year would take into account the amount of consideration paid to acquire, or to subscribe for, the share if the information return described in paragraph 204.81(6)(c) in respect of the share were filed as required under paragraph 127.4(3)(b).

Definition "specified individual" added by 1992 Economic Statement, effective December 3, 1992. The definition accounts for the fact that under 127.4(1)"qualifying trust" and 127.4(3), the LSVCC share can be purchased either by an individual or by that individual's RRSP.

**"start-up period"** of a corporation means

(a) subject to paragraph (c), in the case of a corporation that first issued Class A shares before February 17, 1999, the corporation's taxation year in which it first issued those shares and the four following taxation years,

(b) subject to paragraph (c), in the case of a corporation that first issues Class A shares after February 16, 1999, the corporation's taxation year in which it first issues those shares and the following taxation year, or

(c) where a corporation files an election with its return under this Part for a particular taxation year of the corporation that ends after 1998 and that is referred to in paragraph (a) or (b), the period, if any, consisting of the taxation years referred to in paragraph (a) or (b), as the case may be, other than the particular year and all taxation years following the particular year.

**Notes**: 204.8(1)"start-up period" added by 1999 Budget, effective 1998.

**(2) When venture capital business discontinued** — For the purposes of section 127.4, this Part and Part XII.5, a corporation discontinues its venture capital business

(a) at the time its articles cease to comply with paragraph 204.81(1)(c) and would so cease to comply if it had been incorporated after December 5, 1996;

(b) at the time it begins to wind-up;

(c) immediately before the time it amalgamates or merges with one or more other corporations to form one corporate entity (other than an entity deemed by paragraph 204.85(3)(d) to have been registered under this Part);

(d) at the time it becomes a revoked corporation, if one of the grounds on which the Minister could revoke its registration for the purposes of this Part is set out in paragraph 204.81(6)(a.1); or

(e) at the first time after the revocation of its registration for the purposes of this Part that it fails to comply with any of the provisions of its articles governing its authorized capital, the management of its business and affairs, the reduction of paid-up capital or the redemption or transfer of its Class A shares.

**Related Provisions**: 127.4(1.1) — Application to labour-sponsored funds tax credit; 204.841 — Penalty tax on discontinuance of venture capital business; 211.8(1.1) — Rule applies to 211.8(1).

**Notes**: 204.8(2) added by 1999 Budget, effective February 17, 1999.

**(3) Date of issue of Class A shares** — For the purposes of this Part and subsection 211.8(1), in determining the time of the issue or the original acquisition of Class A shares, identical Class A shares held by a person are deemed to be disposed of by the person in the order in which the shares were issued.

**Related Provisions**: 211.8(1.1) — Rule applies to 211.8(1).

**Notes**: 204.8(3) added by 1999 Budget, effective February 17, 1999.

**Definitions [s. 204.8]**: "active business", "amount", "business" — 248(1); "Canada" — 255, *Interpretation Act* 35(1); "Canadian partnership" — 102, 248(1); "controlled" — 256(6), (6.1); "corporation" — 248(1), *Interpretation Act* 35(1); "eligible business entity", "eligible investment" — 204.8(1); "employed", "employee", "individual", "Minister" — 248(1); "original acquisition" — 127.4(1), 204.8(1); "paid-up capital" — 89(1), 248(1); "person", "prescribed", "property" — 248(1); "province" — *Interpretation Act* 35(1); "related" — 251(2)–(6); "revoked corporation" — 204.8(1); "security" — *Interpretation Act* 35(1); "share", "shareholder" — 248(1); "specified active business" — 204.8(1); "taxable Canadian corporation" — 89(1), 248(1); "taxation year" — 249; "trust" — 104(1), 248(1), (3).

**204.81 (1) Conditions for registration** — The Minister may register a corporation for the purposes of this Part if, in the opinion of the Minister, it complies with the following conditions:

(a) the corporation has applied in prescribed form to the Minister for registration;

(b) the corporation was caused to be incorporated under the *Canada Business Corporations Act* by an eligible labour body; and

(c) the articles of the corporation provide that

(i) the business of the corporation is restricted to assisting the development of eligible business entities and to creating, maintaining and protecting jobs by providing financial and managerial advice to such entities and by investing funds of the corporation in eligible investments and reserves,

(ii) the authorized capital of the corporation shall consist only of

(A) Class A shares that are issuable only to individuals (other than trusts) and trusts governed by registered retirement savings plans, that entitle their holders

(I) to receive notice of and, subject to the *Canada Business Corporations Act*, to attend and vote at all meetings of the shareholders of the corporation,

(II) to receive dividends at the discretion of the board of directors of the corporation, and

(III) to receive, on dissolution of the corporation, all the assets of the corporation that remain after payment of all amounts payable to the holders of all other classes of shares of the corporation,

(B) Class B shares that are issuable only to and may be held only by eligible labour bodies, that entitle each of those shareholders

(I) to receive notice of and, subject to the *Canada Business Corporations Act*, to attend and vote at all meetings of the shareholders of the corporation, and

(II) to receive, on dissolution of the corporation, an amount equal to the amount of the consideration received by the corporation on the issue of the Class B shares,

but that do not entitle them to receive dividends, and

(C) any additional classes of shares that are authorized, if the rights, privileges, restrictions and conditions attached to the shares are approved by the Minister of Finance,

(iii) the business and affairs of the corporation shall be managed by a board of directors, at least ½ of whom are appointed by the Class B shareholders,

(iv) the corporation shall not reduce its paid-up capital in respect of a class of shares (other than Class B shares) otherwise than by way of a redemption of shares of the corporation or in such other manner as is prescribed,

(v) the corporation shall not redeem a Class A share in respect of which an information return described in paragraph (6)(c) has been issued unless

(A) where the share is held by the specified individual in respect of the share, a spouse or common-law partner or former spouse or common-law partner of that individual or a trust governed by a registered retirement savings plan or registered retirement income fund under which that individual, spouse or common-law partner is the annuitant,

(I) a request in writing to redeem the share is made by the holder to the corporation and the information return referred to in paragraph (6)(c) has been returned to the corporation, or

(II) [Repealed]

(III) the corporation is notified in writing that the specified individual in respect of the share became disabled and permanently unfit for work or terminally ill after the share was issued,

(B) there is no specified individual in respect of the share,

(C) [Repealed]

(D) the corporation is notified in writing that the share is held by a person on whom the share has devolved as a consequence of the death of

(I) a holder of the share, or

(II) an annuitant under a trust governed by a registered retirement savings plan or registered retirement income fund that was a holder of the share,

(E) the redemption occurs more than 8 years after the day on which the share was issued, or

(F) the holder of the share has satisfied such other conditions as are prescribed,

**Proposed Amendment — Shares redeemed from Feb. 1 to March 1**

**Department of Finance news release, February 7, 2000**: See under 211.8(1)(a).

(vi) [Repealed]

(vii) the corporation shall not register a transfer of a Class A share by the specified individual in respect of the share, a spouse or common-law partner of the specified individual or a trust governed by a registered retirement savings plan or registered retirement income fund under which the specified individual or spouse or common-law partner is the annuitant, unless

(A) no information return has been issued under paragraph (6)(c) in respect of the share,

(B) [Repealed]

(C) the transfer is to the specified individual, a spouse or common-law partner or former spouse or common-law partner of the specified individual or a trust governed by a registered retirement savings plan or registered retirement income fund under which the specified individual or the spouse or common-law partner or former spouse or common-law partner of the specified individual is the annuitant,

(D) the corporation is notified in writing that the transfer occurs as a consequence of the death of the specified individual or a spouse or common-law partner of the specified individual,

(E) the corporation is notified in writing that the transfer occurs after the specified individual dies,

(F) [Repealed]

(G) the corporation is notified in writing that the specified individual became disabled and permanently unfit for work or terminally ill after the share was issued and before the transfer, or

(H) such other conditions as are prescribed are satisfied;

(viii) the corporation shall not pay any fee or remuneration to a shareholder, director or officer of the corporation unless the payment was approved by a resolution of the directors of the corporation, and

(ix) the corporation shall not make any investment in an eligible business entity with which the corporation or any of the directors of the corporation does not deal at arm's length unless

(A) the corporation would deal at arm's length with the eligible business entity but for the corporation's interest as the holder of eligible investments in such entity, or

(B) the investment was approved by special resolution of the shareholders of the corporation before the investment was made.

**Related Provisions**: 131(8) — Prescribed LSVCC deemed to be a mutual fund corporation; 131(11) — Rules respecting prescribed LSVCCs; 204.81(6)(a), (a.1) — Revocation of registration for failure to comply with conditions; 211.7 — Recovery of credit from provincial LSVCCs; 211.8(1) — Clawback of credit on disposition of approved share; 211.9(a)(ii) — Refund of clawback; 248(1)"registered labour-sponsored venture capital corporation" — Definition of RLSVCC for entire Act; 248(8) — Occurrences as a consequence of death.

**Notes**: See Notes to 248(1)"registered labour-sponsored venture capital corporation".

Opening words of 204.81(1)(c) amended by 1992 Economic Statement, retroactive to its introduction in 1989, to change "articles of incorporation" to "articles".

Opening words of 204.81(1)(c)(ii)(A) amended by 1992 Economic Statement, effective December 3, 1992 (but see exception below), to add reference to trusts governed by RRSPs.

Closing words of 204.81(1)(c)(ii)(A) repealed by 1992 Economic Statement, effective December 3, 1992 (but see exception below). For earlier dates, read:

and that, where an information return described in paragraph (6)(c) was issued in respect thereof, are redeemable or transferable only in the circumstances described in subparagraph (v) or (vii), as the case may be,

204.81(1)(c)(ii)(B) amended by 1996 Budget, effective for corporations incorporated after March 5, 1996, so that Class B shares can be issued to any eligible labour body, not just the eligible labour body that caused the corporation to be incorporated. For corporations incorporated earlier, read the opening and closing words of cl. (B) as:

(B) Class B shares that are issuable only to and may be held only by the eligible labour body that caused the corporation to be incorporated and that entitle the eligible labour body

. . . . .

but that do not entitle the eligible labour body to receive dividends, and

204.81(1)(c)(ii)(C) amended by 1997 Budget, effective 1997. Previously read:

(C) such additional classes of shares without voting rights (except as may be required by law) as are authorized, where the rights, privileges, restrictions and conditions attached to the shares are determined by the board of directors of the corporation and approved by the Minister of Finance,

204.81(1)(c)(iii) amended by 1996 Budget, effective for corporations incorporated after March 5, 1996, to change "appointed by the eligible labour body that caused the corporation to be incorporated" to "appointed by the Class B shareholders". (This allows for the transfer of responsibilities for an LSVCC from an eligible labour body to another eligible labour body.)

Opening words of 204.81(1)(c)(v)(A) amended by 2000 same-sex partners bill to add reference to " common-law partner", effective for the 2001 and later taxation years, or earlier by election (see Notes to 248(1)"common-law partner").

Opening words of 204.81(1)(c)(v) amended by 1996 Budget, effective for corporations incorporated after March 5, 1996. For corporations incorporated earlier, read:

(v) subject to the provision described in subparagraph (vi), the corporation may redeem a Class A share in respect of which an information return described in paragraph (6)(c) has been issued only if

204.81(1)(c)(v)(A)(I) amended and (II) repealed by 1996 Budget, effective for corporations incorporated after March 5, 1996. For corporations incorporated earlier, read:

(I) a request in writing to redeem the share is made by the holder to the corporation within 60 days after the day on which the share was issued to the original purchaser and the information return referred to in paragraph (6)(c) has been returned to the corporation,

(II) the corporation is notified in writing that the specified individual in respect of the share has retired from the workforce or ceased to be resident in Canada, or

204.81(1)(c)(v)(C) repealed by 1996 Budget, effective for corporations incorporated after March 5, 1996. For corporations incorporated earlier, read:

(C) the time of redemption is on or after the day on which the specified individual in respect of the share attained, or would, but for death, have attained the age of 65 years,

204.81(1)(c)(v)(E) amended by 1996 Budget, effective for corporations incorporated after March 5, 1996, to change "5 years" to "8 years".

204.81(1)(c)(vi) repealed by 1996 Budget, effective for corporations incorporated after March 5, 1996. For corporations incorporated earlier, read:

(vi) unless a Class A share has been issued and outstanding for at least 2 years, the corporation shall not be permitted to redeem the share solely because the specified individual in respect of the share attains 65 years of age or the corporation is notified that the specified individual

(A) has retired from the workforce, or

(B) has ceased to be resident in Canada,

204.81(1)(c)(vii) amended by 2000 same-sex partners bill to add reference to "common-law partner", effective for the 2001 and later taxation years, or earlier by election (see Notes to 248(1)"common-law partner").

204.81(1)(c)(vii)(B) repealed by 1996 Budget, effective for corporations incorporated after March 5, 1996. For corporations incorporated earlier, read:

(B) the transfer occurs more than 5 years after the day on which the share was issued,

204.81(1)(c)(vii)(E) amended and (F) repealed by 1996 Budget, effective for corporations incorporated after March 5, 1996. For corporations incorporated earlier, read:

(E) the corporation is notified in writing that the transfer occurs after the specified individual dies, retires from the workforce or ceases to be resident in Canada,

(F) the specified individual attains 65 years of age,

204.81(1)(c)(v) to (vii) amended by 1992 Economic Statement, effective December 3, 1992 (but see exception below). For earlier dates, read:

(v) subject to the provision described in subparagraph (vi), the corporation may redeem a Class A share in respect of which an information return described in paragraph (6)(c) was issued only if the corporation is requested in writing by the holder of the share to redeem it and

(A) where the share is held by the original purchaser,

(I) the request is made within 60 days after the day on which the share was issued to the original purchaser, the information return referred to in paragraph (6)(c) was returned to the corporation and the share is not held as an investment of a registered retirement savings plan, or

(II) the corporation is notified in writing that the original purchaser has retired from the workforce, has attained 65 years of age, has ceased to be a resident of Canada or has, after acquiring the share, become disabled and permanently unfit for work or become terminally ill,

(B) where the holder of the share is not the original purchaser, the time of redemption is on or after the day on which the original purchaser attained, or would, but for death, have attained the age of 65 years,

(C) the share is held by an individual who notifies the corporation in writing that the share has devolved on the individual as a consequence of the death of a shareholder of the corporation,

(D) the share is held as an investment of a registered retirement savings plan under which the original purchaser or the original purchaser's spouse is the annuitant and the original purchaser has died or, where the original purchaser is living, the corporation is notified in writing that the original purchaser

(I) has retired from the workforce or has attained 65 years of age,

(II) has, after acquiring the share, become disabled and permanently unfit for work or become terminally ill, or

(III) has ceased to be a resident of Canada,

(E) the share is held as an investment of a registered retirement savings plan under which the original purchaser or the original purchaser's spouse is not an annuitant and the time of redemption is on or after the day on which the original purchaser attained, or would, but for death, have attained the age of 65 years,

(F) the redemption occurs more than 5 years after the day on which the share was issued, or

(G) the holder of the share has satisfied such other conditions as are prescribed,

(vi) the corporation shall not, because of the original purchaser of a share described in subparagraph (v)

(i) having retired from the workforce,

(ii) having attained 65 years of age, or

(iii) having ceased to be a resident of Canada,

redeem the share until it has been issued and outstanding for at least 2 years,

(vii) the corporation shall not register a transfer by the original purchaser, or by a registered retirement savings plan under which the original purchaser or the original purchaser's spouse is the annuitant, of a Class A share in respect of which an information return described in paragraph (6)(c) was issued, except where the transfer occurs more than 5 years after the day on which the share was issued, or where the corporation is notified in writing that the share is being transferred

(A) to be held as an investment of a registered retirement savings plan under which the original purchaser or the original purchaser's spouse is the annuitant,

(B) as a consequence of the death of the original purchaser,

(C) at a time when the original purchaser

(I) has retired from the workforce or has attained 65 years of age,

(II) has, after acquiring the share, become disabled and permanently unfit for work or become terminally ill, or

(III) has ceased to be a resident of Canada, or

(D) in accordance with such other conditions as are prescribed,

Where a corporation was registered under 204.81(1) before December 3, 1992, the amendments to 204.81(1)(c)(ii), (v), (vi) and (vii) apply to the corporation on and after the earlier of

(a) November 30, 1994, and

(b) the first day after December 2, 1992 on which the articles of incorporation of the corporation are amended.

204.81(1) amended by 1992 technical bill, effective for 1992 and later taxation years. For earlier years, read "national central labour body" in place of "eligible labour body" throughout.

204.81(1)(c)(vi) does not apply to shares purchased before 1991.

**Regulations**: 6706 (prescribed conditions for 204.81(1)(c)(v)(G)).

**Forms**: T5005: Application for registration — registered labour-sponsored venture capital corporation.

**(2) Registration number** — On registering a corporation under subsection (1), the Minister shall assign to it a registration number.

**(3) Successive registrations** — Where an eligible labour body causes more than one corporation to be registered under this Part, for the purposes of paragraph (6)(h) and section 204.82, each of those corporations shall be deemed

(a) to have issued a Class A share at the earliest time any such corporation issued a Class A share, and, where the corporation did not exist at the time referred to in paragraph (a),

(b) to have been in existence during the particular period beginning immediately before that time and ending immediately after the corporation was incorporated, and

(c) to have had, throughout the particular period, fiscal periods ending on the same calendar day in each year in the particular period as the calendar day on which its first fiscal period after it was incorporated ended.

**Notes:** Opening words of 204.81(3) amended by 1992 technical bill, effective for 1992 and later taxation years, to replace "national central labour body" with "eligible labour body".

**(4) Determination of cost** — For the purposes of this Part, the cost at any time to a corporation of an eligible investment that is a guarantee shall be deemed to be 25% of the amount of the debt obligation subject to the guarantee at that time.

**(5) Registration date** — Where the Minister registers a corporation for the purposes of this Part, the corporation shall be deemed to have become so registered on the later of

(a) the day the application for registration of the plan is received by the Minister, and

(b) where in the application for registration a day is specified as the day on which the registration is to take effect, that day.

**(6) Revocation of registration** — The Minister may revoke the registration of a corporation for the purposes of this Part where

(a) the articles of the corporation do not comply with paragraph (1)(c) and would not comply with that paragraph if the corporation had been incorporated after December 5, 1996;

(a.1) the corporation does not comply with any of the provisions of its articles described in paragraph (1)(c), except where there would be no failure to comply if the provisions of its articles were consistent with the articles of a corporation that would be permitted to be registered under this Part if it had been incorporated after December 5, 1996;

(b) an individual acquires or irrevocably subscribes and pays for a Class A share of the capital stock of the corporation in the period beginning on the 61st day of a calendar year and ending on the 60th day of the following calendar year and the corporation fails to file with the Minister an information return in prescribed form containing prescribed information before April of that following calendar year;

(c) an individual acquires or irrevocably subscribes and pays for a Class A share of the capital stock of the corporation in the period beginning on the 61st day of a calendar year and ending on the 60th day of the following calendar year and the corporation fails to issue to the individual before April of that following calendar year an information return in prescribed form stating the amount of the consideration paid for the share in that period;

(d) the corporation issues more than one information return described in paragraph (c) in respect of the same acquisition of or subscription for a Class A share;

(e) the financial statements of the corporation presented to its shareholders are not prepared in accordance with generally accepted accounting principles;

(f) the corporation fails within 6 months after the end of any taxation year to have an independent valuation of its shares made as of the end of that year;

(g) [Repealed.]

(h) the corporation does not pay the tax or penalty payable under section 204.82 by it on or before the day on or before which that tax or penalty is required to be paid;

(i) tax was payable under subsection 204.82(3) by the corporation for 3 or more taxation years;

(j) the corporation provides a guarantee that is an eligible investment and fails to maintain, at any time during the term of the guarantee, a reserve equal to the cost to the corporation of the guarantee at that time;

(k) the corporation pays a fee or commission in excess of a reasonable amount in respect of the offering for sale, or the sale, of its shares; or

(l) the corporation has a monthly deficiency in 18 or more months in any 36-month period.

**Related Provisions**: 127.4(6)(b) — No labour-sponsored funds tax credit unless return under 204.81(6)(c) filed with tax return; 204.8(1)"revoked corporation", 211.7(1)"revoked corporation" — Corporations whose registration has been revoked; 204.81(4) — Determination of cost; 204.81(7), (8) — Notice of intent to revoke registration; 204.81(8.1) — Voluntary de-registration.

**Notes:** 204.81(6)(a) and (a.1) amended by 1996 Budget, effective March 6, 1996. Before that date, read:

(a) the articles of the corporation do not comply with paragraph (1)(c);

(a.1) the corporation does not comply with any of the provisions of its articles of incorporation described in paragraph (1)(c);

204.81(6)(a) re-enacted as (a.1) and para. (a) added by 1992 Economic Statement, retroactive to 1989.

204.81(6)(g) repealed by 1999 Budget, effective February 17, 1999. Before that date, read:

(g) at any time in any of the first 5 taxation years of the corporation beginning with the taxation year in which the corporation first issues a Class A share, the corporation does not have eligible investments or reserves the cost to the corporation of which equals or is greater than 80% of the amount by which the total consideration received by it for Class A shares issued by it before that time exceeds the total of all amounts paid by it before that time to its shareholders as a return of capital on such shares;

**Forms**: T2152: Part X.3 tax return for an LSVCC; T2152 SCH 1: Calculating tax under subsec. 204.82(2); T2152 SCH 2: Calculating tax under subsecs. 204.82(3) and (6) and s. 204.841; T2152A: Part X.3 tax return and request for a refund for an LSVCC; T5006 Summ: Return of Class A shares; T5006 Supp: Statement of registered labour-sponsored venture capital corporation Class A shares.

**(7) Notice of intent to revoke registration** — Where the Minister proposes to revoke the registration of a corporation under subsection (6), the Minister shall, by registered mail, give notice to the corporation of the proposal.

**Related Provisions**: 244(5) — Proof of service by mail; 248(7)(a) — Mail deemed received on day mailed; 204.81(9) — Appeal of decision to revoke registration.

**(8) Idem** — Where the Minister gives notice under subsection (7) to a registered labour-sponsored venture capital corporation, the Minister may, after the expiration of 30 days after the day of mailing of the notice, or after the expiration of such extended period after the day of mailing as the Federal Court of Appeal or a judge thereof, on application made at any time before the determination of any appeal under subsection (9) from the giving of the notice, may fix or allow, publish a copy of the notice in the *Canada Gazette* and, on the publication of a copy of the notice, the registration of the corporation is revoked.

**(8.1) Voluntary de-registration** — Where at any time the Minister receives a certified copy of a resolution of the directors of a corporation seeking the revocation of the corporation's registration under this Part,

(a) the registration is revoked at that time; and

(b) the Minister shall, with all due dispatch, give notice in the *Canada Gazette* of the revocation.

**Related Provisions**: 204.81(6) — Revocation of registration; 204.81(8.2) — Actual date of receipt applies.

**Notes**: 204.81(8.1) added by 1999 Budget, effective for resolutions received by the Minister of National Revenue after June 29, 2000.

**(8.2) Application of subsection 248(7)** — Subsection 248(7) does not apply for the purpose of subsection (8.1).

**Notes**: 204.81(8.2) added by 1999 Budget, effective for resolutions received by the Minister of National Revenue after June 29, 2000.

**(9) Right of appeal** — Where the Minister refuses to accept a corporation for registration under subsection (1) or gives notice of a proposal to revoke the registration of a corporation under subsection (7), the corporation may appeal to the Federal Court of Appeal from the decision or from the giving of the notice.

**Definitions [s. 204.81]**: "amount" — 248(1); "annuitant" — 146(1), 204.8(1); "arm's length" — 251(1); "business" — 248(1); "Canada" — 255, *Interpretation Act* 35(1); "common-law partner" — 248(1); "consequence of the death" — 248(8); "corporation" — 248(1), *Interpretation Act* 35(1); "dividend" — 248(1); "eligible business entity" — 204.8(1); "eligible investment", "eligible labour body" — 204.8(1); "Federal Court" — *Interpretation Act* 35(1); "fiscal period" — 249.1; "individual", "Minister" — 248(1); "month" — *Interpretation Act* 35(1); "officer" — 248(1); "paid-up capital" — 89(1), 248(1); "person", "prescribed", "registered labour-sponsored venture capital corporation" — 248(1); "registered retirement income fund" — 146.3(1), 248(1); "registered retirement savings plan" — 146(1), 248(1); "reserve" — 204.8(1); "share", "shareholder" — 248(1); "specified individual" — 204.8(1); "taxation year" — 249; "trust" — 104(1), 248(1), (3); "writing" — *Interpretation Act* 35(1).

**204.82 (1) Recovery of credit** — Where, at any time that is both in a taxation year included in the start-up period of a corporation that was registered under this Part and before its venture capital business is first discontinued,

(a) 80% of the amount, if any, by which the total consideration received by it for Class A shares issued by it before that time exceeds the total of all amounts paid by it before that time to its shareholders as a return of capital on such shares

exceeds

(b) the total of all amounts each of which is the cost to the corporation of an eligible investment or reserve of the corporation at that time,

the corporation shall pay a tax under this Part for the year equal to the amount determined by the formula

$$(A \times 20\%) - B$$

where

A is the greatest amount by which the amount determined under paragraph (a) exceeds the amount determined under paragraph (b) for the year, and

B is the total of all taxes payable under this subsection by the corporation for preceding taxation years.

**Related Provisions**: 204.81(4) — Determination of cost; 257 — Formula cannot calculate to less than zero.

**Notes**: Opening words of 204.82(1) amended by 1999 Budget, effective for 1989 and later taxation years. For 1989–98, read:

(1) Where, at any time in a taxation year referred to in paragraph 204.81(6)(g) of a corporation that was registered under this Part,

**(2) Liability for tax** — Each corporation that has been registered under this Part shall, in respect of each month that ends before its venture capital business is first discontinued and in a particular taxation year of the corporation that begins after the end of the corporation's start-up period (or, where the corporation has no start-up period, that begins after the time the corporation first issues a Class A share), pay a tax under this Part equal to the amount obtained when the greatest investment shortfall at any time that is in the month and in the particular year (in this section and sections 204.81 and 204.83 referred to as the "monthly deficiency") is multiplied by $1/60$ of the prescribed rate of interest in effect during the month.

**Related Provisions**: 204.82(2.1), (2.2) — Investment shortfall.

**Notes**: 204.82(2) amended by 1999 Budget, effective for 1999 and later taxation years. For taxation years ending from March 1997 through 1998, read:

(2) Each corporation that has been registered under this Part shall, in respect of each month that ends in a particular taxa-

tion year of the corporation that begins after the end of the corporation's last taxation year referred to in paragraph 204.81(6)(g), pay a tax under this Part equal to the amount obtained when the greatest investment shortfall at any time that is in the month and in the particular year (in this section and sections 204.81 and 204.83 referred to as the "monthly deficiency") is multiplied by $\frac{1}{60}$ of the prescribed rate of interest during the month.

204.82(2) amended by 1997 Budget, effective for taxation years that end after February 1997. For taxation years that end from January 1995 through February 1997, read:

(2) Where, at any time in a month in a particular taxation year of a corporation that was registered under this Part that began after the end of the corporation's last taxation year referred to in paragraph 204.81(6)(g), 60% of the least of

(a) the amount of the shareholders' equity in the corporation determined at the end of the taxation year immediately preceding the particular taxation year, without taking into account any unrealized gains or losses in respect of eligible investments of the corporation, and

(a.1) the amount of the shareholders' equity in the corporation determined at the end of the second taxation year before the particular taxation year, without taking into account any unrealized gains or losses in respect of eligible investments of the corporation, and

(b) the amount of the shareholders' equity in the corporation, determined at the end of the particular taxation year, without taking into account any unrealized gains or losses in respect of eligible investments of the corporation,

exceeds

(c) the total of all amounts, each of which is the cost to the corporation of an eligible investment of the corporation at that time,

the corporation shall, in respect of that month, pay a tax under this Part equal to the amount obtained when the greatest such excess in the month (in this section and sections 204.81 and 204.83 referred to as the "monthly deficiency") is multiplied by a percentage equal to $\frac{1}{60}$ of the prescribed rate of interest in effect for the month.

**Regulations**: 4301 (prescribed rate of interest).

**(2.1) Determination of investment shortfall** — Subject to subsection (2.2), a corporation's investment shortfall at any time in a particular taxation year is the amount determined by the formula

$$A - B - C$$

where

A is 60% of the lesser of

(a) the amount, if any, by which the amount of the shareholders' equity in the corporation at the end of the preceding taxation year exceeds the specified adjustment in respect of the shareholders' equity in the corporation at the end of that year, and

(b) the amount, if any, by which the amount of the shareholders' equity in the corporation at the end of the particular taxation year exceeds the specified adjustment in respect of the shareholders' equity in the corporation at the end of the particular year;

B is the greater of

(a) the total of all amounts each of which is the adjusted cost to the corporation of an eligible investment of the corporation at that time, and

(b) 50% of the total of all amounts each of which is

(i) the adjusted cost to the corporation of an eligible investment of the corporation at the beginning of the particular year, or

(ii) the adjusted cost to the corporation of an eligible investment of the corporation at the end of the particular year; and

C is 60% of the amount, if any, by which

(a) the total of all amounts each of which is a tax or penalty under subsection (3) or (4), or a prescribed tax or penalty, paid before that time by the corporation (other than the portion, if any, of that tax or penalty the liability for which resulted in a reduction in the amount of the shareholders' equity at the end of any preceding taxation year)

exceeds

(b) the total of all amounts each of which is a refund before that time of any portion of the total described in paragraph (a).

**Notes [204.82(2.1)C]**: See Notes to 127.4(5) re parallel Ontario changes.

**Related Provisions**: 257 — Formula cannot calculate to less than zero.

**Notes**: 204.82(2.1)A(a) and (b) amended by 1998 Budget, effective for taxation years that begin after 1997, to add the reductions for the specified adjustment. For earlier years, read:

(a) the amount of the shareholders' equity in the corporation at the end of the preceding taxation year, and

(b) the amount of the shareholders' equity in the corporation at the end of the particular year; and

Formula element C added by 1998 Budget, effective for taxation years that begin after 1997.

204.82(2.1) added by 1997 Budget, this version effective for taxation years that end after 1998. For taxation years that end from March 1997 through the end of 1998, ignore 204.82(2)B(b).

**(2.2) Investment shortfall** — For the purpose of this subsection and for the purpose of computing a corporation's investment shortfall under subsection (2.1) at any time in a taxation year (in this subsection referred to as the "relevant year"),

(a) unrealized gains and losses in respect of its eligible investments shall not be taken into account in computing the amount of the shareholders' equity in the corporation;

(b) where

(i) the relevant year ends after 1998, and

(ii) it is expected that a redemption of its Class A shares will occur after the end of a particular taxation year and, as a consequence, the amount of the shareholders' equity in the corporation at the end of the particular year would otherwise be reduced to take into account the expected redemption,

subject to paragraph (c), the amount (or, where the relevant year ends in 1999, 2000, 2001 or 2002, 20%, 40%, 60% or 80%, respectively of the amount) expected to be redeemed shall not be taken into account in determining the amount of the shareholders' equity in the corporation at the end of the particular year;

(c) paragraph (b) does not apply to a redemption expected to be made after the end of a taxation year where

(i) the redemption is made within 60 days after the end of the year, and

(ii) either

(A) tax under Part XII.5 became payable as a consequence of the redemption, or

(B) tax under Part XII.5 would not have become payable as a consequence of the redemption if the redemption had occurred at the end of the year; and

(c.1) the specified adjustment in respect of shareholders' equity in the corporation at the end of a taxation year is the amount determined by the formula

$$(A \times (B/C)) - D$$

where

A is the shareholders' equity at the end of the year,

B is the total of

(i) the fair market value at the end of the year of all Class A shares issued by it before March 6, 1996 and more than five years before the end of the year,

(ii) the fair market value at the end of the year of all Class A shares issued by it after March 5, 1996 and more than eight years before the end of the year,

(iii) the fair market value at the end of the year of all Class A shares issued by it in the last 60 days of the year, and

(iv) if the corporation so elects in writing filed with the Minister not more than six months after the end of the year and is not a revoked corporation at the end of the year, the fair market value at the end of the year of all shares of classes, of the capital stock of the corporation, to which clause 204.81(1)(c)(ii)(C) applies,

C is the fair market value at the end of the year of all shares issued by it, and

D is the amount by which the shareholders' equity in the corporation at the end of the year has been reduced to take into account the expected subsequent redemption of shares of the capital stock of the corporation; and

(d) the adjusted cost to the corporation of an eligible investment of the corporation at any time is

(i) 150% of the cost to the corporation of the eligible investment at that time where the eligible investment is

(A) a property acquired by the corporation after February 18, 1997 (other than a property to which subparagraph (i.1) applies) that would be an eligible investment of the corporation if the reference to "$50,000,000" in paragraph (f) of the definition "eligible investment" in subsection 204.8(1) were read as "$10,000,000", or

(B) a share of the capital stock of a prescribed corporation,

(i.1) 200% of the cost to the corporation of the eligible investment at that time where the eligible investment is a property acquired by the corporation after February 16, 1999 (other than a property described in clause (i)(B)) that would be an eligible investment of the corporation if the reference to "$50,000,000" in paragraph (f) of the definition "eligible investment" in subsection 204.8(1) were read as "$2,500,000", and

(ii) in any other case, the cost to the corporation of the eligible investment of the corporation at that time.

**Related Provisions**: 257 — Formula cannot calculate to less than zero.

**Notes**: 204.82(2.2)(d)(i) amended and (d)(i.1) added by 1999 Budget, effective for 1999 and later taxation years. For taxation years ending from March 1997 through 1998, read:

(i) where the eligible investment is a property acquired by the corporation after February 18, 1997 that would be an eligible investment of the corporation if the reference to "$50,000,000" in paragraph (f) of the definition "eligible investment" in section 204.8 were read as "$10,000,000", 150% of the cost to the corporation of the eligible investment of the corporation at that time, and

Opening words of 204.82(2.2) amended by 1998 Budget to add "For the purpose of this subsection and", effective for taxation years that begin after 1997.

204.82(2.2)(c.1) added by 1998 Budget, effective for taxation years that begin after 1997.

204.82(2.2) added by 1997 Budget, effective for taxation years that end after February 1997.

**(3) Recovery of credit** — Where a corporation is liable under subsection (2) to pay a tax in respect of 12 consecutive months (in this subsection referred to as the "particular period"), the corporation shall pay a tax under this Part for a taxation year in respect of each particular period that ends in the year equal to the total of the amounts determined by the formula

$$\left(\frac{A}{12} \times 20\%\right) - (B - C)$$

where

A is the total of the monthly deficiencies for each month in the particular period;

B  is the total of all taxes payable by the corporation under subsection (1) for preceding taxation years and taxes payable by it under this subsection in respect of a period ending before the end of the particular period; and

C  is the total of all amounts refunded under section 204.83 in respect of the tax paid under this subsection by the corporation for preceding taxation years.

**Related Provisions**: 204.82(4) — Penalty; 204.83(1) — Refund of amount paid; 257 — Formula cannot calculate to less than zero.

**(4) Penalty** — Where a corporation is liable under subsection (3) to pay a tax for a taxation year, the corporation shall pay, in addition to the tax payable under that subsection, a penalty for the year equal to that tax.

**Related Provisions**: 18(1)(t) — Penalty is non-deductible; 204.83(1) — Refund of 80% of penalty; 211.7 — Recovery of credit from shareholder where share redeemed or disposed of.

**Notes**: See Notes to 238(1).

**(5) Provincially registered LSVCCs** — Where

(a) an amount (other than interest on an amount to which this subsection applies or an amount payable under or as a consequence of a prescribed provision of a law of a province) is payable to the government of a province by a corporation,

(b) the amount is payable as a consequence of a failure to acquire sufficient properties of a character described in the law of the province,

(c) the corporation has been prescribed for the purpose of the definition "approved share" in subsection 127.4(1), and

(d) the corporation is not a registered labour-sponsored venture capital corporation or a revoked corporation,

the corporation shall pay a tax under this Part for the taxation year in which the amount became payable equal to that amount.

**Related Provisions**: 204.83(2) — Refund; 204.86(2) — Return and payment of tax.

**Notes**: 204.82(5) added by 1997 Budget, effective for liabilities arising after February 18, 1997. It imposes a new tax on LSVCCs that have been prescribed under the Regulations for the purpose of 127.41(1)"approved share" and that were not registered under Part X.3.

If such an LSVCC is liable to pay an amount to the government of a province because of a failure to acquire enough small business properties as described in the provincial law, the LSVCC is generally liable to pay a tax for the taxation year in which that amount became payable, equal to that amount. However, 204.82(5) does not require the matching of provincially-imposed interest on unpaid provincial amounts payable. Instead, because of 204.87, interest on unpaid Part X.3 tax will be calculated under Reg. 4301.

204.82(5) also does not apply to any amount payable under or a prescribed provision of the provincial law. S. 25.1 of the Ontario *Community Small Business Investment Funds Act* (formerly the *Labour-Sponsored Venture Capital Corporations Act*), which imposes special additional penalties on provincially-registered LSVCCs for the failure to meet provincial investment requirements in respect of certain small businesses, will be prescribed for this purpose.

Under 204.86(2), the LSVCC must file a Part X.3 return for the year in which tax becomes payable under 204.82(5). The tax is payable within 90 days after the end of the taxation year in which the liability arose.

**Regulations**: 6707 (prescribed provision of a law of a province (Ontario)).

**(6) Further matching of amounts payable to a province** — Where

(a) a particular amount is payable (other than interest on an amount to which this subsection applies) by a registered labour-sponsored venture capital corporation or a revoked corporation to the government of a province as a consequence of a failure of a prescribed corporation to acquire sufficient properties of a character described in a law of the province, and

(b) the particular amount became payable before the corporation first discontinued its venture capital business,

the corporation shall pay a tax under this Part for the taxation year in which the particular amount became payable equal to that amount.

**Related Provisions**: 204.83(2) — Refund of tax paid under 204.82(6).

**Notes**: 204.82(6) added by 1999 Budget, effective for 1999 and later taxation years.

**Regulations**: The Department of Finance Technical Notes indicate that prescribed corporations will be corporations registered under Part III.1 of the Ontario *Community Small Business Investment Funds Act*.

**Definitions [s. 204.82]**: "adjusted cost" — 204.82(2.2)(d); "amount" — 248(1); "corporation" — 248(1), *Interpretation Act* 35(1); "eligible investment" — 204.8(1); "investment shortfall" — 204.82(2.1), (2.2); "Minister" — 248(1); "month" — *Interpretation Act* 35(1); "particular period" — 204.82(3); "prescribed" — 248(1); "prescribed rate" — Reg. 4301; "property" — 248(1); "province" — *Interpretation Act* 35(1); "registered labour-sponsored venture capital corporation" — 248(1); "relevant year" — 204.82(2.2); "reserve", "revoked corporation" — 204.8(1); "share", "shareholder" — 248(1); "shareholders' equity" — 204.82(2.2)(a), (b); "specified adjustment" — 204.82(2.2)(c.1); "start-up period" — 204.8(1); "taxation year" — 249; "writing" — *Interpretation Act* 35(1).

**204.83 (1) Refunds for federally registered LSVCCs** — If a corporation is required, under subsections 204.82(3) and (4), to pay a tax and a penalty under this Part for a taxation year, it has no monthly deficiency throughout any period of 12 consecutive months (in this section referred to as the "second period") that begins after the 12-month period in respect of which the tax became payable (in this section referred to as the "first period") and it so requests in an application filed with the Minister in prescribed form, the Minister shall refund to it an amount equal to the total of the amount that was paid under subsection 204.82(3) and 80% of the amount

## S. 204.83(1) — Income Tax Act

that was paid under subsection 204.82(4) in respect of the first period on or before the later of

(a) the 30th day after receiving the application, and

(b) the 60th day after the end of the second period.

**Notes**: 204.83(1) amended by 1998 Budget, effective June 17, 1999, but applications received before that day are deemed to have been received on that day. Before the amendment, read:

(1) If a corporation is required, under subsections 204.82(3) and (4), to pay a tax and a penalty under this Part for a taxation year and, throughout any period of 12 consecutive months (in this section referred to as the "second period") that begins after the 12-month period in respect of which the tax became payable (in this section referred to as the "first period"), the corporation has no monthly deficiency and files with the Minister the return required under this Part for the taxation year in which the second period ends, the Minister shall refund to the corporation an amount equal to the total of the amount that was paid under subsection 204.82(3) and 80% of the amount that was paid under subsection 204.82(4) in respect of the first period.

204.83 renumbered as 204.83(1) by 1997 Budget, effective February 19, 1997, to accommodate the introduction of 204.83(2).

**Forms**: T2152A: Part X.3 tax return and request for a refund for an LSVCC.

**(2) Refunds of amounts payable to provinces** — Where

(a) the government of a province refunds, at any time, an amount to a corporation,

(b) the refund is of an amount that had been paid in satisfaction of a particular amount payable in a taxation year of the corporation, and

(c) tax was payable under subsection 204.82(5) or (6) by the corporation for a taxation year because the particular amount became payable,

the corporation is deemed to have paid at that time an amount equal to the refund on account of its tax payable under this Part for the year.

**Notes**: 204.83(2) added by 1997 Budget, effective February 19, 1997. 204.83(2)(c) amended by 1999 Budget, effective for 1999 and later taxation years, to add reference to 204.82(6).

**Definitions [s. 204.83]**: "amount" — 248(1); "corporation" — 248(1), *Interpretation Act* 35(1); "first period" — 204.83(1); "Minister" — 248(1); "month", "province" — *Interpretation Act* 35(1); "second period" — 204.83(1); "taxation year" — 249.

### 204.84 Penalty
— Every corporation that for a taxation year issues an information return described in paragraph 204.81(6)(c) in respect of

(a) the issuance of a share when the corporation was a revoked corporation, or

(b) a subscription in respect of a share if the share is not issued on or before the day that is 180 days after the day the information return was issued,

is liable to a penalty for the year equal to the amount of the consideration for which the share was or was to be issued.

**Related Provisions**: 18(1)(t) — Penalty is non-deductible.

**Notes**: See Notes to 238(1).

**Definitions [s. 204.84]**: "amount" — 248(1); "corporation" — 248(1), *Interpretation Act* 35(1); "revoked corporation" — 204.8(1); "share" — 248(1); "taxation year" — 249.

### 204.841 Penalty tax where venture capital business discontinued
— Where, at a particular time in a taxation year, a particular corporation that is a registered labour-sponsored venture capital corporation or a revoked corporation first discontinues its venture capital business, the particular corporation shall pay a tax under this Part for the year equal to the total of all amounts each of which is the amount in respect of a Class A share of the capital stock of the particular corporation outstanding immediately before the particular time that is determined by the formula

$$A \times B$$

where

A is

(a) if the original acquisition of the share was before March 6, 1996 and less than five years before the particular time, 4% of the consideration received by the particular corporation for the issue of the share,

(b) if the original acquisition of the share was after March 5, 1996 and less than eight years before the particular time, 1.875% of the consideration received by the particular corporation for the issue of the share, and

(c) in any other case, nil; and

B is

(a) if the original acquisition of the share was before March 6, 1996, the number obtained when the number of whole years throughout which the share was outstanding before the particular time is subtracted from five, and

(b) in any other case, the number obtained when the number of whole years throughout which the share was outstanding is subtracted from eight.

**Related Provisions**: 204.8(2) — Determining when an RLSVCC discontinues its business.

**Notes**: 204.841 added by 1999 Budget, effective for businesses discontinued after February 16, 1999.

**Definitions [s. 204.841]**: "amount", "business" — 248(1); "corporation" — 248(1), *Interpretation Act* 35(1); "discontinues" — 204.8(2); "original acquisition" — 127.4(1), 204.8(1); "registered labour-sponsored venture capital corporation" — 248(1); "revoked corporation" — 204.8(1); "share" — 248(1); "taxation year" — 249.

### 204.85 (1) Dissolution of federally registered LSVCCs
— A registered labour-sponsored venture capital corporation or a revoked corporation that has issued any Class A shares shall send written notification of any proposed amalgamation, merger, liquidation or dissolution of the corporation to the Minister

at least 30 days before the amalgamation, merger, liquidation or dissolution, as the case may be.

Notes: 204.85(1) amended by 1999 Budget, effective for amalgamations, mergers, liquidations and dissolutions that occur after July 29, 2000. Previously read:

> 204.85 (1) Dissolution [or amalgamation] of federally registered LSVCCs — If a registered labour-sponsored venture capital corporation or a revoked corporation has issued any Class A shares, it shall not be amalgamated or merged with another corporation, or be liquidated or dissolved, except with the written permission of the Minister of Finance and on any terms and conditions that are specified by that Minister.

204.85 renumbered as 204.85(1) effective for taxation years that end after February 19, 1997 to accommodate the introduction of 204.85(2), and amended effective August 1997, both by 1997 Budget. Previously read:

> 204.85 Prohibition against dissolution — A registered labour-sponsored venture capital corporation or a revoked corporation shall not, if it has issued any Class A shares, liquidate or dissolve except with the written permission of the Minister of Finance and on such terms and conditions as are specified by that Minister.

(2) **Dissolution of other LSVCCs** — Where

(a) an amount (other than interest on an amount to which this subsection applies or an amount payable under or as a consequence of a prescribed provision of a law of a province) is payable to the government of a province by a corporation,

(b) the amount is payable as a consequence of the amalgamation or merger of the corporation with another corporation, the winding-up or dissolution of the corporation or the corporation ceasing to be registered under a law of the province,

(c) the corporation has been prescribed for the purpose of the definition "approved share" in subsection 127.4(1), and

(d) the corporation is not a registered labour-sponsored venture capital corporation or a revoked corporation,

the corporation shall pay a tax under this Part for the taxation year in which the amount became payable equal to that amount.

Notes: 204.85(2) added by 1997 Budget, effective for taxation years that end after February 19, 1997.

(3) **Amalgamations and mergers** — For the purposes of section 127.4, this Part and Part XII.5, where two or more corporations (each of which is referred to in this subsection as a "predecessor corporation") amalgamate or merge to form one corporate entity (in this subsection referred to as the "new corporation") and at least one of the predecessor corporations was, immediately before the amalgamation or merger, a registered labour-sponsored venture capital corporation or a revoked corporation,

(a) subject to paragraphs (d) and (e), the new corporation is deemed to be the same corporation as, and a continuation of, each predecessor corporation;

(b) where a predecessor corporation was authorized to issue a class of shares to which clause 204.81(1)(c)(ii)(C) applies, the new corporation is deemed to have received approval from the Minister of Finance to issue substantially similar shares at the time of the amalgamation or merger;

(c) where a share of a predecessor corporation (in this paragraph referred to as the "predecessor share") is replaced on the amalgamation or merger by a new share of the new corporation,

(i) the new share

(A) is deemed not to have been issued on the amalgamation or merger, and

(B) is deemed to have been issued by the new corporation at the time the predecessor corporation issued the predecessor share, and

(ii) if the new share was issued to a person who acquired the predecessor share as a consequence of a transfer the registration of which by the predecessor corporation was permitted under paragraph 204.81(1)(c), the issuance of the new share is deemed to be in compliance with the conditions described in paragraph 204.81(1)(c);

**Proposed Amendment — 204.85(3)(c)**
**Letter from Department of Finance, March 14, 2000:**

Dear [xxx]

Thank you for your letter of February 18, 2000, concerning proposed amendments to the *Income Tax Act*, contained in Bill C-25, that apply on the merger or amalgamation of federally-registered labour-sponsored venture capital corporations (LSVCCs).

You have expressed concern that, where upon an amalgamation, an amalgamated corporation issues shares as contemplated by proposed paragraph 204.85(3)(c), the issuance of Class A shares to a non-eligible investor would be in contravention of the provisions of the corporation's articles. This is because, under paragraph 204.81(1)(c) of the Act, one of the conditions for federal registration is that the articles of an LSVCC provide that Class A shares may be issued only to an individual (other than a trust) or a registered retirement savings plan (RRSP) ("eligible investors"). A non-eligible investor may, however, acquire Class A shares in certain circumstances upon transfer from an eligible investor. Accordingly, a non-eligible investor may be a holder of shares to which a new corporation issues shares on an amalgamation.

We have reviewed the application of the proposed legislative amendments regarding the merger or amalgamation of federally-registered LSVCC as they apply in the circumstances described in your letter. From a policy perspective, our view is that the amendments may be too narrow. Consequently, we will recommend changes to the Act to permit a trust governed by a registered retirement income fund that is a holder of shares in a federally-registered LSVCC to be issued shares upon an amalgamation of the LSVCC described in proposed subsection 204.85(3). We will further recommend that this amendment apply as of the same time as proposed 204.85(3) applies.

Thank you for writing on this matter.

Yours sincerely,

Brian Ernewein

Director, Tax Legislation Division, Tax Policy Branch

(d) the Minister is deemed to have registered the new corporation for the purposes of this Part unless

(i) the new corporation is not governed by the *Canada Business Corporations Act*,

(ii) one or more of the predecessor corporations was a registered labour-sponsored venture capital corporation the venture capital business of which was discontinued before the amalgamation or merger,

(iii) one or more of the predecessor corporations was, immediately before the amalgamation or merger, a revoked corporation,

(iv) immediately after the amalgamation or merger, the articles of the new corporation do not comply with paragraph 204.81(1)(c), or

(v) shares other than Class A shares of the capital stock of the new corporation were issued to any shareholder of the new corporation in satisfaction of any share (other than a share to which clause 204.81(1)(c)(ii)(B) or (C) applied) of a predecessor corporation;

(e) where paragraph (d) does not apply, the new corporation is deemed to be a revoked corporation;

(f) subsection 204.82(1) does not apply to the new corporation; and

(g) subsection 204.82(2) shall, in its application to the new corporation, be read without reference to the words "that begins after the end of the corporation's start-up period (or, where the corporation has no start-up period, that begins after the time the corporation first issues a Class A share)".

**Related Provisions**: 87 — General rules for amalgamations; 127.4(1.1) — Application to labour-sponsored funds tax credit; 211.7(2) — Effect of amalgamation on Part XII.5 tax; 211.8(1.1) — Rule applies to 211.8(1).

**Notes**: 204.85(3) added by 1999 budget, effective for amalgamations and mergers that occur after February 16, 1999.

**Definitions [s. 204.85]**: "amount", "business" — 248(1); "Canada" — 255, *Interpretation Act* 35(1); "corporation" — 248(1), *Interpretation Act* 35(1); "Minister", "prescribed" — 248(1); "province" — *Interpretation Act* 35(1); "registered labour-sponsored venture capital corporation" — 248(1); "revoked corporation" — 204.8(1); "share", "shareholder" — 248(1); "start-up period" — 204.8(1); "taxation year" — 249; "written" — *Interpretation Act* 35(1)"writing".

**204.86 (1) Return and payment of tax for federally-registered LSVCCs** — Every registered labour-sponsored venture capital corporation and every revoked corporation shall

(a) on or before its filing-due date for a taxation year, file with the Minister a return for the year under this Part in prescribed form and containing prescribed information, without notice or demand therefor;

(b) estimate in the return the amount of tax and penalties, if any, payable under this Part by it for the year; and

(c) within 90 days after the end of the year, pay to the Receiver General the amount of tax and penalties, if any, payable under this Part by it for the year.

**Related Provisions**: 150.1(5) — Electronic filing.

**Notes**: 204.86 renumbered as 204.86(1) by 1997 Budget (and amended to use the new term "filing-due date", with no substantive change), effective February 19, 1997, to accommodate the introduction of 204.86(2).

**(2) Return and payment of tax for other LSVCCs** — Where tax is payable under this Part for a taxation year by a corporation because of subsection 204.82(5) or 204.85(2), the corporation shall

(a) on or before its filing-due date for the year, file with the Minister a return for the year under this Part in prescribed form and containing prescribed information, without notice or demand therefor;

(b) estimate in the return the amount of tax payable under this Part by it for the year; and

(c) within 90 days after the end of the year, pay to the Receiver General the amount of tax payable under this Part by it for the year.

**Related Provisions**: 150.1(5) — Electronic filing.

**Notes**: 204.86(2) added by 1997 Budget, effective February 19, 1997.

**Definitions [s. 204.86]**: "amount" — 248(1); "corporation" — 248(1), *Interpretation Act* 35(1); "filing-due date", "Minister", "prescribed", "registered labour-sponsored venture capital corporation" — 248(1); "revoked corporation" — 204.8(1); "taxation year" — 249.

**Forms [s. 204.86]**: T2152: Part X.3 tax return for an LSVCC; T2152 SCH 1: Calculating tax under subsec. 204.82(2); T2152 SCH 2: Calculating tax under subsecs. 204.82(3) and (6) and s. 204.841; T2152A: Part X.3 tax return and request for a refund for an LSVCC.

**204.87 Provisions applicable to Part** — Subsection 150(3), sections 152 and 158, subsections 161(1) and (11), sections 162 to 164 and 165 to 167, Division J of Part I and section 227.1 apply to this Part, with such modifications as the circumstances require.

**Notes [Part X.3]**: Part X.3 (204.8–204.87) added by 1991 technical bill, effective 1989 (except for 204.81(1)(c)(vi), which does not apply to shares purchased before 1991).

# PART X.4 — TAX IN RESPECT OF OVERPAYMENTS TO REGISTERED EDUCATION SAVINGS PLANS

**204.9 (1) Definitions** — The definitions in this subsection apply in this Part.

"excess amount" for a year at any time in respect of an individual means the amount, if any, by which the total of all contributions made after February 20, 1990 in the year and before that time into all registered education savings plans by or on behalf of all subscribers in respect of the individual exceeds the lesser of

(a) the RESP annual limit for the year, and

(b) the amount, if any, by which the RESP lifetime limit for the year exceeds the total of all contributions made into registered education savings plans by or on behalf of all subscribers in respect of the individual in all preceding years.

**Related Provisions**: 146.1(2)(k) — Limit on annual RESP contributions; 204.9(2)(a) — Where agreement entered into before February 21, 1990.

**Notes**: "Excess amount" amended by 1997 Budget, effective for determining Part X.4 tax for months that are after 1996. The limit is now $4,000 per year (see 146.1(1)"RESP annual limit") and $42,000 lifetime (204.9"RESP lifetime limit"). For months that end in 1996, read:

"excess amount", for a year at any time in respect of a beneficiary, means the amount, if any, by which the total of all payments made after February 20, 1990 in the year and before that time into all registered education savings plans by or on behalf of all subscribers in respect of the beneficiary exceeds the lesser of

(a) $2,000, and

(b) the amount, if any, by which $42,000 exceeds the total of all payments made into registered education savings plans by or on behalf of all subscribers in respect of the beneficiary in all preceding years;

Paras. (a) and (b) amended by 1996 Budget, effective for months that end after 1995. For 1990-95, read "$1,500" in place of "$2,000", and "$31,500" in place of "$42,000".

For initial enactment see Notes after 204.93.

**"RESP lifetime limit"** for a year means,

(a) for 1990 to 1995, $31,500; and

(b) for 1996 and subsequent years, $42,000.

**Notes**: "RESP lifetime limit" added by 1997 Budget, effective for determining Part X.4 tax for months that are after 1996.

**"subscriber's gross cumulative excess"** at any time in respect of an individual means the total of all amounts each of which is the subscriber's share of the excess amount for a relevant year at that time in respect of the individual and, for the purpose of this definition, a relevant year at any time is a year that began before that time.

**Notes**: "Subscriber's gross cumulative excess" added by 1997 Budget, effective for determining Part X.4 tax for months that are after 1996.

**"subscriber's share of the excess amount"** for a year at any time in respect of an individual means the amount determined by the formula

$$(A/B) \times C$$

where

A is the total of all contributions made after February 20, 1990, in the year and before that time into all registered education savings plans by or on behalf of the subscriber in respect of the individual;

B is the total of all contributions made after February 20, 1990, in the year and before that time into all registered education savings plans by or on behalf of all subscribers in respect of the individual; and

C is the excess amount for the year at that time in respect of the individual.

**Related Provisions**: 204.9(2)(b) — Where agreement entered into before February 21, 1990.

**Notes**: "Subscriber's share of the excess amount" amended by 1997 Budget, effective for determining Part X.4 tax for months that are after 1996, to add "after February 20, 1990" in the descriptions of A and B.

For initial enactment see Notes after 204.93.

**(1.1) Application of subsec. 146.1(1)** — The definitions in subsection 146.1(1) apply to this Part.

**Notes**: 204.9(1.1) added in revised version of 1991 technical bill that is consistent with the R.S.C. (5th Supp.) consolidation. This rule was formerly contained in the opening words of 146.1(1).

**(2) Agreements before February 21, 1990** — Where a subscriber is required, pursuant to an agreement in writing entered into before February 21, 1990, to make payments of specified amounts on a periodic basis into a registered education savings plan in respect of a beneficiary, and the subscriber makes at least one payment under the agreement before that day,

(a) the excess amount for a year in respect of the beneficiary shall be deemed not to exceed the excess amount for the year that would be determined under subsection (1) if the total of all such payments made in the year and, where the agreement so provides, amounts paid in the year in satisfaction of the requirement to make such payments under all such agreements by all such subscribers in respect of the beneficiary were equal to the lesser of the amounts described in paragraphs (a) and (b) of the definition "excess amount" in subsection (1); and

(b) in determining a subscriber's share of an excess amount for a year, any payment included in the total described in paragraph (a) in respect of the year shall be excluded in determining the values for A and B in the definition "subscriber's share of the excess amount" in subsection (1).

**(3) Refunds from unregistered plans** — For the purposes of subsection (1) and section 146.1, where an individual entered into an education savings plan before February 21, 1990, pursuant to a preliminary prospectus issued by a promoter, and the promoter refunds all payments made into the plan and all income accrued thereon to the individual, each payment made by the individual into a registered education savings plan before December 31, 1990 shall be deemed to be a payment made before February 21, 1990, to the extent that the total of all such payments does not exceed the amount so refunded to the individual.

**(4) New beneficiary** — For the purposes of this Part, if at any particular time an individual (in this subsection referred to as the "new beneficiary") becomes a beneficiary under a registered education savings plan in place of another individual (in this subsection referred to as the "former beneficiary") who ceased at or before the particular time to be a beneficiary under the plan,

(a) except as provided by paragraph (b), each contribution made at an earlier time by or on behalf of a subscriber into the plan in respect of the former beneficiary is deemed also to have been made at that earlier time in respect of the new beneficiary;

(b) except for the purpose of applying this subsection to a replacement of a beneficiary after the particular time, applying subsection (5) to a distribution after the particular time and applying subsection 204.91(3) to events after the particular time, paragraph (a) does not apply as a consequence of the replacement at the particular time of the former beneficiary if

(i) the new beneficiary had not attained 21 years of age before the particular time and a parent of the new beneficiary was a parent of the former beneficiary, or

(ii) both beneficiaries were connected by blood relationship or adoption to an original subscriber under the plan and neither had attained 21 years of age before the particular time; and

(c) except where paragraph (b) applies, each contribution made by or on behalf of a subscriber under the plan in respect of the former beneficiary under the plan is, without affecting the determination of the amount withdrawn from the plan in respect of the new beneficiary, deemed to have been withdrawn at the particular time from the plan to the extent that it was not withdrawn before the particular time.

**Notes**: 204.9(4)(b)(ii) added by 1998 Budget, effective for replacements of beneficiaries that occur after 1997.

204.9(4) amended by 1997 Budget, effective for replacements of beneficiaries and distributions that occur after 1996. Previously read:

(4) For the purposes of this Part,

(a) where at any time an individual (in this paragraph referred to as the "new beneficiary") becomes a beneficiary under a registered education savings plan in place of another individual (in this paragraph referred to as the "former beneficiary") who ceases at that time to be a beneficiary under the plan, all payments made before that time into the plan in respect of the former beneficiary shall be deemed to have been made in respect of the new beneficiary; and

(b) where at any time property is transferred from a trust governed by a registered education savings plan (in this paragraph referred to as the "transferor plan") to a trust governed by another registered education savings plan (in this paragraph referred to as the "transferee plan"), unless a beneficiary under the transferee plan was, immediately before that time, a beneficiary under the transferor plan, all payments made before that time in respect of all beneficiaries under the transferor plan shall be deemed to have been made in respect of the beneficiaries under the transferee plan.

For initial enactment see Notes after 204.93.

**(5) Transfers between plans** — For the purposes of this Part, if property held by a trust governed by a registered education savings plan (in this subsection referred to as the "transferor plan") is distributed at a particular time to a trust governed by another registered education savings plan (in this subsection referred to as the "transferee plan"),

(a) except as provided by paragraphs (b) and (c), the amount of the distribution is deemed not to have been contributed into the transferee plan;

(b) subject to paragraph (c), each contribution made at any earlier time by or on behalf of a subscriber into the transferor plan in respect of a beneficiary under the transferor plan is deemed also to have been made at that earlier time by the subscriber in respect of each beneficiary under the transferee plan;

(c) except for the purpose of applying this subsection to a distribution after the particular time, applying subsection (4) to a replacement of a beneficiary after the particular time and applying subsection 204.91(3) to events after the particular time, paragraph (b) does not apply as a consequence of the distribution where

(i) any beneficiary under the transferee plan was, immediately before the particular time, a beneficiary under the transferor plan, or

(ii) a beneficiary under the transferee plan had not attained 21 years of age at the particular time and a parent of the beneficiary was a parent of an individual who was, immediately before the particular time, a beneficiary under the transferor plan;

(d) where subparagraph (c)(i) or (ii) applies in respect of the distribution, the amount of the distribution is deemed not to have been withdrawn from the transferor plan; and

(e) each subscriber under the transferor plan is deemed to be a subscriber under the transferee plan.

**Related Provisions**: 146.1(2)(g.2), (i.2) — Restrictions on transfers between RESPs; 146.1(6.1) — Effect of transfers between RESPs.

**Notes**: 204.9(5) added by 1997 Budget, effective for replacements of beneficiaries and distributions that occur after 1996.

**Definitions**: See Definitions at end of s. 204.93.

**204.91 (1) Tax payable by subscribers** — Every subscriber under a registered education savings plan shall pay a tax under this Part in respect of each month equal to 1% of the amount, if any, by which

(a) the total of all amounts each of which is the subscriber's gross cumulative excess at the end of the month in respect of an individual

exceeds

(b) the total of all amounts each of which is the portion of such an excess that has been withdrawn from a registered education savings plan before the end of the month.

**Notes**: 204.91 amended and renumbered as 204.91(1) by 1997 Budget, effective for determining Part X.4 tax for months that are after 1996. From February 1990 through 1996, read:

> 204.91 **Tax payable by subscribers** — Each subscriber under a registered education savings plan shall, in respect of each month, pay a tax under this Part equal to 1% of the subscriber's share of each excess amount for a year at the end of that month in respect of a beneficiary or former beneficiary under the plan, to the extent that the amount of the share is not withdrawn from the plan before the end of that month.

For initial enactment see Notes after 204.93.

**Regulations**: 103(8) (withholding of tax at source).

(2) **Waiver of tax** — If a subscriber under a registered education savings plan would, but for this subsection, be required to pay a tax in respect of a month under subsection (1) in respect of an individual, the Minister may waive or cancel all or part of the tax where it is just and equitable to do so having regard to all the circumstances, including

(a) whether the tax arose as a consequence of reasonable error;

(b) whether, as a consequence of one or more transactions or events to which subsection 204.9(4) or (5) applies, the tax is excessive; and

(c) the extent to which further contributions could be made into registered education savings plans in respect of the individual before the end of the month without causing additional tax to be payable under this Part if this Part were read without reference to this subsection.

**Notes**: 204.91(2) added by 1997 Budget, effective for determining Part X.4 tax for months that are after January 1990.

(3) **Marriage [or common-law partnership] breakdown** — If at any time an individual (in this subsection referred to as the "former subscriber") ceases to be a subscriber under a registered education savings plan as a consequence of the settlement of rights arising out of, or on the breakdown of, the marriage or common-law partnership of the former subscriber and another individual (in this subsection referred to as the "current subscriber") who is a subscriber under the plan immediately after that time, for the purpose of determining tax payable under this Part in respect of a month that ends after that time, each contribution made before that time into the plan by or on behalf of the former subscriber is deemed to have been made into the plan by the current subscriber and not by or on behalf of the former subscriber.

**Notes**: 204.91(3) amended by 2000 same-sex partners bill to add reference to "common-law partnership", effective for the 2001 and later taxation years, or earlier by election (see Notes to 248(1)"common-law partner").

204.91(3) added by 1997 Budget, effective for determining Part X.4 tax for months that are after 1997.

(4) **Deceased subscribers** — For the purpose of applying this section where a subscriber has died, the subscriber's estate is deemed to be the same person as, and a continuation of, the subscriber for each month that ends after the death.

**Notes**: 204.91(4) added by 1997 Budget, effective for determining Part X.4 tax for months that are after 1997.

**Related Provisions [s. 204.91]**: 18(1)(t) — Tax is non-deductible.

**Definitions [s. 204.91]**: See Definitions at end of s. 204.93.

**204.92 Return and payment of tax** — Every person who is liable to pay tax under this Part in respect of a month in a year shall, within 90 days after the end of the year,

(a) file with the Minister a return for the year under this Part in prescribed form and containing prescribed information, without notice or demand therefor;

(b) estimate in the return the amount of tax, if any, payable under this Part by the person in respect of each month in the year; and

(c) pay to the Receiver General the amount of tax, if any, payable by the person under this Part in respect of each month in the year.

**Related Provisions**: 150.1(5) — Electronic filing.

**Definitions [s. 204.92]**: See Definitions at end of s. 204.93.

**Regulations**: 103(8) (withholding of tax at source).

**Forms**: T1E-OVP: Individual income tax return for RESP overpayments.

**204.93 Provisions applicable to Part** — Subsections 150(2) and (3), sections 152, 158 and 159, subsections 161(1) and (11), sections 162 to 167 and Division J of Part I are applicable to this Part, with such modifications as the circumstances require.

**Notes [Part X.4]**: Part X.4 (204.9 to 204.93) added by 1990 Budget/1991 technical bill, effective for months ending after January 1990, but no return is required to be filed and no payment is required to be made under 204.92 before March 16, 1992.

**Definitions [Part X.4]**: "amount" — 248(1); "beneficiary" — 146.1(1), 204.9(1.1); "common-law partner" — 248(1); "connected" — 251(6); "education savings plan" — 146.1(1), 204.9(1.1); "estate" — 104(1), 248(1); "excess amount" — 204.9(1), (2); "individual" — 248(1); "Minister" — 248(1); "month" — *Interpretation Act* 35(1); "new beneficiary" — 204.9(4); "person" — 248(1); "RESP annual limit" — 146.1(1), 204.9(1.1); "RESP lifetime limit" — 204.9(1); "refund of payments" — 146.1(1), 204.9(1.1); "registered education savings plan" — 146.1(1), 248(1); "subscriber" — 146.1(1), 204.9(1.1); "subscriber's gross cumulative excess" — 204.9(1); "subscriber's share" — 204.9(1), (2); "transferee plan", "transferor plan" — 204.9(5); "trust" — 146.1(1), 204.9(1.1); "writing" — *Interpretation Act* 35(1).

# PART X.5 — PAYMENTS UNDER REGISTERED EDUCATION SAVINGS PLANS

**204.94 (1) Definitions** — The definitions in subsection 146.1(1) apply for the purposes of this Part, except that the definition "subscriber" in that subsection shall be read without reference to paragraph (c).

**Notes**: See Notes at end of 204.94.

**(2) Charging provision** — Every person shall pay a tax under this Part for each taxation year equal to the amount determined by the formula

$$(A + B - C) \times D$$

where

A is the total of all amounts each of which is an accumulated income payment made at any time that is

  (a) either

    (i) under a registered education savings plan under which the person is a subscriber at that time, or

    (ii) under a registered education savings plan under which there is no subscriber at that time, where the person has been a spouse or common-law partner of an individual who was a subscriber under the plan, and

  (b) included in computing the person's income under Part I for the year;

B is the total of all amounts each of which is an accumulated income payment that is

  (a) not included in the value of A in respect of the person for the year, and

  (b) included in computing the person's income under Part I for the year;

C is the lesser of

  (a) the lesser of the value of A in respect of the person for the year and the total of all amounts each of which is an amount deducted under subsection 146(5) or (5.1) in computing the person's income under Part I for the year, and

  (b) the amount, if any, by which $50,000 exceeds the total of all amounts each of which is an amount determined under paragraph (a) in respect of the person for a preceding taxation year; and

D is

  (a) where a tax, similar to the tax provided under this Part, is payable by the person for the year under a law of the province of Quebec, 12%, and

  (b) in any other case, 20%.

**Related Provisions**: 257 — Formula cannot calculate to less than zero.

**Notes**: 204.94(2)A(a)(ii) amended by 2000 same-sex partners bill to add reference to "common-law partner", effective for the 2001 and later taxation years, or earlier by election (see Notes to 248(1)"common-law partner").

Formula in 204.94(2) amended by 1998 Budget to change "0.2" to "D" and add description for D, effective for 1998 and later taxation years. The rate is 12% instead of 20% in Quebec because Quebec imposes its own tax.

204.94(2)C(b) amended by 1998 Budget to change $40,000 to $50,000, effective for 1999 and later taxation years.

See also Notes at end of 204.94.

**Regulations**: 103(8) (withholding of 20% at source).

**(3) Return and payment of tax** — Every person who is liable to pay tax under this Part for a taxation year shall, on or before the person's filing-due date for the year,

  (a) file with the Minister a return for the year under this Part in prescribed form and containing prescribed information, without notice or demand therefor;

  (b) estimate in the return the amount of tax payable under this Part by the person for the year; and

  (c) pay to the Receiver General the amount of tax payable under this Part by the person for the year.

**Related Provisions**: 156.1(1)"net tax owing"(b)A — Part X.5 tax included in calculation of instalment threshold.

**Notes**: See Notes at end of 204.94.

**(4) Administrative rules** — Subsections 150(2) and (3), sections 152, 155 to 156.1 and 158 to 167 and Division J of Part I apply with any modifications that the circumstances require.

**Related Provisions**: 156.1(1)"net tax owing"(b)A — Part X.5 tax included in calculation of instalment threshold.

**Notes**: 204.94 added by 1997 Budget, effective for 1998 and later taxation years. It imposes a special 20% tax on "accumulated income payments" from RESPs. This tax can generally be reduced to the extent the recipient makes deductible RRSP contributions under 146(5) or (5.1) for the year in which the payment is made. The purpose of this tax is to discourage the use of RESPs strictly for their tax deferral advantages, particularly by individuals who already maximize their tax savings through RRSP contributions. See also Notes to 146.1(2).

**Regulations**: 103(8) (withholding of 20% at source).

**Definitions [s. 204.94]**: "accumulated income payment" — 146.1(1), 204.94(1); "amount", "common-law partner", "filing-due date", "individual", "Minister", "person", "prescribed" — 248(1); "registered education savings plan" — 146.1(1), 204.94(1), 248(1); "subscriber" — 204.94; "tax payable" — 248(2); "taxation year" — 249.

# PART XI — TAX IN RESPECT OF CERTAIN PROPERTY ACQUIRED BY TRUSTS, ETC., GOVERNED BY DEFERRED INCOME PLANS

**205. Application of Part** — This Part applies in respect of a taxpayer that is

  (a) a corporation described in paragraph 149(1)(o.1) or (o.2) or a trust described in paragraph 149(1)(o) or (o.4), other than a trust described in paragraph 149(1)(o)

(i) established for the exclusive benefit of non-residents working outside Canada, or

(ii) the only beneficiaries of which are persons whose entitlement thereunder arises by virtue of employment outside Canada;

(b) a trust governed by a registered retirement savings plan;

(c) a trust governed by a deferred profit sharing plan;

(d) [Repealed under former Act]

(e) a trust governed by a registered retirement income fund;

(f) a registered investment; or

(g) any other person, other than a prescribed person, exempt from tax under Part I on its taxable income.

**Related Provisions**: 204.2(2) — Where terminated plan deemed to continue to exist; 206(2.1) — Exemption for master trust or pension fund corporation where proportional holdings election made; 207.1(1) — Tax payable by RRSP; 259(1), (2) — Proportional holdings in trust property.

**Definitions [s. 205]**: "corporation" — 248(1), *Interpretation Act* 35(1); "deferred profit sharing plan" — 147(1), 248(1); "employment", "non-resident" — 248(1); "registered investment" — 204.4(1), 248(1); "registered retirement income fund" — 146.3(1), 248(1); "registered retirement savings plan" — 146(1), 248(1); "taxable income" — 2(2), 248(1); "taxpayer" — 248(1); "trust" — 104(1), 248(1), (3).

**I.T. Application Rules [s. 205]**: 65(1), (1.1), (2), (5).

**Interpretation Bulletins [s. 205]**: IT-412R2: Foreign property of registered plans.

## 206. (1) Definitions — In this Part,

**"affiliate"** of a corporation (in this definition referred to as the "parent corporation") at any time is any other corporation where, at that time,

(a) the parent corporation controls the other corporation,

(b) the parent corporation or a corporation controlled by the parent corporation owns

(i) shares of the capital stock of the other corporation that would give the parent corporation or the corporation controlled by the parent corporation 25% or more of the votes that could be cast under all circumstances at an annual meeting of shareholders of that other corporation, and

(ii) shares of the capital stock of the other corporation having a fair market value of 25% or more of the fair market value of all the issued shares of the capital stock of that other corporation, or

(c) the other corporation is controlled by a particular corporation and the parent corporation or a corporation controlled by the parent corporation owns

(i) shares of the capital stock of the particular corporation that would give the parent corporation or the corporation controlled by the parent corporation 25% or more of the votes that could be cast under all circumstances at an annual meeting of shareholders of the particular corporation, and

(ii) shares of the capital stock of the particular corporation having a fair market value of 25% or more of the fair market value of all the issued shares of the capital stock of the particular corporation;

**Related Provisions**: 256(6), (6.1) — Meaning of "controlled".

**Notes**: "Affiliate" added by 1995-97 technical bill, effective for shares and indebtedness acquired after December 4, 1985 (otherwise than pursuant to an agreement in writing made before 5:00 p.m. E.S.T. on December 4, 1985).

**"carrying value"** of a property of a corporation or partnership at any time means

(a) where a balance sheet of the corporation or the partnership as of that time was presented to the shareholders of the corporation or the members of the partnership and the balance sheet was prepared using generally accepted accounting principles and was not prepared using the equity or consolidation method of accounting, the amount in respect of the property reflected in the balance sheet, and

(b) in any other case, the amount that would have been reflected in a balance sheet of the corporation or the partnership as of that time if the balance sheet had been prepared in accordance with generally acceptable accounting principles and neither the equity nor consolidation method of accounting were used;

**Notes**: "Carrying value" added by 1995-97 technical bill, effective for shares and indebtedness acquired after December 4, 1985 (otherwise than pursuant to an agreement in writing made before 5:00 p.m. E.S.T. on December 4, 1985).

### Proposed Addition — 206(1)"cost amount"

**"cost amount"** at any time of a taxpayer's capital interest in a trust that is foreign property is deemed to be the greater of

(a) the cost amount of the interest, determined without reference to this definition, and

(b) where that time is more than 60 days after the end of a taxation year of the trust, the amount that would be the cost amount of the interest if new units of the trust had been issued in satisfaction of each amount payable

(i) after 2000 and at or before the end of the taxation year, by the trust in respect of the interest,

(ii) to which subparagraph 53(2)(h)(i.1) applies (or would apply if that subparagraph were read without reference to clauses (A) and (B) of that subparagraph), and

(iii) that has not been satisfied at or before that time by the issue of new units of the trust or by a payment of an amount by the trust;

**Related Provisions**: 108(1)"cost amount" — Cost amount of capital interest in a trust.

**Application**: Bill C-43 (First Reading September 20, 2000), subsec. 98(1), will add the definition "cost amount" to subsec. 206(1), applicable to months that end after February 2001.

**Technical Notes**: Part XI of the Act provides a foreign property limit for certain taxpayers, mainly tax-exempt taxpayers such as trusts governed by registered retirement savings plans and registered pension plans. In general, a penalty tax is applied under subsection 206(2) where the total cost amount of foreign property in such a trust or plan exceeds a specified percentage of the total cost amount of all property in the trust or plan.

Where such a taxpayer holds a capital interest in a trust, the income of the trust is usually made payable to the taxpayer so that the income is not taxed at the trust level. Arrangements have been made, however, to "capitalize" income and other amounts payable without the trust issuing new units or otherwise making a payment in satisfaction of the amounts. These arrangements are designed to maximize the indirect foreign property holdings for these unitholders by minimizing the cost amount with regard to these capital interests.

Subsection 206(1) is amended to add a special definition of "cost amount" for the purposes of Part XI. The definition is designed to increase the cost amount of a taxpayer's interest in a trust to reflect capitalized amounts payable to the taxpayer. It is also intended to amend Part L of the Regulations to make it clear that the definition also applies for this purpose.

**Letter from Department of Finance, February 8, 2000**:

Dear [xxx]

This is in reply to your letter of January 19, 2000 concerning the proposed addition of the definition "cost amount" in subsection 206(1) of the *Income Tax Act* that was part of Legislative Proposals on Trusts released by the Department of Finance on December 17, 1999.

We have examined the application of this amendment as it applies in the circumstances raised in your letter. From a tax policy perspective, our view is that the proposed amendment may be too broad. Consequently, we will recommend that the amendment not affect the computation of the "cost amount" of a capital interest in a trust in connection with an amount that became payable by the trust in a taxation year and that is satisfied through payment from the trust not more than 60 days after the end of that year. Thus, a satisfaction of an amount payable through such a payment by a trust would be treated under the amendment in the same manner as a satisfaction of an amount payable through the issue of units by the trust. We will further recommend that this refinement apply as of the same time that the present version of the amendment applies.

Thank you for writing on this matter.

Yours sincerely,

Brian Ernewein
Director, Tax Legislation Division, Tax Policy Branch

**"designated value"** of a property at any time means the greater of

(a) the fair market value at that time of the property, and

(b) the carrying value at that time of the property;

**Notes**: "Designated value" added by 1995-97 technical bill, effective for shares and indebtedness acquired after December 4, 1985 (otherwise than pursuant to an agreement in writing made before 5:00 p.m. E.S.T. on December 4, 1985).

**"excluded share"** means

(a) a share that is of a class of shares listed on a prescribed stock exchange in Canada, where no share of that class has been issued after December 4, 1985 (otherwise than pursuant to an agreement in writing entered into before 5:00 p.m. Eastern Standard Time on December 4, 1985),

(b) a share last acquired after 1995 that is of a class of shares listed on a prescribed stock exchange in Canada, where

(i) no share of that class has been issued after July 20, 1995 (otherwise than pursuant to an agreement in writing made before July 21, 1995), and

(ii) the share would not be foreign property if the expression "primarily from foreign property" in paragraph (d.1) of the definition "foreign property" in this subsection were read as "primarily from portfolio investments in property that is foreign property" and that paragraph were read without reference to "(other than an excluded share)", and

(c) a share last acquired after 1995 as a consequence of the exercise of a right acquired before 1996 where the share would not be foreign property if the expression "primarily from foreign property" in paragraph (d.1) of the definition "foreign property" in this subsection were read as "primarily from portfolio investments in property that is foreign property" and that paragraph were read without reference to "(other than an excluded share)";

**Notes**: "Excluded share" added by 1995-97 technical bill, effective for shares and indebtedness acquired after December 4, 1985 (otherwise than pursuant to an agreement in writing made before 5:00 p.m. E.S.T. on December 4, 1985).

**Regulations**: 3200 (prescribed stock exchange in Canada; will be amended to apply to this definition).

**"foreign property"** means

(a) tangible property situated outside Canada except automotive equipment registered in Canada,

(b) automotive equipment not registered in Canada pursuant to the laws of Canada or a province,

(c) intangible property (other than any property described in paragraphs (d) to (g)) situated outside Canada including, without restricting the generality of the foregoing, any patent under the laws of a country other than Canada and any licence in respect thereof,

(d) any share of the capital stock of a corporation other than a Canadian corporation,

(d.1) except as provided by subsection (1.1), any share (other than an excluded share) of the capital stock of, or any debt obligation issued by, a corporation (other than an investment corporation, mutual fund corporation or registered investment) that is a Canadian corporation, where shares of the corporation can reasonably be considered to derive their value, directly or indirectly, primarily from foreign property,

(e) except as prescribed, any share of the capital stock of a mutual fund corporation or investment corporation that is not a registered investment, other than a share of the capital stock of an investment corporation that was last acquired before October 14, 1971,

(f) any property that, under the terms or conditions thereof or any agreement relating thereto, is convertible into, is exchangeable for or confers a right to acquire, property that is foreign property, but not including property that is

   (i) a share of the capital stock of a Canadian corporation listed on a prescribed stock exchange in Canada, or

   (ii) a right issued before 1984 and listed on a prescribed stock exchange in Canada to acquire a share of the capital stock of a Canadian corporation,

(g) indebtedness of a non-resident person, other than indebtedness issued or guaranteed by

   (i) the International Bank for Reconstruction and Development,

   (i.1) the International Finance Corporation,

   (ii) the Inter-American Development Bank,

   (iii) the Asian Development Bank,

   (iv) the Caribbean Development Bank,

   (iv.1) the European Bank for Reconstruction and Development,

   (iv.2) the African Development Bank, or

   (v) a prescribed person,

> **Proposed Amendment — 206(1) "foreign property"(g)**
>
> (g) indebtedness of a non-resident person, other than
>
>   (i) a deposit with a branch in Canada of an authorized foreign bank, or
>
>   (ii) indebtedness issued or guaranteed by
>
>   (A) the International Bank for Reconstruction and Development,
>
>   (B) the International Finance Corporation,
>
>   (C) the Inter-American Development Bank,
>
>   (D) the Asian Development Bank,
>
>   (E) the Caribbean Development Bank,
>
>   (F) the European Bank for Reconstruction and Development,
>
>   (G) the African Development Bank, or
>
>   (H) a prescribed person,
>
> **Application**: The August 8, 2000 draft legislation, subsec. 21, will amend para. (g) of the definition "foreign property" in subsec. 206(1) to read as above, applicable after June 27, 1999.
>
> **Technical Notes**: Section 206 of the Act imposes a tax on the amount of "foreign property" (as defined in subsection 206(1)) held by pension funds and certain other tax-exempt entities in excess of defined limits.
>
> Subsection 206(1) contains the definition of foreign property. Paragraph (g) of this definition treats as foreign property the indebtedness of a non-resident person other than a prescribed person or any of various international organizations. The paragraph is amended so that a deposit with a Canadian branch of an authorized foreign bank is not foreign property. The amended definition applies after June 27, 1999.

(h) any interest in or right to any property that is foreign property by virtue of paragraphs (a) to (g), and

(i) except as prescribed by regulation, any interest in, or right to acquire an interest in, a trust (other than a registered investment) or a partnership;

> **Proposed Amendment — "foreign property" — segregated fund annuity contracts**
>
> **Department of Finance news release, December 19, 1996**: *(c) Foreign Property*
>
> An interest in an annuity contract will be "foreign property" for the purposes of the Act if the annuity contract is a segregated fund policy and more than 20% of the segregated fund's assets are "foreign property". As a consequence, if an RRSP or RRIF trust or any other taxpayer described in paragraphs 204(1)(a) to (f) of the Act acquires such a foreign property, it will be included in the 20% foreign property limit set out in Part XI of the Act.
>
> If an insurer issues interests in one or more registered annuity policies directly to an RRSP or RRIF annuitant or to a registered pension plan (RPP), the insurer will be likewise liable to pay a monthly foreign property penalty tax in respect of each RRSP annuitant, RRIF annuitant and RPP equal to the amount, if positive, determined by the formula:
>
> $$1\% \times (A - (20\% \times B))$$
>
> where
>
> A is the total of all premiums and other amounts paid on account of the acquisition by the RRSP annuitant, RRIF annuitant or RPP, as the case may be, of such of those interests outstanding at the end of the month as constitute foreign property, and
>
> B is the total of all premiums and other amounts paid on account of the acquisition by the RRSP annuitant, RRIF annuitant or RPP, as the case may be, of such of those interests as are outstanding at the end of the month.
>
> Issuers of segregated fund policies will be allowed to elect to have their segregated funds registered under Part X.2 of the Act. The result of this election would be to exclude in-

terests in registered segregated funds from the "foreign property" definition. However, as a consequence of the election in respect of a segregated fund, the issuer of the segregated fund would be required to pay any penalty tax under Part XI of the Act in respect of foreign property holdings of the segregated fund.

[For the full text of this news release, see under 12.2(1) — ed.]

### Department of Finance news release, October 23, 1997: *Application of Foreign Property Limit to Segregated Funds*

*1. Introduction*

The new foreign property rules for segregated funds will apply in three situations.

First, they will apply where an interest in a segregated fund is held by a tax-exempt taxpayer described in paragraphs 205(a) to (f) of the *Income Tax Act*, such as a registered pension plan (RPP), a trust governed by a registered retirement savings plan (RRSP) or a trust governed by a registered retirement income fund (RRIF). Such taxpayers are subject to tax under Part XI of the Act if they invest too heavily in "foreign property". Under the proposed changes, an interest in a segregated fund will, in some circumstances, become a "foreign property" and the holding of such an interest can result in Part XI tax becoming payable.

A similar penalty tax may apply where an interest in a segregated fund policy is held directly as an RRSP or RRIF (i.e., outside of an RRSP or RRIF trust), or where such an interest is issued under an RPP that is not an RPP trust or corporation. The tax will generally be collected by the insurer that issued the segregated fund policy on behalf of the policyholder that is liable to pay it.

Third, the new rules can result in Part XI tax for an insurer where the Minister accepts a segregated fund administered by the insurer as a "registered investment" under proposed amendments to Part X.2 of the Act.

The application of the proposed rules to these three situations is described below.

*2. Tax payable under Part XI of the Income Tax Act by trusts governed by RRSPs, RRIFs and RPPs*

General

A trust governed by an RRSP, RRIF or RPP is generally liable to pay a penalty tax under subsection 206(2) of the Act in respect of a month where the cost amount to the trust of the "foreign property" (as defined in subsection 206(1)) held by the trust exceeds 20 per cent of the cost amount to the trust of all property held by it.

Under paragraph (i) of the definition "foreign property", an interest in a trust is a foreign property, except where the trust is a "registered investment" or where the interest in the trust is prescribed not to be a foreign property under the *Income Tax Regulations*. Under the proposed amendments, after 1998, an interest in a segregated fund will be treated as an interest in a trust for the purpose of Part XI. As a consequence, a trust governed by an RRSP, RRIF or RPP that holds a segregated fund policy in any month that ends after 1998 may be liable to pay the penalty tax under Part XI.

When is an Interest in a Segregated Fund Prescribed Not to be a Foreign Property?

The proposed amendments include a number of transitional provisions described below. However, section 5000 of the Regulations will prescribe an interest in a segregated fund held at a particular time not to be a foreign property in two cases:

- where the particular time is after 1999 and, throughout the last year that ended before the particular time (or at the end of the year that includes the particular time, if the fund was created in the year that includes the particular time), the total cost amount of all the foreign property held by the segregated fund does not exceed 20 per cent of the cost amount of all the property held by it; or

- where each policyholder holding an interest in the segregated fund at the particular time held an interest in the fund at the end of 1996 or acquired the interest from another policyholder who held an interest in the fund before 1997.

Transitional rules are proposed for 1999, 2000 and 2001 to give insurers an opportunity to shift the properties held by the segregated funds that they administer from foreign properties to non-foreign properties. To this end, an interest in a segregated fund will be prescribed not to be a foreign property in 1999 where:

- the segregated fund was created before 1997 and, at any time in the first 90 days of 1998, the fair market value (FMV) of all the foreign property held by the fund does not exceed 80 per cent of the FMV of all the property held by the fund;

- the segregated fund was created in 1997 or 1998 and, at any time in the first 90 days of its 1998 taxation year, the FMV of all the foreign property held by the fund does not exceed 20 per cent of the FMV of all of the property held by the fund; or

- the segregated fund was created in 1999 and, at the end of 1999, the cost amount of all of the foreign property held by the fund does not exceed 20 per cent of the cost amount of all of the property held by the fund.

In 2000, an interest in a segregated fund will be prescribed not to be a foreign property if the segregated fund was created before 1997 and, throughout 1999, the cost amount of all the foreign property held by the segregated fund does not exceed 60 per cent of the cost amount of all the property held by the fund.

In 2001, an interest in a segregated fund will be prescribed not to be a foreign property if the segregated fund was created before 1997 and, throughout 2000, the cost amount of all the foreign property held by the segregated fund does not exceed 40 per cent of the cost amount of all the property held by the segregated fund.

"Cost Amount" for the Purposes of Part XI of the Act

Under the proposed amendments, where an interest in a segregated fund is, after 1998, treated as "foreign property", the "cost amount" of the interest will be determined on a lagged basis.

Specifically, the "cost amount" of an interest in a segregated fund to an RRSP trust, RRIF trust or RPP will be its adjusted cost base (ACB), except that the ACB adjustments that would otherwise be required in a particular calendar year will not be made until after March of the following calendar year. An interest in a segregated fund will have a known constant ACB throughout each year as ACB adjustments in respect of the year will not be made until the following year, making it possible for taxpayers subject to the foreign property penalty tax to comply with the foreign property limit on an on-going basis.

3. *New Foreign Property Limits with respect to Segregated Fund Policies Issued or Effected as RRSPs or RRIFs and Policies Issued under RPPs*

Segregated Fund Policies Issued or Effected as RRSPs or RRIFs

The new rules will also apply where, after 1998, an individual holds an interest in a segregated fund directly as an RRSP or RRIF (i.e., outside a RRSP or RRIF trust). In general, the policyholder's liability for penalty tax will be determined on a policy-by-policy basis. Where the penalty tax is owing, the insurer that issued the segregated fund will be required to collect the penalty tax on behalf of the policyholder.

A policyholder will be liable to pay the penalty tax in respect of a segregated fund policy for any month where the total cost amount (determined on a lagged basis as described above) at the end of the month of all the interests in segregated funds under the policy that are foreign properties exceeds 20 per cent of the total of

- the cash surrender value of the policy at the end of the month (not including any amount in respect of an interest in a segregated fund), and
- the total cost amount (determined on a lagged basis) at the end of the month of all the interests in segregated funds under the policy.

For this purpose, whether an interest in a segregated fund is a foreign property is determined using the definition of "foreign property" described above.

Where an insurer has issued interests in more than one segregated fund policy, the insurer will be able to treat those policies as one policy for purposes of calculating how much penalty tax is payable. The election will allow policies that derive their value largely from foreign property to be offset by policies that derive their value largely from non-foreign property.

Segregated Fund Policies Issued under RPPs

The administrator of an RPP (other than an RPP trust or corporation) may also be liable to pay foreign property tax where the RPP is funded or partially funded by an interest in a segregated fund policy.

The administrator's liability will be determined on an insurer-by-insurer basis. As a consequence, all the segregated fund policies used to fund the RPP that were issued by a particular insurer will be grouped together for this purpose. The administrator will be liable to pay tax in a given month in respect of the policies issued by a particular insurer where the total cost amount (determined on a lagged basis as described above) at the end of the month of all the interests in segregated funds that arise under the policies and that are foreign properties exceeds 20 per cent of the total of

- the cash surrender values, at the end of the month, of all the policies (not including any amount in respect of an interest in a segregated fund), and
- the total cost amount (determined on a lagged basis) at the end of the month of all the interests in segregated funds that arise under the policies.

For this purpose, whether an interest in a segregated fund is a foreign property will be determined using the definition of "foreign property" described above.

Where an RPP is funded with segregated fund policies issued by more than one insurer, the administrator of the RPP will be able to elect to treat all such insurers as one insurer for purposes of determining its penalty tax liability. Where the policies issued by one insurer have a high foreign property content, the election will make it possible for an administrator to offset that high foreign property content with the non-foreign property content of policies issued by other insurers.

The responsibility for collecting and remitting an administrator's penalty tax falls on the insurer, unless the administrator makes the election to treat all insurers as one. Where this election is made, the responsibility for collecting and remitting the penalty tax falls on the administrator.

[For the full text of this news release, see under 12.2(1) — ed.]

**Notes**: This amendment was reportedly in response to a plan announced by Manulife Financial to offer an RRSP-eligible segregated fund with 100% foreign content. Manulife was the only major insurer that did not voluntarily enforce the 20% foreign content limit. (*Financial Post*, Dec. 20/96, p. 5)

**Department of Finance news release, October 27, 1998**: *Segregated Funds*

Proposed new rules for segregated funds were announced on October 23, 1997. These rules, which are not included in the draft legislation, are intended to put interests in segregated funds offered by life insurers on an equal footing with units in mutual funds for the purposes of the 20% foreign property limit. The October 23, 1997 press release indicated that these rules would begin to apply from January 1999. However, consultation with the insurance industry has indicated the considerable extent of the systems changes that will be required for the insurance industry to monitor these limits, and the need to consider substantial technical amendments to the rules governing the taxation of segregated funds. Given the technical and administrative issues associated with this proposal, the Minister announced that the foreign property rules for segregated funds would apply only as of January 2001.

**Federal budget, supplementary information, February 28, 2000**: *Extension of FPR Rules to Segregated Funds*

Although the FPR currently applies to mutual funds which issue units to deferred income plans, there is currently no legislation providing for its application to segregated funds. Segregated funds are insurance products offered by life insurers which are broadly analogous to mutual funds. As announced by the Minister of Finance by press release on October 27, 1998, proposed rules to extend the FPR to segregated funds were to be effective as of January 2001.

The FPR for segregated funds will contain the same one-year lag as is provided for mutual funds (i.e., an interest in a mutual fund is generally not treated as foreign property during a year, provided the mutual fund satisfied the FPR limit throughout the previous year). In order to provide a better opportunity for insurance companies to institute systems changes to allow foreign property levels to be monitored for segregated funds, the budget proposes that the FPR for segregated funds apply after 2001 (rather than after 2000).

**Department of Finance news release Backgrounder, December 21, 2000**: *Segregated Funds and Foreign Property*

Also under review and development are the tax rules that apply to life insurers' 'segregated fund' investment products. The Department has undertaken extensive consultations with the insurance industry with a view to improving several aspects of these rules, and detailed legislative proposals are expected to be released in 2001.

Among other things, the proposals will include measures that affect the application to segregated funds of the foreign property rule (FPR). The application of the FPR to segregated funds was previously proposed to apply as of 2002, with the result that insurers would have been required to have monitoring systems in place by the beginning of 2001. In recognition of the fact that the specific rules are still under development, and in recognition of the need for the industry to implement associated systems changes, *the FPR will be extended to the funds only as of the second year following the year in which the proposals are finalized.* This deferral will ensure that insurers have the information they need to implement those systems fully and efficiently.

**Related Provisions**: 206(1.1)(d) — Exception where substantial Canadian presence; 206(1.4) — Interpretation; 206(1.5) — Identical property.

**Notes**: Para. (d.1) amended by 1995-97 technical bill, this version effective for shares and indebtedness last acquired in 1996 or later. For shares and indebtedness acquired after December 4, 1985 (otherwise than pursuant to an agreement in writing made before 5:00 p.m. E.S.T. on December 4, 1985) to the end of 1995, read "primarily from foreign property" as "primarily from portfolio investments in property that is foreign property".

Para. (e) amended by 1995-97 technical bill, effective for months that end after June 1995.

Para. (g) amended by 1993 technical bill, effective for months in 1993 or later, to clarify that all forms of indebtedness of a non-resident are foreign property. For November 1985 through December 1992, read:

(g) any bond, debenture, mortgage, note or similar obligation of, or issued by, a person not resident in Canada, except any such bond, debenture, mortgage, note or similar obligation issued or guaranteed by

Subpara. (g)(i.1) added by 1991 technical bill, effective July 14, 1990.

Subpara. (g)(iv.1) added by 1995-97 technical bill, effective for months after March 1991.

Subpara. (g)(iv.2) added by 1995-97 technical bill, effective for months after 1996.

**Regulations**: 221(3) (information return by issuer of share or trust interest claimed not to be foreign property); 3200 (prescribed stock exchange); 5000 (property prescribed not to be foreign property).

**I.T. Application Rules**: 65(5) (amalgamation of mutual fund corporations).

**Interpretation Bulletins**: IT-320R2: RRSP — qualified investments; IT-412R2: Foreign property of registered plans.

**Forms**: T3F: Investments prescribed to be qualified or not to be foreign property information return.

"**investment activity**" of a particular corporation means any business carried on by the corporation, or any holding of property by the corporation otherwise than as part of a business carried on by the corporation, the principal purpose of which is to derive income from, or to derive profits from the disposition of,

(a) shares (other than shares of the capital stock of another corporation in which the particular corporation has a significant interest, where the primary activity of the other corporation is not an investment activity),

(b) interests in trusts,

(c) indebtedness (other than indebtedness owing by another corporation in which the particular corporation has a significant interest, where the primary activity of the other corporation is not an investment activity),

(d) annuities,

(e) commodities or commodities futures purchased or sold, directly or indirectly in any manner whatever, on a commodities or commodities futures exchange (except commodities manufactured, produced, grown, extracted or processed by the corporation or another corporation with which the corporation does not deal at arm's length),

(f) currencies (other than currencies in the form of numismatic coins),

(g) interests in funds or entities other than corporations, partnerships and trusts,

(h) interests or options in respect of property described in any of paragraphs (a) to (g), or

(i) any combination of properties described in any of paragraphs (a) to (h);

**Related Provisions**: 206(4), 251(1) — Meaning of arm's length.

**Notes**: This was called "investment business" in the draft legislation of December 13, 1995.

"Investment activity" added by 1995-97 technical bill, effective 1996.

"**qualified property**" of a corporation means a property (other than a debt obligation or share issued by an affiliate of the corporation or by any corporation related to the corporation) owned by the corporation and used by it or an affiliate of the corporation in a specified active business carried on by it or the affiliate;

**Notes**: "Qualified property" added by 1995-97 technical bill, effective for shares and indebtedness acquired after December 4, 1985 (otherwise than pursuant to an agreement in writing made before 5:00 p.m. E.S.T. on December 4, 1985).

"**significant interest**" has the meaning that would be assigned by section 142.2 if that section were read without reference to paragraphs 142.2(3)(b) and (c);

**Notes**: "Significant interest" added by 1995-97 technical bill, effective 1996.

"**small business investment amount**" of a taxpayer for a month means the greater of

(a) the total of the cost amounts of all small business properties to the taxpayer at the end of the month, and

(b) the quotient obtained when the total of all amounts determined for each of the three preceding months, each of which is the total of the cost amounts of all small business properties to the taxpayer at the end of that preceding month, is divided by three;

**Notes**: Para. (a) (and "the greater of" in the opening words) added by 1999 Budget, effective for months that end after 1997.

**"small business property"** of a taxpayer at a particular time means property acquired by the taxpayer after October 31, 1985 that is at that particular time

(a) a property prescribed to be a small business security,

(b) a share of a class of the capital stock of a corporation prescribed to be a small business investment corporation,

(c) an interest of a limited partner in a partnership prescribed to be a small business investment limited partnership, or

(d) an interest in a trust prescribed to be a small business investment trust,

where

(e) the taxpayer is a prescribed person in respect of the property, or

(f) throughout the period that began at the time the property was first acquired (otherwise than by a broker or dealer in securities) and ends at the particular time, the property was not owned by any person other than

(i) the taxpayer,

(ii) a trust governed by a particular registered retirement income fund or registered retirement savings plan if

(A) the taxpayer is another trust governed by a registered retirement income fund or registered retirement savings plan, and

(B) the annuitant under the particular fund or plan (or the spouse or former spouse of that annuitant) is also the annuitant under the fund or plan referred to in clause (A), or

(iii) an annuitant under a registered retirement income fund or registered retirement savings plan that governs the taxpayer, or a spouse or former spouse of that annuitant;

**Related Provisions**: 252(3) — Extended meaning of "spouse" and "former spouse".

**Notes**: Everything after para. (d) amended by 1999 Budget, effective for months that end after 1997. From November 1986 through 1997, read:

where the taxpayer is

(e) a prescribed person in respect of the property, or

(f) the first person (other than a broker or dealer in securities) to have acquired the property and the taxpayer has owned the property continuously since it was so acquired.

**Regulations**: 5100–5104 (prescribed property).

**"specified active business"** carried on by a corporation, at any time, means a particular business that is carried on by the corporation in Canada where

(a) the corporation employs in the particular business at that time more than 5 full-time employees and at least

(i) 50% of the full-time employees employed by the corporation at that time in the particular business are employed in Canada, and

(ii) 50% of the salaries and wages paid to employees employed at that time in the particular business are reasonably attributable to services rendered in Canada by the employees, or

(b) one or more other corporations associated with the corporation provide, in the course of carrying on one or more other active businesses, managerial, administrative, financial, maintenance or other similar services to the corporation in respect of the particular business and

(i) the corporation could reasonably be expected to require more than 5 full-time employees at that time in respect of the particular business if those services had not been provided,

(ii) at least 50% of the full-time employees employed at that time by the corporation in the particular business and by the other corporations in the other active businesses are employed in Canada, and

(iii) at least 50% of the salaries and wages paid to employees employed at that time by the corporation in the particular business and by the other corporations in the other active businesses are reasonably attributable to services rendered in Canada by the employees,

but does not include a business carried on by the corporation the principal purpose of which is to derive income from, or from the disposition of, shares and debt obligations the value of which can reasonably be considered to derive, directly or indirectly, primarily from foreign property;

**Notes**: It is not clear whether the definition "salary or wages" in 248(1) is intended to apply to the phrase "salaries and wages" in subparas. (a)(ii) and (b)(iii).

The words "more than 5 full-time employees" mean 6 or more, not 5 plus a part-time person. See *Hughes & Co. Holdings Ltd.*, [1994] 2 C.T.C. 170 (FCTD). However, in appropriate cases even 4 hours per day could be "full-time": *Ben Raedarc Holdings Ltd.*, [1998] 1 C.T.C. 2774 (TCC).

"Specified active business" added by 1995-97 technical bill, effective for shares and indebtedness acquired after December 4, 1985 (otherwise than pursuant to an agreement in writing made before 5:00 p.m. E.S.T. on December 4, 1985).

**"specified proportion"** of a member of a partnership for a fiscal period of the partnership means the proportion that the member's share of the total income or loss of the partnership for the partnership's fiscal period is of the partnership's total income or loss for that period and, for the purpose of this definition, where that income or loss for a period is nil, that proportion shall be computed as if the partnership had income for that period in the amount of $1,000,000.

**Notes:** "Specified proportion" added by 1995-97 technical bill, effective for shares and indebtedness acquired after December 4, 1985 (otherwise than pursuant to an agreement in writing made before 5:00 p.m. E.S.T. on December 4, 1985).

**(1.1) Exception where substantial Canadian presence** — Property described in paragraph (d.1) of the definition "foreign property" in subsection (1) does not, at a particular time, include property of a taxpayer that is a share or debt obligation that was issued by a corporation that, at the particular time, is a Canadian corporation where

(a) either at any time in any of the last 15 months beginning before the time (in this subsection referred to as the "acquisition time") when the property was last acquired before the particular time by the taxpayer or at any time in the calendar year that includes the acquisition time, the total of all amounts each of which is the designated value of a qualified property of the corporation or an affiliate of the corporation exceeded $50,000,000;

(b) the particular time is not later than the end of the 15th month ending after the acquisition time and, at any time in any of the last 15 months beginning before the acquisition time, the total of all amounts each of which is the designated value of a qualified property of the corporation or another corporation controlled by the corporation exceeded 50% of the lesser of the fair market value of all of the corporation's property and the carrying value of all of the corporation's property;

(c) the particular time is after the acquisition time and, at any time in any of the first 15 months beginning after the acquisition time, the total of all amounts each of which is the designated value of a qualified property of the corporation or another corporation controlled by the corporation exceeded 50% of the lesser of the fair market value of all of the corporation's property and the carrying value of all of the corporation's property;

(d) the particular time is after 1995 and, at the particular time,

　(i) either

　　(A) the corporation was incorporated or otherwise formed under the laws of Canada or a province, or

　　(B) where the corporation was not required to maintain an office under the laws by or under which it was incorporated, the maintenance of an office in Canada is required under the constitutional documents of the corporation,

　(ii) the corporation maintains an office in Canada, and

　(iii) any of the following conditions applies, namely,

　　(A) the corporation employs more than 5 individuals in Canada full time and those individuals are not employed primarily in connection with

　　　(I) an investment activity of the corporation or another corporation with which the corporation does not deal at arm's length,

　　　(II) a business carried on by the corporation through a partnership of which the corporation is not a majority interest partner, or

　　　(III) a business carried on by another corporation with which the corporation does not deal at arm's length through a partnership of which that other corporation is not a majority interest partner,

　　(B) another corporation that is controlled by the corporation employs more than 5 individuals in Canada full time and those individuals are not employed primarily in connection with

　　　(I) an investment activity of the other corporation or another corporation with which the other corporation does not deal at arm's length,

　　　(II) a business carried on by the other corporation through a partnership of which the other corporation is not a majority interest partner, or

　　　(III) a business carried on by another corporation with which the other corporation does not deal at arm's length through a partnership of which that other corporation is not a majority interest partner,

　　(C) the total amount incurred by the corporation for the services (other than services relating to an investment activity of the corporation or another corporation with which the corporation does not deal at arm's length) of employees and other individuals rendered in Canada in any calendar year that ends in any of the last 15 months that end before the particular time exceeds $250,000,

　　(D) the total amount incurred by another corporation that is controlled by the corporation for the services (other than services relating to an investment activity of the other corporation or another corporation with which the other corporation does not deal at arm's length) of employees and other individuals rendered in Canada in any calendar year that ends in any of the

Part XI — Property Acq'd by Deferred Income Plans        S. 206(2)(a)(iii)

last 15 months that end before the particular time exceeds $250,000, or

(E) in the calendar year that includes the particular time the corporation was continued from a jurisdiction outside Canada, or incorporated or otherwise formed and the total amount incurred in the year by the corporation for the services (other than services relating to an investment activity of the corporation or another corporation with which the corporation does not deal at arm's length) of employees and other individuals rendered in Canada exceeds $250,000; or

(e) the particular time is after 1995 and, at the particular time, all or substantially all of the property of the corporation is not foreign property.

**Related Provisions**: 206(1.2) — Application to partnerships; 256(6), (6.1) — Meaning of "controlled".

**Notes**: 206(1.1) added by 1995-97 technical bill, effective December 5, 1985.

**(1.2) Partnerships** — For the purposes of paragraphs (1.1)(a) to (c) and this subsection,

(a) a member of a partnership

(i) is deemed not to own any interest in the partnership at any time, and

(ii) is deemed to own the member's specified proportion for the partnership's first fiscal period that ends at or after that time of each property that would, if the assumption in paragraph 96(1)(c) were made, be owned by the partnership at that time; and

(b) the carrying value at that time of that specified proportion of a partnership's property is deemed to be that specified proportion of the carrying value at that time to the partnership of that property.

**Notes**: 206(1.2) added by 1995-97 technical bill, effective December 5, 1985.

**(1.3) Interpretation** — For the purpose of paragraph (1.1)(d),

(a) an employee of a corporation is deemed to be employed in Canada where the corporation's permanent establishment (as defined by regulation) to which the employee principally reports is situated in Canada; and

(b) services are deemed to be rendered in Canada to a corporation where the permanent establishment (as defined by regulation) for which the services are rendered is situated in Canada.

**Notes**: 206(1.3) added by 1995-97 technical bill, effective December 5, 1985.

This provision was not included in the draft legislation of December 13, 1995.

**Regulations**: 8201, 8201.1 (permanent establishment).

**(1.4) Rights in respect of foreign property** — For the purpose of determining whether a property owned by a taxpayer is foreign property at any time because of paragraph (f) or (h) of the definition "foreign property" in subsection (1), it shall be assumed that each other property not owned at that time by the taxpayer was acquired immediately before that time by the taxpayer.

**Notes**: 206(1.4) added by 1995-97 technical bill, effective December 5, 1985.

This provision was 206(1.3) in the draft legislation of December 13, 1995.

**(1.5) Identical property** — Notwithstanding paragraphs (d.1), (f) and (h) of the definition "foreign property" in subsection (1), a property shall not be considered to be foreign property at a particular time of a taxpayer because of any of those paragraphs where

(a) the property is

(i) a share or debt obligation issued by a Canadian corporation, or

(ii) an interest in, a right to, a property that is convertible into or a property that is exchangeable for, a share or debt obligation issued by a Canadian corporation; and

(b) the property, or the share or obligation referred to in subparagraph (a)(ii), is identical to another property that is owned at the particular time by the taxpayer and that is not foreign property at the particular time of the taxpayer.

**Related Provisions**: 248(12) — Whether properties are identical.

**Notes**: 206(1.5) added by 1995-97 technical bill, effective December 5, 1985.

This provision was 206(1.4) in the draft legislation of December 13, 1995.

**(2) Tax payable** — Where, at the end of any month,

(a) the amount, if any, by which

(i) the total of all amounts each of which is the cost amount of a foreign property to a taxpayer described in any of paragraphs 205(a) to (f)

exceeds the total of

(ii) where the taxpayer is described in any of paragraphs 205(b), (c) and (e), all amounts each of which is the cost amount to the taxpayer of a foreign property that was not at the end of the month a qualified investment (within the meaning assigned by subsection 146(1) or 146.3(1) or section 204, as the case may be) of the taxpayer, and

(iii) all amounts (other than an amount included in respect of the taxpayer for the month under subparagraph (ii)) each of which is the cost amount to the taxpayer of foreign property that became foreign property of the taxpayer after its last acquisition by the taxpayer and at a time that is not more than 24 months before the end of the month,

1623

**S. 206(2)** — Income Tax Act

exceeds the total of

(b) 30% of the total of all amounts each of which is the cost amount of a property to the taxpayer, and

(c) in the case of a taxpayer described in paragraph 205(a), (b), (c) or (e), other than a taxpayer described in paragraph 149(1)(o.2), the lesser of

(i) three times the small business investment amount of the taxpayer for the month, and

(ii) 20% of the total of all amounts each of which is the cost amount of a property to the taxpayer,

the taxpayer shall, in respect of that month, pay a tax under this Part equal to 1% of the lesser of the excess and the total of all amounts each of which is the cost amount to the taxpayer of each of its foreign properties that was acquired after June 18, 1971.

**Related Provisions**: 107.4(3)(c) — Cost of property after qualifying disposition to trust; 206(2.1) — Limitation — maximum tax payable by registered investment; 206(3.1) — Reorganizations, etc.; 259 — Proportional holdings in trust property.

**Notes**: 206(2)(b) amended by by 2000 first budget bill (C-32) to change 20% to 25% for months in 2000 and to 30% for months after 2000. This increases the foreign property limit for RRSPs and other deferred income plans, as announced in the February 2000 budget, from 20% to 25% and then 30% (and to 45% and 50% where sufficient amounts are invested in small business property; see 206(2)(c)).

206(2)(a)(iii) added by 1992 technical bill, effective for December 1991 and later months. It provides that where property in the portfolio was not foreign property but becomes foreign property, it will not be subject to the foreign property limits for 2 years. (This could happen, for example, for the shares of a Canadian corporation the value of which, at some point, becomes derived primarily from portfolio investments in foreign property.)

206(2)(b) amended by 1990 Budget, this version effective 1994. The maximum percentage of foreign property is limited as follows: months before 1990, 10%; months in 1990, 12%; 1991, 14%; 1992, 16%; 1993, 18%; months in 1994 and later, 20%.

**Regulations**: 5000.

**I.T. Application Rules**: 65.

**Interpretation Bulletins**: IT-320R2: RRSPs — qualified investments; IT-412R2: Foreign property of registered plans.

**Forms**: T3P: Employees' pension plan income tax return.

**(2.01) [Tax payable by] Registered investments** — Notwithstanding subsection (2), the tax payable under this section by a registered investment in respect of a month is equal to the lesser of

(a) the tax that would, but for this subsection, be payable by the registered investment in respect of the month, and

(b) the greater of

(i) 20% of the amount determined under paragraph (a), and

(ii) the amount determined by the formula

$$\$5,000 + (A \times B/C)$$

where

A is equal to the amount determined under paragraph (a),

B is equal to

(A) where the registered investment is a trust, the total of all amounts each of which is the fair market value at the end of the month of an interest in the registered investment that is held at that time by a taxpayer described in any of paragraphs 205(a) to (f) or by a mutual fund corporation, investment corporation, mutual fund trust, prescribed trust or prescribed partnership, and

(B) where the registered investment is a corporation, the total of all amounts each of which is the fair market value at the end of the month of a share of the capital stock of the registered investment that is held at that time by a taxpayer described in any of paragraphs 205(a) to (f) or by a mutual fund corporation, investment corporation, mutual fund trust, prescribed trust or prescribed partnership, and

C is equal to

(A) where the registered investment is a trust, the total of all amounts each of which is the fair market value at the end of the month of an interest in the registered investment that is held at that time, and

(B) where the registered investment is a corporation, the total of all amounts each of which is the fair market value at the end of the month of a share of the capital stock of the registered investment that is held at that time.

**Notes**: 206(2.01) added by 1995-97 technical bill, effective for months that end after 1992.

**Regulations**: 5002 (prescribed trust and prescribed partnership for 206(2.01)(b)(ii)B).

**(2.1) Exemption** — Notwithstanding section 205, subsection (2) does not apply to a trust described in paragraph 149(1)(o.4) or a corporation described in paragraph 149(1)(o.2) in respect of any month that falls within a period for which the trustee or the corporation, as the case may be, elects in accordance with subsections 259(1) and (3).

**Notes**: 206(2.1) amended by 1993 technical bill, effective for 1992 and later taxation years. For 1987 through 1992, read:

(2.1) Notwithstanding section 205, subsection (2) shall not apply in respect of a trust described in paragraph 149(1)(o.4) in respect of any month that falls within a period in respect of which the trustee has elected in accordance with subsection 259(2).

**Interpretation Bulletins**: IT-412R2: Foreign property of registered plans.

**(3) [Repealed]**

**Notes**: 206(3) repealed by 1995-97 technical bill, effective for months that end after June 1995. See now 206(1)"foreign property"(e). For earlier months since 1981, read:

(3) **Shares in investment corporation** — Notwithstanding the definition "foreign property" in subsection (1), a share of the capital stock of an investment corporation (other than a registered investment) acquired after October 13, 1971 by a taxpayer to whom this Part applies and owned by the taxpayer at a particular time shall, except as prescribed by regulation, be deemed to be a foreign property of the taxpayer at that time.

(3.1) **Reorganizations, etc.** — Where

(a) a security (in this subsection referred to as the "new security") is issued at a particular time by a corporation to a taxpayer

(i) in exchange for another security acquired before the particular time by the taxpayer, and

(ii) in the course of

(A) a corporate merger or reorganization of capital, or

(B) a transaction in which control of the corporation that issued the other security is acquired by a person or a group of persons, and

(b) the new security is foreign property at the particular time,

for the purposes of applying subparagraph (2)(a)(iii) to the taxpayer at or after the particular time,

(c) the new security shall be deemed to have been last acquired by the taxpayer at the time the other security was last acquired by the taxpayer,

(d) where the other security was not foreign property immediately before the particular time, the new security shall be deemed to have become foreign property at the particular time, and

(e) where the other security was foreign property immediately before the particular time, the new security shall be deemed to have become foreign property at the time the other security became foreign property.

**Proposed Amendment — 206(3.1), (3.2)**

(3.1) **Acquisition of qualifying security** — For the purpose of applying subparagraph (2)(a)(iii) at or after a particular time, where a qualifying security in relation to another security is acquired at the particular time by the taxpayer referred to in subsection (3.2) in respect of the security, and the security is foreign property at that time,

(a) the qualifying security is deemed to have been last acquired by the taxpayer at the time the other security was last acquired by the taxpayer;

(b) where the other security was not foreign property immediately before the particular time, the qualifying security is deemed to have become foreign property at the particular time; and

(c) where the other security was foreign property immediately before the particular time, the qualifying security is deemed to have become foreign property at the time the other security became foreign property.

(3.2) **Qualifying security** — For the purpose of subsection (3.1), a qualifying security in relation to another security means

(a) a security issued at any time by a corporation to a taxpayer

(i) in exchange for another security acquired before that time by the taxpayer, and

(ii) in the course of

(A) a corporate merger or reorganization of capital,

(B) a transaction or series of transactions in which control of the corporation that issued the other security is acquired by a person or group of persons, or

(C) a transaction or series of transactions in which all or substantially all of the issued and outstanding shares (other than shares held immediately before the transaction or the beginning of the series by a particular person or related group) of the corporation that issued the other security are acquired by the particular person or related group; or

(b) a security acquired by a taxpayer from a corporation pursuant to a distribution with respect to another security that is an eligible distribution described in subsection 86.1(2).

**Application**: The December 21, 2000 draft legislation, s. 89, will amend subsec. 206(3.1) to read as above and add subsec. 206(3.2), applicable to months that end after 1997.

**Technical Notes**: Part XI sets out the rules for the 1% per month penalty tax on deferred income plans and funds, master trusts and registered investments listed in section 205 in respect of their excess foreign property holdings.

Section 206 imposes a tax on certain taxpayers, such as registered retirement savings plans, registered retirement income funds and registered pension plans, which invest more than a specified percentage of their assets in foreign property. Subparagraph 206(2)(a)(iii) provides relief from the imposition of this tax in respect of property that was not foreign property when it was acquired, but that subsequently becomes foreign property, by not treating such property as foreign property for up to 24 months. Subsection 206(3.1) extends the relief provided by that subparagraph where a security that is foreign property is issued to a taxpayer in exchange for another security in the course of a change in control of the corporation that issued the other security or a corporate merger or reorganization of capital. In these circumstances, the new security is likewise not treated as foreign property for up to 24 months if the other security was not foreign property.

Section 206 is amended so that the existing rule in subsection 206(3.1) is reflected in amended subsection 206(3.1) and new subsection 206(3.2).

New subsection 206(3.2) extends the relief provided by subparagraph 206(2)(a)(iii) to include the circumstances where a new security is issued to a taxpayer in exchange for another security in the course of a transaction or series of transactions in which all or substantially all of the issued and outstanding shares of a corporation (other than shares held by a particular person or related group) that issued the other security are acquired by the particular person or related group. This relief applies where the shares of a corporation acquired in the course of the transaction or series represent a minority interest in the corporation.

Subsection 206(3.2) also ensures that the relief provided by subparagraph 206(2)(a)(iii) is available to a taxpayer where a particular security of the taxpayer that became foreign property in circumstances to which that subparagraph applied is, during the period of up to 24 months applicable to the particular security, subject to an "eligible distribution" (as defined in new section 86.1). In these circumstances, the new security (in new section 86.1 referred to as a "spin-off share") acquired by the taxpayer is deemed under subsection 206(3.1) to have been last acquired by the taxpayer at the time the particular security was last acquired by the taxpayer and to have become foreign property at the time the particular security became foreign property. This is intended to ensure that the remaining portion of that period of up to 24 months available in respect of the particular security applies after the eligible distribution to both the particular security and the new security. For more detail on eligible distributions, see the commentary to new section 86.1.

**Letter from Department of Finance, November 17, 1998:**

Dear [xxx]

This is in reply to your letter of November 3, 1998 to Simon Thompson concerning subsection 206(3.1) of the *Income Tax Act*.

We understand that an arrangement of a Canadian corporation is proposed under section 182 of the *Ontario Business Corporations Act*. We understand that all shareholders of the Canadian corporation will be required, if specified levels of shareholder support are achieved in connection with an upcoming vote on the arrangement, to exchange their shares for the capital stock of a corporation resident in the United States or, in the case of dissenting shareholders, for cash. We assume, for this purpose, that the shares of the capital stock of the Canadian corporation are not "foreign property" under Part XI of the *Income Tax Act*.

We agree that, in these circumstances, it would be appropriate to extend subsection 206(3.1) of the *Income Tax Act* so that it applies in all cases to the shares of the U.S. corporation acquired on such an exchange by a taxpayer described in any of paragraphs 205(a) to (f). Such an extension would, in general terms, have the effect pursuant to subparagraph 206(2)(a)(iii) of treating these shares as not being foreign property under Part XI for up to 24 months. We will recommend that this amendment apply for months ending after 1997.

Thank you for writing.

Yours sincerely,

Len Farber
Director General, Tax Legislation Division

**Related Provisions**: 206(3.2) — Qualifying security; 256(6)–(9) — Whether control acquired.

**Notes**: 206(3.1) added by 1992 technical bill, effective for December 1991 and later months.

**Interpretation Bulletins**: IT-412R2: Foreign property of registered plans.

**(4) Non-arm's length transactions** — For the purposes of this Part, where a taxpayer has acquired property from a person with whom the taxpayer was not dealing at arm's length for no consideration or for consideration less than the fair market value thereof at the time of the acquisition, the taxpayer shall be deemed to have acquired the property at that fair market value, and for those purposes, a trust shall be deemed not to deal at arm's length with another trust if any person is beneficially interested in both trusts.

### Proposed Amendment — 206(4)

**(4) Non-arm's length transactions** — For the purposes of this Part, where at any time a taxpayer acquires property, otherwise than pursuant to a transfer of property to which paragraph (f) or (g) of the definition "disposition" in subsection 248(1) applies, from a person with whom the taxpayer does not deal at arm's length for no consideration or for consideration less than the fair market value of the property at that time, the taxpayer is deemed to acquire the property at that fair market value, and for those purposes, a particular trust is deemed not to deal at arm's length with another trust if a person who is beneficially interested in the particular trust is at that time also beneficially interested in the other trust.

**Application**: Bill C-43 (First Reading September 20, 2000), subsec. 98(2), will amend subsec. 206(4) to read as above, applicable in respect of property acquired after December 17, 1999.

**Technical Notes**: Subsection 206(4) provides, for the purposes of Part XI, that property acquired by a taxpayer from a person with whom the taxpayer does not deal at arm's length and for less than fair market value consideration is treated as having been acquired at its fair market value at the time of its acquisition. For these purposes, trusts that have the same beneficiary are considered not to deal with each other at arm's length.

Subsection 206(4) is amended so that it does not apply to a transfer of property to which paragraph (f) or (g) of the definition "disposition" in subsection 248(1) applies. In conjunction with subsection 248(25.1), this amendment is intended to ensure that where a transfer of property is one to which either of those paragraphs applies and that involves a taxpayer to which subsection 206(4) would otherwise apply, the transfer will occur on a rollover basis.

This amendment is part of a set of amendments intended to clarify the tax treatment of transfers of property involving RRSPs and RRIFs. For further detail, see the commentary to paragraphs 107.4(2)(b) and (3)(c), paragraphs (f) and (g) of the new definition "disposition" in subsection 248(1), and subsection 248(25.1).

**Related Provisions [subsec. 206(4)]**: 107.4(3)(c) — Cost of property after qualifying disposition to trust; 248(25) — Meaning of "beneficially interested"; 251 — Arm's length.

**Definitions [s. 206]**: "acquired" — 256(7)–(9); "active business" — 248(1); "affiliate" — 206(1); "amount" — 248(1); "annuitant" — 146(1), 146.3(1); "arm's length" — 206(4), 251(1); "authorized foreign bank" — 248(1); "beneficially interested" — 248(25); "business" — 248(1); "calendar year" — *Interpretation Act* 37(1)(a); "Canada" — 255; "Canadian corporation" — 89(1), 248(1); "capital interest" — 108(1), 248(1); "carrying value" — 206(1); "class of shares" — 248(6); "control" — 256(6)–(9); "controlled" — 256(6), (6.1); "corporation" — 248(1), *Interpretation Act* 35(1); "cost amount" — 206(1), 248(1); "designated value" — 206(1.3); "eligible distribution" — 86.1(2); "employed" — 248(1); "employed in Canada" — 206(1.3); "excluded share" — 206(1); "foreign property" — 206(1); "former spouse" — 252(3); "identical" — 248(12); "individual" — 248(1); "investment activity" — 206(1); "investment corporation" — 130(3)(a), 248(1); "majority interest partner" — 248(1); "month" — *Interpretation Act* 35(1); "mutual fund corporation" — 131(8), 248(1); "non-resident" — 248(1); "partnership" — see Notes to 96(1); "permanent establishment" — Reg. 8201, 8201.1; "person", "prescribed" — 248(1); "prescribed stock exchange in Canada" — Reg. 3200; "property" — 248(1); "qualified property" — 206(1); "qualifying security" — 206(3.2); "province" — *Interpretation Act* 35(1); "registered investment" — 204.4(1), 204.5, 248(1); "registered retirement income fund" — 146.3(1), 248(1); "registered retirement savings plan" — 146(1), 248(1); "regulation" — 248(1); "related" — 251(2); "share", "shareholder" — 248(1); "significant interest", "small business investment amount", "small business property" — 206(1); "specified active business" — 206(1); "spouse" — 252(3); "taxation year" — 249; "taxpayer" — 248(1); "trust" — 248(1), (3); "writing" — *Interpretation Act* 35(1).

**Forms [s. 206]**: T3F: Investments prescribed to be qualified or not to be foreign property information return; T3RI: Registered investment and income tax return.

## 206.1 Tax in respect of acquisition of shares
— Where at any time a taxpayer to which this Part applies makes an agreement (otherwise than as a consequence of the acquisition or writing by it of an option listed on a prescribed stock exchange) to acquire a share of the capital stock of a corporation (otherwise than from the corporation) at a price that may differ from the fair market value of the share at the time the share may be acquired, the taxpayer shall, in respect of each month during which the taxpayer is a party to the agreement, pay a tax under this Part equal to the total of all amounts each of which is the amount, if any, by which

(a) the amount of a dividend paid on the share at a time in the month at which the taxpayer is a party to the agreement

exceeds

(b) the amount, if any, of the dividend that is received by the taxpayer.

**Notes**: 206.1 amended by 1995-97 technical bill, this version effective for agreements entered into after April 25, 1995. For agreements entered into from January 1993 through April 25, 1995, read:

> 206.1 Where at any time a taxpayer to which this Part applies enters into an agreement (otherwise than as a consequence of the acquisition or writing by it of an option listed on a prescribed stock exchange) to acquire a share of the capital stock of a corporation (otherwise than from the corporation) at a price that may differ from the fair market value of the share at the time the share may be acquired, the taxpayer shall, in respect of each month during which the taxpayer is a party to the agreement, pay a tax under this Part equal to the lesser of
>
> (a) the total of all amounts each of which is the amount, if any, by which
>
> (i) the amount of a dividend paid on the share at a time in the month at which the taxpayer is a party to the agreement
>
> exceeds
>
> (ii) the amount, if any, of the dividend that is received by the taxpayer, and
>
> (b) 1% of the fair market value of the share at the time the agreement is entered into

For agreements entered into before 1993, read:

> 206.1 Where at any time a taxpayer to which this Part applies enters into an agreement (otherwise than as a consequence of the acquisition or writing by it of an option listed on a prescribed stock exchange) to acquire a share of the capital stock of a corporation (otherwise than from the corporation) at a price that may differ from the fair market value thereof at the time the share may be acquired, the taxpayer shall, in respect of each month during which the taxpayer is a party to the agreement, pay a tax under this Part equal to 1% of the fair market value of the share at the time that the agreement is entered into.

206.1 amended by 1991 technical bill, effective for agreements entered into after July 13, 1990, to calculate the penalty tax as 1% of the fair market value of the shares transferred rather than of their stipulated purchase price. This prevents taxpayers from avoiding liability under 206.1 by transferring shares at a nominal acquisition price. 206.1 is intended to prevent tax-exempt entities from temporarily transferring shares to corporations that can receive dividends on a tax-favoured basis.

**Definitions [s. 206.1]**: "amount" — 248(1); "corporation" — 248(1), *Interpretation Act* 35(1); "person", "prescribed" — 248(1); "prescribed stock exchange" — Reg. 3200, 3201; "registered investment" — 204.4(1), 248(1); "share", "taxpayer" — 248(1); "writing" — *Interpretation Act* 35(1).

**Regulations [s. 206.1]**: 3200, 3201 (prescribed stock exchanges, both in Canada and outside Canada).

**I.T. Application Rules [s. 206.1]**: 65(1), (1.1) and (5) (property acquired before July 1972).

**Information Circulars [s. 206.1]**: 77-1R4: Deferred profit sharing plans.

**Forms [s. 206.1]**: T3ATH-IND: Amateur athlete trust income tax return; T3P: Employees' pension plan income tax return; T3RI: Registered investment and income tax return; T2000: Calculation of tax on agreements to acquire shares.

## 207. (1) Return and payment of tax
— Within 90 days after the end of each year after 1971, a taxpayer to whom this Part applies shall

(a) file with the Minister a return for the year under this Part in prescribed form and containing prescribed information, without notice or demand therefor;

(b) estimate in the return the amount of tax, if any, payable by the taxpayer under this Part in respect of each month in the year; and

(c) pay to the Receiver General the amount of tax, if any, payable by the taxpayer under this Part in respect of each month in the year.

**Related Provisions**: 150.1(5) — Electronic filing; 207.1(1) — Tax payable by RRSP.

**Interpretation Bulletins**: IT-320R2: RRSP — qualified investments.

**Information Circulars**: 78-14R2: Guidelines for trust companies and others.

**Forms**: T3D: Income tax return for DPSP or revoked DPSP; T3G: Certification of no tax liability by a group of RRSPs, RRIFs, or RESPs; T3IND: T3IND income tax return for RRSP, RRIF, or RESP; T3P: Employees' pension plan income tax return.

**(2) Liability of trustee** — Where the trustee of a taxpayer that is liable to pay tax under this Part does not remit to the Receiver General the amount of the tax within the time specified in subsection (1), the trustee is personally liable to pay on behalf of the taxpayer the full amount of the tax and is entitled to recover from the taxpayer any amount paid by the trustee as tax under this section.

**(3) Provisions applicable to Part** — Subsections 150(2) and (3), sections 152 and 158, subsections 161(1) and (11), sections 162 to 167 and Division J of Part I are applicable to this Part with such modifications as the circumstances require.

**Definitions [s. 207]**: "amount", "Minister", "prescribed", "taxpayer" — 248(1).

**Information Circulars [s. 207]**: 77-1R4: Deferred profit sharing plans.

# PART XI.1 — TAX IN RESPECT OF CERTAIN PROPERTY HELD BY TRUSTS GOVERNED BY DEFERRED INCOME PLANS

**207.1 (1) Tax payable by trust under registered retirement savings plan [holding non-qualified investment]** — Where, at the end of any month, a trust governed by a registered retirement savings plan holds property that is neither a qualified investment (within the meaning assigned by subsection 146(1)) nor a life insurance policy in respect of which, but for subsection 146(11), subsection 146(10) would have applied as a consequence of its acquisition, the trust shall, in respect of that month, pay a tax under this Part equal to 1% of the fair market value of the property at the time it was acquired by the trust of all such property held by it at the end of the month, other than

(a) property, the fair market value of which was included, by virtue of subsection 146(10), in computing the income, for any year, of an annuitant (within the meaning assigned by subsection 146(1)) under the plan; and

(b) property acquired by the trust before August 25, 1972.

**Related Provisions**: 146(10) — Tax on beneficiary when RRSP acquires non-qualified investment; 146(10.1) — Tax on RRSP's income from non-qualified investment; 205 — Application of Part XI — deferred income plan trust property; 206 — Tax payable;

207.2 — Return and payment of tax; 259(1) — Proportional holdings in trust property.

**Notes**: See Notes to 146(10.1).

**Interpretation Bulletins**: IT-320R2: RRSP — qualified investments.

**(2) Tax payable by trust under deferred profit sharing plan [holding non-qualified investment]** — Where, at the end of any month, a trust governed by a deferred profit sharing plan holds property that is neither a qualified investment (within the meaning assigned by section 204) nor a life insurance policy (referred to in paragraphs 198(6)(c) to (e) or subsection 198(6.1)), the trust shall, in respect of that month, pay a tax under this Part equal to 1% of the fair market value of the property at the time it was acquired by the trust of all such property held by it at the end of the month, other than

(a) property in respect of the acquisition of which the trust has paid or is liable to pay a tax under subsection 198(1); and

(b) property acquired by the trust before August 25, 1972.

**Related Provisions**: 198(1) — Tax on acquisition of non-qualified investment; 205 — Application of Part XI — deferred income plan trust property; 206 — Tax payable; 207.2 — Return and payment of tax; 259(1) — Proportional holdings in trust property.

**(3) Tax payable by trust under registered education savings plan [holding non-qualified investment]** — Every trust governed by a registered education savings plan shall, in respect of any month, pay a tax under this Part equal to 1% of the total of all amounts each of which is the fair market value of a property, at the time it was acquired by the trust, that

(a) is not a qualified investment (as defined in subsection 146.1(1)) for the trust; and

(b) is held by the trust at the end of the month.

**Notes**: 207.1(3) added by 1998 Budget, effective for 1999 and later taxation years. It imposes a 1% monthly penalty tax on non-"qualified investments" (as defined in 146.1(1)) held by a RESP. Note that property that a RESP acquired by October 27, 1998 (the release of the draft legislation) is a qualified investment under para. (d) of the definition.

Holding non-qualified investments can also cause the RESP to be revoked, although Revenue Canada will not normally issue a revocation notice unless there is abuse. See 146.1(2.1) and (12.1).

Former 207.1(3), repealed by 1985 Budget, imposed a similar tax on registered home ownership savings plans. See Notes to 146.2.

**(4) Tax payable by trust under registered retirement income fund [holding non-qualified investment]** — Where, at the end of any month after 1978, a trust governed by a registered retirement income fund holds property that is not a qualified investment (within the meaning assigned by subsection 146.3(1)), the trust shall, in respect of that month, pay a tax under this Part equal to 1% of the fair market value of the property at the time it was acquired by the trust of all such property held by it at the end of the month other than property, the fair market value of which was included by virtue of subsection 146.3(7) in computing the income for any year of an annuitant (within the meaning assigned by subsection 146.3(1)) under the fund.

**Related Provisions**: 146.3(7) — Tax on beneficiary when RRIF acquires non-qualified investment; 146.3(9) — Tax on income from non-qualified investments; 205 — Application of Part XI — deferred income plan trust property; 206 — Tax payable; 207.2 — Return and payment of tax; 259(1) — Proportional holdings in trust property.

**Notes**: See Notes to 146.3(9).

**(5)** [Repealed]

**Notes**: 207.1(5) repealed by 1992 Economic Statement, retroactive to its introduction in 1985. Now deemed never to have been in force, it previously read:

(5) Tax on excessive small business property holdings — Where at the end of any month a trust governed by a registered retirement savings plan or registered retirement income fund holds a prescribed property, the trust shall, in respect of that month, pay a tax under this Part equal to 1% of the amount, if any, by which

(a) the total of the fair market values, at the time of acquisition, of all prescribed properties held by the trust at the end of the month

exceeds

(b) 50% of the total of the fair market values, at the time of acquisition, of all properties held by the trust at the end of the month.

**Related Provisions [s. 207.1]**: 205 — Application of Part XI — deferred income plan trust property; 206 — Tax payable; 207.2 — Return and payment of tax; 259(1) — Proportional holdings in trust property.

**Definitions [s. 207.1]**: "deferred profit sharing plan" — 147(1), 248(1); "life insurance policy" — 138(12), 248(1); "property" — 248(1); "registered education savings plan" — 146.1(1), 248(1); "registered retirement income fund" — 146.3(1), 248(1); "registered retirement savings plan" — 146(1), 248(1); "trust" — 104(1), 248(1), (3).

**Regulations [s. 207.1]**: 4901(1.1) (prescribed property).

**Information Circulars [s. 207.1]**: 77-1R4: Deferred profit sharing plans.

## 207.2 (1) Return and payment of tax — Within 90 days after the end of each year, a taxpayer to whom this Part applies shall

(a) file with the Minister a return for the year under this Part in prescribed form and containing prescribed information, without notice or demand therefor;

(b) estimate in the return the amount of tax, if any, payable by it under this Part in respect of each month in the year; and

(c) pay to the Receiver General the amount of tax, if any, payable by it under this Part in respect of each month in the year.

**Related Provisions**: 150.1(5) — Electronic filing.

**Interpretation Bulletins**: IT-320R2: RRSP — qualified investments.

**Information Circulars**: 78-14R2: Guidelines for trust companies and others.

**Forms**: T3D: Income tax return for DPSP or revoked DPSP; T3G: Certification of no tax liability by a group of RRSPs, RRIFs, or RESPs; T3IND: T3IND income tax return for RRSP, RRIF, or RESP.

**(2) Liability of trustee** — Where the trustee of a trust that is liable to pay tax under this Part does not remit to the Receiver General the amount of the tax within the time specified in subsection (1), the trustee is personally liable to pay on behalf of the trust the full amount of the tax and is entitled to recover from the trust any amount paid by the trustee as tax under this section.

**(3) Provisions applicable to Part** — Subsections 150(2) and (3), sections 152 and 158, subsections 161(1) and (11), sections 162 to 167 and Division J of Part I are applicable to this Part with such modifications as the circumstances require.

**Definitions [s. 207.2]**: "amount", "Minister", "prescribed", "taxpayer" — 248(1); "trust" — 104(1), 248(1), (3).

# PART XI.2 — TAX IN RESPECT OF DISPOSITIONS OF CERTAIN PROPERTIES

## 207.3 Tax payable by institution or public authority — Every institution or public authority that, at any time in a year, disposes of an object within 10 years after the object became an object described in subparagraph 39(1)(a)(i.1) shall pay a tax under this Part, in respect of the year, equal to 30% of the object's fair market value at that time, unless the disposition was made to another institution or public authority that was, at that time, designated under subsection 32(2) of the *Cultural Property Export and Import Act* either generally or for a specified purpose related to that object.

**Related Provisions**: 118.1(7.1) — No tax on deemed disposition upon gift of cultural property.

**Notes**: 207.3 amended to change "5 years" to "10 years" by 1998 Budget, effective for dispositions made after February 23, 1998.

207.3 is designed as an incentive to institutions (such as galleries and museums) to keep cultural property for 10 years, in light of the special tax relief given under 118.1(7.1), whereby accrued gains on the property are not taxed when it is donated to the institution.

207.3 amended by 1991 technical bill, effective December 12, 1988 (the day on which the Revised Statutes of Canada, 1985 came into effect for statutes other than the *Income Tax Act*), to update the cross-references to the *Cultural Property Import and Export Act*.

**Interpretation Bulletins**: IT-407R4: Dispositions of cultural property to designated Canadian institutions.

## 207.31 Tax payable by recipient of an ecological gift — Any charity or municipality that, at any time in a taxation year, without the authorization of the Minister of the Environment, or a person designated by that Minister, disposes or changes the use of a property described in paragraph 110.1(1)(d) or in the definition "total ecological gifts" in subsection 118.1(1) and given to the charity or municipality after February 27, 1995 shall, in respect of the year pay a tax under this Part equal to 50% of the fair

market value of the property at the time of the disposition or change.

### Proposed Amendment — 207.31

**207.31 Tax payable by recipient of an ecological gift** — Any charity or municipality that at any time in a taxation year, without the authorization of the Minister of the Environment or a person designated by that Minister, disposes of or changes the use of a property described in paragraph 110.1(1)(d) or in the definition "total ecological gifts" in subsection 118.1(1) and given to the charity or municipality after February 27, 1995 shall, in respect of the year, pay a tax under this Part equal to 50% of the amount that would be determined for the purposes of section 110.1 or 118.1, if this Act were read without reference to subsections 110.1(3) and 118.1(6), to be the fair market value of the property if the property were given to the charity or municipality immediately before the disposition or change.

**Application**: Bill C-43 (First Reading September 20, 2000), s. 99, will amend s. 207.31 to read as above, applicable in respect of dispositions or changes that occur after November 1999.

**Technical Notes**: Section 207.31 imposes a tax on charities and Canadian municipalities where they dispose of or change the use of property donated to them as an ecological gift without the approval of the Minister of the Environment. The tax is equal to 50% of the fair market value of the property at the time of the disposition or change in use. The section is amended to clarify that the fair market value will be that amount that would be determined at that time for a donor for the purposes of section 110.1 or 118.1, as the case may be.

Amended section 207.3 applies where a charity or municipality disposes of or changes the use of an ecological gift after November 30, 1999.

**Related Provisions**: 110.1(5), 118.1(12) — Fair market value of ecological servitude, covenant or easement; 118.1(10.1)–(10.5) — Determination of fair market value by Minister of the Environment; 207.4(1) — Return and payment of tax.

**Notes**: 207.31 added by 1995 Budget, effective February 28, 1995. See Notes to 118.1(1) "total ecological gifts".

**Definitions [s. 207.31]**: "fair market value" — 110.1(5); "property" — 248(1); "taxation year" — 249.

**207.4 (1) Return and payment of tax** — Any institution, public authority, charity or municipality that is liable to pay a tax under subsection 207.3 or 207.31 in respect of a year shall, within 90 days after the end of the year,

(a) file with the Minister a return for the year under this Part in prescribed form and containing prescribed information without notice or demand therefor;

(b) estimate in the return the amount of tax payable by it under this Part in respect of the year; and

(c) pay to the Receiver General the amount of tax payable by it under this Part in respect of the year.

**Related Provisions**: 150.1(5) — Electronic filing.

**Notes**: 207.4(1) amended by 1995 Budget, effective February 28, 1995, to add "charity or municipality" and reference to 207.31.

**Forms**: T913: Part XI.2 tax return — tax for the disposition of certain properties.

**(2) Provisions applicable to Part** — Subsections 150(2) and (3), sections 152 and 158, subsections 161(1) and (11), sections 162 to 167 and Division J of Part I are applicable to this Part with such modifications as the circumstances require.

**Definitions [s. 207.4]**: "Minister", "prescribed" — 248(1).

## PART XI.3 — TAX IN RESPECT OF RETIREMENT COMPENSATION ARRANGEMENTS

**207.5 (1) Definitions** — In this Part,

**"RCA trust"** under a retirement compensation arrangement means

(a) any trust deemed by subsection 207.6(1) to be created in respect of subject property of the arrangement, and

(b) any trust governed by the arrangement;

**"refundable tax"** of a retirement compensation arrangement at the end of a taxation year of an RCA trust under the arrangement means the amount, if any, by which the total of

(a) 50% of all contributions made under the arrangement while it was a retirement compensation arrangement and before the end of the year, and

(b) 50% of the amount, if any, by which

(i) the total of all amounts each of which is the income (determined as if this Act were read without reference to paragraph 82(1)(b)) of an RCA trust under the arrangement from a business or property for the year or a preceding taxation year or a capital gain of the trust for the year or a preceding taxation year,

exceeds

(ii) the total of all amounts each of which is a loss of an RCA trust under the arrangement from a business or property for the year or a preceding taxation year or a capital loss of the trust for the year or a preceding taxation year,

exceeds

(c) 50% of all amounts paid as distributions to one or more persons (including amounts that are required by paragraph 12(1)(n.3) to be included in computing the recipient's income) under the arrangement while it was a retirement compensation arrangement and before the end of the year, other than a distribution paid where it is established, by subsequent events or otherwise, that the distribution was paid as part of a series of payments and refunds of contributions under the arrangement;

**Related Provisions**: 207.5(2) — Deemed refundable tax on election; 207.6(7)(c) — Where amount transferred from one RCA to another. See additional Related Provisions and Definitions at end of Part XI.3.

**"subject property of a retirement compensation arrangement"** means property that is held in connection with the arrangement.

**(2) Election** — Notwithstanding the definition "refundable tax" in subsection (1), where the custodian of a retirement compensation arrangement so elects in the return under this Part for a taxation year of an RCA trust under the arrangement and all the subject property, if any, of the arrangement (other than a right to claim a refund under subsection 164(1) or 207.7(2)) at the end of the year consists only of cash, debt obligations, shares listed on a prescribed stock exchange, or any combination thereof, an amount equal to the total of

(a) the amount of that cash at the end of the year,

(b) the total of all amounts each of which is the greater of the principal amount of such a debt obligation outstanding at the end of the year and the fair market value of the obligation at the end of the year, and

(c) the fair market value of those shares at the end of the year

shall be deemed for the purposes of this Part to be the refundable tax of the arrangement at the end of the year.

**Related Provisions [s. 207.5]**: See Related Provisions at end of Part XI.3.

**Definitions [s. 207.5]**: "amount" — 248(1); "capital gain", "capital loss" — 39(1), 248(1); "person", "prescribed" — 248(1); "prescribed stock exchange" — Reg. 3200, 3201; "property" — 248(1); "RCA trust", "refundable tax" — 207.5(1); "retirement compensation arrangement" — 248(1); "series of transactions" — 248(10); "share" — 248(1); "subject property" — 207.5(1); "taxation year" — 249; "trust" — 104(1), 248(1), (3).

**Regulations [s. 207.5]**: 3200, 3201 (prescribed stock exchanges).

**Forms [s. 207.5]**: T735: Application for a remittance number for tax withheld from an RCA.

**207.6 (1) Creation of trust** — In respect of the subject property of a retirement compensation arrangement, other than subject property of the arrangement held by a trust governed by a retirement compensation arrangement, for the purposes of this Part and Part I, the following rules apply:

(a) an *inter vivos* trust is deemed to be created on the day that the arrangement is established;

(b) the subject property of the arrangement is deemed to be property of the trust and not to be property of any other person; and

(c) the custodian of the arrangement is deemed to be the trustee having ownership or control of the trust property.

**Related Provisions**: 207.6(7) — Transfer from RCA to another RCA. See also Related Provisions and Definitions at end of Part XI.3.

**Forms**: T4041: Retirement compensation arrangements guide.

**(2) Life insurance policies** — For the purposes of this Part and Part I, where by virtue of a plan or arrangement an employer is obliged to provide benefits that are to be received or enjoyed by any person on, after or in contemplation of any substantial change in the services rendered by a taxpayer, the retirement of a taxpayer or the loss of an office or employment of a taxpayer, and where the employer, former employer or a person or partnership with whom the employer or former employer does not deal at arm's length acquires an interest in a life insurance policy that may reasonably be considered to be acquired to fund, in whole or in part, those benefits, the following rules apply in respect of the plan or arrangement if it is not otherwise a retirement compensation arrangement and is not excluded from the definition "retirement compensation arrangement", in subsection 248(1), by any of paragraphs (a) to (l) and (n) thereof:

(a) the person or partnership that acquired the interest is deemed to be the custodian of a retirement compensation arrangement;

(b) the interest is deemed to be subject property of the retirement compensation arrangement;

(c) an amount equal to twice the amount of any premium paid in respect of the interest or any repayment of a policy loan thereunder is deemed to be a contribution under the retirement compensation arrangement; and

(d) any payment received in respect of the interest, including a policy loan, and any amount received as a refund of refundable tax is deemed to be an amount received out of or under the retirement compensation arrangement by the recipient and not to be a payment of any other amount.

**(3) Incorporated employee** — For the purpose of the provisions of this Act relating to retirement compensation arrangements, where

(a) a corporation that at any time carried on a personal services business, or an employee of the corporation, enters into a plan or arrangement with a person or partnership (referred to in this subsection as the "employer") to whom or which the corporation renders services, and

(b) the plan or arrangement provides for benefits to be received or enjoyed by any person on, after or in contemplation of the cessation of, or any substantial change in, the services rendered by the corporation, or an employee of the corporation, to the employer,

the following rules apply:

(c) the employer and the corporation are deemed to be an employer and employee, respectively, in relation to each other, and

(d) any benefits to be received or enjoyed by any person under the plan or arrangement are deemed to be benefits to be received or enjoyed by the person on, after or in contemplation of a substantial change in the services rendered by the corporation.

**Related Provisions**: 18(1)(p) — Limitation on deductions re incorporated employees. See additional Related Provisions and Definitions at end of Part XI.3.

**(4) Deemed contribution** — Where at any time an employee benefit plan becomes a retirement compensation arrangement as a consequence of a change of the custodian of the plan or as a consequence of the custodian ceasing either to carry on business through a fixed place of business in Canada or to be licensed or otherwise authorized under the laws of Canada or a province to carry on in Canada the business of offering to the public its services as trustee,

(a) for the purposes of this Part and Part I, the custodian of the plan is deemed to have made a contribution to the arrangement immediately after that time, in an amount equal to the fair market value at that time of all the properties of the plan; and

(b) for the purposes of section 32.1, that amount is deemed to be a payment made at that time out of or under the plan to or for the benefit of employees or former employees of the employers who contributed to the plan.

**Related Provisions**: See Related Provisions and Defintions at end of Part XI.3.

**(5) Resident's arrangement** — For the purposes of this Act, where a resident's contribution has been made under a plan or arrangement (in this subsection referred to as the "plan"),

(a) the plan is deemed, in respect of its application to all resident's contributions made under the plan and all property that can reasonably be considered to be derived from those contributions, to be a separate arrangement (in this subsection referred to as the "residents' arrangement") independent of the plan in respect of its application to all other contributions and property that can reasonably be considered to derive from those other contributions;

(b) the residents' arrangement is deemed to be a retirement compensation arrangement; and

(c) each person and partnership to whom a contribution is made under the residents' arrangement is deemed to be a custodian of the residents' arrangement.

**Related Provisions**: 207.6(5.1) — Resident's contribution; 252.1 — Where union is employer. See additional Related Provisions and Definitions at end of Part XI.3.

**Notes**: 207.6(5) amended by 1993 technical bill, retroactive to October 9, 1986 (i.e., to the introduction of Part XI.3). The change replaces the description of the contributions to which the subsec. applies with "resident's contribution", now defined in 207.6(5.1). The amendments change the conditions for determining which contributions made to a foreign plan are subject to the rules in 207.6(5).

As well, 207.6(5) was amended to clarify that only one RCA is considered to exist in respect of a foreign plan, regardless of the number of Canadian resident employees who participate in the plan and the number of contributions made to the plan in respect of those employees. This is relevant for compliance with the administrative requirements for RCAs.

**Regulations**: 6804(4)–(6) (prescribed contribution).

**(5.1) Resident's contribution** — For the purpose of subsection (5), "resident's contribution" means such part of a contribution made under a plan or arrangement (in this subsection referred to as the "plan") at a time when the plan would, but for paragraph (l) of the definition "retirement compensation arrangement" in subsection 248(1), be a retirement compensation arrangement as

(a) is not a prescribed contribution; and

(b) can reasonably be considered to have been made in respect of services rendered by an individual to an employer in a period

(i) throughout which the individual was resident in Canada and rendered services to the employer that were primarily services rendered in Canada or services rendered in connection with a business carried on by the employer in Canada (or a combination of such services), and

(ii) at the beginning of which the individual had been resident in Canada throughout at least 60 of the 72 preceding calendar months, where the individual was non-resident at any time before the period and became a member of the plan before the end of the month after the month in which the individual became resident in Canada,

and, for the purpose of this paragraph, where benefits provided to an individual under a particular plan or arrangement are replaced by benefits under another plan or arrangement, the other plan or arrangement shall be deemed, in respect of the individual, to be the same plan or arrangement as the particular plan or arrangement.

**Related Provisions**: 252.1 — Where union is employer.

**Notes**: 207.6(5.1) added by 1993 technical bill, retroactive to October 9, 1986 (i.e., to the introduction of Part XI.3). See Notes to 207.6(5).

**Regulations**: 6804(4)–(6) (prescribed contribution).

**(6) Prescribed plan or arrangement** — For the purposes of the provisions of this Act relating to retirement compensation arrangements, the following rules apply in respect of a prescribed plan or arrangement:

(a) the plan or arrangement shall be deemed to be a retirement compensation arrangement;

(b) an amount credited at any time to the account established in the accounts of Canada or a province in connection with the plan or arrangement shall be, except to the extent that it is in respect of a refund determined under subsection

207.7(2), deemed to be a contribution under the plan or arrangement at that time;

(c) the custodian of the plan or arrangement shall be deemed to be

(i) where the account is established in the accounts of Canada, Her Majesty in right of Canada, and

(ii) where the account is established in the accounts of a province, Her Majesty in right of that province; and

(d) the subject property of the plan or arrangement, at any time, shall be deemed to include an amount of cash equal to the balance at that time in the account.

**Related Provisions**: See Related Provisions and Definitions at end of Part XI.3.

**Notes**: 207.6(6) added by 1992 technical bill, effective 1992.

**Regulations**: 103(7)(a)(ii) (no withholding on transfer under 207.6(6)); 6802 (prescribed plan or arrangement).

**(7) Transfers** — Where an amount (other than an amount that is part of a series of periodic payments) is transferred directly to a retirement compensation arrangement (other than an arrangement the custodian of which is non-resident or which is deemed by subsection (5) to be a retirement compensation arrangement) from another retirement compensation arrangement,

(a) the amount shall not, solely because of the transfer, be included in computing a taxpayer's income under Part I;

(b) no deduction may be made in respect of the amount in computing a taxpayer's income under Part I; and

(c) the amount is considered, for the purpose of the definition "refundable tax" in subsection 207.5(1), to be paid as a distribution to one or more persons under the arrangement from which the amount is transferred and to be a contribution made under the arrangement to which the amount is transferred.

**Related Provisions**: 60(t)(ii)(A), (A.1), (E), 60(u)(ii)(A), (A.1), (E) — Whether amounts transferred under 207.6(7) deductible; 212(1)(j) — Transfer not subject to non-resident withholding tax.

**Notes**: 207.6(7) added by 1995-97 technical bill, effective for amounts transferred after 1995. It provides for the transfer of amounts between RCAs on a tax-neutral basis. It achieves this by providing that there is no inclusion in or deduction from income of any taxpayer where a lump sum amount is transferred directly from one RCA (the "transferor plan") to another RCA (the "transferee plan").

This means that, where the transfer constitutes a payment out of the transferor plan to an employer or an individual, there is no requirement for the employer or the individual to include the payment in income under 12(1)(n.3) or 56(1)(x) or (z). Also, the individual is denied a deduction under 60(t), although consequential amendments to 60(t) and (u) allow for the deduction when payments are ultimately received out of the transferee plan.

Similarly, where such a transfer constitutes a contribution to the transferee plan by an individual or an employee, 207.6(7) denies any deduction that might otherwise be available under 8(1)(m.2) or 20(1)(r).

207.6(7) also clarifies that, for purposes of the 50% refundable RCA tax under Part XI.3, an amount transferred under that 207.6(7) is considered to be a distribution from the transferor plan and a contribution to the transferee plan. This ensures that the obligation for the tax is transferred from the transferor plan to the transferee plan.

Reg. 103(7)(a) provides that, where an amount is transferred under 207.6(7), there is no withholding on the amount when it is paid out of the transferor plan or when it is paid into the transferee plan.

Under its opening words, 207.6(5) does not apply where the transferee plan has a non-resident custodian or is a foreign plan deemed by 207.6(5) to be an RCA in respect of Canadian residents participating in the plan.

**Regulations**: 103(7)(a)(iii) (no withholding on transfer under 207.6(7)); 6802.1(2) (prescribed plans and arrangements).

**Definitions [s. 207.6]**: "amount" — 248(1); "arm's length" — 251(1); "business" — 248(1); "Canada" — 255; "carrying on business" — 253; "corporation" — 248(1), *Interpretation Act* 35(1); "employee", "employee benefit plan", "employer", "employment", "individual" — 248(1); *inter vivos* trust" — 108(1), 248(1); "life insurance policy" — 138(12), 248(1); "non-resident", "office", "person", "prescribed" — 248(1); "prescribed plan or arrangement" — Reg. 6801, 6802, 6802.1, 6803; "property" — 248(1); "province" — *Interpretation Act* 35(1); "refundable tax" — 207.5(1); "resident in Canada" — 250; "residents' arrangement" — 207.6(5)(b); "resident's contribution" — 207.6(5.1); "retirement compensation arrangement" — 248(1); "subject property" — 207.5(1); "taxpayer" — 248(1); "trust" — 104(1), 248(1), (3).

**Forms [s. 207.6]**: T733: Application for an RCA account number.

**207.7 (1) Tax payable** — Every custodian of a retirement compensation arrangement shall pay a tax under this Part for each taxation year of an RCA trust under the arrangement equal to the amount, if any, by which the refundable tax of the arrangement at the end of the year exceeds the refundable tax of the arrangement at the end of the immediately preceding taxation year, if any.

**Related Provisions**: See Related Provisions and Definitions at end of Part XI.3.

**Forms**: T4041: Retirement compensation arrangements guide.

**(2) Refund** — Where the custodian of a retirement compensation arrangement has filed a return under this Part for a taxation year within three years after the end of the year, the Minister

(a) may, on mailing the notice of assessment for the year or a notification that no tax is payable for the year, refund without application therefor an amount equal to the amount, if any, by which the refundable tax of the arrangement at the end of the immediately preceding year exceeds the refundable tax of the arrangement at the end of the year; and

(b) shall, with all due dispatch, make such a refund after mailing the notice of assessment if application therefor has been made in writing by the custodian within three years after the day of mailing of a notice of an original assessment for the year or of a notification that no tax is payable for the year.

**Related Provisions:** 207.6(6) — Prescribed plan or arrangement. See additional Related Provisions and Definitions at end of Part XI.3.

**(3) Payment of tax** — Every custodian of a retirement compensation arrangement shall, within 90 days after the end of each taxation year of an RCA trust under the arrangement,

   (a) file with the Minister a return for the year under this Part in prescribed form and containing prescribed information, without notice or demand therefor;

   (b) estimate in the return the amount of tax, if any, payable by the custodian under this Part for the year; and

   (c) pay to the Receiver General the amount of tax, if any, payable by the custodian under this Part for the year.

**Related Provisions:** 147.1(3) — Postponement of filing deadline where RCA is registered as pension plan; 150.1(5) — Electronic filing; 248(7) — Return deemed received on day mailed. See additional Related Provisions at end of Part XI.3.

**(4) Provisions applicable to Part** — Subsections 150(2) and (3), sections 152 and 158, subsections 161(1) and (11), sections 162 to 167 and Division J of Part I are applicable to this Part with such modifications as the circumstances require.

**Definitions [s. 207.7]:** "amount", "assessment", "Minister", "prescribed" — 248(1); "RCA trust", "refundable tax" — 207.5(1); "retirement compensation arrangement" — 248(1); "tax payable" — 248(2); "taxation year" — 249; "trust" — 104(1), 248(1), (3); "writing" — *Interpretation Act* 35(1).

**Forms [s. 207.7]:** T3-RCA: Part XI.3 tax return; T4A-RCA Summ: Return of distributions from an RCA; T735: Application for a remittance number for tax withheld from an RCA; T737-RCA: Statement of contributions paid to a custodian of an RCA.

**Related Provisions [Part XI.3]:** 8(1)(m.2) — Deduction for employee RCA contributions; 87(2)(j.3) — Amalgamations — continuation of corporation; 107.2 — Distribution by RCA to beneficiary; 149(1)(q.1) — RCA trust exempt from Part I tax; 153(1)(p)–(r) — Withholding of tax at source on contribution to RCA, distribution out of RCA, and purchase of interest in RCA; 160.3 — Joint and several liability — RCA benefits; 227(8.2) — Liability for failure to withhold.

# PART XII — TAX IN RESPECT OF CERTAIN ROYALTIES, TAXES, LEASE RENTALS, ETC., PAID TO A GOVERNMENT BY A TAX EXEMPT PERSON

**208. (1) Tax payable by exempt person** — Where in a taxation year an amount (other than an amount to which paragraph 18(1)(l.1) or (m) applies) was paid, payable, distributed or distributable in any manner whatever by a person (other than a prescribed person) who was exempt from tax under Part I on that person's taxable income to anyone in respect of any production from a Canadian resource property of the person of petroleum, natural gas or other related hydrocarbons or of metals or minerals to any stage that is not beyond the specified stage or in respect of any revenue or income that may reasonably be regarded as attributable to that production, the person shall, in respect of the year, pay a tax under this Part equal to $33^1/_3$% of the lesser of

   (a) the total of all amounts in respect of the property, each of which is

      (i) an amount that became receivable in the year and that was required by paragraph 12(1)(o) to be included in computing the person's income for the year,

      (ii) an amount that was paid or became payable by the person in the year and that by virtue of paragraph 18(1)(l.1) or (m) was not deductible in computing the person's income for the year,

      (iii) an amount by which the person's proceeds of disposition were increased by virtue of subsection 69(6) in the year, or

      (iv) an amount by which the person's cost of acquisition was decreased by virtue of subsection 69(7) in the year, and

   (b) the proportion of the amount determined under paragraph (a) that

      (i) the total of all amounts each of which is an amount (other than an amount to which paragraph 18(1)(l.1) or (m) applies) that was paid, payable, distributed or distributable by the person in the year in any manner whatever to

         (A) another person (other than a person whose taxable income is exempt from tax under Part I), or

         (B) another person whose taxable income is exempt from tax under Part I, where the amount was paid, payable, distributed or distributable as part of a transaction or event or series of transactions or events to which any person whose taxable income is not exempt from tax under Part I was a party

in respect of any production from the property of petroleum, natural gas or other related hydrocarbons or of metals or minerals to any stage that is not beyond the specified stage or in respect of any revenue or income that can reasonably be regarded as attributable to that production

is of

      (ii) the amount, if any, by which the total of

         (A) the income of the person from the property for the year from the production of petroleum, natural gas or other related hydrocarbons or of metals or minerals to any stage that is not beyond the specified stage, computed in accordance with Part I on the assumption that the property was the person's only source of income and that the person was allowed only those deductions in computing income from the property (other than a deduction under paragraph 20(1)(v.1) or section 65) that may reasonably be regarded as applicable to that income from the property, and

    (B) the amount determined under subparagraph (i)

exceeds

    (C) the amount determined under paragraph (a).

**Related Provisions**: 208(1.1) — Meaning of "specified stage"; 248(10) — Series of transactions.

**Notes**: 208(1)(b)(i)(A) and (B) added in place of the word "anyone" by 1991 technical bill, effective 1988, so as to narrow the scope of 208 to target the abuse at which it was aimed.

**Regulations**: 1216 (prescribed person).

**(1.1) Definition of "specified stage"** — For the purpose of subsection (1), "specified stage" means, in respect of the production from a Canadian resource property of a substance,

(a) where the substance is petroleum or related hydrocarbons (other than natural gas), the crude oil stage or its equivalent;

(b) where the substance is natural gas, the stage of natural gas that is acceptable to a common carrier of natural gas;

(c) where the substance is a metal or mineral (other than iron, sulphur or petroleum or related hydrocarbons), the prime metal stage or its equivalent;

(d) where the substance is iron, the pellet stage or its equivalent; and

(e) where the substance is sulphur, the marketable sulphur stage.

**Notes**: 208(1.1) amended by 1996 Budget, effective for taxation years that begin in 1997 or later. For earlier years, read:

  (1.1) For the purpose of subsection (1), "specified stage" means, in respect of the production from a Canadian resource property

    (a) where the production is petroleum, natural gas or related hydrocarbons from an oil or gas well or a mineral resource, the crude oil stage or its equivalent;

    (b) where the production is metal or minerals (other than iron or petroleum or related hydrocarbons) from a mineral resource, the prime metal stage or its equivalent; and

    (c) where the production is iron from a mineral resource, the pellet stage or its equivalent.

The amended version makes explicit reference to the production of sulphur, which is a mineral. In the case of sulphur, the specified stage is the marketable sulphur stage. This amendment is consequential on amendments to 12(1)(o) and 18(1)(m) denying the deductibility of sulphur Crown royalties.

**(2) Return and payment of tax** — A person liable to pay a tax under this Part in respect of a year shall, within 3 months from the end of the year,

(a) file with the Minister a return for the year under this Part in prescribed form and containing prescribed information, without notice or demand therefor;

(b) estimate in the return the amount of tax payable by the person under this Part in respect of the year; and

(c) pay to the Receiver General the tax payable by the person under this Part for the year.

**Related Provisions**: 150.1(5) — Electronic filing.

**Forms**: T2026: Part XII tax return — tax on payments to the Crown by a tax exempt person.

**(3) Liability of trustee** — Where a trustee of a trust liable to pay tax under subsection (1) does not pay to the Receiver General the amount of the tax within the time specified in subsection (2), the trustee is personally liable to pay on behalf of the trust the full amount of the tax and is entitled to recover from the trust any amount paid by the trustee as tax under this section.

**(4) Provisions applicable to Part** — Subsections 150(2) and (3), sections 152 and 158, subsections 161(1) and (11), sections 162 to 167 and Division J of Part I are applicable to this Part with such modifications as the circumstances require.

**Definitions [s. 208]**: "amount" — 248(1); "Canadian resource property" — 66(15), 248(1); "mineral resource", "mineral", "Minister", "person", "prescribed", "property" — 248(1); "series of transactions" — 248(10); "specified stage" — 208(1.1); "tar sands" — 248(1); "taxable income" — 2(2), 248(1); "taxation year" — 249; "trust" — 248(1), (3).

**Notes [Part XII]**: Part XII introduced by 1979 Budget.

An earlier Part XII (208, 209), which imposed a tax on the investment income of life insurers, was repealed in 1977. However, it was re-enacted as Part XII.3 (211–211.5), introduced in 1988.

# PART XII.1 — TAX ON CARVED-OUT INCOME

**209. (1) Definitions** — For the purposes of this Part,

**"carved-out income"** of a person for a taxation year from a carved-out property means the amount, if any, by which

(a) the person's income for the year attributable to the property computed under Part I on the assumption that in computing that income no deduction was allowed under section 20 (other than a deduction under paragraph 20(1)(v.1)), subdivision e of Division B of Part I or section 104,

exceeds the total of

(b) the amount deducted under subsection 66.4(2) in computing the person's income for the year to the extent that it may reasonably be considered to be attributable to the property, and

(c) to the extent that the property is an interest in a bituminous sands deposit or oil shale deposit, the amount deducted under subsection 66.2(2) in computing the person's income for the year to the

**S. 209(1) car** — Income Tax Act

extent that it can reasonably be considered to be attributable to the cost of that interest;

**Related Provisions**: 66(14.6) — Deduction of carved-out income; 209(6) — Partnerships.

**Notes**: Definition amended by 1996 Budget, effective March 7, 1996, to delete the words "oil sands deposit" after "bituminous sands deposit". The change is consequential on the introduction of the definition "bituminous sands" in 248(1).

**"carved-out property"** of a person means

(a) a Canadian resource property where

(i) all or substantially all of the amount that the person is or may become entitled to receive in respect of the property may reasonably be considered to be limited to a maximum amount or to an amount determinable by reference to a stated quantity of production from a mineral resource or an accumulation of petroleum, natural gas or related hydrocarbons,

(ii) the period of time during which the person's interest in the income attributable to the property may reasonably be expected to continue is

(A) where the property is a head lease or may reasonably be considered to derive from a head lease, less than the lesser of 10 years and the remainder of the term of the head lease, and

(B) in any other case, less than 10 years,

(iii) the person's interest in the income attributable to the property, expressed as a percentage of production for any period, may reasonably be expected to be reduced substantially,

(A) where the property is a head lease or may reasonably be considered to derive from a head lease, at any time before

(I) the expiration of a period of 10 years commencing when the property was acquired, or

(II) the expiration of the term of the head lease,

whichever occurs first, and

(B) in any other case, at any time before the expiration of a period of 10 years commencing when the property was acquired, or

(iv) another person has a right under an arrangement to acquire, at any time, the property or a portion thereof or a similar property from the person and it is reasonable to consider that one of the main reasons for the arrangement, or any series of transactions or events that includes the arrangement, was to reduce or postpone tax that would, but for this subparagraph, be payable under this Part, or

(b) an interest in a partnership or trust that holds a Canadian resource property where it is reasonable to consider that one of the main reasons for the existence of the interest is to reduce or postpone the tax that would, but for this paragraph, be payable under this Part,

but does not include

(c) an interest in respect of a property that was acquired by the person solely in consideration of the person's undertaking under an agreement to incur Canadian exploration expense or Canadian development expense in respect of the property and, where the agreement so provides, to acquire gas or oil well equipment (as defined in subsection 1104(2) of the *Income Tax Regulations*) in respect of the property,

(c.1) an interest in respect of a property that was retained by the person under an agreement under which another person obtained an absolute or conditional right to acquire another interest in respect of the property, if the other interest is not carved-out property of the other person because of paragraph (c),

(d) a particular property acquired by the person under an arrangement solely as consideration for the sale of a Canadian resource property (other than a property that, immediately before the sale was a carved-out property of the person) that relates to the particular property except where it is reasonable to consider that one of the main reasons for the arrangement, or any series of transactions or events that includes the arrangement, was to reduce or postpone tax that would, but for this paragraph, be payable under this Act,

(e) a property retained or reserved by the person out of a Canadian resource property (other than a property that, immediately before the transaction by which the retention or reservation is made, was a carved-out property of the person) that was disposed of by the person except where it is reasonable to consider that one of the main reasons for the retention or reservation, or any series of transactions or events in which the property or interest was retained or reserved, was to reduce or postpone tax that would, but for this paragraph, be payable under this Act,

(f) a property acquired by the person from a taxpayer with whom the person did not deal at arm's length at the time of the acquisition and the property was acquired by the taxpayer or a person with whom the taxpayer did not deal at arm's length

(i) pursuant to an agreement in writing to do so entered into before July 20, 1985, or

(ii) under the circumstances described in this paragraph or paragraph (d) or (e),

except where it is reasonable to consider that one of the main reasons for the acquisition of the property, or any series of transactions or events in which the property was acquired, was to reduce or postpone tax that would, but for this paragraph, be payable under this Act, (f.1) where the taxable income of the person is exempt from tax under Part I, a property of the person that

(i) does not relate to property of a person whose taxable income is not exempt from tax under Part I, and

(ii) is not, and does not relate to, property that was at any time a carved-out property of any other person, or

(g) a prescribed property;

**Related Provisions**: 209(6) — Partnerships.

**Notes**: The CCRA takes the position that "all or substantially all", used in para. (a)(i), means 90% or more.

Para. (c) amended by 1991 technical bill, effective for property acquired after July 19, 1985 (the introduction of Part XII.1), to add everything from "and, where the agreement so provides".

Para. (c.1) added by 1991 technical bill, effective for property acquired after July 19, 1985.

Para. (f.1) added by 1991 technical bill, effective for property acquired after 1987.

**Regulations**: 7600 (prescribed property).

**"head lease"** means a contract under which

(a) Her Majesty in right of Canada or a province grants, or

(b) an owner in fee simple, other than Her Majesty in right of Canada or a province, grants for a period of not less than 10 years

any right, licence or privilege to explore for, drill for or take petroleum, natural gas or related hydrocarbons in Canada or to prospect, explore, drill or mine for minerals in a mineral resource in Canada;

**"term"** of a head lease includes all renewal periods in respect of the head lease.

**(2) Tax** — Every person shall pay a tax under this Part for each taxation year equal to 45% of the total of the person's carved-out incomes for the year from carved-out properties.

**Related Provisions**: 18(1)(t) — Tax is non-deductible; 66(14.6) — Deduction of carved-out income.

**Notes**: Tax rate in 209(2) changed from 50% to 45% by 1993 technical bill, effective for 1992 and later taxation years. This rate more closely approximates the combined federal/provincial corporate tax rate (see the table of rates in the introductory pages).

**(3) Return** — Every person liable to pay tax under this Part for a taxation year shall file with the Minister, not later than the day on or before which the person is or would be, if the person were liable to pay tax under Part I for the year, required under section 150 to file a return of the person's income for the year under Part I, a return for the year under this Part in prescribed form containing an estimate of the amount of tax payable by the person under this Part for the year.

**Related Provisions**: 150.1(5) — Electronic filing.

**Forms**: T2096: Part XII.1 tax return — tax on carved-out income.

**(4) Payment of tax** — Where a person is liable to pay tax for a taxation year under this Part, the person shall pay in respect of the year, to the Receiver General

(a) on or before the last day of each month in the year, an amount equal to 1/12 of the amount of tax payable by the person under this Part for the year; and

(b) the remainder, if any, of the tax payable by the person under this Part for the year, on or before the end of the second month following the end of the year.

**(5) Provisions applicable to Part** — Subsections 150(2) and (3) and sections 152, 158 and 159, subsections 161(1), (2) and (11), sections 162 to 167 and Division J of Part I are applicable to this Part with such modifications as the circumstances require.

**(6) Partnerships** — For the purposes of subsection (1), a partnership shall be deemed to be a person and its taxation year shall be deemed to be its fiscal period.

**Definitions [s. 209]**: "amount" — 248(1); "arm's length" — 251(1); "bituminous sands" — 248(1); "Canada" — 255; "Canadian development expense" — 66.2(5), 248(1); "Canadian exploration expense" — 66.1(6), 248(1); "Canadian resource property" — 66(15), 248(1); "carved-out income", "carved-out property" — 209(1); "fiscal period" — 249(2)(b), 249.1; "head lease" — 209(1); "mineral resource", "mineral", "Minister" — 248(1); "partnership" — see Notes to 96(1); "person" — 209(6), 248(1); "prescribed", "property" — 248(1); "province" — *Interpretation Act* 35(1); "series of transactions" — 248(10); "tax payable" — 248(2); "taxable income" — 2(2), 248(1); "taxation year" — 209(6), 249; "taxpayer" — 248(1); "term" — 209(1); "trust" — 104(1), 248(1), (3); "writing" — *Interpretation Act* 35(1).

## PART XII.2 — TAX ON DESIGNATED INCOME OF CERTAIN TRUSTS

**210. Designated beneficiary** — In this Part, a "designated beneficiary" under a trust at any time means a beneficiary under the trust that was, at that time,

(a) a non-resident person;

(b) a non-resident-owned investment corporation;

(c) a person exempt from tax under Part I by reason of subsection 149(1), where that person acquired an interest in the trust after October 1, 1987 directly or indirectly from a beneficiary under the trust except

(i) where the interest was owned continuously since October 1, 1987 or the date on which the interest was created, whichever is later, by persons exempt from tax under Part I by reason of subsection 149(1), or

(ii) where the person was a trust governed by

(A) a registered retirement savings plan, or

(B) a registered retirement income fund,

and acquired the interest, directly or indirectly, from an individual or the spouse or common-law partner or former spouse or common-law partner of the individual who was, immediately after the interest was acquired, a beneficiary under the trust governed by the fund or plan;

(d) a trust resident in Canada (other than a testamentary trust, a mutual fund trust or a trust exempt, because of subsection 149(1), from tax under Part I on all or part of its taxable income), if

(i) a person described in paragraph (a), (b) or (c),

(ii) a partnership described in paragraph (e), or

(iii) a trust (other than a trust resident in Canada that is a testamentary trust)

is, at that time, a beneficiary thereunder; or

(e) a partnership, if a person described in paragraph (a), (b) or (d), a partnership or a person exempt from tax under Part I by reason of subsection 149(1) is, at that time, a member thereof.

**Proposed Amendment — 210**

**Letter from Department of Finance, December 9, 1999:**

Dear [xxx]

Thank you for your letter of October 20, 1999 concerning the definition "designated beneficiary" in section 210 of the *Income Tax Act*. I apologize for the delay in responding to you.

I am attaching a copy of our earlier letter to you of September 3, 1996 in which we agree to recommend changes to the definition "designated beneficiary" so that Part XII.2 tax is not exigible in the circumstances of certain kinds of "tiering" arrangements involving trusts (such as, for example, those arrangements described in your letters of October 20, 1999 and June 10, 1996). It continues to be our intention to recommend inclusion of this amendment in a future technical bill.

Thank you for writing.

Yours sincerely,

Brian Ernewein
Director, Tax Legislation Division, Tax Policy Branch

**Letter from Department of Finance, September 3, 1996:**

Dear [xxx]

This is in reply to your letter of June 10, 1996 to Simon Thompson regarding a suggested change to the definition of "designated beneficiary" in section 210 of the *Income Tax Act*.

Your letter contemplates a structure involving a number of different trusts resident in Canada. Under this structure, registered pension plans and other investors resident in Canada will invest in trust units issued by one unit trust (the "top fund"). The top fund will invest in units issued by other unit trusts (the "bottom funds"). You have asked that section 210 of the Act be amended so the top fund will *not* be a "designated beneficiary" of the bottom funds as a consequence of the top fund having beneficiaries (i.e., registered pension plans) which are exempt from tax under Part I of the Act.

We agree that one of the objectives of Part XII.2 tax is to prevent the minimization of tax on specified Canadian-source income that would otherwise arise where a Canadian trust's income is distributed to a non-resident and is subject only to Part XIII tax. However, Part XII.2 tax is also meant to discourage transactions between taxable and tax-exempt beneficiaries designed to allow "lumpy" taxable income earned by a trust to be flowed-through to tax-exempt beneficiaries after the acquisition of a trust unit by the tax-exempt beneficiary from the taxable beneficiaries.

In view of the second objective of Part XII.2 tax, described above, it would be difficult to recommend the amendment referred to above by itself. However, I understand that you have discussed this matter with one of my staff and are amenable to an additional amendment in this context. The additional amendment would, in effect, provide that the top fund would be a "designated beneficiary" under a bottom fund if it acquired an interest in the bottom fund directly or indirectly from a beneficiary under the bottom fund (except where the interest was owned, at each time after the date on which the bottom fund was created, by the top fund or a person exempt from tax under Part I of the Act because of subsection 149(1) of the Act). The combination of the two amendments would meet the both of the policy objectives. I am prepared to recommend that these amendments be introduced in a future technical bill and be effective from a date that will accommodate the planned structure described in your letter.

Thank you for writing to us on this matter.

Yours sincerely,

Len Farber
Director, Tax Legislation Division

**Related Provisions**: 104(31) — Credit to be included in income of beneficiary; 210.3(2) — Non-resident beneficiary taxed in Canada deemed not to be designated beneficiary; 252(3) — Extended meaning of "spouse" and "former spouse".

**Notes**: 210(c) amended by 2000 same-sex partners bill to add reference to "common-law partner", effective for the 2001 and later taxation years, or earlier by election (see Notes to 248(1)"common-law partner").

Opening words of 210(d) amended by 1993 technical bill, effective for 1993 and later taxation years, to add reference to a mutual fund trust and to add the words "on all or part of its taxable income". A mutual fund trust is now excluded from the definition of "designated beneficiary" regardless of the nature of the mutual fund trust's beneficiaries.

**Definitions [s. 210]**: "common-law partner" — 248(1); "designated income" — 210.2(2); "former spouse" — 252(3); "individual", "non-resident" — 248(1); "non-resident-owned investment corporation" — 133(8), 248(1); "person" — 248(1); "registered retirement income fund" — 146.3(1), 248(1); "registered retirement savings plan" — 146(1), 248(1); "resident in Canada" — 250; "spouse" — 252(3); "testamentary trust" — 108(1), 248(1); "trust" — 104(1), 248(1), (3).

**210.1 Application of Part** — This Part does not apply in a taxation year to a trust that was throughout the year

(a) a testamentary trust;

(b) a mutual fund trust;

(c) a trust that was exempt from tax under Part I by reason of subsection 149(1);

(d) a trust described in paragraph (a) or (c) of the definition of that expression in subsection 108(1); or

> **Proposed Amendment — 210.1(d)**
>
> (d) a trust described in paragraph (a), (a.1) or (c) of the definition "trust" in subsection 108(1); or
>
> **Application**: Bill C-43 (First Reading September 20, 2000), s. 100, will amend para. 210.1(d) to read as above, applicable to 1999 et seq.
>
> **Technical Notes**: Section 210.1 provides a list of trusts to which Part XII.2 does not apply.
>
> Paragraph 210.1(d) is amended to add to the list of exempt trusts a trust described in paragraph (a.1) of the definition "trust" in subsection 108(1). This change is strictly consequential to the introduction of paragraph (a.1) of that definition. For further detail on the amended definition "trust" in subsection 108(1), see the commentary on that provision.

(e) a non-resident trust.

**Related Provisions**: 132(6.2) — Retention of status as mutual fund trust; 253 — Extended meaning of carrying on business.

**Definitions [s. 210.1]**: "mutual fund trust" — 132(6)–(7), 132.2(1)(q), 248(1); "non-resident" — 248(1); "taxation year" — 249; "testamentary trust" — 108(1), 248(1); "trust" — 104(1), 248(1), (3).

**210.2 (1) Tax on income of trust** — Subject to section 210.3, where an amount in respect of the income of a trust for a taxation year is or would, if all beneficiaries under the trust were persons resident in Canada to whom Part I was applicable, be included in computing the income under Part I of a person by reason of subsection 104(13) or 105(2), the trust shall pay a tax under this Part in respect of the year equal to 36% of the least of

(a) the designated income of the trust for the year,

(b) the amount that, but for subsections 104(6) and (30), would be the income of the trust for the year, and

(c) 100/64 of the amount deducted under paragraph 104(6)(b) in computing the trust's income under Part I for the year.

**Related Provisions**: 18(1)(t) — Tax under Part XII.2 is deductible; 104(30) — Part XII.2 tax deductible in computing income of trust; 210.3 — Where no tax payable.

**Information Circulars**: 77-16R4: Non-resident income tax.

**(1.1) Amateur athlete trusts** — Notwithstanding section 210.1, where an amount described in subsection 143.1(2) in respect of an amateur athlete trust would, if Part I were applicable, be required to be included in computing the income for a taxation year of a designated beneficiary under the trust, the trust shall pay a tax under this Part in respect of the year equal to 36% of 100/64 of that amount.

**Notes**: 210.2(1.1) added by 1992 technical bill, effective 1992. It extends Part XII.2 tax to amateur athlete trusts (see 143.1) where amounts are distributed to non-resident beneficiaries.

**Forms**: T3ATH-IND: Amateur athlete trust income tax return.

**(2) Designated income** — For the purposes of subsection (1), the **designated income** of a trust for a taxation year means the amount that, but for subsections 104(6), (12) and (30), would be the income of the trust for the year determined under section 3 if

(a) it had no income other than taxable capital gains from dispositions described in paragraph (b) and incomes from

(i) real properties in Canada (other than Canadian resource properties),

(ii) timber resource properties,

(iii) Canadian resource properties (other than properties acquired by the trust before 1972), and

(iv) businesses carried on in Canada;

(b) the only taxable capital gains and allowable capital losses referred to in paragraph 3(b) were from dispositions of property that would have been taxable Canadian property if, at no time in the year, the trust had been resident in Canada; and

> **Proposed Amendment — 210.2(2)(b)**
>
> (b) the only taxable capital gains and allowable capital losses referred to in paragraph 3(b) were from dispositions of taxable Canadian property; and
>
> **Application**: Bill C-43 (First Reading September 20, 2000), s. 101, will amend para. 210.2(2)(b) to read as above, applicable after October 1, 1996.
>
> **Technical Notes**: The tax under Part XII.2 is calculated with reference to a trust's "designated income" (as determined under subsection 210.2(2)). "Designated income" is calculated with reference to taxable capital gains and allowable capital losses from dispositions of the trust's taxable Canadian property, determined on the assumption that the trust is non-resident.
>
> Paragraph 210.2(2)(b) is amended to remove the assumption described above. The amendment merely simplifies paragraph 210.2(2)(b) and does not represent any policy change.

(c) the only losses referred to in paragraph 3(d) were losses from sources described in subparagraphs (a)(i) to (iv).

**Related Provisions**: 104(7.01)(b)(i) — No deduction under 104(6) for designated income of trust.

**(3) Tax deemed paid by beneficiary** — Where an amount (in this subsection and subsection 210.3(2) referred to as the "income amount") in respect of the income of a trust for a taxation year is, by reason of subsection 104(13) or 105(2), included in computing

(a) the income under Part I of a person who was not at any time in the year a designated beneficiary under the trust, or

**S. 210.2(3)(b)**      Income Tax Act

(b) the income of a non-resident person (other than a person who, at any time in the year, would be a designated beneficiary under the trust if section 210 were read without reference to paragraph 210(a)) that is subject to tax under Part I by reason of subsection 2(3) and is not exempt from tax under Part I by reason of a provision contained in a tax convention or agreement with another country that has the force of law in Canada,

an amount determined by the formula

$$A \times \frac{B}{C}$$

where

A is the tax paid under this Part by the trust for the year,

B is the income amount in respect of the person, and

C is the total of all amounts each of which is an amount that is or would be, if all beneficiaries under the trust were persons resident in Canada to whom Part I was applicable, included in computing the income under Part I of a beneficiary under the trust by reason of subsection 104(13) or 105(2) in respect of the year,

shall, if designated by the trust in respect of the person in its return for the year under this Part, be deemed to be an amount paid on account of the person's tax payable under Part I for the person's taxation year in which the taxation year of the trust ends, on the day that is 90 days after the end of the taxation year of the trust.

**Related Provisions**: 104(31) — Amount deemed payable by trust to beneficiary; 210.3(2) — Where non-resident beneficiary already taxed in Canada.

**Notes**: The amount deemed paid by the beneficiary is credited against the beneficiary's tax obligations, and creates a refund to the extent the beneficiary had no tax to pay.

**Interpretation Bulletins**: IT-342R: Trusts — Income payable to beneficiaries.

**(4) Designations in respect of partnerships** — Where a taxpayer is a member of a partnership in respect of which an amount is designated by a trust for a taxation year of the trust (in this subsection referred to as the "particular year") under subsection (3),

(a) no amount shall be deemed to be paid on account of the partnership's tax payable under Part I by reason of subsection (3) except in the application of that subsection for the purposes of subsection 104(31), and

(b) an amount determined by the formula

$$A \times \frac{B}{C}$$

where

A is the amount so designated,

B is the amount that may reasonably be regarded as the share of the taxpayer in the designated income of the trust received by the partnership in the fiscal period of the partnership in which the particular year ends (that fiscal period being referred to in this subsection as the "partnership's period"), and

C is the designated income received by the partnership from the trust in the partnership's period,

shall be deemed to be an amount paid on account of the taxpayer's tax payable under Part I for the person's taxation year in which the partnership's period ends, on the last day of that year.

**(5) Returns** — A trust shall, within 90 days after the end of each taxation year,

(a) file with the Minister a return for the year under this Part in prescribed form and containing prescribed information, without notice or demand therefor;

(b) estimate in the return the amount of tax, if any, payable by it under this Part for the year; and

(c) pay to the Receiver General the tax, if any, payable by it under this Part for the year.

**Related Provisions**: 150.1(5) — Electronic filing.

**Forms**: T3 SCH 10: Part XII.2 tax and Part XIII non-resident withholding tax.

**(6) Liability of trustee** — A trustee of a trust is personally liable to pay to the Receiver General on behalf of the trust the full amount of any tax payable by the trust under this Part to the extent that the amount is not paid to the Receiver General within the time specified in subsection (5), and the trustee is entitled to recover from the trust any such amount paid by the trustee.

**(7) Provisions applicable to Part** — Subsections 150(2) and (3), sections 152 and 158, subsections 161(1) and (11), sections 162 to 167 and Division J of Part I are applicable to this Part with such modifications as the circumstances require.

**Definitions [s. 210.2]**: "allowable capital loss" — 38(b), 248(1); "amateur athlete trust" — 143.1(1)(a), 248(1); "amount", "business" — 248(1); "Canada" — 255; "Canadian resource property" — 66(15), 248(1); "carrying on business" — 253; "designated beneficiary" — 210; "fiscal period" — 249(2)(b), 249.1; "income amount" — 210.2(3); "Minister", "non-resident", "person", "prescribed", "property" — 248(1); "resident in Canada" — 250; "tax payable" — 248(2); "taxable Canadian property" — 248(1); "taxable capital gain" — 38(a), 248(2); "taxation year" — 249; "taxpayer" — 248(1); "timber resource property" — 13(21), 248(1); "trust" — 104(1), 248(1), (3).

**210.3 (1) Where no designated beneficiaries** — No tax is payable under this Part by a trust for a taxation year in respect of which the trustee has certified in the trust's return under this Part for the year that no beneficiary under the trust was a designated beneficiary in the year.

**(2) Where beneficiary deemed not designated** — Where a trust would, if the trust paid tax under this Part for a taxation year, be entitled to designate an amount under subsection 210.2(3) in respect of a non-resident beneficiary and the income amount in respect of the beneficiary is included in computing the income of the beneficiary which is subject to tax under Part I by reason of subsection 2(3) and is not exempt from tax under Part I by reason of a provision contained in a tax convention or agreement with another country that has the force of law in Canada, for the purposes of subsection (1), the beneficiary shall be deemed not to be a designated beneficiary of the trust at any time in the year.

**Definitions [s. 210.3]**: "amount" — 248(1); "designated beneficiary" — 210; "income amount" — 210.2(3); "non-resident" — 248(1); "taxation year" — 249; "trust" — 104(1), 248(1), (3).

**Notes [Part XII.2]**: Part XII.2 added by 1988 tax reform.

## PART XII.3 — TAX ON INVESTMENT INCOME OF LIFE INSURERS

**Notes**: Life insurance companies are also subject to the financial institutions capital tax under Part VI (190 to 190.21). See also Notes at end of s. 138.

**211. (1) Definitions** — For the purposes of this Part,

**"existing guaranteed life insurance policy"**, at any time, means a non-participating life insurance policy in Canada in respect of which

(a) the amount of every premium that became payable before that time and after December 31, 1989,

(b) the number of premium payments under the policy, and

(c) the amount of each benefit under the policy at that time

were fixed and determined on or before December 31, 1989;

**"life insurance policy"** includes a benefit under

(a) a group life insurance policy, and

(b) a group annuity contract

but does not include

(c) that part of a policy in respect of which the policyholder is deemed by paragraph 138.1(1)(e) to have an interest in a related segregated fund trust, or

(d) a reinsurance arrangement;

**Notes**: Definition "life insurance policy" amended by 1996 Budget, effective for 1996 and later taxation years. For earlier years, read:

"life insurance policy" and "life insurance policy in Canada" do not include

(a) that part of a policy in respect of which the policyholder is deemed by paragraph 138.1(1)(e) to have an interest in a related segregated fund trust, or

(b) a reinsurance arrangement;

The substantive change is that the definition has been extended to include benefits under both group life insurance policies and group annuity contracts.

**"life insurance policy in Canada"** means a life insurance policy issued or effected by an insurer on the life of a person resident in Canada at the time the policy was issued or effected;

**Notes**: Definition "life insurance policy in Canada" amended by 1996 Budget, effective for 1996 and later taxation years. For earlier years, see Notes to "life insurance policy" above. The new explicit definition is needed because it has been repealed from 138(12).

**"net interest rate"**, in respect of a liability, benefit, risk or guarantee under a life insurance policy of an insurer for a taxation year, is the positive amount, if any, determined by the formula

$$(A - B) \times C$$

where

A is the simple arithmetic average determined as of the first day of the year of the average yield (expressed as a percentage per year rounded to 2 decimal points) in each of the 60 immediately preceding months prevailing on all domestic Canadian-dollar Government of Canada bonds outstanding on the last Wednesday of that month that have a remaining term to maturity of more than 10 years,

B is

(a) in the case of a guaranteed benefit provided under the terms and conditions of the policy as they existed on March 2, 1988, other than a policy where, at any time after March 2, 1988, its terms and conditions relating to premiums and benefits were changed (otherwise than to give effect to the terms and conditions that were determined before March 3, 1988), the greater of

(i) the rate of interest (expressed as a percentage per year) used by the insurer in determining the amount of the guaranteed benefit, and

(ii) 4%, and

(b) in any other case, nil, and

C is

(a) in the case of a guaranteed benefit to which paragraph (a) of the description of B applies, 65%, and

(b) in any other case, 55%;

**Related Provisions**: 257 — Formula cannot calculate to less than zero.

**"non-participating life insurance policy"** means a life insurance policy that is not a participating life insurance policy;

**"participating life insurance policy"** has the meaning assigned by subsection 138(12);

**"policy loan"** has the meaning assigned by subsection 138(12);

## S. 211(1) pol — Income Tax Act

**Notes**: "policy loan" was included together with "participating life insurance policy" above, before consolidation in R.S.C. 1985 (5th Supp.).

**"registered life insurance policy"** means a life insurance policy issued or effected

(a) as a registered retirement savings plan, or

(b) pursuant to a registered retirement savings plan, a deferred profit sharing plan or a registered pension plan;

**"reinsurance arrangement"** does not include an arrangement under which an insurer has assumed the obligations of the issuer of a life insurance policy to the policyholder;

**"segregated fund"** has the meaning given that expression in subsection 138.1(1);

**Notes**: "segregated fund" was included under "participating life insurance policy" above, before consolidation in R.S.C. 1985 (5th Supp.).

**"specified transaction or event"**, in respect of a life insurance policy, means

(a) a change in underwriting class,

(b) a change in premium because of a change in frequency of premium payments within a year that does not alter the present value, at the beginning of the year, of the total premiums to be paid under the policy in the year,

(c) an addition under the terms of the policy as they existed on

(i) in the case of an existing guaranteed life insurance policy, December 31, 1989,

(ii) in any other case, March 2, 1988,

of accidental death, dismemberment, disability or guaranteed purchase option benefits,

(d) the deletion of a rider,

(e) redating lapsed policies within the reinstatement period referred to in paragraph (g) of the definition "disposition" in subsection 148(9) or redating for policy loan indebtedness,

(f) a change in premium because of a correction of erroneous information,

(g) the payment of a premium after its due date, or no more than 30 days before its due date, as established on or before

(i) in the case of an existing guaranteed life insurance policy, December 31, 1989, and

(ii) in any other case, March 2, 1988, and

(h) the payment of an amount described in paragraph (a) of the definition "premium" in subsection 148(9);

**"taxable life insurance policy"** of an insurer at any time means a life insurance policy in Canada issued by the insurer (or in respect of which the insurer has assumed the obligations of the issuer of the policy to the policyholder), other than a policy that is at that time

(a) an existing guaranteed life insurance policy,

(b) an annuity contract (including a settlement annuity),

(c) a registered life insurance policy,

(d) a registered pension plan, or

(e) a retirement compensation arrangement.

**(2) Riders and changes in terms** — For the purposes of this Part,

(a) any rider added at any time after March 2, 1988 to a life insurance policy shall be deemed to be a separate life insurance policy issued and effected at that time; and

(b) a change in the terms or conditions of a life insurance policy resulting from a specified transaction or event shall be deemed not to have occurred and not to be a change.

**Notes**: 211(1) completely rewritten by 1991 technical bill, effective for taxation years commencing after 1989 and, where an insurer has elected by notifying Revenue Canada in writing before July 1991, to all taxation years of the insurer to which the election relates. Where such an election is made,

(a) in respect of each taxation year of the insurer to which the election relates, each reference to "December 31, 1989" in the definitions in 211(1), as the reference relates to a life insurance policy, shall be read as a reference to the later of

(i) the day the policy was issued, and

(ii) March 2, 1988; and

(b) notwithstanding 152(4) to (5), such assessments of tax, interest and penalties shall be made as are necessary to give effect to the election to the extent it applies in respect of this section.

In cases where no such election is made, the 1991 technical bill also provides that in the application of the former 211 to taxation years commencing before 1990, it shall be read as though it included a definition "benefits payable under a life insurance policy", not reproduced here.

**Definitions [s. 211]**: "annuity", "business" — 248(1); "Canada" — 255; "carrying on business" — 253; "deferred profit sharing plan" — 147(1); "insurer", "life insurance business" — 248(1); "life insurance policy", "life insurance policy in Canada" — 138(12), 211(1), 248(1); "person" — 248(1); "property", "registered pension plan" — 248(1); "registered retirement savings plan" — 146(1), 248(1); "resident in Canada" — 250; "taxation year" — 249; "trust" — 104(1), 248(1), (3).

**211.1 (1) Tax payable** — Every life insurer shall pay a tax under this Part for each taxation year equal to 15% of its taxable Canadian life investment income for the year.

**Related Provisions**: 18(1)(t) — Tax is non-deductible; 138(3)(g) — Part XII.3 tax deductible by insurer; 190.1(1.1) — Additional capital tax on life insurance corporations.

**Notes**: See Notes at beginning of Part XII.2.

**(2) Taxable Canadian life investment income** — For the purposes of this Part, the taxable Canadian life investment income of a life insurer for a taxation year is the amount, if any, by which its Canadian life investment income for the year exceeds the total of its Canadian life investment losses for such of the 7 taxation years immediately preceding the year that begin after 1989, to the extent that those losses were not deducted in computing its taxable Canadian life investment income for any preceding taxation year.

**Related Provisions**: 87(2.2) — Amalgamation of insurance corporations; 138(11.5)(k) — Transfer of business by non-resident insurer.

**Notes**: 211.1(2) amended by 1991 technical bill to limit the carryforward of Canadian life investment losses to losses arising in 1990 and later years, in view of the significant changes to the design of the Part XII.3 tax.

**(3) Canadian life investment income** — For the purposes of this Part, the Canadian life investment income or loss of a life insurer for a taxation year is the positive or negative amount determined by the formula

$$A + B - C$$

where

A is, subject to subsection (4), the total of all amounts, each of which is in respect of a liability, benefit, risk or guarantee under a life insurance policy that was at any time in the year a taxable life insurance policy of the insurer, determined by multiplying the net interest rate in respect of the liability, benefit, risk or guarantee for the year by $\frac{1}{2}$ of the total of

(a) the maximum amount that would be determined under paragraph 1401(1)(a), (c) or (d) of the *Income Tax Regulations* (other than an amount that would be determined under subparagraph 1401(1)(d)(ii) of those Regulations in respect of a disabled life) in respect of the insurer for the year in respect of the liability, benefit, risk or guarantee if subsection 1401(1) of those Regulations applied to all life insurance policies and if that amount were determined without reference to any policy loan or reinsurance arrangement, and

(b) the maximum amount that would be determined under paragraph 1401(1)(a), (c) or (d) of the *Income Tax Regulations* (other than an amount that would be determined under subparagraph 1401(1)(d)(ii) of those Regulations in respect of a disabled life) in respect of the insurer for the preceding taxation year in respect of the liability, benefit, risk or guarantee if subsection 1401(1) of those Regulations applied to all life insurance policies and if that amount were determined without reference to any policy loan or reinsurance arrangement;

B is the total of all amounts, each of which is the positive or negative amount in respect of a life insurance policy that was at any time in the year a taxable life insurance policy of the insurer, determined by the formula

$$D - E$$

where

D is, subject to subsection (4), the amount determined by multiplying the percentage determined in the description of A in the definition "net interest rate" in subsection 211(1) in respect of the year by $\frac{1}{2}$ of the total of

(a) the maximum amount that would be determined under paragraph 1401(1)(c.1) of the *Income Tax Regulations* in respect of the insurer for the year in respect of the policy if subsection 1401(1) of those Regulations applied to all life insurance policies and if that amount were determined without reference to any policy loan or reinsurance arrangement, and

(b) the maximum amount that would be determined under paragraph 1401(1)(c.1) of the *Income Tax Regulations* in respect of the insurer for the preceding taxation year in respect of the policy if subsection 1401(1) of those Regulations applied to all life insurance policies and if that amount were determined without reference to any policy loan or reinsurance arrangement, and

E is the amount, if any, by which

(a) the total of all amounts determined in respect of the insurer under the description of D in respect of the policy for the year and any preceding taxation years ending after 1989

exceeds the total of

(b) all amounts determined in respect of the insurer under the description of E in respect of the policy for taxation years ending before the year, and

(c) the amount, if any, by which

(i) the maximum amount that would be determined under paragraph 1401(1)(c.1) of the *Income Tax Regulations* in respect of the insurer for the year in respect of the policy if subsection 1401(1) of those Regulations applied to all life insurance policies and if that amount were determined without reference to any policy loan or reinsurance arrangement

exceeds

(ii) the maximum amount that would be determined under paragraph 1401(1)(c.1) of the *Income Tax Regulations* in respect of the insurer for its last 1989 taxation year in respect of the policy if subsection 1401(1) of those Regulations applied to all life insurance policies and if that amount were determined without reference to any policy loan or reinsurance arrangement; and

**S. 211.1(3)**  Income Tax Act

C is the total of all amounts each of which is 100% of the amount required to be included in computing the income of a policyholder under section 12.2 or paragraph 56(1)(j) for which the insurer is required by regulation to prepare an information return in respect of the calendar year ending in the taxation year, in respect of a taxable life insurance policy of the insurer, except that the reference in this description to 100% shall be read as a reference to,

(a) where paragraph (a) of the description of B in the definition "net interest rate" in subsection 211(1) applies for any taxation year in respect of a guaranteed benefit under the policy,

0% for calendar years before 1991,
5% for 1991,
10% for 1992,
15% for 1993,
20% for 1994,
25% for 1995,
30% for 1996,
35% for 1997,
40% for 1998,
45% for 1999, and
50% for calendar years after 1999,

and

(b) where the policy was at any time after 1989 an existing guaranteed life insurance policy,

0% for the calendar year in which it became a taxable life insurance policy of the insurer,
0% for the first following calendar year,
0% for the second following calendar year,
5% for the third following calendar year,
10% for the fourth following calendar year,
15% for the fifth following calendar year,
20% for the sixth following calendar year,
25% for the seventh following calendar year,
30% for the eighth following calendar year,
35% for the ninth following calendar year,
40% for the tenth following calendar year,
45% for the eleventh following calendar year, and
50% for the twelfth following and subsequent calendar years.

**Related Provisions**: 257 — Formula amounts cannot calculate to less than zero.

**Notes**: Opening words of 211.1(3)A and of B:D both amended by 1995-97 technical bill, effective for 1992 and later years, to add "subsection to subsection (4)".

211.1(3)B:D(a) and (b), and 211.1(3)B:E(c)(i) and (ii), all amended by 1996 Budget, effective for 1996 and later taxation years, to add the condition "if subsection 1401(1) of those Regulations applied to all life insurance policies".

211.1(3) completely revised by 1991 technical bill, effective for taxation years commencing in 1990 or later and, if the insurer elects by notifying Revenue Canada in writing before July 1991, to taxation years commencing in 1988 or 1989 to which the election relates. Where such an election is made, each reference to "1989" in 211.1(3) is to be read as the year before the first taxation year to which the election relates; and notwithstanding 152(4) to (5), such assessments of tax, interest and penalties shall be made as are necessary to give effect to the election.

In cases where no such election is made, the 1991 technical bill also provides amendments (not reproduced here) to the descriptions of C and G in the application of the former 211.1(3) to taxation years commencing before 1990.

**Regulations [subsec. 211.1(3)]**: 1900 (for taxation years that began after June 17, 1987 and before 1990 that end after 1987).

**(4) Short taxation year** — Where a taxation year of a life insurer is less than 51 weeks, the values of A and D in subsection (3) for the year are that proportion of those values otherwise so determined that the number of days in the year (other than February 29) is of 365.

**Notes**: 211.1(4) added by 1995-97 technical bill, effective for 1992 and later years.

**Definitions [s. 211.1]**: "allowable capital loss" — 38(b), 248(1); "amount", "annuity", "business" — 248(1); "calendar year" — *Interpretation Act* 37(1)(a); "Canada" — 255; "capital property" — 54, 248(1); "carrying on business" — 253; "insurer", "life insurance business" — 248(1); "life insurance policy" — 138(12), 211, 248(1); "life insurer", "prescribed", "property", "registered pension plan" — 248(1); "taxation year" — 249. See also 211(1).

**211.2 Return** — Every life insurer shall file with the Minister, not later than the day on or before which it is required by section 150 to file its return of income for a taxation year under Part I, a return of taxable Canadian life investment income for that year in prescribed form containing an estimate of the tax payable by it under this Part for the year.

**Related Provisions**: 150.1(5) — Electronic filing.

**Definitions [s. 211.2]**: "life insurer", "Minister", "prescribed" — 248(1); "taxation year" — 249.

**Forms**: T2142: Part XII.3 tax return — tax on investment income of life insurers.

**211.3 (1) Instalments** — Every life insurer shall, in respect of each of its taxation years, pay to the Receiver General on or before the last day of each month in the year, an amount equal to $1/12$ of the lesser of

(a) the amount estimated by the insurer to be the annualized tax payable under this Part by it for the year, and

(b) the annualized tax payable under this Part by the insurer for the immediately preceding taxation year.

**Notes**: See Notes at end of 211.3.

**(2) Annualized tax payable** — For the purposes of subsections (1) and 211.5(2), the annualized tax payable under this Part by a life insurer for a taxation year is the amount determined by the formula

$$(365/A) \times B$$

where

A is

(a) if the year is less than 357 days, the number of days in the year (other than February 29), and

(b) otherwise, 365; and

B is the tax payable under this Part by the insurer for the year.

**Notes**: 211.3 replaced by 211.3(1) and (2) by 1995-97 technical bill, effective for taxation years that begin after 1995. For earlier taxation years since 1988 (beginning after June 18, 1987), read:

211.3 **Instalments** — Every life insurer shall pay to the Receiver General on or before the last day of each three month period, if any, in a taxation year an instalment determined by the formula

$$\frac{A}{B} \times C$$

where

A is the number of months in the year within the three month period;

B is the number of months in the year; and

C is the lesser of

(a) the tax payable under this Part by the insurer for the year, and

(b) the tax payable under this Part by the insurer for the immediately preceding taxation year.

**Definitions [s. 211.3]**: "annualized tax payable" — 211.3(2); "life insurer" — 248(1); "tax payable" — 248(2); "taxation year" — 249.

**211.4 Payment of remainder of tax** — Every life insurer shall pay, on or before the last day of the second month ending after the end of a taxation year, the remainder, if any, of the tax payable under this Part by the insurer for the year.

**Definitions [s. 211.4]**: "insurer", "life insurer" — 248(1); "taxation year" — 249.

**211.5 (1) Provisions applicable to Part** — Section 152, subsection 157(2.1), sections 158 and 159, subsections 161(1), (2), (2.1), (2.2) and (11), sections 162 to 167 and Division J of Part I apply to this Part, with such modifications as the circumstances require.

**Notes**: 211.5 renumbered as 211.5(1) by 1995-97 technical bill, effective for taxation years that begin after 1995.

211.5 amended and 211.6 repealed by 1991 technical bill, effective 1990. 211.5 formerly dealt only with interest (now covered by the references to 161), while 211.6 provided the rest of what is now 211.5.

**(2) Interest on instalments** — For the purposes of subsection 161(2) and section 163.1 as they apply to this Part, a life insurer is, in respect of a taxation year, deemed to have been liable to pay, on or before the last day of each month in the year, an instalment equal to $1/12$ of the lesser of

(a) the annualized tax payable under this Part by the insurer for the year, and

(b) the annualized tax payable under this Part by the insurer for the immediately preceding taxation year.

**Related Provisions**: 211.3(2) — Annualized tax payable.

**Notes**: 211.5(2) added by 1995-97 technical bill, effective for taxation years that begin after 1995.

**Definitions [s. 211.5]**: "annualized tax payable" — 211.3(2); "life insurer" — 248(1); "taxation year" — 249.

## PART XII.4 — TAX ON QUALIFYING ENVIRONMENTAL TRUSTS

**211.6 (1) Charging provision** — Every trust that is a qualifying environmental trust at the end of a taxation year shall pay a tax under this Part for the year equal to 28% of its income under Part I for the year.

**Related Provisions**: 127.41 — Part XII.4 tax credit to beneficiary; 149(1)(z) — No Part I tax on trust.

**Notes**: See at end of 211.6.

**(2) Computation of income** — For the purpose of subsection (1), the income under Part I of a qualifying environmental trust shall be computed as if this Act were read without reference to subsections 104(4) to (31) and sections 105 to 107.

**(3) Return** — Every trust that is a qualifying environmental trust at the end of a taxation year shall file with the Minister on or before its filing-due date for the year a return for the year under this Part in prescribed form containing an estimate of the amount of its tax payable under this Part for the year.

**Related Provisions**: 150.1(5) — Electronic filing.

**Forms**: T3M: Environmental trust income tax return.

**(4) Payment of tax** — Every trust shall pay to the Receiver General its tax payable under this Part for each taxation year on or before its balance-due day for the year.

**(5) Provisions applicable to Part** — Subsections 150(2) and (3), sections 152, 158 and 159, subsections 161(1) and (11), sections 162 to 167 and Division J of Part I apply to this Part, with such modifications as the circumstances require.

**Notes**: 211.6 (Part XII.4) added by 1994 Budget, effective 1994; and amended by 1997 Budget, effective for 1997 and later taxation years, to change all instances of "mining reclamation trust" to "qualifying environmental trust" (QET) (the same change was made throughout the Act). It imposes a special tax on QETs, as defined in 248(1). QETs are exempt from Part I tax under 149(1)(z). Beneficiaries under an QET are generally entitled to a refund under 127.41 for tax payable by the trust under 211.6. See also 107.3(1). There are two reasons for taxing QETs under a separate Part. First, the rate of tax corresponds to the general corporate rate under 123(1)(a) and 124(1), since most QET beneficiaries are corporations. Second, it was anticipated that the provincial governments will establish similar taxes, with tax rates linked to provincial corporate income tax rates.

The amendments to 211.6 by 1997 Budget bill also introduced use of the terms "filing-due date" in 211.6(3) and "balance-due day" in

211.6(4), in place of references to "90 days after the end of the year". These changes were non-substantive. (Both terms are now defined in 248(1).)

For former 211.6, see Notes to 211.5.

**Definitions [s. 211.6]**: "amount"; "balance-due day", "filing-due date" — 248(1); "mining reclamation trust", "Minister", "prescribed", "qualifying environmental trust" — 248(1); "taxation year" — 11(2), 249; "trust" — 104(1), 248(1); "trust's year" — 107.3(1).

# PART XII.5 — RECOVERY OF LABOUR-SPONSORED FUNDS TAX CREDIT

**211.7 (1) Definitions** — The definitions in this section apply for the purposes of this Part.

**Notes**: 211.7 renumbered as 211.7(1) by 1999 Budget, effective February 17, 1999.

**"approved share"** has the meaning assigned by subsection 127.4(1).

**"labour-sponsored funds tax credit"** in respect of a share is

(a) where the original acquisition of the share occurred before 1996, 20% of the net cost of the share on that acquisition; and

(b) in any other case, the amount that would be determined under subsection 127.4(6) in respect of the share if this Act were read without reference to paragraphs 127.4(6)(b) and (d).

**"net cost"** has the meaning assigned by subsection 127.4(1).

**"original acquisition"** has the meaning assigned by subsection 127.4(1).

**"qualifying trust"** has the meaning assigned by subsection 127.4(1).

**"revoked corporation"** means a corporation the registration of which has been revoked under subsection 204.81(6).

**(2) Amalgamations and mergers** — For the purposes of this Part, where two or more corporations (each of which is referred to in this subsection as a "predecessor corporation") amalgamate or merge to form a corporate entity deemed by paragraph 204.85(3)(d) to have been registered under Part X.3, the shares of each predecessor corporation are deemed not to be redeemed, acquired or cancelled by the predecessor corporation on the amalgamation or merger.

**Notes**: 211.7(2) added by 1999 Budget, effective February 17, 1999.

**Notes [211.7]**: 211.7 added by 1996 Budget, effective on the same basis as 211.8(1).

**Definitions [s. 211.7]**: "amount" — 248(1); "corporation" — 248(1), *Interpretation Act* 35(1); "net cost", "original acquisition" — 127.4(1), 211.7(1); "share" — 248(1).

**211.8 (1) Disposition of approved share** — Where an approved share of the capital stock of a registered labour-sponsored venture capital corporation or a revoked corporation is, before the first discontinuation of its venture capital business, redeemed, acquired or cancelled by the corporation less than eight years after the day on which the share was issued (other than in circumstances described in subclause 204.81(1)(c)(v)(A)(I) or (III) or clause 204.81(1)(c)(v)(B) or (D)) or any other share that was issued by any other labour-sponsored venture capital corporation is disposed of, the person who was the shareholder immediately before the redemption, acquisition, cancellation or disposition shall pay a tax under this Part equal to the lesser of

(a) the amount determined by the formula

$$A \times B$$

where

A is

(i) where the share was issued by a registered labour-sponsored venture capital corporation or a revoked corporation, the labour-sponsored funds tax credit in respect of the share, and

(ii) where the share was issued by any other labour-sponsored venture capital corporation and was at any time an approved share, the amount, if any, required to be remitted to the government of a province as a consequence of the redemption, acquisition, cancellation or disposition (otherwise than as a consequence of an increase in the corporation's liability for a penalty under a law of the province), and

B is

(i) nil, where the share was issued by a registered labour-sponsored venture capital corporation or a revoked corporation, the original acquisition of the share was before March 6, 1996 and the redemption, acquisition, cancellation or disposition is

(A) more than 2 years after the day on which it was issued, where the redemption, acquisition, cancellation or disposition is permitted under the articles of the corporation because an individual attains 65 years of age, retires from the workforce or ceases to be resident in Canada, or

(B) more than 5 years after the day on which it was issued,

(ii) one, in any other case where the share was issued by a registered labour-sponsored venture capital corporation or a revoked corporation, and

(iii) in any other case, the quotient obtained when the labour-sponsored fund tax credit in respect of the share is divided by the tax credit provided under a law of a province in respect of any previous acquisition of the share, and

### Proposed Amendment — Shares redeemed from Feb. 1 to March 1

**Department of Finance news release, February 7, 2000**: *Finance Minister Announces Minor Change to the Redemption Requirements for Federal LSVCCs*

Finance Minister Paul Martin today announced that he would propose a minor change affecting federally-registered labour-sponsored venture capital corporations (LSVCCs). The proposed change provides an exemption from the rules governing the recovery of the federal LSVCC tax credit.

Shares in federally-registered LSVCCs that qualify for the federal LSVCC tax credit must be held for a minimum period. Where a share is redeemed prior to the expiry of the minimum period, the federal LSVCC tax credit for the share is generally recovered. In the case of shares issued before March 6, 1996, there is no recovery of the tax credit for a share redeemed more than five years after the day on which the share was issued. For shares issued after March 5, 1996, the recovery applies where a share is redeemed less than eight years after the day on which it was issued.

The proposed change will, for the purpose of the recovery provisions, treat a share redeemed in February or on March 1st as having been redeemed 30 days later. For example, existing LSVCC shares issued on March 1, 1995 and redeemed on February 29, 2000 would be exempt from a recovery of the federal LSVCC tax credit that was associated with the original acquisition of the shares.

This measure is intended to accommodate taxpayers wishing to acquire new LSVCC shares in the first 60 days of a year with the proceeds from the redemption of LSVCC shares. In these circumstances, a taxpayer would generally be entitled to claim a tax credit for the preceding year in respect of an acquisition of the new shares and would not be subject to a tax penalty with respect to the redemption of the existing shares. In addition, any necessary changes will be made to ensure that an LSVCC's registration cannot be revoked as a result of having redeemed LSVCC shares in these circumstances. It is proposed that this change apply from the inception of the rules governing the recovery of the LSVCC tax credit.

For further information: Grant Nash, Tax Policy Branch, (613) 992-5287; Karl Littler, Senior Advisor, Tax Policy, Office of the Minister of Finance, (613) 996-7861; Jean-Michel Catta, Public Affairs and Operations Division, (613) 996-8080.

(b) the amount that would, but for subsection (2), be payable to the shareholder because of the redemption, acquisition, cancellation or disposition (determined after taking into account the amount determined under subparagraph (ii) of the description of A in paragraph (a)).

**Related Provisions**: 204.8(2) — Determining when an RLSVCC discontinues its business; 204.8(3) — Order of disposition of shares; 211.8(1.1) — Rules of application; 211.8(2) — Withholding and remittance of tax; 211.9 — Refund of clawback; 227(10.01) — Assessment of amount payable by resident of Canada; 227(10.1)(c) — Assessment of amount payable by non-resident; Reg. 6706 — Repayment of credit by national LSVCCs.

**Notes**: Opening words of 211.8(1) amended to add "before the first discontinuation of its venture capital business" by 1999 Budget, effective for redemptions, acquisitions, cancellations and dispositions that occur after February 16, 1999.

211.8(1) added by 1996 Budget, effective for redemptions, acquisitions, cancellations and dispositions that occur after November 15, 1995, except that it does not apply

(a) to any redemption that occurs before 1998 of a share of a corporation that was registered under 204.81(1), where an amount determined under the regulations made under 204.81(1)(c)(v)(F) is directed to be remitted to the Receiver General in order to permit the redemption; and

(b) to any disposition that occurs before 1998, where an amount is required to be remitted to the government of a province as a consequence of the disposition and a portion of the amount is in respect of the recovery of a tax credit that is provided under 127.4(2) in respect of the share.

211.8 was 211.7 in the draft legislation of November 15, 1995.

211.8 provides a mechanism for the recovery of a federal tax credit under 127.4 with respect to the original acquisition of a share issued by a labour-sponsored venture capital corporation (LSVCC). The mechanism is a new tax under Part XII.5 all or part of which may be refundable under 211.9. Part XII.5 tax applies to the following:

(1) a disposition after November 15, 1995 of a share issued by an LSVCC, other than an LSVCC (referred to below as a "federally-registered LSVCC") that was never registered under section 204.81,

(2) a disposition of a share issued by a federally-registered LSVCC due to the purchase or acquisition of the share for cancellation by the LSVCC after November 15, 1995, where the share is not redeemed by the LSVCC, and

(3) a redemption after November 15, 1995 of a share issued by a federally-registered LSVCC, other than a redemption before 1998 to which the clawback rules in Reg. 6706 apply.

The tax under Part XII.5 on the disposition of a share of a non-federally-registered LSVCC is equal to a specified percentage of the portion of the provincial LSVCC tax credit that must be repaid due to the disposition. The specified percentage for a share reflects the proportion that the federal LSVCC tax credit (more specifically, the "labour-sponsored funds tax credit" in respect of the share) is to the provincial LSVCC credit available on the acquisition of the share. In addition, the amount of the special tax on the disposition of a share will not exceed the proceeds of disposition (net of any provincial LSVCC tax credit recovery).

The special tax payable with respect to such a disposition of a share issued by a federally-registered LSVCC or a revoked corporation is generally charged where the disposition occurs less than 8 years after the share was issued. The special tax on the disposition is generally equal to the "labour-sponsored funds tax credit" in respect of the share. However, the special tax under Part XII.5 is not charged on a disposition of such a share where:

- the disposition was a redemption in respect of which the information return to claim the LSVCC tax credit was returned to the corporation under 204.81(1)(c)(v)(A)(I),

- the disposition was a redemption that occurred under 204.81(1)(c)(v)(A)(III) because an individual became disabled and permanently unfit for work or terminally ill,

- the disposition was a redemption that occurred due to the unusual circumstances to which 204.81(1)(c)(v)(B) applies (essentially, the acquisition of the share was in circumstances where no one could be entitled to a federal LSVCC tax credit in respect of its acquisition), or

## S. 211.8(1) — Income Tax Act

- most significantly, in the case of a share the original acquisition of which was before March 6, 1996, where the share is disposed of
  - more than 2 years after it was issued where the disposition occurred, pursuant to the terms of the articles of the LSVCC, because an individual attains 65 years of age, retires from the workforce or ceases to be resident in Canada, or
  - more than 5 years after it was issued.

Like the special tax on dispositions of shares of the capital stock of non-federally-registered LSVCCs, Part XII.5 tax on the disposition of a share issued by a federally-registered LSVCC is limited to the proceeds of disposition (net of any provincial tax credit recovery).

**(1.1) Rules of application** — Subsections 204.8(2) and (3) and 204.85(3) apply for the purpose of subsection (1).

**Notes**: 211.8(1.1) added by 1999 Budget, effective for redemptions, acquisitions, cancellations and dispositions that occur after February 16, 1999.

**(2) Withholding and remittance of tax** — Where a person or partnership (in this section referred to as the "transferee") redeems, acquires or cancels a share and, as a consequence, tax is payable under this Part by the person who was the shareholder immediately before the redemption, acquisition or cancellation, the transferee shall

(a) withhold from the amount otherwise payable on the redemption, acquisition or cancellation to the shareholder the amount of the tax;

(b) within 30 days after the redemption, acquisition or cancellation, remit the amount of the tax to the Receiver General on behalf of the shareholder; and

(c) submit with the remitted amount a statement in prescribed form.

**Related Provisions**: 211.8(3) — Liability for failure to withhold; 211.9 — Refund of clawback; 227 — Withholding taxes — administration and enforcement; 227(5)(a.1) — Person who has influence over payment may be liable for failure to withhold; 227(6) — Application of excess amount withheld; 227(8.3)(c) — Interest on amounts not withheld.

**Notes**: 211.8(2) added by 1996 Budget, effective for redemptions, acquisitions and cancellations that occur after April 25, 1997 (Royal Assent).

**Forms**: T1149: Remittance form for labour-sponsored funds tax credits withheld on redeemed shares.

**(3) Liability for tax** — Where a transferee has failed to withhold any amount as required by subsection (2) from an amount paid or credited to a shareholder, the transferee is liable to pay as tax under this Part on behalf of the shareholder the amount the transferee failed to withhold, and is entitled to recover that amount from the shareholder.

**Related Provisions**: 227(10.01) — Assessment of amount payable by resident of Canada; 227(10.1)(c) — Assessment of amount payable by non-resident.

**Notes**: 211.8(3) added by 1996 Budget, effective for redemptions, acquisitions and cancellations that occur after April 25, 1997 (Royal Assent).

**Definitions [s. 211.8]**: "approved share" — 127.4(1), 211.7(1); "business" — 248(1); "corporation" — 248(1), *Interpretation Act* 35(1); "discontinuation" — 204.8(2); "disposition", "individual" — 248(1); "labour-sponsored funds tax credit" — 211.7(1); "original acquisition" — 127.4(1), 211.7(1); "partnership" — see Notes to 96(1); "person", "prescribed" — 248(1); "province" — *Interpretation Act* 35(1); "registered labour-sponsored venture capital corporation" — 248(1); "resident in Canada" — 250; "revoked corporation" — 211.7(1); "share", "shareholder" — 248(1); "transferee" — 211.8(2).

**211.9 Refund** — The Minister may pay to an individual (other than a trust) in respect of the disposition of a share, if application for the payment has been made in writing by the individual and filed with the Minister no later than two years after the end of the calendar year in which the disposition occurred, an amount not exceeding the lesser of

(a) the tax paid under this Part in respect of a disposition of the share, and

(b) 15% of the net cost of the share on the original acquisition by the individual (or by a qualifying trust for the individual in respect of the share).

**Related Provisions**: 127.4(6)(d) — Labour-sponsored funds credit is nil where amount has been refunded under 211.9.

**Notes**: 211.9 amended by 1999 Budget, effective for dispositions that occur after 1998. For earlier disposition, read:

211.9 Refund of clawback — The Minister may pay to an individual (other than a trust) an amount not exceeding the lesser of

(a) either

(i) the tax paid under this Part in respect of a disposition of a share, or

(ii) the amount determined under regulations made for the purpose of clause 204.81(1)(c)(v)(F) that was remitted to the Receiver General in respect of a disposition of an approved share, and

(b) the amount, if any, by which

(i) 15% of the net cost of the share on the original acquisition by the individual (or by a qualifying trust for the individual in respect of the share)

exceeds

(ii) the amount deducted under subsection 127.4(2) in respect of the original acquisition of the share by the individual (or by a qualifying trust for the individual in respect of the share)

if application for the payment has been made in writing by the individual and filed with the Minister no later than 2 years after the end of the calendar year in which the disposition occurred.

211.9 added by 1996 Budget, effective April 26, 1997 (day after Royal Assent), except that

(a) in respect of a disposition of a share the original acquisition of which was before March 6, 1996, read "15%" in 211.9(b)(i) as "20%"; and

(b) any application filed under 211.9 by the end of 1997 is deemed to be filed on a timely basis.

**Definitions [s. 211.9]**: "amount" — 248(1); "approved share" — 127.4(1), 211.7(1); "calendar year" — *Interpretation Act* 37(1)(a); "disposition", "individual", "Minister" — 248(1); "net cost", "original acquisition", "qualifying trust" — 127.4(1), 211.7(1); "regula-

Part XIII — Tax on Non-Resident's Income from Canada    S. 212(1)

tion", "share" — 248(1); "trust" — 104(1), 248(1), (3); "writing" — *Interpretation Act* 35(1).

## PART XII.6 — TAX ON FLOW-THROUGH SHARES

**211.91 (1) Tax imposed** — Every corporation shall pay a tax under this Part in respect of each month (other than January) in a calendar year equal to the amount determined by the formula

$$\left(A + \frac{B}{2} - C - \frac{D}{2}\right) \times \left(\frac{E}{12} + \frac{F}{10}\right)$$

where

A is the total of all amounts each of which is an amount that the corporation purported to renounce in the year under subsection 66(12.6) or (12.601) because of the application of subsection 66(12.66) (other than an amount purported to be renounced in respect of expenses incurred or to be incurred in connection with production or potential production in a province where a tax, similar to the tax provided under this Part, is payable by the corporation under the laws of the province as a consequence of the failure to incur the expenses that were purported to be renounced);

B is the total of all amounts each of which is an amount that the corporation purported to renounce in the year under subsection 66(12.6) or (12.601) because of the application of subsection 66(12.66) and that is not included in the value of A;

C is the total of all expenses described in paragraph 66(12.66)(b) that are

(a) made or incurred by the end of the month by the corporation, and

(b) in respect of the purported renunciations in respect of which an amount is included in the value of A;

D is the total of all expenses described in paragraph 66(12.66)(b) that are

(a) made or incurred by the end of the month by the corporation, and

(b) in respect of the purported renunciations in respect of which an amount is included in the value of B;

E is the rate of interest prescribed for the purpose of subsection 164(3) for the month; and

F is

(a) one, where the month is December, and

(b) nil, in any other case.

**Related Provisions**: 18(1)(t), 20(1)(nn) — Tax under Part XII.6 is deductible; 66(18) — Members of partnerships; 87(4.4)(e)–(h) — Amalgamation of principal-business corporations; 211.91(2) — Return and payment of tax; 257 — Formula cannot calculate to less than zero.

**Notes**: See Notes at end of 211.91.

**Regulations**: 4301(b) (prescribed rate of interest under 164(3), for 211.91(1)E).

**(2) Return and payment of tax** — A corporation liable to tax under this Part in respect of one or more months in a calendar year shall, before March of the following calendar year,

(a) file with the Minister a return for the year under this Part in prescribed form containing an estimate of the tax payable under this Part by it in respect of each month in the year; and

(b) pay to the Receiver General the amount of tax payable under this Part by it in respect of each month in the year.

**(3) Provisions applicable to Part** — Subsections 150(2) and (3), sections 152, 158 and 159, subsections 161(1) and (11), sections 162 to 167 and Division J of Part I apply to this Part, with any modifications that the circumstances require.

**Notes**: Part XII.6 levies a tax on flow-through share issuers that use the 1-year look-back rule under 66(12.66), under which certain CEE and CDE incurred in a calendar year can be flowed through to an investor and treated as if they had been incurred at the end of the preceding calendar year. The Part XII.6 tax compensates the fisc for the acceleration of the deduction resulting from 66(12.66). Due to 18(1)(t) and 20(1)(nn), this tax is deductible in computing an issuer's income. An additional tax under Part XII.6 is levied if the flow-through share funds have not been spent by the end of the calendar year of the renunciation. This is in effect an administrative charge for the extra costs associated with retroactive adjustments caused by excessive renunciations.

211.91 (Part XII.6) added by 1996 Budget, effective for 1997 and later calendar years.

**Definitions [s. 211.91]**: "amount" — 248(1); "calendar year" — *Interpretation Act* 37(1)(a); "corporation" — 248(1), *Interpretation Act* 35(1); "Minister", "prescribed" — 248(1); "province" — *Interpretation Act* 35(1).

## PART XIII — TAX ON INCOME FROM CANADA OF NON-RESIDENT PERSONS

**212. (1) Tax** — Every non-resident person shall pay an income tax of 25% on every amount that a person resident in Canada pays or credits, or is deemed by Part I to pay or credit, to the non-resident person as, on account or in lieu of payment of, or in satisfaction of,

**Related Provisions**: 94(3)(a) [proposed], 104(7.01) — Application to trust deemed resident in Canada; 212(13.3)(a) — Authorized foreign bank deemed resident in Canada; 214(1) — No deductions from tax; 215(1) — Requirement to withhold and remit; 216 — Election to pay tax on net income from rents and timber royalties; 217 — Election to file return under Part I in respect of certain kinds of income; 227 — Withholding taxes — administration and enforcement; Reg. 105 — Withholding on payments to non-residents for services; Reg. 805 — No tax where income attributable to permanent establishment or taxable under 115(1)(a)(iii.3).

**Notes**: The 25% withholding tax rate is reduced by Canada's bilateral tax treaties for certain kinds of payments to residents of many countries. Interest, dividends, royalties and occasionally manage-

## S. 212(1) — Income Tax Act

ment fees are often reduced to 10%, 15% or some other rate. See the table of treaty withholding rates in the introductory pages, as well as the Canada-U.S. and Canada-U.K. treaties reproduced at the end of the book. See also ITAR 10(6), which limits the rate of tax under s. 212 to the limit provided by the treaty.

U.S. charitable organizations and pension trusts are exempt from certain withholding tax under Article XXI of the Canada-U.S. treaty.

No return is filed by non-residents in respect of tax withheld under this section, except where an election is made under section 216 or 217 to file a return and pay regular tax on the net rather than withholding tax on the gross. If tax is wrongly withheld or overwithheld, a refund application may be made under 227(6).

**I.T. Application Rules [subsec. 212(1)]**: 10(4) (application to debts issued before 1976); 10(6) (reduction of 25% rate by treaty).

**Interpretation Bulletins [subsec. 212(1)]**: IT-77R: Securities in satisfaction of income debt; IT-360R2: Interest payable in a foreign currency. See also list at end of s. 212.

**Information Circulars [subsec. 212(1)]**: 76-12R4: Applicable rate of Part XIII tax on amounts paid or credited to persons in treaty countries; 77-16R4: Non-resident income tax.

**I.T. Technical News [subsec. 212(1)]**: No. 11 (reporting of amounts paid out of an employee benefit plan); No. 14 (meaning of "credited" for purposes of Part XIII withholding tax).

**Forms [subsec. 212(1)]**: NR2-UK, NR2A-UK: Statements of amounts paid to non-residents of Canada; NR4 Summ: Return of amounts paid or credited to non-residents of Canada; NR4 Supp: Statement of amounts paid or credited to non-residents of Canada; NR4-OAS: Statement of OAS pension paid or credited to non-residents of Canada; NR601: Non-resident ownership certificate — withholding tax; NR602: Non-resident ownership certificate — no withholding tax; T1141: Information return in respect of transfers to non-resident trusts; T1142: Information return in respect of distributions from and indebtedness owed to a non-resident trust; T4061: Non-resident withholding tax guide.

(a) **management fee** — a management or administration fee or charge;

**Related Provisions**: 212(4) — Meaning of "management or administration fee or charge"; Reg. 105 — Withholding tax on payments to non-residents for services. See additional Related Provisions at beginning of subsec. 212(1).

**Notes**: Under many of Canada's tax treaties, management fees paid to a non-resident are treated as business profits and not subject to Canadian tax at all if the non-resident does not have a permanent establishment in Canada. Thus, the withholding tax does not apply in such cases.

Corporations based in Ontario must pay an additional 5% provincial tax on non-arm's length management and administration fees paid to non-residents. See 11(5)–(8) of the *Corporations Tax Act* (Ontario), reproduced in David M. Sherman, *The Practitioner's Ontario Taxes, Annotated*. Although the 5% tax is economically equivalent to a withholding tax, it is imposed on the corporation and thus not protected by treaty provisions that benefit the non-resident.

For a discussion of methods of calculating management fees charged by a non-resident parent to a Canadian subsidiary, see Emma Purdy & Jeffrey Zanchelli, "Calculating and Supporting Management Fees", 44(1) *Canadian Tax Journal* 157–187 (1996).

**Regulations**: 202(1)(a) (information return); 805 (no tax where income attributable to permanent establishment).

**Interpretation Bulletins**: IT-468R: Management or administrative fees paid to non-residents. See also list at end of s. 212.

**Information Circulars**: 87-2R: International transfer pricing. See also at beginning of subsec. 212(1).

**Forms**: See at beginning of subsec. 212(1).

(b) **interest** — interest except

(i) interest payable by a non-resident-owned investment corporation,

(ii) interest payable on

(A) bonds of or guaranteed by the Government of Canada issued on or before December 20, 1960,

(B) bonds of or guaranteed by the Government of Canada issued after December 20, 1960, and before April 16, 1966, the interest on which is payable to the government or central bank of a country other than Canada or to any international organization or agency prescribed by regulation, or

(C) bonds, debentures, notes, mortgages or similar obligations

(I) of or guaranteed by the Government of Canada,

(II) of the government of a province or an agent thereof,

(III) of a municipality in Canada or a municipal or public body performing a function of government in Canada,

(IV) of a corporation, commission or association not less than 90% of the shares or capital of which is owned by Her Majesty in right of a province or by a Canadian municipality, or of a subsidiary wholly-owned corporation that is subsidiary to such a corporation, commission or association, or

---

**Proposed Amendment — 212(1)(b)(ii)(C)(IV)**

(IV) of a corporation, commission or association to which any of paragraphs 149(1)(d) to (d.6) applies, or

**Application**: Bill C-43 (First Reading September 20, 2000), subsec. 102(1), will amend subcl. 212(1)(b)(ii)(C)(IV) to read as above, applicable to amounts paid or credited after 1998.

**Technical Notes**: Clause 212(1)(b)(ii)(C) provides an exemption from non-resident withholding tax for interest paid on certain government and government-guaranteed debt obligations, as well as debt obligations issued by entities used to be described in paragraph 149(1)(d), before that paragraph was amended and paragraphs 149(1)(d.1) to (d.6) were added, effective for taxation years and fiscal periods that begin after 1998. Clause 212(1)(b)(ii)(C) is, therefore, amended to refer to paragraphs 149(1)(d) to (d.6) consequential on the 1998 amendment to subsection 149(1).

---

(V) of an educational institution or a hospital if repayment of the principal amount thereof and payment of the interest thereon is to be made, or is guaranteed, assured or otherwise specifically provided for or secured by the government of a province,

issued after April 15, 1966,

(iii) interest payable in a currency other than Canadian currency to a person with whom the payer is dealing at arm's length, on

(A) any obligation where the evidence of indebtedness was issued on or before December 20, 1960,

(B) any obligation where the evidence of indebtedness was issued after December 20, 1960, if the obligation was entered into under an agreement in writing made on or before that day, under which the obligee undertook to advance, on or before a specified day, a specified amount at a specified rate of interest or a rate of interest to be determined as provided in the agreement, to the extent that the interest payable on the obligation is payable

(I) in respect of a period ending not later than the earliest day on which, under the terms of the obligation determined as of the time it was entered into, the obligee would be entitled to demand payment of the principal amount of the obligation or the amount outstanding as or on account of the principal amount thereof, as the case may be, if the terms of the obligation determined as of that time provided for that payment on or after a specified day, or

(II) in respect of a period ending not later than one year after the time the obligation was entered into, in any other case,

(C) any bond, debenture or similar obligation issued after December 20, 1960, for the issue of which arrangements were made on or before that day with a dealer in securities, if the existence of the arrangements for the issue of the bond, debenture or similar obligation can be established by evidence in writing given or made on or before that day,

(D) an amount not repayable in Canadian currency deposited with an institution that was at the time the amount was deposited or at the time the interest was paid or credited a prescribed financial institution,

(E) any obligation entered into in the course of carrying on a business in a country other than Canada, to the extent that the interest payable on the obligation is deductible in computing the income of the payer under Part I from a business carried on by the payer in such a country, or that, but for subsection 18(2) or section 21, would have been so deductible, or

(F) any obligation entered into by the payer after December 20, 1960, on assuming an obligation referred to in clause (A) in consideration or partial consideration for the purchase by the payer of property of the vendor that constituted security for that obligation, if the payer on entering into the obligation undertook to pay the same amount of money on or before the same date and at the same rate of interest as the vendor of the property had undertaken in respect of the obligation under which the vendor was the obligor,

(for the purpose of this subparagraph, interest expressed to be computed by reference to Canadian currency shall be deemed to be payable in Canadian currency),

(iv) interest payable on any bond, debenture or similar obligation to a person with whom the payer is dealing at arm's length and to whom a certificate of exemption that is in force on the day the amount is paid or credited was issued under subsection (14),

(v) interest payable to a person with whom the payer is dealing at arm's length on any obligation entered into in the course of carrying on a life insurance business in a country other than Canada,

(vi) [Repealed under former Act]

(vii) interest payable by a corporation resident in Canada to a person with whom that corporation is dealing at arm's length on any obligation where the evidence of indebtedness was issued by that corporation after June 23, 1975 if under the terms of the obligation or any agreement relating thereto the corporation may not under any circumstances be obliged to pay more than 25% of

(A) where the obligation is one of a number of obligations that comprise a single debt issue of obligations that are identical in respect of all rights (in equity or otherwise, either immediately or in the future and either absolutely or contingently) attaching thereto, except as regards the principal amount thereof, the total of the principal amount of those obligations, or

(B) in any other case, the principal amount of the obligation,

within 5 years from the date of issue of that single debt issue or that obligation, as the case may be, except

(C) in the event of a failure or default under the said terms or agreement,

(D) if the terms of the obligation or any agreement relating thereto become unlawful or are changed by virtue of legislation or by a court, statutory board or commission,

(E) if the person exercises a right under the terms of the obligation or any agreement relating thereto to convert the obligation into, or exchange the obligation for, a prescribed security, or

(F) in the event of the person's death;

(viii) interest payable on a mortgage or similar obligation secured by, or on an agreement for sale or similar obligation with respect to, real property situated outside Canada or an interest in any such real property except to the extent that the interest payable on the obligation is deductible in computing the income of the payer under Part I from a business carried on by the payer in Canada or from property other than real property situated outside Canada,

(ix) interest payable in Canadian currency on account of an amount in Canadian currency deposited in a country other than Canada with a branch or office of a payer who

(A) is, or is eligible to become, a member of the Canadian Payments Association, or

(B) is a credit union that is a shareholder or member of a body corporate or organization that is a central for the purposes of the *Canadian Payments Association Act*,

to a person with whom the payer is dealing at arm's length,

(x) interest payable to a prescribed international organization or agency,

(xi) interest payable on an amount deposited with a prescribed financial institution for the period during which the amount was an eligible deposit (within the meaning assigned by subsection 33.1(1)) of the institution, and

(xii) interest payable under a securities lending arrangement by a lender under the arrangement that is a financial institution prescribed for the purpose of clause (iii)(D), or a registered securities dealer resident in Canada, on money provided to the lender either as collateral or as consideration for the particular security lent or transferred under the arrangement where

(A) the particular security is an obligation referred to in subparagraph (ii) or an obligation of the government of any country, province, state, municipality or other political subdivision,

(B) the amount of money so provided at any time during the term of the arrangement does not exceed 110% of the fair market value at that time of the particular security, and

(C) the arrangement was neither intended, nor made as a part of a series of securities lending arrangements, loans or other transactions that was intended, to be in effect for more than 270 days,

and for the purpose of this paragraph, where interest is payable on an obligation, other than a prescribed obligation, and all or any portion of the interest is contingent or dependent on the use of or production from property in Canada or is computed by reference to revenue, profit, cash flow, commodity price or any other similar criterion or by reference to dividends paid or payable to shareholders of any class of shares of the capital stock of a corporation, the interest shall be deemed not to be interest described in subparagraphs (ii) to (vii) and (ix);

**Related Provisions**: 204 — Qualified investment defined; 212(3) — Replacement obligations issued by corporations in financial difficulty; 212(6)–(8) — Reduced tax on interest on pre-1961 provincial bonds; 212(9)(c) — Exemption for interest received by mutual fund trust and paid to non-resident; 212(13.3)(a) — Authorized foreign bank deemed resident in Canada; 212(15) — CD-insured obligations deemed not to be guaranteed by Government of Canada; 212(18) — Return by financial institutions; 212(19) — Tax on dealers re excess amount exempted under securities lending arrangement; 214(2) — Income and capital combined; 214(3)(e) — Deemed payments; 214(4) — Securities; 214(6) — Deemed interest; 214(7), (7.1) — Sale of obligation; 214(11) — Application to payments deemed made by NRO; 214(15) — Deemed interest; 218 — Loan to wholly-owned subsidiary; 240(2) — Interest coupon to be identified; 248(10) — Series of transactions; 248(12) — Identical properties; 260(8) — Securities lending arrangement — deemed payment of interest; Canada-U.S. tax treaty, Art. XI — Taxation of interest. See additional Related Provisions at beginning of 212(1).

**Notes**: Interest payments to residents of countries with which Canada has a tax treaty are usually limited by the treaty to a lower rate, such as 15%. (For the U.S., it is 10%). See ITAR 10(6) and the tables of treaty withholding rates in the introductory pages. Interest on arm's length debt issued before 1976 to residents of prescribed countries is specifically limited to 15% regardless of treaty arrangements. See ITAR 10(4).

212(1)(b)(ii) and (vii) were originally intended to apply to bonds etc. issued before a given year. This limitation, after being extended several times, was removed entirely by 1988 tax reform.

212(1)(b)(iii)(D) was amended in 1986. It does not apply to interest paid or credited on amounts deposited before 1988 with a bank. For interest on such amounts, read:

(D) any debt owing by a bank to which the *Bank Act* applies, as or on account of an amount deposited with that bank that is not repayable in Canadian currency.

212(1)(b)(iv) amended by 1992 technical bill, effective for amounts paid or credited to a person in 1992 or later, except that for obligations acquired by the person or by a person related to the person before 1992, the amendment applies only to amounts paid or credited in 1995 or later. Where the amendment does not apply, ignore the words "with whom the payer is dealing at arm's length".

212(1)(b)(vii)(F) added by 1992 technical bill, effective for amounts paid or credited after 1991.

212(1)(b)(viii) was enacted to deal with personal vacation properties (e.g., a condominium in Florida).

212(1)(b)(xii) added (and amended retroactively by 1994 tax amendments bill (Part VIII) to use the new term "registered securities dealer") added by 1993 technical bill, effective for securities lending arrangements entered into after May 28, 1993 (the date of the press release announcing this change). Note that a securities trader who makes "too much" use of this exemption is subject to a special tax under 212(19). Revenue Canada monitors the exemption through returns required by 212(18).

The closing words of 212(1)(b) are (per amendment in 1986) effective for obligations issued or extended after February 25, 1986 otherwise than pursuant to an agreement in writing made on or before that date. (For the purposes of this rule, where the terms and conditions relating to the computation of interest payable on an obligation are changed at any time pursuant to an agreement made after February 25, 1986, the obligation is not grandfathered.) For earlier obligations, read the closing words as follows:

> and for the purpose of this paragraph, where interest is payable on an obligation entered into after November 12, 1981 (otherwise than pursuant to a commitment in writing made on or before that date) and all or any portion of the interest is contingent or dependent upon the use of or production from property in Canada, the interest shall be deemed not to be interest described in subparagraphs (ii) to (vii) and (ix);

**Regulations**: 202(1)(b) (information return); 806, 806.1 (prescribed international organization or agency); 806.2 (prescribed obligation); 1600 (prescribed countries for ITAR 10(4)); 6208 (prescribed security); 7900 (prescribed financial institutions).

**Remission Orders**: *Churchill Falls (Labrador) Corporation Withholding Tax Remission Order*, P.C. 1968-832 (no withholding on interest on first mortgage bonds sold in the U.S. by Churchill Falls (Labrador) Corp.).

**I.T. Application Rules**: 10(5) (certificate of exemption in force since 1971).

**Interpretation Bulletins**: IT-155R3: Exemption from non-resident tax or interest payable on certain bonds, debentures, notes, hypothecs or similar obligations; IT-265R3: Payments of income and capital combined; IT-320R2: RRSP — qualified investments; IT-360R2: Interest payable in a foreign currency; IT-361R3: Exemption from Part XIII tax on interest payments to non-residents; IT-430R3: Life insurance proceeds received by a private corporation or a partnership as a consequence. See also list at end of s. 212.

**Information Circulars**: See at beginning of subsec. 212(1).

**I.T. Technical News**: No. 9 (exemption from withholding tax under 212(1)(b)(vii)(C)); No. 11 (paragraph 212(1)(b) — postamble); No. 16 (*Crown Forest* case).

**Advance Tax Rulings**: ATR-49: Long-term foreign debt; ATR-69: Withholding tax on interest paid to non-resident persons;.

**Forms**: See at beginning of subsec. 212(1).

(c) **estate or trust income** — income of or from an estate or a trust to the extent that the amount

(i) would, if the non-resident person were a person resident in Canada to whom Part I applied, be included in computing the income of the non-resident person under subsection 104(13), except to the extent that the amount is deemed by subsection 104(21) to be a taxable capital gain of the non-resident person, or

### Proposed Amendment — 212(1)(c)(i)

(i) is included in computing the income of the non-resident person under subsection 104(13), except to the extent that the amount is deemed by subsection 104(21) to be a taxable capital gain of the non-resident person, or

**Application**: Bill C-43 (First Reading September 20, 2000), subsec. 102(2), will amend subpara. 212(1)(c)(i) to read as above, applicable to amounts paid or credited after December 17, 1999.

**Technical Notes**: Paragraph 212(1)(c) generally provides that a non-resident beneficiary is subject to Part XIII withholding tax on trust distributions in connection with the same types of amounts on which a beneficiary resident in Canada is subject to tax under Part I.

Paragraph 212(1)(c) is amended to clarify that the tax consequences of a beneficiary's residence outside Canada will be taken into account in determining the amount subject to tax under paragraph 212(1)(c). These tax consequences include the potential indirect tax consequences to a beneficiary of a trust under subsection 104(13) of the application of subsection 107(5) to the trust because the beneficiary is non-resident.

This amendment, which is linked with new section 250.1, applies to amounts paid or credited after December 17, 1999.

(ii) can reasonably be considered (having regard to all the circumstances including the terms and conditions of the estate or trust arrangement) to be a distribution of, or derived from, an amount received by the estate or trust as, on account of, in lieu of payment of or in satisfaction of, a dividend on a share of the capital stock of a corporation resident in Canada, other than a taxable dividend;

**Related Provisions**: 104(11) — Dividend received from NRO; 212(2)(b) — Withholding tax on capital dividends; 212(9) — Exemptions; 212(10) — Trust established before 1949; 212(11) — Payment to a beneficiary as income of trust; 212(13) — Non-resident payor deemed resident in Canada; 212(17) — No withholding tax on payments from employee benefit plan or employee trust; 214(3)(f), (f.1) — Deemed payments; 250.1(b) — Calculation of income of non-resident person; Canada-U.S. tax treaty, Art. XXII:2 — Estate or trust income. See additional Related Provisions at beginning of subsec. 212(1).

**Notes**: 212(1)(c)(ii) added by 1991 technical bill, effective July 14, 1990, to require withholding tax on a capital distribution by a trust that is attributable to a capital dividend. Other capital distributions to non-residents are, like such distributions to Canadian residents, non-taxable.

**Regulations**: 202(1)(c) (information return).

**Interpretation Bulletins**: IT-342R: Trusts — income payable to beneficiaries; IT-465R: Non-resident beneficiaries of trusts; IT-500R: RRSPs — death of an annuitant; IT-531: Eligible funeral arrangements. See also list at end of s. 212.

**Information Circulars**: See at beginning of subsec. 212(1).

**Forms**: See at beginning of subsec. 212(1).

(d) **rents, royalties, etc.** — rent, royalty or similar payment, including, but not so as to restrict the generality of the foregoing, any payment

(i) for the use of or for the right to use in Canada any property, invention, trade-name, patent, trade-mark, design or model, plan, secret formula, process or other thing whatever,

(ii) for information concerning industrial, commercial or scientific experience where the total amount payable as consideration for that information is dependent in whole or in part on

(A) the use to be made of, or the benefit to be derived from, that information,

## S. 212(1)(d)(ii)(B) — Income Tax Act

(B) production or sales of goods or services, or

(C) profits,

(iii) for services of an industrial, commercial or scientific character performed by a non-resident person where the total amount payable as consideration for those services is dependent in whole or in part on

(A) the use to be made of, or the benefit to be derived from, those services,

(B) production or sales of goods or services, or

(C) profits,

but not including a payment made for services performed in connection with the sale of property or the negotiation of a contract,

(iv) made pursuant to an agreement between a person resident in Canada and a non-resident person under which the non-resident person agrees not to use or not to permit any other person to use any thing referred to in subparagraph (i) or any information referred to in subparagraph (ii), or

(v) that was dependent on the use of or production from property in Canada whether or not it was an instalment on the sale price of the property, but not including an instalment on the sale price of agricultural land,

but not including

(vi) a royalty or similar payment on or in respect of a copyright in respect of the production or reproduction of any literary, dramatic, musical or artistic work,

(vii) a payment in respect of the use by a railway company or by a person whose principal business is that of a common carrier of property that is railway rolling stock as defined in the definition "rolling stock" in section 2 of the *Railway Act*

(A) if the payment is made for the use of that property for a period or periods not expected to exceed in the aggregate 90 days in any 12 month period, or

(B) in any other case, if the payment is made pursuant to an agreement in writing entered into before November 19, 1974;

(viii) a payment made under a *bona fide* cost-sharing arrangement under which the person making the payment shares on a reasonable basis with one or more non-resident persons research and development expenses in exchange for an interest in any or all property or other things of value that may result therefrom,

(ix) a rental payment for the use of or the right to use outside Canada any corporeal property,

(x) any payment made to a person with whom the payer is dealing at arm's length, to the extent that the amount thereof is deductible in computing the income of the payer under Part I from a business carried on by the payer in a country other than Canada, or

(xi) a payment made to a person with whom the payer is dealing at arm's length for the use of or the right to use property that is

(A) an aircraft,

(B) furniture, fittings or equipment attached to an aircraft, or

(C) a spare part for property described in clause (A) or (B);

**Related Provisions**: 212(5) — Motion picture films; 212(9)(b) — Exemption for royalty payment received by trust and paid to non-resident; 216 — Alternative re rents and timber royalties; Canada-U.S. tax treaty, Art. VI — Income from real property; Art. XII — Royalties. See additional Related Provisions at beginning of subsec. 212(1).

**Notes**: Royalty and rental payments to residents of countries with which Canada has a tax treaty are often limited by the treaty to a lower rate, such as 15%. See the tables of treaty withholding rates at the beginning of the book.

An election is available to pay regular tax on net rental income from real property rather than withholding tax on the gross. See 216(1).

The federal government announced in the April 1993 budget that it was prepared to eliminate the withholding tax, in its tax treaty negotiations, on arm's length payments in respect of rights to use patented information or information concerning scientific experience, and on payments made for the use of computer software. This has now been done in recent treaties or Protocols, such as with Algeria, Austria, Denmark, Kyrgyzstan, Luxembourg, The Netherlands and the U.S. See Art. XII(3)(b) of the Canada-U.S. tax treaty.

The exemption for "literary" works in 212(1)(d)(vi) applies to software, as a result of amendments in 1988 to the *Copyright Act* that define "literary work" to include computer programs. The exemption applies only to the right to make copies (not just backup copies) of software, however, and not to payments by end-users to non-residents. See Revenue Canada Round Table, Canadian Tax Foundation 1988 annual conference report, at p. 53:89; and 1993 conference report, Q. 29, at p. 58:15. During 1994 and at the 1994 Canadian Tax Foundation conference, Revenue Canada indicated that a right to use packaged or "shrink-wrapped" software is now considered a sale of goods to which 212(1)(d) does not apply. (The same principle is applied under the GST; see GST Technical Information Bulletin B-037R, in David M. Sherman, *GST Memoranda, Bulletins & Policies* (Carswell, annual).) Payments for custom software are still considered royalties. Related services such as maintenance fees will not be taxable under 212(1)(d) if they are reasonable, but could be subject to withholding under Reg. 105.

Corporations based in Ontario must pay an additional 5% provincial tax on certain non-arm's length royalties paid to non-residents, although this was eliminated in certain cases by the May 1997 Ontario budget. See 11(5)–(8) of the *Corporations Tax Act* (Ontario), reproduced in *The Practitioner's Ontario Taxes Annotated* (Carswell, annual).

212(1)(d)(xi) added by 1992 transportation industry assistance bill, effective for payments made after December 6, 1991 pursuant to agreements entered into after 1990. It extends the exemption from withholding tax for lease payments on aircraft, which already applied under 212(1)(d)(ix) to the extent the aircraft was used in international traffic, to aircraft used in domestic flights.

**Regulations**: 202(1)(d) (information return).

Part XIII — Tax on Non-Resident's Income from Canada   S. 212(1)(h)(v)

**Interpretation Bulletins**: IT-303: Know-how and similar payments to non-residents; IT-393R2: Elections re tax on rents and timber royalties — non-residents; IT-438R2: Crown charges — resource properties in Canada; IT-494: Hire of ships and aircraft from non-residents. See also list at end of s. 212.

**Information Circulars**: See at beginning of subsec. 212(1).

**Forms**: See at beginning of subsec. 212(1).

(e) **timber royalties** — a timber royalty in respect of a timber resource property or a timber limit in Canada (which, for the purposes of this Part, includes any consideration for a right under or pursuant to which a right to cut or take timber from a timber resource property or a timber limit in Canada is obtained or derived, to the extent that the consideration is dependent on, or computed by reference to, the amount of timber cut or taken);

**Related Provisions**: 13(21) — Timber resource property defined; 212(13) — Non-resident payor deemed resident in Canada; 216 — Alternative re rents and timber royalties. See additional Related Provisions at beginning of subsec. 212(1).

**Regulations**: 202(1)(e) (information return).

**Interpretation Bulletins**: IT-393R2: Election re tax on rents and timber royalties — non-residents. See also list at end of s. 212.

**Information Circulars**: See at beginning of subsec. 212(1).

**Forms**: See at beginning of subsec. 212(1).

(f) [Repealed]

**Notes**: 212(1)(f) repealed by 1996 Budget, effective for amounts paid and (or) credited after April 1997. For earlier payments, read:

(f) alimony [or support] — alimony or other payment for the support of the non-resident person, children of the non-resident person or both the non-resident person and children of the non-resident person that would, under paragraph 56(1)(b), (c) or (c.1), be included in computing the non-resident person's income if the non-resident person were resident in Canada;

This withholding tax was repealed at the same time as amendments to 56(1)(b) and 60(b) that eliminated the income inclusion and deduction for certain child support payments. (See Notes to 56(1)(b).) However, the repeal of 212(1)(f) goes much further than was done with domestic payments, which are only non-taxable if they are child (not spousal) support, and only if the agreement was made or varied after April 1997. For payments to non-residents, *all* child and spousal support is now non-taxable. (Under the Canada-U.S. tax treaty Art. XVIII:6(a), such payments were already exempt when paid to a U.S. resident. The same applied to residents of several other countries.)

(g) **patronage dividend** — a patronage dividend, that is, a payment made pursuant to an allocation in proportion to patronage as defined by section 135 or an amount that would, under subsection 135(7), be included in computing the non-resident person's income if that person were resident in Canada;

**Related Provisions**: See Related Provisions at beginning of subsec. 212(1).

**Regulations**: 202(1)(g) (information return).

**Interpretation Bulletins**: IT-362R: Patronage dividends. See also list at end of s. 212.

**Information Circulars**: See at beginning of subsec. 212(1).

**Forms**: See at beginning of subsec. 212(1).

(h) **pension benefits** — a payment of a superannuation or pension benefit, other than

(i), (ii) [Repealed]

(iii) an amount or payment referred to in subsection 81(1) to the extent that that amount or payment would not, if the non-resident person had been resident in Canada throughout the taxation year in which the payment was made, be included in computing that person's income,

(iii.1) the portion of the payment that is transferred by the payer on behalf of the non-resident person, pursuant to an authorization in prescribed form, to a registered pension plan, registered retirement savings plan or registered retirement income fund and that

(A) because of subsection 146(21) or 147.3(9) would not, if the non-resident person had been resident in Canada throughout the taxation year in which the payment was made, be included in computing the non-resident person's income, or

(B) by reason of paragraph 60(j) or (j.2) would, if the non-resident person had been resident in Canada throughout the year, be deductible in computing the non-resident person's income for the year,

(iii.2) an amount referred to in paragraph 110(1)(f) to the extent that the amount would, if the non-resident person had been resident in Canada throughout the taxation year in which the amount was paid, be deductible in computing that person's taxable income or that of the spouse or common-law partner of that person,

(iv) in the case of a payment described in section 57, that portion of the payment that would, by virtue of that section, not be included in the recipient's income for the taxation year in which it was received, if the recipient were resident in Canada throughout that year, or

(iv.1) the portion of the payment that is transferred by the payer on behalf of the non-resident person, pursuant to an authorization in prescribed form, to acquire an annuity contract in circumstances to which subsection 146(21) applies,

except such portion, if any, of the payment as may reasonably be regarded as attributable to services rendered by the person, to or in respect of whom the payment is made, in taxation years

(v) during which the person at no time was resident in Canada, and

1655

## S. 212(1)(h)(vi) — Income Tax Act

(vi) throughout which the person was not employed, or was only occasionally employed, in Canada;

**Related Provisions**: 128.1(4)(b)(iii) [to be repealed], 128.1(10)"excluded right or interest"(a)(viii), (g) — No deemed disposition of pension rights on emigration; 180.2(2)B — Reduction in OAS clawback to reflect non-resident withholding tax; 180.2(4)(b)(ii), 180.2(5)(a)(ii) — No OAS benefits paid to non-resident who has not filed return; 215(5) — Regulations reducing amount to be deducted or withheld; 217 — Election to pay tax under Part I instead of withholding tax; Canada-U.S. tax treaty, Art. XVIII — Pensions and annuities. See additional Related Provisions at beginning of subsec. 212(1).

**Notes**: 212(1)(h)(i) and (ii) repealed by 1995 Budget, effective for payments made after 1995. They read:

(i) a pension or supplement under the *Old Age Security Act* or a similar payment under a law of a province,

(ii) a benefit under the *Canada Pension Plan* or a provincial pension plan as defined in section 3 of that Act,

Thus, OAS, CPP and QPP benefits received by non-residents are now subject to Canadian withholding tax. This change was related to the 1995 Protocol to the Canada-U.S. tax treaty, which amended Art. XVIII(5) so that cross-border social security benefits (including OAS and CPP) became taxed only by the paying country, not the country in which the recipient is resident. The 1997 Protocol to the treaty then retroactively reversed the effect of the 1995 Protocol, so that Canada now no longer imposes withholding tax on payments of OAS and CPP to U.S. residents. (See Art. XVIII of the treaty.) Nevertheless, the repeal of 212(1)(h)(i) and (ii) has remained, so that Canada now taxes such payments to residents of other countries, except where protection is provided by treaty.

A $50 payment to U.S. social security recipients in lieu of interest, to compensate for the time tax was withheld during the above flip-flop, was originally proposed as 122.7. It was instead enacted as Part 2 of the 1998 Budget bill; see under Art. XVIII:5 of the treaty.

212(1)(h)(iii.1) amended by 1990 pension bill, 1992 technical bill and 1993 technical bill. For payments before September 1992, ignore the reference to 146(21). For payments from June 28, 1990 to August 29, 1990, ignore the references to RRIFs. For payments from 1981 to June 27, 1990, read:

(iii.1) the portion thereof that is transferred by the payer on behalf of the non-resident person pursuant to an authorization in prescribed form to a registered pension plan or to a registered retirement savings plan under which the non-resident person is the annuitant (within the meaning assigned by section 146),

212(1)(h)(iii.2) amended by 2000 same-sex partners bill to add reference to "common-law partner", effective for the 2001 and later taxation years, or earlier by election (see Notes to 248(1)"common-law partner").

212(1)(h)(iv.1) added by 1993 technical bill, effective for payments made after August 1992, to accommodate transfers to an RRSP from the Saskatchewan Pension Plan.

The words "only occasionally employed in Canada" in 212(1)(h)(vi) were held to apply to players on U.S. NHL teams who played only a small percentage of their games in Canada: *Lou Nanne & Stan Mikita v. The Queen*, [2000] 1 C.T.C. 2776 (T.C.C.).

**Regulations**: 202(2)(a) (information return).

**Interpretation Bulletins**: IT-76R2: Exempt portion of pension when employee has been a non-resident; IT-163R2: Election by non-resident individuals on certain Canadian source income; IT-397R: Amounts excluded from income — statutory exemptions and certain pensions, allowances and compensations; IT-451R: Deemed disposition and acquisition on ceasing to be or becoming resident in Canada. See also list at end of s. 212.

**Information Circulars**: 79-8R3: Forms to use to directly transfer funds to or between plans, or to purchase an annuity. See also at beginning of 212(1).

**Forms**: NRTA1: Authorization for non-resident tax exemption. See also at beginning of subsec. 212(1).

(i) [Repealed under former Act]

**Notes**: 212(1)(i), repealed in 1976, dealt with Canada Pension Plan and Quebec Pension Plan benefits, which were subsequently exempted under 212(1)(h)(ii), and are now taxable effective 1996.

(j) **benefits** — any benefit described in any of subparagraphs 56(1)(a)(iii) to (vi), any amount described in paragraph 56(1)(x) or (z) (other than an amount transferred under circumstances in which subsection 207.6(7) applies) or the purchase price of an interest in a retirement compensation arrangement;

**Related Provisions**: 128.1(4)(b)(iii) [to be repealed], 128.1(10)"excluded right or interest"(a)(ix), (h) — No deemed disposition of rights on emigration; 214(3)(b.1) — Deemed payments; 215(5) — Regulations reducing amount to be deducted or withheld; 217 — Election to pay tax under Part I instead of withholding tax. See additional Related Provisions at beginning of subsec. 212(1).

**Notes**: Parenthetical exclusion relating to 207.6(7) added to 212(1)(j) by 1995-97 technical bill, effective for amounts paid or credited after 1995.

**Regulations**: 202(2)(b) (information return).

**Interpretation Bulletins**: IT-163R2: Election by non-resident individuals on certain Canadian source income; IT-451R: Deemed disposition and acquisition on ceasing to be or becoming resident in Canada. See also list at end of s. 212.

**Information Circulars**: See at beginning of subsec. 212(1).

**Forms**: See at beginning of subsec. 212(1).

(j.1) **retiring allowances** — a payment of any allowance described in subparagraph 56(1)(a)(ii), except

(i) such portion, if any, of the payment as may reasonably be regarded as attributable to services rendered by the person, to or in respect of whom the payment is made, in taxation years

(A) during which the person at no time was resident in Canada, and

(B) throughout which the person was not employed, or was only occasionally employed, in Canada, and

(ii) the portion of the payment transferred by the payer on behalf of the non-resident person pursuant to an authorization in prescribed form to a registered pension plan or to a registered retirement savings plan under which the non-resident person is the annuitant (within the meaning assigned by subsection 146(1)) that would, if the non-resident person had been resident in Canada throughout the year, be deductible in computing the income of the non-resident person by virtue of paragraph 60(j.1);

**Related Provisions**: 128.1(4)(b)(iii)) [to be repealed], 128.1(10)"excluded right or interest"(d) — No deemed disposition of right to retiring allowance on emigration; 215(5) — Regulations reducing deduction or withholding; 217 — Election to pay tax under Part I instead of withholding tax. See additional Related Provisions at beginning of subsec. 212(1).

**Notes**: This applies to termination pay and severance as well as amounts paid on retirement. See 248(1)"retiring allowance".

**Regulations**: 202(2)(b) (information return).

**Interpretation Bulletins**: IT-163R2: Election by non-resident individuals on certain Canadian source income; IT-337R3: Retiring allowances; IT-451R: Deemed disposition and acquisition on ceasing to be or becoming resident in Canada. See also list at end of s. 212.

**Information Circulars**: 79-8R3: Forms to use to directly transfer funds to or between plans, or to purchase an annuity. See also at beginning of subsec. 212(1).

**Forms**: NRTA1: Authorization for non-resident tax exemption. See also at beginning of subsec. 212(1).

**(k) supplementary unemployment benefit plan payments** — a payment by a trustee under a registered supplementary unemployment benefit plan;

**Related Provisions**: 128.1(4)(b)(iii) [to be repealed], 128.1(10)"excluded right or interest"(a)(xi) — No deemed disposition of rights on emigration; 212(13)(e) — Payment by non-resident deemed made by resident of Canada; 215(5) — Regulations reducing amount to be deducted or withheld; 217 — Election to pay tax under Part I instead of withholding tax. See additional Related Provisions at beginning of 212(1).

**Regulations**: 202(2)(c) (information return).

**Interpretation Bulletins**: IT-451R: Deemed disposition and acquisition on ceasing to be or becoming resident in Canada. See also list at end of s. 212.

**Information Circulars**: See at beginning of subsec. 212(1).

**Forms**: See at beginning of subsec. 212(1).

**(l) registered retirement savings plan payments** — a payment out of or under a registered retirement savings plan or a plan referred to in subsection 146(12) as an "amended plan" that would, if the non-resident person had been resident in Canada throughout the taxation year in which the payment was made, be required by section 146 to be included in computing the income of the non-resident person for the year, other than the portion thereof that

(i) has been transferred by the payer on behalf of the non-resident person pursuant to an authorization in prescribed form

(A) to a registered retirement savings plan under which the non-resident person is the annuitant (within the meaning assigned by subsection 146(1)),

(B) to acquire an annuity described in subparagraph 60(l)(ii) under which the non-resident person is the annuitant, or

(C) to a carrier (within the meaning assigned by subsection 146.3(1)) as consideration for a registered retirement income fund under which the non-resident person is the annuitant (within the meaning assigned by subsection 146.3(1)), and

(ii) would, if the non-resident person had been resident in Canada throughout the year, be deductible in computing the income of the non-resident person for the year by virtue of paragraph 60(l);

**Related Provisions**: 128.1(4)(b)(iii) [to be repealed], 128.1(10)"excluded right or interest"(a)(i) — No deemed disposition of rights on emigration; 146(16) — RRSP — deduction on transfer of funds; 212(13)(e) — Payment by non-resident deemed made by resident of Canada; 214(3)(c) — Deemed payments; 215(5) — Regulations reducing amount to be deducted or withheld; 217 — Election to pay tax under Part I instead of withholding tax; Canada-U.S. tax treaty, Art. XXIX:5 — Election for income accruing in RRSP not to be taxed until paid out; *Income Tax Conventions Interpretation Act* 5.1 — Definition of "pension" for tax treaty purposes. See additional Related Provisions at beginning of subsec. 212(1).

**Notes**: A withdrawal from an RRSP may not be protected by tax treaty provisions that limit withholding tax on pension payments, depending on the wording and the definition of "pension" in the treaty. See the definitions "pension" and "periodic pension payment" in s. 5 of the *Income Tax Conventions Interpretation Act* (reproduced herein, before the treaties). Where "pension" is defined in the treaty to include a "retirement arrangement", as in Article XIII of the Canada-U.S. treaty and Article 17 of the Canada-UK treaty, an RRSP falls into ITCIA 5"pension"(b).

212(1)(l)(i)(C) added by 1990 pension bill, effective for payments made after June 27, 1990.

**Regulations**: 202(2)(d) (information return).

**Interpretation Bulletins**: IT-163R2: Election by non-resident individuals on certain Canadian source income; IT-451R: Deemed disposition and acquisition on ceasing to be or becoming resident in Canada; IT-500R: RRSPs — death of an annuitant. See also list at end of s. 212.

**Information Circulars**: 72-22R9: Registered retirement savings plans; 79-8R3: Forms to use to directly transfer funds to or between plans, or to purchase an annuity. See also at beginning of subsec. 212(1).

**Forms**: NRTA1: Authorization for non-resident tax exemption. See also at beginning of subsec. 212(1).

**(m) deferred profit sharing plan payments** — a payment under a deferred profit sharing plan or a plan referred to in subsection 147(15) as a "revoked plan" that would, if the non-resident person had been resident in Canada throughout the taxation year in which the payment was made, be required by section 147, if it were read without reference to subsections 147(10.1) and (20), to be included in computing the non-resident person's income for the year, other than the portion thereof that is transferred by the payer on behalf of the non-resident person, pursuant to an authorization in prescribed form, to a registered pension plan or registered retirement savings plan and that

(i) by reason of subsection 147(20) would not, if the non-resident person had been resident in Canada throughout the year, be included in computing the non-resident person's income, or

(ii) by reason of paragraph 60(j.2) would, if the non-resident person had been resident in Canada throughout the year, be deductible in computing the non-resident person's income for the year;

**S. 212(1)(m)** — Income Tax Act

**Related Provisions**: 128.1(4)(b)(iii) [to be repealed], 128.1(10)"excluded right or interest"(a)(iv) — No deemed disposition of rights on emigration; 212(13)(e) — Payment by non-resident deemed made by resident of Canada; 214(3)(d) — Deemed payments; 215(5) — Regulations reducing amount to be deducted or withheld; 217 — Election to pay tax under Part I instead of withholding tax. See additional Related Provisions at beginning of subsec. 212(1).

**Notes**: 212(1)(m) amended by 1990 pension bill, effective 1989, except that, in subpara. (ii), for payments made before June 28, 1990, read "60(j)" in place of "60(j.2)".

**Regulations**: 202(2)(e) (information return).

**Interpretation Bulletins**: IT-163R2: Election by non-resident individuals on certain Canadian source income; IT-451R: Deemed disposition and acquisition on ceasing to be or becoming resident in Canada. See also list at end of s. 212.

**Information Circulars**: 79-8R3: Forms to use to directly transfer funds to or between plans, or to purchase an annuity. See also at beginning of subsec. 212(1).

**Forms**: NRTA1: Authorization for non-resident tax exemption. See also at beginning of subsec. 212(1).

(n) **income-averaging annuity contract payments** — a payment under an income-averaging annuity contract, any proceeds of the surrender, cancellation, redemption, sale or other disposition of an income-averaging annuity contract, or any amount deemed by subsection 61.1(1) to have been received by the non-resident person as proceeds of the disposition of an income-averaging annuity contract;

**Related Provisions**: 61 — IAACs; 128.1(4)(b)(iii) [to be repealed], 128.1(10)"excluded right or interest"(f)(ii) — No deemed disposition of rights on emigration; 212(13)(e) — Payment by non-resident deemed made by resident of Canada; 214(3)(b) — Deemed payments. See additional Related Provisions at beginning of 212(1).

**Regulations**: 202(2)(f) (information return).

**Interpretation Bulletins**: IT-451R: Deemed disposition and acquisition on ceasing to be or becoming resident in Canada. See also list at end of s. 212.

**Information Circulars**: See at beginning of subsec. 212(1).

**Forms**: See at beginning of subsec. 212(1).

(o) **other annuity payments** — a payment under an annuity contract (other than a payment in respect of an annuity issued in the course of carrying on a life insurance business in a country other than Canada) to the extent of the amount in respect of the interest of the non-resident person in the contract that, if the non-resident person had been resident in Canada throughout the taxation year in which the payment was made,

(i) would be required to be included in computing the income of the non-resident person for the year, and

(ii) would not be deductible in computing that income;

**Related Provisions**: 56(1)(d) — Annuity payments required to be included in income of resident; 128.1(4)(b)(iii) [to be repealed], 128.1(10)"excluded right or interest"(f)(i) — No deemed disposition of rights on emigration; 240(1) — Taxable and non-taxable obligations defined. See additional Related Provisions at beginning of 212(1).

**Regulations**: 202(2)(g) (information return).

**Interpretation Bulletins**: IT-451R: Deemed disposition and acquisition on ceasing to be or becoming resident in Canada. See also list at end of s. 212.

**Information Circulars**: See at beginning of subsec. 212(1).

**Forms**: See at beginning of subsec. 212(1).

(p) **payments from RHOSP** — a payment out of or under a fund, plan or trust that was at the end of 1985 a registered home ownership savings plan (within the meaning assigned by paragraph 146.2(1)(h) of the *Income Tax Act*, chapter 148 of the Revised Statutes of Canada, 1952, as it read in its application to the 1985 taxation year), other than

(i) the portion of the payment that is a refund of an excess described in paragraph 146.2(7)(a) of that Act (as it read in its application to the 1985 taxation year) made on or before April 30, 1986, and

(ii) the portion of the payment that can reasonably be considered to be income of the fund, plan or trust after 1985;

**Related Provisions**: 128.1(4)(b)(iii) [to be repealed] — No deemed disposition of rights on emigration; 214(3)(g) — Deemed payments. See additional Related Provisions at beginning of 212(1).

**Notes**: See notes to 146.2.

**Regulations**: 202(2)(h) (information return).

**I.T. Application Rules**: 69 (meaning of "*Income Tax Act*, chapter 148 of the Revised Statutes of Canada, 1952").

**Interpretation Bulletins**: IT-451R: Deemed disposition and acquisition on ceasing to be or becoming resident in Canada. See also list at end of s. 212.

**Information Circulars**: See at beginning of subsec. 212(1).

**Forms**: See at beginning of subsec. 212(1).

(q) **registered retirement income fund payments** — a payment out of or under a registered retirement income fund that would, if the non-resident person had been resident in Canada throughout the taxation year in which the payment was made, be required by section 146.3 to be included in computing the non-resident person's income for the year, other than the portion thereof that

(i) has been transferred by the payer on behalf of the non-resident person pursuant to an authorization in prescribed form

(A) to a registered retirement savings plan under which the non-resident person is the annuitant (within the meaning assigned by subsection 146(1)),

(B) to acquire an annuity described in subparagraph 60(l)(ii) under which the non-resident person is the annuitant, or

(C) to a carrier (within the meaning assigned by subsection 146.3(1)) as consideration for a registered retirement income fund under which the non-resident person is the annuitant (within the meaning assigned by subsection 146.3(1)), and

Part XIII — Tax on Non-Resident's Income from Canada    S. 212(2)

(ii) would, if the non-resident person had been resident in Canada throughout the year, be deductible in computing the non-resident person's income for the year by reason of paragraph 60(l);

**Related Provisions**: 128.1(4)(b)(iii) [to be repealed], 128.1(10)"excluded right or interest"(a)(ii) — No deemed disposition of rights on emigration; 212(13)(e) — Payment by non-resident deemed made by resident of Canada; 214(3)(i) — Deemed payments; 215(5) — Regulations reducing amount to be deducted or withheld; 217 — Election to pay tax under Part I instead of withholding tax. See additional Related Provisions at beginning of 212(1).

**Notes**: A RRIF withdrawal in excess of twice the "minimum amount" for the year may not be protected by tax treaty provisions that limit withholding tax on pension payments, due to 5"pension" and 5"periodic pension payment"(c)(i) of the *Income Tax Conventions Interpretation Act*.

Exceptions in 212(1)(q)(i) and (ii) added by 1990 pension bill, effective for payments made after June 27, 1990.

**Regulations**: 202(2)(i) (information return).

**Interpretation Bulletins**: IT-451R: Deemed disposition and acquisition on ceasing to be or becoming resident in Canada. See also list at end of s. 212.

**Information Circulars**: 79-8R3: Forms to use to directly transfer funds to or between plans, or to purchase an annuity. See also at beginning of subsec. 212(1).

**Forms**: NRTA1: Authorization for non-resident tax exemption. See also at beginning of subsec. 212(1).

(r) **registered education savings plan** — a payment that is

(i) required by paragraph 56(1)(q) to be included in computing the non-resident person's income under Part I for a taxation year, and

(ii) not required to be included in computing the non-resident person's taxable income or taxable income earned in Canada for the year;

**Related Provisions**: 214(3)(j) — Deemed payments. See additional Related Provisions at beginning of subsec. 212(1).

**Notes**: 212(1)(r) amended by 1997 Budget, retroactive to amounts paid or credited after February 28, 1979. The amendment was intended to ensure that amounts included in the non-resident's taxable income or taxable income earned in Canada (i.e., subject to tax under Part I) are not subject to Part XIII withholding tax.

**Regulations**: 202(2)(j) (information return).

**Information Circulars**: See at beginning of subsec. 212(1).

**Forms**: See at beginning of subsec. 212(1).

(s) **home insulation or energy conversion grants** — a grant under a prescribed program of the Government of Canada relating to home insulation or energy conversion;

**Related Provisions**: See Related Provisions at beginning of subsec. 212(1).

**Regulations**: 202(2)(k) (information return).

**Information Circulars**: See at beginning of subsec. 212(1).

**Forms**: See at beginning of subsec. 212(1).

(t) **NISA Fund No. 2 payments** — a payment out of a NISA Fund No. 2 to the extent that that amount would, if Part I applied, be required by subsection 12(10.2) to be included in computing the person's income for a taxation year;

**Related Provisions**: 128.1(10)"excluded right or interest"(i) — No deemed disposition on emigration; 214(3)(l) — Deemed payments. See additional Related Provisions at beginning of subsec. 212(1).

**Notes**: 212(1)(t) added by 1992 technical bill, effective for payments made in 1991 or later.

**Regulations**: 202(2.1) (information return).

**Information Circulars**: See at beginning of subsec. 212(1).

**Forms**: See at beginning of subsec. 212(1).

(u) **amateur athlete trust payments** — a payment in respect of an amateur athlete trust that would, if Part I applied, be required by section 143.1 to be included in computing the person's income for a taxation year; or

**Related Provisions**: 214(3)(k) — Deemed payments. See additional Related Provisions at beginning of subsec. 212(1).

**Notes**: 212(1)(u) added by 1992 technical bill, effective for payments made in 1992 or later.

**Information Circulars**: See at beginning of subsec. 212(1).

(v) **payments under an eligible funeral arrangement** — a payment made by a custodian (within the meaning assigned by subsection 148.1(1)) of an arrangement that was, at the time it was established, an eligible funeral arrangement, to the extent that such amount would, if the non-resident person were resident in Canada, be included because of subsection 148.1(3) in computing the person's income.

**Related Provisions**: 212(13)(e) — Payment by non-resident deemed made by resident of Canada.

**Notes**: 212(1)(v) added by 1994 tax amendments bill (Part IV), effective for amounts paid or credited after October 21, 1994. See Notes to 148.1.

**Regulations**: 202(2)(m) (information return); 204(3)(d.1) (cemetery care trust need not file T3 return).

**Information Circulars**: IT-531: Eligible funeral arrangements. See at beginning of subsec. 212(1).

**Related Provisions, I.T. Application Rules, Information Circulars, I.T Technical News, Forms — subsec. 212(1)**: See at beginning of subsec. 212(1), before para. (a).

**(2) Tax on dividends** — Every non-resident person shall pay an income tax of 25% on every amount that a corporation resident in Canada pays or credits, or is deemed by Part I or Part XIV to pay or credit, to the non-resident person as, on account or in lieu of payment of, or in satisfaction of,

(a) a taxable dividend (other than a capital gains dividend within the meaning assigned by subsection 130.1(4), 131(1) or 133(7.1)), or

(b) a capital dividend.

**Related Provisions**: 40(3.7) — Stop-loss rule where non-resident has received dividends; 84 — Deemed dividends; 128.1(1)(c.1) — Deemed dividend to non-resident corporation before it becomes resident in Canada; 139.1(4)(f)(ii) — Dividend deemed received on demutualization of insurance corporation; 212(1)(c)(ii) — Estate or trust income derived from capital dividend; 212(13.3)(a) — Authorized foreign bank deemed resident in Canada; 212.1, 212.2 — Deemed dividends on surplus strips by non-resident; 213(1) — Where tax not payable; 214(1) — No deductions; 214(3)(a) — Deemed payments; 214(12) — Application of subsec. 214(2); 215(1), (1.1) — Requirement to withhold and remit; 219 — Branch tax; 227(10), (10.1) — Assessment; 250(5) — Anti-avoidance rule re corporate residence; 257 — Formula cannot calculate to less than zero; Canada-U.S. tax treaty, Art. X — Taxation of dividends.

**Notes**: Dividend payments to residents of countries with which Canada has a tax treaty are usually limited by the treaty to a lower rate, such as 15%. See ITAR 10(6) and the table of treaty withholding rates at the beginning of this book. "Direct" intercorporate dividends are often limited to 10% and, as announced in the February 1992 Budget, may be reduced to 5%. Canada has so far agreed to reduce the rate to 5% with numerous countries, including Austria, Croatia, Denmark, Estonia, France, Hungary, Iceland, Indonesia, Japan, Kazakhstan, Latvia, Lebanon, Lithuania, Luxembourg, The Netherlands, Slovenia, South Africa, Sweden, Switzerland, Trinidad & Tobago, Ukraine, the United States, Uzbekistan and Vietnam. (However, other recent treaties signed, such as with Algeria, Bulgaria, Chile, India, Jordan, Kyrgyzstan, Portugal and Tanzania, do not have this low rate.)

**Regulations**: 202(1)(g) (information return); 805 (where no withholding tax).

**Interpretation Bulletins**: IT-66R6: Capital dividends; IT-96R6: Options granted by corporations to acquire shares, bonds, or debentures and by trusts to acquire trust units; IT-119R4: Debts of shareholders and certain persons connected with shareholders; IT-421R2: Benefits to individuals, corporations and shareholders from loans or debt; IT-430R3: Life insurance proceeds received by a private corporation or a partnership as a consequence of death; IT-465R: Non-resident beneficiaries of trusts; IT-468R: Management or administration fees paid to non-residents. See also list at end of s. 212.

**Information Circulars**: 77-16R4: Non-resident income tax; 88-2 Supplement, para. 7: General anti-avoidance rule — section 245 of the *Income Tax Act*.

**I.T. Technical News**: No. 14 (meaning of "credited" for purposes of Part XIII withholding tax).

**Forms**: NR2-UK: Statement of amounts paid to non-residents of Canada; NR2A-UK: Statement of amounts paid to non-residents of Canada; NR4 Summ: Return of amounts paid or credited to non-residents of Canada; NR4 Supp: Statement of amounts paid or credited to non-residents of Canada; NR4-OAS: Statement of OAS pension paid or credited to non-residents of Canada; NR601: Non-resident ownership certificate — withholding tax; NR602: Non-resident ownership certificate — no withholding tax; T4061: Non-resident withholding tax guide.

**(3) Replacement obligations** — For the purpose of subparagraph (1)(b)(vii), an obligation (in this subsection referred to as the "replacement obligation") issued by a corporation resident in Canada wholly or in substantial part and either directly or indirectly in exchange or substitution for an obligation or a part of an obligation (in this subsection referred to as the "former obligation") shall, where

(a) the replacement obligation was issued

(i) as part of a proposal to, or an arrangement with, its creditors that was approved by a court under the *Bankruptcy and Insolvency Act*,

(ii) at a time when all or substantially all of its assets were under the control of a receiver, receiver-manager, sequestrator or trustee in bankruptcy, or

(iii) at a time when, because of financial difficulty, the issuing corporation or another corporation resident in Canada with which it does not deal at arm's length was in default, or could reasonably be expected to default, on the former obligation,

(b) the proceeds from the issue of the replacement obligation can reasonably be regarded as having been used by the issuing corporation or another corporation with which it does not deal at arm's length in the financing of its active business carried on in Canada immediately before the time when the replacement obligation was issued, and

(c) all interest on the former obligation was (or would be, if the person to whom that interest was paid or credited were non-resident) exempt from tax under this Part because of subparagraph (1)(b)(vii),

be deemed to have been issued when the former obligation was issued.

**Notes**: 212(3) added by 1993 technical bill, effective for replacement obligations issued after June 1993. It allows a corporation in financial difficulty to restructure its long-term debt by issuing replacement obligations, under the conditions stated, while still preserving the withholding tax exemption that applies to long-term corporate debt under 212(1)(b)(vii).

The CCRA takes the position that "all or substantially all", used in 212(3)(a)(ii), means 90% or more.

Former 212(3), repealed by 1981 Budget, reduced the withholding tax on dividends to non-residents paid by corporations with a "degree of Canadian ownership".

**Interpretation Bulletins**: IT-361R3: Exemption from Part XIII tax on interest payments to non-residents.

**(4) Interpretation of "management or administration fee or charge"** — For the purpose of paragraph (1)(a), "management or administration fee or charge" does not include any amount paid or credited or deemed by Part I to have been paid or credited to a non-resident person as, on account or in lieu of payment of, or in satisfaction of,

(a) a service performed by the non-resident person if, at the time the non-resident person performed the service

(i) the service was performed in the ordinary course of a business carried on by the non-resident person that included the performance of such a service for a fee, and

(ii) the non-resident person and the payer were dealing with each other at arm's length, or

(b) a specific expense incurred by the non-resident person for the performance of a service that was for the benefit of the payer,

to the extent that the amount so paid or credited was reasonable in the circumstances.

**Notes**: See Notes to 212(1)(a).

**Interpretation Bulletins**: IT-468R: Management or administration fees paid to non-residents. See also list at end of s. 212.

**(5) Motion picture films** — Every non-resident person shall pay an income tax of 25% on every amount that a person resident in Canada pays or credits, or is deemed by Part I to pay or credit, to the non-resident person as, on account or in lieu of payment of, or in satisfaction of, payment for a right in or to the use of

(a) a motion picture film, or

(b) a film, video tape or other means of reproduction for use in connection with television (other than solely in connection with and as part of a news program produced in Canada),

that has been or is to be used or reproduced in Canada.

**Related Provisions**: 212(1)(d) — Withholding tax — royalties; 214(1) — No deduction; 215(1) — Requirement to withhold and remit.

**Notes**: The withholding tax under 212(5) technically applies to the full amount of the payment even where part of the payment is in respect of use outside Canada. However, the CCRA is willing to consider excluding the portion relating to use outside Canada on a case-by-case basis. See Revenue Canada Round Table, Canadian Tax Foundation 1993 annual conference report, Q. 30.

**Regulations**: 202(1)(h) (information return).

**Forms**: NR4 Summ: Return of amounts paid or credited to non-residents of Canada; NR4 Supp: Statement of amounts paid or credited to non-residents of Canada.

**(6) Interest on provincial bonds from wholly-owned subsidiaries** — Where an amount described by subsection (1) relates to interest on bonds or other obligations of or guaranteed by Her Majesty in right of a province or interest on bonds or other obligations provision for the payment of which was made by a statute of a provincial legislature, the tax payable under subsection (1) is 5% of that amount.

**Related Provisions**: 212(7) — Application of subsec. 212(6); 240(1) — Taxable and non-taxable obligations defined.

**Notes**: There is no withholding tax on provincial bonds issued after April 15, 1966. See 212(1)(b)(ii)(C)(II) and (IV).

**(7) Where subsec. (6) does not apply** — Subsection (6) does not apply to interest on any bond or other obligation described therein that was issued after December 20, 1960, except any such bond or other obligation for the issue of which arrangements were made on or before that day with a dealer in securities, if the existence of the arrangements for the issue of the bond or other obligation can be established by evidence in writing given or made on or before that day.

**Related Provisions**: 212(8) — Bonds issued in exchange for earlier bonds.

**(8) Bonds issued after December 20, 1960 in exchange for earlier bonds** — For the purposes of this Part, where any bond, except a bond to which clause (1)(b)(ii)(C) applies, was issued after December 20, 1960 in exchange for a bond issued on or before that day, it shall, if the terms on which the bond for which it was exchanged was issued conferred on the holder thereof the right to make the exchange, be deemed to have been issued on or before December 20, 1960.

**Interpretation Bulletins**: IT-360R2: Interest payable in a foreign currency. See also list at end of s. 212.

**(9) Exemptions** — Where

(a) a dividend or interest is received by a trust from a non-resident-owned investment corporation,

(b) an amount (in this subsection referred to as the "royalty payment") is received by a trust as, on account of, in lieu of payment of or in satisfaction of, a royalty on or in respect of a copyright in respect of the production or reproduction of any literary, dramatic, musical or artistic work, or

(c) interest is received by a mutual fund trust maintained primarily for the benefit of non-resident persons

and a particular amount is paid or credited to a non-resident person as income of or from the trust and can reasonably be regarded as having been derived from the dividend, interest or royalty payment, as the case may be, no tax is payable because of paragraph (1)(c) as a consequence of the payment or crediting of the particular amount if no tax would have been payable under this Part in respect of the dividend, interest or royalty payment, as the case may be, if it had been paid directly to the non-resident person instead of to the trust.

**Related Provisions**: 104(10) — Where property owned for non-residents; 104(11) — Dividend received from non-resident-owned investment corporation.

**Notes**: 212(9) amended by 1995-97 technical bill, effective for amounts paid or credited to non-resident persons after April 1995. From April 1977 to April 1995, read:

(9) No tax is payable under paragraph (1)(c) on an amount paid or credited to a non-resident person as income of or from a trust if it may reasonably be regarded as having been derived from

(a) dividends or interest received by the trustee from a non-resident-owned investment corporation, or

(b) amounts received as, on account or in lieu of payment of, or in satisfaction of a royalty on or in respect of a copyright in respect of the production or reproduction of any literary, dramatic, musical or artistic work,

on which no tax would have been payable under this Part if they had been paid by the non-resident-owned investment corporation or person paying the amounts in respect of copyright to the non-resident person instead of to the trustee.

**Interpretation Bulletins**: IT-465R: Non-resident beneficiaries of trusts. See also list at end of s. 212.

**(10) Trust beneficiaries residing outside of Canada** — Where all the beneficiaries of a trust established before 1949 reside, during a taxation year, in one country other than Canada and all amounts included in computing the income of the trust for the taxation year were received from persons resident in that country, no tax is payable under paragraph (1)(c) on an amount paid or credited in the taxation year to a beneficiary as income of or from the trust.

**Interpretation Bulletins**: IT-465R: Non-resident beneficiaries of trusts. See also list at end of s. 212.

**(11) Payment to beneficiary as income of trust** — An amount paid or credited by a trust or an estate to a beneficiary or other person beneficially interested therein shall be deemed, for the purpose of paragraph (1)(c) and without limiting the generality thereof, to have been paid or credited as income of the trust or estate, regardless of the source from which the trust or estate derived it.

**Related Provisions**: 107(5) — Distribution to non-resident; 248(25) — Meaning of "beneficially interested".

**Notes**: 212(11) amended by 1991 technical bill, effective July 14, 1990, to remove an exclusion for "a distribution or payment of capital", so that 212(1)(c)(ii) can be operative.

**Interpretation Bulletins**: IT-465R: Non-resident beneficiaries of trusts. See also list at end of s. 212.

**(11.1), (11.2)** [Repealed under former Act]

**Notes**: 212(11.1) and (11.2), repealed by 1988 tax reform, dealt with distributions by a trust before 1988. See 212(1)(c) now.

**(12) Deemed payments to spouse, etc.** — Where by reason of subsection 56(4) or (4.1) or any of sections 74.1 to 75 of this Act or section 74 of the *Income Tax Act*, chapter 148 of the Revised Statutes of Canada, 1952, there is included in computing a taxpayer's income under Part I for a taxation year an amount paid or credited to a non-resident person in the year, no tax is payable under this section on that amount.

**I.T. Application Rules**: 69 (meaning of "*Income Tax Act*, chapter 148 of the Revised Statutes of Canada, 1952").

**Interpretation Bulletins**: IT-369R: Attribution of trust income to settlor; IT-438R2: Crown charges — resource properties in Canada; IT-440R2: Transfer of rights to income. See also list at end of s. 212.

**(13) Rent and other payments** — For the purposes of this section, where a non-resident person pays or credits an amount as, on account or in lieu of payment of, or in satisfaction of,

(a) rent for the use in Canada of property (other than property that is rolling stock as defined in section 2 of the *Railway Act*),

(b) a timber royalty in respect of a timber resource property or a timber limit in Canada,

(c) a payment of a superannuation or pension benefit under a registered pension plan or of a distribution to one or more persons out of or under a retirement compensation arrangement,

(d) a payment of a retiring allowance or a death benefit to the extent that the payment is deductible in computing the payer's taxable income earned in Canada,

(e) a payment described in any of paragraphs (1)(k) to (n), (q) and (v), or

(f) interest on any mortgage or other indebtedness entered into or issued or modified after March 31, 1977 and secured by real property situated in Canada or an interest therein to the extent that the amount so paid or credited is deductible in computing the non-resident person's taxable income earned in Canada or the amount on which the non-resident person is liable to pay tax under Part I,

the non-resident person shall be deemed in respect of that payment to be a person resident in Canada.

**Related Provisions**: 13(21) — Timber resource property defined.

**Notes**: Reference to 212(1)(v) added to 212(13)(e) by 1994 tax amendments bill (Part IV), effective for amounts paid or credited after October 21, 1994.

**Regulations**: 202(4) (information return).

**(13.1) Application of Part XIII tax where payer or payee is a partnership** — For the purposes of this Part, other than section 216,

(a) where a partnership pays or credits an amount to a non-resident person, the partnership shall, in respect of the portion of that amount that is deductible, or that would but for section 21 be deductible in computing the amount of the income or loss, as the case may be, referred to in paragraph 96(1)(f) or (g) if the references therein to "a particular place" and "that particular place" were read as references to "Canada", be deemed to be a person resident in Canada; and

(b) where a person resident in Canada pays or credits an amount to a partnership (other than a Canadian partnership within the meaning assigned by section 102), the partnership shall be deemed, in respect of that payment, to be a non-resident person.

**Related Provisions**: 212(13.3)(b) — Authorized foreign bank deemed resident for purposes of meaning of "Canadian partnership" in para. (b); 227(15) — Partnership included in "person".

**Regulations**: 202(5) (information return).

**Interpretation Bulletins**: IT-81R: Partnerships — income of non-resident partners. See also list at end of s. 212.

**(13.2) Application of Part XIII tax where non-resident operates in Canada** — For the purposes of this Part, where in a taxation year

(a) a non-resident person whose business was carried on principally in Canada, or

(b) a non-resident person who

(i) manufactures or processes goods in Canada,

(ii) operates an oil or gas well in Canada or extracts petroleum or natural gas from a natural accumulation thereof in Canada, or

(iii) extracts minerals from a mineral resource in Canada

pays or credits an amount (other than an amount to which subsection (13) applies) to another non-resident person, the first-mentioned non-resident person shall be deemed, in respect of the portion of that amount that was deductible in computing that person's taxable income earned in Canada for any taxation year, to be a person resident in Canada.

**Regulations**: 202(6) (information return).

## Proposed Addition — 212(13.3)

**(13.3) Application of Part XIII to authorized foreign bank** — An authorized foreign bank is deemed to be resident in Canada for the purposes of

(a) this Part, in respect of any amount paid or credited to or by the bank in respect of its Canadian banking business; and

(b) the application in paragraph (13.1)(b) of the definition "Canadian partnership" in respect of a partnership interest held by the bank in the course of its Canadian banking business.

**Application**: The August 8, 2000 draft legislation, s. 22, will add subsec. 212(13.3), applicable after June 27, 1999.

**Technical Notes**: Section 212 of the Act imposes a tax of 25% (reduced by many treaties) on certain amounts paid or credited to non-residents by residents of Canada. Pursuant to section 215 of the Act, this tax must be withheld by the resident payer.

New subsection 212(13.3) of the Act provides special rules regarding the application of withholding taxes under Part XIII of the Act to authorized foreign banks. This new subsection treats an authorized foreign bank as being resident in Canada for the purposes of any amount paid or credited to or by the bank with respect to its Canada banking business. An authorized foreign bank is also deemed to be resident in Canada with respect to the application of the definition of Canadian partnership to paragraph 212(13.1)(b) of the Act, with respect to a partnership interest held by the bank in the course of its Canadian banking business.

As a result of this amendment, an authorized foreign bank will not pay tax under section 212 on, for example, interest payments its Canadian banking business receives from residents of Canada. On the other hand, the bank will be responsible for withholding the tax payable by a non-resident to whom it makes a taxable payment.

This new subsection applies after June 27, 1999.

**Related Provisions**: 218.2 — Branch interest tax on authorized foreign banks.

**(14) Certificate of exemption** — The Minister may, on application, issue a certificate of exemption to any non-resident person who establishes to the satisfaction of the Minister that

(a) an income tax is imposed under the laws of the country of which the non-resident person is a resident;

(b) the non-resident person is exempt under the laws referred to in paragraph (a) from the payment of income tax to the government of the country of which the non-resident person is a resident; and

(c) the non-resident person is

(i) a person who is or would be, if the non-resident person were resident in Canada, exempt from tax under section 149,

(ii) a trust or corporation that is operated exclusively to administer or provide superannuation, pension, retirement or employee benefits, or

(iii) a trust, corporation or other organization constituted and operated exclusively for charitable purposes, no part of the income of which is payable to, or is otherwise available for, the personal benefit of any proprietor, member, shareholder, trustee or settlor thereof.

**Related Provisions**: 172(3) — Appeal from refusal to issue certificate; 172(4) — Deemed refusal to register; 212(1)(b)(iv) — No withholding tax where certificate of exemption; Reg. 6804(1) — Definition of "qualifying entity" — same conditions; Canada-U.S. Tax Convention, Art. XXI:2 — Exemption from cross-border income tax.

**Notes**: 212(14)(c)(ii) amended by 1998 Budget, this version effective for applications for certificates of exemption made after 1998. For applications submitted from February 24 through December 31, 1998, read "operated exclusively" as "operated principally". For applications submitted before February 24, 1998, read:

(ii) a trust or corporation established or incorporated principally in connection with, or the principal purpose of which is to administer or provide benefits under, one or more superannuation, pension or retirement funds or plans or any funds or plans established to provide employee benefits, or

The amendment ensures that non-resident trusts or corporations that were established or incorporated to provide pension, retirement or superannuation benefits, but that no longer have this as their exclusive activity, are ineligible for certificates of exemption. This matches the exclusivity requirement for charitable institutions in 212(14)(c)(iii), and for non-resident trusts or corporations that provide these benefits in Art. XXI:2 of the Canada-US tax treaty.

**I.T. Application Rules**: 10(5).

**Information Circulars**: 77-16R4: Non-resident income tax.

**Forms**: NR6A: Application for certificate of exemption.

**(15) Certain obligations** — For the purposes of subparagraph (1)(b)(ii), after November 18, 1974 interest on a bond, debenture, note, mortgage or similar obligation that is insured by the Canada Deposit Insurance Corporation shall be deemed not to be interest with respect to an obligation guaranteed by the Government of Canada.

**Interpretation Bulletins**: IT-155R3: Exemption from non-resident tax on interest payable on certain bonds, debentures, notes, hypothecs or similar obligations. See also list at end of s. 212.

**(16) Payments for temporary use of rolling stock** — Clause (1)(d)(vii)(A) does not apply to a payment in a year for the temporary use of railway rolling stock by a railway company to a person resident in a country other than Canada unless that country grants substantially similar relief for the year to the company in respect of payments received by it for the temporary use by a person resident in that country of railway rolling stock.

**(17) Exception** — This section is not applicable to payments out of or under an employee benefit plan or employee trust.

**Interpretation Bulletins**: IT-502: Employee benefit plans and employee trusts. See also list at end of s. 212.

**(18) Return by financial institutions and registered securities dealers** — Every person who in a taxation year is a prescribed financial insti-

**S. 212(18)** — Income Tax Act

tution for the purpose of clause (1)(b)(iii)(D) or a person resident in Canada who is a registered securities dealer shall

(a) within 6 months after the end of the year file with the Minister a return in prescribed form if in the year the person paid or credited an amount to a non-resident person in respect of which the non-resident person is, because of clause (1)(b)(iii)(D) or subparagraph (1)(b)(xii), not liable to pay tax under this Part; and

(b) on demand from the Minister, served personally or by registered letter, file within such reasonable time as may be stipulated in the demand, an undertaking in prescribed form relating to the avoidance of payment of tax under this Part.

**Related Provisions**: 150.1(5) — Electronic filing; 212(19) — Tax on securities traders; 248(7)(a) — Mail deemed received on day mailed.

**Notes**: 212(18) amended by 1993 technical bill, effective for taxation years that end after May 28, 1993, to add "or a person resident in Canada who is registered or licensed under the laws of a province to trade in securities" and the reference to 212(1)(b)(xii). The amendments require securities traders to report on transactions exempt under 212(1)(b)(xii), so that the CCRA can assess tax under 212(19) where appropriate. Amended by 1994 tax amendments bill (Part VIII), also effective for taxation years that end after May 28, 1993, to use the new term "registered securities dealer".

**Forms**: NR4B Summ: Return of amounts paid or credited to non-residents of Canada; NR4B Supp: Statement of amounts paid or credited to non-residents of Canada; NR67AR: Non-resident tax remittance; NR67BR: Non-resident tax remittance form; NR75: Non-resident tax remitter registration form; NR601: Non-resident ownership certificate — withholding tax; NR602: Non-resident ownership certificate — no withholding tax; T4061: Guide for payers of non-resident tax.

**(19) Tax on registered securities dealers** — Every taxpayer who is a registered securities dealer resident in Canada shall pay a tax under this Part equal to the amount determined by the formula

$$\frac{1}{365} \times .25 \times (A - B) \times C$$

where

A is the total of all amounts each of which is the amount of money provided before the end of a day to the taxpayer (and not returned or repaid before the end of the day) by or on behalf of a non-resident person as collateral or as consideration for a security that was lent or transferred under a securities lending arrangement described in subparagraph (1)(b)(xii),

B is the total of

(a) all amounts each of which is the amount of money provided before the end of the day by or on behalf of the taxpayer (and not returned or repaid before the end of the day) to a non-resident person as collateral or as consideration for a security described in clause (1)(b)(xii)(A) that was lent or transferred under a securities lending arrangement, and

(b) the greater of

(i) 10 times the greatest amount determined under those laws to be the capital employed by the taxpayer at the end of the day, and

(ii) 20 times the greatest amount of capital required under those laws to be maintained by the taxpayer as a margin in respect of securities described in clause (1)(b)(xii)(A) at the end of the day, and

C is the prescribed rate of interest in effect for the day,

and shall remit that amount to the Receiver General on or before the 15th day of the month after the month in which the day occurs.

**Related Provisions**: 212(18) — Return by securities traders; 227(9) — Penalty on tax not paid; 227(9.3) — Interest on tax not paid; 257 — Formula cannot calculate to less than zero.

**Notes**: 212(19) added by 1993 technical bill (and amended retroactively by 1994 tax amendments bill (Part VIII) to use the new term "registered securities dealer"), effective for securities lending arrangements entered into after May 28, 1993. See Notes to 212(1)(b)(xii).

**Definitions [s. 212]**: "active business" — 248(1); "amateur athlete trust" — 143.1(1)(a), 248(1); "amount", "annuity", "authorized foreign bank" — 248(1); "arm's length" — 251(1); "bank" — 248(1), Interpretation Act 35(1); "beneficially interested" — 248(25); "business" — 248(1); "Canada" — 255; "Canadian banking business" — 248(1); "Canadian partnership" — 102, 248(1); "capital dividend" — 83(2), 248(1); "capital gain" — 39(1)(a), 248(1); "capital property" — 54, 248(1); "class of shares", "common-law partner" — 248(1); "corporation" — 248(1), Interpretation Act 35(1); "credit union" — 137(6), 248(1); "death benefit" — 248(1); "deferred profit sharing plan" — 147(1), 248(1); "dividend" — 248(1); "eligible funeral arrangement" — 148.1(1), 248(1); "employed", "employee benefit plan", "employee trust" — 248(1); "estate" — 104(1), 248(1); "identical" — 248(12); "income-averaging annuity contract" — 61(4), 248(1); "legislature" — Interpretation Act 35(1)"legislative assembly"; "management or administration fee or charge" — 212(4); "mineral resource", "Minister", "NISA Fund No. 2", "non-resident" — 212(13.3), 248(1); "non-resident-owned investment corporation" — 133(8), 248(1); "OSFI risk-weighting guidelines", "oil or gas well", "person", "prescribed" — 248(1); "prescribed rate" — Reg. 4301; "principal amount", "property" — 248(1); "province" — Interpretation Act 35(1); "registered education savings plan" — 146.1(1), 248(1); "registered pension plan" — 248(1); "registered retirement income fund" — 146.3(1), 248(1); "registered retirement savings plan" — 146(1), 248(1); "registered securities dealer" — 248(1); "registered supplementary unemployment benefit plan" — 145(1), 248(1); "regulation" — 248(1); "replacement obligation" — 212(3); "resident in Canada" — 212(13.3), 250; "retirement compensation arrangement", "retiring allowance" — 248(1); "securities lending arrangement" — 248(1), 260(1); "series" — 248(10); "share", "shareholder" — 248(1); "subsidiary wholly-owned corporation", "superannuation or pension benefit" — 248(1); "taxable capital gain" — 38(a), 248(1); "taxable dividend" — 89(1), 248(1); "taxable income" — 2(2), 248(1); "taxable income earned in Canada" — 115(1), 248(1); "taxation year" — 249; "taxpayer", "timber resource property" — 13(21), 248(1); "trust" — 104(1), 248(1), (3); "writing" — Interpretation Act 35(1).

**Interpretation Bulletins [s. 212]**: IT-88R2: Stock dividends; IT-109R2: Unpaid amounts; IT-168R3: Athletes and players employed by football, hockey and similar clubs; IT-221R2: Determination of an individual's residence status; IT-280R: Employees profit sharing plans — payments computed by reference to profits. See also list at beginning of 212(1).

## 212.1 (1) Non-arm's length sales of shares by non-residents — If a non-resident person, a designated partnership or a non-resident-owned investment corporation (in this section referred to as the "non-resident person") disposes of shares (in this section referred to as the "subject shares") of any class of the capital stock of a corporation resident in Canada (in this section referred to as the "subject corporation") to another corporation resident in Canada (in this section referred to as the "purchaser corporation") with which the non-resident person does not (otherwise than because of a right referred to in paragraph 251(5)(b)) deal at arm's length and, immediately after the disposition, the subject corporation is connected (within the meaning that would be assigned by subsection 186(4) if the references in that subsection to "payer corporation" and "particular corporation" were read as "subject corporation" and "purchaser corporation", respectively) with the purchaser corporation,

(a) the amount, if any, by which the fair market value of any consideration (other than any share of the capital stock of the purchaser corporation) received by the non-resident person from the purchaser corporation for the subject shares exceeds the paid-up capital in respect of the subject shares immediately before the disposition shall, for the purposes of this Act, be deemed to be a dividend paid at the time of the disposition by the purchaser corporation to the non-resident person and received at that time by the non-resident person from the purchaser corporation; and

(b) in computing the paid-up capital at any particular time after March 31, 1977 of any particular class of shares of the capital stock of the purchaser corporation, there shall be deducted that proportion of the amount, if any, by which the increase, if any, by virtue of the disposition, in the paid-up capital, computed without reference to this section as it applies to the disposition, in respect of all of the shares of the capital stock of the purchaser corporation exceeds the amount, if any, by which

(i) the paid-up capital in respect of the subject shares immediately before the disposition

exceeds

(ii) the fair market value of the consideration described in paragraph (a),

that the increase, if any, by virtue of the disposition, in the paid-up capital, computed without reference to this section as it applies to the disposition, in respect of the particular class of shares is of the increase, if any, by virtue of the disposition, in the paid-up capital, computed without reference to this section as it applies to the disposition, in respect of all of the issued shares of the capital stock of the purchaser corporation.

**Related Provisions**: 54"proceeds of disposition"(k) — Exclusion of deemed dividend from proceeds; 84(7) — When dividend payable; 84.1 — Similar rule for residents of Canada; 212.1 — Deemed dividend on surplus strip to non-resident; 212.2 — Deemed dividend on surplus strip to non-resident insurer.

**Notes**: The object of s. 212.1 is the same as s. 84.1, but where the shareholder is non-resident. See Notes to 84.1(1). Avoidance of 212.1 can trigger GAAR: see Notes to 245(2) re *RMM Canadian Enterprises* (the *Equilease* case).

212.1(1) opening words amended by 1998 Budget to add reference to a designated partnership and to change "another Canadian corporation" to "another corporation resident in Canada" (i.e., relaxing the requirements for the purchaser corporation), effective February 24, 1998.

212.1(1) opening words and 212.1(1)(a) amended by 1978 Budget and 1988 press release. The current version applies to dispositions after February 9, 1988.

For dispositions from April 11, 1978 through February 9, 1988, read:

212.1 (1) Where, after April 10, 1978, a non-resident person disposes of shares (in this section referred to as the "subject shares") of any class of the capital stock of a Canadian corporation (in this section referred to as the "subject corporation") to another Canadian corporation (in this section referred to as the "purchaser corporation") with which the non-resident person does not (otherwise than by virtue of a right referred to in paragraph 251(5)(b)) deal at arm's length and, immediately after the disposition, the subject corporation is connected (within the meaning of subsection 186(4), on the assumption that the references therein to "payer corporation" and to "particular corporation" were read as "subject corporation" and "purchaser corporation" respectively), with the purchaser corporation,

(a) the amount, if any, by which the fair market value of any consideration (other than any share of the capital stock of the purchaser corporation) received by the non-resident person from the purchaser corporation for the subject shares, exceeds the paid-up capital in respect of the subject shares immediately before the disposition shall, for the purposes of this Act, be deemed to be a dividend paid at the time of the disposition by the purchaser corporation to the non-resident person; and

For dispositions from April 1, 1977 through April 10, 1978, read as above for 1978 through 1988, but read the opening words as follows:

212.1 (1) Where after March 31, 1977, a non-resident person disposes of shares (in this section referred to as the "subject shares") of any class of the capital stock of a Canadian corporation (in this section referred to as the "subject corporation") to another Canadian corporation (in this section referred to as the "purchaser corporation") that, immediately after the disposition, does not deal at arm's length with the non-resident person, and immediately after the disposition the purchaser corporation controls (within the meaning of subsection 186(2)) the subject corporation,

**Interpretation Bulletins**: See at end of s. 212.1.

**Information Circulars**: 77-16R4: Non-resident income tax.

**(2) Idem** — In computing the paid-up capital at any particular time after March 31, 1977 of any particular class of shares of the capital stock of a corporation, there shall be added an amount equal to the lesser of

(a) the amount, if any, by which

(i) the total of all amounts each of which is an amount deemed by subsection 84(3), (4) or

(4.1) to be a dividend on shares of the particular class paid after March 31, 1977 and before the particular time by the corporation and received by a non-resident-owned investment corporation or by a person who is not a corporation resident in Canada

exceeds

(ii) the total that would be determined under subparagraph (i) if this Act were read without reference to paragraph (1)(b), and

(b) the total of all amounts each of which is an amount required by paragraph (1)(b) to be deducted in computing the paid-up capital in respect of the particular class of shares after March 31, 1977 and before the particular time.

**(3) Idem** — For the purposes of this section,

(a) in respect of any disposition described in subsection (1) by a non-resident person of shares of the capital stock of a subject corporation to a purchaser corporation, the non-resident person shall, for greater certainty, be deemed not to deal at arm's length with the purchaser corporation if the non-resident person was,

(i) immediately before the disposition, one of a group of less than 6 persons that controlled the subject corporation, and

(ii) immediately after the disposition, one of a group of less than 6 persons that controlled the purchaser corporation, each member of which was a member of the group referred to in subparagraph (i);

(b) for the purposes of determining whether or not a particular non-resident person (in this paragraph referred to as the "taxpayer") referred to in paragraph (a) was a member of a group of less than 6 persons that controlled a corporation at any time, any shares of the capital stock of that corporation owned at that time by

(i) the taxpayer's child (within the meaning assigned by subsection 70(10)), who is under 18 years of age, or the taxpayer's spouse or common-law partner,

(ii) a trust of which the taxpayer, a person described in subparagraph (i) or a corporation described in subparagraph (iii) is a beneficiary,

(iii) a corporation controlled by the taxpayer, a person described in subparagraph (i), a trust described in subparagraph (ii) or any combination thereof, or

(iv) a partnership of which the taxpayer or a person described in one of paragraphs (i) to (iii) is a majority interest partner or a member of a majority interest group of partners (as defined in subsection 251.1(3))

shall be deemed to be owned at that time by the taxpayer and not by the person who actually owned the shares at that time;

(c) a trust and a beneficiary of the trust or a person related to a beneficiary of the trust shall be deemed not to deal with each other at arm's length;

(d) for the purpose of paragraph (a),

(i) a group of persons in respect of a corporation means any 2 or more persons each of whom owns shares of the capital stock of the corporation,

(ii) a corporation that is controlled by one or more members of a particular group of persons in respect of that corporation shall be considered to be controlled by that group of persons, and

(iii) a corporation may be controlled by a person or a particular group of persons notwithstanding that the corporation is also controlled or deemed to be controlled by another person or group of persons;

(e) a "designated partnership" means a partnership of which either a majority interest partner or every member of a majority interest group of partners (as defined in subsection 251.1(3)) is a non-resident person or a non-resident-owned investment corporation; and

(f) in this subsection, a person includes a partnership.

**Related Provisions**: 256(6), (6.1) — Meaning of "controlled".

**Notes**: 212.1(3)(b)(i) amended by 2000 same-sex partners bill to add reference to "common-law partner", effective for the 2001 and later taxation years, or earlier by election (see Notes to 248(1)"common-law partner").

212.1(3) amended by 1978 Budget, by 1991 technical bill, by 1992 technical bill and by 1998 Budget. Current version effective February 24, 1998.

Before February 24, 1998, for dispositions after December 20, 1991, ignore 212.1(3)(b)(iv) and 3(e) and (f).

For dispositions from July 14, 1990 through December 20, 1991, ignore 212.1(3)(d).

For dispositions from April 11, 1978 through July 13, 1990, ignore 212.1(3)(c), and read 212.1(3)(b)(i) to (iii) as follows:

(i) the taxpayer's spouse,

(ii) an *inter vivos* trust of which the taxpayer, his spouse, a corporation described in subparagraph (iii) or any combination thereof is a beneficiary, or

(iii) a corporation controlled by the taxpayer, his spouse, a trust described in subparagraph (ii) or any combination thereof.

For dispositions from April 1, 1977 through April 10, 1978, read the following in place of 212.1(3) and (4):

(3) Where taxpayer not dealing at arm's length — For the purposes of this section, a taxpayer who is one of a group of less than ten persons who act in concert to control a corporation shall be deemed not to deal with the corporation at arm's length.

**(4) Where section does not apply** — Notwithstanding subsection (1), this section does not apply

1666

Part XIII — Tax on Non-Resident's Income from Canada        S. 212.2

in respect of a disposition by a non-resident corporation of shares of a subject corporation to a purchaser corporation that immediately before the disposition controlled the non-resident corporation.

**Related Provisions**: 256(6), (6.1) — Meaning of "controlled".

**Notes**: 212.1(4) added by 1978 Budget, effective for dispositions after April 10, 1978.

**Definitions [s. 212.1]**: "amount" — 248(1); "arm's length" — 212.1(3)(c), 251(1); "Canada" — 255; "Canadian corporation" — 89(1), 248(1); "child" — 70(10), 252(1); "class of shares" — 248(6); "common-law partner" — 248(1); "control" — 212.1(3)(d); "controlled" — 256(6), (6.1); "corporation" — 248(1), *Interpretation Act* 35(1); "designated partnership" — 212.1(3)(e); "dividend" — 248(1); "group" — 212.1(3)(d); "majority interest partner", "non-resident" — 248(1); "non-resident-owned investment corporation" — 133(8), 248(1); "paid-up capital" — 89(1), 248(1); "partnership" — see Notes to 96(1); "person" — 212.1(3)(f), 248(1); "received" — 248(7); "resident in Canada" — 250; "share" — 248(1); "taxpayer" — 248(1); "trust" — 104(1), 108(1), 248(1), (3).

**Interpretation Bulletins [s. 212.1]**: IT-88R2: Stock dividends; IT-109R2: Unpaid amounts; IT-489R: Non-arm's length sale of shares to a corporation.

**212.2 (1) Application** — This section applies where

(a) a taxpayer disposes at a particular time of a share of the capital stock of a corporation resident in Canada (or any property more than 10% of the fair market value of which can be attributed to shares of the capital stock of corporations resident in Canada) to

   (i) a person resident in Canada,

   (ii) a partnership in which any person resident in Canada has, directly or indirectly, an interest, or

   (iii) a person or partnership that acquires the share or the property in the course of carrying on a business through a permanent establishment in Canada, as defined in the *Income Tax Regulations*;

(b) subsection 212.1(1) does not apply to the disposition;

(c) the taxpayer is non-resident at the particular time;

(d) it is reasonable to conclude that the disposition is part of an expected series of transactions or events that includes the issue after December 15, 1998 of a particular share of the capital stock of a particular insurance corporation resident in Canada on the demutualization (within the meaning assigned by subsection 139.1(1)) of the particular corporation and

   (i) after the particular time, the redemption, acquisition or cancellation of the particular share, or a share substituted for the particular share, by the particular corporation or the issuer of the substituted share, as the case may be,

   (ii) after the particular time, an increase in the level of dividends declared or paid on the particular share or a share substituted for the particular share, or

   (iii) the acquisition, at or after the particular time, of the particular share or a share substituted for the particular share by

      (A) a person not dealing at arm's length with the particular corporation or with the issuer of the substituted share, as the case may be, or

      (B) a partnership any direct or indirect interest in which is held by a person not dealing at arm's length with the particular corporation or with the issuer of the substituted share, as the case may be; and

(e) at the particular time, the person described in subparagraph (a)(i) or (iii) or any person who has, directly or indirectly, an interest in the partnership described in subparagraph (a)(ii) or (iii) knew, or ought reasonably to have known, of the expected series of transactions or events described in paragraph (d).

**Notes**: See Notes at end of 212.2.

**(2) Deemed dividend** — For the purposes of this Part, where property is disposed of at any time by a taxpayer to a person or partnership in circumstances in which this section applies,

(a) a taxable dividend is deemed to be paid at that time by the person or partnership to the taxpayer and received at the time by the taxpayer;

(b) the amount of the dividend is deemed to be equal to the amount determined by the formula

$$A - ((A/B) \times C)$$

where

A is the portion of the proceeds of disposition of the property that can reasonably be attributed to the fair market value of shares of a class of the capital stock of a corporation resident in Canada,

B is the fair market value immediately before that time of shares of that class, and

C is the paid-up capital immediately before that time of that class of shares; and

(c) in respect of the dividend, the person or partnership is deemed to be a corporation resident in Canada.

**Related Provisions [subsec. 212.2(2)]**: 54"proceeds of disposition"(k) — Exclusion of deemed dividend from proceeds.

**Notes [212.2]**: 212.2 added by 1999 Budget, effective December 16, 1998. It is an anti-avoidance "surplus stripping" rule designed, in the context of the demutualization of insurance corporations, to discourage transactions designed to allow Canadian corporate surplus to be distributed to non-residents free of Part XIII withholding tax.

**Definitions [s. 212.2]**: "amount" — 248(1); "arm's length" — 251(1); "business" — 248(1); "Canada" — 255, *Interpretation Act* 35(1); "corporation"— 248(1), *Interpretation Act* 35(1); "demutu-

**S. 212.2**  Income Tax Act

alization" — 139.1(1); "disposition", "dividend", "insurance corporation", "non-resident" — 248(1); "paid-up capital" — 89(1), 248(1); "partnership" — see Notes to 96(1); "person", "property" — 248(1); "resident in Canada" — 250; "share" — 248(1); "taxable dividend" — 89(1), 248(1); "taxpayer" — 248(1).

**213. (1) Tax non-payable by non-resident person** — Tax is not payable by a non-resident person under subsection 212(2) on a dividend in respect of a share of the capital stock of a foreign business corporation if not less than 90% of the total of the amounts received or receivable by it that are required to be included in computing its income for the taxation year in which the dividend was paid was received or receivable in respect of the operation by it of public utilities or from mining, transporting and processing of ore in a country in which

(a) if the non-resident person is an individual, the non-resident person resides; or

(b) if the non-resident person is a corporation, individuals who own more than 50% of its share capital (having full voting rights under all circumstances) reside.

**Forms**: T4061: Non-resident withholding tax guide.

**(2) Idem** — For the purposes of this section, if 90% of the total of the amounts received or receivable by a corporation that are required to be included in computing its income for a taxation year was received or receivable in respect of the operation by it of public utilities or from the mining, transporting and processing of ore, an amount received or receivable in that year from that corporation by another corporation shall, if it is required to be included in computing the receiving corporation's income for the year, be deemed to have been received by the receiving corporation in respect of the operation by it of public utilities or from the mining, transporting and processing of ore by it in the country in which the public utilities were operated or the mining, transporting and processing of ore was carried out by the payer corporation.

**(3) Corporation deemed to be foreign business corporation** — For the purposes of this section, a corporation shall be deemed to be a foreign business corporation at a particular time if it would have been a foreign business corporation within the meaning of section 71 of the *Income Tax Act*, chapter 148 of the Revised Statutes of Canada, 1952 (as that section read in its application to the 1971 taxation year), for the taxation year of the corporation in which the particular time occurred, if that section had been applicable to that taxation year.

**I.T. Application Rules**: 69 (meaning of "*Income Tax Act*, chapter 148 of the Revised Statutes of Canada, 1952").

**Definitions [s. 213]**: "amount" — 248(1); "corporation" — 248(1), *Interpretation Act* 35(1); "dividend" — 248(1); "foreign business corporation" — 213(3); "individual", "non-resident", "person" — 248(1); "taxation year" — 249.

**Interpretation Bulletins [s. 213]**: IT-109R2: Unpaid amounts.

**214. (1) No deductions** — The tax payable under section 212 is payable on the amounts described therein without any deduction from those amounts whatever.

**Related Provisions**: 216 — Option to pay tax on the net rather than the gross.

**I.T. Application Rules**: 10(6) (tax limited to treaty rate).

**Interpretation Bulletins**: IT-88R2: Stock dividends; IT-109R2: Unpaid amounts; IT-438R2: Crown charges — resource properties in Canada; IT-465R: Non-resident beneficiaries of trusts.

**(2) Income and capital combined** — Where paragraph 16(1)(b) would, if Part I were applicable, result in a part of an amount being included in computing the income of a non-resident person, that part of the amount shall, for the purposes of this Part, be deemed to have been paid or credited to the non-resident person in respect of property, services or otherwise, depending on the nature of that part of the amount.

**Related Provisions**: 214(12) — Application.

**Interpretation Bulletins**: IT-88R2: Stock dividends; IT-265R3: Payments of income and capital combined.

**(3) Deemed payments** — For the purposes of this Part,

(a) where section 15 or subsection 56(2) would, if Part I were applicable, require an amount to be included in computing a taxpayer's income, that amount shall be deemed to have been paid to the taxpayer as a dividend from a corporation resident in Canada;

(b) where paragraph 56(1)(f) would, if Part I were applicable, require an amount to be included in computing an individual's income, that amount shall be deemed to have been paid to the individual under an income-averaging annuity contract;

(b.1) where paragraph 56(1)(y) would, if Part I were applicable, require an amount to be included in computing a taxpayer's income, that amount shall be deemed to have been paid to the taxpayer to acquire an interest in a retirement compensation arrangement;

(c) where, because of subsection 146(8.1), (8.8), (8.91), (9), (10) or (12), an amount would, if Part I applied, be required to be included in computing a taxpayer's income, that amount shall be deemed to have been paid to the taxpayer as a payment under a registered retirement savings plan or an amended plan (within the meaning assigned by subsection 146(12)), as the case may be;

(d) where, by virtue of subsection 147(10), (13) or (15), an amount would, if Part I were applicable, be required to be included in computing a taxpayer's income, that amount shall be deemed to have been paid to the taxpayer as a payment under a deferred profit sharing plan or a plan referred to in subsection 147(15) as a "revoked plan", as the case may be;

(e) where subsection 130.1(2) would, if Part I were applicable, deem an amount received by a shareholder of a mortgage investment corporation to have been received by the shareholder as interest, that amount shall be deemed to have been paid to the shareholder as interest on a bond issued after 1971;

(f) where subsection 104(13) would, if Part I were applicable, require any part of an amount payable by a trust in its taxation year to a beneficiary to be included in computing the income of the non-resident person who is a beneficiary of the trust, that part shall be deemed to be an amount paid or credited to that person as income of or from the trust on the earlier of

(i) the day on which the amount was paid or credited, and

(ii) the day that is 90 days after the end of the taxation year

and not at any subsequent time when the amount was actually paid or credited;

(f.1) where paragraph 132.1(1)(d) would, if Part I were applicable, require an amount to be included in computing a taxpayer's income for a taxation year by reason of a designation by a mutual fund trust under subsection 132.1(1), that amount shall be deemed to be an amount paid or credited to that person as income of or from the trust on the day of the designation;

(g) where an individual who is a beneficiary under a fund, plan or trust that was a registered home ownership savings plan (within the meanings assigned by subparagraphs 146.2(1)(a) and (h) of the *Income Tax Act*, chapter 148 of the Revised Statutes of Canada, 1952, as they read in their application to the 1985 taxation year) on December 31, 1985 dies, an amount equal to the fair market value of the property in the fund, plan or trust at the time of death shall be deemed, for the purposes of section 212, to have been paid to the individual at the time of death as a payment out of or under a fund, plan or trust that was at the end of 1985 a registered home ownership savings plan;

(h) [Repealed under former Act]

(i) where, because of subsection 146.3(4), (6), (6.1), (7) or (11), an amount would, if Part I applied, be required to be included in computing a taxpayer's income, that amount shall be deemed to have been paid to the taxpayer as a payment under a registered retirement income fund;

(j) [Repealed]

(k) where, because of subsection 143.1(2), an amount distributed at any time by an amateur athlete trust would, if Part I were applicable, be required to be included in computing an individual's income, that amount shall be deemed to have been paid at that time to the individual as a payment in respect of an amateur athlete trust; and

(l) where, because of subsection 12(10.2), an amount would at any particular time, if Part I were applicable, be required to be included in computing a taxpayer's income, that amount shall be deemed to have been paid by Her Majesty in right of Canada at that time to the taxpayer out of the taxpayer's NISA Fund No. 2.

**Related Provisions**: 94(3)(a)(iii) [proposed], 104(7.01) — Trusts that are deemed resident in Canada; 214(3.1) — Time of deemed payment; 227(6.1) — Repayment of non-resident shareholder loan.

**Notes**: 214(3)(c) amended by 1993 technical bill, effective for payments made in 1993 or later, to delete a reference to 146.3(6.1). (It was moved to 214(3)(i).)

214(3)(h) repealed by 1988 tax reform, but still in effect for any one or more transactions, one of which was entered into before April 13, 1988, that were entered into by a taxpayer in the course of an arrangement and in respect of which the taxpayer received from Revenue Canada before April 13, 1988, a confirmation or opinion in writing with respect to the tax consequences thereof. (This parallels the introduction of the general anti-avoidance rule in 245.) For such cases, read:

(h) where subsection 247(1) would, if Part I were applicable, require an amount to be included in computing a taxpayer's income for a taxation year, that amount shall be deemed to have been paid at the end of that taxation year to the taxpayer as a dividend from a corporation resident in Canada;

214(3)(i) amended by 1990 pension bill, effective 1989, to change a reference to 146.3(12) to a reference to 146.3(11); and by 1993 technical bill, effective for payments made in 1993 or later, to add reference to 146.3(6.1) (this reference was formerly in 214(3)(c)).

214(3)(j) repealed by 1997 Budget, effective 1998, due to the repeal of 146.1(14). From December 12, 1979 through 1997, read:

(j) where, by virtue of subsection 146.1(14), an amount would, if Part I were applicable, be required to be included in computing a taxpayer's income, that amount shall be deemed to have been paid to the taxpayer as a payment in respect of a registered education savings plan;

214(3)(k) added by 1992 technical bill, effective for amounts distributed in 1992 or later.

214(3)(l) added by 1992 technical bill, effective 1991.

**I.T. Application Rules**: 69 (meaning of "*Income Tax Act*, chapter 148 of the Revised Statutes of Canada, 1952").

**Interpretation Bulletins**: IT-88R2: Stock dividends; IT-96R6: Options to acquire shares, bonds or debentures and by trusts to acquire trust units; IT-109R2: Unpaid amounts; IT-119R4: Debts of shareholders, certain persons connected with shareholders, etc.; IT-421R2: Benefits to individuals, corporations and shareholders from loans or debt; IT-432R2: Benefits conferred on shareholders; IT-465R: Non-resident beneficiaries of trusts; IT-468R: Management or administration fees paid to non-residents; IT-500R: RRSPs — death of an annuitant.

**Information Circulars**: 77-16R4: Non-resident income tax; 72-22R9: Registered retirement savings plans.

**(3.1) Time of deemed payment** — Except as otherwise expressly provided, each amount deemed by subsection (3) to have been paid shall be deemed to have been paid at the time of the event or transaction as a consequence of which the amount would, if Part I were applicable, be required to be included in computing a taxpayer's income.

## S. 214(4) — Income Tax Act

**(4) Securities** — Where, if section 76 were applicable in computing a non-resident person's income, that section would require an amount to be included in computing the income, that amount shall, for the purpose of this Part, be deemed to have been, at the time the non-resident person received the security, right, certificate or other evidence of indebtedness, paid to the non-resident person on account of the debt in respect of which the non-resident person received it.

**Related Provisions**: 214(5) — Interpretation.

**Interpretation Bulletins**: IT-77R: Securities in satisfaction of an income debt; IT-88R2: Stock dividends; IT-109R2: Unpaid amounts.

**(5) Interpretation** — Subsection (4) is enacted for greater certainty and shall not be construed as limiting the generality of the other provisions of this Part defining amounts on which tax is payable.

**(6) Deemed interest** — Where, in respect of interest stipulated to be payable, on a bond, debenture, bill, note, mortgage or similar obligation that has been assigned or otherwise transferred by a non-resident person to a person resident in Canada, subsection 20(14) would, if Part I were applicable, require an amount to be included in computing the transferor's income, that amount shall, for the purposes of this Part, be deemed to be a payment of interest on that obligation made by the transferee to the transferor at the time of the assignment or other transfer of the obligation, if

(a) the obligation was issued by a person resident in Canada;

(b) the obligation was not an obligation described in paragraph (8)(a) or (b); and

(c) the assignment or other transfer is not an assignment or other transfer referred to in paragraph (7.1)(b).

**Related Provisions**: 214(7.1) — Sale of obligation; 214(9) — Deemed resident; 214(11) — Application to non-resident-owned investment corporation; 214(14) — Deemed assignment of obligation.

**Notes**: The term "bond, debenture, note, bill, mortgage or similar obligation" in 181.2(4)(c) may not include bankers' acceptances. See *Federated Cooperatives Ltd.*, [2000] 2 C.T.C. 2382 (TCC).

214(6) amended in 1973, effective for bonds, debentures, bills, notes or similar obligations issued after July 27, 1973. For earlier obligations, read:

(6) Where, in respect of interest stipulated to be payable on an obligation that has been assigned or otherwise transferred by a non-resident person to a person resident in Canada, subsection 20(14) would, if Part I were applicable, require an amount to be included in computing the transferor's income, that amount shall, for the purposes of this Part, be deemed to be a payment of interest on that obligation made by the transferee to the transferor at the time of the assignment or other transfer of the obligation, if

(a) the obligation was issued after June 18, 1971, and

(b) the obligation was not an obligation referred to in subparagraph (8)(a)(i), (ii) or (iii),

and where the transferee is a non-resident-owned investment corporation, paragraph 212(1)(b) shall be read and construed without reference to subparagraph (i) thereof.

214(6) amended by 1991 technical bill, effective for obligations assigned or transferred after July 13, 1990, to conform to numbering changes in 214(8).

**Interpretation Bulletins**: IT-410R: Debt obligations — accrued interest on transfer.

**Information Circulars**: 77-16R4: Non-resident income tax.

**(7) Sale of obligation** — Where

(a) a non-resident person has at any time assigned or otherwise transferred to a person resident in Canada a bond, debenture, bill, note, mortgage or similar obligation issued by a person resident in Canada,

(b) the obligation was not an excluded obligation, and

(c) the assignment or other transfer is not an assignment or other transfer referred to in paragraph (7.1)(b),

the amount, if any, by which

(d) the price for which the obligation was assigned or otherwise transferred at that time,

exceeds

(e) the price for which the obligation was issued,

shall, for the purposes of this Part, be deemed to be a payment of interest on that obligation made by the person resident in Canada to the non-resident person at that time.

**Related Provisions**: 16(6) — Indexed debt obligations; 214(7.1) — Sale of obligation; 214(8) — Meaning of "excluded obligation"; 214(9) — Deemed resident; 214(10) — Reduction of tax; 214(11) — Application to non-resident-owned investment corporation; 214(14) — Deemed assignment of obligation; 215(5) — Regulations reducing amount to be deducted or withheld.

**Notes**: 214(7) amended in 1973, effective for bonds, debentures, bills, notes or similar obligations issued after July 27, 1973. For earlier obligations, read:

(7) Where a person resident in Canada has issued or sold to a non-resident person a bond, debenture, bill, note, mortgage, hypothec or similar obligation, other than an excluded obligation, issued after June 18, 1971 by a person resident in Canada, an amount equal to $4/3$ of the amount, if any, by which

(a) the principal amount of the obligation

exceeds

(b) the price for which the obligation was issued or sold to the non-resident person,

shall, for the purposes of this Part, be deemed to be a payment of interest made by the person resident in Canada to the non-resident person at the time of the issue or sale of the obligation to the non-resident person, except that where it is established that, at any subsequent time before the maturity of the obligation, the non-resident person has sold the obligation to a person resident in Canada, the amount of the tax under this Part that the non-resident person is liable to pay in respect thereof shall be deemed, for the purpose of subsection 227(6), to be that proportion of the tax he would otherwise have been liable to pay in respect thereof that the number of days in the period commencing with the day the obligation was issued or sold to him and ending with the day the obligation was sold by him is of the number of days in the period commencing with the day the obligation was issued or sold to him and ending with the date of its maturity.

**Interpretation Bulletins**: IT-88R2: Stock dividends; IT-109R2: Unpaid amounts; IT-360R2: Interest payable in a foreign currency.

**Information Circulars**: 77-16R4: Non-resident income tax.

**(7.1) Idem** — Where

(a) a person resident in Canada has at a particular time assigned or otherwise transferred an obligation to a non-resident person,

(b) the non-resident person has at a subsequent time assigned or otherwise transferred the obligation back to the person resident in Canada, and

(c) subsection (6) or (7) would apply with respect to the assignment or other transfer referred to in paragraph (b), if those subsections were read without reference to paragraphs (6)(c) and (7)(c),

the amount, if any, by which

(d) the price for which the obligation was assigned or otherwise transferred at the subsequent time,

exceeds

(e) the price for which the obligation was assigned or otherwise transferred at the particular time,

shall, for the purposes of this Part, be deemed to be a payment of interest on that obligation made by the person resident in Canada to the non-resident person at the subsequent time.

**Related Provisions**: 214(11) — Application to non-resident-owned investment corporation; 214(14) — Deemed assignment of obligation.

**Notes**: 214(7.1) added in 1973, effective for bonds, debentures, bills, notes or similar obligations issued after July 27, 1973.

**Interpretation Bulletins**: IT-88R2: Stock dividends; IT-109R2: Unpaid amounts; IT-410R: Debt obligations — accrued interest on transfer.

**Information Circulars**: 77-16R4: Non-resident income tax.

**(8) Meaning of "excluded obligation"** — For the purposes of subsection (7), "excluded obligation" means any bond, debenture, bill, note, mortgage or similar obligation

(a) the interest on which is exempt from tax under this Part because of subparagraph 212(1)(b)(ii), (iii) or (vii);

(b) that is prescribed to be a public issue security; or

(c) that is not an indexed debt obligation and that was issued for an amount not less than 97% of the principal amount thereof, and the yield from which, expressed in terms of an annual rate on the amount for which the obligation was issued (which annual rate shall, if the terms of the obligation or any agreement relating thereto conferred on the holder thereof a right to demand payment of the principal amount of the obligation or the amount outstanding as or on account of the principal amount thereof, as the case may be, before the maturity of the obligation, be calculated on the basis of the yield that produces the highest annual rate obtainable either on the maturity of the obligation or conditional on the exercise of any such right) does not exceed $4/3$ of the interest stipulated to be payable on the obligation, expressed in terms of an annual rate on

(i) the principal amount thereof, if no amount is payable on account of the principal amount before the maturity of the obligation, and

(ii) the amount outstanding from time to time as or on account of the principal amount thereof, in any other case.

**Notes**: Opening words of 214(8)(c) amended by 1992 technical bill, effective for debt obligations issued after October 16, 1991, to exclude an indexed debt obligation. (Note that 214(7) will, by reason of 214(4), apply where an indexed debt obligation is redeemed or cancelled.)

214(8) amended by 1991 technical bill, effective for obligations assigned or transferred after July 13, 1990. The only two substantive changes are the direct reference to 212(1)(b)(vii), so as to cover, for example, debt obligations exempted under 212(1)(b)(vii)(E); and the reference in 214(8)(a) to interest that "would be exempt", making the definition subject to the proviso in 212(1)(b) that exempted interest may not be contingent on use or production from property or computed by reference to revenue, profit or similar criteria.

For obligations assigned or transferred before July 14, 1990, read:

(8) Definitions — For the purposes of subsection (7),

(a) "excluded obligation" — "excluded obligation" means any bond, debenture, bill, note, mortgage, hypothec or similar obligation,

(i) referred to in subparagraph 212(1)(b)(ii) or (iii),

(ii) if, under the terms of the obligation or any agreement relating thereto, the issuer thereof is not obliged to pay more than 25% of the principal amount thereof within 5 years of the date of its issue except in the event of a failure or default under the said terms or agreement,

(iii) that is prescribed to be a public issue security, or

(iv) that was issued for an amount not less than 97% of the principal amount thereof, and the yield from which, expressed in terms of an annual rate on the amount for which the obligation was issued (which annual rate shall, if the terms of the obligation or any agreement relating thereto conferred upon the holder thereof a right to demand payment of the principal amount of the obligation or the amount outstanding as or on account of the principal amount thereof, as the case may be, before the maturity of the obligation, be calculated on the basis of the yield that produces the highest annual rate obtainable either on the maturity of the obligation or conditional upon the exercise of any such right) does not exceed $4/3$ of the interest stipulated to be payable on the obligation, expressed in terms of an annual rate on

(A) the principal amount thereof, if no amount is payable on account of the principal amount before the maturity of the obligation, or

(B) the amount outstanding from time to time as or on account of the principal amount thereof, in any other case.

(b) [Repealed]

Former 214(8)(b), repealed in 1973, defined "principal amount", a definition now found in 248(1).

**Regulations**: No prescribed public issue security yet under 214(8)(b).

**(9) Deemed resident** — Where

(a) the assignment or other transfer of an obligation to a non-resident person carrying on business in Canada would be described in subsection (6) or (7) if those subsections were read without reference to paragraphs (6)(c) and (7)(c) and if that non-resident person were a person resident in Canada, and

(b) that non-resident person

(i) may deduct, under subsection 20(14), in computing the non-resident person's taxable income earned in Canada for a taxation year an amount in respect of interest on the obligation, or

(ii) may deduct, under Part I, in computing the non-resident person's taxable income earned in Canada for a taxation year an amount in respect of any amount paid on account of the principal amount of the obligation,

the non-resident person shall, with respect to the assignment or other transfer of the obligation, be deemed, for the purposes of this Part, to be a person resident in Canada.

**Related Provisions**: 214(14) — Assignment of obligation.

**Notes**: 214(9) amended in 1973, effective for bonds, debentures, bills, notes or similar obligations issued after July 27, 1973. For earlier obligations, read:

(9) Where, in respect of a transfer or other assignment of an obligation referred to in subsection (6), a non-resident person carrying on business in Canada may deduct, under subsection 20(14), in computing his income from the business for a taxation year an amount in respect of interest on the obligation, the non-resident person shall, with respect to the assignment or other transfer of the obligation, be deemed, for the purposes of this Part, to be a person resident in Canada.

**Interpretation Bulletins**: IT-88R2: Stock dividends; IT-109R2: Unpaid amounts; IT-410R: Debt obligations — accrued interest on transfer.

**(10) Reduction of tax** — Where a non-resident person has assigned or otherwise transferred to a person resident in Canada an obligation

(a) on which an amount of interest was deemed by subsection (6) or (7) to have been paid, and

(b) that the non-resident person had previously acquired from a person resident in Canada,

the amount of the tax under this Part that the non-resident person is liable to pay in respect thereof shall be deemed, for the purpose of subsection 227(6), to be that proportion of the tax the non-resident person would otherwise have been liable to pay in respect thereof that

(c) the number of days in the period commencing with the day the obligation was last acquired by the non-resident person from a person resident in Canada and ending with the day the obligation was last assigned or otherwise transferred by the non-resident person to a person resident in Canada

is of

(d) the number of days in the period commencing with the day the obligation was issued and ending with the day the obligation was last assigned or otherwise transferred by the non-resident person to a person resident in Canada.

**Related Provisions**: 214(14) — Deemed assignment of obligation.

**Notes**: 214(10) amended in 1973, effective for bonds, debentures, bills, notes or similar obligations issued after July 27, 1973. For earlier obligations, read:

(10) Where, in respect of an issue or sale of an obligation referred to in subsection (7), a non-resident person carrying on business in Canada is required, under Part I, to include the price for which the obligation was issued or sold in computing his income from the business for a taxation year, the non-resident person shall, with respect to the issue or sale of the obligation, be deemed, for the purposes of this Part, to be a person resident in Canada.

**Interpretation Bulletins**: IT-88R2: Stock dividends; IT-109R2: Unpaid amounts; IT-410R: Debt obligations — accrued interest on transfer.

**(11) Application of para. 212(1)(b)** — In respect of any payment of interest deemed by subsection (6), (7) or (7.1) to have been made by a non-resident-owned investment corporation on the assignment or other transfer of an obligation, paragraph 212(1)(b) shall be read and construed without reference to subparagraph 212(1)(b)(i).

**Notes**: 214(11) amended in 1973, effective for bonds, debentures, bills, notes or similar obligations issued after July 27, 1973. For earlier obligations, read:

(11) In respect of any payment of interest deemed by subsection (7) to have been made by a non-resident-owned investment corporation on the issue or sale of an obligation, paragraph 212(1)(b) shall be read and construed without reference to subparagraph (i) thereof.

**(12) Where subsec. (2) does not apply** — Subsection (2) does not apply in respect of a payment to a non-resident person under any obligation in respect of which that person is liable to pay tax under this Part by reason of subsection (7) or (7.1).

**Notes**: 214(12) amended in 1973, effective for bonds, debentures, bills, notes or similar obligations issued after July 27, 1973. For earlier obligations, read:

(12) Subsection (2) does not apply in respect of a payment to a non-resident person under any obligation in respect of which that person is liable to pay tax under this Part by virtue of subsection (7).

**(13) Regulations respecting residents** — The Governor in Council may make general or special regulations, for the purposes of this Part, prescribing

(a) who is or has been at any time resident in Canada;

(b) where a person was resident in Canada as well as in some other place, what amounts are taxable under this Part; and

(c) where a non-resident person carried on business in Canada, what amounts are taxable under this Part or what portion of the tax under this Part is payable by that person.

**Regulations**: 802 (amounts taxable).

**(14) Assignment of obligation** — For the purposes of this section, any transaction or event by which an obligation held by a non-resident person is redeemed in whole or in part or is cancelled shall be deemed to be an assignment of the obligation by the non-resident person.

**Notes**: 214(14) added in 1973, effective for bonds, debentures, bills, notes or similar obligations issued after July 27, 1973.

**Interpretation Bulletins**: IT-88R2: Stock dividends; IT-109R2: Unpaid amounts; IT-360R2: Interest payable in a foreign currency.

**(15) Standby charges and guarantee fees** — For the purposes of this Part,

(a) where a non-resident person has entered into an agreement under the terms of which the non-resident person agrees to guarantee the repayment, in whole or in part, of the principal amount of a bond, debenture, bill, note, mortgage or similar obligation of a person resident in Canada, any amount paid or credited as consideration for the guarantee shall be deemed to be a repayment of interest on that obligation; and

(b) where a non-resident person has entered into an agreement under the terms of which the non-resident person agrees to lend money, or to make money available, to a person resident in Canada, any amount paid or credited as consideration for so agreeing to lend money or to make money available shall, if the non-resident person would be liable to tax under this Part in respect of interest payable on any obligation issued under the terms of the agreement on the date it was entered into, be deemed to be a payment of interest.

**Advance Tax Rulings**: ATR-49: Long-term foreign debt.

**Definitions [s. 214]**: "amateur athlete trust" — 143.1(1)(a), 248(1); "amount" — 248(1); "assignment" — 214(14); "business" — 248(1); "Canada" — 255; "corporation" — 248(1), *Interpretation Act* 35(1); "deferred profit sharing plan" — 147(1), 248(1); "dividend" — 248(1); "excluded obligation" — 214(8); "Governor in Council" — *Interpretation Act* 35(1); "income-averaging annuity contract" — 61(4), 248(1); "indexed debt obligation", "individual" — 248(1); "mutual fund trust" — 132(6)–(7), 132.2(1)(q), 248(1); "NISA Fund No. 2", "non-resident" — 248(1); "non-resident-owned investment corporation" — 133(8), 248(1); "person", "prescribed", "principal amount", "property" — 248(1); "registered education savings plan" — 146.1(1), 248(1); "registered retirement income fund" — 146.3(1), 248(1); "registered retirement savings plan" — 146(1), 248(1); "regulation" — 248(1); "resident in Canada" — 250; "retirement compensation arrangement", "shareholder" — 248(1); "taxable income earned in Canada" — 115(1), 248(1); "taxation year" — 249; "taxpayer" — 248(1); "trust" — 104(1), 248(1), (3).

**215. (1) Deduction and payment of tax** — When a person pays or credits or is deemed to have paid or credited an amount on which an income tax is payable under this Part, the person shall, notwithstanding any agreement or law to the contrary, deduct or withhold therefrom the amount of the tax and forthwith remit that amount to the Receiver General on behalf of the non-resident person on account of the tax and shall submit therewith a statement in prescribed form.

**Related Provisions**: 215(1.1) — Limitation on requirement to withhold tax on corporate immigration; 215(5) — Regulations reducing deduction or withholding; 215(6) — Liability for tax; 227 — Withholding taxes — administration and enforcement; 227.1 — Liability of directors; 248(7)(b)(i) — Remittance deemed made when received.

**Regulations**: 105 (withholding of 15% on fees for services); 202 (information return); 805 (where withholding not required); 809 (reduction in withholding).

**Interpretation Bulletins**: IT-88R2: Stock dividends; IT-465R: Non-resident beneficiaries of trusts.

**Information Circulars**: 77-16R4: Non-resident income tax.

**Advance Tax Rulings**: ATR-49: Long-term foreign debt; ATR-69: Withholding tax on interest paid to non-resident persons;.

**I.T. Technical News**: No. 14 (meaning of "credited" for purposes of Part XIII withholding tax).

**Forms**: NR4B Summ: Return of amounts paid or credited to non-residents of Canada; NR7-R: Application for refund of non-resident tax withheld; NR67AR: Non-resident tax remittance; NR67BR: Non-resident tax remittance form; NR75: Non-resident tax remitter registration form; T3 SCH 10: Part XII.2 tax and Part XIII non-resident withholding tax.

**(1.1) Exception — corporate immigration** — Subsection (1) does not apply in respect of a dividend deemed to be paid under paragraph 128.1(1)(c.1) by a corporation to a non-resident corporation with which the corporation was dealing at arm's length.

**Notes**: 215(1.1) added by 1998 Budget, effective February 24, 1998. See Notes to 128.1(1) re 128.1(1)(c.1).

**(2) Idem** — Where an amount on which an income tax is payable under this Part is paid or credited by an agent or other person on behalf of the debtor either by way of redemption of bearer coupons or warrants or otherwise, the agent or other person by whom the amount was paid or credited shall, notwithstanding any agreement or law to the contrary, deduct or withhold and remit the amount of the tax and shall submit therewith a statement in prescribed form as required by subsection (1) and shall thereupon, for purposes of accounting to or obtaining reimbursement from the debtor, be deemed to have paid or credited the full amount to the person otherwise entitled to payment.

**Related Provisions**: 215(5) — Regulations reducing deduction or withholding; 215(6) — Liability for tax; 227(8)–(8.4) — Liabilities arising from failure to withhold or deduct amount; 227.1 — Liability of directors.

**Regulations**: 202(2) (information return); 805 (where withholding not required); 809 (reduction in withholding).

**I.T. Technical News**: No. 14 (meaning of "credited" for purposes of Part XIII withholding tax).

**(3) Idem** — Where an amount on which an income tax is payable under this Part was paid or credited to an agent or other person for or on behalf of the person entitled to payment without the tax having been deducted or withheld under subsection (1), the agent or other person shall, notwithstanding any agreement or law to the contrary, deduct or withhold therefrom the amount of the tax and forthwith remit that amount to the Receiver General on behalf of the person entitled to payment in payment of the tax and shall submit therewith a statement in prescribed form, and the agent or other person shall thereupon, for purposes of accounting to the person entitled to payment, be deemed to have paid or credited that amount to that person.

**Related Provisions**: 215(5) — Regulations reducing deduction or withholding; 215(6) — Liability for tax; 216(4) — Optional method of payment; 227(8)–(8.4) — Liabilities arising from failure to withhold or deduct amount; 227.1 — Liability of directors.

**Notes**: 215(3) typically applies to a property manager who collects rents on behalf of a non-resident landlord. The property manager is required to withhold and remit the 25% withholding tax under 212(1)(d) if the tenant did not withhold. However, see 216(1) and (4) for an election that allows the withholding requirement to be reduced or eliminated.

**Regulations**: 202(3) (information return); 805 (where withholding not required); 809 (reduction in withholding).

**Interpretation Bulletins**: IT-393R2: Election re tax on rents and timber royalties — non-residents.

**I.T. Technical News**: No. 14 (meaning of "credited" for purposes of Part XIII withholding tax).

**Forms**: NR1: Return of income received from sources within the United States on behalf of non-residents of Canada; NR7-R: Application for refund of non-resident tax withheld; NR67AR: Non-resident tax remittance; NR67BR: Non-resident tax remittance form; NR75: Non-resident tax remitter registration form.

**(4) Regulations creating exceptions** — The Governor in Council may make regulations with reference to any non-resident person or class of non-resident persons who carries or carry on business in Canada, providing that subsections (1) to (3) are not applicable to amounts paid to or credited to that person or those persons and requiring the person or persons to file an annual return on a prescribed form and to pay the tax imposed by this Part within a time limited in the regulations.

**Related Provisions**: 162(7) — Penalty for failure to comply with regulation; 227(9) — Penalty on tax not paid; 227(9.3) — Interest on tax not paid; 227.1 — Liability of directors; 235 — Penalty for failure to make returns.

**Regulations**: 800, 801, 803, 805.

**Forms**: T2016: Part XIII tax return — tax on income from Canada of registered non-resident insurers.

**(5) Regulations reducing deduction or withholding** — The Governor in Council may make regulations in respect of any non-resident person or class of non-resident persons to whom any amount is paid or credited as, on account of, in lieu of payment of or in satisfaction of, any amount described in any of paragraphs 212(1)(f), (h), (j) to (m) and (q) reducing the amount otherwise required by any of subsections (1) to (3) to be deducted or withheld from the amount so paid or credited.

**Proposed Amendment — 215(5)**

**(5) Regulations reducing deduction or withholding** — The Governor in Council may make regulations in respect of any non-resident person or class of non-resident persons to whom any amount is paid or credited as, on account of, in lieu of payment of or in satisfaction of, any amount described in any of paragraphs 212(1)(h), (j) to (m) and (q) reducing the amount otherwise required by any of subsections (1) to (3) to be deducted or withheld from the amount so paid or credited.

**Application**: Bill C-43 (First Reading September 20, 2000), s. 103, will amend subsec. 215(5) to read as above, applicable after April 1997.

**Technical Notes**: Subsection 215(5) provides that the Governor in Council may make regulations reducing the tax to be withheld from certain payments made to a non-resident. The amendment to that subsection deletes a reference to paragraph 212(1)(f), which has been previously repealed.

This amendment applies to amounts paid or credited after April 1997, which is the time at which the repeal of paragraph 212(1)(f) came into force.

**Related Provisions**: 190.15(6) — Related financial institution; 212(1) — Tax on Canadian income of non-residents; 212(2) — Tax on dividends; 227.1 — Liability of directors.

**Notes**: 215(5) amended by 1991 technical bill, effective July 14, 1990, to cover 212(1)(j.1) by using the words "(j) to (m)" in place of "(j), (k), (l), (m)".

**Regulations**: 805 (where withholding not required); 809 (reduction in withholding).

**Forms**: NR5: Application by a non-resident of Canada for a reduction in the amount of non-resident tax required to be withheld; NR7-R: Application for refund of non-resident tax withheld; NR67AR: Non-resident tax remittance; NR67BR: Non-resident tax remittance form; NR75: Non-resident tax remitter registration form.

**(6) Liability for tax** — Where a person has failed to deduct or withhold any amount as required by this section from an amount paid or credited or deemed to have been paid or credited to a non-resident person, that person is liable to pay as tax under this Part on behalf of the non-resident person the whole of the amount that should have been deducted or withheld, and is entitled to deduct or withhold from any amount paid or credited by that person to the non-resident person or otherwise recover from the non-resident person any amount paid by that person as tax under this Part on behalf thereof.

**Related Provisions**: 227(8.4) — Parallel provision for other withholding taxes; 227.1 — Liability of directors where corporation fails to withhold.

**Definitions [s. 215]**: "amount" — 248(1); "arm's length" — 251(1); "business" — 248(1); "Canada" — 255; "corporation" — 248(1), *Interpretation Act* 35(1); "dividend" — 248(1); "Governor in Council" — *Interpretation Act* 35(1); "non-resident", "person", "prescribed", "regulation" — 248(1).

**Interpretation Bulletins [s. 215]**: IT-88R2: Stock dividends; IT-109R2: Unpaid amounts; IT-362R: Patronage dividends.

**216. (1) Alternatives re rents and timber royalties** — Where an amount has been paid during a taxation year to a non-resident person or to a partnership of which that person was a member as, on account of, in lieu of payment of or in satisfaction of, rent on real property in Canada or a timber royalty, that person may, within 2 years (or, where that person has filed an undertaking described in subsection (4) in respect of the year, within 6 months) after the end of the year, file a return of income under Part I in the form prescribed for a person resident in Canada for that year and the non-resident person shall, without affecting the liability of the non-resident person for tax otherwise payable under Part I, thereupon be liable, in lieu of paying tax under this Part on that amount, to pay tax under Part I for the year as though

(a) the non-resident person were a person resident in Canada and not exempt from tax under section 149;

(b) the non-resident person's income from the non-resident person's interest in real property in Canada, timber resource properties and timber limits in Canada and the non-resident person's share of the income of a partnership of which the non-resident person was a member from its interest in real property in Canada, timber resource properties and timber limits in Canada were the non-resident person's only income;

(c) the non-resident person were entitled to no deductions from income for the purpose of computing the non-resident person's taxable income; and

(d) the non-resident person were entitled to no deductions under sections 118 to 118.9 in computing the non-resident person's tax payable under Part I for the year.

### Proposed Amendment — Recapture on donation of depreciable property to charity

**Letter from Department of Finance, February 15, 2000**:

Dear [xxx]

The Honourable Paul Martin, Minister of Finance, has forwarded your letter of September 7, 1999 to me for reply. It is my understanding that you have requested amendments to the *Income Tax Act* (the Act) that would address a situation where a resident of Switzerland would be required to pay Canadian income tax as a result of a donation of a Canadian rental building to a charity. More specifically, upon the donation to charity of their Canadian rental buildings, your Swiss clients would be required to pay tax under Part I of the Act on the resulting recaptured capital cost allowance ("CCA"), without the ability to deduct a charitable donations tax credit.

I also understand that Mr. Ed Short of this Department spoke with you in this regard and asked whether you were seeking amendments to the Act that would allow for an elective reduction of the deemed proceeds of disposition as a result of the gift (with a concurrent reduction of the base upon which the charitable donations tax credit is calculated) or amendments that would allow the claim of the charitable donations tax credit against tax on other sources of income. Your letter dated November 1, 1999 suggests that you are seeking both. That is, you have suggested not only that the disposition should (on an elective basis) not give rise to tax but that the charitable donations tax credit should also be allowed to be claimed against tax on other Canadian sources of income that a non-resident may have.

You have indicated that, on an ongoing basis, your Swiss clients have elected under section 216 of the Act to pay Part I tax on their net incomes from rental property, rather than to pay tax at the flat rate on gross rents that otherwise applies to non-residents under Part XIII of the Act. In this regard, they have claimed CCA against their rental revenues. Disposing of the rental properties for proceeds above their undepreciated capital costs would, therefore, result in recaptured CCA and, potentially, capital gains.

As you are aware, the charitable donations tax credit may be claimed by a non-resident individual to offset tax imposed under Part I of the Act on income from a business or employment carried on in Canada. The charitable donations tax credit is also available in respect of certain other sources of income, other than income from property, where the non-resident elects under section 217 of the Act to file a Part I tax return.

Property income of non-residents is, however, taxed under Part XIII, and is generally calculated as a percentage of the gross amount of revenues. The exceptions are rental income from real property and timber royalties, for which a non- resident may elect to pay tax under Part I on net income from the property. Although this election is provided in order to give non-residents some relief from Part XIII tax, the basis of relief is the method of calculating income, not the availability of tax credits. Just as the Part XIII tax on property income may not be reduced by the charitable donations tax credit, the elective Part I tax on property income may not be reduced.

However, an amendment that the Minister of Finance is prepared to support would extend the existing election to report a reduced amount of capital gain on the donation of capital property to also reduce the recaptured CCA that must be reported on the donation of a depreciable capital property. This amendment would apply equally to residents who file under section 152 of the Act and non-residents who are required to file under subsection 216(5). The result of this amendment would be that taxpayers, resident and non-resident alike, would not be required to pay tax on the donation of a depreciable property.

I understand that the Minister of Finance intends to recommend that the requisite amendments to the *Income Tax Act* be effective for donations made after 1999.

Yours sincerely,
Munir A. Sheikh
Senior ADM, Tax Policy Branch

**Related Provisions**: 13(21) — "Timber resource property"; 96 — Partnerships and their members; 120(1) — Additional tax on income not earned in a province; 150.1(5) — Electronic filing; 216(8) — Restriction on deduction; 220(3) — Extension of time for making return; 248(4) — Interest in real property; 250.1(b) — Calculation of income of non-resident person.

**Notes**: 216 allows a non-resident to file a return and pay regular (Part I) tax on the *net* income from real property in Canada (or a timber royalty), rather than paying a flat 25% (or 15% or whatever other rate applies by treaty) on the *gross* income.

Under 216(1)(d), the personal credits are not allowed on such a return; but the graduated tax rates under 117(2) do apply if the non-resident is an individual. Note also that deductions under s. 60, including RRSP contributions and deductible alimony or support, *are* deductible for purposes of 216(1). (They are specifically listed on Form T1159.)

In *Kutlu* (February 21, 1997), T-205-96, 1997 CarswellNat 14, the Federal Court–Trial Division ruled that Revenue Canada could not refuse to accept a late-filed return under 216(1) where it had ac-

## S. 216(1) Income Tax Act

cepted such returns late in the past. (An appeal by the Crown to the FCA was discontinued on March 17/98.)

Opening words of 216(1) amended by 1991 technical bill, effective for taxation years ending after July 13, 1990, to add the words in parentheses limiting the period for filing the return in cases where an undertaking has been filed under 216(4).

**Interpretation Bulletins**: IT-81R: Partnerships — income of non-resident partners; IT-88R2: Stock dividends; IT-109R2: Unpaid amounts; IT-121R3: Election to capitalize cost of borrowed money; IT-393R2: Election re tax on rents and timber royalties — non-residents; IT-434R: Rental of real property by individual.

**Information Circulars**: 77-16R4: Non-resident income tax.

**Forms**: T1 General: Individual income tax return; T2: Corporation income tax return; T2 Short: A simpler return for eligible corporations; T3: Trust income tax and information return; NR6: Undertaking to file an income tax return by a non-resident receiving rent from real property or receiving a timber royalty; T1159: Income tax return electing under s. 216; T4144: Income tax guide for electing under section 216 [guide].

**(2) Idem** — Where a non-resident person has filed a return of income under Part I as permitted by this section, the amount deducted under this Part from

(a) rent on real property or from timber royalties paid to the person, and

(b) the person's share of the rent on real property or from timber royalties paid to a partnership of which the person is a member

and remitted to the Receiver General shall be deemed to have been paid on account of tax under this section and any portion of the amount so remitted to the Receiver General in a taxation year on the person's behalf in excess of the person's liability for tax under this Act for the year shall be refunded to the person.

**(3) Idem** — Part I is applicable, with such modifications as the circumstances require, to payment of tax under this section.

**(4) Optional method of payment** — Where a non-resident person or, in the case of a partnership, each non-resident person who is a member of the partnership files with the Minister an undertaking in prescribed form to file within 6 months after the end of a taxation year a return of income under Part I for the year as permitted by this section, a person who is otherwise required by subsection 215(3) to remit in the year, in respect of the non-resident person or the partnership, an amount to the Receiver General in payment of tax on rent on real property or on a timber royalty may elect under this section not to remit under that subsection, and if that election is made, the elector shall,

(a) when any amount is available out of the rent or royalty received for remittance to the non-resident person or the partnership, as the case may be, deduct 25% of the amount available and remit the amount deducted to the Receiver General on behalf of the non-resident person or the partnership on account of the tax under this Part; and

(b) if the non-resident person or, in the case of a partnership, a non-resident person who is a member of the partnership

(i) does not file a return for the year in accordance with the undertaking, or

(ii) does not pay under this section the tax the non-resident person or member is liable to pay for the year within the time provided for payment,

pay to the Receiver General, on account of the non-resident person's or the partnership's tax under this Part, on the expiration of the time for filing or payment, as the case may be, the full amount that the elector would otherwise have been required to remit in the year in respect of the rent or royalty minus the amounts that the elector has remitted in the year under paragraph (a) in respect of the rent or royalty.

---

**Possible Future Amendment — Requirement for non-resident to post security**

**Letter from Department of Finance, June 17, 1996**:

Mr. Donald H. Watkins, Chair, Taxation Section, The Canadian Bar Association

Mr. Robert Spindler, C.A., Chair, Taxation Committee, Canadian Institute of Chartered Accountants

Dear Messrs. Watkins and Spindler:

At our recent meeting we discussed the possibility of revising the Canadian income tax rules governing the taxation of rental income earned by non-resident owners of Canadian real estate. This letter outlines a proposal that would, if implemented, place the risk of a non-resident's non-compliance with the Canadian tax system on the non-resident rather than the non-resident's Canadian property agent.

In general, Part XIII of the *Income Tax Act* levies a withholding tax of 25% on rental payments made by Canadians to non-resident owners of Canadian real property. Where the non-resident collects the rent through a Canadian agent (who is typically a building or property manager), the agent is responsible for ensuring that 25% of the gross rental payments are remitted to Revenue Canada. An exception to this general rule exists where a non-resident elects, under section 216 of the Act, to file a Canadian income tax return in respect of the rental income and pay tax on the net property income.

To make the election the non-resident and the non-resident's Canadian agent are required to provide an undertaking to Revenue Canada to file an income tax return for the rental income within six months of the end of the relevant year. Where an election is made, the rule requiring the Canadian agent to remit 25% of the gross rental payments to Revenue Canada does not apply; instead, only 25% of the net amount of rent received by the agent need be remitted. However, if the non-resident fails to either file an income tax return or pay his tax liability within the time required under the election, the Canadian agent becomes liable for the amount that the agent would ordinarily have been required to withhold under Part XIII of the Act (ie., 25% of the gross rental payments) less the amount of tax actually remitted. The non-resident's tax liability is placed on the Canadian agent in an attempt to protect the government from the loss of any tax revenue arising from the non-resident's failure to pay the required tax. This mechanism is necessary because, in practice, it would be very difficult to enforce a tax liability on non-resident property owners.

We are considering alternatives to the current system which may reduce the liability of Canadian agents while at the same time protecting Canada's tax base. To achieve these objectives, we are prepared to consider a system which would require non-resident property owners to post security with Revenue Canada in order to take advantage of the election to file an income tax return and avoid having tax withheld on the gross amount of the rental payments. Where the non-resident fails to pay the required amount of tax within the specified time, the government would be able to look to the security; accordingly, the Canadian agent's exposure to tax could be reduced. In this context, acceptable security could be similar to that which is required under section 116 of the Act.

Finance is not, however, committed to this proposal; it remains our view that the current system works reasonably well from the government's viewpoint, and implementation of the alternative proposal would be considered only if it were thought to provide a better system from the taxpayer's perspective. This alternative has been outlined to a number of real estate organizations and other interested parties from whom we hope to gather comments over the course of the coming months.

I would also note that at our recent meeting you raised the possibility of considering changes to the existing time limits for filing a Part I income tax return under subsection 216(4). We would be pleased to receive written comments on your suggestion for modifying those time limits or on the alternative system outlined above.

    Yours sincerely,
    Len Farber
    Director, Tax Legislation Division, Department of Finance

**Related Provisions**: 96 — Partnerships and their members; 216(1) — Alternative re rents and timber royalties.

**Notes**: 216(4) amended by 1995-97 technical bill, retroactive to amounts paid or credited after November 1991 (i.e., on the same basis as the application of the R.S.C. 1985 (5th Supp.)), to correct errors introduced in the 5th Supp. consolidation, whereby "non-resident person or member" was used in certain places instead of "elector". Cosmetic changes to the wording were made as well.

**Forms**: NR6: Undertaking to file an income tax return by a non-resident receiving rent from real property or receiving a timber royalty; T1159: Income tax return electing under s. 216; T4144: Income tax guide for electing under section 216 [guide].

**(5) Disposition by non-resident of interest in real property, timber resource property or timber limit** — Where a person or a trust of which that person is a beneficiary has filed a return of income under Part I for a taxation year as permitted by this section or as required by section 150 and, in computing the amount of the person's income under Part I an amount has been deducted under paragraph 20(1)(a), or is deemed by subsection 107(2) to have been allowed under that paragraph, in respect of real property in Canada, a timber resource property or a timber limit in Canada, the person shall, within the time prescribed by section 150 for filing a return of income under Part I, file a return of income under Part I, in the form prescribed for a person resident in Canada, for any subsequent taxation year in which the person was a non-resident person and in which that real property, timber resource property or timber limit or any interest therein is disposed of, within the meaning of section 13, by the person or by a partnership of which the person is a member, and the person shall, without affecting the person's liability for tax otherwise payable under Part I, thereupon be liable, in lieu of paying tax under this Part on any amount paid, or deemed by this Part to have been paid to the person or to a partnership of which the person is a member in that subsequent taxation year in respect of any interest in real property, timber resource property or timber limit in Canada, to pay tax under Part I for that subsequent taxation year as though

(a) the person were a person resident in Canada and not exempt from tax under section 149;

(b) the person's income from the person's interest in real property, timber resource property or timber limits in Canada and the person's share of the income of a partnership of which the person was a member from its interest in real property, timber resource property or timber limits in Canada were the person's only income;

(c) the person were entitled to no deductions from income for the purpose of computing the person's taxable income; and

(d) the person were entitled to no deductions under sections 118 to 118.9 in computing the person's tax payable under Part I for the year.

**Related Provisions**: 150.1(5) — Electronic filing; 216(6) — Saving provision; 216(7) — Election; 216(8) — Restriction on deduction; 248(4) — Interest in real property.

**(6) Saving provision** — Subsection (5) does not apply to require a non-resident person

(a) to file a return of income under Part I for a taxation year unless, by filing that return, there would be included in computing the non-resident person's income under Part I for that year an amount by virtue of section 13; or

(b) to include in computing the non-resident person's income for a taxation year any amount to the extent that that amount has been included in computing the non-resident person's taxable income earned in Canada for that taxation year by virtue of any provision of this Act other than subsection (5).

**Related Provisions**: 13(1) — Recaptured depreciation.

**(7) Election** — Where, by virtue of subsection (5), a non-resident person is liable to pay tax under Part I for a taxation year, for greater certainty section 61 is not applicable in computing the non-resident person's income for the year.

**(8) Restriction on deduction** — For greater certainty, in determining the amount of tax payable by a non-resident person under Part I for a taxation year by reason of subsection (1) or (5), no deduction in

S. 216(8)                                Income Tax Act

computing the non-resident person's income or tax payable under Part I for the year shall be made to the extent that such a deduction by non-resident persons is not permitted under Part I.

**Definitions [s. 216]**: "amount" — 248(1); "Canada" — 255; "interest" — in real property 248(4); "Minister", "non-resident" — 248(1); "partnership" — see Notes to 96(1); "person", "prescribed", "property" — 248(1); "resident in Canada" — 250; "tax payable" — 248(2); "taxable income" — 2(2), 248(1); "taxation year" — 249; "timber resource property" — 13(21), 248(1).

**Interpretation Bulletins [s. 216]**: See under subsec. 216(1).

**217. (1) Alternative re Canadian benefits** — In this section, a non-resident person's "Canadian benefits" for a taxation year is the total of all amounts each of which is an amount paid or credited in the year and in respect of which tax under this Part would, but for this section, be payable by the person because of any of paragraphs 212(1)(h), (j) to (m) and (q).

**Notes**: See Notes at end of s. 217.

**(2) Part I return** — No tax is payable under this Part in respect of a non-resident person's Canadian benefits for a taxation year if the person

(a) files with the Minister, within 6 months after the end of the year, a return of income under Part I for the year; and

(b) elects in the return to have this section apply for the year.

**Related Provisions**: 150.1(5) — Electronic filing; 217(3)–(6) — Part I tax payable when election made.

**Notes**: See Notes at end of s. 217.

**Forms**: See at end of s. 217.

**(3) Taxable income earned in Canada** — Where a non-resident person elects under paragraph (2)(b) for a taxation year, for the purposes of Part I

(a) the person is deemed to have been employed in Canada in the year; and

(b) the person's taxable income earned in Canada for the year is deemed to be the greater of

(i) the amount that would, but for subparagraph (ii), be the person's taxable income earned in Canada for the year if

(A) paragraph 115(1)(a) included the following subparagraph after subparagraph (i):

"(i.1) the non-resident person's Canadian benefits for the year, within the meaning assigned by subsection 217(1),", and

(B) paragraph 115(1)(f) were read as follows:

"(f) such of the other deductions permitted for the purpose of computing taxable income as can reasonably be considered wholly applicable to the amounts described in subparagraphs (a)(i) to (vi)."; and

(ii) the person's income (computed without reference to subsection 56(8)) for the year minus the total of such of the deductions permitted for the purpose of computing taxable income as can reasonably be considered wholly applicable to the amounts described in subparagraphs 115(1)(a)(i) to (vi).

**Related Provisions**: 2(3) — Tax payable under Part I as a result of being deemed employed in Canada.

**Notes**: 217(3) describes how a non-resident person who elects to have 217 apply computes taxable income earned in Canada (TIEC). The person is deemed to have been employed in Canada, and is deemed to have TIEC equal to the greater of two amounts. The first amount (217(3)(b)(i)) is essentially the amount that would be the person's TIEC if s. 115 included the person's Canadian benefits in TIEC. The second amount (217(3)(b)(ii)) is net income for the year, less any deductions in computing taxable income that can reasonably be considered wholly applicable to the Canadian-source Part I income (not including the Canadian benefits).

This means, for example, that a non-resident person who has $10,000 in Canadian benefits for a year, and $60,000 in foreign-source income, will be deemed under 217(3) to have TIEC of $70,000 (assuming no deductions in computing taxable income). This does not mean that the non-resident will pay Canadian tax on the $60,000 of foreign income: 217(6) provides a special credit to offset the Canadian tax on such income. The effect of this rule is that the Part I tax on the $10,000 applies at high rates.

217(3)(b)(ii) amended by 1997 Budget, effective for 1997 and later taxation years, to add "(computed without reference to subsection 56(8))". Thus, the withholding tax applies to the full amount of any CPP/QPP lump sum payment for purposes of the calculation under s. 217.

See also Notes at end of 217.

**(4) Tax credits — limitation** — Sections 118 to 118.91 and 118.94 do not apply in computing the tax payable under Part I for a taxation year by a non-resident person who elects under paragraph (2)(b) for the year, unless

(a) where section 114 applies to the person for the year, all or substantially all of the person's income for the year is included in computing the person's taxable income for the year; or

(b) in any other case, all or substantially all of the person's income for the year is included in computing the amount determined under subparagraph (3)(b)(i) in respect of the person for the year.

**Notes**: See Notes at end of s. 217. The CCRA takes the position that "all or substantially all" means 90% or more.

**(5) Tax credits allowed** — In computing the tax payable under Part I for a taxation year by a non-resident person to whom neither paragraph (4)(a) nor paragraph (4)(b) applies for the year there may, notwithstanding section 118.94 and subsection (4), be deducted the lesser of

(a) the total of

(i) such of the amounts that would have been deductible under any of section 118.2, subsections 118.3(2) and (3) and sections 118.6, 118.8 and 118.9 in computing the person's tax payable under Part I for the year if the person

1678

had been resident in Canada throughout the year, as can reasonably be considered wholly applicable, and

(ii) the amounts that would have been deductible under any of sections 118 and 118.1, subsection 118.3(1) and sections 118.5 and 118.7 in computing the person's tax payable under Part I for the year if the person had been resident in Canada throughout the year, and

(b) the appropriate percentage for the year of the person's Canadian benefits for the year.

**Notes**: See Notes at end of s. 217.

**(6) Special credit** — In computing the tax payable under Part I for a taxation year by a non-resident who elects under paragraph (2)(b) for the year, there may be deducted the amount determined by the formula

$$A \times \left( \frac{B - C}{B} \right)$$

where

A is the amount of tax under Part I that would, but for this subsection, be payable by the person for the year;

B is the amount determined under subparagraph (3)(b)(ii) in respect of the person for the year; and

C is the amount determined under subparagraph (3)(b)(i) in respect of the person for the year.

**Related Provisions**: 257 — Formula cannot calculate to less than zero.

**Notes**: 217(6) provides a special credit in computing tax payable by a non-resident under Part I for a year as a result of a section 217 election. The effect of the credit is to exclude foreign-source (and non-Part I) income from Canadian tax, while maintaining the appropriate rate of tax on the non-resident's Part I income, including Canadian benefits. See Notes to 217(4).

**Notes [s. 217]**: 217 replaced by 217(1)–(6) by 1996 Budget, effective for 1997 and later taxation years. The changes provide that in determining the Part I tax rate that applies where a non-resident elects under the section, the non-resident's non-Canadian income (and Canadian-source income subject to Part XIII but not eligible for the s. 217 election) is taken into consideration. This will not mean that Canada will tax that other income under Part I, but only that the foreign income may increase the rate of tax that applies to the non-resident's Canadian-source Part I income. See Notes to 217(3).

As well, the requirement that more than half a non-resident's income be included in the non-resident's taxable income earned in Canada, in order for any Part I tax credits to be available, has been deleted.

For 1996, read:

> **217. Election respecting certain payments** — Where by virtue of any one or more of paragraphs 212(1)(f), (h), (j) to (m) and (q) a non-resident person would otherwise be liable to pay tax under this Part on one or more amounts paid or credited to the non-resident person in a taxation year and that person has, within 6 months after the end of the year, filed a return of income under Part I for the year and so elected therein, the following rules apply:
>
> (a) notwithstanding subsection 212(1), no tax under this Part is payable by the non-resident person on those amounts;

> (b) notwithstanding section 115, for the purposes of computing that person's taxable income earned in Canada for the year,
>
> (i) paragraph 115(1)(a) shall be read as though it included the following subparagraph:
>
>> "(i.1) amounts paid or credited to the non-resident person in the year on which that person would, under any of paragraphs 212(1)(f), (h), (j) to (m) and (q) be liable to pay tax under Part XIII if no election were made under section 217,", and
>
> (ii) all that portion of subsection 115(1) following paragraph (c) shall be read as follows:
>
>> "minus the total of such of the deductions from income permitted for the purpose of computing taxable income as may reasonably be considered wholly applicable"; and
>
> (c) notwithstanding sections 118.91 and 118.94, where the non-resident person is an individual more than ½ of whose income for the year is included in the individual's taxable income or taxable income earned in Canada for the year, as the case may be, section 118.94 shall, where the individual so elects in the return, be applied in respect of the individual for the year as if it read as follows:
>
>> "118.94 Sections 118 to 118.91 do not apply for the purpose of computing the tax payable under this Part for a taxation year by an individual who was non-resident at any time in the year, except that for the purpose of computing the tax payable under this Part for the year there may be deducted the total of
>>
>> (a) such of the amounts that would have been deductible under any of section 118.2, subsections 118.3(2) and (3) and sections 118.6, 118.8 and 118.9 for the purpose of computing the individual's tax payable under this Part for the year if the individual had been resident in Canada throughout the year, as can reasonably be considered wholly applicable, and
>>
>> (b) the amounts that would have been deductible under sections 118 and 118.1, subsection 118.3(1) and sections 118.5 and 118.7 for the purpose of computing the individual's tax payable under this Part for the year if the individual had been resident in Canada throughout the year,
>>
>> not exceeding the appropriate percentage for the year of the total of all amounts each of which is an amount paid or credited to the individual in the year on which the individual would, under any of paragraphs 212(1)(f), (h), (j) to (m) and (q) be liable to pay tax under Part XIII if no election were made under section 217."

217(b)(i) and 217(c) amended by 1995 Budget, effective for 1996. For earlier years, read 217(b)(i) as follows:

> (i) there shall be added to the total of the amounts determined under subparagraphs 115(1)(a)(i) to (v) in respect of that person the total of amounts each of which is an amount paid or credited to the non-resident person in the year on which that person would, by virtue of any one or more of paragraphs 212(1)(f), (h), (j) to (m) and (q), be liable to pay tax under this Part if paragraph 212(1)(h) were read without reference to subparagraphs 212(1)(h)(i) and (ii), and
>
> not exceeding the appropriate percentage for the year of the total of all amounts each of which is an amount paid or credited to the individual in the year on which the individual

## S. 217 — Income Tax Act

would, under any of paragraphs 212(1)(f), (h), (j) to (m) and (q), be liable to pay tax under Part XIII if paragraph 212(1)(h) were read without reference to subparagraphs 212(1)(h)(i) and (ii), and no election were made under section 217.

217(c) amended by 1991 technical bill, effective 1991.

**Definitions [s. 217]**: "amount", "appropriate percentage" — 248(1); "Canada" — 255; "Canadian benefits" — 217(1); "individual", "Minister", "non-resident", "person" — 248(1); "resident in Canada" — 250; "tax payable" — 248(2); "taxable income" — 2(2), 248(1); "taxable income earned in Canada" — 115(1), 248(1); "taxation year" — 249.

**Interpretation Bulletins [s. 217]**: IT-88R2: Stock dividends; IT-109R2: Unpaid amounts; IT-163R2: Election by non-resident individuals on certain Canadian source income; IT-171R2: Non-resident individuals — computation of taxable income earned in Canada and non-refundable tax credits; IT-193 SR: Taxable income of individuals resident in Canada during part of a year (Special Release); IT-337R2: Retiring allowances.

**Forms [s. 217]**: NR5: Application by a non-resident of Canada for reduction in the amount of non-resident tax required to be withheld; NR7-R: Application for refund of non-resident tax withheld; T4145: Electing under section 217 of the *Income Tax Act* [guide].

**218. (1) Loan to wholly-owned subsidiary** — For the purposes of this Act, where

(a) a non-resident corporation (in this section referred to as the "parent corporation") is indebted to

    (i) a person resident in Canada, or

    (ii) a non-resident insurance corporation carrying on business in Canada,

(in this section referred to as the "creditor") under an arrangement whereby the parent corporation is required to pay interest in Canadian currency, and

(b) the parent corporation has lent the money in respect of which it is so indebted, or a part thereof, to a subsidiary wholly-owned corporation resident in Canada whose principal business is the making of loans (in this section referred to as the "subsidiary corporation") under an arrangement whereby the subsidiary corporation is required to repay the loan to the parent corporation with interest at the same rate as is payable by the parent corporation to the creditor,

the amount so lent by the parent corporation to the subsidiary corporation shall be deemed to have been borrowed by the parent corporation as agent of the subsidiary corporation and interest paid by the subsidiary corporation to the parent corporation that has been paid by the parent corporation to the creditor shall be deemed to have been paid by the subsidiary corporation to the creditor and not by the subsidiary corporation to the parent corporation or by the parent corporation to the creditor.

**Notes**: 218 allows an exemption from withholding tax where funds are loaned to a non-resident for use by its Canadian subsidiary, where the conditions in 218(1) are met and an election is filed under 218(3). Since the interest payments are going out of Canada and then back into Canada, they are exempt from withholding tax under 212(1)(b) when paid by the Canadian subsidiary to its non-resident parent.

**(2) Idem** — Where a parent corporation has lent money to a subsidiary wholly-owned corporation resident in Canada whose principal business is not the making of loans and the money has been lent by that corporation to a subsidiary corporation wholly-owned by it and resident in Canada whose principal business is the making of loans, the loan by the parent corporation shall be deemed, for the purpose of subsection (1), to have been a loan to a subsidiary wholly-owned corporation whose principal business is the making of loans.

**(3) Election** — This section does not apply in respect of any payment of interest unless the parent corporation and the creditor have executed, and filed with the Minister, an election in prescribed form.

**Forms**: T2023: Election in respect of loans from non-residents.

**(4) Application of election** — An election filed under subsection (3) does not apply in respect of any payment of interest made more than 12 months before the date on which the election was filed with the Minister.

**Related Provisions**: 17 — Inclusion of deemed interest in income of corporation resident in Canada.

**Definitions [s. 218]**: "business" — 248(1); "Canada" — 255; "corporation" — 248(1), *Interpretation Act* 35(1); "insurance corporation", "Minister", "non-resident" — 248(1); "parent corporation" — 218(1)(a); "person", "prescribed" — 248(1); "resident in Canada" — 250; "subsidiary corporation" — 218(1)(b); "subsidiary wholly-owned corporation" — 248(1).

**Interpretation Bulletins [s. 218]**: IT-88R2: Stock dividends; IT-109R2: Unpaid amounts.

**218.1 Application of s. 138.1** — In respect of life insurance policies for which all or any part of an insurer's reserves vary in amount depending on the fair market value of a specified group of properties, the rules contained in section 138.1 apply for the purposes of this Part.

**Notes**: 218.1 added in R.S.C. 1985 (5th Supp.) consolidation. It was previously contained in the opening words of 138.1(1), which applied "for the purposes of this Part and Part XIII". Part XIII is sections 212 to 218.1.

**Definitions [s. 218.1]**: "amount", "insurer", "life insurance policy" — 248(1).

---

**Proposed Addition — Part XIII.1**

# PART XIII.1 — ADDITIONAL TAX ON AUTHORIZED FOREIGN BANKS

**218.2 (1) Branch interest tax** — Every authorized foreign bank shall pay a tax under this Part for each taxation year equal to 25% of its taxable interest expense for the year.

**Related Provisions**: 157(1)(a)(i) — Monthly instalments required; 218.2(2) — Taxable interest expense; 218.2(3), (4) — Effect of treaties on tax rate; 218.2(5) — Administration of Part XIII.1 tax.

**(2) Taxable interest expense** — The taxable interest expense of an authorized foreign bank for a taxation year is 15% of the amount, if any, by which

(a) the total of all amounts on account of interest that are deducted under section 20.2 in computing the bank's income for the year from its Canadian banking business

exceeds

(b) the total of all amounts that are included in paragraph (a) and that are in respect of a liability of the bank to another person or partnership.

**(3) Where tax not payable** — No tax is payable under this Part for a taxation year by an authorized foreign bank if

(a) the bank is resident in a country with which Canada has a tax treaty at the end of the year; and

(b) no tax similar to the tax under this Part would be payable in that country for the year by a bank resident in Canada carrying on business in that country during the year.

**(4) Rate limitation** — Despite any other provision of this Act, the reference in subsection (1) to 25% shall, in respect of a taxation year of an authorized foreign bank that is resident in a country with which Canada has a tax treaty on the last day of the year, be read as a reference to,

(a) if the treaty specifies the maximum rate of tax that Canada may impose under this Part for the year on residents of that country, that rate;

(b) if the treaty does not specify a maximum rate as described in paragraph (a) but does specify the maximum rate of tax that Canada may impose on a payment of interest in the year by a person resident in Canada to a related person resident in that country, that rate; and

(c) in any other case, 25%.

**(5) Provisions applicable to Part** — Sections 150 to 152, 158, 159, 160.1 and 161 to 167 and Division J of Part I apply to this Part with any modifications that the circumstances require.

**Related Provisions**: 157(1)(a)(i) — Monthly instalments required.

**Application**: The August 8, 2000 draft legislation, s. 23, will add s. 218.2, applicable to taxation years that end after June 27, 1999.

**Technical Notes**: New Part XIII.2 of the Act applies a special branch interest tax, in lieu of Part XIII withholding tax, to certain notional interest payments by an "authorized foreign bank." The operation of this new tax is tied to the special interest-deductibility rules that apply to such banks.

In general terms, new section 20.2 of the Act allows an authorized foreign bank to deduct on account of the interest expense of its Canadian banking business for a year one or more of three amounts:

- Interest expense actually incurred by the bank in the year, in relation to liabilities of the Canadian banking business to other persons or partnerships;

- Interest expense notionally incurred by the Canadian banking business in the year, in relation to documented "branch advances" from the bank itself to the business; and

- A residual amount, representing interest for the year on the amount by which 95% of the value of the Canadian banking business's assets exceeds the total of its actual liabilities and its branch advances.

Existing Part XIII of the Act applies withholding tax to certain payments of interest by persons resident in Canada to non-residents. An amendment to Part XIII (new subsection 212(13.3)) treats an authorized foreign bank, in respect of its Canadian banking business, as being resident in Canada for purposes of that Part. As a result, the bank's actual interest payments to non-residents (item 1 above) may attract tax under Part XIII.

New Part XIII.2 complements Part XIII by ensuring the appropriate tax results in respect of an authorized foreign bank's notional and residual interest expenses (items 2 and 3 above). Specifically, new subsection 218.2(1) of the Act imposes a tax equal to 25% (the statutory rate under Part XIII) of an authorized foreign bank's "taxable interest expense" for a year. "Taxable interest expense" for a year is defined in new subsection 218.2(2) of the Act as 15% of the amount by which the bank's interest expense deduction for the year exceeds that part of the deduction that relates to actual liabilities to other persons or partnerships.

Canada's tax treaties have important effects on the taxation of non-residents' Canadian-source income. New Part XIII.2 includes two rules that reflect the influence of tax treaties. First, new subsection 218.2(3) of the Act states that an authorized foreign bank that is resident in a country with which Canada has a tax treaty is exempt from this tax, provided that a Canadian-resident bank that carried on business in that country would not be required to pay a comparable tax. Thus an authorized foreign bank from a treaty country, which country either has no such tax or considers that its tax treaty with Canada precludes it from applying the tax to residents of Canada, is not liable to pay tax under new Part XIII.2.

Second, new subsection 218.2(4) of the Act limits the rate of tax under Part XIII.2 (otherwise 25%) where a tax treaty applies. If the relevant treaty includes a specific rate limit for the Part, that limit governs; if it does not, the applicable rate is the maximum rate that the treaty allows Canada to apply to interest payments between a resident of Canada and a related person in the treaty country.

New Part XIII.2 of the Act applies for taxation years that end after June 27, 1999.

**Notice of Ways and Means Motion (authorized foreign banks), February 11, 1999**: (3) That, for the purposes of Part XIII of the Act, an authorized foreign bank be deemed, in respect of its business in Canada, to be a person resident in Canada.

(4) That an authorized foreign bank be subject to a tax equal to the product of

(a) 25% or such lesser rate as may apply, under an income tax treaty between Canada and the country in which the authorized foreign bank is resident, to interest payable by a person resident in Canada to a person resident in that country, and

**Department of Finance news release, February 11, 1999**: *Withholding Tax on Interest*

(a) Foreign banks deemed resident for purposes of Part XIII tax

Subject to certain exceptions and to tax treaties, Part XIII of the *Income Tax Act* imposes a withholding tax on, among other things, interest paid by residents of Canada to non-residents. To treat Canadian banks and the Canadian branches of foreign banks equally, it is proposed that Part XIII of the Act be amended to treat a Canadian branch of a foreign bank as resident in Canada for the purposes of applying that Part to interest and other payments made to or by the branch.

This change will also have the effect of ensuring that all banks operating in Canada have equal access to the securities lending market.

(b) Tax re: interest on allocated debt

Although it is proposed that Canadian branches of foreign banks be allowed a deduction on account of interest on "allocated debt" (see above [under 20(1)(c) — ed.]), the interest would not, under existing rules, be subject to withholding tax. As Canadian banks would, in some cases, be subject to withholding tax in respect of funds borrowed outside Canada, a new tax is proposed to apply to a portion of the interest deducted by the Canadian branch of a foreign bank in respect of its allocated debt.

**Definitions [s. 218.2]**: "amount", "authorized foreign bank", "bank", "business" — 248(1); "Canada" — 255, *Interpretation Act* 35(1); "Canadian banking business" — 248(1); "partnership" — see Notes to 96(1); "person" — 248(1); "related" — 251(2)–(6); "resident", "resident in Canada" — 250; "tax treaty" — 248(1); "taxable interest expense" — 218.2(2); "taxation year" — 249.

# PART XIV — ADDITIONAL TAX ON NON-RESIDENT CORPORATIONS

**219. (1) Additional tax [branch tax]** — Every corporation that is non-resident in a taxation year shall, on or before its filing-due date for the year, pay a tax under this Part for the year equal to 25% of the amount, if any, by which the total of

(a) the corporation's taxable income earned in Canada for the year (in this subsection referred to as the corporation's "base amount"),

(b) the amount deducted because of section 112 and paragraph 115(1)(d.1) in computing the corporation's base amount,

(c) the amount deducted under paragraph 20(1)(v.1) in computing the corporation's base amount, other than any portion of the amount so deducted that was deductible because of the membership of the corporation in a partnership,

(d) 1/3 of the amount, if any, by which the total of all amounts each of which is a taxable capital gain of the corporation for the year from a disposition of a taxable Canadian property exceeds the total of all amounts each of which is

(i) an allowable capital loss of the corporation for the year from a disposition of a taxable Canadian property, or

(ii) an amount deductible because of paragraphs 111(1)(b) and 115(1)(e) in computing the corporation's base amount,

---

**Proposed Amendment — 219(1)(d)**

**Application**: The December 21, 2000 draft legislation, s. 90, will amend para. 219(1)(d) to delete the expression "1/3 of", applicable to taxation years that end after February 27, 2000 except that, for such taxation years that ended before October 18, 2000, the reference to the expression "the amount" shall be read as a reference to the expression "1/2 of the amount".

**Technical Notes**: Paragraph 219(1)(d) adds to the branch tax base the non-taxable portion of any net gain realized by a non-resident corporation on the disposition of taxable Canadian property used in a Canadian business. Paragraph 219(1)(d) is amended to delete the reference to "1/3 of". The amendment is consequential on the reduction of the inclusion rate for capital gains from 3/4 to 1/2 [see 38(a) — ed.].

The amendment applies to taxation years that end after February 27, 2000 except that, for a taxpayer's taxation year that ends after February 27, 2000 but before October 17, 2000, the reference to the expression "the amount" in that paragraph is to be read as a reference to "1/2 of the amount".

---

(e) the total of all amounts each of which

(i) is an amount in respect of a grant or credit that can reasonably be considered to have been received by the corporation in the year as a reimbursement or repayment of, or as indemnification or compensation for, an amount deducted because of

(A) paragraph (j), as it read in its application to the 1995 taxation year, in computing the amount determined under this subsection for a preceding taxation year that began before 1996, or

(B) paragraph (k) in computing the amount determined under this subsection for the year or for a preceding taxation year that began after 1995, and

(ii) was not included in computing the corporation's base amount for any taxation year,

(f) where, at any time in the year, the corporation has made one or more dispositions described in paragraph (l) of qualified property, the total of all amounts each of which is an amount in respect of one of those dispositions equal to the amount, if any, by which the fair market value of the qualified property at the time of the disposition exceeds the corporation's proceeds of disposition of the property, and

(g) the amount, if any, claimed for the immediately preceding taxation year under paragraph (j) by the corporation,

exceeds the total of

(h) that proportion of the total of

(i) the total of the taxes payable under Parts I, I.3 and VI for the year by the corporation, determined without reference to subsection (1.1), and

(ii) the total of the income taxes payable to the government of a province for the year by the corporation, determined without reference to subsection (1.1),

that the corporation's base amount is of the amount that would, if this Act were read without reference to subsection (1.1), be the corporation's base amount,

(i) the total of all amounts each of which is the amount of interest or a penalty paid by the corporation in the year

(i) under this Act, or

(ii) on or in respect of an income tax payable by it to the government of a province under a law of the province relating to income tax,

to the extent that the interest or penalty was not deductible in computing its base amount for any taxation year,

(j) where the corporation was carrying on business in Canada at the end of the year, the amount claimed by the corporation for the year, not exceeding the amount prescribed to be its allowance for the year in respect of its investment in property in Canada,

(k) the portion of the total of all amounts, each of which is an amount by which the corporation's base amount is increased because of paragraph 12(1)(o) or 18(1)(l.1) or (m) or subsection 69(6) or (7), that is not deductible under paragraph (h) or (j), and

(l) where the corporation has at any time in the year disposed of property (in this paragraph and paragraph (f) referred to as "qualified property") used by it immediately before that time for the purpose of gaining or producing income from a business carried on by it in Canada to a Canadian corporation (in this paragraph referred to as the "purchaser corporation") that was, immediately after the disposition, a qualified related corporation of the corporation for consideration that includes a share of the capital stock of the purchaser corporation, the total of all amounts each of which is an amount in respect of a disposition in the year of a qualified property equal to the amount, if any, by which

(i) the fair market value of the qualified property at the time of the disposition

exceeds the total of

(ii) the amount, if any, by which the paid-up capital in respect of the issued and outstanding shares of the capital stock of the purchaser corporation increased because of the disposition, and

(iii) the fair market value, at the time of receipt, of the consideration (other than shares) given by the purchaser corporation for the qualified property.

**Related Provisions**: 18(1)(t) — Tax is non-deductible; 52(7) — Cost of shares of subsidiary; 115.2 — Non-resident investment or pension fund deemed not to be carrying on business in Canada; 134 — Status of non-resident-owned investment corporation for purposes of s. 219; 142.7(10)(b) — Addition under 219(1)(g) for branch-establishment dividend of foreign entrant bank; 218.2 — Branch interest tax on foreign banks; 219(1.1) — Excluded gains; 219(2) — Exempt corporations; 219.1 — Corporate emigration — 25% tax; 219.2 — Limitation on rate of Part XIV tax to dividend rate under treaties; Canada-U.S. tax treaty, Art. X:6(d) — Exemption for first $500,000 of earnings.

**Notes**: The Part XIV tax is known informally as the "branch tax". It parallels the withholding tax in 212(2) by taxing branch profits not reinvested in Canada at the same rate as dividends. The measurement of "not reinvested in Canada" is intended to approximate the funds remitted to the home base; Canada having no exchange controls or currency controls, there is no other way to measure the actual funds "sent home".

Where the rate on dividends is reduced by treaty, as is usually the case, the branch tax rate is normally correspondingly reduced: see 219.2. (Until 1985, the rule in 219.2 was in ITAR 11(4).)

Note that some of Canada's tax treaties exempt the first $500,000 of a non-resident corporation's income. See for example Article X(6)(d) of the Canada-U.S. tax treaty.

219(1) amended by 1995-97 technical bill, this version effective for taxation years that begin in 1997 or later. For taxation years that began in 1996, read the reference in 219(1)(g) to "paragraph (j)" as "paragraph (h), as it read in its application to the 1995 taxation year, or paragraph (j)". For taxation years that began before 1996, read:

(1) Every corporation carrying on business in Canada at any time in a taxation year (other than a corporation that was, throughout the year, a Canadian corporation) shall, on or before the day on or before which it is required to file a return of income under Part I for the year, pay a tax under this Part for the year equal to 25% of the amount by which the total of

(a) the corporation's amount taxable (within the meaning given that expression in section 123) for the taxation year,

(a.1) the amount deducted by the corporation under section 112 in computing the amount referred to in paragraph (a),

(a.2) the amount deducted by the corporation under subsection 115(1) in computing the amount referred to in paragraph (a) that was an amount the deduction of which was permitted under section 112,

(a.3) the amount deducted under paragraph 20(1)(v.1) by the corporation in computing the amount referred to in paragraph (a), other than any portion of the amount so deducted that was deductible because of the membership of the corporation in a partnership,

(a.4) where, at any time in the taxation year, the corporation has made one or more dispositions as described in paragraph (k) of qualified property, the total of all amounts each of which is an amount in respect of such a disposition equal to the amount, if any, by which the fair market value of the qualified property at the time of the disposition exceeds the amount of the corporation's proceeds of disposition of the property,

(b) the amount claimed by the corporation under paragraph (h) for the immediately preceding taxation year, and

(c) where the corporation was resident in Canada at any time in the year, the amount claimed under paragraph (i) for the immediately preceding taxation year,

exceeds the total of,

(d) where the corporation was, throughout the year, not resident in Canada, the lesser of

(i) the amount, if any, by which the total of amounts each of which is a taxable capital gain of the corporation for the year from a disposition of a taxable Canadian property that was not property used in the year in, or held in the year in the course of, carrying on business in Canada, exceeds the total of amounts each of which is an allowable capital loss of the corporation for the year from a disposition of any such property, and

(ii) the amount that would be determined under subparagraph (i) for the year if it were read without reference to the expression "that was not property used in the year in, or held in the year in the course of, carrying on business in Canada",

(e) the total of the taxes payable by it under Parts I, I.3 and VI for the year less, where the corporation was at no time in the year resident in Canada, that proportion of the tax payable by it under Part I for the year that the amount determined under paragraph (d) in respect of the corporation for the year is of the corporation's amount taxable for the year,

(f) any income taxes payable by the corporation to the government of a province in respect of the year (to the extent that those taxes were not deductible under Part I in computing its income for the year from businesses carried on by it in Canada) less, where the corporation was, at no time in the year, resident in Canada, that proportion thereof that the amount determined under paragraph (d) in respect of the corporation for the year is of the corporation's amount taxable for the year,

(f.1) the total of all amounts each of which is the amount of interest or a penalty paid by it in the year

(i) under this Act, or

(ii) on or in respect of income taxes payable by it to the government of a province under a law of the province relating to income tax,

to the extent that the interest or penalty was not deductible in computing its income under Part I for any taxation year from a business carried on by it in Canada,

(g) where the corporation was resident in Canada at any time in the year

(i) the amount deducted under section 126 from the tax for the year otherwise payable by the corporation under Part I, and

(ii) ½ of the lesser of the corporation's taxable income for the year and the amount, if any, by which

(A) the total of such of its incomes for the year from businesses or properties and its taxable capital gains for the year from disposition of property as were from sources in countries other than Canada

exceeds

(B) the total of such of its losses for the year from businesses or properties and its allowable capital losses for the year from dispositions of property as were from sources in countries other than Canada,

(h) where the corporation was, at the end of the year, carrying on business in Canada, such amount as the corporation may claim for the year, not exceeding the amount prescribed to be its allowance for the year in respect of its investment in property in Canada,

(i) where the corporation was resident in Canada at any time in the year, such amount as the corporation may claim for the year, not exceeding the amount, if any, by which

(i) the total of dividends paid by it after it last became resident in Canada, while it was resident in Canada and before the end of the year

exceeds

(ii) the total of amounts determined under subparagraph (g)(ii) in respect of the corporation for taxation years ending after it last became resident in Canada and not later than the end of the year,

(j) such portion of the total of all amounts, each of which is an amount referred to in paragraph (a) is increased by virtue of paragraph 12(1)(o), 18(1)(l.1) or (m) or subsection 69(6) or (7), as is not deductible under paragraph (f) or (h), and

(k) where, at any time after December 11, 1979, the corporation has, in the taxation year, disposed of property (in this paragraph and paragraph (a.4) referred to as "qualified property") used by it immediately before that time for the purpose of gaining or producing income from a business carried on by it in Canada to a Canadian corporation that was, immediately after the disposition, its subsidiary wholly-owned corporation (in this paragraph referred to as the "purchaser corporation") for consideration that includes shares of the capital stock of the purchaser corporation, the total of all amounts each of which is an amount in respect of a disposition in the year of a qualified property equal to the amount, if any, by which

(i) the fair market value of the qualified property at the time of its disposition

exceeds the total of

(ii) the amount, if any, by which the paid-up capital in respect of the issued and outstanding shares of the capital stock of the purchaser corporation increased by virtue of the disposition, and

(iii) the fair market value, at the time of receipt, of the consideration (other than shares) given by the purchaser corporation for the qualified property.

219(1)(a.3) amended by 1992 technical bill, effective December 21, 1991, to add the words beginning "other than". See Notes to 96(1).

219(1)(e) amended by 1992 technical bill, retroactive to taxation years that end after June 1989, to add reference to taxes under Parts I.3 and VI. Thus, those taxes can be deducted in computing the amount on which the branch-tax liability is based.

219(1)(f.1) added by 1991 technical bill, effective for interest and penalties paid after 1987.

**Regulations**: 808 (allowance in respect of investment in property in Canada).

**Interpretation Bulletins**: See list at end of s. 219.

**(1.1) Excluded gains** — For the purposes of subsection (1), paragraph 115(1)(b) shall be read without reference to subparagraphs (i) and (iii) to (xii).

### Proposed Amendment — 219(1.1)

**(1.1) Excluded gains** — For the purpose of subsection (1), the definition "taxable Canadian property" in subsection 248(1) shall be read without reference to paragraphs (a) and (c) to (k) of that definition and as if the only interests or options referred to in paragraph (l) of that definition were those in respect of property described in paragraph (b) of that definition.

**Application**: Bill C-43 (First Reading September 20, 2000), s. 104, will amend subsec. 219(1.1) to read as above, applicable after October 1, 1996.

**Technical Notes**: Under subsection 219(1), a non-resident corporation's taxable income earned in Canada for a taxation year is one of the elements of the corporation's tax base in respect of the "branch tax" imposed under Part XIV. Subsection 219(1.1) restricts the definition of taxable Canadian property for the purposes of computing a non-resident corporation's branch tax base under subsection 219(1). For those purposes, subsection 219(1.1) directs that the existing definition of taxable Canadian property in paragraph 115(1)(b) is to be read without reference to subparagraphs 115(1)(b)(i) and (iii) to (xii). As a consequence of the relocation of the definition "taxable Canadian property" to subsection 248(1), it is now necessary to amend subsection 219(1.1) to reflect the new definition of taxable Canadian property.

**Notes**: 219(1.1) added by 1995-97 technical bill, effective for taxation years that begin in 1996 or later.

**(2) Exempt corporations** — No tax is payable under this Part for a taxation year by a corporation that was, throughout the year,

(a) a bank;

### Proposed Repeal — 219(2)(a)

**Application**: The August 8, 2000 draft legislation, s. 24, will repeal para. 219(2)(a), applicable to taxation years that end after June 27, 1999.

**Technical Notes**: A non-resident corporation may carry on business in Canada either through a subsidiary corporation or by operating a branch here. Dividends paid by a subsidiary to its non-resident parent company are subject to non-resident withholding tax under Part XIII of the Act, as modified by any applicable tax treaty. In the case of a branch, Part XIV imposes what is intended to be a generally comparable tax: in broad terms, any after-tax Canadian earnings that are not reinvested in the corporation's Canadian business are subject to the so-called branch tax.

Paragraph 219(2)(a) of the Act currently exempts banks from the branch tax. In recent years, non-resident banks have not been permitted to operate branches in Canada in any event, so the exemption has had no practical effect. With changes to the regulatory rules, however, "authorized foreign banks" may now open Canadian branches. Since part of the appropriate tax treatment of these banks is the application to them of the branch tax, paragraph 219(2)(a) is repealed.

This amendment applies for taxation years that end on or after June 28, 1999 — the date on which the relevant *Bank Act* amendments were proclaimed.

Given the extension of the branch tax to authorized foreign banks, it is proposed that the *Income Tax Regulations* be amended to set out, in new subsection 808(8), how the investment allowance of an authorized foreign bank for the purpose of paragraph 219(1)(j) of the Act is calculated.

**Notice of Ways and Means Motion (authorized foreign banks), February 11, 1999**: (6) That an authorized foreign bank be subject to tax under Part XIV of the Act.

**Department of Finance news release, February 11, 1999**: *Branch Tax*

Resident corporations must pay withholding tax on dividends remitted to a non-resident parent. The concept of a dividend is not relevant to a branch office, however, as the non-resident home office is not a separate legal entity from its branches. Part XIV of the *Income Tax Act* imposes a "branch tax" on the earnings of a non-resident corporation carrying on business in Canada through a branch office, to the extent that the earnings of the non-resident corporation are not retained in Canada to fund the Canadian operations. The branch tax is designed to replicate the tax treatment of dividends. For example, the branch tax is reduced in cases where a treaty provides for a reduced withholding rate on dividends.

It is proposed that the branch tax apply to foreign banks. The application of this tax is intended to ensure that Canadian branches of foreign banks are taxed in the same manner on their surplus as Canadian subsidiaries of foreign banks.

(b) a corporation whose principal business was

(i) the transportation of persons or goods,

(ii) communications, or

(iii) mining iron ore in Canada; or

(c) a corporation exempt from tax under section 149.

**(3) Provisions applicable to Part** — Sections 150 to 152, 154, 158, 159 and 161 to 167 and Division J of Part I are applicable to this Part with such modifications as the circumstances require.

**Interpretation Bulletins**: See list at end of s. 219.

**(4) Non-resident insurers** — No tax is payable under subsection (1) for a taxation year by a non-resident insurer, but where it elects, in prescribed manner and within the prescribed time, to deduct, in computing its Canadian investment fund as of the end of the immediately following taxation year, an amount not greater than the amount, if any, by which

(a) the amount, if any, by which the total of

(i) the insurer's surplus funds derived from operations as of the end of the year, and

(i.1) where, in any particular taxation year that began before the end of the year, the insurer transferred to a taxable Canadian corporation with which it did not deal at arm's length any designated insurance property of the insurer for the particular year, and

(A) the property was transferred before December 16, 1987 and subsection 138(11.5) of the *Income Tax Act*, chapter 148 of the Revised Statutes of Canada, 1952, applied in respect of the transfer, or

(B) the property was transferred before November 22, 1985 and subsection 85(1)

of that Act applied in respect of the transfer,

the amount, if any, by which

(C) the total of the fair market value, at the time of the transfer, of all such property

exceeds

(D) the total of the insurer's proceeds of disposition of all such property,

exceeds the total of

(ii) each amount on which the insurer has paid tax under this Part for a previous taxation year,

(iii) the amount, if any, by which the insurer's accumulated 1968 deficit exceeds the amount of the insurer's maximum tax actuarial reserves for its 1968 taxation year for its life insurance policies in Canada,

(iv) the insurer's loss, if any, for each of its 5 consecutive taxation years ending with its 1968 taxation year, from all insurance businesses (other than its life insurance business) carried on by it in Canada (computed without reference to section 30 of the *Income Tax Act*, chapter 148 of the Revised Statutes of Canada, 1952, as it read in its application to those years), except to the extent that any such loss was deductible in computing its taxable income for any of its taxation years ending before 1969, and

(v) the total of all amounts in respect of which the insurer has filed an election under subsection (5.2) for a previous taxation year in accordance with that subsection,

exceeds

(b) the amount of the insurer's attributed surplus for the year,

the insurer shall, on or before the day on or before which it is required to file a return under Part I for the year, pay a tax for the year equal to 25% of the amount, if any, by which the amount it has so elected to deduct exceeds the amount in respect of which it filed an election under subsection (5.2) for the year in accordance with that subsection.

**Related Provisions**: 181.3(3)(d)(i)(A), 190.13(c)(i)(A) — Effect on capital tax.

**Notes**: Opening words of 219(4)(a)(i.1) amended by 1996 Budget, effective for 1997 and later taxation years (changed from 1996 at Second Reading of the Budget bill). The changes reflect the new definition of "designated insurance property" in 138(12). For earlier taxation years, read:

(i.1) where, in any taxation year commencing before the end of the year, the insurer transferred to a taxable Canadian corporation with which it did not deal at arm's length any property used by it in the year in, or held by it in the year in the course of (within the meaning assigned by subsection 138(12)), carrying on an insurance business in Canada, and

**Regulations**: 2403(1) (prescribed manner and time).

**I.T. Application Rules**: 69 (meaning of "*Income Tax Act*, chapter 148 of the Revised Statutes of Canada, 1952").

**Interpretation Bulletins**: See list at end of s. 219.

**(5)** [Repealed under former Act]

**(5.1) Additional tax on insurer** — Where a non-resident insurer ceases in a taxation year to carry on all or substantially all of an insurance business in Canada, it shall, on or before its filing-due date for the year, pay a tax for the year equal to 25% of the amount, if any, by which

(a) that portion of the amount determined under paragraph (4)(a) for the year in respect of the insurer that can reasonably be attributed to the business, including the disposition by it of property that was its designated insurance property in respect of the business for the year in which the disposition occurred,

exceeds

(b) the amount the insurer and a qualified related corporation of the insurer jointly elect in accordance with subsection (5.2) for the year in respect of the business.

**Related Provisions**: 18(1)(t) — Tax is non-deductible.

**Notes**: 219(5.1) amended by 1996 Budget, effective for 1997 and later taxation years (changed from 1996 at Second Reading of the Budget bill). The changes reflect the new definition of "designated insurance property" in 138(12), and use the new term "filing-due date" (defined in 248(1)). For earlier taxation years, read:

(5.1) Where, in a particular taxation year, a non-resident insurer has ceased to carry on all or substantially all of an insurance business in Canada, it shall, on or before the day on or before which it is required to file a return of income under Part I for the particular year, pay a tax for the year equal to 25% of the amount, if any, by which

(a) that portion of the amount determined under paragraph (4)(a) for the particular year in respect of the non-resident insurer that can reasonably be attributed to the business including the disposition by it of property that was, at the time of the disposition, used by it in the year in, or held by it in the year in the course of (within the meaning assigned by subsection 138(12)), carrying on the business

exceeds

(b) the amount in respect of which the non-resident insurer and a qualified related corporation of the insurer have jointly elected in accordance with subsection (5.2) for the particular year in respect of the business.

The CCRA takes the position that "all or substantially all" means 90% or more.

**(5.2) Election by non-resident insurer** — Where

(a) a non-resident insurer has ceased to carry on all or substantially all of an insurance business in Canada in a taxation year, and

(b) the insurer has transferred the business to a qualified related corporation of the insurer and the insurer and the corporation have elected to have subsection 138(11.5) apply in respect of the transfer,

the insurer and the corporation may elect, in prescribed manner and within prescribed time, to reduce the amount in respect of which the insurer would otherwise be liable to pay tax under subsection (5.1) by an amount not exceeding the lesser of

(c) the amount determined under paragraph (5.1)(a) in respect of the insurer in respect of the business, and

(d) the total of the paid-up capital of the shares of the capital stock of the corporation received by the insurer as consideration for the transfer of the business and any contributed surplus arising on the issue of those shares.

**Related Provisions**: 138(11.9) — Computation of contributed surplus; 181.3(3)(d)(i)(A), 190.13(c)(i)(A) — Effect on capital tax.

**Notes**: The CCRA takes the position that "all or substantially all", used in 219(5.2)(a), means 90% or more.

**Regulations**: 2403(2) (prescribed manner and time).

**Interpretation Bulletins**: See list at end of s. 219.

**(5.3) Deemed payment of dividend** — Where, at any time in a taxation year,

(a) a qualified related corporation of a non-resident insurer ceases to be a qualified related corporation of that insurer, or

(b) the tax deferred account of a qualified related corporation of a non-resident insurer exceeds the total of the paid-up capital in respect of all the shares of the capital stock of the corporation and its contributed surplus,

the corporation shall be deemed to have paid, immediately before that time, a dividend to the insurer in an amount equal to

(c) where paragraph (a) is applicable, the balance of the tax deferred account of the corporation at that time, or

(d) where paragraph (b) is applicable, the amount of the excess referred to in that paragraph at that time.

**Related Provisions**: 138(11.9) — Computation of contributed surplus.

**Interpretation Bulletins**: See list at end of s. 219.

**(6) [Repealed under former Act]**

**Notes**: 219(6), which related to non-resident insurers, was repealed in 1978.

**(7) Definitions** — In this Part,

**"accumulated 1968 deficit"** of a life insurer means such amount as can be established by the insurer to be its deficit as of the end of its 1968 taxation year from carrying on its life insurance business in Canada on the assumption that the amounts of its assets and liabilities (including reserves of any kind)

(a) as of the end of any taxation year before its 1968 taxation year, were the amounts thereof determined for the purposes of the Superintendent of Insurance for Canada or other similar officer, and

(b) as of the end of its 1968 taxation year, were

(i) in respect of depreciable property, the capital cost thereof as of the first day of its 1969 taxation year,

(ii) in respect of policy reserves, the insurer's maximum tax actuarial reserves for its 1968 taxation year for life insurance policies issued by it in the course of carrying on its life insurance business in Canada, and

(iii) in respect of other assets and liabilities, the amounts thereof determined as of the end of that year for the purpose of computing its income for its 1969 taxation year;

**Notes**: Definition "accumulated 1968 deficit" amended by 1996 Budget, effective for 1997 and later taxation years (changed from 1996 at Second Reading of the Budget bill). It was previously defined by reference to the definition in 138(12). That definition has been repealed, so the substantive definition was moved here.

219(7)"accumulated 1968 deficit" was 219(7)(b) before consolidation in R.S.C. 1985 (5th Supp.), effective for taxation years ending after November 1991.

**"attributed surplus"** of an insurer for a taxation year has the meaning assigned by regulation;

**Notes**: Term changed from "attributed surplus for the year" to "attributed surplus" by 1996 Budget, effective for 1997 and later taxation years (changed from 1996 at Second Reading of the Budget bill).

219(7)"attributed surplus for the year" was 219(7)(a) before consolidation in R.S.C. 1985 (5th Supp.), effective for taxation years ending after November 1991.

**Regulations**: 2400(4)(b) (draft); 2405(3) (meaning of "attributed surplus for the year").

**"Canadian investment fund"** has the meaning prescribed for that expression;

**Notes**: 219(7)"Canadian investment fund" was 219(7)(a) before consolidation in R.S.C. 1985 (5th Supp.), effective for taxation years ending after November 1991.

**Regulations**: 2400(4)(b) (draft); 2405(3) (meaning of "Canadian investment fund").

**"maximum tax actuarial reserves"** has the meaning assigned by subsection 138(12);

**Notes**: 219(7)"maximum tax actuarial reserves" was 219(7)(b.1) before consolidation in R.S.C. 1985 (5th Supp.), effective for taxation years ending after November 1991.

**"surplus funds derived from operations"** has the meaning assigned by subsection 138(12);

**Notes**: 219(7)"surplus funds derived from operations" was 219(7)(b.2) before consolidation in R.S.C. 1985 (5th Supp.), effective for taxation years ending after November 1991.

**"tax deferred account"** of a qualified related corporation at any time means the amount determined by the formula

$$A - B$$

where

A is the total of all amounts each of which is an amount in respect of which the qualified related corporation and a non-resident insurer have elected jointly before that time in accordance with subsection (5.2), and

B is the total of all amounts each of which is the amount of a dividend deemed by subsection (5.3) to have been paid by the qualified related corporation before that time.

**Related Provisions**: 257 — Formula cannot calculate to less than zero.

**Notes**: 219(7)"tax deferred account" was 219(7)(c) before consolidation in R.S.C. 1985 (5th Supp.), effective for taxation years ending after November 1991. The previous version, identical in meaning, read:

(c) "tax deferred account" of a qualified related corporation at any time means the amount, if any, by which

(i) the aggregate of all amounts each of which is an amount in respect of which the qualified related corporation and a non-resident insurer have elected jointly before that time in accordance with subsection (5.2)

exceeds

(ii) the aggregate of all amounts each of which is the amount of a dividend deemed by subsection (5.3) to have been paid by the qualified related corporation before that time.

**Interpretation Bulletins**: See list at end of s. 219.

## (8) Meaning of "qualified related corporation"

For the purposes of this Part, a corporation is a "qualified related corporation" of a particular corporation if it is resident in Canada and all of the issued and outstanding shares (other than directors' qualifying shares) of its capital stock (having full voting rights under all circumstances) are owned by

(a) the particular corporation,

(b) a subsidiary wholly-owned corporation of the particular corporation,

(c) a corporation of which the particular corporation is a subsidiary wholly-owned corporation,

(d) a subsidiary wholly-owned corporation of a corporation of which the particular corporation is also a subsidiary wholly-owned corporation, or

(e) any combination of corporations each of which is a corporation described in paragraph (a), (b), (c) or (d),

and, for the purpose of this subsection, a subsidiary wholly-owned corporation of a particular corporation includes any subsidiary wholly-owned corporation of a corporation that is a subsidiary wholly-owned corporation of the particular corporation.

**Related Provisions**: 134 — Status of non-resident-owned investment corporation for purposes of s. 219.

**Notes**: 219(8) amended by 1995-97 technical bill, effective for taxation years that begin in 1996 or later. The former version was identical in effect but was worded throughout in terms of a "non-resident insurer" rather than a "particular corporation". The amendment extends its application beyond corporations related to insurers, to apply for other purposes of Part XIV as well. This is relevant to the transfer of Canadian business property by a non-resident under amended 219(1)(f) and (l), which require that the transfer be to a qualified related corporation.

**Definitions [s. 219]**: "accumulated 1968 deficit" — 138(12), 219(7); "allowable capital loss" — 38(b), 248(1); "amount" — 248(1); "arm's length" — 251(1); "attributed surplus" — 219(7), Reg. 2405(3); "base amount" — 219(1)(a); "business" — 248(1); "Canada" — 255; "Canadian corporation" — 89(1), 248(1); "Canadian investment fund" — 219(7), Reg. 2405(3); "carrying on business" — 253; "corporation" — 248(1), *Interpretation Act* 35(1); "depreciable property" — 13(21), 248(1); "designated insurance property" — 138(12), 248(1); "dividend" — 248(1); "filing-due date" — 248(1); "insurer" — 248(1); "life insurance policy" — 138(12), 248(1); "life insurer" — 248(1); "maximum tax actuarial reserve" — 138(12), 219(7); "non-resident" — 248(1); "paid-up capital" — 89(1), 248(1); "person", "prescribed", "property" — 248(1); "province" — *Interpretation Act* 35(1); "qualified property" — 219(1)(l); "qualified related corporation" — 219(8); "qualifying share" — 192(6), 248(1) *[not intended to apply to s. 219]*; "regulation" — 248(1); "resident in Canada" — 250; "share" — 248(1); "subsidiary wholly-owned corporation" — 219(8), 248(1); "surplus funds derived from operations" — 138(12), 219(7); "tax deferred account" — 219(7); "taxable Canadian corporation" — 89(1), 248(1); "taxable Canadian property" — 219(1.1), 248(1); "taxable capital gain" — 38(a), 248(1); "taxable income" — 2(2), 248(1); "taxable income earned in Canada" — 248(1); "taxation year" — 249.

**Interpretation Bulletins [s. 219]**: IT-137R3: Additional tax on certain corporations carrying on business in Canada; IT-393R2: Election re tax on rents and timber royalties — non-residents.

## 219.1 Corporate emigration

Where a taxation year of a corporation is deemed by paragraph 128.1(4)(a) to have ended at any time, the corporation shall, on or before its filing-due date for the year, pay a tax under this Part for the year equal to 25% of the amount, if any, by which

(a) the fair market value of all the property owned by the corporation immediately before that time

exceeds the total of

(b) the paid-up capital in respect of all the issued and outstanding shares of the capital stock of the corporation immediately before that time,

(c) all amounts (other than amounts payable by the corporation in respect of dividends and amounts payable under this section) each of which is a debt owing by the corporation, or an obligation of the corporation to pay an amount, that is outstanding at that time, and

(d) where a tax was payable by the corporation under subsection 219(1) or this section for a preceding taxation year that began before 1996 and after the corporation last became resident in Canada, 4 times the total of all amounts that would, but for sections 219.2 and 219.3 and any agreement or convention between the Government of Canada and the government of any other country that has the force of law in Canada, have been so payable.

**Related Provisions**: 219.3 — Limitation of tax under 219.1 to rate under treaty; Canada-U.S. tax treaty, Art. IV:3 (Protocol) — Continuance in other jurisdiction.

**Notes**: 219.1 amended by 1995-97 technical bill, effective for 1996 and later taxation years. For 1993-95, read:

219.1 Where at any time a corporation ceases to be a Canadian corporation, it shall, on or before the day on or before which it is required to file a return of income under Part I for its last taxation year that began before that time, pay a tax under this Part for that year equal to 25% of the amount, if any, by which the fair market value at that time of all the property owned by the corporation exceeds the total of

(a) the paid-up capital in respect of all the issued and outstanding shares of the capital stock of the corporation at that time, and

(b) all amounts, other than amounts payable by the corporation in respect of dividends and amounts payable under this section, each of which is the amount of any debt owing by the corporation, or any other obligation of the corporation to pay an amount, that is outstanding at that time.

219.1 amended by 1993 technical bill, effective January 1, 1993, but where a corporation continued before 1993 elects for new 250(5.1) to apply earlier (see Notes to 250(5.1)), the amendment is effective from the corporation's "time of continuation". The previous version read:

219.1 Where a taxation year of a corporation is deemed by section 88.1 to have ended, it shall, on or before the day on or before which it is required to file a return of income under Part I for the year, pay a tax under this Part for that year equal to 25% of the amount, if any, by which

(a) the total of all amounts each of which is the proceeds of disposition deemed by virtue of paragraph 88.1(e) to have been received by the corporation

exceeds the total of

(b) the paid-up capital in respect of all the issued and outstanding shares of the capital stock of the corporation immediately before the end of the year, and

(c) all amounts, other than amounts payable by the corporation in respect of dividends, each of which is the amount of any debt owing by the corporation, or any other obligation of the corporation to pay an amount, that was outstanding at the end of the year.

As a result of the amendment, the scope of 219.1 was widened. Before 1993, it applied only to a corporation becoming non-resident by moving to a treaty country. It now applies to a corporation becoming non-resident by moving to any country. Specifically, it applies when a corporation incorporated outside Canada, but which is resident in Canada under the common-law test of "central management and control", becomes non-resident by moving its management to a non-treaty country.

**Definitions [s. 219.1]**: "amount" — 248(1); "Canadian corporation" — 89(1), 248(1); "corporation" — 248(1), *Interpretation Act* 35(1); "dividend" — 248(1); "paid-up capital" — 89(1), 248(1); "property" — 248(1); "share" — 248(1); "taxation year" — 249.

**Interpretation Bulletins**: IT-137R3: Additional tax on certain corporations carrying on business in Canada; IT-451R: Deemed disposition and acquisition on ceasing to be or becoming resident in Canada.

**219.2 Limitation on rate of branch tax** — Notwithstanding any other provision of this Act, where an agreement or convention between the Government of Canada and the government of another country that has the force of law in Canada

(a) does not limit the rate of tax under this Part on corporations resident in that other country, and

(b) provides that, where a dividend is paid by a corporation resident in Canada to a corporation resident in that other country that owns all of the shares of the capital stock of the corporation resident in Canada, the rate of tax imposed on the dividend shall not exceed a specified rate,

any reference in section 219 to a rate of tax shall, in respect of a taxation year of a corporation to which that agreement or convention applies on the last day of that year, be read as a reference to the specified rate.

**Related Provisions**: Canada-U.S. tax treaty, Art. X:2 — Limit on withholding tax rate on dividends.

**Notes**: 219.2 amended by 1993 technical bill, effective for 1985 and later taxation years, so that the rate limitation used is the rate that applies under treaties to wholly-owned corporations rather than the treaty rate that applies to dividends generally. The rate for such so-called "direct dividends" is sometimes lower, and never higher, than the regular rate. See Notes to 212(2) and 219(1).

The rule in 219.2 was originally in ITAR 11(4).

**Definitions [s. 219.2]**: "Canada" — 255; "corporation" — 248(1), *Interpretation Act* 35(1); "dividend" — 248(1); "property" — 248(1); "resident in Canada" — 250; "share" — 248(1); "taxation year" — 249.

**Interpretation Bulletins**: IT-137R3: Additional tax on certain corporations carrying on business in Canada.

**219.3 Effect of tax treaty** — For the purpose of section 219.1, where an agreement or convention between the Government of Canada and the government of another country that has the force of law in Canada provides that the rate of tax imposed on a dividend paid by a corporation resident in Canada to a corporation resident in the other country that owns all of the shares of the capital stock of the corporation resident in Canada shall not exceed a specified rate, the reference in section 219.1 to "25%" shall, in respect of a corporation that ceased to be resident in Canada and to which the agreement or convention applies at the beginning of its first taxation year after its taxation year that is deemed by paragraph 128.1(4)(a) to have ended, be read as a reference to the specified rate unless it can reasonably be concluded that one of the main reasons that the corporation became resident in the other country was to reduce the amount of tax payable under this Part or Part XIII.

**Notes**: 219.3 amended by 1995-97 technical bill, effective for 1996 and later taxation years. For earlier years, read:

219.3 Effect of tax agreement or convention — For the purpose of section 219.1, where an agreement or convention between the Government of Canada and the government of another country that has the force of law in Canada provides that, where a dividend is paid by a corporation resident in Canada to a corporation resident in that other country that owns all of the shares of the capital stock of the corporation resident in Canada, the rate of tax imposed on the dividend shall not exceed a specified rate, the reference in section 219.1 to a rate of tax shall, in respect of a corporation that ceased to be a Canadian corporation and to which the agreement or convention applies on the first day of the taxation year after the taxation year in which the corporation ceased to be a Canadian corporation, be read as a reference to the specified rate unless, having regard to all the circumstances, it can reasonably be concluded that one of the main reasons for the corporation becoming resident in that other country was to reduce the amount of tax payable under this Part or Part XIII.

## S. 219.3 — Income Tax Act

219.3 added by 1993 technical bill, effective for 1985 and later taxation years. However, the anti-avoidance rule at the end (beginning "unless, having regard to...") does not apply to taxation years that end before July 1993.

**Definitions [s. 219.3]:** "Canadian corporation" — 89(1), 248(1); "corporation" — 248(1), *Interpretation Act* 35(1); "dividend" — 248(1); "resident in Canada" — 250; "share" — 248(1); "taxation year" — 249.

# PART XV — ADMINISTRATION AND ENFORCEMENT

## Administration

**220. (1) Minister's duty** — The Minister shall administer and enforce this Act and the Commissioner of Customs and Revenue may exercise all the powers and perform the duties of the Minister under this Act.

**Related Provisions:** 166 — Assessment not to be vacated by reason of CCRA failure to follow proper procedures; 220(2.01) — Delegation of powers; *Canada Customs and Revenue Agency Act* — Establishment of CCRA; *Interpretation Act* 24(2) — Power of others to act for Minister; *Interpretation Act* 31(2) — Ancillary powers granted to enable work to be done.

**Notes:** 220(1) amended by *Canada Customs & Revenue Agency Act*, effective November 1, 1999, to change "Deputy Minister" to "Commissioner of Customs and Revenue" (appointed under s. 25 of that Act). The transition from Revenue Canada to the CCRA took effect on that date. The Commissioner is Rob Wright, who had been Deputy Minister since January 1997.

"Deputy Minister of National Revenue for Taxation" changed to "Deputy Minister of National Revenue" by Department of National Revenue Act amending bill, effective May 12, 1994. See also Notes to 248(1)"Minister".

**Regulations:** 900 (delegation of powers and duties to other officials).

**I.T. Technical News:** No. 8 (publication of advance tax rulings); No. 9 (electronic publication of severed rulings); No. 14 (the Income Tax rulings and Interpretations Directorate — common deficiencies or omissions in requests for advance rulings); No. 18 (The advance income tax rulings process — practical problems and possible solutions).

**(2) Officers, clerks and employees** — Such officers, clerks and employees as are necessary to administer and enforce this Act shall be appointed or employed in the manner authorized by law.

**Related Provisions:** 220(2.01) — Delegation of powers; *Interpretation Act* 23(1) — Public officers hold office during pleasure; *Interpretation Act* 31(2) — Ancillary powers granted to enable work to be done.

**(2.01) Delegation** — The Minister may authorize an officer or a class of officers to exercise powers or perform duties of the Minister under this Act.

**Related Provisions:** *Interpretation Act* 23(1) — Public officers hold office during pleasure; *Interpretation Act* 31(2) — Ancillary powers granted to enable work to be done.

**Notes:** 220(2.01) provides that the Minister of National Revenue may administratively delegate the Minister's powers and duties under the Act or Regulations to an officer or class of officers in the Department. This replaces the requirement under 221(1)(f) that delegation be done by regulation (see Reg. 900). This allows a more timely revision of the delegation of the Minister's powers and duties required by an amendment to the Act or a reorganization within the Department.

A 95-page list of such delegations, signed by the Minister, was released by the CCRA in December 1999. The Schedule is dated September 23, 1999 (see RC991221k on *TaxPartner*).

Note that delegation to a provincial official would likely be valid, as it was found to be for purposes of the GST: *Ricken Leroux Inc. v. Quebec (Minister of Revenue)*, [1998] G.S.T.C. 1 (Que. CA), leave to appeal to SCC denied [1998] G.S.T.C. 24.

220(2.01) added by 1995-97 technical bill, effective June 18, 1998. The amending bill provides that any power or duty of the Minister of National Revenue delegated to an officer or a class of officers by a regulation made under 221(1)(f) before June 18, 1998 continues to be delegated to that officer or that class of officers until an authorization by that Minister made under 220(2.01) changes the delegation of that power or duty. (The above authorization has now done so.)

**(2.1) Waiver of filing of documents** — Where any provision of this Act or a regulation requires a person to file a prescribed form, receipt or other document, or to provide prescribed information, the Minister may waive the requirement, but the person shall provide the document or information at the Minister's request.

**Notes:** 220(2.1) added by 1992 technical bill, effective for 1992 and later taxation years.

An example of a receipt required by the Act to be filed but not required by Revenue Canada's administrative practice is a receipt for child care expenses (see 63(1)).

**Interpretation Bulletins:** IT-495R2: Child care expenses.

**(3) Extensions for returns** — The Minister may at any time extend the time for making a return under this Act.

**Related Provisions:** 127.4(5.1) — Authorization for late LSVCC investments; 146(22) — Authorization for late RRSP contributions; 220(3.2) — Late filing of elections.

**Notes:** In *Kutlu* (February 21, 1997), T-205-96, 1997 CarswellNat 14, the Federal Court–Trial Division ruled that Revenue Canada could not refuse to accept a late-filed return under 216(1) where it had accepted such returns late in the past. (An appeal by the Crown to the FCA was discontinued on March 17/98.)

**(3.1) Waiver of penalty or interest** — The Minister may at any time waive or cancel all or any portion of any penalty or interest otherwise payable under this Act by a taxpayer or partnership and, notwithstanding subsections 152(4) to (5), such assessment of the interest and penalties payable by the taxpayer or partnership shall be made as is necessary to take into account the cancellation of the penalty or interest.

**Related Provisions:** 164(1.5) — Late refund of overpayment; 164(3.2) — Interest on refunds and repayments; 165(1.2) — Limitation of right to object; 225.1(1) — No collection restrictions following assessment.

**Notes:** 220(3.1) added by 1991 technical bill (as part of the "Fairness Package") and amended retroactively by 1992 technical bill, effective for penalty and interest in respect of 1985 and later taxation years.

Note that the CCRA has no jurisdiction to waive tax; the waiver applies only to penalty and interest. However, it appears that tax sometimes is waived even though this is technically not possible. See David M. Sherman, "Revenue Canada Comes Through With

Tax Waiver", *GST & Commodity Tax* newsletter (Carswell), Vol. X, No. 4 (May 1996), pp. 25–26.

Information Circular 92-2 sets out the guidelines for waiver of interest and penalty. In general, waiver will only be granted for (1) events beyond the taxpayer's control, such as death or natural disaster; (2) reliance on incorrect *written* information provided by Revenue Canada; (3) delay on Revenue Canada's part; or (4) inability to pay, where waiver (by Collections) will enable the account to be paid.

- The ice storm of January 1998 qualified as a natural disaster, and interest and penalties caused by it will be waived on request: "Revenue Canada Extends Measures to Assist Canadians Most Affected by Ice Storm", news release, February 18, 1998.
- The spring 1998 forest fires in Alberta and Northern Ontario also qualified for fairness relief: "Revenue Canada Minister Reminds Canadians Affected by Forest Fires about the Department's Fairness Provisions", news release, May 19, 1998.
- Service of Canadian military and police personnel in the Serbia-Kosovo NATO action in spring 1999 also qualifies for fairness relief, so that penalties and interest will not apply if they did not file their returns by April 30: "Revenue Canada Announces Tax Fairness Measures for Canadian Forces Personnel Serving in the Balkans", news release, April 23, 1999.
- The June 2000 E.coli water disaster in Walkerton, Ont. also qualifies for fairness relief: "Tax fairness provisions extended to Walkerton residents", CCRA news release, June 29, 2000.

Judicial review of a failure to grant relief under 220(3.1) is available in the Federal Court — Trial Division, but will be exercised very sparingly. For a review of the jurisprudence see Morley Hirsh, "Fairness Package Update", 1998 Canadian Tax Foundation annual conference proceedings, at pp. 24:10-24:16.

An alternative form of tax relief, in appropriate circumstances, is a remission order granted by the Cabinet under the *Financial Administration Act*. See H.A. Sherman and Jeffrey Sherman, "Income Tax Remission Orders: The Tax Planner's Last Resort or the Ultimate Weapon?", 34(4) *Canadian Tax Journal* 801-827 (1986). A remission order request will have improved chance of success if it refers to, and tracks the requirements of, the CCRA's Remission Guidelines. Remission orders of general interest are reproduced near the end of this book, following the Regulations (and Schedules thereto).

**Information Circulars**: 92-2: Guidelines for the cancellation and waiver of interest and penalties; 98-1R: Collections policies.

**(3.2) Late, amended or revoked elections —** Where

(a) an election by a taxpayer or a partnership under a provision of this Act or a regulation that is a prescribed provision was not made on or before the day on or before which the election was otherwise required to be made, or

(b) a taxpayer or partnership has made an election under a provision of this Act or a regulation that is a prescribed provision,

the Minister may, on application by the taxpayer or the partnership, extend the time for making the election referred to in paragraph (a) or grant permission to amend or revoke the election referred to in paragraph (b).

**Related Provisions**: 60(l), 60(l)(iv) — Minister may accept late rollover of RRSP after death to spouse, child or grandchild; 127.4(5.1) — Authorization for late LSVCC investments; 146(22) — Authorization for late RRSP contributions; 220(3) — Late filing allowed by extending time for return; 220(3.21) — Certain designations deemed to be elections; 220(3.3) — Date of late election, amended election or revocation; 220(3.4) — Consequential assessment; 220(3.5) — Penalty for late filed, amended or revoked elections.

**Notes**: 220(3.2) added by 1991 technical bill, effective for elections in respect of 1985 and later years.

The CCRA does accept some late-filed election forms that are not specifically listed in Reg. 600. However, there is no specific statutory authority for this.

The courts may be willing to allow late filing of some elections and designations in cases where the CCRA does not. See M. Gerard Tompkins, "Emerging Tax Issues", 1995 Canadian Tax Foundation annual conference report, at pp. 9:4-9:10. See also *Nassau Walnut Investments*, [1998] 1 C.T.C. 33 (FCA), where the Court allowed a late designation where the taxpayer was not engaged in retroactive tax planning.

**Regulations**: 600 (prescribed provisions).

**Interpretation Bulletins**: IT-120R5: Principal residence.

**Information Circulars**: 92-1: Guidelines for accepting late, amended or revoked elections.

**(3.21) Designations and allocations —** For the purpose of subsection (3.2),

(a) a designation in any form prescribed for the purpose of paragraph 80(2)(i) or any of subsections 80(5) to (11) or 80.03(7) is deemed to be an election under a prescribed provision of this Act; and

(b) a designation or allocation under subsection 132.11(6) is deemed to be an election under a prescribed provision of this Act.

**Notes**: 220(3.21)(b) added by 1998 Budget, effective June 17, 1999.

220(3.21) added by 1994 tax amendments bill (Part I), effective June 22, 1995 (Royal Assent).

**(3.3) Date of late election, amended election or revocation —** Where, under subsection (3.2), the Minister has extended the time for making an election or granted permission to amend or revoke an election,

(a) the election or the amended election, as the case may be, shall be deemed to have been made on the day on or before which the election was otherwise required to be made and in the manner in which the election was otherwise required to be made, and, in the case of an amendment to an election, that election shall be deemed, otherwise than for the purposes of this section, never to have been made; and

(b) the election that was revoked shall be deemed, otherwise than for the purposes of this section, never to have been made.

**Related Provisions**: 220(3.4) — Assessment to take late filing into account.

**Notes**: 220(3.3) added by 1991 technical bill, effective for elections in respect of 1985 and later years.

**(3.4) Assessments —** Notwithstanding subsections 152(4), (4.01), (4.1) and (5), such assessment of the tax, interest and penalties payable by each taxpayer in respect of any taxation year that began before the day an application is made under subsection (3.2) to the Minister shall be made as is necessary to take into account the election, the amended election or the revocation, as the case may be, referred to in subsection (3.3).

**Related Provisions**: 164(1.5) — Refunds; 164(3.2) — Interest on refunds and repayments; 165(1.1) — Limitation of right to object to assessment or determination; 169(2)(a) — Limitation of right to appeal.

**Notes**: 220(3.4) added by 1991 technical bill, effective for elections in respect of 1985 and later years; and amended retroactive to its introduction by 1995-97 technical bill, to add reference to 152(4.01).

**(3.5) Penalty for late filed, amended or revoked elections** — Where, on application by a taxpayer or a partnership, the Minister extends the time for making an election or grants permission to amend or revoke an election, the taxpayer or the partnership, as the case may be, is liable to a penalty equal to the lesser of

(a) $8,000, and

(b) the product obtained when $100 is multiplied by the number of complete months from the day on or before which the election was required to be made to the day the application was made in a form satisfactory to the Minister.

**Related Provisions**: 220(3.6) — Assessment of penalty.

**Notes**: 220(3.5) added by 1991 technical bill, effective for elections in respect of 1985 and later years.

**(3.6) Unpaid balance of penalty** — The Minister shall, with all due dispatch, examine each election, amended election and revoked election referred to in subsection (3.3), assess any penalty payable and send a notice of assessment to the taxpayer or the partnership, as the case may be, and the taxpayer or the partnership, as the case may be, shall pay forthwith to the Receiver General the amount, if any, by which the penalty so assessed exceeds the total of all amounts previously paid on account of that penalty.

**Related Provisions**: 161(11)(c) — Interest on penalties.

**Notes**: 220(3.6) added by 1991 technical bill, effective for elections in respect of 1985 and later years.

**(3.7) Idem** — The provisions of Divisions I and J of Part I apply, with such modifications as the circumstances require, to an assessment made under this section as though it had been made under section 152.

**Notes**: 220(3.7) added by 1991 technical bill, effective for elections in respect of 1985 and later years.

**(4) Security** — The Minister may, if the Minister considers it advisable in a particular case, accept security for payment of any amount that is or may become payable under this Act.

**Related Provisions**: 159(2) — Certificate before distribution; 222.1 — Application to awards of court costs.

**Regulations**: 2200 (Minister may discharge security).

**(4.1) Idem** — Where a taxpayer has objected to or appealed from an assessment under this Act, the Minister shall, while the objection or appeal is outstanding, accept adequate security furnished by or on behalf of the taxpayer for payment of the amount in controversy except to the extent that the Minister may collect the amount because of subsection 225.1(7).

**Notes**: 220(4.1) amended by 1992 technical bill, effective June 10, 1993. Before that date, ignore the words "except to the extent the Minister may collect the amount because of subsection 225.1(7)".

**(4.2) Surrender of excess security** — Where at any time a taxpayer requests in writing that the Minister surrender any security accepted by the Minister under subsection (4) or (4.1), the Minister shall surrender the security to the extent that the value of the security exceeds the total of amounts payable under this Act by the taxpayer at that time.

**Related Provisions**: 222.1 — Application to awards of court costs.

**(4.3) Security furnished by a member institution of a deposit insurance corporation** — The Minister shall accept adequate security furnished by or on behalf of a taxpayer that is a member institution in relation to a deposit insurance corporation (within the meaning assigned by subsection 137.1(5)) for payment of

(a) the tax payable under this Act by the taxpayer for a taxation year, to the extent that the amount of that tax exceeds the amount that that tax would be if no amount that the taxpayer is obliged to repay to the corporation were included under paragraph 137.1(10)(a) or (b) in computing the taxpayer's income for the year or a preceding taxation year, and

(b) interest payable under this Act by the taxpayer on the amount determined under paragraph (a),

until the earlier of

(c) the day on which the taxpayer's obligation referred to in paragraph (a) to repay the amount to the corporation is settled or extinguished, and

(d) the day that is 10 years after the end of the year.

**Notes**: 220(4.3)(a) amended by 1991 technical bill, effective July 14, 1990, to add the words "or a preceding taxation year" at the end.

**(4.4) Additional security** — The adequacy of security furnished by or on behalf of a taxpayer under subsection (4.3) shall be determined by the Minister and the Minister may require additional security to be furnished from time to time by or on behalf of the taxpayer where the Minister determines that the security that has been furnished is no longer adequate.

**Proposed Addition — 220(4.5)–(4.71)**

**(4.5) Security for departure tax** — If an individual who is deemed by subsection 128.1(4) to have disposed of a property (other than a right to a benefit under, or an interest in a trust governed by, an employee benefit plan) at any particular time in a taxation year (in this section referred to as the individual's "emigration year") elects, in prescribed manner on or before the individual's balance-due day for the emigration year, that this subsection and subsections (4.51) to (4.54) apply in respect of the emigration year,

(a) the Minister shall, until the individual's balance-due day for a particular taxation year that begins after the particular time, accept adequate security furnished by or on behalf of the individual on or before the individual's balance-due day for the emigration year for the lesser of

(i) the total amount of taxes under Parts I and I.1

(A) that would be payable by the individual for the emigration year if the exclusion or deduction of each amount referred to in paragraph 161(7)(a) were not taken into account, but

(B) that would not have been so payable if each property (other than a right to a benefit under, or an interest in a trust governed by, an employee benefit plan) deemed by subsection 128.1(4) to have been disposed of at the particular time, and that has not been subsequently disposed of before the beginning of the particular year, were not deemed by subsection 128.1(4) to have been disposed of by the individual at the particular time, and

(ii) if the particular year does not immediately follow the emigration year, the amount determined under this paragraph in respect of the individual for the taxation year that immediately precedes the particular year; and

(b) except for the purposes of subsections 161(2), (4) and (4.01),

(i) interest under this Act for any period that ends on the individual's balance-due day for the particular year and throughout which security is accepted by the Minister, and

(ii) any penalty under this Act computed with reference to an individual's tax payable for the year that was, without reference to this paragraph, unpaid

shall be computed as if the particular amount for which adequate security has been accepted under this subsection were an amount paid by the individual on account of the particular amount.

**Technical Notes**: Section 220 of the Act sets out a number of rules relating to the administration and enforcement of the Act.

New subsections 220(4.5) to (4.54) of the Act permit an individual to elect, on giving security acceptable to the Minister of National Revenue, to defer payment of an amount of tax that is owing as a result of the deemed disposition of a particular property (other than an employee benefit plan right) in paragraph 128.1(4)(b). If such an election is made, interest does not start to accrue on the amount secured until such time as the amount becomes unsecured, as described below. In addition, relief is provided from a penalty under the Act to the extent that it is computed with reference to the unpaid tax with respect to the amount secured.

New subsection 220(4.5) allows an individual to elect, in prescribed manner, to defer payment of an amount of tax that is owing as a result of the deemed disposition of a particular property in paragraph 128.1(4)(b). It is intended that this deferral also operate in respect of the corresponding provincial taxes for which the Government of Canada has assessment and collection responsibilities, with the settlement of accounts between the governments taking place as the tax is collected. To understand how the subsection works, several points should be noted.

- The security rule is in a mechanical sense applied annually. That is, the Minister of National Revenue's obligation to accept security applies for one year at a time. This does not mean that the emigrant must file a renewed election each year, but only that the Minister will determine on an annual basis whether, and in what amount, the security may remain in place.

- While the election to provide security must ordinarily be made — and the security itself must be provided — on or before the individual's balance-due day for the year of emigration, special accommodation is provided for those who cease to be resident before these amendments receive Royal Assent. Those individuals have until their filing-due date for the taxation year that includes Royal Assent to make the election and provide the security.

- The provision requires the Minister of National Revenue to accept "adequate security." The adequacy of any particular proposal for security is a matter of fact. It is understood, however, that in respect of tax on a gain from the deemed disposition of shares of a corporation, the Minister will not exclude the possibility of accepting some or all of the shares as security.

Where an individual has elected under subsection 220(4.5) and has provided adequate security, the Minister of National Revenue must, for a particular taxation year that begins after the individual ceases to be a resident of Canada, accept adequate security for the lesser of two amounts. The amounts are, in effect:

(i) the individual's taxes under Parts I and I.1 for the emigration year, to the extent those taxes are attributable to the deemed disposition under paragraph 128.1(4)(b) of properties that have not been disposed of before the particular year; and

(ii) if the particular year does not immediately follow the emigration year, the amount for which security was accepted for the preceding taxation year.

Where an individual who emigrated from Canada actually disposes, in a given year, of a property that was the subject of a deemed disposition on emigration, the Minister's obligation to accept security for the tax attributable to the deemed disposition of that property lasts only until the individual's balance-due day for the given year. The amount for which the Minister must accept security, in respect of a given departure from Canada, may thus decrease from year to year as the former emigrant disposes of properties. The amount cannot, however, increase.

An amount of tax may also become unsecured if the security furnished by the taxpayer for the tax has ceased to be adequate. For additional information in respect of inadequate security, see the commentary on subsection 220(4.53).

The effects of the acceptance of security by the Minister under subsection 220(4.5) are, first, that the Minister will not take any action to collect the tax so secured, and second, that for the purpose of computing interest and penalties owing by the taxpayer, the amount secured will be treated as an amount paid on account of the tax liability.

New subsection 220(4.5) generally applies to dispositions that occur after October 1, 1996. However, as noted above, elections made and security furnished under this subsection will be considered timely if effected before the taxpayer's filing-due date for the taxation year that includes the particular day on which these amendments receive Royal Assent.

**Related Provisions**: 128.3 — Shares acquired on rollover deemed to be same shares for 220(4.5); 128.1(6) — Tax cancelled if emigrant returns to Canada; 152(10) — Posted security deemed not to be tax assessed for purposes of administration of provincial tax; 220(4.51) — Exemption for first $25,000 of security; 220(4.52) — Security effective only for departure tax; 220(4.53) — Where security proves inadequate; 220(4.54) — Extension of time for making election; 220(4.7) — Reduction in security for undue hardship.

**Notes**: This was 220.1(1) in the draft legislation (migration) of December 23, 1998.

**(4.51) Deemed security** — If an individual (other than a trust) elects under subsection (4.5) that that subsection apply in respect of a taxation year, for the purposes of subsections (4.5) to (4.54) the Minister is deemed to have accepted at any time after the election is made adequate security for a total amount of taxes payable under Parts I and I.1 by the individual for the emigration year equal to the lesser of

(a) the total amount of those taxes that would be payable for the year by an *inter vivos* trust resident in Canada (other than a trust described in subsection 122(2)) the taxable income for which for the year is $67,000, and

(b) the greatest amount for which the Minister is required to accept security furnished by or on behalf of the individual under subsection (4.5) at that time in respect of the emigration year,

and that security is deemed to have been furnished by the individual before the individual's balance-due day for the emigration year.

**Technical Notes**: New subsection 220(4.5) permits an individual to elect, on giving adequate security to the Minister of National Revenue, to defer payment of an amount of tax that is owing as a result of the deemed disposition of a particular property in paragraph 128.1(4)(b). New subsection 220(4.51) treats an individual (other than a trust) as having furnished acceptable security to the Minister for the lesser of two amounts. The first amount is the total amount of taxes under Parts I and I.1 of the Act that would be payable, at the highest tax rate that applies to individuals, on a taxable capital gain of $67,000. (For administrative simplicity, this amount is described in the provision as the amount of those taxes that an inter vivos trust would pay for a year if the trust's taxable income for the year were $67,000.)

The second amount is the greatest amount of tax for which the Minister is required to accept security under subsection 220(4.5) for any particular taxation year of the individual. The deemed security is treated as having been furnished by the individual before the individual's balance-due day for the year in which the individual ceased to be a resident of Canada.

The effect of this provision is to excuse individual emigrants (other than trusts) from the requirement to provide security for an amount at least equal to the taxes payable on their first $100,000 of capital gains ($67,000 of taxable capital gains) resulting from the deemed disposition on emigration.

New subsection 220(4.51) applies after October 1, 1996. To reflect the three-quarters inclusion rate for capital gains that applies before the 2000 federal budget, a transitional rule provides that the amount "$67,000" in new paragraph 220(4.52)(a) shall be read as "$75,000" in respect of emigration years that are before 2001.

**Notes**: This is a convoluted way of saying that security need not be provided for the tax on up to $75,000 of income ($100,000 of gain) in the top bracket.

This was 220.1(2) in the draft legislation (migration) of December 23, 1998.

**(4.52) Limit** — Notwithstanding subsections (4.5) and (4.51), the Minister is deemed at any time not to have accepted security under subsection (4.5) in respect of an individual's emigration year for any amount greater than the amount, if any, by which

(a) the total amount of taxes that would be payable by the individual under Parts I and I.1 for the year if the exclusion or deduction of each amount referred to in paragraph 161(7)(a), in respect of which the day determined under paragraph 161(7)(b) is after that time, were not taken into account

exceeds

(b) the total amount of taxes that would be determined under paragraph (a) if this Act were read without reference to subsection 128.1(4).

**Technical Notes**: New subsections 220(4.5) and (4.51) set out rules respecting the posting of security for tax that is owing as a result of a deemed disposition of property under paragraph 128.1(4)(b). New subsection 220(4.52) limits the amount of tax that may be so secured to the total tax payable under Parts I and I.1 in respect of the application of paragraph 128.1(4)(b) in the taxation year that the individual ceased to be a resident of Canada (calculated without reference to any of the deductions or exclusions listed in paragraph 161(7)(a)).

New subsection 220(4.52) applies after October 1, 1996.

**Notes**: This is a convoluted way of saying that the security is effective only with respect to the departure tax under 128.1(4).

This was 220.1(3) in the draft legislation (migration) of December 23, 1998.

**(4.53) Inadequate security** — Subject to subsection (4.7), if it is determined at any particular time that security accepted by the Minister under subsection (4.5) is not adequate to secure the particular amount for which it was furnished by or on behalf of an individual,

(a) subject to a subsequent application of this subsection, the security shall be considered after the particular time to secure only the amount for which it is adequate security at the particular time;

(b) the Minister shall notify the individual in writing of the determination and shall accept adequate security, for all or any part of the particular amount, furnished by or on behalf of the individual within 90 days after the day of notification; and

(c) any security accepted in accordance with paragraph (b) is deemed to have been accepted by the Minister under subsection (4.5) on account of the particular amount at the particular time.

**Technical Notes**: New subsection 220(4.5) permits an individual to elect, on giving security acceptable to the Minister of National Revenue, to defer payment of an amount of tax that is owing as a result of the deemed disposition of a particular property in paragraph 128.1(4)(b). If such an election is made, interest and penalties do not accrue on the particular amount secured until such time as the amount becomes unsecured.

If the Minister determines, at any time, that the security accepted under subsection 220(4.5) is not adequate to secure the particular amount for which it was furnished by the individual, new subsection 220(4.53) provides that the security secures the part of the particular amount for which it is adequate security at that particular time; the balance of the particular amount is unsecured. The Minister is required to notify the individual in writing if part of the particular amount becomes unsecured in this manner, and the individual has the opportunity to furnish further security to the Minister within 90 days of being so notified. Where additional security is so furnished, the Minister is deemed to have accepted it in accordance with subsection 220(4.5).

New subsection 220(4.53) applies after October 1, 1996.

**Related Provisions**: 220(4.54)(c) — Extension of 90-day period under (4.53)(b).

**Notes**: This was 220.1(4) in the draft legislation (migration) of December 23, 1998.

**(4.54) Extension of time** — If in the opinion of the Minister it would be just and equitable to do so, the Minister may at any time extend

(a) the time for making an election under subsection (4.5);

(b) the time for furnishing and accepting security under subsection (4.5); or

(c) the 90-day period for the acceptance of security under paragraph (4.53)(b).

**Technical Notes**: New subsection 220(4.5) permits an individual to elect, on giving security acceptable to the Minister of National Revenue, to defer payment of an amount of tax that is owing as a result of the deemed disposition of a particular property in paragraph 128.1(4)(b). This election must be made, and the security furnished, on or before the balance-due date for the taxation year that the individual ceased to be a resident of Canada. New subsection 220(4.53) permits an individual to furnish additional security to the Minister, where the Minister has notified the individual that security previously furnished is no longer adequate. The additional security must be so furnished within 90 days of the Minister's notification.

New subsection 220(4.54) permits the Minister to extend the time available to an individual to make an election or to furnish security under subsection 220(4.5), or to furnish additional security under subsection 220(4.53), where the Minister considers it just and equitable to do so.

New subsection 220(4.54) applies after October 1, 1996.

**Notes**: This was 220.1(5) in the draft legislation (migration) of December 23, 1998.

**(4.6) Security for tax on distributions of taxable Canadian property to non-resident beneficiaries** — Where

(a) solely because of the application of subsection 107(5), paragraphs 107(2)(a) to (c) do not apply to a distribution by a trust in a particular taxation year (in this section referred to as the trust's "distribution year") of taxable Canadian property, and

(b) the trust elects, in prescribed manner on or before the trust's balance-due day for the distribution year, that this subsection and subsections (4.61) to (4.63) apply in respect of the distribution year,

the following rules apply:

(c) the Minister shall, until the trust's balance-due day for a subsequent taxation year, accept adequate security furnished by or on behalf of the trust on or before the trust's balance-due day for the distribution year for the lesser of

(i) the total amount of taxes under Parts I and I.1

(A) that would be payable by the trust for the distribution year if the exclusion or deduction of each amount referred to in paragraph 161(7)(a) were not taken into account, but

(B) that would not have been so payable if the rules in subsection 107(2) (other than the election referred to in that subsection) had applied to each distribution by the trust in the distribution year of property (other than property subsequently disposed of before the beginning of the subsequent year) to which paragraph (a) applies, and

(ii) where the subsequent year does not immediately follow the distribution year, the amount determined under this paragraph in respect of the trust for the taxation year that immediately precedes the subsequent year, and

(d) except for the purposes of subsections 161(2), (4) and (4.01),

(i) interest under this Act for any period ending on the trust's balance-due day for the subsequent year and throughout which security is accepted by the Minister, and

(ii) any penalty under this Act computed with reference to the trust's tax payable for the year that was, without reference to this paragraph, unpaid

shall be computed as if the particular amount for which adequate security has been accepted under this subsection were an amount paid by the trust on account of the particular amount.

**Technical Notes**: New subsections 220(4.6) to (4.63) permit a trust to elect, on the giving of security acceptable to the Minister of National Revenue, to defer payment of an amount of tax that it owes as a result of the distribution of a taxable Canadian property to a non-resident beneficiary. If such an election is made, interest does not start to accrue on the amount secured until such time as the amount becomes unsecured. In addition, relief is provided from a penalty under the Act to the extent that it is computed with reference to the unpaid tax with respect to the amount secured. These subsections are structured in a similar manner to new subsections 220(4.5) to (4.53), and are intended to operate similarly with respect to both federal and provincial taxes.

Subsection 220(4.6) applies where such a distribution is made and, only because of subsection 107(5), the rollover under paragraphs 107(2)(a) to (c) does not apply to the distribution. Provided that the trust makes an election on or before the trust's balance-due day for the distribution year (or at a later time permitted under subsection 220(4.63)) and furnishes security before that balance-due day (or at a later time permitted under subsection 220(4.63)), the Minister is required to accept security in respect of each taxation year after the distribution year of an amount up to the amount specified under paragraph 220(4.6)(c) in respect of that subsequent year. The amount is required to be accepted until the balance-due day for that subsequent year.

The amount specified under paragraph 220(4.6)(c) for a particular taxation year of a trust is equal to the lesser of the following two amounts:

- the portion of the trust's total tax payable under Parts I and I.1 of the Act (determined without reference to loss carrybacks and other amounts specified under paragraph 161(7)(a)) for the distribution year that would not have been payable if each such distribution of taxable Canadian property (other than taxable Canadian property subsequently disposed of before the beginning of the particular year) had not occurred; and

- where the particular year does not immediately follow the distribution year, the amount so specified for the taxation year of the trust that immediately precedes the particular year.

The relief with regard to arrears interest and penalties is provided under new paragraph 220(4.6)(d). This provision provides that interest is generally payable as if the particular amount for which adequate security is accepted at any time under subsection 220(4.6) in a particular period ending on the balance-due day for a taxation year subsequent to the distribution year had actually been paid on account of the trust's taxes under Parts I and I.1 for the distribution year. The particular amount in respect of a period that ends on a trust's balance-due day for a subsequent taxation year cannot exceed the amount specified under paragraph 220(4.6)(c) for the year. In addition, the particular amount is constrained because of the limit under subsection 220(4.61). However, paragraph 220(4.6)(d) does not apply with respect to interest on unpaid tax instalments which is dealt with under new subsection 107(5.1).

Subsection 220(4.61) limits the amount for which the Minister is considered to have accepted security under subsection 220(4.6), in order to take into account reductions as of any day, for the purpose of computing arrears interest, in the calculation of taxes under Parts I and I.1 arising from the carryback of losses and similar amounts. The effect of subsection 220(4.61) is to limit the amount of acceptable security as of any day in respect of a trust's tax payable for a distribution year to:

- the total taxes payable by the trust under those Parts for the distribution year, determined without reference to such reductions that occur after that day

MINUS

- the total taxes payable under those Parts, determined without reference to such reductions and as if the rollover rules in subsection 107(2) had applied to distributions in the distribution year not covered by those rules only because of subsection 107(5).

Subsection 220(4.62) provides rules which apply where security furnished by a trust under subsection 220(4.6) ceases to be adequate. These rules are essentially the same as the rules in subsection 220(4.53). As noted above, subsection 220(4.63) allows for the late filing of elections and the late furnishing of security. Subsection 220(4.63) is essentially the same as subsection 220(4.54).

These amendments apply to distributions that occur after October 1, 1996. However, transitional measures treat elections made, and security furnished, up to the taxpayer's filing-due date for the year in which these amendments receive Royal Assent as having been made at such time as to maximize the benefits under subsection 220(4.6).

**Related Provisions**: 128.3 — Shares acquired on rollover deemed to be same shares for 220(4.6); 152(10) — Posted security deemed not to be tax assessed for purposes of administration of provincial tax; 220(4.61) — Security effective only for tax caused by 107(5); 220(4.62) — Where security proves inadequate; 220(4.63) — Extension of time for making election; 220(4.7) — Reduction in security for undue hardship.

**Notes**: This was 220.2(1) in the draft legislation (migration) of December 23, 1998.

**(4.61) Limit** — Notwithstanding subsection (4.6), the Minister is deemed at any time not to have accepted security under that subsection in respect of a trust's distribution year for any amount greater than the amount, if any, by which

(a) the total amount of taxes that would be payable by the trust under Parts I and I.1 for the year if the exclusion or deduction of each amount referred to in paragraph 161(7)(a), in respect of which the day determined under paragraph 161(7)(b) is after that time, were not taken into account

exceeds

(b) the total amount of taxes that would be determined under paragraph (a) if paragraphs 107(2)(a) to (c) had applied to each distribution by the trust in the year of property to which paragraph (1)(a) applies.

**Technical Notes**: See under 220(4.6).

**Notes**: This was 220.2(2) in the draft legislation (migration) of December 23, 1998.

**(4.62) Inadequate security** — Subject to subsection (4.7), where it is determined at any particular time that security accepted by the Minister under subsection (4.6) is not adequate to secure the particular amount for which it was furnished by or on behalf of a trust,

(a) subject to a subsequent application of this subsection, the security shall be considered after the particular time to secure only the amount for which it is adequate security at the particular time;

(b) the Minister shall notify the trust in writing of the determination and shall accept adequate security, for all or any part of the particular amount, furnished by or on behalf of the trust within 90 days after the notification; and

(c) any security accepted in accordance with paragraph (b) is deemed to have been accepted by the Minister under subsection (4.6) on account of the particular amount at the particular time.

**Technical Notes**: See under 220(4.6).

**Notes**: This was 220.2(3) in the draft legislation (migration) of December 23, 1998.

**(4.63) Extension of time** — Where in the opinion of the Minister it would be just and equitable to do so, the Minister may at any time extend

(a) the time for making an election under subsection (4.6);

(b) the time for furnishing and accepting security under subsection (4.6); or

(c) the 90-day period for the acceptance of the security under paragraph (4.62)(b).

**Technical Notes**: See under 220(4.6).

**Notes**: This was 220.2(4) in the draft legislation (migration) of December 23, 1998.

**(4.7) Undue hardship** — If, in respect of any period of time, the Minister determines that an individual who has made an election under either of subsection (4.5) or (4.6)

(a) cannot, without undue hardship, pay or reasonably arrange to have paid on the individual's behalf, an amount of taxes to which security under that subsection would relate, and

(b) cannot, without undue hardship, provide or reasonably arrange to have provided on the individual's behalf, adequate security under that subsection,

the Minister may, in respect of the election, accept for the period security different from, or of lesser value than, that which the Minister would otherwise accept under that subsection.

**Technical Notes**: In some circumstances, an individual who wishes to provide security under new subsection 220(4.5) or (4.6) may be unable to do so without undue hardship. In such a case, new subsection 220(4.7) authorizes the Minister of National Revenue to accept security different from, or of lesser value than, that which would otherwise be required. The Minister is under no obligation to exercise this discretion, and can in any event do so only if the individual can without undue hardship neither provide security, pay the tax owing, nor reasonably arrange to have the security provided or the tax paid on the individual's behalf.

**Related Provisions**: 220(4.71) — Transactions entered into to create hardship to be ignored.

**Notes**: The term "undue hardship" is interpreted very liberally for purposes of 153(1.1). It may be interpreted more strictly for 220(4.7).

**(4.71) Limit** — In making a determination under subsection (4.7), the Minister shall ignore any transaction that is a disposition, lease, encumbrance, mortgage, or other voluntary restriction by a person or partnership of the person's or partnership's rights in respect of a property, if the transaction can reasonably be considered to have been entered into for the purpose of influencing the determination.

**Technical Notes**: New subsection 220(4.71) provides that in making a determination under subsection 220(4.7), the Minister will ignore any transaction by which a person or partnership limits their rights in respect of a property, if the transaction can reasonably be considered to have been entered into in order to influence the Minister's determination.

These new subsections apply to dispositions and trust distributions that occur after October 1, 1996.

**Application**: Bill C-43 (First Reading September 20, 2000), s. 105, will add subsecs. 220(4.5) to (4.71), applicable to dispositions and distributions that occur at any time after October 1, 1996 except that,

(a) the reference to "$67,000" in para. 220(4.51)(a) shall be read as a reference to "$75,000" in respect of emigration years that are before 2001; and

(b) if an individual ceased to be resident in Canada, or a distribution by a trust occurred to which para. 220(4.6)(a) applies in respect of the trust, before the particular day on which the amending legislation is assented to,

(i) an election by the individual under subsec. 220(4.5), or by the trust under subsec. 220(4.6), as the case may be in respect of the taxation year that includes that time is deemed to have been made in a timely manner if it is made on or before the individual's filing-due date for the taxation year that includes the particular day; and

(ii) security furnished by or on behalf of the individual under subsec. 220(4.5), or by or on behalf of the trust under subsec. 220(4.6), as the case may be is deemed to

S. 220(4.71)  Income Tax Act

have been furnished in a timely manner if it is furnished on or before the individual's filing-due date for the taxation year that includes the particular day.

**Department of Finance news release, September 10, 1999**: *Taxpayer Migration and Trusts: Technical Backgrounder*

Comments received on the December 1998 detailed proposals regarding taxpayer migration and trusts identified two major concerns: the need for flexibility in accepting security for the later payment of any tax arising from the deemed disposition on departure; and possible overlap between Canadian and foreign taxes. This backgrounder describes the government's proposed response to each of these two concerns. These changes, together with modifications to address more technical issues raised in connection with the December 1998 proposals, will be included in the proposals when they are put into bill form with the 1999 budget legislation.

*1. Security for later payment*

Several submissions raised concerns about the provision of security for later payment of any tax arising from the deemed disposition on departure. While this option is a significant relieving measure — it allows the deferral of tax, with no interest, until the property in question is eventually disposed of — a number of submissions have noted that some emigrating individuals may have serious difficulty providing acceptable security. This is not entirely a new issue: since 1972, an emigrant who owns, for example, foreign real property has had to either pay the tax on any gain on the property or provide acceptable security. But with the extension of the deemed disposition on departure to more types of property — notably shares of unlisted Canadian companies — difficulties of this kind may arise more frequently than they have in the past.

For example, an individual emigrant whose only significant property is shares of an unlisted Canadian company may be prohibited from pledging those shares as security because of prior restrictions under a shareholder agreement. Even if the shares can be pledged, their value may already be taken up by a bank as security for a business loan, thus making them inadequate security for the tax arising at the time of emigration. If the individual has no means of paying the tax, and no other means of providing security, he or she may have to sell the shares, and thus give up ownership of the company in order to pay the tax.

Under the December proposals, the Minister of National Revenue would have considerable discretion in the administration of the security provisions. In response to the concern about cases such as the one described above, it is proposed that the Minister's discretion be even broader.

Specifically, in cases of undue hardship, the Minister of National Revenue would be able to accept a lesser value of security than, or security of a different kind from, that which the Minister would normally consider adequate. In an extreme case, this would give the Minister authority to accept very modest security. The individual's tax debt would remain owing, and would be collected when the individual eventually disposed of the property, but, in cases like the example described above, the individual would not necessarily be forced to sell the shares in order to satisfy a tax debt that arose because of emigration from Canada.

Two further points should be noted about this broader discretion. First, the statutory rule would not only require that the individual emigrant personally be unable, without undue hardship, to pay the tax or to provide fully acceptable security, it would also require that the individual be unable to reasonably arrange to have another person pay the tax or provide security. If, for example, the individual referred to above controls in any manner whatsoever a corporation that has sufficient assets, the corporation should provide security and the individual will not be able to rely on the undue hardship rule.

Second, to prevent abuse of this relief, the rule would direct the Minister to ignore any restriction that any person or partnership puts on its rights in respect of a property, if that was done for the purpose of influencing a determination under the rule.

[For the second proposal, "Interaction of Canadian and foreign taxes", see under 126(2.21) — ed.]

**(5) Administration of oaths** — Any officer or servant employed in connection with the administration or enforcement of this Act, if designated by the Minister for the purpose, may, in the course of that employment, administer oaths and take and receive affidavits, declarations and affirmations for the purposes of or incidental to the administration or enforcement of this Act or regulations made thereunder, and every officer or servant so designated has for those purposes all the powers of a commissioner for administering oaths or taking affidavits.

**Related Provisions**: *Interpretation Act* 19 — Administration of oaths.

**(6) Assignment by corporation** — Notwithstanding section 67 of the *Financial Administration Act* and any other provision of a law of Canada or a province, a corporation may assign any amount payable to it under this Act.

**Related Provisions**: 220(7) — Assignment not binding on federal government.

**Notes**: 220(6) and (7) added by 1996 Budget, effective for assignments made after March 5, 1996.

In *Marzetti v. Marzetti*, [1994] 2 S.C.R. 765, the Supreme Court of Canada ruled that an income tax refund could not be assigned, due to s. 67 of the *Financial Administration Act*. 220(6) gets around this prohibition, but only for corporations, provided the CCRA consents (see 220(7)). Since the assignment is not binding on the CCRA, it can only be done effectively to the extent it is permitted by CCRA administrative discretion. It was introduced to permit assignments of film tax credits under 125.4 and R&D investment tax credits under 127(5).

A parallel rule for refunds payable by the Quebec government was introduced by the Quebec budget of March 9, 1999.

See also the *Tax Rebate Discounting Act*, RSC 1985, c. T-3, which permits the assignment of personal income tax refunds in connection with the preparation of personal tax returns; and the *Assignment of Crown Debt Regulations*, reproduced in the *Practitioner's GST Annotated* and the *Canada GST Service*.

**(7) Effect of assignment** — An assignment referred to in subsection (6) is not binding on Her Majesty in right of Canada and, without limiting the generality of the foregoing,

(a) the Minister is not required to pay to the assignee the assigned amount;

(b) the assignment does not create any liability of Her Majesty in right of Canada to the assignee; and

(c) the rights of the assignee are subject to all equitable and statutory rights of set-off in favour of Her Majesty in right of Canada.

**Notes**: See Notes to 220(6).

**Definitions [s. 220]**: "amount" — 248(1); "assessment" — 220; "balance-due day" — 248(1); "Commissioner of Customs and Revenue" — *Canada Customs and Revenue Agency Act* s. 25; "corporation" — 248(1), *Interpretation Act* 35(1); "disposition" — 248(1); "distribution year" — 220(4.6)(a); "emigration year" — 220(4.5); "employed", "employee benefit plan", "employment", "individual", "insurance corporation" — 248(1); "*inter vivos* trust" — 108(1), 248(1); "Minister", "non-resident" — 248(1); "oath" — *Interpretation Act* 35(1); "officer" — 248(1)"office"; "partnership" — see Notes to 96(1); "person", "prescribed", "property" — 248(1); "province" — *Interpretation Act* 35(1); "resident in Canada" — 250; "security" — *Interpretation Act* 35(1); "servant" — 248(1)"employment"; "tax payable" — 248(2); "taxable Canadian property", "taxable income" — 248(1); "taxation year" — 249; "taxpayer" — 248(1); "trust" — 104(1), 248(1), (3); "undue hardship" — 220(4.71); "writing" — *Interpretation Act* 35(1).

**221. (1) Regulations** — The Governor in Council may make regulations

(a) prescribing anything that, by this Act, is to be prescribed or is to be determined or regulated by regulation;

(b) prescribing the evidence required to establish facts relevant to assessments under this Act;

(c) to facilitate the assessment of tax where deductions or exemptions of a taxpayer have changed in a taxation year;

(d) requiring any class of persons to make information returns respecting any class of information required in connection with assessments under this Act;

(d.1) requiring any person or partnership to provide any information including their name, address, Social Insurance Number or business number to any class of persons required to make an information return containing that information;

(e) requiring a person who is, by a regulation made under paragraph (d), required to make an information return to supply a copy of the information return or of a prescribed part thereof to the person to whom the information return or part thereof relates;

(f) [Repealed]

(g) providing for the retention by way of deduction or set-off of the amount of a taxpayer's income tax or other indebtedness under this Act out of any amount or amounts that may be or become payable by Her Majesty to the taxpayer in respect of salary or wages;

(h) defining the classes of persons who may be regarded as dependent for the purposes of this Act;

(i) defining the classes of non-resident persons who may be regarded for the purposes of this Act

(i) as a spouse or common-law partner supported by a taxpayer, or

(ii) as a person dependent or wholly dependent on a taxpayer for support,

and specifying the evidence required to establish that a person belongs to any such class; and

(j) generally to carry out the purposes and provisions of this Act.

**Related Provisions**: 65(2) — Regulations permitting resource allowances; 147.1(18) — Authority for regulations re registered pension plans; 214(13), 215(4), (5) — Regulations re non-resident withholding tax; 221(2) — Effect of regulations; 221(3) — Regulations binding Crown; 233 — Demands for information returns; 244(12) — Judicial notice to be taken of regulations; *Interpretation Act* 31(4) — Power to repeal, amend or vary regulations.

**Notes**: 221(1)(i)(i) amended by 2000 same-sex partners bill to add reference to "common-law partner", effective for the 2001 and later taxation years, or earlier by election (see Notes to 248(1)"common-law partner").

221(1)(d.1) amended by 1995-97 technical bill, effective June 18, 1998, to add reference to the "business number" (see Notes to definition of that term in 248(1)).

221(1)(f) repealed by 1995-97 technical bill, effective June 18, 1998. It read "(f) authorizing a designated officer or class of officers to exercise powers or perform duties of the Minister under this Act". 220(2.01) now provides authority for such delegation, without regulations being needed in each case. (See Reg. 900 for the delegation provided previously by regulation.)

**Regulations**: Part I – Part XCIII. For regulations under paras. 221(1)(d), (e), see Part II; under para. (g), see Part XXV.

**Information Circulars**: 82-2R2: SIN legislation that relates to the preparation of information slips.

**(2) Effect** — A regulation made under this Act shall have effect from the date it is published in the *Canada Gazette* or at such time thereafter as may be specified in the regulation unless the regulation provides otherwise and it

(a) has a relieving effect only;

(b) corrects an ambiguous or deficient enactment that was not in accordance with the objects of this Act or the *Income Tax Regulations*;

(c) is consequential on an amendment to this Act that is applicable before the date the regulation is published in the *Canada Gazette*; or

(d) gives effect to a budgetary or other public announcement, in which case the regulation shall not, except where paragraph (a), (b) or (c) applies, have effect

(i) before the date on which the announcement was made, in the case of a deduction or withholding from an amount paid or credited, and

(ii) before the taxation year in which the announcement is made, in any other case.

**(3) Regulations binding Crown** — Regulations made under paragraph (1)(d) or (e) are binding on Her Majesty in right of Canada or a province.

S. 221(3)  Income Tax Act

**Notes**: 221(3) added by 1991 technical bill, effective 1991.

**(4) Incorporation by reference** — A regulation made under this Act may incorporate by reference material as amended from time to time.

**Notes**: 221(4) added by 1995-97 technical bill, effective for any regulation, regardless of whether it is made before Royal Assent to the enactment of 221(4). It allows regulations to give legal effect to documents (either legislative or non-legislative instruments) and other laws not included directly in the Regulations but that are incorporated as amended from time to time.

**Definitions [s. 221]**: "amount", "assessment", "business number", "common-law partner" — 248(1); "Governor in Council" — *Interpretation Act* 35(1); "Minister", "non-resident" — 248(1); "partnership" — see Notes to 96(1); "person", "prescribed" — 248(1); "province" — *Interpretation Act* 35(1); "regulation", "salary or wages" — 248(1); "taxation year" — 249; "taxpayer" — 248(1).

**221.1 Application of interest** — For greater certainty, where an amendment to this Act or an amendment or enactment that relates to this Act applies to or in respect of any transaction, event or time, or any taxation year, fiscal period or other period of time or part thereof (in this section referred to as the "application time") occurring, or that is, before the day on which the amendment or enactment is assented to or promulgated, for the purposes of the provisions of this Act that provide for payment of, or liability to, any interest, the amendment or enactment shall, unless a contrary intention is evident, be deemed to have come into force at the beginning of the last taxation year beginning before the application time.

**Notes**: 221.1 added by 1991 technical bill, deemed to have come into force on January 1, 1990 and effective for amendments and enactments assented to or promulgated after 1989. It allows interest to be assessed where legislation is retroactive.

**Definitions [s. 221.1]**: "fiscal period" — 249(2)(b), 249.1; "taxation year" — 11(2), 249.

**221.2 Re-appropriation of amounts** — Where a particular amount was appropriated to an amount (in this section referred to as the "debt") that is or may become payable by a person under any enactment referred to in paragraphs 223(1)(a) to (d), the Minister may, on application by the person, appropriate the particular amount, or a part thereof, to another amount that is or may become payable under any such enactment and, for the purposes of any such enactment,

(a) the later appropriation shall be deemed to have been made at the time of the earlier appropriation;

(b) the earlier appropriation shall be deemed not to have been made to the extent of the later appropriation; and

(c) the particular amount shall be deemed not to have been paid on account of the debt to the extent of the later appropriation.

**Related Provisions**: 161.1 — Offsetting of refund interest and arrears interest.

**Notes**: 221.2 added by 1992 technical bill, effective June 10, 1993. It allows the CCRA to transfer amounts between different tax accounts, such as instalments, arrears of tax owing, and employer remittances (payroll deductions), including amounts for CPP, UI and provincial tax withholdings. Where an amount is transferred in this way at the taxpayer's request, it will be treated as though it had never been paid on account of the first account, and had initially been a payment made in respect of the second. Thus, interest that would otherwise accumulate on a deficient account can be reduced or eliminated by using a surplus or overpaid balance from another account.

Since 221.2 refers to amounts owing under 223(1)(a) to (d), it cannot be used for transfers of balances to or from a GST account. However, as an administrative policy, the CCRA does allow taxpayers receiving GST refunds to arrange to have their source withholdings (payroll deductions) account, or any other tax account, credited with their GST net tax refund immediately upon filing their monthly GST return.

Note that it is a general principle of contract law, accepted by the courts for tax purposes, that a debtor has the right to specify which account should be credited when a payment is made. See *Polish Combatants' Association Credit Union Ltd. v. Moge* (1984), 9 D.L.R. (4th) 60 (Man. CA), and *Frankel*, [1984] C.T.C. 259 (FCTD). Where the allocation is not clearly specified, however, the CCRA can choose where to put the remittance.

Two related companies cannot technically transfer balances between them (i.e., use one's refund to offset the other's debt), but in practice this is often allowed by the CCRA on an administrative basis.

The CCRA will also allow two corporations to transfer a refund balance from one to another in unusual circumstances, even where they are not part of the same corporate group. Sometimes this can be done by a direction from one corporation to the CCRA to pay its refund to the other corporation. See 220(6), which permits a corporation's refund to be assigned.

221.1 provides a way around the 3-year limit on refunds where a return is filed late. See Notes to 164(1).

**Definitions [s. 221.2]**: "amount", "Minister", "person" — 248(1).

## Collection

**222. Debts to Her Majesty** — All taxes, interest, penalties, costs and other amounts payable under this Act are debts due to Her Majesty and recoverable as such in the Federal Court of Canada or any other court of competent jurisdiction or in any other manner provided by this Act.

**Related Provisions**: 225.1 — Collection restrictions.

**Notes**: As to enforcement against non-residents, see Notes to 223(3).

**Definitions [s. 222]**: "amount" — 248(1).

**Information Circulars**: 98-1R: Collections policies.

**222.1 Court costs** — Where an amount is payable by a person to Her Majesty because of an order, judgment or award of a court in respect of the costs of litigation relating to a matter to which this Act applies, subsections 220(4) and (4.2) and sections 223, 224 to 225 and 226 apply to the amount as if the amount were a debt owing by the person to Her Majesty on account of tax payable by the person under this Act.

**Notes**: 222.1 added by 1995-97 technical bill, effective for amounts that are payable after June 18, 1998 (Royal Assent to the bill), including amounts that became payable before June 18, 1998.

1700

It allows the CCRA to use its collection powers to recover court costs awarded against a taxpayer.

**Definitions [s. 222.1]:** "amount" — 248(1); "Her Majesty" — *Interpretation Act* 35(1); "person" — 248(1).

### 223. (1) Definition of "amount payable" — For the purposes of subsection (2), an "amount payable" by a person means any or all of

(a) an amount payable under this Act by the person;

(b) an amount payable under the *Employment Insurance Act* by the person;

(b.1) an amount payable under the *Unemployment Insurance Act* by the person;

(c) an amount payable under the *Canada Pension Plan* by the person; and

(d) an amount payable by the person under an Act of a province with which the Minister of Finance has entered into an agreement for the collection of taxes payable to the province under that Act.

**Related Provisions:** 221.2 — Transfers of balances between accounts; 223.1(1) — Application.

**Notes:** 223(1)(a.1), which referred to the *Wage Claim Payment Act*, was never proclaimed in force and was repealed retroactive to its introduction. That Act would have imposed a small payroll tax on all employers to create a fund for unpaid wages of employees of bankrupt corporations.

Reference in 223(1)(b) changed from *Unemployment Insurance Act* to *Employment Insurance Act* by 1996 Employment Insurance bill, effective June 20, 1996. 223(1)(b.1) then added by 1995-97 technical bill, effective June 30, 1996, because proceedings under the UI Act are still underway in respect of past years.

### (2) Certificates — An amount payable by a person (in this section referred to as a "debtor") that has not been paid or any part of an amount payable by the debtor that has not been paid may be certified by the Minister as an amount payable by the debtor.

**Related Provisions:** 222.1 — Application to awards of court costs; 231.2(1) — requirement to provide information or documents for collection purposes; 231.6(1) — foreign-based documents sought for collection purposes.

**Information Circulars:** 98-1R: Collections policies.

### (3) Registration in court — On production to the Federal Court, a certificate made under subsection (2) in respect of a debtor shall be registered in the Court and when so registered has the same effect, and all proceedings may be taken thereon, as if the certificate were a judgment obtained in the Court against the debtor for a debt in the amount certified plus interest thereon to the day of payment as provided by the statute or statutes referred to in subsection (1) under which the amount is payable and, for the purpose of any such proceedings, the certificate shall be deemed to be a judgment of the Court against the debtor for a debt due to Her Majesty, enforceable in the amount certified plus interest thereon to the day of payment as provided by that statute or statutes.

**Related Provisions:** 161(1) — Interest; 161(11) — Interest on penalties; 222.1 — Application to awards of court costs; 223.1(1) — Application; 227.1(2)(a) — Liability of directors; 248(11) — Compound interest.

**Notes:** Unlike court judgments generally, a judgment based on a tax debt will normally not be enforceable in a foreign jurisdiction. Thus, the CCRA has little scope for action against a non-resident with no assets in Canada. See *United States of America v. Harden*, [1963] C.T.C. 450 (SCC); this rule is generally followed in other countries. However, this rule is overridden by Article XXVI A of the Canada-U.S. tax convention, added in 1995, retroactive to tax debts finalized since November 10, 1985, but which generally does not allow the CCRA to use the IRS to collect Canadian tax from a U.S. citizen or U.S.-incorporated corporation. Article 26A of the Canada-Netherlands treaty, added by a protocol signed on August 25, 1997, provides similar "collection assistance" rights, but does not contain an exclusion for Netherlands citizens or corporations.

The fact that an assessment is registered in the Court as a judgment does not entitle a tax debtor to pay the *Federal Court Act* rate of interest, which is lower than the rate under s. 161: *Prodor*, [1997] 3 C.T.C. 179 (FCTD).

223(3) amended by 1992 technical bill, effective June 10, 1993, to clarify that interest is to be calculated at the rate specified in the applicable statute (i.e., the *Income Tax Act, Canada Pension Plan, Employment Insurance Act* or provincial income tax statute). Before June 10, 1993, in place of "by the statute or statutes ... under which the amount is payable", read simply "by law" (which could have been taken to mean the interest rate provided under the *Federal Court Act*).

### (4) Costs — All reasonable costs and charges incurred or paid in respect of the registration in the Court of a certificate made under subsection (2) or in respect of any proceedings taken to collect the amount certified are recoverable in like manner as if they had been included in the amount certified in the certificate when it was registered.

### (5) Charge on property — A document issued by the Federal Court evidencing a certificate in respect of a debtor registered under subsection (3), a writ of that Court issued pursuant to the certificate or any notification of the document or writ (such document, writ or notification in this section referred to as a "memorial") may be filed, registered or otherwise recorded for the purpose of creating a charge, lien or priority on, or a binding interest in, property in a province, or any interest in such property, held by the debtor in the same manner as a document evidencing

(a) a judgment of the superior court of the province against a person for a debt owing by the person, or

(b) an amount payable or required to be remitted by a person in the province in respect of a debt owing to Her Majesty in right of the province

may be filed, registered or otherwise recorded in accordance with or pursuant to the law of the province to create a charge, lien or priority on, or a binding interest in, the property or interest.

**Related Provisions:** 223(11.1) — Where charge registered under *Bankruptcy and Insolvency Act*; 223.1(1) — Application; 248(4) — Interest in real property.

## S. 223(5) — Income Tax Act

**Notes:** 223(5) amended by 1995-97 technical bill (as amended before Third Reading), effective June 18, 1998. Before then, since 1988, read:

> (5) **Charge on land** — A document (in this section referred to as a "memorial") issued by the Federal Court evidencing a certificate in respect of a debtor registered under subsection (3) may be filed, registered or otherwise recorded for the purpose of creating a charge or lien on or otherwise binding land in a province, or any interest therein, held by the debtor in the same manner as a document evidencing a judgment of the superior court of the province against a person for a debt owing by the person may be filed, registered or otherwise recorded in accordance with the law of the province to create a charge or lien on or otherwise bind land, or any interest therein, held by the person.

**(6) Creation of charge** — If a memorial has been filed, registered or otherwise recorded under subsection (5),

(a) a charge, lien or priority is created on, or a binding interest is created in, property in the province, or any interest in such property, held by the debtor, or

(b) such property or interest in the property is otherwise bound,

in the same manner and to the same extent as if the memorial were a document evidencing a judgment referred to in paragraph (5)(a) or an amount referred to in paragraph (5)(b), and the charge, lien, priority or binding interest created shall be subordinate to any charge, lien, priority or binding interest in respect of which all steps necessary to make it effective against other creditors were taken before the time the memorial was filed, registered or otherwise recorded.

**Related Provisions:** 223(11.1) — Where charge registered under *Bankruptcy and Insolvency Act*; 223.1(1) — Application; 248(4) — Interest in real property.

**Notes:** 223(6) amended by 1995-97 technical bill (as amended before Third Reading), effective June 18, 1998. Before then, since 1988, read:

> (6) **Idem** — Where a memorial has been filed, registered or otherwise recorded under subsection (5), a charge or lien is created on land in the province, or any interest therein, held by the debtor, or such land or interest is otherwise bound, in the same manner and to the same extent as if the memorial were a document evidencing a judgment of the superior court of the province.

**(7) Proceedings in respect of memorial** — If a memorial is filed, registered or otherwise recorded in a province under subsection (5), proceedings may be taken in the province in respect of the memorial, including proceedings

(a) to enforce payment of the amount evidenced by the memorial, interest on the amount and all costs and charges paid or incurred in respect of

(i) the filing, registration or other recording of the memorial, and

(ii) proceedings taken to collect the amount,

(b) to renew or otherwise prolong the effectiveness of the filing, registration or other recording of the memorial,

(c) to cancel or withdraw the memorial wholly or in respect of any of the property or interests affected by the memorial, or

(d) to postpone the effectiveness of the filing, registration or other recording of the memorial in favour of any right, charge, lien or priority that has been or is intended to be filed, registered or otherwise recorded in respect of any property or interest affected by the memorial,

in the same manner and to the same extent as if the memorial were a document evidencing a judgment referred to in paragraph (5)(a) or an amount referred to in paragraph (5)(b), except that if in any such proceeding or as a condition precedent to any such proceeding any order, consent or ruling is required under the law of the province to be made or given by the superior court of the province or a judge or official of the court, a like order, consent or ruling may be made or given by the Federal Court or a judge or official of the Federal Court and, when so made or given, has the same effect for the purposes of the proceeding as if it were made or given by the superior court of the province or a judge or official of the court.

**Notes:** 223(7) amended by 1995-97 technical bill (as amended before Third Reading), effective June 18, 1998. Before then, since 1988, read:

> (7) Where a memorial of a certificate in respect of a debtor registered under subsection (3) is filed, registered or otherwise recorded as permitted under subsection (5), proceedings may be taken in respect thereof, including proceedings
>
> (a) to enforce payment of the amount certified in the certificate, interest thereon and all costs and charges paid or incurred in respect of
>
> (i) the filing, registration or other recording of the memorial, and
>
> (ii) proceedings taken to collect the amount,
>
> (b) to renew or otherwise prolong the effectiveness of the filing, registration or other recording of the memorial,
>
> (c) to cancel or withdraw the memorial wholly or in respect of one or more parcels of land or interests in land affected by the memorial, or
>
> (d) to postpone the effectiveness of the filing, registration or other recording of the memorial in favour of any right, charge or lien that has been or is intended to be filed, registered or otherwise recorded in respect of any land or interest in land affected by the memorial,
>
> in the same manner and subject to the same restrictions and limitations as though the memorial were a document evidencing a judgment of the superior court of the province except that, where in any such proceeding or as a condition precedent to any such proceeding any order, consent or ruling is required under the law of the province to be made or given by the superior court of the province or a judge or official thereof, a like order, consent or ruling may be made or given by the Federal Court or a judge or official thereof and, when so made or given, has the same effect for the purposes of the proceeding as though made or given by the superior court of the province or a judge or official thereof.

**(8) Presentation of documents** — If

(a) a memorial is presented for filing, registration or other recording under subsection (5) or a document relating to the memorial is presented for filing, registration or other recording for the purpose of any proceeding described in subsection (7) to any official in the land, personal property or other registry system of a province, it shall be accepted for filing, registration or other recording, or

(b) access is sought to any person, place or thing in a province to make the filing, registration or other recording, the access shall be granted

in the same manner and to the same extent as if the memorial or document relating to the memorial were a document evidencing a judgment referred to in paragraph (5)(a) or an amount referred to in paragraph (5)(b) for the purpose of a like proceeding, as the case may be, except that, if the memorial or document is issued by the Federal Court or signed or certified by a judge or official of the Court, any affidavit, declaration or other evidence required under the law of the province to be provided with or to accompany the memorial or document in the proceedings is deemed to have been provided with or to have accompanied the memorial or document as so required.

**Related Provisions**: 223.1(1) — Application.

**Notes**: 223(8) amended by 1995-97 technical bill (as amended before Third Reading), effective June 18, 1998. Before then, since 1988, read:

(8) Where a memorial of a certificate registered under subsection (3) is presented for filing, registration or other recording as permitted under subsection (5), or any document relating to the memorial is presented for filing, registration or other recording for the purpose of any proceeding described in subsection (7), to any officer of a superior court of a province or to any official in the land registry system of a province, it shall be accepted for filing, registration or other recording as though it were a like document issued from the superior court of the province or prepared in respect of a document evidencing a judgment of the superior court of the province for the purpose of a like proceeding, as the case may be, except that, where the memorial or document is issued by the Federal Court or signed or certified by a judge or official thereof, any affidavit, declaration or other evidence required under the law of the province to be provided with or to accompany the memorial or document in such proceedings shall be deemed to have been provided with or to have accompanied the memorial or document as so required.

**(9) Sale, etc.** — Notwithstanding any law of Canada or of a province, a sheriff or other person shall not, without the written consent of the Minister, sell or otherwise dispose of any property, or publish any notice or otherwise advertise in respect of any sale or other disposition of any property pursuant to any process issued or charge, lien, priority or binding interest created in any proceeding to collect an amount certified in a certificate made under subsection (2), interest on the amount and costs, but if that consent is subsequently given, any property that would have been affected by such a process, charge, lien, priority or binding interest if the Minister's consent had been given at the time the process was issued or the charge, lien, priority or binding interest was created, as the case may be, shall be bound, seized, attached, charged or otherwise affected as it would be if that consent had been given at the time the process was issued or the charge, lien, priority or binding interest was created, as the case may be.

**Related Provisions**: 223.1(1) — Application.

**Notes**: 223(9) amended by 1995-97 technical bill (as amended before Third Reading), effective June 18, 1998. Before then, since 1988, read:

(9) Notwithstanding any law of Canada or of a province, a sheriff or other person shall not, without the written consent of the Minister, sell or otherwise dispose of any property, or publish any notice or otherwise advertise in respect of any sale or other disposition of any property pursuant to any process issued or charge or lien created in any proceeding to collect an amount certified in a certificate made under subsection (2), interest thereon and costs but any property that would have been affected by such a process, charge or lien had the Minister's consent been given at the time the process was issued or the charge or lien was created, as the case may be, shall be bound, seized, attached, charged or otherwise affected as it would be had that consent been given at the time the process was issued or the charge or lien was created, as the case may be.

**(10) Completion of notices, etc.** — If information required to be set out by any sheriff or other person in a minute, notice or document required to be completed for any purpose cannot, by reason of subsection (9), be so set out, the sheriff or other person shall complete the minute, notice or document to the extent possible without that information and, when the consent of the Minister is given under that subsection, a further minute, notice or document setting out all the information shall be completed for the same purpose, and the sheriff or other person having complied with this subsection is deemed to have complied with the Act, regulation or rule requiring the information to be set out in the minute, notice or document.

**Related Provisions**: 223.1(1) — Application.

**Notes**: 223(10) amended by 1995-97 technical bill (as amended before Third Reading), effective June 18, 1998. The changes were purely cosmetic and non-substantive ("under that subsection" instead of "for the purposes of that subsection"; "is deemed" instead of "shall be deemed").

**(11) Application for an order** — A sheriff or other person who is unable, by reason of subsection (9) or (10), to comply with any law or rule of court is bound by any order made by a judge of the Federal Court, on an *ex parte* application by the Minister, for the purpose of giving effect to the proceeding, charge, lien, priority or binding interest.

**Related Provisions**: 223.1(1) — Application.

**Notes**: 223(11) amended by 1995-97 technical bill (as amended before Third Reading), effective June 18, 1998, to add "priority or binding interest" at the end. Other changes were purely cosmetic and non-substantive.

**(11.1) Deemed security** — When a charge, lien, priority or binding interest created under subsection (6) by filing, registering or otherwise recording a memorial under subsection (5) is registered in accor-

S. 223(11.1)                                          Income Tax Act

dance with subsection 87(1) of the *Bankruptcy and Insolvency Act*, it is deemed

    (a) to be a claim that is secured by a security and that, subject to subsection 87(2) of that Act, ranks as a secured claim under that Act; and

    (b) to also be a claim referred to in paragraph 86(2)(a) of that Act.

**Notes**: 223(11.1) added by 1995-97 technical bill (as amended before Third Reading), effective June 18, 1998. Corrected by 2000 GST bill, retroactive to June 18, 1998, to change "security claim" to "secured claim".

**(12) Details in certificates and memorials** — Notwithstanding any law of Canada or of a province, in any certificate made under subsection (2) in respect of a debtor, in any memorial evidencing the certificate or in any writ or document issued for the purpose of collecting an amount certified, it is sufficient for all purposes

    (a) to set out, as the amount payable by the debtor, the total of amounts payable by the debtor without setting out the separate amounts making up that total; and

    (b) to refer to the rate of interest to be charged on the separate amounts making up the amount payable in general terms as interest at the rate prescribed under this Act applicable from time to time on amounts payable to the Receiver General without indicating the specific rates of interest to be charged on each of the separate amounts or to be charged for any particular period of time.

**Related Provisions [subsec. 223(12)]**: 223.1(1) — Application; 225.1 — Collection restrictions.

**Definitions [s. 223]**: "amount" — 248(1); "interest" — in real property 248(4); "memorial" — 223(5); "Minister", "person", "property" — 248(1); "province" — *Interpretation Act* 35(1); "superior court" — *Interpretation Act* 35(1).

**Regulations [s. 223]**: 4301 (prescribed rate of interest).

**223.1 (1) Application of subsecs. 223(1) to (8) and (12)** — Subsections 223(1) to (8) and (12) are applicable with respect to certificates made under section 223 or section 223 of the *Income Tax Act*, chapter 148 of the Revised Statutes of Canada, 1952, after 1971 and documents evidencing such certificates that were issued by the Federal Court and that were filed, registered or otherwise recorded after 1977 under the laws of a province, except that, where any such certificate or document was the subject of an action pending in a court on February 10, 1988 or the subject of a court decision given on or before that date, section 223 shall be read, for the purposes of applying it with respect to that certificate or document, as section 223 of the *Income Tax Act*, chapter 148 of the Revised Statutes of Canada, 1952, read at the time the certificate was registered or the document was issued, as the case may be.

**(2) Application of subsecs. 223(9) to (11)** — Subsections 223(9) to (11) are applicable with respect to certificates made under section 223, or section 223 of the *Income Tax Act*, chapter 148 of the Revised Statutes of Canada, 1952, after September 13, 1988.

**Notes**: 223.1 added in the R.S.C. 1985 (5th Supp.) consolidation, effective after November 1991. This rule was formerly contained in a rule of application in 1988 tax reform (1988, c. 55, s. 168(2)).

**I.T. Application Rules**: 69 (meaning of "*Income Tax Act*, chapter 148 of the Revised Statutes of Canada, 1952").

**Definitions [s. 223.1]**: "province" — *Interpretation Act* 35(1).

**224. (1) Garnishment** — Where the Minister has knowledge or suspects that a person is, or will be within one year, liable to make a payment to another person who is liable to make a payment under this Act (in this subsection and subsections (1.1) and (3) referred to as the "tax debtor"), the Minister may in writing require the person to pay forthwith, where the moneys are immediately payable, and in any other case as and when the moneys become payable, the moneys otherwise payable to the tax debtor in whole or in part to the Receiver General on account of the tax debtor's liability under this Act.

**Related Provisions**: 222.1 — Application to awards of court costs; 224(5), (6) — Service of garnishee; 225.1 — Collection restrictions; 231.2(1) — requirement to provide information or documents for collection purposes; 231.6(1) — foreign-based documents sought for collection purposes; 244(5), (6) — Proof of service by mail or personal service; 248(7)(a) — Mail deemed received on day mailed.

**Notes**: The garnishment notice under 224(1) or (1.1) is also known as a Requirement to Pay or a Third Party Demand. The CCRA usually starts by issuing such notices to the taxpayer's bank to clean out any bank accounts, and often sends notices to employers, clients or other sources of income. However, collection action cannot start where it is restricted by 225.1(1).

Where an RRSP is held in the form of life insurance and no amount is payable to the policyholder until maturity, the RRSP cannot be garnished under 224(1): *Maritime Life Assurance Co.*, [1997] 3 C.T.C. 2561 (TCC).

Garnishment of monthly payments from a registered pension plan is valid, since the federal Crown is not subject to provincial pension benefits legislation that restricts creditors from accessing pension payments: *Sun Life Assurance Co. v. Canada*, [1992] 2 C.T.C. 315 (Sask. QB). Such seizure is not subject to the rule in 225(5) which prevents seizures from applying to goods exempted under provincial law: *Marcoux*, [2000] 4 C.T.C. 143 (FCTD).

224(1) amended by 1993 technical bill, effective for requirements and notifications made in 1993 or later, to change "by registered letter or letter served personally" to "in writing". Also amended by 1993 technical bill, effective for requirements and notifications made after June 15, 1994, to change "within 90 days" to "within one year".

**Information Circulars**: 98-1R: Collections policies.

**(1.1) Idem** — Without limiting the generality of subsection (1), where the Minister has knowledge or suspects that within 90 days

    (a) a bank, credit union, trust company or other similar person (in this section referred to as the "institution") will lend or advance moneys to, or make a payment on behalf of, or make a payment in respect of a negotiable instrument issued by, a tax debtor who is indebted to the institution and who has granted security in respect of the indebtedness, or

(b) a person, other than an institution, will lend or advance moneys to, or make a payment on behalf of, a tax debtor who the Minister knows or suspects

    (i) is employed by, or is engaged in providing services or property to, that person or was or will be, within 90 days, so employed or engaged, or

    (ii) where that person is a corporation, is not dealing at arm's length with that person,

the Minister may in writing require the institution or person, as the case may be, to pay in whole or in part to the Receiver General on account of the tax debtor's liability under this Act the moneys that would otherwise be so lent, advanced or paid and any moneys so paid to the Receiver General shall be deemed to have been lent, advanced or paid, as the case may be, to the tax debtor.

**Related Provisions**: 222.1 — Application to awards of court costs; 224(5), (6) — Service of garnishee; 225.1 — Collection restrictions; 231.2(1) — requirement to provide information or documents for collection purposes; 231.6(1) — foreign-based documents sought for collection purposes; 244(5), (6) — Proof of service by mail or personal service; 248(7)(a) — Mail deemed received on day mailed.

**Notes**: See Notes to 224(1). Such collection action cannot start in respect of regular tax until objection or appeal rights have run out: see 225.1(1). However, it can start immediately for amounts owing for unremitted source deductions.

Closing words of 224(1.1) amended by 1993 technical bill, effective for requirements and notifications made in 1993 or later, to change "by registered letter or letter served personally" to "in writing".

**Information Circulars**: 98-1R: Collections policies.

**(1.2) Idem** — Notwithstanding any other provision of this Act, the *Bankruptcy and Insolvency Act*, any other enactment of Canada, any enactment of a province or any law, but subject to subsections 69(1) and 69.1(1) of the *Bankruptcy and Insolvency Act* and section 11.4 of the *Companies' Creditors Arrangement Act*, where the Minister has knowledge or suspects that a particular person is, or will become within one year, liable to make a payment

(a) to another person (in this subsection referred to as the "tax debtor") who is liable to pay an amount assessed under subsection 227(10.1) or a similar provision, or

(b) to a secured creditor who has a right to receive the payment that, but for a security interest in favour of the secured creditor, would be payable to the tax debtor,

the Minister may in writing require the particular person to pay forthwith, where the moneys are immediately payable, and in any other case as and when the moneys become payable, the moneys otherwise payable to the tax debtor or the secured creditor in whole or in part to the Receiver General on account of the tax debtor's liability under subsection 227(10.1) or the similar provision, and on receipt of that requirement by the particular person, the amount of those moneys that is so required to be paid to the Receiver General shall, notwithstanding any security interest in those moneys, become the property of Her Majesty to the extent of that liability as assessed by the Minister and shall be paid to the Receiver General in priority to any such security interest.

**Related Provisions**: 224(5), (6) — Service of garnishee; 244(5), (6) — Proof of service by mail or personal service; 248(7)(a) — Mail deemed received on day mailed.

**Notes**: 224(1.2) provides an "enhanced garnishment" or "super priority" over funds that are owing by a third party to a tax debtor, where the tax debtor is liable for unremitted source deductions (which under s. 227 are deemed to be funds held in trust for the Crown).

The words "notwithstanding any security interest in those moneys, become the property of Her Majesty", added in 1990, ensure that the enhanced garnishment operates against secured creditors: *Canada Trustco Mortgage Corp. v. Port O'Call Hotel Inc.*, [1996] G.S.T.C. 17 (also known as *The Queen v. Province of Alberta Treasury Branches*, as *Re Country Inns Inc.*, and as *Pigott Project Management Ltd.*, [1996] 1 C.T.C. 395. The Court ruled 3-2 that a general assignment of book debts is a security interest and not an absolute assignment, and thus remains subject to the garnishment under 224(1.2), which takes priority over the bank to whom the assignment was made.

There was a question whether 224(1.2) is constitutionally valid, or is *ultra vires* the federal government by infringing on provincial jurisdiction over ownership of property. However, in *Transgas Ltd. v. Mid-Plains Contractors Ltd.*, [1993] 1 C.T.C. 280, the Saskatchewan Court of Appeal held that it is constitutionally valid. That decision was upheld by the Supreme Court of Canada, under the name *Non-Labour Lien Claimants v. The Queen and TransGas Ltd.*, [1994] 3 S.C.R. 753.

Note that some of the case law on this issue deals with subsection 317(3) of the *Excise Tax Act* (GST legislation), which is virtually identical except with respect to priority over the *Bankruptcy and Insolvency Act*. (See the cases reported on ETA 317(3) in the *Canada GST Cases*, or see the Cases annotation in *The Practitioner's Goods and Services Tax, Annotated*.)

Opening words of 224(1.2) amended by *Companies' Creditors Arrangement Act* amending bill (S.C. 1997, c. 12), effective September 30, 1997, to add reference to s. 11.4 of the CCCA. See below at end of these Notes.

Opening words of 224(1.2) amended by 1993 technical bill, effective for requirements and notifications made after June 15, 1994, to change "within 90 days" to "within one year" and to change references to provisions of the *Bankruptcy and Insolvency Act* from "paragraphs 69(1)(c) and 69.1(1)(c)" to "subsections 69(1) and 69.1(1)".

Closing words of 224(1.2) amended by 1993 technical bill, effective for requirements and notifications made in 1993 or later, to change "by registered letter or letter served personally" to "in writing" and to remove additional references to a "letter". The previous version read:

> the Minister may, by registered letter or by a letter served personally, require the particular person to pay forthwith, where the moneys are immediately payable, and in any other case, as and when the moneys become payable, the moneys otherwise payable to the tax debtor or the secured creditor in whole or in part to the Receiver General on account of the tax debtor's liability under subsection 227(10.1) or a similar provision, and on receipt of that letter by the particular person, the amount of those moneys that is required by that letter to be paid to the Receiver General shall, notwithstanding any security interest in those moneys, become the property of Her Majesty to the extent of that liability as assessed by the Min-

ister and shall be paid to the Receiver General in priority to any such security interest.

Closing words of 224(1.2) amended by 1992 technical bill, effective June 10, 1993. Before that date, ignore the words "to the extent of that liability as assessed by the Minister".

224(1.2) previously amended by 1990 garnishment/collection bill, effective June 27, 1990.

*Companies' Creditors Arrangement Act*

Draft legislation released by the Department of Finance on March 11, 1999 (news release 99-026) and included in the GST bill of December 2, 1999 will apply the super priority rules of 224(1.2) to employer contributions under the *Employment Insurance Act* (s. 99) and the *Canada Pension Plan* (s. 99). (The rules already applied to amounts withheld on account of employee premiums and contributions.) The amendments will also introduce new subsec. 86(3) of the *Bankruptcy and Insolvency Act* (BIA), to provide that BIA 86(1) does not affect the operation of ITA 224(1.2) and (1.3).

Subsection 11.4(1) of the *Companies' Creditors Arrangement Act*, as introduced by Bill C-5 (former C-109) (S.C. 1997, c. 12, Royal Assent April 25, 1997), provides (to be amended by the GST bill tabled December 2, 1999):

> 11.4 (1) **Her Majesty affected** — An order made under section 11 may provide that Her Majesty in right of Canada may not exercise rights under subsection 224(1.2) of the *Income Tax Act* in respect of the company where the company is a tax debtor under that subsection and Her Majesty in right of a province may not exercise rights under provincial legislation substantially similar to that subsection in respect of the company where the company is a tax debtor under the provincial legislation for such period as the court considers appropriate but ending not later than
>
> (a) the expiration of the order;
>
> (b) the refusal of a proposed compromise by the creditors or the court;
>
> (c) six months following the court sanction of a compromise or arrangement;
>
> (d) the default by the company on any term of a compromise or arrangement; or
>
> (e) the performance of a compromise or arrangement in respect of the company.
>
> (2) An order referred to in subsection (1) ceases to be in effect if
>
> (a) the company defaults on payment of any amount that could be subject to a demand under subsection 224(1.2) of the *Income Tax Act* or under any substantially similar provincial legislation and that becomes due to Her Majesty after the order is made; or
>
> (b) any other creditor is or becomes entitled to realize a security on any property that could be claimed by Her Majesty in exercising rights under subsection 224(1.2) of the *Income Tax Act* or under similar provincial legislation.
>
> (3) An order made under section 11, other than an order referred to in subsection (1) of this section, does not affect the operation of any provision of provincial legislation that is substantially similar to subsection 224(1.2) of the *Income Tax Act*.

For discussion of the application of the CCCA to ITA 224(1.2) before the enactment of this legislation, see *Canadian Asbestos Services Ltd. v. Bank of Montreal*, [1992] G.S.T.C. 15, [1993] G.S.T.C. 23, [1995] G.S.T.C. 36 (Ont. Gen. Div.); and *Fine's Flowers Ltd. v. Fine's Flowers Ltd. (Creditors of)* (1993), 16 O.R. (3d) 315 (Ont. CA).

**Information Circulars**: 98-1R: Collections policies.

**I.T. Technical News**: No. 6 (enhanced garnishment takes priority over builders' lien claimants).

**(1.3) Definitions** — In subsection (1.2),

**"secured creditor"** means a person who has a security interest in the property of another person or who acts for or on behalf of that person with respect to the security interest and includes a trustee appointed under a trust deed relating to a security interest, a receiver or receiver-manager appointed by a secured creditor or by a court on the application of a secured creditor, a sequestrator, or any other person performing a similar function;

**Related Provisions**: 227(5.1)(h) — Secured creditor jointly liable for unremitted withholding tax.

**"security interest"** means any interest in property that secures payment or performance of an obligation and includes an interest created by or arising out of a debenture, mortgage, lien, pledge, charge, deemed or actual trust, assignment or encumbrance of any kind whatever, however or whenever arising, created, deemed to arise or otherwise provided for;

**"similar provision"** means a provision, similar to subsection 227(10.1), of any Act of a province that imposes a tax similar to the tax imposed under this Act, where the province has entered into an agreement with the Minister of Finance for the collection of the taxes payable to the province under that Act.

**Notes**: See Notes to 224(1.2).

**(1.4) Garnishment** — Provisions of this Act that provide that a person who has been required to do so by the Minister must pay to the Receiver General an amount that would otherwise be lent, advanced or paid to a taxpayer who is liable to make a payment under this Act, or to that taxpayer's secured creditor, apply to Her Majesty in right of Canada or a province.

**Notes**: 224(1.4) added by 1993 technical bill, effective June 15, 1994.

**(2) Minister's receipt discharges original liability** — The receipt of the Minister for moneys paid as required under this section is a good and sufficient discharge of the original liability to the extent of the payment.

**(3) Idem** — Where the Minister has, under this section, required a person to pay to the Receiver General on account of a liability under this Act of a tax debtor moneys otherwise payable by the person to the tax debtor as interest, rent, remuneration, a dividend, an annuity or other periodic payment, the requirement applies to all such payments to be made by the person to the tax debtor until the liability under this Act is satisfied and operates to require payments to the Receiver General out of each such payment of such amount as is stipulated by the Minister in the requirement.

**Notes**: 224(3) amended by 1993 technical bill, effective for requirements and notifications made in 1993 or later, to change "registered letter or letter served personally" (at the end) to "requirement".

**(4) Failure to comply with subsec. (1), (1.2) or (3) requirement** — Every person who fails to comply with a requirement under subsection (1), (1.2) or (3) is liable to pay to Her Majesty an amount equal to the amount that the person was required under subsection (1), (1.2) or (3), as the case may be, to pay to the Receiver General.

**Related Provisions**: 227(10) — Assessment.

**(4.1) Failure to comply with subsec. (1.1) requirement** — Every institution or person that fails to comply with a requirement under subsection (1.1) with respect to moneys to be lent, advanced or paid is liable to pay to Her Majesty an amount equal to the lesser of

(a) the total of moneys so lent, advanced or paid, and

(b) the amount that the institution or person was required under that subsection to pay to the Receiver General.

**Related Provisions**: 227(10) — Assessments.

**(5) Service of garnishee** — Where a person carries on business under a name or style other than the person's own name, notification to the person of a requirement under subsection (1), (1.1) or (1.2) may be addressed to the name or style under which the person carries on business and, in the case of personal service, shall be deemed to be validly served if it is left with an adult person employed at the place of business of the addressee.

**Notes**: 224(5) amended by 1993 technical bill, effective for requirements and notifications made in 1993 or later, to correspond to the amendment made to 224(1) eliminating the requirement for the garnishment to be by registered letter or letter served personally. Previously read:

(5) Where the person who is or is about to become indebted or liable under this section carries on business under a name or style other than the person's own name, the registered or other letter under subsections (1) and (1.2) may be addressed to the name or style under which the person carries on business and, in the case of personal service, shall be deemed to have been validly served if it has been left with an adult person employed at the place of business of the addressee.

**(6) Idem** — Where persons carry on business in partnership, notification to the persons of a requirement under subsection (1), (1.1) or (1.2) may be addressed to the partnership name and, in the case of personal service, shall be deemed to be validly served if it is served on one of the partners or left with an adult person employed at the place of business of the partnership.

**Related Provisions**: 244(20)(b) — Service of documents on partnerships.

**Notes**: 224(6) amended by 1993 technical bill, effective for requirements and notifications made in 1993 or later, to correspond to the amendment made to 224(1) eliminating the requirement for the garnishment to be by registered letter or letter served personally. Previously read:

(6) Service on partnership — Where the persons who are or are about to become indebted or liable under this section carry on business in partnership, the registered or other letter under subsections (1) and (1.2) may be addressed to the partnership name and, in the case of personal service, shall be deemed to have been validly served if it has been served on one of the partners or left with an adult person employed at the place of business of the partnership.

**Notes [s. 224]**: 224 amended by 1990 garnishment/collection bill, effective June 27, 1990.

**Definitions [s. 224]**: "amount", "annuity" — *Interpretation Act* 35(1); "bank" — 248(1), *Interpretation Act* 35(1); "business" — 248(1); "Canada" — 255; "carrying on business" — 253; "dividend", "employed", "employee", "employer", "Minister", "person", "property" — 248(1); "province" — *Interpretation Act* 35(1); "tax debtor" — 224(1); "tax payable" — 248(2); "trust" — 104(1), 248(1), (3); "writing" — *Interpretation Act* 35(1).

**224.1 Recovery by deduction or set-off** — Where a person is indebted to Her Majesty under this Act or under an Act of a province with which the Minister of Finance has entered into an agreement for the collection of the taxes payable to the province under that Act, the Minister may require the retention by way of deduction or set-off of such amount as the Minister may specify out of any amount that may be or become payable to the person by Her Majesty in right of Canada.

**Related Provisions**: 164(2) — Set-off of refund against other amount owing by the taxpayer to the Crown or a province; 203 — Set-off of Part X refunds; 222.1 — Application to awards of court costs; 225.1 — Collection restrictions; 231.2(1) — requirement to provide information or documents for collection purposes; 231.6(1) — foreign-based documents sought for collection purposes.

**Notes**: Where there is a question as to which taxation year a payment should be allocated to, see Notes to 221.2.

**Definitions [s. 224.1]**: "amount", "Minister", "person" — 248(1); "province" — *Interpretation Act* 35(1).

**Information Circulars**: 98-1R: Collections policies.

**224.2 Acquisition of debtor's property** — For the purpose of collecting debts owed by a person to Her Majesty under this Act or under an Act of a province with which the Minister of Finance has entered into an agreement for the collection of taxes payable to the province under that Act, the Minister may purchase or otherwise acquire any interest in the person's property that the Minister is given a right to acquire in legal proceedings or under a court order or that is offered for sale or redemption and may dispose of any interest so acquired in such manner as the Minister considers reasonable.

**Related Provisions**: 222.1 — Application to awards of court costs; 231.2(1) — requirement to provide information or documents for collection purposes; 231.6(1) — foreign-based documents sought for collection purposes.

**Definitions [s. 224.2]**: "Minister", "person" — 248(1); "province" — *Interpretation Act* 35(1).

**224.3 (1) Payment of moneys seized from tax debtor** — Where the Minister has knowledge or

**S. 224.3(1)**  Income Tax Act

suspects that a particular person is holding moneys that were seized by a police officer in the course of administering or enforcing the criminal law of Canada from another person (in this section referred to as the "tax debtor") who is liable to make a payment under this Act or under an Act of a province with which the Minister of Finance has entered into an agreement for the collection of taxes payable to the province under that Act and that are restorable to the tax debtor, the Minister may in writing require the particular person to turn over the moneys otherwise restorable to the tax debtor in whole or in part to the Receiver General on account of the tax debtor's liability under this Act or under the Act of the province, as the case may be.

**Related Provisions**: 222.1 — Application to awards of court costs; 225.1 — Collection restrictions; 231.2(1) — requirement to provide information or documents for collection purposes; 231.6(1) — foreign-based documents sought for collection purposes; 244(5), (6) — Proof of service by mail or personal service; 248(7)(a) — Mail deemed received on day mailed.

**Notes**: 224.3(1) amended by 1993 technical bill, effective for requirements made in 1993 or later, so that the requirement need not be sent by registered mail or served personally. Previously read:

> (1) Where the Minister has knowledge or suspects that a person is holding moneys that were seized by a police officer in the course of administering or enforcing the criminal law of Canada from another person who is liable to make a payment under this Act or under an Act of a province with which the Minister of Finance has entered into an agreement for the collection of taxes payable to the province under that Act (in this section referred to as the "tax debtor") and that are restorable to the tax debtor, the Minister may, by registered letter or by a letter served personally, require that person to turn over the moneys otherwise restorable to the tax debtor in whole or in part to the Receiver General on account of the tax debtor's liability under this Act or under the Act of the province, as the case may be.

**Information Circulars**: 98-1R: Collections policies.

**(2) Receipt of Minister** — The receipt of the Minister for moneys turned over as required by this section is a good and sufficient discharge of the requirement to restore the moneys to the tax debtor to the extent of the amount so turned over.

**Definitions [s. 224.3]**: "Minister", "person" — 248(1); "province" — *Interpretation Act* 35(1); "tax debtor" — 224.3(1); "writing" — *Interpretation Act* 35(1).

**Forms [s. 224.3]**: T1118; T1118A, B, C, PD-A, PD-B: Requirement to pay.

**225. (1) Seizure of chattels** — Where a person has failed to pay an amount as required by this Act, the Minister may give 30 days notice to the person by registered mail addressed to the person's latest known address of the Minister's intention to direct that the person's goods and chattels be seized and sold, and, if the person fails to make the payment before the expiration of the 30 days, the Minister may issue a certificate of the failure and direct that the person's goods and chattels be seized.

**Related Provisions**: 222.1 — Application to awards of court costs; 225.1 — Collection restrictions; 231.2(1) — requirement to provide information or documents for collection purposes; 231.6(1) — foreign-based documents sought for collection purposes; 244(5) — Proof of service by mail; 248(7) — Mail deemed received on day mailed.

**Notes**: Chattels can also be seized by a sheriff acting under the authority of the Federal Court, once an assessment is registered in that Court, without using section 225.

**Information Circulars**: 98-1R: Collections policies.

**(2) Sale of seized property** — Property seized under this section shall be kept for 10 days at the cost and charges of the owner and, if the owner does not pay the amount owing together with the costs and charges within the 10 days, the property seized shall be sold by public auction.

**(3) Notice of sale** — Except in the case of perishable goods, notice of the sale setting out the time and place thereof, together with a general description of the property to be sold shall, a reasonable time before the goods are sold, be published at least once in one or more newspapers of general local circulation.

**(4) Surplus returned to owner** — Any surplus resulting from the sale after deduction of the amount owing and all costs and charges shall be paid or returned to the owner of the property seized.

**(5) Exemptions from seizure** — Such goods and chattels of any person in default as would be exempt from seizure under a writ of execution issued out of a superior court of the province in which the seizure is made are exempt from seizure under this section.

**Related Provisions**: 226(2) — Taxpayer leaving Canada or defaulting.

**Notes**: 225(5) does not apply to a garnishment under 224(1): *Marcoux*, [2000] 4 C.T.C. 143 (FCTD).

**Definitions [s. 225]**: "assessment", "Minister", "person", "property" — 248(1); "province", "superior court" — *Interpretation Act* 35(1).

**225.1 (1) Collection restrictions** — Where a taxpayer is liable for the payment of an amount assessed under this Act, other than an amount assessed under subsection 152(4.2), 169(3) or 220(3.1), the Minister shall not, for the purpose of collecting the amount,

(a) commence legal proceedings in a court,

(b) certify the amount under section 223,

(c) require a person to make a payment under subsection 224(1),

(d) require an institution or a person to make a payment under subsection 224(1.1),

(e) require the retention of the amount by way of deduction or set-off under section 224.1,

(f) require a person to turn over moneys under subsection 224.3(1), or

(g) give a notice, issue a certificate or make a direction under subsection 225(1)

until after the day that is 90 days after the day of the mailing of the notice of assessment.

**Related Provisions**: 164(1.1) — Refund to taxpayer of amount under objection or appeal; 225.1(6), (7) — Limitations on collection restrictions.

**Notes**: 225.1 effectively means that most taxpayers (but see 225.1(6), (7)) need not pay tax that is under objection or a Tax Court appeal, though interest will continue to accrue. See Notes to 158. If the amount in dispute has already been paid, it can be retrieved by the taxpayer under 164(1.1).

The collection restrictions do not apply in respect of taxes that have been withheld at source (both from employees and from non-residents), as well as certain other amounts. See 225.1(6), as well as the opening words of 225.1(1) (per 1996 amendments). They also do not apply to GST payments or remittances under the *Excise Tax Act*, which can be collected by the CCRA as soon as they are assessed even if the assessment is being appealed. See Information Circular 98-1R for the CCRA's administrative policies as to when collection will be enforced

See also Notes to Canada-U.S. tax treaty, Article XXVI-A(1) and to 223(2), re enforcement by the IRS of a CCRA claim and vice versa.

Opening words of 225.1(1) amended by 1995-97 technical bill, effective June 18, 1998, to add reference to assessments under 152(4.2), 169(3) and 220(3.1). These are relieving assessments that cannot be objected to.

Closing words of 225.1(1) amended by 1992 technical bill, effective June 10, 1993, to change "before" to "until after", thus ensuring that collection proceedings cannot start on the 90th day.

**Information Circulars**: 98-1R: Collections policies.

**(2) Idem** — Where a taxpayer has served a notice of objection under this Act to an assessment of an amount payable under this Act, the Minister shall not, for the purpose of collecting the amount in controversy, take any of the actions described in paragraphs (1)(a) to (g) until after the day that is 90 days after the day on which notice is mailed to the taxpayer that the Minister has confirmed or varied the assessment.

**Related Provisions**: 225.1(6), (7) — Limitations on collection restrictions.

**Notes**: 225.1(2) amended by 1992 technical bill, effective June 10, 1993, to change "before" to "until after", thus ensuring that collection proceedings cannot start on the 90th day.

**(3) Idem** — Where a taxpayer has appealed from an assessment of an amount payable under this Act to the Tax Court of Canada, the Minister shall not, for the purpose of collecting the amount in controversy, take any of the actions described in paragraphs (1)(a) to (g) before the day of mailing of a copy of the decision of the Court to the taxpayer or the day on which the taxpayer discontinues the appeal, whichever is the earlier.

**Related Provisions**: 225.1(6), (7) — Limitations on collection restrictions.

**Notes**: Once a Tax Court decision has been reached against the taxpayer, the CCRA can enforce collection even if the case is further appealed to the Federal Court of Appeal.

**(4) Idem** — Where a taxpayer has agreed under subsection 173(1) that a question should be determined by the Tax Court of Canada, or where a taxpayer is served with a copy of an application made under subsection 174(1) to that Court for the determination of a question, the Minister shall not take any of the actions described in paragraphs (1)(a) to (g) for the purpose of collecting that part of an amount assessed, the liability for payment of which will be affected by the determination of the question, before the day on which the question is determined by the Court.

**Related Provisions**: 225.1(6), (7) — Limitations on collection restrictions.

**(5) Idem** — Notwithstanding any other provision in this section, where a taxpayer has served a notice of objection under this Act to an assessment or has appealed to the Tax Court of Canada from an assessment and agrees in writing with the Minister to delay proceedings on the objection or appeal, as the case may be, until judgment has been given in another action before the Tax Court of Canada, the Federal Court of Appeal or the Supreme Court of Canada in which the issue is the same or substantially the same as that raised in the objection or appeal of the taxpayer, the Minister may take any of the actions described in paragraphs (1)(a) to (g) for the purpose of collecting the amount assessed, or a part thereof, determined in a manner consistent with the decision or judgment of the Court in the other action at any time after the Minister notifies the taxpayer in writing that

(a) the decision of the Tax Court of Canada in that action has been mailed to the Minister,

(b) judgment has been pronounced by the Federal Court of Appeal in that action, or

(c) judgment has been delivered by the Supreme Court of Canada in that action,

as the case may be.

**Notes**: Where many cases depend on the same issue (e.g. certain kinds of investments or tax shelters), it is the CCRA's practice to write to all the taxpayers involved, asking them to agree to hold their objections or appeals "in abeyance" pending resolution of a test case by the courts. Once the test case has been decided, 225.1(5) gives the CCRA the right to proceed with collection action based on that decision — without, of course, prejudicing the taxpayer's right to proceed with the taxpayer's own appeal (possibly on the basis of distinguishable facts, or by pursuing the case to a higher court).

225.1(5) amended by 1991 technical bill, effective January 1, 1991, to delete a reference to the Federal Court–Trial Division.

**(6) Where subsecs. (1) to (4) do not apply** — Subsections (1) to (4) do not apply with respect to

(a) an amount payable under Part VIII;

(b) an amount deducted or withheld, and required to be remitted or paid, under this Act or a regulation made under this Act;

### Proposed Amendment — 225.1(6)(b)

(b) an amount required to be deducted or withheld, or required to be remitted or paid, under this Act or the Regulations;

**Notes**: The new wording, "*or* required to be remitted *or* paid", is extremely broad and could be interpreted so as to emasculate 225.1 completely! The first "or" should probably be "and". This has been brought to the attention of the Dept. of Finance, which will be addressing this concern.

## S. 225.1(6)(b) — Income Tax Act

> **Application**: Bill C-43 (First Reading September 20, 2000), s. 106, will amend para. 225.1(6)(b) to read as above, in force on Royal Assent.
>
> **Technical Notes**: Section 225.1 imposes restrictions on the collection of tax where a taxpayer objects to or appeals from an assessment.
>
> Subsection 225.1(6) provides for an exception to the collection restrictions in limited circumstances. Paragraph 225.1(6)(b) is amended to clarify that the collection restrictions, which do not apply in cases where source deductions were deducted from an employee's remuneration but not remitted to the Receiver General, also do not apply in cases where source deductions were required to be deducted or withheld but were not so deducted or withheld.

(c) an amount of tax required to be paid under section 116 or a regulation made under subsection 215(4) but not so paid;

(d) the amount of any penalty payable for failure to remit or pay an amount referred to in paragraph (b) or (c) as and when required by this Act or a regulation made under this Act; and

(e) any interest payable under a provision of this Act on an amount referred to in this paragraph or any of paragraphs (a) to (d).

**Related Provisions**: 225.2 — Collection in jeopardy.

**Notes**: There are also no collection restrictions on a GST assessment under the *Excise Tax Act*, which is considered analogous to an assessment of a taxpayer who fails to withhold and remit tax on payments to employees.

See Notes to 225.1(1).

**Information Circulars**: 98-1R: Collections policies.

**(7) Idem — large corporations** — Where an amount has been assessed under this Act in respect of a corporation for a taxation year in which it was a large corporation, subsections (1) to (4) do not apply to limit any action of the Minister to collect

(a) at any time on or before the particular day that is 90 days after the day of the mailing of the notice of assessment, ½ of the amount so assessed; and

(b) at any time after the particular day, the amount, if any, by which the amount so assessed exceeds the total of

(i) all amounts collected before that time with respect to the assessment, and

(ii) ½ of the amount in controversy at that time.

**Notes**: 225.1(7) and (8) added by 1992 technical bill, effective June 10, 1993. They require large corporations to pay ½ of the amount in dispute. However, if the assessment that is objected to or appealed from was mailed before 1992, then during 1993, read "½" as "¼" — in other words, for assessments issued before 1992, large corporations had to pay ¼ of the amount in dispute on June 10, 1993 and a further ¼ on January 1, 1994 if the matter was still unresolved.

The proceeds from this provision are supposedly to be used to finance aid to Canadian farmers (Department of Finance news release, December 2, 1991).

**Information Circulars**: 98-1R:: Collections policies.

**(8) Definition of "large corporation"** — For the purposes of this section, a "large corporation" in a particular taxation year means

(a) a corporation by which tax under Part I.3 is payable,

(i) where the particular year ended before July 1989, for its first taxation year that ends after June 1989, or

(ii) where the particular year ended after June 1989, for the particular year,

or would, but for subsection 181.1(4), have been so payable, or

(b) a corporation that, at the end of the particular year, is related (for the purpose of section 181.5, as that section reads in its application to the 1992 taxation year) to a corporation that is a large corporation in its taxation year that includes the end of the particular year,

and, for the purpose of subparagraph (a)(i), a corporation formed as a result of the amalgamation or merger of 2 or more predecessor corporations shall be deemed to be the same corporation as, and a continuation of, each of the predecessor corporations.

**Related Provisions**: 164(1.1) — Repayment on objections and repeals; 165(1.11), (1.13), 169(2.1) — Limitations on objections and appeals by large corporations; 220(4.1) — Security; 225.1(8) — Definition of "large corporation".

**Notes**: 225.1(8) amended by 1993 technical bill, effective June 15, 1994, to correct the reference to 181.1(4) (formerly read "section 181.10"), and to add the qualification "as that section reads in its application to the 1992 taxation year".

See also Notes to 225.1(7).

**Notes [s. 225.1]**: 225.1 amended by 1990 garnishment/collection bill, effective June 27, 1990.

**Definitions [s. 225.1]**: "amount", "assessment" — 248(1); "corporation" — 248(1), *Interpretation Act* 35(1); "large corporation" — 225.1(8); "Minister", "person" — 248(1); "regulation" — 248(1); "taxation year" — 249; "taxpayer" — 248(1); "writing" — *Interpretation Act* 35(1).

**225.2 (1) Definition of "judge"** — In this section, "judge" means a judge or a local judge of a superior court of a province or a judge of the Federal Court.

**(2) Authorization to proceed forthwith** — Notwithstanding section 225.1, where, on *ex parte* application by the Minister, a judge is satisfied that there are reasonable grounds to believe that the collection of all or any part of an amount assessed in respect of a taxpayer would be jeopardized by a delay in the collection of that amount, the judge shall, on such terms as the judge considers reasonable in the circumstances, authorize the Minister to take forthwith any of the actions described in paragraphs 225.1(1)(a) to (g) with respect to the amount.

**Related Provisions**: 164(1.2) — Delay of refund where collection of tax in jeopardy.

**Notes**: The order issued under this subsection is called a "jeopardy order" or a "jeopardy assessment".

In *Steele*, [1996] 2 C.T.C. 279 (Sask. QB), the Court ruled that no assessment under 225.2 could be made against a tax debtor who was transferring assets to her husband — because the husband could be assessed under s. 160! Thus, collection would not be jeopardized.

For discussion of jeopardy assessments under 225.2, see Elaine Sibson, "Revenue Canada's Long Collection Arm", 1998 Canadian Tax Foundation annual conference proceedings, pp. 26:1-26:13.

**Information Circulars**: 98-1R: Collections policies.

**(3) Notice of assessment not sent** — An authorization under subsection (2) in respect of an amount assessed in respect of a taxpayer may be granted by a judge notwithstanding that a notice of assessment in respect of that amount has not been sent to the taxpayer at or before the time the application is made where the judge is satisfied that the receipt of the notice of assessment by the taxpayer would likely further jeopardize the collection of the amount, and for the purposes of sections 222, 223, 224, 224.1, 224.3 and 225, the amount in respect of which an authorization is so granted shall be deemed to be an amount payable under this Act.

**(4) Affidavits** — Statements contained in an affidavit filed in the context of an application under this section may be based on belief with the grounds therefor.

**(5) Service of authorization and of notice of assessment** — An authorization granted under this section in respect of a taxpayer shall be served by the Minister on the taxpayer within 72 hours after it is granted, except where the judge orders the authorization to be served at some other time specified in the authorization, and, where a notice of assessment has not been sent to the taxpayer at or before the time of the application, the notice of assessment shall be served together with the authorization.

**(6) How service effected** — For the purposes of subsection (5), service on a taxpayer shall be effected by

(a) personal service on the taxpayer; or

(b) service in accordance with directions, if any, of a judge.

**Related Provisions**: 244(6) — Proof of personal service.

**(7) Application to judge for direction** — Where service on a taxpayer cannot reasonably otherwise be effected as and when required under this section, the Minister may, as soon as practicable, apply to a judge for further direction.

**(8) Review of authorization** — Where a judge of a court has granted an authorization under this section in respect of a taxpayer, the taxpayer may, on 6 clear days notice to the Deputy Attorney General of Canada, apply to a judge of the court to review the authorization.

**Related Provisions**: *Interpretation Act* 27(1) — Calculation of clear days.

**Notes**: The words "a judge of *the* court" indicate that a judge of the same court must be approached for a review of the first judge's order.

**(9) Limitation period for review application** — An application under subsection (8) shall be made

(a) within 30 days from the day on which the authorization was served on the taxpayer in accordance with this section; or

(b) within such further time as a judge may allow, on being satisfied that the application was made as soon as practicable.

**(10) Hearing *in camera*** — An application under subsection (8) may, on the application of the taxpayer, be heard *in camera*, if the taxpayer establishes to the satisfaction of the judge that the circumstances of the case justify *in camera* proceedings.

**Notes**: See Notes to 179.

**(11) Disposition of application** — On an application under subsection (8), the judge shall determine the question summarily and may confirm, set aside or vary the authorization and make such other order as the judge considers appropriate.

**Related Provisions**: 225.2(13) — No appeal from judge's decision.

**(12) Directions** — Where any question arises as to the course to be followed in connection with anything done or being done under this section and there is no direction in this section with respect thereto, a judge may give such direction with regard thereto as, in the opinion of the judge, is appropriate.

**(13) No appeal from review order** — No appeal lies from an order of a judge made pursuant to subsection (11).

**Notes**: Although there is no appeal, presumably if the judge made an error of law it would be possible to seek judicial review under s. 28 of the *Federal Court Act*.

**Definitions [s. 225.2]**: "amount" — 248(1); "clear days" — *Interpretation Act* 27(1); "Minister" — 248(1); "province" — *Interpretation Act* 35(1); "superior court" — *Interpretation Act* 35(1); "taxpayer" — 248(1).

**Information Circulars [s. 225.2]**: 73-10R3: Tax evasion.

**226. (1) Taxpayer leaving Canada** — Where the Minister suspects that a taxpayer has left or is about to leave Canada, the Minister may, before the day otherwise fixed for payment, by notice served personally or by registered letter addressed to the taxpayer's latest known address, demand payment of the amount of all taxes, interest and penalties for which the taxpayer is liable or would be liable if the time for payment had arrived, and that amount shall be paid forthwith by the taxpayer notwithstanding any other provision of this Act.

**Related Provisions**: 128.1(4) — Tax effects of ceasing to be resident in Canada; 222.1 — Application to awards of court costs; 225.2 — Immediate collection of amounts owing; 231.2(1) — requirement to provide information or documents for collection purposes; 231.6(1) — foreign-based documents sought for collection purposes; 248(7)(a) — Notice deemed received on day mailed.

**Notes**: 226(1) amended by 1991 technical bill to include the case where the taxpayer has already left Canada, effective December 17, 1991.

See Notes to 223(3).

**Information Circulars**: 98-1R: Collections policies.

**(2) Idem** — Where a taxpayer has failed to pay, as required, any tax, interest or penalties demanded under this section, the Minister may direct that the goods and chattels of the taxpayer be seized and subsections 225(2) to (5) apply, with respect to the seizure, with such modifications as the circumstances require.

**Related Provisions**: 222.1 — Application to awards of court costs; 231.2(1) — requirement to provide information or documents for collection purposes; 231.6(1) — foreign-based documents sought for collection purposes.

**Definitions [s. 226]**: "Minister", "taxpayer" — 248(1).

**227. (1) Withholding taxes** — No action lies against any person for deducting or withholding any sum of money in compliance or intended compliance with this Act.

**(2) Return filed with person withholding** — Where a person (in this subsection referred to as the "payer") is required by regulations made under subsection 153(1) to deduct or withhold from a payment to another person an amount on account of that other person's tax for the year, that other person shall, from time to time as prescribed, file a return with the payer in prescribed form.

**Related Provisions**: 162(7) — Failure to comply with regulation; 227(3) — Where return is not filed.

**Regulations**: 107 (deadline for employee to file TD1 return).

**Forms**: TD1: Personal tax credits return; TD1A: Amendment to the personal tax credits return.

**(3) Failure to file return** — Every person who fails to file a return as required by subsection (2) is liable to have the deduction or withholding under section 153 on account of the person's tax made as though the person were a person who is neither married nor in a common-law partnership and is without dependants.

**Notes**: 227(3) amended by 2000 same-sex partners bill, effective for the 2001 and later taxation years, or earlier by election (see Notes to 248(1)"common-law partner"). It formerly read:

(3) Failure to file return — Every person who fails to file a return as required by subsection (2) is liable to have the deduction or withholding under section 153 on account of the person's tax made as though the person were an unmarried person without dependants.

**(4) Trust for moneys deducted** — Every person who deducts or withholds an amount under this Act is deemed, notwithstanding any security interest (as defined in subsection 224(1.3)) in the amount so deducted or withheld, to hold the amount separate and apart from the property of the person and from property held by any secured creditor (as defined in subsection 224(1.3)) of that person that but for the security interest would be property of the person, in trust for Her Majesty and for payment to Her Majesty in the manner and at the time provided under this Act.

**Related Provisions**: 227(4.1) — Extension of trust; 227(4.2) — Meaning of security interest; 227(4.3) — Application to the Crown.

**Notes**: A parallel rule for GST collected but not remitted is found in s. 222 of the *Excise Tax Act*. See *The Practitioner's GST Annotated* or the *Canada GST Service* for reference to the case law under that section.

227(4) amended by 1995-97 technical bill, effective June 15, 1994. These amendments (see also 227(4.1), (4.2)) were first announced by press release on April 7, 1997. They are designed to overturn *Royal Bank v. Sparrow Electric Corp.*, 97 D.T.C. 5089 (SCC), and give Revenue Canada stronger powers of recovery of source deductions. (Parallel amendments were made to the GST legislation, in 222(3)–(4) of the *Excise Tax Act*.) These amendments were applied in the Crown's favour in *Royal Bank v. Tuxedo Transport Ltd.*, [2000] 3 C.T.C. 331 (BCCA). However, the BCSC decision in that case, which the BCCA reversed, was approved in *First Vancouver Finance v. MNR*, [2000] 3 C.T.C. 93 (Sask. CA), which ruled that "after-acquired property" was not subject to the deemed trust.

See also CCRA Accounts Receivable Division Publication 2000-1, "Deemed trust — A responsible application policy" (June 15, 2000), available on *TaxPartner* and from the CCRA's web site.

227(4) amended by 1993 technical bill, effective June 15, 1994. From 1972 through June 14, 1994, read:

(4) Every person who deducts or withholds any amount under this Act shall be deemed to hold the amount so deducted or withheld in trust for Her Majesty.

**Information Circulars**: 98-1R: Collections policies.

**(4.1) Extension of trust** — Notwithstanding any other provision of this Act, the *Bankruptcy and Insolvency Act* (except sections 81.1 and 81.2 of that Act), any other enactment of Canada, any enactment of a province or any other law, where at any time an amount deemed by subsection (4) to be held by a person in trust for Her Majesty is not paid to Her Majesty in the manner and at the time provided under this Act, property of the person and property held by any secured creditor (as defined in subsection 224(1.3)) of that person that but for a security interest (as defined in subsection 224(1.3)) would be property of the person, equal in value to the amount so deemed to be held in trust is deemed

(a) to be held, from the time the amount was deducted or withheld by the person, separate and apart from the property of the person, in trust for Her Majesty whether or not the property is subject to such a security interest, and

(b) to form no part of the estate or property of the person from the time the amount was so deducted or withheld, whether or not the property has in fact been kept separate and apart from the estate or property of the person and whether or not the property is subject to such a security interest

and is property beneficially owned by Her Majesty notwithstanding any security interest in such property and in the proceeds thereof, and the proceeds of such property shall be paid to the Receiver General in priority to all such security interests.

**Related Provisions**: 227(4.2) — Meaning of security interest; 227(4.3) — Application to the Crown.

**Notes**: 227(4.1) added by 1995-97 technical bill, effective June 15, 1994. See Notes to 227(4).

**(4.2) Meaning of security interest** — For the purposes of subsections (4) and (4.1), a security interest does not include a prescribed security interest.

**Related Provisions**: 227(4.3) — Application to the Crown.

**Notes**: 227(4.2) added by 1995-97 technical bill, effective June 15, 1994.

**Regulations**: 2201 (prescribed security interest).

### Proposed Addition — 227(4.3)

**(4.3) Application to Crown** — For greater certainty, subsections (4) to (4.2) apply to Her Majesty in right of Canada or a province where Her Majesty in right of Canada or a province is a secured creditor (within the meaning assigned by subsection 224(1.3)) or holds a security interest (within the meaning assigned by that subsection).

**Application**: Bill C-43 (First Reading September 20, 2000), subsec. 107(1), will add subsec. 227(4.3), in force on Royal Assent.

**Technical Notes**: Section 227 provides special rules relating to source deductions and non-resident withholding tax under sections 153 and 215 respectively, and also deals with the application of certain Parts of the Act to particular persons and entities.

New subsection 227(4.3) clarifies that the deemed trusts in subsections 227(4) and (4.1) relating to unremitted source deductions are binding on Her Majesty in right of Canada or of a province. Accordingly, the deemed trusts will always take priority over any other security interest in favour of the Crown, subject to prescribed security interests as provided in the Regulations.

**(5) Payments by trustees, etc.** — Where a specified person in relation to a particular person (in this subsection referred to as the "payer") has any direct or indirect influence over the disbursements, property, business or estate of the payer and the specified person, alone or together with another person, authorizes or otherwise causes a payment referred to in subsection 135(3) or 153(1), or on or in respect of which tax is payable under Part XII.5 or XIII, to be made by or on behalf of the payer, the specified person

(a) is, for the purposes of subsections 135(3) and 153(1), section 215 and this section, deemed to be a person who made the payment;

(a.1) is, for the purpose of subsection 211.8(2), deemed to be a person who redeemed, acquired or cancelled a share and made the payment as a consequence of the redemption, acquisition or cancellation;

(b) is jointly and severally liable with the payer to pay to the Receiver General

(i) all amounts payable by the payer because of any of subsections 135(3), 153(1) and 211.8(2) and section 215 in respect of the payment, and

(ii) all amounts payable under this Act by the payer because of any failure to comply with any of those provisions in respect of the payment; and

(c) is entitled to deduct or withhold from any amount paid or credited by the specified person to the payer or otherwise recover from the payer any amount paid under this subsection by the specified person in respect of the payment.

**Related Provisions**: 227(5.1) — Specified person; 227(5.2) — "Person" includes partnership.

**Notes**: 227(5) added by 1995 Budget, effective June 20, 1996 (Royal Assent). Amended by 1996 Budget, effective April 25, 1997 (Royal Assent), to add para. (a.1) and references to Part XII.5 and 211.8(2).

Former 227(5) repealed by 1993 technical bill, effective June 15, 1994. From September 13, 1988 through June 14, 1994, read:

(5) **Amount in trust not part of estate** — Notwithstanding any provision of the *Bankruptcy [and Insolvency] Act*, in the event of any liquidation, assignment, receivership or bankruptcy of or by a person, an amount equal to any amount

(a) deemed by subsection (4) to be held in trust for Her Majesty, or

(b) deducted or withheld under an Act of a province with which the Minister of Finance has entered into an agreement for the collection of taxes payable to the province under that Act that is deemed under that Act to be held in trust for Her Majesty in right of the province

shall be deemed to be separate from and form no part of the estate in liquidation, assignment, receivership or bankruptcy, whether or not that amount has in fact been kept separate and apart from the person's own moneys or from the assets of the estate.

**(5.1) Definition of "specified person"** — In subsection (5), a "specified person" in relation to a particular person means a person who is, in relation to the particular person or the disbursements, property, business or estate of the particular person,

(a) a trustee;

(b) a liquidator;

(c) a receiver;

(d) an interim receiver;

(e) a receiver-manager;

(f) a trustee in bankruptcy or other person appointed under the *Bankruptcy and Insolvency Act*;

(g) an assignee;

(h) a secured creditor (as defined in subsection 224(1.3));

(i) an executor or administrator;

(j) any person acting in a capacity similar to that of a person referred to in any of paragraphs (a) to (i);

(k) a person appointed (otherwise than as an employee of the creditor) at the request of, or on the advice of, a secured creditor in relation to the particular person to monitor, or provide advice in respect of, the disbursements, property, business or estate of the particular person under circumstances such that it is reasonable to conclude that the person is appointed to protect or advance the interests of the creditor; or

(l) an agent of a specified person referred to in any of paragraphs (a) to (k).

**S. 227(5.1)**                                    Income Tax Act

**Notes**: 227(5.1) added by 1995 Budget, effective June 20, 1996 (Royal Assent).

**(5.2) "Person" includes partnership** — For the purposes of this section, references in subsections (5) and (5.1) to persons include partnerships.

**Related Provisions**: 227(15) — "Person" includes certain partnerships for all purposes under s. 227.

**Notes**: 227(5.2) added by 1995 Budget, effective June 20, 1996 (Royal Assent).

### Possible Future Amendment — 227(5.2)–(5.4)

**(5.2) Interference with remittance** — Where at any time

  (a) an amount (in this subsection referred to as the "amount to be remitted") that is deducted or withheld from a payment (in this subsection referred to as the "gross payment") is required by a provision of this Act to be remitted by a particular person on account of the tax of another person,

  (b) a secured creditor (as defined in subsection 224(1.3)) in relation to the particular person has influence over the issuance or clearance of the payment of the amount to be remitted, and

  (c) the secured creditor, alone or together with another person, exercises that influence for the purpose of

   (i) postponing the remittance of the amount to be remitted,

   (ii) subordinating the remittance of the amount to be remitted, in favour of the payment of other amounts, or

   (iii) causing the amount to be remitted not to be remitted,

and the remittance of the amount to be remitted is postponed or subordinated or the amount to be remitted is not remitted, as the case may be,

the secured creditor

  (d) is, for the purposes of subsections 135(3) and 153(1), section 215 and this section, deemed to be a person who made the gross payment and is deemed to be a person who deducted or withheld the amount to be remitted from the gross payment,

  (e) is, notwithstanding any other provision of this Act, jointly and severally liable with the particular person to pay to the Receiver General

   (i) all amounts payable by the particular person because of any of subsections 135(3) and 153(1) and section 215 in respect of the gross payment, and

   (ii) all amounts payable under this Act by the particular person because of any failure to comply with any of those provisions in respect of the gross payment, and

  (f) is entitled to deduct or withhold from any amount paid or credited by the secured creditor to the particular person, or otherwise recover from the particular person, any amount paid under this subsection by the secured creditor in respect of the amount to be remitted.

**Technical Notes**: New subsection 227(5.2) provides a new rule for imposing joint and several liability on certain secured creditors who interfere with the remittance of source deductions. Under this new rule it need not be established that a secured creditor actually causes or authorizes a payment — which is subject to source deduction — before joint and several liability arises. It is sufficient to show that an amount is deducted at source from a payment (hereafter referred to as a "gross payment") that the secured creditor has influence over the issuance or clearance of that gross payment and that the secured creditor exercises that influence for the purpose of interfering with the remittance of source deductions. Interference may take place by way of postponing a remittance, subordinating a remittance in favour of another payment or simply causing a remittance not to be made.

A typical example is the situation of a financial institution that has influential control over a person and that, in the course of providing banking services to the person (usually in financial difficulty) who is liable to deduct certain amounts from the remuneration of its employees, interferes with the remittance of these deductions by preventing the issuance of, stopping or refusing to clear a remittance cheque made to the Receiver General while issuing, clearing, or honouring other cheques made to suppliers or other creditors. This might be done in order to enhance trade receivables and limit the secured creditor's own risks.

Generally, it is not intended that the refusal of a cheque or other means of payment for lack of sufficient funds or other legitimate banking reasons be regarded as influence that is exercised for the purpose of interfering with the payment of source deductions. However, it is intended that a secured creditor that refuses to extend credit in respect of a source deduction payment and that subsequently extends credit in respect of other similar payments made to another party, be considered as exercising influence for the purpose of interfering with source deductions.

Where the circumstances described in new subsection 227(5.2) exist, the secured creditor will be deemed to have made the payment and will become jointly and severally liable with the person making the gross payment to pay all amounts payable in respect of the gross payment and all amounts payable by that person for the failure to deduct and remit the amounts payable. This will include the amount of tax not remitted, interest, and penalties. However, exceptions to this rule are contained in new subsections 227(5.3) and (5.4). A specific right to recover amounts paid by the secured creditor on behalf of the person making the gross payment is provided in paragraph 227(5.2)(f).

**(5.3) Exception where all cheques stopped** — Where on a day a secured creditor in relation to a person stops or refuses a cheque or other means of payment or remittance drawn on the secured creditor by the person for an amount to be remitted by the person to the Receiver General,

1714

subsection (5.2) does not apply in respect of that stopping or refusal if, throughout the period that begins at the end of that day and ends when the amount is paid to the Receiver General, the creditor stops or refuses all cheques and all other means of payment or remittance drawn on the creditor by the person (other than cheques payable, or other means of payment or remittance, to the Receiver General and other than cheques certified on or before that day).

**Technical Notes**: New subsections 227(5.3) and (5.4) provide certain exceptions to the joint and several liability rules which apply to secured creditors. Subsection 227(5.3) deals with the case in which a cheque or other means of payment is stopped or refused by the secured creditor. Joint and several liability will not arise in this case if the secured creditor also stops or refuses all other cheques presented and payments made starting immediately after that day, except cheques or payments made to the Receiver General or cheques certified on or before that day. Using the example of the financial institution that stops a remittance cheque (referred to in the commentary on subsection 227(5.2)), no joint and several liability would arise if the financial institution were to stop or refuse (until payment in full of the amount to be paid or remitted) all other cheques made to any other creditor of the person and presented at any time after the day on which it stopped the cheque payable to the Receiver General.

**(5.4) Other exceptions** — Where subsection (5.2) would, but for this subsection, apply to a secured creditor in relation to a person because the creditor has exercised influence in respect of an amount to be remitted by the person to the Receiver General, that subsection does not apply where

(a) the person does not make any payment or disbursement (other than payments or disbursements to the Receiver General) at and after the time referred to in that subsection until the amount to be remitted is paid to the Receiver General;

(b) the exercise of the influence is only a refusal, or an expression of intention to refuse, to supply to the person any further property or services until a payment for property sold or leased or services rendered to the person is received by the creditor; or

(c) the exercise of the influence is pursuant to a decree, order or judgment of a competent tribunal in Canada.

**Technical Notes**: Similarly, new subsection 227(5.4) provides relief from joint and several liability where a person does not make any other payment or disbursement at or after the time the secured creditor exercises influence in respect of an amount to be paid or remitted by the person to the Receiver General.

New paragraph 227(5.4)(b) provides, for greater certainty, that a refusal by a secured creditor to continue to supply property or services because of the non-payment for such property or services will not give rise to joint and several liability.

Under new paragraph 227(5.4)(c), court actions such as collection and conservation measures will not be regarded as exercising influence for the purpose of interfering with a remittance. In addition, where a court orders a secured creditor to make a payment in priority to a remittance, the secured creditor will not be regarded as having exercised influence for the purpose of interfering with a remittance.

**Application**: The December 12, 1995 Notice of Ways and Means Motion would have added subsecs. 227(5.2)–(5.4) as above (and would have numbered what is now 227(5.2) as 227(5.5)), to come into force on Royal Assent. However, these provisions (and the parallel rules in 323.1 of the *Excise Tax Act* for GST remittances) were dropped in the revised Notice of Ways and Means Motion of March 28, 1996 (Bill C-36 — 1995 Budget bill). Officials at the Department of Finance advise that implementation of these rules has been deferred following consultations with the banks and other financial institutions, which have promised voluntary compliance. The CCRA has been monitoring this compliance in order to make a determination as to whether to proceed with these rules. As of January 2001, no decision had yet been made, and the proposals are still "on hold".

**(6) Excess withheld, returned or applied** — Where a person on whose behalf an amount has been paid under Part XII.5 or XIII to the Receiver General was not liable to pay tax under that Part or where the amount so paid is in excess of the amount that the person was liable to pay, the Minister shall, on written application made no later than 2 years after the end of the calendar year in which the amount was paid, pay to the person the amount so paid or such part of it as the person was not liable to pay, unless the person is or is about to become liable to make a payment to Her Majesty in right of Canada, in which case the Minister may apply the amount otherwise payable under this subsection to that liability and notify the person of that action.

**Notes**: 227(6) applies only to non-resident withholding tax (Part XIII) and withholding of Part XII.5 tax relating to the labour-sponsored funds tax credit. For regular employee source withholding, the employee claims amounts withheld at source as a refundable credit on page 4 of the T1 General tax return, and can do so even if the employer never remits the amount withheld: *Manke*, [1999] 1 C.T.C. 2186 (TCC). See also Notes to 153(1).

Reference to Part XII.5 added to 227(6) by 1996 Budget, effective April 25, 1997 (Royal Assent).

227(6) amended by 1993 technical bill, effective June 15, 1994. From 1972 through June 14, 1994, read:

(6) **Withheld money returned or applied otherwise** — Where a person on whose behalf an amount has been paid to the Receiver General after having been deducted or withheld under Part XIII was not liable to pay any tax under that Part or where the amount so paid to the Receiver General on the person's behalf is in excess of the tax that the person was liable to pay, the Minister shall, on application in writing made within two years from the end of the calendar year in which the amount was paid, pay to the person the amount so paid or such part thereof as the person was not liable to pay, unless the person is otherwise liable or about to become liable to make a payment under this Act, in which case the Minister may apply the amount otherwise payable under this subsection to that payment and notify the person of that fact.

**Forms**: NR7-R: Application for refund of non-resident tax withheld.

S. 227(6.1)　　　　　　　　　　　　　　Income Tax Act

**(6.1) Repayment of non-resident shareholder loan** — Where, in respect of a loan from or indebtedness to a corporation or partnership, a person on whose behalf an amount was paid to the Receiver General under Part XIII because of subsection 15(2) and paragraph 214(3)(a) repays the loan or indebtedness or a portion of it and it is established by subsequent events or otherwise that the repayment was not made as part of a series of loans or other transactions and repayments, the Minister shall, on written application made no later than 2 years after the end of the calendar year in which the repayment is made, pay to the person an amount equal to the lesser of

(a) the amount so paid to the Receiver General in respect of the loan or indebtedness or portion of it, as the case may be, and

(b) the amount that would be payable to the Receiver General under Part XIII if a dividend described in paragraph 212(2)(a) equal in amount to the amount of the loan or indebtedness repaid were paid by the corporation or partnership to the person at the time of the repayment,

unless the person is or is about to become liable to make a payment to Her Majesty in right of Canada, in which case the Minister may apply the amount otherwise payable under this subsection to that liability and notify the person of that action.

**Related Provisions**: 227(7.1) — Determination of amount under subsec. (6.1).

**Notes**: 227(6.1) added by 1993 technical bill, effective June 15, 1994.

**Interpretation Bulletins**: IT-119R4: Debts of shareholders and certain persons connected with shareholders.

**(7) Application for assessment** — Where, on application under subsection (6) by or on behalf of a person to the Minister in respect of an amount paid under Part XII.5 or XIII to the Receiver General, the Minister is not satisfied

(a) that the person was not liable to pay any tax under that Part, or

(b) that the amount paid was in excess of the tax that the person was liable to pay,

the Minister shall assess any amount payable under that Part by the person and send a notice of assessment to the person, and sections 150 to 163, subsections 164(1) and (1.4) to (7), sections 164.1 to 167 and Division J of Part I apply with any modifications that the circumstances require.

**Notes**: Reference to Part XII.5 added to 227(7) by 1996 Budget, effective April 25, 1997 (Royal Assent).

227(7) amended by 1993 technical bill, effective June 15, 1994. From 1985 through June 14, 1994, read:

(7) **Idem** — Where, on application by or on behalf of a person to the Minister pursuant to subsection (6) in respect of an amount paid to the Receiver General that was deducted or withheld under Part XIII, the Minister is not satisfied

(a) that the person was not liable to pay any tax under that Part, or

(b) that the amount paid to the Receiver General was in excess of the tax that the person was liable to pay,

the Minister shall assess the person for any amount payable by the person under Part XIII and send a notice of assessment to the person, whereupon sections 150 to 163, subsections 164(1) and (1.4) to (7), sections 164.1 to 167 and Division J of Part I are applicable with such modifications as the circumstances require.

**(7.1) Application for determination** — Where, on application under subsection (6.1) by or on behalf of a person to the Minister in respect of an amount paid under Part XIII to the Receiver General, the Minister is not satisfied that the person is entitled to the amount claimed, the Minister shall, at the person's request, determine, with all due dispatch, the amount, if any, payable under subsection (6.1) to the person and shall send a notice of determination to the person, and sections 150 to 163, subsections 164(1) and (1.4) to (7), sections 164.1 to 167 and Division J of Part I apply with such modifications as the circumstances require.

**Notes**: 227(7.1) added by 1993 technical bill, effective June 15, 1994.

**(8) Penalty** — Subject to subsection (8.5), every person who in a calendar year has failed to deduct or withhold any amount as required by subsection 153(1) or section 215 is liable to a penalty of

(a) 10% of the amount that should have been deducted or withheld; or

(b) where at the time of the failure a penalty under this subsection was payable by the person in respect of an amount that should have been deducted or withheld during the year and the failure was made knowingly or under circumstances amounting to gross negligence, 20% of that amount.

**Related Provisions**: 147.1(3) — Deemed registration; 161(11) — Interest on penalties; 227(8.3) — Interest on amounts not deducted or withheld; 227(8.4) — Non-resident employees and patronage dividends; 227(9) — Penalty; 227(9.5) — Each establishment considered a separate person; 227(10) — Assessment; 227(10.2) — Joint and several liability re contributions to RCA; 252.1 — Where union is employer.

**Notes**: 227(8)(b) amended by 1992 technical bill, effective 1993, except for amounts that were required to be remitted before 1993. Before 1993, ignore the words "and the failure was made knowingly or under circumstances amounting to gross negligence".

**I.T. Application Rules**: 62(2) (subsec. 227(8) applies to interest payable in respect of any period after December 23, 1971).

**Interpretation Bulletins**: IT-494: Hire of ships and aircraft from non-residents.

**Information Circulars**: 77-16R4: Non-resident income tax; 92-2: Guidelines for the cancellation and waiver of interest and penalties.

**(8.1) Joint and several liability** — Where a particular person has failed to deduct or withhold an amount as required under subsection 153(1) or section 215 in respect of an amount that has been paid to a non-resident person, the non-resident person is jointly and severally liable with the particular person to pay any interest payable by the particular person pursuant to subsection (8.3) in respect thereof.

**Related Provisions**: 227(10) — Assessment.

**(8.2) Retirement compensation arrangement deductions** — Where a person has failed to deduct or withhold any amount as required under subsection 153(1) in respect of a contribution under a retirement compensation arrangement, that person is liable to pay to Her Majesty an amount equal to the amount of the contribution, and each payment on account of that amount is deemed to be, in the year in which the payment is made,

(a) for the purposes of paragraph 20(1)(r), a contribution by the person to the arrangement; and

(b) an amount on account of tax payable by the custodian under Part XI.3.

**Related Provisions**: 147.1(3) — Deemed registration; 153(1)(p) — Withholding required; 227(10) — Assessment; 227(10.2) — Joint and several liability re contributions to RCA; 252.1 — Where union is employer.

**(8.3) Interest on amounts not deducted or withheld** — A person who fails to deduct or withhold any amount as required by subsection 135(3), 153(1) or 211.8(2) or section 215 shall pay to the Receiver General interest on the amount at the prescribed rate, computed

(a) in the case of an amount required by subsection 153(1) to be deducted or withheld from a payment to another person, from the fifteenth day of the month immediately following the month in which the amount was required to be deducted or withheld, or from such earlier day as may be prescribed for the purposes of subsection 153(1), to,

(i) where that other person is not resident in Canada, the day of payment of the amount to the Receiver General, and

(ii) where that other person is resident in Canada, the earlier of the day of payment of the amount to the Receiver General and April 30 of the year immediately following the year in which the amount was required to be deducted or withheld;

(b) in the case of an amount required by subsection 135(3) or section 215 to be deducted or withheld, from the day on which the amount was required to be deducted or withheld to the day of payment of the amount to the Receiver General; and

(c) in the case of an amount required by subsection 211.8(2) to be withheld, from the day on or before which the amount was required to be remitted to the Receiver General to the day of payment of the amount to the Receiver General.

**Related Provisions**: 221.1 — Application of interest where legislation retroactive; 227(8.1) — Joint and several liability; 227(10) — Assessment; 227(10.2) — Joint and several liability re contributions to RCA; 248(11) — Compound interest; 252.1 — Where union is employer.

**Notes**: See Notes to 227(8.4).

Reference to 211.8(2) added to opening words of 227(8.3), and para. (c) added, by 1996 Budget, effective April 25, 1997 (Royal Assent).

227(8.3) amended by 1991 technical bill, effective July 14, 1990, to refer to 135(3).

**Regulations**: 4301(a) (prescribed rate of interest).

**Information Circulars**: 92-2: Guidelines for the cancellation and waiver of interest and penalties.

**(8.4) Liability to pay amount not deducted or withheld** — A person who fails to deduct or withhold any amount as required under

(a) subsection 135(3) in respect of a payment made to another person, or

(b) subsection 153(1) in respect of an amount paid to another person who is non-resident or who is resident in Canada solely because of paragraph 250(1)(a)

is liable to pay as tax under this Act on behalf of the other person the whole of the amount that should have been so deducted or withheld and is entitled to deduct or withhold from any amount paid or credited by the person to the other person or otherwise to recover from the other person any amount paid by the person as tax under this Part on behalf of the other person.

**Related Provisions**: 215(6) — Parallel provision for non-resident withholding tax; 227(10) — Assessment.

**Notes**: 227(8.4)(b) does not impose liability on a corporation for the tax not withheld at source from an employee who is resident in Canada (e.g., where the "employer" thought that the "employee" was an independent contractor). Similarly, 227(8.1) applies only to withholdings from non-residents. There are penalty and interest provisions, but no provision in 227 appears to impose liability for the unwithheld tax itself. (This is to be distinguished from tax withheld but not remitted, for which 227(9.4) imposes liability.) However, if the entity not withholding is a corporation, 227.1(1) appears to impose liability on both the corporation and the directors, although it was designed specifically to catch the directors.

227(8.4) amended by 1991 technical bill, effective July 14, 1990, to refer to 135(3).

**(8.5) [Repealed]**

**Notes**: 227(8.5) repealed by 1992 technical bill, effective 1993, except for amounts that were required to be remitted before 1993. It and 227(9.5) were replaced with new 227(9.5).

**(9) Penalty** — Subject to subsection (9.5), every person who in a calendar year has failed to remit or pay as and when required by this Act or a regulation an amount deducted or withheld as required by this Act or a regulation or an amount of tax that the person is, by section 116 or by a regulation made under subsection 215(4), required to pay is liable to a penalty of

(a) 10% of that amount; or

(b) where at the time of the failure a penalty under this subsection was payable by the person in respect of an amount that should have been remitted or paid during the year and the failure was made knowingly or under circumstances amounting to gross negligence, 20% of that amount.

S. 227(9)                    Income Tax Act

**Related Provisions**: 227(8) — Penalty; 227(9.1) — Penalty; 227(9.3) — Interest on certain tax not paid; 227(9.5) — Each establishment considered a separate person; 227(10.1) — Assessment; 227(10.2) — Joint and several liability re contributions to RCA; 248(7) — Receipt of things mailed; 252.1 — Where union is employer.

**Notes**: 227(9)(b) amended by 1992 technical bill, effective 1993, except for amounts that were required to be remitted before 1993. Before 1993, ignore the words "and the failure was made knowingly or under circumstances amounting to gross negligence".

**Regulations**: Part I (amount required to be withheld).

**I.T. Application Rules**: 62(2) (subsec. 227(9) applies to interest payable in respect of any period after December 23, 1971).

**Information Circulars**: 92-2: Guidelines for the cancellation and waiver of interest and penalties.

**(9.1) Penalty** — Notwithstanding any other provision of this Act, any other enactment of Canada, any enactment of a province or any other law, the penalty for failure to remit an amount required to be remitted by a person on or before a prescribed date under subsection 153(1), subsection 21(1) of the *Canada Pension Plan*, subsection 53(1) of the *Unemployment Insurance Act* and subsection 82(1) of the *Employment Insurance Act* shall, unless the person who is required to remit the amount has, knowingly or under circumstances amounting to gross negligence, delayed in remitting the amount or has, knowingly or under circumstances amounting to gross negligence, remitted an amount less than the amount required, apply only to the amount by which the total of all amounts so required to be remitted on or before that date exceeds $500.

**Notes**: 227(9.1) amended by 1996 employment insurance bill and then by 1995-97 technical bill, both effective June 30, 1996. Before that date it referred only to the *Unemployment Insurance Act*; this was first changed to the *Employment Insurance Act*, then changed back to both Acts since procedures under the old UI Act are still ongoing.

227(9.1) amended by 1992 technical bill, effective 1993, except for amounts that were required to be remitted before 1993. Before 1993, read "wilfully" in place of "knowingly or under circumstances amounting to gross negligence" (2 places).

**(9.2) Interest on amounts deducted or withheld but not remitted** — Where a person has failed to remit as and when required by this Act or a regulation an amount deducted or withheld as required by this Act or a regulation, the person shall pay to the Receiver General interest on the amount at the prescribed rate computed from the day on which the person was so required to remit the amount to the day of remittance of the amount to the Receiver General.

**Related Provisions**: 221.1 — Application of interest where legislation retroactive; 227(10.1) — Assessment; 227(10.2) — Joint and several liability re contributions to RCA; 248(11) — Compound interest; 252.1 — Where union is employer.

**Regulations**: 4301(a) (prescribed rate of interest).

**Information Circulars**: 92-2: Guidelines for the cancellation and waiver of interest and penalties.

**(9.3) Interest on certain tax not paid** — Where a person fails to pay an amount of tax that, because of section 116, subsection 212(19) or a regulation made under subsection 215(4), the person is required to pay, as and when the person is required to pay it, the person shall pay to the Receiver General interest on the amount at the prescribed rate computed from the day on or before which the amount was required to be paid to the day of payment of the amount to the Receiver General.

**Related Provisions**: 221.1 — Application of interest where legislation retroactive; 227(10.1) — Assessment; 248(11) — Compound interest.

**Notes**: 227(9.3) amended by 1993 technical bill, effective May 29, 1993, to add reference to 212(19).

**Regulations**: 4301 (prescribed rate of interest).

**(9.4) Liability to pay amount not remitted** — A person who has failed to remit as and when required by this Act or a regulation an amount deducted or withheld from a payment to another person as required by this Act or a regulation is liable to pay as tax under this Act on behalf of the other person the amount so deducted or withheld.

**Related Provisions**: 227(10.1) — Assessment; 227(10.2) — Joint and several liability re contributions to RCA; 252.1 — Where union is employer.

**Notes**: See Notes to 227(8.4).

**(9.5) Payment from same establishment** — In applying paragraphs (8)(b) and (9)(b) in respect of an amount required by paragraph 153(1)(a) to be deducted or withheld, each establishment of a person shall be deemed to be a separate person.

**Notes**: 227(9.5) amended by 1992 technical bill, effective 1993, except for amounts that were required to be remitted before 1993. It provides a similar rule by rewriting 227(9).

**Information Circulars**: 92-2: Guidelines for the cancellation and waiver of interest and penalties.

**(10) Assessment** — The Minister may at any time assess any amount payable under

(a) subsection (8), (8.1), (8.2), (8.3) or (8.4) or 224(4) or (4.1) or section 227.1 or 235 by a person,

(b) subsection 237.1(7.4) by a person or partnership,

(c) subsection (10.2) by a person as a consequence of a failure of a non-resident person to deduct or withhold any amount, or

(d) Part XIII by a person resident in Canada,

and, where the Minister sends a notice of assessment to that person or partnership, Divisions I and J of Part I apply with any modifications that the circumstances require.

**Notes**: 227(10) amended by 1995-97 technical bill, effective December 2, 1994. From June 15 to December 1, 1994, read:

(10) The Minister may assess

(a) any person for any amount payable by that person under subsection (8), (8.1), (8.2), (8.3) or (8.4) or 224(4) or (4.1) or section 227.1 or 235,

(a.1) any person for any amount payable under subsection (10.2) by the person as a consequence of a failure by a non-resident person to deduct or withhold any amount, and

(b) any person resident in Canada for any amount payable by that person under Part XIII,

and, where the Minister sends a notice of assessment to that person, Divisions I and J of Part I are applicable with such modifications as the circumstances require.

227(10)(a.1) added by 1993 technical bill, effective June 15, 1994.

227(10)(a) amended by 1991 technical bill, effective December 17, 1991, to add reference to 235.

**(10.01) Part XII.5 [assessment]** — The Minister may at any time assess any amount payable under Part XII.5 by a person resident in Canada and, where the Minister sends a notice of assessment to that person, Divisions I and J of Part I apply with any modifications that the circumstances require.

Notes: 227(10.01) added by 1996 Budget, effective April 25, 1997 (Royal Assent). It implements the same rules for Part XII.5 (special tax in respect of the labour-sponsored funds tax credit) as applies under 227(10) for Part XIII non-resident withholding tax. It was first proposed as an amendment to 227(10)(b) in the draft legislation of November 15, 1995.

**(10.1) Idem** — The Minister may at any time assess

(a) any amount payable under section 116 or subsection (9), (9.2), (9.3) or (9.4) by any person,

(b) any amount payable under subsection (10.2) by any person as a consequence of a failure by a non-resident person to remit any amount, and

(c) any amount payable under Part XII.5 or XIII by any non-resident person,

and, where the Minister sends a notice of assessment to the person, sections 150 to 163, subsections 164(1) and (1.4) to (7), sections 164.1 to 167 and Division J of Part I apply with such modifications as the circumstances require.

Related Provisions: 224(1.2) — Garnishment of payments redirected to secured creditors.

Notes: Reference in 227(10.1)(a) to section 116 added by 1993 technical bill, effective for amounts that become payable in 1991 or later.

227(10.1)(a.1) (now (b)) added by 1993 technical bill, effective June 15, 1994.

227(10.1)(a), (a.1) and (b) replaced with (a), (b) and (c) by 1996 Budget, effective April 25, 1997 (Royal Assent). The substantive amendment was to add reference to Part XII.5. Before that date, read:

(a) any person for any amount payable under section 116 or subsection (9), (9.2), (9.3) or (9.4) by the person,

(a.1) any person for any amount payable under subsection (10.2) by the person as a consequence of a failure by a non-resident person to remit any amount, and

(b) any non-resident person for any amount payable under Part XIII by the person,

**(10.2) Joint and several liability re contributions to RCA** — Where a non-resident person fails to deduct, withhold or remit an amount as required by subsection 153(1) in respect of a contribution under a retirement compensation arrangement that is paid on behalf of the employees or former employees of an employer with whom the non-resident person does not deal at arm's length, the employer is jointly and severally liable with the non-resident person to pay any amount payable under subsection (8), (8.2), (8.3), (9), (9.2) or (9.4) by the non-resident person in respect of the contribution.

Related Provisions: 227(10)(a.1) — Assessment for failure to deduct or withhold; 227(10.1)(c) — Assessment for failure to remit tax.

Notes: 227(10.2) added by 1993 technical bill, effective June 15, 1994.

**(10.3)–(10.9) [Repealed]**

Notes: Former 227(10.2), and (10.3) to (10.8), enacted in 1986 but never proclaimed into force, repealed by 1992 technical bill. 227(10.9), which was added in the R.S.C. 1985 consolidation, provided that those subsections would come into force on proclamation. It was repealed by the redrafted form of the 1992 technical bill (S.C. 1994, c. 7, Sched. VIII, s. 153).

227(10.2) to (10.8) would have created a priority in favour of Revenue Canada, as against the claims of most other creditors, in respect of amounts owing under the Act by a person as unremitted source deductions. The enhanced garnishment in 224(1.2) and (1.3) is now used instead for the collection of unremitted source deductions. See Notes to 224(1.2)).

**(11) Withholding tax** — Provisions of this Act requiring a person to deduct or withhold an amount in respect of taxes from amounts payable to a taxpayer are applicable to Her Majesty in right of Canada or a province.

**(12) Agreement not to deduct void** — Where this Act requires an amount to be deducted or withheld, an agreement by the person on whom that obligation is imposed not to deduct or withhold is void.

**(13) Minister's receipt discharges debtor** — The receipt of the Minister for an amount deducted or withheld by any person as required by or under this Act is a good and sufficient discharge of the liability of any debtor to the debtor's creditor with respect thereto to the extent of the amount referred to in the receipt.

**(14) Application of other Parts** — Parts IV, IV.1, VI and VI.1 do not apply to any corporation for any period throughout which it is exempt from tax because of section 149.

Related Provisions: 181.1(3)(c) — Exemption from Part I.3 tax; 186.1 — Part IV tax — exempt corporations; 219(2) — Part XIV tax — exempt corporations; 227(16) — Part IV tax — municipal or provincial corporation.

Notes: 227(14) amended by 1991 technical bill, effective 1990, to delete reference to Part III. An exempt corporation can thus be liable for Part III tax, e.g. by making an election under 83(2) where the amount of the dividend payable by it exceeds its capital dividend account.

Interpretation Bulletins: IT-269R3: Part IV tax on taxable dividends received by a private corporation or a subject corporation; IT-347R2: Crown corporations.

**(15) Partnership included in "person"** — In this section, a reference to a "person" with respect to any amount deducted or withheld or required to be deducted or withheld is deemed to include a partnership.

Related Provisions: 96 — Partnerships and their members; 212(13.1) — Application of Part XIII tax to a partnership;

227(5.2) — "Person" includes any partnership for purposes of certain provisions.

**Notes**: 227(15) amended by 1996 Budget, effective April 25, 1997 (Royal Assent), so that it applies for all purposes of withholding (including Part XII.5), rather than just Part XIII. Before that date, read:

> (15) In this section a reference to "person" with respect to any amount or any tax deducted or withheld from an amount under Part XIII shall be deemed to include a partnership that is with respect to that amount deemed for the purposes of that Part to be a person resident in Canada or a non-resident person.

**(16) Municipal or provincial corporation excepted** — A corporation that at any time during the taxation year would be a corporation described in paragraph 149(1)(d) but for a provision of an appropriation Act shall be deemed not to be a private corporation for the purposes of Part IV.

### Proposed Amendment — 227(16)

**(16) Municipal or provincial corporation excepted** — A corporation that at any time in a taxation year would be a corporation described in any of paragraphs 149(1)(d) to (d.6) but for a provision of an appropriation Act is deemed not to be a private corporation for the purposes of Part IV with respect to that year.

**Application**: Bill C-43 (First Reading September 20, 2000), subsec. 107(2), will amend subsec. 227(16) to read as above, applicable to taxation years that begin after 1998.

**Technical Notes**: Subsection 227(16) deems municipal and provincial corporations, which are exempt from tax because of paragraph 149(1)(d), not to be private corporations for the purposes of the Part IV tax. This amendment extends this treatment to corporations that are exempt from tax under any of paragraphs 149(1)(d) to (d.6) and is strictly consequential on the addition of paragraphs 149(1)(d.1) to (d.6) made applicable to taxation years and fiscal periods that begin after 1998.

**Interpretation Bulletins [subsec. 227(16)]**: IT-269R3: Part IV tax on taxable dividends received by a private corporation or a subject corporation; IT-347R2: Crown corporations.

**Definitions [s. 227]**: "amount", "assessment" — 248(1); "calendar year" — *Interpretation Act* 37(1)(a); "Canada" — 255; "common-law partnership" — 248(1); "corporation" — 248(1), *Interpretation Act* 35(1); "employee" — 248(1); "employer" — 248(1); "estate" — 104(1), 248(1); "Minister"; "non-resident" — 248(1); "person" — 227(5.2), (15), 248(1); "prescribed" — 248(1); "prescribed rate" — Reg. 4301; "private corporation" — 89(1), 248(1); "property" — 248(1); "province" — *Interpretation Act* 35(1); "public corporation" — 89(1), 248(1); "regulation" — 248(1); "resident in Canada" — 250; "retirement compensation arrangement", "salary or wages" — 248(1); "secured creditor" — 224(1.3); "security interest" — 227(4.2); "specified person" — 227(5.1); "tax payable" — 248(2); "taxation year" — 249; "taxpayer" — 248(1); "trust" — 104(1), 248(1), (3); "writing" — *Interpretation Act* 35(1).

**227.1 (1) Liability of directors for failure to deduct** — Where a corporation has failed to deduct or withhold an amount as required by subsection 135(3) or section 153 or 215, has failed to remit such an amount or has failed to pay an amount of tax for a taxation year as required under Part VII or VIII, the directors of the corporation at the time the corporation was required to deduct, withhold, remit or pay the amount are jointly and severally liable, together with the corporation, to pay that amount and any interest or penalties relating thereto.

**Related Provisions**: 159(2) — Requirement for clearance certificate before distributing property; 236 — Execution of documents by corporate directors; 242 — Directors guilty of offences of corporation.

**Notes**: Directors are liable for unpaid source withholdings such as employee payroll deductions (s. 153), for unremitted non-resident withholding tax (s. 215) and for three special taxes: withholding relating to patronage (135(3)) and the expired share-purchase and scientific research tax credit taxes (Parts VII and VIII). They are also liable for unremitted CPP and EI withholdings; see s. 21.1 of the *Canada Pension Plan* and s. 83 of the *Employment Insurance Act* (s. 54 of the former *Unemployment Insurance Act*). They are also liable for unremitted GST, whether or not collected from purchasers (*Excise Tax Act* s. 323, reproduced in the *Practitioner's Goods and Services Tax, Annotated* and the *Canada GST Service*); and in some provinces, for unremitted sales taxes (e.g., Ontario *Retail Sales Tax Act* s. 43). Directors are not liable for ordinary unpaid tax of a corporation under Part I, or under other Parts (such as Part IV). The main defences directors have against a 227.1 assessment are "due diligence" (227.1(3)) and the two-year limitation after ceasing to be a director (227.1(4)).

In *Wheeliker and Corsano*, [1999] 2 C.T.C. 395 (FCA), leave to appeal to SCC denied (April 20, 2000), File 27319, the Court ruled that *de facto* directors were liable even where they were not technically legal directors.

A person assessed under 227.1 may challenge the underlying assessment of the corporation even if the corporation did not: *Gaucher*, [2001] 1 C.T.C. 125 (FCA).

**Information Circulars**: 89-2R: Directors' liability — section 227.1 of the *Income Tax Act* and section 323 of the *Excise Tax Act*; 98-1R: Collections policies.

**(2) Limitations on liability** — A director is not liable under subsection (1), unless

(a) a certificate for the amount of the corporation's liability referred to in that subsection has been registered in the Federal Court under section 223 and execution for that amount has been returned unsatisfied in whole or in part;

(b) the corporation has commenced liquidation or dissolution proceedings or has been dissolved and a claim for the amount of the corporation's liability referred to in that subsection has been proved within six months after the earlier of the date of commencement of the proceedings and the date of dissolution; or

(c) the corporation has made an assignment or a receiving order has been made against it under the *Bankruptcy and Insolvency Act* and a claim for the amount of the corporation's liability referred to in that subsection has been proved within six months after the date of the assignment or receiving order.

**(3) Idem** — A director is not liable for a failure under subsection (1) where the director exercised the degree of care, diligence and skill to prevent the failure that a reasonably prudent person would have exercised in comparable circumstances.

**Notes**: There is extensive case law on this "due diligence" defence, going both ways. (Much of the case law is under s. 323 of the *Excise Tax Act*, in the *Canada GST Cases*.) Generally the director must have taken active steps to ensure that the corporation would make its source deduction remittances. Attempting to remedy the problem after the corporation ceased to be a director is normally not enough to excuse the director from liability. An outside director will not be held to the same standard as an inside director, but a director's background and experience in business will be given great weight in determining whether the director has met the due-diligence test.

The most authoritative and complete statement of the law on this issue is in *Soper*, [1997] 3 C.T.C. 242 (FCA). See also *Worrell*, [2000] G.S.T.C. 91 (FCA)

**(4) Limitation period** — No action or proceedings to recover any amount payable by a director of a corporation under subsection (1) shall be commenced more than two years after the director last ceased to be a director of that corporation.

**Notes**: To use this defence, the person must legally have ceased to be a director. Merely losing control of the corporation due to its being put into bankruptcy or receivership is insufficient to start the clock running. See *Kalef*, [1996] 2 C.T.C. 1 (FCA); *Drover*, [1998] G.S.T.C. 45 (FCA); and *Worrell*, [2000] G.S.T.C. 91 (FCA).

**(5) Amount recoverable** — Where execution referred to in paragraph (2)(a) has issued, the amount recoverable from a director is the amount remaining unsatisfied after execution.

**(6) Preference** — Where a director pays an amount in respect of a corporation's liability referred to in subsection (1) that is proved in liquidation, dissolution or bankruptcy proceedings, the director is entitled to any preference that Her Majesty in right of Canada would have been entitled to had that amount not been so paid and, where a certificate that relates to that amount has been registered, the director is entitled to an assignment of the certificate to the extent of the director's payment, which assignment the Minister is hereby empowered to make.

**(7) Contribution** — A director who has satisfied a claim under this section is entitled to contribution from the other directors who were liable for the claim.

**Related Provisions [s. 227.1]**: 227(10) — Assessment; 236 — Execution of documents by corporations; 242 — Officers and directors guilty of corporation's offences.

**Definitions [s. 227.1]**: "amount" — 248(1); "corporation" — 248(1), *Interpretation Act* 35(1); "Minister" — 248(1).

**Information Circulars [s. 227.1]**: 89-2R: Director's liability — s. 227.1 of the *Income Tax Act* and subsection 323 of the *Excise Tax Act*.

**228. Applying payments under collection agreements** — Where a payment is made to the Minister on account of tax under this Act, an Act of a province that imposes a tax similar to the tax imposed under this Act, or any two or more such Acts, such part of that payment as is applied by the Minister in accordance with the provisions of a collection agreement entered into under Part III of the *Federal-Provincial Fiscal Arrangements Act* against the tax payable by a taxpayer for a taxation year under this Act discharges the liability of the taxpayer for that tax only to the extent of the part of the payment so applied, notwithstanding that the taxpayer directed that the payment be applied in a manner other than that provided in the collection agreement or made no direction as to its application.

**Related Provisions**: 154 — Tax transfer payments.

**Definitions [s. 228]**: "Minister" — 248(1); "province" — *Interpretation Act* 35(1); "taxation year" — 249; "taxpayer" — 248(1).

**229. Receipt of taxes by banks** — A chartered bank in Canada shall receive for deposit, without any charge for discount or commission, any cheque made payable to the Receiver General in payment of tax, interest or penalty imposed by this Act, whether drawn on the bank receiving the cheque or on any other chartered bank in Canada.

**Notes**: 229, repealed by 1985 Budget but only on proclamation, required chartered banks to accept income tax payments without charge. Para. 159(2)(c) of the *Financial Administration Act* now provides this rule. See 229.1.

**229.1 (1)** Section 229 is repealed.

**(2)** Subsection (1) shall come into force on a day to be fixed by proclamation.

**Notes**: 229.1 added in R.S.C. 1985 5th Supplement consolidation.

## General

**230. (1) Records and books** — Every person carrying on business and every person who is required, by or pursuant to this Act, to pay or collect taxes or other amounts shall keep records and books of account (including an annual inventory kept in prescribed manner) at the person's place of business or residence in Canada or at such other place as may be designated by the Minister, in such form and containing such information as will enable the taxes payable under this Act or the taxes or other amounts that should have been deducted, withheld or collected to be determined.

**Related Provisions**: 150.1(4) — Record of return filed electronically; 230(4.1) — Requirement to keep electronic records; 238(1) — Punishment for failing to comply.

**Notes**: For detailed discussion of s. 230, see Michael Quigley, "Controlling Tax Information: Limits to Record-Keeping and Disclosure Obligations", 47(1) *Canadian Tax Journal* 1-48 (1999).

**Regulations**: 1800 (prescribed manner of keeping inventory).

**Information Circulars**: 77-9R: Books, records and other requirements for taxpayers having foreign affiliates; 78-10R3: Books and records retention/destruction.

**(1.1) [Repealed under former Act]**

**Notes**: 230(1.1), repealed by 1985 Budget (effective for books and records relating to taxation years ending after 1986), required books and records to be kept by the administrator of an indexed security investment plan.

**(2) Idem** — Every registered charity and registered Canadian amateur athletic association shall keep records and books of account at an address in Canada recorded with the Minister or designated by the Minister containing

(a) information in such form as will enable the Minister to determine whether there are any grounds for the revocation of its registration under this Act;

(b) a duplicate of each receipt containing prescribed information for a donation received by it; and

(c) other information in such form as will enable the Minister to verify the donations to it for which a deduction or tax credit is available under this Act.

**Related Provisions**: 149.1(6.4) — Rules apply to registered national arts service organizations; 168(1)(e) — Notice of intention to revoke registration; 238(1) — Punishment for failing to comply.

**Notes**: 230(2) amended by 1993 technical bill, effective December 22, 1992. From 1977 through December 21, 1992, read:

(2) Every registered charity and registered Canadian amateur athletic association shall keep records and books of account (including a duplicate of each receipt containing prescribed information for a donation received by it) at an address in Canada recorded with the Minister or designated by the Minister in such form and containing such information as will enable the donations to it that are deductible under this Act to be verified.

**Regulations**: 216 (information return); 3502 (prescribed information for receipts).

**Information Circulars**: 80-10R: Registered charities: operating a registered charity.

**Forms**: RC4108: Registered charities and the *Income Tax Act* [guide].

**Registered Charities Newsletters**: 5 (Where and why does the Department require your registered charity to keep books and records?).

**(2.1) Idem, lawyers** — For greater certainty, the records and books of account required by subsection (1) to be kept by a person carrying on business as a lawyer (within the meaning assigned by subsection 232(1)) whether by means of a partnership or otherwise, include all accounting records of the lawyer, including supporting vouchers and cheques.

**(3) Minister's requirement to keep records, etc.** — Where a person has failed to keep adequate records and books of account for the purposes of this Act, the Minister may require the person to keep such records and books of account as the Minister may specify and that person shall thereafter keep records and books of account as so required.

**Related Provisions**: 230.1(3) — Application to political party's or candidate's records; 238(1) — Punishment for failing to comply.

**Notes**: This provision applies only where the person has first failed to keep adequate records, meaning sufficient to enable tax to be determined. That determination is a question of fact to be decided by the courts. See *Empire House (London) Ltd.*, [1966] C.T.C. 681, and *Merchant (2000) Ltd.*, [2000] 3 C.T.C. 291 (FCTD).

**(4) Limitation period for keeping records, etc.** — Every person required by this section to keep records and books of account shall retain

(a) the records and books of account referred to in this section in respect of which a period is prescribed, together with every account and voucher necessary to verify the information contained therein, for such period as is prescribed; and

(b) all other records and books of account referred to in this section, together with every account and voucher necessary to verify the information contained therein, until the expiration of six years from the end of the last taxation year to which the records and books of account relate.

**Related Provisions**: 150.1(4) — Record of return filed electronically; 168(1)(e) — Notice of intention to revoke registration; 230(4.1) — Requirement to keep electronic records; 230.1(3) — Application to political party's or candidate's records; 238(1) — Punishment for failing to comply.

**Regulations**: 5800 (required retention periods).

**Information Circulars**: 78-10R3: Books and records retention/destruction; 80-10R: Registered charities — operating a registered charity.

**Forms**: T137: Request for destruction of books and records; T2213: Receipt for borrowed books, records and documents.

**(4.1) Electronic records** — Every person required by this section to keep records who does so electronically shall retain them in an electronically readable format for the retention period referred to in subsection (4).

**Related Provisions**: 230(4.2) — Exemption from requirement; 238(1) — Punishment for failing to comply.

**Notes**: 230(4.1) added by 1995-97 technical bill, effective June 18, 1998.

**(4.2) Exemptions** — The Minister may, on such terms and conditions as are acceptable to the Minister, exempt a person or a class of persons from the requirement in subsection (4.1).

**Notes**: 230(4.2) added by 1995-97 technical bill, effective June 18, 1998.

**(5) Exception** — Where, in respect of any taxation year, a person referred to in subsection (1) has not filed a return with the Minister as and when required by section 150, that person shall retain every record and book of account that is required by this section to be kept and that relates to that taxation year, together with every account and voucher necessary to verify the information contained therein, until the expiration of six years from the day the return for that taxation year is filed.

**Related Provisions**: 238(1) — Punishment for failing to comply.

**(6) Exception where objection or appeal** — Where a person required by this section to keep records and books of account serves a notice of objection or where that person is a party to an appeal to the Tax Court of Canada under this Act, that person shall retain every record, book of account, account and voucher necessary for dealing with the objection or appeal until, in the case of the serving of a notice of objection, the time provided by section 169 to appeal has elapsed or, in the case of an appeal, until the appeal is disposed of and any further appeal in respect thereof is disposed of or the time for filing any such further appeal has expired.

**Notes:** 230(6) amended by 1988 Tax Court bill, effective January 1, 1991, to delete reference to appeals to the Federal Court.

**Information Circulars:** 78-10R3: Books and records retention/destruction.

**(7) Exception where demand by Minister** — Where the Minister is of the opinion that it is necessary for the administration of this Act, the Minister may, by registered letter or by a demand served personally, require any person required by this section to keep records and books of account to retain those records and books of account, together with every account and voucher necessary to verify the information contained therein, for such period as is specified in the letter or demand.

**Related Provisions:** 244(5), (6) — Proof of service by mail or personal service; 248(7)(a) — Mail deemed received on day mailed.

**Information Circulars:** 78-10R3 Books and records retention/destruction.

**(8) Permission for earlier disposal** — A person required by this section to keep records and books of account may dispose of the records and books of account referred to in this section, together with every account and voucher necessary to verify the information contained therein, before the expiration of the period in respect of which those records and books of account are required to be kept if written permission for their disposal is given by the Minister

**Related Provisions:** 168(1)(e) — Notice of intention to revoke registration; 230.1(3) — Application to political party's or candidate's records; 238(1) — Offences.

**Forms:** T137: Request for destruction of books and records.

**Definitions [s. 230]:** "allowable capital loss" — 38(b), 248(1); "amount", "business" — 248(1); "Canada" — 255; "inventory", "Minister", "person", "prescribed" — 248(1); "record" — 150.1(4), 248(1); "registered Canadian amateur athletic association", "registered charity" — 248(1); "taxable capital gain" — 38(a), 248(1); "taxation year" — 249; "taxpayer" — 248(1).

## 230.1 (1) Records and books re political contributions
— Every registered agent of a registered party and the official agent of each candidate at an election of a member or members to serve in the House of Commons of Canada shall keep records and books of account sufficient to enable the amounts contributed that are received by the agent and expenditures that are made by the agent to be verified (including duplicates of all receipts for amounts contributed, containing prescribed information and signed by the agent) at

(a) in the case of a registered agent, the agent's address recorded in the registry maintained by the Chief Electoral Officer pursuant to subsection 33(1) of the *Canada Elections Act*; and

(b) in the case of an official agent, an address in Canada recorded with or designated by the Minister.

**Related Provisions:** 127(3)–(4.2) — Credit for political contributions; 168(1)(e) — Revocation of registration; 238(1) — Punishment for failing to comply.

**Notes:** Opening words of 230.1(1) amended by 1992 technical bill, effective 1992. Before 1992, in place of "containing prescribed information", read "other than any such duplicate receipts filed by him under subsection (2)". Duplicate receipts no longer need be filed under 230.1(2).

**Regulations:** 2000, 2002 (contents of receipts).

**Information Circulars:** 75-2R4: Contributions to a registered political party or to a candidate at a federal election.

**(2) Return of information** — Each person to whom subsection (1) applies shall,

(a) in the case of a registered agent, at such times, not more frequently than annually, as are prescribed by the Minister, and

(b) in the case of an official agent, within the time within which a return is required to be submitted by the agent to a returning officer under section 228 of the *Canada Elections Act*,

file with the Minister a return of information in prescribed form and containing prescribed information.

**Related Provisions:** 168(1)(e) — Revocation of registration; 230.1(4) — Reports to chief electoral officer; 238(1) — Punishment for failing to comply.

**Notes:** 230.1(2) amended by 1992 technical bill, effective 1992. Before 1992, add the following to the closing words:

> together with duplicates of all receipts referred to in that subsection signed by him since the later of the day any previous such information return was filed by him and the coming into force of this section.

**Regulations:** 2001 (time for filing return).

**Information Circulars:** 75-2R4: Contributions to a registered political party or to a candidate at a federal election.

**Forms:** T2092: Contributions to a registered party — information return; T2093: Contributions to a candidate at an election — information return.

**(3) Application of subsecs. 230(3) to (8)** — Subsections 230(3) to (8) apply, with such modifications as the circumstances require, in respect of the records and books of account required by subsection (1) to be kept and in respect of the persons thereby required to keep them.

**Regulations:** 5800(2) (retention period for records and books of account).

**Information Circulars:** 78-10R: Books and records retention/destruction.

**(4), (5) [Repealed]**

**Notes:** 230.1(4) and (5) repealed by 1993 technical bill, effective June 15, 1994. In view of the extensive public reporting requirements imposed on political parties and candidates by the *Canada Elections Act*, the reporting requirements imposed by these subsections were considered redundant. From 1992 through June 14, 1994, read:

> (4) Reports to chief electoral officer — Notwithstanding section 241, the Minister shall, as soon as is reasonably possible after each election and at such other time as is appropriate

having regard to the time of receipt by the Minister of returns of information under subsection (2), forward to the Chief Electoral Officer a report that is based on all such returns of information as have been received by the Minister since the most recent such report and that sets out the total of amounts contributed to each registered party and the total of amounts contributed to each candidate at an election of a member or members to serve in the House of Commons of Canada since the most recent such report, and, on receipt thereof by the Chief Electoral Officer, the report is a public record and may be inspected by any person on request during normal business hours.

(5) No report to enable identification of contributor — No report under subsection (4) shall contain information that would enable any person to identify a person by whom a contribution to a registered party or candidate was made.

230.1(4) amended by 1992 technical bill, effective 1992, to eliminate a reference to duplicate receipts (which are no longer required by 230.1(2)).

**(6) Definitions** — In this section, the terms "candidate", "official agent", "registered agent" and "registered party" have the meanings assigned to them by section 2 of the *Canada Elections Act*.

**(7) Definition of "amount contributed"** — In this section, "amount contributed" by a taxpayer has the meaning assigned by subsection 127(4.1).

**Notes [subsec. 230.1(7)]**: 230.1(7) added in the R.S.C. 1985 (5th Supp.) consolidation, effective December 1, 1991. This rule of application was formerly contained in the opening words of subsec. 127(4.1).

**Notes [s. 230.1]**: For extracts from the *Canada Elections Act*, see Notes to 127(4).

**Definitions [s. 230.1]**: "amount contributed" — 127(4.1), 230.1(7); "candidate" — 230.1(6); "Minister" — 248(1); "official agent" — 230.1(6); "person", "prescribed", "record" — 248(1); "registered agent", "registered party" — 230.1(6).

**231. Definitions** — In sections 231.1 to 231.6,

> **Proposed Amendment — 231 opening words**
>
> **231. Definitions** — In sections 231.1 to 231.7,
>
> **Application**: Bill C-43 (First Reading September 20, 2000), s. 108, will amend the opening words of s. 231 to read as above, in force on Royal Assent.
>
> **Technical Notes**: Section 231 provides definitions for the purposes of sections 231.1 to 231.6, the provisions that set out the rules relating to the powers of the Canada Customs and Revenue Agency to audit and examine taxpayers' books and records.
>
> Section 231 is amended to provide that the section also applies to new section 231.7, which deals with compliance orders. For commentary on the new compliance orders, see the commentary on new section 231.7.

**"authorized person"** means a person authorized by the Minister for the purposes of sections 231.1 to 231.5;

**"document"** includes money, a security and a record;

**Notes**: Definition "document" enacted to replace "documents" by 1995-97 technical bill, effective June 18, 1998. The previous wording has now been incorporated in the definition of "record" in 248(1). From February 13, 1986 to June 17, 1998, read:

> "documents" includes money, securities and any of the following, whether computerized or not: books, records, letters, telegrams, vouchers, invoices, accounts and statements (financial or otherwise);

**"dwelling-house"** means the whole or any part of a building or structure that is kept or occupied as a permanent or temporary residence and includes

(a) a building within the curtilage of a dwelling-house that is connected to it by a doorway or by a covered and enclosed passageway, and

(b) a unit that is designed to be mobile and to be used as a permanent or temporary residence and that is being used as such a residence;

**"judge"** means a judge of a superior court having jurisdiction in the province where the matter arises or a judge of the Federal Court.

**Related Provisions**: 66(12.72) — Application of sections 231 to 231.3.

**Definitions [s. 231]**: "Minister", "person" — 248(1); "province" — *Interpretation Act* 35(1); "record" — 248(1); "superior court" — *Interpretation Act* 35(1).

**231.1 (1) [Audits,] inspections** — An authorized person may, at all reasonable times, for any purpose related to the administration or enforcement of this Act,

(a) inspect, audit or examine the books and records of a taxpayer and any document of the taxpayer or of any other person that relates or may relate to the information that is or should be in the books or records of the taxpayer or to any amount payable by the taxpayer under this Act, and

(b) examine property in an inventory of a taxpayer and any property or process of, or matter relating to, the taxpayer or any other person, an examination of which may assist the authorized person in determining the accuracy of the inventory of the taxpayer or in ascertaining the information that is or should be in the books or records of the taxpayer or any amount payable by the taxpayer under this Act,

and for those purposes the authorized person may

(c) subject to subsection (2), enter into any premises or place where any business is carried on, any property is kept, anything is done in connection with any business or any books or records are or should be kept, and

(d) require the owner or manager of the property or business and any other person on the premises or place to give the authorized person all reasonable assistance and to answer all proper questions relating to the administration or enforcement of this Act and, for that purpose, require the owner or manager to attend at the premises or place with the authorized person.

Part XV — Administration and Enforcement    S. 231.2(1)

**Related Provisions**: 231.7 — Court order for compliance with audit.

**Notes**: The Audit section of the local Tax Services Office is now called Verification and Enforcement (V&E); the senior official in charge of all local audit work is the Assistant Director Verification and Enforcement (ADVE).

231.1 entitles auditors to request and examine documents including computer records (note the extended definition of "record" in 248(1)). 231.2 is a more formal provision whereby a "demand" or "requirement" is issued. For discussion of these sections, see Michael Quigley, "Controlling Tax Information: Limits to Record-Keeping and Disclosure Obligations", 47(1) *Canadian Tax Journal* 1 at 28-48 (1999).

The CCRA's practice on income tax audits is to do a GST "compliance review"; if problems are found, the matter is forwarded to a GST auditor for a full audit. Similarly, an income tax "compliance review" is done during GST audits.

**(2) Prior authorization** — Where any premises or place referred to in paragraph (1)(c) is a dwelling-house, an authorized person may not enter that dwelling-house without the consent of the occupant except under the authority of a warrant under subsection (3).

**(3) Application** — Where, on *ex parte* application by the Minister, a judge is satisfied by information on oath that

(a) there are reasonable grounds to believe that a dwelling-house is a premises or place referred to in paragraph (1)(c),

(b) entry into the dwelling-house is necessary for any purpose relating to the administration or enforcement of this Act, and

(c) entry into the dwelling-house has been, or there are reasonable grounds to believe that entry will be, refused,

the judge may issue a warrant authorizing an authorized person to enter the dwelling-house subject to such conditions as are specified in the warrant but, where the judge is not satisfied that entry into the dwelling-house is necessary for any purpose relating to the administration or enforcement of this Act, the judge may

(d) order the occupant of the dwelling-house to provide to an authorized person reasonable access to any document or property that is or should be kept in the dwelling-house, and

(e) make such other order as is appropriate in the circumstances to carry out the purposes of this Act,

to the extent that access was or may be expected to be refused and that the document or property is or may be expected to be kept in the dwelling-house.

**Notes [subsec. 231.1(3)]**: 231.1(3) amended by 1993 technical bill, effective June 15, 1994, to change "shall" to "may" in two places between paras. (c) and (d). See Notes to 231.3(3).

See Notes to 231.2(1) re limitations on audits.

**Related Provisions [s. 231.1]**: 66(12.72) — Application of sections 231 to 231.3 to audits of flow-through shares; 168(1)(e) — Revocation of registration; 230 — Requirement to keep books and records; 231.2 — Requirements for information; 231.3 — Search warrants; 231.5(2) — No person shall hinder or molest auditor; 232(3.1) — Examination of documents where privilege claimed; 237.1(8) — Application to tax shelter disclosure rules; 238(1) — Punishment for failing to comply; *Interpretation Act* 31(2) — Ancillary powers granted to enable work to be done.

**Definitions [s. 231.1]**: "amount" — 248(1); "authorized person", "documents", "dwelling-house" — 231; "inventory" — 248(1); "judge" — 231; "Minister", "property", "record", "taxpayer" — 248(1).

**Information Circulars [s. 231.1]**: 71-14R3: The tax audit; 94-4: International transfer pricing — advance pricing agreements (APA).

**Forms [s. 231.1]**: RC4024: Enhancing service for large businesses: the audit protocol; real-time audit, concurrent audit, single-window focus [guide]; T3024: Inspection, audit and examination provisions.

**231.2 (1) Requirement to provide documents or information** — Notwithstanding any other provision of this Act, the Minister may, subject to subsection (2), for any purpose related to the administration or enforcement of this Act, including the collection of any amount payable under this Act by any person, by notice served personally or by registered or certified mail, require that any person provide, within such reasonable time as is stipulated in the notice,

(a) any information or additional information, including a return of income or a supplementary return; or

(b) any document.

**Related Provisions**: 66(12.72) — Application re flow-through shares; 168(1)(e) — Revocation of charity's registration for failure to comply; 231.1(1)(b) — Examination of inventory; 231.5(1) — Copy of taxpayer's document may be used in court proceedings; 231.5(2) — No person shall hinder or molest auditor; 231.7 — Court order for compliance with requirement; 232(2) — Solicitor-client privilege defence; 232(3.1) — Examination of documents where privilege claimed; 237.1(8) — Application to tax shelter disclosure; 238(1) — Punishment for failure to comply; 244(5), (6) — Proof of service by mail or personal service; 244(9) — Copy of taxpayer's document may be used in court proceedings; 248(7)(a) — Mail deemed received on day mailed.

**Notes**: The CCRA's normal administrative practice is to allow 30 days for a reply to a request for information or documents under 231.2(1).

A requirement under 231.2(1) can be challenged by bringing action in Federal Court–Trial Division for judicial review of the Minister's decision to issue the requirement. See Edwin Kroft & Dan Lipetz, "How Does a Taxpayer Contest a Requirement for Information Before the Expiry of Time for Compliance?", VIII(2) *Tax Litigation* (Federated Press) 502–503 (2000). Alternatively, one might ignore the requirement and raise the appropriate defences in any prosecution under 238(1) for failure to comply. See also 232(2) re the defence of solicitor-client privilege.

Once the CCRA has started a criminal investigation, it cannot use the audit and requirement powers to gather information for use in the investigation, due to the *Charter of Rights* protection against self-incrimination and the right to remain silent. See *Norway Insulation Ltd.*, [1995] 2 C.T.C. 451 (Ont. Gen. Div.) ; *R. v. Saplys*, [1999] G.S.T.C. 21 (Ont. Gen. Div.). (However, the Supreme Court of Canada has given leave to appeal (27266, January 27, 2000) in *Gorenko*, a decision of the Quebec Court of Appeal on this issue (500-10-001098, Montreal, February 23, 1999.) It *may* also be unable to use the information for assessment purposes: *O'Neill Motors Ltd.*, [1998] 3 C.T.C. 385 (FCA); *Jurchison (Norway Insulation)*, [2000] 1 C.T.C. 2762 (TCC).

## S. 231.2(1) — Income Tax Act

See also Notes to 231.1(1).

Opening words of 231.2(1) amended by 2000 GST bill, effective October 20, 2000, to add "including the collection of any amount payable under this Act by any person".

**Forms:** T375: Requirement to provide information and documents.

**(2) Unnamed persons** — The Minister shall not impose on any person (in this section referred to as a "third party") a requirement under subsection (1) to provide information or any document relating to one or more unnamed persons unless the Minister first obtains the authorization of a judge under subsection (3).

**Notes:** The scope of "fishing expeditions" by Revenue Canada was limited by the Supreme Court of Canada in *James Richardson & Sons Ltd.*, [1984] C.T.C. 345. See Notes to 231.2(3) re the relaxation of the restrictions in 1995.

**(3) Judicial authorization** — On *ex parte* application by the Minister, a judge may, subject to such conditions as the judge considers appropriate, authorize the Minister to impose on a third party a requirement under subsection (1) relating to an unnamed person or more than one unnamed person (in this section referred to as the "group") where the judge is satisfied by information on oath that

(a) the person or group is ascertainable; and

(b) the requirement is made to verify compliance by the person or persons in the group with any duty or obligation under this Act.

(c), (d) [Repealed]

**Related Provisions:** 66(12.72) — Application re flow-through shares; 168(1)(e) — Revocation of charity's registration for failure to comply; 232(2), (3.1) — Solicitor-client privilege defence; 237.1(8) — Application to tax shelter disclosure; 238(1) — Punishment for failure to comply.

**Notes:** 231.2(3)(c) and (d) repealed by 1995 Budget, effective June 20, 1996 (Royal Assent). They provided the following additional conditions:

> (c) it is reasonable to expect, based on any grounds, including information (statistical or otherwise) or past experience relating to the group or any other persons, that the person or any person in the group may have failed or may be likely to fail to provide information that is sought pursuant to the requirement or to otherwise comply with this Act; and
>
> (d) the information or document is not otherwise more readily available.

The change means that the CCRA can now go on judicially-authorized "fishing expeditions" by demanding information from various sources. The Department of Finance Technical Notes explain the change as follows: "Paragraphs 231.2(3)(c) and (d) are repealed in order to simplify those conditions." However, the 1995 Budget papers put it this way:

> These restrictions, which make it difficult for Revenue Canada to obtain timely information in order to verify compliance with the Act, are being eliminated. This proposed measure will improve Revenue Canada's ability to verify compliance with the self-assessment system with respect to transactions where no information reporting is required.

**(4) Service of authorization** — Where an authorization is granted under subsection (3), it shall be served together with the notice referred to in subsection (1).

**(5) Review of authorization** — Where an authorization is granted under subsection (3), a third party on whom a notice is served under subsection (1) may, within 15 days after the service of the notice, apply to the judge who granted the authorization or, where the judge is unable to act, to another judge of the same court for a review of the authorization.

**(6) Powers on review** — On hearing an application under subsection (5), a judge may cancel the authorization previously granted if the judge is not then satisfied that the conditions in paragraphs (3)(a) and (b) have been met and the judge may confirm or vary the authorization if the judge is satisfied that those conditions have been met.

**Notes:** 231.2(6) amended to change "(3)(a) to (d)" to "(3)(a) and (b)" by 1995 Budget, effective June 20, 1996. See Notes to 231.2(3).

**(7) [Repealed under former Act]**

**Notes:** 231.2(7), repealed by 1988 tax reform effective September 13, 1988, allowed the court to make further compliance orders. It was repealed due to the introduction of a general power to make compliance orders in 238(2).

**Definitions [s. 231.2]:** "documents", "judge" — 231; "Minister", "person" — 248(1); "third party" — 231.2(2).

**Information Circulars [s. 231.2]:** 73-10R3: Tax evasion.

**231.3 (1) Search warrant** — A judge may, on *ex parte* application by the Minister, issue a warrant in writing authorizing any person named therein to enter and search any building, receptacle or place for any document or thing that may afford evidence as to the commission of an offence under this Act and to seize the document or thing and, as soon as practicable, bring it before, or make a report in respect of it to, the judge or, where the judge is unable to act, another judge of the same court to be dealt with by the judge in accordance with this section.

**Related Provisions:** See at end of 231.3.

**Notes:** As an alternative to 231.3, a search warrant can also be obtained under s. 487 of the *Criminal Code*, which is now Revenue Canada's standard practice. See *R. v. 2821109 Canada Inc.*, [1995] G.S.T.C. 67 (NBCA).

See also Notes to 231.2(1).

**Information Circulars:** 73-10R3: Tax evasion.

**(2) Evidence in support of application** — An application under subsection (1) shall be supported by information on oath establishing the facts on which the application is based.

**(3) Evidence** — A judge may issue the warrant referred to in subsection (1) where the judge is satisfied that there are reasonable grounds to believe that

(a) an offence under this Act was committed;

(b) a document or thing that may afford evidence of the commission of the offence is likely to be found; and

(c) the building, receptacle or place specified in the application is likely to contain such a document or thing.

**Related Provisions**: See at end of 231.3.

**Notes**: Opening words of 231.3(3) amended by 1993 technical bill, effective June 15, 1994, to change "shall" to "may". This was in response to the Supreme Court of Canada having ruled, in *Baron*, [1993] 1 C.T.C. 111, that 231.3(3) violated s. 8 of the *Canadian Charter of Rights and Freedoms* because it allowed the judge no discretion as to whether to issue a warrant.

**(4) Contents of warrant** — A warrant issued under subsection (1) shall refer to the offence for which it is issued, identify the building, receptacle or place to be searched and the person alleged to have committed the offence and it shall be reasonably specific as to any document or thing to be searched for and seized.

**(5) Seizure of document** — Any person who executes a warrant under subsection (1) may seize, in addition to the document or thing referred to in that subsection, any other document or thing that the person believes on reasonable grounds affords evidence of the commission of an offence under this Act and shall as soon as practicable bring the document or thing before, or make a report in respect thereof to, the judge who issued the warrant or, where the judge is unable to act, another judge of the same court to be dealt with by the judge in accordance with this section.

**Related Provisions**: 231.5(1) — Copy of document seized may be used in court proceedings; 231.5(2) — Compliance; 244(9) — Copy of document seized may be used in court proceedings.

**Information Circulars**: 73-10R3: Tax evasion.

**(6) Retention of things seized** — Subject to subsection (7), where any document or thing seized under subsection (1) or (5) is brought before a judge or a report in respect thereof is made to a judge, the judge shall, unless the Minister waives retention, order that it be retained by the Minister, who shall take reasonable care to ensure that it is preserved until the conclusion of any investigation into the offence in relation to which the document or thing was seized or until it is required to be produced for the purposes of a criminal proceeding.

**(7) Return of things seized** — Where any document or thing seized under subsection (1) or (5) is brought before a judge or a report in respect thereof is made to a judge, the judge may, of the judge's own motion or on summary application by a person with an interest in the document or thing on three clear days notice of application to the Deputy Attorney General of Canada, order that the document or thing be returned to the person from whom it was seized or the person who is otherwise legally entitled thereto if the judge is satisfied that the document or thing

(a) will not be required for an investigation or a criminal proceeding; or

(b) was not seized in accordance with the warrant or this section.

**Related Provisions**: *Interpretation Act* 27(1) — Meaning of "clear days". See additional Related Provisions and Definitions at end of s. 231.3.

**(8) Access and copies** — The person from whom any document or thing is seized pursuant to this section is entitled, at all reasonable times and subject to such reasonable conditions as may be imposed by the Minister, to inspect the document or thing and to obtain one copy of the document at the expense of the Minister.

**Information Circulars [subsec. 231.3(8)]**: 73-10R3: Tax evasion.

**Related Provisions [s. 231.3]**: 66(12.72) — Application of sections 231 to 231.3; 168(1)(e) — Revocation of registration; 232(3) — Seizure of certain documents where privilege claimed; 237.1(8) — Application to tax shelter disclosure rules; 238(1) — Punishment for failing to comply.

**Definitions [s. 231.3]**: "clear days" — *Interpretation Act* 27(1); "documents", "judge" — 231; "Minister", "person" — 248(1); "writing" — *Interpretation Act* 35(1).

**231.4 (1) Inquiry** — The Minister may, for any purpose related to the administration or enforcement of this Act, authorize any person, whether or not the person is an officer of the Canada Customs and Revenue Agency, to make such inquiry as the person may deem necessary with reference to anything relating to the administration or enforcement of this Act.

**Related Provisions**: 231.5(2) — Compliance. See also Related Provisions and Definitions at end of 231.4.

**Notes**: Inquiries under 231.4 were found not to violate the *Charter of Rights* by the Supreme Court of Canada in *Del Zotto*, [1999] 1 C.T.C. 113 (SCC) overturning the majority decision of the Federal Court of Appeal at [1997] 3 C.T.C. 199.

231.4(1) amended by *Canada Customs & Revenue Agency Act*, effective November 1, 1999, to change "Department of National Revenue" to "Canada Customs and Revenue Agency".

**(2) Appointment of hearing officer** — Where the Minister, pursuant to subsection (1), authorizes a person to make an inquiry, the Minister shall forthwith apply to the Tax Court of Canada for an order appointing a hearing officer before whom the inquiry will be held.

**(3) Powers of hearing officer** — For the purposes of an inquiry authorized under subsection (1), a hearing officer appointed under subsection (2) in relation thereto has all the powers conferred on a commissioner by sections 4 and 5 of the *Inquiries Act* and that may be conferred on a commissioner under section 11 thereof.

**Notes**: Sections 4 and 5 of the *Inquiries Act*, referred to in 231.4(3) and (4), provide:

> 4. The commissioners have the power of summoning before them any witnesses, and of requiring them to
>
> (a) give evidence, orally or in writing, and on oath or, if they are persons entitled to affirm in civil matters on solemn affirmation; and
>
> (b) produce such documents and things as the commissioners deem requisite to the full investigation of the matters into which they are appointed to examine.

S. 231.4(3)          Income Tax Act

5. The commissioners have the same power to enforce the attendance of witnesses and to compel them to give evidence as is vested in any court of record in civil cases.

**(4) When powers to be exercised** — A hearing officer appointed under subsection (2) in relation to an inquiry shall exercise the powers conferred on a commissioner by section 4 of the *Inquiries Act* in relation to such persons as the person authorized to make the inquiry considers appropriate for the conduct thereof but the hearing officer shall not exercise the power to punish any person unless, on application by the hearing officer, a judge of a superior or county court certifies that the power may be exercised in the matter disclosed in the application and the applicant has given to the person in respect of whom the applicant proposes to exercise the power 24 hours notice of the hearing of the application or such shorter notice as the judge considers reasonable.

**(5) Rights of witness at inquiry** — Any person who gives evidence in an inquiry authorized under subsection (1) is entitled to be represented by counsel and, on request made by the person to the Minister, to receive a transcript of the evidence given by the person.

**(6) Rights of person whose affairs are investigated** — Any person whose affairs are investigated in the course of an inquiry authorized under subsection (1) is entitled to be present and to be represented by counsel throughout the inquiry unless the hearing officer appointed under subsection (2) in relation to the inquiry, on application by the Minister or a person giving evidence, orders otherwise in relation to the whole or any part of the inquiry on the ground that the presence of the person and the person's counsel, or either of them, would be prejudicial to the effective conduct of the inquiry.

**Related Provisions [s. 231.4]**: 168(1)(e) — Revocation of registration; 238(1) — Punishment for failing to comply.

**Definitions [s. 231.4]**: "Canada Customs and Revenue Agency" — *Canada Customs and Revenue Agency Act* s. 4(1); "judge" — 231; "Minister", "person" — 248(1).

**Information Circulars [s. 231.4]**: 73-10R3: Tax evasion.

**231.5 (1) Copies** — Where any document is seized, inspected, audited, examined or provided under any of sections 231.1 to 231.4, the person by whom it is seized, inspected, audited or examined or to whom it is provided or any officer of the Canada Customs and Revenue Agency may make, or cause to be made, one or more copies thereof and, in the case of an electronic document, make or cause to be made a print-out of the electronic document, and any document purporting to be certified by the Minister or an authorized person to be a copy of the document, or to be a print-out of an electronic document, made pursuant to this section is evidence of the nature and content of the original document and has the same probative force as the original document would have if it were proven in the ordinary way.

**Related Provisions**: 244(9) — Copy of taxpayer's document may be used in court proceedings.

**Notes**: 231.5(1) amended by *Canada Customs & Revenue Agency Act*, effective November 1, 1999, to change "Department of National Revenue" to "Canada Customs and Revenue Agency".

231.5(1) amended by 1995-97 technical bill, effective for copies and print-outs made after June 18, 1998, to add reference to making print-outs of electronic documents, and to add references to "audited".

**(2) Compliance** — No person shall hinder, molest or interfere with any person doing anything that the person is authorized by or pursuant to subsection (1) or sections 231.1 to 231.4 to do or prevent or attempt to prevent any person doing any such thing and, notwithstanding any other Act or law, every person shall, unless the person is unable to do so, do everything the person is required to do by or pursuant to subsection (1) or sections 231.1 to 231.4.

---

**Proposed Amendment — 231.5(2)**

**(2) Compliance** — No person shall physically or otherwise interfere with, hinder or molest any person who does, or prevent any person from doing, anything that the person is authorized by this Act to do, or attempt to interfere with, hinder or molest any person who does, or attempt to prevent any person from doing, any such thing and every person shall, unless the person is unable to do so, do everything the person is required to do by or pursuant to subsection (1) or sections 231.1 to 231.4.

**Notes**: This amendment is much broader than indicated by the budget proposal or the Technical Notes. It applies not only to acts an *official* (of the CCRA) is authorized to do, but to acts of *any person*. For example, preventing another person from claiming an expense by failing to issue a necessary receipt could become an offence (see 238(1)).

**Application**: The December 21, 2000 draft legislation, s. 91, will amend subsec. 231.5(2) to read as above, in force on Royal Assent.

**Technical Notes**: Subsection 231.5(2) makes it an offence to hinder, molest or interfere with an official who is performing certain administrative and enforcement functions. This provision does not apply in the context of an official who is performing a collection duty, or to attempts to hinder.

Subsection 231.5(2) is amended to apply to a person who interferes with, hinders, molests, or prevents (or attempts to prevent) an official from doing what the official is authorised to do by the Act. This amendment applies after the enacting legislation receives Royal Assent.

**Notice of Ways and Means Motion, federal budget, February 28, 2000**: *Hindering a Federal Tax Official*

(43) That the penalty applying under section 238 of the Act to a person who fails to comply with subsection 231.5(2) of the Act be extended to persons who hinder, molest, interfere with or prevent an official in the performance of a collection function, and to persons who attempt to hinder, molest, interfere with or prevent an official in the performance of a collection function or any other duty to which that subsection currently applies.

**Federal budget, supplementary information, February 28, 2000**: *Administration and Enforcement of the Tax Law*

The *Income Tax Act* and the *Excise Tax Act* make it an offence to hinder, molest or interfere with an official who is performing certain administrative or enforcement functions. The applicable provisions do not apply in the context of an official who is performing a collection duty, nor do they apply to attempts to hinder. Increasingly, some individuals have taken exceptional measures in an attempt to hinder, harass or delay CCRA officials in the performance of their duties.

The budget proposes to amend the *Income Tax Act* to extend the penalty applying under subsection 231.5(2) of the Act to persons who hinder, molest or interfere with an official who is performing a collection function, and to persons who attempt to hinder, molest or interfere with an official in the performance of a collection function or any other duty to which that subsection currently applies. Similarly, the budget proposes changes to the *Customs Act* and the relevant provisions of the *Excise Tax Act* to parallel the penalty proposed for purposes of the *Income Tax Act*.

**Related Provisions [subsec. 231.5(2)]**: 168(1)(e) — Revocation of registration; 231.7 — Court order for compliance with audit or demand; 238(1) — Punishment for failing to comply.

**Definitions [s. 231.5]**: "authorized person", "documents" — 231; "Canada Customs and Revenue Agency" — *Canada Customs and Revenue Agency Act* s. 4(1); "Minister", "person" — 248(1).

**Information Circulars [s. 231.5]**: 73-10R3: Tax evasion.

**Forms [s. 231.5]**: T3024: Inspection, audit and examination provisions.

**231.6 (1) Definition of "foreign-based information or document"** — For the purposes of this section, "foreign-based information or document" means any information or document that is available or located outside Canada and that may be relevant to the administration or enforcement of this Act, including the collection of any amount payable under this Act by any person.

**Notes**: 231.6(1) amended by 2000 GST bill, effective October 20, 2000, to add "including the collection of any amount payable under this Act by any person".

**(2) Requirement to provide foreign-based information** — Notwithstanding any other provision of this Act, the Minister may, by notice served personally or by registered or certified mail, require that a person resident in Canada or a non-resident person carrying on business in Canada provide any foreign-based information or document.

**Related Provisions**: 233.1–233.7 — Requirement to file annual information returns with respect to non-resident dealings; 244(5) — Proof of service by mail; 248(7)(a) — Mail deemed received on day mailed.

**Information Circulars**: 77-9R: Books, records and other requirements for taxpayers having foreign affiliates.

**(3) Notice** — The notice referred to in subsection (2) shall set out

(a) a reasonable period of time of not less than 90 days for the production of the information or document;

(b) a description of the information or document being sought; and

(c) the consequences under subsection (8) to the person of the failure to provide the information or documents being sought within the period of time set out in the notice.

**(4) Review of foreign information requirement** — The person on whom a notice of a requirement is served under subsection (2) may, within 90 days after the service of the notice, apply to a judge for a review of the requirement.

**Notes**: See Notes to 165(1) with respect to time limits and weekends.

**(5) Powers on review** — On hearing an application under subsection (4) in respect of a requirement, a judge may

(a) confirm the requirement;

(b) vary the requirement as the judge considers appropriate in the circumstances; or

(c) set aside the requirement if the judge is satisfied that the requirement is unreasonable.

**(6) Idem** — For the purposes of paragraph (5)(c), the requirement to provide the information or document shall not be considered to be unreasonable because the information or document is under the control of or available to a non-resident person that is not controlled by the person served with the notice of the requirement under subsection (2) if that person is related to the non-resident person.

**Related Provisions**: 256(6), (6.1) — Meaning of "controlled".

**(7) Time during consideration not to count** — The period of time between the day on which an application for review of a requirement is made pursuant to subsection (4) and the day on which the review is decided shall not be counted in the computation of

(a) the period of time set out in the notice of the requirement; and

(b) the period of time within which an assessment may be made pursuant to subsection 152(4).

**(8) Consequence of failure** — If a person fails to comply substantially with a notice served under subsection (2) and if the notice is not set aside by a judge pursuant to subsection (5), any court having jurisdiction in a civil proceeding relating to the administration or enforcement of this Act shall, on motion of the Minister, prohibit the introduction by that person of any foreign-based information or document covered by that notice.

**Related Provisions [subsec. 231.6(8)]**: 143.2(13), (14) — Effect of information outside Canada on tax shelter investments.

## S. 231.6 — Income Tax Act

**Definitions [s. 231.6]**: "Canada" — 255; "carrying on business" — 253; "controlled" — 256(6), (6.1); "documents", "judge" — 231; "Minister", "non-resident", "person" — 248(1); "related" — 251(2); "resident in Canada" — 250.

### Proposed Addition — 231.7

**231.7 (1) Compliance order** — On summary application by the Minister five clear days after the service of the notice of application to the person against whom the order is sought, a judge may, notwithstanding subsection 238(2) but subject to section 232 and such conditions as the judge considers appropriate, order that the person provide such access, assistance, information or document sought by the Minister under section 231.1 or 231.2 where the judge is satisfied that

(a) the person was required under section 231.1 or 231.2 to provide the access, assistance, information or document; and

(b) the person did not provide the access, assistance, information or document as required under section 231.1 or 231.2.

**Related Provisions**: 231.5(2) — Compliance with audit or demand required.

**(2) Contempt of court** — Where a person fails or refuses to comply with an order made under subsection (1), a judge may find the person in contempt of court and the person is subject to the processes and the punishments of the court that made the order.

**(3) Appeal** — An order under subsection (1) may be appealed to the court to which appeals from the court making the order normally lie. An appeal does not suspend the execution of the order unless it is so ordered by a judge of the court to which the appeal is made.

**Application**: Bill C-43 (First Reading September 20, 2000), s. 109, will add s. 231.7, in force on Royal Assent.

**Technical Notes**: Sections 237.1 to 237.6 set out the rules relating to the powers of the Canada Customs and Revenue Agency (CCRA) to audit and examine taxpayers' books and records. In particular, section 231.1 authorizes the inspection, audit and examination of books, records and property, and section 231.2 provides that the CCRA may by notice require that a person provide information or documents relating to the administration or enforcement of the Act. Where a person refuses to comply with section 231.1 or 231.2, the person is subject to criminal prosecution under section 238.

New section 231.7 will allow the Minister of National Revenue to instead seek an order requiring a person to provide the access, assistance, information or document sought under section 231.1 or 231.2 by way of summary application in cases where the Minister has requested that access, assistance, information or document and the person did not comply. The judge hearing the application will have, under subsection 231.7(1), the discretion to allow the order, or to attach such conditions to the order as the judge considers appropriate. Subsection 231.7(2) provides that a person who refuses to comply with the judge's order may be found in contempt of court and will be subject to the processes and punishments of the court that made the order. Subsection 231.7(3) provides that an order made under this new provision may also be appealed to the court to which appeals from the court making the order normally lie, but that the execution of an order is not suspended unless it is so ordered by the court to which the appeal is made.

**Definitions [s. 231.7]**: "clear days" — *Interpretation Act* 27(1); "document", "judge" — 231; "Minister", "person" — 248(1).

**232. (1) [Solicitor-client privilege] Definitions** — In this section,

**"custodian"** means a person in whose custody a package is placed pursuant to subsection (3);

**Related Provisions**: 230(2.1) — Books and records.

**Notes**: 232(1)"custodian" was 232(1)(b) before consolidation in R.S.C. 1985 (5th Supp.), effective for taxation years ending after November 1991.

**"judge"** means a judge of a superior court having jurisdiction in the province where the matter arises or a judge of the Federal Court;

**Notes**: 232(1)"judge" was 232(1)(a) before consolidation in R.S.C. 1985 (5th Supp.), effective December 1, 1991.

**"lawyer"** means, in the province of Quebec, an advocate or notary and, in any other province, a barrister or solicitor;

**Related Provisions**: 248(1)"lawyer" — Definition applies to entire Act.

**Notes**: 232(1)"lawyer" was 232(1)(c) before consolidation in R.S.C. 1985 (5th Supp.), effective December 1, 1991.

**"officer"** means a person acting under the authority conferred by or under sections 231.1 to 231.5;

**Notes**: 232(1)"officer" was 232(1)(d) before consolidation in R.S.C. 1985 (5th Supp.), effective December 1, 1991.

**"solicitor-client privilege"** means the right, if any, that a person has in a superior court in the province where the matter arises to refuse to disclose an oral or documentary communication on the ground that the communication is one passing between the person and the person's lawyer in professional confidence, except that for the purposes of this section an accounting record of a lawyer, including any supporting voucher or cheque, shall be deemed not to be such a communication.

**Notes**: 232(1)"solicitor-client privilege" was 232(1)(e) before consolidation in R.S.C. 1985 (5th Supp.), effective December 1, 1991.

**(2) Solicitor-client privilege defence** — Where a lawyer is prosecuted for failure to comply with a requirement under section 231.2 with respect to information or a document, the lawyer shall be acquitted if the lawyer establishes to the satisfaction of the court

(a) that the lawyer, on reasonable grounds, believed that a client of the lawyer had a solicitor-client privilege in respect of the information or document; and

(b) that the lawyer communicated to the Minister, or some person duly authorized to act for the

Minister, the lawyer's refusal to comply with the requirement together with a claim that a named client of the lawyer had a solicitor-client privilege in respect of the information or document.

**Notes**: There is no "accountant-client" privilege in Canada. Unless solicitor-client privilege can be claimed in respect of documents in an accountant's files, they can be seized by the CCRA. See Joel Nitikman, "Accountant's Privilege — Getting Closer to the Holy Grail?", *Tax Litigation* (Federated Press), Vol. VI, No. 3 (1998), pp. 382-384.

Solicitor-client privilege requires that the client have been seeking legal advice and have intended that the communication be in confidence. It belongs to the client and can be waived by the client, not the lawyer; once waived, the privilege is lost. For more detail see William Lawlor, "Extending Privilege to Accountants: Should We Follow the American Lead?", 1998 Canadian Tax Foundation annual conference report, pp. 4:1–4:22.

See also Gloria Geddes, "The Fragile Privilege: Establishing and Safeguarding Solicitor-Client Privilege", 47(4) *Canadian Tax Journal* 799–843 (1999).

**(3) Seizure of certain documents where privilege claimed** — Where, pursuant to section 231.3, an officer is about to seize a document in the possession of a lawyer and the lawyer claims that a named client of the lawyer has a solicitor-client privilege in respect of that document, the officer shall, without inspecting, examining or making copies of the document,

(a) seize the document and place it, together with any other document in respect of which the lawyer at the same time makes the same claim on behalf of the same client, in a package and suitably seal and identify the package; and

(b) place the package in the custody of the sheriff of the district or county in which the seizure was made or, if the officer and the lawyer agree in writing on a person to act as custodian, in the custody of that person.

**Notes**: Although 232(3) refers to documents "in the possession of the lawyer", the CCRA and the Department of Justice acknowledge that the solicitor-client privilege extends to documents in the possession of the client, where the documents are otherwise protected by privilege. See also Notes to 231.3(1).

**(3.1) Examination of certain documents where privilege claimed** — Where, pursuant to section 231.1, an officer is about to inspect or examine a document in the possession of a lawyer or where, pursuant to section 231.2, the Minister has required provision of a document by a lawyer, and the lawyer claims that a named client or former client of the lawyer has a solicitor-client privilege in respect of the document, no officer shall inspect or examine the document and the lawyer shall

(a) place the document, together with any other document in respect of which the lawyer at the same time makes the same claim on behalf of the same client, in a package and suitably seal and identify the package or, if the officer and the lawyer agree, allow the pages of the document to be initialed and numbered or otherwise suitably identified; and

(b) retain it and ensure that it is preserved until it is produced to a judge as required under this section and an order is issued under this section in respect of the document.

**Notes**: Opening words of 232(3.1) amended by 1995-97 technical bill, effective June 18, 1998. From February 13, 1986 to June 17, 1998, read:

(3.1) Where, pursuant to sections 231.1 and 231.2, an officer is about to inspect or examine a document in the possession of a lawyer and the lawyer claims that a named client of the lawyer has a solicitor-client privilege in respect of that document, the officer shall not inspect or examine the document and the lawyer shall

**(4) Application to judge** — Where a document has been seized and placed in custody under subsection (3) or is being retained under subsection (3.1), the client, or the lawyer on behalf of the client, may

(a) within 14 days after the day the document was so placed in custody or commenced to be so retained apply, on three clear days notice of motion to the Deputy Attorney General of Canada, to a judge for an order

(i) fixing a day, not later than 21 days after the date of the order, and place for the determination of the question whether the client has a solicitor-client privilege in respect of the document, and

(ii) requiring the production of the document to the judge at that time and place;

(b) serve a copy of the order on the Deputy Attorney General of Canada and, where applicable, on the custodian within 6 days of the day on which it was made and, within the same time, pay to the custodian the estimated expenses of transporting the document to and from the place of hearing and of safeguarding it; and

(c) if the client or lawyer has proceeded as authorized by paragraph (b), apply at the appointed time and place for an order determining the question.

**Related Provisions**: *Interpretation Act* 27(1), (2) — Calculation of days and clear days.

**(5) Disposition of application** — An application under paragraph (4)(c) shall be heard *in camera*, and on the application

(a) the judge may, if the judge considers it necessary to determine the question, inspect the document and, if the judge does so, the judge shall ensure that it is repackaged and resealed; and

(b) the judge shall decide the matter summarily and,

(i) if the judge is of the opinion that the client has a solicitor-client privilege in respect of the document, shall order the release of the document to the lawyer, and

(ii) if the judge is of the opinion that the client does not have a solicitor-client privilege in respect of the document, shall order

(A) that the custodian deliver the document to the officer or some other person designated by the Commissioner of Customs and Revenue, in the case of a document that was seized and placed in custody under subsection (3), or

(B) that the lawyer make the document available for inspection or examination by the officer or other person designated by the Commissioner of Customs and Revenue, in the case of a document that was retained under subsection (3.1),

and the judge shall, at the same time, deliver concise reasons in which the judge shall identify the document without divulging the details thereof.

**Notes [s. 232(5)]**: 232(5) amended by *Canada Customs & Revenue Agency Act*, effective November 1, 1999, to change "Deputy Minister of National Revenue" to "Commissioner of Customs and Revenue".

**(6) Order to deliver or make available** — Where a document has been seized and placed in custody under subsection (3) or where a document is being retained under subsection (3.1) and a judge, on the application of the Attorney General of Canada, is satisfied that neither the client nor the lawyer has made an application under paragraph (4)(a) or, having made that application, neither the client nor the lawyer has made an application under paragraph (4)(c), the judge shall order

(a) that the custodian deliver the document to the officer or some other person designated by the Commissioner of Customs and Revenue, in the case of a document that was seized and placed in custody under subsection (3); or

(b) that the lawyer make the document available for inspection or examination by the officer or other person designated by the Commissioner of Customs and Revenue, in the case of a document that was retained under subsection (3.1).

**Notes [s. 232(6)]**: 232(6) amended by *Canada Customs & Revenue Agency Act*, effective November 1, 1999, to change "Deputy Minister of National Revenue" to "Commissioner of Customs and Revenue".

**(7) Delivery by custodian** — The custodian shall

(a) deliver the document to the lawyer

(i) in accordance with a consent executed by the officer or by or on behalf of the Deputy Attorney General of Canada or the Commissioner of Customs and Revenue, or

(ii) in accordance with an order of a judge under this section; or

(b) deliver the document to the officer or some other person designated by the Commissioner of Customs and Revenue

(i) in accordance with a consent executed by the lawyer or the client, or

(ii) in accordance with an order of a judge under this section.

**Notes [s. 232(7)]**: 232(7) amended by *Canada Customs & Revenue Agency Act*, effective November 1, 1999, to change "Deputy Minister of National Revenue" to "Commissioner of Customs and Revenue".

**(8) Continuation by another judge** — Where the judge to whom an application has been made under paragraph (4)(a) cannot for any reason act or continue to act in the application under paragraph (4)(c), the application under paragraph (4)(c) may be made to another judge.

**(9) Costs** — No costs may be awarded on the disposition of any application under this section.

**(10) Directions** — Where any question arises as to the course to be followed in connection with anything done or being done under this section, other than subsection (2), (3) or (3.1), and there is no direction in this section with respect thereto, a judge may give such direction with regard thereto as, in the judge's opinion, is most likely to carry out the object of this section of allowing solicitor-client privilege for proper purposes.

**(11) Prohibition** — The custodian shall not deliver a document to any person except in accordance with an order of a judge or a consent under this section or except to any officer or servant of the custodian for the purposes of safeguarding the document.

**(12) Idem** — No officer shall inspect, examine or seize a document in the possession of a lawyer without giving the lawyer a reasonable opportunity of making a claim under this section.

**(13) Authority to make copies** — At any time while a document is in the custody of a custodian under this section, a judge may, on an *ex parte* application of the lawyer, authorize the lawyer to examine or make a copy of the document in the presence of the custodian or the judge by an order that shall contain such provisions as may be necessary to ensure that the document is repackaged and that the package is resealed without alteration or damage.

**(14) Waiver of claim of privilege** — Where a lawyer has, for the purpose of subsection (2), (3) or (3.1), made a claim that a named client of the lawyer has a solicitor-client privilege in respect of information or a document, the lawyer shall at the same time communicate to the Minister or some person duly authorized to act for the Minister the address of the client last known to the lawyer so that the Minister may endeavour to advise the client of the claim of privilege that has been made on the client's behalf and may thereby afford the client an opportunity, if it is practicable within the time limited by this section, of waiving the claim of privilege before the matter is to be decided by a judge or other tribunal.

**(15) Compliance** — No person shall hinder, molest or interfere with any person doing anything that that person is authorized to do by or pursuant to this section or prevent or attempt to prevent any person doing any such thing and, notwithstanding any other Act or law, every person shall, unless the person is unable to do so, do everything the person is required to do by or pursuant to this section.

**Related Provisions**: 238(1) — Punishment for failing to comply.

**Notes [s. 232]**: "Deputy Minister of National Revenue for Taxation" throughout s. 232 changed to "Deputy Minister of National Revenue" by Department of National Revenue Act amending bill, effective May 12, 1994. (See Notes to 220(1).)

**Definitions [s. 232]**: "clear days" — *Interpretation Act* 27(1); "Commissioner of Customs and Revenue" — *Canada Customs and Revenue Agency Act* s. 25; "county" — *Interpretation Act* 35(1); "custodian", "judge", "lawyer" — 232(1); "Minister" — 248(1); "officer" — 232(1); "person" — 248(1); "province" — *Interpretation Act* 35(1); "record" — 248(1); "servant" — 248(1) (under "employment"); "solicitor-client privilege" — 232(1); "superior court", "writing" — *Interpretation Act* 35(1).

**Information Circulars [s. 232]**: 73-10R3: Tax evasion.

**233. (1) Information return** — Every person shall, on written demand from the Minister served personally or otherwise, whether or not the person has filed an information return as required by this Act or the regulations, file with the Minister, within such reasonable time as is stipulated in the demand, the information return if it has not been filed or such information as is designated in the demand.

**Related Provisions**: 150(2) — Demands for returns; 162 — Penalties; 244(5) — Proof of service by mail; 244(6) — Proof of personal service; 248(7)(a) — Mail deemed received on day mailed.

**Notes**: See Notes at end of s. 233.

**(2) Partnerships** — Every partnership shall, on written demand from the Minister served personally or otherwise on any member of the partnership, file with the Minister, within such reasonable time as is stipulated in the demand, an information return required under section 233.3, 233.4 or 233.6.

**Related Provisions**: 150(2) — Demands for returns; 162 — Penalties; 233(3) — Tiers of partnerships; 244(5) — Proof of service by mail; 244(6) — Proof of personal service; 244(20)(b) — Service of documents on partnerships; 248(7)(a) — Mail deemed received on day mailed.

**Notes**: See Notes at end of s. 233.

**(3) Application to members of partnerships** — For the purposes of this subsection and subsection (2), a person who is a member of a partnership that is a member of another partnership is deemed to be a member of the other partnership.

**Notes**: 233 amended by 1996 Budget, effective for returns required to be filed by April 30, 1998 or later. For earlier returns, read:

> 233. Information return — Every person shall, on written demand from the Minister served personally or otherwise, whether or not the person has filed an information return as required by this Act or a regulation, file with the Minister,

within such reasonable time as is stipulated in the demand, such information as is designated therein.

233 amended by 1992 technical bill, effective June 10, 1993, primarily to broaden its requirements to include an information return required by the regulations.

**Definitions [s. 233]**: "Minister" — 248(1); "partnership" — see Notes to 96(1); "person", "regulation" — 248(1).

**Regulations [s. 233]**: 200–233 (information returns).

**Information Circulars [s. 233]**: 77-9R: Books, records and other requirements for taxpayers having foreign affiliates.

**233.1 (1) Definitions** — The definitions in this subsection apply in this section.

**"reportable transaction"** means

(a) in the case of

(i) a reporting person for a taxation year who is not resident in Canada at any time in the year, or

(ii) a reporting partnership for a fiscal period no member of which is resident in Canada in the period,

a transaction or series of transactions that relate in any manner whatever to a business carried on in Canada by the reporting person or partnership in the year or period or a preceding taxation year or period; and

(b) in any other case, a transaction or series of transactions that relate in any manner whatever to a business carried on by a reporting person (other than a business carried on by a reporting person as a member of a partnership) or partnership in a taxation year or fiscal period.

**Notes**: See Notes at end of 233.1.

**"reporting partnership"** for a fiscal period means a partnership

(a) a member of which is resident in Canada in the period; or

(b) that carries on a business in Canada in the period.

**"reporting person"** for a taxation year means a person who, at any time in the year,

(a) is resident in Canada; or

(b) is non-resident and carries on a business (other than a business carried on as a member of a partnership) in Canada.

**"transaction"** includes an arrangement or event.

**Related Provisions [233.1(1)"transaction"]**: 245(1)"transaction" — Parallel definition under general anti-avoidance rule; 247(1) — Parallel definition re transfer pricing.

**(2) Reporting person's information return** — Subject to subsection (4), a reporting person for a taxation year shall, on or before the reporting person's filing-due date for the year, file with the Minister, in respect of each non-resident person with whom the reporting person does not deal at arm's length in the year and each partnership of which

S. 233.1(2)  Income Tax Act

such a non-resident person is a member, an information return for the year in prescribed form containing prescribed information in respect of the reportable transactions in which the reporting person and the non-resident person or the partnership, as the case may be, participated in the year.

**Related Provisions**: 152(4)(b)(iii) — Reassessment period extended by 3 years re non-arm's length transactions with non-residents; 162(7), (10), (10.1) — Penalty for failure to file; 163(2.4)(a) — Penalty of $24,000 for false statement or omission; 233.2–233.7 — Foreign reporting requirements; 247 — Transfer pricing rules; Canada-U.S. Tax Treaty, Art. IX — Adjustments on non-arm's length transactions.

**Notes**: See Notes at end of 233.1.

**Forms**: T106: Information return of non-arm's length transactions with non-residents.

**(3) Reporting partnership's information return** — Subject to subsection (4), a reporting partnership for a fiscal period shall, on or before the day on or before which a return is required by section 229 of the *Income Tax Regulations* to be filed in respect of the period or would be required to be so filed if that section applied to the reporting partnership, file with the Minister, in respect of each non-resident person with whom the reporting partnership, or a member of the reporting partnership, does not deal at arm's length in the period and each partnership of which such a non-resident person is a member, an information return for the period in prescribed form containing prescribed information in respect of the reportable transactions in which the reporting partnership and the non-resident person or the partnership, as the case may be, participated in the period.

**Related Provisions**: 152(4)(b)(iii) — Reassessment period extended by 3 years re non-arm's length transactions with non-residents; 162(7), (10), (10.1) — Penalty for failure to file; 163(2.4)(a) — Penalty of $24,000 for false statement or omission; 233.1(5) — Tiers of partnerships; 233.2–233.7 — Foreign reporting requirements; 247 — Transfer pricing rules; Canada-U.S. Tax Treaty, Art. IX — Adjustments on non-arm's length transactions.

**Notes**: See Notes at end of 233.1.

**(4) *De minimis* exception** — A reporting person or partnership that, but for this subsection, would be required under subsection (2) or (3) to file an information return for a taxation year or fiscal period is not required to file the return unless the total of all amounts, each of which is the total fair market value of the property or services that relate to a reportable transaction in which the reporting person or partnership and any non-resident person with whom the reporting person or partnership, or a member of the reporting partnership, does not deal at arm's length in the year or period, or a partnership of which such a non-resident person is a member, as the case may be, participated in the year or period, exceeds $1,000,000.

**Notes**: See Notes at end of 233.1.

**(5) Deemed member of partnership** — For the purposes of this section, a person who is a member of a partnership that is a member of another partnership is deemed to be a member of the other partnership.

**Notes [subsec. 233.1(5)]**: This rule looks through tiers of partnerships.

**Notes [s. 233.1]**: Revenue Canada issued the following notice on July 23, 1999:

*Information Return of Non-Arm's Length Transactions with Non-Residents*

Form T106, Information Return of Non-Arm's Length Transactions with Non-Residents, has been revised as the result of amendments to section 233.1 of the *Income Tax Act*. These legislative amendments, which received Royal Assent on June 8, 1998, require that persons, including corporations, individuals and trusts, and partnerships, file form T106 effective for taxation years and fiscal periods beginning after 1997. Previously, only corporations were required to file the form T106.

Corporations may file the previous version of the form T106, known as form T106 (96), or the new version, known as form T106 (98), until September 30, 1999. Effective October 1, 1999, corporations will only be able to file the form T106 (98).

Partnerships, trusts and individuals will have until September 30, 1999 to review and prepare for the new reporting requirements under section 233.1 of the *Income Tax Act*. Effective October 1, 1999, partnerships, trusts and individuals with filing due dates after September 30, 1999 will have to file form T106 (98).

For general enquiries or to obtain a copy of T106 (98), contact the Business Enquiries section of your tax services office. For detailed information about completing T106 (98), contact the International Audit Division of your tax services office.

T106 (98) is also available through the Revenue Canada Web site at www.rc.gc.ca.

233.1 replaced by 1995-97 technical bill, effective for taxation years and fiscal periods that begin in 1998 or later. For earlier taxation years ending after September 13, 1988, read:

> 233.1 Information return with respect to certain non-resident persons — Every corporation that, at any time in a taxation year, was resident in Canada or carried on business in Canada shall, in respect of each non-resident person with whom it was not dealing at arm's length at any time in the year, file with the Minister, within 6 months from the end of the year, an annual information return for the year in prescribed form and containing prescribed information in respect of transactions with that person.

**Definitions [s. 233.1]**: "amount" — 248(1); "arm's length" — 251(1); "business" — 248(1); "Canada" — 255; "carry on business in Canada" — 253; "filing-due date" — 248(1); "fiscal period" — 249.1; "Minister", "non-resident" — 248(1); "partnership" — see Notes to 96(1); "person", "prescribed", "property" — 248(1); "reportable transaction", "reporting partnership", "reporting person" — 233.1(1); "resident in Canada" — 250; "taxation year" — 249; "transaction" — 233.1(1).

**Information Circulars [s. 233.1]**: 87-2R: International transfer pricing; 77-9R: Books, records and other requirements for taxpayers having foreign affiliates.

**233.2 (1) Definitions** — The definitions in this subsection apply in this section.

**"exempt trust"** means

(a) a trust that is governed by a foreign retirement arrangement;

(b) a trust that

(i) is resident in a country under the laws of which an income tax is imposed,

(ii) is exempt under the laws referred to in subparagraph (i) from the payment of income tax to the government of that country,

(iii) is established principally in connection with, or the principal purpose of which is to administer or provide benefits under, one or more superannuation, pension or retirement funds or plans or any funds or plans established to provide employee benefits, and

(iv) is either

(A) maintained primarily for the benefit of non-resident individuals, or

(B) governed by an employees profit sharing plan; or

(c) a trust

(i) where the interest of each beneficiary under the trust is described by reference to units, and

(ii) that complies with prescribed conditions.

**Related Provisions**: 94(1)"exempt foreign trust"(n) — Trust in para. (c) excluded from non-resident trust rules; 233.6(2)(a) — No reporting required on distribution from certain exempt trusts.

**Notes**: "Exempt trust"(b)(iv)(B) added by 1995-97 technical bill, retroactive to the introduction of 233.2 (see Notes at end of 233.2).

**Regulations**: Reg. 4801.1 (prescribed conditions for subpara. (c)(ii)).

**"specified beneficiary"** at any time under a trust means

(a) any person beneficially interested in the trust who is not at that time

(i) a mutual fund corporation,

(ii) a non-resident-owned investment corporation,

(iii) a person (other than a trust) all of whose taxable income for the person's taxation year that includes that time is exempt from tax under Part I,

(iv) a trust all of the taxable income of which for its taxation year that includes that time is exempt from tax under Part I,

(v) a mutual fund trust,

(vi) a trust described in any of paragraphs (a) to (e.1) of the definition "trust" in subsection 108(1),

(vii) a registered investment,

(viii) a trust in which all persons beneficially interested are persons described in subparagraphs (i) to (vii),

(ix) a particular person who is beneficially interested in the trust solely because the particular person is beneficially interested in an exempt trust or a trust described in this subparagraph or any of subparagraphs (iv) to (vi), nor

(x) a particular person who is beneficially interested in the trust only because of a right that is subject to a contingency, where at that time the identity of the particular person as a person beneficially interested in the trust is impossible to determine; or

(b) any person described at that time in any of subparagraphs (a)(i) to (x) who is beneficially interested in the trust, where it is reasonable to consider that the person became beneficially interested in the trust as part of a transaction or event or series of transactions or events one of the purposes of which is to limit the reporting in respect of the trust that would, but for this paragraph, be required under subsection (4).

### Proposed Repeal — 233.2(1) "specified beneficiary"

**Application**: The June 22, 2000 draft legislation, subsec. 22(1), will repeal the definition "specified beneficiary" in subsec. 233.2(1), applicable to returns in respect of taxation years that begin after 2000.

**Technical Notes**: Existing section 233.2 of the Act requires certain persons who have made transfers or loans to a "specified foreign trust", or to a non-resident corporation that is a controlled foreign affiliate of such a trust, to file annual information returns with respect to the trust. A "specified foreign trust", as defined in subsection 233.2, includes a trust with a "specified beneficiary" resident in Canada. As defined in subsection 233.2(1), a "specified beneficiary" is generally any beneficiary under the trust with the exception of persons listed in subparagraphs (a)(i) to (x) of the definition. For a return to be required to be filed as a consequence of a transfer or loan, it is necessary to have a "non-arm's length indicator", as set out in subsection 233.2(2), apply in respect of the transfer or loan. One of the cases where a "non-arm's length indicator" applies in respect of a transfer to a trust is where the transferor is a "specified beneficiary" under the trust. Subsection 233.2(3) provides a look-through rule so that where a partnership transfers property, it is considered to have been transferred by members of the partnership.

New section 94 sets out new rules governing the taxation of non-resident trusts. In order to be consistent with the new rules:

- the definitions "specified beneficiary" and "specified foreign trust" in section 233.2 are repealed,
- there is no longer a requirement for a "non-arm's length indicator", so the existing rule in subsection 233.2(2) is repealed,
- except as described below, the definitions and rules of application in section 94 apply because of amended subsection 233.2(2), and
- there is no longer a requirement for an explicit look-through rule for partnerships in section 233.2, given that the rule in paragraph 94(2)(m) applies because of amended subsection 233.2(2). Consequently, subsection 233.2(3) is repealed.

**Related Provisions**: 248(25) — Extended meaning of "beneficially interested".

**"specified foreign trust"** at any time means a trust (other than an exempt trust) that is non-resident at that time where either

(a) there is a specified beneficiary under the trust who at that time

(i) is resident in Canada,

(ii) is a corporation or trust with which a person resident in Canada does not deal at arm's length, or

(iii) is a controlled foreign affiliate of a person resident in Canada; or

(b) at that time the terms or conditions of the trust or any arrangement in respect of the trust

(i) permit persons (other than persons described in any of subparagraphs (a)(i) to (viii) of the definition "specified beneficiary") who are not beneficially interested in the trust at that time to become, because of the exercise of any discretion by any person or partnership, beneficially interested in the trust after that time, or

(ii) allow property to be distributed, directly or indirectly, to another trust that immediately after the receipt of the distribution can reasonably be expected to be a specified foreign trust.

### Proposed Repeal — 233.2(1)"specified foreign trust"

**Application**: The June 22, 2000 draft legislation, subsec. 22(1), will repeal the definition "specified foreign trust" in subsec. 233.2(1), applicable to returns in respect of taxation years that begin after 2000.

**Technical Notes**: See under 233.2(1)"specified beneficiary".

**Related Provisions**: 248(25) — Extended meaning of "beneficially interested".

**Notes**: "Specified foreign trust"(b) opening words and (b)(i) amended by 1995-97 technical bill, effective December 1997. Previously read, since its enactment (see Notes at end of 233.2):

(b) at that time the terms of the trust

(i) permit persons (other than persons described in any of subparagraphs (a)(i) to (viii) of the definition "specified beneficiary") to be added as beneficiaries under the trust after that time who are not beneficially interested in the trust at that time and who may be resident in Canada at the time of being so added, or

**(2) Non-arm's length indicators** — For the purpose of this section,

(a) a non-arm's length indicator applies to a trust at a particular time with respect to a transfer of property made at an earlier time to the trust or a corporation where

(i) immediately after the earlier time the transferor was

(A) a specified beneficiary under the trust,

(B) a person related to a specified beneficiary under the trust,

(C) an uncle, aunt, nephew or niece of a specified beneficiary under the trust, or

(D) a trust or corporation that had, directly or indirectly in any manner whatever, previously acquired the transferred property from a person described in clause (A), (B) or (C),

(ii) the fair market value at the earlier time of the transferred property was greater than the amount, if any, by which

(A) the total fair market value at the earlier time of the consideration, if any, given to the transferor for the transfer of property at the earlier time

exceeds

(B) the portion of the total described in clause (A) that is attributable to the fair market value of an interest as a beneficiary in the trust or a share or debt issued by the corporation,

(iii) the consideration received by the transferor in respect of the transfer included indebtedness on which

(A) interest was not charged in respect of a period that began before the particular time,

(B) interest was charged in respect of a period that began before the particular time at a rate that was less than the lesser of

(I) the prescribed rate that was in effect at the earlier time, and

(II) the rate that would, having regard to all the circumstances, have been agreed on at the earlier time between parties dealing with each other at arm's length,

(C) any interest that was payable at the end of any calendar year that ended at or before the particular time was unpaid on the day that is 180 days after the end of that calendar year, or

(D) the amount of interest that was payable at the end of any calendar year that ended at or before the particular time was paid on or before the day that is 180 days after the end of that calendar year and it is established, by subsequent events or otherwise, that the payment was made as part of a series of loans or other transactions and repayments,

(iv) the property transferred was a share of the capital stock of a corporation or an interest in another trust and a specified beneficiary under the trust is related to the corporation or the other trust or would be so related if paragraph 80(2)(j) applied for the purposes of this subparagraph, or

(v) the transfer was made as part of a series of transactions or events one of the purposes of which was to avoid the application of this paragraph; and

(b) a non-arm's length indicator applies to a trust at a particular time with respect to a loan made at an earlier time where

(i) interest was not charged on the loan in respect of a period that began before the particular time,

(ii) interest was charged on the loan in respect of a period that began before the particular time at a rate that was less than the lesser of

(A) the prescribed rate that was in effect at the earlier time, and

(B) the rate that would, having regard to all the circumstances, have been agreed on at the earlier time between parties dealing with each other at arm's length,

(iii) any interest on the loan that was payable at the end of any calendar year that ended at or before the particular time was unpaid on the day that is 180 days after the end of that calendar year,

(iv) the amount of interest on the loan that was payable at the end of any calendar year that ended at or before the particular time was paid on or before the day that is 180 days after the end of that calendar year and it is established, by subsequent events or otherwise, that the payment was made as part of a series of loans or other transactions and repayments, or

(v) the loan was made as part of a series of transactions or events one of the purposes of which was to avoid the application of this paragraph.

### Proposed Amendment — 233.2(2)

**(2) Rule of application** — Subsections 94(1) and (2) apply for the purposes of this section (other than paragraph (4.1)(b)) and paragraph 233.5(c.1), except that for these purposes the definition "arm's length transfer" in subsection 94(1) shall be read without reference to subparagraph (a)(v) of that definition.

**Application:** The June 22, 2000 draft legislation, subsec. 22(2), will amend subsec. 233.2(2) to read as above, applicable to returns in respect of taxation years that begin after 2000.

**Technical Notes:** See under 233.2(1) "specified beneficiary".

**Related Provisions:** 233.2(3) — Property transferred or lent by partnership; 248(10) — Series of transactions or events; 252(2) — Extended meaning of "uncle", "aunt", "nephew" and "niece".

**Regulations:** Reg. 4301(c) (prescribed rate of interest for 233.2(2)(a)(iii)(B)(I) and 233.2(2)(b)(ii)(A).

**(3) Partnerships** — For the purpose of this section, where property is transferred or lent at any time by a partnership, the property is deemed to have been transferred or lent at that time by each of the members of the partnership.

### Proposed Repeal — 233.2(3)

**Application:** The June 22, 2000 draft legislation, subsec. 22(2), will repeal subsec. (3), applicable to returns in respect of taxation years that begin after 2000.

**Technical Notes:** See under 233.2(1) "specified beneficiary".

**(4) Filing information on specified foreign trusts** — Where

(a) at any time (in this subsection referred to as the "transfer time") before the end of a trust's taxation year (in this subsection referred to as the "trust's year"), property was transferred or lent, either directly or indirectly in any manner whatever, by any person (in this subsection referred to as the "transferor") to

(i) the trust, or

(ii) a corporation that, at the transfer time, would have been a controlled foreign affiliate of the trust if the trust had been resident in Canada,

(b) the trust was a specified foreign trust at any time in the trust's year, and

(c) a non-arm's length indicator applied to the trust at the end of the trust's year in respect of the transfer or loan,

the following rules apply:

(d) where the transferor is resident in Canada at the end of the trust's year, the transferor shall make an information return in respect of the trust's year in prescribed form and file it with the Minister on or before the transferor's filing-due date for the transferor's taxation year that includes the end of the trust's year, and

(e) where

(i) the transferor was, at the transfer time, a corporation that would have been a controlled foreign affiliate of a particular person if the particular person had been resident in Canada, and

(ii) the particular person is resident in Canada at the end of the trust's year,

the particular person shall make an information return in respect of the trust's year in prescribed form and file it with the Minister on or before the filing-due date for the particular person's taxation year that includes the end of the trust's year.

### Proposed Amendment — 233.2(4), (4.1)

**(4) Filing information on foreign trusts** — Where

(a) a contribution has been made by a person to a particular trust (other than an exempt trust or a trust described in any of paragraphs (c) to (i) of the definition "exempt foreign trust" in subsection 94(1)) at any time in a taxation year of the particular trust or in a preceding taxation year,

(b) the person is

(i) resident in Canada at the end of the particular trust's taxation year, and

(ii) not, at the end of the year,

(A) a mutual fund corporation,

(B) a non-resident-owned investment corporation,

(C) a person (other than a trust) all of whose taxable income for the person's taxation year that includes that time is exempt from tax under Part I,

(D) a trust all of the taxable income of which for its taxation year that includes that time is exempt from tax under Part I,

(E) a mutual fund trust,

(F) a trust described in any of paragraphs (a) to (e.1) of the definition "trust" in subsection 108(1),

(G) a registered investment,

(H) a trust in which all persons beneficially interested are persons described in clauses (A) to (G), or

(I) a person who is a contributor to the particular trust only because of being a contributor to a trust described in any of clauses (D) to (H), and

(c) the particular trust is not resident in Canada at the end of its taxation year,

the person shall file an information return in prescribed form, in respect of the particular trust's taxation year, with the Minister on or before the person's filing-due date for the person's taxation year in which the particular trust's taxation year ends.

**Technical Notes**: Under amended subsection 233.2(4), reporting will generally be required for a taxation year whenever a "contribution" has been made by a person resident in Canada to a non-resident trust at or before the end of the year. Because of amended subsection 233.2(2), the expression "contribution" generally carries the same meaning as in new section 94 with most of the same exceptions for "arm's length transfers" contained in the definition of that expression in subsection 94(1). However, the exception contained in subparagraph (a)(v) of that definition (transfers or loans not undertaken to allow for the conferral of benefits on non-arm's length persons) does not give rise to an exception to the obligations for reporting under subsection 233.2(4). It should be noted that amended subsection 233.2(2) also applies for the purpose of new paragraph 233.5(c.1).

New subparagraph 233.2(4)(b)(ii) sets out a list of persons for whom reporting obligations are not imposed. This list is consistent with the list of beneficiaries who are not treated as "specified beneficiaries" under the existing rules in section 233.2.

Amended subsection 233.2(4) of the Act also exempts contributors from filing information returns with regard to trusts described in paragraphs (c) to (i) of the new definition "exempt foreign trust" in subsection 94(1). For more detail in this regard, see the commentary on that definition.

These amendments apply to returns in respect of taxation years that begin after 2000.

**(4.1) Similar arrangements** — Where

(a) property is at any time, directly or indirectly, transferred or loaned by a person to be held

(i) under an arrangement governed by laws that are not laws of Canada or a province, or

(ii) by a non-resident entity (within the meaning assigned by subsection 94.1(1)),

(b) the transfer or loan would not be an arm's length transfer (within the meaning assigned by the definition "arm's length transfer" in subsection 94(1) if that definition were read without reference to the words "in respect of a trust" and to subparagraph (a)(v)),

(c) the transfer or loan is not solely in exchange for property that would be described in paragraphs (a) to (i) of the definition "specified foreign property" in subsection 233.3(1) if that definition were read without reference to paragraphs (j) to (q),

(d) the entity or arrangement is not a trust in respect of which the person would, but for this subsection, be required to file an information return for a taxation year that includes that time, and

(e) the entity or arrangement is not an exempt foreign trust (within the meaning assigned by subsection 94(1)) or an exempt trust,

for the purposes of this section and sections 162, 163 and 233.5, the person's obligations under subsection (4) (except to the extent that they are waived in writing by the Minister) shall be determined as if the transfer were a contribution to which paragraph (4)(a) applied, the entity or arrangement were a trust not resident in Canada throughout the calendar year that includes that time and the taxation year of the entity or arrangement were that calendar year.

**Technical Notes**: New subsection 94(3) of the Act provides that, where a non-resident trust has a resident contributor or resident beneficiary at the end of the trust's taxation year, the trust is generally taxed on its income in Canada for the year as if the trust were resident in Canada. However, subsection 94(3) applies only to arrangements that are considered to be trusts for Canadian income tax purposes. In some cases, there may be doubt as to whether a given arrangement is a trust for Canadian income tax purposes.

New subsection 233.2(4.1), in combination with new subsection 233.2(4), imposes a filing obligation on contributors to certain entities or arrangements in respect of which reporting is not otherwise required. One of the key objectives of subsection 233.2(4.1) is to ensure that claims that section 94 does not apply can be reviewed by the CCRA.

Part XV — Administration and Enforcement                S. 233.3(1)

More specifically, new subsection 233.2(4.1) applies where property has, directly or indirectly, been transferred or loaned by a person to be held

- under an arrangement governed by laws that are not laws of Canada or a province, or
- by a non-resident entity (as defined in subsection 94.1(1)).

The person must, where certain additional conditions are satisfied, file the information return referred to in amended subsection 233.2(4).

New subsection 233.2(4.1) provides that, except as the Minister of National Revenue otherwise permits in writing, the person has obligations under amended subsection 233.2(4) if all of the following conditions are satisfied:

- the transfer or loan would not be an arm's length transfer (within the meaning assigned by the definition "arm's length transfer" in subsection 94(1) if that definition were read without reference to the words "in respect of a trust" and to subparagraph (a)(v) of that definition);
- the transfer or loan is not solely in exchange for property that would be described in paragraphs (a) to (i) of the definition "specified foreign property" in subsection 233.3(1) if that definition were read without reference to paragraphs (j) to (q) of that definition;
- the entity or arrangement is not a trust in respect of which the person would, without reference to subsection 233.2(4.1) and the explicit exemptions for filing returns contained in subsection 233.2(4), be required to file an information return for a taxation year that includes that time; and
- the entity or arrangement is not an exempt foreign trust (as defined in subsection 94(1)) or an exempt trust (as defined in subsection 233.2(1)).

Where the above conditions are satisfied, the person's obligations under subsection 233.2(4) and related provisions are determined as if:

- the transfer were a contribution to which paragraph 233.2(4)(a) applied;
- the entity or arrangement were a trust not resident in Canada throughout the calendar year that includes the time of the transfer or loan; and
- the taxation year of the entity or arrangement were that calendar year.

These amendments apply to returns in respect of taxation years that begin after 2000.

**Application**: The June 22, 2000 draft legislation, subsec. 22(3), will amend subsec. 233.2(4) to read as above, and add subsec. (4.1), applicable to returns in respect of taxation years that begin after 2000.

**Related Provisions**: 162(10), (10.1) — Penalty for failure to file; 163(2.4)(b) — Minimum $24,000 penalty for false statement or omission; 220(2.1) — Waiver of filing requirement; 220(3) — Extension of time to file return; 233.2(2) — Presence of non-arm's length indicators; 233.2(4.1) — Similar arrangements; 233.2(5) — Election to use other person's information return; 233.3(3) — Requirement to file return re foreign property; 233.5 — Due diligence exception; 233.6(2)(b) — No return required on distribution from trusts where return required under 233.2; 233.7 — No requirement to file in first year of immigration; 248(25.1) — Transfer to non-resident bare trust.

**Notes**: 233.2(4)(c) amended by 1995-97 technical bill, effective December 1997, to remove the initial words "unless paragraph (b) of the definition "specified foreign trust" in subsection (1) applies,". See parallel amendment to 233.1(1)"specified foreign trust".

**Forms**: T1141: Information return re transfers or loans to a non-resident trust.

**(5) Joint filing** — Where information returns in respect of a trust's taxation year would, but for this subsection, be required to be filed under subsection (4) by a particular person and another person, and the particular person identifies the other person in an election filed in writing with the Minister, for the purposes of applying this Act to the particular person

(a) the information return filed by the other person shall be treated as if it had been filed by the particular person;

(b) the information required to be provided with the return by the particular person shall be deemed to be the information required to be provided by the other person with the return;

(c) the day on or before which the return is required to be filed by the particular person is deemed to be the later of the day on or before which

(i) the return would, but for this subsection, have been required to have been filed by the particular person, and

(ii) the return is required to have been filed by the other person; and

(d) each act and omission of the other person in respect of the return is deemed to be an act or omission of the particular person.

**Notes [s. 233.2]**: 233.2 added by 1996 Budget, effective for returns in respect of trusts' taxation years that begin after 1995, except that such a return in respect of a taxation year that ends in 1996, 1997 or 1998 must be filed by the later of

(a) April 30, 1998, and

(b) the day on or before which the return is otherwise required to be filed.

See also Notes to 233.7.

**Definitions [s. 233.2]**: "amount" — 248(1); "arm's length" — 251(1); "aunt" — 252(2)(e); "beneficially interested" — 248(25); "calendar year" — Interpretation Act 37(1)(a); "Canada" — 255; "controlled foreign affiliate" — 95(1), 248(1); "corporation" — 248(1), Interpretation Act 35(1); "exempt foreign trust" — 94(1); "exempt trust" — 233.2(1); "employee" — 248(1); "employees profit sharing plan" — 144(1), 248(1); "filing-due date" — 248(1); "foreign retirement arrangement" — 248(1), Reg. 6803; "individual" — 248(1); "mutual fund corporation" — 131(8), (8.1), 248(1); "Minister" — 248(1); "mutual fund trust" — 132(6)–(7), 132.2(1)(q), 248(1); "nephew"; "niece" — 252(2)(g); "non-arm's length indicator" — 233.2(2); "non-resident" — 248(1); "non-resident-owned investment corporation" — 133(8), 248(1); "partnership" — see Notes to 96(1); "person", "prescribed" — 248(1); "prescribed rate" — Reg. 4301; "property" — 248(1); "registered investment" — 204.4(1), 248(1); "related" — 251(2); "resident in Canada" — 250; "series of transactions" — 248(10); "specified beneficiary", "specified foreign trust" — 233.2(1); "taxation year" — 249; "transfer time", "transferor" — 233.2(4)(a); "trust" — 104(1), 248(1), (3); "trust's year" — 233.2(4)(a); "uncle" — 252(2)(e); "writing" — Interpretation Act 35(1).

**233.3 (1) Definitions** — The definitions in this subsection apply in this section.

**"reporting entity"** for a taxation year or fiscal period means a specified Canadian entity for the year or period where, at any time (other than a time when the entity is non-resident) in the year or period, the total of all amounts each of which is the cost amount to the entity of a specified foreign property of the entity exceeds $100,000.

**Related Provisions:** 233.6(2)(c) — No return required on distribution from certain trusts to reporting entity.

**"specified Canadian entity"** for a taxation year or fiscal period means

(a) a taxpayer resident in Canada in the year that is not

(i) a mutual fund corporation,

(ii) a non-resident-owned investment corporation,

(iii) a person (other than a trust) all of whose taxable income for the year is exempt from tax under Part I,

(iv) a trust all of the taxable income of which for the year is exempt from tax under Part I,

(v) a mutual fund trust,

(vi) a trust described in any of paragraphs (a) to (e.1) of the definition "trust" in subsection 108(1),

(vii) a registered investment, nor

(viii) a trust in which all persons beneficially interested are persons described in subparagraphs (i) to (vii); and

(b) a partnership (other than a partnership all the members of which are taxpayers referred to in any of subparagraphs (a)(i) to (viii)) where the total of all amounts, each of which is a share of the partnership's income or loss for the period of a non-resident member, is less than 90% of the income or loss of the partnership for the period, and, where the income and loss of the partnership are nil for the period, the income of the partnership for the period is deemed to be $1,000,000 for the purpose of determining a member's share of the partnership's income for the purpose of this paragraph.

**Related Provisions:** 94(1)(c)(i) [to be repealed], 94(3)(a) [proposed] — Certain trusts deemed resident in Canada; 248(25) — Meaning of "beneficially interested".

**"specified foreign property"** of a person or partnership means any property of the person or the partnership that is

(a) funds or intangible property which are situated, deposited or held outside Canada,

(b) tangible property situated outside Canada,

(c) a share of the capital stock of a non-resident corporation,

(d) an interest in a non-resident trust or a trust that, but for section 94, would be a non-resident trust for the purpose of this section,

### Proposed Amendment — 233.3(1) "specified foreign property" (d)

(d) an interest in a non-resident trust or in a trust that, but for subparagraph 94(3)(a)(ii), would be non-resident,

**Application:** The June 22, 2000 draft legislation, subsec. 23(1), will amend para. (d) of the definition "specified foreign property" in subsec. 233.3(1) to read as above, applicable to interests in a trust held at any time in taxation years of the trust that begin after 2000.

**Technical Notes:** Section 233.3 of the Act provides reporting requirements in respect of foreign property. In general terms, it provides that certain taxpayers resident in Canada and certain partnerships must file an information return with respect to their "specified foreign property" if the total cost amount of such property exceeds $100,000. For this purpose, "specified foreign property" (as defined in subsection 233.3(1)) includes an interest in a non-resident trust or a trust that would be non-resident were it not for section 94. It does not include an interest in a non-resident trust that was not acquired for consideration by the person or partnership.

Paragraph (d) of the definition "specified foreign property" is amended by changing a cross-reference to section 94 to a cross-reference to new subparagraph 94(3)(a)(ii). This amendment is strictly consequential on amendments to section 94. As a consequence, interests in trusts deemed to be resident of Canada because of section 94 are "specified foreign property" unless otherwise expressly excluded.

### Proposed Addition — 233.3(1) "specified foreign property" (d.1)

(d.1) an interest in an insurance policy that is deemed by subsection 94.2(10) to be a participating interest in a non-resident entity,

**Application:** The June 22, 2000 draft legislation, subsec. 23(2), will add para. (d.1) to the definition "specified foreign property" in subsec. 233.3(1), applicable to returns for taxation years that begin after 2001.

**Technical Notes:** Paragraph (d.1) of the definition is introduced so that specified foreign property includes an interest in an insurance policy issued by a non-resident insurer, if the mark-to-market regime in section 94.2 applies in respect of the interest. For further detail in this regard, see the commentary on new subsection 94.2(10).

(e) an interest in a partnership that owns or holds specified foreign property,

(f) an interest in, or right with respect to, an entity that is non-resident,

(g) indebtedness owed by a non-resident person,

(h) an interest in or right, under a contract, in equity or otherwise, either immediately or in the future and either absolutely or contingently, to any property (other than any property owned by a corporation or trust that is not the person) that is specified foreign property, and

(i) property that, under the terms or conditions thereof or any agreement relating thereto, is convertible into, is exchangeable for or confers a right to acquire, property that is specified foreign property,

but does not include

(j) property that is used or held exclusively in the course of carrying on an active business of the person or partnership (determined as if the person or partnership were a corporation resident in Canada),

(k) a share of the capital stock or indebtedness of a non-resident corporation that is a foreign affiliate of the person or partnership for the purpose of section 233.4,

(l) an interest in, or indebtedness of, a non-resident trust that is a foreign affiliate of the person or partnership for the purpose of section 233.4,

### Proposed Repeal — 233.3(1)"specified foreign property"(l)

**Application**: The June 22, 2000 draft legislation, subsec. 23(3), will repeal para. (l) of the definition "specified foreign property" in subsec. 233.3(1), applicable to interests in a trust held at any time in taxation years of the trust that begin after 2000.

**Technical Notes**: Paragraph (l) of the definition is repealed to eliminate a reference to trusts that are treated as foreign affiliates. This reference is no longer necessary in light of new subsection 94(1), under which non-resident trusts are no longer treated as foreign affiliates.

(m) an interest in a non-resident trust that was not acquired for consideration by either the person or partnership or a person related to the person or partnership,

### Proposed Amendment — 233.3(1)"specified foreign property"(m)

(m) an interest in a non-resident trust (or in a trust that, but for subparagraph 94(3)(a)(ii), would be non-resident) that was not acquired for consideration by the person or partnership or by a person related to the person or partnership,

**Application**: The June 22, 2000 draft legislation, subsec. 23(4), will amend para. (m) of the definition "specified foreign property" in subsec. 233.3(1) to read as above, applicable to interests in a trust held at any time in taxation years of the trust that begin after 2000.

**Technical Notes**: Paragraph (m) of the definition is amended so that the exclusion for non-resident trusts that applies with regard to interests not acquired for consideration also applies to trusts that are deemed to be resident in Canada by subsection 94(3). This amendment is made for consistency.

These amendments generally apply to interests in a trust held in taxation years of the trust that begin after 2000. However, new paragraph (d.1) applies in respect of returns required to be filed for taxation years that begin after 2001, in order to be consistent with new subsection 94.2(10).

(n) an interest in a trust described in paragraph (a) or (b) of the definition "exempt trust" in subsection 233.2(1),

(o) an interest in a partnership that is a specified Canadian entity,

(p) personal-use property of the person or partnership, and

(q) an interest in or right to acquire a property that is described in any of paragraphs (j) to (p).

**Related Provisions**: 94.2(10) — Treatment of foreign insurance policies.

**(2) Application to members of partnerships** — For the purpose of this section, a person who is a member of a partnership that is a member of another partnership

(a) is deemed to be a member of the other partnership; and

(b) the person's share of the income or loss of the other partnership is deemed to be equal to the amount of that income or loss to which the person is directly or indirectly entitled.

**Notes**: This rule looks through tiers of partnerships.

**(3) Returns respecting foreign property** — A reporting entity for a taxation year or fiscal period shall file with the Minister for the year or period a return in prescribed form on or before the day that is

(a) where the entity is a partnership, the day on or before which a return is required by section 229 of the *Income Tax Regulations* to be filed in respect of the fiscal period of the partnership or would be required to be so filed if that section applied to the partnership; and

(b) where the entity is not a partnership, the entity's filing-due date for the year.

**Related Provisions**: 94(1)(c)(i) [to be repealed], 94(3)(a) [proposed] — Application to trust deemed resident in Canada; 162(7), (10), (10.1) — Penalty for failure to file; 163(2.4)(c) — Minimum $24,000 penalty for false statement or omission; 220(2.1) — Waiver of filing requirement; 220(3) — Extension of time to file return; 233(2) — Demand for return by partnership; 233.2(4) — Requirement to file return re transfers to foreign trusts; 233.7 — No requirement to file in first year of immigration.

**Notes [subsec. 233.3(3)]**: Form T1135, as revised when it first became mandatory in 1999, uses what is known as "check-the-box" rules, with limited specifics having to be provided. This was in response to political pressure, particularly from residents of British Columbia, who were concerned about the amount of information required by the form.

**Forms**: T1135: Information return relating to foreign property.

**Notes [s. 233.3]**: 233.3 added by 1996 Budget, effective for returns for taxation years and fiscal periods that begin after 1997 (changed from "after 1995" by 1998 Budget bill, s. 91), except that such a return for a taxation year or fiscal period that ended in 1998 must be filed by the later of

(a) April 30, 1999 (changed from "1998" by 1998 Budget bill, s. 91), and

(b) the day by which the return is otherwise required to be filed.

See also Notes to 233.7.

**Definitions [s. 233.3]**: "active business", "amount" — 248(1); "beneficially interested" — 248(25); "Canada" — 255; "corporation" — 248(1), *Interpretation Act* 35(1); "filing-due date", "Minister", "non-resident" — 248(1); "partnership" — see Notes to 96(1); "personal-use property" — 54, 248(1); "property" — 248(1); "registered investment" — 204.4(1), 248(1); "reporting entity" — 233.3(1); "resident in Canada" — 94(1)(c)(i) [to be repealed], 94(3)(a) [proposed], 250; "share" — 248(1); "specified Canadian entity", "specified foreign property" — 233.3(1); "trust" — 104(1), 248(1), (3); "writing" — *Interpretation Act* 35(1).

**233.4 (1) Reporting entity** — For the purpose of this section, "reporting entity" for a taxation year or fiscal period means

(a) a taxpayer resident in Canada (other than a taxpayer all of whose taxable income for the year is exempt from tax under Part I) of which a non-resident corporation is a foreign affiliate at any time in the year;

(b) a taxpayer resident in Canada (other than a taxpayer all of whose taxable income for the year is exempt from tax under Part I) of which a non-resident trust is a foreign affiliate at any time in the year; and

### Proposed Repeal — 233.4(1)(b)

**Application**: The June 22, 2000 draft legislation, subsec. 24(1), will repeal para. 233.4(1)(b), applicable to taxation years and fiscal periods that begin after 2000.

**Technical Notes**: Section 233.4 of the Act provides reporting requirements in respect of foreign affiliates. In general terms, it provides that taxpayers resident in Canada (or certain partnerships) of which a non-resident corporation or non-resident trust is a foreign affiliate must file an information return in respect of the affiliate.

Subsections 233.4(1) and (2) are amended to eliminate references to foreign affiliates that are non-resident trusts. These references are no longer necessary in light of new subsection 94(1), under which non-resident trusts are no longer treated as foreign affiliates.

These amendments apply to taxation years and fiscal periods that begin after 2000.

(c) a partnership

(i) where the total of all amounts, each of which is a share of the partnership's income or loss for the period of a non-resident member, is less than 90% of the income or loss of the partnership for the period, and, where the income and loss of the partnership are nil for the period, the income of the partnership for the period is deemed to be $1,000,000 for the purpose of determining a member's share of the partnership's income for the purpose of this subparagraph, and

(ii) of which a non-resident corporation or trust is a foreign affiliate of which[31] at any time in the fiscal period.

### Proposed Amendment — 233.4(1)(c)(ii)

(ii) of which a non-resident corporation is a foreign affiliate at any time in the fiscal period.

**Application**: The June 22, 2000 draft legislation, subsec. 24(2), will amend subpara. 233.4(1)(c)(ii) to read as above, applicable to taxation years and fiscal periods that begin after 2000.

**Technical Notes**: See under 233.4(1)(b).

**Related Provisions**: 94(1)(c)(i) [to be repealed], 94(3)(a) [proposed] — Certain trusts deemed resident in Canada.

**(2) Rules of application** — For the purpose of this section, in determining whether a non-resident corporation or trust is a foreign affiliate or a controlled foreign affiliate of a taxpayer resident in Canada or of a partnership

### Proposed Amendment — 233.4(2) opening words

**(2) Rules of application** — For the purpose of this section, in determining whether a non-resident corporation is a foreign affiliate or a controlled foreign affiliate of a taxpayer resident in Canada or of a partnership

**Application**: The June 22, 2000 draft legislation, subsec. 24(3), will amend the opening words of subsec. 233.4(2) to read as above, applicable to taxation years and fiscal periods that begin after 2000.

**Technical Notes**: See under 233.4(1)(b).

(a) paragraph (b) of the definition "equity percentage" in subsection 95(4) shall be read as if the reference to "any corporation" were a reference to "any corporation other than a corporation resident in Canada";

(b) the definitions "direct equity percentage" and "equity percentage" in subsection 95(4) shall be read as if a partnership were a person; and

(c) the definitions "controlled foreign affiliate" and "foreign affiliate" in subsection 95(1) shall be read as if a partnership were a taxpayer resident in Canada.

**Related Provisions**: 94(1)(d) — Trust deemed to be controlled foreign affiliate.

**(3) Application to members of partnerships** — For the purpose of this section, a person who is a member of a partnership that is a member of another partnership

(a) is deemed to be a member of the other partnership; and

(b) the person's share of the income or loss of the other partnership is deemed to be equal to the amount of that income or loss to which the person is directly or indirectly entitled.

**Related Provisions**: 162(7), (10), (10.1) — Penalty for failure to file.

**Notes**: This rule looks through tiers of partnerships.

**(4) Returns respecting foreign affiliates** — A reporting entity for a taxation year or fiscal period shall file with the Minister for the year or period a return in prescribed form in respect of each foreign affiliate of the entity in the year or period within 15 months after the end of the year or period.

**Related Provisions**: 162(10), (10.1) — Penalty for failure to file; 163(2.4)(d) — Minimum $24,000 penalty for false statement or

---

[31] *Sic*. Will be fixed by Proposed Amendment.

omission; 220(2.1) — Waiver of filing requirement; 220(3) — Extension of time to file return; 233(2) — Demand for return by partnership; 233.6(2)(d) — No return required on distribution from trust where return required under 233.4; 233.7 — No requirement to file in first year of immigration.

**Forms**: T1134: Information return relating to foreign affiliates; T1134-A: Information return re foreign affiliates that are not controlled foreign affiliates; T1134-B: Information return re controlled foreign affiliates.

**Notes [s. 233.4]**: 233.4 added by 1996 Budget, effective for returns for taxation years and fiscal periods that begin after 1995, except that such a return for a taxation year or fiscal period that ends in 1996, 1997 or 1998 must be filed by the later of

(a) June 30, 1998, and

(b) the day on or before which the return is otherwise required to be filed.

See also Notes to 233.7.

**Definitions [s. 233.4]**: "amount" — 248(1); "Canada" — 255; "controlled foreign affiliate" — 95(1), 233.4(2), 248(1); "corporation" — 94(1)(d), 248(1), *Interpretation Act* 35(1); "filing-due date" — 248(1); "fiscal period" — 249.1; "foreign affiliate" — 95(1), 233.4(2), 248(1); "non-resident" — 248(1); "partnership" — see Notes to 96(1); "person" — 248(1); "reporting entity" — 233.4(1); "resident in Canada" — 94(1)(c)(i) [to be repealed], 94(3)(a) [proposed], 250; "taxation year" — 249; "trust" — 104(1), 248(1), (3).

**233.5 Due diligence exception** — The information required in a return filed under section 233.2 or 233.4 does not include information that is not available, on the day on which the return is filed, to the person or partnership required to file the return where

(a) there is a reasonable disclosure in the return of the unavailability of the information;

(b) before that day, the person or partnership exercised due diligence in attempting to obtain the information;

(c) if

  (i) the return is required to be filed under section 233.2, or

  (ii) the return is required to be filed under section 233.4 by a person or partnership in respect of a corporation that is a controlled foreign affiliate, for the purpose of that section, of the person or partnership,

it was reasonable to expect, at the time of each transaction, if any, entered into by the person or partnership after March 5, 1996 that gives rise to the requirement to file the return or that affects the information to be reported in the return, that sufficient information would be available to the person or partnership to comply with that section; and

**Proposed Amendment — 233.5(c), (c.1), (c.2)**

(c) if the return is required to be filed under section 233.2 in respect of a trust, at the time of each transaction, if any, entered into by the person or partnership after March 5, 1996 and before June 23, 2000 that gave rise to the requirement to file a return for a taxation year of the trust that began before 2001 or that affects the information to be reported in the return, it was reasonable to expect that sufficient information would be available to the person or partnership to comply with section 233.2 in respect of each taxation year of the trust that began before 2001;

(c.1) if the return is required to be filed under section 233.2, at the time of each contribution (determined with reference to subsection 233.2(2)) made by the person or partnership after June 22, 2000 that gives rise to the requirement to file the return or that affects the information to be reported in the return, it was reasonable to expect that sufficient information would be available to the person or partnership to comply with section 233.2;

(c.2) if the return is required to be filed under section 233.4 by a person or partnership in respect of a corporation that is a controlled foreign affiliate, for the purpose of that section, of the person or partnership, at the time of each transaction, if any, entered into by the person or partnership after March 5, 1996 that gives rise to the requirement to file the return or that affects the information to be reported in the return, it was reasonable to expect that sufficient information would be available to the person or partnership to comply with section 233.4; and

**Application**: The June 22, 2000 draft legislation, s. 25, will amend para. 233.5(c) to read as above, and add paras. (c.1) and (c.2), applicable to returns required to be filed for taxation years that begin after 2000.

**Technical Notes**: Section 233.5 of the Act provides that, where specified conditions set out in paragraphs 233.5 (a) to (d) are met, information required in a return filed under section 233.2 or 233.4 does not include information that is not available to the person or partnership required to file the return. In the case of a return required to be filed by a person or partnership under section 233.2, paragraph 233.5(c) provides that it must be reasonable for the person or partnership to expect, at the time of each transaction entered into by the person or partnership after March 5, 1996 that either gives rise to the requirement to file the return or that affects the information to be reported in the return, that sufficient information would be available to the person or partnership to comply with section 233.2.

Paragraph 233.5(c) is amended so that it only applies in connection with transactions entered into before June 23, 2000. In connection with trust returns required to be filed for trust taxation years that begin after 2000, it must be reasonable for the person or partnership to expect that sufficient information would have been available to the person or partnership to comply with section 233.2 if the proposed amendments to section 94 were not taken into account.

Paragraph 223.5(c) is also amended so that it does not apply to returns required to be filed under section 233.4. It is replaced in this respect by new paragraph 233.5(c.2), without any change in the specified conditions for such returns.

1743

Paragraph 233.5(c.1) is introduced in connection with returns required to be filed under section 233.2 by a person or partnership for a taxation year of the trust that begins after 2000. Where "contributions" (determined with reference to subsection 233.2(2), referred to in the commentary above) are made after June 22, 2000, relief under section 233.5 is available only if it was reasonable for the person or partnership to expect, at the time of each such contribution that either gives rise to the requirement to file the return or that affects the information to be reported in the return, that sufficient information would be available to the person or partnership to comply with section 233.2.

(d) if the information subsequently becomes available to the person or partnership, it is filed with the Minister not more than 90 days after it becomes so available.

**Notes**: 233.5 added by 1996 Budget, effective for returns required to be filed by April 30, 1998 or later.

**Definitions [s. 233.5]**: "corporation" — 248(1), *Interpretation Act* 35(1); "controlled foreign affiliate" — 95(1), 248(1); "Minister" — 248(1); "partnership" — see Notes to 96(1); "person" — 248(1).

**233.6 (1) Returns respecting distributions from non-resident trusts** — Where a specified Canadian entity (as defined by subsection 233.3(1)) for a taxation year or fiscal period receives a distribution of property from, or is indebted to, a non-resident trust (other than a trust that was an excluded trust in respect of the year or period of the entity or an estate that arose on and as a consequence of the death of an individual) in the year or period and the entity is beneficially interested in the trust at any time in the year or period, the entity shall file with the Minister for the year or period a return in prescribed form on or before the day that is

(a) where the entity is a partnership, the day on or before which a return is required by section 229 of the *Income Tax Regulations* to be filed in respect of the fiscal period of the partnership or would be required to be so filed if that section applied to the partnership; and

(b) where the entity is not a partnership, the entity's filing-due date for the year.

**Related Provisions**: 162(7) — Penalty for failure to file; 163(2.4)(e) — Minimum $2,500 penalty for false statement or omission; 220(2.1) — Waiver of filing requirement; 220(3) — Extension of time to file return; 233.5(2) — Meaning of "excluded trust"; 233.7 — No requirement to file in first year of immigration; 248(25) — Extended meaning of "beneficially interested".

**Forms**: T1142: Information return re distributions from and indebtedness to a non-resident trust.

**(2) Excluded trust defined** — For the purpose of subsection (1), an excluded trust in respect of the taxation year or fiscal period of an entity means

(a) a trust described in paragraph (a) or (b) of the definition "exempt trust" in subsection 233.2(1) throughout the portion of the year or period during which the trust was extant;

(b) a trust in respect of which the entity is required by section 233.2 to file a return in respect of each taxation year of the trust that ends in the entity's year;

(c) a trust an interest in which is at any time in the year or period specified foreign property (as defined by subsection 233.3(1)) of the entity, where the entity is a reporting entity (as defined by subsection 233.3(1)) for the year or period; and

(d) a trust in respect of which the entity is required by section 233.4 to file a return for the year or period.

**Related Provisions [subsec. 233.6(2)]**: 233(1) — Demand for return by partnership.

**Notes [s. 233.6]**: 233.6 added by 1996 Budget, effective for returns for taxation years and fiscal periods that begin after 1995, except that (as amended by 1998 Budget bill, s. 91):

(a) such a return for a taxation year or fiscal period that ended in 1996, 1997 or 1998 must be filed by the later of

(i) April 30, 1999, and

(ii) the day by which the return is otherwise required to be filed;

(b) for taxation years and fiscal periods that began before 1998, ignore 233.6(2)(c); and

(c) for returns for taxation years and fiscal periods that began after 1995 and before 1998, "specified Canadian entity" in 233.6(1) has the meaning that it would under 233.3(1) if 233.3(1) applied for those returns.

See also Notes to 233.7.

**Definitions [s. 233.6]**: "beneficially interested" — 248(25); "consequence of the death" — 248(8).

**233.7 Exception for first-year residents** — Notwithstanding sections 233.2, 233.3, 233.4 and 233.6, a person who, but for this section, would be required under any of those sections to file an information return for a taxation year, is not required to file the return if the person is an individual (other than a trust) who first became resident in Canada in the year.

**Notes**: 233.7 added by 1996 Budget, effective for returns required to be filed by April 30, 1998 or later (i.e., all returns under 233.2–233.6).

For a detailed review of the rules in proposed 233.2–233.5 (now 233.2–233.7), see Joel Nitikman, "The New Foreign Property Reporting Rules", 44(2) *Canadian Tax Journal* 425–450 (1996).

**Definitions [s. 233.7]**: "individual", "person" — 248(1); "resident in Canada" — 250; "taxation year" — 249; "trust" — 104(1), 248(1), (3).

**234. (1) Ownership certificates** — Before a bearer coupon or warrant representing either interest or dividends payable by any debtor or cheque representing dividends or interest payable by a non-resident debtor is negotiated by or on behalf of a resident of Canada, there shall be completed by or on behalf of the resident an ownership certificate in prescribed form.

**Related Provisions**: 162(4) — Failure to complete ownership certificate.

**Forms**: NR601: Non-resident ownership certificate — withholding tax; NR602: Non-resident ownership certificate — no withholding tax; T600: Ownership certificate; T600B: Ownership certificate.

**(2) Idem** — An ownership certificate completed pursuant to subsection (1) shall be delivered in such manner, at such time and at such place as may be prescribed.

**Regulations**: 207 (prescribed time).

**Forms**: NR601: Non-resident ownership certificate — withholding tax; NR602: Non-resident ownership certificate — no withholding tax.

**(3) Idem** — The operation of this section may be extended by regulation to bearer coupons or warrants negotiated by or on behalf of non-resident persons.

**(4)–(6)** [Repealed under former Act]

**Notes**: 234(4), repealed by 1988 tax reform, provided a fine for failure to deliver an ownership certificate. This penalty is now provided in 162(4)(b).

234(5) and (6), repealed by 1980 Budget, imposed a requirement to withhold 25% of amounts paid on bearer bonds and warrants (such as Canada Savings Bonds) where the ownership certificate did not disclose a Social Insurance Number.

**Definitions [s. 234]**: "amount", "dividend", "individual", "non-resident", "person", "prescribed", "regulation" — 248(1); "trust" — 104(1), 248(1), (3).

**234.1** [Repealed under former Act]

**Notes**: 234.1, repealed in 1983, dealt with fuel certificates required on the purchase of aviation turbine fuel.

**235. Penalty for failing to file corporate returns [large corporations]** — Every corporation that fails to file a return for a taxation year as and when required by section 150, 181.6 or 190.2 is liable, in addition to any penalty otherwise provided, to a penalty for each such failure equal to the amount determined by the formula

$$.0025 \, A \times B$$

where

A is the total of the taxes that would be payable under Parts I.3 and VI by the corporation for the year if this Act were read without reference to subsections 181.1(4) and 190.1(3); and

B is the number of complete months, not exceeding 40, from the later of

(a) the day on or before which the return was required to be filed, and

(b) December 17, 1991,

to the day on which the return is filed.

**Related Provisions**: 18(1)(t) — No deduction for penalties; 161(11) — Interest on unpaid penalties; 220(3.1) — Waiver of penalty by CCRA; 227(10)(a) — Assessment.

**Notes**: 235 imposes a penalty on large corporations that fail to file their returns on time, even where no tax remained unpaid (see 162(1)). See Notes to 238(1).

Description of "A" amended by 1992 technical bill, effective for 1991 and later taxation years, due to the introduction of 181.1(4) and 190.1(3) (see Notes to 125.2(1)).

235 added by 1991 technical bill (based on January 3, 1991 press release), in force December 17, 1991.

Former 235, repealed by 1988 tax reform, provided a penalty for failure to file certain information returns. That penalty is now found in 162(7).

**Definitions [s. 235]**: "amount" — 248(1); "corporation" — 248(1), *Interpretation Act* 35(1); "taxation year" — 249.

**Information Circulars**: 00-1: Voluntary disclosures program.

**236. Execution of documents by corporations** — A return, certificate or other document made by a corporation pursuant to this Act or a regulation shall be signed on its behalf by the President, Secretary or Treasurer of the corporation or by any other officer or person thereunto duly authorized by the Board of Directors or other governing body of the corporation.

**Related Provisions**: 227.1 — Liability of directors; 242 — officers and directors of corporation guilty of corporate offences.

**Definitions [s. 236]**: "corporation" — 248(1), *Interpretation Act* 35(1); "officer", "person", "regulation" — 248(1).

**237. (1) Social Insurance Number** — Every individual (other than a trust) who was resident or employed in Canada at any time in a taxation year and who files a return of income under Part I for the year, or in respect of whom an information return is to be made by a person pursuant to a regulation made under paragraph 221(1)(d), shall,

(a) on or before the first day of February of the year immediately following the year for which the return of income is filed, or

(b) within 15 days after the individual is requested by the person to provide his[32] Social Insurance Number,

apply to the Minister of Human Resources Development in prescribed form and manner for the assignment to the individual of a Social Insurance Number unless the individual has previously been assigned, or made application to be assigned, a Social Insurance Number.

**Related Provisions**: 162(6) — Penalty for failure to provide Social Insurance Number; 221(1)(d.1) — Regulations may require disclosure of Social Insurance Number; 237(1.1), (2) — Obligations re Social Insurance Number; 239(2.3) — Offence re Social Insurance Number.

**Notes**: Closing words of 237(1) amended by 1995-97 technical bill, effective June 18, 1998, to remove the final words "and shall provide that number in any return filed under this Act or, at the request of any person required to make an information return pursuant to this Act or the regulations requiring the individual's Social Insurance Number, to that person". This requirement is now provided under 237(1.1).

"National Health and Welfare" changed to "Human Resources Development" by S.C. 1996, c. 11, effective July 12, 1996.

---

[32]*Sic.* Should be "the individual's".

**S. 237(1)**  Income Tax Act

**Regulations**: 3800 (how Social Insurance Number to be applied for).

**Information Circulars**: 82-2R2: SIN legislation that relates to the preparation of information slips.

**Forms**: T600: Ownership certificate.

**(1.1) Production of number** — Every person and partnership shall provide

(a) in the case of an individual (other than a trust), the individual's Social Insurance Number, and

(b) in any other case, the person's or partnership's business number

in any return filed under this Act or, at the request of any person required to make an information return pursuant to this Act or the regulations requiring either number, to that person.

**Notes**: 237(1.1) added by 1995-97 technical bill, effective June 18, 1998. This requirement (but only in respect of a SIN) was formerly in the closing words of 237(1).

**(2) Number required in information returns** — For the purposes of this Act and the regulations, a person required to make an information return requiring a Social Insurance Number or a business number of a person or partnership

(a) shall make a reasonable effort to obtain the number from the person or partnership; and

(b) shall not knowingly use, communicate or allow to be communicated, otherwise than as required or authorized under this Act or a regulation, the number without the written consent of the person or partnership.

**Related Provisions**: 162(6) — Failure to provide Social Insurance Number; 237(3) — Communication to related person allowed; 237(4) — Communication allowed to agent during insurance demutualization; 239(2.3) — Offence re Social Insurance Number or business number.

**Notes**: 237(2)(b) amended by 1999 Budget to add "or authorized", effective June 29, 2000.

237(2) amended by 1995-97 technical bill, effective June 18, 1998, to add references to a business number and to a partnership.

**Information Circulars**: 82-2R2: SIN legislation that relates to the preparation of information slips.

**(3) Authority to communicate number** — A particular person may communicate, or allow to be communicated, a Social Insurance Number or business number to another person related to the particular person where the other person is required, by this Act or the Regulations, to make an information return that requires the Social Insurance Number or business number.

**Notes**: 237(3) added by 1999 Budget, effective June 29, 2000.

**(4) Authority to communicate number [for demutualization]** — An insurance corporation may communicate, or allow to be communicated, to another person the Social Insurance Number or business number of a particular person or partnership where

(a) the other person became the holder of a share of the capital stock of the insurance corporation, or of a holding corporation (in this subsection having the meaning assigned by subsection 139.1(1)) in respect of the insurance corporation, on the share's issuance in connection with the demutualization (as defined by subsection 139.1(1)) of the insurance corporation;

(b) the other person became the holder of the share in the other person's capacity as nominee or agent for the particular person or partnership pursuant to an arrangement established by the insurance corporation or a holding corporation in respect of the insurance corporation; and

(c) the other person is required, by this Act or the Regulations, to make an information return, in respect of the disposition of the share or income from the share, that requires the Social Insurance Number or business number.

**Notes**: 237(4) added by 1999 Budget, effective June 29, 2000.

**Definitions [s. 237]**: "business number" — 248(1); "Canada" — 255; "demutualization" — 139.1(1); "employed" — 248(1); "holding corporation" — 139.1(1); "individual" — 248(1); "partnership" — see Notes to 96(1); "person", "prescribed", "regulation" — 248(1); "related" — 251(1)–(6); "taxation year" — 249; "trust" — 104(1), 248(1), (3); "written" — *Interpretation Act* 35(1)"writing".

**237.1 (1) Definitions** — In this section,

**"person"** includes a partnership;

**Notes**: Definition "person" added by 1995-97 technical bill, effective December 1994.

**"promoter"** in respect of a tax shelter means a person who in the course of a business

(a) sells or issues, or promotes the sale, issuance or acquisition of, the tax shelter,

(b) acts as an agent or adviser in respect of the sale or issuance, or the promotion of the sale, issuance or acquisition, of the tax shelter, or

(c) accepts, whether as a principal or agent, consideration in respect of the tax shelter,

and more than one person may be a tax shelter promoter in respect of the same tax shelter;

**Related Provisions**: 163.2 — Penalty for false statement by tax shelter promoter.

**Notes**: Definition "promoter" amended by 1995-97 technical bill, effective December 2, 1994, to add para. (c), and to change "an interest in the tax shelter" to "the tax shelter" in paras. (a) and (b).

**"tax shelter"** means any property (including, for greater certainty, any right to income) in respect of which it can reasonably be considered, having regard to statements or representations made or proposed to be made in connection with the property, that, if a person were to acquire an interest in the property, at the end of a particular taxation year that ends within

4 years after the day on which the interest is acquired,

(a) the total of all amounts each of which is

(i) an amount, or a loss in the case of a partnership interest, represented to be deductible in computing income in respect of the interest in the property (including, where the property is a right to income, an amount or loss in respect of that right that is represented to be deductible) and expected to be incurred by or allocated to the person for the particular year or any preceding taxation year, or

(ii) any other amount represented to be deductible in computing income or taxable income in respect of the interest in the property and expected to be incurred by or allocated to the person for the particular year or any preceding taxation year, other than any amount included in computing a loss described in subparagraph (i),

would equal or exceed

(b) the amount, if any, by which

(i) the cost to the person of the interest in the property at the end of the particular year, determined without reference to section 143.2,

would exceed

(ii) the total of all amounts each of which is the amount of any prescribed benefit that is expected to be received or enjoyed, directly or indirectly, in respect of the interest in the property by the person or another person with whom the person does not deal at arm's length,

but does not include property that is a flow-through share or a prescribed property.

**Related Provisions**: 18.1(1)"tax shelter" — Definition for purposes of matchable expenditure rules; 53(2)(c)(i.3) — Tax shelter excluded from certain ACB reductions; 127.52(1)(c.3) — Minimum tax on tax shelter deductions; 143.2(1)"tax shelter investment"(a) — Definition includes a tax shelter under 237.1(1); 143.2(6) — Limitation on cost of tax shelter; 163.2(1)"excluded activity"(a)(i) — No good-faith reliance defence for advisor assessed third-party penalty re tax shelter; 248(1)"tax shelter" — Definition applies to entire Act; 249.1(5) — Election for non-calendar year-end not permitted for tax shelters; Reg. 1100(20.1) — limitation on CCA claim for computer software tax shelter property.

**Notes**: It is not necessary that there be a "promoter" as defined for there to be statements or representations that create a tax shelter.

The "prescribed benefits" that can cause there to be a tax shelter include revenue guarantees. See Reg. 231(6)(b)(ii).

For more detail on this definition, see Donald Watkins, "The Tax Shelter Rules: An Update", 1998 Canadian Tax Foundation annual conference proceedings, pp. 5:1-5:32.

Definition "tax shelter" amended by 1995-97 technical bill, effective December 1994, to add the following:

- the words "(including, for greater certainty, any right to income)" in the opening words;
- the words "an amount, or a loss in the case of a partnership interest" in place of "a loss", in subpara. (a)(i);
- the parenthesized words ("(including...)") in subpara. (a)(i);

- the words "determined without reference to section 143.2" in subpara. (b)(i).

Subpara. (a)(ii) of "tax shelter" amended by 1991 technical bill, effective for interests acquired after August 1989, to add the words "or any preceding year".

**Regulations**: 231(6), (6.1) (prescribed benefit for subpara. (b)(ii)); 231(7) (prescribed property).

**(2) Application** — A promoter in respect of a tax shelter shall apply to the Minister in prescribed form for an identification number for the tax shelter unless an identification number therefor has previously been applied for.

**Related Provisions**: 237.1(4) — Sale without identification number prohibited; 237.1(7.4) — Penalty for false information or selling shelter without number; 237.2 — Application of s. 237.1.

**Information Circulars**: 89-4: Tax shelter reporting.

**Forms**: T5001: Application for tax shelter identification number and undertaking to keep books and records.

**(3) Identification** — On receipt of an application under subsection (2) for an identification number for a tax shelter, together with prescribed information and an undertaking satisfactory to the Minister that books and records in respect of the tax shelter will be kept and retained at a place in Canada that is satisfactory to the Minister, the Minister shall issue an identification number for the tax shelter.

**Related Provisions**: 237.1(5) — Number is for administrative purposes only.

**Information Circulars**: 89-4: Tax shelter reporting.

**(4) Sales prohibited** — No person shall, whether as a principal or an agent, sell or issue, or accept consideration in respect of, a tax shelter before the Minister has issued an identification number for the tax shelter.

**Related Provisions**: 237.1(7.4) — Penalty for false information or selling shelter without number; 237.2 — Application of s. 237.1.

**Notes**: 237.1(4) amended by 1995-97 technical bill, effective December 2, 1994, to change "towards the acquisition of, an interest in a tax shelter" to "in respect of, a tax shelter".

**Information Circulars**: 89-4: Tax shelter reporting.

**(5) Providing tax shelter number** — Every promoter in respect of a tax shelter shall

(a) make reasonable efforts to ensure that all persons who acquire or otherwise invest in the tax shelter are provided with the identification number issued by the Minister for the tax shelter;

(b) prominently display on the upper right-hand corner of any statement of earnings prepared by or on behalf of the promoter in respect of the tax shelter the identification number issued for the tax shelter; and

(c) on every written statement made after 1995 by the promoter that refers either directly or indirectly and either expressly or impliedly to the issuance by the Canada Customs and Revenue Agency of an identification number for the tax shelter, as well as on the copies of the portion of the information return to be forwarded pursuant to subsection (7.3), prominently display

(i) where the statement or return is wholly or partly in English, the following:

"The identification number issued for this tax shelter shall be included in any income tax return filed by the investor. Issuance of the identification number is for administrative purposes only and does not in any way confirm the entitlement of an investor to claim any tax benefits associated with the tax shelter."

(ii) where the statement or return is wholly or partly in French, the following:

"Le numéro d'inscription attribué à cet abri fiscal doit figurer dans toute déclaration d'impôt sur le revenu produite par l'investisseur. L'attribution de ce numéro n'est qu'une formalité administrative et ne confirme aucunement le droit de l'investisseur aux avantages fiscaux découlant de cet abri fiscal."

and

(iii) where the statement includes neither English nor French, the following:

"The identification number issued for this tax shelter shall be included in any income tax return filed by the investor. Issuance of the identification number is for administrative purposes only and does not in any way confirm the entitlement of an investor to claim any tax benefits associated with the tax shelter.

Le numéro d'inscription attribué à cet abri fiscal doit figurer dans toute déclaration d'impôt sur le revenu produite par l'investisseur. L'attribution de ce numéro n'est qu'une formalité administrative et ne confirme aucunement le droit de l'investisseur aux avantages fiscaux découlant de cet abri fiscal."

**Related Provisions**: 163.2 — Penalty for false statement by tax shelter promoter; 239(2.1) — Incorrect identification number.

**Notes**: 237.1(5) amended by *Canada Customs & Revenue Agency Act*, effective November 1, 1999, to change "Department of National Revenue" to "Canada Customs and Revenue Agency".

237.1(5) amended by 1995-97 technical bill, effective December 2, 1994, effectively to add paras. (b) and (c); these requirements were formerly in Reg. 231(5). Previously read:

(5) Every promoter in respect of a tax shelter shall make reasonable efforts to ensure that all persons who acquire an interest in the tax shelter are provided with the identification number issued by the Minister for the tax shelter.

**Regulations**: 231(5) (disclosure requirements in providing identification number; now incorporated into ITA 237.1(5)).

**Information Circulars**: 89-4: Tax shelter reporting.

**(6) Deductions and claims disallowed** — No amount may be deducted or claimed by a person in respect of a tax shelter unless the person files with the Minister a prescribed form containing prescribed information, including the identification number for the tax shelter.

**Related Provisions**: 143.2 — Limitation on tax shelter expenditure; 237.2 — Application of s. 237.1.

**Notes**: 237.1(6) amended by 1995-97 technical bill, effective December 2, 1994. Previously read:

(6) **Deduction disallowed** — In computing the amount of income, taxable income or taxable income earned in Canada of, or tax or other amount payable by, or refundable to, a taxpayer under this Act for a taxation year, or any other amount that is relevant for the purposes of computing that amount, no amount may be deducted in respect of an interest in a tax shelter unless the taxpayer files with the Minister a prescribed form containing prescribed information, including the identification number for the shelter.

237.1(6) amended by 1991 technical bill, effective for interests acquired after 1990, to require a prescribed form and prescribed information.

**Information Circulars**: 89-4: Tax shelter reporting.

**Forms**: T5004: Statement of tax shelter loss or deduction. See also under subsec. 237.1(7).

**(6.1) Deductions and claims disallowed** — No amount may be deducted or claimed by any person for any taxation year in respect of a tax shelter of the person where any person is liable to a penalty under subsection (7.4) or 162(9) in respect of the tax shelter or interest on the penalty and

(a) the penalty or interest has not been paid; or

(b) the penalty and interest have been paid, but an amount on account of the penalty or interest has been repaid under subsection 164(1.1) or applied under subsection 164(2).

**Related Provisions**: 237.1(6.2) — No time limit on assessment; 237.1(7.4) — Penalty for false information or selling shelter without number.

**Notes**: 237.1(6.1) added by 1995-97 technical bill, effective December 2, 1994.

**(6.2) Assessments** — Notwithstanding subsections 152(4) to (5), such assessments, determinations and redeterminations may be made as are necessary to give effect to subsection (6.1).

**Related Provisions**: 143.2(15) — Late assessment to implement tax shelter deduction rules.

**Notes**: 237.1(6.2) added by 1995-97 technical bill, effective December 2, 1994.

**(7) Information return** — Every promoter in respect of a tax shelter who accepts consideration in respect of the tax shelter or who acts as a principal or agent in respect of the tax shelter in a calendar year shall, in prescribed form and manner, file an information return for the year containing

(a) the name, address and either the Social Insurance Number or business number of each person who so acquires or otherwise invests in the tax shelter in the year,

(b) the amount paid by each of those persons in respect of the tax shelter, and

(c) such other information as is required by the prescribed form

unless an information return in respect of the tax shelter has previously been filed.

**Related Provisions**: 237.1(7.1)–(7.3) — Administrative requirements for returns; 237.2 — Application of s. 237.1.

**Notes**: 237.1(7) amended by 1995-97 technical bill, this version effective June 18, 1998. From December 2, 1994 to June 17, 1998, ignore the reference to "business number" in para. (a). Before December 2, 1994, read:

(7) Every promoter in respect of a tax shelter from whom an interest in the tax shelter was acquired, who accepted a contribution in respect of an acquisition of an interest in the tax shelter or who acted as an agent in respect of an acquisition of an interest in the tax shelter in a calendar year shall, in the prescribed form and manner, make an information return for that year containing

(a) the name, address and Social Insurance Number of each person who so acquired an interest in the tax shelter in the year,

(b) the amount paid by each such person for the interest, and

(c) such other information as may be required by the prescribed form,

unless an information return in respect of the acquisition has previously been made.

The requirement in the closing words to send two copies was formerly in Reg. 231(4).

**Regulations**: 231(2)–(4) (prescribed manner).

**Information Circulars**: 89-4: Tax shelter reporting.

**Forms**: T5003: Tax shelter information returns; T5003 Supp: Statement of tax shelter information; T5004: Statement of tax shelter loss or deduction; T5016: Summary information for tax shelters that are partnerships or for partnerships that allocated renounced resource expenses to their members.

**(7.1) Time for filing return** — An information return required under subsection (7) to be filed in respect of the acquisition of an interest in a tax shelter in a calendar year shall be filed with the Minister on or before the last day of February of the following calendar year.

**Related Provisions**: 237.1(7.2) — Return required within 30 days of discontinuing business or activity.

**Notes**: 237.1(7.1) added by 1995-97 technical bill, effective December 2, 1994.

**(7.2) Time for filing — special case** — Notwithstanding subsection (7.1), where a person is required under subsection (7) to file an information return in respect of a business or activity and the person discontinues that business or activity, the return shall be filed on or before the earlier of

(a) the day referred to in subsection (7.1); and

(b) the day that is 30 days after the day of the discontinuance.

**Notes**: 237.1(7.2) added by 1995-97 technical bill, effective December 2, 1994.

**(7.3) Copies to be provided** — Every person required to file a return under subsection (7) shall, on or before the day on or before which the return is required to be filed with the Minister, forward to each person to whom the return relates 2 copies of the portion of the return relating to that person.

**Notes**: 237.1(7.3) added by 1995-97 technical bill, effective December 2, 1994.

**(7.4) Penalty** — Every person who files false or misleading information with the Minister in respect of an application under subsection (2) or, whether as a principal or as an agent, sells, issues or accepts consideration in respect of a tax shelter before the Minister has issued an identification number for the tax shelter is liable to a penalty equal to the greater of

(a) $500, and

(b) 25% of the total of all amounts each of which is the consideration received or receivable from a person in respect of the tax shelter before the correct information is filed with the Minister or the identification number is issued, as the case may be.

**Related Provisions**: 161(11)(b.1) — Interest on penalty; 163(2.9) — Where partnership is liable to penalty; 227(10)(b) — Assessment of penalty at any time; 237.1(6.1) — No deduction allowed while tax shelter penalty unpaid.

**Notes**: 237.1(7.4) added by 1995-97 technical bill, effective December 2, 1994.

**(8) Application of sections 231 to 231.3** — Without restricting the generality of sections 231 to 231.3, where an application under subsection (2) with respect to a tax shelter has been made, notwithstanding that a return of income has not been filed by any taxpayer under section 150 for the taxation year of the taxpayer in which an amount is claimed as a deduction in respect of the tax shelter, sections 231 to 231.3 apply, with such modifications as the circumstances require, for the purpose of permitting the Minister to verify or ascertain any information in respect of the tax shelter.

**Information Circulars [subsec. 237.1(8)]**: 89-4: Tax shelter reporting.

**Notes [s. 237.1]**: 237.1 added by 1988 tax reform, effective for interests acquired after August 1989 (see 237.2).

**Definitions [s. 237.1]**: "arm's length" — 251(1); "business", "business number" — 248(1); "calendar year" — *Interpretation Act* 37(1)(a); "flow-through share" — 66(15), 248(1); "business", "Minister" — 248(1); "partnership" — see Notes to 96(1); "person" — 237.1(1), 248(1); "prescribed" — 248(1); "promoter" — 237.1(1); "property", "record", "share" — 248(1); "tax shelter" — 237.1(1), 248(1); "taxable income" — 2(2), 248(1); "taxable income earned in Canada" — 115(1), 248(1); "taxation year" — 249; "written" — *Interpretation Act* 35(1)"writing".

**237.2 Application of section 237.1** — Section 237.1 is applicable with respect to interests acquired after August 31, 1989.

**Notes**: 237.2 added in the R.S.C. 1985 (5th Supp.) consolidation, effective December 1, 1991. This rule was formerly contained in the rule of application in 1988 tax reform (S.C. 1988, c. 55, s. 180).

## Offences and Punishment

**238. (1) Offences and punishment** — Every person who has failed to file or make a return as and when required by or under this Act or a regulation or who has failed to comply with subsection 116(3), 127(3.1) or (3.2), 147.1(7) or 153(1), any of sections 230 to 232 or a regulation made under subsection 147.1(18) or with an order made under subsection (2) is guilty of an offence and, in addition to any penalty otherwise provided, is liable on summary conviction to

(a) a fine of not less than $1,000 and not more than $25,000; or

(b) both the fine described in paragraph (a) and imprisonment for a term not exceeding 12 months.

**Related Provisions**: 162, 163 — Penalties; 242 — Where corporation is guilty of offence; 243 — Minimum fine; *Interpretation Act* 34(1) — Indictable and summary conviction offences; *Interpretation Act* 34(2) — *Criminal Code* provisions apply.

**Notes**: The imposition of penalties under sections such as 162 or 163 is merely an administrative action taken by the CCRA. Conviction under sections such as 238 or 239, however, requires a criminal prosecution in provincial court, and the accused must be found guilty beyond a reasonable doubt. Pursuant to s. 34(2) of the *Interpretation Act* (reproduced towards the end of this book), the provisions of the *Criminal Code* apply to proceedings under 238 and 239. Under 244(4), the prosecution must be instituted within 8 years of the offence. The Supreme Court of Canada confirmed in *Knox Contracting Ltd.*, [1990] 2 C.T.C. 262, that offences under s. 239 are matters of criminal law.

238 and 239 can apply to advisors as well as to taxpayers. See Notes to 163(2), which cannot (until enactment of February 1999 budget proposals).

Note that due diligence may be a defence to any of the administrative penalties, even where they purport to apply automatically. See *Consolidated Canadian Contractors Inc.*, [1998] G.S.T.C. 91 (FCA), which upheld the principle established in *Pillar Oilfield Projects Ltd.*, [1993] G.S.T.C. 49 (TCC). Lack of *mens rea* (having the mind to commit the offence) is normally a defence to a criminal prosecution.

The CCRA's practice is to hold off dealing with an objection to a civil assessment while criminal proceedings in respect of the same issue are underway. See 239(4).

**Information Circulars**: 00-1: Voluntary disclosures program.

**(2) Compliance orders** — Where a person has been convicted by a court of an offence under subsection (1) for a failure to comply with a provision of this Act or a regulation, the court may make such order as it deems proper in order to enforce compliance with the provision.

**Related Provisions**: 231.7 — Compliance order for assistance with audit or demand.

**Information Circulars**: 73-10R3: Tax evasion.

**(3) Saving** — Where a person has been convicted under this section of failing to comply with a provision of this Act or a regulation, the person is not liable to pay a penalty imposed under section 162 or 227 for the same failure unless the person was assessed for that penalty or that penalty was demanded from the person before the information or complaint giving rise to the conviction was laid or made.

**Notes**: See under 239(3), which provides a parallel rule for conviction under s. 239.

**Definitions [s. 238]**: "person", "regulation" — 248(1).

**239. (1) Other offences and punishment** — Every person who has

(a) made, or participated in, assented to or acquiesced in the making of, false or deceptive statements in a return, certificate, statement or answer filed or made as required by or under this Act or a regulation,

(b) to evade payment of a tax imposed by this Act, destroyed, altered, mutilated, secreted or otherwise disposed of the records or books of account of a taxpayer,

(c) made, or assented to or acquiesced in the making of, false or deceptive entries, or omitted, or assented to or acquiesced in the omission, to enter a material particular, in records or books of account of a taxpayer,

(d) wilfully, in any manner, evaded or attempted to evade compliance with this Act or payment of taxes imposed by this Act, or

(e) conspired with any person to commit an offence described by paragraphs (a) to (d),

is guilty of an offence and, in addition to any penalty otherwise provided, is liable on summary conviction to

(f) a fine of not less than 50%, and not more than 200%, of the amount of the tax that was sought to be evaded, or

(g) both the fine described in paragraph (f) and imprisonment for a term not exceeding 2 years.

**Related Provisions**: 163(2) — Penalty — false statements; 239(1.1) — Offences re refunds and credits; 239(2) — Prosecution on indictment; 242 — Where corporation is guilty of offence; 243 — Minimum fine; *Interpretation Act* 34(1) — Indictable and summary conviction offences; *Interpretation Act* 34(2) — *Criminal Code* provisions apply.

**Notes**: See Notes to 238(1).

**I.T. Application Rules**: 65.1(b) (where offence committed before December 23, 1971).

**Interpretation Bulletins**: IT-99R5: Legal and accounting fees.

**Information Circulars**: 73-10R3: Tax evasion; 00-1: Voluntary disclosures program.

**(1.1) Offences re refunds and credits** — Every person who obtains or claims a refund or credit under this Act to which the person or any other person is not entitled or obtains or claims a refund or credit under this Act in an amount that is greater than the amount to which the person or other person is entitled

(a) by making, or participating in, assenting to or acquiescing in the making of, a false or deceptive statement in a return, certificate, statement or answer filed or made under this Act or a regulation,

(b) by destroying, altering, mutilating, hiding or otherwise disposing of a record or book of account of the person or other person,

(c) by making, or assenting to or acquiescing in the making of, a false or deceptive entry in a record or book of account of the person or other person,

(d) by omitting, or assenting to or acquiescing in an omission to enter a material particular in a record or book of account of the person or other person,

(e) wilfully in any manner, or

(f) by conspiring with any person to commit any offence under this subsection,

is guilty of an offence and, in addition to any penalty otherwise provided, is liable on summary conviction to

(g) a fine of not less than 50% and not more than 200% of the amount by which the amount of the refund or credit obtained or claimed exceeds the amount, if any, of the refund or credit to which the person or other person, as the case may be, is entitled, or

(h) both the fine described in paragraph (g) and imprisonment for a term not exceeding 2 years.

**Related Provisions**: 239(2) — Prosecution on indictment.

**Notes**: 239(1.1) added by 1995-97 technical bill, effective June 18, 1998.

**(2) Prosecution on indictment** — Every person who is charged with an offence described in subsection (1) or (1.1) may, at the election of the Attorney General of Canada, be prosecuted on indictment and, if convicted, is, in addition to any penalty otherwise provided, liable to

(a) a fine of not less than 100% and not more than 200% of

(i) where the offence is described in subsection (1), the amount of the tax that was sought to be evaded, and

(ii) where the offence is described in subsection (1.1), the amount by which the amount of the refund or credit obtained or claimed exceeds the amount, if any, of the refund or credit to which the person or other person, as the case may be, is entitled; and

(b) imprisonment for a term not exceeding 5 years.

**Related Provisions**: 243 — Minimum fine; *Interpretation Act* 34(1) — Indictable and summary conviction offences; *Interpretation Act* 34(2) — *Criminal Code* provisions apply.

**Notes**: 239(2) amended to refer to 239(1.1), and 239(2)(a)(ii) added, by 1995-97 technical bill, effective June 18, 1998.

See Notes to 238(1).

**Interpretation Bulletins**: IT-99R5: Legal and accounting fees.

**Information Circulars**: 73-10R3: Tax evasion.

**(2.1) Providing incorrect tax shelter identification number** — Every person who wilfully provides another person with an incorrect identification number for a tax shelter is guilty of an offence and, in addition to any penalty otherwise provided, is liable on summary conviction to

(a) a fine of not less than 100%, and not more than 200%, of the cost to the other person of that person's interest in the shelter;

(b) imprisonment for a term not exceeding 2 years; or

(c) both the fine described in paragraph (a) and the imprisonment described in paragraph (b).

**Related Provisions**: 237.1 — Tax shelters; 242 — Where corporation is guilty of offence; 243 — Minimum fine;.

**Notes**: See Notes to 238(1).

**Information Circulars**: 89-4: Tax shelter reporting.

**(2.2) Offence with respect to confidential information** — Every person who

(a) contravenes subsection 241(1), or

(b) knowingly contravenes an order made under subsection 241(4.1)

is guilty of an offence and liable on summary conviction to a fine not exceeding $5,000 or to imprisonment for a term not exceeding 12 months, or to both.

**Related Provisions**: 122.64(4) — Offence; 239(2.21) — Offence with respect to confidential information; 239(2.22) — Definitions; 242 — Where corporation is guilty of offence.

**Notes**: See Notes to 238(1).

239(2.2)(b) amended by 1992 technical bill, effective June 10, 1993. From September 13, 1988 to June 9, 1993, read:

(b) to whom information has been provided pursuant to subsection 241(4) and who knowingly uses, communicates or allows to be communicated such information for any purpose other than that for which it was provided,

**(2.21) Idem** — Every person

(a) to whom taxpayer information has been provided for a particular purpose under paragraph 241(4)(b), (c), (e), (h), (k) or (n), or

(b) who is an official to whom taxpayer information has been provided for a particular purpose under paragraph 241(4)(a), (d), (f), (i) or (j.1)

and who for any other purpose knowingly uses, provides to any person, allows the provision to any person of, or allows any person access to, that information is guilty of an offence and liable on summary conviction to a fine not exceeding $5,000 or to imprisonment for a term not exceeding 12 months, or to both.

**Notes**: 239(2.21) added by 1992 technical bill, effective June 10, 1993. Reference to 241(4)(j.1) added to para. (b) by 1998 first budget bill, effective June 18, 1998. Reference to 241(4)(n) added to para. (a) by 1999 first budget bill, effective June 17, 1999.

**(2.22) Definitions** — In subsection (2.21), "official" and "taxpayer information" have the meanings assigned by subsection 241(10).

**Notes**: See Notes to 238(1).

239(2.22) added by 1992 technical bill, effective June 10, 1993.

**(2.3) Offence with respect to an identification number** — Every person to whom the Social Insurance Number of an individual or to whom the business number of a taxpayer or partnership has been provided under this Act or a regulation, and every officer, employee and agent of such a person, who without written consent of the individual, taxpayer or partnership, as the case may be, knowingly uses, communicates or allows to be communicated the number (otherwise than as required or authorized by law, in the course of duties in connection with the administration or enforcement of this Act or for a purpose for which it was provided by the individual, taxpayer or partnership, as the case may be) is guilty of an offence and liable on summary conviction to a fine not exceeding $5,000 or to imprisonment for a term not exceeding 12 months, or to both.

**Related Provisions**: 237(2)(b) — Social Insurance Number not to be used or communicated without individual's consent; 242 — Where corporation is guilty of offence.

**Notes**: See Notes to 238(1).

References to a business number of a taxpayer or partnership added by 1995-97 technical bill, effective June 18, 1998. However, this amendment is rather silly, since such numbers are disclosed for GST purposes on all of a business's invoices and receipts. See Notes to 248(1)"business number".

239(2.3) amended by 1991 technical bill, effective December 17, 1991, to include officers, employees and agents and to provide the parenthetical exclusion for permitted uses. For actions before December 17, 1991, read:

(2.3) Every person to whom the Social Insurance Number of an individual has been provided pursuant to this Act or a regulation who knowingly uses, communicates, or allows to be communicated, the number for any purpose other than that for which it was so provided or for which the person has been authorized in writing by the individual is guilty of an offence and is liable on summary conviction to a fine not exceeding $5,000 or to imprisonment for a term not exceeding 12 months or to both such fine and imprisonment.

**Information Circulars**: 82-2R2: SIN legislation that relates to the preparation of information slips.

**(3) Penalty on conviction** — Where a person is convicted under this section, the person is not liable to pay a penalty imposed under section 162, 163 or 163.2 for the same contravention unless the penalty is assessed before the information or complaint giving rise to the conviction was laid or made.

**Notes**: 239(3) reverses the decision of the Supreme Court of Canada in *Panko*, [1971] C.T.C. 467.

239(3) does not offer much protection. All the CCRA has to do is assess the penalty before a charge is laid. In *Lavers v. British Columbia*, [1990] 1 C.T.C. 265 (BCCA), the Court ruled that imposition of an administrative penalty plus a criminal fine did not offend para. 11(h) of the *Charter of Rights* by constituting double punishment for the same offence.

239(3) amended by 1999 Budget to add reference to 163.2, effective June 29, 2000.

239(3) amended by 1995-97 technical bill, effective June 18, 1998, to remove a restriction that the conviction be for "wilfully, in any manner, evading or attempting to evade payment of taxes imposed by Part I". The intention was to extend 239(3) to offences under 239(1.1), relating to claiming credits and refunds.

**(4) Stay of appeal** — Where, in any appeal under this Act, substantially the same facts are at issue as those that are at issue in a prosecution under this section, the Minister may file a stay of proceedings with the Tax Court of Canada and thereupon the proceedings before that Court are stayed pending final determination of the outcome of the prosecution.

**Notes**: 239(4) amended by 1988 Tax Court bill, effective 1991, to delete reference to proceedings before the Federal Court.

**Definitions [s. 239]**: "business number" — 248(1); "contravene" — *Interpretation Act* 35(1); "individual", "Minister" — 248(1); "official" — 239(2.22), 241(10); "person", "record", "regulation", "taxpayer" — 248(1); "tax shelter" — 237.1(1), 248(1); "taxpayer information" — 239(2.22), 241(10).

**240. (1) Definition of "taxable obligation" and "non-taxable obligation"** — In this section, "taxable obligation" means any bond, debenture or similar obligation the interest on which would, if paid by the issuer to a non-resident person, be subject to the payment of tax under Part XIII by that non-resident person at the rate provided in subsection 212(1) (otherwise than by virtue of subsection 212(6)), and "non-taxable obligation" means any bond, debenture or similar obligation the interest on which would not, if paid by the issuer to a non-resident person, be subject to the payment of tax under Part XIII by that non-resident person.

**(2) Interest coupon to be identified in prescribed manner — offence and punishment** — Every person who, at any time after July 14, 1966, issues

(a) any taxable obligation, or

(b) any non-taxable obligation

the right to interest on which is evidenced by a coupon or other writing that does not form part of, or is capable of being detached from, the evidence of indebtedness under the obligation is, unless the coupon or other writing is marked or identified in prescribed manner by the letters "AX" in the case of a taxable obligation, and by the letter "F" in the case of a non-taxable obligation, on the face thereof, guilty of an offence and liable on summary conviction to a fine not exceeding $500.

**Regulations [subsec. 240(2)]**: 807 (prescribed manner of identification of obligation).

**Notes [s. 240]**: See Notes to 238(1).

**Definitions [s. 240]**: "non-resident", "person" — 248(1); "writing" — *Interpretation Act* 35(1).

**241. (1) Provision of information** — Except as authorized by this section, no official shall

(a) knowingly provide, or knowingly allow to be provided, to any person any taxpayer information;

(b) knowingly allow any person to have access to any taxpayer information; or

(c) knowingly use any taxpayer information otherwise than in the course of the administration or enforcement of this Act, the *Canada Pension Plan*, the *Unemployment Insurance Act* or the *Employment Insurance Act* or for the purpose for which it was provided under this section.

**Related Provisions**: 122.64(2) — Communication of Child Tax Benefit information to provinces; 122.64(3) — Communication of name and address for enforcement of family support orders; 149.1(15) — Charities — information can be communicated; 230.1(4) — Reports to chief electoral officer; 237(2)(b) — Communication of Social Insurance Number; 239(2.2) — Offence; 241(3) — Communication of information; 241(3.2) — Charities — additional information that may be communicated; 241(4) — Exceptions; 241(11) — Meaning of "this Act".

**Notes**: 241(1) amended by 1992 technical bill, effective June 10, 1993. From December 18, 1987 to June 9, 1993, read:

(1) **Communication of information** — Except as authorized by this section, no official or authorized person shall

(a) knowingly communicate or knowingly allow to be communicated to any person any information obtained by or on behalf of the Minister for the purposes of this Act or the *Petroleum and Gas Revenue Tax Act*,

(b) knowingly allow any person to inspect or to have access to any book, record, writing, return or other document obtained by or on behalf of the Minister for the purposes of this Act or the *Petroleum and Gas Revenue Tax Act*, or

(c) knowingly use, other than in the course of the duties of the official or authorized person in connection with the administration or enforcement of this Act or the *Petroleum and Gas Revenue Tax Act*, any information obtained by or on behalf of the Minister for the purposes of this Act or the *Petroleum and Gas Revenue Tax Act*.

Reference in 241(1)(c) to the *Unemployment Insurance Act* changed to the *Employment Insurance Act* by 1996 Employment Insurance bill, effective June 30, 1996; and then recorrected by 1995-97 technical bill, also effective June 30, 1996, to add Unemployment Insurance Act back (since procedures under the old UI Act are still ongoing).

**Information Circulars**: 94-4: International transfer pricing — advance pricing agreements (APA).

**I.T. Technical News**: No. 8 (publication of advance tax rulings); No. 9 (electronic publication of severed rulings).

**Application Policies**: SR&ED 95-04: Conflict of interest..

**Forms**: T1013: Consent form.

(2) **Idem, in legal proceedings** — Notwithstanding any other Act of Parliament or other law, no official shall be required, in connection with any legal proceedings, to give or produce evidence relating to any taxpayer information.

**Related Provisions**: 149.1(15) — Charities — information may be communicated.

**Notes**: 241(2) amended by 1992 technical bill, effective June 10, 1993. From July 8, 1981 to June 9, 1993, read:

(2) Notwithstanding any other Act or law, no official or authorized person shall be required, in connection with any legal proceedings,

(a) to give evidence relating to any information obtained by or on behalf of the Minister for the purposes of this Act or the *Petroleum and Gas Revenue Tax Act*, or

(b) to produce any book, record, writing, return or other document obtained by or on behalf of the Minister for the purposes of this Act or the *Petroleum and Gas Revenue Tax Act*.

(3) **Communication where proceedings have been commenced** — Subsections (1) and (2) do not apply in respect of

(a) criminal proceedings, either by indictment or on summary conviction, that have been commenced by the laying of an information or the preferring of an indictment, under an Act of Parliament; or

(b) any legal proceedings relating to the administration or enforcement of this Act, the *Canada Pension Plan*, the *Unemployment Insurance Act* or the *Employment Insurance Act* or any other Act of Parliament or law of a province that provides for the imposition or collection of a tax or duty.

**Proposed Addition — 241(3)(c)**

(c) the provision of taxpayer information to a police officer (within the meaning assigned by subsection 462.48(17) of the *Criminal Code*) solely for the purpose of investigating an alleged offence, or the laying of an information or the preferring of an indictment in respect of an alleged offence, where

(i) such information can reasonably be regarded as being relevant for the purpose of ascertaining the circumstances in which an offence under the *Criminal Code* may have been committed, or the identity of the person or persons who may have committed an offence, in respect of an official, or in respect of any person related to that official,

(ii) the official performed or is performing an act which the Act obliges or authorizes the official to perform, and

(iii) the offence can reasonably be considered to be related to that act.

**Application**: The December 21, 2000 draft legislation, subsec. 92(1), will add para. 241(3)(c), in force on Royal Assent.

**Technical Notes**: Subsection 241(3) authorizes the disclosure of taxpayer information in respect of

• criminal proceedings, where charges have been laid, and

• any legal proceeding relating to the administration or enforcement of certain statutes including the *Income Tax Act*.

Subsection 241(3) is amended to authorize the provision of taxpayer information to a police officer solely for the purpose of investigating an alleged offence, where:

• such information can reasonably be regarded as being relevant for the purpose of ascertaining the circumstances in which an offence under the *Criminal Code* may have been committed, or the identity of the person who may have committed an offence, in respect of an official (or a person related to that official),

• the official performed, or is performing, an act which the Act obliges or authorizes the official to perform, and

• the offence can reasonably be considered to be related to that act.

**S. 241(3)(c)**      Income Tax Act

> **Notice of Ways and Means Motion, federal budget, February 28, 2000**: *Communication of Taxpayer Information*
>
> (44) That the provisions of the Act relating to the communication of taxpayer information be amended to permit an official to provide
>
> . . . . .
>
> (b) taxpayer information to a police officer, within the meaning assigned by subsection 462.48(17) of the *Criminal Code*, where
>
> (i) an official has performed or is performing an act which the *Income Tax Act* obliges or authorizes the official to perform,
>
> (ii) such information can reasonably be regarded as necessary to ascertain the identity of a person and the circumstances in which an offence under the *Criminal Code* may have been committed by the person in respect of an official of the Canada Customs and Revenue Agency, or in respect of any person related to that official,
>
> (iii) the offence can reasonably be considered to be related to the official's act, referred to in clause (i), and
>
> (iv) the information is provided solely for the purpose of the investigation or prosecution of the offence.

> **Federal budget, supplementary information, February 28, 2000**: *Provision of Information to Police*
>
> Under current law, it is not clear whether taxpayer information can be provided to the police for the purpose of investigating whether the acts of a person against an official of the Canada Customs and Revenue Agency constitute the commission of an offence, unless charges have first been laid or the circumstances constitute imminent personal danger to the official. The Government proposes to amend the confidentiality provisions of the *Income Tax Act* and the *Excise Tax Act* to permit an official of the CCRA to provide relevant taxpayer information to the police for the purpose of investigating whether the acts of a person against an official of the CCRA, or against a member of the official's family, constitute an offence under the Criminal Code. In the case of sales tax, the proposed amendment would also apply in respect of a provincial official authorized to exercise duties and powers under Part IX of the *Excise Tax Act* pursuant to an administration agreement between the government of the province and the Government of Canada.

**Related Provisions**: 241(11) — Meaning of "this Act".

**Notes**: For a detailed discussion of 241(3), see Patrick Bendin, "The Requirement of Confidentiality under the *Income Tax Act* and Its Effect on the Conduct of Appeals before the Tax Court of Canada", 44(3) *Canadian Tax Journal* 680–722 (1996).

241(3) amended by 1992 technical bill, effective June 10, 1993. From February 19, 1987 to June 9, 1993, read:

> (3) Exception for criminal or tax proceedings — Subsections (1) and (2) do not apply in respect of criminal proceedings, either by indictment or on summary conviction, that have been commenced by the laying of an information, under an Act of Parliament, or in respect of proceedings relating to the administration or enforcement of this Act or the *Petroleum and Gas Revenue Tax Act*.

Reference in 241(3)(b) to the *Unemployment Insurance Act* changed to the *Employment Insurance Act* by 1996 EI bill, effective June 30, 1996; and then recorrected by 1995-97 technical bill, also effective June 30, 1996, to add UI Act back (since procedures under the old UI Act are still ongoing).

**Information Circulars**: 87-2R: International transfer pricing.

**(3.1) Circumstances involving danger** — The Minister may provide to appropriate persons any taxpayer information relating to imminent danger of death or physical injury to any individual.

**Notes**: 241(3.1) added by 1992 technical bill, effective June 10, 1993.

**(3.2) Registered charities** — An official may provide to any person the following taxpayer information relating to a charity that at any time was a registered charity:

> **Proposed Amendment — 241(3.2) opening words**
>
> **(3.2) Registered charities** — An official may provide to any person the following taxpayer information relating to another person that was at any time a registered charity (in this subsection referred to as the "charity"):
>
> **Application**: Bill C-43 (First Reading September 20, 2000), s. 110, will amend the opening words of subsec. 241(3.2) to read as above, in force on Royal Assent.
>
> **Technical Notes**: Subsection 241(3.2) permits the Canada Customs and Revenue Agency to release specified information relating to an organization that was at any time a registered charity under the Act. The amendment clarifies that specified information may be released at a time when the organization is no longer a registered charity, provided that the information to be released relates to a period during which the organization was so registered.

(a) a copy of the charity's governing documents, including its statement of purpose;

(b) any information provided in prescribed form to the Minister by the charity on applying for registration under this Act;

(c) the names of the persons who at any time were the charity's directors and the periods during which they were its directors;

(d) a copy of the notification of the charity's registration, including any conditions and warnings; and

(e) if the registration of the charity has been revoked, a copy of any letter sent by or on behalf of the Minister to the charity relating to the grounds for the revocation.

**Related Provisions**: 149.1(6.4) — Rule applies to registered national arts service organizations; 149.1(15) — Disclosure permitted of information in public information return.

**Notes**: 241(3.2) added by 1997 Budget, effective June 18, 1998.

**Registered Charities Newsletters**: 7 (Increased transparency).

**(4) Where taxpayer information may be disclosed** — An official may

(a) provide to any person taxpayer information that can reasonably be regarded as necessary for the purposes of the administration or enforcement of this Act, the *Canada Pension Plan*, the *Unem-*

*ployment Insurance Act* or the *Employment Insurance Act*, solely for that purpose;

(b) provide to any person taxpayer information that can reasonably be regarded as necessary for the purposes of determining any tax, interest, penalty or other amount that is or may become payable by the person, or any refund or tax credit to which the person is or may become entitled, under this Act or any other amount that is relevant for the purposes of that determination;

(c) provide to the person who seeks a certification referred to in paragraph 147.1(10)(a) the certification or a refusal to make the certification, solely for the purposes of administering a registered pension plan;

(d) provide taxpayer information

(i) to an official of the Department of Finance solely for the purposes of the formulation or evaluation of fiscal policy,

(ii) to an official solely for the purposes of the initial implementation of a fiscal policy or for the purposes of the administration or enforcement of an Act of Parliament that provides for the imposition and collection of a tax or duty,

(iii) to an official solely for the purposes of the administration or enforcement of a law of a province that provides for the imposition or collection of a tax or duty,

(iv) to an official of the government of a province solely for the purposes of the formulation or evaluation of fiscal policy,

(v) to an official of the Department of Natural Resources or of the government of a province solely for the purposes of the administration or enforcement of a program of the Government of Canada or of the province relating to the exploration for or exploitation of Canadian petroleum and gas resources,

(vi) to an official of the government of a province that has received or is entitled to receive a payment referred to in this subparagraph, or to an official of the Department of Natural Resources, solely for the purposes of the provisions relating to payments to a province in respect of the taxable income of corporations earned in the offshore area with respect to the province under the *Canada–Nova Scotia Offshore Petroleum Resources Accord Implementation Act*, chapter 28 of the Statutes of Canada, 1988, the *Canada-Newfoundland Atlantic Accord Implementation Act*, chapter 3 of the Statutes of Canada, 1987, or similar Acts relating to the exploration for or exploitation of offshore Canadian petroleum and gas resources,

(vi.1) to an official of the Department of Natural Resources solely for the purpose of determining whether property is prescribed energy conservation property or whether an outlay or expense is a Canadian renewable and conservation expense,

(vii) to an official solely for the purposes of the administration or enforcement of the *Pension Benefits Standards Act, 1985* or a similar law of a province,

(vii.1) to an official of the Department of Human Resources Development or to a prescribed official solely for the purpose of the administration or enforcement of Part III.1 of the *Department of Human Resources Development Act*,

(viii) to an official of the Department of Veterans Affairs solely for the purposes of the administration of the *War Veterans Allowance Act* or Part XI of the *Civilian War-related Benefits Act*,

(ix) to an official of a department or agency of the Government of Canada or of a province as to the name, address, occupation, size or type of business of a taxpayer, solely for the purposes of enabling that department or agency to obtain statistical data for research and analysis,

(x) to an official of the Canada Employment Insurance Commission or the Department of Employment and Immigration solely for the purpose of the administration or enforcement of, or the evaluation or formation of policy for the purposes of, the *Unemployment Insurance Act*, the *Employment Insurance Act* or an employment program of the Government of Canada,

(xi) to an official of the Department of Agriculture and Agri-Food or of the government of a province solely for the purposes of the administration or enforcement of a program of the Government of Canada or of the province established under an agreement entered into under the *Farm Income Protection Act*,

(xii) to an official of the Department of Canadian Heritage or a member of the Canadian Cultural Property Export Review Board solely for the purposes of administering sections 32 to 33.2 of the *Cultural Property Export and Import Act*,

(xiii) to an official solely for the purposes of setting off against any sum of money that may be due or payable by Her Majesty in right of Canada a debt due to

(A) Her Majesty in right of Canada, or

(B) Her Majesty in right of a province, or

(xiv) to an official solely for the purposes of section 7.1 of the *Federal-Provincial Fiscal Arrangements Act*;

(e) provide taxpayer information, or allow the inspection of or access to taxpayer information, as the case may be, under, and solely for the purposes of,

    (i) subsection 36(2) or section 46 of the *Access to Information Act*,

    (ii) section 13 of the *Auditor General Act*,

    (iii) section 92 of the *Canada Pension Plan*,

    (iv) a warrant issued under subsection 21(3) of the *Canadian Security Intelligence Service Act*,

    (v) an order made under subsection 462.48(3) of the *Criminal Code*,

    (vi) section 26 of the *Cultural Property Export and Import Act*,

    (vii) section 79 of the *Family Orders and Agreements Enforcement Assistance Act*,

    (viii) paragraph 33.11(a) of the *Old Age Security Act*,

    (ix) subsection 34(2) or section 45 of the *Privacy Act*,

    (x) section 24 of the *Statistics Act*,

    (xi) section 9 of the *Tax Rebate Discounting Act*, or

    (xii) a provision contained in a tax convention or agreement between Canada and another country that has the force of law in Canada;

(f) provide taxpayer information solely for the purposes of sections 23 to 25 of the *Financial Administration Act*;

(g) use taxpayer information to compile information in a form that does not directly or indirectly reveal the identity of the taxpayer to whom the information relates;

(h) use, or provide to any person, taxpayer information solely for a purpose relating to the supervision, evaluation or discipline of an authorized person by Her Majesty in right of Canada in respect of a period during which the authorized person was employed by or engaged by or on behalf of Her Majesty in right of Canada to assist in the administration or enforcement of this Act, the *Canada Pension Plan*, the *Unemployment Insurance Act* or the *Employment Insurance Act*, to the extent that the information is relevant for the purpose;

(i) provide access to records of taxpayer information to the National Archivist of Canada or a person acting on behalf of or under the direction of the National Archivist of Canada, solely for the purposes of section 5 of the *National Archives of Canada Act*, and transfer such records to the care and control of such persons solely for the purposes of section 6 of that Act;

(j) use taxpayer information relating to a taxpayer to provide information to the taxpayer;

(j.1) provide taxpayer information to an official or a designated person solely for the purpose of permitting the making of an adjustment to

    (i) a social assistance payment made on the basis of a means, needs or income test, or

    (ii) a payment pursuant to a prescribed law of a province in respect of a child within the meaning of the prescribed law,

where the purpose of the adjustment is to take into account the amount determined for C in subsection 122.61(1) in respect of a person for a taxation year;

(k) provide, or allow inspection of or access to, taxpayer information to or by any person otherwise legally entitled to it under an Act of Parliament solely for the purposes for which that person is entitled to the information;

(l) provide the business number, name, address, telephone number and facsimile number of a holder of a business number to an official of a department or agency of the Government of Canada or of a province solely for the purpose of the administration or enforcement of an Act of Parliament or a law of a province, if the holder of the business number is required by that Act or that law to provide the information (other than the business number) to the department or agency;

(m) provide taxpayer information to an official of the government of a province solely for use in the management or administration by that government of a program relating to payments under subsection 164(1.8); or

(n) provide taxpayer information to any person, solely for the purposes of the administration or enforcement of a law of a province that provides for workers' compensation benefits.

**Proposed Addition — 241(4)(o)**

(o) to provide taxpayer information to any person solely for the purpose of enabling the Chief Statistician, within the meaning assigned by section 2 of the *Statistics Act*, to provide to a statistical agency of a province data concerning business activities carried on in the province, where the information is used by the agency solely for research and analysis and the agency is authorized under the law of the province to collect the same or similar information on its own behalf in respect of such activities.

**Application**: The December 21, 2000 draft legislation, subsec. 92(2), will add para. 241(4)(o), applicable on Royal Assent to information relating to 1997 et seq. and, for the purpose of subsec. 17(2) of the *Statistics Act*, where such information was collected before Royal Assent, the information is deemed to have been collected at the time at which it is provided to a provincial agency pursuant to para. 241(4)(o).

**Technical Notes**: Subsection 241(4) authorizes the communication of information to government officials, outside of the Canada Customs and Revenue Agency, for limited purposes. One of these purposes is the provision of taxpayer information solely for the purposes of section 24 of the *Statistics Act*.

Subsection 241(4) is amended to allow the disclosure of taxpayer information in respect of business activities carried on in a province to provincial statistical agencies. This exception applies only where such information is to be used by the provincial agency solely for research and analysis and that agency is authorized under the law of the province to collect the same or similar information on its own behalf in respect of such business activities. This amendment applies after the enacting legislation receives Royal Assent.

### Notice of Ways and Means Motion, federal budget, February 28, 2000: *Communication of Taxpayer Information*

(44) That the provisions of the Act relating to the communication of taxpayer information be amended to permit an official to provide

(a) taxpayer information, relating to the 1997 and subsequent taxation years, to any person solely for the purpose of enabling the Chief Statistician, as defined by section 2 of the *Statistics Act*, to provide to a statistical agency of a province statistical data that is pertinent to activities carried on in the province and that is to be used by the agency solely for research and analysis, if the information relates to

(i) a corporation, or

(ii) an individual, where the information is solely in respect of the computation of income from the individual's business,

and for the purpose of subsection 17(2) of the *Statistics Act*, where such information was collected before any measure giving effect to this paragraph is assented to, the information shall be deemed to have been collected at the time at which it is so provided to the provincial statistical agency.

### Federal budget, supplementary information, February 28, 2000: *Sharing of Tax Information with Provincial Statistical Agencies*

In the past, Statistics Canada has been striving to minimize the high degree of overlap between business survey data collected by Statistics Canada and taxpayer information on businesses collected by the Canada Customs and Revenue Agency. Businesses have expressed concern about the response burden placed on them and the resources required to comply with these requests for information. Since 1997, Statistics Canada has obtained from tax records much of the information previously collected through survey questionnaires. Authority for the release of taxpayer information to Statistics Canada is provided in the *Income Tax Act*.

When Statistics Canada relied on business surveys conducted jointly by Statistics Canada and the provinces, it applied an authority provided under the *Statistics Act* to share survey business financial information with provincial statistical agencies — which have the statutory authority to obtain this information by means of their own surveys — for purposes of research and analysis. This data sharing helped to reduce the number of surveys and response costs incurred by businesses in completing these surveys. However, the rule which allows the sharing of taxpayer information with Statistics Canada does not allow Statistics Canada to share this information with provincial statistical agencies.

To address this issue and to provide continuity of business data for research and analysis by the provinces, the budget proposes to amend the *Income Tax Act* to allow Statistics Canada to provide taxpayer information in respect of incorporated and unincorporated businesses for the 1997 and subsequent taxation years to provincial statistical agencies solely for use in research and analysis. This amendment will allow provincial needs to be met while keeping the response burden for businesses as low as possible.

The sharing of taxpayer information between federal and provincial statistical agencies will only be permitted once the enabling legislation receives royal assent. Appropriate measures to safeguard the confidentiality of this information will continue to apply. Also, only business-related information can be shared; thus, for unincorporated businesses, information on the business owner which is unrelated to business activities cannot be shared.

### Proposed Amendment — 241(4) — Social Insurance Number disclosure

**Letter from Department of Finance, March 17, 1999**:

Dear [xxx]

This is in reply to your letter of March 12, 1999 to Simon Thompson with respect to the transfer of Social Insurance Numbers and business numbers from [xxx] to a nominee.

We understand that [xxx] plans to put in place an arrangement under which legal ownership of shares will, in many cases, be with a nominee of the shareholders. The nominee will receive dividend payments on the shares for which it is the registered owner, and will then distribute each dividend to the beneficial owners of the shares. As a consequence, the nominee will have an independent tax-reporting obligation under subsection 201(2) of the *Income Tax Regulations*. Under the existing law and the proposed amendments to it that were released on December 15, 1998, we agree that it may not be technically possible for [xxx] to provide Social Insurance Numbers and business numbers of beneficial owners to the nominee.

Given the reasons for the creation of the nominee in these circumstances, and in the interests of ensuring timely and complete reporting with regard to Social Insurance Numbers and business numbers, we are prepared to recommend an amendment to the *Income Tax Act*. The amendment would, in the circumstance set out in your letter, allow the transfer of this information to the nominee for the purpose of allowing the nominee to comply with tax reporting requirements.

Thank you for writing.

Yours sincerely,

Brian Ernewein
Director, Tax Legislation Division, Tax Policy Branch

**Related Provisions**: 37(3) — Consultation with other government departments to determine R&D claims; 122.62(9) — Consultation with Health and Welfare for determining Child Tax Benefit; 122.64(2)(a) — Communication of Child Tax Benefit information to provinces; 122.64(3) — Communication of name and address for enforcement of family support orders; 149.1(15) — Registered charity's information return may be communicated to public; 230.1(4) — Reports to chief electoral officer; 239(2.21) — Offence with respect to confidential information; 241(5) — Disclosure to taxpayer or with taxpayer's consent; 241(11) — Meaning of "this

Act"; Canada-U.S. Tax Treaty, Art. XXVII — Exchange of information with U.S. government (for 241(4)(e)(xii)).

**Notes**: Reference in 241(4)(a), (h) to the *Unemployment Insurance Act* changed to the *Employment Insurance Act* by 1996 EI bill, effective June 30, 1996; and then recorrected by 1995-97 technical bill, also effective June 30, 1996, to add Unemployment Insurance Act back (since procedures under the old UI Act are still ongoing).

241(4)(d)(vi.1) added by 1994 Budget, effective February 22, 1994, and by 1996 Budget, effective April 25, 1997, to add "or whether an outlay or expense is a Canadian renewable and conservation expense".

241(4)(d)(vii.1) added by 1998 first budget bill, effective June 18, 1998.

Reference in 241(4)(d)(viii) changed from *Merchant Navy Veteran and Civilian War-related Benefits Act* to *Civilian War-related Benefits Act* by S.C. 1999, c. 10, effective May 1, 1999 (P.C. 1999-738).

241(4)(d)(x) amended by 1996 Employment Insurance bill, and then recorrected by 1995-97 technical bill, both effective June 30, 1996, to add *Unemployment Insurance Act* back.

241(4)(d)(xi) amended by 1994 Department of Agriculture bill (1994, c. 38), to substitute "Department of Agriculture and Agri-Food" for "Department of Agriculture", effective January 12, 1995.

Reference in 241(4)(d)(xii) to CPEIA section 33 changed to "33.2" by 1995 cultural property bill, effective July 12, 1996. See Notes to 118.1(10). Also changed by 1995 *Department of Canadian Heritage Act*, in force July 12, 1996, to change "Department of Communications" to "Department of Canadian Heritage".

241(4)(d)(xiii)(B) amended by 1995-97 technical bill, effective June 18, 1998. Previously read "Her Majesty in right of a province on account of taxes payable to the province where an agreement exists between Canada and the province under which Canada is authorized to collect the taxes on behalf of the province".

241(4)(e)(vii) amended by 1995-97 technical bill, effective May 1997, to change "section 62" to "section 79".

Reference in 241(4)(e)(viii) changed from "33(3)(a)" to "33.11(a)" by 1998 first budget bill, effective June 18, 1998.

For 241(4)(h), see under 241(4)(a) above.

241(4)(j.1) added by 1998 first budget bill, effective June 18, 1998. (See 241(10) "designated person".)

241(4)(l) added by 1995 Budget, effective June 20, 1996 (Royal Assent). See 241(10) "business number".

241(4)(m) added by 1995-97 technical bill, effective June 18, 1998.

241(4)(n) added by 1999 first budget bill, effective June 17, 1999. It reflects the new role the Canada Customs and Revenue Agency will have in collecting workers' compensation premiums in Nova Scotia and possibly other provinces.

*Pre-1994 amendments*

241(4) amended several times in 1990 and 1991, and by 1992 technical bill, effective June 10, 1993. From December 17, 1991 to June 9, 1993, read:

(4) **Other exceptions** — An official or authorized person may,

(a) in the course of the duties of the official or authorized person in connection with the administration or enforcement of this Act or the *Petroleum and Gas Revenue Tax Act*,

(i) communicate or allow to be communicated to an official or authorized person information obtained by or on behalf of the Minister for the purposes of this Act or the *Petroleum and Gas Revenue Tax Act*, and

(ii) allow an official or authorized person to inspect or to have access to any book, record, writing, return or other document obtained by or on behalf of the Minister for the purposes of this Act or the *Petroleum and Gas Revenue Tax Act*;

(b) under prescribed conditions, communicate or allow to be communicated information obtained under this Act or the *Petroleum and Gas Revenue Tax Act*, or allow inspection of or access to any written statement furnished under this Act or the *Petroleum and Gas Revenue Tax Act*, to the government of any province in respect of which information and written statements obtained by the government of the province, for the purpose of a law of the province that imposes a tax similar to the tax imposed under this Act or the *Petroleum and Gas Revenue Tax Act*, are communicated or furnished on a reciprocal basis to the Minister;

(c) communicate or allow to be communicated information obtained under this Act or the *Petroleum and Gas Revenue Tax Act*, or allow inspection of or access to any book, record, writing, return or other document obtained by or on behalf of the Minister for the purposes of this Act or the *Petroleum and Gas Revenue Tax Act*, to or by any person otherwise legally entitled thereto;

(d) communicate or allow to be communicated to a taxpayer information obtained under this Act or the *Petroleum and Gas Revenue Tax Act* that may reasonably be regarded as necessary for the purposes of determining any tax, interest, penalty or other amount payable by the taxpayer or any refund or tax credit to which the taxpayer is entitled under this Act or the *Petroleum and Gas Revenue Tax Act*;

(e) communicate or allow to be communicated to a taxpayer information obtained under this Act or the *Petroleum and Gas Revenue Tax Act* from a transferor of property to the taxpayer that relates to the cost, capital cost or adjusted cost base to the taxpayer of the property, if, under any provision of this Act or the *Petroleum and Gas Revenue Tax Act* or the *Income Tax Application Rules*, the cost, capital cost or adjusted cost base is an amount other than the consideration paid by the taxpayer for that property;

(e.1) communicate or allow to be communicated to the person who seeks a certification referred to in paragraph 147.1(10)(a) the certification or a refusal to make the certification, for the purposes of administering a registered pension plan;

(f) communicate or allow to be communicated information obtained under this Act or the *Petroleum and Gas Revenue Tax Act*

(i) to an official of the Department of Finance solely for the purposes of evaluating and formulating tax policy,

(ii) to an official of the Department of National Revenue, Customs and Excise, solely for the purposes of administering or enforcing the *Customs Act*, the *Customs Tariff*, the *Excise Tax Act* or the *Excise Act*,

(iii) to an official of the Department of Energy, Mines and Resources or to the government of a province solely for the purposes of administering or enforcing a prescribed program of the Government of Canada or of the province relating to the exploration for or exploitation of Canadian petroleum and gas resources,

(iv) to an official of the appropriate department or agency of the Government of Canada solely for the purpose of administering subsection 127(11.3) and the definitions "approved project" and "approved project property" in subsection 127(9),

(v) to the government of a province that has received or is entitled to receive a payment referred to in this subparagraph or to an official of the Department of Energy, Mines and Resources solely for the purposes of the provisions relating to payments to a province in respect of the taxable income of corporations earned in the offshore area with respect to the province under the *Canada–Nova Scotia Oil and Gas Agreement Act*, chapter 29 of the Statutes of Canada, 1984, the *Canada-Newfoundland Atlantic Accord Implementation Act*, chapter 3 of the Statutes of Canada, 1987, or similar Acts relating to the exploration for or exploitation of offshore Canadian petroleum and gas resources, and

(vi) to an official of the Office of the Superintendent of Financial Institutions solely for the purpose of providing the Minister with advice with respect to any matter relating to pension plans;

(f.1) communicate or allow to be communicated information obtained under this Act or the *Petroleum and Gas Revenue Tax Act* to an official of the Department of Veterans Affairs solely for the purposes of administering the *War Veterans Allowance Act* or Part XI of the *Merchant Navy Veteran and Civilian War-related Benefits Act*;

(g) communicate or allow to be communicated information obtained under this Act or the *Petroleum and Gas Revenue Tax Act* as to the name, address, occupation or size or type of business of a taxpayer to an official of a department or agency of the Government of Canada or of a province, solely for the purpose of enabling that department or agency to obtain statistical data for research and analysis;

(h) communicate or allow to be communicated information obtained under this Act or the *Petroleum and Gas Revenue Tax Act* to an official of the Canada Employment Immigration Commission or the Department of Employment and Immigration solely for the purposes of administering, evaluating or enforcing the *Unemployment Insurance Act* or a prescribed employment program;

(h.1) communicate or allow to be communicated to a taxpayer information obtained under this Act, regarding expenses in respect of which a deduction is denied under subsection 18(2) or (3.1) to any other taxpayer, that is necessary for the purpose of determining the cost or adjusted cost base, as the case may be, to the taxpayer of any property;

(h.2) communicate or allow to be communicated to a taxpayer information obtained under this Act from a corporation that previously owned or had an interest in property of the taxpayer that relates to the control of the corporation or the question whether the corporation was exempt from tax under Part I on its taxable income if it is necessary for the purposes of determining under this Act whether a gain from a disposition of the property accrued while the property was a property of a corporation controlled directly or indirectly in any manner whatever by one or more non-resident persons or of a corporation exempt from tax under Part I on its taxable income;

(i) communicate or allow to be communicated, pursuant to an order made under subsection 462.48(3) of the *Criminal Code*, information obtained under this Act;

(j) communicate or allow to be communicated to an official, solely for the purposes of administering or enforcing the *Pension Benefits Standards Act, 1985* or a similar law of a province,

(i) information obtained under this Act

(A) as to the identity of a pension plan in respect of which application for registration for the purposes of this Act has, at any time, been made,

(B) as to the names and addresses of the persons who are, have been or will be responsible for the administration of a pension plan referred to in clause (A),

(C) as to the names and addresses of the employers who participate, have participated or will participate in a pension plan referred to in clause (A),

(D) as to the terms of a pension plan referred to in clause (A), a trust deed, insurance contract or other document relating to the funding of benefits under such a plan or an amendment or proposed amendment to such a plan or document, or

(E) as to the date of termination or partial termination of a pension plan referred to in clause (A),

(ii) information as to whether a pension plan is or was a registered pension plan,

(iii) the date of registration of a pension plan that is or was a registered pension plan, or

(iv) in the case of a pension plan the registration of which under this Act has been refused or revoked, the date of the refusal or revocation and the reason therefor;

(k) communicate or allow to be communicated information obtained under this Act to an official of the Department of Agriculture or to an official of the government of a province solely for the purposes of administering or enforcing a program of the Government of Canada or of the province established under an agreement entered into pursuant to the *Farm Income Protection Act*;

(l) communicate or allow to be communicated information obtained under this Act to an official of the Department of Communications or a member of the Canadian Cultural Property Export Review Board, solely for the purpose of administering the provisions of sections 32 and 33 of the *Cultural Property Export and Import Act*; or

(m) communicate or allow to be communicated information obtained under this Act to an official or authorized person for the purpose of setting off against any sum of money that is due or payable by Her Majesty in right of Canada a debt due to

(i) Her Majesty in right of Canada, or

(ii) Her Majesty in right of a province on account of taxes payable to the province where an agreement exists between Canada and the province under which Canada is authorized to collect the taxes on behalf of the province.

**Regulations**: 3004 (prescribed law of a province for 241(4)(j.1)(ii)); 8200.1 (prescribed energy conservation property for 241(4)(d)(vi.1)).

**Forms**: T1013 — Consent form.

### (4.1) Measures to prevent unauthorized use or disclosure
— The person who presides at a legal proceeding relating to the supervision, evaluation or discipline of an authorized person may order such measures as are necessary to ensure that taxpayer information is not used or provided to any person for any purpose not relating to that proceeding, including

(a) holding a hearing *in camera*;

(b) banning the publication of the information;

(c) concealing the identity of the taxpayer to whom the information relates; and

(d) sealing the records of the proceeding.

**S. 241(4.1)**      Income Tax Act

**Related Provisions**: 239(2.2) — Offence with respect to confidential information; 238(1) — Punishment for failing to comply.

**Notes**: 241(4.1) added by 1992 technical bill, effective June 10, 1993.

**(5) Disclosure to taxpayer or on consent** — An official may provide taxpayer information relating to a taxpayer

(a) to the taxpayer; and

(b) with the consent of the taxpayer, to any other person.

**Related Provisions**: 238(1) — Punishment for failing to comply; 241(4)(j) — Disclosure to taxpayer permitted.

**Notes**: 241(5) amended by 1992 technical bill, effective June 10, 1993. From July 8, 1981 to June 9, 1993, read:

> (5) Return of copy of books, etc. — Notwithstanding anything in this section, the Minister may permit a copy of any book, record, writing, return or other document obtained by or on behalf of the Minister for the purposes of this Act or the *Petroleum and Gas Revenue Tax Act* to be given to the person from whom the book, record, writing, return or other document was obtained or the legal representative of that person, or to the agent of that person or of the legal representative authorized in writing in that behalf.

**Forms**: T1013 — Consent form.

**(6) Appeal from order or direction** — An order or direction that is made in the course of or in connection with any legal proceedings and that requires an official or authorized person to give or produce evidence relating to any taxpayer information may, by notice served on all interested parties, be appealed forthwith by the Minister or by the person against whom the order or direction is made to

(a) the court of appeal of the province in which the order or direction is made, in the case of an order or direction made by a court or other tribunal established by or pursuant to the laws of the province, whether or not that court or tribunal is exercising a jurisdiction conferred by the laws of Canada; or

(b) the Federal Court of Appeal, in the case of an order or direction made by a court or other tribunal established by or pursuant to the laws of Canada.

**Notes**: Opening words of 241(6) amended by 1992 technical bill, effective June 10, 1993. From July 8, 1981 to June 9, 1993, read:

> (6) An order or direction made in the course of or in connection with any legal proceedings requiring an official or authorized person to give evidence relating to any information or produce any book, record, writing, return or other document obtained by or on behalf of the Minister for the purposes of this Act or the *Petroleum and Gas Revenue Tax Act*, may, by notice served upon all interested parties, be appealed forthwith by the Minister or by the person against whom the order or direction is made to

**(7) Disposition of appeal** — The court to which an appeal is taken pursuant to subsection (6) may allow the appeal and quash the order or direction appealed from or dismiss the appeal, and the rules of practice and procedure from time to time governing appeals to the courts shall apply, with such modifications as the circumstances require, to an appeal instituted pursuant to that subsection.

**(8) Stay of order or direction** — An appeal instituted pursuant to subsection (6) shall stay the operation of the order or direction appealed from until judgment is pronounced.

**(9)** [Repealed under former Act]

**Notes**: 241(9), repealed by 1988 tax reform, provided a fine or imprisonment for contravention of 241. The offence provision is now 239(2.2).

**(10) Definitions** — In this section,

**"authorized person"** means a person who is engaged or employed, or who was formerly engaged or employed, by or on behalf of Her Majesty in right of Canada to assist in carrying out the provisions of this Act, the *Canada Pension Plan*, the *Unemployment Insurance Act* or the *Employment Insurance Act*;

**Related Provisions**: 241(11) — Meaning of "this Act".

**Notes**: Definition "authorized person" amended by 1996 EI bill and then by 1995-97 technical bill, both effective June 30, 1996. Before that date it referred only to the *Unemployment Insurance Act*; this was first changed to the *Employment Insurance Act*, then changed back to both Acts since procedures under the old UI Act are still ongoing.

Definition amended by 1992 technical bill, effective June 10, 1993, to add references to the *Canada Pension Plan* and the *Unemployment Insurance Act*.

**"business number"** — [Repealed]

**Notes**: Definition "business number" repealed by 1995-97 technical bill, effective June 18, 1998. The definition now appears in 248(1). From June 20, 1996 to June 17, 1998, read as now in 248(1) but without the closing words.

**"court of appeal"** has the meaning assigned by the definition "court of appeal" in section 2 of the *Criminal Code*;

**Notes**: Definition "court of appeal" amended by 1992 technical bill, effective June 10, 1993. Before that date, the reference was to paras. 2(a) to (j) of the *Criminal Code*, which did not cover the Yukon and Northwest Territories.

**"designated person"** means any person who is employed in the service of, who occupies a position of responsibility in the service of, or who is engaged by or on behalf of,

(a) a municipality in Canada, or

(b) a public body performing a function of government in Canada,

or any person who was formerly so employed, who formerly occupied such a position or who was formerly so engaged;

**Notes**: Definition "designated person" added by 1998 first budget bill, effective June 18, 1998.

**"official"** means any person who is employed in the service of, who occupies a position of responsibility in the service of, or who is engaged by or on behalf of,

(a) Her Majesty in right of Canada or a province, or

(b) an authority engaged in administering a law of a province similar to the *Pension Benefits Standards Act, 1985*,

or any person who was formerly so employed, who formerly occupied such a position or who was formerly so engaged and, for the purposes of subsection 239(2.21), subsections (1) and (2), the portion of subsection (4) before paragraph (a), and subsections (5) and (6), includes a designated person;

**Notes**: Everything from "and, for the purposes of subsection 239(2.21)..." added by 1998 first budget bill, effective June 18, 1998.

Definition "official" amended by 1992 technical bill, effective June 10, 1993. From 1989 to June 9, 1993, read:

(a) "official" means any person employed in or occupying a position of responsibility

(i) in the service of Her Majesty in right of Canada or a province, or

(ii) in the service of an authority engaged in administering a law of a province similar to the *Pension Benefits Standards Act, 1985*

or any person formerly so employed or formerly occupying a position therein;

**Application Policies**: SR&ED 95-04: Conflict of interest..

**"taxpayer information"** means information of any kind and in any form relating to one or more taxpayers that is

(a) obtained by or on behalf of the Minister for the purposes of this Act, or

(b) prepared from information referred to in paragraph (a),

but does not include information that does not directly or indirectly reveal the identity of the taxpayer to whom it relates.

**Related Provisions**: 122.64(1) — Confidentiality of information; 241(11) — Meaning of "this Act".

**Notes**: Definition "taxpayer information" added by 1992 technical bill, effective June 10, 1993.

**(11) PGRT Act references** — The references in subsections (1), (3), (4) and (10) to "this Act" shall be read as references to "this Act or the *Petroleum and Gas Revenue Tax Act*".

**Definitions [s. 241]**: "adjusted cost base" — 54, 248(1); "authorized person" — 241(10); "business" — 248(1); "business number" — 248(1); "Canada" — 255; "corporation" — 248(1), *Interpretation Act* 35(1); "court of appeal" — 241(10); "designated person" — 241(10); "employed", "employer", "Minister", "Newfoundland offshore area", "non-resident" — 248(1); "official" — 241(10); "prescribed", "property" — 248(1); "province" — *Interpretation Act* 35(1); "record", "registered charity", "registered pension plan" — 248(1); "related" — 251(2)–(6); "taxable income" — 2(2), 248(1); "taxpayer" — 248(1); "taxpayer information" — 241(10); "this Act" — 241(11); "writing" — *Interpretation Act* 35(1).

**242. Officers, etc., of corporations** — Where a corporation commits an offence under this Act, any officer, director or agent of the corporation who directed, authorized, assented to, acquiesced in or participated in the commission of the offence is a party to and guilty of the offence and is liable on conviction to the punishment provided for the offence whether or not the corporation has been prosecuted or convicted.

**Related Provisions**: 227.1 — Liability of directors; 236 — Corporate directors and officers entitled to execute documents.

**Definitions [s. 242]**: "corporation" — 248(1), *Interpretation Act* 35(1); "officer" — 248(1)"office".

**Information Circulars**: 73-10R3: Tax evasion.

**243. Power to decrease punishment** — Notwithstanding the *Criminal Code* or any other statute or law in force on June 30, 1948, the court has, in any prosecution or proceeding under this Act, no power to impose less than the minimum fine or imprisonment fixed by this Act or to suspend sentence.

**Notes**: One judge sidestepped this prohibition by imposing the minimum fine, but making it payable at a rate of $1 per month, with no jail time if the taxpayer defaults.

## Procedure and Evidence

**244. (1) Information or complaint** — An information or complaint under this Act may be laid or made by any officer of the Canada Customs and Revenue Agency, by a member of the Royal Canadian Mounted Police or by any person thereto authorized by the Minister and, where an information or complaint purports to have been laid or made under this Act, it shall be deemed to have been laid or made by a person thereto authorized by the Minister and shall not be called in question for lack of authority of the informant or complainant except by the Minister or by a person acting for the Minister or Her Majesty.

**Notes**: 244(1) amended by *Canada Customs & Revenue Agency Act*, effective November 1, 1999, to change "Department of National Revenue" to "Canada Customs and Revenue Agency".

**(2) Two or more offences** — An information or complaint in respect of an offence under this Act may be for one or more offences and no information, complaint, warrant, conviction or other proceeding in a prosecution under this Act is objectionable or insufficient by reason of the fact that it relates to two or more offences.

**(3) Venue** — An information or complaint in respect of an offence under this Act may be heard, tried or determined by any court, judge or justice if the accused is resident, carrying on business, found or apprehended or is in custody within the territorial jurisdiction of the court, judge or justice, as the case may be, although the matter of the information or complaint did not arise within that jurisdiction.

**(4) Limitation period** — An information or complaint under the provisions of the *Criminal Code* relating to summary convictions, in respect of an offence under this Act, may be laid or made at any time but not later than 8 years after the day on which the matter of the information or complaint arose.

**Notes:** See Notes to 238(1).

**(5) Proof of service by mail** — Where, by this Act or a regulation, provision is made for sending by mail a request for information, notice or demand, an affidavit of an officer of the Canada Customs and Revenue Agency, sworn before a commissioner or other person authorized to take affidavits, setting out that the officer has knowledge of the facts in the particular case, that such a request, notice or demand was sent by registered letter on a named day to the person to whom it was addressed (indicating the address) and that the officer identifies as exhibits attached to the affidavit the post office certificate of registration of the letter or a true copy of the relevant portion thereof and a true copy of the request, notice or demand, shall, in the absence of proof to the contrary, be received as evidence of the sending and of the request, notice or demand.

**Related Provisions**: 244(11) — Presumption that affidavit valid; 244(14) — Mailing date deemed to be date of notice; 248(7)(a) — Mail deemed received on day mailed; *Interpretation Act* 25(1) — Evidence is rebuttable.

**Notes**: 244(5) amended by *Canada Customs & Revenue Agency Act*, effective November 1, 1999, to change "Department of National Revenue" to "Canada Customs and Revenue Agency".

**(6) Proof of personal service** — Where, by this Act or a regulation, provision is made for personal service of a request for information, notice or demand, an affidavit of an officer of the Canada Customs and Revenue Agency sworn before a commissioner or other person authorized to take affidavits setting out that the officer has knowledge of the facts in the particular case, that such a request, notice or demand was served personally on a named day on the person to whom it was directed and that the officer identifies as an exhibit attached to the affidavit a true copy of the request, notice or demand, shall, in the absence of proof to the contrary, be received as evidence of the personal service and of the request, notice or demand.

**Related Provisions**: 244(11) — Presumption that affidavit valid; *Interpretation Act* 25(1) — Evidence is rebuttable.

**Notes**: 244(6) amended by *Canada Customs & Revenue Agency Act*, effective November 1, 1999, to change "Department of National Revenue" to "Canada Customs and Revenue Agency".

**(7) Proof of failure to comply** — Where, by this Act or a regulation, a person is required to make a return, statement, answer or certificate, an affidavit of an officer of the Canada Customs and Revenue Agency, sworn before a commissioner or other person authorized to take affidavits, setting out that the officer has charge of the appropriate records and that after a careful examination and search of those records the officer has been unable to find in a given case that the return, statement, answer or certificate, as the case may be, has been made by that person, shall, in the absence of proof to the contrary, be received as evidence that in that case that person did not make the return, statement, answer or certificate, as the case may be.

**Related Provisions**: 244(11) — Presumption that affidavit valid; *Interpretation Act* 25(1) — Evidence is rebuttable.

**Notes**: 244(7) amended by *Canada Customs & Revenue Agency Act*, effective November 1, 1999, to change "Department of National Revenue" to "Canada Customs and Revenue Agency".

**(8) Proof of time of compliance** — Where, by this Act or a regulation, a person is required to make a return, statement, answer or certificate, an affidavit of an officer of the Canada Customs and Revenue Agency, sworn before a commissioner or other person authorized to take affidavits, setting out that the officer has charge of the appropriate records and that after careful examination of those records the officer has found that the return, statement, answer or certificate was filed or made on a particular day, shall, in the absence of proof to the contrary, be received as evidence that it was filed or made on that day and not prior thereto.

**Related Provisions**: 244(11) — Presumption that affidavit valid; *Interpretation Act* 25(1) — Evidence is rebuttable.

**Notes**: 244(8) amended by *Canada Customs & Revenue Agency Act*, effective November 1, 1999, to change "Department of National Revenue" to "Canada Customs and Revenue Agency".

**(9) Proof of documents** — An affidavit of an officer of the Canada Customs and Revenue Agency, sworn before a commissioner or other person authorized to take affidavits, setting out that the officer has charge of the appropriate records and that a document annexed to the affidavit is a document or true copy of a document, or a print-out of an electronic document, made by or on behalf of the Minister or a person exercising a power of the Minister or by or on behalf of a taxpayer, is evidence of the nature and contents of the document.

**Related Provisions**: 231.5(1) — Copy of document seized or examined may be used in court proceedings; 244(11) — Presumption that affidavit valid; *Interpretation Act* 25(1) — Evidence is rebuttable.

**Notes**: 244(9) amended by *Canada Customs & Revenue Agency Act*, effective November 1, 1999, to change "Department of National Revenue" to "Canada Customs and Revenue Agency".

244(9) amended by 1995-97 technical bill, effective June 18, 1998, primarily to add reference to print-outs of electronic documents. From 1972 until the amendment, read:

> (9) An affidavit of an officer of the Department of National Revenue, sworn before a commissioner or other person authorized to take affidavits, setting out that the officer has charge of the appropriate records and that a document annexed thereto is a document or true copy of a document made by or on behalf of the Minister or a person exercising the powers of the Minister or by or on behalf of a taxpayer, shall, in the absence of proof to the contrary, be received as evidence of the nature and contents of the document and shall be admissible in evidence and have the same probative force as the original document would have if it had been proven in the ordinary way.

**(10) Proof of no appeal** — An affidavit of an officer of the Canada Customs and Revenue Agency, sworn before a commissioner or other person authorized to take affidavits, setting out that the officer has charge of the appropriate records and has knowledge of the practice of the Agency and that an examination of those records shows that a notice of assessment for a particular taxation year or a notice of determination was mailed or otherwise communicated to a taxpayer on a particular day under this Act and that, after careful examination and search of those records, the officer has been unable to find that a notice of objection or of appeal from the assessment or determination or a request under subsection 245(6), as the case may be, was received within the time allowed, shall, in the absence of proof to the contrary, be received as evidence of the statements contained in it.

**Related Provisions**: 244(11) — Presumption that affidavit valid; *Interpretation Act* 25(1) — Evidence is rebuttable.

**Notes**: 244(10) amended by *Canada Customs & Revenue Agency Act*, effective November 1, 1999. From Sept. 13, 1988 through October 1999, read:

(10) An affidavit of an officer of the Department of National Revenue, sworn before a commissioner or other person authorized to take affidavits, setting out that the officer has charge of the appropriate records and has knowledge of the practice of the Department and that an examination of the records shows that a notice of assessment for a particular taxation year or a notice of determination was mailed or otherwise communicated to a taxpayer on a particular day pursuant to this Act and that, after careful examination and search of those records, the officer has been unable to find that a notice of objection or of appeal from the assessment or determination or a request under subsection 245(6), as the case may be, was received within the time allowed therefor, shall, in the absence of proof to the contrary, be received as evidence of the statements contained there

**(11) Presumption** — Where evidence is offered under this section by an affidavit from which it appears that the person making the affidavit is an officer of the Canada Customs and Revenue Agency, it is not necessary to prove the person's signature or that the person is such an officer nor is it necessary to prove the signature or official character of the person before whom the affidavit was sworn.

**Notes**: 244(11) amended by *Canada Customs & Revenue Agency Act*, effective November 1, 1999, to change "Department of National Revenue" to "Canada Customs and Revenue Agency".

**(12) Judicial notice** — Judicial notice shall be taken of all orders or regulations made under this Act without those orders or regulations being specially pleaded or proven.

**(13) Proof of documents** — Every document purporting to have been executed under, or in the course of the administration or enforcement of, this Act over the name in writing of the Minister, the Deputy Minister of National Revenue, the Commissioner of Customs and Revenue or an officer authorized to exercise a power or perform a duty of the Minister under this Act is deemed to have been signed, made and issued by the Minister, the Deputy Minister, the Commissioner or the officer unless it has been called in question by the Minister or by a person acting for the Minister or Her Majesty.

**Notes**: 244(13) amended by *Canada Customs & Revenue Agency Act*, effective November 1, 1999. From June 18, 1998 through October 1999, read:

(13) Every document purporting to have been executed under, or in the course of the administration or enforcement of, this Act over the name in writing of the Minister, the Deputy Minister of National Revenue or an officer authorized to exercise a power or perform a duty of the Minister under this Act is deemed to have been signed, made and issued by the Minister, the Deputy Minister or the officer unless it has been called in question by the Minister or by a person acting for the Minister or Her Majesty.

244(13) amended by 1995-97 technical bill, effective June 18, 1998. The substantive change was to change "authorized by regulation" to "authorized", due to the enactment of 220(2.01). From May 12, 1994 to June 17, 1998, read:

(13) Every document purporting to be an order, direction, demand, notice, certificate, requirement, decision, assessment, discharge of mortgage or other document purporting to have been executed under, or in the course of administration or enforcement of, this Act over the name in writing of the Minister, the Deputy Minister of National Revenue or any officer authorized by regulation to exercise powers or perform duties of the Minister under this Act shall be deemed to be a document signed, made and issued by the Minister, the Deputy Minister or the officer unless it has been called in question by the Minister or by a person acting for the Minister or Her Majesty.

"Deputy Minister of National Revenue for Taxation" changed to "Deputy Minister of National Revenue" by Department of National Revenue Act amending bill, effective May 12, 1994.

244(13) prevents taxpayers from challenging the validity of CCRA documents during court proceedings. The "person acting for the Minister or Her Majesty" would normally be Department of Justice tax litigation counsel, or a CCRA officer appearing as a witness.

**(13.1) [Repealed]**

**Notes**: 244(13.1) repealed by Department of National Revenue Act amending bill, effective May 12, 1994. It allowed "Revenue Canada" to be used in documents to refer to the Department of National Revenue. It was replaced by s. 3.1 of the *Department of National Revenue Act*. That Act has now been replaced by the *Canada Customs and Revenue Agency Act*, effective November 1999.

244(13.1) was originally enacted to override *Re Solway*, [1979] C.T.C. 154 and *Wel Holdings*, [1979] C.T.C. 116, where the Federal Court had held that documents issued under the name "Revenue Canada, Taxation" were a nullity.

See also s. 38 of the *Interpretation Act*.

**(14) Mailing date** — For the purposes of this Act, where any notice or notification described in subsection 149.1(6.3), 152(3.1), 165(3) or 166.1(5) or any notice of assessment or determination is mailed, it shall be presumed to be mailed on the date of that notice or notification.

**Related Provisions**: 244(5) — Proof of service by mail; 244(15) — Assessment deemed made on date of mailing; 248(7)(a) — Mail deemed received on day mailed.

**Notes**: Because the word "presumed" is used, rather than "deemed", the presumption is rebuttable rather than conclusive. See *Hughes*, [1987] 2 C.T.C. 2360 (TCC). However, see 244(15), which uses the word "deemed".

The CCRA does not retain actual copies of many notices of assessment, and thus can only produce "reconstructed" versions from its computer system. This means that the CCRA can often not prove when or whether the assessment was mailed, allowing an otherwise-late Notice of Objection to be considered filed on time: *Sykes*,

[1998] 1 C.T.C. 2639 (TCC). But where an assessment is found to have been mailed, time starts running even if it is never received by the taxpayer: *Schafer*, [2000] G.S.T.C. 82 (FCA)

See also Notes to 244(15).

244(14) amended by 1995-97 technical bill, effective June 18, 1998. From December 17, 1991 to June 17, 1998, read:

> (14) For the purposes of this Act, the day of mailing of any notice or notification described in subsection 149.1(6.3), 152(4) or 166.1(5) or of any notice of assessment shall be presumed to be the date of that notice or notification.

244(14) amended by 1991 technical bill, effective December 17, 1991, to add reference to 166.1(5) and to delete references to now irrelevant 192(8) and 194(7).

**(15) Date when assessment made** — Where any notice of assessment or determination has been sent by the Minister as required by this Act, the assessment or determination is deemed to have been made on the day of mailing of the notice of the assessment or determination.

**Related Provisions**: 244(5) — Proof of service by mail; 244(14) — Date of mailing presumed to be date of notice.

**Notes**: 244(15) provides that once the "day of mailing" of a notice is known, the assessment or determination is deemed to have been made on that date. The word "deemed" is conclusive: *Kushnir*, [1985] 1 C.T.C. 2301 (TCC); it creates a statutory fiction: *Verrette*, [1978] 2 S.C.R. 838 at 845. The determination of the "day of mailing" is done under 244(14): there is a (rebuttable) presumption that a notice was mailed on the date that is printed on it.

244(15) amended by 1995-97 technical bill, effective June 18, 1998, to add references to a determination.

**(16) Forms prescribed or authorized** — Every form purporting to be a form prescribed or authorized by the Minister shall be deemed to be a form authorized under this Act by the Minister unless called in question by the Minister or by a person acting for the Minister or Her Majesty.

**Related Provisions**: *Interpretation Act* 32 — Deviations from a prescribed form.

**Notes**: 244(16) amended by 1991 technical bill, effective December 17, 1991, to deem every form to be a form "authorized" rather than "prescribed" by the Minister. (See the definition of "prescribed" in 248(1).)

**(17) Proof of return in prosecution for offence** — In any prosecution for an offence under this Act, the production of a return, certificate, statement or answer required by or under this Act or a regulation, purporting to have been filed or delivered by or on behalf of the person charged with the offence or to have been made or signed by or on behalf of that person shall, in the absence of proof to the contrary, be received as evidence that the return, certificate, statement or answer was filed or delivered, or was made or signed, by or on behalf of that person.

**Related Provisions**: *Interpretation Act* 25(1) — Evidence is rebuttable.

**(18) Idem, in proceedings under Division J of Part I** — In any proceedings under Division J of Part I, the production of a return, certificate, statement or answer required by or under this Act or a regulation, purporting to have been filed or delivered, or to have been made or signed, by or on behalf of the taxpayer shall in the absence of proof to the contrary be received as evidence that the return, certificate, statement or answer was filed or delivered, or was made or signed, by or on behalf of the taxpayer.

**Related Provisions**: *Interpretation Act* 25(1) — Evidence is rebuttable.

**(19) Proof of statement of non-receipt** — In any prosecution for an offence under this Act, an affidavit of an officer of the Canada Customs and Revenue Agency, sworn before a commissioner or other person authorized to take affidavits, setting out that the officer has charge of the appropriate records and that an examination of the records shows that an amount required under this Act to be remitted to the Receiver General on account of tax for a year has not been received by the Receiver General, shall, in the absence of proof to the contrary, be received as evidence of the statements contained therein.

**Related Provisions**: 244(11) — Presumption that affidavit valid; *Interpretation Act* 25(1) — Evidence is rebuttable.

**Notes**: 244(19) amended by *Canada Customs & Revenue Agency Act*, effective November 1, 1999, to change "Department of National Revenue" to "Canada Customs and Revenue Agency".

**(20) Members of partnerships** — For the purposes of this Act,

> (a) a reference in any notice or other document to the firm name of a partnership shall be read as as a reference to all the members thereof; and
>
> (b) any notice or other document shall be deemed to have been provided to each member of a partnership if the notice or other document is mailed to, served on or otherwise sent to the partnership
>
>> (i) at its latest known address or place of business, or
>>
>> (ii) at the latest known address
>>
>>> (A) where it is a limited partnership, of any member thereof whose liability as a member is not limited, or
>>>
>>> (B) in any other case, of any member thereof.

**Related Provisions**: 96(3) — Election by members; 224(6) — Service of garnishment notice on partnership.

**Notes**: 244(20) added by 1991 technical bill, effective December 17, 1991.

**(21) Proof of return filed** — For the purposes of this Act, a document presented by the Minister purporting to be a print-out of the information in respect of a taxpayer received under section 150.1 by the Minister from a person shall be received as evidence and, in the absence of evidence to the contrary, is proof of the return filed by the person under that section.

**Related Provisions**: *Interpretation Act* 25(1) — Evidence is rebuttable.

**Notes**: 244(21) added by 1992 technical bill, effective for 1992 and later taxation years.

**(22) Filing of information returns** — Where a person who is required by this Act or a regulation to file an information return in prescribed form with the Minister meets the criteria specified in writing by the Minister, the person may at any time file the information return with the Minister by way of electronic filing (within the meaning assigned by subsection 150.1(1)) and the person shall be deemed to have filed the information return with the Minister at that time, and a document presented by the Minister purporting to be a print-out of the information so received by the Minister shall be received as evidence and, in the absence of evidence to the contrary, is proof of the information return so deemed to have been filed.

**Related Provisions**: Reg. 205.1 — Electronic filing of information returns required if more than 500 returns being filed; *Interpretation Act* 25(1) — Evidence is rebuttable.

**Notes**: 244(22) added by 1992 technical bill, effective 1992.

**Definitions [s. 244]**: "assessment", "business" — 248(1); "Canada Customs and Revenue Agency" — *Canada Customs and Revenue Agency Act* s. 4(1); "Commissioner of Customs and Revenue" — *Canada Customs and Revenue Agency Act* s. 25; "day of mailing" — 244(14); "Minister", "person", "prescribed", "record", "regulation" — 248(1); "taxation year" — 249; "taxpayer" — 248(1); "writing" — *Interpretation Act* 35(1).

# PART XVI — TAX AVOIDANCE

**245. [General Anti-Avoidance Rule — GAAR]** — **(1) Definitions** — In this section,

**Notes**: Opening words of 245(1) amended to delete reference to 152(1.11) in R.S.C. 1985 (5th Supp.) consolidation. That rule of application is now in 152(1.111).

**"tax benefit"** means a reduction, avoidance or deferral of tax or other amount payable under this Act or an increase in a refund of tax or other amount under this Act;

**Advance Tax Rulings**: ATR-41: Convertible preferred shares; ATR-44: Utilization of deductions and credits within a related corporate group.

**"tax consequences"** to a person means the amount of income, taxable income, or taxable income earned in Canada of, tax or other amount payable by or refundable to the person under this Act, or any other amount that is relevant for the purposes of computing that amount;

**"transaction"** includes an arrangement or event.

**Related Provisions**: 233.1(1)"transaction" — Parallel definition for reporting non-arm's length transactions with non-residents; 247(1) — Parallel definition re transfer pricing.

**Interpretation Bulletins**: IT-532: Part I.3 — tax on large corporations.

**(2) General anti-avoidance provision [GAAR]** — Where a transaction is an avoidance transaction, the tax consequences to a person shall be determined as is reasonable in the circumstances in order to deny a tax benefit that, but for this section, would result, directly or indirectly, from that transaction or from a series of transactions that includes that transaction.

**Related Provisions**: 56(2) — Indirect payments; 246 — Benefit conferred on a person; 247(2)(b)(ii) — GAAR test in transfer-pricing rules; 248(10) — Series of transactions; Canada-U.S. Tax Convention, Art. XXIX A: Limitations on using treaty benefits.

**Notes**: 245(2), known as GAAR (General Anti-Avoidance Rule), added by 1988 tax reform, effective for transactions entered into on or after September 13, 1988 other than

(a) transactions that are part of a series of transactions (ignore 248(10) for this purpose), commencing before that date and completed by the end of 1988, or

(b) any one or more transactions, one of which was entered into before April 13, 1988, that were entered into by a taxpayer in the course of an arrangement and in respect of which the taxpayer received from Revenue Canada, before April 13, 1988, a confirmation or opinion in writing with respect to the tax consequences thereof.

For transactions that are grandfathered as indicated above, read:

245. (1) **Artificial transactions** — In computing income for the purposes of this Act, no deduction may be made in respect of a disbursement or expense made or incurred in respect of a transaction or operation that, if allowed, would unduly or artificially reduce the income.

(1.1) **Idem** — Where it may reasonably be considered that one of the purposes of a series of transactions or events is that an individual convert into a capital gain from the disposition of property an amount that would

(a) but for one or more of such transactions or events in the series, or

(b) on a disposition by him of property in respect of which the property is a substituted property

otherwise have been received by the individual and included in computing his income under paragraph 3(a), no amount shall be deducted by the individual under section 110.6 in respect of that capital gain.

(2) **Indirect payments or transfers** — Where the result of one or more sales, exchanges, declarations of trust, or other transactions of any kind whatever is that a person confers a benefit on a taxpayer, that person shall be deemed to have made a payment to the taxpayer equal to the amount of the benefit conferred notwithstanding the form or legal effect of the transactions or that one or more other persons were also parties thereto; and, whether or not there was an intention to avoid or evade taxes under this Act, the payment shall, depending upon the circumstances, be

(a) included in computing the taxpayer's income for the purpose of Part I,

(b) deemed to be a payment to a non-resident person to which Part XIII applies, or

(c) deemed to be a disposition by way of gift.

(3) **Arm's length** — Where it is established that a sale, exchange or other transaction was entered into by persons dealing at arm's length, *bona fide* and not pursuant to, or as part of, any other transaction and not to effect payment, in whole or in part, of an existing or future obligation, no party thereto shall be regarded, for the purpose of this section, as having conferred a benefit on a party with whom he was so dealing.

(245(1.1) above applied only to a series of transactions or events commencing after November 21, 1985.)

GAAR was found to apply in the following cases:

- *Michelin Tires (Canada) Ltd.*, [1995] G.S.T.C. 17 (CITT), aff'd [2000] G.S.T.C. 17 (FCTD) (sale of inventory to affiliated company to obtain refund of federal sales tax)

## S. 245(2) — Income Tax Act

- *McNichol*, [1997] 2 C.T.C. 2088 (TCC) (surplus stripping by selling shares of corporation instead of paying dividend) (appeal to FCA discontinued June 29, 1998)
- *RMM Canadian Enterprises (Equilease Corp.)*, [1998] 1 C.T.C. 2300 (TCC) (surplus stripping by selling shares of corporation instead of paying dividend) (appeal to FCA discontinued October 5, 1998)
- *Nadeau*, [1999] 3 C.T.C. 2235 (TCC) (paid-up capital increased)
- *OSFC Holdings Ltd.*, [1999] 3 C.T.C. 2649 (TCC) (sale of assets via partnership to transfer loss to purchaser).
- *Duncan*, (TCC, Jan. 8, 2001, 97-2936(IT)G) (purchase of interest in U.S. partnership in order to claim terminal loss)

GAAR was found not to apply in the following cases:

- *Husky Oil Ltd.*, [1999] 4 C.T.C. 2691 (TCC) (sale of assets via partnership to transfer loss to purchaser)
- *Jabs Construction Ltd.*, [1999] 3 C.T.C. 2556 (TCC) (transfer of capital gain to charity via 110.1(3))
- *Canadian Pacific Ltd.*, 2000 CarswellNat 2097 (TCC) (weak-currency loans à la *Shell Canada*; see now 20.3).

See also *Central Supply Co.*, [1997] 3 C.T.C. 102 (FCA), which dealt with the pre-1988 anti-avoidance rule, but which was dealt with by the Federal Court of Appeal using principles very similar to those applicable under GAAR. But see also *Duha Printers (Western) Ltd.*, [1998] 3 C.T.C. 303; *Continental Bank Leasing Corp.*, [1998] 4 C.T.C. 119; and *Shell Canada Ltd.*, [1999] 4 C.T.C. 143, in all of which (plus others) the Supreme Court of Canada approved artificial tax avoidance in pre-GAAR transactions.

GAAR assessments normally go to the GAAR Committee in Ottawa for approval before they can be issued or formally proposed. However, local Tax Services Office can now assess GAAR on fact situations which have been approved in prior cases by Ottawa.

As of November 1999, the regular GAAR Committee members are: Mike Hiltz (Chair), Ted Harris, Terry Miszaniec, Sharon Gulliver, Gerry Lalonde (Finance), John Bentley (Justice); occasional members are Wayne Adams, Walter Szyc and Anne-Marie Lévesque (Justice). The committee normally meets once a week, but will not, as a committee, meet with taxpayers or their representatives.

**Interpretation Bulletins**: IT-489R: Non-arm's length sale of shares to a corporation.

**Information Circulars**: 88-2 and Supplement: General anti-avoidance rule — section 245 of the *Income Tax Act*.

**I.T. Technical News**: No. 3 (loss utilization within a corporate group); No. 9 (loss consolidation within a corporate group); No. 16 (*Neuman* case; *Duha Printers* case and GAAR statistics; *Continental Bank* case); No. 19 (Change in position in respect of GAAR — section 7).

**Advance Tax Rulings**: ATR-41: Convertible preferred shares; ATR-42: Transfer of shares; ATR-43: Utilization of a non-resident-owned investment corporation as a holding corporation; ATR-44: Utilization of deductions and credits within a related corporate group; ATR-47: Transfer of assets to Realtyco; ATR-50: Structured settlement; ATR-53: Purification of a small business corporation; ATR-54: Reduction of paid-up capital; ATR-55: Amalgamation followed by sale of shares; ATR-56: Purification of a family farm corporation; ATR-57: Transfer of property for estate planning purposes; ATR-58: Divisive reorganization; ATR-60: Joint exploration corporations; ATR-66: Non-arm's length transfer of debt followed by a winding-up and a sale of shares.

**(3) Avoidance transaction** — An avoidance transaction means any transaction

(a) that, but for this section, would result, directly or indirectly, in a tax benefit, unless the transaction may reasonably be considered to have been undertaken or arranged primarily for *bona fide* purposes other than to obtain the tax benefit; or

(b) that is part of a series of transactions, which series, but for this section, would result, directly or indirectly, in a tax benefit, unless the transaction may reasonably be considered to have been undertaken or arranged primarily for *bona fide* purposes other than to obtain the tax benefit.

**Related Provisions**: 248(10) — Series of transactions.

**Notes**: For the case law dealing with GAAR, see Notes to 245(2).

**Information Circulars**: 88-2 and Supplement: General anti-avoidance rule — section 245 of the *Income Tax Act*.

**Advance Tax Rulings**: ATR-41: Convertible preferred shares; ATR-42: Transfer of shares; ATR-44: Utilization of deductions and credits within a related corporate group; ATR-54: Reduction of paid-up capital; ATR-55: Amalgamation followed by sale of shares; ATR-56: Purification of a family farm corporation; ATR-57: Transfer of property for estate planning purposes; ATR-58: Divisive reorganization.

**(4) Where subsec. (2) does not apply** — For greater certainty, subsection (2) does not apply to a transaction where it may reasonably be considered that the transaction would not result directly or indirectly in a misuse of the provisions of this Act or an abuse having regard to the provisions of this Act, other than this section, read as a whole.

**Notes**: The difference between "misuse" and "abuse" in this context is unclear. The French version of 245(4) uses only a single word, "abus".

**I.T. Technical News**: No. 19 (Change in position in respect of GAAR — section 7). Also see under 245(2).

**Advance Tax Rulings**: ATR-42: Transfer of shares; ATR-44: Utilization of deductions and credits within a related corporate group; ATR-54: Reduction of paid-up capital; ATR-55: Amalgamation followed by sale of shares; ATR-56: Purification of a family farm corporation; ATR-58: Divisive reorganization.

**(5) Determination of tax consequences** — Without restricting the generality of subsection (2),

(a) any deduction in computing income, taxable income, taxable income earned in Canada or tax payable or any part thereof may be allowed or disallowed in whole or in part,

(b) any such deduction, any income, loss or other amount or part thereof may be allocated to any person,

(c) the nature of any payment or other amount may be recharacterized, and

(d) the tax effects that would otherwise result from the application of other provisions of this Act may be ignored,

in determining the tax consequences to a person as is reasonable in the circumstances in order to deny a tax benefit that would, but for this section, result, directly or indirectly, from an avoidance transaction.

**(6) Request for adjustments** — Where with respect to a transaction

(a) a notice of assessment, reassessment or additional assessment involving the application of subsection (2) with respect to the transaction has been sent to a person, or

(b) a notice of determination pursuant to subsection 152(1.11) has been sent to a person with respect to the transaction,

any person (other than a person referred to in paragraph (a) or (b)) shall be entitled, within 180 days after the day of mailing of the notice, to request in writing that the Minister make an assessment, reassessment or additional assessment applying subsection (2) or make a determination applying subsection 152(1.11) with respect to that transaction.

**Related Provisions**: 166.1 — Extension of time by Minister; 167(1) — Application to Tax Court of Canada for time extension; 244(10) — Proof that no notice of objection filed.

**(7) Exception** — Notwithstanding any other provision of this Act, the tax consequences to any person, following the application of this section, shall only be determined through a notice of assessment, reassessment, additional assessment or determination pursuant to subsection 152(1.11) involving the application of this section.

**(8) Duties of Minister** — On receipt of a request by a person under subsection (6), the Minister shall, with all due dispatch, consider the request and, notwithstanding subsection 152(4), assess, reassess or make an additional assessment or determination pursuant to subsection 152(1.11) with respect to that person, except that an assessment, reassessment, additional assessment or determination may be made under this subsection only to the extent that it may reasonably be regarded as relating to the transaction referred to in subsection (6).

**Related Provisions**: 165(1.1) — Limitation of right to object to assessments or redetermination; 169(2)(a) — Limitation of right to appeal.

**Notes [s. 245]**: See Notes to 245(2).

**Definitions [s. 245]**: "assessment", "Minister", "person" — 248(1); "series of transactions" — 248(10); "tax benefit", "tax consequences" — 245(1); "taxable income" — 2(2), 248(1); "taxable income earned in Canada" — 115(1), 248(1); "transaction" — 245(1); "writing" — *Interpretation Act* 35(1).

**Information Circulars [s. 245]**: 88-2 and Supplement: General anti-avoidance rule — section 245 of the *Income Tax Act*.

**246. (1) Benefit conferred on a person** — Where at any time a person confers a benefit, either directly or indirectly, by any means whatever, on a taxpayer, the amount of the benefit shall, to the extent that it is not otherwise included in the taxpayer's income or taxable income earned in Canada under Part I and would be included in the taxpayer's income if the amount of the benefit were a payment made directly by the person to the taxpayer and if the taxpayer were resident in Canada, be

(a) included in computing the taxpayer's income or taxable income earned in Canada under Part I for the taxation year that includes that time; or

(b) where the taxpayer is a non-resident person, deemed for the purposes of Part XIII to be a payment made at that time to the taxpayer in respect of property, services or otherwise, depending on the nature of the benefit.

**Related Provisions**: 56(2) — Inclusion in income of indirect payments.

**Interpretation Bulletins**: IT-432R2: Benefits conferred on shareholders.

**(2) Arm's length** — Where it is established that a transaction was entered into by persons dealing at arm's length, *bona fide* and not pursuant to, or as part of, any other transaction and not to effect payment, in whole or in part, of an existing or future obligation, no party thereto shall be regarded, for the purpose of this section, as having conferred a benefit on a party with whom the first-mentioned party was so dealing.

**Interpretation Bulletins [subsec. 246(2)]**: IT-432R2: Benefits conferred on shareholders.

**Related Provisions [s. 246]**: 56(2) — Indirect payments; 245(2) — General anti-avoidance rule.

**Definitions [s. 246]**: "amount" — 248(1); "arm's length" — 251(1); "Canada" — 255; "non-resident", "person", "property" — 248(1); "resident in Canada" — 250; "taxable income earned in Canada" — 115(1), 248(1); "taxation year" — 249; "taxpayer" — 248(1).

# PART XVI.1 — TRANSFER PRICING

**247. (1) Definitions** — The definitions in this subsection apply in this section.

**"arm's length allocation"** means, in respect of a transaction, an allocation of profit or loss that would have occurred between the participants in the transaction if they had been dealing at arm's length with each other.

**Related Provisions**: 9(1) — Normal computation of profit.

**Notes**: Definitions in 247(1) added by 1995-97 technical bill, effective for taxation years and fiscal periods that begin after 1997. For pre-1988 247(1), see Notes at end of 247.

**"arm's length transfer price"** means, in respect of a transaction, an amount that would have been a transfer price in respect of the transaction if the participants in the transaction had been dealing at arm's length with each other.

**Notes**: See under 247(1)"arm's length allocation".

**Information Circulars**: 87-2R: International transfer pricing.

**"documentation-due date"** for a taxation year or fiscal period of a person or partnership means

(a) in the case of a person, the person's filing-due date for the year; or

(b) in the case of a partnership, the day on or before which a return is required by section 229 of the *Income Tax Regulations* to be filed in respect of the period or would be required to be so filed if that section applied to the partnership.

**Notes**: See under 247(1)"arm's length allocation".

**"qualifying cost contribution arrangement"** means an arrangement under which reasonable efforts are made by the participants in the arrangement to establish a basis for contributing to, and to contribute on that basis to, the cost of producing, developing or acquiring any property, or acquiring or performing any services, in proportion to the benefits which each participant is reasonably expected to derive from the property or services, as the case may be, as a result of the arrangement.

**Notes**: The word "derive" as used in this definition should possibly be interpreted broadly; see Notes to 34.2(3).

See under 247(1)"arm's length allocation".

**"tax benefit"** means a reduction, avoidance or deferral of tax or other amount payable under this Act or an increase in a refund of tax or other amount under this Act.

**Notes**: See under 247(1)"arm's length allocation".

**"transaction"** includes an arrangement or event.

**Related Provisions**: 233.1(1)"transaction" — Parallel definition for reporting non-arm's length transactions with non-residents; 245(1) — Parallel definition for general anti-avoidance rule.

**Notes**: See under 247(1)"arm's length allocation".

**"transfer price"** means, in respect of a transaction, an amount paid or payable or an amount received or receivable, as the case may be, by a participant in the transaction as a price, a rental, a royalty, a premium or other payment for, or for the use, production or reproduction of, property or as consideration for services (including services provided as an employee and the insurance or reinsurance of risks) as part of the transaction.

**Notes**: See under 247(1)"arm's length allocation".

**Information Circulars**: 87-2R: International transfer pricing.

**"transfer pricing capital adjustment"** of a taxpayer for a taxation year means the total of

(a) all amounts each of which is

(i) 3/4 of the amount, if any, by which the adjusted cost base to the taxpayer of a capital property (other than a depreciable property) or an eligible capital expenditure of the taxpayer in respect of a business is reduced in the year because of an adjustment made under subsection (2), or

(ii) the amount, if any, by which the capital cost to the taxpayer of a depreciable property is reduced in the year because of an adjustment made under subsection (2); and

(b) all amounts each of which is that proportion of the total of

(i) 3/4 of the amount, if any, by which the adjusted cost base to a partnership of a capital property (other than a depreciable property) or an eligible capital expenditure of a partnership in respect of a business is reduced in a fiscal period that ends in the year because of an adjustment made under subsection (2), and

(ii) the amount, if any, by which the capital cost to a partnership of a depreciable property is reduced in the period because of an adjustment made under subsection (2),

that

(iii) the taxpayer's share of the income or loss of the partnership for the period

is of

(iv) the income or loss of the partnership for the period,

and where the income and loss of the partnership are nil for the period, the income of the partnership for the period is deemed to be $1,000,000 for the purpose of determining a taxpayer's share of the partnership's income for the purpose of this definition.

---

**Proposed Amendment — 247(1)"transfer pricing capital adjustment"**

**"transfer pricing capital adjustment"** of a taxpayer for a taxation year means the total of

(a) all amounts each of which is

(i) 1/2 of the amount, if any, by which the adjusted cost base to the taxpayer of a capital property (other than a depreciable property) is reduced in the year because of an adjustment made under subsection (2)

(ii) 3/4 of the amount, if any, by which the adjusted cost base to the taxpayer of an eligible capital expenditure of the taxpayer in respect of a business is reduced in the year because of an adjustment made under subsection (2), or

(iii) the amount, if any, by which the capital cost to the taxpayer of a depreciable property is reduced in the year because of an adjustment made under subsection (2); and

(b) all amounts each of which is that proportion of the total of

(i) 1/2 of the amount, if any, by which the adjusted cost base to a partnership of a capital property (other than a depreciable property) is reduced in a fiscal period that ends in the year because of an adjustment made under subsection (2),

(ii) 3/4 of the amount, if any, by which the adjusted cost base to a partnership of an eligible capital expenditure of the partnership in respect of a business is reduced in a fiscal period that ends in the year because of an adjustment made under subsection (2), and

(iii) the amount, if any, by which the capital cost to a partnership of a depreciable property is reduced in the period because of an adjustment made under subsection (2),

that

(iv) the taxpayer's share of the income or loss of the partnership for the period

is of

(v) the income or loss of the partnership for the period,

and where the income and loss of the partnership are nil for the period, the income of the partnership for the period is deemed to be $1,000,000 for the purpose of determining a taxpayer's share of the partnership's income for the purpose of this definition.

**Application**: The December 21, 2000 draft legislation, s. 93, will amend the definition "transfer pricing capital adjustment" in subsec. 247(1) to read as above, applicable to taxation years that end after February 27, 2000 except that, for a taxation year of a taxpayer that includes either February 28, 2000 or October 17, 2000, the reference to the fraction "1/2" shall be read as a reference to the fraction in para. 38(a), as amended [by the December 21, 2000 draft legislation], that applies to the taxpayer for that year.

**Technical Notes**: The "transfer pricing capital adjustment of a taxpayer" as defined in subsection 247(1) represents the transfer pricing adjustments made under subsection 247(2) that are in respect of capital property and eligible capital property of the taxpayer. The adjustment includes 3/4 of the adjustments with respect to non-depreciable capital property and eligible capital property and 100% of the adjustment with respect to depreciable capital property.

The definition is amended as a consequence of the reduction of the inclusion rate for capital gains from 3/4 to 1/2 [see 38(a) — ed.], with the result that only 1/2, rather than 3/4, of adjustments made under subsection 247(2) with respect to non-depreciable capital property will be included in the taxpayer's transfer pricing capital adjustment for a year.

The amendment applies to taxation years that end after February 27, 2000 except that, for a taxation year of a taxpayer that includes either February 28, 2000 or October 17, 2000, the reference to "1/2" in the definition "transfer pricing capital adjustment" in subsection 247(1) is to be read as reference to the fraction in paragraph 38(a) that applies to the taxpayer for the year. These modifications are required in order to reflect the capital gains/losses rate for the year.

**Notes**: See under 247(1) "arm's length allocation".

**Information Circulars**: 87-2R: International transfer pricing.

**"transfer pricing capital setoff adjustment"** of a taxpayer for a taxation year means the amount, if any, that would be the taxpayer's transfer pricing capital adjustment for the year if the references, in the definition "transfer pricing capital adjustment", to "reduced" were read as "increased".

**Notes**: See under 247(1) "arm's length allocation".

**"transfer pricing income adjustment"** of a taxpayer for a taxation year means the total of all amounts each of which is the amount, if any, by which an adjustment made under subsection (2) (other than an adjustment included in determining a transfer pricing capital adjustment of the taxpayer for a taxation year) would result in an increase in the taxpayer's income for the year or a decrease in a loss of the taxpayer for the year from a source if that adjustment were the only adjustment made under subsection (2).

**Notes**: See under 247(1) "arm's length allocation".

**"transfer pricing income setoff adjustment"** of a taxpayer for a taxation year means the total of all amounts each of which is the amount, if any, by which an adjustment made under subsection (2) (other than an adjustment included in determining a transfer pricing capital setoff adjustment of the taxpayer for a taxation year) would result in a decrease in the taxpayer's income for the year or an increase in a loss of the taxpayer for the year from a source if that adjustment were the only adjustment made under subsection (2).

**Notes**: See under 247(1) "arm's length allocation".

**(2) Transfer pricing adjustment** — Where a taxpayer or a partnership and a non-resident person with whom the taxpayer or the partnership, or a member of the partnership, does not deal at arm's length (or a partnership of which the non-resident person is a member) are participants in a transaction or a series of transactions and

(a) the terms or conditions made or imposed, in respect of the transaction or series, between any of the participants in the transaction or series differ from those that would have been made between persons dealing at arm's length, or

(b) the transaction or series

(i) would not have been entered into between persons dealing at arm's length, and

(ii) can reasonably be considered not to have been entered into primarily for *bona fide* purposes other than to obtain a tax benefit,

any amounts that, but for this section and section 245, would be determined for the purposes of this Act in respect of the taxpayer or the partnership for a taxation year or fiscal period shall be adjusted (in this section referred to as an "adjustment") to the quantum or nature of the amounts that would have been determined if,

(c) where only paragraph (a) applies, the terms and conditions made or imposed, in respect of the transaction or series, between the participants in the transaction or series had been those that would have been made between persons dealing at arm's length, or

(d) where paragraph (b) applies, the transaction or series entered into between the participants had been the transaction or series that would have been entered into between persons dealing at arm's length, under terms and conditions that

## S. 247(2)(d) — Income Tax Act

would have been made between persons dealing at arm's length.

**Related Provisions**: 115.2(4) — Non-resident investment or pension fund deemed not to deal at arm's length with Canadian service provider; 247(3) — Penalty; 247(6) — Tiers of partnerships; 247(7) — Exclusion for loans to subsidiary; 247(10) — Adjustment only if appropriate; Canada-U.S. tax treaty, Art. IX — Adjustments on transactions between related persons.

**Notes**: The transfer pricing adjustment applies for all purposes of the Act (including, for example, Part XIII withholding tax), not just for Part I tax. The CCRA will follow the OECD transfer pricing guidelines, as per Information Circular 87-2R. The essential requirement is, as far as possible, to follow the "arm's length principle" — i.e., the transaction should be priced at the price that would apply between arm's length parties.

The test in 247(2)(b)(ii) is a GAAR-type test, but without the "no misuse or abuse" defence of 245(4) which the General Anti-Avoidance Rule contains.

For discussion of s. 247, see François Vincent & Ian Freedman, "Transfer Pricing in Canada: The Arm's-Length Principle and the New Tax Rules", 45(6) *Canadian Tax Journal* 1213-1242 (1997).

The transfer pricing rules of the foreign country must also be considered, especially when doing business in the U.S. See Robert Misey, "A Primer on Transfer Pricing for Canadian Companies Conducting Business in the United States", IX(4) *International Tax Planning* (Federated Press), 664–668 (2000).

No assessments will be issued under 247(2) until they have been reviewed by the Transfer Pricing Review Committee at CCRA Headquarters. The CCRA will be issuing a series of Memoranda, with policy on transfer pricing issues. (Reference: Gary Zed.)

Taxpayers may enter into Advance Pricing Agreements with the CCRA and the tax authority of another jurisdiction. Although the CCRA will consider itself administratively bound by such an agreement, it appears not to be legally enforceable: Tom Clearwater, "A Note on the Enforceability of Advance Pricing Agreements Under Canadian Law", VII(2) *Tax Litigation* (Federated Press) 438-442 (1999).

247(2) added by 1995-97 technical bill, effective for taxation years and fiscal periods that begin after 1997. For pre-1988 247(2), see Notes at end of 247.

**Information Circulars**: 87-2R: International transfer pricing; 94-4: International transfer pricing — advance pricing agreements (APA).

**(3) Penalty** — A taxpayer (other than a taxpayer all of whose taxable income for the year is exempt from tax under Part I) is liable to a penalty for a taxation year equal to 10% of the amount determined under paragraph (a) in respect of the taxpayer for the year, where

(a) the amount, if any, by which

(i) the total of

(A) the taxpayer's transfer pricing capital adjustment for the year, and

(B) the taxpayer's transfer pricing income adjustment for the year

exceeds the total of

(ii) the total of all amounts each of which is the portion of the taxpayer's transfer pricing capital adjustment or transfer pricing income adjustment for the year that can reasonably be considered to relate to a particular transaction, where

(A) the transaction is a qualifying cost contribution arrangement in which the taxpayer or a partnership of which the taxpayer is a member is a participant, or

(B) in any other case, the taxpayer or a partnership of which the taxpayer is a member made reasonable efforts to determine arm's length transfer prices or arm's length allocations in respect of the transaction, and to use those prices or allocations for the purposes of this Act, and

(iii) the total of all amounts, each of which is the portion of the taxpayer's transfer pricing capital setoff adjustment or transfer pricing income setoff adjustment for the year that can reasonably be considered to relate to a particular transaction, where

(A) the transaction is a qualifying cost contribution arrangement in which the taxpayer or a partnership of which the taxpayer is a member is a participant, or

(B) in any other case, the taxpayer or a partnership of which the taxpayer is a member made reasonable efforts to determine arm's length transfer prices or arm's length allocations in respect of the transaction, and to use those prices or allocations for the purposes of this Act,

is greater than

(b) the lesser of

(i) 10% of the amount that would be the taxpayer's gross revenue for the year if this Act were read without reference to subsection (2), subsections 69(1) and (1.2) and section 245, and

(ii) $5,000,000.

**Related Provisions**: 247(4) — Requirement for contemporaneous documentation; 247(3) — Determination of partner's gross revenue; 247(9) — Anti-avoidance rule re increases in gross revenue; 247(11) — Payment and assessment of penalty.

**Notes**: See Notes to 238(1).

247(3) added by 1995-97 technical bill, effective with respect to adjustments made under 247(2) for taxation years and fiscal periods that begin after 1998, but it does not apply to transactions completed before September 11, 1997.

**Information Circulars**: 87-2R: International transfer pricing; 94-4: International transfer pricing — advance pricing agreements (APA).

**(4) Contemporaneous documentation** — For the purposes of subsection (3) and the definition "qualifying cost contribution arrangement" in subsection (1), a taxpayer or a partnership is deemed not to have made reasonable efforts to determine and use arm's length transfer prices or arm's length allocations in respect of a transaction or not to have participated in a transaction that is a qualifying cost contribution arrangement, unless the taxpayer or the partnership, as the case may be,

(a) makes or obtains, on or before the taxpayer's or partnership's documentation-due date for the taxation year or fiscal period, as the case may be, in which the transaction is entered into, records or documents that provide a description that is complete and accurate in all material respects of

(i) the property or services to which the transaction relates,

(ii) the terms and conditions of the transaction and their relationship, if any, to the terms and conditions of each other transaction entered into between the participants in the transaction,

(iii) the identity of the participants in the transaction and their relationship to each other at the time the transaction was entered into,

(iv) the functions performed, the property used or contributed and the risks assumed, in respect of the transaction, by the participants in the transaction,

(v) the data and methods considered and the analysis performed to determine the transfer prices or the allocations of profits or losses or contributions to costs, as the case may be, in respect of the transaction, and

(vi) the assumptions, strategies and policies, if any, that influenced the determination of the transfer prices or the allocations of profits or losses or contributions to costs, as the case may be, in respect of the transaction;

(b) for each subsequent taxation year or fiscal period, if any, in which the transaction continues, makes or obtains, on or before the taxpayer's or partnership's documentation-due date for that year or period, as the case may be, records or documents that completely and accurately describe each material change in the year or period to the matters referred to in any of subparagraphs (a)(i) to (vi) in respect of the transaction; and

(c) provides the records or documents described in paragraphs (a) and (b) to the Minister within 3 months after service, made personally or by registered or certified mail, of a written request therefor.

**Related Provisions**: 244(5) — Proof of service by mail or request under 247(4)(c); 248(7) — Mail sent under 247(4)(c) deemed received on day mailed.

**Notes**: The term "records" as used in the opening words of 247(4)(a) includes information stored electronically: see 248(1)"record".

247(4) added by 1995-97 technical bill, effective with respect to adjustments made under 247(2) for taxation years and fiscal periods that begin after 1998, but it does not apply to transactions completed before September 11, 1997.

The enacting legislation provides that a record or document made or obtained or provided to Revenue Canada by a taxpayer or a partnership on or before the taxpayer's or partnership's "documentation-due date" (see 247(1)) for the taxpayer's or partnership's first taxa-tion year or fiscal period, as the case may be, that begins after 1998 is deemed for the purpose of 247(4) to have been made, obtained or provided on a timely basis.

See also Notes to repealed 69(2).

**Information Circulars**: 87-2R: International transfer pricing; 94-4: International transfer pricing — advance pricing agreements (APA).

**(5) Partner's gross revenue** — For the purpose of subparagraph (3)(b)(i), where a taxpayer is a member of a partnership in a taxation year, the taxpayer's gross revenue for the year as a member of the partnership from any activities carried on by means of the partnership is deemed to be that proportion of the amount that would be the partnership's gross revenue from the activities if it were a taxpayer (to the extent that amount does not include amounts received or receivable from other partnerships of which the taxpayer is a member in the year), for a fiscal period of the partnership that ends in the year, that

(a) the taxpayer's share of the income or loss of the partnership from its activities for the period

is of

(b) the income or loss of the partnership from its activities for the period,

and where the income and loss of the partnership from its activities are nil for the period, the income of the partnership from its activities for the period is deemed to be $1,000,000 for the purpose of determining a taxpayer's share of the partnership's income from its activities for the purpose of this subsection.

**Related Provisions**: 247(6) — Tiers of partnerships; 248(1) — Definition of "gross revenue".

**Notes**: 247(5) added by 1995-97 technical bill, effective with respect to adjustments made under 247(2) for taxation years and fiscal periods that begin after 1998, but it does not apply to transactions completed before September 11, 1997.

**(6) Deemed member of partnership** — For the purposes of this section, where a person is a member of a partnership that is a member of another partnership,

(a) the person is deemed to be a member of the other partnership; and

(b) the person's share of the income or loss of the other partnership is deemed to be equal to the amount of that income or loss to which the person is directly or indirectly entitled.

**Notes**: This rule looks through tiers of partnerships.

247(6) added by 1995-97 technical bill, effective for taxation years and fiscal periods that begin after 1997.

**(7) Exclusion for loans to certain controlled foreign affiliates** — Where, in a taxation year of a corporation resident in Canada, a non-resident person owes an amount to the corporation, the non-resident person is a controlled foreign affiliate of the corporation for the purpose of section 17 throughout the period in the year during which the amount is

## S. 247(7) — Income Tax Act

owing and it is established that the amount owing is an amount owing described in paragraph 17(8)(a) or (b), subsection (2) does not apply to adjust the amount of interest paid, payable or accruing in the year on the amount owing.

**Notes**: 247(7) permits a corporation resident in Canada to make an interest-free loan to a controlled foreign affiliate (CFA) or to charge no interest on an amount owing by a CFA without 247(2) applying to deem interest to be payable on the amount owing, provided the affiliate uses the money to earn active business income or the amount owing arose in the course of an active business carried on by the affiliate. Note that, although 247(2) will not apply to the interest payable, it could still apply to any other term of the transaction. For example, 247(2) could apply to adjust the amount actually owing where the amount owing is the unpaid purchase price of goods sold to the non-resident and the purchase price is not one that persons dealing at arm's length would have agreed to.

247(7) amended by 1998 Budget, effective for taxation years that begin after February 23, 1998. For earlier years, read:

> (7) **Exclusion for loans to subsidiary** — Subsection 247 (2) does not apply to a transaction that is a loan referred to in subsection 17(3).

247(7) added by 1995-97 technical bill, effective for taxation years and fiscal periods that begin after 1997.

**(8) Provisions not applicable** — Where subsection (2) would, if this Act were read without reference to sections 67 and 68 and subsections 69(1) and (1.2), apply to adjust an amount under this Act, sections 67 and 68 and subsections 69(1) and (1.2) shall not apply to determine the amount if subsection (2) is applied to adjust the amount.

**Notes**: Put more simply, the transfer-pricing rules in 247 take precedence over 67, 69(1) and 69(1.2).

247(8) added by 1995-97 technical bill, effective for taxation years and fiscal periods that begin after 1997.

**(9) Anti-avoidance** — For the purposes of determining a taxpayer's gross revenue under subparagraph (3)(b)(i) and subsection (5), a transaction or series of transactions is deemed not to have occurred, if one of the purposes of the transaction or series was to increase the taxpayer's gross revenue for the purpose of subsection (3).

**Notes**: 247(9) added by 1995-97 technical bill, effective with respect to adjustments made under 247(2) for taxation years and fiscal periods that begin after 1998, but it does not apply to transactions completed before September 11, 1997.

**(10) No adjustment unless appropriate** — An adjustment (other than an adjustment that results in or increases a transfer pricing capital adjustment or a transfer pricing income adjustment of a taxpayer for a taxation year) shall not be made under subsection (2) unless, in the opinion of the Minister, the circumstances are such that it would be appropriate that the adjustment be made.

**Notes**: One circumstance where Revenue Canada may not find it appropriate to exercise its discretion to make an adjustment under 247(2) is where a taxpayer is entitled to request or has requested relief from double taxation under the mutual agreement procedures of a tax treaty. Note that where a transfer pricing adjustment results in double tax, the taxpayer may request competent authority consideration under the Mutual Agreement article of Canada's tax treaties. See Information Circulars 87-2R and 71-17R4, and Notes to 115.1.

247(10) added by 1995-97 technical bill, effective for taxation years and fiscal periods that begin after 1997.

**Information Circulars**: 87-2R: International transfer pricing.

**(11) Provisions applicable to Part** — Sections 152, 158, 159, 162 to 167 and Division J of Part I apply to this Part, with such modifications as the circumstances require.

**Notes [subsec. 247(11)]**: The draft transfer pricing legislation of September 11, 1997 included s. 247.1, which provided for the payment of penalty and interest to the Receiver General. It was replaced with 247(11), which brings in all the administrative rules from Part I.

247(11) added by 1995-97 technical bill, effective for taxation years and fiscal periods that begin after 1997.

**Notes [former 247]**: Former 247(1) repealed by 1988 tax reform, but still in effect for any one or more transactions, one of which was entered into before April 13, 1988, that were entered into by a taxpayer in the course of an arrangement and in respect of which the taxpayer received from Revenue Canada, before April 13, 1988, a confirmation or opinion in writing with respect to the tax consequences thereof. (This parallels the introduction of the general anti-avoidance rule in 245.) It provided a dividend-stripping rule. Dividend stripping is now dealt with in 84.1 and 212.1. See also Information Circular 88-2, "General anti-avoidance rule", para. 25.

Former 247(2) and (3), repealed by 1988 tax reform (effective 1989–90), set out a rule dealing with corporations deemed to be associated. This rule was re-enacted, with some changes, in 256(2.1).

**Definitions [s. 247]**: "adjusted cost base" — 54, 248(1); "adjustment" — 247(2); "amount" — 248(1); "arm's length" — 115.2(4), 251(1); "arm's length allocation", "arm's length transfer price" — 247(1); "business" — 248(1); "capital property" — 54, 248(1); depreciable property" — 13(21), 248(1); "documentation-due date" — 247(1); "eligible capital expenditure" — 14(5), 248(1); "employee", "filing-due date" — 248(1); "fiscal period" — 249.1; "gross revenue" — 247(5), (9), 248(1); "Minister", "non-resident" — 248(1); "partnership" — see Notes to 96(1); "property" — 248(1); "person" — 248(1); "qualifying cost contribution arrangement" — 247(1); "reasonable efforts" — 247(4); "record" — 248(1); "tax benefit" — 247(1); "taxation year" — 249; "taxpayer" — 248(1); "transaction", "transfer price", "transfer pricing capital adjustment", "transfer pricing capital setoff adjustment", "transfer pricing income adjustment", "transfer pricing income setoff adjustment" — 247(1); "written" — *Interpretation Act* 35(1) ["writing"].

## PART XVII — INTERPRETATION

**248. (1) Definitions** — In this Act,

**"active business"**, in relation to any business carried on by a taxpayer resident in Canada, means any business carried on by the taxpayer other than a specified investment business or a personal services business;

**Related Provisions**: 95(1) — Meaning of "active business" of a foreign affiliate for FAPI purposes; 125(1) — Small business deduction; 125(7)"active business" — Meaning of "active business" for purposes of the small business deduction; 248(1) — Small business corporation.

**Interpretation Bulletins**: IT-73R5: The small business deduction; IT-406R2: Tax payable by an *inter vivos* trust.

**"additional voluntary contribution"** to a registered pension plan means a contribution that is made by a member to the plan, that is used to provide benefits under a money purchase provision (within the meaning assigned by subsection 147.1(1)) of the plan and that is not required as a general condition of membership in the plan;

**Related Provisions**: 60.2 — Refund of undeducted past service AVCs; 147.2(4) — Amount of employee's pension contributions deductible.

**Notes**: "Additional voluntary contribution" added by 1990 pension bill, effective 1986.

**Interpretation Bulletins**: IT-167R6: Registered pension plans — employee's contributions.

**"adjusted cost base"** has the meaning assigned by section 54;

**Related Provisions**: 40(1) — Calculation of gain or loss for capital gain/loss purposes.

**"adjustment time"** has the meaning assigned by subsection 14(5);

**"allowable business investment loss"** has the meaning assigned by section 38;

**Related Provisions**: 3(d) — Income for taxation year — application of allowable business investment losses; 111(1)(a), 111(8)"non-capital loss" — Carryforward of allowable business investment losses.

**"allowable capital loss"** has the meaning assigned by section 38;

**Related Provisions**: 3(b)(ii) — Income for taxation year — application of allowable capital losses.

### Proposed Addition — 248(1)"*alter ego* trust"

"*alter ego* trust" means a trust to which paragraph 104(4)(a) would apply if that paragraph were read without reference to subparagraph 104(4)(a)(iii) and clauses 104(4)(a)(iv)(B) and (C);

**Application**: Bill C-43 (First Reading September 20, 2000), subsec. 112(4), will add the definition "*alter ego* trust" to subsec. 248(1), applicable to trusts created after 1999.

**Technical Notes**: The new definition "*alter ego* trust" in subsection 248(1) refers to a trust to which paragraph 104(4)(a) would apply if that paragraph were read without reference to subparagraph 104(4)(a)(iii) and clause 104(4)(a)(iv)(B). Accordingly, for a trust to be an *alter ego* trust it must satisfy the following conditions:

1. at the time of the trust's creation, the taxpayer creating the trust was alive and had attained 65 years of age;
2. the trust was created after 1999;
3. the taxpayer was entitled to receive all of the income of the trust that arose before the taxpayer's death;
4. no person except the taxpayer could, before the taxpayer's death, receive or otherwise obtain the use of any of the income or capital of the trust; and
5. the trust did not make an election referred to in subparagraph 104(4)(a)(ii.1).

The definitions "*alter ego* trust" and "joint partner trust" apply to trusts created after 1999. The definition "post-1971 partner trust" applies to trusts created after 1971. Other amendments related to the introduction of these definitions include amendments to section 73, subsections 104(5.8), (6) and (15) and subsection 107(4), and the amended definition of "trust" in subsection 108(1). For further detail, see the commentary on those provisions.

**Related Provisions**: 73(1.01)(c)(ii) — Rollover on transfer to alter ego trust; 104(5.8) — Transfers from alter ego trust to another trust; 104(6)(b)(ii.1), (iii) — Deduction from income of trust; 104(15)(a) — Preferred beneficiary election; 107(4)(a)(ii) — Distribution of property to person other than taxpayer; 248(1)"joint partner trust" — Parallel trust where spouse is also a beneficiary.

**Notes**: This means a trust described in 104(4)(a)(iv)(A). *Alter ego* trusts and joint partner trusts are expected to be used as an estate planning tool to avoid probate fees. They effectively extend the spousal-trust rule in 73(1)(c) (draft 73(1.01)) to allow the settlor to be a beneficiary as well. See John Fuke & Mary Anne Bueschkens, "Alter Ego Trust and Joint Spousal Trust", VI(2) *Business Vehicles* (Federated Press) 292-294 (2000).

**"amateur athlete trust"** has the meaning assigned by subsection 143.1(1);

**Notes**: "Amateur athlete trust" added by 1992 technical bill, effective 1988.

**"amortized cost"** of a loan or lending asset at any time to a taxpayer means the amount, if any, by which the total of

(a) in the case of a loan made by the taxpayer, the total of all amounts advanced in respect of the loan at or before that time,

(b) in the case of a loan or lending asset acquired by the taxpayer, the cost of the loan or lending asset to the taxpayer,

(c) in the case of a loan or lending asset acquired by the taxpayer, the part of the amount, if any, by which

(i) the principal amount of the loan or lending asset at the time it was so acquired

exceeds

(ii) the cost to the taxpayer of the loan or lending asset

that was included in computing the taxpayer's income for any taxation year ending at or before that time,

(c.1) the total of all amounts each of which is an amount in respect of the loan or lending asset that was included in computing the taxpayer's income for a taxation year that ended at or before that time in respect of changes in the value of the loan or lending asset attributable to the fluctuation in the value of a currency of a country other than Canada relative to Canadian currency,

(d) where the taxpayer is an insurer, any amount in respect of the loan or lending asset that was deemed by reason of paragraph 142(3)(a) of the *Income Tax Act*, chapter 148 of the Revised Statutes of Canada, 1952, as it read in its application to the 1977 taxation year, to be a gain for any taxation year ending at or before that time, and

(e) the total of all amounts each of which is an amount in respect of the loan or lending asset that was included under paragraph 12(1)(i) in computing the taxpayer's income for any taxation year ending at or before that time

**S. 248(1) amo**          Income Tax Act

exceeds the total of

(f) the part of the amount, if any, by which

(i) the amount referred to in subparagraph (c)(ii)

exceeds

(ii) the amount referred to in subparagraph (c)(i)

that was deducted in computing the taxpayer's income for any taxation year ending at or before that time,

(f.1) the total of all amounts each of which is an amount in respect of the loan or lending asset that was deducted in computing the taxpayer's income for a taxation year that ended at or before that time in respect of changes in the value of the loan or lending asset attributable to the fluctuation in the value of a currency of a country other than Canada relative to Canadian currency,

(g) the total of all amounts that, at or before that time, the taxpayer had received as or on account or in lieu of payment of or in satisfaction of the principal amount of the loan or lending asset,

(h) where the taxpayer is an insurer, any amount in respect of the loan or lending asset that was deemed by reason of paragraph 142(3)(b) of the *Income Tax Act*, chapter 148 of the Revised Statutes of Canada, 1952, as it read in its application to the 1977 taxation year, to be a loss for any taxation year ending at or before that time, and

(i) the total of all amounts each of which is an amount in respect of the loan or lending asset deducted under paragraph 20(1)(p) in computing the taxpayer's income for any taxation year ending at or before that time;

**Related Provisions**: 138(13) — Variation in amortized of certain insurers.

**Notes**: Paras (c.1) and (f.1) added by 1994 tax amendments bill (Part III), retroactive to taxation years that begin after June 17, 1987 and end after 1987.

**I.T. Application Rules**: 69 (meaning of "*Income Tax Act*, chapter 148 of the Revised Statutes of Canada, 1952").

**Interpretation Bulletins**: IT-442R: Bad debts and reserves for doubtful debts.

**"amount"** means money, rights or things expressed in terms of the amount of money or the value in terms of money of the right or thing, except that,

(a) notwithstanding paragraph (b), in any case where subsection 112(2.1), (2.2) or (2.4), or section 187.2 or 187.3 or subsection 258(3) or (5) applies to a stock dividend, the "amount" of the stock dividend is the greater of

(i) the amount by which the paid-up capital of the corporation that paid the dividend is increased by reason of the payment of the dividend, and

(ii) the fair market value of the share or shares paid as a stock dividend at the time of payment,

(b) in any case where section 191.1 applies to a stock dividend, the "amount" of the stock dividend for the purposes of Part VI.1 is the greater of

(i) the amount by which the paid-up capital of the corporation that paid the dividend is increased by reason of the payment of the dividend, and

(ii) the fair market value of the share or shares paid as a stock dividend at the time of payment,

and for any other purpose the amount referred to in subparagraph (i), and

(c) in any other case, the "amount" of any stock dividend is the amount by which the paid-up capital of the corporation that paid the dividend is increased by reason of the payment of the dividend;

**Related Provisions**: 95(7) — "Amount" of stock dividend paid by foreign affiliate.

**Interpretation Bulletins**: IT-88R2: Stock dividends.

**Information Circulars**: 88-2, para. 26: General anti-avoidance rule — section 245 of the *Income Tax Act*.

**"annuity"** includes an amount payable on a periodic basis whether payable at intervals longer or shorter than a year and whether payable under a contract, will or trust or otherwise;

**Related Provisions**: 56(1)(d), 60(a), 212(1)(o) — Annuity payments taxable; 128.1(10) "excluded right or interest"(f) — Emigration — no deemed disposition of right under annuity contract; Canada-U.S. tax treaty, Art. XVIII:4 — Meaning of "annuities" for treaty purposes; *Income Tax Conventions Interpretation Act* 5 — Meaning of "annuity" for treaty purposes.

**"appropriate percentage"** for a taxation year means the lowest percentage referred to in subsection 117(2) that is applicable in determining tax payable under Part I for the year;

**Notes**: This means 17% for 1988-2000 and 16% effective 2001 (per Oct. 18/00 Economic Statement proposals). It is used as the percentage for credits in 118–118.7. The effect is equivalent to a deduction at the lowest marginal rate — a deduction off the "bottom" of one's income instead of off the "top".

**"assessment"** includes a reassessment;

**Related Provisions**: 152 — Assessments; 244(15) — Assessment deemed made on date of mailing.

### Proposed Addition — 248(1) "authorized foreign bank"

**"authorized foreign bank"** has the meaning assigned by section 2 of the *Bank Act*;

**Application**: The August 8, 2000 draft legislation, s. 25(1), will add the definition "authorized foreign bank" to s. 248(1), applicable after June 27, 1999.

**Technical Notes**: Section 248 defines a number of terms that apply for the purposes of the Act, and sets out various rules relating to the interpretation and application of various provisions of the Act.

Subsection 248(1) is amended to add several new definitions, all of which relate to Canadian branches of authorized foreign banks.

An "authorized foreign bank" means the same thing as that term means under section 2 of the *Bank Act* — that is, a foreign bank in respect of which an order under subsection 524(1) of the *Bank Act* has been made.

**Department of Finance news release, August 8, 2000**: *FOREIGN BANK TAX PROPOSALS RELEASED*

Secretary of State (International Financial Institutions) Jim Peterson today released detailed income tax proposals relating to the taxation of foreign banks that operate branches in Canada.

The new rules are presented in the form of proposed amendments to the *Income Tax Act* and Regulations, and are accompanied by comprehensive explanatory notes.

The proposed tax changes follow from amendments to the *Bank Act* enacted in June 1999, which allow foreign banks to establish specialized, commercially focused branches in Canada. Previously, foreign banks could operate in Canada only through Canadian-incorporated subsidiaries.

"These rules will make Canada's taxation of the new foreign bank branches broadly comparable to the taxation of Canadian banks," Mr. Peterson said.

As previously proposed, the rules give foreign banks a time-limited window to move operations from a Canadian subsidiary into a Canadian branch without undue tax consequences. Today's announcement ensures that foreign banks have adequate time to plan such moves by extending the proposed cut-off date for relief eligibility by three months — to March 31, 2001. To be eligible, a bank must apply by that date to the Office of the Superintendent of Financial Institutions to operate a Canadian branch.

Among the proposals in today's announcement are incidental changes in several other tax areas, including a proposal that foreign currency deposits be permitted investments for registered retirement savings plans and other deferred-income plans. The attached annex contains a list of the more significant of these changes, including a number of amendments that apply to branches of non-resident taxpayers other than banks.

Mr. Peterson is inviting taxpayers and their professional advisors to review and comment on today's proposals before they are submitted to Parliament as a bill later this year.

The detailed measures set out in today's proposals were the subject of a Notice of Ways and Means Motion tabled in Parliament on February 11, 1999. The transitional relief for conversion of subsidiaries to branches was announced on May 11, 1999.

The draft legislation and accompanying explanatory notes are available on the Department of Finance's Web site at the address shown below. Printed copies of these documents will be available later this month from the department's Distribution Centre at (613) 943-8665.

References in the proposals to "Announcement Date" should be read as references to today's date.

For further information: Foreign bank branches (taxation), James Greene, Tax Policy Branch, (613) 992-4853; Foreign bank branches (general policy), Eleanor Ryan, Financial Sector Policy Branch, (613) 943-9400; Business Income Tax, Sharmila Khare, Tax Policy Branch, (613) 947-1980; Karl Littler, Executive Assistant to the Secretary of State (International Financial Institutions), (613) 992-6054; Laurette Bergeron, Public Affairs and Operations Division, (613) 996-8080.

**Department of Finance news release, February 11, 1999**: *Authorized Foreign Banks: Income Tax Rules*

Secretary of State (International Financial Institutions) Jim Peterson, on behalf of Finance Minister Paul Martin, today tabled in the House of Commons a Notice of Ways and Means Motion that proposes changes to the *Income Tax Act* as a result of the introduction of legislation that would permit foreign banks to establish specialized, commercially-focused branches in Canada.

"These proposed tax rules were developed in consultation with the industry," Mr. Peterson said. "They will ensure that Canadian branches of foreign banks, Canadian subsidiaries of foreign banks, and domestic banks are all taxed on a similar basis."

The proposed tax rules are described in the attached Notice of Ways and Means Motion and Backgrounder. Legislation to implement the rules will be included in a Bill and tabled in Parliament at an early opportunity. The measures described in the proposals will come into force at the same time as the foreign bank entry legislation introduced today.

For further information: Robin Maley, Tax Legislation Division, (613) 992-4859; Jean-Michel Catta, Public Affairs and Operations Division, (613) 992-1574; Patrick Dion, Special Assistant to the Secretary of State (International Financial Institutions), (613) 996-7861.

BACKGROUNDER

In February 1997, the Secretary of State for International Financial Institutions announced that a new foreign bank entry regime would be implemented to allow foreign banks to carry on business in Canada through branch offices. Currently, a non-resident bank must incorporate a Canadian subsidiary if it wishes to carry on business in Canada.

The proposed *Income Tax Act* changes announced today were developed in consultation with representatives of both domestic and foreign banks, and are intended to place these new Canadian branches of foreign banks in a comparable tax position to Canadian resident banks ("Canadian banks"). In other respects, it is anticipated that Canadian branches of foreign banks will generally be subject to the same provisions of that Act as Canadian banks.

The proposed changes are described in more detail below. Any references to the Bank Act include the proposed amendments included in the Bill introduced today to permit foreign banks to establish branches in Canada. In all cases, the changes will apply on and after the day that subsection 35(1) of that Bill comes into force.

*Definition*

It is proposed that the term "authorized foreign bank" used in the *Bank Act* be adopted in the *Income Tax Act* by reference to the definition in the *Bank Act*.

*Transfer of Loans and Other Assets*

Under the *Income Tax Act*, transfers of loans and other assets between non-arm's length corporations are generally treated as occurring at fair market value. Special rules may also apply to defer the recognition of losses until an asset is transferred to an arm's length party.

A foreign bank may have some discretion in deciding whether to hold specific assets in Canada or in its home jurisdiction. Moreover, the assets of the foreign bank may be transferred between the home jurisdiction and Canada. As the Canadian branch of a foreign bank and its home office are not separate legal entities, new rules are proposed to ensure that transfers of assets between the Canadian branch and its home office are taxed in the same manner as other non-arm's length transfers. The new rules deem such transfers to occur at fair market value, subject to the existing loss deferral rules that prevent the premature realization of losses.

[For other proposals, see under 18(5), 20(1)(c), 126(2), 153(1), 181.3(3), 190.13, 212(1)(b) and 219(1) — ed.]

**Department of Finance news release, May 11, 1999**: *Changes Proposed to Tax Rules relating to the Conversion of Foreign Bank Subsidiaries into Foreign Bank Branches*

Secretary of State (International Financial Institutions) Jim Peterson today announced proposals to change the Income Tax Act to allow special transitional tax rules for foreign banks that establish specialized, commercially focused branches in Canada.

"We are proposing these time-limited, special tax rules to make sure there are no unwarranted impediments to foreign banks that choose to pursue the branching option now being considered by Parliament," Mr. Peterson said. "The foreign bank entry bill, Bill C-67, is intended to sustain and encourage healthy competition in the Canadian financial marketplace, and these tax changes will help that happen."

Foreign banks have historically been required to establish their Canadian operations in the form of Canadian subsidiaries. However, the government has now introduced Bill C-67 to allow foreign banks to operate in the form of branches that will be limited to specific, commercially focused activities.

Under current tax rules, a foreign bank subsidiary that opts to restructure itself as a branch office under Bill C-67 could face a number of significant potential tax liabilities. This could discourage foreign banks currently operating in Canada from pursuing the branching option.

The proposed *Income Tax Act* changes will allow a foreign bank to transfer existing assets and associated tax liabilities of its Canadian banking or trust subsidiary to a newly established branch. This transfer will be allowed to take place, for a limited time, without accelerating certain tax liabilities. Also, where the subsidiary is wound up, the changes will allow the foreign bank to use certain of its former Canadian subsidiary's tax losses.

These transition measures will be available only to foreign banks that carried on business in Canada through a bank or trust company subsidiary prior to the tabling of Bill C-67.

The proposed transitional rules are described in the attached backgrounder. Legislation to implement the rules will be included in a Bill and tabled in Parliament at an early opportunity. The transition measures are intended to come into force at the same time as the proposed foreign bank entry legislation.

For further information:

Robin Maley, Tax Legislation Division, (613) 992-4859

Jean-Michel Catta, Public Affairs and Operations Division, (613) 996-8080

Patrick Dion, Special Assistant to the Secretary of State, (International Financial Institutions), (613) 996-7861

*Backgrounder*

In February 1997, the Honourable Jim Peterson, Secretary of State (International Financial Institutions), announced that a new foreign bank entry regime would be implemented to allow foreign banks to carry on business in Canada through branch offices. This change is expected to enhance competition in the Canadian financial services market. Currently, a non-resident bank must establish a Canadian bank subsidiary or trust company (referred to generally as "subsidiaries") if it wishes to carry on business in Canada.

On February 11, 1999, legislation to implement the new foreign bank entry regime was tabled in the House of Commons as Bill C-67. On the same day, a Notice of Ways and Means Motion was tabled describing the *Income Tax Act* changes to be implemented as a consequence of Bill C-67, to ensure that the new Canadian branches of foreign banks are in a comparable tax position to Canadian resident banks.

It is anticipated that a number of existing foreign banks will wish to convert their subsidiaries to Canadian branch offices. As foreign banks were not permitted to establish their Canadian banking businesses as branch offices in the past, special tax provisions, for a limited time, are being proposed to both enable subsidiaries to convert to branch offices and ensure they will not incur an undue tax liability. In the absence of these changes, the foreign banks could incur significant tax costs in converting their subsidiaries to branch offices, which in turn would act as an impediment to their utilizing the branch option that is being made available to them.

The proposed measures defer the recognition of a subsidiary's tax liability in respect of certain assets. However, they do not forgive any outstanding, or accruing, tax liability of the subsidiary. For example, any accrued gain on property transferred to a branch will be inherited by the branch, and will be subject to tax when the branch disposes of the property or ceases to use it in its Canadian banking business. These transition tax rules will be time-limited and will apply only to foreign banks that carried on a banking business in Canada through a subsidiary prior to the passage of Bill C-67.

The proposed changes are described in more detail below. Any references to the Bank Act include the amendments proposed in Bill C-67. In all cases, the changes will apply as of the day that Bill C-67 comes into force.

**Proposed Relief**

The proposed changes address three specific tax consequences of converting a subsidiary to a non-resident branch office under the current law.

**a) — *Gains on Property of Subsidiary***

The first change relates to the taxation of accrued gains in respect of property owned by a subsidiary. Ordinarily, when a subsidiary transfers property to a branch office of its non-resident parent corporation, the property is treated as having been sold to the non-resident corporation at fair market value. This may give rise to income or a capital gain, and tax may be payable by the subsidiary.

It is proposed that a foreign bank be permitted to elect, on a property-by-property basis, to transfer property from its subsidiary to its new Canadian branch office on a tax-deferred basis. Properties eligible for this election will be those properties used in carrying on the subsidiary's banking business in Canada that would be eligible for transfer under section 85 of the Income Tax Act, if that section applied in respect of the transfer. As a consequence of making the election, the subsidiary's proceeds of disposition in respect of an elected property and the branch office's cost of the property will be equal to the amount that would be the subsidiary's proceeds of disposition in respect of the property had section 85 of the *Income Tax Act* applied. Where the elected property is depreciable property, any latent or future recapture will retain that character to the branch.

This approach will enable the subsidiary to defer any recapture or accrued gains in respect of elected properties or, where the subsidiary wishes to use accrued losses or loss carryovers, to realize only that portion of its gains that may be offset by the losses.

### b) — Retained Earnings of Subsidiary

The second change relates to the taxation of the subsidiary's retained earnings. If a subsidiary distributes retained earnings to the branch office of a non-resident corporation, Part XIII withholding tax would generally be payable on the distribution. Moreover, if a subsidiary winds up into its non-resident parent, it is deemed under the Income Tax Act to have distributed a dividend to its shareholders equal to the difference between the value of property distributed on the winding-up and the paid-up capital of the subsidiary's redeemed shares. The deemed dividend is also subject to withholding tax under Part XIII of the Act. Consequently, a foreign bank that converts its subsidiary to a branch office could be subject to withholding tax on the subsidiary's retained earnings.

It is proposed that a subsidiary be permitted to transfer all or part of its retained earnings on a tax-deferred basis to a Canadian branch office of its foreign parent bank. For the purposes of the "branch tax" imposed under Part XIV of the *Income Tax Act*, the transferred amount would be treated as having been claimed by the foreign bank as its "investment allowance" for a notional year preceding the branch's first year of operation in Canada. The tax deferral in respect of the subsidiary's retained earnings would thereby be maintained only as long as the branch continues to employ those earnings in the Canadian business of the foreign bank.

### Accumulated Losses of Subsidiary

The third change relates to the treatment of the subsidiary's accumulated tax losses. A corporation that incurs losses in a taxation year may generally deduct those losses in computing its taxable income in subsequent taxation years. However, losses may only be deducted by the taxpayer that incurs them and may not be transferred for use by other taxpayers, including related corporations. Thus, a subsidiary would not ordinarily be able to transfer its tax losses to a Canadian branch office.

It is proposed that a foreign bank be able to deduct the net capital and non-capital losses of its subsidiary in computing the taxable income of its Canadian branch office, in circumstances where the foreign bank has wound up the subsidiary as a consequence of transferring the subsidiary's business to the branch office. This would be accomplished by treating the Canadian branch office as having incurred losses equal to the losses of the wound-up subsidiary, in the year in which the subsidiary incurred them.

### Who Qualifies for Relief?

The proposed new rules will apply to foreign banks that carried on a banking business in Canada through a federally regulated bank or trust company on the day that Bill C-67 was introduced in Parliament.

### When is Relief Available?

The proposed relief will be available on a time-limited basis. To qualify for relief, a foreign bank must establish

a) that it complied, on or before December 31, 2000, with paragraphs 1.0(1.1)(b) and (c) of the draft "Guide to Foreign Bank Branching" issued by the Office of the Superintendent of Financial Institutions, in respect of establishing and operating a bank branch in Canada, and

b) that it completed the transaction in respect of which the relief is sought on or before the earlier of

i) the day that is 6 months after the day that the Superintendent of Financial Institutions makes an order in respect of the foreign bank under subsection 534(1) of the *Bank Act*, and

ii) December 31, 2002.

**Related Provisions:** 20.2 — Interest deduction; 115(1)(a)(vii) — Taxable income earned in Canada; 126(1.1) — Foreign tax credit; 142.7 — Conversion of foreign bank affiliate to branch; 181.3(3)(e), (4)(c), 190.13(d), 190.14(1)(c) — Capital tax; 212(13.3) — Application of non-resident withholding tax; 218.2 — Branch interest tax.

**Notes:** Section 2 of the *Bank Act*, as amended by Bill C-67 (S.C. 1999, c. 28), includes the following definition:

"authorized foreign bank" means a foreign bank in respect of which an order under subsection 524(1) has been made;

Section 524, as added by Bill C-67, provides:

524. (1) Order permitting carrying on of business in Canada, etc. — On application by a foreign bank, the Minister may make an order permitting the foreign bank to establish a branch in Canada to carry on business in Canada under this Part.

(2) Restrictions and requirements — The order may be made subject to the restrictions and requirements referred to in subsections 540(1) and (2), respectively.

(3) Reciprocal treatment — The Minister may make an order only if the Minister is satisfied that

(a) the authorized foreign bank will be capable of making a contribution to the financial system in Canada; and

(b) treatment as favourable for banks to which this Act applies exists or will be provided in the jurisdiction in which the authorized foreign bank principally carries on business, either directly or through a subsidiary.

(4) Consultation with Superintendent — The Minister may make an order only if the Minister is of the opinion, after consultation with the Superintendent, that

(a) the applicant is a bank in the jurisdiction under whose laws it was incorporated and is regulated in a manner acceptable to the Superintendent; and

(b) the applicant's principal activity is the provision of services that would be permitted by this Act if they were provided by a bank in Canada.

**"automobile"** means

(a) a motor vehicle that is designed or adapted primarily to carry individuals on highways and streets and that has a seating capacity for not more than the driver and 8 passengers,

**S. 248(1) aut**  Income Tax Act

but does not include

(b) an ambulance,

(c) a motor vehicle acquired primarily for use as a taxi, a bus used in a business of transporting passengers or a hearse used in the course of a business of arranging or managing funerals,

(d) except for the purposes of section 6, a motor vehicle acquired to be sold, rented or leased in the course of carrying on a business of selling, renting or leasing motor vehicles or a motor vehicle used for the purpose of transporting passengers in the course of carrying on a business of arranging or managing funerals, and

(e) a motor vehicle of a type commonly called a van or pick-up truck or a similar vehicle

(i) that has a seating capacity for not more than the driver and 2 passengers and that, in the taxation year in which it is acquired, is used primarily for the transportation of goods or equipment in the course of gaining or producing income, or

(ii) the use of which, in the taxation year in which it is acquired, is all or substantially all for the transportation of goods, equipment or passengers in the course of gaining or producing income;

**Related Provisions**: 248(1) — "motor vehicle", "passenger vehicle".

**Notes**: The CCRA takes the position that "all or substantially all", used in para. (e)(ii), means 90% or more.

Definition of "automobile" amended by 1991 technical bill, retroactive to its introduction in 1988, to exclude

- a bus used in the business of transporting passengers,
- except for the purposes of section 6, a motor vehicle used for the purpose of transporting passengers in the course of carrying on a business of arranging or managing funerals, and
- a motor vehicle of a type commonly called a van or pick-up truck or similar vehicle that is used all or substantially all for the transportation of goods, equipment or passengers in the course of gaining or producing income.

The term "passenger vehicle" is used for the rules relating to automobiles introduced by 1988 tax reform. See Notes to 248(1)"passenger vehicle".

**Interpretation Bulletins**: IT-521R: Motor vehicle expenses claimed by self-employed individuals; IT-522R: Vehicle, travel and sales expenses of employees.

**"balance-due day"** of a taxpayer for a taxation year means,

(a) where the taxpayer is a trust, the day that is 90 days after the end of the year,

(b) where the taxpayer is an individual who died after October in the year and before May in the following taxation year, the day that is 6 months after the day of death,

(c) in any other case where the taxpayer is an individual, April 30 in the following taxation year, and

(d) where the taxpayer is a corporation, the day on or before which the corporation is required under section 157 to pay the remainder of its tax payable under Part I for the year or would be so required if such a remainder were payable;

**Related Provisions**: 87(2)(oo.1) — Balance-due day of amalgamated corporation; 150(1) — Returns; 156.1(4) — Payment of balance — individuals who pay instalments; 157(1)(b) — Payment of balance by corporations; 158 — Payment of balance on assessment; *Interpretation Act* 26 — Deadline on Sunday or holiday extended to next business day.

**Notes**: "Balance-due day" added by 1991 technical bill, effective 1990, and amended by 1996 Budget, effective for 1996 and later taxation years, to extend definition to corporations and add para. (d). It corresponds to the date on which the annual return must be filed under 150(1) and the balance of any tax owing paid under 153(2), 155(1)(b) or 156(2).

**Information Circulars**: 98-1R: Collection policies.

**Proposed Addition — 248(1)"bank"**

**"bank"** means a bank within the meaning assigned by section 2 of the *Bank Act* or an authorized foreign bank;

**Notes**: Section 2 of the *Bank Act*, as amended by Bill C-67 (S.C. 1999, c. 28), includes the following definition:

"bank" means a bank listed in Schedule I or II to the *Bank Act*;

**Application**: The August 8, 2000 draft legislation, s. 25, will add the definition "bank" to s. 248(1), applicable after June 27, 1999.

**Technical Notes**: A "bank" means a bank within the meaning assigned by section 2 of the *Bank Act* (a "Schedule I" or "Schedule II" bank) or an authorized foreign bank.

**"bankrupt"** has the meaning assigned by the *Bankruptcy and Insolvency Act*;

**Related Provisions**: 80(1)"forgiven amount"B(i) — Debt forgiveness rules do not apply when debtor is bankrupt; 128 — Rules on bankruptcy.

**Notes**: Definition "bankrupt" added by 1994 tax amendments bill (Part I), effective for taxation years that end after February 21, 1994. See Notes to 128(3) for definition in the *Bankruptcy and Insolvency Act*.

**"benefit under a deferred profit sharing plan"** received by a taxpayer in a taxation year means the total of all amounts each of which is an amount received by the taxpayer in the year from a trustee under the plan, minus any amounts deductible under subsections 147(11) and (12) in computing the income of the taxpayer for the year;

**Related Provisions**: 56(1)(i), 147(10) — DPSP benefits taxable.

**"bituminous sands"** means sands or other rock materials containing naturally occurring hydrocarbons (other than coal) which hydrocarbons have

(a) a viscosity, determined in a prescribed manner, equal to or greater than 10,000 centipoise, or

(b) a density, determined in a prescribed manner, equal to or less than 12 degrees API;

**Notes**: Definition "bituminous sands" added by 1996 Budget, effective March 7, 1996. References to "oil sands" throughout the Act were eliminated at the same time.

Oil sands are a mixture of sand, clay, water and bitumen. Bitumen is generally described as a form of heavy oil with a density of less than 10 degrees API. In its natural state, bitumen is too viscous to be recovered through a well. Canada's known oil sands are located virtually entirely in Alberta in three well-delineated areas known as the Athabasca-Wabasca, Peace River and Cold Lake deposits.

Oil sands occur at varying depths ranging from surface outcroppings to hundreds of metres below ground level. Deposits more than 80 metres deep can currently be exploited only by "in-situ" extraction. This involves introducing sufficient heat into the oil sands to reduce the viscosity of the bitumen, thus allowing it to flow and be recovered via a well.

**Regulations**: 1107 (prescribed manner for determining viscosity and density).

**"borrowed money"** includes the proceeds to a taxpayer from the sale of a post-dated bill drawn by the taxpayer on a bank;

**Related Provisions**: 15.1(4) — Money borrowed; 15.2(4) — Status of interest; 20(1)(c) — Interest on money borrowed for certain purposes is deductible; 20(2), (3) — Rules re borrowed money.

**Interpretation Bulletins**: IT-121R3: Election to capitalize cost of borrowed money.

**"business"** includes a profession, calling, trade, manufacture or undertaking of any kind whatever and, except for the purposes of paragraph 18(2)(c), section 54.2, subsection 95(1) and paragraph 110.6(14)(f), an adventure or concern in the nature of trade but does not include an office or employment;

**Related Provisions**: 253 — Extended meaning of "carrying on business" in Canada; 253.1 — Certain limited partners deemed not to carry on business for certain purposes.

**Notes**: "Adventure or concern in the nature of trade" has generally been held by the courts to include the purchase of a single property (such as land) with the intention of reselling it. Thus, the gain on such property is usually ordinary income rather than capital gain (which is only ⅔ taxed). See Notes to 54"capital property".

A business that is an "adventure or concern in the nature of trade" cannot write down inventory until it is sold. See 10(1.01). See Notes to 10(1.01) re the meaning of "adventure in the nature of trade" as distinct from "business".

Where a taxpayer claims losses, the CCRA may deny the existence of a "business", and thus the losses, on the grounds that there is no reasonable expectation of profit (REOP). See Notes to 18(1)(h).

See Notes to 248(1)"employee" on the distinction between business and employment.

Reference to 95(1) added by 1994 tax amendments bill (Part II), effective for taxation years that end after 1994.

**Interpretation Bulletins**: IT-153R3: Land developers — subdivision and development costs and carrying charges on land; IT-206R: Separate businesses; IT-218R: Profit, capital gains and losses from the sale of real estate, including farmland and inherited land and conversion of real estate from capital property to inventory and vice versa; IT-371: Rental property — meaning of "principal business"; IT-459: Adventure or concern in the nature of trade.

**Forms**: RC4100: Employee or Self-Employed?.

**"business limit"** of a corporation for a taxation year means the amount determined under section 125 to be its business limit for the year;

**Related Provisions**: 125(2)–(5.1) — Determination of business limit.

**Notes**: Definition "business limit" added by 1996 Budget, retroactive to May 24, 1985. The business limit is the amount of business income that can be earned at the low rate of tax for Canadian-controlled private corporations, in 125(1). The substantive rules defining the business limit are in 125(2)–(5.1). The business limit is normally $200,000, but is shared among associated corporations and reduced for large corporations.

**"business number"** means the number (other than a Social Insurance Number) used by the Minister to identify

(a) a corporation or partnership, or

(b) any other association or taxpayer that carries on a business or is required by this Act to deduct or withhold an amount from an amount paid or credited or deemed to be paid or credited under this Act

and of which the Minister has notified the corporation, partnership, association or taxpayer;

**Notes**: The Business Number takes the form "12345 6789 RC0001", where the "0001" represents multiple accounts of the same taxpayer and can be suppressed if there is only one account of a given type. "RC" is for corporate income tax; "RT" is GST; "RP" is for payroll (source withholdings); "RM" is for import/export (Customs); and "RR" is a charity registration.

While Social Insurance Numbers are private, Business Numbers are not. The BN appears on every GST-registered business's invoices and receipts as its GST registration number, to enable business purchasers to claim an input tax credit for GST paid. Note that individuals who carry on business and are GST-registered have a BN, but that number is not used for income tax purposes except for payroll withholding (para. (b)). For income tax returns, individuals use the SIN. A partnership is not a "person" for income tax purposes, but is a "person" for GST purposes, and has a BN (see Notes to 96(1) and Reg. 229).

As of May 1999, amalgamating corporations can choose to keep the BN of the "dominant" corporation rather than getting a new BN. The Taxation Centre will contact the corporation to ask whether to carry forward one of the old BNs (this may be particularly important for GST purposes, so that invoices need not be reprinted). The old corporations may get an interim BN for their final T2 return (this was a temporary measure applying in 1999–2000).

Revenue Canada announced on August 25, 1999 that federally incorporated businesses will now receive a BN for corporate income tax when incorporation is approved by Industry Canada. They will not need to register separately with Revenue Canada (now the CCRA). Once they have the BN, they can apply to the CCRA for other accounts using Business Registration On-line (BRO) workstations at most CCRA tax services offices, or by telephone, mail or in person.

Definition "business number" added by 1995-97 technical bill, effective June 18, 1998. It was formerly in 241(10), but without the closing words.

### Proposed Addition — 248(1) "Canadian banking business"

**"Canadian banking business"** means the business carried on by an authorized foreign bank through a permanent establishment (as defined by regulation) in Canada;

**Application**: The August 8, 2000 draft legislation, s. 25, will add the definition "Canadian banking business" to s. 248(1), applicable after June 27, 1999.

**Technical Notes**: A "Canadian banking business" is the business carried on by an authorized foreign bank through a permanent establishment in Canada.

**Regulations**: Reg. 8201 (meaning of "permanent establishment").

**"Canadian-controlled private corporation"** has the meaning assigned by subsection 125(7);
**Related Provisions**: 248(1) — "Small business corporation".
**I.T. Application Rules**: 50(1) (status for 1972 taxation year).
**Interpretation Bulletins**: IT-458R2: Canadian-controlled private corporations.

**"Canadian corporation"** has the meaning assigned by subsection 89(1);

**"Canadian development expense"** has the meaning assigned by subsection 66.2(5);

**"Canadian exploration and development expenses"** has the meaning assigned by subsection 66(15);

**"Canadian exploration expense"** has the meaning assigned by subsection 66.1(6);

**"Canadian field processing"** means, except as otherwise prescribed,

(a) the processing in Canada of raw natural gas at a field separation and dehydration facility,

(b) the processing in Canada of raw natural gas at a natural gas processing plant to any stage that is not beyond the stage of natural gas that is acceptable to a common carrier of natural gas,

(c) the processing in Canada of hydrogen sulphide derived from raw natural gas to any stage that is not beyond the marketable sulphur stage,

(d) the processing in Canada of natural gas liquids, at a natural gas processing plant where the input is raw natural gas derived from a natural accumulation of natural gas, to any stage that is not beyond the marketable liquefied petroleum stage or its equivalent,

(e) the processing in Canada of crude oil (other than heavy crude oil recovered from an oil or gas well or a tar sands deposit) recovered from a natural accumulation of petroleum to any stage that is not beyond the crude oil stage or its equivalent, and

(f) prescribed activities

and, for the purposes of paragraphs (b) to (d),

(g) gas is not considered to cease to be raw natural gas solely because of its processing at a field separation and dehydration facility until it is received by a common carrier of natural gas, and

(h) where all or part of a natural gas processing plant is devoted primarily to the recovery of ethane, the plant, or the part of the plant, as the case may be, is considered not to be a natural gas processing plant;

**Notes**: Definition "Canadian field processing" added by 1996 Budget, effective 1997; and para. (g) amended by 1995-97 technical bill, retroactive to its introduction, to add "until it is received by a common carrier of natural gas". See 125.1"manufacturing or processing"(k) and 127(9)"qualified property"(c)(ix). The term is also to be used in Reg. Parts XI and XII.

**"Canadian oil and gas property expense"** has the meaning assigned by subsection 66.4(5);

**"Canadian partnership"** has the meaning assigned by section 102;
**Related Provisions**: 80(1) — "Eligible Canadian partnership".
**Interpretation Bulletins**: IT-123R6: Transactions involving eligible capital property.

**"Canadian resource property"** has the meaning assigned by subsection 66(15);

**"capital dividend"** has the meaning assigned by section 83;

**"capital gain"** for a taxation year from the disposition of any property has the meaning assigned by section 39;

**"capital interest"** of a taxpayer in a trust has the meaning assigned by subsection 108(1);

**"capital loss"** for a taxation year from the disposition of any property has the meaning assigned by section 39;

**"capital property"** has the meaning assigned by section 54;

**"cash method"** has the meaning assigned by subsection 28(1);
**Notes**: Definition "cash method" added to 248(1) by 1991 technical bill, effective 1989. The operative definition has been in 28(1) since 1972.

**"cemetery care trust"** has the meaning assigned by subsection 148.1(1);
**Related Provisions**: 248(1)"disposition"(f)(vi) — Rollover from one trust to another.
**Notes**: Definition "cemetery care trust" added by 1995-97 technical bill, effective 1993.
**Interpretation Bulletins**: IT-531: Eligible funeral arrangements.

**"common-law partner"**, with respect to a taxpayer at any time, means a person who cohabits at that time in a conjugal relationship with the taxpayer and

(a) has so cohabited with the taxpayer for a continuous period of at least one year, or

(b) would be the parent of a child of whom the taxpayer is a parent, if this Act were read without reference to paragraphs 252(1)(c) and (e) and subparagraph 252(2)(a)(iii),

and, for the purposes of this definition, where at any time the taxpayer and the person cohabit in a conjugal relationship, they are, at any particular time after that time, deemed to be cohabiting in a conjugal relationship unless they were not cohabiting at the particular time for a period of at least 90 days that includes the particular time because of a breakdown of their conjugal relationship;

**Notes**: For review of the case law to 1992 interpreting "cohabit in a conjugal relationship", see David M. Sherman, "Till Tax Do Us

Part: The New Definition of Spouse", 1992 Canadian Tax Foundation annual conference report, pp. 20:1–20:33.

The term "common-law partner" has been added throughout the Act wherever "spouse" appears, to cover both common-law spouses and same-sex (homosexual/gay/lesbian) partners. This replaces former 252(4), which provided an extended meaning of (opposite-sex) "spouse" for all purposes.

Definition "common-law partner" added by 2000 same-sex partners bill, effective for 2001 and later taxation years, subject to the following election to have it apply earlier:

> 144. Where a taxpayer and a person who would have been the taxpayer's common-law partner in the 1998, 1999 or 2000 taxation year, if sections 130 to 142 [the amendments adding reference to "common-law partner"] applied to the applicable year, jointly elect in respect of that year by notifying the Minister of National Revenue in prescribed manner on or before their filing due date for the year in which this Act receives royal assent, those sections apply to the taxpayer and the person in respect of the applicable taxation year and subsequent taxation years.

Section 1.1 of the same-sex partners bill, as amended before Third Reading in the House of Commons, provides:

> 1.1 For greater certainty, the amendments made by this Act do not affect the meaning of the word "marriage", that is, the lawful union of one man and one woman to the exclusion of all others.

**"common-law partnership"** means the relationship between two persons who are common-law partners of each other;

**Notes**: Definition "common-law partnership" added by 2000 same-sex partners bill, effective on the same basis as "common-law partner".

**"common share"** means a share the holder of which is not precluded on the reduction or redemption of the capital stock from participating in the assets of the corporation beyond the amount paid up on that share plus a fixed premium and a defined rate of dividend;

**Related Provisions**: 248(1) — "Preferred share".

**Interpretation Bulletins**: IT-116R3: Rights to buy additional shares.

**"controlled foreign affiliate"** has the meaning assigned by subsection 95(1);

**Related Provisions**: 17(15)"controlled foreign affiliate" — Definition applicable to loan by corporation to non-resident.

**Notes**: Definition "controlled foreign affiliate" added by 1996 Budget, effective 1996.

**"corporation"** includes an incorporated company;

**Related Provisions**: 227.1 — Liability of directors; 236 — Execution of documents by corporations; 242 — Officers, directors and agents guilty of corporation's offences; *Interpretation Act* 21(1) — Powers vested in corporation; *Interpretation Act* 35(1) — Corporation does not include partnership that is separate legal entity.

**Notes**: A limited-liability company (LLC) created under U.S. state law is a corporation for Canadian tax purposes, though it may be treated as a partnership for U.S. tax purposes. (See Reg. 5907(11.2)(b) re its being a foreign affiliate.) The same apparently applies to a Nova Scotia unlimited liability corporation (ULC), as per an IRS ruling. For more discussion, see Gabrielle Richards, "Takeovers and Subsection 88(1); Hybrids; Update on LLCs/ULCs", 1996 Canadian Tax Foundation annual conference report, at 6:13-6:27. Note that the benefit of reduced treaty withholding rates may be denied by U.S. regulations for income derived through an entity treated as a partnership for U.S. tax purposes. See *Canadian Tax Highlights* (CTF), Vol. 5 at pp. 50 (July), 58–59 (August) and 69 (September 1997).

The CCRA considers a Delaware Revised Uniform Partnership Act (DRUPA) partnership to be a partnership for Canadian tax purposes: VIEWS docs 2000-005671 (Nov. 20, 2000) and 2000-005776 (Nov. 28, 2000).

**Interpretation Bulletins**: IT-343R: Meaning of the term "corporation" [for purposes of the definition of "foreign affiliate"]; IT-432R2: Benefits conferred on shareholders.

**"corporation incorporated in Canada"** includes a corporation incorporated in any part of Canada before or after it became part of Canada;

**Related Provisions**: 250(5.1) — Corporation continued outside Canada deemed incorporated in new jurisdiction.

**Notes**: 248(1)"corporation incorporated in Canada" added as a separate definition in the R.S.C. 1985 (5th Supp.) consolidation, effective December 1, 1991. This definition was formerly included under the heading for "corporation".

**"cost amount"** to a taxpayer of any property at any time means, except as expressly otherwise provided in this Act,

(a) where the property was depreciable property of the taxpayer of a prescribed class, the amount that would be that proportion of the undepreciated capital cost to the taxpayer of property of that class at that time that the capital cost to the taxpayer of the property is of the capital cost to the taxpayer of all property of that class that had not been disposed of by the taxpayer before that time if subsection 13(7) were read without reference to paragraph 13(7)(e) and if

(i) paragraph 13(7)(b) were read as follows:

"(b) where a taxpayer, having acquired property for some other purpose, has commenced at a later time to use it for the purpose of gaining or producing income, the taxpayer shall be deemed to have acquired it at that later time at a capital cost to the taxpayer equal to the fair market value of the property at that later time;", and

(ii) subparagraph 13(7)(d)(i) were read as follows:

"(i) if the use regularly made by the taxpayer of the property for the purpose of gaining or producing income has increased, the taxpayer shall be deemed to have acquired at that time depreciable property of that class at a capital cost equal to the proportion of its fair market value at that time that the amount of the increase in the use regularly made by the taxpayer of the property for that purpose is of the whole of the use regularly made of the property, and"

(b) where the property was capital property (other than depreciable property) of the taxpayer, its adjusted cost base to the taxpayer at that time,

(c) where the property was property described in an inventory of the taxpayer, its value at that time as determined for the purpose of computing the taxpayer's income,

(c.1) where the taxpayer was a financial institution in its taxation year that includes that time and the property was a mark-to-market property for the year, the cost to the taxpayer of the property,

> **Proposed Addition — 248(1)"cost amount"(c.2)**
>
> (c.2) where the cost at that time to the taxpayer of the property is determined under subsection 94.2(12), the cost so determined,
>
> **Application**: The June 22, 2000 draft legislation, subsec. 26(1), will add para. (c.1) to the definition "cost amount" in subsec. 248(1), applicable after 2000.
>
> **Technical Notes**: Subsection 248(1) of the Act defines "cost amount", which is used throughout the Act, particularly in provisions relating to the transfer of properties to and from corporations, trusts and partnerships.
>
> New paragraph (c.2) of the definition "cost amount" provides that, where a cost of property to a taxpayer is determined as of any time under new subsection 94.2(12), that cost is also the "cost amount", under subsection 248(1), of the property to the taxpayer at that time.
>
> This amendment applies after 2000.

(d) where the property was eligible capital property of the taxpayer in respect of a business, $4/3$ of the amount that would, but for subsection 14(3), be determined by the formula

$$A \times \frac{B}{C}$$

where

A is the cumulative eligible capital of the taxpayer in respect of the business at that time,

B is the fair market value at that time of the property, and

C is the fair market value at that time of all the eligible capital property of the taxpayer in respect of the business,

(d.1) where the property was a loan or lending asset (other than a net income stabilization account or a property in respect of which paragraph (b), (c), (c.1) or (d.2) applies), the amortized cost of the property to the taxpayer at that time,

(d.2) where the taxpayer was a financial institution in its taxation year that includes that time and the property was a specified debt obligation (other than a mark-to-market property for the year), the tax basis of the property to the taxpayer at that time,

(e) where the property was a right of the taxpayer to receive an amount, other than property that is

(i) a debt the amount of which was deducted under paragraph 20(1)(p) in computing the taxpayer's income for a taxation year that ended before that time,

(ii) a net income stabilization account,

(iii) a right in respect of which paragraph (b), (c), (c.1), (d.1) or (d.2) applies, or

(iv) a right to receive production (as defined in subsection 18.1(1)) to which a matchable expenditure (as defined in subsection 18.1(1)) relates,

the amount the taxpayer has a right to receive,

(e.1) where the property was a policy loan (within the meaning assigned by subsection 138(12)) of an insurer, nil,

(e.2) where the property is an interest of a beneficiary under a qualifying environmental trust, nil, and

(f) in any other case, the cost to the taxpayer of the property as determined for the purpose of computing the taxpayer's income, except to the extent that that cost has been deducted in computing the taxpayer's income for any taxation year ending before that time;

and, for the purposes of this definition, "financial institution", "mark-to-market property" and "specified debt obligation" have the meanings assigned by subsection 142.2(1), and "tax basis" has the meaning assigned by subsection 142.4(1);

**Related Provisions**: 13(7) — Rule affecting capital cost of depreciable property; 13(33) — Consideration given for depreciable capital; 52(3) — Cost of stock dividend; 53 — Adjusted cost base — adjustments; 70(14) — Order of disposal of depreciable property on death; 86.1(3) — Cost amount adjustments on foreign spin-off; 108(1) — Meaning of "cost amount" of capital interest in a trust; 206(1)"cost amount" — Meaning of "cost amount" of capital interest in a trust; 248(25.3) — Deemed cost of trust units.

**Notes**: Para. (a) of "cost amount" amended by 1991 technical bill, effective May 23, 1985. Before that date, read:

> (a) where the property was depreciable property of the taxpayer of a prescribed class, that proportion of the undepreciated capital cost to him of property of that class at that time that the capital cost to him of the property is of the capital cost to him of all property of that class,

Para. (c.1) added by 1994 tax amendments bill (Part III), effective for taxation years that begin after October 1994.

Para. (d) amended by 1992 technical bill, effective July 14, 1990. Before that date, for fiscal periods that begin after 1987 (or, for corporations, for taxation years that begin after June 1988 (date amended by 1993 technical bill, s. 138)), read:

> (d) where the property is eligible capital property in respect of business, $4/3$ of the amount that would, but for subsection 14(3), be the cumulative eligible capital of the taxpayer in respect of the business at that time,

Paras. (d.1) and (d.2) added, and para. (e) amended, by 1994 tax amendments bill (Part III), effective for the determination of cost amount after February 22, 1994. Previously read:

> (e) where the property was a debt owing to the taxpayer (other than the amount in respect of such property that was deducted under paragraph 20(1)(p) in computing the taxpayer's income for a taxation year ending before that time or of a net income stabilization account) or any other right of the taxpayer to receive an amount (other than a right to receive an amount in respect of a net income stabilization account), the

amortized cost of the property to the taxpayer at that time or, where the property does not have an amortized cost to the taxpayer, the amount of the debt or right that was outstanding at that time,

Para. (e) amended by 1992 technical bill, effective for 1991 and later taxation years, to add the two references to a net income stabilization account.

Subpara. (e)(iv) added by 1995-97 technical bill, effective November 18, 1996.

Para. (e.2) added by 1994 Budget, effective 1994; and amended by 1997 Budget, effective 1996, to change "mining reclamation trust" to "qualifying environmental trust".

Closing words of the definition added by 1994 tax amendments bill (Part III), effective for the determination of cost amount after February 22, 1994.

**I.T. Application Rules**: 18 (property acquired before 1972).

**Interpretation Bulletins**: IT-142R3: Settlement of debts on the winding-up of a corporation; IT-220R2: CCA — Proceeds of disposition of depreciable property; IT-457R: Election by professionals to exclude work in progress from income; IT-471R: Merger of partnerships; IT-488R2: Winding-up of 90%-owned taxable Canadian corporation; IT-528: Transfers of funds between registered plans.

**"credit union"** has the meaning assigned by subsection 137(6);

**"cumulative eligible capital"** has the meaning assigned by subsection 14(5);

**"death benefit"** means the total of all amounts received by a taxpayer in a taxation year on or after the death of an employee in recognition of the employee's service in an office or employment minus

(a) where the taxpayer is the only person who has received such an amount and who is a surviving spouse or common-law partner of the employee (which person is, in this definition, referred to as the "surviving spouse or common-law partner"), the lesser of

(i) the total of all amounts so received by the taxpayer in the year, and

(ii) the amount, if any, by which $10,000 exceeds the total of all amounts received by the taxpayer in preceding taxation years on or after the death of the employee in recognition of the employee's service in an office or employment, or

(b) where the taxpayer is not the surviving spouse or common-law partner of the employee, the lesser of

(i) the total of all amounts so received by the taxpayer in the year, and

(ii) that proportion of

(A) the amount, if any, by which $10,000 exceeds the total of all amounts received by the surviving spouse or common-law partner of the employee at any time on or after the death of the employee in recognition of the employee's service in an office or employment

that

(B) the amount described in subparagraph (i)

is of

(C) the total of all amounts received by all taxpayers other than the surviving spouse or common-law partner of the employee at any time on or after the death of the employee in recognition of the employee's service in an office or employment;

**Related Provisions**: 56(1)(a)(iii) — Death benefit included in income; 104(28) — Death benefit flowed through trust; 128.1(10)"excluded right or interest"(h) — Emigration — no deemed disposition of right to death benefit.

**Notes**: 248(1)"death benefit" amended by 2000 same-sex partners bill to add reference to "common-law partner", effective for the 2001 and later taxation years, or earlier by election (see Notes to 248(1)"common-law partner").

Opening words of para. (a) of "death benefit" amended by 1992 technical bill, effective for 1993 and later taxation years, due to the introduction of 252(4) and the fact that a person could thus have two "spouses". For 1985-92, read:

(a) Where the taxpayer is the surviving spouse of the employee, the lesser of

**Interpretation Bulletins**: IT-508R: Death benefits.

**"deferred amount"** at the end of a taxation year under a salary deferral arrangement in respect of a taxpayer means

(a) in the case of a trust governed by the arrangement, any amount that a person has a right under the arrangement at the end of the year to receive after the end of the year where the amount has been received, is receivable or may at any time become receivable by the trust as, on account or in lieu of salary or wages of the taxpayer for services rendered in the year or a preceding taxation year, and

(b) in any other case, any amount that a person has a right under the arrangement at the end of the year to receive after the end of the year,

and, for the purposes of this definition, a right under the arrangement shall include a right that is subject to one or more conditions unless there is a substantial risk that any one of those conditions will not be satisfied;

**"deferred profit sharing plan"** has the meaning assigned by subsection 147(1);

**"depreciable property"** has the meaning assigned by subsection 13(21);

**Related Provisions**: See under 13(21)"depreciable property".

**I.T. Application Rules**: 18, 20 (property acquired before 1972).

**"designated insurance property"** has the meaning assigned by subsection 138(12);

**Notes**: Definition "designated insurance property" added by 1996 Budget effective for 1997 and later taxation years (changed from 1996 at Second Reading of the Budget bill).

**"designated surplus"** — [Repealed under former Act]

**Notes**: The concept of "designated surplus" was eliminated effective April 1977.

### Proposed Addition — 248(1) "disposition"

**"disposition"** of any property, except as expressly otherwise provided, includes

(a) any transaction or event entitling a taxpayer to proceeds of disposition of the property,

(b) any transaction or event by which,

(i) where the property is a share, bond, debenture, note, certificate, hypothec, mortgage, agreement of sale or similar property, or an interest in it, the property is redeemed in whole or in part or is cancelled,

(ii) where the property is a debt or any other right to receive an amount, the debt or other right is settled or cancelled,

(iii) where the property is a share, the share is converted because of an amalgamation or merger, and

(iv) where the property is an option to acquire or dispose of property, the option expires,

(c) any transfer of the property to a trust or, where the property is property of a trust, any transfer of the property to any beneficiary under the trust, except as provided by paragraph (f) or (g), and

(d) where the property is, or is part of, a taxpayer's capital interest in a trust, except as provided by paragraph (h) or (i), a payment made after 1999 to the taxpayer from the trust that can reasonably be considered to have been made because of the taxpayer's capital interest in the trust,

but does not include

(e) any transfer of the property as a consequence of which there is no change in the beneficial ownership of the property, except where the transfer is

(i) from a person or a partnership to a trust for the benefit of the person or the partnership,

(ii) from a trust to a beneficiary under the trust, or

(iii) from one trust maintained for the benefit of one or more beneficiaries under the trust to another trust maintained for the benefit of the same beneficiaries,

(f) any transfer of the property as a consequence of which there is no change in the beneficial ownership of the property, where

(i) the transferor and the transferee are trusts,

(ii) the transfer is not by a trust resident in Canada to a non-resident trust,

(iii) the transferee does not receive the property in satisfaction of the transferee's right as a beneficiary under the transferor trust,

(iv) the transferee held no property immediately before the transfer (other than property the cost of which is not included, for the purposes of this Act, in computing a balance of undeducted outlays, expenses or other amounts in respect of the transferee),

(v) the transferee does not file a written election with the Minister on or before the filing-due date for its taxation year in which the transfer is made (or on such later date as is acceptable to the Minister) that this paragraph not apply,

(vi) where the transferor is an amateur athlete trust, a cemetery care trust, an employee trust, an *inter vivos* trust deemed by subsection 143(1) to exist in respect of a congregation that is a constituent part of a religious organization, a related segregated fund trust (in this paragraph having the meaning assigned by section 138.1), a trust described in paragraph 149(1)(o.4) or a trust governed by an eligible funeral arrangement, an employees profit sharing plan, a registered education savings plan or a registered supplementary unemployment benefit plan, the transferee is the same type of trust, and

(vii) the transfer results, or is part of a series of transactions or events that results, in the transferor ceasing to exist and, immediately before the time of the transfer or the beginning of that series, as the case may be, the transferee never held any property or held only property having a nominal value,

(g) any transfer of the property where

(i) the transferor is a trust governed by a registered retirement savings plan or a trust governed by a registered retirement income fund,

(ii) the transferee is a trust governed by a registered retirement savings plan or a trust governed by a registered retirement income fund,

(iii) the annuitant under the plan or fund that governs the transferor is also the annuitant under the plan or fund that governs the transferee,

(iv) the transferee held no property immediately before the transfer (other than property the cost of which is not included, for the purposes of this Act, in computing a balance of undeducted outlays, expenses or other amounts in respect of the transferee),

(v) the transferee does not file a written election with the Minister on or before the filing-due date for its taxation year in which the transfer is made (or on such later day as is acceptable to the Minister) that this paragraph not apply, and

(vi) the transfer results, or is part of a series of transactions or events that results, in the transferor ceasing to exist and, immediately before the time of the transfer or the beginning of that series, as the case may be, the transferee never held any property or held only property having a nominal value,

(h) where the property is part of a capital interest of a taxpayer in a trust (other than a personal trust or a trust prescribed for the purpose of subsection 107(2)) that is described by reference to units issued by the trust, a payment after 1999 from the trust in respect of the capital interest, where the number of units in the trust that are owned by the taxpayer is not reduced because of the payment,

(i) where the property is a taxpayer's capital interest in a trust, a payment to the taxpayer after 1999 in respect of the capital interest to the extent that the payment

(i) is out of the income of the trust (determined without reference to subsection 104(6)) for a taxation year or out of the capital gains of the trust for the year, if the payment was made in the year or the right to the payment was acquired by the taxpayer in the year, or

(ii) is in respect of an amount designated in respect of the taxpayer by the trust under subsection 104(20),

(j) any transfer of the property for the purpose only of securing a debt or a loan, or any transfer by a creditor for the purpose only of returning property that had been used as security for a debt or a loan,

(k) any transfer of the property to a trust as a consequence of which there is no change in the beneficial ownership of the property, where the main purpose of the transfer is

(i) to effect payment under a debt or loan,

(ii) to provide assurance that an absolute or contingent obligation of the transferor will be satisfied, or

(iii) to facilitate either the provision of compensation or the enforcement of a penalty, in the event that an absolute or contingent obligation of the transferor is not satisfied,

(l) any issue of a bond, debenture, note, certificate, mortgage or hypothec, and

(m) any issue by a corporation of a share of its capital stock, or any other transaction that, but for this paragraph, would be a disposition by a corporation of a share of its capital stock;

**Application**: Bill C-43 (First Reading September 20, 2000), subsec. 112(4), will add the definition "disposition" to subsec. 248(1), applicable to transactions and events that occur after December 23, 1998, except that paras. (f) and (g) shall not apply for the purposes of the Act (other than s. 107.4) to a transfer of property, that occurred before 2000, by a trust governed by a registered retirement savings plan to a trust governed by a registered retirement income fund (or to a transfer by a trust governed by a registered retirement income fund to a trust governed by a registered retirement savings plan) unless the transferee trust files a written election with the Minister of National Revenue on or before the filing-due date for its taxation year in which the transfer is made (or on such later day as is acceptable to the Minister) that para. (f) or (g), as the case may be, of that definition apply.

**Technical Notes**: The new definition of "disposition" in subsection 248(1) replaces a definition of the same expression in section 54. The new definition applies for the purposes of the entire Act.

The table below briefly compares the new definition with the former definition, with further detail provided below with regard to the policy changes introduced by the new definition. The first column and second column indicate paragraph references in the new definition and the former definition, respectively. Except as indicated otherwise below, these amendments apply to transactions and events that occur after December 23, 1998.

| New | Old | Description |
|---|---|---|
| (a) | (a) | Disposition of property by a taxpayer includes transaction or event entitling taxpayer to proceeds. No policy change. |
| (b) | (b) | Specified redemptions, cancellations, conversions and expirations of debt, equity and options treated as dispositions. No policy change. |
| (c) | (c) | Except as otherwise specified, dispositions include transfers to and from trusts. No policy change. |
| (d), (h) and (i) | N/A | Circumstances in which distribution by a trust constitutes disposition of a capital interest in a trust. See description below. |
| (e) and (f) | (e) | Circumstances in which a transfer not a "disposition" because no change in beneficial ownership. Under the new rules, these circumstances are narrower. See also amended subsection 104(1). |
| (g) | N/A | Circumstances in which transfers involving RRSPs and RRIFs of the same annuitant not a "disposition". See description below. |
| (j) | (d) | Transfer to secure debt not a disposition. No policy change. |
| (k) | N/A | Other transfers to secure obligations not a disposition. See description below. |
| (l) | (f) | Issue of debt not a disposition. No policy change, but minor technical change. See description below. |

| (m) | (g) | Issue of share not a disposition. No policy change. |

### Transactions involving capital interests in a trust

Paragraph (d) of the new definition applies with respect to capital interests in a trust. Paragraph (d) makes it clear that, except as specifically provided in paragraph (h) or (i), every payment (in kind or otherwise) by a trust to a taxpayer in respect of the taxpayer's capital interest (as defined in subsection 108(1)) in the trust will result in a disposition of all or part of the taxpayer's capital interest in the trust.

The exception under paragraph (h) applies to a payment made by a trust after 1999 where the following conditions are satisfied:

1. the capital interest in the trust is described by reference to units issued by the trust;
2. the payment does not result in a reduction of the number of units in the trust owned by the taxpayer; and
3. the trust is neither a personal trust nor a trust prescribed for the purpose of subsection 107(2).

The exception under paragraph (i) applies to a payment made by a trust after 1999 where the following conditions are satisfied:

1. the payment is made out of the trust's income (determined without reference to subsection 104(6)) or capital gains for a taxation year and the payment was made in the year or the right to the payment was acquired in the year; and
2. the payment is in respect of an amount designated by the trust under subsection 104(20).

Paragraphs (d), (h) and (i) are part of a set of amendments designed to clarify the tax consequences of distributions from trusts to their beneficiaries after 1999. Generally, results achieved under these rules are intended to accord with existing income tax practice. For further detail, see the notes on amendments to subsections 43(2) [now 43(3) — ed.], 52(6), 107(2) and (2.1) and the definition "capital interest" in subsection 108(1).

### Transactions involving no change in beneficial ownership of property

Paragraph (e) of the new definition provides that there is no disposition where a transfer of property does not involve a trust and does not result in a change in the beneficial ownership of the property. Where any of the exceptions in subparagraphs (e)(i) to (iii) apply, paragraph (c) of the definition will ensure a disposition subject to the exceptions in paragraph (c). Paragraph (e) takes into account past interpretations of the definition "disposition" in section 54. For example, the CCRA has taken the position that there is no disposition where an individual's undivided joint ownership interest in real property is converted to a tenancy-in-common interest in the property.

Paragraph (f) of the new definition provides an exception to the general rule in paragraph (c) that a disposition results from any transfer of the property to a trust or, where the property is property of a trust, any transfer of the property to any beneficiary under the trust. Paragraph (f) avoids, unless an election is made to the contrary under subparagraph (f)(v), a disposition in the case of certain very simple trust-to-trust transfers involving no change in beneficial ownership. For this paragraph to apply, the following additional conditions must be satisfied:

1. the transfer is not from a trust resident in Canada to a non-resident trust;
2. the transferee does not receive the property in satisfaction of the transferee's right as a beneficiary under the transferor trust;
3. the transferee does not hold property immediately before the transfer other than property the cost of which is not included, for the purposes of the Act, in computing a balance of undeducted outlays, expenses or other amounts in respect of the transferee (i.e., subject to subparagraph (f)(vii) described in item 6 below, the transferee would be permitted to hold non-depreciable capital property);
4. where the transferor is an amateur athlete trust, a cemetery care trust, an employee trust, an inter vivos trust deemed by subsection 143(1) to exist in respect of a congregation that is a constituent part of a religious organization, a related segregated fund trust (in this paragraph having the meaning assigned by section 138.1), a trust described in paragraph 149(1)(o.4) or a trust governed by an eligible funeral arrangement, an employees profit sharing plan, a registered education savings plan or a registered supplementary unemployment benefit plan, the transferee is the same type of trust;
5. the transfer results, or is part of a series of transactions or events that results, in the transferor ceasing to exist; and
6. at all times before the transfer or before the beginning of that series of transactions or events, as the case may be, the transferee held no property or held only property having a nominal value.

Paragraph (f) generally will not apply to a transfer of property that occurred before 2000 by an RRSP trust to a RRIF trust (or by a RRIF trust to an RRSP trust), unless the transferee trust files a written election with the Minister of National Revenue on or before the filing-due date for its taxation year in which the transfer is made (or on such later day as is acceptable to the Minister) that paragraph (f) of that definition applies. For transfers of property involving RRSPs and RRIFs and that occur after 1999, where the conditions of paragraph (f) are satisfied, that paragraph will apply to avoid a disposition without need for an election. For further detail, see the commentary on paragraph (g) of the definition.

Where paragraph (f) does apply, new subsection 248(25.1) applies with tax consequences described in the commentary on that subsection. Where the paragraph does not apply because the six additional conditions described above are not satisfied (and paragraph (g) also does not apply), the transfer will generally be a qualifying disposition under new subsection 107.4(1).

Paragraph (k) of the new definition also applies to a transfer of property as a consequence of which there is no change in the beneficial ownership of the property. For paragraph (k) to apply with no resulting disposition resulting from the transfer of property, the main purpose of the transfer must be:

- to effect payment under a debt or loan;
- to provide comfort that an absolute or contingent obligation of the transferor will be satisfied; or
- to facilitate either the provision of compensation or the enforcement of a penalty, in the event that an ab-

solute or contingent obligation of the transferor is not satisfied.

Where paragraph (k) applies, new subsection 248(25.2) applies with tax consequences described in the commentary on that subsection.

*Transactions involving RRSPs and RRIFs*

Paragraph (g) also provides an exception to the general rule in paragraph (c) that a disposition results upon the transfer of property to a trust or transfers of property from a trust to a beneficiary of the trust. Paragraph (g) of the new definition avoids, unless an election is made to the contrary under subparagraph (g)(v), a disposition in the case of certain trust-to-trust transfers involving RRSPs and RRIFs. A transfer under this paragraph is not subject to the restriction in paragraph (f) that there be no change in beneficial ownership. For paragraph (g) to apply, the following additional conditions must be satisfied:

1. the transferor is an RRSP trust or RRIF trust;
2. the transferee is an RRSP trust or RRIF trust;
3. the transferee does not hold property immediately before the transfer other than property the cost of which is not included, for the purposes of the Act, in computing a balance of undeducted outlays, expenses or other amounts in respect of the transferee (i.e., subject to subparagraph (g)(vi) described in item 5 below, the transferee would be permitted to hold nondepreciable capital property);
4. the transfer results, or is part of a series of transactions or events that results, in the transferor ceasing to exist; and
5. at all times before the transfer or before the beginning of that series of transactions or events, as the case may be, the transferee held no property or held only property having a nominal value.

Paragraph (g) generally will not apply to a transfer of property that occurred before 2000 by an RRSP trust of an annuitant to a RRIF trust of the same annuitant (or by a RRIF trust of an annuitant to an RRSP trust of the same annuitant), unless the transferee trust files a written election with the Minister of National Revenue on or before the filing-due date for its taxation year in which the transfer is made (or on such later day as is acceptable to the Minister) that paragraph (g) of that definition applies. For transfers of property involving RRSPs and RRIFs that occur after 1999 and that satisfy the requirements of paragraph (g), the paragraph will apply to avoid a disposition without need for an election.

Where paragraph (g) applies, new subsection 248(25.1) applies with tax consequences described in the commentary on that subsection. Where neither paragraph (f) nor (g) applies, the transfer will generally be a qualifying disposition under new subsection 107.4(1) provided the conditions of that provision are met.

**EXAMPLE 1**

Imelda arranged the transfer of properties in November 1999 from the RRSP trust under which she was the annuitant to a RRIF trust under which she was the annuitant. Under the RRSP trust the only named beneficiary was Luc. However, under the RRIF trust, Imelda named Gilbert as a beneficiary.

Results:

1. Because the transfer occurred after December 23, 1998 but before 2000, it will constitute a disposition under paragraph (c) of the definition "disposition", unless the RRIF trust files an election that paragraph (g) of that definition applies (paragraph (f) of that definition is intended not to apply where there is a change in beneficial ownership upon the transfer). If the election is filed and the remaining conditions in paragraph (g) are met, the transfer will not be a disposition. However, because of subsection 206(4), the transfer would be expected to occur on a fair market value basis.

2. If the election referred to in item 1 above is not filed, the transfer will be a "qualifying disposition" if the conditions of subsection 107.4(1) are met. For this purpose, paragraph 107.4(2)(b) deems there to be no change in beneficial ownership if the annuitant under the transferor trust is the same individual as the annuitant under the transferee trust. If the transfer is a "qualifying disposition", under subparagraph 107.4(3)(c)(iii) the transfer will occur on a fair market value basis unless subparagraph 107.4(3)(c)(i) applies.

3. This result reflects the intent that transfers between RRSPs and RRIFs of the same annuitant that occur before 2000 generally occur on a fair market value basis.

**EXAMPLE 2**

Lucie arranged the transfer of properties in March 2000 from the RRSP trust under which she was the annuitant to a RRIF trust under which she was the annuitant. Under the RRSP trust the only named beneficiary was Paulette. However, under the RRIF trust, Lucie named Jamal as the beneficiary.

Results:

1. Because the transfer occurred after 1999, if the conditions of paragraph (g) of the definition "disposition" are met, the transfer will not be a disposition unless an election is filed by the transferee under subparagraph (g)(v). (Paragraph (f) of that definition is intended not to apply where there is a change in beneficial ownership upon the transfer). The combined effect of amended subsection 206(4), which expressly does not apply to a transfer described in paragraph (g) of the definition "disposition", and new subsection 248(25.1), which provides that the transferee trust is a continuation of the transferor trust, will ensure the intended result that the transfer occur on a rollover basis.

2. If the transferee trust elects out of paragraph (g) of the definition "disposition", the transfer will be a "qualifying disposition" if the conditions of subsection 107.4(1) are met. For this purpose, paragraph 107.4(2)(b) deems there to be no change in beneficial ownership if the annuitant under the transferor is the same individual as the annuitant under the transferee. If the transfer is a "qualifying disposition", then under subparagraph 107.4(3)(c)(iv) the transfer will occur on a rollover basis unless subparagraph 107.4(3)(c)(ii) applies.

3. This result reflects the intent that transfers between RRSP and RRIF trusts of the same annuitant that occur after 2000 generally occur on a rollover basis.

Paragraph (g) of the definition is part of a set of amendments intended to clarify the tax treatment of transfers of property involving RRSPs and RRIFs. For further detail, see the commentary to paragraphs 107.4(2)(b) and (3)(c), subsection 206(4), the new definition "disposition" in subsection 248(1) and subsection 248(25.1).

*Other transactions*

Paragraph (l) of the definition replaces paragraph (f) of the definition "disposition" in subsection 54(1), which is repealed. Paragraph (l) adds a reference to "hypothec". This amendment is made to ensure that the Act appropriatly reflects both the civil law of the province of Quebec and the law of other provinces.

Except as indicated otherwise above, these amendments apply to transactions and events that occur after December 23, 1998.

### Letter from Department of Finance, February 18, 1999:

Dear [xxx]

SUBJECT: *December 23, 1998 Draft Legislation Trust proposals*

This is in reply to your letter of February 15, 1999 regarding the applicability of the withholding tax exemption in subparagraph 212(1)(b)(vii) of the *Income Tax Act*.

Your concern relates to debt issued through a trust indenture, pursuant to which a non-resident financial institution acts as the trustee. The main function of the trustee is to administer and enforce the collective rights of a large group of lenders. Additionally, the trustee may act as paying agent for the disbursement of funds to lenders and is expected to receive funds from your client in this capacity, some of which in limited circumstances could be returned to your client. You are concerned about three of the proposed provisions in the December 23, 1998 draft legislation on trust: proposed subparagraph (e)(iii) of the definition "disposition" in subsection 248(1) and proposed paragraphs 248(25.1)(b) and 251(1)(b). You are of the view that these provisions could technically result in the loss of the Part XIII withholding tax exemption provided under subparagraph 212(1)(b)(vii), on the basis that your client could now be construed as making its interest payable to a non-arm's length trust.

We agree that modifications to the draft legislation should be made to address this concern. The draft amendments were not intended to result in a loss of this exemption from withholding tax in the circumstances described above.

Consequently, we will recommend changes to these provisions applying from the date of the release of the draft legislation [to] ensure that the intended policy result is achieved.

Thank you for writing.

Yours sincerely,

Brian Ernewein
Director, Tax Legislation Division, Tax Policy Branch

### Letter from Department of Finance, April 21, 1999:

Dear [xxx]

This is in reply to your letter of April 20, 1999 with regard to the proposed definition "disposition" in the draft taxation proposals on trusts released on December 23, 1998.

From a policy perspective we agree that where property is transferred from a trust to a bare trust acting an agent for the transferor and there is no change in beneficial ownership as a result of the transfer, there should not be a "disposition" for income tax purposes. Accordingly, we will recommend that paragraph (e) of the definition be amended in the manner suggested in your letter.

Thank you for raising this matter with us.

Yours sincerely,

Brian Ernewein
Director, Tax Legislation Division, Tax Policy Branch

### Letter from Department of Finance, December 1, 1999:

Dear [xxx]

This is in reply to your letter of November 8, 1999 requesting that amendments be made to the draft income tax legislation released on December 23, 1998 regarding trusts and to the *Income Tax Regulations* regarding the determination of tax reserves for life insurance policies.

*Draft Legislation on Trusts*

I am prepared to recommend to the Minister of Finance amendments to proposed paragraph (f) of the definition "disposition" in subsection 248(1) of the *Income Tax Act* so that a transfer after December 23, 1998 of all the assets from one related segregated fund trust to a new related segregated fund trust is not precluded from being covered by that paragraph. In these circumstances, as you note, the new related segregated fund trust would be treated as being a continuation of the transferor.

I am also prepared to recommend to the Minister of Finance that subsection 107.4(1) of the Act be amended so as not to preclude the application of that subsection in connection with the transfer after December 23, 1998 of property from one related segregated fund trust to another. However, as you and Simon Thompson have discussed, an additional rule would be required so that any "acquisition fee" otherwise recognized on the transfer may only be recognized once there is a disposition of units in the transferee fund.

. . . . .

Yours sincerely,

Brian Ernewein
Director, Tax Legislation Division, Tax Policy Branch

**Related Provisions**: 43(2) — No capital loss on capital interest of trust on payment out of trust's income or gains; 48.1(1) — Gain when small business corporation becomes public; 49(1) — Granting of option is a disposition; 49(5) — Extension or renewal of option; 49.1 — Satisfaction of obligation is not a disposition of property; 51(1)(c) — Conversion of convertible property deemed not to be a disposition; 53(2)(h)(i.1), (i.2) — Reduction in ACB of capital interest of trust re amount payable before 2000; 69(1)(b)(iii) — Deemed proceeds on disposition to a trust where no change in beneficial ownership; 69(1)(c) — Deemed acquisition at fair market value where disposition with no change in beneficial interest; 70(5) — Deemed disposition on death; 80.03(2), (4) — Deemed capital gain on disposition of property following debt forgiveness; 87(4) — Shares of predecessor corporation; 104(5.3) — Election by trust to postpone deemed disposition; 104(5.8) — Transfer where para. (f) applies; 107(2), (2.1) — Effect of distribution of property by trust; 107.4 — Rollover on "qualifying disposition" to a trust; 128.1(1)(b) — Deemed disposition of property on becoming resident in Canada; 128.1(4) —

Deemed disposition on emigration; 248(25.1) — Where para. (f) applies — continuation of trust; 248(25.2) — Where para. (j) applies — trust deemed to be agent.

**Notes**: In the draft legislation of December 17, 1999, para. (g) was not included; what are now paras. (h)–(l) were numbered (g)–(l).

A trust that Finance and the CCRA call a "protective trust" may be a "blind trust", such as those set up by politicians to hold their interests and manage their affairs without their involvement. The term "protective trust" is used in some jurisdictions to mean a discretionary trust that effectively protects the beneficiary from creditors.

See also Notes to 104(1) re bare trusts.

**Interpretation Bulletins**: IT-65: Stock splits and consolidations; IT-96R6: Options to acquire shares, bonds or debentures and by trusts to acquire trust units; IT-102R2: Conversion of property, other than real property, from or to inventory; IT-124R6: Contributions to registered retirement savings plans; IT-125R4: Dispositions of resource properties; IT-126R2: Meaning of "winding-up"; IT-133: Stock exchange transactions — date of disposition of shares; IT-146R4: Shares entitling shareholders to choose taxable or capital dividends; IT-170R: Sale of property — when included in income computation; IT-182: Compensation for loss of business income or property used in a business; IT-218R: Profit, capital gains and losses from the sale of real estate, including farmland and inherited land and conversion of real estate from capital property to inventory and vice versa; IT-220R2: Capital cost allowance — proceeds of disposition of depreciable property; IT-334R2: Miscellaneous receipts; IT-444R: Corporations — involuntary dissolutions; IT-448: Dispositions — changes in terms of securities; IT-488R2: Winding-up of 90%-owned taxable Canadian corporations; IT-505: Mortgage foreclosures and conditional sales repossessions.

**I.T. Technical News**: No. 3 (loss utilization within a corporate group); No. 7 (revocable living trusts, protective trusts, bare trusts); No. 14 (changes in terms of debt obligations); No. 15 (tax consequences of the adoption of the "euro" currency).

**Advance Tax Rulings**: ATR-1: Transfer of legal title in land to bare trustee corporation — mortgagee's requirements sole reason for transfer; ATR-54: Reduction of paid-up capital.

**"dividend"** includes a stock dividend (other than a stock dividend that is paid to a corporation or to a mutual fund trust by a non-resident corporation);

**Related Provisions**: 15(3), (4) — Interest or dividend on income bond or debenture; 52(3) — Cost of stock dividend; 55(2) — Capital gains stripping — Deemed dividend; 82(1) — Dividends included in income; 84 — Deemed dividend; 90 — Dividend from non-resident corporation; 93(1) — Election re disposition of share in foreign affiliate; 128.1(1)(c.1), (c.2) — Deemed dividends on corporation becoming resident in Canada; 137(4.2) — Credit unions — deemed interest deemed not to be a dividend; 139.1(4)(f) — Deemed dividend on demutualization of insurance corporation; 139.2 — Deemed dividend on distribution by mutual holding corporation; 212.2 — Deemed dividend on surplus strip to non-resident insurer; 258 — Certain amounts deemed to be or not to be dividends.

**Notes**: See Notes to 82(1).

"Dividend" amended by 1991 technical bill to add the parenthetical exclusion, effective for stock dividends paid to a corporation or to a mutual fund trust in 1991 or later. The new definition is also effective for such stock dividends paid from March 24, 1985 through December 31, 1990 if the corporation or trust so elects by notifying Revenue Canada in writing before July 1991. (In such case, notwithstanding 152(4) to (5), such assessments of tax, interest and penalties shall be made as are necessary to give effect to the election.)

**Interpretation Bulletins**: IT-67R3: Taxable dividends from corporations resident in Canada; IT-88R2: Stock dividends; IT-243R4: Dividend refund to private corporations.

**"dividend rental arrangement"** of a person means any arrangement entered into by the person where it may reasonably be considered that

(a) the main reason for the person entering into the arrangement was to enable the person to receive a dividend on a share of the capital stock of a corporation, other than a dividend on a prescribed share or a share described in paragraph (e) of the definition "term preferred share" in this subsection or an amount deemed to be received as a dividend on a share of the capital stock of a corporation by reason of subsection 15(3), and

(b) under the arrangement someone other than that person bears the risk of loss or enjoys the opportunity for gain or profit with respect to the share in any material respect,

and for greater certainty includes any arrangement under which

(c) a corporation at any time receives on a particular share a taxable dividend that would, but for subsection 112(2.3), be deductible in computing its taxable income or taxable income earned in Canada for the taxation year that includes that time, and

(d) the corporation is obligated to pay to another person an amount as compensation for

(i) that dividend,

(ii) a dividend on a share that is identical to the particular share, or

(iii) a dividend on a share that, during the term of the arrangement, can reasonably be expected to provide to a holder of the share the same or substantially the same proportionate risk of loss or opportunity for gain as the particular share,

that, if paid, would be deemed by subsection 260(5) to have been received by that other person as a taxable dividend;

**Related Provisions**: 82(1)(a)(i) — Taxable dividends received; 112(2.3) — Intercorporate dividends — where no deduction permitted; 126(4.2) — No foreign tax credit on short-term securities acquisitions; 260(6.1) — Deductible amount under securities lending arrangement.

**Notes**: "Dividend rental arrangement" added by 1989 Budget, effective May 1989. It describes an arrangement whereby a corporation borrows a share for a short period in order to receive an intercorporate dividend on it, which would normally be tax-free under 112(1). The lender under such an arrangement (e.g. an exempt pension fund) would be indifferent as to whether it received the dividend or an equivalent fee from the corporation for the "use" of the share. Under 112(2.3), the deduction for the intercorporate dividend is denied.

Everything after para. (b) added by 1994 tax amendments bill (Part VIII), effective for dividends received at any time by a corporation on shares acquired

    (a) before that time and after April 1989, where the corporation elects by notifying Revenue Canada in writing by the end of 1995 (see also Notes to 260(6.1) if this election is made); and

    (b) before that time and after June 1994, in any other case.

**Interpretation Bulletins**: IT-67R3: Taxable dividends from corporations resident in Canada.

**"eligible capital amount"** has the meaning assigned by subsection 14(1);

**"eligible capital expenditure"** has the meaning assigned by subsection 14(5);

**"eligible capital property"** has the meaning assigned by section 54;

**"eligible funeral arrangement"** has the meaning assigned by subsection 148.1(1);

**Related Provisions**: 248(1)"disposition"(f)(vi) — Rollover from one trust to another.

**Notes**: Definition "eligible funeral arrangement" added by 1994 tax amendments bill (Part IV), effective 1993.

**Interpretation Bulletins**: IT-531: Eligible funeral arrangements.

**"eligible relocation"** means a relocation of a taxpayer where

    (a) the relocation occurs to enable the taxpayer

        (i) to carry on a business or to be employed at a location in Canada (in section 62 and this subsection referred to as "the new work location"), or

        (ii) to be a student in full-time attendance enrolled in a program at a post-secondary level at a location of a university, college or other educational institution (in section 62 and in this subsection referred to as "the new work location"),

    (b) both the residence at which the taxpayer ordinarily resided before the relocation (in section 62 and this subsection referred to as "the old residence") and the residence at which the taxpayer ordinarily resided after the relocation (in section 62 and this subsection referred to as "the new residence") are in Canada, and

    (c) the distance between the old residence and the new work location is not less than 40 kilometres greater than the distance between the new residence and the new work location

except that, in applying subsections 6(19) to (23) and section 62 in respect of a relocation of a taxpayer who is absent from but resident in Canada, this definition shall be read without reference to the words "in Canada" in subparagraph (a)(i), and without reference to paragraph (b);

**Related Provisions**: 6(19)–(22) — Employer subsidy of housing loss; 6(23) — Employer-provided mortgage subsidy is taxable; 62 — Deduction for moving expenses.

**Notes**: "Eligible relocation" added by 1998 Budget, effective for all taxation years. These conditions were formerly in 62(1) but now apply as well to the taxable-benefit rules in 6(19)–(22). See also 64.1 and 80.4(1.1).

**"employed"** means performing the duties of an office or employment;

**"employee"** includes officer;

**Related Provisions**: 248(1)"employment" — Further meaning of "employee".

**Notes**: The distinction between employee and independent contractor is not always obvious, and there is no one distinguishing factor. The leading case is *Wiebe Door Services Ltd.*, [1986] 2 C.T.C. 200 (FCA). In general, an employer *controls* (or has the right to control) the employee's hours and working conditions; the employee uses the employer's *equipment* and facilities; the employee does not share the employer's *risk*; the employee is an *integral part* of the business; and the employee may receive normal employee *benefits*. Where these factors are missing, the worker is likely an independent contractor. See Joanne Magee, "Whose Business Is It?" 45(3) *Canadian Tax Journal* 584–603 (1997). See also the CCRA's pamphlet, "Employee or Self-Employed?" (RC4110) for a good review of the relevant factors and checklist of questions.

An employee (as opposed to an independent contractor) normally has tax withheld from pay at source (153(1)(a)); can deduct only specifically permitted expenses (8(2)); must file on April 30 instead of June 15 (150(1)(d)); does not collect and remit GST on earnings; is eligible for Employment Insurance; has the employer pay a portion of EI premiums and CPP contributions; and is taxed when income is *received* rather than when it is *earned* (5(1)).

**Interpretation Bulletins**: IT-525: Performing artists.

**Forms**: CPT-1: Request for a ruling as to the status of a worker under the Canada Pension Plan or Unemployment Insurance Act; RC4100: Employee or Self-Employed?.

**"employee benefit plan"** means an arrangement under which contributions are made by an employer or by any person with whom the employer does not deal at arm's length to another person (in this Act referred to as the "custodian" of an employee benefit plan) and under which one or more payments are to be made to or for the benefit of employees or former employees of the employer or persons who do not deal at arm's length with any such employee or former employee (other than a payment that, if section 6 were read without reference to subparagraph 6(1)(a)(ii) and paragraph 6(1)(g), would not be required to be included in computing the income of the recipient), but does not include

    (a) a fund or plan referred to in subparagraph 6(1)(a)(i) or paragraph 6(1)(d) or (f),

    (b) a trust described in paragraph 149(1)(y),

    (c) an employee trust,

    (c.1) a salary deferral arrangement, in respect of a taxpayer, under which deferred amounts are required to be included as benefits under paragraph 6(1)(a) in computing the taxpayer's income,

    (c.2) a retirement compensation arrangement,

    (d) an arrangement the sole purpose of which is to provide education or training for employees of the employer to improve their work or work-related skills and abilities, or

    (e) a prescribed arrangement;

Part XVII — Interpretation  S. 248(1) exe

**Related Provisions**: 6(1)(g) — Amount received from employee benefit plan taxable; 12(11) — Definitions — "investment contract"; 32.1 — Deductions to employer re employee benefit plan; 104(6)(a.1) — Deduction in computing income of employee benefit plan; 104(13)(b) — Income inclusion to trust; 107.1 — Distribution by employee benefit plan; 128.1(10)"excluded right or interest"(a)(v) — No deemed disposition of rights on emigration; 212(17) — No non-resident withholding tax on payments from employee benefit plan.

**Notes**: Para. (e) of "employee benefit plan" changed from "a prescribed fund or plan" to "a prescribed arrangement" by 1993 technical bill, retroactive to 1980, to conform to the wording of Reg. 6800.

**Regulations**: 6800 (prescribed plan, prescribed arrangement).

**Interpretation Bulletins**: IT-502: Employee benefit plans and employee trusts.

**Advance Tax Rulings**: ATR-17: Employee benefit plan — purchase of company shares; ATR-21: Pension benefit from an unregistered pension plan.

**"employee trust"** means an arrangement (other than an employees profit sharing plan, a deferred profit sharing plan or a plan referred to in subsection 147(15) as a "revoked plan") established after 1979

(a) under which payments are made by one or more employers to a trustee in trust solely to provide to employees or former employees of

   (i) the employer, or

   (ii) a person with whom the employer does not deal at arm's length,

benefits the right to which vests at the time of each such payment and the amount of which does not depend on the individual's position, performance or compensation as an employee,

(b) under which the trustee has, since the commencement of the arrangement, each year allocated to individuals who are beneficiaries thereunder, in such manner as is reasonable, the amount, if any, by which the total of all amounts each of which is

   (i) an amount received under the arrangement by the trustee in the year from an employer or from a person with whom the employer does not deal at arm's length,

   (ii) the amount that would, if this Act were read without reference to subsection 104(6), be the income of the trust for the year (other than a taxable capital gain from the disposition of property) from a property or other source other than a business, or

   (iii) a capital gain of the trust for the year from the disposition of property

exceeds the total of all amounts each of which is

   (iv) the loss of the trust for the year (other than an allowable capital loss from the disposition of property) from a property or other source other than a business, or

   (v) a capital loss of the trust for the year from the disposition of property, and

(c) the trustee of which has elected to qualify the arrangement as an employee trust in its return of income filed within 90 days from the end of its first taxation year;

**Related Provisions**: 6(1)(h) — Amounts received from employee trust taxable; 104(6)(a) — Deduction in computing income of employee trust; 107.1 — Distribution by employee trust; 128.1(10)"excluded right or interest"(e)(i) — No deemed disposition on emigration; 212(17) — No non-resident withholding tax on payments from employee trust; 248(1)"disposition"(f)(vi) — Rollover from one trust to another.

**Interpretation Bulletins**: IT-502: Employee benefit plans and employee trusts.

**"employees profit sharing plan"** has the meaning assigned by subsection 144(1);

**"employer"**, in relation to an officer, means the person from whom the officer receives the officer's remuneration;

**Related Provisions**: 6(2) — Definition of "employer" for automobile standby charge; 6(17) — Extended definition for disability insurance top-up payments; 80.4(1)(b)(i) — Definition of "employer" for employee loans; 81(3)(c) — Definition of "employer" for municipal officer's expense allowance; 126.1(1) — Definition of "employer" for UI premium tax credit; 207.6(3)(a) — Definition of "employer" for incorporated employee/RCA rules; 252.1 — Application of pension rules where union is employer.

**Notes**: See Notes to 248(1)"employee".

**Forms**: PD20: Employer registration.

**"employment"** means the position of an individual in the service of some other person (including Her Majesty or a foreign state or sovereign) and **"servant"** or **"employee"** means a person holding such a position;

**Notes**: "Employee" is defined both here and above (in its alphabetical order). See Notes to "employee" above re the distinction between employee and independent contractor.

**Interpretation Bulletins**: IT-525: Performing artists (determining whether self-employed or employed).

**Forms**: CPT-1: Request for a ruling as to the status of a worker under the Canada Pension Plan or Unemployment Insurance Act.

**"estate"** has the meaning assigned by subsection 104(1);

**Related Provisions**: 128(1)(b) — Where corporation bankrupt; 128(2)(b) — Where individual bankrupt.

**"estate of the bankrupt"** has the same meaning as in the *Bankruptcy and Insolvency Act*;

**Notes**: Definition "estate of the bankrupt" added by 1994 tax amendments bill (Part I), effective for taxation years that end after February 21, 1994. See Notes to 128(3).

**"exempt income"** means property received or acquired by a person in such circumstances that it is, because of any provision of Part I, not included in computing the person's income, but does not include a dividend on a share or a support amount (as defined in subsection 56.1(4));

**Related Provisions**: 81 — Amounts not included in income; 149 — Exempt taxpayers.

**Notes**: An intercorporate dividend is included in income and thus is not "exempt income", even though it may be offset by a deduction in computing taxable income, under 112(1) or 113(1). Certain

1791

**S. 248(1) exe**      Income Tax Act

other amounts, such as workers' compensation payments and social assistance (welfare), are also not "exempt income" because they are included in income and then subject to an offsetting deduction. (See 56(1)(u), (v) and 110(1)(f)(ii).)

Definition "exempt income" amended by 1996 Budget, effective 1997, to add the exclusion for a support amount and to delete a redundant reference to "money" (which is included in "property" as defined in 248(1)). Before 1997, read:

> "exempt income" means money or property received or acquired by a person in such circumstances that it is, by reason of any provision in Part I, not included in computing the person's income, but for greater certainty does not include a dividend on a share;

**"farming"** includes tillage of the soil, livestock raising or exhibiting, maintaining of horses for racing, raising of poultry, fur farming, dairy farming, fruit growing and the keeping of bees, but does not include an office or employment under a person engaged in the business of farming;

**Related Provisions**: 28–31 — Rules for computing income from farming.

**Interpretation Bulletins**: IT-156R: Feedlot operators; IT-268R3: *Inter vivos* transfer of farm property to child; IT-433R: Farming or fishing — use of cash method.

**"farm loss"** has the meaning assigned by subsection 111(8);

**Related Provisions**: 31(1), (1.1), 248(1) — Definition of "restricted farm loss"; 111(9) — Farm loss where taxpayer not resident in Canada.

**"filing-due date"** for a taxation year of a taxpayer means the day on or before which the taxpayer's return of income under Part I for the year is required to be filed or would be required to be filed if tax under that Part were payable by the taxpayer for the year;

**Related Provisions**: 150(1) — Due dates for filing returns; *Interpretation Act* 26 — Deadline on Sunday or holiday extended to next business day.

**Notes**: "filing-due date" added by 1995 Budget, effective 1994.

**"fiscal period"** — [Repealed]

**Notes**: "Fiscal period" repealed by 1995 Budget, effective for fiscal periods that begin after 1994. See now 249.1(1) and (7).

**Interpretation Bulletins**: IT-179R: Change of fiscal period.

**Information Circulars**: 80-10R: Registered charities: operating a registered charity; 88-2 para. 21: General anti-avoidance rule — section 245 of the *Income Tax Act*.

**"fishing"** includes fishing for or catching shell fish, crustaceans and marine animals but does not include an office or employment under a person engaged in the business of fishing;

**Interpretation Bulletins**: IT-433R: Farming or fishing use of cash method.

**"flow-through share"** has the meaning assigned by subsection 66(15);

**Notes**: Definition "flow-through share added by 1995-97 technical bill, effective December 1994.

### Proposed Addition — 248(1) "foreign accrual property income"

**"foreign accrual property income"** has the meaning assigned by section 95;

**Application**: The June 22, 2000 draft legislation, subsec. 26(3), will add the definition "foreign accrual property income" to subsec. 248(1), applicable after 2000.

**Technical Notes**: The definition "foreign accrual property income" is introduced so that the definition of this expression in section 95 of the Act applies for the purposes of the Act.

This amendment applies after 2000.

**Related Provisions**: 95(1) "foreign accrual property income", 95(2) — Definition.

**"foreign affiliate"** has the meaning assigned by subsection 95(1);

**Interpretation Bulletins**: IT-343R: Meaning of the term "corporation"; IT-119R4: Debts of shareholders and certain persons connected with shareholders.

### Proposed Addition — 248(1) "foreign currency"

**"foreign currency"** means currency of a country other than Canada;

**Application**: The August 8, 2000 draft legislation, s. 25, will add the definition "foreign currency" to s. 248(1), applicable after June 27, 1999.

**Technical Notes**: "Foreign currency" means currency of a country other than Canada.

**"foreign exploration and development expenses"** has the meaning assigned by subsection 66(15);

### Proposed Addition — 248(1) "foreign resource expense", "foreign resource pool expenses"

**"foreign resource expense"** has the meaning assigned by subsection 66.21(1);

**Technical Notes**: The definition "foreign resource expense" is added to subsection 248(1), applicable for the purposes of the Act. The meaning of the expression is as defined in new subsection 66.21(1). See the commentary on that subsection for information about this new definition. This amendment applies after 2000.

**"foreign resource pool expenses"** of a taxpayer means the taxpayer's foreign resource expenses in respect of all countries and the taxpayer's foreign exploration and development expenses;

**Technical Notes**: The new definition "foreign resource pool expenses" is added to subsection 248(1), applicable for the purposes of the Act. Foreign resource pool expenses comprise all foreign resource expenses in respect of all countries (as defined in the definition "foreign resource expense" in new subsection 66.21(1)) and foreign exploration and development expenses (as defined in subsection 66(15)). This amendment applies after 2000.

**Application**: The December 21, 2000 draft legislation, subsec. 94(2), will add the definitions "foreign resource expense" and "foreign resource pool expenses" to subsec. 248(1), applicable after 2000.

"**foreign resource property**" has the meaning assigned by subsection 66(15);

### Proposed Amendment — 248(1)"foreign resource property"

"**foreign resource property**" has the meaning assigned by subsection 66(15), and a foreign resource property in respect of a country means a foreign resource property that is

(a) a right, licence or privilege to explore for, drill for or take petroleum, natural gas or related hydrocarbons in that country,

(b) a right, licence or privilege to

(i) store underground petroleum, natural gas or related hydrocarbons in that country, or

(ii) prospect, explore, drill or mine for minerals in a mineral resource in that country,

(c) an oil or gas well in that country or real property in that country the principal value of which depends on its petroleum or natural gas content (but not including depreciable property),

(d) a rental or royalty computed by reference to the amount or value of production from an oil or gas well in that country or from a natural accumulation of petroleum or natural gas in that country,

(e) a rental or royalty computed by reference to the amount or value of production from a mineral resource in that country,

(f) a real property in that country the principal value of which depends upon its mineral resource content (but not including depreciable property), or

(g) a right to or interest in any property described in any of paragraphs (a) to (f), other than such a right or interest that the taxpayer has by reason of being a beneficiary of a trust;

**Application**: The December 21, 2000 draft legislation, subsec. 94(1), will amend the definition "foreign resource property" in subsec. 248(1), applicable after 2000.

**Technical Notes**: The new definition "foreign resource property" in respect of a country is added, applicable for the purposes of the Act. The definition is structured in the same way as the amended definition "Canadian resource property" in subsection 66(15), with necessary modifications to reflect the location of the property in a country outside Canada. This amendment applies after 2000.

"**foreign retirement arrangement**" means a prescribed plan or arrangement;

### Proposed Amendment — Income inclusion on conversion of U.S. IRA

**Department of Finance news release, December 18, 1998**: *Qualified RRSP Investments and IRAs*

Finance Minister Paul Martin today announced that he will propose changes to the *Income Tax Act* and the *Income Tax Regulations* to address two issues that have been recently raised with the Department of Finance, in the context of retirement savings decisions currently being made by individuals.

[For the first measure, see Proposed Amendment under Reg. 4900(1) — ed.]

The second issue deals with individual retirement accounts (IRAs) established under the United States Internal Revenue Code. The Minister announced that he will propose an amendment to the *Income Tax Act* in response to recent changes to the Code relating to IRAs.

The changes to the Code have established a new type of IRA, known as a Roth IRA. Under the Code, contributions to a Roth IRA are not deductible, but investment income accrues tax-free and distributions are generally not taxable. Under certain circumstances, an individual may convert an ordinary IRA into a Roth IRA, but is required to include in computing income for the year of conversion the value of the ordinary IRA at the time of conversion. If the conversion is made in 1998, the income inclusion may be spread out over a four-year period.

The proposed amendment to the Act would affect Canadian residents who convert ordinary IRAs into Roth IRAs. It would require that the individual include in income for Canadian tax purposes any amount that must be included in income for U.S. tax purposes. This would ensure that the conversion amount is taxed in Canada, even where the IRA is converted simply by amending its terms. It would also ensure that the amount and timing of the inclusion in Canada matches the amount and timing in the U.S., thus allowing individuals to maximize the use of U.S. taxes paid on conversion as foreign tax credits in computing Canadian income tax payable.

Mr. Martin noted that the deferral opportunities in the U.S. for Roth IRAs are far more generous than the deferral opportunities in the U.S. for ordinary IRAs and the deferral opportunities in Canada for tax-assisted retirement savings. In particular, contributions can be made to a Roth IRA at any age, and there is no requirement for payments under a Roth IRA to begin by a certain age. Accordingly, there are no plans to provide tax assistance by way of an exemption from or deferral of taxation in Canada on earnings within a Roth IRA.

For further information: Tax Legislation Division, (613) 992-1916; Jean-Michel Catta, Public Affairs and Operations Division, (613) 992-1574.

**Related Provisions**: 12(11) — Definitions — "investment contract"; 94(1)"exempt foreign trust"(f) — Arrangement excluded from non-resident trust rules; 128.1(10)"excluded right or interest"(a)(x) — No deemed disposition on emigration.

**Notes**: A foreign retirement arrangement is a U.S. Individual Retirement Account (IRA); see Notes to Reg. 6803. The income earned within it is untaxed (81(1)(r)), while payments from it are taxed (56(1)(a)(i)(C.1)) but can be rolled into an RRSP (60.01). Note that such payments are taxed even when inherited on the death of another person: *Kaiser*, [1994] 2 C.T.C. 2385 (TCC).

"Foreign retirement arrangement" added by 1991 technical bill, effective 1990.

**Regulations**: 6803 (prescribed plan or arrangement is U.S. IRA).

"**former business property**" of a taxpayer means a capital property of the taxpayer that was used by the taxpayer or a person related to the taxpayer primarily for the purpose of gaining or producing income from a business, and that was real property of the taxpayer or an interest of the taxpayer in real property, but does not include

(a) a rental property of the taxpayer,

(b) land subjacent to a rental property of the taxpayer,

(c) land contiguous to land referred to in paragraph (b) that is a parking area, driveway, yard or garden or that is otherwise necessary for the use of the rental property referred to therein, or

(d) a leasehold interest in any property described in paragraphs (a) to (c),

and, for the purpose of this definition, "rental property" of a taxpayer means real property owned by the taxpayer, whether jointly with another person or otherwise, and used by the taxpayer in the taxation year in respect of which the expression is being applied principally for the purpose of gaining or producing gross revenue that is rent (other than property leased by the taxpayer to a person related to the taxpayer and used by that related person principally for any other purpose), but, for greater certainty, does not include a property leased by the taxpayer or the related person to a lessee, in the ordinary course of a business of the taxpayer or the related person of selling goods or rendering services, under an agreement by which the lessee undertakes to use the property to carry on the business of selling or promoting the sale of the goods or services of the taxpayer or the related person;

**Related Provisions**: 13(4), 44(1)(b), 44(6) — Rollovers of former business property replaced by new property; 87(2)(l.3) — Amalgamations — replacement property; 248(4) — Interest in real property.

**Notes**: "Former business property" amended by 1991 technical bill, effective for dispositions after July 13, 1990, to add references to a related person and to add the parenthetical exclusion in the middle of the closing words.

**Interpretation Bulletins**: IT-491: Former business property.

**"goods and services tax"** means the tax payable under Part IX of the *Excise Tax Act*;

**Related Provisions**: 6(1)(e.1), 15(1.4) — Employee and shareholder benefits; 248(15)–(18) — Rules with respect to GST.

**Notes**: "Goods and services tax" added by 1990 GST, effective 1991. GST is imposed by sections 165, 212 and 218 of the *Excise Tax Act*: s. 165 imposes the regular tax on taxable supplies; s. 212 applies to importations of goods; and s. 218 requires self-assessment of tax on certain importations, such as of services and intangible property.

For the GST legislation, see David M. Sherman, *The Practitioner's Goods and Services Tax, Annotated*, (Carswell, annual). It is also found, with detailed commentary, in David M. Sherman, *Canada GST Service* (Carswell, looseleaf) and on Carswell's *GST Partner* CD-ROM.

**"grandfathered share"** means

(a) a share of the capital stock of a corporation issued after 8:00 p.m. Eastern Daylight Saving Time, June 18, 1987 pursuant to an agreement in writing entered into before that time,

(b) a share of the capital stock of a corporation issued after 8:00 p.m. Eastern Daylight Saving Time, June 18, 1987 and before 1988 as part of a distribution to the public made in accordance with the terms of a prospectus, preliminary prospectus, registration statement, offering memorandum or notice filed before 8:00 p.m. Eastern Daylight Saving Time, June 18, 1987 with a public authority pursuant to and in accordance with the securities legislation of the jurisdiction in which the shares are distributed,

(c) a share (in this paragraph referred to as the "new share") of the capital stock of a corporation that is issued after 8:00 p.m. Eastern Daylight Saving Time, June 18, 1987 in exchange for

(i) a share of a corporation that was issued before 8:00 p.m. Eastern Daylight Saving Time, June 18, 1987 or is a grandfathered share, or

(ii) a debt obligation of a corporation that was

(A) issued before 8:00 p.m. Eastern Daylight Saving Time, June 18, 1987, or

(B) issued after 8:00 p.m. Eastern Daylight Saving Time, June 18, 1987 under an agreement in writing entered into before that time, or after that time and before 1988 as part of a distribution to the public made in accordance with the terms of a prospectus, preliminary prospectus, registration statement, offering memorandum or notice filed before that time with a public authority under and in accordance with the securities legislation of the jurisdiction in which the debt obligation is distributed,

where the right to the exchange and all or substantially all the terms and conditions of the new share were established in writing before that time, and

(d) a share of a class of the capital stock of a Canadian corporation listed on a prescribed stock exchange that is issued after 8:00 p.m. Eastern Daylight Saving Time, June 18, 1987 on the exercise of a right that

(i) was issued before that time, that was issued after that time under an agreement in writing entered into before that time or that was issued after that time and before 1988 as part of a distribution to the public made in accordance with the terms of a prospectus, preliminary prospectus, registration statement, offering memorandum or notice filed before that time with a public authority under and in accordance with the securities legislation of the jurisdiction in which the rights were distributed, and

(ii) was listed on a prescribed stock exchange,

where all or substantially all the terms and conditions of the right and the share were established in writing before that time, except that a share that is deemed under the definition "short-term preferred share", "taxable preferred share" or "term preferred share" in this subsection or under subsection 112(2.2) to have been issued at any time shall be deemed after that time not to be a grandfathered share for the purposes of that provision;

### Proposed Amendment — 248(1)"grandfathered share" closing words

except that a share that is deemed under the definition "short-term preferred share", "taxable preferred share" or "term preferred share" in this subsection or under subsection 112(2.22) to have been issued at any time is deemed after that time not to be a grandfathered share for the purposes of that provision;

**Application**: Bill C-43 (First Reading September 20, 2000), subsec. 112(1), will amend the closing words of the definition "grandfathered share" in subsec. 248(1) to read as above, applicable in respect of dividends received after 1998.

**Technical Notes**: The definition "grandfathered share" in subsection 248(1) is amended to correct a cross-reference as a consequence of the movement of the deeming rule in paragraph 112(2.2)(f) to new paragraph 112(2.22)(a).

**Related Provisions**: 87(4.2), (4.3) — Amalgamation.

**Notes**: (c)(ii)(B) and (d)(i) of "grandfathered share" amended by 1991 technical bill, retroactive to the introduction of the definition (June 18, 1987), to add the words from "or after that time and before 1988" through to the end of the clause or subpara.

The CCRA takes the position that "all or substantially all" means 90% or more.

**Regulations**: 3200 (prescribed stock exchange in Canada).

**"gross revenue"** of a taxpayer for a taxation year means the total of

(a) all amounts received in the year or receivable in the year (depending on the method regularly followed by the taxpayer in computing the taxpayer's income) otherwise than as or on account of capital, and

(b) all amounts (other than amounts referred to in paragraph (a)) included in computing the taxpayer's income from a business or property for the year by virtue of paragraph 12(1)(o) or subsection 12(3) or (4) or section 12.2 of this Act or subsection 12(8) of the *Income Tax Act*, chapter 148 of the Revised Statutes of Canada, 1952;

**Related Provisions**: 149(9) — Limitation re gross revenue of non-profit SR&ED corporation; 247(5), (9) — Determination of gross revenue for transfer pricing rules.

**I.T. Application Rules**: 69 (meaning of "*Income Tax Act*, chapter 148 of the Revised Statutes of Canada, 1952").

**"group term life insurance policy"** means a group life insurance policy under which the only amounts payable by the insurer are

(a) amounts payable on the death or disability of individuals whose lives are insured in respect of, in the course of or because of, their office or employment or former office or employment, and

(b) policy dividends or experience rating refunds;

**Related Provisions**: 6(1)(a)(i), 6(4) — $25,000 group term life insurance not a taxable benefit before July 1994; 18(9.01) — Limitation on deduction for premiums paid; 138(15) — Meaning of "group term insurance policy"; Reg. 1408(2) — Definition does not apply to regulations re policy reserves.

**Notes**: Definition "group term life insurance policy" amended by 1994 Budget, effective for insurance provided in respect of periods that are after June 1994. Previously read:

"group term life insurance policy", with respect to a taxpayer, means, subject to subsection 138(15), a group life insurance policy under which no amount is payable to a person other than the group policyholder as a result of contributions made to or under the policy by the employer of the taxpayer before the death or disability of the taxpayer;

For the calculation of the taxable employee benefit on such policies' premiums, see 6(4) and Reg. 2700–2704.

The phrase "subject to subsection 138(15)" added in the R.S.C. 1985 (5th Supp.) consolidation, effective for taxation years ending after November 1991. See Notes to 138(15).

**Interpretation Bulletins**: IT-529: Flexible employee benefit programs.

**"home relocation loan"** means a loan received by an individual or the individual's spouse or common-law partner in circumstances where the individual has commenced employment at a location in Canada (in this definition referred to as the "new work location") and by reason thereof has moved from the residence in Canada at which, before the move, the individual ordinarily resided (in this definition referred to as the "old residence") to a residence in Canada at which, after the move, the individual ordinarily resided (in this definition referred to as the "new residence") if

(a) the distance between the old residence and the new work location is at least 40 kilometres greater than the distance between the new residence and the new work location,

(b) the loan is used to acquire a dwelling, or a share of the capital stock of a cooperative housing corporation acquired for the sole purpose of acquiring the right to inhabit a dwelling owned by the corporation, where the dwelling is for the habitation of the individual and is the individual's new residence,

(c) the loan is received in the circumstances described in subsection 80.4(1), or would have been so received if subsection 80.4(1.1) had applied to the loan at the time it was received, and

(d) the loan is designated by the individual to be a home relocation loan, but in no case shall more than one loan in respect of a particular move, or more than one loan at any particular time, be designated as a home relocation loan by the individual;

**Related Provisions**: 6(23) — Employer-provided mortgage subsidy is taxable; 15(2)(a)(ii) — Housing loan to shareholder; 80.4(4) — Home purchase or relocation loan to employee.

**Notes**: 248(1)"home relocation loan" opening words amended by 2000 same-sex partners bill to add reference to "common-law partner", effective for the 2001 and later taxation years, or earlier by election (see Notes to 248(1)"common-law partner").

Subpara. (c) amended by 1998 Budget, effective February 24, 1998, to add "or would have been so received if subsection 80.4(1.1) had applied to the loan at the time it was received". The reason for the amendment was that because of the case law holding that 80.4(1) did not apply to some loans, it was possible that some loans in respect of eligible relocations would not meet the definition and that no partial offsetting deduction would be available.

Para. (b) of "home relocation loan" amended by 1991 technical bill, retroactive to 1986, to include a share of a co-operative housing corporation.

**Interpretation Bulletins**: IT-421R2: Benefits to individuals, corporations and shareholders from loans or debt.

**"income-averaging annuity contract"** of an individual means, except for the purposes of section 61, a contract

    (a) that is an income-averaging annuity contract within the meaning assigned by subsection 61(4), and

    (b) in respect of which the individual has made a deduction under section 61 in computing the individual's income for a taxation year;

**Related Provisions**: 128.1(10)"excluded right or interest"(f)(ii) — Emigration — no deemed disposition of right under IAAC.

**"income bond"** or **"income debenture"** of a corporation (in this definition referred to as the "issuing corporation") means a bond or debenture in respect of which interest or dividends are payable only to the extent that the issuing corporation has made a profit before taking into account the interest or dividend obligation and that was issued

    (a) before November 17, 1978,

    (b) after November 16, 1978 and before 1980 pursuant to an agreement in writing to do so made before November 17, 1978 (in this definition referred to as an "established agreement"), or

    (c) by an issuing corporation resident in Canada for a term that may not, in any circumstances, exceed 5 years,

        (i) as part of a proposal to or an arrangement with its creditors that had been approved by a court under the *Bankruptcy and Insolvency Act*,

        (ii) at a time when all or substantially all of its assets were under the control of a receiver, receiver-manager, sequestrator or trustee in bankruptcy, or

        (iii) at a time when, by reason of financial difficulty, the issuing corporation or another corporation resident in Canada with which it does not deal at arm's length was in default, or could reasonably be expected to default, on a debt obligation held by a person with whom the issuing corporation or the other corporation was dealing at arm's length and the bond or debenture was issued either wholly or in substantial part and either directly or indirectly in exchange or substitution for that obligation or a part thereof,

and, in the case of a bond or debenture issued after November 12, 1981, the proceeds from the issue may reasonably be regarded as having been used by the issuing corporation or a corporation with which it was not dealing at arm's length in the financing of its business carried on in Canada immediately before the bond or debenture was issued,

and, for the purposes of this definition,

    (d) where the terms or conditions of an established agreement were amended after November 16, 1978, the agreement shall be deemed to have been made after that date, and

    (e) where

        (i) at any particular time the terms or conditions of a bond or debenture issued pursuant to an established agreement or of any agreement relating to such a bond or debenture have been changed,

        (ii) under the terms or conditions of a bond or debenture acquired in the ordinary course of the business carried on by a specified financial institution or a partnership or trust (other than a testamentary trust) or under the terms or conditions of any agreement relating to any such bond or debenture (other than an agreement made before October 24, 1979 to which the issuing corporation or any person related thereto was not a party), the owner thereof could at any particular time after November 16, 1978 require, either alone or together with one or more taxpayers, the repayment, acquisition, cancellation or conversion of the bond or debenture otherwise than by reason of a failure or default under the terms or conditions of the bond or debenture or any agreement that related to, and was entered into at the time of, the issuance of the bond or debenture,

        (iii) at any particular time after November 16, 1978, the maturity date of a bond or debenture was extended or the terms or conditions relating to the repayment of the principal amount thereof were changed,

        (iv) at a particular time a specified financial institution (or a partnership or trust of which a specified financial institution or a person related to the institution is a member or beneficiary) acquires a bond or debenture that

            (A) was issued before November 17, 1978 or under an established agreement,

            (B) was issued to a person other than a corporation that was, at the time of issue,

                (I) described in any of paragraphs (a) to (e) of the definition "specified financial institution", or

(II) a corporation that was controlled by one or more corporations described in subclause (I) and, for the purpose of this subclause, one corporation is controlled by another corporation if more than 50% of its issued share capital (having full voting rights under all circumstances) belongs to the other corporation, to persons with whom the other corporation does not deal at arm's length, or to the other corporation and persons with whom the other corporation does not deal at arm's length,

(C) was acquired from a person that was, at the time the person last acquired the bond or debenture and at the particular time, a person other than a corporation described in any of paragraphs (a) to (f) of that definition, and

(D) was acquired otherwise than under an agreement in writing made before October 24, 1979, or

(v) at a particular time after November 12, 1981, a specified financial institution (or a partnership or trust of which a specified financial institution or a person related to the institution is a member or beneficiary) acquires a bond or debenture that

(A) was not a bond or debenture referred to in paragraph (c),

(B) was acquired from a person that was, at the particular time, a corporation described in any of paragraphs (a) to (f) of the definition "specified financial institution", and

(C) was acquired subject to or conditional on a guarantee agreement (within the meaning that would be assigned by subsection 112(2.2) if the reference in that subsection to a "share" were read as a reference to an "income bond" or "income debenture") that was entered into after November 12, 1981,

the bond or debenture shall, for the purposes of determining at any time after the particular time whether it is an income bond or income debenture, be deemed to have been issued at the particular time otherwise than pursuant to an established agreement;

**Related Provisions**: 15(3), (4) — Payment on income bond deemed to be a dividend; 15.1, 15.2 — Small business bonds and small business development bonds; 248(13) — Interests in trusts and partnerships; 256(2), (6.1) — Meaning of "controlled".

**Notes**: Subparas. (e)(iv) and (v) amended by 1998 Budget, effective for taxation years that begin after 1998, except that for a bond or debenture acquired from a corporation that last acquired the bond or debenture in a taxation year that began before 1999,

(a) read "at the time the person last acquired the bond or debenture and at the particular time, a person other than a corporation described in any of paragraphs (a) to (f)" in cl. (e)(iv)(C) as "at the time the person last acquired the bond or debenture, a corporation described in subclause (B)(I) or (II), and at the particular time, a corporation described in any of paragraphs (a) to (f) of that definition"; and

(b) read "a corporation described in any of paragraphs (a) to (f) of the definition" in cl. (e)(v)(B) as "a corporation described in subclause (iv)(B)(I) or (II)".

From June 19, 1987 through taxation years that began before 1999, read:

(iv) at any particular time after October 23, 1979, a bond or debenture issued before November 17, 1978 or a bond or debenture issued pursuant to an established agreement (other than a bond or debenture issued to a corporation described in any of paragraphs (a) to (f) of the definition "specified financial institution" in this subsection) is acquired (otherwise than pursuant to an agreement in writing made before October 24, 1979) from a person (other than a corporation described in any of paragraphs (a) to (f) of that definition) by a specified financial institution or by a partnership or trust of which a specified financial institution or a person related thereto is a member or beneficiary, or

(v) at any particular time after November 12, 1981, a bond or debenture (other than a bond or debenture referred to in paragraph (c)) is acquired by a specified financial institution or by a partnership or trust of which a specified financial institution or a person related thereto is a member or beneficiary from a corporation described in any of paragraphs (a) to (f) of the definition "specified financial institution" in this subsection and the acquisition is subject to or conditional on a guarantee agreement (within the meaning that would be assigned by subsection 112(2.2) if the reference therein to a "share" were read as a reference to an "income bond" or "income debenture") that was entered into after November 12, 1981,

The CCRA takes the position that "all or substantially all", used in (c)(ii), means 90% or more.

**Interpretation Bulletins**: IT-52R4: Income bonds and income debentures; IT-527: Distress preferred shares.

**"income debenture"** — [See under "income bond".]

**"income interest"** of a taxpayer in a trust has the meaning assigned by subsection 108(1);

**"indexed debt obligation"** means a debt obligation the terms or conditions of which provide for an adjustment to an amount payable in respect of the obligation for a period during which the obligation was outstanding that is determined by reference to a change in the purchasing power of money;

**Related Provisions**: 16(6) — Indexed debt obligations; 142.3(2) — Indexed debt obligation not subject to rules re income from specified debt obligations; 142.4(5)(a)(i) — Disposition of indexed debt obligation.

**Notes**: "indexed debt obligation" added by 1992 technical bill, effective for indexed debt obligations issued after October 16, 1991.

**"indexed security", "indexed security investment plan"** — [Repealed under former Act]

**Notes**: Indexed security investment plans existed from 1983 to 1985, and were repealed by the 1985 Budget with the introduction of the capital gains exemption in 110.6.

**"individual"** means a person other than a corporation;

**Related Provisions**: 104(2) — Trust deemed to be an individual.

**S. 248(1) ind**  Income Tax Act

**Notes**: The definition of individual includes both a human being and a trust (see 104(2)), as well as an exempt non-profit organization that falls within the definition of "person" in 248(1).

**Interpretation Bulletins**: IT-123R6, para. 11: Transactions involving eligible capital property.

**"insurance corporation"** means a corporation that carries on an insurance business;

**Related Provisions**: 138(1) — Corporation deemed to carry on insurance business; 148(10)(a) — Issuer of annuity contracts deemed to be insurer for certain purposes; 186.1(b) — Insurance corporation not liable for Part IV tax.

**"insurance policy"** includes a life insurance policy;

**Notes**: 248(1)"insurance policy" added by 1999 Budget, effective December 16, 1998.

**"insurer"** has the meaning assigned by this subsection to the expression "insurance corporation";

**Related Provisions**: See under "insurance corporation" above.

**Notes**: 248(1)"insurer" added in the R.S.C. 1985 (5th Supp.), effective December 1, 1991. This definition was formerly included in the definition of "insurance corporation".

**"inter vivos trust"** has the meaning assigned by subsection 108(1);

**Related Provisions**: 149(5) — Exception re investment income of certain clubs; 207.6(1) — Definitions (re RCA tax).

**"international traffic"** means, in respect of a non-resident person carrying on the business of transporting passengers or goods, any voyage made in the course of that business where the principal purpose of the voyage is to transport passengers or goods

(a) from Canada to a place outside Canada,

(b) from a place outside Canada to Canada, or

(c) from a place outside Canada to another place outside Canada;

**Related Provisions**: 250(6) — Residence of international shipping corporation; Canada-U.S. tax treaty, Art. III:1(h) — Meaning of "international traffic" for treaty purposes; Art. XV:3 — Exemption for U.S. resident employee; Art. XXIII:3 — Capital tax on ship or aircraft employed in international traffic.

**Interpretation Bulletins**: IT-494: Hire of ships and aircraft from non-residents.

**"inventory"** means a description of property the cost or value of which is relevant in computing a taxpayer's income from a business for a taxation year or would have been so relevant if the income from the business had not been computed in accordance with the cash method and, with respect to a farming business, includes all of the livestock held in the course of carrying on the business;

### Proposed Amendment — 248(1)"inventory"

**"inventory"** means a description of property (other than property to which subsection 94.2(3) applies) the cost or value of which is relevant in computing a taxpayer's income from a business for a taxation year or would have been so relevant if the income from the business had not been computed in accordance with the cash method and, with respect to a farming business, includes all of the livestock held in the course of carrying on the business;

**Application**: The June 22, 2000 draft legislation, subsec. 26(2), will amend the definition "inventory" in subsec. 248(1) to read as above, applicable to fiscal periods that begin after 2000.

**Technical Notes**: A taxpayer's "inventory" is generally described in subsection 248(1) as a description of property the cost or value of which is relevant in computing a taxpayer's income from a business for a taxation year. Rules for "inventory" in section 10 and elsewhere in the Act affect the calculation of a taxpayer's income from business.

The definition "inventory" is amended to exclude descriptions of property to the disposition of which subsection 94.2(3) applies.

This amendment applies to fiscal periods that begin after 2000.

**Related Provisions**: 10(1), (1.01) — Valuation of inventory property; 10(5) — Certain property deemed to be inventory; 66.3(1)(a)(ii) — Certain exploration and development shares deemed to be inventory; 142.5 — Mark-to-market rules for securities held by financial institutions; 142.6(3), (4) — Certain property of financial institution deemed not to be inventory; 231.1(1)(b) — Examination of inventory.

**Notes**: "Inventory" amended by 1991 technical bill, effective for fiscal periods beginning in 1989 or later, to add all the words from "or would have been". The amendment clarifies that a farmer's livestock is included in inventory regardless of whether the farmer uses cash accounting or accrual accounting.

See Notes to 54"capital property".

**Interpretation Bulletins**: IT-51R2: Supplies on hand at the end of a fiscal year; IT-218R: Profit, capital gains and losses from the sale of real estate, including farmland and inherited land and conversion of real estate from capital property to inventory and vice versa; IT-427R: Livestock of farmers; IT-457R: Election by professionals to exclude work in progress from income; IT-473R: Inventory valuation.

**"investment corporation"** has the meaning assigned by subsection 130(3);

**"investment tax credit"** has the meaning assigned by subsection 127(9);

**Notes**: The December 14, 1995 draft legislation proposed to add the definition "joint exploration corporation" to 248(1) with a cross-reference to 66(15); however, the 1995-97 technical bill did not include this addition. The term is used in 53(2)(f) and (f.1) as well as in s. 66.

### Proposed Addition — 248(1)"joint partner trust"

**"joint partner trust"** means a trust to which paragraph 104(4)(a) would apply if that paragraph were read without reference to subparagraph 104(4)(a)(iii) and clause 104(4)(a)(iv)(A);

**Application**: Bill C-43 (First Reading September 20, 2000), subsec. 112(4), will add the definition "joint partner trust" to subsec. 248(1), applicable to trusts created after 1999.

**Technical Notes**: The definition "joint partner trust" refers to a trust to which paragraph 104(4)(a) would apply if that paragraph were read without reference to subparagraph 104(4)(a)(iii) and clause 104(4)(a)(iv)(A). Accordingly, for a trust to be a joint partner trust it generally must satisfy the following conditions:

1. at the time of the trust's creation, the taxpayer creating the trust was alive and had attained 65 years of age;
2. the trust was created after 1999;
3. the taxpayer or the taxpayer's spouse was, in combination with the spouse or the taxpayer, as the case may be, entitled to receive all of the income of the trust that arose before the later of the death of the taxpayer and the death of the spouse; and
4. no other person could, before the later of those deaths, receive or otherwise obtain the use of any of the income or capital of the trust.

The definitions *"alter ego* trust" and "joint partner trust" apply to trusts created after 1999. The definition "post-1971 partner trust" applies to trusts created after 1971. Other amendments related to the introduction of these definitions include amendments to section 73, subsections 104(5.8), (6) and (15) and subsection 107(4), and the amended definition of "trust" in subsection 108(1). For further detail, see the commentary on those provisions.

These amendments also reflect changes proposed under Bill C-23, the *Modernization of Benefits and Obligations Act* [by changing "spousal" to "partner" to cover common-law same-sex partners — ed.].

**Related Provisions**: 73(1.01)(c)(ii) — Rollover on transfer to joint partner trust; 104(5.8) — Transfers from joint partner trust to another trust; 104(6)(b)(ii.1), (iii) — Deduction from income of trust; 104(15)(a) — Preferred beneficiary election; 107(4)(a)(iii) — Distribution of property to person other than taxpayer or partner; 248(1)*"alter ego* trust" — Parallel trust where partner is not a beneficiary.

**Notes**: This means a trust described in 104(4)(a)(iv)(B). *Alter ego* trusts and joint partner trusts (called joint spousal trusts in the draft legislation of December 17, 1999) are expected to be used as an estate planning tool to avoid probate fees. They effectively extend the spousal-trust rule in 73(1)(c) (draft 73(1.01)) to allow the settlor to be a beneficiary as well. For discussion see John Fuke & Mary Anne Bueschkens, "Alter Ego Trust and Joint Spousal Trust", VI(2) *Business Vehicles* (Federated Press 292-294 (2000)).

**"lawyer"** has the meaning assigned by subsection 232(1);

**"legal representative"** of a taxpayer means a trustee in bankruptcy, an assignee, a liquidator, a curator, a receiver of any kind, a trustee, an heir, an administrator, an executor, a committee, or any other like person, administering, winding up, controlling or otherwise dealing in a representative or fiduciary capacity with the property that belongs or belonged to, or that is or was held for the benefit of, the taxpayer or the taxpayer's estate;

**Notes**: Definition "legal representative" added by 1995-97 technical bill, effective June 18, 1998.

**"lending asset"** means a bond, debenture, mortgage, note, agreement of sale or any other indebtedness or a prescribed share, but does not include a prescribed property;

**Related Provisions**: 95(1)"lending of money" closing words — Extended definition for FAPI purposes; 142.2(1) — Definition of "specified debt obligation".

**Notes**: Definition "lending asset" amended to change "prescribed security" to "prescribed property", effective

(a) for taxation years that end after September 1997; and

(b) for taxation years that end after 1995 and before October 1997, if the taxpayer files an election for amended 20(1)(l) to apply to such years (see Notes to 20(1)(l)).

**Regulations**: 6209 (prescribed share, prescribed security, prescribed property).

**Interpretation Bulletins**: IT-442R: Bad debts and reserves for doubtful debts.

**"licensed annuities provider"** has the meaning assigned by subsection 147(1);

**Notes**: Definition "licensed annuities provider" added by 1995-97 technical bill, effective 1997.

**"life insurance business"** includes

(a) an annuities business, and

(b) the business of issuing contracts all or any part of the issuer's reserves for which vary in amount depending on the fair market value of a specified group of assets,

carried on by a life insurance corporation or a life insurer;

**Related Provisions**: 138(1)(b) — Corporation deemed carrying on (life) insurance business.

**"life insurance capital dividend"** has the meaning assigned by subsection 83(2.1);

**Notes**: This reference should be "subsection 83(2.1) of the *Income Tax Act*, chapter 148 of the Revised Statutes of Canada, 1952". The provision in 83(2.1) which allowed a corporation to elect for a dividend to be a life insurance capital dividend was repealed effective for dividends paid after May 23, 1985. However, the definition still applies for limited transitional purposes. See Notes to 83(2.1).

**"life insurance corporation"** means a corporation that carries on a life insurance business that is not a business described in paragraph (a) or (b) of the definition "life insurance business" in this subsection, whether or not the corporation also carries on a business described in either of those paragraphs;

**Related Provisions**: 148(10)(a) — Issuer of annuity contracts deemed to be life insurer for certain purposes.

**"life insurance policy"** has the meaning assigned by subsection 138(12);

**Related Provisions**: 211(1) — Definitions.

**"life insurance policy in Canada"** has the meaning assigned by subsection 138(12);

**"life insurer"** has the meaning assigned by this subsection to the expression "life insurance corporation";

**Notes**: 248(1)"life insurer" added in the R.S.C. 1985 (5th Supp.) consolidation, effective December 1, 1991. This definition was formerly included in the definition of "life insurance corporation".

**"limited partnership loss"** has the meaning assigned by subsection 96(2.1);

**Related Provisions**: 111(9) — Limited partnership loss where taxpayer not resident in Canada.

**"listed personal property"** has the meaning assigned by section 54;

**"majority interest partner"** of a particular partnership at any time means a person or partnership (in this definition referred to as the "taxpayer")

(a) whose share of the particular partnership's income from all sources for the last fiscal period of the particular partnership that ended before that time (or, if the particular partnership's first fiscal period includes that time, for that period) would have exceeded 1/2 of the particular partnership's income from all sources for that period if the taxpayer had held throughout that period each interest in the partnership that the taxpayer or a person affiliated with the taxpayer held at that time, or

(b) whose share, if any, together with the shares of every person with whom the taxpayer is affiliated, of the total amount that would be paid to all members of the particular partnership (otherwise than as a share of any income of the partnership) if it were wound up at that time exceeds 1/2 of that amount;

**Related Provisions**: 251.1 — Affiliated persons.

**Notes**: Definition "majority interest partner" added by 1995-97 technical bill, effective April 27, 1995. This definition was formerly in 97(3.1), but has been amended in two respects. First, it applies on the basis of a partner's entitlement to the partnership's income from all sources, rather than the partner's entitlement to income from each source. Second, it uses the concept of affiliated persons in 251.1.

**"mineral"** includes ammonite gemstone, bituminous sands, calcium chloride, coal, kaolin, oil shale and silica, but does not include petroleum, natural gas or a related hydrocarbon not expressly referred to in this definition;

**Related Provisions**: *Interpretation Act* 8(2.1), (2.2) — Application to exclusive economic zone and continental shelf.

**Notes**: Definition "mineral" amended to delete "oil sands" and add "ammonite gemstone" by 1995-97 technical bill, effective for taxation years and fiscal periods that begin after 1996 except that,

(a) for greater certainty, the definition shall not result in a characterization of expenditures made or costs incurred in a taxation year or fiscal period that began before 1997 as a Canadian exploration expense, Canadian development expense, Canadian exploration and development expense or foreign exploration and development expense or an increase in any amount deductible under s. 65 as a consequence of an expenditure made or cost incurred before 1997; and

(b) where, as a consequence of the application of the definition, a person's property would, but for this paragraph, be recharacterized as Canadian resource property or foreign resource property at the beginning of the person's first taxation year or fiscal period that begins after 1996, for the purposes of the Act the property is deemed

(i) to have been disposed of by the person immediately before that time for proceeds equal to its cost amount to the person at that time, and

(ii) to have been reacquired at that time by the person for the same amount.

"mineral" substituted for "minerals" by 1993 technical bill, this version effective for taxation years that end in 1988 or later. For taxation years that begin in 1985 or later and end in 1985-87, delete "kaolin". For taxation years that began before 1985, the former definition read:

"minerals" does not include petroleum, natural gas or related hydrocarbons (except coal, bituminous sands, oil sands or oil shale);

Among other things, the change allows calcium chloride producers access to the income tax incentives for mining, including the resource allowance. (Department of Finance news release, December 2, 1992.) See also "mineral resource" below.

**Interpretation Bulletins**: IT-125R4: Dispositions of resource properties.

**"mineral resource"** means

(a) a base or precious metal deposit,

(b) a coal deposit,

(c) a bituminous sands deposit or oil shale deposit, or

(d) a mineral deposit in respect of which

(i) the Minister of Natural Resources has certified that the principal mineral extracted is an industrial mineral contained in a non-bedded deposit,

(ii) the principal mineral extracted is ammonite gemstone, calcium chloride, diamond, gypsum, halite, kaolin or sylvite, or

(iii) the principal mineral extracted is silica that is extracted from sandstone or quartzite;

**Related Provisions**: *Interpretation Act* 8(2.1), (2.2) — Application to exclusive economic zone and continental shelf.

**Notes**: Para. (c) of "mineral resource" amended by 1996 Budget, effective March 6, 1997, to delete "oil sands deposit". See now 248(1)"bituminous sands".

Subpara. (d)(ii) amended by 1995-97 to add reference to ammonite gemstone, effective on the same basis as the amendment to 248(1)"mineral".

Subpara. (d)(ii) amended by 1993 technical bill, to add reference to "calcium chloride" effective for taxation years that begin in 1985 or later, and to "diamond" effective for taxation years that end in 1993 or later. The change with respect to diamonds means that exploration for diamond deposits can be financed by flow-through share offerings, since all eligible exploration costs qualify as Canadian exploration expenses. (Department of Finance news release, June 21, 1993.)

**Interpretation Bulletins**: IT-125R4: Dispositions of resource properties.

**"minerals"** — [Repealed]

**Notes**: See under "mineral" above.

**"mining reclamation trust"** — [Repealed]

**Notes**: Definition "mining reclamation trust" repealed by 1997 Budget, effective after 1997 and, if an election is made by a trust under 248(1)"qualifying environmental trust"(i),

(a) the trust is deemed to have never been a mining reclamation trust; and

(b) notwithstanding 152(4) to (5), Revenue Canada may before 2000 make any assessments and reassessments that are necessary to give effect to the election.

The broader term "qualifying environmental trust" has replaced "mining reclamation trust" throughout the Act. See Notes to 107.3(1), 211.6 and 248(1)"qualifying environmental trust".

Definition "mining reclamation trust" added by 1994 Budget, effective 1994. However, it did not apply to a trust the first contribution to which was made before February 23, 1994, and which elected in writing, filed with Revenue Canada by the end of 1995, for the definition not to apply.

See Notes to 248(1)"qualifying environmental trust".

**"Minister"** means the Minister of National Revenue;

**Related Provisions**: 220 — Administration of the Act.

**Notes**: Recent Ministers of National Revenue have been: Otto Jelinek (1989-93); Garth Turner (1993); David Anderson (1993-96); Jane Stewart (1996-97); Herb Dhaliwal (June 11, 1997-August 3, 1999); Martin Cauchon (August 3, 1999-present).

Bill C-43, the *Canada Customs & Revenue Agency Act*, changed Revenue Canada from a department to an agency (CCRA) effective November 1, 1999. See Notes to 220(1). However, the role of the Minister remains unchanged.

**Regulations**: 900 (delegation of authority by the Minister to specific officials).

**"money purchase limit"** for a calendar year has the meaning assigned by subsection 147.1(1);

**Notes**: "Money purchase limit" added by 1990 pension bill, effective 1989.

**"mortgage investment corporation"** has the meaning assigned by subsection 130.1(6);

**"motor vehicle"** means an automotive vehicle designed or adapted to be used on highways and streets but does not include

(a) a trolley bus, or

(b) a vehicle designed or adapted to be operated exclusively on rails;

**Related Provisions**: 248(1) — "automobile", "passenger vehicle".

**Interpretation Bulletins**: IT-521R: Motor vehicle expenses claimed by self-employed individuals; IT-522R: Vehicle, travel and sales expenses of employees.

**"mutual fund corporation"** has the meaning assigned by subsection 131(8);

**Related Provisions**: 131(8.1) — Meaning of "mutual fund corporation".

**"mutual fund trust"** has the meaning assigned by subsection 132(6);

**Related Provisions**: 132(6.1), (6.2), (7); 132.2(1)(q) — Extensions and limitations to definition of mutual fund trust.

**"net capital loss"** has the meaning assigned by subsection 111(8);

**Related Provisions**: 111(1)(b) — Application of net capital losses; 111(9) — Net capital loss of person not resident in Canada.

**"net income stabilization account"** means an account of a taxpayer under the net income stabilization account program under the *Farm Income Protection Act*;

**Related Provisions**: 248(1) — "NISA Fund No. 2".

**Notes**: The NISA program is a voluntary program designed to give farmers improved long-term stability. A farmer can deposit money annually into the farmer's individual NISA account and receive a matching contribution from the federal and provincial governments. By allowing the account to build, the farmer can withdraw funds when needed in lower income years. See guide RC4060 for full details.

"Net income stabilization account" added by 1992 technical bill, effective for 1991 and later taxation years.

**Forms**: RC4060: Farming income and NISA [guide]; T1163: Statement A — NISA account information and statement of farming activities for individuals; T1164: Statement B — NISA account information and statement of farming activities for additional farming operations; T1165: Statement C — statement of farming activities for Ontario self directed risk management (SDRM); T1175 Sched. 1: NISA/Farming — calculation of CCA and business-use-of-home expenses.

**"Newfoundland offshore area"** has the meaning assigned to the expression "offshore area" by the *Canada-Newfoundland Atlantic Accord Implementation Act*, chapter 3 of the Statutes of Canada, 1987;

**"NISA Fund No. 2"** means the portion of a taxpayer's net income stabilization account described in paragraph 8(2)(b) of the *Farm Income Protection Act*;

**Related Provisions**: 248(1) — "net income stabilization account".

**Notes**: "NISA Fund No. 2" added by 1992 technical bill, effective for 1991 and later taxation years. See Notes to 248(1)"net income stabilization account".

**Forms**: RC4060: Farming income and NISA [guide]; T1163: Statement A — NISA account information and statement of farming activities for individuals; T1164: Statement B — NISA account information and statement of farming activities for additional farming operations; T1165: Statement C — statement of farming activities for Ontario self directed risk management (SDRM); T1175 Sched. 1: NISA/Farming — calculation of CCA and business-use-of-home expenses.

**"non-capital loss"** has the meaning assigned by subsection 111(8);

**Related Provisions**: 111(1)(a) — Application of non-capital losses; 111(9) — Non-capital loss of person not resident in Canada.

---

**Proposed Addition — 248(1)"non-discretionary trust"**

**"non-discretionary trust"** has the meaning assigned by subsection 17(15).

**Application**: The June 22, 2000 draft legislation, subsec. 26(3), will add the definitions "foreign accrual property income" and "non-discretionary trust" to subsec. 248(1), applicable after 2000.

**Technical Notes**: The definition "non-discretionary trust" is introduced so that the existing definition of the expression in subsection 17(15) applies for the purposes of the Act. The expression is used in the definition "foreign investment entity" in new subsection 94.1(1).

This amendment applies after 2000.

---

**"non-resident"** means not resident in Canada;

**Related Provisions**: 250 — Resident in Canada.

**"non-resident-owned investment corporation"** has the meaning assigned by subsection 133(8);

**"Nova Scotia offshore area"** has the meaning assigned to the expression "offshore area" by the *Canada-Nova Scotia Offshore Petroleum Resources Accord Implementation Act*, chapter 28 of the Statutes of Canada, 1988;

**Related Provisions**: 124(4)"province" — Taxable income earned in offshore area deemed earned in a province.

### Proposed Addition — 248(1)"OSFI risk-weighting guidelines"

**"OSFI risk-weighting guidelines"** means the guidelines, issued by the Superintendent of Financial Institutions under the authority of section 600 of the *Bank Act*, requiring an authorized foreign bank to provide to the Superintendent on a periodic basis a return of the bank's risk-weighted on-balance sheet assets and off-balance sheet exposures, that apply as of August 8, 2000;

**Application**: The August 8, 2000 draft legislation, s. 25, will add the definition "OSFI risk-weighting guidelines" to s. 248(1), applicable after June 27, 1999.

**Technical Notes**: The "OSFI risk-weighting guidelines" are those issued by the Superintendent of Financial Institutions under section 600 of the *Bank Act*. These guidelines require an authorized foreign bank periodically to provide to the Superintendent a return listing the bank's risk-weighted on-balance sheet assets and off-balance sheet exposures. It is important to note that, as used here, the guidelines are static: they are the guidelines that apply as of August 8, 2000, and not as they may be modified by the Superintendent from time to time.

These new definitions apply after June 27, 1999.

**Notes**: OSFI stands for Office of the Superintendent of Financial Institutions.

**"office"** means the position of an individual entitling the individual to a fixed or ascertainable stipend or remuneration and includes a judicial office, the office of a minister of the Crown, the office of a member of the Senate or House of Commons of Canada, a member of a legislative assembly or a member of a legislative or executive council and any other office, the incumbent of which is elected by popular vote or is elected or appointed in a representative capacity and also includes the position of a corporation director, and **"officer"** means a person holding such an office;

**Interpretation Bulletins**: IT-377R: Director's, executor's or juror's fees.

**"officer"** — [See the final words of "office" above.]

**"oil or gas well"** means any well (other than an exploratory probe or a well drilled from below the surface of the earth) drilled for the purpose of producing petroleum or natural gas or of determining the existence, location, extent or quality of a natural accumulation of petroleum or natural gas, but, for the purpose of applying sections 13 and 20 and any regulations made for the purpose of paragraph 20(1)(a) in respect of property acquired after March 6, 1996, does not include a well for the extraction of material from a deposit of bituminous sands or oil shales;

**Notes**: Definition "oil or gas well" amended by 1996 Budget, effective March 7, 1996, to add all the words beginning "but, for the purpose...".

**Interpretation Bulletins**: IT-125R4: Dispositions of resource properties.

**"overseas Canadian Forces school staff"** means personnel employed outside Canada whose services are acquired by the Minister of National Defence under a prescribed order relating to the provision of educational facilities outside Canada;

**Related Provisions**: 250(1)(d.1) — Optional deemed residence in Canada.

**Regulations**: 6600 (prescribed order).

**"paid-up capital"** has the meaning assigned by subsection 89(1);

**"paid-up capital deficiency"** — [Repealed under former Act]

**"Part VII refund"** has the meaning assigned by subsection 192(2);

**Notes**: 248(1)"Part VII refund" added in the R.S.C. 1985 (5th Supp.) consolidation, effective December 1, 1991.

**"Part VIII refund"** has the meaning assigned by subsection 194(2);

**Notes**: 248(1)"Part VIII refund" added in the R.S.C. 1985 (5th Supp.) consolidation, effective December 1, 1991.

**"participant"** — [Repealed under former Act]

**Notes**: Repealed in 1985. This definition referred to a participant under an indexed security investment plan. The term as used in 67.1(3) (convention or seminar participant) is not defined. The term as used in Reg. 1204(4) is defined in Reg. 1204(5) (by reference to the *Syncrude Remission Order*).

**"passenger vehicle"** means an automobile acquired after June 17, 1987 (other than an automobile acquired after that date pursuant to an obligation in writing entered into before June 18, 1987) and an automobile leased under a lease entered into, extended or renewed after June 17, 1987;

**Notes**: See the definition of "automobile". The special rules dealing with automobiles introduced in 1988 tax reform (such as 13(7)(g), 67.2 and 67.3) are worded in terms of "passenger vehicles" so as not to apply to vehicles acquired before those rules were announced.

**Regulations**: Sch. II:Cl. 10, Sch. II:Cl. 10.1, Sch. II:Cl. 16.

**Interpretation Bulletins**: IT-521R: Motor vehicle expenses claimed by self-employed individuals; IT-522R: Vehicle, travel and sales expenses of employees.

**"past service pension adjustment"** of a taxpayer for a calendar year in respect of an employer has the meaning assigned by regulation;

**Notes**: "past service pension adjustment" added by 1990 pension bill, effective 1989.

**Regulations**: 8303(1).

**Interpretation Bulletins**: IT-528: Transfers of funds between registered plans.

**Forms**: T215 Segment: Breakdown of T215 Supplementaries; T215 Summ: Summary of past service pension adjustments exempt from certification; T215 Supp: Past service pension adjustment exempt from certification; T1004: Application for certification of a provisional past service pension adjustment; T1006: Designating an RRSP withdrawal as a qualifying withdrawal; T4104: Past service pension adjustment guide.

**"pension adjustment"** of a taxpayer for a calendar year in respect of an employer has the meaning assigned by regulation;

**Related Provisions**: 146(5.21) — Anti-avoidance.

**Notes**: "Pension adjustment" added by 1990 pension bill, effective 1989. In simple terms, the pension adjustment for a defined-benefit plan is normally the value of benefits earned times 9, minus $600. See Reg. 8301(6). For a defined-contribution (money purchase) plan it is normally the amount of the contributions (Reg. 8301(4)).

For the pension adjustment *reversal*, see 248(1)"total pension adjustment reversal".

**Regulations**: 8301(1).

**Forms**: T4084: Pension Adjustment Guide.

**"person"**, or any word or expression descriptive of a person, includes any corporation, and any entity exempt, because of subsection 149(1), from tax under Part I on all or part of the entity's taxable income and the heirs, executors, administrators or other legal representatives of such a person, according to the law of that part of Canada to which the context extends;

**Related Provisions**: 33.1(2)(a) — "Person" includes partnership for international banking centre rules; 66(16) — "Person" includes partnership for flow-through share rules; 79(1), 79.1(1) — "Person" includes partnership for rules re seizure of property by creditor; 80(1), 80.01(1) — "Person" includes partnership for debt forgiveness rules; 127.2(9), 127.3(7) — "Person" includes partnership for SPTC and SRTC rules; 139.1(1) — "Person" includes partnership for insurance demutualization; 187.4(c) — "Person" includes partnership for Part IV.1 tax; 209(6) — "Person" includes partnership for purposes of tax on carved-out income; 227(5.2), (15) — "Person" includes partnership for certain purposes re withholding tax; 237.1(1) — "Person" includes partnership for tax shelter identification rules; 251.1(4) — "Person" includes partnership for definition of affiliated persons; Canada-U.S. tax treaty, Art. III:1(e) — Meaning of "person" for treaty purposes.

**Notes**: For all practical purposes, the terms "person" and "taxpayer" are interchangeable. However, see Notes to 248(1)"taxpayer".

"Person" certainly includes a natural person (human being), despite the spurious claims of "tax protestors" that they are not subject to the Act: *Kennedy*, [2000] 4 C.T.C. 186 (Ont. SCJ).

A bare trustee is not considered to be a separate person; rather, the beneficial owner is considered to deal directly with the property to which the bare trustee holds legal title, subject to some legislated exceptions. See Notes to 104(1).

Definition of "person" amended by 1992 technical bill, effective May 5, 1993, to apply to entities exempt under 149(1), such as clubs and associations. The change allows such associations to be required under 149(12) to file information returns. See Notes to 149(12).

**Interpretation Bulletins**: IT-216: Corporation holds property as agent for shareholder; IT-379R: Employees profit sharing plans — allocations to beneficiaries.

**Advance Tax Rulings**: ATR-1: Transfer of legal title in land to bare trustee.

**"personal or living expenses"** includes

(a) the expenses of properties maintained by any person for the use or benefit of the taxpayer or any person connected with the taxpayer by blood relationship, marriage or common-law partnership or adoption, and not maintained in connection with a business carried on for profit or with a reasonable expectation of profit,

(b) the expenses, premiums or other costs of a policy of insurance, annuity contract or other like contract if the proceeds of the policy or contract are payable to or for the benefit of the taxpayer or a person connected with the taxpayer by blood relationship, marriage or common-law partnership or adoption, and

(c) expenses of properties maintained by an estate or trust for the benefit of the taxpayer as one of the beneficiaries;

**Related Provisions**: 18(1)(h), 56(1)(o)(i) — No deduction for personal or living expenses.

**Notes**: See Notes to 18(1)(h).

248(1)"personal or living expenses" amended by 2000 same-sex partners bill to add reference to "common-law partnership", effective for the 2001 and later taxation years, or earlier by election (see Notes to 248(1)"common-law partner").

**"personal services business"** has the meaning assigned by subsection 125(7);

**"personal trust"** means

(a) a testamentary trust, or

(b) an *inter vivos* trust, no beneficial interest in which was acquired for consideration payable directly or indirectly to

(i) the trust, or

(ii) any person who has made a contribution to the trust by way of transfer, assignment or other disposition of property,

and, for the purposes of this paragraph and paragraph 53(2)(h), where all the beneficial interests in a particular *inter vivos* trust acquired by way of the transfer, assignment or other disposition of property to the particular trust were acquired by

(iii) one person, or

(iv) 2 or more persons who would be related to each other if

(A) a trust and another person were related to each other, where the other person is a beneficiary under the trust or is related to a beneficiary under the trust, and

(B) a trust and another trust were related to each other, where a beneficiary under the trust is a beneficiary under the other trust or is related to a beneficiary under the other trust,

any beneficial interest in the particular trust acquired by such a person shall be deemed to have been acquired for no consideration;

**Proposed Amendment — 248(1)"personal trust"**

but, after 1999, does not include a unit trust;

**Application**: Bill C-43 (First Reading September 20, 2000), subsec. 112(2), will amend the portion of the definition "personal trust" after subpara. (b)(ii) to read as above, applicable after December 23, 1998.

**Technical Notes**: A "personal trust" is defined in subsection 248(1) as a testamentary trust or an *inter vivos* trust in which no beneficial interest was acquired for consideration payable to the trust or to a contributor to the trust. A special rule within the definition generally ensures that one person (or two or more related persons) can make contributions to a trust and retain an interest under the trust without the prohibition on consideration being considered to apply. This special rule also applies for the purposes of paragraph 53(2)(h), which deals with the calculation of the adjusted cost bases of certain trust interests.

The definition is amended so that this special rule is removed from the definition. Instead, the special rule is now provided in new subsection 108(7) (as described in the commentary above).

The definition is also amended to expressly exclude, after 1999, unit trusts (as defined in subsection 108(2)). The reference to unit trusts is being made in this context because under the old definition "personal trust" it was arguable (but by no means certain) that an unusual type of personal trust might technically satisfy the definition "unit trust" in subsection 108(2).

**Related Provisions**: 107.4(3)(i) — Trust deemed not to be personal trust; 108(6) — Where terms of trust are varied; 108(7) — Meaning of "acquired for consideration"; 110.6(16) — Extension of definition for purposes of capital gains exemption; 128.1(10)"excluded right or interest"(j) — No deemed disposition on emigration of beneficiary; 251(1)(b) — Trust deemed not at arm's length with beneficiary.

**Notes**: A trust that is not a personal trust is known informally as a "commercial trust" — a trust whose units or interests are bought and sold. See also "unit trust".

Definition of "personal trust" amended by 1992 technical bill, retroactive to 1988, so that any one person may acquire a beneficial interest in a trust for consideration payable to the trust, without disqualifying the trust as a personal trust.

**Interpretation Bulletins**: IT-342R: Trusts — Income payable to beneficiaries; IT-381R3: Trusts — capital gains and losses and the flow-through of taxable capital gains to beneficiaries; IT-385R2: Disposition of an income interest in a trust.

**"personal-use property"** has the meaning assigned by section 54;

### Proposed Addition — 248(1)"post-1971 partner trust"

**"post-1971 partner trust"** means a trust that would be described in paragraph 104(4)(a) if that paragraph were read without reference to subparagraph 104(4)(a)(iv);

**Application**: Bill C-43 (First Reading September 20, 2000), subsec. 112(4), will add the definition "post-1971 partner trust" to subsec. 248(1), applicable to trusts created after 1971.

**Technical Notes**: The new definition "post-1971 partner trust" refers to a trust that would be described in paragraph 104(4)(a) if that paragraph were read without reference to subparagraph 104(4)(a)(iv). Accordingly, a post-1971 partner trust must generally satisfy the following conditions:

1. it is a trust under which only the taxpayer's spouse is entitled to receive all of the income of the trust that arose before the spouse's death; and

2. no person except the spouse could, before the spouse's death, receive or otherwise obtain the use of any of the income or capital of the trust.

Unlike *alter ego* trusts and joint partner trusts (referred to in the commentary above), a post-1971 partner trust may also be created by a taxpayer's will.

The definitions *"alter ego* trust" and "joint partner trust" apply to trusts created after 1999. The definition "post-1971 partner trust" applies to trusts created after 1971. Other amendments related to the introduction of these definitions include amendments to section 73, subsections 104(5.8), (6) and (15) and subsection 107(4), and the amended definition of "trust" in subsection 108(1). For further detail, see the commentary on those provisions.

These amendments also reflect changes proposed under Bill C-23, the *Modernization of Benefits and Obligations Act* [by changing "spousal" to "partner", to cover common-law same-sex partners — ed.].

**Related Provisions**: 104(6)(b)(ii), (iii) — Deduction from income of trust; 104(15)(a) — Preferred beneficiary election; 107(4)(a)(i) — Distribution of property to person other than taxpayer or partner.

**Notes**: This term was "post-1971 spousal trust" in the draft legislation of December 17, 1999.

**"preferred share"** means a share other than a common share;

**"prescribed"** means

(a) in the case of a form, the information to be given on a form or the manner of filing a form, authorized by the Minister,

(a.1) in the case of the manner of making or filing an election, authorized by the Minister, and

(b) in any other case, prescribed by regulation or determined in accordance with rules prescribed by regulation;

**Related Provisions**: 147.1(18) — Regulation re pension plans; 220(3.21) — Certain designations in prescribed form deemed to be elections; 221 — Regulations generally; 244(16) — Forms prescribed or authorized; 248(1) — "Regulation"; *Interpretation Act* 32 — Deviations from prescribed form acceptable.

**Notes**: Notwithstanding para. (a), s. 32 of the *Interpretation Act* (reproduced at the end of this book) allows deviations from a prescribed form that do not affect the substance, provided they are not calculated to mislead.

"Prescribed" amended by 1991 technical bill, effective December 17, 1991. Before that date, ignore (a.1) and read (a) as follows:

(a) in the case of a form or the information to be given on a form, prescribed by order of the Minister, and

**Regulations**: Part I–XCII.

**"principal amount"**, in relation to any obligation, means the amount that, under the terms of the obligation or any agreement relating thereto, is the maximum amount or maximum total amount, as the case may be, payable on account of the obligation by the issuer thereof, otherwise than as or on account of interest or as or on account of any premium payable by the issuer conditional on the exercise by the issuer of a right to redeem the obligation before the maturity thereof;

**Related Provisions**: 80.02(2)(a) — Principal amount of distress preferred share.

**I.T. Application Rules**: 26(1.1) (where obligation was outstanding on January 1, 1972).

**"private corporation"** has the meaning assigned by subsection 89(1);

**"private foundation"** has the meaning assigned by section 149.1;

**Notes**: Definition "private foundation" added by 1997 Budget, effective 1997.

**"private health services plan"** means

(a) a contract of insurance in respect of hospital expenses, medical expenses or any combination of such expenses, or

(b) a medical care insurance plan or hospital care insurance plan or any combination of such plans,

except any such contract or plan established by or pursuant to

(c) a law of a province that establishes a health care insurance plan as defined in section 2 of the *Canada Health Act*, or

(d) an Act of Parliament or a regulation made thereunder that authorizes the provision of a medical care insurance plan or hospital care insurance plan for employees of Canada and their dependants and for dependants of members of the Royal Canadian Mounted Police and the regular force where such employees or members were appointed in Canada and are serving outside Canada;

**Related Provisions**: 6(1)(a)(i) — Employer's contribution to private health services plan not a taxable benefit; 20.01 — Deduction from business income for premiums paid to plan; 118.2(2)(q) — Medical expense credit for premiums paid to private health services plan.

**Notes**: This term includes extended health plans, drug plans and dental plans (see IT-339R2). The premiums are not a taxable employment benefit: 6(1)(a)(i). Premiums paid by self-employed persons may be deductible from business income: 20.01.

Section 2 of the *Canada Health Act* provides:

"health care insurance plan" means, in relation to a province, a plan or plans established by the law of the province to provide for insured health services;

Revenue Canada indicated in a technical interpretation dated November 15, 1996 (VIEWS doc. #9637385) that as a result of a 1996 Canadian Human Rights Tribunal decision, a plan that provides coverage for same-sex couples could meet the definition of a "private health services plan" notwithstanding 252(4). Effective 2001 (or 1998), see 248(1)"common-law partner".

Para. (c) amended by 1998 Budget, effective April 1, 1996. From the 1988 taxation year through March 1996, read:

(c) a law of a province that establishes a health care insurance plan in respect of which the province receives contributions from Canada for insured health services provided under the plan pursuant to the *Federal-Provincial Fiscal Arrangements Act*, or

**Interpretation Bulletins**: IT-339R2: Meaning of "private health services plan"; IT-529: Flexible employee benefit programs.

**Advance Tax Rulings**: ATR-8: Self-insured health and welfare trust fund; ATR-23: Private health services plan.

**"professional corporation"** means a corporation that carries on the professional practice of an accountant, dentist, lawyer, medical doctor, veterinarian or chiropractor;

**Related Provisions**: 249.1(1)(b) — Year-end of professional corporation.

**Notes**: Definition "professional corporation" added by 1995 Budget, effective 1995. See Notes to 249.1(1).

**"profit sharing plan"** has the meaning assigned by subsection 147(1);

**"property"** means property of any kind whatever whether real or personal or corporeal or incorporeal and, without restricting the generality of the foregoing, includes

(a) a right of any kind whatever, a share or a chose in action,

(b) unless a contrary intention is evident, money,

(c) a timber resource property, and

(d) the work in progress of a business that is a profession;

**Related Provisions**: 9(1), 9(3) — Income from property; 79(1), 79.1(1) — Definition of property for purposes of rules re seizure of property by creditor; 248(5) — Meaning of substituted property.

**I.T. Application Rules**: 26(6) (property disposed of and reacquired from June 19 to December 31, 1971).

**Interpretation Bulletins**: IT-334R2: Miscellaneous receipts; IT-432R2: Benefits conferred on shareholders; IT-457R: Election by professionals to exclude work in progress from income.

**Advance Tax Rulings**: ATR-60: Joint exploration corporations.

**"province"** — [Repealed under former Act]

**Notes**: This definition was repealed in 1981. Subsec. 35(1) of the *Interpretation Act* provides:

"province" means a province of Canada, and includes the Yukon Territory, the Northwest Territories and Nunavut.

See also the definition of "province" in 124(4), which applies for purposes of s. 124.

**"public corporation"** has the meaning assigned by subsection 89(1);

**"public foundation"** has the meaning assigned by section 149.1;

**Notes**: Definition "public foundation" added by 1997 Budget, effective 1997.

### Proposed Addition — 248(1)"qualified donee"

**"qualified donee"** has the meaning assigned by subsection 149.1(1).

**Application**: The December 21, 2000 draft legislation, subsec. 94(2), will add the definition "qualified donee" to subsec. 248(1), applicable after 1998.

**Technical Notes**: The definition "qualified donee" is being included in subsection 248(1) so that the existing definition of the expression in subsection 149.1(1) applies for the purposes of the whole Act. This expression is used in new subsections 118.1(5.1), (5.2) and (5.3). The definition "qualified donee" in subsection 149.1(1) refers to specified entities (including registered charities) the gifts to which can give rise to the charitable donations tax credit.

**"qualifying environmental trust"** at any time means a trust resident in a province and maintained at that time for the sole purpose of funding the reclamation of a site in the province that had been used primarily for, or for any combination of, the operation of a mine, the extraction of clay, peat, sand, shale or aggregates (including dimension stone and gravel) or the deposit of waste, where the maintenance of the trust is or may become required under the terms of a contract entered into with Her Majesty in right of Canada or the province or is or may become required under a law of Canada or the province and the contract was entered into or that law was enacted, as the case may be, on or before the later of January 1, 1996 and the day that is one year after the day on which the trust was created, but does not include a trust

(a) that relates at that time to the reclamation of a well,

(b) that is not maintained at that time to secure the reclamation obligations of one or more persons or partnerships that are beneficiaries under the trust,

(c) that at that time has a trustee other than

(i) Her Majesty in right of Canada or the province, or

(ii) a corporation resident in Canada that is licensed or otherwise authorized under the laws of Canada or a province to carry on in Canada the business of offering to the public its services as trustee,

(d) that borrows money at that time,

(e) that acquired at that time any property that is not described in any of paragraphs (a), (b) and (f) of the definition "qualified investment" in section 204,

(f) to which the first contribution was made before 1992,

(g) from which any amount was distributed before February 23, 1994,

(h) if that time is before 1998 and the trust is not a mining reclamation trust at that time,

(i) to which the first contribution was made before 1996,

(ii) from which any amount was distributed before February 19, 1997, or

(iii) any interest in which was disposed of before February 19, 1997,

(i) that elected in writing filed with the Minister, before 1998 or before April of the year following the year in which the first contribution to the trust was made, never to have been a qualifying environmental trust, or

(j) that was at any previous time during its existence not a qualifying environmental trust;

**Related Provisions**: 12(1)(z.1), (z.2) — Income from trust or from sale of interest; 20(1)(ss), (tt) — Deduction for contribution to trust or acquisition of interest; 75(3)(c.1) — Reversionary trust rules do not apply; 107.3(1), (2) — Rules applying to trust; 107.3(3) — Where trust ceases to be qualifying environmental trust; 127.41 — Tax credit to beneficiary of trust; 149(1)(z) — No Part I tax on trust; 211.6 — Part XII.4 tax on trust; 248(1)"cost amount"(e.2) —

Cost amount of interest in trust is zero; 250(7) — Trust deemed resident in province where site is located.

**Notes**: Definition "qualifying environmental trust" added by 1997 Budget, effective 1992. It has replaced the narrower term "mining reclamation trust" throughout the Act. See Notes to 107.3(1) and 211.6 for discussion of how such trusts are treated.

See Brian Carr, "Mining Reclamation Trusts", *1997 Current Issues in Resource Taxation Conference* (Canadian Tax Foundation). A summary of this 52-page article appears in 45(4) *Canadian Tax Journal* 722–725 (1997).

See also John Fuke, "Taxation of Newly Created Qualified Environmental Trusts", IV(3) *Business Vehicles* 198-201 (Federated Press) (1998).

**"qualifying share"** has the meaning assigned by subsection 192(6);

**Notes**: 248(1)"qualifying share" added in the R.S.C. 1985 (5th Supp.) consolidation, effective December 1, 1991.

**"record"** includes an account, an agreement, a book, a chart or table, a diagram, a form, an image, an invoice, a letter, a map, a memorandum, a plan, a return, a statement, a telegram, a voucher, and any other thing containing information, whether in writing or in any other form;

**Notes**: See Notes to 230(1).

Definition "record" added by 1995-97 technical bill, effective June 18, 1998.

**"refundable Part VII tax on hand"** has the meaning assigned by subsection 192(3);

**Notes**: 248(1)"refundable Part VII tax on hand" added in the R.S.C. 1985 (5th Supp.) consolidation, effective December 1, 1991.

**"refundable Part VIII tax on hand"** has the meaning assigned by subsection 194(3);

**Notes**: 248(1)"refundable Part VIII tax on hand" added in the R.S.C. 1985 (5th Supp.) consolidation, effective December 1, 1991.

**"registered Canadian amateur athletic association"** means an association that was created under any law in force in Canada, that is resident in Canada and that

(a) is a person described in paragraph 149(1)(l), and

(b) has, as its primary purpose and its primary function, the promotion of amateur athletics in Canada on a nation-wide basis,

that has applied to the Minister in prescribed form for registration, that has been registered and whose registration has not been revoked under subsection 168(2);

**Related Provisions**: 143.1 — Amateur athletes' reserve funds.

**Interpretation Bulletins**: IT-168R3: Athletes and players employed by football, hockey and similar clubs; IT-496: Non-profit organizations.

**Forms**: T1189: Application to register a Canadian amateur athletic association under the ITA.

**Registered Charities Newsletters**: 2 (Revised publications and forms).

**"registered charity"** at any time means

(a) a charitable organization, private foundation or public foundation, within the meanings assigned by subsection 149.1(1), that is resident in Canada and was either created or established in Canada, or

(b) a branch, section, parish, congregation or other division of an organization or foundation described in paragraph (a), that is resident in Canada and was either created or established in Canada and that receives donations on its own behalf,

that has applied to the Minister in prescribed form for registration and that is at that time registered as a charitable organization, private foundation or public foundation;

**Related Provisions**: 149(1)(f) — No tax on registered charity; 149.1(6.3) — Designation as public foundation, etc; 149.1(6.4) — Registered national arts service organization treated as registered charity; Canada-U.S. tax treaty, Art. XXI — Exempt organizations.

**Notes**: Pursuant to the 1976 legislation that introduced 149.1, an organization that was a registered Canadian charitable organization (as then defined) at the end of 1976 is deemed to be a registered charity until such time, if any, as its registration is revoked. See 1976–77, c. 4, s. 60(3)–(5) and ITAR 75.

For a thorough treatment of charities, see Arthur Drache, *Canadian Taxation of Charities and Donations* (Carswell, looseleaf).

See Notes to 248(1)"business number" re the BN of a charity.

**Interpretation Bulletins**: IT-496: Non-profit organizations.

**Information Circulars**: 80-10R: Registered charities: operating a registered charity.

**Forms**: T2050: Application to register a charity under the ITA; T2095: Canadian charities — application for re-designation; T4063: Registering a charity for income tax purposes [guide].

**Registered Charities Newsletters**: 2 (Revised publications and forms); 8 (Changes in departmental policy on applications for re-registration).

**"registered education savings plan"** has the meaning assigned by subsection 146.1(1);

**"registered home ownership savings plan"** — [Repealed under former Act]

**Notes**: See Notes to 146.2.

**"registered investment"** has the meaning assigned by subsection 204.4(1);

**"registered labour-sponsored venture capital corporation"** means a corporation that was registered under subsection 204.81(1), the registration of which has not been revoked;

**Notes**: Definition "registered labour-sponsored venture capital corporation" added by 1996 Budget, effective 1996. This replaces the definition of the term in 204.8.

For a thorough review of LSVCCs, their tax status, tax treatment of investors, and restrictions on redemptions, transfers and investments, see Andrew Smith, "Labour-Sponsored Venture Capital Corporations: A New Venture Capital Vehicle Matures", *Business Vehicles* (Federated Press), Vol. IV, No. 1 (1997), pp. 162-178.

For another thorough review of LSVCCs, including their history and comparisons of the various provincial rules, see Duncan Osborne and Daniel Sandler, "A Tax Expenditure Analysis of Labour-Sponsored Venture Capital Corporations", 46(3) *Canadian Tax Journal* (1998) 499-574.

**"registered national arts service organization"**, at any time, means a national arts service organization that has been registered by the Minister under subsection 149.1(6.4), which registration has not been revoked;

**Notes**: "Registered national arts service organization" added by 1991 technical bill, effective July 14, 1990.

**"registered pension fund or plan"** — [Repealed under former Act]

**Notes**: "Registered pension fund or plan" repealed by 1990 pension bill, effective 1986. The definition, which depended on administrative rules for registration, has been replaced by "registered pension plan" (see below), which is subject to the rules for registration in 147.1.

**"registered pension plan"** means a pension plan that has been registered by the Minister for the purposes of this Act, which registration has not been revoked;

**Related Provisions**: 147.1(2) — Registration of plan; 147.1(3) — Deemed registration; 128.1(10)"excluded right or interest"(a)(viii) — No deemed disposition of pension rights on emigration.

**Notes**: "Registered pension plan" added by 1990 pension bill, this version effective 1989.

**I.T. Application Rules**: 17(8) (reference to RPP includes reference to approved plan before RPP amendment in 1990).

**Interpretation Bulletins**: IT-167R6: Registered pension plans — employee's contributions; IT-528: Transfers of funds between registered plans.

**Forms**: T510: Application for registration of employees' pension plan.

**"registered retirement income fund"** has the meaning assigned by subsection 146.3(1);

**"registered retirement savings plan"** has the meaning assigned by subsection 146(1);

**"registered securities dealer"** means a person registered or licensed under the laws of a province to trade in securities, in the capacity of an agent or principal, without any restriction as to the types or kinds of securities in which that person may trade;

**Related Provisions**: 142.2(1)"investment dealer", 142.5 — Corporation subject to mark-to-market rules.

**Notes**: Definition "registered securities dealer" added by 1994 tax amendments bill (Part VIII), effective April 27, 1989.

**"registered supplementary unemployment benefit plan"** has the meaning assigned by subsection 145(1);

**"regulation"** means a regulation made by the Governor in Council under this Act;

**Related Provisions**: 65(2) — Regulations allowing resource allowances; 147.1(18) — Regulations re pension plans; 215(5) — Regulations reducing amount to be deducted or withheld; 221 — Regulations generally; 248(1) — "Prescribed".

**Notes**: This definition is redundant. Subsection 41(4) of the *Interpretation Act* already provides this rule.

**"restricted farm loss"** has the meaning assigned by subsection 31(1.1);

**Related Provisions**: 111(1)(c) — Application of restricted farm losses; 111(9) — Restricted farm loss where taxpayer not resident in Canada.

**Notes**: Reference to 31(1) changed to 31(1.1) by 1994 tax amendments bill (Part I), effective for taxation years that end after February 21, 1994.

**"restricted financial institution"** means

(a) a bank,

(b) a corporation licensed or otherwise authorized under the laws of Canada or a province to carry on in Canada the business of offering to the public its services as trustee,

(c) a credit union,

(d) an insurance corporation,

(e) a corporation whose principal business is the lending of money to persons with whom the corporation is dealing at arm's length or the purchasing of debt obligations issued by such persons or a combination thereof,

(e.1) a corporation described in paragraph (g) of the definition "financial institution" in subsection 181(1), or

(f) a corporation that is controlled by one or more corporations described in any of paragraphs (a) to (e.1);

**Related Provisions**: 131(10) — Mutual fund corporation or investment corporation — election not to be restricted financial institution; 142.2(1)"financial institution" — Definition for mark-to-market and related rules; 256(2), (6.1) — Meaning of "controlled".

**Notes**: Para. (e.1) added, and (f) amended to replace "(a) to (e)" with "(a) to (e.1)", by 1998 Budget, effective for taxation years that begin after 1998.

This amendment means that companies such as AVCO and GMAC, which have applied to be financial institutions for purpose of the large corporations tax (see Reg. 8604), will now be stuck with all the negatives of being financial institutions as well.

**Regulations**: 8604 (prescribed financial institutions).

**"retirement compensation arrangement"** means a plan or arrangement under which contributions (other than payments made to acquire an interest in a life insurance policy) are made by an employer or former employer of a taxpayer, or by a person with whom the employer or former employer does not deal at arm's length, to another person or partnership (in this definition and in Part XI.3 referred to as the "custodian") in connection with benefits that are to be or may be received or enjoyed by any person on, after or in contemplation of any substantial change in the services rendered by the taxpayer, the retirement of the taxpayer or the loss of an office or employment of the taxpayer, but does not include

(a) a registered pension plan,

(b) a disability or income maintenance insurance plan under a policy with an insurance corporation,

(c) a deferred profit sharing plan,

(d) an employees profit sharing plan,

(e) a registered retirement savings plan,

(f) an employee trust,

(g) a group sickness or accident insurance plan,

(h) a supplementary unemployment benefit plan,

(i) a vacation pay trust described in paragraph 149(1)(y),

(j) a plan or arrangement established for the purpose of deferring the salary or wages of a professional athlete for [the athlete's] services as such with a team that participates in a league having regularly scheduled games (in this definition referred to as an "athlete's plan"), where

(i) the plan or arrangement would, but for paragraph (j) of the definition "salary deferral arrangement" in this subsection, be a salary deferral arrangement, and

(ii) in the case of a Canadian team, the custodian of the plan or arrangement carries on business through a fixed place of business in Canada and is licensed or otherwise authorized under the laws of Canada or a province to carry on in Canada the business of offering to the public its services as trustee,

(k) a salary deferral arrangement, whether or not deferred amounts thereunder are required to be included as benefits under paragraph 6(1)(a) in computing a taxpayer's income,

(l) a plan or arrangement (other than an athlete's plan) that is maintained primarily for the benefit of non-residents in respect of services rendered outside Canada,

(m) an insurance policy, or

(n) a prescribed plan or arrangement,

and, for the purposes of this definition, where a particular person holds property in trust under an arrangement that, if the property were held by another person, would be a retirement compensation arrangement, the arrangement shall be deemed to be a retirement compensation arrangement of which the particular person is the custodian;

**Related Provisions**: 8(1)(m.2) — Employee RCA contributions; 12(11) — Definitions — "investment contract"; 75(3)(a) — Reversionary trust rules do not apply to RCA ; 94(1)"exempt foreign trust"(e) — RCA excluded from non-resident trust rules; 128.1(10)"excluded right or interest"(a)(ix) — No deemed disposition of right to RCA on emigration; 207.6(2) — Life insurance policies; 207.6(4) — Deemed contribution; 207.6(5) — Resident's arrangement; 252.1(c), (d) — All branches of a union deemed to be a single employer.

**Notes**: Simplified, RCAs work as follows: Contributions to the plan bear a 50% refundable tax (207.7(1), 207.5(1)"refundable tax"(a)), which must be withheld at source (153(1)(p), Reg. 103(7)). Income earned in the in plan is also subject to 50% tax (207.5(1)"refundable tax"(b)); the custodian must file a return within 90 days of year-end (207.7(3)). Employers' contributions to the RCA are deductible (8(1)(m.2)). Employees include in income all receipts from the RCA (56(1)(x)–(z)), with tax withheld at source (153(1)(q), (r)). Payments to employees trigger a refund of the refundable tax to the RCA (207.7(2)).

For a good overview of the operation of an RCA, see Marilyn Lurz, "A Practical Guide to Administering a Retirement Compensation Arrangement", *Taxation of Executive Compensation and Retirement* (Federated Press), Vol. 8 No. 4 (November 1996), pp. 211–215.

"Retirement compensation arrangement" added by 1986 press release, effective October 9, 1986. However, with respect to a plan or arrangement (other than a pension fund or plan the registration of which has been revoked under the Act) established before October 9, 1986 or established after October 8, 1986 pursuant to an agreement between a taxpayer and an employer or former employer of the taxpayer entered into before October 9, 1986 (referred to herein as the "existing arrangement"), for the purposes of the Act,

(a) another plan or arrangement (referred to herein as the "statutory arrangement") is deemed to be established on the day that is the earlier of January 1, 1988, and the day after October 8, 1986 on which the terms of the existing arrangement have been materially altered;

(b) the statutory arrangement is deemed to be a separate arrangement independent of the existing arrangement;

(c) the existing arrangement is deemed not to be a retirement compensation arrangement; and

(d) all contributions made under the existing arrangement after the establishment of the statutory arrangement and all property that can reasonably be considered to derive from those contributions are deemed to be property held in connection with the statutory arrangement and not in connection with the existing arrangement.

**Regulations**: 6802 (prescribed plan or arrangement).

**Interpretation Bulletins**: IT-529: Flexible employee benefit programs.

**Advance Tax Rulings**: ATR-45: Share appreciation rights plan.

**Forms**: T733: Application for "A retirement compensation arrangement" (RCA) identification account; T4041: Retirement compensation arrangements guide.

**"retirement income fund"** has the meaning assigned by subsection 146.3(1);

**"retirement savings plan"** has the meaning assigned by subsection 146(1);

**"retiring allowance"** means an amount (other than a superannuation or pension benefit, an amount received as a consequence of the death of an employee or a benefit described in subparagraph 6(1)(a)(iv)) received

(a) on or after retirement of a taxpayer from an office or employment in recognition of the taxpayer's long service, or

(b) in respect of a loss of an office or employment of a taxpayer, whether or not received as, on account or in lieu of payment of, damages or pursuant to an order or judgment of a competent tribunal,

by the taxpayer or, after the taxpayer's death, by a dependant or a relation of the taxpayer or by the legal representative of the taxpayer;

**Related Provisions**: 56(1)(a)(ii) — Inclusion in income; 60(j.1) — Rollover of retiring allowance to RRSP; 128.1(10)"excluded right or interest"(d) — No deemed disposition of right to retiring allowance on emigration; 248(8) — Occurrences as a consequence of death.

**Notes**: In "retiring allowance", reference to 6(1)(a)(iv) added by 1989 Budget, effective 1988.

Note that a "retiring allowance" includes termination pay and a severance payment, whether awarded by a court or paid in a private settlement. However, payments after termination may also be "salary continuation payments" (not a legally defined term) which are treated as a continuation of salary rather than as a retiring allowance; see Income Tax Technical News No. 19.

A retiring allowance is taxable (56(1)(a)(ii)) and subject to source withholding (153(1)(c)) as a lump sum at rates of 10–30% (25–38% in Quebec) (Reg. 103(4), (6)(e)). If paid to a non-resident, it is subject to withholding tax (212(1)(j.1)). The main advantage of having a payment classified as a retiring allowance rather than as employment income is that a portion of the amount can be rolled into an RRSP under 60(j.1), where the employment began before 1996. (See Notes to 60(j.1).) As well, for a non-resident it will be taxed at only 25% rather than as employment income. If an amount is not a retiring allowance, it may be taxable as employment income under 5(1), 6(1)(a) or 6(3)(b). Alternatively, it may be non-taxable as damages for mental distress or to reimburse the taxpayer for losses: *Bédard*, [1991] 1 C.T.C. 2323 (TCC); *Mendes-Roux*, [1998] 2 C.T.C. 2274 (TCC); *Saardi*, [1999] 4 C.T.C. 2488 (TCC); *Fournier*, [1999] 4 C.T.C. 2247 (TCC).

**Interpretation Bulletins**: IT-99R5: Legal and accounting fees; IT-337R3: Retiring allowances; IT-365R2: Damages, settlements and similar receipts; IT-508R: Death benefits.

**I.T. Technical News**: No. 7 (retiring allowances); No. 19 (Retiring allowances — clarification to Interpretation Bulletin IT-337R3).

**Advance Tax Rulings**: ATR-12: Retiring allowance.

**"RRSP deduction limit"** has the meaning assigned by subsection 146(1);

**Notes**: "RRSP deduction limit" added by 1990 pension bill, effective 1989.

**"RRSP dollar limit"** has the meaning assigned by subsection 146(1);

**Notes**: "RRSP dollar limit" added by 1990 pension bill, effective 1989.

**"salary deferral arrangement"**, in respect of a taxpayer, means a plan or arrangement, whether funded or not, under which any person has a right in a taxation year to receive an amount after the year where it is reasonable to consider that one of the main purposes for the creation or existence of the right is to postpone tax payable under this Act by the taxpayer in respect of an amount that is, or is on account or in lieu of, salary or wages of the taxpayer for services rendered by the taxpayer in the year or a preceding taxation year (including such a right that is subject to one or more conditions unless there is a substantial risk that any one of those conditions will not be satisfied), but does not include

(a) a registered pension plan,

(b) a disability or income maintenance insurance plan under a policy with an insurance corporation,

(c) a deferred profit sharing plan,

(d) an employees profit sharing plan,

(e) an employee trust,

(f) a group sickness or accident insurance plan,

(g) a supplementary unemployment benefit plan,

(h) a vacation pay trust described in paragraph 149(1)(y),

(i) a plan or arrangement the sole purpose of which is to provide education or training for employees of an employer to improve their work or work-related skills and abilities,

(j) a plan or arrangement established for the purpose of deferring the salary or wages of a professional athlete for the services of the athlete as such with a team that participates in a league having regularly scheduled games,

(k) a plan or arrangement under which a taxpayer has a right to receive a bonus or similar payment in respect of services rendered by the taxpayer in a taxation year to be paid within 3 years following the end of the year, or

(l) a prescribed plan or arrangement;

**Related Provisions**: 6(1)(i) — Income inclusion on payment from SDA; 6(11) — Income inclusion on having right to payment from SDA; 12(11) — Definitions — "investment contract"; 56(1)(w) — Income inclusion on payment from SDA; 128.1(10)"excluded right or interest"(a)(vii), (b) — No deemed disposition of right to SDA on emigration.

**Notes**: For a detailed discussion of salary deferral arrangements, see Raymond Murrill, "Taxation of Short-to-Medium-Term Cash Incentives in Canada", 9(7) *Taxation of Executive Compensation & Retirement* (Federated Press), 103–115 (March 1998).

**Regulations**: 6801 (prescribed plan or arrangement).

**Interpretation Bulletins**: IT-109R2: Unpaid amounts; IT-168R3: Athletes and players employed by football, hockey and similar clubs; IT-529: Flexible employee benefit programs.

**I.T. Technical News**: No. 7 (salary deferral arrangement — paragraph (k)).

**Advance Tax Rulings**: ATR-39: Self-funded leave of absence; ATR-45: Share appreciation rights plan; ATR-64: Phantom stock award plan.

**"salary or wages"**, except in sections 5 and 63 and the definition "death benefit" in this subsection, means the income of a taxpayer from an office or employment as computed under subdivision a of Division B of Part I and includes all fees received for services not rendered in the course of the taxpayer's business but does not include superannuation or pension benefits or retiring allowances;

**Interpretation Bulletins**: IT-99R5: Legal and accounting fees.

**Application Policies**: SR&ED 96-06: Directly undertaking, supervising or supporting v. "directly engaged" SR&ED salary and wages..

**"scientific research and experimental development"** means systematic investigation or search that is carried out in a field of science or technology by means of experiment or analysis and that is

(a) basic research, namely, work undertaken for the advancement of scientific knowledge without a specific practical application in view,

(b) applied research, namely, work undertaken for the advancement of scientific knowledge with a specific practical application in view, or

(c) experimental development, namely, work undertaken for the purpose of achieving technological advancement for the purpose of creating new, or improving existing, materials, devices, products or processes, including incremental improvements thereto,

and, in applying this definition in respect of a taxpayer, includes

(d) work undertaken by or on behalf of the taxpayer with respect to engineering, design, operations research, mathematical analysis, computer programming, data collection, testing or psychological research, where the work is commensurate with the needs, and directly in support, of work described in paragraph (a), (b), or (c) that is undertaken in Canada by or on behalf of the taxpayer,

but does not include work with respect to

(e) market research or sales promotion,

(f) quality control or routine testing of materials, devices, products or processes,

(g) research in the social sciences or the humanities,

(h) prospecting, exploring or drilling for, or producing, minerals, petroleum or natural gas,

(i) the commercial production of a new or improved material, device or product or the commercial use of a new or improved process,

(j) style changes, or

(k) routine data collection;

**Related Provisions**: 37(3) — CCRA may obtain advice from certain sources as to whether an activity is SR&ED; 37(8) — Amounts deemed not to be expenditures on SR&ED; 37(13) — Linked work deemed to be SR&ED.

**Notes**: Definition "scientific research and experimental development" added by 1995 Budget (initially simply referring to the regulations) and amended retroactive to its introduction by 1995-97 technical bill, effective for work performed after February 27, 1995 except that, for the purposes of 149(1)(j) and (8)(b), the definition does not apply to work performed pursuant to an agreement in writing entered into before February 28, 1995. For earlier periods, see Reg. 2900.

The draft legislation of July 19, 1995, and the Notice of Ways and Means Motion of December 12, 1995, both proposed this definition with a lengthy exclusion. Scientific research and experimental development would have excluded information technology work done by or on behalf of certain financial institutions. This restriction, which would have applied to work performed after February 27, 1995, was announced in the 1995 federal budget in response to publicity about banks' claims for investment tax credits for software development. However, the restriction was dropped from the 1995 Budget bill before enactment.

For discussion of the tax incentives for SR&ED, see *R&D: Credits Today, Innovation Tomorrow*, proceedings of the Canadian Tax Foundation's 1999 Corporate Management Tax Conference.

**Regulations**: 2900 (meaning of "scientific research and experimental development" (no longer applicable now that the full definition is in the Act).

**Information Circulars**: 86-4R3: Scientific research and experimental development; 86-4R3 Supplement 1: Automotive industry application paper; 86-4R3 Supplement 2: Aerospace industry application paper; 94-1: Plastics industry application paper; 94-2: Machinery and equipment industry application paper; 97-1: Administrative guidelines for software development.

**Application Policies**: SR&ED 94-03: Testing activities on new substances required by the Canadian Protection Act (CEPA);

SR&ED 95-01R: Linked activities — Reg. 2900(1)(d); SR&ED 95-02: Science eligibility guidelines for the oil and gas mining industries; SR&ED 95-03: Claims for ISO 9000 registration; SR&ED 95-04R: Conflict of interest with regard to outside consultants; SR&ED 96-01: Reclassification of SR&ED expenditures per subsec. 127(11.4); SR&ED 96-02: Tests and studies required to meet requirements in regulated industries; SR&ED 96-08: Eligibility of the preparation of new drug submissions; SR&ED 96-09: Eligibility of clinical trials to meet regulatory requirements.

**Forms**: T2 SCH 301: Newfoundland scientific research and experimental development tax credit; T2 SCH 340: Nova Scotia research and development tax credit; T2 SCH 380: Manitoba research and development tax credit; T2 SCH 403: Saskatchewan research and development tax credit; T661 — Claim for SR&ED carried on in Canada; T4088: Claiming scientific research and experimental development expenditures — guide to form T661.

**"scientific research and experimental development financing contract"** has the meaning assigned by subsection 194(6);

**Notes**: 248(1)"scientific research and experimental development financing contract" added in the R.S.C. 1985 (5th Supp.) consolidation, effective December 1, 1991.

**"scientific research and experimental development tax credit"** of a taxpayer for a taxation year has the meaning assigned by subsection 127.3(2);

**Notes**: 248(1)"scientific research and experimental development tax credit" added in the R.S.C. 1985 (5th Supp.) consolidation, effective December 1, 1991.

**"securities lending arrangement"** has the meaning assigned by subsection 260(1);

**Notes**: "securities lending arrangement" added by 1993 technical bill, effective for 1993 and later taxation years. It is needed outside s. 260 because of the rules in 212(1)(b)(xii) and 212(19) dealing with such arrangements.

**"self-contained domestic establishment"** means a dwelling-house, apartment or other similar place of residence in which place a person as a general rule sleeps and eats;

**Interpretation Bulletins**: IT-91R4: Employment at special work sites or remote work locations; IT-352R2: Employee's expenses, including work space in home expenses; IT-513R: Personal tax credits.

**"separation agreement"** includes an agreement by which a person agrees to make payments on a periodic basis for the maintenance of a former spouse or common-law partner, children of the marriage or common-law partnership or both the former spouse or common-law partner and children of the marriage or common-law partnership, after the marriage or common-law partnership has been dissolved whether the agreement was made before or after the marriage or common-law partnership was dissolved;

**Notes**: 248(1)"separation agreement" amended by 2000 same-sex partners bill to add reference to "common-law partner" and "common-law partnership", effective for the 2001 and later taxation years, or earlier by election (see Notes to 248(1)"common-law partner").

**"servant"** — [See under "employment".]

**"share"** means a share or fraction of a share of the capital stock of a corporation and, for greater certainty, a share of the capital stock of a corporation includes a share of the capital of a cooperative corporation (within the meaning assigned by subsection 136(2)) and a share of the capital of a credit union;

**Related Provisions**: 132.2(2) — Definition of "share" for mutual fund rollover rules; 142.2(1)"mark-to-market property"(a), 142.5 — Mark-to-market rules for financial institutions.

**Notes**: "Share" amended by 1991 technical bill, effective 1989, to add everything from "and, for greater certainty" to the end.

**Interpretation Bulletins**: IT-116R3: Rights to buy additional shares.

**Advance Tax Rulings**: ATR-26: Share exchange.

**"shareholder"** includes a member or other person entitled to receive payment of a dividend;

**Interpretation Bulletins**: IT-116R3: Rights to buy additional shares; IT-432R2: Benefits conferred on shareholders.

**"share-purchase tax credit"** of a taxpayer for a taxation year has the meaning assigned by subsection 127.2(6);

**Notes**: 248(1)"share-purchase tax credit" added in the R.S.C. 1985 (5th Supp.) consolidation, effective December 1, 1991.

**"short-term preferred share"** of a corporation at any particular time means a share, other than a grandfathered share, of the capital stock of the corporation issued after December 15, 1987 that at that particular time

(a) is a share where, under the terms and conditions of the share, any agreement relating to the share or any modification of those terms and conditions or that agreement, the corporation or a specified person in relation to the corporation is or may, at any time within 5 years from the date of its issue, be required to redeem, acquire or cancel, in whole or in part, the share (unless the requirement to redeem, acquire or cancel the share arises only in the event of the death of the shareholder or by reason only of a right to convert or exchange the share) or to reduce the paid-up capital of the share, and for the purposes of this paragraph

(i) an agreement in respect of a share of the capital stock of a corporation shall be read without reference to that part of the agreement under which a person agrees to acquire the share for an amount

(A) in the case of a share (other than a share that would, but for that part of the agreement, be a taxable preferred share) the agreement in respect of which provides that the share is to be acquired within 60 days after the day on which the agreement was entered into, that does not exceed the greater of the fair market value of the share at the time the agreement was entered into, determined without reference to the agreement, and the fair market value of the share at the time of the acquisition, determined without reference to the agreement, or

(B) that does not exceed the fair market value of the share at the time of the acquisition, determined without reference to the agreement, or for an amount determined by reference to the assets or earnings of the corporation where that determination may reasonably be considered to be used to determine an amount that does not exceed the fair market value of the share at the time of the acquisition, determined without reference to the agreement, and

(ii) "shareholder" includes a shareholder of a shareholder, or

(b) is a share that is convertible or exchangeable at any time within 5 years from the date of its issue, unless

(i) it is convertible into or exchangeable for

(A) another share of the corporation or a corporation related to the corporation that, if issued, would not be a short-term preferred share,

(B) a right or warrant that, if exercised, would allow the person exercising it to acquire only a share of the corporation or a corporation related to the corporation that, if issued, would not be a short-term preferred share, or

(C) both a share described in clause (A) and a right or warrant described in clause (B), and

(ii) all the consideration receivable for the share on the conversion or exchange is the share described in clause (i)(A) or the right or warrant described in clause (i)(B) or both, as the case may be, and for the purposes of this subparagraph, where a taxpayer may become entitled on the conversion or exchange of a share to receive any particular consideration (other than consideration described in any of clauses (i)(A) to (C)) in lieu of a fraction of a share, the particular consideration shall be deemed not to be consideration unless it may reasonably be considered that the particular consideration was receivable as part of a series of transactions or events one of the main purposes of which was to avoid or limit the application of Part IV.1 or VI.1,

and, for the purposes of this definition,

(c) where at any particular time after December 15, 1987, otherwise than pursuant to a written arrangement to do so entered into before December 16, 1987, the terms or conditions of a share of the capital stock of a corporation that are relevant to any matter referred to in any of paragraphs (a), (b), (f) and (h) are established or modified, or any agreement in respect of any such matter to which the corporation or a specified person in relation to the corporation is a party, is changed or entered into, the share shall be deemed after that particular time to have been issued at that particular time,

(d) where at any particular time after December 15, 1987 a particular share of the capital stock of a corporation has been issued or its terms or conditions have been modified or an agreement in respect of the share is modified or entered into, and it may reasonably be considered, having regard to all the circumstances, including the rate of interest on any debt obligation or the dividend provided on any short-term preferred share, that

(i) but for the existence at any time of such a debt obligation or such a short-term preferred share, the particular share would not have been issued or its terms or conditions modified or the agreement in respect of the share would not have been modified or entered into, and

(ii) one of the main purposes for the issue of the particular share or the modification of its terms or conditions or the modification or entering into the agreement in respect of the share was to avoid or limit the tax payable under subsection 191.1(1),

the particular share shall be deemed after that particular time to have been issued at that particular time and to be a short-term preferred share of the corporation,

(e) where at any particular time after December 15, 1987, otherwise than pursuant to a written arrangement to do so entered into before December 16, 1987, the terms or conditions of a share of the capital stock of a corporation are modified or established or any agreement in respect of the share has been changed or entered into, and as a consequence thereof the corporation or a specified person in relation to the corporation may reasonably be expected to redeem, acquire or cancel (otherwise than by reason of the death of the shareholder or by reason only of a right to convert or exchange the share that would not cause the share to be a short-term preferred share by reason of paragraph (b)), in whole or in part, the share, or to reduce its paid-up capital, within 5 years from the particular time, the share shall be deemed to have been issued at that particular time and to be a short-term preferred share of the corporation after the particular time until the time that such reasonable expectation ceases to exist and, for the purposes of this paragraph,

(i) an agreement in respect of a share of the capital stock of a corporation shall be read without reference to that part of the agreement under which a person agrees to acquire the share for an amount

(A) in the case of a share (other than a share that would, but for that part of the agreement, be a taxable preferred share) the agreement in respect of which provides that the share is to be acquired within 60 days after the day on which the agreement was entered into, that does not exceed the greater of the fair market value of the share at the time the agreement was entered into, determined without reference to the agreement, and the fair market value of the share at the time of the acquisition, determined without reference to the agreement, or

(B) that does not exceed the fair market value of the share at the time of the acquisition, determined without reference to the agreement, or for an amount determined by reference to the assets or earnings of the corporation where that determination may reasonably be considered to be used to determine an amount that does not exceed the fair market value of the share at the time of the acquisition, determined without reference to the agreement, and

(ii) "shareholder" includes a shareholder of a shareholder;

(f) where a share of the capital stock of a corporation was issued after December 15, 1987 and at the time the share was issued the existence of the corporation was, or there was an arrangement under which it could be, limited to a period that was within 5 years from the date of its issue, the share shall be deemed to be a short-term preferred share of the corporation unless the share is a grandfathered share and the arrangement is a written arrangement entered into before December 16, 1987,

(g) where a share of the capital stock of a corporation is acquired at any time after December 15, 1987 by the corporation or a specified person in relation to the corporation and the share is at any particular time after that time acquired by a person with whom the corporation or a specified person in relation to the corporation was dealing at arm's length if this Act were read without reference to paragraph 251(5)(b), from the corporation or a specified person in relation to the corporation, the share shall be deemed after that particular time to have been issued at that particular time,

(h) where at any particular time after December 15, 1987, otherwise than pursuant to a written arrangement to do so entered into before December 16, 1987, as a result of the terms or conditions of a share of the capital stock of a corporation or any agreement entered into by the corporation or a specified person in relation to the corporation, any person (other than the corporation or an individual other than a trust) was obligated, either absolutely or contingently and either immediately or in the future, to effect any undertaking within 5 years after the day on which the share was issued (in this paragraph referred to as a "guarantee agreement") including any guarantee, covenant or agreement to purchase or repurchase the share, and including the lending of funds or the placing of amounts on deposit with, or on behalf of the shareholder or a specified person in relation to the shareholder given

(i) to ensure that any loss that the shareholder or a specified person in relation to the shareholder may sustain, by reason of the ownership, holding or disposition of the share or any other property is limited in any respect, and

(ii) as part of a transaction or event or series of transactions or events that included the issuance of the share,

the share shall be deemed after that particular time to have been issued at the particular time and to be at and immediately after the particular time a short-term preferred share, and for the purposes of this paragraph, where a guarantee agreement in respect of a share is given at any particular time after December 15, 1987, otherwise than pursuant to a written arrangement to do so entered into before December 16, 1987, the share shall be deemed to have been issued at the particular time and the guarantee agreement shall be deemed to have been given as part of a series of transactions that included the issuance of the share,

(i) a share that is, at the time a dividend is paid thereon, a share described in paragraph (e) of the definition "term preferred share" in this subsection during the applicable time period referred to in that paragraph or a prescribed share shall, notwithstanding any other provision of this definition, be deemed not to be a short-term preferred share at that time, and

(j) "specified person" has the meaning assigned by paragraph (h) of the definition "taxable preferred share" in this subsection;

**Related Provisions**: 87(4.2) — Amalgamation; 248(10) — Series of transactions.

**Notes**: The CCRA considers that "convertible or exchangeable" in para. (b) applies to a share that is convertible or exchangeable at the option of either the shareholder or the corporation. (This may not have been the intention of the drafters of the legislation.) See Revenue Canada Round Table, Canadian Tax Foundation 1993 annual conference report, Q. 10.

"Short-term preferred share" amended by 1988 tax reform, effective for shares issued (or deemed to have been issued) after December 15, 1987. For earlier shares, read:

"short-term preferred share" of a corporation (in this definition referred to as the "issuing corporation") means

(a) a share of the capital stock of the issuing corporation issued after November 12, 1981 if

(i) the issuing corporation, any person related to the issuing corporation or any partnership or trust of which the issuing corporation or a person related thereto is a member or beneficiary (each of which is referred to in this definition as "a member of the related issuing group") is or may be required to redeem, acquire or cancel, in whole or in part, the share or to reduce its paid-up capital at any time within 18 months from the date of its issue, and

(ii) the share was issued in order to obtain funds for a member of the related issuing group and the share may reasonably be regarded as having been issued by a member of the related issuing group in lieu of commercial paper or a similar short-term debt instrument that would otherwise have been issued or sold on the money market by a member of the related issuing group had a member of the related issuing group borrowed the funds, or

(b) a share described in subparagraph (a)(ii) that is convertible, directly or indirectly, within 18 months from the date of its issue into debt or into a share that, if issued, would be a share described in subparagraph (a)(i),

but does not include a share of the capital stock of a corporation

(c) that was issued after November 12, 1981 and before 1983 pursuant to an agreement in writing to do so made before November 13, 1981,

(d) that is a share described in paragraph (e) of the definition "term preferred share" in this subsection, or

(e) that is a prescribed share

and for the purposes of this definition,

(f) where, at any particular time after November 12, 1981, in the case of a share issued before November 13, 1981 or a share described in paragraph (c), its redemption date was changed or the terms or conditions relating to

(i) its redemption, acquisition, cancellation, conversion or reduction of its paid-up capital by the issuing corporation, or

(ii) its acquisition by a member of the related issuing group

were changed, the share shall, for the purpose of determining at a subsequent time whether it is a short-term preferred share, be deemed to have been issued at the particular time,

(g) where a person has an interest in a trust, whether directly or indirectly, through an interest in any other trust or in any other manner whatever, the person shall be deemed to be a beneficiary of the trust,

(h) where a particular share of the capital stock of a corporation has been issued or its terms or conditions have been modified and it may reasonably be considered, having regard to all circumstances (including the rate of interest on any debt or the dividend provided on any short-term preferred share), that

(i) but for the existence at any time of the debt or the short-term preferred share, the particular share would not have been issued or its terms or conditions modified, and

(ii) one of the main purposes for the issue of the particular share or the modification of its terms or conditions was to avoid or limit the application of subsection 112(2.3),

the particular share shall, after December 31, 1982, be deemed to be a short-term preferred share of the corporation,

(i) where a share is substituted or exchanged for a short-term preferred share, the share shall be deemed to be a short-term preferred share,

(j) where the terms or conditions of a share of the capital stock of the issuing corporation are modified or established after June 28, 1982 and as a consequence thereof any member of the related issuing group may reasonably be expected to redeem, acquire or cancel, in whole or in part, the share, or to reduce its paid-up capital, within 18 months from the date of its issue, the share shall be deemed as from the date of the modification or as from the date of the establishment, as the case may be, to be a share described in subparagraph (a)(i),

(k) where a share of the capital stock of the issuing corporation was issued after June 28, 1982 and at the time the share was issued the existence of the issuing corporation was, or there was an arrangement under which it could be, limited to a period that was within 18 months from the date of its issue, the share shall be deemed to be a share described in subparagraph (a)(i), and

(l) where a share is issued after November 12, 1981 by a member of the related issuing group to another member of that related issuing group and the share is subsequently sold by any member of the related issuing group to a person with whom such member was, but for paragraph 251(5)(b), dealing at arm's length, the share shall be deemed to have been issued at the time the share was sold by such member;

**Regulations**: 6201(8) (prescribed shares).

**Advance Tax Rulings**: ATR-46: Financial difficulty.

**"small business bond"** has the meaning assigned by section 15.2;

**"small business corporation"**, at any particular time, means, subject to subsection 110.6(15), a particular corporation that is a Canadian-controlled private corporation all or substantially all of the fair market value of the assets of which at that time is attributable to assets that are

(a) used principally in an active business carried on primarily in Canada by the particular corporation or by a corporation related to it,

(b) shares of the capital stock or indebtedness of one or more small business corporations that are at that time connected with the particular corporation (within the meaning of subsection 186(4) on the assumption that the small business corporation is at that time a "payer corporation" within the meaning of that subsection), or

(c) assets described in paragraphs (a) and (b),

including, for the purpose of paragraph 39(1)(c), a corporation that was at any time in the 12 months preceding that time a small business corporation, and, for the purpose of this definition, the fair market value of a net income stabilization account shall be deemed to be nil;

**Related Provisions**: 110.6(2.1) — Capital gains deduction — qualified small business corporation shares; 110.6(14)(b) — Interpretation rule for capital gains exemption purposes; 110.6(15) — Value of assets of corporation; 136(1) — Whether cooperative corporation can be a small business corporation; 137(7) — Whether credit union can be a small business corporation.

**Notes**: Note that a "small business corporation" need not in fact be small, and that "active business" is defined above in 248(1).

The CCRA takes the position that "all or substantially all" means 90% or more.

The CCRA also takes the position that a loan to an employee who is not a shareholder, or a loan to an employee who is a shareholder on the same terms as loans to other employees, is an asset used in an active business. Thus, such a loan will not jeopardize "small business corporation" status. See Revenue Canada Round Table, Canadian Tax Foundation 1993 annual conference report, Q. 45.

Closing words of "small business corporation" amended by 1992 technical bill, effective for 1991 and later taxation years, to add the rule that the fair market value of a net income stabilization account is deemed to be nil for purposes of the definition.

Definition amended by 1991 technical bill, retroactive to 1988, to make a number of changes, most notably by providing that in determining whether an asset is used in an active business carried on in Canada, it is the principal use of the asset that is relevant.

**Interpretation Bulletins**: IT-268R3: *Inter vivos* transfer of farm property to child; IT-484R2: Business investment losses.

**Advance Tax Rulings**: ATR-53: Purification of a small business corporation; ATR-55: Amalgamation followed by sale of shares.

**"small business development bond"** has the meaning assigned by section 15.1;

**"specified employee"** of a person means an employee of the person who is a specified shareholder of the person or who does not deal at arm's length with the person;

**Related Provisions**: 15(2.7) — Meaning of specified employee of a partnership for purpose of shareholder appropriations and loans.

**Notes**: "specified employee" added by 1992 Economic Statement, effective for taxation years ending after December 2, 1992. See 37(9).

**"specified financial institution"**, at any time, means

(a) a bank,

(b) a corporation licensed or otherwise authorized under the laws of Canada or a province to carry on in Canada the business of offering to the public its services as trustee,

(c) a credit union,

(d) an insurance corporation,

(e) a corporation whose principal business is the lending of money to persons with whom the corporation is dealing at arm's length or the purchasing of debt obligations issued by such persons or a combination thereof,

(e.1) a corporation described in paragraph (g) of the definition "financial institution" in subsection 181(1),

(f) a corporation that is controlled by one or more corporations described in any of paragraphs (a) to (e.1) and, for the purpose of this paragraph, one corporation is controlled by another corporation if more than 50% of its issued share capital (having full voting rights under all circumstances) belongs to the other corporation, to persons with whom the other corporation does not deal at arm's length, or to the other corporation and persons with whom the other corporation does not deal at arm's length, or

(g) a corporation that is related to a particular corporation described in any of paragraphs (a) to (f), other than a particular corporation described in paragraph (e) or (e.1) the principal business of which is the factoring of trade accounts receivable that

(i) the particular corporation acquired from a related person,

(ii) arose in the course of an active business carried on by a person (in this paragraph referred to as the "business entity") related at that time to the particular corporation, and

(iii) at no particular time before that time were held by a person other than a person who was related to the business entity;

**Related Provisions**: 248(14) — Related corporations; 256(6), (6.1) — Meaning of "controlled".

**Notes**: Opening words amended by 1998 Budget to add "at any time", effective for determining the status of a corporation as a specified financial institution, for all purposes of the Act, for taxation years of the corporation that begin after 1998.

Para. (e.1) added, para. (f) amended to replace "(a) to (e)" with "(a) to (e.1)", and para. (g) amended to add everything after "paragraphs (a) to (f)", by 1998 Budget, effective on the same basis as the amendment to the opening words.

**Regulations**: 8604 (prescribed financial institutions).

**"specified future tax consequence"** for a taxation year means

(a) the consequence of the deduction or exclusion of an amount referred to in paragraph 161(7)(a),

(b) the consequence of a reduction under subsection 66(12.73) of a particular amount purported to be renounced by a corporation after the beginning of the year to a person or partnership under subsection 66(12.6) or (12.601) because of the application of subsection 66(12.66), determined as if the purported renunciation would, but for subsection 66(12.73), have been effective only where

(i) the purported renunciation occurred in January, February or March of a calendar year,

(ii) the effective date of the purported renunciation was the last day of the preceding calendar year,

(iii) the corporation agreed in that preceding calendar year to issue a flow-though share to the person or partnership,

(iv) the particular amount does not exceed the amount, if any, by which the consideration for which the share is to be issued exceeds the total of all other amounts purported by the corporation to have been renounced under subsection 66(12.6) or (12.601) in respect of that consideration,

(v) paragraphs 66(12.66)(c) and (d) are satisfied with respect to the purported renunciation, and

(vi) the form prescribed for the purpose of subsection 66(12.7) in respect of the purported renunciation is filed with the Minister before May of the calendar year; and

(c) the consequence of an adjustment or a reduction described in subsection 161(6.1);

**Related Provisions**: 127(10.2)A — Effect of specified future tax consequence (SFTC) on investment tax credits; 156.1(1.1), (1.2), 157(2)(c), (d), 157(2.1)(a), 161(4)(a), 161(4.01)(a), 161(4.1)(a) — Effect of SFTC on instalment obligations and instalment interest; 161(6.2) — Flow-through share renunciations and one-year lookback — effect of SFTC on interest; 162(11) — Effect of SFTC on penalties.

**Notes**: Para. (c) added by 1998 Budget, effective for 1998 and later taxation years.

Definition "specified future tax consequence" added by 1996 Budget, effective for 1996 and later taxation years; and, for greater certainty, for taxation years that ended before 1996, there are deemed to be no specified future tax consequences.

The term refers to adjustments from the carryback of losses or similar amounts or because of corrections of certain amounts renounced in connection with the issuance of flow-through shares. Note that there are no "specified future tax consequences" for previous taxation years unless they end after 1995.

**"specified individual"** has the meaning assigned by subsection 120.4(1);

**Notes**: 248(1)"specified individual" added by 1999 Budget, effective for 2000 and later taxation years.

**"specified investment business"** has the meaning assigned by subsection 125(7);

**"specified member"** of a partnership in a fiscal period or taxation year of the partnership, as the case may be, means

(a) any member of the partnership who is a limited partner (within the meaning assigned by subsection 96(2.4)) of the partnership at any time in the period or year, and

(b) any member of the partnership, other than a member who is

(i) actively engaged in those activities of the partnership business that are other than the financing of the partnership business, or

(ii) carrying on a similar business as that carried on by the partnership in its taxation year, otherwise than as a member of a partnership,

on a regular, continuous and substantial basis throughout that part of the period or year during which the business of the partnership is ordinarily carried on and during which the member is a member of the partnership;

**Related Provisions**: 40(3.131), 127.52(2,1) — Anti-avoidance.

**Interpretation Bulletins**: IT-151R5: Scientific research and experimental development expenditures.

**"specified shareholder"** of a corporation in a taxation year means a taxpayer who owns, directly or indirectly, at any time in the year, not less than 10% of the issued shares of any class of the capital stock of the corporation or of any other corporation that is related to the corporation and, for the purposes of this definition,

(a) a taxpayer shall be deemed to own each share of the capital stock of a corporation owned at that time by a person with whom the taxpayer does not deal at arm's length,

(b) each beneficiary of a trust shall be deemed to own that proportion of all such shares owned by the trust at that time that the fair market value at that time of the beneficial interest of the beneficiary in the trust is of the fair market value at that time of all beneficial interests in the trust,

(c) each member of a partnership shall be deemed to own that proportion of all the shares of any class of the capital stock of a corporation that are property of the partnership at that time that the fair market value at that time of the member's interest in the partnership is of the fair market value at that time of the interests of all members in the partnership,

(d) an individual who performs services on behalf of a corporation that would be carrying on a personal services business if the individual or any person related to the individual were at that time a specified shareholder of the corporation shall be deemed to be a specified shareholder of the corporation at that time if the individual, or any person or partnership with whom the individual does not deal at arm's length, is, or by virtue of any arrangement, may become, entitled, directly or indirectly, to not less than 10% of the assets or the shares of any class of the capital stock of the corporation or any corporation related thereto, and

(e) notwithstanding paragraph (b), where a beneficiary's share of the income or capital of the trust depends on the exercise by any person of, or the failure by any person to exercise, any discretionary power, the beneficiary shall be deemed to own each share of the capital stock of a corporation owned at that time by the trust;

**Related Provisions**: 18(5), (5.1) — Alternate definition for thin capitalization rules; 55(3.2)(a), 55(3.3) — Extended meanings for capital gains strip rules; 88(1)(c.2)(iii) — Restriction on definition for windups.

**Notes**: Para. (e) added by 1992 technical bill, effective January 1, 1992.

**Interpretation Bulletins**: IT-73R5: The small business deduction; IT-88R2: Stock dividends; IT-153R3: Land developers — subdivision and development costs and carrying charges on land; IT-421R2: Benefits to individuals, corporations and shareholders from loans or debt; IT-432R2: Benefits conferred on shareholders.

**Advance Tax Rulings**: ATR-36: Estate freeze.

**"split income"** has the meaning assigned by subsection 120.4(1);

**Notes**: 248(1)"split income" added by 1999 Budget, effective for 2000 and later taxation years. See Notes to 120.4.

**"stock dividend"** includes any dividend (determined without reference to the definition "dividend" in this subsection) paid by a corporation to the extent that it is paid by the issuance of shares of any class of the capital stock of the corporation;

**Related Provisions**: 15(1.1) — Where stock dividend designed to confers benefit on shareholder; 52(3) — Cost of stock dividend; 95(7) — Stock dividend received from foreign affiliate; 248(1) —

"Amount" (of stock dividend); 248(5)(b) — Stock dividend is deemed to be substituted property.

**Notes**: "Stock dividend" amended by 1991 technical bill, effective December 17, 1991, to add the parenthetical exclusion so as to avoid circularity in the definition.

**Interpretation Bulletins**: IT-67R3: Taxable dividends from corporations resident in Canada; IT-88R2: Stock dividends.

**Information Circulars**: 88-2 para. 26: General anti-avoidance rule — section 245 of the *Income Tax Act*.

**"subsidiary controlled corporation"** means a corporation more than 50% of the issued share capital of which (having full voting rights under all circumstances) belongs to the corporation to which it is subsidiary;

**Notes**: 248(1)"subsidiary controlled corporation" added in the R.S.C. 1985 (5th Supp.) consolidation, effective December 1, 1991. This definition was formerly included in the definition of "subsidiary wholly-owned corporation".

**"subsidiary wholly-owned corporation"** means a corporation all the issued share capital of which (except directors' qualifying shares) belongs to the corporation to which it is subsidiary;

**Related Provisions**: 87(1.4) — Definition of "subsidiary wholly-owned corporation"; 87(2.11) — Losses, etc., on amalgamation with subsidiary wholly-owned corporation.

**Interpretation Bulletins**: IT-98R2: Investment corporations.

**"superannuation or pension benefit"** includes any amount received out of or under a superannuation or pension fund or plan and, without restricting the generality of the foregoing, includes any payment made to a beneficiary under the fund or plan or to an employer or former employer of the beneficiary thereunder

(a) in accordance with the terms of the fund or plan,

(b) resulting from an amendment to or modification of the fund or plan, or

(c) resulting from the termination of the fund or plan;

**Related Provisions**: 6(1)(g) — Employee benefit plan benefits; 56(1)(a)(i) — Superannuation or pension benefit included in income.

**Interpretation Bulletins**: IT-499R: Superannuation or pension benefits; IT-508R: Death benefits.

**"supplementary unemployment benefit plan"** has the meaning assigned by subsection 145(1);

**"tar sands"** means bituminous sands or oil shales extracted, otherwise than by a well, from a mineral resource, but, for the purpose of applying sections 13 and 20 and any regulations made for the purpose of paragraph 20(1)(a) in respect of property acquired after March 6, 1996, includes material extracted by a well from a deposit of bituminous sands or oil shales;

**Notes**: Definition "tar sands" amended by 1996 Budget, effective March 7, 1996. For 1983 through March 6, 1996, read:

"tar sands" means bituminous sands, oil sands or oil shales extracted, otherwise than by a well, from a mineral resource;

See Notes to 248(1)"bituminous sands".

**"tax shelter"** has the meaning assigned by subsection 237.1(1);

**"tax treaty"** with a country at any time means a comprehensive agreement or convention for the elimination of double taxation on income, between the Government of Canada and the government of the country, which has the force of law in Canada at that time;

**Related Provisions**: 108(1)"exempt property" — Property exempted by tax treaty.

**Notes**: Definition added by 1998 Budget, effective for 1998 and later taxation years.

**"taxable Canadian corporation"** has the meaning assigned by subsection 89(1);

**"taxable Canadian property"** has the meaning assigned by subsection 115(1) except that, for the purposes only of sections 2, 128.1 and 150, the expression "taxable Canadian property" includes

(a) a Canadian resource property,

(b) a timber resource property,

(c) an income interest in a trust resident in Canada,

(d) a right to a share of the income or loss under an agreement referred to in paragraph 96(1.1)(a), and

(e) a life insurance policy in Canada;

### Proposed Amendment — 248(1)"taxable Canadian property"

**"taxable Canadian property"** of a taxpayer at any time in a taxation year means a property of the taxpayer that is

(a) real property situated in Canada,

(b) property used or held by the taxpayer in, eligible capital property in respect of, or property described in an inventory of, a business carried on in Canada, other than

(i) property used in carrying on an insurance business, and

(ii) where the taxpayer is non-resident, ships and aircraft used principally in international traffic and personal property pertaining to their operation if the country in which the taxpayer is resident does not impose tax on gains of persons resident in Canada from dispositions of such property,

(c) if the taxpayer is an insurer, its designated insurance property for the year,

(d) a share of the capital stock of a corporation resident in Canada (other than a non-resident-owned investment corporation if, on the first day of the year, the corporation owns neither taxable Canadian property nor property referred to in any of paragraphs (m) to (o), or a mutual fund corporation) that is not listed on a prescribed stock exchange,

(e) a share of the capital stock of a non-resident corporation that is not listed on a prescribed stock exchange if, at any particular time during the 60-month period that ends at that time,

  (i) the fair market value of all of the properties of the corporation each of which was

    (A) a taxable Canadian property,

    (B) a Canadian resource property,

    (C) a timber resource property,

    (D) an income interest in a trust resident in Canada, or

    (E) an interest in or option in respect of a property described in any of clauses (B) to (D), whether or not the property exists,

was greater than 50% of the fair market value of all of its properties, and

  (ii) more than 50% of the fair market value of the share was derived directly or indirectly from one or any combination of

    (A) real property situated in Canada,

    (B) Canadian resource properties, and

    (C) timber resource properties,

(f) a share that is listed on a prescribed stock exchange and that would be described in paragraph (d) or (e) if those paragraphs were read without reference to the words "that is not listed on a prescribed stock exchange", or a share of the capital stock of a mutual fund corporation, if at any time during the 60-month period that ends at that time the taxpayer, persons with whom the taxpayer did not deal at arm's length, or the taxpayer together with all such persons owned 25% or more of the issued shares of any class of the capital stock of the corporation that issued the share,

(g) an interest in a partnership if, at any particular time during the 60-month period that ends at that time, the fair market value of all of the properties of the partnership each of which was

  (i) a taxable Canadian property,

  (ii) a Canadian resource property,

  (iii) a timber resource property,

  (iv) an income interest in a trust resident in Canada, or

  (v) an interest in or option in respect of a property described in any of subparagraphs (ii) to (iv), whether or not that property exists,

was greater than 50% of the fair market value of all of its properties,

(h) a capital interest in a trust (other than a unit trust) resident in Canada,

  (i) a unit of a unit trust (other than a mutual fund trust) resident in Canada,

(j) a unit of a mutual fund trust if, at any time during the 60-month period that ends at that time, not less than 25% of the issued units of the trust belonged to the taxpayer, to persons with whom the taxpayer did not deal at arm's length, or to the taxpayer and persons with whom the taxpayer did not deal at arm's length,

(k) an interest in a non-resident trust if, at any particular time during the 60-month period that ends at that time,

  (i) the fair market value of all of the properties of the trust each of which was

    (A) a taxable Canadian property,

    (B) a Canadian resource property,

    (C) a timber resource property,

    (D) an income interest in a trust resident in Canada, or

    (E) an interest in or option in respect of a property described in any of clauses (B) to (D), whether or not that property exists

was greater than 50% of the fair market value of all of its properties, and

  (ii) more than 50% of the fair market value of the interest was derived directly or indirectly from one or any combination of

    (A) real property situated in Canada,

    (B) Canadian resource properties, and

    (C) timber resource properties, or

(l) an interest in or option in respect of a property described in any of paragraphs (a) to (k), whether or not that property exists,

and, for the purposes of section 2, subsection 107(2.001) and sections 128.1 and 150, and for the purpose of applying paragraphs 85(1)(i) and 97(2)(c) to a disposition by a non-resident person, includes

(m) a Canadian resource property,

(n) a timber resource property,

(o) an income interest in a trust resident in Canada,

(p) a right to a share of the income or loss under an agreement referred to in paragraph 96(1.1)(a), and

(q) a life insurance policy in Canada;

**Application**: Bill C-43 (First Reading September 20, 2000), subsec. 112(3), will amend the definition "taxable Canadian property" in subsec. 248(1) to read as above, applicable after October 1, 1996 except that, in its application before December 24, 1998, the portion of para. (b) before subpara. (i) shall be read as follows:

  (b) capital property used by the taxpayer in carrying on a business in Canada, other than

**Technical Notes**: One of the key concepts in the Act is the concept of "taxable Canadian property." The term is used for a variety of purposes, mostly but not exclusively to do with the taxation of non-residents and migrants. The scope and functions of the term are, however, less than fully clear, in part because the Act currently includes two definitions. The main definition, in subsection 115(1), appears to apply for all purposes of the Act. A second definition, however, is provided in subsection 248(1). This second definition both confirms the meaning assigned in subsection 115(1) and provides an extended meaning for certain limited purposes.

To clarify the meaning of "taxable Canadian property" and to simplify the Act, the definition in subsection 248(1) is made the only one, and the substance of the existing subsection 115(1) definition is incorporated into it. In addition, certain changes are made to the definition to reflect its policy basis and to harmonize its components.

Under this new single definition, taxable Canadian property of a taxpayer at any time in a taxation year includes property of the taxpayer that is:

(a) real property in Canada,

(b) property used or held by the taxpayer in carrying on a business in Canada (including eligible capital property), or inventory of such a business, other than

  (i) property used in carrying on an insurance business, and

  (ii) where the taxpayer is non-resident, ships and aircraft used principally in international traffic and related personal property, if the country in which the taxpayer is resident does not tax the gains of persons resident in Canada from dispositions of such property,

(c) if the taxpayer is an insurer, its designated insurance property for the year,

(d) unlisted shares of Canadian-resident corporations (other than a non-resident-owned investment corporation, unless on the first day of the year the corporation owns taxable Canadian property, and other than a mutual fund corporation),

(e) unlisted shares of non-resident corporations if, at any time during the 60-month (currently 12-month) period that ends at that time, the value of the company's Canadian real and resource properties made up more than half the fair market value of all of its properties, and more than half of the fair market value of the share was derived directly or indirectly from such properties,

(f) listed shares that would be described in paragraph (d) or (e) if those paragraphs included listed shares, or shares of a mutual fund corporation, if at any time during the 60-month period that ends at that time the taxpayer and non-arm's length persons owned 25% or more of the issued shares of any class of the capital stock of the corporation,

(g) certain partnership interests, if at any time in the 60-month (currently 12-month) period that ends at the time, most of the partnership's value is attributable to Canadian property,

(h) capital interests in trusts (other than unit trusts) that are resident in Canada,

(i) units of unit trusts (other than mutual fund trusts) that are resident in Canada,

(j) units of a mutual fund trust if, at any time during the 60-month period that ends at that time, not less than 25% of the units of the trust belonged to the taxpayer and non-arm's length persons,

(k) interests in a non-resident trust if, at any particular time during the 60-month (currently 12-month) period that ends at that time, the trust met a test comparable to the one described in respect of a non-resident corporation in (e) above, and

(l) interests in, and options in respect of, property described in any of paragraphs (a) to (k), whether or not the property exists.

Two additional points should be noted with respect to this new definition. First, in addition to listing the above types of property, the new definition preserves in its paragraphs (m) to (q) the extended meaning of "taxable Canadian property." That extended meaning now applies for the purposes of section 2, subsection 107(2.001), sections 128.1 and 150 of the Act, and for the purpose of applying paragraphs 85(1)(i) and 97(2)(c) of the Act to a disposition by a non-resident person. For these purposes, "taxable Canadian property" includes Canadian resource properties, timber resource properties, income interests in trusts resident in Canada, rights to a share of the income or loss under an agreement referred to in paragraph 96(1.1)(a) of the Act, and life insurance policies in Canada. Second, the new definition does not include, as the existing one does, property that is not otherwise defined to be taxable Canadian property but that rather is deemed by another provision of the Act to be so. That distinction remains relevant, but the rewording of the definition "excluded property" in subsection 116(6) of the Act makes it unnecessary here.

The amended definition of "taxable Canadian property" generally applies after October 1, 1996. Before December 24, 1998, however, the portion of paragraph (b) of the definition before subparagraph (b)(i) is to be read as though it were confined to capital property used in carrying on a business in Canada.

### Notice of Ways and Means Motion (re taxpayer emigration), October 2, 1996:

*Taxable Canadian property*

(1) That it be clarified that property may be taxable Canadian property of any taxpayer, whether the taxpayer is a Canadian resident or a non-resident.

*Classification of property*

(2) That taxable Canadian property include at any time after October 1, 1996 a property that is

  (a) a share of the capital stock of a non-resident corporation,

  (b) an interest in a partnership, or

  (c) an interest in a non-resident trust

that would be "taxable Canadian property" under paragraph 115(1)(b) of the Act if the Act were amended in accordance with the Notice of Ways and Means Motion to amend the *Income Tax Act* and other Acts tabled in the House of Commons on June 20, 1996, and if the references in subparagraphs 115(1)(b)(v), (vii) and (xi) of the Act, as proposed to be amended in that Motion, to "12-month period" were read as references to "5-year period".

*Trust distributions*

(6) That

  (b) any property that was taxable Canadian property of a trust and that was distributed by the trust to a beneficiary on or before October 1, 1996 be deemed, for greater certainty, to be taxable Canadian property of the beneficiary after that date.

[For resolutions (3)–(6) in the same Notice of Ways and Means Motion, see under 128.1(4) — ed.]

**Technical Background**: [See under 128.1(4) — ed.]

**Letter from Department of Finance, February 12, 1998**:

Dear [xxx]

This is in response to your letter of February 11, 1998 to Davine Roach of the Department regarding a proposed series of transactions under which a public corporation (Opco) in the course of a butterfly reorganization spins-off certain of its property to a new corporation (Newco).

Our understanding of the facts of the proposed transaction is that each common share currently held by an Opco shareholder will be exchanged for a new common share and a special share ("a reorganization share") of Opco. This exchange will be governed by section 86 of the Act. The reorganization shares will not be listed on a prescribed stock exchange. Newco will acquire all the reorganization shares of Opco from the Opco shareholders in exchange for common shares of Opco from the Opco shareholders in exchange for common shares of Newco (the Newco shares). This exchange will be governed by section 85.1 of the Act unless a shareholder elects under subsection 85(1) of the Act. The Newco shares will be listed on a prescribed stock exchange. The reorganization shares will be redeemed by Opco as part of the butterfly reorganization.

Because of the proposed amendment to subparagraph 115(1)(b)(iv) of the Act contained in Bill C-28, the reorganization shares held by a non-resident shareholder will be considered to be taxable Canadian property for the purposes of the Act. [See now 248(1)"taxable Canadian property"(d) — ed.] Under the provisions of sections 85 and 85.1 of the Act, the taxable Canadian property status of the reorganization shares will also cause the Newco shares acquired by the non-resident shareholder in exchange for the non-resident's reorganization shares to be taxable Canadian property, of the non-resident [see 85.1(1)(a) — ed.] even though the Newco shares will be listed on a prescribed stock exchange. In addition, the reorganization shares will not be considered to be excluded property for the purpose of subsection 116(3) of the Act because of proposed amendments to paragraph 116(6)(b) of the Act.

In these circumstances, we agree that the Newco shares held by a non-resident shareholder, which were acquired by the non-resident in exchange for the reorganization shares of Opco in the course of the butterfly reorganization, should not be considered to be taxable Canadian property of the non-resident for the purposes of the Act. Consequently, we are prepared to recommend to the Minister of Finance that the income tax provisions be amended to ensure that any such reorganization shares of Opco held by a non-resident shareholder will not be considered to be taxable Canadian property of the non-resident for the purposes of the Act. We would recommend that such an amendment be effective for such reorganization shares issued by a public corporation after April 26, 1995 where the shares were issued by the corporation as part of the series of transactions or events that included a distribution of property by the corporation in the course of a butterfly reorganization. If the recommendation is acted upon, I would anticipate that such an amendment would be included in a future technical bill.

Yours sincerely,

Len Farber

Director General, Tax Legislation Division

**Letter from Department of Finance, September 30, 1998**:

Dear [xxx]

I am writing in reply to your letter of September 17, 1998, to Davine Roach regarding a proposed series of transactions by which your client ("DCo"), in the course of a butterfly reorganization, transfers certain of its businesses to a new corporation ("TCo").

Our understanding of the facts of the proposed transaction is that the common shares currently held by each DCo shareholder will be exchanged for new common shares and special preferred shares (the "Butterfly Shares") of DCo. The Butterfly Shares will not be listed on a stock exchange prescribed in the Income Tax Regulations (a "prescribed stock exchange"). TCo will acquire all the Butterfly Shares of DCo from the DCo shareholders in exchange for common shares of TCo (the TCo Shares). The TCo Shares will be listed on a prescribed stock exchange. The Butterfly Shares will be redeemed by DCo as part of the butterfly reorganization.

Because of subparagraph 115(1)(b)(iv) of the *Income Tax Act* (the "Act"), the Butterfly Shares will be considered to be taxable Canadian property for the purposes of the Act. Under the provisions of sections 85 and 85.1 of the Act, the taxable Canadian property status of the Butterfly Shares will also cause the TCo Shares acquired in exchange for a shareholder's Butterfly Shares to be taxable Canadian property of the shareholder even though the TCo Shares will be listed on a prescribed stock exchange. In addition, the Butterfly Shares will not be considered to be excluded property for the purpose of subsection 116(3) of the Act because of paragraph 116(6)(b) of the Act.

In these circumstances, we agree that the TCo Shares held by a shareholder, which were acquired by the shareholder in exchange for the Butterfly Shares of DCo in the course of the butterfly reorganization, should not be considered to be taxable Canadian property of the shareholder for the purposes of the Act. Consequently, we will recommend to the Minister of Finance that amendments to the Act be introduced to ensure that any such Butterfly Shares of DCo held by a shareholder will not be considered to be taxable Canadian property of the shareholder for the purposes of the Act. We will recommend that such an amendment be effective for such Butterfly Shares issued by a public corporation after April 26, 1995 where the shares were issued by the corporation as part of the series of transactions or events that included a distribution of property by the corporation in the course of a butterfly reorganization. If the recommendation is acted upon, I would anticipate that such an amendment would be included in the government's next income tax technical bill.

Yours sincerely,

Brian Ernewein
Director
Tax Legislation Division

**Letter from Department of Finance, June 15, 2000**:

Dear [xxx]

This is in response to your letter of May 8, 2000 regarding a proposed reorganisation of [xxx] and the application of paragraph 116(6)(b) of the *Income Tax Act* (the "Act").

You attached a copy of a Canada Customs and Revenue Agency Advance Income Tax Ruling (the "Ruling") dated

March 27, 2000 and a copy of a letter from the Department of Finance dated September 30, 1998 (copy attached). You ask that we confirm that we continue to be of the view expressed in that letter of September 30, 1998 — that we are prepared to recommend that the Act be amended to ensure that, in the circumstances set out therein, the so-called "Butterfly Shares" are not "taxable Canadian property" under the Act.

While we do not express any comments regarding the transactions that are the subject of the Ruling, we confirm our intention to recommend an amendment to the Act, as set out in the attached letter of September 30, 1998.

If that recommendation is acted upon, I would anticipate that such an amendment would be included in a future income tax technical bill.

Yours sincerely,
Brian Ernewein
Director, Tax Legislation Division, Tax Policy Branch

### Proposed Amendment — 248(1)"taxable Canadian property"

**Letter from Department of Finance, June 6, 2000:**

Dear [xxx]

I am writing in response to your letter of March 20, 2000 and further to your telephone conversation with Davine Roach of this Division regarding a proposed butterfly reorganisation in which [xxx], a Canadian public corporation, proposes to distribute the shares of its wholly-owned subsidiary, [xxx] ("Subco"), proportionately amongst [xxx] shareholders. [xxx] shareholders will hold their interest in Subco indirectly through Newco, which will subsequently be amalgamated with Subco.

Our understanding of the facts of the proposed transaction is that the common shares currently held by each [xxx] shareholder will be exchanged for New [xxx] Common Shares and [xxx] Reorganisation Shares. The Reorganisation Shares will not be listed on a stock exchange prescribed in the Income Tax Regulations (a "prescribed stock exchange"). The [xxx] Reorganisation Shares will be exchanged for Newco common shares (the "Newco Shares"). The Newco Shares will be listed on a prescribed stock exchange. [xxx] Reorganisation Shares will be redeemed by [xxx] as part of the butterfly reorganisation.

Because of subparagraph 115(1)(b)(iv) of the *Income Tax Act* (the "Act"), the [xxx] Reorganisation Shares will be considered to be taxable Canadian property for the purposes of the Act. Under the provisions of section 85 and 85.1 of the Act, the taxable Canadian property status of the [xxx] Reorganisation Shares will also cause the Newco Shares acquired in exchange for a shareholder's Reorganisation Shares to be taxable Canadian property of the shareholder even though the Newco Shares will be listed on a prescribed stock exchange. In addition, the [xxx] Reorganisation Shares will not be considered to be excluded property for the purpose of subsection 116(3) of the Act because paragraph 116(6)(b) of the Act will not apply to those shares.

In these circumstances, we agree that the Newco Shares held by a shareholder, which were acquired by the shareholder in exchange for the Reorganisation Shares in the course of the butterfly reorganisation, should not be considered to be taxable Canadian property of the shareholders for the purposes of the Act. Consequently, we will recommend to the Minister of Finance that amendments to the Act be introduced to ensure that the [xxx] Reorganisation Shares held by a shareholder of [xxx] will not be considered to be taxable Canadian property of the shareholder for the purposes of the Act.

You have also expressed a concern that shareholders may be prevented from choosing, under subsection 85.1(1) of the Act, to include in computing their incomes a loss arising from the disposition of their Reorganisation Shares in exchange for Newco Common Shares because of the application of paragraph 40(3.5)(b) of the Act.

The stop-loss rule in subsection 40(3.4) of the Act suspends the loss that would otherwise be realized on a transfer of a non-depreciable capital property to an affiliated person. For the purposes of this rule, paragraph 40(3.5)(b) provides that a share that is acquired in exchange for another share in a transaction to which section 85.1 applies is deemed to be a property identical to the other share. This ensures, for example, that a loss that is deferred on the transfer of a share to an affiliate will not be recognized at the time the share is subsequently replaced by the affiliate in a share-for-share exchange with another corporation under that provision. Even though it may be argued that the former share is no longer held by an affiliated person (since that share no longer exists), paragraph 40(3.5)(b) causes the new share in effect to take its place for this purpose.

We agree that from a policy point of view, in a transaction to which section 85.1 applies, it ought to be possible for the vendor (as defined in that subsection) to realize a loss on the transfer of the exchanged shares to the purchaser corporation in exchange for shares of the purchaser, provided that the purchaser is not affiliated with the vendor. We will recommend that the Act be amended to ensure that this result obtains in the context of the transaction that you have described. We do not, however, anticipate recommending that this change be implemented in the particular manner proposed in your letter — through a new exclusion in subsection 85.1(2). This would have the incidental effect of removing a whole class of transactions from the application of paragraph 85.1(1)(b), a result which we do not believe would be appropriate in policy terms.

We will recommend that the amendments described above be included in a future bill containing technical amendments to the Act. While I cannot, as you know, offer any assurance that either the Minister or Parliament will agree with our recommendations, I hope that this statement of our position is helpful to you.

Yours sincerely,
Len Farber
General Director, Tax Legislation Division, Tax Policy Branch

**Related Provisions**: 87(10) — New share issued on amalgamation of public corporation deemed to be listed on prescribed stock exchange; 107(2)(d.1) — TCP status retained on rollout of trust property to beneficiary; 219(1.1) — Restricted definition for branch tax purposes. See also Related Provisions annotation to 115(1).

**Notes**: In the draft legislation of December 17, 1999, what is now paras. (m)–(q) was subparas. (m)(i)–(iv), with the words now between (l) and (m) forming the opening words of para. (m).

Reference to s. 150 in opening words of "taxable Canadian property" added by 1998 Budget, effective for taxation years that begin after 1998.

Reference to 128.1 in opening words added by 1993 technical bill, effective January 1, 1993, but where a corporation continued before 1993 elects for new 250(5.1) to apply earlier (see Notes to

250(5.1)), the reference applies from the corporation's "time of continuation".

Para. (e) added by 1991 technical bill, effective July 14, 1990, to ensure that a non-resident who disposes of a life insurance policy in Canada will be liable for tax on the disposition in the same manner as a resident of Canada.

**Interpretation Bulletins**: IT-420R3: Non-residents — income earned in Canada.

**Forms**: T2 SCH 91: Information concerning claims for treaty-based exemptions.

**"taxable capital gain"** has the meaning assigned by section 38;

**"taxable dividend"** has the meaning assigned by subsection 89(1);

**"taxable income"** has the meaning assigned by subsection 2(2), except that in no case may a taxpayer's taxable income be less than nil;

**"taxable income earned in Canada"** means a taxpayer's taxable income earned in Canada determined in accordance with Division D of Part I, except that in no case may a taxpayer's taxable income earned in Canada be less than nil;

**Related Provisions**: 2(3) — Tax on taxable income earned in Canada; 115(1) — Non-resident's taxable income earned in Canada.

**"taxable net gain"** from dispositions of listed personal property has the meaning assigned by section 41;

**"taxable preferred share"** at any particular time means

(a) a share issued after December 15, 1987 that is a short-term preferred share at that particular time, or

(b) a share (other than a grandfathered share) of the capital stock of a corporation issued after 8:00 p.m. Eastern Daylight Saving Time, June 18, 1987 where, at that particular time by reason of the terms or conditions of the share or any agreement in respect of the share or its issue to which the corporation, or a specified person in relation to the corporation, is a party,

(i) it may reasonably be considered, having regard to all the circumstances, that the amount of the dividends that may be declared or paid on the share (in this definition referred to as the "dividend entitlement") is, by way of a formula or otherwise

(A) fixed,

(B) limited to a maximum, or

(C) established to be not less than a minimum (including any amount determined on a cumulative basis) and with respect to the dividend that may be declared or paid on the share there is a preference over any other dividend that may be declared or paid on any other share of the capital stock of the corporation,

(ii) it may reasonably be considered, having regard to all the circumstances, that the amount that the shareholder is entitled to receive in respect of the share on the dissolution, liquidation or winding-up of the corporation or on the redemption, acquisition or cancellation of the share (unless the requirement to redeem, acquire or cancel the share arises only in the event of the death of the shareholder or by reason only of a right to convert or exchange the share) or on a reduction of the paid-up capital of the share by the corporation or by a specified person in relation to the corporation (in this definition referred to as the "liquidation entitlement") is, by way of a formula or otherwise

(A) fixed,

(B) limited to a maximum, or

(C) established to be not less than a minimum,

and, for the purposes of this subparagraph, "shareholder" includes a shareholder of a shareholder,

(iii) the share is convertible or exchangeable at any time, unless

(A) it is convertible into or exchangeable for

(I) another share of the corporation or a corporation related to the corporation that, if issued, would not be a taxable preferred share,

(II) a right or warrant that, if exercised, would allow the person exercising it to acquire only a share of the corporation or a corporation related to the corporation that, if issued, would not be a taxable preferred share, or

(III) both a share described in subclause (I) and a right or warrant described in subclause (II), and

(B) all the consideration receivable for the share on the conversion or exchange is the share described in subclause (A)(I) or the right or warrant described in subclause (A)(II) or both, as the case may be, and, for the purposes of this clause, where a taxpayer may become entitled on the conversion or exchange of a share to receive any particular consideration (other than consideration described in any of subclauses (A)(I) to (III)) in lieu of a fraction of a share, the particular consideration shall be deemed not to be consideration unless it may reasonably be considered that the particular consideration was receivable as part of a series of transactions or events one of the main purposes of which was to avoid or limit the application of Part IV.1 or VI.1, or

(iv) any person (other than the corporation) was, at or immediately before that particular time, obligated, either absolutely or contingently, and either immediately or in the future, to effect any undertaking (in this subparagraph referred to as a "guarantee agreement"), including any guarantee, covenant or agreement to purchase or repurchase the share, and including the lending of funds to or the placing of amounts on deposit with, or on behalf of, the shareholder or any specified person in relation to the shareholder given

(A) to ensure that any loss that the shareholder or a specified person in relation to the shareholder may sustain by reason of the ownership, holding or disposition of the share or any other property is limited in any respect, or

(B) to ensure that the shareholder or a specified person in relation to the shareholder will derive earnings by reason of the ownership, holding or disposition of the share or any other property,

and the guarantee agreement was given as part of a transaction or event or a series of transactions or events that included the issuance of the share and, for the purposes of this paragraph, where a guarantee agreement in respect of a share is given at any particular time after 8:00 p.m. Eastern Daylight Saving Time, June 18, 1987, otherwise than pursuant to a written arrangement to do so entered into before 8:00 p.m. Eastern Daylight Saving Time, June 18, 1987, the share shall be deemed to have been issued at the particular time and the guarantee agreement shall be deemed to have been given as part of a series of transactions that included the issuance of the share,

but does not include a share that is at the particular time a prescribed share or a share described in paragraph (e) of the definition "term preferred share" in this subsection during the applicable time period referred to in that paragraph and, for the purposes of this definition,

(c) the dividend entitlement of a share of the capital stock of a corporation shall be deemed not to be fixed, limited to a maximum or established to be not less than a minimum where all dividends on the share are determined solely by reference to the dividend entitlement of another share of the capital stock of the corporation or of another corporation that controls the corporation that would not be a taxable preferred share if

(i) this definition were read without reference to paragraph (f),

(ii) the other share were issued after June 18, 1987, and

(iii) the other share were not a grandfathered share, a prescribed share or a share described in paragraph (e) of the definition "term preferred share" in this subsection,

(d) the liquidation entitlement of a share of the capital stock of a corporation shall be deemed not to be fixed, limited to a maximum or established to be not less than a minimum where all the liquidation entitlement is determinable solely by reference to the liquidation entitlement of another share of the capital stock of the corporation or of another corporation that controls the corporation that would not be a taxable preferred share if

(i) this definition were read without reference to paragraph (f),

(ii) the other share were issued after June 18, 1987, and

(iii) the other share were not a grandfathered share, a prescribed share or a share described in paragraph (e) of the definition "term preferred share" in this subsection,

(e) where at any particular time after 8:00 p.m. Eastern Daylight Saving Time, June 18, 1987, otherwise than pursuant to a written arrangement to do so entered into before 8:00 p.m. Eastern Daylight Saving Time, June 18, 1987, the terms or conditions of a share of the capital stock of a corporation that are relevant to any matter referred to in any of subparagraphs (b)(i) to (iv) are established or modified or any agreement in respect of any such matter, to which the corporation or a specified person in relation to the corporation is a party, is changed or entered into, the share shall, for the purpose of determining after the particular time whether it is a taxable preferred share, be deemed to have been issued at that particular time, unless

(i) the share is a share described in paragraph (b) of the definition "grandfathered share" in this subsection, and

(ii) the particular time is before December 16, 1987 and before the time at which the share is first issued,

(f) an agreement in respect of a share of the capital stock of a corporation shall be read without reference to that part of the agreement under which a person agrees to acquire the share for an amount

(i) in the case of a share the agreement in respect of which provides that the share is to be acquired within 60 days after the day on which the agreement was entered into, that does not exceed the greater of the fair market value of the share at the time the agreement was entered into, determined without reference to the agreement, and the fair market value of the share at the time of the acquisition, determined without reference to the agreement, or

(ii) that does not exceed the fair market value of the share at the time of the acquisition, determined without reference to the agreement, or for an amount determined by reference to the assets or earnings of the corporation where that determination may reasonably be considered to be used to determine an amount that does not exceed the fair market value of the share at the time of the acquisition, determined without reference to the agreement,

(g) where

(i) it may reasonably be considered that the dividends that may be declared or paid to a shareholder at any time on a share (other than a prescribed share or a share described in paragraph (e) of the definition "term preferred share" in this subsection during the applicable time period referred to in that paragraph) of the capital stock of a corporation issued after December 15, 1987 or acquired after June 15, 1988 are derived primarily from dividends received on taxable preferred shares of the capital stock of another corporation, and

(ii) it may reasonably be considered that the share was issued or acquired as part of a transaction or event or series of transactions or events one of the main purposes of which was to avoid or limit the application of Part IV.1 or VI.1,

the share shall be deemed at that time to be a taxable preferred share, and

(h) "specified person", in relation to any particular person, means another person with whom the particular person does not deal at arm's length or any partnership or trust of which the particular person or the other person is a member or beneficiary, respectively;

**Related Provisions**: 87(4.2) — Amalgamation; 248(1) — "Grandfathered share"; 248(10) — Series of transactions; 248(13) — Interest in trust or partnerships.

**Regulations**: 6201(7), (8) (prescribed shares).

**I.T. Technical News**: No. 7 (taxable preferred shares — stock dividend in lieu of cash dividend).

**Advance Tax Rulings**: ATR-46: Financial difficulty.

**"taxable RFI share"** at any particular time means a share of the capital stock of a corporation issued before 8:00 p.m. Eastern Daylight Saving Time, June 18, 1987 or a grandfathered share of the capital stock of a corporation, where at the particular time under the terms or conditions of the share or any agreement in respect of the share,

(a) it may reasonably be considered, having regard to all the circumstances, that the amount of the dividends that may be declared or paid on the share (in this definition referred to as the "dividend entitlement") is, by way of a formula or otherwise

(i) fixed,

(ii) limited to a maximum, or

(iii) established to be not less than a minimum, or

(b) it may reasonably be considered, having regard to all the circumstances, that the amount that the shareholder is entitled to receive in respect of the share on the dissolution, liquidation or winding-up of the corporation (in this definition referred to as the "liquidation entitlement") is, by way of formula or otherwise

(i) fixed,

(ii) limited to a maximum, or

(iii) established to be not less than a minimum,

but does not include a share that is at the particular time a prescribed share, a term preferred share, a share described in paragraph (e) of the definition "term preferred share" in this subsection during the applicable time period referred to in that paragraph or a taxable preferred share and, for the purposes of this definition,

(c) the dividend entitlement of a share of the capital stock of a corporation shall be deemed not to be fixed, limited to a maximum or established to be not less than a minimum where all dividends on the share are determined solely by reference to the dividend entitlement of another share of the capital stock of the corporation or of another corporation that controls the corporation that would not be a taxable preferred share if

(i) the definition "taxable preferred share" in this subsection were read without reference to paragraph (f) of that definition,

(ii) the other share were issued after June 18, 1987, and

(iii) the other share were not a grandfathered share, a prescribed share or a share described in paragraph (e) of the definition "term preferred share" in this subsection,

(d) the liquidation entitlement of a share of the capital stock of a corporation shall be deemed not to be fixed, limited to a maximum or established to be not less than a minimum where all the liquidation entitlement is determinable solely by reference to the liquidation entitlement of another share of the capital stock of the corporation or of another corporation that controls the corporation that would not be a taxable preferred share if

(i) the definition "taxable preferred share" in this subsection were read without reference to paragraph (f) of that definition,

(ii) the other share were issued after June 18, 1987, and

(iii) the other share were not a grandfathered share, a prescribed share or a share described in paragraph (e) of the definition "term preferred share" in this subsection, and

(e) where

(i) it may reasonably be considered that the dividends that may be declared or paid to a shareholder at any time on a share (other than a prescribed share or a share described in paragraph (e) of the definition "term preferred share" in this subsection during the applicable time period referred to in that paragraph) of the capital stock of a corporation issued after December 15, 1987 or acquired after June 15, 1988 are derived primarily from dividends received on taxable RFI shares of the capital stock of another corporation, and

(ii) it may reasonably be considered that the share was issued or acquired as part of a transaction or event or series of transactions or events one of the main purposes of which was to avoid or limit the application of Part IV.1,

the share shall be deemed at that time to be a taxable RFI share;

**Related Provisions**: 87(4.2) — Amalgamation; 187.3(1) — Tax on dividends on taxable RFI share; 248(10) — Series of transactions.

**Regulations**: 6201(4), (5.1), (9)–(11) (prescribed shares).

**Advance Tax Rulings**: ATR-46: Financial difficulty.

**"tax-paid undistributed surplus on hand"** — [Repealed under former Act]

**Notes**: See Notes to this definition (repealed) under 89(1).

**"taxpayer"** includes any person whether or not liable to pay tax;

**Related Provisions**: 143.2(1) — "Taxpayer" includes partnership for tax shelter investment cost rules.

**Notes**: Generally, the terms "person" and "taxpayer" are perceived as interchangeable. However, in *Oceanspan Carriers Ltd.*, [1987] 1 C.T.C. 210, the Federal Court of Appeal ruled that a non-resident corporation with no income from Canadian sources is not liable to pay tax under the Act on its foreign income and hence is not a corporation contemplated by the definition of "taxpayer".

A bare trustee is not considered to be a separate person; rather, the beneficial owner is considered to deal directly with the property to which the bare trustee holds legal title, subject to some legislated exceptions. See Notes to 104(1).

**"term preferred share"** of a corporation (in this definition referred to as the "issuing corporation") means a share of a class of the capital stock of the issuing corporation if the share was issued or acquired after June 28, 1982 and, at the time the share was issued or acquired, the existence of the issuing corporation was, or there was an arrangement under which it could be, limited or, in the case of a share issued after November 16, 1978 if

(a) under the terms or conditions of the share, any agreement relating to the share or any modification of those terms or conditions or that agreement,

(i) the owner thereof may cause the share to be redeemed, acquired or cancelled (unless the owner of the share may cause the share to be redeemed, acquired or cancelled by reason only of a right to convert or exchange the share) or cause its paid-up capital to be reduced,

(ii) the issuing corporation or any other person or partnership is or may be required to redeem, acquire or cancel, in whole or in part, the share (unless the requirement to redeem, acquire or cancel the share arises by reason only of a right to convert or exchange the share) or to reduce its paid-up capital,

(iii) the issuing corporation or any other person or partnership provides or may be required to provide any form of guarantee, security or similar indemnity or covenant (including the lending of funds to or the placing of amounts on deposit with, or on behalf of, the holder thereof or any person related thereto) with respect to the share, or

(iv) the share is convertible or exchangeable unless

(A) it is convertible into or exchangeable for

(I) another share of the issuing corporation or a corporation related to the issuing corporation that, if issued, would not be a term preferred share,

(II) a right or warrant that, if exercised, would allow the person exercising it to acquire only a share of the issuing corporation or a corporation related to the issuing corporation that, if issued, would not be a term preferred share, or

(III) both a share described in subclause (I) and a right or warrant described in subclause (II), and

(B) all the consideration receivable for the share on the conversion or exchange is the share described in subclause (A)(I) or the right or warrant described in subclause (A)(II) or both, as the case may be, and, for the purposes of this clause, where a taxpayer may become entitled on the conversion or exchange of a share to receive any particular consideration (other than consideration described in any of subclauses (A)(I) to (III)) in lieu of a fraction of a share, the particular consideration shall be deemed not to be consideration unless it may reasonably be considered that the particular consideration was receivable as part of a series of transactions or events one of the main purposes of which was to avoid or limit the application of subsection 112(2.1) or 258(3), or

(b) the owner thereof acquired the share after October 23, 1979 and is

(i) a corporation described in any of paragraphs (a) to (e.1) of the definition "specified financial institution",

(ii) a corporation that is controlled by one or more corporations described in subparagraph (i),

(iii) a corporation that acquired the share after December 11, 1979 and is related to a corporation referred to in subparagraph (i) or (ii), or

(iv) a partnership or trust of which a corporation referred to in subparagraph (i) or (ii) or a person related thereto is a member or a beneficiary,

that (either alone or together with any of such corporations, partnerships or trusts) controls or has an absolute or contingent right to control or to acquire control of the issuing corporation,

but does not include a share of the capital stock of a corporation

(c) that was issued after November 16, 1978 and before 1980 pursuant to an agreement in writing to do so made before November 17, 1978 (in this definition referred to as an "established agreement"),

(d) that was issued as a stock dividend

(i) before April 22, 1980 on a share of the capital stock of a public corporation that was not a term preferred share, or

(ii) after April 21, 1980 on a share that was, at the time the stock dividend was paid, a share prescribed for the purposes of paragraph (f),

(d.1) that is listed on a prescribed stock exchange in Canada and was issued before April 22, 1980 by

(i) a corporation referred to in any of paragraphs (a) to (d) of the definition "specified financial institution" in this subsection,

(ii) a corporation whose principal business is the lending of money or the purchasing of debt obligations or a combination thereof, or

(iii) an issuing corporation associated with a corporation described in subparagraph (i) or (ii),

(e) for a period not exceeding ten years and, in the case of a share issued after November 12, 1981, for a period not exceeding five years, from the date of its issuance, which share was issued by a corporation resident in Canada,

(i) as part of a proposal to, or an arrangement with, its creditors that had been approved by a court under the *Bankruptcy and Insolvency Act*,

(ii) at a time when all or substantially all of its assets were under the control of a receiver, receiver-manager, sequestrator or trustee in bankruptcy, or

(iii) at a time when, by reason of financial difficulty, the issuing corporation or another corporation resident in Canada with which it does not deal at arm's length was in default, or could reasonably be expected to default, on a debt obligation held by a person with whom the issuing corporation or the other corporation was dealing at arm's length and the share was issued either wholly or in substantial part and either directly or indirectly in exchange or substitution for that obligation or a part thereof,

and, in the case of a share issued after November 12, 1981, the proceeds from the issue may reasonably be regarded as having been used by the issuing corporation or a corporation with which it was not dealing at arm's length in the financing of its business carried on in Canada immediately before the share was issued,

(f) that is a prescribed share, or

(f.1) that is a taxable preferred share held by a specified financial institution that acquired the share

(i) before December 16, 1987, or

(ii) before 1989 pursuant to an agreement in writing entered into before December 16, 1987,

other than a share deemed by paragraph (c) of the definition "short-term preferred share" in this subsection or by paragraph (i.2) to have been issued after December 15, 1987 or a share that would be deemed by paragraph (e) of the definition "taxable preferred share" in this subsection to have been issued after December 15, 1987 if the references therein to "8:00 p.m. Eastern Daylight Saving Time, June 18, 1987" were read as references to "December 15, 1987",

and, for the purposes of this definition,

(g) where the terms or conditions of an established agreement were amended after November 16, 1978, the agreement shall be deemed to have been made after that date,

(h) where

(i) at any particular time the terms or conditions of a share issued pursuant to an established agreement or of any agreement relating to such a share have been changed,

(ii) under the terms or conditions of

(A) a share of a class of the capital stock of the issuing corporation issued before November 17, 1978 (other than a share that was listed on November 16, 1978 on a prescribed stock exchange in Canada),

(B) a share issued pursuant to an established agreement,

(C) any agreement between the issuing corporation and the owner of a share described in clause (A) or (B), or

(D) any agreement relating to a share described in clause (A) or (B) made after October 23, 1979,

the owner thereof could at any particular time after November 16, 1978 require, either alone or together with one or more taxpayers, the redemption, acquisition, cancellation, conversion or reduction of the paid-up capital of the share otherwise than by reason of a failure or default under the terms or conditions of the share or any agreement that related to, and was entered into at the time of, the issuance of the share,

(iii) in respect of a share issued before November 17, 1978, at any particular time after November 16, 1978 the redemption date was extended or the terms or conditions relating to its redemption, acquisition, cancellation, conversion or reduction of its paid-up capital were changed,

(iv) at a particular time after October 23, 1979 and before November 13, 1981, a specified financial institution (or a partnership or trust of which a specified financial institution or a person related to the institution is a member or beneficiary) acquired a share that

(A) was issued before November 17, 1978 or under an established agreement,

(B) was issued to a person other than a corporation that was, at the time of issue,

(I) described in any of paragraphs (a) to (e) of the definition "specified financial institution", or

(II) a corporation that was controlled by one or more corporations described in subclause (I) and, for the purpose of this subclause, one corporation is controlled by another corporation if more than 50% of its issued share capital (having full voting rights under all circumstances) belongs to the other corporation, to persons with whom the other corporation does not deal at arm's length, or to the other corporation and persons with whom the other corporation does not deal at arm's length,

(C) was acquired from a person that was, at the particular time, a person other than a corporation described in subclause (B)(I) or (II), and

(D) was acquired otherwise than under an agreement in writing made before October 24, 1979,

(v) at any particular time after November 12, 1981

(A) in respect of

(I) a share (other than a share referred to in paragraph (e) or a share listed on November 13, 1981 on a prescribed stock exchange in Canada) issued after November 16, 1978 and before November 13, 1981, or

(II) a share issued after November 12, 1981 and before 1983 pursuant to an agreement in writing to do so made before November 13, 1981 (in this definition referred to as a "specified agreement")

the owner thereof could require, either alone or together with one or more taxpayers, the redemption, acquisition, cancellation, conversion or reduction of the paid-up capital of the share otherwise than by reason of a failure or default under the terms or conditions of the share or any agreement that related to, and was entered into at the time of, the issuance of the share, or

(B) the redemption date of

(I) a share issued after November 16, 1978 and before November 13, 1981 or

(II) a share issued pursuant to a specified agreement

was extended or the terms or conditions relating to its redemption, acquisition, cancellation, conversion or reduction of its paid-up capital were changed, or

(vi) at a particular time after November 12, 1981, a specified financial institution (or a partnership or trust of which a specified financial institution or a person related to the institution is a member or beneficiary) acquired a share (other than a share referred to in paragraph (e)) that

(A) was issued before November 13, 1981 or under a specified agreement,

(B) was acquired from a partnership or person, other than a person that was, at the particular time, a corporation described in any of paragraphs (a) to (f) of the definition "specified financial institution" in this subsection,

(C) was acquired in an acquisition that was not subject to nor conditional on a guarantee agreement, within the meaning assigned by subsection 112(2.2), entered into after November 12, 1981, and

(D) was acquired otherwise than under an agreement in writing made before October 24, 1979 or a specified agreement, the share shall, for the purposes of determining at any time after the particular time whether it is a term preferred share, be deemed to have been issued at the particular time otherwise than pursuant to an established or specified agreement,

(i) where the terms or conditions of a share of the capital stock of the issuing corporation are modified or established after June 28, 1982 and as a consequence thereof the issuing corporation, any person related thereto or any partnership or trust of which the issuing corporation or a person related thereto is a member or a beneficiary may reasonably be expected at any time to redeem, acquire or cancel, in whole or in part, the share or to reduce its paid-up capital, the share shall be deemed as from the date of the modification or as from the date of the establishment, as the case may be, to be a share described in paragraph (a),

(i.1) where

(i) it may reasonably be considered that the dividends that may be declared or paid at any time on a share (other than a prescribed share or a share described in paragraph (e) during the applicable time period referred to in that paragraph) of the capital stock of a corporation issued after December 15, 1987 or acquired after June 15, 1988 are derived primarily from dividends received on term preferred shares of the capital stock of another corporation, and

(ii) it may reasonably be considered that the share was issued or acquired as part of a transaction or event or series of transactions or events one of the main purposes of which was to avoid or limit the application of subsection 112(2.1) or 138(6),

the share shall be deemed at that time to be a term preferred share acquired in the ordinary course of business,

(i.2) where at any particular time after December 15, 1987, otherwise than pursuant to a written arrangement to do so entered into before December 16, 1987, the terms or conditions of a taxable preferred share of the capital stock of a corporation relating to any matter referred to in subparagraphs (a)(i) to (iv) have been modified or established, or any agreement in respect of the share relating to any such matter has been changed or entered into by the corporation or a specified person (within the meaning assigned by paragraph (h) of the definition "taxable preferred share" in this subsection) in relation to the corporation, the share shall be deemed after that particular time to have been issued at that particular time, and,

(j) where a particular share of the capital stock of a corporation has been issued or its terms and conditions have been modified and it may reasonably be considered, having regard to all circumstances (including the rate of interest on any debt or the dividend provided on any term preferred share), that

(i) but for the existence at any time of the debt or the term preferred share, the particular share would not have been issued or its terms or conditions modified, and

(ii) one of the main purposes for the issue of the particular share or for the modification of its terms or conditions was to avoid a limitation provided by subsection 112(2.1) or 138(6) in respect of a deduction,

the particular share shall be deemed after December 31, 1982 to be a term preferred share of the corporation;

**Related Provisions**: 80(1) — Definition of "distress preferred share"; 87(4.1) — Amalgamations — exchanged shares; 112(2.1) — No deduction on intercorporate dividends; 112(2.6)"exempt share"(c) — Distress preferred shares excluded from restrictions on collateralized preferred shares; 248(13) — Interests in trusts or partnerships; 256(1.6) — Fair market valuation; 256(6), (6.1) — Meaning of "controlled"; Canada-U.S. tax treaty, Art. XXIX A:5(c) — Meaning of "debt substitute share".

**Notes**: Term preferred shares result in no deduction under 112(2.1), so intercorporate dividends on such shares are taxable. For discussion see Elinore Richardson, "Term Preferred Shares Revisited", VIII(2) *Corporate Finance* (Federated Press) 726-730 (2000).

In *Citibank Canada*, (TCC, Jan. 15, 2001, 1999-3261(IT)G), preferred shares with a conversion formula, which were drafted to avoid this definition, were held not to be term preferred shares, as they were not similar to debt.

The shares described in para. (e) are generally referred to as "distress preferred" or "financial difficulty" shares. See also 80(1)"distress preferred share" and 80.02.

Subpara. (b)(i) amended by 1998 Budget to replace "(a) to (e)" with "(a) to (e.1)", effective for taxation years that begin after 1998.

Para. (d.1) amended by 1995-97 technical bill, effective February 23, 1994. Previously read:

(d.1) that was issued before April 22, 1980 by a corporation described in any of paragraphs 39(5)(b) to (f) or by an issuing corporation associated with any such corporation and is listed on a prescribed stock exchange in Canada,

Subpara. (h)(iv) amended by 1998 Budget, effective for taxation years that begin after 1998. For earlier taxation years, read:

(iv) a share issued before November 17, 1978 or a share issued pursuant to an established agreement (other than a share issued to a corporation described in any of paragraphs (a) to (f) of the definition "specified financial institution" in this subsection), is, at any particular time after October 23, 1979 and before November 13, 1981 acquired (otherwise than pursuant to an agreement in writing made before October 24, 1979) from a person (other than a corporation described in any of paragraphs (a) to (f) of that definition) by a specified financial institution or by a partnership or trust of which a specified financial institution or a person related thereto is a member or a beneficiary,

Subpara. (h)(vi) amended by 1998 Budget, effective for taxation years that begin after 1998 except that, in its application to a share acquired from a corporation that last acquired the share in a taxation year that began before 1999, read "described in any of paragraphs (a) to (f) of the definition "specified financial institution" in this subsection" as "described in subclause (iv)(B)(I) or (II)".

For earlier years, read:

(vi) a share (other than a share referred to in paragraph (e)) issued before November 13, 1981 or a share issued pursuant to a specified agreement is, at any particular time after November 12, 1981, acquired (otherwise than pursuant to an agreement in writing made before October 24, 1979 or otherwise than pursuant to a specified agreement) from a partnership or person (other than an acquisition from a corporation described in any of paragraphs (a) to (f) of the definition "specified financial institution" in this subsection where that acquisition is neither subject to nor conditional on a guarantee agreement, within the meaning assigned by subsection 112(2.2), entered into after November 12, 1981) by a specified financial institution or by a partnership or trust of which a specified financial institution or a person related thereto is a member or a beneficiary.

"Term preferred share" amended extensively by 1988 tax reform. Some of the changes were effective as of June 19, 1987, and thus the previous version of the legislation is now irrelevant. The following two changes were made effective for shares issued (or deemed to have been issued) after 8:00 pm EDST, June 18, 1987:

> (e)(iii) was reworded slightly, primarily to add "or a part thereof" at the end.

The closing words of the definition were repealed. For shares issued before the above cutoff date, read, after (j):

> "and where after November 12, 1981 a person has an interest in a trust, whether directly or indirectly through an interest in any other trust or in any other manner whatever, the person shall, for the purposes of this definition, the definition "income bond" or "income debenture" in this subsection, subsection 112(2.2) and section 258, be deemed to be a beneficiary of the trust;"

The reference in (j)(ii) to 138(6) was added by the 1985 technical bill, effective for shares issued after May 9, 1985 (and to shares the terms or conditions of which have been modified since that date).

For shares issued from October 24, 1979 through November 12, 1981, read (a)(i) to (iii) as follows:

> (i) the owner thereof may, at any time within 10 years of the date of issue, cause the share to be redeemed, acquired or cancelled or cause its paid-up capital to be reduced,

> (ii) the issuing corporation or any other person is or may be required to redeem, acquire or cancel, in whole or in part, the share or to reduce its paid-up capital at any time within 10 years of the date of issue (otherwise than pursuant to a requirement of the issuing corporation to redeem, acquire or cancel annually not more than 5% of the issued and fully paid shares of that class, and, where the requirement was agreed to after April 21, 1980, it provides that such redemption, acquisition or cancellation of the shares be in proportion to the number of shares of the class or, where such shares are of a series of a class, of that series, registered in the name of each shareholder),

> (iii) the issuing corporation or any other person provides or may be required to provide any form of guarantee, security or similar indemnity or covenant (including the lending of funds to or placing of amounts on deposit with, or on behalf of, the owner thereof or any person related thereto) with respect to the share, or;

For that same period, read the closing words of para. (e) as follows:

> and, in the case of a share issued after October 13, 1979 and before November 13, 1981, the proceeds from the issue may reasonably be regarded as having been used by the issuing corporation or a corporation with which it was not dealing at arm's length in the financing of its business carried on immediately before the share was issued, or.

For shares issued from November 17, 1978 through October 23, 1979, read (a)(i) to (iii) as follows:

> (i) the owner thereof may, at any time within 10 years of the date of issue, cause the share to be redeemed, acquired or cancelled or cause its paid-up capital to be reduced,

> (ii) the corporation or any other person with whom it does not deal at arm's length is or may be required to redeem, acquire or cancel, in whole or in part, the share or reduce its paid-up capital at any time within 10 years of the date of issue (other than pursuant to a requirement of the corporation to redeem, acquire or cancel annually not more than 5% of the issued and fully paid shares of that class),

> (iii) the corporation or any other person is or may be required to provide any form of guarantee, security or similar covenant (including the lending of funds to or placing of amounts on deposit with, or on behalf of, the owner thereof or any person related thereto) with respect to the share, or.

The CCRA takes the position that "all or substantially all", used in (e)(ii), means 90% or more.

**Regulations**: 3200 (prescribed stock exchange in Canada); 6201 (prescribed shares).

**Interpretation Bulletins**: IT-64R3: Corporations: Association and control — after 1988; IT-527: Distress preferred shares.

**Advance Tax Rulings**: ATR-5: Preferred shares exchangeable for common shares; ATR-10: Issue of term preferred shares; ATR-18: Term preferred shares; ATR-46: Financial difficulty.

## "termination payment" — [Repealed under former Act]

**Notes**: "Termination payment" repealed by 1981 Budget. Payments for termination of employment, including severance pay and wrongful dismissal awards, now fall within the definition of "retiring allowance" and are taxed under 56(1)(a)(ii). See Notes to 248(1)"retiring allowance".

## "testamentary trust" has the meaning assigned by subsection 108(1);

**Related Provisions**: 248(3) — Rules applicable in relation to the Province of Quebec.

## "timber resource property" has the meaning assigned by subsection 13(21);

## "total pension adjustment reversal" of a taxpayer for a calendar year has the meaning assigned by regulation;

**Related Provisions**: 147.1(18)(t) — Authorization for regulations determining TPAR.

**Notes**: Definition "total pension adjustment reversal" added by 1997 Budget, effective 1997. See Notes to 146(1)"RRSP deduction limit".

**Regulations**: 8304.1 (pension adjustment reversal).

**Forms**: RC4137: Pension adjustment reversal guide; T4104: Past service pension adjustment guide.

## "Treasury Board" means the Treasury Board established by section 5 of the *Financial Administration Act*;

**Notes**: Sections 5–12 of the *Financial Administration Act* create the Treasury Board and set out its powers.

## "treaty-protected business" of a taxpayer at any time means a business in respect of which any income of the taxpayer for a period that includes that time would, because of a tax treaty with another country, be exempt from tax under Part I;

**Notes**: Definition "treaty-protected business" added by 1998 Budget, effective for 1998 and later taxation years. Note that a business can be a treaty-protected business even if it has generated no treaty-exempt income.

**"treaty-protected property"** of a taxpayer at any time means property any income or gain from the disposition of which by the taxpayer at that time would, because of a tax treaty with another country, be exempt from tax under Part I;

*Related Provisions*: 13(4.1)(d) — Replacement of depreciable property that is not treaty-protected property; 44(5)(d) — Replacement of capital property that is not treaty-protected property.

*Notes*: Definition "treaty-protected property" added by 1998 Budget, effective for 1998 and later taxation years. Note that it is not necessary, for this definition to apply, that there be income or gain from the disposition of the property, or even that the property be disposed of.

**"trust"** has the meaning assigned by subsection 104(1);

*Related Provisions*: 108(1) — Meaning of "trust"; 146.1(1) — RESPs — "Meaning of trust"; 149(5) — Exception re investment income of certain clubs; 207.6(1) — Definitions (re RCA tax); 233.2(4) — Reporting requirement re transfers to foreign trust; 233.6(1) — Reporting requirement re distributions from foreign trust; 248(3) — Deemed trusts in Quebec; 248(5.2) — Trust-to-trust transfers — deemed same trust.

*Notes*: See Notes to 104(1).

**"undepreciated capital cost"** to a taxpayer of depreciable property of a prescribed class has the meaning assigned by subsection 13(21);

**"unit trust"** has the meaning assigned by subsection 108(2);

*Related Provisions*: 248(1)"personal trust" — Unit trust deemed not to be a personal trust.

*Notes*: A definition "unrecognized gains balance" was proposed in the draft trusts legislation of December 23, 1998, but was not included in the revised version of that legislation in December 17, 1999.

**"unused RRSP deduction room"** of a taxpayer at the end of a taxation year has the meaning assigned by subsection 146(1);

*Notes*: "Unused RRSP deduction room" added by 1990 pension bill, effective 1989.

**"unused scientific research and experimental development tax credit"** of a taxpayer for a taxation year has the meaning assigned by subsection 127.3(2);

*Notes*: 248(1) — "unused scientific research and experimental development tax credit" added in the R.S.C. 1985 (5th Supp.) consolidation, effective December 1, 1991.

**"unused share-purchase tax credit"** of a taxpayer for a taxation year has the meaning assigned by subsection 127.2(6);

*Notes*: 248(1)"unused share-purchase tax credit" added in the R.S.C. 1985 (5th Supp.) consolidation, effective December 1, 1991.

**"1971 capital surplus on hand", "1971 undistributed income on hand"** — [Repealed under former Act]

*Notes*: See Notes to "1971 capital surplus on hand" as repealed from 89(1).

**(2) Tax payable** — In this Act, the tax payable by a taxpayer under any Part of this Act by or under which provision is made for the assessment of tax means the tax payable by the taxpayer as fixed by assessment or reassessment subject to variation on objection or on appeal, if any, in accordance with the provisions of that Part.

*Related Provisions*: 117(1) — Meaning of "tax payable" for purposes of sections 117–127.4.

**(3) Rules applicable in relation to the Province of Quebec [deemed trusts]** — For the purposes of the application of this Act in relation to the Province of Quebec,

(a) a usufruct shall be deemed to be a trust, created by will where the usufruct was so established, and property subject to a usufruct shall be deemed to have been transferred to the trust, on the death of the testator and as a consequence thereof where the usufruct arises on death, and to be held in trust and not otherwise;

(b) a right of use or habitation shall be deemed to be a trust, created by will where the right was so established, and property subject to such a right shall be deemed to have been transferred to the trust, on the death of the testator and as a consequence thereof where the right arises on death, and to be held in trust and not otherwise;

(c) a substitution shall be deemed to be a trust, created by will where the substitution was so established, and property subject to a substitution shall be deemed to have been transferred to the trust, on the death of the testator and as a consequence thereof where the substitution arises on death, and to be held in trust and not otherwise;

(d) property subject to rights and obligations under an arrangement (other than a trust) that

(i) is established by or under a written contract that

(A) is governed by the laws of the Province of Quebec, and

(B) provides that, for the purposes of this Act, the arrangement shall be considered to be a trust, and

(ii) creates rights and obligations that are substantially similar to the rights and obligations under a trust (determined without reference to this subsection),

shall be deemed to be held in trust and not otherwise, and such an arrangement shall be deemed to be a trust;

(e) a person who has a right (whether immediate or future and whether absolute or contingent) to receive all or any part of the income or capital in respect of property referred to in paragraph (a), (b), (c) or (d) shall be deemed to be beneficially interested in the trust referred to in that paragraph; and

(f) property in relation to which any person has, at any time,

   (i) the right of ownership,

   (ii) a right as a lessee in an emphyteutic lease, or

   (iii) a right as a beneficiary in a trust

shall, notwithstanding that such property is subject to a servitude, be deemed to be beneficially owned by the person at that time.

**Related Provisions**: 248(5.2) — Turst-to-trust transfers — deemed same trust; 248(8) — Occurrences as a consequence of death; 248(9.1) — Trust created by taxpayer's will; 248(25) — Beneficially interested.

**Notes**: 248(3) is needed because Quebec is governed by the *Civil Code*, which does not have the concept of "trust". The trust was developed by the courts in common-law jurisdictions, including England and all provinces other than Quebec. The Department of Justice is currently engaged in a "bijuralism" project of redrafting all federal legislation to handle both common-law and civil law concepts properly in both French and English (the "four-audience" model). Provisions such as 248(3), and common-law concepts such as real property, trusts and partnerships, are being examined and may be redrafted.

248(3) amended by 1991 technical bill, effective

   (a) 1991 with respect to property the ownership of which was acquired after 1990;

   (b) 1991 with respect to property that became subject to a usufruct, a right of use or habitation, a substitution, an emphyteutic lease or a trust after 1990;

   (c) 1990 with respect to property that became subject to a usufruct, a right of use or habitation or a substitution in 1990, where the persons who so acquire interests in the property elected jointly by notifying Revenue Canada in writing by November 5, 1993 (deadline extended by 1992 technical bill, s. 159); and

   (d) to 1989 and later taxation years, for property that became subject to an arrangement referred to in 248(3)(d) in the 1989 or any later taxation year.

248(3) formerly read:

   (3) References to property beneficially owned and to beneficial owner of property — In its application in relation to the Province of Quebec, a reference in this Act to any property that is or was beneficially owned by any person shall be read as including a reference to property in relation to which any person has or had the full ownership whether or not the property is or was subject to a servitude, or has or had a right as a usufructuary, a lessee in an emphyteutic lease, an institute in a substitution or a beneficiary in a trust; and a reference in this Act to the beneficial owner of any property shall be read as including a reference to a person who has or had, accordingly as the context requires, such ownership as a right in relation to that property.

**Interpretation Bulletins**: IT-305R4: Testamentary spouse trusts; IT-437R: Ownership of property (principal residence).

**(4) Interest in real property** — In this Act, an interest in real property includes a leasehold interest in real property but does not include an interest as security only derived by virtue of a mortgage, agreement for sale or similar obligation.

**Related Provisions**: 43.1(1) — Life estates in real property.

**(5) Substituted property** — For the purposes of this Act, other than paragraph 98(1)(a),

   (a) where a person has disposed of or exchanged a particular property and acquired other property in substitution therefor and subsequently, by one or more further transactions, has effected one or more further substitutions, the property acquired by any such transaction shall be deemed to have been substituted for the particular property; and

   (b) any share received as a stock dividend on another share of the capital stock of a corporation shall be deemed to be property substituted for that other share.

**Notes**: 248(5)(b), enacted in 1986, applies to exchanges of property made after November 21, 1985 and shares received as stock dividends after November 21, 1985 other than shares received as payment of a stock dividend declared on or before that date.

**Interpretation Bulletins**: IT-244R3: Gifts by individuals of life insurance policies as charitable donations; IT-369R: Attribution of trust income to settlor; IT-489R: Non-arm's length sale of shares to a corporation; IT-511R: Interspousal and certain other transfers and loans of property.

**(6) "Class" of shares issued in series** — In its application in relation to a corporation that has issued shares of a class of its capital stock in one or more series, a reference in this Act to the "class" shall be read, with such modifications as the circumstances require, as a reference to a "series of the class".

**Interpretation Bulletins**: IT-328R3: Losses on shares on which dividends have been received.

**(7) Receipt of things mailed** — For the purposes of this Act,

   (a) anything (other than a remittance or payment described in paragraph (b)) sent by first class mail or its equivalent shall be deemed to have been received by the person to whom it was sent on the day it was mailed; and

   (b) the remittance or payment of an amount

      (i) deducted or withheld, or

      (ii) payable by a corporation,

as required by this Act or a regulation shall be deemed to have been made on the day on which it is received by the Receiver General.

**Related Provisions**: 153(1) [closing words] — Certain remittances must be made directly to a financial institution; 204.81(8.2) — Rule in 248(7) does not apply to voluntary de-registration of LSVCC; 244(5) — Proof of service by mail; 244(14) — Mailing date presumed to be date of assessment or notice; Reg. 110 — Certain remittances must be made directly to a financial institution.

**Notes**: The CCRA considers an item entrusted to a courier service for prompt delivery as equivalent to being sent by first-class mail. See Interpretation Bulletin IT-433R, para. 4.

**Interpretation Bulletins**: IT-433R: Farming or fishing — use of cash method.

**(8) Occurrences as a consequence of death** — For the purpose of this Act,

(a) a transfer, distribution or acquisition of property under or as a consequence of the terms of the will or other testamentary instrument of a taxpayer or the taxpayer's spouse or common-law partner or as a consequence of the law governing the intestacy of a taxpayer or the taxpayer's spouse or common-law partner shall be considered to be a transfer, distribution or acquisition of the property as a consequence of the death of the taxpayer or the taxpayer's spouse or common-law partner, as the case may be;

(b) a transfer, distribution or acquisition of property as a consequence of a disclaimer, release or surrender by a person who was a beneficiary under the will or other testamentary instrument or on the intestacy of a taxpayer or the taxpayer's spouse or common-law partner shall be considered to be a transfer, distribution or acquisition of the property as a consequence of the death of the taxpayer or the taxpayer's spouse or common-law partner, as the case may be; and

(c) a release or surrender by a beneficiary under the will or other testamentary instrument or on the intestacy of a taxpayer with respect to any property that was property of the taxpayer immediately before the taxpayer's death shall be considered not to be a disposition of the property by the beneficiary.

**Related Provisions**: 248(9) — Definitions; 248(9.1) — Whether trust created by taxpayer's will.

**Notes**: 248(8) amended by 2000 same-sex partners bill to add reference to "common-law partner", effective for the 2001 and later taxation years, or earlier by election (see Notes to 248(1) "common-law partner").

**Interpretation Bulletins**: IT-305R4: Testamentary spouse trusts; IT-313R2: Eligible capital property — rules where a taxpayer has ceased carrying on a business or has died; IT-349R3: Intergenerational transfers of farm property on death; IT-385R2: Disposition of an income interest in a trust; IT-449R: Meaning of "vested indefeasibly"; IT-500R: RRSPs — death of an annuitant.

**(9) Definitions** — In subsection (8),

"**disclaimer**" includes a renunciation of a succession made under the laws of the Province of Quebec that is not made in favour of any person, but does not include any disclaimer made after the period ending 36 months after the death of the taxpayer unless written application therefor has been made to the Minister by the taxpayer's legal representative within that period and the disclaimer is made within such longer period as the Minister considers reasonable in the circumstances;

**Interpretation Bulletins**: IT-305R4: Testamentary spouse trusts.

"**release or surrender**" means

(a) a release or surrender made under the laws of a province (other than the Province of Quebec) that does not direct in any manner who is entitled to benefit therefrom, or

(b) a gift *inter vivos* made under the laws of the Province of Quebec of an interest in, or right to property of, a succession that is made to the person or persons who would have benefited if the donor had made a renunciation of the succession that was not made in favour of any person,

and that is made within the period ending 36 months after the death of the taxpayer or, where written application therefor has been made to the Minister by the taxpayer's legal representative within that period, within such longer period as the Minister considers reasonable in the circumstances.

**Notes**: 248(9) "disclaimer" amended by 1993 technical bill, effective June 15, 1994, to add everything from "but does not include" to the end. The circumstances described fall into the closing words of "release or surrender".

**Interpretation Bulletins**: IT-305R4: Testamentary spouse trusts; IT-313R2: Eligible capital property — rules where a taxpayer has ceased carrying on a business or has died; IT-349R3: Intergenerational transfers of farm property on death.

**(9.1) How trust created** — For the purposes of this Act, a trust shall be considered to be created by a taxpayer's will if the trust is created

(a) under the terms of the taxpayer's will; or

(b) by an order of a court in relation to the taxpayer's estate made under any law of a province that provides for the relief or support of dependants.

**Related Provisions**: 108(1) "testamentary trust" — Trust created by taxpayer's will is a testamentary trust; 248(3) — Whether usufruct, right of use or habitation or substitution in Quebec deemed to be trust created by taxpayer's will.

**Notes**: 248(9.1) added by 1992 technical bill, effective for 1990 and later taxation years. This rule was formerly in 70(6.1), which applied only for certain specified purposes.

**Interpretation Bulletins**: IT-305R4: Testamentary spouse trusts.

**(9.2) Vested indefeasibly** — For the purposes of this Act, property shall be deemed not to have vested indefeasibly

(a) in a trust under which a taxpayer's spouse or common-law partner is a beneficiary, where the trust is created by the will of the taxpayer, unless the property vested indefeasibly in the trust before the death of the spouse or common-law partner; and

(b) in an individual (other than a trust), unless the property vested indefeasibly in the individual before the death of the individual.

**Related Provisions**: 248(9.1) — Whether trust created by taxpayer's will.

**Notes**: 248(9.2)(a) amended by 2000 same-sex partners bill to add reference to "common-law partner", effective for the 2001 and later taxation years, or earlier by election (see Notes to 248(1) "common-law partner").

248(9.2) added by 1992 technical bill, effective for deaths after December 20, 1991. The amendment ensures that a rollover on death to a qualifying individual or spousal trust is permitted only where appropriate gains will be recognized on the death of the beneficiary spouse or the qualifying individual. 248(9.2) is not a complete definition; the CCRA's administrative definition in IT-449R is still relevant.

**Interpretation Bulletins**: IT-305R4: Testamentary spouse trusts; IT-449R: Meaning of "vested indefeasibly".

**(10) Series of transactions** — For the purposes of this Act, where there is a reference to a series of transactions or events, the series shall be deemed to include any related transactions or events completed in contemplation of the series.

**Advance Tax Rulings**: ATR-56: Purification of a family farm corporation; ATR-57: Transfer of property for estate planning purposes; ATR-58: Divisive reorganization.

**(11) Compound interest** — Interest computed at a prescribed rate under any of subsections 129(2.1) and (2.2), 131(3.1) and (3.2), 132(2.1) and (2.2), 133(7.01) and (7.02), 159(7), 160.1(1), 161(1), (2) and (11), 161.1(5), 164(3) to (4), 181.8(1) and (2) (as those two subsections read in their application to the 1991 and earlier taxation years), 185(2), 187(2) and 189(7), section 190.23 (as it read in its application to the 1991 and earlier taxation years) and subsections 193(3), 195(3), 202(5) and 227(8.3), (9.2) and (9.3) of this Act and subsection 182(2) of the *Income Tax Act*, chapter 148 of the Revised Statutes of Canada, 1952 (as that subsection read in its application to taxation years beginning before 1986) and subsection 191(2) of that Act (as that subsection read in its application to the 1984 and earlier taxation years) shall be compounded daily and, where interest is computed on an amount under any of those provisions and is unpaid or unapplied on the day it would, but for this subsection, have ceased to be computed under that provision, interest at the prescribed rate shall be computed and compounded daily on the unpaid or unapplied interest from that day to the day it is paid or applied and shall be paid or applied as would be the case if interest had continued to be computed under that provision after that day.

**Related Provisions**: 221.1 — Application of interest where legislation retroactive.

**Notes**: 248(11) amended by 1999 Budget to add reference to 161.1(5), effective after 1999.

248(11) amended by 1989 Budget, to add the references to 181.8(1) and (2) and 211.5, and to add the closing words from "and shall be paid" to the end. Interest computed in respect of a period ending before 1987 shall be compounded on and after January 1, 1987. However, in applying this subsection,

(a) in respect of periods ending before September 13, 1988, the reference to "227(8.3), (9.2) or (9.3)" shall be read as a reference to "227(8) or (9)";

(b) in respect of periods ending on or before June 17, 1987, it shall be read without reference to "211.5"; and

(c) in respect of periods in taxation years ending before July 1989, it shall be read without reference to "181.8(1) or (2)".

Amended by 1991 technical bill, effective 1990, to delete reference to 211.5, no longer needed.

Amended by 1992 technical bill, effective for refunds re taxation years that begin in 1992 or later, to add reference to new subsections 129(2.1) and (2.2), 131(3.1) and (3.2), 132(2.1) and (2.2), 133(7.01) and (7.02), and to change all references to "paid" and "unpaid" to "paid or applied" and "unpaid or unapplied".

**Regulations**: 4301 (prescribed rate of interest).

**I.T. Application Rules**: 69 (meaning of "*Income Tax Act*, chapter 148 of the Revised Statutes of Canada, 1952").

**(12) Identical properties** — For the purposes of this Act, one bond, debenture, bill, note or similar obligation issued by a debtor is identical to another such obligation issued by that debtor if both are identical in respect of all rights (in equity or otherwise, either immediately or in the future and either absolutely or contingently) attaching thereto, except as regards the principal amount thereof.

**Related Provisions**: 14(13), 18(16) — Deemed identical properties for superficial loss/pregnant loss rules; 18.1(12) — Identical properties for matchable-expenditure rules; 40(3.5) — Deemed identical properties for superficial loss/pregnant loss rules; 47 — Capital gains treatment of identical properties; 54"superficial loss" [closing words] — Deemed identical properties for superficial loss/pregnant loss rules; 138(11.1) — Identical properties of life insurance corporation; 206(1.5) — Identical property rule for determining foreign property.

**I.T. Application Rules**: 26(8)–(8.4) — Identical properties owned since before 1972.

**Interpretation Bulletins**: IT-387R2: Meaning of "identical properties".

**(13) Interests in trusts and partnerships** — Where after November 12, 1981 a person has an interest in a trust or partnership, whether directly or indirectly through an interest in any other trust or partnership or in any manner whatever, the person shall, for the purposes of the definitions "income bond", "income debenture" and "term preferred share" in subsection (1), paragraph (h) of the definition "taxable preferred share" in that subsection, subsections 84(4.2) and (4.3) and 112(2.6) and section 258, be deemed to be a beneficiary of the trust or a member of the partnership, as the case may be.

**(14) Related corporations** — For the purpose of paragraph (g) of the definition "specified financial institution" in subsection (1), where in the case of 2 or more corporations it can reasonably be considered, having regard to all the circumstances, that one of the main reasons for the separate existence of those corporations in a taxation year is to limit or avoid the application of subsection 112(2.1) or (2.2) or 138(6), the 2 or more corporations shall be deemed to be related to each other and to each other corporation to which any such corporation is related.

**Notes**: 248(14) amended by 1991 technical bill, effective July 14, 1990, to add the closing words "and to each other corporation to which any such corporation is related".

**(15) Goods and services tax — change of use** — For the purposes of this Act, where a liability for the goods and services tax is incurred in respect of a change of use at any time of a property, the liability so incurred shall be deemed to have been incurred immediately after that time in respect of the acquisition of the property.

**Notes**: 248(15) added by 1990 GST, effective 1991.

**(16) Goods and services tax — input tax credit and rebate** — For the purposes of this Act, other than this subsection and subsection 6(8), an amount claimed by a taxpayer as an input tax credit or rebate with respect to the goods and services tax in respect of a property or service shall be deemed to be assistance from a government in respect of the property or service that is received by the taxpayer

(a) where the amount was claimed by the taxpayer as an input tax credit in a return under Part IX of the *Excise Tax Act* for a reporting period under that Act,

(i) at the time the goods and services tax in respect of the input tax credit was paid or became payable, if the tax was paid or became payable in the reporting period, or

(ii) if no such tax was paid or became payable in respect of the input tax credit in the reporting period, at the end of the reporting period; or

(b) where the amount was claimed as a rebate with respect to the goods and services tax, at the time the amount was received or credited.

**Related Provisions**: 8(11) — GST rebate deemed not to be reimbursement for employment expense purposes; 12(1)(x) — Inclusion in income; 12(2.2) — Deemed outlay or expense; 13(7.1) — Deemed capital cost of certain property; 37(1)(d) — Scientific research and experimental development; 53(2)(k) — Reduction in adjusted cost base; 66.1(6)"cumulative Canadian exploration expense"J — Assistance reduces CCEE; 66.2(5)"cumulative Canadian development expense"M — Assistance reduces CCDE; 66.4(5)"cumulative Canadian oil and gas property expense"I — Assistance reduces CCOGPE; 248(17) — Application of 248(16) to passenger vehicles and aircraft; 248(18) — GST — repayment of input tax credit.

**Notes**: 248(16) added by 1990 GST, effective 1991. By being deemed to be government assistance, GST input tax credits and rebates operate (depending on how they arose) to reduce the cost of depreciable property under 13(7.1), reduce eligible capital expenditures under 14(10), reduce the ACB of capital property under 53(2)(k) or reduce the amount of R&D expenditures under 37(1)(d) or the resource pools under 66.1–66.4. Otherwise they are included in income under 12(1)(x). Input tax credits arise under s. 169(1) of the *Excise Tax Act* (see the *Practitioner's Goods and Services Tax, Annotated*).

**Interpretation Bulletins**: IT-273R2: Government assistance — general comments.

**(17) Application of subsec. (16) to passenger vehicles and aircraft** — Where the input tax credit of a taxpayer under Part IX of the *Excise Tax Act* in respect of a passenger vehicle or aircraft is determined with reference to subsection 202(4) of the *Excise Tax Act*, subparagraphs (16)(a)(i) and (ii) shall, as they apply in respect of such property, be read as follows:

"(i) at the beginning of the first taxation year or fiscal period of the taxpayer commencing after the end of the taxation year or fiscal period, as the case may be, in which the goods and services tax in respect of such property was considered for the purposes of determining the input tax credit to be payable, if the tax was considered for the purposes of determining the input tax credit to have become payable in the reporting period, or

(ii) if no such tax was considered for the purposes of determining the input tax credit to have become payable in the reporting period, at the end of the reporting period; or"

**Notes**: 248(17) added by 1990 GST, effective 1991.

**(18) Goods and services tax — repayment of input tax credit** — For the purposes of this Act, where an amount is added at a particular time in determining the net tax of a taxpayer under Part IX of the *Excise Tax Act* in respect of an input tax credit relating to property or a service that had been previously deducted in determining the net tax of the taxpayer, that amount shall be deemed to be assistance repaid at the particular time in respect of the property or service pursuant to a legal obligation to repay all or part of that assistance.

**Related Provisions**: 20(1)(hh) — Deduction for repayment of assistance; 39(13) — Capital loss on repayment of assistance; 53(1)(e)(ix)(B) — Adjusted cost base of partnership interest; 127(10.7) — Investment tax credit — repayment of assistance.

**Notes**: 248(18) added by 1990 GST, effective 1991. Amounts are added to net tax in respect of previously claimed input tax credits for several reasons, including a refund of previously paid GST resulting in a credit note under s. 232(3) of the *Excise Tax Act*, and the restrictions on meals and entertainment (s. 236 of the *Excise Tax Act*).

**(19) When property available for use** — Except as otherwise provided, property shall be considered to have become available for use for the purposes of this Act at the time at which it has, or would have if it were depreciable property, become available for use for the purpose of subsection 13(26).

**Related Provisions**: 13(27)–(31) — Meaning of "available for use"; 37(1.2) — R&D capital expenditures; 127(11.2) — Investment tax credit.

**Notes**: 248(19) added by 1991 technical bill, effective 1990.

**(20) Partition of property** — Subject to subsections (21) to (23), for the purposes of this Act, where at any time a property owned jointly by 2 or more persons is the subject of a partition, the following rules apply, notwithstanding any retroactive or declaratory effect of the partition:

(a) each such person who had an interest in the property immediately before that time shall be deemed not to have disposed at that time of that proportion, not exceeding 100%, of the interest that the fair market value of that person's interest in the property immediately after that time is of the fair market value of that person's interest in the property immediately before that time,

(b) each such person who has an interest in the property immediately after that time shall be deemed not to have acquired at that time that proportion of the interest that the fair market value of that person's interest in the property immediately before that time is of the fair market value of that person's interest in the property immediately after that time,

(c) each such person who had an interest in the property immediately before that time shall be deemed to have had until that time, and to have disposed at that time of, that proportion of the person's interest to which paragraph (a) does not apply,

(d) each such person who has an interest in the property immediately after that time shall be deemed not to have had before that time, and to have acquired at that time, that proportion of the person's interest to which paragraph (b) does not apply, and

(e) paragraphs (a) to (d) do not apply where the interest of the person is an interest in fungible tangible property described in that person's inventory,

and, for the purposes of this subsection, where an interest in the property is an undivided interest, the fair market value of the interest at any time shall be deemed to be equal to that proportion of the fair market value of the property at that time that the interest is of all the undivided interests in the property.

**Related Provisions**: 248(21) — Subdivision of property; 248(22) — Matrimonial regimes.

**Notes**: 248(20) added by 1991 technical bill, effective July 14, 1990. However, it does not apply to a partition effected before 1992

(a) pursuant to the terms of an agreement in writing entered into before July 14, 1990; or

(b) in accordance with a confirmation in writing from Revenue Canada or a provincial department of revenue as to the tax consequences of that partition, where the confirmation is in respect of a written request received by such department before July 14, 1990.

**(21) Subdivision of property** — Where a property that was owned jointly by 2 or more persons is the subject of a partition among those persons and, as a consequence thereof, each such person has, in the property, a new interest the fair market value of which immediately after the partition, expressed as a percentage of the fair market value of all the new interests in the property immediately after the partition, is equal to the fair market value of that person's undivided interest immediately before the partition, expressed as a percentage of the fair market value of all the undivided interests in the property immediately before the partition,

(a) subsection (20) does not apply to the property, and

(b) the new interest of each such person shall be deemed to be a continuation of that person's undivided interest in the property immediately before the partition,

and, for the purposes of this subsection,

(c) subdivisions of a building or of a parcel of land that are established in the course of, or in contemplation of, a partition and that are jointly owned by the same persons who jointly owned the building or the parcel of land, or by their assignee, shall be regarded as one property, and

(d) where an interest in the property is or includes an undivided interest, the fair market value of the interest shall be determined without regard to any discount or premium that applies to a minority or majority interest in the property.

**Related Provisions**: 248(20) — Partition of property; 248(21) — Subdivision of property.

**Notes**: 248(21) added by 1991 technical bill, effective July 14, 1990.

**(22) Matrimonial regimes** — Where at any time property could, as the consequence of the dissolution of a matrimonial regime between 2 spouses or common-law partners, be the subject of a partition, for the purposes of this Act

(a) where that property was owned by one of the spouses or common-law partners immediately before it became subject to that regime and had not subsequently been disposed of before that time, it shall be deemed to be owned at that time by that spouse or common-law partner and not by the other spouse or common-law partner; and

(b) in any other case, the property shall be deemed to be owned by the spouse or common-law partner who has the administration of that property at that time and not by the other spouse or common-law partner.

**Related Provisions**: 248(20) — Partition of property; 248(21) — Subdivision of property; 248(23) — Dissolution of a matrimonial regime; 252(3) — Extended meaning of "spouse".

**Notes**: 248(22) amended by 2000 same-sex partners bill to add reference to "common-law partner", effective for the 2001 and later taxation years, or earlier by election (see Notes to 248(1)"common-law partner").

248(22) added by 1991 technical bill, effective July 14, 1990.

**Interpretation Bulletins**: IT-325R2: Property transfers after separation, divorce and annulment; IT-437R: Ownership of property (principal residence); IT-511R: Interspousal and certain other transfers and loans of property.

**(23) Dissolution of a matrimonial regime** — Where, immediately after the dissolution of a matrimonial regime (other than a dissolution occurring as a consequence of death), the owner of a property that was subject to that regime is not the person, or the estate of the person, who is deemed by subsection (22) to have been the owner of the property immediately before the dissolution, the person shall be deemed for the purposes of this Act to have transferred the property to the person's spouse or common-law partner immediately before the dissolution.

**Related Provisions**: 110.6(14)(g) — Related persons, etc.; 252(3) — Extended meaning of "spouse".

**Notes**: 248(23) amended by 2000 same-sex partners bill to add reference to "common-law partner", effective for the 2001 and later taxation years, or earlier by election (see Notes to 248(1)"common-law partner").

248(23) added by 1991 technical bill, effective July 14, 1990. Amended by 1993 technical bill, effective for dissolutions after December 21, 1992. From July 14, 1990 through December 21, 1992, read:

(23) Where the owner, immediately after the dissolution of a matrimonial regime, of a property that was subject to that re-

gime is not the person, or the estate of the person, who, because of subsection (22), was the owner of the property immediately before the dissolution, that person shall be deemed, for the purposes of this Act, to have transferred the property to that person's spouse immediately before the dissolution or, if the dissolution occurs as a consequence of the death of one of the spouses, immediately before the time that is immediately before the death.

**Interpretation Bulletins**: IT-325R2: Property transfers after separation, divorce and annulment; IT-437R: Ownership of property (principal residence); IT-511R: Interspousal and certain other transfers and loans of property.

**(23.1) Transfers after death** — Where, as a consequence of the laws of a province relating to spouses' and common-law partners' interests in respect of property as a result of marriage or common-law partnership, property is, after the death of a taxpayer,

(a) transferred or distributed to a person who was the taxpayer's spouse or common-law partner at the time of the death, or acquired by that person, the property shall be deemed to have been so transferred, distributed or acquired, as the case may be, as a consequence of the death; or

(b) transferred or distributed to the taxpayer's estate, or acquired by the taxpayer's estate, the property shall be deemed to have been so transferred, distributed or acquired, as the case may be, immediately before the time that is immediately before the death.

**Notes**: 248(23.1) amended by 2000 same-sex partners bill to add reference to "common-law partner" and "common-law partnership", effective for the 2001 and later taxation years, or earlier by election (see Notes to 248(1)"common-law partner").

248(23.1) added by 1993 technical bill, effective for deaths after December 21, 1992.

**Interpretation Bulletins**: IT-313R2: Eligible capital property — rules where a taxpayer has ceased carrying on a business or has died.

**(24) Accounting methods** — For greater certainty, it is hereby declared that, unless specifically required, neither the equity nor the consolidation method of accounting shall be used to determine any amount for the purposes of this Act.

**Related Provisions**: 61.3(1)(b)C(i) — Repetition of rule for purposes of debt forgiveness reserve calculation.

**Notes**: 248(24) added by 1991 technical bill, effective July 14, 1990.

**(25) Beneficially interested** — For the purposes of this Act,

(a) a person or partnership beneficially interested in a particular trust includes any person or partnership that has any right (whether immediate or future, whether absolute or contingent or whether conditional on or subject to the exercise of any discretion by any person or partnership) as a beneficiary under a trust to receive any of the income or capital of the particular trust either directly from the particular trust or indirectly through one or more trusts or partnerships;

(b) except for the purpose of this paragraph, a particular person or partnership is deemed to be beneficially interested in a particular trust at a particular time where

(i) the particular person or partnership is not beneficially interested in the particular trust at the particular time,

(ii) because of the terms or conditions of the particular trust or any arrangement in respect of the particular trust at the particular time, the particular person or partnership might, because of the exercise of any discretion by any person or partnership, become beneficially interested in the particular trust at the particular time or at a later time, and

(iii) at or before the particular time, either

(A) the particular trust has acquired property, directly or indirectly in any manner whatever, from

(I) the particular person or partnership,

(II) another person with whom the particular person or partnership, or a member of the particular partnership, does not deal at arm's length,

(III) a person or partnership with whom the other person referred to in subclause (II) does not deal at arm's length,

(IV) a controlled foreign affiliate of the particular person or of another person with whom the particular person or partnership, or a member of the particular partnership, does not deal at arm's length, or

(V) a non-resident corporation that would, if the particular partnership were a corporation resident in Canada, be a controlled foreign affiliate of the particular partnership, or

(B) a person or partnership described in any of subclauses (A)(I) to (V) has given a guarantee on behalf of the particular trust or provided any other financial assistance whatever to the particular trust; and

(c) a member of a partnership that is beneficially interested in a trust is deemed to be beneficially interested in the trust.

**Related Provisions**: 108(1) — "Beneficiary"; 248(3) — Certain persons in Quebec deemed to be beneficially interested in trust.

**Notes**: If 248(25)(b)(ii) is taken literally, every person in the world is beneficially interested in many trusts.

248(25) amended by 1995-97 technical bill, effectively to add paras. (b) and (c), effective 1998. Previously read:

(25) For the purposes of this Act, a person or partnership beneficially interested in a particular trust includes any person or partnership that has any right (whether immediate or future, whether absolute or contingent or whether conditional on or subject to the exercise of any discretionary power by any person or persons) as a beneficiary under a trust to receive any of

the income or capital of the particular trust either directly from the particular trust or indirectly through one or more other trusts.

248(25) amended by 1996 Budget, effective 1997. The substantive change was the introduction of the word "includes". Since the word "includes" is now used, the normal meaning of the term in question applies as well (see *Storrow*, [1978] C.T.C. 792 at 795). A person or partnership "beneficially interested" in a trust now includes, in addition to any person or partnership explicitly referred to, any other person or partnership otherwise regarded as "beneficially interested" in the trust.

For 1991–1996, read:

(25) For the purposes of this Act, a person or partnership is beneficially interested in a particular trust if the person or partnership has any right (whether immediate or future, whether absolute or contingent or whether conditional on or subject to the exercise of any discretionary power by any person or persons) as a beneficiary under a trust to receive any of the income or capital of the particular trust either directly from the particular trust or indirectly through one or more other trusts.

248(25) added by 1992 technical bill and amended retroactively by 1993 technical bill (to add the words "as a beneficiary under a trust"), both effective 1991. This rule was formerly in 74.5(10) and 94(7), which applied only for certain specified purposes.

A different draft version of 248(25), proposed in October 1991 to deal with indexed debt obligations, is now found in 16(6).

**Interpretation Bulletins**: IT-394R2: Preferred beneficiary election; IT-511R: Interspousal and certain other transfers and loans of property.

### Proposed Addition — 248(25.1)–(25.4)

**(25.1) Trust-to-trust transfers** — Where there is a transfer at a particular time of a property from a trust (in this subsection referred to as the "transferor") to another trust (in this subsection referred to as the "transferee") in circumstances to which paragraph (f) or (g) of the definition "disposition" in subsection (1) applies, without affecting the personal liabilities under this Act of the trustees of either trust or the application of subsection 104(5.8) and paragraph 122(2)(f), the transferee is deemed to be after the particular time the same trust as, and a continuation of, the transferor.

**Technical Notes**: New subsection 248(25.1) applies where there is a transfer of a property from a particular trust to another trust in circumstances to which paragraph (f) or (g) of the definition "disposition" in subsection 248(1) (explained in the notes above) applies. The result of the application of either of those paragraphs is that the transfer does not constitute a disposition. Where this is the case, subsection 248(25.1) deems the other trust after the particular time to be the same trust as, and a continuation of, the particular trust.

The application of subsection 248(25.1) does not affect the personal liabilities under this Act of the trustees of either trust or the application of subsection 104(5.8) or paragraph 122(2)(f).

This amendment applies to transfers that occur after December 23, 1998.

**Related Provisions**: 104(5.8) — Transfers between trusts; 108(1) — Definition of "capital interest"; 233.2(4) — Disclosure of transfer to CCRA; 248(1)"disposition"(c) — Disposition includes transfer to a trust.

**(25.2) Trusts to ensure obligations fulfilled** — Except for the purpose of this subsection, where at any time property is transferred to a trust in circumstances to which paragraph (k) of the definition "disposition" in subsection (1) applies, the trust is deemed to deal with the property as agent for the transferor throughout the period that begins at the time of the transfer and ends at the time of the first change after that time in the beneficial ownership of the property.

**Technical Notes**: Subsection 248(25.2) applies where at any time there is a transfer of property to a trust in circumstances to which paragraph (k) of the definition "disposition" in subsection 248(1) applies. Once the property has been transferred, the trust is deemed to deal with the property as agent for the transferor until there is a subsequent change in its beneficial ownership.

This amendment applies to transfers that occur after December 23, 1998.

**(25.3) Cost of trust interest** — The cost to a taxpayer of a particular unit of a trust is deemed to be equal to the amount described in paragraph (a) where

(a) the trust issues the particular unit to the taxpayer directly in satisfaction of a right to enforce payment of an amount by the trust in respect of the taxpayer's capital interest in the trust;

(b) at the time that the particular unit is issued, the trust is neither a personal trust nor a trust prescribed for the purpose of subsection 107(2); and

(c) either

(i) the particular unit is capital property and subparagraph 53(2)(h)(i.1) applies in respect of the amount described in paragraph (a), or would apply if that subparagraph were read without reference to clauses 53(2)(h)(i.1)(A) and (B), or

(ii) the particular unit is not capital property and subparagraph 53(2)(h)(i.1) does not apply in respect of the amount described in paragraph (a) but would so apply if that subparagraph were read without reference to clauses 53(2)(h)(i.1)(A) and (B).

**Technical Notes**: Subsection 248(25.3) applies where a trust (other than a personal trust or a trust prescribed for the purpose of subsection 107(2)) issues particular units of the trust to a taxpayer directly in satisfaction of a right to a qualifying amount payable from the trust in respect of the taxpayer's capital interest in the trust. Where this is the case, the cost to the taxpayer of the particular units is deemed to equal the amount so payable. In the case of particular units of a trust that are capital property, a qualifying amount payable is one that causes, or but for clauses 53(2)(h)(i.1)(A) and (B) would cause, a reduction under subparagraph 53(2)(h)(i.1) to the adjusted cost base of the taxpayer's capital interest. Where the particular units of a trust are not capital property, a qualifying amount payable is one in respect of which subparagraph 53(2)(h)(i.1) does not apply but to which that subparagraph would apply if it were read without reference to clauses 53(2)(h)(i.1)(A) and (B).

This amendment applies to the 1999 and subsequent taxation years.

**(25.4) Where acquisition by another of right to enforce** — If at a particular time a taxpayer's capital interest in a trust includes a right to enforce payment of an amount by the trust, the amount shall be added at the particular time to the cost otherwise determined to the taxpayer of the capital interest where

(a) immediately after the particular time there is a disposition by the taxpayer of the capital interest;

(b) as a consequence of the disposition, the right to enforce payment of the amount is acquired by another person or partnership; and

(c) if the right to enforce payment of the amount had been satisfied by a payment to the taxpayer by the trust, there would have been no disposition of that right for the purposes of this Act because of the application of paragraph (i) of the definition "disposition" in subsection (1).

**Technical Notes**: Subsection 248(25.4) provides relief from possible double taxation where a taxpayer disposes to another person or a partnership a capital interest in a trust that includes a right to enforce payment of an amount by the trust. If, had the trust satisfied the right, there would have been no disposition of the right because of paragraph (i) of the definition "disposition" in subsection 248(1), the amount is added to the cost otherwise determined immediately before the disposition of the taxpayer's capital interest in the trust.

This amendment applies to transfers that occur after December 23, 1998.

**EXAMPLE**

Stephanie's capital interest in a unit trust initially consists of 1,000 units that Stephanie purchased on December 23, 2000 for $10,000. The trust has not made an election under subsection 132.11(1) to have a December 15 year end. It makes $400 of its income for its 2000 taxation year payable to Stephanie on December 31, 2000. However, prior to the satisfaction of Stephanie's assignable right to enforce payment of the $400 amount payable, Stephanie sells 1/2 of her capital interest in the trust (i.e., 500 units and 1/2 of the right to enforce payment) to a 3rd party for $5,700.

Results:

1. Under subsection 104(13), Stephanie is required to include $400 in computing her income for the 2000 taxation year.

2. The right to enforce payment of the $400 amount by the trust is treated as part of Stephanie's capital interest in the trust under subsection 108(1). Under paragraph (i) of the definition "disposition" in subsection 248(1), a payment by the trust in satisfaction of the right would not be a disposition. However, the sale of the 500 units in the trust is a disposition of part of Stephanie's capital interest that includes a part of her right to enforce payment from the trust.

3. As the ACB of the right disposed of is nil, Stephanie realizes a gain of $200 (i.e., 1/2 of the total amount to which the right to enforce relates) upon its sale to the 3rd party. Subsection 248(25.4) is intended to apply in these circumstances to provide a $200 "bump" in the ACB of her capital interest in the trust otherwise determined immediately before the disposition. Consequently, the total ACB of the 500 units sold is $5,200 (i.e., $5,000 + $200).

4. Consequently, the capital gain realized on the disposition of the 500 units is $500 ($5,700 - $5,200).

**Application**: Bill C-43 (First Reading September 20, 2000), subsec. 112(5), will add subsecs. 248(25.1) to (25.4), subsecs. (25.1), (25.2) and (25.4) applicable to transfers that occur after December 23, 1998, and subsec. (25.3) applicable to 1999 *et seq.*

**Related Provisions**: 107(1.1) — Cost of capital interest in a trust.

**(26) Debt obligations** — For greater certainty, where at any time a person or partnership (in this subsection referred to as the "debtor") becomes liable to repay money borrowed by the debtor or becomes liable to pay an amount (other than interest)

(a) as consideration for any property acquired by the debtor or services rendered to the debtor, or

(b) that is deductible in computing the debtor's income,

for the purposes of applying the provisions of this Act relating to the treatment of the debtor in respect of the liability, the liability shall be considered to be an obligation, issued at that time by the debtor, that has a principal amount at that time equal to the amount of the liability at that time.

**Related Provisions**: 43 — Partial disposition of capital property; 142.4(9) — Partial disposition of specified debt obligation by financial institution.

**Notes**: 248(26) added by 1994 tax amendments bill (Part I), effective for taxation years that end after February 21, 1994.

**(27) Parts of debt obligations** — For greater certainty,

(a) unless the context requires otherwise, an obligation issued by a debtor includes any part of a larger obligation that was issued by the debtor;

(b) the principal amount of that part shall be considered to be the portion of the principal amount of that larger obligation that relates to that part; and

(c) the amount for which that part was issued shall be considered to be the portion of the amount for which that larger obligation was issued that relates to that part.

**Related Provisions**: 43 — Partial disposition of capital property; 142.4(9) — Partial disposition of specified debt obligation by financial institution.

**Notes**: 248(27) added by 1994 tax amendments bill (Part I), effective for taxation years that end after February 21, 1994.

**(28) Limitation respecting inclusions, deductions and tax credits** — Unless a contrary intention is evident, no provision of this Act shall be read or construed

(a) to require the inclusion or permit the deduction, either directly or indirectly, in computing a taxpayer's income, taxable income or taxable income earned in Canada, for a taxation year or in computing a taxpayer's income or loss for a taxation year from a particular source or from sources in a particular place, of any amount to the extent that the amount has already been directly or indirectly included or deducted, as the case may be, in computing such income, taxable income, taxable income earned in Canada or loss, for the year or any preceding taxation year;

(b) to permit the deduction, either directly or indirectly, in computing a taxpayer's tax payable under any Part of this Act for a taxation year of any amount to the extent that the amount has already been directly or indirectly deducted in computing such tax payable for the year or any preceding taxation year; or

(c) to consider an amount to have been paid on account of a taxpayer's tax payable under any Part of this Act for a taxation year to the extent that the amount has already been considered to have been paid on account of such tax payable for the year or any preceding taxation year.

**Related Provisions**: 181(4), 190(2) — Similar rules for Part I.3 and Part VI taxes.

**Notes**: 248(28) added by 1995 Budget, effective for taxation years that end after July 19, 1995. It replaces 4(4), and is somewhat more general.

A different 248(28), "Specified member of a partnership", in the draft legislation of April 26, 1995, was moved before enactment to 40(3.131) and 127.52(2.1). It no longer applies to 143.2(1)"tax shelter investment".

**Definitions [s. 248]**: "active business" — 248(1); "adventure or concern in the nature of trade" — see Notes to 10(1.01); "affiliated" — 251.1; "amateur athlete trust" — 143.1(1), 248(1); "amount" — 248(1); "arm's length" — 251(1); "associated" — 256; "authorized foreign bank" — 248(1); "bank" — 248(1), Interpretation Act 35(1); "bituminous sands", "business" — 248(1); "calendar year" — Interpretation Act 37(1)(a); "Canada" — 255, Interpretation Act 35(1); "Canadian-controlled private corporation" — 125(7); "Canadian resource property" — 66(15), 248(1); "capital gain" — 39(1), 248(1); "capital interest" — 108(1), 248(1); "capital loss" — 39(1)(b), 248(1); "carrying on business" — 253; "cemetery care trust" — 148.1(1), 248(1); "child" — 252(1); "common-law partner", "common-law partnership", "common share" — 248(1); "connected" — 186(4), 251(6); "consequence of the death" — 248(8); "consideration" — 108(7); "controlled" — 256(6), (6.1); "controlled foreign affiliate" — 95(1), 248(1); "corporation" — 248(1), Interpretation Act 35(1); "deferred amount" — 248(1); "deferred profit sharing plan" — 147(1), 248(1); "depreciable property" — 13(21), 248(1); "designated insurance property" — 138(12), 248(1); "disclaimer" — 248(9); "disposition" — 248(1); "eligible capital property" — 54, 248(1); "eligible funeral arrangement" — 148.1(1), 248(1); "employed", "employee trust" — 248(1); "employees profit sharing plan" — 144(1), 248(1); "filing-due date" — 248(1); "fiscal period" — 249(2)(b), 249.1; "foreign exploration and development expenses" — 66(15), 248(1); "foreign resource expense" — 66.21(1), 248(1); "goods and services tax", "grandfathered share", "gross revenue", "income interest", "insurance policy", "insurer" — 248(1); "inter vivos trust" — 108(1), 248(1); "interest in real property" — 248(4); "international traffic",

"inventory", "lending asset" — 248(1); "life insurance policy", "life insurance policy in Canada" — 138(12), 248(1); "mineral" — 248(1); "mineral resouce", "Minister" — 248(1); "mutual fund corporation" — 131(8), 248(1); "mutual fund trust" — 132(6)–(7), 132.2(1)(q), 248(1); "net income stabilization account", "non-resident" — 248(1); "non-resident-owned investment corporation" — 133(8), 248(1); "oil or gas well" — 248(1); "parent" — 252(2)(a); "partnership" — see Notes to 96(1); "passenger vehicle" — 248(1); "permanent establishment" — Reg. 8201; "person" — 248(1); "personal services business" — 125(7), 248(1); "personal trust", "prescribed" — 248(1); "prescribed plan or arrangement" — Reg. 6801, 6802, 6802.1, 6803; "prescribed rate"Reg. 4301; "prescribed stock exchange" — Reg. 3200, 3201; "prescribed stock exchange in Canada" — Reg. 3200; "principal amount", "property" — 248(1); "province" — Interpretation Act 35(1); "qualifying environmental trust" — 248(1); "registered education savings plan" — 146.1(1), 248(1); "registered retirement savings plan" — 146(1), 248(1); "registered securities dealer" — 248(1); "registered supplementary unemployment benefit plan" — 145(1), 248(1); "related" — 248(14), 251; "release or surrender" — 248(9); "resident" — 250; "resident in a province" — 250(7); "resident in Canada" — 250; "restricted financial institution" — 248(1); "salary or wages" — 248(1); "security" — Interpretation Act 35(1); "series of transactions" — 248(10); "share", "specified financial institution" — 248(1); "specified investment business" — 125(7), 248(1); "specified person" — 248(1)"short-term preferred share"(j), 248(1)"taxable preferred share"(h); "spouse" — 252(3); "supplementary unemployment benefit plan" — 145(1), 248(1); "tar sands", "tax treaty", "taxable Canadian property" — 248(1); "taxable income" — 2(2); "taxation year" — 249; "taxpayer" — 248(1); "testamentary trust" — 108(1), 248(1); "timber resource property" — 13(21), 248(1); "trust" — 104(1), 248(1), (3); "unit trust" — 108(2), 248(1); "writing" — Interpretation Act 35(1); "written" — Interpretation Act 35(1)"writing".

**249. (1) Definition of "taxation year"** — For the purpose of this Act, a "taxation year" is

(a) in the case of a corporation, a fiscal period, and

(b) in the case of an individual, a calendar year,

and when a taxation year is referred to by reference to a calendar year, the reference is to the taxation year or years coinciding with, or ending in, that year.

**Related Provisions**: 11(2) — Reference to "taxation year" of individual who carries on a business; 14(4) — Taxation year of individual — eligible capital property rules; 20(16.2) — Taxation year of individual — terminal loss rules; 87(2)(a) — Deemed year-end and new taxation year on amalgamation; 95(1)"taxation year" — Taxation year of foreign affiliate; 96(1)(b) — Taxation year of partnership; 104(23) — Testamentary trusts; 128(2)(d) — Deemed year-end where individual bankrupt; 128.1(1)(a) — Deemed year-end and new taxation year on becoming resident in Canada; 128.1(4)(a) — Deemed year-end and new taxation year on ceasing to be resident in Canada; 132.11 — Election for mutual fund trust to have December 15 year-end; 132.2(1)(b) — Deemed year-end and new taxation year on transfer of property between mutual funds; 144(11) — Deemed year-end on EPSP becoming DPSP; 149(10)(a) — Taxation year of corporation becoming or ceasing to be exempt; 149.1(1) — Taxation year of registered charity; 249(2), (3) — References to "taxation year" and "fiscal period"; 249(4) — Deemed year-end on change of control; 250.1(a) — Taxation year of non-resident person.

**Regulations**: 1104(1) (taxation year of individual for capital cost allowance purposes).

**Interpretation Bulletins**: IT-172R: Capital cost allowance — Taxation year of individuals; IT-184R: Deferred cash purchase tickets issued by Canadian Wheat Board; IT-363R2: Deferred profit

**S. 249(1)**     Income Tax Act

sharing plans — deductibility of employer contributions and taxation of amounts received by a beneficiary.

**(2) References to certain taxation years and fiscal periods** — For the purposes of this Act,

(a) a reference to a taxation year ending in another year includes a reference to a taxation year ending coincidentally with that other year; and

(b) a reference to a fiscal period ending in a taxation year includes a reference to a fiscal period ending coincidentally with that year.

**Related Provisions**: 249(1) — "Taxation year"; 250.1(a) — Taxation year of non-resident person.

**Notes**: 249(2)(b) amended by 1994 Budget, effective for fiscal periods that end after 1993. For earlier fiscal periods since 1985, read:

(b) a reference to a fiscal period of a partnership ending in a taxation year includes a reference to a fiscal period of the partnership ending coincidentally with that year.

**(3) Deemed year end where fiscal period exceeds 365 days** — Notwithstanding subsection (1), where the fiscal period of a corporation exceeds 365 days and by reason thereof the corporation does not have a taxation year that ends in a particular calendar year, for the purposes of this Act, the corporation's first taxation year ending in the immediately following calendar year shall be deemed to end on the last day of the particular calendar year.

**(4) Year end on change of control** — Where at any time control of a corporation (other than a corporation that is a foreign affiliate of a taxpayer resident in Canada and that did not carry on a business in Canada at any time in its last taxation year beginning before that time) is acquired by a person or group of persons, for the purposes of this Act,

(a) subject to paragraph (c), the taxation year of the corporation that would, but for this paragraph, have included that time shall be deemed to have ended immediately before that time;

(b) a new taxation year of the corporation shall be deemed to have commenced at that time;

(c) subject to paragraph 128(1)(d), section 128.1, and paragraphs 142.6(1)(a) and 149(10)(a), and notwithstanding subsections (1) and (3), where the taxation year of the corporation that would, but for this subsection, have been its last taxation year that ended before that time would, but for this paragraph, have ended within the 7-day period that ended immediately before that time, that taxation year shall, except where control of the corporation was acquired by a person or group of persons within that period, be deemed to end immediately before that time where the corporation so elects in its return of income under Part I for that taxation year; and

(d) for the purpose of determining the corporation's fiscal period after that time, the corporation shall be deemed not to have established a fiscal period before that time.

**Related Provisions**: 139.1(18)) — Holding corporation deemed not to acquire control of insurer on demutualization; 149(10) — Exempt corporations; 256(6)–(9) — Whether control acquired.

**Notes**: The deemed year-end on change of control has numerous effects. A return must be filed for the "short" year under 150(1)(a). A loss carryforward year under 111(1)(a) can vanish due to the extra taxation year, as can other carryforward years such as for foreign tax credits (126(2)(a)), ITCs (127(9)"investment tax credit"(c)) and reserves (40(1)(a)(iii), 20(8)). Amounts deducted but unpaid may have to be reincluded in income (78(1)). The due date for the current year's tax balance (157(1)(b)) is moved earlier. See also under "Short taxation year" in the Topical Index for applicable prorating of various kinds. For a more detailed list see Ronit Florence, "Acquisition of Control of Canadian Resident Corporations: Checklist", V(4) *Business Vehicles* (Federated Press) 262-272 (1999).

249(4)(d) has the effect of overriding the rule in 249.1(7).

It has been argued that "acquired" control under 249(4) is not the same as a "change" in control. See Gordon Funt, "Acquisition or Change of Control: Is There a Difference?", V(2) *Business Vehicles* (Federated Press), 234-37 (1999).

Opening words of 249(4) amended by 1991 technical bill, effective July 14, 1990, to add the parenthetical exclusion for foreign affiliates that do not carry on business in Canada, and to clarify that 249(4) applies for purposes of the entire Act.

Reference to 88.1(c) in first line of 249(4)(c) changed to 128.1 by 1993 technical bill, effective 1993. However, where a corporation continued before 1993 elects for new 250(5.1) to apply earlier (see Notes to 250(5.1)), the amendment is effective from the corporation's "time of continuation".

Reference to 142.6(1)(a) at beginning of 249(4)(c) added by 1994 tax amendments bill (Part III), effective February 23, 1994.

**Interpretation Bulletins**: IT-151R5: Scientific research and experimental development expenditures; IT-302R3: Losses of a corporation — the effect that acquisitions of control, amalgamations, and windings-up have on their deductibility — after January 15, 1987.

**I.T. Technical News**: No. 7 (control by a group — 50/50 arrangement).

**Definitions [s. 249]**: "acquired" — 256(7)–(9); "business" — 248(1)"business"; "calendar year" — *Interpretation Act* 37(1)(a); "Canada" — 255; "carry on business in Canada" — 253; "control" — 256(6)–(9); "corporation" — 248(1); "fiscal period" — 248(1), 249(2)(b), 249.1; "foreign affiliate" — 95(1), 248(1); "individual", "person" — 248(1); "taxation year" — 249.

**249.1 (1) Definition of "fiscal period"** — For the purposes of this Act, a "fiscal period" of a business or a property of a person or partnership means the period for which the person's or partnership's accounts in respect of the business or property are made up for purposes of assessment under this Act, but no fiscal period may end

(a) in the case of a corporation, more than 53 weeks after the period began,

(b) in the case of

(i) an individual (other than an individual to whom section 149 or 149.1 applies or a testamentary trust),

(i.1) a fiscal period of an inter vivos trust (other than a fiscal period to which paragraph 132.11(1)(c) applies),

(ii) a partnership of which

(A) an individual (other than a testamentary trust or an individual to whom section 149 or 149.1 applies),

(B) a professional corporation, or

(C) a partnership to which this subparagraph applies,

would, if the fiscal period ended at the end of the calendar year in which the period began, be a member of the partnership in the period, or

(iii) a professional corporation that would, if the fiscal period ended at the end of the calendar year in which the period began, be in the period a member of a partnership to which subparagraph (ii) applies,

after the end of the calendar year in which the period began unless, in the case of a business, the business is not carried on in Canada or is a prescribed business, and

### Proposed Amendment — 249.1(1)(b)

after the end of the calendar year in which the period began unless, in the case of a business, the business is not carried on in Canada, is a prescribed business or is carried on by a prescribed person or partnership, and

**Application**: Bill C-43 (First Reading September 20, 2000), s. 113, will amend the closing words of para. 249.1(1)(b) to read as above, applicable to fiscal periods that begin after 1994.

**Technical Notes**: Subsection 249.1(1) provides the definition "fiscal period" for the purposes of the Act. Paragraph 249.1(1)(b) provides restrictions on the timing of fiscal periods of certain individuals, trusts, partnerships and professional corporations (other than the fiscal period of a business not carried on in Canada or of a prescribed business). For technical reasons related to the promulgation of Regulations, paragraph 249.1(1)(b) is amended so that the exception refers to a business that is "carried on by a prescribed person or partnership" as well as to a "prescribed business".

(c) in any other case, more than 12 months after the period began,

and, for the purpose of this subsection, the activities of a person to whom section 149 or 149.1 applies are deemed to be a business.

### Proposed Amendment — 249.1(1)

**Letter from Department of Finance, 1995**:

Dear [xxx]

Thank you for your letter of April 4, 1995 concerning the business fiscal period measure announced in my budget of February 27, 1995. You have written on behalf of your client, [xxx].

I understand that [xxx] operates an [xxx] storage and transportation system in the province of [xxx]. Being a [xxx], [xxx] is regulated by the [xxx], which establishes [xxx]'s annual return on equity, its authorized equity capital level and the tariff it can charge consumers. You ask, on behalf of [xxx], that it be exempted from the above-mentioned fiscal period measure for reasons that include the administrative complexity the proposal would have on it, given that it is a regulated business, and that its units trade publicly.

I am sympathetic to your request in view of the unique circumstances that arise in the case of [xxx] and am, therefore, prepared to recommend that the Regulations be amended in due course to prescribe [xxx] [as exempt] from the application of the rules which would otherwise require a calendar year fiscal period.

I trust that this information addresses your client's concern.

Sincerely,

The Honourable Paul Martin, P.C., M.P.
Minister of Finance

**Related Provisions**: 25(1) — Optional continuation of year-end after disposing of business; 34.2 — Reserve in respect of 1995 stub period income; 96(1.1) — Allocation of share of income to retiring partner; 99(2) — Optional continuation of original year-end of partnership that ceases to exist; 128.1(4)(a.1) — Deemed end of fiscal period on emigration; 249.1(2), (3) — Interpretation; 249.1(4), (5) — Election for non-calendar year-end.

**Notes**: 249.1(1)(b)(i) amended and (i.1) added by 1998 Budget, effective for fiscal periods that begin after December 15, 1997. The change to subpara. (i) was to correct an ambiguity. For fiscal periods that began from 1995 through December 14, 1997, read:

(i) an individual (other than a testamentary trust or an individual to whom section 149 or 149.1 applies),

See also Notes at end of 249.1.

**I.T. Technical News**: No. 8 (bankrupt corporation — change of fiscal period).

**(2) Not a member of a partnership** — For the purpose of subparagraph (1)(b)(ii) and subsection (4), a person or partnership that would not have a share of any income or loss of a partnership for a fiscal period of the partnership, if the period ended at the end of the calendar year in which the period began, is deemed not to be a member of the partnership in that fiscal period.

**Notes**: See Notes at end of 249.1.

**(3) Subsequent fiscal periods** — Where a fiscal period of a business or a property of a person or partnership ends at any time, the subsequent fiscal period, if any, of the business or property of the person or partnership is deemed to begin immediately after that time.

**Notes**: See Notes at end of 249.1.

**(4) Alternative method** — Paragraph (1)(b) does not apply to a fiscal period of a business carried on, throughout the period of time that began at the beginning of the fiscal period and ended at the end of the calendar year in which the fiscal period began,

(a) by an individual (otherwise than as a member of a partnership), or

(b) by an individual as a member of a partnership, where throughout that period

(i) each member of the partnership is an individual, and

(ii) the partnership is not a member of another partnership,

where

(c) in the case of an individual

(i) who is referred to in paragraph (a), or

(ii) who is a member of a partnership no member of which is a testamentary trust,

an election in prescribed form to have paragraph (1)(b) not apply is filed with the Minister by the individual on or before the individual's filing-due date, and with the individual's return of income under Part I, for the taxation year that includes the first day of the first fiscal period of the business that begins after 1994, and

(d) in the case of an individual who is a member of a partnership a member of which is a testamentary trust, an election in prescribed form to have paragraph (1)(b) not apply is filed with the Minister by the individual on or before the earliest of the filing-due dates of the members of the partnership for a taxation year that includes the first day of the first fiscal period of the business that begins after 1994.

**Related Provisions**: 34.1(1) — Additional income adjustment where election made; 96(1.1) — Allocation of share of income to retiring partner; 96(3) — Election by members of partnership; 249.1(5) — Alternative method not applicable to tax shelter; 249.1(6) — Revocation of election; Reg. 600(b.1) — Late filing of election by January 31, 1998.

**Notes**: See Notes at end of 249.1.

**(5) Alternative method not applicable to tax shelter investments** — Subsection (4) does not apply to a particular fiscal period of a business where, in a preceding fiscal period or throughout the period of time that began at the beginning of the particular period and ended at the end of the calendar year in which the particular period began, the expenditures made in the course of carrying on the business were primarily the cost or capital cost of tax shelter investments (as defined in subsection 143.2(1)).

**Notes**: 249.1(5) prevents tax shelters from electing a non-calendar year-end under 249.1(4). Of course, a tax shelter may have a non-calendar year-end if it is not otherwise subject to 249.1(1).

This rule covers tax shelters as defined in 237.1(1) as well as those under the broader definition in 143.2(1)"tax shelter investment"(b).

249.1(5) amended by 1995-97 technical bill, retroactive to its introduction (see Notes at end of 249.1), to change reference from 237.1(1)"tax shelter" to 143.2(1)"tax shelter investment".

**(6) Revocation of election** — Subsection (4) does not apply to fiscal periods of a business carried on by an individual that begin after the beginning of a particular taxation year of the individual where

(a) an election in prescribed form to revoke an election filed under subsection (4) in respect of the business is filed with the Minister; and

(b) the election to revoke is filed

(i) in the case of an individual

(A) who is not a member of a partnership, or

(B) who is a member of a partnership no member of which is a testamentary trust,

by the individual on or before the individual's filing-due date, and with the individual's return of income under Part I, for the particular taxation year, and

(ii) in [the] case of an individual who is a member of a partnership a member of which is a testamentary trust, by the individual on or before the earliest of the filing-due dates of the members of the partnership for a taxation year that includes the first day of the first fiscal period of the business that begins after the beginning of the particular year.

**Related Provisions**: 96(3) — Election by members of partnership.

**Notes**: See Notes at end of 249.1.

**(7) Change of fiscal period** — No change in the time when a fiscal period ends may be made for the purposes of this Act without the concurrence of the Minister.

**Related Provisions**: 87(2)(j.91), (qq) — Change in fiscal period after amalgamation; 149(10)(a) — Change in fiscal period on becoming or ceasing to be exempt; 249(4)(d) — Change in fiscal period allowed after change in control of corporation.

**Notes**: The requirement for consent of the Minister to a year-end change was formerly in the closing words of 248(1)"fiscal period".

Once a fiscal period has been determined, it cannot be changed without the CCRA's permission. However, after change in control of a corporation, a new fiscal period may be chosen for the corporation: see 249(4)(d). The same applies after an amalgamation (87(2)(j.91)) and after becoming or ceasing to be exempt (149(10)(a)).

**Interpretation Bulletins**: IT-179R: Change of fiscal period.

**Registered Charities Newsletters**: 5 (How can you get the Department's permission to change your charity's fiscal period?).

**Notes [s. 249.1]**: 249.1 added by 1995 Budget, effective for fiscal periods that begin after 1994. The original announcement in February 1995 would have forced all individuals (and most partnerships and professional corporations) to adopt a calendar year-end. An election is now available under 249.1(4) to retain an off-calendar year-end, but where this election is made an additional income inclusion applies each year under 34.1. For the entities that are required to use a calendar year-end if they do not make the 249.1(4) election, see 249.1(1). See also Notes to 34.1 and 34.2.

**Definitions [s. 249.1]**: "business" — 248(1); "calendar year" — *Interpretation Act* 37(1)(a); "Canada" — 255; "carried on in Canada" — 253; "corporation" — 248(1), *Interpretation Act* 35(1); "filing-due date" — 150(1), 248(1); "individual" — 248(1); "member" — of partnership 249.1(2); "Minister" — 248(1); "partnership" — see Notes to 96(1); "person", "prescribed", "professional corporation", "property" — 248(1); "testamentary trust" — 108(1), 248(1).

**250. (1) Person deemed resident** — For the purposes of this Act, a person shall, subject to subsection (2), be deemed to have been resident in Canada throughout a taxation year if the person

(a) sojourned in Canada in the year for a period of, or periods the total of which is, 183 days or more;

(b) was, at any time in the year, a member of the Canadian Forces;

(c) was, at any time in the year,

(i) an ambassador, minister, high commissioner, officer or servant of Canada, or

(ii) an agent-general, officer or servant of a province,

and was resident in Canada immediately prior to appointment or employment by Canada or the province or received representation allowances in respect of the year;

(d) performed services, at any time in the year, in a country other than Canada under a prescribed international development assistance program of the Government of Canada and was resident in Canada at any time in the 3 month period preceding the day on which those services commenced;

(d.1) was, at any time in the year, a member of the overseas Canadian Forces school staff who filed his or her return for the year on the basis that the person was resident in Canada throughout the period during which the person was such a member;

(e) [Repealed]

(f) was at any time in the year a child of, and dependent for support on, an individual to whom paragraph (b), (c), (d) or (d.1) applies and the person's income for the year did not exceed the amount used under paragraph (c) of the description of B in subsection 118(1) for the year;

(g) was at any time in the year, under an agreement or a convention with one or more other countries that has the force of law in Canada, entitled to an exemption from an income tax otherwise payable in any of those countries in respect of income from any source (unless all or substantially all of the person's income from all sources was not so exempt), because at that time the person was related to or a member of the family of an individual (other than a trust) who was resident in Canada.

**Related Provisions**: 6(1)(b)(ii), (iii) — No tax on certain allowances to deemed residents; 14(8) — Deemed residence in Canada for cumulative eligible capital recapture; 64.1 — Application to deemed resident; 94(1)(c)(i) [to be repealed], 94(3)(a) [proposed] — Offshore trust deemed resident in Canada; 110.6(5) — Deemed residence in Canada for capital gains exemption; 115(2) — Certain persons deemed employed in Canada; 118.5(2) — Tuition credit — application to deemed residents; 120(1) — Federal surtax on non-resident's income not earned in a province; 214(13)(a) — Regulations deeming person resident in Canada for purposes of Part XIII; 250(3) — "Resident" includes ordinarily resident; 250(6.1) — Deemed residence of trust that ceases to exist; Canada-U.S. tax treaty, Art. IV:5 — Residence of government employee working in the other country.

**Notes**: Where none of the deeming provisions in 250(1) applies, an individual is resident in Canada if the individual is "ordinarily resident" in Canada (see 250(3)). The courts have held that a Canadian resident must generally cut his or her ties with Canada to become non-resident. the CCRA's position is that the departing taxpayer must intend to remain outside Canada for at least 2 years to become non-resident. See Interpretation Bulletin IT-221R2. (The 2-year rule of thumb has no basis in law, however; see, for example, *Peel*, [1995] 2 C.T.C. 2888 (TCC).) See also Notes to 114. For corporations, see Notes to 250(4).

For a recent case involving an "astronaut" taxpayer who was found not to be resident in Canada despite having many of the ties referred to in IT-221R2, see *Shih*, [2000] 2 C.T.C. 2921 (TCC).

Certain members of armed forces visiting Canada are deemed non-resident and exempt from Canadian income tax (see also 149(1)(a) in this regard). Section 22 of the *Visiting Forces Act*, R.S.C. 1985, c. V-2, provides:

22. (1) **Residence or domicile** — Where the liability for any form of taxation in Canada depends on residence or domicile, a period during which a member of a visiting force is in Canada by reason of his being a member of such visiting force shall, for the purpose of such taxation, be deemed not to be a period of residence in Canada and not to create a change of residence or domicile.

(2) **Salaries** — A member of a visiting force is exempt from taxation in Canada on the salary and emoluments paid to him as such member by a designated state and in respect of any tangible personal property that is in Canada temporarily by reason of his presence in Canada as such member.

(3) **Resident Canadian citizens excepted** — For the purposes of this section, the term "member of a visiting force" does not include a Canadian citizen resident or ordinarily resident in Canada.

250(1)(e) repealed by 1998 Budget, effective after February 23, 1998 except that, where

(a) any person would, but for 250(1)(e),

(i) have been non-resident at any time before February 24, 1998 and

(ii) not have become resident in Canada after that time and before February 24, 1998, and

(b) the person does not elect in writing filed with Revenue Canada with the person's Part I return for 1998 to have the repeal apply after February 23, 1998

the repeal does not apply in respect of the person before the first time after February 23, 1998 that the person would, but for 250(1)(e), cease to be resident in Canada.

Before February 24, 1998, read:

(e) was resident in Canada in any previous year and was, at any time in the year, the spouse of a person described in paragraph 250(1) (b), (c), (d) or (d.1) living with that person;

250(1)(f) amended by 1999 Budget, effective for 1999 and later taxation years, to delete "the total of $500 and" before "the amount used". However, for the 1999 taxation year, instead of "the amount used..." etc., read "$7,044."

250(1)(f) amended to add "the total of $500 and" by 1998 Budget, effective for 1998 and later taxation years. This reflects the supplementary credit under 118(1)B(b.1) that increases the amount of income that can be earned tax-free from $6,456 to $6,956 for 1998.

250(1)(f) amended by 1992 Child Benefit bill and by 1993 technical bill, effective for 1993 and later taxation years. For 1988 through 1992, read:

(f) he was at any time in the year a child of a person described in paragraph (b), (c), (d) or (d.1) and a dependant, as described in paragraph 118(1)(d), of that person.

250(1)(g) added by 1998 Budget, effective February 24, 1998.

**Regulations**: 3400 (prescribed international development assistance program, for 250(1)(d)).

**Remission Orders**: *Income Earned in Quebec Income Tax Remission Order*, P.C. 1989-1204 (remission to certain individuals linked with Quebec but not resident in a province on the last day of the year).

**Interpretation Bulletins**: IT-91R4: Employment at special work sites or remote work locations; IT-106R2: Crown corporation employees abroad; IT-178R3: Moving expenses; IT-193 SR: Taxable income of individuals resident in Canada during part of a year (Special Release); IT-221R2: Determination of an individual's residence status; IT-447: Residence of trust or estate; IT-451R: Deemed disposition and acquisition on ceasing to be or becoming resident in Canada; IT-513R: Personal tax credits; IT-516R2: Tuition tax credit.

**Forms**: NR73: Determination of residency status (leaving Canada); NR74: Determination of residency status (entering Canada).

**(2) Idem** — Where at any time in a taxation year a person described in paragraph (1)(b), (c) or (d) ceases to be a person so described, or a person described in paragraph (1)(d.1) ceases to be a member of the overseas Canadian Forces school staff, that person shall be deemed to have been resident in Canada throughout the part of the year preceding that time and the spouse or common-law partner and child of that person who by reason of paragraph (1)(e) or (f) would, but for this subsection, be deemed to have been resident in Canada throughout the year shall be deemed to have been resident in Canada throughout that part of the year.

**Notes**: 250(2) amended by 2000 same-sex partners bill to add reference to "common-law partner", effective for the 2001 and later taxation years, or earlier by election (see Notes to 248(1) "common-law partner").

**Interpretation Bulletins**: IT-193 SR: Taxable income of individuals resident in Canada during part of a year (Special Release).

**(3) Ordinarily resident** — In this Act, a reference to a person resident in Canada includes a person who was at the relevant time ordinarily resident in Canada.

**Interpretation Bulletins**: IT-193 SR: Taxable income of individuals resident in Canada during part of a year (Special Release); IT-221R2: Determination of a resident's status.

**(4) Corporation deemed resident** — For the purposes of this Act, a corporation shall be deemed to have been resident in Canada throughout a taxation year if

(a) in the case of a corporation incorporated after April 26, 1965, it was incorporated in Canada;

(b) in the case of a corporation that

(i) was incorporated before April 9, 1959,

(ii) was, on June 18, 1971, a foreign business corporation (within the meaning of section 71 of the *Income Tax Act*, chapter 148 of the Revised Statutes of Canada, 1952, as it read in its application to the 1971 taxation year) that was controlled by a corporation resident in Canada,

(iii) throughout the 10 year period ending on June 18, 1971, carried on business in any one particular country other than Canada, and

(iv) during the period referred to in subparagraph (iii), paid dividends to its shareholders resident in Canada on which its shareholders paid tax to the government of the country referred to in that subparagraph,

it was incorporated in Canada and, at any time in the taxation year or at any time in any preceding taxation year commencing after 1971, it was resident in Canada or carried on business in Canada; and

(c) in the case of a corporation incorporated before April 27, 1965 (other than a corporation to which subparagraphs (b)(i) to (iv) apply), it was incorporated in Canada and, at any time in the taxation year or at any time in any preceding taxation year of the corporation ending after April 26, 1965, it was resident in Canada or carried on business in Canada.

**Related Provisions**: 126(1.1)(a) — Authorized foreign bank deemed resident in Canada for foreign tax credit purposes; 128.2 — Predecessor corporations take on residence status of amalgamated corporation; 212(13.3) — Authorized foreign bank deemed resident in Canada for withholding tax purposes; 214(13)(a) — Regulations deeming person resident in Canada for purposes of Part XIII; 250(5) — Corporation deemed not resident; 250(5.1) — Continuance outside Canada; 256(6), (6.1) — Meaning of "controlled".

**Notes**: 250(4) applies to deem a corporation to be resident, most notably by being incorporated under Canadian (federal or provincial) law. However, a corporation can also be resident in Canada under the common-law test of having its "central management and control" (or "mind and management") in Canada. See the case law on the residence of corporations. See also Notes to 219.1.

**I.T. Application Rules**: 69 (meaning of "*Income Tax Act*, chapter 148 of the Revised Statutes of Canada, 1952").

**Interpretation Bulletins**: IT-451R: Deemed disposition and acquisition on ceasing to be or becoming resident in Canada.

**(5) Deemed non-resident** — Notwithstanding any other provision of this Act, a person is deemed not to be resident in Canada at a time if, at that time, the person would, but for this subsection and any tax treaty, be resident in Canada for the purposes of this Act but is, under a tax treaty with another country, resident in the other country and not resident in Canada.

**Related Provisions**: 128.1(4) — Corporation becoming non-resident; 219.1 — Tax payable when corporation becomes non-resident.

**Notes**: 250(5) amended by 1998 Budget, effective after February 24, 1998 except that, if on that day an individual was, under a tax treaty (as defined in 248(1)), resident in another country, the amendment is effective the first time after February 24, 1998 at which the individual becomes, under a tax treaty with a country other than Canada, resident in the other country. [This wording will be clarified; see Proposed Amendment below.] Before February 25, 1998, read:

(5) Corporation deemed not resident — Notwithstanding subsection (4), for the purposes of this Act, a corporation, other than a prescribed corporation, shall be deemed to be not resident in Canada at any time if, by virtue of an agreement or convention between the Government of Canada and the government of another country that has the force of law in Canada, it would at that time, if it had income from a source outside Canada, not be subject to tax on that income under Part I.

The amendment extends the rule from corporations to all persons. It treats as a non-resident any individual who would otherwise be resident in Canada but has become entitled under a tax treaty, as a resident of another country, to an exemption from or reduction in Canadian income tax. This is to prevent an individual from arguing that they are simultaneously resident in Canada under Canadian domestic rules (and therefore not subject to Canadian non-resident tax), and resident in the treaty country under the treaty (and therefore not subject to taxation as a resident of Canada).

The original 250(5) is designed to prevent setting up a corporation incorporated outside Canada and qualifying as non-resident under treaty tie-breaker rules (Article 4 of most tax treaties) but with management and control in Canada, as a mechanism for avoiding withholding tax on dividends under 212(2). Absent 250(5), a dividend paid by a Canadian subsidiary to such a corporation would be exempt from withholding tax because the corporation would be resident in Canada under the "management and control" test. (Dividends from the corporation to its foreign parent will not be subject to Canadian withholding tax because the corporation is resident in the foreign country under the treaty tie-breaker rules.)

**Regulations**: No prescribed corporations to date.

**Interpretation Bulletins**: IT-137R3: Additional tax on certain corporations carrying on business in Canada.

### Proposed Amendment — Application of 1998 Budget amendment to 250(5)

**Application**: Bill C-43 (First Reading September 20, 2000), s. 122, will amend the application of the amendment made to subsec. 250(5) by S.C. 1999, c. 22, s. 82 (1999 Budget bill) so that it is applicable after February 24, 1998 except that, if on that day an individual who would, but for a tax treaty (as defined in subsec. 248(1)), be resident in Canada for the purposes of the *Income Tax Act* is, under the tax treaty, resident in another country, the amendment does not apply to the individual until the first time after February 24, 1998 at which the individual becomes, under a tax treaty, resident in a country other than Canada.

The amendment to the application is deemed to have come into force on June 17, 1999.

**Technical Notes**: Prior to 1998, subsection 250(5) contained a deeming rule applicable to corporations — where a corporation that would otherwise be resident in Canada was, under a tax treaty between Canada and another country, resident in the other country, the rule deemed the corporation not to be resident in Canada for the purposes of the *Income Tax Act*.

Subsections 82(4) and 82(8) of the *Income Tax Amendments Act, 1998* [1995-97 technical bill — ed.] extended this rule to both corporations and other persons — new subsection 250(5) deems a person not to be resident in Canada at a time if, at that time, the person, who would otherwise be resident in Canada under the *Income Tax Act*, "tie-breaks" under a tax treaty as a resident of a treaty country. This new rule was intended to be effective after February 24, 1998, except that an individual who was resident both in Canada and in a treaty country on that day was not to be subject to the new rule until the first time after February 24, 1998 at which that individual "tie-breaks" as a resident of a treaty country other than Canada.

Due to a possible ambiguity in the wording of the coming-into-force provision, subsection 82(8) of the *Income Tax Amendments Act, 1998* is now being clarified to ensure that amended subsection 250(5) applies as described above.

The new coming-into-force provision is deemed to have come into force on June 17, 1999, the day on which the *Income Tax Amendments Act, 1998* received Royal Assent.

### Proposed Amendment — 250(5)

**(5) Deemed non-resident** — Despite any other provision of this Act (other than paragraph 126(1.1)(a)), a person is deemed not to be resident in Canada at a time if, at that time, the person would, but for this subsection and any tax treaty, be resident in Canada for the purposes of this Act but is, under a tax treaty with another country, resident in the other country and not resident in Canada.

**Application**: The August 8, 2000 draft legislation, s. 26, will amend subsec. 250(5) to read as above, applicable after June 27, 1999.

**Technical Notes**: Subsection 250(5) deems a person not to be resident in Canada at a time if, at that time, the person, who would otherwise be resident in Canada under the Act, "tie-breaks" under a tax treaty as a resident of a treaty country.

Although non-resident, an authorized foreign bank may in certain cases claim foreign tax credits under section 126. This is accomplished by an amendment to that section (new paragraph 126(1.1)(a)) that treats the bank as resident in Canada for foreign tax credit purposes.

This amendment to subsection 250(5) ensures that the residence deeming rule in new paragraph 126(1.1)(a) is not overridden by subsection 250(5). That is, an authorized foreign bank may still be deemed to be resident in Canada for foreign tax credit purposes, even if subsection 250(5) confirms that it is resident in another country for other purposes.

This amendment applies after June 27, 1999.

**(5.1) Continued corporation** — Where a corporation is at any time (in this subsection referred to as the "time of continuation") granted articles of continuance (or similar constitutional documents) in a particular jurisdiction, the corporation shall

(a) for the purposes of applying this Act (other than subsection (4)) in respect of all times from the time of continuation until the time, if any, of continuation in a different jurisdiction, be deemed to have been incorporated in the particular jurisdiction and not to have been incorporated in any other jurisdiction; and

(b) for the purpose of applying subsection (4) in respect of all times from the time of continuation until the time, if any, of continuation in a different jurisdiction, be deemed to have been incorporated in the particular jurisdiction at the time of continuation and not to have been incorporated in any other jurisdiction.

**Related Provisions**: 54"superficial loss"(c) — Non-application of superficial loss rule where corporation has elected for 250(5.1) to apply before 1993; 88.1 — Repeal of 88.1 before 1993 where corporation so elects; Canada-U.S. tax treaty Art. IV:3 — Continuation in other jurisdictions.

**Notes**: 250(5.1) added by 1993 technical bill. The date on which a corporation is granted articles of continuation or similar constitutional documents is the corporation's "time of continuation". 250(5.1) applies as follows:

- If the time of continuation is July 1994 or later, 250(5.1) applies.
- If the time of continuation is January 1, 1993 through June 30, 1994, then 250(5.1) applies, unless arrangements evidenced in writing for obtaining the articles or other documents were substantially advanced before December 21, 1992, *and* the corporation elected by notifying Revenue Canada in writing by Decem-

ber 31, 1994 to have 250(5.1) not apply. (This election is under para. 111(4)(b) of the 1993 technical bill, S.C. 1994, c. 21.)

- If the time of continuation is before 1993, then 250(5.1) applies only if the corporation elected by notifying Revenue Canada in writing by December 31, 1994 to have it apply. (This election is under para. 111(4)(a) of the 1993 technical bill.) If this was done, then notwithstanding 152(4) to (5), such assessments and determinations in respect of any taxation year shall be made as are necessary to give effect to the election.

The basic principle of 250(5.1) is that the continued corporation is treated as having been incorporated in the jurisdiction into which it has continued.

**Interpretation Bulletins**: IT-137R3: Additional tax on certain corporations carrying on business in Canada.

## (6) Residence of international shipping corporation

— For the purposes of this Act, a corporation that was incorporated or otherwise formed under the laws of a country other than Canada or of a state, province or other political subdivision of such a country shall be deemed to be resident in that country throughout a taxation year and not to be resident in Canada at any time in the year, where

(a) the corporation

(i) has as its principal business in the year the operation of ships that are used primarily in transporting passengers or goods in international traffic (determined on the assumption that the corporation is non-resident and that, except where paragraph (c) of the definition "international traffic" in subsection 248(1) applies, any port or other place on the Great Lakes or St. Lawrence River is in Canada), or

(ii) holds throughout the year shares of one or more other corporations, each of which

(A) is a subsidiary wholly-owned corporation of the corporation as defined by subsection 87(1.4), and

(B) is deemed by this subsection to be resident in a country other than Canada throughout the year,

and at no time in the year is the total of the cost amounts to the corporation of all those shares less than 50% of the total of the cost amounts to it of all its property;

(b) all or substantially all of the corporation's gross revenue for the year consists of

(i) gross revenue from the operation of ships in transporting passengers or goods in that international traffic,

(ii) dividends from one or more other corporations each of which

(A) is a subsidiary wholly-owned corporation of the corporation, as defined by subsection 87(1.4), and

(B) is deemed by this subsection to be resident in a country other than Canada throughout each of its taxation years that began after February 1991 and before the last time at which it paid any of those dividends, or

(iii) a combination of amounts described in subparagraph (i) or (ii); and

(c) the corporation was not granted articles of continuance in Canada before the end of the year.

**Related Provisions**: 81(1)(c) — Amounts not included in income — ship or aircraft of non-residents; Canada-U.S. tax treaty, Art. VIII — International shipping.

**Notes**: 250(6)(a) and (b) amended by 1995-97 technical bill, effective for 1995 and later taxation years, effectively to add (a)(ii) and (b)(ii). Before the amendment, read:

(a) the corporation's principal business in the year consists of the operation of ships that are used primarily in transporting passengers or goods in international traffic (determined on the assumption that the corporation is non-resident and that, except where paragraph (c) of the definition "international traffic" in subsection 248(1) applies, any port or other place on the Great Lakes or St. Lawrence River is in Canada);

(b) all or substantially all of the corporation's gross revenue for the year is from the operation of ships in transporting passengers or goods in such international traffic; and

250(6) added by 1991 technical bill, effective for taxation years that begin in March 1991 or later.

The CCRA takes the position that "all or substantially all", used in 250(6)(b), means 90% or more.

### Proposed Addition — 250(6.1)

**(6.1) Residence of *inter vivos* trusts** — For the purposes of provisions of this Act that apply to a trust for a taxation year only where the trust has been resident in Canada throughout the year, where a particular trust ceases at any time to exist and the particular trust was resident in Canada immediately before that time, the particular trust is deemed to be resident in Canada throughout the period that begins at that time and ends at the end of the year.

**Application**: Bill C-43 (First Reading September 20, 2000), s. 114, will add subsec. 250(6.1), applicable to 1990 *et seq.*

**Technical Notes**: New subsection 250(6.1) applies where a trust ceases to exist. The subsection provides that a trust that ceases to exist at any time in a calendar year, and that was resident in Canada immediately before it ceased to exist, is deemed to be resident in Canada during the remaining period in the year. The CCRA takes the position that a trust's taxation year is generally not affected by the termination of the trust. Subsection 250(6.1) is meant to avoid unintended consequences of the CCRA's position that arise under a number of provisions of the Act that require a trust to be resident in Canada throughout a taxation year (e.g. flow-through rules under section 104). Subsection 250(6.1) is similar to new subsection 132(6.2), described in the commentary above.

**Related Provisions**: 132(6.2) — Parallel rule for mutual fund trust that ceases to qualify as such.

**Interpretation Bulletins**: IT-447: Residence of trust or estate.

## (7) Residence of a qualifying environmental trust

— For the purposes of this Act, where a trust resident in Canada would be a qualifying environmental trust at any time if it were resident at that time in the province in which the site to which the trust relates is situated, the trust is deemed to be resident at that time in that province and in no other province.

**Notes**: 250(7) added by 1994 Budget, effective 1994; and amended by 1997 Budget, effective 1996, to change "mining reclamation trust" to "qualifying environmental trust". (The same change was made throughout the Act.)

**Definitions [s. 250]**: "amount", "business" — 248(1); "Canada" — 255, *Interpretation Act* 35(1); "child" — 252(1); "common-law partner" — 248(1); "controlled" — 256(6), (6.1); "corporation", "employment", "gross revenue" — 248(1); "incorporated in Canada" — 248(1) "corporation incorporated in Canada"; "individual", "international traffic", "non-resident", "overseas Canadian Forces school staff", "person", "prescribed" — 248(1); "province" — *Interpretation Act* 35(1); "qualifying environmental trust" — 248(1); "related" — 251(2)–(6); "servant" — 248(1) "employment"; "subsidiary wholly-owned corporation" — 87(1.4), 248(1); "tax treaty" — 248(1); "taxation year" — 249; "trust" — 104(1), 248(1), (3).

### Proposed Addition — 250.1

**250.1 Non-resident person's taxation year and income** — For greater certainty, unless the context requires otherwise

(a) a taxation year of a non-resident person shall be determined, except as permitted by the Minister, in the same manner as the taxation year of a person resident in Canada; and

(b) a person for whom income for a taxation year is determined in accordance with this Act includes a non-resident person.

**Application**: Bill C-43 (First Reading September 20, 2000), s. 115, will add s. 250.1, applicable after December 17, 1999.

**Technical Notes**: New section 250.1 contains clarifying rules that apply for greater certainty, unless the context requires otherwise.

New paragraph 250.1(a) provides that, unless the Minister of National Revenue provides otherwise, the taxation year of a non-resident person is determined in the same manner as that of a person resident in Canada.

New paragraph 250.1(b) clarifies that a person for whom "income" for the year is determined in accordance with the Act includes a non-resident person. It is a non-resident person's "taxable income earned in Canada" that is relevant for the purposes of computing the person's tax liability under Part I. However, a non-resident person does, in some narrow cases, have "income" for purposes of the Act. For example, there are references to a non-resident's "income" (rather than "taxable income earned in Canada") in paragraphs 212(1)(c) and 216(1)(b) and subparagraph 217(3)(b)(ii). In addition, the "income" of a non-resident person may affect the tax liability of a person resident in Canada (e.g., subsection 104(13)).

**Related Provisions**: 2(3) — Tax on taxable income earned in Canada of non-resident; 115(1) — Calculation of taxable income earned in Canada of non-resident.

**Definitions [s. 250.1]**: "Minister", "non-resident", "person" — 248(1); "resident in Canada" — 250; "taxation year" — 249.

**251. (1) Arm's length** — For the purposes of this Act,

(a) related persons shall be deemed not to deal with each other at arm's length; and

(b) it is a question of fact whether persons not related to each other were at a particular time dealing with each other at arm's length.

### Proposed Amendment — 251(1)(b), (c)

(b) a taxpayer and a personal trust (other than a trust described in any of paragraphs (a) to (e.1) of the definition "trust" in subsection 108(1)) are deemed not to deal with each other at arm's length if the taxpayer, or any person not dealing at arm's length with the taxpayer, would be beneficially interested in the trust if subsection 248(25) were read without reference to subclauses 248(25)(b)(iii)(A)(II) to (IV); and

(c) where paragraph (b) does not apply, it is a question of fact whether persons not related to each other are at a particular time dealing with each other at arm's length.

**Application**: Bill C-43 (First Reading September 20, 2000), s. 116, will amend para. 251(1)(b) to read as above, and add para. (c), applicable after December 23, 1998, except that para. (b) shall, for the purpose of applying the definition "taxable Canadian property" in subsec. 248(1), not apply in respect of property acquired before December 24, 1998.

**Technical Notes**: Section 251 defines the circumstances in which persons are considered not to deal with each other at arm's length for the purposes of the Act.

Subsection 251(1) is amended to ensure that a taxpayer and a specified personal trust (i.e., a personal trust other than one described in any of paragraphs (a) to (e.1) of the definition "trust" in subsection 108(1)) are deemed not to deal with each other at arm's length if the taxpayer, or any person not dealing at arm's length with the taxpayer, is beneficially interested in the trust. (In determining whether a person is "beneficially interested" in a trust for this purpose, subsection 248(25) is read without reference to subclauses 248(25)(b)(iii)(A)(II) to (IV), which provide an extended meaning of this expression.) The non-arm's length relationship is relevant, for example, in applying amended subsection 69(1).

**Letter from Department of Finance, April 1, 1999**:

Dear [xxx]

This is in reply to your letter of February 23, 1999 concerning a proposed amendment to section 251 of the *Income Tax Act* that was part of the Legislative Proposals on Trusts released by the Department of Finance on December 23, 1999.

We have examined the application of this amendment as it applies in the circumstances raised in your letter and in other circumstances. From a tax policy perspective, our view is that the amendment in its present form may be too broad. Consequently, we will recommend that the application of this amendment be limited to "personal trusts", as defined in subsection 248(1) of the Act.

Thank you for writing on this matter.

Yours sincerely,

Brian Ernewein
Director, Tax Legislation Division, Tax Policy Branch

**Notes**: Note the extremely wide definition of "beneficially interested" in 248(25).

**Related Provisions**: 7(1.11) — Whether mutual fund trust at arm's length with corporation for purposes of stock option rules;

**S. 251(1)**      Income Tax Act

55(4) — Arm's length dealings; 55(5)(e) — Siblings deemed to deal at arm's length for purposes of s. 55; 66(17) — Non-arm's length partnerships; 84.1(2)(b), (d) — Non-arm's length sale of shares; 88(1)(d.2) — Whether parties dealing at arm's length for bump of cost base of property on windup of corporation; 95(2.1) — Whether taxpayer dealing with foreign affiliate at arm's length for certain purposes; 107.4(4) — Certain dispositions by trust deemed not at arm's length; 143.2(14) — Parties deemed not dealing at arm's length for tax shelter cost calculation where information located outside Canada; 212.1(3)(c) — Non-arm's length sales of shares by non-residents; 247 — Calculation of profit on non-arm's length transactions with non-residents (transfer pricing); 248(25) — Meaning of "beneficially interested"; Reg. 1102(20) — Taxpayers deemed at arm's length for certain purposes relating to depreciable property; Reg. 1204(1.2) — Whether partners and partnerships deal at arm's length for purposes of resource allowance.

**Notes**: Despite 251(1)(b) (draft (c)), the Tax Court of Canada has stated that "whether, on the facts, there is in law an arm's-length relationship is necessarily a question of law... All that para. 251(1)(b) means is that in determining whether, as a matter of law, unrelated persons are at arm's length, the factual underpinning of the relationship must be ascertained." *RMM Canadian Enterprises (Equilease Corp.)*, [1998] 1 C.T.C. 2300, per Bowman J.

For the leading cases on the meaning of arm's length, see *Swiss Bank Corp.*, [1972] C.T.C. 614; *Sheldon's Engineering Ltd.*, [1955] C.T.C. 174 (SCC); and *Merritt Estate*, [1969] C.T.C. 207 (Exch. Ct.).

**Interpretation Bulletins**: IT-419R: Meaning of arm's length.

**Information Circulars**: 80-10R: Registered charities: operating a registered charity.

**Advance Tax Rulings**: ATR-58: Divisive reorganization.

**(2) Definition of "related persons"** — For the purpose of this Act, "related persons", or persons related to each other, are

  (a) individuals connected by blood relationship, marriage or common-law partnership or adoption;

  (b) a corporation and

    (i) a person who controls the corporation, if it is controlled by one person,

    (ii) a person who is a member of a related group that controls the corporation, or

    (iii) any person related to a person described in subparagraph (i) or (ii); and

  (c) any two corporations

    (i) if they are controlled by the same person or group of persons,

    (ii) if each of the corporations is controlled by one person and the person who controls one of the corporations is related to the person who controls the other corporation,

    (iii) if one of the corporations is controlled by one person and that person is related to any member of a related group that controls the other corporation,

    (iv) if one of the corporations is controlled by one person and that person is related to each member of an unrelated group that controls the other corporation,

    (v) if any member of a related group that controls one of the corporations is related to each member of an unrelated group that controls the other corporation, or

    (vi) if each member of an unrelated group that controls one of the corporations is related to at least one member of an unrelated group that controls the other corporation.

**Related Provisions**: 55(5)(e) — Siblings deemed not related for purposes of s. 55; 80(2)(j) — Interpretation of "related" for debt forgiveness rules; 104(5.7)(b) — Designated contributor; 190.15(6) — Related financial institution; 248(14) — Corporations deemed related for certain purposes; 251(3) — Corporations related through a third corporation; 251(3.1), (3.2) — Amalgamated corporation deemed related to predecessors; 251(6) — Meaning of blood relationship, marriage and adoption; 256(6), (6.1) — Meaning of "controlled"; Canada-U.S. tax treaty, Art. IX:2 — Meaning of "related" for treaty purposes.

**Notes**: 251(2)(a) amended by 2000 same-sex partners bill to add reference to "common-law partnership", effective for the 2001 and later taxation years, or earlier by election (see Notes to 248(1)"common-law partner").

**Interpretation Bulletins**: IT-363R2: Deferred profit sharing plans — deductibility of employer contributions and taxation of amounts received by a beneficiary; IT-419R: Meaning of arm's length; IT-495R2: Child care expenses; IT-513R: Personal tax credits.

**Information Circulars**: 80-10R: Registered charities: operating a registered charity.

**(3) Corporations related through a third corporation** — Where two corporations are related to the same corporation within the meaning of subsection (2), they shall, for the purposes of subsections (1) and (2), be deemed to be related to each other.

**(3.1) Relation where amalgamation or merger** — Where there has been an amalgamation or merger of two or more corporations and the new corporation formed as a result of the amalgamation or merger and any predecessor corporation would have been related immediately before the amalgamation or merger if the new corporation were in existence at that time, and if the persons who were the shareholders of the new corporation immediately after the amalgamation or merger were the shareholders of the new corporation at that time, the new corporation and any such predecessor corporation shall be deemed to have been related persons.

**Related Provisions**: 251(3.2) — Further deeming on amalgamation of related corporations.

**Interpretation Bulletins**: IT-419R: Meaning of arm's length.

**(3.2) Amalgamation of related corporations** — Where there has been an amalgamation or merger of 2 or more corporations each of which was related (otherwise than because of a right referred to in paragraph (5)(b)) to each other immediately before the amalgamation or merger, the new corporation formed as a result of the amalgamation or merger and each of the predecessor corporations is[33] deemed to have been related to each other.

**Notes**: 251(3.2) added by 1995-97 technical bill, effective for amalgamations and mergers that occur after 1996.

**(4) Definitions concerning groups** — In this Act,

**"related group"** means a group of persons each member of which is related to every other member of the group;

**Notes**: 251(4)"related group" was 251(4)(a) before R.S.C. 1985 (5th Supp.) consolidation, effective December 1, 1991.

**Interpretation Bulletins**: IT-419R: Meaning of arm's length.

**"unrelated group"** means a group of persons that is not a related group.

**Interpretation Bulletins**: IT-419R: Meaning of arm's length.

**Notes**: 251(4)"related group" was 251(4)(a), and "unrelated group" was 251(4)(b), before consolidation in R.S.C. 1985 (5th Supp.), effective December 1, 1991.

**(5) Control by related groups, options, etc.** — For the purposes of subsection (2) and the definition "Canadian-controlled private corporation" in subsection 125(7),

(a) where a related group is in a position to control a corporation, it shall be deemed to be a related group that controls the corporation whether or not it is part of a larger group by which the corporation is in fact controlled;

(b) where at any time a person has a right under a contract, in equity or otherwise, either immediately or in the future and either absolutely or contingently,

(i) to, or to acquire, shares of the capital stock of a corporation or to control the voting rights of such shares, the person shall, except where the right is not exercisable at that time because the exercise thereof is contingent on the death, bankruptcy or permanent disability of an individual, be deemed to have the same position in relation to the control of the corporation as if the person owned the shares at that time,

(ii) to cause a corporation to redeem, acquire or cancel any shares of its capital stock owned by other shareholders of the corporation, the person shall, except where the right is not exercisable at that time because the exercise thereof is contingent on the death, bankruptcy or permanent disability of an individual, be deemed to have the same position in relation to the control of the corporation as if the shares were so redeemed, acquired or cancelled by the corporation at that time,

(iii) to, or to acquire or control, voting rights in respect of shares of the capital stock of a corporation, the person is, except where the right is not exercisable at that time because its exercise is contingent on the death, bankruptcy or permanent disability of an individual, deemed to have the same position in relation to the control of the corporation as if the person could exercise the voting rights at that time, or

(iv) to cause the reduction of voting rights in respect of shares, owned by other shareholders, of the capital stock of a corporation, the person is, except where the right is not exercisable at that time because its exercise is contingent on the death, bankruptcy or permanent disability of an individual, deemed to have the same position in relation to the control of the corporation as if the voting rights were so reduced at that time; and

(c) where a person owns shares in two or more corporations, the person shall as shareholder of one of the corporations be deemed to be related to himself, herself or itself as shareholder of each of the other corporations.

**Related Provisions**: 17(11.1) — Limitation on 251(5)(b) re loans to non-residents; 110.6(14)(b) — Right under share purchase agreement does not trigger 251(5)(b) for purposes of capital gains exemption; 256(6), (6.1) — Meaning of "controlled"; 256(8) — Deemed acquisition of shares.

**Notes**: 251(5)(b) opening words amended by 1995-97 technical bill, effective April 27, 1995, to add the word "at any time".

251(5)(b)(i) and (ii) amended by 1991 technical bill, effective July 14, 1990, primarily to delete the words "the contract provides that" before the words "the right is not exercisable". For taxation years commencing after 1988 and until July 13, 1990, read:

(i) to, or to acquire, shares in a corporation, or to control the voting rights of shares in a corporation, shall, except where the contract provides that the right is not exercisable until the death, bankruptcy or permanent disability of an individual designated therein, be deemed to have the same position in relation to the control of the corporation as if he owned the shares, or

(ii) to cause a corporation to redeem, acquire or cancel any shares of its capital stock owned by other shareholders of the corporation shall, except where the contract provides that the right is not exercisable until the death, bankruptcy or permanent disability of an individual designated therein, be deemed to have the same position in relation to the control of the corporation as if the shares were redeemed, acquired or cancelled by the corporation; and

251(5)(b)(iii) and (iv) added by 1995-97 technical bill, effective April 27, 1995.

**Interpretation Bulletins**: IT-64R3: Corporations: association and control — after 1988; IT-151R5: Scientific research and experimental development expenditures; IT-243R4: Dividend refund to private corporations; IT-302R3: Losses of a corporation — the effect that acquisitions of control, amalgamations, and windings-up have on their deductibility — after January 15, 1987; IT-400: Exploration and development expenses — meaning of principal-business corporation; IT-419R: Meaning of arm's length; IT-458R2: Canadian-controlled private corporation.

**Advance Tax Rulings**: ATR-13: Corporations not associated;.

---

[33]*Sic*. Should be "are" — ed.

**(6) Blood relationship, etc.** — For the purposes of this Act, persons are connected by

(a) blood relationship if one is the child or other descendant of the other or one is the brother or sister of the other;

(b) marriage if one is married to the other or to a person who is so connected by blood relationship to the other; and

(b.1) common-law partnership if one is in a common-law partnership with the other or with a person who is connected by blood relationship to the other; and

(c) adoption if one has been adopted, either legally or in fact, as the child of the other or as the child of a person who is so connected by blood relationship (otherwise than as a brother or sister) to the other.

**Notes**: 251(6)(b.1) added by 2000 same-sex partners bill, effective for the 2001 and later taxation years, or earlier by election (see Notes to 248(1)"common-law partner").

**Interpretation Bulletins**: IT-419R: Meaning of arm's length; IT-495R2: Child care expenses; IT-513R: Personal tax credits.

**Information Circulars**: 80-10R: Registered charities: operating a registered charity.

**Definitions [s. 251]**: "beneficially interested" — 248(25); "brother" — 252(2); "child" — 252(1); "common-law partnership" — 248(1); "connected" — 251(6); "control", "controlled" — 256(6), (6.1); "corporation", "individual" — 248(1); "person" — 248(1); "personal trust" — 251.1; "related group" — 251(4); "share", "shareholder" — 248(1); "sister" — 252(2); "unrelated group" — 251(4).

**251.1 (1) Definition of "affiliated persons"** — For the purposes of this Act, "affiliated persons", or persons affiliated with each other, are

(a) an individual and a spouse or common-law partner of the individual;

(b) a corporation and

(i) a person by whom the corporation is controlled,

(ii) each member of an affiliated group of persons by which the corporation is controlled, and

(iii) a spouse or common-law partner of a person described in subparagraph (i) or (ii);

(c) two corporations, if

(i) each corporation is controlled by a person, and the person by whom one corporation is controlled is affiliated with the person by whom the other corporation is controlled,

(ii) one corporation is controlled by a person, the other corporation is controlled by a group of persons, and each member of that group is affiliated with that person, or

(iii) each corporation is controlled by a group of persons, and each member of each group is affiliated with at least one member of the other group;

(d) a corporation and a partnership, if the corporation is controlled by a particular group of persons each member of which is affiliated with at least one member of a majority-interest group of partners of the partnership, and each member of that majority-interest group is affiliated with at least one member of the particular group;

(e) a partnership and a majority interest partner of the partnership; and

(f) two partnerships, if

(i) the same person is a majority-interest partner of both partnerships,

(ii) a majority-interest partner of one partnership is affiliated with each member of a majority-interest group of partners of the other partnership, or

(iii) each member of a majority-interest group of partners of each partnership is affiliated with at least one member of a majority-interest group of partners of the other partnership.

**Related Provisions**: 251.1(3), (4) — Definitions and interpretation; 256(6), (6.1) — Meaning of "controlled".

**Notes**: See Notes at end of 251.1.

251.1(1) amended by 2000 same-sex partners bill to add reference to "common-law partner", effective for the 2001 and later taxation years, or earlier by election (see Notes to 248(1)"common-law partner").

**I.T. Technical News**: No. 9 (loss consolidation within a corporate group — "affiliated" test to apply).

**(2) Affiliation where amalgamation or merger** — Where at any time 2 or more corporations (in this subsection referred to as the "predecessors") amalgamate or merge to form a new corporation, the new corporation and any predecessor are deemed to have been affiliated with each other where they would have been affiliated with each other immediately before that time if

(a) the new corporation had existed immediately before that time; and

(b) the persons who were the shareholders of the new corporation immediately after that time had been the shareholders of the new corporation immediately before that time.

**Notes**: See Notes at end of 251.1.

**(3) Definitions** — The definitions in this subsection apply in this section.

**"affiliated group of persons"** means a group of persons each member of which is affiliated with every other member.

**Notes**: See Notes at end of 251.1.

**"controlled"** means controlled, directly or indirectly in any manner whatever.

**Related Provisions**: 256(5.1), (6.2) — Controlled directly or indirectly — control in fact.

"**majority-interest group of partners**" of a partnership means a group of persons each of whom has an interest in the partnership such that

(a) if one person held the interests of all members of the group, that person would be a majority interest partner of the partnership; and

(b) if any member of the group were not a member, the test described in paragraph (a) would not be met.

**Notes**: See Notes at end of 251.1.

**(4) Interpretation** — For the purposes of this section,

(a) persons are affiliated with themselves; and

(b) a person includes a partnership.

**Notes [s. 251.1]**: 251.1 added by 1995-97 technical bill, effective April 27, 1995. It was introduced as part of the "suspended pregnant loss" anti-avoidance rules. See Notes to 13(21.2) and 40(3.4).

**Definitions [s. 251.1]**: "affiliated" — 251.1(1), (4)(a); "affiliated group" — 251.1(3); "common-law partner" — 248(1); "control", "controlled" — 256(6), (6.1); "controlled directly or indirectly" — 256(5.1), (6.2); "corporation" — 248(1), *Interpretation Act* 35(1); "individual" — 248(1); "majority-interest group of partners" — 251.1(3); "majority interest partner" — 248(1); "partnership" — see Notes to 96(1); "person" — 248(1), 251.1(4)(b).

**252. (1) Extended meaning of "child"** — In this Act, words referring to a child of a taxpayer include

(a) a person of whom the taxpayer is the natural parent whether the person was born within or outside marriage;

(b) a person who is wholly dependent on the taxpayer for support and of whom the taxpayer has, or immediately before the person attained the age of 19 years had, in law or in fact, the custody and control;

(c) a child of the taxpayer's spouse or common-law partner;

(d) an adopted child of the taxpayer; and

(e) a spouse or common-law partner of a child of the taxpayer.

**Related Provisions**: 70(10) — Extended meaning of "child" for certain purposes; 75.1(2) — Extended meaning of "child"; 110.6(1) — Extended meaning of "child" for purposes of capital gains exemption.

**Notes**: 252(1) amended by 2000 same-sex partners bill to add reference to "common-law partner", effective for the 2001 and later taxation years, or earlier by election (see Notes to 248(1)"common-law partner").

**I.T. Application Rules**: 20(1.11) (extended meaning of "child" re disposition of depreciable property owned since before 1972); 26(20) (extended meaning of "child" re transfer of farmland owned since before 1972).

**Interpretation Bulletins**: IT-268R4: *Inter vivos* transfer of farm property to child; IT-349R3: Intergenerational transfers of farm property on death; IT-394R2: Preferred beneficiary election; IT-495R2: Child care expenses; IT-513R: Personal tax credits; IT-516R2: Tuition tax credit.

**(2) Relationships** — In this Act, words referring to

(a) a parent of a taxpayer include a person

(i) whose child the taxpayer is,

(ii) whose child the taxpayer had previously been within the meaning of paragraph (1)(b), or

(iii) who is a parent of the taxpayer's spouse or common-law partner;

(b) a brother of a taxpayer include a person who is

(i) the brother of the taxpayer's spouse or common-law partner, or

(ii) the spouse or common-law partner of the taxpayer's sister;

(c) a sister of a taxpayer include a person who is

(i) the sister of the taxpayer's spouse or common-law partner, or

(ii) the spouse or common-law partner of the taxpayer's brother;

(d) a grandparent of a taxpayer include a person who is

(i) the grandfather or grandmother of the taxpayer's spouse or common-law partner, or

(ii) the spouse or common-law partner of the taxpayer's grandfather or grandmother;

(e) an aunt or uncle of a taxpayer include the spouse or common-law partner of the taxpayer's aunt or uncle, as the case may be;

(f) a great-aunt or great-uncle of a taxpayer include the spouse or common-law partner of the taxpayer's great-aunt or great-uncle, as the case may be; and

(g) a niece or nephew of a taxpayer include the niece or nephew, as the case may be, of the taxpayer's spouse or common-law partner.

**Related Provisions**: 252(1) — Extended meaning of "child".

**Notes**: 252(2) amended by 2000 same-sex partners bill to add reference to "common-law partner", effective for the 2001 and later taxation years, or earlier by election (see Notes to 248(1)"common-law partner").

252(2)(e) and (f) amended by 2000 same-sex partners bill, effective for the 2001 and later taxation years, or earlier by election (see Notes to 248(1)"common-law partner"). They formerly read:

(e) an aunt or great-aunt of a taxpayer include the spouse of the taxpayer's uncle or great-uncle, as the case may be;

(f) an uncle or great-uncle of a taxpayer include the spouse of the taxpayer's aunt or great-aunt, as the case may be; and

252(2) amended by 1992 technical bill, effective 1993, due to the extended meaning of "spouse" in 252(4). (Terms such as "mother-in-law" are no longer appropriate when a "spouse" can be a common-law spouse.) Before 1993, read:

(2) Definitions concerning parents and other relatives — In this Act, words referring to a parent of a taxpayer include a person whose child the taxpayer is, in the taxation year in respect of which the expression is being employed, within the

meaning of subsection (1) or whose child the taxpayer had previously been within the meaning of paragraph (1)(b), and

(a) "brother" includes brother-in-law;

(b) "grandparent" includes grandmother-in-law and grandfather-in-law;

(c) "parent" includes mother-in-law and father-in-law; and

(d) "sister" includes sister-in-law.

**Interpretation Bulletins**: IT-349R3: Intergenerational transfers of farm property on death; IT-513R: Personal tax credits; IT-516R2: Tuition tax credit.

**(3) Extended meaning of "spouse" and "former spouse"** — For the purposes of paragraphs 56(1)(b) and (c), section 56.1, paragraphs 60(b), (c) and (j), section 60.1, subsections 70(6) and (6.1), 73(1) and (5) and 104(4), (5.1) and (5.4), the definition "pre-1972 spousal trust" in subsection 108(1), subsection 146(16), subparagraph 146.3(2)(f)(iv), paragraph 146.3(14)(b), subsections 147.3(5) and (7) and 148(8.1) and (8.2), the definition "small business property" in subsection 206(1), subparagraph 210(c)(ii) and subsections 248(22) and (23), "spouse" and "former spouse" of a particular individual include another individual of the opposite sex who is a party to a voidable or void marriage with the particular individual.

**Related Provisions**: 147.1(1) — RPP — Definition of spouse; Reg. 8500(5) — Rule in 252(3) applies to Regs. 8500–8520.

**Notes**: 252(3) amended by 1999 Budget to add reference to 206(1)"small business property", effective for 1998 and later taxation years.

252(3) amended by 1992 technical bill, effective for 1991 and later taxation years. For earlier years, ignore references to 70(6), 70(6.1), 73(5), 104(4), 104(5.1), 104(5.4) and 108(1)(f.2) (now 108(1)"pre-1972 spousal trust"), and read the last part of the subsec. as:

"spouse" and "former spouse" include a party to a voidable or void marriage, as the case may be

252(3) amended by 1990 pension bill, effective 1989, and by 1991 technical bill, effective 1990. For 1988, ignore the reference to 147.3(5). For 1989, ignore the references to 148(8.1) and (8.2) and 248(22) and (23).

See 252(4) re a further extended meaning of "spouse", which applied from 1993-2000.

**Interpretation Bulletins**: IT-305R4: Testamentary spouse trusts; IT-307R3: Spousal registered retirement savings plans; IT-325R2: Property transfers after separation, divorce and annulment.

**(4) [Repealed.]**

**Notes**: 252(4) repealed by 2000 same-sex partners bill (S.C. 2000, c. 12), effective for the 2001 and later taxation years, or earlier by election (see Notes to 248(1)"common-law partner"). The bill also replaced all references throughout the Act to "spouse" to read "spouse or common-law partner" (and "marriage" to mean "marriage or common-law partnership"). Thus, the extended meaning of "spouse" in 252(4) is no longer needed.

252(4) read:

(4) Idem — In this Act,

(a) words referring to a spouse at any time of a taxpayer include the person of the opposite sex who cohabits at that time with the taxpayer in a conjugal relationship and

(i) has so cohabited with the taxpayer throughout a 12-month period ending before that time, or

(ii) would be a parent of a child of whom the taxpayer would be a parent, if this Act were read without reference to paragraph (1)(e) and subparagraph (2)(a)(iii)

and, for the purposes of this paragraph, where at any time the taxpayer and the person cohabit in a conjugal relationship, they shall, at any particular time after that time, be deemed to be cohabiting in a conjugal relationship unless they were not cohabiting at the particular time for a period of at least 90 days that includes the particular time because of a breakdown of their conjugal relationship;

(b) references to marriage shall be read as if a conjugal relationship between 2 individuals who are, because of paragraph (a), spouses of each other were a marriage;

(c) provisions that apply to a person who is married apply to a person who is, because of paragraph (a), a spouse of a taxpayer; and

(d) provisions that apply to a person who is unmarried do not apply to a person who is, because of paragraph (a), a spouse of a taxpayer.

252(4) added by 1992 technical bill, effective 1993, to treat common-law couples (who meet the definition) as spouses for all purposes. (This means that a person can have more than one "spouse" at the same time.) This can be either good or bad for taxpayers, depending on their circumstances. For discussion of the effects and review of the case law interpreting "cohabit in a conjugal relationship" to 1992, see David M. Sherman, "Till Tax Do Us Part: The New Definition of Spouse", 1992 Canadian Tax Foundation annual conference report, pp. 20:1–20:33.

252(4)(a)(ii) amended by 1993 technical bill and 1995-97 technical bill, both retroactive to the introduction of 252(4), to add and then amend the exclusion. Without it, two parents from opposite sides of a married (or common-law) couple who begin to live together would instantly be deemed to be spouses without waiting 12 months, because of 252(2)(a)(iii).

252(4)(a) was judicially amended by the Ontario Court of Appeal in *Rosenberg v. Canada* (1998), 38 O.R. (3d) 577, to change "of the opposite sex" to "of the opposite or the same sex", for purposes of pension registration. (This decision was not appealed to the Supreme Court of Canada.) Thus, the definition applies to homosexual couples for this purpose. This rule has been codified by the 2000 amendments adding 248(1)"common-law partner", generally effective 2001.

See also Notes to 248(1)"common-law partner".

**Definitions [s. 252]**: "common-law partner" — 248(1); "former spouse" — 252(3); "person" — 248(1); "taxpayer" — 248(1).

**Interpretation Bulletins [s. 252]**: IT-419R: Meaning of "arm's length".

**Information Circulars [s. 252]**: 80-10R: Registered charities: operating a registered charity.

**252.1 Union [as] employer** — All the structural units of a trade union, including each local, branch, national and international unit, shall be deemed to be a single employer and a single entity for the purposes of the provisions of this Act and the regulations relating to

(a) pension adjustments and past service pension adjustments for years after 1994;

(b) the determination of whether a pension plan is, in a year after 1994, a multi-employer plan or a specified multi-employer plan (within the meanings assigned by subsection 147.1(1));

(c) the determination of whether a contribution made under a plan or arrangement is a resident's contribution (within the meaning assigned by subsection 207.6(5.1)); and

(d) the deduction or withholding and the remittance of any amount as required by subsection 153(1) in respect of a contribution made after 1991 under a retirement compensation arrangement.

**Related Provisions**: Reg. 6804(3) — Election by union re foreign pension plan.

**Notes**: 252.1 added by 1993 technical bill, retroactive to October 9, 1986.

**Definitions [s. 252.1]**: "amount" — 248(1); "multi-employer plan" — 147.1(1), Reg. 8500(1), 8510(1); "past service pension adjustment" — 248(1), Reg. 8303(1); "pension adjustment" — 248(1), Reg. 8301(1); "retirement compensation arrangement" — 248(1); "specified multi-employer plan" — 147.1(1), Reg. 8510(2), (3).

## 253. Extended meaning of "carrying on business" [in Canada] — 
For the purposes of this Act, where in a taxation year a person who is a non-resident person or a trust to which Part XII.2 applies

(a) produces, grows, mines, creates, manufactures, fabricates, improves, packs, preserves or constructs, in whole or in part, anything in Canada whether or not the person exports that thing without selling it before exportation,

(b) solicits orders or offers anything for sale in Canada through an agent or servant, whether the contract or transaction is to be completed inside or outside Canada or partly in and partly outside Canada, or

(c) disposes of

(i) Canadian resource property, except where an amount in respect of the disposition is included under paragraph 66.2(1)(a) or 66.4(1)(a),

(ii) property (other than depreciable property) that is a timber resource property or an interest therein or option in respect thereof, or

(iii) property (other than capital property) that is real property situated in Canada, including an interest therein or option in respect thereof, whether or not the property is in existence,

the person shall be deemed, in respect of the activity or disposition, to have been carrying on business in Canada in the year.

**Related Provisions**: 115.2 — Non-resident investment or pension fund deemed not to be carrying on business in Canada for certain purposes; 248(4) — Meaning of "interest in real property".

**Notes**: Although 253 deems many non-residents to be carrying on business in Canada, in many cases such persons are not required to pay Canadian tax because they do not have a permanent establishment in Canada, and are thus protected by tax treaty. See, e.g., Canada-U.S. tax treaty, Art. VII.

For a detailed discussion of s. 253, see Constantine Kyres, "Carrying on Business in Canada", 45(5) *Canadian Tax Journal* 1629-71 (1995).

253(c) and the closing words "in respect of such activity or disposition" added by 1991 technical bill, effective for the 1990 taxation year. However, ignore 253(c) for dispositions before February 21, 1990, as well as for later dispositions pursuant to agreements in writing entered into before February 21, 1990.

**Definitions [s. 253]**: "amount", "business" — 248(1); "Canada" — 255; "Canadian resource property" — 66(15), 248(1); "capital property" — 54, 248(1); "depreciable property" — 13(21), 248(1); "interest" — in real property 248(4); "non-resident", "person", "property" — 248(1); "servant" — 248(1)"employment"; "taxation year" — 249; "timber resource property" — 13(21), 248(1).

**Interpretation Bulletins [s. 253]**: IT-420R3: Non-residents — income earned in Canada.

### Proposed Addition — 253.1

**253.1 Investments in limited partnerships [deemed not carrying on business]** — For the purposes of subparagraph 108(2)(b)(ii), the definition "non-resident investment fund" in subsection 115.2(1), paragraphs 130.1(6)(b), 131(8)(b) and 132(6)(b), the definition "private holding corporation" in subsection 191(1) and regulations made for the purposes of paragraphs 149(1)(o.3) and (o.4), where a trust, corporation or partnership is a member of a particular partnership and, by operation of any law governing the arrangement in respect of the particular partnership, the liability of the member as a member of the particular partnership is limited, the member is deemed

(a) to undertake an investing of its funds because of its acquisition and holding of its interest as a member of the particular partnership; and

(b) not to carry on any business or other activity of the particular partnership.

**Application**: Bill C-43 (First Reading September 20, 2000), s. 117, will add s. 253.1, applicable after 1992.

**Technical Notes**: New section 253.1 applies for the purposes of subparagraph 108(2)(b)(ii) (definition of "unit trust"), the definition "non-resident investment fund" in subsection 115.2(1), paragraphs 130.1(6)(b) (definition of "mortgage investment corporation"), 131(8)(b) (definition of "mutual fund corporation") and 132(6)(b) (definition of "mutual fund trust") and the definition "private holding corporation" in subsection 191(1), where a trust or corporation holds an interest as a limited partner in a limited partnership. Section 253.1 also applies for the purposes of regulations made for the purpose of paragraph 149(1)(o.3) (i.e., section 5101 of the Regulations) and paragraph 149(o.4) (i.e., section 5001 of the Regulations). These regulations define the expressions "small business investment corporation" and "master trust".

For the purposes of applying the above-noted provisions and definitions where a trust, corporation or partnership is a member of a particular limited partnership, the member is deemed

- to undertake an investing of its funds because of its acquisition and holding of its interest as a member of the particular partnership, and

- not to carry on any business or other activity of the particular partnership.

This amendment ensures that the holding of a limited partnership interest by a trust or corporation will not jeopardize the classification of the trust or corporation under specified definitions of the Act and the Regulations. It responds, in part, to the reasoning of the Federal Court of Appeal in *Robinson (Trustee of) v. R.*, [1998] 1 C.T.C. 272, 98 D.T.C. 6065, which, in another context, clarified that limited partners carry on the business of a partnership. As a consequence of this amendment, the meanings of the specified definitions will be determined with reference to new section 253.1 wherever the definitions are used in the Act or Regulations.

This amendment is not, however, intended to suggest that ownership of a unit as a limited partner in a limited partnership is not otherwise an investment for the purposes of the Act. For example, in applying paragraph 149(1)(o.2), it is intended that an interest held by a corporation as a limited partner in a limited partnership be treated as an investment of the corporation.

**Definitions [s. 253.1]**: "business" — 248(1); "corporation" — 248(1), *Interpretation Act* 35(1); "partnership" — see Notes to 96(1); "regulation" — 248(1); "trust" — 104(1), 248(1), (3).

**254. Contract under pension plan** — Where a document has been issued or a contract has been entered into before July 31, 1997 purporting to create, to establish, to extinguish or to be in substitution for, a taxpayer's right to an amount or amounts, immediately or in the future, out of or under a superannuation or pension fund or plan,

(a) if the rights provided for in the document or contract are rights provided for by the superannuation or pension plan or are rights to a payment or payments out of the superannuation or pension fund, and the taxpayer acquired an interest under the document or in the contract before that day, any payment under the document or contract is deemed to be a payment out of or under the superannuation or pension fund or plan and the taxpayer is deemed not to have received, by the issuance of the document or entering into the contract, an amount out of or under the superannuation or pension fund or plan; and

(b) if the rights created or established by the document or contract are not rights provided for by the superannuation or pension plan or a right to payments out of the superannuation or pension fund, an amount equal to the value of the rights created or established by the document or contract shall be deemed to have been received by the taxpayer out of or under the superannuation or pension fund or plan when the document was issued or the contract was entered into.

**Related Provisions**: 60(j.2) — Transfer to spousal RRSP; 147.3(10) — Taxation of amount transferred; 147.4(2) — Amendment to RPP annuity contract; 147.4(3) — Substitution of new RPP annuity contract; 147.4(4) — Conversion of pension rights before 1997 to annuity contract commencing after age 69.

**Notes**: 254 opening words and 254(a) amended by 1995-97 technical bill, effective July 31, 1997. Before then, read:

254. For greater certainty it is hereby declared that, where a document has been issued or a contract entered into (either before, on or after September 15, 1953) purporting to create, to establish, to extinguish or to be in substitution for, a taxpayer's right to an amount or amounts, immediately or in the future, out of or under a superannuation or pension fund or plan,

(a) if the rights provided for in the document or contract are rights provided for by the superannuation or pension plan or are rights to a payment or payments out of the superannuation or pension fund, any payment under the document or contract is a payment out of or under the superannuation or pension fund or plan and the taxpayer shall be deemed not to have received, by the issuance of the document or entering into the contract, an amount out of or under the superannuation or pension fund or plan; and

**Definitions [s. 254]**: "amount", "taxpayer" — 248(1).

**Interpretation Bulletins**: IT-499R: Superannuation or pension benefits.

**Information Circulars**: 72-13R8: Employees' pension plans; 74-1R5: Form T2037 — Notice of purchase of annuity with "plan" funds.

**Forms**: T2037: Notice of purchase of annuity with "plan" funds.

**255. "Canada"** — For the purposes of this Act, "Canada" is hereby declared to include and to have always included

(a) the sea bed and subsoil of the submarine areas adjacent to the coasts of Canada in respect of which the Government of Canada or of a province grants a right, licence or privilege to explore for, drill for or take any minerals, petroleum, natural gas or any related hydrocarbons; and

(b) the seas and airspace above the submarine areas referred to in paragraph (a) in respect of any activities carried on in connection with the exploration for or exploitation of the minerals, petroleum, natural gas or hydrocarbons referred to in that paragraph.

**Related Provisions**: 127(9) "qualified property" closing words — "Canada" includes prescribed offshore region for certain investment tax credit purposes; 248(1) "corporation incorporated in Canada" — "Canada" includes areas before they were part of Canada; 250 — Extended meaning of "resident in Canada"; 253 — Extended meaning of "carrying on business in Canada"; *Income Tax Conventions Interpretation Act* s. 5 — Meaning of "Canada" for treaty purposes; *Interpretation Act* 8(2.1), (2.2) — Application to exclusive economic zone and continental shelf; *Interpretation Act* 35(1) — "Canada" includes internal waters and territorial seas; Canada-U.S. tax treaty, Art. III:1(a) — Meaning of "Canada" for treaty purposes.

**Notes**: See also subsection 8(2.1) and (2.2) of the *Interpretation Act* (reproduced at the end of this book), which extend the meaning of "Canada" to the exclusive economic zone and the continental shelf for certain purposes.

**Definitions [s. 255]**: "mineral" — 248(1); "province" — *Interpretation Act* 35(1).

**Interpretation Bulletins**: IT-494: Hire of ships and aircraft from non-residents.

**256. (1) Associated corporations** — For the purposes of this Act, one corporation is associated with another in a taxation year if, at any time in the year,

(a) one of the corporations controlled, directly or indirectly in any manner whatever, the other;

(b) both of the corporations were controlled, directly or indirectly in any manner whatever, by the same person or group of persons;

(c) each of the corporations was controlled, directly or indirectly in any manner whatever, by a person and the person who so controlled one of the corporations was related to the person who so controlled the other, and either of those persons owned, in respect of each corporation, not less than 25% of the issued shares of any class, other than a specified class, of the capital stock thereof;

(d) one of the corporations was controlled, directly or indirectly in any manner whatever, by a person and that person was related to each member of a group of persons that so controlled the other corporation, and that person owned, in respect of the other corporation, not less than 25% of the issued shares of any class, other than a specified class, of the capital stock thereof; or

(e) each of the corporations was controlled, directly or indirectly in any manner whatever, by a related group and each of the members of one of the related groups was related to all of the members of the other related group, and one or more persons who were members of both related groups, either alone or together, owned, in respect of each corporation, not less than 25% of the issued shares of any class, other than a specified class of the capital stock thereof.

**Related Provisions**: 13(9.5) — Extended meaning of "associated" for SR&ED specified-employee payment limitation; 18(2.2)–(2.4) — Associated corps share $1,000,000 base level deduction; 125(2)–(4) — Associated corps share $200,000 income limit for small business deduction; 126.1(8)–(11) — Associated employers share $30,000 UI premium tax credit; 127(10.2)–(10.4) — Associated corps share $2,000,000 expenditure limit for investment tax credit; 127.1(2) — Associated corps share $200,000 taxable income limit to be qualifying corps for refundable investment tax credit; 128(1)(f) — Bankrupt corporation deemed not associated; 129(6) — Investment income from associated corporation deemed active business income; 157(1)(b)(i)(B) — Later final payment of tax where associated corps' taxable incomes do not exceed $200,000; 191.1(2)–(4) — Associated corps share dividend allowance for Part VI.1 tax; 256(1.1) — "Specified class" defined; 256(1.2) — Control, etc.; 256(1.5) — Person deemed related to self; 256(5.1), (6.2) — Control in fact; 256(6.1) — Simultaneous control by different persons.

**Notes**: Associated corporations must share various limits, including most notably the small business deduction limit of $200,000 of active business income (see 125(3)–(5)). Note the additional rules in 256, especially 256(2) and (2.1).

For a detailed discussion see Maureen Donnelly and Allister Young, "The Associated Corporation Rules: Getting Tax Reduction Under 'Control' ", 46(3) *Canadian Tax Journal* 589-625 (1998).

**Interpretation Bulletins**: IT-64R3: Corporations: association and control — after 1988.

**Advance Tax Rulings**: ATR-13: Corporations not associated.

**(1.1) Definition of "specified class"** — For the purposes of subsection (1), "specified class" means a class of shares of the capital stock of a corporation where, under the terms or conditions of the shares or any agreement in respect thereof,

(a) the shares are not convertible or exchangeable;

(b) the shares are non-voting;

(c) the amount of each dividend payable on the shares is calculated as a fixed amount or by reference to a fixed percentage of an amount equal to the fair market value of the consideration for which the shares were issued;

(d) the annual rate of the dividend on the shares, expressed as a percentage of an amount equal to the fair market value of the consideration for which the shares were issued, cannot in any event exceed,

(i) where the shares were issued before 1984, the rate of interest prescribed for the purposes of subsection 161(1) at the time the shares were issued, and

(ii) where the shares were issued after 1983, the prescribed rate of interest at the time the shares were issued; and

(e) the amount that any holder of the shares is entitled to receive on the redemption, cancellation or acquisition of the shares by the corporation or by any person with whom the corporation does not deal at arm's length cannot exceed the total of an amount equal to the fair market value of the consideration for which the shares were issued and the amount of any unpaid dividends thereon.

**Related Provisions**: 256(1.2) — Control, etc.; 256(1.5) — Person deemed related to self.

**Notes**: 256(1.1)(d)(i) added by 1991 technical bill, effective 1989, to correct an error (since there was no general prescribed rate of interest before 1984).

**Regulations**: 4301(c) (prescribed rate of interest).

**Interpretation Bulletins**: IT-64R3: Corporations: association and control — after 1988.

**(1.2) Control, etc.** — For the purposes of this subsection and subsections (1), (1.1) and (1.3) to (5),

(a) a group of persons in respect of a corporation means any two or more persons each of whom owns shares of the capital stock of the corporation;

(b) for greater certainty,

(i) a corporation that is controlled by one or more members of a particular group of persons in respect of that corporation shall be considered to be controlled by that group of persons, and

(ii) a corporation may be controlled by a person or a particular group of persons notwithstanding that the corporation is also controlled or deemed to be controlled by another person or group of persons;

(c) a corporation shall be deemed to be controlled by another corporation, a person or a group of persons at any time where

(i) shares of the capital stock of the corporation having a fair market value of more than 50% of the fair market value of all the issued and outstanding shares of the capital stock of the corporation, or

(ii) common shares of the capital stock of the corporation having a fair market value of more than 50% of the fair market value of all the issued and outstanding common shares of the capital stock of the corporation

are owned at that time by the other corporation, the person or the group of persons, as the case may be;

(d) where shares of the capital stock of a corporation are owned, or deemed by this subsection to be owned, at any time by another corporation (in this paragraph referred to as the "holding corporation"), those shares shall be deemed to be owned at that time by any shareholder of the holding corporation in a proportion equal to the proportion of all those shares that

(i) the fair market value of the shares of the capital stock of the holding corporation owned at that time by the shareholder

is of

(ii) the fair market value of all the issued shares of the capital stock of the holding corporation outstanding at that time;

(e) where, at any time, shares of the capital stock of a corporation are property of a partnership, or are deemed by this subsection to be owned by the partnership, those shares shall be deemed to be owned at that time by each member of the partnership in a proportion equal to the proportion of all those shares that

(i) the member's share of the income or loss of the partnership for its fiscal period that includes that time

is of

(ii) the income or loss of the partnership for its fiscal period that includes that time

and for this purpose, where the income and loss of the partnership for its fiscal period that includes that time are nil, that proportion shall be computed as if the partnership had had income for that period in the amount of $1,000,000;

(f) where shares of the capital stock of a corporation are owned, or deemed by this subsection to be owned, at any time by a trust,

(i) in the case of a testamentary trust under which one or more beneficiaries were entitled to receive all of the income of the trust that arose before the date of death of one or the last surviving of those beneficiaries (in this paragraph referred to as the "distribution date") and no other person could, before the distribution date, receive or otherwise obtain the use of any of the income or capital of the trust,

(A) where any such beneficiary's share of the income or capital therefrom depends on the exercise by any person of, or the failure by any person to exercise, any discretionary power, those shares shall be deemed to be owned at any time before the distribution date by the beneficiary, and

(B) where clause (A) does not apply, those shares shall be deemed to be owned at any time before the distribution date by any such beneficiary in a proportion equal to the proportion of all those shares that the fair market value of the beneficial interest in the trust of the beneficiary is of the fair market value of the beneficial interests in the trust of all those beneficiaries,

(ii) where a beneficiary's share of the accumulating income or capital therefrom depends on the exercise by any person of, or the failure by any person to exercise, any discretionary power, those shares shall be deemed to be owned at that time by the beneficiary, except where subparagraph (i) applies and that time is before the distribution date,

(iii) in any case where subparagraph (ii) does not apply, a beneficiary shall be deemed at that time to own the proportion of those shares that the fair market value of the beneficial interest in the trust of the beneficiary is of the fair market value of all beneficial interests in the trust, except where subparagraph (i) applies and that time is before the distribution date, and,

(iv) in the case of a trust referred to in subsection 75(2), the person referred to in that subsection from whom property of the trust or property for which it was substituted was directly or indirectly received shall be deemed to own those shares at that time; and

(g) in determining the fair market value of a share of the capital stock of a corporation, all issued and outstanding shares of the capital stock of the corporation shall be deemed to be non-voting.

**Related Provisions**: 248(5) — Substituted property; 256(1.5) — Person deemed related to self; 256(1.6) — Exception; 256(6.1) — Simultaneous control by different persons.

**Interpretation Bulletins**: IT-64R3: Corporations: association and control — after 1988.

**(1.3) Parent deemed to own shares** — Where at any time shares of the capital stock of a corporation are owned by a child who is under 18 years of age, for the purpose of determining whether the corporation is associated at that time with any other corporation that is controlled, directly or indirectly in any manner whatever, by a parent of the child or by a group of persons of which the parent is a member, the shares shall be deemed to be owned at that time by the parent unless, having regard to all the circumstances, it can reasonably be considered that the child manages the business and affairs of the corporation and does so without a significant degree of influence by the parent.

**Related Provisions**: 256(1.2) — Control, etc.; 256(1.5) — Person deemed related to self; 256(5.1), (6.2) — Control in fact.

**Notes**: 256(1.3) amended by 1991 technical bill, retroactive to its introduction (1989 or 1990 taxation year), to delete the words "or the group, as the case may be" after the words "deemed to be owned by the parent".

**Interpretation Bulletins**: IT-64R3: Corporations: association and control — after 1988.

**(1.4) Options and rights** — For the purpose of determining whether a corporation is associated with another corporation with which it is not otherwise associated, where a person or any partnership in which the person has an interest has a right at any time under a contract, in equity or otherwise, either immediately or in the future and either absolutely or contingently,

(a) to, or to acquire, shares of the capital stock of a corporation, or to control the voting rights of shares of the capital stock of a corporation, the person or partnership shall, except where the right is not exercisable at that time because the exercise thereof is contingent on the death, bankruptcy or permanent disability of an individual, be deemed to own the shares at that time, and the shares shall be deemed to be issued and outstanding at that time; or

(b) to cause a corporation to redeem, acquire or cancel any shares of its capital stock owned by other shareholders of a corporation, the person or partnership shall, except where the right is not exercisable at that time because the exercise thereof is contingent on the death, bankruptcy or permanent disability of an individual, be deemed at that time to have the same position in relation to control of the corporation and ownership of shares of its capital stock as if the shares were redeemed, acquired or cancelled by the corporation.

**Related Provisions**: 256(1.2) — Control, etc.; 256(1.5) — Person deemed related to self; 256(1.6) — Exception; 256(5.1) — Control in fact.

**Notes**: 256(1.4) amended by 1991 technical bill, retroactive to its introduction (1989 or 1990 taxation year), to make minor technical amendments.

**Interpretation Bulletins**: IT-64R3: Corporations: association and control — after 1988.

**(1.5) Person related to himself, herself or itself** — For the purposes of subsections (1) to (1.4) and (1.6) to (5), where a person owns shares in two or more corporations, the person shall as shareholder of one of the corporations be deemed to be related to himself, herself or itself as shareholder of each of the other corporations.

**Related Provisions**: 256(1.2) — Control, etc.

**Interpretation Bulletins**: IT-64R3: Corporations: association and control — after 1988.

**(1.6) Exception** — For the purposes of subsection (1.2) and notwithstanding subsection (1.4), any share that is

(a) described in paragraph (e) of the definition "term preferred share" in subsection 248(1) during the applicable time referred to in that paragraph, or

(b) a share of a specified class within the meaning of subsection (1.1)

shall be deemed not to have been issued and outstanding and not to be owned by any shareholder and an amount equal to the greater of the paid-up capital of the share and the amount, if any, that any holder of the share is entitled to receive on the redemption, cancellation or acquisition of the share by the corporation shall be deemed to be a liability of the corporation.

**Related Provisions**: 256(1.2) — Control, etc.; 256(1.5) — Person deemed related to self.

**(2) Corporations associated through a third corporation** — Where two corporations

(a) would, but for this subsection, not be associated with each other at any time, and

(b) are associated, or are deemed by this subsection to be associated, with the same corporation (in this subsection referred to as the "third corporation") at that time,

they shall, for the purposes of this Act, be deemed to be associated with each other at that time, except that, for the purposes of section 125, where the third corporation is not a Canadian-controlled private corporation at that time or elects, in prescribed form, for its taxation year that includes that time not to be associated with either of the other two corporations, the third corporation shall be deemed not to be associated with either of the other two corporations in that taxation year and its business limit for that taxation year shall be deemed to be nil.

**Related Provisions**: 256(1.2) — Control, etc.; 256(1.5) — Person deemed related to self.

**Notes**: 256(2) provides a "transitivity" rule: if A and B are associated, and A and C are associated, then B and C are associated, unless A elects not to be associated with either — in which case A cannot claim any small business deduction (see 125(2)) but B and C can each claim the full $200,000.

**Interpretation Bulletins**: IT-64R3: Corporations: association and control — after 1988; IT-243R4: Dividend refund to private corporations.

**Advance Tax Rulings**: ATR-13: Corporations not associated.

**Forms**: T2 SCH 28: Election not to be an associated corporation.

**(2.1) Anti-avoidance** — For the purposes of this Act, where, in the case of two or more corporations, it may reasonably be considered that one of the main reasons for the separate existence of those corporations in a taxation year is to reduce the amount of taxes that would otherwise be payable under this Act or to increase the amount of refundable investment tax credit under section 127.1, the two or more corporations shall be deemed to be associated with each other in the year.

**Notes**: This rule was in 247(2) before 1988.

**Interpretation Bulletins**: IT-64R3: Corporations: association and control — after 1988.

**Advance Tax Rulings**: ATR-13: Corporations not associated.

**(3) Saving provision** — Where one corporation (in this subsection referred to as the "controlled corporation") would, but for this subsection, be associated with another corporation in a taxation year by reason of being controlled, directly or indirectly in any manner whatever, by the other corporation or by reason of both of the corporations being controlled, directly or indirectly in any manner whatever, by the same person at a particular time in the year (which corporation or person so controlling the controlled corporation is in this subsection referred to as the "controller") and it is established to the satisfaction of the Minister that

(a) there was in effect at the particular time an agreement or arrangement enforceable according to the terms thereof, under which, on the satisfaction of a condition or the happening of an event that it is reasonable to expect will be satisfied or happen, the controlled corporation will

(i) cease to be controlled, directly or indirectly in any manner whatever, by the controller, and

(ii) be or become controlled, directly or indirectly in any manner whatever, by a person or group of persons, with whom or with each of the members of which, as the case may be, the controller was at the particular time dealing at arm's length, and

(b) the purpose for which the controlled corporation was at the particular time so controlled was the safeguarding of rights or interests of the controller in respect of

(i) any indebtedness owing to the controller the whole or any part of the principal amount of which was outstanding at the particular time, or

(ii) any shares of the capital stock of the controlled corporation that were owned by the controller at the particular time and that were, under the agreement or arrangement, to be redeemed by the controlled corporation or purchased by the person or group of persons referred to in subparagraph (a)(ii),

the controlled corporation and the other corporation with which it would otherwise be so associated in the year shall be deemed, for the purpose of this Act, not to be associated with each other in the year.

**Related Provisions**: 256(1.2) — Control, etc.; 256(1.5) — Person deemed related to self; 256(5.1), (6.2) — Controlled directly or indirectly; 256(6.1) — Simultaneous control by different persons.

**Interpretation Bulletins**: IT-64R3: Corporations: association and control — after 1988.

**(4) Idem** — Where one corporation would, but for this subsection, be associated with another corporation in a taxation year by reason of both of the corporations being controlled by the same trustee or executor and it is established to the satisfaction of the Minister

(a) that the trustee or executor did not acquire control of the corporations as a result of one or more trusts or estates created by the same individual or two or more individuals not dealing with each other at arm's length, and

(b) that the trust or estate under which the trustee or executor acquired control of each of the corporations arose only on the death of the individual creating the trust or estate,

the two corporations shall be deemed, for the purposes of this Act, not to be associated with each other in the year.

**Related Provisions**: 256(1.2) — Control, etc.; 256(1.5) — Person deemed related to self; 256(6.1) — Simultaneous control by different persons.

**Interpretation Bulletins**: IT-64R3: Corporations: association and control — after 1988.

**(5) Idem** — Where one corporation would, but for this subsection, be associated with another corporation in a taxation year, by reason only that the other corporation is a trustee under a trust pursuant to which the corporation is controlled, the two corporations shall be deemed, for the purposes of this Act, not to be associated with each other in the year unless, at any time in the year, a settlor of the trust controlled or is a member of a related group that controlled the other corporation that is the trustee under the trust.

**Related Provisions**: 256(1.2) — Control, etc.; 256(1.5) — Person deemed related to self; 256(6.1) — Simultaneous control by different persons.

**Interpretation Bulletins**: IT-64R3: Corporations: association and control — after 1988.

**(5.1) Control in fact** — For the purposes of this Act, where the expression "controlled, directly or indirectly in any manner whatever," is used, a corporation shall be considered to be so controlled by another corporation, person or group of persons (in this subsection referred to as the "controller") at any time where, at that time, the controller has any direct or indirect influence that, if exercised, would result in control in fact of the corporation, except that, where the corporation and the controller are dealing with each other at arm's length and the influence is derived from a franchise, licence, lease, distribution, supply or management agreement or other similar agreement or arrangement, the main purpose of which is to govern the relationship between the corporation and the controller regarding the manner in which a business carried on by the corporation is to be conducted, the corporation shall not be considered to be controlled, directly or indirectly in any manner whatever, by the controller by reason only of that agreement or arrangement.

**Related Provisions**: 256(6) — Idem.

**Interpretation Bulletins**: IT-64R3: Corporations: association and control — after 1988; IT-236R4: Reserves — disposition of capital property; IT-313R2: Eligible capital property — rules where a taxpayer has ceased carrying on a business or has died; IT-291R2: Transfer of property to a corporation under subsection 85(1); IT-458R2: Canadian-controlled private corporation.

**(6) Idem** — For the purposes of this Act, where a corporation (in this subsection referred to as the "controlled corporation") would, but for this subsection, be regarded as having been controlled or controlled, directly or indirectly in any manner whatever, by a person or partnership (in this subsection referred to as the "controller") at a particular time and it is established that

(a) there was in effect at the particular time an agreement or arrangement enforceable according to the terms thereof, under which, on the satisfaction of a condition or the happening of an event that it is reasonable to expect will be satisfied or happen, the controlled corporation will

(i) cease to be controlled, or controlled, directly or indirectly in any manner whatever, as the case may be, by the controller, and

(ii) be or become controlled, or controlled, directly or indirectly in any manner whatever, as the case may be, by a person or group of persons, with whom or with each of the members of which, as the case may be, the controller was at the particular time dealing at arm's length, and

(b) the purpose for which the controlled corporation was at the particular time so controlled, or controlled, directly or indirectly in any manner whatever, as the case may be, was the safeguarding of rights or interests of the controller in respect of

(i) any indebtedness owing to the controller the whole or any part of the principal amount of which was outstanding at the particular time, or

(ii) any shares of the capital stock of the controlled corporation that were owned by the controller at the particular time and that were, under the agreement or arrangement, to be redeemed by the controlled corporation or purchased by the person or group of persons referred to in subparagraph (a)(ii),

the controlled corporation is deemed not to have been controlled by the controller at the particular time.

**Related Provisions**: 256(5.1), (6.2) — Controlled directly or indirectly; 256(6.1) — Simultaneous control by different persons.

**Notes**: Closing words of 256(6) amended by 1995-97 technical bill, retroactive to taxation years that begin after 1988, to change "shall be deemed, for the purposes of that provision" to "is deemed".

**Interpretation Bulletins**: IT-64R3: Corporations: association and control — after 1988; IT-458R2: Canadian-controlled private corporation.

### Proposed Addition — 256(6.1), (6.2)

**(6.1) Simultaneous control** — For the purposes of this Act and for greater certainty,

(a) where a corporation (in this paragraph referred to as the "subsidiary") would be controlled by another corporation (in this paragraph referred to as the "parent") if the parent were not controlled by any person or group of persons, the subsidiary is controlled by

(i) the parent, and

(ii) any person or group of persons by whom the parent is controlled; and

(b) where a corporation (in this paragraph referred to as the "subject corporation") would be controlled by a group of persons (in this paragraph referred to as the "first-tier group") if no corporation that is a member of the first-tier group were controlled by any person or group of persons, the subject corporation is controlled by

(i) the first-tier group, and

(ii) any group of one or more persons comprised of, in respect of every member of the first-tier group, either the member, or a person or group of persons by whom the member is controlled.

**Technical Notes**: Section 256 provides rules relevant to the determination, for the purposes of the Act, of whether corporations are associated, whether a corporation is controlled by a person or group of persons, and whether control of a corporation has been acquired.

New subsection 256(6.1) specifies, for greater certainty, that a corporation may be controlled simultaneously by persons or groups at more than one level above it in a corporate chain.

Paragraph 256(6.1)(a) specifies that, where a subsidiary would be controlled by its parent if the parent were not itself controlled by any other person or group, the subsidiary is considered to be controlled both by the parent and by the person or group that controls the parent.

Paragraph 256(6.1)(b) is a rule of similar effect that applies where the subject corporation would be controlled by a group (the "first-tier group") if no member of the first-tier group were itself controlled by a third party. In that case, the subject corporation is considered to be controlled both by the first-tier group, and by any higher-tier group which includes, in respect of each member of the first-tier group, either the member or a person or group by whom the member is controlled. If one person controls all members of the first-tier group, that person would constitute a higher-tier group.

The operation of paragraph (b) is illustrated by the following example, in which the percentages represent ownership of voting shares, and the various groups identified are assumed to act in concert in voting their shares.

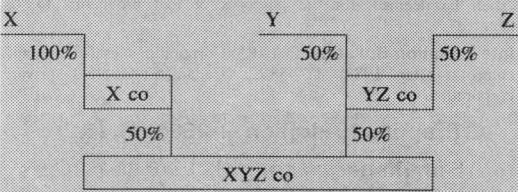

In this example, XYZco is considered to be simultaneously controlled by:

(i) the first-tier group comprised of Xco and YZco,
(ii) the higher-tier group comprised of X, Y and Z,
(iii) the higher-tier comprised of Xco, Y and Z, and
(iv) the higher-tier group comprised of X and YZco.

While the concepts set out in subsection 256(6.1) deal directly only with a corporation and persons in the two levels of ownership immediately above it, application of the provision sequentially from the top of a chain makes it applicable to corporate chains with three or more levels.

**Notes**: 256(6.1) will override *Parthenon Investments Ltd.*, [1997] 3 C.T.C. 152 (FCA), where mid-tier control was ignored on the principle that "control cannot allow for two masters simultaneously". Under 256(6.1), a chain with a Canadian corporation at the bottom, U.S. corporation in the middle and a Canadian parent on top will be considered "controlled" by a non-resident and will not be a Canadian-controlled private corporation.

**(6.2) Application to control in fact** — In its application to subsection (5.1), subsection (6.1) shall be read as if the references in subsection (6.1) to "controlled" were references to "controlled, directly or indirectly in any manner whatever,".

**Technical Notes**: New subsection 256(6.2) specifies that the rule regarding simultaneous control in new subsection 256(6.1) also applies to the concept of *de facto* control, which is set out in subsection 256(5.1).

**Application**: Bill C-43 (First Reading September 20, 2000), s. 118, will add subsecs. 256(6.1) and (6.2), applicable after November 1999.

**(7) Acquiring control** — For the purposes of subsections 10(10), 13(21.2) and (24), 14(12) and 18(15), sections 18.1 and 37, subsection 40(3.4), the definition "superficial loss" in section 54, section 55, subsections 66(11), (11.4) and (11.5), 66.5(3) and 66.7(10) and (11), section 80, paragraph 80.04(4)(h), subsections 85(1.2) and 88(1.1) and (1.2), sections 111 and 127, subsection 249(4) and this subsection,

(a) control of a particular corporation shall be deemed not to have been acquired solely because of

(i) the acquisition at any time of shares of any corporation by

(A) a particular person who acquired the shares from a person to whom the particular person was related (otherwise than because of a right referred to in paragraph 251(5)(b)) immediately before that time,

(B) a particular person who was related to the particular corporation (otherwise than because of a right referred to in paragraph 251(5)(b)) immediately before that time,

(C) an estate that acquired the shares because of the death of a person, or

(D) a particular person who acquired the shares from an estate that arose on the death of another person to whom the particular person was related, or

(ii) the redemption or cancellation at any particular time of, or a change at any particular time in the rights, privileges, restrictions or conditions attaching to, shares of the particular corporation or of a corporation controlling the particular corporation, where each person and each member of each group of persons that controls the particular corporation immediately after the particular time was related (otherwise than because of a right referred to in paragraph 251(5)(b)) to the corporation

(A) immediately before the particular time, or

(B) immediately before the death of a person, where the shares were held immediately before the particular time by an estate that acquired the shares because of the person's death;

(b) where at any time 2 or more corporations (each of which is referred to in this paragraph as a "predecessor corporation") have amalgamated to form one corporate entity (in this paragraph referred to as the "new corporation"),

(i) control of a corporation is deemed not to have been acquired by any person or group of persons solely because of the amalgamation unless it is deemed by subparagraph (ii) or (iii) to have been so acquired,

(ii) a person or group of persons that controls the new corporation immediately after the amalgamation and did not control a predecessor corporation immediately before the amalgamation is deemed to have acquired immediately before the amalgamation control of the predecessor corporation and of each corporation it controlled immediately before the amalgamation (unless the person or group of persons would not have acquired control of the predecessor corporation if the person or group of persons had acquired all the shares of the predecessor corporation immediately before the amalgamation), and

(iii) control of a predecessor corporation and of each corporation it controlled immediately before the amalgamation is deemed to have been acquired immediately before the amalgamation by a person or group of persons

(A) unless the predecessor corporation was related (otherwise than because of a right referred to in paragraph 251(5)(b)) immediately before the amalgamation to each other predecessor corporation,

(B) unless, if one person had immediately after the amalgamation acquired all the shares of the new corporation's capital stock that the shareholders of the predecessor corporation, or of another predecessor corporation that controlled the predecessor corporation, acquired on the amalgamation in consideration for their shares of the predecessor corporation or of the other predecessor corporation, as the case may be, the person would have acquired control of the new corporation as a result of the acquisition of those shares, or

(C) unless this subparagraph would, but for this clause, deem control of each predecessor corporation to have been acquired on the amalgamation where the amalgamation is an amalgamation of

(I) two corporations, or

(II) two corporations (in this subclause referred to as the "parents") and one or more other corporations (each of which is in this subclause referred to as a "subsidiary") that would, if all the shares of each subsidiary's capital stock that were held immediately before the amalgamation by the parents had been held by one person, have been controlled by that person;

(c) subject to paragraph (a), where 2 or more persons (in this paragraph referred to as the "transferors") dispose of shares of the capital stock of a particular corporation in exchange for shares of the capital stock of another corporation (in this paragraph referred to as the "acquiring corporation"), control of the acquiring corporation and of each corporation controlled by it immediately before the exchange is deemed to have been acquired at the time of the exchange by a person or group of persons unless

(i) the particular corporation and the acquiring corporation were related (otherwise than because of a right referred to in paragraph 251(5)(b)) to each other immediately before the exchange, or

(ii) if all the shares of the acquiring corporation's capital stock that were acquired by the transferors on the exchange were acquired at the time of the exchange by one person, the person would not control the acquiring corporation;

(d) where at any time shares of the capital stock of a particular corporation are disposed of to another corporation (in this paragraph referred to as the "acquiring corporation") for consideration that includes shares of the acquiring corporation's capital stock and, immediately after that time, the acquiring corporation and the particular corporation are controlled by a person or group of persons who

(i) controlled the particular corporation immediately before that time, and

(ii) did not, as part of the series of transactions or events that includes the disposition, cease to control the acquiring corporation,

control of the particular corporation and of each corporation controlled by it immediately before that time is deemed not to have been acquired by the acquiring corporation solely because of the disposition; and

(e) where at any time all the shares of the capital stock of a particular corporation are disposed of to another corporation (in this paragraph referred to as the "acquiring corporation") for consideration that consists solely of shares of the acquiring corporation's capital stock and, immediately after that time,

(i) the acquiring corporation is not controlled by any person or group of persons, and

(ii) the fair market value of the shares of the capital stock of the particular corporation is not less than 95% of the fair market value of all the assets of the acquiring corporation,

control of the particular corporation and of each corporation controlled by it immediately before that time is deemed not to have been acquired by the acquiring corporation solely because of the disposition.

**Related Provisions**: 139.1(18) — Control deemed not acquired on demutualization of insurer; 256(8.1) — Corporations without share capital.

**Notes**: Opening words of 256(7) amended by 1995-97 technical bill, effective April 27, 1995, to delete references to 87(2.1), 87(2.11) and 89(1.1) and to add references to 10(10), 13(21.2), 14(12), 18(15), 40(3.4), 54"superficial loss" and 256(7); and to add reference to 18.1 effective November 18, 1996.

Opening words of 256(7) amended by 1994 tax amendments bill (Part I), effective for amalgamations, acquisitions, redemptions and cancellations that occur after February 21, 1994, to add reference to 80 and 80.04(4)(h).

Opening words of 256(7) amended by 1994 Budget, effective for amalgamations, acquisitions, redemptions and cancellations that occur after February 21, 1994, to add reference to s. 55.

Opening words of 256(7) amended by 1993 technical bill, effective for acquisitions, redemptions and cancellations occurring in 1993 or later, to add reference to 87(2.11).

Opening words of 256(7) amended by 1991 technical bill, effective for dispositions after 1984, to add reference to 85(1.2).

## S. 256(7) — Income Tax Act

256(7)(a)(ii) amended by 1995-97 technical bill, effective for 1994 and later taxation years. Previously read:

(ii) the redemption or cancellation at any time of shares of the particular corporation or of a corporation controlling the particular corporation, where the person or each member of the group of persons that controls the corporation immediately after that time was related to the corporation (otherwise than because of a right referred to in paragraph 251(5)(b)) immediately before that time; and

256(7)(a) amended by 1993 technical bill, effective for acquisitions, redemptions and cancellations occurring in 1993 or later. From 1990 to 1992, read:

(a) a person shall be deemed not to have acquired control of a particular corporation, or of any corporation controlled by it, because of the redemption, acquisition or cancellation of shares of the particular corporation if that person

(i) was, immediately before the share redemption, acquisition or cancellation, related (otherwise than because of a right referred to in paragraph 251(5)(b)) to the particular corporation,

(ii) was an executor, administrator or trustee of an estate who acquired the shares by virtue of the death of any other person,

(iii) acquired the shares by way of a distribution from an estate arising on the death of another person with whom the first-mentioned person was related, or

(iv) was a corporation formed by an amalgamation (within the meaning of section 87) of two or more predecessor corporations each of which was related (otherwise than by virtue of a right referred to in paragraph 251(5)(b)) to the particular corporation immediately before the amalgamation; and

Opening words of 256(7)(a) and 256(7)(a)(i) amended by 1991 technical bill, effective for redemptions, dispositions, acquisitions and cancellations of shares after 1989. However, where the person elects by notifying Revenue Canada in writing by November 5, 1993 (deadline extended by 1992 technical bill, s. 159), redemptions and cancellations are only caught after July 13, 1990.

Before 1990, 256(7)(a) and (a)(i) dealt only with acquisition of shares:

(a) where shares of a particular corporation have been acquired by a person after March 31, 1977, that person shall be deemed not to have acquired control of the particular corporation by virtue of such share acquisition if that person

(i) was, immediately before such share acquisition, related (otherwise than by virtue of a right referred to in paragraph 251(5)(b)) to the particular corporation,

256(7)(b) amended by 1995-97 technical bill, effective

(a) for mergers that occur after April 26, 1995, other than a merger that occurs pursuant to a written agreement made before that day where the corporate entity formed by the merger so elects by the end of 1998; and

(b) to a merger that occurred after 1992 and before April 26, 1995 where the corporate entity formed by the merger so elects by the end of 1998.

For earlier mergers, read:

(b) where there has been an amalgamation (within the meaning assigned by section 87) of two or more corporations after November 12, 1981, and a person or group of persons controlled the new corporation immediately after the amalgamation and did not control a particular predecessor corporation immediately before the amalgamation, that person or group of persons shall be deemed to have acquired control of the particular predecessor corporation immediately before the amalgamation unless control would not have been acquired if the person or group of persons that controlled the new corporation immediately after the amalgamation had acquired all of the shares of the particular predecessor corporation immediately before the amalgamation.

256(7)(c) added by 1995-97 technical bill, effective for exchanges that occur after April 26, 1995, other than an exchange that occurs pursuant to a written agreement made before that day.

256(7)(d) added by 1995-97 technical bill, effective April 27, 1995.

256(7)(e) added by 1995-97 technical bill, effective April 27, 1995, but with respect to acquisitions of shares before June 20, 1996 or pursuant to a written agreement made before June 20, 1996, read 256(7)(e)(ii) as:

(ii) all or substantially all of the fair market value of the shares of the acquiring corporation's capital stock is attributable to the shares acquired by it at that time,

**Interpretation Bulletins**: IT-64R3: Corporations: association and control — after 1988; IT-302R3: Losses of a corporation — the effect that acquisitions of control, amalgamations, and windings-up have on their deductibility — after January 15, 1987.

**I.T. Technical News**: No. 7 (control by a group — 50/50 arrangement); No. 16 (*Duha Printers* case).

**Advance Tax Rulings**: ATR-7: Amalgamation involving losses and control.

**(8) Deemed exercise of right** — Where at any time a taxpayer acquires a right referred to in paragraph 251(5)(b) in respect of a share and it can reasonably be concluded that one of the main purposes of the acquisition is

(a) to avoid any limitation on the deductibility of any non-capital loss, net capital loss, farm loss or any expense or other amount referred to in subsection 66(11), 66.5(3) or 66.7(10) or (11),

(b) to avoid the application of subsection 10(10) or 13(24), paragraph 37(1)(h) or subsection 55(2) or 66(11.4) or (11.5), paragraph 88(1)(c.3) or subsection 111(4), (5.1), (5.2) or (5.3), 181.1(7) or 190.1(6),

(c) to avoid the application of paragraph (j) or (k) of the definition "investment tax credit" in subsection 127(9),

(d) to avoid the application of section 251.1, or

(e) to affect the application of section 80,

the taxpayer is deemed to be in the same position in relation to the control of the corporation as if the right were immediate and absolute and as if the taxpayer had exercised the right at that time for the purpose of determining whether control of a corporation has been acquired for the purposes of subsections 10(10) and 13(24), section 37, subsections 55(2), 66(11), (11.4) and (11.5), 66.5(3), 66.7(10) and (11), section 80, paragraph 80.04(4)(h), subparagraph 88(1)(c)(vi), paragraph 88(1)(c.3), sections 111 and 127 and subsections 181.1(7), 190.1(6) and 249(4), and in determining for the purpose of section 251.1 whether a corporation is controlled by any person or group of persons.

**Related Provisions**: 256(8.1) — Corporations without share capital.

**Notes**: 256(8) amended by 1995-97 technical bill, this version effective April 27, 1995. From June 24, 1994 to April 26, 1995, read:

(8) Where at any time a taxpayer acquires a right referred to in paragraph 251(5)(b) in respect of shares and it can reasonably be concluded that one of the main purposes of the acquisition is

(a) to avoid any limitation on the deductibility of any non-capital loss, net capital loss, farm loss or any expense or other amount referred to in subsection 66(11), 66.5(3) or 66.7(10) or (11),

(b) to avoid the application of subsection 13(24), paragraph 37(1)(h), subsection 55(2), 66(11.4) or (11.5), paragraph 88(1)(c.3) or subsection 111(4), (5.1), (5.2) or (5.3),

(c) to avoid the application of paragraph (j) or (k) of the definition "investment tax credit" in subsection 127(9), or

(d) to affect the application of section 80,

the taxpayer is deemed to have acquired the shares at that time for the purpose of determining whether control of the corporation has been acquired for the purposes of subsection 13(24), sections 37 and 55, subsections 66(11), (11.4) and (11.5), 66.5(3) and 66.7(10) and (11), section 80, paragraph 80.04(4)(h) subparagraph 88(1)(c)(vi), paragraph 88(1)(c.3), sections 111 and 127 and subsection 249(4).

From February 22, 1994 to June 23, 1994, read:

(8) Where at any time a taxpayer acquires a right referred to in paragraph 251(5)(b) in respect of shares and it can reasonably be concluded that one of the main purposes of the acquisition is

(a) to avoid any limitation on the deductibility of any non-capital loss, net capital loss, farm loss or any expense or other amount referred to in subsection 66(11), 66.5(3) or 66.7(10) or (11),

(b) to avoid the application of subsection 13(24), paragraph 37(1)(h), subsection 66(11.4) or (11.5), paragraph 88(1)(c.3) or subsection 111(4), (5.1), (5.2) or (5.3),

(c) to avoid the application of paragraph (j) or (k) of the definition "investment tax credit" in subsection 127(9), or

(d) to affect the application of section 80,

the taxpayer is deemed to have acquired the shares at that time for the purpose of determining whether control of the corporation has been acquired for the purposes of subsection 13(24), section 37, subsections 66(11), (11.4) and (11.5), 66.5(3) and 66.7(10) and (11), section 80, paragraph 80.04(4)(h), subparagraph 88(1)(c)(vi), paragraph 88(1)(c.3), sections 111 and 127 and subsection 249(4).

256(8)(d), and reference to 80 and 80.04(4)(h) in closing words of 256(8), added by 1994 tax amendments bill (Part I), effective for acquisitions that occur after February 21, 1994.

Reference to 55(2) in 256(8)(b) and to s. 55 in closing words of 256(8), added by 1994 Budget, effective for acquisitions that occur after June 23, 1994.

**Interpretation Bulletins**: IT-64R3: Corporations: association and control — after 1988.

**(8.1) Corporations without share capital** — For the purposes of subsections (7) and (8),

(a) a corporation incorporated without share capital is deemed to have a capital stock of a single class;

(b) each member, policyholder and other participant in the corporation is deemed to be a shareholder of the corporation; and

(c) the membership, policy or other interest in the corporation of each of those participants is deemed to be the number of shares of the corporation's capital stock that the Minister considers reasonable in the circumstances, having regard to the total number of participants in the corporation and the nature of their participation.

**Notes**: 256(8.1) added by 1995-97 technical bill, effective April 27, 1995.

**(9) Date of acquisition of control** — For the purposes of this Act, where control of a corporation is acquired by a person or group of persons at a particular time on a day, control of the corporation shall be deemed to have been acquired by the person or group of persons, as the case may be, at the commencement of that day and not at the particular time unless the corporation elects in its return of income under Part I filed for its taxation year ending immediately before the acquisition of control not to have this subsection apply.

**Related Provisions**: 249(4) — Deemed year end where change of control occurs; Reg. 6204(4) — Subsec. 256(9) ignored for purposes of "specified person" in determining prescribed shares under 110(1)(d).

**Definitions [s. 256]**: "amount" — 248(1); "arm's length" — 251(1); "associated" — 256; "business" — 248(1); "Canada" — 255; "Canadian-controlled private corporation" — 125(7), 248(1); "child" — 252(1); "class of shares" — 248(6); "common share" — 248(1); "controlled directly or indirectly" — 256(5.1), (6.2); "corporation", "dividend" — 248(1); "estate" — 104(1), 248(1); "farm loss" — 111(8), 248(1); "fiscal period" — 249(2)(b), 249.1; "group" — 256(1.2)(a); "individual" — 248(1); "investment tax credit" — 127(9), 248(1); "Minister" — 248(1); "net capital loss", "non-capital loss" — 111(8), 248(1); "paid-up capital" — 89(1), 248(1); "parent" — 252(2); "person", "prescribed" — 248(1); "prescribed rate"Reg. 4301; "principal amount", "property" — 248(1); "related group" — 251(4); "share", "shareholder" — 248(1); "specified class" — 256(1.1); "substituted property" — 248(5); "taxation year" — 249; "taxpayer" — 248(1); "testamentary trust" — 108(1), 248(1); "trust" — 104(1), 248(1), (3).

**257. Negative amounts** — Except as specifically otherwise provided, where an amount or a number is required under this Act to be determined or calculated by or in accordance with an algebraic formula, if the amount or number when so determined or calculated would, but for this section, be a negative amount or number, it shall be deemed to be nil.

**Related Provisions**: 248(1)"taxable income" — Taxable income cannot be less than nil.

**Notes**: This rule overrides the principle that has been held to apply to calculations not expressed in algebraic or formula terms, but that use the word "minus". In such calculations, the word "minus" may be given its arithmetic or technical sense, so the result of a "minus" can be a negative number. See *Canterra Energy Ltd.*, [1987] 1 C.T.C. 89 (FCA).

It is uncertain whether this rule applies to formulas in the Income Tax Regulations. Arguably, a formula under the Regulations is "required under this Act", since the Act authorizes the Regulations. S. 16 of the *Interpretation Act* (reproduced towards the end of this book) provides that "expressions" used in the Regulations have the same meanings as under the Act, but it is unclear whether a formula is an "expression" with a "meaning". Many of the formulas in the

## S. 257 — Income Tax Act

Regulations are evidently drafted on the assumption that s. 257 applies to them.

**Definitions [s. 257]**: "amount" — 248(1).

**258. (1) [Repealed under former Act]**

**Notes**: 258(1) repealed by 1988 tax reform. This rule, which provided for a deemed dividend on term preferred shares in certain circumstances, was moved to 84(4.2).

**(2) Deemed dividend on term preferred share** — Notwithstanding subsection 15(3), an amount paid or payable after 1978 as interest on or as an amount in lieu of interest in respect of

(a) any interest or dividend payable after November 16, 1978 on an income bond or an income debenture issued before November 17, 1978 or pursuant to an agreement in writing made before that date, or

(b) a dividend that became payable or in arrears after November 16, 1978 on a share of the capital stock of a corporation that is not a term preferred share by reason of having been issued before November 17, 1978 or pursuant to an agreement in writing made before that date,

shall, for the purposes of subsections 112(2.1) and 138(6), be deemed to be a dividend received on a term preferred share.

**Related Provisions**: 248(13) — Interests in trusts and partnerships.

**Interpretation Bulletins**: IT-52R4: Income bonds and income debentures.

**(3) Deemed interest on preferred shares** — Subject to subsection (4), for the purposes of paragraphs 12(1)(c) and (k) and sections 113 and 126, each amount that is a dividend received in a taxation year on

(a) a term preferred share by a specified financial institution resident in Canada from a corporation not resident in Canada, or

(b) any other share that

(i) is a grandfathered share, or

(ii) was issued before 8:00 p.m. Eastern Daylight Saving Time, June 18, 1987 and was not deemed by paragraph 112(2.2)(f) to have been issued after that time

### Proposed Amendment — 258(3)(b)(ii)

(ii) was issued before 8:00 p.m. Eastern Daylight Saving Time, June 18, 1987 and is not deemed by paragraph 112(2.22) to have been issued after that time

**Application**: Bill C-43 (First Reading September 20, 2000), s. 119, will amend subpara. 258(3)(b)(ii) to read as above, applicable in respect of dividends received after 1998.

**Technical Notes**: Section 258 contains deeming provisions that complement the rules set out in section 112, which disallow the intercorporate dividend deduction in respect of dividends paid on certain preferred shares and so-called guaranteed shares.

Subsection 258(3) provides that certain dividends received by a corporation from a corporation not resident in Canada are to be treated for certain purposes as having been received in the form of interest. This subsection is amended to correct a cross-reference as a consequence of the movement of the deeming rule in paragraph 112(2.2)(f) to new paragraph 112(2.22)(a).

by a corporation from a corporation not resident in Canada, if the dividend would have been a dividend in respect of which no deduction could have been made under subsection 112(1) or (2) or 138(6) because of subsection 112(2.2) of the *Income Tax Act*, chapter 148 of the Revised Statutes of Canada, 1952, as it read on June 17, 1987, if the corporation that paid the dividend were a taxable Canadian corporation

shall be deemed to be interest received in the year and not a dividend received on a share of the capital stock of a corporation.

**Related Provisions**: 248(1) — "amount" — stock dividend; 248(13) — Interests in trusts and partnerships.

**Notes**: 258(3)(b) amended by 1992 technical bill, retroactive to dividends received or deemed to be received on shares acquired after 8:00 p.m. EDST, June 18, 1987.

**I.T. Application Rules**: 69 (meaning of "*Income Tax Act*, chapter 148 of the Revised Statutes of Canada, 1952").

**Interpretation Bulletins**: IT-88R2: Stock dividends.

**(4) Exception** — Subsection (3) is not applicable to a dividend described in paragraph (3)(a) if the share on which the dividend was paid was not acquired in the ordinary course of the business carried on by the corporation.

**(5) Deemed interest on certain shares** — For the purposes of paragraphs 12(1)(c) and (k) and sections 113 and 126, a dividend received after June 18, 1987 and in a taxation year from a corporation not resident in Canada, other than a corporation in which the recipient had or would have, if the corporation were a taxable Canadian corporation, a substantial interest (within the meaning assigned by section 191), on a share, if the dividend would have been a dividend in respect of which no deduction could have been made under subsection 112(1) or (2) or 138(6) by reason of subsection 112(2) or (2.4) if the corporation that paid the dividend were a taxable Canadian corporation, shall be deemed to be interest received in the year and not a dividend received on a share of the capital stock of the payer corporation.

**Related Provisions**: 248(1) "amount" — stock dividend; 248(13) — Interests in trusts and partnerships.

**Definitions [s. 258]**: "amount" — 248(1); "Canada" — 255; "corporation", "dividend", "income bond", "grandfathered share", "person" — 248(1); "resident in Canada" — 250; "share" — 248(1); "specified financial institution" — 248(1); "taxable Canadian corporation" — 89(1), 248(1); "taxation year" — 249; "term preferred share" — 248(1); "trust" — 248(1), (3); "writing" — *Interpretation Act* 35(1).

**Interpretation Bulletins [s. 258]**: IT-88R2: Stock dividends.

**259. (1) Proportional holdings in trust property** — For the purposes of subsections 146(6), (10) and (10.1) and 146.3(7), (8) and (9) and Parts X, X.2, XI and XI.1, where at any time a taxpayer described in section 205 acquires, holds or disposes of a particular unit in a qualified trust and the trust elects for any period that includes that time to have the provisions of this subsection apply,

(a) the taxpayer shall be deemed not to acquire, hold or dispose of at that time, as the case may be, the particular unit;

(b) where the taxpayer holds the particular unit at that time, the taxpayer shall be deemed to hold at that time that proportion (referred to in this subsection as the "specified portion") of each property (in this subsection referred to as a "relevant property") held by the trust at that time that one (or, where the particular unit is a fraction of a whole unit, that fraction) is of the number of units of the trust outstanding at that time;

(c) the cost amount to the taxpayer at that time of the specified portion of a relevant property shall be deemed to be equal to the specified portion of the cost amount at that time to the trust of the relevant property;

(d) where that time is the later of

(i) the time the trust acquires the relevant property, and

(ii) the time the taxpayer acquires the particular unit,

the taxpayer shall be deemed to acquire the specified portion of a relevant property at that time;

(e) where that time is the time the specified portion of a relevant property is deemed by paragraph (d) to have been acquired, the fair market value of the specified portion of the relevant property at that time shall be deemed to be the specified portion of the fair market value of the relevant property at the time of its acquisition by the trust;

(f) where that time is the time immediately before the time the trust disposes of a particular relevant property, the taxpayer shall be deemed to dispose of, immediately after that time, the specified portion of the particular relevant property for proceeds equal to the specified portion of the proceeds of disposition to the trust of the particular relevant property;

(g) where that time is the time immediately before the time the taxpayer disposes of the particular unit, the taxpayer shall be deemed to dispose of, immediately after that time, the specified portion of each relevant property for proceeds equal to the specified portion of the fair market value of that relevant property at that time; and

(h) where the taxpayer is deemed because of this subsection

(i) to have acquired a portion of a relevant property as a consequence of the acquisition of the particular unit by the taxpayer and the acquisition of the relevant property by the trust, and

(ii) subsequently to have disposed of the specified portion of the relevant property,

the specified portion of the relevant property shall, for the purposes of determining the consequences under this Act of the disposition and without affecting the proceeds of disposition of the specified portion of the relevant property, be deemed to be the portion of the relevant property referred to in subparagraph (i).

**Related Provisions**: 206(2.1) — Exemption from Part XI tax when election made.

**Notes**: 259(1) added by 1993 technical bill, effective for periods occurring after 1985. See Notes at end of 259 for reference to former section.

**(2) Proportional holdings in corporate property** — Subsection (1) applies to an election by a qualified corporation as if

(a) the reference to "a qualified trust" were read as "the capital stock of a qualified corporation";

(b) the references to "unit" were read as "share"; and

(c) the references to "the trust" were read as "the corporation".

**Notes**: 259(2) added by 1993 technical bill, effective for periods occurring after 1991. See Notes at end of 259 for reference to former section.

**(3) Election** — The election by a trust or a corporation (in this subsection referred to as the "elector") under subsection (1) shall be made by the elector filing a prescribed form with the Minister and shall apply for the period beginning 15 months before the day of filing thereof (or such later time as the elector designates in its election) and ending at such time as the election is revoked by the elector filing with the Minister a notice of revocation (or at such earlier time within the 15-month period before the day on which the notice of revocation is filed with the Minister as the elector designates in its notice of revocation).

**Related Provisions**: 206(2.1) — Exemption from Part XI tax when election made.

**Notes**: 259(3) added by 1993 technical bill, effective for periods occurring after 1985. See Notes at end of 259 for reference to former section.

**Interpretation Bulletins**: IT-412R2: Foreign property of registered plans.

**Forms**: T1024: Election to deem a proportional holding in qualified trust/corporate property.

**(4) Requirement to provide information** — Where a trust or a corporation elects under subsection (1),

(a) it shall, not more than 30 days after making the election, notify each person who, before the election is made and during the period for which the election is made, held a unit in the trust or a share in the capital stock of the corporation, as the case may be, of the election; and

(b) where any person who holds such a unit or share during the period for which the election is made makes a written request to the trust or the corporation for information that is necessary for the purpose of determining the consequences under this Act of the election for that person, the trust or the corporation, as the case may be, shall provide the person with that information not more than 30 days after the receipt of the request.

**Notes**: 259(4) added by 1993 technical bill, effective for elections made after December 21, 1992. See Notes at end of 259 for reference to former section.

**(5) Definitions** — In this section,

**"qualified corporation"** at any time means a corporation described in paragraph 149(1)(o.2) where, at that time,

(a) all the issued and outstanding shares of the capital stock of the corporation are identical to each other, or

(b) all the issued and outstanding shares of the capital stock of the corporation are held by one person;

**Related Provisions**: 248(12) — Identical properties.

**Notes**: 259(5)"qualified corporation" added by 1993 technical bill, effective for periods occurring after 1985. See Notes at end of 259 for reference to former section.

**"qualified trust"** at any time means a trust (other than a registered investment or a trust that is prescribed to be a small business investment trust) where

(a) each trustee of the trust at that time is a corporation that is licensed or otherwise authorized under the laws of Canada or a province to carry on in Canada the business of offering to the public its services as a trustee or a person who is a trustee of a trust governed by a registered pension plan,

(b) all the interests of the beneficiaries under the trust at that time are described by reference to units of the trust all of which are at that time identical to each other,

(c) it has never before that time borrowed money except where the borrowing was for a term not exceeding 90 days and the borrowing was not part of a series of loans or other transactions and repayments, and

(d) it has never before that time accepted deposits.

**Related Provisions**: 149(1)(o.4) — No tax payable by master trust; 248(12) — Identical properties.

**Notes**: 259(5)"qualified trust" added by 1993 technical bill, effective for periods occurring after 1985. See Notes at end of 259 for reference to former section.

**Regulations**: 5103 (prescribed small business investment trust; needs to be amended to apply for 259(5) rather than 259(3)).

**Notes [s. 259]**: Former 259 replaced by the subsections of 259 as above, without a legislated repeal date for the former section as a whole, so the repeal is technically effective as of June 15, 1994, the date of Royal Assent to the 1993 technical bill. However, new 259(1), (3) and (5), which effectively replace all of the former 259, apply to periods after 1985 and so appear to supersede the old version. Former 259 read:

259. (1) **Proportional holdings in trust property** — For the purposes of subsections 146(6), (10) and (10.1) and 146.3(7) to (9) and Parts X, X.2, XI and XI.1 of this Act and subsections 146.2(12), (13) and (14) of the *Income Tax Act*, chapter 148 of the Revised Statutes of Canada, 1952, where at any time a taxpayer described in section 205 acquires, holds or disposes of an interest in a qualified trust and the trust elects for any period that includes that time to have the provisions of this subsection apply, the taxpayer shall be deemed

(a) not to acquire, hold or dispose of at that time, as the case may be, that interest in the trust;

(b) to hold at that time that proportion (in this subsection referred to as the taxpayer's "specified portion") of each property of the trust that the number of units of the trust held by the taxpayer at that time is of the number of units of the trust outstanding at that time, and the cost amount to the trust of the taxpayer's specified portion of each such property shall be deemed to be the cost amount to the taxpayer of the taxpayer's specified portion of the property;

(c) to acquire the taxpayer's specified portion of each property of the trust at the later of

(i) the date the trust acquires the property, and

(ii) the date the taxpayer acquires the interest in the trust,

and the fair market value, at the time of acquisition by the taxpayer, of the taxpayer's specified portion of the property shall be deemed to be the fair market value of that specified portion of the property at the time of its acquisition by the trust; and

(d) to dispose of the taxpayer's specified portion of each property of the trust at the earlier of

(i) the date the trust disposes of the property, and

(ii) the date the taxpayer disposes of the interest in the trust

for proceeds equal to,

(iii) where subparagraph (i) applies, the proceeds of disposition to the trust of the taxpayer's specified portion of the property, and

(iv) where subparagraph (ii) applies, the fair market value, immediately before the disposition of the interest, of the taxpayer's specified portion of the property.

(2) **Election** — The election by a trust under subsection (1) shall be made by the trust filing a prescribed form with the Minister and shall be applicable in respect of the period commencing 15 months before the date of filing thereof (or such later time as the trust may designate in its election) and ending at such time as the election is revoked by the trust filing with the Minister a notice of revocation (or at such earlier time within the 15 month period immediately preceding the

date on which the notice of revocation is filed with the Minister as the trust may designate in its notice of revocation).

**(3) Definition of "qualified trust"** — In this section, "qualified trust" means a trust, other than a registered investment or a trust that is prescribed to be a small business investment trust, where

   (a) each trustee of the trust is a corporation that is licensed or otherwise authorized under the laws of Canada or a province to carry on in Canada the business of offering to the public its services as trustee or a person who is a trustee of a trust governed by a registered pension fund or plan;

   (b) the interests of the beneficiaries under the trust are described by reference to units of the trust that are identical in all respects and any difference between the interest in the trust of each beneficiary and the interest in the trust of each other beneficiary is dependent solely on the difference in the number of units held by those beneficiaries;

   (c) it has never borrowed money except where the borrowing was for a term not exceeding 90 days and was not part of a series of loans or other transactions and repayments;

   (d) it has never accepted deposits; and

   (e) it complies with prescribed conditions.

Former 259(3)(c) amended by 259(3)(c) amended by 1992 technical bill, effective for borrowings after 1990. For earlier borrowings, read simply "it has never borrowed money".

**Definitions [s. 259]**: "business" — 248(1); "Canada" — 255; "corporation" — 248(1), *Interpretation Act* 35(1); "cost amount" — 248(1); "identical" — 248(12); "Minister", "person", "prescribed" — 248(1); "province" — *Interpretation Act* 35(1); "qualified corporation", "qualified trust" — 259(5); "registered investment" — 204.4(1), 248(1); "registered pension plan" — 248(1); "relevant property" — 259(1)(b); "share" — 248(1); "small business investment trust" — Reg. 5103; "series of transactions" — 248(10); "specified portion" — 259(1)(b); "taxpayer" — 248(1); "trust" — 104(1), 248(1), (3); "written" — *Interpretation Act* 35(1) ["writing"].

**Regulations [s. 259]**: 5103 (small business investment trust).

**Interpretation Bulletins [s. 259]**: IT-320R2: RRSPs — qualified investments.

## 260. (1) Definitions — In this section,

**"qualified security"** means

   (a) a share of a class of the capital stock of a corporation that is listed on a prescribed stock exchange or of a class of the capital stock of a corporation that is a public corporation by reason of the designation of the class by the corporation in an election made under subparagraph (b)(i) of the definition "public corporation" in subsection 89(1) or by the Minister in a notice to the corporation under subparagraph (b)(ii) of that definition,

   (b) a bond, debenture, note or similar obligation of a corporation described in paragraph (a) or of a corporation that is controlled by such a corporation,

   (c) a bond, debenture, note or similar obligation of or guaranteed by the government of any country, province, state, municipality or other political subdivision, or a corporation, commission, agency or association controlled by any such person, or

   (d) a warrant, right, option or similar instrument with respect to a share described in paragraph (a);

**Notes**: Definition "qualified security" added by 1989 Budget, effective for transfers, loans and payments made after April 26, 1989.

**Regulations**: 3200, 3201 (prescribed stock exchanges).

**"securities lending arrangement"** means an arrangement under which

   (a) a person (in this section referred to as the "lender") transfers or lends at any particular time a qualified security to another person (in this section referred to as the "borrower") with whom the lender deals at arm's length,

   (b) it may reasonably be expected, at the particular time, that the borrower will transfer or return after the particular time to the lender a security (in this section referred to as an "identical security") that is identical to the security so transferred or lent,

   (c) where the qualified security is a share of the capital stock of a corporation, the borrower is obligated to pay to the lender amounts equal to and as compensation for all dividends, if any, paid on the security that would have been received by the borrower if the borrower had held the security throughout the period beginning after the particular time and ending at the time an identical security is transferred or returned to the lender, and

   (d) the lender's risk of loss or opportunity for gain or profit with respect to the security is not changed in any material respect,

but does not include an arrangement one of the main purposes of which may reasonably be considered to be to avoid or defer the inclusion in income of any gain or profit with respect to the security.

**Related Provisions**: 112(2.3) — Dividend rental arrangements; 248(1)"securities lending arrangement" — Definition applies to entire Act; 248(12) — Identical properties; 256(6), (6.1) — Meaning of "controlled".

**Notes**: Securities lending arrangements are used to facilitate the short-sale market. 260 is designed to recognize that such arrangements are not supposed to be transfers of the securities in question.

Para. (c) of "securities lending arrangement" amended by 1991 technical bill, retroactive to the introduction of s. 260 in 1989, to provide that the obligation to pay compensation for dividends is required only where the security is a share and applies only where the right to receive the dividend arises during the term of the arrangement.

Definition "securities lending arrangement" added by 1989 Budget, effective for transfers, loans and payments made after May 26, 1989. For transfers, loans and payments made from April 27 through May 26, 1989, ignore the words "with whom the person was dealing at arm's length" in para. (a).

**(2) Non-disposition** — Subject to subsections (3) and (4), for the purposes of this Act, any transfer or loan by a lender of a security under a securities lending arrangement shall be deemed not to be a disposition of the security and the security shall be deemed to continue to be property of the lender and, for the purposes of this subsection, a security shall be deemed to include an identical security that has been transferred or returned to the lender under the arrangement.

Notes: 260(2) added by 1989 Budget, effective for transfers, loans and payments made after April 26, 1989.

**(3) Disposition of right** — Where, at any time, a lender receives property (other than an identical security or an amount deemed by subsection (4) to have been received as proceeds of disposition) in satisfaction of or in exchange for the lender's right under a securities lending arrangement to receive the transfer or return of an identical security, for the purposes of this Act the lender shall be deemed to have disposed at that time of the security that was transferred or lent for proceeds of disposition equal to the fair market value of the property received for the disposition of the right (other than any portion thereof that is deemed to have been received by the lender as a taxable dividend), except that section 51, 85.1, 86 or 87, as the case may be, shall apply in computing the income of the lender with respect to any such disposition as if the security transferred or lent had continued to be the lender's property and the lender had received the property directly.

Notes: 260(3) added by 1989 Budget, effective for transfers, loans and payments made after April 26, 1989.

**(4) Idem** — Where, at any time, it may reasonably be considered that a lender would have received proceeds of disposition for a security that was transferred or lent under a securities lending arrangement, if the security had not been transferred or lent, the lender shall be deemed to have disposed of the security at that time for those proceeds of disposition.

Notes: 260(4) added by 1989 Budget, effective for transfers, loans and payments made after April 26, 1989.

**(5) Deemed dividend** — For the purposes of this Act, any amount received (other than an amount received as proceeds of disposition or an amount received by a corporation under an arrangement where it may reasonably be considered that one of the main reasons for the corporation entering into the arrangement was to enable it to receive an amount that would otherwise have been deemed by this subsection to be a dividend)

(a) under a securities lending arrangement from a person resident in Canada, or a person not resident in Canada where the amount was paid in the course of carrying on business in Canada through a permanent establishment as defined by regulation, or

(b) by or from a person who is a registered securities dealer resident in Canada, where the amount is received or paid, as the case may be, in the ordinary course of the business of trading in securities carried on by the dealer,

as compensation for a taxable dividend paid on a share of the capital stock of a public corporation that is a qualified security shall, to the extent of the amount of that dividend, be deemed to have been received as a taxable dividend on the share from the corporation.

Related Provisions: 82(1)(a)(ii)(B) — Amount deemed received by another person excluded from taxable dividends of individual; 248(1)"dividend rental arrangement"(d) — Dividend rental arrangement where 260(5) applies.

Notes: 260(5) added by 1989 Budget, and amended retroactively by 1994 tax amendments bill (Part VIII) to use the new term "registered securities dealer" in 260(5)(b). This version is effective for transfers, loans and payments made after May 26, 1989. For transfers, loans and payments made from April 27 through May 26, 1989, ignore the words "from a person resident in Canada, or a person not resident in Canada where the amount was paid in the course of carrying on business in Canada through a permanent establishment as defined by regulation" in 260(5)(a). 260(5) does not apply to transfers, loans and payments made before April 27, 1989.

Regulations: 8201 (permanent establishment).

Interpretation Bulletins: IT-67R3: Taxable dividends from corporations resident in Canada.

**(6) Non-deductibility** — In computing a taxpayer's income under Part I from a business or property

(a) where the taxpayer is not a registered securities dealer, no deduction shall be made in respect of an amount that, if paid, would be deemed by subsection (5) to have been received by another person as a taxable dividend; and

(b) where the taxpayer is a registered securities dealer, no deduction shall be made in respect of more than $2/3$ of that amount.

Related Provisions: 260(6.1) — Deductible amount.

Notes: 260(6) added by 1989 Budget, but amended retroactively by 1994 tax amendments bill (Part VIII) to add the rule in 260(6)(b), both effective for payments made after June 1989. The $2/3$ deduction in 260(6)(b) was originally a transitional rule of application that was to be in place only to the end of 1992, but it was extended to June 30, 1994 (by the 1993 technical bill) because the tax treatment of dividend compensation payments was under discussion between Finance officials and industry representatives. (See Department of Finance news releases, December 23, 1992 and December 20, 1993.) The $2/3$ deduction has now been made permanent. The transitional rules for the application of 260(6), appearing in 1989 Budget, 1991 technical bill and 1993 technical bill, were therefore all repealed retroactively by 1994 tax amendments bill (Part VIII), so there is only one form and one effective date for 260(6) now.

**(6.1) Deductible amount** — Notwithstanding subsection (6), there may be deducted in computing a corporation's income under Part I from a business or property for a taxation year an amount equal to the lesser of

(a) the amount that the corporation is obligated to pay to another person under an arrangement described in paragraphs (c) and (d) of the definition "dividend rental arrangement" in subsection 248(1) that, if paid, would be deemed by subsection (5) to have been received by another person as a taxable dividend, and

(b) the amount of the dividends received by the corporation under the arrangement that were identified in its return of income under Part I for the year as an amount in respect of which no amount was deductible because of subsection 112(2.3) in computing the taxpayer's taxable income or taxable income earned in Canada.

**Related Provisions**: 260(7)(b) — No dividend refund on amount deductible under 260(6.1).

**Notes**: 260(6.1) added by 1994 tax amendments bill (Part VIII), effective

(a) after April 1989, where the corporation has elected for the definition of "dividend rental arrangement" to apply after April 1989 (see Notes to 248(1)"dividend rental arrangement"), except that, for the purposes of 260(6.1)(b), a dividend received after April 1989 and before July 1994 that was identified in the corporation's Part I income tax return for its first taxation year that ends after June 22, 1995 shall be deemed to have been identified in its return for the taxation year in which the dividend was received; and

(b) after June 1994, in any other case.

**(7) Dividend refund** — For the purposes of section 129,

(a) any amount paid by a corporation that is not a registered securities dealer (other than an amount for which a deduction in computing income may be claimed under subsection (6.1)), and

(b) ⅓ of any amount paid by a corporation that is a registered securities dealer (other than an amount for which a deduction in computing income may be claimed under subsection (6.1))

that is deemed by subsection (5) to have been received by another person as a taxable dividend shall be deemed to have been paid by the corporation as a taxable dividend.

**Notes**: 260(7) added by 1989 Budget, but amended retroactively by 1994 tax amendments bill (Part VIII) to add the rule in 260(7)(b), effective for payments made after June 1989. (The exclusion for an amount claimable under 260(6.1) is effective on the same basis as is 260(6.1); see the Notes thereto.) Other transitional rules for the application of 260(7), appearing in 1989 Budget, 1991 technical bill and 1993 technical bill were all repealed retroactively by 1994 tax amendments bill (Part VIII); see Notes to 260(6).

**Interpretation Bulletins**: IT-243R4: Dividend refund to private corporations.

**(8) Non-resident withholding tax** — For the purposes of Part XIII,

(a) any amount paid or credited under a securities lending arrangement by or on behalf of the borrower to the lender as compensation for any interest or dividend paid in respect of the security shall be deemed to be a payment made by the borrower to the lender of interest, except that where, throughout the term of the securities lending arrangement, the borrower has provided the lender under the arrangement with money in an amount of, or securities described in paragraph (c) of the definition "qualified security" in subsection (1) that have a fair market value of, not less than 95% of the fair market value of the security and the borrower is entitled to enjoy, directly or indirectly, the benefits of all or substantially all income derived from, and opportunity for gain with respect of, the money or securities,

(i) the amount paid or credited shall, to the extent of the amount of the interest or dividend paid in respect of the security, be deemed to be a payment made by the borrower to the lender of interest or a dividend, as the case may be, payable on the security,

(ii) the amount paid or credited shall, to the extent of the amount of the interest, if any, paid in respect of the security, be deemed for the purpose of subparagraph 212(1)(b)(vii) to have been payable by the issuer of the security, and

(iii) the security shall be deemed to be a security described in subparagraph 212(1)(b)(ii) if it is a security described in paragraph (c) of the definition "qualified security" in subsection (1), and

(b) any amount paid or credited under a securities lending arrangement by or on behalf of the borrower to the lender as, on account of, in lieu of payment of or in satisfaction of, a fee for the use of the security shall be deemed to be a payment made by the borrower to the lender of interest and, for the purposes of this paragraph, where the borrower has at any time provided the lender with money, either as collateral or consideration for the security, and the borrower does not under the arrangement pay or credit a reasonable amount to the lender as, on account of, in lieu of payment of or in satisfaction of, a fee for the use of the security, the amount, if any, by which

(i) interest on the money computed at the prescribed rates in effect during the term of the arrangement

exceeds

(ii) the amount, if any, by which any amount that the lender pays or credits to the borrower under the arrangement exceeds the amount of the money

shall be deemed to be an amount paid under the arrangement by the borrower to the lender as a fee for the use of the security, at the time that an identical security is or can reasonably be expected to be transferred or returned to the lender,

and, for the purposes of Part XIII and any agreement or convention between the Government of Canada and the government of another country that has the force of law in Canada, any amount deemed by this subsection (other than subparagraph (a)(i) or (ii)) to be a payment of interest shall be deemed not to be payable on or in respect of the security.

**Related Provisions**: 212(1)(b)(xii) — Exemption from withholding tax; 212(19) — Special tax on securities dealers re non-resident withholding tax exemption.

**Notes**: The CCRA takes the position that "all or substantially all", used in 260(8)(a), means 90% or more.

## S. 260(8) — Income Tax Act

260(8) amended by 1991 technical bill, retroactive to the introduction of 260 in 1989, in part to clarify that, where the borrowed security is a long-term corporate debt obligation, a non-resident lender will continue to be entitled to the exemption from withholding tax under 212(1)(b)(vii) for any compensation payments. The amendment also provides that where a non-resident lender has received money as collateral or consideration for a loaned security and the resident borrower has not paid a reasonable fee for the use of the security, the difference between interest on the money held by the lender (calculated at the prescribed rate) and any amount that is paid by the lender to the borrower (other than as a return of the collateral or consideration) will be considered to be a fee paid for the use of the security.

260(8)(a)(iii) added by 1993 technical bill, effective for securities lending arrangements entered into after May 28, 1993.

260(8) added by 1989 Budget, effective for transfers, loans and payments made after April 26, 1989.

**(9) Restricted financial institution** — For the purposes of subsection 187.3(1), where at any time a dividend is received by a restricted financial institution on a share that was last acquired before that time pursuant to an obligation of a borrower to return or transfer a share under a securities lending arrangement, an acquisition of the share under the arrangement shall be deemed at and after that time not to be an acquisition of the share.

**Notes**: 260(9) added by 1989 Budget, effective for transfers, loans and payments made after April 26, 1989.

**Definitions [s. 260]**: "amount" — 248(1); "arm's length" — 251(1); "business" — 248(1); "carrying on business in Canada" — 253; "class" — 248(6); "class of shares" — 248(6); "controlled" — 256(6), (6.1); "corporation" — 248(1); "disposition" — 54; "dividend" — 248(1); "identical" — 248(12); "permanent establishment" — Reg. 8201; "person" — 248(1); "prescribed stock exchange" — Reg. 3200, 3201; "property" — 248(1); "province" — *Interpretation Act* 35(1); "public corporation" — 89(1), 248(1); "qualified security" — 260(1); "registered securities dealer" — 248(1); "resident in Canada" — 250; "securities lending arrangement" — 248(1), 260(1); "share" — 248(1); "taxable dividend" — 89(1), 248(1).

**Application rule — Grandfathering of amendments announced on April 26, 1995**: The 1995-97 technical bill, s. 247, provides:

> 156. (1) Exception to coming-into-force — Subsections 73(4), 74(5), subsection 18(13) of the Act, as enacted by subsection 79(2) and subsections 89(1), (2) and (6), 94(1) and (2), 95(1), 116(3) to (5), 120(1) and 124(1) and (2) do not apply to the disposition of property by a person or partnership (in this subsection and subsection (2) referred to as the "transferor") that occurred before 1996
>
> (a) to a person who was obliged on April 26, 1995 to acquire the property pursuant to the terms of an agreement in writing made on or before that day; or

> (b) in a transaction, or as part of a series of transactions, the arrangements for which, evidenced in writing, were substantially advanced before April 27, 1995, other than a transaction or series a main purpose of which can reasonably be considered to have been to enable an unrelated person to obtain the benefit of
>
> > (i) any deduction in computing income, taxable income, taxable income earned in Canada or tax payable under the Act, or
> >
> > (ii) any balance of undeducted outlays, expenses or other amounts.
>
> (2) Election — Notwithstanding subsection (1), subsection 18(13) of the Act, as enacted by subsection 79(2), and the other subsections of this Act referred to in subsection (1) apply to a disposition in respect of which the transferor has filed with the Minister of National Revenue before the end of the third month after the month in which this Act is assented to [i.e., before October 1998 — ed.] an election in writing to have those subsections apply.
>
> (3) Interpretation — For the purpose of subsection (1),
>
> > (a) a person shall be considered not to be obliged to acquire property where the person can be excused from the obligation if there is a change to the Act or if there is an adverse assessment under the Act;
> >
> > (b) an "unrelated person" means any person who was not, or a partnership any member of which was not, related (otherwise than because of paragraph 251(5)(b) of the Act) to the transferor at the time of the disposition; and
> >
> > (c) a person is deemed to be related to a partnership of which that person is a majority interest partner.

The following are the provisions of the Act affected by the indicated provisions of the 1995-97 technical bill:

| Amending Bill | ITA Provision |
| --- | --- |
| 73(4) | 13(21.1), (21.2) [new] |
| 74(5) | 14(12), (13) [new] |
| 79(2) | 18(13) [amended] |
| 89(1) | 40(2)(e) [repeal] |
| 89(2) | 40(2)(h)(i) [amended] |
| 89(6) | 40(3.3)–(3.6) [new] |
| 94(1) | 53(1)(f.1), (f.11) [amended] |
| 94(2) | 53(1)(f.2) [amended] |
| 95(1) | 54 "superficial loss" [amended] |
| 116(3) | 85(4) [repeal] |
| 116(4) | 85(5) [amended] |
| 116(5) | 85(5.1) [repeal] |
| 120(1) | 93(4) [amended] |
| 124(1) | 97(2) [amended] |
| 124(2) | 97(3) [repeal], (3.1) [repeal] |

# DETAILED TABLE OF SECTIONS

## INCOME TAX APPLICATION RULES

7 Short title

### PART I — INCOME TAX APPLICATION RULES, 1971
#### Interpretation
8 Definitions

#### Application of 1970-71-72, c. 63, s. 1
9 Application of 1970-71-72, c. 63, s. 1
9.1 [Repealed under former Act]

#### Application of Part XIII of Amended Act
10
10(1)–(3) [Repealed under former Act]
10(4) Application of Part XIII of amended Act
10(5) Certificates of exemption
10(6) Limitation on non-resident's tax rate

#### References and Continuation of Provisions
11 [Repealed under former Act]
12 Definitions
13
13(1) References relating to same subject-matter
14 Part IV of former Act
15 Part VIII of former Act
16 Construction of certain references
17
17(1) *Income War Tax Act*, s. 8
17(2), (3) S.C. 1947, c. 63, s. 16
17(4) Retrospection
17(5) Amount not previously included as income
17(6), (7) S.C. 1949 (2nd S.), c. 25, s. 53
17(8) Registered pension plan
18
18(1), (2) General depreciation provisions
18(3) Provisoes not applicable
18(4) Reference to depreciation
18(5) Deduction deemed depreciation

#### Special Transitional Rules
19
19(1) Income maintenance payments
19(2) Effect of certain changes made in plan established before June 19, 1971
20
20(1) Depreciable property
20(1.1) Where depreciable property disposed of to spouse, common-law partner, trust or child
20(1.11) Extended meaning of "child"
20(1.2) Other transfers of depreciable property
20(1.3) Transfers before 1972 not at arm's length
20(1.4) Depreciable property received as dividend in kind
20(2) Recapture of capital cost allowances
20(3) Depreciable property of partnership of prescribed class
20(4) Definitions
20(5) Other depreciable property of partnership

1871

## Detailed Table of Sections

| | |
|---|---|
| 21 | |
| 21(1)–(2.1) | Goodwill and other nothings |
| 21(2.2) | Amalgamations |
| 21(3) | Definitions |
| 22 | [Repealed under former Act] |
| 23 | |
| 23(1), (2) | [Repealed under former Act] |
| 23(3) | Rules applicable [to professional business] |
| 23(4) | Application of para. (3)(a) |
| 23(4.1) | Certain persons deemed to be carrying on business by means of partnership |
| 23(5) | Definitions |
| 24 | Definition of "valuation day" for capital gains and losses |
| 25 | [Not included in R.S.C. 1985] |
| 26 | |
| 26(1) | Capital gains subject to tax |
| 26(1.1) | Principal amount of certain obligations |
| 26(2) | [Repealed under former Act] |
| 26(3) | Cost of acquisition of capital property owned on Dec. 31, 1971 |
| 26(4) | Determination of cost where property not disposed of |
| 26(5), (5.1) | Where property disposed of in transaction not at arm's length |
| 26(5.2) | Transfer of capital property to a corporation |
| 26(6) | Reacquired property |
| 26(7) | Election re cost |
| 26(8)–(8.4) | Identical properties |
| 26(8.5) | Amalgamation |
| 26(9) | Cost of interest in partnership |
| 26(9.1) | Determination of amount for purposes of subsec. (9) |
| 26(9.2) | Where interest acquired before 1972 and after beginning of 1st fiscal period ending after 1971 |
| 26(9.3) | Amounts deemed to be required to be deducted in respect of interest in partnership |
| 26(9.4) | Application of section 53 of amended Act in respect of interest in partnership |
| 26(10) | Where paragraph 128.1(1)(b) applies |
| 26(11) | Fair market value of publicly-traded securities |
| 26(11.1), (11.2) | Fair market value of share of foreign affiliate |
| 26(12) | Definitions |
| 26(13)–(17) | Meaning of "actual cost" |
| 26(17.1) | Application |
| 26(18) | Transfer of farm land by a farmer to [the farmer's] child at death |
| 26(19) | *Inter vivos* transfer of farm land by a farmer to child |
| 26(20) | Extended meaning of "child" |
| 26(21) | Shares received on amalgamation |
| 26(22) | Options received on amalgamations |
| 26(23) | Obligations received on amalgamations |
| 26(24) | Convertible properties |
| 26(25) | Bond conversion |
| 26(26) | Share for share exchange |
| 26(27), (28) | Reorganization of capital |
| 26(29) | Effect of election under subsection 110.6(19) |
| 26(30) | Additions to taxable Canadian property |
| 26(30) | [Proposed] Additions to taxable Canadian property |
| 26.1 | |
| 26.1(1) | Change of use of property before 1972 |
| 26.1(2) | No capital cost allowance while election in force |
| 27, 28 | [Repealed under former Act] |
| 29 | |
| 29(1) | Deduction from income of petroleum or natural gas corporation |
| 29(2) | Deduction from income of mining corporation |
| 29(3) | Deduction from income of petroleum or natural gas corporation or mining corporation |
| 29(4) | Deduction from income of petroleum corporation, etc. |
| 29(5) | Application of para. (4)(g) |
| 29(6)–(8) | [Repealed effective 2007] |
| 29(9), (10) | Deduction from income from businesses of associations, etc. |

## Detailed Table of Sections

| | |
|---|---|
| 29(11) | Deduction from income of corporation |
| 29(12) | Deduction by individual of exploration expenses |
| 29(13) | Limitation re payments for exploration and drilling rights |
| 29(14), (15) | Exploration and drilling rights; payments deductible |
| 29(16)–(20) | Receipts for exploration or drilling rights included in income |
| 29(21), (22) | Bonus payments |
| 29(23) | Expenses incurred for specified considerations not deductible |
| 29(24) | Exception |
| 29(25) | Successor rule |
| 29(25.1) | Definitions |
| 29(26) | Processing or fabricating corporation |
| 29(27) | Meaning of "drilling and exploration expenses" |
| 29(28) | Deduction from expenses |
| 29(29) | [Repealed under former Act] |
| 29(30) | Inclusion in "drilling and exploration expenses" |
| 29(31) | General limitation |
| 29(32) | Deduction for provincial tax |
| 29(33) | Definition of "provincial statute" |
| 29(34) | Expenses deductible under certain enactments deemed not otherwise deductible |
| 30 | |
| 30(1), (2) | [Repealed under former Act] |
| 30(3) | Reference to this Act in amended Act |
| 31 | Application of section 67 of amended Act |
| 32 | |
| 32(1) | Application of para. 69(1)(a) of amended Act |
| 32(2) | Application of para. 69(1)(b) of amended Act |
| 32(3) | Application of para. 69(1)(c) of amended Act |
| 32.1 | |
| 32.1(1)–(3.2) | [Repealed under former Act] |
| 32.1(4) | Capital dividend account |
| 32.1(5), (6) | [Repealed under former Act] |
| 33 | [Repealed under former Act] |
| 34 | |
| 34(1) | Amalgamations |
| 34(2)–(4) | [Repealed under former Act] |
| 34(5), (6) | [Repealed under former Act] |
| 34(7) | Definition of "amalgamation" |
| 34(8) | [Repealed under former Act] |
| 35 | |
| 35(1), (2) | Foreign affiliates |
| 35(3), (4) | [Repealed under former Act] |
| 35.1 | [Repealed under former Act] |
| 36 | Application of paras. 107(2)(b) to (d) of amended Act |
| 37–39 | [Repealed under former Act] |
| 40 | |
| 40(1) | Payments out of pension funds, etc. |
| 40(2) | Employee not resident in Canada |
| 40(3), (4) | Determination of amount of payment |
| 40(5), (6) | Maximum amount for election |
| 40(7) | Limitation |
| 40(8) | Application rule |
| 41–48 | [Repealed under former Act] |
| 49 | |
| 49(1) | Tax deemed payable under amended Act |
| 49(2) | Application of section 13 |
| 49(3) | Computation of tax deemed payable under amended Act |
| 50 | |
| 50(1) | Status of certain corporations |
| 50(2) | Election to be public corporation |
| 50(3) | Designation by Minister |
| 51–56.1 | [Repealed under former Act] |

## Detailed Table of Sections

| | |
|---|---|
| 57 | |
| 57(1)–(8) | [Repealed under former Act] |
| 57(9) | Capital dividend account |
| 57(10) | [Repealed under former Act] |
| 57(11) | Meaning of "specified personal corporation" |
| 57(12) | [Repealed under former Act] |
| 57.1 | [Repealed under former Act] |
| 58 | |
| 58(1) | Credit unions |
| 58(1.1) | Exception |
| 58(2)–(3.1) | [Repealed under former Act] |
| 58(3.2)–(3.4) | Determination of maximum cumulative reserve at end of taxation year |
| 58(4), (4.1) | [Repealed under former Act] |
| 58(5) | Definitions |
| 59 | |
| 59(1) | [Repealed under former Act] |
| 59(2) | Non-resident-owned investment corporation |
| 60 | [Repealed under former Act] |
| 60.1 | Taxes payable by insurer under Part IA of former Act |
| 61 | |
| 61(1) | Registered retirement savings plans |
| 61(2) | |
| 62 | |
| 62(1) | Assessments |
| 62(2) | Interest |
| 62(3) | [Repealed under former Act] |
| 62(4) | Objections to assessment |
| 62(5) | Appeals |
| 62(6) | Appeals to Federal Court |
| 63–64.3 | [Repealed under former Act] |
| 65 | |
| 65(1), (1.1) | Part XI of amended Act |
| 65(2) | Definition of "foreign investment limit" |
| 65(3) | Foreign property acquired by registered retirement savings plan |
| 65(4) | Definition of "foreign reinvestment limit" |
| 65(5) | Shares of a mutual fund corporation received on amalgamation |
| 65.1 | Part XV of amended Act |
| 66 | |
| 66(1) | Part II of former Act |
| 66(2) | [Repealed under former Act] |
| 67 | |
| 67(1)–(4) | |
| 67(5) | Prescription of unpaid amounts |
| 68 | |

### PART II — TRANSITIONAL CONCERNING THE 1985 STATUTE REVISION

| | |
|---|---|
| 69 | Definitions |

#### Application of the 1971 Acts and the Revised Acts

| | |
|---|---|
| 70 | Application of *Income Tax Application Rules, 1971*, 1970-71-72, c. 63 |
| 71 | Application of this Act |
| 72 | Application of *Income Tax Act*, R.S.C., 1952, c. 148 |
| 73 | Application of *Income Tax Act* |

#### Application of Certain Provisions

| | |
|---|---|
| 74 | Definition of "provision" |
| 75 | Continued effect of amending and application provisions |
| 76 | Application of section 75 |
| 77 | Continued effect of repealed provisions |
| 78 | Application of section 77 |
| 79 | |
| 79(1) | Effect of amendments on former ITA |
| 79(2) | Effect of amendments on former ITAR |

1874

# INCOME TAX APPLICATION RULES

REVISED STATUTES OF CANADA 1985, CHAPTER 2 (5TH SUPPLEMENT), AS AMENDED BY 1994, cc. 7, 21; 1995, cc. 3, 21; 1997, c. 25; 1998, c. 19.

**Notes:** Sections 1 to 6 of 1970-71-72, c. 63 replaced the *Income Tax Act* and amended various other Acts. The *Income Tax Application Rules, 1971* began at section 7. With the consolidation of the Act as R.S.C. 1985, c. 1 (5th Supp.) as of March 1, 1994, the ITARs have been re-enacted with the same numbering as before, as R.S.C. 1985, c. 2 (5th Supp.).

**7. Short title** — This Act may be cited as the *Income Tax Application Rules*.

## PART I — INCOME TAX APPLICATION RULES, 1971

### Interpretation

**8. Definitions** — In this Act,

**"amended Act"** means, according to the context in which that expression appears,

(a) the *Income Tax Act*, chapter 148 of the Revised Statutes of Canada, 1952, as amended by section 1 of chapter 63 of the Statutes of Canada, 1970-71-72, and by any subsequent Act, and

(b) the *Income Tax Act*, as amended from time to time;

**"former Act"** means the *Income Tax Act*, chapter 148 of the Revised Statutes of Canada, 1952, as it was before being amended by section 1 of chapter 63 of the Statutes of Canada, 1970-71-72.

**Notes:** ITAR 8"amended Act" was 8(a) and "former Act" was 8(b), before consolidation in R.S.C. 1985 (5th Supp.), effective for taxation years ending after November 1991.

**Definitions [ITAR 8]:** "Income Tax Act, chapter 148 of the Revised Statutes of Canada, 1952" — ITAR 69.

### Application of 1970-71-72, c. 63, s. 1

**9. Application of 1970-71-72, c. 63, s. 1** — Subject to the amended Act and this Act, section 1 of chapter 63 of the Statutes of Canada, 1970-71-72, applies to the 1972 and subsequent taxation years.

**Related Provisions:** ITAR 65.1 — Part XV of amended Act.

**Notes:** The referenced section repealed the pre-1972 version of the Act and enacted the version that was in force from January 1, 1972 until March 1, 1994.

**Definitions [ITAR 9]:** "amended Act" — ITAR 8; "taxation year" — ITA 249.

**9.1** [Repealed under former Act]

**Notes:** ITAR 9.1, repealed in 1977, provided an application rule for the pre-1978 Part VIII of the Act.

### Application of Part XIII of Amended Act

**10. (1)–(3)** [Repealed under former Act]

**Notes:** ITAR 10(1)–(3), repealed in 1985, provided application rules for the non-resident withholding tax for 1972-75.

**(4) Application of Part XIII of amended Act** — Where an amount is paid or credited by a person resident in Canada to a non-resident person

(a) who is resident in a prescribed country, and

(b) with whom the person resident in Canada was dealing at arm's length,

as, on account or in lieu of payment of or in satisfaction of, interest payable on any bond, debenture, mortgage, note or similar obligation issued before 1976 by the person resident in Canada to the non-resident person, for the purposes of computing the tax under Part XIII of the amended Act payable by the non-resident person on the amount, the reference in subsection 212(1) of that Act to "25%" shall be read as a reference to "15%".

**Regulations:** 1600 (prescribed country).

**(5) Certificates of exemption** — Any certificate of exemption issued by the Minister under subsection 106(9) of the former Act that was in force on December 31, 1971 shall, for the purposes of subparagraph 212(1)(b)(iv) of the amended Act,

(a) be deemed to have been issued under subsection 212(14) of the amended Act; and

(b) be deemed

(i) in respect of interest payable on any bond, debenture or similar obligation acquired on or before December 31, 1971 by the person to whom the certificate was issued, to have been in force on January 1, 1972 and thereafter without interruption,

except that if the person to whom the certificate was issued has ceased at any time after 1971 to be exempt, under the laws of the country of which the person is a resident, from the payment of income tax to the government of that country, the certificate ceases to be in force

(iii) in respect of interest described in subparagraph (i), on the day on which the person first so ceased to be exempt.

**Information Circulars:** 77-16R4: Non-resident income tax.

**(6) Limitation on non-resident's tax rate** — Notwithstanding any provision of the amended Act, where an agreement or convention between the Government of Canada and the government of any other country that has the force of law in Canada provides that where an amount is paid or credited, or deemed to be paid or credited, to a resident of that other country the rate of tax imposed thereon shall not exceed a specified rate,

    (a) any reference in Part XIII of the amended Act to a rate in excess of the specified rate shall, in respect of such an amount, be read as a reference to the specified rate; and

    (b) except where the amount can reasonably be attributed to a business carried on by that person in Canada, that person shall, for the purpose of the agreement or convention in respect of the amount, be deemed not to have a permanent establishment in Canada.

**Definitions [ITAR 10]**: "amended Act" — ITAR 8; "amount", "business" — ITA 248(1); "Canada" — ITA 255, *Interpretation Act* 35(1); "former Act" — ITAR 8; "Minister", "non-resident", "person", "prescribed" — ITA 248(1); "resident", "resident in Canada" — ITA 250.

**11.** [Repealed under former Act]

**Notes**: ITAR 11 repealed in 1985. 11(1)–(3) reduced the branch tax under Part XIV of the Act from 25% to 15% from 1972 to 1975. 11(4) provided that tax treaty provisions reducing the withholding tax on dividends apply to the branch tax as well. This rule is now in 219.2 of the Act.

## References and Continuation of Provisions

**12. Definitions** — In this section and sections 13 to 18,

**"enactment"** has the meaning assigned by section 2 of the *Interpretation Act*;

**"new law"** — [Not included in R.S.C. 1985]

**"old law"** means the *Income War Tax Act*, *The 1948 Income Tax Act*, and the *Income Tax Act*, chapter 148 of the Revised Statutes of Canada, 1952, as amended from time to time otherwise than by section 1 of chapter 63 of the Statutes of Canada, 1970-71-72, or any subsequent Act;

**"The 1948 Income Tax Act"**; means *The Income Tax Act*, chapter 52 of the Statutes of Canada, 1948, together with all Acts passed in amendment thereof.

**Notes**: ITAR 12"enactment" was 12(a), "new law" was 12(b), "old law" was 12(c), "*The 1948 Income Tax Act*" was 12(d), before consolidation in R.S.C. 1985 (5th Supp.), effective for taxation years ending after November 1991.

**Definitions [ITAR 12]**: "Canada" — ITA 255, *Interpretation Act* 35(1); "Income Tax Act, chapter 148 of the Revised Statutes of Canada, 1952" — ITAR 69.

**13. (1) References relating to same subject-matter** — Subject to this Act and unless the context otherwise requires, a reference in any enactment to a particular Part or provision of the amended Act shall be construed, as regards any transaction, matter or thing to which the old law applied, to include a reference to the Part or provision, if any, of the old law relating to, or that may reasonably be regarded as relating to, the same subject-matter.

**Interpretation Bulletins**: IT-474R: Amalgamations of Canadian corporations.

**Definitions [ITAR 13]**: "amended Act" — ITAR 8; "enactment", "old law" — ITAR 12.

**14. Part IV of former Act** — Part IV of the former Act is continued in force but does not apply in respect of gifts made after 1971.

**Definitions [ITAR 14]**: "former Act" — ITAR 8.

**15. Part VIII of former Act** — Part VIII of the former Act is continued in force but as though the references in that Part that, according to the context in which they appear, are references to or to provisions of the *Income Tax Act* were read as references to or to provisions of the *Income Tax Act*, chapter 148 of the Revised Statutes of Canada, 1952, as amended from time to time otherwise than by section 1 of chapter 63 of the Statutes of Canada, 1970-71-72, or any subsequent Act.

**I.T. Application Rules**: 69 (meaning of "*Income Tax Act*, chapter 148 of the Revised Statutes of Canada, 1952").

**Definitions [ITAR 15]**: "former Act" — ITAR 8; "Income Tax Act, chapter 148 of the Revised Statutes of Canada, 1952" — ITAR 69.

**16. Construction of certain references** — In any enactment, a reference by number to any provision of the *Income Tax Act* that, according to the context in which the reference appears, is a reference to

    (a) a provision of Part IV of the former Act,

    (b) a provision of Part VIII of the former Act, or

    (c) a provision of the amended Act having the same number as a provision described in paragraph (a) or (b),

shall, for greater certainty, be read as a reference to the provision described in paragraph (a), (b) or (c), as the case may be, and not to any other provision of the *Income Tax Act* or the *Income Tax Act*, chapter 148 of the Revised Statutes of Canada, 1952, having the same number.

**Definitions [ITAR 16]**: "amended Act" — ITAR 8; "enactment" — ITAR 12; "former Act" — ITAR 8; "Income Tax Act, chapter 148 of the Revised Statutes of Canada, 1952" — ITAR 69.

**I.T. Application Rules**: 69 (meaning of "*Income Tax Act*, chapter 148 of the Revised Statutes of Canada, 1952").

**17. (1) *Income War Tax Act*, s. 8** — A taxpayer may deduct from the tax otherwise payable under Part I of the amended Act for a taxation year such amount as would, if the *Income War Tax Act* applied to the taxation year, be deductible from tax because of subsections 8(6), (7) and (7A) of the *Income War Tax Act*.

Part I — Income Tax Application Rules, 1971    ITAR S. 18(5)

**(2) S.C. 1947, c. 63, s. 16** — There may be deducted in computing income for a taxation year under Part I of the amended Act an amount that would be deductible under section 16 of chapter 63 of the Statutes of Canada, 1947, from income as defined by the *Income War Tax Act* if that Act applied to the taxation year.

**(3) Idem** — There may be deducted from the tax for a taxation year otherwise payable under Part I of the amended Act an amount that would be deductible under section 16 of chapter 63 of the Statutes of Canada, 1947, from the total of taxes payable under the *Income War Tax Act* and *The Excess Profits Tax Act, 1940*, if those Acts applied to the taxation year.

**(4) Retrospection** — Where there is a reference in the amended Act to any act, matter or thing done or existing before a taxation year, it shall be deemed to include a reference to the act, matter or thing, even though it was done or existing before the commencement of that Act.

**(5) Amount not previously included as income** — Where, on the application of a method adopted by a taxpayer for computing income from a business, other than a business that is a profession, or farm or property for a taxation year to which the amended Act applies, an amount received in the year would not be included in computing the taxpayer's income for the year because on the application of that method it would have been included in computing the taxpayer's income for the purposes of the *Income Tax Act* or the *Income Tax Act*, chapter 148 of the Revised Statutes of Canada, 1952, for a preceding taxation year in respect of which it was receivable, if the amount was not included in computing the income for the preceding year, it shall be included in computing the income for the year in which it was received.

**I.T. Application Rules**: 69 (meaning of "*Income Tax Act*, chapter 148 of the Revised Statutes of Canada, 1952").

**(6) S.C. 1949 (2nd S.), c. 25, s. 53** — There may be deducted in computing income for a taxation year under Part I of the amended Act an amount that would be deductible under section 53 of chapter 25 of the Statutes of Canada, 1949 (Second Session), in computing income under *The 1948 Income Tax Act* if that Act applied to the taxation year.

**(7) Idem** — There may be deducted from the tax for a taxation year otherwise payable under Part I of the amended Act an amount that would be deductible under section 53 of chapter 25 of the Statutes of Canada, 1949 (Second Session) from the tax payable under Part I of *The 1948 Income Tax Act* if that Act applied to the taxation year.

**(8) Registered pension plan** — A reference in the amended Act to a registered pension plan shall, in respect of a period while the plan was an approved superannuation or pension fund or plan, be construed as a reference to that approved superannuation or pension fund or plan.

**Definitions [ITAR 17]**: "amended Act" — ITAR 8; "amount", "business" — ITA 248(1); "Canada" — ITA 255, *Interpretation Act* 35(1); "commencement" — *Interpretation Act* 35(1); "Income Tax Act, chapter 148 of the Revised Statutes of Canada, 1952" — ITAR 69; "property", "registered pension plan" — ITA 248(1); "taxation year" — ITA 249; "taxpayer" — ITA 248(1); "The 1948 Income Tax Act" — ITAR 12.

**18. (1) General depreciation provisions** — Where the capital cost to a taxpayer of any depreciable property that was acquired by him before 1972 was required by any provision of the old law to be determined for the purpose of computing the amount of any deduction under any such provision in respect of that property, or would have been required by any provision of the old law to be determined for that purpose if any deduction under any such provision had been claimed by the taxpayer in respect of that property, the amount of the capital cost so required to be determined or that would have been so required to be determined, as the case may be, shall be deemed, for all purposes of the amended Act, to be the capital cost to the taxpayer of that property.

**(2) Idem** — Where a taxpayer has acquired depreciable property before the beginning of the 1949 taxation year, for the purposes of section 13 of the amended Act and any regulations made under paragraph 20(1)(a) of that Act an amount equal to the total of

(a) all deductions allowed in computing the taxpayer's income for the purpose of the *Income War Tax Act* as "special depreciation", "extra depreciation" or allowances in lieu of depreciation for property the taxpayer had at the beginning of the 1949 taxation year (except deductions allowed under subparagraph 6(1)(n)(ii) of that Act), and

(b) ½ of all amounts allowed to the taxpayer under subparagraph 6(1)(n)(ii) of that Act for property that the taxpayer had at the beginning of the 1949 taxation year,

shall be deemed to have been allowed to the taxpayer under regulations made under paragraph 20(1)(a) of the amended Act in computing income for a taxation year before the 1949 taxation year.

**(3) Provisoes not applicable** — The second and third provisoes to paragraph 6(1)(n) of the *Income War Tax Act* do not apply to sales made after the beginning of the 1949 taxation year.

**(4) Reference to depreciation** — Reference in this section to depreciation shall be deemed to include a reference to allowances in respect of depreciable property of a taxpayer made under paragraph 5(1)(a) of the *Income War Tax Act*.

**(5) Deduction deemed depreciation** — An amount deducted under paragraph 5(1)(u) of the *Income War Tax Act* in respect of amounts of a capital nature shall, for the purpose of this section, be deemed to be depreciation taken into account in ascertaining the taxpayer's income for the purpose of that Act or in ascertaining the taxpayer's loss for the taxation year for which it was deducted.

**Definitions [ITAR 18]:** "amended Act" — ITAR 8; "amount" — ITA 248(1); "depreciable property" — ITA 13(21), 248(1); "depreciation" — ITAR 18(4), (5); "old law" — ITAR 12; "property" — ITA 248(1); "taxation year" — ITA 249; "taxpayer" — ITA 248(1).

## Special Transitional Rules

**19. (1) Income maintenance payments** — Notwithstanding section 9, paragraph 6(1)(f) of the amended Act does not apply in respect of amounts received by a taxpayer in a taxation year that were payable to the taxpayer in respect of the loss, in consequence of an event occurring before 1974, of all or any part of the taxpayer's income from an office or employment, under a plan, described in that paragraph, that was established before June 19, 1971.

**(2) Effect of certain changes made in plan established before June 19, 1971** — For the purposes of this section, a plan described in paragraph 6(1)(f) of the amended Act that was in existence before June 19, 1971 does not cease to be a plan established before that date solely because of changes made therein on or after that date for the purpose of ensuring that the plan qualifies as one entitling the employer of persons covered under the plan to a reduction, as provided for by subsection 50(2) of the *Unemployment Insurance Act*, in the amount of the employer's premium payable under that Act in respect of insured persons covered under the plan.

**Interpretation Bulletins:** IT-54: Wage loss replacement plans; IT-85R2: Health and welfare trusts for employees; IT-428: Wage loss replacement plans.

**Definitions [ITAR 19]:** "amended Act" — ITAR 8; "amount", "employer", "employment", "office", "person" — ITA 248(1); "plan" — ITA 6(1)(f), ITAR 19(2); "taxation year" — ITA 249; "taxpayer" — ITA 248(1).

**20. (1) Depreciable property** — Where the capital cost to a taxpayer of any depreciable property acquired by the taxpayer before 1972 and owned by the taxpayer without interruption from December 31, 1971 until such time after 1971 as the taxpayer disposed of it is less than the fair market value of the property on valuation day and less than the proceeds of disposition thereof otherwise determined,

(a) for the purposes of section 13 of the amended Act, subdivision c of Division B of Part I of that Act and any regulations made under paragraph 20(1)(a) of that Act, the taxpayer's proceeds of disposition of the property shall be deemed to be an amount equal to the total of its capital cost to the taxpayer and the amount, if any, by which the proceeds of disposition thereof otherwise determined exceed the fair market value of the property on valuation day;

(b) where the property has, by one or more transactions or events (other than the death of a taxpayer to which subsection 70(5) of the amended Act applies) between persons not dealing at arm's length, become vested in another taxpayer

(i) for the purposes of the amended Act (other than, where paragraph 13(7)(e) of that Act applies in determining the capital cost to that other taxpayer of the property, for the purposes of paragraphs 8(1)(j) and (p) and sections 13 and 20 of that Act), that other taxpayer shall be deemed to have acquired the property at a capital cost equal to the proceeds deemed to have been received for the property by the person from whom that other taxpayer acquired the property, and

(ii) for the purposes of this subsection, that other taxpayer shall be deemed to have acquired the property before 1972 at a capital cost equal to the capital cost of the property to the taxpayer who actually owned the property at the end of 1971, and to have owned it without interruption from December 31, 1971 until such time after 1971 as that other taxpayer disposed of it; and

(c) where the disposition occurred because of an election under subsection 110.6(19) of the amended Act,

(i) for the purposes of that Act (other than paragraphs 8(1)(j) and (p) and sections 13 and 20 of that Act), the taxpayer is deemed to have reacquired the property at a capital cost equal to

(A) where the amount designated in respect of the property in the election did not exceed 110% of the fair market value of the property at the end of February 22, 1994, the taxpayer's proceeds of disposition determined under paragraph (a) in respect of the disposition of the property that immediately preceded the reacquisition minus the amount, if any, by which the amount designated in respect of the property in the election exceeded that fair market value, and

(B) in any other case, the amount otherwise determined under subsection 110.6(19) of that Act to be the cost to the taxpayer of the property immediately after the reacquisition referred to in that subsection minus the amount by which the fair market value of the property on valuation day exceeded the capital cost of the property at the time it was last acquired before 1972, and

(ii) for the purposes of this subsection, the taxpayer's capital cost of the property after the reacquisition shall be deemed to be equal to the taxpayer's capital cost of the property before the reacquisition and the taxpayer shall be considered to have owned the property without interruption from December 31, 1971 until such time after February 22, 1994 as the taxpayer disposes of it.

**Related Provisions**: ITAR 20(1.1) — Rollover to spouse, spouse trust or child; ITAR 20(1.2) — Other rollovers; ITA 257 — Formulas cannot calculate to less than zero [rule does not apply explicitly to the ITARs].

**Notes**: ITAR 20(1)(b)(i) amended by 1994 Budget, retroactive to acquisitions of property that occur after May 22, 1985.

ITAR 20(1)(c) added by 1994 Budget and amended by 1995-97 technical bill, both effective for 1994 and later taxation years.

**Interpretation Bulletins**: IT-209R: *Inter vivos* gifts of capital property to individuals directly or through trusts; IT-217R: Depreciable property owned on December 31, 1971; IT-220R2: CCA — proceeds of disposition of depreciable property; IT-268R4: *Inter vivos* transfer of farm property to child; IT-432R2: Benefits conferred on shareholders; IT-488R2: Winding-up of 90%-owned taxable Canadian corporations.

**(1.1) Where depreciable property disposed of to spouse, common-law partner, trust or child** — Subsection (1) does not apply in any case where

(a) subsection 70(6) or 73(1) of the amended Act applies in respect of the disposition by a taxpayer of any depreciable property of a prescribed class to the spouse, common-law partner, trust or transferee, as the case may be, referred to therein, and

(b) subsection 70(9) of the amended Act applies in respect of the disposition by a taxpayer of any depreciable property of a prescribed class to a child referred to therein,

except that where the spouse, common-law partner, trust, transferee or child, as the case may be, subsequently disposes of the property at any time, subsection (1) applies as if the spouse, common-law partner, trust, transferee or child, as the case may be, had acquired the property before 1972 and owned it without interruption from December 31, 1971 until that time.

**Notes**: ITAR 20(1.1) amended by 2000 same-sex partners bill to add references to "common-law partner", effective for the 2001 and later taxation years, or earlier by election (see Notes to ITA 248(1)"common-law partner").

**Interpretation Bulletins**: IT-209R: *Inter vivos* gifts of capital property to individuals directly or through trusts; IT-217R: Depreciable property owned on December 31, 1971.

**(1.11) Extended meaning of "child"** — For the purposes of subsection (1.1), "child" of a taxpayer includes

(a) a child of the taxpayer's child;

(b) a child of the taxpayer's child's child; and

(c) a person who, at any time before attaining the age of 21 years, was wholly dependent on the taxpayer for support and of whom the taxpayer had, at that time, in law or in fact, the custody and control.

**Related Provisions**: ITA 70(10) — Extended meaning of "child".

**(1.2) Other transfers of depreciable property** — Where, because of a transaction or an event in respect of which any of subsections 70(5), 85(1), (2) and (3), 87(2), section 88, subsections 97(2), 98(3) and (5) and 107(2) of the amended Act applies, a taxpayer has at any particular time after 1971 acquired any depreciable property of a prescribed class from a person who acquired the property before 1972 and owned it without interruption from December 31, 1971 until the particular time, for the purposes of subsection (1) the taxpayer shall be deemed to have acquired the property before 1972 and to have owned it without interruption from December 31, 1971 until such time after 1971 as the taxpayer disposed of it.

**Interpretation Bulletins**: IT-209R: *Inter vivos* gifts of capital property to individuals directly or through trusts; IT-217R: Depreciable property owned on December 31, 1971; IT-488R2: Winding-up of 90%-owned taxable Canadian corporation.

**(1.3) Transfers before 1972 not at arm's length** — Without restricting the generality of section 18, where any depreciable property has been transferred before 1972 in circumstances such that subsection 20(4) of the former Act would, if that provision applied to transfers of property made in the 1972 taxation year, apply, paragraph 69(1)(b) of the amended Act does not apply to the transfer and subsection 20(4) of the former Act applies thereto.

**(1.4) Depreciable property received as dividend in kind** — The capital cost to a taxpayer, as of any particular time after 1971, of any depreciable property (other than depreciable property referred to in subsection (1.3) or deemed by subparagraph (1)(b)(ii) to have been acquired by the taxpayer before 1972) acquired by the taxpayer before 1972 as, on account of, in lieu of payment of or in satisfaction of, a dividend payable in kind (other than a stock dividend) in respect of a share owned by the taxpayer of the capital stock of a corporation, shall be deemed to be the fair market value of that property at the time the property was so received.

**(2) Recapture of capital cost allowances** — In determining a taxpayer's income for a taxation year from farming or fishing, subsection 13(1) of the amended Act does not apply in respect of the disposition by the taxpayer of property acquired by the taxpayer before 1972 unless the taxpayer has elected to make a deduction for that or a preceding taxation year, in respect of the capital cost of property acquired by the taxpayer before 1972, under regulations made under paragraph 20(1)(a) of that Act other than a regulation providing solely for an allowance for computing income from farming or fishing.

**(3) Depreciable property of partnership of prescribed class** — For the purposes of the amended Act, where a partnership had, on December

31, 1971, partnership property that was depreciable property of a prescribed class,

(a) the capital cost to the partnership of each property of that class shall be deemed to be an amount determined as follows:

(i) determine, for each person who, by reason of having been a member of the partnership on the later of June 18, 1971 and the day the partnership was created, and thereafter without interruption until December 31, 1971, can reasonably be regarded as having had an interest in the property of that class on December 31, 1971, the person's acquisition cost in respect of property of that class,

(ii) determine, for each such person, the amount that is that proportion of the person's acquisition cost in respect of property of that class that 100% is of the person's percentage in respect of property of that class,

(iii) select the amount determined under subparagraph (ii) for a person described therein that is not greater than any amount so determined for any other such person,

(iv) determine that proportion of the amount selected under subparagraph (iii) (in this subsection referred to as the "capital cost of that class") that the fair market value on December 31, 1971 of that property is of the fair market value on that day of all property of that class,

and the amount determined under subparagraph (iv) is the capital cost to the partnership of that property;

(b) for the purposes of sections 13 and 20 of the amended Act and any regulations made under paragraph 20(1)(a) of that Act, the undepreciated capital cost to the partnership of property of that class as of any time after 1971 shall be computed as though the amount, if any, by which the capital cost of that class to the partnership exceeds the undepreciated cost to the partnership of that class had been allowed to the partnership in respect of property of that class under regulations made under paragraph 20(1)(a) of the amended Act in computing income for taxation years before that time;

(c) in computing the income for the 1972 and subsequent taxation years of each person who was a member of the partnership on June 18, 1971 and thereafter without interruption until December 31, 1971, there may be deducted such amount as the person claims for the year, not exceeding the amount, if any, by which the total of

(i) the lesser of

(A) the amount, if any, by which the amount that was the capital cost to the person of all property of that class exceeds the percentage, equal to the person's percentage in respect of property of that class, of the capital cost of that class to the partnership, and

(B) the amount that was the undepreciated capital cost to the person of property of that class as of December 31, 1971, and

(ii) the amount, if any, by which

(A) the undepreciated capital cost to the person of property of that class as of December 31, 1971, less the amount, if any, determined under subparagraph (i) in respect of property of that class,

exceeds

(B) the percentage, equal to the person's percentage in respect of property of that class, of the undepreciated cost to the partnership of that class,

exceeds the total of all amounts deducted under this paragraph in computing the person's income for preceding taxation years; and, for the purposes of section 3 of the amended Act, the amount so claimed shall be deemed to be a deduction permitted by subdivision e of Division B of Part I of that Act; and

(d) notwithstanding paragraph (c), a person who became a member of the partnership after June 18, 1971 and who was a member of the partnership thereafter without interruption until December 31, 1971 shall be deemed to be a person described in paragraph (c) and the amount that may be claimed thereunder as a deduction in computing the person's income for any taxation year shall not exceed 10% of the total of the amounts determined under subparagraphs (c)(i) and (ii).

**(4) Definitions** — In subsection (3),

**"acquisition cost"** of a person who was a member of a partnership on December 31, 1971 in respect of depreciable property of a prescribed class that was partnership property of the partnership on December 31, 1971 means the total of the undepreciated capital cost to that person of property of that class as of December 31, 1971 and the total depreciation allowed to the person before 1972 in respect of property of that class;

**"percentage"** of a member of a partnership in respect of any depreciable property of a prescribed class that was partnership property of the partnership on December 31, 1971 means the interest of the member of the partnership in property of that class, expressed as a percentage of the total of the interests of all members of the partnership in property of that class on that day;

**"undepreciated cost to the partnership"** of any class of depreciable property means an amount determined as follows:

(a) determine, for each person who, because of having been a member of the partnership on the later of June 18, 1971 and the day the partnership was created, and thereafter without interruption until December 31, 1971, can reasonably be regarded as having had an interest in property of that class on December 31, 1971, the amount, if any, by which the undepreciated capital cost to the person of property of that class as of December 31, 1971 exceeds the amount, if any, determined under subparagraph (3)(c)(i) for the person in respect of property of that class,

(b) determine, for each such person, the amount that is that proportion of the amount determined under paragraph (a) that 100% is of the person's percentage in respect of property of that class, and

(c) select the amount determined under paragraph (b) for a person described therein that is not greater than any amount so determined for any other such person,

and the amount selected under paragraph (c) is the undepreciated cost to the partnership of that class.

**Notes**: ITAR 20(4)"acquisition cost" was 20(4)(a), "percentage" was 20(4)(b), and "undepreciated cost to the partnership" was 20(4)(c), before consolidation in R.S.C. 1985 (5th Supp.), effective for taxation years ending after November 1991.

**(5) Other depreciable property of partnership** — For the purposes of the amended Act, where a partnership had, on December 31, 1971, any particular partnership property that was depreciable property other than depreciable property of a prescribed class,

(a) the cost to the partnership of the particular property shall be deemed to be the amount that would be determined under paragraph (3)(a) to be the capital cost thereof if

(i) the particular property constituted a prescribed class of property, and

(ii) the acquisition cost of each person described therein in respect of the particular property were its actual cost to the person or the amount at which the person was deemed by subsection 20(6) of the former Act to have acquired it, as the case may be;

(b) for the purposes of sections 13 and 20 of the amended Act and any regulations made under paragraph 20(1)(a) of that Act, the undepreciated capital cost of property of any class as of any particular time after 1971 shall be computed as if the amount, if any, by which

(i) the amount determined under paragraph (a) to have been the cost to the partnership of the particular property,

exceeds

(ii) the amount that would be determined under the definition "undepreciated cost to the partnership" in subsection (4) to be the undepreciated cost to the partnership of any

class of depreciable property comprising the particular property if

(A) paragraph (a) of that definition were read without reference to the words "the later of June 18, 1971 and the day the partnership was created, and thereafter without interruption until",

(B) the amount determined under subparagraph (3)(c)(i) for any person in respect of that class were nil, and

(C) the undepreciated capital cost to each person described in the definition "acquisition cost" in subsection (4) of the particular property as of December 31, 1971 were the amount, if any, by which the amount assumed by subparagraph (a)(ii) to have been the acquisition cost of the person in respect of the property exceeds the total of all amounts allowed to the person in respect of the property under regulations made under paragraph 11(1)(a) of the former Act in computing income for taxation years ending before 1972,

had been allowed to the partnership in respect of the particular property under regulations made under paragraph 20(1)(a) of the amended Act in computing income for taxation years ending before the particular time; and

(c) in computing the income for the 1972 and subsequent taxation years of each person who was, on December 31, 1971, a member of the partnership, there may be deducted such amount as the person claims for the year, not exceeding the amount, if any, by which

(i) the amount by which

(A) the amount assumed by clause (b)(ii)(C) to have been the undepreciated capital cost to the person of the particular property as of December 31, 1971

exceeds

(B) a percentage of the amount determined under subparagraph (b)(ii) in respect of the particular property, equal to the percentage that would be the person's percentage (within the meaning assigned by subsection (4)) in respect of the particular property if that property constituted a prescribed class,

exceeds

(ii) the total of all amounts deducted under this paragraph in computing the person's income for preceding taxation years;

and for the purposes of section 3 of the amended Act the amount so claimed shall be deemed to be a deduction permitted by subdivision e of Division B of Part I of that Act.

**Related Provisions**: Reg. 1701(2) — Maximum CCA deduction from farming or fishing business where ITAR 20(5) applies.

**Definitions [ITAR 20]:** "acquired" — ITAR 20(1)(b)(ii), 20(1.2); "acquisition cost" — ITAR 20(4); "amended Act" — ITAR 8; "amount" — ITA 248(1); "arm's length" — ITA 251(1); "capital cost" — ITAR 20(1)(c)(ii), 20(1.4); "capital cost of that class" — ITAR 20(3)(a)(iv); "child" — ITAR 20(1.11); "common-law partner" — ITA 248(1); "corporation" — ITA 248(1), *Interpretation Act* 35(1); "depreciable property" — ITA 13(21), 248(1); "dividend", "farming", "fishing" — ITA 248(1); "former Act" — ITAR 8; "owned" — ITAR 20(1)(b)(ii), 20(1.2); "partnership" — see Notes to ITA 96(1); "percentage" — ITAR 20(4); "person", "prescribed", "property", "share" — ITA 248(1); "stock dividend" — ITA 248(1); "taxation year" — ITA 249; "taxpayer" — ITA 248(1); "trust" — ITA 104(1), 248(1), (3); "undepreciated capital cost" — ITA 13(21), 248(1); "undepreciated cost to the partnership" — ITAR 20(4); "valuation day" — ITAR 24.

**21. (1) Goodwill and other nothings** — Where as a result of a disposition occurring after 1971 a taxpayer has or may become entitled to receive an amount (in this section referred to as the "actual amount") in respect of a business carried on by the taxpayer throughout the period beginning January 1, 1972 and ending immediately after the disposition occurred, for the purposes of section 14 of the amended Act the amount that the taxpayer has or may become entitled to receive shall be deemed to be the total of

(a) an amount equal to a percentage, equal to 40% plus the percentage (not exceeding 60%) obtained when 5% is multiplied by the number of full calendar years ending in the period and before the transaction occurred, of the amount, if any, by which the actual amount exceeds the portion thereof referred to in subparagraph (b)(i), and

(b) an amount equal to the lesser of

(i) the percentage, described in paragraph (a), of such portion, if any, of the actual amount as may reasonably be considered as being the consideration received by him for the disposition of, or for allowing the expiration of, a government right, and

(ii) the amount, if any, by which the portion described in subparagraph (i) exceeds the greater of

(A) the total of all amounts each of which is an outlay or expenditure made or incurred by the taxpayer as a result of a transaction that occurred before 1972 for the purpose of acquiring the government right, or the taxpayer's original right in respect of the government right, to the extent that the outlay or expenditure was not otherwise deducted in computing the income of the taxpayer for any taxation year and would, if made or incurred by the taxpayer as a result of a transaction that occurred after 1971, be an eligible capital expenditure of the taxpayer, and

(B) the fair market value to the taxpayer as at December 31, 1971 of the taxpayer's specified right in respect of the government right, if no outlay or expenditure was made or incurred by the taxpayer for the purpose of acquiring the right or, if an outlay or expenditure was made or incurred, if that outlay or expenditure would have been an eligible capital expenditure of the taxpayer if it had been made or incurred as a result of a transaction that occurred after 1971.

**Notes:** Opening words of ITAR 21(1) amended by 1988 tax reform, effective for dispositions of property after June 17, 1987 otherwise than pursuant to the terms of an obligation entered into in writing before June 18, 1987. For earlier dispositions, read the opening words as:

(1) Where as a result of a transaction occurring after 1971 an amount (in this section referred to as the "actual amount") has become payable to a taxpayer in respect of a business carried on by him throughout the period commencing January 1, 1972 and ending immediately after the transaction occurred, for the purposes of section 14 of the amended Act the amount that has become so payable to him shall be deemed to be the aggregate of

**Interpretation Bulletins:** IT-268R4: *Inter vivos* transfer of farm property to child; IT-488R2: Winding-up of 90%-owned taxable Canadian corporations. See also list at end of ITAR 21.

**(2) Idem** — Where the taxpayer and the person by whom the actual amount has become payable to the taxpayer were not dealing with each other at arm's length, for the purposes of computing the income of that person the portion of the actual amount in excess of the amount deemed by subsection (1) to be the amount that has become payable to the taxpayer shall be deemed not to have been an outlay, expense or cost, as the case may be, of that person.

**Interpretation Bulletins:** IT-268R4: *Inter vivos* transfer of farm property to child. See also list at end of ITAR 21.

**(2.1) Idem** — Where after 1971 a taxpayer has acquired a particular government right referred to in subsection (1)

(a) from a person with whom the taxpayer was not dealing at arm's length, or

(b) under an agreement with a person with whom the taxpayer was not dealing at arm's length, if under the terms of the agreement that person allowed the right to expire so that the taxpayer could acquire a substantially similar right from the authority that had issued the right to that person,

and an actual amount subsequently becomes payable to the taxpayer as consideration for the disposition by the taxpayer of, or for the taxpayer allowing the expiration of, the particular government right or any other government right acquired by the taxpayer for the purpose of effecting the continuation, without interruption, of rights that are substantially similar to the rights that the taxpayer had under the particular government right, for the purpose of section 14 of the amended Act, the amount that has so become payable to the taxpayer shall be deemed to be the amount that would, if that person and the taxpayer had at all times been the same person, be determined under subsection (1) to be the amount that would have become so payable to the taxpayer.

**Interpretation Bulletins**: See list at end of ITAR 21.

**(2.2) Amalgamations** — For the purposes of this section, an amalgamation (within the meaning of section 87 of the amended Act) of two or more Canadian corporations shall be deemed to be a transaction between persons not dealing at arm's length.

**(3) Definitions** — In this section,

**"government right"** of a taxpayer means a right or licence

(a) that enables the taxpayer to carry on a business activity in accordance with a law of Canada or of a province or Canadian municipality, to an extent to which the taxpayer would otherwise be unable to carry it on in accordance therewith,

(b) that was granted or issued by Her Majesty in right of Canada or a province or a Canadian municipality, or by a department, board, agency or any other body authorized by or under a law of Canada, a province or a Canadian municipality to grant or issue such a right or licence, and

(c) that was acquired by the taxpayer

(i) as a result of a transaction that occurred before 1972, or

(ii) at a particular time for the purpose of effecting the continuation, without interruption, of rights that are substantially similar to the rights that the taxpayer had under a government right held by the taxpayer before the particular time;

**"original right"** of a taxpayer in respect of a government right means a right or licence

(a) described in the definition "government right" in this subsection, and

(b) acquired by the taxpayer as a result of a transaction that occurred before 1972 for a purpose other than the purpose described in subparagraph (c)(ii) of that definition,

if the government right was acquired by the taxpayer for the purpose of effecting the continuation, without interruption, of rights that are substantially similar to the rights that the taxpayer had under the right or licence;

**"specified right"** of a taxpayer in respect of a government right means a right owned by a taxpayer on December 31, 1971 that was

(a) an original right, or

(b) a government right that was acquired by the taxpayer in substitution for the original right or that was one of a series of government rights acquired by the taxpayer for the purpose of effecting the continuation, without interruption, of rights that are substantially similar to the rights that the taxpayer had under the original right.

**Notes**: ITAR 21(3)"government right" was 21(3)(a), "original right" was 21(3)(b), and "specified right" was 21(3)(c), before consolidation in R.S.C. 1985 (5th Supp.), effective for taxation years ending after November 1991.

**Definitions [ITAR 21]**: "actual amount" — ITAR 21(1); "amended Act" — ITAR 8; "amount" — ITA 248(1); "arm's length" — ITAR 21(2.2); "business" — ITA 248(1); "Canada" — ITA 255, *Interpretation Act* 35(1); "Canadian corporation" — ITA 89(1), 248(1); "eligible capital expenditure" — ITA 14(5), 248(1); "government right" — ITAR 21(3); "Her Majesty" — *Interpretation Act* 35(1); "original right" — ITAR 21(3); "person" — ITA 248(1); "province" — *Interpretation Act* 35(1); "specified right" — ITAR 21(3); "taxation year" — ITA 249; "taxpayer" — ITA 248(1).

**Interpretation Bulletins [ITAR 21]**: IT-123R6: Transactions involving eligible capital property; IT-313R2: Eligible capital property — rules where a taxpayer has ceased carrying on a business or has died; IT-474R: Amalgamations of Canadian corporations.

**22. [Repealed under former Act]**

**Notes**: ITAR 22, repealed in 1985, dealt with the application of 18(4) of the Act to 1972 and 1973.

**23. (1), (2) [Repealed under former Act]**

**Notes**: ITAR 23(1) and (2), repealed in 1985, dealt with calculating professional income and work in progress for the 1972 taxation year.

**(3) Rules applicable [to professional business]** — For the purposes of computing the income of a taxpayer for a taxation year ending after 1971 from a business that is a profession,

(a) there may be deducted such amount as the taxpayer claims, not exceeding the lesser of

(i) the amount deducted under this paragraph in computing the taxpayer's income from the business for the preceding taxation year, and

(ii) the taxpayer's investment interest in the business at the end of the year;

(b) where the taxation year is the taxpayer's 1972 taxation year, the amount deducted under paragraph (a) in computing the taxpayer's income for the preceding taxation year from the business shall be deemed to be an amount equal to the taxpayer's 1971 receivables in respect of the business;

(c) there shall be included the amount deducted under paragraph (a) in computing the taxpayer's income for the preceding taxation year from the business; and

(d) there shall be included amounts received by the taxpayer in the year on account of debts in respect of the business that were established by the taxpayer to have become bad debts before the end of the 1971 fiscal period of the business.

**Related Provisions**: ITA 34 — Income from a professional business.

**Interpretation Bulletins**: IT-242R: Retired partners; IT-278R2: Death of a partner or of a retired partner. See also list at end of ITAR 23.

**Forms**: T2032: Statement of professional activities.

**(4) Application of para. (3)(a)** — Paragraph (3)(a) does not apply to allow a deduction in computing the income of a taxpayer from a business that is a profession

   (a) for the taxation year in which the taxpayer died; or

   (b) for any taxation year, if,

      (i) in the case of a taxpayer who at no time in that year was resident in Canada, the taxpayer ceased to carry on the business, or

      (ii) in the case of any other taxpayer, the taxpayer ceased to be resident in Canada and ceased to carry on the business

at any time in that year or the following year.

**Interpretation Bulletins**: IT-242R: Retired partners; IT-278R2: Death of a partner or of a retired partner. See also list at end of ITAR 23.

**(4.1) Certain persons deemed to be carrying on business by means of partnership** — For the purposes of paragraph (a) of the definition "investment interest" in subsection (5),

   (a) where subsection 98(1) of the amended Act applies, the persons who are deemed not to have ceased to be members of a partnership because of that subsection shall be deemed to be carrying on business in Canada by means of that partnership; and

   (b) a taxpayer who has a residual interest in a partnership (within the meaning assigned by section 98.1 of the amended Act) shall be deemed to be carrying on business in Canada by means of that partnership.

**(5) Definitions** — In this section,

**"investment interest"** in a business at the end of a taxation year means

   (a) in the case of a taxpayer other than a corporation, the total of all amounts each of which is an amount in respect of a proprietorship or partnership by means of which the taxpayer carried on that business in Canada in the year, equal to,

      (i) in respect of each such proprietorship, the amount, if any, by which

         (A) the total of such of the amounts that were included in computing the taxpayer's income for that or a preceding taxation year as were receivable by the taxpayer at the end of the fiscal period of the proprietorship ending in the taxation year,

      exceeds

         (B) the amount claimed under paragraph 20(1)(l) of the amended Act as a reserve for doubtful debts in computing the taxpayer's income from the business for the fiscal period of the proprietorship ending in the year, and

      (ii) in respect of each such partnership, the adjusted cost base to the taxpayer of the taxpayer's interest in the partnership immediately after the end of the fiscal period of the partnership ending in the year,

   (b) in the case of a taxpayer that is a corporation, the lesser of

      (i) the amount thereof that would be determined under paragraph (a) in respect of the corporation if that paragraph applied to a taxpayer that is a corporation, and

      (ii) that proportion of its 1971 receivables in respect of the business that

         (A) the amount, if any, by which 10 exceeds the number of its taxation years ending after 1971 and either before or coincidentally with the taxation year,

     is of

         (B) 10;

**Notes**: ITAR 23(5)"investment interest" was 23(5)(a), (b), before consolidation in R.S.C. 1985 (5th Supp.), effective for taxation years ending after November 1991.

**Interpretation Bulletins**: See list at end of ITAR 23.

**"1971 receivables"** in respect of a business of a taxpayer means the total of

   (a) all amounts that became receivable by the taxpayer in respect of property sold or services rendered in the course of the business (within the meaning given that expression in section 34 of the amended Act) in taxation years ending before 1972 and that were not included in computing the taxpayer's income for any such taxation year, other than debts that were established by the taxpayer to have become bad debts before the end of the 1971 fiscal period of the business, and

   (b) the total of all amounts each of which is an amount, in respect of each partnership by means of which the taxpayer carried on that business before 1972, equal to such portion of the total that would be determined under paragraph (a) in respect of the partnership, if the references in that paragraph to "the taxpayer" were read as references to "the partnership", as is designated by the taxpayer in the taxpayer's return of income under Part I of the amended Act for the year to be attributable to the taxpayer, except that where the total of the portions so designated by all members of the partnership is less than the total that would be so determined under paragraph (a) in respect of the partnership, the Minister may designate the portion of that total that is attributable to the taxpayer, in which case the portion so designated by the Minister in respect of the taxpayer shall be deemed to be the portion so designated by the taxpayer.

**Notes**: ITAR 23(5)"1971 receivables" was 23(5)(c), before consolidation in R.S.C. 1985 (5th Supp.), effective for taxation years ending after November 1991.

Part I — Income Tax Application Rules, 1971

**Definitions [ITAR 23]**: "1971 receivables" — ITAR 23(5); "adjusted cost base" — ITA 54, 248(1); "amended Act" — ITAR 8; "amount", "business" — ITA 248(1); "Canada" — ITA 255, *Interpretation Act* 35(1); "carried on that business in Canada" — ITA 253, ITAR 23(4.1); "corporation" — ITA 248(1), *Interpretation Act* 35(1); "fiscal period" — ITA 249.1; "investment interest" — ITAR 23(5); "Minister" — ITA 248(1); "partnership" — see Notes to ITA 96(1); "person", "property" — ITA 248(1); "resident in Canada" — ITA 250; "taxation year" — ITA 249; "taxpayer" — ITA 248(1).

**Interpretation Bulletins [ITAR 23]**: IT-188R: Sale of accounts receivable; IT-189R: Corporations used by practising members of professions; IT-212R3: Income of deceased persons — rights or things.

## 24. Definition of "valuation day" for capital gains and losses — In this Act, "valuation day" means

(a) December 22, 1971, in relation to any property prescribed to be a publicly-traded share or security; and

(b) December 31, 1971, in relation to any other property.

**Regulations**: 4400 (prescribed property).

**Definitions [ITAR 24]**: "prescribed", "property", "share" — ITA 248(1).

## 25. [Not included in R.S.C. 1985]

**Notes**: ITAR 25 provided for proclamations of "valuation day" for ITAR 24. With the reconsolidation of the ITAR in R.S.C. 1985 (5th Supp.), the dates were enacted directly in ITAR 24 and ITAR 25 is no longer needed.

## 26. (1) Capital gains subject to tax — The provisions of subdivision c of Division B of Part I of the amended Act apply to dispositions of property made after 1971 and to transactions or events occurring after 1971 because of which any disposition of property was made or deemed to have been made in accordance with the provisions of that subdivision.

**Interpretation Bulletins**: IT-330R: Dispositions of capital property subject to warranty, covenant, etc. See also list at end of ITAR 26.

### (1.1) Principal amount of certain obligations — For the purposes of subsection 39(3) and section 80 of the amended Act, the principal amount of any debt or other obligation of a taxpayer to pay an amount that was outstanding on January 1, 1972 (in this subsection referred to as an "obligation") shall be deemed to be the lesser of

(a) the principal amount, otherwise determined for the purposes of the amended Act, of the obligation, and

(b) the fair market value, on valuation day, of the obligation,

and in applying paragraph 39(3)(a) of the amended Act to an obligation, the reference in that paragraph to "the amount for which the obligation was issued" shall be read as a reference to "the lesser of the principal amount of the obligation and the amount for which the obligation was issued".

**Related Provisions**: ITAR 26(30) — Disposition by non-resident of taxable Canadian property.

**Interpretation Bulletins**: IT-293R: Debtor's gain on settlement of debt. See also list at end of ITAR 26.

### (2) [Repealed under former Act]

**Notes**: ITAR 26(2), repealed in 1985, dealt with the application of ITA s. 41 from 1972 to 1976.

### (3) Cost of acquisition of capital property owned on Dec. 31, 1971 — For the purpose of computing the adjusted cost base to a taxpayer of any capital property (other than depreciable property or an interest in a partnership) that was owned by the taxpayer on December 31, 1971 and thereafter without interruption until such time as the taxpayer disposed of it, its cost to the taxpayer shall be deemed to be the amount that is neither the greatest nor the least of the following three amounts, namely:

(a) its actual cost to the taxpayer or, if the property was an obligation, its amortized cost to the taxpayer on January 1, 1972,

(b) its fair market value on valuation day, and

(c) the amount, if any, by which the total of

(i) the taxpayer's proceeds of disposition of the property, determined without reference to subsection 13(21.1) of the amended Act,

(ii) all amounts required by subsection 53(2) of the amended Act to be deducted in computing its adjusted cost base to the taxpayer immediately before the disposition, and

(iii) all amounts described in clause (5)(c)(ii)(B) that are relevant in computing its adjusted cost base to the taxpayer immediately before the disposition,

exceeds the total of

(iv) all amounts required by subsection 53(1) of the amended Act (other than paragraphs 53(1)(f.1) to (f.2)) to be added in computing its adjusted cost base to the taxpayer immediately before the disposition, and

(v) all amounts described in clause (5)(c)(i)(B) that are relevant in computing its adjusted cost base to the taxpayer immediately before the disposition,

except that where two or more of the amounts determined under paragraphs (a) to (c) in respect of any property are the same amount, that amount shall be deemed to be its cost to the taxpayer.

**Related Provisions**: ITAR 26(7) — Election for cost to be V-day value; ITAR 26(29) — No tax-free zone following election to trigger capital gains exemption; ITAR 26(30) — Disposition by non-resident of taxable Canadian property; ITAR 35(1) — No application to disposition by foreign affiliate for purposes of FAPI.

**Notes**: ITAR 26(3) provides that the cost of capital property owned since before 1972 is the median value of the actual cost, the V-day value (fair market value at end of 1971) and the proceeds of disposition. The effect is to allow any capital gain accruing to the end of 1971 to remain tax-free (capital gains were not taxed at all before 1972). The difference between the original cost and the value on December 31, 1971 is sometimes referred to as the "tax-free zone".

ITAR 26(3)(c)(iv) amended by 1994 tax amendments bill (Part IX), effective for taxation years that end after February 21, 1994, to change "53(1)(f.1) and (f.2)" to "53(1)(f.1) to (f.2)", thus adding reference to ITA 53(1)(f.11) and (f.12). Note also that the taxpayer can elect under ITAR 26(7) for the V-day value to be used as the deemed cost.

**Regulations**: 4400, Sch. VII (V-day values for publicly-traded shares).

**Interpretation Bulletins**: IT-65: Stock splits and consolidations; IT-78: Capital property owned on December 31, 1971 — identical properties; IT-84: Capital property owned on December 31, 1971 — median rule (tax-free zone); IT-93: Capital property owned on December 31, 1971 — meaning of actual cost and amortized cost; IT-107: Costs of disposition of capital property affected by the median rule; IT-130: Capital property owned on December 31, 1971 — actual cost of property owned by a testamentary trust; IT-209R: *Inter vivos* gifts of capital property to individuals directly or through trusts; IT-268R4: *Inter vivos* transfer of farm property to child; IT-319: Cost of obligations owned on December 31, 1971. See also list at end of ITAR 26.

**Information Circulars**: 72-25R4: Business equity valuations.

**Advance Tax Rulings**: ATR-35: Partitioning of assets to get specific ownership — "butterfly".

**Forms**: T1105: Supplementary schedule for dispositions of capital property acquired before 1972; T2080–T2085, T2090: Capital dispositions supplementary schedules.

**(4) Determination of cost where property not disposed of** — For the purpose of computing the adjusted cost base to a taxpayer of any capital property (other than depreciable property or an interest in a partnership) at any particular time before the taxpayer disposed of it, where the property was owned by the taxpayer on December 31, 1971 and thereafter without interruption until the particular time, its cost to the taxpayer shall be deemed to be the amount that would be determined under subsection (3) to be its cost to the taxpayer if the taxpayer had disposed of it at the particular time and the taxpayer's proceeds of disposition had been its fair market value at that time.

**Related Provisions**: ITAR 26(7) — Election for cost to be V-day value.

**Forms**: T1105: Supplementary schedule for dispositions of capital property acquired before 1972.

**(5) Where property disposed of in transaction not at arm's length** — Where any capital property (other than depreciable property or an interest in a partnership) that was owned by a taxpayer (in this subsection referred to as the "original owner") on June 18, 1971 has, by one or more transactions or events between persons not dealing at arm's length, become vested in another taxpayer (in this subsection referred to as the "subsequent owner") and the original owner has not elected under subsection (7) in respect of the property, notwithstanding the provisions of the amended Act, for the purposes of computing, at any particular time after 1971, the adjusted cost base of the property to the subsequent owner,

(a) the subsequent owner shall be deemed to have owned the property on June 18, 1971 and thereafter without interruption until the particular time;

(b) for the purposes of this section, the actual cost of the property to the subsequent owner or, if the property was an obligation, its amortized cost to him on January 1, 1972 shall be deemed to be the amount that was its actual cost or its amortized cost on January 1, 1972, as the case may be, to the original owner; and

(c) where the property became vested in the subsequent owner after 1971, there shall be added to the cost to the subsequent owner of the property (as determined under subsection (3)) the amount, if any, by which

(i) the total of all amounts each of which is

(A) a capital gain (other than any amount deemed by subsection 40(3) of the amended Act to be a capital gain) from the disposition after 1971 of the property by a person who owned the property before it so became vested in the subsequent owner,

(B) an amount required by subsection 53(1) of the amended Act to be added in computing the adjusted cost base of the property to a person (other than the subsequent owner) described in clause (A),

(C) an amount determined under paragraph 88(1)(d) of the amended Act in computing the cost of the property to the subsequent owner or a person who owned the property before it became vested in the subsequent owner, or

(D) an amount by which a gain otherwise determined of a person who owned the property before it became so vested in the subsequent owner was reduced because of paragraph 40(2)(b) or (c) of the amended Act,

exceeds

(ii) the total of amounts each of which is

(A) a capital loss or an amount that would, but for paragraph 40(2)(e) and subsection 85(4) of the amended Act (as that Act read in its application to property disposed of on or before April 26, 1995) and paragraphs 40(2)(e.1) and (e.2) and subsection 40(3.3) of the amended Act, be a capital loss from the disposition to a corporation after 1971 of the property by a person who owned the property before it became vested in the subsequent owner, or

(B) an amount required by subsection 53(2) of the amended Act to be deducted in computing the adjusted cost base of the property to a person (other than the subsequent owner) described in clause (A),

and there shall be deducted from the cost to the subsequent owner of the property the amount, if any, by which the total determined under subparagraph (ii) exceeds the total determined under subparagraph (i).

**Related Provisions**: ITAR 26(30) — Disposition by non-resident of taxable Canadian property.

**Notes**: ITAR 26(5)(c)(ii)(A) amended by 1995-97 technical bill, effective for dispositions after April 26, 1995, to add reference to ITA 40(3.3) and to reflect ITA 85(4) having been repealed.

ITAR 26(5)(c)(ii)(A) amended by 1994 tax amendments bill (Part IX), effective for taxation years that end after February 21, 1994, to add reference to ITA 40(2)(e.1) and (e.2).

**Interpretation Bulletins**: IT-132R2: Capital property owned on December 31, 1971 — non-arm's length transactions; IT-199: Identical properties: acquired in non-arm's length transactions; IT-209R: *Inter vivos* gifts of capital property to individuals directly or through trusts; IT-268R4: *Inter vivos* transfer of farm property to child; IT-370: Trusts — capital property owned on December 31, 1971; IT-432R2: Benefits conferred on shareholders; IT-488R2: Winding-up of 90%-owned taxable Canadian corporations. See also list at end of ITAR 26.

**Advance Tax Rulings**: ATR-35: Partitioning of assets to get specific ownership — "butterfly".

**(5.1) Idem** — For the purposes of subsection (5), an amalgamation (within the meaning assigned by section 87 of the amended Act) of two or more Canadian corporations shall be deemed to be a transaction between persons not dealing at arm's length.

**(5.2) Transfer of capital property to a corporation** — For the purposes of subsection (5), where a taxpayer has disposed of capital property after May 6, 1974 to a corporation in respect of which an election under section 85 of the amended Act was made, the disposition shall be deemed to be a transaction between persons not dealing at arm's length.

**(6) Reacquired property** — Where a taxpayer has, at any time after June 18, 1971 and before 1972, disposed of any property owned by the taxpayer on that day and has, within 30 days after that time, reacquired the same property or acquired a substantially identical property, for the purposes of this section

(a) the taxpayer shall be deemed to have owned the property so reacquired or the substantially identical property so acquired, as the case may be, on June 18, 1971 and thereafter without interruption until the time when the taxpayer so reacquired or acquired it, as the case may be;

(b) where the property was property so reacquired, its actual cost or its amortized cost on January 1, 1972, as the case may be, to the taxpayer shall be determined as if the taxpayer had not so disposed of and so reacquired it; and

(c) where the property was substantially identical property so acquired, its actual cost or its amortized cost on January 1, 1972, as the case may be, to the taxpayer shall be deemed to be the amount that was the actual cost or the amortized cost on January 1, 1972, as the case may be, to the taxpayer of the property so disposed of by the taxpayer.

**(7) Election re cost** — Where, but for this subsection, the cost to an individual of any property actually owned by the individual on December 31, 1971 would be determined under subsection (3) or (4) otherwise than because of subsection (5) and the individual has so elected, in prescribed manner and not later than the day on or before which the individual is required by Part I of the amended Act to file a return of income for the first taxation year in which the individual disposes of all or any part of the property, other than

(a) personal-use property of the individual that was not listed personal property or real property,

(b) listed personal property, if the individual's gain or loss, as the case may be, from the disposition thereof was, because of subsection 46(1) or (2) of the amended Act, nil,

(c) the individual's principal residence, if the individual's gain from the disposition thereof was, because of paragraph 40(2)(b) of the amended Act, nil,

(d) personal-use property of the individual that was real property (other than the individual's principal residence), if the individual's gain from the disposition thereof was, because of subsection 46(1) or (2) of the amended Act, nil, or

(e) any other property, the proceeds of disposition of which are equal to its fair market value on valuation day,

the cost to the individual of each capital property (other than depreciable property, an interest in a partnership or any property described in any of paragraphs (a) to (e) that was disposed of by the individual before that taxation year) actually owned by the individual on December 31, 1971 shall be deemed to be its fair market value on valuation day.

**Regulations**: 4700 (prescribed manner).

**Interpretation Bulletins**: IT-139R: Capital property owned on December 31, 1971 — fair market value. See also list at end of ITAR 26.

**Forms**: T1105: Supplementary schedule for dispositions of capital property acquired before 1972; T2076: Valuation Day value election for capital properties owned on December 31, 1971.

**(8) Identical properties** — For the purposes of computing, at any particular time after 1971, the adjusted cost base to a taxpayer of any capital property (other than depreciable property or an interest in a partnership) that was owned by the taxpayer on December 31, 1971 and thereafter without interruption until the particular time, if the property was one of a group of identical properties owned by the taxpayer on December 31, 1971,

(a) section 47 of the amended Act does not apply;

(b) where the property was an obligation,

(i) for the purpose of paragraph (3)(a), its amortized cost to the taxpayer on January 1, 1972 shall be deemed to be that proportion of the total of the amortized costs to the taxpayer on January 1, 1972 of all obligations of that group that the principal amount of the obligation is of the total of the principal amounts of all obligations of that group, and

(ii) for the purpose of paragraph (3)(b), its fair market value on valuation day shall be deemed to be that proportion of the fair market value on that day of all obligations of that group that the principal amount of the obligation is of the total of the principal amounts of all obligations of that group;

(c) where the property was not an obligation,

(i) for the purpose of paragraph (3)(a), its actual cost to the taxpayer shall be deemed to be the quotient obtained when the total of the actual costs to the taxpayer of all properties of that group is divided by the number of properties of that group, and

(ii) for the purpose of paragraph (3)(b), its fair market value on valuation day shall be deemed to be the quotient obtained when the fair market value on that day of all properties of that group is divided by the number of properties of that group;

(d) for the purpose of distinguishing any such property from an otherwise identical property acquired and disposed of by the taxpayer before 1972, properties acquired by the taxpayer at any time shall be deemed to have been disposed of by the taxpayer before properties acquired by the taxpayer after that time; and

(e) for the purposes of distinguishing any such property from an otherwise identical property acquired by the taxpayer after 1971, properties owned by the taxpayer on December 31, 1971 shall be deemed to have been disposed of by the taxpayer before properties acquired by the taxpayer at a later time.

**Interpretation Bulletins**: IT-78: Capital property owned on December 31, 1971 — identical properties; IT-115R2: Fractional interest in shares; IT-199: Identical properties acquired in non-arm's length transactions; IT-387R2: Meaning of "identical properties". See also list at end of ITAR 26.

**(8.1) Idem** — For the purposes of subsection (8), any property of a life insurance corporation that would, but for this subsection, be identical to any other property of the corporation shall be deemed not to be identical to that other property unless both properties are

(a) included in the same segregated fund of the corporation;

(b) non-segregated property used in the year in, or held in the course of, carrying on a life insurance business in Canada; or

(c) non-segregated property used in the year in, or held in the course of, carrying on an insurance business in Canada, other than a life insurance business.

**Interpretation Bulletins**: IT-387R2: Meaning of "identical properties". See also list at end of ITAR 26.

**(8.2) Idem** — For the purposes of subsection (8), any bond, debenture, bill, note or other similar obligation issued by a debtor is identical to any other such obligation issued by that debtor if both are identical in respect of all rights (in equity or otherwise, either immediately or in the future and either absolutely or contingently) attaching thereto, except as regards the principal amount thereof.

**Interpretation Bulletins**: IT-387R2: Meaning of "identical properties". See also list at end of ITAR 26.

**(8.3) Idem** — Where a corporation resident in Canada has, after 1971, received a stock dividend in respect of a share owned on June 18, 1971 and December 31, 1971 by it or by a corporation with which it did not deal at arm's length of the capital stock of a foreign affiliate of that corporation and the share or shares received as the stock dividend are identical to the share in respect of which the stock dividend was received, the share or shares received as the stock dividend may, at the option of the corporation, be deemed for the purposes of subsection (5) to be capital property owned by it on June 18, 1971 and for the purposes of this subsection, paragraph (3)(c) and subsection (8) to be capital property owned by it on June 18, 1971 and December 31, 1971 and not to be property acquired by the corporation after 1971 for the purposes of paragraph (8)(e).

**(8.4) Idem** — Where a corporation resident in Canada has, after 1971, received a stock dividend in respect of a share acquired by it after June 18, 1971 from a person with whom it was dealing at arm's length and owned by it on December 31, 1971 of the capital stock of a foreign affiliate of that corporation and the share or shares received as the stock dividend are identical to the share in respect of which the stock dividend was received, the share or shares received as the stock dividend may, at the option of the corporation, be deemed for the purposes of this subsection, paragraph (3)(c) and subsection (8) to be capital property owned by it on December 31, 1971 and not to be property acquired by the corporation after 1971 for the purposes of paragraph (8)(e).

**(8.5) Amalgamation** — For the purposes of subsections (8.3) and (8.4), where there has been an amalgamation (within the meaning of section 87 of the amended Act), the new corporation shall be deemed to be the same corporation as, and a continuation of, each predecessor corporation.

**(9) Cost of interest in partnership** — For the purpose of computing, at any particular time after 1971, the adjusted cost base to a taxpayer of an interest in a partnership of which he was a member on December 31, 1971 and thereafter without interruption until the particular time, the cost to the taxpayer of the interest shall be deemed to be the amount that

Part I — Income Tax Application Rules, 1971   S. 26(9.4)

is neither the greatest nor the least of the following three amounts, namely:

(a) its actual cost to the taxpayer as of the particular time,

(b) the amount determined under subsection (9.1) in respect of the interest as of the particular time, and

(c) the amount, if any, by which the total of the fair market value of the interest at the particular time and all amounts required by subsection 53(2) of the amended Act to be deducted in computing its adjusted cost base to the taxpayer immediately before the particular time exceeds the total of all amounts required by subsection 53(1) of the amended Act to be added in computing its adjusted cost base to the taxpayer immediately before the particular time,

except that where two or more of the amounts determined under paragraphs (a) to (c) in respect of the interest are the same amount, that amount shall be deemed to be its cost to the taxpayer.

**Forms**: T4A-RCA Supp: Statement of amounts paid from an RCA; T2065: Determination of adjusted cost base of a partnership interest.

**(9.1) Determination of amount for purposes of subsec. (9)** — For the purposes of subsection (9), the amount determined under this subsection in respect of a taxpayer's interest in a partnership as of a particular time is the amount, if any, by which the total of

(a) the taxpayer's share, determined at the beginning of the first fiscal period of the partnership ending after 1971, of the tax equity of the partnership at the particular time,

(b) such part of any contribution of capital made by the taxpayer to the partnership (otherwise than by way of loan) before 1972 and after the beginning of the partnership's first fiscal period ending after 1971, as cannot reasonably be regarded as a gift made to, or for the benefit of, any other member of the partnership who was related to the taxpayer, and

(c) the amount of any consideration that became payable by the taxpayer after 1971 to any other person to acquire, after 1971, any right in respect of the partnership, the sole purpose of the acquisition of which was to increase the taxpayer's interest in the partnership,

exceeds the total of

(d) all amounts received by the taxpayer before 1972 and after the beginning of the partnership's first fiscal period ending after 1971 as, on account of, in lieu of payment of or in satisfaction of, a distribution of the taxpayer's share of the partnership profits or partnership capital, and

(e) all amounts each of which is an amount in respect of the disposition by the taxpayer after 1971 and before the particular time of a part of the taxpayer's interest in the partnership, equal to such portion of the adjusted cost base to the taxpayer of the interest immediately before the disposition as may reasonably be regarded as attributable to the part so disposed of.

**(9.2) Where interest acquired before 1972 and after beginning of 1st fiscal period ending after 1971** — Where a taxpayer has, before 1972 and after the beginning of the first fiscal period of a partnership ending after 1971, acquired an interest in the partnership from another person, subsection (9.1) applies as if, for the purposes of paragraphs (a), (b) and (d) thereof, the taxpayer had in respect of the interest, throughout the period beginning at the beginning of that fiscal period and ending at the time the taxpayer acquired the interest, the same position in relation to the partnership as the taxpayer would have had in relation thereto if, throughout that period, the taxpayer had been the owner of the interest.

**(9.3) Amounts deemed to be required to be deducted in respect of interest in partnership** — For the purpose of computing, at any particular time after 1971, the adjusted cost base to a taxpayer of an interest in a partnership of which the taxpayer was a member on December 31, 1971 and thereafter without interruption until the particular time, the lesser of

(a) the amount, if any, by which

(i) the total of all amounts in respect of the interest determined under paragraph (9.1)(d)

exceeds

(ii) the total of

(A) the taxpayer's share, determined at the beginning of the first fiscal period of the partnership ending after 1971, of the tax equity of the partnership at the particular time, and

(B) the amount in respect of the interest determined under paragraph (9.1)(b), and

(b) the amount, if any, by which

(i) the total of all amounts in respect of the interest determined as of the particular time under paragraphs (14)(e) to (g)

exceeds

(ii) the total of all amounts in respect of the interest determined as of the particular time under paragraphs (14)(a) to (d),

shall be deemed to be required by subsection 53(2) of the amended Act to be deducted.

**(9.4) Application of section 53 of amended Act in respect of interest in partnership** — For the purpose of computing, at any particular time after 1971, the adjusted cost base to a taxpayer of an interest in a partnership of which the taxpayer was a member on December 31, 1971 and thereafter without interruption until the particular time,

(a) the reference in clause 53(1)(e)(i)(B) of the amended Act to "relating to" shall be read as a reference to "relating to section 14 or to"; and

(b) clause 53(2)(c)(i)(B) of the amended Act shall be read as follows:

"(B) paragraphs 12(1)(o) and (z.5), 18(1)(m) and 20(1)(v.1), section 31, subsection 40(2), section 55 and subsections 69(6) and (7) of this Act, paragraphs 20(1)(gg) and 81(1)(r) and (s) of the *Income Tax Act*, chapter 148 of the Revised Statutes of Canada, 1952, and the provisions of the *Income Tax Application Rules* relating to section 14, and"

**Notes**: ITAR 26(9.4)(b) amended to add reference to ITA 12(1)(z.5) by 1996 Budget, effective for the purpose of computing the adjusted cost base of property after 1996.

**(10) Where paragraph 128.1(1)(b) applies** — Where subsection 48(3) of the amended Act, as it read in its application before 1993, or paragraph 128.1(1)(b) of the amended Act applies for the purpose of determining the cost to a taxpayer of any property, this section does not apply for that purpose.

**Notes**: ITAR 26(10) amended by 1993 technical bill to add reference to ITA 128.1(1)(b), effective 1993. Where a corporation continued before 1993 elects for ITA 250(5.1) to apply earlier (see Notes to ITA 250(5.1)), the amendment is effective from the corporation's "time of continuation".

**(11) Fair market value of publicly-traded securities** — For the purposes of this section, the fair market value on valuation day of any property prescribed to be a publicly-traded share or security shall be deemed to be the greater of the amount, if any, prescribed in respect of that property and the fair market value of that property, otherwise determined, on valuation day.

**Regulations**: 4400 (prescribed property); Sch. VII (list of fair market values of publicly-traded securities).

**Interpretation Bulletins**: IT-84: Capital property owned on December 31, 1971 — Median rule (Tax-free zone). See also list at end of ITAR 26.

**Information Circulars**: 72-25R4: Business equity valuations.

**(11.1) Fair market value of share of foreign affiliate** — For the purposes of computing the fair market value

(a) on December 31, 1971, or

(b) at any subsequent time for the purposes of subsection (4),

of any shares owned by a taxpayer resident in Canada of the capital stock of a foreign affiliate of the taxpayer, the fair market value at that time of any asset owned by the foreign affiliate at that time

(c) that was subsequently acquired by the taxpayer from the foreign affiliate

(i) as a dividend payable in kind,

(ii) as a benefit the amount of which was deemed by paragraph 80.1(4)(b) of the amended Act to have been received by the taxpayer as a dividend from the foreign affiliate, or

(iii) as consideration for the settlement or extinguishment of an obligation described in subsection 80.1(5) of the amended Act, and

(d) in respect of which subsection 80.1(4) or (5), as the case may be, of the amended Act applies because of an election described in that subsection made by the taxpayer,

shall be deemed to be the principal amount of that asset.

**(11.2) Idem** — For the purposes of computing the fair market value on December 31, 1971 of any shares owned by a taxpayer resident in Canada of the capital stock of a foreign affiliate of the taxpayer, the fair market value on that day of any asset owned by the foreign affiliate on that day

(a) that was subsequently acquired by the taxpayer from the foreign affiliate as described in paragraph 80.1(6)(a) or (b) of the amended Act, and

(b) in respect of which subsection 80.1(1) of the amended Act applies because of an election described in subsection 80.1(6) of that Act made by the taxpayer,

shall be deemed to be the principal amount of that asset.

**(12) Definitions** — In this section,

**"amortized cost"** to a taxpayer of any obligation on January 1, 1972 means

(a) the principal amount of the obligation, if its actual cost to the taxpayer was less than 100% but not less than 95% of that principal amount and the obligation was issued before November 8, 1969,

(b) the actual cost to the taxpayer of the obligation, if the actual cost to the taxpayer thereof was less than 105% but not less than 100% of the principal amount thereof, and

(c) in any other case, the actual cost to the taxpayer of the obligation, plus that proportion of the discount or minus that proportion of the premium, as the case may be, in respect thereof that

(i) the number of full months in the period commencing with the day the taxpayer last acquired the obligation and ending with valuation day,

is of

(ii) the number of full months in the period commencing with the day the taxpayer last acquired the obligation and ending with the date of its maturity;

**Notes**: ITAR 26(12) "amortized cost" was 26(12)(a) before consolidation in R.S.C. 1985 (5th Supp.), effective for taxation years ending after November 1991.

**Interpretation Bulletins**: IT-319: Cost of obligations owned on December 31, 1971. See also list at end of ITAR 26.

**"capital property"** of a taxpayer means any depreciable property of the taxpayer, and any property (other than depreciable property) any gain or loss from the disposition of which would, if the property were disposed of after 1971, be a capital gain or a capital loss, as the case may be, of the taxpayer;

**Notes**: ITAR 26(12)"capital property" was 26(12)(b) before consolidation in R.S.C. 1985 (5th Supp.), effective for taxation years ending after November 1991.

**"discount"** in respect of any obligation owned by a taxpayer means the amount, if any, by which the principal amount thereof exceeds its actual cost to the taxpayer determined without reference to subsection (3);

**Notes**: ITAR 26(12)"discount" was 26(12)(c) before consolidation in R.S.C. 1985 (5th Supp.), effective for taxation years ending after November 1991.

**"eligible capital property"** of a taxpayer means any property, $1/2$ of any amount payable to the taxpayer as consideration for the disposition of which would, if the property were disposed of after 1971, be an eligible capital amount in respect of a business within the meaning assigned by subsection 14(1) of the amended Act;

**Notes**: ITAR 26(12)"eligible capital property" was 26(12)(d) before consolidation in R.S.C. 1985 (5th Supp.), effective for taxation years ending after November 1991.

**"obligation"** means a bond, debenture, bill, note, mortgage or agreement of sale;

**Notes**: ITAR 26(12)"obligation" was 26(12)(e) before consolidation in R.S.C. 1985 (5th Supp.), effective for taxation years ending after November 1991.

**"premium"** in respect of any obligation owned by a taxpayer means the amount, if any, by which its actual cost to the taxpayer determined without reference to subsection (3) exceeds the principal amount thereof;

**Notes**: ITAR 26(12)"premium" was 26(12)(f) before consolidation in R.S.C. 1985 (5th Supp.), effective for taxation years ending after November 1991.

**"tax equity"** of a partnership at any particular time means the amount, if any, by which the total of amounts each of which is

(a) the amount of any money of the partnership on hand at the beginning of its first fiscal period ending after 1971,

(b) the cost amount to the partnership, at the beginning of that fiscal period, of any partnership property other than capital property or eligible capital property,

(c) an amount in respect of any property (other than depreciable property) that was, at the beginning of that fiscal period, capital property of the partnership, equal to,

(i) where the property was disposed of before 1972, the proceeds of disposition thereof,

(ii) where the property was disposed of after 1971 and before the particular time, the amount determined under this section to be its cost to the partnership for the purposes of computing its adjusted cost base to the partnership immediately before it was disposed of, and

(iii) in any other case, the amount determined under this section to be its cost to the partnership for the purposes of computing its adjusted cost base to the partnership immediately before the particular time,

(d) an amount in respect of any prescribed class of depreciable property of the partnership, equal to the amount, if any, by which the total of the undepreciated capital cost to the partnership of property of that class as of January 1, 1972 exceeds the capital cost to the partnership of property of that class acquired by it after the beginning of that fiscal period and before 1972,

(e) an amount in respect of any other depreciable property of the partnership at the beginning of that fiscal period, equal to the amount by which

(i) the actual cost of the property to the partnership, or the amount at which the partnership was deemed to have acquired the property under subsection 20(6) of the Act as it read in its application to the 1971 taxation year, as the case may be,

exceeds

(ii) the total of all amounts in respect of the cost of the property that were allowed under paragraph 11(1)(a) of the Act as it read in computing the income from the partnership of the members thereof for taxation years ending before 1972,

(f) an amount in respect of any property that was, at the beginning of that fiscal period, partnership property that was depreciable property, equal to

(i) where the property was disposed of before 1972, the proceeds of disposition thereof minus the amount, if any, by which the lesser of

(A) the proceeds of disposition thereof, and

(B) the capital cost of the property,

exceeds

(C) in respect of depreciable property of a prescribed class, the undepreciated capital cost of all of the property of that class at the time of the disposition, or

(D) in respect of any other depreciable property, the amount that would be determined under paragraph (e) if the words "at the beginning of that fiscal period" were read as "at the time of the disposition",

(ii) where the property was disposed of after 1971 and before the particular time, the amount, if any, by which the lesser of

(A) the proceeds of disposition thereof, and

(B) the fair market value of the property on valuation day,

exceeds the capital cost to the partnership of the property, and

(iii) in any other case, the amount, if any, by which

(A) the lesser of the fair market value of the property on valuation day and its fair market value at the particular time

exceeds

(B) the capital cost to the partnership of the property, or

(g) an amount in respect of any business carried on by the partnership in its 1971 fiscal period and thereafter without interruption until the particular time, equal to the amount, if any, by which

(i) 2 times the eligible capital amounts (within the meaning assigned by section 14 of the amended Act) in respect of the business (computed without reference to section 21 of this Act) that would have become payable to the partnership

would exceed

(ii) the amount that would be deemed by subsection 21(1) to be the amount that had become payable to the partnership

if the partnership had disposed of the business at the particular time for an amount equal to its fair market value at that time,

exceeds the total of all amounts each of which is the amount of any debt owing by the partnership, or any other obligation of the partnership to pay an amount, that was outstanding at the beginning of the partnership's first fiscal period ending after 1971, minus such part, if any, thereof as would, if the amount had been paid by the partnership in that fiscal period, have been deductible in computing its income for that fiscal period.

**Notes**: ITAR 26(12)"tax equity" was 26(12)(g) before consolidation in R.S.C. 1985 (5th Supp.), effective for taxation years ending after November 1991.

**(13) Meaning of "actual cost"** — For the purposes of this section, the "actual cost" to a person of any property means, except as expressly otherwise provided in this section, the amount, if any, by which

(a) its cost to the person computed without regard to the provisions of this section

exceeds

(b) such part of that cost as was deductible in computing the person's income for any taxation year ending before 1972.

**Interpretation Bulletins**: IT-93: Capital property owned on December 31, 1971 — meaning of actual cost and amortized cost. See also list at end of ITAR 26.

**(14) Idem** — For the purposes of this section, the "actual cost" to a taxpayer, as of any particular time after 1971, of an interest in a partnership of which the taxpayer was a member on December 31, 1971 and thereafter without interruption until the particular time means the amount, if any, by which the total of

(a) the cost to the taxpayer of the interest, computed as of the particular time without regard to the provisions of this section,

(b) the total of all amounts each of which is an amount in respect of a fiscal period of the partnership that ended before 1972, equal to the total of

(i) the amount that the taxpayer's income from the partnership for the taxation year of the taxpayer in which the period ended would have been, if the former Act had been read without reference to subsection 83(5) of that Act, and

(ii) the taxpayer's share, determined at the end of the period, of all profits made from dispositions in the period of capital assets that were partnership property of the partnership, to the extent that those profits were not included in computing the income or loss, as the case may be, from the partnership, of any member thereof,

(c) where the taxpayer had, before 1972, made a contribution of capital to the partnership otherwise than by way of loan, such part of the contribution as cannot reasonably be regarded as a gift made to, or for the benefit of, any other member of the partnership who was related to the taxpayer, and

(d) where, by means of the partnership, the taxpayer carried on before 1972 a business that was a profession, the amount that the taxpayer's 1971 receivables (within the meaning assigned by subsection 23(5)) in respect of the business would have been if, before 1972, the taxpayer had carried on no businesses except by means of the partnership,

exceeds the total of

(e) all amounts each of which is an amount in respect of the disposition by the taxpayer before the particular time of a part of the taxpayer's interest in the partnership, equal to such portion of,

(i) where the disposition was made before 1972, the actual cost to the taxpayer of the interest, and

(ii) in any other case, the adjusted cost base to the taxpayer of the interest immediately before the disposition, as can reasonably be regarded as attributable to the part so disposed of,

(f) all amounts each of which is an amount in respect of a fiscal period of the partnership that ended before 1972, equal to the total of

(i) the amount that would have been the taxpayer's loss from the partnership for the taxation year of the taxpayer in which the period ended if the former Act had been read without reference to subsection 83(5) of that Act,

(ii) the taxpayers' share, determined at the end of the period, of all losses sustained from dispositions in the period of capital assets that were partnership property of the partnership, to the extent that those losses were not included in computing the loss or income, as the case may be, from the partnership, of any member thereof, and

(iii) the taxpayer's share, determined at the end of the period, of such of the drilling and exploration expenses, including all general geological and geophysical expenses incurred by the partnership while the taxpayer was a member thereof, on or in respect of exploring or drilling for petroleum or natural gas in Canada as were incurred in the period and after 1948, to the extent that those expenses were not deducted in computing the taxpayer's income from the partnership for the taxpayer's 1971 or any preceding taxation year, and

(g) all amounts received by the taxpayer before 1972 as, on account of, in lieu of payment of or in satisfaction of, a distribution of the taxpayer's share of the partnership profits or partnership capital.

**(15) Idem** — For the purposes of this section and subsection 88(2.1) of the amended Act, the "actual cost" to a taxpayer, as of any particular time after 1971, of any shares (in this subsection referred to as "new shares") of any class of the capital stock of a new corporation formed as a result of an amalgamation of two or more corporations (within the meaning of section 85I of the former Act as it read in its application to the 1971 taxation year) that were

(a) owned by the taxpayer on December 31, 1971, and thereafter without interruption until the particular time, and

(b) acquired by the taxpayer by the conversion, because of the amalgamation, of shares of the capital stock of a predecessor corporation into shares of the capital stock of the new corporation,

means that proportion of the actual cost to the taxpayer of any shares owned by the taxpayer that were so converted because of the amalgamation that the fair market value, immediately after the amalgamation, of the new shares of that class so acquired by the taxpayer is of the fair market value, immediately after the amalgamation, of all of the shares of the capital stock of the new corporation so acquired by the taxpayer.

**(16) Idem** — For the purposes of this section, the "actual cost" to an individual, as of any particular time after 1971, of any share of the capital stock of a corporation that was

(a) owned by the individual on December 31, 1971 and thereafter without interruption until the particular time, and

(b) acquired by the individual in a taxation year before 1972 under an agreement referred to in subsection 85A(1) of the former Act as it read in its application to that taxation year,

means an amount equal to the greater of

(c) the actual cost to the individual of the share computed without regard to this subsection, and

(d) the fair market value of the share at the time the individual so acquired it.

**(17) Idem** — For the purposes of this section and subsection 88(2.1) of the amended Act, the "actual cost" to a taxpayer, as of any particular time after 1971, of any capital property received by the taxpayer before 1972 and owned by the taxpayer thereafter without interruption until the particular time means,

(a) where the property was so received as, on account of, in lieu of payment of or in satisfaction of, a dividend payable in kind (other than a stock dividend) in respect of a share owned by the taxpayer of the capital stock of a corporation, the fair market value of that property at the time the property was so received;

(b) where the property so received was a share of the capital stock of a corporation received by the taxpayer as a stock dividend, the amount that, because of the receipt of the share, was deemed by subsection 81(3) of the former Act to have been received by the taxpayer as a dividend; and

(c) where the property was so received from a pension fund or plan, an employees profit sharing plan, a retirement savings plan, a deferred profit sharing plan or a supplementary unemployment benefit plan, the fair market value of that property at the time the property was so received.

**(17.1) Application** — Where a taxpayer is deemed to have acquired a property because of subsection 138(11.3) of the amended Act, this section does not apply in respect of any subsequent disposition or deemed disposition of the property.

**Interpretation Bulletins**: IT-88R2: Stock dividends. See also list at end of ITAR 26.

**(18) Transfer of farm land by a farmer to [the farmer's] child at death** — Where

(a) a taxpayer owned, on December 31, 1971 and thereafter without interruption until the taxpayer's death, any land referred to in subsection 70(9) of the amended Act,

(b) the land has, on or after the death of the taxpayer and as a consequence thereof, been transferred or distributed to a child of the taxpayer who was resident in Canada immediately before the death of the taxpayer, and

(c) it can be shown, within the period ending 36 months after the death of the taxpayer or, where written application therefor has been made to the Minister by the legal representative of the taxpayer within that period, within such longer period as the Minister considers reasonable in the circumstances, that the land has become vested indefeasibly in the child,

the following rules apply:

(d) paragraph 70(9)(b) of the amended Act does not apply for the purpose of determining the cost to the child of the land or part thereof, as the case may be, and

(e) subsection (5) applies in respect of the transfer or distribution of the land to the child as if the references in that subsection to "June 18, 1971" were references to "December 31, 1971".

**Related Provisions**: ITAR 26(20) — Extended meaning of "child".

**Interpretation Bulletins**: IT-349R3: Intergenerational transfers of farm property on death; IT-449R: Meaning of "vested indefeasibly". See also list at end of ITAR 26.

**(19) *Inter vivos* transfer of farm land by a farmer to child** — Where a taxpayer owned, on December 31, 1971, and thereafter without interruption until a transfer thereof by the taxpayer to the taxpayer's child, in circumstances to which subsection 73(3) of the amended Act applies, land referred to in that subsection,

(a) paragraph 73(3)(d) of the amended Act does not apply for the purpose of determining the cost to the child of the land; and

(b) subsection (5) shall apply in respect of the transfer of the land to the child as if the references in that subsection to "June 18, 1971" were references to "December 31, 1971".

**Related Provisions**: ITAR 26(20) — Extended meaning of "child".

**Interpretation Bulletins**: IT-268R4: *Inter vivos* transfer of farm property to child. See also list at end of ITAR 26.

**(20) Extended meaning of "child"** — For the purposes of subsections (18) and (19), "child" of a taxpayer includes

(a) a child of the taxpayer's child;

(b) a child of the taxpayer's child's child; and

(c) a person who, at any time before attaining the age of 21 years, was wholly dependent on the taxpayer for support and of whom the taxpayer had, at that time, in law or in fact, the custody and control.

**Related Provisions**: ITA 70(10) — Extended meaning of "child".

**(21) Shares received on amalgamation** — Where, after May 6, 1974, there has been an amalgamation (within the meaning assigned by section 87 of the amended Act) of two or more corporations (each of which is in this subsection referred to as a "predecessor corporation") to form one corporate entity (in this subsection referred to as the "new corporation"), and

(a) any shareholder (except any predecessor corporation) owned shares of the capital stock of a predecessor corporation on December 31, 1971 and thereafter without interruption until immediately before the amalgamation,

(b) any shares referred to in paragraph (a) were shares of one class of the capital stock of a predecessor corporation (in this subsection referred to as the "old shares"),

(c) no consideration was received by the shareholder for the disposition of the old shares on the amalgamation other than shares of one class of the capital stock of the new corporation (in this subsection referred to as the "new shares"), and

(c.1) the cost of the new shares received by the shareholder because of the amalgamation was determined otherwise than because of paragraph 87(4)(e) of the amended Act,

notwithstanding any other provision of this Act or of the amended Act, for the purposes of subsection 88(2.1) of the amended Act and of determining the cost to the taxpayer and the adjusted cost base to the taxpayer of the new shares,

(d) the property that was the old shares shall be deemed not to have been disposed of by the shareholder because of the amalgamation but to have been altered, in form only, because of the amalgamation and to have continued in existence in the form of the new shares, and

(e) the property that is the new shares shall be deemed not to have been acquired by the shareholder because of the amalgamation but to have been in existence prior thereto in the form of the old shares that were altered, in form only, because of the amalgamation.

**Related Provisions**: ITAR 26(30) — Disposition by non-resident of taxable Canadian property.

**(22) Options received on amalgamations** — Where, after May 6, 1974, there has been an amalgamation (within the meaning assigned by section 87 of the amended Act) of two or more corporations (each of which is in this subsection referred to as a "predecessor corporation") to form one corporate entity (in this subsection referred to as the "new corporation") and a taxpayer has acquired an option to acquire capital property that was shares of the capital stock of the new corporation (in this subsection referred to as the "new option") as sole consideration for the disposition on the amalgamation of an option to acquire shares of the capital stock of a predecessor corporation (in this subsection referred to as the "old option") owned by the taxpayer on December 31, 1971 and thereafter without interruption until immediately before the amalgamation, notwithstanding any other provision of this Act or of the amended Act, for the purposes of subsection 88(2.1) of the amended Act and of determining the cost to the taxpayer and the adjusted cost base to the taxpayer of the new option,

(a) the property that was the old option shall be deemed not to have been disposed of by the taxpayer because of the amalgamation but to have been altered, in form only, because of the amalgamation and to have continued in existence in the form of the new option; and

(b) the property that is the new option shall be deemed not to have been acquired by the taxpayer because of the amalgamation but to have been in existence prior thereto in the form of the old option that was altered, in form only, because of the amalgamation.

**(23) Obligations received on amalgamations** — Where, after May 6, 1974, there has been an amalgamation (within the meaning assigned by section 87 of the amended Act) of two or more corporations (each of which is in this subsection referred to as a "predecessor corporation") to form one corporate entity (in this subsection referred to as the "new corporation") and a taxpayer has acquired a capital property that was a bond, debenture, note, mortgage or other similar obligation of the new corporation (in this subsection referred to as the "new obligation") as sole consideration for the disposition on the amalgamation of a bond, debenture, note, mortgage or other similar obligation respectively of a predecessor corporation (in this subsection referred to as the "old obligation") owned by the taxpayer on December 31, 1971 and thereafter without interruption until immediately before the amalgamation, notwithstanding any other provision of this Act or of the amended Act, for the purposes of subsection 88(2.1) of the amended Act and of determining the cost to the taxpayer and the adjusted cost base to the taxpayer of the new obligation,

(a) the property that was the old obligation shall be deemed not to have been disposed of by the taxpayer because of the amalgamation but to have been altered, in form only, because of the amalgamation and to have continued in existence in the form of the new obligation; and

(b) the property that is the new obligation shall be deemed not to have been acquired by the taxpayer because of the amalgamation but to have been in existence prior thereto in the form of the old obligation that was altered, in form only, because of the amalgamation.

**(24) Convertible properties** — Where there has been an exchange to which subsection 51(1) of the amended Act applies on which a taxpayer has acquired shares of one class of the capital stock of a corporation (in this subsection referred to as the "new shares") in exchange for a share, bond, debenture or note of the corporation (in this subsection referred to as the "old property") owned by the taxpayer on December 31, 1971 and thereafter without interruption until immediately before the time of the exchange, notwithstanding any other provision of this Act or of the amended Act, for the purposes of subsection 88(2.1) of the amended Act and, where the exchange occurred after May 6, 1974, for the purposes of determining the cost to the taxpayer and the adjusted cost base to the taxpayer of the new shares,

(a) the property that was the old property shall be deemed not to have been disposed of by the taxpayer because of the exchange but to have been altered, in form only, because of the exchange and to have continued in existence in the form of the new shares; and

(b) the property that is the new shares shall be deemed not to have been acquired by the taxpayer because of the exchange but to have been in existence prior thereto in the form of the old property that was altered, in form only, because of the exchange.

**Interpretation Bulletins**: IT-146R3: Shares entitling shareholders to choose taxable or other kinds of dividends; IT-474R: Amalgamations of Canadian corporations. See also list at end of ITAR 26.

**(25) Bond conversion** — Where, after May 6, 1974, there has been an exchange to which section 51.1 of the amended Act applies on which a taxpayer has acquired a bond of a debtor (in this subsection referred to as the "new bond") in exchange for another bond of the same debtor (in this subsection referred to as the "old bond") owned by the taxpayer on December 31, 1971 and thereafter without interruption until immediately before the exchange, notwithstanding any other provision of this Act or of the amended Act, for the purposes of subsection 88(2.1) of the amended Act and of determining the cost to the taxpayer and the adjusted cost base to the taxpayer of the new bond,

(a) the property that was the old bond shall be deemed not to have been disposed of by the taxpayer because of the exchange but to have been altered, in form only, because of the exchange and to have continued in existence in the form of the new bond; and

(b) the property that is the new bond shall be deemed not to have been acquired by the taxpayer because of the exchange but to have been in existence prior thereto in the form of the old bond that was altered, in form only, because of the exchange.

**Notes**: ITAR 26(25) amended by 1995-97 technical bill, effective for exchanges after October 1994, to change reference from ITA 77 to ITA 51.1.

**(26) Share for share exchange** — Where, after May 6, 1974, there has been an exchange to which subsection 85.1(1) of the amended Act applies on which a taxpayer has acquired shares of any particular class of the capital stock of a corporation (in this subsection referred to as the "new shares") in exchange for shares of any particular class of the capital stock of another corporation (in this subsection referred to as the "old shares") owned by the taxpayer on December 31, 1971 and thereafter without interruption until immediately before the exchange, notwithstanding any other provision of this Act or of the amended Act, for the purposes of subsection 88(2.1) of the amended Act and of determining the cost to the taxpayer and the adjusted cost base to the taxpayer of the new shares,

(a) the property that was the old shares shall be deemed not to have been disposed of by the taxpayer because of the exchange but to have been altered, in form only, because of the exchange and to have continued in existence in the form of the new shares; and

(b) the property that is the new shares shall be deemed not to have been acquired by the taxpayer because of the exchange but to have been in existence prior thereto in the form of the old shares that were altered, in form only, because of the exchange.

**Interpretation Bulletins**: IT-450R: Share for share exchange.

**(27) Reorganization of capital** — Where, after May 6, 1974, there has been a reorganization of the capital of a corporation to which section 86 of the amended Act applies on which a taxpayer has acquired shares of a particular class of the capital stock of the corporation (in this subsection referred to as the "new shares") as the sole consideration for the disposition on the reorganization of shares of another class of the capital stock of the corporation (in this subsection referred to as the "old shares") owned by the taxpayer on December 31, 1971 and thereafter without interruption until immediately before the reorganization and the cost to the taxpayer of the new shares was determined otherwise than because of subsection 86(2) of the amended Act, notwithstanding any other provision of this Act or of the amended Act, for the purposes of subsection 88(2.1) of the amended Act and of determining the cost to the taxpayer and the adjusted cost base to the taxpayer of the new shares,

(a) the property that was the old shares shall be deemed not to have been disposed of by the taxpayer because of the reorganization but to have been altered, in form only, because of the reorganization and to have continued in existence in the form of the new shares; and

(b) the property that is the new shares shall be deemed not to have been acquired by the taxpayer by virtue of the reorganization but to have been in existence prior thereto in the form of the old shares that were altered, in form only, because of the reorganization.

**Advance Tax Rulings**: ATR-22R: Estate freeze using share exchange.

**(28) Idem** — Where a taxpayer acquired a property (in this subsection referred to as the "first property") in circumstances to which any of subsections (5) and (21) to (27) applied and subsequently acquires, in exchange for or in consideration for the disposition of the first property, another property in circumstances to which any of subsections (21) to (27) would apply if the taxpayer had owned the first property on December 31, 1971 and thereafter without interruption until the time of the subsequent acquisition, for the purposes of applying subsections (21) to (27) in respect of that subsequent acquisition, the taxpayer shall be deemed to have owned the first property on December 31, 1971 and thereafter without interruption until the time of the subsequent acquisition.

**Notes**: ITAR 26(28) added by 1991 technical bill, effective for acquisitions after July 13, 1990, and also for acquisitions from May 7, 1974 through July 13, 1990 (with respect to property owned by the taxpayer on July 13, 1990) if the taxpayer elected by notifying the CCRA in writing either before 1993 or in the return for the taxation year in which the taxpayer disposed of the property. The effect of ITAR 26(28) is to provide for the preservation of the tax-free zone and pre-1972 capital surplus on hand on successive applications of ITAR 26(21)–(27) due to more than one reorganization.

**Interpretation Bulletins**: IT-450R: Share for share exchange.

**(29) Effect of election under subsection 110.6(19)** — Where subsection 110.6(19) of the amended Act applies to a particular property, for the purposes of determining the cost and the adjusted cost base to a taxpayer of any property at any time after February 22, 1994, the particular property shall be deemed not to have been owned by any taxpayer on December 31, 1971.

**Related Provisions**: ITAR 26(30) — Disposition by non-resident of taxable Canadian property.

**Notes**: ITAR 26(29) added by 1994 Budget, effective March 26, 1995 (Royal Assent).

**(30) Additions to taxable Canadian property** — Subsections (1.1) to (29) do not apply to a disposition by a non-resident person of a taxable Canadian property that would not be a taxable Canadian property immediately before the disposition if section 115 of the amended Act were read as it applied to dispositions that occurred on April 26, 1995.

**Proposed Amendment — ITAR 26(30)**

**(30) Additions to taxable Canadian property** — Subsections (1.1) to (29) do not apply to a disposition by a non-resident person of a property

(a) that the person last acquired before April 27, 1995;

(b) that would not be a taxable Canadian property immediately before the disposition if section 115 of the amended Act were read as it applied to dispositions that occurred on April 26, 1995; and

(c) that would be a taxable Canadian property immediately before the disposition if section 115 of the amended Act were read as it applied to dispositions that occurred on January 1, 1996.

**Related Provisions**: ITA 40(9) — Gains limited to those accruing after April 1995.

**Application**: Bill C-43 (First Reading September 20, 2000), s. 120, will amend subsec. 26(30) to read as above, applicable to dispositions that occur after October 1, 1996.

**Technical Notes**: Section 26 of the *Income Tax Application Rules* sets out the method for computing the adjusted cost base to a taxpayer of certain capital property owned by the taxpayer at the end of 1971. The general purpose of section 26 is to prevent gains that accrued before 1972 from being subject to tax.

Subsection 26(30) of the Rules provides that dispositions by non-residents persons of certain types of property are not within the application of subsections 26(1.1) to (29) of the rules. Essentially, these are properties that became taxable Canadian properties because of changes to the definition "taxable Canadian property" that took effect in April, 1995. The relief provided by section 26 is not needed for such properties, as subsection 40(9) of the *Income Tax Act* ensures that a non-resident person's gains or losses on the disposition of such properties are limited to those that accrued after April 1995.

This amendment to subsection 26(30) of the rules ensures that the provision does not apply to property that becomes taxable Canadian property as a result of these proposals. The amendment applies to dispositions that occur after October 1, 1996.

**Notes**: ITAR 26(30) added by 1995-97 technical bill, effective for dispositions after April 26, 1995.

**Definitions [ITAR 26]**: "actual cost" — ITAR 26(5)(b), (6)(b), (c), (8)(c)(i), 26(13)–(17); "adjusted cost base" — ITA 54, 248(1); "amended Act" — ITAR 8; "amortized cost" — ITAR 26(5)(b), (6)(b), (c), 26(12); "amount" — ITA 248(1); "arm's length" — ITAR 26(5.1), (5.2); "business" — ITA 248(1); "Canada" — ITA 255, *Interpretation Act* 35(1); "Canadian corporation" — ITA 89(1), 248(1); "capital gain" — ITA 39(1), 248(1); "capital loss" — ITA 39(1)(b), 248(1); "capital property" — ITA 54, ITAR 26(8.3), (8.4), (12); "child" — ITAR 26(20); "consequence" — 248(8); "corporation" — ITA 248(1), ITAR 26(8.5); "cost amount" — ITA 248(1); "deferred profit sharing plan" — ITA 147(1), 248(1); "depreciable property" — ITA 13(21), 248(1); "discount" — ITAR 26(12); "dividend" — ITA 248(1); "eligible capital amount" — ITA 14(1), 248(1); "eligible capital property" — ITAR 26(12); "employees profit sharing plan" — ITA 144(1), 248(1); "fair market value on valuation day" — ITAR 26(8)(b)(ii), (c)(ii), 26(11); "first property" — ITAR 26(28); "fiscal period" — ITA 249.1; "foreign affiliate" — ITA 95(1), 248(1); "former Act" — ITAR 8; "identical" — ITA 248(12), ITAR 26(8.1), (8.2); "Income Tax Act, chapter 148 of the Revised Statutes of Canada, 1952", "Income Tax Application Rules, 1971" — ITAR 69; "individual", "legal representative", "life insurance business", "life insurance corporation" — ITA 248(1); "listed personal property" — ITAR 26(8)(b)(ii), (c)(ii), 26(11); "Minister" — ITA 248(1); "month" — *Interpretation Act* 35(1); "new bond" — ITAR 26(25); "new corporation" — ITAR 26(21)–(23); "new obligation" — ITAR 26(23); "new option" — ITAR 26(22); "new shares" — ITAR 26(21)(c), 26(24), (26), (27); "non-resident" — ITA 248(1); "obligation" — ITAR 26(1.1), (12); "old bond" — ITAR 26(25); "old obligation", "old option" — ITAR 26(22); "old property" — ITAR 26(24); "old shares" — ITAR 26(21)(b), 26(26), (27); "original owner" — ITAR 26(5); "owned" — ITAR 26(6)(a), 26(28); "partnership" — see Notes to ITA 96(1); "person" — ITA 248(1); "personal-use property" — ITA 54, 248(1); "predecessor corporation" — ITAR 26(21)–(23); "premium" — ITAR 26(12); "prescribed", "principal amount", "property" — ITA 248(1); "related" — ITA 251(2)–(6); "resident in Canada" — ITA 250; "retirement savings plan" — ITA 146(1), 248(1); "share", "shareholder", "stock dividend" — ITA 248(1); "subsequent owner" — ITAR 26(5); "supplementary unemployment benefit plan" — ITA 145(1), 248(1); "tax equity" — ITAR 26(12); "taxable Canadian property" — ITA 248(1); "taxation year" — ITA 249; "taxpayer" — ITA 248(1); "undepreciated capital cost" — ITA 13(21), 248(1); "valuation day" — ITAR 24; "writing" — *Interpretation Act* 35(1); "written" — *Interpretation Act* 35(1)"writing".

## 26.1 (1) Change of use of property before 1972 

— For the purposes of paragraph 40(2)(b) and the definition "principal residence" in section 54 of the amended Act, where a taxpayer owned, on December 31, 1971, a property that is a housing unit, a leasehold interest in a housing unit or a share of the capital stock of a cooperative housing corporation, if the housing unit was, or if the share was acquired for the sole purpose of acquiring the right to inhabit, a housing unit owned by the corporation that was ordinarily inhabited by the taxpayer, and the taxpayer began at any time thereafter but before 1972 to use the property for the purpose of gaining or producing income therefrom, or for the purpose of gaining or producing income from a business, and the taxpayer elected in the taxpayer's return of income for the 1974 or 1975 taxation year as if the taxpayer had begun to use the property for the purpose of gaining or producing income therefrom or for the purpose of gaining or producing income from a business on January 1, 1972, the taxpayer shall be deemed to have made an election under subsection 45(2) of the amended Act in the taxpayer's return of income for the 1972 taxation year and to have so begun to use the property.

## (2) No capital cost allowance while election in force 

— Where the taxpayer has made the election described in subsection (1), no amount may be deducted under paragraph 20(1)(a) of the amended Act for the 1974 and subsequent taxation years in respect of property referred to in that subsection while the election remains in force.

**Definitions [ITAR 26.1]**: "amended Act" — ITAR 8; "amount", "business" — ITA 248(1); "corporation" — ITA 248(1), *Interpretation Act* 35(1); "property", "share" — ITA 248(1); "taxation year" — ITA 249; "taxpayer" — ITA 248(1).

## 27, 28. [Repealed under former Act]

**Notes**: ITAR 27 and 28 repealed in 1985. 27 dealt with moving expenses paid before 1972, and 28 provided an exemption for mining income to the end of 1973.

## 29. (1) Deduction from income of petroleum or natural gas corporation 

— A corporation whose principal business is production, refining or marketing of petroleum, petroleum products or natural gas or exploring or drilling for petroleum or natural gas may deduct, in computing its income for a taxation year, the lesser of

(a) the total of such of the drilling and exploration expenses, including all general geological and geophysical expenses, incurred by it on or in respect of exploring or drilling for petroleum or natural gas in Canada as were incurred during the calendar years 1949 to 1952, to the extent that they were not deductible in computing income for a previous taxation year, and

(b) of that total, an amount equal to its income for the taxation year if no deduction were allowed under this section or section 65, 66 or 66.1 of the amended Act minus the deductions allowed for the year under subsections (9), (10) and (25) of this section and sections 112 and 113 of the amended Act.

**Related Provisions**: ITA 87(1.2) — New corporation deemed continuation of predecessor; ITAR 29(31) — Multiple deductions.

**(2) Deduction from income of mining corporation** — A corporation whose principal business is mining or exploring for minerals may deduct, in computing its income for a taxation year, the lesser of

(a) the total of such of the prospecting, exploration and development expenses incurred by it in searching for minerals in Canada as were incurred during 1952, to the extent that they were not deductible in computing income for a preceding taxation year, and

(b) of that total, an amount equal to its income for the taxation year if no deduction were allowed under this section or section 65, 66 or 66.1 of the amended Act minus the deductions allowed for the year under subsections (9), (10) and (25) of this section and sections 112 and 113 of the amended Act,

if the corporation has filed certified statements of those expenses and has satisfied the Minister that it has been actively engaged in prospecting and exploring for minerals in Canada by means of qualified persons and has incurred the expenses for those purposes.

**(3) Deduction from income of petroleum or natural gas corporation or mining corporation** — A corporation whose principal business is

(a) production, refining or marketing of petroleum, petroleum products or natural gas, or exploring or drilling for petroleum or natural gas, or

(b) mining or exploring for minerals,

may deduct, in computing its income for a taxation year, the lesser of

(c) the total of such of

(i) the drilling and exploration expenses, including all general geological and geophysical expenses, incurred by it on or in respect of exploring or drilling for petroleum or natural gas in Canada, and

(ii) the prospecting, exploration and development expenses incurred by it in searching for minerals in Canada,

as were incurred after 1952 and before April 11, 1962, to the extent that they were not deductible in computing income for a previous taxation year, and

(d) of that total, an amount equal to its income for the taxation year if no deduction were allowed under this section or section 65, 66 or 66.1 of the amended Act minus the deductions allowed for the year under subsections (1), (2), (9), (10) and (25) of this section and sections 112 and 113 of the amended Act.

**Related Provisions**: ITAR 29(31) — Multiple deductions.

**(4) Deduction from income of petroleum corporation, etc.** — A corporation whose principal business is

(a) production, refining or marketing of petroleum, petroleum products or natural gas, or exploring or drilling for petroleum or natural gas,

(b) mining or exploring for minerals,

(c) processing mineral ores for the purpose of recovering metals therefrom,

(d) a combination of

(i) processing mineral ores for the purpose of recovering metals therefrom, and

(ii) processing metals recovered from the ores so processed,

(e) fabricating metals, or

(f) operating a pipeline for the transmission of oil or natural gas,

may deduct, in computing its income for a taxation year, the lesser of

(g) the total of such of

(i) the drilling and exploration expenses, including all general geological and geophysical expenses, incurred by it on or in respect of exploring or drilling for petroleum or natural gas in Canada, and

(ii) the prospecting, exploration and development expenses incurred by it on searching for minerals in Canada,

as were incurred after April 10, 1962 and before 1972, to the extent that they were not deductible in computing income for a previous taxation year, and

(h) of that total, an amount equal to its income for the taxation year if no deduction were allowed under this subsection or section 65, 66 or 66.1 of the amended Act minus the deductions allowed for the year under subsection 66(2) and sections 112 and 113 of the amended Act.

**Related Provisions**: ITAR 29(31) — Multiple deductions.

**(5) Application of para. (4)(g)** — In applying paragraph 4(g) to a corporation described in paragraph (4)(f), the reference in paragraph (4)(g) to "April 10, 1962" shall be read as a reference to "June 13, 1963".

**(6), (7), (8)** [Repealed effective 2007]

**Notes**: ITAR 29(6)–(8) repealed by 1996 Budget, effective for renunciations made

(a) after 2006, in respect of a payment or loan received by a joint exploration corporation before March 6, 1996;

(b) after 2006, in respect of a payment or loan received by a joint exploration corporation after March 5, 1996 under an agreement in writing made

(i) by the corporation before March 6, 1996, or

(ii) by another corporation before March 6, 1996, where

(A) the other corporation controlled the corporation at the time the agreement was made, or

(B) the other corporation undertook, at the time the agreement was made, to form the corporation; and

(c) after March 5, 1996, in any other case.

Where they still apply, read:

**(6) Joint exploration corporation may renounce expenses** — A joint exploration corporation may, in any particular taxation year or within 6 months after the end of that year, elect in prescribed form to renounce in favour of another corporation described in subsection (4) an agreed portion of the total of such of

(a) the drilling and exploration expenses, including all general geological and geophysical expenses, incurred by the joint exploration corporation on or in respect of exploring or drilling for petroleum or natural gas in Canada, and

(b) the prospecting, exploration and development expenses incurred by the joint exploration corporation in searching for minerals in Canada,

as were incurred by the joint exploration corporation during a period after 1956 and before April 11, 1962 throughout which the other corporation was a shareholder corporation, to the extent that the total of those expenses exceeds any amount deductible under subsection (3) in respect thereof by the joint exploration corporation in computing its income for any taxation year preceding the particular year, and on the election the agreed portion

(c) shall be deemed, for the purposes of subsection (4) of this section and sections 66, 66.1 and 66.2 of the amended Act, to be expenses described in paragraphs (a) and (b) of this subsection incurred by the other corporation during its taxation year in which the particular taxation year ends, and

(d) shall be subtracted from the total described in paragraph (3)(c) in determining the amount deductible by the joint exploration corporation under subsection (3) in computing its income.

**(7) Idem** — A joint exploration corporation may, in any particular taxation year or within 6 months from the end of that year, elect in prescribed form to renounce in favour of another corporation described in subsection (4) an agreed portion of the total of such of

(a) the drilling and exploration expenses, including all general geological and geophysical expenses, incurred by the joint exploration corporation on or in respect of exploring or drilling for petroleum or natural gas in Canada, and

(b) the prospecting, exploration and development expenses incurred by the joint exploration corporation in searching for minerals in Canada,

as were incurred by the joint exploration corporation during a period after April 10, 1962 and before 1972 throughout which the other corporation was a shareholder corporation, to the extent that the total of those expenses exceeds any amount deductible under subsection (4) in respect thereof by the joint exploration corporation in computing its income for any taxation year preceding the particular year, and on the election the agreed portion

(c) shall be deemed, for the purposes of subsection (4) of this section and sections 66, 66.1 and 66.2 of the amended Act, to be expenses described in paragraphs (a) and (b) of this subsection incurred by the other corporation during its taxation year in which the particular taxation year ends, and

(d) shall be subtracted from the total described in paragraph (4)(g) in determining the amount deductible by the joint exploration corporation under subsection (4) in computing its income.

**(8) Definitions** — For the purposes of subsections (6) and (7),

"agreed portion" in respect of a corporation that was a shareholder corporation of a joint exploration corporation means such amount as is agreed on between the joint exploration corporation and the other corporation not exceeding

(a) the payments referred to in paragraph (c) of the definition "shareholder corporation" in this subsection made by the other corporation to the joint exploration corporation during the period it was a shareholder corporation in respect of the expenses incurred by the joint exploration corporation referred to in paragraphs (6)(a) and (b) or (7)(a) and (b), as the case may be,

minus

(b) the total of the amounts, if any, previously renounced by the joint exploration corporation under subsection (6) or (7), as the case may be, in favour of the other corporation;

"joint exploration corporation" means a corporation

(a) whose principal business is of a class described in paragraph (3)(a) or (b), and

(b) that has not at any time since its incorporation had more than 10 shareholders (not including any individual holding a share for the sole purpose of qualifying as a director);

a "shareholder corporation" of a joint exploration corporation means a corporation that for the period in respect of which the expression is being applied

(a) was a shareholder of the joint exploration corporation,

(b) was a corporation whose principal business was of a class described in subsection (4), and

(c) made payments to the joint exploration corporation in respect of the expenses incurred by the joint exploration corporation referred to in paragraphs (6)(a) and (b) or (7)(a) and (b), as the case may be.

ITAR 29(8)"agreed portion" was 29(8)(c), "joint exploration corporation" was 29(8)(a), and "shareholder corporation" was 29(8)(b), before consolidation in R.S.C. 1985 (5th Supp.), effective for taxation years ending after November 1991.

**(9) Deduction from income from businesses of associations, etc.** — There may be deducted in computing the income of a taxpayer for a taxation year from the businesses of all associations, partnerships or syndicates formed for the purpose of exploring or drilling for petroleum or natural gas and of which the taxpayer was a member or partner, the lesser of

(a) the total of the taxpayer's share of such of the drilling and exploration expenses, including all general geological and geophysical expenses, incurred by all those associations, partnerships or syndicates while the taxpayer was a member or partner thereof, on or in respect of exploring or drilling for petroleum or natural gas in Canada as were incurred after 1948 and before April 11, 1962, to the extent that they were not deductible in computing the taxpayer's income for a preceding taxation year, and

(b) of that total, an amount equal to the taxpayer's income from the businesses of all those associations, partnerships or syndicates for the taxation year, computed before making any deduction under this section or section 65, 66, or 66.1 of the amended Act.

**(10) Idem** — There may be deducted in computing the income of a taxpayer for the taxation year from the businesses of all associations, partnerships or syndicates formed for the purpose of exploring or drilling for petroleum or natural gas and of which the taxpayer was a member or partner, the lesser of

(a) the total of the taxpayer's share of such of the drilling and exploration expenses, including all general geological and geophysical expenses incurred by all those associations, partnerships or syndicates while the taxpayer was a member or partner thereof, on or in respect of exploring or drilling for petroleum or natural gas in Canada as were incurred after April 10, 1962 and before 1972, to the extent that they were not deductible in computing the taxpayer's income for a previous taxation year, and

(b) of that total, an amount equal to the taxpayer's income from the businesses of all those associations, partnerships or syndicates for the taxation year computed before making any deduction under this section or section 65, 66, or 66.1 of the amended Act, minus the deduction allowed for the year under subsection (9) of this section.

**Related Provisions**: 127.52(1)(e) — Limitation on deduction for minimum tax purposes.

**(11) Deduction from income of corporation** — A corporation, other than a corporation described in subsection (4), may deduct, in computing its income for a taxation year, the lesser of

(a) the total of such of

(i) the drilling and exploration expenses, including all general geological and geophysical expenses, incurred by it on or in respect of exploring or drilling for petroleum or natural gas in Canada, and

(ii) the prospecting, exploration and development expenses incurred by it in searching for minerals in Canada,

as were incurred after April 10, 1962 and before 1972, to the extent that they were not deductible in computing income for a preceding taxation year, and

(b) of that total, an amount that would be equal to the total of

(i) its income for the taxation year from operating an oil or gas well in Canada in which the corporation has an interest,

(ii) its income for the taxation year from royalties in respect of an oil or gas well in Canada,

(iii) any amount included in computing its income for the taxation year because of subsection (17), and

(iv) the amount, if any, included under paragraph 59(3.2)(b) or (c) of the amended Act in computing its income for the year,

if no deduction were allowed under this section or section 65, 66 or 66.1 of the amended Act minus the deductions allowed for the year under subsections (9) and (10) of this section and subsection 66(2) of the amended Act.

**Notes**: ITAR 29(11)(b)(iv) amended by 1991 technical bill, retroactive to 1985, in consequence of the repeal of ITA 66(3)(b)(ii)(C) in 1985. Now, amounts included in computing income under ITA 59(3.2)(b) and (c) increase the limit for deductions under ITAR 29(11).

**(12) Deduction by individual of exploration expenses** — There may be deducted, in computing an individual's income for a taxation year, the lesser of

(a) the total of such of

(i) the drilling and exploration expenses, including all general geological and geophysical expenses, incurred by the individual on or in respect of exploring or drilling for petroleum or natural gas in Canada, and

(ii) the individual's share of the drilling and exploration expenses, including all general geological and geophysical expenses incurred by all associations, partnerships or syndicates described in subsection (9), while the individual was a member or partner thereof, on or in respect of exploring or drilling for petroleum or natural gas in Canada,

as were incurred after April 10, 1962 and before 1972, to the extent that they were not deductible in computing the individual's income for a preceding taxation year, and

(b) of that total, an amount that would be equal to the total of

(i) the individual's income for the taxation year from a business that consisted of the operation of an oil or gas well in Canada in which the individual had an interest,

(ii) the individual's income for the taxation year from royalties in respect of an oil or gas well in Canada,

(iii) any amount included in computing the individual's income for the taxation year because of subsection (17), and

(iv) the amount, if any, included under paragraph 59(3.2)(b) or (c) of the amended Act in computing the individual's income for the year,

if no deduction were allowed under this section or section 65, 66 or 66.1 of the amended Act, minus the deductions allowed for the year under subsections (9) and (10) of this section.

**Related Provisions**: 127.52(1)(e) — Limitation on deduction for minimum tax purposes.

**Notes**: ITAR 29(12)(b)(iv) amended by 1991 technical bill, retroactive to 1985, in consequence of the repeal of 66(3)(b)(ii)(C) of the Act in 1985. Now, amounts included in computing income under ITA 59(3.2)(b) and (c) increase the limit for deductions under ITAR 29(12).

**(13) Limitation re payments for exploration and drilling rights** — In computing a deduction under subsection (1), (3) or (9), no amount shall be included in respect of a payment for or in respect of a right, licence or privilege to explore for, drill for or take petroleum or natural gas, acquired before April 11, 1962, other than an annual payment not exceeding $1 per acre.

**(14) Exploration and drilling rights; payments deductible** — Where an association, partnership or syndicate described in subsection (9) or a corporation or individual has, after April 10, 1962 and before 1972, acquired under an agreement or other contract or arrangement a right, licence or privilege to explore for, drill for or take in Canada petroleum, natural gas or other related hydrocarbons (except coal) under which agreement, contract or arrangement there was not acquired any other right to, over or in respect of the land in respect of which such right, licence or privilege was so acquired except the right

(a) to explore for, drill for or take materials and substances (whether liquid or solid and whether hydrocarbons or not) produced in association with the petroleum, natural gas or other related hydrocarbons (except coal) or found in any water contained in an oil or gas reservoir, or

(b) to enter on, use and occupy as much of the land as is necessary for the purpose of exploiting the right, licence or privilege,

an amount paid in respect of the acquisition thereof that was paid

(c) before 1972, shall, for the purposes of subsections (4), (7), (10), (11) and (12), be deemed to be a drilling or exploration expense on or in respect of exploring or drilling for petroleum or natural gas in Canada incurred at the time of its payment,

(d) after 1971 and before May 7, 1974, shall, for the purposes of the amended Act, be deemed to be Canadian exploration and development expenses (within the meaning assigned by subsection 66(15) of the amended Act) incurred at the time of its payment, and

(e) after May 6, 1974, shall, for the purposes of the amended Act, be deemed to be a Canadian development expense (within the meaning assigned by paragraph 66.2(5)(a) of the amended Act) incurred at the time of its payment.

**(15) Idem** — In applying subsection (14) for the purposes of subsection (7), the expression "after April 10, 1962 and before 1972" in subsection (14) shall be read as "after April 10, 1962 and before April 27, 1965".

**(16) Receipts for exploration or drilling rights included in income** — Where a right, licence or privilege to explore for, drill for or take in Canada petroleum, natural gas or other related hydrocarbons (except coal) was disposed of after April 10, 1962 and before October 23, 1968

(a) by a corporation described in subsection (4),

(b) by a corporation, other than a corporation described in subsection (4), that was at the time of acquisition of the right, licence or privilege a corporation described in subsection (4), or

(c) by an association, partnership or syndicate described in subsection (9),

any amount received by the corporation, association, partnership or syndicate as consideration for the disposition thereof shall be included in computing its income for its fiscal period in which the amount was received, unless the corporation, association, partnership or syndicate

(d) acquired the right, licence or privilege by inheritance or bequest, or

(e) acquired the right, licence or privilege before April 11, 1962 and disposed of it before November 9, 1962.

**(17) Idem** — Where a right, licence or privilege to explore for, drill for or take in Canada petroleum, natural gas or other related hydrocarbons (except coal) that was acquired after April 10, 1962 and before 1972 by an individual or a corporation other than a corporation described in subsection (4), was subsequently disposed of before October 23, 1968, any amount received by the taxpayer as consideration for the disposition thereof shall be included in computing the taxpayer's income for the taxation year in which the amount was received, unless the right, licence or privilege was acquired by the taxpayer by inheritance or bequest.

**(18) Idem** — Subsections (16) and (17) do not apply to any disposition by an association, partnership or syndicate described in subsection (9) or a corporation or an individual of any right, licence or privilege described in subsection (14) or (16) unless the right, licence or privilege was acquired by the association, partnership, syndicate or corporation or individual, as the case may be, under an agreement, contract or arrangement described in subsection (14).

**(19) Idem** — For the purposes of subsections (16) and (17),

(a) where an association, partnership or syndicate described in subsection (9) or a corporation or an individual has disposed of any interest in land that includes a right, licence or privilege described in subsection (14) that was acquired under an agreement, contract or arrangement described in that subsection, the proceeds of disposition of the interest shall be deemed to be proceeds of disposition of the right, licence or privilege; and

(b) where an association, partnership or syndicate described in subsection (9) or a corporation or an individual has acquired a right, licence or privilege described in subsection (14) under an agreement, contract or arrangement described in that subsection and subsequently disposes of any interest

(i) in such right, licence or privilege, or

(ii) in the production of wells situated on the land to which the right, licence or privilege relates,

the proceeds of disposition of the interest shall be deemed to be proceeds of disposition of the right, licence or privilege.

**(20) Idem** — Subsections (11), (12) and (17) do not apply in computing the income for a taxation year of a taxpayer whose business includes trading or dealing in rights, licences or privileges to explore for, drill for or take in Canada petroleum, natural gas or other related hydrocarbons (except coal).

**(21) Bonus payments** — Notwithstanding subsection (13), where a corporation whose principal business is of the class described in paragraph (3)(a) or (b) or an association, partnership or syndicate formed for the purpose of exploring or drilling for petroleum or natural gas has after 1952 paid an amount (other than a rental or royalty) to the government of Canada or a province for

(a) the right to explore for petroleum or natural gas on a specified parcel of land in Canada (which right is, for greater certainty, declared to include a right of the type commonly referred to as a "licence", "permit" or "reservation"), or

(b) a legal lease of the right to take or remove petroleum or natural gas from a specified parcel of land in Canada,

and before April 11, 1962 acquired the rights in respect of which the amount was so paid and, before any well came into production on the land in reasonable commercial quantities, the corporation, association, partnership or syndicate surrendered all the rights so acquired (including, in respect of a right of the kind described in paragraph (a), all rights thereunder to any lease and all rights under any lease made thereunder) without receiving any consideration therefor or repayment of any part of the amount so paid, the amount so paid shall, for the purposes of subsections (3), (4), (7), (9) and (10) of this section, and for the purposes of subsections 66(1),(10) and (10.1) and the definitions "Canadian exploration and development expenses" in subsection 66(15) and "Canadian exploration expense" in subsection 66.1(6) of the amended Act, be deemed to have been a drilling or exploration expense on or in respect of exploring or drilling for petroleum or natural gas in Canada or a Canadian exploration expense described in paragraph (a) of the definition "Canadian exploration expense" in subsection 66.1(6) of the amended Act, as the case may be, incurred by the corporation, association, partnership or syndicate during the taxation year in which the rights were so surrendered.

**(22) Idem** — In applying the provisions of subsection (25) to determine the amount that may be deducted by a successor corporation in computing its income for a taxation year, where the predecessor corporation has paid an amount (other than a rental or royalty) to the government of Canada or a province for

(a) the right to explore for petroleum or natural gas on a specified parcel of land in Canada (which is, for greater certainty, declared to include a right of the type commonly referred to as a "licence", "permit" or "reservation"), or

(b) a legal lease of the right to take or remove petroleum or natural gas from a specified parcel of land in Canada,

if, before the predecessor corporation was entitled, by virtue of subsection (21), to any deduction in computing its income for a taxation year in respect of the amount so paid, the property of the predecessor corporation was acquired by the successor corporation before April 11, 1962 in the manner set out in subsection (25), and the successor corporation did, before any well came into production in reasonable commercial quantities on the land referred to in paragraph (a) or (b), surrender all the rights so acquired by the predecessor corporation (including in respect of a right of the kind described in paragraph (a), all rights thereunder to any lease and all rights under any lease made thereunder) without receiving any consideration therefor or payment of any part of the amount so paid by the predecessor corporation, the amount so paid by the predecessor corporation shall be added to the amount determined under paragraph 25(c).

**(23) Expenses incurred for specified considerations not deductible** — For the purposes of this section and section 53 of chapter 25 of the Statutes of Canada, 1949 (Second Session), it is declared that expenses incurred before 1972 by a corporation, association, partnership or syndicate on or in respect of exploring or drilling for petroleum or natural gas in Canada or in searching for minerals in Canada do not and never did include expenses so incurred by that corporation, association, partnership or syndicate under an agreement under which it undertook to incur those expenses in consideration for

(a) shares of the capital stock of a corporation that owned or controlled the mineral rights;

(b) an option to purchase shares of the capital stock of a corporation that owned or controlled the mineral rights; or

(c) a right to purchase shares of the capital stock of a corporation that was to be formed for the purpose of acquiring or controlling the mineral rights.

**(24) Exception** — Notwithstanding subsection (23), a corporation whose principal business is

(a) production, refining or marketing of petroleum, petroleum products or natural gas or exploring or drilling for petroleum or natural gas, or

(b) mining or exploring for minerals,

may deduct, in computing its income for a taxation year, the lesser of

(c) the total of such of

(i) the drilling and exploration expenses, including all general geological and geophysical expenses, incurred by it on or in respect of exploring or drilling for petroleum or natural gas in Canada, and

(ii) the prospecting, exploration and development expenses incurred by it in searching for minerals in Canada,

as were incurred after 1953 and before 1972,

(iii) under an agreement under which it undertook to incur those expenses for a consideration mentioned in paragraph (23)(a), (b) or (c), and

(iv) to the extent that they were not deductible in computing income for a preceding taxation year, and

(d) of that total, an amount equal to its income for the taxation year if no deduction were allowed under this subsection or subsection (4) or under section 65, 66 or 66.1 of the amended Act minus the deductions allowed for the year under subsection 66(2) and sections 112 and 113 of the amended Act,

but where a corporation has incurred expenses in respect of which this subsection authorizes a deduction from income for a taxation year, no deduction in respect of those expenses may be made in computing the income of any other corporation or from the business of an association, partnership or syndicate for any taxation year.

**Related Provisions**: ITAR 29(25) — Successor rule.

**(25) Successor rule** — Notwithstanding subsection (24) and subject to subsections 66.7(6) and (7) of the amended Act, where a corporation (in this subsection referred to as the "successor") whose principal business is

(a) production, refining or marketing of petroleum, petroleum products or natural gas, or exploring or drilling for petroleum or natural gas, or

(b) mining or exploring for minerals,

has, at any time after 1954, acquired a particular Canadian resource property (whether by way of a purchase, amalgamation, merger, winding-up or otherwise) from another person whose principal business was a business described in paragraph (a) or (b), there may be deducted by the successor in computing its income for a taxation year an amount not exceeding the total of all amounts each of which is an amount determined in respect of an original owner of the particular property that is the lesser of

(c) the total of

(i) the drilling and exploration expenses, including all general geological and geophysical expenses, incurred before 1972 by the original owner on or in respect of exploring or drilling for petroleum or natural gas in Canada, and

(ii) the prospecting, exploration and development expenses incurred before 1972 by the original owner in searching for minerals in Canada,

to the extent that those expenses

(iii) were not otherwise deducted in computing the income of the successor for the year, were not deducted in computing the income of the successor for any preceding taxation year and were not deductible by the original owner or deducted by any predecessor owner of the particular property in computing income for any taxation year, and

(iv) would, but for the provisions of any of this subsection and paragraphs (1)(b), (2)(b), (3)(d), (4)(h) and (24)(d), have been deductible in computing the income of the original owner or any predecessor owner of the particular property for the taxation year preceding the taxation year in which the particular property was acquired by the successor, and

(d) the amount, if any, by which

(i) the part of its income for the year that may reasonably be regarded as being attributable to

(A) the amount included in computing its income for the year under paragraph 59(3.2)(c) of the amended Act that can reasonably be regarded as being attributable to the disposition by it in the year or a preceding taxation year of any Canadian resource properties owned by the original owner and each predecessor owner of the particular property before the acquisition of the particular property by the successor to the extent that the proceeds of the disposition have not been included in determining an amount under this clause or clause 66.7(1)(b)(i)(A) or (3)(b)(i)(A) or paragraph 66.7(10)(g) of the amended Act for a preceding taxation year, or

(B) production from the particular property,

computed as if no deduction were allowed under this section or subdivision e of Division B of Part I of the amended Act,

exceeds

(ii) the total of all other amounts deducted under this subsection and subdivision e of Division B of Part I of the amended Act for the year that can reasonably be regarded as attributable to the part of its income for the year described in subparagraph (i) in respect of the particular property.

**Related Provisions**: ITA 66(15) — "predecessor owner"; ITA 66.6 — No application on acquisition from tax-exempt person; ITA 66.7 — Successor rules; ITA 66.7(2.3) — Successor of foreign resource expense — income deemed not attributable to production from Canadian resource property.

**Notes**: ITAR 29(25)(c)(iii) amended by 1991 technical bill, effective for taxation years ending after February 17, 1987, to add the initial words "were not otherwise deducted in computing the income of the successor for the year". The purpose was to ensure that a successor may claim no more than the unused portion of pre-1972 resource expenditures.

**Forms**: T2010: Election to deduct resource expenses upon acquisition of resource property by a corporation.

**(25.1) Definitions** — For the purposes of subsection (25), the terms "Canadian resource property", "original owner", "predecessor owner" and "production" have the same meanings assigned by subsection 66(15) of the amended Act.

**(26) Processing or fabricating corporation** — A reference in subsection (3), (21), (24) or (25) to a corporation whose principal business is mining or exploring for minerals shall, for the purposes of this section, be deemed to include a reference to a corporation whose principal business is

(a) processing mineral ores for the purpose of recovering metals therefrom,

(b) a combination of

(i) processing mineral ores for the purpose of recovering metals therefrom, and

(ii) processing metals recovered from the ores so processed, or

(c) fabricating metals,

but in applying the provisions of this section to any such corporation the references, respectively, in subsections (3), (21), (24) and (25) to the years 1952, 1953 and 1954 shall be read as a reference in each case to the year 1956.

**(27) Meaning of "drilling and exploration expenses"** — For the purposes of this section, "drilling and exploration expenses" incurred on or in respect of exploring or drilling for petroleum or natural gas in Canada include expenses incurred on or in respect of

(a) drilling or converting a well for the disposal of waste liquids from a petroleum or natural gas well in Canada;

(b) drilling for water or gas for injection into a petroleum or natural gas formation in Canada; and

(c) drilling or converting a well for the injection of water or gas to assist in the recovery of petroleum or natural gas from another well in Canada.

**(28) Deduction from expenses** — For the purposes of this section, there shall be deducted in computing

(a) drilling and exploration expenses incurred by a taxpayer on or in respect of exploring or drilling for petroleum or natural gas in Canada, and

(b) prospecting, exploration and development expenses incurred by a taxpayer in searching for minerals in Canada,

any amount paid to the taxpayer before 1972 under the *Northern Mineral Exploration Assistance Regulations* made under an appropriation Act that provides for payments in respect of the Northern Mineral Grants Program, and there shall be included in computing such expenses any amount, except an amount in respect of interest, paid by the taxpayer before 1972 under those Regulations to Her Majesty in right of Canada.

**(29)** [Repealed under former Act]

**Notes**: ITAR 29(29), repealed in 1987, was titled "Property acquired by second successor corporation". The successor corporation rules in ITAR 29(25) were overhauled with the introduction of ITA 66.7.

**(30) Inclusion in "drilling and exploration expenses"** — For the purposes of this section, "drilling and exploration expenses" incurred on or in respect of exploring or drilling for petroleum or natural gas in Canada include an annual payment made for the preservation of a right, licence or privilege described in subsection (14).

**(31) General limitation** — Where a corporation, association, partnership or syndicate has incurred expenses the deduction of which from income is authorized under more than one provision of this section, it is not entitled to make the deduction under more than one provision but is entitled to select the provision under which to make the deduction.

**(32) Deduction for provincial tax** — Where a corporation whose principal business is production, refining or marketing of petroleum, petroleum products or natural gas or exploring or drilling for petroleum or natural gas could have deducted an amount in respect of expenditures of the corporation in connection with exploration or drilling for petroleum or natural gas incurred in a preceding taxation year from the tax payable under a provincial statute for the 1952 or a subsequent taxation year if the provincial statute were applicable to that year, the corporation may deduct from the tax otherwise payable by it under Part I of the amended Act for the year an amount not exceeding the amount that would have been so deductible.

**(33) Definition of "provincial statute"** — For the purposes of subsection (32), "provincial statute" means a statute imposing a tax on the incomes of corporations enacted by the legislature of a province in 1949 and, for the purpose of that subsection, an amount deductible thereunder for one year shall, for the purpose of computing the deduction for a subsequent year, be deemed to have been deductible under the provincial statute.

**(34) Expenses deductible under certain enactments deemed not otherwise deductible** — Where expenses are or have been, under this section, section 8 of the *Income War Tax Act*, section 16 of chapter 63 of the Statutes of Canada, 1947, section 16 of chapter 53 of the Statutes of Canada, 1948, section 53 of chapter 25 of the Statutes of Canada, 1949 (Second Session) or section 83A of the former Act, deductible from or in computing a taxpayer's income, or where any amount is or has been deductible in respect of expenses under any of those provisions from taxes otherwise payable, it is declared that no amount in respect of the same expenses is or has been deductible under any other authority in computing the income or from the income of that taxpayer or any other taxpayer for any taxation year.

Related Provisions [ITAR 29]: ITA 87(1.2) — New corporation deemed continuation of predecessor.

Definitions [ITAR 29]: "amended Act" — ITAR 8; "amount", "business" — ITA 248(1); "Canada" — ITA 255, *Interpretation Act* 35(1); "Canadian development expense" — ITA 66.2(5), 248(1); "Canadian exploration and development expenses" — ITA 66(15), 248(1); "Canadian exploration expense" — ITA 66.1(6), 248(1); "Canadian resource property" — ITA 66(15), ITAR 29(25.1); "corporation" — ITA 248(1), *Interpretation Act* 35(1); "deductible" — ITAR 29(33); "drilling or exploration expense" — ITAR 29(14)(c), 29(27), (30); "expenses incurred before 1972" — ITAR 29(23); "fiscal period" — ITA 249.1; "former Act" — ITAR 8; "Her Majesty" — *Interpretation Act* 35(1); "individual" — ITA 248(1); "legislature" — *Interpretation Act* 35(1)"legislative assembly"; "mineral", "Minister", "oil or gas well" — ITA 248(1); "original owner" — ITA 66(15), ITAR 29(25.1); "partnership" — see Notes to ITA 96(1); "person" — ITA 248(1); "predecessor owner" — ITA 66(15), ITAR 29(25.1); "prescribed" — ITA 248(1); "production" — ITA 66(15), ITAR 29(25.1); "property" — ITA 248(1); "province" — *Interpretation Act* 35(1); "provincial statute" — ITAR 29(33); "related" — ITA 251(2)–(6); "share", "shareholder" — ITA 248(1); "successor" — ITAR 29(25); "taxation year" — ITA 249; "taxpayer" — ITA 248(1); "writing" — *Interpretation Act* 35(1).

**30. (1), (2)** [Repealed under former Act]

**(3) Reference to this Act in amended Act** — In subsection 66(14) of the amended Act, "any amount deductible under the *Income Tax Application Rules*" in respect of that subsection means any amount deductible under section 29 of this Act.

Definitions [ITAR 30]: "amended Act" — ITAR 8; "amount" — ITA 248(1).

**31. Application of section 67 of amended Act** — In respect of any outlay or expense made or incurred by a taxpayer before 1972, section 67 of the amended Act shall be read without reference to the words "in respect of which any amount is".

Definitions [ITAR 31]: "amended Act" — ITAR 8; "amount", "taxpayer" — ITA 248(1).

**32. (1) Application of para. 69(1)(a) of amended Act** — Paragraph 69(1)(a) of the amended Act does not apply to deem a taxpayer by whom anything was acquired at any time before 1972 to have acquired it at its fair market value at that time, unless, if subsection 17(1) of the former Act had continued to apply, that fair market value would have been deemed to have been paid or to be payable therefor for the purpose of computing the taxpayer's income from a business.

**(2) Application of para. 69(1)(b) of amended Act** — Paragraph 69(1)(b) of the amended Act does not apply to deem a taxpayer by whom anything was disposed of at any time before the 1972 taxation year to have received proceeds of disposition therefor equal to its fair market value at that time.

**(3) Application of para. 69(1)(c) of amended Act** — For greater certainty, paragraph 69(1)(c) of the amended Act applies to property acquired by a taxpayer before, at or after the end of 1971.

Definitions [ITAR 32]: "amended Act" — ITAR 8; "business" — ITA 248(1); "former Act" — ITAR 8; "property" — ITA 248(1); "taxation year" — ITA 249; "taxpayer" — ITA 248(1).

**32.1 (1)–(3.2)** [Repealed under former Act]

Notes: ITAR 32.1(1)–(3.2), repealed in 1978 and 1985, dealt with elections on dividends payable before 1975.

**(4) Capital dividend account** — Where a dividend became payable, or was paid if that time was earlier, by a corporation in a taxation year at a particular time that was before May 7, 1974, for the purpose of computing the corporation's capital dividend account immediately before the particular time, all amounts each of which is an amount in respect of a capital loss from the disposition of property in the taxation year and before the particular time shall be deemed to be nil.

**(5), (6)** [Repealed under former Act]

Notes: ITAR 32.1(5) and (6), repealed in 1985, allowed certain elections to be made late if they were filed by the end of June 1975.

**Definitions [ITAR 32.1]**: "amount" — ITA 248(1); "capital dividend" — ITA 83(2)–(2.4), 248(1); "capital loss" — ITA 39(1)(b), 248(1); "corporation" — ITA 248(1), *Interpretation Act* 35(1); "dividend", "property" — ITA 248(1); "taxation year" — ITA 249.

**33.** [Repealed under former Act]

**Notes**: ITAR 33, repealed in 1985, dealt with dividends deemed received as a result of pre-1972 transactions.

**34. (1) Amalgamations** — Notwithstanding section 9, subsections 85I(1) and (2) of the former Act continue to apply with such modifications as, in the circumstances, are necessary by virtue of this Act, in respect of any amalgamation of two or more corporations before 1972.

**(2), (3)** [Repealed under former Act]

**Notes**: ITAR 34(2) and (3) repealed in 1985. 34(2) dealt with taxation in 1972 of corporations that amalgamated in 1971, and 34(3) provided for successor corporation rules in respect of pre-1972 resource expenses, now dealt with in ITAR 29(25) and 29(29).

**(4) Idem** — In applying the provisions of subsection 29(25) to determine the amount that may be deducted by the successor or second successor corporation, as the case may be, in computing its income under Part I of the amended Act for a taxation year, where a predecessor corporation has paid an amount (other than a rental or royalty) to the government of Canada or a province for

   (a) the right to explore for petroleum or natural gas on a specified parcel of land in Canada (which right is, for greater certainty, declared to include a right of the type commonly referred to as a "licence", "permit" or "reservation"), or

   (b) a legal lease of the right to take or remove petroleum or natural gas from a specified parcel of land in Canada,

and before April 11, 1962 acquired the rights in respect of which the amount was so paid, if, before the predecessor corporation was entitled because of subsection 29(21) to any deduction in computing its income for a taxation year in respect of the amount so paid, the property of the predecessor corporation was acquired by the successor or second successor corporation, as the case may be, and at any time, before any well came into production in reasonable commercial quantities on the land referred to in paragraph (a) or (b), the successor or second successor corporation, as the case may be, surrendered all the rights so acquired by the predecessor corporation (including, in respect of a right of the kind described in paragraph (a), all rights thereunder to any lease and all rights under any lease made thereunder) without receiving any consideration therefor or payment of any part of the amount so paid by the predecessor corporation, the amount so paid by the predecessor corporation shall be added at that time to the amount determined under subparagraph 29(25)(c)(i).

**(5), (6)** [Repealed under former Act]

**Notes**: ITAR 34(5) and (6), repealed in 1985, imposed a special tax on a new corporation formed as a result of an amalgamation in 1971.

**(7) Definition of "amalgamation"** — In this section, "amalgamation" has the meaning assigned by section 85I of the former Act.

**(8)** [Repealed under former Act]

**Notes**: ITAR 34(8), repealed in 1985, provided administrative rules for the special tax under ITAR 34(5) and (6).

**Interpretation Bulletins [ITAR 34]**: IT-60R2: 1971 undistributed income on hand.

**Definitions [ITAR 34]**: "amalgamation" — ITAR 34(7); "amended Act" — ITAR 8; "amount" — ITA 248(1); "Canada" — ITA 255, *Interpretation Act* 35(1); "corporation" — ITA 248(1), *Interpretation Act* 35(1); "former Act" — ITAR 8; "property" — ITA 248(1); "province" — *Interpretation Act* 35(1); "taxation year" — ITA 249.

**35. (1) Foreign affiliates** — Section 26 does not apply in determining for the purposes of section 91 of the amended Act the amount of any taxable capital gain or allowable capital loss of a foreign affiliate of a taxpayer.

**(2) Idem** — Any corporation that was a foreign affiliate of a taxpayer on January 1, 1972 shall be deemed, for the purposes of subdivision i of Division B of Part I of the amended Act, to have become a foreign affiliate of the taxpayer on that day.

**(3)** [Repealed under former Act]

**Notes**: ITAR 35(3), repealed in 1985, provided that the inclusion under 91(1) for the foreign accrual property income of a controlled foreign affiliate did not apply before the 1976 taxation year of the affiliate.

**(4) Idem** — Any corporation that was deemed to be a foreign affiliate of a taxpayer at any time prior to May 7, 1974 because of an election made by the taxpayer in accordance with subparagraph 95(1)(b)(iv) of the amended Act, as it read before being amended by chapter 26 of the Statutes of Canada, 1974-75-76, shall be deemed to have been a foreign affiliate of the taxpayer at that time.

**Definitions [ITAR 35]**: "allowable capital loss" — ITA 38(b), 248(1); "amended Act" — ITAR 8; "amount" — ITA 248(1); "Canada" — ITA 255, *Interpretation Act* 35(1); "corporation" — ITA 248(1), *Interpretation Act* 35(1); "foreign affiliate" — ITA 95(1), 248(1); "taxable capital gain" — ITA 38(a), 248(1); "taxpayer" — ITA 248(1).

**35.1** [Repealed under former Act]

**Notes**: ITAR 35.1, repealed in 1985, provided that 94(1)(c)(i) and (ii) of the Act were only effective as of 1976.

**36. Application of paras. 107(2)(b) to (d) of amended Act** — In computing the income of a taxpayer for the taxpayer's 1972 or any subsequent taxation year, paragraphs 107(2)(b) to (d) of the amended Act do not apply in respect of any property of a trust distributed by the trust to the taxpayer at any time before the commencement of the taxpayer's 1972 taxation year.

**Definitions [ITAR 36]**: "amended Act" — ITAR 8; "property" — ITA 248(1); "taxation year" — ITA 249; "taxpayer" — ITA 248(1); "trust" — ITA 104(1), 248(1), (3).

**37–39.** [Repealed under former Act]

**Notes**: ITAR 37 to 39 repealed in 1985. 37 dealt with loss carryovers across the 1971-72 transition. 38 dealt with the transitional rules for general averaging for 1972-75. 39 provided transitional rules for specific income averaging provisions for 1972-75.

**40. (1) Payments out of pension funds, etc.** — In the case of

(a) a single payment

(i) out of or under a superannuation or pension fund or plan

(A) on the death, withdrawal or retirement from employment of an employee or former employee,

(B) on the winding-up of the fund or plan in full satisfaction of all rights of the payee in or under the fund or plan, or

(C) to which the payee is entitled because of an amendment to the plan although the payee continues to be an employee to whom the plan applies,

(ii) upon retirement of an employee in recognition of long service and not made out of or under a superannuation fund or plan,

(iii) under an employees profit sharing plan in full satisfaction of all rights of the payee in or under the plan, to the extent that the amount thereof would otherwise be included in computing the payee's income for the year in which the payment was received, or

(iv) under a deferred profit sharing plan on the death, withdrawal or retirement from employment of an employee or former employee, to the extent that the amount thereof would otherwise be included in computing the payee's income for the year in which the payment was received,

(b) a payment or payments made by an employer to an employee or former employee on or after retirement in respect of loss of office or employment, if made in the year of retirement or within one year after that year, or

(c) a payment or payments made as a death benefit, if made in the year of death or within one year after that year,

the payment or payments made in a taxation year ending after 1971 and before 1974 may, at the option of the taxpayer by whom it is or they are received, be deemed not to be income of the taxpayer for the purpose of Part I of the amended Act, in which case the taxpayer shall pay, in addition to any other tax payable for the year, a tax on the payment or total of the payments equal to the proportion thereof that

(d) the total of the taxes otherwise payable by the employee under that Part for the 3 years immediately preceding the taxation year (before making any deduction under section 120, 121 or 126 or subsection 127(3) of the amended Act),

is of

(e) the total of the employee's incomes for those 3 years.

**(2) Employee not resident in Canada** — Where a taxpayer has elected that a payment or payments of one of the classes described in paragraphs (1)(a) to (c) in respect of an employee or former employee who was not resident in Canada throughout the whole of the 3 years referred to in paragraph (1)(e) shall be deemed not to be income of the taxpayer for the purpose of Part I of the amended Act, the tax payable under this section is that proportion of the amount on which the tax is payable that

(a) the total of the taxes that would have been payable by the employee under that Part for the 3 years referred to in paragraph (1)(e) (before making any deduction under section 120, 121 or 126 or subsection 127(3) of the amended Act) if the employee had been resident in Canada throughout those years and the employee's incomes for those years had been from sources in Canada,

is of

(b) the total of the employee's incomes for those 3 years,

and, in such a case, the election is not valid unless the taxpayer has filed with the election, a return of the employee's incomes for each of the 3 years in the same form and containing the same information as the return that the employee, or the employee's legal representative, would have been required to file under that Part if the employee had been resident in Canada in those years.

**(3) Determination of amount of payment** — In determining the amount of any payment or payments made in a taxation year out of or under a superannuation or pension fund or plan, under a deferred profit sharing plan or as a retiring allowance that is deemed, for the purposes of this section, not to be income of the taxpayer by whom it is or they are received, there shall be subtracted from the amount of the payment or payments so made

(a) the total of all amounts deductible under paragraph 60(j) of the amended Act in computing the taxpayer's income for that year; and

(b) any amount deductible under paragraph 60(m) of the amended Act because of that payment or those payments in computing the taxpayer's income for that year.

**(4) Idem** — In determining the amount of any payment or payments made in a taxation year as a death benefit that is deemed, for the purpose of this section, not to be income of the taxpayer by whom it is or they are received, there shall be subtracted from the amount of the payment or payments so made any amount deductible under paragraph 60(m) of the amended Act because of that payment or those payments in computing the taxpayer's income for that year.

**(5) Maximum amount for election** — For the purpose of determining the amount of any payment or payments of one or more of the classes described in subsection (1) made in a taxation year that may be deemed, for the purposes of this section, not to be income of the taxpayer by whom it is or they are received, the maximum amount in respect of which an election may be made by the taxpayer under subsection (1) for the taxation year in respect of such payment or payments is,

(a) in the case of a payment or payments of a class described in subsection (1) made to the taxpayer on the death of an employee or former employee in respect of whom the payment or payments are made, the amount of the payment or the total amount of the payments, as the case may be, minus any amount subtracted therefrom under subsection (3) or (4);

(b) in the case of one or more single payments of a class described in subparagraph (1)(a)(i), (iii) or (iv), other than a payment described in paragraph (a) of this subsection, the lesser of

(i) the amount of the payment or the total amount of the payments, as the case may be, minus any amount subtracted therefrom under subsection (3), and

(ii) the amount by which

(A) the product obtained by multiplying $1,500 by the number of consecutive 12 month periods included in the period throughout which the taxpayer was a member of any plan or plans described in subparagraph (1)(a)(i), (iii) or (iv) (in this subsection referred to as a "retirement plan"),

(I) out of or under which a payment was made to the taxpayer in the taxation year or a preceding taxation year ending after April 26, 1965, and

(II) to which an employer of the taxpayer has made a contribution on behalf of the taxpayer,

exceeds

(B) the total of all amounts each of which is an amount that, because of a payment to the taxpayer after April 26, 1965,

(I) out of or under a retirement plan to which the employer referred to in subclause (A)(II) made a contribution on behalf of the taxpayer, or

(II) by the employer referred to in subclause (A)(II),

was deemed not to be income of the taxpayer for the purpose of Part I of the amended Act for a preceding taxation year because of an election made by the taxpayer under subsection (1); and

(c) in the case of a payment or payments of the class described in subparagraph (1)(a)(ii) or paragraph (1)(b), other than a payment described in paragraph (a) or (b) of this subsection, the lesser of

(i) the amount of the payment or the total amount of the payments, as the case may be, minus any amount subtracted therefrom pursuant to subsection (3), and

(ii) the amount by which

(A) the product obtained by multiplying $1,000 by the number of years during which the taxpayer was an employee of the employer who made the payment

exceeds

(B) the total of

(I) the total of all amounts each of which is an amount that, because of a payment to the taxpayer after April 26, 1965 by an employer referred to in clause (A) or a payment to the taxpayer after that date out of or under a retirement plan to which such an employer made a contribution on behalf of the taxpayer, was deemed not to be income of the taxpayer for the purpose of Part I of the amended Act for a preceding taxation year by reason of an election made by the taxpayer under subsection (1), and

(II) the total of all amounts each of which is an amount that, because of a payment to the taxpayer after April 26, 1965 out of or under a retirement plan to which an employer referred to in clause (A) made a contribution on behalf of the taxpayer, may be deemed, by subsection (1), not to be income of the taxpayer for the purpose of that Part for the taxation year.

**(6) Idem** — For the purpose of subsection (5),

(a) where all or substantially all of the property used in carrying on the business of a person who was an employer of an employee (in this subsection referred to as the "former employer")

(i) has been purchased by a person who, because of the purchase, or

(ii) has been acquired by bequest or inheritance, or because of an amalgamation (within the meaning assigned by section 85I of the former Act), by a person who, by reason of the acquisition,

became an employer of the employee, and who subsequently made a payment of a class described in paragraph (5)(c) in respect of the employee or former employee, the employee or former employee shall be deemed to have been an employee of that employer throughout the period he or she was an employee of the former employer; and

(b) a taxpayer may, in computing the number of years during which the taxpayer was a member of a superannuation or pension fund or plan (in this subsection referred to as the "subsequent plan"), include the number of years during which the taxpayer was a member of another plan (in this subsection referred to as the "former plan") if the taxpayer had received an amount out of or under the former plan all or part of which amount was deductible under paragraph 60(j) of the amended Act in computing the taxpayer's income for the taxation year in which the amount was received, because of the fact that all or part of the amount, as the case may be, was paid by the taxpayer to or under the subsequent plan as described in clause 60(j)(i)(A) of the *Income Tax Act*, chapter 148 of the Revised Statutes of Canada, 1952, as it read in its application to the 1978 and preceding taxation years.

**Notes:** The CCRA's view is that "all or substantially all" means 90% or more.

**(7) Limitation** — This section applies in respect of any payment or payments described in subparagraph (1)(a)(i) or (iv) made in a taxation year ending after 1973, except that the amount of the payment or the total amount of the payments, as the case may be, shall be deemed to be the lesser of the amount thereof otherwise determined and the total of the amounts that the taxpayer would have received out of or under the plan described in subparagraph (1)(a)(i) or (iv), as the case may be, if

(a) the taxpayer had withdrawn from the plan on January 1, 1972;

(b) there had been no change in the terms and conditions of the plan after June 18, 1971 and before January 2, 1972; and

(c) any term or condition of the plan that would, in the event that the taxpayer had withdrawn from the plan on January 1, 1972, have reduced the amount of any payment or payments that would, if the taxpayer remained a member of the plan for a specified period of time after December 31, 1971, have been made to the taxpayer in respect of years ending before 1972 were not a term or condition of the plan.

**(8) Application rule** — For the purposes of paragraphs (1)(d) and (2)(a), there may be deducted from the total referred to in those paragraphs 9% of the portion of that total that is attributable to the 1974, 1975 or 1976 taxation year.

**Related Provisions [ITAR 40]:** ITA 127.52(1)(j) — ITAR 40 ignored for minimum tax purposes.

**Definitions [ITAR 40]:** "amended Act" — ITAR 8; "amount", "business", "death benefit" — ITA 248(1); "deferred profit sharing plan" — ITA 147(1), 248(1); "employee" — ITA 248(1), ITAR 40(6); "employees profit sharing plan" — ITA 144(1), 248(1); "employer", "employment" — ITA 248(1); "former Act" — ITAR 8; "former employer" — ITAR 40(6)(a); "former plan" — ITAR 40(6)(b); "Income Tax Act, chapter 148 of the Revised Statutes of Canada, 1952" — ITAR 8; "legal representative" — ITA 248(1); "month" — *Interpretation Act* 35(1); "office", "person", "property" — ITA 248(1); "resident in Canada" — ITA 250; "retiring allowance" — ITA 248(1); "subsequent plan" — ITAR 40(6)(b); "taxation year" — ITA 249; "taxpayer" — ITA 248(1).

**Interpretation Bulletins [ITAR 40]:** IT-163R2: Election by non-resident individuals on certain Canadian source income; IT-281R2: Elections on single payments from a deferred profit-sharing plan.

**Information Circulars [ITAR 40]:** 74-21R: Payments out of pension and deferred profit sharing plans.

**41–48.** [Repealed under former Act]

**Notes:** ITAR 41–48 repealed in 1985 (except for 45.1, repealed in 1975). 41 dealt with two fiscal periods of an individual's business ending in the same year before 1974. 42 and 48 provided an election for averaging depreciation recapture for 1972-75. 43 provided an election for averaging an author's copyright income for 1972-73. 44 provided an election for averaging employee benefits before 1974. 45 and 46 provided an election before 1974 for averaging income from sale of inventory or accounts receivable on ceasing to carry on business. 45.1 provided an application rule for interpreting certain provisions before 1975. 47 provided rules for averaging income on a death before 1976.

**49. (1) Tax deemed payable under amended Act** — Where, because of section 40, any tax is payable in addition to or in lieu of any amount of tax payable under Part I of the amended Act for a taxation year, that tax shall be deemed to be payable under Part I of the amended Act for that taxation year.

**(2) Application of section 13** — In applying section 13 to section 40, subsection 13(1) shall be read without reference to the words "subject to this Act and unless the context otherwise requires".

**(3) Computation of tax deemed payable under amended Act** — In computing, under section 40 of this Act or any of section 39 and sections 41 to 48 of the *Income Tax Act*, chapter 148 of the Revised Statutes of Canada, 1952, any tax that is payable in addition to or in lieu of any amount of tax payable under Part I of the amended Act by an individual for a taxation year,

(a) a reference to section 120 of the amended Act does not include a reference to paragraph 33(1)(a) of the former Act; and

(b) for the purposes of paragraph 33(1)(a) of the former Act and subsection 120(1) of the amended Act, all of the income of the individual for that or any preceding taxation year shall be deemed to have been income earned in the year in a province.

**Definitions [ITAR 49]:** "amended Act" — ITAR 8; "amount" — ITA 248(1); "former Act" — ITAR 8; "Income Tax Act, chapter 148 of the Revised Statutes of Canada, 1952" — ITAR 69; "individual" — ITA 248(1); "province" — *Interpretation Act* 35(1); "taxation year" — ITA 249.

**50. (1) Status of certain corporations** — For the purposes of the amended Act, a corporation that was, throughout that portion of its 1972 taxation year that is in 1972, a private corporation, a Canadian-controlled private corporation or a public corporation shall be deemed to have been throughout that taxation year a private corporation, a Canadian-controlled private corporation or a public corporation, as the case may be.

**(2) Election to be public corporation** — For the purposes of the definition "public corporation" in subsection 89(1) of the amended Act, where at any particular time before 1973 a corporation elected in the manner referred to in subparagraph (b)(i) of that definition to be a public corporation and at any time after 1971 and before the time of the election the corporation complied with the conditions referred to in that subparagraph, the corporation shall,

(a) at such time after 1971 and before the particular time as is specified in the election to be the effective date thereof, or

(b) where no time described in paragraph (a) is specified in the election to be the effective date thereof, at the particular time,

be deemed to have elected in the manner referred to in that subparagraph to be a public corporation and to have complied with the conditions referred to therein.

**(3) Designation by Minister** — For the purposes of the definition "public corporation" in subsection 89(1) of the amended Act, where at any particular time before March 22, 1972 the Minister, by notice in writing to a corporation, designated the corporation to be a public corporation or not to be a public corporation, as the case may be, and at the time of the designation the corporation complied with the conditions referred to in subparagraph (b)(i) or (c)(i) of that definition, as the case may be, the corporation shall, at such time as is specified by the Minister in the notice, be deemed

(a) to have been designated by the Minister, by notice in writing to the corporation, to be a public corporation or not to be a public corporation, as the case may be; and

(b) to have complied with the conditions referred to in subparagraph (b)(i) or (c)(i) of that definition, as the case may be.

**Definitions [ITAR 50]:** "amended Act" — ITAR 8; "Canadian-controlled private corporation" — ITA 125(7), 248(1); "corporation" — ITA 248(1), *Interpretation Act* 35(1); "Minister" — ITA 248(1); "private corporation", "public corporation" — ITA 89(1), 248(1); "taxation year" — ITA 249; "writing" — *Interpretation Act* 35(1).

**51–56.1 [Repealed under former Act]**

**Notes:** ITAR 51–56.1 repealed in 1985 (except for 53, repealed in 1975). 51 provided a transitional rule for determining corporate tax for the 1971-72 fiscal year. 52 and 54 provided transitional rules for non-calendar fiscal years from 1972-76. 53 would have provided a deduction from corporate tax for 1977. 55 and 56 provided transitional rules for the foreign-tax carryover and refundable dividend tax on hand for 1972. 56.01 provided transitional rules relating to capital gains dividends payable by a mutual fund corporation in 1973. 56.1 provided a special rule relating to the qualification of a trust as a mutual fund trust in 1972.

**57. (1)–(8) [Repealed under former Act]**

**Notes:** ITAR 57(1)–(7), repealed in 1985, provided rules for "specified personal corporations" for 1972. 57(8), repealed in 1978, dealt with tax-paid undistributed surplus on hand.

**(9) Capital dividend account** — In computing a specified personal corporation's capital dividend account at any time after the end of its 1972 taxation year, there shall be added to the total of the amounts described in paragraphs (a) and (b) of the definition "capital dividend account" in subsection 89(1) of the amended Act the total of its net capital gains (within the meaning assigned by subsection 51(3) of the *Income Tax Application Rules, 1971*, Part III of Chapter 63 of the Statutes of Canada, 1970-71-72, as it read before October 29, 1985) for its 1972 taxation year and that proportion of the total of its incomes for that year, other than

(a) any taxable capital gains of the corporation for the year from dispositions of property, and

(b) any amounts that were, because of subsection 57(3) of the *Income Tax Application Rules, 1971*, Part III of chapter 63 of the Statutes of Canada, 1970-71-72, as it read before October 29, 1985 or under the provisions of subsection 67(1) of the former Act that applied because of subsection 57(12) of those Rules as it read before that date, required to be included in computing the income of the specified personal corporation for its 1972 taxation year,

that the number of days in that portion of the 1972 taxation year that is in 1972 is of the number of days in the whole year.

**Related Provisions:** ITAR 69 (meaning of "*Income Tax Application Rules, 1971*, Part III of chapter 63 of the Statutes of Canada, 1970-71-72").

**(10) [Repealed under former Act]**

**Notes:** ITAR 57(10), repealed in 1985, related to the rules in 57(1) regarding specified personal corporations.

**(11) Meaning of "specified personal corporation"** — For the purposes of this section, a corporation is a specified personal corporation if

(a) part of its 1972 taxation year was before and part thereof after the beginning of 1972; and

(b) during the whole of the period beginning on the earlier of June 18, 1971 and the beginning of its 1972 taxation year and ending at the end of its 1972 taxation year, it was a personal corporation within the meaning assigned by section 68 of the former Act.

**(12)** [Repealed under former Act]

**Notes**: ITAR 57(12), repealed in 1985, provided a transitional rule for 1972 for a personal corporation.

**Definitions [ITAR 57]**: "amended Act" — ITAR 8; "amount" — ITA 248(1); "Canada" — ITA 255, *Interpretation Act* 35(1); "capital dividend" — ITA 83(2)–(2.4), 248(1); "capital gain" — ITA 39(1), 248(1); "corporation" — ITA 248(1), *Interpretation Act* 35(1); "dividend" — ITA 248(1); "former Act" — ITAR 8; "Income Tax Application Rules, 1971" — ITAR 69; "property" — ITA 248(1); "specified personal corporation" — ITAR 57(11); "taxable capital gain" — ITA 38(a), 248(1); "taxation year" — ITA 249.

**57.1** [Repealed under former Act]

**Notes**: ITAR 57.1, repealed in 1985, provided a transitional rule for 1972 for co-operative corporations.

**58. (1) Credit unions** — For the purpose of computing the income of a credit union for the 1972 and subsequent taxation years,

(a) property of the credit union that is a bond, debenture, mortgage or agreement of sale owned by it at the beginning of its 1972 taxation year shall be valued at its actual cost to the credit union,

  (i) plus a reasonable amount in respect of the amortization of the amount by which the principal amount of the property at the time it was acquired by the credit union exceeds its actual cost to the credit union, or

  (ii) minus a reasonable amount in respect of the amortization of the amount by which its actual cost to the credit union exceeds the principal amount of the property at the time it was acquired by the credit union;

(b) property of the credit union that is a debt owing to the credit union (other than property described in paragraph (a) or a debt that became a bad debt before its 1972 taxation year) acquired by it before the beginning of its 1972 taxation year shall be valued at any time at the amount thereof outstanding at that time;

(c) any depreciable property acquired by the credit union in a taxation year ending before 1972 shall be deemed to have been acquired by it on the last day of its 1971 taxation year at a capital cost equal to

  (i) in the case of any building or automotive equipment owned by it on the last day of its 1971 taxation year, the amount, if any, by which the depreciable cost to the credit union of the building or equipment, as the case may be, exceeds the product obtained when the number of full taxation years in the period beginning on the first day of the taxation year following the taxation year in which the building or equipment, as the case may be, was acquired by it and ending with the last day of its 1971 taxation year is multiplied by, in the case of a building, $2\frac{1}{2}\%$, and in the case of equipment, 15%, of its depreciable cost (and for the purposes of this subparagraph, a capital improvement or capital addition to a building owned by a credit union shall be deemed not to be part of the building but to be a separate and distinct building acquired by it, if the cost to the credit union of the improvement or addition, as the case may be, exceeded $10,000),

  (ii) in the case of any leasehold interest, the proportion of the capital cost thereof to the credit union (determined without regard to this subparagraph) that

    (A) the number of months in the period commencing with the first day of the credit union's 1972 taxation year and ending with the day on which the leasehold interest expires

  is of

    (B) the number of months in the period beginning with the day on which the credit union acquired the leasehold interest and ending with the day on which the leasehold interest expires, and

  (iii) in the case of any property (other than a building, automotive equipment or leasehold interest) acquired by the credit union after 1961, the amount, if any, by which the depreciable cost to the credit union of such property exceeds the product obtained when the number of full taxation years beginning with the first day of the taxation year following the taxation year in which the property was acquired by it and ending with the last day of its 1971 taxation year is multiplied by $\frac{1}{2}$ the relevant percentage of the depreciable cost to the credit union of the property; and

(d) the undepreciated capital cost to the credit union as of the first day of its 1972 taxation year of depreciable property of a prescribed class acquired by it before that taxation year is the total of the amounts determined under paragraph (c) to be the capital costs to it as of that day of all property of that class.

**(1.1) Exception** — For the purpose of computing a capital gain from the disposition of depreciable property acquired by a credit union in a taxation year ending before 1972, the capital cost of the property shall be its capital cost determined without reference to paragraph (1)(c).

**(2)–(3.1)** [Repealed under former Act]

**Notes**: ITAR 58(2)–(3.1), repealed in 1985, provided transitional rules for credit unions for 1972-76.

**(3.2) Determination of maximum cumulative reserve at end of taxation year** — Notwith-

**ITAR**
**S. 58(3.2)** — Income Tax Application Rules

standing the definition "maximum cumulative reserve" in subsection 137(6) of the amended Act, for the purposes of section 137 of the amended Act a credit union's maximum cumulative reserve at the end of any particular year is the amount, if any, by which its maximum cumulative reserve at that time, determined under that definition without regard to this subsection, exceeds the lesser of

(a) its maximum cumulative reserve, determined under that definition without regard to this subsection, at the end of its 1971 taxation year, and

(b) the amount, if any, by which its 1971 reserve exceeds the total of the amounts deemed by subsection 58(2) of the *Income Tax Application Rules, 1971*, Part III of chapter 63 of the Statutes of Canada, 1970-71-72, to have been deducted by it in computing its income for its 1971 taxation year.

**Related Provisions**: ITAR 69 (meaning of "*Income Tax Application Rules, 1971*, Part III of chapter 63 of the Statutes of Canada, 1970-71-72").

**(3.3) Idem** — Notwithstanding subsection (3.2), where at any time after May 6, 1974 there has been an amalgamation (within the meaning assigned by section 87 of the amended Act) of two or more credit unions to form a new credit union, the maximum cumulative reserve of the new credit union shall be deemed to be the amount by which its maximum cumulative reserve, determined under the definition of that term in subsection 137(6) of the amended Act, exceeds the total of all amounts, if any, each of which is the lesser of the amounts referred to in paragraphs (3.2)(a) and (b) in respect of each of the predecessor corporations.

**(3.4) Idem** — Notwithstanding subsection (3.2), where a credit union (in this subsection referred to as the acquirer) has, at any time after May 6, 1974, acquired otherwise than by way of amalgamation all or substantially all of the assets of another credit union, the maximum cumulative reserve of the acquirer shall be the amount by which the acquirer's maximum cumulative reserve, determined under the definition of that term in subsection 137(6) of the amended Act, exceeds the total of

(a) the lesser of the amounts determined under paragraphs (3.2)(a) and (b) in respect of the acquirer, and

(b) the lesser of the amounts determined under paragraphs (3.2)(a) and (b) in respect of the other credit union.

**Notes**: The CCRA's view is that "all or substantially all" means 90% or more.

**(4), (4.1)** [Repealed under former Act]

**Notes**: ITAR 58(4) and (4.1), repealed in 1985, provided transitional rules for credit unions for 1972.

**(5) Definitions** — In this section,

"**depreciable cost**" to a credit union of any property means the actual cost to it of the property or the amount at which it is deemed by subsection 13(7) of the amended Act to have acquired the property, as the case may be;

"**relevant percentage**" in relation to a prescribed class of property is the percentage prescribed in respect of that class by any regulations made under paragraph 11(1)(a) of the former Act;

"**1971 reserve**" of a credit union means the amount, if any, by which the total of all amounts each of which is

(a) the amount of any money of the credit union on hand at the beginning of its 1972 taxation year,

(b) an amount in respect of any property described in paragraph (1)(a) or (b), equal to the amount at which it is required by those paragraphs to be valued at the beginning of its 1972 taxation year,

(c) an amount in respect of depreciable property of a prescribed class owned by the credit union on the first day of its 1972 taxation year, equal to the amount determined under paragraph (1)(d) to be the undepreciated capital cost thereof to the credit union as of that day, or

(d) an amount in respect of any capital property (other than depreciable property) owned by the credit union at the beginning of its 1972 taxation year, equal to its cost to the credit union computed without reference to the provisions of section 26,

exceeds the total of all amounts each of which is

(e) the amount of any debt owing by the credit union or of any other obligation of the credit union to pay an amount, that was outstanding at the beginning of its 1972 taxation year, excluding, for greater certainty, any share in the credit union of any member thereof, or

(f) the amount, as of the beginning of the credit union's 1972 taxation year, of any share in the credit union of any member thereof.

**Notes**: ITAR 58(5)"depreciable cost" was 58(5)(a), "relevant percentage" was 58(5)(b), and "1971 reserve" was 58(5)(c), before consolidation in R.S.C. 1985 (5th Supp.), effective for taxation years ending after November 1991.

**Definitions [ITAR 58]**: "1971 reserve" — ITAR 58(5); "amended Act" — ITAR 8; "amount" — ITA 248(1); "Canada" — ITA 255, *Interpretation Act* 35(1); "capital gain" — ITA 39(1), 248(1); "capital property" — ITA 54, 248(1); "corporation" — ITA 248(1), *Interpretation Act* 35(1); "credit union" — ITA 248(1); "depreciable cost" — ITAR 58(5); "depreciable property" — ITA 13(21), 248(1); "former Act" — ITAR 8; "Income Tax Application Rules, 1971" — ITAR 69; "month" — *Interpretation Act* 35(1); "prescribed", "principal amount", "property" — ITA 248(1); "relevant percentage" — ITAR 58(5); "share" — ITA 248(1); "taxation year" — ITA 249; "undepreciated capital cost" — ITA 13(21), 248(1).

**Interpretation Bulletins [ITAR 58]**: IT-483: Credit unions.

**59. (1)** [Repealed under former Act]

**Notes**: ITAR 59(1), repealed in 1985, provided the tax rates for non-resident-owned investment corporations for 1972-75.

**(2) Non-resident-owned investment corporation** — In its application to the 1972 and subsequent taxation years of a corporation, section 133 of the amended Act shall be read as if, in respect of such portion of any period described in the definition "non-resident-owned investment corporation" in subsection 133(8) of that Act as ended before the beginning of the corporation's 1976 taxation year, paragraph (a) of that definition were read as follows:

"(a) at least 95% of the total value of its issued shares, and all of its bonds, debentures and other funded indebtedness, were

   (i) beneficially owned by non-resident persons (other than any foreign affiliate of a taxpayer resident in Canada),

   (ii) owned by trustees for the benefit of non-resident persons or their unborn issue, or

   (iii) owned by a corporation, whether incorporated in Canada or elsewhere, at least 95% of the total value of the issued shares of which and all of the bonds, debentures and other funded indebtedness of which were beneficially owned by non-resident persons or owned by trustees for the benefit of non-resident persons or their unborn issue, or by two or more such corporations;".

**Definitions [ITAR 59]**: "amended Act" — ITAR 8; "Canada" — ITA 255, *Interpretation Act* 35(1); "corporation" — ITA 248(1), *Interpretation Act* 35(1); "foreign affiliate" — ITA 95(1), 248(1); "non-resident", "person" — ITA 248(1); "resident in Canada" — ITA 250; "share" — ITA 248(1); "taxation year" — ITA 249; "taxpayer" — ITA 248(1).

**60.** [Repealed under former Act]

**Notes**: ITAR 60, repealed in 1985, provided rules for phasing out "foreign business corporations" from 1972-76.

**60.1 Taxes payable by insurer under Part IA of former Act** — For the purposes of the description of F in the definition "surplus funds derived from operations" in subsection 138(12) of the amended Act, the reference in that description to "this Part" shall be deemed to be a reference to "this Part and Part IA of the former Act".

**Definitions [ITAR 60.1]**: "amended Act" — ITAR 8.

**61. (1) Registered retirement savings plans** — For the purposes of the definition "non-qualified investment" in subsection 146(1) of the amended Act, property acquired after June 18, 1971 and before 1972 by a trust governed by a registered retirement savings plan shall, if owned or held by the trust on January 1, 1972, be deemed to have been acquired by the trust on January 1, 1972.

**(2)** [Not included in R.S.C. 1985]

**Notes**: ITAR 61(2) not included in R.S.C. 1985 (5th Supp.) consolidation. It dealt with refunds of RRSP premiums where the annuitant died before 1972.

**Definitions [ITAR 61]**: "amended Act" — ITAR 8; "property" — ITA 248(1); "registered retirement savings plan" — ITA 146(1), 248(1); "trust" — ITA 104(1), 248(1), (3).

**62. (1) Assessments** — Subsections 152(4) and (5) of the amended Act apply in respect of any assessment made after December 23, 1971, except that subsection 152(5) of that Act does not apply in respect of any such assessment made in consequence of a waiver filed with the Minister before December 23, 1971 in the form and within the time referred to in subsection 152(4) of that Act.

**(2) Interest** — Subsections 161(1) and (2), 164(3) and (4), 202(5) and 227(8) and (9) of the amended Act, subsection 183(2) of the *Income Tax Act*, chapter 148 of the Revised Statutes of Canada, 1952, and subsection 195(1) of that Act as it read in its application in respect of dividends paid or received before April 1, 1977, in so far as those subsections relate to the rate of interest payable thereunder, apply in respect of interest payable in respect of any period after December 23, 1971.

**(3)** [Repealed under former Act]

**Notes**: ITAR 62(3), repealed in 1988, provided for penalties under s. 163 of the Act to apply to pre-1972 returns that were due in 1972.

**(4) Objections to assessment** — Subsection 165(3) of the amended Act applies in respect of any notice of objection served on the Minister after December 23, 1971.

**(5) Appeals** — Division J of Part I of the amended Act applies in respect of any appeal or application instituted or made, as the case may be, after December 23, 1971.

**(6) Appeals to Federal Court** — Any appeal to the Federal Court instituted, within 2 years after December 23, 1971 and in accordance with Division J of Part I of the former Act and any rules made thereunder (as those rules read immediately before December 23, 1971), shall be deemed to have been instituted in the manner provided by the amended Act, and any document served on the Minister or a taxpayer in connection with an appeal so instituted in the manner provided in that Division and those rules shall be deemed to have been served in the manner provided by the amended Act.

**Definitions [ITAR 62]**: "amended Act" — ITAR 8; "assessment", "dividend" — ITA 248(1); "Federal Court" — *Interpretation Act* 35(1); "former Act" — ITAR 8; "Income Tax Act, chapter 148 of the Revised Statutes of Canada, 1952" — ITAR 69; "Minister", "taxpayer" — ITA 248(1).

**63–64.3** [Repealed under former Act]

**Notes**: ITAR 63, repealed in 1978, dealt with tax-paid undistributed surplus on hand in 1972.

ITAR 64, repealed in 1984, provided a transitional rule for 1972 for calculating the "preferred-rate amount" for purposes of the now-repealed Part VI tax.

ITAR 64.1, repealed in 1977, dealt with a life insurance corporation's control period earnings.

ITAR 64.2, repealed in 1977, provided change-in-control rules for the pre-1978 Parts VII and VII of the Act.

ITAR 64.3, repealed in 1975, provided for retroactive elections under the pre-1978 Part IX of the Act.

**65. (1) Part XI of amended Act** — Where, at any particular time after June 18, 1971 and before July 1, 1972, a taxpayer described in section 205 of the amended Act has acquired a foreign property that was

(a) a share of the capital stock of a corporation that would be a mutual fund corporation if paragraph 131(8)(a) of the amended Act were read without reference to the words "that was a public corporation",

(b) a unit of a trust that would be a mutual fund trust if subsection 132(6) of the amended Act were read without reference to paragraph 132(6)(c), or

(c) an interest, as a beneficiary under a trust, in property held subject to the trust by a trust company incorporated under the laws of Canada or a province, if

(i) throughout the 1971 taxation year of the trust,

(A) all the property of the trust was held in trust for the benefit of not less than 20 beneficiaries, and

(I) not less than 20 of the beneficiaries were taxpayers described in paragraph 205(a) or (c) of the amended Act, or

(II) not less than 100 of the beneficiaries were taxpayers described in paragraph 205(b) of the amended Act,

(B) not less than 80% of all the property of the trust consisted of shares, bonds, mortgages, marketable securities or cash, and

(C) not more than 10% of all the property of the trust consisted of shares, bonds, mortgages or other securities of any one corporation or debtor other than Her Majesty in right of Canada or of a province or a Canadian municipality,

(ii) not less than 95% of the income of the trust for its 1971 taxation year was derived from investments described in clause (i)(B),

(iii) the total value of all such interests owned by all beneficiaries mentioned in clause (i)(A) to which any one employer has made or may make contributions did not exceed, at any time in the 1971 taxation year of the trust, 25% of the value of all the property of the trust at that time, and

(iv) the total value of all such interests owned by all beneficiaries mentioned in subclause (i)(A)(II) to which any one taxpayer has paid or may pay premiums does not exceed, at any time in the 1971 taxation year of the trust, 25% of the value of all the property of the trust at that time,

the property shall, to the extent that the cost to the taxpayer thereof does not exceed the amount, if any, by which the taxpayer's foreign investment limit exceeds the total of the costs to it of all foreign properties described in paragraphs (a) to (c) acquired by the taxpayer after June 18, 1971 and before the particular time, be deemed

(d) for the purposes of Part XI of the amended Act, to have been acquired before June 19, 1971 and not to have been acquired after June 18, 1971, and

(e) where the taxpayer was a trust governed by a registered retirement savings plan, notwithstanding the definition "qualified investment" in subsection 146(1) of the amended Act, to have been a qualified investment for the purposes of section 146 of that Act.

**Regulations:** 221(1)(g) (reporting requirements for trust described under ITAR 65(1)(c)).

**Forms:** T3F: Investments prescribed to be qualified or not to be foreign property information return.

**(1.1) Idem** — Where, at any particular time after October 13, 1971 and before July 1, 1972, a taxpayer to whom Part XI of the amended Act applies has acquired a foreign property that was a share of the capital stock of a corporation that would be an investment corporation if subparagraph 130(3)(a)(i) of the amended Act were read without reference to the words "that was a public corporation", for the purposes of subsection (1) the share so acquired shall be deemed to be a share described in paragraph (1)(a).

**(2) Definition of "foreign investment limit"** — In subsection (1), "foreign investment limit" of a taxpayer means the total of

(a) the taxpayer's income from property for its 1971 taxation year,

(b) where the taxpayer was, throughout its 1971 taxation year, a taxpayer described in paragraph 205(a) of the amended Act, all amounts each of which is such portion of any amount paid or contributed by any person to or under the plan in 1971 as was deductible in computing that person's income for the 1971 taxation year under paragraph 11(1)(g) or (h) of the former Act, or as would have been deductible in computing that income under paragraph 11(1)(i) of the former Act if that paragraph were read (except for the purposes of subparagraph 11(1)(i)(iii) of that Act) without reference to subparagraph 11(1)(i)(ii) of that Act,

(c) where the taxpayer was, throughout its 1971 taxation year, a trust governed by a registered retirement savings plan, all amounts each of which is such portion of any premium paid in 1971 by the annuitant under the plan as was deductible under subsection 79B(5) of the former Act in computing the annuitant's income for the 1971 taxation year, and

(d) where the taxpayer was, throughout its 1971 taxation year, a trust governed by a deferred profit sharing plan, all amounts each of which is such portion of any amount paid by an employer to a trustee under the plan as was deductible under subsection 79C(7) of the former Act in computing the employer's income for the 1971 taxation year.

**(3) Foreign property acquired by registered retirement savings plan** — Where, at any particular time after 1971 and before July 1, 1974, a trust governed by a registered retirement savings plan acquired a foreign property described in paragraph (1)(a) or (b) or a foreign property that would be described in paragraph (1)(c) if the references in that paragraph to the "1971 taxation year" of the trust were read as references to the "1972 and 1973 taxation years" of the trust, the property shall, to the extent that the cost to the trust thereof did not exceed the amount, if any, by which the trust's foreign reinvestment limit exceeded the total of the cost to it of all such foreign properties so acquired by it after 1971 and before the particular time, be deemed

(a) for the purposes of Part XI of the amended Act, to have been acquired before June 19, 1971 and not to have been acquired after June 18, 1971; and

(b) notwithstanding the definition "qualified investment" in subsection 146(1) of the amended Act, to have been a qualified investment for the purposes of section 146 of that Act.

**Forms**: T3F: Investments prescribed to be qualified or not to be foreign property information return.

**(4) Definition of "foreign reinvestment limit"** — In subsection (3), "foreign reinvestment limit" of a trust governed by a registered retirement savings plan means such portion of the total of

(a) the trust's income from property for its 1972 and 1973 taxation years,

(b) all amounts each of which is such portion of any premium paid by the annuitant under the plan as was deductible under subsection 146(5) of the amended Act in computing the annuitant's income for the 1972 or 1973 taxation year,

(c) all amounts each of which is a capital gains dividend (within the meaning assigned by subsection 131(1) of the amended Act) received by the trust in its 1972 or 1973 taxation year, and

(d) 2 times the total of all amounts each of which is, because of subsection 104(21) of the amended Act, deemed to be a taxable capital gain of the trust for its 1972 or 1973 taxation year,

as was, under the terms and conditions of the plan as fixed on or before June 18, 1971, required to be invested by the trust in foreign property described in paragraph (1)(a) or (b) or foreign property that would be described in paragraph (1)(c) if the references in that paragraph to the "1971 taxation year" of the trust were read as references to the "1971 and 1972 taxation years" of the trust.

**(5) Shares of a mutual fund corporation received on amalgamation** — Where, after May 25, 1976, there has been an amalgamation (within the meaning assigned by section 87 of the amended Act) of two or more mutual fund corporations (each of which corporations is in this subsection referred to as a "predecessor corporation") to form one corporate entity (in this subsection referred to as the "new corporation"), and

(a) any shareholder that is a taxpayer described in any of paragraphs 205(a), (b) or (c) of the amended Act owned shares of the capital stock of a predecessor corporation (in this subsection referred to as the "old shares") on June 18, 1971 and thereafter without interruption until immediately before the amalgamation,

(b) any shares referred to in paragraph (a) were foreign property (within the meaning assigned by subsection 206(1) of the amended Act) immediately before the amalgamation, and

(c) no consideration was received by the shareholder for the disposition of the old shares on the amalgamation, other than shares of the capital stock of the new corporation (in this subsection referred to as the "new shares"),

notwithstanding any other provision of this Act or of the amended Act, for the purpose of subsection 206(2) of the amended Act, the taxpayer shall be deemed not to have acquired the new shares after June 18, 1971.

**Notes**: ITAR 65(5) amended by 1991 technical bill, effective November 1985, to update references to 206(1) and 206(2) of the Act to correspond to amendments made to the Act in 1985.

**Definitions [ITAR 65]**: "amended Act" — ITAR 8; "amount" — ITA 248(1); "Canada" — ITA 255, *Interpretation Act* 35(1); "capital gain" — ITA 39(1), 248(1); "corporation" — ITA 248(1), *Interpretation Act* 35(1); "deferred profit sharing plan" — ITA 147(1), 248(1); "dividend", "employer" — ITA 248(1); "foreign investment limit" — ITAR 65(2); "foreign reinvestment limit" — ITAR 65(4); "former Act" — ITAR 8; "Her Majesty" — *Interpretation Act* 35(1); "investment corporation" — ITA 130(3), 248(1); "mutual fund corporation" — ITA 131(8), 248(1); "mutual fund trust" — ITA 132(6)–(7), 132.2(1)(q), 248(1); "new corporation" — ITAR 65(5); "new shares" — ITAR 65(5)(c); "old shares" — ITAR 65(5)(a); "person" — ITA 248(1); "predecessor corporation" — ITAR 65(5); "property" — ITA 248(1); "province" — *Interpretation Act* 35(1); "registered retirement savings plan" — ITA 146(1), 248(1); "share", "shareholder" — ITA 248(1); "taxable capital gain" — ITA 38(a), 248(1); "taxation year" — ITA 249; "taxpayer" — ITA 248(1); "trust" — ITA 104(1), 248(1), (3).

**Interpretation Bulletins [ITAR 65]**: IT-412R2: Foreign property of registered plans.

**65.1 Part XV of amended Act** — For greater certainty,

(a) section 9 does not apply in respect of the repeal, by section 1 of chapter 63 of the Statutes of Canada, 1970-71-72, of Part V of the former Act and the substitution therefor, by that section, of Part XV of the amended Act, and

(b) in its application in respect of any offence described in subsection 239(1) of the amended Act that was committed before December 23, 1971, paragraph 239(1)(f) of the amended Act shall be read as follows:

"(f) a fine of not less than $25 and not more than $10,000 plus, in an appropriate case, an amount not exceeding double the amount of the tax that should have been shown to be payable or that was sought to be evaded, or".

**Definitions [ITAR 65.1]**: "amended Act" — ITAR 8; "amount" — ITA 248(1); "Canada" — ITA 255, *Interpretation Act* 35(1); "former Act" — ITAR 8.

**66. (1) Part II of former Act** — For greater certainty, Part II of the former Act applies only in respect of elections made thereunder before 1972.

**(2)** [Repealed under former Act]

**Notes**: ITAR 66(2), repealed in 1977, dealt with the effect of a pre-1972 election on a corporation's "1971 undistributed income on hand".

**Definitions [ITAR 66]**: "former Act" — ITAR 8.

**67. (1)–(4)** [Not included in R.S.C. 1985]

**Notes**: ITAR 67(1)–(4) dealt with refunds under Part IID of the pre-1972 Act. They were not included in the R.S.C. 1985 (5th Supp.) consolidation.

**(5) Prescription of unpaid amounts** — Her Majesty in right of Canada is not liable, and no action shall be taken, for or in respect of any unrefunded instalment of tax paid under Part IID of the former Act or any interest thereon where

(a) a repayment date with respect to the instalment was prescribed by regulation and reasonable efforts were made thereafter to locate the corporation or trust entitled to the refund;

(b) at least 5 years have elapsed since publication in the *Canada Gazette* of the regulation referred to in paragraph (a); and

(c) no claim whatever has been received by or on behalf of Her Majesty from the corporation or trust entitled to the refund.

**Definitions [ITAR 67]**: "Canada" — ITA 255, *Interpretation Act* 35(1); "corporation" — ITA 248(1), *Interpretation Act* 35(1); "former Act" — ITAR 8; "Her Majesty" — *Interpretation Act* 35(1); "prescribed" — ITA 248(1); "trust" — ITA 104(1), 248(1), (3).

**68.** [Not included in R.S.C. 1985]

**Notes**: ITAR 68 dealt with references in S.C. 1968-69, c. 44, s. 24(3), dealing with the predecessor to ITAR 33. It was not included in the R.S.C. 1985 (5th Supp.) consolidation.

# PART II — TRANSITIONAL CONCERNING THE 1985 STATUTE REVISION

**Notes**: Part II (ITAR 69–78) added in R.S.C. 1985 (5th Supp.) consolidation, to deal with the transition to the new Act that took effect on March 1, 1994.

**69. Definitions** — In this Act and the *Income Tax Act*, unless the context otherwise requires,

"*Income Tax Act*, chapter 148 of the Revised Statutes of Canada, 1952" means that Act as amended by section 1 of chapter 63 of the Statutes of Canada, 1970-71-72, and by any subsequent Act that received royal assent before December, 1991;

"*Income Tax Application Rules, 1971*, Part III of chapter 63 of the Statutes of Canada, 1970-71-72" means that Act as amended by any subsequent Act that received royal assent before December, 1991.

**Definitions [ITAR 69]**: "Canada" — ITA 255, *Interpretation Act* 35(1).

## Application of the 1971 Acts and the Revised Acts

**70. Application of *Income Tax Application Rules, 1971*, 1970-71-72, c. 63** — Subject to this Act and the *Income Tax Act* and unless the context otherwise requires,

(a) sections 7 to 9 and 12 to 68 of the *Income Tax Application Rules, 1971*, Part III of chapter 63 of the Statutes of Canada, 1970-71-72, apply with respect to taxation years that ended before December, 1991; and

(b) section 10 of the *Income Tax Application Rules, 1971*, Part III of chapter 63 of the Statutes of Canada, 1970-71-72, applies with respect to amounts paid or credited before December, 1991.

**Definitions [ITAR 70]**: "amount" — ITA 248(1); "Canada" — ITA 255, *Interpretation Act* 35(1); "Income Tax Application Rules, 1971" — ITAR 69; "taxation year" — ITA 249.

**71. Application of this Act** — Subject to this Act and the *Income Tax Act* and unless the context otherwise requires,

(a) sections 7 to 9 and 12 to 78 of this Act apply with respect to taxation years that end after November, 1991; and

(b) section 10 of this Act applies with respect to amounts paid or credited after November, 1991.

**Definitions [ITAR 71]**: "amount" — ITA 248(1); "taxation year" — ITA 249.

**72. Application of *Income Tax Act*, R.S.C., 1952, c. 148** — Subject to this Act and the *Income*

*Tax Act* and unless the context otherwise requires, the *Income Tax Act*, chapter 148 of the Revised Statutes of Canada, 1952, applies as follows:

(a) Parts I, I.1, I.2, I.3, II.1, IV, IV.1, V, VI, VI.1, VII, VIII, IX, XI.3, XII, XII.1, XII.2, XII.3 and XIV of that Act apply with respect to taxation years that ended before December 1991;

(b) Part III of that Act applies with respect to dividends that became payable before December, 1991;

(c) Parts X, X.1, X.2, XI, XI.1 and XI.2 of that Act apply with respect to calendar years that ended before December, 1991;

(d) Part XIII of that Act applies with respect to amounts paid or credited before December, 1991; and

(e) Parts XV, XVI and XVII of that Act apply before December, 1991.

**Notes**: Reference to Part XII.1 in ITAR 72(a) added by 1993 technical bill, deemed to have come into force on March 1, 1994 (i.e., retroactive to when R.S.C. 1985 (5th Supp.) came into force).

**Definitions [ITAR 72]**: "amount", "dividend" — ITA 248(1); "Income Tax Act, chapter 148 of the Revised Statutes of Canada, 1952" — ITAR 69; "taxation year" — ITA 249.

**73. Application of *Income Tax Act*** — Subject to this Act and the *Income Tax Act* and unless the context otherwise requires, the *Income Tax Act* applies as follows:

(a) Parts I, I.1, I.2, I.3, II.1, IV, IV.1, V, VI, VI.1, VII, VIII, IX, XI.3, XII, XII.1, XII.2, XII.3 and XIV of that Act apply with respect to taxation years that end after November 1991;

(b) Part III of that Act applies with respect to dividends that become payable after November, 1991;

(c) Parts X, X.1, X.2, XI, XI.1 and XI.2 of that Act apply with respect to calendar years that end after November, 1991;

(d) Part XIII of that Act applies with respect to amounts paid or credited after November, 1991; and

(e) Parts XV, XVI and XVII of that Act apply after November, 1991.

**Notes**: Reference to Part XII.1 in ITAR 73(a) added by 1993 technical bill, deemed to have come into force on March 1, 1994 (i.e., retroactive to when R.S.C. 1985 (5th Supp.) came into force).

**Definitions [ITAR 73]**: "amount", "dividend" — ITA 248(1); "taxation year" — ITA 249.

## Application of Certain Provisions

**74. Definition of "provision"** — In sections 75 to 78, "provision" means the whole or part of a provision.

**75. Continued effect of amending and application provisions** — For greater certainty, where an enactment passed after 1971 in amendment of the *Income Tax Application Rules, 1971*, Part III of chapter 63 of the Statutes of Canada, 1970-71-72, or of the *Income Tax Act*, chapter 148 of the Revised Statutes of Canada, 1952, contains an amending, repeal, application or other provision that, immediately before the coming into force of the fifth supplement to the Revised Statutes of Canada, 1985, has any effect on, or in connection with, the application of either or both of those Acts, that provision has, on the coming into force of that supplement, the same effect on, or in connection with, the application of either this Act or the *Income Tax Act* or both.

**Notes**: See also the *Revised Statutes of Canada, 1985 Amendment Act*, S.C. 1987, c. 48, s. 4, which provides that the R.S.C. 1985 (Fifth Supplement) consolidation is not intended to change the law.

**Definitions [ITAR 75]**: "Canada" — ITA 255, *Interpretation Act* 35(1); "Income Tax Act, chapter 148 of the Revised Statutes of Canada, 1952", "Income Tax Application Rules, 1971" — ITAR 69; "provision" — ITAR 74.

**76. Application of section 75** — Section 75 is applicable whether or not this Act or the *Income Tax Act*, as the case may be, contains, or contains the tenor of or any reference to,

(a) the amending, repeal, application or other provision referred to in that section; or

(b) any provision of the *Income Tax Application Rules, 1971*, Part III of chapter 63 of the Statutes of Canada, 1970-71-72, or the *Income Tax Act*, chapter 148 of the Revised Statutes of Canada, 1952, expressed or intended to be the subject of or otherwise affected by that amending, repeal, application or other provision.

**Definitions [ITAR 76]**: "Canada" — ITA 255, *Interpretation Act* 35(1); "Income Tax Act, chapter 148 of the Revised Statutes of Canada, 1952", "Income Tax Application Rules, 1971" — ITAR 69; "provision" — ITAR 74.

**77. Continued effect of repealed provisions** — For greater certainty, where a provision of the *Income Tax Application Rules, 1971*, Part III of chapter 63 of the Statutes of Canada, 1970-71-72, or the *Income Tax Act*, chapter 148 of the Revised Statutes of Canada, 1952, was repealed at any time after 1971 but, immediately before the coming into force of the fifth supplement to the Revised Statutes of Canada, 1985, continues to be applied to any extent or otherwise to have any effect on, or in connection with, the application of either or both of those Acts, the repealed provision, on the coming into force of that supplement, continues to be so applied or to have that effect on, or in connection with, the application of either this Act or the *Income Tax Act* or both.

**Notes**: See Notes to ITAR 75.

**Definitions [ITAR 77]**: "Canada" — ITA 255, *Interpretation Act* 35(1); "Income Tax Act, chapter 148 of the Revised Statutes of Canada, 1952", "Income Tax Application Rules, 1971" — ITAR 69; "provision" — ITAR 74.

# ITAR S. 78

## Income Tax Application Rules

**78. Application of section 77** — Section 77 is applicable whether or not this Act or the *Income Tax Act*, as the case may be, contains any reference to the repealed provision referred to in that section or to the subject-matter of that provision.

**Definitions [ITAR 78]:** "provision" — ITAR 74.

**79. (1) Effect of amendments on former ITA** — Where a provision of an enactment amends the *Income Tax Act* or affects the application of the *Income Tax Act* and the provision applies to or with respect to a period, transaction or event to which the *Income Tax Act*, chapter 148 of the Revised Statutes of Canada, 1952, applies, the *Income Tax Act*, chapter 148 of the Revised Statutes of Canada, 1952, shall be read as if it had been amended or its application had been affected by the provision, with such modifications as the circumstances require, to the extent of the provision's application to or with respect to that period, transaction or event.

**(2) Effect of amendments on former ITAR** — Where a provision of an enactment amends this Act or affects the application of this Act and the provision applies to or with respect to a period, transaction or event to which the *Income Tax Application Rules, 1971*, Part III of chapter 63 of the Statutes of Canada, 1970-71-72, apply, the *Income Tax Application Rules, 1971*, Part III of chapter 63 of the Statutes of Canada, 1970-71-72, shall be read as if they had been amended or their application had been affected by the provision, with such modifications as the circumstances require, to the extent of the provision's application to or with respect to that period, transaction or event.

**Notes:** ITAR 79 added by 1993 technical bill, deemed to have come into force on March 2, 1994 (i.e., the day after the day R.S.C. 1985 (5th Supp.) came into force).

**Definitions [ITAR 79]:** "Canada" — ITA 255, *Interpretation Act* 35(1); "Income Tax Act, chapter 148 of the Revised Statutes of Canada, 1952", "Income Tax Application Rules, 1971" — ITAR 69.

---

Sale of Land + Building (Purchased pre 72)

Purchase  20,000 Land        V-Day  320,000 Land
         160,000 Bldg              640,000 Bldg
         240,000                   960,000

1998 Disposition of Property:
                                              48,000 legal
Proceeds — L  4,800,000    Selling costs → 192,000 commissions
         B    1,600,000    UCC on bldg = 40,000
              6,400,000
              ↳ Cash  1,600,000
                Note  4,800,000

Income Inclusions in 1998

* Approach — Calculate cap. gain + recapture
  — recapture included in income
  — use cap. gains reserve for cap. gain portion

A) Land
ACB median of
Proceeds  4,800,000
V-Day     320,000 *
Cost      80,000

Cap. gain = 4,800,000 − 320,000 = $4,480,000

B) Bldg — ITAR 20(1)(A)

| | | |
|---|---|---|
| Cap cost | | $160,000 |
| Plus the excess | | |
| Proceeds | 1,600,000 | |
| Less V-Day | 640,000 | 960,000 |
| | | 1,120,000 |
| Less - capital cost | | 160,000 |
| Cap. gain | | 960,000 |

Total gain  land  4,480,000
            bldg    960,000  → $5,440,000
            less: expenses   (240,000)
                             5,200,000 * subject to reserve

Recapture: Cap cost − UCC
  160,000 − 40,000
  = 120,000 — full amount include in income

Cap. gain reserve:
  lesser of
  (i) $\frac{\text{proceeds not yet due}}{\text{total proceeds}} \times$ gain

  and (ii) $1/5$ of gain $\times$ (4 − preceding tax years)

  75% × 5,200,000 = 3,900,000 → can take this as reserve
  (20% × 5,200,000) × 4 = 4,160,000

Cap. gain      5,200,000
Less reserve   3,900,000
               1,300,000  × inclusion rate
    + recapture

# DETAILED TABLE OF SECTIONS

## INCOME TAX REGULATIONS

| | |
|---|---|
| 1 | Short title |
| 2 | Interpretation |

### PART I — TAX DEDUCTIONS

| | |
|---|---|
| 100 | Interpretation |
| 100(1) | |
| 100(2) | [Indexing] |
| 100(3) | [Amounts excluded from base for withholding] |
| 100(3.1) | [Northern residents' deduction] |
| 100(3.2) | [Exceptions to subsec. (3)] |
| 100(4) | [Establishment of the employer] |
| 100(5) | [LSVCC share purchase] |
| 101 | Deductions and remittances |
| 102 | Periodic payments |
| 102(1) | [Amount to be withheld] |
| 102(2) | [Commission employees] |
| 102(3), (4) | [Revoked] |
| 102(5) | [Commission employees — exception] |
| 102(6) | [Revoked] |
| 103 | Non-periodic payments |
| 103(1), (2) | [Bonus] |
| 103(3) | [Retroactive pay increase] |
| 103(4) | [Lump sum payment] |
| 103(5) | [Lump sum pension payment] |
| 103(6) | [Lump sum payment] |
| 103(7) | [Retirement compensation arrangement] |
| 103(8) | [RESP payment] |
| 104 | Deductions not required |
| 104(1) | [Sufficient credits on TD1] |
| 104(2) | [Employee not in Canada] |
| 104(3) | [Home Buyers' Plan] |
| 104(3.01) | ["Qualifying homebuyer"] |
| 104(3.1) | ["Owner-occupied home"] |
| 104(4) | ["Home"] |
| 104.1 | Lifelong Learning Plan |
| 104.1(1) | [No amount deducted] |
| 104.1(2) | ["Qualifying educational program"] |
| 105 | Non-residents |
| 105.1 | Fishermen's election |
| 106 | Variations in deductions |
| 107 | Employee's returns |
| 107(1) | [Due date for TD1] |
| 107(2), (3) | [Commission employees] |
| 108 | Remittances to Receiver General |
| 108(1) | [Deadline] |
| 108(1.1) | [Large employers] |
| 108(1.11) | [Option to use preceding year as base] |
| 108(1.12) | [Quarterly remittance] |
| 108(1.2) | ["Average monthly withholding amount"] |
| 108(1.3) | [Where business transferred] |
| 108(2) | [Ceasing to carry on business] |
| 108(3) | [Return] |

## Detailed Table of Sections

| | |
|---|---|
| 108(4) | [Unclaimed dividends, interest on proceeds] |
| 109 | Elections to increase deductions |
| 109(1) | [Filing of election] |
| 109(2) | [Variation] |
| 109(3) | [Time allowed to comply] |
| 110 | Prescribed persons |
| 110(1) | [Large employers] |
| 110(2) | [Average monthly remittance] |

### PART II — INFORMATION RETURNS

| | |
|---|---|
| 200 | Remuneration and benefits |
| 200(1) | [Information return] |
| 200(2) | [Various payments] |
| 200(3) | [Automobile benefits] |
| 200(4) | [Automobile benefits — shareholder] |
| 200(5) | [Proposed] [Employee stock option deferral] |
| 201 | Investment income |
| 201(1) | [Information return] |
| 201(2) | [Nominees and agents] |
| 201(3) | [Bearer coupons, etc.] |
| 201(4) | [Annual interest accrual] |
| 201(4.1) | [Indexed debt obligation] |
| 201(4.2) | [Nominee or agent — debt obligation] |
| 201(5) | [Insurers] |
| 201(6) | [Debt obligation in bearer form] |
| 201(7) | ["Debt obligation in bearer form"] |
| 202 | Payments to non-residents |
| 202(1) | [Information return] |
| 202(2) | [Various payments to non-residents] |
| 202(2.1) | [NISA Fund No. 2] |
| 202(3) | [Nominee or agent] |
| 202(4) | [Non-resident payer deemed resident in Canada] |
| 202(5) | [Partnership payer deemed resident in Canada] |
| 202(6) | [Non-resident payer carrying on business in Canada] |
| 202(7) | [Filing deadline] |
| 202(8) | [Filing deadline — trust or estate] |
| 203 | Certain income in respect of non-residents |
| 204 | Estates and trusts |
| 204(1) | [Trustee to file return] |
| 204(2) | [Filing deadline] |
| 204(3) | [Exceptions] |
| 205 | Date returns to be filed |
| 205(1) | [General] |
| 205(2) | [Where business discontinued] |
| 205.1 | Electronic filing |
| 206 | Legal representatives and others |
| 206(1) | [Filing of return] |
| 206(2) | [Trustee in bankruptcy, etc.] |
| 207 | Ownership certificates |
| 208 | Dispositions of income-averaging annuity contracts |
| 209 | Distribution of taxpayers' portions of returns |
| 210 | Tax deduction information |
| 211 | Accrued bond interest |
| 212 | Employees profit sharing plans |
| 213 | Electric, gas or steam corporations |
| 214 | Registered retirement savings plans |
| 215 | Registered retirement income funds |
| 216 | Registered Canadian amateur athletic associations |
| 217 | Disposition of interest in annuities and life insurance policies |
| 218 | Patronage payments |
| 219 | Family allowances and similar payments |
| 220 | Cash bonus payments on Canada Savings Bonds |

## Detailed Table of Sections

| | |
|---|---|
| 221 | Qualified investments and foreign property |
| 222 | [Repealed] |
| 223 | Registered home ownership savings plans |
| 224 | Canadian home insulation program and Canada oil substitution program |
| 225 | Certified films and video tapes |
| 226 | Scientific research tax credits |
| 227 | Share purchase tax credits |
| 228 | Resource flow-through shares |
| 229 | Partnership return |
| 230 | Security transactions |
| 231 | Information respecting tax shelters |
| 232 | Workers' compensation |
| 233 | Social assistance |
| 234 | Farm support payments |
| 235 | Identifier information |
| 236 | [Members of partnership] |
| 237 | Contract for goods and services [for federal government] |
| 238 | Reporting of payments in respect of construction activities |

### PART III — ANNUITIES AND LIFE INSURANCE POLICIES

| | |
|---|---|
| 300 | Capital element of annuity payments |
| 301 | Life annuity contracts |
| 302 | [Revoked] |
| 303 | Life annuity contracts |
| 304 | Prescribed annuity contracts |
| 305 | Unallocated income accrued before 1982 |
| 306 | Exempt policies |
| 307 | Accumulating funds |
| 308 | Net cost of pure insurance and mortality gains and losses |
| 309 | Prescribed premiums and prescribed increases |
| 310 | Interpretation |

### PART IV — TAXABLE INCOME EARNED IN A PROVINCE BY A CORPORATION

| | |
|---|---|
| 400 | Interpretation |
| 400(1) | [Corporation's taxable income] |
| 400(2) | [Permanent establishment] |
| 401 | Computation of taxable income |
| 402 | General rules |
| 402(4) | [Attribution to permanent establishment] |
| 402.1 | Transitional — Taxable income earned in the 1978 taxation year in the Northwest Territories |
| 402.2 | Transitional — Taxable income earned in the 1980 taxation year in the Yukon Territory |
| 403 | Insurance corporations |
| 404 | Chartered banks |
| 404 | [Proposed] Banks |
| 405 | Trust and loan corporations |
| 406 | Railway corporations |
| 407 | Airline corporations |
| 408 | Grain elevator operators |
| 409 | Bus and truck operators |
| 410 | Ship operators |
| 411 | Pipeline operators |
| 412 | Divided businesses |
| 413 | Non-resident corporations |
| 414 | Nova Scotia offshore area |
| 415 | Idem |

### PART V — NON-RESIDENT-OWNED INVESTMENT CORPORATIONS

| | |
|---|---|
| 500 | Elections |
| 501 | Elections revoked |
| 502 | Certificates of changes of ownership |
| 503 | [Revoked] |

1923

Detailed Table of Sections

## PART VI — ELECTIONS

600 [Prescribed provisions for late elections]

## PART VII — LOGGING TAXES ON INCOME

700 Logging
701 [Revoked]

## PART VIII — NON-RESIDENT TAXES

800 Registered non-resident insurers
801 Filing of returns by non-resident insurers
802 Amounts taxable
803 Payment of tax by non-resident insurers
804 Interpretation
805 Other non-resident persons
806 International organizations and agencies
806.1 [Prescribed international agency]
806.2 Prescribed obligation
807 Identification of obligations
808 Allowances in respect of investment in property in Canada
808(1) [Allowance]
808(1.1) [Resident in Canada]
808(2) ["Qualified investment . . ."]
808(3) ["Allowable liquid assets . . ."]
808(4) ["Qualified investment . . ."]
808(5) ["Qualified investment . . ." of partnership]
808(6) ["Allowable liquid assets . . ." of partnership]
808(7) [Partnerships]
809 Reduction of certain amounts to be deducted or withheld
810 Excluded property of non-resident persons

## PART IX — DELEGATION OF THE POWERS AND DUTIES OF THE MINISTER

900 Powers and duties of the Minister

## PART X — ELECTION IN RESPECT OF DECEASED TAXPAYERS

1000 Property dispositions
1001 Annual instalments

## PART XI — CAPITAL COST ALLOWANCES
### DIVISION I — DEDUCTIONS ALLOWED

1100 Deductions
1100(1)
1100(1)(a) rates
1100(1)(b) Class 13
1100(1)(c) Class 14
1100(1)(d) in lieu of double depreciation
1100(1)(e) timber limits and cutting rights
1100(1)(f) Class 15
1100(1)(g) industrial mineral mines
1100(1)(h) [Revoked]
1100(1)(i) additional allowances — fishing vessels
1100(1)(j), (k) [Repealed]
1100(1)(l) additional allowances — certified productions
1100(1)(m) [Revoked]
1100(1)(m) [Proposed] additional allowance — Canadian film or video production
1100(1)(n) Class 19
1100(1)(o) [Class 19]
1100(1)(p) Class 20
1100(1)(q) Class 21
1100(1)(r), (s), (sa) [Revoked]
1100(1)(sb) additional allowances — grain storage facilities
1100(1)(t) Classes 24, 27, 29 and 34
1100(1)(ta) [Classes 24, 27, 29 and 34]
1100(1)(u) [Revoked]

## Detailed Table of Sections

1100(1)(v)   Canadian vessels
1100(1)(va)   additional allowances — offshore drilling vessels
1100(1)(w), (x)   additional allowances — Class 28
1100(1)(y)   additional allowances — Class 41
1100(1)(ya)   [property for more than one mine]
1100(1)(z)   additional allowances — railway cars
1100(1)(z.1a)   [additional allowance — railway cars]
1100(1)(z.1b)   [railway property]
1100(1)(za)   additional allowances — railway track and related property
1100(1)(za.1)   [railway track and related property]
1100(1)(za.2)   [trestles]
1100(1)(zb)   [trestles]
1100(1)(zc)   additional allowances — railway expansion and modernization property
1100(1)(zd)   Class 38
1100(1)(ze)   Class 39
1100(1)(zf)   Class 40
1100(1)(zg)   additional allowance — year 2000 computer hardware and systems software
1100(1)(zh)   additional allowance — year 2000 computer software
1100(1.1)   [Specified leasing property]
1100(1.11)   ["Specified leasing property"]
1100(1.12)   [Specified leasing property — new property]
1100(1.13)   [Specified leasing property — interpretation]
1100(1.14)   [Specified leasing property — election]
1100(1.15)   [Specified leasing property — term of more than one year]
1100(1.16)   [Specified leasing property — amalgamation]
1100(1.17)   [Specified leasing property — replacement property]
1100(1.18)   [Specified leasing property — breakdown of property]
1100(1.19)   [Specified leasing property — addition or alteration]
1100(1.2)   [Specified leasing property — renogiation of lease]
1100(1.3)   [Specified leasing property — lease of building]
1100(2)   Property acquired in the year [Half-year rule]
1100(2.1)–(2.5)   Exceptions
1100(3)   [Taxation years less than 12 months]
1100(4)–(7)   [Revoked]
1100(8)   Railway sidings
1100(9)   Patents
1100(9.1)   [Class 44]
1100(10)   [Revoked]
1100(11)   Rental properties
1100(12)   [Rental properties — exceptions]
1100(13)   [Rental properties — leasehold interest]
1100(14)   ["Rental property"]
1100(14.1)   ["Gross revenue"]
1100(14.2)   [Gross revenue — exception]
1100(15)   Leasing properties
1100(16)   [Leasing property — exception]
1100(17)   ["Leasing property"]
1100(17.1)   [Deemed use of property]
1100(17.2)   [Deemed rent]
1100(17.3)   [Deemed rent — exception]
1100(18), (19)   [Leasing property — exclusions]
1100(20)   [Leasing property — replacement property]
1100(20.1)   Computer software tax shelter property
1100(20.2)   ["Computer software tax shelter property"]
1100(21)   Certified films and video tapes
1100(21.1)   [Proposed] [Film or videotape — deemed cost reduction]
1100(22)   [Film or tape acquired before 1979]
1100(23)   [Film or tape acquired in 1987 or 1988]
1100(24)   Specified energy property
1100(25)   ["Specified energy property"]
1100(26)   [Specified energy property — exception]

Detailed Table of Sections

1100(27) [Specified energy property — acquisition before 1990]
1100(28) [Specified energy property — exclusion]
1100(29) [Specified energy property — replacement property]
1100A Exempt mining income
1100A(1) [Revoked]
1100A(2)

### DIVISION II — SEPARATE CLASSES

1101
1101(1) Businesses and properties
1101(1a) [Life insurance business deemed corporate business]
1101(1ab) [Partnership property separate]
1101(1ac) [Rental property over $50,000]
1101(1ad) [Rental property over $50,000 — exception]
1101(1ae) [Rental property separate]
1101(1af) [Expensive automobiles]
1101(2) Fishing vessels
1101(2a) Canadian vessels
1101(2b) Offshore drilling vessels
1101(3) Timber limits and cutting rights
1101(4) Industrial mineral mines
1101(4a)–(4d) New or expanded mines properties
1101(5) Lease option agreements
1101(5a) Telecommunication spacecraft
1101(5b) Multiple-unit residential buildings
1101(5c) Leasing properties
1101(5d) Railway cars
1101(5d.1) [Railway property]
1101(5e) Railway track and related property
1101(5e.1) [Railway property]
1101(5e.2), (5f) [Trestles]
1101(5g) Deemed depreciable property
1101(5h) Leasehold interest in real properties
1101(5i) Pipelines
1101(5j) [Election effective forever]
1101(5k) Certified productions
1101(5k.1) [Proposed] Canadian film or video production
1101(5l) Class 38 property and outdoor advertising signs
1101(5m) Specified energy property
1101(5n) [Specified leasing property]
1101(5o) [Exempt leasing properties]
1101(5p) Rapidly depreciating electronic equipment
1101(5q) [Election required]
1101(5r) Computer software tax shelter property
1101(6) Reference

### DIVISION III — PROPERTY RULES

1102
1102(1) Property not included
1102(1)(a) [otherwise deductible]
1102(1)(a.1) [CRCE]
1102(1)(b) [inventory]
1102(1)(c) [no income purpose]
1102(1)(d) [R&D expense]
1102(1)(e), (f) [non-Canadian art]
1102(1)(g) [pre-1972 farming/fishing property]
1102(1)(h) [pre-1966 automobile]
1102(1)(i) [pre-1963 property]
1102(1)(j) [life insurer]
1102(1)(k) [linefill]
1102(1a) Partnership property
1102(2) Land
1102(3) Non-residents

Detailed Table of Sections

| | |
|---|---|
| 1102(4) | Improvements or alterations to leased properties |
| 1102(5) | Buildings on leased properties |
| 1102(5.1) | [Buildings on leased properties] |
| 1102(6) | Leasehold interests acquired before 1949 |
| 1102(7) | River improvements |
| 1102(8) | Electrical plant used for mining |
| 1102(9) | [Generating or distributing equipment] |
| 1102(9.1) | [pre-1970 acquisition] |
| 1102(9.2) | [Property under Reg. 1102(8) or (9)] |
| 1102(10) | Railway companies |
| 1102(11) | Passenger automobiles |
| 1102(12), (13) | [Pre-1966 automobile] |
| 1102(14) | Property acquired by transfer, amalgamation or winding-up |
| 1102(14.1) | [Change in class] |
| 1102(14.2) | Townsite costs |
| 1102(14.3) | Surface construction and bridges |
| 1102(15), (16) | Manufacturing and processing enterprises |
| 1102(17) | Recreational property |
| 1102(18) | [Repealed] |
| 1102(19) | Additions and alterations |
| 1102(20) | Non-arm's length exception |
| 1102(21) | [Class 43.1 property] |

### DIVISION IV — INCLUSIONS IN AND TRANSFERS BETWEEN CLASSES

1103

| | |
|---|---|
| 1103(1) | Elections to include properties in Class 1 |
| 1103(2) | Elections to include properties in Class 2, 4 or 17 |
| 1103(2a) | Elections to include properties in Class 8 |
| 1103(2b) | Elections to include properties in Class 37 |
| 1103(2c), (2d) | Elections to make certain transfers |
| 1103(2e) | Transfers from Class 40 to Class 10 |
| 1103(2f) | Elections to include properties in Class 1, 3 or 6 |
| 1103(2g) | Transfers to Class 8 or Class 10 |
| 1103(2h) | Elections not to include properties in Class 44 |
| 1103(3)–(5) | Election rules |

### DIVISION V — INTERPRETATION

1104

| | |
|---|---|
| 1104(1)–(3) | Definitions |
| 1104(4) | [Revoked] |
| 1104(5) | Mining |
| 1104(5.1)–(6) | ["Gross revenue from a mine"] |
| 1104(6)(a) | ["income from a mine"] |
| 1104(6)(b) | ["mine"] |
| 1104(6.1) | [Repealed] |
| 1104(7) | [Mine] |
| 1104(8) | ["Stone quarry"] |
| 1104(9) | Manufacturing or processing |
| 1104(10) | Certified films and video tapes |
| 1104(11) | Certified Class 34 properties |
| 1104(12) | Amusement parks |
| 1104(13) | Class 43.1 — Energy conservation property |
| 1104(14) | [Class 43.1(c) compliance] |

### DIVISION VI — CLASSES PRESCRIBED

1105      Classes prescribed

### DIVISION VII — CERTIFICATES ISSUED BY MINISTER OF SUPPLY AND SERVICES [REPEALED]
### DIVISION VII — [PROPOSED] CERTIFICATES ISSUED BY MINISTER OF CANADIAN HERITAGE

1106

| | |
|---|---|
| 1106(1) | [Proposed] Definitions |
| 1106(2) | [Proposed] Prescribed taxable Canadian corporation |
| 1106(3) | [Proposed] Canadian film or video production |
| 1106(4) | [Proposed] Creative services |

## Detailed Table of Sections

| | |
|---|---|
| 1106(5) | [Proposed] Lead performer/screenwriter |
| 1106(6) | [Proposed] Documentary production |
| 1106(7) | [Proposed] Prescribed person |
| 1106(8) | [Proposed] Prescribed amount |

### DIVISION VIII — DETERMINATION OF VISCOSITY AND DENSITY

| | |
|---|---|
| 1107 | [Bituminous sands] |

### PART XII — RESOURCE AND PROCESSING ALLOWANCES

| | |
|---|---|
| 1200 | Deduction allowed |
| 1201 | Earned depletion allowances |
| 1202 | Rules |
| 1203 | Mining exploration depletion |
| 1204 | Resource profits |
| 1205 | Earned depletion base |
| 1206 | Interpretation |
| 1206(1) | Definitions |
| 1206(2)–(9) | Interpretation — rules |
| 1207 | Frontier exploration allowances |
| 1208 | Additional allowances in respect of certain oil or gas wells |
| 1209 | Additional allowances in respect of certain mines |
| 1210 | Resource allowance |
| 1210(1) | [Deductible amount] |
| 1210(2) | ["Adjusted resource profits"] |
| 1210(3) | [Partnership] |
| 1210(4) | [Exempt partnership] |
| 1210.1 | [Prescribed resource loss] |
| 1211 | Prescribed amounts |
| 1212 | Supplementary depletion allowances |
| 1213 | Prescribed deductions |
| 1214 | Amalgamations and windings-up |
| 1215 | [Revoked] |
| 1216 | Prescribed persons |
| 1216 | [Proposed] Prescribed persons |
| 1217 | Prescribed Canadian exploration expense |
| 1218 | Prescribed Canadian development expense |
| 1219 | Canadian renewable and conservation expense |

### PART XIII — ELECTIONS IN RESPECT OF TAXPAYERS CEASING TO BE RESIDENT IN CANADA

| | |
|---|---|
| 1300 | Elections to defer capital gains |
| 1301 | Elections to defer payment of taxes |
| 1302 | Elections to realize capital gains |

### PART XIV — INSURANCE BUSINESS POLICY RESERVES

#### DIVISION 1 — POLICY RESERVES

| | |
|---|---|
| 1400 | Non-life insurance business |
| 1400(1) | [Policy reserve] |
| 1400(2) | [Negative reserves] |
| 1400(3) | [Amount of reserve] |
| 1400(4) | [Elements D and E] |
| 1400(5) | [Transitional — Before 2001] |

#### DIVISION 2 — POLICY RESERVES FOR PRE-1996 POLICIES

| | |
|---|---|
| 1401 | Life insurance businesses |
| 1401(1) | [Policy reserves] |
| 1401(1.1) | [Pre-1996 policies only] |
| 1401(2) | [Segregated funds] |
| 1401(3) | [Group life insurance policies] |
| 1401(4) | [Unpaid claims reserve] |

#### DIVISION 3 — SPECIAL RULES

| | |
|---|---|
| 1402 | Non-life and life insurance businesses |
| 1402.1 | [Negative amounts] |
| 1403 | Non-life and life insurance businesses |

Detailed Table of Sections

### DIVISION 4 — POLICY RESERVES FOR POST-1995 POLICIES
1404      Life insurance business
1405      [Unpaid claims reserve]
1406      [Interpretation]
1407      [Negative amounts]

### DIVISION 5 — INTERPRETATION
1408      Insurance businesses
1408(1)      [Definitions]
1408(2)      ["Group term life insurance policy"]
1408(3)      [Interpretation — modified net premium]
1408(4)      ["Premium paid by the policyholder"]
1408(5), (6)      [Riders]
1408(7)      [No change in amount]

## PART XV — PROFIT SHARING PLANS
### DIVISION I — EMPLOYEES PROFIT SHARING PLANS
1500      How elections to be made

### DIVISION II — DEFERRED PROFIT SHARING PLANS
1501      Registration of plans
1502      [Revoked]

### DIVISION III — ELECTIONS IN RESPECT OF CERTAIN SINGLE PAYMENTS
1503      How elections to be made

## PART XVI — PRESCRIBED COUNTRIES
1600      Prescribed countries for ITAR 10(4)

## PART XVII — CAPITAL COST ALLOWANCES, FARMING AND FISHING
### DIVISION I — DEDUCTIONS ALLOWED
1700
1700(1)      Rates
1700(2)      Taxation years less than 12 months
1700(3)      Property disposed of during year
1700(4)      Leasehold interests

### DIVISION II — MAXIMUM DEDUCTIONS
1701      Maximum deductions

### DIVISION III — PROPERTY NOT INCLUDED
1702      Rules

### DIVISION IV — INTERPRETATION
1703
1703(1)      Taxation years for individuals in business
1703(2), (3)      Depreciable cost
1703(4)      Personal use of property
1703(5)      Grants, subsidies or other government assistance
1703(6)      Transactions not at arm's length
1703(7)      Property acquired from a parent
1703(8)      Property acquired by gift

### DIVISION V — APPLICATION OF THIS PART
1704      Application

## PART XVIII — INVENTORIES
1800      Manner of keeping inventories
1801      Valuation
1802      Valuation of animals

## PART XIX — INVESTMENT INCOME TAX
1900

## PART XX — POLITICAL CONTRIBUTIONS
2000      Contents of receipts
2001      Information returns
2002      Interpretation

Detailed Table of Sections

### Part XXI — Elections in respect of Surpluses

| | |
|---|---|
| 2100 | Reduction of tax-paid undistributed surplus on hand or 1971 capital surplus on hand |
| 2101 | Capital dividends and life insurance capital dividends payable by private corporations |
| 2102 | Tax on 1971 undistributed income on hand |
| 2103 | [Revoked] |
| 2104 | Capital gains dividends payable by mutual fund corporations and investment corporations |
| 2104.1 | [Capital gains dividends payable by mortgage investment corporations] |
| 2105 | Capital gains dividends payable by non-resident-owned investment corporations |
| 2106 | Alternative to additional tax on excessive elections [for capital dividends] |
| 2107 | Tax-deferred preferred series |

### Part XXII — Security Interests

| | |
|---|---|
| 2200, 2201 | Minister may discharge security |

### Part XXIII — Principal Residences

| | |
|---|---|
| 2300 | How election to be made |
| 2301 | How designation to be made |

### Part XXIV — Insurers

| | |
|---|---|
| 2400 | |
| 2400(1) | Definitions |
| 2400(2) | Carrying value |
| 2400(3) | Amount or item reported |
| 2400(4) | Application of certain definitions |
| 2400(5) | Deeming rules for certain assets |
| 2400(6) | [Idem] |
| 2400(7) | No double counting |
| 2401 | |
| 2401(1) | Designated insurance property |
| 2401(2) | Designation rules |
| 2401(3) | Order of designation of properties |
| 2401(4) | Equity limit for the year |
| 2401(5) | Exchanged property |
| 2401(6) | Non-investment property |
| 2401(7) | Policy loan excluded from designated property |
| 2402 | Income from participating life insurance businesses |
| 2403 | Branch tax elections |
| 2404 | Currency conversions [inapplicable as of 1999] |
| 2405 | Interpretation [inapplicable as of 1999] |
| 2406 | [ss. 2404 and 2405 inapplicable as of 1999] |
| 2407 | 1977 excess policy dividend deduction |
| 2408 | 1977 carryforward deduction |
| 2409 | Transitional |
| 2410–2412 | Prescribed amount |
| 2412(1) | Mean Canadian investment fund |
| 2412(2) | Cash-flow adjustment |
| 2412(3) | Amounts paid and received |
| 2412(4) | [Meaning of "month"] |

### Part XXV — Special T1 Tax Table for Individuals

| | |
|---|---|
| 2500 | Rules |
| 2501 | Meaning of "amount taxable" |

### Part XXVI — Income Earned in Province by an Individual

| | |
|---|---|
| 2600 | Interpretation |
| 2601 | Residents of Canada |
| 2602 | Non-residents |
| 2603 | Income from business |
| 2604 | Bus and truck operators |
| 2605 | More than one business |
| 2606 | Limitations of business income |
| 2606(1) | [Proposed] Limitations of business income |
| 2606(2) | [Proposed] [Part-year residents] |

Detailed Table of Sections

2607     Dual residence

### Part XXVII — Group Term Life Insurance Benefits
2700     Interpretation
2700(1)     Definitions
2700(2)     Accidental death insurance
2701     Prescribed benefit
2701(1)     [Amount prescribed]
2701(2)     Bankrupt individual
2702     Term insurance benefit
2702(1)     Amount of benefit
2702(2)     Average daily cost of insurance
2702(3)     Survivor income benefits
2702(4)     Determination of present value
2703     Prepaid insurance benefit
2703(1)     Amount of benefit
2703(2)     Taxpayer portion of premiums
2704     Employee-paid insurance
2705     Prescribed premium and insurance

### Part XXVIII — Election in respect of Accumulating Income of Trusts
2800     [Preferred beneficiary election]

### Part XXIX — Scientific Research and Experimental Development
2900     Interpretation
2901, 2902     Prescribed expenditures
2903     Special-purpose buildings

### Part XXX — Communication of Information
3000–3002     [Revoked]
3003, 3004     Prescribed laws of a province

### Part XXXI — [Revoked]

### Part XXXII — Prescribed Stock Exchanges and Contingency Funds
3200     Stock exchanges in Canada
3200     [Proposed] Stock exchanges in Canada
3201     Stock exchanges outside Canada
3201     [Proposed] Stock exchanges outside Canada
3202     Contingency funds

### Part XXXIII — Tax Transfer Payments
3300     Prescribed rate

### Part XXXIV — International Development Assistance Programs
3400     Prescribed programs

### Part XXXV — Receipts for Donations and Gifts
3500     Interpretation
3501     Contents of receipts
3502     Employees' charity trusts
3503     Universities outside Canada
3504     Prescribed donees

### Part XXXVI — Reserves for Surveys
3600
3600(1)     Prescribed amount
3600(2)     Interpretation

### Part XXXVII — Charitable Foundations
3700     Interpretation
3701     Disbursement quota
3702     Determination of value

### Part XXXVIII — Social Insurance Number Applications
3800     How application to be made

Detailed Table of Sections

### PART XXXIX — MINING TAXES ON INCOME

| | |
|---|---|
| 3900 | |
| 3900(1) | Amount deductible Interpretation |
| 3900(2) | Interpretation |
| 3900(3) | Other taxes |

### PART XL — BORROWED MONEY COSTS

| | |
|---|---|
| 4000 | [Revoked] |
| 4001 | Interest on insurance policy loans |

### PART XLI — REPRESENTATION EXPENSES

| | |
|---|---|
| 4100 | How election to be made |

### PART XLII — VALUATION OF ANNUITIES AND OTHER INTERESTS

| | |
|---|---|
| 4200 | How value to be determined |

### PART XLIII — INTEREST RATES

| | |
|---|---|
| 4300 | Interpretation |
| 4301 | Prescribed rate of interest |
| 4302 | Idem |

### PART XLIV — PUBLICLY-TRADED SHARES OR SECURITIES

| | |
|---|---|
| 4400 | Valuation of shares on December 22, 1971 |

### PART XLV — ELECTIONS IN RESPECT OF EXPROPRIATION ASSETS

| | |
|---|---|
| 4500 | How election to be made |

### PART XLVI — INVESTMENT TAX CREDIT

| | |
|---|---|
| 4600 | Qualified property |
| 4601 | Qualified transportation equipment [No longer relevant] |
| 4602 | Certified property |
| 4602(1) | [Prescribed areas] |
| 4602(2) | ["Census divisions"] |
| 4603 | Qualified construction equipment [No longer relevant] |
| 4604 | Approved project property [No longer relevant] |
| 4605 | Prescribed activities [No longer relevant] |
| 4606 | Prescribed amount |
| 4607 | Prescribed designated regions |
| 4608 | Prescribed expenditure for qualified Canadian exploration expenditure [No longer relevant] |
| 4609 | Prescribed offshore region |
| 4610 | Prescribed area |

### PART XLVII — ELECTION IN RESPECT OF CERTAIN PROPERTY OWNED ON DECEMBER 31, 1971

| | |
|---|---|
| 4700 | How election to be made |

### PART XLVIII — STATUS OF CORPORATIONS AND TRUSTS

| | |
|---|---|
| 4800 | Prescribed conditions |
| 4800.1 | Prescribed trusts |
| 4801, 4801.1 | Prescribed conditions |
| 4802 | Prescribed persons |
| 4803 | Interpretation |

### PART XLIX — DEFERRED INCOME PLANS, QUALIFIED INVESTMENTS

| | |
|---|---|
| 4900 | Qualified investments |
| 4900(1) | |
| 4900(1)(a) | [registered investment] |
| 4900(1)(b) | [share of public corporation] |
| 4900(1)(c) | [share of mortgage investment corporation] |
| 4900(1)(c) [Proposed] | [share of mortgage investment corporation] |
| 4900(1)(c.1) | [bond of public corporation] |
| 4900(1)(d) | [unit of mutual fund trust] |
| 4900(1)(d.1) | [bond of mutual fund trust] |
| 4900(1)(e) | [warrant or option] |
| 4900(1)(e.1) | [société d'entraide économique] |
| 4900(1)(f) | [share of credit union] |
| 4900(1)(g) | [bond of credit union] |

## Detailed Table of Sections

| | |
|---|---|
| 4900(1)(g) | [Proposed] [bond of credit union] |
| 4900(1)(h) | [bond of cooperative corporation] |
| 4900(1)(i) | [bonds of certain corporations] |
| 4900(1)(i.1) | [community bond guaranteed by province] |
| 4900(1)(i.11) | [Nova Scotia *Equity Tax Credit Act*] |
| 4900(1)(i.12) | [NWT risk capital investment] |
| 4900(1)(i.2) | [banker's acceptance] |
| 4900(1)(i.2) | [Proposed] [banker's acceptance] |
| 4900(1)(j) | [mortgage] |
| 4900(1)(k) | [pre-1981 qualified investment] |
| 4900(1)(l) | [bond of international organization] |
| 4900(1)(m) | [listed royalty unit] |
| 4900(1)(n) | [listed limited partnership unit] |
| 4900(1)(o) | [bond of foreign government] |
| 4900(1)(p) | [bond of corporation listed outside Canada] |
| 4900(1)(p.1) | [listed depository receipt] |
| 4900(1)(q) | [debt of privatized Crown corporation] |
| 4900(1)(q) | [Proposed] [debt of privatized Crown corporation] |
| 4900(1)(r) | [debt of large non-profit organization] |
| 4900(2) | [Exceptions] |
| 4900(3) | [Annuity contract] |
| 4900(4) | [Mortgage] |
| 4900(4) | [Proposed] [Mortgage] |
| 4900(5) | [RHOSP] |
| 4900(5) | [Proposed] [Registered investment] |
| 4900(6) | [Small business investment] |
| 4900(6)–(11) | [Proposed] [Small business investment] |
| 4900(12) | [Small business corporation] |
| 4900(12) | [Proposed] [Small business corporation] |
| 4900(13) | [Disqualifications] |
| 4901 | Interpretation |

### PART L — DEFERRED INCOME PLANS, FOREIGN PROPERTY

| | |
|---|---|
| 5000 | Foreign property |
| 5001 | [Master trust] |
| 5002 | [Registered investment] |

### PART LI — DEFERRED INCOME PLANS, INVESTMENTS IN SMALL BUSINESS

| | |
|---|---|
| 5100 | Interpretation |
| 5100(1) | [Definitions] |
| 5100(2) | [Small business security] |
| 5100(2.1) | [Prescribed venture capital corporation] |
| 5100(3) | [Debt obligations] |
| 5100(4) | [Prescribed person] |
| 5101 | [Small business investment corporation] |
| 5102 | [Small business investment limited partnership] |
| 5103 | [Small business investment trust] |
| 5104 | Rules |

### PART LII — CANADIAN MANUFACTURING AND PROCESSING PROFITS

| | |
|---|---|
| 5200 | Basic formula |
| 5201 | Small manufacturers' rule |
| 5202 | Interpretation |
| 5203 | Resource income |
| 5204 | Partnerships |

### PART LIII — INSTALMENT BASE

| | |
|---|---|
| 5300 | [Individuals] |
| 5301 | Corporations under Part I of the Act |

### PART LIV — DEBTOR'S GAINS ON SETTLEMENT OF DEBTS

| | |
|---|---|
| 5400 | Order of applying excess |
| 5401 | Limitation |

1933

Detailed Table of Sections

### Part LV — Prescribed Programs and Benefits

| | |
|---|---|
| 5500 | Canadian Home Insulation Program |
| 5501 | Canada Oil Substitution Program |
| 5502 | Benefits under government assistance programs |

### Part LVI — Registered Retirement Savings Plans, Premium Refunds

| | |
|---|---|
| 5600 | How election to be made |

### Part LVII — Medical Devices and Equipment

| | |
|---|---|
| 5700 | Prescribed devices and equipment |

### Part LVIII — Retention of Books and Records

| | |
|---|---|
| 5800 | Required retention periods |

### Part LIX — Foreign Affiliates

| | |
|---|---|
| 5900 | Dividends out of exempt, taxable and pre-acquisition surplus |
| 5901 | Order of surplus distributions |
| 5902 | Election in respect of capital gains |
| 5902(1) | [Proposed] Election in respect of capital gains |
| 5903 | Deductible loss |
| 5904 | Participating percentage |
| 5905 | Special rules |
| 5906 | Carrying on business in a country |
| 5907 | Interpretation |
| 5908 | [Repealed] |
| 5909 | Prescribed circumstances |

### Part LX — Prescribed Activities

| | |
|---|---|
| 6000 | Prescribed activities |

### Part LXI — Related Segregated Fund Trusts

| | |
|---|---|
| 6100 | How election to be made |

### Part LXII — Prescribed Securities and Shares

| | |
|---|---|
| 6200 | Prescribed securities [for election re Canadian securities] |
| 6201 | Prescribed shares |
| 6201(1)–(3) | [Term preferred share] |
| 6201(4) | [Taxable RFI share] |
| 6201(5) | [Term preferred share] |
| 6201(5) | [Proposed] [Term preferred share] |
| 6201(5.1) | [Taxable RFI share — prescribed share] |
| 6201(5.1) | [Proposed] [Taxable RFI share — prescribed share] |
| 6201(6) | [Term preferred share — prescribed share] |
| 6201(7) | [Taxable preferred share — prescribed share] |
| 6201(8) | [Canada Cement Lafarge] |
| 6201(9) | [Time when share acquired] |
| 6201(10) | [Trusts and partnerships] |
| 6201(11) | [Grandfathering] |
| 6202 | [Resource expenditures — prescribed share] |
| 6202.1 | [Flow-through shares — prescribed share] |
| 6202.1(1) | [Idem] |
| 6202.1(2) | [Flow-through shares — prescribed share] |
| 6202.1(3) | [Dividend entitlement and liquidation entitlement] |
| 6202.1(4) | [Agreement deemed not to be undertaking] |
| 6202.1(5) | [Definitions] |
| 6203 | |
| 6204 | Idem |
| 6204(1) | [Employee stock option deduction — prescribed share] |
| 6204(2) | [Rules] |
| 6204(3), (4) | ["Specified person"] |
| 6205 | |
| 6205(1)–(3) | [Capital gains deduction — prescribed share] |
| 6205(4) | [Rules] |
| 6205(5) | [Specified person] |

1934

## Detailed Table of Sections

| | |
|---|---|
| 6206 | [Prescribed share for ITA 84(8)] |
| 6207 | Idem |
| 6208 | Prescribed securities |
| 6208(1) | [Non-resident withholding tax — prescribed security] |
| 6208(2) | [Consideration for fraction of a share] |
| 6208(3) | ["Specified person"] |
| 6209 | [Lending assets — prescribed shares and property] |
| 6210 | [Proposed] [Prescribed debt obligation] |

### Part LXIII — Child Tax Benefits

| | |
|---|---|
| 6300 | Interpretation |
| 6301 | Non-application of presumption |
| 6302 | Factors |

### Part LXIV — Prescribed Dates

| | |
|---|---|
| 6400 | |
| 6400(1) | Child tax credits |
| 6401 | Quebec tax abatement |

### Part LXV — Prescribed Laws

| | |
|---|---|
| 6500 | Interpretation |
| 6501 | Prescribed provisions of the law of a province |
| 6502 | Prescribed class of persons |
| 6503 | Prescribed acts |

### Part LXVI — Prescribed Order

| | |
|---|---|
| 6600 | Prescribed order |

### Part LXVII — Prescribed Venture Capital Corporations, Labour-Sponsored Venture Capital Corporations, Investment Contract Corporations, Qualifying Corporations and Prescribed Stock Savings Plan

| | |
|---|---|
| 6700–6700.2 | Prescribed venture capital corporations |
| 6701 | Prescribed labour-sponsored venture capital corporations |
| 6701 | [Proposed] Prescribed labour-sponsored venture capital corporations |
| 6702 | Prescribed assistance |
| 6703 | Prescribed investment contract corporation |
| 6704 | Prescribed qualifying corporation |
| 6705 | Prescribed stock savings plan |
| 6706 | Prescribed condition |
| 6707 | [Provincially registered LSVCCs] |

### Part LXVIII — Prescribed Plans, Arrangements and Contributions

| | |
|---|---|
| 6800 | Prescribed plan |
| 6801–6803 | Prescribed plan or arrangement |
| 6804 | Contributions to foreign plans |
| 6804(1) | Definitions |
| 6804(2) | Electing employer |
| 6804(3) | Election by union |
| 6804(4) | Contributions made before 1992 |
| 6804(5) | Contributions made in 1992, 1993 or 1994 |
| 6804(6) | Contributions made after 1994 |
| 6804(7) | Replacement plan |

### Part LXIX — Prescribed Offshore Investment Fund Properties

| | |
|---|---|
| 6900 | Prescribed offshore investment fund properties |

### Part LXX — Accrued Interest on Debt Obligations

| | |
|---|---|
| 7000 | Prescribed debt obligations |
| 7001 | Indexed debt obligations |

### Part LXXI — Prescribed Federal Crown Corporations

| | |
|---|---|
| 7100 | Corporations prescribed |

### Part LXXII — Cumulative Deduction Account

| | |
|---|---|
| 7200 | Prescribed addition and reduction |

1935

## Detailed Table of Sections

### Part LXXIII — Prescribed Amounts and Areas

| | |
|---|---|
| 7300, 7301 | [Prescribed amounts] |
| 7302, 7303 | [Revoked] |
| 7303.1 | Prescribed zones |
| 7303.1(1) | [Prescribed northern zone] |
| 7303.1(2) | [Prescribed intermediate zone] |
| 7304 | Travel costs |
| 7304(1) | [Definitions] |
| 7304(2) | [Trip cost] |
| 7304(3) | [Period travel cost] |
| 7304(4) | [Prescribed amounts] |
| 7305 | [Prescribed drought regions] |
| 7305.01 | [Prescribed drought regions — surrounded areas] |
| 7305.1 | [Automobile operating expenses] |
| 7306 | [Tax-free car allowances] |
| 7307 | |
| 7307(1) | [Automobiles — CCA cost limit] |
| 7307(2) | [Automobiles — interest expense limit] [Repealed] |
| 7307(3), (4) | [Automobile — leasing limit] |
| 7308 | Prescribed amounts — RRIF |

### Part LXXIV — Prescribed Tax Treaty Provisions and Election

| | |
|---|---|
| 7400 | Prescribed treaty provisions |

### Part LXXV — Prescribed Film Productions and Revenue Guarantees

| | |
|---|---|
| 7500 | Interpretation |

### Part LXXVI — Carved-Out Property Exclusion

| | |
|---|---|
| 7600 | Prescribed property |

### Part LXXVII — Prescribed Prizes

| | |
|---|---|
| 7700 | Prescribed prizes |

### Part LXXVIII — Prescribed Provincial Pension Plans

| | |
|---|---|
| 7800 | Prescribed provincial pension plan, prescribed amount |

### Part LXXIX — Prescribed Financial Institutions

| | |
|---|---|
| 7900 | Prescribed financial institution |

### Part LXXX — Prescribed Reserve Amount and Recovery Rate

| | |
|---|---|
| 8000 | [Prescribed reserve amount] |
| 8001 | [Repealed] |
| 8002 | [Principal amount, amortized cost] |
| 8003 | [Election] |
| 8004 | [Repealed] |
| 8005 | [Rules — loans and lending assets] |
| 8006 | Interpretation |
| 8007 | [Repealed] |

### Part LXXXI — Transition for Financial Institutions

| | |
|---|---|
| 8100 | Transition deduction in respect of unpaid claims reserve |
| 8101 | Inclusion of transition amount in respect of unpaid claims reserve |
| 8102–8105 | [Repealed] |
| 8102 | [Proposed] Mark-to-market — transition deduction |
| 8103 | [Proposed] Mark-to-market — transition inclusion |
| 8104 | [Proposed] Mark-to-market — transition capital loss |
| 8105 | [Proposed] Mark-to-market — transition capital gains |

### Part LXXXII — Prescribed Properties and Permanent Establishments

| | |
|---|---|
| 8200 | Prescribed properties |
| 8200.1 | [Prescribed energy conservation property] |
| 8201 | Permanent establishments |
| 8201.1 | [Repealed] |

Detailed Table of Sections

**PART LXXXIII — PENSION ADJUSTMENTS, PAST SERVICE PENSION ADJUSTMENTS, PENSION ADJUSTMENT REVERSALS AND PRESCRIBED AMOUNTS**

| | |
|---|---|
| 8300 | Interpretation |
| 8301 | Pension adjustment |
| 8301(1) | Pension adjustment with respect to employer |
| 8301(2) | Pension credit — deferred profit sharing plan |
| 8301(3) | Non-vested termination from DPSP |
| 8301(4) | Pension credit — money purchase provision |
| 8301(4.1) | Money purchase pension credits based on amounts allocated |
| 8301(5) | Pension credit — defined benefit provision of a specified multi-employer plan |
| 8301(6) | Pension credit — defined benefit provision |
| 8301(7) | Pension credit — defined benefit provision of a multi-employer plan |
| 8301(8) | Non-vested termination from RPP |
| 8301(9) | Multi-employer plans |
| 8301(10) | Transition rule — money purchase offsets |
| 8301(11) | Timing of contributions |
| 8301(12) | Indirect contributions |
| 8301(13) | Apportionment of payments |
| 8301(14) | Non-compliance by contributing entity |
| 8301(15) | Transferred amounts |
| 8301(16) | Subsequent events |
| 8302 | Benefit entitlement |
| 8302(1) | Idem |
| 8302(2) | Benefit accrual for year |
| 8302(3) | Normalized pensions |
| 8302(4) | Optional forms |
| 8302(5) | Termination of entitlement to benefits |
| 8302(6) | Defined benefit offset |
| 8302(7) | Offset of specified multi-employer plan benefits |
| 8302(8) | Transition rule — career average benefits |
| 8302(9) | Transition rule — benefit rate greater than 2 per cent |
| 8302(10) | Period of reduced remuneration |
| 8302(11) | Anti-avoidance |
| 8303 | Past service pension adjustment |
| 8303(1) | PSPA with respect to employer |
| 8303(2) | Accumulated PSPA for year |
| 8303(2.1) | 1991 past service events and certifications |
| 8303(3) | Provisional PSPA |
| 8303(4) | Redetermined benefit entitlement |
| 8303(5) | Normalized pension |
| 8303(6) | Qualifying transfers |
| 8303(6) | [Proposed] Qualifying transfers |
| 8303(6.1) | Exclusion for pre-1990 benefits |
| 8303(7) | Deemed payment |
| 8303(7.1) | Excess money purchase transfer |
| 8303(8) | Specified multi-employer plan |
| 8303(9) | Conditional contributions |
| 8303(10) | Benefits in respect of foreign service |
| 8304 | Past service benefits — Additional rules |
| 8304(1) | Replacement of defined benefits |
| 8304(2) | Replacement of money purchase benefits |
| 8304(3) | Past service benefits in year of past service event |
| 8304(4) | Exceptions |
| 8304(5) | Modified PSPA calculation |
| 8304(5.1) | Definitions for subsection (5) |
| 8304(6) | Reinstatement of pre-1997 benefits |
| 8304(7) | Two or more employers |
| 8304(8) | [Repealed] |
| 8304(9) | Specified multi-employer plans |
| 8304.1 | Pension adjustment reversal |
| 8304.1(1) | Total pension adjustment reversal |

## Detailed Table of Sections

| | |
|---|---|
| 8304.1(2) | Termination in 1997 |
| 8304.1(3) | PAR — deferred profit sharing plan |
| 8304.1(4) | PAR — money purchase provision |
| 8304.1(5) | PAR — defined benefit provision |
| 8304.1(6) | Defined benefit pension credits |
| 8304.1(7) | Grossed-up PSPA amount |
| 8304.1(8) | Specified distribution |
| 8304.1(9) | Property made available |
| 8304.1(10) | PA transfer amount |
| 8304.1(11) | Special 1997 PA transfer amount |
| 8304.1(12) | Subsequent membership |
| 8304.1(13) | Termination conditions — deferred profit sharing plan |
| 8304.1(14) | Termination conditions — registered pension plan |
| 8304.1(15) | Marriage breakdown |
| 8305 | Association of benefits with employers |
| 8306 | Exemption from certification |
| 8307 | Certification in respect of past service events |
| 8307(1) | Application for certification |
| 8307(2) | Prescribed condition |
| 8307(3) | Qualifying withdrawals |
| 8307(4) | Eligibility of withdrawn amount for designation |
| 8307(5) | PSPA withdrawals |
| 8307(6) | Prescribed withdrawal |
| 8307(6) | [Proposed] Prescribed withdrawal |
| 8307(7) | Prescribed premium |
| 8308 | Special rules |
| 8308(1) | Benefits provided before registration |
| 8308(2) | Prescribed amount for connected persons |
| 8308(3) | Remuneration for prior years |
| 8308(4) | Period of reduced services — retroactive benefits |
| 8308(5) | Period of reduced services — retroactive contributions |
| 8308(6) | Commitment to make retroactive contributions |
| 8308(7) | Loaned employees |
| 8308(8) | Successor plans |
| 8308(9) | Special downsizing benefits |
| 8308.1 | Foreign plans |
| 8308.1(1) | Definitions |
| 8308.1(2) | Pension credit |
| 8308.1(3) | Pension credit — alternative determination |
| 8308.1(4) | Pension credits for 1992, 1993 and 1994 |
| 8308.1(4.1) | Pension credits — 1996 to 2003 |
| 8308.1(5) | Foreign plan PSPA |
| 8308.1(6) | Foreign plan PSPA — alternative determination |
| 8308.2 | Prescribed amount for member of foreign plan |
| 8308.2(1) | Prescribed amount |
| 8308.2(2) | Prescribed amounts — 1997 to 2004 |
| 8308.3 | Specified retirement arrangements |
| 8308.3(1) | Definition |
| 8308.3(2) | Pension credit |
| 8308.3(3) | Pension credit — alternative determination |
| 8308.3(3.1) | Pension credits — 1996 to 2003 |
| 8308.3(4) | Specified retirement arrangement PSPA |
| 8308.3(5) | Specified retirement arrangement PSPA — alternative determination |
| 8308.4 | Government-sponsored retirement arrangements |
| 8308.4(1) | Definitions |
| 8308.4(2) | Prescribed amount |
| 8309 | Prescribed amount for lieutenant governors and judges |
| 8310 | Minister's powers |
| 8311 | Rounding of amounts |

Detailed Table of Sections

### PART LXXXIV — RETIREMENT AND PROFIT SHARING PLANS — REPORTING AND PROVISION OF INFORMATION

| | |
|---|---|
| 8400 | Definitions |
| 8401 | Pension adjustment |
| 8402 | Past service pension adjustment |
| 8402.01 | Pension adjustment reversal |
| 8402.01(1) | Deferred profit sharing plan |
| 8402.01(2) | Deferred profit sharing plan — employer reporting |
| 8402.01(3) | Benefit provision of a registered pension plan |
| 8402.01(4) | Extended deadline — PA transfer amount |
| 8402.01(5) | Calendar year quarter |
| 8402.1 | Government-sponsored retirement arrangements |
| 8403 | Connected persons |
| 8404 | Reporting to individuals |
| 8405 | Discontinuance of business |
| 8406 | Provision of information |
| 8407 | Qualifying withdrawals |
| 8408 | Requirement to provide Minister with information |
| 8409 | Annual information returns |
| 8410 | Actuarial reports |

### PART LXXXV — REGISTERED PENSION PLANS

| | |
|---|---|
| 8500 | Interpretation |
| 8500(8) | [Proposed] [Member and non-member benefits] |
| 8501 | Prescribed conditions for registration and other conditions applicable to registered pension plans |
| 8501(1) | Conditions for registration |
| 8501(2) | Conditions applicable to registered pension plans |
| 8501(3) | Permissive rules |
| 8501(4) | Supplemental plans |
| 8501(5) | Benefits payable to spouse after marriage breakdown |
| 8501(6) | Indirect contributions |
| 8501(6.1) | [Proposed] Member contributions for unfunded liability |
| 8501(6.2) | [Proposed] Prescribed eligible contributions |
| 8501(7) | Benefits provided with surplus on plan wind-up |
| 8502 | Conditions applicable to all plans |
| 8502(a) | primary purpose |
| 8502(b) | permissible contributions |
| 8502(c) | permissible benefits |
| 8502(d) | permissible distributions |
| 8502(e) | payment of pension |
| 8502(f) | assignment of rights |
| 8502(g) | funding media |
| 8502(h) | investments |
| 8502(i) | borrowing |
| 8502(j) | determination of amounts |
| 8502(k) | transfer of property between provisions |
| 8502(k) | [Proposed] transfer of property between provisions |
| 8502(l) | appropriate pension adjustments |
| 8502(m) | participants in GSRAs |
| 8503 | Defined benefit provisions |
| 8503(1) | Net contribution accounts |
| 8503(2) | Permissible benefits |
| 8503(2)(a) | lifetime retirement benefits |
| 8503(2)(b) | bridging benefits |
| 8503(2)(c) | guarantee period |
| 8503(2)(d) | post-retirement survivor benefits |
| 8503(2)(e) | pre-retirement survivor benefits |
| 8503(2)(f) | pre-retirement survivor benefits — alternative rule |
| 8503(2)(g) | pre-retirement survivor benefits — guarantee period |
| 8503(2)(h) | lump-sum payments on termination |
| 8503(2)(i) | payment of commuted value of benefits on death before retirement |
| 8503(2)(j) | lump sum payments on death |

## Detailed Table of Sections

| | |
|---|---|
| 8503(2)(k) | additional post-retirement death benefits |
| 8503(2)(l) | additional bridging benefits |
| 8503(2)(l.1) | [Proposed] survivor bridging benefits |
| 8503(2)(m) | commutation of benefits |
| 8503(2)(m) | [Proposed] commutation of benefits |
| 8503(2)(n) | [commutation of benefits] |
| 8503(2.1) | [Proposed] Rule for commutation of benefits |
| 8503(3) | Conditions applicable to benefits |
| 8503(3)(a) | eligible service |
| 8503(3)(b) | benefit accruals after pension commencement |
| 8503(3)(c) | early retirement |
| 8503(3)(d) | increased benefits for disabled member |
| 8503(3)(e) | pre-1991 benefits |
| 8503(3)(f) | determination of retirement benefits |
| 8503(3)(g) | benefit accrual rate |
| 8503(3)(h) | increase in accrued benefits |
| 8503(3)(i) | [idem] |
| 8503(3)(j) | offset benefits |
| 8503(3)(k) | bridging benefits — cross-plan restriction |
| 8503(3)(l) | division of benefits on marriage breakdown |
| 8503(4) | Additional conditions |
| 8503(4)(a) | member contributions |
| 8503(4)(b) | pre-payment of member contributions |
| 8503(4)(c) | reduction in benefits and return of contributions |
| 8503(4)(d) | undue deferral of payment |
| 8503(4)(e), (f) | evidence of disability |
| 8503(5) | Waiver of member contribution conditions |
| 8503(6) | Pre-retirement death benefits |
| 8503(7) | Commutation of lifetime retirement benefits |
| 8503(7.1) | [Proposed] Bridging benefits and election |
| 8503(8) | Suspension or cessation of pension |
| 8503(9) | Re-employed member |
| 8503(10) | Re-employed member — special rules not applicable |
| 8503(11) | Re-employed member — anti-avoidance |
| 8503(12) | Limits dependent on Consumer Price Index |
| 8503(13) | Statutory plans — special rules |
| 8503(14) | Artificially reduced pension adjustment |
| 8503(15) | Past service employer contributions |
| 8504 | Maximum benefits |
| 8504(1) | Lifetime retirement benefits |
| 8504(2) | Highest average compensation |
| 8504(3) | Alternative compensation rules |
| 8504(4) | Part-time employees |
| 8504(5) | Retirement benefits before age 65 |
| 8504(6) | Pre-1990 benefits |
| 8504(7) | Limit not applicable |
| 8504(8) | Cross-plan restrictions |
| 8504(9) | Associated defined benefit provisions |
| 8504(10)–(12) | Excluded benefits |
| 8504(13)–(15) | Alternative CPI indexing |
| 8505 | Additional benefits on downsizing |
| 8505(1) | Downsizing program |
| 8505(2) | Applicability of downsizing rules |
| 8505(2.1) | Qualifying individual — exclusion |
| 8505(3) | Additional lifetime retirement benefits |
| 8505(3.1) | Re-employed members |
| 8505(4) | Early retirement reduction |
| 8505(5) | Exception for future benefits |
| 8505(6) | Alternative CPI indexing |
| 8505(7) | Exclusion from maximum pension rules |
| 8505(8) | Exemption from past service contribution rule |

## Detailed Table of Sections

| | |
|---|---|
| 8506 | Money purchase provisions |
| 8506(1) | Permissible benefits |
| 8506(1)(a) | lifetime retirement benefits |
| 8506(1)(b) | bridging benefits |
| 8506(1)(c) | guarantee period |
| 8506(1)(d) | post-retirement surviving spouse benefits |
| 8506(1)(e) | pre-retirement surviving spouse benefits |
| 8506(1)(f) | payment from account |
| 8506(1)(g) | lump-sum payments on death before retirement |
| 8506(1)(h) | commutation of benefits |
| 8506(1)(i) | [idem] |
| 8506(2) | Additional conditions |
| 8506(2)(a) | employer contributions acceptable to minister |
| 8506(2)(b) | employer contributions with respect to particular members |
| 8506(2)(b.1) | allocation of employer contributions |
| 8506(2)(c) | employer contributions not permitted |
| 8506(2)(d) | return of contributions |
| 8506(2)(e) | allocation of earnings |
| 8506(2)(f) | payment or reallocation of forfeited amounts |
| 8506(2)(g) | retirement benefits |
| 8506(2)(h) | undue deferral of payment |
| 8506(2.1) | Alternative method for allocating employer contributions |
| 8506(3) | Reallocation of forfeitures |
| 8507 | Periods of reduced pay |
| 8507(1) | Prescribed compensation |
| 8507(2) | Additional compensation in respect of qualifying period |
| 8507(3) | Qualifying periods and periods of parenting |
| 8507(4) | Cumulative additional compensation fraction |
| 8507(5) | Additional compensation fraction |
| 8507(6) | Exclusion of subperiods |
| 8507(7) | Complete period of reduced pay |
| 8508 | Salary deferral leave plan |
| 8509 | Transition rules |
| 8509(1) | Prescribed conditions applicable before 1992 to grandfathered plan |
| 8509(2) | Conditions applicable after 1991 to benefits under grandfathered plan |
| 8509(3) | Additional prescribed condition for grandfathered plan after 1991 |
| 8509(4) | Defined benefits under grandfathered plan exempt from conditions |
| 8509(4.1) | Benefits under grandfathered plan — pre-1992 disability |
| 8509(5) | Conditions not applicable to grandfathered plan |
| 8509(6) | PA limits for grandfathered plan for 1991 |
| 8509(7) | Limit on pre-age 65 benefits |
| 8509(8) | Benefit accrual rate greater than 2 per cent |
| 8509(9) | Benefits under plan other than grandfathered plan |
| 8509(10) | Money purchase benefits exempt from conditions |
| 8509(10.1) | Stipulation not required for pre-1992 plans |
| 8509(11) | Benefits acceptable to Minister |
| 8509(12) | PA limits — 1996 to 2003 |
| 8509(13) | Maximum benefits indexed before 2005 |
| 8510 | Multi-employer plans and specified multi-employer plans |
| 8510(1) | Definition of "multi-employer plan" |
| 8510(2) | Definition of "specified multi-employer plan" |
| 8510(3) | Qualification as a specified multi-employer plan |
| 8510(4) | Minister's notice |
| 8510(5) | Special rules — multi-employer plan |
| 8510(6) | Special rules — specified multi-employer plan |
| 8510(7) | Additional prescribed conditions |
| 8510(8) | Purchase of additional benefits |
| 8511 | Conditions applicable to amendments |
| 8512 | Registration and amendment |
| 8513 | Designated laws |
| 8514 | Prohibited investments |

## Detailed Table of Sections

| | |
|---|---|
| 8514(1) | [Proposed] Prohibited investments |
| 8515 | Special rules for designated plans |
| 8515(1) | Designated plans |
| 8515(2) | Designated plan in previous year |
| 8515(3) | Exceptions |
| 8515(4) | Specified individuals |
| 8515(5) | Eligible contributions |
| 8515(6) | Funding restriction |
| 8515(7) | Maximum funding valuation |
| 8515(8) | Restricted-funding members |
| 8515(9) | Member contributions |
| 8516 | Eligible contributions |
| 8516(1) | Prescribed contribution |
| 8516(2) | Amortization of excess actuarial surplus |
| 8516(3) | Approval under paragraph 20(1)(s) of the Act |
| 8516(4) | Contributions pursuant to collective bargaining agreement |
| 8516(5) | Contributions pursuant to statute or by-law |
| 8516(6) | Employer not entitled to reduce contributions |
| 8516(7) | Funding on termination basis |
| 8516(8) | Contributions required by pension benefits legislation |
| 8516(9) | Actuarial reports signed before March 6, 1996 |
| 8517 | Transfer — defined benefit to money purchase |
| 8517(1) | Prescribed amount |
| 8517(2) | Minimum prescribed amount |
| 8517(3) | Plan wind-up or replacement |
| 8517(3.1) | Benefits provided with surplus on plan wind-up |
| 8517(4) | Amount of lifetime retirement benefits commuted |
| 8517(5) | Normalized pensions |
| 8517(6) | Optional forms |
| 8517(7) | Replacement benefits |
| 8518 | Pension adjustment limits |
| 8519 | Association of benefits with time periods |
| 8520 | Minister's actions |

### PART LXXXVI — TAXABLE CAPITAL EMPLOYED IN CANADA

| | |
|---|---|
| 8600 | [Definitions] |
| 8601 | [Prescribed proportion of taxable capital] |
| 8602 | [Prescribed proportion of amount under s. 123.2] |
| 8603 | [Definitions] |
| 8604 | [Prescribed corporations] |
| 8605 | [Prescribed corporations — 1991 *et seq.*] |

### PART LXXXVII — NATIONAL ARTS SERVICE ORGANIZATIONS

| | |
|---|---|
| 8700 | Prescribed conditions |

### PART LXXXVIII — DISABILITY-RELATED MODIFICATIONS AND APPARATUS

| | |
|---|---|
| 8800 | Prescribed renovations |
| 8801 | Prescribed equipment |

### PART LXXXIX — PRESCRIBED ORGANIZATIONS

| | |
|---|---|
| 8900 | International and international non-governmental organizations |

### PART XC — FINANCIAL INSTITUTIONS — PRESCRIBED ENTITIES

| | |
|---|---|
| 9000–9003 | [Proposed] Prescribed entities and securities |
| 9004 | Prescribed property |

### PART XCI — FINANCIAL INSTITUTIONS — INCOME FROM SPECIFIED DEBT OBLIGATIONS [PROPOSED]

| | |
|---|---|
| 9100 | [Proposed] Interpretation |
| 9101 | [Proposed] Prescribed inclusions and deductions |
| 9102 | [Proposed] General accrual rules |
| 9102(1) | [Proposed] Fixed payment obligations not in default |
| 9102(2) | [Proposed] Level-yield method |
| 9102(3) | [Proposed] Other obligations |
| 9102(4), (5) | [Proposed] Accrual adjustment |

## Detailed Table of Sections

| | |
|---|---|
| 9102(6) | [Proposed] Special cases and transition |
| 9103 | [Proposed] Accrual rules — special cases and transition |
| 9103(1) | [Proposed] Convertible obligation |
| 9103(2) | [Proposed] Default by debtor [temporary — see below] |
| 9103(3) | [Proposed] Amendment of obligation |
| 9103(4) | [Proposed] Obligations acquired before financial institution rules apply |
| 9103(5) | [Proposed] Prepaid interest — transition rule |
| 9104 | [Proposed] Foreign exchange adjustment |

**PART XCII — FINANCIAL INSTITUTIONS — DISPOSITION OF SPECIFIED DEBT OBLIGATIONS [PROPOSED]**

| | |
|---|---|
| 9200 | [Proposed] Interpretation |
| 9200(1) | [Proposed] Definitions |
| 9200(2) | [Proposed] Amortization date |
| 9201 | [Proposed] Transition amount |
| 9202 | [Proposed] Prescribed debt obligations |
| 9203 | [Proposed] Residual portion of gain or loss |
| 9203(1) | [Proposed] Allocation of residual portion |
| 9203(2) | [Proposed] Proration method |
| 9203(3) | [Proposed] Single proration period |
| 9203(4) | [Proposed] Weighted average amortization date |
| 9204 | [Proposed] Special rules for residual portion of gain or loss |
| 9204(1) | [Proposed] Application of section |
| 9204(2) | [Proposed] Winding-up |
| 9204(2.1) | [Proposed] Winding-up into authorized foreign bank |
| 9204(3) | [Proposed] Transfer of insurance business |
| 9204(4) | [Proposed] Transfer to new partnership |
| 9204(5) | [Proposed] Ceasing to carry on business |
| 9204(5.1) | [Proposed] Non-resident taxpayer |
| 9204(6) | [Proposed] Ceasing to be a financial institution |

**PART XCIII — FILM OR VIDEO PRODUCTION SERVICES TAX CREDIT [PROPOSED]**

| | |
|---|---|
| 9300 | [Proposed] Accredited production |

**SCHEDULE I — (SECS. 100, 102 AND 106) RANGES OF REMUNERATION AND OF TOTAL REMUNERATION**

**SCHEDULE II — CAPITAL COST ALLOWANCES**

**SCHEDULE III — CAPITAL COST ALLOWANCES, CLASS 13**

**SCHEDULE IV — CAPITAL COST ALLOWANCES, CLASS 15**

**SCHEDULE V — CAPITAL COST ALLOWANCES, INDUSTRIAL MINERAL MINES**

**SCHEDULE VI — CAPITAL COST ALLOWANCES, TIMBER LIMITS AND CUTTING RIGHTS**

**SCHEDULE VII — PUBLICLY-TRADED SHARES OR SECURITIES**

**SCHEDULE VIII — UNIVERSITIES OUTSIDE CANADA**

**SCHEDULES IX, X**

# INCOME TAX REGULATIONS
CONSOLIDATED REGULATIONS OF CANADA, CHAPTER 945
(CONSOLIDATED AS OF DECEMBER 31, 1977)
PROCLAIMED IN FORCE AUGUST 15, 1979, AS AMENDED TO FEBRUARY 1, 2001

Note: Editorial annotations have been added in square brackets to update references to the ITA where the numbering of the provision has changed as a result of the R.S.C. 1985, c. 1 (5th Supp.) consolidation. (See Reg. 4900(1) as an example.)

**1. Short title** — These Regulations may be cited as the *Income Tax Regulations*.

**2. Interpretation** — In these Regulations, "Act" means the *Income Tax Act*.

**Notes re Definitions**: Terms used in the regulations should be read with reference to sections 248–260 of the *Income Tax Act*. Section 16 of the *Interpretation Act* provides:

> 16. Words in Regulations — Where an enactment confers power to make regulations, expressions used in the regulations have the same respective meanings as in the enactment conferring the power.

Judicial notice is to be taken of the Regulations; see ITA 244(12).

## PART I — TAX DEDUCTIONS

**100. Interpretation** — (1) In this Part and in Schedule I,

"**employee**" means any person receiving remuneration;

"**employer**" means any person paying remuneration;

"**estimated deductions**" means, in respect of a taxation year, the total of the amounts estimated to be deductible by an employee for the year under any of paragraphs 8(1)(f), (h), (h.1), (i) and (j) of the Act and determined by the employee for the purpose of completing the form referred to in subsection 107(2);

**Notes**: Reference to ITA 8(1)(h.1) added by P.C. 1994-372, effective 1993.

"**exemptions**" — [Revoked]

**Notes**: The definition "exemptions" was revoked effective 1988, when personal exemptions were eliminated from sections 109–110 of the Act. See "personal credits" now.

"**pay period**" includes

(a) a day,

(b) a week,

(c) a two week period,

(d) a semi-monthly period,

(e) a month,

(f) a four week period,

(g) one tenth of a calendar year, or

(h) one twenty-second of a calendar year;

"**personal credits**" means, in respect of a particular taxation year, the aggregate of

(a) the greater of

(i) the amount referred to in paragraph 118(1)(c) of the Act, and

(ii) the aggregate of the credits which the employee would be entitled to claim for the year under

(A) subsections 118(1), (2) and (3) of the Act if the description of A in those subsections were read as "is equal to one",

(B) subsections 118.3(1) and (2) of the Act if the description of A in subsection 118.3(1) of the Act were read as "is equal to one" and if subsection 118.3(1) of the Act were read without reference to paragraph (c) thereof,

(C) subsections 118.5(1) and 118.6(2) of the Act if subsection 118.5(1) of the Act were read without reference to "the product obtained when the appropriate percentage for the year is multiplied by" and the description of A in subsection 118.6(2) of the Act were read as "is equal to one", and after deducting from the aggregate of the amounts determined under those subsections the excess over $500 of the aggregate of amounts that the employee claims to expect to receive in the year on account of a scholarship, fellowship or bursary,

(D) section 118.8 of the Act if the formula $A + B - C$ in that section were read as

$$\frac{A + B}{D}$$

where D is the appropriate percentage for the year, and

(E) subsection 118.9(1) of the Act if the formula $A - B$ in that subsection were read as

$$\frac{A}{C}$$

where C is the appropriate percentage for the year, and

(b) where the remuneration paid by the employer is pension income or qualified pension income of the employee in respect of which subsection 118(3) of the Act would apply if that subsection were read without reference to subparagraphs (b)(ii) and (iii) thereof, a credit equal to the lesser of

(i) $1,000, and

(ii) the employee's pension income or qualified pension income for the year;

**Notes**: Subpara. (a)(ii) amended by P.C. 1994-372, effective 1993. For 1989-92, read:

(ii) the amount by which the aggregate of the credits which the employee would be entitled to claim for the year under

(A) subsections 118(1), (2) and (3) of the Act if the description of A in those subsections were read as "is one",

(B) subsection 118.3(1) of the Act if the description of A in that subsection were read as "is one" and if that subsection were read without reference to paragraph (c) thereof, and

(C) subsections 118.5(1) and 118.6(2) of the Act if subsection 118.5(1) of the Act were read without reference to "the product obtained when the appropriate percentage for the year is multiplied by" and the description of A in subsection 118.6(2) of the Act were read as "is one", and after deducting from the aggregate of the amounts so determined under those subsections the excess over $500 of the aggregate of amounts that the employee claims to expect to receive in the year on account of a scholarship, fellowship or bursary

"**remuneration**" includes any payment that is

(a) in respect of

(i) salary or wages, or

(ii) commissions or other similar amounts fixed by reference to the volume of the sales made or the contracts negotiated (referred to as "commissions" in this Part),

paid to an officer or employee or former officer or employee,

(a.1) in respect of an employee's gratuities required under provincial legislation to be declared to the employee's employer,

(b) a superannuation or pension benefit (including an annuity payment made pursuant to or under a superannuation or pension fund or plan),

(b.1) an amount of a distribution out of or under a retirement compensation arrangement,

(c) a retiring allowance,

(d) a death benefit,

(e) a benefit under a supplementary unemployment benefit plan,

(f) a payment under a deferred profit sharing plan or a plan referred to in section 147 of the Act as a "revoked plan", reduced, if applicable, by amounts determined under subsections 147(10.1), (11) and (12) of the Act,

(g) a benefit under the *Employment Insurance Act*,

(h) an amount that is required by paragraph 56(1)(r) of the Act to be included in computing a taxpayer's income, except the portion of the amount that relates to child care expenses and tuition costs,

(i) a payment made during the lifetime of an annuitant referred to in subparagraph 146(1)(a)(i) [146(1)"annuitant"(a)] of the Act out of or under a registered retirement savings plan of that annuitant, other than

(i) a periodic annuity payment, or

(ii) a payment made by a person who has reasonable grounds to believe that the payment may be deducted under subsection 146(8.2) of the Act in computing the income of any taxpayer,

(j) a payment out of or under a plan referred to in subsection 146(12) of the Act as an "amended plan" other than

(i) a periodic annuity payment, or

(ii) where paragraph 146(12)(a) of the Act applied to the plan after May 25, 1976, a payment made in a year subsequent to the year in which that paragraph applied to the plan, or

(j.1) a payment made during the lifetime of an annuitant referred to in the definition "annuitant" in subsection 146.3(1) of the Act under a registered retirement income fund of that annuitant, other than a particular payment to the extent that

(i) the particular payment is in respect of the minimum amount (in this paragraph having the meaning assigned by subsection 146.3(1) of the Act) under the fund for a year, or

(ii) where the fund governs a trust, the particular payment would be in respect of the minimum amount under the fund for a year if each amount that, at the beginning of the year, is scheduled to be paid after the time of the particular payment and in the year to the trust under an annuity contract that is held by the trust both at the beginning of the year and at the time of the particular payment, is paid to the trust in the year,

(k) a benefit described in section 5502,

(l) an amount as, on account or in lieu of payment of, or in satisfaction of, proceeds of the surrender, cancellation or redemption of an income-averaging annuity contract,

(m) in respect of an amount that can reasonably be regarded as having been received, in whole or in part, as consideration or partial consideration for entering into a contract of service, where the service is to be performed in Canada, or for an undertaking not to enter into such a contract with another party, or

(n) a payment out of a registered education savings plan other than

(i) a refund of payments,

(ii) an educational assistance payment, or

(iii) an amount, up to $50,000, of an accumulated income payment that is made to a subscriber, as defined in subsection 204.94(1) of the Act, or if there is no subscriber at that time, that is made to a person that has been a spouse of an individual who was a subscriber, if

(A) that amount is transferred to an RRSP in which the annuitant is either the recipient of the payment or the recipient's spouse, and

(B) it is reasonable for the person making the payment to believe that that amount is deductible for the year by the recipient of the payment within the limits provided for in subsection 146(5) or (5.1) of the Act;

**Notes:** "Salary or wages" in subpara. (a)(i) includes *all* employment income including benefits calculation under ITA ss. 6 and 7. See ITA 248(1)"salary or wages". Withholding is therefore calculated on the employee's total pay and (taxable) benefit package.

Para. (a.1) added by P.C. 1998-654, effective 1998. It links to a rule that allow tips to qualify for EI where they are required under provincial legislation to be declared to the employer. Quebec is the only province that requires this. See Quebec Government news release of Nov. 26/97, and federal Dept. of Finance news release of Dec. 23/97 (reproduced in *Department of Finance Technical Notes*).

Para. (g) amended by P.C. 1998-2270, effective for 1998 and later taxation years, to change "*Unemployment Insurance Act, 1971*" to "*Employment Insurance*" Act.

Para. (h) amended by P.C. 1998-2270, effective for 1998 and later taxation years. From August 2, 1982 through 1997, read:

(h) a training allowance paid under the *National Training Act*, except to the extent that it was paid to the recipient thereof as or on account of an allowance for his personal or living expenses while he was away from home,

Subpara. (i)(ii) amended by P.C. 1991-2540, effective 1991. For 1990 and earlier years, read:

(ii) a payment received by a taxpayer in a year in respect of an excess amount previously paid under the registered retirement savings plan to the extent that the excess amount may be deducted in computing the taxpayer's income for the year pursuant to subsection 146(8.2) of the Act.

Subpara. (j.1)(ii) added by P.C. 2000-184, effective for 1998 and later taxation years. It provides for exemption from withholding for RRIF distributions based on an estimate of the minimum amount. This is only relevant to RRIF trusts that hold annuity contracts, as permitted under ITA 146.3(1)"qualified investment"(b.1)–(b.2). In such cases, the minimum amount cannot be determined with certainty until the end of the year and an estimate is required to ensure that the exemption applies.

Para. (k) changed from "a benefit under the *Labour Adjustments Benefits Act*" by P.C. 1995-1023, effective for benefits paid after October 1991.

Para. (n) added by P.C. 1998-2275, effective for 1998 and later taxation years.

References to "spouse" are expected to be amended to add "or common-law partner" effective 2001 or earlier by election, as has been done throughout the ITA. See Notes to ITA 248(1)"common-law partner".

"**total remuneration**" means, in respect of a taxation year, the total of all amounts each of which is an amount referred to in paragraph (a) or (a.1) of the definition "remuneration".

**Notes:** Reference to para. (a.1) added by P.C. 1998-654, effective 1998.

**(2) [Indexing]** — Where the amount of any credit referred to in subparagraph (a)(i) or (ii) of the definition "personal credits" in subsection (1) is subject to an annual adjustment under section 117.1 of the Act, such amount shall, in a particular taxation year, be subject to that annual adjustment.

**(3) [Amounts excluded from base for withholding]** — For the purposes of this Part, where an employer deducts or withholds from a payment of remuneration to an employee one or more amounts each of which is

(a) a contribution to or under a registered pension fund or plan,

(b) dues described in subparagraph 8(1)(i)(iv), (v) or (vi) of the Act paid on account of the employee,

(b.1) a contribution by the employee under subparagraph 8(1)(m.2) of the Act,

(c) a premium under a registered retirement savings plan, or

(d) a payment to which paragraph 60(b) of the Act applies, where the payment was made as a result of a garnishee or similar order of a court or competent tribunal received by the employer and dated before May 1997,

the balance remaining after deducting or withholding this amount, as the case may be, shall be deemed to be the amount of that payment of remuneration.

**Related Provisions:** Reg. 100(3.1) — Northern Canada residents; Reg. 100(3.2) — Exceptions to rule in 100(3).

**Notes:** Reg. 100(3)(b.1) added by P.C. 1997-1471, in force October 29, 1997.

Reg. 100(3)(c) and (d) added by P.C. 1994-372, effective 1993. The Ontario Family Support Plan requires support payments to be withheld by the employer at source.

Reg. 100(3)(d) amended by P.C. 1997-1471, effective May 1, 1997. From January 1993 through April 1997, read Reg. 100(3)(d) as:

(d) a payment to which any of paragraphs 60(b) to (c.1) of the Act applies,

The stated reason for this change was that child support is now generally not deductible. However, as a result of this change, *spousal* support withheld by an employer (e.g., under the Ontario Family Support Plan), which is deductible to the payer, will not reduce source withholdings unless special application is made under ITA 153(1.1) (the "undue hardship" rule), or unless there is a Court garnishment issued before May 1997.

**I.T. Technical News:** No. 19 (Retiring allowances — clarification to Interpretation Bulletin IT-337R3 — (d): Deductions at source.

**Forms:** TD2: Tax deduction waiver in respect of funds to be transferred.

**(3.1) [Northern residents' deduction]** — For the purposes of this Part, where an employee has claimed a deduction for a taxation year under paragraph 110.7(1)(b) of the Act as shown on the return most recently filed by the employee with the employee's employer pursuant to subsection 227(2) of the Act, the amount of remuneration otherwise determined, including the amount deemed by subsection (3) to be the amount of that payment of remuneration, paid to the employee for a pay period shall be reduced by an amount equal to the amount of the deduction divided by the maximum number of pay periods in the year in respect of the appropriate pay period.

**Notes**: Reg. 100(3.1) amended by P.C. 1994-372, effective 1993, to update reference from ITA 110.7(1)(e) to 110.7(1)(b).

**(3.2) [Exceptions to subsec. (3)]** — Subsection (3) does not apply to a payment of remuneration that is

(a) a retiring allowance, to the extent that it exceeds the total determined under subparagraph 60(j.1)(ii) of the Act in respect of the retiring allowance; or

(b) a lump sum payment (other than a retiring allowance), within the meaning assigned by subsection 103(6), or a bonus or retroactive payment, if the amount of the payment of remuneration exceeds $10,000.

**Notes**: Reg. 100(3.2) added by P.C. 1997-1471, in force October 29, 1997.

**(4) [Establishment of the employer]** — For the purposes of this Part, where an employee is not required to report for work at any establishment of the employer, he shall be deemed to report for work

(a) in respect of remuneration that is salary, wages or commissions, at the establishment of the employer from which the remuneration is paid; or

(b) in respect of remuneration other than salary, wages or commissions, at the establishment of the employer in the province where the employee resides at the time the remuneration is paid but, if the employer does not have an establishment in that province at that time, he shall, for the purposes of this paragraph, be deemed to have an establishment in that province.

**(5) [LSVCC share purchase]** — For the purposes of this Part, where an employer deducts or withholds from a payment of remuneration to an employee an amount in respect of the acquisition by the employee of an approved share, as defined in subsection 127.4(1) of the Act, there shall be deducted from the amount determined under paragraph 102(1)(e) or (2)(f), as the case may be, in respect of that payment the lesser of

(a) $750, and

(b) 15% of the amount deducted or withheld in respect of the acquisition of an approved share.

**Notes**: Reg. 100(5)(a) and (b) amended by P.C. 1998-2270, effective for 1998 and later taxation years. For 1993-97, read:

(a) $1,000, and

(b) 20 per cent of the cost of the approved share to the employee.

Reg. 100(5) added by P.C. 1994-372, effective 1993.

**Definitions [Reg. 100]**: "accumulated income payment" — ITA 146.1(1); "amount", "annuity" — ITA 248(1); "appropriate percentage" — ITA 248(1); "Canada" — ITA 255, *Interpretation Act* 35(1); "commissions" — Reg. 100(1) "remuneration"(a)(ii); "death benefit" — ITA 248(1); "deferred profit sharing plan" — ITA 147(1), 248(1); "educational assistance payment" — ITA 146.1(1); "employee", "employer" — Reg. 100(1); "income-averaging annuity contract" — ITA 248(1); "month" — *Interpretation Act* 35(1); "officer" — ITA 248(1); "pay period" — Reg. 100(1); "person" — ITA 248(1); "personal credits" — Reg. 100(1); "personal or living expenses" — ITA 248(1); "province" — *Interpretation Act* 35(1); "refund of payments" — ITA 146.1(1); "registered education savings plan" — ITA 146.1(1), 248(1); "registered pension fund or plan" — ITA 248(1); "registered retirement income fund" — ITA 146.3(1), 248(1); "registered retirement savings plan" — ITA 146.1(1), 248(1); "remuneration" — Reg. 100(1); "retirement compensation arrangement", "retiring allowance", "salary or wages", "share" — ITA 248(1); "subscriber" — ITA 146.1(1); "supplementary unemployment benefit plan" — ITA 145(1), 248(1); "taxation year" — ITA 249; "taxpayer" — ITA 248(1); "trust" — ITA 104(1), 248(1), (3).

**101. Deductions and remittances** — Every person who makes a payment described in subsection 153(1) of the Act in a taxation year shall deduct or withhold therefrom, and remit to the Receiver General, such amount, if any, as is determined in accordance with rules prescribed in this Part.

**Related Provisions**: ITA 227 — Obligations with respect to amounts withheld.

**Definitions [Reg. 101]**: "amount", "person", "prescribed" — ITA 248(1); "taxation year" — ITA 249.

**102. Periodic payments — (1) [Amount to be withheld]** — Except as otherwise provided in this Part, the amount to be deducted or withheld by an employer

(a) from any payment of remuneration (in this subsection referred to as the "payment") made to an employee in his taxation year where he reports for work at an establishment of the employer in a province, in Canada beyond the limits of any province or outside Canada, and

(b) for any pay period in which the payment is made by the employer

shall be determined for each payment in accordance with the following rules:

(c) an amount that is a notional remuneration for the year in respect of

(i) a payment to the employee, and

(ii) the amount, if any, of gratuities referred to in paragraph (a.1) of the definition "remuneration" in subsection 100(1)

is deemed to be the amount determined by the formula

$$A \times B$$

where

A is the amount that is deemed for the purpose of this paragraph to be the mid-point of the applicable range of remuneration for the pay period, as provided in Schedule I, in which falls the total of

(A) the payment referred to in subparagraph (i) made in the pay period, and

(B) the amount of gratuities referred to in subparagraph (ii) declared by the employee for the pay period, and

B is the maximum number of such pay periods in that year;

(d) if the employee is not resident in Canada at the time of the payment, no personal credits will be allowed for the purposes of this subsection and if the employee is resident in Canada at the time of the payment, the employee's personal credits for the year shall be established as, where they fall within a range of amounts recorded on the return for the year referred to in subsection 107(1) that is in respect of

(i) one of claim codes 2 to 10 on that return, the midpoint of the applicable range, or

(ii) claim code 1 on that return, the amount determined for the year under paragraph (a) of the definition "personal credits" in subsection 100(1);

(e) an amount (in this subsection referred to as the "notional tax for the year") shall be computed in respect of that employee by

(i) calculating the amount of tax payable for the year, as if that amount were calculated under subsection 117(2) of the Act and adjusted annually pursuant to section 117.1 of the Act, on the amount determined in accordance with paragraph (c) as if that amount represented the employee's amount taxable for that year,

and deducting the aggregate of

(ii) the amount determined in accordance with paragraph (d) multiplied by the appropriate percentage for the year,

(iii) an amount equal to

(A) the amount determined in accordance with paragraph (c) multiplied by the employee's premium rate for the year under the *Employment Insurance Act*, not exceeding the maximum amount of the premiums payable by the employee for the year under that Act,

multiplied by

(B) the appropriate percentage for the year, and

(iv) an amount equal to

(A) the product obtained when the difference between the amount determined in accordance with paragraph (c) and the amount determined under section 20 of the *Canada Pension Plan* for the year is multiplied by the employee's contribution rate for the year under the *Canada Pension Plan* or under a provincial pension plan as defined in subsection 3(1) of that Act, not exceeding the maximum amount of such contributions payable by the employee for the year under the plan,

multiplied by

(B) the appropriate percentage for the year;

(f) the amount determined in accordance with paragraph (e) shall be increased by

(i) where applicable, an additional tax of 52 per cent of that amount as provided for in subsection 120(1) of the Act, and

(ii) an amount equal to the amount that would be determined under subsection 180.1(1) of the Act for the year in respect of the employee if the amount determined in accordance with paragraph (e) were that employee's tax payable under Part I of the Act for that year;

(g) where the amount of notional remuneration for the year is income earned in the Province of Quebec, the amount determined in accordance with paragraph (e) shall be reduced by an amount that is the aggregate of

(i) the amount that is deemed to be paid under subsection 120(2) of the Act as if there were no other source of income or loss for the year, and

(ii) the amount by which the amount referred to in subparagraph (i) is increased by virtue of section 27 of the *Federal-Provincial Fiscal Arrangements Act*; and

(h) [Revoked]

(i) the amount to be deducted or withheld shall be computed by

(i) dividing the amount of the notional tax for the year by the maximum number of pay periods for the year in respect of the appropriate pay period, and

(ii) rounding the amount determined under subparagraph (i) to the nearest multiple of five cents or, if such amount is equidistant from two such multiples, to the higher multiple.

**Related Provisions**: Reg. 102(5) — Commission employees — exception.

**Notes**: Reg. 102(1)(c) amended by P.C. 1998-654, effective 1998. From July 1989 through 1997, read:

(c) an amount that is a notional remuneration for the year in respect of a payment to that employee shall be established by multiplying the amount of the payment that is deemed for the purposes of this paragraph to be the mid-point of the applicable range of remuneration for the pay period, as provided for in Schedule I, in which that payment falls, made in the pay period by the maximum number of such pay periods in that year;

Reg. 102(1)(d) reworded by P.C. 1994-372, effective 1993. The only substantive change was "claim code(s)" in place of "net claim code(s)".

Reg. 102(1)(e)(iii)(A) and (iv)(A) amended by P.C. 1991-142, P.C. 1992-2347 (effective 1992) and P.C. 1994-372; and (iii)(A) amended by P.C. 1998-2270, effective for 1998 and later taxation years, to change "*Unemployment Insurance Act*" to "*Employment Insurance Act*".

Reg. 102(1)(h) revoked by P.C. 1992-2347. Before 1992, read:

(h) reducing, with the approval of the Minister, the notional tax for the year otherwise determined in respect of the employee by an amount equal to the proportion of the notional tax for the year otherwise determined in respect of the employee that the lesser of the amounts determined under paragraphs 122.3(1)(c) and (d) of the Act in respect of the employee for the year is of the amount determined under paragraph 122.3(1)(e) of the Act in respect of the employee for the year; and

**Remission Orders**: *Income Earned in Quebec Income Tax Remission Order*, P.C. 1989-1204 (reduction in withholdings for certain income related to Quebec).

**Forms**: T4001: Employers' Guide to Payroll Deductions — Basic Information (guide).

**(2) [Commission employees]** — Where an employee has elected pursuant to subsection 107(2) and has not revoked such election, the amount to be deducted or withheld by the employer from any payment of remuneration (in this subsection referred to as the "payment") that is

(a) a payment in respect of commissions or is a combined payment of commissions and salary or wages, or

(b) a payment in respect of salary or wages where that employee receives a combined payment of commissions and salary or wages,

made to that employee in his taxation year where he reports for work at an establishment of the employer in a province, in Canada beyond the limits of any province or outside Canada, shall be determined for each payment in accordance with the following rules:

(c) the amount of that employee's total remuneration in respect of the year as recorded by him on the form referred to in subsection 107(2) (in this subsection referred to as "the form") shall be determined;

(d) the amount of that employee's personal credits and expenses in respect of the year as recorded by that employee on the form shall be determined as the aggregate of

(i) the amount that is either

(A) the employee's estimated deductions for that year, or

(B) the employee's total actual deductions under any of paragraphs 8(1)(f), (h), (h.1), (i) and (j) of the Act for the immediately preceding year, and

(ii) the amount determined by the formula

$$(A - B) \times \frac{C}{D}$$

where

A is the amount determined under paragraph (a) of the definition "personal credits" in subsection 100(1),

B is the amount referred to in paragraph 118(1)(c) of the Act,

C is the appropriate percentage for the year, and

D is

(A) 17 per cent, where the amount of the employee's total remuneration for the year, less the employee's expenses for the year as determined under subparagraph (i), does not exceed the amount taxable referred to in paragraph 117(2)(a) of the Act, as adjusted annually pursuant to section 117.1 of the Act,

(B) 26 per cent, where the amount of the employee's total remuneration for the year, less the employee's expenses for the year as determined under subparagraph (i), exceeds the amount referred to in clause (A) but does not exceed the amount taxable referred to in paragraph 117(2)(c) of the Act, as adjusted annually pursuant to section 117.1 of the Act, and

(C) 29 per cent, where the amount of the employee's total remuneration for the year, less the employee's expenses for the year as determined under subparagraph (i), exceeds the amount taxable referred to in paragraph 117(2)(c) of the Act, as adjusted annually pursuant to section 117.1 of the Act,

and the resulting amount shall be rounded to two places after the decimal, such that if the third digit is five or greater, the second digit will be increased by one, and if the third digit is less than five, the third digit will be dropped;

(e) where the amount determined under paragraph (c) in respect of that employee for the year falls within a range of remuneration provided for in section 2 of Schedule I, an amount (in this subsection referred to as the "notional net remuneration for the year") shall be calculated in respect of that employee by deducting from the mid-point of that range the greater of

(i) where the amount of that employee's personal credits and expenses for the year determined under paragraph (d) falls within a range of personal credits and expenses provided for in section 3 of Schedule I, the mid-point of that range, and

(ii) where the amount of that employee's personal credits and expenses for the year determined under paragraph (d) is less than $1,500, $1,500;

(f) an amount (in this subsection referred to as the "notional tax for the year") shall be calculated in respect of that employee by using the formula

$$A - [(B + C + D) \times E] + (F + G) - H$$

where

A is the amount of tax payable for the year, calculated as if that amount of tax were computed under subsection 117(2) of the Act and adjusted annually pursuant to section 117.1 of the Act, on the amount that would be determined in accordance with paragraph (e) if paragraph (d) were read without reference to subparagraph (ii) thereof, as if that amount represented the employee's amount taxable for that year,

B is the amount referred to in paragraph 118(1)(c) of the Act,

C is the mid-point of the range of remuneration referred to in paragraph (e) multiplied by the employee's premium rate for the year under the *Employment Insurance Act*, not exceeding the maximum amount of the premiums payable by the employee for the year under that Act,

D is the mid-point of the range of remuneration referred to in paragraph (e) less the amount for the year determined under section 20 of the *Canada Pension Plan* multiplied by the employee's contribution rate for the year under that Act or under a provincial plan as defined in section 3 of that Act, not exceeding the maximum amount of such contributions payable by the employee for the year under the plan,

E is the appropriate percentage for the year,

F is, where applicable, an additional tax of 52 per cent of that amount as provided for in subsection 120(1) of the Act,

G is an amount equal to the amount that would be determined under subsection 180.1(1) of the Act with respect to the employee if the amount that would be the notional tax for the year for the employee were determined without reference to the elements F, G and H in this formula and that tax were that employee's tax payable under Part I of the Act for that year, and

H is, where the amount of notional net remuneration for the year is income earned in the Province of Quebec, an amount equal to the aggregate of

(i) the amount that would be deemed to have been paid under subsection 120(2) of the Act with respect to the employee if the notional tax for the year for the employee were determined without reference to the elements F, G and H in this formula and if that tax were that employee's tax payable under Part I of the Act for that year, as if there were no other source of income or loss for the year, and

(ii) the amount by which the amount referred to in subparagraph (i) is increased by virtue of section 27 of the *Federal-Provincial Fiscal Arrangements Act*;

(g) that employee's notional rate of tax for a year shall be expressed as a decimal fraction and calculated by dividing the amount of the notional tax for the year by the mid-point of the range of remuneration referred to in paragraph (e) in respect of that employee and where the quotient results in more than two digits after the decimal in the decimal fraction

(i) the second digit shall be rounded to the nearest multiple of one hundredth, and

(ii) where the third digit is equidistant from two such multiples, the second digit shall be rounded to the higher thereof; and

(h) the amount to be deducted or withheld in respect of any payment made to that employee shall be determined by multiplying the payment by the appropriate decimal fraction determined pursuant to paragraph (g).

**Related Provisions**: ITA 257 — Negative amounts in formulas; Reg. 102(5) — Commission employees — exception.

**Notes**: Reg. 102(2)(d)(ii)B and 102(2)(f)B both amended by P.C. 1994-1370 to change reference from Reg. 100(1)"personal credits"(a)(i) to ITA 118(1)(c) (non-substantive amendment, since the reference is the same).

Reference to ITA 8(1)(h.1) in Reg. 102(2)(d)(i)(B) added by P.C. 1994-372, effective 1993.

Reg. 102(2)(d)(ii) amended by P.C. 1991-1643 and P.C. 1992-2347, effective 1992.

Reg. 102(2)(e) and (f) amended by P.C. 1992-2347, effective 1992.

Reg. 102(2)(f) amended by P.C. 1998-2270, effective for 1998 and later taxation years, to change "*Unemployment Insurance Act*" to "*Employment Insurance Act*".

Opening words of Reg. 102(2)(g) amended by P.C. 1992-2347, effective 1992.

**Remission Orders**: *Income Earned in Quebec Income Tax Remission Order*, P.C. 1989-1204 (reduction in withholdings for certain income related to Quebec).

**(3), (4)** [Revoked]

**(5) [Commission employees — exception]** — Notwithstanding subsections (1) and (2), no amount shall be deducted or withheld in the year by an employer from a payment of remuneration to an employee in respect of commissions earned by the employee in the immediately preceding year where those commissions were previously reported by the employer as remuneration of the employee in respect of that year on an information return.

**(6)** [Revoked]

**Definitions [Reg. 102]**: "amount", "appropriate percentage" — ITA 248(1); "Canada" — ITA 255, *Interpretation Act* 35(1); "commissions", "remuneration"(a)(ii); "employee", "employer" — Reg. 100(1); "estimated deductions" — Reg. 100(1); "form" — Reg. 102(2)(c); "notional net remuneration for the year" — Reg. 102(2)(e); "notional tax for the year" — Reg. 102(1)(e), 102(2)(f); "pay period" — Reg. 100(1); "payment" — Reg. 102(1)(a), 102(2); "personal credits" — Reg. 100(1); "province" — *Interpretation Act* 35(1); "remuneration" — Reg. 100(1); "resident in Canada" — ITA 250; "salary or wages" — ITA 248(1); "taxation year" — ITA 249; "total remuneration" — Reg. 100(1).

**103. Non-periodic payments — (1)** Where a payment in respect of a bonus or retroactive increase in remuneration is made by an employer to an employee whose total remuneration from the employer (including the bonus or retroactive increase) may reasonably be expected not to exceed $5,000 in the taxation year of the employee in which the payment is made, the employer shall deduct or withhold, in the case of an employee who reports for work at an establishment of the employer

(a) in Newfoundland, 100/162 of 15 per cent,

(b) in Prince Edward Island, 200/313 of 15,

(c) in Nova Scotia, 200/315 of 15 per cent,

(d) in New Brunswick, 100/157 of 15 per cent,

(e) in Quebec, 10 per cent,

(f) in Ontario, 200/273 of 15 per cent,

(g) in Manitoba, 100/160 of 15 per cent,

(h) in Saskatchewan, 100/157 of 15 per cent,

(i) in Alberta, 100/146 of 15 per cent for the payments made during the period beginning on July 1, 1998 and ending on December 31, 1998, and, after that period, 200/295 of 15 per cent,

(j) in British Columbia, 100/150 of 15 per cent for the payments made during the period beginning on July 1, 1998 and ending on December 31, 1998, and, after that period, 200/299 of 15 per cent,

(k) in the Yukon Territory, 100/148 of 15 per cent,

(l) in the Northwest Territories, 100/145 of 15 per cent,

(m) in Nunavut, 100/145 of 15 per cent, or

(n) in Canada beyond the limits of any province or outside Canada, 15 per cent,

of such payment in lieu of the amount determined under section 102.

**Notes**: The strange fractions reflect the provincial tax, which before 2000 was calculated as a percentage of federal tax (e.g., 62% in Newfoundland), for all provinces other than Quebec.

Reg. 103(1) amended by P.C. 2000-1334 to reflect changes in provincial personal tax rates effective January and July 2000. Previously amended by P.C. 1999-2205, 1998-2271, 1997-1774, 1996-1557, 1996-500, 1994-1370, 1994-372, 1993-1552, 1992-2347, 1992-291 and 1991-1643. Nunavut was added (and former (m) renumbered as (n)) effective April 1999 by P.C. 1999-2205.

From July 1999 through June 2000, the fractions were: Newfoundland, 100/162 (100/169 July–Dec. 1999); PEI, 200/317 (200/315 July–Dec. 1999); Nova Scotia, 200/315; New Brunswick, 100/160; Ontario, 200/277; Manitoba, 100/160; Saskatchewan, 100/167; Alberta, 200/295; BC, 200/299; Yukon, 100/150; NWT and Nunavut, 103/148.

From July 1998–June 1999, the fractions were: Nfld. 100/169; PEI 200/319; NS 200/315; NB 100/160 (103/161 July–Dec. 1998); Ont. 200/281; Man. 100/163; Sask. 100/167; Alta. 200/295 (100/146 Jul–Dec. 1998); BC 200/299 (100/150 July–Dec. 1998); Yukon 100/150; NWT 103/148.

From July 1997–June 1998, the fractions were: Nfld. 103/172; PEI 206/325; NS 206/321; NB 103/164 (103/165 July–Dec. 1997); Ontario 103/148 (103/150 July–Dec. 1997); Manitoba 103/168; Sask. 103/172; Alberta 103/152; BC 103/154; Yukon 103/153; NWT 103/148.

From July 1996–June 1997, NS was 206/325, NB 103/167, and Ontario 103/152. Before July 1996, Ontario was 103/164 and BC 206/311. From July 1993–June 1995, Saskatchewan was 103/173. From Jan.–June 1993, the fractions were: Nfld. 103/172; PEI & NS 206/325; NB 103/163; Ont. 103/158; Man. 103/168; Sask. 103/173; Alta. 103/152; BC 206/311. From July–Dec. 1992: Nfld. 104/171; PEI 208/327; NS 208/327; NB 104/164; Ont. 104/160; Man. 104/169; Sask. 104/174; Alta. 208/299; BC 208/313; Yukon 104/149; NWT 104/148. From Jan. 1991–June 1992: Nfld. 105/167; PEI 105/164 (Jan.–June 1991), 105/164 (July–Dec. 1991) and 210/329 (Jan.–June 1992); NS 210/329; NB 105/165; Ont. & Man. 105/158; Sask. 105/170; Alta. 105/156; BC 210/313; Yukon 105/150; NWT 105/149.

The extra 3 points in both the numerator and denominator before July 1998 (e.g., 103/172 for 69%) reflect the former 3% federal surtax in ITA 180.1(1)(a).

**Remission Orders**: *Income Earned in Quebec Income Tax Remission Order*, P.C. 1989-1204 (reduction in withholdings for certain income related to Quebec).

**(2) [Bonus]** — Where a payment in respect of a bonus is made by an employer to an employee whose total remuneration from the employer (including the bonus) may reasonably be expected to exceed $5,000 in the taxation year of the employee in which the payment is made, the amount to be deducted or withheld therefrom by the employer is

(a) the amount determined under section 102 in respect of an assumed remuneration equal to the aggregate of

(i) the amount of regular remuneration paid by the employer to the employee in the pay period in which the remuneration is paid, and

(ii) an amount equal to the bonus payment divided by the number of pay periods in the taxation year of the employee in which the payment is made

minus

(b) the amount determined under section 102 in respect of the amount of regular remuneration paid by the employer to the employee in the pay period

multiplied by

(c) the number of pay periods in the taxation year of the employee in which the payment is made.

**(3) [Retroactive pay increase]** — Where a payment in respect of a retroactive increase in remuneration is made by an employer to an employee whose

Part I — Tax Deductions  
Reg. S. 103(4)(c)(x)

total remuneration from the employer (including the retroactive increase) may reasonably be expected to exceed $5,000 in the taxation year of the employee in which the payment is made, the amount to be deducted or withheld therefrom by the employer is

(a) the amount determined under section 102 in respect of the new rate of remuneration

minus

(b) the amount determined under section 102 in respect of the previous rate of remuneration

multiplied by

(c) the number of pay periods in respect of which the increase in remuneration is retroactive.

**(4) [Lump sum payment]** — Subject to subsection (5), where a lump sum payment is made by an employer to an employee who is a resident of Canada,

(a) if the payment does not exceed $5,000, the employer shall deduct or withhold therefrom, in the case of an employee who reports for work at an establishment of the employer

(i) in Newfoundland, 100/162 of 10 per cent,

(ii) in Prince Edward Island, 200/313 of 10 per cent,

(iii) in Nova Scotia, 200/315 of 10 per cent,

(iv) in New Brunswick, 100/157 of 10 per cent,

(v) in Quebec, 5 per cent,

(vi) in Ontario, 200/273 of 10 per cent,

(vii) in Manitoba, 100/160 of 10 per cent,

(viii) in Saskatchewan, 100/157 of 10 per cent,

(ix) in Alberta, 100/146 of 10 per cent for the payments made during the period beginning on July 1, 1998 and ending on December 31, 1998, and, after that period, 200/295 of 10 per cent,

(x) in British Columbia, 100/150 of 10 per cent for the payments made during the period beginning on July 1, 1998 and ending on December 31, 1998, and, after that period, 200/299 of 10 per cent,

(xi) in the Yukon Territory, 100/148 of 10 per cent,

(xii) in the Northwest Territories, 100/145 of 10 per cent,

(xiii) in Nunavut, 100/145 of 10 per cent, or

(xiv) in Canada beyond the limits of any province or outside Canada, 10 per cent,

of such payment in lieu of the amount determined under section 102;

(b) if the payment exceeds $5,000 but does not exceed $15,000, the employer shall deduct or withhold therefrom, in the case of an employee who reports for work at an establishment of the employer

(i) in Newfoundland, 100/162 of 20 per cent,

(ii) in Prince Edward Island, 200/313 of 20 per cent,

(iii) in Nova Scotia, 200/315 of 20 per cent,

(iv) in New Brunswick, 100/157 of 20 per cent,

(v) in Quebec, 10 per cent,

(vi) in Ontario, 200/273 of 20 per cent,

(vii) in Manitoba, 100/160 of 20 per cent,

(viii) in Saskatchewan, 100/157 of 20 per cent,

(ix) in Alberta, 100/146 of 20 per cent for the payments made during the period beginning on July 1, 1998 and ending on December 31, 1998, and, after that period, 200/299 of 20 per cent,

(x) in British Columbia, 100/150 of 20 per cent for the payments made during the period beginning on July 1, 1998 and ending on December 31, 1998, and, after that period, 200/299 of 20 per cent,

(xi) in the Yukon Territory, 100/148 of 20 per cent,

(xii) in the Northwest Territories, 100/145 of 20 per cent,

(xiii) in Nunavut, 100/145 of 20 per cent, or

(xiv) in Canada beyond the limits of any province or outside Canada, 20 per cent,

of such payment in lieu of the amount determined under section 102; and

(c) if the payment exceeds $15,000, the employer shall deduct or withhold therefrom, in the case of an employee who reports for work at an establishment of the employer

(i) in Newfoundland, 100/162 of 30 per cent,

(ii) in Prince Edward Island, 200/313 of 30 per cent,

(iii) in Nova Scotia, 200/315 of 30 per cent,

(iv) in New Brunswick, 100/157 of 30 per cent,

(v) in Quebec, 15 per cent,

(vi) in Ontario, 200/273 of 30 per cent,

(vii) in Manitoba, 100/160 of 30 per cent,

(viii) in Saskatchewan, 100/157 of 30 per cent,

(ix) in Alberta, 100/146 of 30 per cent for the payments made during the period beginning on July 1, 1998 and ending on December 31, 1998, and, after that period, 200/295 of 30 per cent,

(x) in British Columbia, 100/150 of 30 per cent for the payments made during the period

**Reg. S. 103(4)(c)(x)**     Income Tax Regulations

beginning on July 1, 1998 and ending on December 31, 1998, and, after that period, 200/299 of 30 per cent,

(xi) in the Yukon Territory, 100/148 of 30 per cent,

(xii) in the Northwest Territories, 100/145 of 30 per cent,

(xiii) in Nunavut, 100/145 of 30 per cent, or

(xiv) in Canada beyond the limits of any province or outside Canada, 30 per cent,

of such payment in lieu of the amount determined under section 102.

**Notes**: The rates in Reg. 103(4) are grossed up to the full 10%, 20% or 30% by the parallel provincial tax (see Notes to Reg. 103(1)). These rates apply, *inter alia*, to payment of a "retiring allowance", including settlement of a wrongful dismissal claim. See Reg. 103(6)(e).

In Quebec, in addition to the 5%/10%/15% federal withholding, there is provincial withholding (*Taxation Act* Reg. 1015R9), of 20% up to $5,000 and 23% over $5,000; so the combined rates are 25/33/38% instead of 10/20/30% as in other provinces.

A withdrawal from a RRIF in excess of twice the "minimum amount" for the year is not protected by tax treaty provisions that limit withholding tax on pension payments, due to s. 5"periodic pension payment"(c)(i) of the *Income Tax Conventions Interpretation Act*. See Notes to Article XVIII(2) of the Canada-U.S. tax treaty.

Reg. 103(4) applies to "retiring allowances", which include severance pay. See Reg. 103(6)(e).

Reg. 103(4) amended by P.C. 2000-1334 to introduce new fractions effective July 2000 (January 2000 for Newfoundland). Previously amended by P.C. 1999-2205 (also added Nunavut, renumbering each subpara. (xiii) as (xiv)), 1998-2271, 1997-1774, 1996-1557, 1996-500, 1994-1370, 1994-372, 1993-1552, 1992-2347, 1992-291 and 1991-1643. For the earlier fractions, see Notes to Reg. 103(1).

**Remission Orders**: *Income Earned in Quebec Income Tax Remission Order*, P.C. 1989-1204 (reduction in withholdings for certain income related to Quebec).

**Forms**: T1036: Home buyers' plan — request to withdraw funds from an RRSP.

**(5) [Lump sum pension payment]** — Where the payment referred to in subsection (4) would be pension income or qualified pension income of the employee in respect of which subsection 118(3) of the Act would apply if the definition "pension income" in subsection 118(7) of the Act were read without reference to subparagraphs (a)(ii) and (iii) thereof, the payment shall be deemed to be the amount of the payment minus

(a) where the payment does not exceed the amount taxable referred to in paragraph 117(2)(a) of the Act, as adjusted annually pursuant to section 117.1 of the Act, the lesser of $1,000 and the amount of the payment;

(b) where the payment exceeds the amount referred to in paragraph (a) but does not exceed the amount taxable referred to in paragraph 117(2)(c) of the Act, as adjusted annually pursuant to section 117.1 of the Act, $654; and

(c) where the payment exceeds the amount taxable referred to in paragraph 117(2)(c) of the Act, as adjusted annually pursuant to section 117.1 of the Act, $586.

**Notes**: Reg. 103(5)(a)–(c) amended by P.C. 1992-2347, effective 1992. Before 1992, specific numbers were used (and amended each year) instead of referring to ITA 117(2).

**(6) [Lump sum payment]** — For the purposes of subsection (4), a "lump sum payment" means a payment that is

(a) a payment described in subparagraph 40(1)(a)(i) or (iii) or paragraph 40(1)(c) of the *Income Tax Application Rules*,

(b) a payment under a deferred profit sharing plan or a plan referred to in section 147 of the Act as a "revoked plan", except a payment referred to in subparagraph 147(2)(k)(v) of the Act,

(c) a payment made during the lifetime of an annuitant referred to in subparagraph 146(1)(a)(i) [146(1)"annuitant"(a)] of the Act out of or under a registered retirement savings plan of that annuitant, other than

(i) a periodic annuity payment, or

(ii) a payment made by a person who has reasonable grounds to believe that the payment may be deducted under subsection 146(8.2) of the Act in computing the income of any taxpayer,

(d) a payment out of or under a plan referred to in subsection 146(12) of the Act as an "amended plan" other than

(i) a periodic annuity payment, or

(ii) where paragraph 146(12)(a) of the Act applied to the plan after May 25, 1976, a payment made in a year subsequent to the year in which that paragraph applied to the plan,

(d.1) a payment made during the lifetime of an annuitant referred to in paragraph 146.3(1)(a) [146.3(1)"annuitant"] of the Act under a registered retirement income fund of that annuitant, other than a payment to the extent that it is in respect of the minimum amount (within the meaning assigned by paragraph 146.3(1)(b.1) [146.3(1)"minimum amount"] of the Act) under the fund for a year,

(e) a retiring allowance,

(f) a payment of an amount as, on account or in lieu of payment of, or in satisfaction of, proceeds of the surrender, cancellation or redemption of an income-averaging annuity contract, or

(g) a payment described in paragraph (n) of the definition "remuneration" in subsection 100(1).

**Related Provisions**: Reg. 100(3)(c) — No source withholding required where amount paid directly to employee's RRSP by employer.

Part I — Tax Deductions  Reg. S. 104(3)

**Notes**: Reg. 103(6)(c)(ii) amended by P.C. 1991-2540, effective 1991. For 1990 and earlier years, read:

(ii) a payment received by a taxpayer in a year in respect of an excess amount previously paid under the registered retirement savings plan to the extent that the excess amount may be deducted in computing the taxpayer's income for the year pursuant to subsection 146(8.2) of the Act.

Reg. 103(6)(g) added by P.C. 1998-2275, effective for 1998 and later taxation years. See Reg. 103(4) and (8) for withholding rates.

**(7) [Retirement compensation arrangement]** — For the purposes of subsection 153(1) of the Act, the amount to be deducted or withheld by a person shall be 50 per cent

(a) of the contribution made by the person under a retirement compensation arrangement, other than

(i) a contribution made by the person as an employee,

(ii) a contribution made to a plan or arrangement that is a prescribed plan or arrangement for the purposes of subsection 207.6(6) of the Act, or

(iii) a contribution made by way of a transfer from another retirement compensation arrangement under circumstances in which subsection 207.6(7) of the Act applies; or

(b) of the payment by the person to a resident of Canada of an amount on account of the purchase price of an interest in a retirement compensation arrangement.

**Notes**: Reg. 103(7)(a) amended, effectively to add subpara. (ii), by P.C. 1999-2211, retroactive to 1992 (but subpara. (iii) does not apply to contributions made before 1996).

Reg. 103(7)(a) amended by P.C. 1998-2770, effective for amounts transferred after 1995, to add "or a contribution that is received under a transfer pursuant to subsection 207.6(7) of the Act".

**Forms**: T4041: Retirement Compensation Arrangements Guide (guide).

**(8) [RESP payment]** — Every employer making a payment described in paragraph (n) of the definition "remuneration" in subsection 100(1) shall withhold — in addition to any other amount required to be withheld under Part I of these Regulations — on account of the tax payable under Part X.5 of the Act, an amount equal to

(a) where the amount is paid in the province of Quebec, 12 per cent of the payment, and

(b) in any other case, 20 per cent of the payment.

**Notes**: Reg. 103(8) applies only to certain payments out of a RESP; see Reg. 103(4) for regular withholding on "lump sum" amounts.

Reg. 103(8) added by P.C. 1998-2275, effective for 1998 and later taxation years; and amended by P.C. 1999-2205, effective June 17, 1999, to add the 12% rate for Quebec. Before June 17, 1999, read:

(8) Every person making a payment described in paragraph (n) of the definition "remuneration" in subsection 100(1) shall withhold an amount equal to 20% of that payment on account of the tax payable under Part X.5 of the Act, in addition to any other amount required to be withheld under Part I of these Regulations.

**Definitions [Reg. 103]**: "amount", "annuity" — ITA 248(1); "Canada" — ITA 255, *Interpretation Act* 35(1); "deferred profit sharing plan" — ITA 147(1), 248(1); "employee", "employer" — Reg. 100(1); "income-averaging annuity contract" — ITA 248(1); "lump sum payment" — Reg. 103(6); "pay period" — Reg. 100(1); "person" — ITA 248(1); "province" — *Interpretation Act* 35(1); "registered retirement income fund" — ITA 146.3(1), 248(1); "registered retirement savings plan" — ITA 146(1), 248(1); "remuneration" — Reg. 100(1); "resident" — ITA 250; "retirement compensation arrangement", "retiring allowance" — ITA 248(1); "taxation year" — ITA 249; "taxpayer" — ITA 248(1); "total remuneration" — Reg. 100(1).

**104. Deductions not required — (1) [Sufficient credits on TD1]** — No amount shall be deducted or withheld from a payment in accordance with section 102 or 103 with respect to an employee who has filed with the employee's employer a return referred to in subsection 107(1) for a year claiming that the employee's income from employment for the year will be less than the claim amount for the year as reported on that return for the year.

**Notes**: Reg. 104(1) amended by P.C. 1992-2347 and 1994-372. For 1992, read:

(1) No amount shall be deducted or withheld from a payment in accordance with section 102 or 103 with respect to an employee who has filed with the employee's employer a return in the prescribed form claiming that the employee's income for the year will be less than the net claim amount for the year as reported on the return for the year referred to in subsection 107(1).

Before 1992, read, in place of "the employee's income": "the employee's income (other than an amount required to be included in the employee's income by reason of subsection 56(5) of the Act) from all sources".

**Forms**: TD1: Personal tax credits return; TD1A: Amendment to the personal tax credits return.

**(2) [Employee not in Canada]** — No amount shall be deducted or withheld from a payment in accordance with section 102 or 103 in respect of an employee who was neither employed nor resident in Canada at the time of payment except in respect of

(a) remuneration described in subparagraph 115(2)(e)(i) of the Act that is paid to a non-resident person who has in the year, or had in any previous year, ceased to be resident in Canada; or

(b) remuneration reasonably attributable to the duties of any office or employment performed or to be performed in Canada by the non-resident person.

**Notes**: Reg. 104(2)(b) amended by P.C. 1997-1471, in force October 29, 1997, to change "*a* non-resident person" to "*the* non-resident person".

**Interpretation Bulletins**: IT-161R3: Non-residents — Exemption from tax deductions at source on employment income.

**(3) [Home Buyers' Plan]** — No amount shall be deducted or withheld from a payment made by a person during the lifetime of an annuitant referred to in paragraph (a) of the definition "annuitant" in subsection 146(1) of the Act out of or under a registered retirement savings plan of the annuitant where, at the

1955

time of the payment, the annuitant has certified in prescribed form to the person that

(a) a written agreement has been entered into to acquire a home by either

(i) the annuitant, or

(ii) a disabled person who is related to the annuitant and who is entitled to the credit for mental or physical impairment under subsection 118.3 (1) of the Act;

(b) the annuitant intends that the home be used as a principal place of residence in Canada for the annuitant or the disabled person, as the case may be, within one year after its acquisition;

(c) the home has not been previously owned by the annuitant, the annuitant's spouse, the disabled person or the spouse of that person;

(d) the annuitant was resident in Canada;

(e) the total amount of the payment and all other such payments received by the annuitant in respect of the home at or before the time of payment does not exceed $20,000;

(f) except where the annuitant certifies that he or she is a disabled person entitled to the credit for mental or physical impairment under subsection 118.3(1) of the Act or certifies that the payment is being withdrawn for the benefit of such a disabled person, the annuitant is a qualifying homebuyer at the time of the certification; and

(g) where the annuitant has withdrawn an eligible amount, within the meaning assigned by subsection 146.01(1) of the Act, before the calendar year of the certification, the total of all eligible amounts received by the annuitant before that calendar year does not exceed the total of all amounts previously designated under subsection 146.01(3) of the Act or included in computing the annuitant's income under subsection 146.01(4) or (5) of the Act.

**Related Provisions:** Reg. 104(3.01), (3.1), (4) — Interpretation.

**Notes:** Reg. 104(3) allows funds to be withdrawn from an RRSP under the Home Buyers' Plan (ITA 146.01) without the financial institution withholding funds at source.

Reg. 104(3) amended by P.C. 1998-2272, effective for payments made after 1998. From March 2, 1994 through 1998, read:

(3) The amount to be deducted or withheld from a payment made by a person during the lifetime of an annuitant referred to in paragraph (a) of the definition "annuitant" in subsection 146(1) of the Act out of or under a registered retirement savings plan of the annuitant is nil where, at the time of the payment, the annuitant has certified in prescribed form to the person that the annuitant has entered into a written agreement to acquire a home and that

(a) the annuitant intends to use the home as a principal place of residence in Canada within one year after its acquisition;

(b) the home has not previously been owned by the annuitant or the annuitant's spouse;

(b.1) the annuitant had no owner-occupied home in the period

(i) commencing at the beginning of the fourth preceding calendar year ending before the time of the payment, and

(ii) ending on the 31st day before the time of the payment;

(b.2) the annuitant's spouse, in the period referred to in paragraph (b.1), had no owner-occupied home that was inhabited by the annuitant at any time during the marriage of the spouse and the annuitant;

(c) the annuitant was resident in Canada at the time of the payment; and

(d) the total amount of the payment and all other such payments in respect of the home to the annuitant at or before that time does not exceed $20,000.

Reg. 104(3) added by P.C. 1992-480; opening words amended to extend the deadline from March 1, 1993 to March 1, 1994 by P.C. 1993-271. Opening words further amended to extend the deadline indefinitely, and Reg. 104(3)(b.1) and (b.2) added, by P.C. 1994-438, effective for payments made after March 1, 1994. This implements the proposals in the February 22, 1994 federal budget even before the legislation has been enacted (see proposed amendments to ITA 146.01).

References to "spouse" are expected to be amended to add "or common-law partner" effective 2001 or earlier by election, as has been done throughout the ITA. See Notes to ITA 248(1)"common-law partner".

**(3.01) ["Qualifying homebuyer"]** — For the purpose of subsection (3), the annuitant is a qualifying homebuyer at a particular time unless

(a) the annuitant had an owner-occupied home in the period beginning on January 1 of the fourth calendar year preceding the particular time, and ending on the thirty-first day before the particular time; or

(b) the annuitant's spouse, in the period referred to in paragraph (a), had an owner-occupied home that was inhabited by the annuitant at any time during the marriage of the spouse and the annuitant.

**Notes:** Reg. 104(3.01) added by P.C. 1998-2272, effective for payments made after 1998.

References to "spouse" are expected to be amended to add "or common-law partner" effective 2001 or earlier by election, as has been done throughout the ITA. See Notes to ITA 248(1)"common-law partner".

**(3.1) ["Owner-occupied home"]** — For the purpose of subsection (3.01), an individual shall be considered to have had an owner-occupied home at any time where the home was owned, whether jointly with another person or otherwise, by the individual at that time and inhabited by the individual as the individual's principal place of residence at that time.

**Notes:** Reg. 104(3.1) added by P.C. 1994-438, effective for payments made after March 1, 1994; and amended by P.C. 1998-2272, effective for payments made after 1998, to change reference to "(3)" to "(3.01)".

**(4) ["Home"]** — For the purposes of subsections (3), (3.01) and (3.1), "home" means

(a) a housing unit;

(b) a share of the capital stock of a cooperative housing corporation, where the holder of the share is entitled to possession of a housing unit; and

(c) where the context so requires, the housing unit to which a share described in paragraph (b) relates.

**Notes**: Reg. 104(4) added by P.C. 1992-480; reference to subsec. (3.1) added by P.C. 1994-438, effective for payments made after March 1, 1994; reference to subsec. (3.01) added by P.C. 1998-2772, effective for payments made after 1998.

**Definitions [Reg. 104]**: "amount" — ITA 248(1); "annuitant" — ITA 146.1(1); "Canada" — ITA 255, *Interpretation Act* 35(1); "corporation" — ITA 248(1), *Interpretation Act* 35(1); "eligible amount" — ITA 146.01(1); "employed", "employee", "employer" — Reg. 100(1); "employment" — ITA 248(1); "home" — Reg. 104(4); "individual" — ITA 248(1); "non-resident", "office" — ITA 248(1); "owner-occupied home" — Reg. 104(3.1); "person", "prescribed" — ITA 248(1); "qualifying homebuyer" — Reg. 104(3.01); "registered retirement savings plan" — ITA 146(1), 248(1); "remuneration" — Reg. 100(1); "resident in Canada" — ITA 250; "share" — ITA 248(1); "written" — *Interpretation Act* 35(1)"writing".

## 104.1 Lifelong Learning Plan — (1) No amount shall be deducted or withheld from a payment made by a person during the lifetime of an annuitant referred to in paragraph (a) of the definition "annuitant" in subsection 146(1) of the Act out of or under a registered retirement savings plan of the annuitant where, at the time of the payment, the annuitant has certified in prescribed form to the person that

(a) at the time of certification, the annuitant or the annuitant's spouse

(i) is a full-time student in a qualifying educational program,

(ii) is a part-time student in a qualifying educational program and is entitled to the credit for mental or physical impairment under subsection 118.3(1) of the Act, or

(iii) has received notification in writing of his or her entitlement, either absolutely or conditionally, to enrol before March of the year that follows the year of certification as

(A) a full-time student in a qualifying educational program, or

(B) a part-time student in a qualifying educational program where the annuitant or the annuitant's spouse is entitled to the credit for mental or physical impairment under subsection 118.3(1) of the Act;

(b) the annuitant is resident in Canada;

(c) the total amount of the payment and all other such payments received by the annuitant for a year at or before that time does not exceed $10,000; and

(d) the total payments received by the annuitant do not exceed $20,000 throughout the period in which the annuitant participates in the Lifelong Learning Plan.

**Related Provisions**: Reg. 104.1(2) — Interpretation.

**Notes**: See at end of Reg. 104.1.

**Forms**: LLP — request to withdraw funds from an RRSP.

**(2) ["Qualifying educational program"]** — For the purpose of subsection (1), a "qualifying educational program" means a qualifying educational program at a designated educational institution (as those expressions are defined in subsection 118.6(1) of the Act), except that a reference to a "qualifying educational program" shall be read

(a) without reference to paragraphs (a) and (b) of that definition; and

(b) as if the reference to "3 consecutive weeks" in that definition were a reference to "3 consecutive months".

**Notes [Reg. 104.1]**: Reg. 104.1 allows funds to be withdrawn from an RRSP under the Lifelong Learning Plan (ITA 146.02) without the financial institution withholding funds at source.

Reg. 104.1 added by P.C. 1998-2272, effective for payments made after 1998.

References to "spouse" are expected to be amended to add "or common-law partner" effective 2001 or earlier by election, as has been done throughout the ITA. See Notes to ITA 248(1)"common-law partner".

**Definitions [Reg. 104.1]**: "amount" — ITA 248(1); "annuitant" — ITA 146(1); "prescribed" — ITA 248(1); "qualifying educational program" — Reg. 104.1(2); "registered retirement savings plan" — ITA 146(1), 248(1); "resident in Canada" — ITA 250.

## 105. Non-residents — (1) Every person paying to a non-resident person a fee, commission or other amount in respect of services rendered in Canada, of any nature whatever, shall deduct or withhold 15 per cent of such payment.

(2) Subsection (1) does not apply to a payment described in the definition "remuneration" in subsection 100(1).

**Related Provisions [Reg. 105]**: ITA 212(1)(a) — Withholding tax on fees for management services; Canada-U.S. tax treaty Art. XIV — Independent personal services; Canada-U.S. tax treaty Art. XVII — Limitation on withholding re U.S. residents.

**Notes**: If the service is rendered in Quebec, a further 9% must be withheld and remitted to Revenu Québec: Reg 1015R8 under the *Quebec Taxation Act*, reproduced on *Provincial TaxPartner* and in *La Loi du Practicien Annotée* (Carswell, annual).

A treaty-based waiver of withholding is available in certain circumstances. See Information Circular 75-6R, paras. 10–16. The administrative conditions for waiver were recently under review by the CCRA and discussion with the Joint Committee on Taxation of the Canadian Bar Association and Canadian Institute of Chartered Accountants. See also Albert Baker & Mark Briggs, "Revenue Canada Provides Increased Guidance on Waivers From Withholding Under Regulation 105", VIII(4) *International Tax Planning* (Federated Press) 596-601 (1999).

New guidelines were issued by the CCRA on November 15, 1999 (*Canadian Tax Highlights*, Canadian Tax Foundation, December 28, 1999). See also Shannon Baker & Dale Meister, "Non-Residents Rendering Services in Canada: Regulation 105 and Other Issues", 47(5) *Canadian Tax Journal* 1321-1341 (1999).

**Information Circulars [Reg. 105]**: 75-6R: Required withholding from amounts paid to non-resident persons performing services in Canada.

**Forms [Reg. 105]**: T4A-NR Summ: Summary of fees (etc.) paid to non-residents for services rendered in Canada; T4A-NR Supp: Statement of fees, etc., paid to non-residents to which subsection 105(1) of the Regulations applies.

**Definitions [Reg. 105]**: "amount" — ITA 248(1); "Canada" — ITA 255, *Interpretation Act* 35(1); "commission" — Reg. 100(1)"remuneration"(a)(ii); "non-resident", "person" — ITA 248(1); "remuneration" — Reg. 100(1).

## 105.1 Fishermen's election — (1) Notwithstanding section 100, in this section,

"**amount of remuneration**" paid to a fisherman means

(a) where a boat crewed by one or more fishermen engaged in making a catch is owned, together with the gear, by a person, other than a member of the crew, to whom the catch is to be delivered for subsequent sale or other disposition, such portion of the proceeds from the disposition of the catch that is payable to the fisherman in accordance with an arrangement under which the proceeds of disposition of the catch are to be distributed (in this section referred to as a "share arrangement");

(b) where the boat or gear used in making a catch is owned or leased by a fisherman who alone or with another individual engaged under a contract of service makes the catch, such portion of the proceeds from the disposition of the catch that remains after deducting therefrom

  (i) the amount in respect of any portion of the catch not caught by the fisherman or the other individual,

  (ii) the amount payable to the other individual under the contract of service, and

  (iii) the amount of such proportionate share of the catch as is attributable to the expenses of the operation of the boat or its gear pursuant to their share arrangement;

(c) where a crew includes the owner of the boat or gear (in this paragraph referred to as the "owner") and any other fisherman engaged in making a catch, such portion of the proceeds from the disposition of the catch that remains after deducting therefrom

  (i) in the case of an owner,

   (A) the amount in respect of that portion of the catch not caught by the crew or an owner,

   (B) the aggregate of all amounts each of which is an amount payable to a crew member (other than the owner) pursuant to their share arrangement or to an individual engaged under a contract of service, and

   (C) the amount of such proportionate share of the catch as is attributable to the expenses of the owner's operation of the boat or its gear pursuant to their share arrangement, or

  (ii) in the case of any other crew member, such proceeds from the disposition of the catch as is payable to him in accordance with their share arrangement; or

(d) in any other case, the proceeds of disposition of the catch payable to the fisherman;

"**catch**" means a catch of shell fish, crustaceans, aquatic animals or marine plants caught or taken from any body of water;

"**crew**" means one or more fishermen engaged in making a catch;

"**fisherman**" means an individual engaged in making a catch other than under a contract of service.

(2) Every person paying at any time in a taxation year an amount of remuneration to a fisherman who, pursuant to paragraph 153(1)(n) of the Act, has elected for the year in prescribed form in respect of all such amounts shall deduct or withhold 20% of each such amount paid to the fisherman while the election is in force.

**Definitions [Reg. 105.1]**: "amount" — ITA 248(1); "amount of remuneration" — Reg. 105.1(1); "catch", "crew" — Reg. 105.1(1)(d); "disposition" — ITA 248(1); "fisherman" — Reg. 105.1(1)(d); "individual" — ITA 248(1); "owner" — Reg. 105.1(1)(c); "person", "prescribed" — ITA 248(1); "remuneration" — Reg. 100(1); "share" — ITA 248(1); "share arrangement" — Reg. 105.1(1)(a); "taxation year" — ITA 249.

## 106. Variations in deductions — (1) Where an employer makes a payment of remuneration to an employee in his taxation year

(a) for a period for which no provision is made in Schedule I,

(b) for a pay period referred to in Schedule I in an amount that is greater than any amount provided for therein,

(c) whose total remuneration in respect of the year is greater than any amount of total remuneration provided for in Schedule I, or

(d) whose personal credits and estimated deductions in respect of the year are greater than $58,999.99,

the amount to be deducted or withheld by the employer from any such payment is that proportion of the payment that the tax that may reasonably be expected to be payable under the Act by the employee with respect to the aggregate of all remuneration that may reasonably be expected to be paid by the employer to the employee in respect of that taxation year is of such aggregate.

(2), (3) [Revoked]

**Definitions [Reg. 106]**: "amount", "employee", "employer", "estimated deductions", "pay period", "personal credits", "remuneration" — Reg. 100(1); "taxation year" — ITA 249; "total remuneration" — Reg. 100(1).

## 107. Employee's returns — (1) [Due date for TD1] — The return required to be filed by an em-

ployee under subsection 227(2) of the Act shall be filed by the employee with the employer when the employee commences employment with that employer and a new return shall be filed thereunder within 7 days of the date on which a change occurs that may reasonably be expected to result in a change in the employee's personal credits for the year.

**Related Provisions**: Reg. 104 — No deduction required where employee claims no tax payable.

**Forms**: TD1: Personal tax credits return; TD1A: Amendment to the personal tax credits return.

**(2) [Commission employees]** — Notwithstanding subsection (1), where, in a year, an employee receives payments in respect of commissions or in respect of commissions and salary or wages, and he elects to file a prescribed form for a year in addition to the return referred to in that subsection, that form shall be filed with his continuing employer on or before January 31 of the year and, where applicable, within one month after he commences his employment with a new employer or within one month of the date on which a change occurs that may reasonably be expected to result in

(a) a change in the employee's personal credits for the year, or

(b) a substantial change in his estimated total remuneration for the year or estimated deductions for the year.

**Related Provisions**: Reg. 102(2) — Amount to be withheld.

**Forms**: TD1X: Statement of remuneration and expenses (for use by commission remunerated employees).

**(3)** Where, in a taxation year, an employee has elected to file the prescribed form referred to in subsection (2) and has filed such form with his employer, the employee may at any time thereafter in the year revoke that election and such revocation is effective from the date that he notifies his employer in writing of his intention.

**Definitions [Reg. 107]**: "commissions" — Reg. 100(1)"remuneration"(a)(ii); "employee", "employer" — Reg. 100(1); "employment" — ITA 248(1); "estimated deductions" — Reg. 100(1); "month" — *Interpretation Act* 35(1); "personal credits" — Reg. 100(1); "prescribed", "salary or wages" — ITA 248(1); "taxation year" — ITA 249; "total remuneration" — Reg. 100(1); "writing" — *Interpretation Act* 35(1).

**108. Remittances to Receiver General — (1) [Deadline]** — Subject to subsections (1.1), (1.11) and (1.12), amounts deducted or withheld in a month under subsection 153(1) of the Act shall be remitted to the Receiver General on or before the 15th day of the following month.

**Notes**: Reg. 108(1) amended to add reference to 108(1.12) by P.C. 1997-1473, effective for amounts and contributions required to be remitted to the Receiver General after October 1997.

**Forms**: RC4163: Employers' guide-remitting payroll deductions; T4001: Employers' guide to payroll deductions — basic information (guide). See also under ITA 153(1).

**(1.1) [Large employers]** — Subject to subsection (1.11), where the average monthly withholding amount of an employer for the second calendar year preceding a particular calendar year is

(a) equal to or greater than $15,000 and less than $50,000, all amounts deducted or withheld from payments described in the definition "remuneration" in subsection 100(1) that are made in a month in the particular calendar year by the employer shall be remitted to the Receiver General

(i) in respect of payments made before the 16th day of the month, on or before the 25th day of the month, and

(ii) in respect of payments made after the 15th day of the month, on or before the 10th day of the following month; or

(b) equal to or greater than $50,000, all amounts deducted or withheld from payments described in the definition "remuneration" in subsection 100(1) that are made in a month in the particular calendar year by the employer shall be remitted to the Receiver General on or before the third day, not including a Saturday or holiday, after the end of the following periods in which the payments were made,

(i) the period beginning on the first day and ending on the 7th day of the month,

(ii) the period beginning on the 8th day and ending on the 14th day of the month,

(iii) the period beginning on the 15th day and ending on the 21st day of the month, and

(iv) the period beginning on the 22nd day and ending on the last day of the month.

**Notes**: The word "holiday", used in Reg. 108(1.1)(b), is defined in subsec. 35(1) of the *Interpretation Act* to include every Sunday as well as the federal statutory holidays (New Year's, Good Friday, Easter Monday, Christmas Day, Victoria Day, Canada Day, Labour Day, Remembrance Day, Thanksgiving), and any day proclaimed or appointed by federal, provincial or civic authorities as a holiday.

**(1.11) [Option to use preceding year as base]** — Where an employer referred to in paragraph (1.1)(a) or (b) would otherwise be required to remit in accordance with that paragraph the amounts withheld or deducted under subsection 153(1) of the Act in respect of a particular calendar year, the employer may elect to remit those amounts

(a) in accordance with subsection (1), if the average monthly withholding amount of the employer for the calendar year preceding the particular calendar year is less than $15,000 and the employer has advised the Minister that the employer has so elected; or

(b) if the average monthly withholding amount of the employer for the calendar year preceding the particular calendar year is equal to or greater than $15,000 and less than $50,000 and the employer has advised the Minister that the employer has so elected,

    (i) in respect of payments made before the 16th day of a month in the particular calendar year, on or before the 25th day of the month, and

    (ii) in respect of payments made after the 15th day of a month in [the] particular calendar year, on or before the 10th day of the following month.

**Notes**: Reg. 108(1.11) added, and 108(1) and (1.1) amended to accommodate it, by P.C. 1993-321, effective March 11, 1993. 108(1.11) allows employers to use the previous year's base for determining instalment remittance deadlines, rather than the second preceding year, where that is to the employer's advantage. It was introduced in response to complaints from employers that had downsized during the recession.

**(1.12) [Quarterly remittance]** — If at any time

    (a) the average monthly withholding amount in respect of an employer for either the first or the second calendar year before the particular calendar year that includes that time is less than $1,000,

    (b) throughout the 12-month period before that time, the employer has remitted, on or before the day on or before which the amounts were required to be remitted, all amounts each of which was required to be

        (i) deducted or withheld under subsection 153(1) of the Act, or

        (ii) remitted under Part IX of the *Excise Tax Act*, and

    (c) throughout the 12-month period before that time, the employer has filed all returns each of which was required to be filed under this Act or Part IX of the *Excise Tax Act* on or before the day on or before which those returns were required to be filed under those Acts,

all amounts deducted or withheld from payments described in the definition "remuneration" in subsection 100(1) that are made by the employer in a month that ends after that time and that is in the particular calendar year may be remitted to the Receiver General

    (d) in respect of such payments made in January, February and March of the particular calendar year, on or before the 15th day of April of the particular year,

    (e) in respect of such payments made in April, May and June of the particular calendar year, on or before the 15th day of July of the particular year,

    (f) in respect of such payments made in July, August and September of the particular calendar year, on or before the 15th day of October of the particular year, and

    (g) in respect of such payments made in October, November and December of the particular calendar year, on or before the 15th day of January of the year following the particular year.

**Notes**: Reg. 108(1.12) added by P.C. 1997-1473, effective for amounts and contributions required to be remitted to the Receiver General after October 1997. This gives effect to an announcement, in the February 18, 1997 federal budget, that small employers would be allowed to remit source deductions quarterly instead of monthly. Employers must have a perfect compliance record (both filing and remitting) for source deductions and GST remittances over the past 12 months (Reg. 108(1.12)(b)), and average monthly withholding of less than $1,000 for either the first or second preceding year (Reg. 108(1.12)(a)) to qualify.

**Forms**: RC4163: Employers' guide-remitting payroll deductions. See also under ITA 153(1).

**(1.2) ["Average monthly withholding amount"]** — For the purposes of this section, average monthly withholding amount, in respect of an employer for a particular calendar year, is the quotient obtained when

    (a) the aggregate of all amounts each of which is an amount required to be remitted with respect to the particular year under

        (i) subsection 153(1) of the Act and a similar provision of a law of a province which imposes a tax upon the income of individuals, where the province has entered into an agreement with the Minister of Finance for the collection of taxes payable to the province, in respect of payments described in the definition "remuneration" in subsection 100(1),

        (ii) subsection 21(1) of the *Canada Pension Plan*, or

        (iii) subsection 82(1) of the *Employment Insurance Act* or subsection 53(1) of the *Unemployment Insurance Act*,

by the employer or, where the employer is a corporation, by each corporation associated with the corporation in a taxation year of the employer ending in the second calendar year following the particular year

is divided by

    (b) the number of months in the particular year, not exceeding twelve, for which such amounts were required to be remitted by the employer and, where the employer is a corporation, by each corporation associated with it in a taxation year of the employer ending in the second calendar year following the particular year.

**Related Provisions**: Reg. 108(1.3) — Where business transferred.

**Notes**: Reg. 108(1.2)(a)(iii) amended by P.C. 1998-2270, effective for 1998 and later taxation years, to add reference to 82(1) of the *Employment Insurance Act*.

**(1.3) [Where business transferred]** — For the purposes of subsection (1.2), where a particular employer that is a corporation has acquired in a taxation year of the corporation ending in a particular calendar year all or substantially all of the property of another employer used by the other employer in a business

(a) in a transaction in respect of which an election was made under subsection 85(1) or (2) of the Act,

(b) by virtue of an amalgamation within the meaning assigned to that term by section 87 of the Act, or

(c) as the result of a winding-up in respect of which subsection 88(1) of the Act is applicable,

the other employer shall be deemed to be a corporation associated with the particular employer in the taxation year and each taxation year ending at any time in the next two following calendar years.

**(2) [Ceasing to carry on business]** — Where an employer has ceased to carry on business, any amount deducted or withheld under subsection 153(1) of the Act that has not been remitted to the Receiver General shall be paid within 7 days of the day when the employer ceased to carry on business.

**(3) [Return]** — Remittances made to the Receiver General under subsection 153(1) of the Act shall be accompanied by a return in prescribed form.

**(4) [Unclaimed dividends, interest on proceeds]** — Amounts deducted or withheld under subsection 153(4) of the Act shall be remitted to the Receiver General within 60 days after the end of the taxation year subsequent to the 12-month period referred to in that subsection.

**Definitions [Reg. 108]**: "amount" — ITA 248(1); "associated" — ITA 256, Reg. 108(1.3); "average monthly withholding amount" — Reg. 108(1.2); "business" — ITA 248(1); "Canada" — ITA 255, *Interpretation Act* 35(1); "corporation" — ITA 248(1), *Interpretation Act* 35(1); "employer" — Reg. 100(1); "holiday" — *Interpretation Act* 35(1); "individual", "Minister" — ITA 248(1); "month" — *Interpretation Act* 35(1); "prescribed", "property" — ITA 248(1); "province" — *Interpretation Act* 35(1); "remuneration" — Reg. 100(1); "taxation year" — ITA 249.

**109. Elections to increase deductions — (1)** Any election under subsection 153(1.2) of the Act shall be made by filing with the person making the payment or class of payments referred to therein (in this section referred to as the "payer") the form prescribed by the Minister for that purpose.

**(2) [Variation]** — A taxpayer who has made an election in the manner prescribed by subsection (1) may require that the amount deducted or withheld pursuant to that election be varied by filing with the payer the form prescribed by the Minister for that purpose.

**(3) [Time allowed to comply]** — An election made in the manner prescribed by subsection (1) or a variation made pursuant to subsection (2) need not be taken into account by the payer in respect of the first payment to be made to the taxpayer after the election or variation, as the case may be, unless the election or variation, as the case may be, is made within such time, in advance of the payment, as may reasonably be required by the payer.

**Definitions [Reg. 109]**: "amount", "Minister" — ITA 248(1); "payer" — Reg. 109(1); "person", "prescribed", "taxpayer" — ITA 248(1).

**110. Prescribed persons — (1) [Large employers]** — The following are prescribed persons for the purposes of subsection 153(1) of the Act:

(a) an employer who is required, under subsection 153(1) of the Act and in accordance with paragraph 108(1.1)(b), to remit amounts deducted or withheld; and

(b) a person or partnership who, acting on behalf of one or more employers, remits the following amounts in a particular calendar year and whose average monthly remittance, in respect of those amounts, for the second calendar year preceding the particular calendar year, is equal to or greater than $50,000,

(i) amounts required to be remitted under subsection 153(1) of the Act and a similar provision of a law of a province that imposes a tax on the income of individuals, where the province has entered into an agreement with the Minister of Finance for the collection of taxes payable to the province, in respect of payments described in the definition "remuneration" in subsection 100(1),

(ii) amounts required to be remitted under subsection 21(1) of the *Canada Pension Plan*, and

(iii) amounts required to be remitted under subsection 82(1) of the *Employment Insurance Act* or subsection 53(1) of the *Unemployment Insurance Act*.

**Notes**: Reg. 110(1)(b)(iii) amended by P.C. 1998-2270, effective for 1998 and later taxation years, to add reference to 82(1) of the *Employment Insurance Act*. See also Notes at end of Reg. 110.

**(2) [Average monthly remittance]** — For the purposes of paragraph (1)(b), the average monthly remittance made by a person or partnership on behalf of all the employers for whom that person or partnership is acting, for the second calendar year preceding the particular calendar year, is the quotient obtained when the aggregate, for that preceding year, of all amounts referred to in subparagraphs (1)(b)(i) to (iii) remitted by the person or partnership on behalf of those employers is divided by the number of months, in that preceding year, for which the person or partnership remitted those amounts.

**Notes [Reg. 110]**: Reg. 110 added by P.C. 1993-1947, effective for remittances made after 1992.

Subsection 159(2) of the *Financial Administration Act* requires banks to accept payments of taxes.

**Definitions [Reg. 110]**: "amount" — ITA 248(1); "average monthly remittance" — Reg. 110(2); "Canada" — ITA 255, *Interpretation Act* 35(1); "employer" — Reg. 100(1); "individual" — ITA 248(1); "Minister" — ITA 248(1); "month" — *Interpretation*

**Reg. S. 110** — Income Tax Regulations

*Act* 35(1); "person", "prescribed" — ITA 248(1); "province" — *Interpretation Act* 35(1); "remuneration" — Reg. 100(1).

# PART II — INFORMATION RETURNS

**Notes [Part II]**: The requirement for reporting the values of assets owned on emigrating from Canada is in ITA 128.1(8). The requirement for an annual return by a RESP trustee is in 146.1(13.1). The requirement for an annual form from a non-profit R&D corporation is in ITA 149(7). The requirement for an information return by a registered charity is in ITA 149.1(14). The requirement for annual returns of income (tax returns) is in ITA 150(1). The requirement for information returns with respect to non-arm's length transactions with non-residents, and holdings in foreign property or foreign trusts, is found in ITA 233–233.7. An annual information return by the administrator of a registered pension plan is required by Reg. 8409, while other pension-related information returns are required by Regs. 8400-8410. See also Proposed Amendments at end of this Part.

**Information Circulars**: 82-2R2: Social insurance number legislation that relates to the preparation of information slips.

**200. Remuneration and benefits** — (1) Every person who makes a payment described in subsection 153(1) of the Act (other than an annuity payment in respect of an interest in an annuity contract to which subsection 201(5) applies) shall make an information return in prescribed form in respect of such payment unless an information return in respect of such payment has been made under section 202 or 214.

**Related Provisions**: Reg. 205 — Date return due; Reg. 205.1 — Electronic filing required if more than 500 returns; Reg. 209 — Two copies to be sent to taxpayer.

**Notes**: For information about magnetic media filing of T4-related information slips, call Revenue Canada at 1-800-665-5164. For electronic filing generally, see ITA 150.1.

**I.T. Technical News**: No. 11 (reporting of amounts paid out of an employee benefit plan).

**Forms**: See at end of Reg. 200.

(2) **[Various payments]** — Every person who makes a payment as or on account of, or who confers a benefit or allocates an amount that is,

(a) a scholarship, fellowship or bursary, or a prize for achievement in a field of endeavour ordinarily carried on by the recipient thereof (other than a prize prescribed by section 7700),

(b) a grant to enable the recipient thereof to carry on research or any similar work,

(c) an amount that is required by paragraph 56(1)(r) of the Act to be included in computing a taxpayer's income,

(d) a benefit under regulations made under an *Appropriation Act* providing for a scheme of transitional assistance benefits to persons employed in the production of products to which the *Canada-United States Agreement on Automotive Products*, signed on January 16, 1965, applies,

(e) a benefit described in section 5502,

(f) an amount payable to a taxpayer on a periodic basis in respect of the loss of all or any part of his income from an office or employment, pursuant to

(i) a sickness or accident insurance plan,

(ii) a disability insurance plan, or

(iii) an income maintenance insurance plan,

to or under which his employer has made a contribution,

(g) an amount or benefit the value of which is required by paragraph 6(1)(a), (e) or (h) or subsection 6(9) of the Act to be included in computing a taxpayer's income from an office or employment, other than a payment referred to in subsection (1),

(h) a benefit the amount of which is required by virtue of subsection 15(5) of the Act to be included in computing a shareholder's income,

(i) a benefit deemed by subsection 15(9) of the Act to be a benefit conferred on a shareholder by a corporation, or

(j) a payment out of a registered education savings plan, other than a refund of payments,

shall make an information return in prescribed form in respect of such payment or benefit except where subsection (3) or (4) applies with respect to the payment or benefit.

**Related Provisions**: Reg. 205 — Date return due; Reg. 205.1 — Electronic filing required if more than 500 returns; Reg. 209 — Two copies to be sent to taxpayer.

**Notes**: Reg. 200(2)(c) amended by P.C. 1998-2270, effective for 1998 and later taxation years. From November 18, 1983 through 1997, read:

(c) a training allowance paid under the *National Training Act*, except to the extent that it was paid to the recipient thereof as or on account of an allowance for his personal or living expenses while he was away from home,

Reg. 200(2)(e) changed from "a benefit under the *Labour Adjustments Benefits Act*" by P.C. 1995-1023, effective for benefits paid after October 1991.

Reg. 200(2)(j) added by P.C. 1998-2275, effective for 1998 and later taxation years.

**Interpretation Bulletins**: IT-75R3: Scholarships, fellowships, bursaries, prizes, and research grants; IT-421R2: Benefits to individuals, corporations and shareholders from loans or debt.

**I.T. Technical News**: No. 11 (reporting of amounts paid out of an employee benefit plan).

**Forms**: See at end of Reg. 200.

(3) **[Automobile benefits]** — Where a benefit is included in computing a taxpayer's income from an office or employment pursuant to paragraph 6(1)(a) or (e) of the Act in respect of an automobile made available to the taxpayer or to a person related to the taxpayer by a person related to the taxpayer's employer, the employer shall make an information return in prescribed form in respect of the benefit.

**Related Provisions**: Reg. 205 — Date return due; Reg. 205.1 — Electronic filing required if more than 500 returns; Reg. 209 — Two copies to be sent to taxpayer.

**(4) [Automobile benefits — shareholder]** — Where a benefit is included in computing the income of a shareholder of a corporation by virtue of subsection 15(5) of the Act in respect of an automobile made available to the shareholder or to a person related to the shareholder by a person related to the corporation, the corporation shall make an information return in prescribed form in respect of the benefit.

**Related Provisions**: Reg. 205 — Date return due; Reg. 205.1 — Electronic filing required if more than 500 returns; Reg. 209 — Two copies to be sent to taxpayer.

### Proposed Addition — Reg. 200(5)

**(5) [Employee stock option deferral]** — Where a particular qualifying person (within the meaning assigned by subsection 7(7) of the Act) has agreed to sell or issue a security (within the meaning assigned by subsection 7(7) of the Act) of the particular qualifying person (or of a qualifying person with which it does not deal at arm's length) to a taxpayer who is an employee of the particular qualifying person (or of a qualifying person with which the particular qualifying person does not deal at arm's length) and the taxpayer has acquired the security under the agreement in circumstances to which subsection 7(8) of the Act applied, each of the particular qualifying person, the qualifying person of which the security is acquired and the qualifying person which is the taxpayer's employer shall, for the particular taxation year in which the security is acquired, make an information return in prescribed form in respect of the benefit from employment that the taxpayer would be deemed to have received in the particular taxation year in respect of the acquisition of the security if the Act were read without reference to subsection 7(8) and, for this purpose, an information return made by one of the qualifying persons in respect of the taxpayer's acquisition of the security is deemed to have been made by each of the qualifying persons.

**Application**: The December 21, 2000 draft regulations, s. 1, will add subsec. 200(5), applicable to 2000 et seq.

**Technical Notes**: New subsection 200(5) of the *Income Tax Regulations* contains special reporting requirements relating to securities acquired under employee option agreements in circumstances to which new subsection 7(8) of the *Income Tax Act* applies. Under that subsection 7(8), taxation of the employment benefit arising from the acquisition of an employee option security after February 27, 2000 is deferred until the employee disposes of the security, provided certain conditions are met. Although taxation is deferred, new subsection 200(5) of the Regulations requires that an information return reporting the deferred amount be filed with the Minister of National Revenue in the year in which the employee acquires the security.

Under subsection 200(5), each of the following parties is jointly liable for filing the information return: the employer, the entity that granted the option under which the security is acquired and the entity whose security is acquired under the option. However, each of the parties is considered to have satisfied the filing requirement if one of the parties satisfies the requirement. This allows the parties involved in the agreement to determine who should be responsible for reporting the deferred employment benefit.

Subsection 200(5) requires that the information return be made in prescribed form as determined by the Minister of National Revenue. The prescribed form will be the employee's T4 slip for the year in which the security is acquired, and the deferred amount will be reported as a separate item on that slip.

It should be noted that this requirement is the only reporting requirement relating to the deferred employment benefit that is imposed on the parties involved in the option agreement. The onus is on the employee to include the deferred amount in computing employment income when filing the tax return for the year in which the security is disposed of.

**Definitions [Reg. 200]**: "amount", "annuity" — ITA 248(1); "arm's length" — ITA 251(1); "automobile" — ITA 248(1); "corporation" — ITA 248(1), *Interpretation Act* 35(1); "employed" — ITA 248(1); "employee", "employer", "employment", "office", "person", "personal or living expenses", "prescribed" — ITA 248(1); "refund of payments" — ITA 146.1(1); "registered education savings plan" — ITA 146.1(1), 248(1); "related" — ITA 251(2)–(6); "shareholder", "taxpayer" — ITA 248(1); "taxation year" — ITA 249.

**Forms [Reg. 200]**: RC4157(E): Employers' Guide: Filing the T4A Slip and Summary Form; T4: Segment; T4 Summ: Summary of remuneration paid; T4 Supp: Statement of remuneration paid; T4A Summ: Summary of remuneration paid (pension, retirement, annuity, and other income); T4A Supp: Statement of pension, retirement, annuity and other income; T4A-NR Summ: Summary of fees (etc.) paid to non-residents for services rendered in Canada; T4A-NR Supp: Statement of fees, etc., paid to non-residents of Canada to which s. 105(1) of the Regulations applies; T4A-RCA Summ: Return of distributions from an RCA; T4A-RCA Supp: Statement of amounts paid from an RCA; T475: Magnetic media filing transmittal — service bureau customer; T695: T4A/T4A-NR data tape transmittal; T709: Magnetic media filing program — filing tips for service bureau customers; T730: Preparation of T4-T4A summaries and supplementaries; T737-RCA Summ: Return of contributions paid to a custodian of an RCA; T737-RCA Supp: Statement of contributions paid to a custodian of an RCA; T4001: Employers' Guide to Payroll Deductions — Basic Information (guide); T5021: T5 filing transmittal.

**201. Investment income — (1)** Every person who makes a payment to a resident of Canada as or on account of

(a) a dividend or an amount deemed by the Act to be a dividend (other than a dividend deemed to have been paid to a person under any of subsections 84(1) to (4) of the Act where, pursuant to subsection 84(8) of the Act, those subsections do not apply to deem the dividend to have been received by the person),

(b) interest (other than the portion of the interest to which any of subsections (4) to (4.2) applies)

   (i) on a fully registered bond or debenture,

   (ii) in respect of

      (A) money on loan to,

      (B) money on deposit with, or

(C) property of any kind deposited or placed with,

a corporation, association, organization or institution,

(iii) in respect of an account with an investment dealer or broker,

(iv) paid by an insurer in connection with an insurance policy or an annuity contract, or

(v) on an amount owing in respect of compensation for property expropriated,

(c) a royalty payment in respect of the use of a work or invention or a right to take natural resources,

(d) a payment referred to in subsection 16(1) of the Act that can reasonably be regarded as being in part a payment of interest or other payment of an income nature and in part a payment of a capital nature, where the payment is made by a corporation, association, organization or institution,

(e) an amount paid from a person's NISA Fund No. 2, or

(f) an amount that is required by subsection 148.1(3) of the Act to be added in computing a person's income for a taxation year

shall make an information return in prescribed form in respect of the portion of such payment for which an information return has not previously been made under this section.

**Related Provisions**: Reg. 205 — Date return due; Reg. 205.1 — Electronic filing required if more than 500 returns; Reg. 209 — Two copies to be sent to taxpayer.

**Notes**: Although Reg. 201(1)(b) requires all interest and dividends to be reported, the CCRA administratively states that no T5 need be provided where the total for a recipient for the year is less than $50: T5 Guide (T4015).

Reg. 201(1)(b) amended by P.C. 1996-1419, effective for debt obligations issued after October 16, 1991, to add exclusion of Reg. 201(4.1) and (4.2).

Reg. 201(1)(e) added by P.C. 1993-1939, effective after 1993 in respect of amounts paid after 1992. Reg. 201(1)(f) added by P.C. 1996-765, effective for payments made after 1995.

**Interpretation Bulletins**: IT-531: Eligible funeral arrangements.

**Forms**: RC4157(E): Employers' Guide: Filing the T4A Slip and Summary Form; T1 Sched. 4: Statement of investment income; T3 Sched. 8: Statement of investment income and calculation of gross-up amount of dividends retained by trust; T4A Supp: Statement of pension, retirement, annuity and other income; T5 Segment; T5 Summ: Return of investment income; T5 Supp: Statement of investment income; T619: Magnetic media transmittal; T4015: T5 Guide — return of investment income (guide); T4031: Computer specifications for data filed on Magnetic Media — T5, T5008, T4RSP, T4RIF, NR4, and T3; T4126: How to file the T5 return of investment income (guide).

**(2) [Nominees and agents]** — Every person who receives as nominee or agent for a person resident in Canada a payment to which subsection (1) applies shall make an information return in prescribed form in respect of such payment.

> **Proposed Amendment — Reg. 201(2) — Social Insurance Number disclosure**
> **Letter from Department of Finance, March 17, 1999**: See under ITA 241(4).

**Related Provisions**: Reg. 205 — Date return due; Reg. 205.1 — Electronic filing required if more than 500 returns; Reg. 209 — Two copies to be sent to taxpayer.

**Forms**: T5 Supp: Statement of investment income;.

**I.T. Technical News**: No. 11 (U.S. spin-offs (divestitures) — dividends in kind).

**(3) [Bearer coupons, etc.]** — Where a person negotiates a bearer coupon, warrant or cheque representing interest or dividends referred to in subsection 234(1) of the Act for another person resident in Canada and the name of the beneficial owner of the interest or dividends is not disclosed on an ownership certificate completed pursuant to that subsection, the person negotiating the coupon, warrant or cheque, as the case may be, shall make an information return in prescribed form in respect of the payment received.

**Related Provisions**: Reg. 205 — Date return due; Reg. 205.1 — Electronic filing required if more than 500 returns; Reg. 209 — Two copies to be sent to taxpayer.

**(4) [Annual interest accrual]** — A person or partnership that is indebted in a calendar year under a debt obligation in respect of which subsection 12(4) of the Act and paragraph (1)(b) apply with respect to a taxpayer shall make an information return in prescribed form in respect of the amount that would, if the year were a taxation year of the taxpayer, be included as interest in respect of the debt obligation in computing the taxpayer's income for the year.

**Related Provisions**: Reg. 205 — Date return due; Reg. 205.1 — Electronic filing required if more than 500 returns; Reg. 209 — Two copies to be sent to taxpayer.

**Notes**: Reg. 201(4) amended by P.C. 1996-1419, effective for debt obligations issued after October 16, 1991. For earlier investment contracts last acquired or materially altered after 1989, read:

> (4) A person or partnership that is indebted under, or holds as nominee or agent for a person resident in Canada, an investment contract described in any of subparagraphs (1)(b)(i) to (v) in respect of which subsection 12(4) of the Act requires an amount to be included in computing a taxpayer's income for a taxation year ending in a calendar year shall, for each such taxpayer and calendar year, make an information return in prescribed form in respect of the amount of interest that would be required by that subsection to be included in computing the income of that taxpayer for the year in respect of the investment contract of that taxation year were the calendar year.

Reg. 201(4) amended by P.C. 1991-172, effective for investment contracts acquired or materially altered after 1989 (Department of Finance officials have confirmed this should be changed to "last acquired after 1989", to be consistent with changes in 1991 technical bill). For investment contracts last acquired before 1990, read:

> (4) Every person who is indebted under, or holds as nominee or agent for a person resident in Canada, an interest in an investment contract (other than a Canada Savings Bond or a debt obligation in bearer form) described in any of subparagraphs (1)(b)(i) to (v) in respect of which subsection 12(4) of the Act applies, or would apply but for an election made in respect thereof under subsection 12(8) of the Act, for a taxa-

tion year ending in a calendar year shall make an information return in prescribed form in respect of the amount of interest that would, but for subsection 12(8) of the Act, be included in computing the income for the year of a taxpayer in respect of the investment contract if the taxpayer's taxation year were the calendar year.

**(4.1) [Indexed debt obligation]** — A person or partnership that is indebted in a calendar year under an indexed debt obligation in respect of which paragraph (1)(b) applies shall, for each taxpayer who holds an interest in the debt obligation at any time in the year, make an information return in prescribed form in respect of the amount that would, if the year were a taxation year of the taxpayer, be included as interest in respect of the debt obligation in computing the taxpayer's income for the year.

**Related Provisions**: Reg. 205.1 — Electronic filing required if more than 500 returns; Reg. 209 — Two copies to be sent to taxpayer.

**Notes**: Reg. 201(4.1) added by P.C. 1996-1419, effective for debt obligations issued after October 16, 1991.

**(4.2) [Nominee or agent — debt obligation]** — Where, at any time in a calendar year, a person or partnership holds, as nominee or agent for a taxpayer resident in Canada, an interest in a debt obligation referred to in paragraph (1)(b) that is

(a) an obligation in respect of which subsection 12(4) of the Act applies with respect to the taxpayer, or

(b) an indexed debt obligation,

that person or partnership shall make an information return in prescribed form in respect of the amount that would, if the year were a taxation year of the taxpayer, be included as interest in respect of the debt obligation in computing the taxpayer's income for the year.

**Related Provisions**: Reg. 205.1 — Electronic filing required if more than 500 returns; Reg. 209 — Two copies to be sent to taxpayer.

**Notes**: Reg. 201(4.2) added by P.C. 1996-1419, effective for debt obligations issued after October 16, 1991.

**(5) [Insurers]** — Every insurer (within the meaning assigned by paragraph 148(10)(a) of the Act) who is a party to a life insurance policy (within the meaning assigned by paragraph 138(12)(f) [138(12)"life insurance policy"] of the Act) in respect of which an amount is to be included in computing a taxpayer's income pursuant to subsection 12.2(1), (3) or (5) or paragraph 56(1)(d.1) of the Act shall make an information return in prescribed form in respect of that amount.

**Related Provisions**: Reg. 205 — Date return due; Reg. 205.1 — Electronic filing required if more than 500 returns; Reg. 209 — Two copies to be sent to taxpayer.

**Notes**: Reg. 201(5) amended by P.C. 1991-172, effective for investment contracts acquired or materially altered after 1989 (Department of Finance officials have confirmed this will be changed to "last acquired after 1989", to be consistent with changes in 1991 technical bill).

For investment contracts last acquired before 1990, add a reference to 12.2(4) of the Act along with 12.2(1), (3) and (5).

**(6) [Debt obligation in bearer form]** — Every person who makes a payment to, or acts as a nominee or agent for, an individual resident in Canada in respect of the disposition or redemption of a debt obligation in bearer form shall make an information return in prescribed form in respect of the transaction indicating the proceeds of disposition or the redemption amount and such other information as may be required by the prescribed form.

**Related Provisions**: Reg. 205 — Date return due; Reg. 205.1 — Electronic filing required if more than 500 returns; Reg. 209 — Two copies to be sent to taxpayer.

**Forms**: T-BD(1) Supp: Statement of disposition — debt obligation in bearer form (single transaction); T-BD(2) Supp: Statement of disposition — debt obligations in bearer form (multiple transactions); T-BD(3) Summ and T-BD(4) Int Summ: Return of investment income debt obligations; T4031: Computer specifications for data filed on Magnetic Media — T5, T5008, T4RSP, T4RIF, NR4, and T3; T4091: Return of securities transactions [guide]; T5008 and T5008S Segment; T5008 Summ: Return of securities transactions; T5008 and T5008S Supp: Statement of securities transactions.

**(7) ["Debt obligation in bearer form"]** — For the purposes of subsection (6), "debt obligation in bearer form" means any debt obligation in bearer form other than

(a) a debt obligation that is redeemed for the amount for which the debt obligation was issued;

(b) a debt obligation described in paragraph 7000(1)(b); and

(c) a coupon, warrant or cheque referred to in subsection 207(1).

**Definitions [Reg. 201]**: "amount", "annuity" — ITA 248(1); "Canada" — ITA 255, *Interpretation Act* 35(1); "corporation" — ITA 248(1), *Interpretation Act* 35(1); "debt obligation in bearer form" — Reg. 201(7); "disposition", "dividend", "indexed debt obligation", "individual", "insurance policy", "insurer" — ITA 248(1); "life insurance policy" — ITA 138(12), 248(1); "person", "prescribed", "property" — ITA 248(1); "resident", "resident in Canada" — ITA 250; "taxation year" — ITA 249; "taxpayer" — ITA 248(1).

**202. Payments to non-residents** — **(1)** Every person resident in Canada who pays or credits, or is deemed by Part I or Part XIII of the Act to pay or credit, to a non-resident person an amount as, on account or in lieu of payment of, or in satisfaction of,

(a) a management or administration fee or charge,

(b) interest,

(c) income of or from an estate or trust,

(d) rent, royalty or a similar payment referred to in paragraph 212(1)(d) of the Act, including any payment described in any of subparagraphs 212(1)(d)(i) to (viii) of the Act,

(e) a timber royalty as described in paragraph 212(1)(e) of the Act,

(f) alimony or other payment referred to in paragraph 212(1)(f) of the Act,

(g) a dividend, including a patronage dividend as described in paragraph 212(1)(g) of the Act, or

(h) a payment for a right in or to the use of

(i) a motion picture film, or

(ii) a film or video tape for use in connection with television,

shall, in addition to any other return required by the Act or these Regulations, make an information return in prescribed form in respect of such amount.

**Related Provisions**: Reg. 202(7), (8) — Date return due; Reg. 205.1 — Electronic filing required if more than 500 returns; Reg. 209 — Two copies to be sent to taxpayer.

**Forms**: NR2-UK, NR2A-UK: Statement of amounts paid to non-residents of Canada; NR4 Supp: Statement of amounts paid or credited to non-residents of Canada; NR4 Summ: Return of amounts paid or credited to non-residents of Canada; NR4-OAS: Statement of OAS pension paid or credited to non-residents of Canada; NR14: Formal demand for non-resident tax information return; NR67AR: Non-resident tax remittance; NR67BR: Non-resident tax remittance form; NR75: Non-resident tax remitter registration forms; T4031: Computer specifications for data filed on Magnetic Media — T5, T5008, T4RSP, T4RIF, NR4, and T3.

**(2) [Various payments to non-residents]** — Every person resident in Canada who pays or credits, or is deemed by Part I or Part XIII of the Act to pay or credit, to a non-resident person an amount as, on account or in lieu of payment of, or in satisfaction of,

(a) a payment of a superannuation or pension benefit,

(b) a payment of any allowance or benefit described in any of subparagraphs 56(1)(a)(ii) to (vi) of the Act,

(c) a payment by a trustee under a registered supplementary unemployment benefit plan,

(d) a payment out of or under a registered retirement savings plan or a plan referred to in subsection 146(12) of the Act as an amended plan,

(e) a payment under a deferred profit sharing plan or a plan referred to in subsection 147(15) of the Act as a revoked plan,

(f) a payment under an income-averaging annuity contract, any proceeds of the surrender, cancellation, redemption, sale or other disposition of an income-averaging annuity contract, or any amount deemed by subsection 61.1(1) of the Act to have been received by the non-resident person as proceeds of the disposition of an income-averaging annuity contract,

(g) an annuity payment not described in any other paragraph of this subsection or subsection (1),

(h) a payment or a portion thereof, to which paragraph 212(1)(p) of the Act applies, out of or under a fund, plan, or trust that was on December 31, 1985 a registered home ownership savings plan (within the meaning assigned by paragraph 146.2(1)(h) of the Act as it read in its application to the 1985 taxation year),

(i) a payment out of or under a registered retirement income fund,

(j) a payment that is or that would be, if paragraph 212(1)(r) of the Act were read without reference to subparagraph 212(1)(r)(ii), a payment described in that paragraph in respect of a registered education savings plan,

(k) a grant under a program prescribed for the purposes of paragraph 212(1)(s) of the Act,

(l) a payment described in paragraph 212(1)(j) of the Act in respect of a retirement compensation arrangement, or

(m) a payment described in paragraph 212(1)(v) of the Act,

shall, in addition to any other return required by the Act or these Regulations, make an information return in prescribed form in respect of such amount.

**Related Provisions**: Reg. 202(7), (8) — Date return due; Reg. 205.1 — Electronic filing required if more than 500 returns; Reg. 209 — Two copies to be sent to taxpayer.

**Notes**: Reg. 202(2)(j) amended by P.C. 1998-2275, effective for 1998 and later taxation years. For earlier years, read simply "a payment described in paragraph 212(1)(r) of the Act in respect of a registered education savings plan".

Reg. 202(2)(m) added by P.C. 1999-2212, effective for payments made or credited after 1999.

**Forms**: NR4 Supp: Statement of amounts paid or credited to non-residents of Canada; NR4 Summ: Return of amounts paid or credited to non-residents of Canada; NR4A-RCA: Statement of amounts paid to non-residents of Canada to which para. 212(1)(j) applies; NR14: Formal demand for non-resident tax information return.

**(2.1) [NISA Fund No. 2]** — Every person resident in Canada who pays an amount to a non-resident person from a NISA Fund No. 2 shall, in addition to any other return required by the Act or these Regulations, make an information return in prescribed form in respect of the amount.

**Related Provisions**: Reg. 202(7), (8) — Date return due; Reg. 205.1 — Electronic filing required if more than 500 returns; Reg. 209 — Two copies to be sent to taxpayer.

**Notes**: Reg. 202(2.1) added by P.C. 1993-1939, effective after 1993 in respect of amounts paid after 1992.

**(3) [Nominee or agent]** — Every person who is paid or credited with an amount referred to in subsection (1), (2) or (2.1) for or on behalf of a non-resident person shall make an information return in prescribed form in respect of the amount.

**Related Provisions**: Reg. 202(7), (8) — Date return due; Reg. 205.1 — Electronic filing required if more than 500 returns; Reg. 209 — Two copies to be sent to taxpayer.

**Notes**: Reference to Reg. 202(2.1) in Reg. 202(3) added by P.C. 1993-1939, effective after 1993 in respect of amounts paid after 1992.

**(4) [Non-resident payer deemed resident in Canada]** — A non-resident person who is deemed, under subsection 212(13) of the Act, to be a person resident in Canada for the purposes of section 212 of the Act shall be deemed, in the same circumstances,

Part II — Information Returns | Reg. S. 204

to be a person resident in Canada for the purposes of subsections (1) and (2).

**(5) [Partnership payer deemed resident in Canada]** — A partnership that is deemed, under paragraph 212(13.1)(a) of the Act, to be a person resident in Canada for the purposes of Part XIII of the Act shall be deemed, in the same circumstances, to be a person resident in Canada for the purposes of subsections (1) and (2).

**(6) [Non-resident payer carrying on business in Canada]** — A non-resident person who is deemed, under subsection 212(13.2) of the Act, to be a person resident in Canada for the purposes of Part XIII of the Act shall be deemed, in the same circumstances, to be a person resident in Canada for the purposes of subsections (1) and (2).

**(7) [Filing deadline]** — Subject to subsection (8), an information return required under this section shall be filed on or before March 31 and shall be in respect of the preceding calendar year.

**(8) [Filing deadline — trust or estate]** — Where an amount referred to in subsection (1) or (2) is income of or from an estate or trust, the information return required under this section in respect thereof shall be filed within 90 days from the end of the taxation year of the estate or trust in which the amount was paid or credited and shall be in respect of that taxation year.

**Definitions [Reg. 202]**: "amount" — ITA 248(1); "deferred profit sharing plan" — ITA 147(1), 248(1); "disposition", "dividend" — ITA 248(1); "estate" — ITA 104(1), 248(1); "income-averaging annuity contract", "non-resident", "person", "prescribed" — ITA 248(1); "registered education savings plan" — ITA 146.1(1), 248(1); "registered home ownership savings plan" — ITA 248(1); "registered retirement income fund" — ITA 146.3(1), 248(1); "registered retirement savings plan" — ITA 146(1), 248(1); "registered supplementary unemployment benefit plan" — ITA 145(1), 248(1); "resident" — ITA 250, Reg. 202(4), (5), (6); "resident in Canada" — ITA 250; "retirement compensation arrangement", "superannuation or pension benefit" — ITA 248(1); "taxation year" — ITA 249; "trust" — ITA 104(1), 248(1), (3).

**Forms [Reg. 202]**: NR4 Supp: Statement of amounts paid or credited to non-residents of Canada; NR4 Summ: Return of amounts paid or credited to non-residents of Canada.

**203. Certain income in respect of non-residents** — **(1)** Every person in Canada who, as a nominee, agent, or custodian receives income derived from a source within the United States on behalf of a person whose address is outside Canada shall make an information return in prescribed form in respect of such income.

**Related Provisions**: Reg. 205.1 — Electronic filing required if more than 500 returns.

**Forms**: NR1: Return of income received from sources within the United States on behalf of non-residents of Canada.

**(2)** The return required under this section shall be filed on or before March 15, and shall be in respect of the preceding calendar year.

**Definitions [Reg. 203]**: "Canada" — ITA 255, *Interpretation Act* 35(1); "person", "prescribed" — ITA 248(1); "United States" — *Interpretation Act* 35(1).

**204. Estates and trusts** — **(1) [Trustee to file return]** — Every person having the control of, or receiving income, gains or profits in a fiduciary capacity, or in a capacity analogous to a fiduciary capacity, shall make a return in prescribed form in respect thereof.

**Related Provisions**: ITA 150(1)(c) — Trust tax return; Reg. 205.1 — Electronic filing required if more than 500 returns; Reg. 209 — Two copies to be sent to taxpayer.

**Interpretation Bulletins**: IT-531: Eligible funeral arrangements.

**Information Circulars**: 78-5R3: Communal organizations; 78-14R2: Guidelines for trust companies, etc.

**Forms**: T3: Trust income tax and information return; T3 Summ: Summary of trust income allocations and designations; T3 Supp: Statement of trust income allocations; also in certain cases; T3ATH-IND: Amateur athlete trust income tax return; T3D: Deferred profit sharing plan or revoked plan information return and income tax return; T3F: Mutual fund, pooled fund and investment corporation information return; T3G: Certification of no tax liability by a group of RRSPs, RRIFs, or RESPs; T3IND: T3IND income tax return for RRSP, RRIF, or RESP; T3P: Employee's pension plan income tax return; T3S: Supplementary unemployment benefit plan — income tax return; T4031: Computer specifications for data filed on Magnetic Media — T5, T5008, T4RSP, T4RIF, NR4, and T3.

**(2) [Filing deadline]** — The return required under this section shall be filed within 90 days from the end of the taxation year and shall be in respect of the taxation year.

**Interpretation Bulletins**: IT-531: Eligible funeral arrangements.

**(3) [Exceptions]** — Subsection (1) does not require a trust to make a return for a taxation year at the end of which it is

(a) governed by a deferred profit sharing plan or by a plan referred to in subsection 147(15) of the Act as a revoked plan;

(b) governed by an employees profit sharing plan;

(c) a registered charity;

(d) governed by an eligible funeral arrangement;

(d.1) a cemetery care trust; or

(e) governed by a registered education savings plan.

**Related Provisions**: ITA 148.1 — Eligible funeral arrangements; ITA 149.1(14) — Charity information return; Reg. 201(1)(f) — Eligible funeral arrangement information return; Reg. 212 — EPSP information return.

**Notes**: Opening words of Reg. 204(3) changed from "This section does not apply in respect of a trust that is", and para. (d) added, by P.C. 1996-765, effective 1993.

Reg. 204(3)(d.1) added by P.C. 1999-2212, effective for 1998 and later taxation years.

Reg. 204(3)(e) added by P.C. 1998-2275, effective for 1998 and later taxation years.

**Interpretation Bulletins**: IT-531: Eligible funeral arrangements.

**Definitions [Reg. 204]**: "deferred profit sharing plan" — ITA 147(1), 248(1); "employees profit sharing plan" — ITA 144(1),

248(1); "person", "prescribed", "registered charity" — ITA 248(1); "taxation year" — ITA 249; "trust" — ITA 104(1), 248(1), (3).

**205. Date returns to be filed** — **(1)** All returns required under this Part shall be filed with the Minister without notice or demand and, unless otherwise specifically provided, on or before the last day of February in each year and shall be in respect of the preceding calendar year.

**Related Provisions**: Reg. 202(7), (8), 203(2), 204(2), 205(2) — Exceptions.

**(2) [Where business discontinued]** — Where a person who is required to make a return under this Part discontinues his business or activity, the return shall be filed within 30 days of the day of the discontinuance of the business or activity and shall be in respect of any calendar year or a portion thereof prior to the discontinuance of the business or activity for which a return has not previously been filed.

**Definitions [Reg. 205]**: "business", "Minister", "person" — ITA 248(1).

**205.1 Electronic filing** — A person who is required to make an information return under this Part, or who files an information return on behalf of a person who is required to make an information return under this Part, shall file the information return with the Minister in an electronic format if more than 500 such returns are to be filed for the calendar year.

**Related Provisions**: ITA 244(22) — Electronic filing permitted.

**Notes**: Reg. 205.1 added by P.C. 1998-2273, effective for returns required to be filed for the 1999 and later calendar years. It appears that the words "such returns" mean that a person is required to file all information returns electronically if they have more than 500 returns, even though there may be fewer than 500 of any given type.

**Definitions [Reg. 205.1]**: "Minister", "person" — ITA 248(1).

**206. Legal representatives and others** — **(1)** Where a person, who is required to make a return under this Part, has died, such return shall be filed by his legal representative within 90 days of the date of death and shall be in respect of any calendar year or a portion thereof prior to the date of death for which a return has not previously been filed.

**(2) [Trustee in bankruptcy, etc.]** — Every trustee in bankruptcy, assignee, liquidator, curator, receiver, trustee or committee and every agent or other person administering, managing, winding-up, controlling or otherwise dealing with the property, business, estate or income of a person who has not filed a return as required by this Part shall file such return.

**Definitions [Reg. 206]**: "legal representative", "person", "property" — ITA 248(1).

**207. Ownership certificates** — **(1)** An ownership certificate completed pursuant to section 234 of the Act shall be delivered to the debtor or encashing agent at the time the coupon, warrant or cheque referred to in that section is negotiated.

**(2)** The debtor or encashing agent to whom an ownership certificate has been delivered pursuant to subsection (1) shall forward it to the Minister on or before the 15th day of the month following the month the coupon, warrant or cheque, as the case may be, was negotiated.

**(3)** The operation of section 234 of the Act is extended to a bearer coupon or warrant negotiated by or on behalf of a non-resident person who is subject to tax under Part XIII of the Act in respect of such a coupon or warrant.

**Forms**: T600, T600B: Ownership certificate; NR601: Non-resident ownership certificate — withholding tax; NR602: Non-resident ownership certificate — no withholding tax.

**Definitions [Reg. 207]**: "Minister" — ITA 248(1); "month" — *Interpretation Act* 35(1); "non-resident", "person" — ITA 248(1).

**208. Dispositions of income-averaging annuity contracts** — Every person who carries on a business referred to in paragraph 61(4)(b) [61(4)"income-averaging annuity contract"] of the Act shall make an information return in prescribed form in respect of

(a) any amount paid by that person to a resident of Canada as, on account or in lieu of payment of, or in satisfaction of, proceeds of the surrender, cancellation, redemption, sale or other disposition of an income-averaging annuity contract; or

(b) any amount deemed by subsection 61.1(1) of the Act to have been received by an individual resident in Canada as proceeds of the disposition of an income-averaging annuity contract that was made with that person.

**Related Provisions**: Reg. 205 — Date return due; Reg. 205.1 — Electronic filing required if more than 500 returns; Reg. 209 — Two copies to be sent to taxpayer.

**Definitions [Reg. 208]**: "amount", "annuity", "business" — ITA 248(1); "Canada" — ITA 255, *Interpretation Act* 35(1); "disposition", "income-averaging annuity contract", "individual", "person", "prescribed" — ITA 248(1); "resident", "resident in Canada" — ITA 250.

**Forms**: T4A: Statement of pension, retirement, annuity and other income.

**209. Distribution of taxpayers' portions of returns** — **(1)** Every person who is required by section 200, 201, 202, 204, 208, 212, 214, 215, 217, 218, 223, 226, 227, 228, 229, 230, 232, 233 or 234 to make an information return shall forward to each taxpayer to whom the return relates two copies of the portion of the return that relates to that taxpayer.

**(2)** The copies referred to in subsection (1) shall be sent to the taxpayer at his last known address or delivered to him in person, on or before the date the return is required to be filed with the Minister.

**Notes**: Reference to Regs. 232 and 233 added to Reg. 209 by P.C. 1992-1567, effective 1991; reference to Reg. 234 added by P.C. 1993-1939, effective after 1993 in respect of amounts paid after 1992.

**Definitions [Reg. 209]**: "Minister", "person", "taxpayer" — ITA 248(1).

**210. Tax deduction information** — Every person who makes or has at any time made a payment described in section 153 of the Act and every person who pays or credits or has at any time paid or credited, or is deemed by Part I or Part XIII of the Act to pay or credit or to have at any time paid or credited, an amount described in Part XIII of the Act shall, on demand by registered letter from the Minister make an information return in prescribed form containing the information required therein and shall file the return with the Minister within such reasonable time as may be stipulated in the registered letter.

**Definitions [Reg. 210]**: "amount", "Minister", "person", "prescribed" — ITA 248(1).

**Forms**: T4-T4A: Summary of remuneration paid; T730: Preparation of T4-T4A summaries and supplementaries.

**211. Accrued bond interest** — (1) Every financial company making a payment in respect of accrued interest by virtue of redemption, assignment or other transfer of a bond, debenture or similar security (other than an income bond, an income debenture or an investment contract in respect of which subsection 201(4) applies), shall make an information return in prescribed form.

**Related Provisions**: Reg. 205.1 — Electronic filing required if more than 500 returns.

**Notes**: Reg. 211(1) amended by P.C. 1991-172, effective for investment contracts acquired or materially altered after 1989 (Department of Finance officials have confirmed this will be changed to "last acquired after 1989", to be consistent with changes in 1991 technical bill).

For investment contracts last acquired before 1990, ignore the words "or an investment contract in respect of which subsection 201(4) applies".

(2) The return referred to in subsection (1) shall be forwarded to the Minister on or before the 15th day of the month following the month in which the payment referred to in subsection (1) is made.

(3) For the purposes of this section, a financial company includes a bank, an investment dealer, a stockbroker, a trust company and an insurance company.

(4) The provisions of subsection (1) do not apply to a payment made by one financial company to another financial company.

**Definitions [Reg. 211]**: "bank" — ITA 248(1), *Interpretation Act* 35(1); "financial company" — Reg. 211(3); "income bond", "Minister" — ITA 248(1); "month" — *Interpretation Act* 35(1); "prescribed" — ITA 248(1); "trust" — ITA 104(1), 248(1), (3).

**Forms**: T600 or T600B: Ownership certificate.

**212. Employees profit sharing plans** — (1) Every trustee of an employees profit sharing plan shall make an information return in prescribed form.

**Related Provisions**: Reg. 205.1 — Electronic filing required if more than 500 returns; Reg. 209 — Two copies to be sent to taxpayer.

(2) Notwithstanding subsection (1), the return required under this section may be filed by the employer instead of by the trustee.

**Related Provisions**: Reg. 205 — Date return due.

**Definitions [Reg. 212]**: "employees profit sharing plan" — ITA 144(1), 248(1); "employer", "prescribed" — ITA 248(1).

**Forms**: T4PS Segment; T4PS Summ: Return of allocations and payments under employees profit sharing plan; T4PS Supp: Statement of employees' profit sharing plan allocations and payments.

**213. Electric, gas or steam corporations** — (1) Every corporation engaged in the distribution or generation of electrical energy, gas or steam shall make an information return in prescribed form in respect of each taxation year of the corporation.

(2) The return required under this section shall be filed within 6 months from the end of the taxation year in respect of which the return is made.

**Definitions [Reg. 213]**: "corporation" — ITA 248(1), *Interpretation Act* 35(1); "month" — *Interpretation Act* 35(1); "prescribed" — ITA 248(1); "taxation year" — ITA 249.

**Forms**: T2025: Return of information — Electric, gas or steam corporations.

**214. Registered retirement savings plans** — (1) Every person who pays an amount that is required by subsection 146(8) of the Act to be included in computing the income of a taxpayer for a taxation year shall make an information return in prescribed form.

**Related Provisions**: Reg. 205 — Date return due; Reg. 205.1 — Electronic filing required if more than 500 returns; Reg. 209 — Two copies to be sent to taxpayer.

**Forms**: See at end of Reg. 214.

(2) Where, in a taxation year, subsection 146(6), (7), (9), or (10) of the Act is applicable in respect of a trust governed by a registered retirement savings plan, the trustee of such a plan shall make an information return in prescribed form.

**Related Provisions**: Reg. 205 — Date return due; Reg. 205.1 — Electronic filing required if more than 500 returns; Reg. 209 — Two copies to be sent to taxpayer.

**Forms**: See at end of Reg. 214.

(3) Where, in respect of an amended plan referred to in subsection 146(12) of the Act, an amount is required to be included in computing the income of a taxpayer for a taxation year, the issuer of the plan shall make an information return in prescribed form.

**Related Provisions**: Reg. 205 — Date return due; Reg. 205.1 — Electronic filing required if more than 500 returns; Reg. 209 — Two copies to be sent to taxpayer.

**Forms**: See at end of Reg. 214.

(4) Where subsection 146(8.8) of the Act deems an amount to be received by an annuitant as a benefit out of or under a registered retirement savings plan and such amount is required by subsection 146(8) of the Act to be included in computing the income of that annuitant for a taxation year, the issuer of the

Reg.
S. 214(4)                            Income Tax Regulations

plan shall make an information return in prescribed form.

**Related Provisions**: Reg. 205 — Date return due; Reg. 205.1 — Electronic filing required if more than 500 returns; Reg. 209 — Two copies to be sent to taxpayer.

**Forms**: See at end of Reg. 214.

**(5)** Where in a taxation year a transfer or payment of funds is made from a registered retirement savings plan under which the taxpayer is the annuitant to another registered retirement savings plan under which the taxpayer's spouse or former spouse or an individual who is party to a void or voidable marriage is the annuitant and subsection 146(16) of the Act applies in respect of the payment or transfer, the issuer of each such plan and each annuitant shall jointly make an information return in prescribed form.

**Related Provisions**: Reg. 205 — Date return due; Reg. 205.1 — Electronic filing required if more than 500 returns; Reg. 209 — Two copies to be sent to taxpayer.

**Notes**: References to "spouse" are expected to be amended to add "or common-law partner" effective 2001 or earlier by election, as has been done throughout the ITA. See Notes to ITA 248(1) "common-law partner".

**Forms**: See at end of Reg. 214.

**(6)** The return referred to in subsection (5) in respect of a particular payment or transfer described therein shall, within 30 days of the payment or transfer, be filed by the issuer of the registered retirement savings plan from which the payment or transfer was made.

**(7)** In this section,

**"annuitant"** has the meaning assigned by paragraph 146(1)(a) [146(1)"annuitant"] of the Act;

**"issuer"** has the meaning assigned by paragraph 146(1)(c.1) [146(1)"issuer"] of the Act;

**"spouse"** has the meaning assigned by subsection 146(1.1) of the Act.

**Notes**: Reg. 214(7) needs to be updated to correspond to amendment to the Act. The terms "annuitant" and "issuer" are now defined in ITA 146(1); "spouse" is no longer specifically defined for purposes of ITA 146 because ITA 252(4) provided, for 1993–2000 a definition that applies for all purposes of the Act and includes certain common-law spouses.

Reference to "spouse" is expected to be amended to add "or common-law partner" effective 2001 or earlier by election, as has been done throughout the ITA. See Notes to ITA 248(1)"common-law partner".

**Definitions [Reg. 214]**: "amount" — ITA 248(1); "annuitant" — ITA 146(1), Reg. 214(7); "individual" — ITA 248(1); "issuer" — ITA 146(1), Reg. 214(7); "person", "prescribed" — ITA 248(1); "registered retirement savings plan" — ITA 146(1), 248(1); "spouse" — ITA 146(1.1), Reg. 214(7); "taxation year" — ITA 249; "taxpayer" — ITA 248(1); "trust" — ITA 104(1), 248(1), (3).

**Forms [Reg. 214]**: T4RSP Segment; T4RSP Summ: Return of registered retirement savings plan income; T4RSP Supp: Statement of registered retirement savings plan income; T4031: Computer specifications for data filed on Magnetic Media — T5, T5008, T4RSP, T4RIF, NR4, and T3; T4079: T4RSP and T4RIF guide.

## 215. Registered retirement income funds —
**(1)** In this section,

**"annuitant"** has the meaning assigned by paragraph 146.3(1)(a) [146.3(1)"annuitant"] of the Act;

**"carrier"** has the meaning assigned by paragraph 146.3(1)(b) [146.3(1)"carrier"] of the Act.

**(2)** Every carrier of a registered retirement income fund who pays out of or under it an amount any portion of which is required under subsection 146.3(5) of the Act to be included in computing the income of a taxpayer shall make an information return in prescribed form in respect of the amount.

**Related Provisions**: Reg. 205 — Date return due; Reg. 205.1 — Electronic filing required if more than 500 returns; Reg. 209 — Two copies to be sent to taxpayer.

**Forms**: T4RIF Summ: Return of income out of a registered retirement income fund; T4RIF Supp: Statement of income out of a registered retirement income fund; T4031: Computer specifications for data filed on Magnetic Media — T5, T5008, T4RSP, T4RIF, NR4, and T3; T4079: T4RSP and T4RIF guide.

**(3)** Where subsection 146.3(4), (7), (8) or (10) of the Act applies in respect of any transaction or event with respect to property of a registered retirement income fund, the carrier of the fund shall make an information return in prescribed form in respect of the transaction or event.

**Related Provisions**: Reg. 205 — Date return due; Reg. 205.1 — Electronic filing required if more than 500 returns; Reg. 209 — Two copies to be sent to taxpayer.

**Forms**: T4RIF Summ: Return of income out of a registered retirement income fund; T4RIF Supp: Statement of income out of a registered retirement income fund; T4031: Computer specifications for data filed on Magnetic Media — T5, T5008, T4RSP, T4RIF, NR4, and T3; T4079: T4RSP and T4RIF guide.

**(4)** Where an amount is deemed under subsection 146.3(6) or (12) of the Act to be received by an annuitant out of or under a registered retirement income fund, the carrier of the fund shall make an information return in prescribed form in respect of the amount.

**Related Provisions [Reg. 215(4)]**: Reg. 205 — Date return due; Reg. 205.1 — Electronic filing required if more than 500 returns; Reg. 209 — Two copies to be sent to taxpayer.

**Forms [Reg. 215(4)]**: T4RIF Summ: Return of income out of a registered retirement income fund; T4RIF Supp: Statement of income out of a registered retirement income fund; T4031: Computer specifications for data filed on Magnetic Media — T5, T5008, T4RSP, T4RIF, NR4, and T3; T4079: T4RSP and T4RIF guide.

**Definitions [Reg. 215]**: "amount" — ITA 248(1); "annuitant" — ITA 146.3(1), Reg. 215(1); "carrier" — ITA 146.3(1), Reg. 215(1); "prescribed", "property" — ITA 248(1); "registered retirement income fund" — ITA 146.3(1), 248(1); "taxpayer" — ITA 248(1).

## 216. Registered Canadian amateur athletic associations — 
**(1)** Every registered Canadian amateur athletic association shall make an information return in prescribed form for each fiscal period of the association within six months after the end of the fiscal period.

(2) For the purposes of this section, "fiscal period" means the period for which the accounts of the registered Canadian amateur athletic association have been ordinarily made up and, in the absence of an established practice, the fiscal period is that adopted by the association but no such fiscal period shall exceed 12 months.

**Definitions [Reg. 216]**: "fiscal period" — Reg. 216(2); "month" — *Interpretation Act* 35(1); "prescribed", "registered Canadian amateur athletic association" — ITA 248(1).

**Forms [Reg. 216]**: T2052: Registered charities and registered Canadian amateur athletic associations — Return of information.

## 217. Disposition of interest in annuities and life insurance policies — (1) In this section,

"**disposition**" has the meaning assigned by paragraph 148(9)(c) [148(9)"disposition"] of the Act and includes anything deemed to be a disposition of a life insurance policy under subsection 148(2) of the Act;

"**insurer**" has the meaning assigned by paragraph 148(10)(a) of the Act;

"**life insurance policy**" has the meaning assigned by paragraph 138(12)(f) [138(12)"life insurance policy"] of the Act.

(2) Where by reason of a disposition of an interest in a life insurance policy an amount is required, pursuant to paragraph 56(1)(j) of the Act, to be included in computing the income of a taxpayer and the insurer that is the issuer of the policy is a party to, or is notified in writing of, the disposition, the insurer shall make an information return in prescribed form in respect of the amount.

**Related Provisions**: Reg. 205 — Date return due; Reg. 205.1 — Electronic filing required if more than 500 returns; Reg. 209 — Two copies to be sent to taxpayer.

**Definitions [Reg. 217]**: "amount" — ITA 248(1); "disposition" — ITA 248(1), Reg. 217(1); "insurer" — ITA 148(10)(a), Reg. 217(1); "life insurance policy" — ITA 138(12), Reg. 217(1); "prescribed", "taxpayer" — ITA 248(1); "writing" — *Interpretation Act* 35(1).

**Forms**: T5 Segment; T5 Summ: Return of investment income; T5 Supp: Statement of investment income.

## 218. Patronage payments — (1) Every person who, within the meaning of section 135 of the Act, makes payments to residents of Canada pursuant to an allocation in proportion to patronage shall make an information return in prescribed form in respect of payments so made.

**Related Provisions**: Reg. 205.1 — Electronic filing required if more than 500 returns; Reg. 209 — Two copies to be sent to taxpayer.

(2) Every person who receives a payment referred to in subsection (1) as nominee or agent for another person resident in Canada shall make an information return in prescribed form in respect of the payment so received.

**Related Provisions**: Reg. 205 — Date return due; Reg. 205.1 — Electronic filing required if more than 500 returns; Reg. 209 — Two copies to be sent to taxpayer.

**Definitions [Reg. 218]**: "Canada" — ITA 255, *Interpretation Act* 35(1); "person", "prescribed" — ITA 248(1); "resident", "resident in Canada" — ITA 250.

**Forms [Reg. 218]**: RC4157(E): Employers' Guide: Filing the T4A Slip and Summary Form; T4A: Statement of pension, retirement, annuity and other income.

## 219. Family allowances and similar payments — Where an allowance referred to in paragraph 56(5)(a) or (b) of the Act has been paid to a person and, in respect of that allowance, an amount is required to be included in computing the income of any taxpayer for a taxation year, the payer of the allowance shall

(a) make an information return in prescribed form in respect of such payment; and

(b) forward to the person at his latest known address, on or before the date the return is required to be filed with the Minister, three copies of the portion of the return relating to that person.

**Related Provisions**: Reg. 205 — Date return due; Reg. 209 — Two copies to be sent to taxpayer.

**Notes**: Family allowances were discontinued after 1992. The replacement Child Tax Benefit payments to lower-income families (see ITA 122.61) are non-taxable.

**Definitions [Reg. 219]**: "amount", "Minister", "person", "prescribed" — ITA 248(1); "taxation year" — ITA 249; "taxpayer" — ITA 248(1).

## 220. Cash bonus payments on Canada Savings Bonds — (1) Every person authorized to redeem Canada Savings Bonds (in this section referred to as the "redemption agent") who pays an amount in respect of a Canada Savings Bond as a cash bonus that the Government of Canada has undertaken to pay (other than any amount of interest, bonus or principal agreed to be paid at the time of the issue of the bond under the terms of the bond) shall make an information return in prescribed form in respect of such payment.

**Related Provisions**: Reg. 205.1 — Electronic filing required if more than 500 returns.

(2) Every redemption agent required by subsection (1) to make an information return shall

(a) issue to the payee, at the time the cash bonus is paid, two copies of the portion of the return relating to him; and

(b) file the return with the Minister on or before the 15th day of the month following the month in which the cash bonus was paid.

**Notes**: See ITA 12.1.

**Forms**: T1-CSB: Annual accrual form for compound interest Canada Savings Bonds; T600C: Statement of cash bonus payment Canada Savings Bonds.

**Definitions [Reg. 220]**: "amount" — ITA 248(1); "Canada" — ITA 255, *Interpretation Act* 35(1); "Minister" — ITA 248(1); "month" — *Interpretation Act* 35(1); "person", "prescribed" — ITA 248(1); "redemption agent" — Reg. 220(1).

**Reg. S. 221** — Income Tax Regulations

## 221. Qualified investments and foreign property

— (1) In this section, "reporting person" means

(a) a mutual fund corporation;

(b) an investment corporation;

(c) a mutual fund trust;

(d) a pooled fund trust (within the meaning assigned by subsection 5000(7));

(e) a resource property trust (within the meaning assigned by subsection 5000(7));

(f) a trust that would be a mutual fund trust if Part XLVIII were read without reference to paragraph 4801(b);

(g) a trust described in paragraph 65(1)(c) of the *Income Tax Application Rules*;

(h) a small business investment trust (within the meaning assigned by subsection 5103(1)); or

(i) a trust described in paragraph 149(1)(o.4) of the Act.

(2) Where in any taxation year a reporting person (other than a registered investment) claims that a share of its capital stock issued by it, or an interest of a beneficiary under it, is a qualified investment under section 146, 146.3 or 204 of the Act, the reporting person shall, in respect of the year and within 90 days after the end of the year, make an information return in prescribed form.

### Proposed Amendment — Reg. 221(2)

(2) Where in any taxation year a reporting person (other than a registered investment) claims that a share of its capital stock issued by it, or an interest as a beneficiary under it, is a qualified investment under section 146, 146.1, 146.3 or 204 of the Act, the reporting person shall, in respect of the year and within 90 days after the end of the year, make an information return in prescribed form.

**Application**: The October 27, 1998 draft regulations, s. 1, will amend subsec. 221(2) to read as above, applicable to 1999 *et seq.*

**Technical Notes**: [These] proposed regulations reflect the introduction of new rules in section 146.1 of the *Income Tax Act*, which limit the types of investments that registered education savings plans (RESPs) are permitted to hold.

Subsection 221(2) of the *Income Tax Regulations* requires certain types of corporations and trusts to file an information return in respect of a taxation year, where the corporation or the trust claims that a share of its capital stock, or an interest of a beneficiary under it, is a qualified investment for an registered retirement savings plan (RRSP), registered retirement income fund (RRIF) or deferred profit sharing plan (DPSP). The requirement for the information return is limited to the types of corporations and trusts described in subsection 221(1) of the Regulations that are not registered investments.

Subsection 221(2) is amended to extend the requirement for filing an information return to a corporation or a trust that claims that a share of its capital stock, or an interest of a beneficiary under it, is a qualified investment for an RESP

[section 146.1 — ed.]. This amendment is consequential on the introduction of qualified investment rules for RESPs.

**Related Provisions**: Reg. 205.1 — Electronic filing required if more than 500 returns.

(3) Where in any taxation year a reporting person (other than a registered investment) claims that a share of its capital stock issued by it, or that an interest of a beneficiary under it, is not foreign property for the purpose of section 206 of the Act, the reporting person shall, in respect of the year and within 90 days after the end of the year, make an information return in prescribed form.

**Related Provisions**: Reg. 205.1 — Electronic filing required if more than 500 returns.

**Notes [221]**: Reg. 221 amended and 222 repealed by P.C. 2000-183, effective for taxation years that begin after 1995. The amendment consolidates the two into one section and narrows their scope to conform with CCRA administrative practice. For taxation years beginning before 1996, read:

> 221. Qualified investments — Where in any taxation year a taxpayer is
>
> (a) a corporation that claims that a share of its capital stock is a qualified investment for the purposes of section 146, 146.2, 146.3 or 204 of the Act; or
>
> (b) a trust that claims that an interest of a beneficiary thereunder is a qualified investment for the purposes of section 146, 146.2, 146.3 or 204 of the Act,
>
> the taxpayer shall, in respect of that taxation year and within 90 days thereafter, make an information return in prescribed form.
>
> 222. Foreign property — Where in any taxation year a taxpayer is
>
> (a) a corporation that claims that a share of its capital stock is not foreign property for the purposes of section 206 of the Act, or
>
> (b) a trustee of a trust who claims that an interest as a beneficiary of the trust is not foreign property for the purposes of section 206 of the Act,
>
> the taxpayer shall, in respect of that taxation year and within 90 days thereafter, make an information return in prescribed form.

**Definitions [Reg. 221]**: "business" — ITA 248(1); "corporation" — ITA 248(1), *Interpretation Act* 35(1); "investment corporation" — ITA 130(3), 248(1); "mutual fund corporation" — ITA 131(8), 248(1); "mutual fund trust" — ITA 132(6)–(7), 132.2(1)(q), 248(1); "person", "prescribed", "property" — ITA 248(1); "registered investment" — ITA 204.4(1), 248(1); "reporting person" — Reg. 221(1); "share" — ITA 248(1); "taxation year" — ITA 249; "taxpayer" — ITA 248(1); "trust" — ITA 104(1), 248(1), (3).

**Information Circulars**: 78-14R2: Guidelines for trust companies and other persons responsible for filing T3R-IND, T3R-G, T3RIF-IND, T3RIF-G, T3H-IND, T3H-G, T3D, T3P, T3S, T3RI and T3F returns.

**Forms**: T3F: Investments prescribed to be qualified or not to be foreign property information return.

## 222. [Repealed]

**Notes**: See Notes to Reg. 221.

## 223. Registered home ownership savings plans — [No longer relevant]

**Notes**: RHOSPs no longer exist. See Notes to ITA 146.2.

**Definitions [Reg. 223]**: "amount" — ITA 248(1); "beneficiary" — Reg. 223(5); "Canada" — ITA 255, *Interpretation Act* 35(1); "depositary" — Reg. 223(5); "person", "prescribed" — ITA 248(1); "registered home ownership savings plan" — Reg. 223(5); "resident" — ITA 250; "taxation year" — ITA 249; "taxpayer" — ITA 248(1); "trust" — ITA 104(1), 248(1), (3).

**224. Canadian home insulation program and Canada oil substitution program** — Where an amount has been paid to a person pursuant to a program prescribed for the purposes of paragraph 12(1)(u), 56(1)(s) and 212(1)(s) of the Act, the payor shall

(a) make an information return in prescribed form in respect of such payment; and

(b) forward to the person at his latest known address on or before the date the return is required to be filed with the Minister two copies of the portion of the return relating to that person.

**Related Provisions**: Reg. 205 — Date return due; Reg. 205.1 — Electronic filing required if more than 500 returns.

**Definitions [Reg. 224]**: "amount", "Minister", "person", "prescribed" — ITA 248(1).

**225. Certified films and video tapes** — (1) Where principal photography or taping of a film or tape (within the meanings assigned by subsection 1100(21)) has occurred during a year or has been completed within 60 days after the end of the year, the producer of the film or tape or production company that produced the film or tape, or an agent of the producer or production company, shall

(a) make an information return in prescribed form in respect of any person who owns an interest in the film or tape at the end of the year; and

(b) forward to the person referred to in paragraph (a) at his latest known address on or before the date the return is required to be filed with the Minister two copies of the portion of the return relating to that person.

**Related Provisions**: Reg. 205.1 — Electronic filing required if more than 500 returns.

(2) The return required under this section shall be filed on or before March 31 and shall be in respect of the preceding calendar year.

**Definitions [Reg. 225]**: "Minister", "person", "prescribed" — ITA 248(1).

**Forms**: T1-CP Summ: Return in respect of certified productions.

**226. Scientific research tax credits** — (1) In this section,

"**administrator**" has the meaning assigned by paragraph 47.1(1)(a) of the Act;

"**designated security**" means a security issued or granted by a corporation in respect of which the corporation has designated an amount pursuant to subsection 194(4) of the Act;

"**first purchaser**" in relation to a designated security, means the first person (other than a trader or dealer in securities) to be the registered holder of the designated security;

"**security**" means

(a) a share of the capital stock of a corporation,

(b) a debt obligation issued by a corporation, or

(c) a right granted by a corporation under a scientific research financing contract;

"**trader or dealer in securities**" has the meaning assigned by paragraph 47.1(1)(l) of the Act.

(2) Each corporation that has designated an amount under subsection 194(4) of the Act in respect of a security issued or granted by it shall make an information return in prescribed form in respect of each such security.

(3) Each trader or dealer in securities who has acquired and disposed of a designated security during the course of the primary distribution thereof pursuant to a public offering shall make an information return in prescribed form in respect of each such designated security.

(4) Each bank, credit union and trust company that, as agent, acquired a designated security for the first purchaser thereof shall make an information return in prescribed form in respect of each such designated security.

(5) Each trader or dealer in securities who, as administrator of an indexed security investment plan, acquired a designated security for the first purchaser thereof shall make an information return in prescribed form in respect of each such designated security.

(6) Notwithstanding subsection 205(1), any return required to be made

(a) under subsection (2), in respect of a security issued by a corporation before March 1, 1984,

(b) under subsection (3), in respect of a designated security disposed of as described in subsection (3) before March 1, 1984, or

(c) under subsection (4) or (5), in respect of a designated security acquired as described in subsection (4) or (5), as the case may be, before March 1, 1984,

shall be filed on or before March 31, 1984.

**Notes**: See Notes to ITA 127.3(1).

**Definitions [Reg. 226]**: "administrator" — ITA 47.1(1)(a), Reg. 226(1); "amount" — ITA 248(1); "corporation" — ITA 248(1), *Interpretation Act* 35(1); "designated security" — Reg. 226(1); "disposed" — ITA 248(1)"disposition"; "first purchaser" — Reg. 226(1); "prescribed" — ITA 248(1); "security", "trader or dealer in securities" — Reg. 226(1); "trust" — ITA 104(1), 248(1), (3).

**227. Share purchase tax credits** — (1) In this section,

"administrator" has the meaning assigned by paragraph 47.1(1)(a) of the Act;

"designated share" means a share of the capital stock of a corporation in respect of which the corporation has designated an amount pursuant to subsection 192(4) of the Act;

"first purchaser", in relation to a designated share, means the first person (other than a trader or dealer in securities) to be the registered holder of the share;

"trader or dealer in securities" has the meaning assigned by paragraph 47.1(1)(l) of the Act.

(2) Each corporation that has designated an amount under subsection 192(4) of the Act in respect of a share issued by it shall make an information return in prescribed form in respect of each such share.

(3) Each trader or dealer in securities who has acquired and disposed of a designated share during the course of the primary distribution thereof pursuant to a public offering shall make an information return in prescribed form in respect of each such designated share.

(4) Each bank, credit union and trust company that, as agent, acquired a designated share for the first purchaser thereof shall make an information return in prescribed form in respect of each such designated share.

(5) Each trader or dealer in securities who, as administrator of an indexed security investment plan, acquired a designated share for the first purchaser thereof shall make an information return in prescribed form in respect of each such designated share.

**Notes**: See Notes to 127.2(1).

**Definitions [Reg. 227]**: "administrator" — ITA 47.1(1)(a), Reg. 227(1); "amount" — ITA 248(1); "corporation" — ITA 248(1), *Interpretation Act* 35(1); "designated share" — Reg. 227(1); "disposed" — ITA 248(1)"disposition"; "first purchaser" — Reg. 227(1); "indexed security investment plan" — ITA 47.1 [repealed]; "prescribed" — ITA 248(1); "share" — ITA 248(1); "trader or dealer in securities" — Reg. 227(1); "trust" — ITA 104(1), 248(1), (3).

### 228. Resource flow-through shares — (1) Each corporation that has renounced an amount under subsection 66(12.6), (12.601), (12.62) or (12.64) of the Act to a person shall make an information return in prescribed form in respect of the amount renounced.

(2) The return required under subsection (1) shall be filed with the Minister together with the prescribed form required to be filed under subsection 66(12.7) of the Act in respect of the amount renounced.

**Notes**: Reference to ITA 66(12.601) added to Reg. 228(1) by P.C. 1996-494, effective December 3, 1992.

**Definitions [Reg. 228]**: "amount" — ITA 248(1); "corporation" — ITA 248(1), *Interpretation Act* 35(1); "Minister"; "person", "prescribed" — ITA 248(1).

**Forms**: T101: Flow-through share — Summary of renunciation, reduction of amount previously renounced, allocation of assistance and calculation of Part XII.6 tax; T101 Supp: Statement — Renunciation of resource expense, reduction of amount previously renounced and allocation of assistance; T102 Summ: Summary — Allocation to members of a partnership of renounced resource expenses, reduction of amounts previously renounced and amount of assistance; T102 Supp: Statement of renounced resource expenses/assistance attributable to members of partnership.

### 229. Partnership return — (1) Every member of a partnership that carries on a business in Canada, or that is a Canadian partnership, at any time in a fiscal period of the partnership shall make for that period an information return in prescribed form containing the following information:

(a) the income or loss of the partnership for the fiscal period;

(b) the name, address and, in the case of an individual, the social insurance number of each member of the partnership who is entitled to a share referred to in paragraph (c) or (d) for the fiscal period;

(c) the share of each member of the income or loss of the partnership for the fiscal period;

(d) the share of each member for the fiscal period of each deduction, credit or other amount in respect of the partnership that is relevant in determining the member's income, taxable income, tax payable or other amount under the Act;

(e) the prescribed information contained in the form prescribed for the purposes of subsection 37(1) of the Act, where the partnership has made an expenditure in respect of scientific research and experimental development in the fiscal period; and

(f) such other information as may be required by the prescribed form.

**Related Provisions**: ITA 96(1) — Taxation of partnership income; ITA 152(1.4) — Determination by CCRA of income or loss of partnership; ITA 233.1(3) — Information return for partnership re non-arm's length transactions with non-residents; ITA 233.3 — Requirement to file information return re foreign property; Reg. 205.1 — Electronic filing required if more than 500 returns; Reg. 209 — Two copies to be sent to taxpayer; Reg. 236 — Partners to provide information.

**Notes**: Under the CCRA's administrative policy, certain partnerships are not required to file, including: (a) partnerships with five or fewer members throughout the fiscal period where no member is another partnership; (b) certain limited partnerships whose only activity is investment in flow-through shares; and (c) partnerships whose members are all status Indians whose income from the partnership is exempt under s. 87 of the *Indian Act* (see Notes to 81(1)(a)). See Information Circular 89-5R, para. 11, as amended by Special Release of December 1, 1994.

Where no return is required, it is still advisable for partnerships to file, to start time running under ITA 152(1.4)(b). Otherwise the partnership income may be open for assessment indefinitely: ITA 152(1.7)(b) and CCRA VIEWS docs 9726115 and 2000-0010935.

See Notes to ITA 150(1)(c) re an extension of the deadline for the 1994 return for certain partnerships (and testamentary trusts) to March 31, 1995.

**Information Circulars**: 82-2R2: SIN legislation that relates to the preparation of information slips; 89-5R: Partnership information return.

**Forms**: T4068: Guide for the partnership information return; T5011: Application for filer identification number; T5013 Summ: Partnership information return; T5013 Supp: Statement of partnership income; T5014: Partnership capital cost allowance schedule; T5015: Reconciliation of partner's capital account; T5016: Summary information for tax shelters that are partnerships or for partnerships that allocated renounced resource expenses to their members; T5017: Calculation of deduction for cumulative eligible capital of a partnership.

**(2)** For the purposes of subsection (1), an information return made by any member of a partnership shall be deemed to have been made by each member of the partnership.

**(3)** Every person who holds an interest in a partnership as nominee or agent for another person shall make an information return in prescribed form in respect of that interest.

**Related Provisions**: Reg. 205.1 — Electronic filing required if more than 500 returns; Reg. 209 — Two copies to be sent to taxpayer.

**(4)** [Revoked]

**Notes**: Reg. 229(4) repealed by P.C. 1993-1691, effective September 8, 1993. It allowed the Minister to exempt the members of a partnership or class of partnerships from Reg. 229. ITA 220(2.1) now provides authority for the Minister to waive documentary requirements in general.

**(5)** Subject to subsection (6), a return required by this section shall be filed with the Minister without notice or demand

(a) in the case of a fiscal period of a partnership all the members of which are corporations throughout the fiscal period, within five months after the end of the fiscal period;

(b) in the case of a fiscal period of a partnership all the members of which are individuals throughout the fiscal period, on or before the last day of March in the calendar year immediately following the calendar year in which the fiscal period ended or with which the fiscal period ended coincidentally; and

(c) in the case of any other fiscal period of a partnership, on or before the earlier of

(i) the day that is five months after the end of the fiscal period, and

(ii) the last day of March in the calendar year immediately following the calendar year in which the fiscal period ended or with which the fiscal period ended coincidentally.

**Forms**: See under Reg. 229(1).

**(6)** Where a partnership discontinues its business or activity, the return required under this section shall be filed, in respect of any fiscal period or portion thereof prior to the discontinuance of the business or activity for which a return has not previously been filed under this section, on or before the earlier of

(a) the day that is 90 days after the discontinuance of the business or activity, and

(b) the day the return is required to be filed under subsection (5).

**Definitions [Reg. 229]**: "amount", "business" — ITA 248(1); "Canada" — ITA 255, *Interpretation Act* 35(1); "corporation" — ITA 248(1), *Interpretation Act* 35(1); "fiscal period" — ITA 249.1; "individual", "Minister" — ITA 248(1); "month" — *Interpretation Act* 35(1); "person", "prescribed", "scientific research and experimental development", "share", "taxable income" — ITA 248(1).

**230. Security transactions** — **(1)** In this section,

**"publicly traded"** means, with respect to any security,

(a) a security that is listed or posted for trading on a stock exchange, commodity exchange, futures exchange or any other exchange, or

(b) a security in respect of the sale and distribution of which a prospectus, registration statement or similar document has been filed with a public authority;

**"sale"** includes the granting of an option and a short sale;

**"security"** means

(a) a publicly traded share of the capital stock of a corporation,

(b) a publicly traded debt obligation,

(c) a debt obligation of or guaranteed by

(i) the Government of Canada,

(ii) the government of a province or an agent thereof,

(iii) a municipality in Canada,

(iv) a municipal or public body performing a function of government in Canada, or

(v) the government of a foreign country or of a political subdivision of a foreign country or a local authority of such a government,

(d) a publicly traded interest in a trust,

(e) a publicly traded interest in a partnership,

(f) an option or contract in respect of any property described in any of paragraphs (a) to (e), or

(g) a publicly traded option or contract in respect of any property including any commodity, financial futures, foreign currency or precious metal or in respect of any index relating to any property;

**"trader or dealer in securities"** means

(a) a person who is registered or licensed under the laws of a province to trade in securities, or

(b) a person who in the ordinary course of business makes sales of securities as agent on behalf of others.

**(2)** Every trader or dealer in securities who, in a calendar year, purchases a security as principal or sells a security as agent for any vendor shall make an information return for the year in prescribed form in respect of the purchase or sale.

**Related Provisions**: Reg. 205.1 — Electronic filing required if more than 500 returns; Reg. 209 — Two copies to be sent to taxpayer.

**Forms**: T5008 Summ: Return of securities transactions; T5008 Supp: Statement of securities transactions.

(3) Every person (other than an individual who is not a trust) who in a calendar year redeems, acquires or cancels in any manner whatever any securities issued by that person shall make an information return for the year in prescribed form in respect of each such transaction, other than a transaction to which section 51, 86 (where there is no consideration receivable other than new shares) or 87 or subsection 98(3) or (6) of the Act applies.

**Related Provisions**: Reg. 205.1 — Electronic filing required if more than 500 returns; Reg. 209 — Two copies to be sent to taxpayer.

(4) Subsection (3) applies to

(a) Her Majesty in right of Canada or a province;

(b) a municipal or public body performing a function of government in Canada; and

(c) an agent of a person referred to in paragraph (a) or (b).

(5) Every person who, in the ordinary course of a business of buying and selling precious metals in the form of certificates, bullion or coins, makes a payment in a calendar year to another person in respect of a sale by that other person of any such property shall make an information return for that year in prescribed form in respect of each such sale.

**Related Provisions**: Reg. 205.1 — Electronic filing required if more than 500 returns; Reg. 209 — Two copies to be sent to taxpayer.

(6) Every person who, while acting as nominee or agent for another person in respect of a sale or other transaction to which subsection (2), (3) or (5) applies, receives the proceeds of the sale or other transaction shall, where the transaction is carried out in the name of the nominee or agent, make an information return in prescribed form in respect of the sale or other transaction.

**Related Provisions**: Reg. 205.1 — Electronic filing required if more than 500 returns; Reg. 209 — Two copies to be sent to taxpayer.

(7) This section does not apply in respect of

(a) a purchase of a security by a trader or dealer in securities from another trader or dealer in securities other than a non-resident trader or dealer in securities;

(b) a sale of currencies or precious metals in the form of jewellery, works of art or numismatic coins;

(c) a sale of precious metals by a person who, in the ordinary course of business, produces or sells precious metals in bulk or in commercial quantities;

(d) a sale of securities by a trader or dealer in securities on behalf of a person who is exempt from tax under Part I of the Act; or

(e) a redemption by the issuer or an agent of the issuer of a debt obligation where

(i) the debt obligation was issued for its principal amount,

(ii) the redemption satisfies all of the issuer's obligations in respect of the debt obligation,

(iii) each person with an interest in the debt obligation is entitled in respect thereof to a proportion of all payments of principal equal to the proportion to which the person is entitled of all payments other than principal, and

(iv) an information return is required under another section of this Part to be made as a result of the redemption in respect of each person with an interest in the debt obligation.

**Related Provisions**: Reg. 205 — Date return due.

**Notes**: Reg. 230 added by P.C. 1989-2156, effective 1991.

**Definitions [Reg. 230]**: "business" — ITA 248(1); "Canada" — ITA 255, *Interpretation Act* 35(1); "corporation" — ITA 248(1), *Interpretation Act* 35(1); "Her Majesty" — *Interpretation Act* 35(1); "individual", "non-resident", "person", "prescribed", "principal amount", "property" — ITA 248(1); "province" — *Interpretation Act* 35(1); "publicly traded", "sale", "security" — Reg. 230(1); "share" — ITA 248(1); "trader or dealer in securities" — Reg. 230(1); "trust" — ITA 104(1), 248(1), (3).

## 231. Information respecting tax shelters — (1)
In this section, "promoter" in respect of a tax shelter and "tax shelter" have the meanings assigned by subsection 237.1(1) of the Act.

(2) An information return made under subsection 237.1(7) of the Act in respect of the acquisition of an interest in a tax shelter in a calendar year shall be filed with the Minister on or before the last day of February of the immediately following calendar year.

**Related Provisions**: Reg. 205.1 — Electronic filing required if more than 500 returns.

**Forms**: T5003: Tax shelter information return; T5004: Statement of tax shelter loss or deduction; T5016: Summary information for tax shelters that are partnerships or for partnerships that allocated renounced resource expenses to their members.

(3) Where a person who is required to make an information return under subsection 237.1(7) of the Act discontinues the business or activity by reason of which the person is required to make the return, the return shall be filed within 30 days after the day of the discontinuance of the business or activity in respect of any calendar year or portion thereof prior to the discontinuance for which such a return has not previously been filed.

(4) [Repealed]

**Notes**: Reg. 231(4) repealed by P.C. 2000-1000, effective 1996. Before 1996, read:

(4) Every person required to make a return under subsection 237.1(7) of the Act shall, on or before the day on or before

which the return is required to be filed with the Minister, forward to each person to whom the return relates two copies of the portion of the return relating to that person.

This rule now appears in ITA 237.1(7.3) instead.

**(5) [Repealed]**

**Notes**: Reg. 231(5) repealed by P.C. 2000-1000, effective 1996. Before 1996, read:

(5) Every promoter with respect to a tax shelter shall

(a) on every written statement made by the promoter that refers either directly or indirectly and either expressly or impliedly to the issuance by the Department of National Revenue of an identification number for the tax shelter, as well as on the copies of the portion of the information return to be forwarded pursuant to subsection (4), include the following statement:

"The identification number issued for this tax shelter shall be included in any income tax return filed by the investor. Issuance of the identification number is for administrative purposes only and does not in any way confirm the entitlement of an investor to claim any tax benefits associated with the tax shelter"; and

(b) prominently display on the upper right-hand corner of any statement of earnings prepared by the promoter in respect of the tax shelter the identification number issued for the tax shelter.

This rule now appears in ITA 237.1(5) instead.

**(6)** For the purposes of paragraph (b) of the definition "tax shelter" in subsection 237.1(1) of the Act, "prescribed benefit" in respect of an interest in a property means any amount that may reasonably be expected, having regard to statements or representations made in respect of the interest, to be received or enjoyed by a person (in this subsection referred to as "the purchaser") who acquires the interest, or a person with whom the purchaser does not deal at arm's length, which receipt or enjoyment would have the effect of reducing the impact of any loss that the purchaser may sustain in respect of the interest, and includes such an amount

(a) that is, either immediately or in the future, owed to any other person by the purchaser or a person with whom the purchaser does not deal at arm's length, to the extent that

(i) liability to pay that amount is contingent,

(ii) payment of that amount is or will be guaranteed by, security is or will be provided by, or an agreement to indemnify the other person to whom the amount is owed is or will be entered into by

(A) a promoter in respect of the interest,

(B) a person with whom the promoter does not deal at arm's length, or

(C) a person who is to receive a payment (other than a payment made by the purchaser) in respect of the guarantee, security or agreement to indemnify,

(iii) the rights of that other person against the purchaser, or against a person with whom the purchaser does not deal at arm's length, in respect of the collection of all or part of the purchase price are limited to a maximum amount, are enforceable only against certain property, or are otherwise limited by agreement, or

(iv) payment of that amount is to be made in a foreign currency or is to be determined by reference to its value in a foreign currency and it may reasonably be considered, having regard to the history of the exchange rate between the foreign currency and Canadian currency, that the aggregate of all such payments, when converted to Canadian currency at the exchange rate expected to prevail at the date on which each such payment would be required to be made, will be substantially less than that aggregate would be if each such payment was converted to Canadian currency at the time that each such payment became owing,

(b) that the purchaser or a person with whom the purchaser does not deal at arm's length is entitled at any time to receive, directly or indirectly, or to have available

(i) as a form of assistance from a government, municipality or other public authority, whether as a grant, subsidy, forgiveable loan, deduction from tax or investment allowance, or as any other form of assistance, or

(ii) by reason of a revenue guarantee or other agreement in respect of which revenue may be earned by the purchaser or a person with whom the purchaser does not deal at arm's length, to the extent that the revenue guarantee or other agreement may reasonably be considered to ensure that the purchaser or person will receive a return of all or a portion of the purchaser's outlays in respect of the interest,

(c) that is the proceeds of disposition to which the purchaser may be entitled by way of an agreement or other arrangement under which the purchaser has a right, either absolutely or contingently, to dispose of the interest (otherwise than as a consequence of the purchaser's death), including the fair market value of any property that the agreement or arrangement provides for the acquisition of in exchange for all or any part of the interest, and

(d) that is owed to a promoter, or a person with whom the promoter does not deal at arm's length, by the purchaser or a person with whom the purchaser does not deal at arm's length in respect of the interest,

but, except as otherwise provided in subparagraph (b)(ii), does not include profits earned in respect of the interest.

**Notes**: Reg. 231(6) amended by P.C. 2000-1000, effective for taxation years ending after July 5, 2000, effectively to change references to a "tax shelter" to an "interest in a property", and to change "received or made available" to "received or enjoyed". For earlier years, read the portion before (a)(ii)(A) and after (b)(i) as:

(6) For the purposes of paragraph (b) of the definition "tax shelter" in subsection 237.1(1) of the Act, "prescribed benefit" in relation to a tax shelter means any amount that may reasonably be expected, having regard to statements or representations made in respect of the tax shelter, to be received by or made available to a person (in this subsection referred to as "the purchaser") who acquires an interest in the tax shelter, or a person with whom the purchaser does not deal at arm's length, which receipt or availability would have the effect of reducing the impact of any loss that the purchaser may sustain by virtue of acquiring, holding or disposing of the interest in the tax shelter, and includes such an amount

(a) that is, either immediately or in the future, owed to any other person by the purchaser or a person with whom the purchaser does not deal at arm's length, to the extent that

(i) liability to pay that amount is contingent,

(ii) payment of that amount is or will be guaranteed by, security is or will be provided by, or an agreement to indemnify the other person to whom the amount is owed is or will be entered into by

. . . . .

(ii) by reason of a revenue guarantee or other agreement in respect of which revenue may be earned by the purchaser or a person with whom the purchaser does not deal at arm's length, to the extent that the revenue guarantee or other agreement may reasonably be considered to ensure that the purchaser or person will receive a return of all or a portion of the purchaser's outlays in respect of the tax shelter,

(c) that is the proceeds of disposition to which the purchaser may be entitled by way of an agreement or other arrangement under which the purchaser has a right, either absolutely or contingently, to dispose of the interest in the tax shelter (otherwise than as a consequence of the purchaser's death), including the fair market value of any property that the agreement or arrangement provides for the acquisition of in exchange for all or any part of the interest in the tax shelter, and

(d) that is owed to a promoter, or a person with whom the promoter does not deal at arm's length, by the purchaser or a person with whom the purchaser does not deal at arm's length in respect of the acquisition of an interest in the tax shelter

but, except as otherwise provided in subparagraph (b)(ii), does not include profits earned in respect of the tax shelter.

(6.1) For the purpose of paragraph (b) of the definition "tax shelter" in subsection 237.1(1) of the Act, "prescribed benefit" in respect of an interest in a property includes an amount that is a limited-recourse amount because of subsection 143.2(1), (7) or (13) of the Act, but does not include an amount of indebtedness that is a limited-recourse amount

(a) solely because it is not required to be repaid within 10 years from the time the indebtedness arose where the debtor would, if the interest were acquired by the debtor immediately after that time, be

(i) a partnership

(A) at least 90% of the fair market value of the property of which is attributable to the partnership's tangible capital property located in Canada, and

(B) at least 90% of the value of all interests in which are held by limited partners (within the meaning assigned by subsection 96(2.4) of the Act) of the partnership,

except where it is reasonable to conclude that one of the main reasons for the acquisition of one or more properties by the partnership, or for the acquisition of one or more interests in the partnership by limited partners, is to avoid the application of this subsection, or

(ii) a member of a partnership having fewer than six members, except where

(A) the partnership is a member of another partnership,

(B) there is a limited partner (within the meaning assigned by subsection 96(2.4) of the Act) of the partnership,

(C) less than 90% of the fair market value of the partnership's property is attributable to the partnership's tangible capital property located in Canada, or

(D) it is reasonable to conclude that one of the main reasons for the existence of one of two or more partnerships, one of which is the partnership, or the acquisition of one or more properties by the partnership, is to avoid the application of this section to the member's indebtedness,

(b) of a partnership

(i) where

(A) the indebtedness is secured by and used to acquire the partnership's tangible capital property located in Canada (other than rental property, within the meaning assigned by subsection 1100(14), leasing property, within the meaning assigned by subsection 1100(17), or specified energy property, within the meaning assigned by subsection 1100(25)), and

(B) the person to whom the indebtedness is repayable is a member of the Canadian Payments Association, and

(ii) throughout the period during which any amount is outstanding in respect of the indebtedness,

(A) at least 90% of the fair market value of the property of which is attributable to tangible capital property located in Canada of the partnership,

(B) at least 90% of the value of all interests in which are held by limited partners (within the meaning assigned by subsection 96(2.4) of the Act) that are corporations, and

(C) the principal business of each such limited partner is related to the principal business of the partnership,

except where it is reasonable to conclude that one of the main reasons for the acquisition of one or more properties by the partnership, or for the acquisition of one or more interests in the partnership by limited partners, is to avoid the application of this subsection, or

(c) of a corporation where the amount is a *bona fide* business loan made to the corporation for the purpose of financing a business that the corporation operates and the loan is made pursuant to a loan program of the Government of Canada or of a province the purpose of which is to extend financing to small- and medium-sized businesses.

**Notes**: Reg. 231(6.1) added by P.C. 2000-1000, effective December 1994.

**(7)** For the purposes of the definition "tax shelter" in subsection 237.1(1) of the Act, "prescribed property" in relation to a tax shelter means property that is a registered pension plan, a registered retirement savings plan, a deferred profit sharing plan, a registered retirement income fund, a registered education savings plan or a property in respect of which paragraph 40(2)(i) of the Act is applicable.

**Definitions [Reg. 231]**: "amount" — ITA 248(1); "arm's length" — ITA 251(1); "associated" — ITA 256; "business" — ITA 248(1); "Canada" — ITA 255, *Interpretation Act* 35(1); "capital property" — ITA 54, 248(1); "consequence of the purchaser's death" — ITA 248(8); "corporation" — ITA 248(1), *Interpretation Act* 35(1); "deferred profit sharing plan" — ITA 147(1), 248(1); "disposes" — ITA 248(1)"disposition"; "disposition" — ITA 248(1); "Minister", "person" — ITA 248(1); "promoter" — ITA 237.1(1), Reg. 231(1); "property" — ITA 248(1); "registered education savings plan" — ITA 146.1(1), 248(1); "registered pension plan" — ITA 248(1); "related" — ITA 251(2)–(6); "security" — *Interpretation Act* 35(1); "tax shelter" — ITA 237.1(1), Reg. 231(1); "written" — *Interpretation Act* 35(1)"writing".

**232. Workers' compensation** — **(1)** Every person who pays an amount in respect of compensation described in subparagraph 110(1)(f)(ii) of the Act shall make an information return in prescribed form in respect of that payment.

**Related Provisions**: Reg. 205.1 — Electronic filing required if more than 500 returns; Reg. 209 — Two copies to be sent to taxpayer.

**Forms**: T4115: T5007 guide — return of benefits (guide); T5007 Summ: Return of benefit payments — summary; T5007 Supp: Statement of benefits.

**(2)** Where a workers' compensation board, or a similar body, adjudicates a claim for compensation described in subparagraph 110(1)(f)(ii) of the Act and stipulates the amount of the award, that board or body shall make an information return in prescribed form in respect of the amount of the award.

**Related Provisions**: Reg. 205.1 — Electronic filing required if more than 500 returns; Reg. 209 — Two copies to be sent to taxpayer.

**(3)** A return required under this section must be filed on or before the last day of February of each year and shall be in respect of

(a) the preceding calendar year, if the return is required under subsection (1); and

(b) the amount of the award that pertains to the preceding calendar year, if the return is required under subsection (2).

**(4)** Subsections (1) and (2) are not applicable in respect of a payment or an award in respect of

(a) medical expenses incurred by or on behalf of the employee;

(b) funeral expenses in respect of the employee;

(c) legal expenses in respect of the employee;

(d) job training or counselling of the employee; or

(e) the death of the employee, other than periodic payments made after the death of the employee.

**Notes**: Reg. 232 added by P.C. 1992-1567, effective 1991.

**Definitions [Reg. 232]**: "amount", "employee", "person", "prescribed" — ITA 248(1).

**233. Social assistance** — **(1)** Every person who makes a payment described in paragraph 56(1)(u) of the Act shall make an information return in prescribed form in respect of the payment.

**Related Provisions**: Reg. 205.1 — Electronic filing required if more than 500 returns; Reg. 209 — Two copies to be sent to taxpayer.

**Forms**: T4115: T5007 guide — return of benefits (guide); T5007 Summ: Return of benefit payments — summary; T5007 Supp: Statement of benefits.

**(2)** Subsection (1) is not applicable in respect of a payment that

(a) is in respect of medical expenses incurred by or on behalf of the payee;

(b) is in respect of child care expenses, within the meaning assigned by paragraph 63(3)(a) [63(3)"child care expense"] of the Act, incurred by or on behalf of the payee or a person related to the payee;

(c) is in respect of funeral expenses in respect of a person related to the payee;

(d) is in respect of legal expenses incurred by or on behalf of the payee or a person related to the payee;

(e) is in respect of job training or counselling of the payee or a person related to the payee;

(f) is paid in a particular year as a part of a series of payments, the total of which in the particular year does not exceed $500; or

(g) is not a part of a series of payments.

**Related Provisions**: Reg. 205 — Date return due.

**Notes**: Reg. 233 added by P.C. 1992-1567, effective 1991.

**Definitions [Reg. 233]**: "child" — ITA 252(1); "person", "prescribed" — ITA 248(1); "related" — ITA 251(2)–(6).

**234. Farm support payments** — **(1)** Every government, municipality or municipal or other public body (in sections 235 and 236 referred to as the "government payer") or producer organization or association that makes a payment of an amount that is a farm support payment (other than an amount paid out of a net income stabilization account) to a person or partnership shall make an information return in prescribed form in respect of the amount.

**Related Provisions**: Reg. 205.1 — Electronic filing required if more than 500 returns; Reg. 209 — Two copies to be sent to taxpayer.

**Forms**: AGR-1: Return of farm support payments.

**(2)** For the purposes of subsection (1) "farm support payment" includes

(a) a payment that is computed with respect to an area of farm land;

(b) a payment that is made in respect of a unit of farm commodity grown or disposed of or a farm animal raised or disposed of; and

(c) a rebate of, or compensation for, all or a portion of

(i) a cost or capital cost incurred in respect of farming, or

(ii) unsowed or unplanted land or crops, or destroyed crops, farm animals or other farm output.

**Related Provisions**: Reg. 205 — Date return due; Reg. 235, 236 — Identification of recipients.

**Notes**: Reg. 234 added by P.C. 1993-1939, effective after 1993 in respect of amounts paid after 1992. The farm support payments described may be taxable under ITA 12(1)(p) or 12(1)(x).

**Definitions [Reg. 234]**: "amount" — ITA 248(1); "disposed" — ITA 248(1)"disposition"; "farm support payment" — Reg. 234(2); "farming", "net income stabilization account", "prescribed" — ITA 248(1).

**235. Identifier information** — Every corporation or trust for which an information return is required to be made under these Regulations by a government payer or by a producer organization or association shall provide its legal name, address and income tax identification number to the government payer or the producer organization or association, as the case may be.

**Notes**: Reg. 235 added by P.C. 1993-1939, effective after 1993 in respect of amounts paid after 1992.

**Definitions [Reg. 235]**: "corporation" — ITA 248(1), *Interpretation Act* 35(1); "government payer" — Reg. 234(1); "trust" — ITA 104(1), 248(1), (3).

**236. [Members of partnership]** — Every person who is a member of a partnership for which an information return is required to be made under these Regulations by a government payer or by a producer organization or association shall provide the government payer or the producer organization or association, as the case may be, with the following information:

(a) the person's legal name, address and Social Insurance Number, or, where the person is a trust or is not an individual, the person's income tax identification number; and

(b) the partnership's name and business address.

**Related Provisions**: Reg. 229 — Partnership information return.

**Notes**: Reg. 236 added by P.C. 1993-1939, effective after 1993 in respect of amounts paid after 1992. See also Notes at beginning of Part II.

**Definitions [Reg. 236]**: "business" — ITA 248(1); "government payer" — Reg. 234(1); "individual""person" — ITA 248(1); "trust" — ITA 104(1), 248(1), (3).

**Information Circulars**: 82-2R2: SIN legislation that relates to the preparation of information slips.

**237. Contract for goods and services [for federal government]** — **(1)** The definitions in this subsection apply in this section.

**"federal body"** means a department or a Crown corporation, within the meaning of section 2 of the *Financial Administration Act*.

**Notes**: The *Financial Administration Act* defines "Crown corporation" and "department" as follows:

2. *"Crown corporation"* has the meaning assigned by subsection 83(1); ... 83.(1) *"Crown corporation"* means a parent Crown corporation or a wholly-owned subsidiary; ... *"parent Crown corporation"* means a corporation that is wholly owned directly by the Crown, but does not include a departmental corporation; ... *"wholly-owned subsidiary"* means a corporation that is wholly owned by one or more parent Crown corporations directly or indirectly through any number of subsidiaries each of which is wholly owned directly or indirectly by one or more parent Crown corporations.

2. *"department"* means

(a) any of the departments named in Schedule I,

(b) any other division or branch of the public service of Canada, including a commission appointed under the Inquiries Act, designated by the Governor in Council as a department for the purposes of this Act,

(c) the staffs of the Senate, the House of Commons and the Library of Parliament, and

(d) any departmental corporation;

*"departmental corporation"* means a corporation named in Schedule II;

Schedule I lists all the regular federal Departments, such as Finance, Industry, Justice, etc., and the Treasury Board. Schedule II lists: Canada Customs and Revenue Agency; Canada Employment Insurance Commission; Canadian Centre for Management Development; Canadian Centre for Occupational Health and Safety; Canadian Food Inspection Agency; Canadian Nuclear Safety Commission; Canadian Polar Commission; Canadian Transportation Accident Investigation and Safety Board; Director of Soldier Settlement; The Director, The Veterans' Land Act; Fisheries Prices Support Board; Law Commission of Canada; Medical Research Council; The National Battlefields Commission; National Research Council of Canada; National Round Table on the Environment and the Economy; Natural Sciences and Engineering Research Council; Social Sciences and Humanities Research Council.

Definition "federal body" added by P.C. 1998-2274, this version effective for amounts paid or credited after 1998. For amounts paid or credited in 1998, ignore the words "or a Crown corporation".

"payee" means a person or partnership to whom an amount is paid or credited in respect of goods for sale or lease, or services rendered, by or on behalf of the person or the partnership.

**Notes**: See at end of Reg. 237.

**(2)** A federal body that pays or credits an amount to a payee shall file an information return in prescribed form in respect of the amount on or before March 31 in each year in respect of the preceding calendar year.

**Related Provisions**: Reg. 205 — Date return due; Reg. 205.1 — Electronic filing required if more than 500 returns; Reg. 209 — Two copies to be sent to taxpayer.

**Notes**: See at end of Reg. 237.

**(3)** Subsection (2) does not apply in respect of an amount

(a) all or substantially all of which is paid or credited in the year in respect of goods for sale or lease by the payee;

(b) to which section 153 or 212 of the Act applies;

(c) that is not required to be included in computing the income of the payee, if the payee is an employee of the federal body;

(d) that is paid or credited in respect of services rendered outside Canada by a payee who was not resident in Canada during the period in which the services were rendered; or

(e) that is paid or credited in respect of a program administered under the *Witness Protection Program Act* or any other similar program.

**Notes [Reg. 237]**: Reg. 237 added by P.C. 1998-2274, effective for amounts paid or credited after 1997.

Proposed Reg. 237 in draft regulations of October 21, 1994, which would have imposed a requirement for an information return with respect to eligible funeral arrangements, was moved to Reg. 201(1)(f).

**Definitions [Reg. 237]**: "calendar year" — *Interpretation Act* 35(1); "Canada" — ITA 255, *Interpretation Act* 35(1); "employee" — ITA 248(1); "federal body" — Reg. 237(1); "partnership" — see Notes to ITA 96(1); "payee" — Reg. 237(1); "person" — ITA 248(1); "prescribed" — ITA 248(1).

## 238. Reporting of payments in respect of construction activities

**(1)** In this section, "construction activities" includes the erection, excavation, installation, alteration, modification, repair, improvement, demolition, destruction, dismantling or removal of all or any part of a building, structure, surface or sub-surface construction, or any similar property.

**Notes [Reg. 238(1)]**: Excavation by the operator of a landfill site is likely not "excavation" requiring contract payment reporting: CCRA VIEWS doc 2000-0013055.

**Forms**: T5018 Summ: Summary of contract payments; T5018 Supp: Statement of contract payments.

**(2)** Every person or partnership that pays or credits, in a reporting period, an amount in respect of goods or services rendered on their behalf in the course of construction activities shall make an information return in the prescribed form in respect of that amount, if the person's or partnership's business income for that reporting period is derived primarily from those activities.

**Notes [Reg. 238(2)]**: See at end of Reg. 238.

**Forms**: T5018 Summ: Summary of contract payments; T5018 Supp: Statement of contract payments.

**(3)** The reporting period may be either on a calendar year basis or a fiscal period basis. Once a period is chosen, it cannot be changed for subsequent years, unless the Minister authorizes it.

**(4)** The return shall be filed within six months after the end of the reporting period to which it pertains.

**(5)** Subsection (2) does not apply in respect of an amount

(a) all of which is paid or credited in the reporting period in respect of goods for sale or lease by the person or partnership;

(b) to which section 153 or 212 of the Act applies; or

(c) that is paid or credited in respect of services rendered outside Canada by a person or partnership who was not resident in Canada during the period in which the services were rendered.

**Notes [Reg. 238]**: Reg. 238 added by P.C. 1999-2204, effective for reporting periods (see Reg. 238(3)) that begin after 1998, except that the information return for the first reporting period is not required until June 30, 2000.

Reg. 238 implements a proposal first made in the February 1995 federal budget and then repeated in the February 1998 federal budget. It is designed to catch the underground economy by requiring construction contractors to report all payments to subcontractors. The CCRA provided further details by news release on December 13, 1999:

- A business whose principal activity is construction must record and keep the name of every subcontractor, along with the subcontractor's Business Number (or Social Insurance Number) and the amounts paid to the subcontractor. Although contractors are encouraged to obtained subcontractor's addresses, that will not be mandatory.

- Contractors will be able to choose between two ways of filing this information:
  — a T5018 information return, attaching copies of the T5018 information slips given to subcontractors, or
  — reporting the required information on a line-by-line basis in a column format with a summary total.

Although the information slips do not have to be given to subcontractors, the CCRA is encouraging contractors to do so.

The CCRA continues to consult with the construction industry about these measures, and to review the effectiveness of the new system.

For other information returns not in Part II of the Regulations, see the Notes at the beginning of Part II.

**Definitions [Reg. 238]**: "business" — ITA 248(1); "Canada" — ITA 255; "construction activities" — Reg. 238(1); "month" — *Interpretation Act* 35(1); "partnership" — See Notes to 96(1); "person", "prescribed", "property" — ITA 248(1); "reporting period" — Reg. 238(3).

# PART III — ANNUITIES AND LIFE INSURANCE POLICIES

**300. Capital element of annuity payments —**
**(1)** For the purposes of paragraphs 32.1(3)(b) and 60(a) of the Act, where an annuity is paid under a contract (other than an income-averaging annuity contract or an annuity contract purchased pursuant to a deferred profit sharing plan or pursuant to a plan referred to in subsection 147(15) of the Act as a "revoked plan") at a particular time, that part of the annuity payment determined in prescribed manner to be a return of capital is that proportion of a taxpayer's interest in the annuity payment that the adjusted purchase price of the taxpayer's interest in the contract at that particular time is of his interest, immediately before the commencement under the contract of payments to which paragraph 56(1)(d) of the Act applies, in the total of the payments

(a) to be made under the contract, in the case of a contract for a term of years certain; or

(b) expected to be made under the contract, in the case of a contract under which the continuation of the payments depends in whole or in part on the survival of an individual.

**(1.1)** For the purposes of subsections (1) and (2), "annuity payment" does not include any portion of a payment under a contract the amount of which cannot be reasonably determined immediately before the commencement of payments under the contract except where the payment of such portion cannot be so determined because the continuation of the annuity payments under the contract depends in whole or in part on the survival of an individual.

**Notes**: Reg. 300(1.1) added by P.C. 1982-1421, effective for annuity contracts under which annuity payments commence after 1981.

**(2)** For the purposes of this section and section 305,

(a) where the continuation of the annuity payments under any contract depends in whole or in part on the survival of an individual, the total of the payments expected to be made under the contract

   (i) shall, in the case of a contract that provides for equal payments and does not provide for a guaranteed period of payment, be equal to the product obtained by multiplying the aggregate of the annuity payments expected to be received throughout a year under the contract by the complete expectations of life using the table of mortality known as the *1971 Individual Annuity Mortality Table* as published in Volume XXIII of the *Transactions of the Society of Actuaries*, or

   (ii) shall, in any other case, be calculated in accordance with subparagraph (i) with such modifications as the circumstances may require;

(b) except as provided in subsections (3) and (4), "adjusted purchase price" of a taxpayer's interest in an annuity contract at a particular time means the amount that would be determined at that time in respect of that interest under paragraph 148(9)(a) [148(9)"adjusted cost basis"] of the Act if that paragraph were read without reference to subparagraph (viii) [k] thereof;

(c) where the continuation of the annual payments under any contract depends on the survival of a person, the age of that person on any date as of which a calculation is being made shall be determined by subtracting the calendar year of his birth from the calendar year in which such date occurs; and

(d) where the continuance of the annual payments under any contract depends on the survival of a person, and where, in the event of the death of that person before the annual payments aggregate a stated sum, the contract provides that the unpaid balance of the stated sum shall be paid, either in a lump sum or instalments, then, for the purpose of determining the expected term of the contract, the contract shall be deemed to provide for the continuance of the payments thereunder for a minimum term certain equal to the nearest integral number of years required to complete the payment of the stated sum;

(e) [Revoked]

**Notes**: Reg. 300(2) amended by P.C. 1982-1421, effective for annuity contracts under which annuity payments commence after 1981.

**(3)** Where

(a) an annuity contract is a life annuity contract entered into before November 17, 1978 under which the annuity payments commence on the death of an individual,

(a.1) [Revoked]

(b) an annuity contract (other than an annuity contract described in paragraph (a)) is

   (i) a life annuity contract entered into before October 23, 1968, or

   (ii) any other annuity contract entered into before January 4, 1968,

under which the annuity payments commence

   (iii) on the expiration of a term of years, and

   (iv) before the later of January 1, 1970 or the tax anniversary date of the annuity contract,

the adjusted purchase price of a taxpayer's interest in the annuity contract shall be

(c) the lump sum, if any, that the person entitled to the annuity payments might have accepted in lieu thereof, at the date the annuity payments commence;

(d) if no lump sum described in paragraph (c) is provided for in the contract, the sum ascertainable from the contract as the present value of the annuity at the date the annuity payments commence; and

(e) if no lump sum described in paragraph (c) is provided for in the contract and no sum is ascertainable under paragraph (d),

(i) in the case of a contract issued under the *Government Annuities Act*, the premiums paid, accumulated with interest at the rate of four per cent per annum to the date the annuity payments commence, and

(ii) in the case of any other contract, the present value of the annuity payments at the date on which payments under the contract commence, computed by applying

(A) a rate of interest of four per cent per annum where the payments commence before 1972 and $5\frac{1}{2}$ per cent per annum where the payments commence after 1971, and

(B) the provisions of subsection (2) where the payments depend on the survival of a person.

(4) Where an annuity contract would be described in paragraph (3)(b) if the reference in subparagraph (iv) thereof to "before the later of" were read as a reference to "on or after the later of", the adjusted purchase price of a taxpayer's interest in the annuity contract at a particular time shall be the greater of

(a) the aggregate of

(i) the amount that would be determined in respect of that interest under paragraph (3)(c), (d) or (e), as the case may be, if the date referred to therein was the tax anniversary date of the contract and not the date the annuity payments commence, and

(ii) the adjusted purchase price that would be determined in respect of that interest if the words "and after the tax anniversary date" were inserted in each of subparagraphs 148(9)(a)(i) to (iii.1) and (vi) [148(9)"adjusted cost basis"A to D and H] of the Act immediately following the words "before that time" in each of those subparagraphs; and

(b) the amount determined under paragraph (2)(b) in respect of that interest.

**Notes**: Reg. 300(4) added by P.C. 1982-1421, effective for annuity contracts under which annuity payments commence after 1981.

**Definitions [Reg. 300]**: "adjusted purchase price" — Reg. 300(2)(b), 300(3), (4); "amount", "annuity" — ITA 248(1); "annuity payment" — Reg. 300(1.1); "commencement" — *Interpretation Act* 35(1); "deferred profit sharing plan" — ITA 147(1), 248(1); "income-averaging annuity contract", "individual" — ITA 248(1); "life annuity contract" — Reg. 301(1), (2); "person", "prescribed" — ITA 248(1); "tax anniversary date" — Reg. 310; "taxpayer" — ITA 248(1); "total of the payments" — Reg. 300(2)(a).

**301. Life annuity contracts** — (1) For the purposes of this Part and section 148 of the Act, "life annuity contract" means any contract under which a person authorized under the laws of Canada or a province to carry on in Canada an annuities business agrees to make annuity payments to an individual (in this section referred to as "the annuitant") or jointly to two or more individuals (each of whom is referred to as "the annuitant" in this section), which payments are, by the terms of the contract,

(a) to be paid annually or at more frequent periodic intervals;

(b) to commence on a specified day; and

(c) to continue throughout the lifetime of the annuitant or one or more of the annuitants.

**Notes**: Reg. 301(1) amended by P.C. 1982-1421, effective for annuity contracts under which annuity payments commence after 1981.

(2) For the purposes of subsection (1), a contract shall not fail to be a life annuity contract by reason that

(a) the contract provides that the annuity payments may be assigned by the annuitant or owner;

(b) the contract provides for annuity payments to be made for a period ending upon the death of the annuitant or for a specified period of not less than 10 years, whichever is the lesser;

(c) the contract provides for annuity payments to be made for a specified period or throughout the lifetime of the annuitant, whichever is longer, to the annuitant and thereafter, if the specified period is the longer, to a specified person;

(d) the contract provides, in addition to the annuity payments to be made throughout the lifetime of the annuitant, for a payment to be made upon the annuitant's death;

(e) the contract provides that the date

(i) on which the annuity payments commence, or

(ii) on which the contract holder becomes entitled to proceeds of the disposition,

may be changed with respect to the whole contract or any portion thereof at the option of the annuitant or owner; or

(f) the contract provides that all or a portion of the proceeds payable at any particular time under the contract may be received in the form of an annuity contract other than a life annuity contract.

**Notes**: Reg. 301(2) amended by P.C. 1982-1421, effective for annuity contracts under which annuity payments commence after 1981.

**Definitions [Reg. 301]**: "annuitant" — Reg. 301(1); "annuity", "business" — ITA 248(1); "Canada" — ITA 255, *Interpretation Act* 35(1); "individual" — ITA 248(1); "life annuity contract" — Reg. 301(1), (2); "person" — ITA 248(1); "proceeds of the disposition" — ITA 148(9), Reg. 310; "province" — *Interpretation Act* 35(1).

**302.** [Revoked]

**303. (1)** Where in a taxation year the rights of a holder under an annuity contract cease upon termination or cancellation of the contract and

(a) the aggregate of all amounts, each of which is an amount in respect of the contract that was included in computing the income of the holder for the year or any previous taxation year by virtue of subsection 12(3) of the Act

exceeds the aggregate of

(b) such proportion of the amount determined under paragraph (a) that the annuity payments made under the contract before the rights of the holder have ceased is of the total of the payments expected to be made under the contract, and

(c) the aggregate of all amounts, each of which is an amount in respect of the contract that was deductible in computing the income of the holder for the year or any previous year by virtue of subsection (2),

the amount of such excess may be deducted by the holder under subsection 20(19) of the Act in computing his income for the year.

**(2)** For the purposes of subsection 20(19) of the Act, where an annuity contract was acquired after December 19, 1980 and annuity payments under the contract commenced before 1982, the amount that may be deducted by a holder under that subsection in respect of an annuity contract for a taxation year is that proportion of

(a) the aggregate of all amounts, each of which is an amount that was included in computing the income of the holder for any previous taxation year by virtue of subsection 12(3) of the Act in respect of the contract

that

(b) the aggregate of all annuity payments received by the holder in the year in respect of the contract

is of

(c) the total of the payments determined under paragraph 300(1)(a) or (b) in respect of the holder's interest in the contract.

**Definitions [Reg. 303]**: "amount", "annuity" — ITA 248(1); "taxation year" — ITA 249.

**304. Prescribed annuity contracts — (1)** For the purposes of this Part and subsections 12.2(1), (3) and (4) and paragraph 148(2)(b) of the Act, prescribed annuity contract for a taxation year means

(a) an annuity contract purchased pursuant to a registered pension plan, a registered retirement savings plan, a deferred profit sharing plan or a plan referred to in subsection 147(15) of the Act as a revoked plan;

(b) an annuity contract described in paragraph 148(1)(c) or (e) of the Act; and

(c) an annuity contract

(i) under which annuity payments have commenced in the taxation year or a preceding taxation year,

(ii) issued by a corporation described in any of paragraphs 39(5)(b) to (d) or clause 146(1)(j)(ii)(B) [146(1)"retirement savings plan"(b)(ii)] of the Act, a life insurance corporation, a registered charity or a corporation (other than a mutual fund corporation or a mortgage investment corporation) the principal business of which is the making of loans (which corporation or charity is in this section referred to as an "issuer"),

**Proposed Amendment — Reg. 304(1)(c)(ii)**

(ii) issued by a life insurance corporation, a registered charity, a corporation referred to in any of paragraphs (a) to (c) of the definition "specified financial institution" in subsection 248(1) of the Act or subparagraph (b)(ii) of the definition "retirement savings plan" in subsection 146(1) of the Act or a corporation (other than a mutual fund corporation or a mortgage investment corporation) the principal business of which is the making of loans (which corporation or charity is referred to in this section as the "issuer"),

**Application**: The June 1, 1995 draft regulations (securities held by financial institutions), s. 1, will amend subpara. 304(1)(c)(ii) to read as above, applicable after February 22, 1994.

**Technical Notes**: Section 304 prescribes certain annuity contracts for exclusion from the rules in the *Income Tax Act* that require income from insurance policies to be reported on an accrual basis. Paragraph 304(1)(c) provides an exclusion for an annuity under which payments have commenced if a number of other conditions are also satisfied. Subparagraph 304(1)(c)(ii) requires that the annuity have been issued by a person specified in that provision. Acceptable issuers include corporations described in any of paragraphs 39(5)(b) to (d) of the Act — banks, trust companies and credit unions.

Subsection 39(5) of the Act is being amended to replace several of its paragraphs by a reference to "financial institutions" (as defined in subsection 142.2(1) of the Act). Consequently, subparagraph 304(1)(c)(ii) is amended to refer to corporations referred to in any of paragraphs (a) to (c) of the definition of "specified financial institution" in subsection 248(1) of the Act, which are the same corporations as were referred to in paragraphs 39(5)(b) to (d).

(iii) each holder of which

(A) is an individual, other than a trust that is neither a testamentary trust nor a trust described in paragraph 104(4)(a) of the Act (in this paragraph referred to as a "spouse trust"),

(B) is an annuitant under the contract, and

(C) throughout the taxation year, dealt at arm's length with the issuer,

Part III — Annuities and Life Insurance Policies    Reg. S. 304(2)(c)

(iv) the terms and conditions of which require that, from the time the contract meets the requirements of this paragraph,

(A) all payments made out of the contract be equal annuity payments made at regular intervals but not less frequently than annually, subject to the holder's right to vary the frequency and quantum of payments to be made out of the contract in any taxation year without altering the present value at the beginning of the year of the total payments to be made in that year out of the contract,

(B) the annuity payments thereunder continue for a fixed term or

(I) where the holder is an individual (other than a trust), for the life of the first holder or until the later of the death of the first holder and the death of any one of the spouse, brothers and sisters (in this subparagraph referred to as "the survivor") of the first holder, or

(II) where the holder is a spouse trust, for the life of the spouse who is entitled to receive the income of the trust;

(C) where the annuity payments are to be made over a term that is guaranteed or fixed, the guaranteed or fixed term not [to] extend beyond the time at which

(I) in the case of a joint and last survivor annuity, the younger of the first holder and the survivor,

(II) where the holder is a spouse trust, the spouse who is entitled to receive the income of the trust,

(III) where the holder is a testamentary trust other than a spouse trust, the youngest beneficiary under the trust,

(IV) where the contract is held jointly, the younger of the first holders, or

(V) in any other case, the first holder,

would, if he survived, attain the age of 91 years,

(D) no loans exist under the contract and the holder's rights under the contract not be disposed of otherwise than on the holder's death or, where the holder is a spouse trust, on the death of the spouse who is entitled to receive the income of the trust, and

(E) no payments be made out of the contract other than as permitted by this section,

(v) none of the terms and conditions of which provide for any recourse against the issuer for failure to make any payment under the contract, and

(vi) where annuity payments under the contract have commenced

(A) before 1987, in respect of which a holder thereof has notified the issuer in writing, before the end of the taxation year, that the contract is to be treated as a prescribed annuity contract,

(B) after 1986, in respect of which a holder thereof has not notified the issuer in writing, before the end of the taxation year in which the annuity payments under the contract commenced, that the contract is not to be treated as a prescribed annuity contract, or

(C) after 1986, in respect of which a holder thereof has notified the issuer in writing, before the end of the taxation year in which the annuity payments under the contract commenced, that the contract is not to be treated as a prescribed annuity contract and a holder thereof has rescinded the notification by so notifying the issuer in writing before the end of the taxation year.

**Proposed Amendment — Reg. 304(1)**

**Department of Finance news release, December 19, 1996**: An annuity contract issued as a RRIF will not be subject to the accrual rules under section 12.2 of the Act.

This amendment will be implemented by way of an amendment to subsection 304(1) of the Regulations. It is contemplated that it will apply to taxation years that begin after 1986, given that the original amendments to the Act that gave rise to the need for this amendment applied after 1986.

[For the full text of this news release, see under 12.2(1) — ed.]

**Department of Finance news release, October 23, 1997**: [See under ITA 12.2(1) — ed.]

(2) Notwithstanding subsection (1), an annuity contract shall not fail to be a prescribed annuity contract by reason that

(a) where the contract provides for a joint and last survivor annuity or is held jointly, the terms and conditions thereof provide that there will be a decrease in the amount of the annuity payments to be made under the contract from the time of death of one of the annuitants thereunder;

(b) the terms and conditions thereof provide that where the holder thereof dies at or before the time he attains the age of 91 years, the contract will terminate and an amount will be paid out of the contract not exceeding the amount, if any, by which the total premiums paid under the contract exceeds the total annuity payments made under the contract;

(c) where the annuity payments are to be made over a term that is guaranteed or fixed, the terms and conditions thereof provide that as a consequence of the death of the holder thereof during

1985

**Reg. S. 304(2)(c)**     Income Tax Regulations

the guaranteed or fixed term any payments that, but for the death of the holder, would be made during the term may be commuted into a single payment; or

(d) the terms and conditions thereof, as they read on December 1, 1982 and at all subsequent times, provide that the holder participates in the investment earnings of the issuer and that the amount of such participation is to be paid within 60 days after the end of the year in respect of which it is determined.

(3) For the purposes of this section, the annuitant under an annuity contract is deemed to be the holder of the contract where

(a) the contract is held by another person in trust for the annuitant; or

(b) the contract was acquired by the annuitant under a group term life insurance policy under which life insurance was effected on the life of another person in respect of, in the course of, or by virtue of the office or employment or former office or employment of that other person.

(4) In this section,

**"annuitant"** under an annuity contract, at any time, means a person who, at that time, is entitled to receive annuity payments under the contract;

**"spouse"** of a particular person means

(a) a person of the opposite sex who is married to the particular person or who is a party to a void or voidable marriage with the particular person, or

(b) a person of the opposite sex who is cohabiting with the particular person in a conjugal relationship and has so cohabited for a period of at least one year.

**Notes**: Reg. 304 should be amended to apply for purposes of ITA 20(20) as well.

Reg. 304 added by P.C. 1982-1421 and amended several times, effective for annuity contracts under which annuity payments commence after 1981. Reference to ITA 12.2(1) added to opening words of Reg. 304(1) by P.C. 1994-940, effective 1990 (see Notes to Reg. 307(4)).

References to "spouse" are expected to be amended to add "or common-law partner" effective 2001 or earlier by election, as has been done throughout the ITA. See Notes to ITA 248(1)"common-law partner".

**Definitions [Reg. 304]**: "amount" — ITA 248(1); "annuitant" — Reg. 304(4); "annuity" — ITA 248(1); "Canada" — ITA 255, *Interpretation Act* 35(1); "consequence of the death" — ITA 248(8); "corporation" — ITA 248(1), *Interpretation Act* 35(1); "deferred profit sharing plan" — ITA 147(1), 248(1); "disposed" — ITA 248(1)"disposition"; "employment", "group term life insurance policy" — ITA 248(1); "holder" — Reg. 304(3); "individual" — ITA 248(1); "issuer" — Reg. 304(1)(c)(ii); "life insurance corporation" — ITA 248(1); "mortgage investment corporation" — ITA 130.1(6), 248(1); "mutual fund corporation" — ITA 131(8), 248(1); "office", "person", "prescribed" — ITA 248(1); "prescribed annuity contract" — Reg. 304(1), (2); "registered pension plan" — ITA 248(1); "spouse" — Reg. 304(4); "spouse trust" — Reg. 304(1)(c)(iii)(A); "survivor" — Reg. 304(1)(c)(iv)(B)(I); "taxation year" — ITA 249; "testamentary trust" — ITA 108(1), 248(1); "trust" — ITA 104(1), 248(1), (3); "writing" — *Interpretation Act* 35(1).

**Interpretation Bulletins**: IT-87R2: Policyholders' income from life insurance policies.

**305. Unallocated income accrued before 1982** — (1) For the purposes of section 12.2 and paragraph 56(1)(d.1) of the Act, the amount at any time of "unallocated income accrued in respect of the interest before 1982, as determined in prescribed manner", in respect of a taxpayer's interest in an annuity contract (other than an interest last acquired after December 1, 1982) or in a life insurance policy referred to in subsection (3), means the amount, if any, by which

(a) the accumulating fund at December 31, 1981 in respect of the interest

exceeds the aggregate of

(b) his adjusted cost basis (within the meaning assigned by paragraph 148(9)(a) [148(9)"adjusted cost basis"] of the Act) at December 31, 1981 in respect of the interest; and

(c) that proportion of the amount, if any, by which the amount determined under paragraph (a) exceeds the amount determined under paragraph (b) that

(i) the aggregate of all amounts each of which is the amount of an annuity payment received before that time in respect of the interest

is of

(ii) the taxpayer's interest, immediately before the commencement of payments under the contract, in the total of the annuity payments

(A) to be made under the contract, in the case of a contract for a term of years certain, or

(B) expected to be made under the contract, in the case of a contract under which the continuation of the payments depends in whole or in part on the survival of an individual.

(2) For the purposes of paragraph (1)(c), "annuity payment" does not include any portion of a payment under a contract the amount of which cannot be reasonably determined immediately before the commencement of payments under the contract except where such portion cannot be so determined because the continuation of the annuity payments under the contract depends in whole or in part on the survival of an individual.

(3) For the purposes of this section, an interest in an annuity contract to which subsection 12.2(9) of the Act applies shall be deemed to be a continuation of the interest in the life insurance policy in respect of which it was issued.

**Definitions [Reg. 305]**: "amount", "annuity" — ITA 248(1); "annuity payment" — Reg. 305(2); "commencement" — *Interpretation*

Act 35(1); "continuation" — Reg. 305(3); "individual" — ITA 248(1); "life insurance policy" — ITA 138(12), Reg. 310; "prescribed", "taxpayer" — ITA 248(1); "total of the payments" — Reg. 300(2)(a).

**Interpretation Bulletins**: IT-87R2: Policyholders' income from life insurance policies.

**306. Exempt policies** — **(1)** For the purposes of this Part and subsection 12.2(11) of the Act, "exempt policy" at any time means a life insurance policy (other than an annuity contract or a deposit administration fund policy) in respect of which the following conditions are met at that time:

(a) if that time is a policy anniversary of the policy, the accumulating fund of the policy at that time (determined without regard to any policy loan) does not exceed the total of the accumulating funds at that time of the exemption test policies issued at or before that time in respect of the policy;

(b) assuming that the terms and conditions of the policy do not change from those in effect on the last policy anniversary of the policy at or before that time and, where necessary, making reasonable assumptions about all other factors (including, in the case of a participating life insurance policy within the meaning assigned by subsection 138(12) of the Act, the assumption that the amounts of dividends paid will be as shown in the dividend scale), it is reasonable to expect that the condition in paragraph (a) will be met on each policy anniversary of the policy on which the policy could remain in force after that time and before the date determined under subparagraph (3)(d)(ii) with respect to the exemption test policies issued in respect of the policy;

(c) the condition in paragraph (a) was met on all policy anniversaries of the policy before that time; and

(d) the condition in paragraph (b) was met at all times on and after the first policy anniversary of the policy and before that time.

**Notes**: Reg. 306(1) amended by P.C. 1994-940 (see Notes to Reg. 307(4)), effective

(a) for life insurance policies issued after March 26, 1992, other than a policy for which written application was made by that date, and

(b) for life insurance policies amended at any time after March 26, 1992 to increase the amount of the benefit on death.

For policies to which the new version does not apply, read:

306. (1) For the purposes of this Part and paragraph 12.2(11)(a) of the Act, "exempt policy" at any time means a life insurance policy (other than an annuity contract or a deposit administration fund policy)

(a) in respect of which

(i) on the policy anniversary thereof, if any, occurring at that time, and

(ii) assuming that the terms and conditions of the policy do not change from those in effect on the last policy anniversary at or before that time and, where necessary, making reasonable assumptions about all other factors (including, in the case of a participating life insurance policy within the meaning assigned by paragraph 138(12)(k) [138(12)"participating life insurance policy"] of the Act, the assumption that the amounts of dividends paid will be shown in the dividend scale), on each policy anniversary after that time on which the policy could remain in force and before the date determined under subparagraph (3)(d)(ii) with respect to any exemption test policy issued in respect of the policy,

the accumulating fund (determined without regard to any policy loan) does not exceed (or, in the case of subparagraph (ii), would not exceed) the aggregate of the accumulating funds of the exemption test policies in respect of the life insurance policy at the time; and

(b) that has met the requirements of paragraph (a) on and after the date of its first policy anniversary.

**Interpretation Bulletins**: IT-87R2: Policyholders' income from life insurance policies.

**(2)** For the purposes of subsection (1), a life insurance policy that is an exempt policy on its first policy anniversary shall be deemed to have been an exempt policy from the time of its issue until that anniversary.

**Notes**: Reg. 306(2) amended by P.C. 1994-940, effective on the same basis as the amendments to Reg. 306(1) above. For policies to which the new version does not apply, read:

(2) For the purposes of subsection (1), any life insurance policy that meets the requirements of paragraph (1)(a) on its first policy anniversary shall be deemed to have been an exempt policy from the time of its issue until that anniversary.

**(3)** For the purposes of this section and section 307, a separate exemption test policy shall be deemed to have been issued to a policyholder in respect of a life insurance policy

(a) on the date of issue of the life insurance policy, and

(b) on each policy anniversary of the life insurance policy where the amount of the benefit on death thereunder exceeds 108 per cent of the amount of the benefit on death thereunder on the later of the date of its issue and the date of its preceding anniversary, if any,

and, for the purpose of determining whether the accumulating fund of the life insurance policy on any particular policy anniversary meets the condition in paragraph (1)(a), each such exemption test policy shall be deemed

(c) to have a benefit on death that is uniform throughout the term of the exemption test policy and equal to

(i) where the exemption test policy is the first such policy issued in respect of the life insurance policy, the amount on that policy anniversary of the benefit on death of the life insurance policy less the total of all amounts each of which is the amount on that policy anniversary of the benefit on death of another exemption test policy issued on or before that policy anniversary in respect of the life insurance policy, and

(ii) in any other case, the amount by which the benefit on death of the life insurance policy on the date the exemption test policy was issued exceeds 108 per cent of the amount of the benefit on death of the life insurance policy on the later of the date of issue of the life insurance policy and the date of its preceding policy anniversary, if any;

(d) to pay the amount of its benefit on death on the earlier of

(i) the date of death of the person whose life is insured under the life insurance policy, and

(ii) the later of

(A) ten years after the date of issue of the life insurance policy, and

(B) the date that the person whose life is insured would, if he survived, attain the age of 85 years; and

(e) to be a life insurance policy in Canada issued by a life insurer that carried on its life insurance business in Canada.

**Notes**: Reg. 306(3) amended by P.C. 1994-940, effective on the same basis as the amendments to Reg. 306(1) above. For policies to which the new version does not apply, read everything after para. (b) and before subpara. (c)(ii) as:

and each such exemption test policy shall be deemed

(c) to have at any time a benefit on death equal to,

(i) where the exemption test policy is the first such policy issued in respect of the life insurance policy, the amount at that time of the benefit on death of the life insurance policy in respect of which it was issued less the aggregate of all amounts each of which is an amount determined under subparagraph (ii) at or before that time, or

**(4)** Notwithstanding subsections (1) to (3),

(a) where at any particular time the amount of the benefit on death of a life insurance policy is reduced, an amount equal to such reduction (such amount is in this paragraph referred to as "the reduction") shall be applied at that time to reduce the amount of the benefit on death of exemption test policies issued before that time in respect of the life insurance policy (other than the exemption test policy issued in respect thereof pursuant to paragraph (3)(a)), in the order in which the dates of their issuance are proximate to the particular time, by an amount equal to the lesser of

(i) the portion, if any, of the reduction not applied to reduce the benefit on death of one or more other such exemption test policies, and

(ii) the amount, immediately before that time, of the benefit on death of the relevant exemption test policy;

(b) where on the tenth or on any subsequent policy anniversary of a life insurance policy, the accumulating fund thereof (computed without regard to any policy loan then outstanding in respect of the policy) exceeds 250 per cent of the accumulating fund thereof on its third preceding policy anniversary (computed without regard to any policy loan then outstanding in respect of the policy), each exemption test policy deemed by subsection (3) to have been issued before that time in respect of the life insurance policy shall be deemed to have been issued on the later of the date of that third preceding policy anniversary and the date on which it was deemed by subsection (3) to have been issued; and

(c) where at one or more times after December 1, 1982

(i) a prescribed premium has been paid by a taxpayer in respect of an interest in a life insurance policy (other than an annuity contract or a deposit administration fund policy) last acquired on or before that date, or

(ii) an interest in a life insurance policy (other than an annuity contract or a deposit administration fund policy) issued on or before that date has been acquired by a taxpayer from the person who held the interest continuously since that date,

the policy shall be deemed to have been an exempt policy from the date of its issue until the earliest of those times that occurred after December 1, 1982; and

(d) a life insurance policy that ceases to be an exempt policy (other than by reason of its conversion into an annuity contract) on a policy anniversary shall be deemed to be an exempt policy on that anniversary

(i) if, had that anniversary occurred 60 days after the date on which it did in fact occur, the policy would have been an exempt policy on that later date, or

(ii) if the person whose life is insured under the policy dies on that anniversary or within 60 days thereafter.

**Definitions [Reg. 306]**: "accumulating fund" — Reg. 307(1); "amount", "annuity" — ITA 248(1); "benefit on death" — Reg. 310; "Canada" — ITA 255, *Interpretation Act* 35(1); "dividend" — ITA 248(1); "exempt policy" — Reg. 306(1), (2), 306(4)(d); "life insurance business" — ITA 248(1); "life insurance policy" — ITA 138(12), Reg. 310; "life insurance policy in Canada" — ITA 138(12), 248(1); "life insurer", "person" — ITA 248(1); "policy anniversary" — Reg. 310; "policy loan" — ITA 148(9), Reg. 310; "prescribed" — ITA 248(1); "prescribed premium" — Reg. 309(1); "reduction" — Reg. 306(4)(a); "taxpayer" — ITA 248(1).

**307. Accumulating funds** — **(1)** For the purposes of this Part and section 12.2, paragraph 56(1)(d.1) and section 148 of the Act, "accumulating fund" at any particular time means,

(a) in respect of a taxpayer's interest in an annuity contract (other than a contract issued by a life insurer), the amount that is the greater of

(i) the amount, if any, by which the cash surrender value of his interest at that time exceeds the amount payable, if any, in respect of a loan outstanding at that time made under the contract in respect of the interest, and

(ii) the amount, if any, by which

(A) the present value at that time of future payments to be made out of the contract in respect of his interest

exceeds the aggregate of

(B) the present value at that time of future premiums to be paid under the contract in respect of his interest, and

(C) the amount payable, if any, in respect of a loan outstanding at that time, made under the contract in respect of his interest;

(b) in respect of a taxpayer's interest in a life insurance policy (other than an exemption test policy or an annuity contract to which paragraph (1)(a) applies), the product obtained when,

(i) where the policy is not a deposit administration fund policy and the particular time is immediately after the death of any person on whose life the life insurance policy is issued or effected, the aggregate of the maximum amounts that could be determined by the life insurer immediately before the death in respect of the policy under paragraph 1401(1)(c) and subparagraph 1401(1)(d)(i) if the mortality rates used were adjusted to reflect the assumption that the death would occur at the time and in the manner that it did occur, and

(ii) in any other case, the maximum amount that could be determined at that particular time by the life insurer under paragraph 1401(1)(a), computed as though there were only one deposit administration fund policy, or under paragraph 1401(1)(c), as the case may be, in respect of the policy

is multiplied by

(iii) the taxpayer's proportionate interest in the policy,

assuming for the purposes of this paragraph that the life insurer carried on its life insurance business in Canada, its taxation year ended at the particular time and the policy was a life insurance policy in Canada; and

(c) in respect of an exemption test policy,

(i) where the policy was issued at least 20 years before the particular time, the amount that would be determined at that particular time by the life insurer under clause 1401(1)(c)(ii)(A) in respect of the policy if the insurer's taxation year ended at that particular time, and

(ii) in any other case, the product obtained when the amount that would be determined under subparagraph (i) in respect of the policy on its twentieth policy anniversary is multiplied by the quotient obtained when the number of years since the policy was issued is divided by 20.

Notes: See under Reg. 307(4).

(2) For the purposes of subsection (1), when computing the accumulating fund of an interest described in

(a) paragraph (1)(a), the amounts determined under clauses (1)(a)(ii)(A) and (B) shall be computed using,

(i) where an interest rate for a period used by the issuer when the contract was issued in determining the terms of the contract was less than any rate so used for a subsequent period, the single rate that would, if it applied for each period, have produced the same terms, and

(ii) in any other case, the rates used by the issuer when the contract was issued in determining the terms of the contract;

(b) paragraph (1)(b), where an interest rate used for a period by a life insurer in computing the relevant amounts in paragraph 1403(1)(a) or (b) is determined under paragraph 1403(1)(c), (d) or (e), as the case may be, and that rate is less than an interest rate so determined for a subsequent period, the single rate that could, if it applied for each period, have been used in determining the premiums for the policy shall be used; and

(c) paragraph (1)(c)

(i) the rates of interest and mortality used and the age of the person whose life is insured shall be the same as those used in computing the amounts described in paragraph 1403(1)(a) or (b) in respect of the life insurance policy in respect of which the exemption test policy was issued except that

(A) where the life insurance policy is one to which paragraph 1403(1)(e) applies and the amount determined under subparagraph 1401(1)(c)(i) in respect of that policy is greater than the amount determined under subparagraph 1401(1)(c)(ii) in respect thereof, the rates of interest and mortality used may be those used in computing the cash surrender values of that policy, and

(B) where an interest rate for a period otherwise determined under this subparagraph in respect of that interest is less than an interest rate so determined for a subsequent period, the single rate that could, if it applied for each period, have been used in determining the premiums for the life insurance policy shall be used, and

(ii) notwithstanding subparagraph (i),

(A) where the rates referred to in subparagraph (i) do not exist, the minimum guaranteed rates of interest used under the life insurance policy to determine cash surrender values and the rates of mortality under the *Commissioners 1958 Standard Ordinary Mortality Table*, as published in Volume X of the *Transactions of the Society of Actuaries*, relevant to the person whose life is insured under the life insurance policy shall be used, or

(B) where, in respect of the life insurance policy in respect of which the exemption test policy was issued, the period over which the amount determined under clause 1401(1)(c)(ii)(A) does not extend to the date determined under subparagraph 306(3)(d)(ii), the weighted arithmetic mean of the interest rates used to determine such amount shall be used for the period that is after that period and before that date.

(3) Notwithstanding paragraph (2)(c),

(a) in the case of a life insurance policy issued after April 30, 1985, no rate of interest used for the purpose of determining the accumulating fund in respect of an exemption test policy issued in respect thereof shall be less than 4 per cent per annum; and

(b) in the case of a life insurance policy issued before May 1, 1985, no rate of interest used for the purpose of determining the accumulating fund in respect of an exemption test policy issued in respect thereof shall be less than 3 per cent per annum.

(4) For the purposes of paragraph (1)(c),

(a) where on the date of issue of an exemption test policy the person whose life is insured has attained the age of 75 years, the references in paragraph (1)(c) to "20" and "twentieth" shall be read as references to "10" and "tenth" respectively; and

(b) where on the date of issue of an exemption test policy the person whose life is insured has attained the age of 66 years but not the age of 75 years, the references in paragraph (1)(c) to "20" and "twentieth" shall be read as references to

(i) the number obtained when the number of years by which the age of the person whose life is insured exceeds 65 years is subtracted from 20, and

(ii) the adjectival form of the number obtained by performing the computation described in subparagraph (i),

respectively.

**Notes**: Draft regulations of March 26, 1992 proposed to revoke Reg. 307(4) and to amend Reg. 307(1)(c). These proposals were replaced by amendments in 1994 to Reg. 304(1), 306 and 308, which achieved the goals intended by the 1992 draft amendments.

(5) In this section, any amount determined by reference to section 1401 shall be determined

(a) without regard to section 1402;

(b) as if each reference therein to the term "policy loan" were read as if that term had the meaning assigned by paragraph 148(9)(e) [148(9)"policy loan"] of the Act; and

(c) as if clauses 1401(1)(c)(i)(B) and 1401(1)(c)(ii)(C) were read without reference to the expression "or the interest thereon that has accrued to the insurer at the end of the year".

**Definitions [Reg. 307]**: "accumulating fund" — Reg. 307(1); "amount" — ITA 248(1); "amount payable" — ITA 138(12), Reg. 310; "annuity" — ITA 248(1); "Canada" — ITA 255, *Interpretation Act* 35(1); "cash surrender value" — ITA 148(9), Reg. 310; "insurer", "life insurance business" — ITA 248(1); "life insurance policy", "life insurance policy in Canada" — ITA 138(12), Reg. 310; "life insurer", "person" — ITA 248(1); "policy anniversary" — Reg. 310; "policy loan" — ITA 148(9), Reg. 310; "taxation year" — ITA 249; "taxpayer" — ITA 248(1).

**Interpretation Bulletins**: IT-87R2: Policyholders' income from life insurance policies.

**308. Net cost of pure insurance and mortality gains and losses** — (1) For the purposes of subparagraph 20(1)(e.2)(ii) and paragraph (a) of the description of L in the definition "adjusted cost basis" in subsection 148(9) of the Act, the net cost of pure insurance for a year in respect of a taxpayer's interest in a life insurance policy is the product obtained when the probability, computed on the basis of the rates of mortality under the 1969-75 mortality tables of the Canadian Institute of Actuaries published in Volume XVI of the Proceedings of the Canadian Institute of Actuaries or on the basis described in subsection (1.1), that a person who has the same relevant characteristics as the person whose life is insured will die in the year is multiplied by the amount by which

(a) the benefit on death in respect of the taxpayer's interest at the end of the year

exceeds

(b) the accumulating fund (determined without regard to any policy loan outstanding) in respect of the taxpayer's interest in the policy at the end of the year or the cash surrender value of such interest at the end of the year, depending on the method regularly followed by the life insurer in computing net cost of pure insurance.

**Notes**: Opening words of Reg. 308(1) amended by P.C. 1994-940; reference to ITA 20(1)(e.2)(ii) added effective for years ending after 1989, and reference to ITA 148(9)(a)(ix) changed to 148(9)"adjusted cost basis"L(a), to correspond to R.S.C. 1985 (5th Supp.) renumbering of the Act, effective for taxation years ending after November 1991.

**Interpretation Bulletins**: IT-87R2: Policyholders' income from life insurance policies; IT-309R2: Premiums on life insurance used as collateral.

**(1.1)** Where premiums for a particular class of life insurance policy offered by a life insurer do not depend directly on smoking or sex classification, the probability referred to in subsection (1) may be determined using rates of mortality otherwise determined provided that for each age for such class of life insurance policy, the expected value of the aggregate net cost of pure insurance, calculated using such rates of mortality, is equal to the expected value of the aggregate net cost of pure insurance, calculated using the rates of mortality under the 1969-75 mortality tables of the Canadian Institute of Actuaries published in Volume XVI of the Proceedings of the Canadian Institute of Actuaries.

(2) Subject to subsection (4), for the purposes of this section and subparagraph 148(9)(a)(v.1) [148(9)"adjusted cost basis"G] of the Act, a "mortality gain" immediately before the end of any calendar year after 1982 in respect of a taxpayer's interest in a life annuity contract means such reasonable amount in respect of his interest therein at that time that the life insurer determines to be the increase to the accumulating fund in respect of the interest that occurred during that year as a consequence of the survival to the end of the year of one or more of the annuitants thereunder.

(3) Subject to subsection (4), for the purposes of this section and subparagraph 148(9)(a)(xi) [148(9)"adjusted cost basis"(c)] of the Act, a "mortality loss" immediately before a particular time after 1982 in respect of an interest in a life annuity contract disposed of immediately after that particular time as a consequence of the death of an annuitant thereunder means such reasonable amount that the life insurer determines to be the decrease, as a consequence of the death, in the accumulating fund in respect of the interest assuming that, in determining such decrease, the accumulating fund immediately after the death is determined in the manner described in subparagraph 307(1)(b)(i).

(4) In determining an amount for a year in respect of an interest in a life annuity contract under subsection (2) or (3), the expected value of the mortality gains in respect of the interest for the year shall be equal to the expected value of the mortality losses in respect of the interest for the year and the mortality rates for the year used in computing those expected values shall be those that would be relevant to the interest and that are specified under such of paragraphs 1403(1)(c), (d) and (e) as are applicable.

**Definitions [Reg. 308]**: "accumulating fund" — Reg. 307(1); "amount", "annuity" — ITA 248(1); "benefit on death" — Reg. 310; "cash surrender value" — ITA 148(9), Reg. 310; "consequence of the death" — ITA 248(8); "disposed" — ITA 248(1)"disposition"; "life annuity contract" — Reg. 301(1), (2); "life insurance policy" — ITA 138(12), Reg. 310; "life insurer" — ITA 248(1); "mortality gain" — Reg. 308(2); "mortality loss" — Reg. 308(3); "person" — ITA 248(1); "policy loan" — ITA 148(9), Reg. 310; "probability" — Reg. 308(1.1); "taxpayer" — ITA 248(1).

**309. Prescribed premiums and prescribed increases** — (1) For the purposes of subsections 12.2(9) and 89(2) of the Act, section 306 and this section, a premium at any time under a life insurance policy is a "prescribed premium" if the total amount of one or more premiums paid at that time under the policy exceeds the amount of premium that, under the policy, was scheduled to be paid at that time and that was fixed and determined on or before December 1, 1982, adjusted for such of the following transactions and events that have occurred after that date in respect of the policy:

(a) a change in underwriting class;

(b) a change in premium due to a change in frequency of premium payments within a year that does not alter the present value, at the beginning of the year, of the total premiums to be paid under the policy in the year;

(c) an addition or deletion of accidental death or guaranteed purchase option benefits or disability benefits that provide for annuity payments or waiver of premiums;

(d) a premium adjustment as a result of interest, mortality or expense considerations, or of a change in the benefit on death under the policy relating to an increase in the Consumer Price Index (as published by Statistics Canada under the authority of the *Statistics Act*) where such adjustment

(i) is made by the life insurer on a class basis pursuant to the policy's terms as they read on December 1, 1982, and

(ii) is not made as a result of the exercise of a conversion privilege under the policy;

(e) a change arising from the provision of an additional benefit on death under a participating life insurance policy (within the meaning assigned by paragraph 138(12)(k) [138(12)"participating life insurance policy"] of the Act) as, on account of or in lieu of payment of, or in satisfaction of

(i) policy dividends or other distributions of the life insurer's income from its participating life insurance business as determined under section 2402, or

(ii) interest earned on policy dividends that are held on deposit by the life insurer;

(f) redating lapsed policies within the reinstatement period referred to in subparagraph 148(9)(c)(vi) [148(9)"disposition"(g)] of the Act or redating for policy loan indebtedness;

(g) a change in premium due to a correction of erroneous information contained in the application for the policy;

(h) payment of a premium after its due date, or payment of a premium no more than 30 days before its due date, as established on or before December 1, 1982; and

(i) the payment of an amount described in subparagraph 148(9)(e.1)(i) [148(9)"premium"(a)] of the Act.

(2) For the purposes of subsections 12.2(9) and 89(2) of the Act, a "prescribed increase" in a benefit on death under a life insurance policy has occurred at any time where the amount of the benefit on death under the policy at that time exceeds the amount of the benefit on death at that time under the policy that was fixed and determined on or before December 1, 1982, adjusted for such of the following transactions and events that have occurred after that date in respect of the policy:

(a) an increase resulting from a change described in paragraph (1)(e);

(b) a change as a result of interest, mortality or expense considerations, or an increase in the Consumer Price Index (as published by Statistics Canada under the authority of the *Statistics Act*) where such change is made by the life insurer on a class basis pursuant to the policy's terms as they read on December 1, 1982;

(c) an increase in consequence of the prepayment of premiums (other than prescribed premiums) under the policy where such increase does not exceed the aggregate of the premiums that would otherwise have been paid;

(d) an increase in respect of a policy for which

(i) the benefit on death was, at December 1, 1982, a specific mathematical function of the policy's cash surrender value or factors including the policy's cash surrender value, and

(ii) that function has not changed since that date,

unless any part of such increase is attributable to a prescribed premium paid in respect of a policy or to income earned on such a premium; and

(e) an increase that is granted by the life insurer on a class basis without consideration and not pursuant to any term of the contract.

(3) For the purposes of subsections (1) and (2), a life insurance policy that is issued as a result of the exercise of a renewal privilege provided under the terms of another policy as they read on December 1, 1982 shall be deemed to be a continuation of that other policy.

(4) For the purposes of subsection (2), a life insurance policy that is issued as a result of the exercise of a conversion privilege provided under the terms of another policy as they read on December 1, 1982 shall be deemed to be a continuation of that other policy except that any portion of the policy relating to the portion of the benefit on death, immediately before the conversion, that arose as a consequence of an event occurring after December 1, 1982 and described in paragraph (1)(e) shall be deemed to be a separate life insurance policy issued at the time of the conversion.

**Definitions [Reg. 309]**: "amount", "annuity" — ITA 248(1); "benefit on death" — Reg. 310; "Canada" — ITA 255, *Interpretation Act* 35(1); "cash surrender value" — ITA 148(9), Reg. 310; "continuation" — Reg. 309(3), (4); "dividend", "insurer", "life insurance business" — ITA 248(1); "life insurance policy" — ITA 138(12), Reg. 310; "life insurer" — ITA 248(1); "policy loan" — ITA 148(9), Reg. 310; "prescribed" — ITA 248(1); "prescribed premium" — Reg. 309(1).

**Interpretation Bulletins**: IT-66R6: Capital dividends; IT-87R2: Policyholders' income from life insurance policies.

**310. Interpretation** — For the purposes of sections 300, 301 and 304 to 309 and this section,

"**amount payable**" has the meaning assigned by paragraph 138(12)(b.1) [138(12)"amount payable"] of the Act;

"**benefit on death**" does not include policy dividends or any interest thereon held on deposit by an insurer or any additional amount payable as a result of accidental death;

"**cash surrender value**" has the meaning assigned by paragraph 148(9)(b) [148(9)"cash surrender value"] of the Act;

"**life insurance policy**" has the meaning assigned by paragraph 138(12)(f) [138(12)"life insurance policy"] of the Act;

"**life insurance policy in Canada**" has the meaning assigned by paragraph 138(12)(g) [138(12)"life insurance policy in Canada"] of the Act;

"**policy anniversary**" includes, where a life insurance policy was in existence throughout a calendar year and there would not otherwise be a policy anniversary in the year in respect of the policy, the end of the calendar year;

"**policy loan**" has the meaning assigned by paragraph 148(9)(e) [148(9)"policy loan"] of the Act;

"**proceeds of the disposition**" has the meaning assigned by paragraph 148(9)(e.2) [148(9)"proceeds of the disposition"] of the Act;

"**tax anniversary date**" in relation to an annuity contract means the second anniversary date of the contract to occur after October 22, 1968.

**Definitions [Reg. 310]**: "amount" — ITA 248(1); "amount payable" — ITA 138(12), Reg. 310; "annuity", "dividend", "insurer" — ITA 248(1); "life insurance policy" — ITA 138(12), Reg. 310.

# PART IV — TAXABLE INCOME EARNED IN A PROVINCE BY A CORPORATION

**Notes**: Part IV allocates a corporation's income among the provinces. For the equivalent rules for individuals (including trusts), see Part XXVI (Reg. 2600–2607).

**400. Interpretation** — (1) For the purposes of paragraph 124(4)(a) [124(4)"taxable income earned in the year in a province"] of the Act, a corporation's "taxable income earned in the year in a province" means the aggregate of the taxable incomes of the

Part IV — Taxable Income Earned in a Province   Reg. S. 402(3)

corporation earned in the year in each of the provinces.

**(2) [Permanent establishment]** — For the purposes of this Part, "permanent establishment" in respect of a corporation means a fixed place of business of the corporation, including an office, a branch, a mine, an oil well, a farm, a timberland, a factory, a workshop or a warehouse, and

(a) where the corporation does not have any fixed place of business it means the principal place in which the corporation's business is conducted;

(b) where a corporation carries on business through an employee or agent, established in a particular place, who has general authority to contract for his employer or principal or who has a stock of merchandise owned by his employer or principal from which he regularly fills orders which he receives, the corporation shall be deemed to have a permanent establishment in that place;

(c) an insurance corporation is deemed to have a permanent establishment in each province and country in which the corporation is registered or licensed to do business;

(d) where a corporation, otherwise having a permanent establishment in Canada, owns land in a province, such land shall be deemed to be a permanent establishment;

(e) where a corporation uses substantial machinery or equipment in a particular place at any time in a taxation year it shall be deemed to have a permanent establishment in that place;

(f) the fact that a corporation has business dealings through a commission agent, broker or other independent agent or maintains an office solely for the purchase of merchandise shall not of itself be held to mean that the corporation has a permanent establishment; and

(g) the fact that a corporation has a subsidiary controlled corporation in a place or a subsidiary controlled corporation engaged in trade or business in a place shall not of itself be held to mean that the corporation is operating a permanent establishment in that place.

**Related Provisions**: Reg. 5906 — Carrying on business in a country.

**Notes**: Reg. 400(2) amended by P.C. 1994-139, effective 10:00 p.m. EDST, April 26, 1989, to no longer apply for purposes of ITA 112(2). "Permanent establishment" for purposes of that provision is now defined in Reg. 8201.

**Interpretation Bulletins**: IT-177R2: Permanent establishment of a corporation in a province and of a foreign enterprise in Canada; IT-393R2: Election re tax on rents and timber royalties — non-residents.

**I.T. Technical News**: No. 2 (permanent establishment in province through an agent).

**Definitions [Reg. 400]**: "business" — ITA 248(1); "Canada" — ITA 255, *Interpretation Act* 35(1); "corporation" — ITA 248(1), *Interpretation Act* 35(1); "employee", "employer", "insurance corporation", "office" — ITA 248(1); "permanent establishment" — Reg. 400(2); "province" — *Interpretation Act* 35(1); "subsidiary controlled corporation" — ITA 248(1); "taxable income" — Reg. 413(1); "taxation year" — ITA 249.

**401. Computation of taxable income** — The amount of taxable income of a corporation earned in a year in a particular province shall be determined in accordance with the provisions of this Part.

**Definitions [Reg. 401]**: "amount" — ITA 248(1); "corporation" — ITA 248(1), *Interpretation Act* 35(1); "province" — *Interpretation Act* 35(1); "taxable income" — Reg. 413(1).

**402. General rules** — (1) Where, in a taxation year, a corporation had a permanent establishment in a particular province and had no permanent establishment outside that province, the whole of its taxable income for the year shall be deemed to have been earned therein.

(2) Where, in a taxation year, a corporation had no permanent establishment in a particular province, no part of its taxable income for the year shall be deemed to have been earned therein.

(3) Except as otherwise provided, where, in a taxation year, a corporation had a permanent establishment in a province and a permanent establishment outside that province, the amount of its taxable income that shall be deemed to have been earned in the year in the province is

(a) in any case other than a case specified in paragraph (b) or (c), $1/2$ the aggregate of

(i) that proportion of its taxable income for the year that the gross revenue for the year reasonably attributable to the permanent establishment in the province is of its total gross revenue for the year, and

(ii) that proportion of its taxable income for the year that the aggregate of the salaries and wages paid in the year by the corporation to employees of the permanent establishment in the province is of the aggregate of all salaries and wages paid in the year by the corporation;

(b) in any case where the gross revenue for the year of the corporation is nil, that proportion of its taxable income for the year that the aggregate of the salaries and wages paid in the year by the corporation to employees of the permanent establishment in the province is of the aggregate of all salaries and wages paid in the year by the corporation; and

(c) in any case where the aggregate of the salaries and wages paid in the year by the corporation is nil, that proportion of its taxable income for the year that the gross revenue for the year reasonably attributable to the permanent establishment in the province is of its total gross revenue for the year.

**Forms**: T2S-TC: Tax calculation supplementary — corporations.

**(4) [Attribution to permanent establishment]** — For the purpose of determining the gross revenue for the year reasonably attributable to a permanent establishment in a province or country other than Canada, within the meaning of subsection (3), the following rules shall apply:

(a) where the destination of a shipment of merchandise to a customer to whom the merchandise is sold is in the particular province or country, the gross revenue derived therefrom shall be attributable to the permanent establishment in the province or country;

(b) except as provided in paragraph (c), where the destination of a shipment of merchandise to a customer to whom the merchandise is sold is in a province or country other than Canada in which the taxpayer has no permanent establishment, if the person negotiating the sale may reasonably be regarded as being attached to the permanent establishment in the particular province or country, the gross revenue derived therefrom shall be attributable to that permanent establishment;

(c) where the destination of a shipment of merchandise to a customer to whom the merchandise is sold is in a country other than Canada in which the taxpayer has no permanent establishment,

(i) if the merchandise was produced or manufactured or produced and manufactured, entirely in the particular province by the taxpayer, the gross revenue derived therefrom shall be attributable to the permanent establishment in the province, or

(ii) if the merchandise was produced or manufactured, or produced and manufactured, partly in the particular province and partly in another place by the taxpayer, the gross revenue derived therefrom attributable to the permanent establishment in the province shall be that proportion thereof that the salaries and wages paid in the year to employees of the permanent establishment in the province where the merchandise was partly produced or manufactured (or partly produced and manufactured) is of the aggregate of the salaries and wages paid in the year to employees of the permanent establishments where the merchandise was produced or manufactured (or produced and manufactured);

(d) where a customer to whom merchandise is sold instructs that shipment be made to some other person and the customer's office with which the sale was negotiated is located in the particular province or country, the gross revenue derived therefrom shall be attributable to the permanent establishment in the province or country;

(e) except as provided in paragraph (f), where a customer to whom merchandise is sold instructs that shipment be made to some other person and the customer's office with which the sale was negotiated is located in a province or country other than Canada in which the taxpayer has no permanent establishment, if the person negotiating the sale may reasonably be regarded as being attached to the permanent establishment in the particular province or country, the gross revenue derived therefrom shall be attributable to that permanent establishment;

(f) where a customer to whom merchandise is sold instructs that shipment be made to some other person and the customer's office with which the sale was negotiated is located in a country other than Canada in which the taxpayer has no permanent establishment,

(i) if the merchandise was produced or manufactured, or produced and manufactured, entirely in the particular province by the taxpayer, the gross revenue derived therefrom shall be attributable to the permanent establishment in the province, or

(ii) if the merchandise was produced or manufactured, or produced and manufactured, partly in the particular province and partly in another place by the taxpayer, the gross revenue derived therefrom attributable to the permanent establishment in the province shall be that proportion thereof that the salaries and wages paid in the year to employees of the permanent establishment in the province where the merchandise was partly produced or manufactured (or partly produced and manufactured) is of the aggregate of the salaries and wages paid in the year to employees of the permanent establishments where the merchandise was produced or manufactured (or produced and manufactured);

(g) where gross revenue is derived from services rendered in the particular province or country, the gross revenue shall be attributable to the permanent establishment in the province or country;

(h) where gross revenue is derived from services rendered in a province or country other than Canada in which the taxpayer has no permanent establishment, if the person negotiating the contract may reasonably be regarded as being attached to the permanent establishment of the taxpayer in the particular province or country, the gross revenue shall be attributable to that permanent establishment;

(i) where standing timber or the right to cut standing timber is sold and the timber limit on which the timber is standing is in the particular province or country, the gross revenue from such sale shall be attributable to the permanent establishment of the taxpayer in the province or country; and

(j) gross revenue which arises from leasing land owned by the taxpayer in a province and which is included in computing its income under Part I of

Part IV — Taxable Income Earned in a Province  Reg. S. 402

the Act shall be attributable to the permanent establishment, if any, of the taxpayer in the province where the land is situated.

**(4.1)** For the purposes of subsections (3) and (4), where, in a taxation year,

(a) the destination of a shipment of merchandise to a customer to whom the merchandise is sold by a corporation is in a country other than Canada or the customer to whom merchandise is sold by a corporation instructs that the shipment of merchandise be made by the corporation to another person and the customer's office with which the sale was negotiated is located in a country other than Canada,

(b) the corporation has a permanent establishment in the other country, and

(c) the corporation is not subject to taxation on its income under the laws of the other country, or its gross revenue derived from the sale is not included in computing the income or profit or other base for income or profits taxation by the other country, because of

(i) the provisions of any taxing statute of the other country, or

(ii) the operation of any tax treaty or convention between Canada and the other country,

the following rules apply:

(d) with respect to the gross revenue derived from the sale,

(i) paragraphs 4(a) and (d) do not apply,

(ii) that portion of paragraph 4(c) preceding subparagraph (i) thereof shall be read as follows:

"(c) where the destination of a shipment of merchandise to a customer to whom the merchandise is sold is in a country other than Canada," and

(iii) that portion of paragraph 4(f) preceding subparagraph (i) thereof shall be read as follows:

"(f) where a customer to whom the merchandise is sold instructs that shipment be made to some other person and the customer's office with which the sale was negotiated is located in a country other than Canada,"; and

(e) for the purposes of subparagraph (3)(a)(ii), paragraph (3)(b) and subparagraphs (4)(c)(ii) and (f)(ii), salaries and wages paid in the year to employees of any permanent establishment of the corporation located in that other country shall be deemed to be nil.

**Notes**: Reg. 402(4.1) added by P.C. 1994-662, effective for taxation years that begin in 1993 or later. Where the corporation elected by notifying Revenue Canada in writing by November 30, 1994, it applies to taxation years that end in 1992 as well. It alleviates the problem resulting from Reg. 402(4) where goods are shipped to a foreign destination, the foreign jurisdiction does not impose tax, and the provincial taxing statutes treat the income as having been earned in the province, leading to double taxation. Reg. 402(4.1) ensures that the income neither escapes provincial taxation nor is double-taxed.

**(5)** For the purposes of subsection (3), "gross revenue" does not include interest on bonds, debentures or mortgages, dividends on shares of capital stock, or rentals or royalties from property that is not used in connection with the principal business operations of the corporation.

**(6)** For the purposes of subsection (3), where part of the corporation's operations were conducted in partnership with one or more other persons

(a) the corporation's gross revenue for the year, and

(b) the salaries and wages paid in the year by the corporation,

shall include, in respect of those operations, only that proportion of

(c) the total gross revenue of the partnership for its fiscal period ending in or coinciding with the year, and

(d) the total salaries and wages paid by the partnership in its fiscal period ending in or coinciding with the year,

respectively, that

(e) the corporation's share of the income or loss of the partnership for the fiscal period ending in or coinciding with the year,

is of

(f) the total income or loss of the partnership for the fiscal period ending in or coinciding with the year.

**(7)** Where a corporation pays a fee to another person under an agreement pursuant to which that other person or employees of that other person perform services for the corporation that would normally be performed by employees of the corporation, the fee so paid shall be deemed to be salary paid in the year by the corporation and that part of the fee that may reasonably be regarded as payment in respect of services rendered at a particular permanent establishment of the corporation shall be deemed to be salary paid to an employee of that permanent establishment.

**(8)** For the purposes of subsection (7), a fee does not include a commission paid to a person who is not an employee of the corporation.

**Definitions [Reg. 402]**: "amount", "business" — ITA 248(1); "Canada" — ITA 255, *Interpretation Act* 35(1); "corporation" — ITA 248(1), *Interpretation Act* 35(1); "dividend", "employee" — ITA 248(1); "fee" — Reg. 402(8); "fiscal period" — ITA 249.1; "gross revenue" — Reg. 402(4), (5), (6); "office" — ITA 248(1); "permanent establishment" — Reg. 400(2); "person", "property" — ITA 248(1); "province" — *Interpretation Act* 35(1); "salaries and wages paid in the year" — Reg. 413(1); "share" — ITA 248(1); "taxable income" — Reg. 413(1); "taxation year" — ITA 249; "taxpayer" — ITA 248(1); "total gross revenue for the year" — Reg. 413(2).

**Interpretation Bulletins**: IT-177R2: Permanent establishment of corporation in province and of foreign enterprise in Canada.

### 402.1 Transitional — Taxable income earned in the 1978 taxation year in the Northwest Territories — [No longer relevant]

### 402.2 Transitional — Taxable income earned in the 1980 taxation year in the Yukon Territory — [No longer relevant]

### 403. Insurance corporations — (1) Notwithstanding subsections 402(3) and (4), the amount of taxable income that shall be deemed to have been earned in a taxation year in a particular province by an insurance corporation is that proportion of its taxable income for the year that the aggregate of

(a) its net premiums for the year in respect of insurance on property situated in the province, and

(b) its net premiums for the year in respect of insurance, other than on property, from contracts with persons resident in the province,

is of the total of such of its net premiums for the year as are included in computing its income for the purposes of Part I of the Act.

**(2)** In this section, "net premiums" of a corporation for a taxation year means the aggregate of the gross premiums received by the corporation in the year (other than consideration received for annuities), minus the aggregate for the year of

(a) premiums paid for reinsurance,

(b) dividends or rebates paid or credited to policyholders, and

(c) rebates or returned premiums paid in respect of the cancellation of policies,

by the corporation.

**(3)** For the purposes of subsection (1), where an insurance corporation had no permanent establishment in a taxation year in a particular province,

(a) each net premium for that year in respect of insurance on property situated in the particular province shall be deemed to be a net premium in respect of insurance on property situated in the province in which the permanent establishment of the corporation to which the net premium is reasonably attributable is situated; and

(b) each net premium for that year in respect of insurance, other than on property, from contracts with persons resident in the particular province shall be deemed to be a net premium in respect of insurance, other than on property, from contracts with persons resident in the province in which the permanent establishment of the corporation to which the net premium is reasonably attributable is situated.

**Definitions [Reg. 403]**: "amount" — ITA 248(1); "corporation" — ITA 248(1), Interpretation Act 35(1); "dividend", "insurance corporation" — ITA 248(1); "net premiums" — Reg. 403(2), (3); "permanent establishment" — Reg. 400(2); "property" — ITA 248(1); "province" — Interpretation Act 35(1); "taxable income" — Reg. 413(1); "taxation year" — ITA 249.

### 404. Chartered banks — (1) Notwithstanding subsections 402(3) and (4), the amount of taxable income that shall be deemed to have been earned by a chartered bank in a taxation year in a province in which it had a permanent establishment is 1/3 of the aggregate of

> **Proposed Amendment — Reg. 404(1) opening words**
>
> **404. Banks — (1)** Despite subsections 402(3) and (4), the amount of taxable income that is deemed to have been earned by a bank in a taxation year in a province in which it had a permanent establishment is 1/3 of the total of
>
> **Application**: The August 8, 2000 draft regulations, s. 1, will amend the heading that precedes s. 404, and the opening words of subsec. 404(1), to read as above, applicable after June 27, 1999.

(a) that proportion of its taxable income for the year that the aggregate of the salaries and wages paid in the year by the bank to employees of its permanent establishment in the province is of the aggregate of all salaries and wages paid in the year by the bank, and

(b) twice that proportion of its taxable income for the year that the aggregate amount of loans and deposits of its permanent establishment in the province for the year is of the aggregate amount of all loans and deposits of the bank for the year.

**Related Provisions**: Reg. 413(3) — Application to authorized foreign bank.

**(2)** For the purposes of subsection (1), the amount of loans for a taxation year is 1/12 of the aggregate of the amounts outstanding, on the loans made by the bank, at the close of business on the last day of each month in the year.

**(3)** For the purposes of subsection (1), the amount of deposits for a taxation year is 1/12 of the aggregate of the amounts on deposit with the bank at the close of business on the last day of each month in the year.

**(4)** For the purposes of subsections (2) and (3), loans and deposits do not include bonds, stocks, debentures, items in transit and deposits in favour of Her Majesty in right of Canada.

**Definitions [Reg. 404]**: "all loans and deposits of the bank for the year" — Reg. 413(3); "amount" — ITA 248(1); "bank" — ITA 248(1), Interpretation Act 35(1); "business" — ITA 248(1); "Canada" — ITA 255, Interpretation Act 35(1); "deposits" — Reg. 404(3), (4); "employee" — ITA 248(1); "Her Majesty" — Interpretation Act 35(1); "loans" — Reg. 404(2), (4); "month" — Interpretation Act 35(1); "permanent establishment" — Reg. 400(2); "province" — Interpretation Act 35(1); "salaries and wages paid in the year" — Reg. 413(1); "taxable income" — Reg. 413(1); "taxation year" — ITA 249.

**405. Trust and loan corporations** — (1) Notwithstanding subsections 402(3) and (4), the amount of taxable income that shall be deemed to have been earned in a taxation year by a trust and loan corporation, trust corporation or loan corporation in a province in which it had a permanent establishment is that proportion of its taxable income for the year that the gross revenue for the year of its permanent establishment in the province is of the total gross revenue for the year of the corporation.

(2) In subsection (1), "gross revenue for the year of its permanent establishment in the province" means the aggregate of the gross revenue of the corporation for the year arising from

(a) loans secured by lands situated in the province;

(b) loans, not secured by land, to persons residing in the province;

(c) loans

(i) to persons residing in a province or country other than Canada in which the corporation has no permanent establishment, and

(ii) administered by a permanent establishment in the province,

except loans secured by land situated in a province or country other than Canada in which the corporation has a permanent establishment; and

(d) business conducted at the permanent establishment in the province, other than revenue in respect of loans.

Definitions [Reg. 405]: "amount", "business" — ITA 248(1); "Canada" — ITA 255, *Interpretation Act* 35(1); "corporation" — ITA 248(1), *Interpretation Act* 35(1); "gross revenue" — ITA 248(1); "gross revenue for the year of its permanent establishment in the province" — Reg. 405(2); "permanent establishment" — Reg. 400(2); "person" — ITA 248(1); "province" — *Interpretation Act* 35(1); "taxable income" — Reg. 413(1); "taxation year" — ITA 249; "trust" — ITA 104(1), 248(1), (3).

**406. Railway corporations** — (1) Notwithstanding subsections 402(3) and (4), the amount of taxable income that shall be deemed to have been earned by a railway corporation in a taxation year in a province in which it had a permanent establishment is, unless subsection (2) applies, ½ the aggregate of

(a) that proportion of the taxable income of the corporation for the year that the equated track miles of the corporation in the province is of the equated track miles of the corporation in Canada; and

(b) that proportion of the taxable income of the corporation for the year that the gross ton miles of the corporation for the year in the province is of the gross ton miles of the corporation for the year in Canada.

(2) Where a corporation to which subsection (1) would apply, if this subsection did not apply thereto, operates an airline service, ships or hotels or receives substantial revenues that are petroleum or natural gas royalties, or does a combination of two or more of those things, the amount of its taxable income that shall be deemed to have been earned in a taxation year in a province in which it had a permanent establishment is the aggregate of the amounts computed

(a) by applying the provisions of section 407 to that part of its taxable income for the year that may reasonably be considered to have arisen from the operation of the airline service;

(b) by applying the provisions of section 410 to that part of its taxable income for the year that may reasonably be considered to have arisen from the operation of the ships;

(c) by applying the provisions of section 402 to that part of its taxable income for the year that may reasonably be considered to have arisen from the operation of the hotels;

(d) by applying the provisions of section 402 to that part of its taxable income for the year that may reasonably be considered to have arisen from the ownership by the taxpayer of petroleum or natural gas rights or any interest therein; and

(e) by applying the provisions of subsection (1) to the remaining portion of its taxable income for the year.

(3) In this section, "equated track miles" in a specified place means the aggregate of

(a) the number of miles of first main track,

(b) 80 per cent of the number of miles of other main tracks, and

(c) 50 per cent of the number of miles of yard tracks and sidings,

in that place.

(4) For the purpose of making an allocation under paragraph (2)(b), a reference in section 410 to "salaries and wages paid in the year by the corporation to employees" shall be read as a reference to salaries and wages paid by the corporation to employees employed in the operation of permanent establishments (other than ships) maintained for the shipping business.

(5) For the purpose of making an allocation under paragraph (2)(c),

(a) a reference in section 402 to "gross revenue for the year reasonably attributable to the permanent establishment in the province" shall be read as a reference to the gross revenue of the taxpayer from operating hotels therein;

(b) a reference in section 402 to "total gross revenue for the year" shall be read as a reference to the total gross revenue of the taxpayer for the year from operating hotels; and

(c) a reference in section 402 to "salaries and wages paid in the year by the corporation to employees" shall be read as a reference to salaries and wages paid to employees engaged in the operations of its hotels.

**(6)** Notwithstanding subsection 402(5), for the purpose of making an allocation under paragraph (2)(d),

(a) a reference in section 402 to "gross revenue for the year reasonably attributable to the permanent establishment in the province" shall be read as a reference to the gross revenue of the taxpayer from the ownership by the taxpayer of petroleum and natural gas rights in lands in the province and any interest therein;

(b) a reference in section 402 to "total gross revenue for the year" shall be read as a reference to the total gross revenue of the taxpayer from ownership by the taxpayer of petroleum and natural gas rights and any interest therein; and

(c) a reference in section 402 to "salaries and wages paid in the year by the corporation to employees" shall be read as a reference to salaries and wages paid to employees employed in connection with the corporation's petroleum and natural gas rights and interests therein.

**Definitions [Reg. 406]:** "amount", "business" — ITA 248(1); "Canada" — ITA 255, *Interpretation Act* 35(1); "corporation" — ITA 248(1), *Interpretation Act* 35(1); "employed", "employee" — ITA 248(1); "equated track miles" — Reg. 406(3); "gross revenue" — ITA 248(1); "permanent establishment" — Reg. 400(2); "province" — *Interpretation Act* 35(1); "taxable income" — Reg. 413(1); "taxation year" — ITA 249; "taxpayer" — ITA 248(1).

**407. Airline corporations** — **(1)** Notwithstanding subsections 402(3) and (4), the amount of taxable income that shall be deemed to have been earned in a taxation year by an airline corporation in a province in which it had a permanent establishment is the amount that is equal to ¼ of the aggregate of

(a) that proportion of its taxable income for the year that the capital cost of all the corporation's fixed assets, except aircraft, in the province at the end of the year is of the capital cost of all its fixed assets, except aircraft, in Canada at the end of the year; and

(b) that proportion of its taxable income for the year that three times the number of revenue plane miles flown by its aircraft in the province during the year is of the total number of revenue plane miles flown by its aircraft in Canada during the year other than miles flown in a province in which the corporation had no permanent establishment.

**Notes:** Reg. 407(1)(b) amended by P.C. 1994-662, effective for taxation years that begin in 1993 or later, to add the words "other than miles flown in a province in which the corporation had no permanent establishment".

**(2)** For the purposes of this section, "revenue plane miles flown" shall be weighted according to take-off weight of the aircraft operated.

**(3)** For the purposes of this section, "take-off weight" of an aircraft means

(a) for an aircraft in respect of which an application form for a Certificate of Airworthiness has been submitted to and accepted by the Department of Transport, the maximum permissible take-off weight, in pounds, shown on the form; and

(b) for any other aircraft, the weight, in pounds, that may reasonably be considered to be the equivalent of the weight referred to in paragraph (a).

**Definitions [Reg. 407]:** "amount" — ITA 248(1); "Canada" — ITA 255, *Interpretation Act* 35(1); "corporation" — ITA 248(1), *Interpretation Act* 35(1); "permanent establishment" — Reg. 400(2); "province" — *Interpretation Act* 35(1); "revenue plane miles flown" — Reg. 407(2); "take-off weight" — Reg. 407(3); "taxable income" — Reg. 413(1); "taxation year" — ITA 249.

**408. Grain elevator operators** — Notwithstanding subsections 402(3) and (4), the amount of taxable income of a corporation whose chief business is the operation of grain elevators that shall be deemed to have been earned by that corporation in a taxation year in a province in which it had a permanent establishment is ½ of the aggregate of

(a) that proportion of its taxable income for the year that the number of bushels of grain received in the year in the elevators operated by the corporation in the province is of the total number of bushels of grain received in the year in all the elevators operated by the corporation; and

(b) that proportion of its taxable income for the year that the aggregate of salaries and wages paid in the year by the corporation to employees of its permanent establishment in the province is of the aggregate of all salaries and wages paid in the year by the corporation.

**Definitions [Reg. 408]:** "amount", "business" — ITA 248(1); "corporation" — ITA 248(1), *Interpretation Act* 35(1); "employee" — ITA 248(1); "permanent establishment" — Reg. 400(2); "province" — *Interpretation Act* 35(1); "salaries and wages paid in the year", "taxable income" — Reg. 413(1); "taxation year" — ITA 249.

**409. Bus and truck operators** — Notwithstanding subsections 402(3) and (4), the amount of taxable income of a corporation whose chief business is the transportation of goods or passengers (other than by the operation of a railway, ship or airline service) that shall be deemed to have been earned by that corporation in a taxation year in a province in which it had a permanent establishment is ½ of the aggregate of

(a) that proportion of its taxable income for the year that the number of kilometres driven by the corporation's vehicles, whether owned or leased, on roads in the province in the year is of the total number of kilometres driven by those vehicles in the year on roads other than roads in provinces or countries in which the corporation had no permanent establishment; and

(b) that proportion of its taxable income for the year that the aggregate of salaries and wages paid in the year by the corporation to employees of its permanent establishment in the province is of the aggregate of all salaries and wages paid in the year by the corporation.

**Definitions [Reg. 409]**: "amount", "business" — ITA 248(1); "corporation" — ITA 248(1), *Interpretation Act* 35(1); "employee" — ITA 248(1); "permanent establishment" — Reg. 400(2); "province" — *Interpretation Act* 35(1); "salaries and wages paid in the year", "taxable income" — Reg. 413(1); "taxation year" — ITA 249.

**410. Ship operators** — (1) Notwithstanding subsections 402(3) and (4), the amount of taxable income of a corporation whose chief business is the operation of ships that shall be deemed to have been earned by the corporation in a taxation year in a province in which it had a permanent establishment is the aggregate of,

(a) that portion of its allocable income for the year that its port-call-tonnage in the province is of its total port-call-tonnage in all the provinces in which it had a permanent establishment; and

(b) if its taxable income for the year exceeds its allocable income for the year, that proportion of the excess that the aggregate of the salaries and wages paid in the year by the corporation to employees of the permanent establishment (other than a ship) in the province is of the aggregate of salaries and wages paid in the year by the corporation to employees of its permanent establishments (other than ships) in Canada.

(2) In this section,

(a) "allocable income for the year" means that proportion of the taxable income of the corporation for the year that its total port-call-tonnage in Canada is of its total port-call-tonnage in all countries; and

(b) "port-call-tonnage" in a province or country means the aggregate of the products obtained by multiplying, for each ship operated by the corporation, the number of calls made in the year by that ship at ports in that province or country by the number of tons of the registered net tonnage of that ship.

**Definitions [Reg. 410]**: "allocable income for the year" — Reg. 410(2)(a); "amount", "business" — ITA 248(1); "Canada" — ITA 255, *Interpretation Act* 35(1); "corporation" — ITA 248(1), *Interpretation Act* 35(1); "employee" — ITA 248(1); "permanent establishment" — Reg. 400(2); "port-call tonnage" — Reg. 410(2)(b); "province" — *Interpretation Act* 35(1); "salaries and wages paid in the year by the corporation to employees" — Reg. 406(4); "taxable income" — Reg. 413(1); "taxation year" — ITA 249.

**411. Pipeline operators** — Notwithstanding subsections 402(3) and (4), the amount of taxable income of a corporation whose chief business is the operation of a pipeline that shall be deemed to have been earned by that corporation in a taxation year in a province in which it had a permanent establishment is $1/2$ of the aggregate of

(a) that proportion of its taxable income for the year that the number of miles of pipeline of the corporation in the province is of the number of miles of pipeline of the corporation in all the provinces in which it had a permanent establishment; and

(b) that proportion of its taxable income for the year that the aggregate of the salaries and wages paid in the year by the corporation to employees of its permanent establishment in the province is of the aggregate of salaries and wages paid in the year by the corporation to employees of its permanent establishments in Canada.

**Notes**: For the CCRA's administrative definition of "pipeline", see Interpretation Bulletin IT-482.

**Definitions [Reg. 411]**: "amount", "business" — ITA 248(1); "Canada" — ITA 255, *Interpretation Act* 35(1); "corporation" — ITA 248(1), *Interpretation Act* 35(1); "employee" — ITA 248(1); "permanent establishment" — Reg. 400(2); "province" — *Interpretation Act* 35(1); "salaries and wages paid in the year", "taxable income" — Reg. 413(1); "taxation year" — ITA 249.

**Interpretation Bulletins**: IT-482: Pipelines.

**412. Divided businesses** — Where part of the business of a corporation for a taxation year, other than a corporation described in section 403, 404, 405, 406, 407, 408, 409, 410 or 411, consisted of operations normally conducted by a corporation described in one of those sections, the corporation and the Minister may agree to determine the amount of taxable income deemed to have been earned in the year in a particular province to be the aggregate of the amounts computed

(a) by applying the provisions of such of those sections as would have been applicable if it had been a corporation described therein to the portion of its taxable income for the year that might reasonably be considered to have arisen from that part of the business; and

(b) by applying the provisions of section 402 to the remaining portion of its taxable income for the year.

**Definitions [Reg. 412]**: "amount", "business" — ITA 248(1); "corporation" — ITA 248(1), *Interpretation Act* 35(1); "Minister" — ITA 248(1); "province" — *Interpretation Act* 35(1); "taxable income" — Reg. 413(1); "taxation year" — ITA 249.

**413. Non-resident corporations** — (1) For the purposes of this Part, where a corporation is not resident in Canada, **"salaries and wages paid in the year"** by the corporation does not include salaries and wages paid to employees of a permanent establishment outside Canada and "taxable income" shall be deemed to refer to taxable income earned in Canada as determined under section 115 of the Act.

(2) For the purposes of paragraph 402(3)(a), where a corporation is not resident in Canada, **"total gross revenue for the year"** of the corporation does not include gross revenue reasonably attributable to a permanent establishment outside Canada.

> **Proposed Addition — Reg. 413(3)**
>
> (3) For the purpose of paragraph 404(1)(b), in the case of an authorized foreign bank, **"all loans and deposits of the bank for the year"** shall be read as a reference to "all loans and deposits of the bank for the year in respect of its Canadian banking business".
>
> **Application**: The August 8, 2000 draft regulations, s. 2, will add subsec. 413(3) to read as above, applicable after June 27, 1999.

**Definitions [Reg. 413]**: "authorized foreign bank" — ITA 248(1); "Canada" — ITA 255, *Interpretation Act* 35(1); "Canadian banking business" — ITA 248(1); "corporation" — ITA 248(1), *Interpretation Act* 35(1); "employee", "gross revenue" — ITA 248(1); "permanent establishment" — Reg. 400(2); "resident in Canada" — ITA 250; "taxable income" — Reg. 413(1); "taxable income earned in Canada" — ITA 248(1).

**414. Nova Scotia offshore area** — For the purpose of subsection 123(2) of the Act, the "amount taxable earned by the corporation in the year in the Nova Scotia offshore area", in respect of a corporation for a taxation year, means the amount of taxable income of the corporation earned in the year that would be allocated under this Part to the Nova Scotia offshore area if the reference to the word "province" in this Part were read as "Nova Scotia offshore area".

**Notes**: ITA 123(2) has been repealed.

**Definitions [Reg. 414]**: "corporation" — ITA 248(1), *Interpretation Act* 35(1); "Nova Scotia offshore area" — Reg. 415; "taxation year" — ITA 249.

**415.** For the purposes of this Part and subsection 123(2) of the Act, "Nova Scotia offshore area" has the meaning assigned to the expression "offshore area" by subsection 63(1) of the *Canada-Nova Scotia Oil and Gas Agreement Act*.

**Notes**: ITA 123(2) has been repealed.

## PART V — NON-RESIDENT-OWNED INVESTMENT CORPORATIONS

**500. Elections** — Any election by a corporation to be taxed under section 133 of the Act shall be made by forwarding by registered mail to the Director–Taxation at the District Office of the Department of National Revenue, Taxation that serves the area in which the head office of the corporation is located the following documents:

(a) a letter stating that the corporation elects to be taxed under the said section 133;

(b) a certified copy of the resolution of the directors of the corporation authorizing the election to be made; and

(c) a certified list showing

(i) the names and addresses of the registered shareholders and the number of shares of each class held by each,

(ii) the names and addresses of the holders of the corporation's bonds, debentures, or other funded indebtedness, if any, and

(iii) the names and addresses of the beneficial owners of shares, bonds, debentures, or other funded indebtedness in cases where the registered shareholders or holders, as the case may be, are not the beneficial owners.

**Definitions [Reg. 500]**: "corporation" — ITA 248(1), *Interpretation Act* 35(1); "office", "share", "shareholder" — ITA 248(1).

**501. Elections revoked** — Any election to be taxed under section 133 of the Act shall be revoked by a corporation by forwarding by registered mail to the Deputy Minister of National Revenue for Taxation at Ottawa the following documents in duplicate:

(a) a letter stating that the corporation revokes its election; and

(b) a certified copy of the resolution of the directors of the corporation authorizing the election to be revoked.

**Definitions [Reg. 501]**: "corporation" — ITA 248(1), *Interpretation Act* 35(1); "Minister" — ITA 248(1).

**502. Certificates of changes of ownership** — A corporation which is taxable under section 133 of the Act shall attach to its return of income required under subsection 150(1) of the Act, a certified statement showing any changes during the taxation year in the information referred to in paragraph 500(c).

**Definitions [Reg. 502]**: "corporation" — ITA 248(1), *Interpretation Act* 35(1); "taxation year" — ITA 249.

**503.** [Revoked]

## PART VI — ELECTIONS

**600. [Prescribed provisions for late elections]** — For the purposes of paragraphs 220(3.2)(a) and (b) of the Act, the following are prescribed provisions:

(a) section 21 of the Act;

(b) subsections 13(4) and (7.4), 14(6), 44(1) and (6), 45(2) and (3), 50(1), 53(2.1), 70(6.2), (9), (9.1), (9.2) and (9.3), 72(2), 73(1), 80(3), 80.1(4), 82(3), 83(2), 104(5.3) and (14), 110.4(2), 146.01(7), 164(6) and 184(3) of the Act;

(b.1) [Repealed]

(c) paragraphs 48(1)(a) and (c), 66.7(7)(c), (d) and (e) and (8)(c), (d) and (e), 80.01(4)(c) and 128.1(4)(d) of the Act;

> **Proposed Amendment — Reg. 600(c)**
>
> (c) paragraphs 48(1)(a) and (c), 66.7(7)(c), (d) and (e) and (8)(c), (d) and (e), 80.01(4)(c) and 128.1(4)(d), (6)(a) and (c) and (7)(c) of the Act;
>
> **Notes**: Due to renumbering of proposed amendments to ITA 128.1 between December 17/99 and June 5/00 (later Bill C-43), the reference to ITA 128.1(7)(c) will be changed to 128.1(8)(c). Also expected to be added are new 128.1(7)(d) and (g).
>
> **Application**: The December 17, 1999 draft regulations (taxpayer migration), s. 1, will amend Reg. 600(c) to read as above, applicable after October 1, 1996.
>
> **Technical Notes**: Subsection 220(3.2) of the Act allows the Minister of National Revenue to extend the time for the filing of, or allow the amendment or revocation of, certain elections under the Act and Regulations. The list of those elections, in Part VI of the Regulations, is amended to include the elections contemplated by new paragraphs 128.1(6)(a) and (c) and (7)(c) of the Act. This amendment applies after October 1, 1996.

(c.1) subparagraph 128.1(4)(b)(iv) of the Act; and

(d) subsections 1103(1), (2) and (2d) and 5907(2.1) of these Regulations.

**Notes**: Part VI added by P.C. 1992-914, effective December 17, 1991. It prescribes the elections that may be made, amended or revoked late under ITA 220(3.2).

Reference to ITA paragraphs 48(1)(a) and (c) and subsections 13(7.4), 45(2), 45(3), 83(2), 110.4(2), 164(6) and 184(3) added to Reg. 600(b) and (c) by P.C. 1993-1942, effective December 15, 1993.

Reference to ITA 50(1)(b), 53(2.1), 82(3), 128.1(4)(b)(iv), 128.1(4)(d) and 146.01(7) and Reg. 5907(2.1) added by P.C. 1995-1210, effective August 9, 1995.

Reference to ITA 80.01(4)(c), 80.1(4) and 104(5.3) added by P.C. 1996-214, effective March 6, 1996.

Para. (b.1) added, and reference to 50(1)(b) changed to 50(1) (and thus moved from para. (c) to para. (b)) by P.C. 1997-1472, in force October 29, 1997. The deadline under para. (b.1) for the election under ITA 249.1(4) is January 31, 1998. Para. (b.1) then repealed effective February 1, 1998 by P.C. 1998-2270.

The Department of Finance's Technical Notes describe the provisions added in 1991 as follows:

> ITA 13(4), 14(6) and 44(1) allow a taxpayer or partnership to elect to defer an income inclusion or the recognition of a capital gain where a replacement property is acquired for a property that was stolen, expropriated or destroyed or for a former business property that was sold.
>
> ITA 21 allows a taxpayer or partnership to elect to treat interest as a capital cost instead of an expense.
>
> ITA 66.7(7)(c), (d) and (e) and (8)(c), (d) and (e) allow a predecessor corporation and a successor corporation to elect to transfer the unused pools of resource expenses from the predecessor to the successor.
>
> ITA 70(6.2) allows a taxpayer's legal representative to elect to have the rollover rules under ITA 70(6) not apply, thus causing the assets transferred to a taxpayer's spouse on the death of the taxpayer to be considered to be transferred at fair market value for tax purposes.
>
> ITA 70(9) allows a taxpayer's legal representative to elect an amount, within limits, as proceeds of disposition for farm property transferred to a child on the taxpayer's death.
>
> ITA 70(9.1) allows a spousal trust to elect an amount, within limits, as proceeds of disposition for farm property transferred from the trust to a child on the spouse's death.
>
> ITA 70(9.2) allows a taxpayer's legal representative to elect an amount, within limits, as proceeds of disposition for a share in a family farm corporation or an interest in a family farm partnership transferred to a child on the taxpayer's death.
>
> ITA 70(9.3) allows a spousal trust to elect an amount, within limits, as proceeds of disposition for a share in a family farm corporation or an interest in a family farm partnership transferred from the trust to a child on the spouse's death.
>
> ITA 72(2) permits a legal representative of a deceased taxpayer to elect to claim a deduction for certain reserves provided that the amount so deducted is subsequently included in the income of the taxpayer's spouse or a spousal trust.
>
> ITA 73(1) allows a taxpayer to elect to have the rollover provisions in respect of an inter-vivos transfer of assets to a spouse or spousal trust not apply, thus causing the assets to be considered to be transferred at fair market value for tax purposes.
>
> ITA 104(14) allows a trust and its preferred beneficiaries to elect to have the income of the trust included in the income of the preferred beneficiaries instead of being taxes as income of the trust.
>
> Reg. 1103(1) allows a taxpayer or partnership to elect, for capital cost allowance purposes, to include in Class 1 all properties included in Classes 2 to 12.
>
> Reg. 1103(2) allows a taxpayer or partnership to elect, for capital cost allowance purposes, to include in Class 2, 4 or 17 all properties included in any other classes where Class 2, 4 or 17 are the classes in which the chief depreciable properties of the taxpayer or partnership are included.
>
> Reg. 1103(2d) allows a taxpayer or partnership to elect to defer a capital cost allowance recapture by transferring the property disposed of to a new class of which the taxpayer or partnership has property where the property disposed of would have been a property of the new class if it had been acquired when the property of the new class was acquired.

The CCRA does accept some late-filed election forms that are not specifically listed above.

**Definitions [Reg. 600]**: "Canada" — ITA 255, *Interpretation Act* 35(1); "Minister" — ITA 248(1); "month" — *Interpretation Act* 35(1); "prescribed" — ITA 248(1).

**Information Circulars**: 92-1: Guidelines for accepting late, amended or revoked elections.

# PART VII — LOGGING TAXES ON INCOME

**700. Logging** — **(1)** Except as provided in subsection (2), for the purposes of paragraph 127(2)(a) [127(2)"income for the year from logging operations in the province"] of the Act "income for the year from logging operations in the province" means the aggregate of

(a) where standing timber is cut in the province by the taxpayer or logs cut from standing timber in the province are acquired by the taxpayer and the logs so obtained are sold by the taxpayer in the province before or on delivery to a sawmill, pulp or paper plant or other place for processing logs, the taxpayer's income for the year from the sale, other than any portion thereof that was included in computing the taxpayer's income from logging operations in the province for a previous year;

(b) where standing timber in the province or the right to cut standing timber in the province is sold by the taxpayer, the taxpayer's income for the year from the sale, other than any portion thereof that was included in computing the taxpayer's income from logging operations in the province for a previous year;

(c) where standing timber is cut in the province by the taxpayer or logs cut from standing timber in the province are acquired by the taxpayer, if the logs so obtained are

(i) exported from the province and are sold by him prior to or on delivery to a sawmill, pulp or paper plant or other place for processing logs, or

(ii) exported from Canada,

the amount computed by deducting from the value, as determined by the province, of the logs so exported in the year, the aggregate of the costs of acquiring, cutting, transporting and selling the logs; and

(d) where standing timber is cut in the province by the taxpayer or logs cut from standing timber in the province are acquired by the taxpayer, if the logs are processed by the taxpayer or by a person on his behalf in a sawmill, pulp or paper plant or other place for processing logs in Canada, the income of the taxpayer for the year from all sources minus the aggregate of

(i) his income from sources other than logging operations carried on in Canada and other than the processing in Canada by him or on his behalf and sale by him of logs, timber and products produced therefrom,

(ii) each amount included in the aggregate determined under this subsection by virtue of paragraph (a), (b) or (c), and

(iii) an amount equal to eight per cent of the original cost to him of properties described in Schedule II used by him in the year in the processing of logs or products derived therefrom or, if the amount so determined is greater than 65 per cent of the income remaining after making the deductions under subparagraphs (i) and (ii), 65 per cent of the income so remaining or, if the amount so determined is less than 35 per cent of the income so remaining, 35 per cent of the income so remaining.

**Notes:** Reg. 700(1)(a) and (b) amended by P.C. 1992-1862, effective for taxation years beginning in 1991 and later, to revise the wording and to refer to "income" instead of "net profits", making the legislation consistent with British Columbia and Quebec logging tax legislation.

**(2)** Where the taxpayer cuts standing timber or acquires logs cut from standing timber in more than one province, for the purposes of paragraph 127(2)(a) [127(2)"income for the year from logging operations in the province"] of the Act "income for the year from logging operations in the province" means the aggregate of

(a) the amounts determined in respect of that province in accordance with paragraphs (1)(a), (b) and (c); and

(b) where the logs are processed by the taxpayer or by a person on his behalf in a sawmill, pulp or paper plant or other place for processing logs in Canada, an amount equal to the proportion of the income of the taxpayer for the year from all sources minus the aggregate of

(i) his income from sources other than logging operations carried on in Canada and other than the processing in Canada by him or on his behalf and sale by him of logs, timber and products produced therefrom,

(ii) the aggregate of amounts determined in respect of each province in accordance with paragraphs (1)(a), (b) and (c), and

(iii) an amount equal to eight per cent of the original cost to him of properties described in Schedule II used by him in the year in the processing of logs or products derived therefrom or, if the amount so determined is greater than 65 per cent of the income remaining after making the deductions under subparagraphs (i) and (ii), 65 per cent of the income so remaining or, if the amount so determined is less than 35 per cent of the income so remaining, 35 per cent of the income so remaining,

that

(iv) the quantity of standing timber cut in the province in the year by the taxpayer and logs cut from standing timber in the province acquired by the taxpayer in the year,

is of

(v) the total quantity of standing timber cut and logs acquired in the year by the taxpayer.

**Forms:** T2 SCH 21: Federal foreign income tax credits and federal logging tax credit.

**(3)** For the purposes of paragraph 127(2)(b) [127(2)"logging tax"] of the Act, the tax imposed by the legislature of

(a) the Province of British Columbia under the *Logging Tax Act* of that province, and

(b) [Revoked]

(c) the Province of Quebec under Part VII of the *Taxation Act* of that province,

are each declared to be a tax of general application on income from logging operations.

**Definitions [Reg. 700]:** "amount" — ITA 248(1); "Canada" — ITA 255, *Interpretation Act* 35(1); "legislature" — *Interpretation Act* 35(1)"legislative assembly"; "person" — ITA 248(1); "province" — *Interpretation Act* 35(1); "taxpayer" — ITA 248(1).

**701.** [Revoked]

# PART VIII — NON-RESIDENT TAXES

**800. Registered non-resident insurers** — For the purposes of subsection 215(4) of the Act, subsections 215(1), (2) and (3) of the Act do not apply to amounts paid or credited to a registered non-resident insurer.

**Definitions [Reg. 800]**: "amount", "insurer", "non-resident" — ITA 248(1); "registered non-resident insurer" — Reg. 804.

**801. Filing of returns by non-resident insurers** — For the purposes of subsection 215(4) of the Act, where a taxpayer is a registered non-resident insurer in a taxation year, the taxpayer shall file a return in respect thereof in prescribed form with the Minister within the six month period immediately following the end of the year.

**Definitions [Reg. 801]**: "insurer", "Minister" — ITA 248(1); "month" — *Interpretation Act* 35(1); "non-resident", "prescribed" — ITA 248(1); "registered non-resident insurer" — Reg. 804; "taxation year" — ITA 249; "taxpayer" — ITA 248(1).

**Forms**: T2016: Part XIII tax return — tax on income from Canada of registered non-resident insurers.

**802. Amounts taxable** — For the purposes of paragraph 214(13)(c) of the Act, the amounts taxable under Part XIII of the Act in a relevant taxation year of a taxpayer are amounts paid or credited to the taxpayer in the relevant taxation year other than amounts included pursuant to Part I of the Act in computing the taxpayer's income from a business carried on by it in Canada.

**Definitions [Reg. 802]**: "amount", "business" — ITA 248(1); "Canada" — ITA 255, *Interpretation Act* 35(1); "taxation year" — ITA 249; "taxpayer" — ITA 248(1).

**803. Payment of tax by non-resident insurers** — For the purposes of subsection 215(4) of the Act, a taxpayer shall pay to the Receiver General, on or before the last day on which the return in respect of a relevant taxation year is required to be filed pursuant to section 801, the tax payable by the taxpayer under Part XIII of the Act on amounts referred to in section 802 in respect of the relevant taxation year.

**Definitions [Reg. 803]**: "amount" — ITA 248(1); "taxation year" — ITA 249; "taxpayer" — ITA 248(1).

**804. Interpretation** — In this Part, "registered non-resident insurer" means a non-resident corporation approved to carry on business in Canada under the *Insurance Companies Act*.

**Notes**: Reg. 804 amended by P.C. 2000-1714, retroactive to June 1992, to replace references to older legislation with the *Insurance Companies Act*.

**Definitions [Reg. 804]**: "business" — ITA 248(1); "Canada" — ITA 255, *Interpretation Act* 35(1); "corporation" — ITA 248(1), *Interpretation Act* 35(1); "non-resident" — ITA 248(1).

**805. Other non-resident persons** — (1) Every non-resident person who carries on business in Canada shall be taxable under Part XIII of the Act on all amounts otherwise taxable under that Part except those amounts that

(a) may reasonably be attributed to the business carried on by him through a permanent establishment (within the meaning assigned by subsection 400(2) or that would be assigned by that subsection if he were a corporation) in Canada; or

(b) are required by subparagraph 115(1)(a)(iii.3) of the Act to be included in computing his taxable income earned in the year in Canada.

(2) Where the Minister is satisfied that under subsection (1) an amount is not taxable under Part XIII of the Act, he may permit payment to be made to the non-resident person without any deduction being made under section 215 of the Act.

(3) Subsections (1) and (2) do not apply in respect of amounts upon which tax under Part XIII of the Act is payable in a relevant taxation year by a taxpayer required by section 801 to file the return described in that section in respect of that year.

**Definitions [Reg. 805]**: "amount", "business" — ITA 248(1); "Canada" — ITA 255, *Interpretation Act* 35(1); "carries on business in Canada" — ITA 253; "corporation" — ITA 248(1), *Interpretation Act* 35(1); "non-resident", "person", "taxable income" — ITA 248(1); "taxation year" — ITA 249; "taxpayer" — ITA 248(1).

**Interpretation Bulletins [Reg. 805]**: IT-420R3: Non-residents — income earned in Canada; IT-438R2: Crown charges — resource properties in Canada.

**806. International organizations and agencies** — For the purposes of clause 212(1)(b)(ii)(B) of the Act, the following international organizations and agencies are hereby prescribed:

(a) Bank for International Settlements;

(b) European Fund;

(c) International Bank for Reconstruction and Development;

(d) International Development Association;

(e) International Finance Corporation; and

(f) International Monetary Fund.

**806.1** For the purposes of subparagraph 212(1)(b)(x) of the Act, the Bank for International Settlements and the European Bank for Reconstruction and Development are prescribed international agencies.

**Notes**: Reference to the EBRD added by P.C. 1994-270, effective 1991. (That agency is exempt from Canadian tax anyway under the *European Bank for Reconstruction and Development Agreement Act*, S.C. 1991, c. 12, Article 53 of the Schedule.)

**806.2 Prescribed obligation** — For the purpose of paragraph 212(1)(b) of the Act, an obligation is a prescribed obligation if it is an indexed debt obligation and no amount payable in respect of it is

(a) contingent or dependent upon the use of, or production from, property in Canada; or

(b) computed by reference to

(i) revenue, profit, cash flow, commodity price or any other similar criterion, other than a change in the purchasing power of money, or

(ii) dividends paid or payable to shareholders of any class of shares.

**Notes**: Reg. 806.2 added by P.C. 1993-1331 and amended retroactively by P.C. 1996-1419, effective for debt obligations issued after October 16, 1991. The 1996 amendment effectively restricts the exception for a change in the purchasing power of money to subpara. (b)(i), rather than applying to the entire provision.

**Definitions [Reg. 806.2]**: "amount" — ITA 248(1); "Canada" — ITA 255, *Interpretation Act* 35(1); "dividend", "indexed debt obligation", "prescribed", "property", "share", "shareholder" — ITA 248(1).

**Interpretation Bulletins**: IT-361R3: Exemption from Part XIII tax on interest payments to non-residents.

**807. Identification of obligations** — For the purposes of subsection 240(2) of the Act, the letters "AX" or the letter "F" as the case may be, shall be clearly and indelibly printed in gothic or similar style capital letters of seven point or larger size either as a prefix to the coupon number or on the lower right hand corner of each coupon or other writing issued in evidence of a right to interest on an obligation referred to in that subsection.

**Definitions [Reg. 807]**: "writing" — *Interpretation Act* 35(1).

**808. Allowances in respect of investment in property in Canada** — **(1) [Allowance]** — For the purposes of paragraph 219(1)(h) of the Act, a corporation's allowance for a taxation year in respect of its investment in property in Canada is hereby prescribed to be the amount, if any, by which

### Proposed Amendment — Reg. 808(1) opening words

**808. (1)** For the purposes of paragraph 219(1)(j) of the Act, the allowance of a corporation (other than an authorized foreign bank) for a taxation year in respect of its investment in property in Canada is prescribed to be the amount, if any, by which

**Application**: The August 8, 2000 draft regulations, subsec. 3(1), will amend the opening words of subsec. 808(1) to read as above, applicable to taxation years that begin after 1995.

(a) the corporation's qualified investment in property in Canada at the end of the year,

exceeds

(b) the aggregate of

(i) all allowances computed under this section as it read in its application to each of the taxation years of the corporation that ended before 1972 to the extent that for those taxation years such allowances reduced the amount on which the corporation was taxable under subsection 110B(1) of the Act as it read in its application to those taxation years, and

(ii) the capital investment of the corporation in property in Canada at the end of the corporation's 1960 taxation year, determined under this section as it read in its application to the 1961 taxation year.

**Interpretation Bulletins**: IT-137R3: Additional tax on certain corporations carrying on business in Canada.

### Proposed Addition — Reg. 808(1.1)

**(1.1)** Notwithstanding subsection (1), if a corporation becomes resident in Canada at a particular time, the corporation's allowance in respect of its investment in property in Canada for its last taxation year that ended before the particular time is prescribed to be nil.

**Notes**: See Notes to ITA 128.1(1) re 128(1)(c.1).

**Application**: The October 27, 1998 draft regulations, s. 1, will add 808(1.1), applicable to corporations that become resident in Canada after February 23, 1998.

**Technical Notes**: Subsection 808(1) of the Regulations specifies the amount of a corporation's allowance in respect of investment in property in Canada for the purposes of the "branch tax" imposed under Part XIV of the Act.

New subsection 808(1.1) provides that where a corporation becomes resident in Canada, the corporation's investment allowance for the taxation year that is deemed to end immediately before immigration is nil. Since the corporation will be unable to claim an investment allowance, it will be liable to pay branch tax on any unremitted profits of a Canadian branch arising in the year or deferred in respect of previous years. Effectively, for an immigrating corporation, unremitted profits of a Canadian branch are treated similarly to the undistributed surplus of a Canadian corporation in which the immigrating corporation holds shares, which is deemed to be distributed as a dividend by paragraph 128.1(1)(c.1) of the Act.

New subsection 808(1.1) applies to corporations that become resident in Canada after February 23, 1998.

**(2) ["Qualified investment ..."]** — For the purposes of subsection (1), where, at the end of a taxation year, a corporation is not a member of a partnership that was carrying on business in Canada at any time in the year, the corporation's "qualified investment in property in Canada at the end of the year" is the amount, if any, by which the aggregate of

(a) the cost amount to the corporation, at the end of the year, of land in Canada owned by it at that time for the purpose of gaining or producing income from a business carried on by it in Canada, other than land that is

(i) described in the corporation's inventory,

(ii) depreciable property,

(iii) a Canadian resource property, or

(iv) land the cost of which is or was deductible in computing the corporation's income,

(b) an amount equal to the aggregate of the cost amount to the corporation, immediately after the end of the year, of each depreciable property in Canada owned by it for the purpose of gaining or

Part VIII — Non-Resident Taxes    Reg. S. 808(2)(h)

producing income from a business carried on by it in Canada,

(c) an amount equal to ⁴/₃ of the cumulative eligible capital of the corporation immediately after the end of the year in respect of each business carried on by it in Canada,

(d) where the corporation is not a principal-business corporation, within the meaning assigned by paragraph 66(15)(h) [66(15)"principal-business corporation"] of the Act, an amount equal to the aggregate of the corporation's

(i) Canadian exploration and development expenses, within the meaning assigned by paragraph 66(15)(b) [66(15)"Canadian exploration and development expenses"] of the Act, incurred by the corporation before the end of the year except to the extent that such expenses were deducted by the corporation in computing its income for the year or for a previous taxation year, and

(ii) cumulative Canadian exploration expense, within the meaning assigned by paragraph 66.1(6)(b) [66.1(6)"cumulative Canadian exploration expense"] of the Act, at the end of the year minus any deduction under subsection 66.1(3) of the Act in computing the corporation's income for the year,

(d.1) an amount equal to the corporation's cumulative Canadian development expense, within the meaning assigned by paragraph 66.2(5)(b) [66.2(5)"cumulative Canadian development expense"] of the Act, at the end of the year minus any deduction under subsection 66.2(2) of the Act in computing the corporation's income for the year,

(d.2) an amount equal to the corporation's cumulative Canadian oil and gas property expense, within the meaning assigned by paragraph 66.4(5)(b) [66.4(5)"cumulative Canadian oil and gas property expense"] of the Act, at the end of the year minus any deduction under subsection 66.4(2) of the Act in computing the corporation's income for the year,

### Proposed Amendment — Reg. 808(2)(d)–(d.2)

(d) where the corporation is not a principal-business corporation, within the meaning assigned by subsection 66(15) of the Act, an amount equal to the total of the corporation's

(i) Canadian exploration and development expenses, within the meaning assigned by subsection 66(15) of the Act, incurred by the corporation before the end of the year, except to the extent that such expenses were deducted in computing the corporation's income for the year or for a previous taxation year, and

(ii) cumulative Canadian exploration expense, within the meaning assigned by subsection 66.1(6) of the Act, at the end of the year minus any deduction under subsection 66.1(3) of the Act in computing the corporation's income for the year,

(d.1) an amount equal to the corporation's cumulative Canadian development expense, within the meaning assigned by subsection 66.2(5) of the Act, at the end of the year minus any deduction under subsection 66.2(2) of the Act in computing the corporation's income for the year,

(d.2) an amount equal to the corporation's cumulative Canadian oil and gas property expense, within the meaning assigned by subsection 66.4(5) of the Act, at the end of the year minus any deduction under subsection 66.4(2) of the Act in computing the corporation's income for the year,

**Application**: The August 8, 2000 draft regulations, subsec. 3(2), will amend paras. 808(2)(d) to (d.2) to read as above, applicable to taxation years that end after November 1991.

(e) an amount equal to the aggregate of the cost amount to the corporation at the end of the year of each debt owing to it, or any other right of the corporation to receive an amount, that was outstanding as a result of the disposition by it of property in respect of which an amount would be included, by virtue of paragraph (a), (b), (c) or (h), in its qualified investment in property in Canada at the end of the year if the property had not been disposed of by it before the end of that year,

(f) an amount equal to the aggregate of the cost amount to the corporation at the end of the year of each property, other than a Canadian resource property, that was described in the corporation's inventory in respect of a business carried on by it in Canada,

(g) an amount equal to the aggregate of the cost amount to the corporation at the end of the year of each debt (other than a debt referred to in paragraph (e) or a debt the amount of which was deducted under paragraph 20(1)(p) of the Act in computing the corporation's income for the year) owing to it

(i) in respect of any transaction by virtue of which an amount has been included in computing its income for the year or for a previous year from a business carried on by it in Canada, or

(ii) where any part of its ordinary business carried on in Canada was the lending of money, in respect of a loan made by the corporation in the ordinary course of that part of its business,

(h) where the corporation was resident in Canada at any time in the year, an amount equal to the aggregate of the cost amount to the corporation at the end of the year of any property in Canada owned by it

(i) the cost amount of which is not included in its qualified investment in property in Canada at the end of the year by virtue of paragraph (a) or (b) or subparagraph (g)(i), but would be so included if those provisions were read without the phrase "from a business carried on by it in Canada",

(ii) that is a share of the capital stock of a corporation that was not described in the corporation's inventory in respect of a business carried on by it in Canada, or

(iii) that is a bond, debenture, bill, note, mortgage or similar obligation that was not described in the corporation's inventory in respect of a business carried on by it in Canada (other than an obligation referred to in subparagraph (3)(a)(iii), a debt referred to in paragraph (e) or (g) or a debt the amount of which was deducted under paragraph 20(1)(p) of the Act in computing the corporation's income for the year), and

### Proposed Repeal — Reg. 808(2)(h)

**Application**: The August 8, 2000 draft regulations, subsec. 3(3), will repeal para. 808(2)(h), applicable to taxation years that begin after 1995.

(i) an amount equal to the allowable liquid assets of the corporation at the end of the year,

exceeds the aggregate of

(j) an amount equal to the aggregate of each amount deducted by the corporation under paragraph 20(1)(l), (l.1) or (n) or subsection 64(1), (1.1) or (1.2) of the Act in computing its income for the year from a business carried on by it in Canada;

(k) an amount equal to the aggregate of all amounts each of which is an amount deducted by the corporation in the year under subparagraph 40(1)(a)(iii) or 44(1)(e)(iii) of the Act in respect of a debt referred to in paragraph (e);

(l) an amount equal to the aggregate of each amount owing by the corporation at the end of the year on account of

(i) the purchase price of property that is referred to in paragraph (a), (b), (f) or (h) or that would be so referred to but for the fact that it has been disposed of before the end of the year,

### Proposed Amendment — Reg. 808(2)(l)(i)

(i) the purchase price of property that is referred to in paragraph (a), (b) or (f) or that would be so referred to but for the fact that it has been disposed of before the end of the year,

**Application**: The August 8, 2000 draft regulations, subsec. 3(4), will amend subpara. 808(2)(l)(i) to read as above, applicable to taxation years that begin after 1995.

(ii) Canadian exploration and development expenses, Canadian exploration expense, Canadian development expense or Canadian oil and gas property expense, within the meanings assigned by paragraphs 66(15)(b) [66(15)"Canadian exploration and development expenses"], 66.1(6)(a) [66.1(6)"Canadian exploration expense"], 66.2(5)(a) [66.2(5)"Canadian development expense"] and 66.4(5)(a) [66.4(5)"Canadian oil and gas property expense"] of the Act, respectively,

### Proposed Amendment — Reg. 808(2)(l)(ii)

(ii) Canadian exploration and development expenses, Canadian exploration expense, Canadian development expense or Canadian oil and gas property expense, within the meanings assigned by subsections 66(15), 66.1(6), 66.2(5) and 66.4(5) of the Act, respectively,

**Application**: The August 8, 2000 draft regulations, subsec. 3(5), will amend subpara. 808(2)(l)(ii) to read as above, applicable to taxation years that end after November 1991.

(iii) an eligible capital expenditure made or incurred by the corporation before the end of the year in respect of a business carried on by it in Canada, or

(iv) any other outlay or expense made or incurred by the corporation to the extent that it was deducted in computing its income for the year or for a previous taxation year from a business carried on by it in Canada;

(m) an amount equal to the aggregate of all amounts each of which is an amount equal to that proportion of the amount owing (other than an amount owing on account of an outlay or expense referred to in paragraph (l)) by the corporation at the end of the year on account of an obligation outstanding at any time in the year in respect of which interest is stipulated to be payable by it that

(i) the interest paid or payable on the obligation by the corporation in respect of the year that is deductible, or would be deductible but for subsection 18(2), (3.1) or (4) or section 21 of the Act, in computing its income for the year from a business carried on by it in Canada,

is of

(ii) the interest paid or payable on the obligation by the corporation in respect of the year;

(n) the amount, if any, by which

(i) the amount (referred to in this paragraph as "Part I liability"), if any, by which the tax payable for the year by the corporation under

Part I of the Act exceeds the amount, if any, paid by the corporation before the end of the year on account thereof,

exceeds

(ii) where the corporation was, throughout the year, not resident in Canada, that proportion of the Part I liability that the amount, if any, determined under paragraph 219(1)(d) of the Act in respect of the corporation for the year is of the corporation's amount taxable (within the meaning given to that expression in section 123 of the Act) for the year, or

(iii) in any other case, nil;

> **Proposed Amendment — Reg. 808(2)(n)(ii), (iii)**
>
> (ii) that proportion of the Part I liability that the amount, if any, in respect of the corporation for the year that is the lesser of
>
> (A) the amount, if any, by which the total of all amounts each of which is a taxable capital gain of the corporation for the year from a disposition of a taxable Canadian property that was not used or held by it in the year in the course of carrying on business in Canada exceeds the total of all amounts each of which is an allowable capital loss of the corporation for the year from a disposition of such a property, and
>
> (B) the amount that would be determined under clause (A) for the year if it were read without reference to the expression "that was not used or held by it in the year in the course of carrying on business in Canada",
>
> is of the corporation's taxable income earned in Canada for the year; and
>
> **Application:** The August 8, 2000 draft regulations, subsec. 3(6), will amend subpara. 808(2)(n)(ii) to read as above, and repeal subpara. (iii), applicable to taxation years that begin after 1995.

(o) the amount, if any, by which

(i) the amount (referred to in this paragraph as "provincial tax liability"), if any, by which any income taxes payable for the year by the corporation to the government of a province (to the extent that such taxes were not deductible under Part I of the Act in computing the corporation's income for the year from a business carried on by it in Canada) exceeds the amount, if any, paid by the corporation before the end of the year on account thereof,

exceeds

(ii) where the corporation was, throughout the year, not resident in Canada, that proportion of the provincial tax liability that the amount, if any, determined under paragraph 219(1)(d) of the Act in respect of the corporation for the year is of the corporation's amount taxable (within the meaning given to that expression in section 123 of the Act) for the year, or

(iii) in any other case, nil; and,

> **Proposed Amendment — Reg. 808(2)(o)(ii), (iii)**
>
> (ii) that proportion of the provincial tax liability that the amount, if any, in respect of the corporation for the year that is the lesser of
>
> (A) the amount, if any, by which the total of all amounts each of which is a taxable capital gain of the corporation for the year from a disposition of a taxable Canadian property that was not used or held by it in the year in the course of carrying on business in Canada exceeds the total of all amounts each of which is an allowable capital loss of the corporation for the year from a disposition of such a property, and
>
> (B) the amount that would be determined under clause (A) for the year if it were read without reference to the expression "that was not used or held by it in the year in the course of carrying on business in Canada"
>
> is of the corporation's taxable income earned in Canada for the year.
>
> **Application:** The August 8, 2000 draft regulations, subsec. 3(7), will amend subpara. 808(2)(o)(ii) to read as above, and repeal subpara. (iii), applicable to taxation years that begin after 1995.

(p) where the corporation was resident in Canada at any time in the year, an amount equal to the aggregate of

(i) an amount equal to the aggregate of each amount deducted by the corporation in the year under paragraph 20(1)(l) or (l.1) or subsection 64(1), (1.1) or (1.2) of the Act in computing its income for the year from a source other than

(A) a business carried on by it in Canada, or

(B) a property situated outside Canada,

(ii) an amount equal to the aggregate of each amount owing by the corporation at the end of the year on account of any outlay or expense made or incurred by the corporation to the extent that it was deducted in computing its income for the year or for a previous taxation year from a source other than

(A) a business carried on by it in Canada, or

(B) a property situated outside Canada, and

(iii) an amount equal to the aggregate of all amounts each of which is an amount equal to that proportion of the amount owing (other than an amount owing on account of an outlay or expense referred to in subparagraph (ii) or paragraph (l)) by the corporation at the end of the year on account of an obligation outstanding at any time in the year in respect of which interest is stipulated to be payable by it that

(A) the interest paid or payable on the obligation by the corporation in respect of the year that is deductible, or would be deductible but for subsection 18(2), (3.1) or (4) or section 21 of the Act, in computing its income for the year from a source other than

(I) a business carried on by it in Canada, or

(II) a property situated outside Canada,

is of

(B) the interest paid or payable on the obligation by the corporation in respect of the year.

### Proposed Repeal — Reg. 808(2)(p)

**Application**: The August 8, 2000 draft regulations, subsec. 3(8), will repeal para. 808(2)(p), applicable to taxation years that end after November 1991.

**Notes**: Reg. 808(2)(h)(iii) amended to change "mortgage, hypothec" to "mortgage" by P.C. 1994-1817, effective November 30, 1994. The change was intended to be non-substantive.

**(3) ["Allowable liquid assets . . . "]** — For the purposes of paragraph (2)(i), the "allowable liquid assets of the corporation at the end of the year" is an amount equal to the lesser of

(a) the aggregate of

(i) the amount of Canadian currency owned by the corporation at the end of that year,

(ii) the balance standing to the credit of the corporation at the end of that year as or on account of amounts deposited with a branch or other office in Canada of

(A) a bank,

(B) a corporation licensed or otherwise authorized under the laws of Canada or a province to carry on in Canada the business of offering to the public its services as trustee, or

(C) a credit union, and

(iii) an amount equal to the aggregate of the cost amount to the corporation at the end of that year of each bond, debenture, bill, note, mortgage or similar obligation that was not described in the corporation's inventory in respect of a business carried on by it in Canada (other than a debt referred to in paragraph (2)(e) or (g) or a debt the amount of which was deducted under paragraph 20(1)(p) of the Act in computing the corporation's income for the year), that was issued by a person resident in Canada with whom the corporation was dealing at arm's length and that matures within one year after the date on which it was acquired by the corporation,

to the extent that such amounts are attributable to the profits of the corporation from carrying on a business in Canada, or are used or held by the corporation in the year in the course of carrying on a business in Canada; and

(b) an amount equal to $4/3$ of the quotient obtained by dividing

(i) the aggregate of all amounts that would otherwise be determined under subparagraphs (a)(i), (ii) and (iii) if the references therein to "at the end of that year" were read as references to "at the end of each month in that year",

by

(ii) the number of months in that year.

**Notes**: Closing words of Reg. 808(3)(a) added by P.C. 1993-1548, effective for taxation years ending after August 11, 1993, to clarify that allowable liquid assets of a corporation do not include amounts that were not either generated by the Canadian branch operation or intended for the use of the Canadian branch.

**(4) ["Qualified investment . . . "]** — For the purposes of subsection (1), where, at the end of a taxation year, a corporation is a member of a partnership that was carrying on business in Canada at any time in that year, the corporation's qualified investment in property in Canada at the end of the year is an amount equal to the aggregate of

(a) the amount, if any, that would be determined under subsection (2) if the corporation were not, at the end of the year, a member of a partnership that was carrying on business in Canada at any time in the year; and

(b) an amount equal to the portion of the amount of the partnership's qualified investment in property in Canada at the end of the last fiscal period of the partnership ending in the taxation year of the corporation that may reasonably be attributed to the corporation, having regard to all the circumstances including the rights the corporation would have, if the partnership ceased to exist, to share in the distribution of the property owned by the partnership for the purpose of gaining or producing income from a business carried on by it in Canada.

**(5) ["Qualified investment . . . " of partnership]** — For the purposes of subsection (4), a partnership's "qualified investment in property in Canada" at the end of a fiscal period is the amount, if any, by which the aggregate of

(a) the cost amount to the partnership, at the end of the fiscal period, of land in Canada owned by it at that time for the purpose of gaining or producing income from a business carried on by it in Canada, other than land that is

(i) described in the inventory of the partnership,

(ii) depreciable property,

(iii) a Canadian resource property, or

(iv) land the cost of which is or was deductible in computing the income of the partnership or the income of a member of the partnership,

(b) an amount equal to the aggregate of the cost amount to the partnership immediately after the end of the fiscal period, of each depreciable property in Canada owned by it for the purpose of gaining or producing income from a business carried on by it in Canada,

(c) an amount equal to $4/3$ of the cumulative eligible capital of the partnership immediately after the end of the fiscal period in respect of each business carried on by it in Canada,

(d) an amount equal to the aggregate of the cost amount to the partnership at the end of the fiscal period of each debt owing to it, or any other right of the partnership to receive an amount, that was outstanding as a result of the disposition by it of property in respect of which an amount would be included, by virtue of paragraph (a), (b) or (c), in its qualified investment in property in Canada at the end of the fiscal period if the property had not been disposed of by it before the end of that fiscal period,

(e) an amount equal to the aggregate of the cost amount to the partnership at the end of the fiscal period of each property, other than a Canadian resource property, that was described in the partnership's inventory in respect of a business carried on by it in Canada,

(f) an amount equal to the aggregate of the cost amount to the partnership at the end of the fiscal period of each debt (other than a debt referred to in paragraph (d) or a debt the amount of which was deducted under paragraph 20(1)(p) of the Act in computing the partnership's income for the fiscal period) owing to it

(i) in respect of any transaction by virtue of which an amount has been included in computing its income for the fiscal period or for a previous fiscal period or in computing the income of a member of the partnership for a previous taxation year from a business carried on in Canada by the partnership, or

(ii) where any part of its ordinary business carried on in Canada was the lending of money, in respect of a loan made by the partnership in the ordinary course of that part of its business, and

(g) an amount equal to the allowable liquid assets of the partnership at the end of the fiscal period,

exceeds the aggregate of

(h) an amount equal to the aggregate of each amount deducted by the partnership under paragraph 20(1)(l), (1.1) or (n) or subsection 64(1), (1.1) or (1.2) of the Act in computing its income for the fiscal period from a business carried on by it in Canada;

(i) an amount equal to the aggregate of all amounts each of which is an amount deducted by the partnership in the fiscal period under subparagraph 40(1)(a)(iii) or 44(1)(e)(iii) of the Act in respect of a debt referred to in paragraph (d);

(j) an amount equal to the aggregate of each amount owing by the partnership at the end of the fiscal period on account of

(i) the purchase price of property that is referred to in paragraph (a), (b) or (e) or that would be so referred to but for the fact that it has been disposed of before the end of the fiscal period,

(ii) Canadian exploration and development expenses, Canadian exploration expense, Canadian development expense or Canadian oil and gas property expense, within the meanings assigned by paragraphs 66(15)(b) [66(15)"Canadian exploration and development expenses"], 66.1(6)(a) [66.1(6)"Canadian exploration expense"] and 66.2(5)(a) [66.2(5)"Canadian development expense"] and 66.4(5)(a) [66.4(5)"Canadian oil and gas property expense"] of the Act, respectively,

**Proposed Amendment — Reg. 808(5)(j)(ii)**

(ii) Canadian exploration and development expenses, Canadian exploration expense, Canadian development expense or Canadian oil and gas property expense, within the meanings assigned by subsections 66(15), 66.1(6), 66.2(5) and 66.4(5) of the Act, respectively,

**Application**: The August 8, 2000 draft regulations, subsec. 3(9), will amend subpara. 808(5)(j)(ii) to read as above, applicable to taxation years that begin after 1995.

(iii) an eligible capital expenditure made or incurred by the partnership before the end of the fiscal period in respect of a business carried on by it in Canada, or

(iv) any other outlay or expense made or incurred by the partnership to the extent that it was deducted in computing its income for the fiscal period or for a previous fiscal period, or in computing the income of a member of the partnership for a previous taxation year, from a business carried on in Canada by the partnership; and

(k) an amount equal to the aggregate of all amounts each of which is an amount equal to that proportion of the amount owing (other than an

**Reg. S. 808(5)(k)** — Income Tax Regulations

amount owing on account of an outlay or expense referred to in paragraph (j)) by the partnership at the end of the fiscal period on account of an obligation outstanding at any time in the period in respect of which interest is stipulated to be payable by it that

(i) the interest paid or payable on the obligation by the partnership in respect of the fiscal period that is deductible, or would be deductible but for subsection 18(2) or (3.1) or section 21 of the Act, in computing its income for the fiscal period from a business carried on by it in Canada,

is of

(ii) the interest paid or payable on the obligation by the partnership in respect of the fiscal period.

**(6) ["Allowable liquid assets . . ." of partnership]** — For the purposes of paragraph (5)(g), the "allowable liquid assets of the partnership at the end of the fiscal period" is an amount equal to the lesser of

(a) the aggregate of

(i) the amount of Canadian currency owned by the partnership at the end of that fiscal period,

(ii) the balance standing to the credit of the partnership at the end of that fiscal period as or on account of amounts deposited with a branch or other office in Canada of

(A) a bank,

(B) a corporation licensed or otherwise authorized under the laws of Canada or a province to carry on in Canada the business of offering to the public its services as trustee, or

(C) a credit union, and

(iii) an amount equal to the aggregate of the cost amount to the partnership at the end of that fiscal period of each bond, debenture, bill, note, mortgage, hypothec or similar obligation that was not described in the partnership's inventory in respect of a business carried on by it in Canada (other than a debt referred to in paragraph (5)(d) or (f) or a debt the amount of which was deducted under paragraph 20(1)(p) of the Act in computing the partnership's income for the fiscal period), that was issued by a person resident in Canada with whom all the members of the partnership were dealing at arm's length and that matures within one year after the date on which it was acquired by the partnership; and

**Proposed Addition — Reg. 808(6)(a) closing words**

to the extent that such amounts are attributable to the profits of the partnership from carrying on a business in Canada, or are used or held by the partnership in the year in the course of carrying on a business in Canada; and

**Application**: The August 8, 2000 draft regulations, subsec. 3(10), will amend the closing words of para. 808(6)(a) to read as above, applicable to taxation years that end after August 11, 1993.

(b) an amount equal to $4/3$ of the quotient obtained by dividing

(i) the aggregate of all amounts that would otherwise be determined under subparagraphs (a)(i), (ii) and (iii) if the references therein to "at the end of that fiscal period" were read as references to "at the end of each month in that fiscal period",

by

(ii) the number of months in that fiscal period.

**(7) [Partnerships]** — Subsections (4) to (6) shall be read and construed as if each of the assumptions in paragraphs 96(1)(a) to (g) of the Act were made.

**Proposed Addition — Reg. 808(8)**

(8) For the purpose of paragraph 219(1)(j) of the Act, the allowance of an authorized foreign bank for a taxation year in respect of its investment in property in Canada is prescribed to be the amount, if any, by which

(a) the average of all amounts, each of which is the amount for a calculation period (within the meaning assigned by subsection 20.2(1) of the Act) of the bank for the year that is the greater of

(i) the amount determined by the formula

$$0.05 \times A$$

where

A is the amount of the element A in the formulae in subsection 20.2(3) of the Act for the period, and

(ii) the amount by which

(A) the total of the cost amount to the bank, at the end of the period (or, in the case of depreciable property or eligible capital property, immediately after the end of the year), of each asset in respect of the bank's Canadian banking business that is an asset recorded in the books of account of the business in a manner consistent with the manner in which it is required to be treated for the purpose of the branch financial statements (within the meaning assigned by subsection 20.2(1) of the Act) for the year

exceeds

(B) the amount equal to the total of

(I) the amount determined by the formula

$$L + BA$$

2010

where

L is the amount of the element L in the formulae in subsection 20.2(3) of the Act for the period, and

BA is the amount of the element BA in the formulae in subsection 20.2(3) of the Act for the period, and

(II) the amount claimed by the bank under clause 20.2(3)(b)(ii)(A) of the Act

exceeds

(b) the total of all amounts each of which is an amount that would be determined under paragraph (2)(j), (k), (n) or (o) if that provision applied to the bank for the year, except to the extent that the amount reflects a liability of the bank that has been included in the element L in the formulae in subsection 20.2(3) of the Act for the bank's last calculation period for the year.

**Application**: The August 8, 2000 draft regulations, subsec. 3(11), will add subsec. 808(8), applicable to taxation years that end after June 27, 1999.

**Definitions [Reg. 808]**: "allowable capital loss" — ITA 38(b), 248(1); "allowable liquid assets of the corporation at the end of the year" — Reg. 808(3); "allowable liquid assets of the partnership at the end of the fiscal period" — Reg. 808(6); "amount" — ITA 248(1); "arm's length" — ITA 251(1); "authorized foreign bank" — ITA 248(1); "bank" — ITA 248(1), *Interpretation Act* 35(1); "business" — ITA 248(1); "Canada" — ITA 255, *Interpretation Act* 35(1); "Canadian banking business" — ITA 248(1); "Canadian development expense" — ITA 66.2(5), 248(1); "Canadian exploration and development expenses" — ITA 66(15), 248(1); "Canadian exploration expense" — ITA 66.1(6), 248(1); "Canadian oil and gas property expense" — ITA 66.4(5), 248(1); "corporation" — ITA 248(1), *Interpretation Act* 35(1); "cost amount", "credit union" — ITA 248(1); "cumulative eligible capital" — ITA 14(5), 248(1); "depreciable property" — ITA 13(21), 248(1); "disposed" — ITA 248(1)"disposition"; "disposition" — ITA 248(1); "eligible capital expenditure" — ITA 14(5), 248(1); "fiscal period" — ITA 249.1; "inventory" — ITA 248(1); "month" — *Interpretation Act* 35(1); "office" — ITA 248(1); "Part I liability" — Reg. 808(2)(n)(i); "partnership" — see Notes to ITA 96(1) ; "person", "prescribed", "property" — ITA 248(1); "province" — *Interpretation Act* 35(1); "provincial tax liability" — Reg. 808(2)(o)(i); "qualified investment in property in Canada at the end of the fiscal period" — Reg. 808(5); "qualified investment in property in Canada at the end of the year" — Reg. 808(2), (4); "resident in Canada" — ITA 250; "share", "taxable Canadian property" — ITA 248(1); "taxable capital gain" — ITA 38(a), 248(1); "taxable income earned in Canada" — ITA 248(1); "taxation year" — ITA 249.

**Interpretation Bulletins [Reg. 808]**: IT-137R3: Additional tax on certain corporations carrying on business in Canada.

**809. Reduction of certain amounts to be deducted or withheld** — **(1)** Subject to subsection (2), where a non-resident person (in this section referred to as the "payee") has filed with the Minister the payee's required statement for the year, the amount otherwise required by subsections 215(1) to (3) of the Act to be deducted or withheld from any qualifying payment paid or credited by a person resident in Canada (in this section referred to as the "payer") to the payee in the year and after the required statement for the year was so filed is hereby reduced by the amount determined in accordance with the following rules:

(a) determine the amount by which

(i) the amount that would, if the payee does not make an election in respect of the year under section 217 of the Act, be the tax payable by the payee under Part XIII of the Act on the aggregate of the amounts estimated by him in his required statement for the year pursuant to paragraph (a) of the definition "required statement" in subsection (4),

exceeds

(ii) the amount that would, if the payee makes the election referred to in subparagraph (i), be the tax payable (on the assumption that no portion of the payee's income for the year was income earned in the year in a province) by the payee under Part I of the Act on his estimated taxable income calculated by him in his required statement for the year pursuant to paragraph (b) of the definition "required statement" in subsection (4),

(b) determine the percentage that the amount determined under paragraph (a) is of the aggregate of the amounts estimated by him in his required statement for the year pursuant to paragraph (a) of the definition "required statement" in subsection (4),

(c) where the determination of a percentage under paragraph (b) results in a fraction, disregard the fraction for the purposes of paragraph (d),

(d) multiply the percentage determined under paragraph (b) by the amount of the qualifying payment,

and the product obtained under paragraph (d) is the amount by which the amount required to be deducted or withheld is reduced.

**Forms**: NR5: Application by a non-resident of Canada for a reduction in the amount of non-resident tax required to be withheld; NR7-R: Application for refund of non-resident tax withheld.

**(2)** Subsection (1) does not apply to reduce the amount to be deducted or withheld from a qualifying payment if, after the qualifying payment has been paid or credited by the payer, the aggregate of all qualifying payments that the payer has paid or credited to the payee in the year would exceed the amount estimated, in respect of that payer, by the payee in his required statement for the year pursuant to paragraph (a) of the definition "required statement" in subsection (4).

**(3)** Where a payee has filed with the Minister a written notice indicating that certain information or estimates in the payee's required statement for the year are incorrect and setting out the correct information or estimates that should be substituted therefor or

Reg. S. 809(3)      Income Tax Regulations

where the Minister is satisfied that certain information or estimates in a payee's required statement for the year are incorrect and that the Minister has the correct information or estimates that should be substituted therefor, for the purposes of making the calculations in subsection (1) with respect to any qualifying payment paid or credited to the payee after the time when he has filed that notice or after the time when the Minister is so satisfied, as the case may be, the incorrect information or estimates shall be disregarded and the required statement for the year shall be deemed to contain only the correct information or estimates.

(4) In this section,

"**qualifying payment**" in relation to a non-resident person means any amount

(a) paid or credited, or to be paid or credited, to him as, on account or in lieu of payment of, or in satisfaction of, any amount described in paragraph 212(1)(f) or (h) or in any of paragraphs 212(1)(j), (k), (l), (m) or (q) of the Act, and

(b) on which tax under Part XIII of the Act is, or would be, but for an election by him under section 217 of the Act, payable by him;

"**required statement**" of a payee for a taxation year means a written statement signed by him that contains, in respect of the payee,

(a) the name and address of each payer of a qualifying payment in the year and, in respect of each such payer, an estimate by the payee of the aggregate of such qualifying payments, and

(b) a calculation by him of his estimated taxable income earned in Canada for the year, on the assumption that he makes the election in respect of the year under section 217 of the Act, and such information as may be necessary for the purpose of estimating such income.

**Definitions [Reg. 809]**: "amount", "Minister", "non-resident" — ITA 248(1); "payee", "payer" — Reg. 809(1); "person" — ITA 248(1); "province" — *Interpretation Act* 35(1); "qualified insurance corporation" — Reg. 810(2); "qualifying payment", "required statement" — Reg. 809(4); "resident in Canada" — ITA 250; "taxable income" — ITA 248(1); "taxable income earned in Canada" — ITA 248(1); "taxation year" — ITA 249; "written" — *Interpretation Act* 35(1)"writing".

**810. Excluded property of non-resident persons** — (1) For the purposes of paragraph 116(6)(e) of the Act, any property that is

(a) property of a non-resident insurer that is a qualified insurance corporation,

(b) an option in respect of property referred to in any of paragraphs 116(6)(a) to (d) of the Act and paragraph (a) whether or not such property is in existence, or

(c) an interest in property referred to in paragraph 116(6)(a), (c) or (d) of the Act or paragraph (a) or (b),

is prescribed to be excluded property.

(2) For the purposes of this section, a non-resident insurer is a "qualified insurance corporation" throughout the period during which it

(a) was licensed or otherwise authorized under the laws of Canada or a province to carry on an insurance business in Canada; and

(b) carried on an insurance business, within the meaning of subsection 138(1) of the Act, in Canada.

**Definitions [Reg. 810]**: "business" — ITA 248(1); "Canada" — ITA 255, *Interpretation Act* 35(1); "insurance corporation", "insurer", "non-resident", "prescribed", "property" — ITA 248(1); "province" — *Interpretation Act* 35(1).

## PART IX — DELEGATION OF THE POWERS AND DUTIES OF THE MINISTER

> **Proposed Repeal — Part IX**
>
> **Application**: Reg. 900 is to be repealed. ITA 220(2.01) now permits delegation by the Minister without a requirement for regulations.
>
> Delegation by the Minister was permitted even where no specific official is authorized by Reg. 900: *Doyle*, [1989] 2 C.T.C. 270 (FCTD).
>
> In December 1999, the CCRA released a 95-page list of delegations, signed by the Minister under ITA 220.01. The Schedule is dated September 27, 1999. It is available on TaxPartner under "Ministerial Delegations".

**900. (1)** An official holding a position of Assistant Deputy Minister of National Revenue for Taxation may exercise all the powers and perform all the duties of the Minister under the Act.

**Notes**: A Deputy Minister needs no authorization from the Act or Regulations to perform the duties of the Minister. See 24(2)(c) of the *Interpretation Act*, reproduced at the end of this book. The Deputy Minister has been replaced by the Commissioner (of Customs and Revenue) anyway.

**(2)** An official holding a position of Director — Taxation in a District Office of the Department of National Revenue, Taxation, may exercise the powers and perform the duties of the Minister under

(a) sections 48, 221.2, 224, 224.1, 224.3 and 233 of the Act;

(b) subsections 10(2.1), (3) and (7), 13(6), 15.1(5), the definition "small business bond" in subsection 15.2(3), subsections 15.2(5), 18(2.4), 28(3), 45(3), 58(5), 65(3), 66(12.72), (12.73), (12.74) and (14.4), 70(6), (6.1), (9), (9.2) and (9.4), 74(5), 83(3.1), 85(7.1), 91(2), 93(5.1), 96(5.1), 104(2), 116(2), (4) and (5.2), 118.3(3) and (4), 125(4), 126(5.1), 127(10), (10.4) and (10.5), 127.53(3), 131(1.2), 146.01(3), 149.1(15), 150(2), 153(1.1), 159(2), (4), (5) and (6.1), 162(5) and (6), 164(1.2), (1.3), (2) and (3.2), 181.5(3), 190.15(3), 191.1(5), 204.1(4), 204.81(1), (2), (6) and (7), 220(2.1) and (3) to

(5), 223(2), (9) and (11), 224(1.2), 225.2(2), (5) and (7), 226(1), 227(10.5), 230(1), (1.1), (3), (7) and (8), 230.1(3) (with respect to the application of subsections 230(3), (7) and (8) of the Act), 231.1(3), 231.2(1) and (3), 231.3(1) and (6), 231.6(2) and (8), 241(3.1), 244(21) and (22), 247(2) and 248(9) of the Act;

(c) the definition "fiscal period" in subsection 248(1) of the Act;

(d) paragraphs 15.2(8)(b), 34(b), 70(5.2)(d) and (f) and (9.5)(f), 73(5)(c), 85(1)(e.1) and (5.1)(f), 89(1)(g) [89(1)"public corporation"] and (3)(b), 104(23)(a), 118(4)(e), 118.1(6)(b), 118.4(1)(b), 133(7.2)(b), 149(1)(l), 150(1)(e) and 184(3.1)(e) and (3.2)(c) of the Act;

(d.1) the definition "small business development bond" in subsection 15.1(3), subparagraph 15.1(10)(b)(i) as it read on June 9, 1993 and subparagraphs 39(1)(a)(i.1), 110.6(15)(b)(ii) and 184(3.1)(c)(iii) and (d)(ii) and (3.2)(a)(ii) of the Act;

(e) subsection 39(3a) of the Act as it read in its application to the 1971 and previous taxation years;

(f) paragraphs 23(5)(c) and 26(18)(c) of the *Income Tax Application Rules*;

(g) sections 106, 210, 412 and 2200 of these Regulations;

(h) subsections 805(2), 809(3), 1403(2), (5) and (6) and 1802(2) of these Regulations;

(i) paragraphs 1802(3)(b) and 2400(1)(f) of these Regulations;

(i.1) paragraphs 2400(1)(e) of these Regulations as it applies to taxation years other than taxation years beginning after June 17, 1987 and ending after December 31, 1987; and

(j) subparagraphs 102(1)(f)(v), (2)(f)(v) and (3)(f)(v) and 1401(1)(d)(viii) of these Regulations.

Notes: The "District Offices" are now called "Tax Services Offices".

(3) The Director, Appeals and Referrals Division, or the Director, Policy and Programs Division, of the Department of National Revenue, Taxation, may exercise the powers and perform the duties of the Minister under

(a) sections 174 and 179.1 of the Act; and

(b) subsections 164(4.1), 165(3), (3.1), (3.2) and (6), 166.1(5), 220(3.1) and (3.2) and 239(4) of the Act.

(4) An official holding a position of Chief of Appeals in a District Office or in a Taxation Centre of the Department of National Revenue, Taxation, may exercise the powers and perform the duties of the Minister under

(a) subsections 165(3), (3.1) and (3.2); and

(b) subsections 165(6), 166.1(5), 220(3.1) and (3.2) and 239(4) of the Act.

(5) The Director, Audit Technical Support Division, of the Department of National Revenue, Taxation, may exercise the powers and perform the duties of the Minister under

(a) subsections 150(2), 152(1.11), 220(3.1) and (3.2), 230(1) and (3), 231.1(3), 231.2(1) and (3), 231.3(1) and (6), 237.1(3) and 241(3.1) of the Act;

(b) subsections 1403(2), (5) and (6) of these Regulations;

(c) paragraph 2400(1)(e) of these Regulations as it applies to taxation years other than taxation years commencing after June 17, 1987 and ending after 1987; and

(d) subparagraph 1401(1)(d)(viii) of these Regulations.

(6) The Director General, Revenue Collection Programs Directorate, of the Department of National Revenue, Taxation, may exercise the powers and perform the duties of the Minister under

(a) sections 221.2, 223 and 224.2 of the Act;

(b) subsections 164(2), 220(2.1), (3.1), (3.2), (4), (4.1) and (4.2), 225(1), 226(1) and (2), 227(10.5), 227.1(6), 231.2(1), 241(3.1) and 244(22) of the Act;

(c) section 2200 of these Regulations; and

(d) subsection 809(3) of these Regulations.

(7) The Director General, Audit Directorate, of the Department of National Revenue may exercise the powers and perform the duties of the Minister under

(a) section 115.1 of the Act;

(b) subsections 150(2), 152(1.11), 220(3.1) and (3.2), 230(1) and (3), 231.1(3), 231.2(1) and (3), 231.3(1) and (6), 237.1(3) and 241(3.1) of the Act;

(c) subsections 1403(2), (5) and (6) of these Regulations;

(d) paragraph 2400(1)(e) of these Regulations as it applies to taxation years other than taxation years beginning after June 17, 1987 and ending after December 31, 1987; and

(e) paragraph 1401(1)(d) of these Regulations.

(8) The Director, Charities Division of the Department of National Revenue, Taxation, may exercise the powers and perform the duties of the Minister under

(a) subsections 149.1(1.2), (2), (3), (4), (4.1), (5), (6.3), (6.4), (7), (8), (13) and (15), 168(1) and (2) and 230(2) and (3), paragraph 230.1(1)(b) and subsection 231.2(1) of the Act;

(b) the definition "fiscal period" (with respect to registered charities only) in subsection 248(1) of the Act;

(c) paragraphs 110(8)(b) and (c) and 149(1)(l) of the Act; and

(d) Part XXXVII of these Regulations.

(9) The Director, Registered Plans Division, of the Department of National Revenue, Taxation, may exercise the powers and perform the duties of the Minister under

(a) sections 145, 146, 146.1, 146.3, 147, 147.1, 147.2, 147.3, 204.4 and 204.5 of the Act;

(b) the definition "registered pension plan" in subsection 248(1) of the Act;

(c) paragraph 20(1)(s) of the Act; and

(d) Parts LXXXIII, LXXXIV and LXXXV of these Regulations.

(10) An official holding the position of Director in a Taxation Centre of the Department of National Revenue, Taxation, may exercise the powers and perform the duties of the Minister under

(a) sections 221.2, 224 and 233 of the Act;

(b) subsections 18(2.4), 58(5), 66(12.68), (12.74) and (14.4), 118.3(3), 125(4), 126(5.1), 127(10.4) and (10.5), 127.53(3), 146.01(3), 150(2), 159(2) and (6.1), 162(5) and (6), 164(2) and (3.2), 181.5(3), 190.15(3), 191.1(5), 192(8), 194(7), 204.1(4), 204.81(1) and (2), 220(2.1), (3), (3.1), (3.2) and (5), 230(1.1), 231.2(1), 237.1(3), 241(3.1) and 244(21) and (22) of the Act;

(c) paragraphs 118.4(1)(b), 147.1(10)(a) and 150(1)(e) of the Act;

(d) section 210 of these Regulations; and

(e) subparagraphs 102(1)(f)(v), (2)(f)(v) and (3)(f)(v) of these Regulations.

(11) The Director General, International Tax Programs Directorate of the Department of National Revenue, Taxation, may exercise the powers and perform the duties of the Minister under

(a) sections 115.1 and 233 of the Act;

(b) subsections 152(1.11), 153(1.1), 220(3.1), (3.2) and (5), 231.2(1) and (3), 231.6(2) and (8) and 241(3.1) of the Act; and

(c) section 210 of these Regulations.

(12) The Director General, Assessment of Returns Directorate, of the Department of National Revenue, Taxation, may exercise the powers and perform the duties of the Minister under

(a) subsections 118.3(4), 150(2), 150.1(2), 164(2) and (3.2), 204.1(4), 220(2.1), (3.1) and (3.2), 231.2(1), 241(3.1) and 244(22) of the Act;

(a.1) paragraph 118.4(1)(b) of the Act;

(b) section 412 of these Regulations.

(13) The Director, Accounts Receivable Division, of the Department of National Revenue, Taxation, may exercise the powers and perform the duties of the Minister under

(a) sections 221.2 and 224.2 of the Act;

(b) subsections 164(2), 220(2.1), (3.1), (3.2), (4), (4.1) and (4.2), 223(2), 225(1), 226(1) and (2), 227(10.5), 227.1(6) and 241(3.1) of the Act; and

(c) section 2200 of these Regulations.

(14) The Director, Source Deductions Division, of the Department of National Revenue, Taxation, may exercise the powers and perform the duties of the Minister under subsections 153(1.1), 220(3) and (3.1) and 241(3.1) of the Act and subsection 809(3) of these Regulations.

(15) The Director, International Taxation Office, of the Department of National Revenue, may exercise the powers and perform the duties of the Minister under

(a) sections 48, 115.1, 221.2, 224, 224.1 and 233 of the Act;

(b) subsections 10(2.1), (3) and (7), 13(6) and 15.2(5), 18(2.4), 28(3), 45(3), 58(5), 65(3), 66(12.68), (12.72), (12.73), (12.74) and (14.4), 70(6), (9) and (9.2), 83(3.1), 85(7.1), 91(2), 96(5.1), 104(2), 116(2), (4) and (5.2), 118.3(3) and (4), 126(5.1), 127(10), 127.53(3), 146.01(3), 149.1(15), 150(2), 153(1.1), 159(2), (4), (5) and (6.1), 164(1.2), (1.3), (2) and (3.2), 181.5(3), 190.15(3), 204.1(4), 220(2.1) and (3) to (5), 223(2), (9) and (11), 226(1), 230(1), (3), (7) and (8), 230.1(3) (with respect to the application of subsections 230(3), (7) and (8) of the Act), 231.2(1), 231.6(2) and (8), 237.1(3), 241(3.1) and 244(21) and (22) of the Act;

(c) the definition

(i) "small business bond" in subsection 15.2(3) of the Act,

(ii) "fiscal period" in subsection 248(1) of the Act,

(iii) "release or surrender" in subsection 248(9) of the Act;

(d) paragraphs 15.2(8)(b), 34(1)(b), 70(5.2)(d) and (f), 73(5)(c), 85(1)(e.1) and (5.1)(f), 104(23)(a), 118(4)(e), 118.1(6)(b), 118.4(1)(b), 147.1(10)(a), 149(1)(l), 150(1)(e) and 164(3.1)(c) of the Act;

(e) subparagraph 15.1(10)(b)(i) as it read on June 9, 1993 and subparagraphs 39(1)(a)(i.1), 110.6(15)(b)(ii) and 184(3.1)(c)(iii) of the Act;

(f) paragraphs 23(5)(c) and 26(18)(c) of the *Income Tax Application Rules*;

(g) sections 210 and 412 of these Regulations;

(h) subsections 805(2), 809(3) and 1802(2) of these Regulations;

(i) paragraphs 1802(3)(b) and 2400(1)(f) of these Regulations; and

(j) paragraph 2400(1)(e) of these Regulations as it applies to taxation years other than taxation years beginning after June 17, 1987 and ending after December 31, 1987.

**(16)** The Director General, Client Assistance Directorate, of the Department of National Revenue, may exercise the powers and perform the duties of the Minister under

(a) section 221.2 of the Act;

(b) subsections 150(2), 204.1(4), 220(2.1), (3), (3.1) and (3.2), 231.2(1) and 241(3.1) of the Act; and

(c) paragraph 118.4(1)(b) of the Act.

**(17)** The powers and the duties of the Minister under subsections 204.1(4), 220(3), (3.1) and (3.2) of the Act may be exercised and performed by an official of the Department of National Revenue in a District Taxation Office who holds the position of

(a) Assistant Director, Revenue Collections;

(b) Assistant Director, Client Assistance; or

(c) Assistant Director, Audit.

**(18)** The powers and the duties of the Minister under subsections 204.1(4), 220(3), (3.1) and (3.2) of the Act may be exercised and performed by an official of the Department of National Revenue in a Taxation Centre who holds the position of

(a) Assistant Director, Finance and Administration;

(b) Assistant Director, Individual and Estates;

(c) Assistant Director, Enquiries and Adjustments;

(d) Assistant Director, Corporation Services; or

(e) Assistant Director, Employer Services.

**Notes**: Reg. 900 most recently amended by P.C. 1991-50, P.C. 1991-731, P.C. 1992-290, P.C. 1993-1043 and P.C. 1994-1132.

**Definitions [Reg. 900]**: "business", "Minister" — ITA 248(1); "taxation year" — ITA 249.

## PART X — ELECTION IN RESPECT OF DECEASED TAXPAYERS

**1000. Property dispositions** — **(1)** Any election under subsection 164(6) of the Act shall be made by the legal representative of a deceased taxpayer by filing with the Minister the following documents:

(a) a letter from the legal representative specifying

(i) the part of the one or more capital losses from the disposition of properties, if any, under paragraph 164(6)(c) of the Act, and

(ii) the part of the amount, if any, under paragraph 164(6)(d) of the Act

in respect of which the election is made;

(b) where an amount is specified under subparagraph (a)(i), a schedule of the capital losses and capital gains referred to in paragraph 164(6)(a) of the Act;

(c) where an amount is specified under subparagraph (a)(ii),

(i) a schedule of the amounts of undepreciated capital cost described in paragraph 164(6)(b) of the Act,

(ii) a statement of the amount that, but for subsection 164(6) of the Act, would be the non-capital loss of the estate for its first taxation year, and

(iii) a statement of the amount that, but for subsection 164(6) of the Act, would be the farm loss of the estate for its first taxation year.

**(2)** The documents referred to in subsection (1) shall be filed not later than the day that is the later of

(a) the last day provided by the Act for the filing of a return that the legal representative of a deceased taxpayer is required or has elected to file under the Act in respect of the income of that deceased taxpayer for the taxation year in which he died; and

(b) the day the return of the income for the first taxation year of the deceased taxpayer's estate is required to be filed under paragraph 150(1)(c) of the Act.

**Definitions [Reg. 1000]**: "amount" — ITA 248(1); "capital gain" — ITA 39(1), 248(1); "disposition" — ITA 248(1); "estate" — ITA 104(1), 248(1); "farm loss" — ITA 111(8), 248(1); "legal representative", "Minister" — ITA 248(1); "non-capital loss" — ITA 111(8), 248(1); "taxation year" — ITA 249; "taxpayer" — ITA 248(1); "undepreciated capital cost" — ITA 13(21), 248(1).

**1001. Annual instalments** — Any election by a deceased taxpayer's legal representative under subsection 159(5) of the Act shall be made by filing with the Minister the prescribed form on or before the day on or before which payment of the first of the "equal consecutive annual instalments" referred to in that subsection is required to be made.

**Definitions [Reg. 1001]**: "legal representative", "Minister", "prescribed", "taxpayer" — ITA 248(1).

**Forms**: T2075: Election under subsection 159(5) by a deceased taxpayer's legal representative to defer payment of income tax.

## PART XI — CAPITAL COST ALLOWANCES

**Proposed Amendment — Capital cost allowance**

**Federal budget, supplementary information, February 28, 2000**: *Adjustments to the Capital Cost Allowance System*

A portion of the capital cost of depreciable property is deductible as capital cost allowance (CCA) each year. The

> maximum CCA rate for each type of property is set out in the *Income Tax Regulations*. The Government attempts to ensure that these CCA rates reflect, as closely as possible, the useful lives of the assets.
>
> Various factors affect the useful lives of capital assets, including technological obsolescence and changing market conditions. The CCA regime is reviewed on an ongoing basis to ensure that the CCA rates are appropriate and do not impede the ability of Canadian firms to invest and compete. As a result of this review, the budget proposes several adjustments to improve the CCA system. Proposed changes include
>
> - an increase in the CCA rate for certain rail assets [see under Class 35 — ed.];
> - an extension of the separate class election to include manufacturing and processing equipment; and [see under Reg. 1101(5p) — ed.]
> - an increase in the CCA rates for certain electrical generating equipment, and for production and distribution equipment of a distributor of water or heat [see under Class 1 — ed.].

**Related Provisions [Part XI]**: ITA 20(1.1) — Definitions in ITA 13(21) apply to regulations.

**Interpretation Bulletins [Part XI]**: IT-285R2: Capital cost allowance — general comments.

**Forms [Part XI]**: T776: Statement of real estate rentals; T777: Statement of employment expenses; T2041: Capital cost allowance schedule for self-employed persons; T2132: Capital cost allowance schedule (depreciation); T5014: Partnership capital cost allowance schedule.

## DIVISION I — DEDUCTIONS ALLOWED

**1100.** (1) For the purposes of paragraphs 8(1)(j) and (p) and 20(1)(a) of the Act, the following deductions are allowed in computing a taxpayer's income for each taxation year:

(a) **rates** — subject to subsection (2), such amount as he may claim in respect of property of each of the following classes in Schedule II not exceeding in respect of property

(i) of Class 1, 4 per cent,

**Related Provisions**: Reg. 1100(1)(zc).

(ii) of Class 2, 6 per cent,

**Related Provisions**: Reg. 1101(5i) — Separate class.

(iii) of Class 3, 5 per cent,

**Related Provisions**: Reg. 1100(1)(sb), (zc).

(iv) of Class 4, 6 per cent,

(v) of Class 5, 10 per cent,

(vi) of Class 6, 10 per cent,

**Related Provisions**: Reg. 1100(1)(sb), (zc).

(vii) of Class 7, 15 per cent,

(viii) of Class 8, 20 per cent,

**Related Provisions**: Reg. 1100(1)(sb), (zc).

(ix) of Class 9, 25 per cent,

(x) of Class 10, 30 per cent,

**Related Provisions**: Reg. 1100(1)(m) — Additional allowance — Canadian film or video production; Reg. 1100(1)(zc) —

Additional allowance — railway expansion and modernization property; Reg. 1100(21) — Certified films and video tapes — limitation on CCA; Reg. 1100(21.1) — Non-certified films and video tapes — limitation on CCA; Reg. 1101(5a), (5k), (5k.1) — Separate classes for telecommunications spacecraft, certified productions and Canadian film or video productions.

(x.1) of Class 10.1, 30 per cent,

**Related Provisions**: Reg. 1101(1af) — Separate class.

(xi) of Class 11, 35 per cent,

(xii) of Class 12, 100 per cent,

**Related Provisions**: Reg. 1100(1)(l), 1100(21), (21.1), (22).

(xiii) of Class 16, 40 per cent,

(xiv) of Class 17, 8 per cent,

(xv) of Class 18, 60 per cent,

(xvi) of Class 22, 50 per cent,

(xvii) of Class 23, 100 per cent,

(xviii) of Class 25, 100 per cent,

(xix) of Class 26, 5 per cent,

(xx) of Class 28, 30 per cent,

**Related Provisions**: Reg. 1100(1)(w), 1100(1)(zc)(i)(H).

(xxi) of Class 30, 40 per cent,

**Related Provisions**: Reg. 1101(5a) — Separate class.

(xxii) of Class 31, 5 per cent,

**Related Provisions**: Reg. 1101(5b) — Separate class.

(xxiii) of Class 32, 10 per cent,

**Related Provisions**: Reg. 1101(5b) — Separate class.

(xxiv) of Class 33, 15 per cent,

(xxv) of Class 35, 7 per cent,

**Related Provisions**: Reg. 1100(1)(zc).

(xxvi) of Class 37, 15 per cent,

(xxvii) of Class 41, 25 per cent,

**Related Provisions**: Reg. 1100(1)(y), (ya).

(xxviii) of Class 42, 12 per cent,

(xxix) of Class 43, 30 per cent,

(xxix.1) of Class 43.1, 30 per cent, and

(xxx) of Class 44, 25 per cent,

of the undepreciated capital cost to him as of the end of the taxation year (before making any deduction under this subsection for the taxation year) of property of the class;

**Related Provisions [Reg. 1100(1)(a)]**: Reg. 1100(2) — Half-year rule; 1100(3) — Short taxation year; Reg. 1700 — CCA rates for farming or fishing property acquired before 1972. See also list at end of Reg. 1100(1).

**Notes [Reg. 1100(1)(a)]**: Reg. 1100(1)(a)(xxviii), for fibre optic cable, added by P.C. 1994-139, effective for property acquired after December 23, 1991, other than property acquired pursuant to an agreement in writing entered into by the taxpayer before December 24, 1991. However, if the taxpayer elected in a letter filed with Revenue Canada by August 8, 1994 or in a letter filed with the taxpayer's return for the first taxation year ending after December 23, 1991, then it, new Classes 3(j) and (l) (Schedule II) and Class 42 apply to property acquired after the beginning of that taxation year.

Reg. 1100(1)(a)(xxix), for property in manufacturing and processing, added by P.C. 1994-230, effective for property acquired after February 25, 1992.

Division I — Deductions Allowed    Reg. S. 1100(1)(i)(i)

Reg. 1100(1)(a)(xxix.1), for energy conservation equipment, added by P.C. 1997-1033, effective February 22, 1994.

Reg. 1100(1)(a)(xxx), for patents or rights to use patented information, added by P.C. 1994-231, effective for property acquired after April 26, 1993.

**Interpretation Bulletins [Reg. 1100(1)(a)]**: IT-285R2: CCA — General comments; IT-521R: Motor vehicle expenses claimed by self-employed individuals; IT-522R: Vehicle, travel and sales expenses of employees.

**Information Circulars [Reg. 1100(1)(a)]**: 84-1: Revision of capital cost allowance claims and other permissive deductions.

(b) **Class 13** — such amount as the taxpayer may claim in respect of the capital cost to the taxpayer of property of Class 13 in Schedule II, not exceeding

(i) where the capital cost of the property, other than property described in subparagraph (2)(a)(v), (vi) or (vii), was incurred in the taxation year and after November 12, 1981, 50 per cent of the amount for the year calculated in accordance with Schedule III, and

(ii) in any other case, the amount for the year calculated in accordance with Schedule III,

and, for the purposes of this paragraph and Schedule III, the capital cost to a taxpayer of a property shall be deemed to have been incurred at the time at which the property became available for use by the taxpayer;

**Related Provisions**: Reg. 1102(4), (5) — Improvements or alterations to leased properties; Reg. 1700(4) — Property of a farmer owned since before 1972.

**Notes**: Reference to Reg. 1100(2)(a)(vii) and closing words of Reg. 1100(1)(b) added by P.C. 1994-139, effective for property acquired after 1989. Reference to Reg. 1100(2)(a)(v) and (vi) added by P.C. 1991-465, effective for taxation years ending after April 26, 1989.

**Interpretation Bulletins**: IT-324: CCA — Emphyteutic lease; IT-464R: CCA — Leasehold interests.

(c) **Class 14** — such amount as he may claim in respect of property of Class 14 in Schedule II not exceeding the lesser of

(i) the aggregate of the amounts for the year obtained by apportioning the capital cost to him of each property over the life of the property remaining at the time the cost was incurred, and

(ii) the undepreciated capital cost to him as of the end of the taxation year (before making any deduction under this subsection for the taxation year) of property of the class;

**Related Provisions**: Reg. 1100(1)(a)(xxx) — 25% CCA rate for certain patents; Reg. 1100(3) — Short taxation year rule does not apply to Reg. 1100(1)(c); Reg. 1100(9) — Patents.

**Interpretation Bulletins**: IT-143R2: Meaning of "eligible capital expenditure"; IT-477: CCA — Patents, franchises, concessions and licences.

(d) **in lieu of double depreciation** — such additional amount as he may claim not exceeding

in the case of property described in each of the classes in Schedule II, the lesser of

(i) one-half the amount that would have been allowed to him in respect of property of that class under subparagraph 6(n)(ii) of the *Income War Tax Act* if that Act were applicable to the taxation year, and

(ii) the undepreciated capital cost to him as of the end of the taxation year (before making any deduction under this paragraph for the taxation year) of property of the class;

(e) **timber limits and cutting rights** — such amount as he may claim not exceeding the amount calculated in accordance with Schedule VI in respect of the capital cost to him of a property, other than a timber resource property, that is a timber limit or a right to cut timber from a limit;

**Related Provisions**: Reg. 1100(3) — Short taxation year rule does not apply to Reg. 1100(1)(e); Reg. 1101(3) — Separate class; Reg. 5202"cost of capital"(a), 5204"cost of capital"(a) — Manufacturing and processing credit.

**Interpretation Bulletins**: IT-481: Timber resource property and timber limits.

(f) **Class 15** — such amount as he may claim not exceeding the amount calculated in accordance with Schedule IV, in respect of the capital cost to him of property of Class 15 in Schedule II;

**Related Provisions**: Reg. 1100(3) — Short taxation year rule does not apply to Reg. 1100(1)(f); Reg. 1102(7) — River improvements; Reg. 1102(17) — Recreational property; Reg. 5202"cost of capital"(a), 5204"cost of capital"(a) — Manufacturing and processing credit.

(g) **industrial mineral mines** — such amount as he may claim not exceeding the amount calculated in accordance with Schedule V in respect of the capital cost to him of a property that is an industrial mineral mine or a right to remove industrial minerals from an industrial mineral mine;

**Related Provisions**: Reg. 1100(3) — Short taxation year rule does not apply to Reg. 1100(1)(g); Reg. 1101(4) — Separate class; Reg. 1104(3) — "Industrial mineral mine"; Reg. 3900(2)"income derived from mining operations" — Deduction for mining taxes on income; Reg. 5202"cost of capital"(a), 5204"cost of capital"(a) — Manufacturing and processing credit.

**Notes**: "Industrial minerals" are considered by Revenue Canada to be non-metallic minerals, such as gravel, clay, stone, limestone, sand and feldspar (IT-145R, para. 11).

**Interpretation Bulletins**: IT-423: Sale of sand, gravel or top soil; IT-492: Industrial mineral mines.

(h) [Revoked]

(i) **additional allowances — fishing vessels** — such additional amount as he may claim in the case of property of a separate class prescribed by subsection 1101(2) not exceeding the lesser of

(i) the amount by which the depreciation that could have been taken on the property, if the Orders in Council referred to in that subsection were applicable to the taxation year, exceeds the amount allowed under paragraph (a) in respect of the property, and

(ii) the undepreciated capital cost to him as of the end of the taxation year (before making any deduction under this paragraph for the taxation year) of property of the class;

**Interpretation Bulletins:** IT-267R2: CCA — vessels.

(j), (k) [Repealed]

**Notes:** Reg. 1100(1)(j) and (k) repealed by P.C. 1995-775, effective May 31, 1995. They provided an additional allowance for property in respect of which a certificate was issued by the Minister of Supply and Services under Reg. 1106. Such certificates were introduced during the Korean War in 1951 and have not been used for many years.

(l) **additional allowances — certified productions** — such additional amount as he may claim in respect of property for which a separate class is prescribed by subsection 1101(5k) not exceeding the lesser of

(i) the aggregate of his income for the year from that property and from property described in paragraph (n) of Class 12 in Schedule II, determined before making any deduction under this paragraph, and

(ii) the undepreciated capital cost to him of property of that separate class as of the end of the year before making any deduction under this paragraph for the year;

**Proposed Amendment — Reg. 1100(1)(l)**

**Federal budget, Supplementary Information, February 27, 1995:** The elements of the existing film tax incentive to be eliminated for films acquired after 1995 (and films acquired in 1995 in respect of which the new credit is claimed) include the following:

.....

• eligibility of Canadian certified productions for an additional CCA (up to income from Canadian certified productions) in Income Tax Regulation 1100(1)(l); ...

**Notes:** This will be accomplished by having a new definition of "Canadian film or video production". See Reg. 1100(1)(m), 1101(5k.1), 1106 and Class 10(x). See also repealed ITA 96(2.2)(d)(ii).

**Related Provisions:** Reg. 1100(3) — Short taxation year rule does not apply to Reg. 1100(1)(l).

(m) [Revoked]

**Proposed Addition — Reg. 1100(1)(m)**

(m) **additional allowance — Canadian film or video production** — such additional amount as the taxpayer claims in respect of property for which a separate class is prescribed by subsection 1101(5k.1) not exceeding the lesser of

(i) the taxpayer's income for the year from the property, determined before making any deduction under this paragraph, and

(ii) the undepreciated capital cost to the taxpayer of the property of that separate class at the end of the year (before making any deduction under this paragraph for the year);

**Notes:** See Notes to Reg. 1100(1)(l).

**Application:** The December 12, 1995 draft regulations (Canadian film tax credit), subsec. 1(1), will add para. 1100(1)(m), applicable to 1995 et seq.

**Federal budget, Supplementary Information, February 27, 1995:** The elements of the existing film tax incentive to be eliminated for films acquired after 1995 (and films acquired in 1995 in respect of which the new credit is claimed) include the following:

.....

• eligibility of Canadian certified productions for an additional CCA (up to income from Canadian certified productions) in Income Tax Regulation 1100(1)(l); ...

(n) **Class 19** — where the taxpayer is a corporation that had a degree of Canadian ownership in the taxation year, or is an individual who was resident in Canada in the taxation year for not less than 183 days, such amount as he may claim in respect of property of Class 19 in Schedule II that was acquired in a particular taxation year not exceeding the lesser of

(i) 50 per cent of the capital cost thereof to him, and

(ii) the amount by which the capital cost thereof to him exceeds the aggregate of the amounts deducted in respect thereof in computing his income for previous taxation years,

but the aggregate of amounts deductible for a taxation year in respect of property acquired in each of the particular taxation years, under this paragraph, shall not exceed the undepreciated capital cost to him as of the end of the taxation year (before making any deduction under this subsection for the taxation year) of property of the class;

**Related Provisions:** Reg. 1100(1)(o).

(o) **[Class 19]** — where the taxpayer is not entitled to make a deduction under paragraph (n) in computing his income for a taxation year, such amount as he may claim in respect of property of Class 19 in Schedule II not exceeding 20 per cent of the undepreciated capital cost to him as of the end of the taxation year (before making any deduction under this subsection for the taxation year) of property of the class;

(p) **Class 20** — such amount as he may claim in respect of property of Class 20 in Schedule II that was acquired in a particular taxation year not exceeding the lesser of

(i) 20 per cent of the capital cost thereof to him, and

(ii) the amount by which the capital cost thereof to him exceeds the aggregate of the amounts deducted in respect thereof in computing his income for previous taxation years, but the aggregate of amounts deductible for a taxation year in respect of property acquired in each of the particular taxation years, under this paragraph, shall not exceed the undepreciated capital cost to him as of the end of the taxation year (before making any deduction under this subsection for the taxation year) of property of the class;

(q) **Class 21** — such amount as he may claim in respect of property of Class 21 in Schedule II that was acquired in a particular taxation year not exceeding the lesser of

    (i) 50 per cent of the capital cost thereof to him, and

    (ii) the amount by which the capital cost thereof to him exceeds the aggregate of the amounts deducted in respect thereof in computing his income for previous taxation years,

but the aggregate of amounts deductible for a taxation year in respect of property acquired in each of the particular taxation years, under this paragraph, shall not exceed the undepreciated capital cost to him as of the end of the taxation year (before making any deduction under this subsection for the taxation year) of property of the class;

(r), (s), (sa) [Revoked]

(sb) **additional allowances — grain storage facilities** — such additional amount as he may claim in respect of property included in Class 3, 6 or 8 in Schedule II

    (i) that is

        (A) a grain elevator situated in that part of Canada that is defined in section 2 of the *Canada Grain Act* as the "Eastern Division" the principal use of which

            (I) is the receiving of grain directly from producers for storage or forwarding or both,

            (II) is the receiving and storing of grain for direct manufacture or processing into other products, or

            (III) has been certified by the Minister of Agriculture to be the receiving of grain that has not been officially inspected or weighed,

        (B) an addition to a grain elevator described in clause (A),

        (C) fixed machinery installed in a grain elevator in respect of which, or in respect of an addition to which, an additional amount has been or may be claimed under this paragraph,

        (D) fixed machinery, designed for the purpose of drying grain, installed in a grain elevator described in clause (A),

        (E) machinery designed for the purpose of drying grain on a farm, or

        (F) a building or other structure designed for the purpose of storing grain on a farm,

    (ii) that was acquired by the taxpayer in the taxation year or in one of the three immediately preceding taxation years, at a time that was after April 1, 1972 but before August 1, 1974, and

    (iii) that was not used for any purpose whatever before it was acquired by the taxpayer,

not exceeding the lesser of

    (iv) where the property is included in Class 3, 22 per cent of the capital cost thereof, where the property is included in Class 6, 20 per cent of the capital cost thereof or where the property is included in Class 8,

        (A) 14 per cent of the capital cost thereof in the case of property referred to in clause (i)(C), (D) or (F), and

        (B) 14 per cent of the lesser of $15,000 and the capital cost thereof in the case of property described in clause (i)(E), and

    (v) the undepreciated capital cost to him as of the end of the taxation year (before making any deduction under this paragraph for the taxation year) of property of the class;

(t) **Classes 24, 27, 29 and 34** — [applies only to the taxation year that includes November 12, 1981]

**Related Provisions**: Reg. 1100(24) — Specified energy property.

(ta) **[Classes 24, 27, 29 and 34]** — for taxation years commencing after November 12, 1981, such amount as he may claim in respect of property of each of Classes 24, 27, 29 and 34 in Schedule II not exceeding the aggregate of

    (i) the aggregate of

        (A) the lesser of

            (I) 50 per cent of the capital cost to him of all designated property of the class acquired by him in the year, and

            (II) the undepreciated capital cost to him of property of the class as of the end of the year (before making any deduction under this paragraph for the year and, where any of the property referred to in subclause (I) was acquired by virtue of a specified transaction, computed as if no amount were included in respect of property, other than designated property of the class acquired by him in the year), and

        (B) 25 per cent of the lesser of

            (I) the undepreciated capital cost to him of property of the class as of the end of the year (computed as if no amount were included in respect of designated property of the class acquired by him in the year and before making any deduction under this paragraph for the year), and

(II) the capital cost to him of all property, other than designated property, of the class acquired by him in the year, and

(ii) the lesser of

(A) the amount, if any, by which

(I) the undepreciated capital cost to him of property of the class as of the end of the year (before making any deduction under this paragraph for the year)

exceeds

(II) the capital cost to him of all property of the class acquired by him in the year, and

(B) an amount equal to the aggregate of

(I) 50 per cent of the capital cost to him of all property of the class acquired by him in the immediately preceding taxation year, other than designated property of the class acquired in a specified transaction, and

(II) the amount, if any, by which the amount determined under clause (A) for the year with respect to the class exceeds the aggregate of 75 per cent of the capital cost to him of all property, other than designated property, of the class acquired by him in the immediately preceding taxation year and 50 per cent of the capital cost to him of designated property of the class acquired by him in the immediately preceding taxation year, other than designated property of the class acquired in a specified transaction,

and for the purposes of this paragraph and paragraph (t), "designated property" of a class means

(iii) property of the class acquired by him before November 13, 1981,

(iv) property deemed to be designated property of the class by virtue of paragraph (2.1)(g) or (2.2)(j), and

(v) property described in subparagraph (2)(a)(v), (vi) or (vii),

and, for the purposes of this paragraph,

(vi) "specified transaction" means a transaction to which subsection 85(5), 87(1), 88(1), 97(4) or 98(3) or (5) of the Act applies, and

(vii) subject to paragraph (2.2)(j), a property shall be deemed to have been acquired by a taxpayer at the time at which the property became available for use by the taxpayer;

**Related Provisions**: Reg. 1100(2.2)(j); Reg. 1100(24) — Specified energy property.

**Notes**: Reg. 1100(1)(ta)(vii) and reference to Reg. 1100(2)(a)(vii) in Reg. 1100(1)(ta)(v) added by P.C. 1994-139, effective for property acquired after 1989. Reg. 1100(1)(ta)(v) added by P.C. 1991-465, effective for taxation years ending after April 26, 1989.

**Interpretation Bulletins**: IT-147R3: CCA — Accelerated write-off of manufacturing and processing machinery and equipment; IT-336R: CCA — Pollution control property.

(u) [Revoked]

(v) **Canadian vessels** — such amount as the taxpayer may claim in respect of property that is

(i) a vessel described in subsection 1101(2a),

(ii) included in a separate prescribed class because of subsection 13(14) of the Act, or

(iii) a property that has been constituted a prescribed class by subsection 24(2) of Chapter 91 of the Statutes of Canada, 1966-67,

not exceeding the lesser of

(iv) where the property, other than property described in subparagraph (2)(a)(v), (vi) or (vii), was acquired in the taxation year and after November 12, 1981, 16 $^2/_3$ per cent of the capital cost thereof to the taxpayer and, in any other case, 33 $^1/_3$ per cent of the capital cost thereof to the taxpayer, and

(v) the undepreciated capital cost to the taxpayer as of the end of the taxation year (before making any deduction under this paragraph for the taxation year) of property of the class,

and, for the purposes of subparagraph (iv), a property shall be deemed to have been acquired by a taxpayer at the time at which the property became available for use by the taxpayer for the purposes of the Act;

**Notes**: Reg. 1100(1)(v)(i) and (ii) amended, reference to Reg. 1100(2)(a)(vii) in Reg. 1100(1)(v)(iv) added, and closing words of Reg. 1100(1)(v) added by P.C. 1994-139, effective for property acquired after 1989. However, for property acquired before July 14, 1990, read Reg. 1100(1)(v)(i) as:

(i) a vessel in respect of which the Minister of Industry, Trade and Commerce has certified as provided in subsection 1101(2a);

Accelerated CCA for vessels and conversion costs is now verified by Revenue Canada as part of the normal audit process.

Parenthetical exclusion in Reg. 1100(1)(v)(iv) added by P.C. 1991-465, effective for taxation years ending after April 26, 1989.

**Interpretation Bulletins**: IT-267R2: CCA — Vessels.

**Advance Tax Rulings**: ATR-52: Accelerated rate of CCA for vessels.

(va) **additional allowances — offshore drilling vessels** — such additional amount as he may claim in respect of property for which a separate class is prescribed by subsection 1101(2b) not exceeding 15 per cent of the undepreciated capital cost to him of property of that class as of the end of the taxation year (before making any deduction under this subsection for the taxation year);

**Interpretation Bulletins**: IT-267R2: CCA — vessels.

(w) **additional allowances — Class 28** — subject to section 1100A, such additional amount as he may claim in respect of property described in Class 28 acquired for the purpose of gaining or producing income from a mine or in respect of property acquired for the purpose of gaining or producing income from a mine and for which a separate class is prescribed by subsection 1101(4a), not exceeding the lesser of

(i) the taxpayer's income for the year from the mine, determined without reference to paragraph 12(1)(z.5) of the Act and before making any deduction under this paragraph, paragraph (x), (y) or (ya), paragraph 20(1)(v.1) of the Act, section 65, 66, 66.1, 66.2 or 66.7 of the Act or section 29 of the *Income Tax Application Rules*, and

(ii) the undepreciated capital cost to him of property of that class as of the end of the taxation year (before making any deduction under this paragraph for the taxation year);

**Related Provisions**: Reg. 1100(3) — Short taxation year rule does not apply to Reg. 1100(1)(w); Reg. 1104(5), (6.1) — Income from a mine.

**Notes**: Reg. 1100(1)(w)(i) amended by P.C. 1999-629, effective for taxation years that begin after 1996, to add reference to ITA 12(1)(z.5).

(x) subject to section 1100A, such additional amount as he may claim in respect of property acquired for the purpose of gaining or producing income from more than one mine and for which a separate class is prescribed by subsection 1101(4b), not exceeding the lesser of

(i) the taxpayer's income for the year from the mines, determined without reference to paragraph 12(1)(z.5) of the Act and before making any deduction under this paragraph, paragraph (ya), paragraph 20(1)(v.1) of the Act, section 65, 66, 66.1, 66.2 or 66.7 of the Act or section 29 of the *Income Tax Application Rules*, and

(ii) the undepreciated capital cost to him of property of that class as of the end of the taxation year (before making any deduction under this paragraph for the taxation year);

**Related Provisions**: Reg. 1100(3) — Short taxation year rule does not apply to Reg. 1100(1)(x); Reg. 1104(5), (6.1) — Income from a mine; Reg. 1104(7) — Interpretation.

**Notes**: Reg. 1100(1)(x)(i) amended by P.C. 1999-629, effective for taxation years that begin after 1996, to add reference to ITA 12(1)(z.5).

(y) **additional allowances — Class 41** — such additional amount as the taxpayer may claim in respect of property acquired for the purpose of gaining or producing income from a mine and for which a separate class is prescribed by subsection 1101(4c), not exceeding the lesser of

(i) the taxpayer's income for the year from the mine, determined without reference to paragraph 12(1)(z.5) of the Act and before making any deduction under this paragraph, paragraph (x) or (ya), paragraph 20(1)(v.1) of the Act, section 65, 66, 66.1, 66.2 or 66.7 of the Act or section 29 of the *Income Tax Application Rules*, and

(ii) the undepreciated capital cost to the taxpayer of property of that class as of the end of the taxation year (computed without reference to subsection (2) and before making any deduction under this paragraph for the taxation year);

**Related Provisions**: Reg. 1100(3) — Short taxation year rule does not apply to Reg. 1100(1)(y); Reg. 1104(5), (6.1) — Income from a mine; Reg. 1104(7) — Interpretation.

**Notes**: Reg. 1100(1)(y)(i) amended by P.C. 1999-629, effective for taxation years that begin after 1996, to add reference to ITA 12(1)(z.5).

Reg. 1100(1)(y)(ii) amended by P.C. 1992-2335, to correct "end of a taxation year" to "end of the taxation year", effective 1988.

(ya) **[property for more than one mine]** — such additional amount as the taxpayer may claim in respect of property acquired for the purpose of gaining or producing income from more than one mine and for which a separate class is prescribed by subsection 1101(4d), not exceeding the lesser of

(i) the taxpayer's income for the year from the mines, determined without reference to paragraph 12(1)(z.5) of the Act and before making any deduction under this paragraph, paragraph 20(1)(v.1) of the Act, section 65, 66, 66.1, 66.2 or 66.7 of the Act or section 29 of the *Income Tax Application Rules*, and

(ii) the undepreciated capital cost to the taxpayer of property of that class as of the end of the taxation year (computed without reference to subsection (2) and before making any deduction under this paragraph for the taxation year);

**Related Provisions**: Reg. 1100(3) — Short taxation year rule does not apply to Reg. 1100(1)(ya); Reg. 1104(5), (6.1) — Income from a mine; Reg. 1104(7) — Interpretation.

**Notes**: Reg. 1100(1)(ya)(i) amended by P.C. 1999-629, effective for taxation years that begin after 1996, to add reference to ITA 12(1)(z.5).

(z) **additional allowances — railway cars** — such additional amount as the taxpayer may claim in respect of property for which a separate class is prescribed by paragraph 1101(5d)(c) not exceeding eight per cent of the undepreciated capital cost to the taxpayer of property of that class as of the end of the taxation year (before making any deduction under this subsection for the taxation year);

**Notes**: Reg. 1100(1)(z) amended by P.C. 1991-465, effective April 27, 1989, to refer to Reg. 1101(5d)(c) rather than Reg. 1101(5d).

(z.1a) **[additional allowance — railway cars]** — such additional amount as the taxpayer may claim in respect of property for which a separate class is prescribed by paragraph

**Reg. S. 1100(1)(z.1a)**      Income Tax Regulations, Part XI

1101(5d)(d), (e) or (f), not exceeding six per cent of the undepreciated capital cost to the taxpayer of property of that class as of the end of the taxation year (before making any deduction under this subsection for the taxation year);

**Notes**: Reg. 1100(1)(z.1a) added by P.C. 1991-465, effective

(a) for property acquired by a taxpayer after April 26, 1989 for rent or lease to another person;

(b) for property acquired by a taxpayer before April 27, 1989 for rent or lease to another person, except that the 6% rate applies only as of the 1994 taxation year. For 1990, the rate is 7-²/₃%; for 1991, it is 7-¹/₃%; for 1992, it is 7%; for 1993, it is 6-²/₃%;

(c) in respect of property acquired by a taxpayer after February 2, 1990, other than

    (i) property acquired for rent or lease to another person,

    (ii) property acquired pursuant to an agreement in writing entered into before February 3, 1990, or

    (iii) property under construction by or on behalf of the taxpayer before February 3, 1990.

(z.1b) **[railway property]** — where throughout the taxation year the taxpayer was a common carrier that owned and operated a railway, such additional amount as the taxpayer may claim in respect of property for which a separate class is prescribed by subsection 1101(5d.1), not exceeding three per cent of the undepreciated capital cost to the taxpayer of property of that class as of the end of the year (before making any deduction under this subsection for the year);

**Notes**: Reg. 1100(z.1b) added by P.C. 1994-139, effective for property acquired after December 6, 1991.

(za) **additional allowances — railway track and related property** — such additional amount as he may claim in respect of property for which a separate class is prescribed by subsection 1101(5e) not exceeding four per cent of the undepreciated capital cost to him of property of that class as of the end of the taxation year (before making any deduction under this subsection for the taxation year);

(za.1) **[railway track and related property]** — where throughout the taxation year the taxpayer was a common carrier that owned and operated a railway, such additional amount as the taxpayer may claim in respect of property for which a separate class is prescribed by subsection 1101(5e.1), not exceeding six per cent of the undepreciated capital cost to the taxpayer of property of that class as of the end of the year (before making any deduction under this subsection for the year);

**Notes**: Reg. 1100(1)(za.1) added by P.C. 1994-139, effective for property acquired after December 6, 1991.

(za.2) **[trestles]** — where throughout the taxation year the taxpayer was a common carrier that owned and operated a railway, such additional amount as the taxpayer may claim in respect of property for which a separate class is prescribed by subsection 1101(5e.2), not exceeding five per cent of the undepreciated capital cost to the taxpayer of property of that class as of the end of the year (before making any deduction under this subsection for the year);

**Notes**: Reg. 1100(1)(za.2) added by P.C. 1994-139, effective for property acquired after December 6, 1991.

(zb) **[trestles]** — such additional amount as he may claim in respect of property for which a separate class is prescribed by subsection 1101(5f) not exceeding three per cent of the undepreciated capital cost to him of property of that class as of the end of the taxation year (before making any deduction under this subsection for the taxation year);

(zc) **additional allowances — railway expansion and modernization property** — where the taxpayer owns and operates a railway as a common carrier, such additional amount as he may claim in respect of property of a class in Schedule II (in this paragraph referred to as "designated property" of the class)

    (i) that is

        (A) included in Class 1 in Schedule II by virtue of paragraph (h) or (i) of that Class,

        (B) a bridge, culvert, subway or tunnel included in Class 1 in Schedule II that is ancillary to railway track and grading,

        (C) a trestle included in Class 3 in Schedule II that is ancillary to railway track and grading,

        (D) included in Class 6 in Schedule II by virtue of paragraph (j) of that Class,

        (E) machinery or equipment included in Class 8 in Schedule II that is ancillary to

            (I) railway track and grading, or

            (II) railway traffic control or signalling equipment, including switching, block signalling, interlocking, crossing protection, detection, speed control or retarding equipment, but not including property that is principally electronic equipment or systems software therefor,

        (F) machinery or equipment included in Class 8 in Schedule II that

            (I) was acquired principally for the purpose of maintaining or servicing, or

            (II) is ancillary to and used as part of,

a railway locomotive or railway car,

        (G) included in Class 10 in Schedule II by virtue of subparagraph (m)(i), (ii) or (iii) of that Class,

        (H) included in Class 28 in Schedule II by virtue of subparagraph (d)(ii) of that Class (other than property referred to in subparagraph (m)(iv) of Class 10), or

        (I) included in Class 35 in Schedule II,

(ii) that was acquired by him principally for use in or is situated in Canada,

(iii) that was acquired by him in respect of the railway in the taxation year or in one of the four immediately preceding taxation years, at a time that was after April 10, 1978 but before 1988, and

(iv) that was not used for any purpose whatever before it was acquired by him,

not exceeding the lesser of

(v) six per cent of the aggregate of the capital cost to him of the designated property of the class, and

(vi) the undepreciated capital cost to him as of the end of the taxation year (after making all deductions claimed by him under other provisions of this subsection for the taxation year but before making any deduction under this paragraph for the taxation year) of property of the class;

(zd) **Class 38** — such amount as the taxpayer may claim in respect of property of Class 38 in Schedule II not exceeding that percentage which is the aggregate of

(i) that proportion of 40 per cent that the number of days in the taxation year that are in 1988 is of the number of days in the taxation year that are after 1987,

(ii) that proportion of 35 per cent that the number of days in the taxation year that are in 1989 is of the number of days in the taxation year, and

(iii) that proportion of 30 per cent that the number of days in the taxation year that are after 1989 is of the number of days in the taxation year

of the undepreciated capital cost to the taxpayer of property of that class as of the end of the taxation year (before making any deduction under this paragraph for the taxation year);

(ze) **Class 39** — such amount as the taxpayer may claim in respect of property of Class 39 in Schedule II not exceeding that percentage which is the aggregate of

(i) that proportion of 40 per cent that the number of days in the taxation year that are in 1988 is of the number of days in the taxation year that are after 1987,

(ii) that proportion of 35 per cent that the number of days in the taxation year that are in 1989 is of the number of days in the taxation year,

(iii) that proportion of 30 per cent that the number of days in the taxation year that are in 1990 is of the number of days in the taxation year, and

(iv) that proportion of 25 per cent that the number of days in the taxation year that are after 1990 is of the number of days in the taxation year

of the undepreciated capital cost to the taxpayer of property of that class as of the end of the taxation year (before making any deduction under this paragraph for the taxation year);

**Interpretation Bulletins**: IT-147R3: CCA — Accelerated write-off of manufacturing and processing machinery and equipment.

(zf) **Class 40** — such amount as the taxpayer may claim in respect of property of Class 40 in Schedule II not exceeding that percentage which is the aggregate of

(i) that proportion of 40 per cent that the number of days in the taxation year that are in 1988 is of the number of days in the taxation year that are after 1987,

(ii) that proportion of 35 per cent that the number of days in the taxation year that are in 1989 is of the number of days in the taxation year, and

(iii) that proportion of 30 per cent that the number of days in the taxation year that are in 1990 is of the number of days in the taxation year

of the undepreciated capital cost to the taxpayer of property of that class as of the end of the taxation year (before making any deduction under this paragraph for the taxation year);

**Interpretation Bulletins [Reg. 1100(1)(zf)]**: IT-147R3: CCA — Accelerated write-off of manufacturing and processing machinery and equipment.

(zg) **additional allowance — year 2000 computer hardware and systems software** — where the taxpayer

(i) has elected for the year in prescribed manner,

(ii) was not in the year a large corporation, as defined in subsection 225.1(8) of the Act, or a partnership any member of which was such a corporation in a taxation year that included any time that is in the partnership's year, and

(iii) acquired property included in paragraph (f) of Class 10 in Schedule II

(A) in the year,

(B) after 1997 and before November 1999, and

(C) for the purpose of replacing property that was acquired before 1998 that has a material risk of malfunctioning because of the change of the calendar year to 2000 and that is described in paragraph (f) of Class 10, or paragraph (o) of Class 12, in Schedule II, such additional amount as the taxpayer claims in respect of all property described in subparagraph (iii) not exceeding the least of

    (iv) the amount, if any, by which $50,000 exceeds the total of

        (A) the total of all amounts each of which is an amount claimed by the taxpayer under this paragraph for a preceding taxation year,

        (B) the total of all amounts each of which is an amount claimed by the taxpayer for the year or a preceding taxation year under paragraph (zh), and

        (C) the total of all amounts each of which is an amount claimed under this paragraph or paragraph (zh) by a corporation for a taxation year in which it was associated with the taxpayer,

    (v) 85% of the capital cost to the taxpayer of all property described in subparagraph (iii), and

    (vi) the undepreciated capital cost to the taxpayer as of the end of the year (computed without reference to subsection (2) and after making all deductions claimed under other provisions of this subsection for the year but before making any deduction under this paragraph for the year) of property included in Class 10 in Schedule II; and

**Notes**: Reg. 1100(1)(zg) added by P.C. 2000-1000, effective for 1998 and later taxation years. As announced by the Department of Finance in news release on June 11, 1998 and June 2, 1999, paras. (zg) and (zh) allow accelerated CCA to small- and medium-sized businesses for an immediate full writeoff of computer equipment and software acquired by October 31, 1999 to replace systems that were not Y2K compliant.

**I.T. Technical News**: No. 14 (millennium bug expenditures).

(zh) **additional allowance — year 2000 computer software** — where the taxpayer

    (i) has elected for the year in prescribed manner,

    (ii) was not in the year a large corporation, as defined in subsection 225.1(8) of the Act, or a partnership any member of which was such a corporation in a taxation year that included any time that is in the partnership's year, and

    (iii) acquired property included in paragraph (o) of Class 12 in Schedule II

        (A) in the year,

        (B) after 1997 and before November 1999, and

        (C) for the purpose of replacing property that was acquired before 1998 that has a material risk of malfunctioning because of the change of the calendar year to 2000 and that is described in paragraph (f) of Class 10, or paragraph (o) of Class 12, in Schedule II,

such additional amount as the taxpayer claims in respect of all property described in subparagraph (iii) not exceeding the least of

    (iv) the amount, if any, by which $50,000 exceeds the total of

        (A) the total of all amounts each of which is an amount claimed by the taxpayer under this paragraph for a preceding taxation year,

        (B) the total of all amounts each of which is an amount claimed by the taxpayer for the year or a preceding taxation year under paragraph (zg), and

        (C) the total of all amounts each of which is an amount claimed under this paragraph or paragraph (zg) by a corporation for a taxation year in which it was associated with the taxpayer,

    (v) 50% of the capital cost to the taxpayer of all property described in subparagraph (iii), and

    (vi) the undepreciated capital cost to the taxpayer as of the end of the year (computed without reference to subsection (2) and after making all deductions claimed under other provisions of this subsection for the year but before making any deduction under this paragraph for the year) of property included in Class 12 in Schedule II.

**Notes**: Reg. 1100(1)(zh) added by P.C. 2000-1000, effective for 1998 and later taxation years. See Notes to Reg. 1100(1)(zg).

**I.T. Technical News**: No. 14 (millennium bug expenditures).

**Related Provisions [Reg. 1100(1)]**: Reg. 1100(1.1) — Specified leasing property; Reg. 1100(3) — Taxation year less than 12 months; Reg. 1100(11) — Rental properties; Reg. 1100(15) — Leasing properties; ITA 20(1.1) — Definitions in ITA 13(21) apply to regulations.

**Interpretation Bulletins [Reg. 1100(1)]**: See also at beginning of Reg. Part XI.

**Forms [Reg. 1100(1)]**: See at beginning of Reg. Part XI.

**(1.1) [Specified leasing property]** — Notwithstanding subsections (1) and (3), the amount deductible by a taxpayer for a taxation year in respect of a property that is a specified leasing property at the end of the year is the lesser of

    (a) the amount, if any, by which the aggregate of

        (i) all amounts that would be considered to be repayments in the year or a preceding year on account of the principal amount of a loan made by the taxpayer if

            (A) the taxpayer had made the loan at the time that the property last became a specified leasing property and in a principal amount equal to the fair market value of the property at that time,

            (B) interest had been charged on the principal amount of the loan outstanding from time to time at the rate, determined in accordance with section 4302, in effect at the earlier of

(I) the time, if any, before the time referred to in subclause (II), at which the taxpayer last entered into an agreement to lease the property, and

(II) the time that the property last became a specified leasing property

(or, where a particular lease provides that the amount paid or payable by the lessee of the property for the use of, or the right to use, the property varies according to prevailing interest rates in effect from time to time, and the taxpayer so elects, in respect of all of the property that is the subject of the particular lease, in the taxpayer's return of income under Part I of the Act for the taxation year of the taxpayer in which the particular lease was entered into, the rate determined in accordance with section 4302 that is in effect at the beginning of the period for which the interest is being calculated), compounded semi-annually not in advance, and

(C) the amounts that were received or receivable by the taxpayer before the end of the year for the use of, or the right to use, the property before the end of the year and after the time it last became a specified leasing property were blended payments of principal and interest, calculated in accordance with clause (B), on the loan applied firstly on account of interest on principal, secondly on account of interest on unpaid interest, and thirdly on account of principal, and

(ii) the amount that would have been deductible under this section for the taxation year (in this subparagraph referred to as the "particular year") that includes the time (in this subparagraph referred to as the "particular time") at which the property last became a specified leasing property of the taxpayer, if

(A) the property had been transferred to a separate prescribed class at the later of

(I) the beginning of the particular year, and

(II) the time at which the property was acquired by the taxpayer,

(B) the particular year had ended immediately before the particular time, and

(C) where the property was not a specified leasing property immediately before the particular time, subsection (3) had applied,

exceeds

(iii) the aggregate of all amounts deducted by the taxpayer in respect of the property by reason of this subsection before the commence-

ment of the year and after the time at which it last became a specified leasing property; and

(b) the amount, if any, by which,

(i) the aggregate of all amounts that would have been deducted by the taxpayer under this Part in respect of the property under paragraph 20(1)(a) of the Act in computing the income of the taxpayer for the year and all preceding taxation years had this subsection and subsections (11) and (15) not applied, and had the taxpayer, in each such year deducted under paragraph 20(1)(a) of the Act the maximum amount allowed under this Part, read without reference to this subsection and subsection (11) and (15), in respect of the property,

exceeds

(ii) the total depreciation allowed to the taxpayer before the commencement of the year in respect of the property.

**Related Provisions**: ITA 16.1 — Election to treat lease as a sale; Reg. 1100(1.11) — Meaning of "specified leasing property"; Reg. 1100(1.12); Reg. 4302 — Prescribed rate of interest.

**Notes**: See Notes to Reg. 1100(1.3).

Prescribed interest rate for purposes of Reg. 1100(1.1) is set in Reg. 4302, unlike the general prescribed rate in Reg. 4301.

**(1.11) ["Specified leasing property"]** — In this section and subsection 1101(5n), "specified leasing property" of a taxpayer at any time means depreciable property (other than exempt property) that is

(a) used at that time by the taxpayer or a person with whom the taxpayer does not deal at arm's length principally for the purpose of gaining or producing gross revenue that is rent or leasing revenue,

(b) the subject of a lease at that time to a person with whom the taxpayer deals at arm's length and that, at the time the lease was entered into, was a lease for a term of more than one year, and

(c) the subject of a lease of property where the tangible property, other than exempt property, that was the subject of the lease had, at the time the lease was entered into, an aggregate fair market value in excess of $25,000,

but, for greater certainty, does not include intangible property (including systems software and property referred to in paragraph (w) of Class 10 or paragraph (n) or (o) of Class 12 in Schedule II).

**Related Provisions**: Reg. 1100(1.12)–(1.3), (17.2) — Interpretation; Reg. 1101(5n) — Separate class.

**(1.12) [Specified leasing property — new property]** — Notwithstanding subsections (1) and (1.1), where, in a taxation year, a taxpayer has acquired a property that was not used by the taxpayer for any purpose in that year and the first use of the property by the taxpayer is a lease of the property in respect of which subsection (1.1) applies, the amount allowed to the taxpayer under subsection (1) in re-

**Reg. S. 1100(1.12)** — Income Tax Regulations, Part XI

spect of the property for the year shall be deemed to be nil.

**(1.13) [Specified leasing property — interpretation]** — For the purposes of this section,

(a) **"exempt property"** means

(i) general purpose office furniture or office equipment included in Class 8 in Schedule II (including, for greater certainty, mobile office equipment such as cellular telephones and pagers) or general purpose electronic data processing equipment and ancillary data processing equipment, included in paragraph (f) of Class 10 in Schedule II, other than any individual piece thereof having a capital cost to the taxpayer in excess of $1,000,000,

(ii) furniture, appliances, television receivers, radio receivers, telephones, furnaces, hot-water heaters and other similar properties, designed for residential use,

(iii) a property that is a motor vehicle that is designed or adapted primarily to carry individuals on highways and streets and that has a seating capacity for not more than the driver and eight passengers, or a motor vehicle of a type commonly called a van or pick-up truck, or a similar vehicle,

(iv) a truck or tractor that is designed for hauling freight on highways,

(v) a trailer that is designed for hauling freight and to be hauled under normal operating conditions by a truck or tractor described in subparagraph (iv),

(vi) a building or part thereof included in Class 1, 3, 6, 20, 31 or 32 in Schedule II (including component parts such as electric wiring, plumbing, sprinkler systems, air-conditioning equipment, heating equipment, lighting fixtures, elevators and escalators) other than a building or part thereof leased primarily to a lessee that is

(A) a person who is exempt from tax by reason of section 149 of the Act,

(B) a person who uses the building in the course of carrying on a business the income from which is exempt from tax under Part I of the Act by reason of any provision of the Act, or

(C) a Canadian government, municipality or other Canadian public authority,

who owned the building or part thereof at any time before the commencement of the lease (other than at any time during a period ending not later than one year after the later of the date the construction of the building or part thereof was completed and the date the building or part thereof was acquired by the lessee),

(vii) vessel mooring space, and

(viii) property that is included in Class 35 in Schedule II,

and for the purposes of subparagraph (i), where a property is owned by two or more persons or partnerships, or any combination thereof, the capital cost of the property to each such person or partnership shall be deemed to be the total of all amounts each of which is the capital cost of the property to such a person or partnership;

(b) property shall be deemed to be the subject of a lease for a term of more than one year at any time where, at that time

(i) the property had been leased by the lessee thereunder, a person with whom the lessee does not deal at arm's length, or any combination thereof, for a period of more than one year ending at that time, or

(ii) it is reasonable, having regard to all the circumstances, to conclude that the lessor thereunder knew or ought to have known that the lessee thereunder, a person with whom the lessee does not deal at arm's length, or any combination thereof, would lease the property for more than one year; and

(c) for the purposes of paragraph (1.11)(c), where it is reasonable, having regard to all the circumstances, to conclude that one of the main reasons for the existence of two or more leases was to avoid the application of subsection (1.1) by reason of each such lease being a lease of property where the tangible property, other than exempt property, that was the subject of the lease had an aggregate fair market value, at the time the lease was entered into, not in excess of $25,000, each such lease shall be deemed to be a lease of tangible property that had, at the time the lease was entered into, an aggregate fair market value in excess of $25,000.

**Related Provisions**: Reg. 1100(1.14); Reg. 8200 — Prescribed property for leasing rules.

**Notes**: Reg. 1100(1.13)(a)(iii) amended by P.C. 1994-139, effective for taxation years and fiscal periods that start after June 17, 1987 and end after 1987.

Reg. 1100(1.13)(a)(viii) amended by P.C. 1994-139, effective for property acquired after December 23, 1991, other than property acquired by the taxpayer before 1993

(a) pursuant to an agreement in writing entered into before December 24, 1991, or

(b) that was under construction by or on behalf of the taxpayer on December 23, 1991.

For earlier acquisitions, read (viii) "a railway car".

See Notes to Reg. 1100(1.3).

**(1.14) [Specified leasing property — election]** — For the purposes of subsection (1.11) and notwithstanding subsection (1.13), where a taxpayer referred to in subsection (16) so elects in the taxpayer's return of income under Part I of the Act for a taxation year in respect of the year and all subsequent taxation years, all of the property of the taxpayer that is the subject of leases entered into in those years shall be deemed not to be exempt property for those years and the aggregate fair market value of all of the tangible property that is the subject of each such lease shall be deemed to have been, at the time the lease was entered into, in excess of $25,000.

**(1.15) [Specified leasing property — term of more than one year]** — Subject to subsection (1.16) and for the purposes of subsection (1.11), where at any time a taxpayer acquires property that is the subject of a lease with a remaining term at that time of more than one year from a person with whom the taxpayer was dealing at arm's length, the taxpayer shall be deemed to have entered into a lease of the property at that time for a term of more than one year.

**(1.16) [Specified leasing property — amalgamation]** — Where, at any time, a taxpayer acquires from a person with whom the taxpayer is not dealing at arm's length, or by virtue of an amalgamation (within the meaning assigned by subsection 87(1) of the Act), property that was specified leasing property of the person from whom the taxpayer acquired it, the taxpayer shall, for the purposes of paragraph (1.1)(a) and for the purpose of computing the income of the taxpayer in respect of the lease for any period after the particular time, be deemed to be the same person as, and a continuation of, that person.

**(1.17) [Specified leasing property — replacement property]** — For the purposes of subsections (1.1) and (1.11), where at any particular time a property (in this subsection referred to as a "replacement property") is provided by a taxpayer to a lessee for the remaining term of a lease as a replacement for a similar property of the taxpayer (in this subsection referred to as the "original property") that was leased by the taxpayer to the lessee, and the amount payable by the lessee for the use of, or the right to use, the replacement property is the same as the amount that was so payable in respect of the original property, the following rules apply:

(a) the replacement property shall be deemed to have been leased by the taxpayer to the lessee at the same time and for the same term as the original property;

(b) the amount of the loan referred to in clause (1.1)(a)(i)(A) shall be deemed to be equal to the amount of that loan determined in respect of the original property;

(c) the amount determined under subparagraph (1.1)(a)(ii) in respect of the replacement property shall be deemed to be equal to the amount so determined in respect of the original property;

(d) all amounts received or receivable by the taxpayer for the use of, or the right to use, the original property before the particular time shall be deemed to have been received or receivable, as the case may be, by the taxpayer for the use of, or the right to use, the replacement property; and

(e) the original property shall be deemed to have ceased to be subject to the lease at the particular time.

**(1.18) [Specified leasing property — breakdown of property]** — For the purposes of subsection (1.1), where for any period of time any amount that would have been received or receivable by a taxpayer during that period in respect of the use of, or the right to use, a property of the taxpayer during that period is not received or receivable by the taxpayer as a consequence of a breakdown of the property during that period and before the lease of that property is terminated, that amount shall be deemed to have been received or receivable, as the case may be, by the taxpayer.

**(1.19) [Specified leasing property — addition or alteration]** — For the purposes of subsections (1.1) and (1.11), where at any particular time

(a) an addition or alteration (in this subsection referred to as "additional property") is made by a taxpayer to a property (in this subsection referred to as the "original property") of the taxpayer that is a specified leasing property at the particular time, and

(b) as a consequence of the addition or alteration, the aggregate amount receivable by the taxpayer after the particular time for the use of, or the right to use, the original property and the additional property exceeds the amount so receivable in respect of the original property,

the following rules apply:

(c) the taxpayer shall be deemed to have leased the additional property to the lessee at the particular time,

(d) the term of the lease of the additional property shall be deemed to be greater than one year,

(e) the prescribed rate in effect at the particular time in respect of the additional property shall be deemed to be equal to the prescribed rate in effect in respect of the lease of the original property at the particular time,

(f) subsection (1.11) shall be read without reference to paragraph (c) thereof in respect of the additional property, and

(g) the excess described in paragraph (b) shall be deemed to be an amount receivable by the taxpayer for the use of, or the right to use, the additional property.

**(1.2) [Specified leasing property — renogiation of lease]** — For the purposes of subsections (1.1) and (1.11), where at any time

(a) a lease (in this subsection referred to as the "original lease") of property is in the course of a *bona fide* renegotiation, and

(b) as a result of the renegotiation, the amount paid or payable by the lessee of the property for the use of, or the right to use, the property is altered in respect of a period after that time (otherwise than by reason of an addition or alteration to which subsection (1.19) applies),

the following rules apply:

(c) the original lease shall be deemed to have expired and the renegotiated lease shall be deemed to be a new lease of the property entered into at that time, and

(d) paragraph (1.13)(b) shall not apply in respect of any period before that time during which the property was leased by the lessee or a person with whom the lessee did not deal at arm's length.

**(1.3) [Specified leasing property — lease of building]** — For the purposes of subsections (1.1) and (1.11), where a taxpayer leases to another person a building or part thereof that is not exempt property, the references to "one year" in paragraphs (1.11)(b) and (1.13)(b), subsection (1.15) and paragraph (1.19)(d) shall in respect of that building or part thereof be read as references to "three years".

**Related Provisions**: Reg. 1100(1.13) — Meaning of "exempt property".

**Notes**: Reg. 1100(1.1)–(1.3) added by P.C. 1991-465, effective for leases entered into after 10:00 p.m. EDST, April 26, 1989, other than leases entered into pursuant to an agreement in writing entered into before that time under which the lessee thereunder has the right to require the lease of the property (and for these purposes a lease in respect of which a material change has been agreed to by the parties thereto effective at any particular time that is after 10:00 p.m. EDST, April 26, 1989 is deemed to have been entered into at that particular time), except that

(a) Reg. 1100(1.12) is effective for property acquired after April 26, 1989;

(b) in its application to leases entered into before February 3, 1990 or after February 2, 1990 pursuant to an agreement in writing entered into before February 3, 1990 under which the lessee thereunder has the right to require the lease of the property,

(i) Reg. 1100(1.3) does not apply,

(ii) read Reg. 1100(1.13)(a)(vi) as follows:

"(vi) a building or part thereof (including component parts such as electric wiring, plumbing, sprinkler systems, air-conditioning equipment, heating equipment, lighting fixtures, elevators and escalators),", and

(iii) in Reg. 1100(1.1)(a)(i)(B), ignore subclause (I) and the words "the earlier of";

(c) in their application to leases entered into on or before March 14, 1991 or after that day pursuant to an agreement in writing entered into on or before that day under which the lessee thereunder has the right to require the lease of the property, read Regs. 1100(1.13)(a)(iv) and (v) as follows:

"(iv) a truck or tractor that is designed for use on highways,

(v) a trailer that is designed to be hauled under normal operating conditions by a truck or tractor described in subparagraph (iv),"; and

(d) any election made under Reg. 1100(1.1)(a)(i)(B) or 1100(1.14) by September 23, 1991 (i.e., 180 days from publication in the *Canada Gazette*) is deemed to be a valid election.

Reg. 1100(1.17)(b) amended by P.C. 1992-2335, to delete the word "so" before "determined", effective on the same basis as the introduction of Regs. 1100(1.1) to (1.3).

**(2) Property acquired in the year [Half-year rule]** — Where at the end of a taxation year of a taxpayer

(a) the aggregate of all amounts, each of which is an amount added

(i) by reason of subparagraph 13(21)(f)(i) [13(21)"undepreciated capital cost"A] of the Act in respect of a property acquired in the year or that became available for use by the taxpayer in the year, or

(ii) by reason of subparagraph 13(21)(f)(ii.1) [13(21)"undepreciated capital cost"C] or (ii.2) [D] of the Act in respect of an amount repaid in the year

to the undepreciated capital cost to the taxpayer of property of a class in Schedule II, other than

(iii) property included in paragraph (1)(v), paragraph (w) of Class 10 or any of paragraphs (a) to (c), (e) to (i), (k), (l), (p), (q) and (s) of Class 12,

**Proposed Amendment — Reg. 1100(2)(a)(iii)**

(iii) property included in paragraph (1)(v), paragraph (w) of Class 10 or any of paragraphs (a) to (c), (e) to (i), (k), (l) and (p) to (s) of Class 12,

**Application**: The December 12, 1995 draft regulations (Canadian film tax credit), subsec. 1(2), will amend subpara. 1100(2)(a)(iii) to read as above, applicable to property acquired after December 12, 1995.

**Notes**: By extending exclusion of the half-year rule to para. (r), this amendment allows rental videotapes and DVDs to be fully written off in the year they are acquired.

**Letter from Department of Finance, August 4, 1995**:

Dear [xxx]:

Thank you for your letter of December 13, 1994 concerning the application of the half-year capital cost allowance rule to rental video-cassettes.

I understand that [xxx], Director of your [xxx], met with my officials to discuss this issue. I am sympathetic to your concerns and am prepared to recommend an amendment of the tax regulations in this regard at the next available opportunity. [This was done by changing "(p), (q) and (s)" to "(p) to (s)" in Reg. 1100(2)(a)(iii), thus covering para. (r) — ed.]

Thank you for bringing this matter to my attention.

Sincerely,

The Honourable Paul Martin, P.C., M.P.

(iv) property included in any of Classes 13, 14, 15, 23, 24, 27, 29 and 34,

Division I — Deductions Allowed  Reg. S. 1100(2.1)(g)

(v) where the taxpayer was a corporation described in subsection (16) throughout the year, property that was specified leasing property of the taxpayer at that time,

(vi) property that was deemed to have been acquired by the taxpayer in a preceding taxation year by reason of the application of paragraph 16.1(1)(b) of the Act in respect of a lease to which the property was subject immediately before the time at which the taxpayer last acquired the property, and

(vii) property considered to have become available for use by the taxpayer in the year by reason of paragraph 13(27)(b) or (28)(c) of the Act

exceeds

(b) the aggregate of all amounts, each of which is an amount deducted

(i) by virtue of subparagraph 13(21)(f)(iv) [13(21)"undepreciated capital cost"F] or (v) [G] of the Act in respect of property disposed of in the year, or

(ii) by virtue of subparagraph 13(21)(f)(viii) [13(21)"undepreciated capital cost"J] of the Act in respect of an amount the taxpayer received or was entitled to receive in the year

from the undepreciated capital cost to him of property of the class,

the amount that the taxpayer may deduct for the year under subsection (1) in respect of property of the class shall be determined as if the undepreciated capital cost to him as of the end of the year (before making any deduction under subsection (1) for the year) of property of the class were reduced by an amount equal to 50 per cent of the amount by which the aggregate determined under paragraph (a) exceeds the aggregate determined under paragraph (b).

**Proposed Amendment — Reg. 1100(2)**

**Federal budget, Supplementary Information, February 27, 1995**: The elements of the existing film tax incentive to be eliminated for films acquired after 1995 (and films acquired in 1995 in respect of which the new credit is claimed) include the following:

.....

- exemption of Canadian certified productions from the half-year CCA rule that generally applies to property in the year of its acquisition pursuant to Regulation 1100(2); ...

**Notes**: This will be accomplished by having a new definition of "Canadian film or video production", defined in Reg. 1106 and listed in Class 10(x), which is not included in Reg. 1100(2)(a)(iii) as is Class 10(w). See also repealed ITA 96(2.2)(d)(ii).

**Related Provisions**: Reg. 1100(1)(ta)(v), Reg. 1100(2.1) — Grandfathering for property acquired before 1983; Reg. 1100(2.2), (2.3) — Half-year rule does not apply to acquisition on butterfly or from related person who owned it for a year; Reg. 1100(2.21) — Effect of deemed disposition and reacquisition; Reg. 1100(2.4) — Rental automobiles.

**Notes**: Reg. 1100(2) is known informally as the "half-year rule" or "first-year rule". The amount of CCA allowed for the first year in which an asset is acquired is normally ½ of the amount that would otherwise be allowed. The exceptions are listed in Reg. 1100(2)(a)(iii) to (vii). There is a further reduction for a short taxation year; see Reg. 1100(3).

The words "or that became available for use by the taxpayer in the year" added to Reg. 1100(2)(a)(i), and Reg. 1100(2)(a)(vii) added, by P.C. 1994-139, effective for property acquired after 1989.

Reg. 1100(2)(a) amended by P.C. 1991-465, effective for taxation years ending after April 26, 1989.

**Interpretation Bulletins**: IT-283R2: CCA — Videotapes, videotape cassettes, films, computer software and master recording media; IT-469R: CCA — Earth-moving equipment; IT-521R: Motor vehicle expenses claimed by self-employed individuals; IT-522R: Vehicle, travel and sales expenses of employees; IT-525R: Performing artists.

**Advance Tax Rulings**: ATR-11: "50% rule" on non-arm's length transactions.

**Forms**: T2 SCH 8: Capital cost allowance.

**(2.1)** Where a taxpayer has, after November 12, 1981 and before 1983, acquired or incurred a capital cost in respect of a property of a class in Schedule II and

(a) he was obligated to acquire the property under the terms of an agreement in writing entered into before November 13, 1981 (or, where the property is a property described in Class 31 in Schedule II, before 1982),

(b) he or a person with whom he was not dealing at arm's length commenced the construction, manufacture or production of the property before November 13, 1981 (or, where the property is a property described in Class 31 in Schedule II, before 1982),

(c) he or a person with whom he was not dealing at arm's length had made arrangements, evidenced in writing for the construction, manufacture or production of the property that were substantially advanced before November 13, 1981 and the construction, manufacture or production commenced before June 1, 1982, or

(d) he was obligated to acquire the property under the terms of an agreement in writing entered into before June 1, 1982 where arrangements, evidenced in writing, for the acquisition or leasing of the property were substantially advanced before November 13, 1981,

the following rules apply:

(e) no amount shall be included under paragraph (2)(a) in respect of the property;

(f) where the property is a property to which paragraph (1)(b) applies, that paragraph shall be read, in respect of the property, as "such amount, not exceeding the amount for the year calculated in accordance with Schedule III, as he may claim in respect of the capital cost to him of property of Class 13 in Schedule II";

(g) where the property is a property of a class to which paragraph (1)(t) or (ta) applies, the property shall be deemed to be designated property of the class; and

(h) where the property is a property described in paragraph (1)(v), subparagraph (iv) thereof shall be read, in respect of the property, as "$33^1/_3$ per cent of the capital cost thereof to him, and".

(2.2) Where a property of a class in Schedule II is acquired by a taxpayer

(a) in the course of a reorganization in respect of which, if a dividend were received by a corporation in the course of the reorganization, subsection 55(2) of the Act would not be applicable to the dividend by reason of the application of paragraph 55(3)(b) of the Act, or

(b), (c), (d) [Revoked]

(e) from a person with whom the taxpayer was not dealing at arm's length (otherwise than by virtue of a right referred to in paragraph 251(5)(b) of the Act) at the time the property was acquired,

and where

(f) the property was depreciable property of the person from whom it was acquired and was owned continuously by that person for the period from

(i) a day that was at least 364 days before the end of the taxation year of the taxpayer during which he acquired the property, or

(ii) November 12, 1981

to the day it was acquired by the taxpayer, or

(g) the rules provided in subsection (2.1) or this subsection applied in respect of the property for the purpose of determining the allowance under subsection (1) to which the person from whom the taxpayer acquired the property was entitled,

the following rules apply:

(h) no amount shall be included under paragraph (2)(a) in respect of the property;

(i) where the property is a property to which paragraph (1)(b) applies, that paragraph shall be read, in respect of the property, as "such amount, not exceeding the amount for the year calculated in accordance with Schedule III, as he may claim in respect of the capital cost to him of property of Class 13 in Schedule II";

(j) where the property is a property of a class to which paragraph (1)(ta) applies,

(i) the property shall be deemed to be designated property of the class,

(ii) for the purposes of computing the amount determined under paragraph (1)(ta) for any taxation year of the taxpayer ending after the time the property was actually acquired by the taxpayer, the property shall be deemed, other than for the purposes of paragraph (f), to have been acquired by the taxpayer immediately after the commencement of the taxpayer's first taxation year that commenced after the time that is the earlier of

(A) the time the property was last acquired by the transferor of the property, and

(B) where the property was transferred in a series of transfers to which this subsection applies, the time the property was last acquired by the first transferor in that series,

unless

(C) where clause (A) applies, the property was acquired by the taxpayer before the end of the taxation year of the transferor of the property that includes the time at which that transferor acquired the property, or

(D) where clause (B) applies, the property was acquired by the taxpayer before the end of the taxation year of the first transferor that includes the time at which that transferor acquired the property;

(iii) where the taxpayer is a corporation that was incorporated or otherwise formed after the end of the transferor's, or where applicable, the first transferor's, taxation year in which the transferor last acquired the property, the taxpayer shall be deemed, for the purposes of subparagraph (ii),

(A) to have been in existence throughout the period commencing immediately before the end of that year and ending immediately after the taxpayer was incorporated or otherwise formed, and

(B) to have had, throughout the period referred to in clause (A), fiscal periods ending on the day of the year on which the taxpayer's first fiscal period ended; and

(iv) the property shall be deemed to have become available for use by the taxpayer at the earlier of

(A) the time it became available for use by the taxpayer, and

(B) if applicable,

(I) the time it became available for use by the person from whom the taxpayer acquired the property, determined without reference to paragraphs 13(27)(c) and (28)(d) of the Act, or

(II) the time it became available for use by the first transferor in a series of transfers of the same property to which this subsection applies, determined without reference to paragraphs 13(27)(c) and (28)(d) of the Act; and

(k) where the property is a property described in paragraph (1)(v), subparagraph (iv) thereof shall

Division I — Deductions Allowed  Reg. S. 1100(8)

be read, in respect of the property, as "33 1/3 per cent of the capital cost thereof to him, and".

**Related Provisions**: Reg. 1100(2.21) — Effect of deemed disposition and reacquisition; Reg. 1100(2.3) — No inclusion under Reg. 1100(2)(b); Reg. 1102(20) — Non-arm's length exception.

**Notes**: Reg. 1100(2.2)(j) amended by P.C. 1994-139, effective for property acquired after 1987. Reg. 1100(2.2)(j)(iv) added by P.C. 1995-775, effective for property acquired after 1989.

**Interpretation Bulletins [Reg. 1100(2.1), (2.2)]**: IT-302R3: Losses of a corporation — the effect that acquisitions of control, amalgamations, and windings-up have on their deductibility — after January 15, 1987; IT-464R: CCA — Leasehold interests.

**Advance Tax Rulings**: ATR-11: "50% rule" on non-arm's length transactions.

(2.21) Where a taxpayer is deemed by a provision of the Act to have disposed of and acquired or reacquired a property,

(a) for the purposes of paragraph (2.2)(e) and subsections (19), 1101(1ad) and 1102(14) and (14.1), the acquisition or reacquisition shall be deemed to have been from a person with whom the taxpayer was not dealing at arm's length at the time of the acquisition or reacquisition; and

(b) for the purposes of paragraphs (2.2)(f) and (g), the taxpayer shall be deemed to be the person from whom the taxpayer acquired or reacquired the property.

(2.3) Where a taxpayer has disposed of a property and, by virtue of paragraph (2.2)(h), no amount is required to be included under paragraph (2)(a) in respect of the property by the person that acquired the property, no amount shall be included by the taxpayer under paragraph (2)(b) in respect of the disposition of the property.

**Advance Tax Rulings**: ATR-11: "50% rule" on non-arm's length transactions.

(2.4) For the purposes of subsection (2), where a taxpayer has disposed of property described in Class 10 of Schedule II that would qualify as property described in paragraph (e) of Class 16 of Schedule II if the property had been acquired by the taxpayer after November 12, 1981, the proceeds of disposition of the property shall be deemed to be proceeds of disposition of property described in Class 16 of Schedule II and not of property described in Class 10 of Schedule II.

(2.5) Where in a particular taxation year a taxpayer disposes of a property included in Class 10.1 in Schedule II that was owned by the taxpayer at the end of the immediately preceding taxation year,

(a) the deduction allowed under subsection (1) in respect of the property in computing the taxpayer's income for the year shall be determined as if the property had not been disposed of in the particular year and the number of days in the particular year were one-half of the number of days in the particular year otherwise determined; and

(b) no amount shall be deducted under subsection (1) in respect of the property in computing the taxpayer's income for any subsequent taxation year.

**Notes**: Reg. 1100(2.5) added by P.C. 1994-103, effective for taxation years that start after June 18, 1987 and end after 1987. Since ITA 20(16.1) prevents a terminal loss from being claimed in the year of disposition of an automobile in Class 10.1, this provision was introduced to allow a claim in the year of disposition of 1/2 of the CCA that would have been allowed. The "1/2" effect is provided by Reg. 1100(3), which prorates the CCA for a short taxation year.

**Interpretation Bulletins**: IT-521R: Motor vehicle expenses claimed by self-employed individuals; IT-522R: Vehicle, travel and sales expenses of employees.

(3) **[Taxation years less than 12 months]** — Where a taxation year is less than 12 months, the amount allowed as a deduction under this section, other than under paragraph (1)(c), (e), (f), (g), (l), (w), (x), (y), (ya), (zg) or (zh), shall not exceed that proportion of the maximum amount otherwise allowable that the number of days in the taxation year is of 365.

**Proposed Amendment — Reg. 1100(3)**

**Notes**: The Department of Finance has indicated that a reference to Reg. 1100(1)(m) will be added to Reg. 1100(3), to come into force at the same time as proposed Reg. 1100(1)(m).

**Related Provisions**: Reg. 1100(1.1) — Specified leasing property; Reg. 1104(1) — "taxation year".

**Notes**: The CCRA takes the position that the "short taxation year" rule does not apply to income from property, since the taxation year for such purposes is the calendar year. See Interpretation Bulletin IT-172R, para. 2. Tax shelters involving the co-ownership of depreciable assets (such as computer software) were often based on this reasoning before the introduction of the CSTSP restrictions in Reg. 1100(20.1), (20.2).

Reference to 1100(1)(l), (w), (x), (y) and (ya) in Reg. 1100(3) added by P.C. 1994-139, retroactive to 1986.

Reference to Reg. 1100(1)(zg) and (zh) added by P.C. 2000-1000, effective for 1998 and later taxation years.

**Interpretation Bulletins**: IT-147R3: CCA — Accelerated write-off of manufacturing and processing machinery and equipment; IT-172R: CCA — Taxation year of individuals; IT-434R: Rental of real property by individual; IT-441: Certified feature productions and certified short productions.

(4)–(7) [Revoked]

(8) **Railway sidings** — Where a taxpayer, other than an operator of a railway system, has made a capital expenditure pursuant to a contract or arrangement with an operator of a railway system under which a railway siding that does not become the taxpayer's property is constructed to provide service to the taxpayer's place of business or to a property acquired by the taxpayer for the purpose of gaining or producing income, there is hereby allowed to the taxpayer, in computing income for the taxation year from the business or property, as the case may be, a deduction equal to such amount as he may claim not exceeding four per cent of the amount remaining, if any, after deducting from the capital expenditure the

## Reg. S. 1100(8)  Income Tax Regulations, Part XI

aggregate of all amounts previously allowed as deductions in respect of the expenditure.

**(9) Patents** — Where a part or all of the cost of a patent is determined by reference to the use of the patent, in lieu of the deduction allowed under paragraph (1)(c), a taxpayer, in computing his income for a taxation year from a business or property, as the case may be, may deduct such amount as he may claim in respect of property of Class 14 in Schedule II not exceeding the lesser of

(a) the aggregate of

(i) that part of the capital cost determined by reference to the use of the patent in the year, and

(ii) the amount that would be computed under subparagraph (1)(c)(i) if the capital cost of the patent did not include the amounts determined by reference to the use of the patent in that year and previous years; and

(b) the undepreciated capital cost to him as of the end of the taxation year (before making any deduction under this subsection for the taxation year) of property of the class.

**Interpretation Bulletins**: IT-477: CCA — Patents, franchises, concessions and licences.

**(9.1) [Class 44]** — Where a part or all of the capital cost to a taxpayer of property that is a patent, or a right to use patented information, is determined by reference to the use of the property and that property is included in Class 44 in Schedule II, in lieu of the deduction allowed under paragraph (1)(a), there may be deducted in computing the taxpayer's income for a taxation year from a business or property such amount as the taxpayer may claim in respect of property of the class not exceeding the lesser of

(a) the total of

(i) that part of the capital cost that is determined by reference to the use of the property in the year, and

(ii) the amount that would be deductible for the year by reason of paragraph (1)(a) in respect of property of the class if the capital cost of the property of the class did not include the amounts determined under subparagraph (i) for the year and preceding taxation years; and

(b) the undepreciated capital cost to the taxpayer as of the end of the taxation year (before making any deduction under this subsection for the taxation year) of property of the class.

**Related Provisions**: Reg. 1100(1)(a)(xxx) — Alternative 25% write-off for patents.

**Notes**: Reg. 1100(9.1) added by P.C. 1994-231, effective for property acquired after April 26, 1993.

**(10)** [Revoked]

**(11) Rental properties** — Notwithstanding subsection (1), in no case shall the aggregate of deductions, each of which is a deduction in respect of property of a prescribed class owned by a taxpayer that includes rental property owned by him, otherwise allowed to the taxpayer by virtue of subsection (1) in computing his income for a taxation year, exceed the amount, if any, by which

(a) the aggregate of amounts each of which is

(i) his income for the year from renting or leasing a rental property owned by him, computed without regard to paragraph 20(1)(a) of the Act, or

(ii) the income of a partnership for the year from renting or leasing a rental property of the partnership, to the extent of the taxpayer's share of such income,

exceeds

(b) the aggregate of amounts each of which is

(i) his loss for the year from renting or leasing a rental property owned by him, computed without regard to paragraph 20(1)(a) of the Act, or

(ii) the loss of a partnership for the year from renting or leasing a rental property of the partnership, to the extent of the taxpayer's share of such loss.

**Related Provisions**: ITA 127.52(3)"rental or leasing property" — Minimum tax; Reg. 1100(12) — Exceptions; Reg. 1100(14) — Meaning of "rental property".

**Interpretation Bulletins**: IT-195R4: Rental property — CCA restrictions; IT-274R: Rental properties — Capital cost of $50,000 or more; IT-304R2: Condominiums; IT-367R3: Capital cost allowance — multiple-unit residential buildings; IT-434R: Rental of real property by individual.

**Forms**: T776: Statement of real estate rentals.

**(12) [Rental properties — exceptions]** — Subject to subsection (13), subsection (11) does not apply in respect of a taxation year of a taxpayer that was, throughout the year,

(a) a life insurance corporation, or a corporation whose principal business was the leasing, rental, development or sale, or any combination thereof, of real property owned by it; or

(b) a partnership each member of which was a corporation described in paragraph (a).

**Related Provisions**: Reg. 1100(13) — Exception.

**Interpretation Bulletins**: IT-195R4: Rental property — CCA restrictions; IT-371: Meaning of "principal business".

**(13) [Rental properties — leasehold interest]** — For the purposes of subsection (11), where a taxpayer or partnership has a leasehold interest in a property that is property of Class 1, 3 or 6 in Schedule II by virtue of subsection 1102(5) and the property is leased by the taxpayer or partnership to a person who owns the land, an interest therein or an option in respect thereof, on which the property is situated, this section shall be read without reference to subsection (12) with respect to that property.

**Related Provisions**: Reg. 1101(5h) — Separate classes.

**Interpretation Bulletins**: IT-195R4: Rental property — CCA restrictions.

**(14) ["Rental property"]** — In this section and section 1101, "rental property" of a taxpayer or a partnership means

(a) a building owned by the taxpayer or the partnership, whether owned jointly with another person or otherwise, or

(b) a leasehold interest in real property, if the leasehold interest is property of Class 1, 3, 6 or 13 in Schedule II and is owned by the taxpayer or the partnership,

if, in the taxation year in respect of which the expression is being applied, the property was used by the taxpayer or the partnership principally for the purpose of gaining or producing gross revenue that is rent, but, for greater certainty, does not include a property leased by the taxpayer or the partnership to a lessee, in the ordinary course of the taxpayer's or partnership's business of selling goods or rendering services, under an agreement by which the lessee undertakes to use the property to carry on the business of selling, or promoting the sale of, the taxpayer's or partnership's goods or services.

**Related Provisions**: ITA 127.52(3)"rental or leasing property" — Minimum tax; Reg. 1100(14.1) — Interpretation; Reg. 1101(1ac), (1ae) — Separate classes; Reg. 2411(4)B(e) — Insurers.

**Notes**: Reg. 1100(14)(a) amended by P.C. 1989-2464. For taxation years before 1994, read as "(a) a building, other than property of Class 31 or 32 in Schedule II, owned by ...".

**Interpretation Bulletins**: IT-195R4: Rental property — CCA restrictions; IT-274R: Rental properties — Capital cost of $50,000 or more; IT-304R2: Condominiums; IT-367R3: Capital cost allowance — multiple-unit residential buildings.

**(14.1) ["Gross revenue"]** — For the purposes of subsection (14), gross revenue derived in a taxation year from

(a) the right of a person or partnership, other than the owner of a property, to use or occupy the property or a part thereof, and

(b) services offered to a person or partnership that are ancillary to the use or occupation by the person or partnership of the property or the part thereof

shall be considered to be rent derived in that year from the property.

**Related Provisions**: Reg. 1100(14.2) — Exception.

**Interpretation Bulletins**: IT-195R4: Rental property — CCA restrictions.

**(14.2)** Subsection (14.1) does not apply in any particular taxation year to property owned by

(a) a corporation, where the property is used in a business carried on in the year by the corporation;

(b) an individual, where the property is used in a business carried on in the year by the individual in which he is personally active on a continuous basis throughout that portion of the year during which the business is ordinarily carried on; or

(c) a partnership, where the property is used in a business carried on in the year by the partnership if at least $2/3$ of the income or loss, as the case may be, of the partnership for the year is included in the determination of the income of

(i) members of the partnership who are individuals that are personally active in the business of the partnership on a continuous basis throughout that portion of the year during which the business is ordinarily carried on, and

(ii) members of the partnership that are corporations.

**Interpretation Bulletins**: IT-195R4: Rental property — CCA restrictions.

**(15) Leasing properties** — Notwithstanding subsection (1), in no case shall the aggregate of deductions, each of which is a deduction in respect of property of a prescribed class that is leasing property owned by a taxpayer, otherwise allowed to the taxpayer under subsection (1) in computing his income for a taxation year, exceed the amount, if any, by which

(a) the aggregate of amounts each of which is

(i) his income for the year from renting, leasing, or earning royalties from, a leasing property or a property that would be a leasing property but for subsection (18), (19) or (20) where such property is owned by him, computed without regard to paragraph 20(1)(a) of the Act, or

(ii) the income of a partnership for the year from renting, leasing or earning royalties from, a leasing property or a property that would be a leasing property but for subsection (18), (19) or (20) where such property is owned by the partnership, to the extent of the taxpayer's share of such income,

exceeds

(b) the aggregate of amounts each of which is

(i) his loss for the year from renting, leasing or earning royalties from, a property referred to in subparagraph (a)(i), computed without regard to paragraph 20(1)(a) of the Act, or

(ii) the loss of a partnership for the year from renting, leasing or earning royalties from, a property referred to in subparagraph (a)(ii), to the extent of the taxpayer's share of such loss.

**Related Provisions**: Reg. 1100(16) — Exception; Reg. 1100(17), (18) — Meaning of "leasing property".

**Interpretation Bulletins**: IT-147R3: CCA — Accelerated write-off of manufacturing and processing machinery and equipment; IT-195R4: Rental property — CCA restrictions; IT-283R2: CCA — Video tapes, videotape cassettes, films, computer software and master recording media; IT-434R: Rental of real property by individual; IT-443: Leasing property — CCA restrictions.

**(16) [Leasing property — exception]** — Subsection (15) does not apply in respect of a taxation year of a taxpayer that was, throughout the year,

(a) a corporation whose principal business was

(i) renting or leasing of leasing property or property that would be leasing property but for subsection (18), (19) or (20), or

(ii) renting or leasing of property referred to in subparagraph (i) combined with selling and servicing of property of the same general type and description,

if the gross revenue of the corporation for the year from such principal business was not less than 90 per cent of the gross revenue of the corporation for the year from all sources; or

(b) a partnership each member of which was a corporation described in paragraph (a).

**Related Provisions**: Reg. 1100(1.14) — Election; Reg. 1100(2)(a)(v) — Half-year rule inapplicable to specified leasing property.

**Interpretation Bulletins**: IT-267R2: CCA — vessels.

**(17) ["Leasing property"]** — Subject to subsection (18), in this section and section 1101, "leasing property" of a taxpayer or a partnership means depreciable property other than

(a) rental property,

(b) computer software tax shelter property, or

(c) property referred to in paragraph (w) of Class 10 or in paragraph (n) of Class 12 in Schedule II,

where such property is owned by the taxpayer or the partnership, whether jointly with another person or otherwise, if, in the taxation year in respect of which the expression is being applied, the property was used by the taxpayer or the partnership principally for the purpose of gaining or producing gross revenue that is rent, royalty or leasing revenue, but for greater certainty, does not include a property leased by the taxpayer or the partnership to a lessee, in the ordinary course of the taxpayer's or partnership's business of selling goods or rendering services, under an agreement by which the lessee undertakes to use the property to carry on the business of selling, or promoting the sale of, the taxpayer's or partnership's goods or services.

**Proposed Amendment — Reg. 1100(17)(c)**

**Federal budget, Supplementary Information, February 27, 1995**: The elements of the existing film tax incentive to be eliminated for films acquired after 1995 (and films acquired in 1995 in respect of which the new credit is claimed) include the following:

.....

- exemption of Canadian certified productions from the leasing-property rules in Income Tax Regulation 1100(15); ...

**Notes**: This will be accomplished by having a new definition of "Canadian film or video production", defined in Reg. 1106 and listed in Class 10(x), which is not included in Reg. 1100(17)(c) as is Class 10(w). See also repealed ITA 96(2.2)(d)(ii).

**Related Provisions**: Reg. 1100(14) — Meaning of "rental property"; Reg. 1100(17.1), (17.2), (18), (19), (20) — Interpretation; Reg. 1100(20.1) — limitation on CCA claims for computer software tax shelter property; Reg. 1101(5c) — Separate class; Reg. 2411(4)B(e) — Insurers.

**Notes**: Reg. 1100(17)(b) added by P.C. 2000-1000, effective on the same basis as Reg. 1100(20.1).

Former Reg. 1100(17)(b) revoked by P.C. 1989-2464, effective as of the 1994 taxation year. For years before 1994, read:

(b) property of Class 31 or 32 in Schedule II and furniture, fixtures and equipment, if any, located within and ancillary thereto, or

**Interpretation Bulletins**: IT-195R4: Rental property — CCA restrictions; IT-283R2: CCA — Videotapes, videotape cassettes, films, computer software and master recording media.

**(17.1) [Deemed use of property]** — For the purposes of subsection (17), where, in a taxation year, a taxpayer or a partnership has acquired a property

(a) that was not used for any purpose in that year, and

(b) the first use of the property by the taxpayer or the partnership was principally for the purpose of gaining or producing gross revenue that is rent, royalty or leasing revenue,

the property shall be deemed to have been used in the taxation year in which it was acquired principally for the purpose of gaining or producing gross revenue that is rent, royalty or leasing revenue.

**(17.2) [Deemed rent]** — For the purposes of subsections (1.11) and (17), gross revenue derived in a taxation year from

(a) the right of a person or partnership, other than the owner of a property, to use or occupy the property or a part thereof, and

(b) services offered to a person or partnership that are ancillary to the use or occupation by the person or partnership of the property or the part thereof

shall be considered to be rent derived in the year from the property.

**Related Provisions**: Reg. 1100(17.3) — Exception.

**Notes**: Reg. 1100(17.2) amended by P.C. 1991-465, effective for leases entered into after 10:00 p.m. EDST, April 26, 1989, other than leases entered into pursuant to an agreement in writing entered into before that time under which the lessee thereunder has the right to require the lease of the property (and for these purposes a lease in respect of which a material change has been agreed to by the parties thereto effective at any particular time that is after 10:00 p.m. EDST, April 26, 1989 is deemed to have been entered into at that particular time).

**(17.3) [Deemed rent — exception]** — Subsection (17.2) does not apply in any particular taxation year to property owned by

(a) a corporation, where the property is used in a business carried on in the year by the corporation;

(b) an individual, where the property is used in a business carried on in the year by the individual in which he is personally active on a continuous

Division I — Deductions Allowed  Reg. S. 1100(20.1)(b)(ii)

basis throughout that portion of the year during which the business is ordinarily carried on;

(c) a partnership, where the property is used in a business carried on in the year by the partnership if at least ⅔ of the income or loss, as the case may be, of the partnership for the year is included in the determination of the income of

(i) members of the partnership who are individuals that are personally active in the business of the partnership on a continuous basis throughout that portion of the year during which the business is ordinarily carried on, and

(ii) members of the partnership that are corporations.

**(18) [Leasing property — exclusions]** — Leasing property of a taxpayer or a partnership referred to in subsection (17) does not include

(a) property that the taxpayer or the partnership acquired before May 26, 1976 or was obligated to acquire under the terms of an agreement in writing entered into before May 26, 1976;

(b) property the construction, manufacture or production of which was commenced by the taxpayer or the partnership before May 26, 1976 or was commenced under an agreement in writing entered into by the taxpayer or the partnership before May 26, 1976; or

(c) property that the taxpayer or the partnership acquired on or before December 31, 1976 or was obligated to acquire under the terms of an agreement in writing entered into on or before December 31, 1976, if

(i) arrangements, evidenced by writing, respecting the acquisition, construction, manufacture or production of the property had been substantially advanced before May 26, 1976, and

(ii) the taxpayer or the partnership had before May 26, 1976 demonstrated a *bona fide* intention to acquire the property for the purpose of gaining or producing gross revenue that is rent, royalty or leasing revenue.

**(19) [Leasing property — exclusions]** — Notwithstanding subsection (17), a property acquired by a taxpayer

(a) in the course of a reorganization in respect of which, if a dividend were received by a corporation in the course of the reorganization, subsection 55(2) of the Act would not be applicable to the dividend by reason of the application of paragraph 55(3)(b) of the Act, or

(b) from a person with whom the taxpayer was not dealing at arm's length (otherwise than by virtue of a right referred to in paragraph 251(5)(b) of the Act) at the time the property was acquired,

that would otherwise be leasing property of the taxpayer, shall be deemed not to be leasing property of the taxpayer if immediately before it was so acquired by the taxpayer, it was, by virtue of subsection (18) or (20) or this subsection, not a leasing property of the person from whom the property was so acquired.

**Related Provisions**: Reg. 1100(2.21)(a); Reg. 1100(17), (18) — Meaning of "leasing property"; Reg. 1102(20) — Non-arm's length exception.

**Interpretation Bulletins**: IT-443: Leasing property — CCA restrictions.

**(20) [Leasing property — replacement property]** — Notwithstanding subsection (17), a property acquired by a taxpayer or partnership that is a replacement property (within the meaning assigned by subsection 13(4) of the Act), that would otherwise be a leasing property of the taxpayer or partnership, shall be deemed not to be a leasing property of the taxpayer or partnership if the property replaced, referred to in paragraph 13(4)(a) or (b) of the Act, was, by reason of subsection (18) or (19) or this subsection, not a leasing property of the taxpayer or partnership immediately before it was disposed of by the taxpayer or partnership.

**Related Provisions**: Reg. 1100(17), (18) — Meaning of "leasing property".

**Notes**: The words "or this subsection" added to Reg. 1100(20) by P.C. 1994-139, retroactive to 1986, so as to allow a second or subsequent replacement property to qualify as not being a leasing property.

**(20.1) Computer software tax shelter property** — The total of all amounts each of which is a deduction in respect of computer software tax shelter property allowed to the taxpayer under subsection (1) in computing a taxpayer's income for a taxation year shall not exceed the amount, if any, by which

(a) the total of all amounts each of which is

(i) the taxpayer's income for the year from a business in which computer software tax shelter property owned by the taxpayer is used, computed without reference to any deduction under subsection (1) in respect of such property, or

(ii) the income of a partnership from a business in which computer software tax shelter property owned by the partnership is used, to the extent of the taxpayer's share of such income that is included in computing the taxpayer's income for the year,

exceeds

(b) the total of all amounts each of which is

(i) a loss of the taxpayer from a business in which computer software tax shelter property is used, computed without reference to any deduction under subsection (1) in respect of such property, or

(ii) a loss of a partnership from a business in which computer software tax shelter property is used, to the extent of the taxpayer's share of such loss that is included in computing the taxpayer's income for the year.

**Related Provisions**: Reg. 1100(20.2) — Definition of "computer software tax shelter property"; Reg. 1101(5r) — Separate class for all computer software tax shelter property.

**Notes**: Reg. 1100(20.1) added by P.C. 2000-1000, effective for taxation years and fiscal periods that end after August 5, 1997, but not in respect of computer software for taxation years and fiscal periods of a taxpayer of partnership that end in 1997 or 1998 where

(a) the taxpayer's or partnership's interest in the computer software

(i) is acquired before August 6, 1997,

(ii) is acquired before 1998 pursuant to an agreement in writing made by the taxpayer or partnership before August 6, 1997, or

(iii) is, or is associated with, a tax shelter investment (as defined by ITA 143.2(1)) that is acquired by a taxpayer or partnership before 1998 pursuant to

(A) the terms of a document that is a prospectus, preliminary prospectus or registration statement where

(I) the document was filed before August 6, 1997 with a public authority in Canada pursuant to and in accordance with the securities legislation of Canada or of any province and, where required by law, accepted for filing by the public authority before August 6, 1997,

(II) the particular computer software is

1. identified in the document, or

2. acquired before November 29, 1997 from a person that is resident in Canada and that developed the software, and

(III) all the funds raised pursuant to the document are raised before 1998 and all or substantially all of the tax shelter investments that can reasonably be considered to be associated with the computer software are acquired before 1998 by a person who is not

1. a promoter, or an agent of a promoter, of the securities,

2. a vendor of the property,

3. a broker or dealer in securities, or

4. a person who does not deal at arm's length with a person referred to in sub-subclause 1 or 2 [above], or

(B) the terms of an offering memorandum distributed as part of an offering of securities where

(I) the memorandum contained a complete or substantially complete description of the securities contemplated in the offering as well as the terms and conditions of the offering,

(II) the memorandum was distributed before August 6, 1997,

(III) solicitations in respect of the sale of the securities contemplated by the memorandum were made before August 6, 1997,

(IV) the sale of the securities was substantially in accordance with the memorandum,

(V) the particular computer software is

1. identified in the memorandum, or

2. acquired before November 29, 1997 from a person that is resident in Canada and that developed the software, and

(VI) all the funds raised pursuant to the memorandum were raised before 1998 and all or substantially all of the tax shelter investments that can reasonably be considered to be associated with the computer software are acquired before 1998 by a person who is not

1. a promoter, or an agent of a promoter, of the securities,

2. a vendor of the property,

3. a broker or dealer in securities, or

4. a person who does not deal at arm's length with a person referred to in sub-subclause 1 or 2 [above];

(b) there is no agreement or other arrangement under which any of the following obligations can be changed, reduced or waived if there is a change to the Act or if there is an adverse assessment under the Act:

(i) the obligation of the taxpayer or the partnership, with respect to the computer software, or

(ii) the obligation of another taxpayer or partnership that acquires a tax shelter investment (as defined by ITA 143.2(1)) that is associated with computer software, with respect to the tax shelter investment;

(c) the computer software is, or is associated with, one or more tax shelters sold or offered for sale at a time and in circumstances in which ITA 237.1 requires an identification number to have been obtained and the identification number was obtained before that time; and

(d) the computer software (including computer software to which subparagraph (a)(i) or (ii) applies) is, or is associated with, a tax shelter investment (as defined by ITA 143.2(1)) sold or offered for sale pursuant to a document or offering memorandum described in subparagraph (a)(iii) and either

(i) the total amount of securities sold in 1997 pursuant to the document or offering memorandum does not exceed $100,000,000, or

(ii) at least 10% of the securities authorized to be sold in 1997 pursuant to the document or offering memorandum were in 1997 and before August 6, 1997 sold to, or subscribed for by, a person who is not

(A) a promoter, or an agent of a promoter, of the securities,

(B) a vendor of the computer software,

(C) a broker or dealer in securities, or

(D) a person who does not deal at arm's length with any person referred to in clause (A) or (B).

For purposes of the above rule, computer software is deemed to be acquired by a taxpayer or partnership no earlier than the time and only to the extent that its cost is considered to be an expenditure made or incurred by the taxpayer or partnership for the purposes of the ITA, determined without reference to Reg. 1100(20.1).

## (20.2) ["Computer software tax shelter property"] — For the purpose of this Part, computer software tax shelter property is computer software that is depreciable property of a prescribed class of a person or partnership where

(a) the person's or partnership's interest in the property is a tax shelter investment (as defined by subsection 143.2(1) of the Act) determined without reference to subsection (20.1); or

Division I — Deductions Allowed  Reg. S. 1100(21)(d)

(b) an interest in the person or partnership is a tax shelter investment (as defined by subsection 143.2(1) of the Act) determined without reference to subsection (20.1).

**Related Provisions**: Reg. 1100(20.1) — Limitation on CCA claim; Reg. 1101(5r) — Separate class for all computer software tax shelter property; Reg. 1104(2) — Definition of "computer software".

**Notes**: Reg. 1100(20.2) added by P.C. 2000-1000, effective on the same basis as Reg. 1100(20.1).

**(21) Certified films and video tapes** — Notwithstanding subsection (1), where a taxpayer (in this subsection and subsection (22) referred to as the "investor") has acquired property of Class 10 or 12 in Schedule II that is a certified feature film or certified production (in this subsection and subsection (22) referred to as the "film or tape"), in no case shall the deduction in respect of property of that class otherwise allowed to the investor by virtue of subsection (1) in computing the investor's income for a particular taxation year exceed the amount that it would be if the capital cost to the investor of the film or tape were reduced by the aggregate of amounts, each of which is

(a) where the principal photography or taping of the film or tape is not completed before the end of the particular taxation year, the amount, if any, by which

(i) the capital cost to the investor of the film or tape as of the end of the year

exceeds the aggregate of

(ii) where the principal photography or taping of the film or tape is completed within 60 days after the end of the year, the amount that may reasonably be considered to be the investor's proportionate share of the production costs incurred in respect of the film or tape before the end of the year,

(iii) where the principal photography or taping of the film or tape is not completed within 60 days after the end of the year, the amount that may reasonably be considered to be the investor's proportionate share of the lesser of

(A) the production costs incurred in respect of the film or tape before the end of the year, and

(B) the proportion of the production costs incurred to the date the principal photography or taping is completed that the percentage of the principal photography or taping completed as of the end of the year, as certified by the Minister of Communications, is of 100 per cent, and

(iv) the aggregate of amounts determined under paragraphs (b), (c) and (d) in respect of the film or tape as of the end of the year;

(b) where, at any time before the later of

(i) the date the principal photography or taping of the film or tape is completed, and

(ii) the date the investor acquired the film or tape,

a revenue guarantee (other than a revenue guarantee that is certified by the Minister of Communications to be a guarantee under which the person who agrees to provide the revenue is a licensed broadcaster or *bona fide* film or tape distributor) is entered into in respect of the film or tape whereby it may reasonably be considered certain, having regard to all the circumstances, that the investor will receive revenue under the terms of the revenue guarantee, the amount, if any, that may reasonably be considered to be the portion of the revenue that has not been included in the investor's income in the particular taxation year or a previous taxation year;

(c) where, at any time, a revenue guarantee, other than

(i) a revenue guarantee in respect of which paragraph (b) applies, or

(ii) a revenue guarantee under which the person (in this subsection referred to as the "guarantor") who agrees to provide the revenue under the terms of the guarantee is a person who does not deal at arm's length with either the investor or the person from whom the investor acquired the film or tape (in this subsection referred to as the "vendor") and in respect of which the Minister of Communications certifies that

(A) the guarantor is a licensed broadcaster or *bona fide* film or tape distributor, and

(B) the cost of the film or tape does not include any amount for or in respect of the guarantee,

is entered into in respect of the film or tape, the amount, if any, that may reasonably be considered to be the portion of the revenue that is to be received by the investor under the terms of the revenue guarantee that has not been included in the investor's income in the particular taxation year or a preceding taxation year, if

(iii) the guarantor and the investor are not dealing at arm's length,

(iv) the vendor and the guarantor are not dealing at arm's length, or

(v) the vendor or a person not dealing at arm's length with the vendor undertakes in any way, directly or indirectly, to fulfil all or any part of the guarantor's obligations under the terms of the revenue guarantee; and

(d) where, at any time, a revenue guarantee, other than a revenue guarantee in respect of which paragraph (b) or (c) applies, is entered into in respect of the film or tape, the amount, if any, that may

**Reg. S. 1100(21)(d)** — Income Tax Regulations, Part XI

reasonably be considered to be the portion of the revenue that is to be received by the investor under the terms of the revenue guarantee that

(i) is not due to the investor until a time that is more than four years after the first day on which the guarantor has the right to the use of the film or tape, and

(ii) has not been included in the investor's income in the particular taxation year or a previous taxation year.

### Proposed Addition — Reg. 1100(21)(e)

(e) the portion of any debt obligation of the investor outstanding at the end of the particular year that is convertible into an interest in the film or tape or in the investor.

**Application**: The September 27, 1994 draft legislation (tax shelters and CCA — films and video tape) will add para. 1100(21)(e), applicable to property acquired by a taxpayer or partnership after February 21, 1994, other than property so acquired before 1995

(a) by a taxpayer or a partnership pursuant to the terms of a written agreement entered into by the taxpayer or partnership before February 22, 1994,

(b) by a partnership pursuant to the terms of a prospectus, preliminary prospectus or registration statement filed before February 22, 1994 with a public authority in Canada pursuant to and in accordance with the securities legislation of Canada or of any province, and, where required by law, accepted for filing by such public authority, or

(c) by a partnership pursuant to the terms of an offering memorandum distributed as part of an offering of securities where

(i) the memorandum contained a complete or substantially complete description of the securities contemplated in the offering as well as the terms and conditions of the offering,

(ii) the memorandum was distributed before February 22, 1994,

(iii) solicitations in respect of the sale of the securities contemplated by the memorandum were made before February 22, 1994,

(iv) the sale of the securities was substantially in accordance with the memorandum, and

(v) the funds raised pursuant to the terms of the memorandum are so raised before 1995.

Notwithstanding the above,

(a) para. 1100(21)(e) applies after 1994 in respect of property acquired at any time by a partnership where [draft] ITA subsec. 40(3.1) does not apply to a member of the partnership before the end of the partnership's fifth fiscal period ending after 1994 by reason only of the application of Bill C-59, subsec. 12(6) (the coming-into-force of subsec. 40(3.1)), and

(b) para. 1100(21)(e) applies after 1994 in respect of property acquired after February 21, 1994 and before 1995 by a partnership pursuant to an agreement in writing entered into by the partnership after February 21, 1994 and before 1995, where

(i) paras. 1100(21)(1)(a) to (c) do not otherwise apply,

(ii) the partnership interests are acquired before 1995,

(iii) all or substantially all of the property (other than money) of the partnership is a film production or an interest in one or more partnerships all or substantially all of the property of which is a film production,

(iv) the principal photography of the production (or in the case of a production that is a television series, an episode of the series) commences before 1995,

(v) the funds used to produce the film production are raised before 1995 and the principal photography of the production is completed, and the funds are expended, before 1995 (or, in the case of a film production prescribed for the purpose of ITA subpara. 96(2.2)(d)(ii), the principal photography of the production is completed, and the funds are expended, before March 2, 1995),

and either

(vi) the producer of the production has, before February 22, 1994, entered into a written agreement for the pre-production, distribution, broadcasting, financing or acquisition of the production or the acquisition of the screenplay for the production (or has entered into a written contract before February 22, 1994 with a screenwriter to write the screenplay for the production),

(vii) the producer of the production receives before 1995 a commitment for funding or other government assistance (or an advance ruling or active status letter in respect of eligibility for such funding or other government assistance) for the production from a federal or provincial government agency the mandate of which is related to the provision of assistance to film productions in Canada, or

(viii) the production is a continuation of a television series an episode of which satisfies the requirements of subpara. (vi).

**Technical Notes**: Subsection 1100(21) requires that the depreciable cost of a taxpayer's interest in a certified feature film or certified production be reduced by certain amounts, including certain revenue guarantees provided in respect of the investment.

Subsection 1100(21) is amended to require that the depreciable cost of such an interest be reduced by the portion of any debt obligation of the investor outstanding at the end of a particular year that is convertible into an interest in the film or tape or the taxpayer.

**Federal budget, Supplementary Information, February 22, 1994**: The federal government is committed to the continued viability of the Canadian film industry. Currently, assistance is provided to the industry through direct expenditure programs as well as income tax incentives for certified Canadian films. The government is concerned, however, that film financing mechanisms have been developed to provide tax benefits to investors in excess of those contemplated when the incentives were introduced and in a manner inconsistent with the limited partnership at-risk rules. Generally, these financings depend on an overallocation of benefits to investors through the use of convertible debt.

In particular, some film limited partnerships have raised debt that is convertible into interests in the partnership. After the tax benefits and cash distributions have been allocated to the original limited partners, the lender converts its loan into a partnership interest. In effect, proceeds from convertible loans are used to acquire films or video tapes at a capital cost which is, when allocated to the original limited partners in the form of capital cost allowance (CCA), in excess of the amount that would otherwise be allocated to such limited partners if the lender were considered to be a partner from the time the loan was made. The combination of this excess allocation of CCA to the original limited partners and the distribution of revenue to those partners ensures that the original limited partners have little or no investment risk.

Accordingly, this budget proposes to amend the *Income Tax Regulations* to reduce the capital cost of a film or video tape acquired after February 22, 1994 by the amount of any loan that is convertible into an interest in the film or a partnership that holds the film or video tape until such time as the convertible loan is exchanged for a partnership interest or repaid. Transitional relief will be provided for property acquired pursuant to an agreement in writing entered into before February 22, 1994 or pursuant to a prospectus, preliminary prospectus, registration statement or offering memorandum filed before February 22, 1994 and where required by law, accepted for filing by a public authority in Canada pursuant to and in accordance with securities legislation of Canada or of any province.

### Proposed Amendment — Reg. 1100(21)

**Federal budget, Supplementary Information, February 27, 1995**: The elements of the existing film tax incentive to be eliminated for films acquired after 1995 (and films acquired in 1995 in respect of which the new credit is claimed) include the following:

. . . . .

- exemption from the reduction of CCA in respect of certain revenue guarantees under Income Tax Regulation 1100(21).

**Notes**: This will be accomplished by having a new definition of "Canadian film or video production", defined in Reg. 1106 and listed in Class 10(x), which is not a "certified production" as listed in the opening words of Reg. 1100(21). See also repealed 96(2.2)(d)(ii).

**Related Provisions**: ITA 125.4(4) — No Canadian film/video production credit to corporation if investor can claim deduction; Reg. 225(1) — Information return; Reg. 1100(21.1) — Depreciable cost reduced by outstanding debt obligation; Reg. 1100(23); Reg. 1104(2) — "certified feature film", "certified production"; Reg. 1104(10) — Interpretation.

**Notes**: The *Department of Canadian Heritage Act* (S.C. 1995, c. 11), in force July 12, 1996, provides:

46. Other references — Every reference made to the Minister of Communications, the Minister of Multiculturalism and Citizenship and the Secretary of State of Canada in relation to any matter to which the powers, duties and functions of the Minister of Canadian Heritage extend by virtue of this Act, in any other Act of Parliament or in any order, regulation or other instrument made under any Act of Parliament shall, unless the context otherwise requires, be read as a reference to the Minister of Canadian Heritage.

**Forms**: T1-CP Summ: Return in respect of certified productions.

### Proposed Addition — Reg. 1100(21.1)

**(21.1) [Film or videotape — deemed cost reduction]** — Notwithstanding subsection (1), where a taxpayer has acquired property described in paragraph (s) of Class 10, in Schedule II, or in paragraph (m) of Class 12, in Schedule II, in no case shall the deduction in respect of the property otherwise allowed to the taxpayer under subsection (1) in computing the taxpayer's income for a taxation year exceed the amount that it would be if the capital cost to the taxpayer of the property were reduced by the portion of any debt obligation of the taxpayer outstanding at the end of the year that is convertible into an interest in the property or the taxpayer.

**Application**: The September 27, 1994 draft legislation (tax shelters and CCA) will add subsec. 1100(21.1), applicable to property acquired by a taxpayer or partnership after February 21, 1994, other than property so acquired before 1995

(a) by a taxpayer or a partnership pursuant to the terms of a written agreement entered into by the taxpayer or partnership before February 22, 1994,

(b) by a partnership pursuant to the terms of a prospectus, preliminary prospectus or registration statement filed before February 22, 1994 with a public authority in Canada pursuant to and in accordance with the securities legislation of Canada or of any province, and, where required by law, accepted for filing by such public authority, or

(c) by a partnership pursuant to the terms of an offering memorandum distributed as part of an offering of securities where

(i) the memorandum contained a complete or substantially complete description of the securities contemplated in the offering as well as the terms and conditions of the offering,

(ii) the memorandum was distributed before February 22, 1994,

(iii) solicitations in respect of the sale of the securities contemplated by the memorandum were made before February 22, 1994,

(iv) the sale of the securities was substantially in accordance with the memorandum, and

(v) the funds raised pursuant to the terms of the memorandum are so raised before 1995.

Notwithstanding the above,

(a) subsec. 1100(21.1) applies after 1994 in respect of property acquired at any time by a partnership where [draft] ITA subsec. 40(3.1) does not apply to a member of the partnership before the end of the partnership's fifth fiscal period ending after 1994 by reason only of the application of Bill C-59, subsection 12(6) (the coming-into-force of subsec. 40(3.1)), and

(b) subsec. 1100(21.1) applies after 1994 in respect of property acquired after February 21, 1994 and before 1995 by a partnership pursuant to an agreement in writing entered into by the partnership after February 21, 1994 and before 1995, where

(i) paras. 1100(21)(1)(a) to (c) do not otherwise apply,

(ii) the partnership interests are acquired before 1995,

(iii) all or substantially all of the property (other than money) of the partnership is a film production or an interest in one or more partnerships all or substantially all of the property of which is a film production,

(iv) the principal photography of the production (or in the case of a production that is a television series, an episode of the series) commences before 1995,

(v) the funds used to produce the film production are raised before 1995 and the principal photography of the production is completed, and the funds are expended, before 1995 (or, in the case of a film production prescribed for the purpose of ITA subpara. 96(2.2)(d)(ii), the principal photography of the production is completed, and the funds are expended, before March 2, 1995),

and either

(vi) the producer of the production has, before February 22, 1994, entered into a written agreement for the pre-production, distribution, broadcasting, financing or acquisition of the production or the acquisition of the screenplay for the production (or has entered into a writ-

**Reg. S. 1100(21.1)** — Income Tax Regulations, Part XI

ten contract before February 22, 1994 with a screenwriter to write the screenplay for the production),

(vii) the producer of the production receives before 1995 a commitment for funding or other government assistance (or an advance ruling or active status letter in respect of eligibility for such funding or other government assistance) for the production from a federal or provincial government agency the mandate of which is related to the provision of assistance to film productions in Canada, or

(viii) the production is a continuation of a television series an episode of which satisfies the requirements of subpara. (vi).

**Technical Notes**: New subsection 1100(21.1) requires that the depreciable cost of a taxpayer's interest in a non-certified motion picture film or video tape, or motion picture film or video tape that is a television commercial message, be reduced by the portion of any debt obligation of the taxpayer outstanding at the end of a particular year that is convertible into an interest in the film or tape or the taxpayer.

**(22) [Film or tape acquired before 1979]** — Notwithstanding subsection (1), where an investor has acquired a film or tape after his 1977 taxation year and before 1979 and the principal photography or taping in respect of the film or tape is completed after a particular taxation year and not later than March 1, 1979, in no case shall the deduction in respect of property of Class 12 in Schedule II otherwise allowed to the investor by virtue of subsection (1) in computing his income for the particular taxation year exceed the amount, otherwise determined, if the capital cost to the investor of the film or tape were reduced by the amount, if any, by which

(a) the capital cost to the investor of the film or tape as of the end of the year

exceeds

(b) the amount that may reasonably be considered to be the investor's proportionate share of the production costs incurred in respect of the film or tape to March 1, 1979.

**Related Provisions**: Reg. 1100(21) — Meaning of "investor" and "film or tape".

**Interpretation Bulletins**: IT-441: CCA — Certified feature film productions and certified short productions.

**Forms**: T1-CP Summ: Return in respect of certified productions.

**(23) [Film or tape acquired in 1987 or 1988]** — For the purposes of paragraph (21)(a),

(a) in respect of a film or tape acquired in 1987, other than a film or tape in respect of which paragraph (b) applies, the references in paragraph (21)(a) to "within 60 days after the end of the year" shall be read as references to "before July, 1988"; and

(b) in respect of a film or tape acquired in 1987 or 1988 that is included in paragraph (n) of Class 12 in Schedule II and that is part of a series of films or tapes that includes another property included in that paragraph, the references in paragraph (21)(a) to "within 60 days after the end of the year" shall be read as references to "before 1989".

**(24) Specified energy property** — Notwithstanding subsection (1), in no case shall the total of deductions, each of which is a deduction in respect of property of Class 34 or Class 43.1 in Schedule II that is specified energy property owned by a taxpayer, otherwise allowed to the taxpayer under subsection (1) in computing the taxpayer's income for a taxation year, exceed the amount, if any, by which

(a) the total of all amounts each of which is

(i) the total of

(A) the amount that would be the income of the taxpayer for the year from property described in Class 34 or 43.1 in Schedule II (other than specified energy property), or from the business of selling the product of that property, if that income were calculated after deducting the maximum amount allowable in respect of the property for the year under paragraph 20(1)(a) of the Act, and

(B) the taxpayer's income for the year from specified energy property or from the business of selling the product of that property, computed without regard to paragraph 20(1)(a) of the Act, or

(ii) the total of

(A) the taxpayer's share of the amount that would be the income of a partnership for the year from property described in Class 34 or 43.1 in Schedule II (other than specified energy property), or from the business of selling the product of that property, if that income were calculated after deducting the maximum amount allowable in respect of the property for the year under paragraph 20(1)(a) of the Act, and

(B) the income of a partnership for the year from specified energy property or from the business of selling the product of that property of the partnership, to the extent of the taxpayer's share of that income,

exceeds

(b) the total of all amounts each of which is

(i) the taxpayer's loss for the year from specified energy property or from the business of selling the product of that property, computed without regard to paragraph 20(1)(a) of the Act, or

(ii) the loss of a partnership for the year from specified energy property or from the business of selling the product of that property of the partnership, to the extent of the taxpayer's share of that loss.

**Related Provisions**: Reg. 1100(25) — Meaning of "specified energy property"; Reg. 1100(26) — Exception.

**Notes**: Reg. 1100(24) amended by P.C. 1997-1033, effective February 22, 1994. The essence of the change was to add references to Class 43.1 in addition to Class 34. Before that date, for taxation years ending after February 9, 1988, read Reg. 1100(24)(a)(i)(A) as "the taxpayer's designated Class 34 income for the year, and"; read Reg. 1100(24)(a)(ii)(A) as "the designated Class 34 income of a partnership for the year, to the extent of the taxpayer's share of such income, and"; and read the following closing words at the end of 1100(24):

> and, for the purpose of this subsection, "designated Class 34 income" means the amount that would be the income of the taxpayer or partnership, as the case may be, from property described in Class 34 (other than specified energy property) or from the business of selling the product of such property, if that income were calculated after deducting the maximum amount allowable in respect thereof for the year under paragraph 20(1)(a) of the Act.

**(25) ["Specified energy property"]** — Subject to subsections (27) to (29), in this section and section 1101, "specified energy property" of a taxpayer or partnership (in this subsection referred to as "the owner") for a taxation year means property of Class 34 or Class 43.1 in Schedule II that was acquired by the owner after February 9, 1988 other than a particular property

(a) acquired to be used by the owner primarily for the purpose of gaining or producing income from a business carried on in Canada (other than the business of selling the product of the particular property) or from another property situated in Canada, or

(b) leased in the year, in the ordinary course of carrying on a business of the owner in Canada, to

(i) a person who can reasonably be expected to use the property primarily for the purpose of gaining or producing income from a business carried on in Canada (other than the business of selling the product of the particular property) or from another property situated in Canada, or

(ii) a corporation or partnership described in subsection (26),

where the owner was

(iii) a corporation whose principal business was, throughout the year,

(A) the renting or leasing of leasing property or property that would be leasing property but for subsection (18), (19) or (20),

(B) the renting or leasing of property referred to in clause (A) combined with the selling and servicing of property of the same general type and description, or

(C) the manufacturing of property described in Class 34 or Class 43.1 in Schedule II that it sells or leases,

and the gross revenue of the corporation for the year from that principal business was not less than 90 per cent of the gross revenue of the corporation for the year from all sources, or

(iv) a partnership each member of which was a corporation described in subparagraph (iii) or paragraph (26)(a).

**Related Provisions**: Reg. 1101(5m) — Separate class.

**Notes**: References to Class 43.1 added to opening words and to Reg. 1100(25)(b)(iii)(C) by P.C. 1997-1033, effective February 22, 1994.

**(26) [Specified energy property — exception]** — Subsection (24) does not apply to a taxation year of a taxpayer that was, throughout the year,

(a) a corporation whose principal business throughout the year was

(i) manufacturing or processing,

(ii) mining operations, or

(iii) the sale, distribution or production of electricity, natural gas, oil, steam, heat or any other form of energy or potential energy; or

(b) a partnership each member of which was a corporation described in paragraph (a).

**Related Provisions**: Reg. 1104(9) — Meaning of "manufacturing and processing".

**Notes**: Reg. 1100(26)(a)(i) and (ii) added by P.C. 1997-1033, effective for taxation years ending after March 6, 1996.

**(27) [Specified energy property — acquisition before 1990]** — Specified energy property of a person or partnership does not include property acquired by the person or partnership after February 9, 1988 and before 1990

(a) pursuant to an obligation in writing entered into by the person or partnership before February 10, 1988;

(b) pursuant to the terms of a prospectus, preliminary prospectus, registration statement or offering memorandum filed before February 10, 1988 with a public authority in Canada pursuant to and in accordance with the securities legislation of any province;

(c) pursuant to the terms of an offering memorandum distributed as part of an offering of securities where

(i) the offering memorandum contained a complete or substantially complete description of the securities contemplated in the offering as well as the terms and conditions of the offering of the securities,

(ii) the offering memorandum was distributed before February 10, 1988,

(iii) solicitations in respect of the sale of the securities contemplated by the offering memorandum were made before February 10, 1988, and,

(iv) the sale of the securities was substantially in accordance with the offering memorandum; or

(d) as part of a project where, before February 10, 1988,

(i) some of the machinery or equipment to be used in the project had been acquired, or agreements in writing for the acquisition of that machinery or equipment had been entered into, by or on behalf of the person or partnership, and

(ii) an approval had been received by or on behalf of the person or partnership from a government environmental authority in respect of the location of the project.

**Related Provisions**: Reg. 1100(17) — Meaning of "leasing property".

**(28) [Specified energy property — exclusion]** — A property acquired by a taxpayer

(a) in the course of a reorganization in respect of which, if a dividend were received by a corporation in the course of the reorganization, subsection 55(2) of the Act would not be applicable to the dividend by reason of the application of paragraph 55(3)(b) of the Act, or

(b) from a person with whom the taxpayer was not dealing at arm's length (otherwise than by virtue of a right referred to in paragraph 251(5)(b) of the Act) at the time the property was acquired

that would otherwise be specified energy property of the taxpayer shall be deemed not to be specified energy property of the taxpayer if, immediately before it was so acquired by the taxpayer, it was not, by virtue of subsection (27), this subsection or subsection (29), specified energy property of the person from whom the property was so acquired.

**(29) [Specified energy property — replacement property]** — A property acquired by a taxpayer or partnership that is a replacement property (within the meaning assigned by subsection 13(4) of the Act), that would otherwise be specified energy property of the taxpayer or partnership, shall be deemed not to be specified energy property of the taxpayer or partnership if the property replaced, referred to in paragraph 13(4)(a) or (b) of the Act, was, by virtue of subsection (27), (28) or this subsection, not specified energy property of the taxpayer or partnership immediately before it was disposed of by the taxpayer or partnership.

**Definitions [Reg. 1100]**: "additional property" — Reg. 1100(1.19)(a); "amount" — ITA 248(1); "arm's length" — ITA 251(1), Reg. 1102(20); "associated" — ITA 256; "broadcasting" — Interpretation Act 35(1); "business" — ITA 248(1); "Canada" — ITA 255, Interpretation Act 35(1); "Canadian" — Reg. 1104(10)(a), (c.2); "capital cost" — Reg. 1100(1)(b), 1100(1.13), 1102(4), (7); "certified feature film", "certified production" — Reg. 1104(2); "class" — Reg. 1101(6), 1102(1)–(3), (14), (14.1); "commencement" — Interpretation Act 35(1); "computer software" — Reg. 1100(2); "computer software tax shelter property" — Reg. 1100(20.2); "corporation" — ITA 248(1), Interpretation Act 35(1); "depreciable property" — ITA 13(21), 248(1); "designated property" — Reg. 1100(1)(ta), (zc); "disposed" — ITA 248(1)"disposition"; "disposes" — ITA 248(1)"disposition"; "disposition" — ITA 248(1); "dividend" — ITA 248(1); "end of the taxation year" — Reg. 1104(1); "exempt property" — Reg. 1100(1.13)(a); "film or tape" — Reg. 1100(21); "fiscal period" — ITA 249.1; "gross revenue" — ITA 248(1); "guarantor" — Reg. 1100(21)(c)(ii); "income from a mine" — Reg. 1104(5), (6.1)(a); "individual" — ITA 248(1); "industrial mineral mine" — Reg. 1104(3); "investor" — Reg. 1100(21); "leasing property" — Reg. 1100(17)–(20); "life insurance corporation" — ITA 248(1); "manufacturing or processing" — Reg. 1104(9); "mine" — Reg. 1104(7); "mineral", "mining" — Reg. 1104(3); "Minister" — ITA 248(1); "month" — Interpretation Act 35(1); "motor vehicle", "office" — ITA 248(1); "original lease" — Reg. 1100(1.2)(a); "original property" — Reg. 1100(1.17), (1.19)(a); "owner" — Reg. 1100(25); "Parliament" — Interpretation Act 35(1); "particular time", "particular year" — Reg. 1100(1.1)(a)(ii); "person" — ITA 248(1), Reg. 1100(1.16); "prescribed" — ITA 248(1); "prescribed rate" — Reg. 4301, 4302; "principal amount", "property" — ITA 248(1); "province" — Interpretation Act 35(1); "radio" — Interpretation Act 35(1); "railway system" — Reg. 1104(2); "received or receivable" — Reg. 1100(1.18); "related" — ITA 251(2)–(6); "remuneration" — Reg. 1104(10)(c); "rent" — Reg. 1100(14.1), (17.2); "rental property" — Reg. 1100(14); "replacement property" — Reg. 1100(1.17); "resident in Canada" — ITA 250; "revenue guarantee" — Reg. 1104(10)(c.1); "share" — Reg. 1100(1.11); "specified energy property" — Reg. 1100(25), (27)–(29); "specified leasing property" — Reg. 1100(1.11); "systems software" — Reg. 1104(2); "tax shelter" — ITA 237.1(1), 248(1); "taxation year" — ITA 249, Reg. 1104(1); "taxpayer" — ITA 248(1); "undepreciated capital cost" — ITA 13(21), 248(1); "unit of production" — Reg. 1104(10)(d); "vendor" — Reg. 1100(21)(c)(ii); "within 60 days after the end of the year" — Reg. 1100(23)(a), (b); "writing", "written" — Interpretation Act 35(1)"writing".

**Interpretation Bulletins [Reg. 1100]**: IT-474R: Amalgamations of Canadian corporations.

## 1100A. Exempt mining income — (1) [Revoked]

(2) Any election under subparagraph 13(21)(f)(vi) [13(21)"undepreciated capital cost"H] of the Act in respect of property of a prescribed class acquired by a corporation for the purpose of gaining or producing income from a mine shall be made by filing with the Minister, not later than the day on or before which the corporation is required to file a return of income pursuant to section 150 of the Act for its taxation year in which the exempt period in respect of the mine ended, one of the following documents in duplicate:

(a) where the directors of the corporation are legally entitled to administer the affairs of the corporation, a certified copy of their resolution authorizing the election to be made in respect of that class; and

(b) where the directors of the corporation are not legally entitled to administer the affairs of the corporation, a certified copy of the authorization of the making of the election in respect of that class by the person or persons legally entitled to administer the affairs of the corporation.

**Related Provisions**: Reg. 1100(1)(w), (x).

**Definitions [Reg. 1100A]**: "class" — Reg. 1101(6), 1102(1)–(3), (14), (14.1); "corporation" — ITA 248(1), Interpretation Act 35(1); "Minister", "person", "prescribed", "property" — ITA 248(1); "taxation year" — ITA 249, Reg. 1104(1).

## DIVISION II — SEPARATE CLASSES

**Notes**: Reg. 1101 prescribes property to be in a "separate class", and not pooled with other property that would otherwise be in the same class in Schedule II. The principal effect is that on disposition of such a property, recapture of depreciation (under ITA 13(1)) or a terminal loss (under ITA 20(16)) is available for the property without regard to the other properties of the same class that the taxpayer owns. See also ITA 37(6) re R&D expenditures.

Separate classes are also deemed into existence under ITA 13(5)(b)(ii), 13(5.2)(c), 13(14), 13(21.2)(e)(ii) and 37(6).

**1101. (1) Businesses and properties** — Where more than one property of a taxpayer is described in the same class in Schedule II and where

(a) one of the properties was acquired for the purpose of gaining or producing income from a business, and

(b) one of the properties was acquired for the purpose of gaining or producing income from another business or from the property,

a separate class is hereby prescribed for the properties that

(c) were acquired for the purpose of gaining or producing income from each business, and

(d) would otherwise be included in the class.

**Related Provisions**: Reg. 1101(1a) — Insurance businesses.

**Interpretation Bulletins**: IT-206R: Separate businesses; IT-218R: Profit, capital gains and losses from the sale of real estate, including farmland and inherited land and conversion of real estate from capital property to inventory and vice versa.

**(1a) [Life insurance business deemed corporate business]** — For the purposes of subsection (1),

(a) a life insurance business, and

(b) an insurance business other than a life insurance business,

shall each be regarded as a separate business.

**(1ab) [Partnership property separate]** — Where, at the end of 1971, more than one property of a taxpayer who was a member of a partnership at that time is described in the same class in Schedule II and where

(a) one of the properties can reasonably be regarded to be the interest of the taxpayer in a depreciable property that is partnership property of the partnership, and

(b) one of the properties is property other than property referred to in paragraph (a),

a separate class is hereby prescribed for all properties each of which

(c) is a property referred to in paragraph (a); and

(d) would otherwise be included in the class.

**(1ac) [Rental property over $50,000]** — Subject to subsection (5h), where more than one property of a taxpayer is described in the same class in Schedule II, and one or more of the properties is a rental property of the taxpayer the capital cost of which to the taxpayer was not less than $50,000, a separate class is hereby prescribed for each such rental property of the taxpayer that would otherwise be included in the same class, other than a rental property that was acquired by the taxpayer before 1972 or that is

(a) a building or an interest therein, or

(b) a leasehold interest acquired by the taxpayer by reason of the fact that the taxpayer erected a building on leased land,

erection of which building was commenced by the taxpayer before 1972 or pursuant to an agreement in writing entered into by the taxpayer before 1972.

**Related Provisions**: Reg. 1100(14) — Meaning of "rental property"; Reg. 1101(1ad) — Exceptions.

**Interpretation Bulletins**: IT-274R: Rental property — Capital cost of $50,000 or more; IT-304R2: Condominiums.

**(1ad) [Rental property over $50,000 — exception]** — Notwithstanding subsection (1ac), a rental property acquired by a taxpayer

(a) in the course of a reorganization in respect of which, if a dividend were received by a corporation in the course of the reorganization, subsection 55(2) of the Act would not be applicable to the dividend by reason of the application of paragraph 55(3)(b) of the Act, or

(b) from a person with whom the taxpayer was not dealing at arm's length (otherwise than by virtue of a right referred to in paragraph 251(5)(b) of the Act) at the time the property was acquired,

that would otherwise be rental property of the taxpayer of a separate class prescribed under subsection (1ac), shall be deemed not to be property of a separate class prescribed under that subsection if, immediately before it was so acquired by the taxpayer, it was a rental property of the person from whom the property was so acquired of a prescribed class other than a separate class prescribed under that subsection.

**Related Provisions**: Reg. 1100(2.21)(a); Reg. 1100(14) — Meaning of "rental property"; Reg. 1102(20) — Non-arm's length exception.

**Interpretation Bulletins**: IT-274R: Rental properties — Capital cost of $50,000 or more.

**(1ae) [Rental property separate]** — Except in the case of a corporation or partnership described in subsection 1100(12), where more than one property of a taxpayer is described in the same class in Schedule II and where

(a) one of the properties is a rental property other than a property of a separate class prescribed under subsection (1ac), and

(b) one of the properties is a property other than rental property,

a separate class is hereby prescribed for properties that

(c) are described in paragraph (a); and

(d) would otherwise be included in the class.

**Related Provisions**: Reg. 1100(14) — Meaning of "rental property".

**Interpretation Bulletins**: IT-195R4: Rental property — CCA restrictions; IT-304R2: Condominiums.

**(1af) [Expensive automobiles]** — A separate class is hereby prescribed for each property included in Class 10.1 in Schedule II.

**Notes**: See Notes to ITA 13(7)(g).

**Interpretation Bulletins**: IT-521R: Motor vehicle expenses claimed by self-employed individuals; IT-522R: Vehicle, travel and sales expenses of employees.

**(2) Fishing vessels** — Where a property of a taxpayer that would otherwise be included in Class 7 in Schedule II is a property in respect of which a depreciation allowance could have been taken under Order in Council

(a) P.C. 2798 of April 10, 1942,

(b) P.C. 7580 of August 26, 1942, as amended by P.C. 3297 of April 22, 1943, or

(c) P.C. 3979 of June 1, 1944,

if those Orders in Council were applicable to the taxation year, a separate class is hereby prescribed for each property, including the furniture, fittings and equipment attached thereto.

**Related Provisions**: Reg. 1100(1)(i).

**(2a) Canadian vessels** — A separate class is hereby prescribed for each vessel of a taxpayer, including the furniture, fittings, radiocommunication equipment and other equipment attached thereto, that

(a) was constructed in Canada;

(b) is registered in Canada; and

(c) had not been used for any purpose whatever before it was acquired by the taxpayer.

**Related Provisions**: Reg. 1100(1)(v) — additional allowance; Reg. 4601(e)(iii) — Investment tax credit — qualified transportation equipment.

**Notes**: Opening words of Reg. 1101(2a) amended by P.C. 1994-139, effective July 14, 1990, to change "in respect of which the Minister of Industry, Trade and Commerce certifies that the vessel" to "that". Accelerated CCA for vessels and conversion costs is now verified by Revenue Canada as part of the normal audit process.

**Interpretation Bulletins**: IT-267R2: CCA — vessels.

**Advance Tax Rulings**: ATR-52: Accelerated rate of CCA for vessels.

**(2b) Offshore drilling vessels** — A separate class is hereby prescribed for all vessels described in Class 7 in Schedule II, including the furniture, fittings, radiocommunication equipment and other equipment attached thereto, acquired by a taxpayer

(a) after May 25, 1976 and designed principally for the purpose of

(i) determining the existence, location, extent or quality of accumulations of petroleum or natural gas (other than mineral resources); or

(ii) drilling oil or gas wells; or

(b) after May 22, 1979 and designed principally for the purpose of determining the existence, location, extent or quality of mineral resources.

**Related Provisions**: Reg. 1100(1)(va).

**Interpretation Bulletins**: IT-267R2: CCA — Vessels; IT-317R: Radio and television equipment.

**(3) Timber limits and cutting rights** — For the purposes of this Part and Schedules IV and VI, each property of a taxpayer that is

(a) a timber limit other than a timber resource property, or

(b) a right to cut timber from a limit other than a right that is a timber resource property,

is hereby prescribed to be a separate class of property.

**Related Provisions**: Reg. 1100(1)(e) — Capital cost allowance.

**Interpretation Bulletins**: IT-469R: CCA — Earth-moving equipment; IT-481: Timber resource property and timber limits.

**(4) Industrial mineral mines** — For the purposes of this Part and Schedule V, where a taxpayer has

(a) more than one industrial mineral mine in respect of which he may claim an allowance under paragraph 1100(1)(g),

(b) more than one right to remove industrial minerals from an industrial mineral mine in respect of which he may claim an allowance under that paragraph, or

(c) both such a mine and a right,

each such industrial mineral mine and each such right to remove industrial minerals from an industrial mineral mine is hereby prescribed to be a separate class of property.

**Related Provisions**: Reg. 1104(3) — Meaning of "industrial mineral mine".

**Notes**: "Industrial minerals" are considered by Revenue Canada to be non-metallic minerals, such as gravel, clay, stone, limestone, sand and feldspar (IT-145R, para. 11).

**(4a) New or expanded mines properties** — Where more than one property of a taxpayer is described in Class 28 in Schedule II and

(a) one of the properties was acquired for the purpose of gaining or producing income from only one mine, and

(b) one of the properties was acquired for the purpose of gaining or producing income from another mine,

a separate class is hereby prescribed for the properties that

(c) were acquired for the purpose of gaining or producing income from each mine;

(d) would otherwise be included in the class; and

(e) are not included in a separate class by virtue of subsection (4b).

**Related Provisions**: Reg. 1100(1)(w), 1104(5), 1104(7); Reg. 1104(5), (6.1) — Income from a mine; Reg. 1104(7) — Interpretation.

**(4b) New or expanded mines properties** — Where more than one property of a taxpayer is described in Class 28 in Schedule II and

(a) one of the properties was acquired for the purpose of gaining or producing income from particular mines, and

(b) one of the properties was acquired for the purpose of gaining or producing income from only one mine or more than one mine other than any of the particular mines,

a separate class is hereby prescribed for the properties that

(c) were acquired for the purpose of gaining or producing income from the particular mines; and

(d) would otherwise be included in the class.

**Related Provisions**: Reg. 1100(1)(x), 1104(5), 1104(7); Reg. 1104(5), (6.1) — Income from a mine; Reg. 1104(7) — Interpretation.

**(4c) New or expanded mines properties** — Where one or more properties of a taxpayer are described in paragraph (a), (a.1), or (a.2) of Class 41 of Schedule II and

(a) where all of the properties were acquired for the purposes of gaining or producing income from only one mine, or

(b) where

(i) one or more of the properties were acquired for the purpose of gaining or producing income from a particular mine, and

(ii) one or more of the properties were acquired for the purpose of gaining or producing income from another mine,

a separate class is hereby prescribed for the properties that

(c) were acquired for the purpose of gaining or producing income from each mine,

(d) would otherwise be included in the class, and

(e) are not included in a separate class by reason of subsection (4d).

**Related Provisions**: Reg. 1100(1)(y), 1104(5), 1104(7); Reg. 1104(5), (6.1) — Income from a mine; Reg. 1104(7) — Interpretation.

**Notes**: Reference to Cl. 41(a.1) and (a.2) added by P.C. 1998-49, effective March 7, 1996.

**(4d) New or expanded mines properties** — Where more than one property of a taxpayer is described in paragraph (a), (a.1), or (a.2) of Class 41 of Schedule II and

(a) one of the properties was acquired for the purpose of gaining or producing income from particular mines, and

(b) one of the properties was acquired for the purpose of gaining or producing income from only one mine or more than one mine other than any of the particular mines,

a separate class is hereby prescribed for the properties that

(c) were acquired for the purpose of gaining or producing income from the particular mines, and

(d) would otherwise be included in the class.

**Related Provisions**: Reg. 1100(1)(ya), 1104(5), 1104(7); Reg. 1104(5), (6.1) — Income from a mine; Reg. 1104(7) — Interpretation.

**Notes**: Reference to Cl. 41(a.1) and (a.2) added by P.C. 1998-49, effective March 7, 1996.

**(5) Lease option agreements** — Where, by virtue of an agreement, contract or arrangement entered into on or after May 31, 1954, a taxpayer is deemed by section 18 of the *Income Tax Act*, as enacted by the Statutes of Canada, 1958, Chapter 32, subsection 8(1), to have acquired a property, a separate class is hereby prescribed for each such property and if the taxpayer subsequently actually acquires the property it shall be included in the same class.

**(5a) Telecommunication spacecraft** — For the purposes of this Part, each property of a taxpayer that is an unmanned telecommunication spacecraft described in paragraph (f.2) of Class 10 or in Class 30 in Schedule II is hereby prescribed to be a separate class of property.

**(5b) Multiple-unit residential buildings** — For the purposes of this Part, when any property of a taxpayer is a property of Class 31 or 32 in Schedule II and the capital cost of that property to the taxpayer was not less than $50,000, a separate class is hereby prescribed for each such property of the taxpayer that would otherwise be included in the same class.

**Interpretation Bulletins**: IT-274R: Rental properties — Capital cost of $50,000 or more; IT-367R3: Capital cost allowance — multiple-unit residential buildings.

**Forms**: TX87: Application for a copy of a MURB certificate.

**(5c) Leasing properties** — For the purposes of this Part, except in the case of a corporation or partnership described in subsection 1100(16), where more than one property of a taxpayer is described in the same class in Schedule II and where

(a) one of the properties is a leasing property, and

(b) one of the properties is a property other than a leasing property,

a separate class is hereby prescribed for properties that

(c) are described in paragraph (a); and

(d) would otherwise be included in the class.

**Related Provisions**: Reg. 1100(17), (18) — Meaning of "leasing property".

**Interpretation Bulletins**: IT-443: Leasing property — CCA restrictions.

**(5d) Railway cars** — Where more than one property of a taxpayer is a railway car included in Class 35 in Schedule II that was rented, leased or used by the taxpayer in Canada in the taxation year, other

**Reg. S. 1101(5d)** — Income Tax Regulations, Part XI

than a railway car owned by a corporation, or a partnership any member of which is a corporation, that

(a) was at any time in that taxation year a common carrier that owned or operated a railway, or

(b) rented or leased the railway cars at any time in that taxation year, by one or more transactions between persons not dealing at arm's length, to an associated corporation that was, at that time, a common carrier that owned or operated a railway,

a separate class is prescribed

(c) for all such properties acquired by the taxpayer before February 3, 1990 (other than such properties acquired for rent or lease to another person),

(d) for all such properties acquired by the taxpayer after February 2, 1990 (other than such properties acquired for rent or lease to another person),

(e) for all such properties acquired by the taxpayer before April 27, 1989 for rent or lease to another person, and

(f) for all such properties acquired by the taxpayer after April 26, 1989 for rent or lease to another person.

**Related Provisions**: Reg. 1100(1)(z), (z.1a).

**Notes**: Reg. 1101(5d) substituted by P.C. 1991-465, effective April 27, 1989; but ignore (5d)(d) and the words "before February 3, 1990" in (5d)(c) for property

(a) acquired by the taxpayer after April 26, 1989 and before February 3, 1990,

(b) acquired by the taxpayer after February 2, 1990 pursuant to an agreement in writing entered into by the taxpayer before February 3, 1990, or

(c) under construction by or on behalf of the taxpayer before February 3, 1990.

**(5d.1) [Railway property]** — A separate class is hereby prescribed for all property included in Class 35 in Schedule II acquired at a time after December 6, 1991 by a taxpayer that was at that time a common carrier that owned and operated a railway.

**Related Provisions**: Reg. 1100(1)(z.1b) — Additional allowance.

**Notes**: Reg. 1101(5d.1) added by P.C. 1994-139, effective for property acquired after December 6, 1991.

**(5e) Railway track and related property** — A separate class is hereby prescribed for all property included in Class 1 in Schedule II acquired by a taxpayer after March 31, 1977 and before 1988 that is

(a) railway track and grading, including components such as rails, ballast, ties and other track material;

(b) railway traffic control or signalling equipment, including switching, block signalling, interlocking, crossing protection, detection, speed control or retarding equipment, but not including property that is principally electronic equipment or systems software therefor; or

(c) a bridge, culvert, subway or tunnel that is ancillary to railway track and grading.

**Related Provisions**: Reg. 1100(1)(za), (za.1) — Additional allowance.

**(5e.1) [Railway property]** — A separate class is hereby prescribed for all property included in Class 1 in Schedule II acquired at a time after December 6, 1991 by a taxpayer that was at that time a common carrier that owned and operated a railway, where the property is

(a) railway track and grading, including components such as rails, ballast, ties and other track material;

(b) railway traffic control or signalling equipment, including switching, block signalling, interlocking, crossing protection, detection, speed control or retarding equipment, but not including property that is principally electronic equipment or systems software therefor; or

(c) a bridge, culvert, subway or tunnel that is ancillary to railway track and grading.

**Related Provisions**: Reg. 1100(1)(za.1) — Additional allowance.

**Notes**: Reg. 1101(5e.1) added by P.C. 1994-139, effective for property acquired after December 6, 1991.

**(5e.2) [Trestles]** — A separate class is hereby prescribed for all trestles included in Class 3 in Schedule II acquired at a time after December 6, 1991 by a taxpayer that was at that time a common carrier that owned and operated a railway, where the trestles are ancillary to railway track and grading.

**Related Provisions**: Reg. 1100(1)(za.2) — Additional allowance.

**Notes**: Reg. 1101(5e.2) added by P.C. 1994-139, effective for property acquired after December 6, 1991.

**(5f) [Trestles]** — A separate class is hereby prescribed for all trestles included in Class 3 in Schedule II acquired by a taxpayer after March 31, 1977 and before 1988 that are ancillary to railway track and grading.

**Related Provisions**: Reg. 1100(1)(zb).

**(5g) Deemed depreciable property** — A separate class is hereby prescribed for each property of a taxpayer described in Class 36 in Schedule II.

**(5h) Leasehold interest in real properties** — For the purposes of this Part, where more than one property of a taxpayer is described in the same class in Schedule II and where

(a) one of the properties is a leasehold interest in real property described in subsection 1100(13), and

(b) one of the properties is a property other than a leasehold interest in real property described in subsection 1100(13),

a separate class is hereby prescribed for properties that

(c) are described in paragraph (a); and

(d) would otherwise be included in the class.

Division II — Separate Classes  Reg. S. 1101(5p)

**(5i) Pipelines** — A separate class is hereby prescribed for each property of a taxpayer described in Class 2 in Schedule II that is

(a) a pipeline the construction of which was commenced after 1984 and completed after September 1, 1985 and the capital cost of which to the taxpayer is not less than $10,000,000,

(b) a pipeline that has been extended or converted where the extension or conversion was completed after September 1, 1985 and the capital cost to the taxpayer of the extension or the cost to him of the conversion, as the case may be, is not less than $10,000,000, or

(c) a pipeline that has been extended and converted as part of a single program of extension and conversion of the pipeline where the program was completed after September 1, 1985 and the aggregate of the capital cost to the taxpayer of the extension and the cost to him of the conversion is not less than $10,000,000,

and in respect of which the taxpayer has, by letter attached to the return of his income filed with the Minister in accordance with section 150 of the Act for the taxation year in which the construction, extension, conversion or program, as the case may be, was completed, elected that this subsection apply.

**Related Provisions**: Reg. 1101(5j) — Effect of election.
**Interpretation Bulletins**: IT-482: Pipelines.

**(5j) [Election effective forever]** — An election under subsection (5i), (5l) or (5o) shall be effective from the first day of the taxation year in respect of which the election is made and shall continue to be effective for all subsequent taxation years.

**Notes**: Reg. 1101(5j) amended by P.C. 1991-465, effective for taxation years ending after April 26, 1989.

**(5k) Certified productions** — A separate class is hereby prescribed for all property of a taxpayer included in Class 10 in Schedule II by reason of paragraph (w) thereof.

**Related Provisions**: Reg. 1100(1)(l).
**Interpretation Bulletins**: IT-283R2: CCA — Videotapes, videotape cassettes, films, computer software and master recording media.

**Proposed Addition — Reg. 1101(5k.1)**

**(5k.1) Canadian film or video production** — A separate class is hereby prescribed for all property of a corporation included in Class 10 in Schedule II because of paragraph (x) thereof that is property

(a) in respect of which the corporation is deemed under subsection 125.4(3) of the Act to have paid an amount, or

(b) acquired by the corporation from another corporation where

(i) the other corporation acquired the property in circumstances to which paragraph (a) applied, and

(ii) the corporations were related to each other throughout the period that began when the other corporation acquired the property and ended when the other corporation disposed of the property to the corporation.

**Application**: The December 12, 1995 draft regulations (Canadian film tax credit), s. 2, will add subsec. 1101(5k.1), applicable to 1995 et seq.
**Related Provisions**: 1100(1)(m) — Additional allowance.

**(5l) Class 38 property and outdoor advertising signs** — A separate class is hereby prescribed for each property of a taxpayer described in Class 38 in Schedule II or in paragraph (l) of Class 8 in Schedule II in respect of which the taxpayer has, by letter attached to the return of income of the taxpayer filed with the Minister in accordance with section 150 of the Act for the taxation year in which the property was acquired, elected that this subsection apply.

**Related Provisions**: Reg. 1101(5j) — Effect of election.
**Interpretation Bulletins**: IT-469R: CCA — Earth-moving equipment.

**(5m) Specified energy property** — Where, for any taxation year, a property of a taxpayer or partnership is a specified energy property, a separate class is prescribed in respect of that property for that and subsequent taxation years.

**Related Provisions**: Reg. 1100(25) — Meaning of "specified energy property".

**(5n) [Specified leasing property]** — Notwithstanding subsection (5c), where at the end of any taxation year a property of a taxpayer is specified leasing property, a separate class is prescribed in respect of that property (including any additions or alterations to that property included in the same class in Schedule II) for that year and all subsequent taxation years.

**Related Provisions**: Reg. 1100(1.1), (1.11) — Specified leasing property.
**Notes**: Reg. 1101(5n) added by P.C. 1991-465, effective for taxation years ending after April 26, 1989.

**(5o) [Exempt leasing properties]** — A separate class is prescribed for one or more properties of a class in Schedule II that are exempt properties, as defined in paragraph 1100(1.13)(a), of a taxpayer referred to in subsection 1100(16) in respect of which the taxpayer has, by letter attached to the return of income of the taxpayer filed with the Minister in accordance with section 150 of the Act for the taxation year in which the property or properties were acquired, elected that this subsection apply.

**Related Provisions**: Reg. 1101(5j) — Effect of election.
**Notes**: Reg. 1101(5o) added by P.C. 1991-465, effective for property acquired after April 26, 1989; an election is valid if made by September 23, 1991.

**(5p) Rapidly depreciating electronic equipment** — Subject to subsection (5q), a separate class is prescribed for one or more properties of a taxpayer

Reg. S. 1101(5p)

acquired in a taxation year and included in the year in Class 8 in Schedule II, or for one or more properties of a taxpayer acquired in a taxation year and included in the year in Class 10 in Schedule II, where each of the properties has a capital cost to the taxpayer of at least $1,000 and is

(a) general-purpose electronic data processing equipment and systems software therefor, including ancillary data processing equipment, included in paragraph (f) of Class 10 in Schedule II;

(b) computer software;

(c) a photocopier; or

(d) office equipment that is electronic communications equipment, such as a facsimile transmission device or telephone equipment.

**Related Provisions**: Reg. 1101(5q) — Election for Reg. 1101(5p) to apply; Reg. 1103(2g) — Property transferred back to pool if still owned after 5 years.

**Notes**: Reg. 1101(5p) added by P.C. 1994-231, effective for property acquired after April 26, 1993. It implements a proposal in the 1993 federal budget to allow a terminal loss for certain office equipment that can depreciate rapidly, at the taxpayer's election (see Reg. 1101(5q)). If the equipment is not disposed of after 5 years, it returns to the pool rather than being treated as a separate item. See Reg. 1103(2g).

**Proposed Amendment — Separate class for manufacturing and processing equipment**

**Federal budget, supplementary information, February 28, 2000**: *Separate Class Election for Manufacturing and Processing Equipment*

In general, the CCA system groups properties into a limited number of broad classes with specified depreciation rates that apply on a diminishing balance basis. In most cases, this system works well and is simple to administer. The use of a class system provides, on average, deductions for tax purposes that reflect the useful life of the property. However, the rate at which any particular piece of equipment depreciates can vary significantly depending on how it is used and the progress of technological change. In some circumstances, the CCA system does not adequately reflect variations in depreciation experience resulting from technological change. In response to this, the 1993 budget introduced a separate class election for computer equipment and certain types of office communication and electronic equipment.

The separate class election allows taxpayers to place eligible property in a separate class for CCA purposes. Although the separate class election does not change the specified CCA rate, it ensures that, upon the disposition of all the property in the class, any remaining undepreciated balance can be fully deducted as a terminal loss.

The useful life of manufacturing equipment can vary widely. To address situations where certain types of equipment have an unusually short economic life, the budget proposes that the separate class election be extended to include manufacturing and processing property included in Class 43 of Schedule II to the *Income Tax Regulations* costing more than $1,000. This measure will apply to property acquired after February 27, 2000. The proposed election must be filed with the income tax return for the taxation year in which the property is acquired.

As with the 1993 provision, the undepreciated capital cost (UCC) in each separate class created pursuant to this measure, that is remaining after five years, must be transferred into the general Class 43 UCC pool.

**(5q) [Election required]** — Subsection (5p) applies only in respect of a property or properties of a taxpayer in respect of which the taxpayer has (by letter attached to the return of income of the taxpayer filed with the Minister in accordance with section 150 of the Act for the taxation year in which the property or properties were acquired) elected that the subsection apply.

**Notes**: Reg. 1101(5q) added by P.C. 1994-231, effective for property acquired after April 26, 1993. Any election under Reg. 1101(5q) was on time if filed by August 31, 1994.

**(5r) Computer software tax shelter property** — For the purpose of this Part, where

(a) more than one property of a taxpayer is described in the same class in Schedule II,

(b) one of the properties is computer software tax shelter property, and

(c) one of the properties is a property other than computer software tax shelter property,

for properties that are described in paragraph (b) and that would otherwise be included in the class, a separate class is prescribed.

**Related Provisions**: Reg. 1100(20.1) — Limitation on CCA claim for computer software tax shelter property; Reg. 1100(20.2) — Definition of "computer software tax shelter property".

**Notes**: Reg. 1101(5r) added by P.C. 2000-1000, effective on the same basis as Reg. 1100(20.1).

**(6) Reference** — A reference in this Part to a class in Schedule II includes a reference to the corresponding separate classes prescribed by this section.

**Interpretation Bulletins**: IT-474R: Amalgamations of Canadian corporations.

**Notes [Reg. 1101]**: See at beginning of Reg. 1101.

**Definitions [Reg. 1101]**: "amount" — ITA 248(1); "arm's length" — ITA 251(1); Reg. 1102(20); "business" — Reg. 1101(1a); "Canada" — ITA 255, *Interpretation Act* 35(1); "class" — Reg. 1101(6), 1102(1)–(3), (14), (14.1); "computer software" — Reg. 1104(2); "computer software tax shelter property" — Reg. 1100(20.2); "corporation" — ITA 248(1), *Interpretation Act* 35(1); "depreciable property" — ITA 13(21), 248(1); "disposed" — ITA 248(1)"disposition"; "dividend" — ITA 248(1); "general-purpose electronic data processing equipment" — Reg. 1104(2); "income from a mine" — Reg. 1104(5), (6.1)(a); "industrial mineral mine" — Reg. 1104(3); "leasing property" — Reg. 1100(17-20); "life insurance business" — ITA 248(1); "mine" — Reg. 1104(7); "mineral" — Reg. 1104(3); "mineral resource", "Minister", "office", "person" — ITA 248(1); "pipeline" — Reg. 1104(2); "prescribed", "property" — ITA 248(1); "related" — ITA 251(2)–(6); "rental property" — Reg. 1100(14); "specified energy property" — Reg. 1100(25), (27)–(29); "specified leasing property" — Reg. 1100(1.11); "systems software" — Reg. 1104(2); "taxation year" — ITA 249, Reg. 1104(1); "taxpayer" — ITA 248(1); "timber resource property" — ITA 13(21), 248(1); "writing" — *Interpretation Act* 35(1).

# DIVISION III — PROPERTY RULES

**1102. (1) Property not included** — The classes of property described in this Part and in Schedule II shall be deemed not to include property

(a) **[otherwise deductible]** — the cost of which would be deductible in computing the taxpayer's income if the Act were read without reference to sections 66 to 66.4 of the Act;

> **Proposed Amendment — Reg. 1102(1)(a)**
>
> **Application**: The July 23, 1999 draft regulations, s. 1, will amend para. 1102(1)(a) to read as it presently does, but applicable to 1988 et seq.
>
> **Technical Notes**: Subsection 1102(1) provides that certain properties are excluded as depreciable properties under Schedule II to the Regulations. Paragraph 1102(1)(a) excludes a taxpayer's property for this purpose if its cost would, ignoring sections 66 to 66.4 of the Act, be deductible in computing the taxpayer's income. This version of paragraph 1102(1)(a) applies to taxation years that end after December 5, 1996.
>
> Paragraph 1102(1)(a) is amended so that this version of paragraph 1102(1)(a) applies to the 1988 and subsequent taxation years. The amendment is consequential to proposed paragraph (k.1) of the CEE definition in subsection 66.1(6) of the Act and proposed paragraph (i.1) of the CDE definition in subsection 66.2(5) of the Act, which are explained in the commentary above.

**Notes**: Reg. 1102(1)(a) amended by P.C. 1999-629, effective for taxation years that end after December 5, 1996. For earlier years since before 1972, read: "(a) the cost of which is deductible in computing the taxpayer's income".

(a.1) **[CRCE]** — the cost of which is included in the taxpayer's Canadian renewable and conservation expense (within the meaning assigned by section 1219);

**Notes**: Reg. 1102(1)(a.1) added by P.C. 2000-1331, effective for expenses incurred after December 5, 1996. CRCE is fully deductible under ITA 66.1(1)"Canadian exploration expense"(g.1), and so is excluded from CCA pools.

(b) **[inventory]** — that is described in the taxpayer's inventory;

(c) **[no income purpose]** — that was not acquired by the taxpayer for the purpose of gaining or producing income;

**I.T. Technical News**: No. 3 (loss utilization within a corporate group; use of a partner's assets by a partnership.

(d) **[R&D expense]** — that was acquired by an expenditure in respect of which the taxpayer is allowed a deduction in computing income under section 37 of the Act;

**Related Provisions**: Reg. 5202"cost of capital"(a), 5204"cost of capital"(a) — Manufacturing and processing credit.

**Interpretation Bulletins**: IT-151R4: Scientific research and experimental development expenditures. See also list at end of Reg. 1102(1).

(e) **[non-Canadian art]** — that was acquired by the taxpayer after November 12, 1981, other than property acquired from a person with whom the taxpayer was not dealing at arm's length (otherwise than by virtue of a right referred to in paragraph 251(5)(b) of the Act) at the time the property was acquired if the property was acquired in the circumstances where subsection (14) applies, and is

(i) a print, etching, drawing, painting, sculpture, or other similar work of art, the cost of which to the taxpayer was not less than $200,

(ii) a hand-woven tapestry or carpet or a handmade appliqué, the cost of which to the taxpayer was not less than $215 per square metre,

(iii) an engraving, etching, lithograph, woodcut, map or chart, made before 1900, or

(iv) antique furniture, or any other antique object, produced more than 100 years before the date it was acquired, the cost of which to the taxpayer was not less than $1,000,

other than any property described in subparagraph (i) or (ii) where the individual who created the property was a Canadian (within the meaning assigned by paragraph 1104(10)(a)) at the time the property was created;

(f) that is property referred to in paragraph 18(1)(l) of the Act acquired after December 31, 1974, an outlay or expense for the use or maintenance of which is not deductible by virtue of that paragraph;

**Related Provisions**: Reg. 1102(17) — Grandfathering to November 13, 1974.

(g) **[pre-1972 farming/fishing property]** — in respect of which an allowance is claimed and permitted under Part XVII;

**Related Provisions**: Reg. 5202"cost of capital"(a), 5204"cost of capital"(a) — Manufacturing and processing credit.

(h) **[pre-1966 automobile]** — that is a passenger automobile acquired after June 13, 1963 and before January 1, 1966, the cost to the taxpayer of which, minus the initial transportation charges and retail sales tax in respect thereof, exceeded $5,000, unless the automobile was acquired by a person before June 14, 1963 and has by one or more transactions between persons not dealing at arm's length become vested in the taxpayer;

**Related Provisions**: Reg. 1102(11)–(13) — Interpretation.

(i) **[pre-1963 property]** — that was deemed by section 18 of the *Income Tax Act*, as enacted by the Statutes of Canada, 1958, Chapter 32, subsection 8(1), to have been acquired by the taxpayer and that did not vest in the taxpayer before the 1963 taxation year;

(j) **[life insurer]** — of a life insurer, that is property used by it in, or held by it in the course of, carrying on an insurance business outside Canada; or

(k) **[linefill]** — that is linefill in a pipeline.

**Notes**: A proposed definition of "pipeline" in Reg. 1104(2), released December 23, 1991, has been abandoned. See Interpretation Bulletin IT-482 for the CCRA's administrative definition.

Reg. 1102(1)(k) added by P.C. 1994-139, effective for property acquired after December 23 1991, other than property acquired before 1993

(a) pursuant to an agreement in writing entered into before December 24, 1991, or

(b) that was under construction by or on behalf of the taxpayer on December 23, 1991.

**Interpretation Bulletins [Reg. 1102(1)]**: IT-128R: CCA — Depreciable property; IT-148R3: Recreational properties and club dues; IT-218R: Profit, capital gains and losses from the sale of real estate, including farmland and inherited land and conversion of real estate from capital property to inventory and vice versa; IT-220R2: CCA — Proceeds of disposition of depreciable property; IT-350R: Investigation of site; IT-482: Pipelines.

**(1a) Partnership property** — Where the taxpayer is a member of a partnership, the classes of property described in this Part and in Schedule II shall be deemed not to include any property that is an interest of the taxpayer in depreciable property that is partnership property of the partnership.

**(2) Land** — The classes of property described in Schedule II shall be deemed not to include the land upon which a property described therein was constructed or is situated.

**(3) Non-residents** — Where the taxpayer is a non-resident person, the classes of property described in this Part and in Schedule II shall, except for the purpose of determining the foreign accrual property income of the taxpayer for the purposes of subdivision i of Division B of Part I of the Act, be deemed not to include property that is situated outside Canada.

**(4) Improvements or alterations to leased properties** — Subject to subsection (5), "capital cost" for the purposes of paragraph 1100(1)(b) includes any amount expended by a taxpayer for or in respect of an improvement or alteration to a leased property.

**(5) Buildings on leased properties** — Where the taxpayer has a leasehold interest in a property, a reference in Schedule II to a property that is a building or other structure shall include a reference to that leasehold interest to the extent that that interest

(a) was acquired by reason of the fact that the taxpayer

   (i) erected a building or structure on leased land,

   (ii) made an addition to a leased building or structure, or

   (iii) made alterations to a leased building or structure that substantially changed the nature of the property; or

(b) was acquired after 1975 or, in the case of any property of Class 31 or 32, after November 18, 1974, from a former lessee who had acquired it by reason of the fact that he or a lessee before him

   (i) erected a building or structure on leased land,

   (ii) made an addition to a leased building or structure, or

   (iii) made alterations to a leased building or structure that substantially changed the nature of the property.

**Related Provisions**: Reg. 1102(4) — Improvements or alterations to leased property; Reg. 1102(5.1) — References to "building".

**Interpretation Bulletins**: IT-79R3: CCA — Buildings or other structures; IT-195R4: Rental property — CCA restrictions; IT-324: CCA — Emphyteutic lease; IT-367R3: Capital cost allowance — multiple-unit residential buildings; IT-464R: Leasehold interests.

**(5.1) [Buildings on leased properties]** — Where a taxpayer has acquired a property that would, if the property had been acquired by a person with whom the taxpayer was not dealing at arm's length at the time the property was acquired by the taxpayer, be described in paragraph (5)(a) or (b) in respect of that person, a reference in Schedule II to a property that is a building or other structure shall, in respect of the taxpayer, include a reference to that property.

**Notes**: Reg. 1102(5.1) added by P.C. 1994-139, effective for property acquired after December 23, 1991, other than property acquired before 1993

(a) pursuant to an agreement in writing entered into before December 24, 1991, or

(b) that was under construction by or on behalf of the taxpayer on December 23, 1991.

**(6) Leasehold interests acquired before 1949** — For the purposes of paragraphs 2(a) and (b) of Schedule III, where an item of capital cost has been incurred before the commencement of the taxpayer's 1949 taxation year, there shall be added to the capital cost of each item the amount that has been allowed in respect thereof as depreciation under the *Income War Tax Act* and has been deducted from the original cost to arrive at the capital cost of the item.

**(7) River improvements** — For the purposes of paragraph 1100(1)(f), capital cost includes an amount expended on river improvements by the taxpayer for the purpose of facilitating the removal of timber from a timber limit.

**(8) Electrical plant used for mining** — Where the generating or distributing equipment and plant (including structures) of a producer or distributor of electrical energy were acquired for the purpose of providing power to a consumer for use by the consumer in the operation in Canada of a mine, ore mill, smelter, metal refinery or any combination thereof and at least 80 per cent of the producer's or distributor's output of electrical energy

(a) for his 1948 and 1949 taxation years, or

Division III — Property Rules  Reg. S. 1102(10)

(b) for his first two taxation years in which he sold power,

whichever period is later, was sold to the consumer for that purpose, the property shall be included in

(c) Class 10 in Schedule II if it is property acquired

(i) before 1988, or

(ii) before 1990

(A) pursuant to an obligation in writing entered into by the taxpayer before June 18, 1987,

(B) that was under construction by or on behalf of the taxpayer on June 18, 1987, or

(C) that is machinery or equipment that is a fixed and integral part of the building, structure, plant facility or other property that was under construction by or on behalf of the taxpayer on June 18, 1987, or

(d) Class 41 in Schedule II in any other case, except where the property would otherwise be included in Class 43.1 in Schedule II and the taxpayer has, by letter filed with the return of income of the taxpayer filed with the Minister in accordance with section 150 of the Act for the taxation year in which the property was acquired, elected to include the property in Class 43.1.

**Related Provisions**: Reg. 1102(9.1) — Acquisition before November 8, 1969; Reg. 1102(9.2) — Acquisition not at arm's length; Reg. 1103(4) — When election under para. (d) effective; Reg. 1104(7) — Interpretation.

**Notes**: Generally, Reg. 1102(8) provides that, where 80% or more of the power generated by electrical generating equipment of a taxpayer is used to provide power to a consumer at a mine, ore mill, smelter, or metal refinery operated in Canada by the consumer, the taxpayer's generating and distribution equipment and plant (including structures) acquired after 1987 is to be included in Class 41. Where it would otherwise be included in Class 43, the taxpayer may elect to include the property in that Class.

Reg. 1102(8) amended by P.C. 1997-1033, effective for property acquired after February 21, 1994. A taxpayer who acquired property from February 22, 1994 through August 20, 1997 may file the election under Reg. 1102(8)(d) by notifying Revenue Canada in writing before the end of February 1998.

For property acquired since 1988 and before February 22, 1994, read "customer" instead of "consumer" in the words between paras. (b) and (c) (this was a drafting error which should have been corrected retroactive to 1988 but was not), and read Reg. 1102(8)(d) as simply "Class 41 in Schedule II in any other case".

**(9) [Generating or distributing equipment]** — Where a taxpayer has acquired generating or distributing equipment and plant (including structures) for the purpose of providing power for his own consumption in operating a mine, ore mill, smelter, metal refinery or any combination thereof and at least 80 per cent of the output of electrical energy was so used

(a) in his 1948 and 1949 taxation years, or

(b) in the first two taxation years in which he so produced power,

whichever period is the later, the property shall be included in

(c) Class 10 in Schedule II if it is property acquired

(i) before 1988, or

(ii) before 1990

(A) pursuant to an obligation in writing entered into by the taxpayer before June 18, 1987,

(B) that was under construction by or on behalf of the taxpayer on June 18, 1987, or

(C) that is machinery or equipment that is a fixed and integral part of a building, structure, plant facility or other property that was under construction by or on behalf of the taxpayer on June 18, 1987, or

(d) Class 41 in Schedule II in any other case, except where the property would otherwise be included in Class 43.1 in Schedule II and the taxpayer has, by a letter filed with the return of income of the taxpayer filed with the Minister in accordance with section 150 of the Act for the taxation year in which the property was acquired, elected to include the property in Class 43.1.

**Related Provisions**: Reg. 1102(9.1) — Acquisition before November 8, 1969; Reg. 1102(9.2) — Acquisition not at arm's length; Reg. 1103(4) — When election under para. (d) effective; Reg. 1104(7) — Interpretation.

**Notes**: Reg. 1102(9)(d) amended by P.C. 1997-1033, effective for property acquired after February 21, 1994. A taxpayer who acquired property from February 22, 1994 through August 20, 1997 may file the election under Reg. 1102(9)(d) by notifying Revenue Canada in writing before the end of February 1998.

For property acquired since 1988 and before February 22, 1994, read Reg. 1102(9)(d) as simply "Class 41 in Schedule II in any other case".

**(9.1) [pre-1970 acquisition]** — In their application to generating or distributing equipment and plant (including structures) that were acquired by the taxpayer before November 8, 1969, subsections (8) and (9) shall be read without reference to a "metal refinery".

**(9.2) [Property under Reg. 1102(8) or (9)]** — Where a taxpayer acquires property after November 7, 1969 from a person with whom he was not dealing at arm's length that is property referred to in subsection (8) or (9), notwithstanding those subsections, that property shall not be included in Class 10 in Schedule II by the taxpayer unless the property had been included in that class by the person from whom it was acquired, by virtue of subsection (8) or (9) as it read in its application before November 8, 1969.

**(10) Railway companies** — For the purposes of section 36 of the Act, where a taxpayer is deemed to have acquired depreciable property of a prescribed class at the time a repair, replacement, alteration or renovation expenditure described therein was incurred,

(a) if the expenditure was incurred by the taxpayer before May 26, 1976, the class hereby prescribed is Class 4 in Schedule II; and

(b) if the expenditure was incurred by the taxpayer after May 25, 1976, the class hereby prescribed is the class in Schedule II in which the depreciable property that was repaired, replaced, altered or renovated would be included if such property had been acquired at the time the expenditure was incurred.

**(11) Passenger automobiles** — In paragraph (1)(h),

"**cost to the taxpayer**" of an automobile means, except as provided in subsections (12) and (13),

(a) except in any case coming under paragraph (b) or (c), the capital cost to the taxpayer of the automobile,

(b) except in any case coming under paragraph (c), where the automobile was acquired by a person (in this section referred to as the "original owner") after June 13, 1963, and has, by one or more transactions between persons not dealing at arm's length, become vested in the taxpayer, the greater of

(i) the actual cost to the taxpayer, and

(ii) the actual cost to the original owner, and

(c) where the automobile was acquired by the taxpayer outside Canada for use in connection with a permanent establishment, as defined for the purposes of Part IV or Part XXVI, outside Canada, the lesser of

(i) the actual cost to the taxpayer, and

(ii) the amount that such an automobile would ordinarily cost the taxpayer if he purchased it from a dealer in automobiles in Canada for use in Canada;

"**initial transportation charges**" in respect of an automobile means the costs incurred by a dealer in automobiles for transporting the automobile (before it had been used for any purpose whatever) from,

(a) in the case of an automobile manufactured in Canada, the manufacturer's plant, and

(b) in any other case, to the place in Canada, if any, at which the automobile was received or stored by a wholesale distributor,

to the dealer's place of business;

"**passenger automobile**" means a vehicle, other than an ambulance or hearse, that was designed to carry not more than nine persons, and that is

(a) an automobile designed primarily for carrying persons on highways and streets except an automobile that

(i) is designed to accommodate and is equipped with auxiliary folding seats installed between the front and the rear seats,

(ii) was acquired by a person carrying on the business of operating a taxi or automobile rental service, or arranging and managing funerals, for use in such business, and

(iii) is not a vehicle described in paragraph (b), or

(b) a station wagon or substantially similar vehicle;

"**retail sales tax**" in respect of an automobile means the aggregate of municipal and provincial retail sales taxes payable in respect of the purchase of the automobile by the taxpayer.

**(12) [Pre-1966 automobile]** — For the purposes of paragraph (1)(h), where an automobile is owned by two or more persons or by partners, a reference to "cost to the taxpayer" shall be deemed to be a reference to the aggregate of the cost, as defined in subsection (11), to each such person or partner.

**(13) [Pre-1966 automobile]** — In determining cost to a taxpayer for the purposes of paragraph (1)(h), subsection 13(7) of the Act shall not apply unless the automobile was acquired by gift.

**(14) Property acquired by transfer, amalgamation or winding-up** — For the purposes of this Part and Schedule II, where a property is acquired by a taxpayer

(a) in the course of a reorganization in respect of which, if a dividend were received by a corporation in the course of the reorganization, subsection 55(2) of the Act would not be applicable to the dividend by reason of the application of paragraph 55(3)(b) of the Act, or

(b), (c) [Revoked]

(d) from a person with whom the taxpayer was not dealing at arm's length (otherwise than by virtue of a right referred to in paragraph 251(5)(b) of the Act) at the time the property was acquired, and

(e) [Revoked]

the property, immediately before it was so acquired by the taxpayer, was property of a prescribed class or a separate prescribed class of the person from whom it was so acquired, the property shall be deemed to be property of that same prescribed class or separate prescribed class, as the case may be, of the taxpayer.

**Related Provisions:** Reg. 1100(2.21)(a); Reg. 1102(20) — Non-arm's length exception.

**Interpretation Bulletins**: IT-147R3: CCA — Accelerated write-off of manufacturing and processing machinery and equipment; IT-267R2: CCA — vessels; IT-481: Timber resource property and timber limits; IT-488R2: Winding-up of 90%-owned taxable Canadian corporations.

**(14.1) [Change in class]** — For the purposes of this Part and Schedule II, where a taxpayer has acquired, after May 25, 1976, property of a class in Schedule II (in this subsection referred to as the "present class") that had been previously owned before May 26, 1976 by the taxpayer or by a person with whom the taxpayer was not dealing at arm's length (otherwise than by virtue of a right referred to in paragraph 251(5)(b) of the Act) at the time the property was acquired, and at the time the property was previously so owned it was a property of a different class in Schedule II (in this subsection referred to as the "former class"), the property shall be deemed to be property of the former class and not property of the present class.

**Related Provisions**: Reg. 1100(2.21)(a).

**Interpretation Bulletins**: IT-147R3: CCA — Accelerated write-off of manufacturing and processing machinery and equipment; IT-267R2: CCA — vessels.

**(14.2) Townsite costs** — For the purpose of paragraph 13(7.5)(a) of the Act, a property is prescribed in respect of a taxpayer where the property would, if it had been acquired by the taxpayer, be property included in Class 10 in Schedule II because of paragraph (l) of that Class.

**Notes**: Reg. 1102(14.2) added by P.C. 1999-629, effective March 7, 1996. These "townsite costs" under Class 10(l) were previously eligible under Reg. 1102(18) for depreciable property treatment.

**(14.3) Surface construction and bridges** — For the purpose of paragraph 13(7.5)(b) of the Act, prescribed property is any of

(a) a road (other than a specified temporary access road), sidewalk, airplane runway, parking area, storage area or similar surface construction;

(b) a bridge; and

(c) a property that is ancillary to any property described in paragraph (a) or (b).

**Related Provisions**: Reg. 1104(2) — Definition of "specified temporary access road".

**Notes**: Reg. 1102(14.3) added by P.C. 1999-629, effective March 7, 1996.

**(15) Manufacturing and processing enterprises** — For the purposes of subsection 13(10) of the Act,

(a) property is hereby prescribed that is

(i) a building included in Class 3 or 6 in Schedule II, or

(ii) machinery or equipment included in Class 8 in Schedule II,

except

(iii) property that may reasonably be regarded as having been acquired for the purpose of producing coal from a coal mine or oil, gas, metals or industrial minerals from a resource referred to in section 1201 as it read immediately before it was repealed by section 2 of Order in Council P.C. 1975-1323 of June 12, 1975, or

(iv) property acquired for use outside Canada; and

(b) a business carried on by the taxpayer is hereby prescribed as a manufacturing or processing business if,

(i) for the fiscal period in which the property was acquired, or

(ii) for the fiscal period in which a reasonable volume of business was first carried on,

whichever was later, the revenue received by the taxpayer, in the course of carrying on the business from

(iii) the sale of goods processed or manufactured by the taxpayer in Canada,

(iv) the leasing or renting of goods that were processed or manufactured by the taxpayer in Canada,

(v) advertisements in a newspaper or magazine that was produced by the taxpayer in Canada, and

(vi) construction carried on by the taxpayer in Canada,

was not less than $2/3$ of the revenue of the business for the period.

**Related Provisions**: Reg. 1102(16) — Meaning of "revenue".

**(16)** For the purposes of paragraph (15)(b), "revenue" means gross revenue minus the aggregate of

(a) amounts that were paid or credited in the period, to customers of the business, in relation to such revenue as a bonus, rebate or discount or for returned or damaged goods; and

(b) amounts included therein by virtue of section 13 or subsection 23(1) of the Act.

**(17) Recreational property** — Property referred to in paragraph (1)(f) does not include

(a) any property that the taxpayer was obligated to acquire under the terms of an agreement in writing entered into before November 13, 1974; or

(b) any property the construction of which was

(i) commenced by the taxpayer before November 13, 1974 or commenced under an agreement in writing entered into by the taxpayer before November 13, 1974, and

(ii) completed substantially according to plans and specifications agreed to by the taxpayer before November 13, 1974.

**Interpretation Bulletins**: IT-148R3: Recreational properties and club dues.

**(18)** [Repealed]

**Reg.**
**S. 1102(18)**      Income Tax Regulations, Part XI

**Notes**: Reg. 1102(18) repealed by P.C. 1999-629, effective for payments required to be made under the terms of contracts made after March 6, 1996. See now ITA 13(7.5)(a) and Reg. 1102(14.2). For payments under earlier contracts, read:

(18) **Townsite costs** — For the purposes of this Part and Schedule II, where under the terms of a contract a taxpayer is required to make a payment to Her Majesty in right of Canada, to a province or to a Canadian municipality in respect of costs incurred or to be incurred by the recipient to acquire property that would qualify as property described in paragraph (l) of Class 10 in Schedule II if it had been acquired by the taxpayer, the taxpayer shall be deemed to have acquired property described in that paragraph

(a) at a capital cost equal to the portion of the payment that can reasonably be regarded as being in respect of such costs; and

(b) at the time the payment is made or the time at which the costs are incurred, whichever is the later.

(19) **Additions and alterations** — For the purposes of this Part and Schedule II, where

(a) a taxpayer acquired a property that is included in a class in Schedule II (in this subsection referred to as the "actual class"),

(b) the taxpayer acquires property that is an addition or alteration to the property referred to in paragraph (a),

(c) the property that is the addition or alteration referred to in paragraph (b) would have been property of the actual class if it had been acquired by the taxpayer at the time he acquired the property referred to in paragraph (a), and

(d) the property referred to in paragraph (a) would have been property of a class in Schedule II (in this subsection referred to as the "present class") that is different from the actual class if it had been acquired by the taxpayer at the time he acquired the addition or alteration referred to in paragraph (b),

the addition or alteration referred to in paragraph (b) shall, except as otherwise provided in this Part or in Schedule II, be deemed to be an acquisition by the taxpayer of property of the present class.

**Interpretation Bulletins**: IT-79R3: CCA — Buildings or other structures.

(20) **Non-arm's length exception** — For the purposes of subsections 1100(2.2) and (19), 1101(1ad) and 1102(14) (in this subsection referred to as the "relevant subsections"), where, but for this subsection, a taxpayer would be considered to be dealing not at arm's length with another person as a result of a transaction or series of transactions the principal purpose of which may reasonably be considered to have been to cause one or more of the relevant subsections to apply in respect of the acquisition of a property, the taxpayer shall be considered to be dealing at arm's length with the other person in respect of the acquisition of that property.

**Interpretation Bulletins**: IT-267R2: CCA — vessels; IT-474R: Amalgamations of Canadian corporations; IT-488R2: Winding-up of 90%-owned taxable Canadian corporations.

(21) **[Class 43.1 property]** — Where a taxpayer has acquired a property described in Class 43.1 of Schedule II in circumstances in which clauses (b)(iii)(A) and (B) or (e)(iii)(A) and (B) of that class apply,

(a) the portion of the property, determined by reference to capital cost, that is equal to or less than the capital cost of the property to the person from whom the property was acquired, is included in that class; and

(b) the portion of the property, if any, determined by reference to capital cost, that is in excess of the capital cost of the property to the person from whom it was acquired, shall not be included in that class.

**Notes**: Reg. 1102(21) added by P.C. 2000-1331, effective for property acquired after June 26, 1996.

**Definitions [Reg. 1102]**: "actual class" — Reg. 1102(19)(a); "amount" — ITA 248(1); "arm's length" — ITA 251(1), Reg. 1102(20); "automobile", "business" — ITA 248(1); "Canada" — ITA 255, *Interpretation Act* 35(1); "class" — Reg. 1101(6), 1102(1)–(3), (14), (14.1); "commencement" — *Interpretation Act* 35(1); "corporation" — ITA 248(1), *Interpretation Act* 35(1); "cost to the taxpayer" — Reg. 1102(11), (12); "depreciable property" — ITA 13(21), 248(1); "disposed" — ITA 248(1) "disposition"; "dividend" — ITA 248(1); "fiscal period" — ITA 249.1; "foreign accrual property income" — ITA 95(1), (2), 248(1); "former class" — Reg. 1102(14.1); "gross revenue" — ITA 248(1); "Her Majesty" — *Interpretation Act* 35(1); "individual" — ITA 248(1); "initial transportation charges" — Reg. 1102(11); "inventory" — ITA 248(1); "mine" — Reg. 1104(7); "mineral" — Reg. 1104(3); "Minister", "non-resident" — ITA 248(1); "ore" — Reg. 1104(2); "original owner" — Reg. 1102(11)(c); "passenger automobile" — Reg. 1102(11); "person" — ITA 248(1); "pipeline" — Reg. 1104(2); "prescribed" — ITA 248(1); "present class" — Reg. 1102(14.1), (19)(d); "property" — ITA 248(1); "relevant subsections" — Reg. 1102(20); "retail sales tax" — Reg. 1102(11); "revenue" — Reg. 1102(16); "specified temporary access road" — Reg. 1104(2); "taxation year" — ITA 249, Reg. 1104(1); "taxpayer" — ITA 248(1); "writing" — *Interpretation Act* 35(1).

## DIVISION IV — INCLUSIONS IN AND TRANSFERS BETWEEN CLASSES

**1103. (1) Elections to include properties in Class 1** — In respect of properties otherwise included in Classes 2 to 10, 11 and 12 in Schedule II, a taxpayer may elect to include in Class 1 in Schedule II all such properties acquired for the purpose of gaining or producing income from the same business.

**Related Provisions**: ITA 220(3.2), Reg. 600(d) — Late filing of election or revocation; Reg. 1103(3)–(5) — How election made and when effective.

**Interpretation Bulletins**: IT-274R: Rental properties — capital cost of $50,000 or more.

**Information Circulars**: 92-1: Guidelines for accepting late, amended or revoked elections.

**(2) Elections to include properties in Class 2, 4 or 17** — Where the chief depreciable properties of a taxpayer are included in Class 2, 4 or 17 in Schedule II, the taxpayer may elect to include in Class 2, 4 or 17 in Schedule II, as the case may be, a property that would otherwise be included in another class in Schedule II and that was acquired by him before May 26, 1976 for the purpose of gaining or producing income from the same business as that for which those properties otherwise included in the said Class 2, 4 or 17 were acquired.

**Related Provisions**: ITA 220(3.2), Reg. 600(d) — Late filing of election or revocation; Reg. 1103(3)–(5) — How election made and when effective.

**Information Circulars**: 92-1: Guidelines for accepting late, amended or revoked elections.

**(2a) Elections to include properties in Class 8** — In respect of properties otherwise included in Class 19 or 21 in Schedule II, a taxpayer may, by letter attached to the return of his income for a taxation year filed with the Minister in accordance with section 150 of the Act, elect to include in Class 8 in Schedule II all properties of the said Class 19 or all properties of the said Class 21, as the case may be, owned by him at the commencement of the year.

**Related Provisions**: Reg. 1103(3)–(5) — How election made and when effective.

**(2b) Elections to include properties in Class 37** — In respect of properties that would have been included in Class 37 in Schedule II had they been acquired after the date on which Class 37 became effective, a taxpayer may, by letter attached to the return of his income for a taxation year filed with the Minister in accordance with section 150 of the Act, elect to include in Class 37 all such properties acquired by the taxpayer before that date.

**Related Provisions**: Reg. 1103(3)–(5) — How election made and when effective.

**(2c) Elections to make certain transfers** — Where a taxpayer has acquired, after May 25, 1976, all or any part of a property of a class in Schedule II (in this subsection referred to as the "present class") and the property or part thereof, if it had been acquired before May 26, 1976, would have been property of a different class in Schedule II (in this subsection referred to as the "former class") and

(a) he was obligated to acquire the property under the terms of an agreement in writing entered into before May 26, 1976,

(b) he commenced the construction, manufacture or production of the property before May 26, 1976 or the construction, manufacture or production of the property was commenced under an agreement in writing entered into by him before May 26, 1976, or

(c) he acquired the property on or before December 31, 1976 or he was obligated to acquire the property under the terms of an agreement in writing entered into on or before December 31, 1976, if

(i) arrangements, evidenced by writing, respecting the acquisition, construction, manufacture or production of the property had been substantially advanced before May 26, 1976, and

(ii) he had, before May 26, 1976, demonstrated a *bona fide* intention to acquire the property,

the taxpayer may, by letter attached to the return of his income filed with the Minister in accordance with section 150 of the Act, for the taxation year in which the property was acquired or for the immediately following taxation year, elect to transfer in the year of acquisition

(d) the property or the part thereof, acquired after May 25, 1976, from the present class to the former class; or

(e) the part of the property acquired before May 26, 1976, from the former class to the present class.

**Related Provisions**: Reg. 1103(3)–(5) — How election made and when effective.

**(2d)** Where a taxpayer has

(a) disposed of a property (in this subsection referred to as the "former property") of a class in Schedule II (in this subsection referred to as the "former class"), and

(b) before the end of the taxation year in which the former property was disposed of, acquired property (in this subsection referred to as the "new property") of a class in Schedule II (in this subsection referred to as the "present class") and the present class is neither

(i) the former class, nor

(ii) a separate class described in section 1101, other than subsection 1101(5d),

such that

(c) if the former property had been acquired at the time that the new property was acquired and from the person from whom the new property was acquired, the former property would have been included in the present class, and

(d) if the new property had been acquired at the time that the former property was acquired and from the person from whom the former property was acquired, the new property would have been included in the former class,

the taxpayer may, by letter attached to the return of income of the taxpayer filed with the Minister in accordance with section 150 of the Act in respect of the taxation year in which the former property was disposed of, elect to transfer the former property from the former class to the present class in the year of its disposition and, for greater certainty, the transfer shall be considered to have been made before the disposition of the property.

**Related Provisions**: ITA 220(3.2), Reg. 600(d) — Late filing of election or revocation; Reg. 1103(3)–(5) — How election made and when effective.

**Notes**: Reg. 1103(2d)(b)(ii) amended by P.C. 1991-465, effective April 27, 1989, to add the reference to Reg. 1101(5d).

**Interpretation Bulletins**: IT-147R3: CCA — Accelerated write-off of manufacturing and processing machinery and equipment; IT-469R: CCA — Earth-moving equipment.

**Information Circulars**: 92-1: Guidelines for accepting late, amended or revoked elections.

**(2e) Transfers from Class 40 to Class 10** — For the purposes of this Part and Schedule II, where property of a taxpayer would otherwise be included in Class 40 in Schedule II, all such properties owned by the taxpayer shall be transferred from Class 40 to Class 10 immediately after the commencement of the first taxation year of the taxpayer commencing after 1989.

**Related Provisions**: Reg. 1103(3)–(5) — How election made and when effective.

**Interpretation Bulletins**: IT-147R3: CCA — Accelerated write-off of manufacturing and processing machinery and equipment; IT-283R2: CCA — Videotapes, videotape cassettes, films, computer software and master recording media.

**(2f) Elections to include properties in Class 1, 3 or 6** — In respect of properties otherwise included in Class 20 in Schedule II, a taxpayer may, by letter attached to the return of income of the taxpayer for a taxation year filed with the Minister in accordance with section 150 of the Act, elect to include in Class 1, 3 or 6 in Schedule II, as specified in the letter, all properties of Class 20 in Schedule II owned by the taxpayer at the commencement of the year.

**Related Provisions**: ITA 220(3.2) — Late, amended or revoked elections; Reg. 1103(3)–(5) — How election made and when effective.

**(2g) Transfers to Class 8 or Class 10** — For the purposes of this Part and Schedule II, where one or more properties of a taxpayer are included in a separate class pursuant to an election filed by the taxpayer in accordance with subsection 1101(5q), all the properties included in that class immediately after the beginning of the taxpayer's fifth taxation year beginning after the end of the first taxation year in which a property of the class became available for use by the taxpayer for the purposes of subsection 13(26) of the Act shall be transferred immediately after the beginning of that fifth taxation year from the separate class to the class in which the property would, but for the election, have been included.

**Related Provisions**: Reg. 1103(3)–(5) — How election made and when effective.

**Notes**: Reg. 1103(2g) added by P.C. 1994-231, effective for property acquired after April 26, 1993.

**(2h) Elections not to include properties in Class 44** — A taxpayer may, by letter attached to the taxpayer's return of income filed with the Minister in accordance with section 150 of the Act for the taxation year in which a property was acquired, elect not to include the property in Class 44 in Schedule II.

**Related Provisions**: Reg. 1103(3)–(5) — How election made and when effective.

**Notes**: When this election is made, the property will normally go into Class 14.

Reg. 1103(2h) added by P.C. 1994-231, effective for property acquired after April 26, 1993. An election under Reg. 1103(2h) is on time if filed by August 31, 1994.

**(3) Election rules** — To be effective in respect of a taxation year, an election under this section must be made not later than the last day on which the taxpayer may file a return of his income for the taxation year in accordance with section 150 of the Act.

**(4)** An election under paragraph 1102(8)(d) or (9)(d) or this section shall be effective from the first day of the taxation year in respect of which the election is made and shall continue to be effective for all subsequent taxation years.

**Notes**: References to Reg. 1102(8)(d) and (9)(d) added to Reg. 1103(4) by P.C. 1997-1033, effective February 22, 1994.

**(5)** An election under subsection (1) or (2) shall be made by registered letter addressed to the District Office at which the taxpayer customarily files the returns required by section 150 of the Act.

**Definitions [Reg. 1103]**: "business" — ITA 248(1); "class" — Reg. 1101(6), 1102(1)–(3), (14), (14.1); "commencement" — *Interpretation Act* 35(1); "disposed" — ITA 248(1)"disposition"; "disposition" — ITA 248(1); "end of the taxation year" — Reg. 1104(1); "former class" — Reg. 1103(2c), (2d)(a); "former property" — Reg. 1103(2d)(b); "Minister" — ITA 248(1); "new property" — Reg. 1103(2d)(b); "person" — ITA 248(1); "present class" — Reg. 1103(2c), (2d)(b); "property" — ITA 248(1); "taxation year" — ITA 249, Reg. 1104(1); "taxpayer" — ITA 248(1); "writing" — *Interpretation Act* 35(1).

**Interpretation Bulletins [Reg. 1103]**: IT-190R2: CCA — transferred and misclassified property; IT-327: Elections under Regulation 1103; IT-478R2: CCA — Recapture and terminal loss.

## DIVISION V — INTERPRETATION

**1104. (1) Definitions** — Where the taxpayer is an individual and his income for the taxation year includes income from a business the fiscal period of which does not coincide with the calendar year, in respect of the depreciable properties acquired for the purpose of gaining or producing income from the business, a reference in this Part to

**"end of the taxation year"** shall be deemed to be a reference to the end of the fiscal period of the business; and

**"taxation year"** shall be deemed to be a reference to the fiscal period of the business.

**Interpretation Bulletins**: IT-172R: CCA — Taxation year of individuals.

**(2)** In this Part and Schedule II,

**"certified feature film"** means a motion picture film certified by the Minister of Communications to be a film of not less than 75 minutes running time in respect of which all photography or art work specifically required for the production thereof and all film editing therefor were commenced after November 18, 1974, and either the film was completed before May 26, 1976, or the photography or art work was commenced before May 26, 1976, and certified by him to be

(a) a film the production of which is contemplated in a coproduction agreement entered into between Canada and another country, or

(b) a film in respect of which

(i) the person who performed the duties of producer was a Canadian,

(ii) no fewer than ⅔ in number of all the persons each of whom

(A) was a person who performed the duties of director, screenwriter, music composer, art director, picture editor or director of photography, or

(B) was the individual in respect of whose services as an actor or actress in respect of the film the highest remuneration or the second highest remuneration was paid or payable,

were Canadians,

(iii) not less than 75 per cent of the aggregate of the remuneration paid or payable to persons for services provided in respect of the film (other than remuneration paid or payable to or in respect of the persons referred to in subparagraphs (i) and (ii) or remuneration paid or payable for processing and final preparation of the film) was paid or payable to Canadians,

(iv) not less than 75 per cent of the aggregate of costs incurred for processing and final preparation of the film including laboratory work, sound recording, sound editing and picture editing (other than remuneration paid or payable to or in respect of persons referred to in subparagraphs (i), (ii) and (iii)), was incurred in respect of services rendered in Canada, and

(v) the copyright protecting its use in Canada is beneficially owned

(A) by a person who is either a Canadian or a corporation incorporated under the laws of Canada or a province, or

(B) jointly or otherwise by two or more persons described in clause (A),

other than a film

(c) acquired after the day that is the earlier of

(i) the day of its first commercial use, and

(ii) 12 months after the day the principal photography thereof is completed, or

(d) in respect of which certification under this definition has been revoked by the Minister of Communications as provided in paragraph (10)(b);

**Related Provisions**: ITA 127.52(1)(c) — Add-back of CCA on film properties for minimum tax purposes; Reg. 1104(10) — Interpretation.

**Notes**: The *Department of Canadian Heritage Act* (S.C. 1995, c. 11), in force July 12, 1996, provides:

46. Other references — Every reference made to the Minister of Communications, the Minister of Multiculturalism and Citizenship and the Secretary of State of Canada in relation to any matter to which the powers, duties and functions of the Minister of Canadian Heritage extend by virtue of this Act, in any other Act of Parliament or in any order, regulation or other instrument made under any Act of Parliament shall, unless the context otherwise requires, be read as a reference to the Minister of Canadian Heritage.

**"certified production"**, in respect of a particular taxation year, means a motion picture film or video tape certified by the Minister of Communications to be a film or tape in respect of which all photography, taping or art work required specifically for the production thereof and all film or tape editing therefor were commenced after May 25, 1976, certified by him to be a film or tape in respect of which the principal photography or taping thereof was commenced before the end of the particular taxation year or was completed no later than 60 days after the end of that year and certified by him to be

(a) a film or tape the production of which is contemplated in a coproduction agreement entered into between Canada and another country, or

(b) a film or tape in respect of which

(i) the individual who performed the duties of producer was a Canadian,

(ii) the Minister of Communications has allotted not less than an aggregate of six units of production, not less than two of which were allotted by virtue of clause (A) or (B) and not less than one of which was allotted by virtue of clause (C) or (D), for individuals who provided services in respect of the film or tape, in the following manner:

(A) for the director, two units of production,

(B) for the screenwriter, two units of production,

(C) for the actor or actress in respect of whose services for the film or tape the highest remuneration was paid or payable (unless in the opinion of the Minister of Communications the individual did not perform a major role in the film or tape), one unit of production,

(D) for the actor or actress in respect of whose services for the film or tape the second highest remuneration was paid or payable (unless in the opinion of the Minister of Communications the individual did not perform a major role in the film or tape), one unit of production,

(E) for the art director, one unit of production,

(F) for the director of photography, one unit of production,

(G) for the music composer, one unit of production, and

(H) for the picture editor, one unit of production,

shall be allotted, provided the individual in respect of such allotment was a Canadian,

(iii) not less than 75 per cent of the aggregate of all costs (other than costs determined by reference to the amount of income from the film or tape) paid or payable to persons for services provided in respect of producing the film or tape (other than remuneration paid or payable to, or in respect of, individuals referred to in subparagraph (i) or (ii), costs referred to in subparagraph (iv) incurred for processing and final preparation of the film or tape, and amounts paid or payable in respect of insurance, financing, brokerage, legal and accounting fees and similar amounts) was paid or payable to, or in respect of services provided by, Canadians, and

(iv) not less than 75 per cent of the aggregate of all costs (other than costs determined by reference to the amount of income from the film or tape) incurred for processing and final preparation of the film or tape, including laboratory work, sound re-recording, sound editing and picture editing (other than remuneration paid or payable to, or in respect of, individuals referred to in subparagraph (i) or (ii)) was incurred in respect of services provided in Canada,

other than a film or tape

(c) acquired after the day that is the earlier of

(i) the day of its first commercial use, and

(ii) 12 months after the day the principal photography or taping thereof is completed,

(d) acquired by a taxpayer who has not paid in cash, as of the end of the particular taxation year, to the person from whom he acquired the film or tape, at least 5 per cent of the capital cost to the taxpayer of the film or tape as of the end of the year,

(e) acquired by a taxpayer who has issued in payment or part payment thereof, a bond, debenture, bill, note, mortgage or similar obligation in respect of which an amount is not due until a time that is more than four years after the end of the taxation year in which the taxpayer acquired the film or tape,

(f) acquired from a non-resident, or

(g) in respect of which certification under this definition has been revoked by the Minister of Communications as provided in paragraph (10)(b),

and, for the purposes of the application of this definition,

(h) in respect of a film or tape acquired in 1987, other than a film or tape in respect of which paragraph (i) applies, the reference in this definition to "commenced before the end of the particular taxation year or was completed no later than 60 days after the end of that year" shall be read as a reference to "commenced before the end of 1987 or was completed before July, 1988", and

(i) in respect of a film or tape acquired in 1987 or 1988 that is included in paragraph (n) of Class 12 in Schedule II and that is part of a series of films or tapes that includes another property included in that paragraph, the reference in this definition to "commenced before the end of the particular taxation year or was completed no later than 60 days after the end of that year" shall be read as a reference to "completed before 1989";

**Related Provisions**: ITA 127.52(1)(c) — Add-back of CCA on film properties for minimum tax purposes; Reg. 1104(10) — Interpretation; Reg. 7500 — "prescribed film production".

**Notes**: The *Department of Canadian Heritage Act* (S.C. 1995, c. 11), in force July 12, 1996, provides:

> 46. Other references — Every reference made to the Minister of Communications, the Minister of Multiculturalism and Citizenship and the Secretary of State of Canada in relation to any matter to which the powers, duties and functions of the Minister of Canadian Heritage extend by virtue of this Act, in any other Act of Parliament or in any order, regulation or other instrument made under any Act of Parliament shall, unless the context otherwise requires, be read as a reference to the Minister of Canadian Heritage.

Para. (e) amended to change "mortgage, hypothec" to "mortgage" by P.C. 1994-1817, effective November 30, 1994. The change was intended to be non-substantive.

As a result of the February 27, 1995 federal budget, a new credit for "Canadian film or video production" is now available. See the definition in Reg. 1106; Class 10(x); and the credit in ITA 125.4.

**Interpretation Bulletins**: IT-441: CCA — Certified feature productions and certified short productions.

**"certified short production"** — [Revoked]

**Notes**: This definition was revoked in 1986.

**"computer software"** includes systems software and a right or licence to use computer software;

**Interpretation Bulletins**: IT-283R2: CCA — Videotapes, videotape cassettes, films, computer software and master recording media.

**"designated overburden removal cost"** of a taxpayer means any cost incurred by him in respect of clearing or removing overburden from a mine in Canada owned or operated by him where the cost

(a) was incurred after November 16, 1978 and before 1988,

(b) was incurred after the mine came into production in reasonable commercial quantities,

(c) as of the end of the taxation year in which the cost was incurred, has not been deducted by the taxpayer in computing his income, and

(d) is not deductible, in whole or in part, by the taxpayer in computing his income for a taxation year subsequent to the taxation year in which the cost was incurred, other than by virtue of paragraph 20(1)(a) of the Act;

**"designated underground storage cost"** of a taxpayer means any cost incurred by him after December 11, 1979 in respect of developing a well, mine or other similar underground property for the storage in Canada of petroleum, natural gas or other related hydrocarbons;

**"gas or oil well equipment"** includes

(a) equipment, structures and pipelines, other than a well casing, acquired to be used in a gas or oil field in the production therefrom of natural gas or crude oil, and

(b) a pipeline acquired to be used solely for transmitting gas to a natural gas processing plant,

but does not include

(c) equipment or structures acquired for the refining of oil or the processing of natural gas including the separation therefrom of liquid hydrocarbons, sulphur or other joint products or by-products, or

(d) a pipeline for removal or for collection for immediate removal of natural gas or crude oil from a gas or oil field except a pipeline referred to in paragraph (b);

**Interpretation Bulletins**: IT-476: CCA — Gas and oil exploration and production equipment; IT-482: Pipelines.

**"general-purpose electronic data processing equipment"** means electronic equipment that, in its operation, requires an internally stored computer program that

(a) is executed by the equipment,

(b) can be altered by the user of the equipment,

(c) instructs the equipment to read and select, alter or store data from an external medium such as a card, disk or tape, and

(d) depends upon the characteristics of the data being processed to determine the sequence of its execution;

**"ore"** includes ore from a mineral resource that has been processed to any stage that is prior to the prime metal stage or its equivalent;

**"railway system"** includes a railway owned or operated by a common carrier, together with all buildings, rolling stock, equipment and other properties pertaining thereto, but does not include a tramway;

**"specified temporary access road"** means

(a) a temporary access road to an oil or gas well in Canada, and

(b) a temporary access road the cost of which would, if the definition "Canadian exploration expense" in subsection 66.1(6) of the Act were read without reference to paragraph (l) of that definition, be a Canadian exploration expense because of paragraph (f) or (g) of that definition;

**Related Provisions**: Reg. 1102(14.3)(a) — Exclusion from prescribed property; Reg. Sch. II:Cl. 8(i)(vi), 17(c) — Specified temporary access road excluded from other classes.

**Notes**: Definition "specified temporary access road" added by P.C. 1999-629, effective March 7, 1997. The intent of the special rule for such roads is to not preclude the costs of temporary access roads in the oil and gas and mining sectors from qualifying as CEE or CDE. (Depreciable property is excluded from CEE and CDE under 66.1(6)"Canadian exploration expense"(l) and 66.2(5)"Canadian development expense"(j).)

**"systems software"** means a combination of computer programs and associated procedures, related technical documentation and data that

(a) performs compilation, assembly, mapping, management or processing of other programs,

(b) facilitates the functioning of a computer system by other programs,

(c) provides service or utility functions such as media conversion, sorting, merging, system accounting, performance measurement, system diagnostics or programming aids,

(d) provides general support functions such as data management, report generation or security control, or

(e) provides general capability to meet widespread categories of problem solving or processing requirements where the specific attributes of the work to be performed are introduced mainly in the form of parameters, constants or descriptors rather than in program logic,

and includes a right or licence to use such a combination of computer programs and associated procedures, related technical documentation and data;

**"tar sands ore"** means ore extracted from a deposit of bituminous sands or oil shales;

**Notes**: Definition "tar sands ore" amended by P.C. 1998-49, effective March 7, 1996. Before that date, read:

"tar sands ore" means ore extracted, other than through a well, from a mineral resource that is a deposit of bituminous sand, oil sand or oil shale;

The amendment was consequential on the 1996 budget proposal that all oil sands projects, whether surface mining or *in-situ*, be treated as mines for CCA purposes.

**"telegraph system"** includes the buildings, structures, general plant and communication and other equipment pertaining thereto;

**"telephone system"** includes the buildings, structures, general plant and communication and other equipment pertaining thereto;

**"television commercial message"** means a commercial message as defined in the *Television Broadcasting Regulations, 1987* made under the *Broadcasting Act*;

**Reg. S. 1104(2) tel**  Income Tax Regulations, Part XI

**Notes**: Definition "television commercial message" amended by P.C. 1995-775, retroactive to January 9, 1987, to correct the reference to the relevant regulations.

**"tramway or trolley bus system"** includes the buildings, structures, rolling stock, general plant and equipment pertaining thereto and where buses other than trolley buses are operated in connection therewith includes the properties pertaining to those bus operations.

**Related Provisions**: Reg. 1100(20.1), (20.2) — Limitation on CCA claim for computer software tax shelter property.

**(3)** Except as otherwise provided in subsection (6), in this Part and Schedules II and V,

**"industrial mineral mine"** includes a peat bog or deposit of peat but does not include a mineral resource;

**"mineral"** includes peat;

**"mining"** includes the harvesting of peat.

**(4)** [Revoked]

**(5) Mining** — For the purposes of paragraphs 1100(1)(w) to (ya), subsections 1101(4a) to (4d) and Classes 10, 28 and 41 of Schedule II, a taxpayer's "income from a mine", or any expression referring to a taxpayer's income from a mine, includes income reasonably attributable to

(a) the processing by the taxpayer of

(i) ore (other than iron ore or tar sands ore) all or substantially all of which is from a mineral resource owned by the taxpayer to any stage that is not beyond the prime metal stage or its equivalent,

(ii) iron ore all or substantially all of which is from a mineral resource owned by the taxpayer to any stage that is not beyond the pellet stage or its equivalent,

(iii) tar sands ore all or substantially all of which is from a mineral resource owned by the taxpayer to any stage that is not beyond the crude oil stage or its equivalent, or

(iv) material extracted by a well, all or substantially all of which is from a deposit of bituminous sands or oil shales owned by the taxpayer, to any stage that is not beyond the crude oil stage or its equivalent;

(b) the production by the taxpayer of material from a deposit of bituminous sands or oil shales; and

(c) the transportation by the taxpayer of

(i) output, other than iron ore or tar sands ore, from a mineral resource owned by the taxpayer that has been processed by him to any stage that is not beyond the prime metal stage or its equivalent,

(ii) iron ore from a mineral resource owned by the taxpayer that has been processed by him to any stage that is not beyond the pellet stage or its equivalent, or

(iii) tar sands ore from a mineral resource owned by the taxpayer that has been processed by him to any stage that is not beyond the crude oil stage or its equivalent,

to the extent that such transportation is effected through the use of property of the taxpayer that is included in Class 10 in Schedule II because of paragraph (m) thereof or that would be so included if that paragraph were read without reference to subparagraph (v) thereof and if Class 41 in Schedule II were read without the reference therein to that paragraph.

**Related Provisions**: Reg. 1104(2) — "Ore"; Reg. 1104(3) — "Mineral", "mining"; Reg. 1104(6.1) — Income from a mine excludes income from services.

**Notes**: Revenue Canada's view is that "all or substantially all", used in para. (a), means 90% or more.

Reg. 1104(5) amended, replacing everything up to the opening words of para. (c), by P.C. 1998-49, effective March 7, 1996. Before that date, read:

For the purposes of paragraphs 1100(1)(w) to (ya), subsections 1101(4a) to (4d) and Classes 10 and 28 in Schedule II, "income from a mine", or any expression referring to income from a mine, includes income reasonably attributable to

(a) the processing of

(i) ore, other than iron ore or tar sands ore, from a mineral resource owned by the taxpayer to any stage that is not beyond the prime metal stage or its equivalent,

(ii) iron ore from a mineral resource owned by the taxpayer to any stage that is not beyond the pellet stage or its equivalent, or

(iii) tar sands ore from a mineral resource owned by the taxpayer to any stage that is not beyond the crude oil stage or its equivalent;

(b) the production (other than production from a well) of crude oil from bituminous sand, oil sand or oil shale; or

(c) the transportation of

The amendments accommodate the 1996 budget proposal to treat oil sands projects as mines regardless of whether they are open pit mines or *in-situ* projects.

Opening words of Reg. 1104(5) amended by P.C. 1994-230, effective for property acquired after February 25, 1992, to delete reference to Class 41.

Closing words of Reg. 1104(5)(c) amended by P.C. 1994-230, effective for 1988 and later taxation years, to add the words "and if Class 41 in Schedule II were read without the reference therein to that paragraph".

**Interpretation Bulletins**: IT-469R: CCA — Earth-moving equipment; IT-492: CCA — Industrial mineral mines.

**(5.1) ["Gross revenue from a mine"]** — For the purpose of Class 41 of Schedule II, a taxpayer's "gross revenue from a mine" includes

(a) revenue reasonably attributable to the processing by the taxpayer of

(i) ore (other than iron ore or tar sands ore) from a mineral resource owned by the taxpayer to any stage that is not beyond the prime metal stage or its equivalent,

Division V — Interpretation

(ii) iron ore from a mineral resource owned by the taxpayer to any stage that is not beyond the pellet stage or its equivalent,

(iii) tar sands ore from a mineral resource owned by the taxpayer to any stage that is not beyond the crude oil stage or its equivalent, and

(iv) material extracted by a well from a mineral resource owned by the taxpayer that is a deposit of bituminous sands or oil shales to any stage that is not beyond the crude oil stage or its equivalent;

(b) the amount, if any, by which any revenue reasonably attributable to the processing by the taxpayer of

(i) ore (other than iron ore or tar sands ore) from a mineral resource not owned by the taxpayer, to any stage that is not beyond the prime metal stage or its equivalent,

(ii) iron ore from a mineral resource not owned by the taxpayer to any stage that is not beyond the pellet stage or its equivalent,

(iii) tar sands ore from a mineral resource not owned by the taxpayer to any stage that is not beyond the crude oil stage or its equivalent, and

(iv) material extracted by a well from a mineral resource not owned by the taxpayer that is a deposit of bituminous sands or oil shales to any stage that is not beyond the crude oil stage or its equivalent

exceeds the cost to the taxpayer of the ore or material processed; and

(c) revenue reasonably attributable to the production by the taxpayer of material from a deposit of bituminous sands or oil shales.

**Related Provisions**: Reg. 1104(5.2) — Interpretation.

**Notes**: Reg. 1104(5.1) added by P.C. 1998-49, effective March 7, 1996. It includes revenue from custom processing (less the cost of the ore or material processed) in the "gross revenue from a mine", a concept introduced by the 1996 budget for accelerated CCA for Class 41 property.

**(5.2) ["Gross revenue from a mine"]** — For the purpose of subsection (5.1), "gross revenue from a mine" does not include revenue reasonably attributable to the addition of diluent, for the purpose of transportation, to material extracted from a deposit of bituminous sands or oil shales.

**Notes**: Reg. 1104(5.2) added by P.C. 1998-49, effective March 7, 1996.

**(6)** For the purposes of Class 10 in Schedule II,

(a) **["income from a mine"]** — "income from a mine" includes income reasonably attributable to the processing of

(i) ore, other than iron ore or tar sands ore, from a mineral resource not owned by the taxpayer to any stage that is not beyond the prime metal stage or its equivalent,

(ii) iron ore from a mineral resource not owned by the taxpayer to any stage that is not beyond the pellet stage or its equivalent, or

(iii) tar sands ore from a mineral resource not owned by the taxpayer to any stage that is not beyond the crude oil stage or its equivalent; and

(iv) material extracted by a well from a mineral resource not owned by the taxpayer that is a deposit of bituminous sands or oil shales to any stage that is not beyond the crude oil stage or its equivalent; and

(b) **["mine"]** — "mine" includes a well for the extraction of material from a deposit of bituminous sands or oil shales or from a deposit of calcium chloride, halite or sylvite.

**Related Provisions**: Reg. 1104(6.1) — Income from a mine excludes income from services.

**Notes**: Opening words of Reg. 1104(6) amended by P.C. 1994-230, effective for property acquired after February 25, 1992, to delete reference to para. (b) of Class 41.

Reg. 1104(6)(a)(iv) added by P.C. 1998-49, effective March 7, 1996.

Reference to calcium choloride added to Reg. 1104(6)(b) by P.C. 1996-495, retroactive to property acquired in taxation years that begin after 1984.

Reference to bituminous sands and oil shales added to Reg. 1104(6)(b) by P.C. 1998-49, effective March 7, 1996.

**Interpretation Bulletins**: IT-469R: CCA — Earth-moving equipment.

**(6.1)** [Repealed]

**Notes**: Reg. 1104(6.1) added by P.C. 1996-1488, effective for taxation years that begin after March 6, 1996, and then repealed retroactive to its introduction by P.C. 1999-629. Now deemed never to have been in force, it read:

(6.1) ["Income from a mine"] — Notwithstanding subsections (5) and (6),

(a) for the purposes of paragraphs 1100(1)(w) to (ya), subsections 1101(4a) to (4d) and Class 28 in Schedule II, "income from a mine", or any expression referring to a taxpayer's income from a mine, does not include income that can reasonably be attributed to a service rendered by the taxpayer; and

(b) for the purpose of Class 10 in Schedule II, "income from a mine" does not include income that can reasonably be attributed to a service rendered by the taxpayer other than the processing of ore.

**(7) [Mine]** — For the purposes of paragraphs 1100(1)(w) to (ya), subsections 1101(4a) to (4d) and 1102(8) and (9), section 1107 and Classes 12, 28 and 41 of Schedule II,

(a) "mine" includes

(i) a well for the extraction of material from a deposit of bituminous sands or oil shales or from a deposit of calcium chloride, halite or sylvite, and

(ii) a pit for the extraction of kaolin or tar sands ore,

but does not include

(iii) an oil or gas well, or

(iv) a sand pit, gravel pit, clay pit, shale pit, peat bog, deposit of peat or a stone quarry (other than a kaolin pit or a deposit of bituminous sands or oil shales);

(b) all wells of a taxpayer for the extraction of material from one or more deposits of calcium chloride, halite or sylvite, the material produced from which is sent to the same plant for processing, are deemed to be one mine of the taxpayer; and

(c) all wells of a taxpayer for the extraction of material from a deposit of bituminous sands or oil shales that the Minister, in consultation with the Minister of Natural Resources, determines constitute one project, are deemed to be one mine of the taxpayer.

**Related Provisions**: Reg. 1104(8) — "Stone quarry".

**Notes**: Reg. 1104(7) amended by P.C. 1998-49, effective March 7, 1996. Before that date read:

(7) For the purposes of paragraphs 1100(1)(w) to (ya), subsections 1101(4a) to (4d) and 1102(8) and (9) and Classes 12 and 28 in Schedule II,

(a) "mine" includes a well for the extraction of material from a deposit of calcium chloride, halite or sylvite, but does not include any oil well or gas well, sand pit, gravel pit, clay pit, shale pit, peat bog, deposit of peat or stone quarry (other than a deposit of bituminous sand, oil sand or oil shale or a kaolin pit); and

(b) all wells of a taxpayer for the extraction of material from one or more deposits of calcium chloride, halite or sylvite, the material produced from which is sent to the same plant for processing, shall be deemed to be one mine of the taxpayer.

Opening words of Reg. 1104(7) amended by P.C. 1994-230, effective for 1988 and later taxation years, to delete reference to Class 41.

References to calcium chloride added to Reg. 1104(7)(a) and (b) by P.C. 1996-495, retroactive to property acquired in taxation years that begin after 1984. (The references to a kaolin pit only apply to taxation years that end after 1987.)

**(8) ["Stone quarry"]** — For the purposes of subsection (7), "stone quarry" includes a mine producing dimension stone or crushed rock for use as aggregates or for other construction purposes.

**(9) Manufacturing or processing** — For the purposes of subsection 1100(26) and Class 29 in Schedule II, "manufacturing or processing" does not include

(a) farming or fishing;

(b) logging;

(c) construction;

(d) operating an oil or gas well or extracting petroleum or natural gas from a natural accumulation thereof;

(e) extracting minerals from a mineral resource;

(f) processing of

(i) ore, other than iron ore or tar sands ore, from a mineral resource to any stage that is not beyond the prime metal stage or its equivalent,

(ii) iron ore from a mineral resource to any stage that is not beyond the pellet stage or its equivalent, or

(iii) tar sands ore from a mineral resource to any stage that is not beyond the crude oil stage or its equivalent;

(g) producing industrial minerals;

(h) producing or processing electrical energy or steam, for sale;

(i) processing natural gas as part of the business of selling or distributing gas in the course of operating a public utility;

(j) processing heavy crude oil recovered from a natural reservoir in Canada to a stage that is not beyond the crude oil stage or its equivalent; or

(k) Canadian field processing.

**Related Provisions**: ITA 125.1(2)(a) — Credit for generating electrical energy for sale; ITA 125.1(3) — Definition of "manufacturing or processing" for M&P credit purposes.

**Notes**: Opening words of Reg. 1104(9) amended by P.C. 1994-230, effective for property acquired after February 25, 1992, to delete reference to Class 39, and amended by P.C. 1997-1033, effective for taxation years ending after March 6, 1996, to add application to Reg. 1100(26).

Reg. 1104(9)(g) amended by P.C. 1999-629 to remove the words "other than sulphur produced by processing natural gas" from the end, effective for taxation years that begin after 1996.

Reg. 1104(9)(i) and (j) amended, and (k) added, by P.C. 1999-629, effective for taxation years that begin after 1996. Paras. (i) and (j) previously read:

(i) processing gas, if such gas is processed as part of the business of selling or distributing gas in the course of operating a public utility; or

(j) processing in Canada of heavy crude oil recovered from a natural reservoir in Canada to a stage that is not beyond the crude oil stage or its equivalent.

**Interpretation Bulletins**: IT-147R3: CCA — Accelerated write-off of manufacturing and processing machinery and equipment; IT-411R: Meaning of "construction".

**(10) Certified films and video tapes** — For the purposes of subsection 1100(21) and the definitions "certified feature film" and "certified production" in subsection (2),

(a) "Canadian" means an individual who was, at all relevant times,

(i) a Canadian citizen as defined in the *Citizenship Act*, or

(ii) a permanent resident within the meaning of the *Immigration Act, 1976*;

(b) a motion picture film or video tape that has been certified by

(i) the Secretary of State, or

(ii) the Minister of Communications

Division V — Interpretation     Reg. S. 1104(13) eli

as a certified feature film or certified production, as the case may be, may have its certification revoked by the Minister of Communications where an incorrect statement was made in the furnishing of information for the purpose of obtaining that certification and a certification that has been so revoked is void from the time of its issue;

(c) "remuneration" does not include an amount determined by reference to the amount of income from a motion picture film or video tape;

(c.1) "revenue guarantee" means a contract or other arrangement under the terms of which a taxpayer has a right to receive a minimum rental revenue or other fixed revenue in respect of a right to the use, in any manner whatever, of a certified feature film or certified production;

(c.2) a screenwriter shall be deemed to be an individual who is a Canadian where

(i) each individual involved in the preparation of the screenplay is a Canadian, or

(ii) the principal screenwriter is an individual who is a Canadian and

(A) the screenplay for the motion picture film or video tape is based upon a work authored by a Canadian,

(B) copyright in the work subsists in Canada, and

(C) the work is published in Canada;

(d) "unit of production" means a measure used by the Minister of Communications in determining the weight to be given for each individual Canadian referred to in subparagraph (b)(ii) of the definition "certified production" in subsection (2) who provides services in respect of a motion picture film or video tape; and

(e) where each individual who performed a service in respect of a motion picture film or video tape as the

(i) director,

(ii) screenwriter,

(iii) actor or actress in respect of whose services for the film or tape the highest remuneration was paid or payable,

(iv) actor or actress in respect of whose services for the film or tape the second highest remuneration was paid or payable,

(v) art director,

(vi) director of photography,

(vii) music composer, or

(viii) picture editor

was a Canadian, the Minister of Communications shall be deemed to have allotted six units of production in respect of the film or tape for the purposes of the definition "certified production" in subsection (2).

**Notes**: The *Department of Canadian Heritage Act* (S.C. 1995, c. 11), in force July 12, 1996, provides:

46. Other references — Every reference made to the Minister of Communications, the Minister of Multiculturalism and Citizenship and the Secretary of State of Canada in relation to any matter to which the powers, duties and functions of the Minister of Canadian Heritage extend by virtue of this Act, in any other Act of Parliament or in any order, regulation or other instrument made under any Act of Parliament shall, unless the context otherwise requires, be read as a reference to the Minister of Canadian Heritage.

**(11) Certified Class 34 properties** — For the purposes of paragraph (h) of Class 34 in Schedule II, a certificate issued under

(a) subparagraph (d)(i) of that class may be revoked by the Minister of Industry, Trade and Commerce, or

(b) subparagraph (d)(ii) or paragraph (g) of that class, as the case may be, may be revoked by the Minister of Energy, Mines and Resources

where

(c) an incorrect statement was made in the furnishing of information for the purpose of obtaining the certificate, or

(d) the taxpayer does not conform to the plan described in subparagraph (d)(i) or (d)(ii) of that class, as the case may be,

and a certificate that has been so revoked shall be void from the time of its issue.

**(12) Amusement parks** — For the purposes of Class 37 in Schedule II, "amusement park" means a park open to the public where amusements, rides and audio-visual attractions are permanently situated.

**(13) Class 43.1 — Energy conservation property** — The definitions in this subsection apply for the purposes of this subsection and subsection (14) and Class 43.1 in Schedule II.

**"digester gas"** means a mixture of gases that are produced from the decomposition of organic waste in a digester and that are extracted from an eligible sewage treatment facility for that organic waste.

**"distribution equipment"** means equipment (other than transmission equipment) used to distribute electrical energy generated by electrical generating equipment.

**"eligible landfill site"** means a landfill site that is situated in Canada, or a former landfill site that is situated in Canada, and, if a permit or license in respect of the site is or was required under any law of Canada or of a province, for which the permit or license has been issued.

**"eligible sewage treatment facility"** means a sewage treatment facility that is situated in Canada and for which a permit or license is issued under any law of Canada or of a province.

2063

**"eligible waste management facility"** means a waste management facility that is situated in Canada and for which a permit or license is issued under any law of Canada or of a province.

**"enhanced combined cycle system"** means an electrical generating system in which thermal waste from one or more natural gas compressor systems is recovered and used to contribute at least 20 per cent of the energy input of a combined cycle process in order to enhance the generation of electricity, but does not include the natural gas compressor systems.

**"fossil fuel"** means a fuel that is petroleum, natural gas or related hydrocarbons, coal, coal gas, coke, lignite or peat.

**"landfill gas"** means a mixture of gases that are produced from the decomposition of organic waste and that are extracted from an eligible landfill site.

**"municipal waste"** means the combustible portion of waste material (other than waste material that is considered to be toxic or hazardous waste pursuant to any law of Canada or of a province) that is generated in Canada and that is accepted at an eligible landfill site or an eligible waste management facility and that, when burned to generate energy, emits only those fluids or other emissions that are in compliance with the law of Canada or of a province.

**"solution gas"** means a fossil fuel that is gas that would otherwise be flared and has been extracted from a solution of gas and produced oil.

**Notes**: Definition "solution gas" added by P.C. 2000-1331, effective February 17, 1999.

**"thermal waste"** means heat energy extracted from a distinct point of rejection in an industrial process.

**"transmission equipment"** means equipment used to transmit more than 75 per cent of the annual electrical energy generated by electrical generating equipment, but does not include a building.

**"wood waste"** includes scrap wood, sawdust, wood chips, bark, limbs, saw-ends and hog fuel, but does not include residuals (known as "black liquor") from wood pulp operations and any waste that no longer has the physical or chemical properties of wood.

**Notes**: Reg. 1104(13) added by P.C. 1997-1033, effective February 22, 1994.

**(14) [Class 43.1(c) compliance]** — Where property of a taxpayer is not operating in the manner required by paragraph (c) of Class 43.1 in Schedule II solely because of a deficiency, failing or shutdown — that is beyond the control of the taxpayer — of the system of which it is part and that previously operated in the manner required by that paragraph, that property is deemed, for the purpose of that paragraph, to be operating in the manner required under that paragraph during the period of the deficiency, failing or shutdown, if the taxpayer makes all reasonable efforts to rectify the circumstances within a reasonable time.

**Notes**: Reg. 1104(14) added by P.C. 1997-1033, effective February 22, 1994.

**Related Provisions [Reg. 1104]**: ITA 20(1.1) — Definitions in ITA 13(21) apply to regulations.

**Definitions [Reg. 1104]**: "amount" — ITA 248(1); "associated" — ITA 256; "bituminous sands", "business" — ITA 248(1); "Canada" — ITA 255, *Interpretation Act* 35(1); "Canadian" — Reg. 1104(10)(a), (c.2); "Canadian exploration expense" — ITA 66.1(6), 248(1); "Canadian field processing" — ITA 248(1); "certified feature film", "certified production" — Reg. 1104(2); "class" — Reg. 1101(6), 1102(1)–(3), (14), (14.1); "coal mine operator", "computer software" — Reg. 1104(2); "corporation" — ITA 248(1), *Interpretation Act* 35(1); "digester gas", "distribution equipment", "eligible landfill site", "eligible sewage treatment facility", "eligible waste management facility" — Reg. 1104(13); "end of the taxation year" — Reg. 1104(1); "enhanced combined cycle system" — Reg. 1104(13); "farming" — ITA 248(1); "fiscal period" — ITA 249.1; "fishing" — ITA 248(1); "fossil fuel" — Reg. 1104(13); "individual" — ITA 248(1); "landfill gas" — Reg. 1104(13); "mineral" — Reg. 1104(3); "mineral resource", "Minister" — ITA 248(1); "month" — *Interpretation Act* 35(1); "municipal waste" — Reg. 1104(13); "non-resident", "oil or gas well" — ITA 248(1); "ore" — Reg. 1104(2); "Parliament" — *Interpretation Act* 35(1); "person" — ITA 248(1); "pipeline" — Reg. 1104(2); "property" — ITA 248(1); "province" — *Interpretation Act* 35(1); "related" — ITA 251(2)–(6); "remuneration" — Reg. 1104(10)(c); "resident" — ITA 250; "revenue guarantee" — Reg. 1104(10)(c.1); "security" — *Interpretation Act* 35(1); "stone quarry" — Reg. 1104(8); "systems software", "tar sands ore" — Reg. 1104(2); "taxation year" — ITA 249, Reg. 1104(1); "taxpayer" — ITA 248(1); "thermal waste", "transmission equipment" — Reg. 1104(13); "unit of production" — Reg. 1104(10)(d); "wood waste" — Reg. 1104(13).

## DIVISION VI — CLASSES PRESCRIBED

**1105.** The classes of property provided in this Part and in Schedule II are hereby prescribed for the purposes of the Act.

**Notes**: Reg. 1105 amended by P.C. 1996-571, effective for taxation years that end after February 21, 1994, to apply for all purposes of the Act instead of just ITA 13, 20(1)(a) and 59(3.3). This ensures it applies for purposes of ITA 80.

**Definitions [Reg. 1105]**: "class" — Reg. 1101(6), 1102(1)–(3), (14), (14.1); "prescribed", "property" — ITA 248(1).

## DIVISION VII — CERTIFICATES ISSUED BY MINISTER OF SUPPLY AND SERVICES [REPEALED]

**Notes**: Former Reg. 1106 (Division VII of Part XI) repealed by P.C. 1995-775, effective for property acquired after May 30, 1995. It allowed the Minister of Supply and Services to issue a certificate in respect of property that would then be entitled to an additional allowance under Reg. 1100(1)(j) or (k). Such certificates were introduced during the Korean War in 1951 and have not been used for many years.

## Proposed Addition — Reg. 1106

### DIVISION VII — CERTIFICATES ISSUED BY MINISTER OF CANADIAN HERITAGE

**1106. (1) Definitions** — For the purposes of this section and paragraph (x) of Class 10 in Schedule II,

**"Canadian"** means a person that is

(a) a Canadian citizen as defined in the *Citizenship Act*,

(b) a permanent resident within the meaning assigned by the *Immigration Act*, or

(c) a corporation that is Canadian-controlled, as determined for the purposes of sections 26 to 28 of the *Investment Canada Act*;

*Related Provisions*: Reg. 1106(5)(c) — Principal screenwriter deemed not Canadian.

**"Canadian government film agency"** means a federal or provincial government agency the mandate of which is related to the provision of assistance to film productions in Canada;

**"excluded production"** means a film or video production of a prescribed taxable Canadian corporation

(a) in respect of which

(i) the Minister of Canadian Heritage has not issued a certificate of completion, within 30 months after the end of the corporation's taxation year in which the production's principal photography began, certifying that the production was completed within two years after the end of the year,

(ii) where the production is not a treaty co-production, neither the corporation nor another prescribed taxable Canadian corporation related to the corporation

(A) is, except to the extent of an interest in the production held by a prescribed taxable Canadian corporation as a co-producer of the production or by a prescribed person (within the meaning assigned by subsection 1106(7)), the exclusive worldwide copyright owner in the production for all commercial exploitation purposes for the 25-year period that begins at the first time the production had been completed and is commercially exploitable,

(B) controls the initial licensing of commercial exploitation, and

(C) retains a share of revenues, that is acceptable to the Minister of Canadian Heritage, from the exploitation of the production in non-Canadian markets,

(iii) there is not an agreement in writing for consideration at the fair market value with

(A) a corporation that is a Canadian and is a distributor of film or video productions, or

(B) a corporation that holds a broadcasting license issued by the Canadian Radio-television and Telecommunications Commission for television markets,

to have the production shown in Canada within the two-year period that begins at the first time the production has been completed and is commercially exploitable, or

(iv) a distribution is made in Canada within that two-year period by a person who is not a Canadian, or

(b) that is

(i) news, current events or public affairs programming, or a programme that includes weather or market reports,

(ii) a talk show,

(iii) a production in respect of a game, questionnaire or contest (other than a production directed primarily at minors),

(iv) a sports event or activity,

(v) a gala presentation or an awards show,

(vi) a production that solicits funds,

(vii) reality television,

(viii) pornography,

(ix) advertising,

(x) a production produced primarily for industrial, corporate or institutional purposes,

(xi) a production, other than a documentary, all or substantially all of which consists of stock footage, or

(xii) a production for which public financial support would, in the opinion of the Minister of Canadian Heritage, be contrary to public policy;

**Technical Notes, June 20, 1996**: Proposed Regulation 1106(1) provides the definition of "excluded production", which is a film or video production that is not considered to be an eligible production for the purposes of the Canadian film or video production tax credit regime. Generally, proposed clause (a)(ii)(A) of that definition provides that a prescribed taxable Canadian corporation's film or video production will be an excluded production if the corporation (or a related prescribed taxable Canadian corporation) is not the exclusive worldwide copyright owner of the production for 5 years. This amendment would lengthen the required ownership period to 25 years. However, an exception from the exclusive worldwide copyright rule in respect of a production is made for copyright in the production held by a co-producer of the production that is a prescribed taxable Canadian corporation or by a prescribed person (see the commentary to proposed Regulation 1106(7)).

**Reg. S. 1106(1) exc**  Income Tax Regulations, Part XI, Division VII

This amendment applies to the 1995 and subsequent taxation years except that the reference to the "25-year period" in that clause shall be read as a "5-year period" in the case of a film or video production for which a Canadian film or video production certificate is obtained before 1997. The change to a 25-year ownership requirement has been made upon recommendation of the Department of Canadian Heritage.

**Related Provisions**: Reg. 1106(2) — Prescribed taxable Canadian corporation; Reg. 1106(7) — Prescribed person.

**Notes**: The CCRA's view is that "all or substantially all", used in subpara. (b)(xi), means 90% or more.

**"producer"** of a film or video production does not include a person unless the person is the individual

(a) who controls and is the central decision maker in respect of the production,

(b) who is directly responsible for the acquisition of the production story or screenplay and the development, creative and financial control and exploitation of the production, and

(c) who is identified in the production as being the producer of the production;

**"remuneration"** does not include an amount determined by reference to profits or revenues;

**"treaty co-production"** means a film or video production the production of which is contemplated in a co-production treaty entered into between Canada and another country.

**(2) Prescribed taxable Canadian corporation** — For the purposes of section 125.4 of the Act and this section, "prescribed taxable Canadian corporation" means a taxable Canadian corporation that is a Canadian, other than a corporation that is

(a) controlled directly or indirectly in any manner whatever by one or more persons all or part of whose taxable income is exempt from tax under Part I of the Act; or

(b) a prescribed labour-sponsored venture capital corporation.

**Related Provisions**: ITA 256(5.1), (6.2) — Meaning of "controlled directly or indirectly"; Reg. 6701 — Prescribed labour-sponsored venture capital corporation.

**(3) Canadian film or video production** — For the purposes of section 125.4 of the Act, this Part and Schedule II, "Canadian film or video production" means a film or video production, other than an excluded production, of a prescribed taxable Canadian corporation and that is

(a) a treaty co-production, or

(b) a film or video production

(i) at all times during the production of which the producer of which is a Canadian,

(ii) in respect of which the Minister of Canadian Heritage has allotted not less than six points in accordance with subsection (4),

(iii) in respect of which not less than 75% of the total of all costs for services provided in respect of producing the production (other than excluded costs) was payable to, and in respect of services provided by individuals who are, Canadians, and for the purpose of this subparagraph, excluded costs are

(A) costs determined by reference to the amount of income from the production,

(B) remuneration payable to, or in respect of, the producer or individuals described in any of clauses (4)(a)(i)(A) to (H) and (ii)(A) to (F) and subparagraph 4(a)(iii),

(C) amounts payable in respect of insurance, financing, brokerage, legal and accounting fees, and similar amounts, and

(D) costs described in subparagraph (iv), and

(iv) in respect of which not less than 75% of the total of all costs incurred for the post-production of the production, including laboratory work, sound re-recording, sound editing and picture editing (other than costs determined by reference to the amount of income from the production and remuneration payable to, or in respect of, the producer or individuals described in any of clauses (4)(a)(i)(A) to (H) and (ii)(A) to (F) and subparagraph 4(a)(iii)) was incurred in respect of services provided in Canada,

other than a production the certification of which has been revoked under subsection 125.4(6) of the Act by the Minister of Canadian Heritage.

**Related Provisions**: Reg. 1101(5k.1) — Separate class for certain property under Class 10(x); Reg. 1106(1) — Definitions; Reg. 1106(4) — Points for creative services; Reg. Sch. II:Cl. 10(x) — CCA class for Canadian film or video production.

**(4) Creative services** — For the purposes of subsection (3) and this subsection,

(a) there shall be allotted in the case of a film or video production

(i) that is not an animation production,

(A) for the director, two points,

(B) for the principal screenwriter, two points,

(C) for the lead performer for whose services the highest remuneration was payable, one point,

(D) for the lead performer for whose services the second highest remuneration was payable, one point,

(E) for the art director, one point,

(F) for the director of photography, one point,

(G) for the music composer, one point, and

(H) for the picture editor, one point,

if that person is an individual who is a Canadian,

(ii) that is an animation production,

(A) for the director, one point,

(B) for the lead voice for which the highest or second highest remuneration was payable, one point,

(C) for the design supervisor, one point,

(D) for the camera operator where the camera operation is done in Canada, one point,

(E) for the music composer, one point, and

(F) for the picture editor, one point,

if that person is an individual who is a Canadian, and

(iii) that is an animation production, one point where both the principal screenwriter and storyboard supervisor are individuals who are Canadians; and

(iv) that is an animation production

(A) for the place where the layout and background work is done, one point,

(B) for the place where the key animation is done, one point,

(C) for the place where the assistant animation and in-betweening is done, one point,

if the place is in Canada;

(b) a production that is not an animation production is deemed not to be a Canadian film or video production unless there are allotted in respect of the production two points under clause (a)(i)(A) or (B) and one point under clause (a)(i)(C) or (D); and

(c) an animation production is deemed not to be a Canadian film or video production unless there are allotted in respect of the production

(i) one point under clause (a)(ii)(A) or subparagraph (a)(iii),

(ii) one point under clause (a)(ii)(B), and

(iii) one point under clause (a)(iv)(B).

**Related Provisions**: Reg. 1106(1) — Definitions; Reg. 1106(5) — Lead performer/screenwriter; Reg. 1106(6) — Documentary production.

**(5) Lead performer/screenwriter** — For the purposes of subsections (4) and (6),

(a) a lead performer in respect of a production is an actor or actress who has a leading role in the production having regard to the performer's remuneration, billing and time on screen;

(b) a lead voice in respect of an animation production is the voice of the individual who has a leading role in the production having regard to the length of time that the individual's voice is heard in the production and the individual's remuneration;

(c) the principal screenwriter of a production is not a Canadian unless

(i) each individual involved in the preparation of the screenplay for the production is otherwise a Canadian, or

(ii) the principal screenwriter is an individual who otherwise is a Canadian and

(A) the screenplay for the production is based upon a work authored by a Canadian, and

(B) the work is published in Canada.

**(6) Documentary production** — Notwithstanding subsection (4), a documentary production that is not an excluded production is deemed to be a Canadian film or video production if all creative positions in respect of the production are occupied by individuals who are Canadians.

**(7) Prescribed person** — For the purpose of section 125.4 of the Act, "prescribed person" means

(a) a corporation that holds a television broadcasting licence issued by the Canadian Radio-television and Telecommunications Commission,

(b) a person to whom paragraph 149(1)(l) of the Act applies where the person has a fund which is used to finance Canadian film or video productions,

(c) a Canadian government film agency, or

(d) in respect of a film or video production, a non-resident person who does not carry on a business in Canada where the person's interest in the production is acquired to comply with the certificate requirements of a treaty co-production twinning arrangement.

**Technical Notes, June 20, 1996**: Draft Regulation 1106(7), which defines "prescribed person" for the purposes of the proposed Canadian film or video production tax credit ("CFVPTC"), is relevant for two purposes. First, a prescribed person is not considered to be an "investor" under subsection 125.4(1). A qualifying corporation will, therefore, not be precluded by subsection 125.4(4) from claiming a CFVPTC in respect of a film or video production solely because a "prescribed person" has an interest in the production.

Second, the definition "prescribed person" is relevant for the purpose of determining whether a production is an "excluded production" under proposed Regulation 1106(1). Subsection 1106(7) of the Regulations applies to the 1995 and subsequent taxation years.

**Related Provisions**: ITA 253 — Extended meaning of "carry on business in Canada".

**Notes**: This definition applies for purposes of 125.4(1) "investor" and Reg. 1106(1) "excluded production".

**(8) Prescribed amount** — For the purpose of the definition "assistance" in subsection 125.4(1)

**Reg. S. 1106(8)**  Income Tax Regulations, Part XI, Division VII

of the Act, "prescribed amount" means an amount paid or payable to a taxpayer under the License Fee Program of the Canada Television and Cable Production Fund or the Canada Television Fund/Fonds canadien de télévision.

**Application**: The October 27, 1998 draft regulations, s. 1, will add subsec. 1106(8), applicable to amounts received after February 23, 1998.

**Technical Notes**: Section 1106 of the *Income Tax Regulations* provides rules related to the Canadian Film or Video Production Tax Credit.

New subsection 1106(8) prescribes amounts paid or payable under the License Fee Program of the Canada Television and Cable Production Fund for the purpose of the definition "assistance" in subsection 125.4(1) of the *Income Tax Act*. As a result, such payments will not be considered assistance for the purposes of the Canadian Film or Video Production Tax Credit provided under section 125.4 of the Act.

New subsection 1106(8) applies to amounts received after February 23, 1998.

**Letter from Department of Finance, July 14, 1998**:

Dear [xxx]

Thank you for your letter dated June 25, 1998 requesting further transitional relief for payments received from the Canada Television and Cable Production fund (CCTCPF) from the 1998 Budget proposal regarding indirect assistance.

I have been informed that the CTCPF has been unable to reorganize itself in such a way as to ensure that its funding is not considered indirect assistance for income tax purposes. I also understand that the positions taken by both the representatives of the CTCPF and Revenue Canada are reasonable in the circumstances.

Therefore, in light of this government's intention that the 1998 Budget proposal not apply to treat funding of CTCPF as assistance for income tax purposes, I have instructed my officials to draft the legislation implementing this Budget measure in a manner which will ensure that payments made to film producers from the CTCPF as licence fee top-ups are excluded from categorization as assistance for the purposes of the Canadian Film or Video Production Tax Credit.

Based on the foregoing, it would appear that no further transitional relief will be necessary to achieve the CTCPF's goal. Should you require additional information, please contact Mr. Len Farber at (613) 992-3024.

Sincerely,

The Honourable Paul Martin, P.C., M.P.

**Application**: The December 12, 1995 draft regulations (Canadian film tax credit), s. 3, will add s. 1106 (Div. VII), applicable to 1995 et seq. The June 20, 1996 Notice of Ways and Means Motion will amend cl. (a)(ii)(A) of the definition "excluded production" in subsec. 1106(1) and add subsec. 1106(7), applicable to 1995 et seq., except that the reference to the "25-year period" in cl. (a)(ii)(A) shall be read as a "5-year period" in the case of a film or video production for which a Canadian film or video production certificate is obtained before 1997. For subsec. 1106(8), see Application note above.

**Definitions [Reg. 1106]**: "amount" — ITA 248(1); "broadcasting" — *Interpretation Act* 35(1); "business" — ITA 248(1); "Canada" — ITA 255, *Interpretation Act* 35(1); "Canadian" — Reg. 1106(1), (5)(c); "Canadian film or video production" — Reg. 1106(3), (4)(b), (c), 1106(6); "Canadian government film agency" — Reg. 1106(1); "controlled directly or indirectly" — ITA 256(5.1), (6.2); "corporation" — ITA 248(1), *Interpretation Act* 35(1); "excluded production" — Reg. 1106(1); "individual" — ITA 248(1); "lead performer" — Reg. 1106(5)(a); "lead voice" — Reg. 1106(5)(b); "Minister" — ITA 248(1); "month" — *Interpretation Act* 35(1); "non-resident", "person", "prescribed" — ITA 248(1); "prescribed labour-sponsored venture capital corporation" — Reg. 6701; "prescribed taxable Canadian corporation" — Reg. 1106(2); "producer" — Reg. 1106(1); "related" — ITA 251(2)–(6); "remuneration" — Reg. 1106(1); "resident" — ITA 250; "share" — ITA 248(1); "taxable Canadian corporation" — ITA 89(1), 248(1); "taxable income" — ITA 248(1); "taxation year" — ITA 249, Reg. 1104(1); "treaty co-production" — Reg. 1106(1); "writing" — *Interpretation Act* 35(1).

## Proposed Amendment — Reg. 1106(7)

**Letter from Department of Finance, April 29, 1998**:

Dear [xxx]

I am writing in response to your facsimile letter of March 31, 1998, in which you suggested that any registered charity that has a fund to finance Canadian film or video productions be included in the list of investors prescribed by draft paragraph 1106(7)(b) of the *Income Tax Regulations*.

It is my understanding, however, that your submission relates to the Independent Production Fund ("the Fund") in particular. You have indicated that the Fund is a charity which makes equity investments in film and television productions which amount to no more than 5-10% of any given production budget. Your concern is that the presence of such an investment could disqualify a film from qualifying for a Canadian Film or Video Production Tax Credit ("CFVPTC") by reason of subsection 125.4(4) of the *Income Tax Act*.

Leaving aside the issue of whether the "charity" is engaging in an ineligible activity, your particular example poses little difficulty from a CFVPTC policy perspective. However, your proposed solution is not constrained to similar fact situations. In particular, it is constrained neither to nominal interests, nor ownership interests, nor funding that could be traced to persons that might otherwise be considered to be prescribed investors in their own right. From a tax policy perspective, the intent of the CFVPTC legislation, as it stands, is to allow the CFVPTC to a producer only where no other person is able to claim a deduction in respect of the production. This is because the deduction itself is considered to already provide a tax benefit in respect of the production. It is not intended that a tax credit be given in addition to this benefit.

As you may know, however, we have discussed with the industry the possibility of excluding from the definition "investor" a person where, in respect of the investment, the person is subject to the matchable expenditure rules in section 18.1 of the *Income Tax Act*, on condition that the "investment" be considered assistance to the producer or otherwise excluded from the producer's eligible cost. If I understand your issue correctly, however, the fund could not claim that the investment was a matchable expenditure because it, in fact, takes an actual percentage ownership in the film (rather than a right to production).

You have also noted that an exemption has been provided in respect of non-profit funds that have been established to fund Canadian film or video productions. As you know, the only such fund in existence receives amounts only from the Government of Canada and persons who would otherwise be prescribed persons. Further, while registered charities are similar to non-profit organizations such as the Canadian Television and Cable Production Fund, charities have one materially distinct characteristic: they can offer tax credits or deductions to their donors. In the absence of any constraint on eligible donors, therefore, it would be difficult to recommit a blanket exemption for funds operated by any charity.

In view of the above, we could recommend a modified version of your proposal under which eligible charities would be constrained to those charities that

- are constated to provide funding for film or video productions, all or substantially all of which funding is provided by way of a direct ownership interest in the production, and
- have not received donations after 1996, other than from persons who are otherwise prescribed persons.

In this regard, you should be aware that we have already proposed to recommend that the list of prescribed persons be expanded to include corporations that hold a specialty or pay-television broadcasting licence issued by the Canadian Radio-television and Telecommunications Commission ("CRTC"), or that hold a broadcast undertaking licence and provide production funding as a result of "significant benefits" commitment given to the CRTC.

Please advise us if these proposals would resolve your concerns. Thank you for bringing your concerns to my attention.

Sincerely,

Len Farber
Director General
Tax Legislation Division

## DIVISION VIII — DETERMINATION OF VISCOSITY AND DENSITY

**1107. (1)** For the purpose of the definition "bituminous sands" in section 248(1) of the Act, viscosity or density of hydrocarbons shall be determined using a number of individual samples (constituting a representative sampling of that deposit or those deposits, as the case may be, from which the taxpayer is committed to produce by means of one mine) tested

(a) at atmospheric pressure;

(b) at a temperature of 15.6 degrees Celsius; and

(c) free of solution gas.

**Notes**: Reg. 1107 added by P.C. 1998-49, effective March 7, 1996.

**Definitions [Reg. 1107]**: "individual" — ITA 248(1); "solution gas" — Reg. 1104(13); "taxpayer" — ITA 248(1).

## PART XII — RESOURCE AND PROCESSING ALLOWANCES

**1200.** For the purposes of section 65 of the Act, there may be deducted in computing the income of a taxpayer for a taxation year such of the amounts determined in accordance with sections 1201 to 1209 and 1212 as are applicable.

**Definitions [Reg. 1200]**: "amount" — ITA 248(1); "taxation year" — ITA 249; "taxpayer" — ITA 248(1).

**1201. Earned depletion allowances** — In computing a taxpayer's income for a taxation year there may be deducted such amount as he may claim not exceeding the lesser of

(a) the aggregate of

(i) 25 per cent of the amount, if any, by which the taxpayer's resource profits for the year exceed four times the total of amounts, if any, deducted under subsection 1202(2) in computing the taxpayer's income for the year, and

(ii) the amount, if any, by which the aggregate of amounts included in computing the taxpayer's income for the year under paragraphs 59(3.3)(a) and (b) of the Act exceeds the aggregate of amounts, if any, that may reasonably be considered to have been deducted under subsection 1202(2) by reason of subparagraph (b)(ii) thereof in computing the taxpayer's income for the year; and

(b) the aggregate of

(i) the taxpayer's earned depletion base as of the end of the year, and

(ii) the amount, if any, by which

(A) the aggregate determined under paragraph 1202(4)(a) in respect of the taxpayer for the year

exceeds

(B) the amount, if any, by which

(I) the aggregate of all amounts that would be determined under paragraphs 1205(1)(e) to (k)

exceeds

(II) 33 $^1/_3$ per cent of the aggregate of all amounts that would be determined under paragraphs 1205(1)(a) to (d.2)

in computing the taxpayer's earned depletion base as of the end of the year.

**Notes**: Reg. 1201(a)(i) amended by P.C. 1999-629, effective for 1999 and later taxation years, to delete the words "(other than that portion of such amounts that may reasonably be considered to have been deducted by reason of subparagraph (b)(ii) thereof)" before "in computing...".

**Definitions [Reg. 1201]**: "amount" — ITA 248(1); "earned depletion base" — Reg. 1202(1), 1205(1); "resource profits" — Reg. 1204(1.1); "successor" — Reg. 1202(7); "taxation year" — ITA 249; "taxpayer" — ITA 248(1).

**1202. (1)** For the purposes of computing the earned depletion base of a corporation, control of which has been acquired under circumstances described in subsection 66(11) of the Act, the amount by which the earned depletion base of the corporation at the time referred to in that subsection exceeds the aggregate of amounts otherwise deducted under section 1201 in computing its income for taxation years ending after that time and before control was so acquired shall be deemed to have been deducted under section 1201

**Reg. S. 1202(1)** — Income Tax Regulations

by the corporation in computing its income for taxation years ending before such acquisition of control.

**(2)** Subject to subsections (5) and (6), where after November 7, 1969 a corporation (in this subsection referred to as the "successor") acquired a particular property (whether by way of a purchase, amalgamation, merger, winding-up or otherwise), there may be deducted by the successor in computing its income for a taxation year an amount not exceeding the aggregate of all amounts each of which is an amount determined in respect of an original owner of the particular property that is the lesser of

(a) the earned depletion base of the original owner immediately after the original owner disposed of the particular property (determined as if, in the case of a disposition after April 28, 1978 as a result of an amalgamation described in section 87 of the Act, the original owner existed after the time of disposition and no property was acquired or disposed of in the course of the amalgamation) to the extent of the amount thereof that was not

(i) deducted by the original owner or any predecessor owner of the particular property in computing income for any taxation year,

(ii) deducted by the successor in computing income for a preceding taxation year, or

(iii) otherwise deducted by the successor in computing income for the taxation year, and

(b) 25 per cent of the amount, if any, by which

(i) the part of the successor's income for the year that can reasonably be regarded as attributable to

(A) the part of any amount included under paragraph 59(3.2)(c) of the Act in computing its income for the year that can reasonably be regarded as attributable to the disposition by it in the year or a preceding taxation year of any interest in or right to the particular property, to the extent that the proceeds of the disposition have not been included in determining an amount under this clause, paragraph (7)(g), clause 29(25)(d)(i)(A) of the *Income Tax Application Rules* or clause 66.7(1)(b)(i)(A) or (3)(b)(i)(A) or paragraph 66.7(10)(g) of the Act for a preceding taxation year,

(B) its reserve amount for the year in respect of the original owner and each predecessor owner, if any, of the particular property,

(C) production from the particular property, or

(D) processing described in subparagraph 1204(1)(b)(iii), (iv) or (v) with the particular property

computed as if no deduction were allowed under section 29 of the *Income Tax Application Rules* or under any of sections 65 to 66.7 of the Act and as if that income did not include any amount designated under clause 66.7(2)(b)(ii)(A) of the Act,

exceeds

(ii) the total of

(A) four times the total of all other amounts deducted under this subsection for the year that can reasonably be regarded as attributable to the part of the successor's income for the year described in subparagraph (i), and

(B) the total of all amounts each of which is an amount deducted under subsection 66.7(1), (3), (4) or (5) of the Act or subsection 29(25) of the *Income Tax Application Rules* for the year that can reasonably be regarded as attributable to the part of the successor's income for the year described in subparagraph (i).

**Notes:** Reg. 1202(2)(b) amended by P.C. 1999-629, effective for 1999 and later taxation years. For earlier taxation years generally since 1987, read:

(b) the amount, if any, by which the aggregate of

(i) 25 per cent of the part of the successor's income for the year that may reasonably be regarded as attributable to

(A) the amount included in computing its income for the year under paragraph 59(3.2)(c) of the Act that may reasonably be regarded as attributable to the disposition by it in the year or a preceding taxation year of any interest in or right to the particular property, to the extent that the proceeds of the disposition have not been included in determining an amount under this clause, paragraph (7)(g), clause 29(25)(d)(i)(A) of the *Income Tax Application Rules*, clause 66.7(1)(b)(i)(A) or (3)(b)(i)(A) of the Act or paragraph 66.7(10)(g) of the Act for a preceding taxation year,

(B) its reserve amount for the year in respect of the original owner and each predecessor owner, if any, of the particular property,

(C) production from the particular property, or

(D) such processing as is described in subparagraph 1204(1)(b)(iii), (iv) or (v) with the particular property

computed as if no deduction were allowed under section 29 of the *Income Tax Application Rules* or under sections 65 to 66.7 of the Act and as if that income did not include any portion thereof designated under clause 66.7(2)(b)(ii)(A) of the Act,

(ii) the aggregate of all amounts each of which is a particular amount included in its income for the year under paragraph 59(3.3)(a) or (b) of the Act in respect of an amount added in computing the earned depletion base of the original owner, and

(iii) where the successor, the original owner or a predecessor owner of the particular property received in the year or in the year became entitled to receive, or in a subsequent year becomes entitled to receive an amount of assistance or benefit

(A) in respect of Canadian exploration expenses or Canadian development expenses, or

(B) that may reasonably be related to Canadian exploration activities or Canadian development activities,

by way of a grant, subsidy, rebate, forgivable loan, deduction from royalty or tax, rebate of royalty or tax, investment allowance or any other form of assistance or benefit, 33⅓ per cent of the aggregate of all amounts each of which is in respect of such a particular amount of assistance or benefit and equal to

(C) the stated percentage (determined, in respect of an amount of Canadian exploration expense or Canadian development expense added in computing the earned depletion base of the original owner by reason of subparagraph 1205(1)(a)(ii) or clause 1205(1)(a)(vi)(B) or (B.1), for the calendar year in which the original owner incurred the expense) of the particular amount of the assistance or benefit (other than an amount in respect of which an amount was added in computing an amount under this subparagraph for a preceding taxation year), where the particular amount of the assistance or benefit was in respect of the amount of that expense, or

(D) the specified percentage (determined, in respect of an amount of Canadian oil and gas exploration expense added in computing the earned depletion base of the original owner by reason of subparagraph 1205(1)(a)(v) or clause 1205(1)(a)(vi)(A), for the calendar year in which the original owner incurred the expense) of the particular amount of the assistance or benefit (other than an amount in respect of which an amount was added in computing an amount under this subparagraph for a preceding taxation year), where the particular amount of the assistance or benefit was in respect of the amount of that expense

exceeds the aggregate of all other amounts deducted under this subsection, subsections 66.7(1), (3), (4) or (5) of the Act or subsection 29(25) of the *Income Tax Application Rules* for the year that may reasonably be regarded as attributable to those parts of the successor's income for the year described in subparagraph (i) or (ii) or to the amount determined in respect of the successor for the year under subparagraph (iii).

For earlier amendments see Notes at end of Reg. 1202.

**(3)** Where in a taxation year ending after February 17, 1987 an original owner of a property disposes of the property in circumstances in which subsection (2) applies,

(a) the amount of the earned depletion base of the original owner determined immediately after the time of that disposition shall be deducted in determining the earned depletion base of the original owner at any time after the time that is immediately after the disposition;

(b) for the purposes of paragraph (2)(a), the earned depletion base of the original owner determined immediately after the original owner disposed of the property that was deducted in computing the original owner's income for the year shall be deemed to be equal to the lesser of

(i) the amount deducted in respect of the disposition under paragraph (a), and

(ii) the amount, if any, by which

(A) the specified amount determined under subsection (4) in respect of the original owner for the year

exceeds

(B) the aggregate of all amounts each of which is an amount determined under this paragraph in respect of any disposition made by the original owner before the disposition and in the year; and

(c) for greater certainty, any amount (other than the amount determined under paragraph (b)) that was deducted under section 1201 by the original owner for the year or a subsequent taxation year shall, for the purposes of paragraph (2)(a), be deemed not to be in respect of the earned depletion base of the original owner determined immediately after the original owner disposed of the particular property.

**(4)** Where in a taxation year ending after February 17, 1987 an original owner of a property disposes of the property in circumstances in which subsection (2) applies, the lesser of

(a) the total of all amounts each of which is the amount, if any, by which

(i) an amount deducted under paragraph (3)(a) in respect of such a disposition in the year by the original owner

exceeds

(ii) the amount, if any, designated by the original owner in a prescribed form filed with the Minister within six months after the end of the year in respect of the amount determined under subparagraph (i), and

(b) the amount, if any, deducted under section 1201 in computing the income of the original owner for the taxation year

is the specified amount in respect of the original owner for the year for the purposes of paragraphs (3)(b) and 1205(1)(d.2).

**Advance Tax Rulings**: ATR-19: Earned depletion base and cumulative Canadian development expense.

**(5)** Subsections (2), 1203(3), 1207(7) and 1212(4) do not apply

(a) in respect of a property acquired by way of an amalgamation or winding-up to which section 1214 applies;

(b) to permit, in respect of the acquisition by a corporation before February 18, 1987 of a property, a deduction by the corporation of an amount that the corporation would not have been entitled to deduct under this Part, if this Part, as it read in its application to taxation years ending before February 18, 1987, applied to taxation years ending after February 17, 1987; or

(c) in respect of a property acquired at any time after July 19, 1985, by purchase, amalgamation, merger, winding-up or otherwise, from a person who is exempt from tax under Part I of the Act on that person's taxable income (other than a corporation that is referred to in paragraph 149(1)(d) of the Act and that is a principal-business corporation), except where the property was acquired before 1987 pursuant to an agreement in writing made before July 20, 1985.

### Proposed Amendment — Reg. 1202(5)(c)

(c) in respect of a property acquired by purchase, amalgamation, merger, winding-up or otherwise, from a person who is exempt from tax under Part I of the Act on that person's taxable income.

**Application**: The November 30, 2000 draft regulations (miscellaneous), s. 1 (pre-published in the *Canada Gazette*, Part I, December 9, 2000), will amend para. 1202(5)(c) to read as above, applicable to acquisitions that take place after April 26, 1995, other than an acquisition that takes place before 1996 and that was required by an agreement in writing entered into before April 26, 1995.

**Regulatory Impact Analysis Statement**: The amendment to paragraph 1202(5)(c) of the Regulations implements a 1995 announcement and was last published in draft form in June 1996. As a result of this amendment, where a person acquires, either after 1995 in the case of an acquisition made pursuant to an agreement in writing entered into before April 26, 1995, or after April 26, 1995, in any other case, property from a tax-exempt corporation, the person will not benefit from the corporation's earned depletion allowances, mining exploration base, frontier exploration base and supplementary allowances in respect of the property. This amendment removes an exemption which allowed those tax attributes to be acquired with the property in certain cases.

**June 20, 1996 Technical Notes**: Part XII of the *Income Tax Regulations* sets out a number of rules with respect to resource and processing allowances. These rules include provision for the inheritance by a corporation (the "successor") of another taxpayer's earned depletion allowances, mining exploration base, frontier exploration base and supplementary depletion allowances. Subsection 1202(5) provides that this successoring is not available in certain circumstances, including (in paragraph 1202(5)(c)) the acquisition of property from a person that is exempt from tax under Part I of the Act. The paragraph includes an exception, however: where the exempt person from whom the property is acquired is a corporation described in paragraph 149(1)(d) — broadly, a Crown or municipal corporation — that is also a principal-business corporation, the successor rules will apply. Paragraph 1202(5)(c) is amended to remove this exception.

**(6)** Subsections (2), 1203(3), 1207(7) and 1212(4) apply only to a corporation that has acquired a particular property

(a) where it acquired the particular property in a taxation year commencing before 1985 and, at the time it acquired the particular property, the corporation acquired the specified property of the person from whom it acquired the particular property;

(b) where it acquired the particular property from a person in a taxation year commencing after 1984 and, at the time it acquired the particular property, the corporation acquired

(i) all or substantially all of the Canadian resource properties of that person, or

(ii) where subparagraph (i) does not apply, the specified property of the person;

(c) where it acquired (other than in circumstances in which subparagraph (b)(ii) applies) the particular property after November 16, 1978 and in a taxation year ending before February 18, 1987 by any means other than by way of an amalgamation or winding-up and it and the person from whom it acquired the particular property have filed with the Minister a joint election under and in accordance with any of subsections 66(6), 66.1(4), 66.1(5), 66.2(3), 66.2(4), 66.4(3), and 66.4(4) of the Act as those subsections read in their application to that year;

(d) where it acquired the particular property after June 5, 1987 by way of an amalgamation or winding-up (other than in circumstances in which subparagraph (b)(ii) applies) and it has filed an election in the form prescribed for the purposes of paragraph 66.7(7)(c) of the Act with the Minister on or before the day on or before which the corporation is required to file a return of income pursuant to section 150 of the Act for its taxation year in which it acquired the particular property;

(e) where it acquired the particular property (other than by means of an amalgamation or winding-up or in circumstances in which subparagraph (b)(ii) applies) in a taxation year ending after February 17, 1987 and it and the person from whom it acquired the particular property have filed a joint election in the form prescribed for the purposes of paragraph 66.7(7)(e) of the Act with the Minister on or before the earlier of the days on or before which either of them is required to file a return of income pursuant to section 150 of the Act in respect of their respective taxation years that include the time of acquisition of the particular property; and

(f) where it acquired (other than by way of an amalgamation or winding-up) the particular property in circumstances in which subparagraph (b)(ii) applies and it and the person from whom it acquired the particular property agree to have subsection (2), 1203(3), 1207(7) or 1212(4), as the case may be, apply to them and notify the Minister in writing of the agreement in their returns of income under Part I of the Act for their respective taxation years that include the time of acquisition of the particular property.

**Notes**: Revenue Canada's view is that "all or substantially all", used in Reg. 1202(6)(b)(i), means 90% or more.

**(7)** Where at any time after November 12, 1981

(a) control of a corporation is considered for the purposes of subsection 66.7(10) of the Act to have been acquired by a person or group of persons, or

(b) a corporation ceases to be exempt from tax under Part I of the Act on its taxable income,

for the purposes of section 1201, this section and section 1205,

(c) the corporation shall be deemed after that time to be a successor (within the meaning assigned by subsection (2)) that had, at that time, acquired all the properties owned by the corporation immediately before that time from an original owner thereof;

(d) a joint election shall be deemed to have been filed in accordance with subsection (6) in respect of the acquisition;

(e) the earned depletion base of the corporation immediately before that time shall be deemed not to be the earned depletion base of the corporation immediately after that time but to be the earned depletion base of the original owner immediately after that time;

(f) [Revoked]

(g) where the corporation (in this paragraph referred to as the "transferee") was, immediately before and at that time,

(i) a parent corporation (within the meaning assigned by subsection 87(1.4) of the Act), or

(ii) a subsidiary wholly-owned corporation (within the meaning assigned by subsection 87(1.4) of the Act)

of a particular corporation (in this paragraph referred to as the "transferor"), if both corporations agree to have this paragraph apply to them in respect of a taxation year of the transferor ending after that time and notify the Minister in writing of the agreement in the return of income under Part I of the Act of the transferor for that year, the transferor may, if throughout that year the transferee was such a parent corporation or subsidiary wholly-owned corporation of the transferor, designate in favour of the transferee, in respect of that year, for the purpose of making a deduction under subsection (2) in respect of expenditures incurred by the transferee before that time and when it was such a parent corporation or subsidiary wholly-owned corporation of the transferor, an amount not exceeding such portion of the amount that would be its income for the year, if no deductions were allowed under any of section 29 of the *Income Tax Application Rules* and sections 65 to 66.7 of the Act, [as] may reasonably be regarded as being attributable to

(iii) the production from Canadian resource properties owned by the transferor immediately before that time,

(iv) the disposition in the year of any Canadian resource properties owned by the transferor immediately before that time, and

(v) such processing as is described in subparagraph 1204(1)(b)(iii), (iv), or (v) with property owned by the transferor immediately before that time

to the extent that such portion of the amount so designated is not designated under this paragraph in favour of any other taxpayer or under paragraph 66.7(10)(g) of the Act in favour of any taxpayer, and the amount so designated shall be deemed, for the purposes of determining the amount under subsection (2),

(vi) to be income from the sources described in subparagraph (iii), (iv) or (v), as the case may be, of the transferee for its taxation year in which that taxation year of the transferor ends, and

(vii) not to be income from the sources described in subparagraph (iii), (iv) or (v), as the case may be, of the transferor for that year;

(h) where, immediately before and at that time, the corporation (in this paragraph referred to as the "transferee") and another corporation (in this paragraph referred to as the "transferor") were both subsidiary wholly-owned corporations (within the meaning assigned by subsection 87(1.4) of the Act) of a particular parent corporation (within the meaning assigned by subsection 87(1.4) of the Act), if the transferee and the transferor agree to have this paragraph apply to them in respect of a taxation year of the transferor ending after that time and notify the Minister in writing of the agreement in the return of income under Part I of the Act of the transferor for that year, paragraph (g) shall apply for that year to the transferee and transferor as though one were the parent corporation (within the meaning assigned by subsection 87(1.4) of the Act) of the other; and

(i) where that time is after January 15, 1987 and at that time the corporation was a member of a partnership that owned a property at that time,

(i) for the purposes of paragraph (c), the corporation shall be deemed to have owned immediately before that time that portion of the property owned by the partnership at that time that is equal to its percentage share of the aggregate of amounts that would be paid to all members of the partnership if it were wound up at that time, and

(ii) for the purposes of clauses (2)(b)(i)(C) and (D) for a taxation year ending after that time, the lesser of

(A) its share of the part of the income of the partnership for the fiscal period of the partnership ending in the year that may reasonably be regarded as being attributable to the production from the property or to such processing as is described in subparagraph 1204(1)(b)(iii), (iv) or (v) with the property, and

(B) an amount that would be determined under clause (A) for the year if its share of the income of the partnership for the fiscal year of the partnership were determined on the basis of the percentage share referred to in subparagraph (i)

shall be deemed to be income of the corporation for the year that may reasonably be attributable to production from the property or to such processing as is described in subparagraph 1204(1)(b)(iii), (iv) or (v) with the property.

**Notes**: See at end of Reg. 1202.

**(8)** For the purposes of subsections (1) and (7), where a corporation acquired control of another corporation after November 12, 1981 and before 1983 by reason of the acquisition of shares of the other corporation pursuant to an agreement in writing concluded on or before November 12, 1981, the corporation shall be deemed to have acquired such control on or before November 12, 1981.

**(9)** Where, at any time,

(a) control of a taxpayer that is a corporation has been acquired by a person or group of persons,

(b) a taxpayer has disposed of all or substantially all of the taxpayer's Canadian resource properties, or

(c) a taxpayer has disposed of the specified property of the taxpayer,

and, before that time, the taxpayer or a partnership of which the taxpayer was a member acquired a property and it may reasonably be considered that one of the main purposes of the acquisition was to avoid any limitation provided in subsection (2) on the deduction in respect of the earned depletion base of the taxpayer or of a corporation referred to as a transferee in paragraph (7)(g) or (h), the taxpayer or the partnership, as the case may be, shall be deemed, for the purposes of applying subsection (2) to or in respect of the taxpayer, not to have acquired the property.

**Related Provisions**: ITA 256(6)–(9) — Whether control acquired.

**Notes**: Revenue Canada's view is that "all or substantially all", used in Reg. 1202(9)(b), means 90% or more.

**(10)** Where in a particular taxation year a predecessor owner of a property disposes of it to a corporation in circumstances in which subsection (2) applies, for the purposes of applying subsection (2) to the predecessor owner for a taxation year ending after February 17, 1987 in respect of its acquisition of the property, the predecessor owner shall be deemed, after the disposition, never to have acquired the property except for the purposes of making a deduction under subsection (2) for the particular year.

**(11)** Where at any time a property is acquired by a person in circumstances in which subsection (2) does not apply, every person who was an original owner or predecessor owner of the property by reason of having disposed of the property before that time shall, for the purposes of applying this Part to or in respect of the person or any other person who after that time acquires the property, be deemed after that time not to be an original owner or predecessor owner of the property by reason of having disposed of the property before that time.

**Notes [Reg. 1202]**: Regs. 1202(2) to (6) amended and (7) to (11) added by P.C. 1990-2780, effective (except for 1202(2)(b)(i)(C) and 1202(9)) to taxation years ending after February 17, 1987 except that the Minister of National Revenue shall be deemed to have been notified in circumstances satisfying the condition in 1202(7)(g) or (h) if the Minister is notified in writing of the agreement referred to therein before July 16, 1991.

Reg. 1202(2)(b)(i) amended and 1202(7)(f) revoked by P.C. 1993-415, both retroactive to taxation years ending after February 17, 1987.

Reg. 1202(4)(a)(ii) added by P.C. 1993-415, effective for dispositions in taxation years commencing after March 23, 1993, or, where an election is filed, for dispositions in taxation years ending after February 17, 1987. Such an election must be filed with Revenue Canada by

(a) the taxpayer, and

(b) each corporation that, before the end of the taxpayer's taxation year that includes March 24, 1993, acquired the property or any other property that was disposed of by the taxpayer in a taxation year ending after February 17, 1987 as part of a transaction or an event as a consequence of which that corporation was or, but for the amendment, would be entitled to deduct an amount under Reg. 1202(2) in respect of an expenditure of the taxpayer.

The deadline for such election is 180 days after the end of the taxpayer's taxation year that includes March 24, 1993, and waivers under ITA 152(4)(a)(ii) must be filed by the taxpayer in respect of taxation years beginning before March 24, 1993 with respect to the consequences of the election.

See also Notes to Reg. 1201 and Reg. 1202(2).

**Definitions [Reg. 1202]**: "acquired" — Reg. 1202(8), (9); "amount" — ITA 248(1); "Canadian development expense" — ITA 66.2(5), 248(1); "Canadian exploration expense" — ITA 66.1(6), 248(1); "Canadian oil and gas exploration expense" — Reg. 1206(1); "control" — ITA 256(6)–(9); "corporation" — ITA 248(1), *Interpretation Act* 35(1); "disposed", "disposes" — ITA 248(1)"disposition", "disposition" — ITA 248(1); "earned depletion base" — Reg. 1202(1), 1205(1); "fiscal period" — ITA 249.1; "Minister" — ITA 248(1); "month" — *Interpretation Act* 35(1); "original owner" — Reg. 1206(1); "parent" — Reg. 1214(3); "person" — ITA 248(1); "predecessor owner" — Reg. 1206(1); "prescribed", "property" — ITA 248(1); "related" — ITA 251(2)–(6); "resource" — Reg. 1206(1); "share" — ITA 248(1); "specified percentage", "specified property", "stated percentage" — Reg. 1206(1); "subsidiary wholly-owned corporation" — ITA 248(1); "successor" — Reg. 1202(2). 1202(7); "taxable income" — ITA 248(1); "taxation year" — ITA 249; "taxpayer" — ITA 248(1); "transferee", "transferor" — Reg. 1202(7)(g), (h); "writing" — *Interpretation Act* 35(1).

**1203. Mining exploration depletion** — **(1)** In computing a taxpayer's income for a taxation year there may be deducted such amount as he may claim not exceeding the lesser of

(a) the amount if any, by which

(i) the aggregate of

(A) 25 per cent of his income for the year, computed in accordance with Part I of the Act without reference to paragraph 59(3.3)(f) thereof and on the assumption that no deduction were allowed under section 65 thereof, and

(B) the amount, if any, included in computing his income for the year by virtue of paragraph 59(3.3)(f) of the Act

exceeds

(ii) the aggregate of amounts deducted under sections 1201, 1202, 1207 and 1212 in computing his income for the year; and

(b) his mining exploration depletion base as of the end of the year (before making any deduction under this subsection for the year).

(2) For the purposes of this section, "mining exploration depletion base" of a taxpayer as of a particular time means the amount by which the aggregate of

(a) $33^1/_3$ per cent of the amount by which

(i) the aggregate of all amounts each of which was the stated percentage of an expenditure that is, or but for paragraph 66(12.61)(b) of the Act would be, incurred by the taxpayer after April 19, 1983 and before the particular time and each of which was a Canadian exploration expense

(A) described in subparagraph 66.1(6)(a)(iii) of the Act, or

(B) that would have been described in subparagraph 66.1(6)(a)(iv) [66.1(6)"Canadian exploration expense"(h)] or (v) [subpara. (i)] of the Act if the references in those subparagraphs to "any of subparagraphs (i) to (iii.1)" were read as "subparagraph (iii)",

other than an expense described in clause (A) or (B) that was

(C) an expense renounced by the taxpayer under subsection 66(10.1) or (12.6) of the Act,

(D) an amount that was a Canadian exploration and development overhead expense of the taxpayer,

(E) an amount that was in respect of financing, including any cost incurred prior to the commencement of carrying on a business, or

(F) an eligible expense within the meaning of the *Canadian Exploration Incentive Program Act* in respect of which the taxpayer, a partnership of which the taxpayer was a member or a principal-business corporation of which the taxpayer was a shareholder, has received, is deemed to have received, is entitled to receive or may reasonably be expected to receive at any time an incentive under that Act,

exceeds

(ii) the aggregate of all amounts each of which is the stated percentage of an amount of assistance (within the meaning assigned by paragraph 66(15)(a.1) [66(15)"assistance"] of the Act) that any person has received, is entitled to receive or, at any time, becomes entitled to receive in respect of an expense that would be described in subparagraph (i) if that subparagraph were read without reference to clause (C) thereof, other than such an amount in respect of an expense renounced under subsection 66(10.1) or (12.6) of the Act

(A) by a corporation in favour of the taxpayer, where the amount of that assistance is excluded from the aggregate in respect of which the expense is so renounced, or

(B) by the taxpayer, where the amount of that assistance is not excluded from the aggregate in respect of which the expense is so renounced, and

(b) where the taxpayer is a successor corporation, any amount required by paragraph (3)(a) to be added before the particular time in computing the taxpayer's mining exploration depletion base

exceeds the aggregate of

(c) all amounts each of which is an amount deducted by the taxpayer under subsection (1) in computing his income for a taxation year ending before the particular time; and

(d) where the taxpayer is a predecessor, all amounts required by paragraph (3)(b) to be deducted before the particular time in computing the taxpayer's mining exploration depletion base.

(3) Subject to subsections 1202(5) and (6), where a corporation (in this section referred to as the "successor corporation") has at any time (in this subsection referred to as the "time of acquisition") after April 19, 1983 and in a taxation year (in this subsection referred to as the "transaction year") acquired a property from another person (in this subsection referred to as the "predecessor") the following rules apply:

(a) for the purpose of computing the mining exploration depletion base of the successor corporation as of any time after the time of acquisition, there shall be added an amount equal to the amount required by paragraph (b) to be deducted in computing the mining exploration depletion base of the predecessor; and

(b) for the purpose of computing the mining exploration depletion base of the predecessor as of any time after the transaction year of the predecessor, there shall be deducted the amount, if any, by which

(i) the mining exploration depletion base of the predecessor immediately after the time of acquisition (assuming for this purpose that, in the case of an acquisition as a result of an amalgamation described in section 87 of the Act, the predecessor existed after the time of acquisition and no property was acquired or disposed of in the course of the amalgamation)

exceeds

(ii) the amount, if any, deducted under subsection (1) in computing the income of the predecessor for the transaction year of the predecessor.

**(3.1)** [Revoked]

**(4)** For greater certainty, where an expense incurred before a particular time is included in the aggregate calculated under subparagraph (2)(a)(i) in respect of a taxpayer and subsequent to the particular time any person becomes entitled to receive an amount of assistance (within the meaning assigned by paragraph 66(15)(a.1) [66(15)"assistance"] of the Act) that is included in the aggregate calculated under subparagraph (2)(a)(ii), the stated percentage of the amount of assistance shall be included in the amounts referred to in subparagraph (2)(a)(ii) in respect of the taxpayer at the time the expense was incurred.

**Definitions [Reg. 1203]**: "amount", "business" — ITA 248(1); "Canadian development expense" — ITA 66.2(5), 248(1), Reg. 1206(4)(a); "Canadian exploration and development expenses" — ITA 66(15), 248(1), Reg. 1206(4)(a); "Canadian exploration and development overhead expense" — Reg. 1206(1), (4.1); "Canadian exploration expense" — ITA 66.1(6), 248(1), Reg. 1206(4)(a); "commencement" — *Interpretation Act* 35(1); "corporation" — ITA 248(1), *Interpretation Act* 35(1); "disposition" — ITA 248(1); "mining exploration depletion base" — Reg. 1203(2), (3); "person" — ITA 248(1); "predecessor" — Reg. 1203(3); "property", "shareholder" — ITA 248(1); "stated percentage" — Reg. 1206(1); "successor corporation" — Reg. 1203(3); "taxation year" — ITA 249; "taxpayer" — ITA 248(1); "time of acquisition", "transaction year" — Reg. 1203(3).

**1204. Resource profits** — **(1)** For the purposes of this Part, "gross resource profits" of a taxpayer for a taxation year means the amount, if any, by which the total of

(a) the amount, if any, by which the aggregate of

(i) the aggregate of amounts, if any, that would be included in computing the taxpayer's income for the year by virtue of subsection 59(2) and paragraphs 59(3.2)(b) and 59.1(b) of the Act if subsection 59(2) were read without reference to subsection 64(1) therein, and

(i.1) the amount, if any, by which the amount included in computing his income for the year by virtue of paragraph 59(3.2)(c) of the Act exceeds the proceeds of disposition of property described in clause 66(15)(c)(ii)(A) [66(15)"Canadian resource property"(b)(i)] of the Act that became receivable in the year or a preceding taxation year and after December 31, 1982 to the extent that such proceeds have not been deducted in determining the amount under this subparagraph for a preceding taxation year

exceeds

(ii) the aggregate of amounts, if any, deducted in computing his income for the year by virtue of paragraph 59.1(a) and subsections 64(1.1) and (1.2) of the Act,

(b) the amount, if any, of the aggregate of his incomes for the year from

(i) the production of petroleum, natural gas, related hydrocarbons or sulphur from

(A) oil or gas wells in Canada operated by the taxpayer, or

(B) natural accumulations (other than mineral resources) of petroleum or natural gas in Canada operated by the taxpayer,

(ii) the production and processing in Canada of

(A) ore, other than iron ore or tar sands ore, from mineral resources in Canada operated by him to any stage that is not beyond the prime metal stage or its equivalent,

(B) iron ore from mineral resources in Canada operated by him to any stage that is not beyond the pellet stage or its equivalent, and

(C) tar sands ore from mineral resources in Canada operated by him to any stage that is not beyond the crude oil stage or its equivalent,

(iii) the processing in Canada of

(A) ore, other than iron ore or tar sands ore, from mineral resources in Canada not operated by him to any stage that is not beyond the prime metal stage or its equivalent,

(B) iron ore from mineral resources in Canada not operated by him to any stage that is not beyond the pellet stage or its equivalent, and

(C) tar sands ore from mineral resources in Canada not operated by him to any stage that is not beyond the crude oil stage or its equivalent,

(iv) the processing in Canada of

(A) ore, other than iron ore or tar sands ore, from mineral resources outside Canada to any stage that is not beyond the prime metal stage or its equivalent,

Part XII — Resource and Processing Allowances    S. 1204(1.1)(a)(v)(B)

(B) iron ore from mineral resources outside Canada to any stage that is not beyond the pellet stage or its equivalent, and

(C) tar sands ore from mineral resources outside Canada to any stage that is not beyond the crude oil stage or its equivalent,

(v) the processing in Canada of heavy crude oil recovered from an oil or gas well in Canada to any stage that is not beyond the crude oil stage or its equivalent, and

(vi) Canadian field processing,

(b.1) the total of all amounts (other than an amount included because of paragraph (b) in computing the taxpayer's gross resource profits for the year) each of which is an amount included in computing the taxpayer's income for the year as a rental or royalty computed by reference to the amount or value of production from a natural accumulation of petroleum or natural gas in Canada, an oil or gas well in Canada or a mineral resource in Canada, and

(c) if the taxpayer owns all the issued and outstanding shares of the capital stock of a railway company throughout the year, the amount that may reasonably be considered to be the railway company's income for its taxation year ending in the year from the transportation of such of the taxpayer's ore as is described in clause (b)(ii)(A), (B) or (C),

exceeds the aggregate of the taxpayer's losses for the year from the sources described in paragraph (b), where the taxpayer's incomes and losses are computed in accordance with the Act on the assumption that the taxpayer had during the year no incomes or losses except from those sources and was allowed no deductions in computing the taxpayer's income for the year other than

(d) amounts deductible under section 66 of the Act (other than amounts in respect of foreign exploration and development expenses) or subsection 17(2) or (6) or section 29 of the *Income Tax Application Rules*, for the year;

(e) the amounts deductible or deducted, as the case may be, under section 66.1, 66.2 (other than an amount that is in respect of a property described in clause 66(15)(c)(ii)(A) [66(15)"Canadian resource property"(b)(i)] of the Act), 66.4, 66.5 or 66.7 (other than subsection (2) thereof) of the Act for the year; and

(f) any other deductions for the year that can reasonably be regarded as applicable to the sources of income described in paragraph (b) or (b.1), other than a deduction under paragraph 20(1)(ss) or (tt) of the Act or section 1201 or subsection 1202(2), 1203(1), 1207(1) or 1212(1).

**Notes**: Opening words of Reg. 1204(1) changed to define "gross resource profits" instead of "resource profits" by P.C. 1996-1488, retroactive to taxation years that begin after December 20, 1991. See Notes to 1204(1.1).

Reg. 1204(1)(b)(i) opening words amended by P.C. 1999-629, effective for taxation years that begin after 1996, to add reference to sulphur.

Reg. 1204(1)(b)(i)(B) amended by P.C. 1996-1488, retroactive to taxation years that end after March 1985.

Reg. 1204(1)(b)(vi) added by P.C. 1999-629, effective for taxation years that begin after 1996.

Reg. 1204(1)(b.1) amended by P.C. 1996-1488, retroactive to taxation years that begin after 1990. See Notes to Reg. 1204(6).

Reg. 1204(1)(f) amended by P.C. 1996-1488, retroactive to taxation years that end after February 22, 1994, to add reference to ITA 20(1)(ss) and (tt).

**(1.1)** For the purposes of this Part, "resource profits" of a taxpayer for a taxation year means the amount, if any, by which the taxpayer's gross resource profits for the year exceeds the total of

(a) all amounts deducted in computing the taxpayer's income for the year other than

(i) an amount deducted in computing the taxpayer's gross resource profits for the year,

(ii) an amount deducted under any of section 8, paragraphs 20(1)(ss) and (tt), sections 60 to 64 and subsections 66(4), 66.7(2) and 104(6) and (12) of the Act and section 1201 and subsections 1202(2), 1203(1), 1207(1) and 1212(1) in computing the taxpayer's income for the year,

(iii) an amount deducted under section 66.2 of the Act in computing the taxpayer's income for the year, to the extent that it is attributable to any right, licence or privilege to store underground petroleum, natural gas or related hydrocarbons in Canada,

(iv) an amount deducted in computing the taxpayer's income for the year from a business, or other source, that does not include any resource activity of the taxpayer, and

(v) an amount deducted in computing the taxpayer's income for the year, to the extent that the amount

(A) relates to an activity

(I) that is not a resource activity of the taxpayer, and

(II) that is

1. the production, processing, manufacturing, distribution, marketing, transportation or sale of any property,

2. carried out for the purpose of earning income from property, or

3. the rendering of a service by the taxpayer to another person for the purpose of earning income of the taxpayer, and

(B) does not relate to a resource activity of the taxpayer,

2077

**Reg. S. 1204(1.1)(b)**     Income Tax Regulations

(b) all amounts each of which is the amount, if any, by which

  (i) the amount that would have been charged to the taxpayer by a person or partnership with whom the taxpayer was not dealing at arm's length if the taxpayer and that person or partnership had been dealing at arm's length

    (A) for the use after March 6, 1996 and in the year of a property (other than money) owned by that person or partnership, or

    (B) for the provision after March 6, 1996 and in the year by that person or partnership of a service to the taxpayer

exceeds the total of

  (ii) the amount charged to the taxpayer for the use of that property or the provision of that service in that period, and

  (iii) the portion of the amount described in subparagraph (i) that, if it had been charged, would not have been deductible in computing the taxpayer's resource profits, and

(c) where the year ends after February 21, 1994, all amounts added under subsection 80(13) of the Act in computing the taxpayer's gross resource profits for the year.

**Notes**: Reg. 1204(1.1) added by P.C. 1996-1488, this version effective for taxation years that begin after July 23, 1992.

For taxation years that begin after December 20, 1991 and before July 24, 1992, the amount determined under Reg. 1204(1.1)(a) is determined by the formula

$$A \times \frac{B}{C}$$

where

A    is the total that would otherwise be determined under Reg. 1204(1.1)(a),

B    is the number of days in the year that are after July 23, 1992, and

C    is the number of days in the year.

New Reg. 1204(1.1), and the change in 1204(1) from defining "resource profits" to "gross resource profits", are in response to the *Gulf Canada Ltd.* case, [1992] 1 C.T.C. 183 (FCA). See also amendments to Reg. 1210. These changes were first issued as draft regulations on July 23, 1992.

**(1.2)** For the purposes of paragraph (1.1)(b) and this subsection,

(a) a taxpayer is considered not to deal at arm's length with a partnership where the taxpayer does not deal at arm's length with any member of the partnership;

(b) a partnership is considered not to deal at arm's length with another partnership where any member of the first partnership does not deal at arm's length with any member of the second partnership;

(c) where a taxpayer is a member, or is deemed by this paragraph to be a member, of a partnership that is a member of another partnership, the taxpayer is deemed to be a member of the other partnership; and

(d) the provision of a service to a taxpayer does not include the provision of a service by an individual in the individual's capacity as an employee of the taxpayer.

**Notes**: Reg. 1204(1.2) added by P.C. 1996-1488, effective for taxation years that end after March 6, 1996. (That is the date of the 1996 federal budget, when this amendment was first released. This amendment was originally proposed as effective for taxation years ending after December 20, 1991, along with the amendments to Reg. 1204(1) and introduction of Reg. 1204(1.1).)

**(2)** For greater certainty, for the purposes of this section, in computing the income or loss of a trust for a taxation year from the sources described in paragraphs (1)(b) and (b.1), no deduction shall be made in respect of amounts deductible by the trust pursuant to subsection 104(6) or (12) of the Act.

**(3)** A taxpayer's income or loss from a source described in paragraph (1)(b) does not include

(a) any income or loss derived from transporting, transmitting or processing (other than processing described in clause (1)(b)(ii)(C), (iii)(C) or (iv)(C) or subparagraph (1)(b)(v) or (vi)) petroleum, natural gas or related hydrocarbons or sulphur from a natural accumulation of petroleum or natural gas;

(b) any income or loss arising because of the application of paragraph 12(1)(z.1) or (z.2) or (z.5) or section 107.3 of the Act; and

(c) any income or loss that can reasonably be attributable to a service rendered by the taxpayer (other than processing described in subparagraph (1)(b)(iii), (iv), (v) or (vi) or activities carried out by the taxpayer as a coal mine operator).

**Notes**: Reg. 1204(3)(a) amended by P.C. 1999-629, effective for taxation years that begin after 1996, to add "or (vi)" and the words "or sulphur from a natural accumulation of petroleum or natural gas".

Reg. 1204(3)(b) amended by P.C. 1999-629, effective for taxation years that begin after 1996, to add reference to ITA 12(1)(z.5).

Reg. 1204(3)(b) added by P.C. 1996-1488, effective for taxation years that end after February 22, 1994.

Reg. 1204(3)(c) amended by P.C. 1999-629, effective for taxation years that begin after March 6 1996, to add "or (vi) or activities carried out by the taxpayer as a coal mine operator".

Reg. 1204(3)(c) added by P.C. 1996-1488, effective for taxation years that begin after March 6, 1996.

**(4)** Notwithstanding any other provision in this Part, for the purposes of this Part, the income or loss of a taxpayer for a taxation year shall be computed on the assumption that paragraphs 12(1)(o) and 18(1)(m) and subsections 69(6) to (10) of the Act were not applicable to

(a) amounts receivable and the fair market value of any property receivable by the Crown as a royalty, tax, rental or levy with respect to the Syncrude Project, or as an amount however described, that may reasonably be regarded as being in lieu of any of the preceding amounts,

(b) dispositions of leased substances to the Crown by the participant, and

(c) acquisitions of leased substances from the Crown by the participant,

where the taxpayer has been granted a remission of tax for the year pursuant to subsection 3(1) of the *Syncrude Remission Order*.

**(5)** For the purposes of subsection (4), "Crown", "leased substances", "participant" and "Syncrude Project" have the meanings assigned by section 2 of the *Syncrude Remission Order*.

**Notes:** The *Syncrude Remission Order* is reproduced in the "Remission Orders" section, following the Regulations.

**(6)** [Repealed]

**Notes:** Reg. 1204(6) repealed by P.C. 1996-1488, retroactive to taxation years that begin after 1990. Along with Reg. 1204(1)(b.1), it provided an exclusion relating to tax-exempt persons that no longer applies. However, tax-exempt persons are subject to a penalty tax under ITA 208 re certain interests in resource property in which taxable and tax-exempt persons each have an interest. This amendment is consequential upon the expiration of transitional relief under ITA 208 effective 1990.

**Definitions [Reg. 1204]:** "amount" — ITA 248(1); "arm's length" — ITA 251(1), Reg. 1204(1.2)(a), (b); "business" — ITA 248(1); "Canada" — ITA 255, *Interpretation Act* 35(1); "Canadian development expense" — ITA 66.2(5), 248(1), Reg. 1206(4)(b); "Canadian exploration and development expenses" — ITA 66(15), 248(1), Reg. 1206(4)(b); "Canadian exploration expense" — ITA 66.1(6), 248(1), Reg. 1206(4)(b); "Canadian field processing" — ITA 248(1); "coal mine operator" — Reg. 1206(1); "crown leased substances" — Reg. 1204(5); "disposition", "employee" — ITA 248(1); "foreign exploration and development expenses" — ITA 66(15), 248(1); "gross resource profits" — Reg. 1204(1); "individual" — ITA 248(1); "member" — Reg. 1204(1.2)(c); "mineral resource", "oil or gas well" — ITA 248(1); "ore" — Reg. 1206(1); "participant" — Reg. 1204(5); "person" — ITA 248(1); "proceeds of disposition" — Reg. 1206(1); "property" — ITA 248(1); "provision of a service" — Reg. 1204(1.2)(d); "related" — ITA 251(2)–(6); "resource", "resource activity" — Reg. 1206(1); "resource profits" — Reg. 1204(1.1); "share" — ITA 248(1); "Syncrude Project" — Reg. 1204(5); "tar sands ore" — Reg. 1206(1); "taxation year" — ITA 249; "taxpayer" — ITA 248(1); "trust" — ITA 104(1), 248(1), (3).

**1205. Earned depletion base** — **(1)** For the purposes of this Part "earned depletion base" of a taxpayer as of a particular time means the amount by which $33^1/_3$ per cent of the aggregate of

(a) all amounts, in respect of expenditures (other than expenditures to acquire property under circumstances that entitled the taxpayer to a deduction under section 1202 or would so entitle the taxpayer if the amounts referred to in paragraphs 1202(2)(a) and (b) were sufficient for the purpose) incurred by the taxpayer after November 7, 1969 and before the particular time, each of which was

(i) a Canadian exploration and development expense or would have been such an expense if it had been incurred after 1971 and was actually incurred before May 7, 1974, other than

(A) a cost of borrowing capital, including any cost incurred prior to the commencement of carrying on a business, that was a Canadian exploration expense or an exploration, prospecting and development expense, as the case may be, of the taxpayer,

(B) the cost to the taxpayer of any Canadian resource property acquired by the taxpayer,

(C) a Canadian exploration and development expense that was incurred after a mine had come into production in reasonable commercial quantities and may reasonably be considered to be related to the mine or to a potential or actual extension thereof,

(D) an expense that would have been described in clause (C) if it had been incurred after 1971,

(E) an expense renounced by the taxpayer under subsection 66(10) of the Act or subsection 29(7) of the *Income Tax Application Rules*,

(F) an amount that, by virtue of subparagraph 66(15)(b)(iv) [66(15)"Canadian exploration and development expenses"(d)] of the Act, was a Canadian exploration and development expense or would have been such an expense if it had been incurred after 1971, if such amount was a cost or expense referred to in clause (A), (B), (C), (D) or (E) that was incurred by an association, partnership or syndicate referred to in that subparagraph, or

(G) an amount that, by virtue of subparagraph 66(15)(b)(v) [66(15)"Canadian exploration and development expenses"(e)] of the Act, was a Canadian exploration and development expense or would have been such an expense if it had been incurred after 1971, if such amount was a cost or expense referred to in clause (A), (B), (C), (D) or (E) that the taxpayer incurred pursuant to an agreement referred to in that subparagraph,

(ii) the stated percentage of a Canadian exploration expense other than

(A) a cost of borrowing capital, including any cost incurred prior to the commencement of carrying on a business, that was a Canadian exploration expense of the taxpayer,

(B) an expense renounced by the taxpayer under subsection 66(10.1) of the Act,

(C) an amount that, by virtue of subparagraph 66.1(6)(a)(iv) [66.1(6)"Canadian ex-

Reg.
S. 1205(1)(a)(ii)(C)      Income Tax Regulations

ploration expense"(h)] of the Act, was a Canadian exploration expense, if such amount was an expense referred to in clause (A), (B), (E), (F), (G) or (H) that was incurred by a partnership referred to in that subparagraph,

(D) an amount that, by virtue of subparagraph 66.1(6)(a)(v) [66.1(6)"Canadian exploration expense"(i)] of the Act, was a Canadian exploration expense, if such amount was an expense referred to in clause (A), (B), (E), (F), (G) or (H) that the taxpayer incurred pursuant to an agreement referred to in that subparagraph,

(E) an amount described in clause 66.1(6)(a)(ii)(B) [66.1(6)"Canadian exploration expense"(c)(ii)] or (ii.1)(B) [subpara. (d)(ii)] of the Act,

(F) an amount that was a Canadian exploration and development overhead expense of the taxpayer,

(G) an amount that was a Canadian oil and gas exploration expense of the taxpayer, or

(H) an expense described in subparagraph 66.1(6)(a)(iii) [66.1(6)"Canadian exploration expense"(f)] of the Act incurred after April 19, 1983,

(iii) a Canadian development expense incurred before 1981 other than

(A) a cost of borrowing capital, including any cost incurred prior to the commencement of carrying on a business, that was a Canadian development expense of the taxpayer,

(B) an expense renounced by the taxpayer under subsection 66(10.2) of the Act,

(C) an amount referred to in subparagraph 66.2(5)(a)(iii) [66.2(5)"Canadian development expense"(e)] of the Act,

(D) an amount that, by virtue of subparagraph 66.2(5)(a)(iv) [66.2(5)"Canadian development expense"(f)] of the Act, was a Canadian development expense, if such amount was an expense referred to in clause (A), (B) or (C) that was incurred by a partnership referred to in that subparagraph, or

(E) an amount that, by virtue of subparagraph 66.2(5)(a)(v) [66.2(5)"Canadian development expense"(g)] of the Act, was a Canadian development expense, if such amount was an expense referred to in clause (A), (B) or (C) that the taxpayer incurred pursuant to an agreement referred to in that subparagraph,

(iv) the stated percentage of the capital cost to the taxpayer of any processing property acquired by the taxpayer principally for the purpose of

(A) processing in Canada

(I) ore, other than iron ore or tar sands ore, from a qualified resource to any stage that is not beyond the prime metal stage or its equivalent,

(II) iron ore from a qualified resource to any stage that is not beyond the pellet stage or its equivalent, or

(III) tar sands ore from a qualified resource to any stage that is not beyond the crude oil stage or its equivalent, or

(B) processing in Canada

(I) ore, other than iron ore or tar sands ore, from an exporting resource beyond the furthest stage to which such ore or similar ore from that resource was ordinarily processed in Canada before such acquisition but not beyond the prime metal stage or its equivalent,

(II) iron ore from an exporting resource beyond the furthest stage to which such ore or similar ore from that resource was ordinarily processed in Canada before such acquisition but not beyond the pellet stage or its equivalent, or

(III) tar sands ore from an exporting resource beyond the furthest stage to which such ore or similar ore from that resource was ordinarily processed in Canada before such acquisition but not beyond the crude oil stage or its equivalent,

(v) where the taxpayer is a corporation that incurred a Canadian oil and gas exploration expense in respect of conventional lands in a calendar year after 1980 and before 1984, the specified percentage for that year of such expense to the extent that it is not an amount or expense referred to in clause (ii)(A), (B) or (F) or an expense that would be referred to in clause (ii)(C) or (D) if the references in those clauses to "clause (A), (B), (E), (F), (G) or (H)" were read as "clause (A), (B) or (F)", or

(vi) where the taxpayer is a corporation,

(A) the specified percentage in respect of a Canadian oil and gas exploration expense in respect of non-conventional lands incurred in a calendar year after 1980 and before 1985 to the extent that it is not an amount or expense referred to in clause (ii)(A), (B) or (F) or an expense that would be referred to in clause (ii)(C) or (E) if the references in those clauses to "clause (A), (B), (E), (F), (G) or (H)" were read as "clause (A), (B) or (F)",

(B) the stated percentage of a Canadian development expense incurred after 1980 in respect of a qualified tertiary oil recovery project of the taxpayer to the extent that such expense is not

(I) an amount or expense described in any of clauses (iii)(A) to (E),

(II) an amount that was a Canadian exploration and development overhead expense of the taxpayer, or

(III) an eligible expense within the meaning of the *Canadian Exploration and Development Incentive Program Act* in respect of which the taxpayer, a partnership of which the taxpayer was a member, a principal-business corporation of which the taxpayer was a shareholder or a joint exploration corporation of which the taxpayer was a shareholder corporation has received, is entitled to receive or may reasonably be expected to receive at any time an incentive under that Act,

(B.1) the stated percentage of a Canadian exploration expense incurred after 1981 in respect of a qualified tertiary oil recovery project of the taxpayer that

(I) would be referred to in subparagraph 66.1(6)(a)(ii) [66.1(6)"Canadian exploration expense"(c)] or (ii.1) [para. (d)] of the Act if subparagraph 66.1(6)(a)(ii) [66.1(6)"Canadian exploration expense"(c)] were read without reference to clause (B) [subpara. (ii)] thereof, or

(II) would be referred to in subparagraph 66.1(6)(a)(iv) or (v) [66.1(6)"Canadian exploration expense"(h) or (i)] of the Act if the Act were read without reference to clause 66.1(6)(a)(ii)(B) [66.1(6)"Canadian exploration expense"(c)(ii)] and subparagraphs 66.1(6)(a)(i), (i.1), (ii.2), (iii) and (iii.1) [66.1(6)"Canadian exploration expense"(a), (b), (e), (f) and (g)],

other than the portion of such expense referred to in subclause (I) or (II) that is

(III) described in any of clauses (ii)(A) to (D) and (F),

(IV) included in the amount determined under subparagraph (v) or clause (vi)(A),

(V) described in subclause (B)(III), or

(VI) an eligible expense within the meaning of the *Canadian Exploration Incentive Program Act* in respect of which the taxpayer, a partnership of which the taxpayer was a member or a principal-business corporation of which the taxpayer was a shareholder corporation, has received, is entitled to receive or may reasonably be expected to receive at any time an incentive under that Act,

(C) the stated percentage of the capital cost to it of property that is tertiary recovery equipment, and

(D) the stated percentage of the capital cost to it of property that is, or but for Class 41 of Schedule II would be, included in Class 10 in Schedule II by virtue of paragraph (u) of the description of that Class, other than the capital cost to it of property that had, before the property was acquired by it, been used for any purpose whatever by any person with whom it was not dealing at arm's length,

(b) all amounts, in respect of expenditures (other than expenditures referred to in paragraph (a) or expenditures to acquire property under circumstances that entitled the taxpayer to a deduction under section 1202 or would so entitle the taxpayer if the amounts referred to in paragraphs 1202(2)(a) and (b) were sufficient for the purpose) incurred by the taxpayer after May 8, 1972 and before the particular time, each of which was the stated percentage of the capital cost to the taxpayer of property that is or, but for Class 41, would be included in Class 10 in Schedule II because of paragraph (k) of the description of that Class and that was acquired for the purpose of processing in Canada

(i) ore (other than iron ore or tar sands ore), after its extraction from a mineral resource, to any stage that is not beyond the prime metal stage or its equivalent,

(ii) iron ore, after its extraction from a mineral resource, to any stage that is not beyond the pellet stage or its equivalent, or

(iii) tar sands ore, after its extraction from a mineral resource, to any stage that is not beyond the crude oil stage or its equivalent,

other than the capital cost to him of property that had, before the property was acquired by the taxpayer, been used for any purpose whatever by any person with whom the taxpayer was not dealing at arm's length,

(c) all amounts, in respect of expenditures (other than expenditures referred to in paragraph (a) or (b) or expenditures to acquire property under circumstances that entitled the taxpayer to a deduction under section 1202 or would so entitle the taxpayer if the amounts referred to in paragraphs 1202(2)(a) and (b) were sufficient for the purpose) incurred by the taxpayer before the particular time, each of which was the stated percentage of the capital cost to the taxpayer of property (other than property that had, before it was acquired by the taxpayer, been used for any purpose whatever by any person with whom the taxpayer was not dealing at arm's length) that is included in Class 28 or paragraph (a) of Class 41, in Schedule II, other than property so included

 (i) by virtue of the first reference in Class 28 to paragraph (l) of Class 10 in Schedule II, where the property was acquired by the taxpayer before November 17, 1978,

 (ii) by virtue of the reference in Class 28 to paragraph (m) of Class 10 in Schedule II,

 (iii) that is bituminous sands equipment acquired by an individual, or

 (iv) that is bituminous sands equipment acquired by a corporation before 1981,

(d) all expenditures (other than expenditures referred to in paragraph (a), (b) or (c)) each of which was incurred by him before November 8, 1969 relating to a mine that came into production in reasonable commercial quantities before that date and that were incurred for the purpose of

 (i) exploration in respect of, or

 (ii) development of the mine for the purpose of gaining or producing income from the extraction of material from,

a bituminous sands deposit, an oil sands deposit or an oil shale deposit,

(d.1) three times the total of all amounts each of which is an amount equal to the lesser of

 (i) the amount that would be determined under subsection 1210(1) in computing the taxpayer's income for a taxation year that ends before the particular time, if the amount determined for C under that subsection were nil, and

 (ii) the amount determined for C under subsection 1210(1) in respect of the taxpayer for that year, and

(d.2) three times the aggregate of all amounts each of which is the specified amount determined under subsection 1202(4) in respect of the taxpayer for a taxation year ending after February 17, 1987 and before the particular time,

exceeds the aggregate of

(e) all amounts deducted by the taxpayer under section 1201 in computing his income for all taxation years ending after May 6, 1974 and before the particular time;

(f) $33^1/_3$ per cent of the aggregate of all amounts, each of which is the stated percentage of a cost of borrowing capital, including any cost incurred prior to the commencement of carrying on a business, that was

 (i) included in the capital cost to him of depreciable property described in subparagraph (a)(iv), clause (a)(vi)(C) or (D) or paragraph (b) or (c), or

 (ii) an expenditure described in paragraph (d);

(g) $33^1/_3$ per cent of the aggregate of all amounts, each of which is an amount

 (i) that became receivable by the taxpayer after April 28, 1978 and before the earlier of December 12, 1979 and the particular time, and

 (ii) in respect of which the consideration given by the taxpayer therefor was a property (other than a share, or a property that would have been a Canadian resource property if it had been acquired by the taxpayer at the time the consideration was given) or services, the cost of which may reasonably be regarded as having been primarily an expenditure that was added in computing

  (A) the taxpayer's earned depletion base by reason of subparagraph (a)(i), (ii) or (iii) or paragraph (d), or

  (B) the earned depletion base of an original owner of a property by reason of subparagraph (a)(i), (ii) or (iii) or paragraph (d) as it applied to the original owner, where the taxpayer acquired the property in circumstances in which subsection 1202(2) applies,

(h) $33^1/_3$ per cent of the aggregate of all amounts, each of which is

 (i) an amount in respect of a disposition of property (other than a disposition of property that had been used by the taxpayer to any person with whom the taxpayer was not dealing at arm's length) of the taxpayer after April 28, 1978 and before the earlier of December 12, 1979 and the particular time, the capital cost of which was added in computing

  (A) the taxpayer's earned depletion base by reason of subparagraph (a)(iv) or paragraph (b) or (c), or

  (B) the earned depletion base of an original owner of a property by reason of subparagraph (a)(iv) or paragraph (b) or (c) as it applied to the original owner, where the taxpayer acquired the property in circumstances in which subsection 1202(2) applies, and

 (ii) equal to the lesser of

  (A) the proceeds of disposition of the property, and

  (B) the capital cost of the property to the taxpayer, where clause (i)(A) applies, or the original owner, where clause (i)(B) applies, computed as if no amount had been included therein that is a cost of borrowing capital, including any cost incurred prior to

Part XII — Resource and Processing Allowances     Reg. S. 1205

the commencement of carrying on a business,

(i) any amount required by paragraph 1202(2)(b) (as it read in its application to taxation years ending before February 18, 1987) or paragraph 1202(3)(a) to be deducted at or before the particular time in computing the taxpayer's earned depletion base,

(j) $33^1/_3$ per cent of the aggregate of all amounts, each of which is in respect of an amount of assistance or benefit in respect of Canadian exploration expenses or Canadian development expenses or that may reasonably be related to Canadian exploration activities or Canadian development activities, whether such amount is by way of a grant, subsidy, rebate, forgivable loan, deduction from royalty or tax, rebate of royalty or tax, investment allowance or any other form of assistance or benefit that

(i) the taxpayer before the particular time has received or was entitled to receive, or that the taxpayer at or after the particular time becomes entitled to receive, or

(ii) an original owner or predecessor owner of a property before the particular time has received or was entitled to receive, or at or after the particular time becomes entitled to receive, where the original owner or the predecessor owner received, became entitled to receive or becomes entitled to receive that amount

(A) at or after the time at which the property was acquired by the taxpayer in circumstances in which subsection 1202(2) applies, and

(B) before the time at which the taxpayer becomes a predecessor owner of the property,

and that is equal to

(iii) where the assistance or benefit was in respect of an amount added by reason of subparagraph (a)(ii) or clause (a)(vi)(B) or (B.1) in computing

(A) the earned depletion base of the taxpayer (other than such portion thereof included in determining an amount described in paragraph 1202(2)(a) before the particular time), or

(B) the portion of the earned depletion base of the original owner included in determining an amount described in paragraph 1202(2)(a) before the particular time,

the stated percentage of the amount of the assistance or benefit, and

(iv) where the assistance or benefit was in respect of an amount of Canadian oil and gas exploration expense added by reason of subparagraph (a)(v) or clause (a)(vi)(A) in computing

(A) the earned depletion base of the taxpayer (other than such portion thereof included in determining an amount described in paragraph 1202(2)(a) before the particular time), or

(B) the portion of the earned depletion base of the original owner included in determining an amount described in paragraph 1202(2)(a) before the particular time,

the amount equal to the product obtained when the amount of the assistance or benefit is multiplied by the specified percentage in respect of the expense for the calendar year in which the taxpayer or the original owner, as the case may be, incurred the expense, and

(k) the amount, if any, by which

(i) the aggregate of all amounts that would be determined under paragraphs 1212(3)(d) to (i)

exceeds

(ii) the aggregate of all amounts that would be determined under paragraphs 1212(3)(a) to (c)

in computing his supplementary depletion base at the particular time.

**Notes:** Opening words of Reg. 1205(1)(b) amended by P.C. 1996-1488 to add reference to Class 41, effective for taxation years that end after 1987.

Reg. 1205(1)(d.1) amended by P.C. 1996-1488, effective for taxation years that begin after December 20, 1991, to refer to variables in the formula in Reg. 1210 as a result of the restructuring of Reg. 1210.

(2) Where an expense is incurred before the particular time referred to in subsection (1) and a person at or after the particular time becomes entitled to receive an amount of assistance or benefit in respect of the expense, the amount of such assistance or benefit shall be included in "the amount of the assistance or benefit" referred to in subparagraphs (1)(j)(iii) and (iv) as of the particular time.

**Definitions [Reg. 1205]:** "amount" — ITA 248(1); "arm's length" — ITA 251(1); "bituminous sands" — ITA 248(1); "bituminous sands equipment" — Reg. 1206(1); "business" — ITA 248(1); "Canada" — ITA 255, *Interpretation Act* 35(1); "Canadian development expense" — ITA 66.2(5), 248(1), Reg. 1206(4)(a); "Canadian exploration and development expenses" — ITA 66(15), 248(1), Reg. 1206(4)(a); "Canadian exploration and development overhead expense" — Reg. 1206(1), (4.1); "Canadian exploration expense" — ITA 66.1(6), 248(1), Reg. 1206(4)(a); "Canadian oil and gas exploration expense" — Reg. 1206(1); "Canadian resource property" — ITA 66(15), 248(1); "commencement" — *Interpretation Act* 35(1); "conventional lands" — Reg. 1206(1); "corporation" — ITA 248(1), *Interpretation Act* 35(1); "depreciable property" — ITA 13(21), 248(1); "disposition" — ITA 248(1); "disposition of property" — Reg. 1206(1); "earned depletion base" — Reg. 1202(1), 1205(1); "exporting resource" — Reg. 1206(1); "individual" — ITA 248(1); "mine" — Reg. 1206(1); "mineral resource" — ITA 248(1); "non-conventional lands", "ore", "original owner" — Reg. 1206(1); "person" — ITA 248(1); "predecessor owner", "proceeds of disposition", "processing property" — Reg. 1206(1); "property" — ITA 248(1); "qualified resource", "qualified tertiary oil recovery project" — Reg. 1206(1); "related" — ITA 251(2)–(6); "resource" — Reg. 1206(1); "share", "shareholder" — ITA 248(1); "specified percentage", "stated percentage" — Reg. 1206(1); "successor" — Reg. 1202(7); "tar sands ore" — Reg. 1206(1); "taxation year" — ITA 249; "taxpayer" — ITA 248(1); "tertiary recovery equipment" — Reg. 1206(1).

**1206. Interpretation** — **(1)** In this Part,

**"bituminous sands equipment"** means property of a taxpayer that

    (a) is included in Class 28 or in paragraph (a) of Class 41 in Schedule II, other than property so included

        (i) by virtue of the first reference in Class 28 to paragraph (l) of Class 10 in Schedule II, where the property was acquired by the taxpayer before November 17, 1978, or

        (ii) by virtue of the reference in Class 28 to paragraph (m) of Class 10 in Schedule II, and

    (b) was acquired by the taxpayer after April 10, 1978 principally for the purpose of gaining or producing income from one or more mines, each of which is a location in a bituminous sands deposit, oil sands deposit or oil shale deposit from which material is extracted;

**"Canadian exploration and development overhead expense"** of a taxpayer means a Canadian exploration expense or a Canadian development expense of the taxpayer made or incurred after 1980 that is not a Canadian renewable and conservation expense (in this definition having the meaning assigned by subsection 66.1(6) of the Act) nor a taxpayer's share of a Canadian renewable and conservation expense incurred by a partnership and

    (a) that was in respect of the administration, management or financing of the taxpayer,

    (b) that was in respect of the salary, wages or other remuneration or related benefits paid in respect of a person employed by the taxpayer whose duties were not all or substantially all directed towards exploration or development activities,

    (c) that was in respect of the upkeep or maintenance of, taxes or insurance in respect of, or rental or leasing of, property other than property all or substantially all of the use of which by the taxpayer was for the purposes of exploration or development activities, or

    (d) that may reasonably be regarded as having been in respect of

        (i) the use of or the right to use any property in which any person who was connected with the taxpayer had an interest,

        (ii) compensation for the performance of a service for the benefit of the taxpayer by any person who was connected with the taxpayer, or

        (iii) the acquisition of any materials, parts or supplies from any person who was connected with the taxpayer

to the extent that the expense exceeds the least of amounts, each of which was the aggregate of the costs incurred by a person who was connected with the taxpayer

        (iv) in respect of the property,

        (v) in respect of the performance of the service, or

        (vi) in respect of the materials, parts or supplies;

**Notes**: Opening words of definition amended by P.C. 2000-1331, effective for expenses incurred after December 5, 1996, to add everything from "that is not...".

Revenue Canada's view is that "all or substantially all", used in paras. (b) and (c), means 90% or more.

**"Canadian oil and gas exploration expense"** of a taxpayer means an outlay or expense made or incurred after 1980 that would be a Canadian exploration expense of the taxpayer within the meaning assigned by paragraph 66.1(6)(a) [66.1(6)"Canadian exploration expense"] of the Act if that paragraph were read without reference to subparagraphs (iii) and (iii.1) [paras. (f) and (g)] thereof and if the reference in subparagraphs (iv) and (v) [paras. (h) and (i)] thereof to "any of subparagraphs (i) to (iii.1) [paras. (a) to (g)]" were read as a reference to "any of subparagraphs (i) to (ii.2) [paras. (a) to (e)]", other than an outlay or expense that was a Canadian exploration expense by virtue of clause 66.1(6)(a)(ii)(B) or (ii.1)(B) [66.1(6)"Canadian exploration expense"(c)(ii) or (d)(ii)] of the Act that was in respect of a qualified tertiary oil recovery project;

**"coal mine operator"** means a person who undertakes all or substantially all of the activities involved in the production of coal from a resource;

**Related Provisions**: Reg. 1104(2)"coal mine operator" — Same definition for capital cost allowance.

**Notes**: Revenue Canada's view is that "all or substantially all" means 90% or more.

"Coal mine operator" added by P.C. 1999-629, effective March 7, 1996.

**"conventional lands"** means lands situated in Canada other than non-conventional lands;

**"disposition of property"** has the meaning assigned by paragraph 13(21)(c) [13(21)"disposition of property"] of the Act;

**"enhanced recovery equipment"** means property of a taxpayer that

    (a) is included in Class 10 in Schedule II by virtue of paragraph (j) of the description of that Class, and

    (b) was acquired by the taxpayer after April 10, 1978 and before 1981 for use in the production of oil, from a reservoir or a deposit of bituminous sand, oil sand or oil shale in Canada operated by the taxpayer, that is incremental to oil that would be recovered using primary recovery techniques alone,

other than property

(c) used by the taxpayer as part of a primary recovery process prior to the use described in paragraph (b),

(d) that had, before it was acquired by the taxpayer, been used for any purpose whatever by any person with whom the taxpayer was not dealing at arm's length, or

(e) that has been used by any person before April 11, 1978 in the production of oil, from a reservoir in Canada, that is incremental to oil that would be recovered using primary recovery techniques alone;

"exempt partnership" in respect of a taxpayer at a particular time means a partnership of which the taxpayer was a member throughout the period beginning on December 20, 1991 and ending at the particular time, where all or substantially all of the fair market value of the property of the partnership at the particular time is attributable to property held in connection with one or more working interests that were held by the partnership on December 20, 1991 for the production of minerals, petroleum, natural gas or related hydrocarbons, unless

(a) any of the depreciable property acquired after December 20, 1991 and before the particular time by the partnership in connection with one of the working interests had, before the time of the acquisition, been owned by the taxpayer (or any other person with whom the taxpayer did not deal at arm's length) and been used by the taxpayer (or that other person) in connection with that working interest, or

(b) it is reasonable to consider that, before the particular time, amounts were charged to the partnership that would not have been so charged if section 1210 were read without reference to subsection (4) of that section;

Notes: Revenue Canada's view is that "all or substantially all" means 90% or more.

"Exempt partnership" added by P.C. 1996-1488, effective for partnership fiscal periods that begin after December 20, 1991.

"exporting resource" means, in relation to a particular processing property of a taxpayer, a resource the ore or any portion thereof produced from which during the year immediately preceding the day on which the property was acquired by the taxpayer was ordinarily processed outside Canada to any stage that is not beyond the prime metal stage or its equivalent;

"mine" means any location where material is extracted from a resource but does not include a well for the extraction of material from a deposit of bituminous sand, oil sand or oil shale;

"non-conventional lands" means lands that belong to Her Majesty in right of Canada, or in respect of which Her Majesty in right of Canada has the right to dispose of or exploit the natural resources, situated in

(a) the Yukon Territory, the Northwest Territories, or Sable Island, or

(b) those submarine areas, not within a province, adjacent to the coast of Canada and extending throughout the natural prolongation of the land territory of Canada to the outer edge of the continental margin or to a distance of two hundred nautical miles from the baselines from which the breadth of the territorial sea of Canada is measured, whichever is the greater;

Notes: Para. (a) will need to be amended to refer to Nunavut, effective April 1999.

"ore" includes ore from a mineral resource that has been processed to any stage that is prior to the prime metal stage or its equivalent;

"original owner" of a property means a person

(a) who owned the property and disposed of it to a corporation that acquired it in circumstances in which subsection 1202(2) applies, or would apply if the corporation had continued to own the property, to the corporation in respect of the property, and

(b) who would, but for paragraph 1202(2)(b) (as it read in its application to taxation years ending before February 18, 1987) or paragraph 1202(3)(a), as the case may be, be entitled in computing the person's income for a taxation year ending after the person disposed of the property to a deduction under section 1201 in respect of expenditures that were incurred by the person before the person disposed of the property;

"predecessor owner" of a property means a corporation

(a) that acquired the property in circumstances in which subsection 1202(2) applies, or would apply if the corporation had continued to own the property, to the corporation in respect of the property,

(b) that disposed of the property to another corporation that acquired it in circumstances in which subsection 1202(2) applies, or would apply if the other corporation had continued to own the property, to the other corporation in respect of the property, and

(c) that would, but for subsection 1202(10), be entitled in computing its income for a taxation year after it disposed of the property to a deduction under subsection 1202(2) in respect of expenditures incurred by an original owner of the property;

"primary recovery" means the recovery of oil from a reservoir as a result of utilizing the natural energy of the reservoir to move the oil toward a producing well;

**"proceeds of disposition"** of property has the meaning assigned by paragraph 13(21)(d) [13(21)"proceeds of disposition"] of the Act;

**"processing property"** means property

(a) that is included in Class 10 of Schedule II because of paragraph (g) of the description of that Class or would be so included if that paragraph were read without reference to subparagraph (ii) of that paragraph and Schedule II were read without reference to Class 41, or

(b) that is included in Class 10 in Schedule II because of paragraph (k) of the description of that Class or would be so included if that paragraph were read without reference to the words following subparagraph (ii) of that paragraph and Schedule II were read without reference to Class 41,

other than property that had, before it was acquired by a taxpayer, been used for any purpose whatever by any person with whom the taxpayer was not dealing at arm's length;

**Notes**: "Processing property" amended by P.C. 1996-1488 to add reference to Class 41, effective for taxation years that end after 1987.

**"production royalty"** means an amount in respect of a particular Canadian resource property included in computing the income of a taxpayer as a rental or royalty computed by reference to the amount or value of petroleum, natural gas or related hydrocarbons produced after 1981 from a natural accumulation of petroleum or natural gas in Canada (other than a resource) or from an oil or gas well in Canada or produced after June, 1988 from a resource that is a bituminous sands deposit, oil sands deposit or oil shale deposit, if

(a) the taxpayer has a Crown royalty in respect of

(i) such production, or

(ii) the ownership of property to which such production relates where the Crown royalty is computed by reference to an amount of production from the accumulation, oil or gas well or resource,

and it is reasonable to consider that the taxpayer would have had the Crown royalty if the taxpayer's only source of income had been the rental or royalty in respect of the particular property, or

(b) the taxpayer would, but for an exemption or allowance (other than a rate of nil) that is provided, pursuant to a statute, by a person referred to in subparagraph 18(1) (m) (i), (ii) or (iii) of the Act, have a Crown royalty in respect of which paragraph (a) is applicable;

**Notes**: Subpara. (a)(ii) amended by P.C. 1996-1488 to add the words "oil or gas well or resource". The change is a correction to add words inadvertently omitted when the definition was last updated, and is effective re rentals and royalties computed by reference to the amount or value of petroleum, natural gas or related hydrocarbons produced after June 30, 1988.

Para. (b) amended by P.C. 1992-2335, to change "pursuant to a statute" to "by statute", effective December 2, 1992.

**"qualified resource"** means, in relation to a particular processing property of a taxpayer, a resource that, within a reasonable time after the property was acquired by him,

(a) came into production in reasonable commercial quantities, or

(b) was the subject of a major expansion whereby the greatest designed capacity, measured in weight of input of ore, of the mill that processed ore from the resource was not less than 25% greater in the year immediately following the expansion than it was in the year immediately preceding the expansion;

**Notes**: Para. (b) amended by P.C. 2000-1331, effective for expansions commencing after September 13, 2000, to change "tons of input" to "weight of input".

**"qualified tertiary oil recovery project"** in respect of an expense incurred in a taxation year means a project that uses a method (including a method that uses carbon dioxide miscible, hydrocarbon miscible, thermal or chemical processes but not including a secondary recovery method) that is designed to recover oil from an oil well in Canada that is incremental to oil that would be recovered therefrom by primary recovery and a secondary recovery method, if

(a) a specified royalty provision applies in the year or in the immediately following taxation year in respect of the production, if any, or any portion thereof from the project or in respect of the ownership of property to which such production relates,

(b) the project is on a reserve within the meaning of the *Indian Act*, or

(c) the project is located in the Province of Ontario;

**"resource"** means any mineral resource in Canada;

**"resource activity"** of a taxpayer means

(a) the production by the taxpayer of petroleum, natural gas or related hydrocarbons or sulphur from

(i) an oil or gas well in Canada, or

(ii) a natural accumulation (other than a mineral resource) of petroleum or natural gas in Canada,

(b) the production and processing in Canada by the taxpayer or the processing in Canada by the taxpayer of

(i) ore (other than iron ore or tar sands ore) from a mineral resource in Canada to any stage that is not beyond the prime metal stage or its equivalent,

(ii) iron ore from a mineral resource in Canada to any stage that is not beyond the pellet stage or its equivalent, and

(iii) tar sands ore from a mineral resource in Canada to any stage that is not beyond the crude oil stage or its equivalent,

(c) the processing in Canada by the taxpayer of heavy crude oil recovered from an oil or gas well in Canada to any stage that is not beyond the crude oil stage or its equivalent,

(c.1) Canadian field processing carried on by the taxpayer,

(d) the processing in Canada by the taxpayer of

(i) ore (other than iron ore or tar sands ore) from a mineral resource outside Canada to any stage that is not beyond the prime metal stage or its equivalent,

(ii) iron ore from a mineral resource outside Canada to any stage that is not beyond the pellet stage or its equivalent, and

(iii) tar sands ore from a mineral resource outside Canada to any stage that is not beyond the crude oil stage or its equivalent, or

(e) the ownership by the taxpayer of a right to a rental or royalty computed by reference to the amount or value of production from a natural accumulation of petroleum or natural gas in Canada, an oil or gas well in Canada or a mineral resource in Canada,

and, for the purposes of this definition,

(f) the production of a substance by a taxpayer includes exploration and development activities of the taxpayer with respect to the substance, whether or not extraction of the substance has begun or will ever begin,

(g) the production or the processing, or the production and processing, of a substance by a taxpayer includes activities performed by the taxpayer that are ancillary to, or in support of, the production or the processing, or the production and processing, of that substance by the taxpayer,

(h) the production or processing of a substance by a taxpayer includes an activity (including the ownership of property) that is undertaken before the extraction of the substance and that is undertaken for the purpose of extracting or processing the substance,

(i) the production or the processing, or the production and processing, of a substance by a taxpayer includes activities that the taxpayer undertakes as a consequence of the production or the processing, or the production and processing, of that substance, whether or not the production, the processing or the production and processing of the substance has ceased, and

(j) notwithstanding paragraphs (a) to (i), the production, the processing or the production and processing of a substance does not include any activity of a taxpayer that is part of a source described in paragraph 1204(1)(b), where

(i) the activity

(A) is the transporting, transmitting or processing (other than processing described in subparagraph 1206(1)"resource activity"(b) (iii), paragraph 1206(1)"resource activity"(c) or (c.1) or subparagraph 1206(1)"resource activity"(d) (iii)) of petroleum, natural gas or related hydrocarbons or of sulphur, or

(B) can reasonably be attributed to a service rendered by the taxpayer, and

(ii) revenues derived from the activity are not taken into account in computing the taxpayer's gross resource profits;

Notes: Para. (a) amended by P.C. 1999-629, effective for taxation years that begin after 1996, to add reference to sulphur.

Para. (c.1) added by P.C. 1999-629, effective for taxation years that begin after 1996.

Cl. (j)(i)(A) amended by P.C. 1999-629, effective for taxation years that begin after 1996, to add references to para. (c.1) and to sulphur.

"Resource activity" added by P.C. 1996-1488, effective for taxation years that begin after December 20, 1991.

"secondary recovery method" means a method to recover from a reservoir oil that is incremental to oil that would be recovered therefrom by primary recovery, by supplying energy to supplement or replace the natural energy of the reservoir through the use of technically proven methods, including waterflooding;

"specified development well" — [Revoked]

"specified percentage" for a calendar year

(a) in respect of a Canadian oil and gas exploration expense of a taxpayer for that year incurred in respect of conventional lands means,

(i) for the 1981 calendar year, 100 per cent,

(ii) for the 1982 calendar year, 60 per cent, and

(iii) for the 1983 calendar year, 30 per cent, and

(b) in respect of a Canadian oil and gas exploration expense of a taxpayer for that year incurred in respect of non-conventional lands means,

(i) for the 1981 and 1982 calendar years, 100 per cent,

(ii) for the 1983 calendar year, 60 per cent, and

(iii) for the 1984 calendar year, 30 per cent;

"specified property" of a person means all or substantially all of the property used by the person in carrying on in Canada such of the businesses described in subparagraphs 66(15)(h)(i) to (vii) [66(15)"principal-business corporation"(a) to (g)] of the Act as were carried on by the person;

**Reg.**
**S. 1206(1) spe**                                Income Tax Regulations

**Notes**: Revenue Canada's view is that "all or substantially all" means 90% or more.

**"specified royalty"** means a royalty created after December 5, 1996 (otherwise than pursuant to an agreement in writing made before on or before that date) where

(a) the cost of the royalty was a Canadian development expense, and

(b) the royalty was created as part of a transaction or event or series of transactions or events as a consequence of which depreciable property was acquired at a capital cost that was less than its fair market value (determined without regard to the royalty);

**Notes**: "Specified royalty" added by P.C. 1999-629, effective March 7, 1996, except that, with respect to a royalty created from March 7 through December 5, 1996 (or through the end of 1997 pursuant to an agreement in writing made before December 6, 1996) where any of the parties to the royalty so elect in writing filed with Revenue Canada before July 1998, read:

"specified royalty" means a royalty (other than a production royalty) created after March 6, 1996 (otherwise than pursuant to an agreement in writing made before March 7, 1996) where

(a) any amount paid or payable to the holder of the royalty because of the holder's interest in the royalty is calculated with reference to any expense, or

(b) an arrangement involving the reimbursement of, contribution to or allowance for, any expense has been made after March 6, 1996 and it is reasonable to consider that one of the reasons for the arrangement is to avoid the application of paragraph (a) in respect of the royalty;

Under Reg. 1210(2), payments made under a "specified royalty" reduce "adjusted resource profits" and thus the resource allowance. However, only 50% of payments received under a "specified royalty" are included in adjusted resource profits.

The impetus for these amendments was that the resource allowance rules allowed creation of certain royalties (especially net profit interests), which could be used to significantly increase the overall resource allowance available. By carving out a net profit interest from a working interest, the holder of the working interest could substantially decrease the amount paid for depreciable properties associated with the working interest. Thus, the amount of the resource profits qualifying for the resource allowance could be increased due to overall lower resulting CCA (which reduces adjusted resource profits) and higher CDE (which generally does not). Where the cost of a royalty is COGPE (rather than CDE) and is thus not a "specified royalty", there was no concern in this context because the 10% write-off for COGPE tends to be less than the rate for depreciable properties in the oil and gas sector.

**"stated percentage"** means

(a) where the taxpayer is an individual other than a trust, in respect of subparagraph 1203(2)(a)(i),

(i) 100 per cent in respect of an expenditure incurred before 1989,

(ii) 50 per cent in respect of an expenditure incurred after 1988 and before 1990, and

(iii) 0 per cent in respect of an expenditure incurred after 1989,

(b) in respect of subparagraph 1203(2)(a)(i) (where paragraph (a) is not applicable) and paragraphs 1205(1)(a), (b), (c) and (f)

(i) 100 per cent in respect of an expenditure incurred or a cost incurred in borrowing capital before July 1, 1988,

(ii) 50 per cent in respect of an expenditure incurred or a cost incurred in borrowing capital after June 30, 1988 and before 1990, and

(iii) 0 per cent in respect of an expenditure incurred or a cost incurred in borrowing capital after 1989,

(c) where the taxpayer is an individual other than a trust, in respect of subparagraph 1203(2)(a)(ii) and subsection 1203(4),

(i) 100 per cent in respect of any assistance that relates to expenditures incurred before 1989,

(ii) 50 per cent in respect of any assistance that relates to expenditures incurred after 1988 and before 1990, and

(iii) 0 per cent in respect of any assistance that relates to expenditures incurred after 1989, and

(d) in respect of subparagraph 1203(2)(a)(ii) (if paragraph (c) is not applicable), subsection 1203(4) (if paragraph (c) is not applicable) and subparagraph 1205(1)(j)(iii),

(i) 100 per cent in respect of any assistance or benefit that relates to expenditures incurred before July 1, 1988,

(ii) 50 per cent in respect of any assistance or benefit that relates to expenditures incurred after June 30, 1988 and before 1990, and

(iii) 0 per cent in respect of any assistance or benefit that relates to expenditures incurred after 1989;

**Notes**: Opening words of para. (d) amended by P.C. 1999-629, effective for 1999 and later taxation years, to delete a reference to Reg. 1202(2)(b)(iii).

**"tar sands ore"** means ore extracted, other than through a well, from a mineral resource that is a deposit of bituminous sand, oil sand or oil shale;

**"tertiary recovery equipment"** means property of a taxpayer that

(a) is, or but for Class 41 in Schedule II would be, included in Class 10 in Schedule II by virtue of paragraph (j) of the description of that Class,

(b) was acquired by the taxpayer after 1980 for use in a qualified tertiary oil recovery project,

other than property

(c) used by the taxpayer for another use prior to the use described in paragraph (b), or

(d) that had, before it was acquired by the taxpayer, been used for any purpose whatever by

Part XII — Resource and Processing Allowances    Reg. S. 1206(4.1)

any person with whom the taxpayer was not dealing at arm's length.

(2) In this Part, "joint exploration corporation", "principal-business corporation", "production" from a Canadian resource property, "reserve amount" and "shareholder corporation" have the meanings assigned by subsection 66(15) of the Act.

(3) For the purposes of sections 1201 to 1209 and 1212, where at the end of a fiscal period of a partnership, a taxpayer was a member thereof

(a) the resource profits of the partnership for the fiscal period, to the extent of the taxpayer's share thereof, shall be included in computing his resource profits for his taxation year in which the fiscal period ended;

(b) any property acquired or disposed of by the partnership shall be deemed to have been acquired or disposed of by the taxpayer to the extent of his share thereof;

(c) any property deemed by paragraph (b) to have been acquired or disposed of by the taxpayer shall be deemed to have been acquired or disposed of by him on the day the property was acquired or disposed of by the partnership;

(d) any amount that has become receivable by the partnership and in respect of which the consideration given by the partnership therefor was property (other than property referred to in paragraph 59(2)(a), (c) or (d) of the Act or a share or interest therein or right thereto) or services, all or part of the original cost of which to the partnership may reasonably be regarded primarily as an exploration or development expense of the taxpayer, shall be deemed to be an amount receivable by the taxpayer to the extent of his share thereof, and the consideration so given by the partnership shall, to the extent of the taxpayer's share thereof, be deemed to have been given by the taxpayer for the amount deemed to be receivable by him;

(e) any expenditure incurred or deemed to have been incurred by the partnership shall be deemed to have been incurred by the taxpayer to the extent of the taxpayer's share thereof; and

(f) any amount or expenditure deemed by paragraph (d) or (e) to have been receivable or incurred, as the case may be, by the taxpayer shall be deemed to have become receivable or been incurred, as the case may be, by the taxpayer on the day the amount became receivable or the expenditure was incurred or deemed to have been incurred by the partnership.

(3.1) For the purposes of sections 1201 to 1203, 1205, 1217 and 1218, where a taxpayer was a member of a partnership at the end of a fiscal period of the partnership, the taxpayer shall be deemed to receive or to become entitled to receive any amount of assistance or benefit, whether such amount is by way of a grant, subsidy, rebate, forgivable loan, deduction from royalty or tax, rebate of royalty or tax, investment allowance or any other form of assistance or benefit, that the partnership at any time receives or becomes entitled to receive in respect of expenses incurred in that fiscal period of the partnership, to the extent of,

(a) where the partnership in the fiscal period receives or becomes entitled to receive the amount, the taxpayer's share thereof, or

(b) where the partnership after the fiscal period becomes entitled to receive the amount, what would have been the taxpayer's share thereof if the partnership had in the fiscal period received or become entitled to receive the amount,

and the time at which the taxpayer is deemed to receive or become entitled to receive such share of the amount shall be the time that the partnership receives or becomes entitled to receive the amount.

(4) Where an expense incurred after November 7, 1969 that was a Canadian exploration and development expense or that would have been such an expense if it had been incurred after 1971 (other than an amount included therein that is in respect of financing or the cost of any Canadian resource property acquired by a joint exploration corporation or any property acquired by a joint exploration corporation that would have been a Canadian resource property if it had been acquired after 1971), a Canadian exploration expense (other than an amount included therein that is in respect of financing) or a Canadian development expense (other than an amount included therein that is in respect of financing or an amount referred to in subparagraph 66.2(5)(a)(iii) [66.2(5)"Canadian development expense"(e)] of the Act) has been renounced in favour of a taxpayer and was deemed to be an expense of the taxpayer for the purposes of subsection 66(10), (10.1) or (10.2) of the Act or subsection 29(7) of the *Income Tax Application Rules*, the expense shall,

(a) for the purposes of sections 1203 and 1205, be deemed to have been such an expense incurred by the taxpayer at the time the expense was incurred by the joint exploration corporation; and

(b) for the purposes of sections 1204 and 1210 and paragraphs 1217(2)(e) and 1218(2)(e), be deemed to have been such an expense incurred by the taxpayer at the time it was deemed to have been incurred by the taxpayer for the purposes of subsection 66(10), (10.1) or (10.2) of the Act or subsection 29(7) of the *Income Tax Application Rules*, as the case may be.

(4.1) An expense that is a Canadian exploration and development overhead expense of the joint exploration corporation referred to in subsection (4), or would be such an expense if the references to "connected with the taxpayer" in paragraph (d) of the definition "Canadian exploration and development overhead expense" in subsection (1) were read as "connected with the shareholder corporation in favour of whom the expense was renounced for the purposes of subsection 66(10.1) or (10.2) of the Act", that may reasonably be considered to be included in a Canadian exploration expense or Canadian development expense that is deemed by subsection (4) to be a Canadian exploration expense or Canadian development expense of the shareholder corporation, shall be deemed to be a Canadian exploration and development overhead expense of the shareholder corporation incurred by it at the time the expense was deemed by subsection (4) to have been incurred by it and shall be deemed at and after that time not to be a Canadian exploration and development overhead expense incurred by the joint exploration corporation.

**Notes**: Reg. 1206(4.1) added by P.C. 1985-465, effective for expenses renounced after March 6, 1985.

**(4.2)** For the purposes of paragraphs 66(12.6)(b), (12.601)(d) and (12.62)(b) of the Act, a prescribed Canadian exploration and development overhead expense of a corporation is

(a) a Canadian exploration and development overhead expense of the corporation;

(b) an expense that would be a Canadian exploration and development overhead expense of the corporation if the references to "connected with the taxpayer" in paragraph (d) of the definition "Canadian exploration and development overhead expense" in subsection (1) were read as "connected with the person to whom the expense is renounced under subsection 66(12.6), (12.601) or (12.62) of the Act"; and

(c) an expense that would be a Canadian exploration and development overhead expense of the corporation if the references to "person who was connected with the taxpayer" in paragraph (d) of the definition "Canadian exploration and development overhead expense" in subsection (1) were read as "person to whom the expense is renounced under subsection 66(12.6), (12.601) or (12.62) of the Act".

**Notes**: All references to ITA (12.601) added to Reg. 1206(4.2) by P.C. 1996-494, effective for expenses incurred after December 2, 1992.

Regs. 1206(4.2) added by P.C. 1990-2256, effective for expenditures or expenses incurred after February 1986.

**(4.3)** For the purposes of subsections (4.2) and (5), a partnership shall be deemed to be a person and its taxation year shall be deemed to be its fiscal period.

**Notes**: Reg. 1206(4.3) added by P.C. 1990-2256, effective for expenditures or expenses incurred after February 1986.

**(5)** For the purposes of subsection (6) and the definition "Canadian exploration and development overhead expense" in subsection (1),

(a) a person and a particular corporation are connected with each other if

(i) the person and the particular corporation are not dealing at arm's length,

(ii) the person has an equity percentage in the particular corporation that is not less than 10 per cent, or

(iii) the person is a corporation in which another person has an equity percentage that is not less than 10 per cent and the other person has an equity percentage in the particular corporation that is not less than 10 per cent;

(a.1) a person and another person that is not a corporation are connected with each other if they are not dealing at arm's length; and

(b) "costs incurred by a person" shall not include

(i) an outlay or expense described in any of paragraphs (a) to (c) of that definition made or incurred by the person if the references in those paragraphs to "taxpayer" were read as references to "person",

(ii) an outlay or expense made or incurred by the person to the extent that it is not reasonably attributable to the use of a property by, the performance of a service for, or any materials, parts, or supplies acquired by, the taxpayer referred to in that definition, and

(iii) an amount in respect of the capital cost to the person of a property, other than, where the property is a depreciable property of the person, that proportion of the capital allowance of the person for his taxation year in respect of the property that may reasonably be considered attributable to the use of the property by, or in the performance of a service for, the taxpayer referred to in that definition.

**Notes**: Reg. 1206(5)(a.1) added by P.C. 1990-2256, effective for expenditures or expenses incurred after February 1986.

**(6)** For the purpose of subparagraph (5)(b)(iii), the "capital allowance" of a person (in this subsection referred to as the "owner") for his taxation year in respect of a property owned by him means that proportion of an amount not exceeding 20 per cent of the amount that is

(a) in the case of a property owned by the owner on December 31, 1980, the lesser of

(i) the capital cost of the property to the owner computed as if no amount had been included therein that is a cost of borrowing capital, including any cost incurred prior to the commencement of carrying on a business, and

(ii) the fair market value of the property on December 31, 1980,

(b) in the case of a property acquired by the owner after December 31, 1980 that was previously owned by a person connected with the owner, the lesser of

(i) the capital cost of the property, computed as if no amount had been included therein that is a cost of borrowing capital, including any cost incurred prior to the commencement of carrying on a business, to the person, who was connected with the owner, who was the first person to acquire the property from a person with whom the owner was not connected, and

(ii) the fair market value of the property at the time it was acquired by the owner, and

(c) in any other case, the capital cost of the property to the owner computed as if no amount had been included therein that is a cost of borrowing capital, including any cost incurred prior to the commencement of carrying on a business,

that the number of days in the taxation year during which the property was owned by the owner is of 365.

(7) For the purposes of paragraph (5)(a), "equity percentage" has the meaning assigned by paragraph 95(4)(b) [95(4)"equity percentage"] of the Act.

(8) For the purposes of the definition "qualified tertiary oil recovery project" in subsection (1), a "specified royalty provision" means:

(a) the *Experimental Project Petroleum Royalty Regulation* of Alberta (Alta. Reg. 36/79);

(b) *The Experimental Oil Sands Royalty Regulations* of Alberta (Alta. Reg. 287/77);

(c) section 4.2 of the *Petroleum Royalty Regulations* of Alberta (Alta. Reg. 93/74);

(d) section 58A of the *Petroleum and Natural Gas Regulations, 1969* of Saskatchewan (Saskatchewan Regulation 8/69);

(e) section 204 of *The Freehold Oil and Gas Production Tax Regulations, 1983* of Saskatchewan (Saskatchewan Regulation 11/83);

(f) item 9 of section 2 of the *Petroleum and Natural Gas Royalty Regulations* of British Columbia (B.C. Reg. 549/78);

(g) the *Freehold Mineral Taxation Act* of Alberta;

(h) the *Freehold Mineral Rights Tax Act* of Alberta;

(i) Order in Council 427/84 pursuant to section 9(a) of the *Mines and Minerals Act* of Alberta;

(j) Order in Council 966/84 pursuant to section 9 of the *Mines and Minerals Act* of Alberta; or

(k) Order in Council 870/84 pursuant to section 9 of the *Mines and Minerals Act* of Alberta.

(8.1) For the purposes of paragraph (a) of the definition of "qualified tertiary oil recovery project" in subsection (1), where at a particular time unconditional approval is given by a person referred to in subparagraph 18(1)(m)(i), (ii) or (iii) of the Act for a specified royalty provision to apply at a time after the particular time, the specified royalty provision shall be deemed to apply as of the particular time.

(9) For the purposes of the definition "production royalty" in subsection (1), a "Crown royalty" of a taxpayer in respect of the production of petroleum, natural gas or related hydrocarbons from a natural accumulation of petroleum or natural gas in Canada, an oil or gas well in Canada, a resource that is a bituminous sands deposit, oil sands deposit or oil shale deposit or in respect of the ownership of a natural reservoir of gas or petroleum in Canada means an amount

(a) that would be included in computing his income for a taxation year by virtue of paragraph 12(1)(o) of the Act in respect of such production or ownership if that paragraph were read without reference to the words "or a prescribed amount",

(b) that would not be deductible in computing his income for a taxation year by virtue of paragraph 18(1)(m) of the Act in respect of such production or ownership if that paragraph were read without reference to the words "other than a prescribed amount",

(c) by which his proceeds of disposition of such production are increased by virtue of subsection 69(6) of the Act, or

(d) by which his cost of acquisition of such production is reduced by virtue of subsection 69(7) of the Act,

less, in respect of an amount described in paragraph (a) or (b), the amount of any reimbursement, contribution or allowance referred to in section 80.2 of the Act received or receivable by the taxpayer in respect of that amount.

**Notes**: Closing words of Reg. 1206(9) amended by P.C. 1996-1488 to add the words "contribution or allowance", effective February 1990.

**Definitions [Reg. 1206]**: "amount" — ITA 248(1); "arm's length" — ITA 251(1); "bituminous sands", "business" — ITA 248(1); "Canada" — ITA 255, *Interpretation Act* 35(1); "Canadian development expense" — ITA 66.2(5), 248(1); "Canadian exploration and development overhead expense" — Reg. 1206(1), (4.1); "Canadian exploration expense" — ITA 66.1(6), 248(1); "Canadian field processing" — ITA 248(1); "Canadian oil and gas exploration expense" — Reg. 1206(1); "Canadian resource property" — ITA 66(15), 248(1); "capital allowance" — Reg. 1206(6); "commencement" — *Interpretation Act* 35(1); "connected" — Reg. 1206(5); "conventional lands" — Reg. 1206(1); "corporation" — ITA 248(1), *Interpretation Act* 35(1); "cost incurred by a person" — Reg. 1206(5)(b); "Crown royalty" — Reg. 1206(9); "depreciable property" — ITA 13(21), 248(1); "disposed", "disposes" — ITA 248(1)"disposition"; "disposition", "employed" — ITA 248(1); "equity percentage" — Reg. 1206(7); "fiscal period" — ITA 249.1; "gross resource profits" — Reg. 1204(1); "Her Majesty" — *Interpretation Act* 35(1); "individual" — ITA 248(1); "mine" — Reg. 1206(1); "mineral", "mineral resource" — ITA 248(1); "non-conventional lands" — Reg. 1206(1); "oil or gas well" — ITA 248(1); "ore", "original owner" — Reg. 1206(1); "owner" — Reg. 1206(5);

"person" — ITA 248(1), Reg. 1206(4.3); "prescribed" — ITA 248(1); "primary recovery", "proceeds of disposition" — Reg. 1206(1); "processing property" — Reg. 1206(1); "property" — ITA 248(1); "province" — Interpretation Act 35(1); "qualified tertiary oil recovery project" — Reg. 1206(1); "related" — ITA 251(2)–(6); "resource" — Reg. 1206(1); "resource profits" — Reg. 1204(1.1); "secondary recovery method" — Reg. 1206(1); "share", "shareholder" — ITA 248(1); "specified royalty" — Reg. 1206(1); "specified royalty provision" — Reg. 1206(8), (8.1); "tar sands ore" — Reg. 1206(1); "taxation year" — ITA 249; "taxpayer" — ITA 248(1); "territorial sea", "territory" — Interpretation Act 35(1); "trust" — ITA 104(1), 248(1), (3); "writing" — Interpretation Act 35(1).

**1207. Frontier exploration allowances** — (1) A taxpayer may deduct in computing his income for a taxation year such amount as he may claim not exceeding the lesser of

(a) his income for the year, computed in accordance with Part I of the Act, if no deduction were allowed under this subsection; and

(b) his frontier exploration base as of the end of the year (before making any deduction under this subsection for the year).

(2) For the purposes of this section, the "frontier exploration base" of a taxpayer as of a particular time means the amount by which the aggregate of

(a) the aggregate of all amounts, each of which is an amount in respect of a particular oil or gas well in Canada equal to 66⅔ per cent of the amount by which

(i) expenses incurred after March, 1977 and before April, 1980 and before the particular time in respect of the well (other than expenses that may reasonably be regarded as having been incurred as consideration for services rendered to the taxpayer after March, 1980) if those expenses would be included in the Canadian exploration expense of the taxpayer within the meaning of paragraph 66.1(6)(a) [66.1(6)"Canadian exploration expense"] of the Act (if that paragraph were read without reference to subparagraphs (iii) and (iii.1) [paras. (f) and (g)] thereof and without reference to the words "within six months after the end of the year, the drilling of the well is completed and" in subparagraph (ii) [para. (c)] thereof, and if the reference in subparagraphs (iv) and (v) [paras. (h) and (i)] thereof to "any of subparagraphs (i) to (iii.1) [paras. (a) to (g)]" were read as a reference to "subparagraph (i) or (ii) [para. (a) or (c)]") other than

(A) a cost of borrowing capital, including any cost incurred prior to the commencement of carrying on a business, that was a Canadian exploration expense of the taxpayer,

(B) an expense renounced by the taxpayer under subsection 66(10.1) of the Act,

(C) an amount that, by virtue of subparagraph 66.1(6)(a)(iv) [66.1(6)"Canadian exploration expense"(h)] of the Act, was a Canadian exploration expense, if such amount was an expense referred to in clause (A) or (B) that was incurred by a partnership referred to in that subparagraph, or

(D) an amount that, by virtue of subparagraph 66.1(6)(a)(v) [66.1(6)"Canadian exploration expense"(i)] of the Act, was a Canadian exploration expense, if such amount was an expense referred to in clause (A) or (B) that the taxpayer incurred pursuant to an agreement referred to in that subparagraph,

exceeds

(ii) the taxpayer's threshold amount in respect of the well, minus the amount that would be determined under subparagraph (i) in respect of the taxpayer for the well if the reference therein to "after March, 1977 and before April, 1980" were read as "after June, 1976 and before April, 1977", and

(a.1) where the taxpayer is a successor corporation, any amount required by paragraph (7)(a) to be added before the particular time in computing the taxpayer's frontier exploration base,

exceeds the aggregate of

(b) all amounts deducted by the taxpayer under subsection (1) in computing his income for taxation years ending before the particular time,

(c) 66⅔ per cent of the aggregate of all amounts, each of which is an amount that became receivable by the taxpayer after March 28, 1979 and before the earlier of December 12, 1979 and the particular time, and in respect of which the consideration given by the taxpayer therefor was a property (other than a share, or a property that would have been a Canadian resource property if it had been acquired by the taxpayer at the time the consideration was given) or services the cost of which may reasonably be regarded as having been primarily an expenditure in respect of an oil or gas well for which an amount was added in computing the taxpayer's frontier exploration base by virtue of paragraph (a) or in computing the frontier exploration base of a predecessor by virtue of paragraph (a) as it applied to the predecessor where the taxpayer is a successor corporation to the predecessor, as the case may be; and

(d) where the taxpayer is a predecessor, any amount required by paragraph (7)(b) to be deducted before the particular time in computing the taxpayer's frontier exploration base.

(3) For the purposes of subparagraph (2)(a)(ii), a taxpayer's "threshold amount" in respect of an oil or gas well means

(a) where the taxpayer and one or more other persons have filed an agreement with the Minister in prescribed form in respect of the well and

(i) the amount allocated to each such person in the agreement does not exceed the amount that would be determined, at the time the agreement is filed, under subparagraph (2)(a)(i) in respect of that person for the well, if the reference in that subparagraph to "March, 1977" were read as "June, 1976", and

(ii) the aggregate of the amounts allocated by the agreement is $5 million,

the amount allocated to the taxpayer in the agreement, but if no amount is allocated to the taxpayer in the agreement, nil;

(b) where such an agreement has been filed in respect of the well by one or more persons other than the taxpayer, nil; or

(c) where no such agreement has been filed in respect of the well, $5 million.

**Forms:** T3015: Allocation agreement to determine a taxpayer's threshold amount in respect of an oil or gas well.

(4) Where as a result of mechanical or geological difficulties the drilling of a particular oil or gas well does not achieve its stated geological objectives under the drilling authority issued by the relevant government body and a further well, including a relief well, is drilled on the same geological formation and may reasonably be regarded as a continuation of or a substitution for the particular oil or gas well, the expenses in respect of the drilling of the further well shall, for the purposes of this section, be deemed to be expenses in respect of the drilling of the particular oil or gas well.

(5) For the purposes of this section,

(a) when a shareholder corporation is deemed to have incurred a Canadian exploration expense by virtue of an election made by a joint exploration corporation pursuant to subsection 66(10.1) of the Act, that expense shall be deemed to have been incurred by the shareholder corporation at the time when it was incurred by the joint exploration corporation; and

(b) when a member of a partnership is deemed to have incurred a Canadian exploration expense by virtue of subparagraph 66.1(6)(a)(iv) [66.1(6)"Canadian exploration expense"(h)] of the Act, that expense shall be deemed to have been incurred by the member at the time when it was incurred by the partnership.

(6) For the purposes of this section, "oil or gas well" means any well drilled for the purpose of producing petroleum or natural gas or of determining the existence, location, extent or quality of an accumulation of petroleum or natural gas, other than a mineral resource.

(7) Subject to subsections 1202(5) and (6), where a corporation (in this section referred to as the "successor corporation") has at any time (in this subsection referred to as the "time of acquisition") after April 19, 1983 and in a taxation year (in this subsection referred to as the "transaction year") acquired a property from another person (in this subsection referred to as the "predecessor"), the following rules apply:

(a) for the purpose of computing the frontier exploration base of the successor corporation as of any time after the time of acquisition, there shall be added an amount equal to the amount required by paragraph (b) to be deducted in computing the frontier exploration base of the predecessor; and

(b) for the purpose of computing the frontier exploration base of the predecessor as of any time after the transaction year of the predecessor, there shall be deducted the amount, if any, by which

(i) the frontier exploration base of the predecessor immediately before the time of acquisition (assuming for this purpose that, in the case of an acquisition as a result of an amalgamation described in section 87 of the Act, the predecessor existed after the time of acquisition and no property was acquired or disposed of in the course of the amalgamation)

exceeds

(ii) the amount, if any, deducted under subsection (1) in computing the income of the predecessor for the transaction year of the predecessor.

(8) [Revoked]

**Notes:** Reg. 1207(8) revoked by P.C. 1990-2780, effective for taxation years ending after February 17, 1987.

**Definitions [Reg. 1207]:** "amount", "business" — ITA 248(1); "Canada" — ITA 255, *Interpretation Act* 35(1); "Canadian exploration expense" — Reg. 1207(5); "Canadian resource property" — ITA 66(15), 248(1); "commencement" — *Interpretation Act* 35(1); "corporation" — ITA 248(1), *Interpretation Act* 35(1); "disposed" — ITA 248(1)"disposition"; "expenses" — Reg. 1207(4); "frontier exploration base" — Reg. 1207(2); "mineral resource", "Minister" — ITA 248(1); "month" — *Interpretation Act* 35(1); "oil or gas well" — Reg. 1207(6); "person" — ITA 248(1); "predecessor" — Reg. 1203(3); "prescribed", "property", "share", "shareholder" — ITA 248(1); "successor corporation" — Reg. 1203(3); "taxation year" — ITA 249; "taxpayer" — ITA 248(1); "threshold amount" — Reg. 1207(3); "time of acquisition", "transaction year" — Reg. 1203(3).

## 1208. Additional allowances in respect of certain oil or gas wells — (1) Subject to subsections (3) and (4) where a taxpayer has income for a taxation year from an oil or gas well that is outside Canada, or where an individual has income for a taxation year from an oil or gas well in Canada, in com-

puting his income for the year he may deduct the lesser of

(a) the aggregate of drilling costs incurred by him in that year and previous taxation years in respect of the well (not including the cost of land, leases or other rights and not including indirect expenses such as general exploration, geological and geophysical expenses) minus the aggregate of all amounts deductible in respect thereof in computing his income for previous years; and

(b) that part of his income for the year that may reasonably be regarded as income from the well.

(2) Where a taxpayer has more than one oil or gas well to which subsection (1) applies, the allowance in respect of the drilling costs of each well shall be computed separately.

(3) Where an individual has income for a taxation year from an oil or gas well in Canada, no deduction may be made under this section in computing such income in respect of drilling costs of that well incurred after April 10, 1962.

(4) Where a taxpayer has income for a taxation year from an oil or gas well that is outside Canada, no deduction may be made under this section in computing such income in respect of drilling costs of that well incurred after 1971.

**Definitions [Reg. 1208]**: "amount" — ITA 248(1); "Canada" — ITA 255, *Interpretation Act* 35(1); "individual", "oil or gas well" — ITA 248(1); "taxation year" — ITA 249; "taxpayer" — ITA 248(1).

**1209. Additional allowances in respect of certain mines** — (1) Subject to subsection (3), where a taxpayer operates in Canada a mine for the production of materials from a resource he may deduct, in computing his income for a taxation year, such amount as he may claim not exceeding 25 per cent of the amount computed under subsection (2).

(2) The amount referred to in subsection (1) is the aggregate of all expenditures made or incurred by the taxpayer before 1972 that are reasonably attributable to the prospecting and exploration for and the development of the mine prior to the coming into production of the mine in reasonable commercial quantities, except to the extent that the expenditures were

(a) expenditures in respect of which a deduction from, or in computing, a taxpayer's income tax or excess profits tax was provided by section 8 of the *Income War Tax Act*;

(b) expenditures in respect of which an amount was deducted in computing a taxpayer's income under section 16 of chapter 63, S.C., 1947 or section 16 of chapter 53, S.C., 1947-48 or, if the expenditure was incurred prior to 1953, under section 53 of chapter 25, S.C., 1949 (Second Session);

(c) expenditures incurred after 1952 in respect of which a deduction was or is provided by section 53 of chapter 25, S.C., 1949, (Second Session), section 83A of the Act as it read in its application to the 1971 taxation year or section 29 of the *Income Tax Application Rules*;

(d) expenditures deducted in computing the income of the taxpayer in the year they were incurred;

(e) the cost to the taxpayer of property in respect of which an allowance is provided under paragraph 20(1)(a) of the Act; or

(f) the cost to the taxpayer of a leasehold interest.

(3) The amount deductible under subsection (1) shall not exceed the amount computed under subsection (2) minus the aggregate of

(a) amounts deducted under subsection (1) in computing the income of the taxpayer for previous taxation years; and

(b) similar amounts deducted in computing the income of the taxpayer for the purposes of the *Income War Tax Act* and *The 1948 Income Tax Act* (as defined in paragraph 12(d) of the *Income Tax Application Rules*).

**Definitions [Reg. 1209]**: "amount" — Reg. 1209(2); "Canada" — ITA 255, *Interpretation Act* 35(1); "mine" — Reg. 1206(1); "property" — ITA 248(1); "resource" — Reg. 1206(1); "taxation year" — ITA 249; "taxpayer" — ITA 248(1).

**1210. Resource allowance** — (1) For the purpose of paragraph 20(1)(v.1) of the Act, there may be deducted in computing the income of a taxpayer for a taxation year the amount determined by the formula

$$.25 (A - B) - C$$

where

A   is the taxpayer's adjusted resource profits for the year;

B   is the total of all amounts each of which is a Canadian exploration and development overhead expense made or incurred by the taxpayer in the year, other than an amount included therein because of subsection 21(2) or (4) of the Act; and

C   is the amount, if any, by which

(a) the total of all amounts determined under paragraphs 1205(1)(e) to (k) in computing the taxpayer's earned depletion base at the end of the year, other than any portion of that total determined under paragraph 1205(1)(i) as a consequence of a disposition in the year of property in circumstances to which subsection 1202(2) applies

exceeds

(b) 33 $\frac{1}{3}$ per cent of the total of all amounts determined under paragraphs 1205(1)(a) to (d.2) in computing the taxpayer's earned depletion base at the end of the year.

**Related Provisions**: ITA 257 — Negative amounts in formulas.

Part XII — Resource and Processing Allowances

**(2) ["Adjusted resource profits"]** — For the purposes of this section, "adjusted resource profits" of a taxpayer for a taxation year is the amount, which may be positive or negative, determined by the formula

$$A + B - C$$

where

A is the amount that would be the taxpayer's resource profits for the year if the following assumptions were made:

(a) the amount determined under paragraph 1204(1)(a) were nil,

(b) subsection 1204(1) were read without reference to subparagraph 1204(1)(b)(iv) and the definition "resource activity" in subsection 1206(1) were read without reference to paragraph (d) of that definition,

(c) the following amounts were not deducted in computing the taxpayer's gross resource profits for the year and were not deducted in computing the taxpayer's resource profits for the year:

(i) each amount deducted in computing the taxpayer's income for the year in respect of a rental or royalty paid or payable by the taxpayer (other than an amount prescribed by section 1211, an amount that is a production royalty or an amount paid or payable in respect of a specified royalty) computed by reference to the amount or value of petroleum, natural gas or related hydrocarbons

(A) produced from a natural accumulation (other than a resource) of petroleum or natural gas in Canada or an oil or gas well in Canada, or

(B) produced from a resource that is a bituminous sands deposit, oil sands deposit or oil shale deposit,

(ii) each amount deducted in computing the taxpayer's income for the year

(A) under any of paragraphs 20(1)(e), (e.1), (e.2) and (f) of the Act, or

(B) as, on account of or in lieu of, interest in respect of a debt owed by the taxpayer, and

(iii) each amount deducted under any of paragraph 20(1)(v.1) and sections 65 to 66.7 of the Act and subsections 17(2) and (6) and section 29 of the *Income Tax Application Rules*,

(d) each amount that is the taxpayer's share of the income or loss of a partnership from any source were not taken into account, and

(e) subsections 1204(1) and (1.1) provided for the computation of negative amounts where the amounts subtracted in computing gross resource profits and resource profits exceed the amounts added in computing those amounts;

B is the total of all amounts each of which is the taxpayer's share of the adjusted resource profits of a partnership for the year, as determined under subsection (3) or (4); and

C is the amount, if any, by which the total of

(a) the total of all amounts each of which is an amount included in the taxpayer's gross resource profits for the year as a rental or royalty (other than a production royalty or a specified royalty) computed by reference to the amount or value of petroleum, natural gas or related hydrocarbons produced from

(i) a natural accumulation (other than a resource) of petroleum or natural gas in Canada or an oil or gas well in Canada, or

(ii) a resource that is a bituminous sands deposit or oil shale deposit, and

(b) 50 per cent of all amounts included in computing the taxpayer's gross resource profits for the year in respect of specified royalties

exceeds

(c) if the year ends after March 6, 1996, the total of all outlays and expenses that were made or incurred in respect of the total described in paragraph (a) to the extent that the outlays and expenses were deducted in computing the taxpayer's gross resource profits for the year.

**Related Provisions**: ITA 257 — Negative amounts in formulas.

**Notes [Reg. 1210(2)]**: Reg. 1210(2)A(c)(i) amended by P.C. 1999-629, effective for taxation years that end after March 6, 1996, to add "an amount paid or payable in respect of a specified royalty".

Reg. 1210(2)C amended by P.C. 1999-629, effective for taxation years that end after March 6, 1996. For earlier taxation years, read:

C is the amount, if any, by which

(a) the total of all amounts each of which is an amount included in the taxpayer's gross resource profits for the year as a rental or royalty (other than a production royalty) computed by reference to the amount or value of petroleum, natural gas or related hydrocarbons produced from

(i) a natural accumulation (other than a resource) of petroleum or natural gas in Canada or an oil or gas well in Canada, or

(ii) a resource that is a bituminous sands deposit, oil sands deposit or oil shale deposit

exceeds

(b) where the year ends after March 6, 1996, the total of all outlays and expenses that were made or incurred in respect of the total described in paragraph (a) to the extent that the outlays and expenses were deducted in computing the taxpayer's gross resource profits for the year.

See Notes to Reg. 1206(1)"specified royalty" for explanation of these amendments.

See also Notes at end of Reg. 1210.

**(3) [Partnership]** — Where a taxpayer is a member of a partnership in a fiscal period of the partnership that ends in a taxation year of the taxpayer, the taxpayer's share of the partnership's adjusted resource profits for the year is

(a) nil, where the fiscal period began before December 21, 1991; and

(b) in any other case, the amount, which may be positive or negative, that could, if this subsection did not apply, reasonably be considered to represent the taxpayer's share of the partnership's adjusted resource profits for the fiscal period, determined on the assumption that each partnership is a taxpayer the fiscal period of which is a taxation year.

**(4) [Exempt partnership]** — Notwithstanding subsection (3), where a taxpayer is a member of an exempt partnership in a fiscal period of the partnership that begins before 2000 and ends in a taxation year of the taxpayer and the taxpayer's share of the partnership's adjusted resource profits for the year would, if this subsection did not apply, be a negative amount, the taxpayer's share of the partnership's adjusted resource profits for the year is the amount, which may be positive or negative, determined by the formula

$$A \times B$$

where

A is the amount that would, if this subsection did not apply, be the taxpayer's share of the partnership's adjusted resource profits for the year; and

B is

(a) nil, where

(i) the partnership is an exempt partnership in respect of the taxpayer at the end of the fiscal period, and

(ii) at the end of the fiscal period, all or substantially all of the assets of the partnership were held in connection with one or more working interests

(A) the production from which began in reasonable commercial quantities before December 21, 1991, or

(B) the production from which was to begin in reasonable commercial quantities after December 20, 1991 in accordance with an agreement in writing made before December 21, 1991, and

(b) in any other case, the lesser of one and the amount determined by the formula

$$\frac{C}{D}$$

where

C is the amount that would be the partnership's adjusted resource profits for the fiscal period if the partnership did not have any working interest described in subparagraph (a)(ii), and

D is the partnership's adjusted resource profits for the fiscal period.

**Notes [Reg. 1210(4)]**: Revenue Canada's view is that "all or substantially all", used in Reg. 1210(4)B(a)(ii), means 90% or more.

**Notes [Reg. 1210]**: Reg. 1210 amended by P.C. 1996-1448, this version effective for taxation years that begin after March 18, 1993. For taxation years that begin from December 21, 1991 to March 18, 1993, read as above, except:

(a) read 1210(1)B as follows:

B is the total of all amounts each of which is a Canadian exploration and development overhead expense made or incurred by the taxpayer in the year, other than each amount included therein in respect of financing, deducted in computing the taxpayer's income for the year,

and

(b) read 1210(2)A(c)(ii) as follows:

(ii) each amount in respect of financing deducted in computing the taxpayer's income for the year,

The amendments were partly in response to the *Gulf Canada Ltd.* case, [1992] 1 C.T.C. 183 (FCA). See also Notes to 1204(1.1).

Opening words of Reg. 1210(1)(a)(i) amended by P.C. 1993-415, retroactive to taxation years ending after February 17, 1987, so that the computation of resource profits includes the income of a wholly-owned railway company from the transportation of the taxpayer's mineral ore.

**Definitions [Reg. 1210]**: "adjusted resource profits" — Reg. 1210(2); "amount", "bituminous sands" — ITA 248(1); "Canada" — ITA 255, *Interpretation Act* 35(1); "Canadian development expense" — ITA 66.2(5), 248(1), Reg. 1206(4)(b); "Canadian exploration and development expenses" — ITA 66(15), 248(1), Reg. 1206(4)(b); "Canadian exploration and development overhead expense" — Reg. 1206(1), (4.1); "Canadian exploration expense" — ITA 66.1(6), 248(1), Reg. 1206(4)(b); "disposition" — ITA 248(1); "earned depletion base" — Reg. 1202(1), 1205(1); "exempt partnership" — Reg. 1206(1); "fiscal period" — ITA 249.1; "gross resource profits" — Reg. 1204(1); "oil or gas well", "prescribed" — ITA 248(1); "production royalty" — Reg. 1206(1); "property" — ITA 248(1); "related" — ITA 251(2)–(6); "resource" — Reg. 1206(1); "resource profits" — Reg. 1204(1.1); "share" — ITA 248(1); "specified royalty" — Reg. 1206(1); "taxation year" — ITA 249; "taxpayer" — ITA 248(1); "writing" — *Interpretation Act* 35(1).

**1210.1 [Prescribed resource loss]** — For the purpose of paragraph 12(1)(z.5) of the Act, a taxpayer's prescribed resource loss for a taxation year is the amount determined by the formula

$$A - B$$

where

A is the total of all amounts each of which is a Canadian exploration and development overhead expense made or incurred by the taxpayer in the year, other than an amount included therein because of subsection 21(2) or (4) of the Act, and

B is the taxpayer's adjusted resource profits for the year (as defined by subsection 1210(2)).

**Related Provisions**: ITA 257 — Negative amounts in formulas.

**Notes**: Reg. 1210.1 added by P.C. 1999-629, effective for taxation years that begin after 1996.

**Definitions [Reg. 1210.1]:** "amount" — ITA 248(1); "Canadian exploration and development overhead expense" — Reg. 1206(1), (4.1); "prescribed" — ITA 248(1); "resource" — Reg. 1206(1); "resource profits" — Reg. 1204(1.1); "taxation year" — ITA 249; "taxpayer" — ITA 248(1).

## 1211. Prescribed amounts

The following amounts are hereby prescribed for the purposes of paragraphs 12(1)(o) and 18(1)(m) of the Act:

(a) an amount paid to, an amount that became payable to, or an amount that became receivable by

(i) Her Majesty in right of Canada for the use and benefit of a band or bands as defined in the *Indian Act*, or

(ii) Petro-Canada;

(b) an amount paid to, an amount that became payable to, or an amount that became receivable by any of the persons referred to in any of subparagraphs 18(1)(m)(i) to (iii) of the Act

(i) that is an amount that may reasonably be regarded as being in respect of a rental for any property described in clause 66(15)(c)(ii)(B) [66(15)"Canadian resource property"(b)(ii)] or subparagraph 66(15)(c)(vi) [66(15)"Canadian resource property"(f)] of the Act,

(ii) that was paid, became payable, or became receivable prior to the commencement of production of minerals from the property referred to in subparagraph (i) in reasonable commercial quantities, and

(iii) that was paid, became payable, or became receivable, after December 11, 1979, in respect of a period commencing after that date;

(c) an amount paid to, an amount that became payable to, or an amount that became receivable by any of the persons referred to in any of subparagraphs 18(1)(m)(i) to (iii) of the Act

(i) that may reasonably be regarded as being in respect of a rental for a right, licence or privilege to store underground petroleum, natural gas or other related hydrocarbons in Canada, and

(ii) that was paid, became payable, or became receivable, after December 11, 1979, in respect of a period commencing after that date;

(d) an amount equal to the lesser of

(i) an amount that

(A) became payable to or receivable by any of the persons referred to in any of subparagraphs 18(1)(m)(i) to (iii) of the Act as a rental for property described in subparagraph 66(15)(c)(i) [66(15)"Canadian resource property"(a)] of the Act or for a portion of such property, and

(B) became payable or receivable

(I) in a taxation year in which there was no taking of petroleum, natural gas or related hydrocarbons in relation to the property or portion thereof, as the case may be, to which the rental relates, if the amount became payable or receivable after 1984, or

(II) prior to the taking of petroleum, natural gas or related hydrocarbons in relation to the property or portion thereof, as the case may be, to which the rental relates, if the amount became payable or receivable after October 31, 1982 and before 1985, and

(ii) an amount equal to $2.50 per year per hectare times the number of hectares to which the amount referred to in subparagraph (i) relates; and

(e) an amount paid under section 49 of the *Canada Oil and Gas Act*.

**Definitions [Reg. 1211]:** "amount" — ITA 248(1); "Canada" — ITA 255, *Interpretation Act* 35(1); "commencement", "Her Majesty" — *Interpretation Act* 35(1); "mineral", "person", "prescribed", "property" — ITA 248(1); "related" — ITA 251(2)–(6); "resource" — Reg. 1206(1); "taxation year" — ITA 249.

**Interpretation Bulletins:** IT-438R2: Crown charges — resource properties in Canada.

## 1212. Supplementary depletion allowances

(1) In computing a taxpayer's income for a taxation year there may be deducted

(a) where the taxpayer is a corporation, such amount as it may claim not exceeding the lesser of

(i) the aggregate of

(A) 50 per cent of its income for the year, computed in accordance with Part I of the Act without reference to paragraphs 59(3.3)(c) and (d) thereof, if no deduction were allowed under this subsection or subsection 1207(1), and

(B) the amount, if any, included in its income for the year by virtue of paragraphs 59(3.3)(c) and (d) of the Act, and

(ii) its supplementary depletion base as of the end of the year (before making any deduction under this subsection for the year); and

(b) where the taxpayer is not a corporation, such amount as he may claim not exceeding the lesser of

(i) the aggregate of

(A) 25 per cent of the amount, if any, by which his resource profits for the year exceed four times the amount, if any, deducted by virtue of subparagraph 1201(a)(i) in computing his income for the year, and

(B) the amount, if any, included in his income for the year by virtue of paragraphs 59(3.3)(c) and (d) of the Act, and

**Reg. S. 1212(1)(b)(ii)**      Income Tax Regulations

(ii) his supplementary depletion base as of the end of the year (before making any deduction under this subsection for the year).

(2) For the purpose of computing the supplementary depletion base of a corporation, where, after the corporation last ceased to carry on active business, control of the corporation is considered, for the purposes of subsection 66(11) of the Act, to have been acquired by a person or persons who did not control the corporation at the time when it so ceased to carry on active business, the amount by which the supplementary depletion base of the corporation at the time it last ceased to carry on active business exceeds the aggregate of amounts otherwise deducted under subsection (1) in computing its income for taxation years ending after that time and before control was so acquired, shall be deemed to have been deducted under subsection (1) by the corporation in computing its income for taxation years ending before control was so acquired.

(3) For the purposes of this section, "supplementary depletion base" of a taxpayer as of a particular time means the amount by which the aggregate of

(a) 50 per cent of the aggregate of all expenditures each of which was incurred by him before the particular time and each of which was the capital cost to him of property that is enhanced recovery equipment,

(b) 33⅓ per cent of the aggregate of all expenditures each of which was incurred by him before the particular time and each of which was the capital cost to him of property (other than property that had, before it was acquired by him, been used for any purpose whatever by any person with whom he was not dealing at arm's length) that is bituminous sands equipment acquired by him before 1981, and

(c) where the taxpayer is a successor corporation, any amount required by paragraph (4)(a) to be added before the particular time in computing the taxpayer's supplementary depletion base,

exceeds the aggregate of

(d) all amounts deducted by the taxpayer under subsection (1) in computing his income for taxation years ending before the particular time;

(e) 50 per cent of the aggregate of all amounts, each of which is a cost of borrowing capital, including any cost incurred prior to the commencement of carrying on a business, included in the capital cost to him of depreciable property described in paragraph (a);

(f) 33⅓ per cent of the aggregate of all amounts, each of which is a cost of borrowing capital, including any cost incurred prior to the commencement of carrying on a business, included in the capital cost to him of depreciable property described in paragraph (b);

(g) 50 per cent of the aggregate of all amounts, each of which is an amount in respect of a disposition of property (other than a disposition of property, that had been used by the taxpayer, to any person with whom the taxpayer was not dealing at arm's length) of the taxpayer before the earlier of December 12, 1979 and the particular time, the capital cost of which was added in computing the taxpayer's supplementary depletion base by virtue of paragraph (a) or in computing the supplementary depletion base of a predecessor by virtue of paragraph (a) as it applied to the predecessor where the taxpayer is a successor corporation to the predecessor, as the case may be, and each of which is the amount that is equal to the lesser of

(i) the proceeds of disposition of the property, and

(ii) the capital cost of the property to the taxpayer or the predecessor, as the case may be, computed as if no amount had been included therein that is a cost of borrowing capital, including a cost incurred prior to the commencement of carrying on a business;

(h) 33⅓ per cent of the aggregate of all amounts, each of which is an amount in respect of a disposition of property (other than a disposition of property, that had been used by the taxpayer, to any person with whom the taxpayer was not dealing at arm's length) of the taxpayer before the earlier of December 12, 1979 and the particular time, the capital cost of which was added in computing the taxpayer's supplementary depletion base by virtue of paragraph (b) or in computing the supplementary depletion base of a predecessor by virtue of paragraph (b) as it applied to the predecessor where the taxpayer is a successor corporation to the predecessor, as the case may be, and each of which is the amount that is equal to the lesser of

(i) the proceeds of disposition of the property, and

(ii) the capital cost of the property to the taxpayer or the predecessor, as the case may be, computed as if no amount had been included therein that is a cost of borrowing capital, including any cost incurred prior to the commencement of carrying on a business; and

(i) where the taxpayer is a predecessor, any amount required by paragraph (4)(b) to be deducted before the particular time in computing the taxpayer's supplementary depletion base.

(4) Subject to subsections 1202(5) and (6), where a corporation (in this section referred to as the "successor corporation") has at any time (in this subsection referred to as the "time of acquisition") after April 19, 1983 and in a taxation year (in this subsection referred to as the "transaction year") acquired a property from another person (in this subsection re-

ferred to as the "predecessor"), the following rules apply:

(a) for the purpose of computing the supplementary depletion base of the successor corporation as of any time after the time of acquisition, there shall be added an amount equal to the amount required by paragraph (b) to be deducted in computing the supplementary depletion base of the predecessor; and

(b) for the purpose of computing the supplementary depletion base of the predecessor as of any time after the transaction year of the predecessor, there shall be deducted the amount, if any, by which

(i) the supplementary depletion base of the predecessor immediately after the time of acquisition (assuming for this purpose that, in the case of an acquisition as a result of an amalgamation described in section 87 of the Act, the predecessor existed after the time of acquisition and no property was acquired or disposed of in the course of the amalgamation)

exceeds

(ii) the amount, if any, deducted under subsection (1) in computing the income of the predecessor for the transaction year of the predecessor.

**(5)** [Revoked]

**Definitions [Reg. 1212]**: "active business", "amount" — ITA 248(1); "arm's length" — ITA 251(1); "business" — ITA 248(1); "commencement" — *Interpretation Act* 35(1); "corporation" — ITA 248(1), *Interpretation Act* 35(1); "deducted" — Reg. 1212(2); "depreciable property" — ITA 13(21), 248(1); "disposed" — ITA 248(1)"disposition"; "disposition" — ITA 248(1); "disposition of property", "enhanced recovery equipment" — Reg. 1206(1); "person" — ITA 248(1); "predecessor" — Reg. 1203(3); "proceeds of disposition" — Reg. 1206(1); "property" — ITA 248(1); "successor corporation" — Reg. 1203(3); "supplementary depletion base" — Reg. 1212(3); "taxation year" — ITA 249; "taxpayer" — ITA 248(1); "time of acquisition", "transaction year" — Reg. 1203(3).

**1213. Prescribed deductions** — For the purposes of subparagraph 66.1(2)(a)(ii) of the Act, "prescribed deduction" in respect of a corporation for a taxation year means an amount deducted under subsection 1202(2) by the corporation in computing its income for the year.

**Definitions [Reg. 1213]**: "amount" — ITA 248(1); "corporation" — ITA 248(1), *Interpretation Act* 35(1); "taxation year" — ITA 249.

**1214. Amalgamations and windings-up — (1)** Where a particular corporation amalgamates with another corporation to form a new corporation, or the assets of a subsidiary are transferred to its parent corporation on the winding-up of the subsidiary, and subsection 87(1.2) or 88(1.5) of the Act is applicable to the new corporation or the parent corporation, as the case may be, the new corporation or the parent corporation, as the case may be, shall be deemed to be the same corporation as, and a continuation of, the particular corporation or the subsidiary, as the case may be, for the purposes of

(a) computing the mining exploration depletion base (within the meaning assigned by subsection 1203(2)), the earned depletion base, the frontier exploration base (within the meaning assigned by subsection 1207(2)) and the supplementary depletion base (within the meaning assigned by subsection 1212(3)) of the new corporation or the parent corporation, as the case may be; and

(b) determining the amounts, if any, that may be deducted under subsection 1202(2) in computing the income of the new corporation or the parent corporation, as the case may be, for a particular taxation year.

**(2)** Where there has been an amalgamation (within the meaning assigned by subsection 87(1) of the Act) of two or more particular corporations to form one corporate entity, that entity shall be deemed to be the same corporation as, and a continuation of, each of the particular corporations for the purposes of subsection 1202(9).

**(3)** Where a taxable Canadian corporation (in this subsection referred to as the "subsidiary") has been wound up in circumstances in which subsection 88(1) of the Act applies in respect of the subsidiary and another taxable Canadian corporation (in this subsection referred to as the "parent"), the parent shall be deemed to be the same corporation as, and a continuation of, the subsidiary for the purposes of subsection 1202(9).

**Definitions [Reg. 1214]**: "amount" — ITA 248(1); "corporation" — ITA 248(1), *Interpretation Act* 35(1); "earned depletion base" — Reg. 1202(1), 1205(1); "parent", "subsidiary" — Reg. 1214(3); "taxable Canadian corporation" — ITA 89(1), 248(1); "taxation year" — ITA 249.

**1215.** [Revoked]

**1216. Prescribed persons** — For the purposes of subsection 208(1) of the Act, "prescribed person" means a person described in paragraph 149(1)(d) of the Act.

> **Proposed Amendment — Reg. 1216**
>
> **1216. Prescribed persons** — For the purposes of subsection 208(1) of the Act, "prescribed person" means a person described in any of paragraphs 149(1)(d) to (d.6) of the Act.
>
> **Application**: The November 30, 2000 draft regulations (miscellaneous), s. 2 (pre-published in the *Canada Gazette*, Part I, December 9, 2000), will amend s. 1216 to read as above, applicable after 1998.
>
> **Regulatory Impact Analysis Statement**: Section 1216 of the Regulations is amended consequentially to amendments to paragraph 149(1)(d) of the *Income Tax Act* (the Act) and the addition to the Act of paragraphs 149(1)(d.1) to (d.6) related to tax-exempt Crown corporations and other public authorities. Prior to 1998, para-

graph 149(1)(d) exempted from tax the taxable income of any corporation, commission or association of which the federal government, provincial government or a Canadian municipality owned at least 90 percent of the shares. The exemption also applied to wholly-owned subsidiaries of these corporations commissions or associations. Paragraph 149(1)(d) was amended for fiscal periods beginning after 1998, by creating paragraphs (d) to (d.6), to clarify the scope of the exemption where an entity or a combination of entities owns either 100 percent or at least 90 percent of the shares or capital of a corporation, commission or association.

**Definitions [Reg. 1216]**: "person" — ITA 248(1).

## 1217. Prescribed Canadian exploration expense

**— (1)** For the purposes of subsection 66(14.1) of the Act, the prescribed Canadian exploration expense of a corporation for a taxation year is the amount, if any, by which its total specified exploration expenses for the year exceed its total exploration assistance for the year.

**(2)** For the purposes of subsection (1), the total specified exploration expenses of a particular corporation for a particular taxation year are the aggregate of

(a) all expenses (other than expenses referred to in paragraph (b) or (c)) that are described in any of subparagraphs 66.1(6)(a)(i) to (ii) of the Act and that were incurred by the particular corporation in the particular year and after March 1985 and before October 1986,

(b) where the particular corporation is a shareholder corporation of a joint exploration corporation, all expenses described in any of subparagraphs 66.1(6)(a)(i) to (ii) of the Act that were incurred by the joint exploration corporation after March 1985 and before October 1986 and in the taxation year of the joint exploration corporation ending in the particular year and that were deemed under paragraph 66(10.1)(c) of the Act to be Canadian exploration expenses incurred by the particular corporation in the particular year, and

(c) all expenses that would be described in subparagraph 66.1(6)(a)(iv) or (v) of the Act if the references in those subparagraphs to "any of subparagraphs (i) to (iii.1) incurred" were read as "any of subparagraphs (i) to (ii) incurred after March 1985 and before October 1986" and that were incurred by the particular corporation in the particular year or by a partnership in a fiscal period of the partnership that ended in the particular year if, at the end of that fiscal period, the particular corporation was a member of the partnership

other than

(d) expenses renounced by the corporation at any time under subsection 66(10.1) or (12.6) of the Act,

(e) Canadian exploration and development overhead expenses of the corporation or of a partnership of which the corporation was a member, or

(f) expenses incurred or deemed to have been incurred by the corporation in a period during which it was exempt from tax on its taxable income under Part I of the Act.

**(3)** For the purposes of subsection (1), the total exploration assistance of a corporation for a taxation year is the aggregate of all amounts each of which is an amount of assistance or benefit that the corporation has received or is entitled to receive in the year from a government, municipality or other public authority in respect of an expense that is included in its total specified exploration expenses for the year by virtue of paragraph (2)(a) or (c), whether such amount is by way of a grant, subsidy, rebate, forgivable loan, deduction from royalty or tax, rebate of royalty or tax, investment allowance or any other form of assistance or benefit.

**Definitions [Reg. 1217]**: "amount" — ITA 248(1); "Canadian development expense" — ITA 66.2(5), 248(1), Reg. 1206(4)(b); "Canadian exploration and development expenses" — ITA 66(15), 248(1), Reg. 1206(4)(b); "Canadian exploration and development overhead expense" — Reg. 1206(1), (4.1); "Canadian exploration expense" — ITA 66.1(6), 248(1), Reg. 1206(4)(b); "corporation" — ITA 248(1), *Interpretation Act* 35(1); "fiscal period" — ITA 249.1; "prescribed", "shareholder", "taxable income" — ITA 248(1); "taxation year" — ITA 249; "total development assistance" — Reg. 1218(3); "total exploration assistance" — Reg. 1217(3); "total specified development expenses" — Reg. 1218(2); "total specified exploration expenses" — Reg. 1217(2).

## 1218. Prescribed Canadian development expense

**— (1)** For the purposes of subsection 66(14.2) of the Act, prescribed Canadian development expense of a corporation for a taxation year is the amount, if any, by which its total specified development expenses for the year exceed its total development assistance for the year.

**(2)** For the purposes of subsection (1), the total specified development expenses of a particular corporation for a particular taxation year is the aggregate of

(a) all expenses (other than expenses referred to in paragraph (b) or (c)) that are described in subparagraph 66.2(5)(a)(i) or (i.1) [66.2(5)"Canadian development expense"(a) or (b)] of the Act and that were incurred by the corporation in the particular year and after March 1985 and before October 1986,

(b) where the particular corporation is a shareholder corporation of a joint exploration corporation, all expenses that are described in subparagraph 66.2(5)(a)(i) or (i.1) [66.2(5)"Canadian development expense"(a) or (b)] of the Act, that were incurred by the joint exploration corporation after March 1985 and before October 1986 and in the taxation year of the joint exploration corporation ending in the particular year and that were deemed under paragraph 66(10.2)(c) of the Act to be Canadian development expenses incurred by the particular corporation in the particular year, and

(c) all expenses that would be described in subparagraph 66.2(5)(a)(iv) or (v) [66.2(5)"Canadian development expense"(f) or (g)] of the Act if the references in those subparagraphs to "any of subparagraphs (i) to (iii) incurred" were read as "subparagraph (i) or (i.1) incurred after March 1985 and before October 1986" and that were incurred by the particular corporation in the particular year or by a partnership in a fiscal period of the partnership that ended in the particular year if, at the end of that fiscal period, the particular corporation was a member of the partnership,

other than

(d) expenses renounced by the corporation at any time under subsection 66(10.2), (12.601) or (12.62) of the Act,

(e) Canadian exploration and development overhead expenses of the corporation or of a partnership of which the corporation was a member, or

(f) expenses incurred or deemed to have been incurred by the corporation in a period during which it was exempt from tax on its taxable income under Part I of the Act.

**Notes**: Reference to ITA 66(12.601) added to Reg. 1218(2)(d) by P.C. 1996-494, effective December 3, 1992.

(3) For the purposes of subsection (1), the total development assistance of a corporation for a taxation year is the aggregate of all amounts each of which is an amount of assistance or benefit that the corporation has received or is entitled to receive in the year from a government, municipality or other public authority in respect of an expense that is included in its total specified development expenses for the year by virtue of paragraph (2)(a) or (c), whether such amount is by way of a grant, subsidy, rebate, forgivable loan, deduction from royalty or tax, rebate of royalty or tax, investment allowance or any other form of assistance or benefit.

**Definitions [Reg. 1218]**: "amount" — ITA 248(1); "Canadian development expense" — ITA 66.2(5), 248(1), Reg. 1206(4)(b); "Canadian exploration and development expenses" — ITA 66(15), 248(1), Reg. 1206(4)(b); "Canadian exploration and development overhead expense" — Reg. 1206(1), (4.1); "Canadian exploration expense" — ITA 66.1(6), 248(1), Reg. 1206(4)(b); "corporation" — ITA 248(1), *Interpretation Act* 35(1); "fiscal period" — ITA 249.1; "prescribed", "shareholder", "taxable income" — ITA 248(1); "taxation year" — ITA 249.

**1219. Canadian renewable and conservation expense** — (1) Subject to subsection (2), for the purpose of subsection 66.1(6) of the Act, "Canadian renewable and conservation expense" means an expense incurred by a taxpayer, and payable to a person or partnership with whom the taxpayer is dealing at arm's length, in respect of the development of a project for which it is reasonable to expect that at least 50% of the capital cost of the depreciable property to be used in the project would be the capital cost of any property that is described in Class 43.1 of Schedule II or that would be such property but for this subsection, and includes such an expense incurred by the taxpayer

(a) for the purpose of making a service connection to the project for the transmission of electricity to a purchaser of the electricity, to the extent that the expense so incurred was not incurred to acquire property of the taxpayer;

(b) for the construction of a temporary access road to the project site;

(c) for a right of access to the project site before the earliest time at which a property described in Class 43.1 of Schedule II is used in the project for the purpose of earning income;

(d) for clearing land to the extent necessary to complete the project;

(e) for process engineering for the project, including

   (i) collection and analysis of site data,

   (ii) calculation of energy, mass, water, or air balances,

   (iii) simulation and analysis of the performance and cost of process design options, and

   (iv) selection of the optimum process design;

(f) for the drilling or completion of a well for the project; or

(g) for the taxpayer's test wind turbine for the project.

**Notes**: See at end of Reg. 1219.

(2) **[Exclusions]** — A Canadian renewable and conservation expense does not include any expense that

(a) is described in paragraphs 20(1)(c), (d), (e) or (e.1) of the Act; or

(b) is incurred by a taxpayer directly or indirectly and is

   (i) for the acquisition of, or the use of or the right to use, land, except as provided by paragraph (1)(b), (c) or (d);

   (ii) for grading or levelling land or for landscaping, except as provided by paragraph (1)(b);

   (iii) payable to a non-resident person or a partnership other than a Canadian partnership (other than an expense described in paragraph (1)(g));

   (iv) included in the capital cost of property that, but for this section, would be depreciable property, except as provided by paragraph (1)(b), (d), (e), (f) or (g);

   (v) an expenditure that, but for this section, would be an eligible capital expenditure, except as provided by any of paragraphs (1)(a) to (e);

   (vi) included in the cost of inventory of the taxpayer;

(vii) an expenditure on or in respect of scientific research and experimental development;

(viii) a Canadian development expense or a Canadian oil and gas property expense;

(ix) incurred, for a project, in respect of any time at or after the earliest time at which a property described in Class 43.1 of Schedule II was used in the project for the purpose of earning income;

(x) incurred in respect of the administration or management of a business of the taxpayer;

(xi) a cost attributable to the period of the construction, renovation or alteration of depreciable property, other than property described in Class 43.1 of Schedule II, that relates to

(A) the construction, renovation or alteration of the property (except as provided by paragraph (1)(b), (f), or (g)), or

(B) the ownership of land during the period (except as provided by paragraph (1)(b), (c) or (d)).

(3) For the purpose of paragraph (1)(g), "test wind turbine" means a fixed location device that is a wind energy conversion system that would, but for this section, be property included in Class 43.1 of Schedule II because of subparagraph (d)(v) thereof, and in respect of which the Minister, in consultation with the Minister of Natural Resources, determines that

(a) the device will be the first such device installed at the taxpayer's site for a proposed wind energy conversion system; and

(b) the primary purpose of the device is to test the level of energy production at the site.

**Related Provisions [Reg. 1219]**: Reg. 1102(1)(a.1) — CRCE ineligible for capital cost allowance.

**Notes [Reg. 1219]**: Reg. 1219 added by P.C. 2000-1331, effective for expenses incurred after December 5, 1996. CRCE is deductible by being included in CEE: see 66.1(6)"Canadian exploration expense"(g.1).

See Notes to ITA 66.1(6)"Canadian renewable and conservation expense."

**Definitions [Reg. 1219]**: "arm's length" — ITA 251(1); "business" — ITA 248(1); "Canadian development expense" — ITA 66.2(5), 248(1); "Canadian oil and gas property expense" — ITA 66.4(5), 248(1); "Canadian partnership" — ITA 102, 248(1); "depreciable property" — ITA 13(21), 248(1); "eligible capital expenditure" — ITA 14(5), 248(1); "inventory", "Minister", "non-resident", "person", "property", "scientific research and experimental development", "taxpayer" — ITA 248(1); "test wind turbine" — Reg. 1219(3).

# PART XIII — ELECTIONS IN RESPECT OF TAXPAYERS CEASING TO BE RESIDENT IN CANADA

**1300. Elections to defer capital gains** — (1) Any election by an individual under paragraph 48(1)(c) of the Act shall be made by filing with the Minister the prescribed form on or before the day on or before which the return of income for the year in which the taxpayer ceased to be resident in Canada is required to be filed under section 150 of the Act.

(2) Any election by a Canadian corporation under paragraph 48(1)(c) of the Act shall be made by filing with the Minister, on or before the day on or before which the return of income for the year in which the corporation ceased to be resident in Canada is required to be filed under section 150 of the Act, the following documents in duplicate:

(a) the form prescribed by the Minister;

(b) where the directors of the corporation are legally entitled to administer the affairs of the corporation, a certified copy of their resolution authorizing the election to be made; and

(c) where the directors of the corporation are not legally entitled to administer the affairs of the corporation, a certified copy of the authorization of the making of the election by the person or persons legally entitled to administer the affairs of the corporation.

**Notes**: Regs. 1300(1) and (2) are expected to be amended to refer to ITA 128.1(4)(b)(iv), which was enacted by the 1993 technical bill in place of ITA 48(1)(c).

**Definitions [Reg. 1300]**: "Canadian corporation" — ITA 89(1), 248(1); "corporation" — ITA 248(1), *Interpretation Act* 35(1); "individual", "Minister", "person", "prescribed" — ITA 248(1); "resident in Canada" — ITA 250; "taxpayer" — ITA 248(1).

**Interpretation Bulletins**: IT-434R: Rental of real property by individual; IT-451R: Deemed disposition and acquisition on ceasing to be or becoming resident in Canada.

**Forms**: T2061: Election by an emigrant to defer deemed disposition of property and capital gains thereon.

**1301. Elections to defer payment of taxes** — (1) Any election by an individual under subsection 159(4) of the Act shall be made by filing with the Minister the prescribed form on or before the day on or before which the return of income for the year in which the taxpayer ceased to be resident in Canada is required to be filed under section 150 of the Act.

**Forms**: T2074: Election under subsection 159(4) to defer payment of income tax on the deemed disposition of property.

(2) Any election by a Canadian corporation under subsection 159(4) of the Act shall be made by filing with the Minister, on or before the day on or before which the return of income for the year in which the corporation ceased to be resident in Canada is required to be filed under section 150 of the Act, the following documents in duplicate:

(a) the form prescribed by the Minister;

(b) where the directors of the corporation are legally entitled to administer the affairs of the corporation, a certified copy of their resolution authorizing the election to be made; and

(c) where the directors of the corporation are not legally entitled to administer the affairs of the corporation, a certified copy of the authorization of the making of the election by the person or persons legally entitled to administer the affairs of the corporation.

**Forms [Reg. 1301(2)]**: T2074: Election under subsection 159(4) to defer payment of income tax on the deemed disposition of property.

**Definitions [Reg. 1301]**: "Canadian corporation" — ITA 89(1), 248(1); "corporation" — ITA 248(1), *Interpretation Act* 35(1); "individual", "Minister", "person", "prescribed" — ITA 248(1); "resident in Canada" — ITA 250; "taxpayer" — ITA 248(1).

**1302. Elections to realize capital gains** — Any election by an individual under paragraph 48(1)(a) of the Act shall be made by filing with the Minister the prescribed form on or before the day on or before which the return of income for the year in which the taxpayer ceased to be resident in Canada is required to be filed under section 150 of the Act.

**Notes**: Reg. 1302 is expected to be amended to refer to ITA 128.1(4)(d) enacted by the 1993 technical bill, in place of ITA 48(1)(a).

**Definitions [Reg. 1302]**: "individual", "Minister", "prescribed" — ITA 248(1); "resident in Canada" — ITA 250; "taxpayer" — ITA 248(1).

# PART XIV — INSURANCE BUSINESS POLICY RESERVES

## DIVISION 1 — POLICY RESERVES

**1400. Non-life insurance business — (1) [Policy reserve]** — For the purpose of paragraph 20(7)(c) of the Act, the amount prescribed in respect of an insurer for a taxation year is

(a) the amount determined under subsection (3) in respect of the insurer for the year, where that amount is greater than nil, and

(b) nil, in any other case.

**Notes**: See at end of Reg. 1400.

**(2) [Negative reserves]** — For the purpose of paragraph 12(1)(e.1) of the Act, the amount prescribed in respect of an insurer for a taxation year is

(a) the absolute value of the amount determined under subsection (3) in respect of the insurer for the year, where that amount is less than nil, and

(b) nil, in any other case.

**Related Provisions**: Reg. 1402.1 — Negative amounts.

**Notes**: See at end of Reg. 1400.

**(3) [Amount of reserve]** — For the purposes of paragraphs (1)(a) and (2)(a), the amount determined under this subsection in respect of an insurer for a taxation year is the amount, which may be positive or negative, determined by the formula

$$A + B + C + D + E + F + G + H + I + J + K + L$$

where

A is the total of all amounts each of which is the unearned portion at the end of the year of the net premium for a policy, (other than a policy that insures a risk in respect of

(a) a financial loss of a lender on a loan made on the security of real property,

(b) a home warranty,

(c) a lease guarantee, or

(d) an extended motor vehicle warranty),

which is determined by apportioning the net premium equally over the period to which that premium relates;

---

**Proposed Amendment — Reg. 1400(3)A**

**Application**: The November 30, 1999 draft regulations (insurance business policy reserves), subsec. 1(1)(a), will amend the description of A in subsec. 1400(3) by replacing "net premium" with "premium paid by the policyholder", applicable to 2000 *et seq.* and, where the taxpayer elects under the coming-into-force provision for the amendments to section 18 of the Act, as released in draft form on November 30, 1999, to the taxpayer's 1998 and 1999 taxation years.

**Technical Notes**: Part XIV of the *Income Tax Regulations* provides rules in respect of insurance business policy reserves.

Part XIV is amended to replace the term "net premium" wherever it appears with the term "premium paid by the policyholder". The change is consequential on newly added subsection 18(9.02) of the Act which denies a deduction on a current basis of acquisition costs of insurance policies (other than a non-cancellable or guaranteed renewable accident and sickness insurance policy, or a life insurance policy that is not a group term life insurance policy that provides coverage for a period of 12 months or less). This amendment ensures that deductions in respect of policy reserves remain consistent with the tax treatment of policy acquisition costs.

This amendment applies to the 2000 and subsequent taxation years and, if a taxpayer files an election in respect of amended subparagraph 18(9)(a)(ii) and new subsection 18(9.02) of the Act, the amendment also applies to the taxpayer's 1998 and 1999 taxation years.

---

B is the total of all amounts each of which is an amount determined in respect of a policy referred to in paragraph (a), (b), (c) or (d) of the description of A equal to the lesser of

(a) the amount of the reported reserve of the insurer at the end of the year in respect of the unearned portion at the end of the year of the net premium for the policy, and

(b) a reasonable amount as a reserve determined as at the end of the year in respect of the unearned portion at the end of the year of the net premium for the policy;

> **Proposed Amendment — Reg. 1400(3)B(a), (b)**
>
> **Application**: The November 30, 1999 draft regulations (insurance business policy reserves), subsec. 1(1)(b), will amend paras. (a) and (b) of the description of B in subsec. 1400(3) by replacing "net premium" with "premium paid by the policyholder", applicable to 2000 et seq. and, where the taxpayer elects under the coming-into-force provision for the amendments to section 18 of the Act, as released in draft form on November 30, 1999, to the taxpayer's 1998 and 1999 taxation years.
>
> **Technical Notes**: See under Reg. 1400(3)A.

C is the total of all amounts each of which is the amount in respect of a policy, where all or a portion of a risk under the policy was reinsured, equal to the unearned portion at the end of the year of a reinsurance commission in respect of the policy determined by apportioning the reinsurance commission equally over the period to which it relates;

D is the amount, in respect of policies (other than policies in respect of which an amount can be determined under the description of E) under which

    (a) a claim that was incurred before the end of the year has been reported to the insurer before the end of the year and in respect of which the insurer is, or may be, required to make a payment or incur an expense after the year, or

    (b) there may be a claim incurred before the end of the year that has not been reported to the insurer before the end of the year,

equal to 95% of the lesser of

    (c) the total of the reported reserves of the insurer at the end of the year in respect of such claims or possible claims, and

    (d) the total of the claim liabilities of the insurer at the end of the year in respect of such claims or possible claims;

E is the amount, in respect of policies under which

    (a) a claim that was incurred before the end of the year has been reported to the insurer before the end of the year,

    (b) the claim is in respect of damages for personal injury or death, and

    (c) the insurer has agreed to a structured settlement of the claim,

equal to the lesser of

    (d) the total of the reported reserves of the insurer at the end of the year in respect of such claims, and

    (e) the total of the claim liabilities of the insurer at the end of the year in respect of such claims;

F is an additional amount, in respect of policies that insure a fidelity risk, a surety risk, a nuclear risk, or a risk related to a financial loss of a lender on a loan made on the security of real property, equal to the lesser of

    (a) the total of the reported reserves of the insurer at the end of the year in respect of such risks (other than an amount included in determining the value of A, B, C, D, E, G, H, I, J, K or L), and

    (b) a reasonable amount as a reserve determined as at the end of the year in respect of such risks (other than an amount included in determining the value of A, B, C, D, E, G, H, I, J, K or L);

G is the amount of a guarantee fund at the end of the year provided for under an agreement in writing between the insurer and Her Majesty in right of Canada under which Her Majesty has agreed to guarantee the obligations of the insurer under a policy that insures a risk related to a financial loss of a lender on a loan made on the security of real property;

H is the amount in respect of risks under pre-1996 non-cancellable or guaranteed renewable accident and sickness policies equal to

    (a) where the amounts determined under subparagraphs (i) and (ii) are greater than nil, the lesser of

        (i) the total of the reported reserves of the insurer at the end of the year in respect of such risks (other than an amount included in determining the value of A, B, C, D, E, F, G, I, J, K or L), and

        (ii) a reasonable amount as a reserve determined as at the end of the year in respect of such risks (other than an amount included in determining the value of A, B, C, D, E, F, G, I, J, K or L), and

    (b) nil, in any other case;

I is the amount in respect of risks under post-1995 non-cancellable or guaranteed renewable accident and sickness policies equal to the lesser of

    (a) the total of the reported reserves of the insurer at the end of the year in respect of such risks (other than an amount included in determining the value of A, B, C, D, E, F, G, H, J, K or L), and

    (b) the total of the policy liabilities of the insurer at the end of the year in respect of such risks (other than an amount included in determining the value of A, B, C, D, E, F, G, H, J, K or L);

J is the total of all amounts (other than an amount deductible under subsection 140(1) of the Act) each of which is the amount, which is the least of P, Q and R, in respect of a dividend, refund of premiums or refund of premium deposits pro-

Division 1 — Policy Reserves

Reg. S. 1400

vided for under the terms of a group accident and sickness insurance policy that will be

(a) used by the insurer to reduce or eliminate a future adverse claims experience under the policy,

(b) paid or unconditionally credited to the policyholder by the insurer, or

(c) applied in discharge, in whole or in part, of a liability of the policyholder to pay premiums to the insurer under the policy,

where

P is a reasonable amount as a reserve determined as at the end of the year in respect of the dividend, refund of premiums or refund of premium deposits,

Q is 25% of the amount of the premium payable under the terms of the policy for the 12-month period ending

(i) if the policy is terminated in the year, on the day the policy is terminated, and

(ii) in any other case, at the end of the year, and

R is the reported reserve of the insurer at the end of the year in respect of the dividend, refund of premiums or refund of premium deposits; and

K is the total of all amounts each of which is the amount, in respect of a policy under which a portion of the particular amount paid or payable by the policyholder for the policy before the end of the year is deducted under paragraph 1408(4)(b), equal to the portion of that particular amount that the insurer has determined will, after the end of the year, be returned to, or credited to the account of the policyholder on the termination of the policy; and

L is an amount in respect of policies that insure earthquake risks in Canada equal to the lesser of

(a) the portion of the reported reserve of the insurer at the end of the year in respect of those risks that is attributable to accumulations from premiums in respect of those risks (other than an amount included in determining the value of A, B, C, D, E, F, G, H, I, J, or K), and

(b) a reasonable amount as a reserve determined as at the end of the year in respect of those risks (other than an amount included in determining the value of A, B, C, D, E, F, G, H, I, J, or K).

**Related Provisions**: Reg. 1400(4) — Where actuarial principles not required for element D or E; Reg. 1400(5) — Transitional — before 2001; Reg. 1402 — All amounts to be net of reinsurance ceded; Reg. 1402.1 — Amounts in Reg. 1400 may be less than zero.

**Notes**: The tax treatment of recipients of payments from a structured settlement (Reg. 1400(3)E) is discussed in Interpretation Bulletin IT-365R2, para. 5, and in various published Advance Tax Rulings.

Formula element L allows earthquake reserves, as proposed in the February 1998 federal budget. It applies to 1998 and later taxation years.

The rest of Reg. 1400(3) applies to 1996 and later taxation years (i.e., for 1996 and 1997, "L" is zero). See Notes at end of Reg. 1400.

**(4) [Elements D and E]** — Where the relevant authority does not require an insurer (other than an insurer that is required by law to report to the Superintendent of Financial Institutions) to determine its liabilities in respect of claims referred to in the description of D or E in subsection (3) in accordance with actuarial principles,

(a) the value of D is deemed to be 95% of the amount determined under paragraph (c) of the description of D; and

(b) the value of E is deemed to be the amount determined under paragraph (d) of the description of E.

**(5) [Transitional — Before 2001]** — Notwithstanding subsection (3), the amount determined under that subsection in respect of an insurer (other than a life insurer) for a taxation year that ends before 2001 is deemed to be the amount determined by the formula

$$A + (B \times (C - D))$$

where

A is the amount that would, but for this subsection, be the amount determined under subsection (3) in respect of the insurer for the year;

B is, where the year ends in

(a) 1996, 100%

(b) 1997, 80%

(c) 1998, 60%

(d) 1999, 40%, and

(e) 2000, 20%;

C is the total of all amounts each of which is the absolute value of any amount that is less than nil and that is used in computing the amount that is the lesser of the totals determined for the year under the description of I in subsection (3), in respect of a risk under a post-1995 non-cancellable or guaranteed renewable accident and sickness policy; and

D is the lesser of

(a) 5% of the total of all amounts each of which is a premium received by the insurer in the year or any preceding taxation year ending after 1995 in respect of a non-cancellable or guaranteed renewable accident and sickness policy, and

(b) the value of C.

**Related Provisions**: Reg. 1402.1 — Negative amounts.

**Notes [Reg. 1400]**: Reg. 1400 replaced with Reg. 1400(1)–(5) by P.C. 1999-1154, this version effective for 1998 and later taxation years. For the 1996 and 1997 years, "L" in Reg. 1400(3) is nil. For

**Reg. S. 1400** — Income Tax Regulations, Part XIV

1994 and 1995 taxation years that end after February 22, 1994 (paras. (e) and (e.1) amended by P.C. 1999-1154), read:

**1400. Non-life insurance businesses** — For the purposes of paragraph 20(7)(c) of the Act, an insurance corporation in computing its income for a taxation year may deduct, in accordance with the following rules, in respect of

(a) a policy, other than a policy that insures a risk in respect of

(i) a financial loss of a lender on a loan made on the security of real property,

(ii) a home warranty, or

(iii) a lease guarantee,

such amount as the corporation may claim not exceeding the unearned portion of the net premium for the policy at the end of the year determined by apportioning the net premium equally over the period to which that premium pertains;

(b) a policy referred to in subparagraph (a)(i), (ii) or (iii), such amount as the corporation may claim not exceeding the lesser of

(i) the amount of the unearned portion, if any, of the net premium for the policy at the end of the year, calculated in the manner required for the purposes of the corporation's annual report for the year to the relevant authority or, where the corporation was subject to the supervision of the relevant authority throughout the year but was not required to file an annual report with the relevant authority for the year, the amount thereof reported in its financial statements for the year, and

(ii) the unearned portion, if any, calculated in the manner required for the purposes of the corporation's annual report for the 1977 fiscal period to the relevant authority, of the net premium for the policy;

(c) a policy where all or a portion of a risk thereunder was reinsured, such amount as the corporation may claim not exceeding the unearned portion at the end of the year of the aggregate of amounts, each of which is a reinsurance commission in respect of the policy, determined by apportioning that aggregate equally over the period to which the reinsurance commission pertains;

(d) a policy where all or a portion of a risk thereunder was assumed by the corporation pursuant to a reinsurance contract and all or a portion of the risk assumed was subsequently reinsured, such amount as the corporation may claim not exceeding the unearned portion at the end of the year of the aggregate of amounts, each of which is a reinsurance commission in respect of the policy, determined by apportioning that aggregate equally over the period to which the reinsurance commission pertains;

(e) policies (other than a policy in respect of which an amount can be determined under paragraph (e.1) under which

(i) a claim that was incurred before the end of the year has been reported to the corporation before the end of the year and in respect of which the corpporation is, or may be, required to make a pyment or incur an expense after the year, or

(ii) there may be a claim incurred before the end of the year that has not been reported to the corporation before the end of the year,

such amount as the corporation may claim not exceeding 95% of the lesser of

(iii) the total of all amounts each of which is the corporation's actuarial liability at the end of the year in respect of such claims or possible claims, and

(iv) the total of all amounts each of which is the corporation's reported reserve at the end of the year in respect of such claims or possible claims;

(e.1) policies under which

(i) a claim that was incurred before the end of the year has been reported to the corporation before the end of the year,

(ii) the claim is in respect of damages for personal injury or death, and

(iii) the corporation has agreed to a structured settlement of the claim,

such amount as the corporation may claim not exceeding the lesser of

(iv) the total of all amounts each of which is the corporation's actuarial liability at the end of the year in respect of such claims, and

(v) the total of all amounts each of which is the corporation's reported reserve at the end of the year in respect of such claims;

(f) a policy that insures

(i) a fidelity risk,

(ii) a surety risk,

(iii) a nuclear risk, or

(iv) a risk related to a financial loss of a lender on a loan made on the security of real property,

such amount as the corporation may claim, other than an amount claimed under any other paragraph of this section, in respect of a supplementary reserve not exceeding the lesser of

(v) the amount of that reserve calculated in the manner required for the purposes of the corporation's annual report for the year to the relevant authority or, where the corporation was subject to the supervision of the relevant authority throughout the year but was not required to file an annual report with the relevant authority for the year, the amount of that reserve reported in its financial statements for the year, and

(vi) the amount in respect of a provision for such a reserve calculated in the manner required for the purposes of the annual report for the 1977 fiscal period to the Superintendent of Insurance for Canada;

(f.1) a guarantee fund provided for under an agreement in writing between the corporation and Her Majesty in right of Canada under which Her Majesty has agreed to guarantee the obligations of the corporation under a policy that insures a risk related to a financial loss of a lender on a loan made on the security of real property, any amount that the corporation claims not exceeding the amount of the guarantee fund at the end of the year;

(g) a non-cancellable or guaranteed renewable accident and sickness policy, such amount as the corporation may claim, in addition to any amount claimed under any other paragraph of this section, not exceeding the lesser of

(i) a reasonable amount in respect of a risk under the policy as at the end of the year, and

(ii) the reserve in respect of that risk reported by the corporation in its annual report for the year to the relevant authority or, where the corporation was subject to the supervision of the relevant authority throughout the year but was not required to file an annual report with the relevant authority for the year, the reserve in respect of that risk reported in its financial statements for the year;

(g.1) a group accident and sickness insurance policy, such amount as the corporation may claim as an amount

## Division 1 — Policy Reserves

## Reg. S. 1400

(other than an amount in respect of which a deduction may be claimed by the corporation pursuant to subsection 140(1) of the Act in computing its income for the year) in respect of a dividend, refund of premiums or refund of premium deposits provided for under the terms of the policy that will be used by the insurer to reduce or eliminate a future adverse claims experience under the policy or that will be paid or unconditionally credited to the policyholder by the corporation or applied in discharge, in whole or in part, of a liability of the policyholder to pay premiums to the corporation, not exceeding the least of

(i) a reasonable amount in respect of such a dividend, refund of premiums or refund of premium deposits,

(ii) 25 per cent of the amount of the premium payable under the terms of the policy for the 12-month period ending

(A) if the policy is terminated in the year, on the day the policy is terminated, and

(B) in any other case, at the end of the year, and

(iii) the amount of the reserve or liability in respect of such a dividend, refund of premiums or refund of premium deposits reported by the corporation in its annual report for the year to the relevant authority or, where the corporation was throughout the year subject to the supervision of the relevant authority for the year but was not required to file an annual report with the relevant authority for the year, in its financial statements for the year;

(h) group accident and sickness policies, such amount as the corporation may claim, in addition to any amount claimed under any other paragraph of this section, not exceeding the product obtained when

(i) the amount deducted by the corporation pursuant to paragraph 20(7)(c) of the Act in computing its income for the 1977 taxation year (other than an amount deducted in respect of a reserve for unpaid claims or unearned premiums) in respect of those policies

is multiplied by

(ii) the proportion that

(A) the number of months in the period commencing on the first day of the corporation's taxation year and ending on the last day of its 1986 taxation year

is of

(B) 120; and

(i) a policy in which a portion of the amount paid or payable by the policyholder for the policy represents an amount described in paragraph 1404(5)(b), the amount, if any, by which the amount deducted under that paragraph exceeds any portion of the amount deducted under that paragraph that the insurer has determined will not be returned to the policyholder, or credited to the account of the policyholder, on the cancellation or expiration of the policy.

A previous amendment by P.C. 1996-1452, amending para. (e) and adding (e.1), was superseded by the above. The amendments to para. (e) deal with reserves for structured settlements; see Notes to Reg. 1400(3).

For taxation years since 1988 that end before February 23, 1994, read:

(e) a policy where an event has occurred before the end of the year that has given or is likely to give rise to a claim under the policy (in this paragraph referred to as "the liability"), and

(i) where the amount of the reserve in respect of the liability (other than a liability referred to in subparagraph (iii)) reported by the corporation in its annual report for the year to the relevant authority or, where the corporation was throughout the year subject to the supervision of the relevant authority but was not required to file an annual report with the relevant authority for the year, in its financial statements for the year was computed as the present value as at the end of the year of the amount of the liability, such amount as it may claim, not exceeding the lesser of

(A) a reasonable amount in respect of the present value of the liability as at the end of the year, and

(B) 95 per cent of the amount of the reserve in respect of the liability reported by the corporation in its annual report or financial statements, as the case may be,

(ii) where the amount of the reserve in respect of the liability other than a liability referred to in subparagraph (iii)) reported by the corporation in its annual report for the year to the relevant authority or, where the corporation was throughout the year subject to the supervision of the relevant authority but was not required to file an annual report with the relevant authority for the year, in its financial statements for the year was not computed as the present value as at the end of the year of the liability, such amount as it may claim not exceeding the amount determined in respect of the liability at the end of the year by the formula

$$A - \frac{1}{3} \times (A - B)$$

where

A is the lesser of a reasonable amount in respect of the liability (other than the present value thereof) as at the end of the year and the amount of the reserve in respect of the liability reported by the corporation in the annual report or financial statements for the year, as the case may be, and

B is the present value of the reasonable amount in respect of the liability as at the end of the year, computed using an interest rate that was reasonable in the circumstances, and

(iii) where the liability is in respect of a structured settlement in respect of damages for personal injury or death, such amount as the corporation may claim not exceeding the present value of the amount of the reserve in respect of the liability reported by the corporation in its annual report for the year to the relevant authority or, where the corporation was throughout the year subject to the supervision of the relevant authority but was not required to file an annual report with the relevant authority for the year, in its financial statements for the year;

**Definitions [Reg. 1400]**: "amount" — ITA 248(1), Reg. 1402.1; "claim liability" — Reg. 1408(1); "dividend" — ITA 248(1); "extended motor vehicle warranty" — Reg. 1408(1); "Her Majesty" — *Interpretation Act* 35(1); "insurance policy", "insurer", "life insurer" — ITA 248(1); "month" — *Interpretation Act* 35(1); "net premium" — Reg. 1408(1); "non-cancellable or guaranteed renewable accident and sickness policy" — Reg. 1408(1), (6); "policy liability", "post-1995 non-cancellable or guaranteed renewable" — Reg. 1408(1); "pre-1996 non-cancellable or guaranteed renewable" — Reg. 1408(1), (7); "premium paid by the policyholder" — Reg. 1408(4); "prescribed" — ITA 248(1); "reinsurance commission", "relevant authority", "reported reserve" — Reg. 1408(1); "security" — *Interpretation Act* 35(1); "taxation year" — ITA 249; "writing" — *Interpretation Act* 35(1).

## DIVISION 2 — POLICY RESERVES FOR PRE-1996 POLICIES

**1401. Life insurance businesses — (1) [Policy reserves]** — For the purpose of subparagraph 138(3)(a)(i) of the Act, in computing a life insurer's income for a taxation year from carrying on its life insurance business in Canada, there may be deducted in respect of

(a) deposit administration fund policies, such amount as the insurer may claim that is a reasonable amount in respect of the aggregate of the insurer's liabilities under the policies as at the end of the year and does not exceed the aggregate of the insurer's liabilities under those policies calculated in the manner required for the purposes of the insurer's annual report to the relevant authority for the year or, where the insurer was throughout the year subject to the supervision of the relevant authority but was not required to file an annual report with the relevant authority for the year, in its financial statements for the year;

(b) a group term life insurance policy that provides coverage for a period not exceeding 12 months, such amount as the insurer may claim not exceeding the unearned portion of the net premium for the policy at the end of the year determined by apportioning the net premium equally over the period to which that premium pertains;

> **Proposed Amendment — Reg. 1401(1)(b)**
>
> **Application**: The November 30, 1999 draft regulations (insurance business policy reserves), subsec. 1(1)(c), will amend para. 1401(1)(b) by replacing "net premium" with "premium paid by the policyholder", applicable to 2000 *et seq.* and, where the taxpayer elects under the coming-into-force provision for the amendments to section 18 of the Act, as released in draft form on November 30, 1999, to the taxpayer's 1998 and 1999 taxation years.
>
> **Technical Notes**: See under Reg. 1400(3)A.

(c) a life insurance policy, other than a policy referred to in paragraph (a) or (b), such amount as the insurer may claim not exceeding the greater of

  (i) the amount, if any, by which

   (A) the cash surrender value of the policy at the end of the year

  exceeds

   (B) the aggregate of all amounts each of which is an amount payable in respect of a policy loan outstanding at the end of the year in respect of the policy or the interest thereon that has accrued to the insurer at the end of the year, and

  (ii) the amount, if any, by which

   (A) the present value at the end of the year of the future benefits provided by the policy

  exceeds the aggregate of

   (B) the present value at the end of the year of any future modified net premiums in respect of the policy, and

   (C) the aggregate of all amounts each of which is an amount payable in respect of a policy loan outstanding at the end of the year in respect of the policy or the interest thereon that has accrued to the insurer at the end of the year;

(c.1) a group life insurance policy, such amount as the insurer may claim as an amount (other than an amount in respect of which a deduction may be claimed by the insurer pursuant to subsection 140(1) of the Act by reason of subparagraph 138(3)(a)(v) of the Act in computing its income for the year) in respect of a dividend, refund of premiums or refund of premium deposits provided for under the terms of the policy that will be used by the insurer to reduce or eliminate a future adverse claims experience under the policy or that will be paid or unconditionally credited to the policyholder by the insurer or applied in discharge, in whole or in part, of a liability of the policyholder to pay premiums to the insurer, not exceeding the least of

  (i) a reasonable amount in respect of such a dividend, refund of premiums or refund of premium deposits,

  (ii) 25 per cent of the amount of the premium payable under the terms of the policy for the 12-month period ending

   (A) if the policy is terminated in the year, on the day the policy is terminated, and

   (B) in any other case, at the end of the year, and

  (iii) the amount of the reserve or liability in respect of such a dividend, refund of premiums or refund of premium deposits reported by the insurer in its annual report for the year to the relevant authority or, where the insurer was throughout the year subject to the supervision of the relevant authority for the year but was not required to file an annual report with the relevant authority for the year, in its financial statements for the year;

(d) a policy, other than a policy referred to in paragraph (a), such amount as the insurer may claim, in respect of a benefit, risk or guarantee that is

  (i) an accidental death benefit,

  (ii) a disability benefit,

  (iii) an additional risk as a result of insuring a substandard life,

  (iv) an additional risk in respect of the conversion of a term policy or the conversion of the benefits under a group policy into another policy after the end of the year,

(v) an additional risk under a settlement option,

(vi) an additional risk under a guaranteed insurability benefit,

(vii) a guarantee in respect of a segregated fund policy, or

(viii) any other benefit that is ancillary to the policy, subject to the prior approval of the Minister on the advice of the Superintendent of Insurance for Canada,

but is not

(ix) a benefit, risk or guarantee in respect of which an amount has been claimed under any other paragraph of this subsection, other than paragraphs (d.1) and (d.2), by the insurer as a deduction in computing its income for the year,

not exceeding the lesser of

(x) a reasonable amount in respect of the benefit, risk or guarantee, and

(xi) the reserve in respect of the benefit, risk or guarantee, reported by the insurer in its annual report to the relevant authority for the year or, where the insurer was throughout the year subject to the supervision of the relevant authority but was not required to file an annual report with the relevant authority for the year, in its financial statements for the year;

(d.1) a policy referred to in paragraph (b), where, after the end of the year, a claim under the policy is made in respect of a death that occurred before the end of the year, such amount as the insurer may claim, not exceeding the lesser of

(i) the present value, at the end of the year, of the payments to be made in respect of the claim made under the policy or such estimate of such payments to be made in respect of the claim as is reasonable in the circumstances, and

(ii) 95 per cent of the amount of the reserve in respect of the claim reported by the insurer in its annual report to the relevant authority for the year or, where the insurer was throughout the year subject to the supervision of the relevant authority for the year but was not required to file an annual report with the relevant authority for the year, in its financial statements for the year;

(d.2) a policy referred to in paragraph (c), where, after the end of the year, a claim under the policy is made in respect of a death that occurred before the end of the year, such amount as the insurer may claim, not exceeding the lesser of

(i) the amount, if any, by which

(A) the present value, at the end of the year, of the payments to be made in respect of the claim made under the policy or such estimate of such payments to be made in respect of the claim as is reasonable in the circumstances

exceeds

(B) the maximum amounts that may be claimed by the insurer for the year in respect of the policy under paragraph (c) or (d), and

(ii) 95 per cent of the amount of the reserve in respect of the claim reported by the insurer in its annual report to the relevant authority for the year or, where the insurer was throughout the year subject to the supervision of the relevant authority but was not required to file an annual report with the relevant authority for the year, in its financial statements for the year; and

(e) a qualified annuity, such amount as the insurer may claim not exceeding the amount, if any, by which

(i) the amount that would have been determined pursuant to paragraph (c) for the year if the rate of interest used (or deemed by section 1403 to have been used) by the insurer in determining the premium for the annuity were reduced by one-half of one percentage point,

exceeds

(ii) the maximum amount that may be claimed by the insurer in respect of the annuity under paragraph (c).

**Related Provisions**: Reg. 211.1(3) — Effect of Reg. 1401(1) on Part XII.3 tax; Reg. 1401(1.1) — Reg. 1401 applies to pre-1996 policies only; Reg. 1402 — All amounts to be net of reinsurance ceded; Reg. 1403(1) — Rules for computation; Reg. 1408 — Definitions.

**Notes**: Opening words of Reg. 1401(1) amended by P.C. 1999-1154, effective for 1996 and later taxation years. For 1978-95, read:

1401. (1) For the purposes of subparagraph 138(3)(a)(i) of the Act, a life insurer in computing its income for a taxation year may, in respect of its life insurance policies in Canada, deduct in respect of

Reg. 1401(1)(c)(ii)(B) amended by P.C. 1999-1154 to change "for" to "in respect of" (to ensure that the new definition "net premium for the policy" in Reg. 1408(1) does not apply), effective for 1996 and later taxation years.

Reg. 1401(1)(c.1)(ii) amended by P.C. 1994-940, effective for taxation years ending after June 15, 1994. For earlier years, read:

(ii) 25 per cent of the amount of the premium for the year payable under the terms of the policy, unless the policy is terminated in the year, in which case 25 per cent of the greater of

**(1.1) [Pre-1996 policies only]** — An amount may be deducted under subsection (1) only in respect of a life insurance policy in Canada that is a pre-1996 life insurance policy.

**Related Provisions**: Reg. 1404 — Policy reserves for post-1995 policies.

**Notes**: Reg. 1401(1.1) added by P.C. 1999-1154, effective for 1996 and later taxation years. Policy reserves for post-1995 policies are now covered in Reg. 1404.

Reg. S. 1401(2)    Income Tax Regulations, Part XIV

**(2) [Segregated funds]** — For the purposes of subsection (1), (except in respect of subparagraph (d)(vii) thereof), any amount claimed by an insurer for the year shall not include an amount in respect of a liability of a segregated fund (within the meaning assigned "segregated fund" by section 138.1 of the Act).

**(3) [Group life insurance policies]** — In computing the amount that a life insurer may deduct under subparagraph 138(3)(a)(i) of the Act in computing its taxable income for a taxation year, there shall be deducted from the aggregate of the amounts determined under subsection (1), the aggregate of all amounts each of which is the lesser of the following amounts determined in respect of a life insurance policy referred to in paragraph (1)(c):

(a) the amount, if any, by which

(i) the amount that would be determined under subclause (1)(c)(i)(B) in respect of the policy

exceeds

(ii) the amount that would be determined under subclause (1)(c)(i)(A) in respect of the policy, and

(b) the amount, if any, by which

(i) the aggregate of the amounts that would be determined under subclauses (1)(c)(ii)(B) and (C) in respect of the policy

exceeds

(ii) the amount that would be determined under subclause (1)(c)(ii)(A) in respect of the policy.

**(4) [Unpaid claims reserve]** — For the purpose of subparagraph 138(3)(a)(ii) of the Act, there may be deducted, in computing a life insurer's income for a taxation year, the amount it claims as a reserve in respect of unpaid claims received by it before the end of the year under life insurance policies in Canada that are pre-1996 life insurance policies, not exceeding the present value at the end of the year, computed using a rate of interest that is reasonable in the circumstances, of a reasonable amount in respect of those unpaid claims.

**Related Provisions**: ITA 20(26) — Deduction for unpaid claims reserve adjustment; Reg. 1401(4) — Unpaid claims reserve re post-1995 policies; Reg. 1402 — All amounts to be net of reinsurance ceded; Reg. 8100, 8101 — Unpaid claims reserve adjustment.

**Notes**: Reg. 1401(4) amended by P.C. 1999-1154, effective for 1996 and later taxation years, to limit its application to pre-1996 policies. (For post-1995 policies, see Reg. 1405.) From 1988–95, read:

(4) For the purposes of subparagraph 138(3)(a)(ii) of the Act, a life insurer may, in computing its income for a taxation year, deduct an amount as a reserve in respect of unpaid claims under life insurance policies in Canada at the end of the year received by the insurer before the end of the year equal to the present value at the end of the year, computed using a rate of interest that is reasonable in the circumstances, of a reasonable amount in respect of such claims.

**Definitions [Reg. 1401]**: "amount" — ITA 248(1); "amount payable" — ITA 138(12), Reg. 1408(1); "benefit" — Reg. 1408(1); "Canada" — ITA 255, *Interpretation Act* 35(1); "cash surrender value" — ITA 148(9), Reg. 1408(1); "dividend" — ITA 248(1); "group term life insurance policy" — Reg. 1408(2); "insurer" — ITA 248(1); "interest" — ITA 138(12), Reg. 1408(1); "life insurance business" — ITA 248(1); "life insurance policy" — ITA 138(12), 248(1), Reg. 1408(5); "life insurance policy in Canada" — Reg. 1408(1); "life insurer", "Minister" — ITA 248(1); "modified net premium" — Reg. 1408(1), (3); "month" — *Interpretation Act* 35(1); "net premium" — Reg. 1408(1); "policy loan" — ITA 138(12), Reg. 1408(1); "pre-1996 life insurance policy" — Reg. 1408(1), (7); "premium paid by the policyholder" — Reg. 1408(4); "qualified annuity", "relevant authority" — Reg. 1408(1); "segregated fund", "segregated fund policy" — ITA 138.1(1), Reg. 1408(1); "taxable income" — ITA 248(1); "taxation year" — ITA 249.

**Interpretation Bulletins**: IT-87R2: Policyholders' income from life insurance policies.

## DIVISION 3 — SPECIAL RULES

**1402. Non-life and life insurance businesses** — Any amount determined under section 1400 or 1401 shall be determined on a net of reinsurance ceded basis.

**Notes**: Reg. 1402(2) repealed, and 1402(1) renumbered as 1402, by P.C. 1999-1154, effective for 1996 and later taxation years. Previously read:

1402. **Special rules** — (1) For the purposes of sections 1400 and 1401, any amounts determined under those sections shall be determined on a net of reinsurance ceded basis.

(2) For the purposes of sections 1400 and 1401, where an insurer is a foreign affiliate of a taxpayer resident in Canada and the amounts to be determined under those sections are in respect of a business that is

(a) an investment business of the affiliate, as defined in subsection 95(1) of the Act, or

(b) a separate business, other than an active business, of the affiliate that the affiliate is deemed, under paragraph 95(2)(a.2) or (b) of the Act, to carry on,

the amounts determined under those sections in respect of the business shall not exceed an amount that is reasonable having regard to all the circumstances and shall be determined as if the business were carried on in Canada and the affiliate were subject to the supervision of the Superintendent of Financial Institutions.

(Reg. 1402(2) is now considered unnecessary, since the Canadian rules for policy reserves must be followed for a foreign affiliate due to ITA 95(2)(k) and Reg. 1408(1)"reported reserve".)

Reg. 1402 amended by P.C. 1997-1670, effective for taxation years of a foreign affiliate that begin after 1994, except that the amendment applies to taxation years of a foreign affiliate that end after 1994 where there has been a change in the foreign affiliate's taxation year in 1994 after February 22, 1994, unless

(i) the foreign affiliate had requested that change in taxation year in writing before February 22, 1994 from the income tax authority of the country in which is was resident and subject to income taxation, or

(ii) the first taxation year of the foreign affiliate that began after 1994 began at a time in 1995 that is earlier than the time when it would have begun had there not been the change in taxation year.

**Definitions [Reg. 1402]**: "amount" — ITA 248(1).

**1402.1 [Negative amounts]** — For greater certainty, any amount referred to or determined under section 1400 may be equal to, or less than, nil.

**Notes**: Reg. 1402.1 added by P.C. 1999-1154, effective for 1996 and later taxation years. It effectively overrides ITA 257 for each individual element of the formula in Reg. 1400(3).

**Definitions [Reg. 1402.1]**: "amount" — ITA 248(1).

**1403. (1)** For the purposes of paragraph 1401(1)(c) and subject to subsections (2) and (3), a modified net premium and an amount claimed by an insurer for a taxation year shall be computed

(a) in the case of a lapse-supported policy effected after 1990, based on rates of interest, mortality and policy lapse only, and

(b) in any other case, based on rates of interest and mortality only,

using

(c) in respect of the modified net premiums and benefits (other than a benefit described in paragraph (d)) of a participating life insurance policy (other than an annuity contract) under the terms of which the policyholder is entitled to receive a specified amount in respect of the policy's cash surrender value, the rates used by the insurer when the policy was issued in computing the cash surrender values of the policy;

(d) in respect of any benefit provided

(i) in lieu of a cash settlement on the termination or maturity of a policy, or

(ii) in satisfaction of a dividend on a policy,

the rates used by the insurer in determining the amount of such benefit; and

(e) in respect of all or part of any other policy, the rates used by the insurer in determining the premiums for the policy.

**Notes**: Reg. 1403(1) amended by P.C. 1994-940, effective for taxation years beginning after 1990. If an insurer elected by notifying Revenue Canada in writing before 1991, the amendment also applies to the insurer's taxation years beginning after 1987, 1988 or 1989 (as specified in the election), in which case,

(i) if the insurer so indicated in the election, ignore the words "effected after 1990" in Reg. 1403(1)(a), and

(ii) if not, read those words as "effected after [the calendar year preceding the first taxation year to which the election relates]".

**(2)** For the purposes of subsection (1), where a rate of mortality or other probability used by an insurer in determining the premium for a policy is not reasonable in the circumstances, the Minister on the advice of the Superintendent of Insurance for Canada may make such revision to the rate as is reasonable in the circumstances and the revised rate shall be deemed to have been used by the insurer in determining the premium.

**(3)** For the purposes of subsection (1), where the present value of the premiums for a policy as at the date of issue of the policy is less than the aggregate of

(a) the present value, at that date, of the benefits provided for by the policy, and

(b) the present value, at that date, of all outlays and expenses made or incurred by the insurer or outlays and expenses that the insurer reasonably estimates it will make or incur in respect of the policy (except outlays and expenses to maintain the policy after all premiums under the policy have been paid and for which explicit provision has not been made in calculating the premiums) and such part of any other outlays and expenses made or incurred by the insurer that may reasonably be regarded as applicable thereto,

an increased rate of interest shall be determined by multiplying the rate of interest used in determining the premiums by a constant factor so that when the increased rate of interest is used,

(c) the present value of the premiums at the date of issue of the policy

shall equal

(d) the aggregate of the present values of the benefits, outlays and expenses referred to in paragraphs (a) and (b),

and the increased rate of interest shall be deemed to have been used by the insurer in determining the premiums for the policy.

**Related Provisions**: Reg. 1403(4) — Computation of present value.

**(4)** For the purposes of subsection (3), a "present value" referred to in that subsection shall be computed by using the rates of mortality and other probabilities used by the insurer in determining its premiums, after making any revision required by subsection (2).

**(5)** For the purposes of subsection (1), where a record of the rate of interest or mortality used by an insurer in determining the premiums for a policy is not available,

(a) the insurer may, if the policy was issued before 1978, make a reasonable estimate of the rate; and

(b) the Minister, on the advice of the Superintendent of Insurance for Canada, may

(i) if the policy was issued before 1978 and the insurer has not made the estimate referred to in paragraph (a), or

(ii) if the policy was issued after 1977,

make a reasonable estimate of the rate.

**(6)** Notwithstanding paragraph 1401(1)(c), a life insurer in computing its income for a taxation year may, in respect of any class of life insurance policies issued before its 1988 taxation year, other than policies referred to in paragraph 1401(1)(a) or (b), use a method of approximation to convert the reserve in respect of such policies reported by the insurer in its annual report to the relevant authority for the year to an amount that is a reasonable estimate of the amount that would otherwise be determined for such policies under paragraph 1401(1)(c), provided that that method of approximation is acceptable to the Minister on the advice of the relevant authority.

(7) For the purposes of subsection (1) and notwithstanding any other provision of this section, where

(a) an individual annuity contract was issued prior to 1969 by a life insurer, or

(b) a benefit was purchased prior to 1969 under a group annuity contract issued by a life insurer, and

the contract

(c) is a policy in respect of which the provisions of paragraph 1401(1)(c) as it read in its application to the insurer's 1977 taxation year applied,

the rates of interest and mortality used by the insurer in computing its reserve for the policy under that paragraph for its 1977 taxation year shall be used by the insurer in respect of that policy.

(8) For the purposes of subsection (1), where

(a) in a taxation year of an insurer, there has been a disposition to the insurer by another person with whom the insurer was dealing at arm's length in respect of which subsection 138(11.92) of the Act applied,

(b) as a result of the disposition, the insurer assumed obligations under life insurance policies (in this subsection referred to as the "transferred policies") in respect of which an amount may be claimed by the insurer as a reserve under paragraph 1401(1)(c) for the taxation year,

(c) the amount, if any, by which

(i) the aggregate of all amounts received or receivable by the insurer from the other person in respect of the transferred policies referred to in paragraph (b)

exceeds

(ii) the aggregate of all amounts paid or payable by the insurer to the other person in respect of commissions in respect of the amounts referred to in subparagraph (i)

exceeds the total of the maximum amounts that may be claimed by the insurer as a reserve under paragraph 1401(1)(c) (determined without reference to this subsection) in respect of the transferred policies for the taxation year, and

(d) the amount determined under paragraph (c) (in this subsection referred to as "reserve deficiency") can reasonably be attributed to the fact that the rates of interest or mortality used by the issuer of the transferred policies in determining the cash surrender values or premiums under such policies are no longer reasonable in the circumstances,

the Minister, on the request of the insurer and with the advice of the relevant authority, may make such revision to the rates of interest or mortality to eliminate all or any part of that reserve deficiency, and those revised rates shall be deemed to have been used by the issuer of the transferred policies in determining the cash surrender value or premiums under the policies.

### Proposed Amendment — Reg. 1403(8)

**Letter from Department of Finance, December 1, 1999:**

Dear [xxx]

This is in reply to your letter of November 8, 1999 requesting that amendments be made to the draft income tax legislation released on December 23, 1998 regarding trusts and to the *Income Tax Regulations* regarding the determination of tax reserves for life insurance policies.

*Regulations on Reserves*

You are of the view that subsection 1403(8) of the *Income Tax Regulations* should be amended to allow an insurer that has acquired an insurance business, or a line of an insurance business, from another insurer to revise the lapse rates used by the other insurer for reserve purposes if those rates are no longer reasonable to eliminate all or part of what is referred to in subsection 1403(8) as a reserve deficiency (the "Reserve Deficiency"). From a policy perspective, we agree. Consequently, we are prepared to recommend to the Minister of Finance that subsection 1403(8) be amended to allow for revisions to lapse rates to eliminate all or part of a Reserve Deficiency if the deficiency is attributable to the fact that the lapse rates used by the issuer of the transferred policies are no longer reasonable in the circumstances.

Your second concern in regard to subsection 1403(8) of the *Income Tax Regulations* is that it provides the Minister of National Revenue with too much discretion in determining whether, and to what extent, rates can be changed to eliminate all or part of a Reserve Deficiency. We agree that subsection 1403(8) may be too broad in this regard. Consequently, we are prepared to recommend to the Minister of Finance that subsection 1403(8) be amended to better ensure that the Ministerial discretion be limited to the approval of adjusted rates provided the adjustments are reasonable.

We would also recommend that the amendments to subsection 1403(8) of the *Income Tax Regulations* be effective for dispositions occurring after November 1999. If the recommendation is acted upon, it is anticipated that the amendments would be included in a future technical bill.

I appreciate you taking the time to bring your concerns to my attention.

Yours sincerely,

Brian Ernewein
Director, Tax Legislation Division, Tax Policy Branch

**Definitions [Reg. 1403]**: "amount", "annuity" — ITA 248(1); "arm's length" — ITA 251(1); "benefit" — Reg. 1408(1); "cash surrender value" — ITA 148(9), Reg. 1408(1); "disposition", "dividend", "insurer" — ITA 248(1); "lapse-supported policy" — Reg. 1408(1); "life insurance policy" — ITA 138(12), 248(1), Reg.

1408(5); "life insurer", "Minister" — ITA 248(1); "modified net premium" — Reg. 1408(1), (3); "participating life insurance policy" — ITA 138(12), Reg. 1404(1); "person" — ITA 248(1); "present value" — Reg. 1403(4); "record" — ITA 248(1); "relevant authority" — Reg. 1408(1); "reserve deficiency" — Reg. 1403(8)(d); "taxation year" — ITA 249.

## DIVISION 4 — POLICY RESERVES FOR POST-1995 POLICIES

**1404. Life insurance business** — **(1)** For the purpose of subparagraph 138(3)(a)(i) of the Act, there may be deducted, in computing a life insurer's income from carrying on its life insurance business in Canada for a taxation year in respect of its life insurance policies in Canada that are post-1995 life insurance policies, the amount the insurer claims, not exceeding

(a) the amount determined under subsection (3) in respect of the insurer for the year, where that amount is greater than nil, and

(b) nil, in any other case.

*Notes*: See at end of Reg. 1404.

**(2)** For the purpose of paragraph 138(4)(b) of the Act, the amount prescribed in respect of an insurer for a taxation year, in respect of its life insurance policies in Canada that are post-1995 life insurance policies, is

(a) the absolute value of the amount determined under subsection (3) in respect of the insurer for the year, where that amount is less than nil, and

(b) nil, in any other case.

*Notes*: See at end of Reg. 1404.

**(3)** For the purposes of paragraphs (1)(a) and (2)(a), the amount determined under this subsection in respect of an insurer for a taxation year, in respect of its life insurance policies in Canada that are post-1995 life insurance policies, is the amount, which may be positive or negative, determined by the formula

$$A + B + C + D - M$$

where

A is the amount (except to the extent the amount is determined in respect of a claim, premium, dividend or refund in respect of which an amount is included in determining the value of B, C or D), in respect of the insurer's life insurance policies in Canada that are post-1995 life insurance policies, equal to the lesser of

(a) the total of the reported reserves of the insurer at the end of the year in respect of those policies, and

(b) the total of the policy liabilities of the insurer at the end of the year in respect of those policies;

B is the amount, in respect of the insurer's life insurance policies in Canada that are post-1995 life insurance policies under which there may be claims incurred before the end of the year that have not been reported to the insurer before the end of the year, equal to 95% of the lesser of

(a) the total of the reported reserves of the insurer at the end of the year in respect of the possibility that there are such claims, and

(b) the total of the policy liabilities of the insurer at the end of the year in respect of the possibility that there are such claims;

C is the total of all amounts each of which is the unearned portion at the end of the year of the net premium for the policy where the policy is a group term life insurance policy that

(a) provides coverage for a period that does not exceed 12 months,

(b) is a life insurance policy in Canada, and

(c) is a post-1995 life insurance policy,

determined by apportioning the net premium equally over the period to which that premium relates;

### Proposed Amendment — Reg. 1404(3)C

**Application**: The November 30, 1999 draft regulations (insurance business policy reserves), subsec. 1(1)(d), will amend the description of C in subsec. 1404(3) by replacing "net premium" with "premium paid by the policyholder", applicable to 2000 *et seq.* and, where the taxpayer elects under the coming-into-force provision for the amendments to section 18 of the Act, as released in draft form on November 30, 1999, to the taxpayer's 1998 and 1999 taxation years.

**Technical Notes**: See under Reg. 1400(3)A.

D is the total of all amounts (other than an amount deductible under subparagraph 138(3)(a)(v) of the Act) each of which is the amount, which is the least of P, Q and R, in respect of a dividend, refund of premiums or refund of premium deposits provided for under the terms of a group life insurance policy that is a life insurance policy in Canada that is a post-1995 life insurance policy that will be

(a) used by the insurer to reduce or eliminate a future adverse claims experience under the policy,

(b) paid or unconditionally credited to the policyholder by the insurer, or

(c) applied in discharge, in whole or in part, of a liability of the policyholder to pay premiums to the insurer under the policy,

where

P is a reasonable amount as a reserve eetermined as at the end of the year in respect of the dividend, refund of premiums or refund of premium deposits provided for under the terms of the policy,

**Reg. S. 1404(3)**

Q is 25% of the amount of the premium under the terms of the policy for the 12-month period ending

    (i) on the day the policy is terminated, if the policy is terminated in the year, and

    (ii) at the end of the year, in any other case, and

R is the amount of the reported reserve of the insurer at the end of the year in respect of the dividend, refund of premiums or refund of premium deposits provided for under the terms of the policy; and

M is the total of all amounts determined in respect of a life insurance policy in Canada that is a post-1995 life insurance policy each of which is

    (a) an amount payable in respect of a policy loan under the policy, or

    (b) interest that has accrued to the insurer to the end of the year in respect of a policy loan under the policy.

**Related Provisions**: ITA 257 — Negative amounts in formulas; Reg. 1406 — All amounts to be net of reinsurance ceded and ignoring seg funds; Reg. 1407 — Amounts in Reg. 1404 may be less than zero.

**Notes**: See at end of Reg. 1404.

**(4)** Notwithstanding subsection (3), the amount determined under that subsection in respect of an insurer for a taxation year that ends before 2001 is deemed to be the amount determined by the formula

$$A + (B \times (C - D))$$

where

A is the amount that would, but for this subsection, be the amount determined under subsection (3) in respect of the insurer for the year;

B is, where the year ends in

    (a) 1996, 100%,

    (b) 1997, 80%,

    (c) 1998, 60%,

    (d) 1999, 40%, and

    (e) 2000, 20%;

C is the total of all amounts each of which is the absolute value of any amount that is less than nil and that is used in computing

    (a) the amount that is the lesser of the totals determined for the year under the description of I in subsection 1400(3), in respect of a risk under a post-1995 non-cancellable or guaranteed renewable accident and sickness policy, or

    (b) the amount that is the lesser of the totals determined for the year under the description of A in subsection (3), in respect of a liability or risk under a life insurance policy in Canada of the insurer that is a post-1995 life insurance policy; and

D is the lesser of

    (a) 5% of the total of all amounts each of which is a premium received by the insurer in the year or any preceding taxation year ending after 1995 in respect of

        (i) a non-cancellable or guaranteed renewable accident and sickness policy, or

        (ii) a life insurance policy in Canada, and

    (b) the value of C.

**Notes**: Reg. 1404 replaced by P.C. 1999-1154, effective for 1996 and later taxation years. The former version provided definitions for Part XIV; those definitions are now in Reg. 1408(1). It provided:

1404. **Interpretation** — (1) In this Part "amount payable", "life insurance policy in Canada", "participating life insurance policy" and "policy loan" have the meanings assigned by subsection 138(12) of the Act.

(2) In this Part,

"acquisition costs" of a policy for a taxation year means, where the policy

    (a) is a policy other than

        (i) a group policy,

        (ii) a policy that insures a risk described in subparagraph 1400(a)(i),

        (iii) a policy issued under an arrangement with a person (other than an insurer or an insurance agent or broker) with whom the insurer does not deal at arm's length whereby a customer of that person is referred to the insurer,

        (iii.1) a policy issued to a member of a credit union as a consequence of an arrangement with a credit union, where

            (A) the insurer was established primarily to provide insurance to members of credit unions,

            (B) the policyholder was referred to the insurer, and

            (C) the principal business of the insurer is the provision of insurance to members of credit unions, or

        (iv) a policy issued to a policyholder that is a corporation with which the insurer does not deal at arm's length,

an amount equal to 20 per cent of the premium paid by the policyholder for the policy, except that in applying this paragraph with respect to a premium paid in a taxation year ending

        (v) before 1978, the reference in this paragraph to 20 per cent shall be read as a reference to nil, or

        (vi) after 1977 and before 1987, the reference in this paragraph to 20 per cent shall be read as a reference to 2 per cent for the 1978 taxation year, 4 per cent for the 1979 taxation year, 6 per cent for the 1980 taxation year, 8 per cent for the 1981 taxation year, 10 per cent for the 1982 taxation year, 12 per cent for the 1983 taxation year, 14 per cent for the 1984 taxation year, 16 per cent for the 1985 taxation year and 18 per cent for the 1986 taxation year, and

    (b) is a policy other than a policy referred to in paragraph (a), an amount equal to the lesser of

        (i) the amount that would have been determined under paragraph (a) if that paragraph had applied in respect of the policy, and

(ii) an amount equal to 5 per cent of the premium paid by the policyholder for the policy;

"actuarial liability" of an insurer at a particular time means

(a) in respect of a claim incurred before that time under an insurance policy, a reasonable estimate, determined in accordance with actuarial principles, of

(i) the present value at that time of the insurer's future payments and claim adjustment expenses in respect of the claim

minus

(ii) the present value at that time of amounts that the insurer will recover after that time in respect of the claim because of salvage, subrogation or any other reason, and

(b) in respect of the possibility that there are claims under an insurance policy incurred before that time that have not been reported to the insurer, a reasonable estimate, determined in accordance with actuarial principles, of

(i) the present value at that time of the insurer's payments and claim adjustment expenses in respect of those claims

minus

(ii) the present value at that time of amounts that the insurer will recover after that time in respect of those claims because of salvage, subrogation or any other reason;

"benefit" includes

(a) a policy dividend in respect of a policy to the extent that the dividend was specifically treated as a benefit by the insurer in determining a premium for the policy, and

(b) an expense of maintaining a policy after all premiums in respect thereof have been paid to the extent that the expense was specifically provided for by the insurer in determining a premium for the policy,

but does not include

(c) a policy dividend in respect of a policy described in paragraph 1403(1)(c),

(d) a policy loan,

(e) interest on funds left on deposit with the insurer under the terms of a policy, or

(f) any other benefit under a policy in respect of which a specific provision was not made by the insurer in determining a premium for the policy;

"cash surrender value" has the meaning assigned by paragraph 148(9)(b) [148(9)"cash surrender value"] of the Act;

"lapse-supported policy" means a life insurance policy that would require materially higher premiums if premiums were determined using lapse rates that are zero after the fifth policy year;

"life insurance policy" includes

(a) an annuity contract, and

(b) a benefit under

(i) a group life insurance policy, or

(ii) a group annuity contract;

"modified net premium", in respect of the particular premium under a policy (other than a prepaid premium under a policy that cannot be refunded except on termination or cancellation of the policy), means

(a) where benefits (other than policy dividends) and premiums (other than the frequency of payment thereof) in respect of the policy are determined at the date of issue of the policy, the amount determined by the formula

$$A \times \frac{(B + C)}{(D + E)}$$

where

A is the amount of the premium,

B is the present value, at the date of the issue of the policy, of the amount of the benefits to be provided under the terms of the policy after a time that is one year after the date of the issue of the policy,

C is the present value, at the date of the issue of the policy, of the amount of the benefits to be provided under the terms of the policy after a time that is two years after the date of the issue of the policy,

D is the present value, at the date of the issue of the policy, of the amount of the premiums payable under the terms of the policy on or after a time that is one year after the date of the issue of the policy, and

E is the present value, at the date of the issue of the policy, of the amount of the premiums payable under the terms of the policy on or after a time that is two years after the date of the issue of the policy,

except that the amount determined by the formula in respect of the premium for the second year of a policy shall be deemed to be the amount that is ½ of the aggregate of

(i) the amount that would be determined under the formula, and

(ii) the amount of a one-year term insurance premium (determined without regard to the frequency of payment thereof) that would be payable under the policy, and

(b) where the amount of the benefits or premiums in respect of the policy are not determined at the date of issue of the policy, the amount that would be determined under paragraph (a) if it were adjusted in a manner that is reasonable in the circumstances;

"net premium for the policy" for a taxation year means the amount by which the premium paid by the policyholder for a policy exceeds the acquisition costs of the policy;

"qualified annuity" means an annuity contract issued before 1982, other than a policy referred to in paragraph 1401(1)(a) or subsection 1403(7),

(a) in respect of which regular periodic annuity payments have commenced,

(b) in respect of which a contract or certificate has been issued that provides for regular periodic annuity payments to commence within one year from the date of issue of the contract or certificate,

(c) that is not issued as, under or pursuant to a registered retirement savings plan, registered pension plan or deferred profit sharing plan and that

(i) does not provide for a guaranteed cash surrender value at any time, and

(ii) provides for regular periodic annuity payments to commence not later than the attainment of age 71 by the annuitant, or

(d) that is issued as, under or pursuant to a registered retirement savings plan, registered pension fund or plan or deferred profit sharing plan, provided that the interest rate is guaranteed for at least 10 years and the plan does not provide for any participation in profits, directly or indirectly;

"reinsurance commission" in respect of a policy means

(a) where the risk under the policy is fully reinsured, the amount, if any, by which

(i) the net premium for the policy

exceeds

    (ii) the consideration payable by the insurer in respect of the reinsurance of the risk, and

(b) where the risk under the policy is not fully reinsured, the amount, if any, by which

    (i) the portion of the net premium for the policy that may reasonably be considered to be in respect of the portion of the risk that is reinsured with a particular reinsurer

exceeds

    (ii) the consideration payable by the insurer to the particular reinsurer in respect of the risk assumed by that reinsurer,

and for the purposes of this definition, "net premium" means the amount determined under the rules applicable to the 1987 and subsequent taxation years;

"relevant authority" means

    (a) the Superintendent of Financial Institutions, if the insurer is required by law to report to the Superintendent of Financial Institutions,

    (a.1) in the case of Canada Mortgage and Housing Corporation, the Superintendent of Financial Institutions, who shall be deemed to supervise that corporation, or

    (b) in any other case, the Superintendent of Insurance or other similar officer or authority of the province under whose laws the insurer is incorporated.

"reported reserve" of an insurer at the end of a taxation year means the amount equal to

    (a) where the insurer was required to file an annual report with the relevant authority for a period ending coincidentally with the year, the amount of the reserve reported in that annual report,

    (b) where the insurer was, throughout the year, subject to the supervision of the relevant authority and paragraph (a) does not apply, the amount of the reserve reported in its financial statements for the year, and

    (c) in any other case (including, for greater certainty, where there is no relevant authority in respect of the insurer), nil.

(3) In construing the meaning of the expression "group term life insurance policy" in this Part, subsection 248(1) of the Act does not apply.

(4) For the purposes of calculating the proportion referred to in the definition "modified net premium" in subsection (2), an insurer may assume that premiums are payable annually in advance.

(5) For the purposes of this Part,

    (a) a reference to a "premium paid by the policyholder" at any particular time shall, depending on the method regularly followed by the insurer in computing its income, be read as a reference to a "premium paid or payable by the policyholder" at that time; and

    (b) in determining the premium paid by a policyholder for a policy, there may be deducted by the insurer the amount, if any, of the premium that

        (i) may reasonably be considered, at the time the policy is issued, to be a deposit that, pursuant to the terms of the policy or the by-laws of the insurer, will be returned to the policyholder, or credited to the account of the policyholder, by the insurer on the cancellation or expiration of the policy, and

        (ii) was not otherwise deducted under section 140 of the Act.

(6) For the purposes of this Part, any rider that is attached to a life insurance policy and that provides for additional life insurance or for an annuity is a separate life insurance policy.

Subpara. (a)(iii.1) of "acquisition costs" added by P.C. 1993-2025, effective for 1991 and later taxation years.

Definition "actuarial liability" added by P.C. 1996-1452, effective for taxation years that end after February 22, 1994.

Definition "lapse-supported policy" added by P.C. 1994-940, effective for taxation years beginning in 1991 or later, or earlier on the same basis as the amendments to 1403(1) if the insurer elected (see Notes to 1403(1)).

Para. (a.1) of "relevant authority" added by P.C. 1993-2025, effective for 1991 and later taxation years.

Definition "reported reserve" added by P.C. 1996-1452, effective for taxation years that end after February 22, 1994.

**Definitions [Reg. 1404]**: "amount" — ITA 248(1), Reg. 1406, 1407; "amount payable" — ITA 138(12), Reg. 1408(1); "business" — ITA 248(1); "Canada" — ITA 255, *Interpretation Act* 35(1); "dividend" — ITA 248(1); "group term life insurance policy" — Reg. 1408(2); "insurer" — ITA 248(1); "interest" — ITA 138(12), Reg. 1408(1); "life insurance business" — ITA 248(1); "life insurance policy" — ITA 138(12), 248(1), Reg. 1408(5); "life insurance policy in Canada" — ITA 138(12), Reg. 1408(1); "life insurer" — ITA 248(1); "month" — *Interpretation Act* 35(1); "net premium for the policy" — Reg. 1408(1); "non-cancellable or guaranteed renewable accident and sickness policy" — Reg. 1408(1), (6); "policy liability" — Reg. 1408(1); "policy loan" — ITA 138(12), Reg. 1408(1); "post-1995 non-cancellable or guaranteed renewable accident and sickness policy" — Reg. 1408(1); "premium paid by the policyholder" — Reg. 1408(4); "prescribed" — ITA 248(1); "reported reserve" — Reg. 1408(1); "taxation year" — ITA 249.

**1405. [Unpaid claims reserve]** — For the purpose of subparagraph 138(3)(a)(ii) of the Act, there may be deducted in computing a life insurer's income for a taxation year the amount it claims as a reserve in respect of an unpaid claim received by the insurer before the end of the year under a life insurance policy in Canada that is a post-1995 life insurance policy, not exceeding the lesser of

    (a) the reported reserve of the insurer at the end of the year in respect of the claim, and

    (b) the policy liability of the insurer at the end of the year in respect of the claim.

**Related Provisions [Reg. 1405]**: ITA 20(26) — Deduction for unpaid claims reserve adjustment; Reg. 1401(4) — Unpaid claims reserve re pre-1996 policies; Reg. 1406 — All amounts to be net of reinsurance ceded and ignoring seg funds; Reg. 1407 — Amounts in Reg. 1405 may be less than zero; Reg. 8100, 8101 — Unpaid claims reserve adjustment.

**Notes**: Reg. 1405 replaced by P.C. 1999-1154, effective for 1996 and later taxation years. (For unpaid claims in respect of pre-1996 policies, see Reg. 1401(4).) The former Reg. 1405 provided:

1405. Transitional — Notwithstanding paragraph 1400(b) as it applied to a corporation's 1977 taxation year, for the purposes of paragraph 20(7)(c) of the Act for the 1977 taxation year, the prescribed amount (other than an amount in respect of unpaid claims or unearned premiums) in respect of group sickness and accident policies is the amount (other than an amount in respect of unpaid claims or unearned premiums), if any, as was, in the corporation's return of income required by subsection 150(1) of the Act to be filed for the 1976 taxation year, deducted in respect of such policies pursuant to paragraph 20(7)(c) of the Act.

**Definitions [Reg. 1405]:** "amount" — ITA 248(1), Reg. 1406, 1407; "insurer" — ITA 248(1); "life insurance policy" — ITA 138(12), 248(1), Reg. 1408(5); "life insurance policy in Canada" — ITA 138(12), Reg. 1408(1); "life insurer" — ITA 248(1); "policy liability", "post-1995 life insurance policy", "reported reserve" — Reg. 1408(1); "taxation year" — ITA 249.

**1406. [Interpretation]** — Any amount determined under section 1404 or 1405 shall be determined

(a) on a net of reinsurance ceded basis; and

(b) without reference to any liability in respect of a segregated fund (other than a liability in respect of a guarantee in respect of a segregated fund policy).

**Notes:** Reg. 1406 replaced by P.C. 1999-1154, effective for 1996 and later taxation years. The former Reg. 1406 provided:

1406. For the purposes of subparagraph 138(3)(a)(ii) of the Act, the amount allowed by regulation to an insurer for its 1977 taxation year shall not exceed the amount, if any, as was, in the insurer's return of income required by subsection 150(1) of the Act to be filed for the 1976 taxation year, deducted in computing its income pursuant to section 1403 as it applied to that year.

**Definitions [Reg. 1406]:** "amount" — ITA 248(1); "segregated fund", "segregated fund policy" — ITA 138.1(1), Reg. 1408(1).

**1407. [Negative amounts]** — For greater certainty, any amount referred to in or determined under section 1404 or 1405 may be equal to, or less than, nil.

**Notes:** Reg. 1407 added by P.C. 1999-1154, effective for 1996 and later taxation years. It effectively overrides ITA 257 for each individual element of the calculations in Reg. 1404 and 1405.

**Definitions [Reg. 1407]:** "amount" — ITA 248(1).

## DIVISION 5 — INTERPRETATION

**1408. Insurance businesses — (1)** The definitions in this subsection apply in this Part.

**"acquisition costs"** in respect of a policy of an insurer, consistency [*sic*] means

(a) 5% of the premium paid by a policyholder for the policy where the policy is

(i) a group policy,

(ii) a policy that insures a risk in respect of a financial loss of a lender on a loan made on the security of real property,

(iii) a policy issued under an arrangement with a person (other than an insurer or an insurance agent or broker) with whom the insurer does not deal at arm's length whereby a customer of the person is referred to the insurer,

(iv) a policy issued to a member of a credit union as a consequence of an arrangement with a credit union, where

(A) the insurer was established primarily to provide insurance to members of credit unions,

(B) the policyholder was referred to the insurer, and

(C) the principal business of the insurer is the provision of insurance to members of credit unions, or

(v) a policy issued to a policyholder that is a corporation with which the insurer does not deal at arm's length; and

(b) in any other case, 20% of the premium paid by the policyholder for the policy.

> **Proposed Repeal — Reg. 1408(1)"acquisition costs"**
>
> **Application:** The November 30, 1999 draft regulations (insurance business policy reserves), subsec. 1(2), will repeal the definition "acquisition costs" in subsec. 1408(1), applicable to 2000 *et seq.* and, where the taxpayer elects under the coming-into-force provision for the amendments to section 18 of the Act, as released in draft form on November 30, 1999, to the taxpayer's 1998 and 1999 taxation years.
>
> **Technical Notes:** Subsection 1408(1) of the Regulations defines the term "acquisition costs" to mean a percentage of the premium paid for the policy. The percentages (either 20% or 5%) were based on assumptions relating to the average industry costs for selling, or otherwise distributing, insurance policies. The definition "acquisition costs" is repealed. The change addresses the insurance industry's concern that amounts deemed incurred as acquisition costs (generally 20% of premiums) under the old definition no longer reflect the real acquisition costs being incurred by insurers.
>
> This amendment applies to the 2000 and subsequent taxation years and, if a taxpayer files an election in respect of amended subparagraph 18(9)(a)(ii) and new subsection 18(9.02) of the Act, the amendment also applies to the taxpayer's 1998 and 1999 taxation years.

**Related Provisions:** Reg. 1408(4) — Determination of premium paid by the policyholder.

**Notes:** See Notes at end of Reg. 1408. For the pre-1996 version of this definition, see former Reg. 1404(2) in Notes to Reg. 1404.

**"amount payable"**, in respect of a policy loan at a particular time, means the amount of the policy loan and the interest that is outstanding on the policy loan at that time.

**Notes:** See Notes at end of Reg. 1408. For the pre-1996 version of this definition, see former Reg. 1404(1) in Notes to Reg. 1404.

**"benefit"**, in respect of a policy, includes

(a) a policy dividend (other than a policy dividend in respect of a policy described in paragraph 1403(1)(c)) in respect of the policy to the extent that the dividend was specifically treated as a benefit by the insurer in determining a premium for the policy, and

(b) an expense of maintaining the policy after all premiums in respect of the policy have been paid to the extent that the expense was specifically provided for by the insurer in determining a premium for the policy,

but does not include

(c) a policy loan,

(d) interest on funds left on deposit with the insurer under the terms of the policy, and

(e) any other amount under the policy that was not specifically provided for by the insurer in determining a premium for the policy.

**Notes**: See Notes at end of Reg. 1408. For the pre-1996 version of this definition, see former Reg. 1404(2) in Notes to Reg. 1404.

"**capital tax**" means a tax imposed under Part I.3 or VI of the Act or a similar tax imposed under an Act of the legislature of a province.

**Notes**: See Notes at end of Reg. 1408. This definition did not appear in pre-1996 Reg. 1404.

"**cash surrender value**" has the meaning assigned by subsection 148(9) of the Act.

**Notes**: See Notes at end of Reg. 1408. For the pre-1996 version of this definition, see former Reg. 1404(2) in Notes to Reg. 1404.

"**claim liability**" of an insurer at the end of a taxation year means

(a) in respect of a claim reported to the insurer before that time under an insurance policy, the amount, if any, by which

(i) the present value at that time, computed using a rate of interest that is reasonable in the circumstances, of a reasonable estimate, determined in accordance with accepted actuarial practice, of the insurer's future payments and claim adjustment expenses in respect of the claim

exceeds

(ii) the present value at that time, computed using a rate of interest that is reasonable in the circumstances, of a reasonable estimate, determined in accordance with accepted actuarial practice, of the amounts that the insurer will recover after that time in respect of the claim because of salvage, subrogation or any other reason; and

(b) in respect of the possibility that there are claims under an insurance policy incurred before that time that have not been reported to the insurer before that time, the amount, if any, by which

(i) the present value at that time, computed using a rate of interest that is reasonable in the circumstances, of a reasonable estimate, determined in accordance with accepted actuarial practice, of the insurer's payments and claim adjustment expenses in respect of those claims

exceeds

(ii) the present value at that time, computed using a rate of interest that is reasonable in the circumstances, of a reasonable estimate, determined in accordance with accepted actuarial practice, of the amounts that the insurer will recover in respect of those claims because of salvage, subrogation or any other reason.

**Notes**: See Notes at end of Reg. 1408. This definition did not appear in pre-1996 Reg. 1404.

"**extended motor vehicle warranty**" means an agreement under which a person agrees to provide goods or render services in respect of the repair or maintenance of a motor vehicle manufactured by the person or a corporation related to the person where

(a) the agreement is in addition to a basic or limited warranty in respect of the vehicle;

(b) the basic or limited warranty has a term of 3 or more years, although it may expire before the end of such term on the vehicle's odometer registering a specified number of kilometres or miles;

(c) more than 50% of the expenses to be incurred under the agreement are reasonably expected to be incurred after the expiry of the basic or limited warranty; and

(d) the person's risk under the agreement is insured by an insurer that is subject to the supervision of a relevant authority.

**Notes**: See Notes at end of Reg. 1408. This definition did not appear in pre-1996 Reg. 1404.

"**general amending provision**", of an insurance policy, means a provision of the policy that allows it to be amended with the consent of the policyholder.

**Notes**: See Notes at end of Reg. 1408. This definition did not appear in pre-1996 Reg. 1404.

"**interest**", in relation to a policy loan, has the meaning assigned by subsection 138(12) of the Act.

**Notes**: See Notes at end of Reg. 1408. This definition did not appear in pre-1996 Reg. 1404.

"**lapse-supported policy**" means a life insurance policy that would require materially higher premiums if premiums were determined using policy lapse rates that are zero after the fifth policy year.

**Notes**: See Notes at end of Reg. 1408. This definition was in Reg. 1404(2) before 1996.

"**life insurance policy in Canada**" means a life insurance policy issued or effected by an insurer on the life of a person resident in Canada at the time the policy was issued or effected.

**Notes**: See Notes at end of Reg. 1408. For the pre-1996 version of this definition, see former Reg. 1404(1) in Notes to Reg. 1404.

"**modified net premium**", in respect of a premium under a policy (other than a prepaid premium under a policy that cannot be refunded except on termination of the policy), means

(a) where all benefits (other than policy dividends) and premiums (other than the frequency of payment of premiums) in respect of the policy are determined at the date of issue of the policy, the amount determined by the formula

$$A \times [(B + C)/(D + E)]$$

where

A   is the amount of the premium,

## Division 5 — Interpretation

B is the present value, at the date of the issue of the policy, of the benefits to be provided under the terms of the policy after the day that is one year after the date of the issue of the policy,

C is the present value, at the date of the issue of the policy, of the benefits to be provided under the terms of the policy after the day that is two years after the date of the issue of the policy,

D is the present value, at the date of the issue of the policy, of the premiums payable under the terms of the policy on or after the day that is one year after the date of the issue of the policy, and

E is the present value, at the date of the issue of the policy, of the premiums payable under the terms of the policy on or after the day that is two years after the date of the issue of the policy,

except that the amount determined by the formula in respect of the premium for the second year of a policy is deemed to be the amount that is 50% of the total of

(i) the amount that would otherwise be determined under the formula, and

(ii) the amount of a one-year term insurance premium (determined without regard to the frequency of payment of the premium) that would be payable under the policy; and

(b) in any other case, the amount that would be determined under paragraph (a) if that paragraph applied and the amount were adjusted in a manner that is reasonable in the circumstances.

**Related Provisions**: Reg. 1408(3) — Interpretation.

**Notes**: See Notes at end of Reg. 1408. For the (essentially identical) pre-1996 version of this definition, see former Reg. 1404(2) in Notes to Reg. 1404.

**"net premium for the policy"** means the amount by which the premium paid by a policyholder for the policy exceeds the acquisition costs of the policy.

### Proposed Repeal — Reg. 1408(1) "net premium for the policy"

**Application**: The November 30, 1999 draft regulations (insurance business policy reserves), subsec. 1(2), will repeal the definition "net premium for the policy" in subsec. 1408(1), applicable to 2000 et seq. and, where the taxpayer elects under the coming-into-force provision for the amendments to section 18 of the Act, as released in draft form on November 30, 1999, to the taxpayer's 1998 and 1999 taxation years.

**Technical Notes**: The definition "net premium for the policy" in subsection 1408(1) is also repealed. The definition is repealed because Part XIV no longer determines any amount on the basis of the unearned portion of a net premium for a policy.

This amendment applies to the 2000 and subsequent taxation years and, if a taxpayer files an election in respect of amended subparagraph 18(9)(a)(ii) and new subsection 18(9.02) of the Act, the amendment also applies to the taxpayer's 1998 and 1999 taxation years.

**Related Provisions**: Reg. 1408(4) — Determination of premium paid by the policyholder.

**Notes**: See Notes at end of Reg. 1408. This definition was in Reg. 1404(2) before 1996.

**"non-cancellable or guaranteed renewable accident and sickness policy"** includes a non-cancellable or guaranteed renewable accident and sickness benefit under a group policy.

**Related Provisions**: Reg. 1408(6) — Riders.

**Notes**: See Notes at end of Reg. 1408. This definition did not appear in pre-1996 Reg. 1404.

**"participating life insurance policy"** has the meaning assigned by subsection 138(12) of the Act.

**Notes**: See Notes at end of Reg. 1408. For the pre-1996 version of this definition, see former Reg. 1404(1) in Notes to Reg. 1404.

**"policy liability"** of an insurer at the end of the taxation year in respect of an insurance policy or a claim, possible claim or risk under an insurance policy means the positive or negative amount of the insurer's reserve in respect of its potential liability in respect of the policy, claim, possible claim or risk at the end of the year determined in accordance with accepted actuarial practice, but without reference to projected income and capital taxes (other than the tax payable under Part XII.3 of the Act).

**Notes**: See Notes at end of Reg. 1408. This definition did not appear in pre-1996 Reg. 1404.

**"policy loan"** has the meaning assigned by subsection 138(12) of the Act.

**Notes**: See Notes at end of Reg. 1408. This definition did not appear in pre-1996 Reg. 1404.

**"post-1995 life insurance policy"** means a life insurance policy that is not a pre-1996 life insurance policy.

**Notes**: See Notes at end of Reg. 1408. This definition did not appear in pre-1996 Reg. 1404.

**"post-1995 non-cancellable or guaranteed renewable accident and sickness policy"** means a non-cancellable or guaranteed renewable accident and sickness policy that is not a pre-1996 non-cancellable or guaranteed renewable accident and sickness policy.

**Notes**: See Notes at end of Reg. 1408. This definition did not appear in pre-1996 Reg. 1404.

**"pre-1996 life insurance policy"**, at any time, means a life insurance policy where

(a) the policy was issued before 1996; and

(b) before that time and after 1995 there has been no change, except in accordance with the provisions (other than a general amending provision) of the policy as they existed on December 31, 1995, to

(i) the amount of any benefit under the policy,

(ii) the amount of any premium or other amount payable under the policy, or

(iii) the number of premium or other payments under the policy.

**Related Provisions**: Reg. 1408(7) — Interpretation.

**Notes**: See Notes at end of Reg. 1408. This definition did not appear in pre-1996 Reg. 1404.

**"pre-1996 non-cancellable or guaranteed renewable accident and sickness policy"**, at any time, means a non-cancellable or guaranteed renewable accident and sickness policy where

(a) the policy was issued before 1996; and

(b) before that time and after 1995 there has been no change, except in accordance with the provisions (other than a general amending provision) of the policy as they existed on December 31, 1995, to

(i) the amount of any benefit under the policy,

(ii) the amount of any premium or other amount payable under the policy, or

(iii) the number of premium or other payments under the policy.

**Related Provisions**: Reg. 1408(7) — Interpretation.

**Notes**: See Notes at end of Reg. 1408. This definition did not appear in pre-1996 Reg. 1404.

**"qualified annuity"** means an annuity contract issued before 1982, other than a deposit administration fund policy or a policy referred to in paragraph 1403(7)(c),

(a) in respect of which regular periodic annuity payments have commenced;

(b) in respect of which a contract or certificate has been issued that provides for regular periodic annuity payments to commence within one year after the date of issue of the contract or certificate;

(c) that is not issued as or under a registered retirement savings plan, registered pension plan or deferred profit sharing plan and that

(i) does not provide for a guaranteed cash surrender value at any time, and

(ii) provides for regular periodic annuity payments to commence not later than the attainment of age 71 by the annuitant; or

(d) that is issued as or under a registered retirement savings plan, registered pension plan or deferred profit sharing plan, if the interest rate is guaranteed for at least 10 years and the plan does not provide for any participation in profits, directly or indirectly.

**Notes**: See Notes at end of Reg. 1408. For the (essentially identical) pre-1996 version of this definition, see former Reg. 1404(2) in Notes to Reg. 1404.

**"reinsurance commission"**, in respect of a policy, means

(a) where the risk under the policy is fully reinsured, the amount, if any, by which

(i) the net premium for the policy

exceeds

(ii) the consideration payable by the insurer in respect of the reinsurance of the risk; and

(b) where the risk under the policy is not fully reinsured, the amount, if any, by which

(i) the portion of the net premium for the policy that may reasonably be considered to be in respect of the portion of the risk that is reinsured with a particular reinsurer

exceeds

(ii) the consideration payable by the insurer to the particular reinsurer in respect of the risk assumed by the reinsurer.

**Proposed Amendment — Reg. 1408(1)"reinsurance commission"**

**Application**: The November 30, 1999 draft regulations (insurance business policy reserves), subsec. 1(1)(e), will amend the definition "reinsurance commission" in subsec. 1408(1) by replacing "net premium" with "premium paid by the policyholder", applicable to 2000 et seq. and, where the taxpayer elects under the coming-into-force provision for the amendments to section 18 of the Act, as released in draft form on November 30, 1999, to the taxpayer's 1998 and 1999 taxation years.

**Technical Notes**: See under Reg. 1400(3)A.

**Notes**: See Notes at end of Reg. 1408. For the pre-1996 version of this definition, which was identical except for a clarification as to the meaning of "net premium", see former Reg. 1404(2) in Notes to Reg. 1404.

**"relevant authority"** of an insurer means

(a) the Superintendent of Financial Institutions, if the insurer is required by law to report to the Superintendent of Financial Institutions; and

(b) in any other case, the Superintendent of Insurance or other similar officer or authority of the province under whose laws the insurer is incorporated.

**Notes**: See Notes at end of Reg. 1408. For the pre-1996 version of this definition, which was identical except for a para. (a.1) for Canada Mortgage & Housing Corp., see former Reg. 1404(2) in Notes to Reg. 1404.

**"reported reserve"** of an insurer at the end of a taxation year in respect of an insurance policy or a claim, possible claim, risk, dividend, refund of premiums or refund of premium deposits under an insurance policy means the amount equal to

(a) where the insurer is required to file an annual report with its relevant authority for a period ending coincidentally with the year, the positive or negative amount of the reserve that would be reported in that report in respect of the insurer's potential liability under the policy if the reserve were determined without reference to projected income and capital taxes (other than the tax payable under Part XII.3 of the Act);

(b) where the insurer is, throughout the year, subject to the supervision of its relevant authority and paragraph (a) does not apply, the positive or negative amount of the reserve that would be reported in its financial statements for the year in respect of the insurer's potential liability under the policy if

(i) those statements were prepared in accordance with generally accepted accounting principles, and

(ii) the reserve were determined without reference to projected income and capital taxes (other than the tax payable under Part XII.3 of the Act);

(c) where the insurer is the Canada Mortgage and Housing Corporation or a foreign affiliate of a taxpayer resident in Canada, the positive or negative amount of the reserve that would be reported in its financial statements for the year in respect of the insurer's potential liability under the policy if

(i) those statements were prepared in accordance with generally accepted accounting principles, and

(ii) the reserve were determined without reference to projected income and capital taxes (other than the tax payable under Part XII.3 of the Act); and

(d) in any other case, nil.

Notes: See Notes at end of Reg. 1408. For the pre-1996 version of this definition, see former Reg. 1404(2) in Notes to Reg. 1404.

**"segregated fund"** has the meaning assigned by subsection 138.1(1).

Notes: See Notes at end of Reg. 1408. This definition did not appear in pre-1996 Reg. 1404.

**"segregated fund policy"** has the meaning assigned by subsection 138.1(1).

Notes: See Notes at end of Reg. 1408. This definition did not appear in pre-1996 Reg. 1404.

**(2) ["Group term life insurance policy"]** — The definition "group term life insurance policy" in subsection 248(1) of the Act does not apply to this Part.

Notes: See Notes at end of Reg. 1408.

**(3) [Interpretation — modified net premium]** — For the purpose of the formula referred to in the definition "modified net premium" in subsection (1), it may be assumed that premiums are payable annually in advance.

Notes: See Notes at end of Reg. 1408.

**(4) ["Premium paid by the policyholder"]** — For the purposes of this Part,

(a) a reference to a "premium paid by the policyholder" shall, depending on the method regularly followed by the insurer in computing its income, be read as a reference to a "premium paid or payable by the policyholder"; and

(b) in determining the premium paid by a policyholder for a policy, there may be deducted by the insurer the portion, if any, of the premium that

(i) can reasonably be considered, at the time the policy is issued, to be a deposit that, pursuant to the terms of the policy or the by-laws of the insurer, will be returned to the policyholder, or credited to the account of the policyholder, by the insurer on the termination of the policy, and

(ii) was not otherwise deducted under section 140 of the Act.

Notes: See Notes at end of Reg. 1408.

**(5) [Riders]** — For the purposes of this Part, any rider that is attached to a life insurance policy and that provides for additional life insurance or for an annuity is a separate life insurance policy.

Notes: See Notes at end of Reg. 1408.

**(6) [Riders]** — For the purposes of this Part, any rider that is attached to a policy and that provides for additional non-cancellable or guaranteed renewable accident and sickness insurance, as the case may be, is a separate non-cancellable or guaranteed renewable accident and sickness policy.

Notes: See Notes at end of Reg. 1408.

**(7) [No change in amount]** — For the purposes of the definitions "pre-1996 life insurance policy" and "pre-1996 non-cancellable or guaranteed renewable accident and sickness policy" in subsection (1), a change in the amount of any benefit or in the amount or number of any premiums or other amounts payable under a policy is deemed not to have occurred where the change results from

(a) a change in underwriting class;

(b) a change in frequency of premium payments within a year that does not alter the present value, at the beginning of the year, of the total premiums to be paid under the policy in the year;

(c) the deletion of a rider;

(d) the correction of erroneous information;

(e) the reinstatement of the policy after its lapse, if the reinstatement occurs not later than 60 days after the end of the calendar year in which the lapse occurred;

(f) the redating of the policy for policy loan indebtedness; or

(g) a change in the amount of a benefit under the policy that is granted by the insurer on a class basis, where

(i) no consideration was payable by the policyholder or any other person for the change, and

Reg. S. 1408(7)(g)(ii)　　Income Tax Regulations, Part XIV

(ii) the change was not made because of the terms or conditions of the policy or any other policy or contract to which the insurer is a party.

**Notes [Reg. 1408]:** Reg. 1408 added by P.C. 1999-1154, effective for 1996 and later taxation years. The definitions for previous years were in former Reg. 1404.

**Definitions [Reg. 1408]:** "acquisition costs" — Reg. 1408(1); "amount" — ITA 248(1); "amount payable" — ITA 138(12), Reg. 1408(1); "annuity" — ITA 248(1); "arm's length" — ITA 251(1); "benefit" — Reg. 1408(1); "business" — ITA 248(1); "capital tax" — Reg. 1408(1); "cash surrender value" — ITA 148(9), Reg. 1408(1); "corporation" — ITA 248(1), *Interpretation Act* 35(1); "credit union" — ITA 248(1); "deferred profit sharing plan" — ITA 147(1), 248(1); "dividend" — ITA 248(1); "foreign affiliate" — ITA 95(1), 248(1); "general amending provision" — Reg. 1408(1); "insurance policy", "insurer" — ITA 248(1); "interest" — ITA 138(12), Reg. 1408(1); "legislature" — *Interpretation Act* 35(1)"legislative assembly"; "life insurance policy" — ITA 138(12), 248(1), Reg. 1408(5); "motor vehicle" — ITA 248(1); "net premium for the policy" — Reg. 1408(1); "non-cancellable or guaranteed renewable accident and sickness policy" — Reg. 1408(1), (6); "officer", "person" — ITA 248(1); "policy loan" — ITA 138(12), Reg. 1408(1); "pre-1996 life insurance policy", "pre-1996 non-cancellable or guaranteed renewable accident and sickness policy" — Reg. 1408(1), (7); "property" — ITA 248(1); "province" — *Interpretation Act* 35(1); "premium paid by the policyholder" — Reg. 1408(4); "registered pension plan" — ITA 248(1); "registered retirement savings plan" — ITA 146(1), 248(1); "related" — ITA 251(2)–(6); "relevant authority" — Reg. 1408(2); "resident in Canada" — ITA 250; "security" — *Interpretation Act* 35(1); "taxation year" — ITA 249; "taxpayer" — ITA 248(1).

# PART XV — PROFIT SHARING PLANS

## DIVISION I — EMPLOYEES PROFIT SHARING PLANS

**1500. (1)** An election under subsection 144(4.1) of the Act by the trustee of a trust governed by an employees profit sharing plan shall be made by filing with the Minister the prescribed form in duplicate.

**(2)** An election under subsection 144(4.2) of the Act by the trustee of a trust governed by an employees profit sharing plan shall be made by filing with the Minister the prescribed form in duplicate on or before the last day of a taxation year of the trust in respect of any capital property deemed to have been disposed of in that taxation year by virtue of the election.

**(3)** An election under subsection 144(10) of the Act shall be made by forwarding by registered mail to the Deputy Minister of National Revenue for Taxation at Ottawa the following documents:

(a) a letter from the employer stating that he elects to have the arrangement qualify as an employees profit sharing plan;

(b) if the employer is a corporation,

(i) where the directors of the corporation are legally entitled to administer the affairs of the corporation, a certified copy of their resolution authorizing the election to be made, and

(ii) where the directors of the corporation are not legally entitled to administer the affairs of the corporation, a certified copy of the authorization of the making of the election by the person or persons legally entitled to administer the affairs of the corporation; and

(c) a copy of the agreement and any supplementary agreement setting out the plan.

**Definitions [Reg. 1500]:** "capital property" — ITA 54, 248(1); "corporation" — ITA 248(1), *Interpretation Act* 35(1); "disposed" — ITA 248(1)"disposition"; "employees profit sharing plan" — ITA 144(1), 248(1); "employer", "Minister", "person", "prescribed" — ITA 248(1); "taxation year" — ITA 249; "trust" — ITA 104(1), 248(1), (3).

**Interpretation Bulletins:** IT-280R: Employees profit sharing plans — payments computed by reference to profits.

**Forms:** T3009: Election for deemed disposition and reacquisition of capital property of a trust governed by an employees profit sharing plan under subsection 144(4.2).

## DIVISION II — DEFERRED PROFIT SHARING PLANS

**1501. Registration of plans** — For the purposes of the definition "deferred profit sharing plan" in subsection 147(1) of the Act, an application for registration of a plan shall be made by forwarding by registered mail to the Deputy Minister of National Revenue for Taxation at Ottawa the following documents:

(a) a letter from the trustee and the employer whereby the trustee and the employer apply for the registration of the plan as a deferred profit sharing plan;

(b) if the employer is a corporation, a certified copy of a resolution of the directors authorizing the application to be made; and

(c) a copy of the agreement and any supplementary agreement setting out the plan.

**Notes:** Opening words of Reg. 1501 amended by P.C. 1991-2540, s. 4, December 16, 1991, effective 1991, purely to correspond to a change in the definition of "deferred profit sharing plan" in the Act (no substantive change).

**Definitions [Reg. 1501]:** "corporation" — ITA 248(1), *Interpretation Act* 35(1); "deferred profit sharing plan" — ITA 147(1), 248(1); "employer", "Minister" — ITA 248(1).

**Information Circulars:** 77-1R4: Deferred profit sharing plans.

**Forms:** T2214: Application for registration as a deferred profit sharing plan.

**1502.** [Revoked]

**Notes:** Reg. 1502, revoked in 1981, prescribed qualified investments for deferred profit sharing plans and revoked plans. These rules are now found in Reg. 4900.

## Division III — Elections in Respect of Certain Single Payments

**1503.** Any election by a beneficiary under subsection 147(10.1) of the Act shall be made by filing the prescribed form in duplicate as follows:

(a) one form shall be filed by the beneficiary with the trustee of the deferred profit sharing plan not later than 60 days after the end of the taxation year in which the beneficiary received the payment referred to in subsection 147(10.1) of the Act; and

(b) the other form shall be filed by the beneficiary with the Minister on or before the day on which the beneficiary is required to file a return of income pursuant to section 150 of the Act for the taxation year in which the beneficiary received the payment referred to in subsection 147(10.1) of the Act.

**Definitions [Reg. 1503]**: "deferred profit sharing plan" — ITA 147(1), 248(1); "Minister", "prescribed" — ITA 248(1); "taxation year" — ITA 249.

**Interpretation Bulletins**: IT-281R2: Elections on single payments from a deferred profit sharing plan.

**Forms**: Election under subsec. 147(10.1) re a single payment received from a deferred profit sharing plan.

## Part XVI — Prescribed Countries

**1600.** For the purposes of subsection 10(4) of the *Income Tax Application Rules*, the following countries are hereby prescribed:

(a) Commonwealth of Australia;

(b) Kingdom of Denmark;

(c) Republic of Finland;

(d) French Republic;

(e) Federal Republic of Germany;

(f) Ireland;

(g) Jamaica;

(h) Japan;

(i) Kingdom of the Netherlands;

(j) New Zealand;

(k) Kingdom of Norway;

(l) Republic of South Africa;

(m) Kingdom of Sweden;

(n) Trinidad and Tobago;

(o) United Kingdom of Great Britain and Northern Ireland; and

(p) United States of America.

**Definitions [Reg. 1600]**: "prescribed" — ITA 248(1); "United Kingdom", "United States" — *Interpretation Act* 35(1).

## Part XVII — Capital Cost Allowances, Farming and Fishing

**Notes**: The CCA rates in this Part apply only to property owned continuously since before 1972. See Reg. 1702(1)(k). For property acquired since 1972, see Part XI and Schedule II.

**Interpretation Bulletins [Part XVII]**: IT-268R4: *Inter vivos* transfer of farm property to child; IT-349R3: Intergenerational transfers of farm property on death.

**Forms [Part XVII]**: T2041: CCA schedule for self-employed persons.

### Division I — Deductions Allowed

**1700. (1) Rates** — For the purposes of paragraph 20(1)(a) of the Act, there is hereby allowed to a taxpayer, in computing his income from farming or fishing, as the case may be, a deduction for each taxation year in respect of each property that was used for the purpose of gaining or producing income from farming or fishing equal to such amount as he may claim, not exceeding in the case of

(a) a building or other structure, not described elsewhere in this subsection, including component parts such as electric wiring, plumbing, sprinkler systems, air-conditioning equipment, heating equipment, lighting fixtures, elevators and escalators, 2½%

(b) a building or other structure of

(i) frame,

(ii) log,

(iii) stucco on frame,

(iv) galvanized iron, or

(v) corrugated iron

construction, including component parts such as electric wiring, plumbing, sprinkler systems, air-conditioning equipment, heating equipment, lighting fixtures, elevators and escalators, 5%

(c) a fence, 5%

(d) a scow or a vessel, including furniture, fittings or equipment attached thereto, but not including radio communication equipment, 7½%

(e) nonautomotive equipment and machinery, 10%

(f) automotive equipment, a sleigh or a wagon, 15%

(g) radiocommunication equipment, 15%

(h) tile drainage acquired before the 1965 taxation year, 10%

(i) a water storage tank, 5%

(j) a gas well that is part of the equipment of a farm and from which the gas produced is not sold, 10%

(k) a tool costing less than $100, 100%

of the depreciable cost to the taxpayer of the property.

**(2) Taxation years less than 12 months** — Where the taxation year is less than 12 months, the amount allowed as a deduction under subsection (1) shall not exceed that proportion of the maximum amount otherwise allowable that the number of days in the taxation year is of 365.

**(3) Property disposed of during year** — Where a taxpayer has disposed of a property before the end of a taxation year, the amount allowed as a deduction under subsection (1) in respect of that property for the year shall not exceed that proportion of the maximum amount otherwise allowable that the number of months in the taxation year during which the property was owned by the taxpayer is of 12.

**(4) Leasehold interests** — Where a taxpayer has property that was used for the purpose of gaining or producing income from farming or fishing and that would be included in Class 13 in Schedule II if he had claimed an allowance under Part XI, he may deduct, in computing his income from farming or fishing for a taxation year, an amount not exceeding the amount he could have deducted in respect of that property for the year under paragraph 1100(1)(b).

**Definitions [Reg. 1700]**: "amount" — ITA 248(1); "depreciable cost" — Reg. 1703(2)–(8); "disposed" — ITA 248(1)"disposition"; "end of a taxation year" — Reg. 1703(1)(b); "farming", "fishing" — ITA 248(1); "month" — *Interpretation Act* 35(1); "property" — ITA 248(1); "radio" — *Interpretation Act* 35(1); "taxation year" — Reg. 1703(1)(a); "taxpayer" — ITA 248(1).

## DIVISION II — MAXIMUM DEDUCTIONS

**1701. (1)** The amount allowed as a deduction under section 1700 in respect of a property shall not exceed the amount by which the capital cost of the property to the taxpayer exceeds the aggregate of the deductions from income allowed under this Part in respect of the property for previous taxation years.

**(2)** In respect of the 1972 and subsequent taxation years, where subsection 20(5) of the *Income Tax Application Rules* applies to a particular property, notwithstanding subsection (1), the amount allowed as a deduction under section 1700 in respect of the property shall not exceed the amount by which

(a) the amount determined to be the undepreciated capital cost of the property, under paragraph 20(5)(b) of the *Income Tax Application Rules*

exceeds

(b) the aggregate of the deductions from income allowed under this Part in respect of the property for previous taxation years ending after 1971.

**Definitions [Reg. 1701]**: "amount", "property" — ITA 248(1); "taxation year" — ITA 249; "taxation years" — Reg. 1703(1)(a); "taxpayer" — ITA 248(1); "undepreciated capital cost" — ITA 13(21), 248(1).

## DIVISION III — PROPERTY NOT INCLUDED

**1702. (1)** Nothing in this Part shall be construed as allowing a deduction in respect of a property

(a) the cost of which is deductible in computing the taxpayer's income;

(b) that is described in the taxpayer's inventory;

(c) that was acquired by an expenditure in respect of which the taxpayer is allowed a deduction from income under section 37 of the Act;

(d) that has been constituted a prescribed class by subsection 24(2) of chapter 91, S.C. 1966-67;

(e) that is included in a separate prescribed class established under subsection 13(14) of the Act;

(f) that was not used in the business during the year;

(g) that is

(i) an animal, or

(ii) a tree, shrub, herb or similar growing thing;

(h) that was not acquired by the taxpayer for the purpose of gaining or producing income from farming or fishing;

(i) that has been included at any time by the taxpayer in a class prescribed under Part XI;

(j) that is a passenger automobile acquired after June 13, 1963, and before January 1, 1966, the cost to the taxpayer of which, minus the initial transportation charges and retail sales tax in respect thereof, exceeded $5,000, unless the automobile was acquired by a person before June 14, 1963 and has, by one or more transactions between persons not dealing at arm's length, become vested in the taxpayer; or

(k) that was acquired by the taxpayer after 1971.

**(2)** Where a taxpayer is a member of a partnership, the properties referred to in this Part shall be deemed not to include any property that is an interest of the taxpayer in depreciable property that is partnership property of the partnership.

**(3)** The properties referred to in section 1700 shall be deemed not to include the land upon which a property described therein was constructed or is situated.

**(4)** Where the taxpayer is a non-resident person, the properties referred to in section 1700 shall be deemed not to include property that is situated outside Canada.

**(5)** The provisions of subsections 1102(11), (12) and (13) are applicable *mutatis mutandis* to paragraph (1)(j).

**Definitions [Reg. 1702]**: "arm's length" — ITA 251(1); "automobile", "business" — ITA 248(1); "Canada" — ITA 255, *Interpretation Act* 35(1); "depreciable property" — ITA 13(21), 248(1);

"farming", "fishing", "inventory", "non-resident" — ITA 248(1); "partnership" — see Notes to ITA 96(1); "person", "prescribed", "property", "taxpayer" — ITA 248(1).

## DIVISION IV — INTERPRETATION

**1703. (1) Taxation years for individuals in business** — Where a taxpayer is an individual and his income for the taxation year includes income from a business the fiscal period of which does not coincide with the calendar year, in respect of depreciable properties acquired for the purpose of gaining or producing income from the business, a reference in this Part to

(a) "the taxation year" shall be deemed to be a reference to the fiscal period of the business; and

(b) "the end of the taxation year" shall be deemed to be a reference to the end of the fiscal period of the business.

**(2) Depreciable cost** — In this Part, "depreciable cost" to a taxpayer of property means, except as otherwise provided, the actual cost of the property to the taxpayer or the amount at which he is deemed under subsection 13(7) of the Act to have acquired the property, as the case may be.

**(3)** Notwithstanding the other provisions of this section, in the case of property the cost of which to a partnership has been determined under paragraph 20(5)(a) of the *Income Tax Application Rules*, the depreciable cost to the taxpayer of the property for the purposes of this Part shall be deemed to be an amount equal to the cost to the partnership of the particular property as determined under that paragraph.

**(4) Personal use of property** — Where a taxpayer has, in a taxation year, regularly used a property in part for the purpose of gaining or producing income from farming or fishing and in part for a purpose other than gaining or producing income, the depreciable cost to the taxpayer of the property for the purposes of this Part is the proportion of the amount that would otherwise be the depreciable cost that the use regularly made of the property for the purpose of gaining or producing income from farming or fishing is of the whole use regularly made of the property.

**(5) Grants, subsidies or other government assistance** — Where a taxpayer has received or is entitled to receive a grant, subsidy or other assistance from a government, municipality or other public authority in respect of or for the acquisition of property, the depreciable cost to the taxpayer of the property for the purposes of this Part is the amount that would otherwise be the depreciable cost minus the amount of the grant, subsidy or other assistance.

**(6) Transactions not at arm's length** — Where property did belong to a person (in this subsection referred to as the "original owner") and has, by one or more transactions between persons not dealing at arm's length, become vested in a taxpayer, the depreciable cost to the taxpayer of the property for the purposes of this Part is the lesser of

(a) the actual capital cost of the property to the taxpayer; and

(b) the amount by which the actual capital cost of the property to the original owner exceeds the aggregate of

(i) the total amount of depreciation for the property that, since the commencement of 1917, has been or should have been taken into account in accordance with the practice of the Department of National Revenue in ascertaining the income of the original owner and all intervening owners for the purposes of the *Income War Tax Act* or in ascertaining a loss for a year where there was no income under that Act,

(ii) any accumulated depreciation reserves that the original owner or an intervening owner had for the property at the commencement of 1917 and that were recognized by the Minister for the purposes of the *Income War Tax Act*, and

(iii) the aggregate of the deductions, if any, allowed under this Part in respect of the property to the original owner and all intervening owners.

**(7) Property acquired from a parent** — Notwithstanding subsection (6), where depreciable property has been acquired by a taxpayer under such circumstances that the provisions of section 85H of the Act as it read in its application to the 1971 and prior taxation years are applicable for the determination of the capital cost of the property, the depreciable cost to the taxpayer of the property for the purposes of this Part is the capital cost as determined under that section.

**(8) Property acquired by gift** — Subsection (6) does not apply in respect of property which a taxpayer has acquired by gift.

**Definitions [Reg. 1703]**: "amount" — ITA 248(1); "arm's length" — ITA 251(1); "business" — ITA 248(1); "commencement" — *Interpretation Act* 35(1); "depreciable cost" — Reg. 1703(2)–(8); "depreciable property" — ITA 13(21), 248(1); "farming" — ITA 248(1); "fiscal period" — ITA 249.1; "fishing", "individual", "Minister" — ITA 248(1); "original owner" — Reg. 1703(6); "partnership" — see Notes to ITA 96(1); "person", "property" — ITA 248(1); "taxation year" — Reg. 1703(1)(a); "taxpayer" — ITA 248(1).

## DIVISION V — APPLICATION OF THIS PART

**1704.** This Part shall apply only to a taxpayer who, in computing his income, has never claimed an allowance under Part XI in respect of a property at a time when an allowance could have been claimed under this Part in respect of that property, other than an allowance claimed by the taxpayer under Part XI that may be claimed in respect of a property described in

(a) paragraph 1100(1)(r) as enacted by Order in Council P.C. 1965-1118 of June 18, 1965 and as amended by Order in Council P.C. 1965-2320 of December 29, 1965;

(b) paragraph 1100(1)(sa) as enacted by Order in Council P.C. 1968-2261 of December 10, 1968;

(c) paragraph 1100(1)(v); or

(d) Class 20 in Schedule II.

**Definitions [Reg. 1704]:** "property", "taxpayer" — ITA 248(1).

**Interpretation Bulletins:** See at beginning of Part XVII.

**Forms:** See at beginning of Part XVII.

## PART XVIII — INVENTORIES

**1800. Manner of keeping inventories** — For the purposes of section 230 of the Act, an inventory shall show quantities and nature of the properties that should be included therein in such a manner and in sufficient detail that the property may be valued in accordance with this Part or section 10 of the Act.

**Definitions [Reg. 1800]:** "inventory", "property" — ITA 248(1).

**1801. Valuation** — Except as provided by section 1802, for the purpose of computing the income of a taxpayer from a business, all the property described in all the inventories of the business may be valued at its fair market value.

**Related Provisions:** ITA 10(1), (1.01) — Rules for valuing inventory.

**Definitions [Reg. 1801]:** "business", "inventory", "property", "taxpayer" — ITA 248(1).

**Interpretation Bulletins:** IT-98R2: Investment corporations; IT-473R: Inventory valuation; IT-504R2: Visual artists and writers.

**1802. Valuation of animals** — (1) Except as provided in subsection (2), a taxpayer who is carrying on a business that includes the breeding and raising of animals may elect in prescribed form for a taxation year and subsequent taxation years to value each animal of a particular species (except a registered animal, an animal purchased for feedlot or similar operations, or an animal purchased by a drover or like person for resale) included in his inventory in respect of the business at a unit price determined in accordance with this section.

**Forms:** T2034: Election to establish inventory unit prices for animals.

(2) An election made in accordance with subsection (1) may be revoked in writing by the taxpayer, but where a taxpayer has made a revocation in accordance with this subsection a further election may not be made under subsection (1) except with the concurrence of the Minister.

(3) The unit price with respect to an animal of a particular class of animal shall be determined in accordance with the following rules:

(a) where animals of a particular class of animal were included in the inventory of a taxpayer at the end of the taxation year immediately preceding the first year in respect of which the taxpayer elected under subsection (1), the unit price of an animal of that class shall be computed by dividing the total value of all animals of the class in the inventory of the preceding year by the number of animals of the class described in that inventory, and

(b) in any other case, the unit price of an animal of a class shall be determined by the Minister, having regard, among other things, to the unit prices of animals of a comparable class of animal used in valuing the inventories of other taxpayers in the district.

(4) Notwithstanding subsection (1), where the aggregate value of the animals of a particular class determined in accordance with that subsection exceeds the market value of those animals, the animals of that class may be valued at fair market value.

(5) In this section

**"class of animal"** means a group of animals of a particular species segregated on the basis of age, breed or other recognized division, as determined by the taxpayer at the time of election under this section;

**"district"** means the territory served by a District Office of the Taxation Division of the Department of National Revenue;

**"registered animal"** means an animal for which a certificate of registration has been issued by the registrar of the breed to which the animal belongs or by the registrar of the Canadian National Livestock Records;

a reference to **"taxation year"** shall be deemed to be a reference to the fiscal period of a business.

**Definitions [Reg. 1802]:** "business" — ITA 248(1); "class of animal", "district" — Reg. 1802(5); "fiscal period" — ITA 249.1; "inventory", "Minister", "person", "prescribed" — ITA 248(1); "registered animal", "taxation year" — Reg. 1802(5); "taxpayer" — ITA 248(1); "territory" — *Interpretation Act* 35(1); "unit price" — Reg. 1802(3); "writing" — *Interpretation Act* 35(1).

## PART XIX — INVESTMENT INCOME TAX

**1900. (1)–(10)** [No longer relevant]

**Notes:** Reg. 1900 added by P.C. 1994-619, effective for taxation years that begin after June 17, 1987 but before 1990 and that end in 1988 or later. It prescribes amounts for ITA 211.1(3). It no longer applies for current years because ITA 211.1(3) has been revised.

Former Part XIX, revoked effective October 29, 1985, was titled "Exempt Mines". It prescribed conditions for the exemption from tax for mining income under ITAR 28 before 1974.

# PART XX — POLITICAL CONTRIBUTIONS

**2000. Contents of receipts** — **(1)** Every official receipt issued by a registered agent of a registered party shall contain a statement that it is an official receipt for income tax purposes and shall, in a manner that cannot readily be altered, show clearly

(a) the full name of the registered party;

(b) the serial number of the receipt;

(c) the name of the registered agent as recorded in the registry maintained by the Chief Electoral Officer pursuant to subsection 13.1(1) of the *Canada Elections Act*;

(d) the day on which the receipt was issued;

(e) where the person making the contribution is

(i) a person other than an individual, the day on which the contribution was received where that day differs from the day referred to in paragraph (d), or

(ii) an individual, the calendar year during which the contribution was received;

(f) the place or locality where the receipt was issued;

(g) the name and address of the person making the contribution including, in the case of an individual, his first name or initial;

(h) the amount of the contribution; and

(i) the signature of the registered agent.

**(2)** Subject to subsection (3), every official receipt issued by an official agent of an officially nominated candidate shall contain a statement that it is an official receipt for income tax purposes and shall, in a manner that cannot readily be altered, show clearly

(a) the name of the officially nominated candidate;

(b) the serial number of the receipt;

(c) the name of the official agent as recorded with the Minister;

(d) the day on which the receipt was issued;

(e) the day on which the contribution was received where that day differs from the day referred to in paragraph (d);

(f) the polling day;

(g) the name and address of the person making the contribution including, in the case of an individual, his first name or initial;

(h) the amount of the contribution; and

(i) the signature of the official agent.

**(3)** The information required by paragraph (2)(f) may be shown by use of a code on an official receipt form issued by the Chief Electoral Officer, provided that the Minister is advised of the meaning of the code used.

**(4)** For the purposes of subsections (1) and (2), an official receipt issued to replace an official receipt previously issued shall show clearly that it replaces the original receipt and, in addition to its own serial number, shall show the serial number of the receipt originally issued.

**(5)** A spoiled official receipt form shall be marked "cancelled" and such form, together with the duplicate thereof, shall be filed by the registered agent or the official agent, as the case may be, together with the duplicates of receipts required to be filed with the Minister pursuant to subsection 230.1(2) of the Act.

**(6)** Every official receipt form on which

(a) the day on which the contribution was received,

(b) the year during which the contribution was received, or

(c) the amount of the contribution

was incorrectly or illegibly entered shall be regarded as spoiled.

**Definitions [Reg. 2000]**: "amount" — ITA 248(1); "Canada" — ITA 255, *Interpretation Act* 35(1); "contribution" — ITA 127(4.1), Reg. 2002(1); "individual", "Minister" — ITA 248(1); "official receipt" — Reg. 2000(4), 2002; "official receipt form" — Reg. 2002(1); "officially nominated candidate" — Reg. 2002(2); "person" — ITA 248(1); "polling day" — Reg. 2002(2); "registered agent", "registered party" — Reg. 2002(1).

**2001. Information returns** — The return of information referred to in subsection 230.1(2) of the Act shall be filed by a registered agent on or before the last day of March in each year and shall be in respect of the preceding calendar year.

**Definitions [Reg. 2001]**: "registered agent" — Reg. 2002(1).

**Forms**: T2092: Contributions to a registered party — information return; T2093: Contributions to a candidate at an election — information return.

**2002. Interpretation** — **(1)** In this Part,

**"contribution"** means an amount contributed within the meaning assigned by subsection 127(4.1) of the Act;

**"official receipt"** means a receipt for the purposes of subsection 127(3) of the Act containing information as provided in subsection 2000(1) or (2), as the case may be;

**"official receipt form"** means any printed form that a registered agent or an official agent, as the case may be, has that is capable of being completed, or that originally was intended to be completed, as an official receipt of the registered agent or official agent, as the case may be.

(2) In this Part, "official agent", "polling day", "registered agent" and "registered party" have the meanings assigned to them by section 2 of the *Canada Elections Act* and "officially nominated candidate" means a person in respect of whom a nomination paper and deposit have been filed as referred to in the definition "official nomination" in that section of that Act.

**Definitions [Reg. 2002]**: "amount" — ITA 248(1); "Canada" — ITA 255, *Interpretation Act* 35(1); "official agent" — Reg. 2002(2); "official receipt" — Reg. 2002(1); "person" — ITA 248(1); "registered agent" — Reg. 2002(1).

## PART XXI — ELECTIONS IN RESPECT OF SURPLUSES

**2100. Reduction of tax-paid undistributed surplus on hand or 1971 capital surplus on hand** — [No longer relevant]

**Notes**: Reg. 2100 provides rules for an election under ITA 83(1) in respect of a dividend payable before 1979.

**2101. Capital dividends and life insurance capital dividends payable by private corporations** — Any election under subsection 83(2) of the Act in respect of a dividend payable by a private corporation shall be made by filing with the Minister the following documents:

(a) the form prescribed by the Minister;

(b) where the directors of the corporation are legally entitled to administer the affairs of the corporation, a certified copy of their resolution authorizing the election to be made;

(c) where the directors of the corporation are not legally entitled to administer the affairs of the corporation, a certified copy of the authorization of the making of the election by the person or persons legally entitled to administer the affairs of the corporation;

(d) where the election has been made under subsection 83(2) of the Act and paragraph (e) is not applicable, schedules showing the computation of the amount, immediately before the election, of the corporation's

   (i) capital dividend account, and

   (ii) 1971 undistributed income on hand, if any, if the dividend was payable on or prior to March 31, 1977; and

(e) where the election has been made under subsection 83(2) of the Act and subsection 83(3) of the Act is applicable, schedules showing the computation of the amount, immediately before the dividend became payable, of the corporation's

   (i) capital dividend account, and

   (ii) 1971 undistributed income on hand, if any, if the dividend was payable on or prior to March 31, 1977.

**Interpretation Bulletins**: IT-66R6: Capital dividends.

**Forms**: T2054: Election in respect of a capital dividend under subsection 83(2).

**2102. Tax on 1971 undistributed income on hand** — (1) [Revoked]

(2) [No longer relevant]

**Notes**: Reg. 2102(2) provides rules for making a retroactive election under 196(1.1) (now repealed) in respect of a dividend payable before 1979.

**Definitions [Reg. 2102]**: "amount" — ITA 248(1); "corporation" — ITA 248(1), *Interpretation Act* 35(1); "dividend", "Minister", "person", "prescribed" — ITA 248(1).

**2103.** [Revoked]

**2104. Capital gains dividends payable by mutual fund corporations and investment corporations** — Any election under subsection 131(1) of the Act in respect of a dividend payable by a mutual fund corporation or an investment corporation shall be made by filing with the Minister the following documents:

(a) the form prescribed by the Minister;

(b) where the directors of the corporation are legally entitled to administer the affairs of the corporation, a certified copy of their resolution authorizing the election to be made;

(c) where the directors of the corporation are not legally entitled to administer the affairs of the corporation, a certified copy of the authorization of the making of the election by the person or persons legally entitled to administer the affairs of the corporation;

(d) where paragraph (f) is not applicable, a schedule showing the computation of the amount, immediately before the election, of the corporation's capital gains dividend account; and

(e) [Revoked]

(f) where subsection 131(1.1) of the Act is applicable, a schedule showing the computation of the amount, immediately before the earlier of

   (i) the date the dividend became payable, and

   (ii) the first day on which any part of the dividend was paid,

of the corporation's capital gains dividend account.

**Definitions [Reg. 2104]**: "amount" — ITA 248(1); "capital gain" — ITA 39(1), 248(1); "corporation" — ITA 248(1), *Interpretation Act* 35(1); "dividend" — ITA 248(1); "investment corporation" — ITA 130(3), 248(1); "Minister" — ITA 248(1); "mutual fund corporation" — ITA 131(8), 248(1); "person", "prescribed" — ITA 248(1).

**Forms**: T2055: Election in respect of a capital gains dividend under subsection 131(1).

**2104.1 [Capital gains dividends payable by mortgage investment corporations]** — Any election under subsection 130.1(4) of the Act in respect of a dividend payable by a mortgage investment corporation shall be made by filing with the Minister the following documents:

(a) the documents referred to in paragraphs 2104(a) to (c); and

(b) a schedule showing the computation of the capital gains dividend in accordance with paragraph 130.1(4)(a) of the Act.

**Definitions [Reg. 2104.1]**: "capital gain" — ITA 39(1), 248(1); "dividend", "Minister" — ITA 248(1); "mortgage investment corporation" — ITA 130.1(6), 248(1).

**Forms**: T2012: Election in respect of a capital gains dividend under subsection 130.1(4); T2143: Election not to be a restricted financial institution.

**2105. Capital gains dividends payable by non-resident-owned investment corporations** — Any election under subsection 133(7.1) of the Act in respect of a dividend payable by a non-resident-owned investment corporation shall be made by filing with the Minister the following documents:

(a) the form prescribed by the Minister;

(b) where the directors of the corporation are legally entitled to administer the affairs of the corporation, a certified copy of their resolution authorizing the election to be made;

(c) where the directors of the corporation are not legally entitled to administer the affairs of the corporation, a certified copy of the authorization of the making of the election by the person or persons legally entitled to administer the affairs of the corporation;

(d) where paragraph (e) is not applicable, a schedule showing the computation of the amount, immediately before the election, of the corporation's capital gains dividend account; and

(e) where subsection 133(7.3) of the Act is applicable, a schedule showing the computation of the amount, immediately before the earlier of

(i) the date the dividend became payable, and

(ii) the first day on which any part of the dividend was paid,

of the corporation's capital gains dividend account.

**Definitions [Reg. 2105]**: "amount" — ITA 248(1); "capital gain" — ITA 39(1), 248(1); "corporation" — ITA 248(1), *Interpretation Act* 35(1); "dividend", "Minister" — ITA 248(1); "non-resident-owned investment corporation" — ITA 133(8), 248(1); "person", "prescribed" — ITA 248(1).

**Forms**: T2053: Election by a Canadian corporation in respect of a dividend out of tax-paid undistributed surplus on hand, and/or 1971 capital surplus on hand; T2054: Election by a private corporation in respect of a dividend out of capital dividend account; T2055: Election to pay a capital gains dividend under subsection 131(1); T2056: Election to pay tax on 1971 undistributed income on hand; T2063:

Election in respect of a capital gains dividend under subsection 133(7.1).

**2106. Alternative to additional tax on excessive elections [for capital dividends]** — Any election under subsection 184(3) of the Act in respect of a dividend that was paid or payable by a corporation shall be made by

(a) filing with the Minister the following documents:

(i) a letter stating that the corporation elects under subsection 184(3) of the Act in respect of the said dividend,

(ii) where the directors of the corporation are legally entitled to administer the affairs of the corporation, a certified copy of

(A) their resolution authorizing the election to be made, and

(B) their declaration that the election is made with the concurrence of all shareholders who received or were entitled to receive all or any portion of the said dividend and whose addresses were known to the corporation,

(iii) where the directors of the corporation are not legally entitled to administer the affairs of the corporation, a certified copy of

(A) the authorization of the making of the election, and

(B) the declaration that the election is made with the concurrence of all shareholders who received or were entitled to receive all or any portion of the said dividend and whose addresses were known to the corporation,

by the person or persons legally entitled to administer the affairs of the corporation,

(iv) a schedule showing the following information:

(A) the date of the notice of assessment of the tax that would, but for the election, have been payable under Part III of the Act,

(B) the full amount of the said dividend,

(C) the date the said dividend became payable, or the first day on which any part of the said dividend was paid if that day is earlier,

(D) the portion, if any, of the said dividend described in paragraph 184(3)(a) of the Act,

(E) the portion, if any, of the said dividend that the corporation is claiming for the purposes of an election in respect thereof under subsection 83(1) or (2), 130.1(4) or 131(1) of the Act pursuant to paragraph 184(3)(b) of the Act, and

(F) the portion, if any, of the said dividend that is deemed by paragraph 184(3)(c) of the Act to be a separate dividend that is a taxable dividend; and

(b) making an election in prescribed manner and prescribed form in respect of any amount claimed under paragraph 184(3)(b) of the Act.

**Definitions [Reg. 2106]:** "amount", "assessment" — ITA 248(1); "corporation" — ITA 248(1), *Interpretation Act* 35(1); "dividend", "Minister", "person", "prescribed", "shareholder" — ITA 248(1); "taxable dividend" — ITA 89(1), 248(1).

**Interpretation Bulletins:** IT-66R6: Capital dividends.

**2107. Tax-deferred preferred series** — The following series of classes of capital stock are hereby prescribed for the purposes of subsection 83(6) of the Act to be tax-deferred preferred series:

(a) The Algoma Steel Corporation, Limited, 8% Tax Deferred Preference Shares Series A;

(b) Aluminum Company of Canada, Limited, $2.00 Tax Deferred Retractable Preferred Shares;

(c) Brascan Limited, 8½% Tax Deferred Preferred Shares Series A;

(d) Canada Permanent Mortgage Corporation, 6¾% Tax Deferred Convertible Preference Shares Series A; and

(e) Cominco Ltd., $2.00 Tax Deferred Exchangeable Preferred Shares Series A.

**Definitions [Reg. 2107]:** "Canada" — ITA 255, *Interpretation Act* 35(1); "prescribed" — ITA 248(1).

## PART XXII — SECURITY INTERESTS

**2200.** Where under subsection 220(4) of the Act the Minister has accepted, as security for payment of taxes, a mortgage or other security or guarantee, he may, by a document in writing, discharge such mortgage or other security or guarantee.

**Notes:** Reg. 2200 amended to change "mortgage, hypothec" to "mortgage" by P.C. 1994-1817, effective November 30, 1994. The change was intended to be non-substantive.

**Definitions [Reg. 2200]:** "Minister" — ITA 248(1); "security", "writing" — *Interpretation Act* 35(1).

**2201. (1)** For the purpose of subsection 227(4.2) of the Act, **"prescribed security interest"**, in relation to an amount deemed by subsection 227(4) of the Act to be held in trust by a person, means that part of a mortgage securing the performance of an obligation of the person, that encumbers land or a building, where the mortgage is registered pursuant to the appropriate land registration system before the time the amount is deemed to be held in trust by the person.

**(2)** For the purpose of subsection (1), where, at any time after 1999, the person referred to in subsection (1) fails to pay an amount deemed by subsection 227(4) of the Act to be held in trust by the person, as required under the Act, the amount of the prescribed security interest referred to in subsection (1) is deemed not to exceed the amount by which the amount, at that time, of the obligation outstanding secured by the mortgage exceeds the total of

(a) all amounts each of which is the value determined at the time of the failure, having regard to all the circumstances including the existence of any deemed trust for the benefit of Her Majesty pursuant to subsection 227(4) of the Act, of all the rights of the secured creditor securing the obligation, whether granted by the person or not, including guarantees or rights of set-off but not including the mortgage referred to in subsection (1), and

(b) all amounts applied after the time of the failure on account of the obligation,

so long as any amount deemed under any enactment administered by the Minister, other than the *Excise Tax Act*, to be held in trust by the person, remains unpaid.

**(3)** For greater certainty, a prescribed security interest includes the amount of insurance or expropriation proceeds relating to land or a building that is the subject of a registered mortgage interest, adjusted after 1999 in accordance with subsection (2), but does not include a lien, a priority or any other security interest created by statute, an assignment or hypothec of rents or leases, or a mortgage interest in any equipment or fixtures that a mortgagee or any other person has the right absolutely or conditionally to remove or dispose of separately from the land or building.

**Notes:** Reg. 2201 added by P.C. 1999-1341, effective June 15, 1994. (The heading for Part XXII was also changed from "Discharge of Security for Taxes" at the same time.)

See Notes to ITA 227(4).

## PART XXIII — PRINCIPAL RESIDENCES

**2300.** Any election by a taxpayer under subparagraph 40(2)(c)(ii) of the Act shall be made by attaching to the return of income required by section 150 of the Act to be filed by him for his taxation year in which the disposition of the land, including the property that was his principal residence, occurred, a letter signed by the taxpayer

(a) stating that he is electing under that subparagraph;

(b) stating the number of taxation years ending after the acquisition date (within the meaning assigned by paragraph 40(2)(b) of the Act) for which the property was his principal residence and during which he was resident in Canada; and

(c) giving a description of the property sufficient to identify it with the property designated as his principal residence.

**Definitions [Reg. 2300]:** "disposition" — ITA 248(1); "property" — ITA 248(1); "resident in Canada" — ITA 250; "taxation year" — ITA 249; "taxpayer" — ITA 248(1).

**2301.** Any designation by a taxpayer under subparagraph 54(g)(iii) [54"principal residence"(c)] of the Act shall be made in the return of income required by section 150 of the Act to be filed by him for any taxation year of the taxpayer in which

(a) he has disposed of a property that is to be designated as his principal residence; or

(b) he has granted an option to acquire such property.

**Definitions [Reg. 2301]:** "disposed" — ITA 248(1)"disposition"; "property" — ITA 248(1); "taxation year" — ITA 249; "taxpayer" — ITA 248(1).

**Interpretation Bulletins:** IT-120R5: Principal residence.

**Forms:** T1079: Designation of a property as a principal residence by a personal trust; T1079-WS: Principal residence worksheet; T2091: Designation of a property as a principal residence by an individual; T2091(IND)WS: Principal residence worksheet.

# PART XXIV — INSURERS

**2400. (1) Definitions** — The definitions in this subsection apply in this Part.

**"attributed surplus"** of a non-resident insurer for a taxation year is the total of

(a) the insurer's property and casualty surplus for the year; and

(b) either,

(i) if the insurer elects for the year in prescribed form and manner, 50% of the total of

(A) the amount that would have been determined at the end of the year in respect of the insurer under subparagraph (a)(ii) of the definition "Canadian investment fund", and

(B) the amount that would have been determined at the end of the preceding taxation year in respect of the insurer under subparagraph (a)(ii) of the definition "Canadian investment fund",

each amount being calculated as if throughout the year and the preceding taxation year the insurer had been a life insurer resident in Canada and had not carried on any insurance business other than a life insurance business or an accident and sickness insurance business, or

(ii) if the insurer does not elect under subparagraph (i) for the year, 120% of the total of all amounts each of which is 50% of the amount determined in accordance with regulations or guidelines made under Part XIII of the *Insurance Companies Act* to be the margin of assets in Canada over liabilities in Canada required to be maintained by the insurer as at the end of the year or as at the end of the preceding taxation year in respect of an insurance business carried on in Canada (other than a property and casualty insurance business).

**"Canadian business property"** of an insurer for a taxation year in respect of an insurance business means

(a) if the insurer was resident in Canada throughout the year and did not carry on an insurance business outside Canada in the year, the property used or held by it in the year in the course of carrying on the business in Canada; and

(b) in any other case, designated insurance property of the insurer for the year in respect of the business.

**"Canadian equity property"** of a person or partnership (in this definition referred to as the "taxpayer") at any time means property of the taxpayer that is

(a) a share of the capital stock of, or an income bond, income debenture, small business development bond or small business bond issued by, a person (other than a corporation affiliated with the taxpayer) resident in Canada or a Canadian partnership; or

(b) that proportion of property that is shares of the capital stock of an entitiy that is a corporation affiliated with the taxpayer or an interest in an entity that is a partnership or trust that

(i) the total value for the taxation year that includes that time of Canadian equity property of the entity,

is of

(ii) the total value for the year or period of all property of the entity.

**Related Provisions:** Reg. 2400(7) — No double counting.

**"Canadian investment fund"** of an insurer at the end of a taxation year means

(a) in the case of a life insurer resident in Canada, the total of

(i) the amount determined by the formula

$$A - B$$

where

A is the amount of the insurer's Canadian reserve liabilities as at the end of the year (to the extent that the amount exceeds the amount of surplus appropriations included in that amount), and

B is the amount of the insurer's Canadian outstanding premiums and policy loans as at the end of the year (to the extent that the amount of the premiums and loans are in respect of policies referred to in paragraphs (a) to (c) of the definition "Canadian reserve liabilities" and were not otherwise deducted in computing the amount of the insurer's Canadian reserve liabilities as at the end of the year), and

(ii) the greater of

(A) the amount determined by the formula

$$C + ((D - E + F) \times (G/H))$$

where

C is 8% of the amount determined under subparagraph (i),

D is the total of all amounts each of which is the amount of a deferred realized net gain or an amount expressed as a negative number of a deferred realized net loss of the insurer as at the end of the year,

E is the total of all amounts each of which is the amount of an item reported as an asset that is owned by the insurer at the end of the year and is a share of the capital stock of, or a debt owing to the insurer by, a financial institution affiliated with the insurer,

F is the total of all amounts each of which is the amount as at the end of the year of a debt assumed or incurred by the insurer in respect of the acquisition of an asset described in E (or another property for which an asset described in E is a substituted property),

G is the amount of the insurer's weighted Canadian liabilities as at the end of the year, and

H is the amount of the insurer's weighted total liabilities as at the end of the year, and

(B) the amount determined by the formula

$$(I - J + K + L) \times (M/N)$$

where

I is the total of all amounts each of which is the amount of an item reported as an asset of the insurer as at the end of the year (other than an item that at no time in the year was used or held by the insurer in the course of carrying on an insurance business),

J is the total of all amounts each of which is the amount of an item reported as a liability of the insurer (other than a liability that was at any time in the year connected with an asset that was not used or held by the insurer in the course of carrying on an insurance business at any time in the year) as at the end of the year in respect of an insurance business carried on by the insurer in the year,

K is the total of all amounts each of which is an amount of an item reported by the insurer as at the end of the year as a general provision or allowance for impairment in respect of investment property of the insurer for the year,

L is the total of all amounts each of which is an amount of a deferred realized net gain or an amount expressed as a negative number of a deferred realized net loss of the insurer as at the end of the year,

M is the amount of the insurer's weighted Canadian liabilities as at the end of the year, and

N is the amount of the insurer's weighted total liabilities as at the end of the year; and

(b) in the case of a non-resident insurer, the total of

(i) the amount, if any, by which the amount of the insurer's Canadian reserve liabilities as at the end of the year exceeds the total of

(A) the amount of the insurer's Canadian outstanding premiums, policy loans and reinsurance recoverables as at the end of the year (to the extent that the amount of the premiums, loans or recoverables are in respect of policies referred to in paragraphs (a) to (c) of the definition "Canadian reserve liabilities" and were not otherwise deducted in computing the amount of the insurer's Canadian reserve liabilities as at the end of the year), and

(B) the amount of the insurer's deferred acquisition expenses as at the end of the year in respect of its property and casualty insurance business carried on in Canada, and

(ii) the greatest of

(A) the total of

(I) 8% of the amount determined under subparagraph (i), and

(II) the total of all amounts each of which is an amount of a deferred realized net gain or an amount expressed as a negative number of a deferred realized net loss of the insurer as at the end of the year in respect of an insurance business carried on by the insurer in Canada,

(B) the amount, if any, by which the total of

(I) the amount of the insurer's surplus funds derived from operations as at the end of its preceding taxation year,

(II) the total determined under subclause (A)(II) to the extent not included in subclause (I), and

(III) the total of all amounts in respect of which the insurer made an election under subsection 219(4) or (5.2) of the Act, each of which is an amount included in the total determined in respect of the insurer under subparagraph 219(4)(a)(i.1) of the Act as at the end of its preceding taxation year

exceeds

(IV) the total of amounts determined in respect of the insurer under subparagraphs 219(4)(a)(ii), (iii), (iv) and (v) of the Act, as at the end of the year, and

(C) the total of

(I) the amount of the insurer's attributed surplus for the year, and

(II) if the amount under subclause (I) was determined without the taxpayer electing under subparagraph (b)(i) of the definition "attributed surplus", the amount determined under subclause (A)(II).

**Related Provisions**: Reg. 2400(6) — Interpretation for cl. (a)(ii)(B).

**"Canadian investment property"** of an insurer for a taxation year means an investment property of the insurer for the year (other than, if the insurer is non-resident, property established by the insurer as not being effectively connected with its Canadian insurance businesses carried on in Canada in the year) that is, at any time in the year

(a) real property situated in Canada;

(b) depreciable property situated in Canada or leased to a person resident in Canada for use inside and outside of Canada;

(c) a mortgage, a hypothec, an agreement of sale or any other form of indebtedness in respect of property described in paragraph (a) or (b);

(d) a Canadian equity property;

(e) a Canadian resource property;

(f) a deposit balance of the insurer that is in Canadian currency;

(g) a bond, debenture or other form of indebtedness, in Canadian currency, issued by

(i) a person resident in Canada or a Canadian partnership, or

(ii) the government of Canada, a province or any of their political subdivisions; or

(h) a property that is

(i) a share of the capital stock of a corporation resident in Canada that is affiliated with the insurer, if at least 75% of the total value for the year of all property of the corporation is attributable to property that would be Canadian investment property if it were owned by an insurer, or

(ii) an interest in a Canadian partnership, or a trust resident in Canada, if at least 75% of the total value for the year of all property of the partnership or trust, as the case may be, is attributable to property that would be Canadian investment property if it were owned by an insurer; or

(i) an amount due or an amount accrued to the insurer on account of income that

(i) is from designated insurance property for the year that is Canadian investment property of the insurer for the year because of any of paragraphs (a) to (h), and

(ii) was assumed in computing the insurer's Canadian reserve liabilities for the year.

**"Canadian outstanding premiums"** of an insurer at any time means the total of all amounts each of which is the amount of an outstanding premium of the insurer with respect to an insurance policy at that time, to the extent that the amount of the premium has been assumed to have been paid in computing the insurer's Canadian reserve liabilities as at that time.

**"Canadian reserve liabilities"** of an insurer as at the end of a taxation year means the total amount of the insurer's liabilities and reserves (other than liabilities and reserves in respect of a segregated fund) in respect of

(a) life insurance policies in Canada;

(b) fire insurance policies issued or effected in respect of property situated in Canada; or

(c) insurance policies of any other class covering risks ordinarily within Canada at the time the policy was issued or effected.

**"deposit balance"** of an insurer means an amount standing to the insurer's credit as or on account of amounts deposited with a corporation authorized to accept deposits or to carry on the business of offering to the public its services as a trustee.

**"equity limit"** of an insurer for a taxation year means

(a) in respect of a life insurer resident in Canada, that proportion of the total of all amounts each of which is the value for the year of an equity property of the insurer that

(i) the insurer's weighted Canadian liabilities as at the end of the year

is of

(ii) the insurer's weighted total liabilities as at the end of the year;

2133

(b) in respect of a non-resident insurer (other than a life insurer), 25% of the total of

(i) the amount, if any, by which the insurer's mean Canadian reserve liabilities for the year exceeds the total of

(A) 50% of the total of its premiums receivable and deferred acquisition expenses as at the end of the year and its premiums receivable and deferred acquisition expenses as at the end of its preceding taxation year to the extent that those amounts were included in the insurer's Canadian reserve liabilities for the year or the preceding taxation year, as the case may be, in respect of the insurer's business in Canada, and

(B) 50% of the total of its reinsurance recoverables as at the end of the year and its reinsurance recoverables as at the end of the preceding taxation year that are in respect of policies referred to in paragraphs (b) and (c) of the definition "Canadian reserve liabilities", and

(ii) the insurer's property and casualty surplus for the year; and

(c) in respect of a non-resident life insurer, the total of

(i) either

(A) if the insurer makes an election referred to in subparagraph (b)(i) of the definition "attributed surplus" for the year, the greater of

(I) that proportion of the total of all amounts each of which is the value for the year of an equity property of the insurer that

1. the insurer's weighted Canadian liabilities as at the end of the year

is of

2. the insurer's weighted total liabilities as at the end of year, and

(II) 8% of the insurer's mean Canadian investment fund for the year, or

(B) if the insurer does not make this election for the year, 8% of the insurer's mean Canadian investment fund for the year,

(ii) 25% of the amount, if any, by which

(A) the insurer's mean Canadian reserve liabilities for the year (determined on the assumption that the insurer's property and casualty insurance business carried on in Canada during the year was its only insurance business carried on in Canada that year)

exceeds

(B) 50% of the total of its premiums receivable and deferred acquisition expenses as at the end of the year and its premiums receivable and deferred acquisition expenses as at the end of its preceding taxation year, to the extent that those amounts were included in the insurer's Canadian reserve liabilities as at the end of the year or the preceding taxation year, as the case may be, (determined on the assumption that the insurer's property and casualty insurance business carried on in Canada during the year was its only insurance business carried on in Canada that year), and

(iii) 25% of the insurer's property and casualty surplus for the year.

**"equity property"** of a person or partnership (in this definition referred to as the "taxpayer") at any time means property of the taxpayer that is

(a) a share of the capital stock of, or an income bond, income debenture, small business development bond or small business bond issued by, another person (other than a corporation affiliated with the taxpayer) or partnership; or

(b) that proportion of property that is shares of the capital stock of a corporation affiliated with the taxpayer or an interest in a partnership or trust that

(i) the total value for the taxation year or fiscal period of the corporation, partnership or trust that includes that time of equity property of the corporation, partnership or trust, as the case may be,

is of

(ii) the total value for the year or period of all property of the corporation, partnership or trust, as the case may be.

**Related Provisions**: Reg. 2400(7) — No double counting.

**"financial institution"** means a corporation that is

(a) a corporation described in any of paragraphs (a) to (e) of the definition "restricted financial institution" in subsection 248(1) of the Act; or

(b) a particular corporation all or substantially all of the value of the assets of which is attributable to shares or indebtedness of one or more corporations described in paragraph (a) to which the particular corporation is affiliated.

**"foreign policy loan"** means an amount advanced by an insurer to a policyholder in accordance with the terms and conditions of a life insurance policy, other than a life insurance policy in Canada.

**"gross Canadian life investment income"** of a life insurer for a taxation year means the amount, if any, by which

(a) the total of all amounts each of which is

(i) the insurer's gross investment revenue for the year, to the extent that the revenue is from Canadian business property of the insurer for the year in respect of the insurer's life insurance business,

(ii) the amount included in computing the insurer's income for the year under paragraph 138(9)(b) of the Act,

(iii) the portion of the amount deducted under paragraph 20(1)(l) of the Act in computing the insurer's income for its preceding taxation year that was in respect of Canadian business property of the insurer for that year in respect of the insurer's life insurance business,

(iv) the amount included under section 142.4 of the Act in computing the insurer's income for the year in respect of property disposed of by the insurer that was, in the taxation year of disposition, Canadian business property of the insurer for that year in respect of the insurer's life insurance business,

(v) the insurer's gain for the year from the disposition of a Canadian business property of the insurer for the year in respect of the insurer's life insurance business, other than a capital property or a property in respect of the disposition of which section 142.4 of the Act applies, or

(vi) the insurer's taxable capital gain for the year from the disposition of a Canadian business property of the insurer for the year in respect of the insurer's life insurance business

exceeds

(b) the total of all amounts each of which is

(i) the portion of the amount deducted under paragraph 20(1)(l) of the Act in computing the insurer's income for the year that is in respect of Canadian business property of the insurer for the year in respect of the insurer's life insurance business,

(ii) the amount deductible under section 142.4 of the Act in computing the insurer's income for the year in respect of a property disposed of by the insurer that was, in the taxation year of disposition, a Canadian business property of the insurer for that year in respect of the insurer's life insurance business,

(iii) the insurer's loss for the year from the disposition of a Canadian business property of the insurer for the year in respect of the insurer's life insurance business, other than a capital property or a property in respect of the disposition of which section 142.4 of the Act applies, or

(iv) the insurer's allowable capital loss for the year from the disposition of a Canadian business property of the insurer for the year in respect of the insurer's life insurance business.

**"investment property"** of an insurer for a taxation year means non-segregated property owned by the insurer, other than a policy loan payable to the insurer, at any time in the year that is

(a) property acquired by the insurer for the purpose of earning gross investment revenue in the year, other than property that is

(i) property, a proportion of which is investment property of the insurer for the year because of paragraph (b),

(ii) a share of the capital stock of, or a debt owing to the insurer by, a corporation affiliated with the insurer, or

(iii) an interest in a partnership or trust;

(b) that proportion, if any, of property of the insurer that is land, depreciable property or property that would have been depreciable property if it had been situated in Canada and used or held by the insurer in the year in the course of carrying on an insurance business in Canada, that

(i) the use made of the property by the insurer in the year for the purpose of earning gross investment revenue in the year

is of

(ii) the whole use made of the property by the insurer in the year;

(c) if the insurer is a life insurer, property described in any of paragraphs 138(4.4)(a) to (d) of the Act;

(d) either

(i) a share of the capital stock of, or a debt owing to the insurer by, a corporation (other than a corporation that is a financial institution) affiliated with the insurer, if the total value for the year of all investment property of the corporation for the year is not less than 75% of the total value for the year of all its property, or

(ii) an interest in a partnership or trust, if the total value for the year of all investment property of the partnership or trust, as the case may be, for the year is not less than 75% of the total value for the year of all its property,

and for the purpose of this paragraph (other than for the purpose of determining whether a corporation is a financial institution) every corporation, partnership and trust is deemed to be an insurer; or

(e) an amount due or an amount accrued to the insurer on account of income that

(i) is from designated insurance property for the year that is investment property of the insurer for the year because of any of paragraphs (a) to (d), and

(ii) was assumed in computing the insurer's Canadian reserve liabilities for the year.

"**mean Canadian outstanding premiums**" of an insurer for a taxation year means 50% of the total of

(a) its Canadian outstanding premiums as at the end of the year, and

(b) its Canadian outstanding premiums as at the end of its preceding taxation year.

"**mean Canadian reserve liabilities**" of an insurer for a taxation year means 50% of the total of

(a) its Canadian reserve liabilities as at the end of the year, and

(b) its Canadian reserve liabilities as at the end of its preceding taxation year.

"**mean maximum tax actuarial reserve**" in respect of a particular class of life insurance policies of an insurer for a taxation year means 50% of the total of

(a) its maximum tax actuarial reserve for that class of policies for the year, and

(b) its maximum tax actuarial reserve for that class of policies for its preceding taxation year.

"**mean policy loans**" of an insurer for a taxation year means 50% of the total of

(a) its policy loans as at the end of the year, and

(b) its policy loans as at the end of its preceding taxation year.

"**outstanding premiums**" of an insurer with respect to an insurance policy at any time means premiums due to the insurer under the policy at that time but unpaid.

"**property and casualty surplus**" of an insurer for a taxation year means the total of

(a) 7.5% of the total of

(i) its unearned premium reserve as at the end of the year (net of reinsurance recoverables in respect of the reserve) in respect of its property and casualty insurance business,

(ii) its unearned premium reserve as at the end of its preceding taxation year (net of reinsurance recoverables in respect of the reserve) in respect of its property and casualty insurance business,

(iii) its provision for unpaid claims and adjustment expenses as at the end of the year (net of reinsurance recoverables in respect of the provision) in respect of its property and casualty insurance business, and

(iv) its provision for unpaid claims and adjustment expenses as at the end of its preceding taxation year (net of reinsurance recoverables in respect of the provision) in respect of its property and casualty insurance business,

and

(b) 50% of the total of

(i) its investment valuation reserve as at the end of the year in respect of its property and casualty insurance business, and

(ii) its investment valuation reserve as at the end of its preceding taxation year in respect of its property and casualty insurance business.

"**reinsurance recoverable**" means

(a) in respect of an insurance business (other than a life insurance business) of a non-resident insurer, the total of all amounts each of which is an item reported as an asset of the insurer as at the end of a taxation year in respect of an amount recoverable from a reinsurer for unearned premiums or unpaid claims and adjustment expenses in respect of the reinsurance of a policy that was issued in the course of carrying on the insurance business to the extent that the amount is included in the insurer's Canadian reserve liabilities at that time and the amount is not an outstanding premium, policy loan or investment property; and

(b) in any other case, nil.

"**value**" for a taxation year of a property of a person or partnership (in this definition referred to as the "owner") means

(a) in the case of a property that is a mortgage, hypothec, an agreement of sale or an investment property that is a deposit balance, the amount, if any, by which

(i) the amount obtained when the gross investment revenue of the owner for the year from the property is divided by the average rate of interest earned by the owner (expressed as an annual rate) on the amortized cost of the property during the year

exceeds

(ii) the amount obtained when the interest payable by the owner, for the period in the year during which the property was held by the owner, on debt assumed or incurred by the owner in respect of the acquisition of the property (or another property for which the property is a substituted property) is divided by the average rate of interest payable by the owner (expressed as an annual rate) on the debt for the year;

(b) in the case of a property that is an amount due or an amount accrued to the owner, the total of the amounts due or accrued at the end of each day in the year divided by the number of days in the year;

(c) in the case of a property (other than a property referred to in paragraph (a) or (b)) that was not owned by the owner throughout the year, the amount, if any, by which

(i) that proportion of

(A) the carrying value of the property as at the end of the preceding taxation year, if the property was owned by the owner at that time,

(B) the carrying value of the property as at the end of the year, if the property was owned by the owner at that time and not at the end of the preceding taxation year, and

(C) in any other case, the cost of the property to the owner when it was acquired,

that the number of days that are in the year and at the end of which the owner owned the property is of the number of days in the year,

exceeds

(ii) the amount obtained when the interest payable by the owner, for the period in the year during which the property was held by the owner, on debt assumed or incurred by the owner in respect of the acquisition of the property (or another property for which the property is a substituted property) is divided by the average rate of interest payable by the owner (expressed as an annual rate) on the debt for the year; and

(d) in the case of any other property, the amount, if any, by which

(i) 50% of the total of

(A) the carrying value of the property as at the end of the year, and

(B) the carrying value of the property as at the end of the preceding taxation year

exceeds

(ii) the amount obtained when the interest payable by the owner, for the period in the year during which the property was held by the owner, on debt assumed or incurred by the owner in respect of the acquisition of the property (or another property for which the property is a substituted property) is divided by the average rate of interest payable by the owner (expressed as an annual rate) on the debt for the year.

**"weighted Canadian liabilities"** of an insurer as at the end of a taxation year means the total of

(a) 300% of the amount, if any, by which

(i) the total of all amounts each of which is an amount that is in respect of an insurance business carried on by the insurer in Canada and that is reported as a liability (other than a liability in respect of an amount payable out of a segregated fund) of the insurer in respect of a life insurance policy in Canada (other than an annuity) or an accident and sickness insurance policy as at the end of the year

exceeds

(ii) the total of the insurer's policy loans (other than policy loans in respect of annuities) as at the end of the year, and

(b) the amount, if any, by which

(i) the total of all amounts each of which is an amount in respect of an insurance business carried on by the insurer in Canada that is reported as a liability of the insurer as at the end of the year, except to the extent that the amount is

(A) in respect of an insurance policy (other than an annuity) described in subparagraph (a)(i),

(B) a liability in respect of an amount payable out of a segregated fund, or

(C) a debt incurred or assumed by the insurer to acquire a property of the insurer,

exceeds

(ii) the total of the insurer's policy loans in respect of annuities as at the end of the year.

**"weighted total liabilities"** of an insurer as at the end of a taxation year means the total of

(a) 300% of the amount, if any, by which

(i) the total of all amounts each of which is an amount that is in respect of an insurance business carried on by the insurer and that is reported as a liability (other than a liability in respect of an amount payable out of a segregated fund) of the insurer in respect of a life insurance policy (other than an annuity) or an accident and sickness insurance policy

exceeds

(ii) the total of the insurer's policy loans and foreign policy loans (other than policy loans and foreign policy loans in respect of annuities) as at the end of the year, and

(b) the amount of any, by which

(i) the total of all amounts each of which is an amount that is in respect of an insurance business carried on by the insurer and that is reported as a liability of the insurer as at the end of the year, except to the extent that the amount is

(A) in respect of an insurance policy (other than an annuity) described in subparagraph (a)(i),

(B) a liability in respect of an amount payable out of a segregated fund, or

(C) a debt incurred or assumed by the insurer to acquire a property of the insurer,

exceeds

(ii) the total of the insurer's policy loans and foreign policy loans in respect of annuities as at the end of the year.

(2) **Carrying value** — For the purposes of this Part, the carrying value of a taxpayer's property for a taxation year, except as otherwise provided in this Part, means

(a) if the taxpayer is an insurer, the amounts reflected in the taxpayer's non-consolidated balance sheet as at the end of the taxation year accepted (or, if that non-consolidated balance sheet was not prepared, the taxpayer's non-consolidated balance sheet as at the end of the year that would have been accepted) by the Superintendent of Financial Institutions, in the case of an insurer that is required under the *Insurance Companies Act* to report to that Superintendent, or by the superintendent of insurance or other similar officer or authority of the province under the laws of which the insurer is incorporated or otherwise formed, in the case of an insurer that is required by law to report to that officer or authority; and

(b) in any other case, the amounts that would be reflected in the taxpayer's non-consolidated balance sheet as at the end of the taxation year if that balance sheet were prepared in accordance with generally accepted accounting principles.

(3) **Amount or item reported** — A reference in this Part to an amount or item reported as an asset or a liability of a taxpayer as at the end of a taxation year means an amount or item that is reported as a liability in the taxpayer's non-consolidated balance sheet as at the end of the year accepted (or, if that non-consolidated balance sheet was not prepared, the taxpayer's non-consolidated balance sheet as at the end of the year that would have been accepted) by the Superintendent of Financial Institutions, in the case of an insurer that is required under the *Insurance Companies Act* to report to that Superintendent, or by the superintendent of insurance or other similar officer or authority of the province under the laws of which the insurer is incorporated or otherwise formed, in the case of an insurer that is required by law to report to that officer or authority.

(4) **Application of certain definitions** — For the purposes

(a) of subsection 138(14) of the Act, the expressions **"Canadian investment fund for a taxation year"**, **"specified Canadian assets"** and **"value for the taxation year"** have the meanings prescribed for them by subsection 2404(1) as it read in its application to the 1977 taxation year; and

(b) of subsection 219(7) of the Act, the expressions **"attributed surplus"** and **"Canadian investment fund"** have the meaning prescribed for them by subsection (1).

(5) **Deeming rules for certain assets** — For the purposes of this Part, other than subsection 2401(6), an asset of an insurer is deemed not to have been used or held by the insurer in a taxation year in the course of carrying on an insurance business if the asset

(a) is owned by the insurer at the end of the year; and

(b) is a share of the capital stock of, or a debt owing to the insurer by, a financial institution affiliated with the insurer during each of the days in the year during which the insurer owned the asset.

(6) **[Idem]** — For the purposes of clause (a)(ii)(B) of the definition "Canadian investment fund" in subsection (1), an asset of an insurer is deemed not to have been used or held by the insurer in a taxation year in the course of carrying on an insurance business if the asset

(a) is owned by the insurer at the end of the year; and

(b) is

(i) goodwill which arose as a result of an amalgamation, a winding-up of an affiliated financial institution, or the assumption by the insurer of any obligation of another insurer with which the insurer deals at arm's length if a reserve in respect of the obligation

(A) may be claimed by the insurer under paragraph 20(7)(c) or subparagraph 138(3)(a)(i) or (ii) of the Act, or

(B) could be claimed by the insurer under paragraph 20(7)(c) or subparagraph 138(3)(a)(i) or (ii) of the Act if the obligations were insurance policies in Canada, or

(ii) real property (or the portion of real property) owned by the insurer and occupied by the insurer for the purposes of carrying on an insurance business.

(7) **No double counting** — For greater certainty, a particular property or a particular proportion of a property shall not, directly or indirectly, be used or included more than once in determining, for a particular taxation year, the Canadian equity property or the equity property of a person or partnership.

Notes [Reg. 2400]: Reg. 2400 replaced by P.C. 2000-1714, effective for 1999 and later taxation years. For earlier years, since November 1994, read:

2400. Property used in insurance businesses in Canada — (1) For the purposes of paragraph 138(12)(l) [138(12)"property used by it in the year in, or held by it in the year in the course of"] of the Act, "property used by it in the year in, or held by it in the year in the course of" carrying on an insurance business in Canada (in this Part referred to as the "particular insurance business") means the property (in this Part referred to as "insurance property") of an insurer that is designated or required to be designated by the insurer in respect of a taxation year, and for that purpose the following rules apply:

(a) such investment property owned by the insurer at the beginning of the year that was insurance property in respect of another insurance business in Canada in the immediately preceding taxation year and that was used by

## Part XXIV — Insurers

the insurer in the year in, or held by it in the year in the course of (determined without reference to this subsection), carrying on the particular insurance business shall be designated by the insurer in respect of the particular insurance business for the year;

(b) where the amount of the insurer's mean Canadian reserve liabilities for the year in respect of the particular insurance business exceeds the total of

(i) the aggregate value for the year of all investment property of the insurer required to be designated by the insurer under paragraph (a) in respect of the particular insurance business for the year,

(ii) where the particular insurance business is a life insurance business in Canada, the aggregate of the mean policy loans of the insurer for the year and $\frac{1}{2}$ of the aggregate of outstanding premiums of the insurer in respect of that insurance business in Canada as determined for the purposes of the relevant authority at the end of the year and the immediately preceding taxation year,

(iii) where the particular insurance business is an accident and sickness insurance business in Canada, $\frac{1}{2}$ of the aggregate of outstanding premiums of the insurer in respect of that insurance business in Canada as determined for the purposes of the relevant authority at the end of the year and the immediately preceding taxation year, and

(iv) where the particular insurance business is an insurance business in Canada, other than a life insurance business in Canada or an accident and sickness insurance business in Canada, $\frac{1}{2}$ of the total of

(A) the aggregate of all amounts each of which is an amount of a deferred acquisition expense or a premium receivable (to the extent included in the insurer's Canadian reserve liabilities) of the insurer in respect of that insurance business in Canada as determined for the purposes of the relevant authority at the end of the immediately preceding taxation year, and

(B) the aggregate of all amounts each of which is an amount of a deferred acquisition expense or a premium receivable (to the extent included in the insurer's Canadian reserve liabilities) of the insurer in respect of that insurance business in Canada as determined for the purposes of the relevant authority at the end of the year,

such investment property (other than investment property required to be designated by the insurer pursuant to paragraph (a) in respect of another insurance business in Canada of the insurer for the year, when that paragraph is applied in respect of that other business) owned by the insurer at the beginning of the year that was insurance property in respect of the particular insurance business in the immediately preceding taxation year, the value for the year of which is not less than the amount of that excess, shall be designated by the insurer in respect of the particular insurance business for the year;

(c) where

(i) the amount of the excess determined under paragraph (b) in respect of the particular insurance business for the year

exceeds

(ii) the aggregate value for the year of insurance property in the immediately preceding taxation year in respect of the particular insurance business required to be designated by the insurer pursuant to paragraph (b) in respect of the particular insurance business for the year,

such investment property (other than investment property designated or required to be designated by the insurer under paragraph (a) or (b) for the year) owned by the insurer at any time in the year, the value for the year of which is not less than the amount of that excess, shall be designated by the insurer in respect of the particular insurance business for the year;

(d) where

(i) the amount of the insurer's Canadian investment fund for the year

exceeds

(ii) the aggregate value for the year of all investment property designated or required to be designated by the insurer under paragraphs (a), (b) and (c) in respect of all insurance businesses in Canada for the year,

such investment property (other than investment property designated or required to be designated by the insurer under paragraph (a), (b) or (c) for the year) owned by the insurer at any time in the year, the value for the year of which is not less than the amount of that excess, shall be designated by the insurer in respect of a particular insurance business for the year;

(e) such non-segregated property or portion thereof (other than investment property) owned by the insurer at any time in the year and used by it in the year in, or held by it in the year in the course of (determined without reference to this subsection), carrying on an insurance business in Canada shall be deemed to have been designated by the insurer for the year; and

(f) where the insurer has failed to designate property required to be designated for the year under any of paragraphs (a) to (d), such property owned by the insurer at any time in the year may, notwithstanding subsection (5), be designated by the Minister on behalf of the insurer for the purposes of those paragraphs, and the designated property by the Minister shall be deemed to have been designated by the insurer for the year, except that the aggregate value for the year of the designated property shall not exceed that required to be designated by the insurer under those paragraphs.

(2) For the purposes of this section, where in a taxation year an insurer carries on a life insurance business in Canada and an insurance business in Canada other than a life insurance business (in this Part referred to as the "other than life insurance business"), the following rules apply:

(a) paragraphs (1)(a), (b) and (c) shall be applied in designating the insurance property of the insurer in respect of its other than life insurance business before they are applied in designating the insurance property of the insurer in respect of its life insurance business;

(b) property that is designated under subsection (1) in respect of an insurance business of the insurer for a taxation year shall not be designated in respect of another insurance business of the insurer for the year; and

(c) investment property that is designated in respect of an insurance business of the insurer for a taxation year pursuant to paragraph (1)(d) or (f) shall,

(i) where paragraph (1)(d) is applicable, be designated in respect of the insurance business in Canada of the insurer as specified by the insurer for the year, and

(ii) where paragraph (1)(f) is applicable, be designated in respect of the insurance business in Canada

2139

**Reg. S. 2400** — Income Tax Regulations

of the insurer as specified by the Minister for the year.

(3) For the purposes of subsection (1), property acquired by an insurer in a taxation year by reason of

(a) a transaction to which any of sections 51, 51.1, 85.1 or 86 of the Act applies,

(b) a transaction in respect of which an election was made under subsection 85(1) or (2) of the Act,

(c) an amalgamation of two or more corporations (within the meaning assigned by subsection 87(1) of the Act), or

(d) a winding-up of a corporation (in respect of which subsection 88(1) of the Act applied),

as consideration for or in exchange for property of the insurer that was, in respect of the year, insurance property in respect of a particular insurance business in the immediately preceding taxation year shall be deemed to be insurance property in respect of that particular insurance business in that immediately preceding taxation year.

(4) Notwithstanding subsection (1) or (6), the aggregate value for the year of Canadian equity property that may be designated in respect of all the insurer's insurance businesses in Canada for a taxation year shall not exceed the insurer's equity limit for the year.

(5) Where investment property owned by the insurer at any time in the year was not insurance property in respect of an insurance business in Canada of the insurer at the end of the immediately preceding taxation year, and was used by the insurer in, or held by the insurer in the course of carrying on an insurance business outside Canada in the year, the property may not be designated by the insurer under subsection (1) for any period in the year, in respect of an insurance business in Canada of the insurer.

(6) For the purposes of subsection (1), investment property of the insurer shall be designated by the insurer in respect of a taxation year in respect of its insurance businesses in Canada in the following order to the extent thereof and to the extent required:

(a) investment property owned by the insurer at any time in the year that was insurance property in respect of an insurance business in Canada of the insurer at the end of the immediately preceding taxation year;

(b) subject to subsection (5), investment property (other than an investment property referred to in paragraph (a)) owned by the insurer at any time in the year that was Canadian investment property except that such investment property shall be designated in the following order:

(i) land and depreciable property situated in Canada,

(ii) mortgages, agreements of sale and other forms of indebtedness in respect of property referred to in subparagraph (i), and

(iii) other property; and

(c) subject to subsection (5), other investment property owned by the insurer at any time in the year.

(7) The insurer or the Minister may designate for a taxation year a portion of a particular investment property pursuant to paragraph (1)(b), (c), (d) or (f) where the designation of the entire investment property would result in a designation of investment property with an aggregate value for the year exceeding that required to be designated by the insurer pursuant to subsection (1).

The CCRA's view is that "all or substantially all" in "financial institution" means 90% or more.

Reference to ITA 51.1 added to Reg. 2400(3)(a) by P.C. 2000-1714, effective for transactions occurring after October 1994.

Reg. 2400(6)(b)(ii) amended to change "mortgages, hypothecs" to "mortgages" by P.C. 1994-1817, effective November 30, 1994.

**Definitions [Reg. 2400]**: "affiliated" — ITA 251.1; "allowable capital loss" — ITA 38(b), 248(1); "amortized cost", "amount" — ITA 248(1); "amount payable" — ITA 138(12), Reg. 2405(1); "annuity" — ITA 248(1); "attributed surplus for the year" — Reg. 2405(3); "business" — ITA 248(1); "Canada" — ITA 255, *Interpretation Act* 35(1); "Canadian business property", "Canadian equity property", "Canadian investment property" — Reg. 2400(1), 2405(3); "Canadian outstanding premiums" — Reg. 2400(1); "Canadian partnership" — ITA 102, 248(1); "Canadian reserve liabilities" — Reg. 2400(1), 2405(3); "Canadian resource property" — ITA 66(15), 248(1); "capital property" — ITA 54, 248(1); "carrying value" — Reg. 2400(2); "corporation" — ITA 248(1), *Interpretation Act* 35(1); "deposit balance" — Reg. 2400(1); "depreciable property" — ITA 13(21), 248(1); "designated insurance property" — ITA 138(12), 248(1); "equity property" — Reg. 2400(1), 2405(3); "financial institution", "financial institution allowance" — Reg. 2400(1); "fiscal period" — ITA 249.1; "foreign policy loan" — Reg. 2400(1), 2405(1); "gross investment revenue" — ITA 138(12), Reg. 2405(1); "income bond", "income debenture", "insurance policy" — ITA 248(1); "insurance property" — Reg. 2400(1), 2406; "insurer" — ITA 248(1); "investment property" — Reg. 2400(1), 2405(3), 2406; "item reported" — Reg. 2400(3); "liability" — Reg. 2400(3); "life insurance business" — ITA 248(1); "life insurance policy", "life insurance policy in Canada" — ITA 138(12), Reg. 2405(1); "life insurer" — ITA 248(1); "maximum tax actuarial reserve" — ITA 138(12), Reg. 2405(1); "mean Canadian investment fund" — Reg. 2400(1); "mean Canadian reserve liabilities" — Reg. 2400(1), 2405(3); "non-resident" — ITA 248(1); "non-segregated property" — ITA 138(12), Reg. 2405(1); "officer" — ITA 248(1); "partnership" — see Notes to ITA 96(1); "person" — ITA 248(1); "policy loan" — ITA 138(12), Reg. 2405(1); "prescribed", "property" — ITA 248(1); "property and casualty surplus" — Reg. 2400(1), 2405(3); "province" — *Interpretation Act* 35(1); "reinsurance recoverable" — Reg. 2400(2); "reported" — Reg. 2400(3); "resident", "resident in Canada" — ITA 250; "segregated fund" — ITA 138.1(1), 2405(1); "share" — ITA 248(1); "small business bond" — ITA 15.2(3), 248(1); "small business development bond" — ITA 15.1(3), 248(1); "surplus funds derived from operations" — ITA 138(12), Reg. 2405(1); "taxable capital gain" — ITA 38(a), 248(1); "taxation year" — ITA 249; "taxpayer" — ITA 248(1); "trust" — ITA 104(1), 248(1), (3); "valuation" — Reg. 2405(3); "value" — Reg. 2400(1); "value for the year" — Reg. 2405(3); "weighted Canadian liabilities", "weighted total liabilities" — Reg. 2400(1).

## 2401. (1) Designated insurance property

For the purposes of the definition "designated insurance property" in subsection 138(12) of the Act, "designated insurance property" of an insurer for a taxation year means property that is designated in accordance with subsections (2) to (7) for the year

(a) by the insurer in its return of income under Part I of the Act for the year; or

(b) if the Minister determines that the insurer has not made a designation that is in accordance with the prescribed rules found in this section, by the Minister.

**(2) Designation rules** — For the purposes of subsection (1), an insurer, or the Minister if paragraph (1)(b) applies,

(a) shall designate for a taxation year investment property of the insurer for the year with a total value for the year equal to the amount, if any, by which the insurer's mean Canadian reserve liabilities for the year in respect of its life insurance business in Canada exceeds the total of the insurer's mean Canadian outstanding premiums and mean policy loans for the year in respect of that business (to the extent that the amount of the mean policy loans was not otherwise deducted in computing the insurer's mean Canadian reserve liabilities for the year);

(b) shall designate for a taxation year investment property of the insurer for the year with a total value for the year equal to the amount, if any, by which the insurer's mean Canadian reserve liabilities for the year in respect of its accident and sickness insurance business in Canada exceeds the total of

(i) the insurer's mean Canadian outstanding premiums for the year in respect of that business, and

(ii) 50% of the total of all amounts, each of which is its total reinsurance recoverables, as at the end of the year or as at the end of the preceding taxation year, that are in respect of that business;

(c) shall designate for a taxation year in respect of the insurer's insurance business in Canada (other than a life insurance business or an accident and sickness insurance business) investment property of the insurer for the year with a total value for the year equal to the amount, if any, by which the insurer's mean Canadian reserve liabilities for the year in respect of that business exceeds the total of

(i) 50% of the total of all amounts each of which is the amount, as at the end of the year or as at the end of its preceding taxation year, of a premium receivable or a deferred acquisition expense (to the extent that it is included in the insurer's Canadian reserve liabilities as at the end of the year or preceding taxation year, as the case may be) of the insurer in respect of that business, and

(ii) 50% of the total of all amounts, each of which is its total reinsurance recoverables, as at the end of the year or as at the end of the preceding taxation year, that are in respect of that business;

(d) if

(i) the insurer's mean Canadian investment fund for a taxation year

exceeds

(ii) the total value for the year of all property required to be designated under paragraph (a), (b) or (c) for the year,

shall designate for the year, in respect of a particular insurance business that the insurer carries on in Canada, investment property of the insurer for the year with a total value for the year equal to that excess;

(e) for greater certainty, under each of paragraphs (a), (b), (c) and (d), shall designate for the taxation year investment property with a total value for the year equal to the amount, if any, determined under each of those paragraphs, and no investment property, or portion of investment property, designated for the year under any of paragraphs (a) to (d) may be designated for the year under any other paragraph; and

(f) may designate for a taxation year a portion of a particular investment property if the designation of the entire property would result in a designation of property with a total value for the year exceeding that required to be designated under paragraphs (a) to (d) for the year.

(3) **Order of designation of properties** — For the purpose of subsection (2), investment property of an insurer for a taxation year shall be designated for the year in respect of the insurer's insurance businesses carried on by it in Canada in the following order:

(a) Canadian investment property of the insurer for the year owned by the insurer at the beginning of the year that was designated insurance property of the insurer for its preceding taxation year, except that such property shall be designated in the following order:

(i) real and depreciable property,

(ii) mortgages, hypothecs, agreements of sale and other forms of indebtedness in respect of real property situated in Canada or depreciable property situated in Canada or depreciable property leased to a person resident in Canada for use inside and outside of Canada, and

(iii) other property;

(b) investment property (other than Canadian investment property of the insurer for the year) owned by the insurer at the beginning of the year that was designated insurance property of the insurer for its preceding taxation year;

(c) Canadian investment property of the insurer for the year (other than property included in paragraph (a)) in the order set out in subparagraphs (a)(i) to (iii); and

(d) other investment property.

(4) **Equity limit for the year** — Notwithstanding subsections (2) and (3),

(a) the total value for the year of Canadian equity property of an insurer that may be designated in respect of the insurer's insurance businesses for a taxation year shall not exceed the insurer's equity limit for the year; and

(b) for a taxation year a portion of a particular Canadian equity property of an insurer may be designated if the designation of the entire property would result in a designation of Canadian equity property of the insurer for the year with a to-

Reg. S. 2401(4)(b)   Income Tax Regulations

tal value for the year exceeding the insurer's equity limit for the year.

**(5) Exchanged property** — For the purposes of subsection (3), property acquired by an insurer in a particular taxation year is deemed to be designated insurance property of the insurer in respect of a particular business of the insurer for its preceding taxation year and to have been owned by the insurer at the beginning of the particular taxation year if the property was acquired

(a) by reason of

(i) a transaction to which any of sections 51, 51.1, 85.1 and 86 of the Act applies,

(ii) a transaction in respect of which an election is made under subsection 85(1) or (2) of the Act,

(iii) an amalgamation (within the meaning assigned by subsection 87(1) of the Act), or

(iv) a winding-up of a corporation to which subsection 88(1) of the Act applies, and

(b) as consideration for or in exchange for property of the insurer that was designated insurance property of the insurer in respect of the particular insurance business for its preceding taxation year.

**(6) Non-investment property** — Non-segregated property owned by an insurer at any time in a taxation year (other than investment property of the insurer for the year) that is used or held by the insurer in the year in the course of carrying on an insurance business in Canada is deemed to be designated insurance property of the insurer for the year in respect of the business.

**(7) Policy loan excluded from designated property** — Notwithstanding any other provision in this Part, a policy loan payable to an insurer is not designated insurance property of the insurer.

**Notes [Reg. 2401]**: Reg. 2401 replaced by P.C. 2000-1714, effective for 1999 and later taxation years. For earlier years read:

2401. Non-resident life insurers — (1) An election referred to in paragraph (a) of the definition "life surplus factor" in subsection 2405(3) shall be made by a non-resident life insurer in respect of a taxation year by filing, with its return of income required by subsection 150(1) of the Act to be filed for the year, the following documents in duplicate:

(a) a letter stating that the insurer elects under paragraph (a) of the definition "life surplus factor" in subsection 2405(3); and

(b) a schedule providing the following information:

(i) the amount determined under subparagraph (a)(i) of the definition "life surplus factor" in subsection 2405(3) in respect of the year,

(ii) the amount that is the aggregate value for the year of all the insurer's equity property,

(iii) information adequate to enable the Minister to verify the amounts referred to in subparagraphs (i) and (ii), and

(iv) where subsection (3) applies, the position and jurisdiction of the insurance officer or authority referred to therein.

(2) Where an insurer has made an election referred to in subsection (1) and the information that is required to be provided pursuant to subparagraph (1)(b)(iii) is not adequate, in the opinion of the Minister on the advice of the Superintendent of Insurance for Canada, to enable the Minister to verify an amount referred to in that subparagraph, the insurer's life surplus factor shall be determined pursuant to paragraph (c) of the definition "life surplus factor" in subsection 2405(3).

(3) Notwithstanding the definition "relevant authority" in subsection 2405(3), where an insurer has made an election referred to in subsection (1), it may, if it so provides in its election, determine the amount referred to in subparagraph (1)(b)(i) as if "relevant authority" were read as "insurance officer or authority of the country or the political subdivision thereof to whom the insurer is required to report its reserves in respect of its insurance businesses carried on in all countries and territories".

**Definitions [Reg. 2401]**: "amount", "business" — ITA 248(1); "Canada" — ITA 255, *Interpretation Act* 35(1); "Canadian equity property", "Canadian investment property", "Canadian reserve liabilities" — Reg. 2400(1), 2405(3); "corporation" — ITA 248(1), *Interpretation Act* 35(1); "depreciable property" — ITA 13(21), 248(1); "designated insurance property" — ITA 138(12), 248(1); "equity limit for the year" — Reg. 2405(3); "insurer" — ITA 248(1); "investment property" — Reg. 2400(1), 2405(3), 2406; "life insurance business" — ITA 248(1); "mean Canadian investment fund", "mean Canadian outstanding premiums" — Reg. 2400(1); "mean Canadian reserve liabilities", "mean policy loans" — Reg. 2400(1), 2405(3); "Minister" — ITA 248(1); "particular insurance business" — Reg. 2400(1); "person", "property" — ITA 248(1); "resident in Canada" — ITA 250; "taxation year" — ITA 249; "value for the year" — Reg. 2405(3).

**2402. Income from participating life insurance businesses** — For the purposes of clause 138(3)(a)(iii)(B) of the Act and subparagraph 309(1)(e)(i), in computing a life insurer's income for a taxation year from its participating life insurance business carried on in Canada,

(a) there shall be included that proportion of the insurer's gross Canadian life investment income for the year that

(i) the aggregate of the insurer's mean maximum tax actuarial reserve for the year in respect of participating life insurance policies in Canada and the mean amount on deposit with the insurer for the year in respect of those policies

is of

(ii) the aggregate of amounts, each of which is

(A) the insurer's mean maximum tax actuarial reserve for the year in respect of a class of life insurance policies in Canada, or

(B) the mean amount on deposit with the insurer for the year in respect of a class of policies described in clause (A);

**Proposed Addition — Reg. 2402(a.1)**

(a.1) there shall be included the amount determined by the formula

$$(A + B) \times \frac{C}{D}$$

Part XXIV — Insurers  Reg. S. 2402(e)

where

A is the amount required by subsection 142.5(5) of the Act to be included in computing the insurer's income for the year,

B is the amount deemed by subsection 142.5(7) of the Act to be a taxable capital gain of the insurer for the year from the disposition of property,

C is the amount determined under subparagraph (a)(i) for the taxation year of the insurer that includes October 31, 1994, and

D is the amount determined under subparagraph (a)(ii) for the taxation year of the insurer that includes October 31, 1994;

**Application**: The June 1, 1995 draft regulations (securities held by financial institutions), subsec. 2(1), will add para. 2402(a.1), applicable to taxation years that end after October 30, 1994.

**Technical Notes**: Section 2402 contains rules for determining a life insurer's income for a year from carrying on its participating life insurance business in Canada. This income is relevant for subparagraph 138(3)(a)(iii) of the Act, which permits an insurer to deduct policy dividends to the extent that the total amount of dividends paid after its 1968 taxation year does not exceed the total amount of its participating business income after that year. Section 2402 is amended to reflect the new rules in the Act for the tax treatment of securities held by financial institutions, and to delete provisions which are no longer applicable.

New paragraph 2402(a.1) includes in an insurer's income from its participating business for a taxation year an amount in respect of the transition adjustments for the mark-to-market requirement for shares. The amount included is equal to a proportion of the transition amount for non-capital gains included in the insurer's income for the year by subsection 142.5(5) of the Act, plus the same proportion of the insurer's deemed taxable capital gain for the year under subsection 142.5(7). The ratio used for this purpose is equal to the ratio used under paragraph 2402(a) in determining the proportion of the insurer's gross Canadian life investment income for its taxation year that includes October 31, 1994 that is included in its income from its participating business. Paragraph 2402(a.1) applies to taxation years ending after October 30, 1994.

(b) there shall be included

(i) the amount deducted by the insurer under subparagraph 138(3)(a)(iv) of the Act in computing its income for the immediately preceding taxation year,

(ii) the insurer's maximum tax actuarial reserve for the immediately preceding taxation year in respect of participating life insurance policies in Canada,

(iii) the maximum amount deductible by the insurer under subparagraph 138(3)(a)(ii) of the Act in computing its income for the immediately preceding taxation year in respect of participating life insurance policies in Canada, and

(iv) that proportion of the amount included in income by the insurer for the year under section 12.3 that

(A) the amount determined under clause (f)(iii)(A) for its first taxation year that commences after June 17, 1987 and ends after 1987

is of

(B) the amount determined under clause (f)(iii)(B) for its first taxation year that commences after June 17, 1987 and ends after 1987;

### Proposed Repeal — Reg. 2402(b)(iv)

**Application**: The June 1, 1995 draft regulations (securities held by financial institutions), subsec. 2(2), will repeal subpara. 2402(b)(iv), applicable to taxation years that begin after 1992.

**Technical Notes**: Subparagraph 2402(b)(iv) relates to a transitional provision introduced in conjunction with the 1987 tax reform measures. The transitional provision, and subparagraph 2402(b)(iv), last applied to taxation years that began in 1992. The subparagraph is repealed since it is no longer applicable.

(c) there shall not be included any amount in respect of the insurer's participating life insurance policies in Canada that was deducted under subparagraphs 138(3)(a)(i) or (ii) of the Act in computing its income for the immediately preceding taxation year;

(d) except as otherwise provided in paragraph (a), there shall not be included any amount as a reserve that was deducted under paragraph 20(1)(l) of the Act in computing the insurer's income for the immediately preceding taxation year;

(e) except as otherwise provided in paragraph (a), there shall not be included

(i) any amount that was included in income for the year by the insurer pursuant to 138(4)(b) or (c) of the Act, or

(ii) any amount that was included in computing the insurer's gains or taxable capital gains for the year from the disposition of property;

### Proposed Amendment — Reg. 2402(e)

(e) except as provided in paragraph (a), there shall not be included any amount that was included in determining the insurer's gross Canadian life investment income for the year;

**Application**: The June 1, 1995 draft regulations (securities held by financial institutions), subsec. 2(3), will amend para. 2402(e) to read as above, applicable to taxation years that end after February 22, 1994.

**Technical Notes**: Paragraph 2402(e) provides that certain amounts are not included in computing an insurer's income from its participating life insurance business, except as provided by paragraph 2402(a). Paragraph 2402(e) is amended so that it applies with respect to all amounts included in determining an insurer's gross Canadian life investment income. This amendment is made for purposes of clarification, and because of the introduction of the new rules for

## Reg. S. 2402(e) — Income Tax Regulations

the taxation of securities held by financial institutions. In this latter regard, subparagraph 2402(e)(i) refers to paragraphs 138(4)(b) and (c) of the Act, which are being repealed.

### Proposed Addition — Reg. 2402(e.1), (e.2)

(e.1) except as provided in paragraph (a.1), there shall not be included the amounts referred to in the descriptions of A and B in that paragraph;

(e.2) where the year includes October 31, 1994, there shall be deducted the amount determined by the formula

$$(A + B) \times \frac{C}{D}$$

where

A is the amount deducted under subsection 142.5(4) of the Act in computing the insurer's income for the year,

B is the amount deemed by subsection 142.5(6) of the Act to be an allowable capital loss of the insurer for the year from the disposition of property,

C is the amount determined under subparagraph (a)(i) for the year, and

D is the amount determined under subparagraph (a)(ii) for the year;

**Application**: The June 1, 1995 draft regulations (securities held by financial institutions), subsec. 2(4), will add paras. 2402(e.1) and (e.2), applicable to taxation years that end after October 30, 1994.

**Technical Notes**: New paragraph 2402(e.1) provides that the transition amounts associated with the introduction of the mark-to-market requirement for shares are not to be included in an insurer's income from its participating life insurance business, except as provided by new paragraph 2402(a.1).

New paragraph 2402(e.2) provides for a deduction in computing an insurer's income from its participating business in respect of the transition deductions associated with the introduction of the mark-to-market requirement for shares. This deduction applies for the insurer's taxation year that includes October 31, 1994. The deducted amount is equal to a proportion of the transition deduction for non-capital gains claimed by the insurer under subsection 142.5(4) of the Act, plus the same proportion of the allowable capital loss claimed by the insurer under subsection 142.5(6). The ratio used for this purpose is equal to the ratio used under paragraph 2402(a) in determining the proportion of the insurer's gross Canadian life investment income for its taxation year that includes October 31, 1994 that is included in its income from its participating business.

(f) there shall be deducted

(i) the insurer's maximum tax actuarial reserve for the year in respect of participating life insurance policies in Canada,

(ii) the maximum amount deductible by the insurer under subparagraph 138(3)(a)(ii) of the Act in computing its income for the year in respect of participating life insurance policies in Canada, and

(iii) that proportion of the amount deducted from income by the insurer for the year under subsection 20(26) that

(A) the amount determined in respect of the insurer for the year under subparagraph (a)(i),

is of

(B) the amount determined in respect of the insurer for the year under subparagraph (a)(ii);

### Proposed Repeal — Reg. 2402(f)(iii)

**Application**: The June 1, 1995 draft regulations (securities held by financial institutions), subsec. 2(5), will repeal subpara. 2402(f)(iii), applicable to taxation years that begin after 1992.

**Technical Notes**: Subparagraph 2402(f)(iii) relates to a transitional deduction provided in conjunction with the 1987 tax reform measures. The transitional deduction, and subparagraph 2402(f)(iii), applied to an insurer's first taxation year that began after June 17, 1987 and ended after 1987. The subparagraph is repealed since it is no longer applicable.

(g) no deduction shall be made in respect of any amount deductible under subparagraph 138(3)(a)(iii) or (iv) of the Act in computing the insurer's income for the year;

(h) except as as otherwise provided in paragraph (a), no deduction shall be made in respect of

(i) any amount deductible under paragraph 138(3)(b) or (d) of the Act in computing the insurer's income for the year,

(ii) any amount deductible as a reserve under paragraph 20(1)(l) of the Act in computing the insurer's income for the year, or

(iii) any amount included in computing the insurer's losses or allowable capital losses for the year from the disposition of property;

### Proposed Amendment — Reg. 2402(h)

(h) except as provided in paragraph (a), no deduction shall be made in respect of

(i) any amount taken into account in determining the insurer's gross Canadian life investment income for the year, or

(ii) any amount deductible under paragraph 20(1)(l) of the Act in computing the insurer's income for the year;

**Application**: The June 1, 1995 draft regulations (securities held by financial institutions), subsec. 2(6), will amend para. 2402(h) to read as above, applicable to taxation years that end after February 22, 1994.

**Technical Notes**: Paragraph 2402(h) provides that certain amounts are not deducted in computing an insurer's income from its participating life insurance business, except as provided by paragraph 2402(a). Paragraph 2402(h) is amended so that it applies with respect to all amounts that are included in determining an insurer's gross Canadian life investment income. This amendment is made for purposes of clarification and because of the introduction of the new rules for the taxation of securities held by financial institutions. In this latter regard, subparagraph 2402(h)(i) refers to paragraphs 138(3)(b) and (d) of the Act, which are being repealed.

### Proposed Addition — Reg. 2402(h.1)

(h.1) except as provided in paragraph (e.2), no deduction shall be made in respect of the amounts referred to in the descriptions of A and B in paragraph (e.2);

**Application**: The June 1, 1995 draft regulations (securities held by financial institutions), subsec. 2(7), will add para. 2402(h.1), applicable to taxation years that end after October 30, 1994.

**Technical Notes**: New paragraph 2402(h.1) provides that the transition amounts deducted by an insurer in connection with the introduction of the mark-to-market requirement for shares are not to be deducted in computing the insurer's income from its participating life insurance business, except as provided by new paragraph 2402(e.2).

(i) except as otherwise provided in paragraph (f), no deduction shall be made in respect of a reserve deductible under subparagraph 138(3)(a)(i) or (ii) of the Act in computing the insurer's income for the year; and

(j) except as otherwise provided in this section, the provisions of the Act relating to the computation of income from a source shall apply.

**Definitions [Reg. 2402]**: "allowable capital loss" — ITA 38(b), 248(1); "amount" — ITA 248(1); "Canada" — ITA 255, *Interpretation Act* 35(1); "gross Canadian life investment income" — Reg. 2400(1), 2405(3); "immediately preceding taxation year" — Reg. 2409(1), (4); "insurer", "life insurance business" — ITA 248(1); "life insurance policy" — ITA 138(12), Reg. 2405(1); "life insurer" — ITA 248(1); "maximum tax actuarial reserve" — ITA 138(12), Reg. 2405(1); "mean amount on deposit" — Reg. 2405(3); "mean maximum tax actuarial reserve" — Reg. 2400(1), 2405(3); "participating life insurance policy" — ITA 138(12), Reg. 2405(1); "property" — ITA 248(1); "taxable capital gain" — ITA 38(a), 248(1); "taxation year" — ITA 249.

**2403. Branch tax elections** — (1) An election referred to in subsection 219(4) of the Act shall be made by a non-resident insurer in respect of a taxation year by filing, with its return of income required by subsection 150(1) of the Act to be filed for the year, a letter in duplicate stating

(a) the insurer elects under subsection 219(4) of the Act; and

(b) the amount the insurer elects to deduct under subsection 219(4) of the Act.

(2) Where a joint election referred to in subsection 219(5.2) of the Act is made by a non-resident insurer and a qualified related corporation (within the meaning assigned by subsection 219(8) of the Act) of the non-resident insurer in respect of a taxation year of the non-resident insurer, it shall be made by filing, with the non-resident insurer's return of income required by subsection 150(1) of the Act to be filed for the year in which the event to which the election relates occurred, a letter in duplicate signed by an authorized officer of the non-resident insurer and an authorized officer of the qualified related corporation stating

(a) whether paragraphs 219(5.2)(a) and (b) of the Act apply; and

(b) the amount elected under subsection 219(5.2) of the Act.

**Notes**: Reg. 2403(2)(a) amended by P.C. 2000-1714, effective for 1999 and later taxation years, to change "(a) or (b)... is applicable" to "(a) *and* (b)... apply".

**Definitions [Reg. 2403]**: "amount" — ITA 248(1); "corporation" — ITA 248(1), *Interpretation Act* 35(1); "insurer", "non-resident", "officer" — ITA 248(1); "related" — ITA 251(2)–(6); "taxation year" — ITA 249.

**2404. Currency conversions [inapplicable as of 1999]** — For the purposes of this Part, where any amount is determined in a currency other than Canadian currency, that amount shall be converted to Canadian currency using the current rate of exchange, as required for the purposes of the relevant authority, on the date in respect of which the amount is determined.

**Related Provisions**: Reg. 2406 — Reg. 2404 does not apply as of 1999.

**Definitions [Reg. 2404]**: "amount" — ITA 248(1); "relevant authority" — Reg. 2405(3).

**2405. Interpretation [inapplicable as of 1999]** — (1) In this Part,

(a) "total depreciation" has the meaning assigned by paragraph 13(21)(e) [13(21)"total depreciation"] of the Act;

(b) "accumulated 1968 deficit", "amount payable", "gross investment revenue", "life insurance policy", "life insurance policy in Canada", "maximum tax actuarial reserve", "non-segregated property", "participating life insurance policy", "policy loan" and "surplus funds derived from operations" have the meanings assigned by subsection 138(12) of the Act; and

(c) "segregated fund" and "segregated fund policies" have the meaning assigned by subsection 138.1(1) of the Act.

**Related Provisions**: Reg. 2406 — Reg. 2405 does not apply as of 1999.

(2) For the purposes of subsection 138(14) of the Act, the expressions "Canadian investment fund for a taxation year", "specified Canadian assets" and "value for the taxation year" have the meanings prescribed therefor by subsection 2404(1) as it read in its application to the 1977 taxation year.

**Related Provisions**: Reg. 2406 — Reg. 2405 does not apply as of 1999.

(3) In this Part and for the purposes of paragraph 219(7)(a) [219(7)"attributed surplus for the year"] of the Act,

**Reg. S. 2405(3) att** — Income Tax Regulations

"**attributed surplus for the year**", for a taxation year in respect of a non-resident insurer, means the aggregate of

(a) its property and casualty surplus for the year, and

(b) an amount equal to the percentage (that is the life surplus factor for the year) of the amount for the year determined under clause (a)(i)(B) of the definition "life surplus factor" in this subsection;

**Related Provisions**: Reg. 2406 — Reg. 2405 does not apply as of 1999.

### Proposed Addition — Reg. 2405(3)"Canadian business property" [temporary]

"**Canadian business property**" of an insurer for a taxation year in respect of an insurance business means

(a) where the insurer was resident in Canada throughout the year and either did not carry on a life insurance business in the year or did not carry on an insurance business outside Canada in the year, the property used by it in the year in, or held by it in the year in the course of, carrying on the business in Canada, and

(b) in any other case, the property designated under subsection 2400(1) for the year by the insurer in respect of the business;

**Application**: The June 1, 1995 draft regulations (securities held by financial institutions), subsec. 3(10), will add the definition "Canadian business property" to subsec. 2405(3), applicable to taxation years that end after February 22, 1994. Reg. 2405 no longer applies as of 1999; see Reg. 2406.

**Technical Notes**: A definition of "Canadian business property" is added to subsection 2405(3). This expression is used in the definition of "gross Canadian life investment income", which is also in subsection 2405(3).

In the case of an insurer that is required to designate property under subsection 2400(1), the "Canadian business property" of the insurer for a taxation year in respect of an insurance business is the property designated for the year in respect of the business. (The designation rules apply to non-resident insurers, and to multinational resident life insurers.)

The "Canadian business property" of any other insurer for a taxation year in respect of an insurance business is the property that is factually determined to have been used by the insurer in the year in, or held by it in the year in the course of, carrying on the business in Canada.

**Related Provisions**: Reg. 2406 — Reg. 2405 does not apply as of 1999.

"**Canadian equity property**" means

(a) a share of the capital stock of, or an income bond, income debenture, small business development bond or a small business bond issued by, a person (other than a designated corporation) or partnership, as the case may be, resident in Canada, or

(b) that proportion of shares of the capital stock of a designated corporation or an interest in a partnership or trust that

(i) the aggregate value for the year of Canadian equity property owned by the designated corporation or the partnership or trust, as the case may be,

is of

(ii) the aggregate value for the year of all property owned by the designated corporation, or partnership or trust, as the case may be;

**Related Provisions**: Reg. 2406 — Reg. 2405 does not apply as of 1999.

"**Canadian investment fund**", as at the end of a taxation year, in respect of

(a) a life insurer resident in Canada, means the positive amount determined by the formula

$$\left[\frac{A}{B} \times (C - D)\right] - E$$

where

A is the amount of the insurer's Canadian reserve liabilities as at the end of the year,

B is the amount of the insurer's total reserve liabilities as at the end of the year,

C is the total of

(i) the aggregate amount of policy loans and foreign policy loans of the insurer as at the end of the year, and

(ii) the valuation of all property of the insurer as at the end of the year each of which is

(A) an investment property,

(B) money, or

(C) a balance (other than a property included under (A) or (B)) standing to the insurer's credit as or on account of amounts deposited with a corporation authorized to accept deposits or to carry on the business of offering to the public its services as a trustee,

D is the total of

(i) the aggregate of all amounts each of which is an amount outstanding as at the end of the year in respect of a debt (other than a debt referred to in paragraph (h) of the definition "valuation" in this subsection or an amount referred to in subparagraph (ii)) owing by the insurer in respect of money borrowed by the insurer (other than money used by the insurer for the purpose of earning income from a source that is not an insurance business), and

(ii) the aggregate of all amounts each of which is the amount of a cheque outstanding at the end of the year drawn on an account of the insurer maintained with a corporation authorized to accept deposits or to carry on the business of offering to the public its services as a trustee, and

E is the aggregate amount of the policy loans of the insurer as at the end of the year, and

(b) a non-resident insurer, means the amount, if any, by which the aggregate of amounts each of which is

(i) a maximum tax actuarial reserve of the insurer for the year,

(i.1) the maximum amount that the insurer is entitled to claim under subparagraph 138(3)(a)(ii) of the Act for the year,

(ii) the maximum amount that the insurer is entitled to deduct under paragraph 20(7)(c) of the Act in computing its income for the year determined on the assumption that it carried on no other than life insurance business other than an accident and sickness insurance business,

(iii) the amount of policy dividends, to the extent that such dividends were not included under subparagraph (i) or (ii), that will, according to the annual report of the insurer filed with the relevant authority for the year or, where the insurer was throughout the year subject to the supervision of the relevant authority but was not required to file an annual report with the relevant authority for the year, according to its financial statements for the year, as at the end of the year, become payable by the insurer in the immediately following year under its participating life insurance policies,

(iv) a liability (other than a debt referred to in paragraph (h) of the definition "valuation" in this subsection) or a reserve (other than the insurer's investment valuation reserve) as reported by the insurer in its annual report for the year to the relevant authority or, where the insurer was throughout the year subject to the supervision of the relevant authority but was not required to file an annual report with the relevant authority for the year, in its financial statements for the year, that was incurred or provided for in the course of carrying on the insurer's property and casualty insurance business in Canada except to the extent those amounts are already included under subparagraph (ii),

(v) a debt (other than a debt referred to in paragraph (h) of the definition "valuation" in this subsection) owing by the insurer at that time that was incurred in the course of carrying on an insurance business (other than a property and casualty insurance business) in Canada, except to the extent those amounts are already included under subparagraph (i), (i.1) or (iii), or

(vi) the amount that is the greater of

(A) the amount, if any, by which the aggregate of

(I) the insurer's surplus funds derived from operations computed as at the end of the immediately preceding taxation year, and

(II) the aggregate of amounts in respect of which the insurer has made an election under subsection 219(4) or (5.2) of the Act, each of which is an amount included in the aggregate determined in respect of the insurer under subparagraph 219(4)(a)(i.1) of the Act at the end of the immediately preceding taxation year

exceeds

(III) the aggregate of amounts determined in respect of the insurer under subparagraphs 219(4)(a)(ii), (iii), (iv) and (v) of the Act, as at the end of the taxation year, and

(B) the insurer's attributed surplus for the year,

exceeds the aggregate of

(vii) the aggregate valuation of all non-segregated property referred to in paragraph 2400(1)(e) at the end of the year in respect of all the insurer's insurance businesses carried on in Canada other than property that is

(A) money, or

(B) a balance standing to the insurer's credit as or on account of amounts deposited with a corporation authorized to accept deposits or to carry on the business of offering to the public its services as a trustee, and

(viii) the aggregate amount of the insurer's deferred acquisition expenses in respect of its property and casualty insurance business in Canada reported by the insurer in its annual report for the year to the relevant authority or, where the insurer was throughout the year subject to the supervision of the relevant authority but was not required to file an annual report with the relevant authority for the year, in its financial statements for the year;

**Related Provisions**: ITA 257 — Negative amounts in formulas; Reg. 2405(5) — Mark-to-market rule to be ignored.

**"Canadian investment fund for the year"**, for a taxation year in respect of a life insurer resident in Canada and a non-resident insurer, means the amount determined under section 2412;

**Related Provisions**: Reg. 2406 — Reg. 2405 does not apply as of 1999.

**"Canadian investment property"** of an insurer for a taxation year means an investment property (unless the insurer is a non-resident insurer and it is established by the insurer that the investment property is not effectively connected with its Canadian insurance businesses) that is

(a) land or depreciable property situated in Canada and, for that purpose, depreciable property of an insurer leased by a person resident in Canada for use inside and outside of Canada shall be deemed to be depreciable property situated in Canada,

(b) a Canadian equity property,

(c) a Canadian resource property,

(d) a mortgage, an agreement of sale or any other form of indebtedness in respect of property referred to in paragraph (a),

(e) an amount in Canadian currency standing to the insurer's credit as or on account of amounts deposited with a corporation resident in Canada authorized to accept deposits or to carry on the business of offering to the public its services as a trustee,

(f) a bond, debenture or other form of indebtedness (other than a property described in paragraph (d) or (e)) in Canadian currency issued by

(i) a person resident in Canada, a Canadian partnership or a partnership an interest in which is an investment property described in paragraph (g),

(ii) the Government of Canada,

(iii) the government of a province of Canada, or

(iv) any other political subdivision of Canada or of any province of Canada, or

(g) a property (to the extent it is not a property described in paragraph (b)) that is

(i) a share of a designated corporation resident in Canada,

(ii) an interest in a partnership, or

(iii) an interest in a trust resident in Canada,

where not less than 75 per cent of the aggregate value for the year of all property of the corporation, partnership or trust, as the case may be, is in respect of property each of which is property described in paragraphs (a) to (f);

**Related Provisions**: Reg. 2406 — Reg. 2405 does not apply as of 1999.

**Notes**: Para. (d) amended to change "a mortgage, hypothec" to "a mortgage" by P.C. 1994-1817, effective November 30, 1994. The change is intended to be non-substantive.

**"Canadian reserve liabilities"** of an insurer, as at the end of a taxation year, means the aggregate amount of the insurer's liabilities and reserves (other than liabilities and reserves in respect of amounts payable out of segregated funds) in respect of its insurance policies in Canada, as determined for the purposes of the relevant authority at the end of the year or as would be determined at that time if the relevant authority required such a determination;

**Related Provisions**: Reg. 2406 — Reg. 2405 does not apply as of 1999.

**"designated corporation"**, in respect of an insurer, at any time in a taxation year, means a corporation in respect of which the insurer or the insurer and persons or partnerships that do not deal at arm's length with the insurer held, at any time in the year, shares that represented 30 per cent or more of the common shares of the corporation outstanding at that time;

**Related Provisions**: Reg. 2406 — Reg. 2405 does not apply as of 1999.

**"equity limit for the year"**, for a taxation year, means

(a) in respect of a life insurer resident in Canada, the greater of

(i) that proportion of the aggregate value for the year of all the insurer's equity property that

(A) the amount, if any, by which the insurer's mean Canadian reserve liabilities exceed the aggregate of the insurer's mean policy loans for the year and $1/2$ of the aggregate of outstanding premiums of the insurer in respect of its insurance businesses in Canada as determined for the purposes of the relevant authority at the end of the year and the immediately preceding taxation year,

is of

(B) the amount, if any, by which the insurer's mean total reserve liabilities exceed the aggregate of the insurer's mean policy loans and foreign policy loans for the year and $1/2$ of the aggregate of outstanding premiums of the insurer in respect of its insurance businesses as determined for the purposes of the relevant authority at the end of the year and the immediately preceding taxation year, and

(ii) 8 per cent of the insurer's Canadian investment fund for the year,

(b) in respect of a non-resident insurer (other than a life insurer), $1/4$ of the aggregate of

(i) the amount, if any, by which the insurer's mean Canadian reserve liabilities exceed $1/2$ of the aggregate of the amounts of the insurer's deferred acquisition expenses and premiums receivable at the end of the year and the immediately preceding year to the extent that those amounts were included in the insurer's Canadian reserve liabilities for those years in respect of the insurer's business in Canada as determined for the purposes of the relevant authority, and

(ii) the insurer's property and casualty surplus for the year, and

(c) in respect of a non-resident life insurer, the aggregate of

(i) the insurer's life equity limit for the year, and

(ii) ¼ of the aggregate of

(A) the amount, if any, by which the insurer's mean Canadian reserve liabilities for the year exceed ½ of the aggregate of the amounts of the insurer's deferred acquisition expenses and premiums receivable at the end of the year and the immediately preceding year in respect of the insurer's business in Canada as determined for the purposes of the relevant authority to the extent that those amounts were included in the insurer's Canadian reserve liabilities for those years (determined on the assumption that the only insurance business carried on in Canada by the insurer was a property and casualty insurance business), and

(B) the insurer's property and casualty surplus for the year;

**Related Provisions**: Reg. 2406 — Reg. 2405 does not apply as of 1999.

**"equity property"** means

(a) a share of the capital stock of, or an income bond, income debenture, small business development bond or small business bond issued by, a person (other than a designated corporation) or partnership, as the case may be, or

(b) that proportion of shares of the capital stock of a designated corporation or an interest in a partnership or trust that

(i) the aggregate value for the year of equity property owned by the designated corporation or the partnership or trust, as the case may be,

is of

(ii) the aggregate value for the year of all property owned by the designated corporation or the partnership or trust, as the case may be;

**Related Provisions**: Reg. 2406 — Reg. 2405 does not apply as of 1999.

**"foreign policy loan"** means an amount advanced at a particular time by an insurer to a policyholder in accordance with the terms and conditions of a life insurance policy, other than a life insurance policy in Canada;

**Related Provisions**: Reg. 2406 — Reg. 2405 does not apply as of 1999.

**"gross Canadian life investment income"** of a life insurer for a taxation year means the amount, if any, by which the aggregate of

(a) the insurer's gross investment revenue for the year to the extent that that revenue is from non-segregated property of the insurer used by it in the year in, or held by it in the year in the course of, carrying on its life insurance business in Canada,

(b) the amount included in computing the insurer's income for the year under paragraph 138(9)(b) of the Act,

(c) the amounts included in computing the insurer's income for the year under paragraphs 138(4)(b) and (c) of the Act,

(d) that portion of the amount included in computing the insurer's income for the year under paragraph 12(1)(d) of the Act in respect of amounts deducted in computing the insurer's income under paragraph 20(1)(l) of the Act in the immediately preceding taxation year in respect of a Canada security (within the meaning assigned by paragraph 138(12)(c) [138(12)"Canada security"] of the Act) owned by the insurer,

(e) the amount included in computing the insurer's gains for the year from the disposition of property (other than a Canada security or capital property),

(f) the amount included in computing the insurer's taxable capital gains for the year from the disposition of property, and

(g) the amount deducted in computing the insurer's income for the immediately preceding taxation year under paragraph 138(3)(c) of the Act (as it read in its application to taxation years commencing before June 17, 1987 or ending before 1988),

exceeds the aggregate of

(h) the amounts deducted in computing the insurer's income for the year under paragraphs 138(3)(b) and (d) of the Act,

(i) the amount deducted in computing the insurer's income for the year under paragraph 20(1)(l) of the Act in respect of a Canada security (within the meaning assigned by paragraph 138(12)(c) [138(12)"Canada security"] of the Act) owned by the insurer,

(j) the amount included in computing the insurer's losses for the year from the disposition of property (other than a Canada security or capital property), and

(k) the amount included in computing the insurer's allowable capital losses for the year from the disposition of property;

**Proposed Amendment — Reg. 2405(3)"gross Canadian life investment income" [temporary]**

**"gross Canadian life investment income"** of a life insurer for a taxation year means the amount, if any, by which the aggregate of

(a) the insurer's gross investment revenue for the year, to the extent that the revenue is from Canadian business property of the insurer for the year in respect of the insurer's life insurance business,

(b) the amount included in computing the insurer's income for the year under paragraph 138(9)(b) of the Act,

(c) [Proposed repeal]

(d) the portion of the amount deducted under paragraph 20(1)(l) of the Act in computing the insurer's income for the preceding taxation year that was in respect of Canadian business property of the insurer for that year in respect of the insurer's life insurance business,

(d.1) the total of all amounts each of which is an amount included under section 142.4 of the Act in the insurer's income for the year in respect of a property disposed of by the insurer that was, in the taxation year of disposition, a Canadian business property of the insurer for that year in respect of the insurer's life insurance business,

(e) the total of all amounts each of which is the insurer's gain for the year from the disposition of a Canadian business property of the insurer for the year in respect of the insurer's life insurance business, other than a capital property or a property in respect of which section 142.4 of the Act applies, and

(f) the total of all amounts each of which is the insurer's taxable capital gain for the year from the disposition of a Canadian business property of the insurer for the year in respect of the insurer's life insurance business,

(g) [Proposed repeal]

exceeds the aggregate of

(h) [Proposed repeal]

(i) the portion of the amount deducted under paragraph 20(1)(l) of the Act in computing the insurer's income for the year that is in respect of debt obligations that are Canadian business property of the insurer for the year in respect of the insurer's life insurance business,

(i.1) the total of all amounts each of which is an amount deductible under section 142.4 of the Act in computing the insurer's income for the year in respect of a property disposed of by the insurer that was, in the taxation year of disposition, a Canadian business property of the insurer for that year in respect of the insurer's life insurance business,

(j) the total of all amounts each of which is the insurer's loss for the year from the disposition of a Canadian business property of the insurer for the year in respect of the insurer's life insurance business, other than a capital property or a property in respect of which section 142.4 of the Act applies, and

(k) the total of all amounts each of which is the insurer's allowable capital loss for the year from the disposition of a Canadian business property of the insurer for the year in respect of the insurer's life insurance business;

**Application**: The June 1, 1995 draft regulations (securities held by financial institutions), subsecs. 3(1) to (9), will amend paras. (a), (d), (e), (f), (i), (j) and (k) of the definition "gross Canadian life investment income" in subsec. 2405(3) to read as above, will add paras. (d.1) and (i.1), and will repeal paras. (c), (g) and (h); para. (a) applicable (see also Reg. 2406) to taxation years that end after June 1, 1995, paras. (c), (d), (g), (h) and (i) applicable to taxation years that begin after February 22, 1994, paras. (d.1) and (e) applicable to dispositions of property that occur after February 22, 1994 except that in its application to property disposed of in a taxation year that ends on or before June 1, 1995, para. (e) shall be read as follows:

(e) the amount included in computing the insurer's gains for the year from the disposition of property (other than capital property or property in respect of which section 142.4 of the Act applies),

para. (f) applicable to taxation years that end after October 30, 1994 except that in its application to property disposed of in a taxation year that ends on or before June 1, 1995, para. (f) shall be read as follows:

(f) the amount included in computing the insurer's taxable capital gains for the year from the disposition of property (other than an amount included because of subsection 142.5(7) of the Act),

paras. (i.1) and (j) applicable to dispositions of property that occur after February 22, 1994 except that in its application to property disposed of in a taxation year that ends on or before June 1, 1995, para. (j) shall be read as follows:

(j) the amount included in computing the insurer's losses for the year from the disposition of property (other than capital property or property in respect of which section 142.4 of the Act applies),

para. (k) applicable to taxation years that end after October 30, 1994 except that in its application to property disposed of in a taxation year that ends on or before June 1, 1995, para. (k) shall be read as follows:

(k) the amount included in computing the insurer's allowable capital losses for the year from the disposition of property (other than an amount included because of subsection 142.5(6) of the Act);

**Technical Notes**: Subsection 2405(3) defines a number of expressions used in Part XXIV.

The expression "gross Canadian life investment income" is defined for the purpose of section 2402, which contains rules for determining an insurer's income for a year from carrying on its participating life insurance business in Canada. Several amendments are made to this definition:

- Paragraph (a) is amended to use the newly-defined term "Canadian business property", which is defined in subsection 2405(3). Gross investment revenue from such property held in respect of an insurer's life insurance business is included by paragraph (a) in determining the insurer's gross Canadian life investment income. This amendment applies to taxation years that end after June 1, 1995.

- Paragraph (c) is repealed. This paragraph includes, in determining an insurer's gross Canadian life investment income, the amounts included in the insurer's income by paragraphs 138(4)(b) and (c) of the Act (profit on disposition of a Canada security, and amortization of discount on such a security). This amendment is consequential on the repeal of paragraphs 138(4)(b) and (c).

- Paragraphs (d) and (i), which deal with doubtful debt reserves, are amended as a consequence of the repeal of the definition of "Canada security" in subsection 138(12) of the Act. The amended paragraphs refer to debt obligations that are "Canadian business property" of the insurer in respect of the insurer's life insurance business.

- New paragraph (d.1) includes in an insurer's gross Canadian life investment income the amounts that are included in the insurer's income by section 142.4 of the Act in respect of property disposed of by the insurer that was "Canadian business property" of the insurer in respect of its life insurance business. New paragraph (i.1) is a corresponding rule for deductions. New section 142.4 of the Act contains rules for the measurement and the timing of recognition of gains and losses from the disposition of specified debt obligations.

- Paragraph (e), which includes certain non-capital gains in an insurer's gross Canadian life investment income, is amended to exclude from its scope property in respect of which section 142.4 of the Act applies. Gains from the disposition of this property are taken into account by new paragraph (d.1). Paragraph (e) is also amended, for dispositions of property in taxation years ending after June 1, 1995, to clarify that it applies only to the property of an insurer's Canadian life insurance business. Similar changes are made to the rule in paragraph (j) for certain non-capital losses.

- Paragraph (f), which includes an insurer's taxable capital gains in its gross Canadian life investment income, is amended so that it does not include amounts deemed by subsection 142.5(7) of the Act to be taxable capital gains of the insurer. That subsection contains a transition rule relating to the introduction of the mark-to-market requirement. Paragraph (f) is also amended, for dispositions of property in taxation years ending after June 1, 1995, to clarify that it applies only to the property of an insurer's Canadian life insurance business. Similar changes are made to the rule in paragraph (k) for allowable capital losses.

- Paragraph (g) is repealed since the provision to which it refers — paragraph 138(3)(c) of the Act (investment reserve) — was repealed in the tax reform of 1987.

- Paragraph (h) is repealed. This paragraph deducts in determining an insurer's gross Canadian life investment income the amounts deducted under paragraphs 138(3)(b) and (d) of the Act (loss on disposition of a Canada security, and amortization of premium on such a security) in computing an insurer's income. This amendment is consequential on the repeal of paragraphs 138(3)(b) and (d).

**Related Provisions**: Reg. 2406 — Reg. 2405 does not apply as of 1999.

**Notes**: Parenthetical qualification (beginning "as it read ...") added to para. (g) by P.C. 1992-2335, effective for taxation years and fiscal periods beginning after June 17, 1987 and ending after 1987.

**"insurance policy in Canada"**, in respect of an insurer, means, in the case of

(a) a life insurance policy, a life insurance policy in Canada,

(b) a fire insurance policy, a policy issued or effected upon property situated in Canada, and

(c) any other class of insurance policy, a policy where the risks covered by the policy were ordinarily within Canada at the time the policy was issued or effected;

**Related Provisions**: Reg. 2406 — Reg. 2405 does not apply as of 1999.

**"investment property"** of an insurer for a taxation year means non-segregated property that is

(a) property acquired by the insurer for the purpose of earning gross investment revenue, other than property that is

(i) property, a portion of which is investment property pursuant to paragraph (b) or (c),

(ii) a share of a designated corporation,

(iii) a debt owing to the insurer by a designated corporation,

(iv) an interest in a partnership, or

(v) an interest in a trust,

(b) the portion, if any, of property of the insurer (other than property a portion of which is investment property pursuant to paragraph (c)) that is

(i) land,

(ii) depreciable property, or

(iii) property that would have been depreciable property if it had been situated in Canada and used in the year in, or held in the year in the course of, carrying on an insurance business in Canada,

that

(iv) the use made of the property in the year for the purpose of earning gross investment revenue therefrom

is of

(v) the whole use made of the property in the year,

(c) the portion, if any, of property of the insurer that is not used in the year for the purpose of earning gross investment revenue that is

(i) land,

(ii) depreciable property, or

(iii) property that would be depreciable property if it had been situated in Canada and used in the year in, or held in the year in the course of, carrying on an insurance business in Canada,

to the extent that the property is held for resale or development or is expected to be used in a subsequent taxation year for the purpose of earning gross investment revenue, or

(d) property of the insurer that is

(i) a share of, or a debt owing to the insurer by a designated corporation other than a corporation that carries on a business of insurance, banking or offering its services to the public as a trustee or whose principal business is the making of loans,

(ii) an interest in a partnership, or

(iii) an interest in a trust,

if

(iv) the aggregate value for the year of all investment property of the corporation, partnership or trust, as the case may be, is not less than 75 per cent of the aggregate value for the year of all its property, and

(v) the gross investment revenue for the year from the investment property referred to in subparagraph (iv) (other than gross investment revenue from persons with whom the corporation, partnership or trust, as the case may be, did not deal at arm's length) is not less than 90 per cent of the gross revenue for the year of the corporation, partnership or trust, as the case may be,

assuming for the purposes of subparagraphs (iv) and (v) that the definition "gross investment revenue" in paragraph 138(12)(e) [138(12)"gross investment revenue"] of the Act and this definition apply to a corporation, partnership or trust, referred to in those subparagraphs, as though the corporation, partnership or trust, as the case may be, were an insurer;

**Related Provisions**: Reg. 2406 — Reg. 2405 does not apply as of 1999.

"**life equity limit**" of a non-resident life insurer for a taxation year means

(a) where the insurer makes an election in respect of its life surplus factor for the year in the manner described in subsection 2401(1), the amount that would have been the insurer's equity limit for the year if the insurer had been a life insurer resident in Canada registered under the *Canadian and British Insurance Companies Act* to carry on an insurance business in Canada and it had carried on no other than life insurance business other than an accident and sickness insurance business,

(b) where the insurer does not make an election referred to in paragraph (a) in respect of the year, but

(i) has made such an election in respect of one of the four immediately preceding taxation years, and

(ii) the insurer's life surplus factor for the year is not determined pursuant to paragraph (c) of the definition "life surplus factor" in this subsection,

the amount that would have been the insurer's equity limit for the year if the insurer had been a life insurer resident in Canada registered under the *Canadian and British Insurance Companies Act* to carry on an insurance business in Canada and it had carried on no other than life insurance business other than an accident and sickness insurance business, using the amount, in respect of the most recent taxation year for which such an election was made, determined under subparagraph (a)(i) of the definition, in this subsection, "equity limit for the year",

(c) in any other case, 8 per cent of the amount of the insurer's Canadian investment fund for the year;

**Related Provisions**: Reg. 2406 — Reg. 2405 does not apply as of 1999.

"**life surplus factor**" of a non-resident life insurer for a taxation year means

(a) subject to subsection 2401(2), where the insurer elects in respect of the year in the manner described in subsection 2401(1), the proportion (expressed as a percentage) that

(i) the amount, if any, by which

(A) the amount that would have been the insurer's Canadian investment fund for the year if the insurer had been a life insurer resident in Canada registered under the *Canadian and British Insurance Companies Act* to carry on an insurance business in Canada and it had carried on no other than life insurance business other than an accident and sickness insurance business

exceeds

(B) the amount, if any, by which $\frac{1}{2}$ of the aggregate of

(I) the aggregate of the amounts described in subparagraphs (b)(i), (i.1), (ii), (iii) and (v) of the definition "Canadian investment fund" in this subsection in respect of a non-resident insurer, as at the end of the year, and

(II) the aggregate of those amounts as at the end of the immediately preceding taxation year,

exceeds the aggregate value for the year of all the insurer's non-segregated property referred to in paragraph 2400(1)(e) in respect of all the insurer's insurance businesses (other than its property and casualty insurance business) carried on in Canada, other than property that is

(III) money, or

(IV) a balance standing to the insurer's credit as or on account of amounts deposited with a corporation authorized to accept deposits or to carry on the business of offering to the public its services as a trustee

is of

(ii) the amount determined under clause (i)(B),

(b) where the insurer does not make an election referred to in paragraph (a) in respect of the year, but

(i) has made such an election in respect of one of the four immediately preceding taxation years, and

(ii) has not, since making the most recent election referred to in subparagraph (i), selected pursuant to this paragraph the percentage referred to in paragraph (c) as its life surplus factor for a year prior to the taxation year,

the percentage, as shall be selected by the insurer, that is the percentage

(iii) determined under paragraph (a) in respect of the most recent taxation year for which the insurer made an election, or

(iv) referred to in paragraph (c), and

(c) in any other case, 10 per cent;

**Related Provisions**: Reg. 2406 — Reg. 2405 does not apply as of 1999.

**"mean amount on deposit"** with an insurer for a taxation year in respect of life insurance policies means $1/2$ of the aggregate of

(a) all amounts on deposit with the insurer as at the end of the year in respect of those policies, and

(b) all amounts on deposit with the insurer as at the end of the immediately preceding taxation year in respect of those policies;

**Related Provisions**: Reg. 2406 — Reg. 2405 does not apply as of 1999.

**"mean Canadian reserve liabilities"** of an insurer for a taxation year means $1/2$ of the aggregate of

(a) the insurer's Canadian reserve liabilities as at the end of the year, and

(b) the insurer's Canadian reserve liabilities as at the end of the immediately preceding taxation year;

**Related Provisions**: Reg. 2406 — Reg. 2405 does not apply as of 1999.

**"mean maximum tax actuarial reserve"**, in respect of a particular class of life insurance policies of an insurer for a taxation year, means $1/2$ of the aggregate of

(a) the insurer's maximum tax actuarial reserve for that class of policies for the year, and

(b) the insurer's maximum tax actuarial reserve for that class of policies for the immediately preceding taxation year;

**Related Provisions**: Reg. 2406 — Reg. 2405 does not apply as of 1999.

**"mean policy loans"**, of an insurer for a taxation year, means $1/2$ of the aggregate of

(a) the insurer's policy loans as at the end of the year, and

(b) the insurer's policy loans as at the end of the immediately preceding taxation year;

**Related Provisions**: Reg. 2406 — Reg. 2405 does not apply as of 1999.

**"mean policy loans and foreign policy loans"**, of an insurer for a taxation year, means $1/2$ of the aggregate of

(a) the insurer's policy loans and foreign policy loans as at the end of the year, and

(b) the insurer's policy loans and foreign policy loans as at the end of the immediately preceding taxation year;

**Related Provisions**: Reg. 2406 — Reg. 2405 does not apply as of 1999.

**"mean total reserve liabilities"** of an insurer for a taxation year means $1/2$ of the aggregate of

(a) the insurer's total reserve liabilities as at the end of the year, and

(b) the insurer's total reserve liabilities as at the end of the immediately preceding taxation year;

**Related Provisions**: Reg. 2406 — Reg. 2405 does not apply as of 1999.

**"property and casualty surplus"** of an insurer for a taxation year means the aggregate of

(a) 15 per cent of $1/2$ of the aggregate of

(i) the insurer's unearned premium reserve as at the end of the year, and

(ii) the insurer's unearned premium reserve as at the end of the immediately preceding taxation year,

as reported to the relevant authority in respect of its property and casualty insurance business,

(b) 15 per cent of $1/2$ of the aggregate of

(i) the insurer's provision for unpaid claims and adjustment expenses as at the end of the year, and

(ii) the insurer's provision for unpaid claims and adjustment expenses as at the end of the immediately preceding taxation year,

as reported to the relevant authority in respect of its property and casualty insurance business, and

(c) $1/2$ of the aggregate of

(i) the insurer's investment valuation reserve as at the end of the year, and

(ii) the insurer's investment valuation reserve as at the end of the immediately preceding taxation year,

as reported to the relevant authority in respect of its property and casualty insurance business;

**Related Provisions**: Reg. 2406 — Reg. 2405 does not apply as of 1999.

**"property of the insurer in the course of development"** — [Revoked]

**"relevant authority"** means

(a) the Superintendent of Financial Institutions, if the insurer is required by law to report to the Superintendent of Financial Institutions, or

(b) in any other case, the Superintendent of Insurance or other similar officer or authority of the province under whose laws the insurer is incorporated;

*Related Provisions*: Reg. 2406 — Reg. 2405 does not apply as of 1999.

**"total reserve liabilities"** of an insurer, as at the end of a taxation year, means the aggregate amount of the insurer's liabilities and reserves (other than liabilities and reserves in respect of amounts payable out of segregated funds) in respect of all its insurance policies, as determined for the purposes of the relevant authority at the end of the year;

*Related Provisions*: Reg. 2406 — Reg. 2405 does not apply as of 1999.

**"valuation"**, in respect of a property of an insurer, designated corporation, partnership or trust (in this definition referred to as an "owner") at a particular time, means, in the case of

(a) land, the cost thereof to the owner,

(b) depreciable property of a prescribed class (other than a property referred to in paragraph (f)), the proportion of the owner's undepreciated capital cost at that time of property of the class that

(i) the owner's capital cost of the property

is of

(ii) the owner's capital cost of all property of the class,

(c) property that would have been depreciable property of a prescribed class if it had been situated in Canada and used in the year in, or held in the year in the course of, carrying on an insurance business in Canada, the amount, if any, by which

(i) the owner's capital cost of the property

exceeds

(ii) the amount that would have been the total depreciation allowed to the owner before the particular time in respect of the property if it had been the owner's only depreciable property of the class and the owner had claimed the maximum amount allowable under paragraph 20(1)(a) of the Act in respect of property of that class for each year in which the owner owned the property,

(d) a share of a corporation (other than a designated corporation), the cost thereof to the owner,

(e) a bond, debenture, mortgage, hypothec or agreement of sale (other than a property referred to in paragraph (f)), the book value thereof in the accounts of the owner as determined for the purposes of the relevant authority or that would have been so determined if the owner had been a life insurer resident in Canada and registered under the *Canadian and British Insurance Companies Act* to carry on an insurance business in Canada,

(e.1) a balance standing to the owner's credit as or on account of amounts deposited with a corporation authorized to accept deposits or to carry on the business of offering to the public its services as a trustee, the amount thereof,

(f) a property acquired and disposed of in a taxation year, the cost thereof to the owner, and

(g) a property (other than a property referred to in any of paragraphs (a) to (f)), the maximum value of the property as determined for the purposes of the relevant authority or that would have been so determined if the owner had been a life insurer resident in Canada and registered under the *Canadian and British Insurance Companies Act* to carry on an insurance business in Canada,

minus

(h) in respect of a particular property referred to in any of paragraphs (a) to (g), the amount of any debt that was incurred or assumed by the owner to acquire that particular property and that was owing by the owner at that time;

*Related Provisions*: Reg. 2406 — Reg. 2405 does not apply as of 1999.

**"value for the year"**, in respect of a property of an insurer, designated corporation, partnership or trust (in this definition referred to as an "owner") for a taxation year, means, in the case of

(a) a property that is a mortgage, a hypothec, an agreement of sale or an investment property that is a balance standing to the insurer's credit as or on account of amounts deposited with a corporation authorized to accept deposits or to carry on the business of offering to the public its services as a trustee, the amount, if any, by which

(i) the amount obtained when the gross investment revenue for the year from the property is divided by the average rate of interest earned by the owner (expressed as an annual rate) on the amortized cost of the property during the year if that rate of interest were expressed as a fraction

exceeds

(ii) the amount obtained when the interest paid or payable for the year on a debt incurred for the purposes of acquiring the property is divided by the average rate of interest paid or payable by the owner (expressed as an annual rate) on the debt for the year if that rate of interest were expressed as a fraction,

(b) a property (other than a property referred to in paragraph (a)) that was not owned by the owner throughout the year, the proportion of

   (i) the valuation of the property as at the end of the immediately preceding taxation year, where the property was owned by the owner at that time, and

   (ii) the valuation of the property, where it was acquired by the owner during the year,

that

   (iii) the number of days that the property may reasonably be considered to have been owned by the owner during the taxation year

is of

   (iv) the number of days in the taxation year, and

(c) a property (other than a property referred to in paragraph (a) or (b)), ½ of the aggregate of

   (i) the valuation of the property as at the end of the year, and

   (ii) the valuation of the property as at the end of the immediately preceding taxation year.

**Related Provisions**: Reg. 2406 — Reg. 2405 does not apply as of 1999.

**Related Provisions [Reg. 2405(3)]**: Reg. 2405(5) — Mark-to-market rule to be ignored.

**(4)** For the purposes of the definition in subsection (3), "Canadian investment fund" in respect of a life insurer resident in Canada, notwithstanding the definitions "Canadian reserve liabilities" and "total reserve liabilities" in that subsection, the insurer shall determine its liabilities and reserves in respect of its insurance policies outside Canada in a manner consistent with that used in determining its liabilities and reserves in respect of its insurance policies in Canada.

**Related Provisions**: Reg. 2406 — Reg. 2405 does not apply as of 1999.

### Proposed Addition — Reg. 2405(5) [temporary]

**(5)** For the purposes of subsection (3), the cost of a property shall be determined without regard to subsection 142.5(2) of the Act.

**Related Provisions**: Reg. 2406 — Reg. 2405 does not apply as of 1999.

**Application**: The June 1, 1995 draft regulations (securities held by financial institutions), subsec. 3(11), would add subsec. 2405(5), applicable to taxation years that end after October 30, 1994. Reg. 2405 no longer applies as of 1999; see Reg. 2406.

**Technical Notes**: New subsection 2405(5) contains a rule for the purposes of the definitions in subsection 2405(3). It provides that the cost of property is to be determined without regard to the mark-to-market requirement in subsection 142.5(2) of the Act. Thus, the cost of mark-to-market property will not change each year for the purpose of the definitions in subsection 2405(3). This rule is relevant for determining the "valuation" of shares, and hence the "value for the year" of shares. As a consequence of this rule, the original cost of shares to an insurer will generally be used in measuring the Canadian investment fund, designating property, and determining any additional investment revenue prescribed by section 2411.

**Definitions [Reg. 2405]**: "allowable capital loss" — ITA 38(b), 248(1); "amortized cost", "amount" — ITA 248(1); "arm's length" — ITA 251(1); "attributed surplus for the year" — Reg. 2405(3); "business" — ITA 248(1); "Canada" — ITA 255, Interpretation Act 35(1); "Canada security" — ITA 138(12); "Canadian business property", "Canadian equity property" — Reg. 2400(1), 2405(3); "Canadian investment fund for the year" — Reg. 2405(3); "Canadian partnership" — ITA 102, 248(1); "Canadian reserve liabilities" — Reg. 2400(1), 2405(3); "Canadian resource property" — ITA 66(15), 248(1); "capital property" — ITA 54, 248(1); "common share" — ITA 248(1); "corporation" — ITA 248(1), Interpretation Act 35(1); "depreciable property" — ITA 13(21), 248(1); "designated corporation" — Reg. 2405(3); "dividend" — ITA 248(1); "equity limit for the year" — Reg. 2405(3); "equity property", "foreign policy loan" — Reg. 2400(1), 2405(3); "gross investment revenue" — ITA 138(12), Reg. 2405(1); "gross revenue" — ITA 248(1); "immediately preceding taxation year" — Reg. 2409(1), (4); "income bond", "income debenture", "insurance policy", "insurer" — ITA 248(1); "investment property" — Reg. 2400(1), 2405(3), 2406; "life equity limit" — Reg. 2405(3); "life insurance business" — ITA 248(1); "life insurance policy", "life insurance policy in Canada" — ITA 138(12), Reg. 2405(1); "life insurer" — ITA 248(1); "life surplus factor" — Reg. 2405(3); "maximum tax actuarial reserve" — ITA 138(12), Reg. 2405(1); "mean Canadian reserve liabilities", "mean policy loans" — Reg. 2400(1), 2405(3); "mean policy loans and foreign policy loans", "mean total reserve liabilities" — Reg. 2405(3); "non-resident" — ITA 248(1); "non-segregated property" — ITA 138(12), Reg. 2405(1); "officer" — ITA 248(1); "other than life insurance business" — Reg. 2400(2); "outstanding premiums" — Reg. 2400(1); "owner" — Reg. 2405(3); "participating life insurance policy" — ITA 138(12), Reg. 2405(1); "partnership" — see Notes to ITA 96(1); "person" — ITA 248(1); "policy loan" — ITA 138(12), Reg. 2405(1); "prescribed", "property" — ITA 248(1); "property and casualty surplus" — Reg. 2400(1), 2405(3); "province" — Interpretation Act 35(1); "relevant authority" — Reg. 2405(3); "resident in Canada" — ITA 250; "segregated fund" — ITA 138.1(1), Reg. 2400(1), 2405(1); "share" — ITA 248(1); "small business bond" — ITA 15.2(3), 248(1); "small business development bond" — ITA 15.1(3), 248(1); "surplus funds derived from operations" — ITA 138(12), Reg. 2405(1); "taxable capital gain" — ITA 38(a), 248(1); "taxation year" — ITA 249; "total depreciation" — ITA 13(21), Reg. 2405(1); "total reserve liabilities" — Reg. 2405(3); "trust" — ITA 104(1), 248(1), (3); "undepreciated capital cost" — ITA 13(21), 248(1); "valuation" — Reg. 2405(3); "value" — Reg. 2400(1); "value for the year" — Reg. 2405(3).

**2406.** Sections 2404 and 2405 do not apply to the 1999 and subsequent taxation years.

**Notes**: Reg. 2406 replaced by P.C. 2000-1714, effective for 1999 and later taxation years. For years before 1999, the definitions now in 2400(1) were in Reg. 2405(3), and read Reg. 2406 as:

> 2406. Notwithstanding any other provision in this Part, an insurance property or an investment property, in respect of an insurer, does not include a policy loan payable to the insurer.

**Definitions [Reg. 2406]**: "insurance property" — Reg. 2400(1), 2406; "insurer" — ITA 248(1); "investment property" — Reg. 2400(1), 2405(3), 2406; "policy loan" — ITA 138(12), Reg. 2405(1).

**2407. 1977 excess policy dividend deduction** — For the purposes of paragraph 138(3.1)(b) of the Act, a life insurer's 1977 excess policy dividend is hereby prescribed to be the amount that is the lesser of

(a) the amount, if any, by which

(i) the amount determined under clause 138(3)(a)(iii)(A) of the Act for the insurer's 1977 taxation year (determined without reference to paragraph 138(3.1)(b) of the Act),

exceeds

(ii) the amount determined under clause 138(3)(a)(iii)(B) of the Act for the insurer's 1977 taxation year; and

(b) the amount, if any, by which

(i) the insurer's maximum tax actuarial reserve for its participating life insurance policies in Canada for its 1977 taxation year,

exceeds the aggregate of

(ii) the amount that would have been the insurer's maximum tax actuarial reserve for its participating life insurance policies in Canada for its 1977 taxation year if that reserve had been determined on the basis of the rules applicable to its 1978 taxation year,

(iii) the aggregate of all amounts payable to the insurer in respect of policy loans outstanding at the end of its 1977 taxation year in respect of participating life insurance policies in Canada, and

(iv) the amount, if any, by which

(A) the insurer's maximum tax actuarial reserve for its participating life insurance policies in Canada for its 1968 taxation year,

exceeds the aggregate of

(B) the amount that would have been the insurer's maximum tax actuarial reserve for its participating life insurance policies in Canada for its 1968 taxation year if that reserve had been determined on the basis of the rules applicable to its 1978 taxation year, and

(C) the aggregate of all amounts payable to the insurer in respect of policy loans outstanding at the end of its 1968 taxation year in respect of participating life insurance policies in Canada.

**Definitions [Reg. 2407]**: "amount" — ITA 248(1); "Canada" — ITA 255, *Interpretation Act* 35(1); "dividend", "insurer", "life insurer" — ITA 248(1); "maximum tax actuarial reserve", "participating life insurance policy", "policy loan" — ITA 138(12), Reg. 2405(1); "prescribed" — ITA 248(1); "taxation year" — ITA 249.

**2408. 1977 carryforward deduction** — For the purposes of subparagraph 138(4.2)(a)(iv) of the Act, a life insurer's 1977 carryforward deduction is hereby prescribed to be the amount, if any, by which

(a) the aggregate of

(i) the aggregate of amounts, each of which is an amount determined under paragraph 13(23)(b) of the Act in respect of property of a prescribed class of the insurer,

(ii) the aggregate of amounts each of which is a non-capital loss of the insurer for a taxation year ending after 1972 and before 1978 that would have been deductible by the insurer in computing its taxable income for a taxation year ending after 1977 if the Act were read without reference to subsection 111(7.2) thereof,

(iii) the amount prescribed by section 2407 to be the insurer's 1977 excess policy dividend deduction,

(iv) the amount determined under subparagraph 138(4.2)(b)(ii) of the Act in respect of the insurer,

(v) the amount determined under subparagraph 138(4.2)(c)(ii) of the Act in respect of the insurer,

(vi) the amount, if any, by which

(A) the aggregate of the insurer's maximum tax actuarial reserves for its 1977 taxation year,

exceeds

(B) the aggregate of the amounts deducted by the insurer for its 1977 taxation year under subparagraph 138(3)(a)(i) of the Act, and

(vii) the amount, if any, by which

(A) the maximum amount deductible by the insurer for its 1977 taxation year under subparagraph 138(3)(a)(ii) of the Act,

exceeds

(B) the amount deducted by the insurer for its 1977 taxation year under subparagraph 138(3)(a)(ii) of the Act,

exceeds

(b) the amount, if any, by which the aggregate of

(i) the lesser of

(A) the insurer's accumulated 1968 deficit, and

(B) the amount, if any, determined under subparagraph (vi),

(ii) the aggregate of the insurer's maximum tax actuarial reserves for its 1977 taxation year, other than reserves or any portions thereof in respect of segregated fund policies, and

(iii) the maximum amount deductible by the insurer for its 1977 taxation year under subparagraph 138(3)(a)(ii) of the Act,

exceeds the aggregate of

(iv) the aggregate of the amounts that would have been the insurer's maximum tax actuarial reserves for its 1977 taxation year if those reserves had been determined on the basis of the rules applicable to its 1978 taxation year,

(v) the aggregate of all amounts payable to the insurer in respect of policy loans outstanding at the end of its 1977 taxation year, and

(vi) the amount, if any, by which

(A) the aggregate of the insurer's maximum tax actuarial reserves for its 1968 taxation year, other than reserves or any portions thereof in respect of segregated fund policies,

exceeds the aggregate of

(B) the aggregate of the amounts that would have been the insurer's maximum tax actuarial reserves for its 1968 taxation year if those reserves had been determined on the basis of the rules applicable to its 1978 taxation year, and

(C) the aggregate of all amounts payable to the insurer in respect of policy loans outstanding at the end of its 1968 taxation year.

**Definitions [Reg. 2408]**: "accumulated 1968 deficit" — ITA 138(12), Reg. 2405(1); "amount", "dividend", "insurer", "life insurer" — ITA 248(1); "maximum tax actuarial reserve" — ITA 138(12), Reg. 2405(1); "non-capital loss" — ITA 111(8), 248(1); "policy loan" — ITA 138(12), Reg. 2405(1); "prescribed", "property" — ITA 248(1); "segregated fund policies" — ITA 138.1(1), Reg. 2405(1); "taxable income" — ITA 248(1); "taxation year" — ITA 249.

**2409. Transitional** — (1) For the purposes of this Part, except as expressly otherwise provided therein, where the expression "immediately preceding taxation year" refers to an insurer's 1977 taxation year, this Part shall be read as though the definitions therein applied to the insurer's 1977 taxation year.

(2), (3) [Apply to the 1978 taxation year only.]

(4) Except as expressly otherwise provided in this Part, where the expression "immediately preceding taxation year" occurs in a provision of this Part (other than section 2402) and refers to the insurer's 1987 taxation year, the provision shall be read as though the definitions in this Part applied to the insurer's 1987 taxation year.

**Definitions [Reg. 2409]**: "amount", "business" — ITA 248(1); "Canada" — ITA 255, *Interpretation Act* 35(1); "Canadian equity property" — Reg. 2400(1), 2405(3); "Canadian investment fund" — Reg. 2400(1), 2405(3), (4); "Canadian reserve liabilities", "equity property" — Reg. 2400(1), 2405(3); "insurance property" — Reg. 2400(1), 2406; "insurer" — ITA 248(1); "investment property" — Reg. 2400(1), 2405(3), 2406; "life insurance business" — ITA 248(1); "life insurance policy" — ITA 138(12), Reg. 2405(1); "life insurer" — ITA 248(1); "maximum tax actuarial reserve" — ITA 138(12), Reg. 2405(1); "mean Canadian reserve liabilities" — Reg. 2400(1), 2405(3); "non-resident" — ITA 248(1); "other than life insurance business" — Reg. 2400(2); "participating life insurance policy" — ITA 138(12), Reg. 2405(1); "particular insurance business" — Reg. 2400(1); "property" — ITA 248(1); "resident in Canada" — ITA 250; "taxation year" — ITA 249; "valuation", "value for the year" — Reg. 2405(3).

**2410. Prescribed amount** — For the purpose of subsection 138(4.4) of the Act, the amount prescribed in respect of an insurer's cost or capital cost, as the case may be, of a property for a period in a taxation year is the amount determined by the formula

$$[(A \times B) \times C/365] - D$$

where

A is the average annual rate of interest determined by reference to rates of interest prescribed in section 4301 for the months or portion thereof in the period;

B is the amount, if any, by which, the average cost or average capital cost, as the case may be, of the property for the period exceeds the average amount of debt relating to the acquisition of the property outstanding during the period that bears a fair market interest rate and, for this purpose,

(a) the average cost or average capital cost, as the case may be, of a property is the total of

(i) the aggregate of all amounts each of which is the cost or capital cost, as the case may be, if any, immediately before the beginning of the period in respect of the property, and

(ii) the aggregate of all amounts each of which is the proportion of any expenditure incurred on any day in the period in respect of the cost or capital cost, as the case may be, of the property that

(A) the number of days from that day to the end of the period

is of

(B) the number of days in the period, and

(b) the average amount of debt relating to the acquisition of a property is the amount, if any, by which the total of

(i) the aggregate of all amounts each of which is an indebtedness relating to the acquisition that was outstanding at the beginning of the period, and

(ii) the aggregate of all amounts each of which is the proportion of an indebtedness relating to the acquisition that was incurred on any day in the period that

(A) the number of days from that day to the end of the period

is of

(B) the number of days in the period,

exceeds

(iii) the aggregate of all amounts each of which is the proportion of an amount that was paid in respect of any indebtedness referred to in subparagraph (i) or (ii) on any day in the period (other than a payment of interest in respect thereof) that

(A) the number of days from that day to the end of the period

is of

(B) the number of days in the period;

C is the number of days in the period; and

D is the income derived from the property in the period by the person or partnership that owned the property.

**Related Provisions**: ITA 257 — Negative amounts in formulas.

**Notes**: Reg. 2410(1) amended (and renumbered 2410) by P.C. 2000-1714, effective for 1999 and later taxation years. For earlier years, read the opening words as:

(1) The amount prescribed for the purposes of subsection 138(4.4) of the Act shall be computed for a taxation year as the aggregate of all amounts each of which is the specified percentage for the year of the amount determined, in respect of a property for a period in the year referred to in that subsection by the formula

$$\left[ (A \times B) \times \frac{C}{D} \times \frac{E}{365} \right] - F$$

where

and, in place of the descriptions of C and D, read:

C is the amount, if any, by which the Canadian reserve liabilities of the life insurer at the end of a taxation year that includes the period exceed the aggregate of the policy loans and the outstanding premiums under insurance policies in Canada of the insurer at the end of the year, as determined for the purposes of the relevant authority;

D is

(a) where the insurer is a life insurer that does not carry on an insurance business outside Canada, the amount, if any, by which

(i) the valuation of all property that is owned by the insurer at the end of the taxation year that includes the period and that is

(A) an investment property,

(B) money, or

(C) a balance (other than a property included under (A) or (B)) standing to the insurer's credit as or on account of amounts deposited with a corporation authorized to accept deposits or to carry on the business of offering to the public its services as a trustee,

exceeds the total of

(ii) the aggregate of all amounts each of which is an amount outstanding at the end of the year in respect of a debt (other than a debt referred to in paragraph (h) of the definition "valuation" in subsection 2405(3) or an amount referred to in subparagraph (iii)) owing by the insurer in respect of money borrowed by the insurer (other

than money used by the insurer for the purpose of earning income from a source that is not an insurance business), and

(iii) the aggregate of all amounts each of which is the amount of a cheque outstanding at the end of the year drawn on an account of the insurer maintained with a corporation authorized to accept deposits or to carry on the business of offering to the public its services as a trustee, or

(b) where the insurer is a life insurer not referred to in paragraph (a), the amount of the insurer's Canadian investment fund as at the end of the taxation year that includes the period;

E is the aggregate of the number of days in the period; and

F is the amount, if any, of the income of the person or partnership that owned the property in the period that was derived from the property for the taxation year that includes the period.

Reg. 2410(2) repealed by P.C. 2000-1714, effective for 1999 and later taxation years. For earlier years read:

(2) The specified percentage for a taxation year in respect of an amount determined in respect of property under subsection (1) for a taxation year is the aggregate of

(a) that proportion of 20 per cent that the number of days in the taxation year that are after 1987 and before 1989 is of the number of days in the taxation year;

(b) that proportion of 40 per cent that the number of days in the taxation year that are after 1988 and before 1990 is of the number of days in the taxation year;

(c) that proportion of 60 per cent that the number of days in the taxation year that are after 1989 and before 1991 is of the number of days in the taxation year;

(d) that proportion of 80 per cent that the number of days in the taxation year that are after 1990 and before 1992 is of the number of days in the taxation year; and

(e) that proportion of 100 per cent that the number of days in the taxation year that are after 1991 is of the number of days in the taxation year.

**Definitions [Reg. 2410]**: "amount", "business" — ITA 248(1); "Canada" — ITA 255, *Interpretation Act* 35(1); "Canadian investment fund" — Reg. 2400(1), 2405(3), (4); "Canadian reserve liabilities" — Reg. 2400(1), 2405(3); "corporation" — ITA 248(1), *Interpretation Act* 35(1); "insurance policy", "insurer" — ITA 248(1); "investment property" — Reg. 2400(1), 2405(3), 2406; "life insurer" — ITA 248(1); "month" — *Interpretation Act* 35(1); "outstanding premiums" — Reg. 2400(1); "partnership" — see Notes to ITA 96(1); "person" — ITA 248(1); "policy loan" — ITA 138(12), Reg. 2405(1); "prescribed", "property" — ITA 248(1); "relevant authority" — Reg. 2405(3); "taxation year" — ITA 249; "valuation" — Reg. 2405(3).

**2411. (1)** Subject to subsection (2), the amount prescribed in respect of an insurer for a taxation year for the purposes of paragraph 138(9)(b) of the Act shall be the amount determined by the formula

$$A - (B + B.1 + C)$$

where

A is the positive or negative amount, as the case may be, determined in respect of the insurer for the year under subsection (3);

B is the positive or negative amount, as the case may be, determined in respect of the insurer for the year under subsection (4) in respect of the insurer's investment property for the year that is designated insurance property of the insurer for the year;

B.1 is the positive or negative amount, as the case may be, determined in respect of the insurer for the year under subsection (4.1) in respect of property disposed of by the insurer in a taxation year for which it was designated insurance property of the insurer; and

C is the amount claimed by the insurer for the year in respect of any balance of its cumulative excess account at the end of the year.

**Related Provisions**: ITA 257 — Negative amounts in formulas.

**Notes**: Formula element B amended by P.C. 2000-1714, effective for 1999 and later taxation years. For earlier years, read:

> B is the positive or negative amount, as the case may be, determined in respect of the insurer for the year under subsection (4) in respect of investment property designated by the insurer for the year pursuant to subsection 2400(1) as investment property used by it in the year in, or held by it in the year in the course of, carrying on an insurance business in Canada; and

Formula element B.1 added by P.C. 2000-1714, this version effective for 1999 and later taxation years. For 1995–1998 taxation years, read:

> B.1 is the positive or negative amount, as the case may be, determined in respect of the insurer for the year under subsection (4.1) in respect of property disposed of by the insurer that was, in the taxation year of disposition, investment property designated by the insurer under subsection 2400(1) as property used by it in the year in, or held by it in the year in the course of, carrying on an insurance business in Canada; and

**(2)** Where an amount computed under subsection (1) in respect of an insurer is a negative amount, that amount shall be deemed to be nil.

**(3)** The positive or negative amount, as the case may be, determined under this subsection in respect of an insurer for a taxation year shall be

(a) if the value for the year of the insurer's foreign investment property that is designated insurance property for the year is not greater than 5% of the amount of the insurer's mean Canadian investment fund for the year and the insurer so elects in its return of income under Part I of the Act for the year, the amount determined by the formula

$$\left[\frac{(A + A.1)}{B} \times (C + J)\right] + \frac{(D \times F)}{E}$$

or

(b) in any other case, the amount determined by the formula

$$\left(\frac{(A + A.1)}{B} \times C\right) + \left(\frac{D \times F}{E}\right) + \left(\frac{(G + G.1)}{H} \times J\right)$$

where

A is the positive or negative amount, as the case may be, determined in respect of the insurer for the year under subsection (4) in respect of Canadian investment property (other than Canadian equity property) owned by the insurer at any time in the year;

A.1 is the positive or negative amount, as the case may be, determined in respect of the insurer for the year under subsection (4.1) in respect of Canadian investment property (other than Canadian equity property) disposed of by the insurer in the year or preceding year;

B is the total value for the year of Canadian investment property (other than Canadian equity property) owned by the insurer at any time in the year;

C is the total value for the year of the insurer's Canadian investment property for the year (other than Canadian equity property and any property described in paragraph (i) of the definition "Canadian investment property" in subsection 2400(1)) that is designated insurance property of the insurer for the year;

D is the positive or negative amount, as the case may be, determined in respect of the insurer for the year under subsection (4) in respect of Canadian investment property that is Canadian equity property owned by the insurer at any time in the year;

E is the total value for the year of Canadian investment property that is Canadian equity property owned by the insurer at any time in the year;

F is the total value for the year of the insurer's Canadian investment property (other than any property described in paragraph (i) of the definition "Canadian investment property" in subsection 2400(1)) for the year that is Canadian equity property that is designated insurance property of the insurer for the year;

G is the positive or negative amount, as the case may be, determined in respect of the insurer for the year under subsection (4) in respect of foreign investment property owned by the insurer at any time in the year;

G.1 is the positive or negative amount, as the case may be, determined in respect of the insurer for the year under subsection (4.1) in respect of foreign investment property disposed of by the insurer in the year or a preceding taxation year;

H is the total value for the year of foreign investment property owned by the insurer at any time in the year; and

J is the total value for the year of the insurer's foreign investment property (other than any property described in paragraph (e) of the definition 'investment property' in subsection 2400(1)) that is designated insurance property of the insurer for the year.

**Reg. S. 2411(3)**  
**Income Tax Regulations**

**Notes**: Reg. 2411(3) amended by P.C. 2000-1714, this version effective for 1999 and later taxation years. For 1995–1998 taxation years, read:

(3) The positive or negative amount, as the case may be, determined under this subsection in respect of an insurer for a taxation year shall be

(a) if the value for the year of the insurer's foreign investment property designated by the insurer for the year pursuant to subsection 2400(1) as investment property used by it in the year in, or held by it in the year in the course of, carrying on an insurance business in Canada is not greater than 5% of the amount of the insurer's mean Canadian investment fund for the year and the insurer so elects, the amount determined by the formula

$$\left[\frac{(A + A.1)}{B} \times (C + J)\right] + \frac{(D \times F)}{E}$$

or

(b) in any other case, the amount determined by the formula

$$\left[\frac{(A + A.1)}{B} \times C\right] + \left(\frac{D \times F}{E}\right) + \left(\frac{(G + G.1)}{H} \times J\right)$$

where

A  is the positive or negative amount, as the case may be, determined in respect of the insurer for the year under subsection (4) in respect of Canadian investment property (other than Canadian equity property) owned by the insurer at any time in the year;

A.1  is the positive or negative amount, as the case may be, determined in respect of the insurer for the year under subsection (4.1) in respect of Canadian investment property (other than Canadian equity property) disposed of by the insurer in the year or a preceding taxation year;

B  is the total value for the year of Canadian investment property (other than Canadian equity property) owned by the insurer at any time in the year;

C  is the total value for the year of Canadian investment property (other than Canadian equity property) designated by the insurer for the year pursuant to subsection 2400(1) as investment property used by it in the year in, or held by it in the year in the course of, carrying on an insurance business in Canada;

D  is the positive or negative amount, as the case may be, determined in respect of the insurer for the year under subsection (4) in respect of Canadian investment property that is Canadian equity property owned by the insurer at any time in the year;

E  is the total value for the year of Canadian investment property that is Canadian equity property owned by the insurer at any time in the year;

F  is the total value for the year of Canadian investment property that is Canadian equity property designated by the insurer for the year pursuant to subsection 2400(1) as investment property used by it in the year in, or held by it in the year in the course of, carrying on an insurance business in Canada;

G  is the positive or negative amount, as the case may be, determined in respect of the insurer for the year under subsection (4) in respect of foreign investment property owned by the insurer at any time in the year;

G.1  is the positive or negative amount, as the case may be, determined in respect of the insurer for the year under subsection (4.1) in respect of foreign investment property disposed of by the insurer in the year or a preceding taxation year;

H  is the total value for the year of foreign investment property owned by the insurer at any time in the year; and

J  is the total value for the year of foreign investment property designated by the insurer for the year pursuant to subsection 2400(1) as investment property used by it in the year in, or held by it in the year in the course of, carrying on an insurance business in Canada.

For taxation years before 1995, read:

(3) The positive or negative amount, as the case may be, determined under this subsection in respect of an insurer for a taxation year shall be the amount determined by the formula

$$\left(\frac{A}{B} \times C\right) + \left(\frac{D}{E} \times F\right) + \left(\frac{G}{H} \times J\right)$$

or, where the value for the year of foreign investment property designated by the insurer for the year pursuant to subsection 2400(1) as investment property used by it in the year in, or held by it in the year in the course of, carrying on an insurance business in Canada is not greater than 5 per cent of the amount of the Canadian investment fund for the year of the insurer and the insurer so elects, the amount determined by the formula

$$\left(\frac{A}{B} \times (C + J)\right) + \left(\frac{D}{E} \times F\right)$$

where

A  is the positive or negative amount, as the case may be, determined in respect of the insurer for the year under subsection (4) in respect of Canadian investment property (other than Canadian equity property) owned by the insurer at any time in the year;

B  is the total value for the year of Canadian investment property (other than Canadian equity property) owned by the insurer at any time in the year;

C  is the total value for the year of Canadian investment property (other than Canadian equity property) designated by the insurer for the year pursuant to subsection 2400(1) as investment property used by it in the year in, or held by it in the year in the course of, carrying on an insurance business in Canada;

D  is the positive or negative amount, as the case may be, determined in respect of the insurer for the year under subsection (4) in respect of Canadian investment property that is Canadian equity property owned by the insurer at any time in the year;

E  is the total value for the year of Canadian investment property that is Canadian equity property owned by the insurer at any time in the year;

F  is the total value for the year of Canadian investment property that is Canadian equity property designated by the insurer for the year pursuant to subsection 2400(1) as investment property used by it in the year in, or held by it in the year in the course of, carrying on an insurance business in Canada;

G  is the positive or negative amount, as the case may be, determined in respect of the insurer for the year under subsection (4) in respect of foreign investment property owned by the insurer at any time in the year;

H  is the total value for the year of foreign investment property owned by the insurer at any time in the year; and

J  is the total value for the year of foreign investment property designated by the insurer for the year pursuant to subsection 2400(1) as investment property used by it in the year in, or held by it in the year in the course of, carrying on an insurance business in Canada.

**(4)** The positive or negative amount, as the case may be, determined under this subsection in respect of an insurer for a taxation year in respect of property shall be the amount determined by the formula

$$A - B$$

where

A is the total of the following amounts determined in respect of the property for the year, or that would be determined in respect of the property for the year if the property were designated insurance property of the insurer in respect of an insurance business in Canada for each taxation year in which the property was held by the insurer:

(a) the insurer's gross investment revenue for the year (other than taxable dividends that were or would be deductible in computing the insurer's taxable income for the year under subsection 138(6) of the Act) derived from the property,

(b) all amounts that were or would be included in computing the insurer's income for the year under paragraph 138(4)(b) and (c) of the Act in respect of the property,

(c) all amounts that were or would be included in computing the insurer's taxable capital gains for the year from the disposition of the property,

(d) all amounts that were or would be included in computing the insurer's gains for the year from the disposition of the property (other than a Canada security or capital property),

(e) all amounts that were or would be included in computing the insurer's income for the year under subsection 13(1) of the Act in respect of the property,

(f) all amounts that were or would be included in computing the insurer's income for the year under paragraph 12(1)(d), (d.1) or (i) of the Act in respect of the property,

(g) all amounts that were or would be included in computing the insurer's income for the year under subsection 59(3.2) or (3.3) of the Act in respect of the property,

(h) all amounts that were or would be included in computing the insurer's income for the year under subsection 14(1) of the Act in respect of the property, and

(i) all other amounts that were or would be included in computing the insurer's income for the year in respect of the property; and

B is the aggregate of the following amounts determined in respect of the property for the year or that would be determined in respect of the property for the year if it were insurance property of the insurer for the year in respect of an insurance business in Canada:

(a) all amounts that were or would be included in computing the insurer's allowable capital losses for the year from the disposition of the property,

(b) all amounts that were or would be included in computing the insurer's losses for the year from the disposition of the property (other than a Canada security or capital property),

(c) all amounts that were or would be deductible in computing the insurer's income for the year under paragraph 138(3)(b) and (d) of the Act in respect of the property,

(d) all amounts that were or would be deductible in computing the insurer's income for the year under paragraph 20(1)(a) of the Act in respect of the capital cost of the property or under paragraphs 20(1)(c) and (d) of the Act in respect of interest paid or payable on borrowed money used to acquire the property,

(e) where any such property is rental property or leasing property (within the meaning assigned by subsections 1100(14) and (17), respectively), all amounts that were or would be deductible in computing the insurer's income for the year in respect of expenses directly related to the earning of rental income derived from the property,

(f) all amounts that were or would be deductible by the insurer in computing the insurer's income for the year under paragraph 20(1)(l), (l.1) or (p) of the Act as reserve or bad debt in respect of the property,

(g) all amounts that were deducted or would be deductible in computing the insurer's income for the year under section 66, 66.1, 66.2 or 66.4 of the Act in respect of the property,

(h) all amounts that were or would be deductible in computing the insurer's income for the year under paragraph 20(1)(b) of the Act in respect of the property, and

(i) all amounts that were or would be deductible in computing the insurer's income for the year in respect of other expenses directly related to the earning of gross investment revenue derived from the property.

**Proposed Amendment — Reg. 2411(4)**

**(4)** The positive or negative amount, as the case may be, determined under this subsection in respect of an insurer for a taxation year in respect of property shall be the amount determined by the formula

$$A - B$$

where

Reg. S. 2411(4)  Income Tax Regulations

A is the total of the following amounts determined in respect of the property for the year, or that would be determined in respect of the property for the year if it were insurance property of the insurer for the year in respect of an insurance business in Canada and if it had been insurance property of the insurer in respect of an insurance business in Canada for each preceding taxation year in which it was held by the insurer:

(a) the insurer's gross investment revenue for the year (other than taxable dividends that were or would be deductible in computing the insurer's taxable income for the year under subsection 138(6) of the Act) derived from the property,

(b) [Proposed repeal]

(c) all amounts that were or would be included in computing the insurer's taxable capital gains for the year from the disposition of the property,

(c.1) all amounts that were or would be included under paragraph 142.4(5)(e) of the Act in respect of the property in computing the insurer's income for the year,

(d) all amounts that were or would be included in computing the insurer's income for the year as gains from the disposition of such of the property as is not capital property or a specified debt obligation (as defined in subsection 142.2(1) of the Act),

(e) all amounts that were or would be included in computing the insurer's income for the year under subsection 13(1) of the Act in respect of the property,

(f) all amounts that were or would be included in computing the insurer's income for the year under paragraph 12(1)(d), (d.1) or (i) of the Act in respect of the property,

(g) all amounts that were or would be included in computing the insurer's income for the year under subsection 59(3.2) or (3.3) of the Act in respect of the property,

(h) all amounts that were or would be included in computing the insurer's income for the year under subsection 14(1) of the Act in respect of the property, and

(i) all other amounts that were or would be included in computing the insurer's income for the year in respect of the property otherwise than because of subsection 142.4(4) of the Act; and

B is the total of the following amounts determined in respect of the property for the year, or that would be determined in respect of the property for the year if it were insurance property of the insurer for the year in respect of an insurance business in Canada and if it had been insurance property of the insurer in respect of an insurance business in Canada for each preceding taxation year in which it was held by the insurer:

(a) all amounts that were or would be included in computing the insurer's allowable capital losses for the year from the disposition of the property,

(a.1) all amounts that were or would be deductible under paragraph 142.4(5)(f) of the Act in respect of the property in computing the insurer's income for the year,

(b) all amounts that were or would be deductible in computing the insurer's income for the year as losses from the disposition of such of the property as is not capital property or a specified debt obligation (as defined in subsection 142.2(1) of the Act),

(c) [Proposed repeal]

(d) all amounts that were or would be deductible in computing the insurer's income for the year under paragraph 20(1)(a) of the Act in respect of the capital cost of the property or under paragraphs 20(1)(c) and (d) of the Act in respect of interest paid or payable on borrowed money used to acquire the property,

(e) where any such property is rental property or leasing property (within the meaning assigned by subsections 1100(14) and (17), respectively), all amounts that were or would be deductible in computing the insurer's income for the year in respect of expenses directly related to the earning of rental income derived from the property,

(f) all amounts that were or would be deductible by the insurer in computing the insurer's income for the year under paragraph 20(1)(l), (l.1) or (p) of the Act as reserve or bad debt in respect of the property,

(g) all amounts that were deducted or would be deductible in computing the insurer's income for the year under section 66, 66.1, 66.2 or 66.4 of the Act in respect of the property,

(h) all amounts that were or would be deductible in computing the insurer's income for the year under paragraph 20(1)(b) of the Act in respect of the property, and

(i) all amounts that were or would be deductible in computing the insurer's income for the year in respect of other expenses directly related to the earning of gross investment revenue derived from the property.

**Application**: The June 1, 1995 draft regulations (securities held by financial institutions), subsecs. 4(7) to (13), will amend the opening words of the descriptions of A and B in subsec. 2411(4), will amend paras. (d) and (i) of the description of A and (b) of the description of B, will add paras. (c.1) to the description of A and (a.1) to the description of B, and will repeal paras. (b) of the description of A and (c) of the description of B; the opening words of the descriptions of A and B applicable to taxation years that end after June 1, 1995, paras. (b) and (i) of the description of A and para. (c) of the description of B applicable to taxation years that begin after February 22, 1994, paras. (d) and (c.1) to the description of A and paras. (a.1) and (b) to the description of B, applicable to dispositions of property that occur after February 22, 1994.

**Technical Notes**: Subsection 2411(4) provides that an insurer's net investment revenue from property of a particular class is determined by the formula "A - B", where A is the total of the gross investment revenue from the property, gains from the disposition of the property and other income inclusions in respect of the property, and B is losses from the property and other deductions in respect of the property. The amounts included in A and B in respect of property that has not been designated as property of an insurance business carried on by the insurer in Canada are determined as if the property had been so designated. Several changes are made to the determination of amounts A and B.

The descriptions of both A and B are amended to clarify that, in determining the amounts to be taken into account in respect of property that has not been designated, the property is to be treated as if it had been designated for each year from the time it was acquired.

The other changes to A are as follows:

- Paragraph (b) is repealed. This paragraph includes in A the amounts included in the insurer's income under paragraphs 138(4)(b) and (c) of the Act (profit on disposition of a Canada security, and amortization of discount on such a security). This amendment is consequential on the repeal of paragraphs 138(4)(b) and (c).

- New paragraph (c.1) includes in A the amounts that are included in the insurer's income by subsection 142.4(5) of the Act. That subsection includes in income the gain from the disposition of specified debt obligations after February 22, 1994 where the gain is not required to be amortized.

- Paragraph (d), which includes certain non-capital gains in A, is amended to replace the exclusion for gains from Canada securities by an exclusion for gains from specified debt obligations. Those gains are dealt with, in some cases, by new paragraph (c.1) and in other cases by new subsection 2411(4.1).

- Paragraph (i), which includes in A all amounts that are included in the insurer's income in respect of the property, but that are not specifically referred to in the preceding paragraphs, is amended so that it does not apply to amounts that are included in income by subsection 142.4(4) of the Act. New subsection 2411(4.1), in conjunction with amendments to subsections 2411(1) and (3), provides for subsection 142.4(4) amounts to be taken into account.

The changes to B, in addition to the change described [to A] above, are as follows:

- New paragraph (a.1) includes in B the amounts that are deductible under subsection 142.4(5) of the Act in computing the insurer's income. That subsection provides a deduction for the loss from the disposition of specified debt obligations after February 22, 1994 where the loss is not required to be amortized.

- Paragraph (b), which includes certain non-capital losses in B, is amended to replace the exclusion for losses from Canada securities by an exclusion for losses from specified debt obligations. Those losses are dealt with, in some cases, by new paragraph (a.1) and in other cases by new subsection 2411(4.1).

- Paragraph (c) is repealed. This paragraph includes in B the amounts that are deductible under paragraphs 138(3)(b) and (d) of the Act (loss on disposition of a Canada security, and amortization of premium on such a security). This amendment is consequential on the repeal of paragraphs 138(3)(b) and (d).

**Related Provisions**: ITA 257 — Negative amounts in formulas.

**Notes**: Opening words of formula element A amended by P.C. 2000-1714, this version effective for 1999 and later taxation years. For taxation years ending from June 2, 1995 through 1998, read:

A  is the total of the following amounts determined in respect of the property for the year, or that would be determined in respect of the property for the year if it were insurance property of the insurer for the year in respect of an insurance business in Canada and if it had been insurance property of the insurer in respect of an insurance business in Canada for each preceding taxation year in which it was held by the insurer:

For taxation years ending before June 2, 1995, read:

A  is the aggregate of the following amounts determined in respect of the property for the year or that would be determined in respect of the property for the year if it were insurance property of the insurer for the year in respect of an insurance business in Canada:

**(4.1)** The positive or negative amount, as the case may be, determined under this subsection in respect of an insurer for a taxation year in respect of property disposed of by the insurer in the year or a preceding taxation year is the amount determined by the formula

$$A - B$$

where

A  is the total of the amounts included under paragraphs 142.4(4)(a) and (c) of the Act in the insurer's income for the year in respect of the property, or that would be so included if the property were designated insurance property of the insurer in respect of an insurance business in Canada for each taxation year in which it was held by the insurer; and

B  is the total of the amounts deductible under paragraphs 142.4(4)(b) and (d) of the Act in respect of the property in computing the insurer's income for the year, or that would be so deductible if the property were designated insurance property of the insurer in respect of an insurance business in Canada for each taxation year in which it was held by the insurer.

**Related Provisions**: ITA 257 — Negative amounts in formulas.

**Notes**: Reg. 2411(4.1) added by P.C. 2000-1714, this version effective for 1999 and later taxation years. For 1995–1998 taxation years, read A and B as:

- A is the total of the amounts included under paragraphs 142.4(4)(a) and (c) of the Act in the insurer's income for the year in respect of the property, or that would be so included if the property had been insurance property of the insurer in respect of an insurance business in Canada for each taxation year in which it was held by the insurer; and

- B is the total of the amounts deductible under paragraphs 142.4(4)(b) and (d) of the Act in respect of the property in computing the insurer's income for the year, or that would be so deductible if the property had been insurance property of the insurer in respect of an insurance business in Canada for each taxation year in which it was held by the insurer.

**(5)** For the purposes of subsection (4), a property that has not been designated by the insurer for the year pursuant to subsection 2400(1) as investment property used by it in the year in, or held by it in the year in the course of, carrying on an insurance business in Canada shall be deemed to be a property used by it in the year in, or held by it in the year in the course of, carrying on that insurance business in respect of which the property has been reported by the insurer in its annual report for the year to the relevant authority or, where the insurer was throughout the year subject to the supervision of the relevant authority but was not required to file an annual report with the relevant authority for the year, that insurance business in respect of which the property would have been reported by the insurer in an annual report for the year if it had been so required by the relevant authority.

**Proposed Repeal — Reg. 2411(5)**

**Application**: The June 1, 1995 draft regulations (securities held by financial institutions), subsec. 4(15), will repeal subsec. 2411(5), applicable to taxation years that begin after February 22, 1994.

**Technical Notes**: Where property has not been designated as property used or held in a Canadian insurance business, subsection 2411(4) applies on the assumption that the property had been so designated. Subsection 2411(5) contains an additional rule for this purpose. It provides that the property is to be considered property of the business in respect of which it is reported in the insurer's annual report. This rule was required because of the special rules for the tax treatment of debt obligations (referred to as Canada securities) that are property of a life insurance business. Subsection 2411(5) is repealed, for taxation years beginning after February 22, 1994, as a consequence of the repeal of the special rules for Canada securities.

**(6)** For the purposes of subsection (1), the balance of an insurer's cumulative excess account at the end of a taxation year shall be determined as the amount, if any, by which

(a) the aggregate of all amounts each of which is a positive amount, if any, determined in respect of each of such of its seven immediately preceding taxation years that began after June 17, 1987 and ended after 1987 by the formula

$$B - A$$

where A and B are the amounts determined under subsection (1) in respect of the insurer for such immediately preceding taxation year,

exceeds

(b) the aggregate of all amounts each of which is an amount claimed by the insurer under subsection (1) in respect of its cumulative excess account for a preceding taxation year that can be attributed to a positive amount determined under paragraph (a) for that year and, for the purpose of this paragraph, a positive amount determined in respect of a taxation year shall be deemed to have been claimed before a positive amount determined in respect of any subsequent taxation year.

**Related Provisions**: ITA 257 — Negative amounts in formulas.

**(7)** [Repealed]

**Notes**: Reg. 2411(7) repealed by P.C. 2000-1714, effective for 1999 and later taxation years. For earlier years, read:

(7) For the purposes of subsection (3),

(a) where the aggregate value for the year of property designated by the insurer for the year pursuant to paragraphs 2400(1)(a) to (d) exceeds the minimum value for the year of property required to be designated by the insurer for the year pursuant to those paragraphs, the aggregate value for the year of the property determined for the year under each of C, F and J of the formula set out in subsection (3) shall not exceed that minimum value for the year of such property that is required to be designated by the insurer for the year pursuant to paragraphs 2400(1)(a) to (d); and

(b) for the purposes of paragraph (a), the value for the year of property required to be designated by the insurer for the year under F in the formula set out in subsection (3) shall be deemed to be the value for the year of such property designated by the insurer for the year.

**(8)** For the purposes of this section, "foreign investment property" of an insurer means investment property of the insurer (unless the insurer is a non-resident insurer and it is established by the insurer that the investment property is not effectively connected with its Canadian insurance businesses) that is not Canadian investment property of the insurer.

**Definitions [Reg. 2411]**: "allowable capital loss" — ITA 38(b), 248(1); "balance" — Reg. 2411(6); "borrowed money", "business" — ITA 248(1); "Canada" — ITA 255, *Interpretation Act* 35(1); "Canada security" — ITA 138(12); "Canadian equity property" — Reg. 2400(1), 2405(3); "Canadian investment fund for the year" — Reg. 2405(3); "Canadian investment property" — Reg. 2400(1), 2405(3); "capital property" — ITA 54, 248(1); "designated insurance property" — ITA 138(12), 248(1); "disposed" — ITA 248(1)"disposition"; "disposition" — ITA 248(1); "foreign investment property" — Reg. 2411(8); "gross investment revenue" — ITA 138(12), Reg. 2405(1); "immediately preceding taxation year" — Reg. 2409(1), (4); "insurance property" — Reg. 2400(1), 2406; "insurer" — ITA 248(1); "investment property" — Reg. 2400(1), 2405(3), 2406; "mean Canadian investment fund" — Reg. 2400(1); "non-resident", "prescribed", "property" — ITA 248(1); "related" — ITA 251(2)–(6); "relevant authority" — Reg. 2405(3);

"taxable capital gain" — ITA 38(a), 248(1); "taxable dividend" — ITA 89(1), 248(1); "taxable income" — ITA 248(1); "taxation year" — ITA 249; "value for the year" — Reg. 2405(3), 2411(7)(b)"amount" — ITA 248(1); "mean Canadian investment fund" — Reg. 2400(1), 2411(5).

**2412. (1) Mean Canadian investment fund** — For the purposes of this Part, the mean Canadian investment fund of an insurer for a particular taxation year is the total of

(a) 50% of the total of

(i) its Canadian investment fund at the end of the particular year, and

(ii) either,

(A) if the insurer is resident in Canada, its Canadian investment fund at the end of its preceding taxation year, or

(B) if the insurer is non-resident, its Canadian investment fund at the end of its preceding taxation year determined as if its attributed surplus for that preceding taxation year were its attributed surplus for the particular year, and

(b) the insurer's cash-flow adjustment for the particular year.

**(2) Cash-flow adjustment** — An insurer's cash-flow adjustment for a taxation year is the amount equal to

(a) if the year ended two months or more after it began, the positive or negative amount determined by the formulaa

$$50\% \times (A - B/C)$$

where

A is the total of all amounts each of which is the amount determined under subsection (3) in respect of a full month in the year (or in respect of the part of the month that ends after the last full month in the year, if that part is greater than 15 days),

B is the total of all amounts each of which is the amount determined in respect of a full month in the year (or in respect of the part of the month that ends after the last full month in the year, if that part is greater than 15 days) by the formula

$$D \times (1 + 2E)$$

where

D is the amount determined under subsection (3) in respect of the month or part of the month, and

E is the number of months in the year that ended before the beginning of the month or part of the month, and

C is the number of full months in the year (plus 1, if the year ends more than 15 days after the end of the last full month in the year); and

(b) if the year ended less than two months after it began, nil.

**Related Provisions**: ITA 257 — Negative amounts in formulas.

**(3) Amounts paid and received** — The amount determined in respect of an insurer for a particular month or part of a month (in this subsection referred to as a "month") in a taxation year is the positive or negative amount determined by the formula

$$G - H$$

where

G is the total of all amounts each of which is

(a) the amount of a premium or consideration received by the insurer in the month in respect of a contract of insurance (including a settlement annuity) entered into in the course of carrying on its insurance businesses in Canada,

(b) an amount received by the insurer in the month in respect of interest on or a repayment in respect of a policy loan made under a life insurance policy in Canada, or

(c) an amount received by the insurer in the month in respect of reinsurance (other than reinsurance undertaken to effect a transfer of a business in respect of which subsection 138(11.5), (11.92) or (11.94) of the Act applies) arising in the course of carrying on its insurance businesses in Canada; and

H is the total of all amounts each of which is

(a) the amount of a claim or benefit (including a payment under an annuity or settlement annuity, a payment of a policy dividend and an amount paid on a lapsed or terminated policy), a refund of premiums, a premium or a commission paid by the insurer in the month under a contract of insurance in the course of carrying on its insurance businesses in Canada,

(b) the amount of a policy loan made by the insurer in the month under a life insurance policy in Canada, or

(c) an amount paid by the insurer in the month in respect of reinsurance (other than reinsurance undertaken to effect a transfer of a business in respect of which subsection 138(11.5), (11.92) or (11.94) of the Act applies) in the course of carrying on its insurance businesses in Canada.

**Related Provisions**: ITA 257 — Negative amounts in formulas.

**(4) [Meaning of "month"]** — A reference to a "month" in this section means

(a) if an insurer's taxation year does not begin on the first day of a calendar month and the insurer elects to have this paragraph apply for the year, the period beginning on the day in a calendar month that has the same calendar number as the particular day on which the taxation year began and ending

(i) on the day immediately before the day in the next calendar month that has the same calendar number as the particular day, or

(ii) if the next calendar month does not have a day that has the same calendar number as the particular day, the last day of that next calendar month; and

(b) in any other case, a calendar month.

**Related Provisions**: ITA 257 — Negative amounts in formulas.

**Notes [Reg. 2412]**: Reg. 2412 amended by P.C. 2000-1714, effective for 1999 and later taxation years. For earlier years, read:

2412. (1) The amount of the Canadian investment fund for the year for a taxation year in respect of an insurer shall be determined by the formula

$$A + B$$

where

A  is the mean Canadian investment fund for the year for the taxation year in respect of the insurer; and

B  is the amount determined under subsection (2) in respect of the insurer for the taxation year.

(2) Subject to subsection (3), the amount determined under this subsection in respect of an insurer for the taxation year shall be determined by the formula

$$\frac{1}{2}\left[A - \frac{(B + 3C + 5D + 7E)}{F}\right]$$

where

A  is the aggregate of B, C, D and E;

B  is the positive or negative amount, as the case may be, determined under subsection (4) in respect of the insurer for the first three month period in the taxation year of the insurer;

C  is the positive or negative amount, as the case may be, determined under subsection (4) in respect of the insurer for the second three month period in the taxation year of the insurer;

D  is the positive or negative amount, as the case may be, determined under subsection (4) in respect of the insurer for the third three month period in the taxation year of the insurer;

E  is the positive or negative amount, as the case may be, determined under subsection (4) in respect of the insurer for the fourth three month period in the taxation year of the insurer; and

F  is the result obtained when the number of calendar months in the taxation year is divided by 3 and, where that result is not a whole number, it shall be rounded down to the next lower whole number.

(3) Where the taxation year of an insurer does not contain any three month period, the amount determined under subsection (2) in respect of the insurer shall be deemed to be nil.

(4) The positive or negative amount, as the case may be, determined in respect of an insurer for a particular three month period in a taxation year of the insurer shall be determined by the formula

$$A - B$$

where

A  is the aggregate of all amounts each of which is

(a) an amount of a premium or consideration received by the insurer in the period in respect of a contract of insurance or an annuity (including a settlement annuity) entered into in the course of carrying on its insurance businesses in Canada,

(b) an amount received by the insurer in the period in respect of interest on or a repayment in respect of a policy loan made under a life insurance policy in Canada, or

(c) an amount received by the insurer in the period in respect of reinsurance (other than reinsurance undertaken to effect a transfer of a business in respect of which subsection 138(11.5), (11.92) or (11.94) of the Act applies) arising in the course of carrying on its insurance businesses in Canada and not otherwise included in paragraph (a) or (b); and

B  is the aggregate of all amounts each of which is

(a) an amount of a claim or benefit (including a payment under an annuity or settlement annuity, a payment of a policy dividend and an amount paid on a lapsed or terminated policy) or a refund of premiums paid by the insurer in the period under a contract of insurance or an annuity in the course of carrying on its insurance businesses in Canada,

(b) an amount of a policy loan made by the insurer in the period under a life insurance policy in Canada,

(c) a premium or commission paid by the insurer in the period in respect of a contract of insurance or an annuity in the course of carrying on its insurance businesses in Canada, or

(d) an amount paid by the insurer in the period in respect of reinsurance (other than reinsurance undertaken to effect a transfer of a business in respect of which subsection 138(11.5), (11.92) or (11.94) of the Act applies) in the course of carrying on its insurance businesses in Canada and not otherwise included in paragraph (a), (b) or (c).

(5) For the purposes of this section, "mean Canadian investment fund for the year", means

(a) for a taxation year in respect of a life insurer resident in Canada, ½ of the aggregate of

(i) its Canadian investment fund as at the end of the year, and

(ii) its Canadian investment fund as at the end of the immediately preceding taxation year; and

(b) for a taxation year in respect of a non-resident insurer, ½ of the aggregate of

(i) its Canadian investment fund as at the end of the year, and

(ii) the amount that would be its Canadian investment fund as at the end of the immediately preceding taxation year if the insurer's attributed surplus for the year for that preceding year were its attributed surplus for the year for that taxation year.

**Definitions [Reg. 2412]**: "affiliated" — ITA 251.1; "amount", "annuity" — ITA 248(1); "attributed surplus" — Reg. 2400(1); "attributed surplus for the year" — Reg. 2405(3); "business" — ITA 248(1); "Canada" — ITA 255, *Interpretation Act* 35(1); "Canadian investment fund" — Reg. 2400(1), 2405(3), (4); "Canadian investment fund for the year" — Reg. 2405(3); "dividend" — ITA 248(1); "immediately preceding taxation year" — Reg. 2409(1), (4); "insurer" — ITA 248(1); "life insurance policy in Canada" — ITA 138(12), Reg. 2405(1); "life insurer" — ITA 248(1); "mean Canadian investment fund" — Reg. 2400(1); "month" — Reg. 2412(4); "non-resident" — ITA 248(1); "partnership" — see Notes to ITA 96(1); "person" — ITA 248(1); "policy dividend" — ITA 139,1(8)(a); "policy loan" — ITA 138(12), Reg. 2405(1); "property" — ITA 248(1); "resident in Canada" — ITA 250; "share", "shareholder" — ITA 248(1); "taxation year" — ITA 249; "weighted Canadian liabilities", "weighted total liabilities" — Reg. 2400(1).

## PART XXV — SPECIAL T1 TAX TABLE FOR INDIVIDUALS

**2500. (1)** For the purposes of subsection 117(6) of the Act,

(a) $55,605, adjusted for each taxation year after 1989 in the manner set out in subsection 117.1(1) of the Act, is the prescribed amount; and

(b) an "individual of a prescribed class" for a taxation year is

(i) an estate or trust,

(ii) an individual who was a non-resident person throughout the year, other than an individual

(A) whose amount taxable for the year was from

(I) the duties of an office or employment performed in one province,

(II) the carrying on of a business in one province, or

(III) any combination of sources described in subclauses (I) and (II) if all of those sources are located in one province, and

(B) who was not subject to any other provision of this subsection,

(iii) an individual who, on the last day of the year, resided in a province and had income for the year from a business with a permanent establishment, as defined in subsection 2600(2), outside the province,

(iv) an individual whose tax otherwise payable for the year under Part I of the Act is reduced by virtue of any of the following provisions of the Act:

(A) subsection 117(7),

(B) section 121,

(C) section 122.3, or

(D) section 126,

(v) an individual who makes an election in respect of the year under subsection 119(1) of the Act,

(vi) an individual eligible to pay tax at a reduced rate pursuant to subsection 40(7) of the *Income Tax Application Rules* on a payment made to him in the year, or

(vii) an individual who makes an election in respect of the year under subsection 110.4(2) of the Act.

**Notes**: The $55,605 figure for 1989 corresponded to the threshold for the top marginal rate of federal tax.

**(2)** For the purposes of subsection 117(6) of the Act, a table of the tax payable for a taxation year shall be prepared in accordance with the following rules:

(a) the table shall be divided into ranges of amounts taxable not exceeding $10 each and shall specify the tax payable in respect of each range;

(b) the tax payable on an amount taxable within any range referred to in paragraph (a) shall be equal to the tax payable thereon for the year computed under subsection 117(2) of the Act and, where applicable, adjusted annually pursuant to section 117.1 of the Act; and

(c) the tax payable referred to in paragraph (b) shall be calculated as if the amount taxable is equal to the average of the highest and lowest amounts taxable in the range and, where the resulting tax payable is not a multiple of one dollar, it shall be rounded to the nearest multiple of one dollar or, if it is equidistant from two such multiples, to the higher thereof.

**(3)** For the purposes of subsection 117(6) of the Act, a table of the additional tax for income not earned in a province, the individual surtax and the refundable Quebec abatement for a taxation year shall be prepared in accordance with the following rules:

(a) the table shall be divided into ranges of tax payable not exceeding $2 each and shall specify, in respect of each range,

(i) the individual surtax payable,

(ii) where applicable, the additional tax for income not earned in a province, and

(iii) where applicable, the refundable Quebec abatement,

on every amount taxable within each such range;

(b) the tax payable referred to in paragraph (a) is the tax payable determined by the table prepared pursuant to subsection (2) less the allowable non-refundable credits under sections 118 to 118.9 of the Act;

(c) the individual surtax in respect of an amount of tax payable within any range referred to in paragraph (a) shall be the amount that is equal to the surtax thereon computed under subsection 180.1(1) of the Act;

(d) the additional tax for income not earned in a province in respect of an amount of tax payable within any range referred to in paragraph (a) shall be the amount that is equal to the tax determined thereon under subsection 120(1) of the Act;

(e) the refundable Quebec abatement in respect of an amount of tax payable within any range referred to in paragraph (a) shall be the amount that is equal to the abatement determined under subsection 120(2) of the Act and in accordance with section 27 of the *Federal-Provincial Fiscal Arrangements Act*;

(f) the amount referred to in paragraph (c) or (d) shall be calculated as if the tax payable is equal to the average of the highest and lowest amounts in the range and, where the resulting amount is not a multiple of one dollar, it shall be rounded to the nearest multiple of one dollar or, if it is equidistant from two such multiples, to the higher thereof; and

(g) the amount referred to in paragraph (e) shall be calculated as if the tax payable is equal to the average of the highest and lowest amounts in the range and, where the resulting amount is not a multiple of one tenth of one dollar, it shall be rounded to the nearest multiple of one tenth of one dollar or, if it is equidistant from two such multiples, to the higher thereof.

**Notes**: Tax tables are no longer used. ITA 117(6) has been repealed.

**Definitions [Reg. 2500]**: "amount" — ITA 248(1); "amount taxable" — ITA 117(2), Reg. 2501; "business", "employment" — ITA 248(1); "estate" — ITA 104(1), 248(1); "individual", "non-resident", "office", "person", "prescribed" — ITA 248(1); "province" — *Interpretation Act* 35(1); "taxation year" — ITA 249; "trust" — ITA 104(1), 248(1), (3).

**Forms [Reg. 2500]**: Table A and Table B, 1994 T1 General Tax Guide. Since the 1995 return, these tables are no longer used, in order to save printing costs. (Revenue Canada news release and Fact Sheet, November 22, 1995.).

**2501.** In this Part, "amount taxable" has the meaning assigned by subsection 117(2) of the Act.

# PART XXVI — INCOME EARNED IN PROVINCE BY AN INDIVIDUAL

**Notes [Part XXVI]**: Part XXVI allocates an individual's (including a trust's) income among the provinces. For the equivalent rules for corporations, see Reg. 400–413.

**2600. Interpretation** — (1) For the purposes of paragraph 120(4)(a) [120(4)"income earned in the year in a province"] of the Act, "income earned in the year in a province" by an individual means the aggregate of his incomes earned in the taxation year in each province, as determined in accordance with this Part.

(2) In this Part, "permanent establishment" means a fixed place of business of the individual including an office, a branch, a mine, an oil well, a farm, a timberland, a factory, a workshop or a warehouse, and

(a) where an individual carries on business through an employee or agent, established in a particular place, who has general authority to contract for his employer or principal or who has a stock of merchandise owned by his employer or principal from which he regularly fills orders which he receives, the individual shall be deemed to have a permanent establishment in that place;

(b) where an individual uses substantial machinery or equipment in a particular place at any time in a taxation year he shall be deemed to have a permanent establishment in that place; and

(c) the fact that an individual has business dealings through a commission agent, broker, or other independent agent or maintains an office solely for the purchase of merchandise, shall not of itself be held to mean that the individual has a permanent establishment.

**Interpretation Bulletins**: IT-242R: Retired partners.

(3) [Revoked]

**Definitions [Reg. 2600]**: "business", "employee", "employer", "individual", "office" — ITA 248(1); "permanent establishment" — Reg. 2600(2); "province" — *Interpretation Act* 35(1); "taxation year" — ITA 249.

**2601. Residents of Canada** — (1) Where an individual resided in a particular province on the last day of a taxation year and had no income for the year from a business with a permanent establishment outside the province, his income earned in the taxation year in the province is his income for the year.

(2) Where an individual resided in a particular province on the last day of a taxation year and had income for the year from a business with a permanent establishment outside the province, his income earned in the taxation year in the province is the amount, if any, by which

(a) his income for the year

exceeds

(b) the aggregate of his income for the year from carrying on business earned in each other province and each country other than Canada determined as hereinafter set forth in this Part.

(3) Where an individual, who resided in Canada on the last day of a taxation year and who carried on business in a particular province at any time in the year, did not reside in the province on the last day of the year, his income earned in the taxation year in the province is his income for the year from carrying on business earned in the province, determined as hereinafter set forth in this Part.

(4) Where an individual resided in Canada on the last day of a taxation year and carried on business in another country at any time in the year, his income earned in the taxation year in that other country is his income for the year from carrying on business earned in the other country, determined as hereinafter set forth in this Part.

(5) In this section, a reference to the "last day of a taxation year" shall

(a) in the case of an individual who resided in Canada at any time in the year but ceased to reside in Canada before the end of the year, be deemed to be a reference to the "last day in the year on which he resided in Canada"; and

(b) in the case of an individual described in paragraph 250(1)(d.1) of the Act or his spouse or child who

(i) resided in Canada at any time in the year,

(ii) would, but for paragraph 250(1)(d.1), (e) or (f) of the Act, have ceased to reside in Canada before the end of the year, and

(iii) is, by virtue of paragraph 250(1)(d.1), (e) or (f) of the Act, deemed to have been resident in Canada throughout the year,

be deemed to be a reference to the "day in the year on which he would have so ceased to reside in Canada".

**Notes [Reg. 2601]**: References to "spouse" are expected to be amended to add "or common-law partner" effective 2001 or earlier by election, as has been done throughout the ITA. See Notes to ITA 248(1)"common-law partner".

**Definitions [Reg. 2601]**: "amount", "business" — ITA 248(1); "Canada" — ITA 255, *Interpretation Act* 35(1); "child" — ITA 252(1); "individual" — ITA 248(1); "last day of a taxation year" — Reg. 2601(5); "permanent establishment" — Reg. 2600(2); "province" — *Interpretation Act* 35(1); "resident in Canada" — ITA 250; "taxation year" — ITA 249.

**Remission Orders [Reg. 2601]**: *Income Earned in Quebec Income Tax Remission Order*, P.C. 1989-1204, as amended by P.C. 1991-1661 and P.C. 1992-2593 (special interpretation of Reg. 2601(1) and (2) for residents of Quebec).

**Forms [Reg. 2601]**: T691A: Minimum tax supplement — multiple jurisdictions; T2203: Calculation of tax in respect of multiple jurisdictions.

**2602. Non-residents** — **(1)** Except as provided in subsection (2), where an individual did not reside in Canada at any time in a taxation year, his income earned in the taxation year in a particular province is the aggregate of

(a) that part of the amount of his income from an office or employment, that is included in computing his taxable income earned in Canada for the year by virtue of subparagraph 115(1)(a)(i) of the Act, that is reasonably attributable to the duties performed by him in the province; and

(b) his income for the year from carrying on business earned in the province, determined as hereinafter set forth in this Part.

**Remission Orders**: *Income Earned in Quebec Income Tax Remission Order*, P.C. 1989-1204, as amended by P.C. 1991-1661 and P.C. 1992-2593 (special interpretation of Reg. 2602(1) for Quebec).

**Interpretation Bulletins**: IT-393R2: Election re tax on rents and timber royalties — non-residents; IT-434R: Rental of real property by individual.

**(2)** Where the aggregate of the amounts of an individual's income as determined under subsection (1) for all provinces for a taxation year exceeds the aggregate of the amounts of his income described in subparagraphs 115(1)(a)(i) and (ii) of the Act, the amount of his income earned in the taxation year in a particular province shall be that proportion of his income so described that the amount of his income earned in the taxation year in the province as determined under subsection (1) is of the aggregate of all such amounts.

**Definitions [Reg. 2602]**: "amount", "business" — ITA 248(1); "Canada" — ITA 255, *Interpretation Act* 35(1); "employment", "individual", "office" — ITA 248(1); "province" — *Interpretation Act* 35(1); "taxable income earned in Canada" — ITA 248(1); "taxation year" — ITA 249.

**2603. Income from business** — **(1)** Where, in a taxation year, an individual had a permanent establishment in a particular province or a country other than Canada and had no permanent establishment outside that province or country, the whole of his income from carrying on business for the year shall be deemed to have been earned therein.

**(2)** Where, in a taxation year, an individual had no permanent establishment in a particular province or country other than Canada, no part of his income for the year from carrying on business shall be deemed to have been earned therein.

**(3)** Except as otherwise provided, where, in a taxation year, an individual had a permanent establishment in a particular province or country other than Canada and a permanent establishment outside that province or country, the amount of his income for the year from carrying on business that shall be deemed to have been earned in the province or country is $\frac{1}{2}$ the aggregate of

(a) that proportion of his income for the year from carrying on business that the gross revenue for the fiscal period ending in the year reasonably attributable to the permanent establishment in the province or country is of his total gross revenue for that period from the business; and

(b) that proportion of his income for the year from carrying on business that the aggregate of the salaries and wages paid in the fiscal period ending in the year to employees of the permanent establishment in the province or country is of the aggregate of all salaries and wages paid in that period to employees of the business.

**(4)** For the purpose of determining the gross revenue for the year reasonably attributable to the permanent establishment in a particular province or country other than Canada within the meaning of paragraph (3)(a), the following rules shall apply:

(a) where the destination of a shipment of merchandise to a customer to whom the merchandise is sold is in the particular province or country, the gross revenue derived therefrom shall be attributable to the permanent establishment in the province or country;

(b) except as provided in paragraph (c), where the destination of a shipment of merchandise to a customer to whom the merchandise is sold is in a province or country other than Canada in which the taxpayer has no permanent establishment, if the person negotiating the sale may reasonably be regarded as being attached to the permanent establishment in the particular province or country, the gross revenue derived therefrom shall be attributable to that permanent establishment;

(c) where the destination of a shipment of merchandise to a customer to whom the merchandise is sold is in a country other than Canada in which the taxpayer has no permanent establishment,

(i) if the merchandise was produced or manufactured, or produced and manufactured, entirely in the particular province by the taxpayer, the gross revenue derived therefrom shall be attributable to the permanent establishment in the province, or

(ii) if the merchandise was produced or manufactured, or produced and manufactured, partly in the particular province and partly in another place by the taxpayer, the gross revenue derived therefrom attributable to the permanent establishment in the province shall be that proportion thereof that the salaries and wages paid in the year to employees of the permanent establishment in the province where the merchandise was partly produced or manufactured (or partly produced and manufactured) is of the aggregate of the salaries and wages paid in the year to employees of the permanent establishments where the merchandise was produced or manufactured (or produced and manufactured);

(d) where a customer to whom merchandise is sold instructs that shipment be made to some other person and the customer's office with which the sale was negotiated is located in the particular province or country, the gross revenue derived therefrom shall be attributable to the permanent establishment in the province or country;

(e) except as provided in paragraph (f), where a customer to whom merchandise is sold instructs that shipment be made to some other person and the customer's office with which the sale was negotiated is located in a province or country other than Canada in which the taxpayer has no permanent establishment, if the person negotiating the sale may reasonably be regarded as being attached to the permanent establishment in the particular province or country, the gross revenue derived therefrom shall be attributable to that permanent establishment;

(f) where a customer to whom merchandise is sold instructs that shipment be made to some other person and the customer's office with which the sale was negotiated is located in a country other than Canada in which the taxpayer has no permanent establishment,

(i) if the merchandise was produced or manufactured, or produced and manufactured, entirely in the particular province by the taxpayer, the gross revenue derived therefrom shall be attributable to the permanent establishment in the province, or

(ii) if the merchandise was produced or manufactured, or produced and manufactured, partly in the particular province and partly in another place by the taxpayer, the gross revenue derived therefrom attributable to the permanent establishment in the province shall be that proportion thereof that the salaries and wages paid in the year to employees of the permanent establishment in the province where the merchandise was partly produced or manufactured (or partly produced and manufactured) is of the aggregate of the salaries and wages paid in the year to employees of the permanent establishments where the merchandise was produced or manufactured (or produced and manufactured);

(g) where gross revenue is derived from services rendered in the particular province or country, the gross revenue shall be attributable to the permanent establishment in the province or country;

(h) where gross revenue is derived from services rendered in a province or country other than Canada in which the taxpayer has no permanent establishment, if the person negotiating the contract may reasonably be regarded as being attached to the permanent establishment of the taxpayer in the particular province or country, the gross revenue shall be attributable to that permanent establishment;

(i) where standing timber or the right to cut standing timber is sold and the timber limit on which the timber is standing is in the particular province or country, the gross revenue from such sale shall be attributable to the permanent establishment of the taxpayer in the province or country; and

(j) where land is a permanent establishment of the taxpayer in the particular province, the gross revenue which arises from leasing the land shall be attributable to that permanent establishment.

(5) Where an individual pays a fee to another person under an agreement pursuant to which that other person or employees of that other person perform services for the individual that would normally be performed by employees of the individual, the fee so paid shall be deemed to be salary paid by the individual and that part of the fee that may reasonably be regarded as payment in respect of services rendered at a particular permanent establishment of the individual shall be deemed to be salary paid to an employee of that permanent establishment.

(6) For the purposes of subsection (5), a fee does not include a commission paid to a person who is not an employee of the individual.

**Definitions [Reg. 2603]:** "amount" — ITA 248(1); "business" — Reg. 2606(3)(a); "Canada" — ITA 255, *Interpretation Act* 35(1); "employee" — ITA 248(1); "fee" — Reg. 2603(6); "fiscal period" — ITA 249.1; "gross revenue" — ITA 248(1); "income for the year from carrying on business" — Reg. 2606(1), 2606(3)(b); "individual", "office" — ITA 248(1); "permanent establishment" — Reg. 2600(2); "person" — ITA 248(1); "province" — *Interpretation Act* 35(1); "salaries and wages paid in the year" — Reg. 2606(3)(c); "taxation year" — ITA 249; "taxpayer" — ITA 248(1); "total gross revenue for the year" — Reg. 2606(3)(d).

**2604. Bus and truck operators** — Notwithstanding subsections 2603(3) and (4), the amount of income that shall be deemed to have been earned in a particular province or country other than Canada by an individual from carrying on the business of transportation of goods or passengers (other than by the operation of a railway, ships or an airline service) is ½ of the aggregate of

(a) that proportion of his income therefrom for the year that the number of miles travelled by his vehicles in the province or country in the fiscal period ending in the year is of the total number of miles travelled by his vehicles in that period; and

(b) that proportion of his income therefrom for the year that the aggregate of salaries and wages paid in the fiscal period ending in the year to employees of the permanent establishment in the province or country is of the aggregate of all salaries and wages paid in that period to employees of the business.

**Definitions [Reg. 2604]:** "amount" — ITA 248(1); "business" — Reg. 2606(3)(a); "Canada" — ITA 255, *Interpretation Act* 35(1); "employee" — ITA 248(1); "fiscal period" — ITA 249.1; "income for the year from carrying on business" — Reg. 2606(1), 2606(3)(b); "individual" — ITA 248(1); "permanent establishment" — Reg. 2600(2); "province" — *Interpretation Act* 35(1); "salaries and wages paid in the year" — Reg. 2606(3)(c); "total gross revenue for the year" — Reg. 2606(3)(d).

**2605. More than one business** — Where an individual operates more than one business, the provisions of sections 2603 and 2604 shall be applied in respect of each business and the amount of income for the year from carrying on business earned in a particular province or country in the year is the aggregate of the amounts so determined.

**Definitions [Reg. 2605]:** "amount" — ITA 248(1); "business" — Reg. 2606(3)(a); "income for the year from carrying on business" — Reg. 2606(1), 2606(3)(b); "individual" — ITA 248(1); "province" — *Interpretation Act* 35(1); "salaries and wages paid in the year" — Reg. 2606(3)(c); "total gross revenue for the year" — Reg. 2606(3)(d).

**Interpretation Bulletins:** IT-206R: Separate businesses.

**2606. Limitations of business income** — (1) Where, in the case of an individual to whom section 2601 applies, the aggregate of the amounts otherwise determined as his income for the taxation year from carrying on business earned in all provinces and countries other than Canada is greater than his income for the year, his income for the year from carrying on business earned in a particular province or country shall be deemed to be that proportion of his income for the year that

(a) his income for the year from carrying on business in the province or country as otherwise determined,

is of

(b) that aggregate.

(2) Where section 114 of the Act is applicable for the purpose of determining the taxable income of an individual for the taxation year, a reference in subsection (1) to "his income for the taxation year" shall be construed as a reference to the amount of his income as determined for the purposes of section 114 of the Act and, for the purpose of this Part, his income for the taxation year from carrying on a business in any place shall be computed by reference only to a business the income from which is included in computing his taxable income for the purposes of section 114 of the Act.

**Proposed Amendment — Reg. 2606(1), (2)**

**(1) Limitations of business income** — If, in the case of an individual to whom section 2601 applies, the total of the amounts otherwise determined as the individual's income for a taxation year from carrying on business earned in all provinces and countries other than Canada is greater that the individual's income for the year, the individual's income for the year from carrying on business earned in a particular province or country is deemed to be that proportion of the individual's income for the year that

(a) the individual's income for the year from carrying on business in the province or country as otherwise determined,

is of

(b) that total.

**(2) [Part-year residents]** — If section 114 of the Act applies in respect of an individual for a taxation year, the reference in subsection (1) to "the individual's income for a taxation year" shall be read as a reference to the amount of the individual's taxable income for the year and, for the purpose of this Part, the individual's income for the year from carrying on a business in any place shall be computed by reference only to a business the income from which is included in computing the individual's taxable income for the year.

**Application:** The December 17, 1999 draft regulations (taxpayer migration), s. 2, will amend the portion of Reg. 2606 before subsec. (3) to read as above, applicable to 1998 *et seq.*

**Technical Notes:** Part XXVI of the Income Tax Regulations sets out rules for computing an individual's income earned in a taxation year in a particular province.

Subsection 2606(1) of the Regulations provides for an adjustment to an individual's income earned in a particular province where the sum of the individual's incomes earned

Reg. S. 2606 — Income Tax Regulations

> in each province and in countries other than Canada exceeds the individual's income for the year. Subsection 2606(2) of the Regulations provides a further adjustment for the purposes of subsection (1) where the individual is non-resident for part of a taxation year only.
>
> Subsection 2606(2) of the Regulations is amended, with application to the 1998 and subsequent taxation years, to reflect amendments to section 114 of the Act (see the commentary on section 114 for further details). In addition, subsections 2606(1) and (2) are amended to update their language.

(3) For the purposes of sections 2603 to 2605, where an individual's taxable income for the taxation year is computed in accordance with section 115 of the Act

(a) a reference to a "business" shall be deemed to refer only to a business that was wholly or partly carried on in Canada;

(b) a reference to "income for the year from carrying on business" shall be deemed to refer only to income for the year from carrying on a business in Canada as determined for the purposes of section 115 of the Act;

(c) a reference to "salaries and wages paid in the year" shall be deemed to be a reference to salaries and wages paid to employees of his permanent establishments in Canada; and

(d) a reference to "total gross revenue for the year" from the business shall be deemed to be a reference to total gross revenue reasonably attributable to his permanent establishments in Canada.

**Definitions [Reg. 2606]**: "amount", "business" — ITA 248(1); "Canada" — ITA 255, *Interpretation Act* 35(1); "employee", "gross revenue" — ITA 248(1); "his income for the taxation year" — Reg. 2606(2); "individual" — ITA 248(1); "permanent establishment" — Reg. 2600(2); "province" — *Interpretation Act* 35(1); "taxable income" — ITA 248(1); "taxation year" — ITA 249.

**2607. Dual residence** — Where an individual was resident in more than one province on the last day of the taxation year, for the purposes of this Part, he shall be deemed to have resided on that day only in that province which may reasonably be regarded as his principal place of residence.

**Definitions [Reg. 2607]**: "individual" — ITA 248(1); "province" — *Interpretation Act* 35(1); "resident" — ITA 250; "taxation year" — ITA 249.

## PART XXVII — GROUP TERM LIFE INSURANCE BENEFITS

**2700. Interpretation — (1) Definitions** — The definitions in this subsection apply in this Part.

**"lump-sum premium"** in relation to a group term life insurance policy means a premium for insurance under the policy on the life of an individual where all or part of the premium is for insurance that is (or would be if the individual survived) in respect of a period that ends more than 13 months after the earlier of the day on which the premium becomes payable and the day on which it is paid.

**"paid-up premium"** in relation to a group term life insurance policy means a premium for insurance under the policy on the life of an individual where the insurance is for the remainder of the lifetime of the individual and no further premiums will be payable for the insurance.

**"premium category"** in relation to term insurance provided under a group term life insurance policy means,

(a) where the premium rate applicable in respect of term insurance on the life of an individual depends on the group to which the individual belongs, any of the groups for which a premium rate is established, and

(b) in any other case, all individuals on whose lives term insurance is in effect under the policy,

and, for the purpose of this definition, a single premium rate is deemed to apply for all term insurance under a policy in respect of periods in 1994, and where individuals are divided into separate groups solely on the basis of their age, sex, or both, the groups are deemed to be a single group for which a premium rate is established.

**"term insurance"** in relation to an individual and a group term life insurance policy means insurance under the policy on the life of the individual, other than insurance in respect of which a lump-sum premium has become payable or been paid.

**(2) Accidental death insurance** — For greater certainty, a premium for insurance on the life of an individual does not include an amount for accidental death insurance.

**Notes [Reg. 2700]**: Reg. 2700 added by P.C. 1997-1623, effective for 1994 and later taxation years.

**Definitions [Reg. 2700]**: "amount", "group term life insurance policy", "individual" — ITA 248(1); "lump-sum premium" — Reg. 2700(1); "month" — *Interpretation Act* 35(1); "term insurance" — Reg. 2700(1).

**2701. Prescribed benefit — (1)** Subject to subsection (2), for the purpose of subsection 6(4) of the Act, the amount prescribed for a taxation year in respect of insurance under a group term life insurance policy on the life of a taxpayer is the total of

(a) the taxpayer's term insurance benefit under the policy for the calendar year in which the taxation year ends,

(b) the taxpayer's prepaid insurance benefit under the policy for that calendar year, and

(c) the total of all sales and excise taxes payable in respect of premiums paid under the policy in that calendar year for insurance on the life of the taxpayer, other than

    (i) taxes paid, directly or by way of reimbursement, by the taxpayer, and

    (ii) taxes in respect of premiums for term insurance that, if the taxpayer were to die, would be paid otherwise than

        (A) to the taxpayer,

        (B) for the benefit of the taxpayer,

        (C) as a benefit that the taxpayer desired to have conferred on any person.

**Related Provisions**: ITA 139.1(15) — Effect of demutualization of insurance corporation.

**(2) Bankrupt individual** — Where a taxpayer who has become a bankrupt has two taxation years ending in a calendar year, for the purpose of subsection 6(4) of the Act, the amount prescribed for the first taxation year in respect of insurance under a group term life insurance policy on the life of the taxpayer is nil.

**Notes [Reg. 2701]**: Reg. 2701 added by P.C. 1997-1623, effective with respect to insurance provided in respect of periods after June 1994. However, with respect to insurance provided in respect of periods that are in 1994 and after June 1994, read "in 1994 and after June 1994" in place of "in that calendar year" in the opening words of Reg. 2701(1)(c).

**Definitions [Reg. 2701]**: "amount", "bankrupt", "group term life insurance policy", "person" — ITA 248(1); "prepaid insurance benefit" — Reg. 2703(1); "prescribed" — ITA 248(1); "taxation year" — ITA 249; "taxpayer" — ITA 248(1); "term insurance" — Reg. 2700(1); "term insurance benefit" — Reg. 2702(1).

**2702. Term insurance benefit — (1) Amount of benefit** — Subject to section 2704, for the purpose of paragraph 2701(1)(a), a taxpayer's term insurance benefit under a group term life insurance policy for a calendar year is

(a) where

    (i) the policyholder elects to determine, under this paragraph, the term insurance benefit for the year of each individual whose life is insured under the policy,

    (ii) no premium rate that applies for term insurance provided under the policy on the life of an individual in respect of the year depends on the age or sex of the individual,

    (iii) no amounts are payable under the policy for term insurance on the lives of individuals in respect of the year other than premiums payable on a regular basis that are based on the amount of term insurance in force in the year for each individual, and

    (iv) the year is after 1995,

the amount determined by the formula

$$A - B$$

where

A  is the total of the premiums payable for term insurance provided under the policy on the taxpayer's life in respect of periods in the year, to the extent that each such premium is in respect of term insurance that, if the taxpayer died in the year, would be paid to or for the benefit of the taxpayer or as a benefit that the taxpayer desired to have conferred on any person, and

B  is the total amount paid by the taxpayer in respect of term insurance under the policy on the taxpayer's life in respect of the year; and

(b) in any other case, the amount, if any, by which

    (i) the total of all amounts each of which is, for a day in the year on which term insurance is in effect under the policy on the taxpayer's life, the amount determined by the formula

$$A \times B$$

where

A  is the amount of term insurance in effect on that day under the policy on the taxpayer's life, except the portion, if any, of the amount that, if the taxpayer were to die on that day, would be paid otherwise than

    (A) to the taxpayer,

    (B) to benefit of the taxpayer, or

    (C) as a benefit that the taxpayer desired to have conferred on any person, and

B  is the average daily cost of insurance for the year for the premium category in which the taxpayer is included on that day

exceeds

    (ii) the total amount paid by the taxpayer in respect of term insurance under the policy on the taxpayer's life in respect of the year.

**Related Provisions**: ITA 257 — Negative amounts in formulas.

**(2) Average daily cost of insurance** — The average daily cost of insurance under a group term life insurance policy for a calendar year for a premium category is

(a) subject to paragraph (b), the amount determined by the formula

$$\frac{(A + B - C)}{D}$$

where

A  is the total of the premiums payable for term insurance provided under the policy on the lives of individuals in respect of periods in the year while they are in the premium category,

B  is the total of the amounts paid in the year under the policy for term insurance in respect of periods in preceding years (other than amounts that have otherwise been taken into account for the purpose of subsection 6(4) of the Act), to the extent that the total can reasonably be considered to relate to term insurance provided on the lives of individuals in the premium category,

C is the total amount of policy dividends and experience rating refunds paid in the year under the policy and not distributed to individuals whose lives are insured under the policy, to the extent that the total can reasonably be considered to relate to term insurance provided on the lives of individuals in the premium category, and

D is the total of all amounts each of which is the amount of term insurance in force on a day in the year on the lives of individuals in the premium category on that day; or

(b) the amount that the policyholder determines using a reasonable method that is substantially similar to the method set out in paragraph (a).

**Related Provisions**: ITA 257 — Negative amounts in formulas.

**(3) Survivor income benefits** — For the purposes of this section, where the proceeds of term insurance on the life of an individual are payable in the form of periodic payments, and the periodic payments are not an optional form of settlement of a lump-sum amount, the amount of term insurance in effect on the individual's life on any day is the present value, on that day, of the periodic payments that would be made if the individual were to die on that day.

**(4) Determination of present value** — For the purpose of subsection (3), the present value on a day in a calendar year

(a) shall be determined using assumptions that are reasonable at some time in the year; and

(b) may be determined assuming that an individual on whose life the present value depends is the same age on that day as on another day in the year.

**Notes [Reg. 2702]**: Reg. 2702 added by P.C. 1997-1623, effective with respect to insurance provided in respect of periods after June 1994. However, with respect to insurance provided in respect of periods that are in 1994 and after June 1994:

(a) read "in the year 1994 that is after June 1994" in place of "in the year" in Reg. 2702(1)(b)(i) before the formula; and

(b) read "in respect of the period in the year 1994 that is after June 1994" in place of "in respect of the year" in Reg. 2702(1)(b)(ii) before the formula.

**Definitions [Reg. 2702]**: "amount" — ITA 248(1); "amount of term insurance" — Reg. 2702(3); "dividend", "group term life insurance policy", "individual", "person" — ITA 248(1); "premium category" — Reg. 2700(1); "present value" — Reg. 2702(4); "taxpayer" — ITA 248(1); "term insurance" — Reg. 2700(1).

**2703. Prepaid insurance benefit — (1) Amount of benefit** — Subject to section 2704, for the purpose of paragraph 2701(1)(b), a taxpayer's prepaid insurance benefit under a group term life insurance policy for a calendar year is

(a) where the taxpayer is alive at the end of the year, the total of all amounts each of which is

(i) a lump-sum premium (other than the taxpayer portion) paid in the year and after February 1994 in respect of insurance under the policy on the life of the taxpayer, other than a paid-up premium paid before 1997, or

(ii) $1/3$ of a paid-up premium (other than the taxpayer portion) in respect of insurance under the policy on the life of the taxpayer that was paid

(A) after February 1994 and before 1997, and

(B) in the year or one of the two preceding years; and

(b) where the taxpayer died after June 1994 and in the year, the amount, if any, by which

(i) the total of all amounts each of which is a lump-sum premium (other than the taxpayer portion) paid under the policy after February 1994 in respect of insurance on the life of the taxpayer

exceeds

(ii) the portion of that total that was included in computing the taxpayer's prepaid insurance benefit under the policy for preceding years.

**Related Provisions**: ITA 18(9.01) — Matching deduction for employer.

**(2) Taxpayer portion of premiums** — For the purpose of subsection (1), the taxpayer portion of a premium is the portion, if any, of the premium that the taxpayer paid, either directly or by way of reimbursement.

**Notes [Reg. 2703]**: Reg. 2703 added by P.C. 1997-1623, effective with respect to insurance provided in respect of periods after June 1994.

**Definitions [Reg. 2703]**: "amount", "group term life insurance policy" — ITA 248(1); "lump-sum premium", "paid-up premium" — Reg. 2700(1); "portion" — Reg. 2703(2); "taxpayer" — ITA 248(1).

**2704. Employee-paid insurance — (1)** For the purpose of subsection 2701(1), where the full cost of insurance under a group term life insurance policy in a calendar year is borne by the individuals whose lives are insured under the policy, each individual's term insurance benefit and prepaid insurance benefit under the policy for the year is deemed to be nil.

**(2)** Where the premiums for part of the life insurance (in this subsection referred to as the "additional insurance") under a group term life insurance policy are determined separately from the premiums for the rest of the life insurance under the policy, and it is reasonable to consider that the individuals on whose lives the additional insurance is provided bear the full cost of the additional insurance, the additional insurance, the premiums, policy dividends and experience rating refunds in respect of that insurance, and the amounts paid in respect of that insurance by the individuals whose lives are insured, shall not be taken into account for the purposes of this Part.

**Notes [Reg. 2704]**: Reg. 2704 added by P.C. 1997-1623, effective with respect to insurance provided in respect of periods after June 1994.

**Definitions [Reg. 2704]**: "additional insurance" — Reg. 2704(2); "amount", "dividend", "group term life insurance policy", "individual" — ITA 248(1); "term insurance" — Reg. 2700(1).

**2705. Prescribed premium and insurance** — For the purpose of subsection 6(4) of the Act, as it applies to insurance provided in respect of periods that are in 1994 and before July 1994,

(a) a lump-sum premium paid under a group term life insurance policy after February 1994 in respect of an individual who is alive at the end of June 1994 is a prescribed premium; and

(b) insurance in respect of which a premium referred to in paragraph (a) is paid is prescribed insurance.

**Notes [Reg. 2705]**: Reg. 2705 added by P.C. 1997-1623, effective with respect to insurance provided in respect of periods that are in 1994 and before July 1994.

**Definitions [Reg. 2705]**: "group term life insurance policy", "individual" — ITA 248(1); "lump-sum premium" — Reg. 2700(1); "prescribed" — ITA 248(1).

**Notes [Part XXVII]**: Part XXVII added by P.C. 1997-1623, effective as per Notes above. See Notes to ITA 6(4).

Former Part XXVII, "Employer Contributions to Registered Pension Plans", revoked by P.C. 1991-2540, effective for taxation years that begin after 1990. The limits for employer contributions to pension plans are now determined under ITA 147.2(1).

# PART XXVIII — ELECTION IN RESPECT OF ACCUMULATING INCOME OF TRUSTS

**2800. [Preferred beneficiary election]** — (1) Any election under subsection 104(14) of the Act in respect of a taxation year shall be made by filing with the Minister the following documents:

(a) a statement

  (i) making the election in respect of the year,

  (ii) designating the part of the accumulating income in respect of which the election is being made, and

  (iii) signed by the preferred beneficiary and a trustee having the authority to make the election; and

(b) a statement signed by the trustee showing the computation of the amount of the preferred beneficiary's share in the accumulating income of the trust for the year in accordance with paragraph 104(15)(a), (b) or (c) of the Act, as the case may be, together with such information concerning the provisions of the trust and its administration as is necessary for this purpose.

**Interpretation Bulletins**: IT-394R2: Preferred beneficiary election.

(2) The documents referred to in subsection (1) shall be filed within 90 days from the end of the trust's taxation year in respect of which the election referred to in subsection (1) is made.

### Proposed Amendment — Application of Reg. 2800(2)

**Application**: The August 8, 1994 draft regulations (capital gains exemption), s. 1, will amend the application of subsec. 2800(2), such that in applying the *Income Tax Act* to the taxation year of a trust that includes February 22, 1994, subsec. 2800(2) shall be read as follows:

(2) The documents referred to in subsection (1) shall be filed

(a) where the trust elects under subsection 110.6(19) of the Act, on or before the day on or before which the election under that subsection is required to be filed with the Minister, and

(b) in any other case, within 90 days after the end of the trust's taxation year in respect of which the election referred to in subsection (1) is made.

**Technical Notes**: Section 2800 of the *Income Tax Regulations* sets out rules relating to preferred beneficiary elections made under subsection 104(14) of the *Income Tax Act*. Subsection 2800(2) establishes the time limit for the filing of such elections. In applying this subsection to a trust's taxation year that includes February 22, 1994, where the trust elects under subsection 110.6(19) of the Act, the normal filing deadline for the documents relating to the preferred beneficiary election is extended to coincide with the filing deadline for the capital gains election under subsection 110.6(19).

**Related Provisions**: ITA 104(14.01) — Extension of filing deadline where capital gains election filed.

**Notes**: ITA 220(3.2) and Reg. 600(b) permit the election to be filed late, if the CCRA accepts it. However, Agency officials are generally reluctant to accept a late preferred beneficiary election, particularly if it appears the taxpayer is attempting retroactive tax planning. See Information Circular 92-1.

(3) For the purposes of paragraph 104(15)(c) of the Act, the discretionary share of a particular preferred beneficiary under a trust of the trust's accumulating income for a taxation year shall be an amount determined as follows:

(a) where the settlor of the trust is an individual and his spouse, both of whom are alive at the end of the year and both of whom may be entitled to share in the accumulating income of the trust, the discretionary share

  (i) of the individual is that proportion of the accumulating income of the trust for the year that the fair market value of the property contributed by the individual is of the aggregate of the fair market value of the property contributed by the individual and the fair market value of the property contributed by his spouse (such fair market values being determined in respect of each contribution at the time of the making of that contribution),

(ii) of the spouse is that proportion of the accumulating income of the trust for the year that the fair market value of the property contributed by the spouse is of the aggregate of the fair market value of the property contributed by the individual and the fair market value of the property contributed by his spouse (such fair market values being determined in respect of each contribution at the time of the making of that contribution), and

(iii) of any other beneficiary who is a preferred beneficiary under the trust is nil;

(b) where the settlor of the trust is an individual and his spouse, both of whom are alive at the end of the year but only one of whom may be entitled to share in the accumulating income of the trust, the discretionary share

(i) of the individual or his spouse, as the case may be, who may be entitled to share in the accumulating income of the trust is the accumulating income of the trust for the year, and

(ii) of any other beneficiary who is a preferred beneficiary under the trust is nil;

(c) where the settlor of the trust is an individual and his spouse, only one of whom is alive at the end of the year, and the one who is alive may be entitled to share in the accumulating income of the trust, the discretionary share

(i) of the individual or his spouse, as the case may be, who is alive at the end of the year is the accumulating income of the trust for the year, and

(ii) of any other beneficiary who is a preferred beneficiary under the trust is nil;

(d) where, in any case not described in paragraph (a), (b) or (c), the settlor of the trust may be entitled to share in the accumulating income of the trust and is alive at the end of the year, the discretionary share

(i) of the settlor is the accumulating income of the trust for the year, and

(ii) of any other beneficiary who is a preferred beneficiary under the trust is nil;

(e) where, in any case not described in paragraph (a), (b) or (c), the spouse of the settlor of the trust may be entitled to share in the accumulating income of the trust, but the settlor may not, and the spouse is alive at the end of the year, the discretionary share

(i) of the spouse is the accumulating income of the trust for the year, and

(ii) of any other beneficiary who is a preferred beneficiary under the trust is nil; and

(f) in any other case, the discretionary share of a preferred beneficiary alive at the end of the year is the amount obtained by dividing the accumulating income of the trust for the year by the number of preferred beneficiaries under the trust alive at the end of the year who may be entitled to share in the accumulating income of the trust.

**Notes:** References to "spouse" are expected to be amended to add "or common-law partner" effective 2001 or earlier by election, as has been done throughout the ITA. See Notes to ITA 248(1)"common-law partner".

**Interpretation Bulletins:** IT-394R2: Preferred beneficiary election.

**Advance Tax Rulings:** ATR-30: Preferred beneficiary election on accumulating income of estate; ATR-34: Preferred beneficiary's election.

**(4)** In paragraphs (3)(a) to (e), the phrase "entitled to share in the accumulating income of the trust" does not include any entitlement that arises by reason of the death of any individual who would otherwise be entitled to share in the accumulating income of the trust.

**Definitions [Reg. 2800]:** "amount" — ITA 248(1); "entitled to share in the accumulating income of the trust" — Reg. 2800(4); "individual", "Minister", "property", "share" — ITA 248(1); "taxation year" — ITA 249; "trust" — ITA 104(1), 248(1), (3).

# PART XXIX — SCIENTIFIC RESEARCH AND EXPERIMENTAL DEVELOPMENT

**2900. (1)** [Repealed.]

**Related Provisions:** ITA 37(13) — Linked work under non-arm's length contract deemed to be SR&ED.

**Notes:** Reg. 2900(1) repealed by P.C. 2000-1095, effective for work performed after February 27, 1995, except that, for purposes of ITA 149(1)(j) and 149(8)(b), it still applies to work performed pursuant to an agreement in writing made before February 28, 1995. The definition has been moved to ITA 248(1).

Before its repeal, for the 1995 and later taxation years, read:

(1) For the purposes of this Part and section 37 of the Act, "scientific research and experimental development" means systematic investigation or search carried out in a field of science or technology by means of experiment or analysis, that is to say,

(a) basic research, namely, work undertaken for the advancement of scientific knowledge without a specific practical application in view,

(b) applied research, namely, work undertaken for the advancement of scientific knowledge with a specific practical application in view,

(c) experimental development, namely, work undertaken for the purposes of achieving technological advancement for the purposes of creating new, or improving existing, materials, devices, products or processes, including incremental improvements thereto, or

(d) work with respect to engineering, design, operations research, mathematical analysis, computer programming, data collection, testing and psychological research where that work is commensurate with the needs, and directly in support, of the work described in paragraph (a), (b) or (c), but does not include work with respect to

(e) market research or sales promotion,

(f) quality control or routine testing of materials, devices, products or processes,

(g) research in the social sciences or the humanities,

(h) prospecting, exploring or drilling for, or producing, minerals, petroleum or natural gas,

(i) the commercial production of a new or improved material, device or product or the commercial use of a new or improved process,

(j) style changes, or

(k) routine data collection.

Opening words of Reg. 2900(1) amended by P.C. 2000-1095, effective for 1995 and later taxation years, to delete application to ITA 37.1.

Reg. 2900(1) previously amended by P.C. 1995-16, effective for taxation years ending after December 2, 1992. The changes were generally clarifying and not intended to be changes in policy.

For discussion of the abandoned restrictions on SR&ED claims for computer software development by banks and other financial institutions, see Notes to 248(1)"scientific research and experimental development".

**Interpretation Bulletins**: See at end of Reg. 2900.

**Information Circulars**: See at end of Reg. 2900.

**Application Policies**: SR&ED 95-01R: Linked activities — Reg. 2900(1)(d); SR&ED 95-02: Science eligibility guidelines for the oil and gas and mining industries; SR&ED 96-02: Tests and studies required to meet requirements in regulated industries; SR&ED 96-07: Prototypes, custom products, commercial assets, pilot plants and experimental production; SR&ED 96-08: Eligibility of the preparation of new drug submissions; SR&ED 96-09: Eligibility of clinical trials to meet regulatory requirements.

**(2)** For the purposes of clause 37(8)(a)(i)(B) and subclause 37(8)(a)(ii)(A)(II) of the Act, the following expenditures are directly attributable to the prosecution of scientific research and experimental development:

(a) the cost of materials consumed or transformed in such prosecution;

(b) where an employee directly undertakes, supervises or supports such prosecution, the portion of the amount incurred for salary or wages of the employee that can reasonably be considered to be in respect of such prosecution; and

(c) other expenditures, or those portions of other expenditures, that are directly related to such prosecution and that would not have been incurred if such prosecution had not occurred.

**Related Provisions**: ITA 127(27) — ITC recapture.

**Notes**: Reg. 2900(2)(a) amended by P.C. 2000-1095 to add the words "or transformed", effective for costs incurred after February 23, 1998. Note that on a subsequent disposition of any materials that still exist, there may be recapture under ITA 127(27).

Opening words of Reg. 2900(2) amended by P.C. 1995-16, effective for taxation years ending after December 2, 1992, to change references from ITA 37(7)(c) to 37(8)(a), consistent with the renumbering of the Act in R.S.C. 1985 (5th Supp.).

Reg. 2900(2)(b) amended by P.C. 1995-16, effective for 1990 and later taxation years, so that an amount need only be "incurred" in respect of salary or wages, rather than paid.

Reg. 2900(2)(c) amended by P.C. 1995-16, effective for 1990 and later taxation years, to add the words "or those portions of other expenditures".

**Application Policies**: SR&ED 96-01: Reclassification of SR&ED expenditures per subsec. 127(11.4); SR&ED 96-06: Directly undertaking, supervising or supporting v. "directly engaged" SR&ED salary and wages; SR&ED 96-07: Prototypes, custom products/commercial assets, pilot plants and experimental production; SR&ED 2000-01: Cost of materials.

**Information Circulars**: See at end of Reg. 2900.

**(3)** For the purposes of subclause 37(8)(a)(ii)(A)(II) of the Act, the following expenditures are directly attributable to the provision of premises, facilities or equipment for the prosecution of scientific research and experimental development:

(a) the cost of the maintenance and upkeep of such premises, facilities or equipment; and

(b) other expenditures, or those portions of other expenditures, that are directly related to that provision and that would not have been incurred if those premises or facilities or that equipment had not existed.

**Notes**: Opening words of Reg. 2900(3) amended by P.C. 1995-16, effective for taxation years ending after December 2, 1992, to change reference from ITA 37(7)(c) to 37(8)(a), consistent with the renumbering of the Act in R.S.C. 1985 (5th Supp.).

Reg. 2900(3)(b) amended by P.C. 1995-16, effective for 1990 and later taxation years, to add the words "or those portions of other expenditures".

**(4)** For the purposes of the definition "qualified expenditure" in subsection 127(9) of the Act, the prescribed proxy amount of a taxpayer for a taxation year, in respect of a business, in respect of which the taxpayer elects under clause 37(8)(a)(ii)(B) of the Act is 65% of the total of all amounts each of which is that portion of the amount incurred in the year by the taxpayer in respect of salary or wages of an employee of the taxpayer who is directly engaged in scientific research and experimental development carried on in Canada that can reasonably be considered to relate to the scientific research and experimental development having regard to the time spent by the employee on the scientific research and experimental development.

**Related Provisions**: Reg. 2900(5)–(7) — Additional rules re prescribed proxy amount.

**Notes**: Reg. 2900(4) amended and 2900(5)–(10) added by P.C. 1995-16, effective for taxation years that end after December 2, 1992. For taxation years that end from May 24, 1985 to December 2, 1992, read:

(4) For the purposes of subsections (2) and (3), an expenditure does not include remuneration based on profits or a bonus paid to a person that does not deal at arm's length with the payor or that is a specified shareholder of the payor.

A taxpayer was permitted to revoke an election made before May 12, 1994 by so requesting in writing by September 28, 1994: Department of Finance news release, June 30, 1994.

**Application Policies**: SR&ED 96-06: Directly undertaking, supervising or supporting v. "directly engaged" SR&ED salary and wages.

**(5)** Subject to subsections (6) to (8), where in subsection (4) the portion of an expenditure is all or substantially all of the expenditure, that portion shall be replaced by the amount of the expenditure.

**Notes**: See under Reg. 2900(4). Revenue Canada considers that "substantially all" means 90% or more.

**Application Policies**: SR&ED 96-06: Directly undertaking, supervising or supporting v. "directly engaged" SR&ED salary and wages.

**(6)** The amount determined under subsection (4) as the prescribed proxy amount of a taxpayer for a taxation year in respect of a business shall not exceed the amount, if any, by which

(a) the total of all amounts deducted in computing the taxpayer's income for the year from the business,

exceeds the total of all amounts each of which is

(b) an amount deducted in computing the income of the taxpayer for the year from the business under any of sections 20, 24, 26, 30, 32, 37, 66 to 66.8 and 104 of the Act, or

(c) an amount incurred by the taxpayer in the year in respect of any outlay or expense made or incurred for the use of, or the right to use, a building other than a special-purpose building.

**Notes**: See under Reg. 2900(4).

**(7)** In determining the prescribed proxy amount of a taxpayer for a taxation year, the portion of the amount incurred in the year by the taxpayer in respect of salary or wages of a specified employee of the taxpayer that is included in computing the total described in subsection (4) shall not exceed the lesser of

(a) 75% of the amount incurred by the taxpayer in the year in respect of salary or wages of the employee, and

(b) the amount determined by the formula

$$2.5 \times A \times \frac{B}{365}$$

where

A is the Year's Maximum Pensionable Earnings (as determined under section 18 of the *Canada Pension Plan*) for the calendar year in which the taxation year ends, and

B is the number of days in the taxation year in which the employee is an employee of the taxpayer.

**Notes**: See under Reg. 2900(4).

The Year's Maximum Pensionable Earnings for 2001 is $38,300, so the maximum in the formula is $95,750 for 2001. See the table of CPP contribution rates in the introductory pages for other years.

**(8)** Where

(a) a taxpayer is a corporation,

(b) the taxpayer employs in a taxation year ending in a calendar year an individual who is a specified employee of the taxpayer,

(c) the taxpayer is associated with another corporation (referred to as the "associated corporation") in a taxation year of the associated corporation ending in the calendar year, and

(d) the individual is an employee of the associated corporation in the taxation year of the associated corporation ending in the calendar year,

the total of all amounts that may be included in computing the total described in subsection (4) in respect of salaries or wages of the individual by the taxpayer in its taxation year ending in the calendar year and by all associated corporations in their taxation years ending in the calendar year shall not exceed the amount that is 2.5 times the Year's Maximum Pensionable Earnings (as determined under section 18 of the *Canada Pension Plan*) for the calendar year.

**Notes**: See under Reg. 2900(4).

**(9)** For the purposes of subsections (4) and (7), an amount incurred in respect of salary or wages of an employee in a taxation year does not include

(a) an amount described in section 6 or 7 of the Act;

(b) an amount deemed under subsection 78(4) of the Act to have been incurred;

(c) bonuses; or

(d) remuneration based on profits.

**Notes**: See under Reg. 2900(4).

**Application Policies**: SR&ED 96-06: Directly undertaking, supervising or supporting v. "directly engaged" SR&ED salary and wages.

**(10)** For the purpose of subsection (8),

(a) an individual related to a particular corporation, and

(b) a partnership any member of which is an individual related to a particular corporation or is a corporation associated with a particular corporation,

shall be deemed to be a corporation associated with the particular corporation.

**Notes**: See under Reg. 2900(4).

**(11)** The depreciable property of a taxpayer that is prescribed for the purposes of the definition "first term shared-use-equipment" in subsection 127(9) of the Act is

(a) a building of the taxpayer;

(b) a leasehold interest of the taxpayer in a building;

(c) a property of the taxpayer if, at the time it was acquired by the taxpayer, the taxpayer or a person related to the taxpayer intended that it would be used in the prosecution of scientific research and experimental development during the assembly, construction or commissioning of a facility, plant or line for commercial manufacturing, commercial processing or other commercial purposes (other than scientific research and experimental development) and intended

(i) that it would be used during its operating time in its expected useful life primarily for purposes other than scientific research and experimental development, or

(ii) that its value would be consumed primarily in activities other than scientific research and experimental development; and

(d) part of a property of the taxpayer if, at the time the part was acquired by the taxpayer, the taxpayer or a person related to the taxpayer intended that the part would be used in the prosecution of scientific research and experimental development during the assembly, construction or commissioning of a facility, plant or line for commercial manufacturing, commercial processing or other commercial purposes (other than scientific research and experimental development), and intended

(i) that it would be used during its operating time in its expected useful life primarily for purposes other than scientific research and experimental development, or

(ii) that its value would be consumed primarily in activities other than scientific research and experimental development.

**Notes**: Reg. 2900(11) added by P.C. 1995-16, effective for property acquired after December 2, 1992.

**Application Policies**: SR&ED 96-07: Prototypes, custom products/commercial assets, pilot plants and experimental production.

**Definitions [Reg. 2900]**: "amount" — ITA 248(1); "amount incurred" — Reg. 2900(9); "associated" — Reg. 2900(10)(b); "associated corporation" — Reg. 2900(8)(c); "business" — ITA 248(1); "Canada" — ITA 255, *Interpretation Act* 35(1); "corporation" — ITA 248(1), *Interpretation Act* 35(1); "depreciable property" — ITA 13(21), 248(1); "employee", "individual", "mineral" — ITA 248(1); "partnership" — see Notes to ITA 96(1); "person", "prescribed", "property" — ITA 248(1); "related" — ITA 251(2)–(6); "salary or wages" — ITA 248(1); "scientific research and experimental development" — Reg. 2900(1); "specified employee" — ITA 248(1); "taxation year" — ITA 249; "taxpayer" — ITA 248(1); "total of all amounts" — Reg. 2900(8).

**Interpretation Bulletins [Reg. 2900]**: IT-151R4: Scientific research and experimental development expenditures.

**Information Circulars [Reg. 2900]**: 86-4R3: Scientific research and experimental development; 94-2: Machinery and equipment industry application paper; 97-1: SR&ED — Administrative guidelines for software development.

**2901. Prescribed expenditures** — [No longer relevant]

**Notes**: Reg. 2901 prescribes expenditures for ITA 37.1(5)(c) ("qualified expenditure") It is irrelevant because ITA 37.1 been repealed.

**Definitions [Reg. 2901]**: "amount", "business" — ITA 248(1); "corporation" — ITA 248(1), *Interpretation Act* 35(1); "person", "prescribed", "property" — ITA 248(1); "related" — ITA 251(2)–(6); "salary or wages" — ITA 248(1); "scientific research and experimental development" — Reg. 2900(1).

**Interpretation Bulletins**: IT-151R4: Scientific research and experimental development expenditures.

**2902.** For the purposes of the definition "qualified expenditure" in subsection 127(9) of the Act, a prescribed expenditure is

(a) an expenditure of a current nature incurred by a taxpayer in respect of

(i) the general administration or management of a business, including

(A) administrative salary or wages and related benefits in respect of a person whose duties are not all or substantially all directed to the prosecution of scientific research and experimental development, except to the extent that such expenditure is described in subsection 2900(2) or (3),

(B) a legal or accounting fee,

(C) an amount described in any of paragraphs 20(1)(c) to (g) of the Act,

(D) an entertainment expense,

(E) an advertising or selling expense,

(F) a conference or convention expense,

(G) a due or fee in respect of membership in a scientific or technical society or organization, and

(H) a fine or penalty, or

(ii) the maintenance and upkeep of premises, facilities or equipment to the extent that such expenditure is not attributable to the prosecution of scientific research and experimental development;

(b) an expenditure of a capital nature incurred by a taxpayer in respect of

(i) the acquisition of property, except any such expenditure that at the time it was incurred

(A) was for first term shared-use-equipment or second term shared-use-equipment, or

(B) was for the provision of premises, facilities or equipment if, at the time of the acquisition of the premises, facilities or equipment, it was intended

(I) that the premises, facilities or equipment would be used during all or substantially all of the operating time of the premises, facilities or equipment in the expected useful life of the premises, facilities or equipment for the prosecution of scientific research and experimental development in Canada, or

(II) that all or substantially all of the value of the premises, facilities or equipment would be consumed in the prosecution of scientific research and experimental development in Canada,

(ii) the acquisition of property that is qualified property within the meaning assigned by subsection 127(9) of the Act, or

(iii) the acquisition of property that has been used, or acquired for use or lease, for any purpose whatever before it was acquired by the taxpayer;

(c) an expenditure made to acquire rights in, or arising out of, scientific research and experimental development; or

(d) an expenditure on scientific research and experimental development in respect of which an amount is deductible under section 110.1 or section 118.1 of the Act; or

(e) an expenditure of a current or capital nature, to the extent that the taxpayer has received or is entitled to receive a reimbursement in respect thereof from

### Proposed Amendment — Reg. 2902(e) opening words

(e) for the purpose of sections 194 and 195 of the Act, an expenditure of a current or capital nature, to the extent that the taxpayer has received or is entitled to receive a reimbursement in respect of the expenditure from

**Notes**: Even though other portions of the October 27, 1998 draft regulations were promulgated and this one was not, the Dept. of Finance has advised (Jan. 31/01) that this measure is still to be considered as a proposed amendment.

**Application**: The October 27, 1998 draft regulations, s. 2, will amend the opening words of para. 2902(e) to read as above, applicable to amounts that become receivable after December 20, 1991.

**Technical Notes**: Section 2902 defines a prescribed expenditure for the purposes of subsection 127(9) of the *Income Tax Act*. Prescribed expenditures are not eligible for investment tax credits.

Paragraph 2902(e) of the *Income Tax Regulations* is amended consequential on the amendments to the definition "contract payment" in subsection 127(9) of the Act. Those amendments provided that a contract payment included certain payments for scientific research and experimental development that is performed for or on behalf of a person entitled to a deduction in respect of the amount because of subparagraph 37(1)(a)(i) or (i.1) of the Act. Contract payments received reduce the base upon which a taxpayer's ITC in respect of SR&ED is calculated. Those amendments were effective for amounts that became payable after December 20, 1991. In view of the amended definition of "contract payment" applicable to ITCs in respect of SR&ED, the provisions of paragraph 2902(e) became redundant for ITC purposes. However, paragraph 2902(e) of the Regulations is still relevant in respect of claims for refunds of Part VIII Refundable Tax on Corporations in Respect of the Scientific Research and Experimental Development Tax Credit. Regulation 2902(e) is, therefore, amended to apply only for the purposes of the Part VIII Refundable Tax.

(i) a person resident in Canada, other than

(A) Her Majesty in right of Canada or a province,

(B) an agent of Her Majesty in right of Canada or a province,

(C) a corporation, commission or association that is controlled, directly or indirectly in any manner whatever, by Her Majesty in right of Canada or a province or by an agent of Her Majesty in right of Canada or a province, or

(D) a municipality in Canada or a municipal or public body performing a function of government in Canada, or

(ii) a person not resident in Canada to the extent that the said reimbursement is deductible by the person in computing his taxable income earned in Canada for any taxation year.

**Related Provisions**: ITA 256(5.1), (6.2) — Meaning of "controlled directly or indirectly".

**Notes**: Revenue Canada's view is that "all or substantially all" means 90% or more.

Reg. 2902(a)(i)(F) amended by P.C. 1995-16, effective January 26, 1995, to add the words "conference or".

Closing words of Reg. 2902(a) repealed by P.C. 1995-16, effective for taxation years that begin after February 22, 1994. For taxation years that end after May 23, 1985 and end before February 23, 1994, read the following as overriding para. (a):

except any such expenditure incurred by a corporation that derives all or substantially all of its revenue from the prosecution of scientific research and experimental development or the sale of rights in or arising out of scientific research and experimental development carried on by it.

The exception applied to what were known informally as "sole-purpose SR&ED performers". It was considered no longer necessary because of other legislative and administrative initiatives that have streamlined the system of SR&ED tax incentives, such as the proxy method of determining the credit for overhead costs (see ITA 127(9)"qualified expenditure" and Reg. 2900(4)).

Reg. 2902(d) amended by P.C. 1994-139, effective for 1988 and later taxation years, to change reference from ITA 110 to ITA 110.1 and 118.1, which are now the provisions dealing with charitable donations.

**Definitions [Reg. 2902]**: "amount", "business" — ITA 248(1); "Canada" — ITA 255, *Interpretation Act* 35(1); "controlled directly or indirectly" — ITA 256(5.1), (6.2); "corporation" — ITA 248(1), *Interpretation Act* 35(1); "Her Majesty" — *Interpretation Act* 35(1); "person", "prescribed", "property" — ITA 248(1); "province" — *Interpretation Act* 35(1); "related" — ITA 251(2)–(6); "resident in Canada" — ITA 250; "salary or wages" — ITA 248(1); "scientific research and experimental development" — Reg. 2900(1); "taxable income earned in Canada" — ITA 248(1); "taxation year" — ITA 249; "taxpayer" — ITA 248(1).

**Interpretation Bulletins**: IT-104R2: Deductibility of fines or penalties; IT-151R4: Scientific research and experimental development expenditures.

**Application Policies**: SR&ED 94-02: Expenditures of sole-purpose SR&ED performers — para. 37(8)(a) of the Act and 2902(a) of the Regulations.

**2903. Special-purpose buildings** — For the purposes of this Part and paragraph 37(8)(d) of the Act, a special-purpose building is a building the working areas of which are designed and constructed to have a displacement in any direction of not more than .02

micrometre and to have, per .028 cubic metre of interior airspace,

(a) not more than 350 airborne particles of a size less than or equal to .1 micrometre in diameter and no airborne particles of a size greater than .1 micrometre in diameter,

(b) not more than 75 airborne particles of a size less than or equal to .2 micrometre in diameter and no airborne particles of a size greater than .2 micrometre in diameter,

(c) not more than 30 airborne particles of a size less than or equal to .3 micrometre in diameter and no airborne particles of a size greater than .3 micrometre in diameter, or

(d) not more than 10 airborne particles of a size less than or equal to .5 micrometre in diameter and no airborne particles of a size greater than .5 micrometre in diameter.

**Interpretation Bulletins**: IT-151R4: Scientific research and experimental development expenditures.

## PART XXX — COMMUNICATION OF INFORMATION

**3000–3002.** [Revoked]

**Notes**: Regs. 3000–3002 revoked by P.C. 1993-1943, effective December 15, 1993. They identified government programs in respect of which information obtained in the course of administering the ITA could be communicated. These rules are now provided directly in ITA 241.

**3003. Prescribed laws of a province** — For the purposes of paragraph 122.64(2)(a) of the Act, the following are prescribed laws of a province:

(a) in respect of the Province of Quebec,

(i) *An Act Respecting Family Benefits*, S.Q. 1997, c. 57,

(ii) *An Act Respecting the Québec Pension Plan*, R.S.Q. 1977, c. R-9; and

(iii) *An Act Respecting Income Security*, R.S.Q. 1977, c. S-3.1.1, as it relates to the additional amounts for dependent children;

(b) in respect of the Province of Manitoba,

(i) *The Social Services Administration Act*, C.C.S.M., c. S165, as it relates to the Child Related Income Support Program,

(ii) *The Social Allowances Act*, C.C.S.M., c. S160, as it relates to

(A) the Social Allowances Program, and

(B) the Municipal Assistance Program, and

(iii) *The Community Child Day Care Standards Act*, C.C.S.M., c. S158, as it relates to the Child Day Care Program;

(c) in respect of the Province of Saskatchewan,

(i) *The Child Care Act*, S.S. 1989-90, c. C-7.3,

(ii) *The Saskatchewan Assistance Act*, R.S.S. 1978, c. S-8, as it relates to

(A) the Family Income Plan, and

(B) the Saskatchewan Assistance Plan, and

(iii) *The Saskatchewan Income Plan Act*, S.S. 1986, c. S-25.1;

(d) in respect of the Province of British Columbia, the *Guaranteed Available Income for Need Act*, R.S.B.C. 1979, c. 158; and

(e) in respect of the Province of Alberta, the *Social Development Act*, R.S.A. 1980, c. S-16.

**Notes**: Reg. 3003(a)(i), (b)(i) and (c) added by P.C. 1992-2653, effective December 21, 1992. Reg. 3003(a)(ii) added by P.C. 1993-538, effective April 7, 1993. Reg. 3003(a)(i) amended and 3003(a)(iii) added by P.C. 1997-1688, effective for information provided after June 19, 1997; previously, read 3003(a)(i) as "*An Act Respecting Family Assistance Allowances*, R.S.Q. 1977, c. A-17".

Reg. 3003(b)(ii) and (iii) added by P.C. 1994-560, effective April 14, 1994.

Reg. 3003(d) and (e) added by P.C. 1994-1658, effective October 19, 1994.

**Definitions [Reg. 3003]**: "amount", "prescribed" — ITA 248(1); "province" — *Interpretation Act* 35(1).

**3004.** For the purposes of subparagraph 241(4)(j.1)(ii) of the Act, *An Act Respecting Family Benefits*, S.Q. 1997, c. 57, is, in respect of the Province of Quebec, a prescribed law of a province.

**Definitions [Reg. 3004]**: "prescribed" — ITA 248(1); "province" — *Interpretation Act* 35(1).

## PART XXXI — [REVOKED]

**Notes**: Part XXXI, revoked in 1984, set out rules for establishing a "degree of Canadian ownership" under former s. 257 of the Act. Where a corporation was more than 25% Canadian-owned, the withholding tax on dividends was reduced. Reduction of withholding tax on dividends is provided in most of Canada's bilateral tax treaties. See ITA 212(2), the notes thereto, and the table of tax treaty withholding rates in the introductory pages.

## PART XXXII — PRESCRIBED STOCK EXCHANGES AND CONTINGENCY FUNDS

**3200. Stock exchanges in Canada** — The following stock exchanges in Canada are hereby prescribed for the purposes of paragraph 13(27)(f), clause 19(5)(b)(v)(C) [19(5)"Canadian newspaper or periodical"(e)(iii)], paragraph 47.1(28)(c), subparagraph 48.1(1)(a)(ii), sections 87 and 89, subsection 112(2.2), sections 146, 146.3, 149.1, 187.3 and 204, subsection 206(1) and sections 206.1 and 207.5 of the Act, and of the definitions "grandfathered share" and "term preferred share" in subsection 248(1) of the Act and the definition "qualified security" in subsection 260(1) of the Act and paragraphs 4900(1)(b) and (e):

Reg. S. 3200

Income Tax Regulations

## Proposed Amendment — Reg. 3200 opening words

**3200. Stock exchanges in Canada** — For the purposes of the Act, the following are prescribed stock exchanges in Canada:

**Application**: The November 30, 2000 draft regulations (miscellaneous), s. 3 (pre-published in the *Canada Gazette*, Part I, December 9, 2000), will amend the opening words of s. 3200 to read as above, applicable after 1991.

**Regulatory Impact Analysis Statement**: Sections 3200 and 3201 of the Regulations list the stock exchanges inside and outside Canada that are prescribed for various purposes of the Act. For example, whether a particular share is taxable Canadian property, a qualified investment for registered retirement savings plans, or a qualified security for the purposes of the rules applying to securities lending arrangements, may depend upon whether the share is listed on a prescribed stock exchange.

Sections 3200 and 3201 of the Regulations are amended by replacing their preambles. Currently, each preamble contains a list of sections to which the regulation applies. To simplify the application of the Regulations, the cross-referencing is deleted and the preambles modified such that each regulation applies for all purposes of the Act. This streamlines the legislation so that each time a section in the Act is amended to add or modify a reference to a prescribed stock exchange, no longer must the preambles of these Regulations be amended as well. Also, taxpayers will no longer have to confirm that a particular section is contained in the preamble to these regulations for the lists to apply to that section. It will now be clear that those regulations apply to the whole Act, including provisions that were not previously cross-referenced, and that would have had to have been added to the preamble if the preambles were not restructured.

**Letter from Department of Finance, October 9, 1998**: This is in response to your telephone call respecting new paragraph 38(a.1) of the *Income Tax Act*, which was introduced as part of the 1997 federal budget.

New paragraph 38(a.1), which provides a preferential inclusion rate in respect of taxable capital gains realized by taxpayers who make charitable gifts of certain properties, including shares or debt listed on a prescribed stock exchange, applies after February 18, 1997. However, you have noted that neither Income Tax Regulation 3200, which lists the prescribed Canadian stock exchanges, nor Regulation 3201, which lists the prescribed foreign stock exchange, currently applies for the purposes of this new paragraph.

I can confirm that we intend to recommend that Regulations 3200 and 3201 be amended to apply for the purposes of new paragraph 38(a.1) of the Act. We will recommend that the amendments apply after February 18, 1997.

If you would like to discuss this matter in more detail, please feel free to contact Robin Maley (613-992-4859) of the Tax Legislation Division directly.

Yours sincerely,

Len Farber
Director General, Tax Legislation Division

(a) Alberta Stock Exchange;
(b) Montreal Stock Exchange;
(c) Toronto Stock Exchange;
(d) Vancouver Stock Exchange; and
(e) Winnipeg Stock Exchange.

## Proposed Addition — Canadian Venture Exchange

**Department of Finance news release, December 16, 1999**: *Addition of the Canadian Venture Exchange to the List of Prescribed Stock Exchanges in Canada*

Secretary of State (International Financial Institutions) Jim Peterson today announced that he intends to recommend an amendment to Part XXXII of the *Income Tax Regulations* to include on the list of prescribed stock exchanges in Canada, The Canadian Venture Exchange, which was created by the merger of the Vancouver and Alberta stock exchanges.

"Both the Vancouver and Alberta exchanges were prescribed for income tax purposes," Mr. Peterson observed. "This amendment will simply reflect the evolution of Canada's capital markets."

Part XXXII of the *Income Tax Regulations* prescribes stock exchanges in Canada and outside Canada for various provisions in the *Income Tax Act*. In particular, shares listed on a prescribed stock exchange are eligible investments for registered retirement savings plans (RRSPs), registered retirement income funds (RRIFs) and deferred profit-sharing plans (DPSPs). Such shares are also qualified securities for rules pertaining to securities lending arrangements and are excluded from the application of withholding requirements under section 116 of the Act.

The prescription will apply as of the date the new exchange started operations, which was November 29, 1999, and will have effect for taxation years ending after that date.

For further information: Lisa Zannese, Tax Legislation Division, (613) 996-5155; Jean-Michel Catta, Public Affairs and Operations Division, (613) 996-8080; Karl Littler, Executive Assistant to the Secretary of State (International Financial Institutions), (613) 996-7861.

**Department of Finance news release Backgrounder, December 21, 2000**: *Canadian Venture Exchange*

A Department of Finance news release dated December 16, 1999, announced that the Canadian Venture Exchange would be added to the list of prescribed stock exchanges in Canada contained in Section 3200 of the *Income Tax Regulations*. This decision was based on the fact that this new stock exchange was created through a merger of two existing stock exchanges, Alberta and Vancouver, both of which are on the list of prescribed stock exchanges in Canada. Tiers 1 and 2 of the Canadian Venture Exchange include the stocks that were previously listed on the Alberta and Vancouver stock exchanges, and thus will be recommended for addition to the list of prescribed stock exchanges in Canada.

Recently, the Canadian Venture Exchange began operations of a new tier, Tier 3, to accommodate the transfer of stocks from the Canadian Dealing Network, Canada's over-the-counter market. The Canadian Dealing Network was not on the list of prescribed stock exchanges in Canada. Consistent with the past treatment of the stocks listed on the Canadian Dealing Network, it is *not currently proposed that Tier 3 of the Canadian Venture Exchange be added to the list of prescribed stock exchanges* in Canada.

Part XXXII — Prescribed Stock Exchanges/Contingency Funds    Reg. S. 3201(w)

[Shares can generally remain in Tier 3 for a period of time, after which they move up to Tier 1 or 2 or become de-listed — ed.]

**Related Provisions**: ITA 87(10) — Share deemed listed on prescribed stock exchange following amalgamation; Canada-U.S. tax treaty, Art. XXIX A:5(a)(ii) — Meaning of "recognized stock exchange".

**Notes**: The amendment changing the opening words to "For the purposes of the Act" will cause Reg. 3200 to apply automatically to all instances in the ITA of "prescribed stock exchange" or "prescribed stock exchange in Canada".

Opening words of Reg. 3200 amended by P.C. 1994-139 to delete a reference to ITA section 70 effective 1986 taxation year, and to add references to: ITA 13(27)(f) effective 1990; 19(5)(b)(v)(C) effective 1989; 47.1(28)(c) effective 1986; 48.1(1)(a)(ii) effective 1991 taxation year; section 87 (previously covered only 87(4.3)) effective 1986; 207.5 effective October 9, 1986; 260(1)"qualified security" effective April 27, 1989; and Reg. 4900(1)(b) and (e) effective 1986. The effective dates are generally retroactive to when the references to "prescribed stock exchange" were added to the Act. The references to Reg. 4900(1)(b) and (e) are now obsolete, as those paras. no longer refer to a prescribed stock exchange.

**Definitions [Reg. 3200]**: "Canada" — ITA 255, *Interpretation Act* 35(1); "prescribed" — ITA 248(1).

**Interpretation Bulletins**: IT-458R2: Canadian-controlled private corporation.

**3201. Stock exchanges outside Canada —** The following stock exchanges in countries other than Canada are hereby prescribed for the purposes of paragraph 13(27)(f) and sections 149.1, 204, 206.1 and 207.5 of the Act, and of the definition "grandfathered share" in subsection 248(1) of the Act and the definition "qualified security" in subsection 260(1) of the Act:

### Proposed Amendment — Reg. 3201 opening words

**3201. Stock exchanges outside Canada —** For the purposes of the Act, the following are prescribed stock exchanges outside Canada:

**Application**: The November 30, 2000 draft regulations (miscellaneous), subsec. 4(1) (pre-published in the *Canada Gazette*, Part I, December 9, 2000), will amend the opening words of s. 3201 to read as above, applicable after 1991.

**Regulatory Impact Analysis Statement**: See under Reg. 3200 opening words.

**Letter from Department of Finance, October 9, 1998**: See under Reg. 3200.

(a) in Australia, the Australian Stock Exchange;
(b) in Belgium, the Brussels Stock Exchange;
(c) in France, the Paris Stock Exchange;
(d) in Germany, the Frankfurt Stock Exchange;
(e) in Hong Kong, the Hong Kong Stock Exchange;
(f) in Italy, the Milan Stock Exchange;
(g) in Japan, the Tokyo Stock Exchange;
(h) in Mexico, the Mexico City Stock Exchange;
(i) in the Netherlands, the Amsterdam Stock Exchange;
(j) in New Zealand, the New Zealand Stock Exchange;
(k) in Singapore, the Singapore Stock Exchange;
(l) in Spain, the Madrid Stock Exchange;
(m) in Switzerland, the Zurich Stock Exchange;
(n) in the United Kingdom, the London Stock Exchange;
(o) in the United States,
  (i) the American Stock Exchange,
  (ii) the Boston Stock Exchange,
  (iii) the Chicago Board of Options,
  (iv) the Chicago Board of Trade,
  (v) the Cincinnati Stock Exchange,
  (vi) the Intermountain Stock Exchange,
  (vii) the Midwest Stock Exchange,
  (viii) the National Association of Securities Dealers Automated Quotation System,
  (ix) the New York Stock Exchange,
  (x) the Pacific Stock Exchange,
  (xi) the Philadelphia Stock Exchange, and
  (xii) the Spokane Stock Exchange; and
(p) in Ireland, the Irish Stock Exchange.

### Proposed Addition — Reg. 3201(q)–(w)

(q) in Israel, the Tel Aviv Stock Exchange;
(r) in Austria, the Vienna Stock Exchange;
(s) in Denmark, the Copenhagen Stock Exchange;
(t) in Finland, the Helsinki Stock Exchange;
(u) in Norway, the Oslo Stock Exchange;
(v) in South Africa, the Johannesburg Stock Exchange; and
(w) in Sweden, the Stockholm Stock Exchange.

**Application**: The November 30, 2000 draft regulations (miscellaneous), subsec. 4(2) (pre-published in the *Canada Gazette*, Part I, December 9, 2000), will add paras. 3201(q) to (w), applicable after July 22, 1998 except that, for the purposes of s. 116 of the Act, it applies to a sale of shares completed after April 1998 and before July 23, 1998, the gains from which are exempt from income tax otherwise payable in Canada under a tax treaty, unless the vendor of the shares otherwise elects in writing filed with the Minister of National Revenue on or before the balance-due day for the taxation year of the vendor in which the sale of shares was completed.

**Regulatory Impact Analysis Statement**: In addition, section 3201 is amended by adding seven new stock exchanges to its list of prescribed foreign exchanges. These additions were requested by taxpayers and were announced publicly on July 22, 1998, in the form of a press release.

The list of prescribed stock exchanges in countries outside Canada in section 3201 of the Regulations is amended to add the following seven additional stock exchanges:

• in Israel, the Tel Aviv Stock Exchange;
• in Austria, the Vienna Stock Exchange;

- in Denmark, the Copenhagen Stock Exchange;
- in Finland, the Helsinki Stock Exchange;
- in Norway, the Oslo Stock Exchange;
- in South Africa, the Johannesburg Stock Exchange; and
- in Sweden, the Stockholm Stock Exchange.

**Department of finance news release, July 22, 1998**: *Proposed Additions to the List of Prescribed Stock Exchanges Outside Canada*

Secretary of State Jim Peterson today announced that he intends to recommend amendments to Part XXXII of the *Income Tax Regulations*.

Part XXXII of the *Income Tax Regulations* prescribes various stock exchanges for the purposes of a number of provisions in the *Income Tax Act*. In particular, shares listed on a prescribed stock exchange automatically constitute eligible investments for registered retirement savings plans (RRSPs), registered retirement income funds (RRIFs) and deferred profit savings plans (DPSPs), are qualified securities for rules pertaining to securities lending arrangements and are excluded from the application of withholding requirements under section 116 of the Act. The Secretary of State indicated that the following stock exchanges would be added to those already prescribed in Part XXXII:

- in Denmark, the Copenhagen Stock Exchange;
- in Finland, the Helsinki Stock Exchange;
- in South Africa, the Johannesburg Stock Exchange;
- in Norway, the Oslo Stock Exchange;
- in Sweden, the Stockholm Stock Exchange;
- in Israel, the Tel Aviv Stock Exchange; and
- in Austria, the Vienna Stock Exchange.

For most purposes, the prescriptions will apply after today's date. For purposes of the withholding requirements imposed under section 116 of the Act, however, the prescriptions will apply to share sales after April 1998 that were exempt from tax payable under the Act because a tax treaty applied. This retroactive relief, which will apply unless the vendor of the shares elects otherwise, recognizes that in such cases, the section 116 obligation serves an administrative function only.

For further information: Robin Maley, Tax Legislation Division, (613) 992-4859.

**Related Provisions**: ITA 87(10) — Share deemed listed on prescribed stock exchange following amalgamation; Canada-U.S. tax treaty, Art. XXIX A:5(a)(ii) — Meaning of "recognized stock exchange".

**Notes**: The amendment changing the opening words to "For the purposes of the Act" will cause Reg. 3201 to apply automatically to all instances in the ITA of "prescribed stock exchange" that do not continue with "in Canada". The Department of Finance has confirmed that all such references are intended to refer to both Canadian and foreign stock exchanges, even where Reg. 3201 had not previously applied to these references.

Opening words of Reg. 3201 amended by P.C. 1994-139 to delete unnecessary references to ITA sections 146 and 146.3 effective October 9, 1986, and to add references to: ITA 13(27)(f) effective 1990; 207.5 effective October 9, 1986; and 260(1)"qualified security" effective April 27, 1989.

Exchanges listed in Reg. 3201(a)–(b) and (d)–(m) added by P.C. 1992-2334 and P.C. 1994-101, effective for 1991 and later taxation years.

Reg. 3201(p) added by P.C. 1997-1145, effective for 1995 and later taxation years. The Irish Stock Exchange separated from the London Stock Exchange in the U.K. and obtained its own independent status.

**Definitions [Reg. 3201]**: "Canada" — ITA 255, *Interpretation Act* 35(1); "prescribed" — ITA 248(1); "United Kingdom", "United States" — *Interpretation Act* 35(1).

**Interpretation Bulletins**: IT-458R2: Canadian-controlled private corporation.

**3202. Contingency funds** — For the purposes of subparagraph 47.1(1)(l)(i) of the Act [repealed], the National Contingency Fund is a prescribed contingency fund.

**Definitions [Reg. 3202]**: "prescribed" — ITA 248(1).

# PART XXXIII — TAX TRANSFER PAYMENTS

**3300.** For the purposes of subsection 154(2) of the Act, a rate of 40 per cent is hereby prescribed.

**Notes**: Rate changed to 40% from 45% effective 1999 by P.C. 1998-2270.

**Definitions [Reg. 3300]**: "prescribed" — ITA 248(1).

# PART XXXIV — INTERNATIONAL DEVELOPMENT ASSISTANCE PROGRAMS

**3400.** For the purposes of paragraphs 122.3(1)(a) and 250(1)(d) of the Act, each international development assistance program of the Canadian International Development Agency that is financed with funds (other than loan assistance funds) provided under External Affairs Vote 30a, *Appropriation Act No. 3, 1977-78*, or another vote providing for such financing, is hereby prescribed as an international development assistance program of the Government of Canada.

**Definitions [Reg. 3400]**: "Canada" — ITA 255, *Interpretation Act* 35(1); "prescribed" — ITA 248(1).

**Interpretation Bulletins**: IT-497R3: Overseas employment tax credit.

# PART XXXV — RECEIPTS FOR DONATIONS AND GIFTS

**Interpretation Bulletins**: IT-110R3: Gifts and official donation receipts; IT-171R2: Non-resident individuals — computation of taxable income earned in Canada and non-refundable tax credits; IT-226R: Gift to a charity of a residual interest in real property or an equitable interest in a trust; IT-288R2: Gifts of tangible capital properties to a charity and others; IT-504R2: Visual artists and writers.

**3500. Interpretation** — In this Part,

**"employees' charity trust"** means a registered charity that is organized for the purpose of remitting, to other registered charities, donations that are collected from employees by an employer;

Notes: Definition "employees' charity trust" amended by P.C. 1994-139, retroactive to 1986, to delete a requirement that donations collected by the employer be "by means of payroll deductions".

**"official receipt"** means a receipt for the purposes of subsection 110.1(2) or (3) or 118.1(2), (6) or (7) of the Act, containing information as required by section 3501 or 3502;

Notes: Definition "official receipt" amended by P.C. 1994-139, effective 1988, to change references from provisions of ITA 110 to the provisions that now deal with gifts.

**"official receipt form"** means any printed form that a registered organization or other recipient of a gift has that is capable of being completed, or that originally was intended to be completed, as an official receipt by it; and

**"other recipient of a gift"** means a person, to whom a gift is made by a taxpayer, referred to in any of subparagraphs 110.1(1)(a)(iii) to (vii), paragraphs 110.1(1)(b) and (c), subparagraph 110.1(3)(a)(ii), paragraphs (c) to (g) of the definition "total charitable gifts" in subsection 118.1(1), the definition "total Crown gifts" in subsection 118.1(1), paragraph (b) of the definition "total cultural gifts" in subsection 118.1(1) and paragraph 118.1(6)(b) of the Act;

Notes: Definition "other recipient of a gift" amended by P.C. 1994-139, effective 1988 except that in its application before December 12, 1988 the reference to "paragraph (b) of the definition "total cultural gifts" " shall be read as "paragraph (c) of the definition "total cultural gifts" ". The definition was amended to change references from provisions of ITA 110 to the provisions that now deal with gifts.

**"registered organization"** means a registered charity, a registered Canadian amateur athletic association or a registered national arts service organization.

Notes: Reference to registered national arts service organization added to definition of "registered organization" by P.C. 1994-139, effective July 14, 1990.

**Definitions [Reg. 3500]**: "employee", "employer" — ITA 248(1); "official receipt", "other recipient of a gift" — Reg. 3500; "person", "registered Canadian amateur athletic association", "registered charity", "registered national arts service organization" — ITA 248(1); "registered organization" — Reg. 3500; "taxpayer" — ITA 248(1).

**3501. Contents of receipts — (1)** Every official receipt issued by a registered organization shall contain a statement that it is an official receipt for income tax purposes, and shall show clearly, in such a manner that it cannot readily be altered,

(a) the name and address in Canada of the organization as recorded with the Minister;

(b) the registration number assigned by the Minister to the organization;

(c) the serial number of the receipt;

(d) the place or locality where the receipt was issued;

(e) where the donation is a cash donation, the day on which or the year during which the donation was received;

(e.1) where the donation is a gift of property other than cash

(i) the day on which the donation was received,

(ii) a brief description of the property, and

(iii) the name and address of the appraiser of the property if an appraisal is done;

(f) the day on which the receipt was issued where that day differs from the day referred to in paragraph (e) or (e.1);

(g) the name and address of the donor including, in the case of an individual, his first name and initial;

(h) the amount that is

(i) the amount of a cash donation, or

(ii) where the donation is a gift of property other than cash, the amount that is the fair market value of the property at the time that the gift was made; and

(i) the signature, as provided in subsection (2) or (3), of a responsible individual who has been authorized by the organization to acknowledge donations.

Notes: Some charities are authorized to issue electronic receipts for gifts paid via the Internet. See Arthur Drache, "Electronic Donation Receipting", 8(3) *Canadian Not-for-Profit News* (Carswell) 23-24 (March 2000).

**Information Circulars**: 80-10R: Registered charities: operating a registered charity.

**Forms**: RC4108: Registered charities and the Income Tax Act [guide].

**(1.1)** Every official receipt issued by another recipient of a gift shall contain a statement that it is an official receipt for income tax purposes and shall show clearly in such a manner that it cannot readily be altered,

(a) the name and address of the other recipient of the gift;

(b) the serial number of the receipt;

(c) the place or locality where the receipt was issued;

(d) where the donation is a cash donation, the day on which or the year during which the donation was received;

(e) where the donation is a gift of property other than cash,

(i) the day on which the donation was received,

(ii) a brief description of the property, and

(iii) the name and address of the appraiser of the property if an appraisal is done;

(f) the day on which the receipt was issued where that day differs from the day referred to in paragraph (d) or (e);

(g) the name and address of the donor including, in the case of an individual, his first name and initial;

(h) the amount that is

(i) the amount of a cash donation, or

(ii) where the donation is a gift of property other than cash, the amount that is the fair market value of the property at the time that the gift was made; and

(i) the signature, as provided in subsection (2) or (3.1), of a responsible individual who has been authorized by the other recipient of the gift to acknowledge donations.

**Information Circulars**: 84-3R5: Gifts to certain charitable organizations outside Canada.

(2) Except as provided in subsection (3) or (3.1), every official receipt shall be signed personally by an individual referred to in paragraph (1)(i) or (1.1)(i).

(3) Where all official receipt forms of a registered organization are

(a) distinctively imprinted with the name, address in Canada and registration number of the organization,

(b) serially numbered by a printing press or numbering machine, and

(c) kept at the place referred to in subsection 230(2) of the Act until completed as an official receipt,

the official receipts may bear a facsimile signature.

(3.1) Where all official receipt forms of another recipient of the gift are

(a) distinctively imprinted with the name and address of the other recipient of the gift,

(b) serially numbered by a printing press or numbering machine,

(c) if applicable, kept at a place referred to in subsection 230(1) of the Act until completed as an official receipt,

the official receipts may bear a facsimile signature.

(4) An official receipt issued to replace an official receipt previously issued shall show clearly that it replaces the original receipt and, in addition to its own serial number, shall show the serial number of the receipt originally issued.

(5) A spoiled official receipt form shall be marked "cancelled" and such form, together with the duplicate thereof, shall be retained by the registered organization or the other recipient of a gift as part of its records.

(6) Every official receipt form on which

(a) the day on which the donation was received,

(b) the year during which the donation was received, or

(c) the amount of the donation,

was incorrectly or illegibly entered shall be regarded as spoiled.

**Definitions [Reg. 3501]**: "amount" — ITA 248(1); "Canada" — ITA 255, *Interpretation Act* 35(1); "individual", "Minister" — ITA 248(1); "official receipt", "official receipt form", "other recipient of a gift" — Reg. 3500; "property", "record" — ITA 248(1); "registered organization" — Reg. 3500.

**Information Circulars**: 80-10R: Registered charities: operating a registered charity.

**3502. Employees' charity trusts** — Where

(a) a registered organization

(i) is an employees' charity trust, or

(ii) has appointed an employer as agent for the purpose of remitting, to that registered organization, donations that are collected by the employer from the employer's employees, and

(b) each copy of the return required by section 200 to be filed for a year by an employer of employees who donated to the registered organization in that year shows

(i) the amount of each employee's donations to the registered organization for the year collected by the employer, and

(ii) the registration number assigned by the Minister to the registered organization,

section 3501 shall not apply and the copy of the portion of the return, relating to each employee who made a donation to the registered organization in that year, that is required by section 209 to be distributed to the employee for filing with the employee's income tax return shall be an official receipt.

**Notes**: Reg. 3502 amended by P.C. 1994-139, retroactive to 1986, to allow for direct collection and distribution by employers of employees' charitable donations without going through an employees' charity trust.

**Definitions [Reg. 3502]**: "amount", "employee" — ITA 248(1); "employees' charity trust" — Reg. 3500; "employer", "Minister" — ITA 248(1); "official receipt", "registered organization" — Reg. 3500.

**3503. Universities outside Canada** — For the purposes of subparagraph 110.1(1)(a)(vi) and paragraph (f) of the definition "total charitable gifts" in subsection 118.1(1) of the Act, the universities outside Canada named in Schedule VIII are hereby prescribed to be universities the student body of which ordinarily includes students from Canada.

**Related Provisions**: Canada-U.S. tax treaty, Art. XXI:6 — Gifts to U.S. universities.

**Definitions [Reg. 3503]**: "Canada" — ITA 255, *Interpretation Act* 35(1); "classification society", "estimate of the expenses of survey", "inspector" — Reg. 3600(2); "prescribed" — ITA 248(1); "quadrennial survey", "survey", "surveyor" — Reg. 3600(2).

**3504. Prescribed donees** — For the purposes of subparagraph 110.1(3)(a)(ii) and paragraph 118.1(6)(b) of the Act, The Nature Conservancy, a charity established in the United States, is a prescribed donee.

**Notes**: Reg. 3504 amended by P.C. 1994-139, effective 1988, to change reference from former ITA 110(2.2)(a)(ii) to the provisions that now deal with gifts.

**Definitions [Reg. 3504]**: "prescribed" — ITA 248(1); "United States" — *Interpretation Act* 35(1).

**Interpretation Bulletins**: Regs. 3500–3504 — See at beginning of Part XXXV.

## PART XXXVI — RESERVES FOR SURVEYS

**3600. (1)** For the purpose of paragraph 20(1)(o) of the Act, the amount hereby prescribed is

(a) for the third taxation year preceding the taxation year during which a survey is scheduled to occur, the amount that is $1/4$ of the estimate of the expenses of the survey;

(b) for the second taxation year preceding the taxation year during which a survey is scheduled to occur, the amount that is $1/2$ of the estimate of the expenses of the survey;

(c) for the first taxation year preceding the taxation year during which a survey is scheduled to occur, the amount that is $3/4$ of the estimate of the expenses of the survey; and

(d) for the taxation year during which a survey is scheduled to occur, if the quadrennial or other special surveys have not, at the end of the year, been completed to the extent that the vessel is permitted to proceed on a voyage, the amount remaining after deducting from the estimate of the expenses of the survey the amount of expenses actually incurred in the year in carrying out the survey.

**(2)** In this section,

**"classification society"** means a society or association for the classification and registry of shipping approved by the Minister of Transport under the *Canada Shipping Act*.

**"estimate of the expenses of survey"** means a fair and reasonable estimate, made by a taxpayer at the time of filing his return of income for the third taxation year preceding the taxation year in which a quadrennial survey is scheduled to occur, of the costs, charges and expenses which might be expected to be necessarily incurred by him by reason of that survey and in respect of which he does not have or possess nor is he likely to have or possess any right of reimbursement, recoupment, recovery or indemnification from any other person or source;

**"inspector"** means a steamship inspector appointed under Part VIII of the *Canada Shipping Act*.

**"quadrennial survey"** means a periodical survey, not being an annual survey nor a survey coinciding as to time with the construction of a vessel, in accordance with the rules of a classification society or, an extended inspection, not being an annual inspection nor an inspection coinciding as to time with the construction of a vessel, pursuant to the provisions of the *Canada Shipping Act*, and the regulations thereunder;

**"survey"** means the drydocking of a vessel, the examination and inspection of its hull, boilers, machinery, engines and equipment by an inspector or a surveyor and everything done to such vessel, its hull, boilers, machinery, engines and equipment pursuant to an order, requirement or recommendation given or made by the inspector or surveyor as the result of the examination and inspection so that a safety and inspection certificate might be issued in respect of the vessel pursuant to the provisions of the *Canada Shipping Act*, and the regulations thereunder or, as the case may be, so that the vessel might be entitled to retain the character assigned to it in the registry book of a classification society;

**"surveyor"** means a surveyor to a classification society.

**Definitions [Reg. 3600]**: "Canada" — ITA 255, *Interpretation Act* 35(1); "classification society", "estimate of the expenses of survey", "inspector" — Reg. 3600(2); "Minister", "person", "prescribed" — ITA 248(1); "quadrennial survey", "survey" — Reg. 3600(2); "surveyor" — Reg. 3600(2)"amount" — ITA 248(1); "taxation year" — ITA 249; "taxpayer" — ITA 248(1).

## PART XXXVII — CHARITABLE FOUNDATIONS

**3700. Interpretation** — In this Part,

**"charitable foundation"** has the meaning assigned by paragraph 149.1(1)(a) [149.1(1)"charitable foundation"] of the Act;

**"limited-dividend housing company"** means a limited-dividend housing company described in paragraph 149(1)(n) of the Act;

**"non-qualified investment"** has the meaning assigned by paragraph 149.1(1)(e.1) [149.1(1)"non-qualified investment"] of the Act;

**"prescribed stock exchange"** means a stock exchange referred to in Part XXXII;

**"taxation year"** has the meaning assigned by paragraph 149.1(1)(l) [149.1(1)"taxation year"] of the Act.

**3701. Disbursement quota** — **(1)** For the purposes of clause 149.1(1)(e)(iv)(A) [149.1(1)"disbursement quota"D] of the Act, the prescribed amount referred to therein for a taxation year of a charitable foundation shall be determined in accordance with the following rules:

(a) choose a number, not less than two and not more than eight, of equal and consecutive periods that total twenty-four months and that end immediately before the beginning of the year;

(b) aggregate for each period chosen under paragraph (a) all amounts, each of which is the value, determined in accordance with section 3702, of property or a portion thereof owned by the foundation, and not used directly in charitable activities or administration, on the last day of the period;

(c) aggregate all amounts, each of which is the aggregate of values determined for each period under paragraph (b); and

(d) divide the aggregate amount determined under paragraph (c) by the number of periods chosen under paragraph (a).

(2) For the purposes of subsection (1) and subject to subsection (3),

(a) the number of periods chosen by a charitable foundation under paragraph (1)(a) shall, unless otherwise authorized by the Minister, be used for the taxation year and for all subsequent taxation years; and

(b) a charitable foundation shall be deemed to have existed on the last day of each of the periods chosen by it.

(3) The number of periods chosen under paragraph (1)(a) may be changed by the foundation for its first taxation year commencing after 1986 and the new number shall, unless otherwise authorized by the Minister, be used for that taxation year and all subsequent taxation years.

**Definitions [Reg. 3701]**: "amount" — ITA 248(1); "charitable foundation" — ITA 149.1(1), Reg. 3700; "Minister" — ITA 248(1); "month" — *Interpretation Act* 35(1); "prescribed"; "property" — ITA 248(1); "taxation year" — ITA 149.1(1), Reg. 3700.

**3702. Determination of value** — (1) For the purposes of subsection 3701(1), the value of property or a portion thereof owned by a charitable foundation, and not used directly in charitable activities or administration, on the last day of a period shall be determined as of that day and shall be

(a) in the case of a non-qualified investment, the greater of its fair market value on that day and its cost amount to the foundation;

(b) subject to paragraph (c), in the case of property other than a non-qualified investment that is

(i) a share of a corporation that is listed on a prescribed stock exchange, the closing price or the average of the bid and asked prices of that share on that day or, if there is no closing price or bid and asked prices on that day, on the last preceding day for which there was a closing price or bid and asked prices,

(ii) a share of a corporation that is not listed on a prescribed stock exchange, the fair market value of that share on that day,

(iii) an interest in real property, the fair market value on that day of the interest less the amount of any debt of the foundation incurred in respect of the acquisition of the interest and secured by the real property or the interest therein, where the debt bears a reasonable rate of interest,

(iv) a contribution that is the subject of a pledge, nil,

(v) an interest in property where the foundation does not have the present use or enjoyment of the interest, nil,

(vi) a life insurance policy, other than an annuity contract, that has not matured, nil, and

(vii) a property not described in any of subparagraphs (i) to (vi), the fair market value of the property on that day; and

(c) in the case of any property described in paragraph (b)

(i) that is owned in connection with the charitable activities of the foundation and is a share of a limited-dividend housing company or a loan,

(ii) that has ceased to be used for charitable purposes and is being held pending disposition or for use in charitable activities, or

(iii) that has been acquired for use in charitable activities,

the lesser of the fair market value of the property on that day and an amount determined by the formula

$$\frac{A}{.045} \times \frac{12}{B}$$

where

A is the income earned on the property in the period, and

B is the number of months in the period.

(2) For the purposes of subsection (1), a method that the Minister may accept for the determination of the fair market value of property or a portion thereof on the last day of a period is an independent appraisal made

(a) in the case of property described in subparagraph (1)(b)(ii) or (iii), not more than three years before that day; and

(b) in the case of property described in paragraph (1)(a), subparagraph (1)(b)(vii) or paragraph (1)(c), not more than one year before that day.

**Definitions [Reg. 3702]**: "amount", "annuity" — ITA 248(1); "charitable foundation" — ITA 149.1(1), Reg. 3700; "corporation" — ITA 248(1), *Interpretation Act* 35(1); "cost amount" — ITA 248(1); "disposition" — ITA 248(1); "interest in real property" — ITA 248(4); "life insurance policy" — ITA 138(12),

248(1); "Minister" — ITA 248(1); "month" — *Interpretation Act* 35(1); "non-qualified investment" — ITA 149.1(1), Reg. 3700; "prescribed stock exchange" — Reg. 3700; "property", "share" — ITA 248(1).

## PART XXXVIII — SOCIAL INSURANCE NUMBER APPLICATIONS

**3800.** Every individual who is required by subsection 237(1) of the Act to apply to the Minister of Human Resources Development for assignment to him of a Social Insurance Number shall do so by delivering or mailing to the local office of the Canada Employment Insurance Commission nearest to the individual's residence, a completed application in the form prescribed by the Minister for that purpose.

**Notes**: Reg. 3800 amended by S.C. 1996, c. 11, to change "National Health and Welfare" to "Human Resources Development", and "Canada Employment and Immigration Commission" to "Canada Employment Insurance Commission", effective July 12, 1996.

**Definitions [Reg. 3800]**: "Canada" — ITA 255, *Interpretation Act* 35(1); "individual", "Minister", "office", "prescribed" — ITA 248(1).

**Information Circulars**: 82-2R2: SIN legislation that relates to the preparation of information slips.

## PART XXXIX — MINING TAXES ON INCOME

**3900. (1)** In computing his income for a taxation year, a taxpayer may deduct, under paragraph 20(1)(v) of the Act, an amount equal to the lesser of

(a) the aggregate of the taxes paid, in respect of his income derived from mining operations in a province for the year,

(i) to the province, and

(ii) to a municipality in the province in lieu of taxes on property or any interest in property (other than his residential property or any interest therein); and

(b) that proportion of such taxes that his income derived from mining operations in the province for the year is of his income in respect of which the taxes were so paid.

**(2)** In this section,

**"income derived from mining operations"** in a province for a taxation year by a taxpayer means,

(a) where the taxpayer has no source of income other than mining operations, the amount that would otherwise be his income for the year if no amount had been deducted in computing his income under paragraph 20(1)(v) of the Act or paragraph 1100(1)(g) of these Regulations, and

(b) in any other case, the amount that would otherwise be his income for the year if no amount had been deducted in computing his income under paragraph 20(1)(v) of the Act or paragraph 1100(1)(g) of these Regulations, minus the aggregate of

(i) his income for the year from all sources other than mining, processing and sale of mineral ores, minerals and products produced therefrom, and

(ii) an amount equal to eight per cent of the original cost to him of properties described in Schedule II used by him in the year in the processing of mineral ores, minerals or products derived therefrom or, if the amount so determined is greater than 65 per cent of the income remaining after deducting the amount determined under subparagraph (i), 65 per cent of the income so remaining or, if the amount so determined is less than 15 per cent of the income so remaining, 15 per cent of the income so remaining;

**"mine"** includes any work or undertaking in which mineral ore is extracted or produced, including a quarry;

**"mineral ores"** includes all unprocessed minerals or mineral bearing substances;

**"minerals"** means minerals other than minerals obtained from a mineral resource but does not include petroleum, natural gas or related hydrocarbons;

**"mining operations"** means the extraction or production of mineral ore from or in any mine or its transportation to or over any part of the distance to the point of egress from the mine, including processing thereof prior to or in the course of such transportation but not including any processing thereof after removal from the mine;

**"processing"** as applied to mineral ores includes all forms of beneficiation, smelting and refining, transportation and distributing but does not include any of these operations that are performed with respect to mineral ore before it is removed from the mine.

**(3)** Nothing in this section shall be construed as allowing a taxpayer to deduct an amount in respect of taxes imposed under a statute or bylaw that is not restricted to the taxation of persons engaged in mining operations.

**Definitions [Reg. 3900]**: "amount", "mineral", "mineral resource", "person", "property" — ITA 248(1); "province" — *Interpretation Act* 35(1); "related" — ITA 251(2)–(6); "taxation year" — ITA 249; "taxpayer" — ITA 248(1).

## PART XL — BORROWED MONEY COSTS

**4000.** [Revoked]

**Notes**: Reg. 4000, revoked effective 1979-80, provided a prescribed manner for making an election under s. 21 of the Act. The election no longer needs to be made in prescribed manner.

**4001. Interest on insurance policy loans** — For the purposes of subsection 20(2.1) of the Act, the amount of interest to be verified by the insurer in respect of a taxpayer shall be verified in prescribed form no later than the last day on which the taxpayer is required to file his return of income under section 150 of the Act for the taxation year in respect of which the interest was paid.

**Definitions [Reg. 4001]**: "amount", "insurer", "prescribed" — ITA 248(1); "taxation year" — ITA 249; "taxpayer" — ITA 248(1).

**Forms**: T2210: Verification of policy loan interest by the insurer.

## PART XLI — REPRESENTATION EXPENSES

**4100.** For the purposes of subsection 20(9) of the Act, an election shall be made by filing with the Minister the following documents in duplicate:

(a) a letter from the taxpayer specifying the amount in respect of which the election is being made; and

(b) where the taxpayer is a corporation, a certified copy of the resolution of the directors authorizing the election to be made.

**Definitions [Reg. 4100]**: "amount" — ITA 248(1); "corporation" — ITA 248(1), *Interpretation Act* 35(1); "Minister", "taxpayer" — ITA 248(1).

## PART XLII — VALUATION OF ANNUITIES AND OTHER INTERESTS

**4200.** For the purposes of subparagraph 115E(f)(i) of the former Act (within the meaning assigned by paragraph 8(b) of the *Income Tax Application Rules*), the value of any income right, annuity, term of years, life or other similar estate or interest in expectancy shall be determined in accordance with the rules and standards, including standards as to mortality and interest, as are prescribed by the *Estate Tax Regulations* pursuant to the provisions of subparagraph 58(1)(s)(i) of the *Estate Tax Act*.

**Notes**: The *Estate Tax Act* was repealed in 1972.

**Definitions [Reg. 4200]**: "annuity" — ITA 248(1); "estate" — ITA 104(1), 248(1); "prescribed" — ITA 248(1).

## PART XLIII — INTEREST RATES

**4300. Interpretation** — For the purposes of this Part, "quarter" means any of the following periods in a calendar year:

(a) the period beginning on January 1 and ending on March 31;

(b) the period beginning on April 1 and ending on June 30;

(c) the period beginning on July 1 and ending on September 30; and

(d) the period beginning on October 1 and ending on December 31.

**Interpretation Bulletins**: IT-421R2: Benefits to individuals, corporations and shareholders from loans or debt.

**4301. Prescribed rate of interest** — Subject to section 4302, for the purposes of

(a) every provision of the Act that requires interest at a prescribed rate to be paid to the Receiver General, the prescribed rate in effect during any particular quarter is the total of

(i) the rate that is the simple arithmetic mean, expressed as a percentage per year and rounded to the next higher whole percentage where the mean is not a whole percentage, of all amounts each of which is the average equivalent yield, expressed as a percentage per year, of Government of Canada Treasury Bills that mature approximately three months after their date of issue and that are sold at auctions of Government of Canada Treasury Bills during the first month of the quarter preceding the particular quarter, and

(ii) 4 per cent;

(b) every provision of the Act that requires interest at a prescribed rate to be paid or applied on an amount payable by the Minister to a taxpayer, the prescribed rate in effect during any particular quarter is the total of

(i) the rate determined under subparagraph (a)(i) in respect of the particular quarter, and

(ii) 2 per cent; and

(c) every other provision of the Act in which reference is made to a prescribed rate of interest or to interest at a prescribed rate, the prescribed rate in effect during any particular quarter is the rate determined under subparagraph (a)(i) in respect of the particular quarter.

**Notes**: Reg. 4301 amended by P.C. 1989-1792, effective for interest in respect of periods after September 1989, to increase the rate by 2% for amounts owing *to* and *by* the government; and amended by P.C. 1995-926, effective for interest in respect of periods after June 1995, to increase the rate by a further 2% for amounts owing *to* the government. (This change was announced in the 1995 federal budget.)

Reg. 4301(a)(i) amended effective December 31, 1997 to change "weekly average" to "average", and "a weekly auction" to "auctions", to reflect the change in the cycle of treasury bill auctions that took effect September 18, 1997 (Dept. of Finance news release 97-67, Aug. 5/97).

There are now three rates:

(a) applies for interest payable by a taxpayer to Revenue Canada (i.e., *late payments of tax*), and to "offset interest" credited to a taxpayer for early payments of instalments. Examples: ITA 129(2.2), 161(1), (2), (2.2).

(b) applies for interest payable by Revenue Canada to a taxpayer (i.e., *late refunds*). Examples: ITA 129(2.1), 164(3), (3.2).

(c) applies for provisions that require a prescribed rate of interest to be paid by one party to another in order for there not to be a *deemed benefit*, or that use a prescribed rate of interest as a

Part XLIII — Interest Rates   Reg. S. 4302

measure of a fair return on capital. Examples: ITA 17(1), 18(2.2), 18(9.7), 56(4.2), 74.4(2)(d), 74.5(1), 74.5(2), 80.4(1), 80.4(2), 94.1(1)(f)(ii), 143.2(7)(b).

Note that for the *leasing rules* in ITA 16.1, Reg. 4302 applies instead of Reg. 4301.

*Prescribed Interest Rates Per Annum*

| Year | Quarter | Reg. 4301(c) Benefits % | Reg. 4301(b) Refunds % | Reg. 4301(a) Late Tax % |
|---|---|---|---|---|
| 1984 | 1st, 2nd | 10 | 10 | 10 |
|  | 3rd | 11 | 11 | 11 |
|  | 4th | 13 | 13 | 13 |
| 1985 | 1st | 12 | 12 | 12 |
|  | 2nd, 3rd, 4th | 10 | 10 | 10 |
| 1986 | 1st | 9 | 9 | 9 |
|  | 2nd | 11 | 11 | 11 |
|  | 3rd | 10 | 10 | 10 |
|  | 4th | 9 | 9 | 9 |

[Compounding under 248(11) applies effective Jan. 1/87]

| 1987 | 1st | 9 | 9 | 9 |
|---|---|---|---|---|
|  | 2nd, 3rd | 8 | 8 | 8 |
|  | 4th | 9 | 9 | 9 |
| 1988 | 1st, 2nd, 3rd | 9 | 9 | 9 |
|  | 4th | 10 | 10 | 10 |
| 1989 | 1st | 11 | 11 | 11 |
|  | 2nd | 12 | 12 | 12 |
|  | 3rd | 13 | 13 | 13 |
|  | 4th | 13 | 15 | 15 |
| 1990 | 1st, 2nd | 13 | 15 | 15 |
|  | 3rd, 4th | 14 | 16 | 16 |
| 1991 | 1st | 13 | 15 | 15 |
|  | 2nd | 11 | 13 | 13 |
|  | 3rd | 10 | 12 | 12 |
|  | 4th | 9 | 11 | 11 |
| 1992 | 1st | 9 | 11 | 11 |
|  | 2nd | 8 | 10 | 10 |
|  | 3rd | 7 | 9 | 9 |
|  | 4th | 6 | 8 | 8 |
| 1993 | 1st | 8 | 10 | 10 |
|  | 2nd | 7 | 9 | 9 |
|  | 3rd | 6 | 8 | 8 |
|  | 4th | 5 | 7 | 7 |
| 1994 | 1st | 5 | 7 | 7 |
|  | 2nd | 4 | 6 | 6 |
|  | 3rd | 6 | 8 | 8 |
|  | 4th | 7 | 9 | 9 |
| 1995 | 1st | 6 | 8 | 8 |
|  | 2nd | 8 | 10 | 10 |
|  | 3rd | 9 | 11 | 13 |
|  | 4th | 7 | 9 | 11 |
| 1996 | 1st | 7 | 9 | 11 |
|  | 2nd | 6 | 8 | 10 |
|  | 3rd, 4th | 5 | 7 | 9 |
| 1997 | 1st | 4 | 6 | 8 |
|  | 2nd | 3 | 5 | 7 |
|  | 3rd, 4th | 4 | 6 | 8 |
| 1998 | 1st | 4 | 6 | 8 |
|  | 2nd, 3rd, 4th | 5 | 7 | 9 |
| 1999 | 1st–4th | 5 | 7 | 9 |

| Year | Quarter | Reg. 4301(c) Benefits % | Reg. 4301(b) Refunds % | Reg. 4301(a) Late Tax % |
|---|---|---|---|---|
| 2000 | 1st | 5 | 7 | 9 |
|  | 2nd, 3rd, 4th | 6 | 8 | 10 |
| 2001 | 1st | 6 | 8 | 10 |

**Interpretation Bulletins**: IT-153R3: Land developers — Subdivision and development costs and carrying charges on land; IT-243R4: Dividend refund to private corporations; IT-421R2: Benefits to individuals, corporations and shareholders from loans or debt.

**Definitions [Reg. 4301]**: "amount" — ITA 248(1); "Canada" — ITA 255, *Interpretation Act* 35(1); "Minister" — ITA 248(1); "month" — *Interpretation Act* 35(1); "prescribed" — ITA 248(1); "quarter" — Reg. 4300; "taxpayer" — ITA 248(1).

**4302.** Notwithstanding section 4301, for the purposes of paragraph 16.1(1)(d) of the Act and subsection 1100(1.1), the interest rate in effect during any month is the rate that is one percentage point greater than the rate that was, during the month before the immediately preceding month, the average yield, expressed as a percentage per year rounded to two decimal points, prevailing on all outstanding domestic Canadian-dollar Government of Canada bonds on the last Wednesday of that month with a remaining term to maturity of over 10 years, as first published by the Bank of Canada.

**Notes**: Reg. 4302 added by P.C. 1991-465, effective for leases entered into after 10:00 p.m. EDST, April 26, 1989, other than leases entered into pursuant to an agreement in writing entered into before that time under which the lessee thereunder has the right to require the lease of the property (and for these purposes a lease in respect of which a material change has been agreed to by the parties thereto effective at any particular time that is after 10:00 p.m. EDST, April 26, 1989 is deemed to have been entered into at that particular time).

*Prescribed Interest Rates for Leasing Rules*

For leases entered into before July 1989, the prescribed rate is 11.2%. The rates applicable for leases entered into after that date are as follows:

|  | 1989 | 1990 | 1991 | 1992 | 1993 | 1994 |
|---|---|---|---|---|---|---|
| Jan. | — | 10.80 | 11.70 | 10.18 | 9.66 | 8.45 |
| Feb. | — | 10.69 | 11.51 | 9.97 | 9.54 | 8.12 |
| March | — | 11.04 | 11.22 | 9.92 | 9.67 | 7.86 |
| April | 11.20 | 11.64 | 10.89 | 9.97 | 9.19 | 8.33 |
| May | 11.20 | 11.91 | 10.88 | 10.28 | 9.27 | 9.25 |
| June | 11.20 | 12.54 | 10.91 | 10.51 | 9.27 | 9.18 |
| July | 10.85 | 11.86 | 10.91 | 10.17 | 9.12 | 9.55 |
| Aug. | 10.60 | 11.72 | 11.36 | 9.87 | 8.96 | 10.29 |
| Sept. | 10.62 | 11.78 | 11.17 | 9.21 | 8.79 | 10.50 |
| Oct. | 10.62 | 11.83 | 10.97 | 9.19 | 8.40 | 9.89 |
| Nov. | 10.91 | 12.54 | 10.59 | 9.53 | 8.55 | 10.04 |
| Dec. | 10.54 | 12.15 | 10.12 | 9.33 | 8.35 | 10.29 |

|  | 1995 | 1996 | 1997 | 1998 | 1999 | 2000 |
|---|---|---|---|---|---|---|
| Jan. | 10.24 | 8.44 | 7.42 | 6.78 | 6.35 | 7.12 |
| Feb. | 10.16 | 8.43 | 7.77 | 6.84 | 6.08 | 7.25 |
| March | 10.41 | 8.35 | 8.07 | 6.63 | 6.08 | 7.36 |
| April | 9.86 | 8.84 | 7.78 | 6.64 | 6.37 | 6.98 |
| May | 9.70 | 8.94 | 7.97 | 6.54 | 6.23 | 6.96 |
| June | 9.44 | 9.07 | 7.97 | 6.64 | 6.34 | 7.03 |

| | | | | | |
|---|---|---|---|---|---|
| July | 9.11 | 8.92 | 7.95 | 6.49 | 6.54 | 6.94 |
| Aug. | 9.02 | 8.98 | 7.49 | 6.45 | 6.63 | 6.90 |
| Sept. | 9.50 | 8.86 | 7.11 | 6.56 | 6.74 | 6.83 |
| Oct. | 9.24 | 8.60 | 7.38 | 6.78 | 6.69 | 6.79 |
| Nov. | 9.11 | 8.48 | 6.99 | 6.15 | 6.92 | 6.83 |
| Dec. | 9.11 | 7.81 | 6.80 | 6.27 | 7.38 | 6.79 |

2001

Jan. 6.63
Feb. 6.59

For updates to this list, contact Rick Owen, (613) 954-2504. The rates are also posted on the CCRA's website: http://www.ccra-adrc.gc.ca.

**Definitions [Reg. 4302]**: "Canada" — ITA 255, *Interpretation Act* 35(1); "month" — *Interpretation Act* 35(1).

## PART XLIV — PUBLICLY-TRADED SHARES OR SECURITIES

**4400. (1)** For the purpose of section 24 and subsection 26(11) of the *Income Tax Application Rules*,

(a) a share or security named in Schedule VII is hereby prescribed to be a publicly-traded share or security; and

(b) for each such share or security, the amount set out in Column II of Schedule VII opposite that share or security is hereby prescribed as the amount, if any, prescribed in respect of that property.

**(2)** In Schedule VII, the abbreviation

(a) "Cl" means "Class";

(b) "Com" means "Common";

(c) "Cv" means "Convertible";

(d) "Cu" means "Cumulative";

(e) "Pc" means "Per Cent";

(f) "Pr" means "Preferred" or "Preference" as the case may be;

(g) "Pt" means "Participating";

(h) "Rt" means "Right"; and

(i) "Wt" means "Warrant".

**Notes**: Schedule VII, which lists the December 23, 1971 share values of all publicly listed shares, is not reproduced. See the *Stikeman Income Tax Act* or TaxPartner.

**Definitions [Reg. 4400]**: "amount", "prescribed", "property" — ITA 248(1); "share" — ITA 248(1).

## PART XLV — ELECTIONS IN RESPECT OF EXPROPRIATION ASSETS

**4500.** Any election by a taxpayer under subsection 80.1(1), (2), (4), (5), (6) or (9) of the Act shall be made on or before the day on or before which the return of income is required to be filed pursuant to section 150 of the Act for the taxation year in which the assets referred to in the particular election were acquired by him.

**Definitions [Reg. 4500]**: "taxation year" — ITA 249; "taxpayer" — ITA 248(1).

**Forms**: T2079: Elections re expropriation assets.

## PART XLVI — INVESTMENT TAX CREDIT

**Forms**: T2038 (Ind.): Investment tax credit (Individuals); T2038 (Corp): Investment tax credit (Corporations).

**4600. Qualified property** — **(1)** Property is a prescribed building for the purposes of the definition "qualified property" in subsection 127(9) of the Act if it is depreciable property of the taxpayer that is a building or grain elevator and it is erected on land owned or leased by the taxpayer,

(a) that is included in Class 1, 3, 6, 20, 24 or 27 or paragraph (c), (d) or (e) of Class 8 in Schedule II; or

(b) that is included or would, but for Class 28 or 41 in Schedule II, be included in paragraph (g) of Class 10 in Schedule II.

**(2)** Property is prescribed machinery and equipment for the purposes of the definition "qualified property" in subsection 127(9) of the Act if it is depreciable property of the taxpayer (other than property referred to in subsection (1)) that is

(a) a property included in paragraph (k) of Class 1 or paragraph (a) of Class 2 in Schedule II;

(b) an oil or water storage tank;

(c) a property included in Class 8 in Schedule II (other than railway rolling stock);

(d) a vessel, including the furniture, fittings and equipment attached thereto;

(e) a property included in paragraph (a) of Class 10 or Class 22 or 38 in Schedule II (other than a car or truck designed for use on highways or streets);

(f) notwithstanding paragraph (e), a logging truck acquired after March 31, 1977 to be used in the activity of logging and having a weight, including the weight of property the capital cost of which is included in the capital cost of the truck at the time of its acquisition (but for greater certainty not including the weight of fuel), in excess of 16,000 pounds;

(g) a property included in any of paragraphs (b) to (f), (h), (j), (k), (o), (r), (t) or (u) of Class 10 in Schedule II, or property included in paragraph (b) of Class 41 in Schedule II and that would otherwise be included in paragraph (j), (k), (r), (t) or (u) of Class 10 in Schedule II;

(h) a property included in paragraph (n) of Class 10, or Class 15, in Schedule II (other than a roadway);

Part XLVI — Investment Tax Credit       Reg. S. 4604

(i) a property included in any of paragraphs (a) to (f) of Class 9 in Schedule II;

(j) a property included in Class 28 or paragraph (a), (a.1), (a.2) or (a.3) of Class 41 in Schedule II that would, but for Class 28 or 41, as the case may be, be included in paragraph (k) or (r) of Class 10 of Schedule II;

(k) a property included in any of Classes 21, 24, 27, 29, 34, 39, 40 and 43 in Schedule II; or

(l) a property included in paragraph (c) or (d) of Class 41 in Schedule II.

**Notes**: Reg. 4600(2)(k) amended by P.C. 1998-49, effective in respect of property acquired after March 6, 1996, to add reference to Cl. 41(a.1)–(a.3) and to change "but for that class or classes" to "but for Class 28 or 41".

Reference to Class 43 in Reg. 4600(2)(k) added by P.C. 1994-230, effective for property acquired after February 25, 1992.

Reg. 4600(2)(l) added by P.C 1999-629, effective for taxation years that begin after 1996.

**Interpretation Bulletins**: IT-411R: Meaning of "construction".

**Definitions [Reg. 4600]**: "depreciable property" — ITA 13(21), 248(1); "prescribed", "property", "taxpayer" — ITA 248(1).

## 4601. Qualified transportation equipment —
[No longer relevant]

**Notes**: Reg. 4601 prescribes property for purposes of ITA 127(9)"qualified transportation equipment", now repealed.

Reg. 4601(c)(i)(A) amended by P.C. 1995-775, effective for property acquired after December 2, 1992.

## 4602. Certified property — (1) For the purposes of the definition "certified property" in subsection 127(9) of the Act, each of the following areas is a prescribed area:

(a) that portion of the Province of Newfoundland comprising the census divisions 2 to 4 and 7 to 10;

(b) that portion of the Province of Prince Edward Island comprising the Kings census division;

(c) that portion of the Province of Nova Scotia comprising the census divisions of

(i) Cape Breton,

(ii) Guysborough,

(iii) Inverness,

(iv) Richmond, and

(v) Victoria;

(d) that portion of the Province of New Brunswick comprising the census divisions of

(i) Gloucester,

(ii) Kent,

(iii) Madawaska,

(iv) Northumberland, and

(v) Restigouche;

(e) that portion of the Province of Quebec comprising

(i) all of the area north of the 50th parallel of latitude, other than the area within the limits of the city of Sept-Iles,

(ii) the Magdalen Islands, and

(iii) the census divisions of

(A) Bonaventure,

(B) Gaspé-Est,

(C) Gaspé-Ouest,

(D) Matane,

(E) Matapédia,

(F) Rimouski, other than the area within the limits of the city of Rimouski,

(G) Rivière-du-Loup, and

(H) Témiscouata;

(f) that portion of the Province of Ontario that is north of the 50th parallel of latitude;

(g) that portion of the Province of Manitoba comprising the census divisions 19 and 21 to 23, other than the area within the limits of the city of Thompson;

(h) that portion of the Province of Saskatchewan comprising the census division of Northern Saskatchewan;

(i) that portion of the Province of Alberta comprising the census division of Peace River, other than the area within the limits of the city of Grande Prairie;

(j) that portion of the Province of British Columbia comprising the Peace River-Liard census division; and

(k) all of the Yukon Territory and the Northwest Territories.

**(2) ["Census divisions"]** — For the purposes of subsection (1), the expression "census divisions" has the same meaning as in the *Dictionary of 1971 Census Terms*, Statistics Canada Catalogue Number 12-540, and the *Census Divisions and Subdivisions*, Statistics Canada Catalogues Numbered 92-704, 92-705, 92-706 and 92-707.

**Definitions [Reg. 4602]**: "Canada" — ITA 255, *Interpretation Act* 35(1); "census divisions" — Reg. 4602(2); "prescribed" — ITA 248(1).

## 4603. Qualified construction equipment —
[No longer relevant]

**Notes**: Reg. 4603 prescribes property for purposes of ITA 127(9)"qualified construction equipment", now repealed.

## 4604. Approved project property — [No longer relevant]

**Notes**: Reg. 4604 prescribes property for purposes of ITA 127(9)"approved project property", now repealed.

Reference to Class 43 in Reg. 4604(2)(j) added by P.C. 1994-230, effective for property acquired after February 25, 1992.

**4605. Prescribed activities** — [No longer relevant]

**Notes**: Reg. 4605 prescribes activities for ITA 127(9)"approved project property", now repealed.

**4606. Prescribed amount** — For the purposes of paragraph (b) of the definition "contract payment" in subsection 127(9) of the Act, a prescribed amount is an amount received from the Canadian Commercial Corporation in respect of an amount received by that Corporation from a government, municipality or other public authority other than the government of Canada or of a province, a Canadian municipality or other Canadian public authority.

**Definitions [Reg. 4606]**: "amount" — ITA 248(1); "Canada" — ITA 255, *Interpretation Act* 35(1); "prescribed" — ITA 248(1); "province" — *Interpretation Act* 35(1).

**Interpretation Bulletins**: IT-151R4: Scientific research and experimental development expenditures.

**4607. Prescribed designated regions** — For the purposes of the definition "specified percentage" in subsection 127(9) of the Act, "prescribed designated region" means a region of Canada, other than the Gaspé peninsula and the provinces of Nova Scotia, New Brunswick, Prince Edward Island, and Newfoundland, including Labrador, that was a designated region on December 31, 1984, under the *Regional Development Incentives Designated Region Order, 1974*.

**Definitions [Reg. 4607]**: "Canada" — ITA 255, *Interpretation Act* 35(1); "province" — *Interpretation Act* 35(1).

**4608. Prescribed expenditure for qualified Canadian exploration expenditure** — [No longer relevant]

**Notes**: Reg. 4608 prescribes expenditures for ITA 127(9)"qualified Canadian exploration expenditure", now repealed.

**4609. Prescribed offshore region** — For the purposes of the definition "specified percentage" in subsection 127(9) of the Act, the following region is a prescribed offshore region:

(a) that submarine area, not within a province, adjacent to the coast of Canada and extending throughout the natural prolongation of that portion of the land territory of Canada comprising the Gaspé Peninsula and the provinces of Newfoundland, Prince Edward Island, Nova Scotia and New Brunswick to the outer edge of the continental margin or to a distance of two hundred nautical miles from the baselines from which the territorial sea of Canada is measured, whichever is the greater; and

(b) the waters above the submarine area referred to in paragraph (a).

**Definitions [Reg. 4609]**: "Canada" — ITA 255, *Interpretation Act* 35(1); "prescribed" — ITA 248(1); "province", "territorial sea", "territory" — *Interpretation Act* 35(1).

**4610. Prescribed area** — For the purpose of paragraph (c.1) of the definition "qualified property" in subsection 127(9) of the Act, the area prescribed is the area comprising the Provinces of Nova Scotia, New Brunswick, Prince Edward Island and Newfoundland and the Gaspé Peninsula.

**Notes**: Reg. 4610 added by P.C. 1995-775, effective for property acquired after 1991.

**Definitions [Reg. 4610]**: "prescribed" — ITA 248(1).

## PART XLVII — ELECTION IN RESPECT OF CERTAIN PROPERTY OWNED ON DECEMBER 31, 1971

**4700.** Any election by an individual under subsection 26(7) of the *Income Tax Application Rules* shall be made by filing with the Minister the form prescribed.

**Definitions [Reg. 4700]**: "individual", "Minister", "prescribed" — ITA 248(1).

**Interpretation Bulletins**: IT-139R: Capital property owned on December 31, 1971 — Fair market value.

**Forms**: T1105: Supplementary schedule for dispositions of capital property acquired before 1972; T2076: Valuation day value election for capital properties owned on December 31, 1971.

## PART XLVIII — STATUS OF CORPORATIONS AND TRUSTS

**4800. (1)** For the purposes of subparagraph 89(1)(g)(ii) [89(1)"public corporation"(b)] of the Act, the following conditions are hereby prescribed in respect of a corporation other than a cooperative corporation (within the meaning assigned by section 136 of the Act) or a credit union:

(a) a class of shares of the capital stock of the corporation designated by the corporation in its election or by the Minister in his notice to the corporation, as the case may be, shall be qualified for distribution to the public;

(b) there shall be no fewer than

(i) where the shares of that class are equity shares, 150, and

(ii) in any other case, 300

persons, other than insiders of the corporation, each of whom holds

(iii) not less than one block of shares of that class, and

(iv) shares of that class having an aggregate fair market value of not less than $500; and

(c) insiders of the corporation shall not hold more than 80 per cent of the issued and outstanding shares of that class.

**Forms**: T2073: Election to be a public corporation.

**(2)** For the purposes of subparagraph 89(1)(g)(iii) [89(1)"public corporation"(c)] of the Act, the fol-

Part XLVIII — Status of Corporations and Trusts  Reg. S. 4800.1

lowing conditions are hereby prescribed in respect of a corporation:

(a) insiders of the corporation shall hold more than 90 per cent of the issued and outstanding shares of each class of shares of the capital stock of the corporation that

(i) was, at any time after the corporation last became a public corporation, listed on a stock exchange in Canada prescribed for the purposes of section 89 of the Act, or

(ii) was a class, designated as described in paragraph (1)(a), by virtue of which the corporation last became a public corporation;

(b) in respect of each class of shares described in subparagraph (a)(i) or (ii), there shall be fewer than

(i) where the shares of that class are equity shares, 50, and

(ii) in any other case, 100

persons, other than insiders of the corporation, each of whom holds

(iii) not less than one block of shares of that class, and

(iv) shares of that class having an aggregate fair market value of not less than $500; and

(c) there shall be no class of shares of the capital stock of the corporation that is qualified for distribution to the public and complies with the conditions described in paragraphs (1)(b) and (c).

**Forms**: T2067: Election not to be a public corporation.

(3) Where, by virtue of an amalgamation (within the meaning assigned by section 87 of the Act) of predecessor corporations any one or more of which was, immediately before the amalgamation, a public corporation, shares of any class of the capital stock of any such public corporation that was

(a) at any time after the corporation last became a public corporation, listed on a stock exchange in Canada prescribed for the purposes of section 89 of the Act, or

(b) the class, designated as described in paragraph (1)(a), by virtue of which the corporation last became a public corporation,

are converted into shares of any class (in this subsection referred to as the "new class") of the capital stock of the new corporation, the new class shall, for the purposes of subsection (2), be deemed to be a class, designated as described in paragraph (1)(a), by virtue of which the new corporation last became a public corporation.

(4) Any election under clause 89(1)(g)(ii)(A) or (iii)(A) [89(1)"public corporation"(b)(i) or (c)(i)] of the Act shall be made by a corporation by filing with the Minister the following documents:

(a) the form prescribed by the Minister;

(b) where the directors of the corporation are legally entitled to administer the affairs of the corporation, a certified copy of their resolution authorizing the election to be made;

(c) where the directors of the corporation are not legally entitled to administer the affairs of the corporation, a certified copy of the authorization of the making of the election by the person or persons legally entitled to administer the affairs of the corporation; and

(d) a statutory declaration made by a director of the corporation stating that, after reasonable inquiry for the purpose of informing himself in that regard, to the best of his knowledge the corporation complies with all the prescribed conditions that must be complied with at the time the election is made.

**Definitions [Reg. 4800]**: "block of shares" — Reg. 4803(1); "Canada" — ITA 255, *Interpretation Act* 35(1); "class of shares" — Reg. 4803(2); "corporation" — ITA 248(1), *Interpretation Act* 35(1); "credit union" — ITA 248(1); "equity share" — ITA 204, Reg. 4803(1); "Minister" — ITA 248(1); "new class" — Reg. 4800(3); "person" — Reg. 4803(3); "prescribed" — ITA 248(1); "public corporation" — ITA 89(1), 248(1); "share" — ITA 248(1); "statutory declaration" — *Interpretation Act* 35(1).

**Interpretation Bulletins**: IT-320R2: RRSP — qualified investments; IT-391R: Status of corporations.

**Forms**: T2067: Election not to be a public corporation; T2073: Election to be a public corporation.

**4800.1** For the purposes of paragraph 107(1)(a), subsections 107(2) and (4.1) and paragraph 108(1)(c) [108(1)"capital interest"] of the Act, the following are prescribed trusts;

(a) a trust maintained primarily for the benefit of employees of a corporation or two or more corporations which do not deal at arm's length with each other, where one of the main purposes of the trust is to hold interests in shares of the capital stock of the corporation or corporations, as the case may be, or any corporation not dealing at arm's length therewith;

(b) a trust established exclusively for the benefit of one or more persons each of whom was, at the time the trust was created, either a person from whom the trust received property or a creditor of that person, where one of the main purposes of the trust is to secure the payments required to be made by or on behalf of that person to such creditor; and

(c) a trust all or substantially all of the properties of which consist of shares of the capital stock of a corporation, where the trust was established pursuant to an agreement between two or more shareholders of the corporation and one of the main purposes of the trust is to provide for the exercise of voting rights in respect of those shares pursuant to that agreement.

**Related Provisions**: ITA 107.4(3)(i) — Trust deemed not to be prescribed trust.

**Notes**: Revenue Canada's view is that "all or substantially all", used in para. (c), means 90% or more.

Reference to ITA 107(1)(a) in opening words of Reg. 4800.1 added by P.C. 1992-2338, effective January 1, 1988.

The Department of Finance Technical Notes of December 17, 1999, to ITA 107(1.1) state:

> Subsection 107(1.1) is amended so that it appplies only to trusts that are personal trusts and prescribed trusts. It is intended that trusts described in section 4800.1 of the Regulations be prescribed for this purpose.

**Definitions [Reg. 4800.1]**: "arm's length" — ITA 251(1); "corporation" — ITA 248(1), *Interpretation Act* 35(1); "employee", "person", "prescribed", "property", "share", "shareholder" — ITA 248(1); "trust" — ITA 104(1), 248(1), (3).

**4801.** For the purposes of paragraph 132(6)(c) of the Act, the following conditions are hereby prescribed in respect of a trust:

(a) a class of the units of the trust shall be qualified for distribution to the public; and

(b) in respect of any one class of units described in paragraph (a), there shall be no fewer than 150 beneficiaries of the trust, each of whom holds

(i) not less than one block of units of the class, and

(ii) units of the class having an aggregate fair market value of not less than $500.

**Related Provisions**: Reg. 221(1)(f) — Reporting requirements.

**Definitions [Reg. 4801]**: "block of units" — Reg. 4803(1); "class of units" — Reg. 4803(2); "person" — Reg. 4803(3); "prescribed" — ITA 248(1); "trust" — ITA 104(1), 248(1), (3).

**4801.1** For the purpose of paragraph (c) of the definition "exempt trust" in subsection 233.2(1) of the Act, the following conditions are hereby prescribed in respect of a trust:

(a) at least 150 beneficiaries of the trust are beneficiaries in respect of the same class of units of the trust; and

(b) at least 150 of the beneficiaries in respect of that class each hold

(i) at least one block of units of that class, and

(ii) units of that class having a total fair market value of at least $500.

**Notes**: Reg. 4801.1 added by P.C. 1998-1573, effective for taxation years that begin after 1995.

**4802.** **(1)** For the purposes of clause 149(1)(o.2)(iv)(D) of the Act, the following are prescribed persons:

(a) a trust all the beneficiaries of which are trusts described in clause 149(1)(o.2)(iv)(B) of the Act;

(b) a corporation incorporated before November 17, 1978 solely in connection with, or for the administration of, a registered pension plan;

(c) a trust or corporation established by or arising by virtue of an act of a province the principal activities of which are to administer, manage or invest the monies of a pension fund or plan that is established pursuant to an act of the province or an order or regulation made thereunder;

(d) a trust or corporation established by or arising by virtue of an act of a province in connection with a scheme or program for the compensation of workers injured in an accident arising out of or in the course of their employment;

(e) Her Majesty in right of a province;

(f) a trust all of the beneficiaries of which are any combination of

(i) registered pension plans,

(ii) trusts described in clause 149(1)(o.2)(iv)(B) or (C) of the Act, and

(iii) persons described in this subsection; and

(g) a corporation all of the shares of the capital stock of which are owned by one or more of the following:

(i) registered pension plans,

(ii) trusts described in clause 149(1)(o.2)(iv)(B) or (C) of the Act, and

(iii) persons described in this subsection.

**Notes**: Reg. 4802(1)(e) amended and (f) added by P.C. 1992-2338, effective for taxation years commencing after 1991. For earlier years, read:

> (e) Her Majesty in right of a province acting in connection with or in the administration of a pension fund or plan established pursuant to an act of the province.

Reg. 4802(1)(f)(iii) amended by P.C. 1996-569, effective for 1994 and later taxation years. For 1992-93, read: "(iii) persons described in any of paragraphs (a) to (e)".

Reg. 4802(1)(g) added by P.C. 1996-569, effective for 1994 and later taxation years.

**(2)** For the purposes of paragraph 149(1)(t) of the Act, the following are prescribed insurers:

(a) Union Québécoise, compagnie d'assurances générales inc.;

(b) Les Clairvoyants Compagnie d'Assurance Générale Inc.; and

(c) Laurentian Farm Insurance Company Inc.

**Notes**: Reg. 4802(2) added by P.C. 1994-785, effective for 1989 and later taxation years.

**Definitions [Reg. 4802]**: "corporation" — ITA 248(1), *Interpretation Act* 35(1); "employment" — ITA 248(1); "Her Majesty" — *Interpretation Act* 35(1); "insurer", "person", "prescribed" — ITA 248(1); "province" — *Interpretation Act* 35(1); "registered pension plan", "share" — ITA 248(1); "trust" — ITA 104(1), 248(1), (3).

**4803.** **(1)** In this Part,

**"block of shares"** means, with respect to any class of the capital stock of a corporation,

(a) 100 shares, if the fair market value of one share of the class is less than $25,

(b) 25 shares, if the fair market value of one share of the class is $25 or more but less than $100, and

(c) 10 shares, if the fair market value of one share of the class is $100 or more;

"block of units" means, with respect to any class of units of a trust,

(a) 100 units, if the fair market value of one unit of the class is less than $25,

(b) 25 units, if the fair market value of one unit of the class is $25 or more but less than $100, and

(c) 10 units, if the fair market value of one unit of the class is $100 or more;

"equity share" has the meaning assigned by section 204 of the Act;

"insider of a corporation" has the meaning that would be assigned by section 100 of the *Canada Corporations Act* if the references therein to "public company" and to "equity shares" were read as references to "corporation" and "shares" respectively, except that a person who is an employee of the corporation, or of a person who does not deal at arm's length with the corporation, and whose right to sell or transfer any share of the capital stock of the corporation, or to exercise the voting rights, if any, attaching to the share, is restricted by

(a) the terms and conditions attaching to the share, or

(b) any obligation of the person, under a contract, in equity or otherwise, to the corporation or to any person with whom the corporation does not deal at arm's length,

shall be deemed to hold the share as an insider of the corporation.

(2) For the purposes of this Part, a class of shares of the capital stock of a corporation or a class of units of a trust is qualified for distribution to the public only if

(a) a prospectus, registration statement or similar document has been filed with, and, where required by law, accepted for filing by, a public authority in Canada pursuant to and in accordance with the law of Canada or of any province and there has been a lawful distribution to the public of shares or units of that class in accordance with that document;

(b) the class is a class of shares, any of which were issued by the corporation at any time after 1971 while it was a public corporation in exchange for shares of any other class of the capital stock of the corporation that was, immediately before the exchange, qualified for distribution to the public;

(c) in the case of any class of shares, any of which were issued and outstanding on January 1, 1972, the class complied on that date with the conditions described in paragraphs 4800(1)(b) and (c); or

(d) in the case of any class of units, any of which were issued and outstanding on January 1, 1972, the class complied on that date with the condition described in paragraph 4801(b).

(3) For the purposes of paragraphs 4800(1)(b), 4800(2)(b) and 4801(b), where a group of persons holds

(a) not less than one block of shares of any class of shares of the capital stock of a corporation or one block of units of any class of a trust, as the case may be, and

(b) shares or units, as the case may be, of that class having an aggregate fair market value of not less than $500,

that group shall, subject to subsection (4), be deemed to be one person for the purposes of determining the number of persons who hold shares or units, as the case may be, of that class.

(4) In determining under subsection (3) the persons who belong to a group for the purposes of determining the number of persons who hold shares or units, as the case may be, of a particular class, the following rules apply:

(a) no person shall be included in more than one group;

(b) no person shall be included in a group if he holds

(i) not less than one block of shares or one block of units, as the case may be, of that class, and

(ii) shares or units, as the case may be, of that class having an aggregate fair market value of not less than $500; and

(c) the membership of each group shall be determined in the manner that results in the greatest possible number of groups.

**Interpretation Bulletins**: IT-391R: Status of corporations.

**Definitions [Reg. 4803]**: "arm's length" — ITA 251(1); "block of shares", "block of units" — Reg. 4803(1); "Canada" — ITA 255, *Interpretation Act* 35(1); "class of shares", "class of units" — Reg. 4803(2); "corporation" — ITA 248(1), *Interpretation Act* 35(1); "employee" — ITA 248(1); "group" — Reg. 4803(4); "person" — ITA 248(1); "province" — *Interpretation Act* 35(1); "public corporation" — ITA 89(1), 248(1); "share" — ITA 248(1); "trust" — ITA 104(1), 248(1), (3).

# PART XLIX — DEFERRED INCOME PLANS, QUALIFIED INVESTMENTS

**4900.** (1) For the purposes of subparagraphs 146(1)(g)(iv) [146(1)"qualified investment"(d)], 146.2(1)(g)(iv) [repealed], 146.3(1)(d)(iii) [146.3(1)"qualified investment"(c)] and 204(e)(x) [204"qualified investment"(i)] of the Act, subject to subsection (2), each of the following investments is hereby prescribed to be a qualified investment for a plan trust at a particular time if at that time it is

### Proposed Amendment — Reg. 4900(1) opening words

**4900. (1)** Subject to subsection (2), for the purposes of paragraph (d) of the definition "qualified investment" in subsection 146(1) of the Act, paragraph (e) of the definition "qualified investment" in subsection 146.1(1) of the Act, paragraph (c) of the definition "qualified investment" in subsection 146.3(1) of the Act and paragraph (i) of the definition "qualified investment" in section 204 of the Act, each of the following investments is prescribed to be a qualified investment for a plan trust at a particular time if at that time it is

**Application**: The October 27, 1998 draft regulations, subsec. 2(1), will amend the opening words of subsec. 4900(1) to read as above, applicable to property acquired after October 27, 1998.

**Technical Notes**: Part XLIX of the Regulations lists a number of qualified investments for RRSPs, RRIFs and DPSPs. Part XLIX is amended to reflect the introduction of qualified investment rules for RESPs. Generally, the types of property that will qualify for an RESP are those that qualify for an RRSP.

All of the amendments described below to Part XLIX of the Regulations apply to property acquired after the date on which the changes are released to the public [October 27, 1998].

Subsection 4900(1) of the Regulations lists a number of types of property that are qualified investments for a trust governed by an RRSP, RRIF or DPSP.

The preamble to subsection 4900(1) is amended so that the listed types of property are also qualified investments for a trust governed by an RESP [section 146.1 — ed.]. It is also amended to delete an obsolete reference to section 146.2 of the Act, which dealt with registered home ownership savings plans.

(a) **[registered investment]** — an interest in a trust or a share of the capital stock of a corporation that was a registered investment for the plan trust during the calendar year in which the particular time occurs or the immediately preceding year;

(b) **[share of public corporation]** — a share of the capital stock of a public corporation other than a mortgage investment corporation;

(c) **[share of mortgage investment corporation]** — a share of the capital stock of a mortgage investment corporation that does not hold as part of its property at any time during the calendar year in which the particular time occurs any indebtedness, whether by way of mortgage or otherwise, of a person who is an annuitant, a beneficiary or an employer, as the case may be, under the governing plan of the plan trust or of any other person who does not deal at arm's length with that person;

### Proposed Amendment — Reg. 4900(1)(c)

(c) **[share of mortgage investment corporation]** — a share of the capital stock of a mortgage investment corporation that does not hold as part of its property at any time during the calendar year in which the particular time occurs any indebtedness, whether by way of mortgage or otherwise, of a person who is an annuitant, a beneficiary, an employer or a subscriber under the governing plan of the plan trust or of any other person who does not deal at arm's length with that person;

**Application**: The October 27, 1998 draft regulations, subsec. 2(2), will amend para. 4900(1)(c) to read as above, applicable to property acquired after October 27, 1998.

**Technical Notes**: Paragraph 4900(1)(c) allows a share of a mortgage investment corporation (as defined in subsection 130.1(6) of the Act) to be a qualified investment, provided the RRSP or RRIF annuitant or any beneficiary or employer under the DPSP is not indebted to the corporation. Paragraph 4900(1)(c) is amended so that the restriction on indebtedness also applies to RESP subscribers and beneficiaries.

(c.1) **[bond of public corporation]** — a bond, debenture, note or similar obligation of a public corporation other than a mortgage investment corporation;

(d) **[unit of mutual fund trust]** — a unit of a mutual fund trust;

### Proposed Amendment — Reg. 4900(1)(d)

**Letter from Department of Finance, December 10, 1998**:

Dear [xxx]

This is in reply to your memorandum to me dated November 5, 1998.

You have drawn our attention to a case where units of trusts are issued to institutional investors and high net worth individuals, without any requirement for a prospectus, registration statement or similar document to be filed with provincial securities regulators. You have advised us that these trusts would, if a prospectus or similar document had been filed, have been mutual fund trusts for the purposes of the *Income Tax Act*.

We agree that, in these circumstances, it would be appropriate to treat units in these trusts in the same manner as mutual fund trusts for the purpose of the qualified investment rules for trusts governed by registered retirement savings plans, registered retirement income funds and deferred profit sharing plans. Consequently, I am prepared to recommend to the Minister of Finance an amendment to the Income Tax Regulations to effect the above noted treatment. If this recommendation is supported, we would propose its application be for acquisitions after 1993.

Thank you for raising this issue with us.

Yours sincerely,

Len Farber
Director General, Tax Legislation Division

(d.1) **[bond of mutual fund trust]** — a bond, debenture, note or similar obligation issued by a mutual fund trust the units of which are listed on a stock exchange referred to in section 3200;

(e) **[warrant or option]** — a warrant or right giving the owner thereof the right to acquire either immediately or in the future property all of which is a qualified investment for the plan trust;

(e.1) **[société d'entraide économique]** — a share of, or deposit with, a société d'entraide économique;

(f) **[share of credit union]** — a share of, or similar interest in a credit union;

(g) **[bond of credit union]** — a bond, debenture, note or similar obligation (in this paragraph referred to as the "obligation") issued by, or a deposit with, a credit union that has not at any time during the calendar year in which the particular time occurs granted any benefit or privilege to a person who is an annuitant, a beneficiary or an employer, as the case may be, under the governing plan of the plan trust, or to any other person who does not deal at arm's length with that person, as a result of the ownership by

> **Proposed Amendment — Reg. 4900(1)(g) opening words**
>
> (g) **[bond of credit union]** — a bond, debenture, note or similar obligation (in this paragraph referred to as the "obligation") issued by, or a deposit with, a credit union that has not at any time during the calendar year in which the particular time occurs granted any benefit or privilege to a person who is an annuitant, a beneficiary, an employer or a subscriber under the governing plan of the plan trust, or to any other person who does not deal at arm's length with that person, as a result of the ownership by
>
> **Application**: The October 27, 1998 draft regulations, subsec. 2(3), will amend the opening words of para. 4900(1)(g) to read as above, applicable to property acquired after October 27, 1998.
>
> **Technical Notes**: Paragraph 4900(1)(g) prescribes, as a qualified investment, a bond, debenture, note or similar obligation issued by, or a deposit with, a credit union that has not at any time in the year granted a benefit, resulting from the investment, to the RRSP or RRIF annuitant or any beneficiary or employer under the DPSP. Paragraph 4900(1)(g) is amended so that the restriction on granting a benefit also applies to RESP subscribers and beneficiaries.

(i) the plan trust of a share or obligation of, or a deposit with, the credit union, or

(ii) a registered investment of a share or obligation of, or a deposit with, the credit union if the plan trust has invested in that registered investment,

and a credit union shall be deemed to have granted a benefit or privilege to a person in a year if at any time in that year that person continues to enjoy a benefit or privilege that was granted in a prior year;

(h) **[bond of cooperative corporation]** — a bond, debenture, note or similar obligation (in this paragraph referred to as the "obligation") issued by a cooperative corporation (within the meaning assigned by subsection 136(2) of the Act)

(i) that throughout the taxation year of the cooperative corporation immediately preceding the year in which the obligation was acquired by the plan trust had not less than 100 shareholders or, if all its shareholders were corporations, not less than 50 shareholders,

(ii) whose obligations were, at the end of each month of

(A) the last taxation year, if any, of the cooperative corporation prior to the date of acquisition of the obligation by the plan trust, or

(B) the period commencing three months after the date an obligation was first acquired by any plan trust and ending on the last day of the taxation year of the cooperative corporation in which that period commenced,

whichever of the periods referred to in clause (A) or (B) commences later, held by plan trusts the average number of which is not less than 100 computed on the basis that no two plan trusts shall have the same individual as an annuitant or a beneficiary, as the case may be, and

(iii) that has not at any time during the calendar year in which the particular time occurs granted any benefit or privilege to a person who is an annuitant, a beneficiary or an employer, as the case may be, under the governing plan of the plan trust, or to any other person who does not deal at arm's length with that person, as a result of the ownership by

> **Proposed Amendment — Reg. 4900(1)(h)(iii) opening words**
>
> (iii) that has not at any time during the calendar year in which the particular time occurs granted any benefit or privilege to a person who is an annuitant, a beneficiary, an employer or a subscriber under the governing plan of the plan trust, or to any other person who does not deal at arm's length with that person, as a result of the ownership by
>
> **Application**: The October 27, 1998 draft regulations, subsec. 2(4), will amend the opening words of subpara. 4900(1)(h)(iii) to read as above, applicable to property acquired after October 27, 1998.
>
> **Technical Notes**: Paragraph 4900(1)(h) prescribes, as a qualified investment, a bond, debenture, note or similar obligation issued by a cooperative corporation (as defined in subsection 136(2) of the Act) provided certain conditions are met. One of the conditions is that the cooperative corporation has not at any time in the year granted a benefit, resulting from the investment, to the RRSP or RRIF annuitant or any beneficiary or employer under the DPSP. Paragraph 4900(1)(h) is amended so that the restriction on

granting a benefit also applies to RESP subscribers and beneficiaries.

    (A) the plan trust of a share or obligation of the cooperative corporation, or

    (B) a registered investment of a share or obligation of the cooperative corporation if the plan trust has invested in that registered investment,

and a cooperative corporation shall be deemed to have granted a benefit or privilege to a person in a year if at any time in that year that person continues to enjoy a benefit or privilege that was granted in a prior year;

(i) **[bonds of certain corporations]** — a bond, debenture, note or similar obligation (in this paragraph referred to as the "obligation") of a Canadian corporation

    (i) if payment of the principal amount of the obligation and the interest thereon is guaranteed by a corporation or a mutual fund trust whose shares or units, as the case may be, are listed on a prescribed stock exchange in Canada,

    (ii) if the corporation is controlled directly or indirectly by

        (A) one or more corporations,

        (B) one or more mutual fund trusts, or

        (C) one or more corporations and mutual fund trusts

whose shares or units, as the case may be, are listed on a prescribed stock exchange in Canada, or

    (iii) if, at the time the obligation is acquired by the plan trust, the corporation that issued the obligation is

        (A) a corporation that, in respect of its capital stock, has issued and outstanding share capital carried in its books at not less than $25 million, or

        (B) a corporation that is controlled by a corporation described in clause (A),

and has issued and outstanding bonds, debentures, notes or similar obligations having in the aggregate a principal amount of at least $10 million that are held by at least 300 different persons and were issued by the corporation by means of one or more offerings, provided that in respect of each such offering a prospectus, registration statement or similar document was filed with and, where required by law, accepted for filing by a public authority in Canada pursuant to and in accordance with the laws of Canada or a province and there was a lawful distribution to the public of those bonds, debentures, notes or similar obligations in accordance with that document;

(i.1) **[community bond guaranteed by province]** — a security of a Canadian corporation

    (i) that was issued pursuant to *The Community Bonds Act*, chapter C-16.1 of the Statutes of Saskatchewan, 1990, *The Rural Development Bonds Act*, chapter 47 of the Statutes of Manitoba, 1991-92, the *Community Economic Development Act, 1993*, chapter 26 of the Statutes of Ontario, 1993, or the New Brunswick Community Development Bond Program through which financial assistance is provided under the *Economic Development Act*, chapter E-1.11 of the Acts of New Brunswick, 1975, and

    (ii) the payment of the principal amount of which is guaranteed by Her Majesty in right of a province;

(i.11) **[Nova Scotia *Equity Tax Credit Act*]** — a share of the capital stock of a Canadian corporation that is registered under section 11 of the *Equity Tax Credit Act*, chapter 3 of the Statutes of Nova Scotia, 1993, the registration of which has not been revoked under that Act;

(i.12) **[NWT risk capital investment]** — a share of the capital stock of a Canadian corporation that is registered under section 39 of the *Risk Capital Investment Tax Credits Act*, chapter 22 of the Statutes of the Northwest Territories, 1998, the registration of which has not been revoked under that Act;

(i.2) **[banker's acceptance]** — indebtedness of a Canadian corporation (other than a corporation that does not deal at arm's length with a person who is an annuitant, a beneficiary or an employer under the governing plan of the plan trust) represented by a bankers' acceptance;

---

**Proposed Amendment — Reg. 4900(1)(i.2)**

(i.2) **[banker's acceptance]** — indebtedness of a Canadian corporation (other than a corporation that does not deal at arm's length with a person who is an annuitant, a beneficiary, an employer or a subscriber under the governing plan of the plan trust) represented by a bankers' acceptance;

**Application**: The October 27, 1998 draft regulations, subsec. 2(5), will amend para. 4900(1)(i.2) to read as above, applicable to property acquired after October 27, 1998.

**Technical Notes**: Paragraph 4900(1)(i.2) allows the indebtedness of a Canadian corporation represented by a bankers' acceptance to be a qualified investment, provided the corporation deals at arm's length with the RRSP or RRIF annuitant or each person who is a beneficiary or an employer under the DPSP. Paragraph 4900(1)(i.2) is amended so that the restriction on non-arm's length dealings also applies to RESP subscribers and beneficiaries.

(j) **[mortgage]** — a mortgage in respect of real property situated in Canada insured

(i) under the *National Housing Act*, or

(ii) by a corporation offering its services to the public in Canada as an insurer of mortgages

and administered by an approved lender under the *National Housing Act*;

(k) **[pre-1981 qualified investment]** — an investment, other than a qualified investment described in paragraphs (a) to (j), that

(i) was, at the end of 1980, a qualified investment for a trust pursuant to subparagraph 204(e)(v) of the Act or section 1502, this Part or section 5800, as the case may be, as those provisions read at that time,

(ii) was held on December 31, 1980 and continuously thereafter by the trust until the particular time,

(iii) would have continued to be a qualified investment of the trust from December 31, 1980 until the particular time had the provisions referred to in subparagraph (i) been in force throughout that period of time, and

(iv) was not, at any time before the particular time, an interest in a registered investment;

(l) **[bond of international organization]** — a bond, debenture, note or similar obligation issued or guaranteed by

(i) the International Bank for Reconstruction and Development,

(i.1) the International Finance Corporation,

(ii) the Inter-American Development Bank,

(iii) the Asian Development Bank,

(iv) the Caribbean Development Bank,

(v) the European Bank for Reconstruction and Development, or

(vi) the African Development Bank;

(m) **[listed royalty unit]** — a royalty unit that is listed on a prescribed stock exchange in Canada and the value of which is derived solely from Canadian resource properties;

(n) **[listed limited partnership unit]** — a limited partnership unit listed on a stock exchange referred to in section 3200;

(o) **[bond of foreign government]** — a bond, a debenture, note or similar obligation issued by the government of a country other than Canada and that had, at the time of purchase, an investment grade rating with a bond rating agency that in the ordinary course of its business rates the debt obligations issued by that government;

(p) **[bond of corporation listed outside Canada]** — a bond, debenture, note or similar obligation of a corporation the shares of which are listed on a stock exchange referred to in section 3201;

(p.1) **[listed depository receipt]** — a right to a share of the capital stock of a corporation where the right is evidenced by a depository receipt that is listed on a stock exchange referred to in section 3200 or 3201;

(q) **[debt of privatized Crown corporation]** — a debt issued by a Canadian corporation (other than a corporation with share capital or a corporation that does not deal at arm's length with a person who is an annuitant, a beneficiary or an employer under the governing plan of the plan trust) where

> **Proposed Amendment — Reg. 4900(1)(q) opening words**
>
> (q) **[debt of privatized Crown corporation]** — a debt issued by a Canadian corporation (other than a corporation with share capital or a corporation that does not deal at arm's length with a person who is an annuitant, a beneficiary, an employer or a subscriber under the governing plan of the plan trust) where
>
> **Application**: The October 27, 1998 draft regulations, subsec. 2(6), will amend the opening words of para. 4900(1)(q) to read as above, applicable to property acquired after October 27, 1998.
>
> **Technical Notes**: Paragraph 4900(1)(q) allows a debt issued by certain Canadian corporations without share capital that are exempt from Part I tax under the Act to be a qualified investment, provided the corporation deals at arm's length with the RRSP or RRIF annuitant or each person who is a beneficiary or employer under the DPSP. Paragraph 4900(1)(q) is amended so that the restriction on non-arm's length dealings also applies to RESP subscribers and beneficiaries.

(i) the taxable income of the corporation is exempt from tax under Part I of the Act because of paragraph 149(1)(l) of the Act, and

(ii) either

(A) before the particular time and after 1995, the corporation

(I) acquired, for a total consideration of not less than $25 million, property from Her Majesty in right of Canada or a province, and

(II) put that property to a use that is the same as or similar to the use to which the property was put before the acquisition described in subclause (I), or

(B) at the time of the acquisition of the debt by the plan trust, it was reasonable to expect that clause (A) would apply in respect of the debt no later than one year after the time of the acquisition; or

(r) **[debt of large non-profit organization]** — a debt issued by a Canadian corporation (other than a corporation with share capital or a corporation that does not deal at arm's length with a person who is an annuitant, a beneficiary

**Reg. S. 4900(1)(r)**

or an employer under the governing plan of the plan trust) if

(i) the taxable income of the corporation is exempt from tax under Part I of the Act because of paragraph 149(1)(l) of the Act, and

(ii) either

(A) the debt is issued by the corporation as part of an issue of debt by the corporation for an amount of at least $25 million,

or

(B) at the time of the acquisition of the debt by the plan trust, the corporation had issued debt as part of a single issue for an amount of at least $25 million.

### Proposed Addition — Foreign Stock Exchange Index Units

**Department of Finance news release, December 18, 1998**: *Qualified RRSP Investments and IRAs*

Finance Minister Paul Martin today announced that he will propose changes to the *Income Tax Act* and the *Income Tax Regulations* to address two issues that have been recently raised with the Department of Finance, in the context of retirement savings decisions currently being made by individuals.

The first issue relates to foreign stock exchange index units. The Minister announced that he would propose changes to the *Income Tax Regulations* to ensure that these units are qualified investments for trusts governed by registered retirement savings plans, registered retirement income funds and deferred profit sharing plans. Qualifying units will include Standard & Poor 500 Depositary Receipts (SPDRs), units valued on the basis of the Dow Jones Industrial Average (known as DIAMONDs) and units for a particular country (known as WEBs) valued on the basis of the Morgan Stanley Capital Investment Index.

It is understood that industry practice for a number of years has been to treat these units as qualified investments. The proposed amendments would accommodate industry practice and recognize that index units can be part of a balanced portfolio of retirement assets for many individuals.

It is proposed that these amendments to the Regulations would apply to property acquired after 1993. This ensures that the regulatory framework conforms to the long-standing industry practice.

[For the second measure, dealing with Roth IRAs, see Proposed Amendment under ITA 248(1)"foreign retirement arrangement" — ed.]

For further information: Tax Legislation Division, (613) 992-1916; Jean-Michel Catta, Public Affairs and Operations Division, (613) 992-1574.

### Proposed Non-Amendment — Exchange-Traded Futures Contracts

**Letter from Department of Finance, July 4, 2000**: [See under ITA 204.4(2)(a)(ii)(A) — ed.]

**Related Provisions**: Reg. 221 — Information return where entity claims that its shares or units are qualified investments.

**Notes**: Many qualified investments are listed in ITA 204"qualified investment"(a), (b), (d), (f), (g) or (h) rather than in Reg. 4900. See ITA 146(1)"qualified investment"(a), 146.1(1)"qualified investment"(a), and 146.3(1)"qualified investment"(a).

Note that some investments are allowed as qualified investments but, for RRSP, RRIF and DPSP purposes, are "foreign property" which is limited to 30% of the plan (see 206(2)). This applies not only to genuinely "foreign" properties but also to certain other investments such as limited partnership units (206(1)"foreign property"(i)). The foreign property limit does not apply to RESPs.

A proposal to add annuity contracts to Reg. 4900(1), in a Dept. of Finance news release of December 19, 1996, was enacted instead in ITA 146(1)"qualified investment"(c.1), (c.2) and 146.3(1)"qualified investment"(b.1), (b.2).

Reg. 4900(1)(b) amended by P.C. 1994-1074, effective 1993, to change "other than a share of a mortgage investment corporation that is not listed on a prescribed stock exchange in Canada" to "other than a mortage investment corporation". The change is non-substantive, since a mortgage investment corporation that is listed on a Canadian stock exchange is covered under 204"qualified investment"(d) anyway.

Reg. 4900(1)(c.1) added by P.C. 1994-1074, effective 1993.

Reg. 4900(1)(d.1) added by P.C. 1998-629, effective for property acquired after 1996. (For bonds of mutual fund corporations, see 4900(1)(c.1).)

Reg. 4900(1)(e) amended by P.C. 1994-1074, effective 1993, to remove a requirement that the warrant or right be listed on an exchange. The change allows RRSPs, RRIFs and DPSPs to acquire shares that are qualified investments together with warrants with respect to such shares.

Reg. 4900(1)(i.1) added by P.C. 1992-2334, effective for property acquired after June 1991, applying to a "bond, debenture, note or similar obligation of a Canadian corporation" issued under the Saskatchewan or Manitoba statutes. Amended to add reference to the Ontario and New Brunswick statutes, and the opening words changed to "a security of a Canadian corporation", by P.C. 1994-1075, effective for property acquired after August 1993.

Reg. 4900(1)(i.11) added by P.C. 1996-1487, effective for property acquired after 1995. It refers to Community Economic Development Corporations under Nova Scotia's *Equity Tax Credit Act*.

Reg. 4900(1)(i.12) added by P.C. 1999-249, effective for property acquired August 1998.

Reg. 4900(1)(i.2) added by P.C. 1994-1074, effective 1993.

Reg. 4900(1)(j) allows investment by the RRSP in the taxpayer's mortgage. See also Reg. 4900(4). For discussion of the administrative rules that apply in addition to the Regulations, see Wayland Chau, "Financing the Executive Home with RRSPs", *Taxation of Executive Compensation and Retirement* (Federated Press), Vol. 8 No. 7 (March 1997), pp. 265-270.

Reg. 4900(1)(l)(i.1) added by P.C. 1994-1074, effective July 14, 1990.

Reg. 4900(1)(l)(v) added by P.C. 1994-1075, effective for months beginning after March 1991.

Reg. 4900(1)(l)(vi) added by P.C. 1999-133, effective 1997.

Reg. 4900(1)(m) added by P.C. 1992-2334, effective for property acquired after July 16, 1992.

Reg. 4900(1)(n) added by P.C. 1994-1074, effective 1993.

Reg. 4900(1)(o) and (p) added by P.C. 1994-1075, effective for property acquired after June 21, 1993. Reg. 4900(1)(o) permits RRSPs to hold Israel Bonds as well as debts of certain other countries.

Reg. 4900(1)(p.1) added by P.C. 1998-629, effective for 1997 and later taxation years.

Reg. 4900(1)(q) added by P.C. 1996-1487 effective for property acquired after 1995. It is designed to accommodate certain situations where provincial or federal Crown assets are privatized, so that Crown corporations are issuing debt to the public. The specific case

Part XLIX — Deferred Income Plans, Qualified Investments     Reg. S. 4900(5)

contemplated was that of Nav Canada (air traffic control operations).

Reg. 4900(1)(r) added by P.C. 1999-133, effective March 1998.

**Interpretation Bulletins**: IT-320R2: RRSP — qualified investments.

**(2)** Notes, bonds, debentures, bankers' acceptances or similar obligations of

(a) an employer by whom payments are made in trust to a trustee under a deferred profit sharing plan or a revoked plan for the benefit of beneficiaries under the plan, or

(b) a corporation with whom that employer does not deal at arm's length

are not qualified investments for the trust.

**Notes**: Reg. 4900(2) amended by P.C. 1994-1074, effective 1993.

**(3) [Annuity contract]** — For the purpose of paragraph (i) of the definition "qualified investment" in section 204 of the Act, a contract with a licensed annuities provider for an annuity payable to an employee who is a beneficiary under a deferred profit sharing plan beginning not later than the end of the year in which the employee attains 69 years of age, the guaranteed term of which, if any, does not exceed 15 years, is prescribed as a qualified investment for a trust governed by such a plan or revoked plan.

**Notes**: Reg. 4900(3) amended by P.C. 1998-2256, effective for annuity contracts acquired after 1996, except that

(a) the amendment does not apply to a contract where the annuitant turned 70 before 1997; and

(b) in applying it to a contract where the annuitant turned 69 in 1996, read "69" as "70".

For contracts acquired earlier, read:

(3) For the purposes of subparagraph 204(e)(x) [204"qualified investment"(i)] of the Act, a contract with a person licensed or otherwise authorized under the laws of Canada or a province to carry on in Canada an annuities business for an annuity payable to an employee or other beneficiary under a deferred profit sharing plan commencing not later than a day 71 years after the day of his birth, the guaranteed term of which, if any, does not exceed 15 years is a qualified investment for a trust governed by such a plan or revoked plan.

This is consistent with the 1996 Budget amendment to ITA 147(2)(k).

**(4) [Mortgage]** — For the purposes of subparagraphs 146(1)(g)(iv) [146(1)"qualified investment"(d)] and 146.3(1)(d)(iii) [146.3(1)"qualified investment"(c)] of the Act, a mortgage secured by real property situated in Canada, or an interest therein, is a qualified investment for a registered retirement savings plan or a registered retirement income fund unless the mortgagor is the annuitant under the plan or fund, as the case may be, or is a person with whom the annuitant does not deal at arm's length.

**Proposed Amendment — Reg. 4900(4)**

**(4) [Mortgage]** — For the purposes of paragraph (d) of the definition "qualified investment" in subsection 146(1) of the Act, paragraph (e) of the definition "qualified investment" in subsection 146.1(1) of the Act and paragraph (c) of the definition "qualified investment" in subsection 146.3(1) of the Act, a mortgage secured by real property situated in Canada, or an interest therein, is a qualified investment for a registered retirement savings plan, a registered education savings plan and a registered retirement income fund unless the mortgagor is a person who is an annuitant, a beneficiary or a subscriber under the plan or fund or any other person who does not deal at arm's length with that person.

**Application**: The October 27, 1998 draft regulations, subsec. 2(7), will amend subsec. 4900(4) to read as above, applicable to property acquired after October 27, 1998.

**Technical Notes**: Subsection 4900(4) of the Regulations allows a mortgage secured by real property situated in Canada, or an interest therein, to be a qualified investment for RRSPs and RRIFs, if the mortgagor deals at arm's length with the RRSP or RRIF annuitant.

Subsection 4900(4) is amended so that such a mortgage is also a qualified investment for an RESP, provided the mortgagor deals at arm's length with each person who is a subscriber or beneficiary under the RESP.

**Related Provisions**: Reg. 4900(1)(j) — Mortgage as qualified investment.

**(5) [RHOSP]** — For the purposes of subparagraph 146.2(1)(g)(iv) of the Act, a contract between a trust governed by a registered home ownership savings plan and a person licensed or otherwise authorized under the laws of Canada or a province to carry on in Canada an annuities business is a qualified investment for that trust if the trust is entitled to receive from the person, on demand, an amount in settlement of the contract that is not less than the amount by which the aggregate of

(a) all the amounts paid as consideration by the trust under the contract, and

(b) interest on the amounts described in paragraph (a) at a rate that is not less than that guaranteed under the contract

exceeds

(c) such amount as may be specified in the contract.

**Proposed Amendment — Reg. 4900(5)**

**(5) [Registered investment]** — For the purposes of paragraph (e) of the definition "qualified investment" in subsection 146.1(1) of the Act, a property is a qualified investment for a trust governed by a registered education savings plan at any time if at that time the property is an interest in a trust or a share of the capital stock of a corporation that was a registered investment for a trust governed by a registered retirement savings plan during the calendar year in which the time occurs or the preceding year.

**Application**: The October 27, 1998 draft regulations, subsec. 2(8), will amend subsec. 4900(5) to read as above, applicable to property acquired after October 27, 1998.

# Reg. S. 4900(5) — Income Tax Regulations

**Technical Notes**: Subsection 4900(5) of the Regulations prescribes certain annuity contracts to be qualified investments for registered home ownership savings plans (RHOSPs). Since the provisions relating to RHOSPs were repealed, effective after 1985, existing subsection 4900(5) is obsolete. It is being replaced by a provision relating to RESPs.

Amended subsection 4900(5) prescribes, as a qualified investment for an RESP, an interest in a trust or a share of a corporation that was a registered investment (as defined in subsection 204.4(1) of the Act) for an RRSP during the calendar year or the immediately preceding year.

**Notes**: ITA 146.2 has been repealed.

**(6) [Small business investment]** — For the purposes of subparagraphs 146(1)(g)(iv) [146(1)"qualified investment"(d)] and 146.3(1)(d)(iii) [146.3(1)"qualified investment"(c)] of the Act, except as provided in subsections (8) and (9), a property is a qualified investment for a trust governed by a registered retirement savings plan or a registered retirement income fund at any time if at that time the property is

(a) a share of the capital stock of an eligible corporation (within the meaning assigned by subsection 5100(1)), unless the annuitant under the plan or fund is a designated shareholder of the corporation;

### Proposed Amendment — Reg. 4900(6)

**(6) [Small business investment]** — For the purposes of paragraph (d) of the definition "qualified investment" in subsection 146(1) of the Act, paragraph (e) of the definition "qualified investment" in subsection 146.1(1) of the Act and paragraph (c) of the definition "qualified investment" in subsection 146.3(1) of the Act, except as provided in subsections (8) and (9), a property is a qualified investment for a trust governed by a registered retirement savings plan, a registered education savings plan and a registered retirement income fund at any time if at that time the property is

(a) a share of the capital stock of an eligible corporation (within the meaning assigned by subsection 5100(1)), unless a person who is an annuitant, a beneficiary or a subscriber under the plan or fund is a designated shareholder of the corporation;

**Application**: The October 27, 1998 draft regulations, subsec. 2(9), will amend the portion of subsec. 4900(6) before para. (b) to read as above, applicable to property acquired after October 27, 1998.

**Technical Notes**: Subsection 4900(6) of the Regulations prescribes the following types of property to be qualified investments for RRSPs and RRIFs:

- a share in the capital stock of an "eligible corporation", provided the annuitant under the RRSP or RRIF is not a "designated shareholder" of the corporation;
- an interest of a limited partner in a small business investment limited partnership; and
- an interest in an small business investment trust

The expressions "designated shareholder", "eligible corporation", "small business investment limited partnership" and "small business investment trust" are defined in subsections 4901(2), 5100(1), 5102(1) and 5103(1) of the Regulations, respectively.

Subsection 4900(6) is amended so that the types of investments described therein also qualify for an RESP. In the case of a share of an eligible corporation, each person who is a subscriber or beneficiary under the RESP must not be a "designated shareholder" of the corporation.

Subsection 4900(6) is subject to the rules in subsections 4900(8) and (9). These rules provide that an investment that would otherwise qualify under subsection 4900(6) will not be a qualified investment in certain circumstances. Subsection 4900(10) provides a special interpretative rule that applies for the purposes of subsection 4900(9).

Subsections 4900(8) to (10) are amended to reflect the extension of subsection 4900(6) to RESPs.

(b) an interest of a limited partner in a small business investment limited partnership; or

(c) an interest in a small business investment trust.

**Related Provisions**: Reg. 4900(12) — Alternative definition of qualified investment; Reg. 4901(2) — Meaning of "designated shareholder", "small business investment limited partnership"; "small business investment trust".

**Notes**: Reg. 4900(6) and (12) provide overlapping mechanisms for investments in small businesses by RRSPs. Although the conditions are similar, it is usually preferable to qualify under Reg. 4900(12) because it is a *one-time* test measured at the time the property is acquired. For a useful discussion see William Holmes, "Qualifying Investments in Private Corporations for an RRSP", *RRSP Planning* (Federated Press), Vol. III No. 4 (1996), pp. 206-212.

**Interpretation Bulletins**: IT-320R2: RRSP — qualified investments.

**(7)** For the purposes of subparagraph 204(e)(x) [204"qualified investment"(i)] of the Act, except as provided in subsection (11), a property is a qualified investment for a trust governed by a deferred profit sharing plan or revoked plan at any time if at that time the property is an interest

(a) of a limited partner in a small business investment limited partnership; or

(b) in a small business investment trust.

**(8)** For the purposes of subsection (6), where

(a) a trust governed by a registered retirement savings plan or a registered retirement income fund holds

### Proposed Amendment — Reg. 4900(8)(a) opening words

(a) a trust governed by a registered retirement savings plan, a registered education savings plan or a registered retirement income fund holds

**Application**: The October 27, 1998 draft regulations, subsec. 2(10), will amend the opening words of para. 4900(8)(a) to read as above, applicable to property acquired after October 27, 1998.

**Technical Notes**: See under 4900(6).

(i) a share of the capital stock of an eligible corporation (within the meaning assigned by subsection 5100(1)),

(ii) an interest in a small business investment limited partnership that holds a small business security, or

(iii) an interest in a small business investment trust that holds a small business security, and

(b) the annuitant under the plan or fund provides services to or for the issuer of the share or small business security, as the case may be, or a person related to that issuer and it may reasonably be considered, having regard to all the circumstances, including the terms and conditions of the share or small business security, as the case may be, or any agreement relating thereto and the rate of interest or the dividend provided on the share or small business security, as the case may be, that any amount received in respect of the share or small business security, as the case may be, is on account, in lieu or in satisfaction of payment for the services,

### Proposed Amendment — Reg. 4900(8)(b)

(b) a person who is an annuitant, a beneficiary or a subscriber under the plan or fund provides services to or for the issuer of the share or small business security, or to or for a person related to that issuer, and it can reasonably be considered, having regard to all the circumstances (including the terms and conditions of the share or small business security or of any related agreement, and the rate of interest or the dividend provided on the share or small business security), that any amount received in respect of the share or small business security is on account, in lieu or in satisfaction of payment for the services,

**Application**: The October 27, 1998 draft regulations, subsec. 2(11), will amend para. 4900(8)(b) to read as above, applicable to property acquired after October 27, 1998.

**Technical Notes**: See under 4900(6).

the property referred to in subparagraph (a)(i), (ii) or (iii) held by the plan or fund shall, immediately before that amount is received, cease to be and shall not thereafter be a qualified investment for the trust governed by the plan or fund.

(9) For the purposes of subsection (6), where

(a) a trust governed by a registered retirement savings plan or a registered retirement income fund holds

### Proposed Amendment — Reg. 4900(9)(a) opening words

(a) a trust governed by a registered retirement savings plan, a registered education savings plan or a registered retirement income fund holds

(i) an interest in a small business investment limited partnership, or

(ii) an interest in a small business investment trust

that holds a small business security (referred to in this subsection as the "designated security") of a corporation, and

(b) the annuitant under the plan or fund is a designated shareholder of the corporation,

### Proposed Amendment — Reg. 4900(9)(b)

(b) a person who is an annuitant, a beneficiary or a subscriber under the plan or fund is a designated shareholder of the corporation,

**Application**: The October 27, 1998 draft regulations, subsec. 2(13), will amend para. 4900(9)(b) to read as above, applicable to property acquired after October 27, 1998.

**Technical Notes**: See under 4900(6).

the interest shall not be a qualified investment for the trust governed by the plan or fund unless

(c) the designated security is a share of the capital stock of an eligible corporation,

(d) the partnership or trust, as the case may be, has no right to set off, assign or otherwise apply, directly or indirectly, the designated security against the interest,

(e) no person is obligated in any way, either absolutely or contingently, under any undertaking the intent or effect of which is

(i) to limit any loss that the plan or fund may sustain by virtue of the ownership, holding or disposition of the interest, or

(ii) to ensure that the plan or fund will derive earnings by virtue of the ownership, holding or disposition of the interest,

(f) in the case of the partnership, there are more than 10 limited partners and no limited partner or group of limited partners who do not deal with each other at arm's length holds more than 10 per cent of the units of the partnership, and

(g) in the case of the trust, there are more than 10 beneficiaries and no beneficiary or group of beneficiaries who do not deal with each other at arm's length holds more than 10 per cent of the units of the trust.

(10) For the purposes of paragraphs (9)(f) and (g), a trust governed by a plan or fund shall be deemed not to deal at arm's length with a trust governed by another plan or fund if the annuitant of the plan or fund is the same person as, or does not deal at arm's length with, the annuitant of the other plan or fund.

### Proposed Amendment — Reg. 4900(10)

**(10)** For the purposes of paragraphs (9)(f) and (g), a trust governed by a plan or fund shall be deemed not to deal at arm's length with a trust governed by another plan or fund if a person who is an annuitant or a subscriber under the plan or fund is the same person as, or does not deal at arm's length with, the annuitant or subscriber under the other plan or fund.

**Application**: The October 27, 1998 draft regulations, subsec. 2(14), will amend subsec. 4900(10) to read as above, applicable to property acquired after October 27, 1998.

**Technical Notes**: See under 4900(6).

---

**(11)** For the purposes of subsection (7), where

(a) a trust governed by a deferred profit sharing plan or revoked plan holds

(i) an interest in a small business investment limited partnership, or

(ii) an interest in a small business investment trust

that holds a small business security of a corporation,

(b) payments have been made in trust to a trustee under the deferred profit sharing plan or revoked plan for the benefit of beneficiaries thereunder by the corporation or a corporation related thereto, and

(c) the small business security is not an equity share described in paragraph 204(e)(vi) [204"qualified investment"(e)] of the Act,

the interest referred to in subparagraphs (a)(i) and (ii) shall not be a qualified investment for the trust referred to in paragraph (a).

**(12) [Small business corporation]** — For the purposes of paragraph (d) of the definition "qualified investment" in subsection 146(1) of the Act and paragraph (c) of the definition "qualified investment" in subsection 146.3(1) of the Act, a property is a qualified investment for a trust governed by a registered retirement savings plan or a registered retirement income fund at any time if, at the time the property was acquired by the trust,

### Proposed Amendment — Reg. 4900(12) opening words

**(12) [Small business corporation]** — For the purposes of paragraph (d) of the definition "qualified investment" in subsection 146(1) of the Act, paragraph (e) of the definition "qualified investment" in subsection 146.1(1) of the Act and paragraph (c) of the definition "qualified investment" in subsection 146.3(1) of the Act, a property is a qualified investment for a trust governed by a registered retirement savings plan, a registered education savings plan or a registered retirement income fund at any time if, at the time the property was acquired by the trust,

**Application**: The October 27, 1998 draft regulations, subsec. 2(15), will amend the opening words of subsec. 4900(12) to read as above, applicable to property acquired after October 27, 1998.

**Technical Notes**: Subsection 4900(12) of the Regulations allows certain shares of small business corporations, venture capital corporations and cooperative corporations to be qualified investments for RRSPs and RRIFs, provided the RRSP or RRIF annuitant is not a "connected shareholder" of the corporation. The expression "connected shareholder" is defined in subsection 4901(2).

Subsection 4900(12) is amended so that such shares also qualify for an RESP, if each person who is a subscriber or beneficiary under the RESP is not a "connected shareholder" of the corporation.

---

(a) the property was a share of the capital stock of a corporation (other than a cooperative corporation) that would, at that time or at the end of the last taxation year of the corporation ending before that time, be a small business corporation if the expression "Canadian-controlled private corporation" in the definition "small business corporation" in subsection 248(1) of the Act were read as "Canadian corporation (other than a corporation controlled at that time, directly or indirectly in any manner whatever, by one or more non-resident persons)",

(b) the property was a share of the capital stock of a prescribed venture capital corporation described in any of sections 6700, 6700.1 or 6700.2, or

(c) the property was a qualifying share in respect of a specified cooperative corporation and the plan or fund

and, immediately after the time the property was acquired by the trust, the annuitant under the plan or fund at that time was not a connected shareholder of the corporation.

### Proposed Amendment — Reg. 4900(12) closing words

and, immediately after the time the property was acquired by the trust, each person who is an annuitant, a beneficiary or a subscriber under the plan or fund at that time was not a connected shareholder of the corporation.

**Application**: The October 27, 1998 draft regulations, subsec. 2(16), will amend the closing words of subsec. 4900(12) to read as above, applicable to property acquired after October 27, 1998.

**Technical Notes**: See under 4900(12).

**Related Provisions**: ITA 256(5.1), (6.2) — Meaning of "controlled directly or indirectly"; Reg. 4900(6) — Alternative definition of qualified investment; Reg. 4901(2) — Meaning of "connected shareholder", "qualifying share" and "specified cooperative corporation".

**Notes**: See Notes to Reg. 4900(6).

Reference to Reg. 6700.1 and 6700.2 added by P.C. 1999-249, effective for property acquired after August 1998.

Reg. 4900(12) added by P.C. 1994-1074, and para. (c) amended by P.C. 1995-1820, both effective December 3, 1992.

**I.T. Technical News**: No. 9 (qualified investments — whether shareholders deal at arm's length).

**(13)** Notwithstanding subsection (12), where

(a) a share that is otherwise a qualified investment for the purposes of paragraph (d) of the definition "qualified investment" in subsection 146(1) of the Act or paragraph (c) of the definition "qualified investment" in subsection 146.3(1) of the Act solely because of subsection (12) is held by a trust governed by a registered retirement savings plan or registered retirement income fund,

### Proposed Amendment — Reg. 4900(13)(a)

(a) a share that is otherwise a qualified investment for the purposes of paragraph (d) of the definition "qualified investment" in subsection 146(1) of the Act, paragraph (e) of the definition "qualified investment" in subsection 146.1(1) of the Act and paragraph (c) of the definition "qualified investment" in subsection 146.3(1) of the Act solely because of subsection (12) is held by a trust governed by a registered retirement savings plan, registered education savings plan or registered retirement income fund,

**Application**: The October 27, 1998 draft regulations, subsec. 2(17), will amend para. 4900(13)(a) to read as above, applicable to property acquired after October 27, 1998.

**Technical Notes**: Subsection 4900(13) of the Regulations is an anti-avoidance rule intended to ensure that amounts received in respect of any shares described in subsection 4900(12) by an RRSP or RRIF trust must be in the nature of a return from an investment.

Subsection 4900(13) is amended so that it also applies for the purposes of an RESP trust.

(b) an individual

(i) provides services to or for,

(ii) acquires goods from, or

(iii) is provided services by

the issuer of the share or a person related to that issuer,

(c) an amount is received in respect of the share by the trust, and

(d) the amount can reasonably be considered, having regard to all the circumstances, including the terms and conditions of the share, or any agreement relating thereto and any dividend provided on the share to be

(i) on account of, or in lieu or in satisfaction of, payment for the services to or for the issuer or the person related to the issuer, or

(ii) in respect of the acquisition of the goods from, or the services provided by, the issuer or the person related to the issuer,

the share shall, immediately before the amount is received, cease to be and shall not thereafter be a qualified investment for the trust.

**Notes**: Reg. 4900(13) added by P.C. 1994-1074, effective December 3, 1992. It is intended to ensure that amounts received in respect of shares qualifying under Reg. 4900(12) must be in the nature of a return from an investment.

**Definitions [Reg. 4900]**: "amount", "annuity" — ITA 248(1); "arm's length" — Reg. 4900(10); "business" — ITA 248(1); "Canada" — ITA 255, *Interpretation Act* 35(1); "Canadian corporation" — ITA 89(1), 248(1); "Canadian resource property" — ITA 66(15), 248(1); "connected shareholder" — Reg. 4901(2), (2.1), (2.2); "controlled" — ITA 256(6), (6.1); "controlled directly or indirectly" — ITA 256(5.1), (6.2); "corporation" — ITA 248(1), *Interpretation Act* 35(1); "credit union" — ITA 248(1); "deferred profit sharing plan" — ITA 147(1), 248(1); "designated shareholder" — Reg. 4901(2), (2.3); "disposition", "dividend", "employee", "employer" — ITA 248(1); "governing plan" — Reg. 4901(2); "Her Majesty" — *Interpretation Act* 35(1); "individual", "insurer" — ITA 248(1); "licensed annuities provider" — ITA 147(1), 248(1); "month" — *Interpretation Act* 35(1); "mortgage" — Reg. 4901(3)(a); "mortgage investment corporation" — ITA 130.1(6), 248(1); "mortgagor" — Reg. 4901(3)(b); "mutual fund trust" — ITA 132(6)–(7), 132.2(1)(q), 248(1); "non-resident" — ITA 248(1); "obligation" — Reg. 4900(1)(g), (h), (i); "partnership" — see Notes to ITA 96(1); "person" — ITA 248(1); "plan trust" — Reg. 4901(2); "prescribed" — ITA 248(1); "prescribed stock exchange", "prescribed stock exchange in Canada" — Reg. 3200; "prescribed venture capital corporation" — Reg. 6700; "principal amount", "property" — ITA 248(1); "province" — *Interpretation Act* 35(1); "public corporation" — ITA 89(1), 248(1); "qualifying share" — Reg. 4901(2); "registered home ownership savings plan" — ITA 248(1); "registered investment" — ITA 204.4(1), 248(1); "registered retirement income fund" — ITA 146.3(1), 248(1); "registered retirement savings plan" — ITA 146(1), 248(1); "related" — ITA 251(2)–(6); "revoked plan" — ITA 204, Reg. 4901(2); "share", "shareholder", "small business corporation" — ITA 248(1); "small business investment limited partnership" — Reg. 4901(2), 5102(1); "small business investment trust" — Reg. 4901(2), 5103(1); "small business security" — Reg. 4901(2), 5100(2); "specified cooperative corporation" — ITA 136(2), Reg. 4901(2); "taxable income" — ITA 248(1); "taxation year" — ITA 249; "trust" — ITA 104(1), 248(1), (3).

**Interpretation Bulletins [Reg. 4900]**: IT-320R2: RRSP — qualified investments.

**4901. Interpretation** — **(1)** For the purposes of paragraphs 204.4(2)(b), (d) and (f) and subsection 204.6(1) of the Act, a "prescribed investment" for a corporation or trust, as the case may be, means a property that is a qualified investment for the plan or fund described in paragraphs 204.4(1)(a) to (d) of the Act in respect of which the corporation or trust is seeking registration or has been registered, as the case may be.

**(1.1)** [Revoked]

**Notes**: Reg. 4901(1.1) revoked by P.C. 1994-1074, retroactive to its introduction (as of November 1985). It prescribed property for purposes of ITA 207.1(5), also repealed retroactive to its introduction, which imposed a penalty tax on excessive holdings of small business properties by an RRSP or RRIF.

**(2)** In this Part,

**"allocation in proportion to patronage"** has the meaning assigned by subsection 135(4) of the Act;

**Notes**: Definition "allocation in proportion to patronage" added by P.C. 1995-1820, effective December 3, 1992.

**"connected shareholder"** of a corporation at any time is a person (other than an exempt person in respect of the corporation) who owns, directly or indirectly, at that time, not less than 10% of the issued shares of any class of the capital stock of the corporation or of any other corporation that is related to the corporation and, for the purposes of this definition,

(a) paragraphs (a) to (e) of the definition "specified shareholder" in subsection 248(1) of the Act apply, and

(b) an exempt person in respect of a corporation is a person who deals at arm's length with the corporation where the total of all amounts, each of which is the cost amount of any share of the capital stock of the corporation, or of any other corporation that is related to it, that the person owns or is deemed to own for the purposes of the definition "specified shareholder" in subsection 248(1) of the Act, is less than $25,000;

**Related Provisions**: Reg. 4901(2.1), (2.2) — Additional rules.

**Notes**: See Reg. 4900(12). Definition "connected shareholder" added by P.C. 1994-1074 and amended by P.C. 1995-1820, effective December 3, 1992. However, where

- a property was acquired by a trust governed by an RRSP or RRIF before November 30, 1994, and
- the annuitant under the RRSP or RRIF would, if this version of the definition and Reg. 4901(2.1)–(2.3) applied, be a connected shareholder of the corporation immediately after that time,

read the definition as:

"connected shareholder" of a corporation is a person who is a specified shareholder of the corporation or a person who would be a specified shareholder of the corporation if

(a) a share in the capital of a specified cooperative corporation and all other shares in the capital of that corporation that have attributes identical to the attributes of that share were shares of a class of the capital stock of the corporation, and

(b) each person or partnership that has a right under a contract, in equity or otherwise, either immediately or in the future and either absolutely or contingently, to acquire a share of a class of the capital stock of a corporation owned the share;

**"consumer goods or services"** has the meaning assigned by subsection 135(4) of the Act;

**Notes**: Definition "consumer goods or services" added by P.C. 1995-1820, effective December 3, 1992.

**"designated shareholder"** of a corporation at any time means a taxpayer who at that time

(a) is, or is related to, a person (other than an exempt person) who owns, directly or indirectly, not less than 10% of the issued shares of any class of the capital stock of the corporation or of any other corporation that is related to the corporation and, for the purposes of this definition,

(i) paragraphs (a) to (e) of the definition "specified shareholder" in subsection 248(1) of the Act apply, and

(ii) an exempt person in respect of a corporation is a person who deals at arm's length with the corporation where the total of all amounts, each of which is the cost amount of any share of the capital stock of the corporation, or of any other corporation that is related to it, that the person owns or is deemed to own for the purposes of the definition "specified shareholder" in subsection 248(1) of the Act, is less than $25,000;

(b) is or is related to a member of a partnership that controls the corporation,

(c) is or is related to a beneficiary under a trust that controls the corporation,

(d) is or is related to an employee of the corporation or a corporation related thereto, where any group of employees of the corporation or of the corporation related thereto, as the case may be, controls the corporation, except where the group of employees includes a person or a related group that controls the corporation, or

(e) does not deal at arm's length with the corporation;

**Related Provisions**: Reg. 4901(2.3) — Deemed designated shareholder.

**Notes**: Para. (a) of "designated shareholder" amended by P.C. 1995-1820, effective for property acquired after November 29, 1994. For property acquired earlier, read:

(a) is or is related to

(i) a specified shareholder of the corporation, or

(ii) a person who would be a specified shareholder of the corporation if, in applying the definition "specified shareholder" in subsection 248(1) of the Act, a person who has a right under a contract, in equity or otherwise, either immediate or in the future and either absolutely or contingently, to or to acquire share of the capital stock of a corporation were deemed to own those shares, and one of the main reasons for the existence of the right may reasonably be considered to be that the person not be regarded as a specified shareholder of the corporation,

unless the aggregate of amounts, each of which is the cost amount of any share of the capital stock of the corporation or any other corporation that is related thereto that the taxpayer owns or is deemed to own for the purposes of the definition "specified shareholder" is less than $25,000,

**"governing plan"** means a registered retirement savings plan, a registered home ownership savings plan, a registered retirement income fund, a deferred profit sharing plan or a revoked plan;

**Proposed Amendment — Reg. 4901(2) "governing plan"**

**"governing plan"** means a registered retirement savings plan, a registered education savings plan, a registered retirement income fund, a deferred profit sharing plan or a revoked plan;

**Application**: The October 27, 1998 draft regulations, subsec. 3(1), will amend the definition "governing plan" in subsec. 4901(2) to read as above, applicable to property acquired after October 27, 1998.

**Technical Notes**: Subsection 4901(2) defines a number of terms that apply for the purposes of Part XLIX.

A "governing plan" is defined as an RRSP, RRIF, RHOSP, DPSP or revoked plan. The expression is used in describing conditions that apply to various types of investments that

Part XLIX — Deferred Income Plans, Qualified Investments  Reg. S. 4901(2.3)

qualify for these plans under subsection 4900(1) of the Regulations.

The definition is amended to add a reference to "registered education savings plan" and to remove an obsolete reference to "registered home ownership savings plan".

**"plan trust"** means a trust governed by a governing plan;

**"qualifying share"**, in respect of a specified cooperative corporation and a registered retirement savings plan or registered retirement income fund, means a share of the capital or capital stock of the corporation where

(a) ownership of the share or a share identical to the share is not a condition of membership in the corporation, or

(b) the annuitant under the plan or fund (or any person related to the annuitant)

### Proposed Amendment — Reg. 4901(2)"qualifying share"

**"qualifying share"**, in respect of a specified cooperative corporation and a registered retirement savings plan, registered education savings plan or registered retirement income fund, means a share of the capital or capital stock of the corporation where

(a) ownership of the share or a share identical to the share is not a condition of membership in the corporation, or

(b) a person who is an annuitant, a beneficiary or a subscriber under the plan or fund (or any other person related to that person)

**Application**: The October 27, 1998 draft regulations, subsec. 3(2), will amend the portion of the definition "qualifying share" in subsec. 4901(2) before subpara. (b)(i) to read as above, applicable to property acquired after October 27, 1998.

**Technical Notes**: The definition "qualifying share" is relevant for the purposes of determining whether a share of a cooperative corporation is a qualified investment under paragraph 4900(12)(c) of the Regulations for an RRSP or RRIF.

The definition is amended to reflect the extension of subsection 4900(12) to RESPs.

(i) has not received a payment from the corporation after November 29, 1994 pursuant to an allocation in proportion to patronage in respect of consumer goods or services, and

(ii) can reasonably be expected not to receive a payment, after the acquisition of the share by the trust governed by the plan or fund, from the corporation pursuant to an allocation in proportion to patronage in respect of consumer goods or services;

**Notes**: Definition "qualifying share" added by P.C. 1995-1820, effective December 3, 1992. However, with respect to property acquired before November 30, 1994, read para. (a) as:

(a) the share is not required to be purchased as a condition of membership in the corporation, or

**"revoked plan"** has the meaning assigned by paragraph 204(f) [204"revoked plan"] of the Act;

**"small business investment limited partnership"** has the meaning assigned by subsection 5102(1);

**"small business investment trust"** has the meaning assigned by subsection 5103(1); and

**"small business security"** has the meaning assigned by subsection 5100(2).

**"specified cooperative corporation"** means

(a) a cooperative corporation within the meaning assigned by subsection 136(2) of the Act, or

(b) a corporation that would be a cooperative corporation within the meaning assigned by subsection 136(2) of the Act if the purpose described in that subsection were the purpose of providing employment to the corporation's members or customers.

**Notes**: Definition "specified cooperative corporation" added by P.C. 1994-1074, effective December 3, 1992 (see Reg. 4900(12)).

**(2.1)** For the purposes of the definition "connected shareholder" in subsection (2) and of subsection (2.2), each share of the capital of a specified cooperative corporation and all other shares of the capital of the corporation that have attributes identical to the attributes of that share shall be deemed to be shares of a class of the capital stock of the corporation.

**Notes**: Reg. 4901(2.1) added by P.C. 1995-1820, effective December 3, 1992. However, it does not apply where

- a property was acquired by a trust governed by an RRSP or RRIF before November 30, 1994, and
- the annuitant under the RRSP or RRIF would, if Reg. 4901(2.1)–(2.3) and the amended version of 4901(2)"connected shareholder" applied, be a connected shareholder of the corporation immediately after that time.

**(2.2)** For the purpose of this Part, a person is deemed to be a connected shareholder of a corporation at any time where the person would be a connected shareholder of the corporation at that time if, at that time,

(a) the person had each right that the person would be deemed to own at that time for the purposes of the definition "specified shareholder" in subsection 248(1) of the Act if that right were a share of the capital stock of a corporation;

(b) the person owned each share of a class of the capital stock of a corporation that the person had a right at that time under a contract, in equity or otherwise, either immediately or in the future and either absolutely or contingently, to acquire; and

(c) the cost amount to the person of a share referred to in paragraph (b) were the cost amount to the person of the right to which the share relates.

**Notes**: Reg. 4901(2.2) added by P.C. 1995-1820, effective on the same basis as Reg. 4901(2.1) (see Notes thereto).

**(2.3)** For the purpose of this Part, a person is deemed to be a designated shareholder of a corporation at any time if the person would be a designated share-

**Reg. S. 4901(2.3)** — Income Tax Regulations

holder of the corporation at that time if, at that time, paragraphs (2.2)(a) to (c) applied in respect of that person.

**Notes**: Reg. 4901(2.3) added by P.C. 1995-1820, effective for property acquired after November 29, 1994.

**(3)** For greater certainty, a reference in this Part to

(a) a mortgage includes a reference to a charge, hypothec or similar instrument pertaining to real property, or to an interest therein; and

(b) a mortgagor includes a reference to a hypothecator or a debtor under any instrument referred to in paragraph (a).

**Definitions [Reg. 4901]**: "allocation in proportion to patronage" — ITA 135(4), Reg. 4901(2); "amount" — ITA 248(1); "arm's length" — ITA 251(1); "connected shareholder" — Reg. 4901(2), (2.1), (2.2); "consumer goods or services" — ITA 135(4), Reg. 4901(2); "corporation" — ITA 248(1), *Interpretation Act* 35(1); "cost amount" — ITA 248(1); "deferred profit sharing plan" — ITA 147(1), 248(1); "designated shareholder" — Reg. 4901(2), (2.3); "employee", "employment" — ITA 248(1); "governing plan" — Reg. 4901(2); "mortgage" — Reg. 4901(3)(a); "mortgagor" — Reg. 4901(3)(b); "partnership" — see Notes to ITA 96(1); "person", "property", "registered home ownership savings plan" — ITA 248(1); "registered retirement income fund" — ITA 146.3(1), 248(1); "registered retirement savings plan" — ITA 146(1), 248(1); "related" — ITA 251(2)–(6); "revoked plan" — ITA 204, Reg. 4901(2); "share" — Reg. 4901(2.1); "specified cooperative corporation" — ITA 136(2), Reg. 4901(2); "taxpayer" — ITA 248(1); "trust" — ITA 104(1), 248(1), (3).

## PART L — DEFERRED INCOME PLANS, FOREIGN PROPERTY

**Interpretation Bulletins**: IT-320R2: RRSP — qualified investments; IT-412R: Foreign property of registered plans.

**5000. (1)** Where a taxpayer holds a share of the capital stock of a mutual fund corporation (other than an investment corporation) or an interest in, or a right to acquire an interest in,

(a) a mutual fund trust,

(b) a pooled fund trust,

(c) a trust that would be a mutual fund trust if Part XLVIII were read without reference to paragraph 4801(b) thereof, or

(c.1) a resource property trust,

that share, interest or right, as the case may be, shall not be foreign property for the purpose of computing the tax payable by the taxpayer under Part XI of the Act in respect of any particular month, if

(d) the corporation or trust, as the case may be, has not acquired any foreign property after June 30, 1971; or

(e) at no time during the relevant period for the particular month did the cost amount to the corporation or to the trust, as the case may be, of all foreign property held by it exceed 20 per cent of the cost amount to it of all property held by it.

**Proposed Amendment — Foreign Property Limit Increase**
Letter from Department of Finance, April 13, 2000: [See under Reg. 5000(2)(c) — ed.]

**Proposed Addition — Segregated funds**
Department of Finance news releases, December 19, 1996 and October 23, 1997: [See under ITA 12.2(1).]

**Notes**: Reg. 5000(1)(e) amended by P.C. 1992-258, this version effective 1994. The maximum percentage of foreign property was limited as follows: months before 1990, 10%; months in 1990, 12%; 1991, 14%; 1992, 16%; 1993, 18%; months in 1994 and later, 20%. See the parallel limitation in ITA 206(2)(b).

**(1.1)** For the purposes of paragraph (i) of the definition "foreign property" in subsection 206(1) of the Act, the following interests are hereby prescribed not to be foreign property;

(a) an interest of a limited partner in a small business investment limited partnership (within the meaning assigned by subsection 5102(1));

(b) an interest in a small business investment trust (within the meaning assigned by subsection 5103(1));

(c) an interest of a limited partner in a qualified limited partnership;

(d) an interest in a specified international finance trust; and

(e) an interest of a limited partner in a designated limited partnership.

**Related Provisions**: Reg. 5000(7) — Definitions of "specified international finance trust" and "designated limited partnership".

**Notes**: Reg. 5000(1.1)(d) and (e) added by P.C. 2000-725, para. (d) effective for months that end after 1998 and para. (e) effective for months that end after 1997. These changes were announced in a Department of Finance news release dated January 28, 1999.

**(1.2)** For the purposes of paragraph (i) of the definition "foreign property" in subsection 206(1) of the Act, a property of a beneficiary that is an interest under a trust described in paragraph 149(1)(o.4) of the Act is prescribed not to be foreign property of the beneficiary at a time where

(a) no other property of the beneficiary is foreign property at that time; or

(b) the trust does not own any foreign property at that time.

**(2)** Where

(a) a share of the capital stock of a corporation referred to in subsection (1) or an interest in, or a right to acquire an interest in, a trust referred to in that subsection would, but for this subsection, be foreign property for the purpose of computing the tax payable by a taxpayer under Part XI of the Act in respect of a particular month,

(b) the relevant period for the particular month in relation to property held by the trust or corporation is its taxation year that includes the end of the particular month, and

2210

Part L — Deferred Income Plans, Foreign Property    Reg. S. 5000(7) des

(c) at the end of the relevant period for the particular month, the cost amount to the corporation or to the trust, as the case may be, of all foreign property held by it did not exceed 20 per cent of the cost amount to it of all property held by it,

### Proposed Amendment — Foreign Property Limit Increase

**Letter from Department of Finance, April 13, 2000:**

Dear [xxx]

Thank you for your letter of March 30, 2000, concerning the 2000 budget proposal to increase the foreign property limit for pension and deferred income plans to 25% for 2000 and to 30% after 2000 [see ITA 200(2)(b) — ed.].

I can confirm that Department's intention is to recommend amendments to Part 50 of the *Income Tax Regulations* to reflect the increase in the foreign property limit. The recommended amendments will be similar to those regulatory amendments made as a consequence of the foreign property limit increasing to 20% from 1990 to 1994. For example, one of the consequences of these proposed amendments is that a unit in a mutual fund trust will not be treated as foreign property in 2001, provided its foreign content level does not exceed 25% throughout 2000. Similarly, a unit in such a trust will not be treated as foreign property in a calendar year that is after 2001, provided its foreign content level does not exceed 30% during the preceding calendar year.

Thank you for writing.

Sincerely yours,

Kevin G. Lynch
Deputy Minister

that share, interest or right shall not be foreign property for the purpose of computing the tax payable by the taxpayer under Part XI of the Act in respect of the particular month.

**Notes**: Reg. 5000(2) amended by P.C. 1992-258, effective 1990. However, the 20% figure in 5000(2)(c) is effective 1994. The maximum percentage of foreign property was limited as follows: months before 1990, 10%; months in 1990, 12%; 1991, 14%; 1992, 16%; 1993, 18%; months in 1994 and later, 20%. See the parallel limitation in ITA 206(2)(b).

(3) Where a taxpayer holds a share of the capital stock of an investment corporation, subsections (1), (2) and (7) apply in respect of that share as if

(a) the reference in subsection (1) to "mutual fund corporation (other than an investment corporation)" were read as a reference to an "investment corporation"; and

(b) the reference in subsection (1) to "June 30, 1971" were read as a reference to "October 13, 1971".

(4) Where a taxpayer holds a share of the capital stock of an investment corporation, that share shall not be foreign property for the purpose of computing the tax payable by the taxpayer under Part XI of the Act in respect of a particular month if the share would otherwise be foreign property solely by reason of the acquisition by the corporation of foreign property before October 16, 1971.

(5) Where a mutual fund corporation or a mutual fund trust holds a share of the capital stock of a mutual fund corporation (other than an investment corporation) or an interest in, or a right to acquire an interest in, a mutual fund trust, the share or the interest, as the case may be, shall not be foreign property for the purpose of computing the tax payable by a taxpayer under Part XI of the Act in respect of a particular month if the last-mentioned corporation or trust, as the case may be, complies with

(a) paragraph (1)(d);

(b) paragraph (1)(e) in respect of the particular month; or

(c) paragraphs (2)(b) and (c) in respect of the particular month.

(6) Where a mutual fund corporation or a mutual fund trust holds a share of the capital stock of an investment corporation, the share shall not be foreign property for the purpose of computing the tax payable by a taxpayer under Part XI of the Act in respect of a particular month if the investment corporation

(a) would comply with paragraph (1)(d) if the reference therein to "June 30, 1971" were read as a reference to "October 16, 1971";

(b) complies with paragraph (1)(e) in respect of the particular month; or

(c) complies with paragraphs (2)(b) and (c) in respect of the particular month.

**Notes**: Regs. 5000(3)–(6) amended by P.C. 1992-258, effective 1990.

(7) In this Part,

**Notes**: Reg. 5000(7) amended to change "In this section" to "In this Part" by P.C. 2000-183, effective 1993.

**"designated limited partnership"** means a limited partnership that complies with the following conditions:

(a) the interests of the limited partners are described by reference to a single class of units of the partnership listed on a stock exchange prescribed under section 3200,

(b) that class was listed before 1999 on a stock exchange prescribed under section 3200,

(c) at least 80% of the full-time employees employed by the partnership are employed in Canada,

(d) the total of all amounts each of which is the cost amount to the partnership of a property used in its activities carried on in Canada is not less that 80% of the total of all amounts each of which is the cost amount to the partnership of a property of the partnership,

(e) the principal activity of the partnership is

(i) the production of goods in Canada,

(ii) the sale of goods in Canada,

(iii) the provision of services in Canada, or

(iv) any combination of the activities described in subparagraphs (i) to (iii), and

(f) the revenue from that principal activity is regulated by a public authority governed by the laws of Canada or a province;

**Related Provisions**: Reg. 5000(8)–(11) — Interpretation rules.

**Notes**: Definition "designated limited partnership" added by P.C. 2000-725, effective for months that end after 1997. See Department of Finance news release 99-009 and Annex of January 28, 1999.

**"foreign property"** has the meaning assigned by section 206 of the Act;

**"pooled fund trust"** means, with respect to a particular taxpayer who owns an interest in the trust, a trust the trustee of which is a trust company incorporated under the laws of Canada or a province and that complies with the following conditions:

(a) throughout the taxation year of the trust (in this subsection referred to as the "first relevant year") in which the taxpayer acquired the interest or the first taxation year of the trust (in this subsection referred to as the "second relevant year") commencing more than one year after the taxpayer acquired the interest, the total, at any time, of

(i) the cost amount to the trust of

(A) shares,

(B) any property that, under its terms or conditions or any agreement relating to it, is convertible into, is exchangeable for or confers a right to acquire, shares,

(C) bonds, debentures, mortgages, notes and other similar obligations,

(D) marketable securities,

(E) cash,

(F) life insurance policies in Canada (other than annuity contracts), and

(G) annuity contracts issued by persons licensed or otherwise authorized under the laws of Canada or a province to carry on in Canada an annuities business, and

(ii) the amount by which the cost amount to the trust of real property that can reasonably be regarded as being held for the purpose of producing income from property exceeds the total of amounts each of which was owing by the trust at that time on account of its acquisition of the real property and was included at that time in the cost amount to the trust of the real property,

was not less than 80 per cent of the amount by which the cost amount to the trust of all property at that time exceeds the total of amounts each of which was owing by it at that time on account of its acquisition of real property and was included at that time in the cost amount to it of real property,

(b) throughout the first relevant year or the second relevant year, the cost amount to the trust at any time of shares, bonds, mortgages and other securities of any one corporation or debtor, other than bonds, mortgages and other securities of or guaranteed by Her Majesty in right of Canada, a province or a Canadian municipality, was not more than 10 per cent of the amount by which the cost amount to the trust of all property at that time exceeds the total of all amounts each of which was owing by the trust at that time on account of the trust's acquisition of real property and was included at that time in the cost amount to the trust of real property,

(c) throughout the first relevant year or the second relevant year, the amount by which

(i) the cost amount to the trust of any one real property at any time

exceeds

(ii) the total of amounts each of which was owing by the trust at that time on account of its acquisition of the real property and was included at that time in the cost amount to it of the real property

was not more than 10 per cent of the amount by which the cost amount to the trust of all property at that time exceeds the total of amounts each of which was owing by the trust at that time on account of its acquisition of real property and was included at that time in the cost amount to the trust of real property, and

(d) not less than 95 per cent of the income of the trust (determined without reference to subsections 49(2.1) and 104(6) of the Act) for the first relevant year or the second relevant year was derived from, or from the dispositions of, investments described in paragraph (a);

**Notes**: Subpara. (a)(i) amended by P.C. 2000-183, effective 1996. Before 1996, (D)–(G) were numbered (E)–(H), and in place of (C), read: "(C) bonds, (D) mortgages".

Cl. (a)(i)(B) added by P.C. 1997-100, effective 1996. (All of subara. (a)(i) was previously one stream of words, not broken into clauses.

Definition "pooled fund trust" amended by P.C. 1994-1074, retroactive to 1990. The substantive changes were the introduction of the "second relevant year" throughout the definition, and the addition of references to ITA 49(2.1) and 104(6) in para. (d).

**"qualified limited partnership"**, at a particular time after 1985, means a limited partnership that at all times after it was formed and before the particular time complied with the following conditions:

(a) it had only one general partner,

(b) the share of the general partner, as general partner, in any income of the partnership from any source in any place, for any period, was the same as his share, as general partner, in

(i) the income of the partnership from that source in any other place,

Part L — Deferred Income Plans, Foreign Property     Reg. S. 5000(7) res

(ii) the income of the partnership from any other source,

(iii) the loss of the partnership from any source,

(iv) any capital gain of the partnership, and

(v) any capital loss of the partnership

for that period, except that the share of the general partner, as general partner, in the income or loss of the partnership from specified properties (within the meaning assigned by subsection 5100(1)) may differ from his share, as general partner, in the income or loss of the partnership from other sources,

(c) the share of the general partner, as general partner, in any income or loss of the partnership for any period was not less than his share, as general partner, in the income or loss of the partnership for any preceding period,

(d) the interests of the limited partners were described by reference to units of the partnership that were identical in all respects,

(e) no limited partner or group of limited partners who did not deal with each other at arm's length held more than 30 per cent of the units of the partnership and, for the purposes of this paragraph,

(i) the general partner shall be deemed not to hold any unit of the partnership as a limited partner, and

(ii) where a limited partner of a partnership is a qualified trust (within the meaning assigned by subsection 259(3) of the Act) for any period in respect of which subsection 259(1) of the Act is applicable, the qualified trust shall be deemed not to hold any unit of the partnership for that period,

(f) its only undertaking was the investing of its funds and its investments consisted solely of

(i) shares of the capital stock of corporations (other than shares that were issued to the partnership and that are shares described in section 66.3 of the Act or shares in respect of which amounts have been designated under subsection 192(4) of the Act),

(ii) rights, or warrants that grant the owner thereof rights, to acquire shares of the capital stock of corporations,

(iii) put or call options in respect of shares of the capital stock of corporations,

(iv) debt obligations of corporations,

(v) specified properties (within the meaning assigned by subsection 5100(1)), or

(vi) any combination of the properties described in subparagraphs (i) to (v),

(g) no election has been made under subsection 97(2) of the Act on the acquisition of any property by it,

(h) it has not borrowed money except for the purpose of earning income from its investments and the amount of any such borrowings at any time did not exceed 20 per cent of the partnership capital at that time, and

(i) the cost amount to it of all foreign property held by it

(i) before 1990 and the particular time did not exceed 10 per cent,

(ii) before 1991 and the particular time did not exceed 12 per cent,

(iii) before 1992 and the particular time did not exceed 14 per cent,

(iv) before 1993 and the particular time did not exceed 16 per cent,

(v) before 1994 and the particular time did not exceed 18 per cent, and

(vi) before the particular time did not exceed 20 per cent

of the cost amount to it of all property held by it.

### Proposed Amendment — Foreign Property Limit Increase
**Letter from Department of Finance, April 13, 2000:**
[See under Reg. 5000(2)(c) — ed.]

**Notes**: Definition "qualified limited partnership" amended by P.C. 1992-258, effective 1990.

**"relevant period for the particular month"** means, in relation to property held by a particular corporation or particular trust,

(a) its most recent taxation year ending before the end of the particular month, and

(b) its taxation year that includes the end of the particular month, where paragraph (a) does not apply.

**"resource property trust"** means a trust the trustee of which is a trust company that is incorporated under the laws of Canada or a province and that complies with the following conditions:

(a) the trust, at all times after the later of November 12, 1981 and the time at which it was created,

(i) has limited its activities to

(A) acquiring Canadian resource properties by purchase or by incurring Canadian exploration expense or Canadian development expense, or

(B) holding, exploring, developing, maintaining, improving, managing, operating or disposing of its Canadian resource properties,

(ii) has made no investments other than

(A) in Canadian resource properties,

(B) in property to be used in connection with Canadian resource properties described in clause (i)(A),

(C) in loans secured by Canadian resource properties for the purpose of carrying out any activity described in subparagraph (i) with respect to Canadian resource properties,

(D) in corporations described in subparagraph 149(1)(o.2)(ii.1) of the Act, or

(E) investments that a pension fund or plan is permitted to make under the *Pension Benefits Standards Act* or a similar law of a province, and

(iii) has not borrowed money except for the purpose of earning income from Canadian resource properties, and

(b) the beneficiaries of the trust, at all times after the later of November 12, 1981 and the time at which it was created, were

(i) registered pension plans, or

(ii) trusts all the beneficiaries of which were registered pension plans.

**"specified international finance trust"** at a particular time means a trust that complies with the following conditions:

(a) the trust was created principally for the purpose of investing in property described in subparagraph (c)(i),

(b) throughout the period that began at the time the trust was created and ends at the particular time, the trust was resident in Canada, and

(c) throughout the period that began 30 days after the time the trust was created and ends at the particular time, the total of all amounts each of which is the cost amount to the trust of the following property was not less that 90% of the total of all amounts each of which is the cost amount to the trust of a property of the trust:

(i) debt issued to and acquired from

(A) the African Development Bank,

(B) the Asian Development Bank,

(C) the Caribbean Development Bank,

(D) the European Bank for Reconstruction and Development,

(E) the Export Development Corporation,

(F) the Inter-American Development Bank,

(G) the International Bank for Reconstruction and Development, or

(H) the International Finance Corporation, and

(ii) shares and debt that are not foreign property of the trust.

**Notes**: Definition "specified international finance trust" added by P.C. 2000-725, effective for months that end after 1998. See Department of Finance news release 99-009 and Annex of January 28, 1999.

(8) For the purposes of the definition "designated limited partnership" in subsection (7) and for the purposes of this subsection, if a particular partnership is a member of another partnership at the end of a fiscal period of the other partnership (in this subsection referred to as the "relevant time"), throughout the period that begins at the relevant time and ends at the earlier of the time that is immediately before the end of the following fiscal period of the other partnership and the time that the other partnership ceases to exist

(a) the particular partnership is deemed to employ an additional number of full-time employees, or full-time employees employed in Canada, as the case may be, equal to the product of

(i) the specified fraction of the particular partnership at the relevant time in respect of the other partnership, and

(ii) the number of full-time employees employed, or employed in Canada, as the case may be, at the relevant time by the other partnership,

(b) each property used, or used in activities carried on in Canada, as the case may be, at the relevant time by the other partnership is deemed to be used, or to be used in activities carried on in Canada, as the case may be, by the particular partnership and is deemed to have a cost amount to the particular partnership equal to the product of

(i) the specified fraction of the particular partnership at the relevant time in respect of the other partnership, and

(ii) the cost amount of the property at the relevant time to the other partnership, and

(c) the particular partnership is, to the degree that can reasonably be considered to reflect the specified fraction of the particular partnership at the relevant time in respect of the other partnership, deemed to carry on each of the activities carried on by the other partnership.

**Related Provisions**: Reg. 5000(9) — Meaning of "specified fraction"; Reg. 5000(11) — Application of ITA 96(1)(a)–(g).

(9) For the purposes of subsection (8), the specified fraction of the particular partnership in respect of the other partnership at the end of a fiscal period of the other partnership is the quotient obtained by dividing the particular partnership's share of the income or loss of the other partnership for the fiscal period by the income or loss of the other partnership for the fiscal period.

**Related Provisions**: Reg. 5000(10) — Where income and loss are nil; Reg. 5000(11) — Application of ITA 96(1)(a)–(g).

(10) For the purposes of subsection (9), if the income and loss of the other partnership for the fiscal period are nil, the quotient referred to in that subsection shall be calculated as if the other partnership had in-

come for the fiscal period in the amount of $1,000,000.

**Related Provisions**: Reg. 5000(11) — Application of ITA 96(1)(a)–(g).

**(11)** The definition "designated limited partnership" in subsection (7) and subsections (8) to (10) shall be read and construed as if each of the assumptions set out in paragraphs 96(1)(a) to (g) of the Act were made.

**Notes [Reg. 5000(8)–(11)]**: Reg. 5000(8) to (11) added by P.C. 2000-725, effective for months that end after 1997. See Department of Finance news release 99-009 and Annex of January 28, 1999.

**Definitions [Reg. 5000]**: "amount", "annuity" — ITA 248(1); "arm's length" — ITA 251(1); "borrowed money", "business" — ITA 248(1); "Canada" — ITA 255, *Interpretation Act* 35(1); "Canadian development expense" — ITA 66.2(5), 248(1); "Canadian exploration expense" — ITA 66.1(6), 248(1); "Canadian resource property" — ITA 66(15), 248(1); "capital gain" — ITA 39(1), 248(1); "capital loss" — ITA 39(1)(b), 248(1); "corporation" — ITA 248(1), *Interpretation Act* 35(1); "cost amount" — ITA 248(1); "designated limited partnership" — Reg. 5000(7), (8)–(11); "disposition" — ITA 248(1); "employed", "employee" — ITA 248(1); "first relevant year" — Reg. 5000(7)(a); "fiscal period" — ITA 249.1; "foreign property" — ITA 206, Reg. 5000(7); "Her Majesty" — *Interpretation Act* 35(1); "investment corporation" — ITA 130(3), 248(1); "life insurance policy" — ITA 138(12), 248(1); "month" — *Interpretation Act* 35(1); "mutual fund corporation" — ITA 131(8), 248(1); "mutual fund trust" — ITA 132(6)–(7), 132.2(1)(q), 248(1); "partnership" — see Notes to ITA 96(1); "person" — ITA 248(1); "pooled fund trust" — Reg. 5000(7); "prescribed", "property" — ITA 248(1); "province" — *Interpretation Act* 35(1); "qualified limited partnership" — Reg. 5000(7); "registered pension plan" — ITA 248(1); "relevant period for the particular month" — Reg. 5000(7); "resident in Canada" — ITA 250; "resource property trust" — Reg. 5000(7); "second relevant year" — Reg. 5000(7)(a); "share" — ITA 248(1); "specified fraction" — Reg. 5000(9); "specified international finance trust" — Reg. 5000(7); "taxation year" — ITA 249; "taxpayer" — ITA 248(1); "trust" — ITA 104(1), 248(1), (3).

**Interpretation Bulletins**: IT-412R2: Foreign property of registered plans.

**5001. [Master trust]** — For the purposes of paragraph 149(1)(o.4) of the Act, a trust is a master trust at any time if, at all times after it was created and before that time,

(a) it was resident in Canada;

(b) its only undertaking was the investing of its funds;

(c) it never borrowed money except where the borrowing was for a term not exceeding 90 days and it is established that the borrowing was not part of a series of loans or other transactions and repayments;

(d) it never accepted deposits; and

(e) each of the beneficiaries of the trust was a trust governed by a registered pension fund or plan or a deferred profit sharing plan.

**Related Provisions**: ITA 253.1 — Deeming rule re investments in limited partnerships.

**Definitions [Reg. 5001]**: "borrowed money" — ITA 248(1); "deferred profit sharing plan" — ITA 147(1), 248(1); "registered pension fund or plan" — ITA 248(1); "resident in Canada" — ITA 250; "trust" — ITA 104(1), 248(1), (3); "undertaking" — ITA 253.1(a).

**5002. [Registered investment]** — For the purpose of subparagraph 206(2.01)(b)(ii) of the Act,

(a) a prescribed trust is,

(i) a pooled fund trust,

(ii) a trust that would be a mutual fund trust if Part XLVIII were read without reference to paragraph 4801(b),

(iii) a resource property trust, or

(iv) a master trust, as described in section 5001; and

(b) a prescribed partnership is a qualified limited partnership.

**Notes**: Reg. 5002 added by P.C. 2000-183, effective for months that end after 1992.

**Definitions [Reg. 5002]**: "master trust" — Reg. 5001; "mutual fund trust" — ITA 132(6), 248(1); "partnership" — see Notes to ITA 96(1); "pooled fund trust" — Reg. 5000(7); "prescribed", "property" — ITA 248(1); "qualified limited partnership", "resource property trust" — Reg. 5000(7); "trust" — ITA 104(1), 248(1), (3).

# PART LI — DEFERRED INCOME PLANS, INVESTMENTS IN SMALL BUSINESS

**5100. (1)** In this Part,

**"designated rate"**, at any time, means 150 per cent of the highest of the prime rates generally quoted at that time by the banks to which Schedule A to the *Bank Act* applies;

**"eligible corporation"**, at any time, means

(a) a particular corporation that is a taxable Canadian corporation all or substantially all of the property of which is at that time

(i) used in a qualifying active business carried on by the particular corporation or by a corporation controlled by it,

(ii) shares of the capital stock of one or more eligible corporations that are related to the particular corporation, or debt obligations issued by those eligible corporations,

(iii) any combination of the properties described in subparagraph (i) and (ii),

(a.1) a specified holding corporation, or

(b) a prescribed venture capital corporation described in section 6700,

but does not include

(c) a corporation (other than a mutual fund corporation) that is

(i) a trader or dealer in securities,

(ii) a bank,

(iii) a corporation licensed or otherwise authorized under the laws of Canada or a province to carry on in Canada the business of offering to the public its services as a trustee,

(iv) a credit union,

(v) an insurance corporation, or

(vi) a corporation the principal business of which is the lending of money or the purchasing of debt obligations or a combination of them,

(d) a corporation controlled by one or more non-resident persons, or

(e) a venture capital corporation, other than a prescribed venture capital corporation described in section 6700;

**Related Provisions**: ITA 256(6), (6.1) — Meaning of "controlled".

**Notes**: Para. (c) amended by P.C. 1999-249, retroactive to 1991 and later taxation years, to add exclusion for a mutual fund corporation, and effective for taxation years that end after February 22, 1994, to change "a taxpayer described in subsection 39(5) of the Act" to subparas. (i)–(vi).

The exclusion of mutual fund corporations from the definition of "eligible corporation" was first announced in a letter from Len Farber, Director General, Tax Legislation Division to the CBA/CICA Joint Taxation Committee on June 18, 1997, and in the Technical Notes of July 31, 1997 to ITA 39(5), which stated that this would be retroactive to 1991.

Revenue Canada's view is that "all or substantially all", used in para. (a), means 90% or more.

**"qualifying active business"**, at any time, means any business carried on primarily in Canada by a corporation, but does not include

(a) a business (other than a business of leasing property other than real property) the principal purpose of which is to derive income from property (including interest, dividends, rent and royalties), or

(b) a business of deriving gains from the disposition of property (other than property in the inventory of the business),

and, for the purposes of this definition, a business carried on primarily in Canada by a corporation, at any time, includes a business carried on by the corporation if, at that time,

(c) at least 50 per cent of the full time employees of the corporation and all corporations related thereto employed in respect of the business are employed in Canada, or

(d) at least 50 per cent of the salaries and wages paid to employees of the corporation and all corporations related thereto employed in respect of the business are reasonably attributable to services rendered in Canada;

**"qualifying obligation"**, at any time, means a bond, debenture, mortgage, note or other similar obligation of a corporation described in paragraph 149(1)(o.2) or (o.3) of the Act, if

(a) the obligation was issued by the corporation after October 31, 1985,

(b) the corporation used all or substantially all of the proceeds of the issue of the obligation within 90 days after the receipt thereof to acquire

(i) small business securities,

(ii) interests of a limited partner in small business investment limited partnerships,

(iii) interests in small business investment trusts, or

(iv) any combination of the properties described in subparagraphs (i) to (iii)

and, except as provided in subsection 5104(1), the corporation was the first person (other than a broker or dealer in securities) to have acquired the properties and the corporation has owned the properties continuously since they were so acquired,

(c) the corporation does not hold, and no group of persons who do not deal with each other at arm's length and of which it is a member holds, more than 30 per cent of the outstanding shares of any class of voting stock of another corporation, except where all or any part of those shares were acquired in specified circumstances, within the meaning of subsection 5104(2),

(d) the recourse of the holder of the obligation against the corporation with respect to the obligation is limited to the properties acquired with the proceeds of the issue of the obligation and any properties substituted therefor, and

(e) the properties acquired with the proceeds of the issue of the obligation have not been disposed of, unless the disposition occurred within the 90 day period immediately preceding that time;

**Notes**: The CCRA's view is that "all or substantially all", used in para. (b), means 90% or more.

Opening words of the definition amended to change "mortgage, hypothec" to "mortgage" by P.C. 1994-1817, effective November 30, 1994. The change is intended to be non-substantive.

**"specified holding corporation"**, at any time, means a taxable Canadian corporation where

(a) all or substantially all of the collective property of the corporation and of all other corporations controlled by it (each of which other corporations is referred to in this definition as a "controlled corporation"), other than shares in the capital stock of the corporation or of a corporation related to it and debt obligations issued by it or by a corporation related to it, is at that time used in a qualifying active business carried on by the corporation, and

(b) all or substantially all of the property of the corporation is at that time

(i) property used in a qualifying active business carried on by the corporation or a controlled corporation,

(ii) shares of the capital stock of one or more controlled corporations or eligible corporations related to the corporation,

(iii) debt obligations issued by one or more controlled corporations or eligible corporations related to the corporation, or

(iv) any combination of the properties described in subparagraphs (i), (ii) and (iii),

and in a determination of whether property is used in a qualifying active business for the purposes of paragraph (a),

(c) where a business is carried on by a controlled corporation,

(i) the business shall be deemed to be a business carried on only by the corporation, and

(ii) the controlled corporation shall be deemed to be the corporation in the application of paragraphs (c) and (d) of the definition "qualifying active business", and

(d) if a business of the corporation is substantially similar to one or more other businesses of the corporation, all those businesses shall be deemed collectively to be one business of the corporation.

**Related Provisions**: ITA 256(6), (6.1) — Meaning of "controlled".

**Notes**: The CCRA's view is that "all or substantially all", used in para. (b), means 90% or more.

**"specified property"** means property described in any of subparagraphs 204(e)(i), (ii), (iii), (vii) and (viii) [204"qualified investment"(a), (b), (c), (f) and (g)] of the Act.

(2) **[Small business security]** — For the purposes of this Part and paragraph (a) of the definition "small business property" in subsection 206(1) of the Act, a small business security of a person, at any time, is the property of that person that is, at that time,

(a) a share of the capital stock of an eligible corporation,

(b) a debt obligation of an eligible corporation (other than a prescribed venture capital corporation described in section 6700) that does not by its terms or any agreement related to the obligation restrict the corporation from incurring other debts and that is

(i) secured solely by a floating charge on the assets of the corporation and that by its terms or any agreement related thereto is subordinate to all other debt obligations of the corporation (other than a small business security issued by the corporation, or a debt obligation that is owing by the corporation to a shareholder of the corporation or a person related to a shareholder of the corporation and that is not secured in any manner whatever), or

(ii) not secured in any manner whatever,

other than a debt obligation that

(iii) where the debt obligation specifies an invariant rate of interest, has an effective annual rate of return that exceeds the designated rate for the day on which the obligation was issued, and

(iv) in any other case, may have an effective annual rate of return at a particular time that exceeds the designated rate at the particular time,

(c) an option or right granted by an eligible corporation in conjunction with the issue of a share or debt obligation that qualifies as a small business security to acquire a share of the capital stock of the corporation, or

(d) an option or right granted for no consideration by an eligible corporation to a holder of a share that qualifies as a small business securities to acquire a share of the capital stock of the corporation

if, immediately after the time of acquisition thereof,

(e) the aggregate of the cost amounts to the person of all shares, options, rights and debt obligations of the eligible corporation and all corporations associated therewith held by the person does not exceed $10,000,000, and

(f) the total assets (determined in accordance with generally accepted accounting principles, on a consolidated or combined basis, where applicable) of the eligible corporation and all corporations associated with it do not exceed $50,000,000

and includes

(g) property of the person that is, at that time,

(i) a qualifying obligation,

(ii) the proportion of the interest of the person as a limited partner in a qualified limited partnership (within the meaning assigned by subsection 5000(7)) at that time that

(A) the aggregate of the cost amounts to the partnership of all properties held by the partnership at that time that would be small business properties (within the meaning assigned by subsection 206(1) of the Act) if the partnership were a person,

is of

(B) the aggregate of the cost amounts to the partnership of all properties held by the partnership at that time, or

(iii) a security (in this subparagraph referred to as the "new security") described in any of paragraphs (a) to (d), where the new security was issued at a particular time

(A) in exchange for, on the conversion of, or in respect of rights pertaining to a security (in this paragraph referred to as the "former security") that would, if this subsection were read without reference to this subparagraph and paragraph (h), be a small business security of the person immediately before the particular time, and

(B) pursuant to an agreement entered into before the particular time and at or before the time that the former security was last acquired by the person, or

(h) where the person is a small business investment corporation, small business investment limited partnership or small business investment trust, property of the person that is, at that time, a security (in this paragraph referred to as the "new security") described in any of paragraphs (a) to (d), where the new security was issued at a particular time not more than 5 years before that time in exchange for, on the conversion of, or in respect of rights pertaining to a security that would, if this subsection were read without reference to this paragraph, be a small business security of the person immediately before the particular time.

**Related Provisions:** ITA 204.8(1)"eligible investment"(f).

**Notes:** Reg. 5100(2)(b) amended by P.C. 1998-782 to add the parenthesized exclusion and to change "thereto" to "to the obligation", effective for debt obligations issued after December 5, 1996, other than debt obligations that were required to be issued pursuant to agreements in writing made on or before that date.

Reg. 5100(2)(b) amended by P.C. 1990-1837, effective for debt obligations issued after September 12, 1990 other than debt obligations that were required to be issued pursuant to agreements in writing entered into on or before that date.

Reg. 5100(2)(f) amended by P.C. 1994-1074, effective 1992, to change the limit from $35 million to $50 million. This was proposed in the February 1992 budget papers, and is consistent with 204.8(1)"eligible investment"(f).

Reg. 5100(2)(g)(iii) and (h) added by P.C. 1992-258, effective for property acquired after 1989.

**Interpretation Bulletins:** IT-320R2: RRSP — qualified investments.

**(2.1) [Prescribed venture capital corporation]** — Where all or part of the property of a person consists of the shares of the capital stock of a prescribed venture capital corporation within the meaning assigned by section 6700, options or rights granted by the corporation, or debt obligations of the corporation,

(a) the aggregate of the cost amounts to the person of all such property shall be deemed for the purposes of paragraph (2)(e) not to exceed $10,000,000; and

(b) the total assets (determined in accordance with generally accepted accounting principles, on a consolidated or combined basis, where applicable) of the corporation and all corporations associated with it shall be deemed for the purposes of paragraph (2)(f) not to exceed $50,000,000.

**Notes:** Reg. 5100(2.1)(b) amended by P.C. 1994-1074, effective 1992, to change $35 million to $50 million. See Notes to Reg. 5100(2)(f).

**(3)** For the purposes of subsection (2),

(a) in determining the effective annual rate of return in respect of a debt obligation of an eligible corporation, the value of any right to convert the debt obligation or any part thereof into, or to exchange the debt obligation or any part thereof for, shares of the capital stock of the corporation or an option or right to acquire such shares shall not be considered; and

(b) a corporation shall be deemed not to be associated with another at any time where the corporation would not be associated with the other if

(i) the references to "controlled, directly or indirectly, in any manner whatever" in section 256 of the Act (other than subsection (5.1) thereof) were read as references to "controlled", and

(ii) such rights described in subsection 256(1.4) of the Act and shares, as were held at that time by a small business investment corporation, small business investment limited partnership or small business investment trust, were disregarded.

**(4) [Prescribed person]** — For the purposes of paragraph (e) of the definition "small business property" in subsection 206(1) of the Act, a taxpayer is a prescribed person in respect of a property at any time where

(a) the following conditions are met:

(i) the taxpayer is a beneficiary of a trust that has elected pursuant to subsection 259(1) of the Act for a period that includes that time,

(ii) the property is deemed to be held by the taxpayer at that time by virtue of subsection 259(1) of the Act, and

(iii) the trust referred to in subparagraph (i) is the first person (other than a broker or dealer in securities) to have acquired the property and has owned the property continuously since it was so acquired, except where the property is a small business security acquired in cases described in subsection 5104(1);

(b) the taxpayer is a limited partner in a qualified limited partnership (within the meaning assigned by subsection 5000(7)) and the property is that proportion of the taxpayer's interest in the partnership that, pursuant to subparagraph (2)(g)(ii), is a small business security of the taxpayer at that time;

(c) the taxpayer is a holder of property that at that time is a small business security acquired in cases described in subsection 5104(1);

(d) the taxpayer is a limited partner in a small business investment limited partnership the units of which are listed on a stock exchange prescribed under section 3200 and the property consists of the taxpayer's units in that partnership; or

(e) the taxpayer is a beneficiary under a small business investment trust the units of which are listed on a stock exchange prescribed under section 3200 and the property consists of the taxpayer's units in that trust.

**Notes**: Reg. 5100(4)(d) and (e) added by P.C. 1990-1837, effective 1990.

**Definitions [Reg. 5100]**: "arm's length" — ITA 251(1); "associated" — Reg. 5100(3)(b); "bank" — ITA 248(1), *Interpretation Act* 35(1); "business" — ITA 248(1); "Canada" — ITA 255, *Interpretation Act* 35(1); "controlled" — ITA 256(6), (6.1); "corporation" — ITA 248(1), *Interpretation Act* 35(1); "cost amount", "credit union" — ITA 248(1); "designated rate" — Reg. 5100(1); "disposed" — ITA 248(1)"disposition"; "disposition" — ITA 248(1); "dividend" — ITA 248(1); "eligible corporation" — Reg. 5100(1); "employed", "employee" — ITA 248(1); "former security" — Reg. 5100(2)(g)(iii)(A); "insurance corporation", "inventory" — ITA 248(1); "new security" — Reg. 5100(2)(g)(iii), 5100(2)(h); "non-resident" — ITA 248(1); "partnership" — see Notes to ITA 96(1); "person" — ITA 248(1), Reg. 5104(6); "prescribed" — ITA 248(1); "prescribed venture capital corporation" — Reg. 6700; "property" — ITA 248(1); "province" — *Interpretation Act* 35(1); "qualifying active business" — Reg. 5100(1); "qualifying obligation" — ITA 149(1)(o.2), (o.3), Reg. 5100(1); "related" — ITA 251(2)–(6); "share", "shareholder" — ITA 248(1); "small business investment corporation" — Reg. 5101(1); "small business investment limited partnership" — Reg. 5102(1); "small business security" — Reg. 5100(2), 5104(3), (5); "specified circumstances" — Reg. 5104(2); "specified holding corporation" — Reg. 5100(1); "substituted" — ITA 248(5); "taxable Canadian corporation" — ITA 89(1), 248(1); "taxpayer" — ITA 248(1); "trust" — ITA 104(1), 248(1), (3).

**5101. [Small business investment corporation]** — **(1)** Subject to subsection (4), for the purposes of this Part and paragraph 149(1)(o.3) and paragraph (b) of the definition "small business property" in subsection 206(1) of the Act, a corporation is a small business investment corporation at any time if it is a Canadian corporation incorporated after May 22, 1985 and at all times after it was incorporated and before that time

(a) all of the shares, and rights to acquire shares, of the capital stock of the corporation were owned by

(i) one or more registered pension plans,

(ii) one or more trusts all the beneficiaries of which were registered pension plans,

(iii) one or more related segregated fund trusts (within the meaning assigned by paragraph 138.1(1)(a) of the Act) all the beneficiaries of which were registered pension plans, or

(iv) one or more persons prescribed by section 4802 for the purposes of clause 149(1)(o.2)(iv)(D) of the Act;

(b) its only undertaking was the investing of its funds and its investments consisted solely of

(i) small business securities,

(ii) interests of a limited partner in small business investment limited partnerships,

(iii) interests in small business investment trusts,

(iv) property (other than small business securities) described in any of subparagraphs (f)(i) to (iv) of the definition "qualified limited partnership" in subsection 5000(7),

(v) specified properties, or

(vi) any combination of properties described in any of subparagraphs (i) to (v)

and, except as provided in subsection 5104(1), with respect to properties referred to in any of subparagraphs (i) to (iii), the corporation was the first person (other than a broker or dealer in securities) to have acquired the properties and the corporation has owned the properties continuously since they were so acquired;

(c) it has complied with subsection (2);

(d) it did not hold, and no group of persons who did not deal with each other at arm's length and of which it was a member held, more than 30 per cent of the outstanding shares of any class of voting stock of a corporation, except where

(i) all or any part of those shares were acquired in specified circumstances within the meaning of subsection 5104(2), or

(ii) those shares were of any class of voting stock of a prescribed venture capital corporation within the meaning assigned by section 6700;

(e) it has not borrowed money except from its shareholders; and

(f) it has not accepted deposits.

**Related Provisions**: ITA 253.1 — Deeming rule re investments in limited partnerships.

**Notes**: Reg. 5101(1)(b)(iv) added by P.C. 1994-1074, effective 1991. (Subparas. (v) and (vi) were previously numbered (iv) and (v).)

**Interpretation Bulletins**: IT-320R2: RRSP — qualified investments.

**(2)** Every small business investment corporation shall at all times hold properties referred to in subparagraphs (1)(b)(i) to (iii), the aggregate of the cost amounts of which is not less than 75 per cent of the amount, if any, by which

(a) the aggregate of all amounts each of which is the amount of consideration for the issue of shares of its capital stock or debt to its shareholders or the amount of a contribution of capital by its shareholders received by it more than 90 days before that time

exceeds

(b) the aggregate of

(i) all amounts paid by it before that time to its shareholders as a return of capital or a repayment of debt, and

(ii) the amount, if any, by which the aggregate of its losses from the disposition of properties disposed of before that time exceeds the aggregate of its gains from the disposition of properties disposed of before that time.

(3) For the purposes of subsection (2), where a small business investment corporation disposes of a property referred to in subparagraphs (1)(b)(i) to (iii), it shall be deemed to continue to hold the investment for a period of 90 days following the date of the disposition.

(4) For the purposes of paragraph 149(1)(o.3) of the Act, where a small business investment corporation holds an interest in a partnership or trust that qualified as a small business investment limited partnership or small business investment trust, as the case may be, when the interest was acquired and that, but for this subsection, would cease at a subsequent time to so qualify, the interest in the partnership or trust shall be deemed to be an interest in a small business investment limited partnership or small business investment trust, as the case may be, for the 24 months immediately following the subsequent time.

**Definitions [Reg. 5101]:** "amount" — ITA 248(1); "arm's length" — ITA 251(1); "borrowed money", "business" — ITA 248(1); "Canadian corporation" — ITA 89(1), 248(1); "corporation" — ITA 248(1), Interpretation Act 35(1); "cost amount" — ITA 248(1); "disposed", "disposes" — ITA 248(1)"disposition", "disposition" — ITA 248(1); "month" — Interpretation Act 35(1); "partnership" — see Notes to ITA 96(1); "person" — ITA 248(1), Reg. 5104(6); "prescribed" — ITA 248(1); "prescribed venture capital corporation" — Reg. 6700; "property", "registered pension plan" — ITA 248(1); "related" — ITA 251(2)–(6); "share", "shareholder" — ITA 248(1); "small business investment corporation" — Reg. 5101(1); "small business investment limited partnership" — Reg. 5102(1); "small business security" — Reg. 5100(2), 5104(3), (5); "specified circumstances" — Reg. 5104(2); "specified property" — ITA 204(a), (b), (c), (f), (g), Reg. 5100(1); "trust" — ITA 104(1), 248(1), (3); "undertaking" — ITA 253.1(a).

**5102. [Small business investment limited partnership]** — **(1)** For the purposes of this Part and paragraph (c) of the definition "small business property" in subsection 206(1) of the Act, a partnership is a small business investment limited partnership at any time if at all times after it was formed and before that time

(a) it had only one general partner,

(b) the share of the general partner, as general partner, in any income of the partnership from any source in any place, for any period, was the same as his share, as general partner, in

(i) the income of the partnership from that source in any other place,

(ii) the income of the partnership from any other source,

(iii) the loss of the partnership from any source,

(iv) any capital gain of the partnership, and

(v) any capital loss of the partnership

for that period, except that the share of the general partner, as general partner, in the income or loss of the partnership from specified properties may differ from his share, as general partner, in the income or loss of the partnership from other sources,

(c) the share of the general partner, as general partner, in any income or loss of the partnership for any period was not less than his share, as general partner, in the income or loss of the partnership for any preceding period;

(d) the interests of the limited partners were described by reference to units of the partnership that were identical in all respects,

(e) no limited partner or group of limited partners who did not deal with each other at arm's length held more than 30 per cent of the units of the partnership and, for the purposes of this paragraph,

(i) a small business investment corporation that has not borrowed money and in which no shareholder or group of shareholders who did not deal with each other at arm's length held more than 30 per cent of the outstanding shares of any class of voting stock shall be deemed not to be a limited partner, and

(ii) the general partner shall be deemed not to hold any unit of the partnership as a limited partner, and

(f) its only undertaking was the investing of its funds and its investments consisted solely of

(i) small business securities where, except as provided in subsection 5104(1), the partnership was the first person (other than a broker or dealer in securities) to have acquired the securities and it has owned the securities continuously since they were so acquired,

(ii) property (other than small business securities) described in any of subparagraphs (f)(i) to (iv) of the definition "qualified limited partnership" in subsection 5000(7),

(iii) specified properties, or

(iv) any combination of properties described in any of subparagraphs (i) to (iii),

(g) it has complied with subsection (2),

(h) it has not borrowed money except for the purpose of earning income from its investments and the amount of any such borrowings at any time did not exceed 20 per cent of the partnership capital at that time, and

(i) it has not accepted deposits.

**Notes**: Reg. 5102(1)(f)(ii) added by P.C. 1994-1074, effective 1991. (Subparas. (iii) and (iv) were previously numbered (ii) and (iii).)

**Interpretation Bulletins**: IT-320R2: RRSP — qualified investments.

(2) The aggregate of the cost amounts to a small business investment limited partnership of small business securities held by it at any time shall not be less than the amount, if any, by which the aggregate of

(a) 25 per cent of the amount, if any, by which

(i) the aggregate of all amounts received by it more than 12 months before that time and not more than 24 months before that time as consideration for the issue of its units or in respect of its units

exceeds

(ii) the aggregate of all amounts paid by it before that time to its members and designated by the partnership as a return of the consideration referred to in subparagraph (i),

(b) 50 per cent of the amount, if any, by which

(i) the aggregate of all amounts received by it more than 24 months before that time and not more than 36 months before that time as consideration for the issue of its units or in respect of its units

exceeds

(ii) the aggregate of all amounts paid by it before that time to its members and designated by the partnership as a return of the consideration referred to in subparagraph (i), and

(c) 75 per cent of the amount, if any, by which

(i) the aggregate of all amounts received by it more than 36 months before that time as consideration for the issue of its units or in respect of its units

exceeds

(ii) the aggregate of all amounts paid by it before that time to its members and designated by the partnership as a return of the consideration referred to in subparagraph (i),

exceeds 75 per cent of the amount, if any, by which the aggregate of its losses from the disposition of properties disposed of before that time exceeds the aggregate of its gains from the disposition of properties disposed of before that time.

(3) For the purposes of subsection (2), where a small business investment limited partnership disposes of a small business security it shall be deemed to continue to hold the investment for a period of 90 days following the date of the disposition.

**Definitions [Reg. 5102]**: "amount" — ITA 248(1); "arm's length" — ITA 251(1); "borrowed money", "business" — ITA 248(1); "capital gain" — ITA 39(1), 248(1); "capital loss" — ITA 39(1)(b), 248(1); "cost amount" — ITA 248(1); "disposed", "disposes" — ITA 248(1)"disposition"; "disposition" — ITA 248(1); "month" — *Interpretation Act* 35(1); "partnership" — see Notes to ITA 96(1); "person" — ITA 248(1), Reg. 5104(6); "property" — ITA 248(1); "share", "shareholder" — ITA 248(1); "small business investment corporation" — Reg. 5101(1); "small business investment limited partnership" — Reg. 5102(1); "small business security" — Reg. 5100(2), 5104(3), (5); "specified property" — ITA 204(a), (b), (c), (f), (g), Reg. 5100(1).

**5103. [Small business investment trust] — (1)** For the purposes of this Part, paragraph (d) of the definition "small business property" in subsection 206(1) of the Act and subsection 259(3) of the Act, a trust is a small business investment trust at any time if at all times after it was created and before that time

(a) it was resident in Canada;

(b) the interests of the beneficiaries under the trust were described by reference to units of the trust that were identical in all respects; and

(c) no beneficiary or group of beneficiaries who did not deal with each other at arm's length held more than 30% of the units of the trust and, for the purposes of this paragraph, a small business investment corporation that has not borrowed money and in which no shareholder or group of shareholders who did not deal with each other at arm's length held more than 30 per cent of the outstanding shares of any class of voting stock shall be deemed not to be a beneficiary;

(d) its only undertaking was the investing of its funds and its investments consisted solely of

(i) small business securities where, except as provided in subsection 5104(1), the trust was the first person (other than a broker or dealer in securities) to have acquired the securities and it has owned the securities continuously since they were so acquired,

(ii) property (other than small business securities) described in any of subparagraphs (f)(i) to (iv) of the definition "qualified limited partnership" in subsection 5000(7),

(iii) specified properties, or

(iv) any combination of properties described in subparagraphs (i) to (iii);

(e) it has complied with subsection (2);

(f) it has not borrowed money except for the purpose of earning income from its investments and the amount of any such borrowings at any time did not exceed 20 per cent of the trust capital at that time; and

(g) it has not accepted deposits.

**Notes**: Reg. 5103(1)(d)(ii) added by P.C. 1994-1074, effective 1991. (Subparas. (iii) and (iv) were previously numbered (ii) and (iii).)

**Interpretation Bulletins**: IT-320R2: RRSP — qualified investments.

(2) The aggregate of the cost amounts to a small business investment trust of small business securities held by it at any time shall not be less than the amount, if any, by which the aggregate of

(a) 25 per cent of the amount, if any, by which

(i) the aggregate of all amounts received by it more than 12 months before that time and not more than 24 months before that time as con-

**Reg. S. 5103(2)(a)(i)**      Income Tax Regulations

sideration for the issue of its units or in respect of its units

exceeds

(ii) the aggregate of all amounts paid by it before that time to its beneficiaries and designated by the trust as a return of the consideration referred to in subparagraph (i),

(b) 50 per cent of the amount, if any, by which

(i) the aggregate of all amounts received by it more than 24 months before that time and not more than 36 months before that time as consideration for the issue of its units or in respect of its units

exceeds

(ii) the aggregate of all amounts paid by it before that time to its beneficiaries and designated by the trust as a return of the consideration referred to in subparagraph (i), and

(c) 75 per cent of the amount, if any, by which

(i) the aggregate of all amounts received by it more than 36 months before that time as consideration for the issue of its units or in respect of its units

exceeds

(ii) the aggregate of all amounts paid by it before that time to its beneficiaries and designated by the trust as a return of the consideration referred to in subparagraph (i)

exceeds 75 per cent of the amount, if any, by which the aggregate of its losses from the disposition of properties disposed of before that time exceeds the aggregate of its gains from the disposition of properties disposed of before that time.

(3) For the purposes of subsection (2), where a small business investment trust disposes of a small business security it shall be deemed to continue to hold the investment for a period of 90 days following the date of disposition.

**Definitions [Reg. 5103]:** "amount" — ITA 248(1); "arm's length" — ITA 251(1); "borrowed money", "business", "cost amount" — ITA 248(1); "disposed", "disposes" — ITA 248(1)"disposition"; "disposition" — ITA 248(1); "month" — *Interpretation Act* 35(1); "person" — ITA 248(1), Reg. 5104(6); "property" — ITA 248(1); "resident in Canada" — ITA 250; "share", "shareholder" — ITA 248(1); "small business investment corporation" — Reg. 5101(1); "small business security" — Reg. 5100(2), 5104(3), (5); "specified property" — ITA 204(a), (b), (c), (f), (g), Reg. 5100(1); "trust" — ITA 104(1), 248(1), (3).

**5104. (1)** Notwithstanding paragraph (b) of the definition "qualifying obligation" in subsection 5100(1) and paragraphs 5101(1)(b), 5102(1)(f) and 5103(1)(d), the corporation, partnership or trust, as the case may be, may acquire a small business security that another person (other than a broker or dealer in securities) had previously acquired if

(a) the small business security is a share of the capital stock of an eligible corporation having full voting rights under all circumstances; and

(b) except where the share was acquired in specified circumstances within the meaning of subsection (2), the share was acquired from an officer or employee of the eligible corporation or a person related to the officer or employee.

(2) For the purposes of this Part,

(a) where a person acquires a share of a corporation

(i) as part of a proposal to, or an arrangement with, the corporation's creditors that has been approved by a court under the *Bankruptcy [and Insolvency] Act* or the *Companies' Creditors Arrangement Act*,

(ii) at a time when all or substantially all of the corporation's assets were under the control of a receiver, receiver-manager, sequestrator or trustee in bankruptcy, or

(iii) at a time when, by reason of financial difficulty, the corporation was in default, or could reasonably be expected to default, on a debt obligation held by a person with whom the corporation was dealing at arm's length,

the person shall be deemed, at any time within 36 months after he acquired the share, to have acquired it in specified circumstances;

(b) where a person acquires a share of a corporation for the purposes of facilitating the disposition of the entire investment of the person in the corporation, the person shall be deemed, at any time within 12 months after he acquired the share, to have acquired it in specified circumstances; and

(c) a qualified trust (within the meaning assigned by subsection 259(3) of the Act) is deemed not to hold any property for any period in respect of which subsection 259(1) of the Act is applicable.

**Notes**: The CCRA's view is that "all or substantially all", used in Reg. 5104(2)(a)(ii), means 90% or more.

(3) Where the purchaser of a property that, but for this subsection, would at the time of its acquisition be a small business security (or, where the purchaser is a partnership, a member thereof) knew at the time of acquisition that the issuer of the security would, within the immediately following 12 months, cease to qualify as an eligible corporation, the property shall be deemed never to have been a small business security of the purchaser.

(4) Where a person who holds a share of or an interest in a corporation, partnership or trust that, but for this subsection, would be a small business investment corporation, small business investment limited partnership or small business investment trust knew

at the time of issue of the share or interest, as the case may be, or at the time of making any contribution in respect of the share or interest, that

(a) a substantial portion of

(i) the consideration for the issue of the share or interest, or

(ii) the contribution in respect of the share or interest

would not be invested by the corporation, partnership or trust, as the case may be, directly or indirectly in small business securities, and

(b) all or substantially all of

(i) the consideration for the issue of the share or interest, or

(ii) the contribution in respect of the share or interest

would be returned to the purchaser within the immediately following 24 months,

the corporation, partnership or trust shall be deemed to have ceased at that time to be a small business investment corporation, small business investment limited partnership or small business investment trust.

**Notes**: The CCRA's view is that "all or substantially all", used in para. (b), means 90% or more.

(5) Where, but for this subsection, a property that qualified as a small business security when it was acquired would cease at a subsequent time to so qualify, the property shall be deemed to be a small business security for the 24 months immediately following the subsequent time.

(6) For the purposes of this Part, a partnership shall be deemed to be a person.

**Definitions [Reg. 5104]**: "arm's length" — ITA 251(1); "business" — ITA 248(1); "corporation" — ITA 248(1), *Interpretation Act* 35(1); "disposition" — ITA 248(1); "eligible corporation" — Reg. 5100(1); "employee" — ITA 248(1); "month" — *Interpretation Act* 35(1); "officer" — ITA 248(1); "partnership" — see Notes to ITA 96(1); "person" — ITA 248(1), Reg. 5104(6); "property" — ITA 248(1); "related" — ITA 251(2)–(6); "share" — ITA 248(1); "small business investment corporation" — Reg. 5101(1); "small business investment limited partnership" — Reg. 5102(1); "small business security" — Reg. 5100(2), 5104(3), (5); "specified circumstances" — Reg. 5104(2), (2)(b); "trust" — ITA 104(1), 248(1), (3).

# PART LII — CANADIAN MANUFACTURING AND PROCESSING PROFITS

**5200. Basic formula** — Subject to section 5201, for the purposes of paragraph 125.1(3)(a) [125.1(3)"Canadian manufacturing and processing profits"] of the Act, "Canadian manufacturing and processing profits" of a corporation for a taxation year are hereby prescribed to be that proportion of the corporation's adjusted business income for the year that

(a) the aggregate of its cost of manufacturing and processing capital for the year and its cost of manufacturing and processing labour for the year,

is of

(b) the aggregate of its cost of capital for the year and its cost of labour for the year.

**Definitions [Reg. 5200]**: "adjusted business income" — Reg. 5202, 5203(1); "corporation" — ITA 248(1), *Interpretation Act* 35(1); "cost of capital", "cost of labour" — Reg. 5202, 5203(1), 5204; "cost of manufacturing and processing capital", "cost of manufacturing and processing labour" — Reg. 5202, 5204; "prescribed" — ITA 248(1); "taxation year" — ITA 249.

**Interpretation Bulletins**: IT-145R: Canadian manufacturing and processing profits — reduced rate of corporate tax.

**5201. Small manufacturers' rule** — For the purposes of paragraph 125.1(3)(a) [125.1(3)"Canadian manufacturing and processing profits"] of the Act, "Canadian manufacturing and processing profits" of a corporation for a taxation year are hereby prescribed to be equal to the corporation's adjusted business income for the year where

(a) the activities of the corporation during the year were primarily manufacturing or processing in Canada of goods for sale or lease;

(b) the aggregate of

(i) the aggregate of all amounts each of which is the income of the corporation for the year from an active business minus the aggregate of all amounts each of which is the loss of the corporation for the year from an active business, and

(ii) if the corporation is associated in the year with a Canadian corporation, the aggregate of all amounts each of which is the income of the latter corporation from an active business for its taxation year coinciding with or ending in the year,

did not exceed $200,000;

(c) the corporation was not engaged in any of the activities listed in subparagraphs 125.1(3)(b)(i) to (ix) [125.1(3)"manufacturing or processing"(a) to (k)] of the Act at any time during the year;

(c.1) the corporation was not engaged in the processing of ore (other than iron ore or tar sands) from a mineral resource located outside Canada to any stage that is not beyond the prime metal stage or its equivalent;

(c.2) the corporation was not engaged in the processing of iron ore from a mineral resource located outside Canada to any stage that is not beyond the pellet stage or its equivalent;

(c.3) the corporation was not engaged in the processing of tar sands located outside Canada to any stage that is not beyond the crude oil stage or its equivalent; and

(d) the corporation did not carry on any active business outside Canada at any time during the year.

**Notes**: Reg. 5201(c.1) to (c.3) added by P.C. 1994-230, effective for 1990 and later taxation years.

**Definitions [Reg. 5201]**: "active business" — ITA 248(1); "adjusted business income" — Reg. 5202, 5203(1); "amount" — ITA 248(1); "associated" — ITA 256; "Canada" — ITA 255, *Interpretation Act* 35(1); "Canadian corporation" — ITA 89(1), 248(1); "corporation" — ITA 248(1), *Interpretation Act* 35(1); "mineral resource", "prescribed", "tar sands" — ITA 248(1); "taxation year" — ITA 249.

**5202. Interpretation** — In this Part, except as otherwise provided in section 5203 or 5204,

**"adjusted business income"** of a corporation for a taxation year means the amount, if any, by which

(a) the aggregate of all amounts each of which is the income of the corporation for the year from an active business carried on in Canada

exceeds

(b) the aggregate of all amounts each of which is the loss of the corporation for the year from an active business carried on in Canada;

**"Canadian resource profits"** has the meaning that would be assigned to the expression "resource profits" by section 1204 if

(a) section 1204 were read without reference to subparagraph 1204(1)(b)(iv), and

(b) the definition "resource activity" in subsection 1206(1) were read without reference to paragraph (d) of that definition;

**Notes**: Definition "Canadian resource profits" added by P.C. 1994-230, effective for 1990 and later taxation years. Amended by P.C. 1996-1488 to refer to "section 1204" rather than "subsection 1204(1)", effective for taxation years that begin after December 20, 1991.

**"cost of capital"** of a corporation for a taxation year means an amount equal to the aggregate of

(a) 10 per cent of the aggregate of all amounts each of which is the gross cost to the corporation of a property referred to in paragraph 1100(1)(e), (f), (g) or (h), paragraph 1102(1)(d) or (g) or Schedule II that

(i) was owned by the corporation at the end of the year, and

(ii) was used by the corporation at any time during the year, and

(b) the aggregate of all amounts each of which is the rental cost incurred by the corporation during the year for the use of any property a portion of the gross cost of which would be included by virtue of paragraph (a) if the property were owned by the corporation at the end of the year,

but for the purposes of this definition, the gross cost of a property or rental cost for the use of any property does not include that portion of those costs that reflects the extent to which the property was used by the corporation during the year

(c) in an active business carried on outside Canada, or

(d) to earn Canadian investment income or foreign investment income as defined in subsection 129(4) of the Act;

**"cost of labour"** of a corporation for a taxation year means an amount equal to the aggregate of

(a) the salaries and wages paid or payable during the year to all employees of the corporation for services performed during the year, and

(b) all other amounts each of which is an amount paid or payable during the year for the performance during the year, by any person other than an employee of the corporation, of functions relating to

(i) the management or administration of the corporation,

(ii) scientific research and experimental development, or

(iii) a service or function that would normally be performed by an employee of the corporation,

but for the purposes of this definition, the salaries and wages referred to in paragraph (a) or other amounts referred to in paragraph (b) do not include that portion of those amounts that

(c) was included in the gross cost to the corporation of a property (other than a property that was manufactured by the corporation and leased during the year by the corporation to another person) that was included in computing the cost of capital of the corporation for the year, or

(d) was related to an active business carried on outside Canada by the corporation;

**Notes**: "Cost of labour"(b)(ii) amended by P.C. 2000-1095, effective for costs incurred after February 27, 1995, to refer to SR&ED instead of "scientific research as defined in section 2900". The definition of SR&ED has been moved from Reg. 2900(1) to ITA 248(1).

**"cost of manufacturing and processing capital"** of a corporation for a taxation year means 100/85 of that portion of the cost of capital of the corporation for that year that reflects the extent to which each property included in the calculation thereof was used directly in qualified activities of the corporation during the year, but the amount so calculated shall not exceed the cost of capital of the corporation for the year;

**"cost of manufacturing and processing labour"** of a corporation for a taxation year means 100/75 of that portion of the cost of labour of the corporation for that year that reflects the extent to which

(a) the salaries and wages included in the calculation thereof were paid or payable to persons for the portion of their time that they were directly engaged in qualified activities of the corporation during the year, and

(b) the other amounts included in the calculation thereof were paid or payable to persons for the performance of functions that would be directly related to qualified activities of the corporation during the year if those persons were employees of the corporation,

but the amount so calculated shall not exceed the cost of labour of the corporation for the year;

**"gross cost"** to a particular person of a property at any time means, in respect of property that has become available for use by the particular person for the purposes of subsection 13(26) of the Act, the capital cost to the particular person of the property computed without reference to subsections 13(7.1), (7.4) and (10), sections 21 and 80 and paragraph 111(4)(e) of the Act and, in respect of any other property, nil, and where the particular person acquired the property

(a) in the course of a reorganization in respect of which, if a dividend were received by the particular person in the course of the reorganization, subsection 55(2) of the Act would not apply to the dividend by reason of the application of paragraph 55(3)(b) of the Act, or

(b) from another person with whom the particular person was not dealing at arm's length (otherwise than by reason of a right referred to in paragraph 251(5)(b) of the Act) immediately after the property was acquired,

the capital cost to the particular person of the property for the purposes of this definition shall be computed as if the property had been acquired at a capital cost equal to the gross cost of the property to the person from whom the property was acquired by the particular person;

**Notes**: Definition "gross cost" amended by P.C. 1994-139, effective for 1985 and later taxation years. If the taxpayer elected by notifying Revenue Canada by the return due date for the first taxation year that ended after February 9, 1994,

(i) for taxation years that ended before January 16, 1987: ignore the reference to ITA 111(4)(e), and

(ii) for taxation years ending before February 9, 1994: ignore the words "in respect of property that has become available for use by the particular person for the purposes of subsection 13(26) of the Act"; and ignore the words "and, in respect of any other property, nil".

If no such election was made, then

(i) for taxation years ending before January 16, 1987, read:

"gross cost" of a property means the capital cost of the property computed without reference to subsections 13(7.1), (7.4) and (10) and sections 21 and 80 of the Act;

(ii) for taxation years ending after January 15, 1987 and before February 9, 1994, read:

"gross cost" of a property means the capital cost of the property computed without reference to subsections 13(7.1), (7.4) and (10), sections 21 and 80 and paragraph 111(4)(e) of the Act.

**"qualified activities"** means

(a) any of the following activities, when they are performed in Canada in connection with manufacturing or processing (not including the activities listed in subparagraphs 125.1(3)(b)(i) to (ix) [125.1(3)"manufacturing or processing"(a) to (k)] of the Act) in Canada of goods for sale or lease:

(i) engineering design of products and production facilities,

(ii) receiving and storing of raw materials,

(iii) producing, assembling and handling of goods in process,

(iv) inspecting and packaging of finished goods,

(v) line supervision,

(vi) production support activities including security, cleaning, heating and factory maintenance,

(vii) quality and production control,

(viii) repair of production facilities, and

(ix) pollution control,

(b) all other activities that are performed in Canada directly in connection with manufacturing or processing (not including the activities listed in subparagraphs 125.1(3)(b)(i) to (ix) [125.1(3)"manufacturing or processing"(a) to (k)] of the Act) in Canada of goods for sale or lease, and

(c) scientific research and experimental development, as defined in section 2900, carried on in Canada,

but does not include any of

(d) storing, shipping, selling and leasing of finished goods,

(e) purchasing of raw materials,

(f) administration, including clerical and personnel activities,

(g) purchase and resale operations,

(h) data processing, and

(i) providing facilities for employees, including cafeterias, clinics and recreational facilities;

**Notes**: Definition "qualified activities" amended by P.C. 1994-139, to add the words "and experimental development" and "carried on in Canada", effective for SR&ED done or carried on after December 23, 1991, other than SR&ED done or carried on by or on behalf of a taxpayer pursuant to an agreement in writing entered into by the taxpayer before December 24, 1991.

**"rental cost"** of a property means the rents incurred for the use of that property;

**"resource profits"** has the meaning assigned by section 1204;

**Notes**: Definition "resource profits" added by P.C. 1994-230, effective for 1990 and later taxation years. Amended by P.C. 1996-1488 as a result of amendments to Reg. 1204, effective for taxation years that begin after December 20, 1991. For earlier years, read "subsection 1204(1)" in place of "section 1204".

"salaries and wages" means salaries, wages and commissions, but does not include any other type of remuneration, any superannuation or pension benefits, any retiring allowances or any amount referred to in section 6 or 7 of the Act;

"specified percentage" for a taxation year means

(a) where the year commences after 1998, 100%, and

(b) in any other case, the total of

(i) that proportion of 10% that the number of days in the year that are in 1990 is of the number of days in the year,

(ii) that proportion of 20% that the number of days in the year that are in 1991 is of the number of days in the year,

(iii) that proportion of 30% that the number of days in the year that are in 1992 is of the number of days in the year,

(iv) that proportion of 50% that the number of days in the year that are in 1993 is of the number of days in the year,

(v) that proportion of 64.3% that the number of days in the year that are in 1994 is of the number of days in the year,

(vi) that proportion of 71.4% that the number of days in the year that are in 1995 is of the number of days in the year,

(vii) that proportion of 78.6% that the number of days in the year that are in 1996 is of the number of days in the year,

(viii) that proportion of 85.7% that the number of days in the year that are in 1997 is of the number of days in the year,

(ix) that proportion of 92.9% that the number of days in the year that are in 1998 is of the number of days in the year, and

(x) that proportion of 100% that the number of days in the year that are in 1999 is of the number of days in the year.

**Notes**: Definition "specified percentage" added by P.C. 1994-230, effective for 1990 and later taxation years.

**Definitions [Reg. 5202]**: "active business", "amount" — ITA 248(1); "arm's length" — ITA 251(1); "Canada" — ITA 255, *Interpretation Act* 35(1); "corporation" — ITA 248(1), *Interpretation Act* 35(1); "cost of capital", "cost of labour" — Reg. 5202, 5203(1), 5204; "dividend", "employee" — ITA 248(1); "gross cost" — Reg. 5202, 5204; "person", "property" — ITA 248(1); "qualified activities" — Reg. 5202; "related" — ITA 251(2)–(6); "rental cost" — Reg. 5202; "retiring allowance" — ITA 248(1); "salaries and wages" — ITA 248(1), Reg. 5202; "scientific research and experimental development" — ITA 248(1); "superannuation or pension benefit" — ITA 248(1); "taxation year" — ITA 249.

## 5203. Resource income — (1) Where a corporation has resource activities for a taxation year the following rules apply, except as otherwise provided in section 5204

"adjusted business income" of the corporation for the year means the amount, if any, by which

(a) the amount otherwise determined under section 5202 to be the adjusted business income of the corporation for the year

exceeds the total of

(b) the amount, if any, by which the corporation's net resource income for the year exceeds the corporation's net resource adjustment for the year,

(c) all amounts each of which is an amount in respect of refund interest included in computing the taxpayer's income for the year, to the extent that the amount is included in the amount otherwise determined to be the adjusted business income, within the meaning of section 5202, of the corporation for the year, and

(d) all amounts each of which is included under paragraph 12(1)(z.5) in computing the taxpayer's income for the year;

**Related Provisions**: Reg. 5203(3.1) — Net resource adjustment.

**Notes**: Para. (b) amended by P.C. 1999-629, effective for taxation years that begin after December 20, 1991, to add reference to the net resource adjustment.

Para. (c) added by P.C. 1996-1488, effective for taxation years that end after March 6, 1996.

Para. (d) added by P.C 1999-629, effective for taxation years that begin after 1996.

"cost of capital" of the corporation for the year means the amount, if any, by which

(a) the amount otherwise determined under section 5202 to be the cost of capital of the corporation for the year

exceeds

(b) that portion of the gross cost of property or rental cost for the use of property included in computing the cost of capital of the corporation for the year that reflects the extent to which the property was used by the corporation during the year,

(i) in activities engaged in for the purpose of earning Canadian resource profits of the corporation, or

(ii) in activities referred to in subparagraph 66(15)(b)(i), (ii) or (v) [66(15)"Canadian exploration and development expenses"(a), (b) or (e)], subparagraph 66(15)(e)(i) or (ii) [66(15)"foreign exploration and development expenses"(a) or (b)], subparagraph 66.1(6)(a)(i), (ii), (iii) or (v) [66.1(6)"Canadian exploration expense"(a), (c), (f) or (i)] or subparagraph 66.2(5)(a)(i), (ii) or (v) [66.2(5)"Canadian development expense"(a), (c) or (g)] of the Act;

**Notes**: Subpara. (b)(i) amended by P.C. 1994-230, effective for 1990 and later taxation years, to change "resource profits (within the meaning assigned by section 1204)" to "Canadian resource profits" (a term now defined in Reg. 5202).

"**cost of labour**" of the corporation for the year means the amount, if any, by which

(a) the amount otherwise determined under section 5202 to be the cost of labour of the corporation for the year

exceeds

(b) that portion of the salaries and wages and other amounts included in computing the cost of labour of the corporation for the year that,

(i) was related to the activities engaged in for the purpose of earning Canadian resource profits of the corporation, or

(ii) was included in the Canadian exploration and development expenses, foreign exploration and development expenses, Canadian exploration expense or Canadian development expense, within the meanings assigned by paragraphs 66(15)(b) and (e) [66(15)"Canadian exploration and development expenses" and "foreign exploration and development expenses"], paragraph 66.1(6)(a) [66.1(6)"Canadian exploration expense"] and 66.2(5)(a) [66.2(5)"Canadian development expense"] of the Act respectively, of the corporation.

**Notes**: Subpara. (b)(i) amended by P.C. 1994-230, effective for 1990 and later taxation years, to change "resource profits (within the meaning assigned by section 1204)" to "Canadian resource profits" (now defined in Reg. 5202).

(2) For the purposes of subsection (1), a corporation has "resource activities" for a taxation year if

(a) in computing its income for the year, an amount is deductible pursuant to paragraph 20(1)(v.1) or section 65, 66, 66.1 or 66.2 of the Act;

(b) the corporation was at any time during the year engaged in activities for the purpose of earning resource profits of the corporation; or

(c) in computing the corporation's income for the year, an amount was included pursuant to section 59 of the Act.

**Notes**: Reg. 5203(2)(b) amended by P.C. 1994-230, effective for 1990 and later taxation years, to change "resource profits (within the meaning assigned by section 1204)" to "resource profits". (See definition in Reg. 5202.)

(3) In subsection (1), "net resource income" of a corporation for a taxation year means the amount, if any, by which the total of

(a) the resource profits of the corporation for the year, and

(b) the amount, if any, by which

(i) the total of amounts included in computing the income of the corporation for the year, from an active business carried on in Canada, pursuant to section 59 of the Act (other than amounts that may reasonably be regarded as having been included in computing the resource profits of the corporation for the year),

exceeds

(ii) the total of amounts deducted in computing the income of the corporation for the year under section 64 of the Act, as that section applies with respect to dispositions occurring before November 13, 1981 and to dispositions occurring after November 12, 1981 pursuant to the terms in existence on that date of an offer or agreement in writing made or entered into on or before that date, except those amounts that may reasonably be regarded as having been deducted in computing the resource profits of the corporation for the year,

exceeds the total of

(c) the total of amounts deducted in computing the income of the corporation for the year under section 65 of the Act (other than amounts that may reasonably be regarded as having been deducted in computing the resource profits of the corporation for the year), and

(d) the specified percentage for the year of the amount, if any, by which

(i) the corporation's resource profits for the year

exceeds the total of

(ii) the corporation's Canadian resource profits for the year, and

(iii) the earned depletion base (within the meaning assigned by subsection 1205(1)) of the corporation at the beginning of its immediately following taxation year.

**Notes**: Reg. 5203(3) amended by P.C. 1994-230, effective for 1990 and later taxation years, in order to allow a portion of a corporation's foreign ore processing income for a taxation year (net of its earned depletion base at the beginning of the next year) to qualify as its adjusted business income for the year.

(3.1) In subsection (1), the net resource adjustment of a corporation for a taxation year is the amount determined by the formula

$$A - B$$

where

A is the amount of Canadian resource profits of the corporation for the year, and

B is the amount that would be the Canadian resource profits of the corporation for the year if

(a) subsections 1204(1) and (1.1) provided for the computation of negative amounts where the amounts subtracted in computing gross resource profits (as defined by subsection 1204(1)) and resource profits exceed the amounts added in computing those amounts, and

(b) paragraph 1206(3)(a) applied so that a negative amount of resource profits of a partnership for a fiscal period that ended in the year were, to the extent of the corporation's share thereof, deducted in computing the corporation's resource profits for the year.

**Related Provisions**: ITA 257 — Negative amounts in formulas.

**Notes**: Reg. 5203(3.1) added by P.C. 1999-629, effective for taxation years that begin after December 20, 1991.

**(4)** For the purpose of subsection 5203(1), "refund interest" means an amount that is received, or that becomes receivable, after March 6, 1996

(a) from an authority (including a government or municipality) situated in Canada as a consequence of the overpayment of a tax that was not deductible under the Act in computing any taxpayer's income and that was imposed by an Act of Canada or a province or a bylaw of a municipality;

(b) from a person described in subparagraph 18(1)(m)(i), (ii) or (iii) of the Act as a consequence of the overpayment of an amount that, because of paragraph 18(1)(m) of the Act, was not deductible under the Act in computing any taxpayer's income; or

(c) from a person described in subparagraph 18(1)(m)(i), (ii) or (iii) of the Act as a consequence of the receipt of an amount that was in excess of the amount to which the person was entitled and in respect of an amount that was required to be included in computing any taxpayer's income because of paragraph 12(1)(o) of the Act.

**Notes**: Reg. 5203(4) added by P.C. 1996-1488, effective for taxation years that end after March 6, 1996.

**Definitions [Reg. 5203]**: "active business" — ITA 248(1); "adjusted business income" — Reg. 5202, 5203(1); "amount" — ITA 248(1); "Canada" — ITA 255, *Interpretation Act* 35(1); "Canadian development expense" — ITA 66.2(5), 248(1); "Canadian exploration and development expenses" — ITA 66(15), 248(1); "Canadian exploration expense" — ITA 66.1(6), 248(1); "Canadian resource profits" — Reg. 5202; "corporation" — ITA 248(1), *Interpretation Act* 35(1); "cost of capital", "cost of labour" — Reg. 5202, 5203(1), 5204; "disposition" — ITA 248(1); "foreign exploration and development expenses" — ITA 66(15), 248(1); "gross cost" — Reg. 5202, 5204; "net resource adjustment" — Reg. 5203(3.1); "person", "property" — ITA 248(1); "province" — *Interpretation Act* 35(1); "related" — ITA 251(2)–(6); "rental cost", "resource profits" — Reg. 5202; "salaries and wages" — ITA 248(1), Reg. 5202; "specified percentage" — Reg. 5202; "taxation year" — ITA 249; "taxpayer" — ITA 248(1); "writing" — *Interpretation Act* 35(1).

**5204. Partnerships** — Where a corporation is a member of a partnership at any time in a taxation year of the corporation, the following rules apply:

**"cost of capital"** of the corporation for the year means an amount equal to the aggregate of

(a) 10 per cent of the aggregate of all amounts each of which is the gross cost to the corporation of a property referred to in paragraph 1100(1)(e), (f), (g) or (h), paragraph 1102(1)(d) or (g) or Schedule II that

(i) was owned by the corporation at the end of the year, and

(ii) was used by the corporation at any time during the year,

(b) the aggregate of all amounts each of which is the rental cost incurred by the corporation during the year for the use of any property a portion of the gross cost of which would be included by virtue of paragraph (a) if the property were owned by the corporation at the end of the year, and

(c) that proportion of the aggregate of the amounts that would be determined under paragraphs (a) and (b) in respect of the partnership for its fiscal period coinciding with or ending in the taxation year of the corporation if the references in those paragraphs to "the corporation" were read as references to "the partnership" and the references in those paragraphs to "the year" were read as references to "the fiscal period of the partnership coinciding with or ending in the year", that

(i) the corporation's share of the income or loss of the partnership for that fiscal period

is of

(ii) the income or loss of the partnership for that fiscal period, as the case may be,

but for the purposes of this definition, the gross cost of a property or rental cost for the use of any property does not include that portion of those costs that reflects the extent to which the property was used by the corporation during the year or by the partnership during its fiscal period coinciding with or ending in the year

(d) in an active business carried on outside Canada,

(e) to earn Canadian investment income or foreign investment income as defined in subsection 129(4) of the Act on the assumption that subsection 129(4) of the Act applied to a partnership as well as to a corporation,

(f) in activities engaged in for the purpose of earning Canadian resource profits of the corporation or the partnership, as the case may be, or

(g) in activities referred to in subparagraph 66(15)(b)(i), (ii) or (v) [66(15)"Canadian exploration and development expenses"(a), (b) or (e)], subparagraph 66(15)(e)(i) or (ii) [66(15)"foreign exploration and development expenses"(a) or (b)], subparagraph 66.1(6)(a)(i), (ii), (iii) or (v) [66.1(6)"Canadian exploration expense"(a), (c), (f) or (i)] or subparagraph 66.2(5)(a)(i), (ii) or (v) [66.2(5)"Canadian development expense"(a), (c) or (g)] of the Act;

**Notes**: Para. (f) amended by P.C. 1994-230, effective for 1990 and later taxation years, to change "resource profits (within the meaning assigned by section 1204)" to "Canadian resource profits" (now defined in Reg. 5202).

"**cost of labour**" of the corporation for the year means an amount equal to the aggregate of

(a) the salaries and wages paid or payable during the year to all employees of the corporation for services performed during the year,

(b) all other amounts each of which is an amount paid or payable during the year for the performance during the year, by any person other than an employee of the corporation, of functions relating to

(i) the management or administration of the corporation,

(ii) scientific research as defined in section 2900, or

(iii) a service or function that would normally be performed by an employee of the corporation, and

(c) that proportion of the aggregate of the amounts that would be determined under paragraphs (a) and (b) in respect of the partnership for its fiscal period coinciding with or ending in the taxation year of the corporation if the references in those paragraphs to the "corporation" were read as references to "the partnership" and the references in those paragraphs to "the year" were read as references to "the fiscal period of the partnership coinciding with or ending in the year", that

(i) the corporation's share of the income or loss of the partnership for that fiscal period

is of

(ii) the income or loss of the partnership for that fiscal period, as the case may be,

but for the purposes of this definition, the salaries and wages referred to in paragraph (a) or other amounts referred to in paragraph (b), of the corporation or the partnership, as the case may be, do not include that portion of those amounts that

(d) was included in the gross cost to the corporation or partnership of a property (other than a property that was manufactured by the corporation or partnership and leased during the year by the corporation or the partnership to another person) that was included in computing the cost of capital of the corporation for the year,

(e) was related to an active business carried on outside Canada by the corporation or the partnership,

(f) was related to the activities engaged in for the purpose of earning Canadian resource profits of the corporation or the partnership, as the case may be, or

(g) was included in the Canadian exploration and development expenses, foreign exploration and development expenses, Canadian exploration expense or Canadian development expense, within the meanings assigned by paragraphs 66(15)(b) and (e) [66(15)"Canadian exploration and development expenses" and "foreign exploration and development expenses"], 66.1(6)(a) [66.1(6)"Canadian exploration expense"] and 66.2(5)(a) [66.2(5)"Canadian development expense"] of the Act respectively, of the corporation;

**Notes**: Para. (f) amended by P.C. 1994-230, effective for 1990 and later taxation years, to change "resource profits (within the meaning assigned by section 1204)" to "Canadian resource profits" (now defined in Reg. 5202).

"**cost of manufacturing and processing capital**" of the corporation for the year means 100/85 of that portion of the cost of capital of the corporation for that year that reflects the extent to which each property included in the calculation thereof was used directly in qualified activities

(a) of the corporation during the year, or

(b) of the partnership during its fiscal period coinciding with or ending in the year, as the case may be,

but the amount so calculated shall not exceed the cost of capital of the corporation for the year;

"**cost of manufacturing and processing labour**" of the corporation for the year means 100/75 of that portion of the cost of labour of the corporation for that year that reflects the extent to which

(a) the salaries and wages included in the calculation thereof were paid or payable to persons for the portion of their time that they were directly engaged in qualified activities

(i) of the corporation during the year, or

(ii) of the partnership during its fiscal period coinciding with or ending in the year, and

(b) the other amounts included in the calculation thereof were paid or payable to persons for the performance of functions that would be directly related to qualified activities

(i) of the corporation during the year, or

(ii) of the partnership during its fiscal period coinciding with or ending in the year,

if those persons were employees of the corporation or the partnership, as the case may be,

but the amount so calculated shall not exceed the cost of labour of the corporation for the year;

"**gross cost**" of a property at any time means

(a) in respect of a property that has become available for use by the partnership for the purposes of subsection 13(26) of the Act, the capital cost to the partnership of the property computed without reference to subsections 13(7.1), (7.4) and (10) and sections 21 and 80 of the Act, and

(b) in respect of any other property of the partnership, nil

and, for the purposes of paragraph (a), where the partnership acquired the property from a person who was a majority interest partner of the partnership (within the meaning assigned by subsection 97(3.1) of the Act) immediately after the property was acquired, the capital cost to the partnership of the property shall be computed as if the property had been acquired at a capital cost equal to the gross cost to the person of the property, except that where the property was partnership property on December 31, 1971, its gross cost shall be its capital cost to the partnership as determined under subsection 20(3) or (5) of the *Income Tax Application Rules*.

**Notes**: Definition "gross cost" amended by P.C. 1994-139. If the taxpayer elected by notifying Revenue Canada by the return due date for the first taxation year that ended after February 9, 1994, then for taxation years ending before February 9, 1994, read as follows:

"gross cost" of a property at any time means in respect of a property of the partnership, the capital cost to the partnership of the property computed without reference to subsections 13(7.1), (7.4) and (10) and sections 21 and 80 of the Act, and, where the partnership acquired the property from a person who was a majority interest partner of the partnership (within the meaning assigned by subsection 97(3.1) of the Act) immediately after the property was acquired, the capital cost to the partnership of the property shall be computed as if the property had been acquired at a capital cost equal to the gross cost to the person of the property, except that where the property was partnership property on December 31, 1971 its gross cost shall be its capital cost to the partnership as determined under subsection 20(3) or (5) of the *Income Tax Application Rules, 1971*.

If no such election was made, then

(i) for taxation years ending from January 1, 1985 through January 15, 1987, read:

"gross cost" of a property means the capital cost of the property computed without reference to subsections 13(7.1), (7.4) and (10) and sections 21 and 80 of the Act, except that where a property was partnership property on December 31, 1971, its gross cost shall be its capital cost to the partnership as determined under subsection 20(3) or (5) of the *Income Tax Application Rules, 1971*;

(ii) for taxation years ending after January 15, 1987 and before February 9, 1994, read:

"gross cost" of a property means the capital cost of the property computed without reference to subsections 13(7.1), (7.4) and (10), sections 21 and 80 and paragraph 111(4)(e) of the Act, except that where a property was partnership property on December 31, 1971, its gross cost shall be its capital cost to the partnership as determined under subsection 20(3) or (5) of the *Income Tax Application Rules, 1971*.

**Definitions [Reg. 5204]**: "active business", "amount" — ITA 248(1); "Canada" — ITA 255, *Interpretation Act* 35(1); "Canadian development expense" — ITA 66.2(5), 248(1); "Canadian exploration and development expenses" — ITA 66(15), 248(1); "Canadian exploration expense" — ITA 66.1(6), 248(1); "Canadian resource profits" — Reg. 5202; "corporation" — ITA 248(1), *Interpretation Act* 35(1); "cost of capital", "cost of labour" — Reg. 5202, 5203(1), 5204; "employee" — ITA 248(1); "fiscal period" — ITA 249.1; "foreign exploration and development expenses" — ITA 66(15), 248(1); "gross cost" — Reg. 5202, 5204; "majority interest partner" — ITA 248(1); "partnership" — see Notes to ITA 96(1); "person" — ITA 248(1); "qualified activities" — Reg. 5202; "related" — ITA 251(2)–(6); "rental cost" — Reg. 5202; "salaries and wages" — ITA 248(1), Reg. 5202; "share" — ITA 248(1); "taxation year" — ITA 249.

## PART LIII — INSTALMENT BASE

**5300. [Individuals]** — For the purposes of subsections 155(2), 156(3) and 161(9) of the Act, the instalment base of an individual for a taxation year is the amount by which

(a) the individual's tax payable under Part I of the Act for the year, determined before taking into consideration the specified future tax consequences for the year

exceeds

(b) the amount deemed by subsection 120(2) of the Act to have been paid on account of the individual's tax under Part I of the Act for the year, determined before taking into consideration the specified future tax consequences for the year.

**Related Provisions**: ITA 248(1) — Definition of "specified future tax consequence".

**Notes**: Reg. 5300 amended by P.C. 1999-196, effective for computing instalments for the 1997 and later taxation years. For 1987-96, read:

5300. (1) For the purposes of subsections 155(2) and 156(3) of the Act, the instalment base of an individual for the 1977 and subsequent taxation years shall be the amount by which the aggregate of

(a) the tax payable by him for the taxation year under Part I of the Act, computed without reference to sections 127.2 and 127.3 thereof and before taking into consideration any amount referred to in any of subparagraphs 161(7)(a)(i) to (vii) thereof that was excluded or deducted, as the case may be, for the year, and

(b) the amount deducted by him for the taxation year under subsection 127(13) of the Act

exceeds the aggregate of

(c) the amount estimated by him to be his deduction under subsection 127(13) of the Act for the immediately following taxation year, and

(d) the amount deemed by subsection 120(2) of the Act to be an amount paid on account of his tax under Part I of the Act for the taxation year.

(2) For the purposes of subsection 161(9) of the Act, the instalment base of an individual for the 1977 and subsequent taxation years shall have the meaning prescribed by subsection (1) if paragraph (c) thereof were read as "the amount deducted by him under subsection 127(13) of the Act for the immediately following taxation year".

**Definitions [Reg. 5300]**: "amount", "individual", "prescribed", "specified future tax consequence" — ITA 248(1); "taxation year" — ITA 249.

### 5301. Corporations under Part I of the Act —
**(1)** Subject to subsections 5301 (6) and (8), for the purposes of subsections 157(4) and 161(9) of the Act, the first instalment base of a corporation for a particular taxation year means the product obtained when the aggregate of

(a) the tax payable under Part I of the Act by the corporation for its taxation year preceding the particular year, and

(b) the total of the taxes payable by the corporation under Parts I.3, VI and VI.1 of the Act for its taxation year preceding the particular year

**Proposed Amendment — Reg. 5301(1)(b)**

(b) the total of the taxes payable by the corporation under Parts I.3, VI, VI.1 and XIII.1 of the Act for its taxation year preceding the particular year

**Application**: The August 8, 2000 draft regulations, subsec. 4(1), will amend para. 5301(1)(b) to read as above, applicable to 2001 *et seq*.

is multiplied by the ratio that 365 is of the number of days in that preceding year.

**Related Provisions**: Reg. 5301(10) — Tax payable under Part I.

**Notes**: Reg. 5301(1)(a) amended by P.C. 1994-556 to replace the details of how to calculate "tax payable" with reference to Reg. 5301(10), effective for taxation years that end after June 30, 1989. Amended by P.C. 1999-196, effective for 1996 and later taxation years, to take out explicit reference to 5301(10), which still defines "tax payable under Part I" for this purpose.

Reference to Parts I.3 and VI added to Reg. 5301(1)(b) by P.C. 1994-556, effective for taxation years that end after 1991.

(2) Subject to subsections (6) and (8), for the purposes of subsections 157(4) and 161(9) of the Act, the "second instalment base" of a corporation for a particular taxation year means the amount of the first instalment base of the corporation for the taxation year immediately preceding the particular year.

(3) For the purposes of subsection (1), where the number of days in the taxation year of a corporation immediately preceding the particular taxation year referred to therein is less than 183, the amount determined for the corporation under that subsection shall be the greater of

(a) the amount otherwise determined for it under subsection (1); and

(b) the amount that would be determined for it under subsection (1) if the reference in that subsection to "its taxation year preceding the particular year" were read as a reference to "its last taxation year, preceding the particular year, in which the number of days exceeds 182".

**Notes**: Reg. 5301(3)(b) amended by P.C. 1999-196, retroactive to 1989, to correct a referencing error (changed "immediately preceding" to "preceding").

(4) Notwithstanding subsections (1) and (2), for the purposes of subsections 157(4) and 161(9) of the Act,

(a) where a particular taxation year of a new corporation that was formed as a result of an amalgamation (within the meaning assigned by section 87 of the Act) is its first taxation year,

(i) its "first instalment base" for the particular year means the total of all amounts each of which is equal to the product obtained when the total of

(A) the tax payable under Part I of the Act, and

(B) the total of the taxes payable under Parts I.3, VI and VI.1 of the Act

**Proposed Amendment — Reg. 5301(4)(a)(i)(B)**

(B) the total of the taxes payable under Parts I.3, VI, VI.1 and XIII.1 of the Act

**Application**: The August 8, 2000 draft regulations, subsec. 4(2), will amend cl. 5301(4)(a)(i)(B) to read as above, applicable to 2001 *et seq*.

by a predecessor corporation (as defined in section 87 of the Act) for its last taxation year is multiplied by the ratio that 365 is of the number of days in that year, and

(ii) its "second instalment base" for the particular year means the aggregate of all amounts each of which is an amount equal to the amount of the first instalment base of a predecessor corporation for its last taxation year; and

(b) where a particular taxation year of a new corporation referred to in paragraph (a) is its second taxation year,

(i) its "first instalment base" for the particular year means

(A) where the number of days in its first taxation year is greater than 182, the amount that would, but for this subsection, be determined under subsection (1) for the year, and

(B) in any other case, the greater of the amount that would, but for this subsection, be determined under subsection (1) for the year and its first instalment base for its first taxation year, and

(ii) its "second instalment base" for the particular year means the amount of the first instalment base of the new corporation for its first taxation year.

**Notes**: Reg. 5301(4)(a)(i)(A) amended by P.C. 1994-556 to replace the details of how to calculate "tax payable" with reference to Reg. 5301(10), effective for taxation years that end after June 30, 1989. Amended by P.C. 1999-196, effective for 1996 and later taxation years, to take out explicit reference to 5301(10), which still defines "tax payable under Part I" for this purpose.

Reference to Parts I.3 and VI added to Reg. 5301(4)(a)(i)(B) by P.C. 1994-556, effective for taxation years that end after 1991.

(5) For the purposes of subsection (4), where the number of days in the last taxation year of a predecessor corporation is less than 183, the amount deter-

mined under subparagraph (4)(a)(i) in respect of the predecessor corporation shall be the greater of

(a) the amount otherwise determined under subparagraph (4)(a)(i) in respect of the predecessor corporation; and

(b) the amount of the first instalment base of the predecessor corporation for its last taxation year.

(6) Subject to subsection (7), where a subsidiary within the meaning of subsection 88(1) of the Act is winding up, and, at a particular time in the course of the winding up, all or substantially all of the property of the subsidiary has been distributed to a parent within the meaning of subsection 88(1) of the Act, the following rules apply:

(a) there shall be added to the amount of the parent's first instalment base for its taxation year that includes the particular time the amount of the subsidiary's first instalment base for its taxation year that includes the particular time;

(b) there shall be added to the amount of the parent's second instalment base for its taxation year that includes the particular time the amount of the subsidiary's second instalment base for its taxation year that includes the particular time;

(c) there shall be added to the amount of the parent's first instalment base for its taxation year immediately following its taxation year referred to in paragraph (a) the amount that is the proportion of the subsidiary's first instalment base for its taxation year referred to in paragraph (a) that

(i) the number of complete months that ended at or before the particular time in the taxation year of the parent that includes the particular time

is of

(ii) 12; and

(d) there shall be added to the amount of the parent's second instalment base for its taxation year immediately following its taxation year referred to in paragraph (a) the amount of the subsidiary's first instalment base for its taxation year that includes the particular time.

**Notes**: The CCRA's view is that "all or substantially all" means 90% or more.

(7) The amount of an instalment of tax for the taxation year referred to in paragraphs (6)(a) and (b) that a parent is deemed under subsection 161(4.1) of the Act to have been liable to pay before the particular time referred to in subsection (6) shall be determined as if subsection (6) were not applicable in respect of a distribution of property described in that subsection occurring after the day on or before which the instalment was required to be paid.

(8) Subject to subsection (9), where at a particular time a corporation (in this subsection referred to as the "transferor") has disposed of all or substantially all of its property to another corporation with which it was not dealing at arm's length (in this subsection and subsection (9) referred to as the "transferee") and subsection 85(1) or (2) of the Act applied in respect of the disposition of any of the property, the following rules apply:

**Proposed Amendment — Reg. 5301(8) opening words**

(8) Subject to subsection (9), if at a particular time a corporation (in this subsection referred as the "transferor") has disposed of all or substantially all of its property to another corporation with which it was not dealing at arm's length (in this subsection and subsection (9) referred to as the "transferee") and subsection 85(1), (2) or 142.7(3) of the Act applied in respect of the disposition of any of the property, the following rules apply:

**Application**: The August 8, 2000 draft regulations, subsec. 4(3), will amend the opening words of subsec. 5301(8) to read as above, applicable after June 27, 1999.

(a) there shall be added to the amount of the transferee's first instalment base for its taxation year that includes the particular time the amount of the transferor's first instalment base for its taxation year that includes the particular time;

(b) there shall be added to the amount of the transferee's second instalment base for its taxation year that includes the particular time the amount of the transferor's second instalment base for its taxation year that includes the particular time;

(c) there shall be added to the amount of the transferee's first instalment base for its taxation year immediately following its taxation year referred to in paragraph (a) the amount that is the proportion of the transferor's first instalment base for its taxation year referred to in paragraph (a) that

(i) the number of complete months that ended at or before the particular time in the taxation year of the transferee that includes the particular time

is of

(ii) 12; and

(d) there shall be added to the amount of the transferee's second instalment base for its taxation year immediately following its taxation year referred to in paragraph (a) the amount of the transferor's first instalment base for its taxation year that includes the particular time.

**Notes**: The CCRA's view is that "all or substantially all" means 90% or more.

(9) The amount of an instalment of tax for the taxation year referred to in paragraphs (8)(a) and (b) that a transferee is deemed under subsection 161(4.1) of the Act to have been liable to pay before the particular time referred to in subsection (8) shall be determined as if subsection (8) were not applicable in re-

spect of a disposition of property described in that subsection occurring after the day on or before which the instalment was required to be paid.

(10) For the purpose of this section, tax payable under Part I, I.3 or VI of the Act by a corporation for a taxation year means the corporation's tax payable for the year under the relevant Part, determined before taking into consideration the specified future tax consequences for the year.

**Proposed Amendment — Reg. 5301(10)**

(10) For the purpose of this section, tax payable under Part I, I.3, VI or XIII.1 of the Act by a corporation for a taxation year means the corporation's tax payable for the year under the relevant Part, determined before taking into consideration the specified future tax consequences for the year.

*Application*: The August 8, 2000 draft regulations, subsec. 4(4), will amend subsec. 5301(10) to read as above, applicable to 2001 *et seq.*

*Related Provisions*: ITA 248(1) — Definition of "specified future tax consequence".

*Notes*: Reg. 5301(10) amended by P.C. 1999-196, effective for 1996 and later taxation years. For taxation years that began after February 29, 1992 and ended before 1996, read:

(10) For the purposes of this section, "tax payable under Part I of the Act" by a corporation for a taxation year means the tax payable under Part I of the Act by the corporation for the year before taking into consideration any amount referred to in any of subparagraphs 161(7)(a)(ii) to (x) of the Act that is excluded or deducted, as the case may be, for the year.

Reg. 5301(10) added by P.C. 1994-556, the above version effective for taxation years that begin after February 29, 1992.

*Definitions [Reg. 5301]*: "amount" — ITA 248(1); "arm's length" — ITA 251(1); "corporation" — ITA 248(1), *Interpretation Act* 35(1); "disposed" — ITA 248(1)"disposition"; "disposition" — ITA 248(1); "month" — *Interpretation Act* 35(1); "property", "specified future tax consequence" — ITA 248(1); "taxation year" — ITA 249.

# PART LIV — DEBTOR'S GAINS ON SETTLEMENT OF DEBTS

**Proposed Repeal — Part LIV**

Technical Notes to ITA 80–80.04, 1994 tax amendment bill (Bill C-70), February 16, 1995: The new rules for debt forgiveness are entirely contained in the Act [in subsecs. 80(5) and (6) — ed.]. As a consequence, Part LIV of the Regulations is no longer relevant, except in the cases where grandfathering applies.

**5400.** (1) Subject to section 5401, the excess referred to in paragraph 80(1)(b) of the Act, after deducting the portion thereof required to be applied as provided in paragraph 80(1)(a) of the Act, shall be applied at the time the debt or obligation is settled or extinguished, in the following order to reduce to the maximum extent possible

(a) the capital cost of depreciable property of a prescribed class or prescribed classes, as the case may be;

(b) the capital cost of depreciable property other than depreciable property of a prescribed class;

(c) the adjusted cost base at that time of capital property, other than depreciable property and personal-use property;

(d) the adjusted cost base at that time of capital property that is listed personal property; and

(e) the adjusted cost base at that time of capital property that is personal-use property, other than listed personal property.

(2) Where an amount is to be applied pursuant to subsection (1), the taxpayer may choose any particular property to make the reduction in the order specified therein.

*Definitions [Reg. 5400]*: "adjusted cost base" — ITA 54, 248(1); "amount" — ITA 248(1); "capital property" — ITA 54, 248(1); "depreciable property" — ITA 13(21), 248(1); "listed personal property", "personal-use property" — ITA 54, 248(1); "prescribed", "property", "taxpayer" — ITA 248(1).

**5401.** (1) For the purposes of paragraph 5400(1)(a), the amount to be applied to reduce the capital cost of a property shall not exceed the lesser of

(a) the amount by which

(i) the capital cost of the property

exceeds

(ii) all amounts that would have been allowed to the taxpayer in respect of the property, if it had been the only property that was included in a prescribed class, at the rate that was allowed to him in respect of property of the class in which it was included under regulations made under paragraph 20(1)(a) of the Act for the taxation years prior to the year in which the debt or obligation was settled or extinguished; and

(b) the amount by which

(i) the undepreciated capital cost of the class at the time the debt or obligation was settled or extinguished

exceeds

(ii) the amount or the aggregate of amounts, if any, that has already been determined under this subsection in respect of another property of the class at the time referred to in subparagraph (i).

(2) For the purposes of paragraph 5400(1)(b), the amount to be applied to reduce the capital cost of a property shall not exceed

(a) the amount by which the capital cost of the property

exceeds

(b) the amount that was allowed to the taxpayer by virtue of Part XVII in respect of the property before the debt or the obligation was settled or extinguished.

**Reg. S. 5401(3)** — Income Tax Regulations

(3) For the purposes of paragraphs 5400(1)(c), (d) and (e), the amount to be applied to reduce the adjusted cost base of a property shall not exceed the amount by which

(a) the aggregate of the cost to the taxpayer of the property and all amounts required by subsection 53(1) of the Act to be included in computing the adjusted cost base to him of that property

exceeds

(b) the aggregate of all amounts required by subsection 53(2) of the Act (except paragraph (c) thereof) to be deducted in computing the adjusted cost base to him of that property,

at the time the debt or obligation was settled or extinguished.

**Definitions [Reg. 5401]:** "adjusted cost base" — ITA 54, 248(1); "amount", "prescribed", "property" — ITA 248(1); "taxation year" — ITA 249; "taxpayer" — ITA 248(1); "undepreciated capital cost" — ITA 13(21), 248(1).

## PART LV — PRESCRIBED PROGRAMS AND BENEFITS

**5500. Canadian Home Insulation Program** — For the purposes of paragraphs 12(1)(u), 56(1)(s) and 212(1)(s) of the Act, the Canadian Home Insulation Program, as authorized and described in Vote 11a of *Appropriation Act No. 3, 1977–78*, as amended, Energy, Mines and Resources Vote 35, Main Estimates, 1981-82 as authorized by *Appropriation Act No. 1, 1981–82*, as amended, or the *Canadian Home Insulation Program Act*, is hereby prescribed to be a program of the Government of Canada relating to home insulation.

**Definitions [Reg. 5500]:** "Canada" — ITA 255, *Interpretation Act* 35(1); "prescribed" — ITA 248(1).

**5501. Canada Oil Substitution Program** — For the purposes of paragraphs 12(1)(u), 56(1)(s) and 212(1)(s) of the Act, the Canada Oil Substitution Program, as authorized and described in paragraph (a) or (b) of Energy, Mines and Resources Vote 45, Main Estimates, 1981-82 as authorized by *Appropriation Act No. 1, 1981–82*, as amended, or the *Oil Substitution and Conservation Act* is hereby prescribed to be a program of the Government of Canada relating to energy conversion.

**Definitions [Reg. 5501]:** "Canada" — ITA 255, *Interpretation Act* 35(1); "prescribed" — ITA 248(1).

**5502. Benefits under government assistance programs** — For the purposes of subparagraph 56(1)(a)(vi) and paragraph 153(1)(m) of the Act, the following benefits are prescribed:

(a) benefits under the *Labour Adjustment Benefits Act*;

(b) benefits under programs to provide income assistance payments, established pursuant to agreements under section 5 of the *Department of Labour Act*; and

(c) benefits under programs to provide income assistance payments, administered pursuant to agreements under section 5 of the *Department of Fisheries and Oceans Act*.

**Notes:** Reg. 5502 added by P.C. 1995-1023, June 23, 1995, effective for benefits received after October 1991 (for ITA 56(1)(a)(vi)), and for benefits paid after October 1991 (for ITA 153(1)(m)). The referenced programs include the Program for Older Worker Adjustment, the Plant Worker Adjustment Program, the Northern Cod Adjustment and Recovery Program, the Atlantic Groundfish Adjustment Program and the Atlantic Groundfish Strategy.

In *Layton*, [1995] 2 C.T.C. 2408 and *Law*, [1996] 1 C.T.C. 2252D (both decided March 14, 1995 before Reg. 5502 existed), the Tax Court of Canada ruled that payments received in 1993 were not taxable because they were not (yet) prescribed.

**Definitions [Reg. 5502]:** "prescribed" — ITA 248(1).

## PART LVI — REGISTERED RETIREMENT SAVINGS PLANS, PREMIUM REFUNDS

**5600.** Any election under subsection 61(2) of the *Income Tax Application Rules* in respect of a refund of premiums referred to in that subsection shall be made by the taxpayer on or before the day on or before which he is required to file a return of income pursuant to section 150 of the Act for the taxation year in which the refund was received.

**Definitions [Reg. 5600]:** "taxation year" — ITA 249; "taxpayer" — ITA 248(1).

## PART LVII — MEDICAL DEVICES AND EQUIPMENT

**5700.** For the purposes of paragraph 118.2(2)(m) of the Act, a device or equipment is prescribed if it is a

(a) wig made to order for individuals who have suffered abnormal hair loss owing to disease, medical treatment or accident;

(b) needle or syringe designed to be used for the purpose of giving an injection;

(c) device or equipment, including a replacement part, designed exclusively for use by an individual suffering from a severe chronic respiratory ailment or a severe chronic immune system disregulation, but not including an air conditioner, humidifier, dehumidifier, heat pump or heat or air exchanger;

(c.1) air or water filter or purifier for use by an individual who is suffering from a severe chronic respiratory ailment or a severe chronic immune system disregulation to cope with or overcome that ailment or disregulation;

(c.2) electric or sealed combustion furnace acquired to replace a furnace that is neither an electric furnace nor a sealed combustion furnace, where the replacement is necessary solely because of a severe chronic respiratory ailment or a severe chronic immune system disregulation;

(c.3) air conditioner acquired for use by an individual to cope with the individual's severe chronic ailment, disease or disorder, to the extent of the lesser of $1,000 and 50% of the amount paid for the air conditioner;

(d) device or equipment designed to pace or monitor the heart of an individual who suffers from heart disease;

(e) orthopaedic shoe or boot and an insert for a shoe or boot made to order for an individual in accordance with a prescription to overcome a physical disability of the individual;

(f) power-operated guided chair installation, for an individual, that is designed to be used solely in a stairway;

(g) mechanical device or equipment designed to be used to assist an individual to enter or leave a bathtub or shower or to get on or off a toilet;

(h) hospital bed including such attachments thereto as may have been included in a prescription therefor;

(i) device that is designed to assist an individual in walking where the individual has a mobility impairment;

(j) external breast prosthesis that is required because of a mastectomy;

(k) teletypewriter or similar device, including a telephone ringing indicator, that enables a deaf or mute individual to make and receive telephone calls;

(l) optical scanner or similar device designed to be used by a blind individual to enable him to read print;

(m) power-operated lift or transportation equipment designed exclusively for use by, or for, a disabled individual to allow the individual access to different areas of a building or to assist the individual to gain access to a vehicle or to place the individual's wheelchair in or on a vehicle;

(n) device designed exclusively to enable an individual with a mobility impairment to operate a vehicle;

(o) device or equipment, including a synthetic speech system, braille printer and large print-on-screen device, designed exclusively to be used by a blind individual in the operation of a computer;

(p) electronic speech synthesizer that enables a mute individual to communicate by use of a portable keyboard;

(q) device to decode special television signals to permit the script of a program to be visually displayed;

(q.1) a visual or vibratory signalling device, including a visual fire alarm indicator, for an individual with a hearing impairment;

(r) device designed to be attached to infants diagnosed as being prone to sudden infant death syndrome in order to sound an alarm if the infant ceases to breathe;

(s) infusion pump, including disposable peripherals, used in the treatment of diabetes or a device designed to enable a diabetic to measure the diabetic's blood sugar level;

(t) electronic or computerized environmental control system designed exclusively for the use of an individual with a severe and prolonged mobility restriction;

(u) extremity pump or elastic support hose designed exclusively to relieve swelling caused by chronic lymphedema;

(v) inductive coupling osteogenesis stimulator for treating non-union of fractures or aiding in bone fusion; and

(w) talking textbook prescribed by a medical practitioner for use by an individual with a perceptual disability, in connection with the individual's enrolment at an educational institution in Canada.

**Notes**: For a detailed discussion of the eligible expenses, see David M. Sherman, *Taxes, Health & Disabilities* (Carswell, 1995).

Some of the devices in Reg. 5700 also qualify as fully deductible business expenses even though they would otherwise be capital purchases for a business. See ITA 20(1)(qq) and (rr).

In *Brown (N.)*, [1995] 1 C.T.C. 208, the Federal Court–Trial Division ruled that Reg. 5700(i) can apply to an air conditioner needed by a person with multiple sclerosis. An appeal by the Crown to the Federal Court of Appeal was discontinued. It is unclear whether new Reg. 5700(c.3), which allows only 50% of the cost and only up to $1,000, will now limit the use of Reg. 5700(i) for this purpose.

Reg. 5700(c.1), (c.2) added by P.C. 1994-271, effective December 17, 1991. Reg. 5700(q.1) added by P.C. 1994-271, effective for 1992 and later taxation years.

Reg. 5700(c.3) added by P.C. 1999-1767, effective 1997 (this measure was proposed in the February 1997 federal budget).

Reg. 5700(w) added by P.C. 2000-1770, effective for 1999 and later taxation years. (This measure was proposed in the February 1999 federal budget.)

**Definitions [Reg. 5700]**: "Canada" — ITA 255, *Interpretation Act* 35(1); "individual" — ITA 248(1); "medical practitioner" — ITA 118.4(2); "prescribed" — ITA 248(1).

**Interpretation Bulletins**: IT-519R2: Medical expense and disability tax credits.

# PART LVIII — RETENTION OF BOOKS AND RECORDS

**5800. (1)** For the purposes of paragraph 230(4)(a) of the Act, the required retention periods for records and books of account of a person are prescribed as follows:

(a) in respect of

(i) any record of the minutes of meetings of the directors of a corporation,

(ii) any record of the minutes of meetings of the shareholders of a corporation,

(iii) any record of a corporation containing details with respect to the ownership of the shares of the capital stock of the corporation and any transfers thereof,

(iv) the general ledger or other book of final entry containing the summaries of the year-to-year transactions of a corporation, and

(v) any special contracts or agreements necessary to an understanding of the entries in the general ledger or other book of final entry referred to in subparagraph (iv),

the period ending on the day that is two years after the day that the corporation is dissolved;

(b) in respect of all records and books of account that are not described in paragraph (a) of a corporation that is dissolved and in respect of the vouchers and accounts necessary to verify the information in such records and books of account, the period ending on the day that is two years after the day that the corporation is dissolved;

(c) in respect of

(i) the general ledger or other book of final entry containing the summaries of the year-to-year transactions of a business of a person (other than a corporation), and

(ii) any special contracts or agreements necessary to an understanding of the entries in the general ledger or other book of final entry referred to in subparagraph (i),

the period ending on the day that is six years after the last day of the taxation year of the person in which the business ceased;

(d) in respect of

(i) any record of the minutes of meetings of the executive of a registered charity or registered Canadian amateur athletic association,

(ii) any record of the minutes of meetings of the members of a registered charity or registered Canadian amateur athletic association,

(iii) all documents and by-laws governing a registered charity or registered Canadian amateur athletic association, and

(iv) all records of any donations received by a registered charity that were subject to a direction by the donor that the property given be held by the charity for a period of not less than 10 years,

the period ending on the day that is two years after the date on which the registration of the registered charity or the registered Canadian amateur athletic association under the Act is revoked;

(e) in respect of all records and books of account that are not described in paragraph (d) and that relate to a registered charity or registered Canadian amateur athletic association whose registration under the Act is revoked, and in respect of the vouchers and accounts necessary to verify the information in such records and books of account, the period ending on the day that is two years after the date on which the registration of the registered charity or the registered Canadian amateur athletic association under the Act is revoked;

(f) in respect of duplicates of receipts for donations (other than donations referred to in subparagraph (d)(iv)) that are received by a registered charity or registered Canadian amateur athletic association and are required to be kept by that charity or association pursuant to subsection 230(2) of the Act, the period ending on the day that is two years from the end of the last calendar year to which the receipts relate; and

(g) notwithstanding paragraphs (c) to (f), in respect of all records, books of account, vouchers and accounts of a deceased taxpayer or a trust in respect of which a clearance certificate is issued pursuant to subsection 159(2) of the Act with respect to the distribution of all the property of such deceased taxpayer or trust, the period ending on the day that the clearance certificate is issued.

(2) For the purposes of subsection 230.1(3) of the Act, with respect to the application of paragraph 230(4)(a) of the Act, the required retention period for records and books of account that are required to be kept pursuant to section 230.1 of the Act is prescribed to be the period ending on the day that is two years after the end of the last calendar year to which the records or books of account relate.

**Definitions [Reg. 5800]:** "business" — ITA 248(1); "corporation" — ITA 248(1), *Interpretation Act* 35(1); "person", "prescribed", "property", "record", "registered Canadian amateur athletic association", "registered charity", "share", "shareholder" — ITA 248(1); "taxation year" — ITA 249; "taxpayer" — ITA 248(1); "trust" — ITA 104(1), 248(1), (3).

**Information Circulars [Reg. 5800]:** 78-10R3: Books and records retention/destruction.

# PART LIX — FOREIGN AFFILIATES

**5900. Dividends out of exempt, taxable and pre-acquisition surplus** — (1) Where at any time a corporation resident in Canada or a foreign affiliate of the corporation receives a dividend on a share of any class of the capital stock of a foreign affiliate of the corporation,

(a) for the purposes of this Part and paragraph 113(1)(a) of the Act, the portion of the dividend paid out of the exempt surplus of the affiliate is prescribed to be that proportion of the dividend received that

(i) such portion of the whole dividend paid by the affiliate on the shares of that class at that time as was deemed by section 5901 to have been paid out of the affiliate's exempt surplus in respect of the corporation

is of

(ii) the whole dividend paid by the affiliate on the shares of that class at that time;

(b) for the purposes of this Part and subsection 91(5) and paragraphs 113(1)(b) and (c) of the Act, the portion of the dividend paid out of the taxable surplus of the affiliate is prescribed to be that portion of the dividend received that

(i) such portion of the whole dividend paid by the affiliate on the shares of that class at that time as was deemed by section 5901 to have been paid out of the affiliate's taxable surplus in respect of the corporation

is of

(ii) the whole dividend paid by the affiliate on the shares of that class at that time;

(c) for the purposes of this Part and paragraph 113(1)(d) of the Act, the portion of the dividend paid out of the pre-acquisition surplus of the affiliate is prescribed to be that proportion of the dividend received that

(i) such portion of the whole dividend paid by the affiliate on the shares of that class at that time as was deemed by section 5901 to have been paid out of the affiliate's pre-acquisition surplus in respect of the corporation

is of

(ii) the whole dividend paid by the affiliate on the shares of that class at that time; and

(d) for the purposes of this Part and paragraph 113(1)(b) of the Act, the foreign tax applicable to the portion of the dividend prescribed to have been paid out of the taxable surplus of the affiliate is prescribed to be that proportion of the underlying foreign tax applicable, in respect of the corporation, to the whole dividend paid by the affiliate on the shares of that class at that time that

(i) the amount of the dividend received by the corporation or the affiliate, as the case may be, on that share at that time

is of

(ii) the whole dividend paid by the affiliate on the shares of that class at that time.

(2) Notwithstanding paragraphs (1)(a) and (b), where at any time a foreign affiliate of a corporation resident in Canada pays a dividend on a share of a class of its capital stock (other than a share in respect of which an election is made under subsection 93(1) of the Act) to the corporation, the corporation may, in its return of income under Part I of the Act for its taxation year in which the dividend was received by it, designate an amount not exceeding the portion of the dividend received that would, but for this subsection, be prescribed to have been paid out of the affiliate's exempt surplus in respect of the corporation and that amount

### Proposed Amendment — Reg. 5900(2) opening words

(2) Notwithstanding paragraphs (1)(a) and (b), where at any time a foreign affiliate of a corporation resident in Canada pays a dividend on a share of a class of its capital stock (other than a dividend referred to in subsection 93(1) or (1.2) of the Act) to the corporation, the corporation may, in its return of income under Part I of the Act for its taxation year in which the dividend was received by it, designate an amount not exceeding the portion of the dividend received that would, but for this subsection, be prescribed to have been paid out of the affiliate's exempt surplus in respect of the corporation and that amount

**Application**: The November 30, 1999 draft regulations (foreign affiliates — partnerships), subsec. 1(1), will amend the opening words of subsec. 5900(2) to read as above, applicable to dividends received after November 30, 1999.

**Technical Notes**: Subsection 5900(2) allows a corporation resident in Canada to elect to have a dividend paid by a foreign affiliate of the corporation to be treated as having been paid out of the taxable surplus rather than out of the exempt surplus of the affiliate. This election is not available where the corporation has elected under subsection 93(1) of the Act to treat proceeds of disposition of a share of a foreign affiliate as a dividend. The amendment ensures that the election in subsection 5900(2) will not apply where the corporation has elected under new subsection 93(1.2) of the Act to treat all or a portion of its gain from a partnership arising on the disposition of a share of a foreign affiliate by the partnership as a dividend.

(a) is prescribed to have been paid out of the affiliate's taxable surplus in respect of the corporation and not to have been paid out of that exempt surplus; and

(b) for the purposes of paragraph (1)(d) and the definitions "underlying foreign tax" and "underlying foreign tax applicable" in subsection 5907(1) is deemed to have been paid by the affiliate to the corporation as a separate whole dividend on the shares of that class of the capital stock immediately after that time, and that whole dividend is deemed to have been paid out of the affiliate's taxable surplus in respect of the corporation.

**Notes**: Reg. 5900(2)(a) and (b) amended by P.C. 1997-1670, effective on the same basis as the amendment to Reg. 5903(1). The amendments were non-substantive, updating references to definitions in Reg. 5907(1), and changing "shall be" prescribed/deemed to "is" prescribed/deemed.

(3) For the purposes of subsection 91(5) of the Act, where at any time an individual resident in Canada

receives a dividend on a share of any class of the capital stock of a foreign affiliate of that individual, the affiliate shall be deemed to have an amount of taxable surplus in respect of the individual and the portion of the dividend paid out of the taxable surplus of the affiliate in respect of the individual is prescribed to be an amount equal to the dividend received.

### Proposed Amendment — Reg. 5900(3)

(3) For the purpose of subsection 91(5) of the Act, where at any time a person (other than a corporation) resident in Canada receives a dividend on a share of any class of the capital stock of a foreign affiliate of that person, the affiliate is deemed to have an amount of taxable surplus in respect of the person and the portion of the dividend paid out of the taxable surplus of the affiliate in respect of the person is prescribed to be an amount equal to the dividend received.

**Application**: The November 30, 1999 draft regulations (foreign affiliates — partnerships), subsec. 1(2), will amend subsec. 5900(3) to read as above, applicable to dividends received after November 30, 1999.

**Technical Notes**: Subsection 5900(3) applies where an individual resident in Canada receives a dividend from a foreign affiliate. For the purpose of subsection 91(5) of the Act, subsection 5900(3) deems the individual to have received all dividends out of the taxable surplus of the affiliate. Subsection 91(5) of the Act permits deductions in respect of dividends paid out of the taxable surplus of an affiliate to the extent that that surplus is represented by foreign accrual property income of the affiliate that has been taxed in the hands of the dividend recipient.

The amendment to subsection 5900(3) replaces the word "individual" with the phrase "person (other than a corporation)". This amendment clarifies that, for the purpose of subsection 91(5), where a partnership is deemed to be a person under section 96 of the Act the partnership is deemed to have received all dividends out of taxable surplus.

**Definitions [Reg. 5900]**: "amount" — ITA 248(1), Reg. 5907(7); "corporation" — ITA 248(1), *Interpretation Act* 35(1); "dividend" — ITA 248(1); "exempt surplus" — Reg. 5902(1)–(3), 5907(1); "foreign affiliate" — Reg. 5907(3); "foreign tax applicable" — Reg. 5900(1)(d); "individual", "prescribed" — ITA 248(1); "pre-acquisition surplus" — Reg. 5900(1)(c); "resident in Canada" — ITA 250; "share" — ITA 248(1); "taxable surplus" — Reg. 5902(1)–(3), 5907(1); "taxation year" — ITA 249; "underlying foreign tax applicable", "whole dividend" — Reg. 5907(1).

**Interpretation Bulletins**: IT-392: Meaning of term "share".

### 5901. Order of surplus distributions — (1)
Where at any time in its taxation year a foreign affiliate of a corporation resident in Canada has paid a whole dividend on the shares of any class of its capital stock, for the purposes of this Part

(a) the portion of the whole dividend deemed to have been paid out of the affiliate's exempt surplus in respect of the corporation at that time is an amount equal to the lesser of

(i) the amount of the whole dividend, and

(ii) the amount by which that exempt surplus exceeds the affiliate's taxable deficit in respect of the corporation at that time;

(b) the portion of the whole dividend deemed to have been paid out of the affiliate's taxable surplus in respect of the corporation at that time is an amount equal to the lesser of

(i) the amount, if any, by which the amount of the whole dividend exceeds the portion determined under paragraph (a), and

(ii) the amount by which that taxable surplus exceeds the affiliate's exempt deficit in respect of the corporation at that time; and

(c) the portion of the whole dividend deemed to have been paid out of the affiliate's pre-acquisition surplus in respect of the corporation at that time is the amount by which the whole dividend exceeds the aggregate of the portions determined under paragraphs (a) and (b).

(2) Notwithstanding subsection (1), where a foreign affiliate of a corporation resident in Canada pays a whole dividend (other than a whole dividend referred to in subsection 5902(1)) at any particular time in its taxation year that is more than 90 days after the commencement of that year or at any particular time in its 1972 taxation year that is before January 1, 1972, the portion of the whole dividend that would, but for this subsection, be deemed to have been paid out of the affiliate's pre-acquisition surplus in respect of the corporation is deemed to have been paid out of the exempt surplus and taxable surplus of the affiliate in respect of the corporation to the extent that it would have been deemed to have been so paid if, immediately after the end of that year, that portion were paid as a separate whole dividend before any whole dividend paid after the particular time and after any whole dividend paid before the particular time by the affiliate, and for the purposes of determining the exempt deficit, exempt surplus, taxable deficit, taxable surplus and underlying foreign tax of the affiliate in respect of the corporation at any time, that portion is deemed to have been paid as a separate whole dividend immediately following the end of the year and not to have been paid at the particular time.

**Notes**: Reg. 5901(2) amended by P.C. 1997-1670, effective on the same basis as the amendment to Reg. 5903(1). The amendments were non-substantive, simply modernizing the wording and updating references to Reg. 5907(1). The old version read:

(2) Notwithstanding subsection (1), where a foreign affiliate of a corporation resident in Canada pays a whole dividend (other than a whole dividend referred to in subsection 5902(1)) at any particular time in its taxation year that is more than 90 days after the commencement of that year or at any particular time in its 1972 taxation year that is prior to January 1, 1972, the portion thereof that would, but for this subsection, be deemed to have been paid out of the affiliate's pre-acquisition surplus in respect of the corporation shall be deemed to have been paid out of the exempt surplus and taxable surplus of the affiliate in respect of the corporation to the extent that it would have been deemed to have been so paid

if, immediately following the end of that year, that portion were paid as a separate whole dividend before any whole dividend paid after the particular time and after any whole dividend paid before the particular time by the affiliate and for the purposes of determining the amounts under paragraphs 5907(1)(d), (k) and (l) at any time that portion shall be deemed to have been paid as a separate whole dividend immediately following the end of the year and not to have been paid at the particular time.

(3) Notwithstanding subsections (1) and (2), for the purposes of the definitions "exempt deficit", "exempt surplus", "taxable deficit" and "taxable surplus" in subsection 5907(1), any amount designated pursuant to subsection 5900(2) in respect of a dividend paid by a foreign affiliate of a corporation resident in Canada increases the portion of the whole dividend deemed to have been paid out of the affiliate's taxable surplus in respect of the corporation and decrease the portion of the whole dividend deemed to have been paid out of the affiliate's exempt surplus in respect of the corporation.

**Notes**: Reg. 5901(3) amended by P.C. 1997-1670, effective on the same basis as the amendment to Reg. 5903(1). The amendments were non-substantive, simply modernizing the wording and updating references to Reg. 5907(1).

**Definitions [Reg. 5901]**: "amount" — ITA 248(1), Reg. 5907(7); "commencement" — *Interpretation Act* 35(1); "corporation" — ITA 248(1), *Interpretation Act* 35(1); "dividend" — ITA 248(1); "exempt deficit", "exempt surplus" — Reg. 5902(1)–(3), 5907(1); "foreign affiliate" — Reg. 5907(3); "pre-acquisition surplus" — Reg. 5900(1)(c); "resident in Canada" — ITA 250; "share" — ITA 248(1); "taxable deficit", "taxable surplus" — Reg. 5902(1)–(3), 5907(1); "taxation year" — ITA 249; "underlying foreign tax" — Reg. 5902(1)–(3), 5907(1); "whole dividend" — Reg. 5907(1).

**5902. Election in respect of capital gains —** (1) Where at any time a dividend is, by virtue of an election made under subsection 93(1) of the Act in respect of a disposition, deemed to have been received on one or more shares of a class of the capital stock of a particular foreign affiliate of a corporation resident in Canada, the following rules apply:

**Proposed Amendment — Reg. 5902(1) opening words**

**(1) Election in respect of capital gains —** Where at any time a dividend is, because of an election made under subsection 93(1) or (1.2) of the Act in respect of a disposition, deemed to have been received on one or more shares of a class of the capital stock of a particular foreign affiliate of a corporation resident in Canada, the following rules apply:

**Application**: The November 30, 1999 draft regulations (foreign affiliates — partnerships), subsec. 2(1), will amend the opening words of subsec. 5902(1) to read as above, applicable to dispositions that occur after November 30, 1999.

**Technical Notes**: Section 5902 applies where a corporation elects to treat proceeds of disposition of a share of a foreign affiliate as a dividend under subsection 93(1) of the Act. Subsection 5902(1) computes a foreign affiliate's surplus accounts and the amount of a whole dividend used in applying subsection 5901(1) for the purposes of subsection 5900(1) of the Regulations. The amendment to subsection 5902(1) ensures that the subsection will also apply where the corporation resident in Canada has elected under new subsection 93(1.2) of the Act to treat a gain from a partnership arising on the disposition of a share of a foreign affiliate of the corporation by the partnership as a dividend.

(a) determine the amounts that would be the particular affiliate's exempt surplus or exempt deficit, taxable surplus or taxable deficit, underlying foreign tax and net surplus in respect of the corporation at that time if

(i) each other foreign affiliate of the corporation in which the affiliate had an equity percentage had immediately before that time paid a dividend equal to its net surplus in respect of the corporation immediately before the dividend was paid, and

(ii) any dividend referred to in subparagraph (i) that any other foreign affiliate would have received had been received by it immediately before any such dividend that it would have paid;

(b) determine the amount that would have been received on the shares (of that class) in respect of which an election is made, if the particular affiliate had at that time paid dividends the aggregate of which on all shares of its capital stock was equal to the amount of its net surplus referred to in paragraph (a); and

(c) for the purposes only of subsection 5900(1), in applying the provisions of subsection 5901(1)

(i) the particular affiliate's exempt surplus or exempt deficit, taxable surplus or taxable deficit and underlying foreign tax in respect of the corporation shall be deemed to be the respective amounts thereof referred to in paragraph (a), and

(ii) the particular affiliate shall be deemed to have paid a whole dividend at that time on the shares of that class of its capital stock in an amount equal to the product obtained when the aggregate of amounts so deemed by subsection 93(1) of the Act to have been received as dividends on shares of that class is multiplied by the greater of

**Proposed Amendment — Reg. 5902(1)(c)(ii) opening words**

(ii) the particular affiliate is deemed to have paid a whole dividend at that time on the shares of that class of its capital stock in an amount equal to the product obtained when the total of amounts so deemed by subsection 93(1) or (1.2) of the Act to have been received as dividends on shares of that class is multiplied by the greater of

**Application**: The November 30, 1999 draft regulations (foreign affiliates — partnerships), subsec. 2(2), will amend the opening words of subpara. 5902(1)(c)(ii) to read as above, applicable to dispositions that occur after November 30, 1999.

**Technical Notes**: See under Reg. 5902(1) opening words.

(A) one, and

(B) the proportion that the amount of the particular affiliate's net surplus determined under paragraph (a) is of the amount determined under paragraph (b), except that where the amount determined under paragraph (b) is less than one, the amount determined under paragraph (b) is deemed for the purpose of this clause to be one.

**Notes**: Reg. 5902(1)(c)(ii)(B) amended by P.C. 1997-1670, effective for 1996 and later taxation years, to add everything beginning "except that..."

(2) For the purposes of paragraphs (1)(a) and (b),

(a) in determining the exempt surplus or exempt deficit, the taxable surplus or taxable deficit, the underlying foreign tax and the net surplus of a particular foreign affiliate of a taxpayer resident in Canada in which any other foreign affiliate of the taxpayer has an equity percentage, no amount shall be included in respect of any distribution that would be received by the particular affiliate from such other affiliate; and

(b) if any foreign affiliate of a corporation resident in Canada has issued shares of more than one class of its capital stock, the amount that would be paid as a dividend on the shares of any class is such portion of its exempt surplus or exempt deficit and its taxable surplus (including underlying foreign tax applicable) or taxable deficit (and thus net surplus) as, in the circumstances, it might reasonably be expected to have paid on all the shares of that class.

(3) Where an election under subsection 93(1) of the Act is made by a corporation resident in Canada in respect of the disposition of a share of the capital stock of a foreign affiliate of the corporation, no adjustment shall be made to the affiliate's exempt surplus, exempt deficit, taxable surplus, taxable deficit or underlying foreign tax in respect of the corporation as a consequence of the election except as provided in subsections 5905(2), (5) and (8).

### Proposed Amendment — Reg. 5902(3)

(3) Where an election under subsection 93(1) or (1.2) of the Act is made by a corporation resident in Canada in respect of the disposition of a share of the capital stock of a foreign affiliate of the corporation, no adjustment shall be made to the affiliate's exempt surplus, exempt deficit, taxable surplus, taxable deficit or underlying foreign tax in respect of the corporation as a consequence of the election except as provided in subsections 5905(2), (5) and (8).

**Application**: The November 30, 1999 draft regulations (foreign affiliates — partnerships), subsec. 2(3), will amend subsec. 5902(3) to read as above, applicable to dispositions that occur after November 30, 1999.

**Technical Notes**: Subsection 5902(3) indicates that where an election is made under subsection 93(1) of the Act, no adjustment shall be made to the affiliate's exempt surplus, exempt deficit, taxable surplus, taxable deficit or underlying foreign tax in respect of the corporation as a consequence of the election except as provided in subsections 5905(2), (5) and (8). The amendment to subsection 5902(3) extends the application of the provision to elections made under new subsection 93(1.2) of the Act.

(4) [Revoked]

(5) Any election under subsection 93(1) of the Act by a corporation resident in Canada in respect of any share of the capital stock of a foreign affiliate of the corporation disposed of by it or by another foreign affiliate of the corporation shall be made by filing the prescribed form with the Minister on or before the day that is the later of

(a) December 31, 1989; and

(b) where the election is made

(i) in respect of a share disposed of by the corporation, the day on or before which the corporation's return of income for its taxation year in which the disposition was made is required to be filed pursuant to subsection 150(1) of the Act, or

(ii) in respect of a share disposed of by another foreign affiliate of the corporation, the day on or before which the corporation's return of income for its taxation year, in which the taxation year of the foreign affiliate in which the disposition was made ends, is required to be filed pursuant to subsection 150(1) of the Act,

as the case may be.

### Proposed Amendment — Reg. 5902(5)

(5) Any election under subsection 93(1) or (1.2) of the Act by a corporation resident in Canada in respect of any share of the capital stock of a foreign affiliate of the corporation disposed of by it, by a foreign affiliate of the corporation or by a partnership shall be made by filing the prescribed form with the Minister on or before the day that is,

(a) where the election is made in respect of a share disposed of by the corporation, the corporation's filing-due date for its taxation year in which the disposition was made;

(b) where the election is made in respect of a share disposed of by a foreign affiliate of the corporation, the corporation's filing-due date for its taxation year in which the taxation year of the foreign affiliate in which the disposition was made ends; and

(c) where the election is made in respect of a share disposed of by a partnership, and

(i) the disposing corporation referred to in subsection 93(1.2) of the Act is the corporation, the corporation's filing-due date for its

Part LIX — Foreign Affiliates    Reg. S. 5903(1)

taxation year in which the fiscal period of the partnership in which the disposition was made ends, or

(ii) the disposing corporation referred to in subsection 93(1.2) of the Act is a foreign affiliate of the corporation, the corporation's filing-due date for its taxation year in which the taxation year of the foreign affiliate which includes the last day of the fiscal period of the partnership in which the disposition was made ends.

**Application**: The November 30, 1999 draft regulations (foreign affiliates — partnerships), subsec. 2(4), will amend subsec. 5902(5) to read as above, applicable to dispositions that occur after November 30, 1999.

**Technical Notes**: Subsection 5902(5) provides that any election under subsection 93(1) of the Act must be made by filing the prescribed form by the corporation's filing-due date for the relevant year. Where the disposition is made by the corporation, the relevant year is the taxation year of the corporation in which the disposition was made. Where the disposition is made by a foreign affiliate of the corporation, the relevant year is the taxation year of the corporation in which the taxation year of the foreign affiliate in which the disposition was made ends.

The amendments to subsection 5902(5) extend its application to include elections made under new subsection 93(1.2) of the Act. Where the disposition is made by a partnership, the relevant year depends on whether the "disposing corporation" in subsection 93(1.2) of the Act is the corporation or a foreign affiliate of the corporation. Where the disposing corporation is the corporation, the relevant year is the taxation year of the corporation in which the fiscal period of the partnership in which the disposition was made ends. Where the disposing corporation is a foreign affiliate of the corporation, the relevant year is the taxation year of the corporation in which the taxation year of the affiliate which includes the last day of the fiscal period of the partnership in which the disposition was made ends.

(6) Where at any time a corporation resident in Canada is deemed by virtue of subsection 93(1.1) of the Act to have made an election under subsection 93(1) of the Act in respect of a share of the capital stock of a particular foreign affiliate of the corporation disposed of by another foreign affiliate of the corporation, the amount deemed to have been designated in the election is hereby prescribed to be the lesser of

(a) the capital gain, if any, otherwise determined in respect of the disposition of the share; and

(b) the amount that could reasonably be expected to have been received in respect of the share if the particular affiliate had at that time paid dividends the aggregate of which on all shares of its capital stock was equal to the amount determined under paragraph 5902 (1)(a) to be its net surplus in respect of the corporation for the purposes of the election.

**Proposed Amendment — Reg. 5902(6)**

(6) Where at any time a corporation resident in Canada is deemed by of subsection 93(1.1) or (1.3)

of the Act to have made an election under subsection 93(1) or (1.2) of the Act in respect of a share of the capital stock of a particular foreign affiliate of the corporation disposed of by a foreign affiliate of the corporation or by a partnership, the amount deemed to have been designated in the election is prescribed to be the lesser of

(a) the capital gain (or where subsection 93(1.2) of the Act applies, the taxable capital gain), if any, otherwise determined in respect of the disposition of the share; and

(b) the amount (or where subsection 93(1.2) of the Act applies, 3/4 of the amount) that could reasonably be expected to have been received in respect of the share if the particular affiliate had at that time paid dividends the aggregate of which on all shares of its capital stock was equal to the amount determined under paragraph 5902 1(a) to be its net surplus in respect of the corporation for the purposes of the election.

**Application**: The November 30, 1999 draft regulations (foreign affiliates — partnerships), subsec. 2(5), will amend subsec. 5902(6) to read as above, applicable to dispositions that occur after November 30, 1999.

**Technical Notes**: Subsection 5902(6) applies where subsection 93(1.1) of the Act deems a corporation to have made an election under subsection 93(1) to treat proceeds of disposition of a share of a foreign affiliate as a dividend. Subsection 5902(6) deems the amount designated in the deemed election to be the lesser of the capital gain otherwise determined in respect of the disposition of the share and the amount that could reasonably be expected to have been received on the share if the affiliate had paid its net surplus in respect of the corporation as a dividend.

Subsection 5902(6) is amended to ensure that the subsection will apply where new subsection 93(1.3) of the Act deems a corporation resident in Canada to have made an election under proposed subsection 93(1.2) of the Act in respect of a taxable capital gain from a deemed disposition of a share of a foreign affiliate of the corporation disposed of by a partnership of which another foreign affiliate of the corporation is a member.

**Definitions [Reg. 5902]**: "amount" — ITA 248(1), Reg. 5907(7); "capital gain" — ITA 39(1), 248(1); "corporation" — ITA 248(1), *Interpretation Act* 35(1); "disposed" — ITA 248(1)"disposition"; "disposition" — ITA 248(1); "dividend" — ITA 248(1); "exempt deficit", "exempt surplus" — Reg. 5902(1)–(3), 5907(1); "foreign affiliate" — Reg. 5907(3); "Minister" — ITA 248(1); "net surplus" — Reg. 5902(1)–(3), 5907(1); "prescribed" — ITA 248(1); "resident in Canada" — ITA 250; "share" — ITA 248(1); "taxable deficit", "taxable surplus" — Reg. 5902(1)–(3), 5907(1); "taxation year" — ITA 249; "taxpayer" — ITA 248(1); "underlying foreign tax" — Reg. 5902(1)–(3), 5907(1); "underlying foreign tax applicable", "whole dividend" — Reg. 5907(1).

**Forms**: T2107: Election for a share disposition in a foreign affiliate.

**5903. Deductible loss** — (1) For the purpose of the description of F in the definition "foreign accrual property income" in subsection 95(1) of the Act, the amount prescribed to be the deductible loss of a particular foreign affiliate of a taxpayer for a taxation year and the five immediately preceding taxation years (each of which preceding taxation years is referred to in this subsection as a "preceding year") is the amount, if any, by which

(a) the total of all amounts each of which is the amount, if any, determined in respect of the particular affiliate in respect of a preceding year during which it was a controlled foreign affiliate of the taxpayer or of a person described in any of subparagraphs 95(2)(f)(iv) to (vii) of the Act, by which

(i) the total of the amounts determined for D and E in the definition "foreign accrual property income" in subsection 95(1) of the Act in respect of the particular affiliate for the preceding year

exceeds

(ii) the total of the amounts determined for A, B and C in the definition "foreign accrual property income" in subsection 95(1) of the Act in respect of the particular affiliate for the preceding year

exceeds the total of

(b) the total of all amounts each of which is an amount determined in respect of the particular affiliate in respect of a preceding year during which it was a controlled foreign affiliate of the taxpayer or of a person described in any of subparagraphs 95(2)(f)(iv) to (vii) of the Act and equal to the lesser of

(i) the amount that would be determined for F in the definition "foreign accrual property income" in subsection 95(1) of the Act in respect of the particular affiliate for the preceding year if that amount did not take into account any amount determined for any of A, B, C, D or E in the definition "foreign accrual property income" in subsection 95(1) of the Act in respect of the particular affiliate for any taxation year that is not a preceding taxation year, and

(ii) the amount that would be the foreign accrual property income of the particular affiliate for the preceding year if the formula in the definition "foreign accrual property income" in subsection 95(1) of the Act were read without reference to the variable F; and

(c) where a payment has been received by the particular foreign affiliate and the payment can reasonably be considered to relate to a payment described in subsection 5907(1.3) made by another foreign affiliate of the taxpayer in respect of a loss, or any portion of a loss, of the particular affiliate described in the description of D or E of the definition "foreign accrual property income" in subsection 95(1) of the Act in respect of any preceding year of the particular affiliate, the amount of that loss or portion.

**Proposed Amendment — Reg. 5903(1)**
See at end of Reg. 5903.

**Related Provisions**: ITA 152(6.1) — Reassessment to apply FAPI loss carryback.

**Notes**: Reg. 5903(1) amended by P.C. 1997-1670, effective for taxation years of a foreign affiliate that begin after 1994, except that the amendment applies to taxation years of a foreign affiliate that end after 1994 where there has been a change in the foreign affiliate's taxation year in 1994 after February 22, 1994, unless

(i) the foreign affiliate had requested that change in taxation year in writing before February 22, 1994 from the income tax authority of the country in which is was resident and subject to income taxation, or

(ii) the first taxation year of the foreign affiliate that began after 1994 began at a time in 1995 that is earlier than the time when it would have begun had there not been the change in taxation year.

For earlier years, read:

(1) For the purpose of subparagraph 95(1)(b)(v) [95(1)"foreign accrual property income"F] of the Act, the amount prescribed to be the deductible loss of a foreign affiliate of a taxpayer for a taxation year and the five immediately preceding taxation years is the amount, if any, by which the aggregate of

(a) the aggregate of all amounts each of which is the amount, if any, for each of the five immediately preceding taxation years of the affiliate during which it was a foreign affiliate of the taxpayer or of a person described in any of subparagraphs 95(2)(f)(iv) to (vii) of the Act, by which

(i) the aggregate of the amounts determined under subparagraphs 95(1)(b)(iii) and (iv) [95(1)"foreign accrual property income"D and E] of the Act in respect of the affiliate for that preceding year

exceeds

(ii) the aggregate of the amounts determined under subparagraphs 95(1)(b)(i) and (ii) [95(1)"foreign accrual property income"A and B] of the Act in respect of the affiliate for that preceding year, and

(b) the amount, if any, by which the aggregate of

(i) each amount determined under clause 5907(1)(c)(ii)(A) and subparagraphs 5907(1)(c)(iii) and (iv) in respect of an exempt loss of the affiliate for those years, and

(ii) each amount determined under clause 5907(1)(j)(ii)(A) in respect of a taxable loss of the affiliate for those years but not including any amount included in the affiliate's exempt loss for those years

exceeds the aggregate of

(iii) each amount determined under subparagraphs 5907(1)(b)(ii), (iii), (iv) and (v) in respect of the exempt earnings of the affiliate for those years less such portion of the income or profits tax payable to the government of a country for any of those years by the affiliate as may reasonably be regarded as payable in respect of an amount referred to in subparagraph 5907(1)(b)(iii) or clause (1)(b)(iv)(B), and

(iv) each amount determined under clauses 5907(1)(i)(ii)(A) and (C) in respect of the taxable earnings of the affiliate for those years but not including any amount included in the affiliate's exempt earnings for those years

exceeds the aggregate of

(c) the aggregate of all amounts each of which is an amount deducted by virtue of subparagraph 95(1)(b)(v)

[95(1)"foreign accrual property income"F] of the Act by the taxpayer or a person described in any of subparagraphs 95(2)(f)(iv) to (vii) of the Act in respect of any of the five immediately preceding taxation years of the affiliate to the extent that such amount relates to a loss for any of those years and assuming that no amount is deductible under that subparagraph for any year until the maximum amount for preceding years has been deducted; and

(d) where a payment has been received by the foreign affiliate that may reasonably be considered to relate to a payment described in subsection 5907(1.3) made by another foreign affiliate of the taxpayer in respect of a loss, or any portion thereof, included in computing the amount referred to in paragraph (a) or (b) in respect of the affiliate, the amount of such loss or portion thereof.

The amendments to Reg. 5903(1) and (2) ensure that losses will be included in a deductible loss of a foreign affiliate only where the affiliate is a controlled foreign affiliate of the taxpayer during the year the loss was incurred. As well, they provide that active business losses will not form part of a deductible loss of a foreign affiliate and will therefore no longer be available to reduce FAPI.

(2) For the purpose of subsection 5903(1), each amount referred to in paragraph 5903(1)(c) in respect of a controlled foreign affiliate of a taxpayer resident in Canada that is not otherwise determined in Canadian currency shall be converted to Canadian currency at the rate of exchange prevailing on the last day of the affiliate's taxation year in respect of which the amount determined under subsection 5903(1) is being used to determine the foreign affiliate's foreign accrual property income as defined in subsection 95(1) of the Act.

**Proposed Amendment — Reg. 5903(2)**

See at end of Reg. 5903.

**Notes**: Reg. 5903(2) amended by P.C. 1997-1670, effective on the same basis as the amendment to Reg. 5903(1). For earlier years, read:

(2) For the purposes of subsection (1), each amount referred to in paragraph (1)(b) or (d) in respect of a controlled foreign affiliate of a taxpayer resident in Canada that is not otherwise determined in Canadian currency shall be converted to Canadian currency at the rate of exchange prevailing on the last day of the affiliate's taxation year referred to in paragraph 95(1)(b) [95(1)"foreign accrual property income"] of the Act.

See Notes to Reg. 5903(1).

**Interpretation Bulletins**: IT-95R: Foreign exchange gains and losses.

**Information Circulars**: 77-9R: Books, records and other requirements for taxpayers having foreign affiliates.

(3) Where

(a) there has been a foreign merger (within the meaning assigned by subsection 87(8.1) of the Act) of two or more foreign affiliates of a taxpayer resident in Canada in respect of each of which the taxpayer's surplus entitlement percentage was not less than 90 per cent immediately before the merger (in this subsection referred to as "predecessor affiliates") to form a new foreign affiliate in respect of which the taxpayer's surplus entitlement percentage immediately after the merger was not less than 90 per cent (in this subsection referred to as the "successor affiliate"), or

(b) there has been a dissolution of a foreign affiliate (in this subsection referred to as the "predecessor affiliate") of a taxpayer resident in Canada and on the dissolution property of the predecessor affiliate, the fair market value of which was not less than 90 per cent of the fair market value of all property of the predecessor affiliate immediately before the dissolution, was distributed to another foreign affiliate (in this subsection referred to as the "successor affiliate") of the taxpayer,

the successor affiliate shall, in respect of such part of the amount determined under subsection 5903(1) to be the deductible loss of a predecessor affiliate at the time of the foreign merger or dissolution as may reasonably be considered to have arisen while the taxpayer, a person or persons referred to in any of subparagraphs 95(2)(f)(iv) to (vii) of the Act, or the taxpayer together with such a person or persons, had a surplus entitlement percentage in respect of such predecessor affiliate that was not less than 90 per cent, be considered to be the same corporation as, and a continuation of, such predecessor affiliate.

**Proposed Amendment — Reg. 5903**

**5903. (1)** For the purpose of the description of F in the definition "foreign accrual property income" in subsection 95(1) of the Act, the deductible loss of a foreign affiliate of a taxpayer for a particular taxation year of the affiliate is the amount claimed by the taxpayer not exceeding the foreign accrual property loss of the affiliate for the seven taxation years of the affiliate preceding and the three taxation years of the affiliate following the particular year.

**(2)** In determining the deductible loss of a foreign affiliate of a taxpayer for a particular taxation year of the affiliate

(a) the amount claimed under subsection (1) in respect of a foreign accrual property loss of the affiliate for a taxation year of the affiliate shall not exceed the amount by which that loss exceeds the total of all amounts each of which was an amount claimed by any taxpayer in respect of that loss in computing the deductible loss of the affiliate for taxation years of the affiliate before the particular year; and

(b) no amount may be claimed in respect of a foreign accrual property loss of a foreign affiliate for a taxation year of the affiliate until the foreign accrual property losses of the affiliate for preceding taxation years have been fully claimed.

**(3)** For the purpose of this section, and subject to subsection (4), "foreign accrual property loss" of a

Reg. S. 5903(3)    Income Tax Regulations

foreign affiliate of a taxpayer for a taxation year means

(a) where at the end of the year the foreign affiliate was a controlled foreign affiliate of the taxpayer, the amount, if any, by which

(i) the total of the amounts determined for D and E in the definition "foreign accrual property income" in subsection 95(1) of the Act in respect of the affiliate for the year

exceeds

(ii) the total of the amounts determined for A, B, and C in the definition "foreign accrual property income" in subsection 95(1) of the Act in respect of the affiliate for the year, or

(b) where, at the end of the year, the foreign affiliate was not a controlled foreign affiliate of the taxpayer but was a controlled foreign affiliate of a person described in any of subparagraphs 95(2)(f)(iv) to (vii) of the Act, the amount determined under paragraph (a) for the year.

(4) In computing the foreign accrual property loss of a particular foreign affiliate of a taxpayer for a taxation year of the affiliate, where the particular affiliate or another corporation has received a payment described in subsection 5907(1.3) from another foreign affiliate of the taxpayer which payment can reasonably be considered to relate to a loss or portion of a loss of the particular affiliate for the year described in the description of D or E of the definition "foreign accrual property income" in subsection 95(1) of the Act, the amount of the loss or portion of the loss for the year is deemed to be nil.

(5) For the purpose of this section, where there has been a foreign merger (within the meaning assigned by subsection 87(8.1) of the Act) of two or more foreign affiliates of a taxpayer resident in Canada in respect of each of which the taxpayer's surplus entitlement percentage immediately before the merger was not less than 90 percent (each of which is in this subsection referred to as a "predecessor affiliate") to form a new foreign affiliate in respect of which the taxpayer's surplus entitlement percentage immediately after the merger was not less than 90 percent (in this section referred to as the "successor affiliate"), the successor is deemed to be the same corporation as, and a continuation of, each predecessor affiliate.

(6) For the purpose of this section, where there has been a winding-up of one or more foreign affiliates of a taxpayer resident in Canada in respect of which the taxpayer's surplus entitlement percentage immediately before the winding-up was not less than 90 percent (each of which is in this subsection referred to as a "predecessor affiliate") into another foreign affiliate of the taxpayer in respect of which the taxpayer's surplus entitlement percentage immediately before and after the winding-up was not less than 90 percent (in this subsection referred to as the "successor affiliate"), the successor affiliate is deemed to be the same corporation as, and a continuation of, each predecessor affiliate.

**Application**: The November 30, 1999 draft regulations (FAPI), subsec. 1(1), will amend s. 5903 to read as above, applicable to taxation years of foreign affiliates that begin after 1998, except that para. 5903(2)(b) applies to foreign affiliate taxation years that begin after 2000.

**Technical Notes**: The description of F in the definition "foreign accrual property income" in subsection 95(1) of the Act allows foreign accrual property income of an affiliate for a year to be reduced by the amount prescribed by section 5903 of the *Income Tax Regulations* to be the deductible loss of the affiliate for the year and the five immediately preceding taxation years. The amendments to section 5903 and the description of F in the definition "foreign accrual property income" in subsection 95(1) of the Act provide that deductible losses may include foreign accrual property losses for the three taxation years following and the seven taxation years preceding the year.

Amended subsection 5903(1) allows a taxpayer to include in the deductible loss of a foreign affiliate an amount not exceeding the foreign accrual property loss of the affiliate for the seven taxation years immediately preceding and the three taxation years immediately following the particular year. Losses for other taxation years will not be included in the deductible loss of the foreign affiliate.

Amended subsection 5903(2) of the Regulations provides that, in determining the deductible loss of a foreign affiliate of a taxpayer for a particular taxation year, the amount claimed under subsection 5903(1) in respect of a foreign accrual property loss of the affiliate for a taxation year of the affiliate cannot exceed the total of amounts previously claimed by any taxpayer in respect of that loss. Also, no amount may be claimed in respect of a foreign accrual property loss until the foreign accrual property loss for preceding taxation years has been fully claimed.

Amended subsection 5903(3) of the Regulations defines foreign accrual property loss of a foreign affiliate of a taxpayer for a taxation year. Where, at the end of a taxation year, a foreign affiliate is a controlled foreign affiliate of the taxpayer or a person related to the taxpayer, the foreign accrual property loss of the affiliate is the amount, if any, by which (D + E) exceeds (A + B + C) in the definition "foreign accrual property income" in subsection 95(1) of the Act.

New subsection 5903(4) of the Regulations provides that, where a foreign affiliate of a taxpayer received a payment described in subsection 5907(1.3) of the Regulations from another affiliate or another corporation, which payment was related to a loss or portion of a loss of the affiliate, the amount of the loss or portion of the loss for the year shall be deemed to be nil.

New subsections 5903(5) and (6) of the Regulations provides that a predecessor affiliate's deductible loss may flow through to a successor affiliate following a foreign merger or a winding-up of one or more affiliates of a taxpayer provided the taxpayer's surplus entitlement percentage exceeds 90 percent in each predecessor affiliate and in the successor affiliate.

**Definitions [Reg. 5903]**: "amount" — ITA 248(1), Reg. 5907(7); "controlled foreign affiliate" — ITA 95(1), Reg. 5907(1); "corporation" — ITA 248(1), *Interpretation Act* 35(1); "foreign accrual property income" — ITA 95(1), (2), 248(1); "foreign affiliate" — Reg. 5907(3); "loss" — Reg. 5907(1); "person", "prescribed", "property" — ITA 248(1); "resident in Canada" — ITA 250; "surplus entitlement percentage" — Reg. 5905(13); "taxation year" — ITA 249; "taxpayer" — ITA 248(1).

## 5904. Participating percentage — (1) For the purpose of subparagraph (b)(ii) of the definition "participating percentage" in subsection 95(1) of the Act, the participating percentage of a particular share owned by a taxpayer of the capital stock of a corporation in respect of any foreign affiliate of the taxpayer that was, at the end of its taxation year, a controlled foreign affiliate of the taxpayer is prescribed to be the percentage that would be the taxpayer's equity percentage in the affiliate at that time on the assumption that

(a) the taxpayer owned no shares other than the particular share;

(b) the direct equity percentage of a person in any foreign affiliate of the taxpayer, for which the total of the distribution entitlements of all the shares of all classes of the capital stock of the affiliate was greater than nil, was determined by the following rules and not by the rules contained in the definition "direct equity percentage" in subsection 95(4) of the Act:

(i) for each class of the capital stock of the affiliate, determine that amount that is the proportion of the distribution entitlement of all the shares of that class that the number of shares of that class owned by that person is of all the issued shares of that class, and

(ii) determine the proportion that

(A) the aggregate of the amounts determined under subparagraph 5904(1)(b) (i) for each class of the capital stock of the affiliate

is of

(B) the aggregate of the distribution entitlements of all the issued shares of all classes of the capital stock of the affiliate

and the proportion determined under subparagraph 5904(1)(b) (ii) when expressed as a percentage is that person's direct equity percentage in the affiliate; and

(c) the direct equity percentage of a person in any foreign affiliate of the taxpayer, for which the total of the distribution entitlements of all the shares of all classes of the capital stock of the affiliate was not greater than nil, was determined by the rules contained in the definition "direct equity percentage" in subsection 95(1) of the Act.

**Notes**: Reg. 5904(1) amended by P.C. 1997-1670, effective on the same basis as the amendment to Reg. 5903(1). The amendments were non-substantive, simply modernizing the wording and updating references to Reg. 5907(1). As well, 5904(1)(a) contained the following wording [presumably removed because it was superfluous]: "(but in no case shall that assumption be made for the purpose of determining whether or not a corporation is a foreign affiliate of the taxpayer)".

(2) For the purposes of this section, the distribution entitlement of all the shares of a class of the capital stock of a foreign affiliate of the taxpayer at the end of its taxation year is the aggregate of

(a) the distributions made during the year by the affiliate to holders of shares of that class; and

(b) the amount that the affiliate might reasonably be expected to distribute to holders of shares of that class immediately after the end of the year if at that time it had distributed to its shareholders an amount equal to the aggregate of

(i) the amount, if any, by which the net surplus of the affiliate in respect of the taxpayer at the end of the year, computed as though any adjustments resulting from the provisions of sections 5902 and 5905 and subsections 5907(2.1) and (2.2) and any references thereto during the year were ignored, exceeds the net surplus of the affiliate in respect of the taxpayer at the end of its immediately preceding taxation year, and

(ii) the amount that the affiliate would receive if at that time each controlled foreign affiliate of the taxpayer in which the affiliate had an equity percentage had distributed to its shareholders an amount equal to the aggregate of

(A) the amount that would be determined under subparagraph 5904(2)(b)(i) for the controlled foreign affiliate if the controlled foreign affiliate were the foreign affiliate referred to in subparagraph 5904(2)(b) (i), for each of the taxation years of the controlled foreign affiliate ending in the taxation year of the affiliate, and

(B) each such amount that the controlled foreign affiliate would receive from any other controlled foreign affiliate of the taxpayer in which it had an equity percentage.

(3) For the purposes of subsection 5904 (2),

(a) the net surplus of a foreign affiliate of a taxpayer who is an individual, in respect of that individual, shall be computed as if that individual were a corporation resident in Canada;

(b) in computing the net surplus of a particular foreign affiliate of a taxpayer resident in Canada in which any other foreign affiliate of the taxpayer has an equity percentage, no amount shall be included in respect of any distribution that would be received by the particular affiliate from such other affiliate;

(c) if any controlled foreign affiliate of a taxpayer resident in Canada has issued shares of more than one class of its capital stock, the amount that would be distributed to the holders of shares of

**Reg. S. 5904(3)(c)**      Income Tax Regulations

any class is such portion of the amount determined under subparagraph 5904 (2)(b)(ii) as, in the circumstances, it might reasonably be expected to distribute to the holders of those shares; and

(d) in determining the distribution entitlement

(i) of a class of shares of the capital stock of a foreign affiliate that is entitled to cumulative dividends, the amount of any distribution referred to in paragraph (2)(a) shall be deemed not to include any distribution in respect of such class that is, or would, if it were made, be referable to profits of a preceding taxation year, and

(ii) of any other class of shares of the capital stock of the affiliate, the net surplus of the affiliate at the end of the year referred to in subparagraph (2)(b)(i) shall be deemed not to have been reduced by any distribution described in subparagraph (i) with respect to a class of shares that is entitled to cumulative dividends to the extent that the distribution was referable to profits of a preceding taxation year.

**Definitions [Reg. 5904]**: "amount" — ITA 248(1), Reg. 5907(7); "controlled foreign affiliate" — ITA 95(1), Reg. 5907(1); "corporation" — ITA 248(1), *Interpretation Act* 35(1); "dividend" — ITA 248(1); "foreign affiliate" — Reg. 5907(3); "individual" — ITA 248(1); "net surplus" — Reg. 5902(1)–(3), 5907(1); "person", "prescribed" — ITA 248(1); "resident in Canada" — ITA 250; "share", "shareholder" — ITA 248(1); "taxation year" — ITA 249; "taxpayer" — ITA 248(1).

**5905. Special rules** — **(1)** Where at any time, other than in the course of a transaction to which subsection (2) or (5) applies, a corporation resident in Canada or a foreign affiliate of such a corporation acquires in any manner whatever shares of the capital stock of another corporation that was a foreign affiliate of the corporation immediately before that time (in this subsection referred to as the "acquired affiliate") and as a result thereof the surplus entitlement percentage of the corporation in respect of the acquired affiliate increases, for the purposes of this Part, the exempt surplus or exempt deficit, the taxable surplus or taxable deficit and the underlying foreign tax, in respect of the corporation, of the acquired affiliate and of each other foreign affiliate of the corporation in which the acquired affiliate has an equity percentage (in this subsection referred to as the "other affiliate"), other than an acquired affiliate or other affiliate in respect of which subsection (8) applies, shall at that time be reduced to the proportion of the amount thereof otherwise determined that

(a) the surplus entitlement percentage immediately before that time of the corporation in respect of the acquired affiliate or the other affiliate, as the case may be, determined on the assumption that the taxation year of the acquired affiliate or the other affiliate, as the case may be, that otherwise would have included that time had ended immediately before that time,

is of

(b) the surplus entitlement percentage immediately after that time of the corporation in respect of the acquired affiliate or the other affiliate, as the case may be, determined on the assumption that the taxation year of the acquired affiliate or the other affiliate, as the case may be, that otherwise would have included that time had ended immediately after that time,

and, for the purposes of the definitions "exempt deficit", "exempt surplus", "taxable deficit", "taxable surplus" and "underlying foreign tax" in subsection 5907(1), those reduced amounts are referred to as the opening exempt deficit, opening exempt surplus, opening taxable deficit, opening taxable surplus and opening underlying foreign tax, as the case may be, of each of those affiliates in respect of the corporation.

**Notes**: Closing words of Reg. 5905(1) amended by P.C. 1997-1670, effective on the same basis as the amendment to Reg. 5903(1). The amendments were non-substantive, simply modernizing the wording and updating references to Reg. 5907(1).

**(2)** Where at any time a foreign affiliate of a corporation resident in Canada redeems, acquires or cancels in any manner whatever (otherwise than by way of a winding-up) any of the shares of any class of its capital stock (other than shares redeemed or cancelled that the affiliate had previously purchased or acquired and that were held by it until that time and in respect of which an adjustment has previously been made under this subsection or subsection (1) as it read prior to November 13, 1981), the following rules apply:

(a) where, by virtue of an election made by the corporation under subsection 93(1) of the Act, a dividend is deemed to have been received on one or more of the shares of the foreign affiliate that were disposed of by the corporation or another foreign affiliate of the corporation (in this paragraph referred to as the "transferor") by virtue of the redemption, acquisition or cancellation of such share or shares by the foreign affiliate, for the purposes of the adjustment required by paragraph (b),

**Proposed Amendment — Reg. 5905(2)(a) opening words**

(a) where, because of an election made by the corporation under subsection 93(1) or (1.2) of the Act, a dividend is deemed to have been received on one or more of the shares of the foreign affiliate that were disposed of by the corporation or by another foreign affiliate of the corporation (in this paragraph referred to as the "transferor") because of the redemption, acquisition or cancellation of such share or shares by the foreign affiliate, for the purposes of the adjustment required by paragraph (b),

Part LIX — Foreign Affiliates     Reg. S. 5905(3)

**Application**: The November 30, 1999 draft regulations (foreign affiliates — partnerships), subsec. 3(1), will amend the opening words of para. 5905(2)(a) to read as above, applicable after November 30, 1999.

**Technical Notes**: Subsection 5905(2) applies where shares of a foreign affiliate of a corporation resident in Canada are redeemed or cancelled (otherwise than by way of a winding-up). If the corporation has made an election under subsection 93(1) of the Act or if the corporation's surplus entitlement percentage in the affiliate changes, then the affiliate's surplus balances are adjusted to offset the change in the surplus entitlement percentage. The amendments to subsection 5905(2) ensure that the subsection will also apply where an election is made under subsection 93(1.2) of the Act.

(i) immediately before that time there is included under subparagraph (v) of the description of B in the definition "exempt surplus" in subsection 5907(1) in computing the affiliate's exempt surplus or exempt deficit, as the case may be, in respect of the corporation an amount equal to the product obtained when the specified adjustment factor in respect of the disposition is multiplied by the total of all amounts each of which is the portion of any such dividend that is prescribed by paragraph 5900(1)(a) to have been paid out of the exempt surplus of the affiliate,

(ii) immediately before that time there is included under subparagraph (v) of the description of B in the definition "taxable surplus" in subsection 5907(1) in computing the affiliate's taxable surplus or taxable deficit, as the case may be, in respect of the corporation an amount equal to the product obtained when the specified adjustment factor in respect of the disposition is multiplied by the total of all amounts each of which is the portion of any such dividend that is prescribed by paragraph 5900(1)(b) to have been paid out of the taxable surplus of the affiliate, and

(iii) immediately before that time there shall be deducted from the amount, if any, otherwise determined to be the underlying foreign tax of the affiliate in respect of the corporation an amount equal to the product obtained when the specified adjustment factor in respect of the disposition is multiplied by the aggregate of all amounts each of which is the amount prescribed by paragraph 5900(1)(d) to be the foreign tax applicable to such portion of any such dividend as is prescribed by paragraph 5900(1)(b) to have been paid out of the taxable surplus of the affiliate,

and, for the purposes of subparagraphs (i) to (iii), the specified adjustment factor in respect of the disposition is the amount equal to the quotient obtained when,

(iv) where the transferor is the corporation, 100 per cent, and

(v) where the transferor is another foreign affiliate of the corporation, the surplus entitlement percentage of the corporation in respect of the transferor immediately before the disposition,

is divided by

(vi) the surplus entitlement percentage of the corporation in respect of the foreign affiliate immediately before the disposition;

(b) the exempt surplus or exempt deficit, the taxable surplus or taxable deficit and the underlying foreign tax, in respect of the corporation, of the affiliate and of each other foreign affiliate of the corporation in which the affiliate has an equity percentage (in this subsection referred to as the "other affiliate") shall at that time be adjusted to the proportion of the amount thereof otherwise determined that

(i) the surplus entitlement percentage immediately before that time of the corporation in respect of the affiliate or the other affiliate, as the case may be, determined on the assumption that the taxation year of the affiliate or the other affiliate, as the case may be, that otherwise would have included that time had ended immediately before that time,

is of

(ii) the surplus entitlement percentage immediately after that time of the corporation in respect of the affiliate or the other affiliate, as the case may be, determined on the assumption that the taxation year of the affiliate or the other affiliate, as the case may be, that otherwise would have included that time had ended immediately after that time; and

(c) for the purposes of the definitions "exempt deficit", "exempt surplus", "taxable deficit", "taxable surplus" and "underlying foreign tax" in subsection 5907(1), the amounts determined under paragraph (b) are referred to as the opening exempt deficit, opening exempt surplus, opening taxable deficit, opening taxable surplus and opening underlying foreign tax, as the case may be, of the affiliate and each other affiliate in respect of the corporation resident in Canada.

**Notes**: Reg. 5905(2)(a)(i), (ii) and (c) amended by P.C. 1997-1670, effective on the same basis as the amendment to Reg. 5903(1). The amendments were non-substantive, simply modernizing the wording and updating references to Reg. 5907(1).

**(3)** Where at any time a foreign affiliate of a corporation resident in Canada has been formed as a result of a foreign merger (within the meaning assigned by subsection 87(8.1) of the Act) of two or more corporations (each of which in this subsection and subsection (4) is referred to as a "predecessor corporation"), for the purposes of this Part, the following rules apply:

(a) in respect of the foreign affiliate,

(i) its opening exempt surplus in respect of the corporation shall be the amount, if any, by which the aggregate of all amounts each of which is the exempt surplus of a predecessor corporation that was a foreign affiliate of the corporation immediately before the merger exceeds the aggregate of all amounts each of which is the exempt deficit of a predecessor corporation that was a foreign affiliate of the corporation immediately before the merger,

(ii) its opening exempt deficit in respect of the corporation shall be the amount, if any, by which the aggregate of all amounts each of which is the exempt deficit of a predecessor corporation that was a foreign affiliate of the corporation immediately before the merger exceeds the aggregate of all amounts each of which is the exempt surplus of a predecessor corporation that was a foreign affiliate of the corporation immediately before the merger,

(iii) its opening taxable surplus in respect of the corporation shall be the amount, if any, by which the aggregate of all amounts each of which is the taxable surplus of a predecessor corporation that was a foreign affiliate of the corporation immediately before the merger exceeds the aggregate of all amounts each of which is the taxable deficit of a predecessor corporation that was a foreign affiliate of the corporation immediately before the merger,

(iv) its opening taxable deficit in respect of the corporation shall be the amount, if any, by which the aggregate of all amounts each of which is the taxable deficit of a predecessor corporation that was a foreign affiliate of the corporation immediately before the merger exceeds the aggregate of all amounts each of which is the taxable surplus of a predecessor corporation that was a foreign affiliate of the corporation immediately before the merger, and

(v) its opening underlying foreign tax in respect of the corporation shall be the aggregate of all amounts each of which is the underlying foreign tax of a predecessor corporation that was a foreign affiliate of the corporation immediately before the merger; and

(b) in respect of any other foreign affiliate of the corporation, other than a predecessor corporation, in which a predecessor corporation had an equity percentage immediately before the merger, the exempt surplus or exempt deficit, the taxable surplus or taxable deficit and the underlying foreign tax of the other affiliate in respect of the corporation shall at that time be adjusted to the propor-

tion of the amount thereof otherwise determined that

(i) the surplus entitlement percentage immediately before that time of the corporation in respect of the other affiliate, determined on the assumption that the taxation year of the other affiliate that otherwise would have included that time had ended immediately before that time,

is of

(ii) the surplus entitlement percentage immediately after that time of the corporation in respect of the other affiliate, determined on the assumption that the taxation year of the other affiliate that otherwise would have included that time had ended immediately after that time,

and, for the purposes of the definitions "exempt deficit", "exempt surplus", "taxable deficit", "taxable surplus" and "underlying foreign tax" in subsection 5907(1), the adjusted amounts are referred to as the opening exempt deficit, opening exempt surplus, opening taxable deficit, opening taxable surplus and opening underlying foreign tax, as the case may be, of the other affiliate in respect of the corporation resident in Canada.

**Notes**: Closing words of Reg. 5905(3)(b) amended by P.C. 1997-1670, effective on the same basis as the amendment to Reg. 5903(1). The amendments were non-substantive, simply modernizing the wording and updating references to Reg. 5907(1).

(4) For the purposes of paragraph (3)(a), the exempt surplus, exempt deficit, taxable surplus, taxable deficit and underlying foreign tax of each predecessor corporation immediately before the foreign merger shall be deemed to be the proportion of the amount thereof otherwise determined that

(a) the surplus entitlement percentage of the corporation resident in Canada immediately before the merger in respect of the predecessor corporation, determined on the assumption that the taxation year of the predecessor corporation that otherwise would have included the time of the merger had ended immediately before that time,

is of

(b) the percentage that would be the surplus entitlement percentage of the corporation resident in Canada immediately after the merger in respect of the foreign affiliate of the corporation formed as a result of the merger if the net surplus of such foreign affiliate were the aggregate of all amounts, each of which is the net surplus of a predecessor corporation immediately before the merger.

(5) Where at any time

(a) there is a disposition by a corporation resident in Canada (in this subsection referred to as the "predecessor corporation") of any of the shares owned by it of the capital stock of a particular foreign affiliate of it to a taxable Canadian corporation with which the predecessor corporation was not dealing at arm's length (in this subsection referred to as the "acquiring corporation"),

(b) there is an amalgamation, to which section 87 of the Act applies, of two or more corporations (each of which in this subsection is referred to as a "predecessor corporation") to form a new corporation (in this subsection referred to as the "acquiring corporation") as a result of which shares of the capital stock of a particular foreign affiliate of a predecessor corporation become the property of the acquiring corporation, or

(c) there is a winding-up, to which subsection 88(1) of the Act applies, of a corporation (in this subsection referred to as the "predecessor corporation") into another corporation (in this subsection referred to as the "acquiring corporation") as a result of which shares of the capital stock of a particular foreign affiliate of the predecessor corporation become the property of the acquiring corporation,

the following rules apply for the purposes of this Part in respect of the particular affiliate and each other foreign affiliate of the predecessor corporation in which the particular affiliate has an equity percentage:

(d) its opening exempt surplus in respect of the acquiring corporation shall be the amount, if any, by which the aggregate of its exempt surplus in respect of each predecessor corporation and in respect of the acquiring corporation immediately before any of the transactions referred to in paragraph (a), (b) or (c) exceeds the aggregate of its exempt deficit in respect of each predecessor corporation and in respect of the acquiring corporation immediately before any of the transactions referred to in paragraph (a), (b) or (c);

(e) its opening exempt deficit in respect of the acquiring corporation shall be the amount, if any, by which the aggregate of its exempt deficit in respect of each predecessor corporation and in respect of the acquiring corporation immediately before any of the transactions referred to in paragraph (a), (b) or (c) exceeds the aggregate of its exempt surplus in respect of each predecessor corporation and in respect of the acquiring corporation immediately before any of the transactions referred to in paragraph (a), (b) or (c);

(f) its opening taxable surplus in respect of the acquiring corporation shall be the amount, if any, by which the aggregate of its taxable surplus in respect of each predecessor corporation and in respect of the acquiring corporation immediately before any of the transactions referred to in paragraph (a), (b) or (c) exceeds the aggregate of its taxable deficit in respect of each predecessor corporation and in respect of the acquiring corporation immediately before any of the transactions referred to in paragraph (a), (b) or (c);

(g) its opening taxable deficit in respect of the acquiring corporation shall be the amount, if any, by which the aggregate of its taxable deficit in respect of each predecessor corporation and in respect of the acquiring corporation immediately before any of the transactions referred to in paragraph (a), (b) or (c) exceeds the aggregate of its taxable surplus in respect of each predecessor corporation and in respect of the acquiring corporation immediately before any of the transactions referred to in paragraph (a), (b) or (c); and

(h) its opening underlying foreign tax in respect of the acquiring corporation shall be the aggregate of its underlying foreign tax in respect of each predecessor corporation and in respect of the acquiring corporation immediately before any of the transactions referred to in paragraph (a), (b) or (c).

(6) For the purposes of subsection (5), the following rules apply:

(a) where paragraph (5)(a) is applicable and the predecessor corporation is, by virtue of an election made under subsection 93(1) of the Act, deemed to have received a dividend on one or more of the shares of the particular affiliate disposed of in the transaction, for the purposes of the adjustment required by paragraph (b),

**Proposed Amendment — Reg. 5905(6)(a) opening words**

(a) where paragraph (5)(a) applies and the predecessor corporation is, because of an election made under subsection 93(1) or (1.2) of the Act, deemed to have received a dividend on one or more of the shares of the particular affiliate disposed of in the transaction, for the purposes of the adjustment required by paragraph (b),

**Application:** The November 30, 1999 draft regulations, subsec. 3(2) (foreign affiliates — partnerships), will amend the opening words of para. 5905(6)(a) to read as above, applicable after November 30, 1999.

**Technical Notes:** Paragraph 5905(6)(a) of the Regulations applies for the purpose of paragraph 5905(5)(a) to adjust the surplus balances of a particular foreign affiliate of a corporation resident in Canada where the corporation has made an election under subsection 93(1) of the Act. The amendment to paragraph 5905(6)(a) ensures that the paragraph will also apply where the corporation has made an election under new subsection 93(1.2) of the Act.

(i) immediately before the time of the transaction there shall be included under subparagraph (v) of the description of B in the definition "exempt surplus" in subsection 5907(1) in computing the particular affiliate's exempt surplus or exempt deficit, as the case may be, in respect of the predecessor corporation an amount equal to the quotient obtained when

(A) such portion of the dividend as is prescribed by paragraph 5900(1)(a) to have been paid out of the exempt surplus of the particular affiliate

is divided by

(B) the surplus entitlement percentage of the predecessor corporation in respect of the particular affiliate immediately before the disposition, determined on the assumption that the shares disposed of by the predecessor corporation were the only shares owned by it immediately before the time of the transaction,

(ii) immediately before the time of the transaction there shall be included under subparagraph (v) of the description of B in the definition "taxable surplus" in subsection 5907(1) in computing the particular affiliate's taxable surplus or taxable deficit, as the case may be, in respect of the predecessor corporation an amount equal to the quotient obtained when

(A) such portion of the dividend as is prescribed by paragraph 5900(1)(b) to have been paid out of the taxable surplus of the particular affiliate

is divided by

(B) the surplus entitlement percentage referred to in clause (i)(B), and

(iii) immediately before the time of the transaction there shall be deducted from the amount, if any, otherwise determined to be the underlying foreign tax of the particular affiliate in respect of the predecessor corporation an amount equal to the quotient obtained when

(A) the amount prescribed by paragraph 5900(1)(d) to be the foreign tax applicable to such portion of the dividend as is prescribed by paragraph 5900(1)(b) to have been paid out of the taxable surplus of the particular affiliate

is divided by

(B) the surplus entitlement percentage referred to in clause (i)(B); and

(b) the exempt surplus, exempt deficit, taxable surplus, taxable deficit and underlying foreign tax of an affiliate in respect of a predecessor corporation (within the meaning assigned by subsection (5)) and the acquiring corporation (within the meaning assigned by subsection (5)) shall be deemed to be the proportion of the amount thereof otherwise determined that

(i) the surplus entitlement percentage immediately before the time of the latest of the transactions referred to in paragraph (5)(a), (b) or (c) of the predecessor corporation or the acquiring corporation, as the case may be, in respect of the affiliate, determined on the assumption

(A) that the taxation year of the affiliate that otherwise would have included that time had ended immediately before that time, and

(B) where the transaction is one referred to in paragraph (5)(a), that the shares referred to therein were the only shares owned by the predecessor corporation immediately before that time,

is of

(ii) the surplus entitlement percentage immediately after the time of the latest of the transactions referred to in paragraph (5)(a), (b) or (c) of the acquiring corporation in respect of the affiliate, determined on the assumption that the taxation year of the affiliate that otherwise would have included that time had ended immediately after that time.

Notes: Opening words of each of Reg. 5905(6)(a)(i) and (ii) amended by P.C. 1997-1670, effective on the same basis as the amendment to Reg. 5903(1). The amendments were non-substantive, simply updating references to Reg. 5907(1).

(7) Where at any time there has been a dissolution of a foreign affiliate (in this subsection referred to as the "dissolved affiliate") of a corporation resident in Canada and paragraph 95(2)(e.1) of the Act is applicable in respect of the dissolution, each other foreign affiliate of the corporation that had a direct equity percentage in the dissolved affiliate immediately before that time shall, for the purposes of computing its exempt surplus or exempt deficit, taxable surplus or taxable deficit and underlying foreign tax in respect of the corporation, be deemed to have received dividends immediately before that time the aggregate of which is equal to the amount it might reasonably have expected to receive if the dissolved affiliate had, immediately before that time, paid dividends the aggregate of which on all shares of its capital stock was equal to the amount of its net surplus in respect of the corporation immediately before that time, determined on the assumption that the taxation year of the dissolved affiliate that otherwise would have included that time had ended immediately before that time.

(8) Where at any time a dividend is, by virtue of an election made by a corporation under subsection 93(1) of the Act, deemed to have been received on one or more shares of a class of the capital stock of a particular foreign affiliate of the corporation disposed of to the corporation or another foreign affiliate of the corporation, the following rules apply:

**Proposed Amendment — Reg. 5905(8) opening words**

(8) Where at any time a dividend is, because of an election made by a corporation under subsection 93(1) or (1.2) of the Act, deemed to have been re-

ceived on one or more shares of a class of the capital stock of a particular foreign affiliate of the corporation disposed of to the corporation or to another corporation that was a foreign affiliate of the corporation immediately after the disposition, the following rules apply:

**Application**: The November 30, 1999 draft regulations (foreign affiliates — partnerships), subsec. 3(3), will amend the opening words of subsec. 5905(8) to read as above, applicable after November 30, 1999.

**Technical Notes**: Subsection 5905(8) reduces the surplus accounts of a particular foreign affiliate of a corporation resident in Canada where a dividend is deemed to have been received from the particular affiliate following an election under subsection 93(1) of the Act. The amendment to subsection 5905(8) ensures that the subsection will also apply where a dividend is deemed to have been received from the particular affiliate following an election under new subsection 93(1.2) of the Act.

(a) for the purposes of the adjustment required by paragraph (b),

(i) immediately before that time there shall be included under subparagraph (v) of the description of B in the definition "exempt surplus" in subsection 5907(1 in computing the particular affiliate's exempt surplus or exempt deficit, as the case may be, in respect of the corporation an amount equal to the product obtained when the specified adjustment factor in respect of the disposition is multiplied by the total of all amounts each of which is the portion of any such dividend that is prescribed by paragraph 5900(1)(a) to have been paid out of the exempt surplus of the particular affiliate,

(ii) immediately before that time there shall be included under subparagraph (v) of the description of B in the definition "taxable surplus" in subsection 5907(1) in computing the particular affiliate's taxable surplus or taxable deficit, as the case may be, in respect of the corporation an amount equal to the product obtained when the specified adjustment factor in respect of the disposition is multiplied by the total of all amounts each of which is the portion of any such dividend that is prescribed by paragraph 5900(1)(b) to have been paid out of the taxable surplus of the particular affiliate, and

(iii) immediately before that time there shall be deducted from the amount, if any, otherwise determined to be the underlying foreign tax of the particular affiliate in respect of the corporation an amount equal to the product obtained when the specified adjustment factor in respect of the disposition is multiplied by the aggregate of all amounts each of which is the amount prescribed by paragraph 5900(1)(d) to be the foreign tax applicable to such portion of any such dividend as is prescribed by paragraph 5900(1)(b) to have been paid out of the taxable surplus of the particular affiliate,

and, for the purposes of subparagraphs (i) to (iii), the specified adjustment factor in respect of the disposition is the amount equal to the quotient obtained when

(iv) where the person disposing of the shares is the corporation, 100 per cent, and

(v) where the person disposing of the shares is another foreign affiliate of the corporation, the surplus entitlement percentage of the corporation in respect of that affiliate immediately before the disposition,

is divided by

(vi) the surplus entitlement percentage of the corporation in respect of the particular foreign affiliate immediately before that disposition;

(b) the exempt surplus or exempt deficit, the taxable surplus or taxable deficit and the underlying foreign tax in respect of the corporation of the particular affiliate and of each other foreign affiliate of the corporation in which the particular affiliate has an equity percentage (in this subsection referred to as the "other affiliate") shall at that time be adjusted to the proportion of the amount thereof otherwise determined that

(i) the surplus entitlement percentage immediately before that time of the corporation in respect of the particular affiliate or the other affiliate, as the case may be, determined on the assumption that the taxation year of the particular affiliate or the other affiliate, as the case may be, that otherwise would have included that time had ended immediately before that time,

is of

(ii) the surplus entitlement percentage immediately after that time of the corporation in respect of the particular affiliate or the other affiliate, as the case may be, determined on the assumption that the taxation year of the particular affiliate or the other affiliate, as the case may be, that otherwise would have included that time had ended immediately after that time; and

(c) for the purposes of the definitions "exempt deficit", "exempt surplus", "taxable deficit", "taxable surplus" and "underlying foreign tax" in subsection 5907(1), the amounts determined under paragraph (b) are referred to as the opening exempt deficit, opening exempt surplus, opening taxable deficit, opening taxable surplus and opening underlying foreign tax, as the case may be, of the particular affiliate and each other affiliate in respect of the corporation resident in Canada.

**Notes**: Reg. 5905(8)(a)(i), (ii) and (c) amended by P.C. 1997-1670, effective on the same basis as the amendment to Reg. 5903(1). The amendments were non-substantive, simply modernizing the wording and updating references to Reg. 5907(1).

**Reg. S. 5905(9)** — Income Tax Regulations

(9) Where at any time a foreign affiliate of a corporation resident in Canada (in this subsection referred to as the "issuing affiliate") issues shares of a class of its capital stock to a person other than the corporation or another foreign affiliate of the corporation and as a result thereof the surplus entitlement percentage of the corporation in respect of the issuing affiliate decreases, for the purposes of this Part, the exempt surplus or exempt deficit, the taxable surplus or taxable deficit and the underlying foreign tax, in respect of the corporation, of the issuing affiliate and of each other foreign affiliate of the corporation in which the issuing affiliate has an equity percentage (in this subsection referred to as the "other affiliate") shall at that time be increased to the proportion of the amount thereof otherwise determined that

(a) the surplus entitlement percentage immediately before that time of the corporation in respect of the issuing affiliate or the other affiliate, as the case may be, determined on the assumption that the taxation year of the issuing affiliate or the other affiliate, as the case may be, that otherwise would have included that time had ended immediately before that time,

is of

(b) the surplus entitlement percentage immediately after that time of the corporation in respect of the issuing affiliate or other affiliate, as the case may be, determined on the assumption that the taxation year of the issuing affiliate or the other affiliate, as the case may be, that otherwise would have included that time had ended immediately after that time,

and, for the purposes of the definitions "exempt deficit", "exempt surplus", "taxable deficit", "taxable surplus" and "underlying foreign tax" in subsection 5907(1), those increased amounts are referred to as the opening exempt deficit, opening exempt surplus, opening taxable deficit, opening taxable surplus and opening underlying foreign tax, as the case may be, of each of those affiliates in respect of the corporation resident in Canada.

**Notes**: Closing words of Reg. 5905(9) amended by P.C. 1997-1670, effective on the same basis as the amendment to Reg. 5903(1). The amendments were non-substantive, simply modernizing the wording and updating references to Reg. 5907(1).

(10) For the purposes of this section, the surplus entitlement at any time of a share owned by a corporation resident in Canada of the capital stock of a foreign affiliate of the corporation in respect of a particular foreign affiliate of the corporation is the portion of

(a) the amount that would have been received on the share if the foreign affiliate had at that time paid dividends the aggregate of which on all shares of its capital stock was equal to the amount that would be its net surplus in respect of the corporation at that time assuming that

(i) each other foreign affiliate of the corporation in which the foreign affiliate had an equity percentage had immediately before that time paid a dividend equal to its net surplus in respect of the corporation immediately before the dividend was paid, and

(ii) any dividend referred to in subparagraph (i) that would be received by another foreign affiliate was received by such other foreign affiliate immediately before any such dividend that it would have paid,

that may reasonably be considered to relate to

(b) the amount that would be the net surplus of the particular affiliate in respect of the corporation at that time assuming that

(i) each other foreign affiliate of the corporation in which the particular affiliate had an equity percentage had immediately before that time paid a dividend equal to its net surplus in respect of the corporation immediately before the dividend was paid, and

(ii) any dividend referred to in subparagraph (i) that would be received by another foreign affiliate was received by such other foreign affiliate immediately before any such dividend that it would have paid.

(11) For the purposes of subsection (10),

(a) in determining the net surplus of, or the amount of a dividend received by, a particular foreign affiliate of a taxpayer resident in Canada in which any other foreign affiliate of the taxpayer has an equity percentage, no amount shall be included in respect of any distribution that would be received by the particular affiliate from such other affiliate; and

(b) if any foreign affiliate of a corporation resident in Canada has issued shares of more than one class of its capital stock, the amount that would be paid as a dividend on the shares of any class is such portion of its net surplus as, in the circumstances, it might reasonably be expected to have paid on all the shares of that class.

(12) Notwithstanding any other provision of this Part, for the purposes of determining under subsection (10) the net surplus of a foreign affiliate of a corporation resident in Canada in respect of the corporation at any time in a taxation year of the affiliate that would otherwise have included that time (in this subsection referred to as the "normal year"), the exempt earnings or loss and the taxable earnings or loss required to be included in computing the net surplus in respect of any taxation year of the affiliate that is assumed for the purposes of a provision of this section to have ended at that time shall be deemed to be that proportion of such amounts determined for the normal year that the number of days in

Part LIX — Foreign Affiliates     Reg. S. 5905(14)

the taxation year assumed to have ended at that time is of the number of days in the normal year.

**(13)** For the purposes of the definition "surplus entitlement percentage" in subsection 95(1) of the Act and of this Part, the surplus entitlement percentage at any time of a corporation resident in Canada in respect of a particular foreign affiliate of the corporation is,

  (a) where the particular affiliate and each corporation that is relevant to the determination of the corporation's equity percentage in the particular affiliate have only one class of issued shares at that time, the percentage that is the corporation's equity percentage in the particular affiliate at that time, and

  (b) in any other case, the proportion of 100 that

    (i) the aggregate of all amounts, each of which is the surplus entitlement at that time of a share owned by the corporation of the capital stock of a foreign affiliate of the corporation in respect of the particular foreign affiliate of the corporation

is of

    (ii) the amount determined under paragraph (10)(b) to be the net surplus of the particular affiliate in respect of the corporation at that time,

except that where the amount determined under subparagraph (ii) is nil, the percentage determined under this paragraph shall be the corporation's equity percentage in the particular affiliate at that time,

and, for the purposes of this subsection, "equity percentage" has the meaning that would be assigned by subsection 95(4) of the Act if the reference in paragraph (b) of the definition "equity percentage" in that subsection to any corporation" were read as a reference to "any corporation other than a corporation resident in Canada".

**Notes**: Opening and closing words of Reg. 5905(13) amended by P.C. 1997-1670, effective on the same basis as the amendment to Reg. 5903(1). The amendments were non-substantive, simply modernizing the wording and updating references to Reg. 5907(1).

### Proposed Addition — Reg. 5905(14), (15)

**(14)** For the purpose of this section, where the number of shares of a class of the capital of the capital stock of a foreign affiliate of a corporation resident in Canada deemed by subsection 93.1(1) of the Act to be owned by a person at a particular time is different from the number so deemed immediately before the particular time

  (a) if the number of shares of that class deemed to be owned by the person has decreased, the person is deemed to have disposed of, at the particular time, the number of shares of that class equal to the amount of the decrease;

  (b) if the number of shares of that class deemed to be owned by the person has increased, the person is deemed to have acquired, at the particular time, the number of shares of that class equal to the amount of the increase;

  (c) a person (in this paragraph referred to as the "seller") that is deemed by paragraph (a) to have disposed of, at a particular time, shares of a class is deemed to have disposed of those shares to the persons (in this paragraph referred to as the "acquirers") deemed in paragraph (b) to have acquired shares of that class at that time and the number of shares of that class deemed to have been acquired at that time by a particular acquirer from the seller shall be determined by the formula

$$A(B/C)$$

where

A   is the number of shares of that class acquired by the particular acquirer at that time,

B   is the number of shares of that class disposed of by the seller at that time, and

C   is the number of shares of that class acquired by all acquirers at that time; and

  (d) persons (in this paragraph referred to as the "acquirers") that are deemed by paragraph (b) to have acquired, at a particular time, shares of a class are deemed to have acquired those shares from a person (in this paragraph referred to as the "seller") deemed in paragraph (a) to have disposed of shares of that class at that time and the number of shares of that class deemed to have been disposed of by the seller to a particular acquirer at that time shall be determined by the formula

$$A(B/C)$$

where

A   is the number of shares of that class disposed of by the seller,

B   is the number of shares of that class acquired by the particular acquirer at that time, and

C   is the number of shares of that class time disposed of by all sellers at that time.

**Technical Notes**: New subsection 93.1(1) of the Act deems, for certain purposes, a member of a partnership to own its proportionate number of shares of a non-resident corporation held by a partnership. New subsection 5905(14) of the Regulations applies where the number of shares of a foreign affiliate of a corporation resident in Canada deemed to be owned by a person under subsection 93.1(1) increases or decreases.

Where the number of shares deemed to be held by the person has decreased, the person is deemed to have disposed of shares to the extent of the decrease. Where the number of shares deemed to be held by the person has increased, the person is deemed to have acquired shares to the extent of the increase. Persons that are treated as having acquired shares of class are treated as having ac-

Reg. S. 5905(14)     Income Tax Regulations

quired those shares proportionately from persons that are treated as having disposed of shares of that class and vice versa.

(15) In determining,

(a) for the purpose of this Part (other than section 5904), the equity percentage at any time of a person in a corporation,

(b) for the purpose of this section, the surplus entitlement at any time of a share owned by a corporation resident in Canada of the capital stock of a foreign affiliate of the corporation in respect of a particular foreign affiliate of the corporation, and

(c) for the purposes of this Part and of the definition "surplus entitlement percentage" in subsection 95(1) of the Act, the surplus entitlement percentage at any time of a corporation resident in Canada in respect of a particular foreign affiliate of the corporation,

where at any time shares of a class of the capital stock of a corporation are owned by a partnership or are deemed under this subsection to be owned by a partnership, those shares are deemed to be owned at that time by each member of the partnership in a proportion equal to the proportion of all such shares that

(d) the fair market value of the member's interests in the partnership at that time

is of

(e) the fair market value of all members' interest in the partnership at that time.

**Technical Notes**: New subsection 5905(15) of the Regulations applies to determine the equity percentage (other than for section 5904), surplus entitlement of a share and the surplus entitlement percentage at any time of a corporation resident in Canada in respect of a particular foreign affiliate of the corporation where the shares of the foreign affiliate are property of a partnership. Each member of the partnership is deemed to own that proportion of the number of the shares held by the partnership that the fair market value of the member's interest in the partnership is of the fair market value of all the members' interests in the partnership.

**Application**: The November 30, 1999 draft regulations (foreign affiliates — partnerships), subsec. 3(4), will add subsecs. 5905(14) and (15), applicable after November 30, 1999.

**Definitions [Reg. 5905]**: "amount" — ITA 248(1), Reg. 5907(7); "arm's length" — ITA 251(1); "corporation" — ITA 248(1), Interpretation Act 35(1); "disposed", "disposes" — ITA 248(1) "disposition"; "disposition" — ITA 248(1); "dividend" — ITA 248(1); "exempt deficit" — Reg. 5902(1)–(3), 5907(1); "exempt earnings" — Reg. 5907(1), (10); "exempt surplus" — Reg. 5902(1)–(3), 5907(1); "foreign affiliate" — Reg. 5907(3); "foreign tax applicable" — Reg. 5900(1)(d); "loss" — Reg. 5907(1); "net surplus" — Reg. 5902(1)–(3), 5907(1); "opening exempt deficit" — Reg. 5905(5)(e); "opening exempt surplus" — Reg. 5905(5)(d); "opening taxable deficit" — Reg. 5905(5)(g); "opening taxable surplus" — Reg. 5905(5)(f); "opening underlying foreign tax" — Reg. 5905(5)(h); "partnership" — see Notes to ITA 96(1); "person", "prescribed", "property" — ITA 248(1); "resident", "resident in Canada" — ITA 250; "share" — ITA 248(1); "surplus entitlement percentage" — Reg. 5905(13); "taxable Canadian corporation" — ITA 89(1),

248(1); "taxable deficit" — Reg. 5902(1)–(3), 5907(1); "taxable earnings" — Reg. 5907(1), (10); "taxable surplus" — Reg. 5902(1)–(3), 5907(1); "taxation year" — ITA 249; "taxpayer" — ITA 248(1); "underlying foreign tax" — Reg. 5902(1)–(3), 5907(1).

### 5906. Carrying on business in a country — (1)
For the purposes of this Part, where a foreign affiliate of a corporation resident in Canada carries on an active business, it shall be deemed to carry on that business

(a) in a country other than Canada only to the extent that such business is carried on through a permanent establishment situated therein; and

(b) in Canada only to the extent that its income therefrom is subject to tax under Part I of the Act.

(2) Where the Government of Canada has concluded an agreement or convention with the government of another country for the avoidance of double taxation that has the force of law in Canada and in which the expression "permanent establishment" is given a particular meaning, for the purposes of subsection (1), that expression has that meaning with respect to a business carried on in that country and, in any other case, has the meaning assigned by subsection 400(2).

**Definitions [Reg. 5906]**: "active business" — ITA 95(1), Reg. 5907(1); "business" — ITA 248(1); "Canada" — ITA 255, Interpretation Act 35(1); "corporation" — ITA 248(1), Interpretation Act 35(1); "foreign affiliate" — Reg. 5907(3); "resident in Canada" — ITA 250.

### 5907. Interpretation — (1) For the purposes of this Part,

"**active business**" has the meaning assigned by subsection 95(1) of the Act;

**Notes**: Definition "active business" added by P.C. 1997-1670, effective on the same basis as the amendment to Reg. 5903(1).

"**controlled foreign affiliate**" has the meaning assigned by subsection 95(1) of the Act;

**Notes**: Definition "controlled foreign affiliate" added by P.C. 1997-1670, effective on the same basis as the amendment to Reg. 5903(1).

"**earnings**" of a foreign affiliate of a taxpayer resident in Canada for a taxation year of the affiliate from an active business means

(a) in the case of an active business carried on by it in a country,

(i) the income or profit from the active business for the year computed in accordance with the income tax law of the country in which the affiliate is resident, in any case where the affiliate is required by that law to compute that income or profit,

(ii) the income or profit from the active business for the year computed in accordance with the income tax law of the country in which the business is carried on, in any case not described in subparagraph (i) where the affiliate is required by that law to compute that income or profit, and

(iii) in any other case, the amount that would be the income from the active business for the year under Part I of the Act if the business were carried on in Canada, the affiliate were resident in Canada and the Act were read without reference to subsections 80(3) to (12), (15) and (17) and 80.01(5) to (11) and sections 80.02 to 80.04,

adjusted in each case in accordance with subsections (2), (2.1), (2.2) and (2.9) and, for the purposes of this Part, to the extent that the earnings of an affiliate from an active business carried on by it cannot be attributed to a permanent establishment in any particular country, they shall be attributed to the permanent establishment in the country in which the affiliate is resident and, if the affiliate is resident in more than one country, to the permanent establishment in the country that may reasonably be regarded as the affiliate's principal place of residence, and

(b) in any other case, the total of the amounts by which the income for the year from an active business of an affiliate is increased because of paragraph 95(2)(a) of the Act;

**Notes**: Definition "earnings" added by P.C. 1997-1670, effective on the same basis as the amendment to Reg. 5903(1); this was formerly Reg. 5907(1)(a). With the change from being a paragraph to a subsection-level definition, subparas. moved up to the para. level, etc., and the wording was modernized (e.g., "total" for "aggregate"). For the former version, see Notes at end of Reg. 5907(1). The only substantive changes were:

- the closing words of para. (a) [former 5907(1)(a)(i)] referred to adjustment in accordance with subsection (2), but not (2.1), (2.2) and (2.9); and

- para. (b) [former 5907(1)(a)(ii)] continued with the words: "after deducting the aggregate of the expenses reasonably attributable thereto".

**"exempt deficit"** of a foreign affiliate of a corporation in respect of the corporation at any time means the amount, if any, by which

(a) the total of all amounts each of which is an amount determined at that time under any of subparagraphs (i) to (vi) of the description of B in the definition "exempt surplus" in this subsection

exceeds

(b) the total of all amounts each of which is an amount determined at that time under any of subparagraphs (i) to (vii) of the description of A in that definition;

**Notes**: Definition "exempt deficit" added by P.C. 1997-1670, effective on the same basis as the amendment to Reg. 5903(1); this was formerly included at the tail end of Reg. 5907(1)(d), which defined "exempt surplus", and referred to the subparagraphs of that definition. The change is non-substantive.

**"exempt earnings"** of a particular foreign affiliate of a particular corporation for a taxation year of the particular affiliate is the total of all amounts each of which is

(a) the amount by which the capital gains of the particular affiliate for the year exceed the total of

(i) the amount of the taxable capital gains for the year referred to in the description of B in the definition "foreign accrual property income" in subsection 95(1) of the Act,

(ii) the amount of the taxable capital gains for the year referred to in subparagraphs (c)(i) and (d)(iii) of the definition "net earnings" in this subsection, and

(iii) the portion of any income or profits tax paid to the government of a country for the year by the particular affiliate that can reasonably be regarded as tax in respect of the amount by which the capital gains of the particular affiliate for the year exceed the total of the amounts referred to in subparagraphs (i) and (ii),

and for the purpose of this paragraph, where the particular affiliate has disposed of capital property that was shares of the capital stock of another foreign affiliate of the particular corporation to any corporation that was, immediately after the disposition, a foreign affiliate of the particular corporation, the capital gains of the particular affiliate for the year shall not include the portion of those gains that is the total of all amounts each of which is an amount equal to the excess of the fair market value at the end of the particular affiliate's 1975 taxation year of one of those shares disposed of over the adjusted cost base of that share,

(b) where the year is the 1975 or any preceding taxation year of the particular affiliate, the total of all amounts each of which is the particular affiliate's net earnings for the year,

(c) where the year is the 1975 or any preceding taxation year of the particular affiliate, the earnings as determined in paragraph (b) of the definition "earnings" in this subsection to the extent that those earnings have not been included because of paragraph (b) or deducted in determining an amount included in subparagraph (b)(i) of the definition "exempt loss" in this subsection,

(d) where the year is the 1976 or any subsequent taxation year of the particular affiliate and the particular affiliate is resident in a designated treaty country, each amount that is

(i) the particular affiliate's net earnings for the year from an active business carried on by it in Canada or a designated treaty country, or

(ii) the earnings of the particular affiliate for the year from an active business to the extent that they derive from

(A) amounts by which the income of the particular affiliate from an active business for the year is increased because of subparagraph 95(2)(a)(i) of the Act that are derived by the particular affiliate from activities that could reasonably be considered to be directly related to business activities carried on by a non-resident corporation, to which the particular affiliate and the particular corporation are related throughout the year, in the course of an active business carried on by the non-resident corporation the income from which would, if the non-resident corporation were a foreign affiliate of a corporation, be included in computing the non-resident corporation's exempt earnings or exempt loss,

(B) where the particular corporation is a life insurance corporation resident in Canada throughout the year and the particular affiliate is a foreign affiliate in respect of which the particular corporation has a qualifying interest throughout the year, amounts by which the income of the particular affiliate from an active business for the year is increased because of subparagraph 95(2)(a)(i) of the Act that are derived by the particular affiliate from activities that could reasonably be considered to be directly related to business activities carried on by the particular corporation in the course of an active business carried on by the particular corporation in a country other than Canada, the income from which would, if the particular corporation were a foreign affiliate of another corporation and were resident in the country other than Canada in which that active business of the particular corporation is carried on, be included in computing the particular corporation's exempt earnings or exempt loss,

(C) amounts by which the income of the particular affiliate from an active business for the year is increased because of clause 95(2)(a)(ii)(A) of the Act that are derived from amounts paid or payable, directly or indirectly, to it or a partnership of which it is a member by a non-resident corporation to which the particular affiliate and the particular corporation are related throughout the year, to the extent that, if the non-resident corporation were a foreign affiliate of a corporation, the amounts paid or payable by the non-resident corporation would be deductible in the year or a subsequent taxation year in computing its exempt earnings or exempt loss,

(D) where a non-resident corporation to which the particular affiliate and the particular corporation are related throughout the year is a member of a particular partnership (other than where the non-resident corporation is a specified member of the particular partnership at any time in a fiscal period of the particular partnership ending in the year), amounts by which the income of the particular affiliate from an active business for the year is increased because of clause 95(2)(a)(ii)(A) of the Act that are derived from amounts paid or payable, directly or indirectly, to it or another partnership of which it is a member by the particular partnership to the extent that, if the particular partnership were a foreign affiliate of a corporation and were resident in the country in which the non-resident corporation is resident and subject to income taxation, the amounts paid or payable by the particular partnership would be deductible in the year or a subsequent taxation year in computing its exempt earnings or exempt loss,

(E) amounts by which the income of the particular affiliate from an active business for the year is increased because of clause 95(2)(a)(ii)(B) of the Act that are derived from amounts paid or payable, directly or indirectly, to it or a partnership of which it is a member by another foreign affiliate of the particular corporation in respect of which the particular corporation has a qualifying interest throughout the year, to the extent that the amounts paid or payable by the other foreign affiliate are deductible in the year or a subsequent taxation year in computing its exempt earnings or exempt loss,

(F) where another foreign affiliate of the particular corporation in respect of which the particular corporation has a qualifying interest throughout the year is a member of a particular partnership (other than where the other foreign affiliate is a specified member of the particular partnership at any time in a fiscal period of the particular partnership ending in the year), amounts by which the income of the particular affiliate from an active business for the year is increased because of clause 95(2)(a)(ii)(B) of the Act that are derived from amounts paid or payable, directly or indirectly, to it or another partnership of which it is a member by the particular partnership, to the extent that, if the particular partnership were a foreign affiliate of a corporation and were resident in the country in which the other foreign affiliate is resident and subject to income taxation, the amounts paid or payable by the particular partnership would be deductible in the year or a subsequent taxation year in computing its exempt earnings or exempt loss,

(G) where the particular affiliate is a member of a particular partnership (other than where the particular affiliate is a specified member of the particular partnership at any time in a fiscal period of the particular partnership ending in the year), amounts by which the income of the particular affiliate from an active business for the year is increased because of clause 95(2)(a)(ii)(C) of the Act that are derived from amounts paid or payable, directly or indirectly, to it or another partnership of which it is a member by the particular partnership, to the extent that, if the particular partnership were a foreign affiliate of a corporation and were resident in the country in which the particular affiliate is resident and subject to income taxation, the amounts paid or payable by the particular partnership would be deductible in the year or a subsequent taxation year in computing its exempt loss,

(H) amounts by which the income of the particular affiliate from an active business for the year is increased because of clause 95(2)(a)(ii)(D) of the Act that are derived from amounts paid or payable, directly or indirectly, to it or a partnership of which it is a member by another foreign affiliate (in this clause referred to as the "second affiliate") of the particular corporation to which the particular affiliate and the particular corporation are related throughout the year, to the extent that the amounts paid or payable

(I) are on account of interest on borrowed money used for the purpose of earning income from property or interest on an amount payable for property, where

1. the property is shares of a foreign affiliate (in this clause referred to as the "third affiliate") of the particular corporation in respect of which the particular corporation has a qualifying interest throughout the year and that are excluded property, and

2. the second affiliate, the third affiliate and each other affiliate relevant for the purpose of determining whether the shares of the third affiliate are excluded property are resident and subject to income taxation in a designated treaty country, and

(II) are relevant in computing the liability for income taxes, in the designated treaty country in which the second and third affiliates are resident, of the members of a group of corporations composed of the second affiliate and one or more other foreign affiliates (the shares of which are excluded property) of the particular corporation that are resident in that country and in respect of which the particular corporation has a qualifying interest throughout the year,

and, for the purposes of this clause, "excluded property" has the meaning assigned by subsection 95(1) of the Act, except that for that purpose,

(III) the definition "excluded property" in subsection 95(1) of the Act shall be read without reference to amounts receivable referred to in paragraph (c) of that definition where the interest on the amounts is not, or would not if interest were payable on the amounts, be deductible in computing the debtor's exempt earnings or exempt loss, and

(IV) the shares of a foreign affiliate (in this subclause referred to as the "non-qualifying affiliate") that is not resident and subject to income taxation in a designated treaty country are not considered relevant for the purpose of determining whether shares of the third affiliate are excluded property unless the shares of the third affiliate would not have been excluded property if the shares of all such non-qualifying affiliates were not excluded property,

(I) where the particular corporation is a life insurance corporation resident in Canada and the particular affiliate is a foreign affiliate in respect of which the particular corporation has a qualifying interest throughout the year, amounts by which the income of the particular affiliate from an active business for the year is increased because of clause 95(2)(a)(ii)(E) of the Act that are derived from amounts paid or payable, directly or indirectly, to it or a partnership of which it is a member by the particular corporation in the course of the particular corporation carrying on its life insurance business outside Canada, to the extent that, if the particular corporation were a foreign affiliate of another corporation and were resident in the country in which the particular corporation carried on its life insurance business outside Canada, the amounts paid or payable by the particular corporation would be deductible in the year or in a subsequent taxation year in computing its exempt earnings or exempt loss,

(J) amounts by which the income of the particular affiliate from an active business for the year is increased because of subparagraph 95(2)(a)(iii) of the Act that are derived from the factoring of trade accounts receivable acquired by the particular affiliate, or by a partnership of which the particular affiliate was a member, from a non-resident corporation to which the particular affiliate and the particular corporation are related throughout the year, to the extent that the trade accounts receivable arose in the course of an active business carried on by the non-resident corporation any income from which would be included in the exempt earnings of the non-resident corporation if it were a foreign affiliate of a corporation, or

(K) amounts by which the income of the particular affiliate from an active business for the year is increased because of subparagraph 95(2)(a)(iv) of the Act that are derived from loans or lending assets acquired by the particular affiliate, or a partnership of which the particular affiliate was a member from a non-resident corporation to which the particular affiliate and the particular corporation are related throughout the year, to the extent that the loans or lending assets arose in the course of an active business carried on by the non-resident corporation any income from which would be included in the exempt earnings of the non-resident corporation if it were a foreign affiliate of a corporation, or

(e) where the year is the 1976 or any subsequent taxation year of the particular affiliate, each amount that is included in the particular affiliate's exempt earnings for the year because of subsection (10),

minus the portion of any income or profits tax paid to the government of a country for the year by the particular affiliate that can reasonably be regarded as tax in respect of the earnings referred to in paragraph (c) or in subparagraph (d)(ii);

**Notes**: Definition "exempt earnings" added by P.C. 1997-1670, effective on the same basis as the amendment to Reg. 5903(1), except that in applying the definition for taxation years of a foreign affiliate that begin before 1996 and in respect of which new Reg. 5907(11)–(11.2) do not apply, read the references to "designated treaty country" as "country listed in subsection (11)". This definition was formerly Reg. 5907(1)(b), but extensive changes were made. For the former version, see Notes at end of Reg. 5907(1).

"**exempt loss**" of a foreign affiliate of a corporation for a taxation year of the affiliate is the total of all amounts each of which is

(a) the amount by which the capital losses of the affiliate for the year exceed the total of

(i) the amount of the allowable capital losses for the year referred to in the description of E in the definition "foreign accrual property income" in subsection 95(1) of the Act,

(ii) the amount of the allowable capital losses for the year referred to in subparagraphs (c)(i) and (d)(iii) of the definition "net loss" in this subsection, and

(iii) the portion of any income or profits tax refunded by the government of a country for the year to the affiliate that can reasonably be regarded as tax refunded in respect of the amount by which the capital losses of the affiliate for the year exceed the total of the amounts referred to in subparagraphs (i) and (ii),

(b) where the year is the 1975 or any preceding taxation year of the affiliate, the total of all amounts each of which is

(i) the affiliate's net loss for the year from an active business carried on by it in a country, or

(ii) the amount, if any, for the year by which

(A) the amount determined under the description of D in the definition "foreign accrual property income" in subsection 95(1) of the Act for the year

exceeds

(B) the amount determined under the description of A in the definition "foreign accrual property income" in subsection 95(1) of the Act for the year,

(c) where the year is the 1976 or any subsequent taxation year of the affiliate and the affiliate is resident in a designated treaty country, each amount that is the affiliate's net loss for the year from an active business carried on by it in Canada or in a designated treaty country, or

(d) where the year is the 1976 or any subsequent taxation year of the affiliate, each amount that is included in the affiliate's exempt loss for the year because of subsection (10);

**Notes**: Definition "exempt loss" added by P.C. 1997-1670, effective on the same basis as the amendment to Reg. 5903(1); this was formerly Reg. 5907(1)(c). With the change from being a paragraph to a subsection-level definition, subparas. moved up to the para. level, etc., and the wording was modernized (e.g., "total" for "aggregate"). For the former version, see Notes at end of Reg. 5907(1). The only substantive change was in para. (c) [former 5907(1)(c)(iii)], changing "country listed in subsection (11)" to "designated treaty country"; this amendment applies on the same basis as new Reg. 5907(11).

"**exempt surplus**" of a foreign affiliate (in this definition referred to as the "subject affiliate") of a corporation in respect of the corporation is, at any particular time, the amount determined by the formula

$$A - B$$

in respect of the period beginning with the time that is the latest of

(a) the first day of the taxation year of the subject affiliate in which it last became a foreign affiliate of the corporation,

(b) where the corporation is an acquiring corporation referred to in subsection 5905(5) and the subject affiliate is a particular affiliate referred to in that subsection or another foreign affiliate in which such a particular affiliate had an equity percentage at the time referred to in that subsection, the last time at which that subsection was applicable in respect of the affiliate, and

(c) where the subject affiliate is a foreign affiliate referred to in subsection 5905(1), (2), (8) or (9) or paragraph 5905(3)(b), the last time at which any of those subsections or that paragraph was applicable in respect of the subject affiliate

and ending with the particular time, where

A is the total of all amounts, in respect of the period, each of which is

(i) the opening exempt surplus of the subject affiliate as determined under subsection 5905(1), (2), (3), (5), (8) or (9), at the time established in paragraph (a), (b) or (c),

(ii) the exempt earnings of the subject affiliate for any of its taxation years ending in the period,

(iii) the portion of any dividend received in the period and before the particular time by the subject affiliate from another foreign affiliate of the corporation (including, for greater certainty, any dividend deemed by subsection 5905(7) to have been received by the subject affiliate) that was prescribed by paragraph 5900(1)(a) to have been paid out of the payer affiliate's exempt surplus in respect of the corporation,

(iv) the portion of any income or profits tax refunded by or the amount of a tax credit paid by the government of a country to the subject affiliate that can reasonably be regarded as having been refunded or paid in respect of any amount referred to in subparagraph (iii) and that was not deducted in determining any amount referred to in subparagraph (iii) of the description of B,

(v) the portion of any taxable dividend received in the period and before the particular time by the subject affiliate that would, if the dividend were received by the corporation, be deductible by it under section 112 of the Act,

(vi) an amount added to the exempt surplus of the subject affiliate or deducted from its exempt deficit in the period and before the particular time under any provision of subsection (1.1) or (1.2), or

(vii) an amount added, in the period and before the particular time, to the exempt surplus of the subject affiliate under paragraph (7.1)(d), and

B is the total of those of the following amounts that apply in respect of the period:

(i) the opening exempt deficit of the subject affiliate as determined under subsection 5905(1), (2), (3), (5), (8) or (9), at the time established in paragraph (a), (b) or (c),

(ii) the exempt loss of the subject affiliate for any of its taxation years ending in the period,

(iii) the portion of any income or profits tax paid to the government of a country by the subject affiliate that may reasonably be regarded as having been paid in respect of any amount referred to in subparagraph (iii), (iv) or (vi) of the description of A,

(iv) the portion of any whole dividend paid by the subject affiliate in the period and before the particular time deemed by paragraph 5901(1)(a) to have been paid out of the subject affiliate's exempt surplus in respect of the corporation,

(v) each amount that is determined under paragraph 5902(4)(a) or subparagraph 5905(2)(a)(i), (6)(a)(i) or (8)(a)(i) in the period and before the particular time, or

(vi) an amount, in the period and before the particular time, deducted from the exempt surplus of the subject affiliate or added to its exempt deficit under any provision of subsection (1.1) or (1.2);

**Related Provisions**: ITA 257 — Negative amounts in formulas.

**Notes**: Definition "exempt surplus" added by P.C. 1997-1670, effective on the same basis as the amendment to Reg. 5903(1); this was formerly Reg. 5907(1)(d). With the change from being a paragraph to a subsection-level definition, subparas. moved up to the para. level, etc., and the wording was modernized (e.g., "total" for "aggregate"); also, the calculation was changed to be in formula format. All the changes are non-substantive. For the former version, see Notes at end of Reg. 5907(1).

**"loss"** of a foreign affiliate of a taxpayer resident in Canada for a taxation year of the affiliate from an active business carried on by it in a country is the amount of its loss for the year from that active business carried on in that country computed by applying the provisions of paragraph (a) of the definition "earnings" in this subsection respecting the computation of earnings from that active business carried on in that country, with any modifications that the cricumstances require;

**Notes**: Definition "loss" added by P.C. 1997-1670, effective on the same basis as the amendment to Reg. 5903(1); this was formerly Reg. 5907(1)(e). The wording changes are non-substantive. For the former version, see Notes at end of Reg. 5907(1).

**"net earnings"** of a foreign affiliate of a corporation for a taxation year of the affiliate

(a) from an active business carried on by it in a country is the amount of its earnings for the year from that active business carried on in that country minus the portion of any income or profits tax paid to the government of a country for the year by the affiliate that can reasonably be regarded as tax in respect of those earnings,

(b) in respect of foreign accrual property income is the amount that would be its foreign accrual property income for the year, if the formula in the definition "foreign accrual property income" in subsection 95(1) of the Act were read without reference to the variable F in that formula, minus the portion of any income or profits tax paid to the government of a country for the year by the affiliate that can reasonably be regarded as tax in respect of that income,

(c) from dispositions of property used or held by it principally for the purpose of gaining or producing income from an active business carried on by it in a country that is not a designated treaty country (other than Canada) is the amount, if any, by which

(i) the portion of the affiliate's taxable capital gains for the year from those dispositions that can reasonably be considered to have accrued after November 12, 1981

exceeds

(ii) the portion of any income or profits tax paid to the government of a country for the year by the affiliate that can reasonably be regarded as tax in respect of the amount determined under subparagraph (i), and

(d) from dispositions of

(i) shares of the capital stock of another foreign affiliate of the corporation that were excluded property of the affiliate (other than dispositions to which paragraph 95(2)(c), (d) or (e) of the Act was applicable), or

(ii) partnership interests that were excluded property of the affiliate

is the amount, if any, by which

(iii) the portion of the affiliate's taxable capital gains for the year from such dispositions that can reasonably be considered to have accrued after its 1975 taxation year

exceeds

(iv) the portion of any income or profits tax paid to the government of a country for the year by the affiliate that can reasonably be regarded as tax in respect of the amount determined under subparagraph (iii);

**Notes**: Definition "net earnings" added by P.C. 1997-1670, effective on the same basis as the amendment to Reg. 5903(1); this was formerly Reg. 5907(1)(f). With the change from being a paragraph to a subsection-level definition, subparas. moved up to the para. level, etc., and the wording was modernized (e.g., "total" for "aggregate"). For the former version, see Notes at end of Reg. 5907(1). The only substantive change was in the opening words of para. (c) [former 5907(1)(f)(iii)], changing "country not listed in subsection (11)" to "country that is not a designated treaty country"; this amendment applies on the same basis as new Reg. 5907(11).

**"net loss"** of a foreign affiliate of a corporation for a taxation year of the affiliate

(a) from an active business carried on by it in a country is the amount of its loss for the year from that active business carried on in that country minus the portion of any income or profits tax refunded by the government of a country for the year to the affiliate that can reasonably be regarded as tax refunded in respect of that loss,

(b) in respect of foreign accrual property income is the amount, if any, by which

(i) the amount, if any, by which

(A) the total of the amounts determined under the descriptions of D, E and G in the definition "foreign accrual property income" in subsection 95(1) of the Act for the year

exceeds

(B) the total of the amounts determined under the descriptions of A, A.1, A.2, B and C in the definition "foreign accrual property income" in subsection 95(1) of the Act for the year

exceeds

(ii) the portion of any income or profits tax refunded by the government of a country for the year to the affiliate that can reasonably be regarded as tax refunded in respect of the amount determined under subparagraph (i),

(c) from dispositions of property used or held by it principally for the purpose of gaining or producing income from an active business carried on by it in a country that is not a designated treaty country (other than Canada) is the amount, if any, by which

(i) the portion of the affiliate's allowable capital losses for the year from those dispositions that can reasonably be considered to have accrued after November 12, 1981

exceeds

(ii) the portion of any income or profits tax refunded by the government of a country for the year to the affiliate that can reasonably be regarded as tax refunded in respect of the amount determined under subparagraph (i), and

(d) from dispositions of

(i) shares of the capital stock of another foreign affiliate of the corporation that were excluded property of the affiliate (other than dispositions to which paragraph 95(2)(c), (d) or (e) of the Act was applicable), or

(ii) partnership interests that were excluded property of the affiliate

is the amount, if any, by which

(iii) the portion of the affiliate's allowable capital losses for the year from those dispositions that can reasonably be considered to have accrued after its 1975 taxation year

Part LIX — Foreign Affiliates    Reg. S. 5907(1) tax

exceeds

(iv) the portion of any income or profits tax refunded by the government of a country for the year to the affiliate that can reasonably be regarded as tax refunded in respect of the amount determined under subparagraph (iii);

**Notes**: Definition "net loss" added by P.C. 1997-1670, effective on the same basis as the amendment to Reg. 5903(1); this was formerly Reg. 5907(1)(g). With the change from being a paragraph to a subsection-level definition, subparas. moved up to the para. level, etc., and the wording was modernized (e.g., "total" for "aggregate"). For the former version, see Notes at end of Reg. 5907(1). The only substantive changes were:

- in the opening words of para. (c) [former 5907(1)(f)(iii)], changing "country not listed in subsection (11)" to "country that is not a designated treaty country" (this amendment applies on the same basis as new Reg. 5907(11)); and

- in cls. (b)(i)(A) and (B) [former 5907(1)(g)(ii)(A)(I) and (II)], adding reference to formula items G, A.1, A.2 and C.

**"net surplus"** of a foreign affiliate of a corporation resident in Canada in respect of the corporation is, at any particular time,

(a) if the affiliate has no exempt deficit and no taxable deficit, the amount that is the total of its exempt surplus and taxable surplus in respect of the corporation,

(b) if the affiliate has no taxable surplus, the amount, if any, by which its exempt surplus exceeds its taxable deficit in respect of the corporation, or

(c) if the affiliate has no exempt surplus, the amount, if any, by which its taxable surplus exceeds its exempt deficit in respect of the corporation,

as the case may be, at that time;

**Notes**: Definition "net surplus" added by P.C. 1997-1670, effective on the same basis as the amendment to Reg. 5903(1); this was formerly Reg. 5907(1)(h). The wording changes are non-substantive. For the former version, see Notes at end of Reg. 5907(1).

**"taxable deficit"** of a foreign affiliate of a corporation in respect of the corporation at any time is the amount, if any, by which

(a) the total of all amounts each of which is an amount determined at that time under any of subparagraphs (i) to (vi) of the description of B in the definition "taxable surplus" in this subsection

exceeds

(b) the total of all amounts each of which is an amount determined at that time under any of subparagraphs (i) to (v) of the description of A in that definition;

**Notes**: Definition "taxable deficit" added by P.C. 1997-1670, effective on the same basis as the amendment to Reg. 5903(1); this was formerly included at the tail end of Reg. 5907(1)(k), which defined "taxable surplus", and referred to the subparagraphs of that definition. The change is non-substantive.

**"taxable earnings"** of a foreign affiliate of a corporation for a taxation year of the affiliate is

(a) where the year is the 1975 or any preceding taxation year of the affiliate, nil, and

(b) in any other case, the total of all amounts each of which is

(i) the affiliate's net earnings for the year from an active business carried on by it in a country,

(ii) the affiliate's net earnings for the year in respect of its foreign accrual property income,

(iii) to the extent that they have not been included under subparagraph (i) or deducted in determining an amount included under subparagraph (b)(i) of the definition "taxable loss" in this subsection, the earnings for the year as determined under paragraph (b) of the definition "earnings" in this subsection minus the portion of any income or profits tax paid to the government of a country for the year by the affiliate that can reasonably be regarded as tax in respect of those earnings,

(iv) the affiliate's net earnings for the year from dispositions of property used or held by it principally for the purpose of gaining or producing income from an active business carried on by it in a country that is not a designated treaty country (other than Canada), or

(v) the affiliate's net earnings for the year from dispositions of shares of the capital stock of another foreign affiliate of the corporation that were excluded property of the affiliate (other than dispositions to which paragraph 95(2)(c), (d) or (e) of the Act was applicable) or dispositions of partnership interests that were excluded property of the affiliate,

but does not include any amount included in the affiliate's exempt earnings for the year;

**Notes**: Definition "taxable earnings" added by P.C. 1997-1670, effective on the same basis as the amendment to Reg. 5903(1); this was formerly Reg. 5907(1)(i). With the change from being a paragraph to a subsection-level definition, subparas. moved up to the para. level, etc., and the wording was modernized (e.g., "total" for "aggregate"). For the former version, see Notes at end of Reg. 5907(1). The only substantive change was in subpara. (b)(iv) [former 5907(1)(i)(ii)(D)], changing "country not listed in subsection (11)" to "country that is not a designated treaty country"; this amendment applies on the same basis as new Reg. 5907(11).

**"taxable loss"** of a foreign affiliate of a corporation for a taxation year of the affiliate is

(a) where the year is the 1975 or any preceding taxation year of the affiliate, nil, and

(b) in any other case, the total of all amounts each of which is

(i) the affiliate's net loss for the year from an active business carried on by it in a country,

(ii) the affiliate's net loss for the year in respect of foreign accrual property income,

(iii) the affiliate's net loss for the year from dispositions of property used or held by it principally for the purpose of gaining or producing income from an active business carried on by it in a country that is not a designated treaty country (other than Canada), or

(iv) the affiliate's net loss for the year from dispositions of shares of the capital stock of another foreign affiliate of the corporation that were excluded property of the affiliate (other than dispositions to which paragraph 95(2)(c), (d) or (e) of the Act was applicable) or dispositions of partnership interests that were excluded property of the affiliate,

but does not include any amount included in the affiliate's exempt loss for the year;

**Notes**: Definition "taxable loss" added by P.C. 1997-1670, effective on the same basis as the amendment to Reg. 5903(1); this was formerly Reg. 5907(1)(j). With the change from being a paragraph to a subsection-level definition, subparas. moved up to the para. level, etc., and the wording was modernized (e.g., "total" for "aggregate"). For the former version, see Notes at end of Reg. 5907(1). The only substantive change was in subpara. (b)(iii) [former 5907(1)(j)(ii)(C)], changing "country not listed in subsection (11)" to "country that is not a designated treaty country"; this amendment applies on the same basis as new Reg. 5907(11).

**"taxable surplus"** of a foreign affiliate (in this definition referred to as the "subject affiliate") of a corporation in respect of the corporation is, at any particular time, the amount determined by the formula

$$A - B$$

in respect of the period beginning with the time that is the latest of

(a) the first day of the taxation year of the affiliate in which it last became a foreign affiliate of the corporation,

(b) where the corporation is an acquiring corporation referred to in subsection 5905(5) and the subject affiliate is a particular affiliate referred to in that subsection or another foreign affiliate in which such a particular affiliate had an equity percentage at the time referred to in that subsection, the last time at which that subsection was applicable in respect of the subject affiliate, and

(c) where the subject affiliate is a foreign affiliate referred to in subsection 5905(1), (2), (8) or (9) or paragraph 5905(3)(b), the last time at which any of those subsections or that paragraph was applicable in respect of the subject affiliate

and ending with the particular time, where

A is the total of all amounts, in respect of the period, each of which is

(i) the opening taxable surplus of the subject affiliate as determined under subsection 5905(1), (2), (3), (5), (8) or (9) at the time established in paragraph (a), (b) or (c),

(ii) the taxable earnings of the subject affiliate for any of its taxation years ending in the period,

(iii) the portion of any dividend received in the period and before the particular time by the subject affiliate from another foreign affiliate of the corporation (including, for greater certainty, any dividend deemed by subsection 5905(7) to have been received by the subject affiliate) that was prescribed by paragraph 5900(1)(b) to have been paid out of the payer affiliate's taxable surplus in respect of the corporation,

(iv) an amount added to the taxable surplus of the subject affiliate or deducted from its taxable deficit in the period and before the particular time under any provision of subsection (1.1) or (1.2),

(v) an amount added, in the period and before the particular time, to the subject affiliate's taxable surplus under paragraph (7.1)(e), and

B is the total of those of the following amounts that apply in respect of the period:

(i) the opening taxable deficit of the subject affiliate as determined under subsection 5905(1), (2), (3), (5), (8) or (9), at the time established in paragraph (a), (b) or (c),

(ii) the taxable loss of the subject affiliate for any of its taxation years ending in the period,

(iii) the portion of any income or profits tax paid to the government of a country by the subject affiliate that can reasonably be regarded as having been paid in respect of that portion of a dividend referred to in subparagraph (iii) of the description of A,

(iv) the portion of any whole dividend paid by the subject affiliate in the period and before the particular time deemed by paragraph 5901(1)(b) to have been paid out of the subject affiliate's taxable surplus in respect of the corporation,

(v) each amount that is determined under paragraph 5902(4)(b) or subparagraph 5905(2)(a)(ii), (6)(a)(ii) or (8)(a)(ii) in the period and before the particular time, or

(vi) an amount, in the period and before the particular time, deducted from the taxable surplus of the subject affiliate or added to its taxable deficit under any provision of subsection (1.1) or (1.2);

**Related Provisions**: ITA 257 — Negative amounts in formulas.

**Notes**: Definition "taxable surplus" added by P.C. 1997-1670, effective on the same basis as the amendment to Reg. 5903(1); this was formerly Reg. 5907(1)(k). With the change from being a paragraph to a subsection-level definition, subparas. moved up to the para. level, etc., and the wording was modernized (e.g., "total" for "aggregate"); also, the calculation was changed to be in formula format. All the changes are non-substantive. For the former version, see Notes at end of Reg. 5907(1).

**"underlying foreign tax"** of a foreign affiliate (in this definition referred to as the "subject affiliate") of a corporation in respect of the corporation is, at any particular time, the amount, determined by the formula

$$A - B$$

in respect of the period beginning with the time that is the latest of

(a) the first day of the taxation year of the subject affiliate in which it last became a foreign affiliate of the corporation,

(b) where the corporation is an acquiring corporation referred to in subsection 5905(5) and the subject affiliate is a particular affiliate referred to in that subsection or another foreign affiliate in which such a particular affiliate had an equity percentage at the time referred to in that subsection, the last time at which that subsection was applicable in respect of the subject affiliate, and

(c) where the subject affiliate is a foreign affiliate referred to in subsection 5905(1), (2), (8) or (9) or paragraph 5905(3)(b), the last time at which any of those subsections or that paragraph was applicable in respect of the subject affiliate

and ending with the particular time, where

A is the total of all amounts, in respect of the period, each of which is

(i) the opening underlying foreign tax of the subject affiliate as determined under subsection 5905(1), (2), (3), (5), (8) or (9), at the time established in paragraph (a), (b) or (c),

(ii) the portion of any income or profits tax paid to the government of a country by the subject affiliate that can reasonably be regarded as having been paid in respect of the taxable earnings of the affiliate for a taxation year ending in the period,

(iii) the portion of any income or profits tax referred to in subparagraph (iii) of the description of B in the definition "taxable surplus" in this subsection paid by the subject affiliate in respect of a dividend received from any other foreign affiliate of the corporation,

(iv) each amount that was prescribed by paragraph 5900(1)(d) to have been the foreign tax applicable to the portion of any dividend received in the period and before the particular time by the subject affiliate from another foreign affiliate of the corporation (including, for greater certainty, any dividend deemed by subsection 5905(7) to have been received by the subject affiliate) that was prescribed by paragraph 5900(1)(b) to have been paid out of the payer affiliate's taxable surplus in respect of the corporation, or

(v) the amount by which the subject affiliate's underlying foreign tax is required to be increased by any provision of subsection (1.1) or (1.2),

B is the total of those of the following amounts that apply in respect of the period:

(i) the portion of any income or profits tax refunded by the government of a country to the affiliate that can reasonably be regarded as having been refunded in respect of the taxable loss of the subject affiliate for a taxation year ending in the period,

(ii) the underlying foreign tax applicable to any whole dividend paid by the subject affiliate in the period and before the particular time deemed by paragraph 5901(1)(b) to have been paid out of the subject affiliate's taxable surplus in respect of the corporation before that time,

(iii) each amount that is required by paragraph 5902(4)(c) or subparagraph 5905(2)(a)(iii), (6)(a)(iii) or (8)(a)(iii) to be deducted in the period and before the particular time in computing the subject affiliate's underlying foreign tax, or

(iv) the amount by which the subject affiliate's underlying foreign tax is required to be decreased in the period and before the particular time by any provision of subsection (1.1) or (1.2);

**Related Provisions:** ITA 257 — Negative amounts in formulas.

**Notes:** Definition "underlying foreign tax" added by P.C. 1997-1670, effective on the same basis as the amendment to Reg. 5903(1); this was formerly Reg. 5907(1)(l). With the change from being a paragraph to a subsection-level definition, subparas. moved up to the para. level, etc., and the wording was modernized (e.g., "total" for "aggregate"); also, the calculation was changed to be in formula format. All the changes are non-substantive. For the former version, see Notes at end of Reg. 5907(1).

**"underlying foreign tax applicable"** in respect of a corporation to a whole dividend paid at any time on the shares of any class of the capital stock of a foreign affiliate of the corporation by the affiliate is the total of

(a) the proportion of the underlying foreign tax of the affiliate at that time in respect of the corporation that

(i) the portion of the whole dividend deemed to have been paid out of the affiliate's taxable surplus in respect of the corporation

is of

(ii) the affiliate's taxable surplus at that time in respect of the corporation, and

(b) except with respect to any whole dividend referred to in section 5902, in any case where throughout the taxation year of the affiliate in which the whole dividend was paid

(i) there is no more than one class of shares of the capital stock of the affiliate issued and outstanding,

(ii) the surplus entitlement percentage of the corporation in respect of the affiliate is 100 per cent, or

(iii) there is not more than one shareholder who owns shares of the capital stock of the affiliate,

any additional amount in respect of the whole dividend that the corporation claims in its return of income under Part I of the Act in respect of the whole dividend, not exceeding the amount that is the lesser of

(iv) the amount by which the portion of the whole dividend deemed to have been paid out of the affiliate's taxable surplus in respect of the corporation exceeds the amount determined under paragraph (a), and

(v) the amount by which the underlying foreign tax of the affiliate in respect of the corporation immediately before the whole dividend was paid exceeds the amount determined under paragraph (a);

**Notes**: Definition "underlying foreign tax applicable" added by P.C. 1997-1670, effective on the same basis as the amendment to Reg. 5903(1); this was formerly Reg. 5907(1)(m). With the change from being a paragraph to a subsection-level definition, subparas. moved up to the para. level, etc., and the wording was modernized (e.g., "total" for "aggregate"). All the changes are non-substantive. For the former version, see Notes at end of Reg. 5907(1).

**"whole dividend"** paid at any time on the shares of a class of the capital stock of a foreign affiliate of a taxpayer resident in Canada is the total of all amounts each of which is the dividend paid at that time on a share of that class except that

(a) where a dividend is paid at the same time on shares of more than one class of the capital stock of an affiliate, for the purpose only of section 5900, the whole dividend referred to in section 5901 paid at that time on the shares of a class of the capital stock of the affiliate is deemed to be the total of all amounts each of which is the dividend paid at that time on a share of the capital stock of the affiliate,

(b) where a whole dividend is deemed by paragraph 5902(1)(c) to have been paid at the same time on shares of more than one class of the capital stock of an affiliate, for the purpose only of that paragraph, the whole dividend deemed to have been paid at that time on the shares of a class of the capital stock of the affiliate is deemed to be the total of all amounts each of which is a whole dividend deemed to have been paid at that time on the shares of a class of the capital stock of the affiliate, and

(c) where more than one whole dividend is deemed by paragraph 5900(2)(b) to have been paid at the same time on shares of a class of the capital stock of an affiliate, for the purposes only of paragraph 5900(1)(d) and the definitions "underlying foreign tax" and "underlying foreign tax applicable" in this subsection, the whole dividend deemed to have been paid at that time on the shares of a class of the capital stock of the affiliate is deemed to be the total of all amounts each of which is a whole dividend deemed to have been paid at that time on the shares of a class of the capital stock of the affiliate and all of that whole dividend shall be deemed to have been paid out of the affiliate's taxable surplus in respect of the corporation.

**Notes**: Definition "whole dividend" added by P.C. 1997-1670, effective on the same basis as the amendment to Reg. 5903(1); this was formerly Reg. 5907(1)(n). With the change from being a paragraph to a subsection-level definition, subparas. moved up to the para. level, and the wording was modernized (e.g., "total" for "aggregate"). All the changes are non-substantive. For the former version, see Notes at end of Reg. 5907(1).

**Notes [Reg. 5907(1)]**: Reg. 5907(1) amended by P.C. 1997-1670, effective on the same basis as the amendment to Reg. 5903(1), to turn all paragraph definitions into subsection-level definitions (which allows them to be in alphabetical order in both English and French). See Notes to individual definitions above. The application to ITA 113, formerly in the opening words to Reg. 5907(1), is now in 5907(1.01). Formerly read:

(1) For the purposes of this Part and sections 95 and 113 of the Act,

(a) "earnings" — "earnings" of a foreign affiliate of a taxpayer resident in Canada for a taxation year of the affiliate from an active business means

(i) in the case of an active business carried on by it in a country

(A) the income or profit therefrom for the year computed in accordance with the income tax law of the country in which the affiliate is resident in any case where the affiliate is required by such law to compute that income or profit,

(B) the income or profit therefrom for the year computed in accordance with the income tax law of the country in which the business is carried on in any case not described in clause (A) where the affiliate is required by such law to compute that income or profit, and

(C) in any other case, the amount that would be the income therefrom for the year under Part I of the Act if the business were carried on in Canada, the affiliate were resident in Canada and the Act were read without reference to subsections 80(3) to (12), (15) and (17) and 80.01(5) to (11) and sections 80.02 to 80.04;

adjusted in each case in accordance with the provisions of subsection (2) and for the purposes of this Part, to the extent that the earnings of an affiliate from an active business carried on by it cannot be attributed to a permanent establishment in any particular country they shall be attributed to the permanent establishment in the country in which the affiliate is resident and if the affiliate is resident in more than one country, to the permanent establishment in the country that may reasonably be regarded as the affiliate's principal place of residence, and

(ii) in any other case, the aggregate of the amounts by which the income for the year from an active business of an affiliate is increased by virtue of paragraph 95(2)(a) of the Act, after deducting the aggregate of the expenses reasonably attributable thereto;

(b) "exempt earnings" — "exempt earnings" of a foreign affiliate of a corporation for a taxation year of the affiliate is the aggregate of all amounts each of which is

(i) the amount by which the capital gains of the affiliate for the year exceed the aggregate of

(A) the amount of the taxable capital gains for the year referred to in subparagraph 95(1)(b)(ii) [95(1)"foreign accrual property income"B] of the Act,

(B) the amount of the taxable capital gains for the year referred to in clauses (f)(iii)(A) and (f)(iv)(C), and

(C) such portion of any income or profits tax paid to the government of a country for the year by the affiliate as may reasonably be regarded as tax in respect of the amount by which the capital gains of the affiliate for the year exceed the aggregate of the amounts referred to in clauses (A) and (B),

and for the purposes of this subparagraph where the affiliate (in this subparagraph referred to as the "disposing affiliate") has disposed of capital property that was shares of the capital stock of another foreign affiliate of the corporation (in this subparagraph referred to as the "shares disposed of") to any corporation that was, immediately following the disposition, a foreign affiliate of the corporation, the capital gains of the disposing affiliate for the year shall not include the portion of any such gains that is the aggregate of all amounts each of which is an amount equal to the excess of the fair market value at the end of the disposing affiliate's 1975 taxation year of a share disposed of over the adjusted cost base of that share,

(ii) for its 1975 or any preceding taxation year, the aggregate of all amounts each of which is the affiliate's net earnings for the year,

(iii) for its 1975 or any preceding taxation year, the earnings as determined in subparagraph (a)(ii) to the extent that such earnings have not been included by virtue of subparagraph (ii) or deducted in determining an amount included in clause (c)(ii)(A),

(iv) for the 1976 or any subsequent taxation year where the affiliate is resident in a country listed in subsection (11), each amount that is

(A) the affiliate's net earnings for the year from an active business carried on by it in Canada or in a country listed in subsection (11), or

(B) to the extent that they have not been included by virtue of clause (A) or deducted in determining an amount included in subparagraph (c)(iii), the earnings for the year from an active business of the affiliate to the extent that they derive from

(I) amounts determined under subparagraph 95(2)(a)(i) of the Act that pertain to or are incident to an active business carried on in a country listed in subsection (11), or

(II) amounts determined under subparagraph 95(2)(a)(ii) of the Act that are paid or payable to it by another foreign affiliate of the corporation or any other non-resident corporation with which the corporation does not deal at arm's length, to the extent that they are or would be, if the non-resident corporation were a foreign affiliate of the corpora-

tion, deductible in computing its exempt earnings, or

(v) for the 1976 or any subsequent taxation year, each amount that is included in the exempt earnings of the affiliate by virtue of subsection (10),

minus such portion of any income or profits tax paid to the government of a country for the year by the affiliate as may reasonably be regarded as tax in respect of the earnings referred to in subparagraph (iii) or in clause (iv)(B);

(c) "exempt loss" — "exempt loss" of a foreign affiliate of a corporation for a taxation year of the affiliate is the aggregate of all amounts each of which is

(i) the amount by which the capital losses of the affiliate for the year exceed the aggregate of

(A) the amount of the allowable capital losses for the year referred to in subparagraph 95(1)(b)(iv) [95(1)"foreign accrual property income"E] of the Act,

(B) the amount of the allowable capital losses for the year referred to in clauses (g)(iii)(A) and (g)(iv)(C), and

(C) such portion of any income or profits tax refunded by the government of a country for the year to the affiliate as may reasonably be regarded as tax refunded in respect of the amount by which the capital losses of the affiliate for the year exceed the aggregate of the amounts referred to in clauses (A) and (B),

(ii) for its 1975 or any preceding taxation year, the aggregate of all amounts each of which is

(A) the affiliate's net loss for the year from an active business carried on by it in a country, or

(B) the amount, if any, for the year by which

(I) the amount determined under subparagraph 95(1)(b)(iii) [95(1)"foreign accrual property income"D] of the Act for that year

exceeds

(II) the amount determined under subparagraph 95(1)(b)(i) [95(1)"foreign accrual property income"A] of the Act for that year,

(iii) for the 1976 or any subsequent taxation year where the affiliate is resident in a country listed in subsection (11), each amount that is the affiliate's net loss for the year from an active business carried on by it in Canada or in a country listed in subsection (11), or

(iv) for the 1976 or any subsequent taxation year, each amount that is included in the exempt loss of the affiliate by virtue of subsection (10);

(d) "exempt surplus" — "exempt surplus" of a foreign affiliate of a corporation in respect of the corporation is, at any particular time, the amount, if any, by which the aggregate of all amounts in respect of the period commencing with the time that is the latest of

(i) the first day of the taxation year of the affiliate in which it last became a foreign affiliate of the corporation,

(ii) where the corporation is an acquiring corporation referred to in subsection 5905(5) and the affiliate is a particular affiliate referred to in that subsection or another foreign affiliate in which such particular affiliate had an equity percentage at the time referred to in that subsection, the last time at which that subsection was applicable in respect of the affiliate, and

(iii) where the affiliate is a foreign affiliate referred to in subsection 5905(1), (2), (8) or (9) or paragraph 5905(3)(b), the last time at which any such subsection or paragraph was applicable in respect of the affiliate

and ending with the particular time each of which is

(iv) the opening exempt surplus of the affiliate as determined under subsection 5905(1), (2), (3), (5), (8) or (9), at the time established in subparagraph (i), (ii) or (iii),

(v) the exempt earnings of the affiliate for any of its taxation years ending in the period,

(vi) the portion of any dividend received in the period and before the particular time by the affiliate from another foreign affiliate of the corporation (including, for greater certainty, any dividend deemed to have been received by the affiliate by virtue of subsection 5905(7)) that was prescribed by paragraph 5900(1)(a) to have been paid out of the payer affiliate's exempt surplus in respect of the corporation,

(vi.1) the portion of any income or profits tax refunded by or the amount of a tax credit paid by the government of a country to the affiliate that may reasonably be regarded as having been refunded or paid in respect of any amount referred to in subparagraph (vi) and that was not deducted in determining any amount referred to in subparagraph (x),

(vii) the portion of any taxable dividend received in the period and before the particular time by the affiliate that would, if the dividend were received by the corporation, be deductible by it under section 112 of the Act,

(vii.1) an amount added to the affiliate's exempt surplus or deducted from the affiliate's exempt deficit in the period and before the particular time by virtue of any provision of subsection (1.1) or (1.2), or

(vii.2) an amount added, in the period and before the particular time, to the affiliate's exempt surplus by virtue of paragraph (7.1)(d),

exceeds the aggregate of such of the following amounts in respect of the period as are applicable,

(viii) the opening exempt deficit of the affiliate as determined under subsection 5905(1), (2), (3), (5), (8) or (9), at the time established in subparagraph (i), (ii) or (iii),

(ix) the exempt loss of the affiliate for any of its taxation years ending in the period,

(x) the portion of any income or profits tax paid to the government of a country by the affiliate that may reasonably be regarded as having been paid in respect of any amount referred to in subparagraph (vi), (vi.1) or (vii),

(xi) the portion of any whole dividend paid by the affiliate in the period and before the particular time deemed by paragraph 5901(1)(a) to have been paid out of the affiliate's exempt surplus in respect of the corporation,

(xii) each amount that is determined under paragraph 5902(4)(a) or subparagraph 5905(2)(a)(i), (6)(a)(i) or (8)(a)(i) in the period and before the particular time, or

(xii.1) an amount, in the period and before the particular time, deducted from the affiliate's exempt surplus or added to the affiliate's exempt deficit by virtue of any provision of subsection (1.1) or (1.2)

and the "exempt deficit" of the affiliate of the corporation in respect of the corporation at the particular time is the amount, if any, by which

(xiii) the aggregate of all amounts each of which is an amount determined under subparagraph (viii), (ix), (x), (xi), (xii) or (xii.1)

exceeds

(xiv) the aggregate of all amounts each of which is an amount determined under subparagraph (iv), (v), (vi), (vi.1), (vii), (vii.1) or (vii.2);

(e) "loss" — "loss" of a foreign affiliate of a taxpayer resident in Canada for a taxation year of the affiliate from an active business carried on by it in a country is the amount of its loss for the year from that active business carried on in that country computed by applying the provisions of subparagraph (a)(i) respecting the computation of earnings from that active business carried on in that country, *mutatis mutandis*;

(f) "net earnings" — "net earnings" of a foreign affiliate of a corporation for a taxation year of the affiliate

(i) from an active business carried on by it in a country is the amount of its earnings for the year from that active business carried on in that country minus such portion of any income or profits tax paid to the government of a country for the year by the affiliate as may reasonably be regarded as tax in respect of such earnings,

(ii) in respect of foreign accrual property income is the amount that would be its foreign accrual property income for the year if paragraph 95(1)(b) [95(1)"foreign accrual property income"] of the Act were read without reference to subparagraph (v) [the description of F] thereof minus such portion of any income or profits tax paid to the government of a country for the year by the affiliate as may reasonably be regarded as tax in respect of such income,

(iii) from dispositions of property used or held by it principally for the purpose of gaining or producing income from an active business carried on by it in a country not listed in subsection (11) (other than Canada) is the amount, if any, by which

(A) such portion of the affiliate's taxable capital gains for the year from such dispositions as may reasonably be considered to have accrued after November 12, 1981

exceeds

(B) such portion of any income or profits tax paid to the government of a country for the year by the affiliate as may reasonably be regarded as tax in respect of the amount determined under clause (A), and

(iv) from dispositions of

(A) shares of the capital stock of another foreign affiliate of the corporation that were excluded property of the affiliate (other than dispositions to which any of paragraphs 95(2)(c), (d) or (e) of the Act were applicable), or

(B) partnership interests that were excluded property of the affiliate

is the amount, if any, by which

(C) the portion of the affiliate's taxable capital gains for the year from such dispositions as may reasonably be considered to have accrued after its 1975 taxation year

exceeds

(D) such portion of any income or profits tax paid to the government of a country for the year by the affiliate as may reasonably be regarded as tax in respect of the amount determined under clause (C);

(g) "net loss" — "net loss" of a foreign affiliate of a corporation for a taxation year of the affiliate

(i) from an active business carried on by it in a country is the amount of its loss for the year from that active business carried on in that country minus such portion of any income or profits tax refunded by the government of a country for the year to the affiliate as may reasonably be regarded as tax refunded in respect of such loss,

(ii) in respect of foreign accrual property income is the amount, if any, by which

(A) the amount, if any, by which

(I) the aggregate of the amounts determined under subparagraphs 95(1)(b)(iii) and (iv) [95(1)"foreign accrual property income"D and E] of the Act for the year

exceeds

(II) the aggregate of the amounts determined under subparagraphs 95(1)(b)(i) and (ii) [95(1)"foreign accrual property income"A and B] of the Act for the year

exceeds

(B) such portion of any income or profits tax refunded by the government of a country for the year to the affiliate as may reasonably be regarded as tax refunded in respect of the amount determined under clause (A),

(iii) from dispositions of property used or held by it principally for the purpose of gaining or producing income from an active business carried on by it in a country not listed in subsection (11) (other than Canada) is the amount, if any, by which

(A) such portion of the affiliate's allowable capital losses for the year from such dispositions as may reasonably be considered to have accrued after November 12, 1981

exceeds

(B) such portion of any income or profits tax refunded by the government of a country for the year to the affiliate as may reasonably be regarded as tax refunded in respect of the amount determined under clause (A), and

(iv) from dispositions of

(A) shares of the capital stock of another foreign affiliate of the corporation that were excluded property of the affiliate (other than dispositions to which any of paragraphs 95(2)(c), (d) or (e) of the Act were applicable), or

(B) partnership interests that were excluded property of the affiliate

is the amount, if any, by which

(C) the portion of the affiliate's allowable capital losses for the year from such dispositions as may reasonably be considered to have accrued after its 1975 taxation year

exceeds

(D) such portion of any income or profits tax refunded by the government of a country for the year to the affiliate as may reasonably be re-

garded as tax refunded in respect of the amount determined under clause (C);

(h) "net surplus" — "net surplus" of a foreign affiliate of a corporation resident in Canada in respect of the corporation is, at any particular time,

(i) if the affiliate has no exempt deficit and no taxable deficit, the amount that is the aggregate of its exempt surplus and taxable surplus in respect of the corporation,

(ii) if the affiliate has no taxable surplus, the amount, if any, by which its exempt surplus exceeds its taxable deficit in respect of the corporation, or

(iii) if the affiliate has no exempt surplus, the amount, if any, by which its taxable surplus exceeds its exempt deficit in respect of the corporation,

as the case may be, at that time;

(i) "taxable earnings" — "taxable earnings" of a foreign affiliate of a corporation for a taxation year of the affiliate is

(i) for the 1975 or any preceding taxation year, nil, and

(ii) in any other case, the aggregate of all amounts each of which is

(A) the affiliate's net earnings for the year from an active business carried on by it in a country,

(B) the affiliate's net earnings for the year in respect of its foreign accrual property income,

(C) to the extent that they have not been included by virtue of clause (A) or deducted in determining an amount included in clause (j)(ii)(A), the earnings for the year as determined under subparagraph (a)(ii) minus such portion of any income or profits tax paid to the government of a country for the year by the affiliate as may reasonably be regarded as tax in respect of such earnings,

(D) the affiliate's net earnings for the year from dispositions of property used or held by it principally for the purpose of gaining or producing income from an active business carried on by it in a country not listed in subsection (11) (other than Canada), or

(E) the affiliate's net earnings for the year from dispositions of shares of the capital stock of another foreign affiliate of the corporation that were excluded property of the affiliate (other than dispositions to which any of paragraphs 95(2)(c), (d) or (e) of the Act were applicable) or dispositions of partnership interests that were excluded property of the affiliate,

but does not include any amount included in the affiliate's exempt earnings for the year;

(j) "taxable loss" — "taxable loss" of a foreign affiliate of a corporation for a taxation year of the affiliate is

(i) for the 1975 or any preceding taxation year, nil, and

(ii) in any other case, the aggregate of all amounts each of which is

(A) the affiliate's net loss for the year from an active business carried on by it in a country,

(B) the affiliate's net loss for the year in respect of foreign accrual property income,

(C) the affiliate's net loss for the year from dispositions of property used or held by it principally for the purpose of gaining or producing income from an active business carried on by it in a country not listed in subsection (11) (other than Canada), or

(D) the affiliate's net loss for the year from dispositions of shares of the capital stock of another foreign affiliate of the corporation that were excluded property of the affiliate (other than dispositions to which any of paragraphs 95(2)(c), (d) or (e) of the Act were applicable) or dispositions of partnership interests that were excluded property of the affiliate,

but does not include any amount included in the affiliate's exempt loss for the year;

(k) "taxable surplus" and "taxable deficit" — "taxable surplus" of a foreign affiliate of a corporation in respect of the corporation is, at any particular time, the amount, if any, by which the aggregate of all amounts in respect of the period commencing with the time that is the latest of

(i) the first day of the taxation year of the affiliate in which it last became a foreign affiliate of the corporation,

(ii) where the corporation is an acquiring corporation referred to in subsection 5905(5) and the affiliate is a particular affiliate referred to in that subsection or another foreign affiliate in which such particular affiliate had an equity percentage at the time referred to in that subsection, the last time at which that subsection was applicable in respect of the affiliate, and

(iii) where the affiliate is a foreign affiliate referred to in subsection 5905(1), (2), (8) or (9) or paragraph 5905(3)(b), the last time at which any such subsection or paragraph was applicable in respect of the affiliate

and ending with the particular time each of which is

(iv) the opening taxable surplus of the affiliate as determined under subsection 5905(1), (2), (3), (5), (8) or (9) at the time established in subparagraph (i), (ii) or (iii),

(v) the taxable earnings of the affiliate for any of its taxation years ending in the period,

(vi) the portion of any dividend received in the period and before the particular time by the affiliate from another foreign affiliate of the corporation (including, for greater certainty, any dividend deemed to have been received by the affiliate by virtue of subsection 5905(7)) that was prescribed by paragraph 5900(1)(b) to have been paid out of the payer affiliate's taxable surplus in respect of the corporation,

(vi.1) an amount added to the affiliate's taxable surplus or deducted from the affiliate's taxable deficit in the period and before the particular time by virtue of any provision of subsection (1.1) or (1.2), or

(vi.2) an amount added, in the period and before the particular time, to the affiliate's taxable surplus by virtue of paragraph (7.1)(e),

exceeds the aggregate of such of the following amounts in respect of the period as are applicable,

(vii) the opening taxable deficit of the affiliate as determined under subsection 5905(1), (2), (3), (5), (8) or (9), at the time established in subparagraph (i), (ii) or (iii),

(viii) the taxable loss of the affiliate for any of its taxation years ending in the period,

(ix) the portion of any income or profits tax paid to the government of a country by the affiliate that may reasonably be regarded as having been paid in respect of that portion of a dividend referred to in subparagraph (vi),

(x) the portion of any whole dividend paid by the affiliate in the period and before the particular time deemed by paragraph 5901(1)(b) to have been paid out of the affiliate's taxable surplus in respect of the corporation,

(xi) each amount that is determined under paragraph 5902(4)(b) or subparagraph 5905(2)(a)(ii), (6)(a)(ii) or (8)(a)(ii) in the period and before the particular time, or

(xi.1) an amount, in the period and before the particular time, deducted from the affiliate's taxable surplus or added to the affiliate's taxable deficit by virtue of any provision of subsection (1.1) or (1.2),

and the "taxable deficit" of the affiliate of the corporation in respect of the corporation at the particular time is the amount, if any, by which

(xii) the aggregate of all amounts each of which is an amount determined under subparagraph (vii), (viii), (ix), (x), (xi) or (xi.1)

exceeds

(xiii) the aggregate of all amounts each of which is an amount determined under subparagraph (iv), (v), (vi), (vi.1) or (vi.2);

(l) "underlying foreign tax" — "underlying foreign tax" of a foreign affiliate of a corporation in respect of the corporation is, at any particular time, the amount, if any, by which the aggregate of all amounts in respect of the period commencing with the time that is the latest of

(i) the first day of the taxation year of the affiliate in which it last became a foreign affiliate of the corporation,

(ii) where the corporation is an acquiring corporation referred to in subsection 5905(5) and the affiliate is a particular affiliate referred to in that subsection or another foreign affiliate in which such particular affiliate had an equity percentage at the time referred to in that subsection, the last time at which that subsection was applicable in respect of the affiliate, and

(iii) where the affiliate is a foreign affiliate referred to in subsection 5905(1), (2), (8) or (9) or paragraph 5905(3)(b), the last time at which any such subsection or paragraph was applicable in respect of the affiliate

and ending with the particular time each of which is

(iv) the opening underlying foreign tax of the affiliate as determined under subsection 5905(1), (2), (3), (5), (8) or (9), at the time established in subparagraph (i), (ii) or (iii),

(v) the portion of any income or profits tax paid to the government of a country by the affiliate that may reasonably be regarded as having been paid in respect of the taxable earnings of the affiliate for a taxation year ending in the period,

(vi) the portion of any income or profits tax referred to in subparagraph (k)(ix) paid by the affiliate in respect of a dividend received from any other foreign affiliate of the corporation,

(vii) each amount that was prescribed by paragraph 5900(1)(d) to have been the foreign tax applicable to the portion of any dividend received in the period and before the particular time by the affiliate from another foreign affiliate of the corporation (including, for greater certainty, any dividend deemed to have been received by the affiliate by virtue of subsection 5905(7)) that was prescribed by paragraph 5900(1)(b) to have been paid out of the payer affiliate's taxable surplus in respect of the corporation, or

(vii.1) the amount by which the affiliate's underlying foreign tax is required to be increased by virtue of any provision of subsection (1.1) or (1.2),

exceeds the aggregate of such of the following amounts in respect of the period as are applicable,

(viii) the portion of any income or profits tax refunded by the government of a country to the affiliate that may reasonably be regarded as having been refunded in respect of the taxable loss of the affiliate for a taxation year ending in the period,

(ix) the underlying foreign tax applicable to any whole dividend paid by the affiliate in the period and before the particular time deemed by paragraph 5901(1)(b) to have been paid out of the affiliate's taxable surplus in respect of the corporation before that time,

(x) each amount that is required by paragraph 5902(4)(c) or subparagraph 5905(2)(a)(iii), (6)(a)(iii) or (8)(a)(iii) to be deducted in the period and before the particular time in computing the affiliate's underlying foreign tax, or

(xi) the amount by which the affiliate's underlying foreign tax is required to be decreased in the period and before the particular time by virtue of any provision of subsection (1.1) or (1.2);

(m) "**underlying foreign tax applicable**" — "underlying foreign tax applicable" in respect of a corporation to a whole dividend paid at any time on the shares of any class of the capital stock of a foreign affiliate of the corporation by the affiliate is the aggregate of

(i) the proportion of the underlying foreign tax of the affiliate at that time in respect of the corporation that

(A) the portion of the whole dividend deemed to have been paid out of the affiliate's taxable surplus in respect of the corporation

is of

(B) the affiliate's taxable surplus at that time in respect of the corporation, and

(ii) except with respect to any whole dividend referred to in section 5902, in any case where throughout the taxation year of the affiliate in which the whole dividend was paid there is no more than one class of shares of the capital stock of the affiliate issued and outstanding, the surplus entitlement percentage of the corporation in respect of the affiliate is 100 per cent or there is not more than one shareholder who owns shares of the capital stock of the affiliate, such additional amount in respect of the whole dividend as the corporation claims in its return of income under Part I of the Act in respect of the whole dividend, not exceeding the amount that is the lesser of

(A) the amount by which the portion of the whole dividend deemed to have been paid out of the affiliate's taxable surplus in respect of the corporation exceeds the amount determined under subparagraph (i), and

(B) the amount by which the underlying foreign tax of the affiliate in respect of the corporation immediately before the whole dividend was paid exceeds the amount determined under subparagraph (i); and

(n) "**whole dividend**" — "whole dividend" paid at any time on the shares of a class of the capital stock of a foreign affiliate of a taxpayer resident in Canada is the aggregate of all amounts each of which is the dividend paid at that time on a share of that class except that

(i) where a dividend is paid at the same time on shares of more than one class of the capital stock of an affiliate, for the purposes only of section 5900, the whole dividend referred to in section 5901 paid at that time on the shares of a class of the capital stock of the affiliate shall be deemed to be the aggregate of all amounts each of which is the dividend paid at that time on a share of the capital stock of the affiliate,

(ii) where a whole dividend is deemed by paragraph 5902(1)(c) to have been paid at the same time on shares of more than one class of the capital stock of an affiliate, for the purposes only of that paragraph, the whole dividend deemed to have been paid at that time on the shares of a class of the capital stock of the affiliate shall be deemed to be the aggregate of all amounts each of which is a whole dividend deemed to have been paid at that time on the shares of a class of the capital stock of the affiliate, and

(iii) where more than one whole dividend is deemed by paragraph 5900(2)(b) to have been paid at the same time on shares of a class of the capital stock of an affiliate, for the purposes only of paragraph 5900(1)(d) and paragraphs 5907(1)(l) and (m), the whole dividend deemed to have been paid at that time on the shares of a class of the capital stock of the affiliate shall be deemed to be the aggregate of all amounts each of which is a whole dividend deemed to have been paid at that time on the shares of a class of the capital stock of the affiliate and all of any such whole dividend shall be deemed to have been paid out of the affiliate's taxable surplus in respect of the corporation.

Reg. 5907(1)(a)(i)(C) amended by P.C. 1996-571, effective for taxation years that end after February 21, 1994, to add the exclusion of provisions in ITA 80–80.04.

Coming-into-force provision for earlier amendment amended by P.C. 1994-1129, so that Reg. 5907(1)(m)(ii) is effective in respect of whole dividends paid after 1987.

**(1.01)** For the purpose of section 113 of the Act, "exempt surplus" and "taxable surplus" have the meanings assigned by subsection (1).

**Notes**: Reg. 5907(1.01) added by P.C. 1997-1670, effective on the same basis as the amendment to Reg. 5903(1). Reg. 5907(1), by its opening words, previously applied for purposes of ITA s. 113, so this change is non-substantive.

**(1.02)** In paragraph (d) of the definition "exempt earnings" in subsection (1), the determination of whether a corporation

(a) has a "qualifying interest" in respect of a foreign affiliate throughout a taxation year, or

(b) is related to another corporation throughout a taxation year

shall be made as it would for the purpose of paragraph 95(2)(a) of the Act.

**Notes**: Reg. 5907(1.02) added by P.C. 1997-1670, effective on the same basis as the amendment to Reg. 5903(1). This was 5907(1.01) in the draft regulations of January 23, 1995.

**Reg. S. 5907(1.1)**

(1.1) For the purposes of this Part, where, pursuant to the income tax law of a country other than Canada, a group of two or more foreign affiliates (in this subsection referred to as the "consolidated group") of a corporation resident in Canada that are resident in that country determine their liabilities for income or profits tax payable to the government of that country for a taxation year on a consolidated or combined basis and one of the affiliates (in this subsection referred to as the "primary affiliate") is responsible for paying, or claiming a refund of, such tax on behalf of itself and the other members of the consolidated group (hereinafter referred to as the "secondary affiliates"), the following rules apply:

(a) in respect of the primary affiliate,

(i) any such income or profits tax paid by the primary affiliate for the year shall be deemed not to have been paid and any refund to the primary affiliate of income or profits tax otherwise payable by it for the year shall be deemed not to have been made,

(ii) any such income or profits tax that would have been payable by the primary affiliate for the year if the primary affiliate had no other taxation year and had not been a member of the consolidated group shall be deemed to have been paid for the year,

(iii) to the extent that

(A) the income or profits tax that would otherwise have been payable by the primary affiliate for the year on behalf of the consolidated group is reduced by virtue of any loss of the primary affiliate for the year or any previous taxation year, or

(B) the primary affiliate receives, in respect of a loss of the primary affiliate for the year or a subsequent taxation year, a refund of income or profits tax otherwise payable for the year by the primary affiliate on behalf of the consolidated group,

the amount of such reduction or refund, as the case may be, shall be deemed to have been received by the primary affiliate as a refund for the year of the loss of income or profits tax in respect of the loss,

(iv) any such income or profits tax that would have been payable by a secondary affiliate for the year if the secondary affiliate had no other taxation year and had not been a member of the consolidated group shall at the end of the year,

(A) to the extent that such income or profits tax would otherwise have reduced the net earnings included in the exempt earnings of the secondary affiliate, be deducted from the exempt surplus or added to the exempt deficit, as the case may be, of the primary affiliate, and

(B) to the extent that such income or profits tax would otherwise have reduced the net earnings included in the taxable earnings of the secondary affiliate,

(I) be deducted from the taxable surplus or added to the taxable deficit, as the case may be, of the primary affiliate, and

(II) be added to the underlying foreign tax of the primary affiliate,

(v) to the extent that

(A) the income or profits tax that would otherwise have been payable by the primary affiliate for the year on behalf of the consolidated group is reduced by virtue of a loss of a secondary affiliate for the year or a previous taxation year, or

(B) the primary affiliate receives, in respect of a loss of a secondary affiliate for the year or a subsequent taxation year, a refund of income or profits tax otherwise payable for the year by the primary affiliate on behalf of the consolidated group,

the amount of such reduction or refund, as the case may be, shall at the end of the year of the loss,

(C) where such loss reduces the exempt surplus or increases the exempt deficit, as the case may be, of the secondary affiliate, be added to the exempt surplus or deducted from the exempt deficit, as the case may be, of the primary affiliate, and

(D) where such loss reduces the taxable surplus or increases the taxable deficit, as the case may be, of the secondary affiliate,

(I) be added to the taxable surplus or deducted from the taxable deficit, as the case may be, of the primary affiliate, and

(II) be deducted from the underlying foreign tax of the primary affiliate; and

(b) where by virtue of the primary affiliate being responsible for paying, or claiming a refund of, income or profits tax for the year on behalf of the consolidated group,

(i) an amount is paid to the primary affiliate by a secondary affiliate in respect of the income or profits tax that would have been payable by the secondary affiliate for the year had it not been a member of the group,

(A) in respect of the secondary affiliate, the amount so paid shall be deemed to be a payment of such income or profits tax for the year, and

(B) in respect of the primary affiliate,

(I) such portion of the amount so paid as may reasonably be regarded as relating to an amount included in the exempt surplus or deducted from the exempt deficit, as the case may be, of the secondary affiliate shall at the end of the year be added to the exempt surplus or deducted from the exempt deficit, as the case may be, of the primary affiliate, and

(II) such portion of the amount so paid as may reasonably be regarded as relating to an amount included in the taxable surplus or deducted from the taxable deficit, as the case may be, of the secondary affiliate shall at the end of the year be added to the taxable surplus or deducted from the taxable deficit, as the case may be, of the primary affiliate and be deducted from the underlying foreign tax of the primary affiliate, or

(ii) an amount is paid by the primary affiliate to a secondary affiliate in respect of a reduction or refund by virtue of a loss of the secondary affiliate for a taxation year of the income or profits tax that would otherwise have been payable by the primary affiliate for the year on behalf of the consolidated group,

(A) in respect of the primary affiliate,

(I) such portion of the amount so paid as may reasonably be regarded as relating to an amount deducted from the exempt surplus or included in the exempt deficit, as the case may be, of the secondary affiliate shall at the end of the year of the loss be deducted from the exempt surplus or added to the exempt deficit, as the case may be, of the primary affiliate, and

(II) such portion of the amount so paid as may reasonably be regarded as relating to an amount deducted from the taxable surplus or included in the taxable deficit, as the case may be, of the secondary affiliate shall at the end of the year of the loss be deducted from the taxable surplus or added to the taxable deficit, as the case may be, of the primary affiliate and be added to the underlying foreign tax of the primary affiliate, and

(B) in respect of the secondary affiliate, the amount shall be deemed to be a refund to the secondary affiliate for the year of the loss of income or profits tax in respect of the loss,

and, for the purposes of this paragraph, any amount paid by a particular secondary affiliate to another secondary affiliate in respect of any income or profits tax that would have been payable by the particular secondary affiliate for the year had it not been a member of the consolidated group shall be deemed to have been paid in respect of such tax by the particular secondary affiliate to the primary affiliate and to have been paid in respect of such tax by the primary affiliate to the other secondary affiliate.

**(1.2)** For the purposes of this Part, where, pursuant to the income tax law of a country other than Canada, a corporation resident in that country that is a foreign affiliate of a corporation resident in Canada (in this subsection referred to as the "taxpaying affiliate") deducts, in computing its income or profits tax payable for a taxation year to a government of that country, a loss of another corporation resident in that country that is a foreign affiliate of the corporation resident in Canada (in this subsection referred to as the "loss affiliate"), the following rules apply:

(a) any such income or profits tax paid by the taxpaying affiliate for the year shall be deemed not to have been paid;

(b) any such income or profits tax that would have been payable by the taxpaying affiliate for the year if the taxpaying affiliate had not been allowed to deduct such loss shall be deemed to have been paid for the year;

(c) to the extent that the income or profits tax that would otherwise have been payable by the taxpaying affiliate for the year is reduced by virtue of such loss, the amount of such reduction shall at the end of the year,

(i) where such loss reduces the exempt surplus or increases the exempt deficit, as the case may be, of the loss affiliate, be added to the exempt surplus or deducted from the exempt deficit, as the case may be, of the taxpaying affiliate, and

(ii) where such loss reduces the taxable surplus or increases the taxable deficit, as the case may be, of the loss affiliate,

(A) be added to the taxable surplus or deducted from the taxable deficit, as the case may be, of the taxpaying affiliate, and

(B) be deducted from the underlying foreign tax of the taxpaying affiliate; and

(d) where an amount is paid by the taxpaying affiliate to the loss affiliate in respect of the reduction, by virtue of such loss, of the income or profits tax that would otherwise have been payable by the taxpaying affiliate for the year,

(i) in respect of the taxpaying affiliate,

(A) such portion of the amount as may reasonably be regarded as relating to an amount deducted from the exempt surplus or included in the exempt deficit, as the case may be, of the loss affiliate shall at the end of the year be deducted from the exempt surplus or added to the exempt deficit, as the case may be, of the taxpaying affiliate, and

(B) such portion of the amount as may reasonably be regarded as relating to an amount deducted from the taxable surplus or included in the taxable deficit, as the case may be, of the loss affiliate shall at the end of the year be deducted from the taxable surplus or added to the taxable deficit, as the case may be, of the taxpaying affiliate and be added to the underlying foreign tax of the taxpaying affiliate, and

(ii) in respect of the loss affiliate, the amount shall be deemed to be a refund to the loss affiliate of income or profits tax in respect of the loss for the taxation year of the loss.

**(1.3)** For the purposes of paragraph (b) of the definition "foreign accrual tax" in subsection 95(1) of the Act,

### Proposed Amendment — Reg. 5907(1.3) opening words

**(1.3)** For the purpose of paragraph (b) of the definition "foreign accrual tax" in subsection 95(1) of the Act and subject to subsection (1.4),

**Application**: The November 30, 1999 draft regulations (FAPI), subsec. 2(1), will amend the opening words of subsec. 5907(1.3) to read as above, applicable to taxation years that begin after November 30, 1999.

**Technical Notes**: Subsection 91(4) of the Act provides for a deduction in the computation of a taxpayer's income in respect of foreign accrual tax that is attributable to an amount of foreign accrual property income included in the computation of the taxpayer's income. Subsection 95(1) of the Act defines foreign accrual tax to include amounts prescribed to be foreign accrual tax.

In circumstances where the loss of another corporation in a particular group of foreign affiliates of a taxpayer is relevant in the computation of the tax liability of the group to a foreign government, paragraphs 5907(1.3)(a) and (b) of the Regulations provides that an amount paid by the particular corporation to the other corporation in the group in respect of the use of a loss of any other corporation in the computation of the group's tax liability to the foreign government is foreign accrual tax. These provisions apply where the loss of the other corporation is an active business loss or a capital loss resulting from the disposition of excluded property as well as where the loss is a foreign accrual loss as defined in subsection 5903(3) of the Regulations. Subsection 5907(1.3), which applies to taxation years that begin after November 30, 1999, is amended as a consequence of the introduction of subsection 5907(1.4) of the Regulations.

(a) where, pursuant to the income tax law of the country in which a particular foreign affiliate is resident, the particular affiliate and one or more other corporations, each of which is resident in that country, determine their liabilities for income or profits tax payable to the government of that country for a taxation year on a consolidated or combined basis, any amount paid by the particular affiliate to any of the other corporations to the extent that it may reasonably be regarded as being in respect of income or profits tax that would otherwise have been payable by the particular affiliate in respect of a particular amount included in computing the taxpayer's income by virtue of subsection 91(1) of the Act for a taxation year in respect of the particular affiliate, had the tax liability of the particular affiliate and the other corporations not been determined on a consolidated or combined basis, is hereby prescribed to be foreign accrual tax applicable to the particular amount; and

(b) where, pursuant to the income tax law of the country in which a particular foreign affiliate of a taxpayer is resident, the particular affiliate, in computing its income or profits subject to tax in that country for a taxation year, deducts an amount in respect of a loss of another corporation resident in that country, any amount paid by the particular affiliate to the other corporation to the extent that it may reasonably be regarded as being in respect of income or profits tax that would otherwise have been payable by the particular affiliate in respect of a particular amount included in computing the taxpayer's income by virtue of subsection 91(1) of the Act for a taxation year in respect of the particular affiliate, had the tax liability of the particular affiliate been determined without deducting the loss of the other corporation, is hereby prescribed to be foreign accrual tax applicable to the particular amount.

**Notes**: Opening words of Reg. 5907(1.3) amended by P.C. 1997-1670, effective on the same basis as the amendment to Reg. 5903(1), to change "95(1)(c)(ii)" to the current reference. (This change was non-substantive.)

### Proposed Addition — Reg. 5907(1.4)

**(1.4)** Any amount paid by a particular affiliate described in paragraph (1.3)(a) or (b) does not include any amount paid by the particular affiliate to any other corporation where the amount paid can reasonably be considered to be in respect of a loss of any other corporation and such loss would not be a foreign accrual property loss of the other corporation (as defined in subsection 5903(3)) without taking into account the particular payment.

**Application**: The November 30, 1999 draft regulations (FAPI), subsec. 2(2), will add subsec. 5907(1.4), applicable to taxation years that begin after November 30, 1999.

**Technical Notes**: New subsection 5907(1.4) ensures that in such circumstances the amount paid by the particular affiliate to the other corporation will only be foreign accrual tax to the extent that the amount paid is in respect of a foreign accrual property loss of any other corporation. This is consistent with the fact that, under section 5903 of the Regulations, active business losses and capital losses resulting from the disposition of excluded property of a foreign affiliate of a taxpayer are not included in the computation of a deductible loss which may be used to reduce foreign accrual property income of that affiliate in a particular taxation year.

(2) In computing the earnings of a foreign affiliate of a taxpayer resident in Canada for a taxation year of the affiliate from an active business carried on by it in a country, there shall be added to the amount thereof determined under subparagraph (a)(i) or (ii) of the definition "earnings" in subsection (1) (in this subsection referred to as the "earnings amount") such portion of the following amounts as was deducted or was not included, as the case may be, in computing the earnings amount,

(a) any income or profits tax paid to the government of a country by the affiliate so deducted,

(b) if established by the taxpayer, the amount by which any amount so deducted in respect of an expenditure made by the affiliate exceeds the amount, if any, by which

(i) the amount of the expenditure

exceeds

(ii) the aggregate of all other deductions in respect of that expenditure made by the affiliate in computing the earnings amounts for preceding taxation years,

(c) any loss of the affiliate referred to in the description of D in the definition "foreign accrual property income" in subsection 95(1) of the Act so deducted,

(d) any capital loss of the affiliate in respect of the disposition of capital property so deducted (for greater certainty, capital property of the affiliate for the purposes of this paragraph includes all the property of the affiliate other than property referred to in subparagraph 39(1)(b)(i) or (ii) of the Act on the assumption for this purpose that the affiliate is a corporation resident in Canada),

(e) any loss of the affiliate for a preceding or a subsequent taxation year so deducted,

(f) any revenue, income or profit (other than an amount referred to in paragraph (f.1), (h) or (i)) of the affiliate derived in the year from such business carried on in that country to the extent that such revenue, income or profit

(i) is not otherwise required to be included in computing the earnings amount of the affiliate for any taxation year by the income tax law that is relevant in computing that amount, and

(ii) does not arise with respect to a disposition (other than a disposition to which subsection (9) applies) by the affiliate of property to another foreign affiliate of the taxpayer or to a person with whom the taxpayer does not deal at arm's length, to which a tax deferral, rollover or similar tax postponement provision of the income tax law that is relevant in computing the earnings amount of the affiliate applied, and

(f.1) any assistance from a government, municipality or other public authority (other than any such assistance that reduced the amount of an expenditure for purposes of computing the earnings amount for any taxation year) that the affiliate received or became entitled to receive in the year in connection with such business carried on in that country that is not otherwise required to be included in computing the earnings amount for the year or for any other taxation year,

and there shall be deducted such portion of the following amounts as were included or were not deducted, as the case may be, in computing the earnings amount,

(g) any income or profits tax refunded by the government of a country to the affiliate so included;

(h) any capital gain of the affiliate in respect of the disposition of capital property so included (for greater certainty, capital property of the affiliate for the purposes of this paragraph includes all the property of the affiliate other than property referred to in any of subparagraphs 39(1)(a)(i) to (iv) of the Act on the assumption for this purpose that the affiliate is a corporation resident in Canada);

(i) any amount that is included in the foreign accrual property income of the affiliate so included;

(j) any loss, outlay or expense made or incurred in the year by the affiliate for the purpose of gaining or producing such earnings amount to the extent that

(i) such loss, outlay or expense is not otherwise permitted to be deducted in computing the earnings amount of the affiliate for any taxation year by the income tax law that is relevant in computing that amount, or

(ii) such outlay or expense can reasonably be regarded as applicable to any revenue added to the earnings amount of the affiliate under paragraph (f),

where such loss, outlay or expense

(iii) does not arise with respect to a disposition (other than a disposition to which subsection (9) applies) by the affiliate of property to another foreign affiliate of the taxpayer or to a person with whom the taxpayer does not deal at arm's length, to which a loss deferral or similar loss postponement provision of the income tax law that is relevant in computing the earnings amount of the affiliate applied, and

(iv) is not

(A) a loss referred to in paragraph (c) or (d),

(B) a capital expenditure other than interest, or

(C) income or profits tax paid to the government of a country;

(k) any outlay made in the year in repayment of an amount referred to in paragraph (f.1); and

(l) where any property of the affiliate acquired from another foreign affiliate of the taxpayer or from any foreign affiliate of a person resident in Canada with whom the taxpayer does not deal at arm's length has been disposed of, such amount in respect of that property as may reasonably be considered as having been included by virtue of paragraph (f) in computing the earnings amount of any foreign affiliate of the taxpayer or of a person resident in Canada with whom the taxpayer does not deal at arm's length.

**Notes**: Opening words of Reg. 5907(2) and Reg. 5907(2)(c) amended by P.C. 1997-1670, effective on the same basis as the amendment to Reg. 5903(1). The amendments were non-substantive, simply modernizing the wording and updating references to Reg. 5907(1). Formerly read:

(2) In computing the earnings of a foreign affiliate of a taxpayer resident in Canada for a taxation year of the affiliate from an active business carried on by it in a country, there shall be added to the amount thereof determined under clause (1)(a)(i)(A) or (B) (in this subsection referred to as the "earnings amount") such portion of the following amounts as were deducted or were not included, as the case may be, in computing the earnings amount,

.....

(c) any loss of the affiliate referred to in subparagraph 95(1)(b)(iii) [95(1)"foreign accrual property income"D] of the Act so deducted,

**(2.1)** In computing the earnings of a foreign affiliate of a corporation resident in Canada for a taxation year of the affiliate from an active business carried on by it in Canada or in a designated treaty country, where the affiliate is resident in a designated treaty country and the corporation, together with all other corporations resident in Canada with which the corporation does not deal at arm's length and in respect of which the affiliate is a foreign affiliate, have so elected in respect of the business for the taxation year or any preceding taxation year of the affiliate, the following rules apply:

(a) there shall be added to the amount determined under subparagraph (a)(i) of the definition "earnings" in subsection (1) after adjustment in accordance with the provisions of subsection (2) (in this subsection and in subsection (2.2) referred to as the "adjusted earnings amount") the total of all amounts each of which is the amount, if any, by which

(i) the amount that can reasonably be regarded as having been deducted in respect of the cost of a capital property or foreign resource property of the affiliate in computing the adjusted earnings amount

exceeds

(ii) the amount that may reasonably be regarded as having been deducted in respect of the cost of that capital property or foreign resource property in computing income or profit of the affiliate for the year from that business in its financial statements prepared in accordance with the laws of the country in which the affiliate is resident;

(b) there shall be deducted from the adjusted earnings amount the aggregate of all amounts each of which is the amount, if any, by which

(i) the amount determined under subparagraph (a)(ii) in respect of that capital property or foreign resource property

exceeds

(ii) the amount determined under subparagraph (a)(i) in respect of that capital property or foreign resource property;

(c) where any capital property or foreign resource property of the affiliate has been disposed of in the taxation year,

(i) there shall be added to the adjusted earnings amount the aggregate of the amounts deducted pursuant to paragraphs (b) and (2.2)(b) for preceding taxation years of the affiliate in respect of that capital property or foreign resource property, and

(ii) there shall be deducted from the adjusted earnings amount the aggregate of the amounts added pursuant to paragraphs (a) and (2.2)(a) for the preceding taxation years of the affiliate in respect of that capital property or foreign resource property; and

(d) for the purposes of paragraph (c), where the affiliate has merged with one or more corporations to form a new corporation, any capital property or foreign resource property of the affiliate that becomes a property of the new corporation shall be deemed to have been disposed of by the affiliate in its last taxation year before the merger.

**Related Provisions**: ITA 220(3.2), Reg. 600(d) — Late filing of election or revocation.

**Notes**: Opening words of Reg. 5907(2.1) and Reg. 5907(2.1)(a), (c) and (d) amended by P.C. 1997-1670, the change to the opening words effective on the same basis as the amendments to Reg. 5907(11), and the other changes effective on the same basis as the amendment to Reg. 5903(1). In the opening words, "country listed in subsection (11)" was changed to "designated treaty country". The other amendments were non-substantive, simply modernizing the wording and updating references to Reg. 5907(1). Formerly read:

(2.1) In computing the earnings of a foreign affiliate of a corporation resident in Canada for a taxation year of the affiliate from an active business carried on by it in Canada or in a country listed in subsection (11), where the affiliate is resident in a country listed in subsection (11) and the corporation, together with all other corporations resident in Canada with which the corporation does not deal at arm's length and in respect of which the affiliate is a foreign affiliate, have so elected in respect of the business for the taxation year or any preceding taxation year of the affiliate, the following rules apply:

(a) there shall be added to the amount determined under clause (1)(a)(i)(A) after adjustment in accordance with the provisions of subsection (2) (in this subsection and in subsection (2.2) referred to as the "adjusted earnings amount") the aggregate of all amounts each of which is the amount, if any, by which

    (i) the amount that may reasonably be regarded as having been deducted in respect of the cost of a capital property or foreign resource property (within the meaning assigned by paragraph 66(15)(f) [66(15)"foreign resource property"] of the Act) of the affiliate in computing the adjusted earnings amount

exceeds

    (ii) the amount that may reasonably be regarded as having been deducted in respect of the cost of that capital property or foreign resource property in computing income or profit of the affiliate for the year from that business in its financial statements prepared in accordance with the laws of the country in which the affiliate is resident;

(b) there shall be deducted from the adjusted earnings amount the aggregate of all amounts each of which is the amount, if any, by which

    (i) the amount determined under subparagraph (a)(ii) in respect of that capital property or foreign resource property

exceeds

    (ii) the amount determined under subparagraph (a)(i) in respect of that capital property or foreign resource property;

(c) where any capital property or foreign resource property (within the meaning assigned by paragraph 66(15)(f) [66(15)"foreign resource property"] of the Act) of the affiliate has been disposed of in the taxation year,

    (i) there shall be added to the adjusted earnings amount the aggregate of the amounts deducted pursuant to paragraphs (b) and (2.2)(b) for preceding taxation years of the affiliate in respect of that capital property or foreign resource property, and

    (ii) there shall be deducted from the adjusted earnings amount the aggregate of the amounts added pursuant to paragraphs (a) and (2.2)(a) for the preceding taxation years of the affiliate in respect of that capital property or foreign resource property; and

(d) for the purposes of paragraph (c), where the affiliate has merged with one or more corporations to form a new corporation, any capital property or foreign resource property (within the meaning assigned by paragraph 66(15)(f) [66(15)"foreign resource property"] of the Act) of the affiliate that becomes a property of the new corporation shall be deemed to have been disposed of by the affiliate in its last taxation year before the merger.

**Information Circulars**: 77-9R: Books, records and other requirements for taxpayers having foreign affiliates.

**(2.2)** Where the taxation year of a foreign affiliate of a particular corporation resident in Canada for which the particular corporation has made an election under subsection (2.1) in respect of an active business carried on by the affiliate is not the first taxation year of the affiliate in which it carried on the business and in which it was a foreign affiliate of the particular corporation or of another corporation resident in Canada with which the particular corporation was not dealing at arm's length at any time (hereinafter referred to as the "non-arm's length corporation"), in computing the earnings of the affiliate from the business for the taxation year for which the election is made,

the following rules, in addition to those set out in subsection (2.1), apply:

(a) there shall be added to the adjusted earnings amount the aggregate of all amounts each of which is an amount that would have been determined under paragraph (2.1)(a) or subparagraph (2.1)(c)(i)

    (i) for any preceding taxation year of the affiliate in which it was a foreign affiliate of the particular corporation if the particular corporation had made an election under subsection (2.1) for the first taxation year of the affiliate in which it was a foreign affiliate of the particular corporation and carried on the business, and

    (ii) for any preceding taxation year of the affiliate (other than a taxation year referred to in subparagraph (i)) in which it was a foreign affiliate of the non-arm's length corporation if the non-arm's length corporation had made an election under subsection (2.1) for the first taxation year of the affiliate in which it was a foreign affiliate of the non-arm's length corporation and carried on the business; and

(b) there shall be deducted from the adjusted earnings amount the aggregate of all amounts each of which is an amount that would have been determined under paragraph (2.1)(b) or subparagraph (2.1)(c)(ii)

    (i) for any preceding taxation year of the affiliate in which it was a foreign affiliate of the particular corporation if the particular corporation had made an election under subsection (2.1) for the first taxation year of the affiliate in which it was a foreign affiliate of the particular corporation and carried on the business, and

    (ii) for any preceding taxation year of the affiliate (other than a taxation year referred to in subparagraph (i)) in which it was a foreign affiliate of the non-arm's length corporation if the non-arm's length corporation had made an election under subsection (2.1) for the first taxation year of the affiliate in which it was a foreign affiliate of the non-arm's length corporation and carried on the business.

**(2.3)** For the purposes of this subsection and subsections (2.1) and (2.2), where an election under subsection (2.1) has been made by a corporation resident in Canada (in this subsection and in subsection (2.4) referred to as the "electing corporation") in respect of an active business of a foreign affiliate of the electing corporation and the affiliate subsequently becomes a foreign affiliate of another corporation resident in Canada (in this subsection and in subsection (2.4) referred to as the "subsequent corporation") that does not deal at arm's length with the electing corporation, in computing the earnings of the affiliate from such business in respect of the subsequent corporation for any taxation year of the affiliate ending after the affiliate so became a foreign affiliate of the subsequent corporation, the subsequent corporation shall be deemed to have made an election under subsection (2.1) in respect of the business of the affiliate for the first such taxation year and for the purposes of paragraph (2.1)(d), the earnings of the affiliate for all of the preceding taxation years shall be deemed to have been adjusted in accordance with subsections (2.1) and (2.2) in the same manner as if the subsequent corporation had been the electing corporation.

Notes: Reg. 5907(2.3) amended by P.C. 1997-1670, effective on the same basis as the amendment to Reg. 5903(1), to delete a reference to 5907(2.5) [the definition of "subsequent" corporation applied to it] and to change "paragraph (2.1)(c)" to "paragraph (2.1)(d)".

**(2.4)** For the purposes of subsection (2.3)

(a) a corporation formed as a result of a merger, to which section 87 of the Act applies, of the electing corporation and one or more other corporations, or

(b) a corporation that has acquired shares of the capital stock of a foreign affiliate, in respect of which an election under subsection (2.1) has been made, from the electing corporation in a transaction in respect of which an election under section 85 of the Act was made

shall be deemed to be a subsequent corporation that does not deal at arm's length with the electing corporation.

**(2.5)** [Repealed]

Notes: Reg. 5907(2.5) repealed by P.C. 1997-1670, effective on the same basis as the amendment to Reg. 5903(1). It read:

(2.5) The adjustments set out in subsections (2.1) and (2.2) are only relevant in determining the earnings of a foreign affiliate for a taxation year from an active business carried on by it in a country, relative to a corporation that has elected under subsection (2.1) in respect of the business, or a subsequent corporation, and with regard to any such corporation subparagraph (1)(a)(i) shall be read as if the reference therein to "subsection (2)" were a reference to "subsections (2), (2.1) and (2.2)".

**(2.6)** A corporation resident in Canada, and all other corporations resident in Canada with which the corporation does not deal at arm's length, shall each be considered to have elected under subsection (2.1) in respect of an active business carried on by a non-resident corporation that is a foreign affiliate of each such corporation for a taxation year if there is filed with the Minister on or before the day that is the later of

(a) June 30, 1986, and

(b) the earliest of the days on or before which any one of the said corporations is required to file a return of income pursuant to section 150 of the Act for its taxation year following the taxation year in which the taxation year of the affiliate in respect of which the election is made ends,

the following information:

(c) a description of the active business sufficient to identify the business, and

(d) a statement on behalf of each such corporation, signed by an authorized official of the corporation on behalf of which the statement is made, that the corporation is electing under subsection (2.1) in respect of the business.

**(2.7)** Notwithstanding any other provision of this Part, where

(a) an amount is included in computing the income or loss from an active business of a particular foreign affiliate of a taxpayer for a particular taxation year under subparagraph 95(2)(a)(i) or (ii) of the Act, and

(b) the amount included is in respect of an amount paid or payable (other than an amount paid or payable that is described in clause 95(2)(a)(ii)(D) of the Act) by another non-resident corporation described in subparagraph 95(2)(a)(i) or (ii) of the Act or by a partnership of which such a corporation is a member,

the amount (in respect of which an amount was included in the income or loss from an active business of the particular affiliate for the paticular year) paid or payable by the non-resident corporation or the partnership shall, except where it has been deducted under paragraph (2)(j) in computing the non-resident corporation's earnings or loss from an active business, be deducted in computing the earnings or loss of the non-resident corporation or the partnership, as the case may be, from the active business for its earliest taxation year in which the amount was paid or payabble and shall not be deducted in computing its earnings or loss from the active business for any other taxation year.

Notes: Reg. 5907(2.7) added by P.C. 1997-1670, effective on the same basis as the amendment to Reg. 5903(1).

**(2.8)** Notwithstanding any other provision of this Part, where

(a) an amount is included in computing the income from an active business of a particular foreign affiliate of a taxpayer or a person related to the taxpayer for a particular taxation year under clause 95(2)(a)(ii)(D) of the Act, and

(b) the amount included is in respect of an amount of interest paid or payable by another non-resident corporation (in this subsection referred to as the "second affiliate") to which the particular affiliate and the taxpayer are related

the following rules apply:

(c) that amount of interest shall be deducted in computing the second affiliate's income or loss, from an active business carried on by it in a country in which it is resident and subject to income taxation, for its earliest taxation year in which the amount was paid or payable,

(d) the second affiliate is deemed to have carried on an active business in a country in which it was resident and subject to income taxation for each taxation year referred to in paragraph (c) in which such an active business was not otherwise carried on by it, and

(e) in computing the second affiliate's income for a taxation year from any source, no amount shall be deducted in respect of an amount paid or payable by it that is referred to in paragraph (c) except as is required under that paragraph.

**Notes**: Reg. 5907(2.8) added by P.C. 1997-1670, effective on the same basis as the amendment to Reg. 5903(1).

**(2.9)** In computing the earnings from an active business of a foreign affiliate of a corporation resident in Canada for the affiliate's taxation year immediately before the particular taxation year of the affiliate referred to in paragraph 95(2)(k) of the Act,

(a) there shall be added to the amount determined under subparagraph (a)(i) or (ii) of the definition "earnings" in subsection (1) after adjustment in accordance with subsections (2), (2.1) and (2.2) the total of

(i) the amount, if any, by which the total determined in respect of the affiliate in clause (b)(i)(B) for the year exceeds the total determined in respect of the affiliate in clause (b)(i)(A) for the year,

(ii) where, at the end of the year, the affiliate was deemed because of paragraphs 95(2)(k) and 138(11.91)(e) of the Act to have disposed of property owned by it that was used or held by it in the course of a carrying on the active business in the year, the amount that is the total of all amounts each of which is the amount, if any, by which

(A) the lesser of the fair market value and the cost to the affiliate at the end of the year of a capital property (referred to in this subparagraph and subparagraph (b)(ii) as a particular "depreciable asset") owned by it that

(I) was used or held by it in the course of carrying on the active business in the year,

(II) was deemed because of paragraphs 95(2)(k) and 138(11.91)(e) of the Act to have been disposed of at the end of the year, and

(III) was property in respect of the cost of which amounts were, at any time, deductible in computing the earnings from the active business under subparagraph (a)(i) or (ii) of the definition "earnings" in subsection (1)

exceeds

(B) the amount, if any, by which the cost to the affiliate of the particular depreciable asset exceeds the total of all amounts each of which is an amount that can reasonably be regarded as having been deducted in respect of the cost of the particular depreciable asset in computing the earnings (as would be defined in subsection (1) if that definition were read as if the reference in that definition to this subsection did not exist) of the affiliate from the active business in the year or in any preceding taxation year of the affiliate in which it was a foreign affiliate of the corporation or of another corporation resident in Canada which the corporation was not dealing with at arm's length at any time, and

(iii) where, at the end of the year, the affiliate was deemed because of paragraphs 95(2)(k) and 138(11.91)(e) of the Act to have disposed of property (other than capital property) owned by it that was used or held by it in the course of carrying on the active business in the year, the amount that is the total of all amounts each of which is an amount, if any, by which the fair market value of such a property exceeds the cost to the affiliate of the property at the time that is immediately before the end of the year; and

(b) there shall be deducted from the amount determined under subparagraph (a)(i) or (ii) of the definition "earnings" in subsection (1) after adjustment in accordance with subsections (2), (2.1) and (2.2) the total of

(i) the amount, if any, by which

(A) the total of all amounts each of which is a maximum amount deemed because of paragraphs 95(2)(k) and 138(11.91)(d) of the Act to have been claimed under subparagraphs 138(3)(a)(i), (ii) and (iv) and paragraphs 20(1)(l) and (l.1) and 20(7)(c) of the Act (each of which provisions is referred to in this subparagraph as a "reserve provision") in the year

exceeds

(B) the total of all amounts each of which is an amount actually claimed by the affiliate as a reserve in the year that can reasonably be considered to be in respect of amounts in respect of which a reserve could have been claimed under a reserve provision on the assumption that the affiliate could have claimed amounts in respect of the reserve provisions in the year,

(ii) the amount that is the total of all amounts each of which is the amount, if any, by which the amount determined under clause (a)(ii)(B) in respect of a particular depreciable asset described in clause (a)(ii)(A) exceeds the fair market value of the particular depreciable asset at the end of the year, and

(iii) where, at the end of the year, the affiliate was deemed because of paragraphs 95(2)(k) and 138(11,91)(e) of the Act to have disposed of propety (other than capital property) owned by it that was used or held by it in the course of carrying on the active business in the year, the amount that is the total of all amounts each of which is an amount, if any, by which the cost to the affiliate of such a property at the time that is immediately before the end of the year exceeds the fair market value of the property at the end of the year.

**Notes**: Reg. 5907(2.9) added by P.C. 1997-1670, effective on the same basis as the amendment to Reg. 5903(1). Unlike 5907(2.7) and (2.8), this was not included in the draft regulations of January 23, 1995.

**(3)** For the purposes of this Part, any corporation that was, on January 1, 1972, a foreign affiliate of a taxpayer shall be deemed to have become a foreign affiliate of the taxpayer on that day.

**(4)** For the purposes of this Part, "government of a country" includes the government of a state, province or other political subdivision of that country.

**(5)** For the purposes of this section, each capital gain and each capital loss of a foreign affiliate of a taxpayer from the disposition of property shall be computed in accordance with the rules set out in subsection 95(2) of the Act and, for the purposes of subsection (6), where any such gain or loss is required to be computed in Canadian currency, the amount of such gain or loss shall be converted from Canadian currency into the currency referred to in subsection (6) at the rate of exchange prevailing on the date of disposition of the property.

**(5.1)** Notwithstanding subsection (5) and except as provided in subsection (9), where, under the income tax law of a country other than Canada that is relevant in computing the earnings of a foreign affiliate of a taxpayer resident in Canada from an active business carried on by it in a country, no gain or loss is recognized in respect of a disposition by the affiliate of a capital property used or held principally for the purpose of gaining or producing income from an active business to a person (in this subsection referred to as the "transferee") that is another foreign affiliate of the taxpayer or that is a foreign affiliate of another person with whom the taxpayer does not deal at arm's length, for the purposes of this section,

(a) the affiliate's proceeds of disposition of the property shall be deemed to be an amount equal to the aggregate of the adjusted cost base to the affiliate of the property immediately before the disposition and any outlays and expenses to the extent they were made or incurred by the affiliate for the purpose of making the disposition;

(b) the cost to the transferee of the property acquired from the affiliate shall be deemed to be an amount equal to the affiliate's proceeds of disposition, as determined under paragraph (a); and

(c) the transferee shall be deemed to have acquired the property on the date that it was acquired by the affiliate.

**(6)** All amounts referred to in subsections (1) and (2) shall be maintained on a consistent basis from year to year in the currency of the country in which the foreign affiliate of the corporation resident in Canada is itself resident or such currency, other than Canadian currency, as is reasonable in the circumstances.

**Information Circulars**: 77-9R: Books, records and other requirements for taxpayers having foreign affiliates.

**(7)** For the purposes of this Part, the amount of any stock dividend paid by a foreign affiliate of a corporation resident in Canada on a share of a class of its capital stock shall be deemed to be nil.

**(7.1)** Where, at any time in a taxation year of a corporation resident in Canada, a foreign affiliate of the corporation (in this subsection referred to as the "payor affiliate") pays a dividend on the shares of any class of its capital stock to the corporation (in this subsection referred to as the "particular dividend") and as a result of the payment the corporation is entitled to a tax credit from the government of the country in which the payor affiliate is resident,

(a) if the particular dividend was paid on or after the day on which this subsection comes into force, or

(b) if the particular dividend was paid before the day on which this subsection comes into force and in a taxation year commencing after 1978 and the corporation elects in respect of the tax credit in its return of income for the 1985, 1986, 1987, 1988 or 1989 taxation year required to be filed pursuant to subsection 150(1) of the Act,

for the purpose of this Part, the following rules apply:

(c) the tax credit shall be deemed to be a dividend paid at that time by the payor affiliate on the shares of that class of its capital stock to the corporation,

(d) immediately before that time there shall be added to the exempt surplus of the payor affiliate an amount equal to the proportion of the tax credit that

(i) the portion of the particular dividend that would, were the corporation not entitled to the tax credit, be deemed by subsection 5900(1) to have been paid out of the payor affiliate's exempt surplus in respect of the corporation

is of

(ii) the particular dividend,

(e) immediately before that time, there shall be added to the taxable surplus of the payor affiliate an amount equal to the proportion of the tax credit that

(i) the portion of the particular dividend that would, were the corporation not entitled to the tax credit, be deemed by subsection 5900(1) to have been paid out of the payor affiliate's taxable surplus in respect of the corporation

is of

(ii) the particular dividend, and

(f) the foreign tax applicable to the aggregate of

(i) the portion of the particular dividend determined under subparagraph (e)(i), and

(ii) the portion of any amount deemed to be a dividend by virtue of paragraph (c) that is deemed by subsection 5900(1) to have been paid out of the payor affiliate's taxable surplus in respect of the corporation

shall, notwithstanding paragraph 5900(1)(d), be equal to the amount determined under paragraph 5900(1)(d) in respect of the amount referred to in subparagraph (i), less the amount determined under paragraph (e).

(8) For the purposes of computing the various amounts referred to in this section, the first taxation year of a foreign affiliate formed as a result of a merger in the manner described in subsection 5905(3) shall be deemed to have commenced at the time of the merger, and a taxation year of a predecessor corporation (within the meaning assigned by subsection 5905(3)) that would otherwise have ended after the merger shall be deemed to have ended immediately before the merger.

(9) Where a foreign affiliate of a taxpayer resident in Canada has been dissolved and paragraph 95(2)(e.1) of the Act does not apply, for the purpose of computing the various amounts referred to in this section, the following rules apply:

(a) where, at a particular time in the course of the dissolution, all or substantially all of the property owned by the affiliate immediately before that time was distributed to the shareholders of the affiliate, the taxation year of the affiliate that otherwise would have included the particular time shall be deemed to have ended immediately before the particular time;

(b) except as provided in paragraph 88(3)(a) and subparagraph 95(2)(e)(i) of the Act,

(i) each property of the affiliate that was distributed to the shareholders in the course of the dissolution shall be deemed to have been disposed of immediately before the end of the affiliate's taxation year deemed to have ended by paragraph (a) for proceeds of disposition equal to the fair market value thereof immediately before the particular time, and

(ii) each property of the affiliate that was otherwise disposed of in the course of the dissolution shall be deemed to have been disposed of by the affiliate for proceeds of disposition equal to the fair market value thereof at the time of disposition; and

(c) except as provided in subparagraph 95(2)(e)(i) of the Act, each property of the dissolved affiliate that was disposed of or distributed in the course of the dissolution to another foreign affiliate of the taxpayer resident in Canada shall be deemed to have been acquired by that other foreign affiliate at a cost equal to the proceeds of disposition of that property to the dissolved affiliate, as determined in paragraph (b).

Notes: Revenue Canada's view is that "all or substantially all" means 90% or more.

(10) Where

(a) the net earnings or net loss for a taxation year of a foreign affiliate of a corporation resident in Canada from an active business carried on in a country other than Canada would otherwise be included in the affiliate's taxable earnings or taxable loss, as the case may be, for the year,

(b) the rate of the income or profits tax to which any earnings of that active business of the affiliate are subjected by the government of that country is, by virtue of a special exemption from or reduction of tax (other than an export incentive) that is provided under a law of such country to promote investments or projects in pursuance of a program of economic development, less than the rate of such tax that would, but for such exemption or reduction, be paid by the affiliate, and

(c) the affiliate qualified for such exemption from or reduction of tax in respect of an investment made by it in that country before January 1, 1976 or in respect of an investment made by it or a project undertaken by it in that country pursuant to an agreement in writing entered into before January 1, 1976,

for the purposes of this Part, such net earnings or net loss shall be included in the affiliate's exempt earnings or exempt loss, as the case may be, for the year and not in the affiliate's taxable earnings or taxable loss, as the case may be, for the year.

Notes: Reg. 5907(10)(b) refers to what is generally known as "tax sparing", where the host country exempts or reduces tax on income from an investment for incentive purposes. However, such protection from "taxable surplus" treatment applies only for pre-1976 investments (see para. (c)), preserving such treatment from the days when dividends from foreign affiliates were not taxed at all.

There is no need for tax sparing in respect of dividends received by Canadian corporations from countries listed or designated under Reg. 5907(11), since the dividends are not taxed. Tax sparing of Canadian tax on income earned abroad directly (such as through a branch or joint venture), or as dividends received by Canadian resident individuals, is provided in some of Canada's tax treaties with developing countries.

(11) For the purposes of this Part, a country is a "designated treaty country" for a taxation year of a foreign affiliate of a corporation where Canada and

**Reg. S. 5907(11)** — Income Tax Regulations

that country have entered into a comprehensive agreement or convention for the elimination of double taxation on income that has entered into force and has effect for that taxation year of the affiliate but, any territory, possession, department, dependency or area of that country to which that agreement or convention does not apply is not included in that designated treaty country.

**Notes**: Reg. 5907(11) amended by P.C. 1997-1670, effective for taxation years of a corporation's foreign affiliate that begin after 1995, except that, where the corporation notifies Revenue Canada, in its return for its first taxation year that begins after 1994 or for a taxation year in which a dividend was paid by the foreign affiliate, of its election to have new Reg. 5907(11) (as amended), (11.1) and (11.2) apply to a taxation year of the foreign affiliate that begins before 1996,

(a) the amendments apply to that taxation year and each later taxation year of the foreign affiliate; and

(b) read all references in Reg. 5907 to "listed in subsection (11)" as "designated treaty country" for that taxation year and later taxation years of the foreign affiliate.

For years where the amendment does not apply, since 1986, read:

(11) The following countries are hereby listed for the purposes of paragraphs (1)(b) and (c):

Antigua
Argentina
Australia
Austria, Republic of
Bangladesh, People's Republic of
Barbados
Belgium
Belize
Brazil, Federative Republic of
Cameroon, United Republic of
China, People's Republic of
Cyprus, Republic of
Denmark, Kingdom of
Dominica
Dominican Republic
Egypt, Arab Republic of
Finland, Republic of
French Republic, European Departments, the Territorial Authority of Saint-Pierre and Miquelon and the following overseas Departments, namely,
    Guadeloupe
    Guyane
    Martinique
    Réunion
but not including overseas Territories.
Germany, Federal Republic of
Guyana, Cooperative Republic of
India
Indonesia
Ireland
Israel, State of
Italy
Ivory Coast, Republic of
Jamaica
Japan
Kenya
Korea, Republic of
Liberia
Malaysia
Malta
Montserrat
Morocco, Kingdom of
Netherlands, Kingdom of the, but for greater certainty, not including the Netherlands Antilles
New Zealand, but for greater certainty, not including the Cook Islands, Niue or Tokelau
Norway, Kingdom of, but for greater certainty, not including Svalbard (including Bear Island), Jan Mayen and the Norwegian dependencies outside Europe
Pakistan, Islamic Republic of
Philippines, Republic of the
Portugal
Romania, Socialist Republic of
Saint Kitts and Nevis-Anguilla
Saint Lucia
Saint Vincent
Senegal, Republic of
Singapore, Republic of
Spain
Sri Lanka, Democratic Socialist Republic of
Sweden
Switzerland
Thailand, Kingdom of
Trinidad and Tobago
Tunisia, Republic of
Union of Soviet Socialist Republics
United Kingdom of Great Britain and Northern Ireland
United States of America, but for greater certainty, not including its Territories
Zambia, Republic of

Under the new 5907(11), only for countries with which Canada has tax treaties will dividends paid out of earnings be effectively exempt from tax in the hands of the Canadian corporate shareholders.

For a list of countries with which Canada currently has or is negotiating tax treaties, see at the end of this book, after the Canada-U.S. and Canada-U.K. treaties and before the *Interpretation Act*.

**(11.1)** For the purpose of subsection (11), where a comprehensive agreement or convention between Canada and another country for the elimination of double taxation on income has entered into force, that convention or agreement is deemed to have entered into force and have effect in respect of a taxation year of a foreign affiliate of a corporation any day of which is in the period that begins on the day on which the agreement or convention was signed and that ends on the last day of the last taxation year of the affiliate for which the agreement or convention is effective.

**Notes**: Reg. 5907(11.1) added by P.C. 1997-1670, effective on the same basis as the amendment to Reg. 5907(11).

**(11.2)** For the purposes of this Part, a foreign affiliate of a corporation is, at any time, deemed not to be resident in a country with which Canada has entered into a comprehensive agreement or convention for the elimination of double taxation on income unless

(a) the affiliate is, at that time, a resident of that country for the purpose of the agreement or convention;

(b) the affiliate would, at that time, be a resident of that country for the purpose of the agreement or convention if the affiliate were treated, for the purpose of income taxation in that country, as a body corporate;

(c) where the agreement or convention entered into force before 1995, the affiliate would, at that time, be a resident of that country for the purpose of the agreement or convention but for a provision in the agreement or convention that has not been amended after 1994 and that provides that the agreement or convention does not apply to the affiliate; or

(d) the affiliate would, at that time, be a resident of that country, as provided by paragraph (a), (b) or (c) if the agreement or convention had entered into force.

**Notes:** Reg. 5907(11.2) added by P.C. 1997-1670, effective on the same basis as the amendment to Reg. 5907(11).

**I.T. Technical News:** No. 16 (U.S. S-Corps and LLCs).

(12) For the purposes of paragraph 95(2)(j) of the Act, the adjusted cost base to a foreign affiliate of a taxpayer of an interest in a partnership at any time is prescribed to be the cost thereof otherwise determined at that time except that

(a) there shall be added to that cost such of the following amounts as are applicable, namely,

(i) any amount included in the earnings of the affiliate for a taxation year ending after 1971 and before that time that may reasonably be considered to relate to profits of the partnership,

(ii) the affiliate's incomes as described by the description of "A" in the definition "foreign accrual property income" in subsection 95(1) of the Act for a taxation year ending after 1971 and before that time that can reasonably be considered to relate to profits of the partnership,

(iii) any amount included in computing the exempt earnings or taxable earnings, as the case may be, of the affiliate for a taxation year ending after 1971 and before that time that may reasonably be considered to relate to a capital gain of the partnership,

(iv) where the affiliate has, at any time before that time and in a taxation year ending after 1971, made a contribution of capital to the partnership otherwise than by way of a loan, such part of the amount of the contribution as cannot reasonably be regarded as a gift made to or for the benefit of any other member of the partnership who was related to the affiliate, and

(v) such portion of any income or profits tax refunded before that time by the government of a country to the partnership as may reasonably be regarded as tax refunded in respect of an amount described in any of subparagraphs (b)(i) to (iii), and

(b) there shall be deducted from that cost such of the following amounts as are applicable, namely,

(i) any amount included in the loss of the affiliate for a taxation year ending after 1971 that may reasonably be considered to relate to a loss of the partnership,

(ii) the affiliate's losses as described by the description of D in the definition "foreign accrual property income" in subsection 95(1) of the Act for a taxation year ending after 1971 and before that time that can reasonably be considered to relate to the losses of the partnership,

(iii) any amount included in computing the exempt loss or taxable loss, as the case may be, of the affiliate for a taxation year ending after 1971 and before that time that may reasonably be considered to relate to a capital loss of the partnership,

(iv) any amount received by the affiliate before that time and in a taxation year ending after 1971 as, on account or in lieu of payment of, or in satisfaction of, a distribution of his share of the partnership profits or partnership capital, and

(v) such portion of any income or profits tax paid before that time to the government of a country by the partnership as may reasonably be regarded as tax paid in respect of an amount described in any of subparagraphs (a)(i) to (iii),

and, for greater certainty, where any interest of a foreign affiliate in a partnership was reacquired by the affiliate after having been previously disposed of, no adjustment that was required to be made under this subsection before such reacquisition shall be made under this subsection to the cost to the affiliate of the interest as reacquired property of the affiliate.

**Notes:** Reg. 5907(12)(a)(ii) and (b)(ii) amended by P.C. 1997-1670, effective on the same basis as the amendment to Reg. 5903(1), to update references to ITA 95 to use the R.S.C. 1985 (5th Supp.) references. Opening words of Reg. 5907(12)(b) corrected by P.C. 1997-1670, retroactive to November 13, 1981, to add the word "applicable".

(13) For the purpose of subparagraph 128.1(1)(d)(ii) of the Act, the amount prescribed to be included in the foreign accrual property income of a foreign affiliate of a taxpayer for a taxation year is the amount, if any, by which

(a) the taxable surplus of the affiliate in respect of the taxpayer at the end of the year other than the affiliate's net earnings for the year in respect of the affiliate's foreign accrual property income

exceeds the total of

(b) the amount determined by the formula

$$(A - B) \times (C - 1)$$

where

A is the total of the underlying foreign tax of the affiliate in respect of the taxpayer at the end of the year and the amount, to the extent that it is not otherwise included in that underlying foreign tax, that would have been added to that underlying foreign tax if each disposition deemed by paragraph 128.1(1)(b) of the Act had been an actual disposition,

B is the part of the value of A that can reasonably be considered to relate to the affiliate's net earnings for the year in respect of the affiliate's foreign accrual property income, and

C is the relevant tax factor, as defined in subsection 95(1) of the Act, and

(c) the amount, if any, by which

(i) the total of all amounts required by paragraph 92(1)(a) of the Act to be added at any time in a preceding taxation year in computing the adjusted cost base to the taxpayer of the shares of the affiliate owned by the taxpayer at the end of the year

exceeds

(ii) the total of all amounts required by paragraph 92(1)(b) of the Act to be deducted at any time in a preceding taxation year in computing the adjusted cost base to the taxpayer of the shares of the affiliate owned by the taxpayer at the end of the year.

**Notes**: Reg. 5907(13) amended by P.C. 1997-1670, effective after 1992, except that where a corporation elected in accordance with para. 111(4)(a) of the 1993 technical bill (S.C. 1994, c. 21), the amendment applies to the corporation from its time of continuation (see Notes to ITA 250(5.1) re this election). Formerly read:

(13) For the purposes of paragraph 48(5)(c) [subpara. 128.1(1)(d)(ii)] of the Act, the amount prescribed to be included in the foreign accrual property income of a foreign affiliate of a taxpayer for a taxation year is the aggregate of

(a) the amount that would have been included in the foreign accrual property income of the affiliate for the year if immediately before the end thereof the foreign affiliate had disposed of all its capital property, other than

(i) property that would be property described in paragraph 48(1)(a) of the Act if the affiliate had disposed of it immediately before the end of the year, or

(ii) property described in paragraph 48(1)(c) of the Act in respect of which the corporation had previously made an election under that paragraph in respect of the last preceding time the affiliate ceased to be resident in Canada,

and had received therefor proceeds of disposition equal to the fair market value thereof at that time;

(b) the amount, if any, by which

(i) the amount that would have been included in computing the taxable surplus of the affiliate in respect of the taxpayer immediately before the end of the year if at that time the affiliate had disposed of all its excluded property for proceeds of disposition equal to the fair market value thereof at that time

exceeds

(ii) the product obtained when the amount that would be included in the underlying foreign tax of the affiliate in respect of the taxpayer immediately before the end of the year by virtue of the disposition described in subparagraph (i) is multiplied by the amount by which

(A) the relevant tax factor (as defined by paragraph 95(1)(f) [95(1)"relevant tax factor"] of the Act)

exceeds

(B) one; and

(c) the amount, if any, by which

(i) the taxable surplus of the affiliate in respect of the taxpayer at the end of the year other than an amount included in the taxable earnings of the affiliate for the year under clause (l)(i)(ii)(B)

exceeds the aggregate of

(ii) the product obtained when the underlying foreign tax of the affiliate in respect of the taxpayer at that time less such part of such underlying foreign tax as may reasonably be considered to relate to the taxable earnings of the affiliate for the year under clause (l)(i)(ii)(B) is multiplied by the amount by which

(A) the relevant tax factor (as defined by paragraph 95(1)(f) [95(1)"relevant tax factor"] of the Act)

exceeds

(B) one, and

(iii) the amount, if any, by which

(A) the aggregate of all amounts required by paragraph 92(1)(a) of the Act to be added at any time in a previous taxation year in computing the adjusted cost base to the taxpayer of the shares of the affiliate owned by him at the end of the year

exceeds

(B) the aggregate of all amounts required by paragraph 92(1)(b) of the Act to be deducted at any time in a previous taxation year in computing the adjusted cost base to the taxpayer of the shares of the affiliate owned by him at the end of the year.

**Interpretation Bulletins**: IT-451R: Deemed disposition and acquisition on ceasing to be or become a registrant in Canada.

**Definitions [Reg. 5907]**: "active business" — ITA 95(1), Reg. 5907(1); "adjusted cost base" — ITA 54, 248(1); "allowable capital loss" — ITA 38(b), 248(1); "amount" — ITA 248(1), Reg. 5907(7); "arm's length" — ITA 251(1); "borrowed money", "business" — ITA 248(1); "Canada" — ITA 255, *Interpretation Act* 35(1); "capital gain" — ITA 39(1), 248(1); "capital loss" — ITA 39(1)(b), 248(1); "capital property" — ITA 54, 248(1); "corporation" — ITA 248(1), *Interpretation Act* 35(1); "designated treaty country" — Reg. 5907(11); "disposed" — ITA 248(1)"disposition"; "disposition" — ITA 248(1); "dividend" — ITA 248(1); "earnings" — Reg. 5907(1); "exempt deficit" — Reg. 5902(1)–(3), 5907(1); "exempt earnings", "exempt loss" — Reg. 5907(1), (10); "exempt surplus" — Reg. 5902(1)–(3), 5907(1); "fiscal period" — ITA 249.1; "foreign accrual property income" — ITA 95(1), (2), 248(1); "foreign affiliate" — Reg. 5907(3); "foreign resource property" — ITA 66(15), 248(1); "foreign tax applicable" — Reg. 5900(1)(d); "government of a country" — Reg. 5907(4); "lending asset", "life insurance business", "life insurance corporation" — ITA 248(1); "loss" — Reg. 5907(1); "Minister" — ITA 248(1); "net earnings", "net loss" — Reg. 5907(1); "non-resident" — ITA 248(1); "opening exempt deficit" — Reg. 5905(5)(e); "opening exempt surplus" — Reg. 5905(5)(d); "opening taxable deficit" — Reg. 5905(5)(g); "opening taxable surplus" — Reg. 5905(5)(f); "opening underlying foreign tax" — Reg. 5905(5)(h); "particular dividend" — Reg. 5907(7.1); "partnership" — see Notes to ITA 96(1); "payor affiliate" — Reg. 5907(7.1); "person", "prescribed", "property" — ITA 248(1); "province" — *Interpretation Act* 35(1); "related" — ITA 251(2)–(6); "relevant tax factor" — ITA 95(1); "resident", "resident in Canada" — ITA 250; "share", "shareholder", "specified member", "stock dividend" — ITA 248(1); "surplus entitlement percentage" — Reg. 5905(13); "taxable capital gain" — ITA 38(a), 248(1); "taxable deficit" — Reg. 5902(1)–(3), 5907(1); "taxable dividend" — ITA 89(1), 248(1); "taxable earnings", "taxable loss" — Reg. 5907(1), (10); "taxable surplus" — Reg. 5902(1)–(3), 5907(1); "taxation year" — ITA 249; "taxpayer" — ITA 248(1); "territory" — *Interpretation Act* 35(1); "underlying foreign tax" — Reg. 5902(1)–(3), 5907(1); "underlying foreign tax applicable", "whole dividend" — Reg. 5907(1); "writing" — *Interpretation Act* 35(1).

**5908. (1), (2) [Repealed]**

**Notes**: Reg. 5908 repealed by P.C. 1997-1670, effective December 10, 1997. It provided for elections, filed with a taxpayer's 1982, 1983 or 1984 returns, to have different rules apply in respect of foreign affiliates' taxation years ending after 1975 and beginning before February 27, 1980.

**5909. Prescribed circumstances** — For the purposes of subparagraph 94(1)(b)(i) of the Act, property shall be considered to have been acquired in prescribed circumstances where it is acquired by virtue of the repayment of a loan.

**Definitions [Reg. 5909]**: "prescribed", "property" — ITA 248(1).

## PART LX — PRESCRIBED ACTIVITIES

**6000.** For the purpose of clause 122.3(1)(b)(i)(C) of the Act, a prescribed activity is an activity performed under contract with the United Nations.

**Notes**: Reg. 6000 added by P.C. 1995-1723, effective 1994. Former Reg. 6000 provided rules for determining the employment tax credit under ITA 127(16), which was repealed by 1988 tax reform effective 1989.

**Definitions [Reg. 6000]**: "prescribed" — ITA 248(1).

## PART LXI — RELATED SEGREGATED FUND TRUSTS

**6100.** An election under subsection 138.1(4) of the Act by the trustee of a related segregated fund trust shall be made by filing with the Minister the prescribed form within 90 days from the end of the taxation year of the trust in respect of any capital property deemed to have been disposed of in that taxation year by virtue of the election.

**Definitions [Reg. 6100]**: "capital property" — ITA 54, 248(1); "disposed" — ITA 248(1)"disposition"; "Minister", "prescribed" — ITA 248(1); "related" — ITA 251(2)–(6); "taxation year" — ITA 249; "trust" — ITA 104(1), 248(1), (3).

**Forms**: T3018: Election for deemed disposition and reacquisition of capital property of a life insurance segregated fund under subsection 138.1(4).

## PART LXII — PRESCRIBED SECURITIES AND SHARES

**Proposed Amendment — Part LXII**

**Prescribed Securities, Shares and Debt Obligations**

**Application**: The November 30, 2000 draft regulations (miscellaneous), s. 5 (pre-published in the *Canada Gazette*, Part I, December 9, 2000), will amend the heading of Part LXII to read as above, applicable after February 18, 1997.

**6200. Prescribed securities [for election re Canadian securities]** — For the purposes of subsection 39(6) of the Act, a prescribed security is, with respect to the taxpayer referred to in subsection 39(4) of the Act,

(a) a share of the capital stock of a corporation, other than a public corporation, the value of which is, at the time it is disposed of by that taxpayer, a value that is or may reasonably be considered to be wholly or primarily attributable to

(i) real property, an interest therein or an option in respect thereof,

(ii) Canadian resource property or a property that would have been a Canadian resource property if it had been acquired after 1971,

(iii) foreign resource property or a property that would have been a foreign resource property if it had been acquired after 1971, or

(iv) any combination of properties described in subparagraphs (i) to (iii)

owned by

(v) the corporation,

(vi) a person other than the corporation, or

(vii) a partnership;

(b) a bond, debenture, bill, note, mortgage or similar obligation, issued by a corporation, other than a public corporation, if at any time before that taxpayer disposes of the security he does not deal at arm's length with the corporation;

(c) a security that is

(i) a share, or

(ii) a bond, debenture, bill, note, mortgage or similar obligation

that was acquired by the taxpayer from a person with whom the taxpayer does not deal at arm's length (other than from a person subject to subsection 39(4) of the Act for the person's taxation year that includes the time of the acquisition);

(c.1) a security described in subparagraph (c)(i) or (ii) that was acquired by the taxpayer from a person (other than from a person subject to subsection 39(4) of the Act for the person's taxation year that includes the time of the acquisition) in circumstances to which subsection 85(1) or (2) of the Act applied;

(d) a share acquired by that taxpayer under circumstances referred to in section 66.3 of the Act; or

(e) a security described in subparagraph (c)(i) or (ii) that was acquired by the taxpayer

(i) as proceeds of disposition for a security of the taxpayer to which paragraph (a), (b), (c) or (d) applied in respect of the taxpayer, or

(ii) as a result of one or more transactions that can reasonably be considered to have been an exchange or substitution of a security of the taxpayer to which paragraph (a), (b), (c) or (d) applied in respect of the taxpayer.

**Notes**: Reg. 6200(c) and (e) amended and (c.1) added by P.C. 1998-1449, effective for 1993 and later taxation years. For earlier years, read:

(c) a security that is

(i) a share, or

(ii) a bond, debenture, bill, note, mortgage or similar obligation

that was acquired by that taxpayer in a transaction

(iii) in which that taxpayer was not dealing at arm's length, or

(iv) to which the provisions of syubsection 85(1) or (2) of the Act applied;

. . . . .

(e) a security that is

(i) a share, or

(ii) a bond, debenture, bill, note, mortgage or similar obligation,

that was acquired by that taxpayer

(iii) as proceeds of disposition for or

(iv) as a result of one or more transactions that may reasonably be considered to have been an exchange or substitution of the security for, a security described in any of paragraphs (a) to (d).

Reg. 6200(b), (c)(ii) and (e)(ii) amended to change "mortgage, hypothec" to "mortgage" by P.C. 1994-1817, effective November 30, 1994. The change is intended to be non-substantive

**Definitions [Reg. 6200]**: "arm's length" — ITA 251(1); "Canadian resource property" — ITA 66(15), 248(1); "corporation" — ITA 248(1), *Interpretation Act* 35(1); "disposed", "disposes" — ITA 248(1)"disposition"; "foreign resource property" — ITA 66(15), 248(1); "partnership" — see Notes to ITA 96(1); "person", "prescribed", "property" — ITA 248(1); "public corporation" — ITA 89(1), 248(1); "share" — ITA 248(1); "substitution" — ITA 248(5); "taxpayer" — ITA 248(1).

**Interpretation Bulletins**: IT-479R: Transactions in securities.

**6201. Prescribed shares — (1) [Term preferred share]** — For the purposes of paragraph (f) of the definition "term preferred share" in subsection 248(1) of the Act, a share last acquired before June 29, 1982 and of a class of the capital stock of a corporation that is listed on a stock exchange referred to in section 3200 is a prescribed share unless more than 10 per cent of the issued and outstanding shares of that class are owned by

(a) the owner of that share; or

(b) the owner of that share and persons related to him.

**(2) [Term preferred share]** — For the purposes of paragraph (f) of the definition "term preferred share" in subsection 248(1) of the Act, a share acquired after June 28, 1982 and of a class of the capital stock of a corporation that is listed on a stock exchange referred to in section 3200 is a prescribed share at any particular time with respect to another corporation that receives a dividend at the particular time in respect of the share unless

(a) where the other corporation is a restricted financial institution,

(i) the share is not a taxable preferred share,

(ii) dividends (other than dividends received on shares prescribed under subsection (5)) are received at the particular time by the other corporation or by the other corporation and restricted financial institutions with which the other corporation does not deal at arm's length, in respect of more than 5 per cent of the issued and outstanding shares of that class, and

(iii) a dividend is received at the particular time by the other corporation or a restricted financial institution with which the other corporation does not deal at arm's length, in respect of a share (other than a share prescribed under subsection (5)) of that class acquired after December 15, 1987 and before the particular time;

(b) where the other corporation is a restricted financial institution, the share

(i) is not a taxable preferred share,

(ii) was acquired after December 15, 1987 and before the particular time, and

(iii) was, by reason of subparagraph (h)(i), (ii), (iii) or (v) of the definition "term preferred share" in subsection 248(1) of the Act, deemed to have been issued after December 15, 1987 and before the particular time; or

(c) in any case, dividends (other than dividends received on shares prescribed under subsection (5)) are received at the particular time by the other corporation or by the other corporation and persons with whom the other corporation does not deal at arm's length in respect of more than 10 per cent of the issued and outstanding shares of that class.

**(3) [Term preferred share]** — For the purposes of paragraph 112(2.2)(g) of the Act and paragraph (f) of the definition "term preferred share" in subsection 248(1) of the Act, a share of any of the following series of preferred shares of the capital stock of Massey-Ferguson Limited issued after July 15, 1981 and before March 23, 1982 is a prescribed share:

(a) $25 Cumulative Redeemable Retractable Convertible Preferred Shares, Series C;

(b) $25 Cumulative Redeemable Retractable Preferred Shares, Series D; or

(c) $25 Cumulative Redeemable Retractable Convertible Preferred Shares, Series E.

**(4) [Taxable RFI share]** — For the purposes of the definition "taxable RFI share" in subsection 248(1) of the Act, a share of a class of the capital stock of a corporation that is listed on a stock exchange referred to in section 3200 is a prescribed share at any particular time with respect to another corporation that is a restricted financial institution that receives a dividend at the particular time in respect of the share unless dividends (other than dividends received on shares prescribed under subsection (5.1)) are received at that time by the other corporation, or by the other corporation and restricted financial institutions with which the other corporation does not deal at arm's length, in respect of more than

(a) 10 per cent of the shares of that class that were issued and outstanding at the last time, before the particular time, at which the other corporation or a restricted financial institution with which the other corporation does not deal at arm's length acquired a share of that class, where no dividend is received at the particular time by any such corporation in respect of a share (other than a share prescribed under subsection (5.1)) of that class acquired after December 15, 1987 and before the particular time; or

(b) 5 per cent of the shares of that class that were issued and outstanding at the last time, before the particular time, at which the other corporation or a restricted financial institution with which the other corporation does not deal at arm's length acquired a share of that class, where a dividend is received at the particular time by any such corporation in respect of a share (other than a share prescribed under subsection (5.1)) of that class acquired after December 15, 1987 and before the particular time.

Notes: Reg. 6201(4) amended by P.C. 1995-1198, effective for dividends received after December 20, 1991, essentially to measure a financial institution's percentage holding of a class of shares as relative to the shares outstanding when the shares were last acquired by the institution (or another member of the same corporate group), rather than by measuring percentage ownership on the date a dividend is received. (The former rule could lead to problems where other persons' shares had been redeemed in the interim.) For dividends received before December 21, 1991, read the reference to subsec. (5.1) in the opening words as being to subsec. (5), and read paras. (a) and (b) as:

(a) 10 per cent of the issued and outstanding shares of that class where no dividend is received at that time by the other corporation or a restricted financial institution with which the other corporation does not deal at arm's length in respect of a share (other than a share prescribed under subsection (5)) of that class acquired after December 15, 1987 and before the particular time; or

(b) 5 per cent of the issued and outstanding shares of that class where a dividend is received at the particular time by the other corporation or a restricted financial institution with which the other corporation does not deal at arm's length in respect of a share (other than a share prescribed under subsection (5)) of that class acquired after December 15, 1987 and before the particular time.

(5) [Term preferred share] — For the purposes of paragraph (f) of the definition "term preferred share" in subsection 248(1) of the Act, a share of a class of the capital stock of a corporation that is listed on a stock exchange referred to in section 3200 is a prescribed share at any particular time with respect to another corporation that is registered or licensed under the laws of a province to trade in securities and that holds the share as inventory of the business ordinarily carried on by it unless

### Proposed Amendment — Reg. 6201(5) opening words

(5) [Term preferred share] — For the purpose of paragraph (f) of the definition "term preferred share" in subsection 248(1) of the Act, a share of a class of the capital stock of a corporation that is listed on a stock exchange referred to in section 3200 is a prescribed share at any particular time with respect to another corporation that is registered or licensed under the laws of a province to trade in securities and that holds the share for the purpose of sale in the course of the business ordinarily carried on by it unless

Application: The June 1, 1995 draft regulations (securities held by financial institutions), subsec. 6(1), will amend the opening words of subsec. 6201(5) to read as above, applicable to dividends received in taxation years that begin after October 1994.

Technical Notes: Subsections 6201(5) and (5.1) prescribe certain shares held by securities dealers as shares that are excluded from being "term preferred shares" and "taxable RFI shares". One of the requirements for the exclusion to apply to a share is that it be held as inventory of the business ordinarily carried on by the securities dealer. This requirement is replaced by a requirement that the share be held for the purpose of sale in the course of the business ordinarily carried on by the securities dealer. This amendment is made as a consequence of the introduction of subsection 142.6(3) of the Act, which provides that certain property held by a financial institution is considered not to be inventory. The new requirement is intended to be the same, in substance, as the former requirement.

The amendments to subsections 6201(5) and (5.1) apply to dividends received in taxation years that begin after October 1994.

(a) it may reasonably be considered that the share was acquired as part of a series of transactions or events one of the main purposes of which was to avoid or limit the application of subsection 112(2.1) of the Act; or

(b) the share was not acquired by the other corporation in the course of an underwriting of shares of that class to be distributed to the public and

(i) dividends are received at the particular time by the other corporation or by the other corporation and corporations controlled by the other corporation in respect of more than 10 per cent of the issued and outstanding shares of that class,

(ii) the other corporation is a restricted financial institution and

(A) the share is not a taxable preferred share,

(B) dividends are received at the particular time by the other corporation or by the other corporation and corporations controlled by the other corporation in respect of more than 5 per cent of the issued and outstanding shares of that class, and

(C) a dividend is received at the particular time by the other corporation or a corporation controlled by the other corporation in respect of a share of that class acquired after December 15, 1987 and before the particular time, or

(iii) the other corporation is a restricted financial institution and the share

(A) is not a taxable preferred share,

(B) was acquired after December 15, 1987 and before the particular time, and

(C) was, by reason of subparagraph (h)(i), (ii), (iii) or (v) of the definition "term preferred share" in subsection 248(1) of the Act, deemed to have been issued after December 15, 1987 and before the particular time.

**Related Provisions:** ITA 256(6), (6.1) — Meaning of "controlled".

**Notes:** Reg. 6201(5) amended by P.C. 1995-1198 (effectively split into subsecs. (5) and (5.1), effective for dividends received after December 20, 1991 (see Notes to Reg. 6201(4)). For earlier dividends, read:

(5) For the purposes of the definition "taxable RFI share" and paragraph (f) of the definition "term preferred share" in subsection 248(1) of the Act, a share of a class of the capital stock of a corporation that is listed on a stock exchange referred to in section 3200 is a prescribed share at any particular time with respect to another corporation that is registered or licensed under the laws of a province to trade in securities and that holds the share as inventory of the business ordinarily carried on by it unless

(a) it may reasonably be considered that the share was acquired as part of a series of transactions or events one of the main purposes of which was to avoid or limit the application of subsection 112(2.1) or section 187.3 of the Act; or

(b) the share was not acquired by the other corporation in the course of an underwriting of shares of that class to be distributed to the public and

(i) dividends are received at the particular time by the other corporation or by the other corporation and corporations controlled by the other corporation in respect of more than 10 per cent of the issued and outstanding shares of that class,

(ii) the other corporation is a restricted financial institution and

(A) the share is not a taxable preferred share,

(B) dividends are received at the particular time by the other corporation or by the other corporation and corporations controlled by the other corporation in respect of more than 5 per cent of the issued and outstanding shares of that class, and

(C) a dividend is received at the particular time by the other corporation or a corporation controlled by the other corporation in respect of a share of that class acquired after December 15, 1987 and before the particular time, or

(iii) the other corporation is a restricted financial institution and the share

(A) is not a taxable preferred share,

(B) was acquired after December 15, 1987 and before the particular time, and

(C) was, by reason of subparagraph (h)(i), (ii), (iii) or (v) of the definition "term preferred share" in subsection 248(1) of the Act, deemed to have been issued after December 15, 1987 and before the particular time.

**(5.1) [Taxable RFI share — prescribed share]** — For the purposes of the definition "taxable RFI share" in subsection 248(1) of the Act, a share of a class of the capital stock of a corporation that is listed on a stock exchange referred to in section 3200 is a prescribed share at any particular time with respect to another corporation that is registered or licensed under the laws of a province to trade in securities and that holds the share as inventory of the business ordinarily carried on by it unless

**Proposed Amendment — Reg. 6201(5.1)**

**(5.1) [Taxable RFI share — prescribed share]** — For the purpose of the definition "taxable RFI share" in subsection 248(1) of the Act, a share of a class of the capital stock of a corporation that is listed on a stock exchange referred to in section 3200 is a prescribed share at any particular time with respect to another corporation that is registered or licensed under the laws of a province to trade in securities and that holds the share for the purpose of sale in the course of the business ordinarily carried on by it unless

**Application:** The June 1, 1995 draft regulations (securities held by financial institutions), subsec. 6(2), will amend the opening words of subsec. 6201(5.1) to read as above, applicable to dividends received in taxation years that begin after October 1994.

**Technical Notes:** See under Reg. 6201(5) opening words.

(a) it may reasonably be considered that the share was acquired as part of a series of transactions or events one of the main purposes of which was to avoid or limit the application of section 187.3 of the Act; or

(b) the share was not acquired by the other corporation in the course of an underwriting of shares of that class to be distributed to the public and

(i) dividends are received at the particular time by the other corporation, or by the other corporation and corporations controlled by the other corporation, in respect of more than 10 per cent of the shares of that class issued and outstanding at the last time before the particular time at which any such corporation acquired a share of that class,

(ii) the other corporation is a restricted financial institution and

(A) dividends are received at the particular time by the other corporation, or by the other corporation and corporations controlled by the other corporation, in respect of more than 5 per cent of the shares of that class issued and outstanding at the last time before the particular time at which any such corporation acquired a share of that class, and

(B) a dividend is received at the particular time by the other corporation, or a corporation controlled by the other corporation, in respect of a share of that class acquired after December 15, 1987 and before the particular time, or

(iii) the other corporation is a restricted financial institution and the share

(A) was acquired after December 15, 1987 and before the particular time, and

(B) was, because of subparagraph (h)(i), (ii), (iii) or (v) of the definition "term preferred share" in subsection 248(1) of the Act, deemed to have been issued after December 15, 1987 and before the particular time.

**Related Provisions**: ITA 256(6), (6.1) — Meaning of "controlled".

**Notes**: Reg. 6201(5.1) added by P.C. 1995-1198, effective for dividends received after December 20, 1991. For earlier dividends, see Notes to Reg. 6201(5).

**(6) [Term preferred share — prescribed share]** — For the purposes of paragraph (f) of the definition "term preferred share" in subsection 248(1) of the Act, a share of the capital stock of a corporation that is a member institution of a deposit insurance corporation, within the meaning assigned by section 137.1 of the Act, is a prescribed share with respect to the deposit insurance corporation and any subsidiary wholly-owned corporation of the deposit insurance corporation deemed by subsection 137.1(5.1) of the Act to be a deposit insurance corporation.

**(7) [Taxable preferred share — prescribed share]** — For the purposes of the definition "taxable preferred share" in subsection 248(1) of the Act, the following shares are prescribed shares at any particular time:

(a) the 8.5 per cent Cumulative Redeemable Convertible Class A Preferred Shares of St. Marys Paper Inc. issued on July 7, 1987, where such shares are not deemed, by reason of paragraph (e) of the definition "taxable preferred share" in subsection 248(1) of the Act, to have been issued after that date and before the particular time; and

(b) the Cumulative Redeemable Preferred Shares of CanUtilities Holdings Ltd. issued before July 1, 1991, unless the amount of the consideration for which all such shares were issued exceeds $300,000,000 or the particular time is after July 1, 2001.

**(8) [Canada Cement Lafarge]** — For the purposes of paragraph 112(2.2)(d) of the Act, paragraph (i) of the definition "short-term preferred share", the definition "taxable preferred share" and paragraph (f) of the definition "term preferred share" in subsection 248(1) of the Act, the Exchangeable Preference Shares of Canada Cement Lafarge Ltd. (in this subsection referred to as the "subject shares"), the Exchangeable Preference Shares of Lafarge Canada Inc. and the shares of any corporation formed as a result of an amalgamation or merger of Lafarge Canada Inc. with one or more other corporations are prescribed shares at any particular time where the terms and conditions of such shares at the particular time are the same as, or substantially the same as, the terms and conditions of the subject shares as of June 18, 1987 and, for the purposes of this subsection, the amalgamation or merger of one or more corporations with another corporation formed as a result of an amalgamation or merger of Lafarge Canada Inc. with one or more other corporations shall be deemed to be an amalgamation of Lafarge Canada Inc. with another corporation.

**(9) [Time when share acquired]** — For the purposes of determining under subsections (2), (4), (5) and (5.1) the time at which a share of a class of the capital stock of a corporation was acquired by a taxpayer, shares of that class acquired by the taxpayer at any particular time before a disposition by the taxpayer of shares of that class shall be deemed to have been disposed of before shares of that class acquired by the taxpayer before that particular time.

**Notes**: Reference to Reg. 6201(5.1) added to Reg. 6201(9) by P.C. 1995-1198, effective for dividends received after December 20, 1991.

**(10) [Trusts and partnerships]** — For the purposes of subsections (2), (4), (5) and (5.1) and this subsection,

(a) where a taxpayer is a beneficiary of a trust and an amount in respect of the beneficiary has been designated by the trust in a taxation year pursuant to subsection 104(19) of the Act, the taxpayer shall be deemed to have received the amount so designated at the time it was received by the trust; and

(b) where a taxpayer is a member of a partnership and a dividend has been received by the partnership, the taxpayer's share of the dividend shall be deemed to have been received by the taxpayer at the time the dividend was received by the partnership.

**Notes**: Reference to Reg. 6201(5.1) added to opening words of Reg. 6201(10) by P.C. 1995-1198, effective for dividends received after December 20, 1991.

**(11) [Grandfathering]** — For the purposes of subsections (2), (4), (5) and (5.1),

(a) a share of the capital stock of a corporation acquired by a person after December 15, 1987 pursuant to an agreement in writing entered into

Reg. S. 6201(11)(a)

Income Tax Regulations

before December 16, 1987 shall be deemed to have been acquired by that person before December 16, 1987;

(b) a share of the capital stock of a corporation acquired by a person after December 15, 1987 and before July, 1988 as part of a distribution to the public made in accordance with the terms of a prospectus, preliminary prospectus, registration statement, offering memorandum or notice filed before December 16, 1987 with a public authority pursuant to and in accordance with the securities legislation of the jurisdiction in which the shares were distributed shall be deemed to have been acquired by that person before December 16, 1987;

(c) where a share that was owned by a particular restricted financial institution on December 15, 1987 has, by one or more transactions between related restricted financial institutions, been transferred to another restricted financial institution, the share shall be deemed to have been acquired by the other restricted financial institution before that date and after June 28, 1982 unless at any particular time after December 15, 1987 and before the share was transferred to the other restricted financial institution the share was owned by a shareholder who, at that particular time, was a person other than a restricted financial institution related to the other restricted financial institution; and

(d) where at any particular time there has been an amalgamation (within the meaning assigned by section 87 of the Act) and

(i) each of the predecessor corporations (within the meaning assigned by section 87 of the Act) was a restricted financial institution throughout the period beginning December 16, 1987 and ending at the particular time and the predecessor corporations were related to each other throughout that period, or

(ii) each of the predecessor corporations and the new corporation (within the meaning assigned by section 87 of the Act) is a corporation described in any of paragraphs (a) to (d) of the definition "restricted financial institution" in subsection 248(1) of the Act,

a share acquired by the new corporation from a predecessor corporation on the amalgamation shall be deemed to have been acquired by the new corporation at the time it was acquired by the predecessor corporation.

**Notes**: Reference to Reg. 6201(5.1) added to opening words of Reg. 6201(11) by P.C. 1995-1198, effective for dividends received after December 20, 1991.

**Definitions [Reg. 6201]**: "amount" — ITA 248(1); "arm's length" — ITA 251(1); "business" — ITA 248(1); "Canada" — ITA 255, *Interpretation Act* 35(1); "controlled" — ITA 256(6), (6.1); "corporation" — ITA 248(1), *Interpretation Act* 35(1); "disposed" — ITA 248(1)"disposition"; "disposition" — ITA 248(1); "dividend", "insurance corporation", "inventory" — ITA 248(1); "partnership" — see Notes to ITA 96(1); "person", "preferred share", "prescribed" — ITA 248(1); "province" — *Interpretation Act* 35(1); "related" — ITA 251(2)–(6); "restricted financial institution" — ITA 248(1); "share", "shareholder", "subsidiary wholly-owned corporation", "taxable preferred share" — ITA 248(1); "taxation year" — ITA 249; "taxpayer" — ITA 248(1); "trust" — ITA 104(1), 248(1), (3); "writing" — *Interpretation Act* 35(1).

## 6202. [Resource expenditures — prescribed share] — (1) For the purposes of paragraph 66(15)(d.1) [66(15)"flow-through share"] and subparagraphs 66.1(6)(a)(v) [66.1(6)"Canadian exploration expense"(i)], 66.2(5)(a)(v) [66.2(5)"Canadian development expense"(g)] and 66.4(5)(a)(iii) [66.4(5)"Canadian oil and gas property expense"(c)] of the Act, a share of a class of the capital stock of a corporation (in this section referred to as the "issuing corporation") is a prescribed share if it was issued after December 31, 1982 and

(a) the issuing corporation, any person related to the issuing corporation or of whom the issuing corporation has effective management or control or any partnership or trust of which the issuing corporation or a person related thereto is a member or beneficiary (each of which is referred to in this section as a "member of the related issuing group") is or may be required to redeem, acquire or cancel, in whole or in part, the share or to reduce its paid-up capital at any time within five years from the date of its issue,

(b) a member of the related issuing group provides or may be required to provide any form of guarantee, security or similar indemnity with respect to the share (other than a guarantee, security or similar indemnity with respect to any amount of assistance or benefit from a government, municipality or other public authority in Canada or with respect to eligibility for such assistance or benefit) that could take effect within five years from the date of its issue,

(c) the share (referred to in this section as the "convertible share") is convertible under its terms or conditions at any time within five years from the date of its issue directly or indirectly into debt, or into a share (referred to in this section as the "acquired share") that is, or if issued would be, a prescribed share,

(d) immediately after the share was issued, the person to whom the share was issued or a person related to the person to whom the share was issued (either alone or together with a related person, a related group of persons of which he is a member or a partnership or trust of which he is a member or beneficiary) controls directly or indirectly, or has an absolute or contingent right to control directly or indirectly or to acquire direct or indirect control of, the issuing corporation and the issuing corporation has the right under the terms and conditions in respect of which the share was issued to redeem, purchase or otherwise acquire the share within five years from the date of its issue,

2288

(e) at the time the share was issued, the existence of the issuing corporation was, or there was an arrangement (other than an amalgamation within the meaning assigned by subsection 87(1) of the Act) under which the existence of the issuing corporation could be, limited to a period that ends within five years from the date of its issue, or

(f) the terms or conditions of the share (referred to in this paragraph as the "first share") or of an agreement in existence at the time of its issue provide that a share (referred to in this section as the "substituted share") that is, or if issued would be, a prescribed share may be substituted or exchanged for the first share within five years from the date of issue of the first share,

but does not include a share of the capital stock of a corporation

(g) that was issued after December 31, 1982 pursuant to an agreement or offering in writing made on or before December 31, 1982 or in accordance with a prospectus, registration statement or similar document that was filed with and, where required by law, accepted for filing by, a public authority in Canada pursuant to and in accordance with the laws of Canada or of any province on or before December 31, 1982,

(h) that would be a prescribed share solely by virtue of one or more of the terms or conditions of an agreement if such terms or conditions are not effective or exercisable until the death, disability or bankruptcy of the person to whom the share is issued,

(i) that is

　(i) convertible under its terms into one or more shares of a class of the capital stock of the corporation for no consideration other than the share or shares,

　(ii) described in paragraph (a) solely because

　　(A) it is to be cancelled on the conversion within five years from the date of its issue,

　　(B) its paid-up capital is to be reduced on the conversion within five years from the date of its issue, or

　　(C) both clauses (A) and (B) apply, and

　(iii) not described in paragraph (c), or

(j) that

　(i) may have a share substituted or exchanged for it pursuant to its terms or the terms or conditions of an agreement in existence at the time of its issue and no consideration is to be received or receivable for it in respect of the substitution or exchange other than the share substituted or exchanged for it,

　(ii) is described in paragraph (a) solely because it is to be redeemed, acquired or cancelled on the substitution or exchange within five years from the date of its issue, and

　(iii) is not a share to which paragraph (f) applies,

and for the purposes of this section,

(k) where a person has an interest in a trust, whether directly or indirectly, through an interest in any other trust or in any other manner whatever, the person shall be deemed to be a beneficiary of the trust;

(l) in determining whether an acquired share would be a prescribed share if issued,

　(i) the references in paragraphs (a), (b), (d) and (e) to "date of its issue" shall be read as "date of the issue of the convertible share",

　(ii) the reference in paragraph (f) to "issue of the first share" shall be read as "issue of the convertible share", and

　(iii) this section shall be read without reference to paragraph (g) and to the words "after December 31, 1982";

(m) in determining whether a substituted share would be a prescribed share if issued,

　(i) the references in paragraphs (a) to (e) to "date of its issue" shall be read as "date of the issue of the first share", and

　(ii) this section shall be read without reference to paragraph (g) and to the words "after December 31, 1982";

(m.1) an excluded obligation in relation to a share of a class of the capital stock of the issuing corporation and an obligation that would be an excluded obligation in relation to the share if the share had been issued after June 17, 1987, shall be deemed not to be a guarantee, security or similar indemnity with respect to the share for the purposes of paragraph (b);

(n) a guarantee, security or similar indemnity referred to in paragraph (b) shall, for greater certainty, not be considered to take effect within five years from the date of issue of a share if the effect of the guarantee, security or indemnity is to provide that a member of the related issuing group will be able to redeem, acquire or cancel the share at a time that is not within five years from the date of issue of the share; and

(o) where an expense is incurred partly in consideration for shares (referred to in this section as "first corporation shares") of the capital stock of one corporation and partly in consideration for an interest in, or right to, shares (referred to in this paragraph as "second corporation shares") of the capital stock of another corporation, in determining whether the second corporation shares are prescribed shares, the references in paragraphs (a), (d) and (e) to "date of its issue" shall be read as "date of the issue of the first corporation shares".

(2) For the purposes of paragraph 66(15)(d.1) [66(15)"flow-through share"] of the Act, subsection (1) does not apply in respect of a share of the capital stock of an issuing corporation that is a new share.

**Definitions [Reg. 6202]:** "amount" — ITA 248(1); "Canada" — ITA 255, *Interpretation Act* 35(1); "corporation" — ITA 248(1), *Interpretation Act* 35(1); "paid-up capital" — ITA 89(1), 248(1); "partnership" — see Notes to ITA 96(1); "person", "prescribed", "property" — ITA 248(1); "province" — *Interpretation Act* 35(1); "related" — ITA 251(2)–(6); "security" — *Interpretation Act* 35(1); "share" — ITA 248(1); "substituted", "substitution" — ITA 248(5); "trust" — ITA 104(1), 248(1), (3); "writing" — *Interpretation Act* 35(1).

**6202.1 [Flow-through shares — prescribed share]** — (1) For the purposes of the definition "flow-through share" in subsection 66(15) of the Act, a new share of the capital stock of a corporation is a prescribed share if, at the time it is issued,

(a) under the terms or conditions of the share or any agreement in respect of the share or its issue,

(i) the amount of the dividends that may be declared or paid on the share (in this section referred to as the "dividend entitlement") may reasonably be considered to be, by way of a formula or otherwise,

(A) fixed,

(B) limited to a maximum, or

(C) established to be not less than a minimum (including any amount determined on a cumulative basis), where with respect to the dividends that may be declared or paid on the share there is a preference over any other dividends that may be declared or paid on any other share of the capital stock of the corporation,

(ii) the amount that the holder of the share is entitled to receive in respect of the share on the dissolution, liquidation or winding-up of the corporation, on a reduction of the paid-up capital of the share or on the redemption, acquisition or cancellation of the share by the corporation or by specified persons in relation to the corporation (in this section referred to as the "liquidation entitlement") may reasonably be considered to be, by way of a formula or otherwise, fixed, limited to a maximum or established to be not less than a minimum,

(iii) the share is convertible or exchangeable into another security issued by the corporation unless

(A) it is convertible or exchangeable only into

(I) another share of the corporation that, if issued, would not be a prescribed share,

(II) a right, including a right conferred by a warrant that, if exercised, would allow the person exercising it to acquire only a share of the corporation that, if issued, would not be a prescribed share, or

(III) both a share described in subclause (I) and a right or warrant described in subclause (II), and

(B) all the consideration receivable by the holder on the conversion or exchange of the share is the share described in subclause (A)(I) or the right or warrant described in subclause (A)(II), or both, as the case may be, or

(iv) the corporation has, either absolutely or contingently, an obligation to reduce, or any person or partnership has, either absolutely or contingently, an obligation to cause the corporation to reduce, the paid-up capital in respect of the share (other than pursuant to a conversion or exchange of the share, where the right to so convert or exchange does not cause the share to be a prescribed share under subparagraph (iii));

(b) any person or partnership has, either absolutely or contingently, an obligation (other than an excluded obligation in relation to the share)

(i) to provide assistance,

(ii) to make a loan or payment,

(iii) to transfer property, or

(iv) otherwise to confer a benefit by any means whatever, including the payment of a dividend,

either immediately or in the future, that may reasonably be considered to be, directly or indirectly, a repayment or return by the corporation or a specified person in relation to the corporation of all or part of the consideration for which the share was issued or for which a partnership interest was issued in a partnership that acquires the share;

(c) any person or partnership has, either absolutely or contingently, an obligation (other than an excluded obligation in relation to the share) to effect any undertaking, either immediately or in the future, with respect to the share or the agreement under which the share is issued (including any guarantee, security, indemnity, covenant or agreement and including the lending of funds to or the placing of amounts on deposit with, or on behalf of, the holder of the share or, where the holder is a partnership, the members thereof or specified persons in relation to the holder or the members of the partnership, as the case may be) that may reasonably be considered to have been given to ensure, directly or indirectly, that

(i) any loss that the holder of the share and, where the holder is a partnership, the members thereof or specified persons in relation to the holder or the members of the partnership, as the case may be, may sustain by reason of the holding, ownership or disposition of the share or any other property is limited in any respect, or

(ii) the holder of the share and, where the holder is a partnership, the members thereof or specified persons in relation to the holder or the members of the partnership, as the case may be, will derive earnings, by reason of the holding, ownership or disposition of the share or any other property;

(d) the corporation or a specified person in relation to the corporation may reasonably be expected

(i) to acquire or cancel the share in whole or in part otherwise than on a conversion or exchange of the share that meets the conditions set out in clauses (a)(iii)(A) and (B),

(ii) to reduce the paid-up capital of the corporation in respect of the share otherwise than on a conversion or exchange of the share that meets the conditions set out in clauses (a)(iii)(A) and (B), or

(iii) to make a payment, transfer or other provision (otherwise than pursuant to an excluded obligation in relation to the share), directly or indirectly, by way of a dividend, loan, purchase of shares, financial assistance to any purchaser of the share or, where the purchaser is a partnership, the members thereof or in any other manner whatever, that may reasonably be considered to be a repayment or return of all or part of the consideration for which the share was issued or for which a partnership interest was issued in a partnership that acquires the share,

within 5 years after the date the share is issued, otherwise than as a consequence of an amalgamation of a subsidiary wholly-owned corporation, a winding-up of a subsidiary wholly-owned corporation to which subsection 88(1) of the Act applies or the payment of a dividend by a subsidiary wholly-owned corporation to its parent;

(e) any person or partnership can reasonably be expected to effect, within 5 years after the date the share is issued, any undertaking which, if it were in effect at the time the share was issued, would result in the share being a prescribed share by reason of paragraph (c); or

(f) it may reasonably be expected that, within 5 years after the date the share is issued,

(i) any of the terms or conditions of the share or any existing agreement relating to the share or its issue will thereafter be modified, or

(ii) any new agreement relating to the share or its issue will be entered into,

in such a manner that the share would be a prescribed share if it had been issued at the time of the modification or at the time when the new agreement is entered into.

(2) **[Flow-through shares — prescribed share]** — For the purposes of the definition "flow-through share" in subsection 66(15) of the Act, a new share of the capital stock of a corporation is a prescribed share if

(a) the consideration for which the share is to be issued is to be determined more than 60 days after entering into the agreement pursuant to which the share is to be issued;

(b) the corporation or a specified person in relation to the corporation, directly or indirectly,

(i) provided assistance,

(ii) made or arranged for a loan or payment,

(iii) transferred property, or

(iv) otherwise conferred a benefit by any means whatever, including the payment of a dividend,

for the purpose of assisting any person or partnership in acquiring the share or any person or partnership in acquiring an interest in a partnership acquiring the share (otherwise than by reason of an excluded obligation in relation to the share); or

(c) the holder of the share or, where the holder is a partnership, a member thereof, has a right under any agreement or arrangement entered into under circumstances where it is reasonable to consider that the agreement or arrangement was contemplated at or before the time when the agreement to issue the share was entered into,

(i) to dispose of the share, and

(ii) through a transaction or event or a series of transactions or events contemplated by the agreement or arrangement, to acquire a share (referred to in this paragraph as the "acquired share") of the capital stock of another corporation that would be a prescribed share under subsection (1) if the acquired share were issued at the time the share was issued, other than a share that would not be a prescribed share if subsection (1) were read without reference to subparagraphs (a)(iv) and (d)(i) and (ii) thereof where the acquired share is a share

(A) of a mutual fund corporation, or

(B) of a corporation that becomes a mutual fund corporation within 90 days after the acquisition of the acquired share.

**Notes**: Regs. 6202.1(2)(a) and (b) added by P.C. 1990-51, effective for shares issued after December 15, 1987, other than a share issued at a particular time

(a) pursuant to an agreement in writing entered into before December 16, 1987;

(b) as part of a distribution of shares to the public made in accordance with the terms of a prospectus, preliminary prospectus, registration statement, offering memorandum or notice, required by law to be filed before distribution of the shares begins, filed before December 16, 1987 with a public authority in Canada in accordance with the securities legislation of the province in which the shares were distributed; or

(c) to a partnership in which interests were issued as part of a distribution to the public made in accordance with the terms of a prospectus, preliminary prospectus, registration statement, offering memorandum or notice, required by law to be filed before distribution of the interests begins, filed before December 16, 1987 with a public authority in Canada in accordance with the securities legislation of the province in which the interests were distributed, where all interests in the partnership issued at or before the particular time were issued as part of the distribution or prior to the beginning of the distribution.

(3) **[Dividend entitlement and liquidation entitlement]** — For the purposes of subsection (1),

(a) the dividend entitlement of a share of the capital stock of a corporation shall be deemed not to be fixed, limited to a maximum or established to be not less than a minimum where all dividends on the share are determined solely by reference to a multiple or fraction of the dividend entitlement of another share of the capital stock of the corporation, or of another corporation that controls the corporation, where the dividend entitlement of that other share is not described in subparagraph (1)(a)(i); and

(b) the liquidation entitlement of a share of the capital stock of a corporation shall be deemed not to be fixed, limited to a maximum or established to be not less than a minimum where all the liquidation entitlement is determinable solely by reference to the liquidation entitlement of another share of the capital stock of the corporation, or of another corporation that controls the corporation, where the liquidation entitlement of that other share is not described in subparagraph (1)(a)(ii).

(4) **[Agreement deemed not to be undertaking]** — For the purposes of paragraphs (1)(c) and (e), an agreement entered into between the first holder of a share and another person or partnership for the sale of the share to that other person or partnership for its fair market value at the time the share is acquired by the other person or partnership (determined without regard to the agreement) shall be deemed not to be an undertaking with respect to the share.

(5) For the purposes of section 6202 and this section,

**"excluded obligation"**, in relation to a share issued by a corporation, means

(a) an obligation of the corporation

(i) with respect to eligibility for, or the amount of, any assistance under the *Canadian Exploration and Development Incentive Program Act*, the *Canadian Exploration Incentive Program Act*, the *Ontario Mineral Exploration Program Act, 1989*, Statutes of Ontario 1989, c. 40, or the *Mineral Exploration Incentive Program Act (Manitoba)*, Statutes of Manitoba 1990-91, c. 45, or

(ii) with respect to the making of an election respecting such assistance and the flowing out of such assistance to the holder of the share in accordance with any of those Acts,

(a.1) an obligation of the corporation, in respect of the share, to distribute an amount that represents a payment out of assistance to which the corporation is entitled

(i) under section 25.1 of the *Income Tax Act*, Revised Statutes of British Columbia, 1996, c. 215, and

(ii) as a consequence of the corporation making expenditures funded by consideration received for shares issued by the corporation in respect of which the corporation purports to renounce an amount under subsection 66(12.6) of the Act, and

(b) an obligation of any person or partnership to effect an undertaking to indemnify a holder of the share or, where the holder is a partnership, a member thereof, for an amount not exceeding the amount of any tax payable under the Act or the laws of a province by the holder or the member of the partnership, as the case may be, as a consequence of

(i) the failure of the corporation to renounce an amount to the holder in respect of the share, or

(ii) a reduction, under subsection 66(12.73) of the Act, of an amount purported to be renounced to the holder in respect of the share;

**Notes**: "Excluded obligation"(a.1) added by P.C. 2000-1096, effective August 1998. It accommodates a program under which a corporation performing mining exploration can qualify for a BC mining exploration tax credit.

Subpara. (b)(ii) amended to add "purported to be" by P.C. 1999-196, effective for renunciations purported to be made after 1996.

Reference to *Ontario Mineral Exploration Program Act* added to subpara. (a)(i) by P.C. 1991-2475, effective for shares issued after May 3, 1990. Reference to *Mineral Exploration Incentive Program Act (Manitoba)* added by P.C. 1994-618, effective for shares issued after February 1992. See also Notes at end of Reg. 6202.1.

**"new share"** means a share of the capital stock of a corporation issued after June 17, 1987, other than a share issued at a particular time before 1989

(a) pursuant to an agreement in writing entered into before June 18, 1987,

(b) as part of a distribution of shares to the public made in accordance with the terms of a prospectus, preliminary prospectus, registration statement, offering memorandum or notice, required by law to be filed before distribution of the shares begins, filed before June 18, 1987 with a public authority in Canada in accordance with the securities legislation of the province in which the shares were distributed, or

(c) to a partnership in which interests were issued as part of a distribution to the public made in accordance with the terms of a prospectus, preliminary prospectus, registration statement, offering memorandum or notice, required by law to be filed before distribution of the interests begins, filed before June 18, 1987 with a public authority in Canada in accordance with the securities legislation of the province in which the interests were distributed, where all interests in the partnership issued at or before the particular time were issued as part of the distribution or prior to the beginning of the distribution;

"**specified person**", in relation to any particular person, means another person with whom the particular person does not deal at arm's length or any partnership or trust of which the particular person or the other person is a member or beneficiary, respectively.

**Related Provisions**: ITA 96(2.2)(d)(vii) — Exclusion from limited partnership at-risk rules; ITA 143.2(3)(b)(iv) — Exclusion from tax shelter at-risk adjustments.

**Notes**: Reg. 6202.1 added by P.C. 1990-51, effective (other than 6202.1(2)(a) and (b) — see Notes thereto) for shares issued after June 17, 1987.

**Definitions [Reg. 6202.1]**: "amount" — ITA 248(1); "arm's length" — ITA 251(1); "Canada" — ITA 255, *Interpretation Act* 35(1); "corporation" — ITA 248(1), *Interpretation Act* 35(1); "disposition" — ITA 248(1); "dividend" — ITA 248(1); "mutual fund corporation" — ITA 131(8), 248(1); "paid-up capital" — ITA 89(1), 248(1); "partnership" — see Notes to ITA 96(1); "person", "prescribed", "property" — ITA 248(1); "province", "security" — *Interpretation Act* 35(1); "share", "subsidiary wholly-owned corporation" — ITA 248(1); "trust" — ITA 104(1), 248(1), (3); "undertaking" — Reg. 6202.1(4); "writing" — *Interpretation Act* 35(1).

**Interpretation Bulletins**: IT-503: Exploration and development shares.

**6203. (1)–(3)** [No longer relevant.]

**Notes**: Reg. 6203 prescribes shares for purposes of ITA 192(6), the share-purchase tax credit, which applied before 1987.

**6204. (1) [Employee stock option deduction — prescribed share]** — For the purposes of paragraph 110(1)(d) of the Act, a share is a prescribed share of the capital stock of a corporation at the time of its sale or issue, as the case may be, where, at that time,

> **Proposed Amendment — Reg. 6204(1) opening words**
>
> (1) For the purposes of paragraph 110(1)(d) and section 44.1 of the Act, a share is a prescribed share of the capital stock of a corporation at the time of its sale or issue, as the case may be, where, at that time,
>
> **Application**: The December 21, 2000 draft regulations, s. 2, will amend the opening words of subsec. 6204(1) to read as above, applicable in respect of dispositions that occur after February 27, 2000.
>
> **Technical Notes**: Subsection 6204(1) of the *Income Tax Regulations* prescribes a common share for the purposes of paragraph 110(1)(d) of the *Income Tax Act*. The subsection is amended to have it also apply for the purposes of section 44.1 of the Act.

(a) under the terms or conditions of the share or any agreement in respect of the share or its issue,

(i) the amount of the dividends (in this section referred to as the "dividend entitlement") that the corporation may declare or pay on the share is not limited to a maximum amount or fixed at a minimum amount at that time or at any time thereafter by way of a formula or otherwise,

(ii) the amount (in this section referred to as the "liquidation entitlement") that the holder of the share is entitled to receive on the share on the dissolution, liquidation or winding-up of the corporation is not limited to a maximum amount or fixed at a minimum amount by way of a formula or otherwise,

(iii) the share cannot be converted into any other security, other than into another security of the corporation or of another corporation with which it does not deal at arm's length that is, or would be at the date of conversion, a prescribed share,

(iv) the holder of the share cannot at that time or at any time thereafter cause the share to be redeemed, acquired or cancelled by the corporation or any specified person in relation to the corporation, except where the redemption, acquisition or cancellation is required pursuant to a conversion that is not prohibited by subparagraph (iii),

(v) no person or partnership has, either absolutely or contingently, an obligation to reduce, or to cause the corporation to reduce, at that time or at any time thereafter, the paid-up capital in respect of the share, except where the reduction is required pursuant to a conversion that is not prohibited by subparagraph (iii), and

(vi) neither the corporation nor any specified person in relation to the corporation has, either absolutely or contingently, the right or obligation to redeem, acquire or cancel, at that time or any later time, the share in whole or in part other than for an amount that approximates the fair market value of the share (determined without reference to any such right or obligation) or a lesser amount;

(b) the corporation or a specified person in relation to the corporation cannot reasonably be expected to, within two years after the time the share is sold or issued, as the case may be,

(i) redeem, acquire or cancel the share in whole or in part, or

(ii) reduce the paid-up capital of the corporation in respect of the share;

otherwise than as a consequence of an amalgamation of a subsidiary wholly-owned corporation or

**Reg. S. 6204(1)(b)** — Income Tax Regulations

of a winding-up to which subsection 88(1) of the Act applies; and

(c) it cannot reasonably be expected that any of the terms or conditions of the share or any existing agreement in respect of the share or its sale or issue will be modified or amended, or that any new agreement in respect of the share, its sale or issue will be entered into, within two years after the time the share is sold or issued, in such a manner that the share would not be a prescribed share if it had been sold or issued at the time of such modification or amendment or at the time the new agreement is entered into.

**Notes**: Reg. 6204(1)(a)(vi) amended by P.C. 1997-1146, effective for shares issued or sold after 1994, to add the final words "or a lesser amount", and to change "at any time thereafter" to "at any later time".

Reg. 6204(1)(b)(i) amended by P.C. 1994-618 to add the word "redeem", retroactive to 1985 and later taxation years.

Closing words of Reg. 6204(1)(b) added by P.C. 1997-1146, effective for 1996 and later taxation years.

**(2) [Rules]** — For the purposes of subsection (1),

(a) the dividend entitlement of a share of the capital stock of a corporation shall be deemed not to be limited to a maximum amount or fixed at a minimum amount where it may reasonably be considered that all or substantially all of the dividend entitlement is determinable by reference to the dividend entitlement of another share of the capital stock of the corporation that meets the requirements of subparagraph (1)(a)(i);

(b) the liquidation entitlement of a share of the capital stock of a corporation shall be deemed not to be limited to a maximum amount or fixed at a minimum amount where it may reasonably be considered that all or substantially all of the liquidation entitlement is determinable by reference to the liquidation entitlement of another share of the capital stock of the corporation that meets the requirements of subparagraph (1)(a)(ii); and

(c) the determination of whether a share of the capital stock of a corporation is a prescribed share shall be made without reference to a right or obligation to redeem, acquire or cancel the share or to cause the share to be redeemed, acquired or cancelled where

(i) the share was issued or sold pursuant to an employee share purchase agreement (in this paragraph referred to as "the agreement") to an employee (in this paragraph referred to as "the holder") of the corporation or of another corporation with which the corporation was not dealing at arm's length,

(ii) the holder was dealing at arm's length with each corporation referred to in subparagraph (i) at the time the share was issued or sold, and

(iii) having regard to all the circumstances, including the terms of the agreement, it can reasonably be considered that

(A) the amount payable on the redemption, acquisition or cancellation (in this clause and in clause (B) referred to as the "acquisition") of the share will not exceed

(I) the adjusted cost base to the holder of the share immediately before the acquisition, where the acquisition was provided for in the agreement and the principal purpose for its provision was to protect the holder against any loss in respect of the share, or

(II) the fair market value of the share immediately before the acquisition, where the acquisition was provided for in the agreement and the principal purpose for its provision was to provide the holder with a market for the share, and

(B) no portion of the amount payable on the acquisition of the share is directly determinable by reference to the profits of the corporation, or of another corporation with which the corporation does not deal at arm's length, for all or any part of the period during which the holder owned the share or had a right to acquire the share, unless the reference to the profits of the corporation or the other corporation is only for the purpose of determining the fair market value of the share pursuant to a formula set out in the agreement.

**Notes**: Revenue Canada's view is that "all or substantially all" means 90% or more.

Reg. 6204(2)(c) added by P.C. 1994-618, retroactive to 1985 and later taxation years, and amended retroactively to its introduction by P.C. 1997-1146 to change "issued" to "issued or sold" in subparas. (i) and (ii).

**(3) ["Specified person"]** — For the purposes of subsection (1), "specified person", in relation to a corporation, means

(a) any person or partnership with whom the corporation does not deal at arm's length otherwise than because of a right referred to in paragraph 251(5)(b) of the Act that arises as a result of an offer by the person or partnership to acquire all or substantially all of the shares of the capital stock of the corporation, or

(b) any partnership or trust of which the corporation (or a person or partnership with whom the corporation does not deal at arm's length) is a member or beneficiary, respectively.

**Notes**: Revenue Canada's view is that "all or substantially all" means 90% or more.

Reg. 6204(3) amended by P.C. 1994-618, retroactive to 1985 and later taxation years. Amended non-substantively by P.C. 1997-1146, effective for 1996 and later taxation years (wording reorganized but sense unchanged).

Part LXII — Prescribed Securities and Shares    Reg. S. 6205(1)(b)

**(4)** For the purposes of subsection (3), the Act shall be read without reference to subsection 256(9) of the Act.

**Notes:** Reg. 6204(4) added by P.C. 1997-1146, effective for 1996 and later taxation years.

**Definitions [Reg. 6204]:** "adjusted cost base" — ITA 54, 248(1); "amount" — ITA 248(1); "arm's length" — ITA 251(1); "corporation" — ITA 248(1), *Interpretation Act* 35(1); "dividend", "employee" — ITA 248(1); "paid-up capital" — ITA 89(1), 248(1); "partnership" — see Notes to ITA 96(1); "person", "prescribed" — ITA 248(1); "share", "subsidiary wholly-owned corporation" — ITA 248(1); "trust" — ITA 104(1), 248(1), (3).

**Interpretation Bulletins:** IT-113R4: Benefits to employees — stock options; IT-171R2: Non-resident individuals — computation of taxable income earned in Canada and non-refundable tax credits.

**6205. (1) [Capital gains deduction — prescribed share]** — For the purposes of subsections 110.6(8) and (9) of the Act and subject to subsection (3), a prescribed share is a share of the capital stock of a corporation where

(a) under the terms or conditions of the share or any agreement in respect of the share or its issue,

(i) at the time the share is issued,

(A) the amount of the dividends (in this section referred to as the "dividend entitlement") that the corporation may declare or pay on the share is not limited to a maximum amount or fixed at a minimum amount at that time or at any time thereafter by way of a formula or otherwise,

(B) the amount (in this section referred to as the "liquidation entitlement") that the holder of the share is entitled to receive on the share on the dissolution, liquidation or winding-up of the corporation is not limited to a maximum amount or fixed at a minimum amount by way of a formula or otherwise,

(C) the share cannot be converted into any other security, other than into another security of the corporation that is, or would be at the date of conversion, a prescribed share,

(D) the holder of the share does not, at that time or at any time thereafter, have the right or obligation to cause the share to be redeemed, acquired or cancelled by the corporation or a specified person in relation to the corporation, except where the redemption, acquisition or cancellation is required pursuant to a conversion that is not prohibited by clause (C),

(E) no person or partnership has, either absolutely or contingently, an obligation to reduce, or to cause the corporation to reduce, at that time or at any time thereafter, the paid-up capital in respect of the share, otherwise than by way of a redemption, acquisition or cancellation of the share that is not prohibited by this section,

(F) no person or partnership has, either absolutely or contingently, an obligation (other than an excluded obligation in relation to the share, as defined in subsection 6202.1(5)) at that time or any time thereafter to

(I) provide assistance to acquire the share,

(II) make a loan or payment,

(III) transfer property, or

(IV) otherwise confer a benefit by any means whatever, including the payment of a dividend,

that may reasonably be considered to be, directly or indirectly, a repayment or return by the corporation or a specified person in relation to the corporation of all or part of the consideration for which the share was issued, and

(G) neither the corporation nor any specified person in relation to the corporation has, either absolutely or contingently, the right or obligation to redeem, acquire or cancel, at that time or at any time thereafter, the share in whole or in part, except where the redemption, acquisition or cancellation is required pursuant to a conversion that is not prohibited by clause (C),

(ii) no person or partnership has, either absolutely or contingently, an obligation (other than an excluded obligation in relation to the share, as defined in subsection 6202.1(5)) to provide, at any time, any form of undertaking with respect to the share (including any guarantee, security, indemnity, covenant or agreement and including the lending of funds to or the placing of amounts on deposit with, or on behalf of, the holder of the share or any specified person in relation to that holder) that may reasonably be considered to have been given to ensure that

(A) any loss that the holder of the share may sustain by virtue of the holding, ownership or disposition of the share is limited in any respect, or

(B) the holder of the share will derive earnings by virtue of the holding, ownership or disposition of the share; and

(b) at the time the share is issued, it cannot reasonably be expected, having regard to all the circumstances, that any of the terms or conditions of the share or any existing agreement in respect of the share or its issue will thereafter be modified or amended or that any new agreement in respect of the share or its issue will be entered into, in such a manner that the share would not be a prescribed share if it had been issued at the time of such modification or amendment or at the time the new agreement is entered into.

**(2) [Capital gains deduction — prescribed share]** — For the purposes of subsections 110.6(8) and (9) of the Act and subject to subsection (3), a prescribed share is a share of the capital stock of a particular corporation where

(a) it is a particular share that is owned by a person and that was issued by the particular corporation as part of an arrangement to that person, to a spouse or parent of that person or, where the person is a trust described in paragraph 104(4)(a) of the Act, to the person who created the trust or by whose will the trust was created or, where the person is a corporation, to another person owning all of the issued and outstanding shares of the capital stock of the corporation or to a spouse or parent of that other person, and

(i) the main purpose of the arrangement was to permit any increase in the value of the property of the particular corporation to accrue to other shares that would, at the time of their issue, be prescribed shares if this section were read without reference to this subsection, and

(ii) at the time of the issue of the particular share or at the end of the arrangement,

(A) the other shares were owned by

(I) the person to whom the particular share was issued (in this paragraph referred to as the "original holder"),

(II) a person who did not deal at arm's length with the original holder,

(III) a trust none of the beneficiaries of which were persons other than the original holder or a person who did not deal at arm's length with the original holder, or

(IV) any combination of persons described in subclause (I), (II) or (III),

(B) the other shares were owned by employees of the particular corporation or of a corporation controlled by the particular corporation, or

(C) the other shares were owned by any combination of persons each of whom is described in clause (A) or (B); or

(b) it is a share that was issued by a mutual fund corporation.

**Related Provisions**: ITA 256(6), (6.1) — Meaning of "controlled".

**Notes**: Opening words of Reg. 6205(2)(a) amended, Reg. 6205(2)(a)(i) amended and 6205(2)(a)(ii)(C) added by P.C. 1994-618, retroactive to 1985 and later taxation years, except that for taxation years ending before May 5, 1994, read the word "subsection" at the end of Reg. 6205(2)(a)(i) as "paragraph".

References to "spouse" are expected to be amended to add "or common-law partner" effective 2001 or earlier by election, as has been done throughout the ITA. See Notes to ITA 248(1)"common-law partner".

**(3) [Capital gains deduction — prescribed share]** — For the purposes of subsections 110.6(8) and (9) of the Act, a prescribed share does not include a share of the capital stock issued by a mutual fund corporation (other than an investment corporation) the value of which can reasonably be considered to be, directly or indirectly, derived primarily from investments made by the mutual fund corporation in one or more corporations (in this subsection referred to as an "investee corporation") connected with it (within the meaning of subsection 186(4) of the Act on the assumption that the references in that subsection to "payer corporation" and "particular corporation" were read as references to "investee corporation" and "mutual fund corporation", respectively).

**(4) [Rules]** — For the purposes of this section,

(a) the dividend entitlement of a share of the capital stock of a corporation shall be deemed not to be limited to a maximum amount or fixed at a minimum amount where it may reasonably be considered that

(i) all or substantially all of the dividend entitlement is determinable by reference to the dividend entitlement of another share of the capital stock of the corporation that meets the requirements of clause (1)(a)(i)(A), or

(ii) the dividend entitlement cannot be such as to impair the ability of the corporation to redeem another share of the capital stock of the corporation that meets the requirements of paragraph (2)(a);

(b) the liquidation entitlement of a share of the capital stock of a corporation shall be deemed not to be limited to a maximum amount or fixed at a minimum amount where it may reasonably be considered that all or substantially all of the liquidation entitlement is determinable by reference to the liquidation entitlement of another share of the capital stock of the corporation that meets the requirements of clause (1)(a)(i)(B);

(c) where two or more corporations (each of which is referred to in this paragraph as a "predecessor corporation") have merged or amalgamated, the corporation formed as a result of the merger or amalgamation (in this paragraph referred to as the "new corporation") shall be deemed to be the same corporation as, and a continuation of, each of the predecessor corporations and a share of the capital stock of the new corporation issued on the merger or amalgamation as consideration for a share of the capital stock of a predecessor corporation shall be deemed to be the same share as the share of the predecessor corporation for which it was issued, but this paragraph does not apply if the share issued on the merger or amalgamation is not a prescribed share at the time of its issue and either

(i) the terms and conditions of that share are not identical to those of the share of the predecessor corporation for which it was issued, or

(ii) at the time of its issue the fair market value of that share is not the same as that of the share of the predecessor corporation for which it was issued;

(d) a reference in clauses (1)(a)(i)(D) and (G) and subparagraph (1)(a)(ii) to a right or obligation of the corporation or a person or partnership does not include a right or obligation provided in a written agreement among shareholders of a private corporation owning more than 50% of its issued and outstanding share capital having full voting rights under all circumstances to which the corporation, person or partnership is a party unless it may reasonably be considered, having regard to all the circumstances, including the terms of the agreement and the number and relationship of the shareholders, that one of the main reasons for the existence of the agreement is to avoid or limit the application of subsection 110.6(8) or (9) of the Act;

(e) where at any particular time after November 21, 1985, the terms or conditions of a share are changed or any existing agreement in respect thereof is changed or a new agreement in respect of the share is entered into, the share shall, for the purpose of determining whether it is a prescribed share, be deemed to have been issued at that particular time; and

(f) the determination of whether a share of the capital stock of a corporation is a prescribed share for the purposes of subsection (1) shall be made without reference to a right or obligation to redeem, acquire or cancel the share or to cause the share to be redeemed, acquired or cancelled where

(i) the share was issued pursuant to an employee share purchase agreement (in this paragraph referred to as "the agreement") to an employee (in this paragraph referred to as "the holder") of the corporation or of a corporation with which it did not deal at arm's length,

(ii) the holder was dealing at arm's length with each corporation referred to in subparagraph (i) at the time the share was issued, and

(iii) having regard to all the circumstances including the terms of the agreement, it may reasonably be considered that

(A) the amount payable on the redemption, acquisition or cancellation (in this clause and in clause (B) referred to as the "acquisition") of the share will not exceed

(I) the adjusted cost base of the share to the holder immediately before the acquisition, where the acquisition was provided for in the agreement and the principal purpose for its provision was to protect the holder against any loss in respect of the share, or

(II) the fair market value of the share immediately before the acquisition, where the acquisition was provided for in the agreement and the principal purpose for its provision was to provide the holder with a market for the share, and

(B) no portion of the amount payable on the acquisition of the share is directly determinable by reference to the profits of the corporation, or of another corporation with which it does not deal at arm's length, for all or any part of the period during which the holder owned the share or had a right to acquire the share, unless the reference to the profits of the corporation or the other corporation is only for the purpose of determining the fair market value of the share pursuant to a formula set out in the agreement.

**Notes**: The CCRA's view is that "all or substantially all" means 90% or more.

Reg. 6205(4)(c) amended by P.C. 1994-618, retroactive to mergers and amalgamations occurring after 1984.

**(5)** For the purposes of this section, "specified person", in relation to a corporation or a holder of a share, as the case may be (in this subsection referred to as the "taxpayer"), means any person or partnership with whom the taxpayer does not deal at arm's length or any partnership or trust of which the taxpayer (or a person or partnership with whom the taxpayer does not deal at arm's length) is a member or beneficiary, respectively.

**Definitions [Reg. 6205]**: "adjusted cost base" — ITA 54, 248(1); "amount" — ITA 248(1); "arm's length" — ITA 251(1); "controlled" — ITA 256(6), (6.1); "corporation" — ITA 248(1), *Interpretation Act* 35(1); "disposition" — ITA 248(1); "dividend", "employee" — ITA 248(1); "investment corporation" — ITA 130(3), 248(1); "mutual fund corporation" — ITA 131(8), 248(1); "paid-up capital" — ITA 89(1), 248(1); "partnership" — see Notes to ITA 96(1); "person", "prescribed" — ITA 248(1); "private corporation" — ITA 89(1), 248(1); "property" — ITA 248(1); "security" — *Interpretation Act* 35(1); "share", "shareholder" — ITA 248(1); "taxpayer" — ITA 248(1); "trust" — ITA 104(1), 248(1), (3); "written" — *Interpretation Act* 35(1)"writing".

**6206. [Prescribed share for ITA 84(8)]** — The Class I Special Shares of Reed Stenhouse Companies Limited, issued before January 1, 1986, are prescribed for the purposes of subsection 84(8) of the Act.

**Reg. S. 6207**

**6207.** [No longer relevant]

**Notes**: Reg. 6207 defines a prescribed share for purposes of 183.1(4)(c) of the Act, which set out an anti-avoidance rule that was repealed with the introduction of the general anti-avoidance rule in ITA 245(2), effective September 13, 1988 (with certain grandfathering to the end of 1988).

**6208. (1) [Non-resident withholding tax — prescribed security]** — For the purposes of clause 212(1)(b)(vii)(E) of the Act, a prescribed security with respect to an obligation of a corporation is

(a) a share of the capital stock of the corporation unless

(i) under the terms and conditions of the share, any agreement relating to the share or any modification of such terms, conditions or agreement, the corporation or a specified person in relation to the corporation is or may, at any time within 5 years after the date of the issue of the obligation, be required to redeem, acquire or cancel, in whole or in part, the share (unless the share is or may be required to be redeemed, acquired or cancelled by reason only of a right to convert the share into, or exchange the share for, another share of the corporation that, if issued, would be a prescribed security) or to reduce its paid-up capital,

(ii) as a result of the modification or establishment of the terms or conditions of the share or the changing or entering into of any agreement in respect of the share, the corporation or a specified person in relation to the corporation may, within 5 years after the date of the issue of the obligation, reasonably be expected to redeem, acquire or cancel, in whole or in part, the share (unless the share is or may be required to be redeemed, acquired or cancelled by reason only of a right to convert the share into, or exchange the share for, another share of the corporation that, if issued, would be a prescribed security) or to reduce its paid-up capital, or

(iii) as a result of the terms or conditions of the share or any agreement entered into by the corporation or a specified person in relation to the corporation or any modification of such terms, conditions or agreement, any person is required, either absolutely or contingently, within 5 years after the date of the issue of the obligation, to effect any undertaking, including any guarantee, covenant or agreement to purchase or repurchase the share, and including a loan of funds to or the placing of amounts on deposit with, or on behalf of, the shareholder or a specified person in relation to the shareholder given

(A) to ensure that any loss that the shareholder or a specified person in relation to

the shareholder may sustain, by reason of the ownership, holding or disposition of the share or any other property, is limited in any respect, and

(B) as part of a transaction or event or series of transactions or events that included the issuance or acquisition of the obligation,

and for the purposes of this subparagraph, where such an undertaking in respect of a share is given at any particular time after the date of the issue of the obligation, the obligation shall be deemed to have been issued at the particular time and the undertaking shall be deemed to have been given as part of a series of transactions that included the issuance or acquisition of the obligation, and

(b) a right or warrant to acquire a share of the capital stock of the corporation that would, if issued, be a prescribed security with respect to the obligation,

where all the consideration receivable upon a conversion or exchange of the obligation or the prescribed security, as the case may be, is a share of the capital stock of the corporation described in paragraph (a) or a right or warrant described in paragraph (b), or both, as the case may be.

**Interpretation Bulletins**: IT-361R3: Exemption from Part XIII tax on interest payments to non-residents.

**(2) [Consideration for fraction of a share]** — For the purposes of this section, where a taxpayer may become entitled upon the conversion or exchange of an obligation or a prescribed security to receive consideration in lieu of a fraction of a share, that consideration shall be deemed not to be consideration unless it may reasonably be considered to be receivable as part of a series of transactions or events one of the main purposes of which is to avoid or limit the application of Part XIII of the Act.

**(3) ["Specified person"]** — In this section, "specified person", in relation to a corporation or a shareholder, means any person with whom the corporation or the shareholder, as the case may be, does not deal at arm's length or any partnership or trust of which the corporation or the shareholder, as the case may be, or the person is a member or beneficiary, respectively.

**Definitions [Reg. 6208]**: "amount" — ITA 248(1); "arm's length" — ITA 251(1); "corporation" — ITA 248(1), *Interpretation Act* 35(1); "disposition" — ITA 248(1); "paid-up capital" — ITA 89(1), 248(1); "partnership" — see Notes to ITA 96(1); "person", "prescribed", "property" — ITA 248(1); "share", "shareholder", "taxpayer" — ITA 248(1); "trust" — ITA 104(1), 248(1), (3).

**6209. [Lending assets — prescribed shares and property]** — For the purposes of the definition "lending asset" in subsection 248(1) of the Act,

(a) a share owned by a bank is a prescribed share for a taxation year where it is a preferred share of the capital stock of a corporation that is dealing at arm's length with the bank that may reasonably be considered to be, and is reported as, a substitute or alternative for a loan to the corporation, or another corporation with whom the corporation does not deal at arm's length, in the bank's annual report for the year to the relevant authority or, where the bank was throughout the year subject to the supervision of the relevant authority but was not required to file an annual report for the year with the relevant authority, in its financial statements for the year; and

(b) a property is a prescribed property for a taxation year where

(i) in the case of a security held by a bank, the security is reported as part of the bank's trading account in its annual report for the year to the relevant authority or, where the bank was throughout the year subject to the supervision of the relevant authority but was not required to file an annual report for the year with the relevant authority, in its financial statements for the year,

(ii) in the case of a security held by a taxpayer other than a bank, the security is at any time in the year a property described in an inventory of the taxpayer, or

### Proposed Amendment — Reg. 6209(b)(i), (ii)

(i) the security is a mark-to-market property (as defined in subsection 142.2(1) of the Act) for the year of a financial institution (as defined in that subsection), or

(ii) the security is at any time in the year a property described in an inventory of a taxpayer.

**Application**: The June 1, 1995 draft regulations (securities held by financial institutions), s. 7, will amend subparas. 6209(b)(i) and (ii) to read as above, applicable to taxation years that end after February 22, 1994.

**Technical Notes**: Section 6209 prescribes certain shares and other securities for the purpose of the definition of "lending asset" in subsection 248(1) of the Act. Securities prescribed by paragraph 6209(b) are excluded from being lending assets. Paragraph 6209(b) prescribes a security if it is included in the trading account of a bank or in the inventory of a taxpayer other than a bank.

Paragraph 6209(b) is amended to provide that a security is prescribed if it is a mark-to-market property or is included in a taxpayer's inventory. "Mark-to-market property", which is defined in new subsection 142.2(1) of the Act, includes most shares and some debt obligations.

As a consequence of this amendment, a specified debt obligation (as defined in subsection 142.2(1) of the Act) held by a bank in its trading account will be treated as a lending asset if it is not a mark-to-market property. This observation applies, in particular, to the debt obligations of a country that has been designated by the Office of the Superintendent of Financial Institutions and to the United Mexican States Collateralized Par or Discount Bonds Due 2019.

(iii) the property is a direct financing lease, or is any other financing arrangement, of a taxpayer that is reported as a loan in the taxpayer's financial statement for the year prepared in accordance with generally accepted accounting principles and an amount is deductible under paragraph 20(1)(a) of the Act in respect of the property that is the subject of the lease or arrangement in computing the taxpayer's income for the year.

**Notes**: Opening words of Reg. 6209 amended to change "security" to "property" (twice), and Reg. 6209(b)(iii) added, by P.C. 1999-195, effective

(a) for taxation years that end after September 1997, and

(b) for taxation years that end in 1996 or January–September 1997, if the taxpayer elects to have the 1995-97 technical bill amendments to ITA 20(1)(l) apply (see Notes to ITA 20(1)(l)).

**Definitions [Reg. 6209]**: "amount" — ITA 248(1); "arm's length" — ITA 251(1); "bank" — ITA 248(1), *Interpretation Act* 35(1); "corporation" — ITA 248(1), *Interpretation Act* 35(1); "inventory", "preferred share", "prescribed", "property" — ITA 248(1); "share" — ITA 248(1); "taxation year" — ITA 249; "taxpayer" — ITA 248(1).

### Proposed Addition — Reg. 6210

**6210.** For the purposes of paragraph 38(a.1) of the Act, a prescribed debt obligation is a bond, debenture, note, mortgage or similar obligation

(a) of or guaranteed by the Government of Canada; or

(b) of the government of a province or an agent of that government.

**Application**: The November 30, 2000 draft regulations (miscellaneous), s. 6 (pre-published in the *Canada Gazette*, Part I, December 9, 2000), will add s. 6210, applicable after February 18, 1997.

**Regulatory Impact Analysis Statement**: Part LXII of the Regulations is amended by adding section 6210 to prescribe debt obligations for the purpose of paragraph 38(a.1) of the Act, which halves the inclusion rate of capital gains arising from charitable donations of prescribed debt obligations and shares listed on prescribed stock exchanges. Prescribed debt obligations are bonds, debentures, notes, mortgages or similar obligations of or guaranteed by the Government of Canada or similar obligations of the Government of a Province or an Agent of a Government of a Province.

# PART LXIII — CHILD TAX BENEFITS

**6300. Interpretation** — In this Part, "qualified dependant" has the meaning assigned by section 122.6 of the Act.

**6301. Non-application of presumption** — (1) For the purposes of paragraph (g) of the definition "eligible individual" in section 122.6 of the Act, the presumption referred to in paragraph (f) of that definition does not apply in the circumstances where

(a) the female parent of the qualified dependant declares in writing to the Minister that the male parent, with whom she resides, is the parent of the qualified dependant who primarily fulfils the responsibility for the care and upbringing of each of the qualified dependants who reside with both parents;

(b) the female parent is a qualified dependant of an eligible individual and each of them files a notice with the Minister under subsection 122.62 (1) of the Act in respect of the same qualified dependant;

(c) there is more than one female parent of the qualified dependant who resides with the qualified dependant and each female parent files a notice with the Minister under subsection 122.62 (1) of the Act in respect of the qualified dependant; or

(d) more than one notice is filed with the Minister under subsection 122.62 (1) of the Act in respect of the same qualified dependant who resides with each of the persons filing the notices if such persons live at different locations.

Notes: Reg. 6301(1)(a)–(d) amended by P.C. 1998-2770, effective August 28, 1995, to change "Minister of Human Resources Development" (previously changed from "Minister of National Health and Welfare" by 1996, c. 11, effective July 12, 1996) to "Minister [of National Revenue]".

(2) For greater certainty, a person who files a notice referred to in paragraph (1)(b), (c) or (d) includes a person who is not required under subsection 122.62(3) of the Act to file such a notice.

Notes: Reg. 6301(2) amended by by P.C. 1998-2770, effective August 28, 1995, to delete the final words "and a person for whom the requirement to file such a notice has been waived by the Minister of Human Resources Development [changed from National Health and Welfare by 1996, c. 11] under subsection 122.62(5) of the Act". A general waiver of filing requirements by Revenue Canada is provided in ITA 220(2.1).

Definitions [Reg. 6301]: "individual", "Minister" — ITA 248(1); "parent" — ITA 252(2); "person" — ITA 248(1); "qualified dependant" — Reg. 6300; "writing" — Interpretation Act 35(1).

**6302. Factors** — For the purposes of paragraph (h) of the definition "eligible individual" in section 122.6 of the Act, the following factors are to be considered in determining what constitutes care and upbringing of a qualified dependant:

(a) the supervision of the daily activities and needs of the qualified dependant;

(b) the maintenance of a secure environment in which the qualified dependant resides;

(c) the arrangement of, and transportation to, medical care at regular intervals and as required for the qualified dependant;

(d) the arrangement of, participation in, and transportation to, educational, recreational, athletic or similar activities in respect of the qualified dependant;

(e) the attendance to the needs of the qualified dependant when the qualified dependant is ill or otherwise in need of the attendance of another person;

(f) the attendance to the hygienic needs of the qualified dependant on a regular basis;

(g) the provision, generally, of guidance and companionship to the qualified dependant; and

(h) the existence of a court order in respect of the qualified dependant that is valid in the jurisdiction in which the qualified dependant resides.

Definitions [Reg. 6302]: "person" — ITA 248(1); "qualified dependant" — Reg. 6300.

Notes: Part LXIII added by P.C. 1992-2714, effective 1993.

# PART LXIV — PRESCRIBED DATES

**6400. (1) Child tax credits** — For the purposes of subsection 122.2(1) of the Act, the prescribed date for each of the 1978 and subsequent taxation years is December 31 of that year.

Definitions [Reg. 6400]: "prescribed" — ITA 248(1); "taxation year" — ITA 249.

**6401. Quebec tax abatement** — For the purposes of subsection 120(2) of the Act, the prescribed date for each of the 1980 and subsequent taxation years is December 31 of that year.

Definitions [Reg. 6401]: "prescribed" — ITA 248(1); "taxation year" — ITA 249.

# PART LXV — PRESCRIBED LAWS

**6500. (1)** For the purposes of paragraph 73(1)(d) and subparagraph 148(8)(a)(iii) of the Act,

**"prescribed class of persons"** means persons referred to in subparagraph 14(b)(i) of *The Family Law Reform Act, 1978*, S.O. 1978, c. 2, of the Province of Ontario; and

**"prescribed provisions of the law of a province"** means paragraph 19(1)(c) and section 52 of *The Family Law Reform Act, 1978*, S.O. 1978, c. 2, of the Province of Ontario.

Notes: Reg. 6500(1) applies only in respect of transfers until July 13, 1990. For transfers after that date, ITA 73(1)(d) was amended by 1991 technical bill to eliminate the requirement for provisions of provincial law to be prescribed. 148(8)(a) was similarly amended for transfers after 1989.

**(2)** For the purposes of subsection 73(1.1) of the Act, "prescribed provisions of the law of a province" means

(a) sections 7 and 9 of *The Matrimonial Property Act*, S.A. 1978, c. 22, of the Province of Alberta;

Part LXV — Prescribed Laws  Reg. S. 6503

(b) sections 43, 51 and 52 of the *Family Relations Act*, R.S.B.C. 1979, c. 121, of the Province of British Columbia;

(c) sections 13, 16 and 17 of *The Marital Property Act*, S.M. 1978, C. 24-Cap. M45 of the Province of Manitoba;

(d) sections 4, 6, 7 and 8 and paragraph 19(1)(c) of *The Family Law Reform Act, 1978*, S.O. 1978, c. 2, of the Province of Ontario;

(e) sections 5, 7, 8 and 9 of the *Family Law Reform Act*, S.P.E.I. 1978, c. 6, of the Province of Prince Edward Island; and

(f) sections 5, 8, 21 and 22, subsection 23(4) and sections 26 and 42 of *The Matrimonial Property Act*, S.S. 1979, c. M-6.1, of the Province of Saskatchewan.

**Definitions [Reg. 6500]:** "person" — ITA 248(1).

**Interpretation Bulletins:** IT-325R2: Property transfers after separation, divorce and annulment.

**6501.** For the purposes of paragraph 81(1)(q) of the Act, "prescribed provision of the law of a province" means

(a) in respect of the Province of Alberta

(i) subsections 7(1) and 14(1) of *The Criminal Injuries Compensation Act*, R.S.A. 1970, c. 75, and

(ii) subsections 8(3), 10(2) and 13(8) of *The Motor Vehicle Accident Claims Act*, R.S.A. 1970, c. 243;

(b) in respect of the Province of British Columbia

(i) paragraphs 3(1)(a) and (b) and section 9 of the *Criminal Injury Compensation Act*, R.S.B.C. 1979, c. 83, and

(ii) subsection 106(1) of the *Motor-vehicle Act*, R.S.B.C. 1960, c. 253, as amended by S.B.C. 1965, c. 27;

(c) in respect of the Province of Manitoba

(i) subsection 6(1) of *The Criminal Injuries Compensation Act*, S.M. 1970, c. 56, and

(ii) subsections 7(9) and 12(11) of *The Unsatisfied Judgement Fund Act*, R.S.M. 1970, c. U70;

(d) in respect of the Province of New Brunswick

(i) subsections 3(1) and (2) of the *Compensation for Victims of Crime Act*, R.S.N.B. 1973, c. C-14, and

(ii) subsections 319(3), (10) and 321(1) of the *Motor Vehicle Act*, R.S.N.B. 1973, c. M-17;

(e) in respect of the Province of Newfoundland

(i) subsection 27(1) of the *Criminal Injuries Compensation Act*, R.S.N. 1970, c. 68, and

(ii) subsection 106(2) of *The Highway Traffic Act*, R.S.N. 1970, c. 152;

(f) in respect of the Northwest Territories, subsections 3(1) and 5(2) and section 13 of the *Criminal Injuries Compensation Ordinance*, R.O.N.W.T. 1974, c. C-23;

(g) in respect of the Province of Nova Scotia, subsections 190(5) and 191(2) of the *Motor Vehicle Act*, R.S.N.S. 1967, c. 191;

(h) in respect of the Province of Ontario

(i) section 5, subsection 7(2) and section 14 of *The Compensation for Victims of Crime Act, 1971*, S.O. 1971, c. 51, and

(ii) subsections 5(3) and 6(1) and section 18 of *The Motor Vehicle Accident Claims Act*, R.S.O. 1970, c. 281;

(i) in respect of the Province of Prince Edward Island, subsection 351(3) of the *Highway Traffic Act*, R.S.P.E.I. 1974, c. H-6;

(j) in respect of the Province of Quebec

(i) sections 5, 5b and 14 of the *Crime Victims Compensation Act*, S.Q. 1971, c. 18, and

(ii) sections 13 and 26, subsection 37(1) and sections 44 and 54 of the *Automobile Insurance Act*, S.Q. 1977, c. 68;

(k) in respect of the Province of Saskatchewan

(i) subsection 10(1) of *The Criminal Injuries Compensation Act*, R.S.S. 1978, c. C-47, and

(ii) subsections 23(1) to (4) and (7), 24(2) to (7) and (9), 25(1), 26(1), 27(1) and (2), 27(5), 51(8) and (9), 54(3) and 55(1) of *The Automobile Accident Insurance Act*, R.S.S. 1978, c. A-35; and

(l) in respect of the Yukon Territory, subsection 3(1) of the *Compensation for the Victims of Crime Ordinance*, O.Y.T. 1975 (1st), c. 2 as amended by O.Y.T. 1976 (1st), c. 5.

**6502.** For the purposes of paragraph 56(1)(c.1), section 56.1, paragraph 60(c.1) and section 60.1 of the Act, the class of individuals

(a) who were parties, whether in a personal capacity or by representation, to proceedings giving rise to an order made in accordance with the laws of the Province of Ontario, and

(b) who, at the time the application for the order was made, were persons described in subclause 14(b)(i) of the *Family Law Reform Act*, Revised Statutes of Ontario 1980, c. 152,

is prescribed as a class of persons described in the laws of a province.

**Definitions [Reg. 6502]:** "individual", "person", "prescribed" — ITA 248(1); "province" — *Interpretation Act* 35(1).

**6503.** For the purposes of paragraphs 60(j.02) to (j.04) of the Act, subsections 39(7) and 42(8) of the *Public Service Superannuation Act* and subsection 24(6) of the *Royal Canadian Mounted Police Superannuation Act* are prescribed.

**Notes:** Reg. 6503 added by P.C. 1994-738, effective for 1990 and later taxation years (for ITA 60(j.02) and (j.04)) and 1991 and later taxation years (for ITA 60(j.03)). The Department of Finance Technical Notes released with the draft regulations had indicated that similar provisions in the *Members of Parliament Retiring Allowances Act* and the *Canadian Forces Superannuation Act* would be prescribed. It was subsequently determined that the former is covered by regulations made under the *Public Service Superannuation Act*, and the latter is not needed because no one moves from the public service to the Canadian Forces late in their career.

**Definitions [Reg. 6503]:** "prescribed" — ITA 248(1).

## PART LXVI — PRESCRIBED ORDER

**6600.** For the purposes of the definition "overseas Canadian Forces school staff" in subsection 248(1) of the Act, the prescribed order is the "Canadian Forces Overseas Schools Order" made by Order in Council P.C. 1975-3/1054 of 6 May, 1975.

**Definitions [Reg. 6600]:** "prescribed" — ITA 248(1).

## PART LXVII — PRESCRIBED VENTURE CAPITAL CORPORATIONS, LABOUR-SPONSORED VENTURE CAPITAL CORPORATIONS, INVESTMENT CONTRACT CORPORATIONS, QUALIFYING CORPORATIONS AND PRESCRIBED STOCK SAVINGS PLAN

**Interpretation Bulletins [Part LXVII]:** IT-73R5: The small business deduction; IT-269R3: Part IV tax on taxable dividends received by a private corporation or a subject corporation.

**6700.** For the purposes of paragraph 40(2)(i), clause 53(2)(k)(i)(C), paragraph 89(1)(f) [89(1)"private corporation"], subsection 125(6.2), paragraph 125(7)(b) [125(7)"Canadian-controlled private corporation"], section 186.2 and subsection 191(1) of the Act, and in this Part, "prescribed venture capital corporation" means at any particular time

(a) a corporation that is at that time registered under the provisions of

(i) *An Act Respecting Corporations for the Development of Quebec Business Firms*, Statutes of Quebec 1976, c. 33,

(ii) the *Small Business Development Corporations Act, 1979*, Statutes of Ontario 1979, c. 22,

(iii) *Manitoba Regulation 194/84*, being a regulation made under *The Loans Act, 1983(2)*, Statutes of Manitoba 1982-83-84, c. 36,

(iv) *The Venture Capital Tax Credit Act*, Statutes of Saskatchewan 1983-84, c. V-4.1,

(v) the *Small Business Equity Corporations Act*, Statutes of Alberta 1984, c. S-13.5,

(vi) the *Small Business Venture Capital Act*, Statutes of British Columbia 1985, c. 56,

(vii) *An Act respecting Quebec business investment companies*, Statutes of Quebec 1985, c. 9,

(viii) *The Venture Capital Act*, Statutes of Newfoundland 1988, c. 15,

(ix) *The Labour-sponsored Venture Capital Corporations Act*, Statutes of Saskatchewan 1986, c. L-0.2,

(x) Part 2 of the *Employee Investment Act*, Chapter 24 of the Statutes of British Columbia, 1989,

(xi) Part III of the *Community Small Business Investment Funds Act*, chapter 18 of the Statutes of Ontario, 1992,

(xii) *The Labour-Sponsored Venture Capital Corporations Act*, Continuing Consolidation of the Statutes of Manitoba c. L12; or

(xiii) Part II of the *Risk Capital Investment Tax Credits Act*, chapter 22 of the Statutes of the Northwest Territories, 1998;

(b) the corporation established by *An Act to Establish the Fonds de solidarité des travailleurs du Québec (F.T.Q.)*, Revised Statutes of Quebec, F-3.2.1;

(c) a corporation that is at that time registered with the Department of Economic Development and Tourism of the Government of the Northwest Territories pursuant to the Venture Capital Policy and Directive issued by the Government of the Northwest Territories on June 27, 1985;

(d) a corporation that is at that time a registered labour-sponsored venture capital corporation;

(e) the corporation established by *The Manitoba Employee Ownership Fund Corporation Act*, Continuing Consolidation of the Statutes of Manitoba, c. E95;

(f) the corporation established by *An Act to establish Fondaction, le Fonds de développement de la Confédération des syndicats nationaux pour la coopération et l'emploi*, Statutes of Quebec 1995, c. 48; or

(g) a corporation that is at that time registered under Part II of the *Equity Tax Credit Act*, Statutes of Nova Scotia 1993, c. 3.

**Notes [Reg. 6700]:** Reg. 6700(a)(x) added by P.C. 1992-1306, effective for taxation years ending after Sept. 26, 1989. 6700(a)(xi) added by P.C. 1993-1549, effective for 1991 and later taxation years, and amended by P.C. 1999-249, effective May 8, 1997 for the 1997 and later taxation years, to change reference from *Labour-Sponsored Venture Capital Corporations Act, 1992* to the CSBIF Act.. 6700(a)(xii) added by P.C. 1997-1943, effective for 1997 and later taxation years. 6700(a)(xiii) added by P.C. 1999-249, effective for 1998 and later taxation years. 6700(b) amended by P.C. 1993-1549 to refer to the Revised Statutes of Quebec (i.e., as amended from time to time), effective June 20, 1986. 6700(d) added by P.C. 1992-1307, effective 1989, and amended non-substantively by P.C. 1998-782, effective 1996, to delete the final words "within the

Part LXVII — Prescribed Venture Capital Corporations etc.    Reg. S. 6701(f.1)

meaning assigned by section 204.8 of the Act". 6700(e) added by P.C. 1993-1549, effective for 1992 and later taxation years. 6700(f) added by P.C. 1996-436, effective for 1995 and later taxation years. 6700(g) added by P.C. 1997-1669, effective for 1997 and later taxation years. 6700(g) amended by P.C. 1999-249, effective May 8, 1997 for the 1997 and later taxation years, to change reference from *Labour-Sponsored Venture Capital Corporations Act, 1992* to the CSBIF Act, and effective for the 1998 and later taxation years to add reference to the *Risk Capital Investment Tax Credits Act*.

**Definitions [Reg. 6700]:** "business" — ITA 248(1); "corporation" — ITA 248(1), *Interpretation Act* 35(1); "registered labour-sponsored venture capital corporation" — ITA 248(1).

**Interpretation Bulletins:** IT-458R2: Canadian-controlled private corporation.

**6700.1** For the purposes of paragraph 40(2)(i) and clause 53(2)(k)(i)(C) of the Act, a "prescribed venture capital corporation" at any time includes a corporation that at that time has an employee share ownership plan registered under the provisions of Part 1 of the *Employee Investment Act*, chapter 24 of the Statutes of British Columbia, 1989.

**Notes:** Reg. 6700.1 added by P.C. 1992-1036, effective for taxation years ending after Sept. 26, 1989.

**Definitions [Reg. 6700.1]:** "corporation" — ITA 248(1), *Interpretation Act* 35(1).

**6700.2** For the purposes of paragraph 40(2)(i) and clause 53(2)(k)(i)(C) of the Act, "prescribed venture capital corporation" at any time includes a corporation that at that time is a corporation registered under the provisions of Part II of the *Community Small Business Investment Funds Act*, chapter 18 of the Statutes of Ontario, 1992, or of Part II of the *Risk Capital Investment Tax Credits Act*, chapter 22 of the Statutes of the Northwest Territories, 1998.

**Notes:** Reg. 6700.2 added by P.C. 1993-1549, effective for 1991 and later taxation years. Amended by P.C. 1999-249, effective May 8, 1997 for the 1997 and later taxation years, to change reference from *Labour-Sponsored Venture Capital Corporations Act, 1992* to the CSBIF Act, and effective for the 1998 and later taxation years to add reference to the *Risk Capital Investment Tax Credits Act*.

**Definitions [Reg. 6700.2]:** "corporation" — ITA 248(1), *Interpretation Act* 35(1).

**6701.** For the purposes of paragraph 40(2)(i), clause 53(2)(k)(i)(C), the definition "approved share" in subsection 127.4(1), subsections 131(8) and (11), section 186.1 and subsection 191(1) of the Act, and in this Part, "prescribed labour-sponsored venture capital corporation" means at any particular time

**Proposed Amendment — Reg. 6701 opening words**

**6701.** For the purposes of paragraph 40(2)(i), clause 53(2)(k)(i)(C), the definition "approved share" in subsection 127.4(1), subsections 131(8) and (11), section 186.1 and subsection 191(1) of the Act, this Part and subsection 1106(2), "prescribed labour-sponsored venture capital corporation" means at any particular time

**Application:** The December 12, 1995 draft regulations (Canadian film tax credit), s. 4, will amend the opening words of s. 6701 to read as above, applicable to 1995 *et seq*.

**Notes:** This change adds reference to Reg. 1106(2).

**Proposed Amendment — Reg. 6701 opening words — Application to ITA 125(7) "specified investment business"**

**Technical Notes to draft legislation, June 20, 1996:** Section 6701 of the *Income Tax Regulations*, which provides the meaning of "prescribed labour-sponsored venture capital corporation" for a number of provisions of the Act, will be amended to apply for the purpose of the definition "specified investment business" in subsection 125(7).

**Proposed Amendment — Reg. 6701 opening words — Application to ITA 89(1) "public corporation" and 204.8 "eligible investment"(f)(i)**

**Department of Finance Technical Notes to ITA 89(1) "public corporation", July 31, 1997:** The definition is amended to provide that a prescribed labour-sponsored venture capital corporation is not a public corporation for the purposes of the Act unless a class of its shares becomes listed on a prescribed stock exchange in Canada. For this purpose, it is intended that section 6701 of the Regulations will be amended to add a cross reference to this definition.

**Department of Finance Technical Notes to ITA 204.8 "eligible investment"(f)(i), July 31, 1997:** The definition is also amended so that a prescribed LSVCC that is related to the eligible entity is ignored for the purpose of the second condition. It is intended that section 6701 of the Regulations will be amended to add a cross reference to the definition.

(a) the corporation established by the *Act to establish the Fonds de solidarité des travailleurs du Québec 1983*, c. 58,

(b) a corporation that is registered under the provisions of *The Labour-sponsored Venture Capital Corporations Act*, Statutes of Saskatchewan 1986, c. L-0.2,

(c) a corporation that is registered under Part 2 of the *Employee Investment Act*, chapter 24 of the Statutes of British Columbia, 1989,

(d) a registered labour-sponsored venture capital corporation,

(e) a corporation that is registered under Part III of the *Community Small Business Investment Funds Act*, chapter 18 of the Statutes of Ontario, 1992;

(f) the corporation established by *The Manitoba Employee Ownership Fund Corporation Act*, Continuing Consolidation of the Statutes of Manitoba, c. E95,

(f.1) a corporation that is registered under *The Labour-Sponsored Venture Capital Corporations Act*, Continuing Consolidation of the Statutes of Manitoba c. L12, or

2303

(g) the corporation established by *An Act to establish Fondaction, le Fonds de développement de la Confédération des syndicats nationaux pour la coopération et l'emploi*, Statutes of Québec 1995, c. 48;

(h) a corporation that is registered under Part II of the *Equity Tax Credit Act*, Statutes of Nova Scotia 1993, c. 3, or

(i) a corporation that is registered under Part II of the *Risk Capital Investment Tax Credits Act*, chapter 22 of the Statutes of Northwest Territories, 1998.

**Notes**: Reg. 6701(c) added by P.C. 1992-1306, effective for taxation years ending after Sept. 26, 1989. 6701(d) added by P.C. 1992-1307, effective 1989, and amended non-substantively by P.C. 1998-782, effective 1996, to delete the final words "within the meaning assigned by section 204.8 of the Act". 6701(e) and (f) added by P.C. 1993-1549, para. (e) effective for 1991 and later taxation years and para. (f) effective for 1992 and later taxation years. 6701(e) then amended by P.C. 1999-249, effective May 8, 1997 for the 1997 and later taxation years, to change reference from *Labour-Sponsored Venture Capital Corporations Act, 1992* to the CSBIF Act. 6701(f.1) added by P.C. 1997-1943, effective for 1997 and later taxation years. 6701(g) added by P.C. 1996-436, effective for 1995 and later taxation years. 6701(h) added by P.C. 1997-1669, effective for 1997 and later taxation years. 6701(i) added by P.C. 1999-249, effective for the 1998 and later taxation years.

**Definitions [Reg. 6701]**: "corporation" — ITA 248(1), *Interpretation Act* 35(1); "registered labour-sponsored venture capital corporation" — ITA 248(1).

**6702.** For the purposes of subparagraph 40(2)(i)(ii) and clause 53(2)(k)(i)(C) of the Act, "prescribed assistance" means

(a) the amount of any assistance received from a province that has been provided in respect of, or for the acquisition of, a share of the capital stock of a prescribed venture capital corporation;

(a.1) the amount of any assistance provided under the *Employee Investment Act*, chapter 24 of the Statutes of British Columbia, 1989, in respect of, or for the acquisition of, a share of the capital stock of a corporation described in section 6700.1;

(a.2) the amount of any assistance provided under the *Community Small Business Investment Funds Act*, chapter 18 of the Statutes of Ontario, 1992, or the *Risk Capital Investment Tax Credits Act*, chapter 22 of the Statutes of the Northwest Territories, 1998, in respect of, or for the acquisition of, a share of the capital stock of a corporation described in section 6700.2;

(b) the amount of any tax credit provided in respect of, or for the acquisition of, a share of a prescribed labour-sponsored venture capital corporation; and

(c) the amount of any tax credit provided by a province in respect of, or for the acquisition of, a share of the capital stock of a taxable Canadian corporation (other than a share of the capital stock of a corporation in respect of which an amount has been renounced by the corporation under subsection 66(12.6), (12.601), (12.62) or (12.64) of the Act) that is held in a prescribed stock savings plan.

**Related Provisions**: Reg. 7300(b) — Prescribed assistance under Reg. 6702 is a prescribed amount for ITA 12(1)(x).

**Notes**: Reg. 6702(a.1) added by P.C. 1992-1306, effective for taxation years ending after Sept. 26, 1989. 6702(a.2) added by P.C. 1993-1549, effective for 1991 and later taxation years. 6702(a.2) amended by P.C. 1999-249, effective May 8, 1997 for the 1997 and later taxation years, to change reference from *Labour-Sponsored Venture Capital Corporations Act, 1992* to the CSBIF Act, and effective for the 1998 and later taxation years to add reference to the *Risk Capital Investment Tax Credits Act*.

Reference to ITA 66(12.601) added to Reg. 6702(c) by P.C. 1996-494 effective December 3, 1992.

**Definitions [Reg. 6702]**: "amount" — ITA 248(1); "corporation" — ITA 248(1), *Interpretation Act* 35(1); "prescribed labour-sponsored venture capital corporation" — Reg. 6701; "prescribed stock savings plan" — Reg. 6705; "prescribed venture capital corporation" — Reg. 6700; "province" — *Interpretation Act* 35(1); "share" — ITA 248(1); "taxable Canadian corporation" — ITA 89(1), 248(1).

**6703.** For the purposes of section 186.1 of the Act, a "prescribed investment contract corporation" means a corporation described in clause 146(1)(j)(ii)(B) [146(1)"retirement savings plan"(b)(ii)] of the Act.

**Definitions [Reg. 6703]**: "corporation" — ITA 248(1), *Interpretation Act* 35(1).

**6704.** For the purposes of section 186.2 of the Act, a corporation is a prescribed qualifying corporation in respect of dividends received by a shareholder on shares of its capital stock if, when the shares were acquired by the shareholder, they constituted

(a) an investment described in sections 33 and 34 of the Act referred to in subparagraph 6700(a)(i);

(b) an eligible investment under the provisions of an Act referred to in subparagraph 6700(a)(ii), (iv), (v), (vi) or (viii) or the regulation referred to in subparagraph 6700(a)(iii);

(c) a qualified investment under the provisions of the Act referred to in subparagraph 6700(a)(vii); or

(d) an investment in an eligible business under the Venture Capital Policy and Directive referred to in paragraph 6700(c).

**Notes**: Reg. 6704(b), (d) amended, (e) revoked, by P.C. 1993-1549, effective for dividends received after February 18, 1987 (para. (b)) and after September 26, 1989 (para. (d)).

**Definitions [Reg. 6704]**: "business" — ITA 248(1); "corporation" — ITA 248(1), *Interpretation Act* 35(1); "dividend", "prescribed", "share", "shareholder" — ITA 248(1).

**6705.** For the purposes of paragraph 40(2)(i) and clause 53(2)(k)(i)(C) of the Act, and in this Part, "prescribed stock savings plan" means a stock savings plan as defined in

(a) the *Alberta Stock Savings Plan Act*, Statutes of Alberta 1986, c. A-37.7;

## Part LXVII — Prescribed Venture Capital Corporations etc.

(b) *The Stock Savings Tax Credit Act*, Statutes of Saskatchewan 1986, c. S-59.1;

(c) the *Nova Scotia Stock Savings Plan Act*, Statutes of Nova Scotia 1987, c. 6; and

(d) *The Stock Savings Tax Credit Act*, Statutes of Newfoundland 1988, c. 14.

**6706.** For the purpose of clause 204.81(1)(c)(v)(F) of the Act, a prescribed condition is that, in respect of a redemption of a Class A share of a corporation's capital stock, the shareholder requires the corporation to withhold an amount in respect of the redemption in accordance with Part XII.5 of the Act.

**Related Provisions**: ITA 204.81 — Conditions for registration; ITA 211.7 — Recovery of credit from provincial LSVCCs; ITA 211.8(1) — Disposition of approved share.

**Notes**: Reg. 6706 replaced by P.C. 1998-782, effective for redemptions that occur after 1997. See ITA 211.7. For earlier redemptions, read

6706. Qualifying corporations — (1) Interpretation — In this section,

"net cost" has the meaning assigned by subsection 127.4(1) of the Act;

"qualifying Class A share" in the capital stock of a corporation means a share in respect of which an information return described in paragraph 204.81(6)(c) of the Act was provided by the corporation, where the information return was not returned pursuant to subclause 204.81(1)(c)(v)(A)(I) of the Act, but does not include a share the consideration for which is not taken into account in determining the labour-sponsored funds tax credit (as defined in subsection 127.4(1) of the Act) for any taxation year of any individual other than a trust;

"specified percentage" in respect of a share of the capital stock of a corporation means

(a) where a provincial tax credit is available to the original owner of the share with respect to the acquisition of the share and the corporation, the original owner of the share and any subsequent owner of the share would, but for this section, not be obliged to repay the provincial tax credit or an amount in respect thereof, 40 per cent, and

(b) in any other case, 20 per cent.

(2) For the purposes of this section,

(a) any acquisition of shares by a person in the person's capacity as a broker or dealer in securities shall be disregarded for the purposes of determining by whom the shares were originally acquired;

(b) a share shall be deemed to have been acquired by an individual at such time as it is irrevocably subscribed and paid for by the individual; and

(c) where a share was originally acquired by a qualifying trust (as defined in subsection 127.4(1) of the Act) for an individual in respect of the share for any taxation year, the trust shall be deemed in respect of the acquisition to have been an agent for that individual.

(3) For the purposes of subparagraph 204.81(1)(c)(v) of the Act, a corporation may, at a particular time, redeem one or more qualifying Class A shares in the capital stock of the corporation originally acquired at the same time (in this subsection referred to as the "acquisition time") by an individual (in this subsection referred to as the "original owner") where the holder of those shares by written instrument before the particular time

(a) directs the corporation to remit an amount on behalf of the holder to the Receiver General no later than 30 days after the particular time equal to the least of

(i) the amount that represents the specified percentage of the net cost to the original owner of those shares,

(ii) the amount that would be the tax credit balance of the original owner with respect to any one of those shares if other Class A shares in the capital stock of the corporation that were

(A) originally acquired by the original owner at the acquisition time, and

(B) redeemed by the corporation before the particular time

had been acquired immediately before the acquisition time, and

(iii) the amount, if any, by which the amount for which those shares are to be redeemed exceeds the total of all amounts each of which is a repayment (otherwise than under this section) of a provincial tax credit available to the original owner with respect to the acquisition of those shares; and

(b) irrevocably gives the corporation authority to withhold from the amount for which those shares are to be redeemed, and remit on behalf of the holder to the Receiver General, the amount determined in respect of the redemption under paragraph (a).

(4) For the purposes of subsection (3), the tax credit balance of an individual with respect to a particular qualifying Class A share in the capital stock of a corporation originally acquired by the individual at a particular time in a taxation year of the individual means the amount determined by the formula

$$A + B - C$$

where

A is

(a) where the particular time is in the first 60 days of the year, the specified percentage of the amount, if any, by which $5,000 (or, if the particular time is before 1993, $3,500) exceeds the amount, if any, by which

(i) the total of all amounts each of which is the net cost to the individual of a qualifying Class A share in the capital stock of the corporation acquired in the preceding taxation year

exceeds

(ii) such portion of the total described in subparagraph (i) as may reasonably be considered to result in an increase in the amount that would be the tax credit balance of the individual with respect to a qualifying Class A share in the capital stock of the corporation acquired in the first 60 days of the preceding taxation year if the amount used as the value of C in computing such balance were nil, and

(b) in any other case, nil;

B is the specified percentage of the lesser of

(a) $5,000 (or, where the particular time is before 1992, $3,500), and

(b) the amount, if any, by which

(i) the net cost to the individual of all qualifying Class A shares in the capital stock of the corporation acquired by the individual at or before the particular time and in the year

exceeds

(ii) the amount that would be used as the value of A in determining the individual's tax credit balance with respect to the particular share if the description of A were read without reference to the words "the specified percentage of"; and

C is the specified percentage of the total of all amounts each of which is the net cost to the individual of a qualifying Class A share

(a) acquired by the individual before the particular time and in the year, and

(b) redeemed by the corporation before the particular share is to be redeemed.

Reg. 6706(1)"qualifying Class A share" amended by P.C. 1996-437, effective December 3, 1992, to add the words beginning "but does not include...".

Reg. 6706(2)(c) added by P.C. 1996-437, effective December 3, 1992.

Reference to ITA 204.81(1)(c)(v)(G) in Reg. 6706(3) changed to 204.81(1)(c)(v) by P.C. 1996-437, effective December 3, 1992.

Reg. 6706 originally added by P.C. 1992-1307, effective for shares redeemed in 1992 or later.

**Definitions [Reg. 6706]**: "amount" — ITA 248(1); "corporation" — ITA 248(1), *Interpretation Act* 35(1); "prescribed", "share", "shareholder" — ITA 248(1).

**Forms**: T1149: Remittance form for labour-sponsored funds tax credits withheld on redeemed shares; T2152: Part X.3 tax return for a labour-sponsored venture capital corporation; T5006 Summ: Return of Class A shares; T5006 Supp: Statement of registered labour-sponsored venture capital corporation Class A shares.

**6707. [Provincially registered LSVCCs]** — For the purpose of subsection 204.82(5) of the Act, a "prescribed provision of a law of a province" means section 25.1 of the *Community Small Business Investment Funds Act*, chapter 18 of the Statutes of Ontario, 1992.

**Notes**: Reg. 6707 added by P.C. 1999-249, effective May 8, 1997.

## PART LXVIII — PRESCRIBED PLANS, ARRANGEMENTS AND CONTRIBUTIONS

**6800.** For the purpose of paragraph (e) of the definition "employee benefit plan" in subsection 248(1) of the Act, each of the following is a prescribed arrangement:

(a) the Major League Baseball Players Benefit Plan;

(b) an arrangement under which all contributions are made pursuant to a law of Canada or a province, where one of the main purposes of the law is to enforce minimum standards with respect to wages, vacation entitlement or severance pay; and

(c) an arrangement under which all contributions are made in connection with a dispute regarding the entitlement of one or more persons to benefits to be received or enjoyed by the person or persons.

**Notes**: Reg. 6800(b) and (c) added by P.C. 1996-911, effective 1980.

**Definitions [Reg. 6800]**: "Canada" — ITA 255, *Interpretation Act* 35(1); "person", "prescribed" — ITA 248(1); "province" — *Interpretation Act* 35(1).

**6801.** For the purposes of paragraph (l) of the definition "salary deferral arrangement" in subsection 248(1) of the Act, a prescribed plan or arrangement is an arrangement in writing

(a) between an employer and an employee that is established on or after July 28, 1986 where

(i) it is reasonable to conclude, having regard to all the circumstances, including the terms and conditions of the arrangement and any agreement relating thereto, that the arrangement is not established to provide benefits to the employee on or after retirement but is established for the main purpose of permitting the employee to fund, through salary or wage deferrals, a leave of absence from the employee's employment of not less than

(A) where the leave of absence is to be taken by the employee for the purpose of permitting the full-time attendance of the employee at a designated educational institution (within the meaning assigned by subsection 118.6(1) of the Act, three consecutive months, or

(B) in any other case, six consecutive months

that is to commence immediately after a period (in this section referred to as the "deferral period") not exceeding six years after the date on which the deferrals for the leave of absence commence,

(ii) the amount of salary or wages deferred by the employee under all such arrangements for the services rendered by the employee to the employer in a taxation year does not exceed $33\frac{1}{3}$ per cent of the amount of the salary or wages that the employee would, but for the arrangements, reasonably be expected to have received in the year in respect of the services,

(iii) the arrangement provides that throughout the period of the leave of absence the employee does not receive any salary or wages from the employer, or from any other person or partnership with whom the employer does not deal at arm's length, other than

(A) the amount by which the employee's salary or wages under the arrangement was deferred or is to be reduced or, amounts that are based on a percentage of the salary or wage scale of employees of the employer, which percentage is fixed in re-

Part LXVIII — Prescribed Plans/Arrangements/Contributions    Reg. S. 6802

spect of the employee for the deferral period and the leave of absence, and

(B) the reasonable fringe benefits that the employer usually pays to or on behalf of employees,

(iv) the arrangement provides that the amounts deferred in respect of the employee under the arrangement

(A) are held by or for the account of a trust governed by a plan or arrangement that is an employee benefit plan within the meaning of the definition thereof in subsection 248(1) of the Act, and provides that the amount that may reasonably be considered to be the income of the trust for a taxation year that has been earned by it for the benefit of the employee shall be paid in the year to the employee, or

(B) are held by or for the account of any person other than a trust referred to in clause (A), and provides that the amount in respect of interest or other additional amounts that may reasonably be considered to have accrued to or for the benefit of the employee to the end of a taxation year shall be paid in the year to the employee,

(v) the arrangement provides that the employee is to return to his regular employment with the employer or an employer that participates in the same or a similar arrangement after the leave of absence for a period that is not less than the period of the leave of absence, and

(vi) subject to subparagraph (iv), the arrangement provides that all amounts held for the employee's benefit under the arrangement shall be paid to the employee out of or under the arrangement no later than the end of the first taxation year that commences after the end of the deferral period;

(b) between an employer and an employee that is established before July 28, 1986 where it is reasonable to conclude, having regard to all the circumstances, including the terms and conditions of the arrangement and any agreement relating thereto, that the arrangement is not established to provide benefits on or after retirement but is established for the main purpose of permitting the employee to fund, through salary or wage deferrals, a leave of absence from the employment and under which the deferrals in respect of the leave of absence commenced before 1987;

(c) that is established for the purpose of deferring the salary or wages of a professional on-ice official for his services as such with the National Hockey League if, in the case of an official resident in Canada, the trust or other person who has custody and control of any funds, investments or other property under the arrangement is resident in Canada; or

(d) between a corporation and an employee of the corporation or a corporation related thereto under which the employee (or, after the employee's death, a dependant or relation of the employee or the legal representative of the employee) may or shall receive an amount that may reasonably be attributable to duties of an office or employment performed by the employee on behalf of the corporation or a corporation related thereto where

(i) all amounts that may be received under the arrangement shall be received after the time of the employee's death or retirement from, or loss of, the office or employment and no later than the end of the first calendar year commencing thereafter, and

(ii) the aggregate of all amounts each of which may be received under the arrangement depends on the fair market value of shares of the capital stock of the corporation or a corporation related thereto at a time within the period that commences one year before the time of the employee's death or retirement from, or loss of, the office or employment and ends at the time the amount is received,

unless, by reason of the arrangement or a series of transactions that includes the arrangement, the employee or a person with whom the employee does not deal at arm's length is entitled, either immediately or in the future, either absolutely or contingently, to receive or obtain any amount or benefit granted or to be granted for the purpose of reducing the impact, in whole or in part, of any reduction in the fair market value of the shares of the corporation or a corporation related thereto.

**Related Provisions**: Reg. 8508 — Effect of salary deferral leave plan on registered pension plan.

**Notes**: The arrangement described in Reg. 6801(a) is commonly referred to as a "sabbatical" arrangement. Such arrangements are often used by teachers and professors. For a discussion of such plans, see Elizabeth Brown, "Executive Sabbaticals and the Deferred Salary Leave Program", 9(2) *Taxation of Executive Compensation and Retirement* (Federated Press) 24–32 (1997).

**Definitions [Reg. 6801]**: "amount" — ITA 248(1); "arm's length" — ITA 251(1); "corporation" — ITA 248(1), *Interpretation Act* 35(1); "deferral period" — Reg. 6801(a)(i); "employee", "employee benefit plan", "employer", "employment", "legal representative" — ITA 248(1); "month" — *Interpretation Act* 35(1); "office" — ITA 248(1); "partnership" — see Notes to ITA 96(1); "person", "prescribed", "property" — ITA 248(1); "related" — ITA 251(2)–(6); "resident in Canada" — ITA 250; "salary or wages", "share" — ITA 248(1); "taxation year" — ITA 249; "trust" — ITA 104(1), 248(1), (3); "writing" — *Interpretation Act* 35(1).

**I.T. Technical News**: No. 11 (reporting of amounts paid out of an employee benefit plan.

**Advance Tax Rulings**: ATR-39: Self-funded leave of absence.

**6802.** For the purposes of paragraph (n) of the definition "retirement compensation arrangement" in subsection 248(1) of the Act, a prescribed plan or arrangement is

(a) the plan instituted by the *Canada Pension Plan*;

(b) a provincial pension plan as defined in section 3 of the *Canada Pension Plan*;

(c) a plan instituted by the *Unemployment Insurance Act*;

(d) a plan pursuant to an agreement in writing that is established for the purpose of deferring the salary or wages of a professional on-ice official for the official's services as such with the National Hockey League if, in the case of an official resident in Canada, the trust or other person who has custody and control of any funds, investments or other property under the plan is resident in Canada;

(e) an arrangement under which all contributions are made pursuant to a law of Canada or a province, where one of the main purposes of the law is to enforce minimum standards with respect to wages, vacation entitlement or severance pay;

(f) an arrangement under which all contributions are made in connection with a dispute regarding the entitlement of one or more persons to benefits to be received or enjoyed by the person or persons; or

(g) a plan or arrangement instituted by the social security legislation of a country other than Canada or of a state, province or other political subdivision of such a country.

**Related Provisions**: ITA 207.6(6) — Rules applicable to a prescribed plan or arrangement.

**Notes**: Reg. 6802(c) needs to be amended to refer to the *Employment Insurance Act*.

Reg. 6802(e) replaced and (f) and (g) added by P.C. 1996-911, effective October 9, 1996. The rules formerly under Reg. 6802(e) have been incorporated in new Reg. 6804.

**Definitions [Reg. 6802]**: "Canada" — ITA 255, *Interpretation Act* 35(1); "person", "prescribed", "property" — ITA 248(1); "province" — *Interpretation Act* 35(1); "resident in Canada" — ITA 250; "salary or wages" — ITA 248(1); "trust" — ITA 104(1), 248(1), (3); "writing" — *Interpretation Act* 35(1).

**6802.1 (1)** For the purpose of paragraph 8(1)(m.2) of the Act, each of the following is a prescribed plan:

(a) the pension plan established as a consequence of the establishment, by section 27 of the *Members of Parliament Retiring Allowances Act*, of the Members of Parliament Retirement Compensation Arrangements Account; and

(b) the pension plan established by the *Retirement Compensation Arrangements Regulations, No. 1*.

**(2)** For the purpose of subsection 207.6(6) of the Act, each of the following is a prescribed plan or arrangement:

(a) the pension plan established as a consequence of the establishment, by section 27 of the *Members of Parliament Retiring Allowances Act*, of the Members of Parliament Retirement Compensation Arrangements Account;

(b) the pension plan established by the *Retirement Compensation Arrangements Regulations, No. 1*; and

(c) the pension plan established by the *Retirement Compensation Arrangements Regulations, No. 2*.

**Notes [Reg. 6802.1]**: Reg. 6802.1 added by P.C. 1999-2211, paras. (1)(a) and (2)(a) effective 1992; paras. (1)(b) and (2)(b) effective December 15, 1994; and para. (2)(c) effective April 1995.

**Definitions [Reg. 6802.1]**: "Parliament" — *Interpretation Act* 35(1); "prescribed" — ITA 248(1).

**6803.** For the purposes of the definition "foreign retirement arrangement" in subsection 248(1) of the Act, a prescribed plan or arrangement is a plan or arrangement to which subsection 408(a), (b) or (h) of the United States *Internal Revenue Code of 1986*, as amended from time to time, applies.

**Notes**: Reg. 6803 added by P.C. 1992-2416, effective 1990. Subsection 408(a) of the U.S. *Internal Revenue Code* defines "individual retirement account" (IRA) as a trust that meets certain conditions, including permitting contributions of up to $2,000 per year. Subsection 408(b) defines "individual retirement annuity", which is similar but is an annuity or endowment contract issued by an insurer. Subsection 408(h) defines a "custodial account" as an account held by a bank or other person that meets all of the other conditions for an IRA, and which is treated as a trust and therefore effectively deemed to be an IRA.

See also Notes to ITA 248(1)"foreign retirement arrangement".

**Definitions [Reg. 6803]**: "prescribed" — ITA 248(1); "United States" — *Interpretation Act* 35(1).

**6804. Contributions to foreign plans — (1) Definitions** — The definitions in this subsection apply in this section.

**"foreign non-profit organization"** means,

(a) at any time before 1995, an organization

(i) that at that time meets the conditions in subparagraphs (b)(i) to (iii), or

(ii) that at that time is not operated for the purpose of profit, and whose assets are situated primarily outside Canada throughout the calendar year that includes that time, and

(b) at any time after 1994, an organization that at that time

(i) is not operated for the purpose of profit,

(ii) has its main place of management outside Canada, and

(iii) carries on its activities primarily outside Canada.

"**foreign plan**" means a plan or arrangement (determined without regard to subsection 207.6(5) of the Act) that would, but for paragraph (l) of the definition "retirement compensation arrangement" in subsection 248(1) of the Act, be a retirement compensation arrangement.

"**qualifying entity**" means a non-resident entity that holds all or part of the assets of a foreign plan where the following conditions are satisfied:

(a) the entity is resident in a country under the laws of which an income tax is imposed, and

(b) where those laws provide an exemption from tax, a reduced rate of tax or other favourable tax treatment for entities that hold assets of pension or other retirement plans, the entity qualifies for the favourable treatment.

**(2) Electing employer** — For the purposes of this section, an employer is an electing employer for a calendar year with respect to a foreign plan where

(a) the employer has sent or delivered to the Minister a letter stating that the employer elects to have this section apply with respect to contributions to the foreign plan, and

(b) the letter was sent or delivered on or before

(i) the last day of February in the year following the first calendar year after 1991 in which a contribution that is or would be if subsection 207.6(5.1) of the Act were read without reference to paragraph (a) of that subsection, a resident's contribution (as defined in that subsection) was made under the foreign plan in respect of services rendered by an individual to the employer, or

(ii) any later date that is acceptable to the Minister,

except that an employer is not an electing employer for a year with respect to a foreign plan if the Minister has granted written permission for the employer to revoke, for the year or a preceding calendar year, the election made under paragraph (a) in respect of the foreign plan.

**(3) Election by union** — Except as otherwise permitted in writing by the Minister, an election made by a trade union for the purpose of subsection (2) is valid only if it is made by the highest-level structural unit of the union.

**(4) Contributions made before 1992** — For the purpose of paragraph 207.6(5.1)(a) of the Act, a contribution made under a foreign plan by a person or body of persons in a calendar year before 1992 is a prescribed contribution where

(a) the contribution is paid to a qualifying entity;

(b) each employer (in this subsection referred to as a "contributor") that makes a contribution under the foreign plan in the year is

(i) a non-resident corporation throughout the year,

(ii) a partnership that makes contributions under the foreign plan primarily in respect of services rendered outside Canada to the partnership by non-resident employees, or

(iii) a foreign non-profit organization throughout the year;

(c) if a corporation or partnership (other than a corporation or partnership that is a foreign non-profit organization throughout the year) is a contributor, no individual who is entitled (either absolutely or contingently) to benefits under the foreign plan is a member of a registered pension plan, or a beneficiary under a deferred profit sharing plan, to which a contributor, or a person or body of persons not dealing at arm's length with a contributor, makes, or is required to make, contributions in relation to the year;

(d) contributions made in the year under the foreign plan for the benefit of individuals resident in Canada are reasonable in relation to contributions made under the plan for the benefit of non-resident individuals; and

(e) the foreign plan is not a pension plan the registration of which under the Act has been revoked.

**(5) Contributions made in 1992, 1993 or 1994** — For the purpose of paragraph 207.6(5.1)(a) of the Act, a contribution made under a foreign plan by a person or body of persons at any time in 1992, 1993 or 1994 in respect of services rendered by an individual to an employer is a prescribed contribution where

(a) the contribution is paid to a qualifying entity;

(b) the employer is an electing employer for the year with respect to the foreign plan;

(c) if the employer is not at that time a foreign non-profit organization, the individual is not a member of a registered pension plan (other than a specified multi-employer plan, as defined in subsection 147.1(1) of the Act), or a deferred profit sharing plan, in which the employer, or a person or body of persons that does not deal at arm's length with the employer, participates; and

(d) either

(i) the employer is

(A) a corporation that is not resident in Canada at that time,

(B) a partnership that makes contributions under the foreign plan primarily in respect of services rendered outside Canada to the partnership by non-resident employees, or

(C) a foreign non-profit organization at that time, or

(ii) the individual was non-resident at any time before the contribution is made and became a member of the foreign plan before the end of the month after the month in which the individual became resident in Canada.

**(6) Contributions made after 1994** — For the purposes of paragraph 207.6(5.1)(a) of the Act, a contribution made under a foreign plan by a person or body of persons at any time in a calendar year after 1994 in respect of services rendered by an individual to an employer is a prescribed contribution where

(a) the contribution is paid to a qualifying entity;

(b) the employer is an electing employer for the year with respect to the foreign plan;

(c) if the employer is at that time a foreign non-profit organization,

(i) the amount that, if subsection 8301(1) were read without reference to paragraph (b) of that subsection, would be the individual's pension adjustment for the year in respect of the employer is nil, or

(ii) the amount that would be the individual's pension adjustment for the year in respect of the employer if

(A) all contributions made under the foreign plan in the year in respect of the individual were prescribed by this subsection,

(B) where the year is 1996, section 8308.1 were read without reference to subsection (4.1), and

(C) where the year is 1997, subparagraph 8308.1(2)(b)(v) were read as:

"(v) the amount, if any, by which 18% of the individual's resident compensation from the employer for the year exceeds $1,000, and"

does not exceed the lesser of

(D) the money purchase limit for the year, and

(E) 18% of the individual's compensation (as defined in subsection 147.1(1) of the Act) for the year from the employer;

(d) if

(i) the employer is at that time a foreign non-profit organization, and

(ii) a period in the year throughout which the individual rendered services to the employer would be, under paragraph 8507(3)(a), a qualifying period of the individual with respect to another employer if that paragraph were read without reference to subparagraph (iv) of that paragraph,

subsection 8308(7) applies with respect to the determination of the individual's pension adjustment for the year with respect to each employer; and

(e) if the employer is not at that time a foreign non-profit organization,

(i) the individual was non-resident at any time before the contribution is made,

(ii) the individual became a member of the foreign plan before the end of the month after the month in which the individual became resident in Canada, and

(iii) the individual is not a member of a registered pension plan, or a deferred profit sharing plan, in which the employer, or a person or body of persons that does not deal at arm's length with the employer, participates.

Notes: Reg. 6804(6)(c)(ii) amended by P.C. 1998-2256, effective 1996 (thus overriding its enactment; see Notes at end of Reg. 6804). The amendment effectively added cls. (B) and (C).

**(7) Replacement plan** — For the purposes of subparagraphs (5)(d)(ii) and (6)(e)(ii), where benefits provided to an individual under a particular plan or arrangement are replaced by benefits under another plan or arrangement, the other plan or arrangement is deemed, in respect of the individual, to be the same plan or arrangement as the particular plan or arrangement.

Notes [Reg. 6804]: Reg. 6804 added by P.C. 1996-911, effective October 9, 1996. (To some extent these rules were formerly in Reg. 6802(e).) Prescribed contributions under Reg. 6804(4)–(6) are excluded from the definition of "resident's contributions" in ITA 207.6(5.1). They are thus exempted from the rules in ITA 207.6(5) which treat certain contributions to foreign pension plans as RCA contributions.

Definitions [Reg. 6804]: "amount" — ITA 248(1); "arm's length" — ITA 251(1); "Canada" — ITA 255, *Interpretation Act* 35(1); "contributor" — Reg. 6804(4); "corporation" — ITA 248(1), *Interpretation Act* 35(1); "deferred profit sharing plan" — ITA 147(1), 248(1); "electing employer" — Reg. 6804(2); "employee", "employer" — ITA 248(1); "foreign non-profit organization", "foreign plan" — Reg. 6804(1); "individual", "Minister" — ITA 248(1); "money purchase limit" — ITA 147.1(1), 248(1); "month" — *Interpretation Act* 35(1); "non-resident" — ITA 248(1); "partnership" — see Notes to ITA 96(1); "pension adjustment", "person", "prescribed" — ITA 248(1); "qualifying entity" — Reg. 6804(1); "registered pension plan" — ITA 248(1); "resident", "resident in Canada" — ITA 250; "retirement compensation arrangement" — ITA 248(1); "specified multi-employer plan" — ITA 147.1(1), Reg. 8510(2), (3); "written" — *Interpretation Act* 35(1)"writing".

# PART LXIX — PRESCRIBED OFFSHORE INVESTMENT FUND PROPERTIES

Notes: An earlier Part LXIX, "Aviation Turbine Fuel", applied from February 1982 to April 1983 for the purposes of (now-repealed) ITA 234.1. Current Part LXIX was added in 1986, effective 1985.

Part LXX — Accrued Interest on Debt Obligations    Reg. S. 7000(2)(c)

**6900.** For the purpose of paragraph 94.1(2)(a) [94.1(2)"designated cost"] of the Act, an offshore investment fund property (within the meaning assigned by subsection 94.1(1) of the Act) of a taxpayer that

(a) was acquired by him by way of bequest or inheritance from a deceased person who, throughout the five years immediately preceding his death, was not resident in Canada,

(b) had not been acquired by the deceased from a person resident in Canada, and

(c) is not property substituted for property acquired by the deceased from a person resident in Canada

is a prescribed offshore investment fund property of the taxpayer.

**Definitions [Reg. 6900]:** "person", "prescribed", "property" — ITA 248(1); "resident", "resident in Canada" — ITA 250; "substituted" — ITA 248(5); "taxpayer" — ITA 248(1).

## PART LXX — ACCRUED INTEREST ON DEBT OBLIGATIONS

**7000. (1) Prescribed debt obligations** — For the purpose of subsection 12(9) of the Act, each of the following debt obligations (other than a debt obligation that is an indexed debt obligation) in respect of which a taxpayer has at any time acquired an interest is a prescribed debt obligation:

(a) a particular debt obligation in respect of which no interest is stipulated to be payable in respect of its principal amount;

(b) a particular debt obligation in respect of which the proportion of the payments of principal to which the taxpayer is entitled is not equal to the proportion of the payments of interest to which he is entitled;

(c) a particular debt obligation, other than one described in paragraph (a) or (b), in respect of which it can be determined, at the time the taxpayer acquired the interest therein, that the maximum amount of interest payable thereon in a year ending after that time is less than the maximum amount of interest payable thereon in a subsequent year; and

(d) a particular debt obligation, other than one described in paragraph (a), (b) or (c), in respect of which the amount of interest to be paid in respect of any taxation year is, under the terms and conditions of the obligation, dependent on a contingency existing after the year,

and, for the purposes of this subsection, a debt obligation includes, for greater certainty, all of the issuer's obligations to pay principal and interest under that obligation.

**Related Provisions:** ITA 18.1(14) — Right to receive production deemed to be debt obligation.

**Notes:** Opening words of Reg. 7000(1) amended by P.C. 1996-1419, effective for debt obligations issued after October 16, 1991, to add the exclusion for indexed debt obligations.

**Advance Tax Rulings:** ATR-61: Interest accrual rules.

**(2)** For the purposes of subsection 12(9) of the Act, the amount determined in prescribed manner that is deemed to accrue to a taxpayer as interest on a prescribed debt obligation in each taxation year during which he holds an interest in the obligation is,

(a) in the case of a prescribed debt obligation described in paragraph (1)(a), the amount of interest that would be determined in respect thereof if interest thereon for that year were computed on a compound interest basis using the maximum of all rates each of which is a rate computed

(i) in respect of each possible circumstance under which an interest of the taxpayer in the obligation could mature or be surrendered or retracted, and

(ii) using assumptions concerning the interest rate and compounding period that will result in a present value, at the date of purchase of the interest, of all the maximum payments thereunder, equal to the cost thereof to the taxpayer;

(b) in the case of a prescribed debt obligation described in paragraph (1)(b), the aggregate of all amounts each of which is the amount of interest that would be determined in respect of his interest in a payment under the obligation if interest thereon for that year were computed on a compound interest basis using the specified cost of his interest therein and the specified interest rate in respect of his total interest in the obligation, and for the purposes of this paragraph,

(i) the "specified cost" of his interest in a payment under the obligation is its present value at the date of purchase computed using the specified interest rate, and

(ii) the "specified interest rate" is the maximum of all rates each of which is a rate computed

(A) in respect of each possible circumstance under which an interest of the taxpayer in the obligation could mature or be surrendered or retracted, and

(B) using assumptions concerning the interest rate and compounding period that will result in a present value, at the date of purchase of the interest, of all the maximum payments to the taxpayer in respect of his total interest in the obligation, equal to the cost of that interest to the taxpayer;

(c) in the case of a prescribed debt obligation described in paragraph (1)(c), other than an obliga-

2311

**Reg. S. 7000(2)(c)**  Income Tax Regulations

tion in respect of which paragraph (c.1) applies, the greater of

(i) the maximum amount of interest thereon in respect of the year, and

(ii) the maximum amount of interest that would be determined in respect thereof if interest thereon for that year were computed on a compound interest basis using the maximum of all rates each of which is a rate computed

(A) in respect of each possible circumstance under which an interest of the taxpayer in the obligation could mature or be surrendered or retracted, and

(B) using assumptions concerning the interest rate and compounding period that will result in a present value, at the date of issue of the obligation, of all the maximum payments thereunder, equal to its principal amount;

(c.1) in the case of a prescribed debt obligation described in paragraph (1)(c) for which

(i) the rate of interest stipulated to be payable in respect of each period throughout which the obligation is outstanding is fixed at the date of issue of the obligation, and

(ii) the stipulated rate of interest applicable at each time is not less than each stipulated rate of interest applicable before that time,

the amount of interest that would be determined in respect of the year if interest on the obligation for that year were computed on a compound interest basis using the maximum of all rates each of which is the compound interest rate that, for a particular assumption with respect to when the taxpayer's interest in the obligation will mature or be surrendered or retracted, results in a present value (at the date the taxpayer acquires the interest in the obligation) of all payments under the obligation after the acquisition by the taxpayer of the taxpayer's interest in the obligation equal to the principal amount of the obligation at the date of acquisition; and

(d) in the case of a prescribed debt obligation described in paragraph (1)(d), the maximum amount of interest thereon that could be payable thereunder in respect of that year.

**Related Provisions**: ITA 18.1(14) — Right to receive production deemed to be debt obligation.

**Notes**: Reg. 7000(2)(c.1) added, and (c) amended to refer to it, by P.C. 1996-570, effective for 1993 and later taxation years.

**Advance Tax Rulings**: ATR-61: Interest accrual rules.

(3) For the purpose of this section, any bonus or premium payable under a debt obligation is considered to be an amount of interest payable under the obligation.

**Notes**: Reg. 7000(3) amended by P.C. 1996-1419, effective for debt obligations issued after October 16, 1991, to apply for purposes of s. 7000 rather than for all of Part LII.

**Advance Tax Rulings**: ATR-61: Interest accrual rules.

(4) For the purposes of this section, where

(a) a taxpayer has an interest in a debt obligation (in this subsection referred to as the "first interest") under which there is a conversion privilege or an option to extend its term upon maturity, and

(b) at the time the obligation was issued (or, if later, at the time the conversion privilege or option was added or modified), circumstances could reasonably be foreseen under which the holder of the obligation would, by exercising the conversion privilege or option, acquire an interest in a debt obligation with a principal amount less than its fair market value at the time of acquisition,

the subsequent interest in any debt obligation acquired by the taxpayer by exercising the conversion privilege or option shall be considered to be a continuation of the first interest.

**Notes**: Reg. 7000(4)(b) added by P.C. 1996-570, effective for debt obligations acquired by reason of the exercise after August 11, 1993 of a conversion privilege or an option to extend the term of another debt obligation.

(5) For the purposes of making the computations referred to in paragraphs (2)(a), (b), (c) and (c.1), the compounding period shall not exceed one year and any interest rate used shall be constant from the date of acquisition or issue, as the case may be, until the time of maturity, surrender or retraction.

**Notes**: Reg. 7000(5) amended by P.C. 1996-570, effective for 1993 and later taxation years, to add reference to Reg. 7000(2)(c.1) and to change "date" to "time" (two places).

(6) For the purpose of the definition "investment contract" in subsection 12(11) of the Act, a registered retirement savings plan or a registered retirement income fund, other than a plan or fund to which a trust is a party, is a prescribed contract throughout a calendar year where an annuitant (as defined in subsection 146(1) or 146.3(1) of the Act, as the case may be) under the plan or fund is alive at any time in the year or was alive at any time in the preceding calendar year.

**Related Provisions**: ITA 142.3(1)(c) — No income accrual from specified debt obligation.

**Notes**: Reg. 7000(6) amended by P.C. 1996-568, effective for 1993 and later taxation years. The effect of the amendment is to extend the exemption from the accrual rules, where an RRSP or RRIF annuitant has died, to after the end of the first calendar year beginning after the death. (This is consistent with amendments to ITA 146(4) and 146.3(3.1) made by 1993 technical bill.) Previously read:

(6) For the purposes of paragraph 12(11)(a) [12(11)"investment contract"] of the Act, a prescribed contract is, at any time in a calendar year, a registered retirement savings plan, a registered home ownership savings plan or a registered retirement income fund, other than such a plan or fund to which a trust is a party, where an annuitant or beneficiary thereunder (within the meaning assigned by paragraph 146(1)(a) [146(1)"annuitant"], 146.2(1)(a) or 146.3(1)(a) [146.3(1)"annuitant"], as the case may be, of the Act) is alive at that time.

**Definitions [Reg. 7000]**: "amount" — ITA 248(1); "debt obligation" — Reg. 7000(1); "first interest" — Reg. 7000(4)(a); "indexed debt obligation", "prescribed", "principal amount" — ITA 248(1);

"registered retirement income fund" — ITA 146.3(1), 248(1); "registered retirement savings plan" — ITA 146(1), 248(1); "specified cost" — Reg. 7000(2)(b)(i); "specified interest rate" — Reg. 7000(2)(b)(ii); "taxation year" — ITA 249; "taxpayer" — ITA 248(1); "trust" — ITA 104(1), 248(1), (3).

**7001. Indexed debt obligations** — **(1)** For the purpose of subparagraph 16(6)(a)(i) of the Act, where at any time in a taxation year a taxpayer holds an interest in an indexed debt obligation, there is prescribed as interest receivable and received by the taxpayer in the year in respect of the obligation the total of

(a) the amount, if any, by which

(i) the total of all amounts each of which is the amount by which the amount payable in respect of the taxpayer's interest in an indexed payment under the obligation (other than a payment that is an excluded payment with respect to the taxpayer for the year) has, because of a change in the purchasing power of money, increased over an inflation adjustment period of the obligation that ends in the year

exceeds the total of

(ii) that portion of the total, if any, determined under subparagraph (i) that is required, otherwise than by subsection 16(6) of the Act, to be included in computing the taxpayer's income for the year or a preceding taxation year, and

(iii) the total of all amounts each of which is the amount by which the amount payable in respect of the taxpayer's interest in an indexed payment under the obligation (other than a payment that is an excluded payment with respect to the taxpayer for the year) has, by reason of a change in the purchasing power of money, decreased over an inflation adjustment period of the obligation that ends in the year, and

(b) where the non-indexed debt obligation associated with the indexed debt obligation is an obligation that is described in any of paragraphs 7000(1)(a) to (d), the amount of interest that would be determined under subsection 7000(2) to accrue to the taxpayer in respect of the non-indexed debt obligation in the particular period that

(i) begins at the beginning of the first inflation adjustment period of the indexed debt obligation in respect of the taxpayer that ends in the year, and

(ii) ends at the end of the last inflation adjustment period of the indexed debt obligation in respect of the taxpayer that ends in the year

if the particular period were a taxation year of the taxpayer and the taxpayer's interest in the indexed debt obligation were an interest in the non-indexed debt obligation.

**(2)** For the purposes of subparagraph 16(6)(a)(ii) of the Act, where at any time in a taxation year a taxpayer holds an interest in an indexed debt obligation, there is prescribed as interest payable and paid by the taxpayer in the year in respect of the obligation the amount, if any, by which

(a) the total of the amounts, if any, determined under subparagraphs (1)(a)(ii) and (iii) for the year in respect of the taxpayer's interest in the obligation

exceeds

(b) the amount, if any, determined under subparagraph (1)(a)(i) for the year in respect of the taxpayer's interest in the obligation.

**(3)** For the purposes of subparagraph 16(6)(b)(i) of the Act, where at any time in a taxation year an indexed debt obligation is an obligation of a taxpayer, there is prescribed as interest payable in respect of the year by the taxpayer in respect of the obligation the amount, if any, that would be determined under paragraph (1)(a) in respect of the taxpayer for the year if, at each time at which the obligation is an obligation of the taxpayer, the taxpayer were the holder of the obligation and not the debtor under the obligation.

**(4)** For the purposes of subparagraph 16(6)(b)(ii) of the Act, where at any time in a taxation year an indexed debt obligation is an obligation of a taxpayer, there is prescribed as interest receivable and received by the taxpayer in the year in respect of the obligation the amount, if any, that would be determined under subsection (2) in respect of the taxpayer for the year if, at each time at which the obligation is an obligation of the taxpayer, the taxpayer were the holder of the obligation and not the debtor under the obligation.

**(5)** For the purpose of determining the amount by which an indexed payment under an indexed debt obligation has increased or decreased over a period because of a change in the purchasing power of money, the amount of the indexed payment at any time shall be determined using the method for computing the amount of the payment at the time it is to be made, adjusted in a reasonable manner to take into account the earlier date of computation.

**(6)** For the purposes of this section, the non-indexed debt obligation associated with an indexed debt obligation is the debt obligation that would result if the indexed debt obligation were amended to eliminate all adjustments determined by reference to changes in the purchasing power of money.

**(7)** In this section,

**"excluded payment"** with respect to a taxpayer for a taxation year means an indexed payment under an indexed debt obligation where

(a) the non-indexed debt obligation associated with the indexed debt obligation provides for the payment, at least annually, of interest at a single fixed rate, and

(b) the indexed payment corresponds to one of the interest payments referred to in paragraph (a), but does not include payments under an indexed debt obligation where, at any time in the year, the taxpayer's proportionate interest in a payment to be made under the obligation after that time differs from the taxpayer's proportionate interest in any other payment to be made under the obligation after that time;

"**indexed payment**" means, in relation to an indexed debt obligation, an amount payable under the obligation that is determined by reference to the purchasing power of money;

"**inflation adjustment period**" of an indexed debt obligation means, in relation to a taxpayer,

(a) where the taxpayer acquires and disposes of the taxpayer's interest in the obligation in the same regular adjustment period of the obligation, the period that begins when the taxpayer acquires the interest in the obligation and ends when the taxpayer disposes of the interest, and

(b) in any other case, each of the following consecutive periods:

(i) the period that begins when the taxpayer acquires the taxpayer's interest in the obligation and ends at the end of the regular adjustment period of the obligation in which the taxpayer acquires the interest in the obligation,

(ii) each succeeding regular adjustment period of the obligation throughout which the taxpayer holds the interest in the obligation, and

(iii) where the taxpayer does not dispose of the interest in the obligation at the end of a regular adjustment period of the obligation, the period that begins immediately after the last period referred to in subparagraphs (i) and (ii) and that ends when the taxpayer disposes of the interest in the obligation;

"**regular adjustment period**" of an indexed debt obligation means

(a) where the terms or conditions of the obligation provide that, while the obligation is outstanding, indexed payments are to be made at regular intervals not exceeding 12 months in length, each of the following periods:

(i) the period that begins when the obligation is issued and ends when the first indexed payment is required to be made, and

(ii) each succeeding period beginning when an indexed payment is required to be made and ending when the next indexed payment is required to be made,

(b) where paragraph (a) does not apply and the obligation is outstanding for less than 12 months, the period that begins when the obligation is issued and ends when the obligation ceases to be outstanding, and

(c) in any other case, each of the following periods:

(i) the 12-month period that begins when the obligation is issued,

(ii) each succeeding 12-month period throughout which the obligation is outstanding, and

(iii) where the obligation ceases to be outstanding at a time other than the end of a 12-month period referred to in subparagraph (i) or (ii), the period that commences immediately after the last period referred to in those subparagraphs and that ends when the obligation ceases to be outstanding.

**Notes**: Reg. 7001 added by P.C. 1996-1419, effective for debt obligations issued after October 16, 1991.

**Definitions [Reg. 7001]**: "amount" — ITA 248(1); "associated" — ITA 256; "debt obligation" — Reg. 7001(6); "disposes" — ITA 248(1)"disposition"; "excluded payment" — Reg. 7001(7); "indexed debt obligation" — ITA 248(1); "indexed payment", "inflation adjustment period" — Reg. 7001(7); "month" — *Interpretation Act* 35(1); "prescribed" — ITA 248(1); "regular adjustment period" — Reg. 7001(7); "taxation year" — ITA 249; "taxpayer" — ITA 248(1).

# PART LXXI — PRESCRIBED FEDERAL CROWN CORPORATIONS

**7100.** For the purposes of section 27 and subsection 124(3) of the Act, the following are hereby prescribed to be federal Crown corporations:

Canada Deposit Insurance Corporation
Canada Development Investment Corporation
Canada Lands Company Limited
Canada Mortgage and Housing Corporation
Canada Post Corporation
Canadian Broadcasting Corporation
Cape Breton Development Corporation
Farm Credit Corporation
Freshwater Fish Marketing Corporation
Petro-Canada
Royal Canadian Mint
Teleglobe Canada
The St. Lawrence Seaway Authority
VIA Rail Canada Inc.

**Notes**: Reg. 7100 was intended to apply to ITA 89(1)"private corporation", according to the May 1991 Department of Finance Technical Notes to then ITA 89(1)(f). However, it has never been amended to apply for that purpose.

See Notes to ITA 27(2).

Canada Post Corporation added by P.C. 1994-930, effective March 27, 1994. Canada Lands Company Limited added by P.C. 1996-1927, effective November 1, 1996. Air Canada deleted by P.C. 1996-1927, effective November 1, 1995. National Railways (as defined in the pre-1966 *CN-CP Act*) deleted by P.C. 1996-1927, effective January 1, 1996.

**Definitions [Reg. 7100]**: "Canada" — ITA 255, *Interpretation Act* 35(1); "corporation" — ITA 248(1), *Interpretation Act* 35(1); "prescribed" — ITA 248(1).

**Interpretation Bulletins**: IT-347R2: Crown corporations.

## PART LXXII — CUMULATIVE DEDUCTION ACCOUNT

**7200. Prescribed addition and reduction** — [No longer relevant]

**Notes**: Reg. 7200 sets out the prescribed addition and reduction for a corporation's cumulative deduction account. The cumulative deduction account, which limited a corporation's lifetime retained earnings eligible for the small business deduction to a fixed dollar amount, was repealed in 1984 as part of simplification of the small business rules in s. 125 of the Act. Large corporations are now prevented from using the small business deduction by ITA 125(5.1).

## PART LXXIII — PRESCRIBED AMOUNTS AND AREAS

**7300. [Prescribed amounts]** — For the purposes of paragraph 12(1)(x) of the Act, "prescribed amount" means

(a) any amount paid to a corporation by the Native Economic Development Board created under Order in Council P.C. 1983-3394 of October 31, 1983 pursuant to the Native Economic Development Program or paid to a corporation under the Aboriginal Capital Corporation Program of the Canadian Aboriginal Economic Development Strategy, where all of the shares of the capital stock of the corporation are

(i) owned by aboriginal individuals,

(ii) held in trust for the exclusive benefit of aboriginal individuals,

(iii) owned by a corporation, all the shares of which are owned by aboriginal individuals, or

(iv) owned or held in a combination of ownership structures described in subparagraph (i), (ii) or (iii)

and the purpose of the corporation is to provide loans, loan guarantees, bridge financing, venture capital, lease financing, surety bonding or other similar financing services to aboriginal enterprises; or

(b) prescribed assistance within the meaning assigned by section 6702.

**Related Provisions**: ITA 80(1)"excluded obligation"(a)(i) — Debt forgiveness rules do not apply to prescribed amount.

**Notes**: Reg. 7300(a)(ii) to (iv) added by P.C. 1991-729, effective May 8, 1991.

**Definitions [Reg. 7300]**: "amount" — ITA 248(1); "corporation" — ITA 248(1), *Interpretation Act* 35(1); "individual", "prescribed", "share" — ITA 248(1); "taxation year" — ITA 249; "trust" — ITA 104(1), 248(1), (3).

**Forms**: T2124: Statement of business activities.

**7301. [No longer relevant]**

**Notes**: Reg. 7301 prescribes an amount for prepayment of the Child Tax Credit for the year 1987, under ITA 164.1. For 1988–92, the amount of the prepayment was determined under the Act. (The Child Tax Credit was discontinued as of January 1993. The Child Tax Benefit is now provided under ITA 122.6 to 122.64.)

**7302, 7303. [Revoked]**

**Notes**: Regs. 7302 and 7303 repealed by P.C. 1993-1688, effective for 1993 and later taxation years. They set out prescribed areas for ITA 110.7 as it applied before 1993.

**7303.1 (1) [Prescribed northern zone]** — An area is a prescribed northern zone for a taxation year for the purposes of section 110.7 of the Act where it is

(a) the Yukon Territory or the Northwest Territories;

(b) those parts of British Columbia, Alberta and Saskatchewan that lie north of 57°30'N latitude;

(c) that part of Manitoba that lies

(i) north of 56°20'N latitude, or

(ii) north of 52°30'N latitude and east of 95°25'W longitude;

(d) that part of Ontario that lies

(i) north of 52°30'N latitude, or

(ii) north of 51°05'N latitude and east of 89°10'W longitude;

(e) that part of Quebec that lies

(i) north of 51°05'N latitude, or

(ii) north of the Gulf of St. Lawrence and east of 63°00'W longitude; or

(f) Labrador, including Belle Isle.

**(2) [Prescribed intermediate zone]** — An area is a prescribed intermediate zone for a taxation year for the purposes of section 110.7 of the Act where it is the Queen Charlotte Islands, Anticosti Island, the Magdalen Islands or Sable Island, or where it is not part of a prescribed northern zone referred to in subsection (1) for the year and is

(a) that part of British Columbia that lies

(i) north of 55°35'N latitude, or

(ii) north of 55°00'N latitude and east of 122°00'W longitude;

(b) that part of Alberta that lies north of 55°00'N latitude;

(c) that part of Saskatchewan that lies

(i) north of 55°00'N latitude,

(ii) north of 54°15'N latitude and east of 107°00'W longitude, or

(iii) north of 53°20'N latitude and east of 103°00'W longitude;

(d) that part of Manitoba that lies

(i) north of 53°20'N latitude,

(ii) north of 52°10'N latitude and east of 97°40'W longitude, or

(iii) north of 51°30'N latitude and east of 96°00'W longitude;

(e) that part of Ontario that lies north of 50°35'N latitude; or

(f) that part of Quebec that lies

(i) north of 50°35'N latitude and west of 79°00'W longitude,

(ii) north of 49°00'N latitude, east of 79°00'W longitude and west of 74°00'W longitude,

(iii) north of 50°00'N latitude, east of 74°00'W longitude and west of 70°00'W longitude,

(iv) north of 50°45'N latitude, east of 70°00'W longitude and west of 65°30'W longitude, or

(v) north of the Gulf of St. Lawrence, east of 65°30'W longitude and west of 63°00'W longitude.

**Notes**: A complete list of places in the provinces which are in the prescribed northern zone and prescribed intermediate zone appears in the CCRA publication *Northern Residents Deductions — Places in Prescribed Zones* (February 2000), available on *TaxPartner* and on the CCRA's web site.

Reg. 7303.1 added by P.C. 1993-1688, effective for 1988 and later taxation years.

**Definitions [Reg. 7303.1]**: "prescribed" — ITA 248(1); "taxation year" — ITA 249.

**Remission Orders [Reg. 7303.1]**: *Prescribed Areas Forward Averaging Remission Order*, P.C. 1994-109 (remission for certain residents of prescribed areas who filed forward averaging elections for 1987).

**Interpretation Bulletins [Reg. 7303.1]**: IT-91R4: Employment at special work sites or remote work locations.

**7304.** (1) In this section,

**"member of the taxpayer's household"** includes the taxpayer;

**"designated city"** means St. John's, Halifax, Moncton, Quebec City, Montreal, Ottawa, Toronto, North Bay, Winnipeg, Saskatoon, Calgary, Edmonton and Vancouver.

(2) **[Trip cost]** — For the purposes of this section, the trip cost to a taxpayer in respect of a trip made by an individual who, at the time the trip was made, was a member of the taxpayer's household is the least of

(a) the aggregate of

(i) the value of travel assistance, if any, provided by the taxpayer's employer in respect of travelling expenses for the trip, and

(ii) the amount, if any, received by the taxpayer from his employer in respect of travelling expenses for the trip,

(b) the aggregate of

(i) the value of travel assistance, if any, provided by the taxpayer's employer in respect of travelling expenses for the trip, and

(ii) travelling expenses incurred by the taxpayer for the trip, and

(c) the lowest return airfare ordinarily available, at the time the trip was made, to the individual for flights between the place in which the individual resided immediately before the trip, or the airport nearest thereto, and the designated city that is nearest to that place.

(3) **[Period travel cost]** — For the purposes of subsection (4), the "period travel cost" to a taxpayer for a period in a taxation year, in respect of an individual who was a member of the taxpayer's household at any time during the period, is the total of the trip costs to the taxpayer in respect of all trips that were made by the individual at a time when the individual was a member of the taxpayer's household where the trips may reasonably be considered to relate to the period.

(4) For the purposes of clause 110.7(1)(a)(i)(A) of the Act, the prescribed amount in respect of a taxpayer for a period in a taxation year is the lesser of

(a) the total of

(i) the value of travel assistance, if any, provided in the period by the taxpayer's employer in respect of travelling expenses for trips, each of which was made by an individual who, at the time the trip was made, was a member of the taxpayer's household, where the trips may reasonably be considered to relate to the period, and

(ii) the amount, if any, received in the period by the taxpayer from the taxpayer's employer in respect of travelling expenses for trips, each of which was made by an individual who, at the time the trip was made, was a member of the taxpayer's household, where the trips may reasonably be considered to relate to the period; and

(b) the total of all the period travel costs to the taxpayer for the period in respect of all individuals who were members of the taxpayer's household at any time in the period.

**Notes**: Reg. 7304(2)(c), (3) and (4) amended by P.C. 1993-1688, effective for 1988 and later taxation years.

**Definitions [Reg. 7304]**: "amount" — ITA 248(1); "designated city" — Reg. 7304(1); "employer", "individual" — ITA 248(1); "member of the taxpayer's household" — Reg. 7304(1); "period travel cost" — Reg. 7304(3); "prescribed" — ITA 248(1); "taxation year" — ITA 249; "taxpayer" — ITA 248(1); "trip cost" — Reg. 7304(2).

**7305. [Prescribed drought regions]** — For the purposes of subsection 80.3(4) of the Act, prescribed drought regions in respect of

(a) the 1995 calendar year are

(i) in Manitoba, the Local Government Districts of Alonsa, Fisher, Grahamdale, Grand Rapids and Mountain (South), the areas designated under The Northern Affairs Act (Manitoba) as the communities of Camperville, Crane River, Duck Bay, Homebrook, Mallard, Meadow Portage, Rock Ridge, Spence Lake and Waterhen, the Rural Municipalities of Eriksdale, Lawrence, Mossey River, Ste. Rose and Siglunes, and Skownan,

Part LXXIII — Prescribed Amounts and Areas    Reg. S. 7305(c)(iv)

(ii) in Saskatchewan, the Rural Municipalities of Antelope Park, Battle River, Beaver River, Biggar, Blaine Lake, Britannia, Buffalo, Cut Knife, Douglas, Eagle Creek, Eldon, Eye Hill, Frenchman Butte, Glenside, Grandview, Grass Lake, Great Bend, Heart's Hill, Hillsdale, Kindersley, Loon Lake, Manitou Lake, Mariposa, Mayfield, Meadow Lake, Medstead, Meeting Lake, Meota, Mervin, Milton, Mountain View, North Battleford, Oakdale, Paynton, Parkdale, Perdue, Pleasant Valley, Prairie, Prairiedale, Progress, Redberry, Reford, Round Hill, Round Valley, Rosemont, Senlac, Spiritwood, Tramping Lake, Turtle River, Wilton and Winslow, and

(iii) in Alberta, the Counties of Beaver, Camrose, Flagstaff, Lamont, Minburn, Paintearth, Smoky Lake, St. Paul, Strathcona, Thorhild, Two Hills and Vermilion River, the Municipal Districts of Bonnyville, MacKenzie, Northern Lights, Provost and Wainwright, and Special Areas 2, 3 and 4;

(b) the 1997 calendar year are

(i) in Ontario, the Counties of Hastings and Renfrew,

(ii) Nova Scotia,

(iii) in Manitoba, the Rural Municipalities of Albert, Alonsa, Archie, Arthur, Birtle, Boulton, Brenda, Cameron, Clanwilliam, Dauphin, Edward, Ellice, Glenella, Grahamdale, Harrison, Lakeview, Langford, Lansdowne, Lawrence, McCreary, Miniota, Minto, Morton, Ochre River, Park (South), Pipestone, Rosedale, Rossburn, Russell, Ste. Rose, Shellmouth, Shoal Lake, Sifton, Siglunes, Silver Creek, Strathclair, Turtle Mountain, Wallace, Westbourne, Whitewater and Winchester,

(iv) in Saskatchewan, the Rural Municipalities of Abernethy, Antelope Park, Antler, Argyle, Baildon, Bengough, Benson, Big Stick, Biggar, Bratt's Lake, Brock, Brokenshell, Browning, Buchanan, Calder, Caledonia, Cambria, Cana, Chester, Chesterfield, Churchbridge, Clinworth, Coalfields, Cote, Cymri, Deer Forks, Elcapo, Elmsthorpe, Emerald, Enniskillen, Enterprise, Estevan, Excel, Eye Hill, Fertile Belt, Fillmore, Foam Lake, Francis, Fox Valley, Garry, Glenside, Golden West, Good Lake, Grandview, Grass Lake, Grayson, Griffin, Happyland, Happy Valley, Hart Butte, Hazelwood, Heart's Hill, Indian Head, Insinger, Ituna Bon Accord, Invermay, Kellross, Key West, Keys, Kingsley, Lajord, Lake Alma, Lake Johnston, Lake of The Rivers, Langenburg, Laurier, Lipton, Livingston, Lomond, Maple Creek, Mariposa, Martin, Maryfield, McLeod, Milton, Montmartre, Moose Creek, Moose Jaw, Moose Mountain, Moosomin, Mountain View, Mount Pleasant,

North Qu'Appelle, Norton, Oakdale, Orkney, Old Post, Poplar Valley, Prairie, Prairiedale, Progress, Reciprocity, Redburn, Reford, Rocanville, Rosemount, St. Philips, Saltcoats, Scott, Silverwood, Sliding Hills, Souris Valley, South Qu'Appelle, Spy Kill, Stanley, Stonehenge, Storthoaks, Surprise Valley, Tecumseh, Terrell, The Gap, Tramping Lake, Tullymet, Wallace, Walpole, Waverley, Wawken, Wellington, Weyburn, Willow Bunch, Willowdale, Winslow and Wolseley, and

(v) in Alberta, the County of Forty Mile, the Municipal Districts of Acadia Valley, Cypress, Pincher Creek, Provost and Willow Creek, and Special Areas 2, 3 and 4;

(c) the 1998 calendar year are

(i) in Ontario, the Counties of Bruce, Grey, Huron and Oxford, and the Districts of Nipissing, Parry Sound, Sudbury and Thunder Bay,

(ii) in Nova Scotia, the Counties of Annapolis, Colchester, Cumberland, Digby, Hants and Kings,

(iii) in Saskatchewan, the Rural Municipalities of Aberdeen, Antelope Park, Arlington, Auvergne, Battle River, Bayne, Beaver River, Biggar, Blaine Lake, Blucher, Bone Creek, Britannia, Buffalo, Canaan, Chaplin, Chesterfield, Clinworth, Corman Park, Coteau, Coulee, Cut Knife, Douglas, Dundurn, Eagle Creek, Eldon, Enfield, Excelsior, Eye Hill, Fertile Valley, Frenchman Butte, Frontier, Glen Bain, Glen McPherson, Glenside, Grandview, Grant, Grass Lake, Grassy Creek, Gravelbourg, Great Bend, Harris, Hart Butte, Heart's Hill, Hillsdale, Kindersley, King George, Lac Pelletier, Lacadena, Laird, Lake of The Rivers, Lawtonia, Lone Tree, Loon Lake, Loreburn, Mankota, Manitou Lake, Maple Bush, Mariposa, Marriott, Mayfield, Meadow Lake, Medstead, Meeting Lake, Meota, Mervin, Milden, Milton, Miry Creek, Monet, Montrose, Morse, Mountain View, Newcombe, North Battleford, Oakdale, Old Post, Parkdale, Paynton, Perdue, Pinto Creek, Pleasant Valley, Poplar Valley, Prairie, Prairiedale, Progress, Redberry, Reford, Reno, Riverside, Rosedale, Rosemount, Round Hill, Round Valley, Rosthern, Rudy, St. Andrews, Saskatchewan Landing, Senlac, Shamrock, Snipe Lake, Stonehenge, Swift Current, Tramping Lake, Turtle River, Val Marie, Vanscoy, Victory, Waverly, Webb, Whiska Creek, White Valley, Willow Bunch, Wilton, Winslow, Wise Creek, and Wood River, and

(iv) in Alberta, the Counties of Beaver, Camrose, Flagstaff, Grande Prairie, Lamont, Minburn, Paintearth, St. Paul, Smoky Lake, Stettler, Two Hills and Vermilion River, the Municipal Districts of Acadia, Big Lakes,

2317

**Reg.**
**S. 7305(c)(iv)**      Income Tax Regulations

Birch Hills, Bonnyville, Clear Hills, East Peace, Fairview, Greenview, Northern Lights, Peace, Provost, Saddle Hills, Smoky River, Spirit River, Starland, Wainwright and Yellowhead, and Special Areas 2, 3 and 4; and

(d) the 1999 calendar year are

(i) in Nova Scotia, the Counties of Annapolis, Colchester, Cumberland, Digby, Hants, Kings and Yarmouth,

(ii) in British Columbia, the Peace River Region,

(iii) in Saskatchewan, the Rural Municipalities of Beaver River and Loon Lake, and

(iv) in Alberta, the Counties of Athabaska, Barrhead, Birch Hills, Grande Prairie, Lac Ste. Anne, Lakeland, Lamont, Saddle Hills, Smoky Lake, St. Paul, Thorhild, Two Hills, Westlock and Woodlands, and the Municipal Districts of Big Lakes, Bonnyville, Clear Hills, East Peace, Fairview, Greenview, Lesser Slave Lake, MacKenzie, Northern Lights, Peace, Smoky River and Spirit River.

(e) [Repealed]

### Proposed Amendment — Prescribed Drought Regions in Saskatchewan

**Agriculture and Agri-food Canada news release, September 20, 2000**: *Tax Deferral added to Government of Canada Response to Help Saskatchewan Farmers*

Agriculture and Agri-Food Minister Lyle Vanclief today announced farmers in 29 Saskatchewan rural municipalities who sell all or part of their breeding livestock due to severe drought conditions will be eligible for tax deferral provisions.

The eligible municipalities were determined based on recommendations by Mr. Vanclief to Finance Minister Paul Martin. A list of areas initially designated eligible for tax deferral throughout the province is attached.

"Weather conditions are causing real hardship for some Saskatchewan farmers," said Mr. Vanclief. "For livestock breeders, too much rain, too little rain, hail and wind have reduced the forage crops they need to feed their livestock. Tax deferral will give farmers who choose to sell cattle tax savings they can use to help re-stock their herds in the spring."

Mr. Vanclief said the tax deferral builds on a number of safety net programs already in place to help producers through this financial crunch, including interim financial options through Net Income Stabilization Account (NISA) and the income disaster program.

"The safety net system of crop insurance for production losses, combined with NISA and the new Canadian Farm Income Program (CFIP) in Saskatchewan, will help offset the effects left by drought, reduced yields, and a weak grains and oilseeds forecast for the 2000 crop year," he said.

Taken together, producers' NISA accounts and crop insurance coverage will offer an estimated $2.1 billion in protection to Saskatchewan farmers this year. As well, farmers whose margins dropped below 70 per cent of their previous years' margin, are encouraged to submit their 1999 AIDA application. At the request of producers, the deadline has been extended to September 29. To date, AIDA has distributed over $13.5 million to Saskatchewan farmers.

Mr. Vanclief described the Canadian farm safety net system as "a true reflection" of strong federal-provincial and industry partnerships that will help to ensure the future of Canadian agriculture and agri-food. The Government of Canada is supporting Saskatchewan's system of programs with an annual investment of over $195 million over the next three years under the newly announced federal-provincial safety net framework agreement.

The tax deferral designation makes livestock producers eligible for deferral of livestock sale proceeds when filing their 2000 income tax returns. Farmers may contact their local Canada Customs and Revenue Agency office for further information on eligibility requirements and deferral on income details. Additional areas that meet eligibility criteria will be added once final area assessments are available later this fall.

For more information, media may contact: Sylvie Millette LeDuc, Press Secretary, Minister Vanclief's Office, Ottawa (613) 759-1761.

Pamela Kujawa, Agriculture and Agri-Food Canada, Prairie Farm Rehabilitation Administration, Regina, SK, (306) 780-6653.

Tax Deferral 2000 Initial Area Designations — Saskatchewan

RM 51 Reno
RM 111 Maple Creek
RM 141 Big Stick
RM 142 Enterprise
RM 171 Fox Valley
RM 231 Happyland
RM 232 Deer Forks
RM 261 Chesterfield
RM 288 Pleasant Valley
RM 290 Kindersley
RM 292 Milton
RM 318 Mountain View
RM 319 Winslow
RM 320 Oakdale
RM 321 Prairiedale
RM 322 Antelope Park
RM 347 Biggar
RM 349 Grandview
RM 350 Mariposa
RM 351 Progress
RM 352 Heart's Hill
RM 378 Rosemount
RM 379 Reford
RM 380 Tramping Lake
RM 381 Grass Lake
RM 382 Eye Hill
RM 409 Buffalo
RM 410 Round Valley
RM 411 Senlac

### Proposed Amendment — Prescribed Drought Regions in Alberta

**Agriculture and Agri-food Canada news release, September 20, 2000**: *Tax Deferral Added to Government of Canada Response to Help Alberta Farmers*

Agriculture and Agri-Food Minister Lyle Vanclief announced today stock growers in 25 Alberta municipalities, municipal districts and counties will be eligible for tax deferral provisions.

Farmers and ranchers who sell all or part of their breeding livestock due to severe drought conditions will be eligible for a one-year tax deferral on those sales.

The eligible municipalities were determined based on recommendations by Mr. Vanclief to Finance Minister Paul Martin. A list of areas initially designated eligible for tax deferral throughout the province is attached.

"The drought has damaged much of southern Alberta's forage and pasture land this year," said Mr. Vanclief. "Tax deferral offers farmers who choose to sell cattle a real tax savings on the income received from the sale of livestock and will allow farmers to use these saved monies when restocking their herds in the spring."

Mr. Vanclief said the tax deferral builds on a number of safety net programs already in place to help producers through this financial crunch.

"The safety net system of crop insurance for production losses and the new Canadian Farm Income Program's (CFIP) contributions to Alberta's Farm Income Disaster Program (FIDP) for income losses will help to offset a grim situation created by drought, reduced yields, and a weak grains and oilseeds forecast," Mr. Vanclief said.

"I have heard from farmers in the southern sections of Alberta who say they are looking to the federal government for help to get them through the current situation," said Senator Joyce Fairbairn. "Today the Government of Canada continues its ongoing response to them with a tax deferral program that will offer real tax savings and allow farmers to keep more money in their pockets."

Taken together, producers' Net Income Stabilization Account (NISA) and crop insurance coverage will offer an estimated $1.1 billion in protection to Alberta farmers this year. Government support for NISA in Alberta is funded 100 per cent by the federal government. As well, farmers whose margins dropped below 70 per cent of their previous years' margin in 1999 are encouraged to apply to Alberta's FIDP program funded through the federal-provincial AIDA program. To date, FIDP has distributed more than $29.7 million to Alberta farmers for the 1999 tax year.

"I am working with my provincial counterpart to ensure safety nets continue to respond to farm income challenges like the current drought," Mr. Vanclief said.

Mr. Vanclief described the Canadian farm safety net system as a true reflection of strong federal-provincial and industry partnerships that will ensure the future of Canadian agriculture and agri-food. The Government of Canada will support this system of programs through an annual investment of over $169 million for the next three years under the new framework agreement.

This tax deferral designation makes livestock producers eligible for deferral of livestock sale proceeds when filing their 2000 income tax returns. Farmers may contact their local Canada Customs and Revenue Agency office for further information on eligibility requirements and deferral on income details. Additional areas that meet eligibility criteria will be added once final area assessments are available later this fall.

For more information, media may contact: Sylvie Millette LeDuc, Press Secretary, Minister Vanclief's Office, Ottawa (613) 759-1761.

Mark Wonneck, Agriculture and Agri-Food Canada, Calgary, AB, (403) 292-4388.

Tax Deferral 2000 Initial Area Designations — Alberta

County of Forty Mile No. 8
County of Lethbridge No. 26
County of Newell No. 4
County of Paintearth No. 18
County of Stettler No. 6
County of Warner No. 5
Cypress County
Flagstaff County
I.D. No. 4 (Waterton)
Kananaskis Improvement District
M.D. of Acadia No. 34
M.D. of Cardston No. 6
M.D. of Foothills No. 31
M.D. of Pincher Creek No. 9
M.D. of Provost No. 52
M.D. of Ranchland No. 66
M.D. of Taber
M.D. of Willow Creek No. 26
Municipality of Crowsnest Pass
Special Area 2
Special Area 3
Special Area 4
Starland County
Vulcan County
Wheatland County

**Related Provisions**: Reg. 7305.01 — Surrounded areas.

**Notes**: Reg. 7305(d) added by P.C. 2000-1769 to list the prescribed regions for 1999.

Former Reg. 7305(a)–(e) replaced by (a)–(c) by P.C. 1999-1057, to add the prescribed regions for 1995, 1997 and 1998. No regions were prescribed for 1993, 1994 or 1996. Former Reg. 7305(a)–(e) (of which (d) was added by P.C. 1992-2542, and (e) by P.C. 1993-1210) listed the regions for 1988-92.

A decision on the regions for each year is usually announced in September of that year. News releases updating this list in advance of the promulgation of regulations are issued by the Prairie Farm Rehabilitation Administration, Agriculture and Agri-Food Canada, Regina, Saskatchewan. Contact: Jill Vaisey, (306) 780-5716. The most recent news releases were on September 20, 2000, as reproduced above.

**Definitions [Reg. 7305]**: "prescribed" — ITA 248(1).

## 7305.01 [Prescribed drought regions — surrounded areas]

— For the purposes of subsection 80.3(4) of the Act, the prescribed drought regions in respect of a year include any particular area that is surrounded by a region or regions prescribed under section 7305 in respect of the year.

**Notes**: Reg. 7305.01 added by P.C. 2000-1769, effective 1988.

## 7305.1 [Automobile operating expenses]

— For the purpose of subparagraph (v) of the description of A in paragraph 6(1)(k) of the Act, the amount prescribed for a taxation year is

(a) if a taxpayer is employed in a taxation year by a particular person principally in selling or leasing automobiles and an automobile is made available in the year to the taxpayer or a person related to the taxpayer by the particular person or a person related to the particular person, 12 cents; and

(b) in any other case, 15 cents.

### Proposed Amendment — Reg. 7305.1
**Department of Finance news release, December 20, 2000**: *Prescribed Rates for the Automobile Operating Expense Benefit*

These are the rates used to determine the value of the benefit received by the employee of having the personal portion of automobile operating expenses paid by the employer when a vehicle is provided to the employee. Employees must include this benefit as income in their tax returns. For 2001, the general prescribed rate will increase from 15¢ to 16¢ per kilometre of personal driving while, in the case of taxpayers employed principally in selling or leasing automobiles, the prescribed rate will increase from 12¢ to 13¢ per kilometre of personal driving.

These rates reflect only operating expenses and do not include depreciation and financing costs. The additional benefit of having an employer-owned vehicle available for personal use (i.e. the automobile standby charge) is calculated separately and is also included in the employee's income.

**Notes**: The Department of Finance announces changes to the "automobile numbers" in Reg. 7305.1, 7306 and 7307 each December for the following year. The operating cost employee benefit per personal-use kilometre under Reg. 7305.1 is:

| Taxation year | Regular employee | Auto Salesperson |
| --- | --- | --- |
| 1993 | 12¢ | 12¢ |
| 1994 | 12¢ | 9¢ |
| 1995 | 12¢ | 9¢ |
| 1996 | 13¢ | 10¢ |
| 1997-99 | 14¢ | 11¢ |
| 2000 | 15¢ | 12¢ |
| 2001 | 16¢ | 13¢ |

Reg. 7305.1 amended by P.C. 2000-1330, this version effective for taxation years ending after 1999. For 1997–99 taxation years (per P.C. 1999-1056), read "11 cents" and "14 cents" in place of 12¢ and 15¢. For the 1996 year, read "10" and "13". For earlier years, the wording was different (there were two subsections) but the substance was identical, using the cents figures in the table above. Reg. 7305.1 originally added by P.C. 1995-775, effective 1993.

**Definitions [Reg. 7305.1]**: "amount", "automobile", "employed", "person", "prescribed" — ITA 248(1); "related" — ITA 251(2)–(6); "taxation year" — ITA 249; "taxpayer" — ITA 248(1).

**I.T. Technical News**: No. 10 (1997 deduction limits and benefit rates for automobiles); No. 12 (1998 deduction limits and benefit rates for automobiles).

**7306. [Tax-free car allowances]** — For the purposes of paragraph 18(1)(r) of the Act, the amount in respect of the use of one or more automobiles in a taxation year by an individual for kilometres driven in the year for the purpose of earning income of the individual is the total of

(a) the product of 31 cents multiplied by the number of those kilometres;

(b) the product of 6 cents multiplied by the lesser of 5,000 and the number of those kilometres; and

(c) the product of 4 cents multiplied by the number of those kilometres driven in the Yukon Territory, the Northwest Territories or Nunavut.

### Proposed Amendment — Reg. 7306
**Department of Finance news release, December 20, 2000**: *Tax-Exempt Kilometre Limit*

This limit restricts the amount an employer can deduct for tax-free allowances paid to employees who use their personal vehicles for business purposes. It reflects the key cost components of owning and operating an automobile, such as depreciation, financing and operating expenses (i.e. gas, maintenance, insurance and licence fees).

For 2001, the limit is increased by 4¢ per kilometre to 41¢ per kilometre for the first 5,000 kilometres and 35¢ per kilometre for each kilometre thereafter. The limit is 4¢ per kilometre higher in the Yukon Territory, Northwest Territories and Nunavut to reflect the higher cost of maintaining and operating a vehicle in these territories.

The limit provides a system that is simple to administer for both businesses and employees by allowing businesses to deduct reasonable reimbursement costs without requiring employees to include the amounts in income or justify their actual automobile operating expenses. These rates do not limit the amount that employers can pay to employees who use their personal vehicles for business purposes. Employers may be able to deduct higher rates if they are judged reasonable and included in the employee's income. In such circumstances, employees fulfilling certain conditions — such as those who must use a vehicle for their work (e.g. salespersons) — could then claim the actual automobile expenses they incur.

**Notes**: The Department of Finance announces changes to the "automobile numbers" in Reg. 7305.1, 7306 and 7307 each December for the following year. The per-kilometre tax-free allowance limits under Reg. 7306 are:

| | All Provinces | | Yukon/NWT/Nunavut | |
| --- | --- | --- | --- | --- |
| When driven | First 5,000 km | Over 5,000 km | First 5,000 km | Over 5,000 km |
| Jan 88-Aug 89 | 27¢ | 21¢ | 31¢ | 25¢ |
| Sept 89-Dec 95 | 31¢ | 25¢ | 35¢ | 29¢ |
| 1996 | 33¢ | 27¢ | 37¢ | 31¢ |
| 1997-99 | 35¢ | 29¢ | 39¢ | 33¢ |
| 2000 | 37¢ | 31¢ | 41¢ | 35¢ |
| 2001 | 41¢ | 35¢ | 45¢ | 39¢ |

For further information contact Bob Morrison at the Department of Finance, (613) 995-9920.

Reg. 7306 amended by P.C. 2000-1330, effective for kilometres driven after 1999. For km driven in 1997–1999 (with the reference to Nunavut added for km driven after March 1999), per P.C. 1999-1056, read "29 cents" in place of 31 cents in para. (a). For earlier years, the amounts in para. (a) were less, to correspond with the table above. For km driven before 1995 the wording was different but the substance was identical, except for the rate changes. For km driven from September 1989 through 1994, read:

> 7306. For the purposes of paragraph 18(1)(r) of the Act, the amount in respect of the use of one or more automobiles in a taxation year by an individual is the aggregate of
>
> (a) in respect of kilometres driven after 1987 for the purpose of earning income of the individual, the aggregate of
>
> (i) 27 cents multiplied by the number of such kilometres, up to and including 5,000, driven in the year,
>
> (ii) 21 cents multiplied by the number of such kilometres in excess of 5,000 driven in the year, and

(iii) 4 cents multiplied by the number of such kilometres driven in the year in the Yukon Territory or the Northwest Territories, and

(b) in respect of kilometres driven after August 1989 for the purpose of earning income of the individual, 4 cents multiplied by the number of such kilometres driven in the year.

For the per-km rates allowed for certain travel expense purposes, see Notes to ITA 62(1).

**Definitions [Reg. 7306]**: "amount", "automobile", "individual" — ITA 248(1); "taxation year" — ITA 249.

**I.T. Technical News**: No. 10 (1997 deduction limits and benefit rates for automobiles); No. 12 (1998 deduction limits and benefit rates for automobiles).

### 7307. (1) [Automobiles — CCA cost limit] —

For the purposes of subsection 13(2), paragraph 13(7)(g), subparagraph 13(7)(h)(iii), subsections 20(4) and (16.1), the description of B in paragraph 67.3(d) and subparagraph 85(1)(e.4)(i) of the Act, the amount prescribed is

(a) with respect to an automobile acquired, or leased under a lease entered into, after August 1989 and before 1991, $24,000; and

(b) with respect to an automobile acquired, or leased under a lease entered into, after 1990, the amount determined by the formula

$$A + B$$

where

A is, with respect to an automobile acquired, or leased under a lease entered into,

(i) before 1997, $24,000,

(ii) in 1997, $25,000,

(iii) in 1998 or 1999, $26,000, or

(iv) after 1999, $27,000, and

B is the sum that would have been payable in respect of federal and provincial sales taxes on the acquisition of the automobile if it had been acquired, at a cost equal to A before the application of the federal and provincial sales taxes, if the automobile

(i) was acquired, at the time of the acquisition, or

(ii) was leased, at the time the lease was entered into.

#### Proposed Amendment — Reg. 7307(1)
**Department of Finance news release, December 20, 2000**: *Capital Cost Ceiling*

This limit restricts the cost of a vehicle on which capital cost allowance (CCA) may be claimed. It reflects the cost of acquiring an automobile that is generally acceptable for business purposes. For 2001, the ceiling on the capital cost of passenger vehicles for CCA purposes will increase by $3,000 to $30,000, plus applicable federal and provincial sales taxes. This increase will simplify the automobile provisions by reducing the number of taxpayers affected by the provisions while still ensuring that deductions related to luxury vehicles are restricted.

**Related Provisions**: Reg. 1100(2.5) — 50% CCA in year of disposition; Reg. Sch. II:Cl. 10.1.

**Notes**: The Department of Finance announces changes to the "automobile numbers" in Reg. 7305.1, 7306 and 7307 each December for the following year. The capital cost limit for an automobile is:

| Acquisition date | Limit on cost |
| --- | --- |
| June 18/87–Aug 31/89 | $20,000 |
| Sept 1/89–Dec 31/90 | $24,000 |
| 1991–1996 | $24,000 plus GST & PST |
| 1997 | $25,000 plus GST/HST & PST |
| 1998–1999 | $26,000 plus GST/HST & PST |
| 2000 | $27,000 plus GST/HST & PST |
| 2001 | $30,000 plus GST/HST & PST |

For further information contact Bob Morrison at the Department of Finance, (613) 995-9920.

Reg. 7307(1)(b)A(iii) amended and (iv) added by P.C. 2000-1330, effective 2000. (Per P.C. 1999-1056, subpara. (iii) previously read "after 1997, $26,000".) The previous wording before P.C. 1999-1056 was different but the substance was identical, except for the changes in the limits. For 1991–96, read:

(b) with respect to an automobile acquired, or leased under a lease entered into, after 1990, the amount equal to the aggregate of

(i) $24,000,

(ii) where the automobile was acquired, the federal and provincial sales taxes that would have been payable on the acquisition of the automobile if it had been acquired at a cost, before those taxes, of $24,000, and

(iii) where the automobile was leased, the federal and provincial sales taxes that would have been payable on the acquisition of the automobile if it had been acquired at the time the lease was entered into at a cost, before those taxes, of $24,000.

Reference to ITA 85(1)(e.4)(i) in opening words of Reg. 7307(1) added by P.C. 1994-103, effective for automobiles acquired or leased under leases entered into after August 31, 1989 (i.e., retroactive to the original effective date of Reg. 7307(1)).

Reference to ITA 20(4) added to opening words of Reg. 7307(1) by P.C. 1995-775, also retroactive to the original effective date.

**Interpretation Bulletins**: IT-478R2: CCA — recapture and terminal loss; IT-522R: Vehicle, travel and sales expenses of employees.

**I.T. Technical News**: No. 10 (1997 deduction limits and benefit rates for automobiles); No. 12 (1998 deduction limits and benefit rates for automobiles).

### (2) [Automobiles — interest expense limit] — [Repealed]

#### Proposed Amendment — Reg. 7307(2)
**Department of Finance news release, December 20, 2000**: *Interest Expense Limit*

This limit restricts the deductibility of interest expenses on funds borrowed to finance the purchase of a vehicle. It reflects the reasonable cost of financing a vehicle that is generally acceptable for business purposes. For 2001, this limit will increase by $50 per month to $300 per month for loans related to vehicles acquired after 2000.

**Notes**: See Notes to Reg. 7307(1). The interest expense deduction limit for money borrowed to purchase an automobile is:

| Acquisition date | Limit on monthly interest |
| --- | --- |
| June 18/87–Aug 31/89 | $250 |
| Sept 1/89–Dec 31/96 | $300 |

**Reg.
S. 7307(2)**                                    Income Tax Regulations

Jan 1/97–Dec 31/00          $250

Reg. 7307(2) repealed by P.C. 1999-1056, effective for automobiles acquired after 1996. The effect was to reduce the rate from $300 to the statutory $250 that appears in ITA 67.2:A. Note that the reduction for 1997–1999 does not apply to interest paid in 1997–1999 on a loan taken to purchase an automobile in 1996.

**I.T. Technical News**: No. 10 (1997 deduction limits and benefit rates for automobiles); No. 12 (1998 deduction limits and benefit rates for automobiles).

**(3) [Automobiles — leasing limit]** — For the purpose of the description of A in paragraph 67.3(c) of the Act, the amount prescribed in respect of a taxation year of a lessee is, with respect to an automobile leased under a lease entered into

(a) after August 1989 and before 1991, $650; and

(b) after 1990, the amount determined by the formula

$$A + B$$

where

A is

   (i) for leases entered into after 1990 but before 1997, $650;

   (ii) for leases entered into in 1997, $550;

   (iii) for leases entered into in 1998 or 1999, $650; and

   (iv) for leases entered into after 1999, $700; and

B is the sum of the federal and provincial sales taxes that would have been payable on a monthly payment under the lease in the taxation year of the lessee if, before those taxes, the lease had required monthly payments equal to A.

---

**Proposed Amendment — Reg. 7307(3)**

**Department of Finance news release, December 20, 2000**: *Leasing Limit*

The deductibility of automobile leasing costs is restricted to the lesser of two amounts:

- actual lease payments (adjusted downward if the value of the automobile exceeds the capital cost ceiling); and
- a prescribed monthly rate.

The first restriction automatically limits the deductibility of the lease payment where the cost of the vehicle, if purchased, would have exceeded the capital cost ceiling. The second amount — the prescribed monthly rate — further limits the deduction of lease payments to ensure that the level of deductions for leased vehicles is comparable to that for purchased vehicles.

For 2001, the prescribed rate will increase by $100 per month to $800 per month plus applicable federal and provincial sales taxes. This increase will ensure that payments under shorter-term commercial vehicle leases are not unduly restricted, while still limiting the deductibility of lease costs to reasonable levels.

---

**Notes**: See Notes to Reg. 7307(1). The deductible lease cost for an automobile is limited to:

| Lease date | Limit on monthly lease expense |
|---|---|
| June 18/87–Aug 31/89 | $600 |
| Sept 1/89–Dec 31/90 | $650 |
| Jan 1/91–Dec 31/96 | $650 + GST + PST |
| Jan 1/97–Dec 31/97 | $550 + GST/HST + PST |
| Jan 1/98–Dec 31/99 | $650 + GST/HST + PST |
| Jan 1/00–Dec 31/00 | $700 + GST/HST + PST |
| Jan 1/01–Dec 31/01 | $800 + GST/HST + PST |

(Note the alternative limit in 67.3(d), however.)

Reg. 7307(3)(b) amended by P.C. 2000-1330, effective 2000. Previously amended by P.C. 1999-1056, effective 1997. The previous wording was different but the substance was identical, except for the changes in the limits. For September 1989 through 1996, read:

   (b) after 1990, the amount equal to the aggregate of

      (i) $650, and

      (ii) the greatest amount of federal and provincial sales taxes that would have been payable on a monthly payment under the lease in the taxation year of the lessee, if the lease has required monthly payments, before those taxes, of $650.

**I.T. Technical News**: No. 10 (1997 deduction limits and benefit rates for automobiles); No. 12 (1998 deduction limits and benefit rates for automobiles).

**(4)** For the purpose of the description of C in paragraph 67.3(d) of the Act, the amount prescribed in respect of an automobile leased under a lease entered into after August 1989 is the amount equal to 100/85 of the amount determined in accordance with subsection (1) in respect of the automobile.

**Notes**: Under this rule, the figure of $23,529 is $28,235 effective September 1, 1989, and $30,588 (100/85 of $26,000) as of 1998.

**Definitions [Reg. 7307]**: "amount", "automobile", "prescribed" — ITA 248(1); "taxation year" — ITA 249.

**Interpretation Bulletins**: IT-521R: Motor vehicle expenses claimed by self-employed individuals.

**7308. (1)** In this section, "carrier" has the meaning assigned by subsection 146.3(1) of the Act.

**(2)** For the purposes of this section, a retirement income fund is a qualifying retirement income fund at a particular time if

(a) the fund was entered into before 1993 and the carrier has not accepted any property as consideration under the fund after 1992 and at or before the particular time, or

(b) the carrier has not accepted any property as consideration under the fund after 1992 and at or before the particular time, other than property transferred from a retirement income fund that, immediately before the time of the transfer, was a qualifying retirement income fund.

**(3)** For the purposes of the definition "minimum amount" in subsection 146.3(1) of the Act, the prescribed factor in respect of an individual for a year in connection with a retirement income fund that was a qualifying retirement income fund at the beginning of the year is the factor, determined pursuant to the following table, that corresponds to the age in whole years (in the table referred to as "X") attained by the individual at the beginning of that year or that would have been so attained by the individual if the individual had been alive at the beginning of that year.

| X | Factor |
|---|---|
| under 79 | 1/(90 - X) |
| 79 | .0853 |
| 80 | .0875 |
| 81 | .0899 |
| 82 | .0927 |
| 83 | .0958 |
| 84 | .0993 |
| 85 | .1033 |
| 86 | .1079 |
| 87 | .1133 |
| 88 | .1196 |
| 89 | .1271 |
| 90 | .1362 |
| 91 | .1473 |
| 92 | .1612 |
| 93 | .1792 |
| 94 or older | .2000 |

(4) For the purposes of the definition "minimum amount" in subsection 146.3(1) of the Act, the prescribed factor in respect of an individual for a year in connection with a retirement income fund other than a fund that was a qualifying retirement income fund at the beginning of the year is the factor, determined pursuant to the following table, that corresponds to the age in whole years (in the table referred to as "Y") attained by the individual at the beginning of that year or that would have been so attained by the individual if the individual had been alive at the beginning of that year.

| Y | Factor |
|---|---|
| under 71 | 1/(90 - Y) |
| 71 | .0738 |
| 72 | .0748 |
| 73 | .0759 |
| 74 | .0771 |
| 75 | .0785 |
| 76 | .0799 |
| 77 | .0815 |
| 78 | .0833 |
| 79 | .0853 |
| 80 | .0875 |
| 81 | .0899 |
| 82 | .0927 |
| 83 | .0958 |
| 84 | .0993 |
| 85 | .1033 |
| 86 | .1079 |
| 87 | .1133 |
| 88 | .1196 |
| 89 | .1271 |
| 90 | .1362 |
| 91 | .1473 |
| 92 | .1612 |
| 93 | .1792 |
| 94 or older | .2000 |

**Notes [Reg. 7308]**: Reg. 7308(3) and (4) amended by P.C. 2000-184, effective for 1998 and later taxation years, to change "prescribed amount" to "prescribed factor" (since "amount" is defined in ITA 248(1) to refer to money or money's worth).

Reg. 7308 added by P.C. 1994-102, effective for 1992 and later taxation years.

Department of Finance officials have advised that the 1/(90 - N) formula for ages below 71 will remain as it is, despite the 1996 budget change that forces an RRSP to be closed out (or converted to a RRIF) by the end of the year that the taxpayer turns 69.

**Definitions [Reg. 7308]**: "amount" — ITA 248(1); "carrier" — Reg. ITA 146.3(1), Reg. 7308(1); "individual", "prescribed", "property" — ITA 248(1); "qualifying retirement income fund" — Reg. 7308(2); "retirement income fund" — ITA 146.3(1), 248(1).

## PART LXXIV — PRESCRIBED TAX TREATY PROVISIONS AND ELECTION

**7400. (1), (2)** [No longer relevant.]

**Notes**: Reg. 7400 applied for purposes of the former version of ITA 115.1, which was repealed in 1993 retroactive to 1985 and replaced with the existing, more general, version.

## PART LXXV — PRESCRIBED FILM PRODUCTIONS AND REVENUE GUARANTEES

**7500.** For the purposes of subparagraph 96(2.2)(d)(ii) of the Act and this Part,

**"prescribed film production"** means a certified production defined in subsection 1104(2);

**"prescribed revenue guarantee"** means a revenue guarantee in respect of a prescribed film production, which guarantee is certified by the Minister of Communications to be a guarantee under which the person who agrees to provide the revenue is a licensed broadcaster or *bona fide* film or tape distributor.

**Notes**: The *Department of Canadian Heritage Act* (S.C. 1995, c. 11), in force July 12, 1996, provides:

46. Other references — Every reference made to the Minister of Communications, the Minister of Multiculturalism and Citizenship and the Secretary of State of Canada in relation to any matter to which the powers, duties and functions of the Minister of Canadian Heritage extend by virtue of this Act, in any other Act of Parliament or in any order, regulation or other instrument made under any Act of Parliament shall, un-

less the context otherwise requires, be read as a reference to the Minister of Canadian Heritage.

**Definitions [Reg. 7500]**: "Minister", "person" — ITA 248(1); "prescribed film production" — Reg. 7500.

## PART LXXVI — CARVED-OUT PROPERTY EXCLUSION

**7600.** For the purposes of paragraph (g) of the definition "carved-out property" in subsection 209(1) of the Act, a prescribed property at any time is

(a) any right, licence or privilege to prospect, explore, drill or mine for minerals in a mineral resource (other than a bituminous sands deposit, oil sands deposit or oil shale deposit) in Canada;

(b) any rental or royalty computed by reference to the amount or value of production of minerals from a mineral resource (other than a bituminous sands deposit, oil sands deposit or oil shale deposit) in Canada;

(c) any real property in Canada the principal value of which depends on its mineral resource content (other than a bituminous sands deposit, oil sands deposit or oil shale deposit);

(d) any right to or interest in any property described in any of paragraphs (a) to (c); or

(e) a property acquired before that time by a taxpayer in the circumstances described in paragraph (c) of the definition "carved-out property" in subsection 209(1) of the Act, except where it is reasonable to consider that one of the main reasons for the acquisition of the property, or any series of transactions or events in which the property was acquired, by the taxpayer was to reduce or postpone tax that would, but for this paragraph, be payable by another taxpayer under Part XII.1 of the Act.

**Definitions [Reg. 7600]**: "amount", "bituminous sands" — ITA 248(1); "Canada" — ITA 255, *Interpretation Act* 35(1); "mineral", "mineral resource", "prescribed", "property", "taxpayer" — ITA 248(1).

## PART LXXVII — PRESCRIBED PRIZES

**7700.** For the purposes of subparagraph 56(1)(n)(i) of the Act, a prescribed prize is any prize that is recognized by the general public and that is awarded for meritorious achievement in the arts, the sciences or service to the public but does not include any amount that can reasonably be regarded as having been received as compensation for services rendered or to be rendered.

**Notes**: The concept of prescribed prizes was introduced by the 1987 federal budget, after a Canadian (John Polanyi) won a Nobel prize in 1986 and questions arose as to whether it was taxable. Reg. 7700 is retroactive to 1983.

The CCRA states in VIEWS doc. #9514155 that the Prime Minister's Award for Teaching Excellence in Science, Technology and Mathematics is a prescribed prize, and in doc. #9300075 that the Governor General's Performing Arts Awards are prescribed prizes. On the other hand, research grants and Canada Council grants, even where they are described as awards or prizes, are generally considered not to be prescribed prizes.

**Definitions [Reg. 7700]**: "amount", "prescribed" — ITA 248(1).

**Interpretation Bulletins**: IT-75R3: Scholarships, fellowships, bursaries, prizes, and research grants; IT-257R: Canada Council grants.

## PART LXXVIII — PRESCRIBED PROVINCIAL PENSION PLANS

**7800. (1)** For the purposes of clause 56(1)(a)(i)(C), subsections 56(2) and (4), paragraph 60(v), subsection 74.1(1) and paragraph 118(8)(e) of the Act, the Saskatchewan Pension Plan is a prescribed provincial pension plan.

**(2)** For the purpose of subparagraph 60(v)(ii) of the Act, the prescribed amount for a taxation year in respect of the Saskatchewan Pension Plan is, for the 1987 taxation year, $1,200, and for the 1988 and subsequent taxation years, $600.

**Definitions [Reg. 7800]**: "amount", "prescribed" — ITA 248(1); "taxation year" — ITA 249.

**Interpretation Bulletins**: IT-124R6: Contributions to registered retirement savings plans; IT-499R: Superannuation or pension benefits; IT-517R: Pension tax credit.

## PART LXXIX — PRESCRIBED FINANCIAL INSTITUTIONS

**7900.** For the purposes of section 33.1, paragraph 95(2)(a.3), clause 212(1)(b)(iii)(D) and subparagraph 212(1)(b)(xi) of the Act, "prescribed financial institution" means

(a) a corporation that is a member of the Canadian Payments Association; or

(b) a credit union that is a shareholder or member of a body corporate or organization that is a central for the purposes of the *Canadian Payments Association Act*.

---

**Proposed Amendment — Reg. 7900**

**7900. (1)** For the purposes of section 33.1, paragraph 95(2)(a.3), the definition "specified deposit" in subsection 95(2.5), clause 212(1)(b)(iii)(D) and subparagraph 212(1)(b)(xi) of the Act, each of the following is a prescribed financial institution:

(a) a corporation that is a member of the Canadian Payments Association, other than an authorized foreign bank; and

(b) a credit union that is a shareholder or member of a body corporate or organization that is a central for the purposes of the *Canadian Payments Association Act*.

(2) For the purposes of paragraph 95(2)(a.3), the definition "specified deposit" in subsection 95(2.5) and clause 212(1)(b)(iii)(D) of the Act, an authorized foreign bank is a prescribed financial institution.

**Application**: The August 8, 2000 draft regulations, s. 5, will amend s. 7900 to read as above, applicable after June 27, 1999.

**Notes**: Application of Reg. 7900 to ITA 95(2)(a.3) added by P.C. 1997-1670, effective on the same basis as the amendment to Reg. 5903(1).

**Definitions [Reg. 7900]**: "authorized foreign bank" — ITA 248(1); "corporation" — ITA 248(1), *Interpretation Act* 35(1); "credit union", "shareholder" — ITA 248(1).

## PART LXXX — PRESCRIBED RESERVE AMOUNT AND RECOVERY RATE

**8000. [Prescribed reserve amount]** — For the purpose of clause 20(1)(l)(ii)(C) of the Act, the prescribed reserve amount for a taxation year means the aggregate of

(a) where the taxpayer is a bank, an amount equal to the lesser of

(i) the amount of the reserve reported in its annual report for the year that is filed with and accepted by the relevant authority or, where the taxpayer was throughout the year subject to the supervision of the relevant authority but was not required to file an annual report for the year with the relevant authority, in its financial statements for the year, as general provisions or as specific provisions, in respect of exposures to designated countries in respect of loans or lending assets of the taxpayer made or acquired by it in the ordinary course of its business, and

(ii) an amount in respect of the loans or lending assets of the taxpayer at the end of the year that were made or acquired by the taxpayer in the ordinary course of its business and reported for the year by the taxpayer to the relevant authority, in accordance with the guidelines established by the relevant authority, as part of the taxpayer's total exposure to designated countries for the purpose of determining the taxpayer's general provisions or specific provisions referred to in subparagraph (i) or that were acquired by the taxpayer after August 16, 1990 and reported for the year by the taxpayer to the relevant authority, in accordance with the guidelines established by the relevant authority, as an exposure to a designated country (in this subparagraph referred to as the "loans") equal to the positive or negative amount, as the case may be, determined by the formula

$$45\% (A + B) - (B + C)$$

where

A is the aggregate of all amounts each of which is the amount that would be the amortized cost of a loan to the taxpayer at the end of the year if the definition "amortized cost" in section 248 of the Act were read without reference to paragraphs (e) and (i) thereof,

B is the aggregate of all amounts each of which is the amount, if any, by which the principal amount of a loan outstanding at the time it was acquired by the taxpayer exceeds the amortized cost of the loan to the taxpayer immediately after the time it was acquired by the taxpayer, and

C is the aggregate of all amounts each of which is

(A) an amount deducted in respect of a loan under clause 20(1)(l)(ii)(B) of the Act in computing the taxpayer's income for the year, or

(B) an amount in respect of a loan determined as the amount, if any, by which

(I) the aggregate of all amounts in respect of the loan deducted under paragraph 20(1)(p) of the Act in computing the taxpayer's income for the year or a preceding taxation year

exceeds

(II) the aggregate of all amounts in respect of the loan included under paragraph 12(1)(i) of the Act in computing the taxpayer's income for the year or a preceding taxation year, and

(a.1) where the taxpayer is a bank, the positive or negative amount that would be determined under the formula in subparagraph (a)(ii) in respect of the specified loans owned by the taxpayer at the end of the year if that subparagraph applied to those loans.

(b) [Repealed]

**Related Provisions**: ITA 257 — Negative amounts in formulas.

**Notes**: Opening words of Reg. 8000 amended by P.C. 1999-195 to change reference from 20(1)(l)(ii)(A) to 20(1)(l)(ii)(C), effective on the same basis as the 1995-97 technical bill amendments to ITA 20(1)(l).

Reg. 8000(a.1) added by P.C. 1999-195, effective (a) for the 1997 and later taxation years, and (b) for the 1992-1996 taxation years, if the taxpayer elects in writing to have 8000(a.1) apply to those years and files the election with Revenue Canada by June 30, 1999.

Reg. 8000(b) repealed by P.C. 1999-195, effective on the same basis as the 1995-97 technical bill amendments to ITA 20(1)(l). Before its repeal, read:

(b) an amount, not exceeding a reasonable amount, of a reserve for the year in respect of doubtful loans or lending assets of the taxpayer (other than a loan or lending described in subparagraph (a)(ii)) computed by

(i) identifying loans or lending assets of the taxpayer with respect to which a reserve could be claimed under clause 20(1)(l)(ii)(B) of the Act,

(ii) segregating particular types of loans or lending assets of the taxpayer referred to in subparagraph (i) into different classes based on the length of time that interest or principal payable to the taxpayer in respect thereof has been in arrears, and

(iii) determining the aggregate of all amounts each of which is the amount determined by multiplying the amortized cost to the taxpayer at the end of the year of loans or lending assets of a class described in subparagraph (ii) by the historical loss experience of the taxpayer in respect of that class.

**Definitions [Reg. 8000]:** "amortized cost", "amount" — ITA 248(1); "bank" — ITA 248(1), *Interpretation Act* 35(1); "business" — ITA 248(1); "designated country", "exposure to a designated country", "general provisions" — Reg. 8006; "lending asset" — ITA 248(1); "loans" — Reg. 8000(a)(ii); "loans or lending assets" — Reg. 8003; "prescribed", "principal amount" — ITA 248(1); "principal amount outstanding" — Reg. 8002(a); "relevant authority", "specific provisions", "specified loan" — Reg. 8006; "taxation year" — ITA 249; "taxpayer" — ITA 248(1).

## 8001. [Repealed]

**Notes:** Reg. 8001 repealed by P.C. 1999-195, effective on the same basis as the 1995-97 technical bill amendments to ITA 20(1)(l). Before its repeal, read:

8001. For the purposes of subclause 20(1)(l)(ii)(B)(II) and subparagraph 20(1)(l.1)(ii) of the Act, the prescribed recovery rate is 10 per cent.

## 8002. [Principal amount, amortized cost] —

For the purposes of paragraph 8000(a),

(a) the principal amount outstanding at any time of a lending asset of a taxpayer that is a share of the capital stock of a corporation is the part of the consideration received by the corporation for the issue of the share that is outstanding at that time;

(b) where

(i) a taxpayer realizes a loss from the disposition of a loan or lending asset described in subparagraph 8000(a)(ii) or a specified loan described in paragraph 8000(a.1) (in this paragraph referred to as the "former loan") for consideration that included another loan or lending asset that was a loan or lending asset described in subparagraph 8000(a)(ii) or paragraph 8000(a.1) (in this paragraph referred to as the "new loan"), and

(ii) in the case of a former loan that is not a specified loan, the loss is included in computing the taxpayer's provisionable assets as reported for the year to the relevant authority, in accordance with the guidelines established by the relevant authority, for the purpose of determining the taxpayer's general provisions or specific provisions in respect of exposures to designated countries,

the principal amount of the new loan outstanding at the time it was acquired by the taxpayer is deemed to be equal to the principal amount of the former loan outstanding immediately before that time; and

(c) where at the end of a particular taxation year a taxpayer owns a specified loan that, at the end of the preceding taxation year, was described in an inventory of the taxpayer, the amortized cost of the specified loan to the taxpayer at the end of the particular year is its value determined under section 10 of the Act at the end of the preceding year for the purpose of computing the taxpayer's income for the preceding year.

**Notes:** Reg. 8002(b) amended and (c) added by P.C. 1999-195, effective on the same basis as the addition of Reg. 8000(a.1). Before the amendment, read:

(b) where a taxpayer

(i) realized a loss on the disposition of a loan or lending asset that was an exposure to a designated country (in this paragraph referred to as the "former loan") for consideration that included another loan or lending asset that was an exposure to that designated country (in this paragraph referred to as the "new loan"), and

(ii) included the loss referred to in subparagraph (i) in the calculation of its provisionable assets as reported in its annual report for the year to the relevant authority, in accordance with the guidelines established by the relevant authority, for the purposes of determining the taxpayer's general provisions or specific provisions in respect of exposures to designated countries,

the principal amount outstanding of the new loan at the time it was acquired by the taxpayer shall be deemed to be equal to the principal amount outstanding of the former loan immediately before that time.

**Definitions [Reg. 8002]:** "amortized cost" — Reg. 8002(c), ITA 248(1); "corporation" — ITA 248(1), *Interpretation Act* 35(1); "designated country" — Reg. 8006; "disposition" — ITA 248(1); "exposure to a designated country" — Reg. 8006; "former loan" — Reg. 8002(b)(i); "general provisions" — Reg. 8006; "inventory", "lending asset" — ITA 248(1); "new loan" — Reg. 8002(b)(i); "principal amount" — Reg. 8002, ITA 248(1); "provisionable assets", "relevant authority" — Reg. 8006; "share" — ITA 248(1); "specific provisions", "specified loan" — Reg. 8006; "taxation year" — ITA 249; "taxpayer" — ITA 248(1).

## 8003. [Election] —

Where a taxpayer elects to have this section apply by notifying the Minister in writing within 90 days after the day on which this section is published in the *Canada Gazette*, the loans or lending assets of the taxpayer that are described in subparagraph 8000(a)(ii) shall not include any loan or lending asset acquired by the taxpayer before November 1988 from a person with whom the taxpayer was dealing at arm's length.

**Notes:** January 16, 1991 was the date on which Reg. 8003 (along with the rest of Part LXXX) was published in the *Canada Gazette*.

**Definitions [Reg. 8003]:** "arm's length" — ITA 251(1); "Canada" — ITA 255, *Interpretation Act* 35(1); "lending asset", "Minister", "person", "taxpayer" — ITA 248(1); "writing" — *Interpretation Act* 35(1).

## 8004. [Repealed]

## Part LXXX — Prescribed Reserve Amount and Recovery Rate

**Reg. S. 8007**

**Notes:** Reg. 8004 repealed by P.C. 1999-195, effective on the same basis as the 1995-97 technical bill amendments to ITA 20(1)(l). Before its repeal, read:

> 8004. For the purposes of paragraph 8000(b), "historical loss experience" of a taxpayer, in respect of a class of loans or lending assets, means a reasonable percentage of the amortized cost to the taxpayer of the loans or lending assets of that class that are included in determining the amount under subparagraph 8000(b)(iii), where that percentage is a representation of the prior years losses net of recoveries in respect of the loans or lending assets of that class.

### 8005. [Rules — loans and lending assets] —

For the purposes of subparagraph 8000(a)(ii), where a loan or lending asset of a person (in this section referred to as the "holder") related to a taxpayer

(a) was reported for the year by the taxpayer to the relevant authority, in accordance with the guidelines established by the relevant authority, as an exposure to a designated country,

(b) was acquired by the holder or another person related to the taxpayer after August 16, 1990 as part of a series of transactions or events in which the taxpayer or a person related to the taxpayer disposed of a loan or lending asset that

   (i) for the taxation year immediately preceding the particular year in which it was disposed of, was a loan or lending asset that was reported by the taxpayer to the relevant authority, in accordance with the guidelines established by the relevant authority, as an exposure to a designated country, and

   (ii) was a loan or lending asset a loss arising on the disposition of which would be a loss in respect of which a deduction is permitted under Part I of the Act to the taxpayer or a person related to the taxpayer, and

(c) had an amortized cost to the holder, immediately after the time it was acquired by the holder, that was less than 55 per cent of its principal amount,

the following rules apply:

(d) the loan or lending asset shall be deemed

   (i) to be a loan or lending asset of the taxpayer at the end of the year,

   (ii) to be a loan or lending asset of the taxpayer that was acquired by the taxpayer at the time it was acquired by the holder, and

   (iii) to have an amortized cost to the taxpayer, at any time, that is equal to its amortized cost to the holder at that time, and

(e) any amount in respect of the loan or lending asset deducted under paragraph 20(1)(p) of the Act or included under paragraph 12(1)(i) of the Act in computing the holder's income for a particular year shall be deemed to have been so deducted or included, as the case may be, in computing the income of the taxpayer for the year in which the particular year ends.

**Definitions [Reg. 8005]:** "amortized cost", "amount" — ITA 248(1); "disposed" — ITA 248(1)"disposition"; "disposition" — ITA 248(1); "exposure to a designated country" — Reg. 8006; "holder" — Reg. 8005; "lending asset", "person", "principal amount" — ITA 248(1); "related" — ITA 251(2)–(6); "relevant authority" — Reg. 8006; "taxation year" — ITA 249; "taxpayer" — ITA 248(1).

**8006.** For the purposes of this Part,

**"designated country"** has the same meaning as in the Guidelines for banks established pursuant to section 175 of the *Bank Act*, as that section read on May 31, 1992, and issued by the Office of the Superintendent of Financial Institutions, as amended from time to time;

**"exposure to a designated country"** has the same meaning as in the Guidelines for banks established pursuant to section 175 of the *Bank Act*, as that section read on May 31, 1992, and issued by the Office of the Superintendent of Financial Institutions, as amended from time to time;

**"general provisions"** has the same meaning as the expression "general country risk provisions" in the Guidelines for banks established pursuant to section 175 of the *Bank Act*, as that section read on May 31, 1992, and issued by the Office of the Superintendent of Financial Institutions, as amended from time to time;

**"provisionable assets"** has the same meaning as in the Guidelines for banks established pursuant to section 175 of the *Bank Act*, as that section read on May 31, 1992, and issued by the Office of the Superintendent of Financial Institutions, as amended from time to time;

**"relevant authority"** means the Superintendent of Financial Institutions;

**"specific provisions"** has the same meaning as in the Guidelines for banks established pursuant to section 175 of the *Bank Act*, as that section read on May 31, 1992, and issued by the Office of the Superintendent of Financial Institutions, as amended from time to time.

**"specified loan"** means

(a) a United Mexican States Collateralized Par Bond due in 2019, or

(b) a United Mexican States Collateralized Discount Bond due in 2019;

**Notes:** These Mexican bonds are known as "Brady bonds".

Definition "specified loan" added by P.C. 1995-195, effective on the same basis as the addition of Reg. 8000(a.1).

**Notes [Reg. 8006]:** Reg. 8006 added by P.C. 1992-2335, effective for taxation years and fiscal period beginning after June 17, 1987 and ending after 1987.

**Definitions [Reg. 8006]:** "bank" — ITA 248(1), *Interpretation Act* 35(1).

**8007.** [Repealed]

**Notes**: Reg. 8007 added and repealed by P.C. 1999-195. It is effective only for taxation years that ended after 1991 and before October 1997 and only where the taxpayer elects in writing to have Reg. 8000(a.1) apply to those years and files the election by June 30, 1999. It read:

> 8007. Paragraph 8000(b) does not apply in respect of a specified loan of a bank.

**Definitions [Reg. 8007]**: "bank" — ITA 248(1), *Interpretation Act* 35(1); "specified loan" — Reg. 8006.

## PART LXXXI — TRANSITION FOR FINANCIAL INSTITUTIONS

**8100. Transition deduction in respect of unpaid claims reserve** — For the purpose of subsection 20(26) of the Act, an insurer's unpaid claims reserve adjustment for its taxation year that includes February 23, 1994 is the amount, if any, by which

(a) the total of all amounts each of which is the maximum amount that, because of paragraph 1400(e), was deductible under paragraph 20(7)(c) of the Act in respect of an insurance policy in computing the insurer's income for its last taxation year that ended before February 23, 1994

exceeds

(b) where the insurer elects, by notifying the Minister in writing, to have this paragraph apply, the total of all amounts each of which is the maximum amount that would, because of paragraph 1400(e), have been deductible under paragraph 20(7)(c) of the Act in respect of an insurance policy in computing the insurer's income for its last taxation year that ended before February 23, 1994 if the amount "$1/3$" in the formula in subparagraph 1400(e)(ii), as it read for that year, were replaced by the amount "1", and

(c) in any other case, the total of all amounts each of which is the maximum amount that would, because of paragraph 1400(e) or (e.1), have been deductible under paragraph 20(7)(c) of the Act in respect of an insurance policy in computing the insurer's income for its last taxation year that ended before February 23, 1994 if paragraph 1400(e.1) had applied to that year and paragraphs 1400(e) and (e.1) were read in their application to that year as they read in their application to the insurer's taxation year that includes February 23, 1994.

**Notes**: See Notes at end of Reg. 8101.

**Definitions [Reg. 8100]**: "amount", "insurance policy", "insurer", "Minister" — ITA 248(1); "taxation year" — ITA 249; "writing" — *Interpretation Act* 35(1).

**8101. Inclusion of transition amount in respect of unpaid claims reserve** — (1) In this section, "transition deduction" of an insurer means the amount deducted under subsection 20(26) of the Act in computing the insurer's income for its taxation year that includes February 23, 1994.

(2) Subject to subsection (3), there is prescribed for the purpose of section 12.3 of the Act in respect of an insurer for a taxation year that ends after February 22, 1994 the amount determined by the formula

$$\left(\frac{(0.05A + 0.10B + 0.15C)}{365}\right) \times D$$

where

A is the total of

(a) the number of days in the taxation year that are in 1994 or 1995, and

(b) where the taxation year includes February 23, 1994, the number of days in 1994 that are before the first day of the taxation year,

B is the number of days in the taxation year (other than February 29) that are in any of 1996 to 2001,

C is the number of days in the taxation year that are in 2002 or 2003, and

D is the insurer's transition deduction minus the amount, if any, required by subsection (4) or paragraph (5)(b) to be subtracted.

(3) Where subsection 88(1) of the Act has applied to the winding-up of an insurer (in this subsection referred to as the "subsidiary"),

(a) the values of A, B, and C in subsection (2) shall be determined in respect of the subsidiary without including any days that are after the day on which the subsidiary's assets were distributed to its parent on the winding-up; and

(b) there is prescribed for the purpose of section 12.3 of the Act in respect of the parent for its taxation year that includes the day referred to in paragraph (a) the total of

(i) the amount that would be determined under subsection (2) in respect of the parent for the year if the parent's transition deduction did not include the subsidiary's transition deduction, and

(ii) the amount that would be determined under subsection (2) in respect of the parent for the year if

(A) the values of A, B, and C in that subsection were determined without including the day referred to in paragraph (a) and any days before that day, and

(B) the value of D in that subsection were equal to the subsidiary's transition deduction.

(4) Where subsection 138(11.5) or (11.94) of the Act has applied to the transfer of an insurance business by an insurer, there shall be subtracted, in determining the value of D in subsection (2) in respect of the insurer for a taxation year ending after the insurer ceased to carry on all or substantially all of the business, the part of the insurer's transition deduction that can reasonably be attributed to the business.

**Notes**: Revenue Canada's view is that "all or substantially all" means 90% or more.

**(5)** Where an insurer ceases to carry on all or substantially all of an insurance business, otherwise than as a result of a merger to which subsection 87(2) of the Act applies, a winding-up to which subsection 88(1) of the Act applies or a transfer of the business to which subsection 138(11.5) or (11.94) of the Act applies,

(a) there is prescribed for the purpose of section 12.3 of the Act in respect of the insurer for its taxation year in which the cessation of business occurs, in addition to the amount prescribed by subsection (2), the amount, if any, by which

(i) the part of the insurer's transition deduction that can reasonably be attributed to the business

exceeds

(ii) that part of the total of the amounts included under section 12.3 of the Act in computing the income of the insurer for preceding taxation years that can reasonably be considered to be in respect of the amount determined under subparagraph (i); and

(b) there shall be subtracted, in determining the value of D in subsection (2) in respect of the insurer for the year or a subsequent taxation year, the amount determined under subparagraph (a)(i).

**Notes [Reg. 8101(5)]**: Revenue Canada's view is that "all or substantially all" means 90% or more.

**Notes [Reg. 8100, 8101]**: Reg. 8100 and 8101 added (in place of former Regs. 8100–8105) by P.C. 1996-1452, effective for taxation years that end after February 22, 1994. For earlier taxation years (since 1988), read:

8100. (1) Subject to subsections (6) and (7), for the purposes of section 12.3 of the Act, the prescribed amount of a taxpayer's net reserve inclusion for a taxation year ending after 1988 and commencing before 1993 is an amount equal to the aggregate of

(a) that proportion of 15 per cent of the amount deducted by the taxpayer under subsection 20(26) of the Act in computing the taxpayer's income for his first taxation year that commences after June 17, 1987 and ends after 1987 (in this section referred to as an "amount of net reserve adjustment") that the number of days in the year that are in 1989 is of 365,

(b) that proportion of 25 per cent of the amount of net reserve adjustment that the number of days in the year that are in 1990 or 1991 is of 365, and

(c) that proportion of 35 per cent of the amount of net reserve adjustment that the number of days in the year that are in 1992 is of 366.

(2) For the purposes of subsection (1), where a new corporation has been formed as a result of an amalgamation of two or more predecessor corporations, within the meaning of section 87 of the Act, and one or more of the predecessor corporations has an amount of net reserve adjustment, the new corporation shall be deemed to have an amount of net reserve adjustment equal to the aggregate of the amounts of net reserve adjustments of all the predecessor corporations.

(3) For the purposes of subsection (1), where there has been a winding-up as described in subsection 88(1) of the Act and the subsidiary referred to in that subsection has an amount of net reserve adjustment, the following rules apply:

(a) the taxation year of the subsidiary that included the time when the property of the subsidiary was transferred to, and the obligations of the subsidiary were assumed by, the parent on the winding-up shall be deemed to have ended immediately before that time;

(b) the parent shall be deemed to have had a taxation year that commenced immediately after the time referred to in paragraph (a);

(c) the parent shall, for taxation years commencing after the time referred to in paragraph (a), include in computing its amount of net reserve adjustment the amount of net reserve adjustment of the subsidiary at the end of its first taxation year that commences after June 17, 1987 and ends after 1987, determined without reference to paragraph (d); and

(d) the subsidiary shall, for taxation years commencing at or after the time referred to in paragraph (a), be deemed to have no amount of net reserve adjustment.

(4) For the purposes of subsection (1), where, by reason of subsection 98(6) of the Act, a new partnership is deemed to be a continuation of the predecessor partnership referred to therein and that predecessor partnership has an amount of net reserve adjustment, the following rules apply:

(a) the fiscal period of the predecessor partnership that included the time when the property of the predecessor partnership was transferred to, and the obligations of the predecessor partnership were assumed by, the new partnership shall be deemed to have ended immediately before that time;

(b) the new partnership shall be deemed to have had a fiscal period that commenced immediately after the time referred to in paragraph (a);

(c) the new partnership shall, for fiscal periods ending after the time referred to in paragraph (a), include in computing its amount of net reserve adjustment the amount of net reserve adjustment of the predecessor partnership at the end of its first taxation year that commences after June 17, 1987 and ends after 1987, determined without reference to paragraph (d); and

(d) the predecessor partnership shall, for fiscal periods commencing at or after the time referred to in paragraph (a), be deemed to have no amount of net reserve adjustment.

(5) For the purposes of subsection (1), where a non-resident insurer that carried on an insurance business in Canada has transferred that business pursuant to subsection 138(11.5) of the Act to another corporation and the non-resident insurer has an amount of net reserve adjustment that can reasonably be attributed to that business, the following rules apply:

(a) the taxation year of the non-resident insurer that included the time when the business was transferred shall be deemed to have ended immediately before that time;

(b) the other corporation shall be deemed to have had a taxation year that commenced immediately after the time referred to in paragraph (a);

(c) the other corporation shall, for taxation years commencing after the transfer of the business, include in computing its amount of net reserve adjustment the amount of net reserve adjustment of the non-resident insurer at the end of the first taxation year that commences after June 17, 1987 and ends after 1981, determined without reference to paragraph (d), that can reasonably be attributed to that business; and

(d) the non-resident insurer shall, for taxation years commencing at or after the time of the transfer of the business, be deemed to have no amount of net reserve adjustment in respect of that business.

(6) For the purposes of section 12.3 of the Act, where a person or a partnership that has an amount of net reserve adjustment that can reasonably be attributed to a business (in this subsection that amount is referred to as the "particular amount") discontinues or transfers that business, otherwise than pursuant to a transaction described in any of subsections (2) to (5), the following rules apply:

(a) the prescribed amount of the net reserve inclusion of the person or partnership in respect of the particular amount for the taxation year of the person or partnership to which the person or partnership discontinued or transferred that business, shall be equal to the amount, if any, by which

(i) the particular amount

exceeds

(ii) the aggregate of all amounts each of which is an amount that was included under section 12.3 of the Act in computing the income of the person or partnership for a preceding taxation year and that can reasonably be attributed to the particular amount; and

(b) the person or partnership shall, for taxation years commencing at or after the time of the discontinuance or the transfer of the business, be deemed to have no amount of net reserve adjustment in respect of that business.

(7) Subject to subsection (6), where a taxpayer that is an insurer deducts in any taxation year that commences after June 17, 1987 and ends before 1992 an amount under subparagraph 138(3)(a)(v) or subsection 140(1) of the Act, as the case may be, that may reasonably be considered to be in respect of an amount that was included in computing the insurer's income under subsection 140(2) of the Act for its first taxation year that commences after June 17, 1987 and ends after 1987 (in this subsection referred to as its "1988 taxation year"), the following rules apply:

(a) the prescribed amount of its net reserve inclusion for its last taxation year that ends in 1990 shall be equal to the aggregate of

(i) the prescribed amount of its net reserve inclusion for that last taxation year determined without reference to this subsection, and

(ii) its 1990 transition adjustment;

(b) the prescribed amount of its net reserve inclusion for its last taxation year that ends in 1991 shall be equal to the amount, if any, by which the aggregate of

(i) the prescribed amount of its net reserve inclusion for that last taxation year determined without reference to this subsection, and

(ii) its 1991 transition adjustment

exceeds

(iii) that proportion of its 1990 transition adjustment that 25 is of 60; and

(c) the prescribed amount of its net reserve inclusion for its last taxation year that ends in 1992 than be equal to the amount, if any, by which

(i) the prescribed amount of its net reserve inclusion for that last taxation year determined without reference to this subsection

exceeds the aggregate of

(ii) that proportion of its 1990 transition adjustment that 35 is of 60, and

(iii) its 1991 transition adjustment.

(8) For the purposes of subsection (7),

"1990 transition adjustment" of a taxpayer that is an insurer is the amount determined by the formula

$$A \times B$$

where

A is 60 per cent, and

B is the lesser of

(a) the aggregate of all amounts each of which is an amount deducted by it in any taxation year that commences after June 17, 1987 and ends before 1991 under subparagraph 138(3)(a)(v) or subsection 140(1) of the Act that may reasonably be considered in be in respect of an amount that was included in computing its income under subsection 140(2) of the Act for its 1988 taxation year, and

(b) the lesser of

(i) the amount of its net reserve adjustment, and

(ii) the amount, if any, by which

(A) the amount included under subsection 140(2) of the Act in computing its income for its 1988 taxation year

exceeds

(B) the aggregate of the amounts deducted by if under paragraph 20(7)(c) of the Act pursuant to paragraph 1400(g.1) or under subparagraph 138(3)(a)(i) of the Act pursuant to paragraph 1401(1)(c.1) in computing its income for its 1988 taxation year;

"1991 transition adjustment"of a taxpayer that is an insurer is the amount determined by the formula

$$(A \times B) - (C \times D)$$

where

A is 35 per cent,

B is the lesser of

(a) the aggregate of all amounts each of which is in amount deducted by it in any taxation year that commences after June 17, 1987 and ends before 1992 under subparagraph 138(3)(a)(v) or subsection 140(1) of the Act that may reasonably be considered to be in respect of an amount that was included in computing its income under subsection 140(2) of the Act for its 1988 taxation year, and

(b) the lesser of

(i) the amount of its net reserve adjustment, and

(ii) the amount, if any, by which

(A) the amount included under subsection 140(2) of the Act in computing its income for its 1988 taxation year

exceeds

(B) the aggregate of the amounts deducted by it under paragraph 20(7)(c) of the Act pursuant to paragraph 1400(g.1) or under subparagraph 138(3)(a)(i) of the Act pursuant to paragraph 1401(1)(c.1) in computing its income for its 1988 taxation year,

C is 35/60, and

D is its 1990 transition adjustment.

8101. (1) For the purposes of subsection 20(26) of the Act, the prescribed amount of net reserve adjustment of a taxpayer means the amount, if any, by which

(a) the taxpayer's preliminary reserve adjustment

## Part LXXXI — Transition for Financial Institutions

exceeds the aggregate of

(b) the total of all amounts each of which is a non-capital loss of the taxpayer for a taxation year before the taxpayer's first taxation year that commences after June 17, 1987 and ends after 1987 that is deductible under paragraph 111(1)(a) of the Act in computing the taxpayer's taxable income for the taxpayer's first taxation year that commences after June 17, 1987 and ends after 1987 or a subsequent taxation year,

(c) where the taxpayer is a bank, the total of

(i) that part of the total of the amounts of the five-year average loan loss experiences of the taxpayer, as determined, or as would be determined if such a determination were required, under the Minister's rules, for all taxation years before its first taxation year that commences after June 17, 1987 and ends after 1987, that was not deducted by the taxpayer under subsection 26(2) of the Act in computing its income for those taxation years,

(ii) that part of the total of the amounts transferred by the taxpayer to its tax allowable appropriations account, as permitted under the Minister's rules, for all taxation years before its first taxation year that commences after June 17, 1987 and ends after 1987, that was not deducted by the taxpayer under subsection 26(2) of the Act in computing its income for those taxation years,

(iii) the amount by which

(A) the amount of the special provision for losses on trans-border claims of the taxpayer, as determined, or as would be determined if such a determination were required, under the Minister's rules, that was deductible by the taxpayer under subsection 26(2) of the Act in computing its income for its last taxation year before its first taxation year that commences after June 17, 1987 and ends after 1987,

exceeds

(B) that part of the amount described in clause (A) that was deducted in computing the income of the taxpayer for that last taxation year,

(iv) where the tax allowable appropriations account of the taxpayer at the end of its last taxation year before its first taxation year that commences after June 17, 1987 and ends after 1987, as determined, or as would be determined if such a determination were required, under the Minister's rules, is a negative amount, that amount expressed as a positive number, and

(v) that part of the total of the amounts calculated in respect of the taxpayer for the purposes of the Minister's rules, or that would be calculated for the purposes of those rules if such a calculation were required, under Procedure 8 of the Procedures for the Determination of the Provision for Loan Losses (as set out in Appendix 1 to those rules), for taxation years before its first taxation year that commences after June 17, 1987 and ends after 1987, that was not deducted by the taxpayer under subsection 26(2) of the Act in computing its income for those taxation years, and

(d) the total of all amounts each of which is an amount in respect of depreciable property of a prescribed class of the taxpayer equal to the amount, if any, by which

(i) the amount that would have been deductible by the taxpayer under paragraph 20(1)(a) of the Act in computing the taxpayer's income for the taxpayer's last taxation year before the taxpayer's first taxation year that commences after June 17, 1987 and ends after 1987 with respect to that class if the taxpayer had claimed the maximum allowable amount under that paragraph in that last taxation year with respect to that class

exceeds

(ii) the amount deducted by the taxpayer under paragraph 20(1)(a) of the Act in computing the taxpayer's income for that last taxation year with respect to that class.

(2) For the purposes of subsection (1), "preliminary reserve adjustment" of a taxpayer means the aggregate of

(a) the amount, if any, by which

(i) the total of all amounts each of which is an amount deducted by the taxpayer under subparagraph 20(1)(i)(ii), subsection 33(1) and paragraph 137(1)(a) or (b), 137.1(3)(c) or 138(3)(c) of the Act in computing the taxpayer's income for the taxpayer's last taxation year before the taxpayer's first taxation year that commences after June 17, 1987 and ends after 1987

exceeds the total of

(ii) the greater of

(A) the maximum amount that would have been deductible in computing the taxpayer's income for the taxpayer's last taxation year before the taxpayer's first taxation year that commences after June 17, 1987 and ends after 1987 under subparagraph 20(1)(l)(ii) or paragraph 20(1)(l.1) of the Act if those provisions had applied to that last taxation year and they were read as they read in their application to the taxpayer's first taxation year that commences after June 17, 1987 and ends after 1987, and

(B) that proportion of the amount determined under subparagraph (i) that

(I) the sum of the maximum amounts deductible by the taxpayer under subparagraph 20(1)(l)(ii) and paragraph 20(1)(l.1) of the Act in computing the taxpayer's income for the taxpayer's first taxation year that commences after June 17, 1987 and ends after 1987

is of

(II) the sum of the maximum amounts that would have been deductible by the taxpayer under subparagraph 20(1)(l)(ii), subsection 33(1) and paragraphs 137(1)(a) and (b), 137.1(3)(c) and 138(3)(c) of the Act in computing the taxpayer's income for the taxpayer's first taxation year that commences after June 17, 1987 and ends after 1987 if those provisions had applied to that year and they were read as they read in respect of the immediately preceding taxation year, and

(iii) where the taxpayer is a credit union, the prescribed amount of its 1971 reserve adjustment,

(b) where the taxpayer is a bank, the amount, if any, by which

(i) the amount included under subsection 26(1) of the Act in computing its income for its first taxation year that commences after June 17, 1987 and ends after 1987

# Reg. S. 8101 — Income Tax Regulations

exceeds

(ii) the sum of the maximum amounts that would have been deductible in computing its income for its last taxation year before its first taxation year that commences after June 17, 1987 and ends after 1987 under subparagraph 20(1)(l)(ii) and paragraph 20(1)(l.1) of the Act if those provisions had applied to that last taxation year and they were read as they read in their application to the taxpayer's first taxation year that commences after June 17, 1987 and ends after 1987, and

(c) where the taxpayer is an insurer, the amount, if any, by which the aggregate of

(i) the total of the amounts deducted under paragraph 20(7)(c) or under subparagraph 138(3)(a)(i) or (iv) of the Act by the insurer in computing its income for its last taxation year before its first taxation year that commences after June 17, 1987 and ends after 1987,

(ii) where the insurer is a life insurer, the total of the amounts deducted by the insurer in computing its income for its last taxation year before its first taxation year that commences after June 17, 1987 and ends after 1987 in respect of claims made under insurance policies that were received before and unpaid at the end of that last taxation year, and

(iii) the amount included under subsection 140(2) of the Act in computing the insurer's income for its first taxation year that commences after June 17, 1987 and ends after 1987

exceeds the total of

(iv) the sum of the maximum amounts that would have been deductible under paragraph 20(7)(c) or under subparagraph 138(3)(a)(i), (ii) or (iv) of the Act in computing its income for its last taxation year before its first taxation year that commences after June 17, 1987 and ends after 1987 if those provisions had applied to that last taxation year and they were read as they read for its first taxation year that commences after June 17, 1987 and ends after 1987,

(v) the amount, if any, by which

(A) the greater of the amounts determined under clauses (a)(ii)(A) and (B) in respect of the insurer

exceeds

(B) the amount determined under subparagraph (a)(i) in respect of the insurer and

(vi) the prescribed amount of the insurer's 1968 reserve adjustment.

(3) Notwithstanding subsection (1), where a person or partnership discontinues or transfers a business in a taxation year ending before 1989, otherwise than pursuant to a transaction described in any of subsections 8100(2) to (5), and that person or partnership has a prescribed amount of net reserve adjustment that can reasonably be attributed to that business, the prescribed amount of net reserve adjustment of the person or partnership shall be deemed to be the amount, if any, by which

(a) the prescribed amount of net reserve adjustment of the person or partnership otherwise determined

exceeds

(b) that portion of the prescribed amount of net reserve adjustment of the person or partnership that can reasonably be attributed to the business that was discontinued or transferred.

8102. For the purposes of this Part and paragraph 137(1)(d) of the Act (as it read in its application to a credit union's first taxation year that commences after June 17, 1987 and ends after 1987), the prescribed amount of a credit union's 1971 reserve adjustment is the amount determined under section 602 as it read in its application to the credit union at the end of its last taxation year before its first taxation year that commences after June 17, 1987 and ends after 1987.

8103. For the purposes of this Part and paragraph 138(4)(a) of the Act, as it read in its application for the first taxation year that commenced after June 17, 1987 and ends after 1987, the prescribed amount of an insurer's 1968 reserve adjustment is an amount equal to the aggregate of

(a) the amount, if any, by which

(i) the total of the amounts that would have been the insurer's maximum tax actuarial reserves for its 1968 taxation year if those reserves had been determined on the basis of the rules applicable to its 1978 taxation year

exceeds

(ii) the total of the amounts that would have been the insurer's maximum tax actuarial reserves for its 1968 taxation year if those reserves had been determined on the basis of the riles applicable to its first taxation year that commences after June 17, 1987 and ends after 1987, on the assumption that those rules were read without reference to paragraph 1401(1)(c.1),

(b) the amount, if any, by which

(i) the amount the insurer was deemed for the purposes of paragraph 68A(4)(a) of the Act, as it read in respect of the insurer's 1969 taxation year, to have deducted under subparagraph 68A(3)(a)(iv) of the Act, as it read in respect of the insurer's 1969 taxation year, in computing its income for its 1968 taxation year from carrying on its life insurance business in Canada in respect of policy dividends under its participating life insurance policies

exceeds

(ii) the maximum amount that would have been deductible under subparagraph 138(3)(a)(iv) of the Act in computing its income for the 1968 taxation year if that subparagraph had applied to that year and it were read as it read in respect of the insurer's first taxation year that commences after June 17, 1987 and ends after 1987, and

(c) the amount, if any, by which

(i) the amount that the insurer was deemed for the purposes of paragraph 68A(4)(a) of the Act, as it read in respect of the insurer's 1969 taxation year, to have deducted under subparagraph 68A(3)(c) of the Act, as it read in respect of the insurer's 1969 taxation year, in computing its income for its 1968 taxation year from carrying on its life insurance business in Canada

exceeds

(ii) that proportion of the amount determined under subparagraph (i) that

(A) the sum of the maximum amounts deductible by the insurer under subparagraph 20(1)(l)(ii) and paragraph 20(1)(l.1) of the Act in computing its income for its first taxation year that commences after June 17, 1987 and ends after 1987

is of

(B) the maximum amount that would have been deductible by the insurer under paragraph 138(3)(c) of the Act in computing its income for its first taxation year that commences after June 17, 1987 and ends after 1987 if that paragraph had applied to that year and it were read as it read in respect of the immediately preceding taxation year.

8104. For the purposes of sections 8101 to 8103, where

(a) a particular corporation has been formed as a result of the amalgamation of two or more predecessor corporations within the meaning of section 87 of the Act,

(b) a subsidiary of a particular corporation has been wound up into the particular corporation pursuant to subsection 88(1) of the Act, or

(c) a non-resident insurer that carried on an insurance business in Canada has transferred that business to a particular corporation in a transaction to which subsection 138(11.5) of the Act applied,

the particular corporation shall be deemed to be the same corporation as, and a continuation of, the predecessor corporations, the subsidiary or the non-resident insurer, as the case may be.

8105. For the purposes of this Part,

"maximum tax actuarial reserve" has the meaning assigned by paragraph 138(12)(h) of the Act;

"Minister's rules" has the meaning assigned by subsection 26(4) of the Act.

**Definitions [Reg. 8101]**: "amount", "business", "insurer", "prescribed" — ITA 248(1); "subsidiary" — Reg. 8101(3); "taxation year" — ITA 249; "transition deduction" — Reg. 8101(1).

## 8102–8105. [Repealed]

**Notes**: See Notes to Reg. 8101.

### Proposed Addition — Reg. 8102–8105

**Technical Notes**: Part LXXXI contains transition rules for the 1987 tax reform changes to the reserves available to financial institutions. On December 8, 1994, draft amendments were announced that would repeal these rules and introduce (in sections 8100 and 8101) new transition rules relating to unpaid claims reserves for non-life insurance policies.

New transition rules are added in sections 8102 to 8105 in connection with the introduction of the mark-to-market requirement for shares and certain debt obligations held by financial institutions. These new rules apply to taxation years ending after October 30, 1994.

Section 8102 prescribes the maximum transition deduction that may be claimed under subsection 142.5(4) of the Act in respect of non-capital properties.

### 8102. Mark-to-market — transition deduction — (1) In this section,

"excluded property" of a taxpayer means a mark-to-market property used in a business of the taxpayer in its taxation year that includes October 31, 1994 where it is reasonable to expect that the property would have been valued at its fair market value for the purpose of computing the taxpayer's income from the business for the year if

(a) the Act were read without reference to subsection 142.5(2), and

(b) the property were held at the end of the year;

**Technical Notes**: "Excluded property" of a taxpayer is property that it is reasonable to consider would have been marked to market for tax purposes in the taxpayer's taxation year that includes October 31, 1994, even if a requirement to do so had not been introduced. The determination of whether property that has been sold during the year is excluded property is to be made assuming that the taxpayer continued to hold the property throughout the year.

"mark-to-market property" has the meaning assigned by subsection 142.2(1) of the Act.

**Technical Notes**: "Mark-to-market property" of a taxpayer has the meaning given by subsection 142.2(1) of the Act. In general terms, it comprises most shares held by the taxpayer and debt obligations that are marked to market for financial statement purposes.

(2) For the purpose of subsection 142.5(4) of the Act, the prescribed amount for a taxpayer's taxation year that includes October 31, 1994 is the amount, if any, by which

(a) the total of all amounts each of which is the taxpayer's profit from the disposition in the year, because of subsection 142.5(2) of the Act, of a property other than a capital property or an excluded property

exceeds the total of

(b) the total of all amounts each of which is the taxpayer's loss from the disposition in the year, because of subsection 142.5(2) of the Act, of a property other than a capital property or an excluded property, and

(c) the amount, if any, by which

(i) the total of all amounts each of which is the taxpayer's loss from the disposition in the year of a mark-to-market property (other than a capital property, an excluded property or a property disposed of because of subsection 142.5(2) of the Act)

exceeds

(ii) the total of all amounts each of which is the taxpayer's profit from the disposition in the year of a mark-to-market property (other than a capital property, an excluded property or a property disposed of because of subsection 142.5(2) of the Act).

**Technical Notes**: Subsection 142.5(4) of the Act contains a transition deduction in respect of the introduction of the requirement that certain property be marked to market for tax purposes. It permits a taxpayer to deduct an amount not exceeding a prescribed amount in its taxation year that includes October 31, 1994. Subsection 8102(2) prescribes the following maximum amount for this purpose:

• the taxpayer's total profits from the disposition of non-capital mark-to-market properties (other than excluded properties, as defined in subsection 8102(1)) that the mark-to-market rules deem the taxpayer to have disposed of in the year

**Reg. S. 8102(2)** — Income Tax Regulations

*minus*

- the taxpayer's total losses from the disposition of non-capital mark-to-market properties (other than excluded properties) that the mark-to-market rules deem the taxpayer to have disposed of in the year, and
- the taxpayer's net losses (i.e., losses minus profits) from actual dispositions in the year of non-capital mark-to-market properties (other than excluded properties) and from deemed dispositions of such properties otherwise than because of the mark-to-market rules.

**Definitions [Reg. 8102]**: "amount", "business" — ITA 248(1); "capital property" — ITA 54, 248(1); "disposed" — ITA 248(1)"disposition"; "disposition" — ITA 248(1); "excluded property" — Reg. 8102(1); "mark-to-market property" — ITA 142.2(1), Reg. 8102(1); "prescribed", "property" — ITA 248(1); "taxation year" — ITA 249; "taxpayer" — ITA 248(1).

### 8103. Mark-to-market — transition inclusion

**(1)** In this section, "transition deduction" of a taxpayer means the amount deducted under subsection 142.5(4) of the Act in computing the taxpayer's income for its taxation year that includes October 31, 1994.

**Technical Notes**: Section 8103 applies where a taxpayer has claimed a deduction under subsection 142.5(4) of the Act in respect of the introduction of the mark-to-market requirement. It prescribes the amount to be included in income each year under subsection 142.5(5) of the Act in respect of the deducted amount. Generally, the deducted amount is required to be included in income over a 5-year period. Section 8103 also contains rules for the income inclusion after certain corporate reorganizations have occurred or where a taxpayer ceases to carry on a business or to be a financial institution.

Subsection 8103(1) defines the "transition deduction" of a taxpayer to be the amount deducted under subsection 142.5(4) of the Act in computing the taxpayer's income for its taxation year that includes October 31, 1994.

Where a taxpayer has been formed by amalgamation, the continuity rule in paragraph 87(2)(g.2) of the Act ensures that any amount deducted by a predecessor corporation under subsection 142.5(4) of the Act is considered to have been deducted by the taxpayer. Therefore, the taxpayer's transition deduction is the sum of the transition deductions of its predecessors.

Similarly, the transition deduction of a taxpayer to which a business has been transferred in a transaction to which subsection 88(1) (winding-up), 138(11.5) (transfer of insurance business by a non-resident insurer) or 138(11.94) (transfer of insurance business by a resident insurer) of the Act applies will include the amount deducted by the transferor under subsection 142.5(4) in respect of the business. The relevant continuity rules are in paragraph 87(2)(g.2) (which applies to a winding-up by reason of paragraph 88(1)(e.2)) and paragraph 138(11.5)(k).

**(2)** Subject to subsections (3), (5) and (7), there is prescribed for the purpose of subsection 142.5(5) of the Act in respect of a taxpayer for a taxation year that ends after October 30, 1994 the amount determined by the formula

$$\frac{A}{1825} \times B$$

where

A is the number of days (other than February 29) in the year that are before the day that is 5 years after the first day of the taxation year of the taxpayer that includes October 31, 1994, and

B is the taxpayer's transition deduction minus the amount, if any, required by subsection (4) or paragraph (6)(b) to be subtracted.

**Technical Notes**: Subsection 8103(2) prescribes the amount to be included in income each year under subsection 142.5(5) of the Act by a taxpayer that has claimed a transition deduction under subsection 142.5(4). The first taxation year for which an amount is prescribed is the taxation year that includes October 31, 1994. The prescribed amount for a taxation year is given by the formula:

$$\frac{A}{1825} \times B$$

where

A = the number of days in the year that are not more than 5 years after the start of the taxpayer's taxation year that includes October 31, 1994 — February 29th is disregarded for this purpose, and

B = the taxpayer's transition deduction minus the amounts specified by subsection 8103(4) and paragraph 8103(6)(b).

Subsections 8103(3), (5) and (7) contain rules that override the determination of the prescribed amount under subsection 8103(2) when a taxpayer undergoes a reorganization, ceases to be a financial institution or ceases to carry on a business.

**(3)** Where subsection 88(1) of the Act has applied to the winding-up of a taxpayer (in this subsection referred to as the "subsidiary"),

(a) the value of A in subsection (2) shall be determined in respect of the subsidiary without including any days that are after the day on which the subsidiary's assets were distributed to its parent on the winding-up; and

(b) there is prescribed for the purpose of subsection 142.5(5) of the Act in respect of the parent for its taxation year that includes the day referred to in paragraph (a) the total of

(i) the amount that would be determined under subsection (2) in respect of the parent for the year if the parent's transition deduction did not include the subsidiary's transition deduction, and

(ii) the amount that would be determined under subsection (2) in respect of the parent for the year if

(A) the value of A in that subsection were determined without including the day referred to in paragraph (a) and any days before that day, and

(B) the value of B in that subsection were equal to the subsidiary's transition deduction.

**Technical Notes**: As noted in the commentary on subsection 8103(1), where a subsidiary is wound up into its parent corporation and subsection 88(1) of the Act applies to the winding-up, the parent will be considered to have deducted the amount deducted by the subsidiary under subsection 142.5(4) of the Act. Thus, this amount will be taken into account in determining the amounts prescribed by subsection 8103(2) in respect of the parent.

Subsection 8103(3) contains additional rules relating to the winding-up of a subsidiary. These rules ensure that no part of the subsidiary's transition deduction is required to be included in both the parent's and the subsidiary's income.

Paragraph 8103(3)(a) provides that the amounts prescribed by subsection 8103(1) for the subsidiary are to be determined ignoring any days after the day on which the subsidiary's assets are distributed to its parent. This rule is relevant only if the subsidiary has a taxation year that ends after the day on which the distribution occurs.

Paragraph 8103(3)(b) prescribes the amount to be included in the parent's income under subsection 142.5(5) of the Act for the taxation year in which it receives the subsidiary's assets. The prescribed amount is equal to the sum of

- the amount that would otherwise be prescribed by subsection 8103(2) if the parent's transition deduction did not include any amount in respect of the subsidiary's transition deduction, and

- the part of the subsidiary's transition deduction that must be recognized in respect of the days in the taxation year after the parent receives the subsidiary's assets.

**(4)** Where subsection 138(11.5) or (11.94) of the Act has applied to the transfer of an insurance business by an insurer, there shall be subtracted, in determining the value of B in subsection (2) in respect of the insurer for a taxation year that ends after the insurer ceased to carry on all or substantially all of the business, the part of the insurer's transition deduction that is included, because of paragraph 138(11.5)(k) of the Act, in the transition deduction of the person to whom the business was transferred.

**Technical Notes**: Subsection 8103(4) applies where an insurer has transferred an insurance business to another corporation on a rollover basis pursuant to subsection 138(11.5) or (11.94) of the Act. It provides that after the transfer of the business, the portion of the transferor's transition deduction that is considered a transition deduction of the transferee because of paragraph 138(11.5)(k) of the Act is to be disregarded in determining the amount prescribed by subsection 8103(2) in respect of the transferor. Paragraph 138(11.5)(k) contains a continuity rule for the portion of the transition amount that is reasonably attributable to the transferred business. Since paragraph 138(11.5)(h) of the Act deems the transferor and transferee to have taxation year ends immediately before the business is transferred, special rules are not required for the taxation year of transfer.

**Notes**: Revenue Canada's view is that "all or substantially all" means 90% or more.

**(5)** Where subsection 98(6) of the Act deems a partnership (in this subsection referred to as the "new partnership") to be a continuation of another partnership (in this subsection referred to as the "predecessor partnership"),

(a) the value of A in subsection (2) shall be determined in respect of the predecessor partnership without including any days that are after the day on which the predecessor partnership's property was transferred to the new partnership; and

(b) there is prescribed for the purpose of subsection 142.5(5) of the Act in respect of the new partnership for its taxation year that includes the day referred to in paragraph (a) the total of

(i) the amount that would be determined under subsection (2) in respect of the new partnership for the year if its transition deduction did not include the predecessor partnership's transition deduction, and

(ii) the amount that would be determined under subsection (2) in respect of the new partnership for the year if

(A) the value of A in that subsection were determined without including the day referred to in paragraph (a) and any days before that day, and

(B) the value of B in that subsection were equal to the predecessor partnership's transition deduction.

**Technical Notes**: Subsection 8103(5) contains rules that apply where a partnership ceases to exist and another partnership replaces it, in circumstances such that the continuity rule in subsection 98(6) of the Act applies. The rules are similar to those in subsection 8103(3) for the winding-up of a taxpayer into its parent corporation.

**(6)** Where a taxpayer ceases to carry on all or substantially all of a business, otherwise than as a result of a merger to which subsection 87(2) of the Act applies, a winding-up to which subsection 88(1) of the Act applies or a transfer of the business to which subsection 98(6) or 138(11.5) or (11.94) of the Act applies,

(a) there is prescribed for the purpose of subsection 142.5(5) of the Act in respect of the taxpayer for its taxation year in which the cessation of business occurs, in addition to the amount prescribed by subsection (2), the amount, if any, by which

(i) the part of the taxpayer's transition deduction that can reasonably be attributed to the business

exceeds

(ii) that part of the total of the amounts included under subsection 142.5(5) of the Act in computing the income of the taxpayer for

**Reg.**
**S. 8103(6)(a)(ii)**                                    Income Tax Regulations

preceding taxation years that can reasonably be considered to be in respect of the amount determined under subparagraph (i); and

(b) there shall be subtracted, in determining the value of B in subsection (2) in respect of the taxpayer for the year or a subsequent taxation year, the amount determined under subparagraph (a)(i).

**Technical Notes**: Subsection 8103(6) applies where a taxpayer ceases to carry on all or substantially all of a business otherwise than because of a merger, winding-up or transfer of the business to which the rollover rules in subsection 87(2), 88(1), 98(6) or 138(11.5) or (11.94) of the Act apply. In general terms, it accelerates the inclusion in income of the portion of the taxpayer's transition deduction that relates to the business.

Subsection 8103(6) prescribes an amount for inclusion, under subsection 142.5(5) of the Act, in the taxpayer's income for its taxation year in which it ceases to carry on the business. The prescribed amount, which is in addition to the amount prescribed for the year by subsection 8103(2), is equal to the portion of the taxpayer's transition deduction that is attributable to the business minus the amount of that portion that has already been included in the taxpayer's income. Subsection 8103(6) also provides that the portion of the taxpayer's transition deduction that is attributable to the business is to be disregarded in determining the amount prescribed by subsection 8103(2) in respect of the taxpayer for the taxation year in which it ceases to carry on the business and for subsequent taxation years.

**Notes**: Revenue Canada's view is that "all or substantially all" means 90% or more.

(7) Where a taxpayer ceases at any time to be a financial institution otherwise than because it ceases to carry on a business,

(a) there is prescribed for the purpose of subsection 142.5(5) of the Act in respect of the taxpayer for its taxation year that ended immediately before that time, the amount, if any, by which

(i) the taxpayer's transition deduction

exceeds

(ii) the total of the amounts included under subsection 142.5(5) of the Act in computing the taxpayer's income for preceding taxation years; and

(b) the amount prescribed for the purpose of subsection 142.5(5) of the Act in respect of the taxpayer for taxation years after the taxation year referred to in paragraph (a) is nil.

**Technical Notes**: Subsection 8103(7) applies where a taxpayer ceases to be a financial institution (as defined in subsection 142.2(1) of the Act) otherwise than because it has ceased to carry on a business. This subsection would apply, for example, where a taxpayer ceases to be a financial institution because of a change in control. Subsection 8103(7) requires the taxpayer to include the remaining amount of its transition deduction in income in the taxation year that ends immediately before it ceases to be a financial institution. (There will always be such a taxation year because of paragraph 142.6(1)(a) of the Act.)

**Definitions [Reg. 8103]**: "amount", "business", "insurer" — ITA 248(1); "partnership" — see Notes to ITA 96(1); "person", "prescribed", "property" — ITA 248(1); "subsidiary" — Reg. 8103(3); "taxation year" — ITA 249; "taxpayer" — ITA 248(1); "transition deduction" — Reg. 8103(1).

**8104. Mark-to-market — transition capital loss** — (1) In this section,

**"excluded property"** of a taxpayer means a mark-to-market property of the taxpayer for its taxation year that includes October 31, 1994 where

(a) the taxpayer had a taxable capital gain or an allowable capital loss for the year from the disposition of the property to which section 142 of the Act applied, or

(b) in the case of a taxpayer that was non-resident in the year, the property was a capital property other than a taxable Canadian property;

**Technical Notes**: Section 8104 prescribes the maximum amount that a taxpayer may claim under subsection 142.5(6) of the Act as an allowable capital loss in respect of the introduction of the mark-to-market requirement.

"Excluded property" of a taxpayer is certain mark-to-market property held by the taxpayer in its taxation year that includes October 31, 1994. This definition is relevant for a taxpayer that is a resident multinational life insurer or a non-resident insurer. In the case of a resident multinational life insurer, excluded property is capital property disposed of by the insurer in the year that was used by the insurer in a foreign insurance business. Excluded property of a non-resident insurer is capital property that is not taxable Canadian property (as defined in subsection 115(1) of the Act). Taxable capital gains and allowable capital losses from excluded property are disregarded in determining the insurer's income.

**"mark-to-market property"** has the meaning assigned by subsection 142.2(1) of the Act.

**Technical Notes**: "Mark-to-market property" of a taxpayer has the meaning given by subsection 142.2(1) of the Act. In general terms, it comprises most shares held by the taxpayer and debt obligations that are marked to market for financial statement purposes.

(2) For the purpose of subsection 142.5(6) of the Act, the prescribed amount for a taxpayer's taxation year that includes October 31, 1994 is the amount, if any, by which

(a) the total of all amounts each of which is the taxable capital gain of the taxpayer for the year from the disposition, because of subsection 142.5(2) of the Act, of a property other than an excluded property

exceeds the total of

(b) the total of all amounts each of which is the allowable capital loss of the taxpayer for the year from the disposition, because of subsection 142.5(2) of the Act, of a property other than an excluded property, and

2336

(c) the amount, if any, by which

(i) the total of all amounts each of which is the allowable capital loss of the taxpayer for the year from the disposition of a mark-to-market property (other than an excluded property or a property disposed of because of subsection 142.5(2) of the Act)

exceeds

(ii) the total of all amounts each of which is the taxable capital gain of the taxpayer for the year from the disposition of a mark-to-market property (other than an excluded property or a property disposed of because of subsection 142.5(2) of the Act).

**Technical Notes**: Subsection 142.5(6) of the Act contains a transition rule in respect of the introduction of the requirement that certain property be marked to market for tax purposes. It permits a taxpayer to claim, for its taxation year that includes October 31, 1994, an allowable capital loss not exceeding a prescribed amount. Subsection 8104(2) prescribes the following maximum amount for this purpose:

- the taxpayer's total taxable capital gains from the disposition of mark-to-market properties (other than excluded properties, as defined in subsection 8101(1)) that the mark-to-market rules deem the taxpayer to have disposed of in the year

*minus*

- the taxpayer's total allowable capital losses from the disposition of mark-to-market properties (other than excluded properties) that the mark-to-market rules deem the taxpayer to have disposed of in the year, and
- the taxpayer's net allowable capital losses (i.e., allowable capital losses minus taxable capital gains) from actual dispositions in the year of mark-to-market properties (other than excluded properties) and from deemed dispositions of such properties otherwise than because of the mark-to-market rules.

**Definitions [Reg. 8104]**: "allowable capital loss" — ITA 38(b), 248(1); "amount" — ITA 248(1); "capital property" — ITA 54, 248(1); "disposition" — ITA 248(1); "excluded property" — Reg. 8104(1); "mark-to-market property" — ITA 142.2(1), Reg. 8104(1); "non-resident", "prescribed", "property", "taxable Canadian property" — ITA 248(1); "taxable capital gain" — ITA 38(a), 248(1); "taxation year" — ITA 249; "taxpayer" — ITA 248(1).

## 8105. Mark-to-market — transition capital gains

— (1) In this section, "transition loss" of a taxpayer means the amount elected by the taxpayer under subsection 142.5(6) of the Act to be an allowable capital loss of the taxpayer for its taxation year that includes October 31, 1994.

**Technical Notes**: Section 8105 applies where a taxpayer has elected to claim an allowable capital loss under subsection 142.5(6) of the Act in respect of the introduction of the mark-to-market requirement. It prescribes the amount that is deemed by subsection 142.5(7) of the Act to be a taxable capital gain for each year. Generally, the prescribed amount for a year is a proportionate amount of the allowable capital loss that was claimed, based on a 5-year transition period.

Subsection 8105(1) defines the "transition loss" of a taxpayer to be the amount claimed by the taxpayer under subsection 142.5(6) of the Act as an allowable capital loss for the taxation year that includes October 31, 1994. The commentary on subsection 8103(1) regarding the effect of various restructurings on the "transition deduction" also applies to the transition loss.

(2) There is prescribed for the purpose of subsection 142.5(7) of the Act in respect of a taxpayer for a taxation year that ends after October 30, 1994 the amounts that would be prescribed in respect of the taxpayer for the year by section 8103 if the references in subsections 8103(2) to (7) to

(a) "subsection 142.5(5)" were read as "subsection 142.5(7)", and

(b) "transition deduction" were read as "transition loss (as defined in subsection 8105(1))".

**Technical Notes**: Subsection 8105(2) provides that prescribed amounts are determined using the rules in section 8103. For this purpose, the references in that section to "transition deduction" are replaced by "transition loss" and to "142.5(5)" are replaced by "142.5(7)". For information on section 8103, see the commentary on that provision.

**Definitions [Reg. 8105]**: "allowable capital loss" — ITA 38(b), 248(1); "amount", "prescribed" — ITA 248(1); "taxation year" — ITA 249; "taxpayer" — ITA 248(1); "transition loss" — Reg. 8105(1).

**Application**: The June 1, 1995 draft regulations (securities held by financial institutions), s. 8, will add ss. 8102 to 8105, applicable to taxation years that end after October 30, 1994.

# PART LXXXII — PRESCRIBED PROPERTIES AND PERMANENT ESTABLISHMENTS

**8200. Prescribed properties** — For the purposes of subsection 16.1(1) of the Act, "prescribed property" means

(a) exempt property, within the meaning assigned by paragraph 1100(1.13)(a), other than property leased on or before February 2, 1990 that is

(i) a truck or tractor that is designed for use on highways and has a "gross vehicle weight rating" (within the meaning assigned that expression by the *Motor Vehicle Safety Regulations*) of 11,778 kilograms or more,

(ii) a trailer that is designed for use on highways and is of a type designed to be hauled under normal operating conditions by a truck or tractor described in subparagraph (i), or

(iii) a railway car,

(b) property that is the subject of a lease where the tangible property, other than exempt property (within the meaning assigned by paragraph 1100(1.13)(a)), that was the subject of the lease had, at the time the lease was entered into, an aggregate fair market value not in excess of $25,000, and

(c) intangible property.

**Notes**: Reg. 8200 added by P.C. 1991-465, effective for leases entered into after 10:00 p.m. EDST, April 26, 1989, other than leases entered into pursuant to an agreement in writing entered into before that time under which the lessee thereunder has the right to require the lease of the property (and for these purposes a lease in respect of which a material change has been agreed to by the parties thereto effective at any particular time that is after 10:00 p.m. EDST, April 26, 1989 is deemed to have been entered into at that particular time).

**Definitions [Reg. 8200]**: "property" — ITA 248(1).

## 8200.1 [Prescribed energy conservation property]
— For the purposes of subsection 13(18.1) and subparagraph 241(4)(d)(vi.1) of the Act, prescribed energy conservation property means property described in Class 43.1 in Schedule II.

**Related Provisions**: ITA 13(18.1) — Dept. of Natural Resources "Technical Guide to Class 43.1" to be determinative.

**Notes**: Reg. 8200.1 added by P.C. 1997-1033, effective February 22, 1994.

**Definitions [Reg. 8200.1]**: "prescribed", "property" — ITA 248(1).

## 8201. Permanent establishments
— For the purposes of subsection 16.1(1), the definition "outstanding debts to specified non residents" in subsection 18(5), subsections 34.2(6), 112(2), 125.4(1) and 125.5(1), the definition "taxable supplier" in subsection 127(9), subsection 206(1.3) and paragraph 260(5)(a) of the Act, a "permanent establishment" of a person or partnership (referred to in this section as the "person") means a fixed place of business of the person, including an office, a branch, a mine, an oil well, a farm, a timberland, a factory, a workshop or a warehouse and, where the person does not have any fixed place of business, the principal place at which the person's business is conducted, and

### Proposed Amendment — Application to ITA 128.1(4)(b)(ii)

**Technical Notes to ITA 128.1(4), June 5, 2000 [Bill C-43, re migration]**: Second, the *Income Tax Regulations* will be amended after these amendments receive Royal Assent, so that the definition "permanent establishment" in Regulation 8201 will apply for the purpose of subparagraph 128.1(4)(b)(ii).

(a) where the person carries on business through an employee or agent, established in a particular place, who has general authority to contract for the person or who has a stock of merchandise owned by the person from which the employee or agent regularly fills orders, the person shall be deemed to have a permanent establishment at that place,

(b) where the person is an insurance corporation, the person is deemed to have a permanent establishment in each country in which the person is registered or licensed to do business,

(c) where the person uses substantial machinery or equipment at a particular place at any time in a taxation year, the person shall be deemed to have a permanent establishment at that place,

(d) the fact that the person has business dealings through a commission agent, broker or other independent agent or maintains an office solely for the purchase of merchandise shall not of itself be held to mean that the person has a permanent establishment, and

(e) where the person is a corporation, the fact that the person has a subsidiary controlled corporation at a place or a subsidiary controlled corporation engaged in trade or business at a place shall not of itself be held to mean that the person is operating a permanent establishment at that place,

except that, where the person is resident in a country with which the Government of Canada has concluded an agreement or convention for the avoidance of double taxation that has the force of law in Canada and in which the expression "permanent establishment" is given a particular meaning, that meaning shall apply.

### Proposed Amendment — Reg. 8201

**8201.** For the purposes of subsection 16.1(1), the definition "outstanding debts to specified non residents" in subsection 18(5), subsection 34.2(6), paragraph 95(2)(a.3), subsections 112(2), 125.4(1) and 125.5(1), the definition "taxable supplier" in subsection 127(9), subparagraph 128.1(4)(b)(ii), paragraphs 181.3(5)(a) and 190.14(2)(b), subsection 206(1.3), the definition "Canadian banking business" in subsection 248(1) and paragraph 260(5)(a) of the Act, a "permanent establishment" of a person or partnership (referred to in this section as the "person") means a fixed place of business of the person, including an office, a branch, a mine, an oil well, a farm, a timberland, a factory, a workshop or a warehouse and, where the person does not have any fixed place of business, the principal place at which the person's business is conducted, and

**Application**: The August 8, 2000 draft regulations, s. 6, will amend the opening words of s. 8201 to read as above, applicable after June 27, 1999.

**Notes**: Opening words of Reg. 8201 amended by P.C. 2000-183, to extend application to partnerships [effective the 1995 taxation year], to 18(5)"outstanding debts..." [effective the 1997 taxation year], 34.2(6) [effective 1995], 125.4(1) [effective the 1995 taxation year], 125.5(1) [effective taxation years that end after October 1997], 127(9)"taxable supplier" [effective taxation years that begin after 1995], and 206(1.3) [effective the 1995 taxation year, but see repealed Reg. 8201.1 for earlier years].

Reg. 8201 added by P.C. 1994-139, effective 10:00 p.m. EDST, April 26, 1989. The definition for purposes of ITA 112(2) was formerly in Reg. 400(2).

**Definitions [Reg. 8201]**: "business" — ITA 248(1); "Canada" — ITA 255, *Interpretation Act* 35(1); "corporation" — ITA 248(1), *Interpretation Act* 35(1); "employee", "insurance corporation", "office" — ITA 248(1); "partnership" — see Notes to ITA 96(1); "person" — ITA 248(1); "resident" — ITA 250; "subsidiary controlled corporation" — ITA 248(1); "taxation year" — ITA 249.

## 8201.1 [Repealed]

**Notes**: Reg. 8201.1 added and repealed by P.C. 2000-183, to be effective only from December 5, 1985 through the 1994 taxation year. (It is now superseded by the more general definition in Reg. 8201.) For the period if applied, read:

> 8201.1 For the purpose of subsection 206(1.3) of the Act, "permanent establishment" of a corporation means a fixed place of business of the corporation, including an office, a branch, a mine, an oil well, a farm, a timberland, a factory, a workshop or a warehouse and, where the corporation does not have any fixed place of business, the principal place at which the corporation's business is conducted, and
>
>> (a) where the corporation carries on business through an employee or agent, established in a particular place, who has general authority to contract for the corporation or who has a stock of merchandise owned by the corporation from which the employee or agent regularly fills orders, the corporation shall be deemed to have a permanent establishment at that place,
>>
>> (b) where the corporation is an insurance corporation, the corporation is deemed to have a permanent establishment in each country in which the corporation is registered or licensed to do business,
>>
>> (c) where the corporation uses substantial machinery or equipment at a particular place at any time in a taxation year, the corporation shall be deemed to have a permanent establishment at that place,
>>
>> (d) the fact that the corporation has business dealings through a commission agent, broker or other independent agent or maintains an office solely for the purchase of merchandise shall not of itself be held to mean that the corporation has a permanent establishment, and
>>
>> (e) the fact that the corporation has a subsidiary controlled corporation at a place or a subsidiary controlled corporation engaged in trade or business at a place shall not of itself be held to mean that the corporation is operating a permanent establishment at that place,
>
> except that, where the corporation is resident in a country with which the Government of Canada has concluded an agreement or convention for the avoidance of double taxation that has the force of law in Canada and in which the expression "permanent establishment" is given a particular meaning, that meaning shall apply.

**Definitions**: "business" — ITA 248(1); "Canada" — ITA 255, *Interpretation Act* 35(1); "corporation" — ITA 248(1), *Interpretation Act* 35(1); "employee", "insurance corporation", "office" — ITA 248(1); "resident" — ITA 250; "subsidiary controlled corporation" — ITA 248(1); "taxation year" — ITA 249.

# PART LXXXIII — PENSION ADJUSTMENTS, PAST SERVICE PENSION ADJUSTMENTS, PENSION ADJUSTMENT REVERSALS AND PRESCRIBED AMOUNTS

**8300. Interpretation** — (1) In this Part,

"**certifiable past service event**", with respect to an individual means a past service event that is required, by reason of subsection 147.1(10) of the Act, to be disregarded, in whole or in part, in determining the benefits to be paid under a registered pension plan with respect to the individual until a certification of the Minister in respect of the event has been obtained;

"**complete period of reduced services**" of an individual means a period of reduced services of the individual that is not part of a longer period of reduced services of the individual;

"**excluded contribution**" to a registered pension plan means an amount that is transferred to the plan in accordance with any of subsections 146(16), 147(19), 147.3(1) to (4) and 147.3(5) to (7) of the Act;

**Notes**: References to ITA 147.3 amended by P.C. 1995-17, retroactive to transfers in 1991 or later, so that a transfer under ITA 147.1(4.1) is not an excluded contribution.

In its application in respect of amounts paid to pension plans before 1991, read the definition as follows:

> "excluded contribution" to a registered pension plan means an amount paid to the plan that is
>
>> (a) transferred to the plan in accordance with any of subsections 146(16), 147(19) and 147.3(1) to (7) of the Act, or
>>
>> (b) deductible, as a consequence of the payment, under paragraph 60(j) or (j.1) of the Act in computing the income of a taxpayer for a taxation year.

"**flat benefit provision**" of a pension plan means a defined benefit provision of the plan under which the amount of lifetime retirement benefits provided to each member is based on the aggregate of all amounts each of which is the product of a fixed rate and either the duration of service of the member or the number of units of output of the member, and, for the purposes of this definition, where

(a) the amount of lifetime retirement benefits provided under a defined benefit provision to each member is subject to a limit based on the remuneration received by the member, and

(b) the limit may reasonably be considered to be included to ensure that the amount of lifetime retirement benefits provided to each member does not exceed the maximum amount of such benefits that may be provided by a registered pension plan,

the limit shall be disregarded for the purpose of determining whether the provision is a flat benefit provision;

"**member**", in relation to a deferred profit sharing plan or a benefit provision of a registered pension plan, means an individual who has a right (either immediate or in the future and either absolute or contingent) to receive benefits under the plan or the provision, as the case may be, other than an individual who has such a right only because of the participation of another individual in the plan or under the provision, as the case may be;

**Notes**: Definition "member" added by P.C. 1998-2256, effective 1990.

"**PA offset**" for a calendar year means

(a) for years before 1997, $1,000, and

Reg. S. 8300(1) PA     Income Tax Regulations

(b) for years after 1996, $600;

Notes: Definition "PA offset" added by P.C. 1998-2256, effective 1990.

"past service event" means any transaction, event or circumstance that occurs after 1989 and as a consequence of which

(a) retirement benefits become provided to an individual under a defined benefit provision of a pension plan in respect of a period before the time that the transaction, event or circumstance occurs,

(b) there is a change to the way in which retirement benefits provided to an individual under a defined benefit provision of a pension plan in respect of a period before the time that the transaction, event or circumstance occurs are determined, including a change that is applicable only in specified circumstances, or

(c) there is a change in the value of an indexing or other automatic adjustment that enters into the determination of the amount of an individual's retirement benefits under a defined benefit provision of a pension plan in respect of a period before the time that the value of the adjustment changes;

Related Provisions: Reg. 8300(2) — Definition applies to ITA 147.1(1).

"period of reduced services" of an individual means, in connection with a defined benefit or money purchase provision of a registered pension plan, a period that consists of one or more periods each of which is

(a) an eligible period of reduced pay or temporary absence of the individual with respect to an employer who participates under the provision, or

(b) a period of disability of the individual;

"refund benefit" means

(a) with respect to an individual and a money purchase or defined benefit provision of a pension plan, a return of contributions made by the individual under the provision, and

(b) with respect to an individual and a deferred profit sharing plan, a return of contributions made by the individual to the plan,

and includes any interest (computed at a rate not exceeding a reasonable rate) payable in respect of those contributions;

"resident compensation" of an individual from an employer for a calendar year means the amount that would be the individual's compensation from the employer for the year if the definition "compensation" in subsection 147.1(1) of the Act were read without reference to paragraphs (b) and (c) of that definition.

Notes: Definition "resident compensation" added by P.C. 1998-2256, effective 1990.

(2) The definition "past service event" in subsection (1) is applicable for the purposes of subsection 147.1(1) of the Act.

(3) All words and expressions used in this Part that are defined in sections 147 or 147.1 of the Act or in Part LXXXV have the meanings assigned in those provisions unless a definition in this Part is applicable.

(4) For the purposes of this Part, an officer who receives remuneration for holding an office shall, for any period that the officer holds the office, be deemed to render services to, and to be in the service of, the person from whom the officer receives the remuneration.

(5) For the purposes of this Part (other than the definition "member" in subsection (1)), where an individual has received an interest in an annuity contract in full or partial satisfaction of the individual's entitlement to benefits under a defined benefit provision of a pension plan, any rights of the individual under the contract are deemed to be rights under the defined benefit provision.

Notes: Reg. 8300(5) amended by P.C. 1998-2256, effective 1990, to add "(other than the definition "member" in subsection (1))".

(6) For the purposes of this Part and subsection 147.1(10) of the Act, and subject to subsection 8308(1), the following rules apply in respect of the determination of the benefits that are provided to an individual under a defined benefit provision of a pension plan at a particular time:

(a) where a term of the defined benefit provision, or an amendment to a term of the provision, is not applicable with respect to the individual before a specified date, the term shall be considered to have been added to the provision, or the amendment shall be considered to have been made to the term, on the specified date;

(b) where an alteration to the benefits provided to the individual is conditional on the requirements of subsection 147.1(10) of the Act being met, those requirements shall be assumed to have been met;

(c) benefits that will be reinstated if the individual returns to employment with an employer who participates in the plan shall be considered not to be provided until the individual returns to employment; and

(d) where benefits under the provision depend on the individual's job category or other circumstances, the only benefits provided to the individual are the benefits that are relevant to the individual's circumstances at the particular time.

(7) For the purposes of subsections 8301(3) and (8), paragraph 8302(3)(c), subsections 8302(5) and 8304(5) and (5.1), paragraphs 8304.1(10)(c) and (11)(c), subparagraph 8306(4)(a)(ii) and subsection 8308(3), the benefits to which an individual is enti-

tled at any time under a deferred profit sharing plan or pension plan include benefits to which the individual has only a contingent right because a condition for the vesting of the benefits has not been satisfied.

**Notes**: Reg. 8300(7) amended by P.C. 1998-2256, effective 1990, to add references to Reg. 8304(5.1), 8304.1, 8306 and 8308.

(8) For the purposes of this Part, such portion of an amount allocated to an individual at any time under a money purchase provision of a registered pension plan as

(a) is attributable to

(i) forfeited amounts under the provision or earnings of the plan that are reasonably attributable to those amounts,

(ii) a surplus under the provision, or

(iii) property transferred to the provision in respect of the actuarial surplus under a defined benefit provision of the plan or another registered pension plan, and

---

**Proposed Addition — Reg. 8300(8)(a)(iv)**

(iv) property transferred to the provision in respect of the surplus under another money purchase provision of the plan or under a money purchase provision of another registered pension plan, and

**Application**: The November 30, 1999 draft regulations (RPPs), s. 1, will add subpara. 8300(8)(a)(iv), applicable to allocations that occur after 1998.

**Technical Notes**: Subsection 8300(8) deems certain amounts allocated to an individual under a money purchase provision of a registered pension plan (RPP) to be employer contributions for the purpose of Part LXXXIII of the Regulations. The subsection applies where

- the allocation is attributable to forfeitures or surplus under the money purchase provision, or to surplus transferred from a defined benefit provision, and
- the allocation is in lieu of an employer contribution.

Subsection 8300(8) will generally not affect the calculation of pension credits. However, it is relevant for the application of subsections 8308(5) and (6) (retroactive contributions in respect of a period of reduced services) and subsection 8308(7) (loaned employee rules).

Subsection 8300(8) is amended so that it also applies with respect to allocations that are attributable to money purchase surplus transferred from another money purchase provision. This amendment is consequential on the introduction of new subsection 147.3(7.1) of the Act, which permits the transfer of surplus from one money purchase plan to another. It should be noted that this amendment is relevant only where money purchase surplus is allocated to an individual at the time of the transfer. Existing subparagraph 8300(8)(a)(ii) would apply with respect to allocations that occur after the time of the transfer.

---

(b) can reasonably be considered to be allocated in lieu of a contribution that would otherwise have been made under the provision by an employer in respect of the individual

shall be deemed to be a contribution made under the provision by the employer with respect to the individual at that time and not to be an amount attributable to anything referred to in paragraph (a).

**Notes**: Reg. 8300(8) added by P.C. 1995-17, effective for amounts allocated after April 5, 1994.

(9) For the purposes of this Part and Part LXXXV, where property held in connection with a particular benefit provision of a pension plan is made available at any time to pay benefits under another benefit provision of the plan, the property is deemed to be transferred at that time from the particular benefit provision to the other benefit provision.

**Notes**: Reg. 8300(9) added by P.C. 1998-2256, effective 1990.

(10) For the purposes of this Part and Parts LXXXIV and LXXXV, and subject to subsection (11), an individual is considered to have terminated from a deferred profit sharing plan or a benefit provision of a registered pension plan when the individual has ceased to be a member in relation to the plan or the provision, as the case may be.

**Notes**: Reg. 8300(10) added by P.C. 1998-2256, effective 1990.

(11) Where the benefits provided with respect to an individual under a particular defined benefit provision of a registered pension plan depend on benefits provided with respect to the individual under one or more other defined benefit provisions of registered pension plans (each of the particular provision and the other provisions being referred to in this subsection as a "related provision"), for the purposes of this Part and Parts LXXXIV and LXXXV,

(a) if the individual ceases, at any particular time after 1996, to be a member in relation to a specific related provision and is, at the particular time, a member in relation to another related provision, the individual is deemed

(i) not to terminate from the specific provision at the particular time, and

(ii) to terminate from the specific provision at the earliest subsequent time when the individual is no longer a member in relation to any of the related provisions;

(b) if the conditions in subsection 8304.1(14) (read without reference to the words "after 1996 and") are not satisfied with respect to the individual's termination from a related provision, the conditions in that subsection are deemed not to be satisfied with respect to the individual's termination from each of the other related provisions; and

(c) a specified distribution (as defined in subsection 8304.1(8)) made at any particular time in respect of the individual and a related provision is deemed, for the purpose of subsection 8304.1(5), also to be a specified distribution made at the particular time in respect of the individual and each of the other related provisions, except to the ex-

**Reg. S. 8300(11)(c)** — Income Tax Regulations

tent that the Minister has waived the application of this paragraph with respect to the distribution.

**Notes**: Reg. 8300(11) added by P.C. 1998-2256, effective 1990.

(12) For the purposes of this Part, where

(a) all or any part of the amounts payable to an individual under a deferred profit sharing plan are paid by a trustee under the plan to a licensed annuities provider to purchase for the individual an annuity described in subparagraph 147(2)(k)(vi) of the Act, or

(b) an individual has acquired, in full or partial satisfaction of the individual's entitlement to benefits under a benefit provision of a registered pension plan (other than benefits to which the individual was entitled only because of the participation of another individual under the provision), an interest in an annuity contract (other than as a consequence of a transfer of property from the provision to a registered retirement savings plan or a registered retirement income fund under which the individual is the annuitant),

the individual is deemed to continue, from the time of the payment or acquisition, as the case may be, until the individual's death, to be a member in relation to the plan or provision, as the case may be.

**Notes**: Reg. 8300(12) added by P.C. 1998-2256, effective 1990.

(13) For the purposes of this Part and Part LXXXV, where a benefit is to be provided, or may be provided, to an individual under a defined benefit provision of a registered pension plan as a consequence of an allocation that is to be made, or may be made, to the individual of all or part of an actuarial surplus under the provision, the individual is considered not to have any right to receive the benefit under the provision until the time at which the benefit becomes provided under the provision.

**Notes [Reg. 8300(13)]**: Reg. 8300(13) added by P.C. 1998-2256, effective 1990.

**Definitions [Reg. 8300]**: "amount", "annuity" — ITA 248(1); "contribution" — Reg. 8300(8), 8302(11), (12); "deferred profit sharing plan" — ITA 147(1), 248(1); "employer", "employment" — ITA 248(1); "flat benefit provision" — Reg. 8300(1); "individual" — ITA 248(1); "lifetime retirement benefits" — Reg. 8304(5)(c); "Minister", "office", "officer" — ITA 248(1); "offset provision" — Reg. 8300(11)(b); "past service event" — Reg. 8300(1), (2); "pension credit" — Reg. 8301, 8308.1(2)–(4), 8308.3(2), (3); "period of reduced services" — Reg. 8300(1); "person", "property", "registered pension plan" — ITA 248(1); "related" — ITA 251(2)–(6); "related provision" — Reg. 8300(12); "render services" — Reg. 8300(4).

## 8301. Pension adjustment — (1) Pension adjustment with respect to employer
— For the purpose of subsection 248(1) of the Act, "pension adjustment" of an individual for a calendar year with respect to an employer means, subject to paragraphs 8308(4)(d) and (5)(c), the total of all amounts each of which is

(a) the individual's pension credit for the year with respect to the employer under a deferred profit sharing plan or under a benefit provision of a registered pension plan;

(b) the individual's pension credit for the year with respect to the employer under a foreign plan, determined under section 8308.1; or

(c) the individual's pension credit for the year with respect to the employer under a specified retirement arrangement, determined under section 8308.3.

**Related Provisions**: Reg. 8301(2) — Pension credit — deferred profit sharing plan; Reg. 8301(3) — Non-vested termination from DPSP; Reg. 8301(4) — Pension credit — money purchase provision; Reg. 8500(8)(c) — Non-member benefits ignored in determining pension adjustment.

**Notes**: Reg. 8301(1)(b) and (c) added by P.C. 1996-911, effective for the determination of pension adjustments for 1992 and later years.

See also Notes to ITA 248(1) "pension adjustment".

**Interpretation Bulletins**: IT-124R6: Contributions to registered retirement savings plans; IT-307R3: Spousal registered retirement savings plans; IT-363R2: Deferred profit sharing plans — deductibility of employer contributions and taxation of amounts received by a beneficiary.

**Forms**: T4084: Pension adjustment guide.

**(2) Pension credit — deferred profit sharing plan** — For the purposes of subsection (1) and Part LXXXV and subsection 147(5.1) of the Act, and subject to subsections (3) and 8304(2), an individual's pension credit for a calendar year with respect to an employer under a deferred profit sharing plan is the aggregate of all amounts each of which is

(a) a contribution made to the plan in the year by the employer with respect to the individual, or

(b) such portion of an amount allocated in the year to the individual as is attributable to forfeited amounts under the plan and earnings of the plan in respect thereof, except to the extent that such portion is

(i) included in determining the individual's pension credit for the year with respect to any other employer who participates in the plan,

(ii) paid to the individual in the year, or

(iii) where the year is 1990, attributable to amounts forfeited before 1990 or earnings of the plan in respect thereof,

except that, where the year is before 1990, the individual's pension credit is nil.

**Related Provisions**: Reg. 8301(15) — Transferred amounts deemed not paid.

**Notes**: Before 1991, ignore the words "and subsection 147(5.1) of the Act" in Reg. 8301(2). See Notes to Reg. 8311.

**Interpretation Bulletins**: IT-124R6: Contributions to registered retirement savings plans; IT-363R2: Deferred profit sharing plans — deductibility of employer contributions and taxation of amounts received by a beneficiary.

**(3) Non-vested termination from DPSP** — For the purposes of subsection (1) and Part LXXXV and subsection 147(5.1) of the Act, where

(a) an individual ceased in a calendar year after 1989 and before 1997 to be employed by an employer who participated in a deferred profit sharing plan for the benefit of the individual,

(b) as a consequence of the termination of employment, the individual ceased in the year to have any rights to benefits (other than a right to a refund benefit) under the plan,

(c) the individual was not entitled to benefits under the plan at the end of the year, or was entitled only to a refund benefit, and

(d) no benefit has been paid under the plan with respect to the individual, other than a refund benefit,

the individual's pension credit under the plan for the year with respect to the employer is nil.

**Related Provisions**: Reg. 8300(7) — Benefits include contingent benefits.

**Notes**: Reg. 8301(3)(a) amended by P.C. 1998-2256, retroactive to 1990, to add "and before 1997".

Before 1991, ignore the words "and subsection 147(5.1) of the Act" in the opening words of Reg. 8301(3). See Notes to Reg. 8311.

**Interpretation Bulletins**: IT-124R6: Contributions to registered retirement savings plans.

**(4) Pension credit — money purchase provision** — For the purposes of subsection (1) and Part LXXXV and subsection 147.1(9) of the Act, and subject to subsections (4.1) and (8) and 8304(2), an individual's pension credit for a calendar year with respect to an employer under a money purchase provision of a registered pension plan is the total of all amounts each of which is

(a) a contribution (other than an additional voluntary contribution made by the individual in 1990, an excluded contribution or a contribution described in paragraph 8308(6)(e) or (g)) made under the provision in the year by

(i) the individual, except to the extent that the contribution was not made in connection with the individual's employment with the employer and is included in determining the individual's pension credit for the year with respect to any other employer who participates in the plan, or

(ii) the employer with respect to the individual, or

(b) such portion of an amount allocated in the year to the individual as is attributable to

(i) forfeited amounts under the provision or earnings of the plan in respect thereof,

(ii) a surplus under the provision, or

(ii.1) property transferred to the provision in respect of the actuarial surplus under a defined benefit provision of the plan or another registered pension plan,

> **Proposed Addition — Reg. 8301(4)(b)(ii.2)**
>
> (ii.2) property transferred to the provision in respect of the surplus under another money purchase provision of the plan or under a money purchase provision of another registered pension plan,
>
> **Application**: The November 30, 1999 draft regulations (RPPs), s. 2, will add subpara. 8301(4)(b)(ii.2), applicable to the determination of pension credits for 1999 et seq.
>
> **Technical Notes**: In general terms, subsection 8301(4) of the Regulations defines the pension credit of an individual for a year in respect of an employer under a money purchase provision of a pension plan to be the total of
>
> - contributions made in the year by the individual or by the employer with respect to the individual, and
>
> - amounts allocated to the individual in the year that are attributable to forfeited amounts, to surplus under the provision or to surplus transferred from a defined benefit provision.
>
> Paragraph 8301(4)(b) is amended to include in an individual's pension credit any amount allocated to the individual that is attributable to surplus transferred to the provision from another money purchase provision. This amendment is consequential to the introduction of subsection 147.3(7.1) of the Act, which permits the transfer of surplus from one money purchase plan to another. It should be noted that this amendment is relevant only where the money purchase surplus is allocated to an individual immediately upon being transferred. Where the allocation is made after the time of the transfer, existing subparagraph 8301(4)(b)(ii) would apply to include the allocated amount in the individual's pension credit.
>
> It should also be noted that, where such an allocation is in lieu of an employer contribution, amended subsection 8300(8) deems the allocated amount to be an employer contribution rather than an amount attributable to surplus. Thus, the amount is included in the individual's pension credit as an employer contribution, and not as an allocation of surplus.

except to the extent that that portion is

(iii) included in determining the individual's pension credit for the year with respect to any other employer who participates in the plan,

(iv) paid to the individual in the year, or

(v) where the year is 1990, attributable to amounts forfeited before 1990 or earnings of the plan in respect thereof,

except that the individual's pension credit is nil where the year is before 1990, and, for the purposes of this subsection, the plan administrator shall determine the portion of a contribution made by an individual or an amount allocated to the individual that is to be included in determining the individual's pension credit with respect to each employer.

**Related Provisions**: Reg. 8301(15) — Transferred amounts deemed not paid.

**Notes**: Opening words of Reg. 8301(4) and of Reg. 8301(4)(a) amended by P.C. 1995-17, this version effective for the determination of pension credits for 1993 and later years. For 1990-92, ignore the reference to Reg. 8301(4.1).

Reg. 8301(4)(b)(ii.1) added by P.C. 1995-17, effective for the determination of pension credits for 1991 and later years.

**Interpretation Bulletins**: IT-124R6: Contributions to registered retirement savings plans.

**Registered Plans Division Newsletters**: 91-4R (Registration rules for money purchase provisions).

**(4.1) Money purchase pension credits based on amounts allocated** — Where,

(a) under the terms of a money purchase provision of a pension plan, the method for allocating contributions is such that contributions made by an employer with respect to a particular individual may be allocated to another individual, and

(b) the Minister has, on the written application of the administrator of the plan, approved in writing a method for determining pension credits under the provision that, for each individual, takes into account amounts allocated to the individual,

each pension credit under the provision is the amount determined in accordance with the method approved by the Minister.

**Notes**: Reg. 8301(4.1) added by P.C. 1995-17, effective for the determination of pension credits for 1993 and later years.

**(5) Pension credit — defined benefit provision of a specified multi-employer plan** — For the purposes of this Part and Part LXXXV and subsection 147.1(9) of the Act, an individual's pension credit for a calendar year with respect to an employer under a defined benefit provision of a registered pension plan that is, in the year, a specified multi-employer plan is the aggregate of

(a) the aggregate of all amounts each of which is a contribution (other than an excluded contribution) made under the provision by the individual

(i) in the year, in respect of

(A) the year, or

(B) a plan year ending in the year (other than in respect of such portion of a plan year as is before 1990), or

(ii) in January of the year (other than in January 1990) in respect of the immediately preceding calendar year,

except to the extent that the contribution was not made in connection with the individual's employment with the employer and is included in determining the individual's pension credit for the year with respect to any other employer who participates in the plan,

(b) the aggregate of all amounts each of which is a contribution made in the year by the employer in respect of the provision, to the extent that the contribution may reasonably be considered to be determined by reference to the number of hours worked by the individual or some other measure that is specific to the individual, and

(c) the amount determined by the formula

$$\frac{A}{B} \times (C - B)$$

where

A is the amount determined under paragraph (b) for the purpose of computing the individual's pension credit,

B is the aggregate of all amounts each of which is the amount determined under paragraph (b) for the purpose of computing the pension credit of an individual for the year with respect to the employer under the provision, and

C is the aggregate of all amounts each of which is a contribution made in the year by the employer in respect of the provision,

except that, where the year is before 1990, the individual's pension credit is nil.

**Related Provisions**: ITA 257 — Negative amounts in formulas.

**(6) Pension credit — defined benefit provision** — Subject to subsections (7), (8) and (10) and sections 8304 and 8308, for the purposes of this Part and Part LXXXV and subsection 147.1(9) of the Act, an individual's pension credit for a calendar year with respect to an employer under a defined benefit provision of a particular registered pension plan (other than a plan that is, in the year, a specified multi-employer plan) is

(a) if the year is after 1989, the amount determined by the formula

$$A - B$$

where

A is 9 times the individual's benefit entitlement under the provision with respect to the employer and the year, and

B is the amount, if any, by which the PA offset for the year exceeds the total of all amounts each of which is the value of B determined under this paragraph for the purpose of computing the individual's pension credit for the year

(i) with respect to the employer under any other defined benefit provision of a registered pension plan,

(ii) with respect to any other employer who at any time in the year does not deal at arm's length with the employer, under a defined benefit provision of a registered pension plan, or

(iii) with respect to any other employer under a defined benefit provision of the particular plan; and

(b) if the year is before 1990, nil.

Part LXXXIII — Pension Adjustments/Prescribed Amounts    Reg. S. 8301(8)(e)

**Related Provisions**: ITA 257 — Negative amounts in formulas; Reg. 8302(1) — Benefit entitlement is portion attributable to employer.

**Notes**: Reg. 8301(6) amended by P.C. 1998-2256, retroactive to 1990, effectively to change $1,000 to "the PA offset", now defined in Reg. 8300(1). (It was also redrafted into formula format.)

**Interpretation Bulletins**: IT-124R6: Contributions to registered retirement savings plans.

**(7) Pension credit — defined benefit provision of a multi-employer plan** — Where a registered pension plan is a multi-employer plan (other than a specified multi-employer plan) in a calendar year, the following rules apply, except to the extent that the Minister has waived in writing their application in respect of the plan, for the purpose of determining the pension credit of an individual for the year under a defined benefit provision of the plan:

(a) where the individual is employed in the year by more than one participating employer, the pension credit of the individual for the year under the provision with respect to a particular employer shall be determined as if the individual were not employed by any other participating employer;

(b) the description of B in paragraph (6)(a) shall be read as

"B is the amount determined by the formula

$$(C \times D) - E$$

where

C is the PA offset for the year,

D is

(i) where the member rendered services on a full-time basis throughout the year to the employer, one, and

(ii) in any other case, the fraction (not greater than one) that measures the services that, for the purpose of determining the member's lifetime retirement benefits under the provision, the member is treated as having rendered in the year to the employer, expressed as a proportion of the services that would have been rendered by the member in the year to the employer if the member had rendered services to the employer on a full-time basis throughout the year, and

E is the total of all amounts each of which is the value of B determined under this paragraph for the purpose of computing the individual's pension credit for the year with respect to the employer under any other defined benefit provision of the plan; and";

(c) where a period in the year is a period of reduced services of the individual, the pension credit of the individual for the year under the provision with respect to each participating employer shall be determined as the aggregate of

(i) the pension credit that would be determined if no benefits (other than benefits attributable to services rendered by the individual) had accrued to the individual in respect of periods of reduced services, and

(ii) the pension credit that would be determined if the only benefits that had accrued to the individual were benefits in respect of periods of reduced services, other than benefits attributable to services rendered by the individual during such periods; and

(d) subsection (10) shall not apply.

**Related Provisions**: ITA 257 — Negative amounts in formulas.

**Notes**: Reg. 8301(7)(b) amended by P.C. 1998-2256, retroactive to 1990, effectively to change $1,000 to "the PA offset", now defined in Reg. 8300(1). (It was also redrafted.) See also Notes to Reg. 8301(6).

**(8) Non-vested termination from RPP** — For the purposes of this Part and Part LXXXV and subsection 147.1(9) of the Act, and subject to subsection (9), where

(a) an individual ceased in a calendar year after 1989 and before 1997 to be employed by an employer who participated in a registered pension plan for the benefit of the individual,

(b) as a consequence of the termination of employment, the individual ceased in the year to have any rights to benefits (other than a right to a refund benefit) under a money purchase or defined benefit provision of the plan,

(c) the individual was not entitled to benefits under the provision at the end of the year, or was entitled only to a refund benefit, and

(d) no benefit has been paid under the provision with respect to the individual, other than a refund benefit,

the individual's pension credit under the provision for the year with respect to the employer is

(e) where the provision is a money purchase provision, the total of all amounts each of which is a contribution (other than an additional voluntary contribution made by the individual in 1990, an excluded contribution or a contribution described in paragraph 8308(6)(e)) made under the provision in the year by the individual, except to the extent that the contribution was not made in connection with the individual's employment with the employer and is included in determining the individual's pension credit for the year with respect to any other employer who participates in the plan, and

(f) where the provision is a defined benefit provision, the lesser of

    (i) the pension credit that would be determined if this subsection were not applicable, and

    (ii) the aggregate of all amounts each of which is a contribution (other than an excluded contribution) made under the provision by the individual in, and in respect of, the year, except to the extent that the contribution was not made in connection with the individual's employment with the employer and is included in determining the individual's pension credit for the year with respect to any other employer who participates in the plan.

**Related Provisions**: Reg. 8300(7) — Benefits include contingent benefits.

**Notes**: Reg. 8301(8)(a) amended by P.C. 1998-2256, retroactive to 1990, to add "and before 1997".

Reg. 8301(8)(e) amended by P.C. 1995-17, effective for the determination of pension credits for 1990 and later years, to add reference to Reg. 8308(6)(e).

**Interpretation Bulletins**: IT-124R6: Contributions to registered retirement savings plans.

**(9) Multi-employer plans** — Subsection (8) is not applicable in respect of a registered pension plan that is a multi-employer plan in a calendar year except, where

    (a) the plan is not a specified multi-employer plan in the year;

    (b) if the plan contains a defined benefit provision, the Minister has waived in writing the application of paragraph (7)(b) in respect of the plan for the year; and

    (c) the Minister has approved in writing the application of subsection (8) in respect of the plan for the year.

**Interpretation Bulletins**: IT-124R6: Contributions to registered retirement savings plans.

**(10) Transition rule — money purchase offsets** — Where,

    (a) throughout the period beginning on January 1, 1981 and ending on December 31 of a particular calendar year after 1989 and before 2000, there has been subtracted, in determining the amount of lifetime retirement benefits under a defined benefit provision of a registered pension plan (other than a specified multi-employer plan), the amount of lifetime retirement benefits under a money purchase provision of the plan or of another registered pension plan,

    (b) lifetime retirement benefits under the defined benefit provision are determined, at the end of the particular year, in substantially the same manner as they were determined at the end of 1989, and

    (c) for each individual and each calendar year before 1990, the amount of employer contributions made under the money purchase provision for the year with respect to the individual did not exceed $3,500,

the pension credit of an individual for the particular year with respect to an employer under the defined benefit provision is equal to the amount, if any, by which

    (d) the amount that would, but for this subsection, be the individual's pension credit

exceeds

    (e) the lesser of

        (i) $2,500, and

        (ii) the amount determined by the formula

$$\frac{1}{10} \times [\, A - (B \times C) \,]$$

where

A is the balance in the individual's account under the money purchase provision at the end of 1989,

B is the aggregate of all amounts each of which is the duration (measured in years, including any fraction of a year) of a period ending before 1990 that is pensionable service of the individual under the defined benefit provision and that is not part of a longer period ending before 1990 that is pensionable service of the individual under the provision, and

C is the amount that would be the individual's pension credit for 1989 with respect to the employer under the defined benefit provision if subsection (6) were read without reference to the words "if the year is after 1989" in paragraph (6)(a) and without reference to paragraph (6)(b).

**Related Provisions**: ITA 257 — Negative amounts in formulas; Reg. 8301(7)(d) — Provisions inapplicable in determining pension credit in multi-employer plan.

**Notes**: Reg. 8301(10)(e)(ii)C amended by P.C. 1998-2256, retroactive to 1990, consequential on amendments to Reg. 8301(6).

**(11) Timing of contributions** — Subject to paragraph (12)(b), for the purposes of this Part, a contribution made by an employer in the first two months of a calendar year to a deferred profit sharing plan, in respect of a money purchase provision of a registered pension plan, or in respect of a defined benefit provision of a registered pension plan that was, in the immediately preceding calendar year, a specified multi-employer plan, shall be deemed to have been made by the employer at the end of the immediately preceding calendar year and not to have been made in the year, to the extent that the contribution can reasonably be considered to relate to a preceding calendar year.

**Notes**: Reg. 8301(11) was amended from its original draft version to apply to contributions that relate to any preceding calendar year (rather than just to those that relate to the immediately preceding year). This change ensures, for example, that a contribution made in January or February of 1992 that relates to a fiscal year starting in

1990 and ending in 1991 will be treated, for PA purposes, as though it were made entirely in 1991. Thus, it will be reflected entirely in the individual's 1991 PA.

**Information Circulars**: 98-2: Prescribed compensation for RPPs, para. 25.

**(12) Indirect contributions** — For the purposes of this Part and Part LXXXIV, where a trade union or association of employers (in this subsection and subsections (13) and (14) referred to as the "contributing entity") makes contributions to a registered pension plan,

(a) such portion of a payment made to the contributing entity by an employer or an individual as may reasonably be considered to relate to the plan (determined in accordance with subsection (13), where that subsection is applicable) shall be deemed to be a contribution made to the plan by the employer or individual, as the case may be, at the time the payment was made to the contributing entity; and

(b) subsection (11) shall not apply in respect of a contribution deemed by paragraph (a) to have been made to the plan.

**(13) Apportionment of payments** — For the purposes of subsection (12), where employers or individuals make payments in a calendar year to a contributing entity to enable the contributing entity to make contributions to a registered pension plan and the payments are not made solely for the purpose of being contributed to the plan, the contributing entity shall

(a) determine, in a manner that is reasonable in the circumstances, the portion of each payment that relates to the plan;

(b) make the determination in such a manner that all contributions made by the contributing entity to the plan, other than contributions made by the contributing entity as an employer or former employer of members of the plan, are considered to be funded by payments made to the contributing entity by employers or individuals;

(c) in the case of payments remitted to the contributing entity by an employer, notify the employer in writing, by January 31 of the immediately following calendar year, of the portion, or of the method for determining the portion, of each such payment that relates to the plan; and

(d) in the case of payments remitted to the contributing entity by an individual, notify the administrator of the plan in writing, by January 31 of the immediately following calendar year, of the total amount of payments made in the year by the individual that relate to the plan.

**(14) Non-compliance by contributing entity** — Where a contributing entity does not comply with the requirements of subsection (13) as they apply in respect of payments made to the contributing entity in a calendar year to enable the contributing entity to make contributions to a registered pension plan,

(a) the plan becomes, on February 1 of the immediately following calendar year, a revocable plan; and

(b) the Minister may make any determinations referred to in subsection (13) that the contributing entity failed to make, or failed to make in accordance with that subsection.

**Related Provisions**: Reg. 8301(12) — Meaning of contributing entity.

**(15) Transferred amounts** — For the purposes of subparagraphs (2)(b)(ii) and (4)(b)(iv), an amount transferred for the benefit of an individual from a registered pension plan or a deferred profit sharing plan directly to a registered pension plan, a registered retirement savings plan, a registered retirement income fund or a deferred profit sharing plan shall be deemed to be an amount that was not paid to the individual.

**Notes**: Reg. 8301(15) amended by P.C. 1995-17, effective for transfers after August 29, 1990, to add reference to transfers to RRIFs.

**(16) Subsequent events** — Except as otherwise expressly provided in this Part, each pension credit of an individual for a calendar year shall be determined without regard to transactions, events and circumstances that occur subsequent to the year.

**Definitions [Reg. 8301]**: "additional voluntary contribution", "amount" — ITA 248(1); "arm's length" — ITA 251(1); "benefits" — Reg. 8300(7); "contributing entity" — Reg. 8301(12); "contribution" — Reg. 8300(8), 8302(11), (12); "deferred profit sharing plan" — ITA 147(1), 248(1); "employed", "employer", "employment" — ITA 248(1); "excluded contribution" — Reg. 8300(1); "individual" — ITA 248(1); "lifetime retirement benefits" — Reg. 8304(5)(c); "Minister" — ITA 248(1); "month" — *Interpretation Act* 35(1); "PA offset" — Reg. 8300(1); "pension credit" — Reg. 8301(2)–(4), (5), (6), (8); "period of reduced services" — Reg. 8300(1); "property" — ITA 248(1); "refund benefit" — Reg. 8300(1); "registered pension plan" — ITA 248(1); "registered retirement income fund" — ITA 146.3(1), 248(1); "registered retirement savings plan" — ITA 146(1), 248(1); "specified multi-employer plan" — ITA 147.1(1), Reg. 8510(2), (3); "written" — *Interpretation Act* 35(1)"writing".

**8302. Benefit entitlement** — **(1)** For the purposes of subsection 8301(6), the benefit entitlement of an individual under a defined benefit provision of a registered pension plan in respect of a calendar year and an employer is the portion of the individual's benefit accrual under the provision in respect of the year that can reasonably be considered to be attributable to the individual's employment with the employer.

**Related Provisions**: Reg. 8302(2) — Meaning of benefit accrual.

**(2) Benefit accrual for year** — For the purposes of subsection (1), and subject to subsections (6), (8) and (9), the benefit accrual of an individual under a defined benefit provision of a registered pension

**Reg. S. 8302(2)**           Income Tax Regulations

plan in respect of a calendar year is the amount computed in accordance with the following rules:

   (a) determine the portion of the individual's normalized pension under the provision at the end of the year that can reasonably be considered to have accrued in respect of the year;

   (b) where the year is after 1989 and before 1995, determine the lesser of the amount determined under paragraph (a) and

      (i) for 1990, $1,277.78,

      (ii) for 1991 and 1992, $1,388.89,

      (iii) for 1993, $1,500.00, and

      (iv) for 1994, $1,611.11; and

   (c) where, in determining the amount of lifetime retirement benefits payable to the individual under the provision, there is deducted from the amount of those benefits that would otherwise be payable the amount of lifetime retirement benefits payable to the individual under a money purchase provision of a registered pension plan or the amount of a lifetime annuity payable to the individual under a deferred profit sharing plan, reduce the amount that would otherwise be determined under this subsection by $1/9$ of the total of all amounts each of which is the pension credit of the individual for the year under such a money purchase provision or deferred profit sharing plan.

**Related Provisions**: Reg. 8302(3) — Meaning of normalized pension.

**Notes**: Reg. 8302(2)(b) and (c) amended by P.C. 1995-17, effective 1992, to postpone the scheduled increase from 1991 by one year (see Notes to ITA 147.1(1)"money purchase limit").

**(3) Normalized pensions** — For the purposes of paragraph (2)(a), and subject to subsection (11), the normalized pension of an individual under a defined benefit provision of a registered pension plan at the end of a particular calendar year is the amount (expressed on an annualized basis) of lifetime retirement benefits that would be payable under the provision to the individual immediately after the end of the particular year if

   (a) where lifetime retirement benefits have not commenced to be paid under the provision to the individual before the end of the particular year, they commenced to be paid immediately after the end of the year;

   (b) where the individual had not attained 65 years of age before the time at which lifetime retirement benefits commenced to be paid (or are assumed by reason of paragraph (a) to have commenced to be paid) to the individual, the individual attained that age at that time;

   (c) all benefits to which the individual is entitled under the provision were fully vested;

   (d) where the amount of the individual's lifetime retirement benefits would otherwise be determined with a reduction computed by reference to the individual's age, duration of service or both, or with any other similar reduction, no such reduction were applied;

**Proposed Addition — Reg. 8302(3)(d.1), (d.2)**

   (d.1) no reduction in the amount of the individual's lifetime retirement benefits were applied in respect of benefits described in any of clauses 8503(2)(a)(vi)(A) to (C);

   (d.2) no adjustment that is permissible under subparagraph 8503(2)(a)(ix) were made to the amount of the individual's lifetime retirement benefits;

**Application**: The November 30, 2000 draft regulations (RPPs) (pre-published in *Canada Gazette*, Part I, December 9, 2000), s. 1, will add paras. 8302(3)(d.1) and (d.2), applicable to the determination of pension credits for 1990 et seq.

**Technical Notes, April 18, 2000**: Subsection 8302(3) of the *Income Tax Regulations* sets out rules for determining the normalized pension of an individual under a defined benefit provision of a pension plan. The normalized pension is used in determining the individual's pension credit under the provision. In general terms, an individual's normalized pension at the end of a year is the total lifetime retirement benefits accrued to the individual to the end of the year, determined on the basis of a number of assumptions.

Subsection 8302(3) is amended to add two new assumptions for the purposes of calculating the normalized pension of an individual. These new assumptions are consequential to certain amendments to paragraph 8503(2)(a), which provide additional exceptions to the requirement that lifetime retirement benefits be payable on an equal periodic basis.

New paragraph 8302(3)(d.1) provides that any reduction to lifetime retirement benefits that applies because a plan member is receiving benefits described in new subparagraph 8503(2)(a)(vi) be disregarded in computing normalized pensions. The types of benefits described in subparagraph 8503(2)(a)(vi) include public disability benefits, workers' compensation and accident, sickness or disability insurance benefits. Since most of these types of benefits cease by age 65, the assumption in paragraph 8302(3)(b) that the individual has attained age 65 means that new paragraph 8302(3)(d.1) will generally not have any effect.

New paragraph 8302(3)(d.2) requires that the normalized pension be determined without regard to any adjustment to lifetime retirement benefits that is permissible under new subparagraph 8503(2)(a)(ix). Subparagraph 8503(2)(a)(ix) allows the amount of lifetime retirement benefits payable to a member while the member is receiving remuneration from a participating employer to be less than the amount that would otherwise be payable if the member were not receiving the remuneration. The assumption in paragraph 8302(3)(d.2) ensures that an individual's normalized pension is determinable in such circumstances.

These amendments apply to the determination of pension credits for 1990 and subsequent years.

   (e) where the amount of the individual's lifetime retirement benefits depends on the remuneration

Part LXXXIII — Pension Adjustments/Prescribed Amounts   S. 8302(3)(j)(i)(A)

received by the individual in a calendar year (in this paragraph referred to as the "other year") other than the particular year, the remuneration received by the individual in the other year were determined in accordance with the following rules:

(i) where the individual was remunerated for both the particular year and the other year as a person who rendered services on a full-time basis throughout each of the years, the remuneration received by the individual in the other year is identical to the remuneration received by the individual in the particular year,

(ii) where subparagraph (i) is not applicable and the individual rendered services in the particular year, the remuneration received by the individual in the other year is the remuneration that the individual would have received in the other year (or a reasonable estimate thereof determined by a method acceptable to the Minister) had the individual's rate of remuneration in the other year been the same as the individual's rate of remuneration in the particular year, and

(iii) where subparagraph (i) is not applicable and the individual did not render services in the particular year, the remuneration received by the individual in the other year is the remuneration that the individual would have received in the other year (or a reasonable estimate thereof determined by a method acceptable to the Minister) had the individual's rate of remuneration in the other year been the amount that it is reasonable to consider would have been the individual's rate of remuneration in the particular year had the individual rendered services in the particular year;

(f) where the amount of the individual's lifetime retirement benefits depends on the individual's remuneration and all or a portion of the remuneration received by the individual in the particular year is treated under the provision as if it were remuneration received in a calendar year preceding the particular year for services rendered in that preceding year, that remuneration were remuneration for services rendered in the particular year;

(g) where the amount of the individual's lifetime retirement benefits depends on the individual's remuneration and the particular year is after 1989 and before 1995, benefits, to the extent that they can reasonably be considered to be in respect of the following range of annual remuneration, were excluded:

(i) where the particular year is 1990, the range from $63,889 to $86,111,

(ii) where the particular year is 1991 or 1992, the range from $69,444 to $86,111,

(iii) where the particular year is 1993, the range from $75,000 to $86,111, and

(iv) where the particular year is 1994, the range from $80,556 to $86,111;

(h) where

(i) the amount of the individual's lifetime retirement benefits depends on the individual's remuneration,

(ii) the formula for determining the amount of the individual's lifetime retirement benefits includes an adjustment to the individual's remuneration for one or more calendar years,

(iii) the adjustment to the individual's remuneration for a year (in this paragraph referred to as the "specified year") consists of multiplying the individual's remuneration for the specified year by a factor that does not exceed the ratio of the average wage for the year in which the amount of the individual's lifetime retirement benefits is required to be determined to the average wage for the specified year (or a substantially similar measure of the change in the wage measure), and

(iv) the adjustment may reasonably be considered to be made to increase the individual's remuneration for the specified year to reflect, in whole or in part, increases in average wages and salaries from that year to the year in which the amount of the individual's lifetime retirement benefits is required to be determined,

the formula did not include the adjustment to the individual's remuneration for the specified year;

(i) where the amount of the individual's lifetime retirement benefits depends on the Year's Maximum Pensionable Earnings for calendar years other than the particular year, the Year's Maximum Pensionable Earnings for each such year were equal to the Year's Maximum Pensionable Earnings for the particular year;

(j) where the amount of the individual's lifetime retirement benefits depends on the actual amount of pension (in this paragraph referred to as the "statutory pension") payable to the individual under the *Canada Pension Plan* or a provincial plan (as defined in section 3 of that Act), the amount of statutory pension (expressed on an annualized basis) were equal to

(i) 25 per cent of the lesser of the Year's Maximum Pensionable Earnings for the particular year and,

(A) in the case of an individual who renders services throughout the particular year on a full-time basis to employers who participate in the plan, the aggregate of all amounts each of which is the individual's remuneration for the particular year from such an employer, and

(B) in any other case, the amount that it is reasonable to consider would be determined under clause (A) if the individual had rendered services throughout the particular year on a full-time basis to employers who participate in the plan, or

(ii) at the option of the plan administrator, any other amount determined in accordance with a method for estimating the statutory pension that can be expected to result in amounts substantially similar to amounts determined under subparagraph (i);

(k) where the amount of the individual's lifetime retirement benefits depends on a pension (in this paragraph referred to as the "statutory pension") payable to the individual under Part I of the *Old Age Security Act*, the amount of statutory pension payable for each calendar year were equal to the aggregate of all amounts each of which is the the full monthly pension payable under Part I of the *Old Age Security Act* for a month in the particular year;

(l) except as otherwise expressly permitted in writing by the Minister, where the amount of the individual's lifetime retirement benefits depends on the amount of benefits (other than public pension benefits or similar benefits of a country other than Canada) payable under another benefit provision of a pension plan or under a deferred profit sharing plan, the amounts of the other benefits were such as to maximize the amount of the individual's lifetime retirement benefits;

(m) where the individual's lifetime retirement benefits would otherwise include benefits that the plan is required to provide by reason of a designated provision of the law of Canada or a province (within the meaning assigned by section 8513), or that the plan would be required to provide if each such provision were applicable to the plan with respect to all its members, such benefits were not included;

(n) where

(i) the individual attained 65 years of age before lifetime retirement benefits commenced to be paid (or are to be assumed by reason of paragraph (a) to have commenced to be paid) to the individual, and

(ii) an adjustment is made in determining the amount of those benefits for the purpose of offsetting, in whole or in part, the decrease in the value of lifetime retirement benefits that would otherwise result by reason of the deferral of those benefits after the individual attained 65 years of age,

that adjustment were not made, except to the extent that the adjustment exceeds the adjustment that would be made on an actuarially equivalent basis;

(o) except as otherwise provided by subsection (4), where the amount of the individual's lifetime retirement benefits depends on

(i) the form of benefits provided with respect to the individual under the provision (whether or not at the option of the individual), including

(A) the benefits to be provided after the death of the individual,

(B) the amount of retirement benefits, other than lifetime retirement benefits, provided to the individual, or

(C) the extent to which the lifetime retirement benefits will be adjusted to reflect changes in the cost of living, or

(ii) circumstances that are relevant in determining the form of benefits,

the form of benefits and the circumstances were such as to maximize the amount of the individual's lifetime retirement benefits on commencement of payment;

(p) where the amount of the individual's lifetime retirement benefits depends on whether the individual is totally and permanently disabled at the time at which retirement benefits commence to be paid to the individual, the individual were not so disabled at that time; and

(q) where lifetime retirement benefits have commenced to be paid under the provision to the individual before the end of the particular year, benefits payable as a consequence of cost-of-living adjustments described in paragraph 8303(5)(k) were disregarded.

**Related Provisions**: Reg. 8300(4) — Officer deemed to render services to employer; Reg. 8300(7) — Benefits include contingent benefits; Reg. 8302(5) — Benefit entitlement terminated — normalized pension calculations; Reg. 8503(2) — Permissible benefits; Reg. 8513 — Designate provision of the law of Canada or a province.

**Notes**: Reg. 8302(3)(g) amended by P.C. 1995-17, effective 1992, to postpone the scheduled increase from 1991 by one year (see Notes to ITA 147.1(1)"money purchase limit" and to Reg. 8302(2)).

For the Year's Maximum Pensionable Earnings for Reg. 8302(3)(i), see the table of CPP rates in the introductory pages.

**(4) Optional forms** — Where the terms of a defined benefit provision of a registered pension plan permit a member to elect to receive additional lifetime retirement benefits in lieu of benefits that would, in the absence of the election, be payable after the death of the member if the member dies after retirement benefits under the provision commence to be paid to the member, paragraph (3)(o) applies as if the following elections were not available to the member:

(a) an election to receive additional lifetime retirement benefits, not exceeding additional benefits determined on an actuarially equivalent basis, in lieu of all or any portion of a guarantee that retirement benefits will be paid for a minimum period of 10 years or less, and

(b) an election to receive additional lifetime retirement benefits in lieu of retirement benefits that would otherwise be payable to a spouse or former spouse (in this paragraph referred to as the "spouse") of the member for a period commencing after the death of the member and ending with the death of the spouse, where

(i) the election may be made only if the life expectancy of the spouse is significantly shorter than normal and has been so certified in writing by a medical doctor licensed to practise under the laws of a province of Canada or of the place where the spouse resides, and

(ii) the additional benefits do not exceed additional benefits determined on an actuarially equivalent basis and on the assumption that the spouse has a normal life expectancy.

**Notes**: References to "spouse" are expected to be amended to add "or common-law partner" effective 2001 or earlier by election, as has been done throughout the ITA. See Notes to ITA 248(1) "common-law partner".

**(5) Termination of entitlement to benefits** — For the purposes of subsection (3), where an individual ceased in a calendar year to be entitled to all or part of the lifetime retirement benefits provided to the individual under a defined benefit provision of a registered pension plan, the normalized pension of the individual under the provision at the end of the year shall be determined on the assumption that the individual continued to be entitled to those benefits immediately after the end of the year.

**Related Provisions**: Reg. 8300(7) — Benefits include contingent benefits.

**(6) Defined benefit offset** — Where the amount of lifetime retirement benefits provided under a particular defined benefit provision of a registered pension plan to a member of the plan depends on the amount of lifetime retirement benefits provided to the member under one or more other defined benefit provisions of registered pension plans, the benefit accrual of the member under the particular provision in respect of a calendar year is the amount, if any, by which

(a) the amount that would, but for this subsection, be the benefit accrual of the member under the particular provision in respect of the year if the benefits provided under the other provisions were provided under the particular provision

exceeds

(b) the amount that would be the benefit accrual of the member under the other provisions in respect of the year if the other provisions were a single provision.

**(7) Offset of specified multi-employer plan benefits** — Where the amount of an individual's lifetime retirement benefits under a defined benefit provision (in this subsection referred to as the "supplemental provision") of a registered pension plan depends on the amount of benefits payable under a defined benefit provision of a specified multi-employer plan, the defined benefit provision of the specified multi-employer plan shall be deemed to be a money purchase provision for the purpose of determining the benefit accruals of the individual under the supplemental provision.

**(8) Transition rule — career average benefits** — Where

(a) on March 27, 1988 lifetime retirement benefits under a defined benefit provision of a pension plan were determined as the greater of benefits computed on a career average basis and benefits computed on a final or best average earnings basis,

(b) the method for determining lifetime retirement benefits under the provision has not been amended after March 27, 1988 and before the end of a particular calendar year, and

(c) it was reasonable to expect, on January 1, 1990, that the lifetime retirement benefits to be paid under the provision to at least 75 per cent of the members of the plan on that date (other than members to whom benefits do not accrue under the provision after that date) will be determined on a final or best average earnings basis,

at the option of the plan administrator, benefit accruals under the provision in respect of the particular year may, where the particular year is before 1992, be determined without regard to the career average formula.

**(9) Transition rule — benefit rate greater than 2 per cent** — Subject to subsection (6), where

(a) the amount of lifetime retirement benefits provided under a defined benefit provision of a registered pension plan to a member of the plan is determined, in part, by multiplying the member's remuneration (or a function of the member's remuneration) by one or more benefit accrual rates, and

(b) the largest benefit accrual rate that may be applicable is greater than 2 per cent,

the member's benefit accrual under the provision in respect of 1990 or 1991 is the lesser of

(c) the member's benefit accrual otherwise determined, and

(d) 2 per cent of the aggregate of all amounts each of which is the amount that would, if the definition "compensation" in subsection 147.1(1) of the Act were read without reference to subparagraphs (a)(iii) and (iv) and paragraphs (b) and (c) thereof, be the member's compensation for the year from an employer who participated in the plan in the year for the benefit of the member.

Reg. S. 8302(9)  Income Tax Regulations

**Related Provisions**: Reg. 8302(10) — Period of reduced remuneration.

**(10) Period of reduced remuneration** — For the purposes of paragraph (9)(d), where a member of a registered pension plan is provided with benefits under a defined benefit provision of the plan in respect of a period in 1990 or 1991

(a) throughout which, by reason of disability, leave of absence, lay-off or other circumstance, the member rendered no services, or rendered a reduced level of services, to employers who participate in the plan, and

(b) throughout which the member received no remuneration, or a reduced rate of remuneration,

the member's compensation shall be determined on the assumption that the member received remuneration for the period equal to the amount of remuneration that it is reasonable to consider the member would have received if the member had rendered services throughout the period on a regular basis (having regard to the services rendered by the member before the period) and the member's rate of remuneration had been commensurate with the member's rate of remuneration when the member did render services on a regular basis.

**(11) Anti-avoidance** — Where the terms of a defined benefit provision of a registered pension plan can reasonably be considered to have been established or modified so that a pension credit of an individual for a calendar year under the provision would, but for this subsection, be reduced as a consequence of the application of paragraph (3)(g), that paragraph shall not apply in determining the individual's normalized pension under the provision in respect of the year.

**Definitions [Reg. 8302]**: "amount", "annuity" — ITA 248(1); "benefit accrual" — Reg. 8302(2); "benefit entitlement" — Reg. 8302(1); "benefits" — Reg. 8300(7); "Canada" — ITA 255, *Interpretation Act* 35(1); "commencement" — *Interpretation Act* 35(1); "contributing entity" — Reg. 8302(12); "deferred profit sharing plan" — ITA 147(1), 248(1); "designated provision of the law of Canada or a province" — Reg. 8513; "employer", "employment", "individual" — ITA 248(1); "lifetime retirement benefits" — Reg. 8304(5)(c); "member's compensation" — Reg. 8302(10); "Minister" — ITA 248(1); "month" — *Interpretation Act* 35(1); "normalized pension" — Reg. 8302(3), (5); "other year" — Reg. 8302(3)(e); "pension credit" — Reg. 8301, 8308.1(2)–(4), 8308.3(2), (3); "person" — ITA 248(1); "province" — *Interpretation Act* 35(1); "registered pension plan" — ITA 248(1); "render services" — Reg. 8300(4); "specified multi-employer plan" — ITA 147.1(1), Reg. 8510(2), (3); "specified year" — Reg. 8302(3)(h)(3); "spouse" — Reg. 8302(4)(b); "statutory pension" — Reg. 8302(3)(j), (k); "supplemental provision" — Reg. 8302(7); "writing" — *Interpretation Act* 35(1).

**8303. Past service pension adjustment — (1) PSPA with respect to employer** — For the purpose of subsection 248(1) of the Act, "past service pension adjustment" of an individual for a calendar year in respect of an employer means the total of

(a) the accumulated past service pension adjustment (in this Part referred to as "accumulated PSPA") of the individual for the year with respect to the employer, determined as of the end of the year,

(b) the total of all amounts each of which is the foreign plan PSPA (determined under subsection 8308.1(5) or (6)) of the individual with respect to the employer associated with a modification of benefits in the year under a foreign plan (as defined in subsection 8308.1(1)), and

(c) the total of all amounts each of which is the specified retirement arrangement PSPA (determined under subsection 8308.3(4) or (5)) of the individual with respect to the employer associated with a modification of benefits in the year under a specified retirement arrangement (as defined in subsection 8308.3(1)).

**Notes**: Reg. 8303(1)(b) and (c) added by P.C. 1996-911, effective for the determination of past service adjustments for 1993 and later years.

**Forms**: T4104: Past service pension adjustment guide.

**(2) Accumulated PSPA for year** — For the purposes of this Part, the accumulated PSPA of an individual for a calendar year with respect to an employer, determined as of any time, is the total of all amounts each of which is the individual's provisional past service pension adjustment (in this Part referred to as "provisional PSPA") with respect to the employer that is associated with

(a) a past service event (other than a certifiable past service event with respect to the individual) that occurred in the year and before that time; or

**Proposed Amendment — Reg. 8303(2)(a)**

(a) a past service event (other than a certifiable past service event with respect to the individual) that occurred in the preceding year; or

**Application**: The November 30, 2000 draft regulations (RPPs) (pre-published in *Canada Gazette*, Part I, December 9, 2000), subsec. 2(1), will amend para. 8303(2)(a) to read as above, applicable to past service events that occur after 2000.

**Regulatory Impact Analysis Statement**: When past service benefits are provided to an individual under a defined benefit registered pension plan (RPP), the individual's RRSP deduction room is reduced by the PSPA associated with those benefits. The PSPA rule in subsection 8303(2) is modified so that PSPAs that are exempt from certification (generally PSPAs that are associated with broad-based benefit improvements) will not reduce RRSP room until the year following the year of the past service event. Under the existing rule, exempt PSPAs reduce RRSP room in the current year.

**Technical Notes, April 18, 2000**: Section 8303 of the Regulations provides rules for determining the past service pension adjustment (PSPA) of an individual for a year. The most common situation in which a PSPA arises is where benefits are provided to an individual under a defined benefit provision of a registered pension plan (RPP) on a past service basis. The PSPA associated with those past service benefits reduces the individual's RRSP deduction room. The year in which a PSPA applies to reduce RRSP room depends on whether the PSPA is required to be certified by the Canada Customs and Revenue Agency (CCRA). PSPAs that are exempt from certification reduce RRSP room immediately, whereas certifiable PSPAs do not reduce RRSP room until such time as CCRA issues the certification (which could be later than the year of the past service event). Section 8306 provides that a PSPA is exempt from having to be certified if the past service benefit improvement applies to all or most members of the plan and certain other conditions are met.

The PSPA rules are modified so that exempt PSPAs do not reduce RRSP deduction room until the year following the year of the past service event. This change is being implemented by amending subsection 8303(2) so that exempt provisional PSPAs are not included in accumulated PSPA until the year following the year of the past service event. This amendment is intended, in particular, to ensure that an exempt PSPA does not affect the deductibility of RRSP contributions that were made before the occurrence of a past service event on the expectation that the contributions would be deductible.

This amendment applies to past service events that occur after 2000.

(b) a certifiable past service event with respect to the individual where the Minister has, in the year and before that time, issued a certification for the purposes of subsection 147.1(10) of the Act in respect of the event and the individual.

**Related Provisions**: Reg. 8303(2.1) — 1991 past service events and certifications.

**Notes**: Opening words of Reg. 8303(2) amended by P.C. 1998-2256, effective 1996, to remove its application to ITA 204.2(1.3).

**(2.1) 1991 past service events and certifications** — For the purposes of subsection (2),

(a) a past service event that occurred in 1991 (including, for greater certainty, a past service event that is deemed by paragraph 8304(3)(b) to have occurred immediately after the end of 1990) shall be deemed to have occurred on January 1, 1992 and not to have occurred in 1991; and

(b) a certification issued by the Minister in 1991 shall be deemed to have been issued on January 1, 1992 and not to have been issued in 1991.

**Notes**: Reg. 8303(2.1) added by P.C. 1995-17, effective 1991. Its effect is to make 1992 the first year for which PSPAs are reported; thus, RRSP deduction room is first reduced by PSPAs in 1992.

**(3) Provisional PSPA** — Subject to subsections (8) and (10) and sections 8304 and 8308, for the purposes of this Part, the provisional PSPA of an individual with respect to an employer that is associated with a past service event that occurs at a particular time in a particular calendar year is the amount determined by the formula

$$A - B - C + D$$

where

A is the aggregate of all amounts each of which is, in respect of a calendar year after 1989 and before the particular year, the amount that would have been the individual's pension credit for the year with respect to the employer under a defined benefit provision of a registered pension plan (other than a plan that is, at the particular time, a specified multi-employer plan) had the individual's benefit entitlement under the provision in respect of the year and the employer been equal to the individual's redetermined benefit entitlement (determined as of the particular time) under the provision in respect of the year and the employer,

B is the aggregate that would be determined for A if the reference in the description of A to "determined as of the particular time" were read as a reference to "determined as of the time immediately before the particular time",

C is such portion of the amount of the individual's qualifying transfers made in connection with the past service event as is not deducted in computing the provisional PSPA of the individual with respect to any other employer, and

D is the total of all amounts each of which is an excess money purchase transfer in relation to the individual and the past service event that is not included in determining any other provisional PSPA of the individual that is associated with the past service event.

**Related Provisions**: ITA 257 — Negative amounts in formulas; Reg. 8303(4) — Meaning of redetermined benefit entitlement; Reg. 8303(6) — Meaning of qualifying transfers; Reg. 8303(7.1) — Excess money purchase transfer amount; Reg. 8500(8)(c) — Non-member benefits ignored in determining pension adjustment.

**Notes**: Formula element D added by P.C. 1998-2256, effective for past service events that occur after 1997.

**Forms**: T1004: Application for certification of a provisional past service pension adjustment.

**(4) Redetermined benefit entitlement** — For the purposes of the description of A in subsection (3), an individual's redetermined benefit entitlement under a defined benefit provision of a registered pension plan in respect of a calendar year and an employer, determined as of a particular time, is the amount that would be determined under section 8302 to be the individual's benefit entitlement under the provision in respect of the year and the employer if, for the purpose of computing the benefit accrual of the individual in respect of the year under the provision and, where subsection 8302(6) is applicable, under any other defined benefit provision, the amount determined under paragraph 8302(2)(a) in respect of a specific provision were equal to such portion of the individual's normalized pension (computed in accordance with subsection (5)) under the specific provision at the particular time, determined with reference to the year, as may reasonably be considered to have accrued in respect of the year.

**(5) Normalized pension** — For the purposes of subsection (4), the normalized pension of an individual under a defined benefit provision of a registered pension plan at a particular time, determined with

Reg. S. 8303(5)

reference to a calendar year (in this subsection referred to as the "pension credit year"), is the amount (expressed on an annualized basis) of lifetime retirement benefits, other than excluded benefits, that would be payable to the individual under the provision immediately after the particular time if

(a) where lifetime retirement benefits have not commenced to be paid under the provision to the individual before the particular time, they commenced to be paid immediately after the particular time,

(b) where the individual had not attained 65 years of age before the time at which lifetime retirement benefits commenced to be paid (or are assumed by reason of paragraph (a) to have commenced to be paid) to the individual, the individual attained that age at that time,

(c) the amount of the individual's lifetime retirement benefits were determined with regard to all past service events occurring at or before the particular time and without regard to past service events occurring after the particular time,

(d) paragraphs 8302(3)(c) to (p) (other than paragraph 8302(3)(g), where subsection 8302(11) was applicable in respect of the pension credit year and the provision or would have been applicable had all benefits provided as a consequence of past service events become provided in the pension credit year) were applied for the purpose of determining the amount of the individual's lifetime retirement benefits and, for the purpose of those paragraphs, the pension credit year were the particular year referred to in those paragraphs, and

(e) where

(i) the amount of the individual's lifetime retirement benefits under the provision depends on the individual's remuneration, and

(ii) all or any part of the individual's lifetime retirement benefits in respect of the pension credit year became provided as a consequence of a past service event, pursuant to terms of the provision that enable benefits to be provided to members of the plan in respect of periods of employment with employers who have not participated under the provision,

the remuneration received by the individual from each such employer in respect of a period of employment in respect of which the individual is provided with benefits under the provision were remuneration received from an employer who has participated under the provision for the benefit of the individual,

and, for the purposes of this subsection, the following benefits are excluded benefits:

(f) where the formula for determining the amount of lifetime retirement benefits payable under the provision to the individual requires the calculation of an amount that is the product of a fixed rate and the duration of all or part of the individual's pensionable service, benefits payable as a direct consequence of an increase in the value of the fixed rate at any time (in this paragraph referred to as the "time of increase") after the pension credit year, other than benefits

(i) provided as a consequence of a second or subsequent increase in the value of the fixed rate after the time that retirement benefits under the provision commenced to be paid to the individual, or

(ii) that would not have become provided had the value of the fixed rate been increased to the amount determined by the formula

$$A \times \frac{B}{C}$$

where

A is the value of the fixed rate immediately before the time of the increase,

B is the average wage for the calendar year that includes the time of the increase, and

C is

(A) if the value of the fixed rate has previously been increased in the calendar year that includes the time of increase, the average wage for that year, or

(B) otherwise, the average wage for the year immediately preceding the calendar year that includes the time of increase,

(g) where

(i) the provision is a flat benefit provision,

(ii) at the particular time, the amount (expressed on an annual basis) of lifetime retirement benefits provided under the provision to each member in respect of pensionable service in each calendar year does not exceed 40 per cent of the defined benefit limit for the year that includes the particular time,

(iii) the conditions in subsection 8306(2) are satisfied in respect of the provision and the past service event in connection with which the normalized pension is being calculated, and

(iv) only one fixed rate is applicable in determining the amount of the individual's lifetime retirement benefits,

benefits provided as a direct consequence of an increase in the value of the fixed rate at any time (in this paragraph referred to as the "time of increase") after the pension credit year, other than benefits

(v) provided as a consequence of a second or subsequent increase in the value of the fixed rate after the time that retirement benefits under the provision commenced to be paid to the individual, or

(vi) that would not have become provided had the value of the fixed rate been increased to the greater of

(A) the greatest of all amounts each of which is an amount determined by the formula

$$A \times \frac{B}{C}$$

where

A is a value of the fixed rate in the period beginning on January 1, 1984 and ending immediately before the time of increase,

B is the average wage for the calendar year that includes the time of increase, and

C is the average wage for the later of 1984 and the calendar year in which the value of the fixed rate used for A was first effective, and

(B) the amount determined by the formula

$$D + (E \times F)$$

where

D is the value of the fixed rate immediately before the time of increase,

E is the amount by which the value of the fixed rate used for D would have to be increased to provide an increase in the individual's annual lifetime retirement benefits equal to $18 for each year of pensionable service, and

F is the duration (measured in years, including any fraction of a year) of the period beginning on the later of January 1, 1984 and the day on which the value of the fixed rate used for D was first effective and ending on the day that includes the time of increase;

(h) where the provision is a flat benefit provision, benefits provided as a direct consequence of an increase at any time (in this paragraph referred to as the "time of increase") after the pension credit year in the value of a fixed rate under the provision where

(i) the value of the fixed rate was increased pursuant to an agreement made before 1992, and

(ii) at the time the agreement was made, it was reasonable to expect that the percentage increase in the value of the fixed rate would approximate or be less than the percentage increase in the average wage from the calendar year in which the value of the fixed rate was last increased before the time of increase (or, if the increase is the first increase, the calendar year in which the initial value of the fixed rate was first applicable) to the calendar year that includes the time of increase,

(i) where the provision is a flat benefit provision under which the amount of each member's retirement benefits depends on the member's job category or rate of pay in such a manner that the ratio of the amount of lifetime retirement benefits to remuneration does not significantly increase as remuneration increases, benefits provided as a direct consequence of a change, after the pension credit year, in the individual's job category or rate of pay,

(j) where

(i) the individual's pensionable service under the provision ends before the particular time,

(ii) the individual's lifetime retirement benefits under the provision have been adjusted by a cost-of-living or similar adjustment in respect of the period (in this paragraph referred to as the "deferral period") beginning at the latest of

(A) the time at which the individual's pensionable service under the provision ends,

(B) if the amount of the individual's lifetime retirement benefits depends on the individual's remuneration, the end of the most recent period for which the individual received remuneration that is taken into account in determining the individual's lifetime retirement benefits,

(C) if the amount of the individual's lifetime retirement benefits depends on the individual's remuneration and the remuneration is adjusted as described in paragraph 8302(3)(h), the end of the period in respect of which the adjustment is made, and

(D) if the formula for determining the amount of the individual's lifetime retirement benefits requires the calculation of an amount that is the product of a fixed rate and the duration of all or part of the individual's pensionable service (or other measure of services rendered by the individual), the time as of which the value of the fixed rate applicable with respect to the individual was established,

and ending at the earlier of the particular time and the time, if any, at which lifetime retirement benefits commenced to be paid under the provision to the individual, and

(iii) the adjustment is warranted, having regard to all prior such adjustments, by the increase in the Consumer Price Index or in the wage measure from the commencement of the deferral period to the time the adjustment was made, benefits payable as a consequence of the adjustment,

(k) benefits payable as a consequence of a cost-of-living adjustment made after the time lifetime retirement benefits commenced to be paid under the provision to the individual, where the adjustment

(i) is warranted, having regard to all prior such adjustments, by the increase in the Consumer Price Index from that time to the time at which the adjustment was made, or

(ii) is a periodic adjustment described in subparagraph 8503(2)(a)(ii), and

(l) such portion of the individual's lifetime retirement benefits as

(i) would not otherwise be excluded in determining the individual's normalized pension,

(ii) may reasonably be considered to be attributable to cost-of-living adjustments or to adjustments made by reason of increases in a general measure of salaries and wages (other than increases in such a measure after the time at which lifetime retirement benefits commenced to be paid under the provision to the individual), and

(iii) is acceptable to the Minister.

**(6) Qualifying transfers** — For the purposes of subsections (3) and 8304(5) and (7), and subject to subsection (6.1), the amount of an individual's qualifying transfers made in connection with a past service event is the total of all amounts each of which is

### Proposed Amendment — Reg. 8303(6) opening words

**(6) Qualifying transfers** — For the purposes of subsections (3) and 8304(5) and (7), and subject to subsection (6.1) and paragraph 8304(2)(h), the amount of an individual's qualifying transfers made in connection with a past service event is the total of all amounts each of which is

**Application**: The November 30, 2000 draft regulations (RPPs) (pre-published in *Canada Gazette*, Part I, December 9, 2000), subsec. 2(2), will amend the opening words of para. 8303(6) to read as above, applicable to the determination of an individual's qualifying transfers that occur after April 18, 2000.

**Technical Notes, April 18, 2000**: Subsection 8303(6) of the Regulations defines, for the purposes of calculating provisional PSPAs under subsections 8303(3) and 8304(5), the amount of an individual's qualifying transfers made in connection with a past service event. It is defined to be the total of the amounts transferred to fund the past service benefits, where the amounts are

- transferred in accordance with subsections 146(16) (transfers from RRSPs), 147(19) (transfers from DPSPs), 147.3(2) (transfers from money purchase provisions of other RPPs), 147.3(3) (in the case of transfers from a specified multi-employer plan) and 147.3(5) and (7) (transfers from other registered plans on marriage breakdown or death) of the Act, or

- transferred from another benefit provision of the same plan, where the transfer would be in accordance with any of subsections 147.3(2), (5) and (7) of the Act if the two provisions were in separate RPPs.

The amount of the individual's qualifying transfers is applied to offset the provisional PSPA associated with the crediting of the past service benefits.

Subsection 8303(6) is amended so that it is subject to amended subsection 8304(2), which restricts the amount that may be counted as a qualifying transfer when money purchase benefits are replaced by defined benefits. For further details, refer to the commentary on subsection 8304(2).

This amendment applies to the determination of an individual's qualifying transfers that occur after [April 18, 2000].

(a) the portion of an amount transferred to a registered pension plan

(i) in accordance with any of subsections 146(16), 147(19) and 147.3(2), (5) and (7) of the Act, or

(ii) from a specified multi-employer plan in accordance with subsection 147.3(3) of the Act

that is transferred to fund benefits provided to the individual as a consequence of the past service event; or

(b) the amount of any property held in connection with a benefit provision of a registered pension plan that is made available to fund benefits provided to the individual under another benefit provision of the plan as a consequence of the past service event, where the transaction by which the property is made so available is such that, if the benefit provisions were in separate registered pension plans, the transaction would constitute a transfer of property from one plan to the other in accordance with any of subsections 147.3(2), (5) and (7) of the Act.

**Notes**: Reg. 8303(6)(b) added, and reference to (6.1) added to the opening words of Reg. 8303(6), by P.C. 1998-2256, effective

(a) for the determination of an individual's qualifying transfers that occur after June 25, 1998, and

(b) where approved by Revenue Canada, for the determination of qualifying transfers that occurred before June 26, 1998.

**(6.1) Exclusion for pre-1990 benefits** — The amount of an individual's qualifying transfers made in connection with a past service event shall be determined under subsection (6) without regard to the portion, if any, of amounts transferred or property made available, as the case may be, that can reasonably be considered to have been transferred or made available to fund benefits provided in respect of periods before 1990.

**Notes**: Reg. 8303(6.1) added by P.C. 1998-2256, effective for the determination of an individual's qualifying transfers that occur after June 25, 1998.

**(7) Deemed payment** — Where

(a) an individual has given an irrevocable direction that

(i) an amount be paid to a registered pension plan, or

(ii) property held in connection with a benefit provision of a registered pension plan be made available to fund benefits provided to the individual under another benefit provision of the plan

in the event that the Minister issues a certification for the purposes of subsection 147.1(10) of the Act with respect to the individual and to benefits provided under a defined benefit provision of the plan as a consequence of a past service event, and

(b) the amount is to be paid or the property is to be made available, as the case may be,

(i) where subparagraph (ii) does not apply, on or before the day that is 90 days after the day on which the certification is received by the administrator of the plan, and

(ii) where the plan was deemed by paragraph 147.1(3)(a) of the Act to be a registered pension plan at the time the direction was given, on or before the day that is 90 days after the later of

(A) the day on which the certification is received by the administrator of the plan, and

(B) the day on which the administrator of the plan receives written notice from the Minister of the registration of the plan for the purposes of the Act,

the amount or property, as the case may be, is deemed, for the purpose of subsection (6), to have been paid or made available, as the case may be, at the time the direction was given.

**Notes**: Reg. 8303(7) amended, effectively to add (a)(ii) and (b)(ii), by P.C. 1998-2256, effective on the same basis as the amendments to Reg. 8303(6).

**(7.1) Excess money purchase transfer** — Where lifetime retirement benefits have, as a consequence of a past service event, become provided to an individual under a defined benefit provision of a registered pension plan (other than a specified multi-employer plan) in respect of a period (in this subsection referred to as the "past service period") that

(a) was previously pensionable service of the individual under a particular defined benefit provision of a registered pension plan (other than a specified multi-employer plan),

(b) ceased to be pensionable service of the individual under the particular provision as a result of the payment of a single amount, all or part of which was transferred on behalf of the individual from the particular provision to a registered retirement savings plan, a registered retirement income fund, a money purchase provision of a registered pension plan or a defined benefit provision of a registered pension plan that was, at the time of the transfer, a specified multi-employer plan,

(c) has not, at any time after the payment of the single amount and before the past service event, been pensionable service of the individual under any defined benefit provision of a registered pension plan (other than a specified multi-employer plan), and

(d) is not, for the purpose of subsection 8304(5), a qualifying past service period in relation to the individual and the past service event,

the amount determined by the formula

$$A - B$$

is, for the purpose of the description of D in subsection (3), an excess money purchase transfer in relation to the individual and the past service event, where

A is the portion of the amount transferred, as described in paragraph (b), that can reasonably be considered to be attributable to benefits in respect of the portion of the past service period that is after 1989, and

B is the total of all amounts each of which is the portion of a pension credit, or the grossed-up amount of a provisional PSPA, of the individual that can reasonably be considered to be attributable to benefits previously provided under the particular provision in respect of the past service period.

**Related Provisions**: ITA 257 — Negative amounts in formulas; Reg. 8304.1(7) — Meaning of grossed-up amount of provisional PSPA.

**Notes**: Reg. 8303(7.1) added by P.C. 1998-2256, effective for past service events that occur after 1997.

**(8) Specified multi-employer plan** — Where, in a calendar year, an individual makes a contribution (other than an excluded contribution) in respect of a defined benefit provision of a registered pension plan that is, in the year, a specified multi-employer plan, and the contribution

(a) is made in respect of a period after 1989 and before the year, and

(b) is not included in determining the individual's pension credit for the year with respect to any employer under the provision,

the individual's provisional PSPA with respect to an employer who participates in the plan, associated with the payment of the contribution, is the portion of the contribution that is not included in the individual's provisional PSPA with respect to any other employer who participates in the plan, and, for the purpose of this subsection, the plan administrator shall determine the portion of the contribution to be included in the provisional PSPA of the individual with respect to each employer.

**Related Provisions**: Reg. 8303(9) — Contributions include conditional contributions.

**(9) Conditional contributions** — For the purpose of subsection (8), a contribution includes an amount paid to a registered pension plan where the right of any person to retain the amount on behalf of the plan is conditional on the Minister issuing a certification for the purposes of subsection 147.1(10) of the Act as it applies with respect to the individual and to benefits provided as a consequence of the payment.

**(10) Benefits in respect of foreign service** — Where as a consequence of a past service event, benefits become provided to an individual under a defined benefit provision of a registered pension plan in respect of a period throughout which the individual was employed outside Canada, and the Minister has consented in writing to the application of this subsection, each provisional PSPA of the individual associated with the past service event shall be determined on the assumption that no benefits were provided in respect of the period.

**Related Provisions**: Reg. 8503(3)(a)(vii) — Eligible service outside Canada.

**Registered Plan Division Newsletters**: 93-2 (Foreign Service Newsletter); 2000-1 (Foreign Service Newsletter Update).

**Definitions [Reg. 8303]**: "accumulated PSPA" — Reg. 8303(1)(a), 8303(2); "amount" — ITA 248(1); "associated" — ITA 256; "Canada" — ITA 255, *Interpretation Act* 35(1); "certifiable past service event" — Reg. 8300(1); "certification" — Reg. 8303(2.1)(b); "commencement" — *Interpretation Act* 35(1); "contribution" — Reg. 8303(9); "deferral period" — Reg. 8303(5)(j)(ii); "employed", "employer", "employment" — ITA 248(1); "excluded contribution", "flat benefit provision" — Reg. 8300(1); "grossed-up amount" — Reg. 8304(7); "individual" — ITA 248(1); "lifetime retirement benefits" — Reg. 8304(5)(c); "Minister" — ITA 248(1); "normalized pension" — Reg. 8303(5); "past service event" — Reg. 8300(1), 8303(2.1)(a); "past service pension adjustment" — ITA 248(1), Reg. 8303(1); "past service period" — Reg. 8303(7.1); "pension credit" — Reg. 8301, 8308.1(2)–(4), 8308.3(2), (3); "pension credit year" — Reg. 8303(5); "person", "property" — ITA 248(1); "provisional PSPA" — Reg. 8303(2), (3), 8308(4)(e); "qualifying transfers" — Reg. 8303(6); "redetermined benefit entitlement" — Reg. 8303(4); "registered pension plan" — ITA 248(1); "registered retirement income fund" — ITA 146.3(1), 248(1); "registered retirement savings plan" — ITA 146(1), 248(1); "specified multi-employer plan" — ITA 147.1(1), Reg. 8510(2), (3); "time of increase" — Reg. 8303(5)(g), (h); "written" — *Interpretation Act* 35(1)"writing".

**Interpretation Bulletins [Reg. 8303]**: IT-124R6: Contributions to registered retirement savings plans.

## 8304. Past service benefits — Additional rules — (1) Replacement of defined benefits — Where

(a) an individual ceased, at any time in a calendar year, to have any rights to benefits under a defined benefit provision of a registered pension plan (in this subsection referred to as the "former provision"),

(b) benefits became provided at that time to the individual under another defined benefit provision of a registered pension plan (in this subsection referred to as the "current provision") in lieu of the benefits under the former provision,

(c) the benefits that became provided at that time to the individual under the current provision in respect of the period in the year before that time are attributable to employment with the same employers as were the individual's benefits in respect of that period under the former provision,

(d) no amount was transferred in the year on behalf of the individual from the former provision to a registered retirement savings plan, a registered retirement income fund or a money purchase provision of a registered pension plan, and

(e) no benefits became provided under the former provision to the individual in the year and after that time,

each pension credit of the individual under the former provision for the year is nil.

**Notes**: Reg. 8304(1)(d) amended by P.C. 1995-17, effective for the determination of pension credits for 1990 and later years, to add reference to transfers to a RRIF.

**Interpretation Bulletins**: IT-124R6: Contributions to registered retirement savings plans; IT-528: Transfers of funds between registered plans.

**Forms**: T4104: Past service pension adjustment guide.

## (2) Replacement of money purchase benefits — Where

(a) an individual ceased, at any time in a calendar year, to have any rights to benefits under a money purchase provision of a registered pension plan or under a deferred profit sharing plan (in this subsection referred to as the "former provision"),

(b) benefits became provided at that time to the individual under a defined benefit provision of a registered pension plan (in this subsection referred to as the "current provision") in lieu of benefits under the former provision,

(c) the benefits that became provided at that time to the individual under the current provision in respect of the period in the year before that time are attributable to employment with the same employers who made contributions under the former provision in respect of that period on behalf of the individual,

(d) no amount was transferred in the year on behalf of the individual from the former provision to a registered retirement savings plan, a registered retirement income fund, a money purchase provision of a registered pension plan or a deferred profit sharing plan, and

(e) no contributions were made under the former provision by or on behalf of the individual, and no other amounts were allocated under the former provision to the individual, in the year and after that time,

each pension credit of the individual under the former provision for the year is nil.

### Proposed Addition — Reg. 8304(2)(f)–(h)

(f) it is reasonable to consider that no excess would, if this subsection did not apply and if the year ended at that time, be determined under any of paragraphs 147(5.1)(a) to (c), 147.1(8)(a) and (b) and (9)(a) and (b) of the Act with respect to the individual for the year,

the following rules apply:

(g) each pension credit of the individual under the former provision for the year is nil, and

(h) the amount, if any, of the individual's qualifying transfers made in connection with the replacement of the individual's benefits shall be determined under subsection 8303(6) without regard to the portion, if any, of amounts transferred from the former provision to the current provision that can reasonably be considered to relate to an amount that, but for paragraph (g), would have been included in determining the individual's pension credit under the former provision for the year.

**Application**: The November 30, 2000 draft regulations (RPPs) (pre-published in *Canada Gazette*, Part I, December 9, 2000), subsec. 3(3), will substitute paras. (f) to (h) for the closing words of subsec. 8304, applicable to the determination of pension credits for 2000 *et seq.* and to the determination of an individual's qualifying transfers that occur after April 18, 2000.

**Regulatory Impact Analysis Statement**: Subsection 8304(2) provides a special PA rule when money purchase benefits are replaced by defined benefits. This subsection is amended to add an anti-avoidance rule and to limit the amount of a transfer that may be counted as a qualifying transfer for purposes of calculating PSPAs.

**Technical Notes, April 18, 2000**: Subsection 8304(2) of the Regulations contains a special rule that applies when an individual's benefits under a money purchase provision of an RPP or under a DPSP (the "former provision") are replaced with benefits under a defined benefit provision of an RPP maintained by the same employer. The subsection provides that, if certain conditions are met, the individual's pension credit under the former provision for the year of replacement is nil.

Subsection 8304(2) is amended in two ways. First, it is amended to provide an anti-avoidance rule intended to ensure that the subsection does not apply to deem an individual's pension credit to be nil if the contributions (and other similar allocations) that would otherwise be included in the individual's pension credit under the former provision in the year of replacement are excessive. For this purpose, contributions made in the year of replacement will be considered excessive if it is reasonable to consider that they would have otherwise resulted in the DPSP contribution limits in subsection 147(5.1) or the pension adjustment limits in subsection 147.1(8) or (9) being violated. This amendment applies to the determination of pension credits for 2000 and subsequent years.

Second, subsection 8304(2) is amended to exclude from an individual's qualifying transfers (determined under subsection 8303(6)) any amounts transferred from the former provision to the current provision that can reasonably be considered to relate to contributions made by or on behalf of the individual (or other similar allocations) under the former provision in the year of replacement. Since these amounts are not included in determining a pension credit for the individual because of subsection 8304(2), it is not appropriate to allow them to offset the provisional PSPA associated with the replacement benefits. This amendment applies to the determination of an individual's qualifying transfers that occur after [April 18, 2000].

**Notes**: Reg. 8304(2)(d) amended by P.C. 1995-17, effective for the determination of pension credits for 1990 and later years, to add reference to transfers to a RRIF.

Reg. 8304(2)(e) amended by P.C. 1995-17, effective for the determination of pension credits for 1993 and later years. Formerly read:

(e) no contributions were made under the former provision in the year and after that time by, or on behalf of, the individual,

However, the amended Reg. 8304(2)(e) does not apply for determining an individual's pension credits for 1993 under a money purchase provision (MPP) of an RPP, or under a DPSP, where the individual ceased before April 6, 1994 to have any rights to any benefits under the MPP or DPSP, and no amounts were allocated to the individual under the MPP or DPSP after April 5, 1994.

**(3) Past service benefits in year of past service event** — Subject to subsection (4), where, as a consequence of a past service event that occurs at a particular time in a calendar year, benefits (in this subsection and subsection (4) referred to as "past service benefits") become provided to an individual under a defined benefit provision of a registered pension plan in respect of a period in the year and before the particular time that, immediately before the past service event, was not pensionable service of the individual under the provision, the following rules apply, except to the extent that the Minister has waived in writing their application in respect of the plan:

(a) each pension credit of the individual under the provision for the year shall be determined as if the past service benefits had not become provided to the individual;

(b) where the year is 1990, the past service event shall be deemed, for the purposes of this Part, to have occurred immediately after the end of the year;

(c) where the year is after 1990, each provisional PSPA of the individual associated with the past service event as a consequence of which the past service benefits became provided shall be determined as if the past service event had occurred immediately after the end of the year;

(d) where information that is required for the computation of a provisional PSPA referred to in paragraph (c) is not determinable until after the time at which the provisional PSPA is computed, reasonable assumptions shall be made in respect of such information; and

(e) subsection 147.1(10) of the Act shall apply in respect of the past service benefits to the extent that that subsection would apply if the past service event had occurred immediately after the end of the year.

**(4) Exceptions** — Subsection (3) does not apply where

(a) the past service benefits become provided in circumstances where subsection (1) or (2) is applicable; or

(b) the period in respect of which the past service benefits are provided was not, at any time before the past service event,

(i) pensionable service of the individual under a defined benefit provision of a registered pension plan, or

(ii) a period in respect of which a contribution was made on behalf of, or an amount (other than an amount in respect of earnings of a plan) was allocated to, the individual under a money purchase provision of a registered pension plan or under a deferred profit sharing plan.

(c) [Repealed]

**Notes:** Reg. 8304(4)(b)(ii) amended by P.C. 1995-17, effective for past service benefits that become provided after April 5, 1994. For earlier past service benefits, read:

(ii) a period in respect of which contributions were made on behalf of the individual to a money purchase provision of a registered pension plan or to a deferred profit sharing plan; or

Reg. 8304(4)(c) repealed, and the words "(in this subsection referred to as the "past service period")" deleted from para. (b) (after "provided"), by P.C. 1998-2256, effective with respect to past service events that occur after 1996. For earlier past service events, read:

(c) the past service period was previously pensionable service of the individual under the defined benefit provision under which the past service benefits are provided, and no amount was transferred in the year on behalf of the individual from the provision to a registered retirement savings plan, a registered retirement income fund or a money purchase provision of a registered pension plan.

Reg. 8304(4)(c) amended by P.C. 1995-17, effective for past service benefits that become provided after August 29, 1990, to add reference to transfers to a RRIF.

**(5) Modified PSPA calculation** — Where

(a) lifetime retirement benefits have, as a consequence of a past service event, become provided to an individual under a defined benefit provision of a registered pension plan in respect of one or more qualifying past service periods in relation to the individual and the past service event, and

(b) the benefits are considered to be attributable to employment of the individual with a single employer,

the provisional PSPA of the individual with respect to the employer that is associated with the past service event is the amount determined by the formula

$$A + B + C - D$$

where

A is the provisional PSPA that would be determined if

(a) this subsection did not apply,

(b) all former benefits in relation to the individual and the past service event had ceased to be provided at the time the past service event occurred,

(c) all former benefits in relation to the individual and the past service event were considered to be attributable to employment of the individual with the employer, and

(d) the value of C in subsection 8303(3) were nil;

B is the total of all amounts each of which is a non-vested PA amount in respect of the individual and the past service event;

C is the total of all amounts each of which is a money purchase transfer in relation to the individual and the past service event; and

D is the amount of the individual's qualifying transfers made in connection with the past service event.

**Related Provisions:** ITA 257 — Negative amounts in formulas; Reg. 8300(7) — Benefits include contingent benefits; Reg. 8303(6) — Meaning of qualifying transfers.

**Notes:** Reg. 8304(5) amended by P.C. 1998-2256, effective for the determination of provisional PSPAs that are associated with past service events that occur after 1997. Before the amendment, read:

(5) Where

(a) lifetime retirement benefits have, as a consequence of a past service event, become provided to an individual under a defined benefit provision (in this subsection referred to as the "current provision") of a registered pension plan in respect of a period (in this subsection referred to as the "past service period") that

(i) immediately before the past service event, was not pensionable service of the individual under the provision, and

(ii) is, or was, pensionable service of the individual under another defined benefit provision (in this subsection referred to as the "former provision") of a registered pension plan,

(b) either

(i) the individual has ceased to be entitled to benefits under the former provision,

(ii) the individual will cease to be entitled to benefits under the former provision when a certification of the Minister is issued for the purposes of subsection 147.1(10) of the Act in respect of benefits provided to the individual as a consequence of the past service event, or

(iii) all benefits to which the individual is entitled under the former provision will be paid within 90 days after a certification of the Minister is issued for the purposes of subsection 147.1(10) of the Act in respect of benefits provided to the individual as a consequence of the past service event,

(c) the lifetime retirement benefits are, for the purposes of this Part, considered to be attributable to employment of the individual with a single employer (in this subsection referred to as the "current employer"), and

(d) lifetime retirement benefits (in this subsection referred to as the "former benefits") to which the individual is or was entitled under the former provision in respect of the past service period have not been taken into account pursuant to this subsection in determining a provisional

PSPA of the individual that is associated with any other past service event,

the provisional PSPA of the individual in respect of the current employer that is associated with the past service event is the amount determined by the formula

$$A + B + C - D$$

where

A is the provisional PSPA that would be determined if

    (a) this subsection were not applicable,

    (b) the former benefits had ceased to be provided at the time the past service event occurred,

    (c) the former benefits were, for the purposes of this Part, considered to be attributable to employment of the individual with the current employer, and

    (d) the value for C in the formula in subsection 8303(3) were nil,

B is

    (a) where subsection 8301(8) has applied, or will apply, in respect of the determination of a pension credit of the individual under the former provision for a year that includes any part of the past service period, the aggregate of all amounts each of which is the amount, if any, by which

        (i) the amount that would be the individual's pension credit under the former provision for the year with respect to an employer if subsection 8301(8) were not applicable

    exceeds

        (ii) the individual's pension credit under the provision for the year with respect to the employer, and

    (b) otherwise, nil,

C is the total of all amounts each of which is an amount transferred on behalf of the individual from the former provision to a registered retirement savings plan, a registered retirement income fund, a money purchase provision of a registered pension plan or a defined benefit provision of a registered pension plan that was, at the time of the transfer, a specified multi-employer plan, to the extent that the amount may reasonably be considered to be the payment of a benefit in respect of such part of the past service period as is after 1989, and

D is the amount of the individual's qualifying transfers made in connection with the past service event, as determined pursuant to subsection 8303(6).

Description of C amended by P.C. 1995-17, effective for past service events occurring after August 29, 1990, to add reference to transfers to a RRIF.

**(5.1) Definitions for subsection (5)** — For the purpose of subsection (5), where

(a) lifetime retirement benefits (in this subsection referred to as "past service benefits") have, as a consequence of a past service event occurring at a particular time, become provided to an individual under a defined benefit provision of a registered pension plan in respect of a period that

    (i) immediately before the particular time, was not pensionable service of the individual under the provision, and

    (ii) is, or was, pensionable service of the individual under another defined benefit provision (in this subsection referred to as the "former provision") of a registered pension plan,

(b) either

    (i) the individual has not, at any time after 1996 and before the particular time, been a member in relation to the former provision,

    (ii) the individual ceased, at the particular time, to be a member in relation to the former provision, or

    (iii) the past service event is a certifiable past service event and the individual is to cease being a member in relation to the former provision no later than 90 days after the day on which a certification of the Minister is issued for the purposes of subsection 147.1(10) of the Act in respect of the past service benefits, and

(c) lifetime retirement benefits to which the individual is or was entitled under the former provision in respect of the period have not been taken into account under subsection (5) as former benefits in determining a provisional PSPA of the individual that is associated with any other past service event,

the following rules apply:

(d) the period is a qualifying past service period in relation to the individual and the past service event,

(e) lifetime retirement benefits to which the individual is or was entitled under the former provision in respect of the period are former benefits in relation to the individual and the past service event,

(f) where subsection 8301(8) has applied in respect of the determination of a pension credit of the individual under the former provision with respect to an employer for a year that includes any part of the period, the amount determined by the formula

$$A - B$$

is a non-vested PA amount in respect of the individual and the past service event, where

A is the amount that would have been the individual's pension credit under the former provision for the year with respect to the employer if subsection 8301(8) had not applied, and

B is the individual's pension credit under the former provision for the year with respect to the employer, and

(g) the amount determined by the formula

$$A - B$$

is a money purchase transfer in relation to the individual and the past service event, where

**Reg. S. 8304(5.1)(g)**     Income Tax Regulations

A is the total of all amounts each of which is

   (i) an amount that was transferred, at or before the particular time, on behalf of the individual from the former provision to a registered retirement savings plan, a registered retirement income fund, a money purchase provision of a registered pension plan or a defined benefit provision of a registered pension plan that was, at the time of the transfer, a specified multi-employer plan, or

   (ii) an amount that is to be paid or otherwise made available under the former provision with respect to the individual after the particular time, other than an amount that is to be transferred to fund the past service benefits or paid directly to the individual,

to the extent that the amount can reasonably be considered to be attributable to benefits in respect of the portion of the period that is after 1989, and

B is the total of all amounts each of which is, in respect of an employer with respect to which a provisional PSPA of the individual that is associated with the past service event is determined under subsection (5), the amount, if any, by which

   (i) the portion of the value determined for B in subsection 8303(3), for the purpose of determining the individual's provisional PSPA with respect to the employer, that can reasonably be considered to be attributable to benefits provided in respect of the period

exceeds

   (ii) the portion of the value determined for A in subsection 8303(3), for the purpose of determining the individual's provisional PSPA with respect to the employer, that can reasonably be considered to be attributable to benefits provided in respect of the period.

**Related Provisions**: ITA 257 — Negative amounts in formulas; Reg. 8300(7) — Benefits include contingent benefits.

**Notes**: Reg. 8304(5.1) added by P.C. 1998-2256, effective for the determination of provisional PSPAs that are associated with past service events that occur after 1997.

**(6) Reinstatement of pre-1997 benefits** — Where lifetime retirement benefits have, as a consequence of a past service event, become provided to an individual under a defined benefit provision of a registered pension plan in respect of a period that

   (a) was previously pensionable service of the individual under the provision,

   (b) ceased to be pensionable service of the individual under the provision as a consequence of the individual ceasing before 1997 to be a member in relation to the provision, and

   (c) has not, at any time after 1996 and before the past service event, been pensionable service of the individual under a defined benefit provision of a registered pension plan,

each provisional PSPA of the individual that is associated with the past service event shall be determined as if all benefits provided to the individual under the provision before 1997 in respect of the period had been provided to the individual under another defined benefit provision of a registered pension plan in relation to which the individual has not, at any time after 1996, been a member.

**Notes**: Reg. 8304(6) amended by P.C. 1998-2256, effective for the determination of provisional PSPAs that are associated with past service events that occur after 1997. Before the amendment, read:

   **(6) Reinstatement of benefits** — Where lifetime retirement benefits have, as a consequence of a past service event, become provided to an individual under a defined benefit provision of a registered pension plan in respect of a period that

      (a) immediately before the past service event, was not pensionable service of the individual under the provision, and

      (b) was previously pensionable service of the individual under the provision,

   the following rules apply for the purpose of determining each provisional PSPA of the individual that is associated with the past service event:

      (c) each provisional PSPA shall be determined as if the lifetime retirement benefits had become provided under another defined benefit provision of a registered pension plan, and

      (d) subsection (5) shall be read without reference to paragraph (b) thereof.

**(7) Two or more employers** — Where

   (a) lifetime retirement benefits (in this subsection referred to as "past service benefits") provided to an individual under a defined benefit provision of a registered pension plan as a consequence of a past service event are attributable to employment of the individual with two or more employers (each of which is, in this subsection, referred to as a "current employer"), and

   (b) subsection (5) would, but for paragraph (5)(b), apply in respect of the determination of each provisional PSPA of the individual that is associated with the past service event,

each such provisional PSPA shall be determined in accordance with the formula set out in subsection (5), except that

   (c) in determining the amount A,

      (i) the former benefits of the individual shall be considered to be attributable to employment of the individual with the individual's current employers, and

      (ii) the portion of the former benefits attributable to employment with each current employer shall be determined by the administra-

Part LXXXIII — Pension Adjustments/Prescribed Amounts     Reg. S. 8304.1(3)(a)

tor of the pension plan under which the past service benefits are provided in a manner that is consistent with the association of the past service benefits with each current employer,

(d) the amounts B and C shall be included in computing only one provisional PSPA of the individual, as determined by the administrator of the pension plan under which the past service benefits are provided, and

(e) the amount D that is deducted in computing the individual's provisional PSPA with respect to a particular employer shall equal such portion of the individual's qualifying transfers made in connection with the past service event as is not deducted in computing the provisional PSPA of the individual with respect to any other employer.

**Related Provisions**: Reg. 8303(6) — Meaning of qualifying transfers.

**Notes**: Reg. 8304(7)(b) amended by P.C. 1998-2256, effective for the determination of provisional PSPAs that are associated with past service events that occur after 1997, to change "but for the condition in paragraph (5)(c)" to "but for paragraph (5)(b)".

**(8) [Repealed]**

**Notes**: Reg. 8304(8) repealed by P.C. 1998-2256, effective for the determination of provisional PSPAs associated with past service events that occur after 1997. From 1990 until its repeal, read:

(8) Additional rules re calculation of PSPA — The following rules apply for the purposes of subsection (5) as it applies in respect of the determination of a provisional PSPA of an individual that is associated with a past service event:

(a) where the individual is entitled to benefits under the former provision at the time at which application is made for a certification of the Minister for the purposes of subsection 147.1(10) of the Act as it applies in respect of benefits provided to the individual as a consequence of the past service event, the amount C in the formula set out in subsection (5) shall be determined on the assumption that all amounts that will be paid under the former provision with respect to the individual after the certification is issued, other than any amount that will be transferred to fund benefits provided as a consequence of the past service event, have been transferred on behalf of the individual to a registered retirement savings plan;

(b) where an amount is credited to the individual under a money purchase provision of a registered pension plan in lieu of benefits to which the individual was entitled under a defined benefit provision of the plan, the amount shall be considered to be the payment of a benefit that was transferred from the defined benefit provision to the money purchase provision;

(c) the amount B in the formula set out in subsection (5) shall be determined on the assumption that no benefits will accrue to the individual under the former provision after the time at which the determination is made; and

(d) where lifetime retirement benefits have, as a consequence of the past service event, become provided to the individual in respect of two or more separate periods, the periods shall be considered to be a single period.

**(9) Specified multi-employer plans** — Except in subparagraph (4)(b)(i), a reference in this section to a defined benefit provision of a registered pension plan at any time does not, unless expressly provided,

include a defined benefit provision of a plan that is, at that time, a specified multi-employer plan.

**Definitions [Reg. 8304]**: "amount" — ITA 248(1); "associated" — ITA 256; "benefits" — Reg. 8300(7); "certifiable past service event" — Reg. 8300(1); "contribution" — Reg. 8300(8), 8302(11), (12); "current employer" — Reg. 8304(5)(c), (7)(a); "current provision" — Reg. 8304(1)(b), (2)(b), (5)(a); "deferred profit sharing plan" — ITA 147(1), 248(1); "defined benefit provision" — Reg. 8304(9); "employer", "employment" — ITA 248(1); "former benefits" — Reg. 8304(5)(d), (5.1)(e); "former provision" — Reg. 8304(1)(a), (2)(a), (5)(a)(ii), (5.1)(a)(ii); "individual" — ITA 248(1); "lifetime retirement benefits" — Reg. 8304(5)(c), (5.1)(a); "Minister" — ITA 248(1); "past service benefits" — Reg. 8304(3), (5.1)(a), (7)(a); "past service event" — Reg. 8300(1); "pension credit" — Reg. 8301, 8308.1(2)–(4), 8308.3(2), (3); "provision" — Reg. 8300(12)(c); "provisional PSPA" — Reg. 8303(2), (3), 8308(4)(e); "qualifying transfers" — Reg. 8303(6); "registered pension plan" — ITA 248(1); "registered retirement income fund" — ITA 146.3(1), 248(1); "registered retirement savings plan" — ITA 146(1), 248(1); "specified multi-employer plan" — ITA 147.1(1), Reg. 8510(2), (3); "writing" — *Interpretation Act* 35(1).

**Interpretation Bulletins [Reg. 8304]**: IT-124R6: Contributions to registered retirement savings plans.

**8304.1 Pension adjustment reversal — (1) Total pension adjustment reversal** — For the purpose of subsection 248(1) of the Act, an individual's "total pension adjustment reversal" for a calendar year means the total of all amounts each of which is the pension adjustment reversal (in this Part and Part LXXXIV referred to as "PAR") determined in connection with the individual's termination in the year from a deferred profit sharing plan or from a benefit provision of a registered pension plan.

**Related Provisions**: Reg. 8304.1(2) — Termination during 1997 deemed to be in 1998.

**Notes**: See Notes at end of Reg. 8304.1.

**Forms**: RC4137: Pension adjustment reversal guide; T4104: Past service pension adjustment guide.

**(2) Termination in 1997** — For the purpose of subsection (1) and the description of R in paragraph 8307(2)(b), where an individual terminates in 1997 from a deferred profit sharing plan or from a benefit provision of a registered pension plan, the termination is deemed to have occurred in 1998.

**Notes**: See Notes at end of Reg. 8304.1.

**(3) PAR — deferred profit sharing plan** — For the purposes of this Part and Part LXXXIV and subject to subsection (12), an individual's PAR determined in connection with the individual's termination from a deferred profit sharing plan is

(a) where the conditions in subsection (13) are satisfied with respect to the termination, the total of all amounts each of which is an amount

(i) included in determining a pension credit of the individual under the plan, and

(ii) to which the individual has ceased, at or before the time of the termination, to have any rights,

but does not include any amount to which a spouse or former spouse of the individual has ac-

2363

quired rights as a consequence of a breakdown of their marriage; and

(b) in any other case, nil.

**Notes**: See Notes at end of Reg. 8304.1.

**(4) PAR — money purchase provision** — For the purposes of this Part and Part LXXXIV and subject to subsection (12), an individual's PAR determined in connection with the individual's termination from a money purchase provision of a registered pension plan is

(a) where the conditions in subsection (14) are satisfied with respect to the termination, the total of all amounts each of which is an amount

(i) included in determining a pension credit of the individual under the provision, and

(ii) to which the individual has ceased, at or before the time of the termination, to have any rights,

but does not include any amount to which a spouse or former spouse of the individual has acquired rights as a consequence of a breakdown of their marriage; and

(b) in any other case, nil.

**Related Provisions**: Reg. 8500(8)(c) — Non-member benefits ignored in determining pension adjustment.

**Notes**: See Notes at end of Reg. 8304.1.

**(5) PAR — defined benefit provision** — For the purposes of this Part and Part LXXXIV and subject to subsections (6) and (12), an individual's PAR determined in connection with the individual's termination from a defined benefit provision of a registered pension plan is

(a) where the conditions in subsection (14) are satisfied with respect to the termination, the amount determined by the formula

$$A + B - C - D$$

where

A is the total of all amounts each of which is, in respect of a particular year that is the year in which the termination occurs or that is a preceding year, the lesser of

(i) the total of all amounts each of which is the pension credit of the individual under the provision for the particular year with respect to an employer, and

(ii) the RRSP dollar limit for the year following the particular year,

B is the total of all amounts each of which is the portion of the grossed-up amount of a provisional PSPA (other than a provisional PSPA determined in accordance with subsection 8303(8)) of the individual that is associated with a past service event occurring before the time of the termination that can reasonably be considered to be attributable to benefits provided under the provision,

C is the total of all amounts each of which is a specified distribution made in respect of the individual and the provision at or before the time of the termination, and

D is the total of all amounts each of which is a PA transfer amount in relation to the individual's termination from the provision; and

(b) in any other case, nil.

**Related Provisions**: ITA 257 — Negative amounts in formulas; Reg. 8300(11)(c) — Deemed specified distribution; Reg. 8304.1(6) — Defined benefit pension credits; Reg. 8304.1(7) — Meaning of grossed-up amount of provisional PSPA; Reg. 8304.1(8) — Meaning of specified distribution; Reg. 8304.1(10) — PA transfer amount; Reg. 8304.1(11) — Special 1997 PA transfer amount; Reg. 8304.1(14) — Terminations conditions; Reg. 8500(8)(c) — Non-member benefits ignored in determining pension adjustment.

**Notes**: See Notes at end of Reg. 8304.1.

**(6) Defined benefit pension credits** — For the purpose of subparagraph (i) of the description of A in paragraph (5)(a), in determining an individual's PAR in connection with the individual's termination from a defined benefit provision of a registered pension plan,

(a) the individual's pension credits under the provision for the year in which the termination occurs shall be determined without regard to benefits provided after the time of the termination; and

(b) the individual's pension credits under the provision for each year in which the plan was a specified multi-employer plan are deemed to be nil.

**(7) Grossed-up PSPA amount** — For the purposes of the descriptions of B in subsection 8303(7.1) and paragraph (5)(a), the grossed-up amount of an individual's provisional PSPA with respect to an employer that is associated with a past service event is the amount that would be the provisional PSPA if

(a) the values of C and D in subsections 8303(3) and 8304(5) were nil; and

(b) the words "at the time the past service event occurred" in paragraph (b) of the description of A in subsection 8304(5) were read as "immediately before the time the past service event occurred".

**(8) Specified distribution** — For the purpose of the description of C in paragraph (5)(a), an amount paid under a defined benefit provision of a registered pension plan with respect to an individual is a specified distribution made in respect of the individual and the provision at the time it is paid, except to the extent that

(a) it can reasonably be considered to be a payment of benefits in respect of any period before 1990;

(b) it is transferred to another registered pension plan (other than a plan that is, at the time of the transfer, a specified multi-employer plan) in accordance with subsection 147.3(3) of the Act;

(c) it is transferred to another defined benefit provision of the plan where the transfer would, if the provision and the other provision were in separate registered pension plans, constitute a transfer in accordance with subsection 147.3(3) of the Act;

(d) it is a payment in respect of an actuarial surplus;

(e) it is

(i) a return of contributions made by the individual under the provision, where the contributions are returned pursuant to an amendment to the plan that also reduces the future contributions that would otherwise be required to be made under the provision by members of the plan and that does not reduce benefits provided under the provision, or

(ii) a payment of interest in respect of contributions that are returned as described in subparagraph (i);

(f) it can reasonably be considered to be a payment of benefits provided in respect of a period throughout which the plan was a specified multi-employer plan; or

(g) it can reasonably be considered to be a payment of benefits provided in respect of a period throughout which the individual was employed outside Canada, where the benefits became provided as a consequence of a past service event in respect of which the Minister had consented to the application of subsection 8303(10) for the purpose of determining the individual's provisional PSPAs.

**Related Provisions**: Reg. 8304.1(9) — Property made available deemed to be paid; Reg. 8304.1(15) — Marriage breakdown — benefits acquired by spouse.

**(9) Property made available** — Where property held in connection with a particular defined benefit provision of a pension plan is made available at any time to provide benefits with respect to an individual under another benefit provision of a pension plan, subsection (8) applies as if the amount of the property had been paid under the particular provision at that time with respect to the individual.

**(10) PA transfer amount** — Where

(a) an individual has terminated, at a particular time after 1996, from a defined benefit provision (in this subsection referred to as the "former provision") of a registered pension plan,

(b) lifetime retirement benefits (in this subsection referred to as the "past service benefits") have, as a consequence of a past service event occurring at or before the particular time, become provided to the individual under another defined benefit provision of a registered pension plan in respect of a period that is or was pensionable service of the individual under the former provision, and

(c) lifetime retirement benefits to which the individual is or was entitled under the former provision in respect of the period have, under subsection 804(5), been taken into account as former benefits in determining a provisional PSPA of the individual that is associated with the past service event

for the purposes of subsection 8406(5) and the description of D in paragraph (5)(a), the lesser of

(d) the portion of the value determined for A in subsection 8303(3), for the purpose of determining the provisional PSPA, that can reasonably be considered to be attributable to the past service benefits, and

(e) the portion of the value determined for B in subsection 8303(3), for the purpose of determining the provisional PSPA, that can reasonably be considered to be attributable to the former benefits

is a PA transfer amount in relation to the individual's termination from the former provision.

**Related Provisions**: Reg. 8300(7) — Benefits include contingent benefits; Reg. 8304.1(11) — Special 1997 PA transfer amount.

**Notes**: See Notes at end of Reg. 8304.1.

**(11) Special 1997 PA transfer amount** — Where

(a) an individual has terminated, at a particular time in 1997, from a particular defined benefit provision of a registered pension plan,

(b) lifetime retirement benefits (in this subsection referred to as the "past service benefits") have, as a consequence of a past service event that occurred after the particular time and before 1998, become provided to the individual under the particular provision, or under another defined benefit provision of a registered pension plan, in respect of a period that was previously pensionable service of the individual under the particular provision, and

(c) lifetime retirement benefits to which the individual was previously entitled under the particular provision in respect of the period have, under subsection 8304(5), been taken into account as former benefits in determining a provisional PSPA of the individual that is associated with the past service event,

for the purposes of subsection 8406(5) and the description of D in paragraph (5)(a), the lesser of

(d) the portion of the value determined for A in subsection 8303(3), for the purpose of determining the provisional PSPA, that can reasonably be considered to be attributable to the past service benefits, and

(e) the portion of the value determined for B in subsection 8303(3), for the purpose of determining the provisional PSPA, that can reasonably be considered to be attributable to the former benefits

is a PA transfer amount in relation to the individual's termination from the particular provision at the particular time.

**Related Provisions**: Reg. 8300(7) — Benefits include contingent benefits.

**(12) Subsequent membership** — Where an individual has ceased at a particular time to be a member in relation to a deferred profit sharing plan or a benefit provision of a registered pension plan and subsequently becomes a member in relation to the plan or the provision, as the case may be, the following rules apply in determining the individual's PAR in connection with any subsequent termination from the plan or the provision, as the case may be:

(a) in the case of a deferred profit sharing plan or money purchase provision, any amounts included in a pension credit of the individual under the plan or provision because of an allocation to the individual before the particular time shall be disregarded; and

(b) in the case of a defined benefit provision,

(i) the value of A in paragraph (5)(a) shall be determined without regard to any pension credit, or portion of a pension credit that is attributable to benefits provided under the provision before the particular time,

(ii) the value of B in paragraph (5)(a) shall be determined without regard to any provisional PSPA that is associated with a past service event that occurred before the particular time, and

(iii) the value of C in paragraph (5)(a) shall be determined without regard to any specified distribution (as defined in subsection (8)) made at or before the particular time

**Notes**: See Notes at end of Reg. 8304.1.

**(13) Termination conditions — deferred profit sharing plan** — For the purpose of paragraph (3)(a), the conditions with respect to an individual's termination from a deferred profit sharing plan are the following

(a) the termination occurs after 1996 and otherwise than because of death; and

(b) no payments described in subparagraph 147(2)(k)(v) of the Act have been made out of or under the plan with respect to the individual.

**(14) Termination conditions — registered pension plan** — For the purposes of paragraphs (4)(a) and (5)(a), the conditions with respect to an individual's termination from a benefit provision of a registered pension plan are the following:

(a) the termination occurs after 1996 and otherwise than because of death; and

(b) no retirement benefits have been paid under the provision with respect to the individual (other than retirement benefits paid with respect to the individual's spouse or former spouse as a consequence of a breakdown of their marriage).

**Related Provisions**: Reg. 8300(11)(b) — Termination conditions deemed not satisfied.

**(15) Marriage breakdown** — Where

(a) before a member terminates from a defined benefit provision of a registered pension plan, there has been a breakdown of the member's marriage, and

(b) as a consequence of the breakdown,

(i) the member has ceased to have rights to all or a portion of the benefits provided under the provision with respect to the member, and

(ii) the member's spouse or former spouse (in this subsection referred to as the "spouse") has acquired rights under the provision in respect of those benefits,

for the purpose of subsection (8),

(c) any amount paid under the provision with respect to the rights acquired by the spouse (other than a single amount paid under the provision at or before the time of the member's termination in full satisfaction of the rights acquired by the spouse) is deemed not to have been paid with respect to the member, and

(d) unless a single amount has been paid under the provision at or before the time of the member's termination in full satisfaction of the rights acquired by the spouse, a single amount equal to the present value (at the time the member terminates from the provision) of the benefits to which the member has ceased to have rights as a consequence of the breakdown is deemed to have been paid to the member at that time under the provision in full satisfaction of those benefits.

**Notes [Reg. 8304.1]**: Reg. 8304.1 added by P.C. 1998-2256, effective 1997. It implements the PAR (pension adjustment reversal) calculation, which was originally included in the 1989 pension reform proposals but was deleted in the interest of reducing complexity. See Notes to ITA 146(1)"RRSP deduction limit".

PAR is determined when an individual terminates (usually by leaving the employment) from a DPSP or RPP, after 1996 and before retirement benefits have started. PAR measures the extent to which RRSP deduction room has been reduced to reflect RPP or DPSP benefits that will not be paid to the individual.

In general, PAR under a DPSP or RPP money purchase provision is the total included in pension credits under the plan since 1990 but not vested in the individual. PAR under a defined benefit provision is the total pension credits and PSPAs under the provision since 1990, minus any lump sum amounts paid out, or transferred to an RRSP or other money purchase type plan, in respect of post-1989 benefits under the provision.

For PAR reporting requirements, see Reg. 8402.01.

References to "spouse" are expected to be amended to add "or common-law partner" effective 2001 or earlier by election, as has been done throughout the ITA. See Notes to ITA 248(1)"common-law partner".

**Definitions [Reg. 8304.1]:** "amount" — Reg. 8304(16)(c), (d); "annuity" — ITA 248(1); "associated" — ITA 256; "Canada" — ITA 255, *Interpretation Act* 35(1); "contribution" — Reg. 8300(8), 8302(11), (12); "deferred profit sharing plan" — ITA 147(1), 248(1); "employed", "employer" — ITA 248(1); "excess money purchase offset" — Reg. 8304.1(12); "former provision" — Reg. 8304.1(10)(a); "grossed-up amount" — Reg. 8304.1(7); "individual" — ITA 248(1); "lifetime retirement benefits" — Reg. 8304(5)(c); "Minister" — ITA 248(1); "offset provision" — Reg. 8304.1(12)(b); "PA transfer amount" — Reg. 8304.1(10), (11); "PAR" — Reg. 8304.1(1), (3)–(6); "past service benefits" — Reg. 8304.1(10)(b), (11)(b); "past service event" — Reg. 8300(1); "pension adjustment" — Reg. 8308(5)(c), 8308(8); "pension credit" — Reg. 8301, 8308.1(2)–(4), 8308.3(2), (3); "property" — ITA 248(1); "provisional PSPA" — Reg. 8303(2), (3), 8308(4)(e); "registered pension plan" — ITA 248(1); "registered retirement income fund" — ITA 146.3(1), 248(1); "registered retirement savings plan", "RRSP dollar limit" — ITA 146(1), 248(1); "specified distribution" — Reg. 8304.1(8); "specified multi-employer plan" — ITA 147.1(1), Reg. 8510(2), (3); "spouse" — Reg. 8304.1(16)(b)(ii); "termination" — Reg. 8304.1(2), (15).

**Forms [Reg. 8304.1]:** RC4137: Pension adjustment reversal guide.

**8305. Association of benefits with employers** — (1) Where, for the purposes of this Part, it is necessary to determine the portion of an amount of benefits provided with respect to a member of a registered pension plan under a defined benefit provision of the plan that is attributable to the member's employment with a particular employer, the following rules apply, subject to subsection 8308(7):

(a) the determination shall be made by the plan administrator;

(b) benefits provided as a consequence of services rendered by the member to an employer who participates in the plan shall be regarded as attributable to employment with that employer, whether the benefits become provided at the time the services are rendered or at a subsequent time; and

(c) the determination shall be made in a manner that

(i) is reasonable in the circumstances,

(ii) is not inconsistent with such determinations made previously, and

(iii) results in the full amount of benefits being attributed to employment with one or more employers who participate in the plan.

(2) Where the administrator of a registered pension plan does not comply with the requirements of subsection (1) in connection with the determination of an amount under this Part at any time,

(a) the plan becomes, at that time, a revocable plan; and

(b) the Minister shall make any determinations referred to in subsection (1) that the administrator fails to make, or fails to make in accordance with that subsection.

**Definitions [Reg. 8305]:** "amount", "employer", "employment", "Minister", "registered pension plan" — ITA 248(1).

**8306. Exemption from certification** — (1) For the purposes of subsection 147.1(10) of the Act as it applies in respect of a past service event and the benefits provided under a defined benefit provision of a registered pension plan with respect to a particular member of the plan, a certification of the Minister is not required where

(a) each provisional PSPA of the member that is associated with the past service event is nil;

(b) the conditions in subsection (2) or (3) are satisfied;

(c) the conditions in subsection (2) or (3) are substantially satisfied and the Minister waives in writing the requirement for certification; or

(d) the past service event is deemed by paragraph 8304(3)(b) to have occurred immediately after the end of 1990.

(2) The following are conditions for the purposes of paragraphs (1)(b) and (c) and 8303(5)(g):

(a) there are more than 9 active members under the provision,

(b) no more than 25 per cent of the active members under the provision are specified active members under the provision;

(c) for all or substantially all of the active members under the provision, the amount of lifetime retirement benefits accrued under the provision has increased as a consequence of the past service event;

(d) where there is a specified active member under the provision;

(i) the amounts C and D in subparagraph (ii) are greater than nil, and

(ii) the amount determined by the formula A/C does not exceed the amount determined by the formula B/D

where

A is the aggregate of all amounts each of which is the amount of lifetime retirement benefits accrued under the provision, immediately after the past service event, to a specified active member under the provision,

B is the aggregate of all amounts each of which is the amount of lifetime retirement benefits accrued under the provision, immediately after the past service event, to an active member (other than a specified active member) under the provision,

C is the aggregate of all amounts each of which is the amount of lifetime retirement benefits accrued under the provision, immediately before the past service event, to a specified active member under the provision, and

D is the aggregate of all amounts each of which is the amount of lifetime retirement benefits accrued under the provision, immediately before the past service event, to an active member (other than a specified active member) under the provision; and

(e) the benefits provided under the provision as a consequence of the past service event to members of the plan who are not active members under the provision are not more advantageous than such benefits provided to active members under the provision.

**Related Provisions**: Reg. 8306(4) — Meaning of active member and specified active member.

**Notes**: Revenue Canada's view is that "all or substantially all", used in para. (c), means 90% or more.

(3) The following are conditions for the purposes of paragraphs (1)(b) and (c):

(a) the past service event consists of the establishment of the provision;

(b) there are more than 9 active members under the provision;

(c) no more than 25 per cent of the active members under the provision are specified active members under the provision;

(d) the member is not a specified active member under the provision;

(e) if the member is not an active member under the provision, for each of the 5 years immediately preceding the calendar year in which the past service event occurs,

(i) the member was not connected at any time in the year with an employer who participates in the plan, and

(ii) the aggregate of all amounts each of which is the remuneration of the member for the year from an employer who participates in the plan did not exceed 2½ times the Year's Maximum Pensionable Earnings for the year; and

(f) the aggregate of all amounts each of which is a provisional PSPA of the member associated with the past service event does not exceed 7/2 of the money purchase limit for the year in which the past service event occurs.

**Related Provisions**: Reg. 8306(4) — Meaning of active member and specified active member.

(4) For the purposes of this section as it applies in respect of a past service event,

(a) a member of a pension plan is an active member under a defined benefit provision of the plan if

(i) lifetime retirement benefits accrue under the provision to the member in respect of a period that immediately follows the time the past service event occurs, or

(ii) the member is entitled, immediately after the time the past service event occurs, to lifetime retirement benefits under the provision in respect of a period before that time and it is reasonable to expect, at that time, that lifetime retirement benefits will accrue under the provision to the member in respect of a period after that time; and

(b) an active member under a defined benefit provision of a pension plan is a specified active member under the provision if

(i) the member is connected, at the time of the past service event, with an employer who participates in the plan, or

(ii) it is reasonable to expect, at the time of the past service event, that the aggregate of all amounts each of which is the remuneration of the member for the calendar year in which the past service event occurs from an employer who participates in the plan will exceed 2½ times the Year's Maximum Pensionable Earnings for the year.

**Related Provisions**: Reg. 8300(7) — Benefits include contingent benefits.

**Definitions [Reg. 8306]**: "active member" — Reg. 8306(4)(a); "amount" — ITA 248(1); "associated" — ITA 256; "benefits" — Reg. 8300(7); "employer" — ITA 248(1); "lifetime retirement benefits" — Reg. 8304(5)(c); "Minister" — ITA 248(1); "money purchase limit" — ITA 147.1(1), 248(1); "past service event" — Reg. 8300(1); "provisional PSPA" — Reg. 8303(2), (3), 8308(4)(e); "registered pension plan" — ITA 248(1); "specified active member" — Reg. 8306(4)(b); "writing" — *Interpretation Act* 35(1).

**Forms**: T215 Segment; T215 Summ: Summary of past service pension adjustments exempt from certification; T215 Supp: Past service pension adjustment exempt from certification.

**8307. Certification in respect of past service events — (1) Application for certification —** Application for a certification of the Minister for the purposes of subsection 147.1(10) of the Act shall be made in prescribed form by the administrator of the registered pension plan to which the certification relates.

**Forms**: T1004: Application for certification of a provisional past service pension adjustment.

**(2) Prescribed condition —** For the purposes of subsection 147.1(10) of the Act in respect of a past service event and benefits with respect to a particular member of a registered pension plan, the prescribed condition is that, at the particular time the Minister issues the certification,

(a) the aggregate of all amounts each of which is the member's provisional PSPA with respect to an employer associated with the past service event

does not exceed

(b) the amount determined by the formula

$$\$8,000 + A + B + C - D + R$$

where

A is the member's unused RRSP deduction room at the end of the year immediately pre-

Part LXXXIII — Pension Adjustments/Prescribed Amounts  S. 8307(4)(b)(ii)

ceding the calendar year (in this paragraph referred to as the "particular year") that includes the particular time,

B is the amount of the member's qualifying withdrawals made for the purposes of the certification, determined as of the particular time,

C is the amount of the member's PSPA withdrawals for the particular year, determined as of the particular time, and

D is the aggregate of all amounts each of which is the accumulated PSPA of the member for the particular year with respect to an employer, determined as of the particular time.

R is the total of all amounts each of which is a PAR determined in connection with the individual's termination in the particular year from a deferred profit sharing plan, or from a benefit provision of a registered pension plan, and in respect of which an information return has been filed under section 8402.01 with the Minister before the particular time.

**Related Provisions**: ITA 257 — Negative amounts in formulas; Reg. 8304.1(2) — Termination during 1997 deemed to be in 1998; Reg. 8307(3) — Meaning of qualifying withdrawals; Reg. 8307(5) — PSPA withdrawals.

**Notes**: Formula element R added by P.C. 1998-2256, effective for 1998 and later calendar years. See Notes at end of Reg. 8304.1.

**(3) Qualifying withdrawals** — For the purposes of paragraph (5)(a) and the description of B in paragraph (2)(b), the amount of an individual's qualifying withdrawals made for the purposes of a certification in respect of a past service event, determined as of a particular time, is the lesser of

(a) the aggregate of all amounts each of which is such portion of an amount withdrawn by the individual from a registered retirement savings plan under which the individual was the annuitant (within the meaning assigned by subsection 146(1) of the Act) at the time of the withdrawal as

(i) is eligible, pursuant to subsection (4), to be designated for the purposes of the certification, and

(ii) is designated by the individual for the purposes of the certification by filing a prescribed form containing prescribed information with the Minister before the particular time, and

(b) the amount, if any, by which

(i) the aggregate of all amounts each of which is the provisional PSPA of the individual with respect to an employer associated with the past service event

exceeds

(ii) the amount, positive or negative, determined by the formula

$$A + C - D + R$$

where A, C, D and R have the same values as they have at the particular time for the purposes of the formula in paragraph (2)(b).

**Related Provisions**: ITA 257 — Negative amounts in formulas.

**Interpretation Bulletins**: IT-124R6: Contributions to registered retirement savings plans.

**Forms**: T1006: Designating an RRSP withdrawal as a qualifying withdrawal.

**(4) Eligibility of withdrawn amount for designation** — An amount withdrawn by an individual from a registered retirement savings plan is eligible to be designated for the purposes of a certification, except to the extent that the following rules provide otherwise:

(a) the amount is not eligible to be designated if the amount was

(i) withdrawn from a registered retirement savings plan in a calendar year other than the year in which the designation would be filed with the Minister or either of the 2 immediately preceding calendar years, or

(ii) withdrawn in circumstances that entitle the individual to a deduction under paragraph 60(l) of the Act; and

(b) the amount is not eligible to be designated to the extent that the amount was

(i) designated by the individual for the purposes of any other certification, or

(ii) deducted under section 60.2 or subsection 146(8.2) of the Act in computing the individual's income for any taxation year.

---

**Proposed Amendment — Reg. 8307(4)(b)(ii)**

(ii) deducted under section 60.2 or subsection 146(8.2) or 147.3(13.1) of the Act in computing the individual's income for any taxation year.

**Application**: The November 30, 2000 draft regulations (RPPs) (pre-published in Canada Gazette, Part I, December 9, 2000), subsec. 4(1), will amend subpara. 8307(4)(b)(ii) to read as above, applicable to 1992 et seq.

**Regulatory Impact Analysis Statement**: Section 8307, which provides rules for purposes of a PSPA certification, is amended as a consequence of the introduction of subsection 147.3(13.1) of the Act. Subsection 147.3(13.1) provides relief from double taxation where an excess transfer to an RRSP or registered retirement income fund is subsequently withdrawn.

**Technical Notes, April 18, 2000**: Section 8307 of the Regulations contains several rules that apply for the purposes of a certification of a provisional PSPA. In some cases, it may be necessary for an individual to withdraw RRSP funds in order for the CCRA to issue a certification of a provisional PSPA. Subsection 8307(4) contains rules limiting the extent to which an RRSP withdrawal may be designated for the purposes of a certification. These rules provide, in part, that a withdrawal is not eligible to be designated to the extent that the individual has claimed a deduction in respect of the withdrawal under certain provisions of the Act.

Paragraph 8307(4)(b) is amended to add a reference to subsection 147.3(13.1) of the Act. Subsection 147.3(13.1) enables an individual on whose behalf an excess transfer has been made to an RRSP or RRIF, and who withdraws the excess or another amount from an RRSP or RRIF, to deduct the withdrawn amount in order to offset the income inclusion resulting from the withdrawal. The amendment to paragraph 8307(4)(b) ensures that an RRSP withdrawal is not eligible to be designated for the purposes of a PSPA certification if the individual has claimed a deduction under subsection 147.3(13.1) in respect of the withdrawal.

This amendment, which applies to 1992 and subsequent years, is consequential to the introduction of subsection 147.3(13.1).

**(5) PSPA withdrawals** — For the purposes of the description of C in paragraph (2)(b) and the description of G in the definition "net past service pension adjustment" in subsection 146(1) of the Act, the amount of an individual's PSPA withdrawals for a calendar year, determined as of a particular time, is

(a) if the Minister has issued, in the year and before the particular time, a certification for the purposes of subsection 147.1(10) of the Act with respect to the individual, the aggregate of all amounts each of which is the amount of the individual's qualifying withdrawals made for the purposes of a certification that the Minister has issued in the year and before the particular time; and

(b) in any other case, nil.

**Related Provisions**: Reg. 8307(3) — Meaning of qualifying withdrawals.

**Notes**: Opening words of Reg. 8307(5) amended by P.C. 1998-2256, effective 1996, to remove its application to ITA 204.2(1.3).

**Interpretation Bulletins**: IT-124R6: Contributions to registered retirement savings plans.

**(6) Prescribed withdrawal** — For the purposes of subsection (7) and subsection 146(8.2) of the Act, a prescribed withdrawal is such portion of an amount withdrawn by an individual from a registered retirement savings plan under which the individual is the annuitant (within the meaning assigned by subsection 146(1) of the Act) as is designated in accordance with subparagraph (3)(a)(iii)[1] for the purposes of a certification in respect of the individual.

### Proposed Amendment — Reg. 8307(6)

**(6) Prescribed withdrawal** — For the purposes of subsection (7) and subsections 146(8.2) and 147.3(13.1) of the Act, a prescribed withdrawal is the portion of an amount withdrawn by an individual from a registered retirement savings plan under which the individual is the annuitant (within the meaning assigned by subsection 146(1) of the Act) that is designated in accordance with subparagraph

---

[1]*Sic*. Should read (3)(a)(ii) — ed.

(3)(a)(ii) for the purposes of a certification in respect of the individual.

**Application**: The November 30, 2000 draft regulations (RPPs) (pre-published in *Canada Gazette*, Part I, December 9, 2000), subsec. 4(2), will amend subsec. 8307(6) to read as above, applicable to 1992 *et seq.*

**Technical Notes, April 18, 2000**: Subsections 146(8.2) and 147.3(13.1) of the Act provide deductions in certain circumstances where an overcontribution to an RRSP, or an excess transfer to an RRSP or RRIF, is subsequently withdrawn. The subsections are intended to provide relief from double taxation. As an exception, the deduction is not available in the case of prescribed withdrawals. Subsection 8307(6) of the Regulations defines a prescribed withdrawal as an amount withdrawn by a taxpayer from an RRSP and designated for the purposes of a PSPA certification.

As subsection 8307(6) currently applies only for the purpose of subsection 146(8.2), it is amended so that it also applies for the purpose of subsection 147.3(13.1). The combined result of subsections 8307(4) and (6) of the Regulations and subsections 146(8.2) and 147.3(13.1) of the Act is that an RRSP withdrawal may be either deducted in computing income (where subsection 146(8.2) or 147.3(13.1) applies) or designated for the purposes of a PSPA certification, but not both.

This amendment, which applies to 1992 and subsequent years, is consequential to the introduction of subsection 147.3(13.1).

**Notes**: Reg. 8307(6) is effective 1991. (See Notes at end of Reg. 8300-8311.)

**Interpretation Bulletins**: IT-124R6: Contributions to registered retirement savings plans; IT-528: Transfers of funds between registered plans.

**(7) Prescribed premium** — For the purpose of subsection 146(6.1) of the Act, a premium paid by a taxpayer under a registered retirement savings plan under which the taxpayer is the annuitant (within the meaning assigned by subsection 146(1) of the Act) at the time the premium is paid is a prescribed premium for a particular taxation year of the taxpayer where the following conditions are satisfied:

(a) the taxpayer withdrew an amount (in this subsection referred to as the "withdrawn amount") in the particular year from a registered retirement savings plan for the purposes of a certification in respect of a past service event;

(b) all or part of the withdrawn amount is a prescribed withdrawal pursuant to subsection (6);

(c) it is subsequently determined that

(i) as a consequence of reasonable error, the taxpayer withdrew a greater amount than necessary for the purposes of the certification, or

(ii) as a consequence of the application of paragraph 147.1(3)(b) of the Act, it was not necessary for the taxpayer to withdraw any amount;

Part LXXXIII — Pension Adjustments/Prescribed Amounts    Reg. S. 8308(3)(b)(ii)

(d) the premium is paid by the taxpayer in the 12-month period immediately following the time at which the determination referred to in paragraph (c) is made;

(e) the amount of the premium does not exceed such portion of the withdrawn amount as is a prescribed withdrawal pursuant to subsection (6) and is determined to have been an unnecessary withdrawal;

(f) the taxpayer files with the Minister, on or before the day on or before which the taxpayer is required (or would be required if tax under Part I of the Act were payable by the taxpayer for the taxation year in which the taxpayer pays the premium) by section 150 of the Act to file a return of income for the taxation year in which the taxpayer pays the premium, a written notice in which the taxpayer designates the premium as a recontribution of all or any portion of the withdrawn amount; and

(g) the taxpayer has not designated, pursuant to paragraph (f), any other premium as a recontribution of all or any portion of the withdrawn amount.

**Notes**: Reg. 8307(7) is effective for the 1991 and later taxation years. (See Notes to Reg. 8311.)

**Definitions [Reg. 8307]**: "accumulated PSPA" — Reg. 8303(1)(a), 8303(2); "amount" — ITA 248(1); "associated" — ITA 256; "employer", "individual", "Minister" — ITA 248(1); "particular year" — Reg. 8307(2)(b)(A); "past service event" — Reg. 8300(1); "prescribed" — ITA 248(1); "prescribed withdrawal" — Reg. 8307(6), "PSPA withdrawal" — Reg. 8307(5); "provisional PSPA" — Reg. 8303(2), (3), 8308(4)(e); "qualifying withdrawal" — Reg. 8307(3); "registered pension plan" — ITA 248(1); "registered retirement savings plan" — ITA 146(1), 248(1); "taxation year" — ITA 249; "taxpayer" — ITA 248(1); "unused RRSP deduction room" — ITA 146(1), 248(1); "withdrawn amount" — Reg. 8307(7)(a); "written" — Interpretation Act 35(1)"writing".

**Interpretation Bulletins**: IT-124R6: Contributions to registered retirement savings plans.

**8308. Special rules — (1) Benefits provided before registration** — For the purposes of this Part and subsection 147.1(10) of the Act, benefits that became provided under a defined benefit provision of a pension plan before the day as of which the plan becomes a registered pension plan shall be deemed to have become provided as a consequence of an event occurring on that day and not to have been provided before that day.

**(2) Prescribed amount for connected persons** — Where

(a) at any particular time in a calendar year after 1990,

(i) an individual becomes a member of a registered pension plan, or

(ii) lifetime retirement benefits commence to accrue to the individual under a defined benefit provision of a registered pension plan following a period in which lifetime retirement benefits did not accrue to the individual,

(b) the individual is connected at the particular time, or was connected at any time after 1989, with an employer who participates in the plan for the benefit of the individual,

(c) the individual did not have a pension adjustment for 1990 that was greater than nil, and

(d) this subsection did not apply before the particular time to prescribe an amount with respect to the individual,

an amount equal to the lesser of $11,500 and 18 per cent of the individual's earned income (within the meaning assigned by paragraph 146(1)(c) [14(1)"earned income"] of the Act) for 1990 is prescribed with respect to the individual for the year for the purpose of the descriptions of B in paragraphs 146(1)(g.1) and (l) [146(1)"RRSP deduction limit" and"unused RRSP deduction room"] and section 204(1.1) of the Act.

**Interpretation Bulletins**: IT-124R6: Contributions to registered retirement savings plans.

**(3) Remuneration for prior years** — Where an individual who is entitled to benefits under a defined benefit provision of a registered pension plan receives remuneration at a particular time in a particular calendar year no part of which is pensionable service of the individual under the provision and the remuneration is treated for the purpose of determining benefits under the provision as if it were remuneration received in one or more calendar years preceding the particular calendar year for services rendered in those preceding years, the following rules apply:

(a) such portion of the remuneration as is treated under the provision as if it were remuneration received in a preceding calendar year for services rendered in that preceding year shall be deemed, for the purpose of determining, as of the particular time and any subsequent time, a redetermined benefit entitlement of the individual under the provision, to have been received in that preceding year for services rendered in that preceding year; and

(b) the pension credit of the individual for the particular year under the provision with respect to an employer is the aggregate of

(i) the amount that would otherwise be the individual's pension credit for the particular year, and

(ii) the amount that would, if the payment of the remuneration were a past service event, be the provisional PSPA (or a reasonable estimate thereof determined in a manner acceptable to the Minister) of the individual with respect to the employer that is associated with the payment of the remuneration.

**Reg. S. 8308(3)**

**Related Provisions**: Reg. 8300(7)) — Benefits include contingent benefits.

**(4) Period of reduced services — retroactive benefits** — Where,

(a) as a consequence of a past service event retirement benefits (in this subsection referred to as "retroactive benefits") become provided under a defined benefit provision of a registered pension plan (other than a plan that is a specified multi-employer plan) to an individual in respect of a period of reduced services of the individual

(b) the period of reduced services was not, before the past service event, pensionable service of the individual under the provision, and

(c) the past service event occurs on or before April 30 of the year immediately following the calendar year in which ends the complete period of reduced services of the individual that includes the period of reduced services,

the following rules apply:

(d) each pension adjustment of the individual with respect to an employer for a year before the calendar year in which the past service event occurs shall be deemed to be, and to always have been, the aggregate of

   (i) the amount that would otherwise be the individual's pension adjustment with respect to the employer for the year, and

   (ii) such portion of the provisional PSPA of the individual with respect to the employer that is associated with the past service event as may reasonably be considered to be attributable to the provision of retroactive benefits in respect of the year, and

(e) each provisional PSPA of the individual with respect to an employer that is associated with the past service event shall be deemed (except for the purposes of this subsection) to be such portion of the amount that would otherwise be the individual's provisional PSPA as may reasonably be considered not to be attributable to the provision of retroactive benefits.

**Interpretation Bulletins**: IT-363R2: Deferred profit sharing plans — deductibility of employer contributions and taxation of amounts received by a beneficiary.

**Information Circulars**: 98-2: Prescribed compensation for RPPs, paras. 23–25.

**(5) Period of reduced services — retroactive contributions** — Where

(a) a contribution (in this subsection referred to as a "retroactive contribution") is made by an individual, or by an employer with respect to the individual, under a money purchase provision of a registered pension plan in respect of a period in a particular calendar year that is a period of reduced services of the individual, and

(b) the retroactive contribution is made after the particular year and on or before April 30 of the year immediately following the calendar year in which ends the complete period of reduced services of the individual that includes the period of reduced services,

the following rules apply:

(c) each pension adjustment of the individual for the particular year with respect to an employer shall be deemed to be, and to always have been, the amount that it would have been had the retroactive contribution been made at the end of the particular year, and

(d) the retroactive contribution shall be deemed, for the purpose of determining pension adjustments of the individual for any year after the particular year, to have been made at the end of the particular year and not to have been made at any subsequent time.

**Interpretation Bulletins**: IT-363R2: Deferred profit sharing plans — deductibility of employer contributions and taxation of amounts received by a beneficiary.

**Information Circulars**: 98-2: Prescribed compensation for RPPs, paras. 23–25.

**(6) Commitment to make retroactive contributions** — Where

(a) an individual enters into a written commitment to make a contribution under a money purchase provision of a registered pension plan,

(b) the commitment is made to the administrator of the plan or to an employer who participates in the plan, and

(c) the rules in subsection (5) would apply in respect of the contribution if the contribution were made at the time at which the individual enters into the commitment,

the following rules apply for the purposes of this Part:

(d) the individual shall be deemed to have made the contribution to the plan at the time at which the individual enters into the commitment,

(e) if the individual subsequently pays all or a part of the contribution to the plan pursuant to the commitment, the amount paid to the plan is, for the purposes of paragraphs 8301(4)(a) and (8)(e), a contribution described in this paragraph,

(f) any contribution that an employer is required to make under the money purchase provision conditional on the individual making the contribution that the individual has committed to pay and in respect of which subsection (5) would apply if the contribution were made by the employer at the time the individual enters into the commitment shall be deemed to have been made by the employer at that time, and

(g) if an employer subsequently pays to the plan all or a part of a contribution in respect of which paragraph (f) applies, the amount paid to the plan is, for the purposes of paragraph 8301(4)(a), a contribution described in this paragraph.

Part LXXXIII — Pension Adjustments/Prescribed Amounts  Reg. S. 8308.1(2)(a)

**Notes**: Reg. 8308(6)(e) and (g) amended by P.C. 1995-17, effective for amounts paid to RPPs after 1989, to refer to Reg. 8301(4)(a) and (8)(e) and thus modify the way in which contributions made under a commitment are excluded in determining pension credits for the year of contribution.

**Information Circulars**: 98-2: Prescribed compensation for RPPs, paras. 23–25.

**(7) Loaned employees** — Where, pursuant to an arrangement between an employer (in this subsection referred to as the "lending employer") who is a participating employer in relation to a pension plan and an employer (in this subsection referred to as the "borrowing employer") who, but for this subsection, would not be a participating employer in relation to the plan,

(a) an employee of the lending employer renders services to the borrowing employer for which the employee receives remuneration from the borrowing employer, and

(b) while the employee renders services to the borrowing employer, benefits continue to accrue under a defined benefit provision of the plan to the employee, or the lending employer continues to make contributions under a money purchase provision of the plan with respect to the employee,

the following rules apply:

(c) for the purpose of the definition "participating employer" in subsection 147.1(1) of the Act as it applies in respect of the plan, the borrowing employer is a prescribed employer,

(d) the determination, for the purposes of this Part, of the portion of the employee's benefit accrual under a defined benefit provision of the plan in respect of a year that can reasonably be considered to be attributable to the employee's employment with each of the lending and borrowing employers shall be made with regard to the remuneration received by the employee for the year from each employer, and

(e) such portion of the contributions made under a money purchase provision of the plan by the lending employer as may reasonably be considered to be in respect of the employee's remuneration from the borrowing employer shall be deemed, for the purposes of this Part, to be contributions made by the borrowing employer.

**Related Provisions**: Reg. 8507(5)E(a) — Additional compensation fraction.

**(8) Successor plans** — Notwithstanding any other provisions of this Part, other than section 8310, where

(a) all benefits with respect to an individual under a defined benefit provision (in this subsection referred to as the "former provision") of a registered pension plan are replaced in a calendar year by identical benefits under a defined benefit provision of another registered pension plan,

(b) the replacement of benefits is consequent on a transfer of the individual's employment from one employer (in this subsection referred to as the "former employer") to another employer (in this subsection referred to as the "successor employer"), and

(c) the Minister consents in writing to the application of this subsection in respect of that replacement of benefits,

the individual's pension adjustments for the year with respect to the former employer and the successor employer shall be the amounts that they would be if all benefits with respect to the individual under the former provision had been attributable to employment with the successor employer and not to employment with the former employer.

**(9) Special downsizing benefits** — Where

(a) lifetime retirement benefits that do not comply with the condition in paragraph 8503(3)(a) are provided to an individual under a defined benefit provision of a registered pension plan, and

(b) the benefits are permissible only by reason of subsection 8505(3),

each pension credit of the individual under the provision and each provisional PSPA of the individual shall be determined without regard to the lifetime retirement benefits.

**Definitions [Reg. 8308]**: "amount" — ITA 248(1); "associated" — ITA 256; "benefits" — Reg. 8300(7); "borrowing employer" — Reg. 8308(7); "complete period of reduced services" — Reg. 8300(1); "contribution" — Reg. 8300(8), 8302(11), (12); "employee", "employer", "employment" — ITA 248(1); "former employer" — Reg. 8308(8)(b); "former provision" — Reg. 8308(8)(a); "individual" — ITA 248(1); "lending employer" — Reg. 8308(7); "lifetime retirement benefits" — Reg. 8304(5)(c); "Minister" — ITA 248(1); "past service event" — Reg. 8300(1); "pension adjustment" — Reg. 8308(5)(c), 8308(8); "pension credit" — Reg. 8301, 8308.1(2)–(4), 8308.3(2), (3); "period of reduced services" — Reg. 8300(1); "prescribed" — ITA 248(1); "provisional PSPA" — Reg. 8303(2), (3), 8308(4)(e); "registered pension plan" — ITA 248(1); "retroactive benefits" — Reg. 8308(4)(a); "retroactive contribution" — Reg. 8308(5)(a); "specified multi-employer plan" — ITA 147.1(1), Reg. 8510(2), (3); "successor employer" — Reg. 8308(8)(b); "written" — Interpretation Act 35(1) "writing".

**Interpretation Bulletins**: IT-528: Transfers of funds between registered plans.

**8308.1 Foreign plans — (1) Definitions** — In this section, "foreign plan" means a plan or arrangement (determined without regard to subsection 207.6(5) of the Act) that would, but for paragraph (l) of the definition "retirement compensation arrangement" in subsection 248(1) of the Act, be a retirement compensation arrangement.

**(2) Pension credit** — Subject to subsections (3) to (4.1), the pension credit of an individual for a calendar year with respect to an employer under a foreign plan is

(a) where paragraph (b) does not apply, nil; and

(b) where

(i) the year is 1992 or a subsequent year,

(ii) the individual became entitled in the year, either absolutely or contingently, to benefits under the foreign plan in respect of services rendered to the employer in a period throughout which the individual was resident in Canada and rendered services to the employer that were primarily services rendered in Canada or services rendered in connection with a business carried on by the employer in Canada, or a combination of those services,

(iii) the individual continued to be entitled at the end of the year, either absolutely or contingently, to all or part of the benefits, and

(iv) either

(A) no contribution was made under the foreign plan in the year in respect of the individual, except where

(I) no contribution was made because the foreign plan had an actuarial surplus, and

(II) had a contribution been made in respect of the benefits referred to in subparagraph (ii), it would have been a resident's contribution (as defined in subsection 207.6(5.1) of the Act), or

(B) a contribution that is not a resident's contribution was made under the foreign plan in the year in respect of the individual,

the lesser of

(v) the amount, if any, by which 18% of the individual's resident compensation from the employer for the year exceeds the PA offset for the year, and

(vi) the amount by which the money purchase limit for the year exceeds the PA offset for the year.

**Notes**: Reg. 8308.1(2) amended by P.C. 1998-2256, retroactive to its introduction in 1992, to make the opening words subject to subsec. (4.1) and to change everything after subpara. (iv) to use "the PA offset" (now defined in Reg. 8300(1)) instead of $1,000.

**(3) Pension credit — alternative determination** — Subject to subsection (4), where the Minister has, on the written application of an employer, approved in writing a method for determining pension credits for a year with respect to the employer under a foreign plan, the pension credits shall be determined in accordance with that method.

**(4) Pension credits for 1992, 1993 and 1994** — The pension credit of an individual for 1992, 1993 or 1994 with respect to an employer under a foreign plan is the lesser of

(a) the amount that would, but for this subsection, be determined as the pension credit for the year, and

(b) the amount, if any, by which the lesser of

(i) 18% of the amount that would be the individual's compensation from the employer for the year if the definition "compensation" in subsection 147.1(1) of the Act were read without reference to paragraphs (b) and (c) of that definition, and

(ii) the money purchase limit for the year

exceeds the total of

(iii) $1,000, and

(iv) the amount that would be the pension adjustment of the individual for the year with respect to the employer if subsection 8301(1) were read without reference to paragraph (b) of that subsection.

**(4.1) Pension credits — 1996 to 2003** — For the purpose of determining the pension credit of an individual for a calendar year after 1995 and before 2004 with respect to an employer under a foreign plan, subparagraph (2)(b)(vi) shall be read as

"(vi) the money purchase limit for the year.".

**Notes**: Reg. 8308.1(4.1) added by P.C. 1998-2256, retroactive to 1992.

**(5) Foreign plan PSPA** — Subject to subsection (6), where the benefits to which an individual is entitled, either absolutely or contingently, under a foreign plan are modified, the foreign plan PSPA of the individual with respect to an employer associated with the modification of benefits is the amount, if any, by which

(a) the total of all amounts each of which is the amount that, if this section were read without reference to subsection (3), would be the pension credit of the individual with respect to the employer under the foreign plan for a calendar year before the year in which the individual's benefits are modified

exceeds the total of all amounts each of which is

(b) the pension credit of the individual with respect to the employer under the foreign plan for a calendar year before the year in which the individual's benefits are modified, or

(c) the foreign plan PSPA of the individual with respect to the employer associated with a previous modification of the individual's benefits under the foreign plan.

**(6) Foreign plan PSPA — alternative determination** — Where the Minister has, on the written application of an employer, approved in writing a method for determining the foreign plan PSPA of an individual with respect to the employer associated with a modification of the individual's benefits under a foreign plan, the individual's foreign plan PSPA shall be determined in accordance with that method.

**Notes**: Reg. 8308.1 added by P.C. 1996-911, effective 1992.

**Definitions [Reg. 8308.1]**: "amount" — ITA 248(1); "associated" — ITA 256; "business" — ITA 248(1); "Canada" — ITA 255, *Interpretation Act* 35(1); "contribution" — Reg. 8300(8), 8302(11), (12); "employer" — ITA 248(1); "foreign plan" — Reg. 8308.1(1); "individual", "Minister" — ITA 248(1); "money purchase limit" — ITA 147.1(1), 248(1); "PA offset" — Reg. 8300(1); "pension adjustment" — Reg. 8308(5)(c), 8308(8); "pension credit" — Reg. 8308.1(2); "resident" — ITA 250; "resident compensation" — Reg. 8300(1); "resident in Canada" — ITA 250; "retirement compensation arrangement" — ITA 248(1); "written" — *Interpretation Act* 35(1)"writing".

## 8308.2 Prescribed amount for member of foreign plan — (1) Prescribed amount —
Where

(a) throughout a period in a particular calendar year after 1992 an individual resident in Canada rendered services to an employer, other than services that were primarily services rendered in Canada or services rendered in connection with a business carried on by the employer in Canada, or a combination of those services,

(b) the individual became entitled in the particular year, either absolutely or contingently, to benefits under a pension plan that is a foreign plan (as defined in subsection 8308.1(1)) in respect of the services, and

(c) the individual continued to be entitled at the end of the particular year, either absolutely or contingently, to all or part of the benefits,

subject to subsection (2), there is prescribed in respect of the individual for the year following the particular year, for the purposes of the descriptions of B in the definitions "RRSP deduction limit" and "unused RRSP deduction room" in subsection 146(1) of the Act and the description of B in paragraph 204.2(1.1)(b) of the Act, the lesser of

(d) the amount by which the money purchase limit for the particular year exceeds the PA offset for the particular year, and

(e) 10% of the portion of the individual's resident compensation from the employer for the particular year that is attributable to services rendered by the individual to the employer in periods throughout which the individual rendered services described in paragraph (a).

**Notes**: Reg. 8308.2(1) added by P.C. 1998-2256, retroactive to 1992 (replacing former 8308.2 which, as added by P.C. 1996-911, had also been effective 1992). The changes primarily use "the PA offset" (now defined in Reg. 8300(1)), and change "compensation" to "resident compensation" (also defined in Reg. 8300(1)).

**(2) Prescribed amounts — 1997 to 2004** — For the purpose of determining the amount prescribed under subsection (1) in respect of an individual for a calendar year after 1996 and before 2005, paragraph (d) of that subsection shall be read as:

"(d) the money purchase limit for the particular year, and".

**Notes**: Reg. 8308.2(2) added by P.C. 1998-2256, retroactive to 1992.

**Definitions [Reg. 8308.2]**: "amount", "business" — ITA 248(1); "Canada" — ITA 255, *Interpretation Act* 35(1); "employer", "individual" — ITA 248(1); "money purchase limit" — ITA 147.1(1), 248(1); "PA offset" — Reg. 8300(1); "prescribed" — ITA 248(1); "resident compensation" — Reg. 8300(1); "resident in Canada" — ITA 250.

## 8308.3 Specified retirement arrangements —
**(1) Definition** — In this section, "specified retirement arrangement" means, in respect of an individual and an employer, a plan or arrangement under which payments that are attributable to the individual's employment with the employer are to be, or may be, made to or for the benefit of the individual after the termination of the individual's employment with the employer, but does not include

(a) a plan or arrangement referred to in any of paragraphs (a) to (k), (m) and (n) of the definition "retirement compensation arrangement" in subsection 248(1) of the Act;

(b) [Repealed]

(c) a plan or arrangement that does not provide in any circumstances for payments to be made to or for the benefit of the individual after the later of the last day of the calendar year in which the individual attains 69 years of age and the day that is 5 years after the day of termination of the individual's employment with the employer;

(d) a plan or arrangement (in this paragraph referred to as the "arrangement") that is, or would be, but for paragraph (l) of the definition "retirement compensation arrangement" in subsection 248(1) of the Act, a retirement compensation arrangement where

(i) the funding of the arrangement is subject to the *Pension Benefits Standards Act, 1985* or a similar law of a province, or

(ii) the arrangement is funded substantially in accordance with the funding requirements that would apply if the arrangement were subject to the *Pension Benefits Standards Act, 1985*;

(e) a plan or arrangement that is deemed by subsection 207.6(6) of the Act to be a retirement compensation arrangement; or

(f) an arrangement established by the *Judges Act* or the *Lieutenant Governors Superannuation Act*.

**Notes**: Reg. 8308.3(1) amended by P.C. 1998-2256, retroactive to its introduction in 1992, to add "(n)" in para. (a); and to repeal para. (b), which referred to a plan or arrangement under Reg. 6802(a)-(f) (which reference was redundant).

Reg. 8308.3(1)(c) amended by P.C. 1998-2256, effective 1998, to change "the day on which the individual attains 71 years" to "the last day of the calendar year in which the individual attains 69 years"; but new para. (c) does not apply in respect of an individual who turned 69 before 1998.

**(2) Pension credit** — Subject to subsections (3) and (3.1), the pension credit of an individual for a

**Reg. S. 8308.3(2)** — Income Tax Regulations

calendar year with respect to an employer under a specified retirement arrangement is

  (a) where paragraph (b) does not apply, nil; and

  (b) where

    (i) the year is 1993 or a subsequent year,

    (ii) the employer is, at any time in the year,

      (A) a person who is exempt, because of section 149 of the Act, from tax under Part I of the Act on all or part of the person's taxable income, or

      (B) the Government of Canada or the government of a province,

    (iii) the individual became entitled in the year, either absolutely or contingently, to benefits under the arrangement in respect of employment with the employer,

    (iv) at the end of the year, the individual is entitled, either absolutely or contingently, to benefits under the arrangement, and

    (v) the amount determined by the formula

$$0.85A - B$$

is greater than nil where

A is the lesser of

  (A) the amount, if any, by which 18% of the individual's resident compensation from the employer for the year exceeds the PA offset for the year, and

  (B) the amount by which the money purchase limit for the year exceeds the PA offset for the year, and

B is the amount that would be the pension adjustment of the individual for the year with respect to the employer if subsection 8301(1) were read without reference to paragraph (c) of that subsection,

the amount that would be determined by the formula in subparagraph (v) if the reference to "0.85" in the formula were replaced by a reference to "1".

**Related Provisions:** ITA 257 — Negative amounts in formulas.

**Notes:** Reg. 8308.3(2) amended by P.C. 1998-2256, retroactive to its introduction in 1992, to add reference to subsec. (3.1) in the opening words; and to change (b)(v) to use "the PA offset" (defined in Reg. 8300(1)) in place of a formula using $1,000.

**(3) Pension credit — alternative determination** — Where the Minister has, on the written application of an employer, approved in writing a method for determining pension credits for a year with respect to the employer under a specified retirement arrangement, the pension credits shall be determined in accordance with that method.

**(3.1) Pension credits — 1996 to 2003** — For the purpose of determining the pension credit of an individual for a calendar year after 1995 and before 2004 with respect to an employer under a specified retirement arrangement, the portion of paragraph (2)(b) after subparagraph (iv) shall be read as

"(v) the amount determined by the formula

$$0.85A - B$$

is greater than nil where

A is the lesser of

  (A) the amount, if any, by which 18% of the individual's resident compensation from the employer for the year exceeds the PA offset for the year, and

  (B) the amount by which $15,500 exceeds the PA offset for the year, and

B is the amount that would be the pension adjustment of the individual for the year with respect to the employer if subsection 8301(1) were read without reference to paragraph (c),

the amount that would be determined by the formula in subparagraph (v) if

  (vi) the reference to "0.85A" in that formula were read as a reference to "A", and

  (vii) clause (B) of the description of A in that subparagraph were read as

    "(B) the money purchase limit for the year, and".".

**Related Provisions:** ITA 257 — Negative amounts in formulas.

**Notes:** Reg. 8308.3(3.1) added by P.C. 1998-2256, effective 1992.

**(4) Specified retirement arrangement PSPA** — Subject to subsection (5), where the benefits to which an individual is entitled, either absolutely or contingently, under a specified retirement arrangement are modified, the specified retirement arrangement PSPA of the individual with respect to an employer associated with the modification of benefits is the amount, if any, by which

  (a) the total of all amounts each of which is the amount that, if this section were read without reference to subsection (3), would be the pension credit of the individual with respect to the employer under the arrangement for a calendar year before the year in which the individual's benefits are modified

exceeds the total of all amounts each of which is

  (b) the pension credit of the individual with respect to the employer under the arrangement for a calendar year before the year in which the individual's benefits are modified, or

  (c) the specified retirement arrangement PSPA of the individual with respect to the employer associated with a previous modification of the individual's benefits under the arrangement.

**(5) Specified retirement arrangement PSPA — alternative determination** — Where the Minister has, on the written application of an employer, approved in writing a method for determining the specified retirement arrangement PSPA of an individual with respect to the employer associated with a modification of the individual's benefits under a specified retirement arrangement, the individual's specified retirement arrangement PSPA shall be determined in accordance with that method.

**Notes**: Reg. 8308.3 added by P.C. 1996-911, effective 1992, except that for the purposes of applying the definition "specified retirement arrangement" in subsec. (1) before 1996, add the following:

(a.1) an unfunded plan or arrangement that is maintained primarily for the benefit of non-residents in respect of services rendered outside Canada,

**Definitions [Reg. 8308.3]**: "amount" — ITA 248(1); "arrangement" — Reg. 8308.3(1)(d); "associated" — ITA 256; "Canada" — ITA 255, *Interpretation Act* 35(1); "employer", "employment" — ITA 248(1); "Governor" — *Interpretation Act* 35(1); "individual", "Minister" — ITA 248(1); "money purchase limit" — ITA 147.1(1), 248(1); "PA offset" — Reg. 8300(1); "pension adjustment" — Reg. 8308(5)(c), 8308(8); "pension credit" — Reg. 8301, 8308.1(2)–(4), 8308.3(2), (3); "person" — ITA 248(1); "province" — *Interpretation Act* 35(1); "resident compensation" — Reg. 8300(1); "retirement compensation arrangement", "taxable income" — ITA 248(1); "written" — *Interpretation Act* 35(1)"writing".

## 8308.4 Government-sponsored retirement arrangements — (1) Definitions — The definitions in this subsection apply in this section.

**"administrator"** means, in respect of a government-sponsored retirement arrangement, the government or other entity that has ultimate responsibility for the administration of the arrangement.

**"government-sponsored retirement arrangement"** means a plan or arrangement established to provide pensions directly or indirectly from the public money of Canada or a province to one or more individuals each of whom renders services in respect of which amounts that are included in computing the income from a business of any person or partnership are paid directly or indirectly from the public money of Canada or a province.

**Notes**: See at end of Reg. 8308.4.

**(2) Prescribed amount** — Where

(a) in a particular calendar year after 1992 an individual renders services in respect of which an amount that is included in computing the income from a business of any person was payable directly or indirectly by the Government of Canada or of a province, and

(b) at the end of the particular year, the individual is entitled, either absolutely or contingently, to benefits under a government-sponsored retirement arrangement that provides benefits in connection with such services,

there is prescribed in respect of the individual for the year following the particular year, for the purposes of the descriptions of B in the definitions "RRSP deduction limit" and "unused RRSP deduction room" in subsection 146(1) of the Act and the description of B in paragraph 204.2(1.1)(b) of the Act,

(c) where the particular year is before 1996, the amount by which the RRSP dollar limit for that following year exceeds $1,000, and

(d) in any other case, the RRSP dollar limit for that following year.

**Notes**: Reg. 8308.4 added by P.C. 1996-911, effective 1993; and subsec. (2) amended retroactive to its introduction by P.C. 1998-2256. The substance of the amendment is that for years after 1996, the prescribed amount is determined without subtracting $1,000 from the RRSP dollar limit; thus, individuals participating in government-sponsored retirement arrangements will have no RRSP deduction room.

**Definitions [Reg. 8308.4]**: "administrator" — Reg. 8308.4(1); "amount", "business" — ITA 248(1); "Canada" — ITA 255, *Interpretation Act* 35(1); "government-sponsored retirement arrangement" — Reg. 8308.4(1); "individual" — ITA 248(1); "partnership" — see Notes to ITA 96(1); "person", "prescribed" — ITA 248(1); "province" — *Interpretation Act* 35(1); "RRSP dollar limit" — ITA 146(1), 248(1).

**Registered Plans Division Newsletters**: 91-4R (Registration rules for money purchase provisions).

## 8309. Prescribed amount for lieutenant governors and judges — (1) Subject to subsection (3), where an individual is, at any time in a particular calendar year after 1989, a lieutenant governor of a province (other than a lieutenant governor who is not a contributor as defined in section 2 of the *Lieutenant Governors Superannuation Act*), there is prescribed in respect of the individual for the year following the particular year, for the purposes of the descriptions of B in the definitions "RRSP deduction limit" and "unused RRSP deduction room" in subsection 146(1) of the Act and the description of B in paragraph 204.2(1.1)(b) of the Act, the lesser of

(a) the amount, if any, by which 18% of the salary received by the individual for the particular year as a lieutenant governor exceeds the PA offset for the particular year, and

(b) the amount by which the money purchase limit for the particular year exceeds the PA offset for the particular year.

**Notes**: Reg. 8309(1) amended by P.C. 1998-2256, retroactive to 1990. The changes primarily use "the PA offset" (now defined in Reg. 8300(1)) in place of $1,000.

**(2)** Subject to subsection (3), where an individual is, at any time in a particular calendar year after 1990, a judge in receipt of a salary under the *Judges Act*, there is prescribed in respect of the individual for the year following the particular year, for the purposes of the descriptions of B in the definitions "RRSP deduction limit" and "unused RRSP deduction room" in subsection 146(1) of the Act and the description of B in paragraph 204.2(1.1)(b) of the Act, the lesser of

(a) the amount, if any, by which 18% of the salary (other than salary that was not received under the *Judges Act*) received by the individual for the particular year as a judge exceeds the PA offset for the particular year, and

(b) the amount by which the money purchase limit for the particular year exceeds the PA offset for the particular year.

**Notes**: Reg. 8309(2) amended by P.C. 1998-2256, retroactive to 1990. The changes primarily use "the PA offset" (now defined in Reg. 8300(1)) in place of $1,000.

**(3)** For the purpose of determining the amount prescribed under subsection (1) or (2) in respect of an individual for a calendar year after 1996 and before 2005, paragraphs (1)(b) and (2)(b) shall be read as:

"(b) the money purchase limit for the particular year.".

**Notes**: Reg. 8309(3) added by P.C. 1998-2256, retroactive to 1990.

**Definitions [Reg. 8309]**: "amount" — ITA 248(1); "Governor" — *Interpretation Act* 35(1); "individual" — ITA 248(1); "lieutenant governor" — *Interpretation Act* 35(1); "money purchase limit" — ITA 147.1(1), 248(1); "PA offset" — Reg. 8300(1); "prescribed" — ITA 248(1); "province" — *Interpretation Act* 35(1).

**8310. Minister's powers** — **(1)** Where more than one method for determining an amount under this Part complies with the rules in this Part, only such of those methods as are acceptable to the Minister shall be used.

**(2)** Where, in a particular case, the rules in this Part require the determination of an amount in a manner that is not appropriate having regard to the provisions of this Part read as a whole and the purposes for which the amount is determined, the Minister may permit or require the amount to be determined in a manner that, in the Minister's opinion, is appropriate.

**(3)** Where, pursuant to subsection (2), the Minister gives permission or imposes a requirement, the permission or requirement is not effective unless it is given or imposed in writing.

**Definitions [Reg. 8310]**: "amount", "Minister" — ITA 248(1); "writing" — *Interpretation Act* 35(1).

**8311. Rounding of amounts** — Where a pension credit, provisional PSPA or PAR of an individual is not a multiple of one dollar, it shall be rounded to the nearest multiple of one dollar or, if it is equidistant from 2 such consecutive multiples, to the higher of the two multiples.

**Notes**: Reference to PAR (pension adjustment reversal; see Reg. 8304.1) added to Reg. 8311 by P.C. 1998-2256, effective 1997.

The PAR was originally included in the pension regulations before they were passed into force, and deleted in 1990 on the grounds that the system was too complicated. See Reg. 8304 in the draft regulations of December 11, 1989.

**Definitions [Reg. 8311]**: "individual" — ITA 248(1); "PAR" — Reg. 8304.1(1), (3)–(5); "pension credit" — Reg. 8301, 8308.1(2)–(4), 8308.3(2), (3); "provisional PSPA" — Reg. 8303(2), (3), 8308(4)(e).

**Notes [Reg. 8300–8311]**: Part LXXXIII added by P.C. 1991-2540, effective 1990, except that

(a) in its application in respect of amounts paid to pension plans before 1991, "excluded contribution" in 8300(1) shall be read as follows:

"excluded contribution" to a registered pension plan means an amount paid to the plan that is

(a) transferred to the plan in accordance with any of subsections 146(16), 147(19) and 147.3(1) to (7) of the Act, or

(b) deductible, as a consequence of the payment, under paragraph 60(j) or (j.1) of the Act in computing the income of a taxpayer for a taxation year;

(b) before 1991, 8301(2) and (3) shall be read without reference to the phrase "and subsection 147(5.1) of the Act";

(c) 8307(6) is applicable after 1990; and

(d) 8307(7) is applicable to 1991 *et seq.*

## PART LXXXIV — RETIREMENT AND PROFIT SHARING PLANS — REPORTING AND PROVISION OF INFORMATION

**8400. Definitions** — **(1)** All words and expressions used in this Part that are defined in subsection 8300(1), 8308.4(1) or 8500(1) or in subsection 147.1(1) of the Act have the meanings assigned in those provisions.

**Notes**: Reference to 8308.4(1) added by P.C. 1996-911, effective 1993.

**(2)** A reference in this Part to a pension credit of an individual means a pension credit of the individual as determined under Part LXXXIII.

**(3)** For the purposes of this Part, where the administrator of a pension plan is not otherwise a person, the administrator shall be deemed to be a person.

**Definitions [Reg. 8400]**: "administrator" — ITA 147.1(1), Reg. 8308.4(1); "individual" — ITA 248(1); "pension credit" — Reg. 8301, 8308.1(2)–(4), 8308.3(2), (3), Reg. 8400(2); "person" — ITA 248(1), Reg. 8400(3).

**8401. Pension adjustment** — **(1)** Where the pension adjustment of an individual for a calendar year with respect to an employer is greater than nil, the employer shall, on or before the last day of February in the immediately following calendar year, file with the Minister an information return in prescribed form reporting the pension adjustment, other than the portion, if any, required by subsection (2) or (3) to be reported by the administrator of a registered pension plan.

**(2)** Where an individual makes a contribution in a particular calendar year to a registered pension plan that is a specified multi-employer plan in the year and the contribution is not remitted to the plan by any participating employer on behalf of the individual, the plan administrator shall, on or before the last day of February in the immediately following calendar year, file with the Minister an information return in prescribed form reporting the aggregate of all amounts each of which is the portion, if any, of the individual's pension adjustment for the particular year with respect to an employer that may reasonably be considered to result from the contribution.

(3) Where the portion of a pension credit of an individual for a calendar year that, pursuant to subsection (4), is reportable by the administrator of a registered pension plan is greater than nil, the administrator shall, on or before the last day of February in the immediately following calendar year, file with the Minister an information return in prescribed form reporting that portion of the pension credit.

(4) For the purpose of subsection (3), where, on application by the administrator of a registered pension plan that is, in a calendar year, a multi-employer plan (other than a specified multi-employer plan), the Minister consents in writing to the application of this subsection with respect to the plan in the year, such portion of each pension credit for the year under a defined benefit provision of the plan as may reasonably be considered to be attributable to benefits provided in respect of a period of reduced services or disability of an individual is, to the extent permitted by the Minister, reportable by the administrator.

(5) Subsections (1) to (3) do not apply to require the reporting of amounts with respect to an individual for the calendar year in which the individual dies.

(6) Where the pension adjustment of an individual for a calendar year with respect to an employer is altered by reason of the application of paragraph 8308(4)(d) or (5)(c) and the amount (in this subsection referred to as the "redetermined amount") that a person would have been required to report based on the pension adjustment as altered exceeds

    (a) if the person has not previously reported an amount in respect of the individual's pension adjustment, nil, and

    (b) otherwise, the amount reported by the person in respect of the individual's pension adjustment,

the person shall, within 60 days after the day on which paragraph 8308(3)(c) or (5)(c), as the case may be, applies to alter the pension adjustment, file with the Minister an information return in prescribed form reporting the redetermined amount.

**Definitions [Reg. 8401]**: "administrator" — ITA 147.1(1), Reg. 8308.4(1); "amount" — ITA 248(1); "contribution" — Reg. 8302(12); "defined benefit provision" — ITA 147.1(1); "employer", "individual", "Minister" — ITA 248(1); "multi-employer plan", "participating employer" — ITA 147.1(1); "pension adjustment" — ITA 248(1); "pension credit" — Reg. 8301, 8308.1(2)–(4), 8308.3(2), (3), Reg. 8400(2); "person" — ITA 248(1), Reg. 8400(3); "prescribed" — ITA 248(1); "redetermined amount" — Reg. 8401(6); "registered pension plan" — ITA 248(1); "specified multi-employer plan" — ITA 147.1(1), Reg. 8510(2), (3); "writing" — *Interpretation Act* 35(1).

**8402. Past service pension adjustment** — (1) Where a provisional PSPA (computed under section 8303, 8304 or 8308) of an individual with respect to an employer that is associated with a past service event (other than a certifiable past service event) is greater than nil, the administrator of each registered pension plan to which the past service event relates shall, within 60 days after the day on which the past service event occurs, file with the Minister an information return in prescribed form reporting such portion of the aggregate of all amounts each of which is the individual's PSPA with respect to an employer that is associated with the past service event as may reasonably be considered to be attributable to benefits provided under the plan, except that a return is not required to be filed by an administrator if the amount that would otherwise be reported by the administrator is nil.

(2) Where a foreign plan PSPA (computed under subsection 8308.1(5) or (6)) of an individual with respect to an employer associated with a modification of benefits under a foreign plan (as defined by subsection 8308.1(1)) is greater than nil, the employer shall, on or before the last day of February in the year following the calendar year in which the individual's benefits were modified, file with the Minister an information return in prescribed form reporting the foreign plan PSPA.

(3) Where a specified retirement arrangement PSPA (computed under subsection 8308.3(4) or (5)) of an individual with respect to an employer associated with a modification of benefits under a specified retirement arrangement (as defined by subsection 8308.3(1)) is greater than nil, the employer shall, on or before the last day of February in the calendar year following the calendar year in which the individual's benefits were modified, file with the Minister an information return in prescribed form reporting the specified retirement arrangement PSPA.

**Notes**: Reg. 8402 renumbered as 8402(1), and 8402(2) and (3) added, by P.C. 1996-911, effective 1992.

See also Notes to Reg. 8410.

**Definitions [Reg. 8402]**: "administrator" — ITA 147.1(1), Reg. 8308.4(1); "amount" — ITA 248(1); "associated" — ITA 256; "certifiable past service event" — Reg. 8300(1); "employer", "individual", "Minister" — ITA 248(1); "past service event" — ITA 147.1(1), Reg. 8300(1); "prescribed", "registered pension plan" — ITA 248(1).

**8402.01 Pension adjustment reversal** — (1) **Deferred profit sharing plan** — Where the PAR determined in connection with an individual's termination from a deferred profit sharing plan is greater than nil, each trustee under the plan shall file with the Minister an information return in prescribed form reporting the PAR

    (a) where the termination occurs in the first, second or third quarter of a calendar year, on or before the day that is 60 days after the last day of the quarter in which the termination occurs, and

(b) where the termination occurs in the fourth quarter of a calendar year, before February of the following calendar year,

and, for this purpose, an information return filed by a trustee under a deferred profit sharing plan is deemed to have been filed by each trustee under the plan.

**Related Provisions**: Reg. 8404(2) — Copy of return must be provided to taxpayer.

**Notes**: See at end of Reg. 8402.01.

**Forms**: T10: Pension adjustment reversal; T10 Segment; T10 Summ: Summary of PARs.

**(2) Deferred profit sharing plan — employer reporting** — Where an amount included in an individual's pension credit in respect of an employer under a deferred profit sharing plan is included in determining a PAR in connection with the individual's termination from the plan, the employer is deemed to be a trustee under the plan for the purpose of reporting the PAR.

**Related Provisions**: Reg. 8404(2) — Copy of return must be provided to taxpayer.

**(3) Benefit provision of a registered pension plan** — Subject to subsection (4), where the PAR determined in connection with an individual's termination from a benefit provision of a registered pension plan is greater than nil, the administrator of the plan shall file with the Minister an information return in prescribed form reporting the PAR

(a) where the termination occurs in the first, second or third quarter of a calendar year, on or before the day that is 60 days after the last day of the quarter in which the termination occurs; and

(b) where the termination occurs in the fourth quarter of a calendar year, before February of the following calendar year.

**Related Provisions**: Reg. 8404(2) — Copy of return must be provided to taxpayer.

**(4) Extended deadline — PA transfer amount** — Where, in determining an individual's PAR in connection with the individual's termination from a defined benefit provision of a registered pension plan, it is reasonable for the administrator of the plan to conclude, on the basis of information provided to the administrator by the administrator of another pension plan or by the individual, that the value of D in paragraph 8304.1(5)(a) in respect of the termination may be greater than nil, the administrator shall file with the Minister an information return in prescribed form reporting the PAR, if it is greater than nil, on or before the later of

(a) the day on or before which it would otherwise be required to be filed; and

(b) the day that is 60 days after the earliest day on which the administrator has all the information required to determine that value.

**Notes**: See at end of Reg. 8402.01.

**(5) Calendar year quarter** — For the purposes of this section,

(a) the first quarter of a calendar year is the period beginning on January 1 and ending on March 31 of the calendar year;

(b) the second quarter of a calendar year is the period beginning on April 1 and ending on June 30 of the calendar year;

(c) the third quarter of a calendar year is the period beginning on July 1 and ending on September 30 of the calendar year; and

(d) the fourth quarter of a calendar year is the period beginning on October 1 and ending on December 31 of the calendar year.

**Notes [Reg. 8402.01]**: Reg. 8402.01 added by P.C. 1998-2256, effective 1997, except that the deadline for any return required by 8402.01 is extended to March 31, 1999 for 1997 or 1998 terminations (such date being later than 60 days after publication in the *Canada Gazette*, which was January 6, 1999) and September 30 for 1999 terminations. It sets out the reporting requirements for PARs (pension adjustment reversals); see Reg. 8304.1.

**Definitions [Reg. 8402.01]**: "administrator" — ITA 147.1(1), Reg. 8308.4(1); "benefit provision" — ITA 147.1(1); "deferred profit sharing plan" — ITA 147(1), 248(1); "defined benefit provision" — ITA 147.1(1); "individual", "Minister" — ITA 248(1); "PAR" — Reg. 8304.1(1), (3)–(5); "prescribed" — ITA 248(1); "quarter" — Reg. 4300; "registered pension plan" — ITA 248(1).

**8402.1** Where an amount is prescribed by subsection 8308.4(2) in respect of an individual for a calendar year because of the individual's entitlement (either absolute or contingent) to benefits under a government-sponsored retirement arrangement (as defined in subsection 8308.4(1)), the administrator of the arrangement shall, on or before the last day of February in the year, file with the Minister an information return in prescribed form reporting the prescribed amount.

**Notes**: Reg. 8402.1 added by P.C. 1996-911, effective 1993.

**Definitions [Reg. 8402.1]**: "administrator" — ITA 147.1(1), Reg. 8308.4(1); "amount", "individual", "Minister", "prescribed" — ITA 248(1).

**8403. Connected persons** — Where, at any particular time after 1990,

(a) an individual becomes a member of a registered pension plan, or

(b) lifetime retirement benefits commence to accrue to the individual under a defined benefit provision of a registered pension plan following a period in which lifetime retirement benefits did not accrue to the individual,

each employer who participates in the plan for the benefit of the individual and with whom the individual is connected (within the meaning assigned by subsection 8500(3)) at the particular time, or was connected at any time after 1989, shall, within 60 days after the particular time, file with the Minister an information return in prescribed form containing prescribed information with respect to the individual unless the employer has previously filed an information return under this section with respect to the individual.

**Notes**: See Notes to Reg. 8410.

**Definitions [Reg. 8403]**: "defined benefit provision" — ITA 147.1(1); "employer", "individual" — ITA 248(1); "lifetime retirement benefits" — Reg. 8500(1); "Minister", "prescribed", "registered pension plan" — ITA 248(1).

**Registered Plans Division Newsletters**: 98-1 (Simplified pension plans).

**Forms**: T1007: Connected person information return.

**8404. Reporting to individuals** — (1) Every person who is required by section 8401 or 8402.1 to file an information return with the Minister shall, on or before the day on or before which the return is required to be filed with the Minister, send to each individual to whom the return relates, two copies of the portion of the return that relates to the individual.

**Notes**: Reference to 8402.1(1) added by P.C. 1996-911, and changed to (all of) 8402.1 by P.C. 1998-2256, both effective 1993.

(2) Every person who is required by section 8402, 8402.01 or 8403 to file an information return with the Minister shall, on or before the day on or before which the return is required to be filed with the Minister, send to each individual to whom the return relates, one copy of the portion of the return that relates to the individual.

**Notes**: Reference to 8402.1(2) added by P.C. 1996-911, effective 1993, and changed to 8402.01 by P.C. 1998-2256, effective 1997.

(3) Every person who obtains a certification from the Minister for the purposes of subsection 147.1(10) of the Act in respect of a past service event and an individual shall, within 60 days after receiving from the Minister the form submitted to the Minister pursuant to subsection 8307(1) in respect of the past service event and the individual, forward to the individual one copy of the form as returned by the Minister.

(4) Every person required by subsection (1), (2) or (3) to forward a copy of an information return or a form to an individual shall send the copy to the individual at the individual's last known address or shall deliver the copy to the individual in person.

**Definitions [Reg. 8404]**: "individual", "Minister" — ITA 248(1); "past service event" — ITA 147.1(1), Reg. 8300(1); "person" — ITA 248(1), Reg. 8400(3).

**8405. Discontinuance of business** — Subsection 205(2) and section 206 are applicable, with such modifications as the circumstances require, in respect of returns required to be filed under this Part.

**8406. Provision of information** — (1) Where a person who is required to file an information return under section 8401 requires information from another person in order to determine an amount that is to be reported or to otherwise complete the return and makes a written request to the other person for the information, the other person shall provide the person with the information that is available to that other person,

(a) where the information return is required to be filed in the calendar year in which the request is received, within 30 days after receipt of the request; or

(b) in any other case, by January 31 of the year immediately following the calendar year in which the request is received.

(2) Where the administrator of a registered pension plan requires information from a person in order to determine a provisional PSPA of an individual under section 8303, 8304 or 8308 and makes a written request to the person for the information, the person shall, within 30 days after receipt of the request, provide the administrator with the information that is available to the person.

(3) Where the administrator of a registered pension plan requires information from a person in order to complete an information return required to be filed under section 8409 and makes a written request to the person for the information, the person shall, within 30 days after receipt of the request, provide the administrator with the information that is available to that person.

(4) Where a person requires information from another person in order to determine a PAR under section 8304.1 in connection with an individual's termination in a calendar year from a deferred profit sharing plan or from a benefit provision of a registered pension plan (other than information that the other person is required to provide to the person under subsection (5)) and makes a written request to the other person for the information, the other person shall provide the person with the information that is available to the other person on or before

(a) if the request is received before December 17 of the year, the day that is 30 days after the day on which the request is received; and

(b) in any other case, the later of the day that is 15 days after the day on which the request is received and January 15 of the year following the year.

**Notes**: Reg. 8406(4) added by P.C. 1998-2256, effective 1997, except that the deadline for notification is extended to March 7, 1999 (which is 60 days after January 6, 1999, the date of publication in the *Canada Gazette*).

(5) Where benefits provided to an individual under a registered pension plan (in this subsection referred to as the "importing plan") as a consequence of a past service event result in a PA transfer amount in relation to the individual's termination from a defined benefit provision of another registered pension plan (in this subsection referred to as the "exporting plan"),

(a) the administrator of the importing plan shall, in writing on or before the day that is 30 days after the day on which the past service event occurred, notify the administrator of the exporting plan of the occurrence of the past service event and of its relevance in determining the individual's PAR in connection with the individual's termination from the defined benefit provision; and

(b) the administrator of the importing plan shall notify the administrator of the exporting plan of the PA transfer amount in writing on or before the day that is 60 days after

(i) in the case of a certifiable past service event, the day on which the Minister issues a certification for the purposes of subsection 147.1(10) of the Act in respect of the past service event and the individual, and

(ii) in any other case, the day on which the past service event occurred.

**Related Provisions**: Reg. 8304.1(10) — PA transfer amount; Reg. 8304.1(11) — Special 1997 PA transfer amount.

**Notes**: Reg. 8406(5) added by P.C. 1998-2256, effective 1997, except that the deadline for notification under para. (a) is extended to September 30, 1998; and the deadline under para. (b) is extended to March 7, 1999 (60 days after publication in the *Canada Gazette*, which was January 6, 1999).

**Definitions [Reg. 8406]**: "administrator" — ITA 147.1(1), Reg. 8308.4(1); "amount" — ITA 248(1); "certifiable past service event" — Reg. 8300(1); "defined benefit provision" — ITA 147.1(1); "exporting plan", "importing plan" — Reg. 8406(4); "individual", "Minister" — ITA 248(1); "PA transfer amount" — Reg. 8304.1(10), (11); "PAR" — Reg. 8304.1(1), (3)–(5); "past service event" — ITA 147.1(1), Reg. 8300(1); "person" — ITA 248(1), Reg. 8400(3); "registered pension plan" — ITA 248(1); "written" — *Interpretation Act* 35(1) "writing".

### 8407. Qualifying withdrawals — Where

(a) an individual who has withdrawn an amount from a registered retirement savings plan under which the individual was the annuitant (within the meaning assigned by paragraph 146(1)(a) [146(1)"annuitant"] of the Act) at the time of the withdrawal provides the issuer (within the meaning assigned by paragraph 146(1)(c.1) [146(1)"issuer"] of the Act) of the plan, in the calendar year in which the amount was withdrawn or in either of the 2 immediately following calendar years, with the prescribed form referred to in subparagraph 8307(3)(a)(ii) accompanied by a request that the issuer complete the form in respect of the withdrawal, and

(b) the issuer has not, at the time of receipt of the request, forwarded to the individual 2 copies of the information return required by subsection 214(1) to be made by the issuer in respect of the withdrawal, and does not, within 30 days after receipt of the request, forward to the individual 2 copies of that return,

the issuer shall, within 30 days after receipt of the request, complete those portions of the form that the form indicates are required to be completed by the issuer in respect of the withdrawal and return the form to the individual.

**Definitions [Reg. 8407]**: "amount", "individual", "prescribed" — ITA 248(1); "registered retirement savings plan" — ITA 146(1), 248(1).

**Forms**: T1006: Designating an RRSP withdrawal as a qualifying withdrawal.

### 8408. Requirement to provide Minister with information — (1) The Minister may, by notice served personally or by registered or certified mail, require that a person provide the Minister, within such reasonable time as is stipulated in the notice, with

(a) information relating to the determination of amounts under Part LXXXIII;

(b) where the person claims that paragraph 147.1(10)(a) of the Act is not applicable with respect to an individual and a past service event by reason of an exemption provided by regulation, information relevant to the claim; or

(c) information for the purpose of determining whether the registration of a pension plan may be revoked.

(2) Where a person fails to provide the Minister with information pursuant to a requirement under subsection (1), each registered pension plan and deferred profit sharing plan to which the information relates becomes a revocable plan as of the day on or before which the information was required to be provided.

**Definitions [Reg. 8408]**: "amount" — ITA 248(1); "deferred profit sharing plan" — ITA 147(1), 248(1); "individual", "Minister" — ITA 248(1); "past service event" — ITA 147.1(1), Reg. 8300(1); "person" — ITA 248(1), Reg. 8400(3); "registered pension plan" — ITA 248(1).

### 8409. Annual information returns — (1) The administrator of a registered pension plan that is administered under the supervision of a government regulator shall file an information return for a fiscal period of the plan in prescribed form and containing prescribed information

(a) where an agreement concerning annual information returns has been entered into by the Minister and the regulator, as identified in subsection (2),

(i) in the case of the agreement with the Pension Commission of Ontario, with the Taxation Data Centre of the Ministry of Finance of Ontario, and

(ii) in any other case, with that regulator,

on or before the day that an information return required by that regulator is to be filed for the fiscal period; and

(b) in any other case, with the Minister on or before the day that is 180 days after the end of the fiscal period.

**Notes**: See Notes at end of Reg. 8409.

Reg. 8409(1) amended by P.C. 1995-17 to change "1990" to "1991", effective 1990; thus, annual information returns were first required to be filed by June 30, 1992.

**Forms**: T244: Registered pension plan annual information return.

**(2)** For the purposes of paragraph (1)(a), the following government regulators have entered into an agreement concerning annual information returns with the Minister:

(a) the Pension Commission of Ontario, Province of Ontario;

(b) the Superintendent of Pensions, Province of Nova Scotia;

(c) the Superintendent of Pensions, Province of New Brunswick;

(d) the Superintendent of Pensions, Province of Manitoba; and

(e) the Superintendent of Pensions, Province of British Columbia.

**(3)** The administrator of a registered pension plan shall, within 60 days after the final distribution of property held in connection with the plan, notify the Minister in writing of the date of the distribution and the method of settlement.

**Notes [Reg. 8409]**: Reg. 8409 replaced by P.C. 1996-213, effective for fiscal periods that end after December 30, 1994.

Neither the new version nor the previous version applies for the 1994 calendar year to an RPP with a fiscal period ending in 1994 before December 31, 1994. The previous version read:

> 8409. Annual information returns — (1) Subject to subsection (2), the administrator of a registered pension plan shall, on or before June 30 in each calendar year after 1991, file with the Minister an information return for the preceding calendar year in prescribed form and containing prescribed information.
>
> (2) Where a final distribution of property held in connection with a registered pension plan is made in a particular calendar year, the administrator of the plan shall file the return required by subsection (1) for the preceding year on or before the earlier of June 30 of the particular year and the day that is 60 days after the final distribution of property.
>
> (3) The administrator of a registered pension plan shall, within 60 days after the final distribution of property held in connection with the plan, file with the Minister an information return in prescribed form and containing prescribed information.

See Notes to Reg. 8410.

The 1996 amendments implemented changes announced by Revenue Canada press releases on December 20, 1994 ("Simplified Filing Requirements for Registered Pension Plan Annual Information Returns"); February 9, 1995 ("Ottawa and New Brunswick Combine Filing Requirements for Registered Pension Plans"); April 6, 1995 ("Ottawa and Nova Scotia Combine Filing Requirements for Registered Pension Plans"); and May 19, 1995 ("Ottawa and British Columbia Combine Filing Requirements for Registered Pension Plans"). The information return can now be filed with the provincial or federal regulator responsible for the supervision of the RPP if the regulator has entered into an agreement with the CCRA regarding RPP information returns. Reg. 8409(2) lists the regulators that have entered into such an agreement.

The CCRA indicates in Registered Plans Division Newsletter 96-2 (June 17, 1996) the circumstances in which it will waive the filing obligation under Reg. 8409 for inactive plans. See the Newsletter, or contact the Registered Plans Division at (613) 954-0419.

**Definitions [Reg. 8409]**: "administrator" — ITA 147.1(1), Reg. 8308.4(1); "fiscal period" — ITA 249.1; "Minister", "prescribed", "property", "registered pension plan" — ITA 248(1); "writing" — *Interpretation Act* 35(1).

**Registered Plans Division Newsletters**: 95-4 (New filing requirements for the registered pension plan annual information return); 95-7 (Quebec simplified pension plans); 96-2 (Waiving the requirement to file a registered pension plan annual information return for an inactive plan).

**8410. Actuarial reports** — The administrator of a registered pension plan that contains a defined benefit provision shall, on demand from the Minister served personally or by registered or certified mail and within such reasonable time as is stipulated in the demand, file with the Minister a report prepared by an actuary on the basis of reasonable assumptions and in accordance with generally accepted actuarial principles and containing such information as is required by the Minister in respect of the defined benefit provisions of the plan.

**Notes [Reg. 8400–8410]**: Part LXXXIV added by P.C. 1991-2540, Regs. 8400 to 8405, 8409 and 8410 effective 1990, with grandfathering of filing dates to February 28, 1991 (for Reg. 8405) and to March 15, 1992 (for deadlines under Reg. 8402, 8403, 8404(2), (3) and 8409(1) and (3)).

**Definitions [Reg. 8410]**: "actuary" — ITA 147.1(1); "administrator" — ITA 147.1(1), Reg. 8308.4(1); "defined benefit provision" — ITA 147.1(1); "Minister", "registered pension plan" — ITA 248(1).

**Registered Plans Division Newsletters**: 95-3 (Actuarial report content); 95-5 (Conversion of a defined benefit provision to a money purchase provision).

# PART LXXXV — REGISTERED PENSION PLANS

**8500. Interpretation** — **(1)** In this Part,

**"active member"** of a pension plan in a calendar year means a member of the plan to whom benefits accrue under a defined benefit provision of the plan in respect of all or any portion of the year or who makes contributions, or on whose behalf contributions are made, in relation to the year under a money purchase provision of the plan;

**Related Provisions**: Reg. 8500(7) — Amount allocated under money purchase provision deemed to be contribution.

**"average Consumer Price Index"** for a calendar year means the amount that is obtained by dividing by 12 the aggregate of all amounts each of which is the Consumer Price Index for a month in the 12-month period ending on September 30 of the immediately preceding calendar year;

**"beneficiary"** of an individual means a person who has a right, by virtue of the participation of the individual in a pension plan, to receive benefits under the plan after the death of the individual;

**"benefit provision"** of a pension plan means a money purchase or defined benefit provision of the plan;

"**bridging benefits**" provided to a member under a benefit provision of a pension plan means retirement benefits payable to the member under the provision for a period ending no later than a date determinable at the time the benefits commence to be paid;

"**Consumer Price Index**" for a month means the Consumer Price Index for the month as published by Statistics Canada under the authority of the *Statistics Act*;

"**defined benefit limit**" for a calendar year means the greater of

(a) $1,722.22, and

(b) 1/9 of the money purchase limit for the year;

**Related Provisions**: Reg. 8509(13), 8516(9) — Grandfathering provisions.

**Notes**: Definition "defined benefit limit" amended by P.C. 1998-2256, effective 1996, except that para. (b) applies

(a) before March 6, 1996 as though the money purchase limit for each year after 1995 were the amount that it would be if ITA 147.1(1)"money purchase limit" applied as it read on December 31, 1995; and

(b) after March 5, 1996 and before 1997 as though the money purchase limit for each year after 1995 were the amount that it would be if ITA 147.1(1)"money purchase limit" applied as it read on January 1, 1997.

Since $1,722.22 is 1/9th of $15,500, the defined benefit limit will remain frozen at $1,722.22 until the money purchase limit exceeds $15,500. Before the amendment, read:

"defined benefit limit" for a calendar year means

(a) for years before 1996, $1,722.22, and

(b) for years after 1995, ⅑ of the money purchase limit for the year [now superseded by the above];

Definition previously amended by P.C. 1995-17, effective 1992, to postpone year references by one year (see Notes to ITA 147.1(1)"money purchase limit"). Thus, the defined benefit limit remained at $1,722.22 for 1995 and was to begin to be indexed in 1996. However, this was further delayed by the March 1996 federal budget; see ITA 147.1(1)"money purchase limit".

See also Reg. 8509(13) and 8516(9), which contain grandfathering provisions for certain RPP benefits and contributions based on indexing of the defined benefit limit before 2005.

"**dependant**" of an individual at the time of the individual's death means a parent, grandparent, brother, sister, child or grandchild of the individual who, at that time, is both dependent on the individual for support and

(a) under 19 years of age and will not attain 19 years of age in the calendar year that includes that time,

(b) in full-time attendance at an educational institution, or

(c) dependent on the individual by reason of mental or physical infirmity;

"**disabled**" means, in relation to an individual, suffering from a physical or mental impairment that prevents the individual from performing the duties of the employment in which the individual was engaged before the commencement of the impairment;

"**eligible period of reduced pay**" of an employee with respect to an employer means a period (other than a period in which the employee is, at any time after 1990, connected with the employer or a period any part of which is a period of disability of the employee)

(a) that begins after the employee has been employed by the employer or predecessor employers to the employer for not less than 36 months,

(b) throughout which the employee renders services to the employer, and

(c) throughout which the remuneration received by the employee from the employer is less than the remuneration that it is reasonable to expect the employee would have received from the employer had the employee rendered services throughout the period on a regular basis (having regard to the services rendered by the employee to the employer before the period) and had the employee's rate of remuneration been commensurate with the employee's rate of remuneration before the period;

**Information Circulars**: 98-2: Prescribed compensation for RPPs, para. 10.

"**eligible period of temporary absence**" of an individual with respect to an employer means a period throughout which the individual does not render services to the employer by reason of leave of absence, layoff, strike, lock-out or any other circumstance acceptable to the Minister, other than a period

(a) a part of which is a period of disability of the individual, or

(b) in which the individual is, at any time after 1990, connected with the employer;

"**eligible survivor benefit period**" in relation to a person who is a dependant of an individual at the time of the individual's death, means the period beginning on the day of death of the individual and ending on the latest of

(a) where the dependant is under 19 years of age throughout the calendar year that includes the day of death of the individual, the earlier of

(i) December 31 of the calendar year in which the dependant attains 18 years of age, and

(ii) the day of death of the dependant,

(b) where the dependant is in full-time attendance at an educational institution on the later of the day of death of the individual and December 31 of the calendar year in which the dependant attains 18 years of age, the day on which the dependant ceases to be in full-time attendance at an educational institution, and

(c) where the dependant is dependent on the individual at the time of the individual's death by reason of mental or physical infirmity, the day on which the dependant ceases to be infirm or, if there is no such day, the day of death of the dependant;

**"existing plan"** means a pension plan that was a registered pension plan on March 27, 1988 or in respect of which an application for registration was made to the Minister before March 28, 1988, and includes a pension plan that was established before March 28, 1988 pursuant to an Act of Parliament that deems member contributions to be contributions to a registered pension plan;

**"forfeited amount"** under a money purchase provision of a pension plan means an amount to which a member of the plan has ceased to have any rights, other than the portion thereof, if any, that is payable

(a) to a beneficiary of the member as a consequence of the member's death, or

(b) to a spouse or former spouse of the member as a consequence of the breakdown of their marriage or other conjugal relationship;

Notes: References to "spouse" are expected to be amended to add "or common-law partner" effective 2001 or earlier by election, as has been done throughout the ITA. See Notes to ITA 248(1)"common-law partner".

**"grandfathered plan"** means

(a) an existing plan that, on March 27, 1988, contained a defined benefit provision, or

(b) a pension plan that was established to provide benefits under a defined benefit provision to one or more individuals in lieu of benefits to which the individuals were entitled under a defined benefit provision of another pension plan that is a grandfathered plan, whether or not benefits are also provided to other individuals;

Related Provisions: Reg. 8509(13) — Grandfathering where plan complied before March 1996 budget date.

**"lifetime retirement benefits"** provided to a member under a benefit provision of a pension plan means retirement benefits provided to the member under the provision that, after they commence to be paid, are payable to the member until the member's death, unless the benefits are commuted or payment of the benefits is suspended;

**"multi-employer plan"** in a calendar year means

(a) a pension plan in respect of which it is reasonable to expect, at the beginning of the year (or at the time in the year when the plan is established, if later), that at no time in the year will more than 95 per cent of the active members of the plan be employed by a single participating employer or by a related group of participating employers, other than a plan where it is reasonable to consider that one of the main reasons there is more than one employer participating in the plan is to obtain the benefit of any of the provisions of the Act or these Regulations that are applicable only with respect to multi-employer plans, or

(b) a pension plan that is, in the year, a specified multi-employer plan,

and, for the purposes of this definition, 2 corporations that are related to each other solely by reason that they are both controlled by Her Majesty in right of Canada or a province shall be deemed not to be related persons;

Related Provisions: ITA 252.1 — Trade union locals and branches deemed to be a single employer; ITA 256(6), (6.1) — Meaning of "controlled".

Regulations: 8510(2), (3) (meaning of "specified multi-employer plan").

**"pensionable service"** of a member of a pension plan under a defined benefit provision of the plan means the periods in respect of which lifetime retirement benefits are provided to the member under the provision;

**"period of disability"** of an individual means a period throughout which the individual is disabled;

**"predecessor employer"** means, in relation to a particular employer, an employer (in this definition referred to as the "vendor") who has sold, assigned or otherwise disposed of all or part of the vendor's business or undertaking or all or part of the assets of the vendor's business or undertaking to the particular employer or to another employer who, at any time after the sale, assignment or other disposition, becomes a predecessor employer in relation to the particular employer, where one or more employees of the vendor have, in conjunction with the sale, assignment or disposition, become employees of the employer acquiring the business, undertaking or assets;

**"public pension benefits"** means amounts payable on a periodic basis under the *Canada Pension Plan*, a provincial pension plan as defined in section 3 of the *Canada Pension Plan*, or Part I of the *Old Age Security Act*, but does not include disability, death or survivor benefits provided under those Acts;

**"public safety occupation"** means the occupation of

(a) firefighter,

(b) police officer,

(c) corrections officer,

(d) air traffic controller, or

(e) commercial airline pilot;

**"retirement benefits"** provided to an individual under a benefit provision of a pension plan means benefits provided to the individual under the provision that are payable on a periodic basis;

**"surplus"** under a money purchase provision of a pension plan at any time means such portion, if any, of the amount held at that time in respect of the provision as has not been allocated to members and is not reasonably attributable to

(a) forfeited amounts under the provision or earnings of the plan that are reasonably attributable to those amounts,

(b) contributions made under the provision by an employer that will be allocated to members as part of the regular allocation of such contributions, or

(c) earnings of the plan (other than earnings that are reasonably attributable to the surplus under the provision before that time) that will be allocated to members as part of the regular allocation of such earnings;

**Related Provisions:** Reg. 8500(1.1) — Definition applies to ITA 147.3(7.1).

**Notes:** Paras. (a) and (b) amended by P.C. 1995-17, retroactive to the introduction of the definition (1989). The amendment recognizes that contributions made by an employer are not necessarily allocated immediately upon being contributed.

**"totally and permanently disabled"** means, in relation to an individual, suffering from a physical or mental impairment that prevents the individual from engaging in any employment for which the individual is reasonably suited by virtue of the individual's education, training or experience and that can reasonably be expected to last for the remainder of the individual's lifetime;

**"Year's Maximum Pensionable Earnings"** for a calendar year has the meaning assigned by section 18 of the *Canada Pension Plan*.

**Notes:** For the Year's Maximum Pensionable earnings, see the table of CPP contribution limits in the introductory pages.

**Interpretation Bulletins:** IT-124R6: Contributions to registered retirement savings plans.

**Registered Plans Division Newsletters:** 91-4R (Registration rules for money purchase provisions); 96-1 (Changes to retirement savings limits).

### Proposed Addition — Reg. 8500(1.1)

**(1.1)** The definition "surplus" in subsection (1) applies for the purpose of subsection 147.3(7.1) of the Act.

**Application:** The November 30, 1999 draft regulations (RPPs), subsec. 3(1), will add subsec. 8500(1.1), applicable after 1998.

**Technical Notes:** New subsection 147.3(7.1) of the Act permits, in certain circumstances, surplus under a money purchase provision of an RPP to be transferred to a money purchase provision of another RPP. Subsection 147.3(7.1) provides that the term "surplus" has the meaning assigned by the Regulations. New subsection 8500(1.1) of the Regulations provides that the definition of "surplus" in subsection 8500(1) of the Regulations applies for this purpose.

(2) All words and expressions used in this Part that are defined in subsection 147.1(1) of the Act have the meanings assigned in that subsection.

(3) For the purposes of this Part, a person is connected with an employer at any time where, at that time, the person

    (a) owns, directly or indirectly, not less than 10 per cent of the issued shares of any class of the capital stock of the employer or of any other corporation that is related to the employer,

    (b) does not deal at arm's length with the employer, or

    (c) is a specified shareholder of the employer by reason of paragraph (d) of the definition "specified shareholder" in subsection 248(1) of the Act,

and, for the purposes of this subsection,

    (d) a person shall be deemed to own, at any time, each share of the capital stock of a corporation owned, at that time, by a person with whom the person does not deal at arm's length,

    (e) where shares of the capital stock of a corporation are owned at any time by a trust,

        (i) if the share of any beneficiary in the income or capital of the trust depends on the exercise by any person of, or the failure by any person to exercise, any discretionary power, each beneficiary of the trust shall be deemed to own, at that time, all the shares owned by the trust, and

        (ii) in any other case, each beneficiary of a trust shall be deemed to own, at that time, that proportion of the shares owned by the trust that the fair market value at that time of the beneficiary's beneficial interest in the trust is of the fair market value at that time of all beneficial interests in the trust,

    (f) each member of a partnership shall be deemed to own, at any time, that proportion of all shares of the capital stock of a corporation that are property of the partnership at that time that the fair market value at that time of the member's interest in the partnership is of the fair market value at that time of the interests of all members in the partnership, and

    (g) a person who, at any time, has a right under a contract, in equity or otherwise, either immediately or in the future and either absolutely or contingently, to, or to acquire, shares of the capital stock of a corporation shall be deemed to own, at that time, those shares if one of the main reasons for the existence of the right may reasonably be considered to be that the person not be connected with an employer.

**Interpretation Bulletins:** IT-124R6: Contributions to registered retirement savings plans.

**Registered Plans Division Newsletters:** 91-4R (Registration rules for money purchase provisions).

(4) For the purposes of this Part, an officer who receives remuneration for holding an office shall, for any period that the officer holds the office, be deemed to render services to, and to be in the service of, the person from whom the officer receives the remuneration.

**Interpretation Bulletins:** IT-167R6: Registered pension plans — employee's contributions.

(5) For the purposes of this Part, any provision that applies with respect to a spouse of a taxpayer also

applies in the same manner with respect to a party to a void or voidable marriage to a taxpayer.

**Notes**: References to "spouse" are expected to be amended to add "or common-law partner" effective 2001 or earlier by election, as has been done throughout the ITA. See Notes to ITA 248(1)"common-law partner".

**Registered Plans Division Newsletters**: 91-4R (Registration rules for money purchase provisions).

(6) Where this Part provides that an amount is to be determined by aggregating the durations of periods that satisfy specified conditions, a period shall be included in determining the aggregate only if it is not part of a longer period that satisfies the conditions.

(7) For the purposes of the definition "active member" in subsection (1), subparagraph 8503(3)(a)(v) and paragraphs 8504(7)(d) and 8507(3)(a), such portion of an amount allocated to an individual at any time under a money purchase provision of a registered pension plan as is attributable to

(a) forfeited amounts under the provision or earnings of the plan that are reasonably attributable to those amounts,

(b) a surplus under the provision, or

(c) property transferred to the provision in respect of the actuarial surplus under a defined benefit provision of the plan or another registered pension plan

### Proposed Addition — Reg. 8500(7)(d)

(d) property transferred to the provision in respect of the surplus under another money purchase provision of the plan or under a money purchase provision of another registered pension plan

**Application**: The November 30, 1999 draft regulations (RPPs), subsec. 3(2), will add para. 8500(7)(d), applicable to allocations that occur after 1998.

**Technical Notes**: Subsection 8500(7) of the Regulations deems certain amounts allocated to an individual under a money purchase provision of an RPP to be contributions made on behalf of the individual for the purposes of a number of provisions in Part LXXXV that depend on whether money purchase contributions are made on behalf of an individual. Subsection 8500(7) applies with respect to allocated amounts that are attributable to forfeited amounts, to surplus under the provision or to surplus transferred from a defined benefit provision.

Subsection 8500(7) is amended so that it also applies with respect to allocations that are attributable to money purchase surplus transferred from another money purchase provision. This amendment is consequential on the introduction of new subsection 147.3(7.1) of the Act, which permits the transfer of surplus from one money purchase plan to another. It should be noted that this amendment is relevant only where money purchase surplus is allocated to an individual at the time of the transfer. Existing paragraph 8500(7)(b) would apply with respect to allocations that occur after the time of the transfer.

shall be deemed to be a contribution made under the provision on behalf of the individual at that time.

**Notes**: Reg. 8500(7) added by P.C. 1995-17, this version effective for amounts allocated before April 6, 1994. For amounts from 1989 to April 5, 1994, ignore the words "and the definition "active member" in subsection (1)"; and, for purposes of Reg. 8507(3)(a)(vi), ignore para. (c). (The rule in Reg. 8500(7) was formerly found in the closing words of Reg. 8507(3)(a).)

### Proposed Addition — Reg. 8500(8)

**(8) [Member and non-member benefits]** — Where an individual who is entitled to receive benefits (in this subsection referred to as "member benefits") under a pension plan because of the individual's membership in the plan is also entitled to receive other benefits (in this subsection referred to as "non-member benefits") under the plan or under any other pension plan solely because of the participation of another individual in the plan or in the other plan, the following rules apply:

(a) for the purpose of determining whether the member benefits are permissible under this Part, the non-member benefits shall be disregarded;

(b) for the purpose of determining whether the non-member benefits are permissible under this Part, the member benefits shall be disregarded; and

(c) for the purpose of determining a pension adjustment, pension adjustment reversal or provisional past service pension adjustment of the individual under Part LXXXIII, the non-member benefits shall be disregarded.

**Application**: The November 30, 2000 draft regulations (RPPs) (pre-published in *Canada Gazette*, Part I, December 9, 2000), s. 5, will add subsec. 8500(8), applicable after 1988, except that before 1997, para. (c) shall be read without reference to the words "pension adjustment reversal".

**Technical Notes, April 18, 2000**: New subsection 8500(8) of the Regulations sets out several rules of interpretation that apply when an individual who is a member of a pension plan is also entitled to receive other benefits (referred to as "non-member benefits") under the plan or under another pension plan because of the participation of another individual in the plan or other plan. Non-member benefits could include, for example, benefits to which the member is entitled because of marriage breakdown or the death of the member's spouse. Subsection 8500(8) provides that the non-member benefits are to be disregarded in determining whether the benefits provided to the individual as a plan member are permissible and in determining a PA, PSPA or PAR of the individual. It also provides that the benefits provided to the individual as a plan member are to be disregarded in determining whether the non-member benefits are permissible.

These rules are relevant, in particular, for large defined benefit RPPs where it is relatively common for two spouses to participate in the same pension plan. The following example will help illustrate these rules. Consider an individual who is a member of a defined benefit RPP and who is receiving post-retirement survivor benefits under the plan because the individual's spouse had also participated in the plan. Subsection 8500(8) ensures that the survivor benefits are disregarded in determining whether benefits can continue to accrue to the individual as a plan member (paragraph 8503(3)(b)), in determining whether benefits payable to the individual as a plan member comply with the maximum pension limit (section 8504) and in determining a PAR for the individual (subsections 8304.1(8) and (14)). It also ensures that the benefits provided to the individual as a plan member are disregarded in determining whether the survivor benefits are permissible (paragraph 8503(2)(d)).

Subsection 8500(8) applies after 1988.

**Definitions [Reg. 8500]**: "active member" — Reg. 8500(1); "amount" — ITA 248(1); "arm's length" — ITA 251(1); "beneficiary", "benefit provision" — Reg. 8500(1); "benefits" — Reg. 8501(5)(c); "business" — ITA 248(1); "Canada" — ITA 255, *Interpretation Act* 35(1); "child" — ITA 252(1); "commencement" — *Interpretation Act* 35(1); "connected" — Reg. 8500(3); "consequence of the member's death" — 248(8); "Consumer Price Index" — Reg. 8500(1); "contribution" — Reg. 8500(7), 8501(6); "controlled" — ITA 256(6), (6.1); "corporation" — ITA 248(1), *Interpretation Act* 35(1); "defined benefit provision" — ITA 147.1(1); "dependant", "disabled" — Reg. 8500(1); "disposed" — ITA 248(1)"disposition"; "employed", "employee", "employer", "employment" — ITA 248(1); "existing plan", "forfeited amount", "grandfathered plan" — Reg. 8500(1); "Her Majesty" — *Interpretation Act* 35(1); "individual" — ITA 248(1); "lifetime retirement benefits" — Reg. 8500(1); "member" — ITA 147.1(1); "Minister" — ITA 248(1); "money purchase limit", "money purchase provision" — ITA 147.1(1); "month" — *Interpretation Act* 35(1); "office" — ITA 248(1); "officer" — Reg. 8500(4); "own" — Reg. 8500(3)(d)–(g); "Parliament" — *Interpretation Act* 35(1); "participating employer" — ITA 147.1(1); "partnership" — see Notes to ITA 96(1); "past service pension adjustment" — ITA 248(1), Reg. 8303(1); "pension adjustment" — ITA 248(1); "period of disability" — Reg. 8500(1); "person" — ITA 248(1); "predecessor employer" — Reg. 8500(1); "property" — ITA 248(1); "province" — *Interpretation Act* 35(1); "provisional past service pension adjustment" — Reg. 8303(2); "registered pension plan" — ITA 248(1); "related" — ITA 251(2)–(6), Reg. 8500(1)"multi-employer plan"; "retirement benefits" — Reg. 8500(1); "share" — ITA 248(1); "specified multi-employer plan" — ITA 147.1(1), Reg. 8510(2), (3); "specified shareholder" — ITA 248(1); "spouse" — ITA 147.1(1); "surplus" — Reg. 8500(1); "taxpayer" — ITA 248(1); "trust" — ITA 104(1), 248(1), (3).

**Forms [Reg. 8500]**: T920: Application for acceptance of an amendment to an RPP.

## 8501. Prescribed conditions for registration and other conditions applicable to registered pension plans — (1) Conditions for registration — For the purposes of section 147.1 of the Act, and subject to sections 8509 and 8510, the prescribed conditions for the registration of a pension plan are

(a) the conditions in paragraphs 8502(a), (c), (e), (f) and (l),

(b) if the plan contains a defined benefit provision, the conditions in paragraphs 8503(4)(a) and (c), and

(c) if the plan contains a money purchase provision, the conditions in paragraphs 8506(2)(a) and (d),

and the following conditions:

(d) there is no reason to expect, on the basis of the documents that constitute the plan and establish the funding arrangements, that

(i) the plan may become a revocable plan pursuant to subsection (2), or

(ii) the conditions in subsection 147.1(10) of the Act may not be complied with, and

(e) there is no reason to expect that the plan may become a revocable plan pursuant to subsection 147.1(8) or (9) of the Act or subsection 8503(15).

**Related Provisions**: Reg. 8501(3) — Conditions inapplicable where inconsistent with 8503(6) and (8) and 8505(3) and (4); Reg. 8501(6) — Rule where contributions made through employer association or trade union from employer or individual.

**Information Circulars**: 98-2: Prescribed compensation for RPPs, paras. 19, 30.

**Registered Plans Division Newsletters**: 91-4R (Registration rules for money purchase provisions).

**(2) Conditions applicable to registered pension plans** — For the purposes of paragraph 147.1(11)(c) of the Act, and subject to sections 8509 and 8510, a registered pension plan becomes a revocable plan at any time that it fails to comply with

(a) a condition set out in any of paragraphs 8502(b), (d), (g) to (k) and (m);

(b) where the plan contains a defined benefit provision, a condition set out in paragraph 8503(3)(a), (b), (d), (j), (k) or (l) or (4)(b), (d), (e) or (f); or

(c) where the plan contains a money purchase provision, a condition set out in any of paragraphs 8506(2)(b) to (c) and (e) to (h).

**Related Provisions**: Reg. 8501(3) — Conditions inapplicable where inconsistent with 8503(6) and (8) and 8505(3) and (4); Reg. 8501(6) — Rule where contributions made through employer association or trade union from employer or individual.

**Notes**: Reg. 8501(2)(a) amended to add reference to 8502(m) by P.C. 1996-911, effective 1994.

Reg. 8501(2)(c) amended by P.C. 1995-17, effective April 6, 1994, to add reference to Reg. 8506(2)(b.1).

**Registered Plans Division Newsletters**: 91-4R (Registration rules for money purchase provisions).

**(3) Permissive rules** — The conditions in this Part do not apply in respect of a pension plan to the extent that they are inconsistent with the provisions of subsections 8503(6) and (8) and 8505(3) and (4).

**Notes**: Reg. 8501(3) amended by P.C. 1995-17, retroactive to its introduction (1989), to add reference to Reg. 8505(4).

**(4) Supplemental plans** — Where

(a) the benefits provided under a pension plan (in this subsection referred to as the "supplemental plan") that contains one defined benefit provision and no money purchase provisions may reasonably be considered to be supplemental to the benefits provided under a defined benefit provision (in this subsection referred to as the "base provision") of another pension plan,

(b) the supplemental plan does not otherwise comply with the condition set out in paragraph 8502(a) or the condition in paragraph 8502(c), and

(c) the Minister has approved the application of this subsection, which approval has not been withdrawn,

for the purpose of determining whether the supplemental plan complies with the conditions in paragraphs 8502(a) and (c), the benefits provided under the base provision shall be considered to be provided under the supplemental plan.

**(5) Benefits payable to spouse after marriage breakdown** — Where

(a) a spouse or former spouse of a member of a registered pension plan is entitled to receive all or a portion of the benefits that would otherwise be payable under the plan to the member, and

(b) the entitlement was created

(i) by assignment of benefits by the member, on or after the breakdown of their marriage or other conjugal relationship, in settlement of rights arising out of their marriage or other conjugal relationship, or

(ii) by a provision of the law of Canada or a province applicable in respect of the division of property between the member and the member's spouse or former spouse, on or after the breakdown of their marriage or other conjugal relationship, in settlement of rights arising out of their marriage or other conjugal relationship,

the following rules apply:

(c) except where paragraph (d) is applicable, the benefits to which the spouse or former spouse is entitled shall, for the purposes of this Part, be deemed to be benefits provided and payable to the member, and

(d) where

(i) the entitlement of the spouse or former spouse was created by a provision of the law of Canada or a province described in subparagraph (b)(ii), and

(ii) that provision

(A) requires that benefits commence to be paid to the spouse or former spouse at a time that may be different from the time benefits commence to be paid to the member, or

(B) gives the spouse or former spouse any rights in respect of the benefits to which the spouse or former spouse is entitled in addition to the rights that the spouse or former spouse would have as a consequence of an assignment by the member, in whole or in part, of the member's right to benefits under the plan,

the benefits to which the spouse or former spouse is entitled shall, for the purposes of this Part, be deemed to be benefits provided and payable to the spouse or former spouse and not provided or payable to the member.

**Notes**: References to "spouse" are expected to be amended to add "or common-law partner" effective 2001 or earlier by election, as has been done throughout the ITA. See Notes to ITA 248(1) "common-law partner".

**(6) Indirect contributions** — Where an employer or an individual makes payments to a trade union or an association of employers (in this subsection referred to as the "contributing entity") to enable the contributing entity to make contributions to a pension plan, such portion of a contribution made by the contributing entity to the plan as is reasonably attributable to a payment made to the contributing entity by an employer or individual shall, for the purposes of the conditions in this Part, be considered to be a contribution made by the employer or individual, as the case may be, and not by the contributing entity.

**Proposed Addition — Reg. 8501(6.1), (6.2)**

**(6.1) Member contributions for unfunded liability** — For the purposes of the conditions in this Part, a contribution made by a member of a pension plan in respect of a defined benefit provision of the plan is deemed to be a current service contribution made by the member in respect of the member's benefits under the provision if

(a) the contribution cannot, but for this subsection, reasonably be considered to be made in respect of the member's benefits under the provision;

(b) the contribution is determined by reference to the actuarial liabilities under the provision in respect of periods before the time of the contribution; and

(c) the contribution is made pursuant to an arrangement

(i) under which all, or a significant number, of the active members of the plan are required to make similar contributions,

(ii) the main purpose of which is to ensure that the plan has sufficient assets to pay benefits under the provision, and

(iii) that is approved by the Minister.

**Technical Notes**: New subsection 8501(6.1) applies where member contributions under a defined benefit provision of a pension plan are made in respect of an unfunded liability, rather than in respect of the member's benefits. The purpose of this subsection is to accommodate arrangements under defined benefit pension plans that require participating employers and plan members to share in the funding of an unfunded liability.

Under some shared-funding arrangements, member contributions that are dedicated towards the plan's unfunded liability are not considered to be made in respect of the member's benefits. Subsection 8501(6.1) provides that, for the purposes of the conditions in Part LXXXV, such contributions are considered to be current service contributions made in respect of the member's benefits under the provision. This ensures that the contributions are not prohibited by the permissible contribution rule in paragraph 8502(b). It also requires that the contributions be taken into account for the purpose of satisfying the current service contribution limit in paragraph 8503(4)(a). It should be noted that subsection 8503(5) may be relevant where the member contribution rate under a shared-funding arrangement is set a level that results in the condition in paragraph 8503(4)(a) not being met. Subsection 8503(5) allows the Minister to waive the condition on maximum member contributions where it is reasonable to expect, on a long-term basis, that the regular current service contributions made by members will fund no more than one-half of the related benefits.

New subsection 8501(6.1) applies where:

- member contributions under a defined benefit provision of a pension plan are determined by reference to the actuarial liabilities under the provision;
- the contributions cannot reasonably be considered to be in respect of the member's benefits;
- the contributions are made pursuant to an arrangement approved by the Minister that requires all or a significant number of the active members of the plan to make similar contributions; and
- the main purpose of the arrangement is to ensure that the plan is adequately funded.

**Notes**: These arrangements are known as "shared-funding arrangements".

**(6.2) Prescribed eligible contributions** — For the purpose of paragraph 147.2(4)(a) of the Act, a contribution described in subsection (6.1) is a prescribed eligible contribution.

**Technical Notes**: New subsection 8501(6.1) applies where member contributions under a defined benefit provision of a pension plan are made in respect of an unfunded liability, rather than in respect of the member's benefits. The purpose of this subsection is to accommodate arrangements under defined benefit pension plans that require participating employers and plan members to share in the funding of an unfunded liability.

Under some shared-funding arrangements, member contributions that are dedicated towards the plan's unfunded liability are not considered to be made in respect of the member's benefits. Subsection 8501(6.1) provides that, for the purposes of the conditions in Part LXXXV, such contributions are considered to be current service contributions made in respect of the member's benefits under the provision. This ensures that the contributions are not prohibited by the permissible contribution rule in paragraph 8502(b). It also requires that the contributions be taken into account for the purpose of satisfying the current service contribution limit in paragraph 8503(4)(a). It should be noted that subsection 8503(5) may be relevant where the member contribution rate under a shared-funding arrangement is set a level that results in the condition in paragraph 8503(4)(a) not being met. Subsection 8503(5) allows the Minister to waive the condition on maximum member contributions where it is reasonable to expect, on a long-term basis, that the regular current service contributions made by members will fund no more than one-half of the related benefits.

New subsection 8501(6.1) applies where:

- member contributions under a defined benefit provision of a pension plan are determined by reference to the actuarial liabilities under the provision;
- the contributions cannot reasonably be considered to be in respect of the member's benefits;
- the contributions are made pursuant to an arrangement approved by the Minister that requires all or a significant number of the active members of the plan to make similar contributions; and
- the main purpose of the arrangement is to ensure that the plan is adequately funded.

New subsection 8501(6.2) of the Regulations provides that contributions described in subsection 8501(6.1) are prescribed eligible contributions for the purpose of the deductibility rules in amended paragraph 147.2(4)(a) of the Act. This ensures that member contributions made pursuant to a shared-funding arrangement are deductible even though they are not considered to relate to a particular year.

**Application**: The November 30, 1999 draft regulations (RPPs), s. 4, will add subsecs. 8501(6.1) and (6.2), applicable to contributions made after 1990.

**(7) Benefits provided with surplus on plan wind-up** — Where

(a) a single amount is paid in full or partial satisfaction of an individual's entitlement to retirement benefits (in this subsection referred to as the "commuted benefits") under a defined benefit provision of a registered pension plan,

(b) other benefits are subsequently provided to the individual under the provision as a consequence of an allocation, on full or partial wind-up of the plan, of an actuarial surplus under the provision,

(c) the other benefits include benefits (in this subsection referred to as "ancillary benefits") that, but for this subsection, would not be permissible under this Part,

(d) if the individual had previously terminated from the provision and the conditions in subsection 8304.1(14) were satisfied with respect to the termination, it is reasonable to consider that all of the ancillary benefits are in respect of periods before 1990, and

(e) the Minister has approved the application of this subsection in respect of the ancillary benefits,

for the purpose of determining whether the ancillary benefits are permissible under this Part, the individual is considered to have an entitlement under the provision to the commuted benefits.

**Notes**: See Q.5 in Notes to Reg. 8503(3).

Reg. 8501(7) added by P.C. 1998-2256, effective for benefits provided after 1996.

**Definitions [Reg. 8501]**: "active member" — Reg. 8500(1); "benefits" — Reg. 8501(5)(c); "Canada" — ITA 255, *Interpretation Act* 35(1); "contributing entity" — Reg. 8501(6); "contribution" — Reg. 8501(6), (7); "defined benefit provision" — ITA 147.1(1); "employer", "individual" — ITA 248(1); "member" — ITA 147.1(1); "Minister" — ITA 248(1); "money purchase provi-

Part LXXXV — Registered Pension Plans      Reg. S. 8502(d)(ii)

sion" — ITA 147.1(1); "prescribed", "property" — ITA 248(1); "province" — *Interpretation Act* 35(1); "registered pension plan" — ITA 248(1); "retirement benefits" — Reg. 8500(1); "single amount", "spouse" — ITA 147.1(1); "supplemental plan" — Reg. 8501(4)(a); "surplus" — Reg. 8500(1).

**8502. Conditions applicable to all plans** — For the purposes of section 8501, the following conditions are applicable in respect of a pension plan:

(a) **primary purpose** — the primary purpose of the plan is to provide periodic payments to individuals after retirement and until death in respect of their service as employees;

(b) **permissible contributions** — each contribution made to the plan after 1990 is an amount that

    (i) is paid by a member of the plan in accordance with the plan as registered, where the amount is credited to the member's account under a money purchase provision of the plan, or is paid in respect of the member's benefits under a defined benefit provision of the plan,

    (ii) is paid in accordance with a money purchase provision of the plan as registered, by an employer with respect to the employer's employees or former employees,

    (iii) is an eligible contribution that is paid in respect of a defined benefit provision of the plan by an employer with respect to the employer's employees or former employees,

    (iv) is transferred to the plan in accordance with any of subsections 146(16), 147(19) and 147.3(1) to (8) of the Act, or

    (v) is acceptable to the Minister and that is transferred to the plan from a pension plan that is maintained primarily for the benefit of non-residents in respect of services rendered outside Canada,

and, for the purposes of this paragraph,

    (vi) an eligible contribution is a contribution that is paid by an employer in respect of a defined benefit provision of a pension plan is where it is an eligible contribution under subsection 147.2(2) of the Act or, in the case of a plan in which Her Majesty in right of Canada or a province is a participating employer, would be an eligible contribution under subsection 147.2(2) of the Act if all amounts held to the credit of the plan in the accounts of Canada or the province were excluded from the assets of the plan, and

    (vii) such portion of the contributions that are made by Her Majesty in right of Canada or a province in respect of a defined benefit provision of the plan as can reasonably be considered to be made with respect to the employees or former employees of another person shall be deemed to be contributions that are made by that other person;

**Related Provisions**: Reg. 8510(6) — Special rules — specified multi-employer plan.

(c) **permissible benefits** — the plan does not provide for, and its terms are such that it will not under any circumstances provide for, any benefits other than benefits

    (i) that are provided under one or more defined benefit provisions and are in accordance with subsection 8503(2), paragraphs 8503(3)(c) and (e) to (i) and section 8504,

    (ii) that are provided under one or more money purchase provisions and are in accordance with subsection 8506(1),

    (iii) that the plan is required to provide by reason of a designated provision of the law of Canada or a province, or that the plan would be required to provide if each such provision were applicable to the plan with respect to all its members, and

    (iv) that the plan is required to provide to a spouse or former spouse of a member of the plan by reason of a provision of the law of Canada or a province applicable in respect of the division of property between the member and the spouse or former spouse, on or after the breakdown of their marriage or other conjugal relationship, in settlement of rights arising out of their marriage or other conjugal relationship;

**Related Provisions**: Reg. 8503(9)(f) — Re-employed member; Reg. 8509(2) — Conditions applicable after 1991 to benefits under grandfathered plan; Reg. 8509(4) — Grandfathered plan — Minister may exempt certain benefits; Reg. 8510(6) — Special rules — specified multi-employer plan; Reg. 8513 — Designated provision of the law of Canada or a province.

**Notes**: References to "spouse" are expected to be amended to add "or common-law partner" effective 2001 or earlier by election, as has been done throughout the ITA. See Notes to ITA 248(1)"common-law partner".

(d) **permissible distributions** — each distribution that is made from the plan is

    (i) a payment of benefits in accordance with the plan as registered,

    (ii) a transfer of property held in connection with a defined benefit provision of the plan to another pension plan to be held in connection with a benefit provision of that other plan, where the transfer is in accordance with subsection 147.3(3), (4.1) or (8) of the Act,

---

**Proposed Amendment — Reg. 8502(d)(ii)**

(ii) a transfer of property held in connection with the plan where the transfer is made in accordance with subsection 147.3(3), (4.1), (7.1) or (8) of the Act,

**Application**: The November 30, 1999 draft regulations (RPPs), subsec. 5(1), will amend subpara. 8502(d)(ii) to read as above, applicable to transactions that occur after 1998.

**Reg. S. 8502(d)(ii)** — Income Tax Regulations

> **Technical Notes:** Paragraph 8502(d) restricts the distributions that may be made out of an RPP.
>
> Paragraph 8502(d) is amended to add to the list of permissible distributions a transfer of property made in accordance with new subsection 147.3(7.1) of the Act. Subsection 147.3(7.1) permits the transfer of surplus from one money purchase plan to another, where the second plan replaces all or part of the first plan.
>
> This amendment, which is consequential to the introduction of subsection 147.3(7.1), applies to transactions that occur after 1998.

(iii) a return of all or a portion of the contributions made by a member of the plan or an employer who participates in the plan, where the payment is made to avoid the revocation of the registration of the plan,

(iv) a return of all or a portion of the contributions made by a member of the plan under a defined benefit provision of the plan, where the return of contributions is pursuant to an amendment to the plan that also reduces the future contributions that would otherwise be required to be made under the provision by members,

(v) a payment of interest (computed at a rate not exceeding a reasonable rate) in respect of contributions that are returned as described in subparagraph (iv),

(vi) a payment in full or partial satisfaction of the interests of a person in an actuarial surplus that relates to a defined benefit provision of the plan,

(vii) a payment to an employer of property held in connection with a money purchase provision of the plan, or

(viii) where the Minister has, under subsection 8506(2.1), waived the application of the condition in paragraph 8506(2)(b.1) in respect of a money purchase provision of the plan, a payment under the provision of an amount acceptable to the Minister;

**Notes:** Reg. 8502(d)(ii) amended by P.C. 1995-17, effective for distributions made from a pension plan after 1990, to add reference to ITA 147.3(4.1).

Reg. 8502(d)(viii) added by P.C. 1995-17, effective April 6, 1994.

(e) **payment of pension** — the plan

(i) requires that the retirement benefits of a member under each benefit provision of the plan commence to be paid not later than

(A) the end of the calendar year in which the member attains 69 years of age, or

(B) in the case of benefits provided under a defined benefit provision, such later time as is acceptable to the Minister, but only if the amount of benefits (expressed on an annualized basis) payable does not exceed the amount of benefits that would be payable if payment of the benefits commenced at the time referred to in clause (A), and

(ii) provides that retirement benefits under each benefit provision are payable not less frequently than annually;

**Notes:** Reg. 8502(e)(i)(A) amended by P.C. 1998-2256 to change "71" to "69", effective 1997, except that

(a) subject to (b) below, in respect of benefits provided to an individual who turned 70 before 1997, read "71", and to one who turned 69 in 1996, read "70"; and

(b) where retirement benefits under a pension plan are provided to an individual by means of an annuity contract issued before March 6, 1996 and, under the terms and conditions of the contract as they read immediately before that day,

(i) the day on which annuity payments are to begin under the contract is fixed and determined and is after the year in which the individual turns

(A) 69, where the individual had not turned 69 before 1997, or

(B) 70, where the individual turned 69 in 1996, and

(ii) the amount and timing of each annuity payment are fixed and determined,

read "71".

(f) **assignment of rights** — the plan includes a stipulation that no right of a person under the plan is capable of being assigned, charged, anticipated, given as security or surrendered, and, for the purposes of this condition,

(i) assignment does not include

(A) assignment pursuant to a decree, order or judgment of a competent tribunal or a written agreement in settlement of rights arising out of a marriage or other conjugal relationship between an individual and the individual's spouse or former spouse, on or after the breakdown of their marriage or other conjugal relationship, or

(B) assignment by the legal representative of a deceased individual on the distribution of the individual's estate, and

(ii) surrender does not include a reduction in benefits to avoid the revocation of the registration of the plan;

(g) **funding media** — the arrangement under which property is held in connection with the plan is acceptable to the Minister;

(h) **investments** — the property that is held in connection with the plan does not include

(i) a prohibited investment under subsection 8514(1),

(ii) at any time that the plan is subject to the *Pension Benefits Standards Act, 1985* or a similar law of a province, an investment that is not permitted at that time under such laws as apply to the plan, or

(iii) at any time other than a time referred to in subparagraph (ii), an investment that would not be permitted were the plan subject to the *Pension Benefits Standards Act, 1985*;

(i) **borrowing** — a trustee or other person who holds property in connection with the plan does

Part LXXXV — Registered Pension Plans  Reg. S. 8502

not borrow money for the purposes of the plan, except where

(i) the borrowing is for a term not exceeding 90 days,

(ii) the borrowing is not part of a series of loans or other transactions and repayments, and

(iii) none of the property that is held in connection with the plan is used as security for the borrowed money (except where the borrowing is necessary to provide funds for the current payment of benefits or the purchase of annuities under the plan without resort to a distressed sale of the property that is held in connection with the plan),

or where

(iv) the money is borrowed for the purpose of acquiring real property that may reasonably be considered to be acquired for the purpose of producing income from property,

(v) the aggregate of all amounts borrowed for the purpose of acquiring the property and any indebtedness incurred as a consequence of the acquisition of the property does not exceed the cost to the person of the property, and

(vi) none of the property that is held in connection with the plan, other than the real property, is used as security for the borrowed money;

(j) **determination of amounts** — except as otherwise provided in this Part, each amount that is determined in connection with the plan is determined, where the amount is based on assumptions, using such reasonable assumptions as are acceptable to the Minister, and, where actuarial principles are applicable to the determination, in accordance with generally accepted actuarial principles;

(k) **transfer of property between provisions** — property that is held in connection with a benefit provision of the plan is not made available to pay benefits under another benefit provision of the plan (including another benefit provision that replaces the first benefit provision), except where the transaction by which the property is made so available is such that if the benefit provisions were in separate registered pension plans, the transaction would constitute a transfer of property from one plan to the other in accordance with any of subsections 147.3(1) to (4.1), (6) and (8) of the Act;

**Proposed Amendment — Reg. 8502(k)**

(k) **transfer of property between provisions** — property that is held in connection with a benefit provision of the plan is not made available to pay benefits under another benefit provision of the plan (including another benefit provision that replaces the first benefit provision), except where the transaction by which the property is made so available is such that if the benefit provisions were in separate registered pension plans, the transaction would constitute a transfer of property from one plan to the other in accordance with any of subsections 147.3(1) to (4.1), (6), (7.1) and (8) of the Act;

**Application**: The November 30, 1999 draft regulations (RPPs), subsec. 5(2), will amend para. 8502(k) to read as above, applicable to transactions that occur after 1998.

**Technical Notes**: Paragraph 8502(k) of the Regulations requires that property held in connection with one benefit provision of an RPP not be made available to pay benefits under another benefit provision of the same plan. The paragraph exempts from this restriction a transfer of property from one provision of a plan to another where the transfer would be in accordance with any of subsections 147.3(1) to (4.1), (6) and (8) of the Act if the two provisions were in separate RPPs.

Paragraph 8502(k) is amended to add to the list of exempted transfers an intra-plan transfer that would be in accordance with new subsection 147.3(7.1) of the Act. That subsection permits the transfer of surplus from one money purchase plan to another, where the second plan replaces all or part of the first plan.

This amendment, which is consequential to the introduction of subsection 147.3(7.1) of the Act, applies to transactions that occur after 1998.

**Notes**: Reg. 8502(k) amended by P.C. 1995-17, effective for transactions occurring in 1991 or later, to add reference to ITA 147.3(4.1).

(l) **appropriate pension adjustments** — the plan terms are not such that an amount that is determined under Part LXXXIII in respect of the plan would be inappropriate having regard to the provisions of that Part read as a whole and the purposes for which the amount is determined; and

(m) **participants in GSRAs** — no individual who, at any time after 1993, is entitled, either absolutely or contingently, to benefits under the plan by reason of employment with an employer with whom the individual is connected is entitled at that time, either absolutely or contingently, to benefits under a government-sponsored retirement arrangement (as defined in subsection 8308.4(1)).

**Notes**: Reg. 8502(m) added by P.C. 1996-911, effective 1994.

**Registered Plans Division Newsletters [Reg. 8502]**: 91-4R (Registration rules for money purchase provisions); 95-5 (Conversion of a defined benefit provision to a money purchase provision); 96-3 (Flexible pension plans); 98-2 (Treating excess member contributions under a registered pension plan).

**Definitions [Reg. 8502]**: "amount", "annuity" — ITA 248(1); "benefit provision" — Reg. 8500(1); "benefits" — Reg. 8501(5)(c); "borrowed money" — ITA 248(1); "Canada" — ITA 255, *Interpretation Act* 35(1); "connected" — Reg. 8500(3); "contribution" — Reg. 8501(6); "defined benefit provision" — ITA 147.1(1); "designated provision of the law of Canada or a province" — Reg. 8513; "eligible contribution" — Reg. 8502(b)(vi), 8510(6)(a); "employee", "employer", "employment" — ITA 248(1); "Her Majesty" — *Interpretation Act* 35(1); "individual" — ITA 248(1); "member" — ITA 147.1(1); "Minister" — ITA 248(1); "money purchase provision" — ITA 147.1(1); "non-resident" — ITA 248(1); "participating employer" — ITA 147.1(1); "person" — ITA 248(1); "prohibited investment" — Reg. 8514(1); "property" — ITA 248(1); "province" — *Interpretation Act* 35(1); "registered pension plan" — ITA 248(1); "retirement benefits" — Reg. 8500(1); "security" — *Interpretation Act* 35(1); "spouse" — ITA 147.1(1); "surplus" — Reg. 8500(1); "written" — *Interpretation Act* 35(1)"writing".

**8503. Defined benefit provisions — (1) Net contribution accounts** — In this section and subsection 8517(2), the net contribution account of a member of a pension plan in relation to a defined benefit provision of the plan is an account that is

(a) credited with

(i) the amount of each contribution that is made by the member to the plan in respect of the provision,

(ii) each amount that is transferred on behalf of the member to the plan in respect of the provision in accordance with any of subsections 146(16), 147(19) and 147.3(2) and (5) to (7) of the Act,

(iii) such portion of each amount that is transferred to the plan in respect of the provision in accordance with subsection 147.3(3) of the Act as may reasonably be considered to derive from contributions that are made by the member to a registered pension plan or interest (computed at a reasonable rate) in respect of such contributions,

(iv) the amount of any property that was held in connection with another benefit provision of the plan and that has been made available to provide benefits under the provision, to the extent that if the provisions were in separate registered pension plans, the amount would be included in the member's net contribution account by reason of subparagraph (ii) or (iii), and

(v) interest (computed at a reasonable rate determined by the plan administrator) in respect of each period throughout which the account has a positive balance; and

(b) charged with

(i) each amount that is paid under the provision with respect to the member, otherwise than in respect of an actuarial surplus under the provision,

(ii) the amount of any property that is held in connection with the provision (other than property that is in respect of an actuarial surplus under the provision) and that is made available to provide benefits with respect to the member under another benefit provision of the plan, and

(iii) interest (computed at a reasonable rate determined by the plan administrator) in respect of each period throughout which the account has a negative balance.

**Notes:** Reg. 8503(1)(b)(i) and (ii) amended by P.C. 1995-17, retroactive to 1989, so that a member's net contribution account is not charged with payments made in respect of an actuarial surplus under the provision.

**(2) Permissible benefits** — For the purposes of paragraph 8502(c), the following benefits may, subject to the conditions set out in respect of each benefit, be provided under a defined benefit provision of a pension plan:

(a) **lifetime retirement benefits** — lifetime retirement benefits provided to a member where the benefits are payable in equal periodic amounts, or are not so payable only by reason that

(i) the benefits payable to a member after the death of the member's spouse are less than the benefits that would be payable to the member were the member's spouse alive,

(ii) the plan provides for periodic cost-of-living adjustments to be made to the benefits, where the adjustments

(A) are determined in such a manner that they do not exceed cost-of-living adjustments warranted by increases in the Consumer Price Index after the benefits commence to be paid,

(B) consist of periodic increases at a rate not exceeding 4 per cent per annum after the time the benefits commence to be paid,

(C) are based on the rates of return on a specified pool of assets after the benefits commence to be paid, or

(D) consist of any combination of adjustments described in clauses (A) to (C),

and, in the case of adjustments described in clauses (C) and (D), the present value (at the time the member's benefits commence to be paid) of additional benefits that can reasonably be expected to be paid as a consequence of the adjustments does not exceed the greater of

(E) the present value (at the time the member's benefits commence to be paid) of additional benefits that could reasonably be expected to be paid as a consequence of adjustments warranted by increases in the Consumer Price Index after the member's benefits commence to be paid, and

(F) the present value (at the time the member's benefits commence to be paid) of additional benefits that would be paid as a consequence of adjustments at a fixed rate of 4 per cent per annum after the time the member's benefits commence to be paid, or

(iii) where the plan does not provide for periodic cost-of-living adjustments to be made to the benefits, or provides only for such adjustments as are described in clause (ii)(A) or (B), the plan provides for cost-of-living adjustments to be made to the benefits from time to time at the discretion of any person, where the adjustments, together with periodic cost-of-living adjustments, if any, are warranted by increases in the Consumer Price Index after the benefits commence to be paid;

### Proposed Addition — Reg. 8503(2)(a)(iv)–(x)

(iv) the amount of the benefits is increased as a consequence of additional lifetime retirement benefits becoming provided to the member under the provision,

(v) the amount of the benefits is determined with a reduction computed by reference to the member's age, duration of service, or both (or with any other similar reduction), and the amount is subsequently adjusted to reduce or eliminate the portion, if any, of the reduction that is not required for the benefits to comply with the conditions in paragraph (3)(c),

(vi) the amount of the benefits is determined with a reduction computed by reference to the following benefits and the amount is subsequently adjusted to reduce or eliminate the reduction:

(A) disability benefits to which the member is entitled under the *Canada Pension Plan* or a provincial pension plan as defined in section 3 of that Act,

(B) benefits to which the member is entitled under an employees' or workers' compensation law of Canada or a province in respect of an injury or disability, or

(C) benefits to which the member is entitled pursuant to a sickness or accident insurance plan or a disability insurance plan,

(vii) the amount of the benefits is determined with a reduction computed by reference to other benefits provided under the provision in respect of the member that are permissible under paragraph (c), (d), (k) or (n), and the amount is subsequently adjusted to reduce or eliminate the reduction,

(viii) the amount of the benefits is reduced as a consequence of benefits that are permissible under paragraph (c), (d), (k) or (n) becoming provided under the provision in respect of the member,

(ix) the amount of the benefits payable to the member while the member is in receipt of remuneration from a participating employer is less than the amount of the benefits that would otherwise be payable to the member if the member were not in receipt of the remuneration, or

(x) the amount of the benefits is adjusted in accordance with plan terms that were submitted to the Minister before April 19, 2000, where the benefits have commenced to be paid before 2003 and the adjustment is approved by the Minister;

**Application**: The November 30, 2000 draft regulations (RPPs) (pre-published in *Canada Gazette*, Part I, December 9, 2000), subsec. 6(1), will add subparas. 8503(2)(a)(iv) to (x), applicable after 1988.

**Regulatory Impact Analysis Statement**: A registration requirement for defined benefit RPPs is that a member's lifetime pension be payable on an equal periodic basis. The requirement is set out in paragraph 8503(2)(a). It is currently subject to two exceptions, which permit a member's pension to be adjusted for inflation or reduced after the death of the member's spouse. Additional exceptions are added to provide greater flexibility to plan sponsors in designing benefit options that serve the needs of their members. Most notably, the exceptions will accommodate adjustments to a member's pension that:

- eliminate the portion of an early retirement reduction that was not required under paragraph 8503(3)(c) of the Regulations;
- eliminate an offset for disability benefits provided to the member under the Canada Pension Plan (CPP) or Quebec Pension Plan (QPP), workers' compensation or private insurance plans;
- eliminate a joint and survivor reduction; and
- allow a plan member who marries after pension commencement to take a reduced pension in exchange for spousal survivor benefits.

**Technical Notes, April 18, 2000**: Section 8503 of the Regulations describes the benefits that may be provided under a defined benefit provision of an RPP and contains conditions that apply to such benefits.

Paragraph 8503(2)(a) of the Regulations permits an RPP to provide lifetime retirement benefits (as defined in subsection 8500(1)) under a defined benefit provision to a plan member, but requires the benefits to be payable in equal periodic amounts. Paragraph 8503(2)(a) currently provides two exceptions to the equal periodic requirement, namely to allow for a reduction after the death of the member's spouse and to allow the member's benefits to be adjusted for inflation.

Paragraph 8503(2)(a) is amended to expand the list of permitted exceptions to the equal periodic requirement. These amendments are intended to provide greater flexibility to plan sponsors in designing benefit options to suit the needs of their plan members. The amendments are also intended to accommodate existing defined benefit plans that provide certain adjustments that are not offensive from a tax policy perspective, but do not technically comply with the current requirements of paragraph 8503(2)(a).

The amendments accommodate the following adjustments to a member's lifetime retirement benefits:

- an increase that takes effect at a future specified date;

- a reduction or elimination of an early retirement reduction to the extent that the early retirement reduction was not required under paragraph 8503(3)(c);
- a reduction or elimination of an offset for disability benefits provided to the member under the Canada or Quebec Pension Plans, workers' compensation or private insurance plans;
- a reduction or elimination of a joint and survivor reduction;
- a reduction to finance the cost of providing a survivor pension after pension commencement; and
- a partial payment of lifetime retirement benefits to reflect remuneration received during a period of re-employment or postponed retirement.

The following is a more detailed description of the amendments.

New subparagraph 8503(2)(a)(iv) allows the terms of a pension plan to set out future increases that will be made to the lifetime retirement benefits payable to retired members, regardless of whether the increases are warranted by cost-of-living increases. For example, a specified multi-employer plan (SMEP) is amended effective January 1, 2000, as a consequence of a collective agreement negotiation, to upgrade the benefit rate for all members (both active and retired) in each of the next three years. In 2000, the amount of lifetime retirement benefits payable is $300 per year of service, in 2001, the amount is $350 per year of service and in 2002 and future years, the amount is $400 per year of service. Subparagraph 8503(2)(a)(iv) ensures that the CCRA can accept the amendment without knowing if the benefit increases will be supported by future increases in the Consumer Price Index. Since the plan is a SMEP, the benefit increases will not give rise to PSPAs.

New subparagraph 8503(2)(a)(v) allows a plan to provide for an adjustment to lifetime retirement benefits where the adjustment reduces or eliminates the portion of an early retirement reduction that was not required to be applied in order to comply with the early retirement rules in paragraph 8503(3)(c).

*Example*

*Under Pension Plan A, members with less than 10 years service are allowed to retire with an unreduced pension at age 65. They can also retire as early as age 60 with a pension that is reduced by 0.5% for each month prior to age 65. At age 65, the pension is increased to 100% of what would have been payable had the member retired at age 65. The pension is not indexed. Since paragraph 8503(3)(c) would have permitted the pension to be paid without reduction at age 60, the adjustment to eliminate the 0.5% per month early retirement reduction is permissible under subparagraph 8503(2)(a)(v).*

*The plan allows members who have completed at least 10 years of service to retire with an unreduced pension at age 62. Such a member is also allowed to retire as early as age 55 with a pension that is reduced by 0.5% for each month prior to age 62. At age 62, the pension is increased to eliminate the portion of the early retirement reduction that was not required in order to comply with the income tax rules. After 11 years of service, Richard retires at age 58 with an accrued pension of $10,000 per year starting at age 62. His immediate pension payable from the plan is $7,600 per year ($10,000 × (1- (0.5% × 48 months))). The maximum annual pension that could have been paid under paragraph 8503(3)(c) from age 58 is $9,400 ($10,000 × (1- (0.25% × 24 months))). At age 62, Richard's pension is increased to that amount.*

A number of defined benefit pension plans provide that a member's pension is to be reduced to reflect disability benefits provided to the member under the Canada or Quebec Pension Plans, workers' compensation or private insurance plans. Normally, the offset to the RPP pension is eliminated when the other benefits cease to be paid. New subparagraph 8503(2)(a)(vi) ensures that an adjustment to lifetime retirement benefits to reduce or eliminate such an offset is permissible. New paragraph 8303(2)(d.1) provides that such an offset is to be disregarded in computing normalized pensions.

Pension benefits legislation generally requires that a joint and survivor pension be provided if a plan member has a spouse at termination or retirement. Often, the cost of the survivor pension is financed by way of a reduction to the member's initial pension. Some pension plans provide an optional form which allows for an adjustment to the member's pension to eliminate a joint and survivor reduction if it is determined that the survivor pension will not be paid. A member might elect such an option, for example, if there is a concern that the spouse might predecease the member, but the couple still wants the financial security of a joint and survivor pension. Subparagraph 8503(2)(a)(vii) is added to ensure that an adjustment that reduces or eliminates a joint and survivor reduction (or other death benefit reduction) is permissible.

New subparagraph 8503(2)(a)(viii) allows a plan to provide an adjustment to lifetime retirement benefits where, after pension commencement, the member foregoes a portion of his or her lifetime retirement benefits to obtain survivor benefits. For example, a member of a pension plan retires and begins receiving a single life pension. Three years later, the member marries and elects to obtain a survivor pension in place of a proportion of the initial pension. Subparagraph 8503(2)(a)(viii) ensures that the reduction to the member's initial pension is permissible.

New subparagraph 8503(2)(a)(ix) allows the amount of lifetime retirement benefits payable to a member while the member is receiving remuneration from a participating employer to be less than the amount that would otherwise be payable if the member were not receiving the remuneration. This exception is intended to accommodate pension plans that require the pension of a member who becomes re-employed after pension commencement to be reduced to reflect the remuneration received during the period of re-employment. Subparagraph 8503(2)(a)(ix) also resolves a conflict with the *Supplemental Pension Plans Act* (Quebec). Section 77 of that Act allows a member of a pension plan who remains employed with a participating employer after normal retirement age to begin receiving a partial pension to reflect any reduction in remuneration during the postponement period. The member is entitled to a full pension when he or she eventually retires. Subparagraph 8503(2)(a)(ix) permits the use of any method of adjustment while a member is receiving remuneration from a participating employer that results in a lesser amount of lifetime retirement benefits being payable to the member during the period of employment. New paragraph 8303(2)(d.2) provides that this type of adjustment is to be disregarded in computing normalized pensions.

New subparagraph 8503(2)(a)(x) contains a grandfathering rule for lifetime retirement benefits that begin to be paid before 2003 and that are adjusted in a manner that would not otherwise comply with paragraph 8503(2)(a). This subparagraph allows the CCRA to approve such an adjustment provided the adjustment is made in accordance with plan terms submitted to the CCRA on or before [April 18, 2000].

These amendments apply after 1988, which is when paragraph 8503(2)(a) first came into force.

(b) **bridging benefits** — bridging benefits provided to a member where

(i) the bridging benefits are payable for a period beginning no earlier than the time lifetime retirement benefits commence to be paid under the provision to the member and ending no later than the end of the month immediately following the month in which the member attains 65 years of age, and

(ii) the amount of the bridging benefits payable for a particular month does not exceed the amount that is determined for that month by the formula

$$A \times (1 - .0025 \times B) \times C \times \frac{D}{10}$$

where

A is the amount (or a reasonable estimate thereof) of public pension benefits that would be payable to the member for the month in which the bridging benefits commence to be paid to the member if

(A) the member were 65 years of age throughout that month,

(B) that month were the first month for which public pension benefits were payable to the member,

(C) the member were entitled to the maximum amount of benefits payable under the *Old Age Security Act*, and

(D) the member were entitled to that proportion, not exceeding 1, of the maximum benefits payable under the *Canada Pension Plan* (or a provincial plan as defined in section 3 of the *Canada Pension Plan*) that the total of the member's remuneration for the 3 calendar years in which the remuneration is the highest is of the total of the Year's Maximum Pensionable Earnings for those 3 years (or such other proportion of remuneration to Year's Maximum Pensionable Earnings as is acceptable to the Minister),

B is

(A) except where clause (B) is applicable, the number of months, if any, from the date on which the bridging benefits commence to be paid to the member to the date on which the member attains 60 years of age, and

(B) where the member is totally and permanently disabled at the time the bridging benefits commence to be paid to the member and the member was not, at any time after 1990, connected with an employer who has participated in the plan, nil,

C is the greatest of all amounts each of which is the ratio of the Consumer Price Index for a month not before the month in which the bridging benefits commence to be paid to the member and not after the particular month, to the Consumer Price Index for the month in which the bridging benefits commence to be paid to the member, and

D is

(A) except where clause (B) is applicable, the lesser of 10 and

(I) where the member was not, at any time after 1990, connected with an employer who has participated in the plan, the aggregate of all amounts each of which is the duration (measured in years, including any fraction of a year) of a period that is pensionable service of the member under the provision, and

(II) in any other case, the aggregate that would be determined under subclause (I) if the duration of each period were multiplied by a fraction (not greater than 1) that measures the services rendered by the member throughout the period to employers who participate in the plan as a proportion of the services that would have been rendered by the member throughout the period to such employers had the member rendered services on a full-time basis, and

(B) where the member is totally and permanently disabled at the time at which the bridging benefits commence to be paid to the member and the member was not, at any time after 1990, connected with an employer who has participated in the plan, 10;

(c) **guarantee period** — retirement benefits (in this paragraph referred to as "continued retirement benefits") provided to one or more beneficiaries of a member who dies after retirement

Reg. S. 8503(2)(c)     Income Tax Regulations

benefits under the provision commence to be paid to the member where

(i) the continued retirement benefits are payable for a period beginning after the death of the member and ending

(A) if retirement benefits permissible under paragraph (d) are provided under the provision to a spouse or former spouse of the member, no later than 5 years, and

(B) in any other case, no later than 15 years

after the day on which retirement benefits commence to be paid under the provision to the member, and

(ii) the aggregate amount of continued retirement benefits payable under the provision for each month does not exceed the amount of retirement benefits that would have been payable under the provision for the month to the member if the member were alive;

(d) **post-retirement survivor benefits** — retirement benefits (in this paragraph referred to as "survivor retirement benefits") provided to one or more beneficiaries of a member who dies after retirement benefits under the provision commence to be paid to the member where

(i) each beneficiary is a spouse, former spouse or dependant of the member at the time of the member's death,

(ii) the survivor retirement benefits provided to a spouse or former spouse are payable for a period beginning after the death of the member and ending with the death of the spouse or former spouse,

(iii) the survivor retirement benefits provided to a dependant are payable for a period beginning after the death of the member and ending no later than at the end of the dependant's eligible survivor benefit period,

(iv) the amount of survivor retirement benefits payable for each month to a beneficiary does not exceed 66⅔ per cent of the amount of retirement benefits that would have been payable under the provision for the month to the member if the member were alive, and

(v) the aggregate amount of survivor retirement benefits and other retirement benefits payable under the provision for each month to beneficiaries of the member does not exceed the amount of retirement benefits that would have been payable under the provision for the month to the member if the member were alive;

(e) **pre-retirement survivor benefits** — retirement benefits (in this paragraph referred to as "survivor retirement benefits") provided to one or more beneficiaries of a member who dies before

retirement benefits under the provision commence to be paid to the member where

(i) no other benefits (other than benefits permissible under paragraphs (g), (j) and (n)) are payable as a consequence of the member's death,

---

**Proposed Amendment — Reg. 8503(2)(e)(i)**

(i) no other benefits (other than benefits permissible under paragraph (g), (j), (l.1) or (n)) are payable as a consequence of the member's death,

**Application**: The November 30, 2000 draft regulations (RPPs) (pre-published in *Canada Gazette*, Part I, December 9, 2000), subsec. 6(2), will amend subpara. 8503(2)(e)(i) to read as above, applicable after June 4, 1997.

**Technical Notes**: See under 8503(2)(f)(i).

---

(ii) each beneficiary is a spouse, former spouse or dependant of the member at the time of the member's death,

(iii) the survivor retirement benefits provided to a spouse or former spouse are payable for a period beginning after the death of the member and ending with the death of the spouse or former spouse,

(iv) the survivor retirement benefits provided to a dependant are payable for a period beginning after the death of the member and ending no later than at the end of the dependant's eligible survivor benefit period,

(v) the amount of survivor retirement benefits payable for a month to a beneficiary does not exceed 66⅔ per cent of the amount that is determined in respect of the month by the formula set out in subparagraph (vi), and

(vi) the aggregate amount of survivor retirement benefits payable under the provision for a particular month to beneficiaries of the member does not exceed the amount that is determined for the particular month by the formula

$$\frac{(A + B)}{12} \times C$$

where

A    is the amount (expressed on an annualized basis) of lifetime retirement benefits that accrued under the provision to the member as of the member's day of death, determined without any reduction computed by reference to the member's age, duration of service, or both, and without any other similar reduction,

B    is, in the case of a member who attains 65 years of age before the member's death or who was, at any time after 1990, connected with an employer who has participated in the plan, nil, and, otherwise, the amount, if any, by which the lesser of

(A) the amount (expressed on an annualized basis) of lifetime retirement benefits that could reasonably be expected to have accrued to the member to the day on which the member would have attained 65 years of age if the member had survived to that day and continued in employment and if the member's rate of remuneration had not increased after the member's day of death, and

(B) the amount, if any, by which $3/2$ of the Year's Maximum Pensionable Earnings for the calendar year in which the member dies exceeds such amount as is required by the Minister to be determined in respect of benefits provided, as a consequence of the death of the member, under other benefit provisions of the plan and under benefit provisions of other registered pension plans

exceeds the amount determined for A, and

C is the greatest of all amounts each of which is the ratio of the Consumer Price Index for a month not before the month in which the member dies and not after the particular month, to the Consumer Price Index for the month in which the member dies;

(f) **pre-retirement survivor benefits — alternative rule** — retirement benefits (in this paragraph referred to as "surviving spouse benefits") provided to a beneficiary of a member who dies before retirement benefits under the defined benefit provision commence to be paid to the member where

(i) no other benefits (other than benefits that are permissible under paragraphs (g), (j) and (n)) are payable as a consequence of the member's death,

### Proposed Amendment — Reg. 8503(2)(f)(i)

(i) no other benefits (other than benefits permissible under paragraph (g), (j), (1.1) or (n)) are payable as a consequence of the member's death,

Application: The November 30, 2000 draft regulations (RPPs) (pre-published in *Canada Gazette*, Part I, December 9, 2000), subsec. 6(3), will amend subpara. 8503(2)(f)(i) to read as above, applicable after June 4, 1997.

Technical Notes, April 18, 2000: Paragraphs 8503(2)(e) and (f) of the Regulations permit an RPP to provide for the payment of certain survivor benefits under a defined benefit provision where a member dies before beginning to receive retirement benefits. Each paragraph sets out a number of conditions that must be met in order for the plan to provide the survivor benefits. One of the conditions, set out in subparagraphs (e)(i) and (f)(i), is that no other retirement benefits (other than benefits permissible under paragraphs 8503(2)(g), (j) or (n)) can be payable as a consequence of the member's death.

Subparagraphs 8503(2)(e)(i) and (f)(i) are amended to add a reference to new paragraph 8503(2)(l.1), which allows a spouse of a deceased member to elect to receive a bridging benefit in place of all or a proportion of his or her survivor benefits.

These amendments apply after June 4, 1997, which is when paragraph 8503(2)(l.1) comes into force.

(ii) the beneficiary is a spouse or former spouse of the member,

(iii) the surviving spouse benefits are payable for a period beginning not later than the later of

(A) the day that is one year after the day of death of the member, and

(B) the end of the calendar year in which the beneficiary attains 69 years of age,

and ending with the death of the beneficiary,

(iv) the surviving spouse benefits would be in accordance with paragraph (a) if the surviving spouse were a member of the plan, and

(v) the present value (at the time of the member's death) of all benefits provided as a consequence of the member's death does not exceed the present value (immediately before the member's death) of all benefits that have accrued under the provision with respect to the member to the day of the member's death;

(g) **pre-retirement survivor benefits — guarantee period** — retirement benefits provided to one or more individuals as a consequence of the death of a person who

(i) is a beneficiary of a member who died before retirement benefits under the provision commenced to be paid to the member,

(ii) was, at the time of the member's death, a spouse or former spouse of the member, and

(iii) dies after the member's death,

where the benefits would be in accordance with paragraph (c) if the person were a member of the plan;

(h) **lump-sum payments on termination** — the payment, with respect to a member in connection with the member's termination from the plan (otherwise than by reason of death), of one or more single amounts where

(i) the payments are the last payments to be made under the provision with respect to the member,

(ii) if subparagraph (iii) is not applicable, each single amount does not exceed the balance in the member's net contribution account immediately before the time of payment of the single amount, and

(iii) if

(A) the Minister has, pursuant to subsection (5), waived the application of the conditions in paragraph (4)(a) in respect of the provision, or

(B) the member's contributions under the provision for each calendar year after 1990 would have been in accordance with paragraph (4)(a) if the reference in clause (i)(B) thereof to "70 per cent" were read as a reference to "50 per cent",

each single amount does not exceed the amount that would be the balance in the member's net contribution account immediately before the time of payment of the single amount if, for each current service contribution made by the member under the provision, the account were credited with an additional amount equal to the amount of the contribution (other than the portion thereof, if any, paid in respect of one or more periods that were not periods of regular employment and that would not have been required to be paid by the member if the periods were periods of regular employment);

**Proposed Amendment — Reg. 8503(2)(h)(iii) closing words**

each single amount does not exceed the amount that would be the balance in the member's net contribution account immediately before the time of the payment of the single amount if, for each current service contribution made by the member under the provision, the account were credited at the time of the contribution with an additional amount equal to the amount of the contribution (other than the portion of the contribution, if any, paid in respect of one or more periods that were not periods of regular employment and that would not have been required to be paid by the member if the periods were periods of regular employment);

**Application**: The November 30, 2000 draft regulations (RPPs) (pre-published in *Canada Gazette*, Part I, December 9, 2000), subsec. 6(4), will amend the closing words of subpara. 8503(2)(h)(iii) to read as above, applicable after 1988.

**Technical Notes, April 18, 2000**: Paragraph 8503(2)(h) of the Regulations permits a lump sum to be paid under a defined benefit provision of an RPP to a member on termination of plan membership (otherwise than by reason of death) equal to the balance in the member's net contribution account (as defined in subsection 8503(1)). In general terms, that balance is equal to the member's contributions under the provision plus interest, less any payments made in respect of the member. In certain cases, a larger payment may be made equal to the amount that would be the balance in the member's net contribution account if that account were credited with twice the current service contributions made by the member. Normally, the amount that may be paid will equal two times employee contributions plus interest.

Paragraph 8503(2)(h) is amended to clarify that the additional crediting to the net contribution account is to occur at the time that each current service contribution is made, rather than at the time that the lump sum payment is made. This ensures that the notional balance in the net contribution account reflects two times the accrued interest on the current service contributions.

This amendment applies after 1988, which is when paragraph 8503(2)(h) first came into force.

(i) **payment of commuted value of benefits on death before retirement** — the payment of one or more single amounts to one or more beneficiaries of a member who dies before retirement benefits under the provision commence to be paid to the member where

(i) no retirement benefits are payable as a consequence of the member's death, and

(ii) the aggregate of all amounts, each of which is such a single amount (other than the portion thereof, if any, that can reasonably be considered to be interest, computed at a rate not exceeding a reasonable rate, in respect of the period from the day of death of the member to the day the single amount is paid), does not exceed the present value, immediately before the death of the member, of all benefits that have accrued under the provision with respect to the member to the day of the member's death;

(j) **lump sum payments on death** — the payment of one or more single amounts after the death of a member where

(i) the payments are the last payments to be made under the provision with respect to the member,

(ii) if the member dies before retirement benefits under the provision commence to be paid to the member and no retirement benefits are payable as a consequence of the member's death, the aggregate amount to be paid at any time complies with whichever of the conditions in subparagraphs (h)(ii) and (iii) would be applicable if the single amounts were paid in connection with the member's termination from the plan otherwise than by reason of death, and

(iii) if subparagraph (ii) is not applicable, the aggregate amount to be paid at any time does not exceed the balance, immediately before that time, in the member's net contribution account in relation to the provision;

(k) **additional post-retirement death benefits** — retirement benefits (in this paragraph referred to as "additional death benefits") payable after the death of a member who dies after retirement benefits under the provision commence to

Part LXXXV — Registered Pension Plans    S. 8503(2)(l)(ii)

be paid to the member where the additional death benefits are

(i) retirement benefits provided to a spouse or former spouse of the member that are in excess of the benefits that are permissible under paragraph (d), but that would be permissible under that paragraph if the reference in subparagraph (iv) thereof to "66⅔ per cent" were read as a reference to "100 per cent",

(ii) retirement benefits provided to one or more beneficiaries of the member that are in excess of the benefits that are permissible under paragraph (c), but that would be permissible under that paragraph if it were read without reference to clause (i)(A) thereof, or

(iii) a combination of retirement benefits described in subparagraphs (i) and (ii),

and where

(iv) the additional death benefits are provided in lieu of a proportion of the lifetime retirement benefits that would otherwise be payable under the provision to the member, and

(v) the present value (at the time retirement benefits under the provision commence to be paid to the member) of all benefits provided under the provision with respect to the member does not exceed the present value (at that time) of the benefits that would be so provided if

(A) the amount of the member's lifetime retirement benefits were determined without any reduction dependent on the benefits payable after the death of the member or on circumstances that are relevant in determining such death benefits, and

(B) the maximum amount of retirement benefits that are permissible under paragraph (d) were payable to the member's spouse or former spouse after the death of the member;

**Proposed Amendment — Reg. 8503(2)(k)(v)**

(v) the present value of all benefits provided under the provision with respect to the member does not exceed the present value of the benefits that would be provided if

(A) the amount of the member's lifetime retirement benefits were determined without any reduction dependent on the benefits payable after the death of the member or on circumstances that are relevant in determining such death benefits,

(B) the maximum amount of retirement benefits that are permissible under paragraph (d) were payable to the member's spouse or former spouse after the death of the member, and

(C) those present values were determined as of

(I) except where subclause (II) applies, the particular time at which retirement benefits under the provision commence to be paid to the member, and

(II) where the additional death benefits become provided after the particular time, the time at which the additional death benefits become provided;

**Application**: The November 30, 2000 draft regulations (RPPs) (pre-published in Canada Gazette, Part I, December 9, 2000), subsec. 6(5), will amend subpara. 8503(2)(k)(v) to read as above, applicable after 1988.

**Technical Notes, April 18, 2000**: Paragraph 8503(2)(k) of the Regulations allows survivor benefits in excess of the benefits permissible under paragraphs 8503(2)(c) and (d) where the survivor benefits are payable to a spouse of a member who dies after beginning to receive retirement benefits. Specifically, paragraph 8503(2)(k) permits a defined benefit RPP to provide up to a 100% joint and survivor pension and up to a 15-year guarantee. To obtain the additional survivor benefits, a member must forgo a portion of his or her lifetime retirement benefits so that the present value of benefits provided in respect of the member does not exceed the present value of the benefits that would be provided if:

- no reduction were applied to the member's lifetime retirement benefits on account of benefits payable after the death of the member; and
- a 66 2/3% survivor benefit were payable to the spouse after the death of the member.

The present values must be determined as of the time retirement benefits begin to be paid to the member.

Subparagraph 8503(2)(k)(iv) is amended so that the present values are determined as of the time the additional death benefits become provided if that time is later than the time retirement benefits begin to be paid to the member. This amendment is consequential to the introduction of new subparagraph 8503(2)(a)(viii), which allows a member to forego a portion of his or her pension after it has begun to be paid in order to obtain survivor benefits.

This amendment applies after 1988, which is when paragraph 8503(2)(k) first came into force.

(l) **additional bridging benefits** — bridging benefits in excess of bridging benefits that are permissible under paragraph (b) (referred to in this paragraph as "additional bridging benefits") provided to a member where

(i) the additional bridging benefits would be permissible under paragraph (b) if the formula set out in subparagraph (ii) thereof were replaced by the formula "A × C",

(ii) the additional bridging benefits are provided in lieu of a proportion of the lifetime retirement benefits that would otherwise be payable under the provision to the member and any benefits related thereto payable after the death of the member, and

2401

### Proposed Amendment — Reg. 8503(2)(l)(i), (ii)

(i) the additional bridging benefits would be permissible under paragraph (b) if

(A) the formula in subparagraph (b)(ii) were replaced by the formula "A/12 multiplied by C", and

(B) the description of A in subparagraph (b)(ii) were read as follows:

"A is 40 per cent of the Year's Maximum Pensionable Earnings for the year in which the bridging benefits commence to be paid to the member,"

(ii) the additional bridging benefits are provided in lieu of all or a proportion of the benefits that would otherwise be payable under the provision with respect to the member, and

**Application**: The November 30, 2000 draft regulations (RPPs) (pre-published in *Canada Gazette*, Part I, December 9, 2000), subsec. 6(6), will amend subparas. 8503(2)(l)(i) and (ii) to read as above, applicable after June 4, 1997.

**Technical Notes, April 18, 2000**: Paragraph 8503(2)(l) of the Regulations permits additional bridging benefits in excess of the bridging benefits permitted by paragraph 8503(2)(b). In general terms, paragraph 8503(2)(b) permits a defined benefit RPP to provide bridging benefits to a member equal to the total public pension benefits (Old Age Security (OAS) and Canada and Quebec Pension Plans (C/QPP)), for the month in which the bridging benefits begin, that the member would receive if he or she were age 65. In subsequent months, the bridging benefits may be adjusted for inflation. The bridging benefits may be paid for a period beginning at the time lifetime retirement benefits begin and ending when the member attains age 65. The bridging benefits are required to be reduced if the member has less than ten years of pensionable service or retires before age 60.

The additional bridging benefits permissible under paragraph 8503(2)(l) can increase a member's total bridging benefits to the amount that would be allowable under paragraph 8503(2)(b) if no reductions on account of short service or age were required. The additional bridging benefits must be provided in place of a proportion of the member's lifetime retirement benefits (with associated survivor benefits), and on a basis that is no more favourable than an actuarial equivalent basis.

Paragraph 8503(2)(l) is amended in two ways. First, it is amended to accommodate the bridging benefits provided for in section 91.1 of Quebec's *Supplemental Pension Plans Act* (QSPPA). To accommodate these benefits, the limit on the amount of bridging benefits that can be provided under paragraph 8503(2)(l) is being increased to allow bridging benefits equal to 40% of the Year's Maximum Pensionable Earnings (YMPE), for the year in which the bridging benefits begin to be paid. YMPE is defined in subsection 8500(1) by way of reference to section 18 of the *Canada Pension Plan*. The new limit is slightly higher than the existing limit, which is based on combined OAS and C/QPP benefits.

Other amendments relating to the bridging benefit provisions of the QSPPA include new paragraph 8503(2)(l.1) (which accommodates spousal bridging benefits) and new subsection 8503(7.1) (which allows a member to forego all lifetime retirement benefits in order to obtain bridging benefits and permits bridging benefit elections to be disregarded in applying the limits on post-retirement survivor benefits). For further details, refer to the commentary on those provisions.

The second amendment to paragraph 8503(2)(l) relates to the condition that the cost of the additional bridging benefits be financed by way of a reduction in the member's lifetime retirement benefits and associated survivor benefits. This condition is amended to allow a member to forego any combination of lifetime retirement benefits and survivor benefits in order to obtain bridging benefits. This will allow, for example, a member to elect to convert lifetime retirement benefits into bridging benefits without adversely affecting the level of survivor benefits payable to the member's spouse.

These amendments apply after June 4, 1997, which is when the bridging benefit provisions of the QSPPA came into force.

(iii) the present value (at the time retirement benefits under the provision commence to be paid to the member) of all benefits provided under the provision with respect to the member does not exceed the present value (at that time) of the benefits that would be so provided if the additional bridging benefits were not provided;

### Proposed Addition — Reg. 8503(2)(l.1)

(l.1) **survivor bridging benefits** — retirement benefits (in this paragraph referred to as "survivor bridging benefits") provided to a beneficiary of a member after the death of the member where

(i) the beneficiary is a spouse or former spouse of the member,

(ii) the survivor bridging benefits are payable at the election of the beneficiary, and

(iii) the survivor bridging benefits would be in accordance with paragraph (l) if the beneficiary were a member of the plan;

**Application**: The November 30, 2000 draft regulations (RPPs) (pre-published in *Canada Gazette*, Part I, December 9, 2000), subsec. 6(7), will add para. 8503(2)(l.1), applicable after June 4, 1997.

**Technical Notes, April 18, 2000**: New paragraph 8503(2)(l.1) of the Regulations permits a spouse or former spouse of a deceased member to elect to receive bridging benefits in place of all or a proportion of his or her survivor benefits. The spousal bridging benefits that are permissible under this paragraph are identical to the bridging benefits that paragraph 8503(2)(l) permits to be provided to a plan member. Paragraph 8503(2)(l.1) is introduced to accommodate the spousal bridging benefits provided for in section 91.1 of the *Supplemental Pension Plans Act* (Quebec).

This amendment applies after June 4, 1997, which is when the spousal bridging benefit provisions of Quebec's legislation came into force.

(m) **commutation of benefits** — the payment with respect to a member of a single amount in full or partial satisfaction of the member's entitlement to other benefits under the provision, where the single amount does not exceed the present value (at the time the single amount is paid) of

(i) the other benefits that, as a consequence of the payment, cease to be provided, and

(ii) benefits, other than benefits referred to in subparagraph (i), that it is reasonable to consider would cease to be provided as a consequence of the payment if

(A) where retirement benefits have not commenced to be paid under the provision to the member at the time the single amount is paid, the plan provided for the retirement benefits that accrued to the member under the provision to be adjusted to reflect the increase in a general measure of wages and salaries from that time to the day on which the benefits commence to be paid, and

(B) the plan provided for periodic cost-of-living adjustments to be made to the retirement benefits payable under the provision to the member to reflect increases in the Consumer Price Index after the retirement benefits commence to be paid (other than increases before the time the single amount is paid); and

### Proposed Amendment — Reg. 8503(2)(m)

(m) **commutation of benefits** — the payment with respect to a member of a single amount in full or partial satisfaction of the member's entitlement to other benefits under the provision, where the single amount does not exceed the total of

(i) the present value (at the particular time determined in accordance with subsection (2.1)) of

(A) the other benefits that, as a consequence of the payment, cease to be provided, and

(B) benefits, other than benefits referred to in clause (A), that it is reasonable to consider would cease to be provided as a consequence of the payment if

(I) where retirement benefits have not commenced to be paid under the provision to the member at the particular time, the plan provided for the retirement benefits that accrued to the member under the provision to be adjusted to reflect the increase in a general measure of wages and salaries from the particular time to the day on which the benefits commence to be paid, and

(II) the plan provided for periodic cost-of-living adjustments to be made to the retirement benefits payable under the provision to the member to reflect increases in the Consumer Price Index after the retirement benefits commence to be paid (other than increases before the particular time), and

(ii) interest (computed at a reasonable rate) from the particular time to the time the single amount is paid; and

**Application**: The November 30, 2000 draft regulations (RPPs) (pre-published in *Canada Gazette*, Part I, December 9, 2000), subsec. 6(8), will amend para. 8503(2)(m) to read as above, applicable after 1988.

**Technical Notes, April 18, 2000**: Paragraph 8503(2)(m) of the Regulations enables an RPP to provide for the commutation of benefits to which a member is entitled under a defined benefit provision of the plan. The lump sum payment cannot exceed the present value (at the time of payment) of the member's foregone benefits. Where the foregone benefits are not indexed, or are only partially indexed, paragraph 8503(2)(m) permits the present value to be determined as if the benefits were fully indexed. The assumed indexing prior to the date of pension commencement can be based on increases in a general measure of wages and salaries, while the assumed indexing thereafter can be based on increases in the Consumer Price Index.

Pension benefits legislation generally requires the commuted value of a member's benefits to be calculated as of the date of termination of plan membership and adjusted for interest between the calculation date and the payment date. However, the present value limit in paragraph 8503(2)(m) is determined as of the payment date and there is no explicit provision for the interest adjustment. This difference in methods can, in some situations, result in the maximum lump sum payment permissible under paragraph 8503(2)(m) being less than the lump sum payment required by the governing pension benefits legislation.

To resolve this conflict and to bring the income tax rules into closer conformity with accepted actuarial practice, paragraph 8503(2)(m) is amended to allow the present value limit to be calculated as of a date prior to the payment date (according to rules set out in new subsection 8503(2.1)) and adjusted for interest between the calculation date and the payment date. Subsection 8503(2.1) permits any calculation date up to two years before the payment date as long as the use of the earlier date is either mandated by pension benefits legislation or is reasonable having regard to accepted actuarial practice and the circumstances in which the member acquires the right to the commutation benefit.

If the calculation date is more than two years before the payment date, the CCRA must approve the use of the calculation date. It is expected that the CCRA would give its approval only where the payment of the lump sum was delayed for valid reasons, for example, if a plan adminis-

**Reg.**
**S. 8503(2)(m)**    Income Tax Regulations

trator was required to obtain regulatory approval of a wind-up report before making the payment. It is also expected that situations in which the CCRA's approval is requested will be relatively uncommon as pension benefits legislation and accepted actuarial practice generally permit the commuted value to be recalculated on the basis of a new calculation date if there is a lengthy delay between the initial calculation date and the payment date.

This amendment applies after 1988, which is when paragraph 8503(2)(m) first came into force.

(n) **[commutation of benefits]** — the payment, with respect to an individual after the death of a member, of a single amount in full or partial satisfaction of the individual's entitlement to other benefits under the provision, where

(i) the individual is a beneficiary of the member,

(ii) the single amount does not exceed the present value (at the time the single amount is paid) of the other benefits that, as a consequence of the payment, cease to be provided, and

### Proposed Amendment — Reg. 8503(2)(n)(ii)

(ii) the single amount does not exceed the total of

(A) the present value (at the particular time determined in accordance with subsection (2.1)) of the other benefits that, as a consequence of the payment, cease to be provided, and,

(B) interest (computed at a reasonable rate) from the particular time to the time the single amount is paid, and

**Application**: The November 30, 2000 draft regulations (RPPs) (pre-published in *Canada Gazette*, Part I, December 9, 2000), subsec. 6(9), will amend subpara. 8503(2)(n)(ii) to read as above, applicable after 1988.

**Technical Notes, April 18, 2000**: Paragraph 8503(2)(n) of the Regulations enables an RPP to provide for the commutation of benefits to which a beneficiary of a member is entitled under a defined benefit provision of the plan. The lump-sum payment cannot exceed the present value (determined at the time of payment) of the beneficiary's foregone benefits.

Paragraph 8503(2)(n) is amended, effective after 1988, in the same manner as paragraph 8503(2)(m). For details, refer to the commentary on paragraph 8503(2)(m).

(iii) if the other benefits in respect of which the single amount is paid include benefits described in paragraph (e) and the beneficiary was a spouse or former spouse of the member at the time of the member's death, the single amount is not transferred from the plan directly to another registered pension plan, a registered retirement savings plan or a registered retirement income fund except with the approval of the Minister.

**Related Provisions**: Reg. 8302(3) — Normalized pensions; Reg. 8503(7.1) — Bridging benefits election.

**Notes**: See Q.10 in Notes to Reg. 8503(3).

Reg. 8503(2)(f)(iii)(B) amended by P.C. 1998-2256 to change "71" to "69", effective on the same basis as the amendment to Reg. 8502(e)(i)(A).

Reg. 8503(2)(n)(iii) amended by P.C. 1995-17, effective for payments made after April 5, 1994, to add reference to transfers to a RRIF.

References to "spouse" are expected to be amended to add "or common-law partner" effective 2001 or earlier by election, as has been done throughout the ITA. See Notes to ITA 248(1)"common-law partner".

**Registered Plans Division Newsletters**: 96-3 (Flexible pension plans); 98-2 (Treating excess member contributions under a registered pension plan).

### Proposed Addition — Reg. 8503(2.1)

**(2.1) Rule for commutation of benefits** — For the purpose of determining the limit on a single amount that can be paid with respect to an individual under paragraph (2)(m) or (n), the particular time referred to in that paragraph is

(a) except where paragraph (b) applies, the time the single amount is paid; and

(b) an earlier time than the time the single amount is paid, where

(i) the amount is based on a determination of the actuarial value (at the earlier time) of the individual's benefits,

(ii) the use of the earlier time in determining the actuarial value

(A) is required by the *Pension Benefits Standards Act, 1985* or a similar law of a province, or

(B) is reasonable having regard to accepted actuarial practice and the circumstances in which the individual acquires the right to the payment, and

(iii) except where clause (ii)(A) applies, the earlier time is no more than two years before the time the single amount is paid.

**Application**: The November 30, 2000 draft regulations (RPPs) (pre-published in *Canada Gazette*, Part I, December 9, 2000), subsec. 6(10), will add subsec. 8503(2.1), applicable after 1988.

**Technical Notes, April 18, 2000**: New subsection 8503(2.1) of the Regulations contains a special rule that applies for the purposes of paragraphs 8503(2)(m) and (n) in determining the present value limit in connection with a commutation of benefits under a defined benefit provision of an RPP. For further details, refer to the commentary on paragraph 8503(2)(m).

Subsection 8503(2.1) applies after 1988, which is when paragraphs 8503(2)(m) and (n) first came into force.

**(3) Conditions applicable to benefits** — For the purposes of subsection 8501(2) and subparagraph 8502(c)(i), the following conditions are applicable with respect to the benefits provided under each defined benefit provision of a pension plan:

(a) **eligible service** — the only lifetime retirement benefits provided under the provision to a member (other than additional lifetime retirement benefits provided to a member because the member is totally and permanently disabled at the time the member's retirement benefits commence to be paid) are lifetime retirement benefits provided in respect of one or more of the following periods, namely,

(i) a period throughout which the member is employed in Canada by, and receives remuneration from, an employer who participates in the plan,

(ii) a period throughout which the member was employed in Canada by, and received remuneration from, a predecessor employer to an employer who participates in the plan,

(iii) an eligible period of temporary absence of the member with respect to an employer who participates in the plan or a predecessor employer to such an employer,

(iv) a period of disability of the member subsequent to a period described in subparagraph (i) where, throughout such part of the period of disability as is after 1990, the member is not connected with an employer who participates in the plan,

(v) a period in respect of which

(A) benefits that are attributable to employment of the member with a former employer accrued to the member under a defined benefit provision of another registered pension plan, or

(B) contributions were made by or on behalf of the member under a money purchase provision of another registered pension plan,

where the member has ceased to be a member of that other plan,

(vi) a period throughout which the member was employed in Canada by a former employer where the period was an eligibility period for the participation of the member in another registered pension plan, and

(vii) a period acceptable to the Minister throughout which the member is employed outside Canada;

(b) **benefit accruals after pension commencement** — benefits are not provided under the provision (in this paragraph referred to as the "particular provision") to a member in respect of a period that is after the day on which retirement benefits commence to be paid to the member under a defined benefit provision of

(i) the plan, or

(ii) any other registered pension plan if

(A) an employer who participated under the particular provision for the benefit of the member, or

(B) an employer who does not deal at arm's length with an employer referred to in clause (A)

has participated under the defined benefit provision of the other plan for the benefit of the member;

(c) **early retirement** — where lifetime retirement benefits commence to be paid under the provision to a member at any time before

(i) in the case of a member whose benefits are provided in respect of employment in a public safety occupation, the earliest of

(A) the day on which the member attains 55 years of age,

(B) the day on which the member has 25 years of early retirement eligibility service in relation to the provision,

(C) the day on which the aggregate of the member's age (measured in years, including any fraction of a year) and years of early retirement eligibility service in relation to the provision is equal to 75, and

(D) if the member was not, at any time after 1990, connected with any employer who has participated in the plan, the day on which the member becomes totally and permanently disabled, and

(ii) in any other case, the earliest of

(A) the day on which the member attains 60 years of age,

(B) the day on which the member has 30 years of early retirement eligibility service in relation to the provision,

(C) the day on which the aggregate of the member's age (measured in years, including any fraction of a year) and years of early retirement eligibility service in relation to the provision is equal to 80, and

(D) if the member was not, at any time after 1990, connected with any employer who has participated in the plan, the day on which the member becomes totally and permanently disabled,

the amount (expressed on an annualized basis) of lifetime retirement benefits payable to the member for each calendar year does not exceed the amount determined for the year by the formula

$$X \times (1 - .0025 \times Y)$$

where

X is the amount (expressed on an annualized basis) of lifetime retirement benefits that would be payable to the member for the year if the benefits were determined without a reduction computed by reference to the member's age, duration of service, or both, and without any other similar reduction, and

Y is the number of months in the period from the day on which lifetime retirement benefits commence to be paid to the member to the earliest of the days that would be determined under clauses (i)(A) to (C) or (ii)(A) to (C), as the case may be, if the member continued in employment with an employer who participates in the plan,

and, for the purposes of this paragraph,

(iii) "early retirement eligibility service" of a member in relation to a defined benefit provision of a pension plan means one or more periods each of which is

(A) a period that is pensionable service of the member under the provision, or

(B) a period throughout which the member was employed by an employer who has participated in the plan or by a predecessor employer to such an employer, and

(iv) "years of early retirement eligibility service" of a member in relation to a defined benefit provision of a pension plan means the aggregate of all amounts each of which is the duration (measured in years, including any fraction of a year) of a period that is early retirement eligibility service of the member in relation to the provision;

(d) **increased benefits for disabled member** — where the amount of lifetime retirement benefits provided under the provision to a member depends on whether the member is physically or mentally impaired at the time (in this paragraph referred to as the "time of commencement") at which retirement benefits under the provision commence to be paid to the member,

(i) the amount of lifetime retirement benefits payable if the member

(A) is not totally and permanently disabled at the time of commencement, or

(B) is totally and permanently disabled at the time of commencement and was, at any time after 1990, connected with an employer who has participated in the plan

satisfies the limit that would be determined by the formula set out in paragraph (c) if the member were not impaired at the time of commencement, and

(ii) the amount of lifetime retirement benefits payable for a particular month to the member if subparagraph (i) is not applicable does not exceed the amount that is determined for the particular month by the formula

$$\frac{(A+B)}{12} \times C$$

where

A is the amount (expressed on an annualized basis) of lifetime retirement benefits that have accrued under the provision to the member to the time of commencement, determined as if the member were not impaired at the time of commencement and without any reduction computed by reference to the member's age, duration of service, or both, and without any other similar reduction,

B is, in the case of a member who attains 65 years of age before the time of commencement, nil, and, otherwise, the amount, if any, by which the lesser of

(A) the amount (expressed on an annualized basis) of lifetime retirement benefits that could reasonably be expected to have accrued to the member to the day on which the member would have attained 65 years of age if the member had survived to that day and continued in employment and if the member's rate of remuneration had not increased after the time of commencement, and

(B) the amount, if any, by which the Year's Maximum Pensionable Earnings for the calendar year that includes the time of commencement exceeds such amount as is required by the Minister to be determined in respect of benefits provided to the member under other benefit provisions of the plan and under benefit provisions of other registered pension plans

exceeds the amount determined for A, and

C is the greatest of all amounts each of which is the ratio of the Consumer Price Index for a month not before the month that includes the time of commencement and not after the particular month, to the Consumer Price Index for the month that includes the time of commencement;

(e) **pre-1991 benefits** — all benefits provided under the provision in respect of periods before 1991 are acceptable to the Minister and, for the purposes of this condition, any benefits in respect of periods before 1991 that become provided after 1988 with respect to a member who is connected with an employer who participates in the plan or was so connected at any time before the benefits become provided shall, unless the Minister is notified in writing that the benefits are provided with respect to the member, be deemed to be unacceptable to the Minister;

(f) **determination of retirement benefits** — the amount of retirement benefits provided under the provision to a member is determined in such a manner that the member's pension credit (as determined under Part LXXXIII) under the provision for a calendar year with respect to an employer is determinable at the end of the year;

(g) **benefit accrual rate** — where the amount of lifetime retirement benefits provided under the provision to a member is determined, in part, by multiplying the member's remuneration (or a function of the member's remuneration) by an annual benefit accrual rate, or in a manner that is equivalent to such a multiplication, the benefit accrual rate or the equivalent benefit accrual rate, as the case may be, does not exceed 2 per cent;

(h) **increase in accrued benefits** — where the amount of lifetime retirement benefits provided to a member in respect of a calendar year depends on

(i) the member's remuneration in subsequent years, or

(ii) the average wage (or other general measure of wages and salaries) for subsequent years,

and this condition has not been waived by the Minister, the formula for determining the amount of lifetime retirement benefits is such that

(iii) the percentage increase from year to year in the amount of lifetime retirement benefits that accrued to the member in respect of the year can reasonably be expected to approximate or be less than the percentage increase from year to year in the member's remuneration or in the average wage (or other general measure of wages and salaries), as the case may be, or

(iv) the condition in subparagraph (iii) is not satisfied only by reason that the formula can reasonably be considered to have been designed taking into account the public pension benefits payable to members,

and, for the purposes of this condition, where in determining the amount of lifetime retirement benefits provided under the provision to a member there is deducted an amount described in subparagraph (j)(i), it shall be assumed that the amount so deducted is nil;

(i) where the amount of lifetime retirement benefits provided to a member in respect of a calendar year depends on the member's remuneration in other years, the formula for determining the amount of the lifetime retirement benefits is such that any increase in the amount of lifetime retirement benefits that accrued to the member in respect of the year that is attributable to increased remuneration is primarily attributable to an increase in the rate of the member's remuneration;

(j) **offset benefits** — where

(i) in determining the amount of lifetime retirement benefits provided under the provision to a member there is deducted

(A) the amount of lifetime retirement benefits provided to the member under a benefit provision of a registered pension plan, or

(B) the amount of a lifetime annuity that is provided to the member under a deferred profit sharing plan, and

(ii) a single amount is paid in full or partial satisfaction of the member's entitlement to benefits under the benefit provision referred to in clause (i)(A) or the deferred profit sharing plan referred to in clause (i)(B),

the amount that is so deducted in determining the amount of the member's lifetime retirement benefits under the defined benefit provision includes the amount of lifetime retirement benefits or lifetime annuity that may reasonably be considered to have been forgone as a consequence of the payment of the single amount;

(k) **bridging benefits — cross-plan restriction** — bridging benefits are not paid under the provision to a member who receives bridging benefits under another defined benefit provision of the plan (in this paragraph referred to as the "particular plan") or under a defined benefit provision of another registered pension plan, except that this condition is not applicable where it is waived by the Minister or where

(i) bridging benefits are paid to the member under only one defined benefit provision of the particular plan,

(ii) the decision to provide bridging benefits under the particular plan to the member was not made by the member, by persons with whom the member does not deal at arm's length or by the member and such persons, and

(iii) each employer who has participated in any registered pension plan (other than the particular plan) under a defined benefit provision of which the member receives bridging benefits

(A) has not participated in the particular plan, and

(B) has always dealt at arm's length with each employer who has participated in the particular plan,

and, for the purposes of this paragraph, bridging benefits do not include benefits that are provided on a basis no more favourable than an actuarially equivalent basis in lieu of lifetime retirement benefits and related death benefits; and

Reg. S. 8503(3)(k)     Income Tax Regulations

### Proposed Amendment — Reg. 8503(3)(k) closing words

and, for the purposes of this paragraph, bridging benefits provided under a defined benefit provision of a registered pension plan to the member do not include benefits that are provided on a basis no more favourable than an actuarially equivalent basis in lieu of all or a proportion of the benefits that would otherwise be payable under the provision with respect to the member; and

**Application**: The November 30, 2000 draft regulations (RPPs) (pre-published in *Canada Gazette*, Part I, December 9, 2000), subsec. 6(11), will amend the closing words of para. 8503(3)(k) to read as above, applicable after June 4, 1997.

**Technical Notes, April 18, 2000**: Paragraph 8503(3)(k) of the Regulations prohibits the payment of bridging benefits under a defined benefit provision of an RPP to a member to whom bridging benefits are paid under another defined benefit provision of the RPP or under a defined benefit provision of another RPP. This rule is intended to prevent the payment of an inappropriately large amount of bridging benefits. The rule does not apply in respect of bridging benefits that are paid in lieu of lifetime retirement benefits and associated survivor benefits, as long as the benefits are converted on a basis no more favourable than an actuarial equivalent basis.

Paragraph 8503(3)(k) is amended so that the rule does not apply in respect of actuarially determined bridging benefits that are provided in place of any benefits otherwise payable with respect to the member. This amendment is consequential to an amendment to paragraph 8503(2)(l), which allows a member to convert any combination of lifetime retirement benefits and survivor benefits into bridging benefits.

This amendment applies after June 4, 1997, which is when the amendment to paragraph 8503(2)(l) comes into force.

(l) **division of benefits on marriage breakdown** — where, by reason of a provision of a law described in subparagraph 8501(5)(b)(ii), a spouse or former spouse of a member becomes entitled to receive all or a portion of the benefits that would otherwise be payable under the defined benefit provision to the member, and paragraph 8501(5)(d) is applicable with respect to the benefits,

  (i) the present value of benefits provided under the provision with respect to the member (including, for greater certainty, benefits provided with respect to the spouse or former spouse) is not increased as a consequence of the spouse or former spouse becoming so entitled to benefits, and

  (ii) the benefits provided under the provision to the member are not, at any time, adjusted to replace, in whole or in part, the portion of the member's benefits to which the spouse or former spouse has become entitled.

**Related Provisions**: Reg. 8500(7) — Amounts allocated under money purchase provision deemed to be contribution; Reg. 8503(13) — Statutory pension plans — special rules; Reg. 8510(5) — Special rules — multi-employer plan; Reg. 8510(6) — Special rules — specified multi-employer plan; Reg. 8510(8) — Purchase of additional benefits — specified multi-employer plan.

**Notes**: Revenue Canada issued the following "Frequently Asked Questions — Registered Pension Plans" in August 1999:

*Question 1*

What is the "growing in" rule and how does it apply to a member who retires early, in accordance with paragraph 8503(3)(c) of the Regulations, but elects a deferred pension?

The early retirement reduction formula in paragraph 8503(3)(c) of the Regulations is:

$$X \times (1 - .0025 \times Y)$$

Variable X is the amount of the member's unreduced lifetime retirement benefits. Variable Y is the number of months from the day lifetime retirement benefits (LRB's) commence to be paid to the day that is the earliest of the day that a member could have retired with an unreduced pension. One of these factors permit a member to retire without reduction if the combination of their age and early retirement eligibility service total 80 points. By combining age and service in reducing the member's LRB's, each month in the period between the day payment of LRB's commence and the day an unreduced pension could have been paid had the member continued in employment counts as two points. The effect, called the growing in rule when it is applied during a deferral period, is that component Y of the reduction is reduced by half when compared to a reduction based only on age or service.

*Example:*

A member retires at age 46 with 12 years of service. The member elects to defer receipt of their pension until age 57. The member's age, combined with the Y factor is equal to 80. (The member is 57, plus 12 years of service, plus another 11 years of deferral, total 80). The legislation does not require the member's pension to be reduced at age 57.

*Question 2*

For the purposes of determining maximum early retirement benefit levels, subparagraph 8503(3)(c)(iii) defines "early retirement eligibility service" to include a "period throughout which the member was employed by an employer who has participated in the plan". Would this period include leaves of temporary absence and periods of layoff, subject to recall?

Subparagraph 8503(3)(c)(iii) of the *Income Tax Act* defines early retirement eligibility service as a period of pensionable service or as a period throughout which the member was employed by an employer who participated in the plan or by a predecessor employer to such an employer.

Subparagraph 8503(3)(a)(iii) of the Regulations permits an eligible period of temporary absence, which includes a leave of absence or a period of layoff, to be included as eligible or pensionable service under a pension plan. If the terms of a plan as registered include in pensionable service periods of lay off and leaves of absence, these periods may be included as pensionable service for early retirement eligibility purposes.

It is a question of fact as to whether the employee/employer relationship has been severed in a particular situation. An opinion as to whether this relationship has been severed would be determined on a case by case basis.

*Question 3*

Can a registered pension plan administrator increase the joint and survivor option from a 60% to a 66 2/3% survivor pension after the member has commenced receiving pension benefits?

The *Income Tax Act* and Regulations does not prevent such an increase when a member has commenced receipt of their pension.

Paragraph 8503(2)(a) provides that lifetime retirement benefits must be payable in equal and periodic amounts. There are some exceptions to this rule, for example, benefits may be adjusted for inflation, or reduced upon the death of the member's spouse.

Paragraph 8503(2)(d) and subparagraph 8503(2)(a)(i) do not provide that the surviving spouse's benefit must meet the equal and periodic rule and do not prevent such an increase. Although the value of the benefit would increase and additional funding would be necessary, the Regulations permit such an increase.

*Question 4*

Paragraph 8503(3)(g) of the Regulations limits the accrual rate of a defined benefit plan to 2%. In a 2% plan that provides a joint and survivor pension with a 5 year guarantee, would Revenue Canada allow a member to choose an optional Life only pension? The actuarial equivalent of this optional form of pension might exceed 2%.

The intent of paragraph 8503(3)(g) is to limit the benefit accrual rate under the normal form of pension payable to two percent. The effective benefit accrual rate, the accrual rate resulting from an optional form of pension that is the actuarial equivalent of the normal form, may exceed two percent. Pension plans that offer an optional form of pension where the effective benefit accrual rate exceeds two percent must state that the optional forms will be the actuarial equivalent of the normal form, and explicitly limit both the normal and optional forms of lifetime retirement benefits paid to the maximum pension limits in Section 8504 of the Regulations.

*Question 5*

A member terminates from their registered pension plan in 1995 and immediately transfers the commuted value of their benefits to an RRSP, in accordance with the *Income Tax Act* and Regulations. In 1999, the plan is wound up and there is an actuarial surplus in the plan. The employer decides to provide ancillary benefits to the plan members with this surplus. Can the member transfer the value of these ancillary benefits to their RRSP, even though they have already transferred the commuted value of their benefits out of the plan?

Subsection 8501(7) of the Regulations, which applies to benefits provided after 1996, contains a provision which generally allows surplus under a defined benefit provision to be used on wind up of the plan to provide for stand alone ancillary benefits to former members. Subsection 8517(3.1) allows the individual to use previously unused transfer room determined under section 8517 to accommodate a rollover of these ancillary benefits. In accordance with paragraph 8501(7)(e) of the Regulations, Ministerial approval is required regarding these transfers. We will require a demonstration indicating that the sum of the commuted value of the new ancillaries plus the commuted value of the original entitlement does not exceed the prescribed amount that was determined at the time of the initial transfer.

If the members had terminated after 1996, they may only have these stand alone ancillary benefits provided in respect of pre-1990 service. This is to ensure that these individuals are not provided with benefits that, had they been provided before the first termination, would have affected the determination of PAR.

*Question 6*

The decision in *Rosenberg (CUPE) v. Canada* changes the definition of spouse as it relates to the registration of pension plans. Will Revenue Canada now register pension plans that provide benefits for same sex partners?

Yes, the Department will register a pension plan that provides benefits to same sex partners. Should plan sponsors wish to have such a pension plan registered, they are encouraged to submit an application to the Registered Plans Division of Revenue Canada. If a previous request has been refused, a new application should be submitted.

*Question 7*

Will this decision apply retroactively to registered pension plans?

Effective April 23, 1998, Revenue Canada will register pension plans that provide for same-sex survivor benefits. These survivor benefits can be attached to benefits accrued in relation to all years of service. The plan sponsor determines what benefits will be provided in their registered pension plan. These amendments will impact future entitlements only.

*Question 8*

Can the survivor benefits be transferred?

No, at the present time, survivor benefits cannot be transferred to a same sex spouse. The *Rosenberg* case only addressed the payment of survivor benefits from the plan.

*Question 9*

The Regulations require that the plan administrator has to report the PAR amount to both Revenue Canada as well as to the employee. What are the plan administrator's obligations if the T10 that was mailed to the employee is returned because of an incorrect address?

Subsection 8404(4) of the Regulations state that the plan administrator "shall send the copy to the individual at the individual's latest known address".

The plan administrator still needs to send a copy to Revenue Canada. Revenue Canada will match the T10 with the employee's Income Tax Return and advise the employee of their increased RRSP room in their notice of assessment.

*Question 10*

Would a plan amendment that alters the amount of pension being paid to retired members violate the "equal and periodic rule" of paragraph 8503(2)(a) of the regulations?

No, a plan amendment that alters the benefits being paid to retirees or their beneficiaries would not violate the equal and periodic rule, provided that the payments were equal and periodic before the amendment, and continue to be equal and periodic after the amendment.

Such an amendment will be accepted only if the change in the amounts of benefits is done on a prospective basis, and do not provide benefits in excess of what the *Income Tax Act* would have permitted at commencement date. Catch up payments will not be accepted.

Built-in plan provisions that would allow pensions in pay to be automatically altered would violate the equal and periodic rule and will not be accepted.

Under Reg. 8503(3)(a)(vii), lifetime retirement benefits may be provided for foreign service only to the extent acceptable to the CCRA. See Information Circular 72-13R8, para. 8(e); *Foreign Service Newsletter* Update 00-1 (Feb. 7, 2000); and B. Bethune A Whiston, "Foreign Service Finally Increases to Five Years", 11(6) *Taxation of Executive Compensation and Retirement* (Federated Press) 239-244 (Feb. 2000).

For discussion of the administrative conditions that apply to Reg. 8503(3)(e) ("acceptable to the Minister"), see Registered Plans Division newsletter 99-1 and Diana Woodhead, "Revenue Canada Imposes New Restrictions on Past Service Benefits", 10(9) *Taxation of Executive Compensation and Retirement* (Federated Press) 140–143 (May 1999).

References to "spouse" are expected to be amended to add "or common-law partner" effective 2001 or earlier by election, as has been done throughout the ITA. See Notes to ITA 248(1)"common-law partner".

**Information Circulars**: 98-2: Prescribed compensation for RPPs, paras. 8, 32.

**Registered Plan Division Newsletters**: 93-2 (Foreign Service Newsletter); 2000-1 (Foreign Service Newsletter Update).

**(4) Additional conditions** — For the purposes of section 8501, the following conditions are applicable in respect of each defined benefit provision of a pension plan:

(a) **member contributions** — where members are required or permitted to make contributions under the provision,

(i) the aggregate amount of current service contributions to be made by a member in respect of a calendar year after 1990, no part of which is a period of disability or an eligible period of reduced pay or temporary absence of the member, does not exceed the lesser of

(A) 9 per cent of the aggregate of all amounts each of which is the member's compensation for the year from an employer who participates in the plan in the year for the benefit of the member, and

(B) the aggregate of $1,000 and 70 per cent of the aggregate of all amounts each of which is the amount that would be the member's pension credit (as determined under Part LXXXIII) for the year under the provision with respect to an employer if section 8302 were read without reference to paragraphs (2)(b) and (3)(g) thereof,

(ii) the method for determining current service contributions to be made by a member in respect of a calendar year that includes a period of disability or an eligible period of reduced pay or temporary absence of the member (referred to in this subparagraph as a "period of reduced services") is consistent with that used for determining contributions in respect of years described in subparagraph (i), except that the member may be permitted or required to make, in respect of a period of reduced services, current service contributions not exceeding the amount reasonably necessary to fund the member's benefits in respect of the period of reduced services, and

(iii) the aggregate amount of contributions to be made by a member in connection with benefits that, as a consequence of a transaction, event or circumstance occurring at a particular time, become provided under the provision in respect of periods before that time does not exceed the amount reasonably necessary to fund such benefits;

(b) **pre-payment of member contributions** — the contributions that are made under the provision by a member in respect of a calendar year are not paid before the year;

(c) **reduction in benefits and return of contributions** — where the plan is not established by an enactment of Canada or a province, it includes a stipulation that permits, for the purpose of avoiding revocation of the registration of the plan,

(i) the plan to be amended at any time to reduce the benefits provided under the provision with respect to a member, and

(ii) a contribution that is made under the provision by a member or an employer to be returned to the person who made the contribution

which stipulation may provide that an amendment to the plan, or a return of contributions, is subject to the approval of the authority administering the *Pension Benefits Standards Act, 1985* or a similar law of a province;

(d) **undue deferral of payment** — each single amount that is payable after the death of a member is paid as soon as is practicable after the member's death (or, in the case of a single amount permitted by reason of paragraph (2)(j), after all other benefits have been paid);

(e) **evidence of disability** — where additional lifetime retirement benefits are provided under the provision to a member because the member is totally and permanently disabled, the additional benefits are not paid before the plan administrator has received from a medical doctor who is licensed to practise under the laws of a province or of the place where the member resides a written report providing the information on the medical condition of the member taken into account by the administrator in determining that the member is totally and permanently disabled; and

(f) where lifetime retirement benefits are provided under the provision to a member in respect of a period of disability of the member, the benefits, to the extent that they would not be in accordance with paragraph (3)(a) if that paragraph were read without reference to subparagraph (iv) thereof, are not paid before the plan administrator has received from a medical doctor who is licensed to practise under the laws of a province or of the place where the member resides a written report providing the information on the medical condition of the member taken into account by the administrator in determining that the period is a period of disability.

**Related Provisions**: Reg. 8503(5) — Minister may waive member contribution conditions; Reg. 8509(10.1) — Conditions inapplicable for pre-1992 plans; Reg. 8510(6) — Special rules — specified multi-employer plan.

**Notes**: Reg. 8503(4)(c) amended by P.C. 1995-17, retroactive to 1989, to exempt legislated plans from the stipulation, and to allow the stipulation to provide that an amendment or return of contribution is subject to the approval of the authority administering the pension benefit standards legislation. (Note also that Reg. 8509(10.1) exempts pre-1992 plans and replacement plans from the stipulation.)

Original Reg. 8503(4)(e) and (f) repealed by P.C. 1995-17 retroactive to their introduction (1989), and new Reg. 8503(4)(e) and (f) added effective for benefits that begin to be paid after April 5, 1994.

**Registered Plans Division Newsletters**: 96-3 (Flexible pension plans).

**(5) Waiver of member contribution conditions** — The Minister may waive the conditions in paragraph (4)(a) where member contributions under a defined benefit provision of a pension plan are determined in a manner acceptable to the Minister and it is reasonable to expect that, on a long-term basis, the aggregate of the regular current service contributions made under the provision by all members will not exceed ½ of the amount that is required to fund the aggregate benefits in respect of which those contributions are made.

**(6) Pre-retirement death benefits** — A pension plan may provide, in the case of a member who dies before retirement benefits under a defined benefit provision of the plan commence to be paid to the member but after becoming eligible to have retirement benefits commence to be paid, benefits under the provision to the beneficiaries of the member where the benefits would be in accordance with subsection (2) if retirement benefits under the provision had commenced to be paid to the member immediately before the member's death.

**Related Provisions**: Reg. 8501(3) — Conditions inapplicable where inconsistent with 8503(6).

**(7) Commutation of lifetime retirement benefits** — Where a pension plan permits a member to receive a single amount in full or partial satisfaction of the member's entitlement to lifetime retirement benefits under a defined benefit provision of the plan, the following rules apply:

(a) the condition in subparagraph (2)(b)(i) that the payment of bridging benefits under the provision not commence before lifetime retirement benefits commence to be paid under the provision to the member is not applicable where, before the member's lifetime retirement benefits commence to be paid, a single amount is paid in full satisfaction of the member's entitlement to the lifetime retirement benefits; and

(b) such part of the member's lifetime retirement benefits as remains payable after a single amount is paid in full satisfaction of the member's entitlement to lifetime retirement benefits that would otherwise be payable after the member attains a particular age shall be deemed, for the purposes of the conditions in this section, to be lifetime retirement benefits and not to be bridging benefits.

**Proposed Addition — Reg. 8503(7.1)**

**(7.1) Bridging benefits and election** — Where a pension plan permits a member, or a spouse or former spouse of the member, to elect to receive benefits described in any of paragraphs (2)(b), (l) or (1.1) under a defined benefit provision of the plan on a basis no more favourable than an actuarially equivalent basis in lieu of all or a proportion of the benefits that would otherwise be payable under the provision with respect to the member, the following rules apply:

(a) the condition in subparagraph (2)(b)(i) that the payment of bridging benefits under the provision not commence before lifetime retirement benefits commence to be paid under the provision to the member does not apply if, as a consequence of the election, no lifetime retirement benefits remain payable under the provision to the member; and

(b) for the purpose of determining whether retirement benefits provided under the provision to beneficiaries of the member are in accordance with paragraphs (2)(c), (d) and (k), the election may be disregarded.

**Application**: The November 30, 2000 draft regulations (RPPs) (pre-published in *Canada Gazette*, Part I, December 9, 2000), subsec. 6(12), will add subsec. 8503(7.1), applicable after June 4, 1997.

**Technical Notes, April 18, 2000**: New subsection 8503(7.1) of the Regulations contains two special rules that apply where an RPP allows a member, or a spouse of a deceased member, to elect to receive bridging benefits in lieu of benefits that would otherwise be payable with respect to the member (including spousal survivor benefits) under a defined benefit provision of the plan. The rules only apply where the conversion is determined on a basis no more favourable than an actuarial equivalent basis. These new rules are intended to accommodate the bridging benefits provided for in section 91.1 of the *Supplemental Pension Plans Act* (Quebec).

The first rule, which is contained in paragraph 8503(7.1)(a), applies where a member fully converts lifetime retirement benefits into bridging benefits. By virtue of the condition in subparagraph 8503(2)(b)(i), bridging benefits must not begin to be paid unless lifetime retirement benefits have begun to be paid. Paragraph 8503(7.1)(a) provides that this condition does not apply where no lifetime retirement benefits remain payable to the member under the provision as a consequence of the member making the bridging benefit election. Therefore, paragraph 8503(7.1)(a) enables a member to fully convert lifetime retirement benefits into bridging benefits, subject to the limit in paragraph 8503(2)(l). Paragraph 8503(7.1)(a) applies in the same manner to enable a surviving spouse to fully convert his or her spousal survivor benefits into bridging benefits in accordance with paragraph 8503(2)(l.1).

Paragraph 8503(7.1)(b) sets out the second rule. This rule applies for the purpose of determining whether post-retirement survivor benefits provided under the provision to beneficiaries of a member are permissible under paragraphs 8503(2)(c), (d) and (k). Paragraph 8503(2)(c) permits a member's retirement benefits to be guaranteed for up to 5 years if a spousal survivor pension is also payable on the death of a member, and otherwise for up to 15 years. For each month of the guarantee, the total retirement benefits payable to beneficiaries must not exceed the retirement benefits (bridging benefits as well as lifetime retirement benefits) that would have been payable to the member if the member were alive. Paragraph 8503(2)(d) permits an RPP to provide post-retirement survivor benefits to a spouse or dependant of a member, provided the survivor benefits satisfy two limits. First, the survivor benefits payable to any one beneficiary must not exceed 66 2/3% of the retirement benefits that would have been payable to the member if the member were alive. Second, the total survivor benefits payable to all beneficiaries, together with any other retirement benefits (such as a guarantee) payable to beneficiaries, must not exceed 100% of the retirement benefits that would have been payable to the member if the member were alive. Paragraph 8503(2)(k) permits a member to forego a portion of his or her lifetime retirement benefits to obtain spousal survivor benefits in excess of the benefits permissible under paragraphs 8503(2)(c) and (d). The additional survivor benefits must not exceed 100% of the retirement benefits that would have been payable to the member if the member were alive, and are subject to a present value test.

Paragraph 8503(7.1)(b) allows a member's bridging benefit election to be disregarded in determining whether the post-retirement survivor benefits provided under a defined benefit provision are permissible. In particular, this rule allows the survivor benefit limits to be based on the amount of retirement benefits that would have been payable to the member if the member were alive and if the member had not converted lifetime retirement benefits into bridging benefits. This enables a member to elect to convert his or her lifetime retirement benefits into bridging benefits, without adversely affecting the level of survivor benefits.

Paragraph 8503(7.1)(b) also allows a spouse's bridging benefit election to be disregarded in determining whether the post-retirement survivor benefits are permissible. This rule is relevant, in particular, for the purpose of applying the second survivor benefit limit in paragraph 8503(2)(d). Paragraph 8503(7.1)(b) ensures that a conversion of spousal survivor benefits into spousal bridging benefits will not jeopardize the status of survivor benefits provided to other beneficiaries of the member (for example, survivor benefits provided to a dependant child of the member).

Subsection 8503(7.1) applies after June 4, 1997, which is when the bridging benefit provisions of Quebec's legislation came into force.

**Notes**: References to "spouse" are expected to be amended to add "or common-law partner" effective 2001 or earlier by election, as has been done throughout the ITA. See Notes to ITA 248(1)"common-law partner".

**(8) Suspension or cessation of pension** — A pension plan may provide for

(a) the suspension of payment of a member's retirement benefits under a defined benefit provision of the plan where

(i) the retirement benefits payable to the member after the suspension are not altered by reason of the suspension, or

(ii) subsection (9) is applicable in respect of the member's retirement benefits; and

(b) the cessation of payment of any additional benefits that are payable to a member under a defined benefit provision of the plan because of a physical or mental impairment of the member or the termination of the member's employment under a downsizing program (within the meaning assigned by subsection 8505(1)).

**Related Provisions**: Reg. 8501(3) — Conditions inapplicable where inconsistent with 8503(8).

**Notes**: Reg. 8503(8)(b) amended by P.C. 1995-17, retroactive to 1989, to add reference to termination under a downsizing program.

**(9) Re-employed member** — Subject to subsection (10), where a pension plan provides, in the case of a member who becomes an employee of a participating employer after the member's retirement benefits under a defined benefit provision of the plan have commenced to be paid, that

(a) payment of the member's retirement benefits under the provision is suspended while the member is employed by a participating employer, and

(b) the amount of retirement benefits payable to the member after the suspension is redetermined

(i) to include benefits in respect of all or any part of the period throughout which payment of the member's benefits was suspended,

(i.1) where the retirement benefits payable under the provision to the member after the suspension are not adjusted by any cost-of-living or similar adjustments in respect of the period throughout which payment of the member's benefits was suspended, to take into account the member's remuneration from the employer for the period throughout which payment of the benefits was suspended,

(ii) where the member was totally and permanently disabled at the time the member's retirement benefits commenced to be paid, to include benefits in respect of all or a part of the period of disability of the member,

(iii) where the amount of the member's retirement benefits was previously determined with a reduction computed by reference to the member's age, duration of service, or both, or with any other similar reduction, by redetermining the amount of the reduction, or

(iv) where payment of the member's retirement benefits resumes after the member attains 65 years of age, by applying an adjustment for the purpose of compensating, in whole or in part, for the payments forgone by the member after attaining 65 years of age,

the following rules apply:

(c) the condition in paragraph (3)(b) is not applicable in respect of benefits provided under the provision to the member in respect of a period throughout which payment of the member's benefits is suspended,

(d) where the member was totally and permanently disabled at the time the member's retirement benefits commenced to be paid, the condition in paragraph (3)(b) is not applicable in respect of benefits provided under the provision to the member in respect of a period of disability of the member,

(e) the conditions in paragraphs (2)(b) and (3)(c) and (d) and section 8504 are applicable in respect of benefits payable under the provision to the member after a suspension of the member's retirement benefits as if the member's retirement benefits had not previously commenced to be paid, and

(f) for the purpose of paragraph 8502(c) as it applies in respect of benefits provided under the provision on the death of the member during or after a period throughout which payment of the member's benefits is suspended, subsections (2) and (6) are applicable as if the member's retirement benefits had not commenced to be paid before the period.

**Notes**: Reg. 8503(9)(b)(i.1) added by P.C. 1995-17, retroactive to 1989.

**(10) Re-employed member — special rules not applicable** — Subsection (9) does not apply in respect of benefits provided under a defined benefit provision of a pension plan to a member unless the terms of the plan that provide for the redetermination of the amount of the member's retirement benefits do not apply where retirement benefits have, at any time, been paid under the provision to the member while the member was an employee of a participating employer.

**(11) Re-employed member — anti-avoidance** — Where a member of a registered pension plan has become an employee of a participating employer after the member's retirement benefits under a defined benefit provision of the plan have commenced to be paid and it is reasonable to consider that one of the main reasons for the employment of the member is to enable the member to benefit from terms of the plan that provide for a redetermination of the amount of the member's retirement benefits provided in respect of a period before the benefits commenced to be paid, the plan becomes a revocable plan at the time the payment of the member's benefits resumes.

**(12) Limits dependent on Consumer Price Index** — Benefits provided under a defined benefit provision of a pension plan that are benefits to which a condition in any of subparagraphs (2)(b)(ii) and (e)(v) and (vi) and (3)(d)(ii) is applicable shall be deemed to comply with the condition where they would so comply if the Consumer Price Index ratio computed as part of the formula that applies for the purpose of the condition were replaced by a substantially similar measure of the change in the Consumer Price Index.

**(13) Statutory plans — special rules** — Notwithstanding subsection (3),

(a) for the purposes of the condition in paragraph (3)(b) as it applies in respect of benefits provided under the pension plan established by the *Public Service Superannuation Act*, the reference to "any other registered pension plan" in subparagraph (3)(b)(ii) does not include the pension plans established by the *Canadian Forces Superannuation Act* and the *Royal Canadian Mounted Police Superannuation Act*; and

(b) the condition in paragraph (3)(c) does not apply in respect of benefits provided under the pension plan established by the *Canadian Forces Superannuation Act*.

**(14) Artificially reduced pension adjustment** — Where

(a) the amount of lifetime retirement benefits provided under a defined benefit provision of a registered pension plan to a member depends on the member's remuneration,

(b) remuneration (in this subsection referred to as "excluded remuneration") of certain types is disregarded for the purpose of determining the amount of the member's lifetime retirement benefits, and

(c) it can reasonably be considered that one of the main reasons that remuneration in the form of excluded remuneration was paid to the member by an employer at any time was to artificially reduce a pension credit of the member under the provision with respect to the employer,

the following rules apply for the purposes of the conditions in subsection 8504(1):

(d) the member shall be deemed to have been connected with the employer while the member was employed by the employer, and

(e) the member shall be deemed not to have received such remuneration as is excluded remuneration.

**(15) Past service employer contributions** — Where

(a) a contribution that is made by an employer to a registered pension plan is made, in whole or in part, in respect of benefits (in this subsection referred to as "past service benefits") provided under the plan to a member in respect of a period before 1990 and before the calendar year in which the contribution is made,

(b) the contribution is made

(i) after December 10, 1989, or

(ii) before December 10, 1989 where the contribution has not, before that date, been approved by the Minister under paragraph 20(1)(s) of the Act, and

(c) it is reasonable to consider that all or substantially all of such portion of the contribution as is

**Reg. S. 8503(15)(c)** — Income Tax Regulations

in respect of past service benefits was paid by the employer, with the consent of the member, in lieu of a payment or other benefit to which the member would otherwise be entitled,

the plan becomes, for the purposes of paragraph 147.1(11)(c) of the Act, a revocable plan on the later of December 11, 1989 and the day immediately before the day on which the contribution is made.

**Related Provisions**: Reg. 8505(8) — Exemption from past service contribution rule.

**Notes**: The CCRA's view is that "all or substantially all" means 90% or more.

For a discussion of Reg. 8503(15), see Randy Bauslaugh & Barbara Austin, "Trading Surplus and Other Benefits for Pension Benefits — the Subsection 8503(15) Anti-Avoidance Rule", 9(6) *Taxation of Executive Compensation and Retirement* (Federated Press) 91–95 (Feb. 1998).

**Definitions [Reg. 8503]**: "additional bridging benefits" — Reg. 8503(2)(l); "additional death benefits" — Reg. 8503(2)(k); "administrator" — ITA 147.1(1); "aggregate" — Reg. 8509(2)(c)(i); "amount" — Reg. 8509(2)(c)(ii); "annuity" — ITA 248(1); "any other registered pension plan" — Reg. 8503(13)(a); "arm's length" — ITA 251(1); "average wage" — ITA 147.1(1); "beneficiary", "benefit provision" — Reg. 8500(1); "benefit year" — Reg. 8504(6); "benefits" — Reg. 8501(5)(c); "bridging benefits" — Reg. 8500(1), 8503(7)(b); "bridging period" — Reg. 8504(5); "Canada" — ITA 255, *Interpretation Act* 35(1); "commencement" — *Interpretation Act* 35(1); "compensation" — ITA 147.1(1); "compensation year" — Reg. 8504(2)(b)J; "connected" — Reg. 8500(3); "consequence of the death", "consequence of the member's death" — ITA 248(8); "Consumer Price Index" — Reg. 8500(1); "continued retirement benefits" — Reg. 8503(2)(c); "contribution" — Reg. 8501(6), (7); "death benefit" — ITA 248(1); "deferred profit sharing plan" — ITA 147(1), 248(1); "defined benefit provision" — ITA 147.1(1), Reg 8504(9); "dependant" — Reg. 8500(1); "early retirement eligibility service" — Reg. 8503(3)(c)(iii); "eligible period of reduced pay", "eligible period of temporary absence", "eligible survivor benefit period" — Reg. 8500(1); "employed", "employee", "employer", "employment" — ITA 248(1); "excluded remuneration" — Reg. 8503(14)(b); "highest average compensation" — Reg. 8504(2); "individual" — ITA 248(1); "lifetime retirement benefits" — Reg. 8500(1), 8503(7)(b), 8504(6); "member" — ITA 147.1(1); "member's total indexed compensation" — Reg. 8504(2); "Minister" — ITA 248(1); "money purchase provision" — ITA 147.1(1); "month" — *Interpretation Act* 35(1); "net contribution account" — Reg. 8503(1); "participating employer" — ITA 147.1(1); "particular plan" — Reg. 8503(3)(k); "particular provision" — Reg. 8503(3)(b); "past service benefits" — Reg. 8503(15)(a); "payment year" — Reg. 8504(6)(a); "pension credit" — Reg. 8301, 8308.1(2)–(4), 8308.3(2), (3); "pensionable service", "period of disability" — Reg. 8500(1); "period of reduced services" — Reg. 8503(4)(a)(ii); "person" — ITA 248(1); "predecessor employer" — Reg. 8500(1); "property" — ITA 248(1); "province" — *Interpretation Act* 35(1); "public pension benefits", "public safety occupation" — Reg. 8500(1); "registered pension plan" — ITA 248(1); "registered retirement income fund" — ITA 146.3(1), 248(1); "registered retirement savings plan" — ITA 146(1), 248(1); "related" — ITA 251(2)–(6); "retirement benefits" — Reg. 8500(1); "single amount" — ITA 147.1(1); "specified year" — Reg. 8504(1)(a)(i); "spouse" — ITA 147.1(1); "surplus" — Reg. 8500(1); "surviving spouse benefits" — Reg. 8503(2)(f); "survivor retirement benefits" — Reg. 8503(2)(d), (e); "time of commencement" — Reg. 8503(3)(d); "totally and permanently disabled" — Reg. 8500(1); "writing" — *Interpretation Act* 35(1); "written" — *Interpretation Act* 35(1)"writing"; "year of commencement" — Reg. 8504(1)(a), 8504(2); "Year's Maximum Pensionable Earnings" — Reg. 8500(1); "years of early retirement eligibility service" — Reg. 8503(3)(c)(iv).

**8504. Maximum benefits** — **(1) Lifetime retirement benefits** — For the purposes of subparagraph 8502(c)(i), the following conditions are applicable in respect of the lifetime retirement benefits provided to a member under a defined benefit provision of a pension plan:

(a) the amount (expressed on an annualized basis) of lifetime retirement benefits payable to the member for the calendar year (in this paragraph referred to as the "year of commencement") in which the lifetime retirement benefits commence to be paid does not exceed the aggregate of

(i) the aggregate of all amounts each of which is, in respect of a calendar year after 1990 (in this paragraph referred to as a "specified year") in which the member was, at any time, connected with an employer who participated in the plan in the year for the benefit of the member, the lesser of

(A) the amount determined by the formula

$$.02 \times A \times \frac{B}{C}$$

where

A is the aggregate of all amounts each of which is the member's compensation for the specified year from an employer who participated under the provision in the year for the benefit of the member,

B is the greatest of all amounts each of which is the average wage for a calendar year not before the specified year and not after the year of commencement, and

C is the average wage for the specified year, and

(B) the amount determined by the formula

$$D \times E$$

where

D is the defined benefit limit for the year of commencement, and

E is the fraction of the specified year that is pensionable service of the member under the provision, and

(ii) the amount determined by the formula

$$F \times G$$

where

F is the lesser of

(A) 2 per cent of the member's highest average compensation (computed under subsection (2)) for the purpose of the provision, indexed to the year of commencement, and

(B) the defined benefit limit for the year of commencement, and;

G is the aggregate of all amounts each of which is the duration (measured in years, including any fraction of a year) of a period that is pensionable service of the member under the provision and no part of which is in a specified year; and

(b) the amount of lifetime retirement benefits payable to the member for a particular calendar year after the year in which the lifetime retirement benefits commence to be paid does not exceed the product of

(i) the aggregate of the amounts determined under subparagraphs (a)(i) and (ii), and

(ii) the greatest of all amounts each of which is the ratio of

(A) the average Consumer Price Index for a calendar year not earlier than the calendar year in which the lifetime retirement benefits commence to be paid and not later than the particular year

to

(B) the average Consumer Price Index for the calendar year in which the lifetime retirement benefits commence to be paid.

**Related Provisions**: Reg. 8503(14) — Rules applicable where pension credit artificially reduced; Reg. 8504(2) — Meaning of highest average compensation; Reg. 8504(3) — Alternative compensation rules; Reg. 8504(4) — Part-time employees; Reg. 8504(10) — Excluded benefits; Reg. 8504(13) — Alternative CPI indexing; Reg. 8505(7) — Exclusion from maximum pension rules; Reg. 8510(5) — Special rules — multi-employer plan.

**Information Circulars**: 98-2: Prescribed compensation for RPPs.

**(2) Highest average compensation** — For the purposes of subsection (1) and paragraph 8505(3)(d), the highest average compensation of a member of a pension plan for the purpose of a defined benefit provision of the plan, indexed to the calendar year (in this subsection referred to as the "year of commencement") in which the member's retirement benefits under the provision commence to be paid, is,

(a) in the case of a member who has been employed for 3 non-overlapping periods of 12 consecutive months each by employers who participated under the provision for the benefit of the member, 1/3 of the greatest of all amounts each of which is the aggregate of the member's total indexed compensation for the purpose of the provision for each of the 36 months in 3 such periods throughout which the member was so employed, and

(b) in any other case, the amount determined by the formula

$$12 \times \frac{H}{I}$$

where

H is the aggregate of all amounts each of which is the member's total indexed compensation for the purpose of the provision for a month throughout which the member was employed by an employer who participated under the provision for the benefit of the member, and

I is the number of months for which total indexed compensation is included in the amount determined for H,

and, for the purposes of this subsection, the member's total indexed compensation for a month for the purpose of the provision is the amount determined by the formula

$$J \times \frac{K}{L}$$

where

J is the aggregate of all amounts each of which is such portion of the member's compensation for the calendar year (in this subsection referred to as the "compensation year") that includes the month from an employer who participated under the provision for the benefit of the member as may reasonably be considered to have been received in the month or to otherwise relate to the month,

K is the greatest of all amounts each of which is the average wage for a calendar year not before the later of the compensation year and 1986 and not after the year of commencement, and

L is the average wage for the later of the compensation year and 1986.

**Related Provisions**: Reg. 8504(3) — Alternative compensation rules; Reg. 8504(4) — Part-time employees.

**(3) Alternative compensation rules** — Lifetime retirement benefits provided to a member under a defined benefit provision of a pension plan shall be deemed to comply with the conditions in subsection (1) where they would so comply if either or both of the following rules were applicable:

(a) determine, for the purpose of subsection (2), the member's compensation from an employer for a calendar year by adding to the compensation otherwise determined such portion of the amount of each bonus and retroactive increase in remuneration paid by the employer to the member after the year as may reasonably be considered to be in respect of the year and by deducting therefrom such portion of the amount of each bonus and retroactive increase in remuneration paid by the employer to the member in the year as may reasonably be considered to be in respect of a preceding year; and

(b) determine, for the purpose of computing the amount J in subsection (2), the portion of the member's compensation from an employer for a calendar year that may reasonably be considered to relate to a month in the year by apportioning the compensation uniformly over the period in the year in respect of which it was paid.

**(4) Part-time employees** — Where the pensionable service of a member under a defined benefit provision of a pension plan includes a period throughout which the member rendered services on a part-time basis to an employer who participates in the plan, the lifetime retirement benefits provided under the provision to the member shall be deemed to comply with the conditions in subsection (1) where they would so comply or be deemed by subsection (3) to so comply if

(a) for the purpose of determining the amount J in subsection (2), the member's compensation from an employer for a calendar year in which the member rendered services on a part-time basis to the employer were the amount that it is reasonable to expect would have been the member's compensation for the year from the employer if the member had rendered services to the employer on a full-time basis throughout the period or periods in the year throughout which the member rendered services to the employer, and

(b) in determining the amount G in subparagraph (1)(a)(ii), the duration of each period were multiplied by a fraction (not greater than 1) that measures the services rendered by the member throughout the period to employers who participate in the plan as a proportion of the services that would have been rendered by the member throughout the period to such employers had the member rendered services on a full-time basis,

and, for the purposes of this subsection,

(c) where a member of a pension plan has rendered services throughout a period to 2 or more employers who participate in the plan, the employers shall be deemed to be, throughout the period, the same employer, and

(d) where a period is

(i) an eligible period of reduced pay or temporary absence of a member of a pension plan with respect to an employer, or

(ii) a period of disability of the member,

the member shall be deemed to have

(iii) rendered services throughout the period on a regular basis (having regard to the services rendered by the employee before the period) to the employer or employers by whom the member was employed before the period, and

(iv) received remuneration throughout the period at a rate commensurate with the member's rate of remuneration before the period.

**(5) Retirement benefits before age 65** — For the purposes of subparagraph 8502(c)(i), the following conditions are applicable in respect of retirement benefits payable under a defined benefit provision of a pension plan to a member of the plan for the period (in this subsection referred to as the "bridging pe-

riod") from the time the benefits commence to be paid to the time the member attains 65 years of age:

(a) the amount (expressed on an annualized basis) of retirement benefits payable to the member for that part of the bridging period that is in the calendar year in which the benefits commence to be paid does not exceed the amount determined by the formula

$$(A \times B) + \left(0.25 \times C \times \frac{D}{35}\right)$$

where

A is the defined benefit limit for the calendar year in which the benefits commence to be paid,

B is the aggregate of all amounts each of which is the duration (measured in years, including any fraction of a year) of a period that is pensionable service of the member under the provision,

C is the average of the Year's Maximum Pensionable Earnings for the year in which the benefits commence to be paid and for each of the 2 immediately preceding years, and

D is the lesser of 35 and the amount determined for B; and

(b) the amount of retirement benefits (expressed on an annualized basis) payable to the member for that part of the bridging period that is in a particular calendar year after the year in which the retirement benefits commence to be paid does not exceed the product of

(i) the amount determined by the formula set out in paragraph (a), and

(ii) the greatest of all amounts each of which is the ratio of

(A) the average Consumer Price Index for a calendar year not earlier than the calendar year in which the retirement benefits commence to be paid and not later than the particular year

to

(B) the average Consumer Price Index for the calendar year in which the retirement benefits commence to be paid.

**Related Provisions**: Reg. 8504(8) — Rule where benefits provided under multiple plans; Reg. 8504(11) — Excluded benefits; Reg. 8504(14) — Alternative CPI indexing; Reg. 8505(7) — Exclusion from maximum pension rules.

**(6) Pre-1990 benefits** — For the purposes of subparagraph 8502(c)(i), and subject to subsection (7), the lifetime retirement benefits provided under a defined benefit provision of a pension plan to a member of the plan in respect of pensionable service in a particular calendar year before 1990 (in this subsection referred to as the "benefit year") are subject to the condition that

(a) the amount (expressed on an annualized basis) of such lifetime retirement benefits payable to the member for a particular calendar year (in this subsection referred to as the "payment year")

does not exceed

(b) the amount determined by the formula

$$\frac{2}{3} \times A \times B \times C$$

where

A is the greater of $1,725 and the defined benefit limit for the year in which the benefits commence to be paid,

B is the aggregate of all amounts each of which is the duration (measured as a fraction of a year) of a period in the benefit year that is pensionable service of the member under the provision, and

C is the greatest of all amounts each of which is the ratio of

(i) the average Consumer Price Index for a calendar year not earlier than the calendar year in which the lifetime retirement benefits commence to be paid and not later than the payment year

to

(ii) the average Consumer Price Index for the calendar year in which the lifetime retirement benefits commence to be paid.

**Related Provisions**: Reg. 8504(8) — Rule where benefits provided under multiple plans; Reg. 8504(12) — Excluded benefits; Reg. 8504(15) — Alternative CPI indexing.

**Registered Plans Division Newsletters**: 95-3 (Actuarial report content).

**(7) Limit not applicable** — The condition in subsection (6) is not applicable with respect to lifetime retirement benefits provided to an individual in respect of periods of pensionable service in a particular calendar year if

(a) at any time before June 8, 1990, a period in the particular year was pensionable service of the individual under a defined benefit provision of a registered pension plan;

(b) on June 7, 1990, the individual was entitled, pursuant to an arrangement in writing, to be provided with lifetime retirement benefits under a defined benefit provision of a registered pension plan in respect of a period in the particular year, whether or not the individual's entitlement was conditional upon the individual making contributions under the provision;

(c) at the commencement of the particular year, a period in a preceding year was pensionable service of the individual under a defined benefit provision of a registered pension plan, and the individual did not, by reason of disability or leave of absence, render services in the particular year to an employer who participated in the plan with respect to the individual;

(d) contributions were made before June 8, 1990 by or on behalf of the individual under a money purchase provision of a registered pension plan in respect of the year; or

(e) contributions were made in the year by or on behalf of the individual to a deferred profit sharing plan.

**Related Provisions**: Reg. 8500(7) — Amounts allocated under money purchase provision deemed to be contribution.

**(8) Cross-plan restrictions** — Where an individual is provided with benefits under more than one defined benefit provision, the determination of whether the benefits provided to the individual under a particular defined benefit provision comply with the conditions in subsections (5) and (6) shall be made on the assumption that benefits provided to the individual under each other defined benefit provision (other than a provision that is not included in a registered pension plan) associated with the particular provision were provided under the particular provision.

**Related Provisions**: Reg. 8504(9) — Associated defined benefit provisions; Reg. 8510(5) — Special rules — multi-employer plan.

**(9) Associated defined benefit provisions** — For the purposes of subsection (8), a defined benefit provision is associated with a particular defined benefit provision if

(a) the provisions are in the same pension plan, or

(b) the provisions are in separate pension plans and

(i) there is an employer who participates in both plans,

(ii) an employer who participates in one of the plans does not deal at arm's length with an employer who participates in the other plan, or

(iii) there is an individual who is provided with benefits under both provisions and the individual, or a person with whom the individual does not deal at arm's length, has the power to determine the benefits that are provided under the particular provision,

unless it is unreasonable to expect the benefits under the particular provision to be coordinated with the benefits under the other provision and the Minister has agreed not to treat the other provision as being associated with the particular provision.

**(10) Excluded benefits** — For the purpose of determining whether lifetime retirement benefits provided under a defined benefit provision of a pension plan comply with the conditions in subsection (1), the following benefits shall be disregarded:

(a) additional lifetime retirement benefits payable to a member because the member is totally and

Reg. S. 8504(10)(a)                Income Tax Regulations

permanently disabled at the time the member's retirement benefits commence to be paid; and

(b) additional lifetime retirement benefits payable to a member whose retirement benefits commence to be paid after the member attains 65 years of age, where the additional benefits result from an adjustment that is made to offset, in whole or in part, the decrease in the value of lifetime retirement benefits that would otherwise result by reason of the deferral of such benefits after the member attains 65 years of age and the adjustment is not more favourable than such an adjustment made on an actuarially equivalent basis.

**(11) [Excluded benefits]** — For the purpose of determining whether retirement benefits provided under a defined benefit provision of a pension plan comply with the conditions in subsection (5), the following benefits shall be disregarded:

(a) additional lifetime retirement benefits described in paragraph (10)(a); and

(b) bridging benefits payable at the election of a member, where the benefits are provided on a basis that is not more favourable than an actuarially equivalent basis in lieu of a proportion of the lifetime retirement benefits that would otherwise be payable under the provision to the member and any benefits related thereto payable after the death of the member.

### Proposed Amendment — 8504(11)(b)

(b) bridging benefits payable at the election of a member, where the benefits are provided on a basis that is not more favourable than an actuarially equivalent basis in lieu of all or a proportion of the benefits that would otherwise be payable under the provision with respect to the member.

**Application:** The November 30, 2000 draft regulations (RPPs) (pre-published in *Canada Gazette*, Part I, December 9, 2000), s. 7, will amend para. 8504(11)(b) to read as above, applicable after June 4, 1997.

**Technical Notes, April 18, 2000:** Subsection 8504(5) of the Regulations restricts the amount of retirement benefits (lifetime retirement benefits plus bridging benefits) that can be paid under a defined benefit provision of an RPP before a member attains age 65. Paragraph 8504(11)(b) exempts from this limit bridging benefits that are paid in lieu of lifetime retirement benefits and associated survivor benefits, as long as the conversion is determined on a basis no more favourable than an actuarial equivalent basis.

Paragraph 8504(11)(b) is amended so that the exemption applies in respect of actuarially determined bridging benefits that are provided in place of any benefits otherwise payable with respect to the member. This amendment is consequential to an amendment to paragraph 8503(2)(l), which allows a member to convert any combination of lifetime retirement benefits and survivor benefits into bridging benefits.

This amendment applies after June 4, 1997, which is when the amendment to paragraph 8503(2)(l) comes into force.

**(12) [Excluded benefits]** — For the purpose of determining whether lifetime retirement benefits provided under a defined benefit provision of a pension plan comply with the condition in subsection (6), additional lifetime retirement benefits that are described in paragraph (10)(b) shall be disregarded.

**(13) Alternative CPI indexing** — The lifetime retirement benefits provided to a member under a defined benefit provision of a pension plan shall be deemed to comply with the condition in paragraph (1)(b) where they would so comply, or would be deemed by subsection (3) or (4) to so comply, if the ratio that is determined under subparagraph (1)(b)(ii) were replaced by a substantially similar measure of the change in the Consumer Price Index.

**(14) [Idem]** — The retirement benefits provided to a member under a defined benefit provision of a pension plan shall be deemed to comply with the condition in paragraph (5)(b) where they would so comply if the ratio that is determined under subparagraph (5)(b)(ii) were replaced by a substantially similar measure of the change in the Consumer Price Index.

**(15) [Idem]** — The lifetime retirement benefits provided to a member under a defined benefit provision of a pension plan shall be deemed to comply with the condition in subsection (6) where they would so comply if the amount C in the formula set out in paragraph (6)(b) were replaced by a substantially similar measure of the change in the Consumer Price Index.

**Definitions [Reg. 8504]:** "amount" — ITA 248(1); "arm's length" — ITA 251(1); "associated" — Reg. 8504(9); "average Consumer Price Index" — Reg. 8500(1); "average wage" — ITA 147.1(1); "benefits" — Reg. 8501(5)(c); "bridging benefits" — Reg. 8500(1); "commencement" — *Interpretation Act* 35(1); "compensation" — ITA 147.1(1); "connected" — Reg. 8500(3); "Consumer Price Index" — Reg. 8500(1); "contribution" — Reg. 8501(6), (7); "deferred profit sharing plan" — ITA 147(1), 248(1); "defined benefit limit" — Reg. 8500(1); "defined benefit provision" — ITA 147.1(1); "eligible period of reduced pay" — Reg. 8500(1); "employed", "employee" — ITA 248(1); "employer" — ITA 248(1), Reg. 8504(4)(c); "highest average compensation" — Reg. 8504(2); "individual" — ITA 248(1); "lifetime retirement benefits" — Reg. 8500(1); "member" — ITA 147.1(1); "Minister" — ITA 248(1); "money purchase provision" — ITA 147.1(1); "month" — *Interpretation Act* 35(1); "pensionable service", "period of disability" — Reg. 8500(1); "person", "registered pension plan" — ITA 248(1); "related" — ITA 251(2)–(6); "retirement benefits", "totally and permanently disabled" — Reg. 8500(1); "writing" — *Interpretation Act* 35(1); "Year's Maximum Pensionable Earnings" — Reg. 8500(1).

**Registered Plans Division Newsletters:** 96-1 (Changes to retirement savings limits).

## 8505. Additional benefits on downsizing — (1) Downsizing program

— For the purposes of this section, "downsizing program" means the actions that are taken by an employer to bring about a reduction in the employer's workforce, including

(a) the termination of the employment of employees; and

(b) the payment of amounts and the provision of special benefits to employees who elect to or are required to terminate their employment.

**(2) Applicability of downsizing rules** — For the purposes of this section,

(a) a downsizing program is an approved downsizing program if the Minister has approved in writing the application of this section in respect of the program;

(b) subject to subsection (2.1), an individual is a qualifying individual in relation to an approved downsizing program if

(i) the employment of the individual is terminated while the downsizing program is in effect,

(ii) the individual was not, at any time before the termination of employment, connected with the employer from whom the individual terminated employment, and

(iii) the Minister has approved in writing the application of this section to the individual; and

(c) the specified day is, in respect of an approved downsizing program,

(i) the day that is designated by the Minister in writing for the purpose of subparagraph (3)(c)(ii), and

(ii) if no such day has been designated, the day that is 2 years after the day on which the Minister approves the application of this section in respect of the downsizing program.

**Notes**: Reference to Reg. 8505(2.1) added to opening words of Reg. 8505(2)(b) by P.C. 1995-17, effective on the same basis as the addition of Reg. 8505(2.1).

**(2.1) Qualifying individual — exclusion** — An individual whose employment is terminated under an approved downsizing program is not a qualifying individual in relation to the program if, at the time the individual's employment is terminated, it is reasonable to expect that

(a) the individual will become employed by, or provide services to,

(i) a person or body of persons from whom the individual terminated employment under the downsizing program, or

(ii) a person or body of persons that does not deal at arm's length with a person or body of persons referred to in subparagraph (i), or

(b) a corporation with which the individual is connected will provide services to a person or body of persons referred to in paragraph (a) and the individual will be directly involved in the provision of the services,

except that this subsection does not apply with respect to an individual where

(c) it is reasonable to expect that

(i) the individual will not be employed or provide services, or

(ii) if paragraph (b) is applicable, the corporation will not provide services,

for a period exceeding 12 months, and

(d) the Minister has waived the application of this subsection with respect to the individual.

**Notes**: Reg. 8505(2.1) added by P.C. 1995-17, effective for an individual whose employment is terminated after February 14, 1992. However, it does not apply if the individual was notified before February 15, 1992 that employment would be terminated or if the individual elected before February 15, 1992 to terminate employment.

**(3) Additional lifetime retirement benefits** — Lifetime retirement benefits (in this section referred to as "special retirement benefits") that do not comply with the condition in paragraph 8503(3)(a) may be provided under a defined benefit provision of a pension plan to a member of the plan who terminates employment after attaining 55 years of age where the following conditions are satisfied:

(a) the special retirement benefits are provided pursuant to an approved downsizing program;

(b) the member is a qualifying individual in relation to the downsizing program;

(c) under the terms of the provision,

(i) retirement benefits will not commence to be paid to the member until the member ceases to be employed by all employers who participate in the plan, and

(ii) retirement benefits will commence to be paid to the member no later than on the specified day;

(d) the amount (expressed on an annualized basis) of special retirement benefits payable to the member for a particular calendar year does not exceed the amount that is determined by the formula

$$A \times B \times C$$

where

A is the lesser of

(i) 2 per cent of the member's highest average compensation (computed under subsection 8504(2)) for the purpose of the provision, indexed to the calendar year (in this paragraph referred to as the "year of commencement") in which retirement benefits commence to be paid under the provision to the member, and

(ii) the defined benefit limit for the year of commencement,

Reg. S. 8505(3)(d)  Income Tax Regulations

B is the lesser of 7 and the amount, if any, by which 65 exceeds the member's age (expressed in years, including any fraction of a year) at termination of employment, and

C is the greatest of all amounts each of which is the ratio of

(i) the average Consumer Price Index for a calendar year not earlier than the year of commencement and not later than the particular year

to

(ii) the average Consumer Price Index for the year of commencement;

(e) [Repealed]

(f) the plan

(i) does not permit the commutation of retirement benefits payable to the member, or

(ii) permits the commutation of retirement benefits payable to the member only if the life expectancy of the member is significantly shorter than normal; and

(g) lifetime retirement benefits that are permissible only by reason of this subsection are not provided to the member under any other defined benefit provision, unless this condition has been waived by the Minister.

**Related Provisions**: Reg. 8501(3) — Conditions inapplicable where inconsistent with 8505(3); Reg. 8505(6) — Alternative CPI indexing.

**Notes**: Reg. 8505(3)(e) repealed retroactive to its introduction (1989) by P.C. 1995-17. (This was a requirement that the additional lifetime retirement benefits terminate if the individual subsequently became employed or otherwise rendered services as described in Reg. 8505(5), as it then read.)

**Information Circulars**: 98-2: Prescribed compensation for RPPs, para. 29.

**(3.1) Re-employed members** — Where

(a) a member of a pension plan becomes an employee of a participating employer after lifetime retirement benefits that are permissible only by reason of subsection (3) have commenced to be paid under a defined benefit provision of the plan to the member, and

(b) payment of the member's retirement benefits under the provision is suspended while the member is so employed,

the condition in paragraph (3)(d) is applicable in respect of benefits payable under the provision to the member after the suspension as if

(c) the member had not become so employed, and

(d) payment of the member's retirement benefits had not been suspended.

**Notes**: Reg. 8505(3.1) added by P.C. 1995-17, effective 1989.

**(4) Early retirement reduction** — Where a member of a pension plan is a qualifying individual in relation to an approved downsizing program, the terms of a defined benefit provision of the plan that determine the amount by which the member's lifetime retirement benefits under the provision are reduced because of the early commencement of the benefits may, under the downsizing program, be modified in such a way that the benefits do not comply with the condition in paragraph 8503(3)(c) but would so comply if the member's benefits were provided in respect of employment in a public safety occupation.

**Related Provisions**: Reg. 8501(3) — Conditions inapplicable where inconsistent with 8505(4); Reg. 8505(5) — Exception for future benefits.

**Notes**: Reg. 8505(4) amended by P.C. 1995-17, effective 1989. (The change eliminated a requirement that the early retirement reduction be redetermined so as to comply with Reg. 8503(3)(c) if the individual subsequently became re-employed or otherwise rendered services as described in Reg. 8505(5), as it then read.)

**(5) Exception for future benefits** — Subsection (4) does not apply with respect to benefits that are provided to an individual in respect of a period that is after the day on which the individual's employment was terminated under an approved downsizing program.

**Notes**: Reg. 8505(5) amended by P.C. 1995-17, effective 1989. (The former version described the re-employment circumstances under which special benefits provided to an individual under a downsizing program must terminate. It was repealed due to the elimination of the requirements in Regs. 8505(3)(e) and (4)(c), and replaced by the present rule, which sets out an exception to Reg. 8505(4).)

**(6) Alternative CPI indexing** — Special retirement benefits provided to a member under a defined benefit provision of a pension plan shall be deemed to comply with the condition in paragraph (3)(d) where they would so comply if the amount C in that paragraph were replaced by a substantially similar measure of the change in the Consumer Price Index.

**(7) Exclusion from maximum pension rules** — For the purpose of determining whether retirement benefits provided under a defined benefit provision of a pension plan comply with the conditions in subsections 8504(1) and (5), lifetime retirement benefits that are permissible only by reason of subsection (3) shall be disregarded.

**(8) Exemption from past service contribution rule** — Subsection 8503(15) does not apply in respect of a contribution that is made in respect of benefits provided to a qualifying individual pursuant to an approved downsizing program.

**Definitions [Reg. 8505]**: "amount" — ITA 248(1); "arm's length" — ITA 251(1); "average Consumer Price Index" — Reg. 8500(1); "benefits" — Reg. 8501(5)(c); "commencement" — *Interpretation Act* 35(1); "compensation" — ITA 147.1(1); "connected" — Reg. 8500(3); "Consumer Price Index" — Reg. 8500(1); "contribution" — Reg. 8501(6); "corporation" — ITA 248(1), *Interpretation Act* 35(1); "defined benefit limit" — Reg. 8500(1); "defined benefit provision" — ITA 147.1(1); "downsizing program" — Reg. 8505(1), (2)(a); "employed", "employee", "employer", "employment" — ITA 248(1); "highest average compensation" — Reg. 8504(2); "individual" — ITA 248(1); "lifetime retirement benefits" — Reg. 8500(1); "member" — ITA 147.1(1); "Minister" — ITA 248(1); "month" — *Interpretation Act* 35(1); "participating employer" — ITA 147.1(1); "person" — ITA 248(1); "public safety occupation" — Reg. 8500(1); "qualifying individual" — Reg. 8505(2)(b); "retirement benefits" — Reg. 8500(1); "special retirement benefits" — Reg. 8505(3); "specified day" — Reg. 8505(2)(c); "writing" — *Interpretation Act* 35(1); "year of commencement" — Reg. 8505(3)(d)(i).

**8506. Money purchase provisions** — **(1) Permissible benefits** — For the purposes of paragraph 8502(c), the following benefits may, subject to the conditions specified in respect of each benefit, be provided under a money purchase provision of a pension plan:

(a) **lifetime retirement benefits** — lifetime retirement benefits provided to a member where the benefits are payable in equal periodic amounts or are not so payable only by reason that

(i) the benefits payable to a member after the death of the member's spouse are less than the benefits that would be payable to the member were the member's spouse alive, or

(ii) the benefits are adjusted, after they commence to be paid, where

(A) in the case of retirement benefits provided in accordance with subparagraph (2)(g)(i), the adjustments would be in accordance with any of subparagraphs 146(3)(b)(iii) to (v) of the Act if the annuity by means of which the lifetime retirement benefits are provided were an annuity under a retirement savings plan, and

(B) in any other case, the adjustments are acceptable to the Minister and are similar in nature to the adjustments permissible under clause (A);

(b) **bridging benefits** — bridging benefits provided to a member where the bridging benefits are payable for a period ending no later than the end of the month following the month in which the member attains 65 years of age;

(c) **guarantee period** — retirement benefits (in this paragraph referred to as "continued retirement benefits") provided to one or more beneficiaries of a member who dies after retirement benefits under the provision commence to be paid to the member where

(i) the continued retirement benefits are payable for a period beginning after the death of the member and ending no later than 15 years after the day on which retirement benefits commence to be paid under the provision to the member, and

(ii) the aggregate amount of continued retirement benefits payable under the provision for each month does not exceed the amount of retirement benefits that would have been payable under the provision for the month to the member if the member were alive;

(d) **post-retirement surviving spouse benefits** — retirement benefits (in this paragraph referred to as "survivor retirement benefits") provided to a beneficiary of a member who dies after retirement benefits under the provision commence to be paid to the member where

(i) the beneficiary is a spouse or former spouse of the member at the time the member's retirement benefits commence to be paid,

(ii) the survivor retirement benefits are payable for a period beginning after the death of the member and ending with the death of the beneficiary, and

(iii) the aggregate amount of survivor retirement benefits and other retirement benefits payable under the provision for each month to beneficiaries of the member does not exceed the amount of retirement benefits that would have been payable under the provision for the month to the member if the member were alive;

(e) **pre-retirement surviving spouse benefits** — retirement benefits provided to a beneficiary of a member who dies before retirement benefits under the provision commence to be paid to the member, and benefits provided to other individuals after the death of the beneficiary, where

(i) the beneficiary is a spouse or former spouse of the member at the time of the member's death,

(ii) the benefits would be permissible under paragraphs (a) to (c) if the beneficiary were a member of the plan, and

(iii) the retirement benefits are payable to the beneficiary beginning no later than on the later of one year after the day of death of the member and the end of the calendar year in which the beneficiary attains 69 years of age;

(f) **payment from account** — the payment with respect to a member of a single amount from the member's account under the provision;

(g) **lump-sum payments on death before retirement** — the payment of one or more single amounts to one or more beneficiaries of a member who dies before retirement benefits under the provision commence to be paid to the member;

(h) **commutation of benefits** — the payment with respect to a member of a single amount in full or partial satisfaction of the member's entitlement to other benefits under the provision, where the single amount does not exceed the present value (at the time the single amount is paid) of the other benefits that, as a consequence of the payment, cease to be provided; and

(i) the payment, with respect to an individual after the death of a member, of a single amount in full or partial satisfaction of the individual's entitlement to other benefits under the provision, where the individual is a beneficiary of the member and the single amount does not exceed the present value (at the time the single amount is paid) of the other benefits that, as a consequence of the payment, cease to be provided.

Notes: Reg. 8506(1)(e)(iii) amended by P.C. 1998-2256 to change "71" to "69", effective on the same basis as the amendment to Reg. 8502(e)(i)(A).

References to "spouse" are expected to be amended to add "or common-law partner" effective 2001 or earlier by election, as has been done throughout the ITA. See Notes to ITA 248(1)"common-law partner".

Registered Plans Division Newsletters: 91-4R (Registration rules for money purchase provisions).

**(2) Additional conditions** — For the purposes of section 8501, the following conditions are applicable with respect to each money purchase provision of a pension plan:

(a) **employer contributions acceptable to minister** — the amount of contributions that are to be made under the provision by each employer who participates in the plan is determined in a manner acceptable to the Minister;

(b) **employer contributions with respect to particular members** — each contribution that is made under the provision by an employer consists only of amounts each of which is an amount that is paid by the employer with respect to a particular member;

(b.1) **allocation of employer contributions** — each contribution that is made under the provision by an employer is allocated to the member with respect to whom it is made;

(c) **employer contributions not permitted** — contributions are not made under the provision by an employer, and property is not transferred to the provision in respect of the actuarial surplus under a defined benefit provision of the plan or another registered pension plan,

(i) at a time when there is a surplus under the provision, or

(ii) at a time after 1991 when an amount that became a forfeited amount under the provision before 1990, or any earnings of the plan that are reasonably attributable to that amount, is being held in respect of the provision and has not been reallocated to members of the plan;

(d) **return of contributions** — where the plan is not established by an enactment of Canada or a province, it includes a stipulation that permits, for the purpose of avoiding revocation of the registration of the plan, a contribution made under the provision by a member or by an employer to be returned to the person who made the contribution, which stipulation may provide that a return of contributions is subject to the approval of the authority administering the *Pension Benefits Standards Act, 1985* or a similar law of a province;

(e) **allocation of earnings** — the earnings of the plan, to the extent that they relate to the provision and are not reasonably attributable to forfeited amounts or a surplus under the provision, are allocated to plan members on a reasonable basis and no less frequently than annually;

(f) **payment or reallocation of forfeited amounts** — each forfeited amount under the provision (other than an amount forfeited before 1990) and all earnings of the plan that are reasonably attributable to the forfeited amount are

(i) paid to participating employers,

(ii) reallocated to members of the plan, or

(iii) paid as or on account of administrative, investment or similar expenses incurred in connection with the plan

on or before December 31 of the year immediately following the calendar year in which the amount is forfeited, or such later time as is permitted by the Minister under subsection (3);

(g) **retirement benefits** — retirement benefits under the provision are provided

(i) by means of annuities that are purchased from a person who is licensed or otherwise authorized under the laws of Canada or a province to carry on in Canada an annuities business, or

(ii) under an arrangement acceptable to the Minister; and

(h) **undue deferral of payment** — each single amount that is payable after the death of a member is paid as soon as is practicable after the member's death.

Related Provisions: Reg. 8509(10.1) — Conditions inapplicable to pre-1992 plans.

Notes: Reg. 8506(2)(b.1) added by P.C. 1995-17, effective for contributions made under a money purchase provision of a pension plan after April 5, 1994.

Reg. 8506(2)(c) amended by P.C. 1995-17, to add everything from the words "and property is not transferred..." to the opening words, and to add the words "is being held in respect of the provision" in subpara. (ii). The amendment is retroactive to the introduction of Reg. 8506 (1989), except that the amended Reg. 8506(2)(c) does not apply with respect to property transferred before April 6, 1994 to a money purchase provision of a pension plan in respect of an actuarial surplus under a defined benefit provision of an RPP.

Reg. 8506(2)(d) amended by P.C. 1995-17, retroactive to its introduction (1989). The amendment exempts legislated plans from the requirement, and permits the stipulation to provide that a return of contributions is subject to the approval of the authority administering the pension benefits standards legislation. (Note also that Reg. 8509(10.1) exempts pre-1992 plans and replacement plans from the stipulation.)

Reg. 8506(2)(f)(iii) added by P.C. 1995-17, effective April 6, 1994 with respect to

(a) forfeited amounts under a money purchase provision (MPP) of a pension plan that arise after April 5, 1994,

(b) earnings of a pension plan after April 5, 1994, and

(c) forfeited amounts under an MPP of a pension plan that arose before April 6, 1994, and earnings of the plan before that date, to the extent that, on April 5, 1994, those amounts were being held in respect of the provision and had not been reallocated to members of the plan.

**Registered Plans Division Newsletters**: 91-4R (Registration rules for money purchase provisions).

**(2.1) Alternative method for allocating employer contributions** — The Minister may, on the written application of the administrator of a pension plan, waive the application of the condition in paragraph (2)(b.1) in respect of a money purchase provision of the plan where contributions made under the provision by an employer are allocated to members of the plan in a manner acceptable to the Minister.

**Notes**: Reg. 8506(2.1) added by P.C. 1995-17, effective April 6, 1994.

**(3) Reallocation of forfeitures** — The Minister may, on the written application of the administrator of a registered pension plan, extend the time for satisfying the requirements of paragraph (2)(f) where

(a) the aggregate of the forfeited amounts that arise in a calendar year is greater than normal because of unusual circumstances; and

(b) the forfeited amounts are to be reallocated on a reasonable basis to a majority of plan members or paid as or on account of administrative, investment or similar expenses incurred in connection with the plan.

**Notes**: Reg. 8506(3)(b) amended by P.C. 1995-17, to add everything from "or paid as or on account of...", effective on the same basis as Reg. 8506(2)(f)(iii) (see Notes thereto).

**Registered Plans Division Newsletters**: 91-4R (Registration rules for money purchase provisions).

**Definitions [Reg. 8506]**: "administrator" — ITA 147.1(1); "amount", "annuity" — ITA 248(1); "beneficiary" — Reg. 8500(1); "benefits" — Reg. 8501(5)(c); "bridging benefits" — Reg. 8500(1); "business" — ITA 248(1); "Canada" — ITA 255, *Interpretation Act* 35(1); "continued retirement benefits" — Reg. 8506(1)(c); "contribution" — Reg. 8501(6); "defined benefit provision" — ITA 147.1(1); "employer" — ITA 248(1); "forfeited amount" — Reg. 8500(1); "individual" — ITA 248(1); "lifetime retirement benefits" — Reg. 8500(1); "member" — ITA 147.1(1); "Minister" — ITA 248(1); "money purchase provision" — ITA 147.1(1); "month" — *Interpretation Act* 35(1); "participating employer" — ITA 147.1(1); "person", "property" — ITA 248(1); "province" — *Interpretation Act* 35(1); "registered pension plan" — ITA 248(1); "retirement benefits" — Reg. 8500(1); "retirement savings plan" — ITA 146(1), 248(1); "single amount", "spouse" — ITA 147.1(1); "surplus" — Reg. 8500(1); "survivor retirement benefits" — Reg. 8506(1)(d); "written" — *Interpretation Act* 35(1)"writing".

**8507. Periods of reduced pay — (1) Prescribed compensation** — For the purposes of paragraph (b) of the definition "compensation" in subsection 147.1(1) of the Act, there is prescribed for inclusion in the compensation of an individual from an employer for a calendar year after 1990

(a) where the individual has a qualifying period in the year with respect to the employer, the amount that is determined under subsection (2) in respect of the period; and

(b) where the individual has a period of disability in the year, the amount that would be determined under paragraph (2)(a) in respect of the period if the period were a qualifying period of the individual with respect to the employer.

**Related Provisions**: Reg. 8508 — Salary deferral leave plan.

**Interpretation Bulletins**: IT-363R2: Deferred profit sharing plans — deductibility of employer contributions and taxation of amounts received by a beneficiary.

**Information Circulars**: 98-2: Prescribed compensation for RPPs.

**(2) Additional compensation in respect of qualifying period** — For the purposes of paragraph (1)(a) and subsection (5), the amount that is determined in respect of a period in a calendar year that is a qualifying period of an individual with respect to an employer is the lesser of

(a) the amount, if any, by which

(i) the amount that it is reasonable to consider would have been the remuneration of the individual for the period from the employer if the individual had rendered services to the employer throughout the period on a regular basis (having regard to the services rendered by the individual to the employer before the complete period of reduced pay of which the period is a part) and the individual's rate of remuneration had been commensurate with the individual's rate of remuneration before the beginning of the complete period of reduced pay

exceeds

(ii) the remuneration of the individual for the period from the employer, and

(b) the amount determined by the formula

$$(5 + A + B - C) \times D$$

where

A is the lesser of 3 and the amount that would be the cumulative additional compensation fraction of the individual with respect to the employer, determined to the time that is immediately before the end of the period, if the individual's only qualifying periods had been periods that are also periods of parenting,

B is

(i) if no part of the period is a period of parenting, nil, and

(ii) otherwise, the lesser of

(A) the amount, if any, by which 3 exceeds the amount determined for A, and

(B) the ratio of

(I) the amount that would be determined under paragraph (a) if the remuneration referred to in subparagraphs (a)(i) and (ii) were the

Reg. S. 8507(2)(b)

Income Tax Regulations

remuneration for such part of the period as is a period of parenting

to

(II) the amount determined for D,

C is the cumulative additional compensation fraction of the individual with respect to the employer, determined to the time that is immediately before the end of the period, and

D is the amount that it is reasonable to consider would have been the individual's remuneration for the year from the employer if the individual had rendered services to the employer on a full-time basis throughout the year and the individual's rate of remuneration had been commensurate with the individual's rate of remuneration before the beginning of the complete period of reduced pay of which the period is a part.

**Related Provisions**: ITA 257 — Negative amounts in formulas; Reg. 8507(7) — Complete period of reduced pay.

**Information Circulars**: 98-2: Prescribed compensation for RPPs.

**(3) Qualifying periods and periods of parenting** — For the purposes of this section,

(a) a period in a calendar year is a qualifying period of an individual in the year with respect to an employer if

(i) the period is an eligible period of reduced pay or temporary absence of the individual in the year with respect to the employer,

(ii) either

(A) lifetime retirement benefits are provided to the individual under a defined benefit provision of a registered pension plan (other than a plan that is, in the year, a specified multi-employer plan) in respect of the period, or

(B) contributions are made by or on behalf of the individual under a money purchase provision of a registered pension plan (other than a plan that is, in the year, a specified multi-employer plan) in respect of the period,

pursuant to terms of the plan that apply in respect of periods that are not regular periods of employment,

(iii) the lifetime retirement benefits or the contributions, as the case may be, exceed the benefits that would otherwise be provided or the contributions that would otherwise be made if the benefits or contributions were based on the services actually rendered by the individual and the remuneration actually received by the individual,

(iv) the individual's pension adjustment for the year with respect to the employer includes an amount in respect of the lifetime retirement benefits or the contributions, as the case may be,

(v) no benefits are provided in respect of the period to the individual under a defined benefit provision of any registered pension plan in which the employer does not participate, and

(vi) no contributions are made by or on behalf of the individual in respect of the period under a money purchase provision of a registered pension plan or a deferred profit sharing plan in which the employer does not participate; and

(b) a period of parenting of an individual is all or a part of a period that begins

(i) at the time of the birth of a child of whom the individual is a natural parent, or

(ii) at the time the individual adopts a child,

and ends 12 months after that time.

**Related Provisions**: Reg. 8500(7) — Amounts allocated under money purchase provision deemed to be contribution.

**Notes**: Closing words of Reg. 8507(3)(a) repealed by P.C. 1995-17, retroactive to their introduction (1989). (They provided that if an amount attributable to forfeitures or surplus was allocated to an individual under a money purchase provision, the amount was deemed to be a contribution made to the provision on behalf of the individual. See now Reg. 8500(7) for this rule.)

**Information Circulars**: 98-2: Prescribed compensation for RPPs.

**(4) Cumulative additional compensation fraction** — For the purposes of this section, the cumulative additional compensation fraction of an individual with respect to an employer, determined to any time, is the aggregate of all amounts each of which is the additional compensation fraction that is associated with a period that ends at or before that time and that is a qualifying period of the individual in a calendar year after 1990 with respect to

(a) the employer;

(b) any other employer who does not deal at arm's length with the employer; or

(c) any other employer who participates in a registered pension plan in which the employer participates for the benefit of the individual.

**Related Provisions**: Reg. 8507(5) — Additional compensation fraction.

**(5) Additional compensation fraction** — For the purposes of subsection (4), the additional compensation fraction associated with a qualifying period of an individual in a calendar year with respect to a particular employer is the amount determined by the formula

$$\frac{E}{D}$$

where

D is the amount determined for D under paragraph (2)(b) in respect of the qualifying period, and

2424

Part LXXXV — Registered Pension Plans  Reg. S. 8509(2)

E is

(a) if

(i) all or a part of the qualifying period is a period throughout which the individual renders services to another employer pursuant to an arrangement in respect of which subsection 8308(7) is applicable,

(ii) the particular employer is a lending employer for the purposes of subsection 8308(7) as it applies in respect of the arrangement, and

(iii) the particular employer and the other employer deal with each other at arm's length,

the amount that would be determined under subsection (2) in respect of the qualifying period if, in the determination of the amount under paragraph (2)(a), no remuneration were included in respect of the portion of the qualifying period referred to in subparagraph (a)(i), and

(b) otherwise, the amount that is determined under subsection (2) in respect of the qualifying period.

**Information Circulars**: 98-2: Prescribed compensation for RPPs, para. 21.

**(6) Exclusion of subperiods** — A reference in this section to a qualifying period of an individual in a calendar year with respect to an employer or to a period of disability of an individual in a calendar year does not include a period that is part of a longer such period.

**(7) Complete period of reduced pay** — In subsection (2), "complete period of reduced pay" of an individual with respect to an employer means a period that consists of one or more periods each of which is

(a) a period of disability of the individual, or

(b) an eligible period of reduced pay or temporary absence of the individual with respect to the employer,

and that is not part of a longer such period.

**Definitions [Reg. 8507]**: "additional compensation fraction" — Reg. 8507(5); "amount" — ITA 248(1); "arm's length" — ITA 251(1); "associated" — ITA 256; "benefits" — Reg. 8501(5)(c); "child" — ITA 252(1); "compensation" — ITA 147.1(1); "complete period of reduced pay" — Reg. 8507(7); "contribution" — Reg. 8501(6), (7); "cumulative additional compensation fraction" — Reg. 8507(4); "deferred profit sharing plan" — ITA 147(1), 248(1); "defined benefit provision" — ITA 147.1(1); "eligible period of reduced pay" — Reg. 8500(1); "employer", "employment", "individual" — ITA 248(1); "lifetime retirement benefits" — Reg. 8500(1); "money purchase provision" — ITA 147.1(1); "month" — *Interpretation Act* 35(1); "pension adjustment" — ITA 248(1); "period of disability" — Reg. 8500(1); "prescribed" — ITA 248(1); "qualifying period" — Reg. 8507(3)(a), 8507(6); "registered pension plan" — ITA 248(1); "specified multi-employer plan" — ITA 147.1(1), Reg. 8510(2), (3).

**Interpretation Bulletins [Reg. 8507]**: IT-363R2: Deferred profit sharing plans — deductibility of employer contributions and taxation of amounts received by a beneficiary.

**Registered Plans Division Newsletters [Reg. 8507]**: 91-4R (Registration rules for money purchase provisions).

**8508. Salary deferral leave plan** — Where an employee and an employer enter into an arrangement in writing described in paragraph 6801(a) or (b),

(a) the period throughout which the employee defers salary or wages pursuant to the arrangement shall be deemed to be an eligible period of reduced pay of the employee with respect to the employer; and

(b) for the purposes of section 8507, the amount that it is reasonable to consider would have been the remuneration of the employee for any period from the employer shall be determined on the basis that the employee's rate of remuneration was the amount that it is reasonable to consider would, but for the arrangement, have been the employee's rate of remuneration.

**Definitions [Reg. 8508]**: "amount" — ITA 248(1); "eligible period of reduced pay" — Reg. 8500(1); "employee", "employer", "salary or wages" — ITA 248(1); "writing" — *Interpretation Act* 35(1).

**Information Circulars**: 98-2: Prescribed compensation for RPPs, para. 22.

**8509. Transition rules — (1) Prescribed conditions applicable before 1992 to grandfathered plan** — The prescribed conditions for the registration of a grandfathered plan are, before 1992,

(a) the condition set out in paragraph 8502(a),

(b) the condition set out in paragraph 8502(c), but only in respect of benefits provided under a money purchase provision of the plan, and

(c) if the plan contains a money purchase provision, the condition set out in paragraph 8506(2)(a),

and the following conditions:

(d) the benefits provided under each defined benefit provision of the plan are acceptable to the Minister and, for the purposes of this condition, any benefits in respect of periods before 1991 that become provided after 1988 with respect to a member who is connected with an employer who participates in the plan, or was so connected at any time before the benefits become provided, shall, unless the Minister is notified in writing that the benefits are provided with respect to the member, be deemed to be unacceptable to the Minister, and

(e) the plan contains such terms as may be required by the Minister.

**(2) Conditions applicable after 1991 to benefits under grandfathered plan** — For the purpose of the condition in paragraph 8502(c) as it applies after 1991 in respect of a grandfathered plan,

(a) the condition in subparagraph 8503(2)(b)(ii) is replaced by the condition that the amount of bridging benefits payable to a member for a particular month does not exceed the amount that is determined in respect of the month by the formula

$$\left(A \times C \times \frac{E}{F}\right) + \left[G \times \left(1 - \frac{E}{F}\right)\right]$$

where

A is the amount determined for A under subparagraph 8503(2)(b)(ii) with respect to the member for the month,

C is the amount determined for C under subparagraph 8503(2)(b)(ii) with respect to the member for the month,

E is the aggregate of all amounts each of which is the duration (measured in years, including any fraction of a year) of a period ending before 1992 that is pensionable service of the member under the provision,

F is the aggregate of all amounts each of which is the duration (measured in years, including any fraction of a year) of a period that is pensionable service of the member under the provision, and

G is the amount determined with respect to the member for the month by the formula in subparagraph 8503(2)(b)(ii);

(b) the conditions in paragraphs 8503(3)(c), (h) and (i) and 8504(1)(a) and (b) apply only in respect of lifetime retirement benefits provided in respect of periods after 1991; and

(c) for the purposes of the conditions in paragraphs 8504(1)(a) and (b),

(i) the aggregate that is determined under subparagraph 8504(1)(a)(i) does not include an amount in respect of 1991, and

(ii) the amount that is determined for G under subparagraph 8504(1)(a)(ii) is based only on periods of pensionable service after 1991.

**(3) Additional prescribed condition for grandfathered plan after 1991** — The prescribed conditions for the registration of a grandfathered plan include, after 1991, the condition that all benefits provided under each defined benefit provision of the plan in respect of periods before 1992 are acceptable to the Minister.

**(4) Defined benefits under grandfathered plan exempt from conditions** — The Minister may, after 1991, exempt from the condition in paragraph 8502(c) the following benefits provided under a defined benefit provision of a grandfathered plan:

(a) benefits that are payable after the death of a member, to the extent that the benefits can reasonably be considered to relate to lifetime retirement benefits provided to the member in respect of periods before 1992; and

(b) bridging benefits in excess of bridging benefits that are permissible under paragraph 8503(2)(b), to the extent that the excess bridging benefits are vested in a member on December 31, 1991.

**(4.1) Benefits under grandfathered plan — pre-1992 disability** — Where benefits are provided under a defined benefit provision of a grandfathered plan to a member of the plan as a consequence of the member having become, before 1992, physically or mentally impaired, the following rules apply:

(a) the conditions in this Part (other than the condition in paragraph (b)) do not apply in respect of the benefits;

(b) the prescribed conditions for the registration of the plan include the condition that the benefits are acceptable to the Minister; and

(c) subsections 147.1(8) and (9) of the Act do not apply to render the plan a revocable plan where those subsections would not so apply if the member's pension credits under the provision were determined without regard to the benefits.

**Notes**: Reg. 8509(4.1) added by P.C. 1995-17, effective 1989.

**(5) Conditions not applicable to grandfathered plan** — Where a pension plan is a grandfathered plan,

(a) the conditions referred to in paragraph 8501(2)(b) do not apply before 1992 in respect of the plan;

(b) the condition in paragraph 8502(d) does not apply in respect of distributions that are made before 1992 under a defined benefit provision of the plan; and

(c) the conditions in paragraphs 8503(3)(a) and (b) do not apply in respect of benefits provided under a defined benefit provision of the plan in respect of periods before 1992.

**(6) PA limits for grandfathered plan for 1991** — Subsections 147.1(8) and (9) of the Act do not apply in respect of a grandfathered plan for a calendar year before 1992 if

(a) the plan does not contain a money purchase provision in that year; or

(b) no contributions are made in respect of that year under the money purchase provisions of the plan.

**(7) Limit on pre-age 65 benefits** — Where a pension plan is a grandfathered plan or would be a grandfathered plan if the references to "March 27, 1988" in the definitions "existing plan" and "grandfathered plan" in subsection 8500(1) were read as references to "June 7, 1990" and the references to "March 28, 1988" in the definition "existing plan" in that subsection were read as references to "June 8, 1990",

(a) the conditions in paragraphs 8504(5)(a) and (b) apply only in respect of retirement benefits provided in respect of periods after 1991; and

(b) the amounts that are determined for B and D under paragraph 8504(5)(a) are based only on periods of pensionable service after 1991.

**(8) Benefit accrual rate greater than 2 per cent** — Where a pension plan is a grandfathered plan or would be a grandfathered plan if the references to "March 27, 1988" in the definitions "existing plan" and "grandfathered plan" in subsection 8500(1) were read as references to "July 31, 1991" and the references to "March 28, 1988" in the definition "existing plan" in that subsection were read as references to "August 1, 1991",

(a) the condition in paragraph 8503(3)(g) applies only in respect of lifetime retirement benefits provided under a defined benefit provision of the plan in respect of periods after 1994; and

(b) subparagraph 8503(3)(h)(iv) is not applicable in respect of lifetime retirement benefits provided under a defined benefit provision of the plan to a member unless the formula for determining the amount of the member's lifetime retirement benefits complies with the condition in paragraph 8503(3)(g) as that condition would, but for this subsection, apply.

**(9) Benefits under plan other than grandfathered plan** — The following rules apply in respect of the benefits provided under a defined benefit provision of a pension plan that is not a grandfathered plan:

(a) the condition in paragraph 8502(c) does not apply in respect of benefits provided with respect to an individual

(i) to whom retirement benefits have commenced to be paid under the provision before 1992, or

(ii) who has died before 1992; and

(b) the prescribed conditions for the registration of the plan include the condition that all benefits referred to in paragraph (a) are acceptable to the Minister.

**(10) Money purchase benefits exempt from conditions** — The Minister may exempt from the condition in paragraph 8502(c) all or a portion of the benefits provided under a money purchase provision of a pension plan with respect to a member that may reasonably be considered to derive from contributions made before 1992 under a money purchase provision of a registered pension plan.

**Registered Plans Division Newsletters**: 91-4R (Registration rules for money purchase provisions).

**(10.1) Stipulation not required for pre-1992 plans** — The conditions in paragraphs 8503(4)(c) and 8506(2)(d) do not apply in respect of a pension plan

(a) that was a registered pension plan on December 31, 1991,

(b) in respect of which an application for registration was made to the Minister before 1992, or

(c) that was established to provide benefits to one or more individuals in lieu of benefits to which the individuals were entitled under another pension plan that is a plan described in paragraph (a) or (b) or this paragraph, whether or not benefits are also provided to other individuals.

**Notes**: Reg. 8509(10.1) added by P.C. 1995-17, effective 1989. (This exemption recognizes that many of these plans either cannot be amended to add the stipulation or can be amended only with the consent of plan members as well as court approval.)

**Registered Plans Division Newsletters**: 91-4R (Registration rules for money purchase provisions).

**(11) Benefits acceptable to Minister** — For greater certainty, where benefits under a defined benefit provision of a pension plan are, by reason of paragraph 8503(3)(e) or subsection (3), subject to the condition that they be acceptable to the Minister, the provisions of this section shall not be considered to limit in any way the requirements that may be imposed by the Minister in respect of the benefits.

**(12) PA limits — 1996 to 2003** — Neither subsection 147.1(8) nor (9) of the Act applies to render a registered pension plan a revocable plan at the end of any calendar year after 1995 and before 2004 solely because a pension adjustment, a total of pension adjustments or a total of pension credits of an individual for the year (each of which is, in this subsection, referred to as a "test amount") is excessive where the subsection would not apply to render the plan a revocable plan at the end of the year if each test amount were decreased by the lesser of

(a) the amount, if any, by which the lesser of

(i) the total of all amounts each of which is

(A) a pension credit under a defined benefit provision of a registered pension plan that is included in determining the test amount, or

(B) a pension credit under a money purchase provision of a registered pension plan or under a deferred profit sharing plan that is included in determining the test amount and that is taken into account, under paragraph 8302(2)(c), in determining a pension credit referred to in clause (A), and

(ii) $15,500

exceeds the money purchase limit for the year, and

(b) the total of all amounts each of which is a pension credit referred to in clause (a)(i)(A).

Reg. S. 8509(12)

**Notes**: Reg. 8509(12) added by P.C. 1998-2256, effective 1996.
**Registered Plans Division Newsletters**: 96-1 (Changes to retirement savings limits).

**(13) Maximum benefits indexed before 2005** — Where

(a) a pension plan is a grandfathered plan or would be a grandfathered plan if the references to "March 27, 1988" in the definitions "existing plan" and "grandfathered plan" in subsection 8500(1) were read as references to "March 5, 1996" and the references to "March 28, 1988" in the definition "existing plan" in that subsection were read as references to "March 6, 1996",

(b) under the terms of the plan as they read immediately before March 6, 1996, the plan provided for benefits that are benefits to which a condition in any of subsections 8504(1), (5) and (6) and paragraph 8505(3)(d) applies and, at that time, the benefits complied with the condition, and

(c) as a consequence of the change in the defined benefit limit effective March 6, 1996, the benefits would, if this Part were read without reference to this subsection, cease to comply with the condition,

the following rules apply:

(d) for the purpose of determining at any time after March 5, 1996 and before 1998 whether the benefits comply with the condition, the defined benefit limit for each year after 1995 is deemed to be the amount that it would be if the definition "money purchase limit" in subsection 147.1(1) of the Act were applied as it read on December 31, 1995, and

(e) for the purpose of determining at any time after 1997 whether the benefits comply with the condition, the defined benefit limit for 1996 and 1997 is deemed to be the amount that it would be if it were determined in accordance with paragraph (d).

**Notes**: Reg. 8509(13) added by P.C. 1998-2256, effective March 6, 1996, except that where

(a) the retirement benefits provided to an individual under a pension plan are provided by means of an annuity contract issued before March 6, 1996, and

(b) under the terms and conditions of the contract as they read immediately before March 6, 1996,

(i) the day on which annuity payments are to begin under the contract is fixed and determined and is after 1997, and

(ii) the amount and timing of each annuity payment are fixed and determined,

ignore para. (e) and the words "and before 1998" in para. (d).

**Definitions [Reg. 8509]**: "amount" — ITA 248(1); "benefits" — Reg. 8501(5)(c); "bridging benefits" — Reg. 8500(1); "connected" — Reg. 8500(3); "contribution" — Reg. 8501(6); "deferred profit sharing plan" — ITA 147(1), 248(1); "defined benefit limit" — Reg. 8500(1); "defined benefit provision" — ITA 147.1(1); "employer" — ITA 248(1); "grandfathered plan" — Reg. 8500(1); "individual" — ITA 248(1); "lifetime retirement benefits" — Reg. 8500(1); "member" — ITA 147.1(1); "Minister" — ITA 248(1); "money purchase limit", "money purchase provision" — ITA 147.1(1); "month" — Interpretation Act 35(1); "pension adjustment" — ITA 248(1); "pension credit" — Reg. 8301, 8308.1(2)–(4), 8308.3(2), (3); "pensionable service" — Reg. 8500(1); "prescribed", "registered pension plan" — ITA 248(1); "retirement benefits" — Reg. 8500(1); "test amount" — Reg. 8509(12); "writing" — Interpretation Act 35(1).

**8510. Multi-employer plans and specified multi-employer plans — (1) Definition of "multi-employer plan"** — The definition "multi-employer plan" in subsection 8500(1) is applicable for the purposes of subsection 147.1(1) of the Act.

**(2) Definition of "specified multi-employer plan"** — For the purposes of this Part and subsection 147.1(1) of the Act, "specified multi-employer plan" in a calendar year means a pension plan

(a) in respect of which the conditions in subsection (3) are satisfied at the beginning of the year (or at the time in the year when the plan is established, if later),

(b) that has, on application by the plan administrator, been designated in writing by the Minister to be a specified multi-employer plan in the year, or

(c) that was, by reason of paragraph (a), a specified multi-employer plan in the immediately preceding calendar year (where that year is after 1989),

but does not include a pension plan where the Minister has, before the beginning of the year, given notice by registered mail to the plan administrator that the plan is not a specified multi-employer plan.

**Related Provisions**: Reg. 8510(4) — Minister's notice concerning specified multi-employer plans.

**(3) Qualification as a specified multi-employer plan** — The conditions referred to in paragraph (2)(a) are the following:

(a) it is reasonable to expect that at no time in the year will more than 95 per cent of the active members of the plan be employed by a single participating employer or by a related group of participating employers;

(b) where the year is 1991 or a subsequent year, it is reasonable to expect that

(i) at least 15 employers will contribute to the plan in respect of the year, or

(ii) at least 10 per cent of the active members of the plan will be employed in the year by more than one participating employer,

and, for the purposes of this condition, all employers who are related to each other shall be deemed to be a single employer;

(c) employers participate in the plan pursuant to a collective bargaining agreement;

(d) all or substantially all of the employers who participate in the plan are persons who are not exempt from tax under Part I of the Act;

(e) contributions are made by employers in accordance with a negotiated contribution formula that does not provide for any variation in contributions determined by reference to the financial experience of the plan;

(f) the contributions that are to be made by each employer in the year are determined, in whole or in part, by reference to the number of hours worked by individual employees of the employer or some other measure that is specific to each employee with respect to whom contributions are made to the plan;

(g) the administrator is a board of trustees or similar body that is not controlled by representatives of employers; and

(h) the administrator has the power to determine the benefits to be provided under the plan, whether or not that power is subject to the terms of a collective bargaining agreement.

**Notes**: Revenue Canada's view is that "all or substantially all", used in para. (c), means 90% or more.

**(4) Minister's notice** — For the purpose of subsection (2), the Minister may give notice that a plan is not a specified multi-employer plan only if the Minister is satisfied that participating employers will be able to comply with all reporting obligations imposed by Part LXXXIV in respect of the plan if it is not a specified multi-employer plan, and

(a) the notice is given at or after a time when the conditions in subsection (3) are not satisfied in respect of the plan; or

(b) the plan administrator has applied to the Minister for the notice.

**(5) Special rules — multi-employer plan** — Where a pension plan is a multi-employer plan in a calendar year,

(a) each member of the plan who is connected at any time in the year with an employer who participates in the plan shall be deemed, for the purposes of applying the conditions in sections 8503 and 8504 in respect of the plan in the year and in each subsequent year, not to be so connected in the year;

(b) paragraph 8503(3)(b) shall, in its application in respect of benefits provided under a defined benefit provision of the plan in respect of a period in the year, be read without reference to subparagraph (ii) thereof; and

(c) the condition in paragraph 8503(3)(k) and the rule in subsection 8504(8) shall apply in the year in respect of the plan without regard to benefits provided under any other pension plan.

**(6) Special rules — specified multi-employer plan** — Where a pension plan is a specified multi-employer plan in a calendar year,

(a) a contribution that is made in the year in respect of a defined benefit provision of the plan by an employer with respect to the employer's employees or former employees in accordance with the plan as registered shall be deemed, for the purpose of paragraph 8502(b), to be an eligible contribution;

(b) subparagraph 8502(c)(i) shall, in its application in the year in respect of the plan, be read as follows:

"(i) benefits that are in accordance with subsection 8503(2), paragraphs 8503(3)(c), (e) and (g) and subsections 8504(5) and (6)"; and

(c) the conditions in paragraphs 8503(3)(j) and (4)(a) do not apply in the year in respect of the plan.

**Proposed Addition — Reg. 8510(6)(d)**

(d) a payment made in the year under a defined benefit provision of the plan with respect to a member is deemed to comply with the conditions in paragraph 8503(2)(h) (in the case of a payment made in connection with the member's termination from the plan otherwise than by reason of death) or (j) (in the case of a payment made after the death of the member) where it would comply if paragraph 8503(2)(h) were read as follows:

"(h) the payment, with respect to a member in connection with the member's termination from the plan (otherwise than by reason of death), of one or more single amounts where

(i) the payments are the last payments to be made under the provision with respect to the member, and

(ii) each single amount does not exceed the amount that would be the balance in the member's net contribution account immediately before the time of payment of the single amount if, for each contribution that is a specified contribution, the account were credited at the time of the specified contribution with an additional amount equal to the amount of the specified contribution and, for this purpose, a specified contribution is

(A) a contribution included in determining a pension credit of the member under the provision because of paragraph 8301(5)(b), or

(B) a contribution made before 1990 in respect of the provision by a participating employer, to the extent that the contribution can reasonably be considered to have been determined by reference to the number of hours worked by the member or some other measure specific to the member;".

**Application**: The November 30, 2000 draft regulations (RPPs) (pre-published in *Canada Gazette*, Part I, December 9, 2000), s. 8, will add para. 8510(6)(d), applicable after 1988.

**Regulatory Impact Analysis Statement**: The registration rules for specified multi-employer plans (SMEPs) are modified to allow SMEPs to provide lump sum payments on termination or death equal to employee and employer contributions plus interest.

The registration rules relating to lump sum commutation benefits under defined benefit RPPs are modified to accommodate the practice of calculating the commuted value as of the date of termination of active membership and adjusting it for interest between the calculation date and the payment date. This will resolve a conflict with pension benefits legislation and bring the tax rules into closer conformity with accepted actuarial practice.

Defined benefit RPPs are permitted to provide members who retire before age 65 with a temporary bridging benefit during the period before they begin receiving benefits under the Old Age Security Program or the CPP or QPP. The registration rules impose a number of conditions that apply to bridging benefits. These rules are modified to accommodate certain provisions of the *Supplemental Pension Plans Act* (Quebec). The amendments allow:

- additional bridging benefits, on an actuarial equivalent basis, of up to 40 percent of the year's maximum pensionable earnings; and
- spousal bridging benefits.

**Technical Notes, April 18, 2000**: Subsection 8510(6) of the Regulations modifies certain registration rules in sections 8502 and 8503 as they apply to a pension plan that is a specified multi-employer plan (SMEP). In general terms, a SMEP is a defined benefit pension plan in which several non-related employers participate pursuant to a collective bargaining agreement. Employer contribution rates are negotiated and based on hours worked by employees or some other employee-specific measure. Typically, SMEPs are established for employees in an industry or trade where there is frequent movement of employees among employers. SMEP is defined in subsection 8510(2).

New paragraph 8510(6)(d) allows a SMEP to provide lump sum payments on termination or death that are based on employee and employer contributions. Specifically, a SMEP may provide a termination benefit to a member or a death benefit to a beneficiary of a member equal to the amount that would be in the member's net contribution account (as defined in subsection 8503(1)) if that account were also credited with each employer contribution made in respect of the member. Normally, the amount that can be paid will equal the total of the member contributions (if any) and employer contributions plus interest, less any payments previously made with respect to the member. This change is implemented by modifying the conditions in paragraphs 8503(2)(h) and (j) as they apply to SMEPs.

New paragraph 8510(6)(d) applies after 1988, which is when subsection 8510(6) first came into force.

**(7) Additional prescribed conditions** — Where a pension plan is a specified multi-employer plan in a calendar year, the prescribed conditions for the registration of the plan include, in that year, the following conditions:

(a) when employer and member contribution rates under the plan were last established, it was reasonable to expect that, for each calendar year beginning with the year in which the contribution rates were last established,

(i) the aggregate of all amounts each of which is the pension credit of an individual for the year with respect to an employer under a benefit provision of the plan

would not exceed

(ii) 18 per cent of the aggregate of all amounts each of which is, for an individual and an employer where the pension credit of the individual for the year with respect to the employer under a benefit provision of the plan is greater than nil, the compensation of the individual from the employer for the year,

except that this condition does not apply for years before 1992 in the case of a pension plan that is a grandfathered plan; and

(b) where the plan contains a money purchase provision,

(i) the plan terms are such that, if subsection 147.1(9) of the Act were applicable in respect of the plan, the plan would not under any circumstances become a revocable plan at the end of the year pursuant to that subsection, or

(ii) if the plan terms do not comply with the condition in subparagraph (i), the only circumstances that would result in the plan becoming a revocable plan at the end of the year pursuant to subsection 147.1(9) of the Act, if that subsection were applicable in respect of the plan, are circumstances acceptable to the Minister.

**Information Circulars**: 98-2: Prescribed compensation for RPPs, para. 6.

**(8) Purchase of additional benefits** — Where, in the case of a pension plan that is a specified multi-employer plan in a calendar year,

(a) the amount of lifetime retirement benefits provided under a defined benefit provision of the plan to each member is determined by reference to the hours of employment of the member with participating employers,

(b) the plan permits a member whose actual hours of employment in a period are fewer than a specified number of hours for the period to make contributions to the plan in order to increase, to an amount not exceeding the specified number of hours for the period, the number of hours that are treated under the provision as hours of employment of the member in the period, and

(c) the specified number of hours for a period does not exceed a reasonable measure of the actual hours of employment of members who render services throughout the period on a full-time basis, the condition in paragraph 8503(3)(a) does not apply in respect of such portion of the lifetime retirement benefits provided under the provision to a member as is determined by reference to hours acquired by the member as a consequence of contributions made to the plan in the year by the member, as described in paragraph (b).

**Definitions [Reg. 8510]**: "active member" — Reg. 8500(1); "administrator" — ITA 147.1(1); "amount" — ITA 248(1); "benefit provision" — Reg. 8500(1); "benefits" — Reg. 8501(5)(c); "compensation" — ITA 147.1(1); "connected" — Reg. 8500(3); "contribution" — Reg. 8501(6); "defined benefit provision" — ITA 147.1(1); "employed", "employee", "employer", "employment" — ITA 248(1); "grandfathered plan" — Reg. 8500(1); "individual" — ITA 248(1); "lifetime retirement benefits" — Reg. 8500(1); "member" — ITA 147.1(1); "Minister" — ITA 248(1); "money purchase provision" — ITA 147.1(1); "multi-employer plan" — ITA 147.1(1), Reg. 8500(1); "participating employer" — ITA 147.1(1); "pension credit" — Reg. 8301, 8308.1(2)–(4), 8308.3(2), (3); "person", "prescribed" — ITA 248(1); "related" — ITA 251(2)–(6); "single amount" — ITA 147.1(1); "specified multi-employer plan" — ITA 147.1(1), Reg. 8510(2), (3); "writing" — *Interpretation Act* 35(1).

**8511. Conditions applicable to amendments — (1)** For the purposes of paragraph 147.1(4)(c) of the Act, the following conditions are prescribed in respect of an amendment to a registered pension plan:

(a) where the amendment increases the accrued lifetime retirement benefits provided to a member under a defined benefit provision of the plan, the increase is not, in the opinion of the Minister, inconsistent with the conditions in paragraphs 8503(3)(h) and (i); and

(b) where the plan is a grandfathered plan and the amendment increases the bridging benefits provided to a member under a defined benefit provision of the plan, the member's bridging benefits, as amended, comply with the condition in subparagraph 8503(2)(b)(ii) that would apply if the plan were not a grandfathered plan.

(2) Where an amendment to a registered pension plan provides for the return to a member of all or a part of the contributions made by the member under a defined benefit provision of the plan, the plan becomes a revocable plan at any time that an amount (other than an amount that may be transferred from the plan in accordance with subsection 147.3(6) of the Act) that is payable to the member as a consequence of the amendment is not paid to the member as soon after the amendment as is practicable.

**Notes**: Reg. 8511(2) amended by P.C. 1995-17, retroactive to its introduction (1989). (The amendments deleted words referring to ITA 147.3(6) as being for transfer to another RPP or an RRSP, consequential on the amendment to that provision permitting transfer to a RRIF.)

**Definitions [Reg. 8511]**: "amount" — ITA 248(1); "bridging benefits" — Reg. 8500(1); "contribution" — Reg. 8501(6); "defined benefit provision" — ITA 147.1(1); "grandfathered plan",  "lifetime retirement benefits" — Reg. 8500(1); "member" — ITA 147.1(1); "Minister", "prescribed", "registered pension plan" — ITA 248(1).

**8512. Registration and amendment — (1)** For the purposes of subsection 147.1(2) of the Act, an application for registration of a pension plan shall be made by forwarding by registered mail to the Deputy Minister of National Revenue for Taxation at Ottawa the following documents:

(a) an application in prescribed form containing prescribed information;

(b) certified copies of the plan text and any other documents that contain terms of the plan;

(c) certified copies of all trust deeds, insurance contracts and other documents that relate to the funding of benefits under the plan;

(d) certified copies of all agreements that relate to the plan; and

(e) certified copies of all resolutions and by-laws that relate to the documents referred to in paragraphs (b) to (d).

**Notes**: Reg. 8512(1) applies as of January 15, 1992. See Notes to Reg. 8520.

**Registered Plans Division Newsletters**: 91-4R (Registration rules for money purchase provisions).

(2) Where, after 1988, an amendment is made to a registered pension plan, to the arrangement for funding benefits under the plan or to a document that has been filed with the Minister in respect of the plan, the plan administrator shall, within 60 days after the day on which the amendment is made, forward to the Deputy Minister of National Revenue for Taxation at Ottawa

(a) a prescribed form containing prescribed information; and

(b) certified copies of all documents that relate to the amendment.

**Notes**: Any form or document otherwise required by Reg. 8512(2) to be forwarded to the Deputy Minister of National Revenue for Taxation before March 15, 1992 is deemed to have been forwarded as required if it is forwarded on or before March 15, 1992.

**Registered Plans Division Newsletters**: 96-1 (Changes to retirement savings limits).

**Forms**: T920: Application for acceptance of an amendment to a registered pension plan.

(3) For the purposes of subsection 147.1(4) of the Act, an application for the acceptance of an amendment to a registered pension plan is made in prescribed manner where the documents that are required by subsection (2) are forwarded by registered mail to the Deputy Minister of National Revenue for Taxation at Ottawa.

**Definitions [Reg. 8512]**: "administrator" — ITA 147.1(1); "benefits" — Reg. 8501(5)(c); "Minister", "prescribed", "registered pension plan" — ITA 248(1); "trust" — ITA 104(1), 248(1), (3).

**8513. Designated laws** — For the purposes of paragraph 8302(3)(m), subparagraph 8502(c)(iii) and paragraph 8517(5)(f), "designated provision of the law of Canada or a province" means subsection 21(2) of the *Pension Benefits Standards Act, 1985* and any provision of a law of a province that is similar to that subsection.

**Definitions [Reg. 8513]**: "province" — *Interpretation Act* 35(1).

**Registered Plans Division Newsletters**: 91-4R (Registration rules for money purchase provisions).

**8514. Prohibited investments** — (1) For the purposes of subparagraph 8502(h)(i), and subject to subsections (2) and (3), a prohibited investment in respect of a registered pension plan is a share of the capital stock of, an interest in, or a debt of

> **Proposed Amendment — Reg. 8514(1) opening words**
>
> **(1) Prohibited investments** — For the purposes of subparagraph 8502(h)(i) and subject to subsections (2), (2.1) and (3), a prohibited investment in respect of a registered pension plan is a share of the capital stock of, an interest in, or a debt of
>
> **Application**: The November 30, 2000 draft regulations (RPPs) (pre-published in *Canada Gazette*, Part I, December 9, 2000), subsec. 9(1), will amend the opening words of subsec. 8514(1) to read as above, applicable to property acquired after September 1999.
>
> **Regulatory Impact Analysis Statement**: The RPP investment rules in section 8514 are modified to provide a limited exclusion for large defined benefit multi-employer plans.
>
> **Technical Notes, April 18, 2000**: Paragraph 8502(h) requires that an RPP avoid holding investments prohibited by subsection 8514(1). In general terms, subsection 8514(1) provides that an investment is a prohibited investment for an RPP if it is a share of the capital stock or a debt obligation of:
> - a plan member;
> - an employer who participates in the plan;
> - a person connected with a participating employer (as defined in subsection 8500(3));
> - a person or partnership that controls a participating employer or that controls a person connected with a participating employer; or
> - a person or partnership that does not deal at arm's length with any of the above.
>
> Subsection 8514(1) is subject to subsection 8514(2), which provides exceptions for government debt, shares and debt of publicly-traded companies, and insured mortgages.
>
> Subsection 8514(1) is amended so that it is also subject to new subsection 8514(2.1), which accommodates certain incidental investment transactions undertaken by large defined benefit multi-employer plans. For more details, see the commentary to subsection 8514(2.1).

(a) an employer who participates in the plan,

(b) a person who is connected with an employer who participates in the plan,

(c) a member of the plan,

(d) a person or partnership that controls, directly or indirectly, in any manner whatever, a person or partnership referred to in paragraph (a) or (b), or

(e) a person or partnership that does not deal at arm's length with a person or partnership referred to in paragraph (a), (b), (c) or (d),

or an interest in, or a right to acquire, such a share, interest or debt.

(2) A prohibited investment does not include

(a) a bond, debenture, note, mortgage or similar obligation described in clause 212(1)(b)(ii)(C) of the Act;

(b) a share listed on a stock exchange referred to in section 3200 or 3201;

(c) a bond, debenture, note or similar obligation of a corporation any shares of which are listed on a stock exchange referred to in section 3200 or 3201;

(d) an interest in, or a right to acquire, property referred to in paragraph (b) or (c); or

(e) a mortgage in respect of real property situated in Canada that

(i) where this condition has not been waived by the Minister and the amount paid for the mortgage, together with the amount of any indebtedness outstanding at the time the mortgage was acquired under any mortgage or hypothec that ranks equally with or superior to the mortgage, exceeds 75 per cent of the fair market value, at that time, of the real property that is subject to the mortgage, is insured under the *National Housing Act* or by a corporation that offers its services to the public in Canada as an insurer of mortgages,

(ii) where the registered pension plan in connection with which the mortgage is held would be a designated plan for the purposes of subsection 8515(5) if subsection 8515(4) were read without reference to paragraph (b) thereof, is administered by an approved lender under the *National Housing Act*, and

(iii) bears a rate of interest that would be reasonable in the circumstances if the mortgagor dealt with the mortgagee at arm's length.

**Notes**: Reg. 8514(2)(a) amended to change "mortgage, hypothec" to "mortgage" by P.C. 1994-1817, effective November 30, 1994. This change is intended to be non-substantive.

> **Proposed Addition — Reg. 8514(2.1), (2.2)**
>
> **(2.1)** Where a share of the capital stock of, an interest in or a debt of, a person who is connected with a particular employer who participates in a registered pension plan that is a multi-employer plan would, but for this subsection, be a prohibited investment in respect of the plan, the property is not a prohibited investment in respect of the plan if
>
> (a) the plan does not contain a money purchase provision;

Part LXXXV — Registered Pension Plans  Reg. S. 8515(1)

(b) at the time the property is acquired by the plan, there are at least 15 employers who participate in the plan, and, for this purpose,

(i) all employers who are related to each other are deemed to be a single employer, and

(ii) all the structural units of a trade union, including each local, branch, national and international unit, are deemed to be a single employer;

(c) at the time the property is acquired by the plan, no more than 10 per cent of the active members of the plan are employed by the particular employer or by any person related to the particular employer;

(d) the property would not be a prohibited investment in respect of the plan if subsection (1) were read without reference to paragraph (1)(b); and

(e) immediately after the time the property is acquired by the plan, the total of all amounts each of which is the cost amount to a person of a property held in connection with the plan that would, but for this subsection, be a prohibited investment in respect of the plan does not exceed 10 per cent of the total of all amounts each of which is the cost amount to a person of a property held in connection with the plan.

**(2.2)** For the purposes of the conditions in paragraphs (2.1)(b) and (c), two corporations that are related to each other solely because they are both controlled by Her Majesty in right of Canada or a province are deemed not to be related to each other.

**Application**: The November 30, 2000 draft regulations (RPPs) (pre-published in *Canada Gazette*, Part I, December 9, 2000), subsec. 9(2), will add subsecs. 8514(2.1) and (2.2), applicable to property acquired after September 1999.

**Technical Notes, April 18, 2000**: New subsection 8514(2.1) of the Regulations provides a limited exclusion for multi-employer plans (as defined in subsection 8500(1)) from the prohibition on lending or investing with related or other closely held parties. Specifically, subsection 8514(2.1) excludes from the list of otherwise prohibited investments for a pension plan that is a multi-employer plan shares and debt of a person who is connected with an employer who participates in the plan. The exclusion applies only if the following conditions are met:

(a) the plan does not contain a money purchase provision;

(b) at the time the property is acquired by the plan, at least 15 non-related employers participate in the plan;

(c) at the time the property is acquired by the plan, no more than 10% of the active members of the plan are employed by the participating employer or by any person related to the participating employer;

(d) the property would not otherwise be a prohibited investment for the plan if subsection 8514(1) were read

without reference to paragraph 8514(1)(b) (in other words, the investment does not involve a person who controls a participating employer or who does not deal at arm's length with a participating employer); and

(e) immediately after acquisition of the property, the total cost amount of all such properties held in connection with the plan does not exceed 10% of the total cost amount of all properties held in connection with the plan.

In determining whether employers are related for the purposes of conditions (b) and (c), reference should be made to section 251 of the Act, which defines "related persons" and other similar expressions. New subsection 8514(2.2) contains a special rule that also applies for the purposes of conditions (b) and (c). It provides that two corporations that are otherwise related to each other solely because they are both controlled by the government of Canada or a province are considered not to be related. This rule is analogous to the rule contained in the definition "multi-employer plan" in subsection 8500(1).

For the purpose of condition (b), a union and its locals and branches are considered to be a single employer. This rule is analogous to the rule in section 252.1 of the Act.

This amendment applies to property acquired after September 1999.

**(3)** A prohibited investment in respect of a registered pension plan does not include an investment that was acquired by the plan before March 28, 1988.

**Related Provisions**: Reg. 8514(4) — When debt obligation deemed to be issued.

**(4)** For the purposes of subsection (3), where at any time after March 27, 1988, the principal amount of a bond, debenture, note, mortgage or similar obligation increases as a consequence of the advancement or lending of additional amounts, or the maturity date of such an obligation is extended, the obligation shall, after that time, be deemed to have been issued at that time.

**Notes**: Reg. 8514(4) amended to change "mortgage, hypothec" to "mortgage" by P.C. 1994-1817, effective November 30, 1994. This change is intended to be non-substantive.

**Definitions [Reg. 8514]**: "active member" — Reg. 8500(1); "amount" — ITA 248(1); "arm's length" — ITA 251(1); "Canada" — ITA 255, *Interpretation Act* 35(1); "connected" — Reg. 8500(3); "corporation" — ITA 248(1), *Interpretation Act* 35(1); "cost amount", "employed", "employer" — ITA 248(1); "Her Majesty" — *Interpretation Act* 35(1); "insurer" — ITA 248(1); "member" — ITA 147.1(1); "Minister" — ITA 248(1); "money purchase provision" — ITA 147.1(1); "multi-employer plan" — ITA 147.1(1), Reg. 8500(1); "partnership" — see Notes to ITA 96(1); "person", "principal amount", "property" — ITA 248(1); "province" — *Interpretation Act* 35(1); "registered pension plan" — ITA 248(1); "related" — ITA 251(2)–(6), Reg. 8514(2.2); "share" — ITA 248(1).

**8515. Special rules for designated plans — (1) Designated plans** — For the purposes of subsections (5) and (9), and subject to subsection (3), a registered pension plan that contains a defined benefit provision is a designated plan throughout a calendar

**Reg. S. 8515(1)** — Income Tax Regulations

year if the plan is not maintained pursuant to a collective bargaining agreement and

(a) the aggregate of all amounts each of which is a pension credit (as determined under Part LXXIII) for the year of a specified individual under a defined benefit provision of the plan

exceeds

(b) 50 per cent of the aggregate of all amounts each of which is a pension credit (as determined under Part LXXXIII) for the year of an individual under a defined benefit provision of the plan.

**Related Provisions**: Reg. 8515(4) — Specified individual.

**(2) Designated plan in previous year** — For the purposes of subsections (5) and (9), a registered pension plan is a designated plan throughout a particular calendar year after 1990 if the plan was a designated plan at any time in the immediately preceding year, except where the Minister has waived in writing the application of this subsection in respect of the plan.

**(3) Exceptions** — A registered pension plan is not a designated plan in a calendar year pursuant to subsection (1) if

(a) the plan would not be a designated plan in the year pursuant to that subsection if the reference in paragraph (1)(b) to "50 per cent" were read as a reference to "60 per cent",

(b) the plan was established before the year, and

(c) the amount determined under paragraph (1)(a) in respect of the plan for the immediately preceding year did not exceed the amount determined under paragraph (1)(b),

or if

(d) there are more than 9 active members of the plan in the year, and

(e) the Minister has given written notice to the administrator of the plan that the plan is not a designated plan in the year.

**(4) Specified individuals** — An individual is a specified individual for the purposes of paragraph (1)(a) in respect of a pension plan and a particular calendar year if

(a) the individual was connected at any time in the year with an employer who participates in the plan; or

(b) the aggregate of all amounts each of which is the remuneration of the individual for the year from an employer who participates in the plan, or from an employer who does not deal at arm's length with a participating employer, exceeds $2\frac{1}{2}$ times the Year's Maximum Pensionable Earnings for the year.

**(5) Eligible contributions** — For the purpose of determining whether a contribution made by an employer to a registered pension plan at a time when the plan is a designated plan is an eligible contribution under subsection 147.2(2) of the Act, a prescribed condition is that

(a) the contribution satisfies the condition in subsection (6), or

(b) the contribution would satisfy the condition in subsection (6) if

(i) paragraph (6)(b) and subparagraph (7)(e)(i) were applicable only in respect of retirement benefits that became provided under the plan after 1990,

(ii) paragraph (6)(c) were applicable only in respect of those benefits payable after the death of a member that relate to retirement benefits that became provided under the plan to the member after 1990, and

(iii) the assumption as to the time retirement benefits (other than retirement benefits that became provided after 1990) will commence to be paid is the same for the purposes of the maximum funding valuation as for the purposes of the actuarial valuation that forms the basis for the recommendation referred to in subsection 147.2(2) of the Act pursuant to which the contribution is made.

**Related Provisions**: Reg. 8515(1)–(3) — Designated plans.

**Notes**: Reg. 8515(5) is applicable

(i) in respect of contributions made after 1991 to a pension plan that was registered by the Minister on or before July 31, 1991 for the purposes of the *Income Tax Act*, and

(ii) in respect of contributions made after 1990 to a pension plan that is registered by the Minister after July 31, 1991 for the purposes of that Act.

**(6) Funding restriction** — The condition referred to in subsection (5) is that the contribution would be required to be made for the plan to have sufficient assets to pay benefits under the defined benefit provisions of the plan, as registered, with respect to the employees and former employees of the employer if

(a) required contributions were determined on the basis of a maximum funding valuation prepared as of the same effective date as the actuarial valuation that forms the basis for the recommendation referred to in subsection 147.2(2) of the Act pursuant to which the contribution is made;

(a.1) each defined benefit provision of the plan provided that, with respect to restricted-funding members, retirement benefits are payable monthly in advance;

(b) each defined benefit provision of the plan provided that, after retirement benefits commence to be paid with respect to a restricted-funding member, the benefits are adjusted annually by a percentage increase for each year that is 1 percentage point less than the percentage increase in the Consumer Price Index for the year, in lieu of any cost-of-living adjustments actually provided;

(c) each defined benefit provision of the plan provided the following benefits after the death of a restricted-funding member who dies after retirement benefits under the provision have commenced to be paid to the member, in lieu of the benefits actually provided:

(i) where the member dies within 5 years after retirement benefits commence to be paid under the provision, the continuation of the retirement benefits for the remainder of the 5 years as if the member were alive, and

(ii) where an individual who is a spouse of the member when retirement benefits commence to be paid under the provision to the member is alive on the later of the day of death of the member and the day that is 5 years after the day on which the member's retirement benefits commence to be paid, retirement benefits payable to the individual for the duration of the individual's life, with the amount of the benefits payable for each month equal to 66$\frac{2}{3}$ per cent of the amount of retirement benefits that would have been payable under the provision for the month to the member if the member were alive;

(d) where more than one employer participates in the plan, assets and actuarial liabilities were apportioned in a reasonable manner among participating employers with respect to their employees and former employees; and

(e) the rule in paragraph 147.2(2)(d) of the Act that provides for the disregard of a portion of the assets of the plan apportioned to the employer with respect to the employer's employees and former employees were applicable for the purpose of determining required contributions pursuant to this subsection.

**Related Provisions**: Reg. 8515(7) — Maximum funding valuation; Reg. 8515(8) — Restricted-funding member.

**Notes**: Reg. 8515(6)(a.1) added by P.C. 1995-17, effective with respect to a contribution made after June 4, 1994, except where the contribution is made pursuant to a valuation report filed with Revenue Canada in accordance with ITA 147.2(3) by June 4, 1994.

References to "spouse" are expected to be amended to add "or common-law partner" effective 2001 or earlier by election, as has been done throughout the ITA. See Notes to ITA 248(1)"common-law partner".

**(7) Maximum funding valuation** — For the purposes of subsection (6), a maximum funding valuation is a valuation prepared by an actuary in accordance with the following rules:

(a) the projected accrued benefit method is used for the purpose of determining actuarial liabilities and current service costs;

(b) the valuation rate of interest is 7.5 per cent per annum;

(c) it is assumed that

(i) the rate of increase in general wages and salaries and in each member's rate of remuneration will be 5.5 per cent per annum, and

(ii) the rate of increase in the Consumer Price Index will be 4 per cent per annum;

(d) each assumption made in respect of economic factors other than those referred to in paragraph (c) is consistent with the assumptions in that paragraph;

(e) in the case of a restricted-funding member, it is assumed that

(i) retirement benefits will commence to be paid to the member no earlier than the day on which the member attains 65 years of age,

(ii) the member will survive to the time the member's retirement benefits commence to be paid,

(iii) where the member is employed by a participating employer as of the effective date of the valuation, the member will continue in employment until the time when the member's retirement benefits commence to be paid, and

(iv) when the member's retirement benefits commence to be paid, the member will be married to a person who is the same age as the member;

(f) the rate of mortality at each age is equal to

(i) in the case of a restricted-funding member, 80 per cent of the average of the rates at that age for males and females in the *1983 Group Annuity Mortality Table*, as published in Volume XXXV of the *Transactions of the Society of Actuaries*, and

(ii) in the case of any other member, 80 per cent of the rate at that age in the mortality table referred to in subparagraph (i) for individuals of the same sex as the member;

(g) it is assumed that where a member has a choice between receiving retirement benefits or a lump sum payment, retirement benefits will be paid to the member; and

(h) the plan's assets are valued at an amount equal to their fair market value as of the effective date of the valuation.

**Related Provisions**: Reg. 8515(8) — Restricted-funding member.

**Notes**: Reg. 8515(7)(e)(i) amended by P.C. 1995-17, retroactive to its introduction (1989). (The amendment deleted an assumption that the member's pension would begin to be paid on the later of the effective date of the valuation and the member's 65th birthday, if the pension had not begun by the time the valuation was prepared. This assumption is inappropriate if the member continues to accrue benefits after age 65.)

Reg. 8515(7)(f) amended by P.C. 1995-17, to limit subpara. (i) to a restricted-funding member and add subpara. (ii). For female members, the amendment is retroactive to the introduction of the rules limiting contributions to designated plans (1989). However, with respect to a contribution made by June 4, 1994, or pursuant to a valuation report filed with Revenue Canada in accordance with ITA 147.2(3) by June 4, 1994, subpara. (i) applies to a male member who is not a restricted-funding member.

**(8) Restricted-funding members** — For the purposes of subsections (6) and (7) as they apply in respect of a contribution made to a registered pension plan, a member of the plan is a restricted-funding member if, at the time the maximum funding valuation is prepared,

(a) the member has a right, whether absolute or contingent, to receive retirement benefits under a defined benefit provision of the plan and the benefits have not commenced to be paid; or

(b) the payment of retirement benefits under a defined benefit provision of the plan to the member has been suspended.

**(9) Member contributions** — Where

(a) a member of a registered pension plan makes a contribution to the plan to fund benefits that have become provided at a particular time under a defined benefit provision of the plan in respect of periods before that time,

(b) the contribution is made at a time when the plan is a designated plan, and

(c) the contribution would not be an eligible contribution under subsection 147.2(2) of the Act if it were made by an employer who participates in the plan on behalf of the member,

the plan becomes, for the purposes of paragraph 147.1(11)(c) of the Act, a revocable plan immediately before the time the contribution is made.

**Related Provisions**: Reg. 8515(1)–(3) — Designated plans.

**Definitions [Reg. 8515]**: "active member" — Reg. 8500(1); "actuary", "administrator" — ITA 147.1(1); "amount" — ITA 248(1); "arm's length" — ITA 251(1); "benefits" — Reg. 8501(5)(c); "connected" — Reg. 8500(3); "Consumer Price Index" — Reg. 8500(1); "contribution" — Reg. 8501(6); "defined benefit provision" — ITA 147.1(1); "designated plan" — Reg. 8515(1)–(3); "employed", "employee", "employer", "employment", "individual" — ITA 248(1); "maximum funding valuation" — Reg. 8515(7); "member" — ITA 147.1(1); "Minister" — ITA 248(1); "month" — *Interpretation Act* 35(1); "participating employer" — ITA 147.1(1); "pension credit" — Reg. 8301, 8308.1(2)–(4), 8308.3(2), (3); "person", "prescribed" — ITA 248(1); "registered pension plan" — Reg. 8515(1), (2); "restricted-funding member" — Reg. 8515(8); "retirement benefits" — Reg. 8500(1); "specified individual" — Reg. 8515(4); "spouse" — ITA 147.1(1); "writing" — *Interpretation Act* 35(1); "written" — *Interpretation Act* 35(1) "writing"; "Year's Maximum Pensionable Earnings" — Reg. 8500(1).

**8516. Eligible contributions — (1) Prescribed contribution** — For the purposes of subsection 147.2(2) of the Act, a contribution described in any of subsections (2) to (9) that is made by an employer to a registered pension plan in respect of the defined benefit provisions of the plan is a prescribed contribution.

**Notes**: Reg. 8516(1) amended to refer to Reg. 8516(7) and (8) by P.C. 1995-17, retroactive to its introduction (1989); and amended by P.C. 1998-225 to add reference to Reg. 8516(9), effective 1996.

**(2) Amortization of excess actuarial surplus** — A contribution that is made by an employer to a registered pension plan is described in this subsection if

(a) it is made to the plan before 1995;

(b) the recommendation pursuant to which the contribution is made is such that the contributions that are required to be made by the employer in respect of the defined benefit provisions of the plan do not exceed the contributions that would be required if

(i) except as provided in subparagraph (ii), the contributions to be made by the employer were determined without regard to the actuarial surplus under the provisions, and

(ii) the contributions to be made by the employer after 1990 were determined on the basis that the excess actuarial surplus under the provisions with respect to the employer becomes available uniformly throughout the period beginning on the later of January 1, 1991 and the effective date of the actuarial valuation prepared in connection with the recommendation and ending December 31, 1994 to fund benefits under the provisions, in lieu of contributions that would otherwise be required to be made by the employer,

and, for the purposes of this paragraph, the amount of the excess actuarial surplus under the defined benefit provisions of a pension plan with respect to an employer is, in relation to a recommendation pursuant to which contributions are made by the employer, the amount, if any, by which the amount of the actuarial surplus under the provisions with respect to the employer exceeds the aggregate of

(iii) the lesser of the amounts determined under subparagraphs 147.2(2)(d)(ii) and (iii) of the Act in relation to the employer and the recommendation, and

(iv) where the effective date of the actuarial valuation prepared in connection with the recommendation is before 1991, the amount, if any, by which

(A) the aggregate amount of current service contributions that would, but for the actuarial surplus, have been required to be made in respect of the provisions by the employer and the employer's employees for the period from the effective date of the actuarial valuation to December 31, 1990

exceeds

(B) the aggregate amount of current service contributions for that period made in the period by the employer and the employer's employees; and

(c) the contribution would be an eligible contribution under subsection 147.2(2) of the Act if no contributions were prescribed for the purposes of that subsection and if that subsection were read without reference to subparagraphs (d)(ii) and (iii) thereof.

**(3) Approval under paragraph 20(1)(s) of the Act** — A contribution that is made by an employer to a registered pension plan is described in this subsection if

(a) the Minister has approved the contribution under paragraph 20(1)(s) of the Act; and

(b) the contribution would have been deductible under paragraph 20(1)(s) of the Act had that paragraph been applicable to the taxation year of the employer in which the contribution was made.

**(4) Contributions pursuant to collective bargaining agreement** — A contribution that is made by an employer to a registered pension plan is described in this subsection if

(a) it is made to the plan before 1994; and

(b) it is made pursuant to a collective bargaining agreement that was entered into before 1990.

**(5) Contributions pursuant to statute or by-law** — A contribution that is made by an employer to a registered pension plan is described in this subsection if

(a) it is made to the plan in 1991;

(b) it is made pursuant to a formula in a statute or by-law that was in existence on March 27, 1988; and

(c) the formula was not amended after March 27, 1988 and before the time the contribution is made.

**(6) Employer not entitled to reduce contributions** — A contribution that is made by an employer to a registered pension plan is described in this subsection if

(a) it is made to the plan before 1994;

(b) either

(i) the terms of the plan require that contributions made by the employer in respect of the defined benefit provisions of the plan be determined without regard to any actuarial surplus under the provisions, or

(ii) there is a dispute as to whether the terms of the plan have the effect described in subparagraph (i) and steps are being taken to resolve the dispute;

(c) the contribution would be an eligible contribution under subsection 147.2(2) of the Act if no contributions were prescribed for the purposes of that subsection and if that subsection were read without reference to subparagraphs (d)(ii) and (iii) thereof; and

(d) the contribution is acceptable to the Minister.

**(7) Funding on termination basis** — A contribution that is made by an employer to a registered pension plan is described in this subsection if

(a) the contribution is made pursuant to a recommendation by an actuary in whose opinion the contribution is required to be made so that, if the plan is terminated immediately after the contribution is made, it will have sufficient assets to pay benefits accrued under the defined benefit provisions of the plan, as registered, to the time the contribution is made;

(b) the recommendation is based on an actuarial valuation that complies with the following conditions:

(i) the effective date of the valuation is not more than 4 years before the day on which the contribution is made,

(ii) all assumptions made for the purposes of the valuation are reasonable at the time the valuation is prepared and at the time the contribution is made,

(iii) the valuation is prepared in accordance with generally accepted actuarial principles applicable with respect to a valuation prepared on the basis that a plan will be terminated, and

(iv) where more than one employer participates in the plan, assets and actuarial liabilities are apportioned in a reasonable manner among participating employers;

(c) the recommendation is approved by the Minister on the advice of the Superintendent of Financial Institutions; and

(d) at the time the contribution is made, the plan is not a designated plan under section 8515.

**Notes:** Reg. 8516(7) added by P.C. 1995-17, effective 1989.

**(8) Contributions required by pension benefits legislation** — A contribution that is made by an employer to a registered pension plan is described in this subsection if

(a) the contribution

(i) is required to be made to comply with the *Pension Benefits Standards Act, 1985* or a similar law of a province,

(ii) is made in respect of benefits under the defined benefit provisions of the plan as registered, and

(iii) is made pursuant to a recommendation by an actuary;

(b) the recommendation is based on an actuarial valuation that complies with the following conditions:

(i) the effective date of the valuation is not more than 4 years before the day on which the contribution is made,

(ii) all assumptions made for the purposes of the valuation are reasonable at the time the

**Reg. S. 8516(8)(b)(ii)** — Income Tax Regulations

valuation is prepared and at the time the contribution is made, and

(iii) where more than one employer participates in the plan, assets and actuarial liabilities are apportioned in a reasonable manner among participating employers;

(c) the recommendation is approved by the Minister on the advice of the Superintendent of Financial Institutions; and

(d) at the time the contribution is made, the plan is not a designated plan under section 8515.

**Notes**: Reg. 8516(8) added by P.C. 1995-17, effective 1989.

**(9) Actuarial reports signed before March 6, 1996** — A contribution that is made by an employer to a registered pension plan is described in this subsection if

(a) the actuarial report containing the recommendation pursuant to which the contribution is made was signed before March 6, 1996;

(b) the contribution is made after March 5, 1996;

(c) the contribution would be an eligible contribution under subsection 147.2(2) of the Act if

(i) no contributions were prescribed for the purposes of that subsection, and

(ii) for the purpose of determining whether the actuarial valuation on which the recommendation is based complies with the condition in subparagraph 147.2(2)(a)(iii) of the Act, the defined benefit limit for each year after 1995 were equal to the amount that it would be if the definition "money purchase limit" in subsection 147.1(1) of the Act applied as it read on December 31, 1995; and

(d) where the contribution is made after 1996, the plan is not a designated plan under section 8515 at the time it is made.

**Notes [Reg. 8516(9)]**: Reg. 8516(9) added by P.C. 1998-2256, effective 1996.

**Definitions [Reg. 8516]**: "actuary" — ITA 147.1(1); "amount" — ITA 248(1); "benefits" — Reg. 8501(5)(c); "contribution" — Reg. 8501(6); "defined benefit limit" — Reg. 8500(1); "defined benefit provision" — ITA 147.1(1); "employee", "employer", "Minister" — ITA 248(1); "participating employer" — ITA 147.1(1); "prescribed" — ITA 248(1); "province" — *Interpretation Act* 35(1); "registered pension plan" — ITA 248(1); "surplus" — Reg. 8500(1); "taxation year" — ITA 249.

**8517. Transfer — defined benefit to money purchase — (1) Prescribed amount** — Subject to subsections (2) to (3.1), for the purpose of applying paragraph 147.3(4)(c) of the Act to the transfer of an amount on behalf of an individual in full or partial satisfaction of the individual's entitlement to benefits under a defined benefit provision of a registered pension plan, the prescribed amount is the amount that is determined by the formula

$$A \times B$$

where

A is the amount of the individual's lifetime retirement benefits under the provision commuted in connection with the transfer, as determined under subsection (4), and

B is

(a) the present value factor that corresponds to the age attained by the individual at the time of the transfer, determined pursuant to the table to this subsection, or

(b) where the present value factor referred to in paragraph (a) is less than the present value factor that corresponds to the next higher age, the present value factor determined by interpolation between those two factors on the basis of the age (expressed in years, including any fraction of a year) of the individual.

| Attained Age | Present Value Factor | Attained Age | Present Value Factor |
| --- | --- | --- | --- |
| Under 50 | 9.0 | 73 | 9.8 |
| 50 | 9.4 | 74 | 9.4 |
| 51 | 9.6 | 75 | 9.1 |
| 52 | 9.8 | 76 | 8.7 |
| 53 | 10.0 | 77 | 8.4 |
| 54 | 10.2 | 78 | 8.0 |
| 55 | 10.4 | 79 | 7.7 |
| 56 | 10.6 | 80 | 7.3 |
| 57 | 10.8 | 81 | 7.0 |
| 58 | 11.0 | 82 | 6.7 |
| 59 | 11.3 | 83 | 6.4 |
| 60 | 11.5 | 84 | 6.1 |
| 61 | 11.7 | 85 | 5.8 |
| 62 | 12.0 | 86 | 5.5 |
| 63 | 12.2 | 87 | 5.2 |
| 64 | 12.4 | 88 | 4.9 |
| 65 | 12.4 | 89 | 4.7 |
| 66 | 12.0 | 90 | 4.4 |
| 67 | 11.7 | 91 | 4.2 |
| 68 | 11.3 | 92 | 3.9 |
| 69 | 11.0 | 93 | 3.7 |
| 70 | 10.6 | 94 | 3.5 |
| 71 | 10.3 | 95 | 3.2 |
| 72 | 10.1 | 96 or over | 3.0 |

**Notes**: Reg. 8517(1) opening words amended by P.C. 1998-2256, effective for amounts transferred in respect of benefits provided after 1996, to make it subject to subsec. (3.1).

Table amended by P.C. 1998-2256, effective for transfers that occur after 1995. The former table used the same numbers for ages 50–71, but read "0.0" for age 72 or over. The change allows a person over 72 to transfer a single amount from a defined benefit RPP to a RRIF (if permitted by the plan to do so), without the negative consequences of ITA 147.3(10) (income inclusion, possible RRSP over-contributions penalty tax) and (12) (potential revocation of the plan's registration). Such a transfer cannot be made to an RRSP or money purchase provision of an RPP because of the registration rules that apply to such plans.

2438

**Interpretation Bulletins**: IT-528: Transfers of funds between registered plans.

**Forms**: T2151: Record of direct transfer of a "single amount".

**(2) Minimum prescribed amount** — Where an amount is transferred in full satisfaction of an individual's entitlement to benefits under a defined benefit provision of a registered pension plan, the prescribed amount for the purposes of paragraph 147.3(4)(c) of the Act in respect of the transfer is the greater of the amount that would, but for this subsection, be the prescribed amount, and the balance, at the time of the transfer, in the individual's net contribution account (within the meaning assigned by subsection 8503(1)) in relation to the provision.

**(3) Plan wind-up or replacement** — Where an amount is transferred before January 1, 1993, or such later date as is acceptable to the Minister, on behalf of an individual as a consequence of the winding-up of a registered pension plan or as a consequence of the replacement of a defined benefit provision of a registered pension plan by a money purchase provision of another registered pension plan and either

(a) the winding-up of the plan or the replacement of the provision commenced at a time (in this subsection referred to as the "time of termination") before 1989,

(b) at the time of termination, the plan had at least 50 members, and

(c) the plan was established at least 5 years before the time of termination,

or the condition in paragraph (a) is satisfied and the Minister waives the conditions in paragraphs (b) and (c), the prescribed amount for the purposes of paragraph 147.3(4)(c) of the Act in respect of the transfer is the amount so transferred.

**(3.1) Benefits provided with surplus on plan wind-up** — Where an amount is transferred in full or partial satisfaction of an individual's entitlement to benefits under a defined benefit provision of a registered pension plan and the benefits include benefits (in this subsection referred to as "ancillary benefits") that are permissible solely because of subsection 8501(7), the prescribed amount for the purpose of paragraph 147.3(4)(c) of the Act in respect of the transfer is the total of

(a) the amount that would, but for this subsection, be the prescribed amount, and

(b) an amount approved by the Minister not exceeding the lesser of

(i) the present value (at the time of the transfer) of the ancillary benefits that, as a consequence of the transfer, cease to be provided, and

(ii) the total of all amounts each of which is, in respect of a previous transfer from the provision to a money purchase provision of a registered pension plan, a registered retirement savings plan or a registered retirement income fund in full or partial satisfaction of the individual's entitlement to other benefits under the defined benefit provision, the amount, if any, by which

(A) the prescribed amount for the purpose of paragraph 147.3(4)(c) of the Act in respect of the previous transfer

exceeds

(B) the amount of the previous transfer.

**Notes**: Reg. 8517(3.1) added by P.C. 1998-2256, effective for amounts transferred in respect of benefits provided after 1996.

**(4) Amount of lifetime retirement benefits commuted** — For the purposes of subsection (1), and subject to subsection (7), the amount of an individual's lifetime retirement benefits under a defined benefit provision of a registered pension plan commuted in connection with the transfer of an amount on behalf of the individual in full or partial satisfaction of the individual's entitlement to benefits under the provision is the aggregate of

(a) where retirement benefits have commenced to be paid under the provision to the individual, the amount (expressed on an annualized basis) by which the individual's lifetime retirement benefits under the provision are reduced as a result of the transfer,

(b) where retirement benefits have not commenced to be paid under the provision to the individual, the amount (expressed on an annualized basis) by which the individual's normalized pension (computed in accordance with subsection (5)) under the provision at the time of the transfer is reduced as a result of the transfer, and

(c) where, in conjunction with the transfer, any other payment (other than an amount that is transferred in accordance with subsection 147.3(5) of the Act or that is transferred after 1991 in accordance with subsection 147.3(3) of the Act) is made from the plan in partial satisfaction of the individual's entitlement to benefits under the provision, the amount (expressed on an annualized basis) by which

(i) if paragraph (a) is applicable, the individual's lifetime retirement benefits under the provision are reduced, and

(ii) if paragraph (b) is applicable, the individual's normalized pension (computed in accordance with subsection (5)) under the provision at the time of the payment is reduced,

as a result of the payment, except to the extent that such reduction is included in determining, for the purposes of subsection (1), the amount of the individual's lifetime retirement benefits under the provision commuted in connection with the transfer of another amount on behalf of the individual.

**(5) Normalized pensions** — For the purposes of subsection (4), the normalized pension of an individual under a defined benefit provision of a registered pension plan at a particular time is the amount (expressed on an annualized basis) of lifetime retirement benefits that would be payable under the provision at the particular time if

(a) lifetime retirement benefits commenced to be paid to the individual at the particular time;

(b) where the individual has not attained 65 years of age before the particular time, the individual attained that age at the particular time;

(c) all benefits to which the individual is entitled under the provision were fully vested;

(d) where the amount of the individual's lifetime retirement benefits would otherwise be determined with a reduction computed by reference to the individual's age, duration of service, or both, or with any other similar reduction, no such reduction were applied;

(e) where the amount of the individual's lifetime retirement benefits depends on the amount of benefits provided under another benefit provision of the plan or under another plan or arrangement, a reasonable estimate were made of those other benefits;

(f) where the individual's lifetime retirement benefits would otherwise include benefits that the plan is required to provide by reason of a designated provision of the law of Canada or a province, or that the plan would be required to provide if each such provision were applicable to the plan with respect to all its members, such benefits were not included; and

(g) except as otherwise provided by subsection (6), where the amount of the individual's lifetime retirement benefits depends on

(i) the form of benefits provided with respect to the individual under the provision (whether or not at the option of the individual), including

(A) the benefits to be provided after the death of the individual,

(B) the amount of retirement benefits, other than lifetime retirement benefits, provided to the individual, or

(C) the extent to which the lifetime retirement benefits will be adjusted to reflect changes in the cost of living, or

(ii) circumstances that are relevant in determining the form of benefits,

the form of benefits and the circumstances were such as to maximize the amount of the individual's lifetime retirement benefits on commencement of payment.

**Related Provisions**: Reg. 8513 — Designated provision of the law of Canada or a province.

**Registered Plans Division Newsletters**: 98-2 (Treating excess member contributions under a registered pension plan).

**(6) Optional forms** — Where

(a) the terms of a defined benefit provision of a registered pension plan permit an individual to elect to receive additional lifetime retirement benefits in lieu of benefits that would, in the absence of the election, be payable after the death of the individual if the individual dies after retirement benefits under the provision commence to be paid to the individual, and

(b) the elections available to the individual include an election

(i) to receive additional lifetime retirement benefits, not exceeding additional benefits determined on an actuarially equivalent basis, in lieu of all or a portion of a guarantee that retirement benefits will be paid for a minimum period of 10 years or less, or

(ii) to receive additional lifetime retirement benefits in lieu of retirement benefits that would otherwise be payable to a spouse or former spouse (in this subparagraph referred to as the "spouse") of the individual for a period commencing after the death of the individual and ending with the death of the spouse, where

(A) the election may be made only if the life expectancy of the spouse is significantly shorter than normal and has been so certified in writing by a medical doctor licensed to practise under the laws of a province or of the place where the spouse resides, and

(B) the additional benefits do not exceed additional benefits determined on an actuarially equivalent basis and on the assumption that the spouse has a normal life expectancy,

paragraph (5)(g) applies as if

(c) the election described in subparagraph (b)(i) were not available to the individual, and

(d) where the particular time the normalized pension of the individual is determined under subsection (5) is after 1991, the election described in subparagraph (b)(ii) were not available to the individual.

**Notes**: References to "spouse" are expected to be amended to add "or common-law partner" effective 2001 or earlier by election, as has been done throughout the ITA. See Notes to ITA 248(1)"common-law partner".

**(7) Replacement benefits** — Where

(a) an amount is transferred on behalf of an individual in full or partial satisfaction of the individual's entitlement to benefits under a defined benefit provision (in this subsection referred to as the "particular provision") of a registered pension plan,

(b) in conjunction with the transfer, benefits become provided to the individual under another defined benefit provision of the plan or under a defined benefit provision of another registered pension plan, and

(c) an employer who participated under the particular provision for the benefit of the individual also participates under the other provision for the individual's benefit,

the amount of the individual's lifetime retirement benefits under the particular provision commuted in connection with the transfer is the amount that would be determined under subsection (4) if the benefits provided under the other provision were provided under the particular provision.

**Definitions [Reg. 8517]**: "amount" — ITA 248(1); "ancillary benefits" — Reg. 8517(3.1); "benefit provision" — Reg. 8500(1); "benefits" — Reg. 8501(5)(c); "Canada" — ITA 255, *Interpretation Act* 35(1); "commencement" — *Interpretation Act* 35(1); "contribution" — Reg. 8501(6); "defined benefit provision" — ITA 147.1(1); "designated provision of the law of Canada or a province" — Reg. 8513; "employer", "individual" — ITA 248(1); "lifetime retirement benefits" — Reg. 8500(1), 8517(4); "member" — ITA 147.1(1); "Minister" — ITA 248(1); "money purchase provision" — ITA 147.1(1); "net contribution account" — Reg. 8503(1); "normalized pension" — Reg. 8517(5); "particular provision" — Reg. 8517(7)(a); "prescribed" — ITA 248(1); "province" — *Interpretation Act* 35(1); "registered pension plan" — ITA 248(1); "registered retirement income fund" — ITA 146.3(1), 248(1); "registered retirement savings plan" — ITA 146(1), 248(1); "retirement benefits" — Reg. 8500(1); "spouse" — ITA 147.1(1); "time of termination" — Reg. 8517(3)(a); "writing" — *Interpretation Act* 35(1).

**Interpretation Bulletins**: IT-528: Transfers of funds between registered plans.

**Registered Plans Division Newsletters**: 95-5 (Conversion of a defined benefit provision to a money purchase provision).

**8518. Pension adjustment limits** — (1) Subsection 147.1(8) of the Act does not apply to render a registered pension plan a revocable plan at the end of a calendar year by reason that a pension adjustment, or an aggregate of pension adjustments, of an individual for the year is excessive where the subsection would not so apply if the individual's pension adjustments for the year were determined without the inclusion of those pension credits, if any, of the individual for the year under deferred profit sharing plans that are described in subsection (2).

(2) For the purposes of subsection (1), a pension credit (as determined under Part LXXXIII) of an individual for a year under a deferred profit sharing plan is described in this subsection if

(a) it is a pension credit with respect to an employer by whom the individual ceased to be employed in the year; and

(b) it includes the amount of a contribution made to the plan in the year by the employer with respect to the individual that was based, in whole or in part, on the individual's remuneration for the preceding year.

**Definitions [Reg. 8518]**: "amount" — ITA 248(1); "contribution" — Reg. 8501(6); "deferred profit sharing plan" — ITA 147(1), 248(1); "employed", "employer", "individual", "pension adjustment" — ITA 248(1); "pension credit" — Reg. 8301,

8308.1(2)–(4), 8308.3(2), (3), 8518(2); "registered pension plan" — ITA 248(1).

**8519. Association of benefits with time periods** — Where, for the purposes of Part LXXXIII or this Part or subsection 147.1(10) of the Act, it is necessary to associate benefits provided under a defined benefit provision of a pension plan with periods of time, the association shall be made in a manner acceptable to the Minister.

**Definitions [Reg. 8519]**: "benefits" — Reg. 8501(5)(c); "defined benefit provision" — ITA 147.1(1); "Minister" — ITA 248(1).

**8520. Minister's actions** — For the purposes of this Part, a waiver, extension of time or other modification of the requirements of this Part granted by the Minister or an approval by the Minister in respect of any matter is not effective unless it is in writing and expressly refers to the requirement that is modified or the matter in respect of which the approval is given.

**Notes [Reg. 8500–8520]**: Part LXXXV added by P.C. 1991-2540, effective 1989, except that:

(a) Reg. 8512(1) is applicable as of January 15, 1992;

(b) any form or document otherwise required by Reg. 8512(2) to be forwarded to the Deputy Minister of National Revenue for Taxation before March 15, 1992 is deemed to have been forwarded as required if it is forwarded on or before March 15, 1992; and

(c) Reg. 8515(5) is applicable

(i) in respect of contributions made after 1991 to a pension plan that was registered by the Minister on or before July 31, 1991 for the purposes of the *Income Tax Act*, and

(ii) in respect of contributions made after 1990 to a pension plan that is registered by the Minister after July 31, 1991 for the purposes of that Act.

**Definitions [Reg. 8520]**: "Minister" — ITA 248(1); "writing" — *Interpretation Act* 35(1).

# PART LXXXVI — TAXABLE CAPITAL EMPLOYED IN CANADA

**8600. [Definitions]** — For the purposes of this Part and Part I.3 of the Act,

**"attributed surplus"** of a non-resident insurer for a taxation year has the meaning assigned by subsection 2400(1);

**Notes**: Definition amended by P.C. 2000-1714, effective for 1999 and later taxation years. For earlier years, read:

"attributed surplus" for a taxation year, in respect of an insurance corporation that was throughout the year not resident in Canada, means the amount determined under subsection 2405(3) to be the corporation's attributed surplus for the year;

**"Canadian assets"** of a corporation that is a financial institution (as defined in subsection 181(1) of the Act) at any time in a taxation year means, in respect of the year, the amount, if any, by which

(a) the total of all amounts each of which is the amount at which an asset of the corporation (which asset is required, or, if the corporation were a bank to which the *Bank Act* applied, would be required, to be reflected in a return under subsection 223(1) of the *Bank Act*, as that Act read on May 31, 1992, if that return were prepared on a non-consolidated basis) would be shown on the corporation's balance sheet at the end of the year if its balance sheet were prepared on a non-consolidated basis

exceeds the total of

(b) the investment allowance of the corporation for the year determined under subsection 181.3(4) of the Act, and

(c) the total of all amounts each of which is the amount outstanding at the end of the year on account of a deposit made by the corporation that is described in paragraph (c) of the definition "eligible loan" in subsection 33.1(1) of the Act;

**"Canadian premiums"** for a taxation year, in respect of an insurance corporation that was resident in Canada at any time in the year and throughout the year did not carry on a life insurance business, means the total of the insurance corporation's net premiums for the year

(a) in respect of insurance on property situated in Canada, and

(b) in respect of insurance, other than on property, from contracts with persons resident in Canada,

and, for the purposes of this definition, "net premiums" has the same meaning as in subsection 403(2), and subsection 403(3) applies as if the references therein to "province" were read as references to "country";

**"Canadian reserve liabilities"** of an insurer as at the end of a taxation year has the meaning assigned by subsection 2400(1);

Notes: Definition amended by P.C. 2000-1714, effective for 1999 and later taxation years. For earlier years, read:

"Canadian reserve liabilities" as at the end of a taxation year, in respect of an insurance corporation that was resident in Canada at any time during the year and carried on a life insurance business at any time in the year, has the same meaning as in subsection 2405(3).

**"permanent establishment"** has the same meaning as in subsection 400(2);

**"total assets"** of a corporation that is a financial institution (as defined in subsection 181(1) of the Act) at any time in a taxation year means, in respect of that year, the amount, if any, by which

(a) the total of all amounts each of which is the amount at which an asset of the corporation would be shown on the corporation's balance sheet at the end of the year if its balance sheet were prepared on a non-consolidated basis

exceeds

(b) the investment allowance of the corporation for the year determined under subsection 181.3(4) of the Act;

**"total premiums"** for a taxation year, in respect of an insurance corporation that was resident in Canada at any time in the year and throughout the year did not carry on a life insurance business, means the total of the corporation's net premiums for the year (as defined in subsection 403(2)) that are included in computing its income under Part I of the Act;

**"total reserve liabilities"** of an insurer as at the end of a taxation year means the total amount as at the end of the year of the insurer's liabilities and reserves (other than liabilities and reserves in respect of a segregated fund) in respect of all its insurance policies, as determined for the purposes of the Superintendent of Financial Institutions, if the insurer is required by law to report to the Superintendent of Financial Institutions, or, in any other case, the superintendent of insurance or other similar officer or authority of the province under the laws of which the insurer is incorporated.

Related Provisions: ITA 248(1) — "Insurance policy" includes "life insurance policy".

Notes: Definition amended by P.C. 2000-1714, effective for 1999 and later taxation years. For earlier years, read:

"total reserve liabilities" as at the end of a taxation year, in respect of an insurance corporation that was resident in Canada at any time during the year and carried on a life insurance business at any time in the year, has the same meaning as in subsection 2405(3).

Notes: Reg. 8600 added by P.C. 1994-556, effective for taxation years that end after June 1989.

Definitions [Reg. 8600]: "amount" — ITA 248(1); "attributed surplus" — Reg. 2400(1), 8600; "bank" — ITA 248(1), *Interpretation Act* 35(1); "Canada" — ITA 255, *Interpretation Act* 35(1); "corporation" — ITA 248(1), *Interpretation Act* 35(1); "insurance corporation", "insurance policy", "insurer", "life insurance business" — ITA 248(1); "net premiums" — Reg. 403(2), (3), Reg. 8600 "Canadian premiums"; "non-resident", "officer", "person", "property" — ITA 248(1); "province" — *Interpretation Act* 35(1); "resident in Canada" — ITA 250; "taxation year" — ITA 249.

**8601. [Prescribed proportion of taxable capital]** — For the purpose of determining the taxable capital employed in Canada of a corporation for a taxation year under subsection 181.2(1) of the Act, the prescribed proportion of the corporation's taxable capital (as determined under Part I.3 of the Act) for the year is the amount determined by the formula

$$A \times \frac{B}{C}$$

where

A is the taxable capital (as determined under Part I.3 of the Act) of the corporation for the year,

B is the total of all amounts each of which is the amount, determined in accordance with Part IV (or, in the case of an airline corporation, that would be so determined if the corporation had a permanent establishment in every province and if paragraphs 407(1)(a) and (b) were read without reference to the words "in Canada"), of the corporation's taxable income earned in the year in a particular province or the amount of its taxable income that would, pursuant to that Part, be earned in the year in a province if all permanent establishments of the corporation in Canada were in a province, and

C is the corporation's taxable income for the year, except that, where the corporation's taxable income for the year is nil, the corporation shall, for the purposes of this section, be deemed to have a taxable income for the year of $1,000.

**Notes**: Reg. 8601 added by P.C. 1994-556, effective for taxation years that end after June 1989.

**Definitions [Reg. 8601]**: "amount" — ITA 248(1); "Canada" — ITA 255, *Interpretation Act* 35(1); "corporation" — ITA 248(1), *Interpretation Act* 35(1); "employed" — ITA 248(1); "permanent establishment" — Reg. 400(2), 8600; "prescribed" — ITA 248(1); "province" — *Interpretation Act* 35(1); "taxable income" — ITA 248(1); "taxation year" — ITA 249.

**8602. [Prescribed proportion of amount under s. 123.2]** — For the purposes of paragraph (b) of the definition "Canadian surtax payable" in subsection 125.3(4) of the Act, the prescribed proportion of the amount determined under section 123.2 of the Act in respect of a corporation for a taxation year is the amount determined by the formula

$$A \times \frac{B}{C}$$

where

A is the amount determined under section 123.2 of the Act in respect of the corporation for the year;

B is

(a) where the corporation carried on a life insurance business at any time in the year, the corporation's taxable capital (as determined under Part I.3 of the Act) for the year, and

(b) in any other case, the corporation's taxable capital employed in Canada (as would be determined under Part I.3 of the Act if that Part were read without reference to paragraphs 181.3(1)(a) and (b) thereof) for the year; and

C is the corporation's taxable capital (as determined under Part I.3 of the Act) for the year.

**Notes**: Reg. 8602 added by P.C. 1994-556, effective for taxation years that end after June 1989.

**Definitions [Reg. 8602]**: "amount" — ITA 248(1); "Canada" — ITA 255, *Interpretation Act* 35(1); "corporation" — ITA 248(1), *Interpretation Act* 35(1); "employed", "life insurance business", "prescribed" — ITA 248(1); "taxation year" — ITA 249.

**8603. [Definitions]** — For the purposes of Part VI of the Act,

(a) "Canadian assets" of a corporation that is a financial institution (as defined in subsection 190(1) of the Act) at any time in a taxation year means, in respect of that year, the amount that would be determined under the definition "Canadian assets" in section 8600 in respect of the corporation for the year if the reference in that definition to "subsection 181(1)" were read as a reference to "subsection 190(1)" and paragraph (b) of that definition were read as follows:

"(b) the total determined under section 190.14 of the Act in respect of the corporation's investments for the year in financial institutions related to it, and";

(b) "total assets" of a corporation that is a financial institution (as defined in subsection 190(1) of the Act) at any time in a taxation year means, in respect of that year, the amount that would be determined under the definition "total assets" in section 8600 in respect of the corporation for the year if the reference in that definition to "subsection 181(1)" were read as a reference to "subsection 190(1)" and paragraph (b) of that definition were read as follows:

"(b) the total determined under section 190.14 of the Act in respect of the corporation's investments for the year in financial institutions related to it;"; and

(c) "attributed surplus", "Canadian reserve liabilities" and "total reserve liabilities" have the same respective meanings as in section 8600.

**Notes**: Reg. 8603 added by P.C. 1994-556, effective for the 1990 and later taxation years.

**Definitions [Reg. 8603]**: "amount" — ITA 248(1); "corporation" — ITA 248(1), *Interpretation Act* 35(1); "related" — ITA 251(2)–(6); "taxation year" — ITA 249.

**8604. [Prescribed corporations]** — For the purposes of paragraph (g) of the definition "financial institution" in subsection 181(1) of the Act, each of the following corporations is a prescribed corporation:

(a) a corporation of which all or substantially all of the assets are shares or indebtedness of financial institutions (as defined in that subsection) to which the corporation is related;

(b) AVCO Financial Services Canada Limited;

(c) AVCO Financial Services Realty Limited;

(d) AVCO Financial Services Quebec Limited;

(e) General Motors Acceptance Corporation of Canada, Limited;

(f) Household Financial Corporation Limited;

(g) Household Finance Corporation of Canada;

(h) Household Realty Corporation Limited;

(i) Merchant Retail Services Limited;

(j) Superior Acceptance Corporation Limited;

(k) Superior Credit Corporation Limited;

(l) Crédit Industriel Desjardins;

(m) Beneficial Canada Inc.;

(n) Beneficial Realty Ltd.;

**Reg. S. 8604(o)** — Income Tax Regulations

(o) RT Mortgage-Backed Securities Limited;

(p) RT Mortgage-Backed Securities II Limited;

(q) T. Eaton Acceptance Co. Limited;

(r) National Retail Credit Services Limited;

(s) Ford Credit Canada Limited;

(t) Principal Fund Incorporated;

(u) Farm Credit Corporation;

(v) Canadian Cooperative Agricultural Financial Services;

(w) CU Credit Inc.;

(x) Household Commercial Canada Inc.;

(y) Canadian Home Income Plan Corporation;

(z) Hudson's Bay Company Acceptance Limited;

(z.1) Bombardier Capital Ltd.;

(z.2) Trans Canada Credit Corporation;

(z.3) Norwest Financial Canada, Inc.;

(z.4) Norwest Financial Capital Canada, Inc.;

(z.5) GE Capital Canada Limited; and

(z.6) GE Capital Canada Retailer Financial Services Company.

**Notes**: These corporations are also deemed to be RFIs by ITA 248(1)"restricted financial institution"(e.1); SFIs by ITA 248(1)"specified financial institution"(e.1); and FIs by ITA 142.2(1)"financial institution"(a)(i).

Revenue Canada's view is that "all or substantially all", used in para. (a), means 90% or more.

Reg. 8604(a)–(v) added by P.C. 1994-556, effective (as modified by P.C. 1998-2046) as set out below.

Opening words and 8604(a) are effective for 1989 and later taxation years.

8604(b)–(k) are effective for 1991 and later taxation years, or, if the corporation elected by notifying Revenue Canada in writing before 1995, to earlier taxation years that end after June 30, 1989 of the corporation and all corporations related to it.

8604(l)–(n) are effective (per 1998 amendment)

(a) for taxation years ending after April 1994; and

(b) for the 1994 and later taxation years of the corporation and all corporations related to it, and

(c) if the corporation elected by notifying Revenue Canada in writing before 1995, to the taxation years ending after June 1989 of the corporation and all related corporations.

8604(o)–(p) are effective for 1992 and later taxation years.

8604(q), (r), (t) and (u) are effective (per 1998 amendment)

(a) for taxation years ending after April 1994;

(b) for the 1994 and later taxation years of the corporation and all corporations related to it;

(c) if the corporation elected by notifying Revenue Canada in writing before 1995, to the 1993 taxation year of the corporation and all related corporations.

8604(s) is effective (per 1998 amendment)

(a) for taxation years ending after April 1994;

(b) for the 1994 and later taxation years of the corporation and all corporations related to it;

(c) if the corporation elected by notifying Revenue Canada in writing before 1999, to taxation years ending after 1989 of the corporation and all related corporations.

8604(v) is effective for taxation years that begin after 1993.

8604(w)–(z.6) added by P.C. 1998-2046, effective for taxation years that begin after May 1998, and, for each of the companies listed, if the company elected by notifying Revenue Canada in writing before 1999, to X and later taxation years of that company and all corporations related to it. For 8604(w), X is 1995; for 8604(x), 1994; (y), 1996; (z), taxation years beginning after 1994; (z.1)–(z.4), 1997; (z.5) and (z.6), taxation years ending after September 1998.

**Definitions [Reg. 8604]**: "Canada" — ITA 255, *Interpretation Act* 35(1); "corporation" — ITA 248(1), *Interpretation Act* 35(1); "prescribed" — ITA 248(1); "related" — ITA 251(2)–(6); "share" — ITA 248(1).

**8605.** (1) For the purposes of subclause 181.3(1)(c)(ii)(A)(II) and clause 190.11(b)(i)(B) of the Act, the amount prescribed in respect of a particular corporation for a taxation year ending at a particular time is the total of all amounts each of which is the amount determined in respect of a corporation that is, at the particular time, a foreign insurance subsidiary of the particular corporation, equal to the amount, if any, by which

(a) the amount by which the total, at the end of the subsidiary's last taxation year ending at or before the particular time, of

(i) the amount of the subsidiary's long-term debt, and

(ii) the amount of the subsidiary's capital stock (or, in the case of an insurance corporation incorporated without share capital, the amount of its member's contributions), retained earnings, contributed surplus and any other surpluses

exceeds the total of

(iii) the amount of the subsidiary's deferred tax debit balance at the end of the year, and

(iv) the amount of any deficit deducted in computing the subsidiary's shareholders' equity at the end of the year

exceeds the total of all amounts each of which is

(b) the carrying value to its owner at the particular time for the taxation year that includes the particular time of a share of the subsidiary's capital stock or its long term debt that is owned at the particular time by

(i) the particular corporation,

(ii) a subsidiary of the particular corporation,

(iii) a corporation

(A) that is resident in Canada,

(B) that carried on a life insurance business in Canada at any time in its taxation year ending at or before the particular time, and

(C) that is

(I) a corporation of which the particular corporation is a subsidiary, or

(II) a subsidiary of a corporation described in subclause (I), or

(iv) a subsidiary of a corporation described in subparagraph (iii), or

(c) an amount included under paragraph (a) in respect of any surplus of the subsidiary contributed by a corporation described in any of subparagraphs (b)(i) to (iv), other than an amount included under paragraph (b).

(d) [Repealed]

**Notes**: Reg. 8605(1)(c) repealed and (d) renumbered as (c) (and changed to delete an exclusion for the now-repealed (c)), all retroactive to the introduction of Reg. 8605 effective 1991 (see Notes at end of 8605). This corrects an error which caused double-counting of long-term debt in determining a life insurer's taxable capital employed in Canada.

(2) For the purposes of subclause 181.3(1)(c)(ii)(A)(III) and clause 190.11(b)(i)(C) of the Act, the amount prescribed in respect of a particular corporation for a taxation year ending at a particular time is the total of all amounts each of which is the amount determined in respect of a corporation that is, at the particular time, a foreign insurance subsidiary of the particular corporation, equal to the amount, if any, by which

(a) the total of the amounts determined under paragraphs (1)(b) and (c) in respect of the subsidiary for the year

exceeds

(b) the amount determined under paragraph (1)(a) in respect of the subsidiary for the year.

(3) For the purposes of subclause 181.3(1)(c)(ii)(A)(V) and clause 190.11(b)(i)(E) of the Act, the amount prescribed in respect of a particular corporation for a taxation year ending at a particular time means the total of all amounts each of which would be the total reserve liabilities of a foreign insurance subsidiary of the particular corporation as at the end of the subsidiary's last taxation year ending at or before the particular time if the subsidiary were required by law to report to the Superintendent of Financial Institutions for that year.

**Notes**: Reg. 8605(3) amended by P.C. 2000-1714, effective for 1999 and later taxation years, to remove a reference defining "total reserve liabilities" as under Reg. 2405(3). (It is now defined in Reg. 8600 by reference to Reg. 2400(1).)

(4) The definitions in this subsection apply in this section.

**"foreign insurance subsidiary"** of a particular corporation at any time means a non-resident corporation that

(a) carried on a life insurance business throughout its last taxation year ending at or before that time,

(b) did not carry on a life insurance business in Canada at any time in its last taxation year ending at or before that time, and

(c) is at that time

(i) a subsidiary of the particular corporation, and

(ii) not a subsidiary of any corporation that

(A) is resident in Canada,

(B) carried on a life insurance business in Canada at any time in its last taxation year ending at or before that time, and

(C) is a subsidiary of the particular corporation.

**"subsidiary"** of a corporation (in this definition referred to as the "parent corporation") means a corporation controlled by the parent corporation where shares of each class of the capital stock of the corporation having a fair market value of not less than 75% of the fair market value of all of the issued and outstanding shares of that class belong to

(a) the parent corporation,

(b) a corporation that is a subsidiary of the parent corporation, or

(c) any combination of corporations each of which is a corporation referred to in paragraph (a) or described in paragraph (b).

**Related Provisions**: Reg. 8500(1.1) — Definition applies to ITA 147.3(7.1).

**Notes [Reg. 8605]**: Reg. 8605(3) amended by P.C. 2000-1714, effective for 1999 and later taxation years, to remove a reference defining "total reserve liabilities" as under Reg. 2405(3). (It is now defined in Reg. 8600 by reference to Reg. 2400(1).)

Reg. 8605 added by P.C. 1996-1597, effective for 1991 and later taxation years. It was first released in draft form on February 19, 1993, and amended somewhat following consultation with the life insurance industry.

**Definitions [Reg. 8605]**: "amount" — ITA 248(1); "Canada" — ITA 255, *Interpretation Act* 35(1); "controlled" — ITA 256(6), (6.1); "corporation" — ITA 248(1), *Interpretation Act* 35(1); "foreign insurance subsidiary" — Reg. 8605(4); "insurance corporation", "life insurance business", "non-resident" — ITA 248(1); "parent corporation" — Reg. 8605(4)"subsidiary"; "prescribed" — ITA 248(1); "resident in Canada" — ITA 250; "share" — ITA 248(1); "subsidiary" — Reg. 8605(4); "taxation year" — ITA 249; "total reserve liabilities" — Reg. 8600.

## PART LXXXVII — NATIONAL ARTS SERVICE ORGANIZATIONS

**8700.** For the purposes of paragraph 149.1(6.4)(d) of the Act, the following conditions are prescribed for a national arts service organization:

(a) the organization is an organization

(i) that is, because of paragraph 149(1)(l) of the Act, exempt from tax under Part I of the Act,

(ii) that represents, in an official language of Canada, the community of artists from one or more of the following sectors of activity in the arts community, that is, theatre, opera, music, dance, painting, sculpture, drawing, crafts, design, photography, the literary arts, film, sound recording and other audio-visual arts, and such other sectors of artistic activity related to the creation or performance of works of art as the Minister of Communications may recognize,

(iii) no part of the income of which may be payable to, or otherwise available for the personal benefit of, any proprietor, member, shareholder, trustee, or settlor of the organization, except where the payment is for services rendered or is an amount to which paragraph 56(1)(n) of the Act applies in respect of the recipient,

(iv) all of the resources of which are devoted to the activities and objects described in its application for its last designation by the Minister of Communications pursuant to paragraph 1491.1(6.4)(a) of the Act,

(v) more than 50 per cent of the directors, trustees, officers or other officials of which deal with each other at arm's length, and

(vi) no more than 50 per cent of the property of which at any time has been contributed or otherwise paid into the organization by one person or by members of a group of persons who do not deal with each other at arm's length and, for the purposes of this subparagraph, a reference to any person or to members of a group does not include a reference to Her Majesty in right of Canada or a province, a municipality, or a registered charity (other than a club, society or association described in paragraph 149(1)(l) of the Act or a private foundation as that term is defined in paragraph 149.1(1)(f) [149.1(1)"private foundation"] of the Act); and

(b) the activities of the organization are confined to one or more of

(i) promoting one or more art forms,

(ii) conducting research into one or more art forms,

(iii) sponsoring arts exhibitions or performances,

(iv) representing interests of the arts community or a sector thereof (but not of individuals) before governmental, judicial, quasi-judicial or other public bodies,

(v) conducting workshops, seminars, training programs and similar development programs relating to the arts for members of the organization, in respect of which the value of benefits received or enjoyed by members of the organization is required by paragraph 56(1)(aa) of the Act to be included in computing the incomes of those members,

(vi) educating the public about the arts community or the sector represented by the organization,

(vii) organizing and sponsoring conventions, conferences, competitions and special events relating to the arts community or the sector represented by the organization,

(viii) conducting arts studies and surveys of interest to members of the organization relating to the arts community or the sector represented by the organization,

(ix) acting as an information centre by maintaining resource libraries and data bases relating to the arts community or the sector represented by the organization,

(x) disseminating information relating to the arts community or the sector represented by the organization, and

(xi) paying amounts to which paragraph 56(1)(n) of the Act applies in respect of the recipient and which relate to the arts community or the sector represented by the organization.

**Notes**: The *Department of Canadian Heritage Act* (S.C. 1995, c. 11), in force July 12, 1996, provides:

46. Other references — Every reference made to the Minister of Communications, the Minister of Multiculturalism and Citizenship and the Secretary of State of Canada in relation to any matter to which the powers, duties and functions of the Minister of Canadian Heritage extend by virtue of this Act, in any other Act of Parliament or in any order, regulation or other instrument made under any Act of Parliament shall, unless the context otherwise requires, be read as a reference to the Minister of Canadian Heritage.

Reg. 8700 added by P.C. 1994-139, effective July 14, 1990. It is essentially identical to the information in the July 13, 1990 Technical Notes that accompanied the release of ITA 149.1(6.4).

**Definitions [Reg. 8700]**: "amount" — ITA 248(1); "arm's length" — ITA 251(1); "Canada" — ITA 255, *Interpretation Act* 35(1); "Her Majesty" — *Interpretation Act* 35(1); "individual", "Minister", "officer", "person", "prescribed" — ITA 248(1); "private foundation" — ITA 149.1(1), 248(1); "property" — ITA 248(1); "province" — *Interpretation Act* 35(1); "registered charity" — ITA 248(1); "related" — ITA 251(2)–(6); "shareholder" — ITA 248(1).

# PART LXXXVIII — DISABILITY-RELATED MODIFICATIONS AND APPARATUS

**8800.** The renovations and alterations that are prescribed for the purposes of paragraph 20(1)(qq) of the Act are

(a) the installation of

(i) an interior or exterior ramp; or

(ii) a hand-activated electric door opener; and

(b) a modification to a bathroom, elevator or doorway to accommodate its use by a person in a wheelchair.

**Notes**: Reg. 8800 added by P.C. 1993-2026, effective for renovations and alterations made after 1990.
**Definitions [Reg. 8800]**: "person", "prescribed" — ITA 248(1).

**8801.** The devices and equipment that are prescribed for the purposes of paragraph 20(1)(rr) of the Act are

(a) an elevator car position indicator, such as a braille panel or an audio signal, for individuals having a sight impairment;

(b) a visual fire alarm indicator, a listening device for group meetings or a telephone device, for individuals having a hearing impairment; and

(c) a disability-specific computer software or hardware attachment.

**Notes**: Reg. 8801 added by P.C. 1993-2026 and para. (c) added by P.C. 1995-579, both effective for amounts paid after February 25, 1992 (the federal budget date).
**Definitions [Reg. 8801]**: "individual", "prescribed" — ITA 248(1).

## PART LXXXIX — PRESCRIBED ORGANIZATIONS

**8900.** For the purposes of paragraph 110(1)(f) of the Act,

(a) the United Nations, and any specialized agency that is brought into relationship with the United Nations in accordance with Article 63 of the Charter of the United Nations, are prescribed international organizations; and

(b) the International Air Transport Association and the International Society of Aeronautical Telecommunications are prescribed international non-governmental organizations.

**Notes**: Reg. 8900 added by P.C. 1995-663, para. (a) effective 1991 and para. (b) effective 1993.
**Definitions [Reg. 8900]**: "prescribed" — ITA 248(1).

## PART XC — FINANCIAL INSTITUTIONS — PRESCRIBED ENTITIES

### Proposed Addition — (Reg. 9000–9003)

**Technical Notes**: New Parts XC to XCII contain provisions relating to the tax treatment of securities held by financial institutions. The purpose of each Part is as follows:

- Part XC prescribes various entities and properties for the purposes of the definitions in subsection 142.2(1) of the Act. It also prescribes properties for certain other rules.
- Part XCI contains the rules for determining income from specified debt obligations.
- Part XCII sets out rules relating to the disposition of specified debt obligations. These include rules for amortizing gains and losses from the disposition of such obligations.

These new Parts apply to taxation years that end after February 22, 1994.

**9000.** For the purpose of paragraph (e) of the definition "financial institution" in subsection 142.2(1) of the Act, a trust that is deemed to exist by paragraph 138.1(1)(a) of the Act is prescribed at a particular time where

(a) the trust was created not more than two years before that time; and

(b) the cost at that time of the trustee's interest in the trust does not exceed $5,000,000.

**Technical Notes**: The definition of "financial institution" in subsection 142.2(1) of the Act excludes a prescribed person or partnership. Section 9000 prescribes for this purpose certain segregated funds maintained by life insurers. A segregated fund is prescribed at a particular time if it was created not more than two years before that time and the insurer's interest in the fund does not exceed $5 million. This exclusion enables an insurer to hold more than 50% of a segregated fund during its start-up phase without having the rules for securities held by financial institutions apply to the fund.

**Definitions [Reg. 9000]**: "prescribed" — ITA 248(1); "trust" — ITA 104(1), 248(1), (3).

**9001. (1)** In this section, "qualified small business corporation", at any time, means a corporation that, at that time, is

(a) a Canadian-controlled private corporation, and

(b) an eligible corporation (as defined in subsection 5100(1)) or a corporation that would be an eligible corporation if the definition "eligible corporation" in subsection 5100(1) were read without reference to paragraph (e),

where, at that time,

(c) the carrying value of the total assets of the corporation and all corporations related to it (determined in accordance with generally accepted accounting principles on a consolidated or combined basis, where applicable) does not exceed $50,000,000, and

(d) the number of employees of the corporation and all corporations related to it does not exceed 500.

**Technical Notes**: The definition of "mark-to-market property" in subsection 142.2(1) of the Act excludes a prescribed property. Section 9001 prescribes certain shares of qualified small business corporations for this purpose.

Subsection 9001(1) provides that a corporation is a "qualified small business corporation" at any time at which:

- the corporation is a Canadian-controlled private corporation;
- the corporation is an eligible corporation (as defined in subsection 5100(1) for the purposes of the deferred income plan rules) or would be an eligible corporation if the exclusion for certain venture capital corporations were disregarded;
- the carrying value of the total assets of the corporation and all related corporations does not exceed $50 million; and

**Reg. S. 9001(1)**  *Income Tax Regulations*

- the corporation and all related corporations have no more than 500 employees.

(2) For the purpose of paragraph (e) of the definition "mark-to-market property" in subsection 142.2(1) of the Act, a share of the capital stock of a corporation is a prescribed property in respect of a taxpayer where

(a) immediately after the time at which the taxpayer acquired the share, the corporation was a qualified small business corporation, and

(i) the corporation continued to be a qualified small business corporation for one year after that time, or

(ii) the taxpayer could not reasonably expect at that time that the corporation would cease to be a qualified small business corporation within one year after that time; or

(b) the share was issued to the taxpayer in exchange for one or more shares of the capital stock of the corporation that were prescribed by this subsection in respect of the taxpayer.

**Technical Notes**: Subsection 9001(2) prescribes a share of a corporation where, immediately after the taxpayer acquired the share, the corporation was a qualified small business corporation. However, a share is not prescribed if the corporation ceases to be a qualified small business corporation within a year, unless the change of status was not reasonably foreseeable.

Subsection 9001(2) also prescribes a share if it was issued to a taxpayer in exchange for one or more shares that were prescribed in respect of the taxpayer. Since the definition of "share" in subsection 248(1) of the Act includes a fraction of a share, subsection 9001(2) applies even if a taxpayer receives less than one share for each share exchanged.

**Letter from Department of Finance, September 14, 2000**:

Dear [xxx]

Thank you for your letter of August 23, 2000 regarding the demutualization of the Montreal Exchange (the "Exchange") and the application of the mark-to-market property rules that apply to investment dealers and other financial institutions.

In your letter, you asked the Department of Finance to amend the *Income Tax Act Regulations* in order to include a share of the corporation that carries on the business of operating the Exchange, ME Inc., as a prescribed property for the purpose of the definition "mark-to-market property" in subsection 142.2(1) of the *Income Tax Act* (the "Act") when held by an investment dealer. This would have the effect of exempting such shares, while held by an investment dealer, from the application of the mark-to-market property rules.

We have previously received representations on a similar issue and have, as a result, recommended to the Minister that the *Income Tax Regulations* be amended to prescribe a share of ME Inc., that is held by an investment dealer, to be a prescribed property for the purpose of the definition "mark-to-market property" in subsection 142.2(1) of the Act. However, in order to prevent the exemption from being used to circumvent the mark-to-market rules, we will suggest that the exemption apply only if ME Inc. restricts its activities (including the ownership of any investment) to running the Exchange.

Based on the information we have received as to the effective date of the demutualization of the Exchange and consequent issuance of ME Inc. shares, we would propose that the recommended amendment apply to the 2000 and subsequent taxation years.

Thank you for bringing this matter to our attention.

Yours sincerely,

Brian Ernewein
Director, Tax Legislation Division, Tax Policy Branch

**Definitions [Reg. 9001]**: "business" — ITA 248(1); "Canadian-controlled private corporation" — ITA 125(7), 248(1); "corporation" — ITA 248(1), *Interpretation Act* 35(1); "employee", "prescribed", "property" — ITA 248(1); "qualified small business corporation" — Reg. 9001(1); "related" — ITA 251(2)–(6); "share", "small business corporation", "taxpayer" — ITA 248(1).

**9002.** (1) For the purposes of

(a) paragraph (e) of the definition "mark-to-market property" in subsection 142.2(1) of the Act, and

(b) subparagraph 142.6(4)(a)(ii) of the Act,

a debt obligation held by a bank is a prescribed property of the bank where the obligation is

(c) an exposure to a designated country (as defined in section 8006), or

(d) a United Mexican States Collateralized Par or Discount Bond Due 2019.

**Technical Notes**: Section 9002 prescribes various properties for exclusion from the definition of "mark-to-market property" in subsection 142.2(1) of the Act.

Subsection 9002(1) prescribes as property excluded from the definition of "mark-to-market property" in subsection 142.2(1) of the Act certain debt obligations held by a bank. A debt obligation is prescribed if it is an exposure to a country that has been designated by the Office of the Superintendent of Financial Institutions or is a United Mexican States Collateralized Par or Discount Bond Due 2019 (a "Brady bond").

Subsection 9002(1) also prescribes such debt obligations for the purpose of subparagraph 142.6(4)(a)(ii) of the Act. This provision contains a rule relating to prescribed debt obligations held by a bank on February 23, 1994 that were inventory of the bank in its last taxation year ending before February 23, 1994. For further information, see the commentary on subsection 142.6(4) of the Act.

**Notes**: A bond referred to in Reg. 9002(1)(d) is also known as a "Brady bond".

(2) For the purpose of paragraph (e) of the definition "mark-to-market property" in subsection 142.2(1) of the Act, a share is a prescribed property of a taxpayer for a taxation year where

(a) the share is a lending asset of the taxpayer in the year; or

(b) immediately after its issuance, the share was a share described in paragraph (e) of the definition "term preferred share" in subsection 248(1) of the Act and, at any time in the year, the share would be a term preferred share if

(i) that definition were read without reference to the portion following paragraph (b), and

(ii) where the share was issued or acquired on or before June 28, 1982, it were issued or acquired after that day.

**Technical Notes**: Subsection 9002(2) prescribes certain preferred shares for exclusion from the definition of "mark-to-market property" in subsection 142.2(1) of the Act.

Paragraph 9002(2)(a) provides for a share to be prescribed if it is a lending asset. By virtue of the definition of a lending asset in subsection 248(1) of the Act and paragraph 6209(a) of the Regulations, a share is a lending asset if it is a preferred share held by a bank that is reported as a loan substitute.

Paragraph 9002(2)(b) provides for a share to be prescribed if it meets two tests. The first is that, immediately after it was issued, it was a share described in paragraph (e) of the definition of "term preferred share" in subsection 248(1) of the Act, i.e., a financial difficulty share. In this regard, it should be noted that the 5- or 10-year period referred to in paragraph (e) is not part of the description of the share. The second test is that the share would be a term preferred share if the portion of the definition of "term preferred share" following paragraph (b) were disregarded and, where the share was issued or acquired on or before June 28, 1982, it had been issued or acquired after that date.

(3) For the purpose of paragraph (e) of the definition "mark-to-market property" in subsection 142.2(1) of the Act, a share of the capital stock of a corporation held by a credit union is a prescribed property of the credit union for a taxation year where, throughout the year,

(a) the corporation is a credit union; or

(b) credit unions hold

(i) shares of the corporation that give the credit unions more than 50% of the votes that could be cast under all circumstances at an annual meeting of shareholders of the corporation, and

(ii) shares of the corporation having a fair market value of more than 50% of the fair market value of all the issued shares of the corporation.

**Technical Notes**: Subsection 9002(3) prescribes certain shares held by credit unions for exclusion from the definition of "mark-to-market property" in subsection 142.2(1) of the Act. A share is prescribed if it is

- a share of a credit union, or
- a share of a corporation in which credit unions hold shares carrying more than 50% of the votes and shares representing more than 50% of the fair market value of all issued shares.

**Definitions [Reg. 9002]**: "bank" — ITA 248(1), *Interpretation Act* 35(1); "corporation" — ITA 248(1), *Interpretation Act* 35(1); "credit union", "lending asset", "prescribed", "property", "share", "shareholder" — ITA 248(1); "taxation year" — ITA 249; "taxpayer", "term preferred share" — ITA 248(1).

**9003.** For the purpose of paragraph 142.2(3)(c) of the Act, a share described in paragraph 9002(2)(b) is prescribed in respect of all taxpayers.

**Technical Notes**: Paragraph 142.2(3)(c) of the Act provides that shares that are prescribed are to be ignored in determining whether a taxpayer has a significant interest in a corporation pursuant to subsection 142.2(2). Section 9003 prescribes for this purpose shares that are described in paragraph 9002(2)(b). These are certain preferred shares issued by a corporation in financial difficulty. More specifically, a share is prescribed if it is a share described in paragraph (e) of the definition of "term preferred share" in subsection 248(1) of the Act and it would be a term preferred share if the portion of the definition following paragraph (b) were disregarded (and, in the case of a share that was issued or acquired on or before June 28, 1982, it had been issued or acquired after that date).

**Definitions [Reg. 9003]**: "prescribed", "share", "taxpayer" — ITA 248(1).

**Application**: The June 1, 1995 draft regulations (securities held by financial institutions), s. 9, will add Part XC (ss. 9000 to 9003), applicable to taxation years that end after February 22, 1994.

**9004.** For the purpose of the definition "specified debt obligation" in subsection 142.2(1) of the Act, a property is a prescribed property throughout a taxation year if the property is a direct financing lease, or any other financing arrangement, of a taxpayer that is reported as a loan in the taxpayer's financial statement for the year prepared in accordance with generally accepted accounting principles and an amount is deductible under paragraph 20(1)(a) of the Act in respect of the property that is the subject of the lease or arrangement in computing the taxpayer's income for the year.

**Notes**: Reg. 9004 added by P.C. 1995-195, effective on the same basis as the 1995-97 technical bill amendments to ITA 20(1)(l).

**Definitions [Reg. 9004]**: "amount", "prescribed", "property" — ITA 248(1); "taxation year" — ITA 249; "taxpayer" — ITA 248(1).

## PART XCI — FINANCIAL INSTITUTIONS — INCOME FROM SPECIFIED DEBT OBLIGATIONS [PROPOSED]

### Proposed Addition — Part XCI (Reg. 9100–9104)

**Technical Notes**: Part XCI contains rules for determining the amounts that a financial institution is required to include and deduct each year in respect of a specified debt obligation in computing its income. These rules apply for the purpose of subsection 142.3(1) of the Act.

**9100. Interpretation** — In this Part,

**"fixed payment obligation"** of a taxpayer means a specified debt obligation under which

(a) the amount and timing of each payment (other than a fee or similar payment or an amount payable because of a default by the debtor) to be made by the debtor were fixed when the taxpayer acquired the obligation and have not been changed, and

(b) all payments are to be made in the same currency;

**Technical Notes**: A "fixed payment obligation" of a taxpayer is a specified debt obligation held by the taxpayer under which the payments to be made by the debtor are all fixed in timing and amount, and are all denominated in the same currency. Fees and similar payments are to be disregarded for the purpose of this definition, as are any additional payments that the debtor will be required to make if the debtor fails to make a payment as required under the obligation.

**"primary currency"** of a specified debt obligation means

(a) the currency with which the obligation is primarily connected, and

(b) where there is no such currency, Canadian currency;

**Technical Notes**: The "primary currency" of a specified debt obligation is the currency with which the obligation is primarily connected. Where there is no such currency, the primary currency is the Canadian dollar.

**"specified debt obligation"** of a taxpayer has the meaning assigned by subsection 142.2(1) of the Act;

**Technical Notes**: "Specified debt obligation" has the meaning given to that term by subsection 142.2(1) of the Act. It should be noted that this term is defined from the perspective of the holder. For example, where a taxpayer holds a coupon that has been stripped from a debt obligation and holds no other interest in the obligation, the specified debt obligation of the taxpayer is just the coupon. It should also be noted that, if a taxpayer disposes of part of a specified debt obligation, subsection 142.4(9) of the Act applies to deem the part disposed of and the retained part to be separate specified debt obligations.

**"tax basis"** of a specified debt obligation at any time to a taxpayer has the meaning assigned by subsection 142.4(1) of the Act;

**Technical Notes**: The "tax basis" of a specified debt obligation to a taxpayer is the amount defined by subsection 142.4(1) of the Act. The tax basis is analogous to the adjusted cost base of capital property.

**"total return"** of a taxpayer from a fixed payment obligation means the amount (measured in the primary currency of the obligation) by which

(a) the total of all amounts each of which is the amount of a payment (other than a fee or similar payment) required to be made by the debtor under the obligation after its acquisition by the taxpayer

exceeds

(b) the cost to the taxpayer of the obligation.

**Technical Notes**: A taxpayer's "total return" from a fixed payment obligation is equal to (i) the total amount of payments required to be made under the obligation by the debtor after the acquisition of the obligation by the taxpayer minus (ii) the cost of the obligation to the taxpayer. Fees and similar payments (such as insurance premiums) are excluded in determining the total return. The total return is to be measured in the primary currency of the obligation. Where the taxpayer's cost was determined in another currency, it should be translated to the primary currency using the spot rate of exchange at the time of acquisition.

**Definitions [Reg. 9100]**: "amount" — ITA 248(1); "fixed payment obligation", "primary currency" — Reg. 9100; "specified debt obligation" — ITA 142.2(1), Reg. 9100; "taxpayer" — ITA 248(1).

## 9101. Prescribed inclusions and deductions — (1) For the purpose of paragraph 142.3(1)(a) of the Act, where a taxpayer holds a specified debt obligation at any time in a taxation year, the amount prescribed in respect of the obligation for the year is the total of

(a) the taxpayer's accrued return from the obligation for the year;

(b) where the taxpayer's accrual adjustment determined under section 9102 in respect of the obligation for the year is greater than nil, the amount of the adjustment; and

(c) where a foreign exchange adjustment is determined under section 9104 in respect of the obligation for the year and is greater than nil, the amount of the adjustment.

**Technical Notes**: Paragraph 142.3(1)(a) of the Act requires a financial institution that holds a specified debt obligation in a taxation year to include a prescribed amount in income in respect of the obligation. Subsection 9101(1) prescribes an amount for this purpose equal to the sum of:

- the accrued return from the obligation for the year;
- the accrual adjustment in respect of the obligation for the year (if this amount is positive); and
- in the case of a foreign-currency obligation, the foreign exchange adjustment in respect of the obligation for the year (if this amount is positive).

**(2)** For the purpose of paragraph 142.3(1)(b) of the Act, where a taxpayer holds a specified debt obligation at any time in a taxation year, the amount prescribed in respect of the obligation is the total of

(a) where the taxpayer's accrual adjustment determined under section 9102 in respect of the obligation for the year is less than nil, the absolute value of the amount of the adjustment; and

(b) where a foreign exchange adjustment is determined under section 9104 in respect of the obligation for the year and is less than nil, the absolute value of the amount of the adjustment.

**Technical Notes**: Paragraph 142.3(1)(b) of the Act provides that a financial institution that holds a specified debt obligation in a taxation year must deduct a prescribed amount in respect of the obligation. Subsection 9101(2) prescribes an amount for this purpose equal to the absolute value of the sum of:

- the accrual adjustment in respect of the obligation for the year (if this amount is negative); and
- in the case of a foreign-currency obligation, the foreign exchange adjustment in respect of the obligation for the year (if this amount is negative).

In general terms, the accrued return for a year is the total expected economic return to the taxpayer (assuming the taxpayer holds the obligation to maturity) that is allocated to the year under accrual principles of income recognition. Sections 9102 and 9103 contain rules relating to the determination of accrued returns.

The accrual adjustment is the amount by which prior years' accrued returns have to be adjusted to reflect subsequent events. For example, the accrued return for a year may have been based on an estimate of the amount of a future payment under the obligation. When the actual amount becomes known, or the estimate needs to be revised, an adjustment would be determined. Subsections 9102(4) and (5) contain rules relating to the determination of accrual adjustments.

The foreign exchange adjustment in respect of a foreign-currency obligation is the amount determined under section 9104. In general terms, this is the amount by which the tax value of the obligation has changed because of a change in the value of the foreign currency relative to the Canadian dollar.

**Definitions [Reg. 9101]**: "accrual adjustment" — Reg. 9102(4), (5); "accrued return" — Reg. 9102(3); "amount" — ITA 248(1); "foreign exchange adjustment" — Reg. 9104(1); "prescribed" — ITA 248(1); "specified debt obligation" — ITA 142.2(1), Reg. 9100; "taxation year" — ITA 249; "taxpayer" — ITA 248(1).

**9102. General accrual rules — (1) Fixed payment obligations not in default** — For the purpose of paragraph 9101(1)(a), a taxpayer's accrued return for a taxation year from a fixed payment obligation, under which each payment required to be made before the end of the year was made by the debtor when it was required to be made, shall be determined in accordance with the following rules:

(a) determine, in the primary currency of the obligation, the portion of the taxpayer's total return from the obligation that is allocated to each day in the year using

(i) the level-yield method described in subsection (2), or

(ii) any other reasonable method that is substantially similar to the level-yield method;

(b) where the primary currency of the obligation is not Canadian currency, translate to Canadian currency the amount allocated to each day in the year, using a reasonable method of translation; and

(c) determine the total of all amounts each of which is the Canadian currency amount allocated to a day, in the year, at the beginning of which the taxpayer holds the obligation.

**Technical Notes**: Section 9102 contains the general rules for determining a financial institution's accrued returns and accrual adjustments in respect of a specified debt obligation. These amounts are included in the amounts prescribed by section 9101. Transition rules and rules for special situations are contained in section 9103. Examples are provided at the end of the commentary on this section.

Section 9102 is organized as follows:

- Subsection 9102(1) provides for the determination of accrued returns from specified debt obligations under which all payments are fixed in timing and amount. Subsection 9102(2) describes the level-yield method that is referred to in subsection 9102(1).
- Subsection 9102(3) provides for the determination of accrued returns from obligations other than those to which subsection 9102(1) applies.
- Subsections 9102(4) and (5) provide for the determination of accrual adjustments.
- Subsection 9102(6) provides that the rules in section 9102 are subject to the rules in section 9103.

Subsection 9102(1) sets out, for the purpose of paragraph 9101(1)(a), the method for determining a taxpayer's accrued return for each taxation year from a specified debt obligation that is a fixed payment obligation under which the debtor has made all required payments. A "fixed payment obligation" is defined in section 9100 as a specified debt obligation under which the payments to be made by the debtor are all fixed in timing and amount, and are all denominated in the same currency.

**(2) Level-yield method** — For the purpose of subsection (1), the level-yield method for allocating a taxpayer's total return from a fixed payment obligation is the method that allocates, to each particular day in the period that begins on the day following the day on which the taxpayer acquired the obligation and that ends on the day on which the obligation matures, the amount determined by the formula

$$(A + B - C) \times D$$

where

A is the cost of the obligation to the taxpayer (measured in the primary currency of the obligation),

B is the total of all amounts each of which is the portion of the taxpayer's total return from the obligation that is allocated to a day before the particular day,

C is the total of all payments required to be made under the obligation after it was acquired by the taxpayer and before the particular day, and

D is the rate of interest per day that, if used in computing the present value (as of the end of the day on which the taxpayer acquired the obligation and based on daily compounding) of all

**Reg.**
**S. 9102(2)**                    Income Tax Regulations

payments to be made under the obligation after it was acquired by the taxpayer, produces a present value equal to the cost to the taxpayer of the obligation (measured in the primary currency of the obligation).

**Technical Notes**: In the case of a Canadian-dollar obligation that a taxpayer holds throughout a taxation year, the accrued return for the year is the total of the amounts allocated to each day in the year in respect of the taxpayer's total return from the obligation. Where the taxpayer does not hold the obligation throughout the year, the accrued return is the total of the amounts allocated to the days in the year at the beginning of which the taxpayer holds the obligation. The amount allocated to each day is to be determined using the level-yield method described in subsection 9102(2), or any other reasonable method that is substantially similar. Generally, a method would be considered reasonable only if it is in accordance with generally accepted accounting practice.

Under the level-yield method described in subsection 9102(2), the internal rate of return of an obligation is used to determine the amount of the taxpayer's total return from the obligation that is allocated to each day. The internal rate of return is the interest rate that produces a present value of payments under the obligation equal to the cost of the obligation to the taxpayer. For this purpose, compounding is on a daily basis. The amount of the total return allocated to a particular day is determined by the formula:

$$(A + B - C) \times D$$

where

A = the cost of the obligation to the taxpayer;

B = the portion of the total return allocated to preceding days;

C = the total payments required to be made under the obligation to the taxpayer before the particular day; and

D = the internal rate of return of the obligation, expressed as a daily rate of interest.

It is recognized that few, if any, taxpayers use precisely this method for financial statement purposes. As noted above, subsection 9102(1) allows the use of any other reasonable method that is substantially similar. For example, a taxpayer could use a method based on semi-annual compounding, in which case a suitable approach to proration between compounding dates would be necessary (where the taxation year end falls between compounding dates).

It is intended that straight-line proration be an acceptable method where it can be used for financial statement purposes and the obligation provides for a level rate of interest. Under this method, any premium or discount on the acquisition of an obligation is recognized on a uniform basis from the acquisition date to the maturity date of the obligation. Similarly, each interest payment is spread over the period to which it relates. An amount paid in respect of accrued interest on the acquisition of the obligation would normally be taken into account by offsetting it against the interest, and then spreading the remainder of the interest over the period from acquisition to the interest payment date.

In the case of a foreign-currency obligation, the first step is to determine, in the currency of the obligation, the total return and the amount of that return allocated to each day. For this purpose, the level-yield method (or any similar method that is permissible) is applied using the foreign currency as the currency in which all computations are done. Next, the amounts allocated to each day in a taxation year are translated to Canadian dollars using a reasonable method of translation. Finally, the Canadian dollar amounts for the days at the beginning of which the taxpayer holds the obligation are totalled. One translation method that would generally be acceptable is to use the average exchange rate for the year. Where this approach is used, it will make no difference whether the amount allocated to each day is totalled before or after being translated to Canadian dollars. Thus, the accrued return for the year could be determined in the foreign currency, and then translated to Canadian dollars.

Subsection 9102(1) is restricted to specified debt obligations under which the debtor has made all required payments. If a debtor is in default, subsection 9102(3) will apply. In general, under subsection 9102(3) the accrued return for a taxation year will equal the amount that would be determined under subsection 9102(1) plus any additional interest that accrues in the year because of the default.

**Related Provisions**: ITA 257 — Negative amounts in formulas.

**(3) Other obligations** — For the purpose of paragraph 9101(1)(a), a taxpayer's accrued return for a taxation year from a specified debt obligation, other than an obligation to which subsection (1) applies, shall be determined

(a) using a reasonable method that,

(i) taking into account the extent to which the obligation differs from fixed payment obligations, is consistent with the principles implicit in the methods that can be used under subsection (1) for fixed payment obligations, and

(ii) is in accordance with generally accepted accounting practice for the measurement of profit from debt obligations; and

(b) on the basis of reasonable assumptions with respect to the timing and amount of any payments to be made by the debtor under the obligation that are not fixed in their timing or amount (measured in the primary currency of the obligation).

**Technical Notes**: Subsection 9102(3) contains rules regarding the determination of accrued returns from specified debt obligations for the purpose of paragraph 9101(1)(a). It applies to obligations other than those to which subsection 9102(1) applies. Generally, subsection 9102(3) should allow a taxpayer to recognize income from an obligation using the same method for tax purposes as it uses for financial statement purposes.

Subsection 9102(3) requires that a taxpayer's accrued return from an obligation for each taxation year be determined using a reasonable method that is consistent with the principles implicit in the methods that subsection 9102(1) allows to be used for fixed payment obligations. The degree of consistency that is required depends on the extent to which the obligation is similar to fixed payment obligations. Subsection 9102(3) also requires that the method for determining the accrued return be in accordance with generally accepted accounting practice. Finally, it provides that reasonable assumptions are to be made with respect to the amount and timing of payments that are not fixed. Each of these requirements is discussed below.

*Consistency with methods for fixed payment obligations*

The following paragaphs describe the main consequences of the requirement that an accrual method used for a particular specified debt obligation be consistent with the principles that are implicit in the methods that can be used for fixed payment obligations.

The first consequence is that the accrued return for each year must be based on the total return that the taxpayer would realize if the obligation were held to maturity. Whether or not particular payments under the obligation are characterized as interest is irrelevant in determining the total return, and thus the amount to be accrued each year. Also, each year's return must include an amount in respect of any discount on the acquisition of the obligation. Conversely, an acquisition premium is to be applied to reduce the amount that would otherwise accrue each year.

Second, to the extent that the total return derives from fixed payments, it must generally accrue at a uniform (or approximately uniform) rate. For example, if the rate of interest for each period is the sum of a fixed rate and a variable rate, and the fixed rate is not the same for all periods, there would have to be a "levelling" of the fixed rates. This requirement to "level the interest rate" is not new. A similar requirement is contained in the accrual rules under subsection 7000(2).

It is not intended that interest be levelled where this would be inappropriate, such as where additional interest is payable because of the default of the debtor. For example, assume that a debt obligation that was acquired at its face amount provides for interest at the rate of 8%, and also provides that where the debtor fails to make a payment as required, interest on the overdue payment accrues at the rate of 11%. In this case, the accrued return for a year would equal the sum of the regular interest that accrues at the rate of 8% and any interest that accrues at 11% on overdue payments.

As indicated above, the consistency requirement is to be applied taking into account the extent to which an obligation differs from fixed payment obligations. This is relevant, in particular, for the levelling principle. For many variable rate debt obligations, it is appropriate to accrue the variable rate interest on the basis of the actual rates for each year. This would apply for example, if a debt obligation provides for interest that is set annually at a rate equal to the 1-year London Interbank Offered Rate (LIBOR) plus ½%. Another example is a debt obligation that provides for interest at a bank's prime rate plus 1%. Of course, any acquisition premium or discount would have to be taken into account in determining the accrued return for each year.

The third consequence of the consistency requirement is that payments of interest in a year are not directly included in the accrued return for the year. In other words, the accrued return is determined on the basis of accrual principles only. (In some circumstances, interest payments may be included in accrual adjustments determined under subsection 9102(5).) However, interest payments, like other payments, would be subtracted from the base on which the return is considered to accrue. Thus, if a debtor prepays interest, the payment has the same tax consequences as a payment of principal (assuming the payment of principal does not constitute a partial disposition of the obligation). In particular, accrued returns continue to be determined throughout the period for which the interest was prepaid.

Fourth, interest that has accrued before a taxpayer acquires an obligation is included in determining the taxpayer's accrued returns only to the extent that the accrued interest exceeds the portion of the cost of the obligation to the taxpayer that is attributable to the interest. This follows from the fact that the amount included in respect of the interest in the taxpayer's total projected return from the obligation is equal to the difference between the amount of the interest and the amount the taxpayer has paid for it.

Finally, in the case of a foreign-currency obligation, the amount that accrues each day is to be determined in the primary currency of the obligation and then translated to Canadian dollars. However, where amounts are translated using the average exchange rate for each year, the same result is obtained by totalling the daily accruals to give the accrued return for the year (measured in the primary currency) before translating to Canadian dollars.

*Generally accepted accounting practice*

One of the requirements imposed by subsection 9102(3) is that a method for determining accrued returns be in accordance with generally accepted accounting practice. The term "practice" is used rather than "principles" to indicate that the Handbook of The Canadian Institute of Chartered Accountants would not be the only source of information for determining what is acceptable.

*Assumptions*

The requirement that assumptions be made with respect to the timing and amount of payments that are not fixed is intended to ensure that a taxpayer reports reasonable accrued returns from an obligation that provides for contingent payments. For example, assume that a taxpayer holds an obligation that provides for interest payments at the rate of 3% per year, and an amount payable at maturity equal to $1,000 adjusted by the change in a stock index from the date of issue to the maturity date. In determining its accrued returns, the taxpayer would have to make a reasonable assumption about the amount that will be paid at maturity. This assumption may change from year to year, depending on the performance of the stock index. (The performance of the stock index may also give rise to accrual adjustments under subsection 9102(5).)

Whether it is actually necessary to make assumptions with respect to contingent payments depends on the method used to determine accrued returns. For example, assume that a 5-year obligation provides for interest that, at issue date and at each anniversary of that date, is set equal to the 1-year LIBOR rate plus 1%. A taxpayer that acquires the obligation at a discount may choose to accrue the discount on a straight-line basis over a reasonable period, and in addition to recognize the actual amount of interest that accrues each year. In this case, there would be no need to make any assumptions about future interest payments.

**(4) Accrual adjustment** — For the purposes of paragraphs 9101(1)(b) and (2)(a), where a taxation

**Reg. S. 9102(4)**

year of a taxpayer is the first taxation year for which subsection 142.3(1) of the Act applies to the taxpayer in respect of a specified debt obligation, the taxpayer's accrual adjustment in respect of the obligation for the year is nil.

**Technical Notes**: Subsections 9102(4) and (5) provide for the determination of accrual adjustments in respect of specified debt obligations. Where an accrual adjustment for a taxation year is positive, it is included in the amount prescribed by subsection 9101(1) in respect of the obligation for the year. A negative accrual adjustment is included in determining the amount prescribed by subsection 9101(2).

In general terms, an accrual adjustment in respect of an obligation for a taxation year is the amount by which prior years' accrued returns have to be adjusted to recognize payments under the obligation in the year that differ from those assumed for the purpose of determining the accrued returns. The adjustment also takes into account changes in assumptions regarding anticipated future payments under the obligation, to the extent that the changed assumptions will not be fully reflected in the determination of accrued returns for the current and future taxation years.

Subsection 9102(4) provides that a taxpayer's accrual adjustment in respect of a specified debt obligation is nil where the adjustment is being determined for the first taxation year for which subsection 142.3(1) of the Act applies with respect to the obligation. In this case, there are no accrued returns to be adjusted.

**(5)** For the purposes of paragraphs 9101(1)(b) and (2)(a), where subsection (4) does not apply to determine a taxpayer's accrual adjustment in respect of a specified debt obligation for a particular taxation year, the taxpayer's accrual adjustment is the positive or negative amount determined by the formula

$$A - B$$

where

A is the total of all amounts each of which is the amount that would be the taxpayer's accrued return from the obligation for a taxation year, before the particular year, for which subsection 142.3(1) of the Act applied to the taxpayer in respect of the obligation if the accrued return were redetermined on the basis of

   (a) the information available at the end of the particular year, and

   (b) the assumptions, if any, with respect to the timing and amount of payments to be made under the obligation after the particular year that were used for the purpose of determining the taxpayer's accrued return from the obligation for the particular year; and

B is the total of

   (a) the amount included under paragraph 9101(1)(a) as the taxpayer's accrued return from the obligation for the taxation year immediately preceding the particular year, and

   (b) where the taxpayer's accrual adjustment in respect of the obligation for that immediately preceding taxation year was determined under this subsection, the value of A for the purpose of determining that accrual adjustment.

**Technical Notes**: Subsection 9102(5), which applies where subsection 9102(4) is not applicable, provides that a taxpayer's accrual adjustment in respect of a specified debt obligation for a particular taxation year is equal to

- the total of the taxpayer's accrued returns from the obligation for previous taxation years, redetermined to take into account all information available at the end of the particular year and to use the same assumptions regarding the timing and amount of payments as are used for the purpose of determining the accrued return for the particular year

minus

- the taxpayer's accrued return for the taxation year preceding the particular year, and

- if subsection 9102(5) applied to that preceding year, the redetermined amounts of the accrued returns that were used in determining the accrual adjustment for that year.

**Related Provisions**: ITA 257 — Negative amounts in formulas.

**(6) Special cases and transition** — The rules in this section for determining accrued returns and accrual adjustments are subject to section 9103.

**Technical Notes**: Subsection 9102(6) provides that the rules in section 9102 for determining accrued returns and accrual adjustments are subject to section 9103. Section 9103 contains rules for convertible obligations, impaired obligations and amended obligations, and also transition rules.

The following examples illustrate acceptable methods for determining accrued returns under subsection 9102(3), and show the calculation of accrual adjustments under subsection 9102(5). It should be noted that other methods may also be acceptable. It has been assumed that all methods are in accordance with generally acceptable accounting practice.

**Example 1**

A debt obligation is issued on January 1, 1996 and matures on January 1, 2001. The obligation has a face amount of $1,000 and provides for an interest payment each January 1st based on the value of 1-year LIBOR on the preceding January 1st minus 2%. The taxpayer acquires the obligation when it is issued, at a cost of $877. The taxpayer's taxation year is the calendar year.

The value of 1-year LIBOR on January 1, 1996 is 6% and on January 1, 1997 is 8%.

The taxpayer has chosen to recognize the discount using a level-yield approach.

*Accrued returns and accrual adjustments:*

1. Using the value of 1-year LIBOR on January 1, 1996 to project the future values produces interest payments of $40 each January 1st. On this basis, the internal rate of return for the obligation is 7%.

2. The taxpayer's accrued return for 1996 is equal to $61.39 (= $877 × .07).

3. The taxpayer's accrued return for 1997 consists of two components. The first is the amount that would be the accrued return if the value of 1-year LIBOR had remained at 6%. This amount is equal to $62.89 (= ($877 + $61.39 - $40) × .07). The second component is equal to the additional interest because of the difference between the assumed and the actual value of LIBOR. This additional interest is $20. Thus, the accrued return for 1997 is $82.89.

4. Accrued returns for 1998 to 2000 would be determined in a similar manner.

5. There are no accrual adjustments.

### Example 2

The facts are the same as in example 1, except that the taxpayer has chosen to accrue the discount using a straight-line approach.

*Accrued returns and accrual adjustments:*

1. The amount of the discount to be accrued each year is $24.60 (= ($1,000 - $877) / 5).

2. The taxpayer's accrued return for 1996 is equal to $64.60 (= $40 + $24.60).

3. The taxpayer's accrued return for 1997 is equal to $84.60 (= $60 + $24.60).

4. Accrued returns for 1998 to 2000 would be determined in a similar manner.

5. There are no accrual adjustments.

### Example 3

A debt obligation is issued on January 1, 1996 and matures on January 1, 1999. The obligation has a face amount of $1,000 and provides for quarterly interest payments. The interest payment for a quarter is based on a 90-day commercial paper rate at the beginning of the quarter, increased or decreased by a specified amount. For the first 4 interest payments, an amount of 1% is subtracted from the commercial paper rate (expressed on an annualized basis). For the next 4 payments, there is an increase of 1%. For the last 4 payments, the commercial paper rate is increased by 3%. The taxpayer acquires the obligation when it is issued, at a cost of $1,000. The taxpayer's taxation year is the calendar year.

The rates for 90-day commercial paper (on an annualized basis) are 6% throughout 1996, 5% throughout 1997 and 7% throughout 1998.

*Accrued returns and accrual adjustments:*

1. The adjustments to the commercial paper rate must be levelled. The average adjustment is an increase of 1% per year (= (-1% + 1% + 3%) / 3).

2. The accrued return for 1996 is $70 (= $1,000 × (.06 + .01)). The accrued returns for 1997 and 1998 are $60 and $80 respectively.

3. There are no accrual adjustments.

### Example 4

A debt obligation is issued on January 1, 1996 and matures on January 1, 2001. The obligation has a face amount of $1,000 and provides for annual interest payments equal to 5% of the face amount. In addition, a bonus is payable on maturity, based on the debtor's cumulative profits over the 5 years. The taxpayer acquires the obligation when it is issued, at a cost of $1,000. The taxpayer's taxation year is the calendar year.

If the debtor had issued a fixed interest rate obligation for the same price, the interest rate would have been 9%.

The amount of the bonus payment is $151.32, and this amount is known before the end of 2000.

*Accrued returns and accrual adjustments:*

1. The taxpayer's accrued return for 1996 is equal to $90 (= $1,000 × .09).

2. For 1997, the amount to which the 9% rate of return is applied is equal to the face amount plus the difference between the accrued return for 1996 and the amount of interest that was paid, i.e. compounding applies to the unpaid portion of the accrued return. Thus, the taxpayer's accrued return for 1997 is equal to $93.60 (= ($1,000 + $90 - $50) × .09).

3. The taxpayer's accrued returns for 1998 and 1999 are $97.52 and $101.80 respectively.

4. Based on the actual bonus payment, the internal rate of return of the obligation to the taxpayer is 7.6%. Computing the taxpayer's accrued return for 2000 on the basis that all accrued returns were determined using this rate gives an accrued return for 2000 equal to $84.85.

5. Redetermining the taxpayer's accrued returns for 1996 to 1999 on the basis of the rate of return of 7.6% gives total accrued returns for those years equal to $316.47. Since the accrued returns that were reported by the taxpayer totalled $382.92, the taxpayer has an accrual adjustment for 2000 equal to -$66.45. Thus, in computing its income for the year 2000, the taxpayer can claim a deduction of $66.45 under paragraph 142.3(1)(b) of the Act.

6. The net amount included in the taxpayer's income for the year 2000 in respect of the obligation is $18.40 (= $84.85 - $66.45). This is equal to the total return of $401.32 minus $382.92 which was included in computing income for previous years.

### Example 5

A debt obligation is issued on January 1, 1996 and matures on January 1, 2001. The amount payable at maturity is equal to $1,000 multiplied by the ratio of the value of a stock index on December 31, 2000 to the value of the index on December 31, 1995. In addition, the obligation provides for interest payments each January 1st equal to $30 multiplied by the ratio of the value of the stock index on the preceding December 31st to the value of the index on December 31, 1995. The taxpayer acquires the obligation when it is issued, at a cost of $1,050. The taxpayer's taxation year is the calendar year.

*Accrued returns and accrual adjustments:*

1. The taxpayer's accrued return from the obligation for each year is equal to

- the increase, if any, in the adjusted face amount from the end of the preceding year to the end of the current year — the adjusted face amount at any time is equal to $1,000 multiplied by the ratio of the value of the stock index at that time to the value of the stock index on December 31, 1995

plus

- the actual interest for the year

minus

- $10 in respect of the $50 premium over the initial face amount.

2. There would be an accrual adjustment for any year in which the stock index declines. The adjustment would be

a negative amount equal to the decrease in the adjusted face amount of the obligation.

**Definitions [Reg. 9102]**: "amount" — ITA 248(1); "fixed payment obligation" — Reg. 9100; "level-yield method" — Reg. 9102(2); "primary currency" — Reg. 9100; "specified debt obligation" — ITA 142.2(1), Reg. 9100; "taxation year" — ITA 249; "taxpayer" — ITA 248(1); "total return" — Reg. 9100.

## 9103. Accrual rules — special cases and transition — (1) Convertible obligation —

For the purposes of section 9102, where the terms of a specified debt obligation of a taxpayer give the taxpayer the right to exchange the obligation for shares of the debtor or of a corporation related to the debtor,

(a) subject to paragraph (b), the right shall be disregarded (whether or not it has been exercised); and

(b) unless less than 5% of the cost of the obligation to the taxpayer is attributable to the right, the cost shall be deemed to equal the amount by which the cost exceeds the portion of the cost attributable to the right.

**Technical Notes**: Section 9103 contains rules that apply with respect to the determination of accrued returns and accrual adjustments under section 9102. There are rules for convertible obligations, impaired obligations and amended obligations, and also transition rules.

Subsection 9103(1) contains two rules that apply with respect to a specified debt obligation that is convertible into shares of the debtor or of a corporation related to the debtor. Paragraph 9103(1)(a) provides that the conversion right is to be disregarded in determining accrued returns and accrual adjustments. Thus, the possibility that the obligation will be settled by way of shares does not enter into the determination of these amounts. In addition, the actual exercise of the conversion right is ignored for the purpose of determining the accrued return and accrual adjustment for the year of exercise. However, any gain from converting to shares is recognized under the rules in section 142.4 of the Act for the disposition of obligations.

Paragraph 9103(1)(b) provides that if 5% or more of the cost of a convertible obligation is attributable to the conversion right, the taxpayer's cost is to be considered to be the actual cost minus the amount that is attributable to the conversion right. This rule has the effect of preventing a taxpayer from deducting the cost of a conversion right, where this cost is a significant amount. The cost attributable to a conversion right can be determined as the difference between the actual cost of the obligation and the estimated fair market value of the obligation without the conversion right.

It should be noted that subsection 9103(1) does not apply where a debt obligation is convertible into shares of a corporation not related to the debtor. In this case, the possibility of conversion must be taken into account in determining accrued returns. Where the value of the conversion right is material, a method for determining accrued returns will generally not be considered reasonable unless it is based on an assumption that the right will be exercised and a reasonable value is assumed for the shares.

**(2) Default by debtor [temporary — see below]** — For the purposes of section 9102, in determining amounts in respect of a specified debt obligation, no reduction shall be made on account of the possible or actual failure of the debtor to make any payments under the obligation.

**Technical Notes**: Subsection 9103(2) provides that accrued returns and accrual adjustments are to be determined in respect of a specified debt obligation without any reduction for the possible or actual failure of the debtor to make any payments under the obligation. Deductions in respect of impaired debts can be claimed under paragraphs 20(1)(l) (doubtful debt reserve) and 20(1)(p) (bad debt deduction) of the Act.

**(3) Amendment of obligation** — For the purposes of determining accrued returns and accrual adjustments under section 9102, where the terms of a specified debt obligation of a taxpayer have been amended to change the timing or amount of any payment to be made under the obligation, the amendment shall be taken into account as if the obligation had been acquired at the time the amendment was made.

**Technical Notes**: Subsection 9103(3) applies where a specified debt obligation has been amended to change the timing or amount of a payment to be made under the obligation. It provides that the amendment is to be taken into account as if the obligation had been acquired when the amendment was made. This means that the amendment affects future accrued returns only. For example, if accrued returns are being determined for a debt obligation using the level-yield method, the rate of return would be redetermined for the period after the amendment, and there would be no accrual adjustment in respect of the amendment.

It should be noted that subsection 9103(3) applies with respect to payments that are not required to be made until after the amendment. If overdue payments are forgiven, a bad debt deduction would generally be available under paragraph 20(1)(p) of the Act.

**(4) Obligations acquired before financial institution rules apply** — Where a taxpayer held a specified debt obligation at the beginning of the taxpayer's first taxation year (in this subsection referred to as the "initial year") for which subsection 142.3(1) of the Act applied to the taxpayer in respect of the obligation, the following rules apply:

(a) the taxpayer's accrued return from the obligation for the initial year or a subsequent taxation year shall not include an amount to the extent that the amount was included in computing the taxpayer's income for a taxation year preceding the initial year; and

(b) where

(i) interest on the obligation in respect of a period before the initial year becomes receivable or is received by the taxpayer in a particular taxation year that is the initial year or a subsequent taxation year, and

(ii) all or part of the interest would not, but for this paragraph, be included in computing the taxpayer's income for any taxation year, there shall be included in determining the taxpayer's accrued return from the obligation for the particular year the amount, if any, by which

(iii) the portion of the interest that would not otherwise be included in computing the taxpayer's income for any taxation year

exceeds

(iv) the portion of the cost of the obligation to the taxpayer that is reasonably attributable to that portion of the interest.

**Technical Notes**: Subsection 9103(4) applies with respect to a specified debt obligation held by a taxpayer at the beginning of its first taxation year to which subsection 142.3(1) of the Act applies. Subsection 9103(4) ensures a proper transition from subsection 12(3) of the Act to subsection 142.3(1). It is expected that there will be few obligations for which subsection 9103(4) is relevant.

Paragraph 9103(4)(a) provides that a taxpayer's accrued return for a taxation year does not include an amount to the extent that the amount was included in computing the taxpayer's income for a taxation year before subsection 142.3(1) commenced to apply. This rule would apply, for example, where prepaid interest has been included in income under subsection 12(3). A reasonable adjustment would be made to the accrued returns that are otherwise determined to allow for the return that has already been recognized. Paragraph 9103(4)(a) would also apply where subsection 16(3) of the Act has required a discount on the issue of a debt obligation to be included in the taxpayer's income.

Paragraph 9103(4)(b) applies with respect to interest that is received or becomes receivable in a taxation year in which subsection 142.3(1) of the Act is applicable, where the interest is in respect of a period before that subsection applied. Paragraph 9103(4)(b) provides that the taxpayer's accrued return for the year from the obligation includes the amount by which (i) the portion of the interest that would not otherwise be taken into account in computing the taxpayer's income for any taxation year exceeds (ii) the portion of the taxpayer's cost of the obligation that is reasonably attributable to that portion of the interest. This paragraph might apply, for example, where a taxpayer receives a contingent interest payment in the first year in which subsection 142.3(1) applies, and part or all of the payment is in respect of a previous taxation year. If the portion of the interest payment that is in respect of the previous year has not been included in computing the taxpayer's income for that year, and would not otherwise be included in the taxpayer's accrued return for the current year, paragraph 9103(4)(b) will include it in the accrued return.

**(5) Prepaid interest — transition rule —** Where, before November 1994 and in a taxation year that ended after February 22, 1994, a taxpayer received an amount under a specified debt obligation in satisfaction, in whole or in part, of the debtor's obligation to pay interest in respect of a period after the year,

(a) the amount may, at the election of the taxpayer, be included in determining the taxpayer's accrued return for the year from the obligation; and

(b) where the amount is so included, the taxpayer's accrued returns for subsequent taxation years from the obligation shall not include any amount in respect of interest that, because of the payment of the amount, the debtor is no longer required to pay.

**Technical Notes**: Subsection 9103(5) applies where a taxpayer received a prepayment of interest on a debt obligation before November 1994 and in a taxation year that ended after February 22, 1994. Subsection 9103(5) allows the taxpayer to include the full amount of the prepaid interest in its accrued return for the year in which it received the prepayment, in which case the taxpayer's accrued returns for subsequent years are to be determined without including any amount in respect of the prepaid interest.

**Definitions [Reg. 9103]**: "amount" — ITA 248(1); "corporation" — ITA 248(1), *Interpretation Act* 35(1); "initial year" — Reg. 9103(4); "related" — ITA 251(2)–(6); "share" — ITA 248(1); "specified debt obligation" — ITA 142.2(1), Reg. 9100; "taxation year" — ITA 249; "taxpayer" — ITA 248(1).

**9104. Foreign exchange adjustment — (1)** For the purposes of paragraphs 9101(1)(c) and (2)(b), where, at the end of a taxation year, a taxpayer holds a specified debt obligation the primary currency of which is not Canadian currency, the taxpayer's foreign exchange adjustment in respect of the obligation for the year is the positive or negative amount determined by the formula

$$(A \times B) - C$$

where

A is the amount that would be the tax basis of the obligation to the taxpayer at the end of the year if

(a) the tax basis were determined using the primary currency of the obligation as the currency in which all amounts are expressed,

(b) the definition "tax basis" in subsection 142.4(1) of the Act were read without reference to paragraphs (f), (h), (o) and (q), and

(c) the taxpayer's foreign exchange adjustment in respect of the obligation for each year were nil,

B is the rate of exchange at the end of the year of the primary currency of the obligation into Canadian currency, and

C is the amount that would be the tax basis of the obligation to the taxpayer at the end of the year if

(a) the definition "tax basis" were read without reference to paragraphs (h) and (q), and

(b) the taxpayer's foreign exchange adjustment in respect of the obligation for the year were nil.

**Technical Notes**: Section 9104 provides for the determination of foreign exchange adjustments in respect of specified debt obligations. Foreign exchange adjustments

**Reg. S. 9104(1)**      Income Tax Regulations

are determined if the primary currency of an obligation is not the Canadian dollar. As defined in section 9100, the primary currency of an obligation is the currency with which the obligation is primarily connected. Where a foreign exchange adjustment for a taxation year is positive, it is included in the amount prescribed by subsection 9101(1) in respect of the obligation for the year. A negative adjustment is included in determining the amount prescribed by subsection 9101(2).

Subsection 9104(1) applies where a taxpayer holds a foreign currency obligation at the end of a taxation year. It provides that the foreign exchange adjustment in respect of the obligation for the year is to be computed as follows:

1. Determine the tax basis of the obligation to the taxpayer at the end of the year, using the primary currency of the obligation as the currency in which all amounts are expressed. For this purpose, the definition of "tax basis" in subsection 142.4(1) of the Act is modified so that it does not include (i) any amounts in respect of the change in value of a foreign currency relative to the Canadian dollar, and (ii) the amounts referred to in paragraphs (f) and (q) of the definition (adjustments in determining the adjusted cost base on February 22, 1994 of an obligation that was a capital property).

2. Translate the tax basis to Canadian dollars using the spot rate of exchange at the end of the year.

3. Subtract the Canadian dollar tax basis at the end of the year, determined on the assumption that the foreign exchange adjustment in respect of the obligation for the year is nil, and without taking into account the amounts referred to in paragraphs (f) and (q) of the definition of "tax basis".

The following example illustrates the operation of subsection 9104(1):

**Example**

*A U.S. dollar debt obligation is issued on December 31, 1995 and matures on December 31, 2000. The obligation has a face amount of US$1,000 and provides for interest at the rate of 6%, payable annually. The taxpayer acquires the obligation when it is issued, at a cost of US$900. The taxpayer's taxation year is the calendar year.*

*The exchange rates (C$/US$) to the end of 1998 are:*

|  | Year-end | Average |
|---|---|---|
| 1995 | $1.36 | — |
| 1996 | 1.30 | $1.34 |
| 1997 | 1.35 | 1.32 |
| 1998 | 1.32 | 1.34 |

*Results for first 3 years:*

| US Dollar Tax Basis | 1996 (US$) | 1997 (US$) | 1998 (US$) |
|---|---|---|---|
| Tax basis (beginning of year) | 900.00 | 916.86 | 935.17 |
| Add: accrued return | 76.86 | 78.30 | 79.87 |
| Deduct: interest received | 60.00 | 60.00 | 60.00 |
| Tax basis (end of year) | 916.86 | 935.17 | 955.03 |

| Foreign Exchange Adjustment | 1996 (C$) | 1997 (C$) | 1998 (C$) |
|---|---|---|---|
| Tax basis (beginning of year) | 1224.00 | 1191.92 | 1262.48 |
| Add: accrued return[1] | 103.00 | 103.36 | 107.02 |
| Deduct: interest received | 78.00 | 81.00 | 79.20 |
| Tax basis (before current year foreign exchange adjustment) | 1249.00 | 1214.28 | 1290.30 |
| US$ tax basis - translated | 1191.92 | 1262.48 | 1260.65 |
| Foreign exchange adjustment | (57.07) | 48.19 | (29.65) |

Notes:

1. Translated using the average exchange rate for the year.

**Related Provisions**: ITA 257 — Negative amounts in formulas.

**I.T. Technical News**: No. 15 (tax consequences of the adoption of the "euro" currency).

**(2)** Where a taxpayer disposes of a specified debt obligation the primary currency of which is not Canadian currency, the taxpayer's foreign exchange adjustment in respect of the obligation for the taxation year in which the disposition occurs is the amount that would be the foreign exchange adjustment if the year had ended immediately before the disposition.

**Technical Notes**: Subsection 9104(2) provides for the determination of a foreign exchange adjustment for the taxation year in which a taxpayer disposes of a foreign currency debt obligation. The foreign exchange adjustment is the amount that would be determined under subsection 9104(1) if the taxation year had ended immediately before the disposition.

**(3)** At the election of a taxpayer, subsection (2) does not apply to specified debt obligations disposed of by the taxpayer before 1996.

**Technical Notes**: Subsection 9104(3) provides that, at the election of a taxpayer, subsection 9104(2) does not apply to dispositions of debt obligations before 1996. Where a taxpayer makes this election, any foreign-exchange-related change in value of an obligation that arises in the year of disposition will be an element in the determination of the total gain or loss from the disposition of the obligation.

**Definitions [Reg. 9104]**: "amount" — ITA 248(1); "disposed", "disposes" — ITA 248(1)"disposition"; "disposition" — ITA 248(1); "primary currency" — Reg. 9100; "specified debt obligation" — ITA 142.2(1), Reg. 9100; "tax basis" — ITA 142.4(1), Reg. 9100; "taxation year" — ITA 249; "taxpayer" — ITA 248(1).

**Application**: The June 1, 1995 draft regulations (securities held by financial institutions), s. 9, will add Part XCI (ss. 9100 to 9104), applicable to taxation years that end after February 22, 1994.

### Proposed Repeal — Reg. 9103(2)

**Application**: The November 14, 1997 draft regulations (impaired loans), s. 9, will repeal subsec. 9103(2), applicable

(a) to taxation years that end after September 1997; and

(b) to taxation years that end after 1995 and before October 1997 where the taxpayer elects under subparagraph 3(5)(b) of the attached draft amendments to the *Income Tax Act*.

**Technical Notes**: Part XCI contains rules for determining the amounts that a financial institution is required to include or deduct each year in respect of a specified debt obligation in computing its income.

Subsection 9103(2) provides that accrued returns and accrual adjustments are to be determined in respect of a specified debt obligation without any reduction for the possible or actual failure of the debtor to make any payments under the obligation. Subsection 9103(2) is repealed as a consequence of the introduction of new subsection 142.3(4) of the *Income Tax Act*. The repeal of subsection 9103(2) applies to taxation years that end after September 1997, and also to taxation years that end after 1995 and before October 1997 where the taxpayer elects to have the reserve provisions in new paragraph 20(1)(l) of the Act apply to those years.

## PART XCII — FINANCIAL INSTITUTIONS — DISPOSITION OF SPECIFIED DEBT OBLIGATIONS [PROPOSED]

### Proposed Addition — Part XCII (Reg. 9200–9204)

**Technical Notes**: Part XCII contains provisions relating to the disposition of specified debt obligations by financial institutions. These include:

- a definition of "transition amount";
- provisions that prescribe certain specified debt obligations for exclusion from the amortization requirement; and
- rules for amortizing gains and losses from the disposition of specified debt obligations.

**9200. Interpretation — (1) Definitions** — In this Part,

**"financial institution"** has the meaning assigned by subsection 142.2(1) of the Act;

**Technical Notes**: "Financial institution" has the meaning given to that term by subsection 142.2(1) of the Act.

**"gain"** of a taxpayer from the disposition of a specified debt obligation means the gain from the disposition determined under paragraph 142.4(6)(a) of the Act;

**Technical Notes**: A taxpayer's "gain" from the disposition of a specified debt obligation is the gain determined under paragraph 142.4(6)(a) of the Act.

**"loss"** of a taxpayer from the disposition of a specified debt obligation means the loss from the disposition determined under paragraph 142.4(6)(b) of the Act;

**Technical Notes**: A taxpayer's "loss" from the disposition of a specified debt obligation is the loss determined under paragraph 142.4(6)(b) of the Act.

**"residual portion"** of a taxpayer's gain or loss from the disposition of a specified debt obligation means the amount determined under subsection 142.4(8) of the Act in respect of the disposition;

**Technical Notes**: The "residual portion" of a taxpayer's gain or loss from the disposition of a specified debt obligation is the amount determined under subsection 142.4(8) of the Act in respect of the disposition. The residual portion is the amount of the gain or loss that is required to be amortized (if the amortization requirement applies to the obligation).

**"specified debt obligation"** of a taxpayer has the meaning assigned by subsection 142.2(1) of the Act;

**Technical Notes**: "Specified debt obligation" has the meaning given to that term by subsection 142.2(1) of the Act. It should be noted that this term is defined from the perspective of the holder. For example, where a taxpayer holds a coupon that has been stripped from a debt obligation and holds no other interest in the obligation, the specified debt obligation of the taxpayer is just the coupon. It should also be noted that, if a taxpayer disposes of part of a specified debt obligation, subsection 142.4(9) applies to deem the part disposed of and the retained part to be separate specified debt obligations.

**"tax basis"** of a specified debt obligation to a taxpayer has the meaning assigned by subsection 142.4(1) of the Act.

**Technical Notes**: The "tax basis" of a specified debt obligation to a taxpayer is the amount defined by subsection 142.4(1) of the Act. The tax basis is analogous to the adjusted cost base of capital property.

**(2) Amortization date** — For the purposes of this Part, the amortization date for a specified debt obligation disposed of by a taxpayer is the day determined as follows:

(a) subject to paragraphs (b) to (d), the amortization date is the later of the day of disposition and the day on which the debtor is required to make the final payment under the obligation, determined without regard to any option respecting the timing of payments under the obligation (other than an option that was exercised before the disposition);

(b) subject to paragraphs (c) and (d), where the day on which the debtor is required to make the final payment under the obligation is not determinable for the purpose of paragraph (a), the amortization date is the day of disposition;

(c) subject to paragraph (d), where

(i) the obligation provides for stipulated interest payments,

(ii) the rate of interest for one or more periods after the issuance of the obligation was not fixed on the day of issue, and

(iii) when the obligation was issued, it was reasonable to expect that the interest rate for each period would equal or approximate a reasonable market rate of interest for that period,

the amortization date is the first day, if any, after the disposition on which the interest rate could change; and

(d) where, for purposes of its financial statements, the taxpayer had a gain or loss from the disposition that is being amortized to profit, the amortization date is the last day of the amortization period.

**Technical Notes**: Subsection 9200(2) contains rules for determining the amortization date for a specified debt obligation disposed of by a taxpayer. This date is used in subsections 9203(2) and (4) to determine the end of the amortization period for an obligation or group of obligations. It is also used in subsection 9202(2) for determining whether an obligation is excluded from the amortization requirement.

Paragraph 9200(2)(a) provides that the amortization date is the day on which the debtor is required to make the final payment under the specified debt obligation or, if later, the day of disposition. The day of disposition would be later where, for example, the debtor has failed to repay borrowed money on the maturity date of the obligation. In determining when the final payment is required to be made, an option to redeem or retract an obligation, or to extend its maturity date, is to be disregarded unless it has been exercised. Paragraph 9200(2)(a) applies only if none of paragraphs 9200(2)(b) to (d) applies.

It should be noted that a specified debt obligation is a taxpayer's interest in a debt obligation issued by the debtor. The amortization date is determined with respect to the taxpayer's interest. Where, for example, the taxpayer holds a coupon stripped from a debt obligation, the amortization date is the payment date for the coupon.

Paragraph 9200(2)(b) applies where the date for the last payment is not determinable, and so paragraph 9200(2)(a) cannot be applied. This would be the case, for example, where the maturity date is based on a contingency. Paragraph 9200(2)(b) provides that, subject to paragraphs 9200(2)(c) and (d), the amortization date is the day of disposition.

Paragraph 9200(2)(c) applies if the obligation is a variable interest rate debt obligation and, at the time the obligation was issued, the interest rate for each period was expected to equal or approximate a reasonable market rate. In this case, the amortization date is the day before the next interest reset date. Paragraph 9200(2)(c) does not apply if there are no interest reset dates after the disposition, or if paragraph 9200(2)(d) is applicable. An example of a debt obligation to which paragraph 9200(2)(c) would apply is an obligation with a 10-year term that provides for the interest rate to be reset every two years to LIBOR plus 1%.

Paragraph 9200(2)(d) applies where, for the purposes of its financial statements, the taxpayer has a gain or loss from the disposition that is being amortized. In this case, the amortization date is the last day of the financial statement amortization period.

**Definitions [Reg. 9200]**: "amortization date" — Reg. 9200(2); "amount" — ITA 248(1); "disposed" — ITA 248(1)"disposition"; "disposition" — ITA 248(1); "gain", "loss" — Reg. 9200(1); "specified debt obligation" — ITA 142.2(1), Reg. 9200(1); "taxpayer" — ITA 248(1).

**9201. Transition amount** — For the purpose of subsection 142.4(1) of the Act, "transition amount" of a taxpayer in respect of the disposition of a specified debt obligation means,

(a) where neither paragraph (b) nor (c) applies, nil;

(b) where

(i) the taxpayer acquired the obligation before its taxation year that includes February 23, 1994,

(ii) neither paragraph 7000(2)(a) nor (b) has applied to the obligation, and

(iii) the principal amount of the obligation exceeds the cost of the obligation to the taxpayer (which excess is referred to in this paragraph as the "discount"),

the amount determined by the formula

$$A - B$$

where

A is the total of all amounts each of which is the amount included in respect of the discount in computing the taxpayer's profit for a taxation year that ended before February 23, 1994, and

B is the total of all amounts each of which is the amount included in respect of the discount in computing the taxpayer's income for a taxation year that ended before February 23, 1994; and

(c) where

(i) the conditions in subparagraphs (b)(i) and (ii) are satisfied, and

(ii) the cost of the obligation to the taxpayer exceeds the principal amount of the obligation (which excess is referred to in this paragraph as the "premium"),

the negative of the amount determined by the formula

$$A - B$$

where

A is the total of all amounts each of which is the amount deducted in respect of the premium in computing the taxpayer's profit for a taxation year that ended before February 23, 1994, and

B is the total of all amounts each of which is the amount deducted in respect of the premium in computing the taxpayer's income for a taxation year that ended before February 23, 1994.

**Technical Notes**: Subsection 142.4(1) of the Act provides that the transition amount of a taxpayer in respect of the disposition of a specified debt obligation is the amount defined by regulation. This amount is relevant if subsection 142.4(4) of the Act applies in respect of the disposition. The transition amount is required to be recognized in the year of disposition.

Section 9201 defines "transition amount" for the purpose of subsection 142.4(1). In general terms, the transition amount is the amount of any premium or discount that has been recognized for financial statement purposes, but not for tax purposes, to the beginning of the taxation year that includes February 23, 1994.

Paragraphs 9201(b) and (c) provide for the determination of the transition amount in respect of the disposition of a specified debt obligation by a taxpayer where the following conditions are satisfied:

- the taxpayer acquired the obligation before its taxation year that includes February 23, 1994,
- the accrual rules in paragraphs 7000(2)(a) and (b) have not applied to the obligation, and
- the principal amount of the obligation differs from its cost to the taxpayer, i.e. the obligation was purchased at a discount or premium.

Paragraph 9201(b), which applies in the case of a discount, provides that the transition amount is equal to the amount of the discount that has been included in determining the taxpayer's financial statement profit for taxation years ending before February 23, 1994 minus the amount of the discount included in determining its income for those years for tax purposes. Thus, the transition amount will be nil if, for tax purposes, the taxpayer has been following its financial statement reporting.

Paragraph 9201(c) contains a similar rule for premiums, except that the transition amount will be negative if it is not nil.

Paragraph 9201(a) provides that if neither of paragraphs 9201(b) and (c) applies, the transition amount is nil.

**Related Provisions**: ITA 257 — Negative amounts in formulas.

**Definitions [Reg. 9201]**: "amount" — ITA 248(1); "discount" — Reg. 9201(b)(iii); "disposition" — ITA 248(1); "premium" — Reg. 9201(c)(ii); "principal amount" — ITA 248(1); "specified debt obligation" — ITA 142.2(1), Reg. 9200(1); "taxation year" — ITA 249; "taxpayer" — ITA 248(1).

## 9202. Prescribed debt obligations — (1) The following rules apply with respect to an election made under subsection (3) or (4) by a taxpayer:

(a) the election applies only if

(i) it is in writing,

(ii) it specifies the first taxation year (in this subsection referred to as the "initial year") of the taxpayer to which it is to apply, and

(iii) either it is received by the Minister within 6 months after the end of the initial year, or the Minister has expressly accepted the later filing of the election;

(b) subject to paragraph (c), the election applies to dispositions of specified debt obligations in the initial year and subsequent taxation years; and

(c) where the Minister has approved, on written application by the taxpayer, the revocation of the election, the election does not apply to dispositions of specified debt obligations in the taxation year specified in the application and in subsequent taxation years.

**Technical Notes**: Subsection 142.4(5) of the Act provides that the full gain or loss from the disposition of certain specified debt obligations is required to be taken into account in the taxation year of disposition. In other words, the amortization rules do not apply to these gains and losses. Obligations to which this subsection applies include obligations prescribed under subparagraph 142.4(5)(a)(ii). Section 9202 prescribes certain debt obligations for this purpose.

Subsections 9202(3) and (4) provide for elections to be made by a taxpayer. An election is made under subsection 9202(3) if a taxpayer does not want subsection 9202(2) to apply. An election is made under subsection 9202(4) if a taxpayer wants that subsection to apply. Subsection 9202(1) sets out the rules that apply with respect to these elections.

An election must (i) be in writing, (ii) specify the first taxation year to which it applies, and (iii) be received by the Minister of National Revenue within 6 months after the end of that first year (unless the Minister accepts a later filing). An election continues to apply until the taxpayer revokes it. A revocation requires the Minister's approval, and written application must be made for that approval.

(2) Subject to subsection (3), for the purpose of subparagraph 142.4(5)(a)(ii) of the Act, a specified debt obligation disposed of by a taxpayer in a taxation year is prescribed in respect of the taxpayer where the amortization date for the obligation is not more than two years after the end of the year.

**Technical Notes**: Subsection 9202(2) prescribes certain specified debt obligations for the purpose of subparagraph 142.4(5)(a)(ii) of the Act. Prescribed obligations are excluded from the amortization rules for gains and losses. An obligation is prescribed by subsection 9202(2) if its amortization date (as determined under subsection 9200(2)) is within two years of the end of the taxation year in which the taxpayer disposed of the obligation. However, subsection 9202(2) does not apply to a taxpayer if the conditions in subsection 9202(3) are satisfied.

(3) Subsection (2) does not apply in respect of a taxpayer for a taxation year where

(a) generally accepted accounting principles require that the taxpayer's gains and losses arising on the disposition of a class of debt obligations be amortized to profit for the purpose of the taxpayer's financial statements;

(b) the taxpayer has elected not to have subsection (2) apply; and

(c) the election applies to dispositions in the year.

**Technical Notes**: Subsection 9202(3) provides that subsection 9202(2) does not apply to a taxpayer if (i) the

**Reg. S. 9202(3)** — Income Tax Regulations

taxpayer is required by generally accepted accounting principles (GAAP) to amortize gains and losses from a class of debt obligations, and (ii) the taxpayer has elected not to have subsection 9202(2) apply. This exclusion enables a taxpayer that is required to amortize some or all of its gains and losses for financial statement purposes to choose to also amortize them for tax purposes even if the amortization period is short. It should be noted that the exclusion applies to all obligations, not just those for which GAAP requires amortization. See subsection 9202(1) for rules regarding elections under subsection 9202(3).

**(4)** For the purpose of subparagraph 142.4(5)(a)(ii) of the Act, a specified debt obligation disposed of by a taxpayer in a taxation year is prescribed in respect of the taxpayer where

(a) the taxpayer has elected to have this subsection apply;

(b) the election applies to dispositions in the year; and

(c) the absolute value of the positive or negative amount determined by the formula

$$A - B$$

does not exceed the lesser of $5,000 and the amount, if any, specified in the election, where

A is the total of all amounts each of which is the residual portion of the taxpayer's gain from the disposition of the obligation or any other specified debt obligation disposed of in the same transaction, and

B is the total of all amounts each of which is the residual portion of the taxpayer's loss from the disposition of the obligation or any other specified debt obligation disposed of in the same transaction.

**Technical Notes**: Subsection 9202(4) prescribes certain specified debt obligations for the purpose of subparagraph 142.4(5)(a)(ii) of the Act. Prescribed obligations are excluded from the amortization rules that apply to gains and losses. Subsection 9202(4) is an elective provision — see subsection 9202(1) for rules relating to elections.

Where subsection 9202(4) applies, a specified debt obligation is prescribed if the taxpayer's net gain or loss from the disposition of the obligation and from other obligations disposed of in the same transaction does not exceed $5,000. A taxpayer may elect to have a lower threshhold for this purpose. Such an election might be made where, for example, the taxpayer is required to amortize gains and losses for financial statement purposes, but does not amortize if the gain or loss is less than $1,000.

**Related Provisions**: ITA 257 — Negative amounts in formulas.

**(5)** For the purpose of subparagraph 142.4(5)(a)(ii) of the Act, a specified debt obligation disposed of by a taxpayer in a taxation year is prescribed in respect of the taxpayer where

(a) the disposition resulted in an extinguishment of the obligation, other than an extinguishment that occurred because of a purchase of the obligation by the debtor in the open market;

(b) the taxpayer had the right to require the obligation to be settled at any time; or

(c) the debtor had the right to settle the obligation at any time.

**Technical Notes**: Subsection 9202(5) prescribes certain specified debt obligations for the purpose of subparagraph 142.4(5)(a)(ii) of the Act. Prescribed obligations are excluded from the amortization rules for gains and losses. A specified debt obligation is prescribed by subsection 9202(5) if the disposition of the obligation results in its extinguishment. An obligation would be prescribed, for example, where the disposition occurs because the debtor settles it, whether at the scheduled maturity date or as a result of the exercise of an option to redeem or retract before that date. As another example, a specified debt obligation would be prescribed where the holder exercises an option to convert it into shares. As an exception, an obligation is not prescribed where the extinguishment occurs because of an open market purchase of the obligation by the debtor.

Subsection 9202(5) also prescribes a specified debt obligation if the obligation is an obligation that was payable on demand or that could be redeemed at any time by the debtor.

**Definitions [Reg. 9202]**: "amortization date" — Reg. 9200(2); "amount" — ITA 248(1); "disposed" — ITA 248(1)"disposition"; "disposition" — ITA 248(1); "election" — Reg. 9202(1); "gain" — Reg. 9200(1); "initial year" — Reg. 9202(1)(a)(ii); "loss" — Reg. 9200(1); "Minister" — ITA 248(1); "month" — *Interpretation Act* 35(1); "prescribed" — ITA 248(1); "residual portion" — Reg. 9200(1); "specified debt obligation" — ITA 142.2(1), Reg. 9200(1); "taxation year" — ITA 249; "taxpayer" — ITA 248(1); "writing" — *Interpretation Act* 35(1); "written" — *Interpretation Act* 35(1)"writing".

**9203. Residual portion of gain or loss — (1) Allocation of residual portion** — Subject to section 9204, where subsection 142.4(4) of the Act applies to the disposition of a specified debt obligation by a taxpayer, the amount allocated to each taxation year in respect of the residual portion of the gain or loss from the disposition shall be determined, for the purpose of that subsection,

(a) by a method that complies with, or is substantially similar to a method that complies with, subsection (2); or

(b) where gains and losses from the disposition of debt obligations are amortized to profit for the purpose of the taxpayer's financial statements, by the method used for the purpose of the taxpayer's financial statements.

**Technical Notes**: Section 9203 contains rules for determining the amount of the residual portion of a gain or loss from the disposition of a specified debt obligation that must be recognized each year under subparagraph 142.4(4)(c)(ii) or (d)(ii) of the Act. These rules are subject to section 9204, which applies after certain reorganizations and other events.

Subsection 9203(1) specifies the methods that are permitted for amortizing the residual portion of a gain or loss from the disposition of a specified debt obligation. Any method may be used if it complies with subsection 9203(2), or is substantially similar to a method that so complies. Subsection 9203(2) provides for the amount allocated to each year to be determined on a straight-line proration basis. It is intended that the reference to substantially similar methods generally include the method that provides for the amount allocated to each year to equal to the difference between (i) the amount that would have accrued in the year in respect of the obligation if the taxpayer had retained it, and (ii) the amount that would have accrued in the year in respect of the obligation if the taxpayer had reacquired the obligation immediately after disposing of it.

Where a taxpayer amortizes gains and losses for the purpose of its financial statements, the taxpayer is permitted to use the same method of amortization for tax purposes. This rule allows the financial statement method to be used for all obligations, including obligations that are not subject to amortization for financial statement purposes.

**(2) Proration method** — For the purpose of subsection (1), a method for allocating to taxation years the residual portion of a taxpayer's gain or loss from the disposition of a specified debt obligation complies with this subsection where the amount allocated to each taxation year is determined by the formula

$$A \times \frac{B}{C}$$

where

A  is the residual portion of the taxpayer's gain or loss;

B  is the number of days in the year that are in the period referred to in the description of C; and

C  is the number of days in the period that,

  (a) where subsection (3) applies in respect of the obligation, is determined under that subsection, and

  (b) in any other case,

   (i) begins on the day on which the taxpayer disposed of the obligation, and

   (ii) ends on the earlier of

    (A) the amortization date for the obligation, and

    (B) the day that is 20 years after the day on which the taxpayer disposed of the obligation.

**Technical Notes**: Subsection 9203(2) sets out, for the purpose of subsection 9203(1), a method for amortizing the residual portion of the gain or loss from the disposition of a specified debt obligation. The method involves prorating the residual portion on a straight-line basis over the amortization period. More specifically, the amount allocated to a particular taxation year is equal to the residual portion of the gain or loss times the proportion of days in the amortization period that are in the year. Generally, the amortization period for an obligation is the period that begins on the day of disposition of the obligation and ends on the earlier of the amortization date determined under subsection 9200(2) and the day that is 20 years after the day of disposition. However, where subsection 9203(3) applies, the amortization period is determined pursuant to that subsection and subsection 9203(4).

**(3) Single proration period** — Where

(a) a taxpayer has elected in its return of income for a taxation year to have this subsection apply in respect of the specified debt obligations disposed of in a transaction in the year,

(b) all the obligations were disposed of at the same time, and

(c) the number of the obligations to which subsection 142.4(4) of the Act applies is at least 50,

the period determined under this subsection in respect of the obligations is the period that begins on the day of disposition of the obligations and ends on the weighted average amortization date for those obligations to which subsection 142.4(4) applies.

**Technical Notes**: Under the amortization method set out in subsection 9203(2), the residual portion of the gain or loss from the disposition of a specified debt obligation is spread on a straight-line basis over the amortization period for the obligation. Subsection 9203(3) allows a taxpayer to use the same amortization period for a group of specified debt obligations that were disposed of at the same time in the same transaction, if there are at least 50 obligations to which subsection 142.4(4) of the Act applies. This enables the net residual gain or loss to be spread as if it were from the disposition of a single obligation.

Where subsection 9203(3) applies, the amortization period starts on the day of disposition of the obligations, and ends on the weighted average amortization date determined under subsection 9203(4) for those obligations to which subsection 142.4(4) applies. In this regard, obligations that are prescribed by section 9202 (obligations excluded from amortization requirement) are not taken into account in determining the weighted average amortization date. In particular, obligations that are prescribed because their amortization dates are not more than two years after the end of the year of disposition are disregarded.

Subsection 9203(3) applies on an elective basis. An election must be made in the tax return for the year in which the obligations were disposed of. No special form is required for the election — it could be made, for example, by including a page with the return that identifies the transaction to which the election applies.

**(4) Weighted average amortization date** — For the purpose of subsection (3), the weighted average amortization date for a group of specified debt obligations disposed of on the same day by a taxpayer is,

(a) where paragraph (b) does not apply, the day that is the number of days after the day of disposition equal to the total of the number of days determined in respect of each obligation by the formula

$$A \times \frac{B}{C}$$

**Reg. S. 9203(4)(a)** — Income Tax Regulations

where

A  is the number of days from the day of disposition to the amortization date for the obligation,

B  is the residual portion of the gain or loss from the disposition of the obligation, and

C  is the total of all amounts each of which is the residual portion of the gain or loss from the disposition of an obligation in the group; and

(b) the day that the taxpayer determines using a reasonable method for estimating the day determined under paragraph (a).

**Technical Notes**: Subsection 9203(3) allows a taxpayer to use a single amortization period for a group of specified debt obligations. The period ends on the weighted average amortization date for the obligations. Subsection 9203(4) specifies how the weighted average amortization date is to be determined for this purpose. A taxpayer is given a choice between using a precisely determined date and a reasonable estimate of that date.

Under paragraph 9203(4)(a), the weighted average amortization date for a group of obligations disposed of on the same day is obtained as follows:

1. For each obligation, determine the number of days from the day of disposition to the amortization date for the obligation — the amortization date is determined under subsection 9200(2).

2. Multiply the number of days by the ratio of the residual portion of the gain or loss from the disposition of the obligation to the total of the residual portions for all the obligations.

3. Compute the total of the amounts determined under step 2 for all the obligations.

4. Determine the day that follows the day of disposition by that total amount.

Paragraph 9203(4)(b) allows a taxpayer to determine the weighted average amortization date for a group of obligations using a reasonable method for estimating the exact date determined under paragraph 9203(4)(a). An example of an approach that would generally be reasonable is to select a random sample of the debt obligations and determine the exact date for that sample.

**Definitions [Reg. 9203]**: "amortization date" — Reg. 9200(2); "amount" — ITA 248(1); "disposed" — ITA 248(1)"disposition"; "disposition" — ITA 248(1); "gain", "loss" — Reg. 9200(1); "residual portion" — Reg. 9200(1), 9203(2); "specified debt obligation" — ITA 142.2(1), Reg. 9200(1); "taxation year" — ITA 249; "taxpayer" — ITA 248(1); "weighted average amortization date" — Reg. 9203(4).

## 9204. Special rules for residual portion of gain or loss — (1) Application of section — This section applies for the purposes of subparagraphs 142.4(4)(c)(ii) and (d)(ii) of the Act.

**Technical Notes**: Section 9204 contains rules relating to the amortization of the residual portion of the gain or loss from the disposition of a specified debt obligation. These rules, which modify the normal rules in section 9203, apply where

- a subsidiary corporation has been wound up into its parent corporation on a rollover basis pursuant to subsection 88(1) of the Act;
- an insurer has transferred an insurance business on a rollover basis pursuant to subsection 138(11.5) or (11.94) of the Act;
- a new partnership is a continuation of another partnership pursuant to subsection 98(6) of the Act;
- a taxpayer ceases to carry on a business; or
- a taxpayer ceases to be a financial institution.

Subsection 9204(1) provides that section 9204 applies for the purpose of subparagraphs 142.4(4)(c)(ii) and (d)(ii) of the Act. Subparagraph 142.4(4)(c)(ii) requires the residual portion of the gain from the disposition of a specified debt obligation to be amortized in accordance with prescribed rules. Subparagraph 142.4(4)(d)(ii) contains a similar requirement with respect to the residual portion of a loss.

**(2) Winding-up** — Where subsection 88(1) of the Act has applied to the winding-up of a taxpayer (in this subsection referred to as the "subsidiary"), the following rules apply in respect of the residual portion of a gain or loss of the subsidiary from the disposition of a specified debt obligation to which subsection 142.4(4) of the Act applies:

(a) the amount of that residual portion allocated to the taxation year of the subsidiary in which its assets were distributed to its parent on the winding-up shall be determined on the assumption that the taxation year ended when the assets were distributed to its parent;

(b) no amount shall be allocated in respect of that residual portion to any taxation year of the subsidiary after its taxation year in which its assets were distributed to its parent; and

(c) the amount of that residual portion allocated to the taxation year of the parent in which the subsidiary's assets were distributed to it shall be determined on the assumption that the taxation year began when the assets were distributed to it.

**Technical Notes**: Where a subsidiary is wound up into its parent corporation and subsection 88(1) of the Act applies to the winding-up, the parent is considered to be a continuation of the subsidiary for the purpose of paragraphs 142.4(4)(c) and (d) of the Act. The relevant continuity provision is paragraph 87(2)(g.2) of the Act, which applies to a winding-up by reason of paragraph 88(1)(e.2). Consequently, amounts may be allocated to the parent in respect of the residual portion of the subsidiary's gains and losses from the disposition of specified debt obligations.

Subsection 9204(2) contains the following rules that ensure that no part of the residual portion of a gain or loss is taken into account in determining the income of both a parent and a subsidiary:

- The amount of the residual portion of a gain or loss allocated to the taxation year of the subsidiary in which its assets were distributed to its parent is to be determined on the assumption that the taxation year ended when the assets were distributed.

- No amount is to be allocated to any subsequent taxation year of the subsidiary.
- The amount of the residual portion of a gain or loss allocated to the taxation year of the parent in which it received the subsidiary's assets is to be determined on the assumption that the taxation year began when the assets were received.

**Related Provisions**: Reg. 9204(2.1) — Winding-up into authorized foreign bank.

### (3) Transfer of insurance business — Where

(a) subsection 138(11.5) or (11.94) of the Act has applied to the transfer of an insurance business by an insurer, and

(b) the person to whom the business was transferred is considered, because of paragraph 138(11.5)(k) of the Act, to be the same person as the insurer in respect of the residual portion of a gain or loss of the insurer from the disposition of a specified debt obligation to which subsection 142.4(4) of the Act applies,

no amount in respect of that residual portion shall be allocated to any taxation year of the insurer that ends after the insurer ceased to carry on all or substantially all of the business.

**Technical Notes**: Where an insurer has transferred an insurance business to another corporation on a rollover basis pursuant to subsection 138(11.5) or (11.94) of the Act, paragraph 138(11.5)(k) provides that, for the purpose of paragraphs 142.4(4)(c) and (d) of the Act, the transferee is considered to be a continuation of the transferor in respect of the transferred business. Consequently, amounts may be allocated to the transferee in respect of the residual portion of the transferor's gains and losses from the disposition of specified debt obligations in the course of the business. Subsection 9204(3) provides that, after the transfer of the business, amounts that are allocated to the transferee are not also to be allocated to the transferor. Since paragraph 138(11.5)(h) of the Act deems the transferor and transferee to have taxation year ends immediately before the business is transferred, special rules are not required for the taxation year of transfer.

**Notes**: Revenue Canada's view is that "all or substantially all" means 90% or more.

### (4) Transfer to new partnership — Where

subsection 98(6) of the Act deems a partnership (in this subsection referred to as the "new partnership") to be a continuation of another partnership (in this subsection referred to as the "predecessor partnership"), the following rules apply in respect of the residual portion of a gain or loss of the predecessor partnership from the disposition of a specified debt obligation to which subsection 142.4(4) of the Act applies:

(a) the amount of that residual portion allocated to the taxation year of the predecessor partnership in which its property was transferred to the new partnership shall be determined on the assumption that the taxation year ended when the property was transferred;

(b) no amount shall be allocated in respect of that residual portion to any taxation year of the predecessor partnership after its taxation year in which its property was transferred to the new partnership; and

(c) the amount of that residual portion allocated to the taxation year of the new partnership in which the predecessor partnership's property was transferred to it shall be determined on the assumption that the taxation year began when the property was transferred to it.

**Technical Notes**: Subsection 9204(4) contains rules that apply where a partnership has ceased to exist and another partnership has replaced it, in circumstances such that the continuity rule in subsection 98(6) of the Act applies. The rules are similar to those in subsection 9204(2) for the winding-up of a taxpayer into its parent corporation.

### (5) Ceasing to carry on business — Where

(a) at any time a taxpayer ceases to carry on all or substantially all of a business, otherwise than as a result of a merger to which subsection 87(2) of the Act applies, a winding-up to which subsection 88(1) of the Act applies or a transfer of the business to which subsection 98(6) or 138(11.5) or (11.94) of the Act applies,

(b) before that time, the taxpayer disposed of a specified debt obligation that was property used in the business, and

(c) subsection 142.4(4) of the Act applies to the disposition of the obligation,

there shall be allocated to the taxpayer's taxation year that includes that time the part, if any, of the residual portion of the taxpayer's gain or loss from the disposition that was not allocated to a preceding taxation year.

**Technical Notes**: Subsection 9204(5) applies where a taxpayer ceases to carry on all or substantially all of a business otherwise than because of a merger, winding-up or transfer of the business to which the rollover rules in subsection 87(2), 88(1), 98(6) or 138(11.5) or (11.94) of the Act apply. It requires the residual portion of the gain or loss from each specified debt obligation disposed of in the course of the business to be recognized in the taxation year in which the cessation occurs, except to the extent that the residual portion has been recognized in a previous year.

**Related Provisions**: Reg. 9204(5.1) — When non-resident taxpayer deemed to cease carrying on business.

**Notes**: Revenue Canada's view is that "all or substantially all" means 90% or more.

### (6) Ceasing to be a financial institution — Where

(a) at any time a taxpayer ceases to be a financial institution otherwise than because it has ceased to carry on a business,

(b) before that time, the taxpayer disposed of a specified debt obligation, and

(c) subsection 142.4(4) of the Act applies to the disposition of the obligation,

there shall be allocated to the taxpayer's taxation year that ends immediately before that time the part, if any, of the residual portion of the taxpayer's gain or loss from the disposition that was not allocated to a preceding taxation year.

**Technical Notes**: Subsection 9204(6) applies where a taxpayer ceases to be a financial institution, as defined in subsection 142.2(1) of the Act, otherwise than because it has ceased to carry on a business. This subsection would apply, for example, where a taxpayer ceases to be a financial institution because of a change in control. Subsection 9204(6) requires the residual portion of the gain or loss from each specified debt obligation that the taxpayer disposed of before it ceased to be a financial institution to be recognized in the taxation year ending immediately before it ceased to be a financial institution, except to the extent that the residual portion has been recognized in a previous year.

**Definitions [Reg. 9204]**: "amount", "business" — ITA 248(1); "disposed" — ITA 248(1)"disposition"; "disposition" — ITA 248(1); "financial institution" — ITA 142.2(1), Reg. 9200(1); "gain" — Reg. 9200(1); "insurer" — ITA 248(1); "loss" — Reg. 9200(1); "new partnership" — Reg. 9204(4); "partnership" — see Notes to ITA 96(1); "person" — ITA 248(1); "predecessor partnership" — Reg. 9204(4); "property" — ITA 248(1); "residual portion" — Reg. 9200(1); "specified debt obligation" — ITA 142.2(1), Reg. 9200(1); "subsidiary" — Reg. 9204(2); "taxation year" — ITA 249; "taxpayer" — ITA 248(1).

**Application**: The June 1, 1995 draft regulations (securities held by financial institutions), s. 9, will add Part XCII (ss. 9200 to 9204), applicable to taxation years that end after February 22, 1994.

### Proposed Addition — Reg. 9204(2.1)

**(2.1) Winding-up into authorized foreign bank** — If subsection 142.7(13) of the Act applies in respect of the winding-up of a Canadian affiliate of an entrant bank, subsection (2) applies with respect to the winding-up and, for this purpose, the references in subsection (2) to "subsection 88(1)", "taxpayer" and "parent" shall be read as references to "subsection 142.7(13)", "Canadian affiliate" and "entrant bank", respectively.

**Application**: The August 8, 2000 draft regulations, subsec. 7(1), will add subsec. 9204(2.1), applicable after June 27, 1999 in respect of an authorized foreign bank, and after August 8, 2000 in any other case.

### Proposed Amendment — Reg. 9204(5)(a)

(a) any time a taxpayer ceases to carry on all or substantially all of a business, otherwise than as a result of a merger to which subsection 87(2) of the Act applies, a winding-up to which subsection 88(1) or 142.7(13) of the Act applies or a transfer of the business to which subsection 98(6), 138(11.5) or (11.94) of the Act applies,

**Application**: The August 8, 2000 draft regulations, subsec. 7(2), will amend para. 9204(5)(a) to read as above, applicable after June 27, 1999 in respect of an authorized foreign bank, and after August 8, 2000 in any other case.

### Proposed Addition — Reg. 9204(5.1)

**(5.1) Non-resident taxpayer** — For the purpose of subsection (5), a non-resident taxpayer is considered to cease to carry on all or substantially all of a business if the taxpayer ceases to carry on, or ceases to carry on in Canada, all or substantially all of the part of the business that was carried on in Canada.

**Application**: The August 8, 2000 draft regulations, subsec. 7(3), will add subsec. 9204(5.1), applicable after June 27, 1999 in respect of an authorized foreign bank, and after August 8, 2000 in any other case.

## PART XCIII — FILM OR VIDEO PRODUCTION SERVICES TAX CREDIT [PROPOSED]

### Proposed Addition — Reg. 9300

**9300. Accredited production** — For the purpose section 125.5 of the Act, accredited production means

(a) a film or video production in respect of which the aggregate expenditures, included in the cost of the production, in the period that ends 24 months after the time that the principal filming or taping of the production began, exceeds $1,000,000, and

(b) a film or video production that is part of a series of television productions that has two or more episodes, or is a pilot program for such a series of episodes, in respect of which the aggregate expenditures included in the cost of each episode in the period that ends 24 months after the time that the principal filming or taping of the production began exceeds

(i) in the case of an episode the running time of which is less than 30 minutes, $100,000, and

(ii) in any other case, $200,000,

but does not include a production that is

(c) news, current events or public affairs programming, or a programme that includes weather or market reports,

(d) a talk show,

(e) a production in respect of a game, questionnaire or contest,

(f) a sports event or activity,

(g) a gala presentation or awards show,

(h) a production that solicits funds,

(i) reality television,

(j) pornography,

(k) advertising, or

Schedule I — Ranges of Remuneration

(l) a production produced primarily for industrial, corporate or institutional purposes.

**Application**: The October 29, 1997 draft regulations (film/video production services tax credit), s. 1, will add s. 9300, applicable on Royal Assent.

**Technical Notes**: See under ITA 125.5.

**Forms [Reg. 9300]**: T1177: Claiming a film or video production service tax credit.

**Definitions [Reg. 9300]**: "month" — *Interpretation Act* 35(1).

# SCHEDULE I — (SECS. 100, 102 AND 106) RANGES OF REMUNERATION AND OF TOTAL REMUNERATION

**1.** For the purposes of paragraph 102(1)(c), the ranges of remuneration for each pay period in a taxation year shall be determined as follows:

(a) in respect of a daily pay period, the ranges of remuneration shall commence at $33 and increase in increments of $1 for each range up to and including $86.99;

(b) in respect of a weekly pay period, the ranges of remuneration shall commence at $148 and increase in increments of

   (i) $2 for each range up to and including $255.99,

   (ii) $4 for each range from $256 to $475.99,

   (iii) $8 for each range from $476 to $915.99,

   (iv) $12 for each range from $916 to $1,575.99,

   (v) $16 for each range from $1,576 to $2,455.99, and

   (vi) $20 for each range from $2,456 to $3,555.99;

(c) in respect of a bi-weekly pay period, the ranges of remuneration shall commence at $296 and increase in increments of

   (i) $4 for each range up to and including $511.99,

   (ii) $8 for each range from $512 to $951.99,

   (iii) $16 for each range from $952 to $1,831.99,

   (iv) $24 for each range from $1,832 to $3,151.99,

   (v) $32 for each range from $3,152 to $4,911.99, and

   (vi) $40 for each range from $4,912 to $7,111.99;

(d) in respect of a semi-monthly pay period, the ranges of remuneration shall commence at $321 and increase in increments of

   (i) $4 for each range up to and including $536.99,

   (ii) $8 for each range from $537 to $976.99,

   (iii) $18 for each range from $977 to $1,966.99,

   (iv) $26 for each range from $1,967 to $3,396.99,

   (v) $34 for each range from $3,397 to $5,266.99, and

   (vi) $44 for each range from $5,267 to $7,686.99;

(e) in respect of 12 monthly pay periods, the ranges of remuneration shall commence at $642 and increase in increments of

   (i) $8 for each range up to and including $1,073.99,

   (ii) $18 for each range from $1,074 to $2,063.99,

   (iii) $34 for each range from $2,064 to $3,933.99,

   (iv) $52 for each range from $3,934 to $6,793.99,

   (v) $70 for each range from $6,794 to $10,643.99, and

   (vi) $86 for each range from $10,644 to $15,373.99;

(f) in respect of 10 monthly pay periods, the ranges of remuneration shall commence at $769 and increase in increments of

   (i) $10 for each range up to and including $1,308.99,

   (ii) $20 for each range from $1,309 to $2,408.99,

   (iii) $42 for each range from $2,409 to $4,718.99,

   (iv) $62 for each range from $4,719 to $8,128.99,

   (v) $84 for each range from $8,129 to $12,748.99, and

   (vi) $104 for each range from $12,749 to $18,468.99;

(g) in respect of four-week pay periods, the ranges of remuneration shall commence at $591 and increase in increments of

   (i) $8 for each range up to and including $1,022.99,

   (ii) $16 for each range from $1,023 to $1,902.99,

   (iii) $32 for each range from $1,903 to $3,662.99,

   (iv) $48 for each range from $3,663 to $6,302.99,

   (v) $64 for each range from $6,303 to $9,822.99, and

   (vi) $80 for each range from $9,823 to $14,222.99; and

(h) in respect of 22 pay periods per annum, the ranges of remuneration shall commence at $350 and increase in increments of

   (i) $5 for each range up to and including $619.99,

   (ii) $10 for each range from $620 to $1,169.99,

   (iii) $18 for each range from $1,170 to $2,159.99,

   (iv) $28 for each range from $2,160 to $3,699.99,

   (v) $38 for each range from $3,700 to $5,789.99, and

   (vi) $48 for each range from $5,790 to $8,429.99.

**Notes**: Paras. 1(a)–(h) amended by P.C. 1999-2205, effective January and July 1999, to implement the 1999 federal budget measures which eliminated the basic supplementary personal tax credit and increased the basic personal exemption amount. For Jan.–June 1999, subtract amounts from each bracket cutoff as follows: para. (a), $3; (b) $14; (c) $27; (d) $30; (e) $59; (f) $70; (g) $54; (h) $32. For July–Dec. 1998, add back these amounts from to bracket cutoff: para. (a), $2; (b) $10; (c) $20; (d) $24; (e) $48; (f) $50; (g) $40; (h) $25.

Paras. 1(a)–(h) amended by P.C. 1998-2771, effective July 1998, to reflect the 1998 federal budget changes that eliminated the federal surtax for most taxpayers. From 1996 through June 1998, subtract amounts from each bracket cutoff as follows: para. (a), $2; (b) $10; (c) $20; (d) $25; (e) $48; (f) $50; (g) $40; (h) $25 (e.g. $331 to $600.99). The increments in each bracket did not change.

Para. 1(d) amended by P.C. 1996-501, effective 1996, to subtract $1 from each bracket cutoff to reflect an increase in CPP contributions and decrease in UI premiums. Previously amended by P.C. 1004-1370 to add $1 to each bracket cutoff effective 1994, to reflect slightly higher CPP contributions and UI premiums. See also Notes at end of Schedule I.

**Definitions**: "pay period", "remuneration" — Reg. 100(1); "taxation year" — ITA 249.

**2.** For the purposes of paragraph 102(2)(e), the ranges of remuneration for a taxation year shall commence at $9,400 and increase in increments of

   (a) $1,000 for each range up to and including $18,399.99;

   (b) $2,000 for each range from $18,400 to $58,399.99;

   (c) $3,000 for each range from $58,400 to $73,399.99;

   (d) $4,000 for each range from $73,400 to $93,399.99;

   (e) $5,000 for each range from $93,400 to $118,399.99;

   (f) $6,000 for each range from $118,400 to $148,399.99;

   (g) $7,000 for each range from $148,400 to $183,399.99;

   (h) $8,000 for each range from $183,400 to $223,399.99;

   (i) $9,000 for each range from $223,400 to $268,399.99;

   (j) $10,000 for each range from $268,400 to $318,399.99;

   (k) $20,000 for each range from $318,400 to $418,399.99; and

   (l) $30,000 for each range from $418,400 to $568,399.99.

**Notes**: S. 2 amended by P.C. 1999-2205, effective January and July 1999, to implement the 1999 federal budget measures. Previously amended by P.C. 1998-2271, effective July 1998, to reflect the 1998 federal budget changes. For Jan.–June 1999, subtract $700 from each bracket. For July–Dec. 1998, add back $400 to each bracket. From 1992 through June 1998, subtract $400 from each bracket (i.e., they go from $8,300 to $567,299.99). See also Notes at end of Schedule I.

**Definitions**: "remuneration" — Reg. 100(1); "taxation year" — ITA 249.

**3.** For the purposes of paragraph 102(2)(e), the ranges of personal credits and expenses for a taxation year shall commence at $1,500 and increase in increments of

   (a) $1,000 for each range up to and including $4,499.99;

   (b) $2,000 for each range from $4,500 to $8,499.99;

   (c) $2,500 for each range from $8,500 to $13,499.99;

   (d) $3,000 for each range from $13,500 to $19,499.99;

   (e) $3,500 for each range from $19,500 to $26,499.99;

   (f) $4,000 for each range from $26,500 to $34,499.99;

   (g) $4,500 for each range from $34,500 to $43,499.99;

   (h) $5,000 for each range from $43,500 to $53,499.99; and

   (i) $5,500 for each range from $53,500 to $58,999.99.

**Definitions [Reg. Sch. I:3]**: "personal credits" — Reg. 100(1); "taxation year" — ITA 249.

**Notes [Schedule I]**: Schedule I amended by P.C. 1992-291, effective July 1, 1991, and by P.C. 1992-2347, effective 1992, to update all of the dollar amounts. The tax rates stayed the same from 1992 to 1999 because inflation did not exceed 3%; see ITA 117.1(1)(d). See also Notes to ss. 1 and 2 above for changes since 1994.

# SCHEDULE II — CAPITAL COST ALLOWANCES

## Class 1 — (4 per cent)

[Reg. 1100(1)(a)(i), 1100(1)(za.1), (zc)(i)(A), (B)]

Property not included in any other class that is

(a) a bridge;

Cl. 1 — (4 per cent)

(b) a canal;

(c) a culvert;

(d) a dam;

(e) a jetty acquired before May 26, 1976;

(f) a mole acquired before May 26, 1976;

(g) a road, sidewalk, airplane runway, parking area, storage area or similar surface construction, acquired before May 26, 1976;

(h) railway track and grading, including components such as rails, ballast, ties and other track material,

    (i) that is not part of a railway system, or

    (ii) that was acquired after May 25, 1976;

(i) railway traffic control or signalling equipment, acquired after May 25, 1976, including switching, block signalling, interlocking, crossing protection, detection, speed control or retarding equipment, but not including property that is principally electronic equipment or systems software therefor;

(j) a subway or tunnel, acquired after May 25, 1976.

(k) electrical generating equipment (except as specified elsewhere in this Schedule);

(l) a pipeline, other than gas or oil well equipment, unless, in the case of a pipeline for oil or natural gas, the Minister, in consultation with the Minister of Energy, Mines and Resources, is or has been satisfied that the main source of supply for the pipeline is or was likely to be exhausted within 15 years after the date on which operation of the pipeline commenced;

(m) the generating or distributing equipment and plant (including structures) of a producer or distributor of electrical energy;

(n) manufacturing and distributing equipment and plant (including structures) acquired primarily for the production or distribution of gas, except

    (i) a property acquired for the purpose of producing or distributing gas that is normally distributed in portable containers,

    (ii) a property acquired for the purpose of processing natural gas, before the delivery of such gas to a distribution system, or

    (iii) a property acquired for the purpose of producing oxygen or nitrogen;

(o) the distributing equipment and plant (including structures) of a distributor of water;

(p) the production and distributing equipment and plant (including structures) of a distributor of heat; or

(q) a building or other structure, or part thereof, including component parts such as electric wiring, plumbing, sprinkler systems, air-conditioning equipment, heating equipment, lighting fixtures, elevators and escalators.

**Notes**: Para. 1(k) amended by P.C. 1997-1033, retroactive to property acquired after 1987, to add the parenthetical exclusion.

### Proposed Amendment — Electrical generating equipment and heat or water production and distribution equipment

**Federal budget, supplementary information, February 28, 2000**: *Electrical Generating Equipment, and Heat or Water Production and Distribution Equipment*

Currently, the electrical generating equipment of a producer of electrical energy is generally eligible for a 4-per-cent CCA rate under Class 1 of Schedule II to the *Income Tax Regulations*. The production and distribution equipment of a distributor of heat or water are also generally eligible for this rate under Class 1.

*Current CCA Treatment*

Class 1 of Schedule II to the *Income Tax Regulations* includes:

- electrical generating equipment described in paragraph (k), or described in paragraph (m) as "generating or distributing equipment and plant (including structures) of a producer or distributor of electrical energy"; and

- production and distribution equipment described in paragraphs (o) as "distributing equipment and plant (including structures) of a distributor of water" or (p) as "production and distributing equipment and plant (including structures) of a distributor of heat."

Industry consultations have established that this rate no longer reflects the estimated useful life of such equipment. The budget proposes that the CCA rate be increased from 4 per cent to 8 per cent for the following equipment currently included in Class 1:

- electrical generating equipment (other than buildings and other structures),

- production and distribution equipment (other than buildings and other structures) of a producer or distributor of heat, and

- distribution equipment (other than buildings and other structures) for a distributor of water (other than for consumption, disposal or treatment).

The 8-per-cent rate will apply to equipment acquired after February 27, 2000, that has not been used or acquired for use prior to that date.

It is further proposed that combustion turbines that generate electricity (and any associated burners and compressors) be eligible for a separate class election. The general rule which would otherwise require the property to be transferred into the general UCC pool after five years will not apply.

The separate class election will only apply to equipment acquired after February 27, 2000, that has not been used or acquired for use prior to that date. The proposed election must be filed with the income tax return for the taxation year in which the property is acquired.

**Related Provisions**: Reg. 1101(5e), (5e.1) — Separate classes; 4600(1)(a), 4600(2)(a) — Qualified property; 4601(a)(i), (ii) — Qualified transportation equipment; 4604(1)(a), 4604(2)(a) — Approved project property.

**Definitions [Reg. Sch. II:Cl. 1]**: "building" — Reg 1102(5), (5.1); "class" — Reg. 1102 (1)–(3), (14), (14.1); "gas or oil well equipment" — Reg. 1104(2); "Minister", "property" — ITA 248(1); "railway system" — Reg. 1104(2); "structure" — Reg 1102(5), (5.1); "systems software" — Reg. 1104(2).

**Interpretation Bulletins**: IT-79R3: CCA — Buildings or other structures; IT-195R4: Rental property — CCA restrictions; IT-304R2: Condominiums; IT-367R3: CCA — multiple-unit residential buildings; IT-482: Pipelines.

## Class 2 — (6 per cent)
[Reg. 1100(1)(a)(ii)]

Property that is

(a) electrical generating equipment (except as specified elsewhere in this Schedule);

(b) a pipeline, other than gas or oil well equipment, unless, in the case of a pipeline for oil or natural gas, the Minister in consultation with the Minister of Energy, Mines and Resources, is or has been satisfied that the main source of supply for the pipeline is or was likely to be exhausted within 15 years from the date on which operation of the pipeline commenced;

(c) the generating or distributing equipment and plant (including structures) of a producer or distributor of electrical energy, except a property included in Class 10, 13, 14, 26 or 28;

(d) manufacturing and distributing equipment and plant (including structures) acquired primarily for the production or distribution of gas, except

(i) a property included in Class 10, 13 or 14

(ii) a property acquired for the purpose of producing or distributing gas that is normally distributed in portable containers,

(iii) a property acquired for the purpose of processing natural gas, before delivery of such gas to a distribution system, or

(iv) a property acquired for the purpose of producing oxygen or nitrogen;

(e) the distributing equipment and plant (including structures) of a distributor of water, except a property included in Class 10, 13 or 14; or

(f) the production and distributing equipment and plant (including structures) of a distributor of heat, except a property included in Class 10, 13 or 14

acquired by the taxpayer

(g) before 1988, or

(h) before 1990

(i) pursuant to an obligation in writing entered into by the taxpayer before June 18, 1987,

(ii) that was under construction by or on behalf of the taxpayer on June 18, 1987, or

(iii) that is machinery or equipment that is a fixed and integral part of a building, structure, plant facility or other property that was under construction by or on behalf of the taxpayer on June 18, 1987.

**Related Provisions**: Reg. 1101(5i) — Separate class for certain pipelines; Reg. 1103(2); 4600(2)(a) — Qualified property; 4604(2)(a) — Approved project property.

**Definitions [Reg. Sch. II:Cl. 2]**: "building" — Reg 1102(5), (5.1); "gas or oil well equipment" — Reg. 1104(2); "Minister", "property" — ITA 248(1); "structure" — Reg 1102(5), (5.1); "taxpayer" — ITA 248(1); "writing" — *Interpretation Act* 35(1).

**Interpretation Bulletins**: IT-482: Pipelines.

## Class 3 — (5 per cent)
[Reg. 1100(1)(a)(iii), 1100(1)(sb), (za.2), (zc)(i)(C)]

Property not included in any other class that is

(a) a building or other structure, or part thereof, including component parts such as electric wiring, plumbing, sprinkler systems, air-conditioning equipment, heating equipment, lighting fixtures, elevators and escalators, acquired by the taxpayer

(i) before 1988, or

(ii) before 1990

(A) pursuant to an obligation in writing entered into by the taxpayer before June 18, 1987,

(B) that was under construction by or on behalf of the taxpayer on June 18, 1987, or

(C) that is a component part of a building that was under construction by or on behalf of the taxpayer on June 18, 1987;

(b) a breakwater;

(c) a dock;

(d) a trestle;

(e) a windmill;

(f) a wharf;

(g) an addition or alteration, made during the period that is after March 31, 1967 and before 1988, to a building that would have been included in this class during that period but for the fact that it was included in Class 20;

(h) a jetty acquired after May 25, 1976;

(i) a mole acquired after May 25, 1976;

(j) telephone, telegraph or data communication equipment, acquired after May 25, 1976, that is a wire or cable;

(k) an addition or alteration, other than an addition or alteration described in paragraph (k) of Class 6, made after 1987, to a building included, in whole or in part,

(i) in this class,

(ii) in Class 6 by virtue of subparagraph (a)(viii) thereof, or

(iii) in Class 20,

to the extent that the aggregate cost of all such additions or alterations to the building does not exceed the lesser of

(iv) $500,000, and

(v) 25 per cent of the aggregate of the amounts that would, but for this paragraph, be the capital cost of the building and any additions or alterations thereto included in this class or Class 6 or 20; or

(l) ancillary to a wire or cable referred to in paragraph (j) or Class 42 and that is supporting equipment such as a pole, mast, tower, conduit, brace, crossarm, guy or insulator.

**Related Provisions**: Reg. 1101(5e.2), (5f) — Railway trestles — separate classes; 1102(15)(a), 1103(2f); 4600(1)(a) — Qualified property; 4601(a)(iii) — Qualified transportation equipment; 4604(1)(a) — Approved project property.

**Notes**: 3(j) amended by P.C. 1994-139, effective for property acquired after December 23, 1991, other than property acquired pursuant to an agreement in writing entered into before December 24, 1991. For earlier property, as well as "(i) a wire or cable", read:

(ii) supporting equipment such as a pole, mast, tower, conduit, brace, crossarm, guy or insulator that is ancillary to a wire or cable referred to in subparagraph (i); or

3(l) added by P.C. 1994-139, effective for property acquired after December 23, 1991, other than property acquired pursuant to an agreement in writing entered into by the taxpayer before December 24, 1991. However, if the taxpayer so elects in a letter filed with Revenue Canada by August 8, 1994 or in a letter filed with the taxpayer's return for the first taxation year ending after December 23, 1991, then Reg. 1100(1)(a)(xxviii), amended Classes 3(j) and (l) and Class 42 apply to property acquired after the beginning of that taxation year. If the taxpayer makes such election, ignore the words "or Class 42" in 3(l) and ignore Class 42, with respect to property acquired before December 24, 1991. In any event, with respect to property acquired from December 24, 1991 through February 8, 1994, ignore the words "or Class 42" in 3(l).

**Definitions [Reg. Sch. II:Cl. 3]**: "amount" — ITA 248(1); "building" — Reg 1102(5), (5.1); "class" — Reg. 1102 (1)–(3), (14), (14.1); "property" — ITA 248(1); "structure" — Reg 1102(5), (5.1); "taxpayer" — ITA 248(1); "writing" — Interpretation Act 35(1).

**Interpretation Bulletins**: IT-79R3: CCA — buildings or other structures; IT-195R4: Rental property — CCA restrictions; IT-367R3: CCA — multiple-unit residential buildings.

## Class 4 — (6 per cent)
[Reg. 1100(1)(a)(iv)]

Property that would otherwise be included in another class in this Schedule that is

(a) a railway system or a part thereof, except automotive equipment not designed to run on rails or tracks, that was acquired after the end of the taxpayer's 1958 taxation year and before May 26, 1976; or

(b) a tramway or trolley bus system or a part thereof, except property included in class 10, 13 or 14.

**Related Provisions**: Reg. 1102(10)(a), 1103(2), 1104(2)"tramway or trolley bus system".

**Definitions [Reg. Sch. II:Cl. 4]**: "class" — Reg. 1102 (1)–(3), (14), (14.1); "property" — ITA 248(1); "railway system" — Reg. 1104(2); "taxation year" — ITA 249; "taxpayer" — ITA 248(1); "tramway or trolley bus system" — Reg. 1104(2).

## Class 5 — (10 per cent)
[Reg. 1100(1)(a)(v)]

Property that is

(a) a chemical pulp mill or ground wood pulp mill including buildings, machinery and equipment, but not including hydro-electric power plants and their equipment, or

(b) an integrated mill producing chemical pulp or ground wood pulp and manufacturing therefrom paper, paper board or pulp board, including buildings, machinery and equipment, but not including hydro-electric power plants and their equipment,

but not including any property that was acquired after the end of the taxpayer's 1962 taxation year.

**Definitions [Reg. Sch. II:Cl. 5]**: "building" — Reg 1102(5), (5.1); "property" — ITA 248(1); "taxation year" — ITA 249; "taxpayer" — ITA 248(1).

## Class 6 — (10 per cent)
[Reg. 1100(1)(a)(vi), 1100(1)(sb), (zc)(i)(D)]

Property not included in any other class that is

(a) a building of

(i) frame,

(ii) log,

(iii) stucco on frame,

(iv) galvanized iron, or

(v) corrugated metal,

construction, including component parts such as electric wiring, plumbing, sprinkler systems, air-conditioning equipment, heating equipment, lighting fixtures, elevators and escalators, if the building

(vi) is used by the taxpayer for the purpose of gaining or producing income from farming or fishing,

(vii) has no footings or any other base support below ground level,

(viii) was acquired by the taxpayer before 1979 and is not a building described in subparagraph (vi) or (vii),

(ix) was acquired by the taxpayer after 1978 under circumstances such that

(A) he was obligated to acquire the building under the terms of an agreement in writing entered into before 1979, and

(B) the installation of footings or any other base support of the building was commenced before 1979, or

(x) was acquired by the taxpayer after 1978 under circumstances such that

(A) he commenced construction of the building before 1979, or

(B) the construction of the building was commenced under the terms of an agreement in writing entered into by him before 1979, and the installation of footings or any other base support of the building was commenced before 1979;

(b) a wooden breakwater;

(c) a fence;

(d) a greenhouse;

(e) an oil or water storage tank;

(f) a railway tank car acquired before May 26, 1976;

(g) a wooden wharf;

(h) an aeroplane hangar acquired after the end of the taxpayer's 1958 taxation year;

(i) an addition or alteration, made

(A) during the period that is after March 31, 1967 and before 1979, or

(B) after 1978 if the taxpayer was obligated to have it made under the terms of an agreement in writing entered into before 1979,

to a building that would have been included in this class during that period but for the fact that it was included in Class 20;

(j) a railway locomotive acquired after May 25, 1976, but not including an automotive railway car; or

**Proposed Amendment — Railway locomotives**
Federal budget, supplementary information, February 28, 2000: [See under Class 35 — ed.]

(k) an addition or alteration, made after 1978 to a building included in this class by virtue of subparagraph (a)(viii), to the extent that the aggregate cost of all such additions and alterations to the building does not exceed $100,000.

**Related Provisions**: Reg. 1102(15)(a), 1103(2f); 4600(1)(a) — Qualified property; 4601(b)(i) — Qualified transportation equipment; 4604(1)(a) — Approved project property.

**Notes**: 6(a)(v) changed from "corrugated iron" to "corrugated metal" by P.C. 1994-139, effective for 1989 and later taxation years with respect to property acquired after 1987.

**Definitions [Reg. Sch. II:Cl. 6]**: "building" — Reg 1102(5), (5.1); "class" — Reg. 1102 (1)–(3), (14), (14.1); "farming", "fishing", "property" — ITA 248(1); "taxation year" — ITA 249; "taxpayer" — ITA 248(1); "writing" — *Interpretation Act* 35(1).

**Interpretation Bulletins**: IT-79R3: CCA — buildings or other structures; IT-195R4: Rental property — CCA restrictions; IT-367R3: CCA — multiple-unit residential buildings.

## Class 7 — (15 per cent)
[Reg. 1100(1)(a)(vii)]

Property that is

(a) a canoe or rowboat;

(b) a scow;

(c) a vessel, but not including a vessel

(i) of a separate class prescribed by subsection 1101(2a), or

(ii) included in Class 41;

(d) furniture, fittings and equipment attached to a property included in this class, but not including radiocommunication equipment;

(e) a spare engine for a property included in this class;

(f) a marine railway; or

(g) a vessel under construction, other than a vessel included in Class 41.

**Related Provisions**: Reg. 1101(2), (2b) — Separate class for certain property in Class 7; Reg. 4601(e)(i), (ii) — Qualified transportation equipment.

**Definitions [Reg. Sch. II:Cl. 7]**: "class" — Reg. 1102(1)–(3), (14), (14.1); "prescribed", "property" — ITA 248(1).

**Interpretation Bulletins**: IT-267R2: CCA — vessels; IT-317R: Radio and television equipment.

## Class 8 — (20 per cent)
[Reg. 1100(1)(a)(viii), 1100(1)(sb), (zc)(i)(E), (F)]

Property not included in Class 1, 2, 7, 9, 11 or 30 that is

**Proposed Amendment — Reg. Sch. II:Cl. 8 opening words**
Letter from Department of Finance, October 1, 1999:

Dear [xxx]

Thank you for your letter of September 23, 1999 to Kerry Harnish of this Division concerning paragraph (q) of Class 1 and Class 8 of Schedule II to the *Income Tax Regulations* (the "Regulations").

In your letter, you ask whether manufacturing or processing property described in Class 8 can include a component part of a building or structure to which Class 1 applies, given that the preamble to Class 8 excludes from Class 8 property included in Class 1. The exclusion of Class 1 property from Class 8 occurs as a result of amendments to Class 1 and Class 8 promulgated in P.C. 1997-1033, SOR/97-377 registered July 28, 1997, applicable to property acquired after 1987.

In your letter, you note that the *Regulatory Impact Assessment Statement* accompanying the 1997 amendments states:

Further, Class 8 is amended to clarify that it does not apply to property included in Class 1. Class 1 was amended as a consequence of the 1987 tax reform to apply to certain property previously included in Class 2 to which Class 8 also cannot apply.

Property previously included in Class 2 includes electrical generating equipment, but after 1987 tax reform such property is included in paragraph (k) of Class 1 (except as specified elsewhere in Schedule II to the Regulations). However, you note in your letter that "buildings and other structures" were previously included in Class 3, but after 1987 tax reform are included in paragraph (q) of Class 1. Given that the 1997 amendments provided that property cannot be included in Class 8 if included in Class 1, you are concerned that the amendments could result in a building or other structure (including component parts) being excluded from Class 8 notwithstanding that such property could be manufacturing or processing property (or a building) otherwise included in Class 8.

Cl. 8 — (20 per cent)   Reg. Cl. 8

With respect to electrical generating equipment and property referred to in paragraphs (m) to (p) of Class 1, including property that is a structure or a component part of a building, we are not prepared to recommend that the Regulations be amended. As mentioned in your letter, the express policy underlying the 1987 amendments was to reduce the capital cost allowance rate from 6% to 4%, computed on a declining balance basis, for such property (except, for example, electrical generating equipment referred to in paragraphs (f), (g), and (h) of Class 8). This policy was confirmed in the changes made to Class 1 and Class 8 by P.C. 1997-1033, S0R/97-377 registered July 28, 1997.

However, with respect to buildings or other structures to which paragraph (q) of Class 1 could apply (including component parts of a building that are not included in paragraphs (k) and (m) to (p) of Class 1), we agree that the preamble to Class 8 should not automatically preclude inclusion in Class 8 if the property is property to which paragraph (a) to (e) of Class 8 applies. This approach is consistent with the overall policy underlying the amendments made in 1987 to property described in Classes 1 to 3 of Schedule II to the Regulations. We are therefore prepared to recommend that the Regulations be amended to address this aspect of your concern, and that this change be applicable to property acquired after 1987.

Thank you for bringing this matter to our attention.

Yours sincerely,

Len Farber

General Director, Tax Legislation Division, Tax Policy Branch

(a) a structure that is manufacturing or processing machinery or equipment;

(b) tangible property attached to a building and acquired solely for the purpose of

   (i) servicing, supporting, or providing access to or egress from, machinery or equipment,

   (ii) manufacturing or processing, or

   (iii) any combination of the functions described in subparagraphs (i) and (ii);

(c) a building that is a kiln, tank or vat, acquired for the purpose of manufacturing or processing;

(d) a building or other structure, acquired after February 19, 1973, that is designed for the purpose of preserving ensilage on a farm;

(e) a building or other structure, acquired after February 19, 1973, that is

   (i) designed to store fresh fruits or fresh vegetables at a controlled level of temperature and humidity, and

   (ii) to be used principally for the purpose of storing fresh fruits or fresh vegetables by or for the person or persons by whom they were grown;

(f) electrical generating equipment acquired after May 25, 1976, if

   (i) the taxpayer is not a person whose business is the production for the use of or distribution to others of electrical energy,

   (ii) the equipment is auxiliary to the taxpayer's main power supply, and

   (iii) the equipment is not used regularly as a source of supply;

(g) electrical generating equipment, acquired after May 25, 1976, that has a maximum load capacity of not more than 15 kilowatts;

(h) portable electrical generating equipment acquired after May 25, 1976;

(i) a tangible capital property that is not included in another class in this Schedule except

   (i) land or any part thereof or any interest therein,

   (ii) an animal,

   (iii) a tree, shrub, herb or similar growing thing,

   (iv) an oil or gas well,

   (v) a mine,

   (vi) a specified temporary access road of the taxpayer,

   (vii) radium,

   (viii) a right of way,

   (ix) a timber limit,

   (x) a tramway track, or

   (xi) property of a separate class prescribed by subsection 1101(2a);

(j) property not included in any other class that is radiocommunication equipment acquired after May 25, 1976;

(k) a rapid transit car that is used for the purpose of public transportation within a metropolitan area and is not part of a railway system;

(l) an outdoor advertising poster panel or bulletin board; or

(m) a greenhouse constructed of a rigid frame and a replaceable, flexible plastic cover.

**Related Provisions**: Reg. 1101(5l), (5p), 1103(2g) — Separate class for certain equipment; Reg. 1102(15)(b), 1103(2a) — Election to include property in Class 8; 1104(2) — Definition of "specified temporary access road"; 4600(2)(c) — Qualified property; 4601(a)(iv), 4601(b)(ii), 4601(c)(ii), 4601(e)(ii), 4601(g) — Qualified transportation equipment; 4604(1)(a), 4604(2)(c) — Approved project property; *Interpretation Act* 35(1) — Definition of "radiocommunication".

**Notes**: 8(i) is the "catch-all" for property (such as furniture) which is not listed in any other class.

Reference to Class 1 added to opening words of Cl. 8 by P.C. 1997-1033, retroactive to property acquired after 1987. (This was due to the amendment to Cl. 1(k).)

8(i)(iv) amended by P.C. 1999-629, effective for property acquired after March 6, 1996, to change "gas well" to "oil or gas well". ("Oil well" was formerly in 8(1)(vi).)

8(i)(vi) amended by P.C. 1999-629, effective for property acquired after March 6, 1996, to change "oil well" to "specified temporary access road of the taxpayer". ("Oil well" was moved to 8(1)(iv).) See Notes to Reg. 1104(2) "specified temporary access road".

8(m) added by P.C. 1994-139, effective for 1989 and later taxation years with respect to property acquired after 1987.

**Definitions [Reg. Sch. II:Cl. 8]**: "building" — Reg 1102(5), (5.1); "business" — ITA 248(1); "capital property" — ITA 54, 248(1); "class" — Reg. 1102 (1)–(3), (14), (14.1); "oil or gas well", "person", "prescribed"; "property" — ITA 248(1); "railway system" — Reg. 1104(2); "specified temporary access road" — Reg. 1104(2); "structure" — Reg 1102(5), (5.1); "taxpayer" — ITA 248(1).

**Interpretation Bulletins**: IT-79R3: CCA — buildings and other structures; IT-317R: Radio and television equipment; IT-472: Class 8 property; IT-482: Pipelines.

### Class 9 — (25 per cent)
[Reg. 1100(1)(a)(ix)]

Property acquired before May 26, 1976, other than property included in Class 30, that is

(a) electrical generating equipment, if

(i) the taxpayer is not a person whose business is the production for the use of or distribution to others of electrical energy,

(ii) the equipment is auxiliary to the taxpayer's main power supply, and

(iii) the equipment is not used regularly as a source of supply,

(b) radar equipment,

(c) radio transmission equipment,

(d) radio receiving equipment,

(e) electrical generating equipment that has a maximum load capacity of not more than 15 kilowatts, or

(f) portable electrical generating equipment,

and property acquired after May 25, 1976 that is

(g) an aircraft;

(h) furniture, fittings or equipment attached to an aircraft; or

(i) a spare part for an aircraft, or for furniture, fittings or equipment attached to an aircraft.

**Related Provisions**: Reg. 4600(2)(i) — Qualified property; 4601(f) — Qualified transportation equipment; 4604(2)(h) — Approved project; *Interpretation Act* 35(1) — Definition of "radio".

**Definitions [Reg. Sch. II:Cl. 9]**: "business", "person", "property" — ITA 248(1); "radio" — *Interpretation Act* 35(1); "taxpayer" — ITA 248(1).

**Interpretation Bulletins**: IT-317R: Radio and television equipment.

### Class 10 — (30 per cent)
[Reg. 1100(1)(a)(x), 1100(1)(zc)(i)(G)]

Property not included in any other class that is

(a) automotive equipment, including a trolley bus, but not including

(i) an automotive railway car acquired after May 25, 1976,

(ii) a railway locomotive, or

(iii) a tramcar,

(b) a portable tool acquired after May 25, 1976, for the purpose of earning rental income for short terms, such as hourly, daily, weekly or monthly, except a property described in Class 12,

(c) harness or stable equipment,

(d) a sleigh or wagon,

(e) a trailer, including a trailer designed to be hauled on both highways and railway tracks,

(f) general-purpose electronic data processing equipment and systems software therefor, including ancillary data processing equipment, acquired after May 25, 1976, but not including property that is principally or is used principally as

(i) electronic process control or monitor equipment,

(ii) electronic communications control equipment,

(iii) systems software for a property referred to in subparagraph (i) or (ii), or

(iv) data handling equipment unless it is ancillary to general-purpose electronic data processing equipment,

(f.1) a designated underground storage cost, or

(f.2) an unmanned telecommunication spacecraft designed to orbit above the earth,

and property (other than property included in Class 41 or property included in Class 43 that is described in paragraph (b) of that Class) that would otherwise be included in another Class in this Schedule, that is

(g) a building or other structure (other than property described in paragraph (l) or (m)) that would otherwise be included in Class 1, 3 or 6 and that was acquired for the purpose of gaining or producing income from a mine, except

(i) a property included in Class 28,

(ii) a property acquired principally for the purpose of gaining or producing income from the processing of ore from a mineral resource that is not owned by the taxpayer,

(iii) an office building not situated on the mine property, or

(iv) a refinery that was acquired by the taxpayer

(A) before November 8, 1969, or

(B) after November 7, 1969 and that had been used before November 8, 1969 by any person with whom the taxpayer was not dealing at arm's length;

(h) contractor's movable equipment, including portable camp buildings, acquired for use in a construction business or for lease to another taxpayer for use in that other taxpayer's construction business, except a property included in

(i) this Class by virtue of paragraph (t),

(ii) a separate class prescribed by subsection 1101(2b), or

(iii) Class 22 or 38;

(i) a floor of a roller skating rink;

(j) gas or oil well equipment;

(k) property (other than a property included in Class 28 or property described in paragraph (l) or (m)) that was acquired for the purpose of gaining or producing income from a mine and that is

(i) a structure that would otherwise be included in Class 8, or

(ii) machinery or equipment,

except a property acquired before May 9, 1972 for the purpose of gaining or producing income from the processing of ore after extraction from a mineral resource that is not owned by the taxpayer;

(l) property acquired after the 1971 taxation year for the purpose of gaining or producing income from a mine and providing services to the mine or to a community where a substantial proportion of the persons who ordinarily work at the mine reside, if such property is

(i) an airport, dam, dock, fire hall, hospital, house, natural gas pipeline, power line, recreational facility, school, sewage disposal plant, sewer, street lighting system, town hall, water pipeline, water pumping station, water system, wharf or similar property,

(ii) a road, sidewalk, aeroplane runway, parking area, storage area or similar surface construction, or

(iii) machinery or equipment ancillary to any of the property described in subparagraph (i) or (ii),

but is not

(iv) a property included in Class 28, or

(v) a railway not situated on the mine property;

(m) property acquired after March 31, 1977, principally for the purpose of gaining or producing income from a mine, if such property is

(i) railway track and grading including components such as rails, ballast, ties and other track material,

(ii) property ancillary to the track referred to in subparagraph (i) that is

(A) railway traffic control or signalling equipment, including switching, block signalling, interlocking, crossing protection, detection, speed control or retarding equipment, or

(B) a bridge, culvert, subway, trestle or tunnel,

(iii) machinery or equipment ancillary to any of the property referred to in subparagraph (i) or (ii), or

(iv) conveying, loading, unloading or storing machinery or equipment, including a structure, acquired for the purpose of shipping output from the mine by means of the track referred to in subparagraph (i),

but is not

(v) property included in Class 28, or

(vi) for greater certainty, rolling stock;

(n) property that was acquired for the purpose of cutting and removing merchantable timber from a timber limit and that will be of no further use to the taxpayer after all merchantable timber that the taxpayer is entitled to cut and remove from the limit has been cut and removed, unless the taxpayer has elected to include another property of this kind in another class in this Schedule;

(o) mechanical equipment acquired for logging operations, except a property included in Class 7;

(p) an access road or trail for the protection of standing timber against fire, insects or disease;

(q) property acquired for a motion picture drive-in theatre;

(r) property included in this class by virtue of subsection 1102(8) or (9), except a property included in Class 28;

(s) a motion picture film or video tape acquired after May 25, 1976, except a property included in paragraph (w) or in Class 12;

> **Proposed Amendment — Class 10(s)**
> (s) a motion picture film or video-tape acquired after May 25, 1976, except a property included in paragraph (w) or (x) or in Class 12,
>
> **Application:** The December 12, 1995 draft regulations (Canadian film tax credit), subsec. 5(1), will amend para. (s) of Class 10 to read as above, applicable to 1995 et seq.

(t) a property acquired after May 22, 1979 that is designed principally for the purpose of

(i) determining the existence, location, extent or quality of accumulations of petroleum or natural gas,

(ii) drilling oil or gas wells, or

(iii) determining the existence, location, extent or quality of mineral resources,

except a property included in a separate class prescribed by subsection 1101(2b);

(u) property acquired after 1980 to be used primarily in the processing in Canada of heavy crude oil recovered from a natural reservoir in Canada to a stage that is not beyond the crude oil stage or its equivalent that is

(i) property that would otherwise be included in Class 8 except railway rolling stock or a property described in paragraph (j) of Class 8,

(ii) an oil or water storage tank,

(iii) a powered industrial lift truck that would otherwise be included in paragraph (a), or

(iv) property that would otherwise be included in paragraph (f);

(v) property acquired after August 31, 1984 that is equipment used for the purpose of effecting an interface between a cable distribution system and electronic products used by consumers of that system and that is designed primarily

(i) to augment the channel capacity of a television receiver or radio,

(ii) to decode pay television or other signals provided on a discretionary basis, or

(iii) to achieve any combination of functions described in subparagraphs (i) and (ii); or

(w) a certified production acquired after 1987.

**Proposed Amendment — Class 10(w), (x)**

(w) a certified production acquired after 1987 and before March 1996, or

(x) a Canadian film or video production.

**Application**: The December 12, 1995 draft regulations (Canadian film tax credit), subsec. 5(2), will amend para. (w) and add para. (x) to Class 10, applicable to 1995 *et seq.*

**Related Provisions**: ITA 127.52(1)(c) — Add-back of CCA on film properties for minimum tax purposes; Reg. 1100(1)(m) — Additional allowance — Canadian film or video production; Reg. 1100(1)(zg) — accelerated CCA for year 2000 compliant hardware; Reg. 1100(2)(a)(iii) — Half-year rule inapplicable to property in para. 10(w); Reg. 1100(21), (21.1) — Certified films and video tapes; Reg. 1101(5a) — Separate class for spacecraft under Class 10(f.2); Reg. 1101(5k) — Separate class for property under Class 10(w); Reg. 1101(5k.1) — Separate class for certain property under Class 10(x); Reg. 1101(5p), 1103(2g) — Separate class for certain equipment under Class 10(f); Reg. 1102(8)(c), 1102(9)(c) — Generating equipment; Reg. 1102(18) — Townsite costs; Reg. 1102(18), 1103(2e); Reg. 1104(2) — Definitions; Reg. 1104(5), (6), (6.1) — Income from a mine; Reg. 1106 — Certificate for Class 10(x); Reg. 1205(1)(a)(vi)(D), 1205(1)(b) — Earned depletion base; Reg. 1206(1)"enhanced recovery equipment"(a), 1206(1)"processing property", 1206(1)"tertiary recovery equipment"; Reg. 4600(1)(b), 4600(2)(e), (g), (h) — Qualified property; Reg. 4601(a)(v), 4601(c)(i), (ii), 4601(d) — Qualified transportation equipment; Reg. 4604(1)(b), 4604(2)(d), (f), (g) — Approved project property; Reg. Sch. II Cl. 16(g) — Large trucks and tractors; Reg. Sch. II Cl. 41.

**Notes**: 10(a) covers cars, but not expensive cars, which are in Class 10.1.

10(e) changed from simply "a trailer" to current wording by P.C. 1994-139, effective for property acquired after December 23, 1991.

Opening words of 10(h) amended by P.C. 1994-139, effective for property acquired after December 23, 1991, other than property acquired before 1993

(a) pursuant to an agreement in writing entered into before December 24, 1991, or

(b) that was under construction by or on behalf of the taxpayer on December 23, 1991.

For earlier acquisitions, read "(h) contractor's movable equipment, including portable camp buildings, except a property included in".

10(n) amended by P.C. 1994-139, effective for 1986 and later taxation years, to add the words "that the taxpayer is entitled to cut and remove". Thus, it can apply where the taxpayer has the right to remove *some* but not *all* of the timber from the timber limit.

Reference to Class 43(b) before 10(g) added by P.C. 1994-230, effective for property acquired after February 25, 1992.

**Definitions [Reg. Sch. II:Cl. 10]**: "arm's length" — ITA 251(1); "building" — Reg 1102(5), (5.1); "business" — ITA 248(1); "Canada" — ITA 255, *Interpretation Act* 35(1); "Canadian film or video production" — Reg. 1106(3); "certified production" — Reg. 1104(2); "class" — Reg. 1102 (1)–(3), (14), (14.1); "designated underground storage cost", "gas or oil well equipment", "general-purpose electronic data processing equipment" — Reg. 1104(2); "income from a mine" — Reg. 1104(5), (6), (6.1)(a), (b); "mine" — Reg. 1104(6)(b); "mineral resource", "office", "oil or gas well", "person", "prescribed", "property" — ITA 248(1); "radio" — *Interpretation Act* 35(1); "structure" — Reg 1102(5), (5.1); "systems software" — Reg. 1104(2); "taxation year" — ITA 249; "taxpayer" — ITA 248(1).

**Interpretation Bulletins**: IT-306R2: Contractor's movable equipment; IT-476: Gas and oil exploration and production equipment; IT-482: Pipelines; IT-501: Logging assets.

**I.T. Technical News**: No. 14 (millennium bug expenditures).

## Class 10.1 — (30 per cent)
[Reg. 1100(1)(a)(x.1)]

Property that would otherwise be included in Class 10 that is a passenger vehicle, the cost of which to the taxpayer exceeds $20,000 or such other amount as may be prescribed for the purposes of subsection 13(2) of the Act.

**Related Provisions**: Reg. 1101(1af) — Separate class; Reg. 1100(2.5) — 50% CCA in year of disposition; Reg. 7307 — Prescribed amount.

**Notes**: See Notes to ITA 13(7)(g) re prescribed amount for each year.

**Definitions [Reg. Sch. II:Cl. 10.1]**: "amount", "passenger vehicle", "prescribed", "property", "taxpayer" — ITA 248(1).

**Interpretation Bulletins**: IT-521R: Motor vehicle expenses claimed by self-employed individuals; IT-522R: Vehicle, travel and sales expenses of employees.

**I.T. Technical News**: No. 10 (1997 deduction limits and benefit rates for automobiles).

## Class 11 — (35 per cent)
[Reg. 1100(1)(a)(xi)]

Property not included in any other class that is used to earn rental income and that is

(a) an electrical advertising sign owned by the manufacturer thereof, acquired before May 26, 1976; or

(b) an outdoor advertising poster panel or bulletin board acquired by the taxpayer

(i) before 1988, or

(ii) before 1990

(A) pursuant to an obligation in writing entered into by the taxpayer before June 18, 1987, or

(B) that was under construction by or on behalf of the taxpayer on June 18, 1987.

**Definitions [Reg. Sch. II:Cl. 11]**: "class" — Reg. 1102 (1)–(3), (14), (14.1); "property", "taxpayer" — ITA 248(1); "writing" — *Interpretation Act* 35(1).

## Class 12 — (100 per cent)
[Reg. 1100(1)(a)(xii), 1100(1)(l)]

Property not included in any other class that is
 (a) a book that is part of a lending library;
 (b) chinaware, cutlery or other tableware;
 (c) a kitchen utensil costing less than
  (i) $100, if acquired before May 26, 1976, or
  (ii) $200, if acquired after May 25, 1976;
 (d) a die, jig, pattern, mould or last;
 (e) a medical or dental instrument costing less than
  (i) $100, if acquired before May 26, 1976, or
  (ii) $200, if acquired after May 25, 1976;
 (f) a mine shaft, main haulage way or similar underground work designed for continuing use, or any extension thereof, sunk or constructed after the mine came into production, to the extent that the property was acquired before 1988;
 (g) linen;
 (h) a tool costing less than
  (i) $100, if acquired before May 26, 1976, or
  (ii) $200, if acquired after May 25, 1976;
 (i) a uniform;
 (j) the cutting or shaping part in a machine;
 (k) apparel or costume, including accessories used therewith, used for the purpose of earning rental income;
 (l) a video tape acquired before May 26, 1976;
 (m) a motion picture film or video tape that is a television commercial message;
 (n) a certified feature film or certified production;
 (o) computer software acquired after May 25, 1976, but not including systems software or property acquired after August 8, 1989 and before 1993 that is described in paragraph (s);
 (p) a metric scale or a scale designed for ready conversion to metric weighing, acquired after March 31, 1977 and before 1984 for use in a retail business and having a maximum weighing capacity of 100 kilograms;
 (q) a designated overburden removal cost; or
 (r) a videotape cassette acquired after February 15, 1984 for the purpose of renting and that is not expected to be rented to any one person for more than 7 days in any 30 day period;

### Proposed Amendment — Class 12(r)
(r) a video-cassette acquired after February 15, 1984, or a video-laser disk acquired after December 12, 1995, for the purpose of renting and that is not expected to be rented to any one person for more than 7 days in any 30-day period;

**Notes**: The amendments also exclude Class (r) property from the half-year rule in Reg. 1100(2), so rental videotapes and DVDs can now be fully written off in the year acquired.

**Application**: The December 12, 1995 draft regulations (Canadian film tax credit), s. 6, will amend para. (r) of Class 12 to read as above, applicable to property acquired after December 12, 1995.

and property that would otherwise be included in another class in this Schedule that is
 (s) acquired by the taxpayer after August 8, 1989 and before 1993, for use in a business of selling goods or providing services to consumers that is carried on in Canada, or for lease to another taxpayer for use by that other taxpayer in such a business, and that is
  (i) electronic bar code scanning equipment designed to read bar codes applied to goods held for sale in the ordinary course of the business,
  (ii) a cash register or similar sales recording device designed with the capability of calculating and recording sales tax imposed by more than one jurisdiction in respect of the same sale,
  (iii) equipment or computer software that is designed to convert a cash register or similar sales recording device to one having the capability of calculating and recording sales tax imposed by more than one jurisdiction in respect of the same sale, or
  (iv) electronic equipment or computer software that is ancillary to property described in subparagraph (i), (ii) or (iii) and all or substantially all the use of which is in conjunction with that property.

**Related Provisions**: ITA 127.52(1)(c) — Add-back of CCA on film properties for minimum tax purposes; ITA 237.1 — Tax shelters; Reg. 1100(1)(zg), (zh) — accelerated CCA for year 2000 compliant software; Reg. 1100(2)(a)(iii) — Half-year rule applies to some Class 12 property; Reg. 1100(20.1) — Limitation on CCA claim for computer software tax shelter property; Reg. 1100(21), (21.1) — Certified films and video tapes; Reg. 1101(5r) — Separate class for all computer software tax shelter property; Reg. 1104(2), (7) — Definitions.

**Notes**: Revenue Canada's view is that "all or substantially all", used in subpara. (s)(iv), means 90% or more.

Revenue Canada announced on November 23, 1994 (at the Canadian Tax Foundation annual conference) that its audit and special investigations staff will be paying particular attention to software tax shelters (Class 12(o)). Issues of concern to the Department include: little or no economic activity; businesses carried on with no reasonable expectation of profit; inflated costs and over-valuation of assets; attempts to circumvent the "at-risk" rules; and, in general, that certain arrangements are crossing the line between acceptable and abusive tax planning. Since then Revenue Canada has vigorously attacked and disallowed most software shelters. Many are likely to reach the Courts. One such case, *Peter Brown v. The Queen*, was heard by the Tax Court during 1999–2000.

For discussion of software tax shelters, see Robin J. Macknight, "Cabbages and Soda: A Skeptic's Review of Tax Shelters", 1993 Canadian Tax Foundation annual conference report, pp. 50:1-50:34, and "Prophecies and Soda: Evolving and Surviving Tax Shelters", 1995 annual conference report, pp. 14:1–14:17.

Many of these shelters, which avoided the "leasing property" rules in Reg. 1100(17) by planning for business income rather than property income from the software, were effectively shut down by the news release of August 6, 1997 and accompanying draft regulations (except where there are no representations made and so they are not "tax shelters" as described). See Reg. 1100(20.1) and (20.2). See also the "matchable expenditure" rules in ITA 18.1.

**Definitions [Reg. Sch. II:Cl. 12]**: "business" — ITA 248(1); "Canada" — ITA 255, *Interpretation Act* 35(1); "certified feature film", "certified production" — Reg. 1104(2); "class" — Reg. 1102 (1)–(3), (14), (14.1); "computer software", "designated overburden removal cost" — Reg. 1104(2); "mine" — Reg. 1104(7)(a); "person", "property" — ITA 248(1); "systems software" — Reg. 1104(2); "taxpayer" — ITA 248(1); "television commercial message" — Reg. 1104(2).

**Interpretation Bulletins**: IT-422: Definition of tools; IT-441: Certified feature productions.

**I.T. Technical News**: No. 12 (millennium bug expenditures); No. 14 (millennium bug expenditures).

## Class 13
[Reg. 1100(1)(b), Schedule III]

Property that is a leasehold interest and property acquired by a taxpayer that would, if that property had been acquired by a person with whom the taxpayer was not dealing at arm's length at the time the property was acquired by the taxpayer, be a leasehold interest of that person, except

(a) an interest in minerals, petroleum, natural gas, other related hydrocarbons or timber and property relating thereto or in respect of a right to explore for, drill for, take or remove minerals, petroleum, natural gas, other related hydrocarbons or timber;

(b) that part of the leasehold interest that is included in another class in this Schedule by reason of subsection 1102(5) or (5.1); or

(c) a property that is included in Class 23.

**Related Provisions**: Reg. 1100(2)(a)(iv) — Half-year rule inapplicable to Class 13 property; Reg. 1700(4) — CCA — Farming/fishing property owned since before 1972: leasehold interests.

**Notes**: Opening words of Class 13 changed from "Property that is a leasehold interest, except", and reference to Reg. 1102(5.1) added to Class 13(b), by P.C. 1994-139, effective for property acquired after December 23, 1991, other than property acquired before 1993

(a) pursuant to an agreement in writing entered into before December 24, 1991, or

(b) that was under construction by or on behalf of the taxpayer on December 23, 1991.

**Definitions [Reg. Sch. II:Cl. 13]**: "arm's length" — ITA 251(1); "class" — Reg. 1102 (1)–(3), (14), (14.1); "mineral" — Reg. 1104(3); "person", "property" — ITA 248(1); "related" — ITA 251(2)–(6); "taxpayer" — ITA 248(1).

**Interpretation Bulletins**: IT-195R4: Rental property — CCA restrictions; IT-324: Emphyteutic lease.

## Class 14
[Reg. 1100(1)(c) — apportioned over the life of the property (see also Class 44)]

Property that is a patent, franchise, concession or licence for a limited period in respect of property, except

(a) a franchise, concession or licence in respect of minerals, petroleum, natural gas, other related hydrocarbons or timber and property relating thereto (except a franchise for distributing gas to consumers or a licence to export gas from Canada or from a province) or in respect of a right to explore for, drill for, take or remove minerals, petroleum, natural gas, other related hydrocarbons or timber;

(b) a leasehold interest;

(c) a property that is included in Class 23;

(d) a licence to use computer software; or

(e) a property that is included in Class 44.

**Related Provisions**: Reg. 1100(2)(a)(iv) — Half-year rule inapplicable to Class 14 property; Reg. 1103(2h) — Election for patent to be in Class 14 instead of Class 44; Reg. Sch. II:Cl. 44 — Patent or right to use patented information.

**Notes**: Para. 14(e) added by P.C. 1994-231, effective for property acquired after April 26, 1993.

**Definitions [Reg. Sch. II:Cl. 14]**: "Canada" — ITA 255, *Interpretation Act* 35(1); "computer software" — Reg. 1104(2); "mineral" — Reg. 1104(3); "property" — ITA 248(1); "province" — *Interpretation Act* 35(1); "related" — ITA 251(2)–(6).

**Interpretation Bulletins**: IT-143R2: Meaning of "eligible capital expenditure"; IT-477: Patents, franchises, concessions and licences.

## Class 15
[Reg. 1100(1)(f)]

Property that would otherwise be included in another class in this Schedule and that

(a) was acquired for the purpose of cutting and removing merchantable timber from a timber limit, and

(b) will be of no further use to the taxpayer after all merchantable timber that the taxpayer is entitled to cut and remove from the limit has been cut and removed,

except

(c) property that the taxpayer has, in the taxation year or a preceding taxation year, elected not to include in this class, or

(d) a timber resource property.

**Related Provisions**: Reg. 1100(2)(a)(iv) — Half-year rule inapplicable to Class 15 property; Reg. 4604(2)(g) — Approved project property.

**Notes**: Class 15 amended by P.C. 1994-139, effective for 1986 and later taxation years, so that it can apply where the taxpayer has the right to remove *some* but not *all* of the timber from the timber limit.

**Definitions [Reg. Sch. II:Cl. 15]**: "class" — Reg. 1102 (1)–(3), (14), (14.1); "property" — ITA 248(1); "taxation year" — ITA 249; "taxpayer" — ITA 248(1); "timber resource property" — ITA 13(21), 248(1).

**Interpretation Bulletins**: IT-501: Logging assets.

## Class 16 — (40 per cent)
[Reg. 1100(1)(a)(xiii)]

Property acquired before May 26, 1976 that is

(a) an aircraft,

(b) furniture, fittings or equipment attached to an aircraft, or

(c) a spare part for a property included in this class,

property acquired after May 25, 1976 that is

(d) a taxicab,

property acquired after November 12, 1981 that is

(e) a motor vehicle that

(i) would be an automobile as that term is defined in subsection 248(1) of the Act, if that definition were read without reference to paragraph (d) thereof,

(ii) was acquired for the purpose of renting or leasing, and

(iii) is not expected to be rented or leased to any person for more than 30 days in any 12 month period,

property acquired after February 15, 1984 that is

(f) a coin-operated video game or pinball machine,

and property acquired after December 6, 1991 that is

(g) a truck or tractor designed for hauling freight, and that is primarily so used by the taxpayer or a person with whom the taxpayer does not deal at arm's length in a business that includes hauling freight, and that has a "gross vehicle weight rating" (as that term is defined in subsection 2(1) of the *Motor Vehicle Safety Regulations*) in excess of 11,788 kg.

**Related Provisions**: Reg. 4601(c)(i)(A) — Qualified transportation equipment.

**Notes**: 16(e)(i) amended by P.C. 1994-139, effective for taxation years and fiscal periods that begin after June 17, 1987 and end after 1987. 16(g) added by P.C. 1994-139, effective December 7, 1991.

**Definitions [Reg. Sch. II:Cl. 16]**: "arm's length" — ITA 251(1); "automobile", "business" — ITA 248(1); "class" — Reg. 1102 (1)–(3), (14), (14.1); "month" — *Interpretation Act* 35(1); "motor vehicle", "person", "property", "taxpayer" — ITA 248(1).

**Interpretation Bulletins**: IT-317R: Radio and television equipment.

## Class 17 — (8 per cent)
[Reg. 1100(1)(a)(xiv)]

Property that would otherwise be included in another class in this Schedule that is

(a) a telephone system, telegraph system, or a part thereof, acquired before May 26, 1976, except

(i) radiocommunication equipment, or

(ii) a property included in Class 10, 13, 14 or 28,

and property not included in any other class, acquired after May 25, 1976, that is

(b) telephone, telegraph or data communication switching equipment, except

(i) equipment installed on customers' premises, or

(ii) property that is principally electronic equipment or systems software therefor; or

(c) a road (other than a specified temporary access road of the taxpayer), sidewalk, airplane runway, parking area, storage area or similar surface construction.

**Related Provisions**: Reg. 1103(2), 1104(2)"specified temporary access road", "telegraph system", "telephone system"; Sch. II:Cl. 29.

**Notes**: 17(c) amended by P.C. 1999-629, effective for property acquired after March 6, 1996, to add reference to a specified temporary access road. See Notes to Reg. 1104(2)"specified temporary access road".

**Definitions [Reg. Sch. II:Cl. 17]**: "class" — Reg. 1102 (1)–(3), (14), (14.1); "property" — ITA 248(1); "specified temporary access road" — Reg. 1104(2); "systems software" — Reg. 1104(2); "taxpayer" — ITA 248(1); "telegraph system", "telephone system" — Reg. 1104(2).

## Class 18 — (60 per cent)
[Reg. 1100(1)(a)(xv)]

Property that is a motion picture film acquired before May 26, 1976, except

(a) a television commercial message; or

(b) a certified feature film.

**Definitions [Reg. Sch. II:Cl. 18]**: "certified feature film" — Reg. 1104(2); "property" — ITA 248(1); "television commercial message" — Reg. 1104(2).

## Class 19 — (50 per cent or 20 per cent)
[Reg. 1100(1)(n), (o)]

Property acquired by the taxpayer after June 13, 1963 and before January 1, 1967 that would otherwise be included in Class 8 if,

(a) in the taxation year in which the property was acquired,

(i) the taxpayer was an individual who was resident in Canada for not less than 183 days, or

(ii) the taxpayer was a corporation that had a degree of Canadian ownership;

(b) the property was acquired for use in Canada in a business carried on by the taxpayer that,

(i) for the fiscal period in which the property was acquired, or

(ii) for the fiscal period in which the business first commenced selling goods in reasonable commercial quantities,

whichever was later, was a business in which the aggregate of

(iii) its net sales, as they would be determined under paragraphs 71A(2)(d) and (f) of the former Act (within the meaning assigned by paragraph 8(b) of the *Income Tax Application Rules*), from the sale of goods processed or manufactured in Canada by the business,

(iv) an amount equal to that part of its gross revenue that is rent from goods processed or manufactured in Canada in the course of the business, and

(v) its gross revenue from advertisements in a newspaper or magazine produced by the business,

was not less than 2/3 of the amount by which the gross revenue from the business for the period exceeded the aggregate of each amount paid or credited in the period to a customer of the business as a bonus, rebate or discount or for returned or damaged goods, and was not a business that was principally

(vi) operating a gas or oil well,

(vii) logging,

(viii) mining,

(ix) construction, or

(x) a combination of two or more of the activities referred to in subparagraphs (vi) to (ix); and

(c) the property had not been used for any purpose whatever before it was acquired by the taxpayer.

**Related Provisions**: Reg. 1103(2a) — Election to include property in Class 8.

**Definitions [Reg. Sch. II:Cl. 19]**: "amount", "business" — ITA 248(1); "Canada" — ITA 255, *Interpretation Act* 35(1); "corporation" — ITA 248(1), *Interpretation Act* 35(1); "fiscal period" — ITA 249.1; "gross revenue", "individual" — ITA 248(1); "mining" — Reg. 1104(3); "property" — ITA 248(1); "resident in Canada" — ITA 250; "taxation year" — ITA 249; "taxpayer" — ITA 248(1).

## Class 20 — (20 per cent)
[Reg. 1100(1)(p)]

Property that would otherwise be included in Class 3 or 6

(a) that was acquired after December 5, 1963 and before April 1, 1967 that is

(i) a building,

(ii) an extension to a building, outside the previously existing walls or roof of the building, if the aggregate cost of the extensions added in the aforementioned period exceeded the lesser of

(A) $100,000, and

(B) 25 per cent of the capital cost to the taxpayer of the building on December 5, 1963, or

(iii) an addition or alteration to a property described in subparagraph (i) or (ii),

and that has been certified by the Minister of Industry, upon application by the taxpayer in such form as may be prescribed by the Minister of Industry,

(iv) to be situated in an area that was a designated area, as determined for the purposes of section 71A of the former Act (within the meaning assigned by paragraph 8(b) of the *Income Tax Application Rules*),

(A) at the time the property was acquired,

(B) in a case where the property was built by the taxpayer, at the time construction was commenced, or

(C) in a case where the property was built for the taxpayer pursuant to a contract entered into by the taxpayer, at the time the contract was entered into, and

(v) to have not been used for any purpose whatever before it was acquired by the taxpayer; or

(b) the capital cost of which was included in the approved capital costs as defined in the *Area Development Incentives Act* upon which approved capital cost the Minister of Industry has based the amount of a development grant authorized under that Act.

**Related Provisions**: Reg. 1103(2f); 1704(d) — CCA — Farming and fishing: leasehold interests; 4600(1)(a) — Qualified property.

**Definitions [Reg. Sch. II:Cl. 20]**: "amount" — ITA 248(1); "building" — Reg 1102(5), (5.1); "Minister", "prescribed", "property", "taxpayer" — ITA 248(1).

## Class 21 — (50 per cent)
[Reg. 1100(1)(q)]

Property that would otherwise be included in Class 8 or 19

(a) that was acquired after December 5, 1963 and before April 1, 1967 and that

(i) was acquired for use in a business carried on by the taxpayer that has been certified by the Minister of Industry, for the purposes of section 71A of the former Act (within the meaning assigned by paragraph 8(b) of the *Income Tax Application Rules*), to be a new manufacturing or processing business in a designated area for the fiscal period in which the property was acquired or for a subsequent fiscal period, and

(ii) had not been used for any purpose whatever before it was acquired by the taxpayer; or

(b) the capital cost of which was included in the approved capital costs as defined in the *Area Development Incentives Act* upon which approved capital cost the Minister of Industry has based the amount of a development grant authorized under that Act.

**Related Provisions**: Reg. 1103(2a) — Election to include property in Class 8; Reg. 4600(2)(k) — Qualified property; 4604(2)(j) — Approved project property.

**Definitions [Reg. Sch. II:Cl. 21]**: "amount", "business" — ITA 248(1); "fiscal period" — ITA 249.1; "Minister", "property", "taxpayer" — ITA 248(1).

## Class 22
[Reg. 1100(1)(a)(xvi)]

Property acquired by the taxpayer after March 16, 1964 and

(a) before 1988, or

(b) before 1990

(i) pursuant to an obligation in writing entered into by the taxpayer before June 18, 1987, or

(ii) that was under construction by or on behalf of the taxpayer on June 18, 1987

that is power-operated movable equipment designed for the purpose of excavating, moving, placing or compacting earth, rock, concrete or asphalt, except a property included in Class 7.

**Related Provisions**: Reg. 4600(2)(e) — Qualified property; 4603(a) — Qualified construction equipment; 4604(2)(d) — Approved project property; Reg. Sch. II:Cl. 38 — Earth-moving equipment acquired after 1987.

**Definitions [Reg. Sch. II:Cl. 22]**: "property", "taxpayer" — ITA 248(1); "writing" — *Interpretation Act* 35(1).

**Interpretation Bulletins**: IT-411R: Meaning of "construction"; IT-469R: CCA — earth-moving equipment.

### Class 23 — (100 per cent)
[Reg. 1100(1)(a)(xvii)]

Property that is

(a) a leasehold interest or a concession in respect of land granted under or pursuant to an agreement in writing with the Canadian Corporation for the 1967 World Exhibition where such leasehold interest or concession is to expire not later than June 15, 1968;

(b) a building or other structure, including component parts, erected on land that is the subject matter of a leasehold interest or concession described in paragraph (a) where such building or other structure, including component parts, is of a temporary nature and is required by the agreement to be removed not later than June 15, 1968;

(c) a leasehold interest or licence in respect of land granted under or pursuant to an agreement in writing with the Expo 86 Corporation where such leasehold interest or licence is to expire not later than January 31, 1987; or

(d) a building or other structure, including component parts, erected on land that is the subject matter of a leasehold interest or licence described in paragraph (c) where such building or other structure, including component parts, is of a temporary nature and is required by the agreement to be removed not later than January 31, 1987.

**Related Provisions**: Reg. 1100(2)(a)(iv) — Half-year rule inapplicable to Class 23 property.

**Notes**: Expo '67 was held in Montreal. Expo '86 was in Vancouver.

**Definitions [Reg. Sch. II:Cl. 23]**: "building" — Reg 1102(5), (5.1); "property" — ITA 248(1); "structure" — Reg 1102(5), (5.1); "writing" — *Interpretation Act* 35(1).

### Class 24 — (50 per cent)
[Reg. 1100(1)(t), (ta)]

Property acquired after April 26, 1965 and before 1971

(a) that would otherwise be included in Class 2, 3, 6 or 8 and that

(i) was acquired primarily for the purpose of preventing, reducing or eliminating pollution of

(A) any of the inland, coastal or boundary waters of Canada, or

(B) any lake, river, stream, watercourse, pond, swamp or well in Canada,

by industrial waste, refuse or sewage created by operations in the course of carrying on a business by the taxpayer or that would be created by such operations if the property had not been acquired and used, and

(ii) had not been used for any purpose whatever before it was acquired by the taxpayer,

but not including property acquired for use in the production of by-products or the recovery of materials unless the by-products are produced from, or the materials are recovered from, materials that after April 26, 1965,

(iii) were being discarded as waste by the taxpayer, or

(iv) were commonly being discarded as waste by other taxpayers who carried on operations of a type similar to the operations carried on by the taxpayer,

and property acquired before 1999

(b) that would otherwise be included in another class in this Schedule

(i) that has not been included by the taxpayer in any other class,

(ii) that had not been used for any purpose whatever before it was acquired by the taxpayer,

(iii) that was acquired by the taxpayer after 1970 primarily for the purpose of preventing, reducing or eliminating pollution of

(A) any of the inland, coastal or boundary waters of Canada, or

(B) any lake, river, stream, watercourse, pond, swamp or well in Canada,

that is caused, or that, if the property had not been acquired and used, would be caused by

(C) operations carried on by the taxpayer at a site in Canada at which operations have been carried on by him from a time that is before 1974,

(D) the operation in Canada of a building or plant by the taxpayer, the construction of which was either commenced before 1974 or commenced under an agreement in writing entered into by him before 1974, or

(E) the operation of transportation or other movable equipment that has been operated by the taxpayer in Canada (including any of the inland, coastal or boundary waters of Canada) from a time that is before 1974,

or that was acquired by him after May 8, 1972, that would otherwise have been property referred to in this subparagraph except that

(F) it was acquired

(I) for the purpose of gaining or producing income from a business by a taxpayer whose business includes the preventing, reducing or eliminating of pollution of a kind referred to in this subparagraph that is caused or that otherwise would be caused primarily by operations referred to in clause (C), (D) or (E) carried on by other taxpayers (not including persons referred to in section 149 of the Act), and

(II) to be used in a business referred to in subclause (I) in the preventing, reducing or eliminating of pollution of a kind referred to in this subparagraph, or

(G) it was acquired

(I) for the purpose of gaining or producing income from a property by a corporation whose principal business is the purchasing of conditional sales contracts, accounts receivable, bills of sale, chattel mortgages, bills of exchange or other obligations representing part or all of the sale price of merchandise or services, the lending of money, or the leasing of property, or any combination thereof, and

(II) to be leased to a taxpayer (other than a person referred to in section 149 of the Act) to be used by him, in an operation referred to in clause (C), (D), (E) or (F), in the preventing, reducing or eliminating of pollution of a kind referred to in this subparagraph, and

(iv) that has, upon application by the taxpayer to the Minister of the Environment, been accepted by that Minister as property the primary use of which is to be the preventing, reducing or eliminating of pollution of a kind referred to in subparagraph (iii),

and for the purposes of paragraphs (a) and (b)

(c) where a corporation (in this paragraph referred to as the "predecessor corporation") has, as a result of an amalgamation within the meaning assigned by subsection 87(1) of the Act, merged at any time after 1973 with one or more other corporations to form one corporate entity (in this paragraph referred to as the "new corporation"),

the new corporation shall be deemed to be the same corporation as, and a continuation of, the predecessor corporation;

(d) where a corporation (in this paragraph referred to as the "subsidiary") has been wound up at any time after 1973 in circumstances to which subsection 88(1) of the Act applies, the parent (within the meaning assigned by that subsection) shall be deemed to be the same corporation as, and a continuation of, the subsidiary; and

(e) this class shall be read without reference to subparagraph (b)(i) where paragraph (c) or (d) applies to the taxpayer and the property was acquired before 1992.

**Related Provisions:** Reg. 1100(2)(a)(iv) — Half-year rule inapplicable to Class 24 property; Reg. 4600(1)(a), 4600(2)(k) — Qualified property; 4604(1)(a), 4604(2)(j) — Approved project property.

**Notes:** The words "acquired before 1999" before para. 24(b) added by P.C. 1997-1033, effective February 22, 1994.

24(c)–(e) added by P.C. 1994-139, retroactive to 1974 and later taxation years.

**Definitions [Reg. Sch. II:Cl. 24]:** "building" — Reg 1102(5), (5.1); "business" — ITA 248(1); "Canada" — ITA 255, *Interpretation Act* 35(1); "class" — Reg. 1102 (1)–(3), (14), (14.1); "corporation" — ITA 248(1), *Interpretation Act* 35(1); "Minister" — ITA 248(1); "new corporation" — Reg. Sch. II Cl. 24(c); "person" — ITA 248(1); "predecessor corporation" — Reg. Sch. II Cl. 24(c); "property" — ITA 248(1); "subsidiary" — Reg. Sch. II Cl. 24(d); "taxpayer" — ITA 248(1); "writing" — *Interpretation Act* 35(1).

**Interpretation Bulletins:** IT-336R: Pollution control property.

## Class 25 — (100 per cent)
[Reg. 1100(1)(a)(xviii)]

Property that would otherwise be included in another class in this Schedule that is property acquired by the taxpayer

(a) before October 23, 1968, or

(b) after October 22, 1968 and before 1974, where the acquisition of the property may reasonably be regarded as having been in fulfilment of an obligation undertaken in an agreement made in writing before October 23, 1968 and ratified, confirmed or adopted by the legislature of a province by a statute that came into force before that date,

if the taxpayer was, on October 22, 1968, a corporation, commission or association to which, on the assumption that October 22, 1968 was in its 1969 taxation year, paragraph 62(1)(c) of the former Act (within the meaning assigned by paragraph 8(b) of the *Income Tax Application Rules*),

(c) would not apply; and

(d) would have applied but for subparagraph (i) or (ii) of that paragraph.

**Definitions [Reg. Sch. II:Cl. 25]:** "class" — Reg. 1102 (1)–(3), (14), (14.1); "corporation" — ITA 248(1), *Interpretation Act* 35(1); "legislature" — *Interpretation Act* 35(1)"legislative assembly"; "property" — ITA 248(1); "province" — *Interpretation Act* 35(1); "taxation year" — ITA 249; "taxpayer" — ITA 248(1); "writing" — *Interpretation Act* 35(1).

## Class 26 — (5 per cent)
[Reg. 1100(1)(a)(xix)]

Property that is

(a) a catalyst; or

(b) deuterium enriched water (commonly known as "heavy water") acquired after May 22, 1979.

**Definitions [Reg. Sch. II:Cl. 26]:** "property" — ITA 248(1).

## Class 27 — (50 per cent)
[Reg. 1100(1)(t), (ta)]

Property acquired before 1999 that would otherwise be included in another Class in this Schedule

(a) that has not been included by the taxpayer in any other class;

(b) that had not been used for any purpose whatever before it was acquired by the taxpayer;

(c) that was acquired by the taxpayer after March 12, 1970 primarily for the purpose of preventing, reducing or eliminating air pollution by

(i) removing particulate, toxic or injurious materials from smoke or gas, or

(ii) preventing the discharge of part or all of the smoke, gas or other air pollutant,

that is discharged or that, if the property had not been acquired and used, would be discharged into the atmosphere as a result of

(iii) operations carried on by the taxpayer at a site in Canada at which operations have been carried on by him from a time that is before 1974,

(iv) the operation in Canada of a building or plant by the taxpayer, the construction of which was either commenced before 1974 or commenced under an agreement in writing entered into by him before 1974, or

(v) the operation of transportation or other movable equipment that has been operated by the taxpayer in Canada (including any of the inland, coastal or boundary waters of Canada) from a time that is before 1974,

or that was acquired by him after May 8, 1972, that would otherwise have been property referred to in this paragraph except that

(vi) it was acquired

(A) for the purpose of gaining or producing income from a business by a taxpayer whose business includes the preventing, reducing or eliminating of air pollution that is caused or that otherwise would be caused primarily by operations referred to in subparagraphs (iii), (iv) or (v) carried on by other taxpayers (not including persons referred to in section 149 of the Act), and

(B) to be used in a business referred to in clause (A) in the preventing, reducing or eliminating of air pollution in a manner referred to in this paragraph, or

(vii) it was acquired

(A) for the purpose of gaining or producing income from a property by a corporation whose principal business is the purchasing of conditional sales contracts, accounts receivable, bills of sale, chattel mortgages, bills of exchange or other obligations representing part or all of the sale price of merchandise or services, the lending of money, or the leasing of property, or any combination thereof, and

(B) to be leased to a taxpayer (other than a person referred to in section 149 of the Act) to be used by him, in an operation referred to in subparagraph (iii), (iv), (v) or (vi), in the preventing, reducing or eliminating of air pollution in a manner referred to in this paragraph; and

(d) that has, upon application by the taxpayer to the Minister of the Environment, been accepted by that Minister as property the primary use of which is to be the preventing, reducing or eliminating of air pollution in a manner referred to in paragraph (c);

and for the purposes of paragraphs (a) to (d),

(e) where a corporation (in this paragraph referred to as the "predecessor corporation") has, as a result of an amalgamation within the meaning assigned by subsection 87(1) of the Act, merged at any time after 1973 with one or more other corporations to form one corporate entity (in this paragraph referred to as the "new corporation"), the new corporation shall be deemed to be the same corporation as, and a continuation of, the predecessor corporation;

(f) where a corporation (in this paragraph referred to as the "subsidiary") has been wound up at any time after 1973 in circumstances to which subsection 88(1) of the Act applies, the parent (within the meaning assigned by that subsection) shall be deemed to be the same corporation as, and a continuation of, the subsidiary; and

(g) this class shall be read without reference to paragraph (a) where paragraph (e) or (f) applies to the taxpayer and the property was acquired before 1992.

**Related Provisions:** Reg. 1100(2)(a)(iv) — Half-year rule inapplicable to Class 27 property; Reg. 4600(1)(a), 4600(2)(k) — Qualified property; 4604(1)(a), 4604(2)(j) — Approved project property.

**Notes:** The words "acquired before 1999" added to the opening words of Cl. 27 by P.C. 1997-1033, effective February 22, 1994.

27(e)–(g) added by P.C. 1994-139, retroactive to 1974 and later taxation years.

**Definitions [Reg. Sch. II:Cl. 27]:** "building" — Reg 1102(5), (5.1); "business" — ITA 248(1); "Canada" — ITA 255, *Interpretation Act* 35(1); "class" — Reg. 1102 (1)–(3), (14), (14.1); "corporation" — ITA 248(1), *Interpretation Act* 35(1); "Minister" — ITA 248(1); "new corporation" — Reg. Sch. II Cl. 27(e); "person" —

ITA 248(1); "predecessor corporation" — Reg. Sch. II Cl. 27(e); "property" — ITA 248(1); "subsidiary" — Reg. Sch. II Cl. 27(f); "taxpayer" — ITA 248(1); "writing" — *Interpretation Act* 35(1).

**Interpretation Bulletins**: IT-336R: Pollution control property.

### Class 28 — (30 per cent)
[Reg. 1100(1)(a)(xx), 1100(1)(w), (zc)(i)(H)]

Property situated in Canada that would otherwise be included in another class in this Schedule that

(a) was acquired by the taxpayer

  (i) before 1988, or

  (ii) before 1990

    (A) pursuant to an obligation in writing entered into by the taxpayer before June 18, 1987,

    (B) that was under construction by or on behalf of the taxpayer on June 18, 1987, or

    (C) that is machinery or equipment that is a fixed and integral part of a building, structure, plant facility or other property that was under construction by or on behalf of the taxpayer on June 18, 1987,

and that

(b) was acquired by the taxpayer principally for the purpose of gaining or producing income from one or more mines operated by the taxpayer and situated in Canada and each of which

  (i) came into production in reasonable commercial quantities after November 7, 1969, or

  (ii) was the subject of a major expansion after November 7, 1969

    (A) whereby the greatest designed capacity, measured in weight of input of ore, of the mill that processed the ore from the mine was not less than 25% greater in the year following the expansion than it was in the year preceding the expansion, or

    (B) where in the one-year period preceding the expansion,

      (I) the Minister, in consultation with the Minister of Natural Resources, determines that the greatest designed capacity of the mine, measured in weight of output of ore, immediately after the expansion was not less than 25% greater than the greatest designed capacity of the mine immediately before the expansion, and

      (II) either

        (1.) no mill processed the ore from the mine at any time, or

        (2.) the mill that processed the ore from the mine processed other ore,

(c) was acquired by the taxpayer

  (i) after November 7, 1969,

  (ii) before the coming into production of the mine or the completion of the expansion of the mine referred to in subparagraph (b)(i) or (ii), as the case may be, and

  (iii) in the case of a mine that was the subject of a major expansion described in subparagraph (b)(ii), in the course of and principally for the purposes of the expansion,

(d) had not, before it was acquired by the taxpayer, been used for any purpose whatever by any person with whom the taxpayer was not dealing at arm's length, and

(e) is any of the following, namely,

  (i) property that was acquired before the mine came into production and that would, but for this class, be included in Class 10 by virtue of paragraph (g), (k), (l) or (r) of that class or would have been so included in that class if it had been acquired after the 1971 taxation year,

  (ii) property that was acquired before the mine came into production and that would, but for this class, be included in Class 10 by virtue of paragraph (m) of that class, or

  (iii) property that was acquired after the mine came into production and that would, but for this class, be included in Class 10 by virtue of paragraph (g), (k), (l) or (r) of that class,

or that would be described in paragraphs (b) to (e) if in those paragraphs each reference to a "mine" were read as a reference to a "mine that is a location in a bituminous sands deposit, oil sands deposit or oil shale deposit from which material is extracted", and each reference to "after November 7, 1969" were read as "before November 8, 1969".

**Related Provisions**: Reg. 1101(4a), (4b) — Separate class for certain property under Class 20; Reg. 1104(5), (6.1) — Income from a mine; 1104(7) — Extended meaning of "mine"; 1205(1)(c) — Earned depletion base — 1206(1)"bituminous sands equipment"; 4600(1)(b), 4600(2)(j) — Qualified property; 4601(a)(vi) — Qualified transportation equipment; 4604(2)(i) — Approved project property.

**Notes**: 28(b)(ii) amended by P.C. 2000-1331, effective for expansions commencing after September 13, 2000, to change "tons of input" to "weight of input", and "Minister was satisfied" to "Minister determines". (The subpara. was also restructured without substantive change.)

28(b)(ii)(B) added by P.C. 1994-139, effective for expansions of mines that begin after June 18, 1987.

**Definitions [Reg. Sch. II:Cl. 28]**: "arm's length" — ITA 251(1); "bituminous sands" — ITA 248(1); "building" — Reg 1102(5), (5.1); "Canada" — ITA 255, *Interpretation Act* 35(1); "class" — Reg. 1102 (1)–(3), (14), (14.1); "income from a mine" — Reg. 1104(5), (6.1)(a); "mine" — Reg. 1104(7)(a); "Minister", "person", "property" — ITA 248(1); "structure" — Reg 1102(5), (5.1); "taxation year" — ITA 249; "taxpayer" — ITA 248(1); "writing" — *Interpretation Act* 35(1).

### Class 29 — (50 per cent)
[Reg. 1100(1)(t), (ta)]

Property not included in Class 41 because of paragraph (c) or (d) of that Class that would otherwise be included in another class in this Schedule

(a) that is property manufactured by the taxpayer, the manufacture of which was completed by him after May 8, 1972, or other property acquired by the taxpayer after May 8, 1972,

(i) to be used directly or indirectly by him in Canada primarily in the manufacturing or processing of goods for sale or lease, or

(ii) to be leased, in the ordinary course of carrying on a business in Canada of the taxpayer, to a lessee who can reasonably be expected to use, directly or indirectly, the property in Canada primarily in Canadian field processing carried on by the lessee or in the manufacturing or processing by the lessee of goods for sale or lease, if the taxpayer is a corporation whose principal business is

(A) leasing property,

(B) manufacturing property that it sells or leases,

(C) the lending of money,

(D) the purchasing of conditional sales contracts, accounts receivable, bills of sale, chattel mortgages, bills of exchange or other obligations representing part or all of the sale price of merchandise or services, or

(E) selling or servicing a type of property that it also leases,

or any combination thereof, unless use of the property by the lessee commenced before May 9, 1972;

(b) that is

(i) property that, but for this class, would be included in Class 8, except railway rolling stock or a property described in paragraph (j) of Class 8,

(ii) an oil or water storage tank,

(iii) a powered industrial lift truck,

(iv) electrical generating equipment described in Class 9, or

(v) property described in paragraph (b) or (f) of Class 10; and

(c) that is property acquired by the taxpayer

(i) before 1988, or

(ii) before 1990

(A) pursuant to an obligation in writing entered into by the taxpayer before June 18, 1987,

(B) that was under construction by or on behalf of the taxpayer on June 18, 1987, or

(C) that is machinery or equipment that is a fixed and integral part of a building, structure, plant facility or other property that was under construction by or on behalf of the taxpayer on June 18, 1987.

**Related Provisions**: Reg. 1100(2)(a)(iv) — Half-year rule inapplicable to Class 29 property; Reg. 1104(9), 4600(2)(k) — Definition of manufacturing or processing; 4604(2)(j) — Approved project property; Reg. Sch. II Cl. 39.

**Notes**: Opening words of Class 29 amended by P.C. 1999-629, effective for taxation years that begin after 1996, to add "not included in Class 41 because of paragraph (c) or (d) of that Class".

29(a)(ii) opening words amended by P.C. 1999-629, effective for taxation years that begin after 1996, to add reference to Canadian field processing carried on by the lessee.

**Definitions [Reg. Sch. II:Cl. 29]**: "building" — Reg 1102(5), (5.1); "business" — ITA 248(1); "Canada" — ITA 255, *Interpretation Act* 35(1); "Canadian field processing" — ITA 248(1); "class" — Reg. 1102 (1)–(3), (14), (14.1); "corporation" — ITA 248(1), *Interpretation Act* 35(1); "manufacturing or processing" — Reg. 1104(9); "property" — ITA 248(1); "structure" — Reg 1102(5), (5.1); "taxpayer" — ITA 248(1); "writing" — *Interpretation Act* 35(1).

**Interpretation Bulletins**: IT-147R3: CCA — Accelerated write-off of manufacturing and processing machinery and equipment; IT-411R: Meaning of "construction".

## Class 30
[Reg. 1100(1)(a)(xxi)]

Property that is an unmanned telecommunication spacecraft designed to orbit above the earth and acquired by the taxpayer

(a) before 1988, or

(b) before 1990

(i) pursuant to an obligation in writing entered into by the taxpayer before June 18, 1987, or

(ii) that was under construction by or on behalf of the taxpayer before June 18, 1987.

**Related Provisions**: Reg. 1101(5a) — Separate class.

**Definitions [Reg. Sch. II:Cl. 30]**: "property", "taxpayer" — ITA 248(1); "writing" — *Interpretation Act* 35(1).

## Class 31 — (5 per cent)
[Reg. 1100(1)(a)(xxii)]

Property that is a multiple-unit residential building in Canada that would otherwise be included in Class 3 or Class 6 and in respect of which

(a) a certificate has been issued by Canada Mortgage and Housing Corporation certifying

(i) in respect of a building that would otherwise be included in Class 3, that the installation of footings or any other base support of the building was commenced

(A) after November 18, 1974 and before 1980, or

(B) after October 28, 1980 and before 1982,

as the case may be, and

(ii) in respect of a building that would otherwise be included in Class 6, that the installation of footings or any other base support of the building was commenced after December 31, 1977 and before 1979,

and that, according to plans and specifications for the building, not less than 80 per cent of the floor space will be used in providing self-contained domestic establishments and related parking, recreation, service and storage areas;

(b) not more than 20 per cent of the floor space is used for any purpose other than the purposes referred to in paragraph (a);

(c) the certificate referred to in paragraph (a) was issued on or before the later of

(i) December 31, 1981, and

(ii) the day that is 18 months after the day on which the installation of footings or other base support of the building was commenced; and

(d) the construction of the building proceeds, after 1982, without undue delay, taking into consideration acts of God, labour disputes, fire, accidents or unusual delay by common carriers or suppliers of materials or equipment;

and that was acquired by the taxpayer

(e) before June 18, 1987, or

(f) after June 17, 1987 pursuant to

(i) an obligation in writing entered into by the taxpayer before June 18, 1987, or

(ii) the terms of a prospectus, preliminary prospectus, registration statement, offering memorandum or notice required to be filed with a public authority in Canada and filed before June 18, 1987 with that public authority.

**Related Provisions**: Reg. 1101(5b) — Separate class where property cost $50,000 or more.

**Definitions [Reg. Sch. II:Cl. 31]**: "building" — Reg 1102(5), (5.1); "Canada" — ITA 255, *Interpretation Act* 35(1); "month" — *Interpretation Act* 35(1); "property" — ITA 248(1); "related" — ITA 251(2)–(6); "self-contained domestic establishment", "taxpayer" — ITA 248(1); "writing" — *Interpretation Act* 35(1).

**Interpretation Bulletins**: IT-195R4: Rental property — CCA restrictions; IT-367R3: CCA — multiple-unit residential buildings.

**Forms**: TX87: Application for a copy of a MURB certificate.

## Class 32 — (10 per cent)
[Reg. 1100(1)(a)(xxiii)]

Property that is a multiple-unit residential building in Canada that would otherwise be included in Class 6 if the reference to "1979" in subparagraph (a)(viii) of that Class were read as a reference to "1980", and in respect of which

(a) a certificate has been issued by Canada Mortgage and Housing Corporation certifying

(i) that the installation of footings or any other base support of the building was commenced after November 18, 1974 and before 1978, and

(ii) that, according to plans and specifications for the building, not less than 80% of the floor space will be used in providing self-contained domestic establishments and related parking, recreation, service and storage areas; and

(b) not more than 20 per cent of the floor space is used for any purpose other than the purposes referred to in subparagraph (a)(ii).

**Definitions [Reg. Sch. II:Cl. 32]**: "building" — Reg 1102(5), (5.1); "Canada" — ITA 255, *Interpretation Act* 35(1); "property" — ITA 248(1); "related" — ITA 251(2)–(6); "self-contained domestic establishment" — ITA 248(1).

**Interpretation Bulletins**: IT-195R4: Rental property — CCA restrictions; IT-367R3: CCA — multiple-unit residential buildings; .

**Forms**: TX87: Application for a copy of a MURB certificate.

## Class 33 — (15 per cent)
[Reg. 1100(1)(a)(xxiv)]

Property that is a timber resource property.

**Definitions [Reg. Sch. II:Cl. 33]**: "property" — ITA 248(1); "timber resource property" — ITA 13(21), 248(1).

**Interpretation Bulletins**: IT-481: Timber resource property and timber limits.

## Class 34 — (50 per cent)
[Reg. 1100(1)(t), (ta)]

Property that would otherwise be included in Class 1, 2 or 8

(a) that is

(i) electrical generating equipment,

(ii) production equipment and pipelines of a distributor of heat,

(iii) steam generating equipment that was acquired by the taxpayer primarily for the purpose of producing steam to operate property described in subparagraph (i), or

(iv) an addition to a property described in subparagraph (i), (ii) or (iii),

but not including buildings or other structures,

(b) that was acquired by the taxpayer after May 25, 1976,

(c) that

(i) was acquired by the taxpayer for use by him in a business carried on in Canada, or

(ii) is to be leased by the taxpayer to a lessee for use by the lessee in Canada, and

(d) that is property in respect of which a certificate has been issued

(i) before December 11, 1979 by the Minister of Industry, Trade and Commerce certifying that the property is part of a plan designed to

(A) produce heat derived primarily from the consumption of wood wastes or municipal wastes,

(B) produce electrical energy by the utilization of fuel that is petroleum, natural gas or related hydrocarbons, coal, coal gas, coke, lignite or peat (in this clause referred

Cl. 34 — (50 per cent)

to as "fossil fuel"), wood wastes or municipal wastes, or any combination thereof, if the consumption of fossil fuel (expressed as the high heat value of the fossil fuel), if any, chargeable to electrical energy on an annual basis in respect of the property is no greater than 7,000 British Thermal Units per kilowatt-hour of electrical energy produced, or

(C) recover heat that is a by-product of an industrial process, or

(ii) after December 10, 1979 by the Minister of Energy, Mines and Resources certifying that the property is part of a plan designed to

(A) produce heat derived primarily from the consumption of natural gas, coal, coal gas, lignite, peat, wood wastes or municipal wastes, or any combination thereof,

(B) produce electrical energy by the utilization of fuel that is petroleum, natural gas or related hydrocarbons, coal, coal gas, coke, lignite or peat (in this clause referred to as "fossil fuel"), wood wastes or municipal wastes, or any combination thereof, if the consumption of fossil fuel (expressed as the high heat value of the fossil fuel), if any, chargeable to electrical energy on an annual basis in respect of the property is no greater than 7,000 British Thermal Units per kilowatt-hour of electrical energy produced, or

(C) recover heat that is a by-product of an industrial process,

and property that was acquired by the taxpayer after December 10, 1979 (other than property described in paragraph (a)) and would otherwise be included in another Class in this Schedule

(e) that is

(i) active solar heating equipment including solar collectors, solar energy conversion equipment, storage equipment, control equipment, equipment designed to interface solar heating equipment with other heating equipment, and solar water heaters, used to

(A) heat a liquid or air to be used directly in the course of manufacturing or processing,

(B) provide space heating when installed in a new building or other new structure at the time of its original construction where that construction commenced after December 10, 1979, or

(C) heat water for a use other than a use described in clause (A) or (B),

(ii) a hydro electric installation of a producer of hydro electric energy with a planned maxi-

Reg. Cl. 34(i)

mum generating capacity not exceeding 15 megawatts upon completion of site development that is the generating equipment and plant (including structures) of that producer including a canal, a dam, a dyke, an overflow spillway, a penstock, a powerhouse complete with generating equipment and other equipment ancillary thereto, control equipment, fishways or fish bypasses and transmission equipment, except distribution equipment and a property included in Class 10 or 17,

(iii) heat recovery equipment that is designed to conserve energy or reduce the requirement to acquire energy by extracting and reusing heat from thermal waste including condensers, heat exchange equipment, steam compressors used to upgrade low pressure steam, waste heat boilers and ancillary equipment such as control panels, fans, instruments or pumps,

(iv) an addition or alteration to a hydro electric installation described in subparagraph (ii) that results in a change in generating capacity if the new maximum generating capacity at the hydro electric installation does not exceed 15 megawatts, or

(v) a fixed location device acquired after February 25, 1986, that is a wind energy conversion system designed to produce electrical energy, consisting of a wind-driven turbine, generating equipment and related equipment, including control and conditioning equipment, support structures, a powerhouse complete with equipment ancillary thereto, and transmission equipment, but not including distribution equipment, equipment designed to store electrical energy or property included in Class 10 or 17,

(f) that

(i) was acquired by the taxpayer for use by him for the purpose of gaining or producing income from a business carried on in Canada or from property situated in Canada, or

(ii) is to be leased by the taxpayer to a lessee for use by the lessee in Canada, and

(g) that is property in respect of which a certificate has been issued by the Minister of Energy, Mines and Resources,

but not including

(h) property in respect of which a certificate issued under paragraph (d), (g) has been revoked pursuant to subsection 1104(11),

(i) property that had been used before it was acquired by the taxpayer unless the property had previously been included in Class 34 for the purpose of computing the income of the person from whom it was acquired,

(j) property acquired by the taxpayer after February 21, 1994 other than

   (i) property acquired by the taxpayer

   (A) pursuant to an agreement of purchase and sale in writing entered into by the taxpayer before February 22, 1994,

   (B) in order to satisfy a legally binding obligation entered into by the taxpayer in writing before February 22, 1994 to sell electricity to a public power utility in Canada,

   (C) that was under construction by or on behalf of the taxpayer on February 22, 1994, or

   (D) that is machinery or equipment that is a fixed and integral part of a building, structure or other property that was under construction by or on behalf of the taxpayer on February 22, 1994, and

   (ii) property acquired by the taxpayer before 1996

   (A) pursuant to an agreement of purchase and sale in writing entered into before 1995 to acquire the property from a person or partnership in circumstances where

   (I) the property was part of a project that was under construction by the person or partnership on February 22, 1994, and

   (II) it is reasonable to conclude, having regard to all of the circumstances, that the person or partnership constructed the project with the intention of transferring all or part of the project to another taxpayer after completion, or

   (B) pursuant to an agreement in writing entered into before 1995 by the taxpayer with a person or partnership where the taxpayer agrees to assume a legally binding obligation entered into by the person or partnership before February 22, 1994 to sell electricity to a public power utility in Canada, or

(k) property in respect of which a certificate has not been issued under paragraph (d) or (g) before the time that is the later of

   (i) the end of 1995, and

   (ii) 2 years after the property is acquired by the taxpayer or, where the property is property acquired in circumstances to which paragraph (j) applies, 2 years after substantial completion of the property.

**Related Provisions**: Reg. 1100(2)(a)(iv) — Half-year rule inapplicable to Class 34 property; Reg. 1100(24), (25) — Limitation on deduction for specified energy property; Reg. 1104(11) — Revocation of certificate; Reg. 4600(2)(k) — Qualified property; Reg. 4604(2)(j) — Approved project property.

**Notes**: Paras. 34(j) and (k) added by P.C. 1997-1033, effective February 22, 1994.

**Definitions [Reg. Sch. II:Cl. 34]**: "building" — Reg 1102(5), (5.1); "business" — ITA 248(1); "Canada" — ITA 255, *Interpretation Act* 35(1); "fossil fuel" — Reg. Sch. II Cl. 34(d)(i)(B), (ii)(B); "Minister" — ITA 248(1); "partnership" — see Notes to ITA 96(1); "person", "property" — ITA 248(1); "related" — ITA 251(2)–(6); "structure" — Reg 1102(5), (5.1); "taxpayer" — ITA 248(1); "writing" — *Interpretation Act* 35(1).

## Class 35 — (7 per cent)
[Reg. 1100(1)(a)(xxv), 1100(1)(z.1b), 1100(1)(zc)(i)(I)]

Property not included in any other class that is

(a) a railway car acquired after May 25, 1976; or

(b) a rail suspension device designed to carry trailers that are designed to be hauled on both highways and railway tracks.

### Proposed Amendment — Railway assets

**Federal budget, supplementary information, February 28, 2000**: *Rail Assets*

Most rail assets owned by common carriers, including railway cars and locomotives, are currently eligible for a 10-per-cent CCA rate.

*Current CCA Treatment*

Class 6 and Class 35 of Schedule II to the Income Tax Regulations include:

- locomotives described in paragraph (j) of Class 6 as "a railway locomotive acquired after May 25, 1976, but not including an automotive railway car";
- railway cars described in paragraph (a) of Class 35 as "a railway car acquired after May 25, 1976"; and
- rail suspension devices described in paragraph (b) of Class 35 as "a rail suspension device designed to carry trailers that are designed to be hauled on both highways and railway tracks."

The budget proposes that the CCA rates for such locomotives, railway cars and rail suspension devices acquired after February 27, 2000, be increased to 15 per cent. This rate will better reflect the estimated useful life of these assets.

In certain instances, Class 35 railway assets that are the subject of a lease are already eligible for a 13-per-cent CCA rate. The proposed 15-per-cent CCA rate will apply to these assets only if the lessor elects to have the "specified leasing property" rules apply to the asset.

**Related Provisions**: Reg. 1100(1.13)(a)(viii) — exclusion from specified leasing property rules; Reg. 1101(5d), (5d.1) — Separate classes.

**Notes**: 35(b) added by P.C. 1994-139, effective for property acquired after December 23, 1991, other than property acquired before 1993

(a) pursuant to an agreement in writing entered into before December 24, 1991, or

(b) that was under construction by or on behalf of the taxpayer on December 23, 1991.

**Definitions [Reg. Sch. II:Cl. 35]**: "class" — Reg. 1102 (1)–(3), (14), (14.1); "property" — ITA 248(1).

### Class 36

Property acquired after December 11, 1979 that is deemed to be depreciable property by virtue of paragraph 13(5.2)(c) of the Act.

**Related Provisions**: Reg. 1101(5g) — Separate class.

**Definitions [Reg. Sch. II:Cl. 36]**: "depreciable property" — ITA 13(21), 248(1); "property" — ITA 248(1).

### Class 37 — (15 per cent)
[Reg. 1100(1)(a)(xxvi)]

Property that would otherwise be included in another class in this Schedule that is property used in connection with an amusement park, including

  (a) land improvements (other than landscaping) for or in support of park activities, including

    (i) roads, sidewalks, parking areas, storage areas, or similar surface constructions, and

    (ii) canals,

  (b) buildings (other than warehouses, administration buildings, hotels or motels), structures and equipment (other than automotive equipment), including

    (i) rides, attractions and appurtenances associated with a ride or attraction, ticket booths and facades,

    (ii) equipment, furniture and fixtures, in or attached to a building included in this class,

    (iii) bridges, and

    (iv) fences or similar perimeter structures, and

  (c) automotive equipment (other than automotive equipment designed for use on highways or streets),

and property not included in another class in this Schedule that is a waterway or a land improvement (other than landscaping, clearing or levelling land) used in connection with an amusement park.

**Related Provisions**: Reg. 1103(2b) — Election to include earlier property in Class 37; Reg. 1104(12) — Meaning of "amusement park"; Reg. 1104(12); 4604(1)(a), 4604(2)(k) — Approved project property.

**Definitions [Reg. Sch. II:Cl. 37]**: "amusement park" — Reg. 1104(12); "associated" — ITA 256; "building" — Reg. 1102(5), (5.1); "class" — Reg. 1102 (1)–(3), (14), (14.1); "property" — ITA 248(1); "structure" — Reg 1102(5), (5.1).

### Class 38
[Reg. 1100(1)(zd)]

Property not included in Class 22 but that would otherwise be included in that class if that class were read without reference to paragraphs (a) and (b) thereof.

**Related Provisions**: Reg. 1101(5l) — Election for separate class; Reg. 4600(2)(e) — Qualified property; 4603(a) — Qualified construction equipment; 4604(2)(d) — Approved project property.

**Definitions [Reg. Sch. II:Cl. 38]**: "class" — Reg. 1102 (1)–(3), (14), (14.1); "property" — ITA 248(1).

**Interpretation Bulletins**: IT-411R: Meaning of "contruction"; IT-469R: CCA — Earth-moving equipment.

### Class 39
[Reg. 1100(1)(ze)]

Property acquired after 1987 and before February 26, 1992 that is not included in Class 29, but that would otherwise be included in that Class if that Class were read without reference to subparagraphs (b)(iii) and (v) and paragraph (c) thereof.

**Related Provisions**: Reg. 1104(9); 4600(2)(k) — Qualified property; 4604(2)(j) — Approved project property; Sch. II:Cl. 43.

**Notes**: Class 39 amended by P.C. 1994-230 to add the words "and before February 26, 1992". Such property is now in Class 43.

**Definitions [Reg. Sch. II:Cl. 39]**: "property" — ITA 248(1).

**Interpretation Bulletins**: IT-147R3: CCA — Accelerated write-off of manufacturing and processing machinery and equipment; IT-411R: Meaning of "construction".

### Class 40
[Reg. 1100(1)(zf)]

Property acquired after 1987 and before 1990 that is a powered industrial lift truck or property described in paragraph (b) or (f) of Class 10 and that is property not included in Class 29 but that would otherwise be included in that class if that class were read without reference to paragraph (c) thereof.

**Related Provisions**: Reg. 1103(2e) — Transfer from Class 40 to Class 10; 4600(2)(k) — Qualified property; 4604(2)(j) — Approved project property.

**Definitions [Reg. Sch. II:Cl. 40]**: "class" — Reg. 1102 (1)–(3), (14.1); "property" — ITA 248(1).

**Interpretation Bulletins**: IT-147R3: CCA — Accelerated write-off of manufacturing and processing machinery and equipment.

### Class 41 — (25 per cent)
[Reg. 1100(1)(a)(xxvii), 1100(1)(y)]

Property

  (a) not included in Class 28 that would otherwise be included in that class if that Class were read without reference to paragraph (a) of that Class, and if subparagraphs (e)(i) to (iii) of that Class were read as follows:

    "(i) property that was acquired before the mine came into production and that would, but for this Class, be included in Class 10 because of paragraph (g), (k), (l) or (r) of that class or would have been so included in that class if it had been acquired after the 1971 taxation year, and property that would, but for this class, be included in Class 41 because of subsection 1102(8) or (9),

    (ii) property that was acquired before the mine came into production and that would, but for this Class, be

  included in Class 10 because of paragraph (m) of that Class, or

    (iii) property that was acquired after the mine came into production and that would, but for this Class, be included in Class 10 because of paragraph (g), (k), (l) or (r) of that Class, and property that would, but for this Class, be included in Class 41 because of subsection 1102(8) or (9);"

(a.1) that is the portion, expressed as a percentage determined by reference to capital cost, of property that

(i) would, but for this Class, be included in Class 10 because of paragraph (g), (k), or (l) of that Class, or that is included in this Class because of subsection 1102(8) or (9),

(ii) is not described in paragraph (a) or (a.2),

(iii) was acquired by the taxpayer principally for the purpose of gaining or producing income from one or more mines that are operated by the taxpayer and situated in Canada, and that became available for use for the purpose of subsection 13(26) of the Act in a taxation year, and

(iv) had not, before it was acquired by the taxpayer, been used for any purpose by any person or partnership with whom the taxpayer was not dealing at arm's length,

where that percentage is determined by the formula

$$100 \times \frac{[A - (B \times 365/C)]}{A}$$

where

A is the total of all amounts each of which is the capital cost of a property of the taxpayer that became available for use for the purpose of subsection 13(26) of the Act in the year and that is described in subparagraphs (i) to (iv) in respect of the mine or mines, as the case may be,

B is 5% of the taxpayer's gross revenue from the mine or mines, as the case may be, for the year, and

C is the number of days in the year;

(a.2) that

(i) is property that would, but for this Class, be included in Class 10 because of paragraph (g), (k), or (l) of that Class or that is included in this Class because of subsection 1102(8) or (9),

(ii) was acquired by the taxpayer in a taxation year principally for the purpose of gaining or producing income from one or more mines each of which

(A) is one or more wells operated by the taxpayer for the extraction of material from a deposit of bituminous sands or oil shales, operated by the taxpayer and situated in Canada,

(B) was the subject of a major expansion after March 6, 1996, and

(C) is a mine in respect of which the Minister, in consultation with the Minister of Natural Resources, determines that the greatest designed capacity of the mine, measured in volume of oil that is not beyond the crude oil stage or its equivalent, immediately after the expansion was not less than 25% greater than the greatest designed capacity of the mine immediately before the expansion,

(iii) was acquired by the taxpayer

(A) after March 6, 1996,

(B) before the completion of the expansion, and

(C) in the course of and principally for the purposes of the expansion, and

(iv) had not, before it was acquired by the taxpayer, been used for any purpose by any person or partnership with whom the taxpayer was not dealing at arm's length;

(a.3) that is property included in this Class because of subsection 1102(8) or (9), other than property described in paragraph (a) or (a.2) or the portion of property described in paragraph (a.1);

(b) that is property

(i) described in paragraph (f.1), (g), (j), (k), (l), (m), (r), (t) or (u) of Class 10 that would be included in that Class if this Schedule were read without reference to this paragraph; or

(ii) that is a vessel, including the furniture, fittings, radio communication equipment and other equipment attached thereto, that is designed principally for the purpose of

(A) determining the existence, location, extent or quality of accumulations of petroleum, natural gas or mineral resources, or

(B) drilling oil or gas wells,

and that was acquired by the taxpayer after 1987 other than property that was acquired before 1990

(iii) pursuant to an obligation in writing entered into by the taxpayer before June 18, 1987,

(iv) that was under construction by or on behalf of the taxpayer on June 18, 1987, or

(v) that is machinery and equipment that is a fixed and integral part of property that was under construction by or on behalf of the taxpayer on June 18, 1987;

(c) acquired by the taxpayer after May 8, 1972, to be used directly or indirectly by the taxpayer in Canada primarily in Canadian field processing, where the property would be included in Class 29 if

(i) Class 29 were read without reference to subparagraphs (b)(iii) and (v) and paragraph (c) of that Class,

2490

(ii) subsection 1104(9) were read without reference to paragraph (k) of that subsection, and

(iii) this Schedule were read without reference to this Class, Class 39 and Class 43; or

(d) acquired by the taxpayer after December 5, 1996 (otherwise than pursuant to an agreement in writing made before December 6, 1996) to be leased, in the ordinary course of carrying on a business in Canada of the taxpayer, to a lessee who can reasonably be expected to use, directly or indirectly, the property in Canada primarily in Canadian field processing carried on by the lessee, where the property would be included in Class 29 if

(i) Class 29 were read without reference to subparagraphs (b)(iii) and (v) and paragraph (c) of that Class, and

(ii) this Schedule were read without reference to this Class, Class 39 and Class 43.

**Related Provisions**: ITA 13(5) — Reclassification of property as a result of change in regulations; ITA 257 — Negative amounts in formulas; Reg. 1101(4c), (4d) — Separate class for certain property under Class 41(a), (a.1) and (a.2); Reg. 1102(8)(d), 1102(9)(d) — Generating equipment; Reg. 1102(18) — Townsite costs; Reg. 1104(5) — Income from a mine; Reg. 1104(5.1), (5.2) — Gross revenue from a mine; Reg. 1104(7) — Meaning of "mine"; Reg. 1104(5), (6), (7), 1205(1)(a)(vi)(D), 1205(1)(c) — Earned depletion base; 1206(1)"bituminous sands equipment", "tertiary recovery equipment"; 4600(1)(b), 4600(2)(g), (j) — Qualified property; 4601(a)(vi) — Qualified transportation equipment; 4604(2)(i) — Approved project property; Reg. Sch. II Cl. 43.

**Notes**: Cl. 41(a) amended to add everything after "without reference to paragraph (a) thereof", and paras. (a.1)–(a.3) added, by P.C. 1998-49. The amendment to para. (a) and para. (a.3) are effective in respect of property acquired after 1987; paras. (a.1) and (a.2) are effective in respect of property acquired after March 6, 1996.

Cl. 41(a.1) implements the 1996 budget proposal for accelerated CCA for Cl. 41 property, that becomes available for use in respect of a mine in a year, in excess of 5% of the gross revenue from the mine for the year. (See Reg. 1104(5.1)–(5.2)).

Cl. 41(a.2) implements the 1996 budget proposal to treat oil sands *in-situ* projects as mines for CCA purposes. It provides a "major mine expansion" test for *in-situ* projects, analogous to the test in Class 28, to determine eligibility for accelerated CCA.

Cl. 41(a.2)(ii)(C) amended by P.C. 2000-1331, effective for expansions commencing after September 13, 2000, to change "barrels of oil" to "volume of oil", and "Minister is satisfied" to "Minister determines".

Cl. 41(a.3) provides a cross-reference for property in Reg. 1102(8) and (9) (electrical plant for mining), which is thus included in Cl. 41. This property is not eligible for accelerated CCA, but is given the same 25% rate as property in Cl. 41(b).

Class 41(b)(i) amended by P.C. 1994-230, effective for property acquired after February 25, 1992 (and amended retroactively by P.C. 1997-1033 to add a missing word "or" at the end). Formerly read:

(i) that would otherwise be included in paragraph (f.1), (g), (j), (k), (l), (m), (r), (t), or (u) of Class 10, or.

41(c) and (d) added by P.C. 1999-629, effective for taxation years that begin after 1996.

**Definitions [Reg. Sch. II:Cl. 41]**: "amount" — ITA 248(1); "arm's length" — ITA 251(1); "bituminous sands", "business" — ITA 248(1); "Canada" — ITA 255, *Interpretation Act* 35(1); "Canadian field processing" — ITA 248(1); "class" — Reg. 1102 (1)–(3), (14), (14.1); "gross revenue" — ITA 248(1); "gross revenue from a mine" — Reg. 1104(5.1); "income from one or more mines" — Reg. 1104(5), (6.1)(a); "mine" — Reg. 1104(7)(a); "mineral resource", "Minister", "oil or gas well" — ITA 248(1); "partnership" — see Notes to ITA 96(1); "person", "property" — ITA 248(1); "radio" — *Interpretation Act* 35(1); "taxation year" — ITA 249; "taxpayer" — ITA 248(1); "writing" — *Interpretation Act* 35(1).

**Interpretation Bulletins**: IT-267R2: CCA — vessels.

## Class 42 — (12 per cent)
[Reg. 1100(1)(a)(xxviii)]

Property that is fibre optic cable.

**Related Provisions**: Reg. Sch. II Cl. 3(l)–Supporting equipment.

**Notes**: Class 42 added by P.C. 1994-139, effective for property acquired after December 23, 1991, other than property acquired pursuant to an agreement in writing entered into by the taxpayer before December 24, 1991. However, if the taxpayer so elected in a letter filed with Revenue Canada by August 8, 1994 or filed with the taxpayer's return for the first taxation year ending after December 23, 1991, then Reg. 1100(1)(a)(xxviii), amended Classes 3(j) and (l) and Class 42 apply to property acquired after the beginning of that taxation year. If the taxpayer made such election, ignore Class 42 with respect to property acquired before December 24, 1991.

**Definitions [Reg. Sch. II:Cl. 42]**: "property" — ITA 248(1).

## Class 43 — (30 per cent)
[Reg. 1100(1)(a)(xxix)]

Property acquired after February 25, 1992 that

(a) is not included in Class 29, but that would otherwise be included in that Class if that Class were read without reference to subparagraphs (b)(iii) and (v) and paragraph (c) thereof; or

(b) is property

(i) that is described in paragraph (k) of Class 10 and that would be included in that Class if this Schedule were read without reference to this paragraph and paragraph (b) of Class 41, and

(ii) that, at the time of its acquisition, can reasonably be expected to be used entirely in Canada and primarily for the purpose of processing ore extracted from a mineral resource located in a country other than Canada.

**Proposed Amendment — Separate class for manufacturing and processing equipment**

**Federal budget, supplementary information, February 28, 2000**: [See under Reg. 1101(5p) — ed.]

**Related Provisions**: Reg. 4600(2)(k), 4604(2)(j) — Investment tax credit.

**Notes**: Class 43 added by P.C. 1994-230, effective for property acquired after February 25, 1992, and para. 43(b) amended retroactive to its introduction by P.C. 1997-1033. Any election under Class 43(b)(i) was on time if filed by August 22, 1994.

**Definitions [Reg. Sch. II:Cl. 43]**: "Canada" — ITA 255, *Interpretation Act* 35(1); "mineral resource", "property" — ITA 248(1).

**Interpretation Bulletins**: IT-411R: Meaning of "construction".

## Class 43.1 — (30 per cent)
[Reg. 1100(1)(a)(xxix.1)]

Property, other than reconditioned or remanufactured equipment, that would otherwise be included in Class 1, 2 or 8

(a) that is

(i) electrical generating equipment, including any heat generating equipment used primarily for the purpose of producing heat energy to operate the electrical generating equipment,

(ii) equipment that generates both electrical and heat energy,

(iii) heat recovery equipment used primarily for the purpose of conserving energy, or reducing the requirement to acquire energy, by

(A) extracting thermal waste that is generated by equipment referred to in subparagraph (i) or (ii), and

(B) reusing the thermal waste to generate electrical energy from equipment referred to in subparagraph (i) or (ii),

(iv) control, feedwater and condensate systems and other equipment, where that property is ancillary to equipment described in subparagraph (i), (ii) or (iii), or

(v) an addition to a property described in any of subparagraphs (i) to (iv),

other than buildings or other structures, heat rejection equipment (such as condensers and cooling water systems), transmission equipment, distribution equipment, fuel storage facilities and fuel handling equipment,

(b) that

(i) is situated in Canada,

(ii) is

(A) acquired by the taxpayer for use by the taxpayer for the purpose of gaining or producing income from a business carried on in Canada or from property situated in Canada, or

(B) leased by the taxpayer to a lessee for the use by the lessee for the purpose of gaining or producing income from a business carried on in Canada or from property situated in Canada, and

(iii) has not been used for any purpose before it was acquired by the taxpayer unless

(A) the property was depreciable property that

(I) was included in Class 34 or 43.1 of the person from whom it was acquired, or

(II) that would have been included in Class 34 or 43.1 of the person from whom it was acquired had the person made a valid election to include the property in Class 43.1 pursuant ot paragraph 1102(8)(d) or 1102(9)(d), and

(B) the property was acquired by the taxpayer not more than five years after it became available for use for the purpose of subsection 13(26) of the Act by the person from whom it was acquired and remains at the same site in Canada as that at which that person used the property, and

(c) that is

(i) part of a system (other than an enhanced combined cycle system) that

(A) is used by the taxpayer, or by a lessee of the taxpayer, to generate electrical energy, or both electrical and heat energy, using only fuel that is fossil fuel, wood waste, municipal waste, landfill gas or digester gas, or any combination of those fuels, and

(B) has a heat rate attributable to fossil fuel (other than solution gas) not exceeding 6,000 BTU per kilowatt-hour of electrical energy generated by the system, which heat rate is calculated as the fossil fuel (expressed as the high heat value of the fossil fuel) used by the system that is chargeable to gross electrical energy output on an annual basis, or

(ii) part of an enhanced combined cycle system that

(A) is used by the taxpayer, or by a lessee of the taxpayer, to generate electrical energy using only a combination of natural gas and waste heat from one or more natural gas compressor systems located on a natural gas pipeline,

(B) has an incremental heat rate not exceeding 6,700 BTU per kilowatt-hour of electricity generated by the system, which heat rate is calculated as the natural gas (expressed as its high heat value) used by the system that is chargeable to gross electrical energy output on an annual basis, and

(C) does not have economically viable access to a steam host,

and property (other than property described in paragraph (a)) that would otherwise be included in another Class in this Schedule

(d) that is

(i) active solar heating equipment used by the taxpayer, or by a lessee of the taxpayer, primarily for the purpose of heating a liquid or gas used directly in an industrial process, including such equipment that consists of solar collectors, solar energy conversion equipment, solar water heaters, energy storage equipment, control equipment and equipment designed to interface solar heating equipment with other

Cl. 43.1 — (30 per cent)    Reg. Cl. 43.1(d)(ix)

heating equipment, but not including buildings,

(ii) a hydro-electric installation of a producer of hydro-electric energy, where that installation

(A) has an annual average generating capacity not exceeding 15 megawatts upon completion of site development, and

(B) is the electrical generating equipment and plant (including structures) of that producer including a canal, a dam, a dyke, an overflow spillway, a penstock, a powerhouse (complete with electrical generating equipment and other ancillary equipment), control equipment, fishways or fish by-passes, and transmission equipment,

other than distribution equipment and property otherwise included in Class 10 or 17,

(iii) an addition or alteration to a hydro-electric installation described in subparagraph (ii) that results in an increase in generating capacity, if the resulting annual average generating capacity of the hydro-electric installation does not exceed 15 megawatts,

(iv) heat recovery equipment used by the taxpayer, or by a lessee of the taxpayer, primarily for the purpose of conserving energy, or reducing the requirement to acquire energy, by

(A) extracting thermal waste that is generated directly in an industrial process (other than in an industrial process that generates or processes electrical energy), and

(B) reusing the thermal waste directly in an industrial process (other than in an industrial process that generates or processes electrical energy),

including such equipment that consists of heat exchange equipment, compressors used to upgrade low pressure steam, vapour or gas, waste heat boilers and other ancillary equipment such as control panels, fans, instruments or pumps, but not including buildings,

(v) a fixed location device that is a wind energy conversion system that

(A) is used by the taxpayer, or by a lessee of the taxpayer, primarily for the purpose of generating electrical energy, and

(B) consists of a wind-driven turbine, electrical generating equipment and related equipment, including

(I) control, conditioning and battery storage equipment,

(II) support structures,

(III) a powerhouse complete with other ancillary equipment, and

(IV) transmission equipment,

other than distribution equipment, auxiliary electrical generating equipment or property otherwise included in Class 10 or 17,

(vi) fixed location photovoltaic equipment that

(A) is used by the taxpayer, or by a lessee of the taxpayer, primarily for the purpose of generating electrical energy from solar energy,

(B) has a peak capacity of not less than 3 kilowatts of electrical output, and

(C) consists of solar cells or modules and related equipment including

(I) control, conditioning and battery storage equipment,

(II) support structures, and

(III) transmission equipment,

other than buildings, distribution equipment, auxiliary electrical generating equipment and property otherwise included in Class 10 or 17,

(vii) above-ground equipment used by the taxpayer, or by a lessee of the taxpayer, primarily for the purpose of generating electrical energy solely from geothermal energy, including such equipment that consists of pumps, heat exchangers, steam separators, electrical generating equipment and ancillary equipment used to collect the geothermal heat, but not including buildings, transmission equipment, distribution equipment, equipment designed to store electrical energy and property otherwise included in Class 10 or 17,

(viii) above-ground equipment used by the taxpayer, or by a lessee of the taxpayer, primarily for the purpose of collecting landfill gas or digester gas, including such equipment that consists of fans, compressors, storage tanks, heat exchangers and other ancillary equipment used to collect the gas, to remove non-combustibles and contaminants from the gas or to store the gas, but not including buildings or property otherwise included in Class 10 or 17,

(ix) equipment used by the taxpayer, or by a lessee of the taxpayer, primarily for the purpose of generating heat energy from the consumption of wood waste, municipal waste, landfill gas or digester gas, if the heat energy is used directly in an industrial process carried on by the taxpayer or lessee, including such equipment that consists of fuel handling equipment used to upgrade the combustible portion of the fuel and control, feedwater and condensate systems, and other ancillary equipment, but not including buildings or other structures, property otherwise included in Class 10 or 17, heat rejection equipment (such as condensers and cooling water systems),

**Reg.**
**Cl. 43.1(d)(ix)**          Income Tax Regulations, Schedule II

fuel storage facilities, fuel handling equipment and electrical generating equipment, or

(x) an expansion engine with one or more turbines, or cylinders, that convert the compression energy in pressurized natural gas into shaft power that generates electricity, including the related electrical generating equipment and ancillary controls, where the expansion engine

(A) is part of a system that is installed

(I) on a distribution line of a distributor of natural gas, or

(II) on a branch distribution line of a taxpayer primarily engaged in the manufacturing or processing of goods for sale or lease if the branch line is used to deliver natural gas directly to the taxpayer's manufacturing or processing facility, and

(B) is used instead of a pressure reducing valve, and

(e) that

(i) is situated in Canada,

(ii) is

(A) acquired by the taxpayer for use by the taxpayer for the purpose of gaining or producing income from a business carried on in Canada or from property situated in Canada, or

(B) leased by the taxpayer to a lessee for the use by the lessee for the purpose of gaining or producing income from a business carried on in Canada or from property situated in Canada, and

(iii) has not been used for any purpose before it was acquired by the taxpayer unless

(A) the property was depreciable property that was

(I) described in Class 34 or 43.1 of the person from whom it was acquired, or

(II) would have been included in Class 34 or 43.1 or the person from whom it was acquired had the person made a valid election to include the property in Class 43.1 pursuant to paragraph 1102(8)(d) or 1102(9)(d), and

(B) the property was acquired by the taxpayer not more than five years after it became available for use for the purpose of subsection 13(26) of the Act by the person from whom it was acquired and remains at the same site in Canada as that at which that person used the property.

**Related Provisions**: ITA 13(18.1) — Energy, Mines and Resources "Technical Guide to Class 43.1" to be determinative; ITA 66(15)"principal-business corporation"(h), (i) — Corporation whose business uses property in Class 43.1; Reg. 1100(24), (25) — Limitation on deduction for specified energy property; Reg.

1102(8)(d), 1102(9)(d) — Generating equipment — election for Class 43.1; Reg. 1102(21) — Limitation where Cl. 43.1(b)(iii)(A) or (B) or 43.1(e)(iii)(A) or (B) applies; Reg. 1104(13) — Definitions; Reg. 1104(14) — Where Cl. 43.1(c) not operating due to deficiency, failing or shutdown; Reg. 1219 — Canadian renewable and conservation expense; Reg. 8200.1 — Cl. 43.1 property is prescribed energy conservation property.

**Notes**: 43.1(b) amended by P.C. 2000-1331, effective for property acquired after June 26, 1996 except that, in respect of property acquired before 1998 pursuant to an agreement in writing made by that date, ignore (b)(i) and (iii). Before the amendment, read:

(b) that has not been used for any purpose whatever before it is acquired by the taxpayer and that is

(i) acquired by the taxpayer for use by the taxpayer for the purpose of gaining or producing income from a business carried on in Canada or from property situated in Canada, or

(ii) leased by the taxpayer to a lessee for use by the lessee for the purpose of gaining or producing income from a business carried on in Canada or from property situated in Canada, and

The systems referred to in 43.1(c)(i) may be called "cogeneration" systems. 43.1(c)(i)(B) amended by P.C. 2000-1331, effective for property acquired after February 16, 1999, to add "(other than solution gas)".

43.1(d)(vi)(B) amended by P.C. 2000-1331, effective for property acquired after February 18, 1997, to change "10 kilowatts" to "3 kilowatts".

43.1(e) amended by P.C. 2000-1331, effective for property acquired after June 26, 1996 except that, in respect of property acquired before 1998 pursuant to an agreement in writing made by that date, ignore (e)(i) and (iii). Before the amendment, read:

(e) that has not been used for any purpose whatever before it was acquired by the taxpayer and that is

(i) acquired by the taxpayer for use by the taxpayer for the purpose of gaining or producing income from a business carried on in Canada or from property situated in Canada, or

(ii) leased by the taxpayer to a lessee for use by the lessee for the purpose of gaining or producing income from a business carried on in Canada or from property situated in Canada.

Class 43.1 added by P.C. 1997-1033, effective for property acquired after February 21, 1994 except that

(a) in respect of property

(i) acquired by the taxpayer pursuant to an agreement of purchase and sale in writing made before September 27, 1994, or

(ii) under construction by or on behalf of the taxpayer before September 27, 1994,

read cl. (c)(ii)(B) as follows:

(B) has a an incremental heat rate not exceeding 7,000 BTU per kilowatt-hour of electricity generated by the system, which heat rate is calculated as the natural gas (expressed as its high heat value) used by the system that is chargeable to the gross electrical energy output on an annual basis, and

and

(b) in respect of property acquired by a taxpayer before June 27, 1996, or acquired before 1998 pursuant to an agreement in writing made by a taxpayer before June 27, 1996,

(i) in the opening words of Class 43.1, ignore the words "other than reconditioned or remanufactured equipment,",

(ii) read the opening words of para. 43.1(b) as follows:

(b) that is

and

(iii) read the opening words of para. 43.1 (e) as follows:

(e) that is

**Definitions [Reg. Sch. II:Cl. 43.1]:** "building" — Reg 1102(5), (5.1); "business" — ITA 248(1); "Canada" — ITA 255, *Interpretation Act* 35(1); "depreciable property" — ITA 13(21), 248(1); "digester gas", "distribution equipment", "enhanced combined cycle system", "fossil fuel", "landfill gas", "municipal waste" — Reg. 1104(13); "person", "property" — ITA 248(1); "related" — ITA 251(2)–(6); "solution gas" — Reg. 1104(13); "structure" — Reg. 1102(5), (5.1); "taxpayer" — ITA 248(1); "thermal waste", "transmission equipment", "wood waste" — Reg. 1104(13).

### Class 44 — (25 per cent)

[Reg. 1100(1)(a)(xxx), 1100(9.1), 1103(2h)]

Property that is a patent, or a right to use patented information for a limited or unlimited period.

**Related Provisions:** Reg. 1103(2h) — Election not to include property in Class 44; Reg. Sch. II:Cl. 14 — Patent for a limited period.

**Notes:** Class 44 added by P.C. 1994-231, effective for property acquired after April 26, 1993.

**Definitions [Reg. Sch. II:Cl. 44]:** "property" — ITA 248(1).

## SCHEDULE III — CAPITAL COST ALLOWANCES, CLASS 13

**1.** For the purposes of paragraph 1100(1)(b), the amount that may be deducted in computing the income of a taxpayer for a taxation year in respect of the capital cost to him of a property of Class 13 in Schedule II is the lesser of

(a) the aggregate of each amount determined in accordance with section 2 of this Schedule that is a prorated portion of the part of the capital cost to him, incurred in a particular taxation year, of a particular leasehold interest; and

(b) the undepreciated capital cost to the taxpayer as of the end of the taxation year (before making any deduction under section 1100) of property of the class.

**Definitions:** "amount" — ITA 248(1); "capital cost" — Reg. 1100(1)(b); "property" — ITA 248(1); "taxation year" — ITA 249; "taxpayer" — ITA 248(1); "undepreciated capital cost" — ITA 13(21), 248(1).

**2.** Subject to section 3 of this Schedule, the prorated portion for the year of the part of the capital cost, incurred in a particular taxation year, of a particular leasehold interest is the lesser of

(a) 1/5 of that part of the capital cost; and

(b) the amount determined by dividing that part of the capital cost by the number of 12-month periods (not exceeding 40 such periods) falling within the period commencing with the beginning of the particular taxation year in which the capital cost was incurred and ending with the day the lease is to terminate.

**Definitions:** "amount" — ITA 248(1); "capital cost" — Reg. 1100(1)(b); "taxation year" — ITA 249.

**3.** For the purpose of determining, under section 2 of this Schedule, the prorated portion for the year of the part of the capital cost, incurred in a particular taxation year, of a particular leasehold interest, the following rules apply:

(a) where an item of the capital cost of a leasehold interest was incurred before the taxation year in which the interest was acquired, it shall be deemed to have been incurred in the taxation year in which the interest was acquired;

(b) where, under a lease, a tenant has a right to renew the lease for an additional term, or for more than one additional term, after the term that includes the end of the particular taxation year in which the capital cost was incurred, the lease shall be deemed to terminate on the day on which the term next succeeding the term in which the capital cost was incurred is to terminate;

(c) the prorated portion for the year of the part of the capital cost, incurred in a particular taxation year, of a particular leasehold interest shall not exceed the amount, if any, remaining after deducting from that part of the capital cost the aggregate of the amounts claimed and deductible in previous years in respect thereof;

(d) where, at the end of a taxation year, the aggregate of

(i) the amounts claimed and deductible in previous taxation years in respect of a particular leasehold interest, and

(ii) the proceeds of disposition, if any, of part or all of that interest

equals or exceeds the capital cost as of that time of the interest, the prorated portion of any part of that capital cost shall, for all subsequent years, be deemed to be nil; and

(e) where, at the end of a taxation year, the undepreciated capital cost to the taxpayer of property of Class 13 in Schedule II is nil, the prorated portion of any part of the capital cost as of that time shall, for all subsequent years, be deemed to be nil.

**Definitions:** "amount" — ITA 248(1); "capital cost" — Reg. 1100(1)(b); "property" — ITA 248(1); "taxation year" — ITA 249; "taxpayer" — ITA 248(1); "undepreciated capital cost" — ITA 13(21), 248(1).

**Interpretation Bulletins:** IT-324: CCA — Emphyteutic lease; IT-464R: CCA — Leasehold interests.

**4.** Where a taxpayer has acquired a property that would, if the property had been acquired by a person with whom the taxpayer was not dealing at arm's length at the time the property was acquired, be a leasehold interest of that person, a reference in this Schedule to a leasehold interest shall, in respect of the taxpayer, include a reference to that property, and the terms and conditions of the leasehold interest of that property in respect of the taxpayer shall be deemed to be the same as those that would have applied in respect of that person had that person acquired the property.

**Notes**: S. 4 added by P.C. 1994-139, effective for property acquired after December 23, 1991, other than property acquired before 1993

(a) pursuant to an agreement in writing entered into before December 24, 1991, or

(b) that was under construction by or on behalf of the taxpayer on December 23, 1991.

**Definitions**: "arm's length" — ITA 251(1); "person", "property", "taxpayer" — ITA 248(1).

## SCHEDULE IV — CAPITAL COST ALLOWANCES, CLASS 15

**1.** For the purposes of paragraph 1100(1)(f), the amount that may be deducted in computing the income of a taxpayer for a taxation year in respect of property described in Class 15 in Schedule II is the lesser of

(a) an amount computed on the basis of a rate per cord, board foot or cubic metre cut in the taxation year; and

(b) the undepreciated capital cost to the taxpayer as of the end of the taxation year (before making any deduction under section 1100 for the taxation year) of property of that class.

**Notes**: Reference to "cubic metre" added to 1(a) by P.C. 1994-139, effective for 1986 and later taxation years.

**Definitions**: "amount", "property" — ITA 248(1); "taxation year" — ITA 249; "taxpayer" — ITA 248(1); "undepreciated capital cost" — ITA 13(21), 248(1).

**2.** Where all the property of the class is used in connection with one timber limit or section thereof, the rate per cord, board foot or cubic metre is the amount determined by dividing

(a) the undepreciated capital cost to the taxpayer as of the end of the taxation year (before making any deduction under section 1100 for the taxation year) of the property

by

(b) the number of cords, board feet or cubic metres of timber in the limit or section thereof as of the commencement of the taxation year, obtained by deducting the quantity cut up to that time from the amount shown by the latest cruise.

**Notes**: Reference to "cubic metres" added to s. 2 by P.C. 1994-139, effective for 1986 and later taxation years.

**Definitions**: "amount" — ITA 248(1); "commencement" — *Interpretation Act* 35(1); "property" — ITA 248(1); "taxation year" — ITA 249; "taxpayer" — ITA 248(1); "undepreciated capital cost" — ITA 13(21), 248(1).

**3.** Where a part of the property of the class is used in connection with one timber limit or a section thereof and a part is used in connection with another limit or section thereof, a separate rate shall be computed for each part of the property, in the manner provided in section 2 of this Schedule, as though each part of the property were the taxpayer's only property of that class.

**Definitions**: "property", "taxpayer" — ITA 248(1).

## SCHEDULE V — CAPITAL COST ALLOWANCES, INDUSTRIAL MINERAL MINES

**1.** For the purposes of paragraph 1100(1)(g), the amount that may be deducted in computing the income of a taxpayer for a taxation year in respect of a property described in that paragraph that is an industrial mineral mine or a right to remove industrial minerals from an industrial mineral mine is the lesser of

(a) an amount computed on the basis of a rate (computed under section 2 or 3 of this Schedule, as the case may be) per unit of mineral mined in the taxation year; and

(b) the undepreciated capital cost to the taxpayer as of the end of the taxation year (before making any deduction under section 1100) of the mine or right.

**Definitions**: "amount" — ITA 248(1); "industrial mineral mine", "mineral" — Reg. 1104(3); "property" — ITA 248(1); "taxation year" — ITA 249; "taxpayer" — ITA 248(1); "undepreciated capital cost" — ITA 13(21), 248(1).

**2.** Where the taxpayer has not been granted an allowance in respect of the mine or right for a previous taxation year, the rate for a taxation year is an amount determined by dividing the capital cost of the mine or right to the taxpayer minus the residual value, if any, by

(a) in any case where the taxpayer has acquired a right to remove only a specified number of units, the specified number of units of material that he acquired a right to remove; and

(b) in any other case, the number of units of commercially mineable material estimated as being in the mine when the mine or right was acquired.

**Definitions**: "amount" — ITA 248(1); "residual value" — Reg. Sch. V s. 5; "taxation year" — ITA 249; "taxpayer" — ITA 248(1).

**3.** Where the taxpayer has been granted an allowance in respect of the mine or right in a previous taxation year, the rate for the taxation year is

(a) where paragraph (b) does not apply, the rate employed to determine the allowance for the most recent year for which an allowance was granted; and

(b) where it has been established that the number of units of material remaining to be mined in the previous taxation year was in fact different from the quantity that was employed in determining the rate for the previous year referred to in paragraph (a), or where it has been established that the capital cost of the mine or right is substantially different from the amount that was employed in determining the rate for that previous year, a rate determined by dividing the undepreciated capital cost to the taxpayer of the mine or right as of the commencement of the year minus the residual value, if any, by

(i) in any case where the taxpayer has acquired a right to remove only a specified number of units, the number of units of commercially mineable material that, at the commencement of the year, he had a right to remove, and

(ii) in any other case, the number of units of commercially mineable material estimated as remaining in the mine at the commencement of the year.

**Definitions**: "amount" — ITA 248(1); "commencement" — *Interpretation Act* 35(1); "employed" — ITA 248(1); "residual value" — Reg. Sch. V s. 5; "taxation year" — ITA 249; "taxpayer" — ITA 248(1); "undepreciated capital cost" — ITA 13(21), 248(1).

**4.** In lieu of the aggregate of deductions otherwise allowable under this Schedule, a taxpayer may elect that the deduction for the taxation year be the lesser of

(a) $100; and

(b) the amount received by him in the taxation year from the sale of mineral.

**Definitions**: "amount" — ITA 248(1); "mineral" — Reg. 1104(3); "taxation year" — ITA 249; "taxpayer" — ITA 248(1).

**5.** In this Schedule, "residual value" means the estimated value of the property if all commercially mineable material were removed.

**Definitions**: "property" — ITA 248(1).

**Interpretation Bulletins [Schedule V]**: IT-423: Sale of sand, gravel or topsoil; IT-492: Industrial mineral mines.

# SCHEDULE VI — CAPITAL COST ALLOWANCES, TIMBER LIMITS AND CUTTING RIGHTS

**1.** For the purposes of paragraph 1100(1)(e), the amount that may be deducted in computing the income of a taxpayer for a taxation year in respect of the capital cost to him of a property, other than a timber resource property, that is a timber limit or a right to cut timber from a limit is the lesser of

(a) the aggregate of

(i) an amount computed on the basis of a rate (determined under section 2 or 3 of this Schedule) per cord, board foot or cubic metre cut in the year, and

(ii) the lesser of

(A) 1/10 of the amount expended by the taxpayer after the commencement of his 1949 taxation year that is included in the capital cost to him of the timber limit or right, for surveys, cruises or preparation of prints, maps or plans for the purpose of obtaining a licence or right to cut timber, and

(B) the amount expended as described in clause (A) minus the aggregate of amounts deducted under this subparagraph in computing the income of the taxpayer in previous years; and

(b) the undepreciated capital cost to the taxpayer as of the end of the year (before making any deduction under section 1100 for the year) of the timber limit or right.

**Notes**: Reference to "cubic metre" added to 1(a)(i) by P.C. 1994-139, effective for 1986 and later taxation years.

**Definitions**: "amount" — ITA 248(1); "commencement" — *Interpretation Act* 35(1); "property" — ITA 248(1); "taxation year" — ITA 249; "taxpayer" — ITA 248(1); "timber resource property", "undepreciated capital cost" — ITA 13(21), 248(1).

**2.** If the taxpayer has not been granted an allowance in respect of the limit or right for a previous taxation year, the rate for a taxation year is an amount determined by dividing

(a) the capital cost of the limit or right to the taxpayer, minus the aggregate of the residual value of the timber limit and any amount expended by the taxpayer after the commencement of his 1949 taxation year that is included in the capital cost to him of the timber limit or right, for surveys, cruises or preparation of prints, maps or plans for the purpose of obtaining a licence or right to cut timber,

by

(b) the quantity of timber in the limit or the quantity of timber the taxpayer has obtained a right to cut, as the case may be, (expressed in cords, board feet or cubic metres) as shown by a cruise.

**Notes**: Reference to "cubic metres" added to 2(b) and "bona fide cruise" changed to "cruise", by P.C. 1994-139, effective for 1986 and later taxation years.

**Definitions**: "amount" — ITA 248(1); "commencement" — *Interpretation Act* 35(1); "residual value" — Reg. Sch. VI s. 5; "taxation year" — ITA 249; "taxpayer" — ITA 248(1).

**3.** If the taxpayer has been granted an allowance in respect of the limit or right in a previous taxation year, the rate for a taxation year is

(a) where paragraph (b) does not apply, the rate employed to determine the allowance for the most recent year for which an allowance was granted; and

(b) where it has been established that the quantity of timber that was in the limit or that the taxpayer had a right to cut was in fact substantially different from the quantity that was employed in determining the rate for the previous year referred to in paragraph (a), or where it has been established that the capital cost of the limit or right is substantially different from the amount that was em-

**Reg. Sch. VI** — Income Tax Regulations

ployed in determining the rate for that previous year, a rate determined by dividing

(i) the undepreciated capital cost to the taxpayer of the limit or right as of the commencement of the year, minus the residual value,

by

(ii) the estimated remaining quantity of timber that is in the limit or that the taxpayer has a right to cut, as the case may be, (expressed in cords, board feet or cubic metres) at the commencement of the year.

**Notes**: Reference to "cubic metres" added to 3(b)(ii) by P.C. 1994-139, effective for 1986 and later taxation years.

**Definitions**: "amount" — ITA 248(1); "commencement" — *Interpretation Act* 35(1); "employed" — ITA 248(1); "residual value" — Reg. Sch. VI s. 5; "taxation year" — ITA 249; "taxpayer" — ITA 248(1); "undepreciated capital cost" — ITA 13(21), 248(1).

**4.** In lieu of the deduction otherwise determined under this Schedule, a taxpayer may elect that the deduction for a taxation year to be the lesser of

(a) $100; and

(b) the amount received by him in the taxation year from the sale of timber.

**Definitions**: "amount" — ITA 248(1); "taxation year" — ITA 249; "taxpayer" — ITA 248(1).

**5.** In this Schedule, "residual value" means the estimated value of the property if the merchantable timber were removed.

**Definitions**: "property" — ITA 248(1).

**Interpretation Bulletins**: IT-481: Timber limits and cutting rights.

## SCHEDULE VII — PUBLICLY-TRADED SHARES OR SECURITIES

[Reg. 4400]

**Notes**: Schedule VII lists the values of publicly-traded shares on valuation day (V-Day), December 22, 1971. That date was used because, at the time, settlement of publicly traded shares normally occurred five business days after purchase or sale. Schedule VII is needed where a taxpayer disposes of publicly-traded shares that have been held continuously since before 1972. Only the gain since V-Day is treated as a capital gain: see ITAR 26(3) and 26(11).

Schedule VII, which fills 25 pages, is not reproduced in the *Practitioner's Income Tax Act* because it is no longer relevant to most taxpayers. For a copy of Schedule VII, consult the *Stikeman Income Tax Act*, the *Canada Tax Service, Tax Regulations Reports*, the *TaxPartner* CD-ROM, or TaxNet.

## SCHEDULE VIII — UNIVERSITIES OUTSIDE CANADA

**Notes**: The institutions listed below, which are prescribed under Reg. 3503 for purposes of ITA 118.1(1)"total charitable gifts"(f) and 110.1(1)(a)(vi), are accepted by the CCRA for purposes of the tuition credit in 118.5(1)(b). See IT-516R2, para. 4.

The CCRA has been reviewing the list in Sch. VIII and has had institutions removed that have not had significant numbers of Canadian residents attend as students. See Drache, "Schedule VIII Universities Under Review", 7(8) *Canadian Not-For-Profit News* (Carswell) (August 1999) 58-59.

**Interpretation Bulletins**: IT-516R2: Tuition tax credit.

**1.** The universities situated in the United States of America that are prescribed by section 3503 are the following:

Abilene Christian University, Abilene, Texas
Adams State College, Alamosa, Colorado
Alfred University, Alfred, New York
American Film Institute Center for Advanced Film and Television Studies, Los Angeles, California
American Graduate School of International Management, Glendale, Arizona
American International College, Springfield, Massachusetts
American University, The, Washington, District of Columbia
American University in Cairo, The, New York, New York
Amherst College, Amherst, Massachusetts
Anderson College, Anderson, South Carolina
Andover Newton Theological School, Newton Centre, Massachusetts
Andrews University, Berrien Springs, Michigan
Antioch College, Yellow Springs, Ohio
Arizona State University, Tempe, Arizona
Asbury Theological Seminary, Wilmore, Kentucky
Associated Mennonite Biblical Seminary, Elkhart, Indiana
Atlantic Union College, South Lancaster, Massachusetts
Augsburg College, Minneapolis, Minnesota
Azusa Pacific College, Azusa, California
Babson College, Babson Park, Massachusetts
Bard College, Annandale-on-Hudson, New York
Barnard College, New York, New York
Bates College, Lewiston, Maine
Bastyr University, Seattle, Washington
Beloit College, Beloit, Wisconsin
Bennington College, Bennington, Vermont
Bentley College, Waltham, Massachusetts
Beth Medrash, Govoha, Lakewood, New Jersey
Bethel College, Mishawaka, Indiana
Bethel College and Seminary, St. Paul, Minnesota
Bethel College, North Newton, Kansas
Biola University, LaMirada, California
Bob Jones University, Greenville, South Carolina
Boston College, Chestnut Hill, Massachusetts
Boston University, Boston, Massachusetts
Bowdoin College, Brunswick, Maine
Bowling Green State University, Bowling Green, Ohio
Brandeis University, Waltham, Massachusetts

2498

## Schedule VIII — Universities outside Canada

Brigham Young University — Hawaii Campus, Laie, Hawaii
Brigham Young University, Provo, Utah
Brown University, Providence, Rhode Island
Bryn Mawr College, Bryn Mawr, Pennsylvania
Bucknell University, Lewisburg, Pennsylvania
California Institute of Technology, Pasadena, California
California Lutheran University, Thousand Oaks, California
Calvin College, Grand Rapids, Michigan
Calvin Theological Seminary, Grand Rapids, Michigan
Canisius College, Buffalo, New York
Carleton College, Northfield, Minnesota
Carnegie-Mellon University, Pittsburgh, Pennsylvania
Carroll College, Helena, Montana
Case Western Reserve University, Cleveland, Ohio
Catholic University of America, The, Washington, District of Columbia
Cedarville College, Cedarville, Ohio
Central Michigan University, Mount Pleasant, Michigan
Central Yeshiva Tomchei Tmimim-Lubavitch, Brooklyn, New York
City University, Bellevue, Washington
Claremont McKenna College, Claremont, California
Clark University, Worcester, Massachusetts
Clarkson University, Potsdam, New York
Colby College, Waterville, Maine
Colby-Sawyer College, New London, New Hampshire
Colgate University, Hamilton, New York
Colgate-Rochester Divinity School, The, Rochester, New York
College of William and Mary, Williamsburg, Virginia
Colorado College, The, Colorado Springs, Colorado
Colorado School of Mines, Golden, Colorado
Colorado State University, Fort Collins, Colorado
Columbia International University, Columbia, South Carolina
Columbia Pacific University, San Rafael, California
Columbia Union College, Takoma Park, Maryland
Columbia University in the City of New York, New York, New York
Concordia College, Moorhead, Minnesota
Connecticut College, New London, Connecticut
Cornell University, Ithaca, New York
Cornerstone College and Grand Rapids Baptist Seminary, Grand Rapids, Michigan
Covenant College, Lookout Mountain, Tennessee
Creighton University, Omaha, Nebraska
Curtis Institute of Music, The, Philadelphia, Pennsylvania
Dallas Theological Seminary, Dallas, Texas
Dartmouth College, Hanover, New Hampshire
Denison University, Granville, Ohio
De Paul University, Chicago, Illinois
Dordt College, Sioux Center, Iowa
Drake University, Des Moines, Iowa
Drew University, Madison, New Jersey
Drury College, Springfield, Missouri
Duke University, Durham, North Carolina
Duquesne University, Pittsburgh, Pennsylvania
Eastern College, St. Davids, Pennsylvania
Eastern Mennonite University, Harrisonburg, Virginia
Eastern Washington University, Cheney, Washington
Eckerd College, St. Petersburg, Florida
Ecumenical Theological Center, Detroit, Michigan
Elmira College, Elmira, New York
Emerson College, Boston, Massachusetts
Emmanuel School of Religion, Johnson City, Tennessee
Emmaus Bible College, Dubuque, Iowa
Emory University, Atlanta, Georgia
Emporia State University, Emporia, Kansas
Ferris State University, Big Rapids, Michigan
Florida Atlantic University, Boca Raton, Florida
Florida State University, Tallahassee, Florida
Fordham University, New York, New York
Franciscan University of Steubenville, Steubenville, Ohio
Fresno Pacific College, Fresno, California
Fuller Theological Seminary, Pasadena, California
Gallaudet College, Washington, District of Columbia
Geneva College, Beaver Falls, Pennsylvania
George Washington University, The, Washington, District of Columbia
Georgia Institute of Technology, Atlanta, Georgia
Goddard College, Plainfield, Vermont
God's Bible School and College, Cincinnati, Ohio
Gonzaga University, Spokane, Washington
Gordon College, Wenham, Massachusetts
Gordon-Conwell Theological Seminary, South Hamilton, Massachusetts
Goshen College, Goshen, Indiana
Grace University, Omaha, Nebraska
Graceland College, Lamoni, Iowa
Greenville College, Greenville, Illinois
Grinnell College, Grinnell, Iowa
Hamilton College, Clinton, New York
Hampshire College, Amherst, Massachusetts
Harvard University, Cambridge, Massachusetts
Hebrew Union College — Jewish Institute of Religion, Cincinnati, Ohio
Herman M. Finch University of Health Sciences, The/The Chicago Medical School, North Chicago, Illinois

Hillsdale College, Hillsdale, Michigan
Holy Trinity Orthodox Seminary, The, Jordanville, New York
Hope College, Holland, Michigan
Houghton College, Houghton, New York
Huntington College, Huntington, Indiana
Illinois Institute of Technology, Chicago, Illinois
Indiana University, Bloomington, Indiana
Iowa State University of Science and Technology, Ames, Iowa
Ithaca College, Ithaca, New York
Jamestown College, Jamestown, North Dakota
Jewish Theological Seminary of America, The, New York, New York
Johns Hopkins University, The, Baltimore, Maryland
Juilliard School, The, New York, New York
Kansas State University, Manhattan, Kansas
Kettering University, Flint, Michigan
Lafayette College, Easton, Pennsylvania
Lake Superior State University, Sault Ste. Marie, Michigan
Lawrence Technological University, Southfield, Michigan
Lehigh University, Bethlehem, Pennsylvania
Leland Stanford Junior University (Stanford University), Stanford, California
Le Moyne College, Syracuse, New York
Le Tourneau College, Longview, Texas
Liberty University, Lynchburg, Virginia
Life University, Marietta, Georgia
Logan College of Chiropractic, St. Louis, Missouri
Loma Linda University, Loma Linda, California
Louisiana State University and Agricultural and Mechanical College, Baton Rouge, Louisiana
Loyola University, Chicago, Illinois
Lutheran Bible Institute of Seattle, Issaquah, Washington
Macalester College, St. Paul, Minnesota
Maharishi University of Management, Fairfield, Iowa
Manhattanville College, Purchase, New York
Mankato State University, Mankato, Minnesota
Marantha Baptist Bible College, Watertown, Wisconsin
Marquette University, Milwaukee, Wisconsin
Massachusetts Institute of Technology, Cambridge, Massachusetts
Mayo Foundation, Rochester, Minnesota
Mayo Graduate School of Medicine, Rochester, Minnesota
Meadville-Lombard Theological School, Chicago, Illinois
Medical College of Pennsylvania and Hahnemann University, The, Philadelphia, Pennsylvania
Mercyhurst College, Erie, Pennsylvania
Mesivta Yeshiva Rabbi Chaim Berlin, Brooklyn, New York
Messiah College, Grantham, Pennsylvania
Miami University, Oxford, Ohio
Michigan State University, Detroit College of Law, East Lansing, Michigan
Michigan State University, East Lansing, Michigan
Michigan Technological University, Houghton, Michigan
Middlebury College, Middlebury, Vermont
Minot State University, Minot, North Dakota
Mirrer Yeshiva Central Institute, Brooklyn, New York
Montana State University, Bozeman, Montana
Montana Tech of the University of Montana, Butte, Montana
Moody Bible Institute, Chicago, Illinois
Moravian College, Bethlehem, Pennsylvania
Mount Holyoke College, South Hadley, Massachusetts
Mount Ida College, Newton Centre, Massachusetts
Multnomah Bible College, Portland, Oregon
Naropa Institute, The, Boulder, Colorado
National College of Chiropractic, The, Lombard, Illinois
Nazarene Theological Seminary, Kansas City, Missouri
Ner Israel Rabbinical College, Baltimore, Maryland
New England College, Henniker, New Hampshire
New York University, New York, New York
Niagara University, Niagara, New York
North American Baptist Seminary, Sioux Falls, South Dakota
North Carolina State University at Raleigh, Raleigh, North Carolina
North Central College, Naperville, Illinois
North Dakota State University of Agriculture and Applied Science, Fargo, North Dakota
Northeastern University, Boston, Massachusetts
Northwest College of the Assemblies of God, Kirkland, Washington
Northwestern College, Orange City, Iowa
Northwestern College, St. Paul, Minnesota
Northwestern University, Evanston, Illinois
Northwood University, Midland, Michigan
Nyack Missionary College, Nyack, New York
Oakland University, Rochester, Michigan
Oakwood College, Huntsville, Alabama
Oberlin College, Oberlin, Ohio
Ohio College of Podiatric Medicine, Cleveland, Ohio
Ohio State University, The, Columbus, Ohio
Ohio University, Athens, Ohio
Old Dominion University, Norfolk, Virginia
Oral Roberts University, Tulsa, Oklahoma
Oregon State University, Corvallis, Oregon
Ottawa University, Ottawa, Kansas
Pace University, New York, New York
Pacific Graduate School of Psychology, Menlo Park, California

## Schedule VIII — Universities outside Canada

Pacific Lutheran University, Tacoma, Washington
Pacific Union College, Angwin, California
Pacific University, Forest Grove, Oregon
Palm Beach Atlantic College, West Palm Beach, Florida
Palmer College of Chiropractic, Davenport, Iowa
Palmer College of Chiropractic-West, Sunnyvale, California
Park College, Kansas City, Missouri
Parsons School of Design, New York, New York
Pennsylvania College of Podiatric Medicine, Philadelphia, Pennsylvania
Pennsylvania State University, The, University Park, Pennsylvania
Philadelphia College of Bible, Langhorne, Pennsylvania
Philadelphia College of Textiles and Science, Philadelphia, Pennsylvania
Pine Manor College, Chestnut Hill, Massachusetts
Pomona College, Claremont, California
Princeton Theological Seminary, Princeton, New Jersey
Princeton University, Princeton, New Jersey
Principia College, The, Elsah, Illinois
Providence College, Providence, Rhode Island
Purdue University, Lafayette, Indiana
Rabbinical College of America, Morristown, New Jersey
Rabbinical College of Long Island, Long Beach, New York
Rabbinical Seminary of America, Forest Hills, New York
Radcliffe College, Cambridge, Massachusetts
Reed College, Portland, Oregon
Reconstructionist Rabbinical College, Wyncote, Pennsylvania
Reformed Bible College, Grand Rapids, Michigan
Rensselaer Polytechnic Institute, Troy, New York
Rice University, Houston, Texas
Roberts Wesleyan College, North Chili, New York
Rochester Institute of Technology, Rochester, New York
Rockefeller University, New York, New York
Rush University, Chicago, Illinois
Rutgers — The State University, New Brunswick, New Jersey
St. John's College, Annapolis, Maryland
St. John's College, Santa Fe, New Mexico
St. John's University, Jamaica, New York
St. Lawrence University, Canton, New York
Saint Louis University, St. Louis, Missouri
St. Mary's University of San Antonio, San Antonio, Texas
Saint Olaf College, Northfield, Minnesota
St. Vladimir's Orthodox Theological Seminary, Crestwood, New York
San Francisco State College, San Francisco, California
San Jose State College, San Jose, California
Santa Clara University, Santa Clara, California
Sarah Lawrence College, Bronxville, New York
Scripps College, Claremont, California
Scripps Research Institute, The, La Jolla, California
Seattle Pacific University, Seattle, Washington
Seattle University, Seattle, Washington
Sherman College of Straight Chiropractic, Spartanburg, South Carolina
Simmons College, Boston, Massachusetts
Simpson College, Indianola, Iowa
Simpson College, Redding, California
Skidmore College, Saratoga Springs, New York
Smith College, The, Northampton, Massachusetts
South Dakota School of Mines and Technology, Rapid City, South Dakota
Southern Adventist University, Collegedale, Tennessee
Southern Illinois University of Carbondale, Carbondale, Illinois
Southern Methodist University, Dallas, Texas
Southwestern Adventist College, Keene, Texas
Spring Arbor College, Spring Arbor, Michigan
Springfield College, Springfield, Massachusetts
State University College at Oswego, Oswego, New York
State University College at Potsdam, Potsdam, New York
State University of New York at Binghamton, Binghamton, New York
State University of New York at Buffalo, Buffalo, New York
State University of New York at Stony Brook, Stony Brook, New York
State University of New York College of Arts and Science at Plattsburgh, Plattsburgh, New York
Stephens College, Columbia, Missouri
Stevens Institute of Technology, Hoboken, New Jersey
Sunbridge College, Chestnut Ridge, New York
Swarthmore College, Swarthmore, Pennsylvania
Syracuse University, Syracuse, New York
Tabor College, Hillsboro, Kansas
Talmudical Yeshiva of Philadelphia, Philadelphia, Pennsylvania
Taylor University, Upland, Indiana
Teachers College, Columbia University, New York, New York
Telshe Yeshiva Rabbinical College of Telshe, Inc., Wickliffe, Ohio
Telshe Yeshiva-Chicago, Rabbinical College of Telshe-Chicago, Inc., Chicago, Illinois
Temple University, Philadelphia, Pennsylvania
Texas Chiropractic College, Pasadena, Texas
Texas Woman's University, Denton, Texas
Thomas Aquinas College, Santa Paula, California
Touro College, New York, New York

Trinity Bible College, Ellendale, North Dakota
Trinity Christian College, Palos Heights, Illinois
Trinity College, Hartford, Connecticut
Trinity Episcopal School for Ministry, Ambridge, Pennsylvania
Trinity Evangelical Divinity School, Deerfield, Illinois
Trinity University, San Antonio, Texas
Tufts University, Medford, Massachusetts
Tulane University, New Orleans, Louisiana
Union College, Lincoln, Nebraska
Union College, Schenectady, New York
Union Institute, The, Cincinnati, Ohio
Union Theological Seminary, New York, New York
University of Alabama at Birmingham, The, Birmingham, Alabama
University of Arizona, The, Tucson, Arizona
University of Arkansas at Little Rock, Little Rock, Arkansas
University of California, Berkeley, California
University of California, Davis, California
University of California, Irvine, California
University of California, Los Angeles, California
University of California, Riverside, California
University of California, San Diego, California
University of California, San Francisco, California
University of California, Santa Barbara, California
University of California, Santa Cruz, California
University of Central Florida, Orlando, Florida
University of Chicago The, Chicago, Illinois
University of Cincinnati, Cincinnati, Ohio
University of Colorado, Boulder, Colorado
University of Delaware, Newark, Delaware
University of Denver, Denver, Colorado
University of Detroit, Detroit, Michigan
University of Florida, Gainesville, Florida
University of Georgia, The, Athens, Georgia
University of Hawaii, Honolulu, Hawaii
University of Houston, Houston, Texas
University of Idaho, Moscow, Idaho
University of Illinois, Urbana, Illinois
University of Iowa, Iowa City, Iowa
University of Judaism, Los Angeles, California
University of Kansas, Lawrence, Kansas
University of Kentucky, Lexington, Kentucky
University of Maine, Orono, Maine
University of Maryland, College Park, Maryland
University of Massachusetts at Amherst, Amherst, Massachusetts
University of Miami, Coral Gables, Florida
University of Michigan, The, Ann Arbor, Michigan
University of Minnesota, Minneapolis, Minnesota
University of Missouri, Columbia, Missouri
University of Missouri, St. Louis, Missouri
University of Montana-Missoula, The, Missoula, Montana
University of Nebraska, The, Lincoln, Nebraska
University of Nevada-Reno, Reno, Nevada
University of North Carolina at Chapel Hill, Chapel Hill, North Carolina
University of North Dakota, Grand Forks, North Dakota
University of North Texas, Denton, Texas
University of Notre Dame du Lac, Notre Dame, Indiana
University of Oklahoma, Norman, Oklahoma
University of Oregon, Eugene, Oregon
University of Pennsylvania, Philadelphia, Pennsylvania
University of Pittsburgh, Pittsburgh, Pennsylvania
University of Portland, Portland, Oregon
University of Rhode Island, Kingston, Rhode Island
University of Rochester, Rochester, New York
University of San Diego, San Diego, California
University of Southern California, Los Angeles, California
University of Texas, Austin, Texas
University of Texas Southwestern Medical Center at Dallas, The, Dallas, Texas
University of the Pacific, Stockton, California
University of Tulsa, Tulsa, Oklahoma
University of Utah, Salt Lake City, Utah
University of Vermont, Burlington, Vermont
University of Virginia, Charlottesville, Virginia
University of Washington, Seattle, Washington
University of Wisconsin, Madison, Wisconsin
University of Wyoming, The, Laramie, Wyoming
Utah State University of Agriculture and Applied Science, Logan, Utah
Valparaiso University, Valparaiso, Indiana
Vanderbilt University, Nashville, Tennessee
Vassar College, Poughkeepsie, New York
Villanova University, Villanova, Pennsylvania
Wake Forest University, Winston-Salem, North Carolina
Walla Walla College, College Place, Washington
Washington and Lee University, Lexington, Virginia
Washington Bible College, Lanham, Maryland
Washington State University, Pullman, Washington
Washington University, St. Louis, Missouri
Wayne State University, Detroit, Michigan
Wellesley College, Wellesley, Massachusetts
Wesleyan University, Middleton, Connecticut
West Virginia University, Morgantown, West Virginia
Western Baptist College, Salem, Oregon
Western Conservative Baptist Seminary, Portland, Oregon
Western Michigan University, Kalamazoo, Michigan
Western States Chiropractic College, Portland, Oregon
Western Washington University, Bellingham, Washington

Westminster Theological Seminary, Philadelphia, Pennsylvania
Westminster Theological Seminary in California, Escondido, California
Wheaton College, Norton, Massachusetts
Wheaton College, Wheaton, Illinois
Wheelock College, Boston, Massachusetts
Whitman College, Walla Walla, Washington
Whittier College, Whittier, California
Whitworth College, Spokane, Washington
William Tyndale College, Farmington Hills, Michigan
Williams College, Williamstown, Massachusetts
Wittenberg University, Springfield, Ohio
Wright State University, Dayton, Ohio
Yale University, New Haven, Connecticut
Yeshiva Ohr Elchonon Chabad/West Coast Talmudic Seminary, Los Angeles, California
Yeshiva University, New York, New York

Notes: Carroll College, Duquesne U, U of Texas SW Medical Center at Dallas, U of Wyoming and Wright State U added by P.C. 2000-726, effective 1997.

Antioch College, Calif. Lutheran U, Cornerstone College, Eastern College, Emporia State U, Juilliard School, Marantha Baptist Bible College, Naropa Inst., SUNY Stony Brook and West Va. U added by P.C. 2000-726, effective 1998.

Texas Woman's U, U of Missouri and Wheelock College added by P.C. 2000-726, effective 1999.

Colgate-Rochester Divinity School, Eastern Mennonite U, Kettering U, Liberty U, Life U, Louisiana State U, Michigan State U, Northwest College of the Assemblies of God, Northwood U, Santa Clara U, Southern Adventist U and U of Vermont added by P.C. 2000-726, effective June 7, 2000.

Ambassador U (Big Sandy TX), American College (Bryn Mawr PA), Anna Maria College (Paxton MA), Baldwin-Wallace College (Berea OH), Bluffton College (Bluffton OH), Carroll College (Waukesha WI), College of New Rochelle (NY), College of Wooster (OH), Dana College (Blair NB), De Pauw U (Greencastle IN), Detroit College of Law, Divinity School (Rochester NY), Earlham College (Richmond IN), Eastern-Baptist Theological Seminary (Philadelphia), Eastern Mennonite College (Harrisonburg VA), Georgetown U (Washington DC), GMI Engineering and Management Inst. (Flint MI), Gustavus Adolphus College (St. Peter MN), Hebrew Union College (Los Angeles), Hebrew Union College (New York), Hobe Sound Bible College (Hobe Sound FL), Hollins College (VA), Hood College (Frederick MD), Liberty Baptist College (Lynchburg VA), Life Chiropractic College (Marietta GA), Louisiana State U (Baton Rouge), Marymont College (Tarrytown NY), Mills College (Oakland CA), Mount Vernon College (Washington DC), Nasson College (Springvale ME), Nazarene Bible College (Colorado Springs), Nebraska Wesleyan U (Lincoln), Northrop Inst. of Technology (Inglewood CA), Northwest College (Kirkland WA), Northwood Inst. (Midland MI), Puget Sound Christian College (Edmonds WA), Reformed Theological Seminary (Jackson MS), Ripon College (Ripon WI), Saint Mary-of-the-Woods College (IN), Saint Mary's College (Notre Dame IN), Southern College of Seventh-Day Adventists (Collegedale TN), Temple Buell College (Denver), Trinity College (Dunedin FL), U of Dubuque (IA), U of Santa Clara (CA), U of the Ozarks (Clarksville, AK), U of the South (Sewanee TN), U of Vermont/State Agricultural College (Burlington), Wagner College (Staten Island NY) and Yeshiva U of Los Angeles deleted by P.C. 2000-726, effective June 7, 2000.

Bastyr U, City U, Columbia Intl. U, Eckerd College, Grace U, Montana Tech, Multnomah Bible College, Parsons School of Design, Herman M. Finch U of Health Sciences/Chicago Medical School, Union College, UC Davis, UC Irvine, UCLA, UC Riverside, UCSD, UC Santa Barbara, UC Santa Cruz, U of Montana-Missoula and U of North Texas added by P.C. 1997-1041, effective 1996.

Antioch U (New York), Bastyr College (Seattle), Briarcliff College (Briarcliff Manor NY), Columbia Bible College & Seminary (Columbia SC), Dropsie U (Philadelphia), George Williams College (Downers Grove IL), Grace College of the Bible (Omaha), Montana College of Mineral Science and Technology (Butte), Multnomah School of the Bible (Portland OR), Ricker College (Houlton ME), Rosemead Graduate School of Psychology (Rosemead CA), U of Health Sciences/Chicago Medical School (Chicago), U of Montana (Missoula), Western Evangelical Seminary (Portland OR) and Westminster Choir College (Princeton NJ) deleted by P.C. 1997-1041, effective 1996.

Alfred U, Colby-Sawyer College, College of New Rochelle, Forida State U, Holy Trinity Orthodox Seminary, Lawrence Technological U, Maharishi U of Management, Medical College of Pa. and Hehnemann U, Mercyhurst College, Rush U, Simpson College, Southern College of 7th-Day Adventists and Westminster Theological Seminary in California added by P.C. 1996-632, effective 1995.

Maharishi International U (Fairfield IA) and Medical College of Pennsylvania (Philadelphia) deleted by P.C. 1996-632, effective 1995.

Ambassador U, Columbia Union College, Detroit College of Law, Divinity School, Emmanuel School of Religion, Meadville-Lombard Theological School, Oakwood College, Scripps Research Institute and U of the South added by P.C. 1995-581, effective 1994.

Associated Mennonite Biblical Seminary, Bluffton College, Clark U, Ecumenical Theological Center, Nebraska Wesleyan U, Northwestern College (Orange City), Sunbridge College, Union Institute, U of Georgia, U of Judaism, Wake Forest U, Wheaton College (Norton) added; and Goshen Biblical Seminary, Mennonite Biblical Seminary and Union for Experimenting Colleges and Universities deleted by P.C. 1994-866, effective 1993.

American Film Institute Center for Advanced Film and Television Studies, Calvin Theological Seminary, St. John's U and Saint Olaf College added by P.C. 1993-901, effective 1992.

Baldwin-Wallace College, Bastyr College, Earlham College, Lutheran Bible Inst. of Seattle, North Central College, Rabbinical College of L.I., Scripps College, Trinity Bible College and U of Calif. at San Francisco added by P.C. 1992-1108, effective 1991.

**2.** The universities situated in the United Kingdom of Great Britain and Northern Ireland that are prescribed by section 3503 are the following:

Aston University, Birmingham, England
Cranfield University, Bedfordshire, England
Gateshead Talmudical College, Gateshead, England
Imperial College of Science, Technology and Medicine, London, England
Queen's University of Belfast, The, Belfast, Northern Ireland
University of Aberdeen, Aberdeen, Scotland
University of Bath, The, Bath, England
University of Birmingham, Birmingham, England
University of Bradford, Bradford, England
University of Bristol, Bristol, England
University of Cambridge, Cambridge, England
University of Dundee, The, Dundee, Scotland
University of Durham, Durham, England
University of Edinburgh, Edinburgh, Scotland
University of Exeter, Exeter, England
University of Glasgow, Glasgow, Scotland
University of Hull, The, Hull, England

University of Lancaster, Lancaster, England
University of Leeds, Leeds, England
University of Liverpool, Liverpool, England
University of London, London, England
University of Manchester, The, Manchester, England
University of Newcastle, The, Newcastle upon Tyne, England
University of Nottingham, The, Nottingham, England
University of Oxford, Oxford, England
University of Reading, Reading, England
University of St. Andrews, St. Andrews, Scotland
University of Sheffield, Sheffield, England
University of Southampton, Southampton, England
University of Strathclyde, Glasgow, Scotland
University of Surrey, Guildford, Surrey, England
University of Sussex, Brighton, England
University of Wales, Cardiff, Wales

Notes: Gateshead Talmudical College added by P.C. 1992-1108, effective 1991. U of Hull added by P.C. 1994-866, effective 1993. Aston U and U of Sussex added by P.C. 1996-632, effective 1995. Cranfield Inst. of Technology changed to Cranfield U, and Victoria U of Manchester changed to U of Manchester, by P.C. 2000-726, effective June 7, 2000. U of Newcastle and U of Surrey added by P.C. 2000-726, effective 1997. Imperial College added by P.C. 2000-726, effective 1998.

**3.** The universities situated in France that are prescribed by section 3503 are the following:

American University in Paris, Paris
Catholic Faculties of Lyon, Lyon
Catholic Institute of Paris, Paris
Catholic University of Lille, The, Lille
École Nationale des Ponts et Chaussées, Paris
European Institute of Business Administration (INSEAD), Fontainebleau
Hautes Études Commerciales, Paris
Paris Graduate School of Management, Paris
University of Aix-Marseilles, Aix-en-Provence
University of Paris, Paris

Notes: Hautes Études Commerciales and Paris Graduate School of Management added by P.C. 1994-866, effective 1993. Catholic Faculties of Lille changed to Catholic U of Lille by P.C. 2000-726, effective June 7, 2000.

**4.** The universities situated in Austria that are prescribed by section 3503 are the following:

University of Vienna, Vienna

**5.** The universities situated in Belgium that are prescribed by section 3503 are the following:

Catholic University of Louvain, Louvain

Notes: Free University of Brussels deleted by P.C. 2000-726, effective June 7, 2000.

**6.** The universities situated in Switzerland that are prescribed by section 3503 are the following:

Franklin College of Switzerland, Sorengo (Lugano)
University of Fribourg, Fribourg
University of Geneva, Geneva
University of Lausanne, Lausanne

Notes: Franklin College added by P.C. 1992-1108, effective 1991.

**7.** The universities situated in Vatican City that are prescribed by section 3503 are the following:

Pontifical Gregorian University

**8.** The universities situated in Israel that are prescribed by section 3503 are the following:

Bar-Ilan University, Ramat-Gan
Ben Gurion University of the Negev, Beersheba
Bezalel-Academy of Arts and Design, Jerusalem
École biblique et archéologique française, Jerusalem
Hebrew University of Jerusalem, The, Jerusalem
Jerusalem College for Women, Bayit-Vegan, Jerusalem
Jerusalem College of Technology, Jerusalem
Technion-Israel Institute of Technology, Haifa
Tel-Aviv University, Tel-Aviv
University of Haifa, Haifa
Weizmann Institute of Science, Rehovot
Yeshivat Aish Hatorah, Jerusalem

Notes: Yeshivat Aish Hatorah added by P.C. 1994-866, effective 1993. École biblique et archéologique française added by P.C. 1996-632, effective 1995.

**9.** The universities situated in Lebanon that are prescribed by section 3503 are the following:

St. Joseph University, Beirut

Notes: American U of Beirut deleted by P.C. 2000-726, effective June 7, 2000.

**10.** The universities situated in Ireland that are prescribed by section 3503 are the following:

National University of Ireland, Dublin
Royal College of Surgeons in Ireland, Dublin
University of Dublin, Dublin

**11.** The universities situated in the Federal Republic of Germany that are prescribed by section 3503 are the following:

Ruprecht-Karls-Universität Heidenberg, Heidenberg
Ukrainian Free University, Munich

Notes: Ruprecht-Karls-Universität Heidenberg added by P.C. 1996-632, effective 1995.

**12.** The universities situated in Poland that are prescribed by section 3503 are the following:

Catholic University of Lublin, Lublin
Jagiellonian University, Krakow

**Notes**: Jagiellonian U added by P.C. 2000-726, effective 1998.

**13.** The universities situated in Spain that are prescribed by section 3503 are the following:

University of Navarra, Pamplona

**14.** The universities situated in the People's Republic of China that are prescribed by section 3503 are the following:

Nanjing Institute of Technology, Nanjing

**15.** The universities situated in Jamaica that are prescribed for the purposes of section 3503 are the following:

University of the West Indies, Mona Campus, Kingston

**16.** The university situated in the Czech and Slovak Federal Republic that is prescribed by section 3503 is the following:

Universita Karlova, Prague

**Notes**: S. 16 added by P.C. 1992-1108, effective 1991. The country is now the Czech Republic.

**17.** The universities situated in Australia that are prescribed by section 3503 are the following:

University of Melbourne, The, Parkville
University of Queensland, The, Brisbane
University of Sydney, The, Sydney
University of Tasmania, Hobart

**Notes**: S. 17 added by P.C. 1993-901, effective 1992. U of Tasmania added by P.C. 1994-866, effective 1993. Flinders U and U of New South Wales added by P.C. 1996-632, effective 1995. Flinders U of South Australia (Adelaide) and U of New South Wales (Sydney) deleted by P.C. 2000-726, effective June 7, 2000. U of Melbourne and U of Queensland added by P.C. 2000-726, effective 1997.

**18.** The university situated in the Republic of Croatia that is prescribed by section 3503 is the following:

University of Zagreb, Zagreb

**Notes**: S. 18 added by P.C. 1994-866, effective 1993.

**19.** The university situated in South Africa that is prescribed by section 3503 is the following:

University of the Witwatersrand, The, Johannesburg

**Notes**: S. 19 added by P.C. 1995-581, effective 1994.

**Interpretation Bulletins**: See at beginning of Schedule.

**20.** The university situated in the Netherlands that is prescribed by section 3503 is the following:

Leiden University, Leiden
Nijenrode University, Breukelon

**Notes**: S. 20 added by P.C. 1996-632, effective 1995. Leiden U added by P.C. 2000-726, effective 1998.

**21.** The university situated in Hong Kong that is prescribed by section 3503 is the following:

Hong Kong University of Science and Technology, The, Kowloon

**Notes**: S. 21 added by P.C. 1996-632, effective 1995.

**22.** The university situated in New Zealand that is prescribed by section 3503 is the following:

Victoria University of Wellington, Wellington

**Notes**: S. 22 added by P.C. 2000-726, effective 1999.

**Notes [Sch. VIII]**: See at beginning of Schedule VIII.

# SCHEDULES IX, X
[Revoked]

**Notes**: Schedules IX and X revoked by P.C. 1993-1688, effective for 1993 and later taxation years. Schedule IX listed prescribed areas under Reg. 7303 for purposes of the northern residents deduction under ITA 110.7. Schedule X contained climatological maps used for the northern residents deduction under Reg. 7303.

# SELECTED REMISSION ORDERS

Remission orders are issued under the authority of the *Financial Administration Act*. They are a mechanism by which the federal Cabinet can "remit" tax or other amounts such as interest and penalties — in other words, pay such amount back to a taxpayer or waive the taxpayer's obligation to pay. Like regulations, they are passed as "orders in council" by the Cabinet. See H. Arnold Sherman and Jeffrey D. Sherman, "Income Tax Remission Orders: The Tax Planner's Last Resort or the Ultimate Weapon?", 34(4) *Canadian Tax Journal* 801–827 (July-August 1986).

Certain Taxpayers Remission Order, 1998-2 ................................................... 2509
Certain Taxpayers Remission Order, 1999-2 ................................................... 2510
Child Care Expense and Moving Expense Remission Order ................................ 2510
Churchill Falls (Labrador) Corporation Remission Order .................................... 2512
Farmer's Income Taxes Remission Order ........................................................ 2513
Government and Long-Term Corporate Debt Obligations Remission Order ............ 2513
Ice Storm Employee Benefits Remission Order ................................................ 2514
Income Earned in Quebec Income Tax Remission Order, 1988 ............................ 2514
Income Tax Paid by Investors, Other Than Promoters Remission Order ................. 2519
Income Tax Remission Order (Yukon Territory Lands) ...................................... 2520
Indian Income Tax Remission Orders
    P.C. 1993-523 ....................................................................................... 2520
    P.C. 1993-1649 ..................................................................................... 2522
Indian Settlements Remission Order (2000) .................................................... 2523
Indians and Bands on certain Indian Settlements Remission Order ....................... 2524
Indians and Bands on Certain Indian Settlements Remission Order (1997) ............. 2527
Indians and the War Lake First Nation Band on the Ilford Indian Settlement Remission Order ..... 2529
[Lionaird Capital Corporation Notes Remission Order] ..................................... 2530
Maintenance Payments Remission Order ......................................................... 2531
Prescribed Areas Forward Averaging Remission Order ...................................... 2532
Syncrude Remission Order ........................................................................... 2533
Telesat Canada Remission Order ................................................................... 2534

# SELECTED REMISSION ORDERS

Remission orders are issued under the authority of the *Financial Administration Act*. They are a mechanism by which the federal Cabinet can "forgive" family tax or other amounts such as interest and penalties — or offer works, pay such amount back to a taxpayer or waive the taxpayer's obligation to pay. Like regulations, they are passed as "orders-in-council" by the Cabinet. See H. Arnold Sherman and Jerome D. Sherman, "Income Tax Remission Orders: The Tax Planner's Last Resort or the Ultimate Weapon?", 34(4) *Canadian Tax Journal* 820–827 (July/August 1986).

| | |
|---|---|
| Certain Taxpayers Remission Order, 1988-2 | 2509 |
| Certain Taxpayers Remission Order, 1990-1 | 2510 |
| Child Care Expense and Moving Expense Remission Order | 2511 |
| Churchill Falls (Labrador) Corporation Remission Order | 2512 |
| Foreign Income Taxes Remission Order | 2513 |
| Government and Lotto Farm Corporate Debt Obligation Remission Order | 2513 |
| Ice Storm Employees Benefits Remission Order | 2514 |
| Income Earned in Quebec Income Tax Remission Order, 1988 | 2514 |
| Interest Tax Paid by Investors Other Than Promoters Remission Order | 2519 |
| Iroquois Tax Remission Order (Yukon Territory Lands) | 2520 |
| Indian Income Tax Remission Orders | |
|     1993-1994 522 | 2520 |
|     1991 1993-1994 | 2533 |
| Indian Settlements Remission Order (2000) | 2536 |
| Indians and Kanesatake Constitutional Settlement Remission Order | 2534 |
| Indians and Hudson Certain Indian Settlements Remission Order, 1999 | 2537 |
| Indians and the Ward Lake First Nation Band on the Third Indian Settlement Remission Order | 2539 |
| Millbank Capital Corporation Notes Remission Order | 2550 |
| Mennonite Payments Remission Order | 2551 |
| Preserved Annuity Forward Averaging Remission Order | 2553 |
| Syncrude Remission Order | 2553 |
| Tarbox Grants Remission Order | 2554 |

2507

# REMISSION ORDERS

## CERTAIN TAXPAYERS REMISSION ORDER, 1998-2

P.C. 1998-2092, November 26, 1998 (SI/98-121)

**1.** Remission is hereby granted to the taxpayers named in column I of an item of the schedule of the amount set out in column II of that item, which represents tax, penalties and interest, including any interest payable thereon, under the *Income Tax Act*, in respect of the taxation year set out in column III of that item.

**2.** Remission is hereby granted of amounts payable under the *Income Tax Act* by a taxpayer who is or was a judge of the Court of Québec, who made an excess contribution not exceeding $7,500 in 1989 or 1990 to a registered retirement savings plan, the deduction of which was disallowed by assessment and that, within one year of the date of this Order, is withdrawn, or has been withdrawn, from the plan, or the judge's spouse, that would not be payable if the excess contribution had not been made and the amount of the withdrawal were not required to be included in computing income, on condition that the taxpayer discontinue or have discontinued all relevant proceedings and undertake forthwith, in a form filed with and acceptable to the Minister of National Revenue, not to institute or proceed with any action, objection, appeal, application or other proceeding of any kind in respect of any contribution in 1989 or 1990 to such a plan.

**3.** Remission is hereby granted of amounts payable under the *Income Tax Act* by Andrew Gorgichuk and Joachim Gorgichuk that would not be payable if expenditures after 1996 and before the 121st day hereafter (not exceeding $62,230) made by their partnership, in the income of which for its 1996 taxation year $62,230 was included contrary to information received from an appropriate official, had been made by it in that 1996 taxation year and not in any other year and such deductions or other claims in respect of the expenditures that would have been permitted under the said Act as the taxpayers may jointly and not severally describe in the form had been made, on condition that they undertake forthwith, in a form filed with and acceptable to the Minister of National Revenue (the "form"), not to make any claim or deduction in respect of any such expenditures in any taxation year or that is inconsistent with this remission.

## SCHEDULE

[Not reproduced]

## EXPLANATORY NOTE

*(This note is not part of the Order.)*

This Order remits income tax and interest on the basis of extreme hardship or financial setback coupled with conditions over which the taxpayer had no control that gave rise to unintended results, including incomes slightly above and below the poverty line, old age, illness, departmental error or delay, and the receipt of retroactive lump-sum payments, such as pension and disability benefits, which, if received in the years in respect of which they were paid, would have resulted in less or no tax liability.

Section 2 of the Order remits tax and interest resulting from 1989 or 1990 excess RRSP contributions by some judges of the Court of Québec who claim discrimination in that Federal judges can contribute greater amounts to RRSPs. One judge has appealed to the Federal Court but some of the judges wish to discontinue their objections if remission is granted provided that the excess contributions be withdrawn.

Section 3 reallocates farm expenses so as to offset farm income which a partnership believed was not taxable on the basis of information furnished by a departmental official.

## CERTAIN TAXPAYERS REMISSION ORDER, 1999-2
P.C. 1999-1855, October 21, 1999 (SI/99-124)

**1.** Remission is hereby granted to the taxpayers named in column I of an item of the schedule of the amount set out in column II of that item, which represents tax, penalties and interest, including any interest payable thereon, under the *Income Tax Act*, in respect of the taxation year set out in column III of that item.

**2.** Remission is hereby granted to Florence Currie of $12,445 payable by her under the *Income Tax Act* for 1997, plus any interest payable thereon, subject to a deduction therefrom required by the Minister of National Revenue (the "Minister") in respect of any deduction claimed or allowed in respect of a relevant retroactive pension payment, on condition that any other relevant relief is waived in a form filed with and acceptable to the Minister.

**3.** Remission is hereby granted of amounts payable under the *Income Tax Act* by a taxpayer who is or was a judge of the Court of Québec, who made an excess contribution not exceeding $7,500 in 1989 or 1990 to a registered retirement savings plan, the deduction of which was disallowed by assessment and that, within one year of the date of this Order, is withdrawn, or has been withdrawn, from a plan or fund to which it was transferred as provided in subsection 146(16) or 146.3(14) of that Act, or the judge's spouse, that would not be payable if the excess contribution had not been made and the amount of the withdrawal were not required to be included in computing income, on condition that the taxpayer discontinue or have discontinued all relevant proceedings and undertake forthwith, in a form filed with and acceptable to the Minister of National Revenue, not to institute or proceed with any action, objection, appeal, application or other proceeding of any kind in respect of any contribution in 1989 or 1990 to such a plan.

### SCHEDULE

*[Not reproduced]*

### EXPLANATORY NOTE
*(This note is not part of the Order.)*

This Order remits income tax and interest on the basis of extreme hardship or financial setback coupled with conditions over which the taxpayer had no control that gave rise to unintended results, including incomes slightly above and below the poverty line, old age, illness, and the receipt of retroactive lump-sum payments due to processing delays, such as pension and disability benefits, which, if received in the years in respect of which they were paid, would have resulted in less or no tax liability.

Section 3 of the Order remits tax and interest resulting from 1989 or 1990 excess RRSP contributions by some judges of the Court of Québec who claim discrimination in that Federal judges can contribute greater amounts to RRSPs. Remission has already been granted to the judges providing for withdrawals from their RRSPs, but they failed to request a remission providing for withdrawals from their RRIFs (*cf.* SI/98-121).

## CHILD CARE EXPENSE AND MOVING EXPENSE REMISSION ORDER

### ORDER RESPECTING THE REMISSION OF INCOME TAX PAYABLE BY CERTAIN CANADIAN RESIDENTS INCURRING CHILD CARE EXPENSES OUTSIDE CANADA OR INCURRING MOVING EXPENSES WHEN MOVING TO OR FROM A LOCATION OUTSIDE CANADA
P.C. 1991-257, February 14, 1991 (SI/91-23), as amended by P.C. 1994-328, February 24, 1994 (SI/94-26).

### SHORT TITLE

**1.** This Order may be cited as the *Child Care Expense and Moving Expense Remission Order*.

## INTERPRETATION

**2.** In this Order,

**"Act"** means the *Income Tax Act*;

**"Minister"** means the Minister of National Revenue.

## REMISSION

**3.** Subject to sections 4 to 6, remission is granted to each taxpayer for each taxation year ending after 1984 and before 1989 of an amount equal to the amount, if any, by which

(a) the taxes, interest and penalties payable by the taxpayer under the Act for the year

exceed

(b) the taxes, interest and penalties that would have been payable by the taxpayer under the Act for the year if all that portion of section 63.1 of the Act preceding paragraph (a) thereof had read as follows for the year:

"63.1 In applying sections 62 and 63 in respect of a taxpayer who is, throughout all or part of a taxation year, absent from but resident in Canada, the following rules apply for the year or that part of the year, as the case may be:"

## CONDITIONS

**4.** The remission granted under section 3 to a taxpayer is on condition that the taxpayer makes an application for the remission in writing to the Minister on or before December 31, 1995.

**5.** The remission granted under section 3 to a taxpayer for a taxation year is on the further condition that, on the day on which the application under section 4 by the taxpayer with respect to that year is received by the Minister,

(a) the Minister was allowed under the Act to make an assessment or a reassessment of tax payable by the taxpayer for the year; or

(b) an objection or appeal by the taxpayer under section 165, 169 or 172 of the Act against an assessment or a reassessment for the year was outstanding or could still have been made or instituted.

**5.1** Where the taxpayer makes the application referred to in section 4 after December 31, 1991 for remission for a taxation year, the remission is on the further condition that, on December 31, 1991, an objection or appeal by the taxpayer under section 165, 169 or 172 of the Act against an assessment or a reassessment for the year was outstanding.

**6.** The remission granted under section 3 to a taxpayer for a taxation year is on the further condition that the taxpayer

(a) within 45 days after the day of mailing to the taxpayer of a notice from the Department of National Revenue, Taxation, setting out the amount to be remitted to the taxpayer pursuant to this Order, withdraws any outstanding action commenced by the taxpayer in any court, and

(b) does not commence any action, claim or objection, or make any complaint to any tribunal,

by which the taxpayer seeks a reduction in the amount of, or any other relief or remedy relating to, taxes payable by the taxpayer for that year in respect of the deductibility in computing the taxpayer's income for the year of moving expenses incurred when moving to or from a location outside Canada or child care expenses incurred outside Canada.

# CHURCHILL FALLS (LABRADOR) CORPORATION REMISSION ORDER
P.C. 1968-832, April 30, 1968

Whereas it has been made to appear that
1. Churchill Falls (Labrador) Corporation is undertaking a very large investment to develop facilities at Churchill Falls in Labrador to produce very large amounts of electric power for sale to provincially-owned power corporations;
2. The said Corporation proposes to finance the construction of facilities to produce and transmit power in part by means of the sale of first mortgage bonds,[1] of which an aggregate principal amount exceeding four hundred million Canadian dollars is expected to be sold in the United States in denominations of United States dollars;
3. The sale of an issue of bonds of this size might well be prevented by the imposition of a Canadian withholding tax on the interest payable on such bonds, since such a large issue must be sold to many institutions which would neither be exempt from tax nor able to offset it against taxes payable to the United States, or if it were not prevented, the rate of interest required to be paid by the Corporation would be significantly increased, in turn materially increasing the cost of power to the provincially-owned power corporations;
4. Interest paid on bonds issued by the provincially-owned power corporations is not subject to Canadian withholding tax, and the Government of Canada has long followed the policy, most recently expressed in the *Public Utilities Income Tax Transfer Act*, of effectively removing or reducing those federal taxes on investor-owned power corporations that materially affect their position *vis-à-vis* provincially-owned power corporations; and
5. The said issue of first mortgage bonds can be sold in the United States exempt from the Interest Equalization Tax of the United States;

And whereas the Governor in Council considers it to be in the public interest that the first mortgage bonds of the said Corporation may be sold in the United States exempt from withholding tax;

Therefore, His Excellency the Governor General in Council on the recommendation of the Treasury Board, pursuant to section 22 of the *Financial Administration Act*, is pleased hereby to remit

(a) the amount of any tax payable by a person under Part III of the *Income Tax Act* on, or such part of the amount of any tax that is or, but for this Order, would be payable by a person under that Part as may reasonably be regarded as attributable to, amounts paid or credited or deemed to have been paid or credited to that person as, on account or in lieu of payment of, or in satisfaction of, interest on first mortgage bonds issued by Churchill Falls (Labrador) Corporation Limited on or after the date of this Order,

   (i) that are in denominations of United States dollars, and

   (ii) that are identified in a manner prescribed by the Minister of Finance for the purposes of this Order as comprising, or as having been issued in exchange or substitution or partial exchange or substitution for bonds comprising, part of a series of first mortgage bonds issued or covenanted to be issued by Churchill Falls (Labrador) Corporation Limited whether in denominations of United States dollars or otherwise, the aggregate principal amount of which (expressed in terms of Canadian dollars) when added to the aggregate principal amount similarly so expressed of all first mortgage bonds previously issued or covenanted to be issued by Churchill Falls (Labrador) Corporation Limited whether in denominations of United States dollars or otherwise, does not exceed six hundred million dollars; and

(b) any tax or penalty payable by a person under the *Income Tax Act* as a result of the failure of such person to deduct or withhold an amount as required by section 109 of that Act from any amount paid or credited or deemed to have been paid or credited by him as, on account or in lieu of payment of, or in satisfaction of, interest as described in paragraph (a).

[Note: The reference in this Order in Council to Section 22 of the *Financial Administration Act* and to section 109 and Part III of the *Income Tax Act* should be construed as references to sections 23 and 215 and Part XIII, respectively, of the present statutes.]

---

[1] Maturity date of the mortgage bonds is in the year 2007.

Remission

# FARMERS' INCOME TAXES REMISSION ORDER
P.C. 1993-1647, August 4, 1993 (SI/93-164)

HIS EXCELLENCY THE GOVERNOR GENERAL IN COUNCIL, considering that the collection of the tax is unreasonable, on the recommendation of the Minister of National Revenue, pursuant to subsection 23(2) of the *Financial Administration Act*, is pleased hereby to remit tax payable by a taxpayer under Parts I to I.2 of the *Income Tax Act* for the 1992 taxation year that would not be payable if that portion of each payment received in 1992 in respect of a gross revenue insurance program established under the *Farm Income Protection Act* that is required to be and is repaid were not included in computing the income of the taxpayer for the 1992 taxation year under paragraph 12(1)(p) of the *Income Tax Act*, and all relevant interest and penalties, on condition that the taxpayer file with the Minister an undertaking in a form acceptable to the Minister in which the taxpayer agrees not to deduct the amount repaid or required to be repaid in computing the taxpayer's income for any taxation year and waives all relevant rights of objection or appeal.

# GOVERNMENT AND LONG-TERM CORPORATE DEBT OBLIGATIONS REMISSION ORDER

ORDER RESPECTING THE REMISSION OF CERTAIN INCOME TAXES PAID OR PAYABLE BY CERTAIN PERSONS IN RESPECT OF INTEREST FROM GOVERNMENT AND LONG-TERM CORPORATE DEBT OBLIGATIONS

P.C. 1985-3480, November 28, 1985 (SI/85-214)

## Short Title

**1.** This Order may be cited as the *Government and Long-Term Corporate Debt Obligations Remission Order*.

## Interpretation

**2.** In this Order, "Act" means the *Income Tax Act*.

## Remission

**3.** Remission is hereby granted to each non-resident person who is liable for tax under Part XIII of the Act in respect of any amount paid or credited to him as, on account or in lieu of payment of, or in satisfaction of, interest of an amount equal to the amount, if any, by which

(a) the tax payable by the non-resident person under Part XIII of the Act in respect of the amount so paid or credited

exceeds

(b) the tax that would be payable by the non-resident person under Part XIII of the Act in respect of the amount so paid or credited if the references to "1986" in subparagraphs 212(1)(b)(ii) and (vii) of the Act were read as references to "1987".

**4.** Where a person required to deduct or withhold a tax payable by a non-resident person under Part XIII of the Act is liable to pay as tax under Part XIII on behalf of the non-resident person the whole of the amount that should have been deducted or withheld, remission is hereby granted to that person of an amount equal to the amount, if any, by which

(a) the tax payable by the person so required to deduct or withhold under Part XIII of the Act

exceeds

(b) the tax that would be payable by the person so required to deduct or withhold under Part XIII of the Act if the references to "1986" in subparagraphs 212(1)(b)(ii) and (vii) of the Act were read as references to "1987".

# ICE STORM EMPLOYEE BENEFITS REMISSION ORDER
P.C. 1998-2047, November 19, 1998

His Excellency the Governor General in Council, considering that it is in the public interest to do so, on the recommendation of the Minister of National Revenue and the Treasury Board pursuant to subsections 23(2) and (2.1) of the *Financial Administration Act*, hereby remits amounts payable under the *Income Tax Act*, the *Canada Pension Plan* and the *Employment Insurance Act* as a result of an amount paid or advanced in 1998 as relief for loss because of the ice storm in January 1998 which caused extended power outages and extensive damage in Ontario, Quebec, New Brunswick and Nova Scotia in respect of which an amount is required to be included in the income from employment of a taxpayer by virtue of paragraph 6(1)(a) or (b) or subsection 6(9) of the *Income Tax Act*, where the employee deals at arm's length with the employer, the payment or advance is voluntary, reasonable in the circumstances and bona fide and does not exceed the damages suffered by the employee net of any other compensation the employee receives or is entitled to receive, is not based on employment factors such as performance, position or years of service or the fact that the employee is a shareholder and is not made in exchange for past or future services or to compensate for loss of income, plus relevant interest and penalties, on condition that the employee waive any benefit or right accruing under the said Acts as a result of the payment or advance.

**Notes**: See Revenue Canada news release, March 11, 1999 for a description of other tax effects of ice storm compensation.

# INCOME EARNED IN QUEBEC INCOME TAX REMISSION ORDER, 1988

## ORDER RESPECTING THE REMISSION OF INCOME TAX IN RESPECT OF CERTAIN INCOME OF INDIVIDUALS EARNED IN THE PROVINCE OF QUEBEC (1988)

P.C. 1989-1204, June 22, 1989 (SI/89-157), as amended by P.C. 1991-1661, September 5, 1991 (SI/91-116); P.C. 1992-2593, December 11, 1992 (SI/92-230); P.C. 1994-567, April 14, 1994 (SI/94-43); P.C. 1998-396, March 19, 1998 (SI/98-47).

### SHORT TITLE

**1.** This Order may be cited as the *Income Earned in Quebec Income Tax Remission Order, 1988*.

### INTERPRETATION

**2.** In this Order,

"**Act**" means the *Income Tax Act*;

"**Regulations**" means the *Income Tax Regulations*.

### REMISSION TO INDIVIDUALS WHO DID NOT RESIDE IN CANADA AT ANY TIME IN A TAXATION YEAR

**3.** Remission is hereby granted to any individual who did not reside in Canada at any time in a taxation year of the amount, if any, by which

(a) the tax, interest and penalties paid or payable under the Act by that individual in respect of that taxation year

exceeds

(b) the tax, interest and penalties that would have been payable by that individual under the Act in respect of that taxation year if, for the purpose of determining that person's income earned in that year in the Province of Quebec, section 2602 of the Regulations read as follows:

"2602. (1) Except as provided in subsection (2), where an individual did not reside in Canada at any time in a taxation year, his income earned in the taxation year in a particular province is the aggregate of

(a) that part of the amount of his income from an office or employment that is included in computing his taxable income earned in Canada for the year by virtue of subparagraph 115(1)(a)(i) of the Act that is reasonably attributable to the duties performed by him in the province,

(b) his income for that year earned in the province as determined in the manner set forth in section 4 of the *Income Earned in Quebec Income Tax Remission Order, 1988*,

(c) his income for that year from carrying on business earned in the province, determined as hereinafter set forth in this Part,

(d) the taxable capital gains in the province included in computing his taxable income earned in Canada for the year by virtue of subparagraph 115(1)(a)(iii) of the Act from dispositions of property, each of which was a disposition of a property or an interest therein that was

(i) real property situated in the province or an option in respect thereof, or

(ii) any other capital property used by him in carrying on a business in the province,

determined as hereinafter set forth in this Part, and

(e) the income of the individual for that year from the disposition of a life insurance policy under which a person resident in the province is, at the time the policy was issued or effected, the person whose life was insured.

(2) Where the aggregate of the amount of an individual's income as determined under subsection (1) for all provinces for a taxation year exceeds his income described in subsection 115(1) of the Act, the amount of his income earned in the taxation year in a particular province shall be that proportion of his income so described that the amount of his income earned in the taxation year in the province as determined under subsection (1) is of the aggregate of all those amounts.

(3) Where, in a taxation year, a non-resident individual has disposed of real property situated in a particular province or an interest therein, or an option in respect thereof, any taxable capital gain from that disposition shall be a taxable capital gain in that particular province.

(4) Except as provided in subsection (5), where, in a taxation year, a non-resident individual has disposed of any capital property, other than property referred to in subsection (3), used by him in carrying on a business in Canada, the proportion of any taxable capital gain from that disposition that

(a) his income for the year from carrying on that business in a particular province

is of

(b) his income for the year from carrying on that business in Canada,

shall be a taxable capital gain in that particular province.

(5) Where in a taxation year a non-resident individual

(a) had no permanent establishment in Canada, and

(b) disposed of any capital property, other than property referred to in subsection (3), used by him in a previous year in carrying on a business in Canada,

the proportion of any taxable capital gain from that disposition that

(c) his income from carrying on that business in a particular province for the last preceding taxation year in which he had income from carrying on that business in a province

is of

(d) his income for the year referred to in paragraph (c), from carrying on that business in Canada,

shall be a taxable capital gain in the particular province."

4. Where an individual who did not reside in Canada at any time in a taxation year was

(a) a student in full-time attendance at an educational institution in the Province of Quebec that is a university, college or other educational institution providing courses at a post-secondary school level,

(b) a student attending, or a teacher teaching at, an educational institution outside Canada that is a university, college or other educational institution providing courses at a post-secondary school level who had, in any previous year, ceased to be resident in the Province of Quebec in the course of or subsequent to moving to attend or to teach at, as the case may be, that institution,

(c) an individual who had, in any previous year, ceased to be resident in the Province of Quebec in the course of or subsequent to moving to carry on research or any similar work under a grant received by him to enable him to carry on that research or work, or

(d) an individual who had, in any previous year, ceased to be resident in the Province of Quebec and who was, in the taxation year, in receipt of remuneration in respect of an office or employment that was paid to him directly or indirectly by

(i) the Province of Quebec,

(ii) any corporation, commission or association the shares, capital or property of which were at least 90 per cent owned by the Province of Quebec, or a wholly-owned subsidiary corporation to such a corporation, commission or association, on condition that no person other than Her Majesty in right of the Province of Quebec had any right to the shares, capital or property of that corporation, commission, association or subsidiary or a right to acquire the shares, capital or property,

(iii) an educational institution, other than an educational institution of the Government of Canada, in the Province of Quebec that was

(A) a university, college or other educational institution providing courses at a post-secondary school level that received or was entitled to receive financial support from the Province of Quebec,

(B) a school operated by the Province of Quebec, or by a municipality thereof or by a public body thereof performing a function of government, or a school operated on behalf of that Province, municipality or public body, or

(C) a secondary school providing courses leading to a certificate or diploma that is a requirement for entrance to a college or university, or

(iv) an institution in the Province of Quebec, other than an institution of the Government of Canada, supplying health services or social services, or both, that received or was entitled to receive financial support from the Province of Quebec,

there shall be included, for the purposes of this Order, in computing his income earned in the taxation year in the Province of Quebec the aggregate of

(e) the amount of any remuneration in respect of an office or employment that was paid to him directly or indirectly by the Province of Quebec or any corporation, commission, association or institution referred to in paragraph (d), other than an institution of the Government of Canada, or by a wholly-owned corporation subsidiary to such corporation, commission or association, and that was received by the individual who did not reside in Canada in the year, except to the extent that such remuneration was attributable to the duties of an office or employment performed by him outside Canada, and that is

(i) is subject to an income or profits tax imposed by the government of a country other than Canada, or

(ii) is paid in connection with the selling of property, the negotiating of contracts or the rendering of services for his employer, or a foreign affiliate of his employer, or any other person with whom his employer does not deal at arm's length, in the ordinary course of a business carried on by his employer, that foreign affiliate or that other person,

(f) amounts that would be required by paragraph 56(1)(n) or (o) of the Act to be included in computing the individual's income for the year if

(i) the individual were resident in Canada throughout the year,

(ii) the references in subparagraph 56(1)(n)(i) and paragraph 56(1)(o) of the Act to "received by the taxpayer in the year" were read as references to "received by the taxpayer in the year from the Province of Quebec or any corporation, commission, association or institution referred to in paragraph 4(d) of the *Income Earned in Quebec Income Tax Remission Order, 1988*, other than an institution of the Government of Canada, or from a wholly-owned corporation subsidiary to such corporation, commission or association", and

(iii) the reference to "$500" in paragraph 56(1)(n) of the Act were read as a reference to "the proportion of $500 that the amount determined under subparagraph (i) is of the amount that would be so determined if the requirements of subparagraphs 4(f)(i) and (ii) of the *Income Earned in Quebec Income Tax Remission Order, 1988* were not taken into account",

(g) amounts that would be required by subsection 56(8) of the Act to be included in computing the individual's income for the year if the individual were resident in Canada throughout the year, and

(h) amounts that would be required by paragraph 56(1)(q) of the Act to be included in computing his income for the year if he were resident in Canada throughout the year,

minus the amount that would be deductible in computing his income for the year by virtue of section 62 of the Act if

(i) that section were read without reference to paragraph (1)(a) thereof,

(j) that section were applicable in computing the taxable income of individuals who did not reside in Canada, and

(k) the amounts described in subparagraph (1)(f)(ii) thereof were the amounts described in paragraph (f).

## REMISSION TO INDIVIDUALS WHO DID NOT RESIDE IN A PROVINCE, THE NORTHWEST TERRITORIES OR THE YUKON TERRITORY ON THE LAST DAY OF THE TAXATION YEAR

**5. (1)** Subject to subsection (2), remission is hereby granted to any individual who did not reside in a province on the last day of a taxation year of the amount, if any, by which

(a) income tax, interest and penalties paid or payable under the Act by that individual in respect of that taxation year,

exceeds

(b) the tax, interest and penalties that would have been payable by that individual under the Act in respect of that taxation year if the individual had resided in the Province of Quebec on the last day of the taxation year.

**(2)** Subsection (1) is applicable to an individual who

(a) sojourned in the Province of Quebec for a period of, or periods the aggregate of which is, 183 days or more and was ordinarily resident outside Canada;

(b) was at any time in the year an agent-general, officer or servant of the Province of Quebec and was resident in that Province immediately prior to his appointment or employment by that Province;

(c) performed services at any time in the year under an international development assistance program prescribed under Part XXXIV of the Regulations and was at any time

   (i) in the three month period preceding the day on which those services commenced, resident in the Province of Quebec, and

   (ii) in the six month period preceding the day on which those services commenced, an officer or servant of

   (A) the Province of Quebec,

   (B) any corporation, commission or association the shares, capital or property of which were at least 90 per cent owned by the Province of Quebec, or a wholly-owned corporation subsidiary to such a corporation, commission or association, on condition that no person other than Her Majesty in right of the Province of Quebec had any right to those shares or that capital or property of such corporation, commission, association or subsidiary or a right to acquire those shares or that capital or property,

   (C) an educational institution, other than an educational institution of the Government of Canada, in the Province of Quebec that was

   (I) a university, college or other educational institution providing courses at a post-secondary school level that received or was entitled to receive financial support from the Province of Quebec,

   (II) a school operated by the Province of Quebec, or by a municipality thereof or by a public body thereof performing a function of government, or a school operated on behalf of that Province, municipality or public body, or

   (III) a secondary school providing courses leading to a certificate or diploma that is a requirement for entrance to a college or university, or

   (D) an institution in the Province of Quebec, other than an institution of the Government of Canada, supplying health services or social services, or both, that received or was entitled to receive financial support from the Province of Quebec;

(d) was resident in Canada in any previous year and was, at any time in the year, the spouse of a person described in paragraph (b) or (c) living with that person; or

(e) was, at any time in the year, a child of a person described in paragraph (b) or (c) and was living with the person in a self-contained domestic establishment that the person, whether alone or jointly with one or more persons, maintained and in which the person lived and actually supported the child who, at that time, was

   (i) wholly dependent for support on the person, or the person and the other person or persons, and

   (ii) either under 18 years of age or so dependent by reason of mental or physical infirmity.

**(3)** Paragraph (2)(d) is not applicable where the spouse of an individual described in paragraph (2)(c) is also an individual described in paragraph (2)(c).

# Remission to Individuals Who Resided in the Province of Quebec on the Last Day of a Taxation Year

**6. (1)** Remission is hereby granted to any individual who resided in the Province of Quebec on the last day of a taxation year of the amount, if any, by which

(a) the tax, interest and penalties payable under the Act by that individual in respect of that taxation year, exceeds

(b) the tax, interest and penalties that would have been payable by that individual in respect of that taxation year if

(i) if subsections 2601(1) and (2) of the Regulations read as follows:

"2601. (1) Notwithstanding subsection (4) and section 2603, where an individual resided in a particular province on the last day of a taxation year and had no income for the year from a business with a permanent establishment in another province, his income earned in the taxation year in the province is his income for the year.

(2) Notwithstanding subsection (4) and section 2603, where an individual resided in a particular province on the last day of a taxation year and had income for the year from a business with a permanent establishment in any other province, his income earned in the taxation year in the province is the amount, if any, by which

(a) his income for the year

exceeds

(b) the aggregate of his income for the year from carrying on business earned in each other province, determined as hereinafter set forth in this Part.",

(ii) if the definition "business-income tax" in subsection 126(7) of the Act read as follows:

" "business-income tax" paid by a taxpayer for a taxation year in respect of businesses carried on by the taxpayer in a country other than Canada (in this definition referred to as the "business country") means such portion of 55% of any income or profits tax paid by the taxpayer for the year to the government of any country other than Canada or to the government of a state, province or other political subdivision of any such country as can reasonably be regarded as tax in respect of the income of the taxpayer from any business carried on by the taxpayer in the business country, but does not include a tax, or the portion of a tax, that can reasonably be regarded as relating to an amount that

(a) any other person or partnership has received or is entitled to receive from that government, or

(b) was deductible under subparagraph 110(1)(f)(i) in computing the taxpayer's taxable income for the year;", and

(iii) if the definition "tax for the year otherwise payable under this Part" in subsection 126(7) of the Act read as follows:

" "tax for the year otherwise payable under this Part" means the the amount determined by the formula

$$A - B$$

where

A is the tax payable under this Part for the year after taking into account the requirements of subparagraph 6(1)(b)(i) of the *Income Earned in Quebec Income Tax Remission Order, 1988*, but before making any deduction under any of sections 121, 122.3, 126.1, 127 and 127.2 to 127.4 and this section, and

B is the amount, if any, deemed by subsection 120(2) to have been paid on account of tax payable under this Part for the year after taking into account the requirements of subparagraph 6(1)(b)(i) of the *Income Earned in Quebec Income Tax Remission Order, 1988*;".

**(2)** In subsection (1), a reference to the last day of a taxation year shall, in the case of an individual who resided in the Province of Quebec at any time in the year and ceased to reside in Canada before the end of the year, be deemed to be a reference to the last day in the year on which the individual resided in Canada.

Explanatory Note

### DEDUCTIONS AND REMITTANCES

**7.** Notwithstanding paragraph 102(1)(a), subsection 102(2), paragraph 103(1)(m) and subparagraphs 103(4)(a)(xiii), (b)(xiii) and (c)(xiii) of the Regulations, the amount to be deducted or withheld by an employer and remitted to the Receiver General pursuant to Part I of the Regulations shall, in the case of

(a) an individual referred to in section 4 in respect of the remuneration referred to in paragraph 4(e), and

(b) an individual referred to in paragraph 5(2)(b), (c), (d) or (e) in respect of remuneration received from the Province of Quebec or from any corporation, commission, association or institution referred to in paragraph 5(2)(c), other than an institution of the Government of Canada, or from a wholly-owned corporation subsidiary to such corporation, commission or association,

be determined as if the employee reported for work at an establishment of the employer in Quebec.

**7.1** Every individual to whom an amount was remitted under section 5 for a taxation year shall reimburse that amount, plus interest thereon to the day of payment, to Her Majesty in right of Canada to the extent of the amount of tax payable under the *Taxation Act*, R.S.Q., c. I-3, for that year that the individual, as a result of an objection served on the Minister of Revenue of the Province of Quebec, a claim filed in any court or a complaint made to any tribunal, was declared not to be liable to pay on the ground that the individual was not subject to the tax levied under that Act because of the individual's place of residence.

**8. (1)** Sections 3 to 6 apply to the 1983 to 1996 taxation years.

**(2)** Section 7 is applicable in respect of the 1989 and subsequent taxation years.

### INCOME TAX PAID BY INVESTORS, OTHER THAN PROMOTERS REMISSION ORDER

P.C. 1996-1274, August 7, 1996 (SI/96-80)

His Excellency the Governor General in Council, considering that is in the public interest to do so, on the recommendation of the Minister of National Revenue, pursuant to subsection 23(2) of the *Financial Administration Act*, hereby remits to each taxpayer, other than a promoter, who has delivered or delivers to the Minister a timely and duly executed agreement letter (referred to in the details of the settlement project regarding general partnerships used as SR&ED tax shelters issued by the Minister on June 30, 1995) accepted by the Minister, amounts payable under the *Income Tax Act* by the taxpayer equal to

(1) the difference between

(a) 50% of the product of each payment made before executing the agreement on account of the tax liability resulting from adjustments made by the Minister to the taxpayer's claim in respect of the tax shelter and the prescribed rate of interest for income tax refunds, for the period from the date of the payment to the date of the assessment of the tax liability made as a result of the agreement, compounded daily, and

(b) refund interest in respect of any such payment,

(2) 50% of the product of that difference and that rate, for the period from the said date of assessment to the date this Order is implemented, so compounded, and

(3) amounts that would not be payable if there were no such refund interest or if this Order were not made.

### EXPLANATORY NOTE

*(This note is not part of the Order.)*

This Order remits amounts of income tax paid by taxpayers who made payments on account of their tax assessments before executing agreement letters (referred to in the details of the settlement project regarding general partnerships used as SR&ED tax shelters issued by Revenue Canada on June 30, 1995), in order that those taxpayers be on even terms with taxpayers who had not made such payments.

**Notes**: Documents obtained under the *Access to Information Act* reveal that this remission order deals with a group of approximately 8,000 taxpayers in Quebec who invested in scientific research partnership tax shelters from 1989-94 and claimed an investment tax credit (ITC) and a partnership loss. Most of these investors disposed of their partnership interest in the year following the year of purchase. Revenue Canada concluded that the investors were not entitled to any ITC or partnership loss.

Remission Orders

Under the settlement project, Revenue Canada (and Revenu Québec) allowed the investors an income loss on the disposal of the partnership interest, and, for an investor who was not a promoter, will cancel the interest owing on the unpaid tax. This proposal applied also to taxpayers who did not file an objection or who had paid their tax debt in full. The settlement proposal was sent to the investors' representatives (over 100 in total) on June 30, 1995, and was to be accepted by September 30, 1995, although it appears that it was still open for acceptance much later.

The total number of taxpayers involved in the settlement is 7,556. Some $103 million of federal tax and interest was at stake, of which about $45.9 million would be eliminated if all taxpayers accept the settlement.

The remission order gives effect to the settlement project, to the extent Revenue Canada was not otherwise authorized under the *Income Tax Act* to implement the settlement. The remission order is expected to apply to 3,282 taxpayers, and will remit a total of approximately $900,000.

## INCOME TAX REMISSION ORDER (YUKON TERRITORY LANDS)

### ORDER RESPECTING THE REMISSION OF INCOME TAX IN RELATION TO CERTAIN LANDS IN THE YUKON TERRITORY
P.C. 1995-197, February 7, 1995 (SI/95-18)

#### SHORT TITLE

**1.** This Order may be cited as the *Income Tax Remission Order (Yukon Territory Lands)*.

#### INTERPRETATION

**2.** In this Order,

"**Act**" means the *Yukon First Nations Self-Government Act*;

"**reserve**" has the same meaning as in subsection 2(1) of the *Indian Act*.

#### REMISSION

**3.** Remission is hereby granted of amounts payable under the *Income Tax Act* that would not be payable if the lands in the Yukon Territory

(a) that are reserved or set aside, as at the day on which this Order comes into force, by notation in the property records of the Department of Indian Affairs and Northern Development, for the use of its Indian and Inuit Affairs Program, were reserves for the period beginning after 1984 and ending on the expiration of the third calendar year after the calendar year in which the Act comes into force;

(b) that were so notated for a period beginning after 1984 and ending before the day on which this Order comes into force, had been a reserve throughout each calendar year of that period; and

(c) that are so notated for a period beginning after the day on which this Order comes into force and ending before the expiration of the third calendar year after the calendar year in which the Act comes into force, were a reserve throughout each calendar year of that period.

## INDIAN INCOME TAX REMISSION ORDER [MARCH 1993]

### ORDER RESPECTING THE REMISSION OF INCOME TAX PAID OR PAYABLE ON INCOME FROM EMPLOYERS RESIDING ON RESERVES AND INDIAN SETTLEMENTS AND ON CERTAIN UNEMPLOYMENT INSURANCE BENEFITS RECEIVED BY INDIANS
P.C. 1993-523, March 16, 1993 (SI/93-44), as amended by P.C. 1994-799, May 12, 1994 (SI/94-69).

#### SHORT TITLE

**1.** This Order may be cited as the *Indian Income Tax Remission Order*.

Remission Orders

## INTERPRETATION

**2.** In this Order,

**"Act"** means the *Income Tax Act*;

**"Indian"** has the same meaning as in subsection 2(1) of the *Indian Act*;

**"Indian settlement"** has the same meaning as in section 2 of the *Indians and Bands on certain Indian Settlements Remission Order*;

**"reserve"** means

(a) a reserve as defined in subsection 2(1) of the *Indian Act*,

(b) Category IA land or Category IA-N land as defined in subsection 2(1) of the *Cree-Naskapi (of Quebec) Act*, and

(c) Sechelt lands as defined in subsection 2(1) of the *Sechelt Indian Band Self-Government Act*.

## REMISSION IN RESPECT OF CERTAIN EMPLOYMENT INCOME

**3. (1)** Remission is hereby granted to a taxpayer who is an Indian of the amounts payable by the taxpayer under Parts I to I.2 of the Act for a taxation year that would not be payable by the taxpayer if, in the calculation of the taxpayer's income for the year, there were not included an amount equal to the product obtained by multiplying the income for the year from each office or employment of the taxpayer by the proportion that

(a) the amounts that are required to be included in the computation of the income from that office or employment for the year and that are payable to the taxpayer by an employer residing on a reserve or Indian settlement

are of

(b) the amounts that are required to be included in the computation of the income from that office or employment for the year.

**(2)** Remission is hereby granted to a person for whom the amounts payable under Parts I to I.2 of the Act for a taxation year would be reduced if, in the calculation of the income of the taxpayer referred to in subsection (1) for the year, there were not included the product obtained under that subsection in respect of each office or employment of the taxpayer, of an amount equal to the amount, if any, by which

(a) the total amount payable by the person under Parts I to I.2 of the Act for the year

exceeds

(b) the total amount that would be payable by the person for the year if, in the calculation of the taxpayer's income for the year, there were not included the product obtained under subsection (1) in respect of each office or employment of the taxpayer.

**(3)** Subsections (1) and (2) apply to the 1992, 1993 and 1994 taxation years except that, in its application to the 1994 taxation year, paragraph (1)(a) shall be read as follows:

"(a) the amounts that are required to be included in the computation of the income from that office or employment for the year and that are payable to the taxpayer by an employer residing on a reserve or Indian settlement, where the office or employment was held continuously since before 1994."

## REMISSION IN RESPECT OF CERTAIN UNEMPLOYMENT INSURANCE BENEFITS

**4. (1)** Subject to section 5, remission is hereby granted to a taxpayer who is an Indian of the amounts payable by the taxpayer under Parts I to I.2 of the Act for a taxation year that would not be payable by the taxpayer if, in the calculation of the taxpayer's income for the year for the purpose of an assessment, there were not included an amount equal to the product obtained by multiplying the total of the benefits referred to in subparagraph 56(1)(a)(iv) of the Act and included in the calculation of the taxpayer's income for the year for the purpose of an assessment, by the proportion that

(a) the income from employment during a relevant qualifying period that was taken into account in determining the amount of those benefits and that is exempt from taxation under subsection 87(1) of the *Indian Act*[2] or in respect of which there is a remission of tax payable under the Act by a taxpayer who is an Indian

is of

(b) the total income from employment during a relevant qualifying period that was taken into account in determining the amount of those benefits.

(2) Subject to section 5, remission is hereby granted to a person for whom the amounts payable under Parts I to I.2 of the Act for a taxation year would be reduced if, in respect of the taxpayer referred to in subsection (1), an amount equal to the amount of the product referred to in that subsection were not included in the calculation of the taxpayer's income for the year for the purpose of an assessment, of an amount equal to the amount, if any, by which

(a) the total amount payable by the person under Parts I to I.2 of the Act for the year

exceeds

(b) the total amount that would be payable by the person for the year if, in respect of the taxpayer, an amount equal to the amount of the product referred to subsection (1) were not included in the calculation of the taxpayer's income for the year for the purpose of an assessment.

(3) Subsections (1) and (2) apply to taxation years 1985 to 1991.

## Condition

**5.** Remission under subsection 4(1) or (2) is granted on condition that an application in writing establishing the applicant's right to that remission be submitted to the Minister of National Revenue.

## Explanatory Note

*(This note is not part of the Order.)*

This Order remits income tax on employment income received by Indians in 1992 and 1993 from employers residing on a reserve or Indian settlement in order to give such taxpayers time to adjust to the 1992 ruling of the Supreme Court of Canada in *Williams v. R* concerning the proper test regarding the exemption from taxation of the personal property of an Indian situated on a reserve.

This Order also remits income tax assessed for taxation years 1985 to 1991 on those unemployment insurance benefits paid to Indians which, according to the Court, are exempt from taxation.

## Indian Income Tax Remission Order [August 1993]

P.C. 1993-1649, August 4, 1993 (SI/93-166)

His Excellency the Governor General in Council, considering that it is in the public interest to do so, on the recommendation of the Minister of National Revenue, pursuant to subsection 23(2) of the *Financial Administration Act*, is pleased hereby to remit amounts that would be remitted if the reference to subsection 87(1) of the *Indian Act* in the *Indian Income Tax Remission Order* included a reference to a provision similar to that subsection in an Act cited in that Order.

## Explanatory Note

*(This note is not part of the Order.)*

The *Indian Income Tax Remission Order* remitted income tax assessed for 1985 to 1991 on unemployment insurance benefits paid to Indians, which the Supreme Court in 1992 held were exempt from taxation under

---

[2] Order in Council P.C. 1993-1649, *Canada Gazette* Part II, August 25, 1993 (SI/93-166 reproduced below) remits amounts that would be remitted if this reference to subsection 87(1) of the *Indian Act* included a reference to a provision similar to that subsection in an Act cited in this Order (ie in the *Cree-Naskapi (of Quebec) Act* or the *Sechelt Indian Band Self-Government Act*).

section 87 of the *Indian Act*. This order extends that remission to unemployment insurance benefits exempt under the *Cree-Naskapi (of Quebec) Act* and the *Sechelt Indian Band Self-Government Act*.

# INDIAN SETTLEMENTS REMISSION ORDER (2000)
P.C. 2000-1112, July 27, 2000 (SI/2000-69)

Her Excellency the Governor General in Council, considering that it is in the public interest to do so, on the recommendation of the Minister of National Revenue, pursuant to subsection 23(2) of the *Financial Administration Act*, hereby makes the annexed *Indian Settlements Remission Order (2000)*.

## INTERPRETATION

**1.** The following definitions apply in this Order.

**"Indian Settlement"** means a settlement named in column 1 of Schedule 1 and described in column 2 of that Schedule.

**"reserve"** has the same meaning as in subsection 2(1) of the *Indian Act*.

## APPLICATION

**2.** This Order applies in respect of an Indian Settlement until all or part of the lands constituting that Indian Settlement are set apart as a reserve by an order of the Governor in Council.

## PART 1 — INCOME TAX

### Interpretation

**3.** In this Part,

(a) **"tax"** means a tax imposed under Part I, I.1 or I.2 of the *Income Tax Act*; and

(b) all other words and expressions not otherwise defined in section 1 have the same meaning as in the *Income Tax Act*.

### Remission of Income Tax

**4.** Remission is hereby granted to a taxpayer whose income is situated on an Indian Settlement, in respect of each taxation year or fiscal period beginning during or after the year set out in column 2 of Schedule 2 in respect of that Indian Settlement, of any amount by which

(a) the taxes, interest and penalties paid or payable by the taxpayer for the taxation year or fiscal period exceed

(b) the taxes, interest and penalties that would have been payable by the taxpayer for the taxation year or fiscal period if the Indian Settlement had been a reserve throughout that taxation year or fiscal period.

## PART 2 — GOODS AND SERVICES TAX

### Interpretation

**5.** In this Part,

(a) **"tax"** means the goods and services tax imposed under Division II of Part IX of the *Excise Tax Act*; and

(b) all other words and expressions not otherwise defined in section 1 have the same meaning as in Part IX of the *Excise Tax Act*.

Remission Orders

## Remission of the Goods and Services Tax

**6.** Subject to sections 7 and 8, remission is hereby granted to a recipient of a taxable supply made on or delivered to an Indian Settlement on or after the date set out in column 3 or 4 of an item of Schedule 2, as the case may be, of tax paid or payable by that person in an amount equal to any amount by which

(a) the tax paid or payable by the recipient

exceeds

(b) the tax that would have been payable by the recipient if the Indian Settlement had been a reserve.

## Conditions

**7.** Remission under section 6 is granted to an individual if

(a) the tax paid or payable has not otherwise been rebated, credited, refunded or remitted under Part IX of the *Excise Tax Act* or the *Financial Administration Act*; and

(b) a claim for the remission is made to the Minister of National Revenue within two years after the day on which the tax was paid or became payable.

**8.** Remission under section 6 is granted to a person other than an individual if

(a) the tax paid or payable has not otherwise been rebated, credited, refunded or remitted under Part IX of the *Excise Tax Act* or the *Financial Administration Act*;

(b) in respect of tax paid on or after the date set out in column 4 of an item of Schedule 2 but before the date set out in column 3 of that item, a claim for the remission is made to the Minister of National Revenue within two years after the latter date; and

(c) in respect of tax paid on or after the date set out in column 3 of an item of Schedule 2, a claim for the remission is made to the Minister of National Revenue within two years after the date on which the tax was paid.

## SCHEDULE 1
*(Section 1)*

[Not reproduced]

## SCHEDULE 2
*(Section 14, 6 and 8)*

[Not reproduced]

# INDIANS AND BANDS ON CERTAIN INDIAN SETTLEMENTS REMISSION ORDER

ORDER RESPECTING THE REMISSION OF CERTAIN INCOME TAXES PAYABLE BY INDIANS AND OF THE GOODS AND SERVICES TAX PAYABLE BY INDIANS OR BY BANDS OR DESIGNATED CORPORATIONS ON CERTAIN INDIAN SETTLEMENTS

P.C. 1992-1052, June 3, 1992 (SI/92-102), as amended by P.C. 1994-2096, December 28, 1994 (SI/94-145).

### SHORT TITLE

**1.** This Order may be cited as the *Indians and Bands on certain Indian Settlements Remission Order*.

### INTERPRETATION

**2.** In this Order,

"**band**" has the same meaning as in subsection 2(1) of the *Indian Act*;

"**designated corporation**" means the Ouje-Bougoumou Development Corporation or the Ouje-Bougoumou Eenuch Association;

"**Indian**" has the same meaning as in subsection 2(1) of the *Indian Act*;

"**Indian settlement**" means an area that is named and described in the schedule but does not include an area that is
   (a) a reserve within the meaning of the *Indian Act*, or
   (b) Category IA land within the meaning of the *Cree-Naskapi (of Quebec) Act*;

"**reserve**" has the same meaning as in subsection 2(1) of the *Indian Act*.

## PART I — INCOME TAXES

### *Interpretation*

**3. (1)** For the purposes of this Part,

"**Act**" means the *Income Tax Act*;

"**tax**" means tax under Parts I, I.1 and I.2 of the Act.

**(2)** All other words and expressions used in this part have the same meaning as in the Act.

### *Remission of Income Tax*

**4.** Remission is hereby granted to a taxpayer who is an Indian in respect of each taxation year after 1992 of the amount, if any, by which the taxes, interest and penalties payable by the taxpayer for the taxation year under the Act exceed the taxes, interest and penalties that would have been payable by the taxpayer for the year under the Act if the Indian settlements were reserves throughout the year.

## PART II — GOODS AND SERVICES TAX

### *Interpretation*

**5. (1)** For the purposes of this Part,

"**Act**" means the *Excise Tax Act*;

"**tax**" means the goods and services tax imposed under Division II of Part IX of the Act.

**(2)** All other words and expressions used in this Part have the same meaning as in Part IX of the Act.

### *Remission of the Goods and Services Tax*

**6.** Subject to section 8, remission of the tax paid or payable on or after the day on which this Order comes into force is hereby granted to an individual who is an Indian and who is the recipient of a taxable supply, in an amount equal to the amount, if any, by which
   (a) the tax paid or payable by the individual under the Act
exceeds
   (b) the tax that would have been payable by the individual if the Indian settlements were reserves.

**7.** Subject to section 8, remission of the tax paid or payable on or after January 1, 1991 is hereby granted to a band or a designated corporation that is the recipient of a taxable supply, in an amount equal to the amount, if any, by which
   (a) the tax paid or payable by the band or designated corporation under the Act
exceeds
   (b) the tax that would have been payable by the band or designated corporation if the Indian settlements were reserves.

Remission Orders

## Condition

**8.** Remission under sections 6 and 7 in respect of tax paid is granted on condition that an application in writing for the remission be submitted to the Minister of National Revenue within four years after the day on which the tax was paid.

# SCHEDULE
# INDIAN SETTLEMENTS
(Section 2)

**1. Ouje-Bougoumou, Quebec** — The settlement is situated on the north shore of Lake Opémisca, 32 km northwest of Chibougamau, Quebec, in Cuvier Township at 49°55' latitude and 74°49' longitude and has an area of 100 km$^2$.

**2. Kanesatake (Oka), Quebec** — The settlement is situated 25 km northwest of Montreal, on the north side of Des Deux Montagnes Lake, and, for the purposes of this Order, comprises the Village of Oka and the areas in the western portion of the Parish of Oka, known as Côte Sainte-Philomène, Côte Saint-Jean, Côte Saint-Ambroise and Côte Sainte-Germaine-Côte-Sud.

**3. Kee-Way-Win Settlement, Ontario** — The settlement is situated on the south side of Sandy Lake, in the District of Kenora, Patricia Portion, at 53°4' latitude and 92°45' longitude, and has an area of approximately 19,030 hectares.

**4. Savant Lake Settlement, Ontario** — The settlement is situated on the north side of Kasheweogama Lake in the Township of McCubbin, District of Thunder Bay, at 50°4' latitude and 90°43' longitude, and has an area of approximately 5,890 hectares.

**5. Long Dog Lake Settlement, Ontario** — The settlement is situated on the south side of Long Dog Lake, District of Kenora, Patricia Portion, at 52°28' latitude and 90°43' longitude, and has an area of 5,305 hectares.

**6. MacDowell Lake Settlement, Ontario** — The settlement is situated at the southwest end of MacDowell Lake, District of Kenora, Patricia Portion, at 52°11' latitude and 92°45' longitude, and has an area of approximately 4,455 hectares.

**7. Slate Falls Settlement, Ontario** — The settlement is situated on the northeast end of North Bamaji Lake, District of Kenora, Patricia Portion, at 51°11' latitude and 91°35' longitude, and has an area of approximately 6,870 hectares.

**8. Aroland Settlement, Ontario** — The settlement is situated on both the north and south sides of King's Highway 643 at Aroland rural community in the Township of Danford, District of Thunder Bay, at 50°14' latitude and 86°59' longitude, extends northwards west and north of Esnagami Lake and has an area of approximately 18,130 hectares.

**9. Grandmother's Point Settlement, Ontario** — The settlement is situated at the southwest end of Attawapiskat Lake, in the District of Kenora, Patricia Portion, at 52°14' latitude and 87°53' longitude, and has an area of approximately 855 hectares.

**10. Cadotte Lake Settlement, Alberta** — The settlement is situated 40 miles east of Peace River, Alberta at Cadotte Lake, on highway 686, comprises portions of Townships 86 and 87, within ranges 15, 16 and 17, and also land bordering on Marten Lake in Townships 86 and 87 within ranges 13 and 14, west of the 5th meridian (but excluding all mines and minerals and the beds and shores of the Cadotte and Otter Rivers), and has an area of approximately 14,245 hectares.

**11. Fort MacKay, Alberta** — The settlement is situated 105 km northwest of Fort McMurray, and comprises the areas of Namur Lake, Namur River and portions of the Hamlet of Fort MacKay. The Hamlet of Fort MacKay is situated on the west side of the Athabaska River and the Fort MacKay Band occupies an area that includes Lots 1 to 7 on Plan 9022250 (but excluding all mines and minerals), as well as a small portion of the East-West Government Road allowance. The Indian settlement has an area of approximately 86.6 hectares.

**12. Little Buffalo Settlement, Alberta** — The settlement is situated in north central Alberta and surrounding Lubicon Lake, and has an area of approximately 24,505 hectares.

**Notes**: See also the *Indians and the War Lake First Nation Band on the Ilford Indian Settlement*.

# INDIANS AND BANDS ON CERTAIN INDIAN SETTLEMENTS REMISSION ORDER (1997)

P.C. 1997-1529, October 23, 1997 (SI/97-127)

## INTERPRETATION

**1.** The definitions in this section apply in this Order.

**"band"** has the same meaning as in subsection 2(1) of the *Indian Act*.

**"Indian"** has the same meaning as in subsection 2(1) of the *Indian Act*.

**"Indian Settlement"** means an area that is named and described in column 2 of the schedule.

**"reserve"** has the same meaning as in subsection 2(1) of the *Indian Act*.

## APPLICATION

**2.** This Order applies to any Indian Settlement until the time when the area of that Indian Settlement is set aside, in whole or in part, as a reserve by Order of the Governor in Council.

## PART 1 — INCOME TAX

### Interpretation

**3. (1)** For the purposes of this Part, "tax" means tax imposed under Parts I, I.1 and I.2 of the *Income Tax Act*.

**(2)** Subject to section 1, all other words and expressions used in this Part have the same meaning as in the *Income Tax Act*.

### Remission of Income Tax

**4.** Remission is hereby granted to a taxpayer who is an Indian whose income is situated on an Indian Settlement, in respect of the taxation year set out in column 3 of the schedule in relation to that Indian Settlement and each taxation year after that year, of the amount, if any, by which

(a) the taxes, interest and penalties paid or payable by the taxpayer for the taxation year under the *Income Tax Act*

exceed

(b) the taxes, interest and penalties that would have been payable by the taxpayer for the taxation year under that Act if the Indian Settlement were a reserve throughout the year.

## PART 2 — GOODS AND SERVICES TAX

### Interpretation

**5. (1)** For the purposes of this Part, "tax" means the goods and services tax imposed under Division II of Part IX of the *Excise Tax Act*.

**(2)** Subject to section 1, all other words and expressions used in this Part have the same meaning as in Part IX of the *Excise Tax Act*.

## Remission of the Goods and Services Tax

**6.** Subject to section 8, remission of the tax paid or payable is hereby granted to an individual who is an Indian who resides on an Indian Settlement and who is the recipient of a taxable supply made on or after the date for remission of the tax set out in column 4 of the schedule, in an amount equal to the amount, if any, by which

(a) the tax paid or payable by the individual

exceeds

(b) the tax that would have been payable by the individual if the Indian Settlement were a reserve.

**7.** Subject to section 9, remission of the tax paid or payable is hereby granted to a band that is established on an Indian Settlement and is the recipient of a taxable supply made on or after the date for remission of the tax set out in column 5 of the schedule, in an amount equal to the amount, if any, by which

(a) the tax paid or payable by the band

exceeds

(b) the tax that would have been payable by the band if the Indian Settlement were a reserve.

**8.** Remission under section 6 in respect of tax paid is granted on the condition that an application in writing for the remission be submitted to the Minister of National Revenue within two years after the date on which the tax was paid.

**9.** Remission under section 7 in respect of tax paid is granted on the condition that an application in writing for the remission be submitted to the Minister of National Revenue

(a) for tax paid on or after the date for remission of the tax set out in column 5 of the schedule but before the date for remission of the tax set out in column 4, within two years after the latter date; and

(b) for tax paid on or after the date for remission of the tax set out in column 4 of the schedule, within two years after the date on which the tax was paid.

## SCHEDULE
(Sections 1, 4, 6, 7 and 9)

| Item | Column 1<br>Band | Column 2<br>Indian Settlement and Legal Description of Settlement Lands | Column 3<br>Taxation Year | Column 4<br>Date for Remission of GST for Individual Indians | Column 5<br>Date for Remission of GST for Bands |
|---|---|---|---|---|---|
| 1. | Nibinamik First Nation | Summer Beaver, Ontario: District of Nakina, Ontario (52 degrees 45 minutes north latitude, 88 degrees 35 minutes west longitude) having an area of approximately 3.5 square miles. (Excluded are locations SN 160 and CL 6298, the sites of the old and new schools.) | 1995 | October 23, 1997 | January 1, 1995 |
| 2. | Long Point First Nation | Winneway, Quebec: North-half portion of of Lots 50 and 51 Range 8, the whole of Lot 46-5 Range 9 and South-east corner of Lot 47 Range 9, 51770 CLSR, and 59890 CLSR, Township of Devlin, having an area of approximately 47 hectares. | 1996 | October 23, 1997 | January 1, 1996 |
| 3. | God's River First Nation | God's River, Manitoba: Parcel 5, Plan 4955 NLTO (situated in projected Township 67, Range 23, East of the principal meridian) having an area of approximately 2.83 acres | 1993 | October 23, 1997 | January 1, 1993 |

Part I — Remission Orders

## EXPLANATORY NOTE

*(This note is not part of the Order.)*

The purpose of this Order is to extend the benefits of relief from income tax and the goods and services tax (GST) to Indians, as though the specified Indian settlements were reserves. This Order applies to settlements for which a public commitment has been made by the Government of Canada to grant reserve status under the Indian Act. The Department of Indian and Northern Affairs has advised the Department of National Revenue of the settlements that have identified boundaries that should be included in this Order.

With respect to income tax, this Order places Indian individuals in the tax position that they would have been in had the Indian settlements been granted reserve status. With respect to the GST, the same relief that has been afforded to Indian individuals and Indian bands for on-reserve and certain off-reserve acquisitions of taxable supplies has also been extended to similar acquisitions made by Indian individuals or bands on or outside of the specified Indian settlements.

## INDIANS AND THE WAR LAKE FIRST NATION BAND ON THE ILFORD INDIAN SETTLEMENT REMISSION ORDER

ORDER RESPECTING THE REMISSION OF CERTAIN INCOME TAXES PAID OR PAYABLE BY INDIANS AND THE GOODS AND SERVICES TAX PAID OR PAYABLE BY INDIANS OR BY THE WAR LAKE FIRST NATION BAND ON THE ILFORD INDIAN SETTLEMENT

P.C. 1994-801, May 12, 1994 (SI/94-71).

### SHORT TITLE

**1.** This Order may be cited as the *Indians and the War Lake First Nation Band on the Ilford Indian Settlement Remission Order*.

### INTERPRETATION

**2.** In this Order,

**"band"** has the same meaning as in subsection 2(1) of the *Indian Act*;

**"Ilford Indian Settlement"** means the settlement that is situated near Ilford in the Province of Manitoba, consisting of parcels of land lettered "A" and "B", which parcels are shown on a plan of survey of part of unsurveyed township 81 in Range 12, east of the principal meridian and contain 2.89 hectares and 3.89 hectares, respectively, and that is not a reserve;

**"Indian"** has the same meaning as in subsection 2(1) of the *Indian Act*;

**"reserve"** has the same meaning as in subsection 2(1) of the *Indian Act*.

## PART I — INCOME TAX

### Interpretation

**3. (1)** For the purposes of this Part, "tax" means tax under Parts I, I.1 and I.2 of the *Income Tax Act*.

**(2)** Subject to section 2, all other words and expressions used in this Part have the same meaning as in the *Income Tax Act*.

### Remission of Income Tax

**4.** Remission is hereby granted to a taxpayer who is an Indian in respect of the 1992 taxation year and each taxation year following that year of the amount, if any, by which the taxes, interest and penalties paid or payable by the taxpayer for the taxation year under the *Income Tax Act* exceed the taxes, interest and penalties that would have been payable by the taxpayer for the year under the Act if the Ilford Indian Settlement were a reserve throughout the year.

## PART II — GOODS AND SERVICES TAX

### Interpretation

**5. (1)** For the purposes of this Part, "tax" means the goods and services tax imposed under Division II of Part IX of the *Excise Tax Act*.

(2) Subject to section 2, all other words and expressions used in this Part have the same meaning as in Part IX of the *Excise Tax Act*.

### Remission of the Goods and Services Tax

**6.** Subject to section 8, remission is hereby granted to an individual who is an Indian and who is the recipient of a taxable supply made on or after the day on which this Order comes into force of the tax paid or payable, in an amount equal to the amount, if any, by which

(a) the tax paid or payable by the individual

exceeds

(b) the tax that would have been payable by the individual if the Ilford Indian Settlement were a reserve.

**7.** Subject to section 8, remission is hereby granted to the War Lake First Nation Band of the tax paid or payable, where the band is the recipient of a taxable supply made on or after January 1, 1992, in an amount equal to the amount, if any, by which

(a) the tax paid or payable by the band

exceeds

(b) the tax that would have been payable by the band if the Ilford Indian Settlement were a reserve.

### Condition

**8.** Remission under sections 6 and 7 in respect of tax paid is granted on condition that an application in writing for the remission be submitted to the Minister of National Revenue within four years after the day on which the tax was paid.

## [LIONAIRD CAPITAL CORPORATION NOTES REMISSION ORDER]
### P.C. 1999-737, April 22, 1999 (SI/99-45)

His Excellency the Governor General in Council, considering that the collection of the tax is unreasonable, on the recommendation of the Minister of National Revenue (the "Minister"), pursuant to subsection 23(2) of the *Financial Administration Act*, hereby remits amounts payable by a taxpayer that would not be payable if the amounts required to be included in computing the taxpayer's income pursuant to subsections 146(10) and 146.3(7) of the *Income Tax Act* (the "Act") in respect of the acquisition in 1997 or 1998 of notes issued by Lionaird Capital Corp. were not so required, on condition that the taxpayer file with the Minister an undertaking, binding upon the taxpayer's heirs, legal representatives, successors and assigns, in a form acceptable to the Minister, in which the taxpayer (1) waives all rights to object to or appeal that part of any assessment resulting from the inclusion from time to time in the computation of income for the year and of the person the Minister considers appropriate of amounts received that result from or in any way relate to, whether as damages, reimbursement, redemption, compensation or otherwise, any such acquisition, including any loss resulting therefrom or otherwise in respect thereof (the "recovered amounts"), except the part thereof that, within one month of its being paid, becomes the property of a trust governed by a registered retirement savings plan or registered retirement income fund under which the taxpayer is the annuitant and in respect of which part the taxpayer is not entitled to any deduction, (2) agrees that no relevant claim will be made at any time under subsection 146(6) or 146.3(8) of the Act and waives all rights to object to or appeal that part of any assessment resulting from the disallowance of any such claim, and (3) furnishes security acceptable to and required by the Minister for the payment of any amount that may become payable in respect of the recovered amounts.

Remission Orders

## EXPLANATORY NOTE

*(This note is not part of the Order.)*

This Order remits amounts payable under the *Income Tax Act* as a result of the acquisition of non-qualified investments (notes issued by Lionaird Capital Corp.) by registered retirement savings plans or income funds since the taxpayers did their best to ascertain the eligibility of the investments which they allege are now worthless.

## MAINTENANCE PAYMENTS REMISSION ORDER

### ORDER RESPECTING THE REMISSION OF INCOME TAX PAYABLE BY CERTAIN TAXPAYERS WHO HAVE MADE MAINTENANCE PAYMENTS

P.C. 1991-256, February 14, 1991 (SI/91-22), as amended by P.C. 1994-622, April 21, 1994 (SI/94-51).

### Short Title

**1.** This Order may be cited as the *Maintenance Payments Remission Order*.

### Interpretation

**2.** In this Order,

**"Act"** means the *Income Tax Act*;

**"Minister"** means the Minister of National Revenue.

### Remission

**3.** Subject to sections 4 to 6, remission is granted to a taxpayer for a taxation year ending after 1978 and before 1989 of an amount equal to the amount, if any, by which

(a) the taxes, interest and penalties payable by the taxpayer under the Act for the year

exceed

(b) the taxes, interest and penalties that would have been payable by the taxpayer under the Act for the year if there were deducted in computing the taxpayer's income for the year the aggregate of all amounts paid by the taxpayer in the year, after December 11, 1979 and before February 11, 1988 pursuant to an order made by a competent tribunal after December 11, 1979 and before February 11, 1988 in accordance with the laws of a province, as an allowance payable on a periodic basis for the maintenance of the recipient thereof, of children of the recipient or of both the recipient and the children of the recipient if, at the time the payment was made and throughout the remainder of the year, the taxpayer was living apart from the recipient.

### Conditions

**4.** The remission granted under section 3 to a taxpayer is on condition that the taxpayer makes an application for the remission in writing to the Minister on or before December 31, 1995.

**5.** Where the taxpayer has made the application referred to in section 4 or before December 31, 1991 for remission for a taxation year, the remission is on the further condition that, on the day on which the application was received by the Minister,

(a) the Minister was allowed under the Act to make an assessment or a reassessment of tax payable by the taxpayer for the year;

(b) an objection or appeal by the taxpayer under section 165, 169 or 172 of the Act against an assessment or reassessment for the year was outstanding or could still have been made or instituted; or

(c) a complaint made in writing by the taxpayer to the Canadian Human Rights Commission at a time when paragraph (a) or (b) applied in respect of the year was outstanding concerning the non-deductibility in the year of amounts described in paragraph 3(b).

**5.1** Where the taxpayer makes the application referred to in section 4 after December 31, 1991 for remission for a taxation year, the remission is on the further condition that, on December 31, 1991,

(a) an objection or appeal by the taxpayer under section 165, 169 or 172 of the Act against an assessment or a reassessment for the year was outstanding; or

(b) a complaint made in writing by the taxpayer to the Canadian Human Rights Commission at a time when paragraph 5(a) or (b) applied in respect of the year was outstanding concerning the non-deductibility in the year of amounts described in paragraph 3(b).

**6.** The remission granted under section 3 to a taxpayer for a taxation year is on the further condition that the taxpayer

(a) within 45 days after the day of mailing to the taxpayer of a notice from the Department of National Revenue, Taxation, setting out the amount to be remitted to the taxpayer pursuant to this Order, discontinues any outstanding action commenced by the taxpayer in any court,

(b) within 45 days after the day of mailing to the taxpayer of a notice from the Department of National Revenue, Taxation, setting out the amount to be remitted to the taxpayer pursuant to this Order, withdraws any outstanding objection served on the Minister, any claim filed in any court and any complaint made to any tribunal, and

(c) does not commence any action, claim or objection or make any complaint to any tribunal

by which the taxpayer seeks a reduction in the amount of, or any other relief or remedy relating to, taxes payable by the taxpayer for that year in respect of the deductibility in computing the taxpayer's income for the year of any of the amounts described in paragraph 3(b).

# PRESCRIBED AREAS FORWARD AVERAGING REMISSION ORDER

ORDER RESPECTING THE REMISSION OF INCOME TAX AND PENALTIES, AND INTEREST THEREON, PAYABLE BY CERTAIN RESIDENTS OF PRESCRIBED AREAS WHO FILED FORWARD AVERAGING ELECTIONS IN RESPECT OF THE 1987 TAXATION YEAR

P.C. 1994-109, January 20, 1994 (SI/94-16)

## SHORT TITLE

**1.** This Order may be cited as the *Prescribed Areas Forward Averaging Remission Order*.

## INTERPRETATION

**2.** In this Order,

"**Act**" means the *Income Tax Act*;

"**averaging amount**" has the meaning assigned by subsection 110.4(1) of the Act as that subsection applied to the 1987 taxation year.

## REMISSION

**3.** Subject to section 4, remission is granted to a taxpayer in respect of the 1987 taxation year of an amount equal to the amount, if any, by which

(a) the total of the taxes and penalties, and interest thereon, payable by the taxpayer for that year under the Act

exceeds

(b) the total of the taxes and penalties, and interest thereon, that would have been payable by the taxpayer for that year under the Act if the taxpayer's averaging amount for that year were reduced by the amount that the taxpayer was entitled to deduct under section 110.7 of the Act in computing the taxpayer's taxable income for that year by reason of having resided in an area prescribed by subsection 7303(5) or (6) of the *Income Tax Regulations*.

## CONDITIONS

**4.** The remission granted under section 3 is on condition that

(a) the taxpayer makes an application for the remission in writing to the Minister of National Revenue on or before December 31, 1995; and

(b) the amount of the reduction determined under paragraph 3(b) in the taxpayer's averaging amount for the 1987 taxation year is excluded in determining the taxpayer's accumulated averaging amount under paragraph 110.4(8)(a) of the Act after 1987.

# SYNCRUDE REMISSION ORDER

## ORDER RESPECTING THE REMISSION OF INCOME TAX FOR THE SYNCRUDE PROJECT

P.C. 1976-1026, May 6, 1976 (C.R.C. 1978, Vol. VII, c. 794)

### SHORT TITLE

**1.** This Order may be cited as the *Syncrude Remission Order*.

### INTERPRETATION

**2.** In this Order,

"**barrels**" means barrels of synthetic crude oil from Leases 17 and 22 pursuant to the Syncrude Project;

"**condition**" means that the fiscal programs as they relate to the Syncrude Project in effect at the commencement of the Syncrude Project have been revised in such a manner as to have significant adverse economic effect on the Syncrude Project;

"**Crown**" means Her Majesty in right of the Province of Alberta;

"**leased substances**" means all substances the participant has recovered pursuant to Leases 17 and 22;

"**Leases 17 and 22**" means Government of Alberta Bituminous Sands Leases Nos 17 and 22, excluding that portion of Lease No 17 that is subject to an Agreement dated September 20, 1972 as amended by an Agreement dated September 26, 1972 whereby Great Canadian Oil Sands Limited was granted a sublease of lands contained in Lease No 17 and includes any other documents or titles that extend the duration of Leases 17 and 22;

"**participant**" means

(a) Canada-Cities Service Ltd, a body corporate, incorporated under the laws of Canada and having its head office at the City of Calgary, in the Province of Alberta,

(b) Imperial Oil Limited, a body corporate, incorporated under the laws of Canada and having its head office at the municipality of Metropolitan Toronto, in the Province of Ontario,

(c) Gulf Oil Canada Limited, a body corporate, incorporated under the laws of Canada and having its head office at the City of Toronto, in the Province of Ontario,

(d) the Crown as represented by the Minister of Energy and Resources for the Province of Alberta,

(e) Her Majesty in right of Canada as represented by the Minister of Energy, Mines and Resources for Canada, and

(f) Ontario Energy Corporation, a body corporate, incorporated by Special Act of the Legislature of the Province of Ontario and having its head office at the City of Toronto, in the Province of Ontario,

or any or all of them or their successors or assignees as long as they retain a share in the Syncrude Project;

"**royalty provisions**" means the provisions contained in paragraphs 12(1)(o) and 18(1)(m), and subsection 69(6) to (10) of the *Income Tax Act*;

"**Syncrude Project**" means the scheme of the participant for the recovery of leased substances from Leases 17 and 22;

"synthetic crude oil" means a mixture, mainly of pentanes and heavier hydrocarbons, that may contain sulphur compounds, that is derived from crude bitumen and that is liquid at the time its volume is measured or estimated.

## REMISSION

**3. (1)** Subject to subsection (2), remission is hereby granted to each participant of any tax payable for a taxation year pursuant to Part I of the *Income Tax Act* as a result of the royalty provisions being applicable to

(a) amounts receivable and the fair market value of any property receivable by the Crown as a royalty, tax, rental or levy with respect to the Syncrude Project, or as an amount however described, that may reasonably be regarded as being in lieu of any of the preceding amounts;

(b) dispositions of leased substances to the Crown by the participant; and

(c) acquisitions of leased substances from the Crown by the participant.

**(2)** No remission shall be granted pursuant to this Order to a participant in respect of a taxation year of that participant that commences after

(a) the recovery of 1.1 billion barrels, where the Governor in Council revokes this Order upon being satisfied on the report of the Minister of Finance that the condition exists prior to the recovery of 1.1 billion barrels,

(b) the recovery of the number of barrels recovered on the date the Governor in Council revokes this Order upon being satisfied on the report of the Minister of Finance that the condition exists if that date is after the recovery of more than 1.1 billion barrels and less than 2.1 billion barrels,

(c) the recovery of 2.1 billion barrels, or

(d) December 31, 2003,

whichever first occurs.

# TELESAT CANADA REMISSION ORDER
P.C. 1999-1335, July 28, 1999 (SI/99-82)

## INTERPRETATION

**1.** The definitions in this section apply in this Order.

**"Act"** means the *Income Tax Act*.

**"former property"** means the Anik E1 satellite in respect of which Telesat Canada has received proceeds of disposition referred to in paragraph 13(4)(a) of the Act.

**"replacement property"** means the property acquired as a replacement for the former property and to which subsection 13(4) of the Act would apply if it were read in accordance with paragraph 2(b) of this Order and if Telesat Canada had made an election under subsection 13(4) of the Act with respect to the replacement property in its return of income for the taxation year in which it acquired the property.

## REMISSION

**2.** Subject to section 3, remission is hereby granted to Telesat Canada in respect of each of the 1996 and subsequent taxation years, of an amount equal to the amount, if any, by which

(a) the total of the tax payable under Part I and Part I.3 of the Act by Telesat Canada for the year and the interest and penalties in respect thereof payable by it under the Act for the year

exceeds

(b) the total of the tax that would be payable under Part I and Part I.3 of the Act by Telesat Canada for the year and the interest and penalties in respect thereof that would be payable by it under the Act for the year if the expression "the second taxation year following the initial year" in clause 13(4)(c)(ii)(A) and paragraph 44(1)(c) of the Act were read as "the taxation year that includes December 31, 1999" and if Telesat Canada had made an election, as and when required, under subsection 13(4) of the Act, with respect to the disposition of the former property and the acquisition of the replacement property.

Explanatory Note

## CONDITIONS

**3.** Remission is granted under section 2 on condition that

(a) in calculating the income or loss of Telesat Canada under the Act in respect of the 1996 and subsequent taxation years, no deduction in respect of the cost of the replacement property is claimed except to the extent that would be allowed if subsection 13(4) and section 44 of the Act were read in accordance with paragraph 2(b) of this Order and if Telesat Canada had made a valid election under subsection 13(4) of the Act with respect to the disposition of the former property and the acquisition of the replacement property; and

(b) if there is a disposition of the replacement property, the Act is treated by Telesat Canada and the person or partnership that acquired the replacement property as applying as if subsection 13(4) and section 44 of the Act were read in accordance with paragraph 2(b) of this Order and as if Telesat Canada had made a valid election under subsection 13(4) of the Act with respect to the disposition of the former property and the acquisition of the replacement property.

## EXPLANATORY NOTE

*(This note is not part of the Order.)*

This Order defers income tax that would otherwise be payable on insurance proceeds received by Telesat Canada in respect of a damaged satellite, by remitting income tax otherwise payable on the initial receipt of those proceeds on the condition that Telesat Canada reduce its adjusted cost base and capital cost in respect of the replacement satellite, in accordance with the replacement property rules in the *Income Tax Act*.

The present value of the net benefit of the Order is approximately $14 million. This is the amount by which the income tax remitted exceeds the present value of future capital cost allowance deductions that would have been available if the replacement satellite were not treated as a replacement property.

# INCOME TAX CONVENTIONS INTERPRETATION ACT

An Act respecting the interpretation of Canada's international conventions relating to income tax and the Acts implementing such conventions.

R.S.C. 1985, c. I-4, AS AMENDED

## Short Title

**Notes [ITCIA]**: For discussion of the principles of tax treaty interpretation as well as the ITCIA, see Jinyan Li & Daniel Sandler, "The Relationship Between Domestic Anti-Avoidance Legislation and Tax Treaties", 45(5) *Canadian Tax Journal* 891-958 (1997).

**1. Short title** — This Act may be cited as the *Income Tax Conventions Interpretation Act*.

## Definition

**2. Definition of "convention"** — In this Act, "convention" means any convention or agreement between Canada and another state relating to tax on income, and includes any protocol or supplementary convention or agreement relating thereto.

## Interpretation

**3. Meaning of undefined terms** — Notwithstanding the provisions of a convention or the Act giving the convention the force of law in Canada, it is hereby declared that the law of Canada is that, to the extent that a term in the convention is

(a) not defined in the convention,

(b) not fully defined in the convention, or

(c) to be defined by reference to the laws of Canada,

that term has, except to the extent that the context otherwise requires, the meaning it has for the purposes of the *Income Tax Act*, as amended from time to time, and not the meaning it had for the purposes of the *Income Tax Act* on the date the convention was entered into or given the force of law in Canada if, after that date, its meaning for the purposes of the *Income Tax Act* has changed.

**Notes**: This section was introduced to overrule *Melford Developments Ltd.*, [1982] C.T.C. 330, in which the Supreme Court of Canada had ruled that an undefined term was to be interpreted as having the meaning it had under the *Income Tax Act* at the time the convention was adopted.

**I.T. Technical News**: No. 18 (*Cudd Pressure* case).

**4. Permanent establishments in Canada** — Notwithstanding the provisions of a convention or the Act giving the convention the force of law in Canada, it is hereby declared that the law of Canada is that where, for the purposes of the application of the convention, the profits from a business activity, including an industrial or commercial activity, attributable or allocable to a permanent establishment in Canada are to be determined for any period,

(a) there shall, except where the convention expressly otherwise provides, be included in the determination of those profits all amounts with respect to that activity that are attributable or allocable to the permanent establishment and that would be required to be included under the *Income Tax Act*, as amended from time to time, by a person resident in Canada carrying on the activity in Canada in the computation of his income from a business for that period; and

(b) there shall, except to the extent that an agreement between the competent authorities of the parties to the convention expressly otherwise provides, not be deducted in the determination of those profits any amount with respect to that activity that is attributable or allocable to the permanent establishment and that would not be deductible under the *Income Tax Act*, as amended from time to time, by a person resident in Canada carrying on the activity in Canada in the computation of his income from a business for that period.

**5. Definitions** — Notwithstanding the provisions of a convention or the Act giving the convention the force of law in Canada, in this section and in the convention,

**"annuity"** does not include any pension payment or any payment under a plan, arrangement or contract described in subparagraphs (a)(i) to (ix) of the definition "pension";

**Notes**: Definition amended by 1998 Budget to delete "(other than a periodic pension payment) arising in Canada" from the end, effective for amounts paid after 1996.

Definition "annuity" added by 1992 technical bill, effective for amounts paid in 1992 or later. It ensures that pension payments that are specifically excluded from the definition of "periodic pension payment" are not eligible for the reduced rate of withholding tax that applies to annuity payments under many of Canada's tax treaties.

See 5.1 below for the meaning of "pension" for purposes of this definition.

**"Canada"** means the territory of Canada, and includes

(a) every area beyond the territorial seas of Canada that, in accordance with international law and the laws of Canada, is an area in respect of which Canada may exercise rights with respect to the seabed and subsoil and their natural resources, and

(b) the seas and airspace above every area described in paragraph (a);

**"immovable property"** and **"real property"**, with respect to such property in Canada, are hereby declared to include

(a) any right to explore for or exploit mineral deposits and sources in Canada and other natural resources in Canada, and

(b) any right to an amount computed by reference to the production, including profit, from, or to the value of production from, mineral deposits and sources in Canada and other natural resources in Canada;

**"pension"** means, in respect of payments that arise in Canada,

(a) if the convention does not include a definition "pension", a payment under any plan, arrangement or contract that is

(i) a registered pension plan,

(ii) a registered retirement savings plan,

(iii) a registered retirement income fund,

(iv) a retirement compensation arrangement,

(v) a deferred profit sharing plan,

(vi) a plan that is deemed by subsection 147(15) of the *Income Tax Act* not to be a deferred profit sharing plan,

(vii) an annuity contract purchased under a plan referred to in subparagraph (v) or (vi),

(viii) an annuity contract where the amount paid by or on behalf of an individual to acquire the contract was deductible under paragraph 60(l) of the *Income Tax Act* in computing the individual's income for any taxation year (or would have been so deductible if the individual had been resident in Canada), or

(ix) a superannuation, pension or retirement plan not otherwise referred to in this paragraph, and

(b) if the convention includes a definition "pension", a payment that is a pension for the purposes of the convention or a payment (other than a payment of social security benefits) that would be a periodic pension payment if the convention did not include a definition "pension";

**Related Provisions**: 5"annuity" — Annuity excludes pension payments and certain other payments.

**Notes**: Definition "pension" added by 1998 Budget, effective for amounts paid after 1996. Before 1997, see 5.1.

**"periodic pension payment"** means, in respect of payments that arise in Canada, a pension payment other than

(a) a lump sum payment, or a payment that can reasonably be considered to be an instalment of a lump sum amount, under a registered pension plan,

(b) a payment before maturity, or a payment in full or partial commutation of the retirement income, under a registered retirement savings plan,

(c) a payment at any time in a calendar year under a registered retirement income fund, where the total of all payments (other than the specified portion of each such payment) made under the fund at or before that time and in the year exceeds the total of

(i) the amount that would be the greater of

(A) twice the amount that, if the value of C in the definition "minimum amount" in subsection 146.3(1) of the *Income Tax Act* were nil, would be the minimum amount under the fund for the year, and

(B) 10% of the fair market value of the property (other than annuity contracts that, at the beginning of the year, are not described in paragraph (b.1) of the definition "qualified investment" in subsection 146.3(1) of the *Income Tax Act*) held in connection with the fund at the beginning of the year

if all property transferred in the year and before that time to the carrier of the fund as consideration for the carrier's undertaking to make payments under the fund had been so transferred immediately before the beginning of the year and if the definition "minimum amount" in subsection 146.3(1) of the *Income Tax Act* applied with respect to all registered retirement income funds, and

(ii) the total of all amounts each of which is an annual or more frequent periodic payment under an annuity contract that is a qualified investment, as defined in subsection 146.3(1) of the *Income Tax Act*, (other than an annuity contract the fair market value of which is taken into account under clause (i)(B)) held by a trust governed by the fund that was paid into the trust in the year and before that time, or

(d) a payment to a recipient at any time in a calendar year under an arrangement, other than a plan or fund referred to in paragraphs (a) to (c), where

(i) the payment is not

(A) one of a series of annual or more frequent payments to be made over the lifetime of the recipient or over a period of at least 10 years,

(B) one of a series of annual or more frequent payments each of which is contingent on the recipient continuing to suffer from a physical or mental impairment, or

(C) a payment to which the recipient is entitled as a consequence of the death of an individual who was in receipt of periodic pension payments under the arrangement, and that is made under a guarantee that a minimum number of payments will be made in respect of the individual, or

(ii) at the time the payment is made, it may reasonably be concluded that

(A) the total amount of payments (other than excluded payments) under the arrangement to the recipient in the year will exceed twice the total amount of payments (other than excluded payments) made under the arrangement to the recipient in the immediately preceding year, otherwise than because of the fact that payments commenced to be made to the recipient in the preceding year and were made for a period of less than twelve months in that year, or

(B) the total amount of payments (other than excluded payments) under the arrangement to the recipient in the year will exceed twice the total amount of payments (other than excluded payments) to be made under the arrangement to the recipient in any subsequent year, otherwise than because of the termination of the series of payments or the reduction in the amount of payments to be made after the death of any individual,

and, for the purposes of this subparagraph, "excluded payment" means a payment that is neither a periodic payment nor a payment described in any of clauses (i)(A) to (C).

**Notes**: Opening words amended by 1998 Budget, effective for amounts paid after 1996. For amounts paid from 1992-96, read:

"periodic pension payment" does not include a pension payment arising in Canada that is

Para. (c) amended by 1995-97 technical bill, effective for amounts paid after 1997. For 1992–1997, read:

(c) a payment at any time in a calendar year under a registered retirement income fund where the total of all payments made under the fund at or before that time and in the year, other than

(i) a payment or portion thereof that is not required by section 146.3 of the *Income Tax Act* to be included in computing the income of any person and that is not included under paragraph 212(1)(q) of that Act in respect of any person, and

(ii) a payment in respect of which a deduction is available under paragraph 60(l) of the *Income Tax Act* in computing the income of any person,

exceeds the greater of

(iii) twice the amount that would be the minimum amount under the fund for the year, and

(iv) ten per cent of the amount that would be the fair market value of the property held in connection with the fund at the beginning of the year,

if all property transferred in the year and before that time to the carrier of the fund as consideration under the fund had been transferred immediately before the beginning of the year and if the definition "minimum amount" in paragraph 146.3(1)(b.1) of the *Income Tax Act* were applicable with respect to all registered retirement income funds, or

Definition "periodic pension payment" added by 1992 technical bill, effective for amounts paid in 1992 or later. It excludes the payments listed in paras. (a) to (d). Thus, such payments do not qualify for the reduced rate of withholding tax that applies to periodic pension payments under many of Canada's tax treaties. They also do not qualify for the reduced rate on annuity payments; see the definition of "annuity" above.

The 1992 technical bill also provides that the amended definition of "minimum amount" in ITA 146.3(1) does not apply for the purposes of section 5 of this Act with respect to payments made before 1993.

See 5 and 5.1 for the meaning of "pension" and "specified portion" for purposes of this definition.

**"real property"** — [see under "immovable" above — ed.]

**5.1 (1)** [Repealed]

**Notes**: See now 5"pension".

**(2) Definition of "specified portion"** — For the purpose of the definition "periodic pension payment" in section 5, the "specified portion" of a payment means the total of

(a) the portion of the payment that is not required by section 146.3 of the *Income Tax Act* to be included in computing the income of any person and that is not included under paragraph 212(1)(q) of that Act in respect of any person; and

(b) the portion of the payment in respect of which a deduction is available under paragraph 60(l) of the *Income Tax Act* in computing the income of any person.

**Notes**: 5.1(2) added by the 1995-97 technical bill, effective for amounts paid after 1997.

**6. Meaning of "interest"** — Notwithstanding section 3, the meaning of the term "interest" in any convention given the force of law in Canada before November 19, 1974 does not include any amount paid or credited, pursuant to an agreement in writing entered into before June 23, 1983, as consideration for a guarantee referred to in paragraph 214(15)(a) of the *Income Tax Act*.

**6.1 Transitional** — Where a taxation year of a taxpayer includes June 23, 1983, the additional tax payable under the *Income Tax Act* (except Part XIII thereof) by the taxpayer for the taxation year by virtue of this Act shall be calculated in accordance with the following formula

$$A = T \times \frac{B}{C}$$

## S. 6.1    Income Tax Conventions Interpretation Act

where

A    is the amount of additional taxes payable under the *Income Tax Act* (except Part XIII thereof) by the taxpayer for the taxation year by virtue of this Act,

T    is the amount of additional taxes payable under the *Income Tax Act* (except Part XIII thereof) by the taxpayer for the taxation year by virtue of this Act (except this section),

B    is the number of days in the taxation year after June 23, 1983, and

C    is the number of days in the taxation year.

**6.2 Partnerships** — Notwithstanding the provisions of a convention between Canada and another state or the Act giving it the force of law in Canada, it is hereby declared that the law of Canada is that, for the purposes of the application of the convention and the *Income Tax Act* to a person who is a resident of Canada, a partnership of which that person is a member is neither a resident nor an enterprise of that other state.

**Notes:** 6.2 added by 1991 technical bill, retroactive to 1983. It was enacted to preclude the application in Canada of the reasoning of the English Court of Appeal in *Padmore v. Inland Revenue Commissioners*, [1989] STC 493, 62 TC 383. The section clarifies that the tax treatment of a Canadian resident partner's share of the income of a partnership is not affected by the fact that a partnership may be considered a resident or enterprise of another country under one of Canada's tax treaties.

**6.3. Gains arising in Canada** — Except where a convention expressly otherwise provides, any amount of income, gain or loss in respect of the disposition of a property that is taxable Canadian property within the meaning assigned by the *Income Tax Act* is deemed to arise in Canada.

**Notes:** 6.3 added by 1998 Budget, effective for dispositions that occur after February 23, 1998. Before its enactment, residents of Australia, New Zealand or Japan who disposed of taxable Canadian property could arrange, in some cases, for the sale to be outside Canada and thus not taxed in Canada due to the treaties with those countries.

## Application

**7. Application** — This Act applies

(a) in the case of tax under Part XIII of the *Income Tax Act*, to amounts paid or credited after June 23, 1983; and

(b) in all other cases, to taxation years ending after June 23, 1983.

# CANADA–UNITED STATES TAX CONVENTION, (1980)

Convention Between Canada and The United States of America With Respect to Taxes on Income and on Capital Signed on September 26, 1980, as Amended by the Protocols Signed on June 14, 1983, March 28, 1984, March 17, 1995 and July 29, 1997

Enacted in Canada by S.C. 1984, c. 20; 1995 Protocol enacted in Canada by S.C. 1995, c. 34, Royal Assent November 8, 1995; 1997 Protocol enacted in Canada by S.C. 1997, c. 38, Royal Assent December 10, 1997

**Notes:**

The Income Tax Convention (treaty) between Canada and the United States was signed on September 26, 1980, and amended before ratification by Protocols signed on June 14, 1983 and March 28, 1984. Instruments of ratification were exchanged on August 16, 1984. This Convention supersedes the former Canada-U.S. Convention, signed in 1942. A third Protocol, signed on March 17, 1995 (replacing one earlier signed on August 31, 1994), came into force with instruments of ratification exchanged on November 9, 1995. A fourth Protocol, signed on July 29, 1997, came into force with instruments of ratification exchanged on December 16, 1997.

On April 26, 1984, the United States Treasury Department released a technical explanation of the Convention. A news release issued by the Canadian Department of Finance on August 16, 1984 states that the technical explanation "accurately reflects understandings reached in the course of negotiations with respect to the interpretation and application of the various provisions in the 1980 Tax Convention as amended".

The Technical Explanation is accepted as valid guidance by the Courts; see, e.g., *Coblentz*, [1996] 3 C.T.C. 295 (FCA). The relevant portion of the technical explanation is reproduced below after each paragraph of the relevant Article. Note, however, that the Federal Court of Appeal stated in *Kubicek Estate*, [1997] 3 C.T.C. 435: "The Technical Explanation is a domestic American document. True, it is stated to have the endorsation of the Canadian Minister of Finance, but in order to bind Canada it would have to amount to another convention, which it does not. From the Canadian viewpoint, it has about the same status as a Revenue Canada interpretation bulletin, of interest to a Court but not necessarily decisive of an issue".

On June 13, 1995, the U.S. Treasury Department released a technical explanation of the March 17, 1995 Protocol. The Canadian Minister of Finance again stated that "Canada agrees that the technical explanation accurately reflects understandings reached in the course of negotiations with respect to the interpretation and application of the various provisions in the Protocol": Department of Finance news release 95-048, June 13, 1995. Similarly, a technical explanation for the Protocol signed on July 29, 1997 was released by the U.S. Treasury Department in December, 1997. The relevant portions of these technical explanations are reproduced below with the text.

Negotiations for a further Protocol to amend the treaty are underway; see Proposed Amendment box below.

[For reference to the Canada-United States Social Security Agreement, see Revenue Canada Information Circular 84-6.]

## Table of Contents

Art. I — Personal Scope
Art. II — Taxes Covered
Art. III — General Definitions
Art. IV — Residence
Art. V — Permanent Establishment
Art. VI — Income from Real Property
Art. VII — Business Profits
Art. VIII — Transportation
Art. IX — Related Persons
Art. X — Dividends
Art. XI — Interest
Art. XII — Royalties
Art. XIII — Gains

Art. XIV — Independent Personal Services
Art. XV — Dependent Personal Services
Art. XVI — Artistes and Athletes
Art. XVII — Withholding of Taxes in Respect of Personal Services
Art. XVIIII — Pensions and Annuities
Art. XIX — Government Service
Art. XX — Students
Art. XXI — Exempt Organizations
Art. XXII — Other Income
Art. XXIII — Capital
Art. XXIV — Elimination of Double Taxation
Art. XXV — Non-Discrimination
Art. XXVI — Mutual Agreement Procedure
Art. XXVI A — Assistance in Collection
Art. XXVII — Exchange of Information
Art. XXVIII — Diplomatic Agents and Consular Officers
Art. XXIX — Miscellaneous Rules
Art. XXIX A — Limitation on Benefits
Art. XXIX B — Taxes Imposed by Reason of Death
Art. XXX — Entry Into Force
Art. XXXI — Termination

Canada and the United States of America, desiring to conclude a Convention for the avoidance of double taxation and the prevention of fiscal evasion with respect to taxes on income and on capital, have agreed as follows:

---

**Proposed Amendment — New Negotiations**

**Department of Finance news release, September 18, 2000**: *Canada and the United States Propose Tax Treaty Changes*

Finance Minister Paul Martin today announced that Canadian and United States negotiators have agreed in principle to recommend changes to the Canada-United States Income Tax Convention (the "tax treaty").

"If approved by the legislatures of the two countries, these changes will make the tax system fairer by limiting the potential for double taxation of individuals who move from one country to another, and by clarifying a rule that some have argued allows corporations to avoid paying tax," said the Minister.

Minister Martin added that the announced measures will, if ratified, apply as of today's date. "We expect the current negotiations to produce other important changes to the tax treaty as well," he noted. "But we and the United States have agreed that these particular initiatives are important for international mobility, and should take effect right away."

*Individuals — Preventing Double Taxation*

For individuals, the changes will ensure the appropriate tax treatment of an emigrant's gains. Specifically, where one country's tax rules treat an individual as having disposed of a property immediately before the individual emigrates to the other country, the individual will be able to choose to be treated under the other country's rules as also having disposed of and reacquired the property at its fair market value.

In most cases, this will mean that no tax is payable in the destination country on any pre-emigration gain. Where tax is payable in the destination country — for example, where the property in question is real estate situated in that country — the new rule will ensure appropriate tax crediting.

*Corporations — Clarifying Residence*

For corporations, the proposals will clarify the effects on a company's residence of "continuance" (or "continuation") from one country into the other.

Laws in both countries allow a company incorporated in one jurisdiction to subject itself to another jurisdiction's corporate law system. A company originally formed in a Canadian province, for example, could continue into a U.S. state and be treated for company law purposes as though it had been incorporated there.

The Canada-U.S. tax treaty treats a company that continues from one country into the other as thereafter being resident in its new home country. However, it has come to the attention of the Canadian and U.S. tax authorities that some have asserted inconsistent positions with respect to a U.S. corporation that has continued into Canada while retaining its status as a U.S. corporation under U.S. internal law. The argument put forward is that the corporation would, by virtue of the treaty, be a resident only of Canada but that it would, for certain other U.S. tax purposes, retain its status as a U.S. corporation under U.S. internal law.

The negotiators agree that it was not contemplated that the continuance provision in the current treaty would be used to avoid taxes in this manner. Accordingly, the revised provision will clarify that a company incorporated in one country that continues into the other will still be treated as a resident of the first country unless that country's internal law no longer treats it as such. For example, a U.S. corporation that continues into Canada but retains its status as a U.S. corporation will, under the treaty, become a Canadian resident while remaining a U.S. resident. Such a corporation will not be entitled to any benefits under the Canada-U.S. tax treaty except to the extent agreed upon by the competent authorities of the two countries.

*Timing*

If approved, the rule for individuals will apply to changes in residence that take place on and after today's date. Similarly, the rule for corporations will apply to continuances effected on and after today's date, although no inference is intended regarding the treatment of such a corporation under current law. These modifications will form part of a package of tax treaty changes that negotiators expect to finalize in 2001.

For further information: Jean-Michel Catta, Public Affairs and Operations Division, (613) 996-8080; Nathalie Gauthier, Press Secretary, (613) 996-7861; Lawrence Purdy, Tax Legislation Division, (613) 996-0602.

## Department of Finance news release, October 2, 1998: *Canada and United States to Consult regarding Modifications to Income Tax Treaty*

Beginning on October 20, 1998, Canada and the United States will consult in Washington regarding modifications to the current Canada-U.S. Income Tax Convention. These consultations are contemplated by Article 20 of the Protocol to the Convention that was signed on March 17, 1995 and entered into force on November 9, 1995. As stipulated in that Protocol, discussions are to include consideration of reductions in the withholding tax rates provided in the Convention and the need for any modifications to the rules in Article XXIX A of the Treaty regarding Limitation on Benefits. It is possible that other issues will also be discussed.

The Department of Finance invites comments from the public regarding the upcoming negotiations. Persons are invited to send their written comments to the Department to the attention of Brian Ernewein, Director, Tax Legislation Division, 17th Floor, East Tower, 140 O'Connor Street, Ottawa, Ontario K1A 0G5.

For further information: Brian Ernewein, Tax Policy Branch, 992-3045.

**Application of the 1995 Protocol**: Future consultations, and the coming into force of the Protocol, are covered in Articles 20 and 21.

Article 20 provides that the appropriate authorities of each country will consult within a three year period with a view to determining whether further reductions in the withholding rates should be introduced and whether amendments to the new limitation of benefits provisions would be appropriate. The authorities will also consult after a three year period to consider giving effect to the new arbitration procedure provided for under Article XXVI (Mutual Agreement Procedure).

Article 20 reads:

1. The appropriate authorities of the Contracting States shall consult within a three-year period from the date on which this Protocol enters into force with respect to further reductions in withholding taxes provided in the Convention, and with respect to the rules in Article XXIX A (Limitation on Benefits) of the Convention.

2. The appropriate authorities of the Contracting States shall consult after a three-year period from the date on which the Protocol enters into force in order to determine whether it is appropriate to make the exchange of notes referred to in Article XXVI (Mutual Agreement Procedure) of the Convention.

Article 21 sets out the mechanism for the entry into force of the Protocol and the application of its provisions. In general, the provisions of the Protocol will be effective for the withholding tax as of the first day of the second month following the entry into force of the Protocol and, for other taxes, for taxable periods beginning on and after the first day of January following the entry into force of the Protocol. However, special rules are provided for a phased reduction of the withholding tax on direct dividends and the branch profits tax and for the provisions of Article XXVI A (Assistance in Collection). The provisions relating to the US estate tax in Article XXIX B (Taxes Imposed by Reason of Death) are effective retroactively for deaths occurring after November 10, 1988.

Article 21 reads:

1. This Protocol shall be subject to ratification in accordance with the applicable procedures in Canada and the United States and instruments of ratification shall be exchanged as soon as possible.

2. The Protocol shall enter into force upon the exchange of instruments of ratification, and shall have effect:

(a) For tax withheld at the source on income referred to in Articles X (Dividends), XI (Interest), XII (Royalties) and XVIII (Pensions and Annuities) of the Convention, except on income referred to in paragraph 5 of Article XVIII of the Convention (as it read before the entry into force of this Protocol), with respect to amounts paid or credited on or after the first day of the second month next following the date on which the Protocol enters into force, except that the reference in paragraph 2(a) of Article X (Dividends) of the Convention, as amended by the Protocol, to "5 per cent" shall be read, in its application to amounts paid or credited on or after that first day:

(i) Before 1996, as "7 per cent"; and

(ii) After 1995 and before 1997, as "6 per cent"; and

(b) For other taxes, with respect to taxable years beginning on or after the first day of January next following the date on which the Protocol enters into force, except that the reference in paragraph 6 of Article X (Dividends) of the Convention, as amended by the Protocol, to "5 per cent" shall be read, in its application to taxable years beginning on or after that first day and ending before 1997, as "6 per cent".

3. Notwithstanding the provisions of paragraph 2, Article XXVI A (Assistance in Collection) of the Convention shall have effect for revenue claims finally determined by a requesting State after the date that is 10 years before the date on which the Protocol enters into force.

4. Notwithstanding the provisions of paragraph 2, paragraphs 2 through 8 of Article XXIX B (Taxes Imposed by Reason of Death) of the Convention (and paragraph 2 of Article II (Taxes Covered) and paragraph 3(a) of Article XXIX (Miscellaneous Rules) of the Convention, as amended by the Protocol, to the extent necessary to implement paragraphs 2 through 8 of Article XXIX B (Taxes Imposed by Reason of Death) of the Convention) shall, notwithstanding any limitation imposed under the law of a Contracting State on the assessment, reassessment or refund with respect to a person's return, have effect with respect to deaths occurring after the date on which the Protocol enters into force and, provided that any claim for refund by reason of this sentence is filed within one year of the date on which the Protocol enters into force or within the otherwise applicable period for filing such claims under domestic law, with respect to benefits provided under any of those paragraphs with respect to deaths occurring after November 10, 1988.

5. Notwithstanding the provisions of paragraph 2, paragraph 2 of Article 3 of the Protocol shall have effect with respect to taxable years beginning on or after the first day of January next following the date on which the Protocol enters into force.

**Notes**: The date of exchange of instruments of ratification was November 9, 1995.

### Technical Explanation [1995 Protocol]:

*Article 20*

Article 20 of the Protocol does not amend the text of the Convention. It states two understandings between the Contracting States regarding future action relating to matters dealt with in the Protocol. Paragraph 1 requires the appropriate authorities of the Contracting

States to consult on two matters within three years from the date on which the Protocol enters into force. First, they will consult with a view to agreeing to further reductions in withholding rates on dividends, interest and royalties under Articles X, XI, and XII, respectively. This provision reflects the fact that, although the Protocol does significantly reduce withholding rates, the United States remains interested in even greater reductions, to further open the capital markets and fulfill the objectives of the North American Free Trade Agreement. Second, the appropriate authorities of the Contracting States will consult about the rules in Article XXIX A (Limitation on Benefits). By that time, both Contracting States will have had an opportunity to observe the operation of the Article, and the United States will have had greater experience with the corresponding provisions in other recent U.S. tax conventions.

Paragraph 2 of Article 20 also requires consultations between the appropriate authorities, after the three-year period from the date on which the Protocol enters into force, to determine whether to implement the arbitration procedure provided for in paragraph 6 of Article XXVI (Mutual Agreement Procedure), added by Article 14 of the Protocol. The three-year period is intended to give the authorities an opportunity to consider how arbitration has functioned in other tax conventions, such as the U.S.-Germany Convention, before implementing it under this Convention.

*Article 21*

Article 21 of the Protocol provides the rules for the entry into force of the Protocol provisions. The Protocol will be subject to ratification according to the normal procedures in both Contracting States and instruments of ratification will be exchanged as soon as possible. Upon the exchange of instruments, the Protocol will enter into force.

Paragraph 2(a) of Article 21 generally governs the entry into force of the provisions of the Protocol for taxes withheld at source, while paragraph 2(b) generally governs for other taxes. Paragraphs 3, 4, and 5 provide special rules for certain provisions.

Paragraph 2(a) provides that the Protocol generally will have effect for taxes withheld at source on dividends, interest, royalties, and pensions and annuities (other than social security benefits), under Articles X, XI, XII, and XVIII, respectively, with respect to amounts paid or credited on or after the first day of the second month following the date on which the Protocol enters into force (i.e., the date on which instruments of ratification are exchanged). However, with respect to direct investment dividends, the 5 percent rate specified in paragraph 2(a) of Article X will be phased in as follows: (1) for dividends paid or credited after the first day of the second month referred to above, and during 1995, the rate of withholding will be 7 percent; (2) for dividends paid or credited after the first day of the second month, and during 1996, the rate will be 6 percent; and (3) for dividends paid or credited after the first day of the second month and after 1996, the rate will be 5 percent.

For taxes other than those withheld at source and for the provisions of the Protocol relating to taxes withheld on social security benefits, the Protocol will have effect with respect to taxable years beginning on or after the first day of January following the date on which the Protocol enters into force. However, the rate of tax applicable to the branch tax under paragraph 6 of Article X (Dividends) will be phased in in a manner similar to the direct investment dividend withholding tax rate; that is, a rate of 6 percent will apply for taxable years beginning in 1996 and a rate of 5 percent will apply for taxable years beginning in 1997 and subsequent years.

Paragraph 3 of Article 21 provides a special effective date for the provisions of the new Article XXVI A (Assistance in Collection) of the Convention, introduced by Article 15 of the Protocol. Collection assistance may be granted by a Contracting State with respect to a request by the other Contracting State for a claim finally determined by the requesting State after the date that is ten years before the date of the entry into force of the Protocol. Thus, for example, if instruments of ratification are exchanged on July 1, 1995, assistance may be given by Canada under Article XXVI A for a claim that was finally determined in the United States at any time after July 1, 1985.

Paragraph 4 of Article 21 provides special effective date provisions for paragraphs 2 through 7 of the new Article XXIX B (Taxes Imposed by Reason of Death) of the Convention, introduced by Article 18 of the Protocol, and certain related provisions elsewhere in the Convention. These special effective date provisions are discussed above in connection with Article 18.

Finally, paragraph 5 of Article 21 provides a special effective date for paragraph 2 of Article 3 of the Protocol, which provides a new residence rule for certain "continued" corporations. Under paragraph 5, the new residence rule for such corporations will have effect for taxable years beginning on or after the first day of January following the date on which the Protocol enters into force.

**Application of the 1995 Protocol**: Future consultations, and the coming into force of the Protocol are covered in Articles 20 and 21.

Article 20 provides that the appropriate authorities of each country will consult within a three year period with a view to determining whether further reductions in the withholding rates should be introduced and whether amendments to the new limitation of benefits provisions would be appropriate. The authorities will also consult after a three year period to consider giving effect to the new arbitration procedure provided for under Article XXVI (Mutual Agreement Procedure).

Article 20 reads:

1. The appropriate authorities of the Contracting States shall consult within a three-year period from the date on which this Protocol enters into force with respect to further reductions in withholding taxes provided in the Convention, and with respect to the rules in Article XXIX A (Limitation on Benefits) of the Convention.

2. The appropriate authorities of the Contracting States shall consult after a three-year period from the date on which the Protocol enters into force in order to determine whether it is appropriate to make the exchange of notes referred to in Article XXVI (Mutual Agreement Procedure) of the Convention.

Article 21 sets out the mechanism for the entry into force of the Protocol and the application of its provisions. In general, the provisions of the Protocol will be effective for the withholding tax as of the first day of the second month following the entry into force of the Protocol and, for other taxes, for taxable periods beginning on and after the first day of January following the entry into force of the Protocol. However, special rules are provided for a phased reduction of the withholding tax on direct dividends and the branch profits tax and for the provisions of Article XXVI A (Assistance in Collection). The provisions relating to the US estate tax in Article XXIX B (Taxes Imposed by Reason of Death) are effective retroactively for deaths occurring after November 10, 1988.

Article 21 reads:

1. This Protocol shall be subject to ratification in accordance with the applicable procedures in Canada and the United States and instruments of ratification shall be exchanged as soon as possible.

2. The Protocol shall enter into force upon the exchange of instruments of ratification, and shall have effect:

(a) For tax withheld at the source on income referred to in Articles X (Dividends), XI (Interest), XII (Royalties) and XVIII (Pensions and Annuities) of the Convention, except on income referred to in paragraph 5 of Article XVIII of the Convention (as it read before the entry into force of this Protocol), with respect to amounts paid or credited on or after the first day of the second month next following the date on which the Protocol enters into force, except that the reference in paragraph 2(a) of Article X (Dividends) of the Convention, as amended by the

Protocol, to "5 per cent" shall be read, in its application to amounts paid or credited on or after that first day:

(i) Before 1996, as "7 per cent"; and

(ii) After 1995 and before 1997, as "6 per cent"; and

(b) For other taxes, with respect to taxable years beginning on or after the first day of January next following the date on which the Protocol enters into force, except that the reference in paragraph 6 of Article X (Dividends) of the Convention, as amended by the Protocol, to "5 per cent" shall be read, in its application to taxable years beginning on or after that first day and ending before 1997, as "6 per cent".

3. Notwithstanding the provisions of paragraph 2, Article XXVI A (Assistance in Collection) of the Convention shall have effect for revenue claims finally determined by a requesting State after the date that is 10 years before the date on which the Protocol enters into force.

4. Notwithstanding the provisions of paragraph 2, paragraphs 2 through 8 of Article XXIX B (Taxes Imposed by Reason of Death) of the Convention and paragraph 2 of Article II (Taxes Covered) and paragraph 3(a) of Article XXIX (Miscellaneous Rules) of the Convention, as amended by the Protocol, to the extent necessary to implement paragraphs 2 through 8 of Article XXIX B (Taxes Imposed by Reason of Death) of the Convention) shall, notwithstanding any limitation imposed under the law of a Contracting State on the assessment, reassessment or refund with respect to a person's return, have effect with respect to deaths occurring after the date on which the Protocol enters into force and, provided that any claim for refund by reason of this sentence is filed within one year of the date on which the Protocol enters into force or within the otherwise applicable period for filing such claims under domestic law, with respect to benefits provided under any of those paragraphs with respect to deaths occurring after November 10, 1988.

5. Notwithstanding the provisions of paragraph 2, paragraph 2 of Article 3 of the Protocol shall have effect with respect to taxable years beginning on or after the first day of January next following the date on which the Protocol enters into force.

## Article I — Personal Scope

This Convention is generally applicable to persons who are residents of one or both of the Contracting States.

**Technical Explanation [1984]:**

Article I provides that the Convention is generally applicable to persons who are residents of either Canada or the United States or both Canada and the United States. The word "generally" is used because certain provisions of the Convention apply to persons who are residents of neither Canada nor the United States.

## Article II — Taxes Covered

**1.** This Convention shall apply to taxes on income and on capital imposed on behalf of each Contracting State, irrespective of the manner in which they are levied.

**Technical Explanation [1984]:**

Paragraph 1 states that the Convention applies to taxes "on income and on capital" imposed on behalf of Canada and the United States, irrespective of the manner in which such taxes are levied. Neither Canada nor the United States presently impose taxes on capital. Paragraph 1 is not intended either to broaden or to limit paragraph 2, which provides that the Convention shall apply, in the case of Canada, to the taxes imposed by the Government of Canada under Parts I, XIII, and XIV of the *Income Tax Act* and, in the case of the United States, to the Federal income taxes imposed by the *Internal Revenue Code* ("the Code").

National taxes not generally covered by the Convention include, in the case of the United States, the estate, gift, and generation-skipping transfer taxes, the Windfall Profits Tax, Federal unemployment taxes, social security taxes imposed under sections 1401, 3101, and 3111 of the Code, and the excise tax on insurance premiums imposed under Code section 4371. The Convention also does not generally cover the Canadian excise tax on net insurance premiums paid by residents of Canada for coverage of a risk situated in Canada, the Petroleum and Gas Revenue Tax (PGRT) and the Incremental Oil Revenue Tax (IORT). However, the Convention has the effect of covering the Canadian social security tax in certain respects because under Canadian domestic tax law no such tax is due if there is no income subject to tax under the *Income Tax Act* of Canada. Taxes imposed by the states of the United States, and by the provinces of Canada, are not generally covered by the Convention. However, if such taxes are imposed in accordance with the provisions of the Convention, a foreign tax credit is ensured by paragraph 7 of Article XXIV (Elimination of Double Taxation).

**2.** Notwithstanding paragraph 1, the taxes existing on March 17, 1995 to which the Convention shall apply are:

(a) in the case of Canada, the taxes imposed by the Government of Canada under the *Income Tax Act*; and

(b) in the case of the United States, the Federal income taxes imposed by the *Internal Revenue Code* of 1986. However, the Convention shall apply to:

(i) the United States accumulated earnings tax and personal holding company tax, to the extent, and only to the extent, necessary to implement the provisions of paragraphs 5 and 8 of Article X (Dividends);

(ii) the United States excise taxes imposed with respect to private foundations, to the extent, and only to the extent, necessary to implement the provisions of paragraph 4 of Article XXI (Exempt Organizations);

(iii) the United States social security taxes, to the extent, and only to the extent, necessary to implement the provisions of paragraph 2 of Article XXIV (Elimination of Double Taxation) and paragraph 4 of Article XXIX (Miscellaneous Rules); and

(iv) the United States estate taxes imposed by the *Internal Revenue Code* of 1986, to the extent, and only to the extent, necessary to implement the provisions of paragraph 3(g) of Article XXVI (Mutual Agreement Procedure) and Article XXIX B (Taxes Imposed by Reason of Death).

**Technical Explanation [1995 Protocol]:**

Article 1 of the Protocol amends Article II (Taxes Covered) of the Convention. Article II identifies the taxes to which the Convention applies. Paragraph 1 of Article 1 replaces paragraphs 2 through 4 of Article II of the Convention with new paragraphs 2 and 3. For each Contracting State, new paragraph 2 of Article II specifies the taxes existing on the date of signature of the Protocol to which the Convention applies. New paragraph 3 provides that the Convention will also apply to taxes identical or substantially similar to those specified in paragraph 2, and to any new capital taxes, that are imposed after the date of signature of the Protocol.

New paragraph 2(a) of Article II describes the Canadian taxes covered by the Convention. As amended by the Protocol, the Convention will apply to all taxes imposed by the Government of Canada under the *Income Tax Act*.

New paragraph 2(b) of Article II amends the provisions identifying the U.S. taxes covered by the Convention in several respects. The Protocol incorporates into paragraph 2(b) the special rules found in paragraph 4 of Article II of the present Convention. New paragraph 2(b)(iii) conforms the rule previously found in paragraph 4(c) of Article II to the amended provisions of Article XXIV (Elimination of Double Taxation), under which Canada has agreed to grant a foreign tax credit for U.S. social security taxes. In addition, the Protocol adds a fourth special rule to reflect the addition to the Convention of new Article XXIX B (Taxes Imposed by Reason of Death) and related provisions in new paragraph 3(g) of Article XXVI (Mutual Agreement Procedure).

Article 1 of the Protocol also makes minor clarifying, non-substantive amendments to paragraphs 2 and 3 of the Article.

**Technical Explanation [1984]:**

Paragraph 2 contrasts with paragraph 1 of the Protocol to the 1942 Convention, which refers to "Dominion income taxes." In addition, unlike the 1942 Convention, the Convention does not contain a reference to "surtaxes and excess-profits taxes."

**Related Provisions**: Art. XXVI A:9 — Cross-border collection assistance applies to other taxes as well.

**Notes**: Art. II(2) amended by 1995 Protocol, generally effective 1996 (see Art. 21(2) and (4) under "Application of the 1995 Protocol" above). For 1985–1995, read:

2. The existing taxes to which the Convention shall apply are:

(a) in the case of Canada, the taxes imposed by the Government of Canada under Parts I, XIII and XIV of the *Income Tax Act*; and

(b) in the case of the United States, the Federal income taxes imposed by the *Internal Revenue Code*.

3. The Convention shall apply also to:

(a) any taxes identical or substantially similar to those taxes to which the Convention applies under paragraph 2; and

(b) taxes on capital;

which are imposed after March 17, 1995 in addition to, or in place of, the taxes to which the Convention applies under paragraph 2.

**Technical Explanation [1995 Protocol]:**

See under para. 2.

**Technical Explanation [1984]:**

Paragraph 3 provides that the Convention also applies to any taxes identical or substantially similar to the taxes on income in existence on September 26, 1980 which are imposed in addition to or in place of the taxes existing on that date. Similarly, taxes on capital imposed after that date are to be covered.

It was agreed that Part I of the *Income Tax Act* of Canada is a covered tax even though Canada has made certain modifications in the *Income Tax Act* after the signature of the Convention and before the signature of the 1983 Protocol. In particular, Canada has enacted a low flat rate tax on petroleum production (the PGRT) which, at the time of the signature of the 1983 Protocol, is imposed generally at a statutory rate of 14.67 percent for the period June 1, 1982 to May 31, 1983, and at 16 percent thereafter, generally reduced to an effective rate of 11 percent or 12 percent after deducting a 25 percent resource allowance. The PGRT is not deductible in computing income for Canadian income tax purposes. This agreement is not intended to have implications for any other convention or for the interpretation of Code sections 901 and 903. Further, the PGRT and IORT are not taxes described in paragraphs 2 or 3.

**Notes**: Art. II(3) amended by 1995 Protocol, generally effective 1996 (see Art. 21(2) under "Application of the 1995 Protocol" above). For 1985–1995, read:

3. The Convention shall apply also to:

(a) any identical or substantially similar taxes on income; and

(b) taxes on capital

which are imposed after the date of signature of the Convention in addition to, or in place of, the existing taxes.

4. [Repealed]

**Technical Explanation [1984]:**

Paragraph 4 provides that, notwithstanding paragraphs 2 and 3, the Convention applies to certain United States taxes for certain specified purposes: the accumulated earnings tax and personal holding company tax are covered only to the extent necessary to implement the provisions of paragraphs 5 and 8 of Article X (Dividends); the excise taxes imposed with respect to private foundations are covered only to the extent necessary to implement the provisions of paragraph 4 of Article XXI (Exempt Organizations); and the social security taxes imposed under sections 1401, 3101, and 3111 of the Code are covered only to the extent necessary to implement the provisions of paragraph 4 of Article XXIX (Miscellaneous Rules). The pertinent provisions of Articles X, XXI, and XXIX are described below. Canada has no national taxes similar to the United States accumulated earnings tax, personal holding company tax, or excise taxes imposed with respect to private foundations.

Article II does not specifically refer to interest, fines and penalties. Thus, each Contracting State may, in general, impose interest, fines, and penalties or pay interest pursuant to its domestic laws. Any question whether such items are being imposed or paid in connection with covered taxes in a manner consistent with provisions of the Convention, such as Article XXV (Non-Discrimination), may, however, be resolved by the competent authorities pursuant to Article XXVI (Mutual Agreement Procedure). See, however, the discussion below of the treatment of certain interest under Articles XXIX (Miscellaneous Rules) and XXX (Entry Into Force).

**Notes**: Art. II(4) repealed by 1995 Protocol, generally effective 1996 (see Art. 21(2) under "Application of the 1995 Protocol" above). For 1985–1995, read:

4. Notwithstanding the provisions of paragraphs 2(b) and 3, the Convention shall apply to:

(a) the United States accumulated earnings tax and personal holding company tax, to the extent, and only to the extent, necessary to implement the provisions of paragraphs 5 and 8 of Article X (Dividends);

(b) the United States excise taxes imposed with respect to private foundations, to the extent, and only to the extent, necessary to implement the provisions of paragraph 4 of Article XXI (Exempt Organizations); and

(c) the United States social security taxes, to the extent, and only to the extent, necessary to implement the provisions of paragraph 4 of Article XXIX (Miscellaneous Rules).

## Article III — General Definitions

**1.** For the purposes of this Convention, unless the context otherwise requires:

(a) when used in a geographical sense, the term **"Canada"** means the territory of Canada, including any area beyond the territorial seas of Canada which, in accordance with international law and the laws of Canada, is an area within which Canada may exercise rights with respect to the seabed and subsoil and their natural resources;

(b) the term **"United States"** means:

(i) the United States of America, but does not include Puerto Rico, the Virgin Islands, Guam or any other United States possession or territory; and

(ii) when used in a geographical sense, such term also includes any area beyond the territorial seas of the United States which, in accordance with international law and the laws of the United States, is an area within which the United States may exercise rights with respect to the seabed and subsoil and their natural resources;

(c) the term **"Canadian tax"** means the taxes referred to in Article II (Taxes Covered) that are imposed on income by Canada;

(d) the term **"United States tax"** means the taxes referred to in Article II (Taxes Covered), other than in subparagraph (b)(i) to (iv) of paragraph 2 thereof, that are imposed on income by the United States;

(e) the term **"person"** includes an individual, an estate, a trust, a company and any other body of persons;

(f) the term **"company"** means any body corporate or any entity which is treated as a body corporate for tax purposes;

(g) the term **"competent authority"** means:

(i) in the case of Canada, the Minister of National Revenue or his authorized representative; and

(ii) in the case of the United States, the Secretary of the Treasury or his delegate;

(h) the term **"international traffic"** with reference to a resident of a Contracting State means any voyage of a ship or aircraft to transport passengers or property (whether or not operated or used by that resident) except where the principal purpose of the voyage is to transport passengers or property between places within the other Contracting State;

(i) the term **"State"** means any national State, whether or not a Contracting State; and

(j) the term **"the 1942 Convention"** means the Convention and Protocol between Canada and the United States for the Avoidance of Double Taxation and the Prevention of Fiscal Evasion in the case of Income Taxes signed at Washington on March 4, 1942, as amended by the Convention signed at Ottawa on June 12, 1950, by the Convention signed at Ottawa on August 8, 1956 and by the Supplementary Convention signed at Washington on October 25, 1966.

**Technical Explanation [1995 Protocol]:**

This Article of the Protocol amends paragraphs 1(c) and 1(d) of Article III (General Definitions) of the Convention. These paragraphs define the terms "Canadian tax" and "United States tax," respectively. The present Convention defines "Canadian tax" to mean the Canadian taxes specified in paragraph 2(a) or 3(a) of Article II (Taxes Covered), i.e., Canadian income taxes. It similarly defines the term "United States tax" to mean the U.S. taxes specified in paragraph 2(b) or 3(a) of Article II, i.e., U.S. income taxes.

As amended by the Protocol, paragraph 2(a) of Article II of the Convention covers all taxes imposed by Canada under its *Income Tax Act*, including certain taxes that are not income taxes. As explained below, paragraph 2(b) is similarly amended by the Protocol to include certain U.S. taxes that are not income taxes. It was, therefore, necessary to amend the terms "Canadian tax" and "United States tax" so that they would continue to refer exclusively to the income taxes imposed by each Contracting State. The amendment to the definition of the term "Canadian tax" ensures, for example, that the Protocol will not obligate the United States to give a foreign tax credit under Article XXIV (Elimination of Double Taxation) for covered taxes other than income taxes.

The definition of "United States tax," as amended, excludes certain United States taxes that are covered in Article II only for certain limited purposes under the Convention. These include the accumulated earnings tax, the personal holding company tax, foundation excise taxes, social security taxes, and estate taxes. To the extent that these are to be creditable taxes in Canada, that fact is specified elsewhere in the Convention. A Canadian income tax credit for U.S. social security taxes is provided in new paragraph 2(a)(ii) of Article XXIV (Elimination of Double Taxation). A Canadian income tax credit for the U.S. estate taxes is provided in paragraph 6 of new Article XXIX B (Taxes Imposed by Reason of Death).

**Technical Explanation [1984]:**

Article III provides definitions and general rules of interpretation for the Convention. Paragraph 1(a) states that the term "Canada," when used in a geographical sense, means the territory of Canada, including any area beyond the territorial seas of Canada which, under international law and the laws of Canada, is an area within which Canada may exercise rights with respect to the seabed and subsoil and their natural resources. This definition differs only in form from the definition of Canada in the 1942 Convention; paragraph 1(a) omits the reference in the 1942 Convention to "the Provinces, the Territories and Sable Island" as unnecessary.

Paragraph 1(b)(i) defines the term "United States" to mean the United States of America. The term does not include Puerto Rico, the Virgin Islands, Guam, or any other United States possession or territory.

Paragraph 1(b)(ii) states that when the term "United States" is used in a geographical sense the term also includes any area beyond the territorial seas of the United States which, under international law and the laws of the United States, is an area within which the United States may exercise rights with respect to the seabed and subsoil and their natural resources.

Paragraph 1(c) defines the term "Canadian tax" to mean the taxes imposed by the Government of Canada under Parts I, XIII, and XIV of the *Income Tax Act* as in existence on September 26, 1980 and any identical or substantially similar taxes on income imposed by the Government of Canada after that date and which are in addition to or in place of the then existing taxes. The term does not extend to capital taxes, if and when such taxes are ever imposed by Canada.

Paragraph 1(d) defines the term "United States tax" to mean the Federal income taxes imposed by the *Internal Revenue Code* as in existence on September 26, 1980 and any identical or substantially similar taxes on income imposed by the United States after that date in addition to or in place of the then existing taxes. The term does not extend to capital taxes, nor to the United States taxes identified in paragraph 4 of Article II (Taxes Covered).

Paragraph 1(e) provides that the term "person" includes an individual, an estate, a trust, a company, and any other body of persons. Although both the United States and Canada do not regard partnerships as taxable entities, the definition in the paragraph is broad enough to include partnerships where necessary.

Paragraph 1(f) defines the term "company" to mean any body corporate or any entity which is treated as a body corporate for tax purposes.

The term "competent authority" is defined in paragraph 1(g) to mean, in the case of Canada, the Minister of National Revenue or his authorized representative and, in the case of the United States, the Secretary of the Treasury or his delegate. The Secretary of the Treasury has delegated the general authority to act as competent authority to the Commissioner of the Internal Revenue Service, who has redelegated such authority to the Associate Commissioner (Operations). The Assistant Commissioner (Examination) has been delegated the authority to administer programs for simultaneous, spontaneous and industrywide exchanges of information. The Director, Foreign Operations District, has been delegated the authority to administer programs for routine and specific exchanges of information and mutual assistance in collection. The Assistant Commissioner (Criminal Investigations) has been delegated the authority to administer the simultaneous criminal investigation program with Canada.

Paragraph 1(h) defines the term "international traffic" to mean, with reference to a resident of a Contracting State, any voyage of a ship or aircraft to transport passengers or property (whether or not operated or used by that resident), except where the principal purpose of the voyage is transport between points within the other Contracting State. For example, in determining for Canadian tax purposes whether a United States resident has derived profits from the operation of ships or aircraft in international traffic, a voyage of a ship or aircraft (whether or not operated or used by that resident) that includes stops in both Contracting States will not be international traffic if the principal purpose of the voyage is to transport passengers or property from one point in Canada to another point in Canada.

Paragraph 1(i) defines the term "State" to mean any national State, whether or not a Contracting State.

Paragraph 1(j) establishes "the 1942 Convention" as the term to be used throughout the Convention for referring to the pre-existing income tax treaty relationship between the United States and Canada.

**Related Provisions**: *Income Tax Conventions Interpretation Act* 3 — Meanings of undefined terms; 5 — Definitions of "annuity", "Canada", "immovable property", "real property", "periodic pension payment"; 6 — Definition of "interest".

**Notes**: Art. III(1)(c), (d) amended by 1995 Protocol, generally effective 1996 (see Art. 21(2) under "Application of the 1995 Protocol" above). For 1985–1995, read:

(c) the term "Canadian tax" means the Canadian taxes referred to in paragraphs 2(a) and 3(a) of Article II (Taxes Covered);

(d) the term "United States tax" means the United States taxes referred to in paragraphs 2(b) and 3(a) of Article II (Taxes Covered);

See Notes to ITA 115.1 re the designated "competent authority".

**2.** As regards the application of the Convention by a Contracting State any term not defined therein shall, unless the context otherwise requires and subject to the provisions of Article XXVI (Mutual Agreement Procedure), have the meaning which it has under the law of that State concerning the taxes to which the Convention applies.

**Technical Explanation [1984]:**
Article III provides definitions and general rules of interpretation for the Convention. Paragraph 1(a) states that the term "Canada," when used in a geographical sense, means the territory of Canada, including any area beyond the territorial seas of Canada which, under international law and the laws of Canada, is an area within which Canada may exercise rights with respect to the seabed and subsoil and their natural resources. This definition differs only in form from the definition of Canada in the 1942 Convention; paragraph 1(a) omits the reference in the 1942 Convention to "the Provinces, the Territories and Sable Island" as unnecessary.

Paragraph 1(b)(i) defines the term "United States" to mean the United States of America. The term does not include Puerto Rico, the Virgin Islands, Guam, or any other United States possession or territory.

Paragraph 1(b)(ii) states that when the term "United States" is used in a geographical sense the term also includes any area beyond the territorial seas of the United States which, under international law and the laws of the United States, is an area within which the United States may exercise rights with respect to the seabed and subsoil and their natural resources.

Paragraph 1(c) defines the term "Canadian tax" to mean the taxes imposed by the Government of Canada under Parts I, XIII, and XIV of the *Income Tax Act* as in existence on September 26, 1980 and any identical or substantially similar taxes on income imposed by the Government of Canada after that date and which are in addition to or in place of the then existing taxes. The term does not extend to capital taxes, if and when such taxes are ever imposed by Canada.

Paragraph 1(d) defines the term "United States tax" to mean the Federal income taxes imposed by the *Internal Revenue Code* as in existence on September 26, 1980 and any identical or substantially similar taxes on income imposed by the United States after that date in addition to or in place of the then existing taxes. The term does not extend to capital taxes, nor to the United States taxes identified in paragraph 4 of Article II (Taxes Covered).

Paragraph 1(e) provides that the term "person" includes an individual, an estate, a trust, a company, and any other body of persons. Although both the United States and Canada do not regard partnerships as taxable entities, the definition in the paragraph is broad enough to include partnerships where necessary.

Paragraph 1(f) defines the term "company" to mean any body corporate or any entity which is treated as a body corporate for tax purposes.

The term "competent authority" is defined in paragraph 1(g) to mean, in the case of Canada, the Minister of National Revenue or his authorized representative and, in the case of the United States, the Secretary of the Treasury or his delegate. The Secretary of the Treasury has delegated the general authority to act as competent authority to the Commissioner of the Internal Revenue Service, who has redelegated such authority to the Associate Commissioner (Operations). The Assistant Commissioner (Examination) has been delegated the authority to administer programs for simultaneous, spontaneous and industrywide exchanges of information. The Director, Foreign Operations District, has been delegated the authority to administer programs for routine and specific exchanges of information and mutual assistance in collection. The Assistant Commissioner (Criminal Investigations) has been delegated the authority to administer the simultaneous criminal investigation program with Canada.

Paragraph 1(h) defines the term "international traffic" to mean, with reference to a resident of a Contracting State, any voyage of a ship or aircraft to transport passengers or property (whether or not operated or used by that resident), except where the principal purpose of the voyage is transport between points within the other Contracting State. For example, in determining for Canadian tax purposes whether a United States resident has derived profits from the operation of ships or aircraft in international traffic, a voyage of a ship or aircraft (whether or not operated or used by that resident) that includes stops in both Contracting States will not be international traffic if the principal purpose of the voyage is to transport passengers or property from one point in Canada to another point in Canada.

Paragraph 1(i) defines the term "State" to mean any national State, whether or not a Contracting State.

Paragraph 1(j) establishes "the 1942 Convention" as the term to be used throughout the Convention for referring to the pre-existing income tax treaty relationship between the United States and Canada.

Paragraph 2 provides that, in the case of a term not defined in the Convention, the domestic tax law of the Contracting State applying to the Convention shall control, unless the context in which the term is used requires a definition independent of domestic tax law or the competent authorities reach agreement on a meaning pursuant to Article XXVI (Mutual Agreement Procedure). The term "context" refers to the purpose and background of the provision in which the term appears.

Pursuant to the provisions of Article XXVI, the competent authorities of the Contracting States may resolve any difficulties or doubts as to the interpretation or application of the Convention. An agreement by the competent authorities with respect to the meaning of a term used in the Convention would supersede conflicting meanings in the domestic laws of the Contracting States.

## Article IV — Residence

**1.** For the purposes of this Convention, the term **"resident of a Contracting State"** means any person that, under the laws of that State, is liable to tax therein by reason of that person's domicile, residence, citizenship, place of management, place of incorporation or any other criterion of a similar nature, but in the case of an estate or trust, only to the extent that income derived by the estate or trust is liable to tax in that State, either in its hands or in the hands of its beneficiaries. For the purposes of this paragraph, an individual who is not a resident of Canada under this paragraph and who is a United States citizen or an alien admitted to the United States for permanent residence (a "green card" holder) is a resident of the United States only if the individual has a substantial presence, permanent home or habitual abode in the United States, and that individual's personal and economic relations are closer to the United States than to any third State. The term "resident" of a Contracting State is understood to include:

(a) the Government of that State or a political subdivision or local authority thereof or any agency or instrumentality of any such government, subdivision or authority, and

(b)

(i) a trust, organization or other arrangement that is operated exclusively to administer or provide pension, retirement or employee benefits; and

(ii) a not-for-profit organization

that was constituted in that State and that is, by reason of its nature as such, generally exempt from income taxation in that State.

**Technical Explanation [1995 Protocol]:**

Article 3 of the Protocol amends Article IV (Residence) of the Convention. It clarifies the meaning of the term "resident" in certain cases and adds a special rule, found in a number of recent U.S. treaties, for determining the residence of U.S. citizens and "green-card" holders.

The first sentence of paragraph 1 of Article IV sets forth the general criteria for determining residence under the Convention. It is amended by the Protocol to state explicitly that a person will be considered a resident of a Contracting State for purposes of the Convention if he is liable to tax in that Contracting State by reason of citizenship. Although the sentence applies to both Contracting States, only the United States taxes its non-resident citizens in the same manner as its residents. Aliens admitted to the United States for permanent residence ("green card" holders) continue to qualify as U.S. residents under the first sentence of paragraph 1, because they are taxed by the United States as residents, regardless of where they physically reside.

U.S. citizens and green card holders who reside outside the United States, however, may have relatively little personal or economic nexus with the United States. The Protocol adds a second sentence to paragraph 1 that acknowledges this fact by limiting the circumstances under which such persons are to be treated, for purposes of the Convention, as U.S. residents. Under that sentence, a U.S. citizen or green card holder will be treated as a resident of the United States for purposes of the Convention, and, thereby, be entitled to treaty benefits, only if (1) the individual has a substantial presence, permanent home, or habitual abode in the United States, and (2) the individual's personal and economic relations with the United States are closer than those with any third country. If, however, such an individual is a resident of both the United States and Canada under the first sentence of the paragraph, his residence for purposes of the Convention is determined instead under the "tie-breaker" rules of paragraph 2 of the Article.

The fact that a U.S. citizen who does not have close ties to the United States may not be treated as a U.S. resident under Article IV of the Convention does not alter the application of the saving clause of paragraph 2 of Article XXIX (Miscellaneous Rules) to that citizen. However, like any other individual that is a resident alien under U.S. law, a green card holder is treated as a resident of the United States for purposes of the saving clause only if he qualifies as such under Article IV.

New paragraph 1(a) confirms that the term "resident" of a Contracting State includes the Government of that State or a political subdivision or local authority of that State, as well as any agency or instrumentality of one of these governmental entities. This is implicit in the current Convention and in other U.S. and Canadian treaties, even where not specified.

New paragraph 1 also clarifies, in subparagraph (b), that trusts, organizations, or other arrangements operated exclusively to provide retirement or employee benefits, and other not-for-profit organizations, such as organizations described in section 501(c) of the *Internal Revenue Code*, are residents of a Contracting State if they are constituted in that State and are generally exempt from income taxation in that State by reason of their nature as described above. This change clarifies that the specified entities are to be treated as residents of one of the Contracting States. This corresponds to the interpretation that had previously been adopted by the Contracting States. Such entities, therefore, will be entitled to the benefits of the Convention with respect to the other Contracting State, provided that they satisfy the requirements of new Article XXIX A (Limitation on Benefits) (discussed below).

**Technical Explanation [1984]:**

Article IV provides a detailed definition of the term "resident of a Contracting State." The definition begins with a person's liability to tax as a resident under the respective taxation laws of the Contracting States. A person who, under those laws, is a resident of one Contracting State and not the other need look no further. However, the Convention definition is also designed to assign residence to one State or the other for purposes of the Convention in circumstances where each of the Contracting States believes a person to be its resident. The Convention definition is, of course, exclusively for purposes of the Convention.

Paragraph 1 provides that the term "resident of a Contracting State" means any person who, under the laws of that State, is liable to tax therein by reason of his domicile, residence, place of management, place of incorporation, or any other criterion of a similar nature. The phrase "any other criterion of a similar nature" includes, for U.S. purposes, an election under the Code to be treated as a U.S. resident. An estate or trust is, however, considered to be a resident of a Contracting State only to the extent that income derived by such estate or trust is liable to tax in that State either in its hands or in the hands of its beneficiaries. To the extent that an estate or trust is considered a resident of a Contracting State under this provision, it can be a "beneficial owner" of items of income specified in other articles of the Convention — e.g. paragraph 2 of Article X (Dividends).

**Related Provisions**: *Income Tax Conventions Interpretation Act* 6.2 — Residence of partnership.

**Notes**: The words "liable to tax" mean fully liable to tax on worldwide income: *Crown Forest Industries Ltd.*, [1995] 2 C.T.C. 64 (SCC).

Art. IV(1) amended by 1995 Protocol, generally effective 1996 (see Art. 21(2) under "Application of the 1995 Protocol" above). For 1985-1995, read:

> 1. For the purposes of this Convention, the term "resident of a Contracting State" means any person who, under the laws of that State, is liable to tax therein by reason of his domicile, residence, place of management, place of incorporation or any other criterion of a similar nature, but in the case of an estate or trust, only to the extent that income derived by such estate or trust is liable to tax in that State, either in its hands or in the hands of its beneficiaries.

**I.T. Technical News**: No. 16 (*Crown Forest Industries* case; U.S. S-Corps and LLCs).

**2.** Where by reason of the provisions of paragraph 1 an individual is a resident of both Contracting States, then his status shall be determined as follows:

(a) he shall be deemed to be a resident of the Contracting State in which he has a permanent home available to him; if he has a permanent home available to him in both States or in neither State, he shall be deemed to be a resident of the Contracting State with which his personal and economic relations are closer (centre of vital interests);

(b) if the Contracting State in which he has his centre of vital interests cannot be determined, he shall be deemed to be a resident of the Contracting State in which he has an habitual abode;

(c) if he has an habitual abode in both States or in neither State, he shall be deemed to be a resident of the Contracting State of which he is a citizen; and

(d) if he is a citizen of both States or of neither of them, the competent authorities of the Contracting States shall settle the question by mutual agreement.

**Technical Explanation [1984]**:

Paragraphs 2, 3, and 4 provide rules to determine a single residence for purposes of the Convention for persons resident in both Contracting States under the rules set forth in paragraph 1. Paragraph 2 deals with individuals. A "dual resident" individual is initially deemed to be a resident of the Contracting State in which he has a permanent home available to him. If the individual has a permanent home available to him in both States or in neither, he is deemed to be a resident of the Contracting State with which his personal and economic relations are closer. If the personal and economic relations of an individual are not closer to one Contracting State than to the other, the individual is deemed to be a resident of the Contracting State in which he has a habitual abode. If he has such an abode in both States or in neither State, he is deemed to be a resident of the Contracting State of which he is a citizen. If the individual is a citizen of both States or of neither, the competent authorities are to settle the status of the individual by mutual agreement.

**Related Provisions**: ITA 250(5) — Corporation not resident in Canada under treaty is deemed not resident under ITA.

**3.** Where by reason of the provisions of paragraph 1 a company is a resident of both Contracting States, then if it was created under the laws in force in a Contracting State, it shall be deemed to be a resident of that State. Notwithstanding the preceding sentence, a company that was created in a Contracting State, that is a resident of both Contracting States and that is continued at any time in the other Contracting State in accordance with the corporate law in that other State shall be deemed while it is so continued to be a resident of that other State.

**Proposed Amendment — U.S. corporations continued into Canada**
**Department of Finance news release, September 18, 2000**: *Canada and the United States Propose Tax Treaty Changes*
[See at beginning of the convention, under heading "Corporations — Clarifying Residence" — ed.]

**Technical Explanation [1995 Protocol]**:

Article 3 of the Protocol adds a sentence to paragraph 3 of Article IV of the current Convention to address the residence of certain dual resident corporations. Certain jurisdictions allow local incorporation of an entity that is already organized and incorporated under the laws of another country. Under Canadian law, such an entity is referred to as having been "continued" into the other country. Although the Protocol uses the Canadian term, the provision operates reciprocally. The new sentence states that such a corporation will be considered a resident of the State into which it is continued. Paragraph 5 of Article 21 of the Protocol governs the effective date of this provision.

**Technical Explanation [1984]**:

Paragraph 3 provides that if, under the provisions of paragraph 1, a company is a resident of both Canada and the United States, then it shall be deemed to be a resident of the State under whose laws (including laws of political subdivisions) it was created. Paragraph 3 does not refer to the State in which a company is organized, thus making clear that the tie-breaker rule for a company is controlled by the State of the company's original creation. Various jurisdictions may allow local incorporation of an entity that is already organized and incorporated under the laws of another country. Paragraph 3 provides certainty in both the United States and Canada with respect to the treatment of such an entity for purposes of the Convention.

**Related Provisions**: ITA 250(5.1) — Continuation in other jurisdiction.

**Notes**: Second sentence of Art. IV(3) added by 1995 Protocol, generally effective 1996 (see Art. 21(5) under "Application of the 1995 Protocol" above).

**4.** Where by reason of the provisions of paragraph 1 an estate, trust or other person (other than an individual or a company) is a resident of both Contracting States, the competent authorities of the States shall by mutual agreement endeavor to settle the question and to determine the mode of application of the Convention to such person.

**Technical Explanation [1984]:**

Paragraph 4 provides that where, by reason of the provisions of paragraph 1, an estate, trust, or other person, other than an individual or a company, is a resident of both Contracting States, the competent authorities of the States shall by mutual agreement endeavor to settle the question and determine the mode of application of the Convention to such person. This delegation of authority to the competent authorities complements the provisions of Article XXVI (Mutual Agreement Procedure), which implicitly grant such authority.

5. Notwithstanding the provisions of the preceding paragraphs, an individual shall be deemed to be a resident of a Contracting State if:

(a) the individual is an employee of that State or of a political subdivision, local authority or instrumentality thereof rendering services in the discharge of functions or a governmental nature in the other Contracting State or in a third State; and

(b) the individual is subjected in the first-mentioned State to similar obligations in respect of taxes on income as are residents of the first-mentioned State.

The spouse and dependent children residing with such an individual and meeting the requirements of subparagraph (b) above shall also be deemed to be residents of the first-mentioned State.

**Technical Explanation [1984]:**

Paragraph 5 provides a special rule for certain government employees, their spouses, and dependent children. An individual is deemed to be a resident of a Contracting State if he is an employee of that State or of a political subdivision, local authority, or instrumentality of that State, is rendering services in the discharge of functions of a governmental nature in any State, and is subjected in the first-mentioned State to "similar obligations" in respect of taxes on income as are residents of the first-mentioned State. Paragraph 5 provides further that a spouse and dependent children residing with a government employee and also subject to "similar obligations" in respect of income taxes as residents of the first-mentioned State are also deemed to be residents of that State. Paragraph 5 overrides the normal tie-breaker rule of paragraph 2. A U.S. citizen or resident who is an employee of the U.S. government in a foreign country or who is a spouse or dependent of such employee is considered to be subject in the United States to "similar obligations" in respect of taxes on income as those imposed on residents of the United States, notwithstanding that such person may be entitled to the benefits allowed by sections 911 or 912 of the Code.

**Related Provisions**: ITA 250(1)(c) — Residence of Canadian ambassador, etc., working outside Canada.

# Article V — Permanent Establishment

1. For the purposes of this Convention, the term **"permanent establishment"** means a fixed place of business through which the business of a resident of a Contracting State is wholly or partly carried on.

**Technical Explanation [1984]:**

Paragraph 1 provides that for the purposes of the Convention the term "permanent establishment" means a fixed place of business through which the business of a resident of a Contracting State is wholly or partly carried on. Article V does not use the term "enterprise of a Contracting State," which appears in the 1942 Convention. Thus, paragraph 1 avoids introducing an additional term into the Convention. The omission of the term is not intended to have any implications for the interpretation of the 1942 Convention.

**I.T. Technical News**: No. 18 (*Dudney* case).

2. The term "permanent establishment" shall include especially:

(a) a place of management;

(b) a branch;

(c) an office;

(d) a factory;

(e) a workshop; and

(f) a mine, an oil or gas well, a quarry or any other place of extraction of natural resources.

**Technical Explanation [1984]:**

Paragraph 2 provides that the term "permanent establishment" includes especially a place of management, a branch, an office, a factory, a workshop, and a mine, oil or gas well, quarry, or any other place of extraction of natural resources.

3. A building site or construction or installation project constitutes a permanent establishment if, but only if, it lasts more than 12 months.

**Technical Explanation [1984]:**

Paragraph 3 adds that a building site or construction or installation project constitutes a permanent establishment if and only if it lasts for more than 12 months.

4. The use of an installation or drilling rig or ship in a Contracting State to explore for or exploit natural resources constitutes a permanent establishment if, but only if, such use is for more than three months in any twelve-month period.

**Technical Explanation [1984]:**

Paragraph 4 provides that a permanent establishment exists in a Contracting State if the use of an installation or drilling rig or drilling ship in that State to explore for or exploit natural resources lasts for more than 3 months in any 12 month period, but not if such activity exists for a lesser period of time. The competent authorities have entered into an agreement under the 1942 Convention setting forth guidelines as to certain aspects of Canadian taxation of drilling rigs owned by U.S. persons that constitute Canadian permanent establishments. The agreement will be renewed when this Convention enters into force.

5. A person acting in a Contracting State on behalf of a resident of the other Contracting State — other than an agent of an independent status to whom paragraph 7 applies — shall be deemed to be a permanent establishment in the first-mentioned State if such person has, and habitually exercises in that State, an authority to conclude contracts in the name of the resident.

**Technical Explanation [1984]:**

Paragraph 5 provides that a person acting in a Contracting State on behalf of a resident of the other Contracting State is deemed to be a permanent establishment of the resident if such person has and habitually exercises in the first-mentioned State the authority to conclude contracts in the name of the resident. This rule does not apply to an agent of independent status, covered by paragraph 7. Under the provisions of paragraph 5, a permanent establishment may exist even in the absence of a fixed place of business. If, however, the activities of a person described in paragraph 5 are limited to the ancillary activities described in paragraph 6, then a permanent establishment does not exist solely on account of the person's activities.

There are a number of minor differences between the provisions of paragraphs 1 through 5 and the analogous provisions of the 1942 Convention. One important deviation is elimination of the rule of the 1942 Convention which deems a permanent establishment to exist in any circumstance where a resident of one State uses substantial equipment in the other State for any period of time. The Convention thus generally raises the threshold for source basis taxation of activities that involve substantial equipment (and that do not otherwise constitute a permanent establishment). Another deviation of some significance is elimination of the rule of the 1942 Convention that considers a permanent establishment to exist where a resident of one State carries on business in the other State through an agent or employee who has a stock of merchandise from which he regularly fills orders that he receives. The Convention provides that a person other than an agent of independent status who is engaged solely in the maintenance of a stock of goods or merchandise belonging to a resident of the other State for the purpose of storage, display or delivery does not constitute a permanent establishment.

**6.** Notwithstanding the provisions of paragraphs 1, 2 and 5, the term "permanent establishment" shall be deemed not to include a fixed place of business used solely for, or a person referred to in paragraph 5 engaged solely in, one or more of the following activities:

(a) the use of facilities for the purpose of storage, display or delivery of goods or merchandise belonging to the resident;

(b) the maintenance of a stock of goods or merchandise belonging to the resident for the purpose of storage, display or delivery;

(c) the maintenance of a stock of goods or merchandise belonging to the resident for the purpose of processing by another person;

(d) the purchase of goods or merchandise, or the collection of information, for the resident; and

(e) advertising, the supply of information, scientific research or similar activities which have a preparatory or auxiliary character, for the resident.

**Technical Explanation [1984]:**

Paragraph 6 provides that a fixed place of business used solely for, or an employee described in paragraph 5 engaged solely in, certain specified activities is not a permanent establishment, notwithstanding the provisions of paragraphs 1, 2, and 5. The specified activities are: a) the use of facilities for the purpose of storage, display, or delivery of goods or merchandise belonging to the resident whose business is being carried on; b) the maintenance of a stock of goods or merchandise belonging to the resident for the purpose of storage, display, or delivery; c) the maintenance of a stock of goods or merchandise belonging to the resident for the purpose of processing by another person; d) the purchase of goods or merchandise, or the collection of information, for the resident; and e) advertising, the supply of information, scientific research, or similar activities which have a preparatory or auxiliary character, for the resident. Combinations of the specified activities have the same status as any one of the activities. Thus, unlike the OECD Model Convention, a combination of the activities described in subparagraphs 6(a) through 6(e) need not be of a preparatory or auxiliary character (except as required by subparagraph 6(e)) in order to avoid the creation of a permanent establishment. The reference in paragraph 6(e) to specific activities does not imply that any other particular activities — for example, the servicing of a patent or a know-how contract or the inspection of the implementation of engineering plans — do not fall within the scope of paragraph 6(e) provided that, based on the facts and circumstances, such activities have a preparatory or auxiliary character.

**7.** A resident of a Contracting State shall not be deemed to have a permanent establishment in the other Contracting State merely because such resident carries on business in that other State through a broker, general commission agent or any other agent of an independent status, provided that such persons are acting in the ordinary course of their business.

**Technical Explanation [1984]:**

Paragraph 7 provides that a resident of a Contracting State is not deemed to have a permanent establishment in the other Contracting State merely because such resident carries on business in the other State through a broker, general commission agent, or any other agent of independent status, provided that such persons are acting in the ordinary course of their business.

**8.** The fact that a company which is a resident of a Contracting State controls or is controlled by a company which is a resident of the other Contracting State, or which carries on business in that other State (whether through a permanent establishment or otherwise), shall not constitute either company a permanent establishment of the other.

**Technical Explanation [1984]:**

Paragraph 8 states that the fact that a company which is a resident of one Contracting State controls or is controlled by a company which is either a resident of the other Contracting State or which is carrying on a business in the other State, whether through a permanent establishment or otherwise, does not automatically render either company a permanent establishment of the other.

**9.** For the purposes of the Convention, the provisions of this Article shall be applied in determining whether any person has a permanent establishment in any State.

**Technical Explanation [1984]:**

Paragraph 9 provides that, for purposes of the Convention, the provisions of Article V apply in determining whether any person has a permanent establishment in any State. Thus, these provisions would determine whether a person other than a resident of Canada or the United States has a permanent establishment in Canada or the United States, and whether a person resident in Canada or the United States has a permanent establishment in a third State.

**Related Provisions:** *Income Tax Conventions Interpretation Act* 4 — Permanent establishment in Canada.

**Interpretation Bulletins:** IT-173R2: Capital gains derived in Canada by residents of the United States.

## Article VI — Income from Real Property

**1.** Income derived by a resident of a Contracting State from real property (including income from agriculture, forestry or other natural resources) situated in the other Contracting State may be taxed in that other State.

**Technical Explanation [1984]:**

Paragraph 1 provides that income derived by a resident of a Contracting State from real property situated in the other Contracting State may be taxed by that other State. Income from real property includes, for purposes of Article VI, income from agriculture, forestry or other natural resources. Also, while "income derived ... from real property" includes income from rights such as an overriding royalty or a net profits interest in a natural resource, it does not include income in the form of rights to explore for or exploit natural resources which a party receives as compensation for services (e.g., exploration services); the latter income is subject to the provisions of Article VII (Business Profits), XIV (Independent Personal Services), or XV (Dependent Personal Services), as the case may be. As provided by paragraph 3, paragraph 1 applies to income derived from the direct use, letting or use in any other form of real property and to income from the alienation of such property.

**2.** For the purposes of this Convention, the term **"real property"** shall have the meaning which it has under the taxation laws of the Contracting State in which the property in question is situated and shall include any option or similar right in respect thereof. The term shall in any case include usufruct of real property, rights to explore for or to exploit mineral deposits, sources and other natural resources and rights to amounts computed by reference to the amount or value of production from such resources; ships and aircraft shall not be regarded as real property.

**Technical Explanation [1984]:**

Generally speaking, the term "real property" has the meaning which it has under the taxation laws of the Contracting State in which the property in question is situated, in accordance with paragraph 2. In any case, the term includes any option or similar right in respect of real property, the usufruct of real property, and rights to explore for or to exploit mineral deposits, sources, and other natural resources. The reference to "rights to explore for or to exploit mineral deposits, sources and other natural resources" includes rights generating either variable (e.g., computed by reference to the amount of value or production) or fixed payments. The term "real property" does not include ships and aircraft.

**Related Provisions**: *Income Tax Conventions Interpretation Act* 5 — Definition of "immovable property" and "real property".

**3.** The provisions of paragraph 1 shall apply to income derived from the direct use, letting or use in any other form of real property and to income from the alienation of such property.

**Technical Explanation [1984]:**

Unlike Article XIII A of the 1942 Convention, Article VI does not contain an election to allow a resident of a Contracting State to compute tax on income from real property situated in the other State on a net basis. Both the *Internal Revenue Code* and the *Income Tax Act* of Canada generally allow for net basis taxation with respect to real estate rental income, although Canada does not permit such an election for natural resource royalties. Also, unlike the 1942 Convention which in Article XI imposes a 15 percent limitation on the source basis taxation of rental or royalty income from real property, Article VI of the Convention allows a Contracting State to impose tax on such income under its internal law. In Canada the rate of tax on resource royalties is 25 percent of the gross amount of the royalty, if the income is not attributable to a business carried on in Canada. In an exchange of notes to the Protocol, the United States and Canada agreed to resume negotiations, upon request by either country, to provide an appropriate limit on taxation in the State of source if either country subsequently increases its statutory tax rate now applicable to such royalties (25 percent in the case of Canada and 30 percent in the case of the United States).

**Interpretation Bulletins**: IT-173R2: Capital gains derived in Canada by residents of the United States.

## Article VII — Business Profits

**1.** The business profits of a resident of a Contracting State shall be taxable only in that State unless the resident carries on business in the other Contracting State through a permanent establishment situated therein. If the resident carries on, or has carried on, business as aforesaid, the business profits of the resident may be taxed in the other State but only so much of them as is attributable to that permanent establishment.

**Technical Explanation [1984]:**

Paragraph 1 provides that business profits of a resident of a Contracting State are taxable only in that State unless the resident carries on business in the other Contracting State through a permanent establishment situated in that other State. If the resident carries on, or has carried on, business through such a permanent establishment, the other State may tax such business profits but only so much of them as are attributable to the permanent establishment. The reference to a prior permanent establishment ("or has carried on") makes clear that a Contracting State in which a permanent establishment existed has the right to tax the business profits attributable to that permanent establishment, even if there is a delay in the receipt or accrual of such profits until after the permanent establishment has been terminated.

Any business profits received or accrued in taxable years in which the Convention has effect, in accordance with Article XXX (Entry Into Force), which are attributable to a permanent establishment that was previously terminated are subject to tax in the Contracting State in which such permanent establishment existed under the provisions of Article VII.

**Related Provisions**: Art. V — Permanent establishment.

**Notes**: See Notes to Art. XIV.

**I.T. Technical News**: No. 18 (*Dudney* case).

**2.** Subject to the provisions of paragraph 3, where a resident of a Contracting State carries on business in the other Contracting State through a permanent establishment situated therein, there shall in each Contracting State be attributed to that permanent establishment the business profits which it might be expected to make if it were a distinct and separate person engaged in the same or similar activities under the same or similar conditions and dealing wholly independently with the resident and with any other person related to the resident (within the meaning of paragraph 2 of Article IX (Related Persons)).

**Technical Explanation [1984]:**

Paragraph 2 provides that where a resident of either Canada or the United States carries on business in the other Contracting State through a permanent establishment in that other State, both Canada and the United States shall attribute to that permanent establishment business profits which the permanent establishment might be expected to make if it were a distinct and separate person engaged in the same or similar activities under the same or similar conditions and dealing wholly independently with the resident and with any other person related to the resident. The term "related to the resident" is to be interpreted in accordance with paragraph 2 of Article IX (Related Persons). The reference to other related persons is intended to make clear that the test of paragraph 2 is not restricted to independence between a permanent establishment and a home office.

**Notes**: For discussion of paras. VII(2) and (3), see David Ward, "Attribution of Income to Permanent Establishments", 48(3) *Canadian Tax Journal* 559-5576(2000).

**3.** In determining the business profits of a permanent establishment, there shall be allowed as deductions expenses which are incurred for the purposes of the permanent establishment, including executive and general administrative expenses so incurred, whether in the State in which the permanent establishment is situated or elsewhere. Nothing in this paragraph shall require a Contracting State to allow the deduction of any expenditure which, by reason of its nature, is not generally allowed as a deduction under the taxation laws of that State.

**Technical Explanation [1984]:**

Paragraph 3 provides that, in determining business profits of a permanent establishment, there are to be allowed as deductions those expenses which are incurred for the purposes of the permanent establishment, including executive and administrative expenses, whether incurred in the State in which the permanent establishment is situated or in any other State. However, nothing in the paragraph requires Canada or the United States to allow a deduction for any expenditure which would not generally be allowed as a deduction under its taxation laws. The language of this provision differs from that of paragraph 1 of Article III of the 1942 Convention, which states that in the determination of net industrial and commercial profits of a permanent establishment there shall be allowed as deductions "all expenses, wherever incurred" as long as such expenses are reasonably allocable to the permanent establishment. Paragraph 3 of Article VII of the Convention is not intended to have any implications for interpretation of the 1942 Convention, but is intended to assure that under the Convention deductions are allowed by a Contracting State which are generally allowable by that State.

**Notes**: See Notes to Article VII(2).

**I.T. Technical News**: No. 18 (*Cudd Pressure* case).

**4.** No business profits shall be attributed to a permanent establishment of a resident of a Contracting State by reason of the use thereof for either the mere purchase of goods or merchandise or the mere provision of executive, managerial or administrative facilities or services for such resident.

**Technical Explanation [1984]:**

Paragraph 4 provides that no business profits are to be attributed to a permanent establishment of a resident of a Contracting State by reason of the use of the permanent establishment for merely purchasing goods or merchandise or merely providing executive, managerial, or administrative facilities or services for the resident. Thus, if a company resident in a Contracting State has a permanent establishment in the other State, and uses the permanent establishment for the mere performance of stewardship or other managerial services carried on for the benefit of the resident, this activity will not result in profits being attributed to the permanent establishment.

**5.** For the purposes of the preceding paragraphs, the business profits to be attributed to a permanent establishment shall be determined by the same method year by year unless there is good and sufficient reason to the contrary.

**Technical Explanation [1984]:**

Paragraph 5 provides that business profits are to be attributed to a permanent establishment by the same method in every taxable period unless there is good and sufficient reason to change such method. In the United States, such a change may be a change in accounting method requiring the approval of the Internal Revenue Service.

**6.** Where business profits include items of income which are dealt with separately in other Articles of this Convention, then the provisions of those Articles shall not be affected by the provisions of this Article.

**Technical Explanation [1984]:**

Paragraph 6 explains the relationship between the provisions of Article VII and other provisions of the Convention. Where business profits include items of income which are dealt with separately in other Articles of the Convention, those other Articles are controlling.

**7.** For the purposes of the Convention, the business profits attributable to a permanent establishment shall include only those profits derived from the assets or activities of the permanent establishment.

**Technical Explanation [1984]:**

Paragraph 7 provides a definition for the term "attributable to." Profits "attributable to" a permanent establishment are those derived from the assets or activities of the permanent establishment. Paragraph 7 does not preclude Canada or the United States from using appropriate domestic tax law rules of attribution. The "attributable to" definition does not, for example, preclude a taxpayer from using the rules of section 1.864-4(c)(5) of the Treasury Regulations to assure for U.S. tax purposes that interest arising in the United States is attributable to a permanent establishment in the United States. (Interest arising outside the United States is attributable to a permanent establishment in the United States based on the principles of Regulations sections 1.864-5 and 1.864-6 and Revenue Ruling 75-253, 1975-2 C.B. 203.) Income that would be taxable under the Code and that is "attributable to" a permanent establishment under paragraph 7 is taxable pursuant to Article VII, however, even if such income might under the Code be treated as fixed or determinable annual or periodical gains or income not effectively connected with the conduct of a trade or business within the United States. The "attributable to" definition means that the limited "force-of-attraction" rule of Code section 864(c)(3) does not apply for U.S. tax purposes under the Convention.

## Article VIII — Transportation

**1.** Notwithstanding the provisions of Articles VII (Business Profits), XII (Royalties) and XIII (Gains), profits derived by a resident of a Contracting State from the operation of ships or aircraft in international traffic, and gains derived by a resident of a Contracting State from the alienation of ships, aircraft or containers (including trailers and related equipment for the transport of containers) used principally in international traffic, shall be exempt from tax in the other Contracting State.

**Technical Explanation [1984]:**

Paragraph 1 provides that profits derived by a resident of a Contracting State from the operation of ships or aircraft in international traffic are exempt from tax in the other Contracting State, even if, under Article VII (Business Profits), such profits are attributable to a permanent establishment. Paragraph 1 also provides that gains derived by a resident of a Contracting State from the alienation of ships, aircraft or containers (including trailers and related equipment for the transport of containers) used principally in international traffic are exempt from tax in the other Contracting State even if, under Article XIII (Gains), those gains would be taxable in that other State. These rules differ from Article V of the 1942 Convention, which conditions the exemption in the State of source on registration of the ship or aircraft in the other State. Paragraph 1 also applies notwithstanding the provisions of Article XII (Royalties). Thus, to the extent that profits described in paragraph 2 would also fall within Article XII (Royalties) (e.g., rent from the lease of a container), the provisions of Article VIII are controlling.

**Related Provisions:** Art. III:1(h) — Meaning of "international traffic"; ITA 81(1)(c) — Exemption for income from ship or aircraft in international traffic.

**2.** For the purposes of this Convention, profits derived by a resident of a Contracting State from the operation of ships or aircraft in international traffic include profits from:

(a) the rental of ships or aircraft operated in international traffic;

(b) the use, maintenance or rental of containers (including trailers and related equipment for the transport of containers) used in international traffic; and

(c) the rental of ships, aircraft or containers (including trailers and related equipment for the transport of containers) provided that such profits are incidental to profits referred to in paragraph 1, 2(a) or 2(b).

**Technical Explanation [1984]:**

Paragraph 2(a) provides that profits covered by paragraph 1 include profits from the rental of ships or aircraft operated in international traffic. Such rental profits are included whether the rental is on a time, voyage, or bareboat basis, and irrespective of the State of residence of the operator.

Paragraph 2(b) provides that profits covered by paragraph 1 include profits derived from the use, maintenance or rental of containers, including trailers and related equipment for the transport of containers, if such containers are used in international traffic.

Paragraph 2(c) provides that profits covered by paragraph 1 include profits derived by a resident of a Contracting State from the rental of ships, aircraft, or containers (including trailers and related equipment for the transport of containers), even if not operated in international traffic, as long as such profits are incidental to profits of such person referred to in paragraphs 1, 2(a), or 2(b).

**Related Provisions:** Art. III:1(h) — Meaning of "international traffic".

**3.** Notwithstanding the provisions of Article VII (Business Profits), profits derived by a resident of a Contracting State from a voyage of a ship where the principal purpose of the voyage is to transport passengers or property between places in the other Contracting State may be taxed in that other State.

**Technical Explanation [1984]:**

Paragraph 3 states that profits derived by a resident of a Contracting State from a voyage of a ship where the principal purpose of the voyage is to transport passengers or property between points in the other Contracting State is taxable in that other State, whether or not the resident maintains a permanent establishment there. Paragraph 3 overrides the provisions of Article VII. Profits from such a voyage do not qualify for exemption under Article VIII by virtue of the definition of "international traffic" in paragraph 1(h) of Article III (General Definitions). However, profits from a similar voyage by aircraft are taxable in the Contracting State of source only if the profits are attributable to a permanent establishment maintained in that State.

**Related Provisions:** Art. XV:3 — Exemption for employees' income.

**4.** Notwithstanding the provisions of Articles VII (Business Profits) and XII (Royalties), profits of a resident of a Contracting State engaged in the operation of motor vehicles or a railway as a common carrier or a contract carrier derived from:

(a) the transportation of passengers or property between a point outside the other Contracting State and any other point; or

(b) the rental of motor vehicles (including trailers) or railway rolling stock, or the use, maintenance or rental of containers (including trailers and related equipment for the transport of containers) used to transport passengers or property between a point outside the other Contracting State and any other point

shall be exempt from tax in that other Contracting State.

**Technical Explanation [1984]:**

Paragraph 4 provides that profits derived by a resident of a Contracting State engaged in the operation of motor vehicles or a railway as a common carrier or contract carrier, and attributable to the transportation of passengers or property between a point outside the other Contracting State and any other point are exempt from tax in that other State. In addition, profits of such a person from the rental of motor vehicles (including trailers) or railway rolling stock, or from the use, maintenance, or rental of containers (including trailers and related equipment for the transport of containers) used to transport passengers or property between a point outside the other Contracting State and any other point are exempt from tax in that other State.

**Related Provisions:** Art. XV:3 — Exemption for employees' income.

**5.** The provisions of paragraphs 1, 3 and 4 shall also apply to profits or gains referred to in those paragraphs derived by a resident of a Contracting State from the participation in a pool, a joint business or an international operating agency.

**Technical Explanation [1984]:**

Paragraph 5 provides that a resident of a Contracting State that participates in a pool, a joint business, or an international operating agency is subject to the provisions of paragraphs 1, 3 and 4 with respect to the profits or gains referred to in paragraphs 1, 3, and 4.

6. Notwithstanding the provisions of Article XII (Royalties), profits derived by a resident of a Contracting State from the use, maintenance or rental of railway rolling stock, motor vehicles, trailers or containers (including trailers and related equipment for the transport of containers) used in the other Contracting State for a period or periods not expected to exceed in the aggregate 183 days in any twelve-month period shall be exempt from tax in the other Contracting State except to the extent that such profits are attributable to a permanent establishment in the other State and liable to tax in the other State by reason of Article VII (Business Profits).

**Technical Explanation [1984]:**

Paragraph 6 states that profits derived by a resident of a Contracting State from the use, maintenance, or rental of railway rolling stock, motor vehicles, trailers, or containers (including trailers and related equipment for the transport of containers) used in the other Contracting State for a period not expected to exceed 183 days in the aggregate in any 12-month period are exempt from tax in that other State except to the extent that the profits are attributable to a permanent establishment, in which case the State of source has the right to tax under Article VII. The provisions of paragraph 6, unlike the provisions of paragraph 4, apply whether or not the resident is engaged in the operation of motor vehicles or a railway as a common carrier or contract carrier. Paragraph 6 overrides the provisions of Article XII (Royalties), which would otherwise permit taxation in the State of source in the circumstances described.

Gains from the alienation of motor vehicles and railway rolling stock derived by a resident of a Contracting State are not affected by paragraph 4 or 6. Such gains would be taxable in the other Contracting State, however, only if the motor vehicles or rolling stock formed part of a permanent establishment maintained there. See paragraphs 2 and 4 of Article XIII.

## Article IX — Related Persons

1. Where a person in a Contracting State and a person in the other Contracting State are related and where the arrangements between them differ from those which would be made between unrelated persons, each State may adjust the amount of the income, loss or tax payable to reflect the income, deductions, credits or allowances which would, but for those arrangements, have been taken into account in computing such income, loss or tax.

**Technical Explanation [1984]:**

Paragraph 1 authorizes Canada and the United States, as the case may be, to adjust the amount of income, loss, or tax payable by a person with respect to arrangements between that person and a related person in the other Contracting State. Such adjustment may be made when arrangements between related persons differ from those that would obtain between unrelated persons. The term "person" encompasses a company resident in a third State with, for example, a permanent establishment in a Contracting State.

**Related Provisions**: ITA 247 — Transfer pricing adjustments.

2. For the purposes of this Article, a person shall be deemed to be related to another person if either person participates directly or indirectly in the management or control of the other, or if any third person or persons participate directly or indirectly in the management or control of both.

**Technical Explanation [1984]:**

Paragraph 2 provides that, for the purposes of Article IX, a person is deemed to be related to another person if either participates directly or indirectly in the management or control of the other or if any third person or persons participate directly or indirectly in the management or control of both. Thus, if a resident of any State controls directly or indirectly a company resident in Canada and a company resident in the United States, such companies are considered to be related persons for purposes of Article IX. Article IX and the definition of "related person" in paragraph 2 may encompass situations that would not be covered by provisions in the domestic laws of the Contracting States. Nor is the paragraph 2 definition controlling for the definition of "related person" or similar terms appearing in other Articles of the Convention. Those terms are defined as provided in paragraph 2 of Article III (General Definitions).

3. Where an adjustment is made or to be made by a Contracting State in accordance with paragraph 1, the other Contracting State shall (notwithstanding any time or procedural limitations in the domestic law of that other State) make a corresponding adjustment to the income, loss or tax of the related person in that other State if:

(a) it agrees with the first-mentioned adjustment; and

(b) within six years from the end of the taxable year to which the first-mentioned adjustment relates, the competent authority of the other State has been notified of the first-mentioned adjustment. The competent authorities, however, may agree to consider cases where the corresponding adjustment would not otherwise be barred by any time or procedural limitations in the other State, even if the notification is not made within the six-year period.

**Technical Explanation [1995 Protocol]:**

Article 4 of the Protocol amends paragraphs 3 and 4 of Article IX (Related Persons) of the Convention. Paragraph 1 of Article IX authorizes a Contracting State to adjust the amount of income, loss, or tax payable by a person with respect to arrangements between that person and a related person in the other Contracting State, when such arrangements differ from those that would obtain between unrelated persons. Under the present Convention, if an adjustment is made or to be made by a Contracting State under paragraph 1, paragraph 3 obligates the other Contracting State to make a corresponding adjustment if two conditions are satisfied: (1) the other Contracting State agrees with the adjustment made or to be made by the first Contracting State, and (2) the competent authority of the other Contracting State has received notice of the first adjustment within six years of the end of the taxable year to which that adjustment relates. If notice is not given within the six-year period, and if the person to whom the first adjustment relates is not notified of the adjustment at least six months prior to the end of the six-year period, paragraph 4 of Article IX of the present Convention requires that the first Contracting State withdraw its adjustment, to the extent necessary to avoid double taxation.

Article 4 of the Protocol amends paragraphs 3 and 4 of Article IX to prevent taxpayers from using the notification requirements of the present Convention to avoid adjustments. Paragraph 4, as amended, eliminates the requirement that a Contracting State withdraw an adjustment if the notification requirement of paragraph 3 has not been met. Paragraph 4 is also amended to delete the requirement that the taxpayer be notified at least six months before expiration of the six-year period specified in paragraph 3.

As amended by the Protocol, Article IX also explicitly authorizes the competent authorities to relieve double taxation in appropriate cases, even if the notification requirement is not satisfied. Paragraph 3 confirms that the competent authorities may agree to a corresponding adjustment if such an adjustment is not otherwise barred by time or procedural limitations such as the statute of limitations. Paragraph 4 provides that the competent authority of the State making the initial adjustment may grant unilateral relief from double taxation in other cases, although such relief is not obligatory.

**Technical Explanation [1984]:**

Paragraph 3 provides that where, pursuant to paragraph 1, an adjustment is made or to be made by a Contracting State, the other Contracting State shall make a corresponding adjustment to the income, loss, or tax of the related person in that other State, provided that the other State agrees with the adjustment and, within six years from the end of the taxable year of the person in the first State to which the adjustment relates, the competent authority of the other State has been notified in writing of the adjustment. The reference to an adjustment which "is made or to be made" does not require a Contracting State to formally propose an adjustment before paragraph 3 becomes pertinent. The notification required by paragraph 3 may be made by any of the related persons involved or by the competent authority of the State which makes or is to make the initial adjustment. The notification must give details regarding the adjustment sufficient to apprise the competent authority receiving the notification of the nature of the adjustment. If the requirements of paragraph 3 are complied with, the corresponding adjustment will be made by the other Contracting State notwithstanding any time or procedural limitations in the domestic law of that State.

**Notes:** Art. IX(3) amended by 1995 Protocol, generally effective 1996 (see Art. 21(2) under "Application of the 1995 Protocol" above). For 1985–1995, read:

> 3. Where an adjustment is made or to be made by a Contracting State in accordance with paragraph 1, the other Contracting State shall (notwithstanding any time or procedural limitations in the domestic law of that other State) make a corresponding adjustment to the income, loss or tax of the related person in that other State if:
>
> (a) it agrees with the first-mentioned adjustment; and
>
> (b) within six years from the end of the taxable year to which the first-mentioned adjustment relates, the competent authority of the other State has been notified of the first-mentioned adjustment.

**4. In the event that the notification referred to in paragraph 3 is not given within the time period referred to therein, and the competent authorities have not agreed to otherwise consider the case in accordance with paragraph 3(b), the competent authority of the Contracting State which has made or is to make the first-mentioned adjustment may provide relief from double taxation where appropriate.**

**Technical Explanation [1995 Protocol]:**

See under para. 3.

**Technical Explanation [1984]:**

Paragraph 4 provides that in a case where the other Contracting State has not been notified as provided in paragraph 3 and if the person whose income, loss, or tax is being adjusted has not received notification of the adjustment within five and one-half years from the end of its taxable year to which the adjustment relates, such adjustment shall not be made to the extent that the adjustment would give rise to double taxation between the United States and Canada. Again, the notification referred to in this paragraph need not be a formal adjustment, but it must be in writing and must contain sufficient details to permit the taxpayer to give the notification referred to in paragraph 3.

If, for example, the Internal Revenue Service proposes to make an adjustment to the income of a U.S. company pursuant to Code section 482, and the adjustment involves an allocation of income from a related Canadian company, the competent authority of Canada must receive written notification of the proposed IRS adjustment within six years from the end of the taxable year of the U.S. company to which the adjustment relates. If such notification is not received in a timely fashion and if the U.S. company does not receive written notification of the adjustment from the IRS within 5½ years from the end of its relevant taxable year, the IRS will unilaterally recede on the proposed section 482 adjustment to the extent that this adjustment would otherwise give rise to double taxation between the United States and Canada. The Internal Revenue Service will determine whether and to what extent the adjustment would give rise to double taxation with respect to income arising in Canada by examining the relevant facts and circumstances such as the amount of foreign tax credits attributable to Canadian taxes paid by the U.S. company, including any carryovers and credits for deemed paid taxes.

**Notes:** Art. IX(4) amended by 1995 Protocol, generally effective 1996 (see Art. 21(2) under "Application of the 1995 Protocol" above). For 1985–1995, read:

> 4. In the event that the notification referred to in paragraph 3 is not given within the time period referred to therein, and if the person to whom the first-mentioned adjustment relates has not received, at least six months prior to the expiration of such time period, notification of such adjustment from the Contracting State which has made or is to make such adjustment that State shall, notwithstanding the provisions of paragraph 1, not make the first-mentioned adjustment to the extent that such adjustment would give rise to double taxation.

**5. The provisions of paragraphs 3 and 4 shall not apply in the case of fraud, willful default or neglect or gross negligence.**

**Technical Explanation [1984]:**

Paragraph 5 provides that neither a corresponding adjustment described in paragraph 3 nor the cancelling of an adjustment described in paragraph 4 will be made in any case of fraud, willful default, neglect, or gross negligence on the part of the taxpayer or any related person.

Paragraphs 3 and 4 of Article IX are exceptions to the "saving clause" contained in paragraph 2 of Article XXIX (Miscellaneous Rules), as provided in paragraph 3(a) of Article XXIX. Paragraphs 3 and 4 of Article IX apply to adjustments made or to be made with respect to taxable years for which the Convention has effect as provided in paragraphs 2 and 5 of Article XXX (Entry Into Force).

**Notes:** For case law interpreting "fraud, wilful default or neglect", see the cases under ITA 152(4)(a)(i). For "gross negligence", see Notes to ITA 163(2).

## Article X — Dividends

**1. Dividends paid by a company which is a resident of a Contracting State to a resident of the other Contracting State may be taxed in that other State.**

**Technical Explanation [1984]:**

Paragraph 1 allows a Contracting State to impose tax on its residents with respect to dividends paid by a company which is a resident of the other Contracting State.

**2. However, such dividends may also be taxed in the Contracting State of which the company paying the dividends is a resident and according to the laws of that State; but if a resident of the other Contracting**

State is the beneficial owner of such dividends, the tax so charged shall not exceed:

(a) 5 per cent of the gross amount of the dividends if the beneficial owner is a company which owns at least 10 per cent of the voting stock of the company paying the dividends;

(b) 15 per cent of the gross amount of the dividends in all other cases.

This paragraph shall not affect the taxation of the company in respect of the profits out of which the dividends are paid.

### Proposed Amendment — Withholding Tax Rates

**Department of Finance news release, October 2, 1998**: *Canada and United States to Consult regarding Modifications to Income Tax Treaty*
[Reproduced before Article I — ed.]

**Technical Explanation [1995 Protocol]**:
See under para. 7.

**Technical Explanation [1984]**:
Paragraph 2 limits the amount of tax that may be imposed on such dividends by the Contracting State in which the company paying the dividends is resident if the beneficial owner of the dividends is a resident of the other Contracting State. The limitation is 10 percent of the gross amount of the dividends if the beneficial owner is a company that owns 10 percent or more of the voting stock of the company paying the dividends; and 15 percent of the gross amount of the dividends in all other cases. Paragraph 2 does not impose any restrictions with respect to taxation of the profits out of which the dividends are paid.

**Notes**: Art. X(2)(a) amended by 1995 Protocol, the 5% rate effective for amounts paid or credited in 1997 or later (see Art. 21(2)(a) under "Application of the 1995 Protocol" above). For 1996, the rate was 6%. From October 1984 through the end of 1995, the rate was 10%.

**3.** The term **"dividends"** as used in this Article means income from shares or other rights, not being debt-claims, participating in profits, as well as income subjected to the same taxation treatment as income from shares by the taxation laws of the State of which the company making the distribution is a resident.

**Technical Explanation [1984]**:
Paragraph 3 defines the term "dividends," as the term is used in this Article. Each Contracting State is permitted to apply its domestic law rules for differentiating dividends from interest and other disbursements.

**4.** The provisions of paragraph 2 shall not apply if the beneficial owner of the dividends, being a resident of a Contracting State, carries on business in the other Contracting State of which the company paying the dividends is a resident, through a permanent establishment situated therein, or performs in that other State independent personal services from a fixed base situated therein, and the holding in respect of which the dividends are paid is effectively connected with such permanent establishment or fixed base. In such case, the provisions of Article VII (Business Profits) or Article XIV (Independent Personal Services), as the case may be, shall apply.

**Technical Explanation [1984]**:
Paragraph 4 provides that the limitations of paragraph 2 do not apply if the beneficial owner of the dividends carries on business in the State in which the company paying the dividends is a resident through a permanent establishment or fixed base situated there, and the stockholding in respect of which the dividends are paid is effectively connected with such permanent establishment or fixed base. In such a case, the dividends are taxable pursuant to the provisions of Article VII (Business Profits) or Article XIV (Independent Personal Services), as the case may be. Thus, dividends paid in respect of holdings forming part of the assets of a permanent establishment or fixed base or which are otherwise effectively connected with such permanent establishment or fixed base (i.e., dividends attributable to the permanent establishment or fixed base) will be taxed on a net basis using the rates and rules of taxation generally applicable to residents of the State in which the permanent establishment or fixed base is situated.

**5.** Where a company is a resident of a Contracting State, the other Contracting State may not impose any tax on the dividends paid by the company, except insofar as such dividends are paid to a resident of that other State or insofar as the holding in respect of which the dividends are paid is effectively connected with a permanent establishment or a fixed base situated in that other State, nor subject the company's undistributed profits to a tax, even if the dividends paid or the undistributed profits consist wholly or partly of profits or income arising in such other State.

**Technical Explanation [1984]**:
Paragraph 5 imposes limitations on the right of Canada or the United States, as the case may be, to impose tax on dividends paid by a company which is a resident of the other Contracting State. The State in which the company is not resident may not tax such dividends except insofar as they are paid to a resident of that State or the holding in respect of which the dividends are paid is effectively connected with a permanent establishment or fixed base in that State. In the case of the United States, such dividends may also be taxed in the hands of a U.S. citizen and certain former citizens, pursuant to the "saving clause" of paragraph 2 of Article XXIX (Miscellaneous Rules). In addition, the Contracting State in which the company is not resident may not subject such company's undistributed profits to any tax. See, however, paragraphs 6, 7, and 8 which, in certain circumstances, qualify the rules of paragraph 5. Neither paragraph 5 nor any other provision of the Convention restricts the ability of the United States to apply the provisions of the Code concerning foreign personal holding companies and controlled foreign corporations.

**6.** Nothing in this Convention shall be construed as preventing a Contracting State from imposing a tax on the earnings of a company attributable to permanent establishments in that State, in addition to the tax which would be chargeable on the earnings of a company which is a resident of that State, provided that any additional tax so imposed shall not exceed 5 per cent of the amount of such earnings which have not been subjected to such additional tax in previous taxation years. For the purposes of this paragraph, the term "earnings" means the amount by which the business profits attributable to permanent establishments in a Contracting State (including gains from the alienation of property forming part of the business property of such permanent establishments) in a year and previous years exceeds the sum of:

(a) business losses attributable to such permanent establishments (including losses from the alienation of property forming part of the business property of such permanent establishments) in such year and previous years;

(b) all taxes, other than the additional tax referred to in this paragraph, imposed on such profits in that State;

(c) the profits reinvested in that State, provided that where that State is Canada, such amount shall be determined in accordance with the existing provisions of the law of Canada regarding the computation of the allowance in respect of investment in property in Canada, and any subsequent modification of those provisions which shall not affect the general principle hereof; and

(d) five hundred thousand Canadian dollars ($500,000) or its equivalent in United States currency, less any amounts deducted by the company, or by an associated company with respect to the same or a similar business, under this subparagraph (d); for the purposes of this subparagraph (d) a company is associated with another company if one company directly or indirectly controls the other, or both companies are directly or indirectly controlled by the same person or persons, or if the two companies deal with each other not at arm's length.

**Technical Explanation [1995 Protocol]:**

See under para. 7.

**Technical Explanation [1984]:**

Paragraph 6 provides that, notwithstanding paragraph 5, a Contracting State in which is maintained a permanent establishment or permanent establishments of a company resident in the other Contracting State may impose tax on such company's earnings, in addition to the tax that would be charged on the earnings of a company resident in that State. The additional tax may not, however, exceed 10 percent of the amount of the earnings which have not been subjected to such additional tax in previous taxation years. Thus, Canada, which has a branch profits tax in force, may impose that tax up to the 10 percent limitation in the case of a United States company with one or more permanent establishments in Canada. This branch profits tax may be imposed notwithstanding other rules of the Convention, including paragraph 6 of Article XXV (Non-Discrimination).

For purposes of paragraph 6, the term "earnings" means the excess of business profits attributable to all permanent establishments for a year and previous years over the sum of: a) business losses attributable to such permanent establishments for such years; b) all taxes on profits, whether or not covered by the Convention (e.g., provincial taxes on profits and provincial resource royalties (which Canada considers "taxes") in excess of the mineral resource allowance provided for under the law of Canada), other than the additional tax referred to in paragraph 6; c) profits reinvested in such State; and d) $500,000 (Canadian, or its equivalent in U.S. dollars) less any amounts deducted under paragraph 6(d) with respect to the same or a similar business by the company or an associated company. The deduction under paragraph 6(d) is available as of the first year for which the Convention has effect, regardless of the prior earnings and tax expenses, if any, of the permanent establishment. The $500,000 deduction is taken into account after other deductions, and is permanent. For the purpose of paragraph 6, references to business profits and business losses include gains and losses from the alienation of property forming part of the business property of a permanent establishment. The term "associated company" includes a company which directly or indirectly controls another company or two companies directly or indirectly controlled by the same person or persons, as well as any two companies that deal with each other not at arm's length. This definition differs from the definition of "related persons" in paragraph 2 of Article IX (Related Persons).

**Related Provisions:** ITA 219 — Branch tax.

**Notes:** Opening words of Art. X(6) amended by 1995 Protocol, the 5% rate effective for taxable years beginning in 1997 or later (see Art. 21(2)(b) under "Application of the Provisions of the Protocol" above). For 1996, the rate was 6%. For 1985–1995, the rate was 10%.

**7.** Notwithstanding the provisions of paragraph 2,

(a) dividends paid by a company that is a resident of Canada and a non-resident-owned investment corporation to a company that is a resident of the United States, that owns at least 10 per cent of the voting stock of the company paying the dividends and that is the beneficial owner of such dividends, may be taxed in Canada at a rate not exceeding 10 per cent of the gross amount of the dividends;

(b) paragraph 2(b) and not paragraph 2(a) shall apply in the case of dividends paid by a resident of the United States that is a Regulated Investment Company; and

(c) Paragraph 2(a) shall not apply to dividends paid by a resident of the United States that is a Real Estate Investment Trust, and paragraph 2(b) shall apply only where such dividends are beneficially owned by an individual holding an interest of less than 10 per cent in the trust; otherwise the rate of tax applicable under the domestic law of the United States shall apply. Where an estate or a testamentary trust acquired its interest in a Real Estate Investment Trust as a consequence of an individual's death, for the purposes of the preceding sentence the estate or trust shall for the five-year period following the death be deemed with respect to that interest to be an individual.

**Technical Explanation [1995 Protocol]:**

Article 5 of the Protocol amends Article X (Dividends) of the Convention. Paragraph 1 of Article 5 amends paragraph 2(a) of Article X to reduce from 10 percent to 5 percent the maximum rate of tax that may be imposed by a Contracting State on the gross amount of dividends beneficially owned by a company resident in the other Contracting State that owns at least 10 percent of the voting stock of the company paying the dividends. The rate at which the branch profits tax may be imposed under paragraph 6 is also reduced by paragraph 1 of Article 5 from 10 percent to 5 percent. Under the entry-into-force provisions of Article 21 of the Protocol, these reductions will be phased in over a three-year period.

Paragraph 2 of Article 5 of the Protocol replaces paragraph 7 of Article X of the Convention with a new paragraph 7. Paragraph 7 of the existing Convention is no longer relevant because it applies only in the case where a Contracting State does not impose a branch profits tax. Both Contracting States now do impose such a tax.

New paragraph 7 makes the 5 percent withholding rate of new paragraph 2(a) inapplicable in certain situations. Under new paragraph 7(b), dividends paid by U.S. regulated investment companies (RICs) are denied the 5 percent withholding rate even if the Canadian shareholder is a corporation that would otherwise qualify as a direct investor by satisfying the 10-percent ownership requirement. Consequently, all RIC dividends to Canadian beneficial owners are subjected to the 15 percent rate that applies to dividends paid to portfolio investors.

Dividends paid by U.S. real estate investment trusts (REITs) to Canadian beneficial owners are also denied the 5 percent rate under the rules of paragraph 7(c). REIT dividends paid to individuals who own less than a 10 percent interest in the REIT are subject to withholding at a maximum rate of 15 percent. Paragraph 7(c) also provides that dividend distributions by a REIT to an estate or a testamentary trust acquiring the interest in the REIT as a consequence of the death of an individual will be treated as distributions to an individual, for the five-year period following the death. Thus, dividends paid to an estate or testamentary trust in respect of a holding of less than a 10 percent interest in the REIT also will be entitled to the 15 percent rate of withholding, but only for up to five years after the death. REIT dividends paid to other Canadian beneficial owners are subject to the rate of withholding tax that applies under the domestic law of the United States (i.e., 30 percent).

The denial of the 5 percent withholding rate at source to all RIC and REIT shareholders, and the denial of the 15 percent rate to most shareholders of REITs, is intended to prevent the use of these nontaxable conduit entities to gain unjustifiable benefits for certain shareholders. For example, a Canadian corporation that wishes to hold a portfolio of U.S. corporate shares may hold the portfolio directly and pay a U.S. withholding tax of 15 percent on all of the dividends that it receives. Alternatively, it may place the portfolio of U.S. stocks in a RIC, in which the Canadian corporation owns more than 10 percent of the shares, but in which there are enough small shareholders to satisfy the RIC diversified ownership requirements. Since the RIC is a pure conduit, there are no U.S. tax costs to the Canadian corporation of interposing the RIC as an intermediary in the chain of ownership. It is unlikely that a 10 percent shareholding in a RIC will constitute a 10 percent shareholding in any company from which the dividends originate. In the absence of the special rules in paragraph 7(b), however, interposition of a RIC would transform what should be portfolio dividends into direct investment dividends taxable at source by the United States only at 5 percent. The special rules of paragraph 7 prevent this.

Similarly, a resident of Canada may hold U.S. real property directly and pay U.S. tax either at a 30 percent rate on the gross income or at the income tax rates specified in the *Internal Revenue Code* on the net income. By placing the real estate holding in a REIT, the Canadian investor could transform real estate income into dividend income and thus transform high-taxed income into much lower-taxed income. In the absence of the special rule, if the REIT shareholder were a Canadian corporation that owned at least a 10 percent interest in the REIT, the withholding rate would be 5 percent; in all other cases, it would be 15 percent. In either event, with one exception, a tax rate of 30 percent or more would be significantly reduced. The exception is the relatively small individual Canadian investor who might be subject to U.S. tax at a rate of only 15 percent on the net income even if he earned the real estate income directly. Under the rule in paragraph 7(c), such individuals, defined as those holding less than a 10 percent interest in the REIT, remain taxable at source at a 15 percent rate.

Subparagraph (a) of paragraph 7 provides a special rule for certain dividends paid by Canadian non-resident-owned investment corporations ("NROs"). The subparagraph provides for a maximum rate of 10 percent (instead of the standard rate of 5 percent) for dividends paid by NROs that are Canadian residents to a U.S. company that owns 10 percent or more of the voting stock of the NRO and that is the beneficial owner of the dividend. This rule maintains the rate available under the current Convention for dividends from NROs. Canada wanted the withholding rate for direct investment NRO dividends to be no lower than the maximum withholding rates under the Convention on interest and royalties, to make sure that a foreign investor cannot transform interest or royalty income subject to a 10 percent withholding tax into direct dividends qualifying for a 5 percent withholding tax by passing it through to an NRO.

### Technical Explanation [1984]:

Paragraph 7 provides that, notwithstanding paragraph 5, a Contracting State that does not impose a branch profits tax as described in paragraph 6 (i.e., under current law, the United States) may tax a dividend paid by a company which is a resident of the other Contracting State if at least 50 percent of the company's gross income from all sources was included in the computation of business profits attributable to one or more permanent establishments which such company had in the first-mentioned State. The dividend subject to such a tax must, however, be attributable to profits earned by the company in taxable years beginning after September 26, 1980 and the 50 percent test must be met for the three-year period preceding the taxable year of the company in which the dividend is declared (including years ending on or before September 26, 1980) or such shorter period as the company had been in existence prior to that taxable year. Dividends will be deemed to be distributed, for purposes of paragraph 7, first out of profits of the taxation year of the company in which the distribution is made and then out of the profits of the preceding year or years of the company. Paragraph 7 provides further that if a resident of the other Contracting State is the beneficial owner of such dividends, any tax imposed under paragraph 7 is subject to the 10 or 15 percent limitation of paragraph 2 or the rules of paragraph 4 (providing for dividends to be taxed as business profits or income from independent personal services), as the case may be.

**Notes:** Art. X(7) amended by 1995 Protocol, effective for amounts paid or credited in 1996 or later (see Art. 21(2)(a) under "Application of the 1995 Protocol" above). From October 1984 through the end of 1995, read:

> 7. Notwithstanding the provisions of paragraph 5, a Contracting State, other than a Contracting State that imposes the additional tax on earnings referred to in paragraph 6, may tax a dividend paid by a company to the extent that the dividend is attributable to profits earned in taxable years beginning after the date of signature of the Convention if, for the three-year period ending with the close of the company's taxable period preceding the declaration of the dividend (or for such part of that three-year period as the company has been in existence, or for the first taxable year if the dividend was declared in that taxable year), at least 50 per cent of such company's gross income from all sources was included in the computation of the business profits attributable to a permanent establishment which such company had in that State; provided that where a resident of the other Contracting State is the beneficial owner of such dividend any tax so imposed on the dividend shall be subject to the limitations of paragraph 2 or the rules of paragraph 4, as the case may be.

**8. Notwithstanding the provisions of paragraph 5, a company which is a resident of Canada and which has income subject to tax in the United States (without regard to the provisions of the Convention) may be liable to the United States accumulated earnings tax and personal holding company tax but only if 50 per cent or more in value of the outstanding voting shares of the company is owned, directly or indirectly, throughout the last half of its taxable year by citizens or residents of the United States (other than citizens of Canada who do not have immigrant status in the United States or who have not been residents in the United States for more than three taxable years) or by residents of a third state.**

**Technical Explanation [1984]:**

Paragraph 8 provides that, notwithstanding paragraph 5, a company which is a resident of Canada and which, absent the provisions of the Convention, has income subject to tax by the United States may be liable for the United States accumulated earnings tax and personal holding company tax. These taxes can be applied, however, only if 50 percent or more in value of the outstanding voting shares of the company is owned, directly or indirectly, throughout the last half of its taxable year by residents of a third State or by citizens or residents of the United States, other than citizens of Canada who are resident in the United States but who either do not have immigrant status in the United States or who have not been resident in the United States for more than three taxable years. The accumulated earnings tax is applied to accumulated taxable income calculated without the benefits of the Convention. Similarly, the personal holding company tax is applied to undistributed personal holding company income computed as if the Convention had not come into force.

Article X does not apply to dividends paid by a company which is not a resident of either Contracting State. Such dividends, if they are income of a resident of one of the Contracting States, are subject to tax as provided in Article XXII (Other Income).

**Information Circulars:** 76-12R4: Applicable rate of part XIII tax on amounts paid or credited to persons in treaty countries.

## Article XI — Interest

1. Interest arising in a Contracting State and paid to a resident of the other Contracting State may be taxed in that other State.

**Technical Explanation [1984]:**

Paragraph 1 allows interest arising in Canada or the United States and paid to a resident of the other State to be taxed in the latter State. Paragraph 2 provides that such interest may also be taxed in the Contracting State where it arises, but if a resident of the other Contracting State is the beneficial owner, the tax imposed by the State of source is limited to 15 percent of the gross amount of the interest.

2. However, such interest may also be taxed in the Contracting State in which it arises, and according to the laws of that State; but if a resident of the other Contracting State is the beneficial owner of such interest, the tax so charged shall not exceed 10 per cent of the gross amount of the interest.

**Proposed Amendment — Withholding Tax Rates**

**Department of Finance news release, October 2, 1998**: *Canada and United States to Consult regarding Modifications to Income Tax Treaty*

[Reproduced before Article I — ed.]

**Technical Explanation [1995 Protocol]:**

Article 6 of the Protocol amends Article XI (Interest) of the Convention. Paragraph 1 of the Article reduces the general maximum withholding rate on interest under paragraph 2 of Article XI from 15 percent to 10 percent.

**Technical Explanation [1984]:**

See Article XI, para. 1.

**Notes:** Art. XI(2) amended by 1995 Protocol, the 10% rate effective for amounts paid or credited in 1996 or later (see Art. 21(2)(a) under "Application of the 1995 Protocol" above). From October 1984 through the end of 1995, the rate was 15%.

3. Notwithstanding the provisions of paragraph 2, interest arising in a Contracting State shall be exempt from tax in that State if:

(a) the interest is beneficially owned by the other Contracting State, a political subdivision or local authority thereof or an instrumentality of such other State, subdivision or authority, and is not subject to tax by that other State;

(b) the interest is beneficially owned by a resident of the other Contracting State and is paid with respect to debt obligations issued at arm's length and guaranteed or insured by that other State or a political subdivision thereof or an instrumentality of such other State or subdivision which is not subject to tax by that other State;

(c) the interest is beneficially owned by a resident of the other Contracting State and is paid by the first-mentioned State, a political subdivision or local authority thereof or an instrumentality of such first-mentioned State, subdivision or authority which is not subject to tax by that first-mentioned State;

(d) the interest is beneficially owned by a resident of the other Contracting State and is paid with respect to indebtedness arising as a consequence of the sale on credit by a resident of that other State of any equipment, merchandise or services except where the sale or indebtedness was between related persons; or

(e) the interest is paid by a company created under the laws in force in the other Contracting State with respect to an obligation entered into before the date of signature of this Convention, provided that such interest would have been exempt from tax in the first-mentioned State under Article XII of the 1942 Convention.

**Technical Explanation [1995 Protocol]:**

Paragraph 3 of Article XI of the Convention provides that, notwithstanding the general withholding rate applicable to interest payments under paragraph 2, certain specified categories of interest are exempt from withholding at source. Paragraph 2 of Article 6 of the Protocol amends paragraph 3(d) of the Convention, which deals with interest paid on indebtedness arising in connection with a sale on credit of equipment, merchandise, or services. The exemption provided by that paragraph in the Convention is broadened under the Protocol to apply to interest that is beneficially owned either by the seller in the underlying transaction, as under the present Convention, or by any beneficial owner of interest paid with respect to an indebtedness arising as a result of the sale on credit of equipment, merchandise, or services. This exemption, however, does not apply in cases where the purchaser is related to the seller or the debtor is related to the beneficial owner of the interest. The negotiators agreed that this exemption is subject, as are the other provisions of the Convention, to any anti-avoidance rules applicable under the respective domestic law of the Contracting States.

The reference to "related persons" in paragraph 3(d) of Article XI of the Convention, as amended, is a change from the present Convention, which refers to "persons dealing at arm's length." The term "related person" as used in this Article is not defined for purposes of the Convention. Accordingly, the meaning of the term, and, therefore, the application of this Article, will be governed by the domestic law of each Contracting State (as is true with the use of the term "arm's-length" under the current Convention) under the interpetative rule of paragraph 2 of Article III (General Definitions). The United States will define the term "related person" as under section 482 of the *Internal Revenue Code*, to include organizations, trades, or businesses (whether or not incorporated, whether or not organized in the United States, and whether or not affiliated) owned or controlled directly or indirectly by the same interests. The Canadian definition of "related persons" is found in section 251 of the *Income Tax Act*.

**Technical Explanation [1984]:**

Paragraph 3 provides a number of exceptions to the right of the source State to impose a 15 percent tax under paragraph 2. The following types of interest beneficially owned by a resident of a Contracting State are exempt from tax in the State of source: a) interest beneficially owned by a Contracting State, a political subdivision, or a local authority thereof, or an instrumentality of such State, subdivision, or authority, which interest is not subject to tax by such State; b) interest beneficially owned by a resident of a Contracting State and paid with respect to debt obligations issued at arm's length which are guaranteed or insured by such State or a political subdivision thereof, or by an instrumentality of such State or subdivision (not by a local authority or an instrumentality thereof), but only if the guarantor or insurer is not subject to tax by that State; c) interest paid by a Contracting State, a political subdivision, or a local authority thereof, or by an instrumentality of such State, subdivision, or authority, but only if the payer is not subject to tax by such State; and d) interest beneficially owned by a seller of equipment, merchandise, or services, but only if the interest is paid in connection with a sale on credit of equipment, merchandise, or services and the sale was made at arm's length. Whether such a transaction is made at arm's length will be determined in the United States under the facts and circumstances. The relationship between the parties is a factor, but not the only factor, taken into account in making this determination. Furthermore, interest paid by a company resident in the other Contracting State with respect to an obligation entered into before September 26, 1980 is exempt from tax in the State of source (irrespective of the State of residence of the beneficial owner), provided that such interest would have been exempt from tax in the Contracting State of source under Article XII of the 1942 Convention. Thus, interest paid by a United States corporation whose business is not managed and controlled in Canada to a recipient not resident in Canada or to a corporation not managed and controlled in Canada would be exempt from Canadian tax as long as the debt obligation was entered into before September 26, 1980. The phrase "not subject to tax by that ... State" in paragraph 3(a), (b), and (c) refers to taxation at the Federal levels of Canada and the United States.

The phrase "obligation entered into before the date of signature of this Convention" means: (1) any obligation under which funds were dispersed prior to September 26, 1980; (2) any obligation under which funds are dispersed on or after September 26, 1980, pursuant to a written contract binding prior to and on such date, and at all times thereafter until the obligation is satisfied; or (3) any obligation with respect to which, prior to September 26, 1980, a lender had taken every action to signify approval under procedures ordinarily employed by such lender in similar transactions and had sent or deposited for delivery to the person to whom the loan is to be made written evidence of such approval in the form of a document setting forth, or referring to a document sent by the person to whom the loan is to be made that sets forth, the principal terms of such loan.

**Notes**: Art. XI(3)(d) amended by 1995 Protocol, effective for amounts paid or credited in 1996 or later (see Art. 21(2)(a) under "Application of the 1995 Protocol" above. From October 1984 through the end of 1995, read:

> (d) the interest is beneficially owned by a seller who is a resident of the other Contracting State and is paid by a purchaser in connection with the sale on credit of any equipment, merchandise or services, except where the sale is made between persons dealing with each other not at arm's length; or

**4.** The term **"interest"** as used in this Article means income from debt-claims of every kind, whether or not secured by mortgage, and whether or not carrying a right to participate in the debtor's profits, and in particular, income from government securities and income from bonds or debentures, including premiums and prizes attaching to such securities, bonds or debentures, as well as income assimilated to income from money lent by the taxation laws of the Contracting State in which the income arises. However, the term "interest" does not include income dealt with in Article X (Dividends).

**Technical Explanation [1984]:**

Paragraph 4 defines the term "interest," as used in Article XI, to include, among other things, debt claims of every kind as well as income assimilated to income from money lent by the taxation laws of the Contracting State in which the income arises. In no event, however, is income dealt with in Article X (Dividends) to be considered interest.

**5.** The provisions of paragraphs 2 and 3 shall not apply if the beneficial owner of the interest, being a resident of a Contracting State, carries on business in the other Contracting State in which the interest arises, through a permanent establishment situated therein, or performs in that other State independent personal services from a fixed base situated therein, and the debt-claim in respect of which the interest is paid is effectively connected with such permanent establishment or fixed base. In such case, the provisions of Article VII (Business Profits) or Article XIV (Independent Personal Services), as the case may be, shall apply.

**Technical Explanation [1984]:**

Paragraph 5 provides that neither the 15 percent limitation on tax in the Contracting State of source provided in paragraph 2 nor the various exemptions from tax in such State provided in paragraph 3 apply if the beneficial owner of the interest is a resident of the other Contracting State carrying on business in the State of source through a permanent establishment or fixed base, and the debt claim in respect of which the interest is paid is effectively connected with such permanent establishment or fixed base (i.e., the interest is attributable to the permanent establishment or fixed base). In this case, interest income is to be taxed in the Contracting State of source as business profits — that is, on a net basis.

**6.** For the purposes of this Article, interest shall be deemed to arise in a Contracting State when the payer is that State itself, or a political subdivision, local authority or resident of that State. Where, however, the person paying the interest, whether he is a resident of a Contracting State or not, has in a State other than that of which he is a resident a permanent establishment or a fixed base in connection with which the indebtedness on which the interest is paid was incurred, and such interest is borne by such permanent establishment or fixed base, then such interest shall be deemed to arise in the State in which the permanent establishment or fixed base is situated and not in the State of which the payer is a resident.

**Technical Explanation [1984]**:

Paragraph 6 establishes the source of interest for purposes of Article XI. Interest is considered to arise in a Contracting State if the payer is that State, or a political subdivision, local authority, or resident of that State. However, in cases where the person paying the interest, whether a resident of a Contracting State or of a third State, has in a State other than that of which he is a resident a permanent establishment or fixed base in connection with which the indebtedness on which the interest was paid was incurred, and such interest is borne by the permanent establishment or fixed base, then such interest is deemed to arise in the State in which the permanent establishment or fixed base is situated and not in the State of the payer's residence. Thus, pursuant to paragraphs 6 and 2, and Article XXII (Other Income), Canadian tax will not be imposed on interest paid to a U.S. resident by a company resident in Canada if the indebtedness is incurred in connection with, and the interest is borne by, a permanent establishment of the company situated in a third State. "Borne by" means allowable as a deduction in computing taxable income.

**7.** Where, by reason of a special relationship between the payer and the beneficial owner or between both of them and some other person, the amount of the interest, having regard to the debt-claim for which it is paid, exceeds the amount which would have been agreed upon by the payer and the beneficial owner in the absence of such relationship, the provisions of this Article shall apply only to the last-mentioned amount. In such case, the excess part of the payments shall remain taxable according to the laws of each Contracting State, due regard being had to the other provisions of the Convention.

**Technical Explanation [1984]**:

Paragraph 7 provides that in cases involving special relationships between persons Article XI does not apply to amounts in excess of the amount which would have been agreed upon between persons having no special relationship; any such excess amount remains taxable according to the laws of Canada and the United States, consistent with any relevant provisions of the Convention.

**8.** Where a resident of a Contracting State pays interest to a person other than a resident of the other Contracting State, that other State may not impose any tax on such interest except insofar as it arises in that other State or insofar as the debt-claim in respect of which the interest is paid is effectively connected with a permanent establishment or a fixed base situated in that other State.

**Technical Explanation [1984]**:

Paragraph 8 restricts the right of a Contracting State to impose tax on interest paid by a resident of the other Contracting State. The first State may not impose any tax on such interest except insofar as the interest is paid to a resident of that State or arises in that State or the debt claim in respect of which the interest is paid is effectively connected with a permanent establishment or fixed base situated in that State. Thus, pursuant to paragraph 8 the United States has agreed not to impose tax on certain interest paid by Canadian companies to persons not resident in the United States, to the extent that such companies would pay U.S.-source interest under Code section 861(a)(1)(C) but not under the source rule of paragraph 6. It is to be noted that paragraph 8 is subject to the "saving clause" of paragraph 2 of Article XXIX (Miscellaneous Rules), so the United States may in all events impose its tax on interest received by U.S. citizens.

**9.** The provisions of paragraphs 2 and 3 shall not apply to an excess inclusion with respect to a residual interest in a Real Estate Mortgage Investment Conduit to which Section 860G of the United States *Internal Revenue Code*, as it may be amended from time to time without changing the general principle thereof, applies.

**Technical Explanation [1995 Protocol]**:

Paragraph 3 of Article 6 of the Protocol adds a new paragraph 9 to Article XI of the Convention. Although the definition of "interest" in paragraph 4 includes an excess inclusion with respect to a residual interest in a real estate mortgage investment conduit (REMIC) described in section 860G of the *Internal Revenue Code*, new paragraph 9 provides that the reduced rates of tax at source for interest provided for in paragraphs 2 and 3 do not apply to such income. This class of interest, therefore, remains subject to the statutory 30 percent U.S. rate of tax at source. The legislation that created REMICs in 1986 provided that such excess inclusions were to be taxed at the full 30 percent statutory rate, regardless of any then-existing treaty provisions to the contrary. The 30 percent rate of tax on excess inclusions received by residents of Canada is consistent with this expression of Congressional intent.

**Notes**: Art. XI(9) added by 1995 Protocol, effective for amounts paid or credited in 1996 or later (see Art. 21(2)(a) under "Application of the Provisions of the Protocol" above).

**Information Circulars [Article XI]**: 76-12R4: Applicable rate of part XIII tax on amounts paid or credited to persons in treaty countries.

## Article XII — Royalties

**1.** Royalties arising in a Contracting State and paid to a resident of the other Contracting State may be taxed in that other State.

**Technical Explanation [1984]**:

Generally speaking, under the 1942 Convention royalties, including royalties with respect to motion picture films, which are derived by a resident of one Contracting State from sources within the other Contracting State are taxed at a maximum rate of 15 percent in the latter State; copyright royalties are exempt from tax in the State of source, if the resident does not have a permanent establishment in that State. See Articles II, III, XIII C, and paragraph 1 of Article XI of the 1942 Convention, and paragraph 6(a) of the Protocol to the 1942 Convention.

Paragraph 1 of Article XII of the Convention provides that a Contracting State may tax its residents with respect to royalties arising in the other Contracting State. Paragraph 2 provides that such royalties may also be taxed in the Contracting State in which they arise, but that if a resident of the other Contracting State is the beneficial owner of the royalties the tax in the Contracting State of source is limited to 10 percent of the gross amount of the royalties.

**2.** However, such royalties may also be taxed in the Contracting State in which they arise, and according to the laws of that State; but if a resident of the other Contracting State is the beneficial owner of such royalties, the tax so charged shall not exceed 10 per cent of the gross amount of the royalties.

**Proposed Amendment — Withholding Tax Rates**
**Department of Finance news release, October 2, 1998**: *Canada and United States to Consult regarding Modifications to Income Tax Treaty*

# Art. XII  Canada–U.S. Tax Convention

[Reproduced before Article I — ed.]

**Technical Explanation [1984]:**

See Article XII, para. 1.

**Notes:** For the meaning of "resident" in this context, see Notes to Art. IV(1).

3. Notwithstanding the provisions of paragraph 2,

(a) copyright royalties and other like payments in respect of the production or reproduction of any literary, dramatic, musical or artistic work (other than payments in respect of motion pictures and works on film, videotape or other means of reproduction for use in connection with television);

(b) payments for the use of, or the right to use, computer software;

(c) payments for the use of, or the right to use, any patent or any information concerning industrial, commercial or scientific experience (but not including any such information provided in connection with a rental or franchise agreement); and

(d) payments with respect to broadcasting as may be agreed for the purposes of this paragraph in an exchange of notes between the Contracting States;

arising in a Contracting State and beneficially owned by a resident of the other Contracting State shall be taxable only in that other State.

**Technical Explanation [1995 Protocol]:**

Article 7 of the Protocol modifies Article XII (Royalties) of the Convention by expanding the classes of royalties exempt from withholding of tax at source. Paragraph 3, as amended by the Protocol, identifies four classes of royalty payments arising in one Contracting State and beneficially owned by a resident of the other that are exempt at source: (1) subparagraph (a) preserves the exemption in paragraph 3 of the present Convention for copyright royalties in respect of literary and other works, other than certain such payments in respect of motion pictures, videotapes, and similar payments; (2) subparagraph (b) specifies that computer software royalties are also exempt; (3) subparagraph (c) adds royalties paid for the use of, or the right to use, patents and information concerning industrial, commercial, and scientific experience, other than payments in connection with rental or franchise agreements; and (4) subparagraph (d) allows the Contracting States to reach an agreement, through an exchange of diplomatic notes, with respect to the application of paragraph 3 of Article XII to payments in respect of certain live broadcasting transmissions.

The specific reference to software in subparagraph (b) is not intended to suggest that the United States views the term "copyright" as excluding software in other U.S. treaties (including the current treaty with Canada).

The negotiators agreed that royalties paid for the use of, or the right to use, designs or models, plans, secret formulas, or processes are included under subparagraph (c) to the extent that they represent payments for the use of, or the right to use, information concerning industrial, commercial, or scientific experience. In addition, they agreed that royalties paid for the use of, or the right to use, "know-how," as defined in paragraph 11 of the Commentary on Article 12 of the OECD Model Income Tax Treaty, constitute payments for the use of, or the right to use, information concerning industrial, commercial, or scientific experience. The negotiators further agreed that a royalty paid under a "mixed contract," "package fee," or similar arrangement will be treated as exempt at source by virtue of paragraph 3 to the extent of any portion that is paid for the use of, or the right to use, property or information with respect to which paragraph 3 grants an exemption.

The exemption granted under subparagraph 3(c) does not, however, extend to payments made for information concerning industrial, commercial, or scientific experience that is provided in connection with a rental or franchise agreement. For this purpose, the negotiators agreed that a franchise is to be distinguished from other arrangements resulting in the transfer of intangible property. They agreed that a license to use intangibles (whether or not including a trademark) in a territory, in and of itself, would not constitute a franchise agreement for purposes of subparagraph 3(c) in the absence of other rights and obligations in the license agreement or in any other agreement that would indicate that the arrangement in its totality constituted a franchise agreement. For example, a resident of one Contracting State may acquire a right to use a secret formula to manufacture a particular product (e.g., a perfume), together with the right to use a trademark for that product and to market it at a non-retail level, in the other Contracting State. Such an arrangement would not constitute a franchise in the absence of any other rights or obligations under that arrangement or any other agreement that would indicate that the arrangement in its totality constituted a franchise agreement. Therefore, the royalty payment under that arrangement would be exempt from withholding tax in the other Contracting State to the extent made for the use of, or the right to use, the secret formula or other information concerning industrial, commercial, or scientific experience; however, it would be subject to withholding tax at a rate of 10 percent, to the extent made for the use of, or the right to use, the trademark.

The provisions of paragraph 3 do not fully reflect the U.S. treaty policy of exempting all types of royalty payments from taxation at source, but Canada was not prepared to grant a complete exemption for all types of royalties in the Protocol. Although the Protocol makes several important changes to the royalty provisions of the present Convention in the direction of bringing Article XII into conformity with U.S. policy, the United States remains concerned about the imposition of withholding tax on some classes of royalties and about the associated administrative burdens. In this connection, the Contracting States have affirmed their intention to collaborate to resolve in good faith any administrative issues that may arise in applying the provisions of subparagraph 3(c). The United States intends to continue to pursue a zero rate of withholding for all royalties in future negotiations with Canada, including discussions under Article 20 of the Protocol, as well as in negotiations with other countries.

As noted above, new subparagraph 3(d) enables the Contracting States to provide an exemption for royalties paid with respect to broadcasting through an exchange of notes. This provision was included because Canada was not prepared at the time of the negotiations to commit to an exemption for broadcasting royalties. Subparagraph 3(d) was included to enable the Senate to give its advice and consent in advance to such an exemption, in the hope that such an exemption could be obtained without awaiting the negotiation of another full protocol. Any agreement reached under the exchange of notes authorized by subparagraph 3(d) would lower the withholding rate from 10 percent to zero and, thus, bring the Convention into greater conformity with established U.S. treaty policy.

**Technical Explanation [1984]:**

Paragraph 3 provides that, notwithstanding paragraph 2, copyright royalties and other like payments in respect of the production or reproduction of any literary, dramatic, musical, or artistic work, including royalties from such works on videotape or other means of reproduction for private (home) use, if beneficially owned by a resident of the other Contracting State, may not be taxed by the Contracting State of source. This exemption at source does not apply to royalties in respect of motion pictures, and of works on film, videotape or other means of reproduction for use in connection with television broadcasting. Such royalties are subject to tax at a maximum rate of 10 percent in the Contracting State in which they arise, as provided in paragraph 2 (unless the provisions of paragraph 5, described below, apply).

## Art. XII — Royalties

**Notes:** Art. XII(3) amended by 1995 Protocol (effectively to add paras. (b)–(d)), effective for amounts paid or credited in 1996 or later (see Art. 21(2)(a) under "Application of the 1995 Protocol" above). From October 1984 through the end of 1995, read:

> 3. Notwithstanding the provisions of paragraph 2, copyright royalties and other like payments in respect of the production or reproduction of any literary, dramatic, musical or artistic work (but not including royalties in respect of motion pictures and works on film, videotape or other means of reproduction for use in connection with television) arising in a Contracting State and beneficially owned by a resident of the other Contracting State shall be taxable only in that other State.

For a thorough overview of these rules, see Catherine Brown, "The 1995 Canada-US Protocol: The Scope of the New Royalty Provisions", 43(3) *Canadian Tax Journal* 592–609 (1995).

**4.** The term **"royalties"** as used in this Article means payments of any kind received as a consideration for the use of, or the right to use, any copyright of literary, artistic or scientific work (including motion pictures and works on film, videotape or other means of reproduction for use in connection with television), any patent, trade mark, design or model, plan, secret formula or process, or for the use of, or the right to use, tangible personal property or for information concerning industrial, commercial or scientific experience, and, notwithstanding the provisions of Article XIII (Gains), includes gains from the alienation of any intangible property or rights described in this paragraph to the extent that such gains are contingent on the productivity, use or subsequent disposition of such property or rights.

**Technical Explanation [1984]:**

Paragraph 4 defines the term "royalties" for purposes of Article XII. "Royalties" means payments of any kind received as consideration for the use of or the right to use any copyright of literary, artistic, or scientific work, including motion pictures, and works on film, videotape or other means of reproduction for use in connection with television broadcasting, any patent, trademark, design or model, plan, secret formula or process, or any payment for the use of or the right to use tangible personal property or for information concerning industrial, commercial, or scientific experience. The term "royalties" also includes gains from the alienation of any intangible property or rights described in paragraph 4 to the extent that such gains are contingent on the productivity, use, or subsequent disposition of such intangible property or rights. Thus, a guaranteed minimum payment derived from the alienation of (but not the use of) any right or property described in paragraph 4 is not a "royalty." Any amounts deemed contingent on use by reason of Code section 871(e) are, however, royalties under paragraph 2 of Article III (General Definitions), subject to Article XXVI (Mutual Agreement Procedure). The term "royalties" does not encompass management fees, which are covered by the provisions of Article VII (Business Profits) or XIV (Independent Personal Services), or payments under a bona fide cost-sharing arrangement. Technical service fees may be royalties in cases where the fees are periodic and dependent upon productivity or a similar measure.

**5.** The provisions of paragraphs 2 and 3 shall not apply if the beneficial owner of the royalties, being a resident of a Contracting State, carries on business in the other Contracting State in which the royalties arise, through a permanent establishment situated therein, or performs in that other State independent personal services from a fixed base situated therein, and the right or property in respect of which the royalties are paid is effectively connected with such permanent establishment or fixed base. In such case the provisions of Article VII (Business Profits) or Article XIV (Independent Personal Services), as the case may be, shall apply.

**Technical Explanation [1984]:**

Paragraph 5 provides that the 10 percent limitation on tax in the Contracting State of source provided by paragraph 2, and the exemption in the Contracting State of source for certain copyright royalties provided by paragraph 3, do not apply if the beneficial owner of the royalties carries on business in the State of source through a permanent establishment or fixed base and the right or property in respect of which the royalties are paid is effectively connected with such permanent establishment or fixed base (i.e., the royalties are attributable to the permanent establishment or fixed base). In that event, the royalty income would be taxable under the provisions of Article VII (Business Profits) or XIV (Independent Personal Services), as the case may be.

**6.** For the purposes of this Article,

(a) royalties shall be deemed to arise in a Contracting State when the payer is a resident of that State. Where, however, the person paying the royalties, whether he is a resident of a Contracting State or not, has in a State a permanent establishment or a fixed base in connection with which the obligation to pay the royalties was incurred, and such royalties are borne by such permanent establishment or fixed base, then such royalties shall be deemed to arise in the State in which the permanent establishment or fixed base is situated and not in any other State of which the payer is a resident; and

(b) where subparagraph (a) does not operate to treat royalties as arising in either Contracting State and the royalties are for the use of, or the right to use, intangible property or tangible personal property in a Contracting State, then such royalties shall be deemed to arise in that State.

**Technical Explanation [1995 Protocol]:**

Paragraph 2 of Article 7 of the Protocol amends the rules in paragraph 6 of Article XII of the Convention for determining the source of royalty payments. Under the present Convention, royalties generally are deemed to arise in a Contracting State if paid by a resident of that State. However, if the obligation to pay the royalties was incurred in connection with a permanent establishment or a fixed base in one of the Contracting States that bears the expense, the royalties are deemed to arise in that State.

The Protocol continues to apply these basic rules but changes the scope of an exception provided under the present Convention. Under the present Convention, a royalty paid for the use of, or the right to use, property in a Contracting State is deemed to arise in that State. Under the Protocol, this "place of use" exception applies only if the Convention does not otherwise deem the royalties to arise in one of the Contracting States. Thus, the "place of use" exception will apply only if royalties are neither paid by a resident of one of the Contracting States nor borne by a permanent establishment or fixed base in either State. For example, if a Canadian resident were to grant franchise rights to a resident of Chile for use in the United States, the royalty paid by the Chilean resident to the Canadian resident for those rights would be U.S. source income under this Article, subject to U.S. withholding at the 10 percent rate provided in paragraph 2.

The rules of this Article differ from those provided under U.S. domestic law. Under U.S. domestic law, a royalty is considered to be from U.S. sources if it is paid for the use of, or the privilege of using, an intangible within the United States; the residence of the payor is irrelevant. If paid to a nonresident alien individual or other foreign person, a U.S. source royalty is generally subject to withholding tax at a rate of 30 percent under U.S. domestic law. By reason of paragraph 1 of Article XXIX (Miscellaneous Rules), a Canadian resident would be permitted to apply the rules of U.S. domestic law to its royalty income if those rules produced a more favorable result in its case than those of this Article. However, under a basic principle of tax treaty interpretation recognized by both Contracting States, the prohibition against so-called "cherry-picking," the Canadian resident would be precluded from claiming selected benefits under the Convention (e.g., the tax rates only) and other benefits under U.S. domestic law (e.g., the source rules only) with respect to its royalties. See, e.g., Rev. Rul. 84-17, 1984-1 C.B. 308. For example, if a Canadian company granted franchise rights to a resident of the United States for use 50 percent in the United States and 50 percent in Chile, the Convention would permit the Canadian company to treat all of its royalty income from that single transaction as U.S. source income entitled to the withholding tax reduction under paragraph 2. U.S. domestic law would permit the Canadian company to treat 50 percent of its royalty income as U.S. source income subject to a 30 percent withholding tax and the other 50 percent as foreign source income exempt from U.S. tax. The Canadian company could choose to apply either the provisions of U.S. domestic law or the provisions of the Convention to the transaction, but would not be permitted to claim both the U.S. domestic law exemption for 50 percent of the income and the Convention's reduced withholding rate for the remainder of the income.

Royalties generally are considered borne by a permanent establishment or fixed base if they are deductible in computing the taxable income of that permanent establishment or fixed base.

Since the definition of "resident" of a Contracting State in Article IV (Residence), as amended by Article 3 of the Protocol, specifies that this term includes the Contracting States and their political subdivisions and local authorities, the source rule does not include a specific reference to these governmental entities.

**Technical Explanation [1984]:**

Paragraph 6 establishes rules to determine the source of royalties for purposes of Article XII. The first rule is that royalties arise in a Contracting State when the payer is that State, or a political subdivision, local authority, or resident of that State. Notwithstanding that rule, royalties arise not in the State of the payer's residence but in any State, whether or not a Contracting State, in which is situated a permanent establishment or fixed base in connection with which the obligation to pay royalties was incurred, if such royalties are borne by such permanent establishment or fixed base. Thus, royalties paid to a resident of the United States by a company resident in Canada for the use of property in a third State will not be subject to tax in Canada if the obligation to pay the royalties is incurred in connection with, and the royalties are borne by, a permanent establishment of the company in a third State. "Borne by" means allowable as a deduction in computing taxable income.

A third rule, which overrides both the residence rule and the permanent establishment rule just described, provides that royalties for the use of, or the right to use, intangible property or tangible personal property in a Contracting State arise in that State. Thus, consistent with the provisions of Code section 861(a)(4), if a resident of a third State pays royalties to a resident of Canada for the use of or the right to use intangible property or tangible personal property in the United States, such royalties are considered to arise in the United States and are subject to taxation by the United States consistent with the Convention. Similarly, if a resident of Canada pays royalties to a resident of a third State, such royalties are considered to arise in the United States and are subject to U.S. taxation if they are for the use of or the right to use intangible property or tangible personal property in the United States. The term "intangible property" encompasses all the items described in paragraph 4, other than tangible personal property.

**Notes**: Art. XII(6) amended by 1995 Protocol, effective for amounts paid or credited in 1996 or later (see Art. 21(2)(a) under "Application of the 1995 Protocol" above). From October 1984 through the end of 1995, read:

> 6. For the purposes of this Article, royalties shall be deemed to arise in a Contracting State when the payer is that State itself, or a political subdivision, local authority or resident of that State. However:
>
> (a) except as provided in subparagraph (b), where the person paying the royalties, whether he is a resident of a Contracting State or not, has in a State other than that of which he is a resident a permanent establishment or a fixed base in connection with which the obligation to pay the royalties was incurred, and such royalties are borne by such permanent establishment or fixed base, then such royalties shall be deemed to arise in the State in which the permanent establishment or fixed base is situated and not in the State of which the payer is a resident; and
>
> (b) where the royalties are for the use of, or the right to use, intangible property or tangible personal property in a Contracting State, then such royalties shall be deemed to arise in that State and not in the State of which the payer is a resident.

**7.** Where, by reason of a special relationship between the payer and the beneficial owner or between both of them and some other person, the amount of the royalties, having regard to the use, right or information for which they are paid, exceeds the amount which would have been agreed upon by the payer and the beneficial owner in the absence of such relationship, the provisions of this Article shall apply only to the last-mentioned amount. In such case, the excess part of the payments shall remain taxable according to the laws of each Contracting State, due regard being had to the other provisions of this Convention.

**Technical Explanation [1984]:**

Paragraph 7 provides that in cases involving special relationships between persons the benefits of Article XII do not apply to amounts in excess of the amount which would have been agreed upon between persons with no special relationship; any such excess amount remains taxable according to the laws of Canada and the United States, consistent with any relevant provisions of the Convention.

**8.** Where a resident of a Contracting State pays royalties to a person other than a resident of the other Contracting State, that other State may not impose any tax on such royalties except insofar as they arise in that other State or insofar as the right or property in respect of which the royalties are paid is effectively connected with a permanent establishment or a fixed base situated in that other State.

**Technical Explanation [1984]:**

Paragraph 8 restricts the right of a Contracting State to impose tax on royalties paid by a resident of the other Contracting State. The first State may not impose any tax on such royalties except insofar as they arise in that State or they are paid to a resident of that State or the right or property in respect of which the royalties are paid is effectively connected with a permanent establishment or fixed base situated in that State. This rule parallels the rule in paragraph 8 of Article XI (Interest) and paragraph 5 of Article X (Dividends).

Again, U.S. citizens remain subject to U.S. taxation on royalties received despite this rule, by virtue of paragraph 2 of Article XXIX (Miscellaneous Rules).

**Information Circulars**: 77-16R4: Non-resident income tax.

## Article XIII — Gains

### Proposed Amendment — Gains following emigration of individual from Canada

**Department of Finance news release, September 18, 2000**: *Canada and the United States Propose Tax Treaty Changes*

. . . . .

For individuals, the changes will ensure the appropriate tax treatment of an emigrant's gains. Specifically, where one country's tax rules treat an individual as having disposed of a property immediately before the individual emigrates to the other country, the individual will be able to choose to be treated under the other country's rules as also having disposed of and reacquired the property at its fair market value.

In most cases, this will mean that no tax is payable in the destination country on any pre-emigration gain. Where tax is payable in the destination country — for example, where the property in question is real estate situated in that country — the new rule will ensure appropriate tax crediting.

. . . . .

*Timing*

If approved, the rule for individuals will apply to changes in residence that take place on and after today's date.

[For the full text of this news release, see at the beginning of the Convention — ed.]

**1.** Gains derived by a resident of a Contracting State from the alienation of real property situated in the other Contracting State may be taxed in that other State.

**Technical Explanation [1984]**:

Paragraph 1 provides that Canada and the United States may each tax gains from the alienation of real property situated within that State which are derived by a resident of the other Contracting State. The term "real property situated in the other Contracting State" is defined for this purpose in paragraph 3 of this article. The term "alienation" used in paragraph 1 and other paragraphs of Article XIII means sales, exchanges and other dispositions or deemed dispositions (e.g., change of use, gifts, distributions, death) that are taxable events under the taxation laws of the Contracting State applying the provisions of the Article.

**Related Provisions**: ITA 115(1)(b) — Taxable Canadian property; ITA 126(2.21), (2.22) — Foreign tax credit to emigrant for tax payable on gain accrued while resident in Canada; ITA 128.1(4)(b)(i) — Real property in Canada excluded from deemed disposition on emigration.

**2.** Gains from the alienation of personal property forming part of the business property of a permanent establishment which a resident of a Contracting State has or had (within the twelve-month period preceding the date of alienation) in the other Contracting State or of personal property pertaining to a fixed base which is or was available (within the twelve-month period preceding the date of alienation) to a resident of a Contracting State in the other Contracting State for the purpose of performing independent personal services, including such gains from the alienation of such a permanent establishment or of such a fixed base, may be taxed in that other State.

**Technical Explanation [1984]**:

Paragraph 2 of Article XIII provides that the Contracting State in which a resident of the other Contracting State "has or had" a permanent establishment or fixed base may tax gains from the alienation of personal property constituting business property if such gains are attributable to such permanent establishment or fixed base. Unlike paragraph 1 of Article VII (Business Profits), paragraph 2 limits the right of the source State to tax such gains to a twelve-month period following the termination of the permanent establishment or fixed base.

**3.** For the purposes of this Article the term **"real property situated in the other Contracting State"**

(a) in the case of real property situated in the United States, means a United States real property interest and real property referred to in Article VI (Income from Real Property) situated in the United States, but does not include a share of the capital stock of a company that is not a resident of the United States; and

(b) in the case of real property situated in Canada means:

(i) real property referred to in Article VI (Income from Real Property) situated in Canada;

(ii) a share of the capital stock of a company that is a resident of Canada, the value of whose shares is derived principally from real property situated in Canada; and

(iii) an interest in a partnership, trust or estate, the value of which is derived principally from real property situated in Canada.

**Technical Explanation [1997]**:

Article 1 of the Protocol amends paragraph 3 of Article XIII (Gains) of the Convention. Paragraph 1 of Article XIII of the Convention provides that gains derived by a resident of a Contracting State from the alienation of real property situated within the other Contracting State may be taxed in that other State. The term "real property situated in the other Contracting State" is defined for this purpose in paragraph 3 of Article XIII of the Convention.

Under paragraph 3(a) of Article XIII of the Convention, real property situated in the United States includes real property (as defined in Article VI (Income from Real Property) of the Convention) situated in the United States and a United States real property interest. Under section 897(c) of the *Internal Revenue Code* (the "Code") the term "United States real property interest" includes shares in a U.S. corporation that owns sufficient U.S. real property interests to satisfy an asset-ratio test on certain testing dates.

Under Paragraph 3(b) of Article XIII of the Convention, real property situated in Canada means real property (as defined in Article VI of the Convention) situated in Canada; shares of stock of a company, the value of whose shares consists principally of Canadian real property; and an interest in a partnership, trust or estate, the value of which consists principally of Canadian real property. The term "principally" means more than 50 percent.

Under the Code, stock of a foreign corporation is not considered a "United States real property interest." Therefore, the United States does not tax a resident of Canada on the sale of stock of a foreign corporation, regardless of the composition of the corporation's assets. Although the Convention permits Canada to tax a U.S. resident on the sale of stock of a company that is not a resident of Canada if the value of the company's shares consists principally of Canadian real property, Canada does not currently impose such a tax. However, on April 26, 1995, amendments were proposed to the Canadian Income Tax Act that would impose Canadian income tax on gains realized on stock of certain companies that are not residents of Canada if (i) more than 50 percent of the fair market value of all of the company's properties consists of any combination of taxable Canadian property, Canadian resource property, timber resource property in Canada and income interests in Canadian trusts, and (ii) more than 50 percent of the fair market value of the shares in question is derived directly or indirectly from any combination of real property located in Canada, Canadian resource property, and timber resource property in Canada. [See ITA 115(1)(b) — ed.] This amendment is proposed to be effective as of April 26, 1995 with proration for gains that accrued before that date. Although the Canadian Parliament was dissolved before these amendments were passed, they are expected to be re-introduced in the current session with the same effective date.

The Protocol amends paragraphs 3(a) and 3(b)(ii) of Article XIII of the Convention to limit each State's right to tax the gains of a resident of the other State from the sale of stock of a real property holding company to cases where the company is resident in that State. Although the United States does not impose and is not currently considering imposing a tax under the Code on gains from the sale of stock of non-resident real property holding companies, the Protocol nevertheless amends the Convention to prohibit the imposition of such a tax on Canadian residents. Although Canada is considering imposing such a tax on gains from the sale of shares of companies that are not residents of Canada, this Protocol provision will cause the proposed amendments to the Canadian *Income Tax Act* to be inapplicable to U.S. residents who derive gains from the sale of stock of real property holding companies that are not residents of Canada. This provision will be retroactively effective to April 26, 1995, the date the previous Canadian legislation was proposed to be effective.

**Technical Explanation [1984]:**

Paragraph 3 provides a definition of the term "real property situated in the other Contracting State." Where the United States is the other Contracting State, the term includes real property (as defined in Article VI (Income from Real Property)) situated in the United States and a United States real property interest. Thus, the United States retains the ability to exercise its full taxing right under the *Foreign Investment in Real Property Tax Act* (Code section 897). (For a transition rule from the 1942 Convention, see paragraph 9 of this Article).

Where Canada is the other Contracting State, the term means real property (as defined in Article VI) situated in Canada; shares of stock of a company, the value of whose shares consists principally of Canadian real property; and an interest in a partnership, trust or estate, the value of which consists principally of Canadian real property. The term "principally" means more than 50 percent. Taxation in Canada is preserved through several tiers of entities if the value of the company's shares or the partnership, trust or estate is ultimately dependent principally upon real property situated in Canada.

**Related Provisions:** *Income Tax Conventions Interpretation Act* 5 — Definition of "real property".

**Notes:** Para. 3(a) amended by 1997 Protocol to add everything from "but does not include ...", and subpara. 3(b)(ii) amended to add "that is a resident of Canada", both amendments effective April 26, 1995.

**4.** Gains from the alienation of any property other than that referred to in paragraphs 1, 2 and 3 shall be taxable only in the Contracting State of which the alienator is a resident.

**Technical Explanation [1984]:**

Paragraph 4 reserves to the Contracting State of residence the sole right to tax gains from the alienation of any property other than property referred to in paragraphs 1, 2, and 3.

**Notes:** This paragraph overrides ITA 115(1)(b) for persons who are resident in the U.S. under the treaty tie-breaker rules (Article IV).

**Advance Tax Rulings:** ATR-43: Utilization of a non-resident-owned investment corporation as a holding corporation. However, see para. 5 below.

**5.** The provisions of paragraph 4 shall not affect the right of a Contracting State to levy tax on gains from the alienation of property derived by an individual who is a resident of the other Contracting State if such individual:

(a) was a resident of the first-mentioned State for 120 months during any period of 20 consecutive years preceding the alienation of the property; and

(b) was a resident of the first-mentioned State at any time during the ten years immediately preceding the alienation of the property;

and if such property (or property for which such property was substituted in an alienation the gain on which was not recognized for the purposes of taxation in the first-mentioned State) was owned by the individual at the time he ceased to be a resident of the first-mentioned State.

**Technical Explanation [1984]:**

Paragraph 5 states that, despite paragraph 4, a Contracting State may impose tax on gains derived by an individual who is a resident of the other Contracting State if such individual was a resident of the first-mentioned State for 120 months (whether or not consecutive) during any period of 20 consecutive years preceding the alienation of the property, and was a resident of that State at any time during the 10-year period immediately preceding the alienation of the property. The property (or property received in substitution in a tax-free transaction in the first-mentioned State) must have been owned by the individual at the time he ceased to be a resident of the first-mentioned State.

**6.** Where an individual (other than a citizen of the United States) who was a resident of Canada became a resident of the United States, in determining his liability to United States taxation in respect of any gain from the alienation of a principal residence in Canada owned by him at the time he ceased to be a resident of Canada, the adjusted basis of such property shall be no less than its fair market value at that time.

**Technical Explanation [1984]:**

Paragraph 6 provides a rule to coordinate Canadian and United States taxation of gains from the alienation of a principal residence situated in Canada. An individual (not a citizen of the United States) who was a resident of Canada and becomes a resident of the United States may determine his liability for U.S. income tax purposes in respect of gain from the alienation of a principal residence in Canada owned by him at the time he ceased to be a resident of Canada by claiming an adjusted basis for such residence in an amount no less than the fair market value of the residence at that time. Under paragraph 2(b) of Article XXX, the rule of paragraph 6 applies to gains realized for U.S. income tax purposes in taxable years beginning on or after the first day of January next following the date when instruments of ratification are exchanged, even if a particular individual described in paragraph 6 ceased to be a resident of Canada prior to such date. Paragraph 6 supplements any benefits available to a taxpayer pursuant to the provisions of the Code, e.g., section 1034.

**7.** Where at any time an individual is treated for the purposes of taxation by a Contracting State as having alienated a property and is taxed in that State by reason thereof and the domestic law of the other Contracting State at such time defers (but does not forgive) taxation, that individual may elect in his annual return of income for the year of such alienation to be liable to tax in the other Contracting State in that year as if he had, immediately before that time, sold and repurchased such property for an amount equal to its fair market value at that time.

**Technical Explanation [1984]:**

Paragraph 7 provides a rule to coordinate U.S. and Canadian taxation of gains in circumstances where an individual is subject to tax in both Contracting States and one Contracting State deems a taxable alienation of property by such person to have occurred, while the other Contracting State at that time does not find a realization or recognition of income and thus defers, but does not forgive, taxation. In such a case the individual may elect in his annual return of income for the year of such alienation to be liable to tax in the latter Contracting State as if he had sold and repurchased the property for an amount equal to its fair market value at a time immediately prior to the deemed alienation. The provision would, for example, apply in the case of a gift by a U.S. citizen or a U.S. resident individual which Canada deems to be an income producing event for its tax purposes but with respect to which the United States defers taxation while assigning the donor's basis to the donee. The provision would also apply in the case of a U.S. citizen who, for Canadian tax purposes, is deemed to recognize income upon his departure from Canada, but not to a Canadian resident (not a U.S. citizen) who is deemed to recognize such income. The rule does not apply in the case of death, although Canada also deems that to be a taxable event, because the United States in effect forgives income taxation of economic gains at death. If in one Contracting State there are losses and gains from deemed alienations of different properties, then paragraph 7 must be applied consistently in the other Contracting State within the taxable period with respect to all such properties. Paragraph 7 only applies, however, if the deemed alienations of the properties result in a net gain.

**8.** Where a resident of a Contracting State alienates property in the course of a corporate or other organization, reorganization, amalgamation, division or similar transaction and profit, gain or income with respect to such alienation is not recognized for the purpose of taxation in that State, if requested to do so by the person who acquires the property, the competent authority of the other Contracting State may agree, in order to avoid double taxation and subject to terms and conditions satisfactory to such competent authority, to defer the recognition of the profit, gain or income with respect to such property for the purpose of taxation in that other State until such time and in such manner as may be stipulated in the agreement.

**Technical Explanation [1995 Protocol]:**

Article 8 of the Protocol broadens the scope of paragraph 8 of Article XIII (Gains) of the Convention to cover organizations, reorganizations, amalgamations, and similar transactions involving either corporations or other entities. The present Convention covers only transactions involving corporations. The amendment is intended to make the paragraph applicable to transactions involving other types of entities, such as trusts and partnerships.

As in the case of transactions covered by the present Convention, the deferral allowed under this provision shall be for such time and under such other conditions as are stipulated between the person acquiring the property and the competent authority. The agreement of the competent authority of the State of source is entirely discretionary and, when granted, will be granted only to the extent necessary to avoid double taxation.

**Technical Explanation [1984]:**

Paragraph 8 concerns the coordination of Canadian and U.S. rules with respect to the recognition of gain on corporate organizations, reorganizations, amalgamations, divisions, and similar transactions. Where a resident of a Contracting State alienates property in such a transaction, and profit, gain, or income with respect to such alienation is not recognized for income tax purposes in the Contracting State of residence, the competent authority of the other Contracting State may agree, pursuant to paragraph 8, if requested by the person who acquires the property, to defer recognition of the profit, gain, or income with respect to such property for income tax purposes. This deferral shall be for such time and under such other conditions as are stipulated between the person who acquires the property and the competent authority. The agreement of the competent authority of the State of source is entirely discretionary and will be granted only to the extent necessary to avoid double taxation of income. This provision means, for example, that the United States competent authority may agree to defer recognition of gain with respect to a transaction if the alienator would otherwise recognize gain for U.S. tax purposes and would not recognize gain under Canada's law. The provision only applies, however, if alienations described in paragraph 8 result in a net gain. In the absence of extraordinary circumstances the provisions of the paragraph must be applied consistently within a taxable period with respect to alienations described in the paragraph that take place within that period.

**Notes:** For discussion of this provision, see François Vincent, "U.S. Revenue Procedure 98-21 and Article XIII(8) of the Canada-U.S. Convention", VI(2) *Corporate Finance* (Federated Press), 505–7 (1998).

Art. XIII(8) amended by 1995 Protocol, generally effective 1996 (see Art. 21 under "Application of the 1995 Protocol" above), to change "corporate" to "corporate or other".

**9.** Where a person who is a resident of a Contracting State alienates a capital asset which may in accordance with this Article be taxed in the other Contracting State and

(a) that person owned the asset on September 26, 1980 and was resident in the first-mentioned State on that date; or

(b) the asset was acquired by that person in an alienation of property which qualified as a non-recognition transaction for the purposes of taxation in that other State;

the amount of the gain which is liable to tax in that other State in accordance with this Article shall be reduced by the proportion of the gain attributable on a monthly basis to the period ending on December 31 of the year in which the Convention enters into force, or such greater portion of the gain as is shown to the satisfaction of the competent authority of the other State to be reasonably attributable to that period. For the purposes of this paragraph the term

# Art. XIII — Canada–U.S. Tax Convention

"**non-recognition transaction**" includes a transaction to which paragraph 8 applies and, in the case of taxation in the United States, a transaction that would have been a non-recognition transaction but for Sections 897(d) and 897(e) of the *Internal Revenue Code*. The provisions of this paragraph shall not apply to

(c) an asset that on September 26, 1980 formed part of the business property of a permanent establishment or pertained to a fixed base of a resident of a Contracting State situated in the other Contracting State;

(d) an alienation by a resident of a Contracting State of an asset that was owned at any time after September 26, 1980 and before such alienation by a person who was not at all times after that date while the asset was owned by such person a resident of that State; or

(e) an alienation of an asset that was acquired by a person at any time after September 26, 1980 and before such alienation in a transaction other than a non-recognition transaction.

### Technical Explanation [1984]:

Paragraph 9 provides a transitional rule reflecting the fact that under Article VIII of the 1942 Convention gains from the sale or exchange of capital assets are exempt from taxation in the State of source provided the taxpayer had no permanent establishment in that State. Paragraph 9 applies to deemed, as well as actual, alienations or dispositions. In addition, paragraph 9 applies to a gain described in paragraph 1, even though such gain is also income within the meaning of paragraph 3 of Article VI. Paragraph 9 will apply to transactions notwithstanding section 1125(c) of the *Foreign Investment in Real Property Tax Act*, Public Law 96-499 ("FIRPTA").

Paragraph 9 applies to capital assets alienated by a resident of a Contracting State if (a) that person owned the asset on September 26, 1980 and was a resident of that Contracting State on September 26, 1980 (and at all times after that date until the alienation), or (b) the asset was acquired by that person in an alienation of property which qualified as a non-recognition transaction for tax purposes in the other Contracting State. For purposes of subparagraph 9(b), a non-recognition transaction is a transaction in which gain resulting therefrom is, in effect, deferred for tax purposes, but is not permanently forgiven. Thus, in the United States, certain tax-free organizations, reorganizations, liquidations and like-kind exchanges will qualify as non-recognition transactions. However, a transfer of property at death will not constitute a non-recognition transaction, since any gain due to appreciation in the property is permanently forgiven in the United States due to the fair market value basis taken by the recipient of the property. If a transaction is a non-recognition transaction for tax purposes, the transfer of non-qualified property, or "boot," which may cause some portion of the gain on the transaction to be recognized, will not cause the transaction to lose its character as a non-recognition transaction for purposes of subparagraph 9(b). In addition, a transaction that would have been a non-recognition transaction in the United States but for the application of sections 897(d) and 897(e) of the Code will also constitute a non-recognition transaction for purposes of subparagraph 9(b). Further, a transaction which is not a non-recognition transaction under U.S. law, but to which non-recognition treatment is granted pursuant to the agreement of the competent authority under paragraph 8 of this Article, is a non-recognition transaction for purposes of subparagraph 9(b). However, a transaction which is not a non-recognition transaction under U.S. law does not become a non-recognition transaction for purposes of subparagraph 9(b) merely because the basis of the property in the hands of the transferee is reduced under section 1125(d) of FIRPTA.

The benefits of paragraph 9 are not available to the alienation or disposition by a resident of a Contracting State of an asset that (a) on September 26, 1980 formed part of the business property of a permanent establishment or pertained to a fixed base which a resident of that Contracting State had in the other Contracting State, (b) was alienated after September 26, 1980 and before the alienation in question in any transaction that was not a non-recognition transaction, as described above, or (c) was owned at any time prior to the alienation in question and after September 26, 1980 by a person who was not a resident of that same Contracting State after September 26, 1980 while such person held the asset. Thus, for example, in order for paragraph 9 to be availed of by a Canadian resident who did not own the alienated asset on September 26, 1980, the asset must have been owned by other Canadian residents continuously after September 26, 1980 and must have been transferred only in transactions which were non-recognition transactions for U.S. tax purposes.

The availability of the benefits of paragraph 9 is illustrated by the following examples. It should be noted that the examples do not purport to fully describe the U.S. and Canadian tax consequences resulting from the transactions described therein. Any condition for the application of paragraph 9 which is not discussed in an example should be assumed to be satisfied.

*Example 1.*

A, an individual resident of Canada, owned an appreciated U.S. real property interest on September 26, 1980. On January 1, 1982, A transferred the U.S. real property interest to X, a Canadian corporation, in exchange for 100 percent of X's voting stock. A's gain on the transfer to X is exempt from U.S. tax under Article VIII of the 1942 Convention. Since the transaction qualifies as a non-recognition transaction for U.S. tax purposes, as described above, X is entitled to the benefits of paragraph 9, pursuant to subparagraph 9(b), upon a subsequent disposition of the U.S. real property interest occurring after the entry into force of this Convention. If A's transfer to X had instead occurred after the entry into force of this Convention, A would be entitled to the benefits of paragraph 9, pursuant to subparagraph 9(a), with respect to U.S. taxation of that portion of the gain resulting from the transfer to X that is attributable on a monthly basis to the period ending on December 31 of the year in which the Convention enters into force (or a greater portion of the gain as is shown to the satisfaction of the U.S. competent authority). X would be entitled to the benefits of paragraph 9 pursuant to subparagraph 9(b), upon a subsequent disposition of the U.S. real property interest.

*Example 2.*

The facts are the same as in Example 1, except that A is a corporation which is resident in Canada. Assuming that the transfer of the U.S. real property interest to X is a section 351 transaction or a tax-free reorganization for U.S. tax purposes, the results are the same as in Example 1.

*Example 3.*

The facts are the same as in Example 1, except that X is a U.S. corporation. If the transfer to X by A took place on January 1, 1982, A's gain on the transfer to X would be exempt from tax under Article VIII of the 1942 Convention and A would be entitled to the benefits of paragraph 9, pursuant to subparagraph 9(b), upon a subsequent disposition of the stock of X occurring after the entry into force of this Convention. If the transfer to X by A took place after the entry into force of this Convention, A would be entitled to the benefits of paragraph 9, pursuant to subparagraph 9(a), with respect to U.S. taxation (if any) of the gain resulting from the transfer to X, and would also be entitled to the benefits of paragraph 9, pursuant to subparagraph 9(b), upon a subsequent disposition of the stock of X. For several reasons, including the fact that X is a U.S. corporation, paragraph 9 has no impact on the U.S. tax consequences of a subsequent disposition by X of the U.S. real property interest in either case.

*Example 4.*

B, a corporation resident in Canada, owns all of the stock of C, which is also a corporation resident in Canada. C owns a U.S. real property interest. After the Convention enters into force, B liquidates C in a section 332 liquidation. The transaction is treated as a non-recognition transaction for U.S. tax purposes under the definition of a non-recognition transaction described above. C is entitled to the benefits of paragraph 9, pursuant to subparagraph 9(a), with respect to gain taxed (if any) under section 897(d), and B is entitled to the benefits of paragraph 9, pursuant to subparagraph 9(b), upon a subsequent disposition of the U.S. real property interest. Generally, the United States would not subject B to tax upon the liquidation of C.

*Example 5.*

The facts are the same as in Example 4, except that C is a U.S. corporation. B is entitled to the benefits of paragraph 9, pursuant to subparagraph 9(a), with respect to U.S. taxation (if any) of the gain resulting from the liquidation of C. B is not entitled to the benefits of paragraph 9 upon a subsequent disposition of the U.S. real property interest since that asset was held after September 26, 1980 by a person who was not a resident of Canada. The U.S. tax consequences to C are governed by the internal law of the United States.

*Example 6.*

D, an individual resident of the United States, owns Canadian real estate. On January 1, 1982, D transfers the Canadian real estate to E, a corporation resident in Canada, in exchange for all of E's stock. This transfer is treated as a taxable transaction under the *Income Tax Act* of Canada. However, D's gain on the transfer is exempt from Canadian tax under Article VIII of the 1942 Convention. D is not entitled to the benefits of subparagraph 9(b) upon a subsequent disposition of the stock of E since the stock was not transferred in a transaction which was a non-recognition transaction for Canadian tax purposes. E is not entitled to Canadian benefits under this paragraph since, *inter alia*, it is a Canadian resident. (However, under Canadian law, both D and E would have a basis for tax purposes equal to the fair market value of the property at the time of D's transfer). If the transfer to E had taken place after entry into force of this Convention, D would be entitled to the benefits of paragraph 9, pursuant to subparagraph 9(a), with respect to Canadian tax resulting from the transfer to E, but would not be entitled to the benefits of subparagraph 9(b) upon a subsequent disposition of the E stock. (Note that E could seek to have the transaction treated as a non-recognition transaction under paragraph 8 of this Article, with the result that, if the competent authority agrees, D will take a carryover basis in the stock of E and be entitled to the benefits of subparagraph 9(b) upon a subsequent disposition thereof).

*Example 7.*

The facts are the same as in Example 6, except that E is a U.S. corporation. This transaction is also a recognition event under Canadian law at the shareholder level. The results are generally the same as in Example 6. However, if the transfer to E had been granted non-recognition treatment in Canada pursuant to paragraph 8, both D and E would be entitled to the benefits of paragraph 9 for Canadian tax purposes, pursuant to subparagraph 9(b), upon subsequent dispositions of the stock of E or the Canadian real estate, respectively.

*Example 8.*

F, an individual resident of the United States, owns all of the stock of G, a Canadian corporation, which in turn owns Canadian real estate. F causes G to be amalgamated in a merger with another Canadian corporation. This is a non-recognition transaction under Canadian law and F is entitled for Canadian tax purposes, to the benefits of paragraph 9, pursuant to subparagraph 9(b), upon a subsequent disposition of the stock of the other Canadian corporation.

*Example 9.*

H, a U.S. corporation, owns all of the stock of J, another U.S. corporation. J owns Canadian real estate. H liquidates J. For Canadian tax purposes, no tax is imposed on H as a result of the liquidation and H receives a fair market value basis in the Canadian real estate. Accordingly, since gain has been forgiven due to the fair market value basis (rather than postponed in a non-recognition transaction), H would not be entitled to the benefits of subparagraph 9(b) upon the subsequent disposition of the Canadian real estate. Canada would impose a tax on J, but J would be entitled to the benefits of paragraph 9, pursuant to subparagraph 9(a), with respect to Canadian tax imposed on the liquidation.

*Example 10.*

The facts are the same as in Example 9, except that J is a Canadian corporation. Paragraph 9 does not affect the Canadian taxation of J. While H is subject to Canadian tax on the liquidation of J, H is entitled to the benefits of paragraph 9, pursuant to subparagraph 9(a), with respect to such Canadian taxation. H will take a fair market value basis (rather than have gain postponed in a non-recognition transaction) in the Canadian real estate for Canadian tax purposes and is thus not entitled to the benefits of paragraph 9 upon a subsequent disposition of the Canadian real estate (since, *inter alia*, the gain has been forgiven due to the fair market value basis).

*Example 11.*

K, a U.S. corporation, owns the stock of L, another U.S. corporation, which in turn owns Canadian real estate. K causes L to be merged into another U.S. corporation. For Canadian tax purposes, such a transaction is treated as a recognition event, but Canada will not impose a tax on K under its internal law. Canada would impose tax on L, but L is entitled to the benefits of paragraph 9, pursuant to subparagraph 9(a), with respect to Canadian taxation of gain resulting from the merger. The acquiring U.S. corporation would take a fair market value basis in the Canadian real estate, and would thus not be entitled to the benefits of subparagraph 9(b) upon a subsequent disposition of the real estate. (Note that the acquiring U.S. corporation could seek to obtain non-recognition treatment under paragraph 8 of this Article, with the result that, if approved by the competent authority, it would obtain a carryover basis in the property and be entitled to the benefits of subparagraph 9(b) upon a subsequent disposition of the Canadian real estate).

Paragraph 9 provides that where a resident of Canada or the United States is subject to tax pursuant to Article XIII in the other Contracting State on gains from the alienation of a capital asset, and if the other conditions of paragraph 9 are satisfied, the amount of the gain shall be reduced for tax purposes in that other State by the amount of the gain attributable to the period during which the property was held up to and including December 31 of the year in which the documents of ratification are exchanged. The gain attributable to such person[1] is normally determined by dividing the total gain by the number of full calendar months the property was held by such person, including, in the case of an alienation described in paragraph 9(b), the number of months in which a predecessor in interest held the property, and multiplying such monthly amount by the number of full calendar months ending on or before December 31 of the year in which the instruments of ratification are exchanged.

Upon a clear showing, however, a taxpayer may prove that a greater portion of the gain was attributable to the specified period. Thus, in the United States the fair market value of the alienated property at the treaty valuation date may be established under paragraph 9 in the manner and with the evidence that is generally required by U.S. Federal income, estate, and gift tax regulations. For this purpose a taxpayer may use valid appraisal techniques for valuing real estate such as the comparable sales approach (see Rev. Proc. 79-24, 1979-1 C.B. 565) and the reproduction cost approach. If more than one property is alienated in a single transaction each property will be considered individually.

---

[1] *Sic.* Should read "period" — ed.

A taxpayer who desires to make this alternate showing for U.S. tax purposes must so indicate on his U.S. income tax return for the year of the sale or exchange and must attach to the return a statement describing the relevant evidence. The U.S. competent authority or his authorized delegate will determine whether the taxpayer has satisfied the requirements of paragraph 9.

The amount of gain which is reduced by reason of the application of paragraph 9 is not to be treated for U.S. tax purposes as an amount of "nontaxed gain" under section 1125(d)(2)(B) of FIRPTA, where that section would otherwise apply. (Note that gain not taxed by virtue of the 1942 Convention is "nontaxed gain").

U.S. residents, citizens and former citizens remain subject to U.S. taxation on gains as provided by the Code notwithstanding the provisions of Article XIII, other than paragraphs 6 and 7. See paragraphs 2 and 3(a) of Article XXIX (Miscellaneous Rules).

**Notes**: The CCRA's view (IT-173R2 para. 14; Income Tax Technical News No. 4) is that the proration under para. 9 applies only to the period since Jan. 1, 1972, since Canada did not tax capital gains accrued before that date (see Notes to ITAR 26(3)). This view has been upheld by the Courts: *Kubicek Estate*, [1997] 3 C.T.C. 435 (FCA); *Haas Estate*, [2000] 1 C.T.C. 2446 (TCC); aff'd (Nov. 3, 2000), file A-709-99 (FCA).

**Interpretation Bulletins**: IT-173R2: Capital gains derived in Canada by residents of the United States.

**I.T. Technical News**: No. 4 (article XIII:9 of the Canada–U.S. tax convention (1980).

## Article XIV — Independent Personal Services

Income derived by an individual who is a resident of a Contracting State in respect of independent personal services may be taxed in that State. Such income may also be taxed in the other Contracting State if the individual has or had a fixed base regularly available to him in that other State but only to the extent that the income is attributable to the fixed base.

**Technical Explanation [1984]**:

Article XIV concerns the taxation of income derived by an individual in respect of the performance of independent personal services. Such income may be taxed in the Contracting State of which such individual is a resident. It may also be taxed in the other Contracting State if the individual has or had a fixed base regularly available to him in the other State for the purpose of performing his activities, but only to the extent that the income is attributable to that fixed base. The use of the term "has or had" ensures that a Contracting State in which a fixed base existed has the right to tax income attributable to that fixed base even if there is a delay between the termination of the fixed base and the receipt or accrual of such income.

Unlike Article VII of the 1942 Convention, which provides a limited exemption from tax at source on income from independent personal services, Article XIV does not restrict the exemption to persons present in the State of source for fewer than 184 days. Furthermore, Article XIV does not allow the $5,000 exemption at source of the 1942 Convention, which was available even if services were performed through a fixed base. However, Article XIV provides complete exemption at source if a fixed base does not exist.

**Related Provisions**: ITA 146(1)"earned income"(c) — Income exempted by tax treaty is not earned income of a non-resident for RRSP purposes.

**Notes**: In *Dudney*, [1999] 1 C.T.C. 2267 (TCC), aff'd [2000] 2 C.T.C. 56 (FCA); leave to appeal denied (Nov. 2, 2000), file 27869 (SCC), the term "fixed base" was interpreted to mean essentially the same as "permanent establishment."

**I.T. Technical News**: No. 18 (*Dudney* case).

## Article XV — Dependent Personal Services

**1.** Subject to the provisions of Articles XVIII (Pensions and Annuities) and XIX (Government Service), salaries, wages and other similar remuneration derived by a resident of a Contracting State in respect of an employment shall be taxable only in that State unless the employment is exercised in the other Contracting State. If the employment is so exercised, such remuneration as is derived therefrom may be taxed in that other State.

**Technical Explanation [1984]**:

Paragraph 1 provides that, in general, salaries, wages, and other similar remuneration derived by a resident of a Contracting State in respect of an employment are taxable only in that State unless the employment is exercised in the other Contracting State. If the employment is exercised in the other Contracting State, the entire remuneration derived therefrom may be taxed in that other State but only if, as provided by paragraph 2, the recipient is present in the other State for a period or periods exceeding 183 days in the calendar year, or the remuneration is borne by an employer who is a resident of that other State or by a permanent establishment or fixed base which the employer has in that other State. However, in all cases where the employee earns $10,000 or less in the currency of the State of source, such earnings are exempt from tax in that State. "Borne by" means allowable as a deduction in computing taxable income. Thus, if a Canadian resident individual employed at the Canadian permanent establishment of a U.S. company performs services in the United States, the income earned by the employee from such services is not exempt from U.S. tax under paragraph 1 if such income exceeds $10,000 (U.S.) because the U.S. company is entitled to a deduction for such wages in computing its taxable income.

**2.** Notwithstanding the provisions of paragraph 1, remuneration derived by a resident of a Contracting State in respect of an employment exercised in a calendar year in the other Contracting State shall be taxable only in the first-mentioned State if:

   (a) such remuneration does not exceed ten thousand dollars ($10,000) in the currency of that other State; or

   (b) the recipient is present in the other Contracting State for a period or periods not exceeding in the aggregate 183 days in that year and the remuneration is not borne by an employer who is a resident of that other State or by a permanent establishment or a fixed base which the employer has in that other State.

**Technical Explanation [1984]**:

See Article XV, para. 1.

**Related Provisions**: ITA 146(1)"earned income"(c) — Income exempted by tax treaty is not earned income of a non-resident for RRSP purposes.

**Notes**: The $10,000 is measured against *each* employment, not total employment in the other country: *Prescott*, [1995] 2 C.T.C. 2068 (TCC).

**3.** Notwithstanding the provisions of paragraphs 1 and 2, remuneration derived by a resident of a Contracting State in respect of an employment regularly exercised in more than one State on a ship, aircraft, motor vehicle or train operated by a resident of that Contracting State shall be taxable only in that State.

**Technical Explanation [1984]:**

Paragraph 3 provides that a resident of a Contracting State is exempt from tax in the other Contracting State with respect to remuneration derived in respect of an employment regularly exercised in more than one State on a ship, aircraft, motor vehicle, or train operated by a resident of the taxpayer's State of residence. The word "regularly" is intended to distinguish crew members from persons occasionally employed on a ship, aircraft, motor vehicle, or train. Only the Contracting State of which the employee and operator are resident has the right to tax such remuneration. However, this provision is subject to the "saving clause" of paragraph 2 of Article XXIX (Miscellaneous Rules), which permits the United States to tax its citizens despite paragraph 3.

Article XV states that its provisions are overridden by the more specific rules of Article XVIII (Pensions and Annuities) and Article XIX (Government Services).

**Related Provisions:** Art. III:1(h) — Meaning of "international traffic"; ITA 146(1)"earned income"(c) — Income exempted by tax treaty is not earned income of a non-resident for RRSP purposes.

## Article XVI — Artistes and Athletes

**1.** Notwithstanding the provisions of Articles XIV (Independent Personal Services) and XV (Dependent Personal Services), income derived by a resident of a Contracting State as an entertainer, such as a theatre, motion picture, radio or television artiste, or a musician, or as an athlete, from his personal activities as such exercised in the other Contracting State, may be taxed in that other State, except where the amount of the gross receipts derived by such entertainer or athlete, including expenses reimbursed to him or borne on his behalf, from such activities do not exceed fifteen thousand dollars ($15,000) in the currency of that other State for the calendar year concerned.

**Technical Explanation [1984]:**

Article XVI concerns income derived by a resident of a Contracting State as an entertainer, such as a theatre, motion picture, radio, or television artiste, or a musician, or as an athlete, from his personal activities as such exercised in the other Contracting State. Article XVI overrides Articles XIV (Independent Personal Services) and XV (Dependent Personal Services) to allow source basis taxation of an entertainer or athlete in cases where the latter Articles would not permit such taxation. Thus, paragraph 1 provides that certain income of an entertainer or athlete may be taxed in the State of source in all cases where the amount of gross receipts derived by the entertainer or athlete, including expenses reimbursed to him or borne on his behalf, exceeds $15,000 in the currency of that other State for the calendar year concerned. For example, where a resident of Canada who is an entertainer derives income from his personal activities as an entertainer in the United States, he is taxable in the United States on all such income in any case where his gross receipts are greater than $15,000 for the calendar year. Article XVI does not restrict the right of the State of source to apply the provisions of Articles XIV and XV. Thus, an entertainer or athlete resident in a Contracting State and earning $14,000 in wages borne by a permanent establishment in the other State may be taxed in the other State as provided in Article XV.

**Related Provisions:** ITA 146(1)"earned income"(c) — Income exempted by tax treaty is not earned income of a non-resident for RRSP purposes.

**2.** Where income in respect of personal activities exercised by an entertainer or an athlete in his capacity as such accrues not to the entertainer or athlete but to another person, that income may, notwithstanding the provisions of Articles VII (Business Profits), XIV (Independent Personal Services) and XV (Dependent Personal Services), be taxed in the Contracting State in which the activities of the entertainer or athlete are exercised. For the purposes of the preceding sentence, income of an entertainer or athlete shall be deemed not to accrue to another person if it is established that neither the entertainer or athlete, nor persons related thereto, participate directly or indirectly in the profits of such other person in any manner, including the receipt of deferred remuneration, bonuses, fees, dividends, partnership distributions or other distributions.

**Technical Explanation [1984]:**

Paragraph 2 provides that where income in respect of personal activities exercised by an entertainer or an athlete accrues not to the entertainer or athlete himself but to another person, that income may, notwithstanding the provisions of Article VII (Business Profits), Article XIV, and Article XV, be taxed in the Contracting State in which the activities are exercised. The anti-avoidance rule of paragraph 2 does not apply if it is established by the entertainer or athlete that neither he nor persons related to him participate directly or indirectly in the profits of the other person in any manner, including the receipt of deferred remuneration, bonuses, fees, dividends, partnership distributions, or other distributions.

Thus, if an entertainer who is a resident of Canada is under contract with a company and the arrangement between the entertainer and the company provides for payments to the entertainer based on the profits of the company, all of the income of the company attributable to the performer's U.S. activities may be taxed in the United States irrespective of whether the company maintains a permanent establishment in the United States. Paragraph 2 does not affect the rule of paragraph 1 that applies to the entertainer or athlete himself.

**3.** The provisions of paragraphs 1 and 2 shall not apply to the income of:

(a) an athlete in respect of his activities as an employee of a team which participates in a league with regularly scheduled games in both Contracting States; or

(b) a team described in subparagraph (a).

**Technical Explanation [1984]:**

Paragraph 3 provides that paragraphs 1 and 2 of Article XVI do not apply to the income of an athlete in respect of an employment with a team which participates in a league with regularly scheduled games in both Canada and the United States, nor do those paragraphs apply to the income of such a team. Such an athlete is subject to the rules of Article XV. Thus, the athlete's remuneration would be exempt from tax in the Contracting State of source if he is a resident of the other Contracting State and earns $10,000 or less in the currency of the State of source, or if he is present in that State for a period or periods not exceeding in the aggregate 183 days in the calendar year, and his remuneration is not borne by a resident of that State or a permanent establishment or fixed base in that State. In addition, a team described in paragraph 3 may not be taxed in a Contracting State under paragraph 2 of this Article solely by reason of the fact that a member of the team may participate in the profits of the team through the receipt of a bonus based, for example, on ticket sales. The employer may be taxable pursuant to other articles of the Convention, such as Article VII.

4. Notwithstanding the provisions of Articles XIV (Independent Personal Services) and XV (Dependent Personal Services) an amount paid by a resident of a Contracting State to a resident of the other Contracting State as an inducement to sign an agreement relating to the performance of the services of an athlete (other than an amount referred to in paragraph 1 of Article XV (Dependent Personal Services) may be taxed in the first-mentioned State, but the tax so charged shall not exceed 15 per cent of the gross amount of such payment.

**Technical Explanation [1984]:**

Paragraph 4 provides that, notwithstanding Articles XIV and XV, an amount paid by a resident of a Contracting State to a resident of the other State as an inducement to sign an agreement relating to the performance of the services of an athlete may be taxed in the first-mentioned State. However, the tax imposed may not exceed 15 per cent of the gross amount of the payment. The provision clarifies the taxation of signing bonuses in a manner consistent with their treatment under U.S. interpretations of the 1942 Convention. Amounts paid as salary or other remuneration for the performance of the athletic services themselves are not taxable under this provision, but are subject to the provisions of paragraphs 1 and 3 of this Article, or Articles XIV or XV, as the case may be. The paragraph covers all amounts paid (to the athlete or another person) as an inducement to sign an agreement for the services of an athlete, such as a bonus to sign a contract not to perform for other teams. An amount described in this paragraph is not to be included in determining the amount of gross receipts derived by an athlete in a calendar year for purposes of paragraph 1. Thus, if an athlete receives a $50,000 signing bonus and a $12,000 salary for a taxable year, the State of source would not be entitled to tax the salary portion of the receipt of the athlete for that year under paragraph 1 of this Article.

## Article XVII — Withholding of Taxes in Respect of Personal Services

1. Deduction and withholding of tax on account of the tax liability for a taxable year on remuneration paid to an individual who is a resident of a Contracting State (including an entertainer or athlete) in respect of the performance of independent personal services in the other Contracting State may be required by that other State, but with respect to the first five thousand dollars ($5,000) in the currency of that other State, paid as remuneration in that taxable year by each payer, such deduction and withholding shall not exceed 10 per cent of the payment.

**Technical Explanation [1984]:**

Article XVII confirms that a Contracting State may require withholding of tax on account of tax liability with respect to remuneration paid to an individual who is a resident of the other Contracting State, including an entertainer or athlete, in respect of the performance of independent personal services in the first-mentioned State. However, withholding with respect to the first $5,000 (in the currency of the State of source) of such remuneration paid in that taxable year by each payor shall not exceed 10 percent of such payment. In the United States, the withholding described in paragraph 1 relates to withholding with respect to income tax liability and does not relate to withholding with respect to other taxes, such as social security taxes. Nor is the paragraph intended to suggest that withholding in circumstances not specifically mentioned, such as withholding with respect to dependent personal services, is precluded by the Convention.

2. Where the competent authority of a Contracting State considers that an amount that would otherwise be deducted or withheld from any amount paid or credited to an individual who is a resident of the other Contracting State in respect of the performance of personal services in the first-mentioned State is excessive in relation to the estimated tax liability for the taxable year of that individual in the first-mentioned State, it may determine that a lesser amount will be deducted or withheld.

**Technical Explanation [1984]:**

Paragraph 2 provides that in any case where the competent authority of Canada or the United States believes that withholding with respect to remuneration for the performance of personal services is excessive in relation to the estimated tax liability of an individual to that State for a taxable year, it may determine that a lesser amount will be deducted or withheld. In the case of independent personal services, paragraph 2 may thus result in a lesser withholding than the maximum authorized by paragraph 1.

3. The provisions of this Article shall not affect the liability of a resident of a Contracting State referred to in paragraph 1 or 2 for tax imposed by the other Contracting State.

**Technical Explanation [1984]:**

Paragraph 3 states that the provisions of Article XVII do not affect the liability of a resident of a Contracting State for taxes imposed by the other Contracting State. The Article deals only with the method of collecting taxes and not with substantive tax liability.

Article XVIIIA of the 1942 Convention authorizes the issuance of regulations to specify circumstances under which residents of the United States temporarily performing personal services in Canada may be exempted from deduction and withholding of United States tax. This provision is omitted from the Convention as unnecessary. The Code and regulations provide sufficient authority to avoid excessive withholding of U.S. income tax. Further, paragraph 2 provides for adjustments in the amount of withholding where appropriate.

## Article XVIII — Pensions and Annuities

1. Pensions and annuities arising in a Contracting State and paid to a resident of the other Contracting State may be taxed in that other State, but the amount of any such pension that would be excluded from taxable income in the first-mentioned State if the recipient were a resident thereof shall be exempt from taxation in that other State.

**Technical Explanation [1984]:**

Paragraph 1 provides that a resident of a Contracting State is taxable in that State with respect to pensions and annuities arising in the other Contracting State. However, the State of residence shall exempt from taxation the amount of any such pension that would be excluded from taxable income in the State of source if the recipient were a resident thereof. Thus, if a $10,000 pension payment arising in a Contracting State is paid to a resident of the other Contracting State and $5,000 of such payment would be excluded from taxable income as a return of capital in the first-mentioned State if the recipient were a resident of the first-mentioned State, the State of residence shall exempt from tax $5,000 of the payment. Only $5,000 would be so exempt even if the first-mentioned State would also grant a personal allowance as a deduction from gross income if the recipient were a resident thereof. Paragraph 1 imposes no such restriction with respect to the amount that may be taxed in the State of residence in the case of annuities.

**Notes**: In *Coblentz*, [1996] 3 C.T.C. 295 (FCA), the Court used the Technical Explanation (above) to assist in interpreting Art. XVIII(1), and ruled that a U.S. itemized deduction was not a "personal allowance" as described in the Technical Explanation.

**2. However:**

(a) pensions may also be taxed in the Contracting State in which they arise and according to the laws of that State; but if a resident of the other Contracting State is the beneficial owner of a periodic pension payment, the tax so charged shall not exceed 15 per cent of the gross amount of such payment; and

(b) annuities may also be taxed in the Contracting State in which they arise and according to the laws of that State; but if a resident of the other Contracting State is the beneficial owner of an annuity payment, the tax so charged shall not exceed 15 per cent of the portion of such payment that would not be excluded from taxable income in the first-mentioned State if the beneficial owner were a resident thereof.

**Technical Explanation [1984]**:

Paragraph 2 provides rules with respect to the taxation of pensions and annuities in the Contracting State in which they arise. If the beneficial owner of a periodic pension payment is a resident of the other Contracting State, the tax imposed in the State of source is limited to 15 percent of the gross amount of such payment. Thus, the State of source is not required to allow a deduction or exclusion for a return of capital to the pensioner, but its tax is limited in amount in the case of a periodic payment. Other pension payments may be taxed in the State of source without limit.

In the case of annuities beneficially owned by a resident of a Contracting State, the Contracting State of source is limited to a 15 percent tax on the portion of the payment that would not be excluded from taxable income (i.e., as a return of capital) in that State if the beneficial owner were a resident thereof.

**Notes**: See Notes to ITA 212(1)(l).

**Information Circulars**: 75-6R: Required withholding from amounts paid to non-resident persons performing services in Canada.

**3.** For the purposes of this Convention, the term **"pensions"** includes any payment under a superannuation, pension or other retirement arrangement, Armed Forces retirement pay, war veterans pensions and allowances and amounts paid under a sickness, accident or disability plan, but does not include payments under an income-averaging annuity contract or, except for the purposes of Article XIX (Government Service), any benefit referred to in paragraph 5.

**Technical Explanation [1997 Protocol]**:

Paragraph 1 of Article 2 of the Protocol amends paragraph 3 of Article XVIII (Pensions and Annuities) of the Convention to clarify that social security benefits paid by one Contracting State in respect of services rendered to that State or a subdivision or authority of that State are subject to the rules set forth in paragraph 5 of Article XVIII, and are not subject to Article XIX (Government Service). Thus, all social security benefits paid by a Contracting State will be subject to the same rules, regardless of whether the services were rendered to a private sector employer, the government, or both.

**Technical Explanation [1995 Protocol]**:

Article 9 of the Protocol amends Article XVIII (Pensions and Annuities) of the Convention. Paragraph 3 of Article XVIII defines the term "pensions" for purposes of the Convention, including the rules for the taxation of cross-border pensions in paragraphs 1 and 2 of the Article, the rules in paragraphs 2 and 3 of Article XXI (Exempt Organizations) for certain income derived by pension funds, and the rules in paragraph 1(b)(i) of Article IV (Residence) regarding the residence of pension funds and certain other entities. The Protocol amends the present definition by substituting the phrase "other retirement arrangement" for the phrase "retirement plan." The purpose of this change is to clarify that the definition of "pensions" includes, for example, payments from Individual Retirement Accounts (IRAs) in the United States and to provide that "pensions" includes, for example, Registered Retirement Savings Plans (RRSPs) and Registered Retirement Income Funds (RRIFs) in Canada. The term "pensions" also would include amounts paid by other retirement plans or arrangements, whether or not they are qualified plans under U.S. domestic law; this would include, for example, plans and arrangements described in section 457 or 414(d) of the *Internal Revenue Code*.

**Technical Explanation [1984]**:

Paragraph 3 defines the term "pensions" for purposes of the Convention to include any payment under a superannuation, pension, or retirement plan, Armed Forces retirement pay, war veterans pensions and allowances, and amounts paid under a sickness, accident, or disability plan. Thus, the term "pension" includes pensions paid by private employers as well as any pension paid by a Contracting State in respect of services rendered to that State. A pension for government service is covered. The term "pensions" does not include payments under an income averaging annuity contract or benefits paid under social security legislation. The latter benefits are taxed, pursuant to paragraph 5, only in the Contracting State paying the benefit. Income derived from an income averaging annuity contract is taxable pursuant to the provisions of Article XXII (Other Income).

**Related Provisions**: *Income Tax Conventions Interpretation Act* 5.1 — Definition of "pension".

**Notes**: Art. XVIII(3) amended by 1995 Protocol, generally effective 1996 (see Art. 21(2)(a) under "Application of the 1995 Protocol" above), to change "or retirement plan" to "or other retirement arrangement".

Art. XVIII(3) amended by 1997 Protocol, effective on the same basis as the amendments to Art. XVIII(5), to add the words "except for the purposes of Article XIX (Government Service)".

**4.** For the purposes of the Convention, the term **"annuities"** means a stated sum paid periodically at stated times during life or during a specified number of years, under an obligation to make the payments in return for adequate and full consideration (other than services rendered), but does not include a payment that is not a periodic payment or any annuity the cost of which was deductible for the purposes of taxation in the Contracting State in which it was acquired.

**Technical Explanation [1984]**:

Paragraph 4 provides that, for purposes of the Convention, the term "annuities" means a stated sum paid periodically at stated times during life or during a specified number of years, under an obligation to make payments in return for adequate and full consideration other than services rendered. The term does not include a payment that is not periodic or any annuity the cost of which was deductible for tax purposes in the Contracting State where the annuity was acquired. Items excluded from the definition of "annuities" are subject to the rules of Article XXII.

**Related Provisions**: *Income Tax Conventions Interpretation Act* 5 — Definition of "annuity".

5. Benefits under the social security legislation in a Contracting State (including tier 1 railroad retirement benefits but not including unemployment benefits) paid to a resident of the other Contracting State shall be taxable only in that other State, subject to the following conditions:

(a) a benefit under the social security legislation in the United States paid to a resident of Canada shall be taxable in Canada as though it were a benefit under the *Canada Pension Plan*, except that 15 per cent of the amount of the benefit shall be exempt from Canadian tax; and

(b) a benefit under the social security legislation in Canada paid to a resident of the United States shall be taxable in the United States as though it were a benefit under the Social Security Act, except that a type of benefit that is not subject to Canadian tax when paid to residents of Canada shall be exempt from United States tax.

**Technical Explanation [1997 Protocol]**:

Paragraph 2 of Article 2 of the Protocol amends paragraph 5 of Article XVIII of the Convention, which provides rules for the taxation of social security benefits (including tier 1 railroad retirement benefits but not including unemployment benefits), and reverses changes made by the third protocol to the Convention, which was signed on March 17, 1995 and generally took effect as of January 1, 1996 (the "1995 Protocol"). Under the Convention prior to amendment by the 1995 Protocol, the State of residence of the recipient of social security benefits had the exclusive right to tax social security benefits paid by the other State on a net basis but exempted 50 percent of the benefit. This was changed by the 1995 Protocol. Under the 1995 Protocol, effective January 1, 1996 benefits paid under the U.S. or Canadian social security legislation to a resident of the other Contracting State (or, in the case of Canadian benefits, paid to a U.S. citizen) are taxable exclusively in the paying State.

Canada and the United States impose different source-basis taxing regimes on social security benefits. Under Code section 871(a)(3), 85 percent of social security benefits paid to a nonresident alien are includible in gross income. The taxable portion of social security benefits is subject to the regular 30 percent withholding tax, with the result that the gross social security benefit is subject to an effective tax rate of 25.5 percent. This is a final payment of tax and Canadian recipients of U.S. social security benefits, regardless of their level of income, may not elect to be taxed in the United States on a net basis at graduated rates.

In Canada, social security benefits paid to nonresidents are subject to a general withholding tax of 25 percent. However, Canada permits U.S. recipients of Canadian benefits to file a Canadian tax return and pay tax at regular graduated rates on their net income. As a result, low-income U.S. recipients of Canadian social security typically pay little or no tax on their benefits.

The Protocol returns to a system of residence-based taxation in which social security benefits are exclusively taxable in the State where the recipient lives. Social security benefits will generally be taxed as if they were benefits paid under the social security legislation in the residence State. Therefore, social security benefits will be taxed on a net basis at graduated rates and low-income recipients will not pay any tax on these benefits. However, the Protocol modifies the residence State's taxation of cross-border benefits in order to take into account how the benefits would have been taxed in the source State if paid to a resident of that State.

In the case of Canadian recipients of U.S. social security benefits, the Protocol provides that only 85 percent of these benefits will be subject to tax in Canada. This reflects the fact that, although in Canada social security benefits are fully includible, a maximum of 85 percent of United States social security benefits are includible in income for U.S. tax purposes. See Code section 86. This is also consistent with the taxation of social security benefits under the Convention prior to the effective date of the 1995 Protocol, since at the time the pre-1996 rule was adopted the United States included a maximum of 50 percent of the social security benefits in income.

In the case of U.S. recipients of Canadian social security benefits, the Protocol provides that the benefits will be taxed as if they were payments under the *Social Security Act*. Therefore, a maximum of 85 percent of the Canadian benefits will be included in the gross income of a U.S. recipient, even though the entire benefit would have been taxed by Canada if received by a Canadian resident. However, if the Canadian benefit is of a type that is not subject to Canadian tax when paid to a resident of Canada, it will not be subject to U.S. tax when received by a resident of the United States. This provision is necessary to take into account certain proposed changes to Canada's Old Age Security benefits. At present, Old Age Security benefits paid to U.S. residents are subject to both ordinary Canadian income tax and an additional "recovery tax" that has the effect of means-testing the benefit. Canada has proposed to change the Old Age Security benefit system so that the benefit would be means-tested at source and not subject to the recovery tax. Because the amount of such future benefits will have already been reduced to take into account the recipient's income, it would not be appropriate to subject such benefits to additional U.S. tax.

*[Application of the Protocol]*

Article 3 of the Protocol contains the rules for bringing the Protocol into force and giving effect to its provisions.

Paragraph 1

Paragraph 1 provides for the ratification of the Protocol by both Contracting States according to their constitutional and statutory requirements and instruments of ratification will be exchanged as soon as possible.

In the United States, the process leading to ratification and entry into force is as follows: Once a protocol has been signed by authorized representatives of the two Contracting States, the Department of State sends the protocol to the President who formally transmits it to the Senate for its advice and consent to ratification, which requires approval by two-thirds of the Senators present and voting. Prior to this vote, however, it generally has been the practice for the Senate Committee on Foreign Relations to hold hearings on the protocol and make a recommendation regarding its approval to the full Senate. Both Government and private sector witnesses may testify at these hearings. After receiving the advice and consent of the Senate to ratification, the protocol is returned to the President for his signature on the ratification document. The President's signature on the document completes the process in the United States.

Paragraph 2

Paragraph 2 of Article 3 provides that the Protocol will enter into force on the date on which the instruments of ratification are exchanged. However, the date on which the Protocol enters into force will not be the date on which its provisions will take effect. Paragraph 2, therefore, also contains rules that determine when the provisions of the Protocol will have effect.

Under paragraph 2(a), Article 1 of the Protocol will have effect as of April 26, 1995. As discussed above, this is the date on which certain proposed amendments to Canadian law would be effective.

Under paragraph 2(b), Article 2 of the Protocol will have effect as of January 1, 1996, which is the date as of which the changes to the taxation of social security benefits that were implemented by the 1995 Protocol became effective. Consequently, the source-basis taxation of social security benefits that was implemented by the 1995 Protocol will be retroactively eliminated and recipients of cross-border social security benefits will be entitled to a refund of any source-State tax withheld on their benefits for 1996 and later years. This return to residence-basis taxation of social security benefits means that some high-income recipients of cross-border benefits may be required to pay additional taxes to their State of residence if their average tax rate on these benefits in their State of residence is higher than the current rate of source-State withholding tax. It is only for future years, however, that such high-income recipients of benefits will be subject to a higher rate of tax. No one will be subject to a higher rate of tax for the retroactive period. If, as a result of the change, the residence-State tax would exceed the amount of the refund otherwise due, there will be neither a refund of source-State tax nor the imposition of additional residence-State tax.

Subparagraphs (b)(i) and (ii) provide rules that determine how the retroactive effect of the Protocol will generally be implemented for the year in which the Protocol enters into effect. As discussed below, these rules are required as a result of administrative limitations on the ability of the relevant Government organizations to effect the payment of refunds. Withholding taxes imposed by the United States on cross-border social security benefits are collected and administered by the Social Security Administration (SSA), not the Internal Revenue Service (IRS). However, any refunds of withholding tax improperly collected on social security benefits are ordinarily paid by the IRS. If the Protocol enters into force prior to September 1 of a calendar year, it is possible for the SSA to pay refunds of the tax withheld for the entire year directly to the individual Canadian recipient. If the Protocol enters into force after August 31 of a calendar year, it will not be possible for SSA to pay refunds of tax withheld for that year and refunds must be paid through the IRS.

Paragraphs 3, 4 and 5 of Article 3 establish administrative procedures to govern the payment of refunds through the IRS, including rules to ensure that benefits will not be subject to a higher rate of tax in the residence State for the retroactive period. The taxes withheld on social security benefits paid for years after 1995 and prior to the calendar year in which the Protocol enters into force (referred to in the Protocol as "source-taxed benefits") will be subject to the refund procedures set forth in paragraphs 3, 4, and 5, regardless of when the Protocol enters into force. Social security benefits paid for calendar years beginning after the Protocol enters into force will not be subject to the refund procedures set forth in paragraphs 3, 4, and 5 because source State tax will not be withheld.

If the Protocol enters into force after August 31 of a calendar year, subparagraph (b)(i) provides that social security benefits paid during such calendar year will be treated as benefits paid for calendar years ending before the year in which the Protocol enters into force (and thus will be treated as "source-taxed benefits"). In this case, the taxes withheld on these benefits will be subject to the refund procedures set forth in paragraphs 3, 4, and 5 of Article 3 and these benefits will not be subject to a higher rate of residence-State tax. If the Protocol enters into force before September 1 of a calendar year, subparagraph (b)(ii) provides that social security benefits paid during such calendar year will be treated as benefits paid for calendar years beginning after the year in which the Protocol enters into force. In this case, the taxes withheld on these benefits will be directly and automatically refunded by the source State and the potentially higher rate of residence-State tax will apply.

Paragraph 3

Paragraph 3 of Article 3 of the Protocol provides rules governing the payment of refunds of source-State tax with respect to "source-taxed benefits." In general, all applications for refund must be made to the competent authority of the source State within three years of entry into force of the Protocol.

Except as set forth in subparagraph (b) of paragraph 2, the retroactive effect of the Protocol is elective and applies only if a recipient of benefits applies for a refund of the tax paid or withheld. Consequently, if a recipient of benefits does not apply for a refund of the tax paid or withheld, the Protocol will not be given retroactive effect, except as set forth in subparagraph (b) of paragraph 2. If the residence-State tax that would be imposed on such source-taxed benefits is greater than the source-State tax imposed on such benefits, it is assumed that the recipient will not apply for a refund of the source-State tax and such benefits will not be subject to the retroactive effect of the Protocol. Because the application for refund may be made on a year-by-year basis, the recipient may elect the most beneficial treatment for each year. Therefore, social security benefits will not be subject to a higher rate of tax for the retroactive period, except as set forth in subparagraph (b) of paragraph 2.

The refund procedure depends on the recipient's State of residence. In the case of U.S. residents who received Canadian social security benefits that were subject to Canadian tax, a U.S. resident who elects to have the Protocol apply retroactively will apply directly to the Canadian competent authority for the refund of any Canadian tax not previously refunded. On the receipt of such refund, the Canadian social security benefits will be includible in the U.S. resident's gross income for the years with respect to which the refund was paid. Consequently, the U.S. recipient may be required to file an amended U.S. income tax return for such years and pay U.S. tax on such benefits. Pursuant to Article XXVII (Exchange of Information) of the Convention, the Canadian competent authority will provide the U.S. competent authority with information regarding the payment of refunds.

In the case of Canadian residents who received U.S. social security benefits, the Canadian competent authority shall be the only person entitled to apply for a refund of the U.S. taxes withheld on such benefits. Individual residents of Canada will not apply directly to the IRS for refunds. However, the Canadian competent authority may base its applications on information received from individual Canadians, as well as on information to be provided by the United State competent authority. The Protocol provides that the Canadian competent authority shall apply for and receive all such refunds on behalf of individual residents of Canada and shall remit such refunds to individual residents of Canada after deducting any additional Canadian tax that may imposed as a result of such social security benefits being subject to tax in Canada. The Canadian competent authority shall make such application for refund on behalf of an individual resident of Canada only if the additional Canadian tax that would be imposed is less than the amount of the U.S. tax to be refunded. If, with respect to an individual resident of Canada, the additional Canadian tax that would be imposed on the individual's social security benefits is equal to or greater than the U.S. tax withheld, the Canadian competent authority shall not apply for a refund of the U.S. tax withheld on the individual's benefits. This provision ensures that refunds of U.S. tax will be paid only when the refund will benefit an individual resident of Canada. A refund of U.S. tax will not be paid if it would simply result in a payment from the U.S. Treasury to the Government of Canada without any portion of the refund being paid to an individual resident of Canada.

Paragraph 4

Paragraph 4 provides that all taxes refunded as a result of the Protocol will be refunded without interest. Correspondingly, any additional taxes assessed as a result of the Protocol will be assessed without interest provided that the additional taxes are paid in a timely manner. However, interest and penalties on underpayments may be assessed for periods beginning after December 31 of the year following the year in which the Protocol enters into force.

Paragraph 5

Paragraph 5 provides that the competent authorities shall establish procedures for making or revoking the application for refund provided for in paragraph 3 and such other procedures as are necessary to ensure the appropriate implementation of the Protocol. It will be necessary to establish procedures for a taxpayer to revoke his application for refund because a taxpayer may apply for a refund and then determine that the residence-State tax imposed on his social security benefits pursuant to Article 2 of the Protocol exceeds the amount of source-State tax refunded. Such a taxpayer (or, in the case of a Canadian resident, the Canadian competent authority acting on behalf of such taxpayer) will be permitted to revoke his application for refund provided that the taxpayer returns the source-State refund and the three-year period established in paragraph 3

### Art. XVIII — Canada–U.S. Tax Convention

has not expired as of the date on which the revocation is filed. The competent authorities will also establish procedures to ensure that duplicate refunds are not paid.

**Technical Explanation [1995 Protocol]:**

Paragraph 2 of Article 9 of the Protocol amends paragraph 5 of Article XVIII to modify the treatment of social security benefits under the Convention. Under the amended paragraph, benefits paid under the U.S. or Canadian social security legislation to a resident of the other Contracting State, or, in the case of Canadian benefits, to a U.S. citizen, are taxable exclusively in the paying State. This amendment brings the Convention into line with current U.S. treaty policy. Social security benefits are defined, for this purpose, to include tier 1 railroad retirement benefits but not unemployment benefits (which therefore fall under Article XXII (Other Income) of the Convention). Pensions in respect of government service are covered not by this rule but by the rules of paragraphs 1 and 2 of Article XVIII.

The special rule regarding U.S. citizens is intended to clarify that only Canada, and not the United States, may tax a social security payment by Canada to a U.S. citizen not resident in the United States. This is consistent with the intention of the general rule, which is to give each Contracting State exclusive taxing jurisdiction over its social security payments. Since paragraph 5 is an exception to the saving clause, Canada will retain exclusive taxing jurisdiction over Canadian social security benefits paid to U.S. residents and citizens, and vice versa. It was not necessary to provide a special rule to clarify the taxation of U.S. social security payments to Canadian citizens, because Canada does not tax on the basis of citizenship and, therefore, does not include citizens within the scope of its saving clause.

**Technical Explanation [1984]:**

Paragraph 5, as amended by the 1984 Protocol, provides that benefits under social security legislation in Canada or the United States paid to a resident of the other Contracting State are taxable only in the State in which the recipient is resident. However, the State of residence must exempt from taxation one-half of the total amount of such benefits paid in a taxable year. Thus, if U.S. social security benefits are paid to a resident of Canada, the United States will exempt such benefits from tax and Canada will exempt one-half of the benefits from taxation. The exemption of one-half of the benefits in the State of residence is an exception to the saving clause under subparagraph 3(a) of Article XXIX (Miscellaneous Rules). The United States will not exempt U.S. social security benefits from tax if the Canadian resident receiving such benefits is a U.S. citizen. If a U.S. citizen and resident receives Canadian social security benefits, Canada will not tax such benefits and the United States will exempt from tax one-half of the total amount of such benefits. The United States will also exempt one-half of Canadian social security benefits from tax if the recipient is a U.S. citizen who is a resident of Canada, under paragraph 7 of Article XXIX. Paragraph 5 encompasses benefits paid under social security legislation of a political subdivision, such as a province of Canada.

**Notes:** S.C. 1999, c. 22 (the 1999 Budget bill), s. 83, applicable to the 1996 and 1997 taxation years, provides special rules for the application of the 1997 Protocol to the Canada-U.S. Income Tax Convention. It reads as follows:

83. (1) **Definitions** — The definitions in this subsection apply in this Part.

"Convention" has the meaning assigned by section 2 of the *Canada-United States Tax Convention Act, 1984*.

"creditable United States tax" of an individual for a taxation year means an amount

(a) that was paid to the government of the United States by or on behalf of the individual, at a time when the individual was resident in Canada, on account of United States tax on the individual's United States social security benefits for the year;

(b) that would have been so payable to that government if the Convention had not been amended by the Protocol signed at Ottawa on July 29, 1997; and

(c) that is refundable by that government under the terms of the Convention.

"United States social security benefits" of an individual for a particular taxation year includes

(a) benefits of the United States Social Security Administration, and

(a) (b) tier 1 railroad benefits of the United States Railroad Retirement Board

paid to or for the benefit of the individual in the particular year (but does not include unemployment benefits) and, for the purpose of this definition, a benefit paid in a taxation year for the following taxation year is deemed to have been paid in that following year.

(2) **Additional Amount** — Each individual who has paid creditable United States tax for a taxation year is deemed to have paid the amount of $50, on the individual's balance-due day for the year, on account of the individual's tax payable under Part I of the *Income Tax Act* for the year.

(3) **Interest** — For the purpose of determining interest payable under the *Income Tax Act* by or to an individual, the individual's creditable United States tax for a taxation year is deemed

(a) to have been paid, on the individual's balance-due day for the year, on account of the individual's tax payable under Part I of the Act for the year; and

(b) to have been refunded to the individual on the first day on which the Minister of National Revenue, in respect of the individual's creditable United States tax,

(i) pays an amount to or for the benefit of the individual, or

(ii) applies an amount to a liability of the individual.

The effect of being deemed under subsec. (2) to have paid the $50 is that this amount becomes refundable to the taxpayer even if no tax is payable for the year. Thus, this is a refundable credit. See Revenue Canada news releases of December 29, 1997 and August 4, 1998.

Art. XVIII(5) amended by 1997 Protocol, generally retroactive to 1996 (but see below). Previously read (i.e., as amended by 1995 Protocol):

5. Benefits under the social security legislation in a Contracting State (including tier 1 railroad benefits but not including unemployment benefits) paid to a resident of the other Contracting State (and in the case of Canadian benefits, to a citizen of the United States) shall be taxable only in the first-mentioned State.

Sections 2–5 of Article 3 of the 1997 Protocol provide:

2. This Protocol shall enter into force upon the exchange of instruments of ratification, and shall have effect as follows:

(a) Article 1 [amendments to Article XIII (Gains)] of this Protocol shall have effect as of April 26, 1995; and

(b) Article 2 [amendments to Article XVIII (Pension and Annuities)] of this Protocol shall have effect with respect to amounts paid or credited to a resident of the other Contracting State after 1995, except that where a Contracting State has, in accordance with the Convention read without reference to this Protocol, imposed a tax on benefits paid or credited under the social security legislation in that State, and those benefits are paid or credited after 1995 and

(i) before the calendar year in which this Protocol enters into force, if this Protocol enters into force before September 1 of that year, or

(ii) before the end of the calendar year in which this Protocol enters into force, if this Protocol enters into force after August 31 of that year,

Article 2 [amendments to Article XVIII (Pension and Annuities)] shall only have effect with respect to such benefits (referred to in this Article as "source-taxed benefits") as described in paragraphs 3, 4 and 5.

3. With respect to source-taxed benefits paid by a Contracting State to a resident of the other Contracting State, Article 2 applies only if the resident has, within three years after the date on which this Protocol enters into force, applied to the competent authority of the first-mentioned Contracting State for a refund of the tax imposed on the benefits. However, with respect to source-taxed benefits paid by the United States to a resident of Canada, the competent authority of Canada shall:

(a) apply for and receive such refund on behalf of the resident;

(b) remit to the resident, in accordance with the law of Canada governing refunds of income tax overpayments, such refund less any tax imposed in Canada on the benefits in accordance with Article 2 of this Protocol; and

(c) make the application referred to in subparagraph (*a*) only if the additional tax that would be imposed in Canada on the benefits, on the assumption that Article 2 of this Protocol applied, would be less than the tax imposed in the United States on the benefits as a result of paragraph 5 of Article XVIII (Pensions and Annuities) of the Convention read without reference to this Protocol.

4. All taxes refunded as a result of this Protocol shall be refunded without interest and interest on any taxes of a resident of a Contracting State assessed as a result of this Protocol shall be computed as though those taxes became payable no earlier than December 31 of the year following the year in which this Protocol enters into force.

5. The competent authorities of the Contracting States shall establish procedures for making or revoking the application referred to in paragraph 3 and shall agree on such additional procedures as are necessary to ensure the appropriate implementation of this Protocol.

Art. XVIII(5) amended by 1995 Protocol, generally effective 1996 (see Art. 21(2) under "Application of the 1995 Protocol" above). For 1985–1995, read:

5. Benefits under the social security legislation in a Contracting State paid to a resident of the other Contracting State shall be taxable as follows:

(a) such benefits shall be taxable only in that other State;

(b) notwithstanding the provisions of subparagraph (a), one-half of the total amount of any such benefit paid in a taxable year shall be exempt from taxation in that other State.

Canada extended the 25% withholding tax under ITA 212(1)(h) to Old Age Security benefits and Canada Pension Plan/Quebec Pension Plan payments effective January 1, 1996. See the 1996 repeal of ITA 212(1)(h)(i) and (ii). However, the 1997 Protocol amendments effectively override this change for U.S. residents.

**6. Alimony and other similar amounts (including child support payments) arising in a Contracting State and paid to a resident of the other Contracting State shall be taxable as follows:**

(a) such amounts shall be taxable only in that other State;

(b) notwithstanding the provisions of subparagraph (a), the amount that would be excluded from taxable income in the first-mentioned State if the recipient were a resident thereof shall be exempt from taxation in that other State.

**Technical Explanation [1984]:**

Paragraph 6(a) provides that only the State of which a person is resident has the right to tax alimony and other similar amounts (including child support payments) arising in the other Contracting State and paid to such person. However, under paragraph 6(b), the state of residence shall exempt from taxation the amount that would be excluded from taxable income in the State of source if the recipient were a resident thereof. Thus, if child support payments are made by a U.S. resident to a resident of Canada, Canada shall exempt from tax the amount of such payments which would be excluded from taxable income under section 71(b) of the *Internal Revenue Code*. Paragraph 6 does not define the term "alimony"; the term is defined pursuant to the provisions of paragraph 2 of Article III (General Definitions).

Article XVIII does not provide rules to determine the State in which pensions, annuities, alimony, and other similar amounts arise. The provisions of paragraph 2 of Article III are used to determine where such amounts arise for purposes of determining whether a Contracting State has the right to tax such amounts.

Paragraphs 1, 3, 4, 5(b) and 6(b) of Article XVIII are, by reason of paragraph 3(a) of Article XXIX (Miscellaneous Rules), exceptions to the "saving clause." Thus, the rules in those paragraphs change U.S. taxation of U.S. citizens and residents.

**Notes:** Canada repealed ITA para. 212(1)(f) effective May 1997, so withholding tax will not apply to alimony and maintenance payments even when no treaty protection is available.

**7. A natural person who is a citizen or resident of a Contracting State and a beneficiary of a trust, company, organization or other arrangement that is a resident of the other Contracting State, generally exempt from income taxation in that other State and operated exclusively to provide pension, retirement or employee benefits may elect to defer taxation in the first-mentioned State, under rules established by the competent authority of that State, with respect to any income accrued in the plan but not distributed by the plan, until such time as and to the extent that a distribution is made from the plan or any plan substituted therefor.**

**Technical Explanation [1995 Protocol]:**

A new paragraph 7 is added to Article XVIII by Article 9 of the Protocol. This paragraph replaces paragraph 5 of Article XXIX (Miscellaneous Rules) of the present Convention. The new paragraph makes reciprocal the rule that it replaced and expands its scope, so that it no longer applies only to residents and citizens of the United States who are beneficiaries of Canadian RRSPs. As amended, paragraph 7 applies to an individual who is a citizen or resident of a Contracting State and a beneficiary of a trust, company, organization, or other arrangement that is a resident of the other Contracting State and that is both generally exempt from income taxation in its State of residence and operated exclusively to provide pension, retirement, or employee benefits. Under this rule, the beneficiary may elect to defer taxation in his State of residence on income accrued in the plan until it is distributed or rolled over into another plan. The new rule also broadens the types of arrangements covered by this paragraph in a manner consistent with other pension-related provisions of the Protocol.

**Notes:** Art. XVIII(7) added by 1995 Protocol, generally effective 1996 (see Art. 21(2)(a) under "Application of the 1995 Protocol" above). This rule is a more generic version of that in former Art. XXIX(5), which applied only to RRSPs.

**Interpretation Bulletins**: IT-122R2: United States social security taxes and benefits.

## Article XIX — Government Service

Remuneration, other than a pension, paid by a Contracting State or a political subdivision or local authority thereof to a citizen of that State in respect of services rendered in the discharge of functions of a governmental nature shall be taxable only in that State. However, the provisions of Article XIV (Independent Personal Services), XV (Dependent Personal Services) or XVI (Artistes and Athletes), as the case may be, shall apply, and the preceding sentence shall not apply, to remuneration paid in respect of services rendered in connection with a trade or business carried on by a Contracting State or a political subdivision or local authority thereof.

**Technical Explanation [1984]**:

Article XIX provides that remuneration, other than a pension, paid by a Contracting State or political subdivision or local authority thereof to a citizen of that State in respect of services rendered in the discharge of governmental functions shall be taxable only in that State. (Pursuant to paragraph 5 of Article IV (Residence), other income of such a citizen may also be exempt from tax, or subject to reduced rates of tax, in the State in which he is performing services, in accordance with other provisions of the Convention.) However, if the services are rendered in connection with a trade or business, then the provisions of Article XIV (Independent Personal Services), Article XV (Dependent Personal Services), or Article XVI (Artistes and Athletes), as the case may be, are controlling. Whether functions are of a governmental nature may be determined by a comparison with the concept of a governmental function in the State in which the income arises.

Pursuant to paragraph 3(a) of Article XXIX (Miscellaneous Rules), Article XIX is an exception to the "saving clause." As a result, a U.S. citizen resident in Canada and performing services in Canada in the discharge of functions of a governmental nature for the United States is taxable only in the United States on remuneration for such services.

This provision differs from the rules of Article VI of the 1942 Convention. For example, Article XIX allows the United States to impose tax on a person other than a citizen of Canada who earns remuneration paid by Canada in respect of services rendered in the discharge of governmental functions in the United States. (Such a person may, however, be entitled to an exemption from U.S. tax as provided in Code section 893.) Also, under the provisions of Article XIX Canada will not impose tax on amounts paid by the United States in respect of services rendered in the discharge of governmental functions to a U.S. citizen who is ordinarily resident in Canada for purposes other than rendering governmental services. Under paragraph 1 of Article VI of the 1942 Convention, such amounts would be taxable by Canada.

**Related Provisions**: Art. XXVIII — Diplomatic agents and consular officials.

## Article XX — Students

Payments which a student, apprentice or business trainee, who is or was immediately before visiting a Contracting State a resident of the other Contracting State, and who is present in the first-mentioned State for the purpose of his full-time education or training, receives for the purpose of his maintenance, education or training shall not be taxed in that State provided that such payments are made to him from outside that State.

**Technical Explanation [1984]**: Article XX provides that a student, apprentice, or business trainee temporarily present in a Contracting State for the purpose of his full-time education or training is exempt from tax in that State with respect to amounts received from outside that State for the purpose of his maintenance, education, or training, if the individual is or was a resident of the other Contracting State immediately before visiting the first-mentioned State. There is no limitation on the number of years or the amount of income to which the exemption applies.

The Convention does not contain provisions relating specifically to professors and teachers. Teachers are treated under the Convention pursuant to the rules established in Articles XIV (Independent Personal Services) and XV (Dependent Personal Services), in the same manner as other persons performing services. In Article VIII A of the 1942 Convention there is a 2-year exemption in the Contracting State of source in the case of a professor or teacher who is a resident of the other Contracting State.

## Article XXI — Exempt Organizations

**1.** Subject to the provisions of paragraph 3, income derived by a religious, scientific, literary, educational or charitable organization shall be exempt from tax in a Contracting State if it is resident in the other Contracting State but only to the extent that such income is exempt from tax in that other State.

**Technical Explanation [1984]**:

Paragraph 1 provides that a religious, scientific, literary, educational, or charitable organization resident in a Contracting State shall be exempt from tax on income arising in the other Contracting State but only to the extent that such income is exempt from taxation in the Contracting State in which the organization is resident. Since this paragraph, and the remainder of Article XXI, deal with entities that are not normally taxable, the test of "resident in" is intended to be similar — but cannot be identical — to the one outlined in paragraph 1 of Article IV (Residence). Paragraph 3 provides that paragraph 1 does not exempt from tax income of a trust, company, or other organization from carrying on a trade or business, or income from a "related person" other than a person referred to in paragraph 1 or 2.

**Notes**: A detailed list of exempt U.S. organizations is in Revenue Canada publication T4016, "Exempt U.S. Organizations".

**2.** Subject to the provisions of paragraph 3, income referred to in Articles X (Dividends) and XI (Interest) derived by:

(a) a trust, company, organization or other arrangement that is a resident of a Contracting State, generally exempt from income taxation in a taxable year in that State and operated exclusively to administer or provide pension, retirement or employee benefits; or

(b) a trust, company, organization or other arrangement that is a resident of a Contracting State, generally exempt from income taxation in a taxable year in that State and operated exclusively to earn income for the benefit of an organization referred to in subparagraph (a);

shall be exempt from income taxation in that taxable year in the other Contracting State.

## Art. XXI — Exempt Organizations

**Technical Explanation [1995 Protocol]:**

Article 10 of the Protocol amends Article XXI (Exempt Organizations) of the Convention. Paragraph 1 of Article 10 amends paragraphs 2 and 3 of Article XXI. The most significant changes are those that conform the language of the two paragraphs to the revised definition of the term "pension" in paragraph 3 of Article XVIII (Pensions and Annuities). The revision adds the term "arrangement" to "trust, company or organization" in describing the residents of a Contracting State that may receive dividend and interest income exempt from current income taxation by the other Contracting State. This clarifies that IRAs, for example, are eligible for the benefits of paragraph 2, subject to the exception in paragraph 3, and makes Canadian RRSPs and RRIFs, for example, similarly eligible (provided that they are operated exclusively to administer or provide pension, retirement, or employee benefits).

The other changes, all in paragraph 2, are intended to improve and clarify the language. For example, the reference to "tax" in the present Convention is changed to a reference to "income taxation." This is intended to clarify that if an otherwise exempt organization is subject to an excise tax, for example, it will not lose the benefits of this paragraph. In subparagraph 2(b), the phrase "not taxed in a taxable year" was changed to "generally exempt from income taxation in a taxable year" to ensure uniformity throughout the Convention; this change was not intended to disqualify a trust or other arrangement that qualifies for the exemption under the wording of the present Convention.

**Technical Explanation [1984]:**

Paragraph 2 provides that a trust, company, or other organization that is resident in a Contracting State and constituted and operated exclusively to administer or provide employee benefits or benefits for the self-employed under one or more funds or plans established to provide pension or retirement benefits or other employee benefits is exempt from taxation on dividend and interest income arising in the other Contracting State, in a taxable year, if the income of such organization is generally exempt from taxation for that year in the Contracting State in which it is resident. In addition, a trust, company, or other organization resident in a Contracting State and not taxed in a taxable year in that State shall be exempt from taxation in the other State in that year on dividend and interest income arising in that other State if it is constituted and operated exclusively to earn income for the benefit of an organization described in the preceding sentence. Pursuant to paragraph 3 the exemption at source provided by paragraph 2 does not apply to dividends or interest from carrying on a trade or business or from a "related person," other than a person referred to in paragraph 1 or 2. The term "related person" is not necessarily defined by paragraph 2 of Article IX (Related Persons).

**Related Provisions:** ITA 212(14)(c) — Certificate of exemption from non-resident withholding tax.

**Notes:** Art. XXI(2) amended by 1995 Protocol, generally effective 1996 (see Art. 21(2) under "Application of the 1995 Protocol" above). For 1985–1995, read:

> 2. Subject to the provisions of paragraph 3, income referred to in Articles X (Dividends) and XI (Interest) derived by:
>
> (a) a trust, company or other organization which is resident in a Contracting State, generally exempt from tax in a taxable year in that State and constituted and operated exclusively to administer or provide benefits under one or more funds or plans established to provide pension, retirement or other employee benefits; or
>
> (b) a trust, company or other organization which is resident in a Contracting State, not taxed in a taxable year in that State and constituted and operated exclusively to earn income for the benefit of an organization referred to in subparagraph (a);
>
> shall be exempt from tax in that taxable year in the other Contracting State.

A detailed list of exempt U.S. organizations is in Revenue Canada publication T4016, "Exempt U.S. Organizations". See also Notes to para. 6 below.

**3.** The provisions of paragraphs 1 and 2 shall not apply with respect to the income of a trust, company, organization or other arrangement from carrying on a trade or business or from a related person other than a person referred to in paragraph 1 or 2.

**Technical Explanation [1995 Protocol]:**

See under para. 2.

**Technical Explanation [1984]:**

See under para. 1.

**Notes:** Art. XXI(3) amended by 1995 Protocol, generally effective 1996 (see Art. 21(2) under "Application of the 1995 Protocol" above). For 1985–1995, read:

> 3. The provisions of paragraphs 1 and 2 shall not apply with respect to the income of a trust, company or other organization from carrying on a trade or business or from a related person other than a person referred to in paragraph 1 or 2.

**4.** A religious, scientific, literary, educational or charitable organization which is resident in Canada and which has received substantially all of its support from persons other than citizens or residents of the United States shall be exempt in the United States from the United States excise taxes imposed with respect to private foundations.

**Technical Explanation [1984]:**

Paragraph 4 provides an exemption from U.S. excise taxes on private foundations in the case of a religious, scientific, literary, educational, or charitable organization which is resident in Canada but only if such organization has received substantially all of its support from persons other than citizens or residents of the United States.

**5.** For the purposes of United States taxation, contributions by a citizen or resident of the United States to an organization which is resident in Canada, which is generally exempt from Canadian tax and which could qualify in the United States to receive deductible contributions if it were resident in the United States shall be treated as charitable contributions; however, such contributions (other than such contributions to a college or university at which the citizen or resident or a member of his family is or was enrolled) shall not be deductible in any taxable year to the extent that they exceed an amount determined by applying the percentage limitations of the laws of the United States in respect of the deductibility of charitable contributions to the income of such citizen or resident arising in Canada. The preceding sentence shall not be interpreted to allow in any taxable year deductions for charitable contributions in excess of the amount allowed under the percentage limitations of the laws of the United States in respect of the deductibility of charitable contributions. For the purposes of this paragraph, a company that is a resident of Canada and that is taxable in the United States as if it were a resident of the United States shall be deemed to be a resident of the United States.

### Technical Explanation [1995 Protocol]:

Paragraph 2 of Article 10 adds a sentence to paragraph 5 of Article XXI of the Convention. The paragraph in the present Convention provides that a U.S. citizen or resident may deduct, for U.S. income tax purposes, contributions made to Canadian charities under certain circumstances. The added sentence makes clear that the benefits of the paragraph are available to a company that is a resident of Canada but is treated by the United States as a domestic corporation under the consolidated return rules of section 1504(d) of the *Internal Revenue Code*. Thus, such a company will be able to deduct, for U.S. income tax purposes, contributions to Canadian charities that are deductible to a U.S. resident under the provisions of the paragraph.

### Technical Explanation [1984]:

Paragraph 5 provides that contributions by a citizen or resident of the United States to an organization which is resident in Canada and is generally exempt from Canadian tax are treated as charitable contributions, but only if the organization could qualify in the United States to receive deductible contributions if it were resident in (i.e., organized in) the United States. Paragraph 5 generally limits the amount of contributions made deductible by the Convention to the income of the U.S. citizen or resident arising in Canada, as determined under the Convention. In the case of contributions to a college or university at which the U.S. citizen or resident or a member of his family is or was enrolled, the special limitation to income arising in Canada is not required. The percentage limitations of Code section 170 in respect of the deductibility of charitable contributions apply after the limitations established by the Convention. Any amounts treated as charitable contributions by paragraph 5 which are in excess of amounts deductible in a taxable year pursuant to paragraph 5 may be carried over and deducted in subsequent taxable years, subject to the limitations of paragraph 5.

**Notes**: The last sentence of Art. XXI(5) added by 1995 Protocol, generally effective 1996 (see Art. 21(2) under "Application of the 1995 Protocol" above).

**Registered Charities Newsletters**: 6a (Canadian charities and their U.S. donors).

6. For the purposes of Canadian taxation, gifts by a resident of Canada to an organization that is a resident of the United States, that is generally exempt from United States tax and that could qualify in Canada as a registered charity if it were a resident of Canada and created or established in Canada, shall be treated as gifts to a registered charity; however, no relief from taxation shall be available in any taxation year with respect to such gifts (other than such gifts to a college or university at which the resident or a member of the resident's family is or was enrolled) to the extent that such relief would exceed the amount of relief that would be available under the *Income Tax Act* if the only income of the resident for that year were the resident's income arising in the United States. The preceding sentence shall not be interpreted to allow in any taxation year relief from taxation for gifts to registered charities in excess of the amount of relief allowed under the percentage limitations of the laws of Canada in respect of relief for gifts to registered charities.

### Technical Explanation [1995 Protocol]:

Paragraph 3 of Article 10 amends paragraph 6 of Article XXI of the Convention to replace references to "deductions" for Canadian tax purposes with references to "relief" from tax. These changes clarify that the provisions of paragraph 6 apply to the credit for charitable contributions allowed under current Canadian law. The Protocol also makes other non-substantive drafting changes to paragraph 6.

### Technical Explanation [1984]:

Paragraph 6 provides rules for purposes of Canadian taxation with respect to the deductibility of gifts to a U.S. resident organization by a resident of Canada. The rules of paragraph 6 parallel the rules of paragraph 5. The current limitations in Canadian law provide that deductions for gifts to charitable organizations may not exceed 20 percent of income. Excess deductions may be carried forward for one year.

The term "family" used in paragraphs 5 and 6 is defined in paragraph 2 of the Exchange of Notes accompanying the Convention to mean an individual's brothers and sisters (whether by whole or half-blood, or by adoption), spouse, ancestors, lineal descendants, and adopted descendants. Paragraph 2 of the Exchange of Notes also provides that the competent authorities of Canada and the United States will review procedures and requirements for organizations to establish their exempt status under paragraph 1 of Article XXI or as an eligible recipient of charitable contributions or gifts under paragraphs 5 and 6 of Article XXI. It is contemplated that such review will lead to the avoidance of duplicative administrative efforts in determining such status and eligibility.

The provisions of paragraph 5 and 6 generally parallel the rules of Article XIII D of the 1942 Convention. However, paragraphs 5 and 6 permit greater deductions for certain contributions to colleges and universities than do the provisions of the 1942 Convention.

**Related Provisions**: ITA 118.1(9) — Commuter's charitable donations.

**Notes**: The CCRA accepts that any organization that qualifies under s. 501(c)(3) of the U.S. Internal Revenue Code will meet the test in this section (VIEWS doc 9900795).

Relief for donations to specific U.S. charities is also available under ITA 118.1(1)"total charitable gifts"(f) (universities in Schedule VIII) and (g) (charities to which the Canadian government has donated).

Art. XXI(6) amended by 1995 Protocol, generally effective 1996 (see Art. 21(2) under "Application of the 1995 Protocol" above). For 1985–1995, read:

> 6. For the purposes of Canadian taxation, gifts by a resident of Canada to an organization which is resident in the United States, which is generally exempt from United States tax and which could qualify in Canada to receive deductible gifts if it were created or established and resident in Canada shall be treated as gifts to a registered charity; however, such gifts (other than such gifts to a college or university at which the resident or a member of his family is or was enrolled) shall not be deductible in any taxable year to the extent that they exceed an amount determined by applying the percentage limitations of the laws of Canada in respect of the deductibility of gifts to registered charities to the income of such resident arising in the United States. The preceding sentence shall not be interpreted to allow in any taxable year deductions for gifts to registered charities in excess of the amount allowed under the percentage limitations of the laws of Canada in respect of the deductibility of gifts to registered charities.

**Registered Charities Newsletters**: 6a (U.S. charities and their Canadian donors).

**Information Circulars [Art. XXI]**: 77-16R4: Non-resident income tax.

**Forms [Art. XXI]**: NR602: Non-resident ownership certificate — no withholding tax.

## Article XXII — Other Income

**1.** Items of income of a resident of a Contracting State, wherever arising, not dealt with in the foregoing Articles of this Convention shall be taxable only in that State, except that if such income arises in the other Contracting State it may also be taxed in that other State.

**Technical Explanation [1984]:**

Paragraph 1 provides that a Contracting State of which a person is a resident has the sole right to tax items of income, wherever arising, if such income is not dealt with in the prior Articles of the Convention. If such income arises in the other Contracting State, however, it may also be taxed in that State. The determination of where income arises for this purpose is made under the domestic laws of the respective Contracting States unless the Convention specifies where the income arises (e.g., paragraph 6 of Article XI (Interest)) for purposes of determining the right to tax, in which case the provisions of the Convention control.

**2.** To the extent that income distributed by an estate or trust is subject to the provisions of paragraph 1, then, notwithstanding such provisions, income distributed by an estate or trust which is a resident of a Contracting State to a resident of the other Contracting State who is a beneficiary of the estate or trust may be taxed in the first-mentioned State and according to the laws of that State, but the tax so charged shall not exceed 15 per cent of the gross amount of the income; provided, however, that such income shall be exempt from tax in the first-mentioned State to the extent of any amount distributed out of income arising outside that State.

**Technical Explanation [1984]:**

Paragraph 2 provides that to the extent that income distributed by an estate or trust resident in one Contracting State is deemed under the domestic law of that State to be a separate type of income "arising" within that State, such income distributed to a beneficiary resident in the other Contracting State may be taxed in the State of source at a maximum rate of 15 percent of the gross amount of such distribution. Such a distribution will, however, be exempt from tax in the State of source to the extent that the income distributed by the estate or trust was derived by the estate or trust from sources outside that State. Thus, in a case where the law of Canada treats a distribution made by a trust resident in Canada as a separate type of income arising in Canada, Canadian tax is limited by paragraph 2 to 15 percent of the gross amount distributed to a U.S. resident beneficiary. Although the Code imposes a tax on certain domestic trusts (e.g., accumulation trusts) and such trusts are residents of the United States for purposes of Article IV (Residence) and paragraph 2 of Article XXII, paragraph 2 does not apply to distributions by such trusts because, pursuant to Code sections 667(e) and 662(b), these distributions have the same character in the hands of a non-resident beneficiary as they do in the hands of the trust. Thus, a distribution by a domestic accumulation trust is not a separate type of income for U.S. purposes. The taxation of such a distribution in the United States is governed by the distribution's character, the provisions of the Code and the provisions of the Convention other than the provision in paragraph 2 limiting the tax at source to 15 percent.

**Interpretation Bulletins:** IT-465R: Non-resident beneficiaries of trusts.

**3.** Losses incurred by a resident of a Contracting State with respect to wagering transactions the gains on which may be taxed in the other Contracting State shall, for the purpose of taxation in that other State, be deductible to the same extent that such losses would be deductible if they were incurred by a resident of that other State.

**Technical Explanation [1995 Protocol]:**

Article 11 of the Protocol adds a new paragraph 3 to Article XXII (Other Income) of the Convention. This Article entitles residents of one Contracting State who are taxable by the other State on gains from wagering transactions to deduct losses from wagering transactions for the purposes of taxation in that other State. However, losses are to be deductible only to the extent that they are incurred with respect to wagering transactions, the gains on which could be taxable in the other State, and only to the extent that such losses would be deductible if incurred by a resident of that other State.

This Article does not affect the collection of tax by a Contracting State. Thus, in the case of a resident of Canada, this Article does not affect, for example, the imposition of U.S. withholding taxes under section 1441 or section 1442 of the *Internal Revenue Code* on the gross amount of gains from wagering transactions. However, in computing its U.S. income tax liability on net income for the taxable year concerned, the Canadian resident may reduce its gains from wagering transactions subject to taxation in the United States by any wagering losses incurred on such transactions, to the extent that those losses are deductible under the provisions of new paragraph 3. Under U.S. domestic law, the deduction of wagering losses is governed by section 165 of the *Internal Revenue Code*. It is intended that the resident of Canada file a nonresident income tax return in order to substantiate the deduction for losses and to claim a refund of any overpayment of U.S. taxes collected by withholding.

**Notes:** Art. XXII(3) added by 1995 Protocol, generally effective 1996 (see Art. 21(2) under "Application of the 1995 Protocol" above).

## Article XXIII — Capital

**1.** Capital represented by real property, owned by a resident of a Contracting State and situated in the other Contracting State, may be taxed in that other State.

**Technical Explanation [1984]:**

Although neither Canada nor the United States currently has national taxes on capital, Article XXIII provides rules for the eventuality that such taxes might be enacted in the future. Paragraph 1 provides that capital represented by real property (as defined in paragraph 2 of Article VI (Income From Real Property)) owned by a resident of a Contracting State and situated in the other Contracting State may be taxed in that other State.

**Related Provisions:** *Income Tax Conventions Interpretation Act* 5 — Definition of "immovable property" and "real property".

**2.** Capital represented by personal property forming part of the business property of a permanent establishment which a resident of a Contracting State has in the other Contracting State, or by personal property pertaining to a fixed base available to a resident of a Contracting State in the other Contracting State for the purpose of performing independent personal services, may be taxed in that other State.

**Technical Explanation [1984]:**

Paragraph 2 provides that capital represented by either personal property forming part of the business property of a permanent establishment or personal property pertaining to a fixed base in a Contracting State may be taxed in that State.

3. Capital represented by ships and aircraft operated by a resident of a Contracting State in international traffic, and by personal property pertaining to the operation of such ships and aircraft, shall be taxable only in that State.

**Technical Explanation [1984]:**

Paragraph 3 provides that capital represented by ships and aircraft operated by a resident of a Contracting State in international traffic and by personal property pertaining to the operation of such ships and aircraft are taxable only in the Contracting State of residence.

**Related Provisions:** Art. III:1(h) — Meaning of "international traffic".

4. All other elements of capital of a resident of a Contracting State shall be taxable only in that State.

**Technical Explanation [1984]:**

Paragraph 4 provides that all elements of capital other than those covered by paragraphs 1, 2, and 3 are taxable only in the Contracting State of residence. Thus, capital represented by motor vehicles or railway cars, not pertaining to a permanent establishment or fixed base in a Contracting State, would be taxable only in the Contracting State of which the taxpayer is a resident.

## Article XXIV — Elimination of Double Taxation

1. In the case of the United States, subject to the provisions of paragraphs 4, 5 and 6, double taxation shall be avoided as follows: In accordance with the provisions and subject to the limitations of the law of the United States (as it may be amended from time to time without changing the general principle hereof), the United States shall allow to a citizen or resident of the United States, or to a company electing to be treated as a domestic corporation, as a credit against the United States tax on income the appropriate amount of income tax paid or accrued to Canada; and, in the case of a company which is a resident of the United States owning at least 10 per cent of the voting stock of a company which is a resident of Canada from which it receives dividends in any taxable year, the United States shall allow as a credit against the United States tax on income the appropriate amount of income tax paid or accrued to Canada by that company with respect to the profits out of which such dividends are paid.

**Technical Explanation [1984]:**

Paragraph 1 provides the general rules that will apply under the Convention with respect to foreign tax credits for Canadian taxes paid or accrued. The United States undertakes to allow to a citizen or resident of the United States, or to a company electing under Code section 1504(d) to be treated as a domestic corporation, a credit against the Federal income taxes imposed by the Code for the appropriate amount of income tax paid or accrued to Canada. In the case of a company which is a resident of the United States owning 10 percent or more of the voting stock of a company which is a resident of Canada (which for this purpose does not include a company electing under Code section 1504(d) to be treated as a domestic corporation), and from which it receives dividends in a taxable year, the United States shall allow as a credit against income taxes imposed by the Code the appropriate amount of income tax paid or accrued to Canada by the Canadian company with respect to the profits out of which such company paid the dividends.

The direct and deemed-paid credits allowed by paragraph 1 are subject to the limitations of the Code as they may be amended from time to time without changing the general principle of paragraph 1. Thus, as is generally the case under U.S. income tax conventions, provisions such as Code sections 901(c), 904, 905, 907, 908, and 911 apply for purposes of computing the allowable credit under paragraph 1. In addition, the United States is not required to maintain the overall limitation currently provided by U.S. law.

The term "income tax paid or accrued" is defined in paragraph 7 of Article XXIV to include certain specified taxes which are paid or accrued. The Convention only provides a credit for amounts paid or accrued. The determination of whether an amount is paid or accrued is made under the Code. Paragraph 1 provides a credit for these specified taxes whether or not they qualify as creditable under Code section 901 or 903. A taxpayer who claims credit under the Convention for Canadian taxes made creditable solely by paragraph 1 is not, as a result of the Protocol, subject to a per-country limitation with respect to Canadian taxes. Thus, credit for such Canadian taxes would be computed under the overall limitation currently provided by U.S. law. (However, see the discussion below of the source rules of paragraphs 3 and 9 for a restriction on the use of third country taxes to offset the U.S. tax imposed on resourced income).

A taxpayer claiming credits for Canadian taxes under the Convention must apply the source rules of the Convention, and must apply those source rules in their entirety. Similarly, a taxpayer claiming credit for Canadian taxes which are creditable under the Code and who wishes to use the source rules of the Convention in computing that credit must apply the source rules of the Convention in their entirety.

2. In the case of Canada, subject to the provisions of paragraphs 4, 5 and 6, double taxation shall be avoided as follows:

(a) subject to the provisions of the law of Canada regarding the deduction from tax payable in Canada of tax paid in a territory outside Canada and to any subsequent modification of those provisions (which shall not affect the general principle hereof)

(i) income tax paid or accrued to the United States on profits, income or gains arising in the United States, and

(ii) in the case of an individual, any social security taxes paid to the United States (other than taxes relating to unemployment insurance benefits) by the individual on such profits, income or gains

shall be deducted from any Canadian tax payable in respect of such profits, income or gains;

(b) subject to the existing provisions of the law of Canada regarding the taxation of income from a foreign affiliate and to any subsequent modification of those provisions — which shall not affect the general principle hereof — for the purpose of computing Canadian tax, a company which is a resident of Canada shall be allowed to deduct in computing its taxable income any dividend received by it out of the exempt surplus of a foreign affiliate which is a resident of the United States; and

(c) notwithstanding the provisions of subparagraph (a), where Canada imposes a tax on gains from the alienation of property that, but for the provisions of paragraph 5 of Article XIII (Gains), would not be taxable in Canada, income tax paid or accrued to the United States on such gains shall be deducted from any Canadian tax payable in respect of such gains.

**Technical Explanation [1995 Protocol]:**

Article 12 of the Protocol amends Article XXIV (Elimination of Double Taxation) of the Convention. Paragraph 1 of Article 12 amends the rules for Canadian double taxation relief in subparagraphs (a) and (b) of paragraph 2 of Article XXIV. The amendment to subparagraph (a) obligates Canada to give a foreign tax credit for U.S. social security taxes paid by individuals. The amendment to subparagraph (b) of paragraph 2 does not alter the substantive effect of the rule, but conforms the language to current Canadian law. Under the provision as amended, Canada generally continues to allow an exemption to a Canadian corporation for direct dividends paid from the exempt surplus of a U.S. affiliate.

**Notes:** Art. XXIV(2) amended by 1995 Protocol, generally effective 1996 (see Art. 21(2) under "Application of the 1995 Protocol" above). For 1985–1995, read:

> 2. In the case of Canada, subject to the provisions of paragraphs 4, 5 and 6, double taxation shall be avoided as follows:
>
>> (a) subject to the provisions of the law of Canada regarding the deduction from tax payable in Canada of tax paid in a territory outside Canada and to any subsequent modification of those provisions (which shall not affect the general principle hereof), and unless a greater deduction or relief is provided under the law of Canada, income tax paid or accrued to the United States on profits, income or gains arising in the United States shall be deducted from any Canadian tax payable in respect of such profits, income or gains;
>>
>> (b) subject to the provisions of the law of Canada regarding the determination of the exempt surplus of a foreign affiliate and to any subsequent modification of those provisions (which shall not affect the general principle hereof), for the purposes of computing Canadian tax, a company which is a resident of Canada shall be allowed to deduct in computing its taxable income any dividend received by it out of the exempt surplus of a foreign affiliate which is a resident of the United States; and
>>
>> (c) notwithstanding the provisions of subparagraph (a), where Canada imposes a tax on gains from the alienation of property that, but for the provisions of paragraph 5 of Article XIII (Gains), would not be taxable in Canada, income tax paid or accrued to the United States on such gains shall be deducted from any Canadian tax payable in respect of such gains.

**Interpretation Bulletins:** IT-173R2: Capital gains derived in Canada by residents of the United States.

3. For the purposes of this Article:

   (a) profits, income or gains (other than gains to which paragraph 5 of Article XIII (Gains) applies) of a resident of a Contracting State which may be taxed in the other Contracting State in accordance with the Convention (without regard to paragraph 2 of Article XXIX (Miscellaneous Rules)) shall be deemed to arise in that other State; and

   (b) profits, income or gains of a resident of a Contracting State which may not be taxed in the other Contracting State in accordance with the Convention (without regard to paragraph 2 of Article XXIX (Miscellaneous Rules)) or to which paragraph 5 of Article XIII (Gains) applies shall be deemed to arise in the first-mentioned State.

**Technical Explanation [1984]:**

Paragraph 3 provides source rules for purposes of applying Article XXIV. Profits, income or gains of a resident of a Contracting State which may be taxed in the other Contracting State in accordance with the Convention, for reasons other than the saving clause of paragraph 2 of Article XXIX (Miscellaneous Rules) (e.g., pensions and annuities taxable where arising pursuant to Article XVIII (Pensions and Annuities)), are deemed to arise in the latter State. This rule does not, however, apply to gains taxable under paragraph 5 of Article XIII (Gains) (i.e., gains taxed by a Contracting State derived from the alienation of property by a former resident of that State). Gains from such an alienation arise, pursuant to paragraph 3(b), in the State of which the alienator is a resident. Thus, if in accordance with paragraph 5 of Article XIII, Canada imposes tax on certain gains of a U.S. resident such gains are deemed, pursuant to paragraphs 2 and 3(b) of Article XXIV, to arise in the United States for purposes of computing the deduction against Canadian tax for the U.S. tax on such gain. Under the Convention such gains arise in the United States for purposes of the United States foreign tax credit. Paragraph 3(b) also provides that profits, income, or gains arise in the Contracting State of which a person is a resident if they may not be taxed in the other Contracting State under the provisions of the Convention (e.g., alimony), other than the "saving clause" of paragraph 2 of Article XXIX.

4. Where a United States citizen is a resident of Canada, the following rules shall apply:

   (a) Canada shall allow a deduction from the Canadian tax in respect of income tax paid or accrued to the United States in respect of profits, income or gains which arise (within the meaning of paragraph 3) in the United States, except that such deduction need not exceed the amount of the tax that would be paid to the United States if the resident were not a United States citizen; and

   (b) for the purposes of computing the United States tax, the United States shall allow as a credit against United States tax the income tax paid or accrued to Canada after the deduction referred to in subparagraph (a). The credit so allowed shall not reduce that portion of the United States tax that is deductible from Canadian tax in accordance with subparagraph (a).

5. Notwithstanding the provisions of paragraph 4, where a United States citizen is a resident of Canada, the following rules shall apply in respect of the items of income referred to in Article X (Dividends), XI (Interest) or XII (Royalties) that arise (within the meaning of paragraph 3) in the United States and that would be subject to United States tax if the resident of Canada were not a citizen of the United States, as long as the law in force in Canada allows a deduction in computing income for the portion of any foreign tax paid in respect of such items which exceeds 15 per cent of the amount thereof:

   (a) the deduction so allowed in Canada shall not be reduced by any credit or deduction for income tax paid or accrued to Canada allowed in computing the United States tax on such items;

(b) Canada shall allow a deduction from Canadian tax on such items in respect of income tax paid or accrued to the United States on such items, except that such deduction need not exceed the amount of the tax that would be paid on such items to the United States if the resident of Canada were not a United States citizen; and

(c) for the purposes of computing the United States tax on such items, the United States shall allow as a credit against United States tax the income tax paid or accrued to Canada after the deduction referred to in subparagraph (b). The credit so allowed shall reduce only that portion of the United States tax on such items which exceeds the amount of tax that would be paid to the United States on such items if the resident of Canada were not a United States citizen.

**Technical Explanation [1995 Protocol]:**

Paragraphs 4 and 5 of Article XXIV of the Convention provide double taxation relief rules, for both the United States and Canada, with respect to U.S. source income derived by a U.S. citizen who is resident in Canada. These rules address the fact that a U.S. citizen resident in Canada remains subject to U.S. tax on his worldwide income at ordinary progressive rates, and may, therefore, be subject to U.S. tax at a higher rate than a resident of Canada who is not a U.S. citizen. In essence, these paragraphs limit the foreign tax credit that Canada is obliged to allow such a U.S. citizen to the amount of tax on his U.S. source income that the United States would be allowed to collect from a Canadian resident who is not a U.S. citizen. They also oblige the United States to allow the U.S. citizen a credit for any income tax paid to Canada on the remainder of his income. Paragraph 4 deals with items of income other than dividends, interest, and royalties and is not changed by the Protocol. Paragraph 5, which deals with dividends, interest, and royalties, is amended by paragraph 2 of Article 12 of the Protocol.

The amendments to paragraph 5 of the Article make that paragraph applicable only to dividend, interest, and royalty income that would be subject to a positive rate of U.S. tax if paid to a Canadian resident who is not a U.S. citizen. This means that the rules of paragraph 4, not paragraph 5, will apply to items of interest and royalties, such as portfolio interest, that would be exempt from U.S. tax if paid to a non-U.S. citizen resident in Canada. Under paragraph 4, Canada will not allow a credit for the U.S. tax on such income, and the United States will credit the Canadian tax to the extent necessary to avoid double taxation.

Paragraph 2 of Article 12 of the Protocol makes further technical amendments to paragraph 5 of Article XXIV of the Convention. The existing Technical Explanation of paragraphs 5 and 6 of Article XXIV of the Convention should be read as follows to reflect the amendments made by the Protocol:

> Paragraph 5 provides special rules for the elimination of double taxation in the case of dividends, interest, and royalties earned by a U.S. citizen resident in Canada. These rules apply notwithstanding the provisions of paragraph 4, but only as long as the law in Canada allows a deduction in computing income for the portion of any foreign tax paid in respect of dividends, interest, or royalties which exceeds 15 percent of the amount of such items of income, and only with respect to those items of income. The rules of paragraph 4 apply with respect to other items of income; moreover, if the law in force in Canada regarding the deduction for foreign taxes is changed so as to no longer allow such a deduction, the provisions of paragraph 5 shall not apply and the U.S. foreign tax credit for Canadian taxes and the Canadian credit for U.S. taxes will be determined solely pursuant to the provisions of paragraph 4.

> The calculations under paragraph 5 are as follows. First, the deduction allowed in Canada in computing income shall be made with respect to U.S. tax on the dividends, interest, and royalties before any foreign tax credit by the United States with respect to income tax paid or accrued to Canada. Second, Canada shall allow a deduction from (credit against) Canadian tax for U.S. tax paid or accrued with respect to the dividends, interest, and royalties, but such credit need not exceed the amount of income tax that would be paid or accrued to the United States on such items of income if the individual were not a U.S. citizen after taking into account any relief available under the Convention. Third, for purposes of computing the U.S. tax on such dividends, interest, and royalties, the United States shall allow as a credit against the U.S. tax the income tax paid or accrued to Canada after the credit against Canadian tax for income tax paid or accrued to the United States. The United States is in no event obliged to give a credit for Canadian income tax which will reduce the U.S. tax below the amount of income tax that would be paid or accrued to the United States on the amount of the dividends, interest, and royalties if the individual were not a U.S. citizen after taking into account any relief available under the Convention.

> The rules of paragraph 5 are illustrated by the following examples.

> *Example B*

> A U.S. citizen who is a resident of Canada has $100 of dividend income arising in the United States. The tentative U.S. tax before foreign tax credit is $40.

> Canada, under its law, allows a deduction for the U.S. tax in excess of 15 percent or, in this case, a deduction of $25 ($40 - $15). The Canadian taxable income is $75 and the Canadian tax on that amount is $35.

> Canada gives a credit of $15 (the maximum credit allowed is 15 percent of the gross dividend taken into Canadian income) and collects a net tax of $20.

> The United States allows a credit for the net Canadian tax against its tax in excess of 15 percent. Thus, the maximum credit is $25 ($40 - $15). But since the net Canadian tax paid was $20, the usable credit is $20.

> To be able to use a credit of $20 requires Canadian source taxable income of $50 (50% of the U.S. tentative tax of $40). Under paragraph 6, $50 of the U.S. dividend is resourced to be of Canadian source. The credit of $20 may then be offset against the U.S. tax of $40, leaving a net U.S. tax of $20.

> The combined tax paid to both countries is $40, $20 to Canada and $20 to the United States.

> *Example C*

> A U.S. citizen who is a resident of Canada receives $200 of income with respect to personal services performed within Canada and $100 of dividend income arising within the United States. Taxable income for U.S. purposes, taking into account the rules of Code section 911, is $220. U.S. tax (before foreign tax credits) is $92. The $100 of dividend income is deemed to bear U.S. tax (before foreign tax credits) of $41.82 ($100/$200 x $92). Under Canadian law, a deduction of $26.82 (the excess of $41.82 over 15 percent of the $100 dividend income) is allowed in computing income. The Canadian tax on $273.18 of income ($300 less the $26.82 deduction) is $130. Canada then gives a credit against the $130 for $15 (the U.S. tax paid or accrued with respect to the dividend, $41.82 but limited to 15 percent of the gross amount of such income, or $15), leaving a final Canadian tax of $115. Of the $115, $30.80 is attributable to the dividend:

$$\frac{\$73.18\ (\$100\ \text{dividend less}\ \$26.82\ \text{deduction})}{\$273.18\ (\$300\ \text{income less}\ \$26.82\ \text{deduction})} \times \$115$$

Of this amount, $26.82 is creditable against U.S. tax pursuant to paragraph 5. (Although the U.S. allows a credit for the Canadian tax imposed on the dividend, $30.80, the credit may not reduce the U.S. tax below 15 percent of the amount of the dividend. Thus, the maximum allowable credit is the excess of $41.82, the U.S. tax imposed on the dividend income, over $15, which is 15 percent of the $100 dividend). The remaining $3.98 (the Canadian tax of $30.80 less the credit allowed of $26.82) is a foreign tax credit carryover for U.S. purposes, subject to the limitations of paragraph 5. (An additional $50.18 of Canadian tax with respect to Canadian source services income is creditable against U.S. tax pursuant to paragraphs 3 and 4(b). The $50.18 is computed as follows: tentative U.S. tax (before foreign tax credits) is $92; the U.S. tax on Canadian source services income is $50.18 ($92 less the U.S. tax on the dividend income of $41.82); the limitation on the services income is:

$$\frac{\$120 \text{ (taxable income from services)}}{\$220 \text{ (total taxable income)}} \times \$92$$

or $50.18. The credit for Canadian tax paid on the services income is therefore $50.18; the remainder of the Canadian tax on the services income, or $34.02, is a foreign tax credit carryover for U.S. purposes, subject to the limitations of paragraph 5.)

Paragraph 6 is necessary to implement the objectives of paragraphs 4(b) and 5(c). Paragraph 6 provides that where a U.S. citizen is a resident of Canada, items of income referred to in paragraph 4 or 5 are deemed for the purposes of Article XXIV to arise in Canada to the extent necessary to avoid double taxation of income by Canada and the United States consistent with the objectives of paragraphs 4(b) and 5(c). Paragraph 6 can override the source rules of paragraph 3 to permit a limited resourcing of income. The principles of paragraph 3 have effect, pursuant to paragraph 3(b) of Article XXX (Entry Into Force) of the Convention, for taxable years beginning on or after January 1, 1976. See the discussion of Article XXX below.

The application of paragraph 6 is illustrated by the following example.

*Example D*

The facts are the same as in Example C. The United States has undertaken, pursuant to paragraph 5(c) and paragraph 6, to credit $26.82 of Canadian taxes on dividend income that has a U.S. source under both paragraph 3 and the *Internal Revenue Code*. (As illustrated in Example C, the credit, however, only reduces the U.S. tax on the dividend income which exceeds the amount of income tax that would be paid or accrued to the United States on such income if the individual were not a U.S. citizen after taking into account any relief available under the Convention. Pursuant to paragraph 6, for purposes of determining the U.S. foreign tax credit limitation under the Convention with respect to Canadian taxes,

$$\$64.13 \left(\frac{A}{\$220} \times \$92 = \$26.82; A = \$64.13\right)$$

of taxable income with respect to the dividends is deemed to arise in Canada.

**Notes**: Art. XXIV(5) amended by 1995 Protocol, generally effective 1996 (see Art. 21(2) under "Application of the 1995 Protocol" above). For 1985–1995, read:

5. Notwithstanding the provisions of paragraph 4, where a United States citizen is a resident of Canada, the following rules shall apply in respect of the items of income referred to in Article X (Dividends), XI (Interest) or XII (Royalties) which arise (within the meaning of paragraph 3) in the United States, as long as the law in force in Canada allows a deduction in computing income for the portion of any foreign tax paid in respect of such items which exceeds 15 per cent of the amount thereof:

(a) the deduction so allowed in Canada shall not be reduced by any credit or deduction for income tax paid or accrued to Canada allowed in computing the United States tax on such items;

(b) Canada shall allow a deduction from the Canadian tax in respect of the income tax paid or accrued to the United States on such items, except that such deduction need not exceed 15 per cent of the gross amount of such items that has been included in computing the income of the citizen for Canadian tax purposes; and

(c) for the purposes of computing the United States tax on such items, the United States shall allow as a credit against United States tax the income tax paid or accrued to Canada after the deduction referred to in subparagraph (b). The credit so allowed shall reduce only that portion of the United States tax on such items which exceeds 15 per cent of the amount thereof included in computing United States taxable income.

6. Where a United States citizen is a resident of Canada, items of income referred to in paragraph 4 or 5 shall, notwithstanding the provisions of paragraph 3, be deemed to arise in Canada to the extent necessary to avoid the double taxation of such income under paragraph 4(b) or paragraph 5(c).

7. For the purposes of this Article, any reference to "income tax paid or accrued" to a Contracting State shall include Canadian tax and United States tax, as the case may be, and taxes of general application which are paid or accrued to a political subdivision or local authority of that State, which are not imposed by that political subdivision or local authority in a manner inconsistent with the provisions of the Convention and which are substantially similar to the Canadian tax or United States tax, as the case may be.

**Technical Explanation [1995 Protocol]**:

Paragraph 3 of Article 12 of the Protocol makes a technical amendment to paragraph 7 of Article XXIV. It conforms the reference to U.S. and Canadian taxes to the amended definitions of "United States tax" and "Canadian tax" in subparagraphs (c) and (d) of paragraph 1 of Article III (General Definitions). No substantive change in the effect of the paragraph is intended.

**Notes**: Art. XXIV(7) amended by 1995 Protocol, generally effective 1996 (see Art. 21(2) under "Application of the 1995 Protocol" above), to change "the taxes of that State referred to in paragraphs 2 and 3(a) of Article II (Taxes Covered)" to "the Canadian tax or United States tax, as the case may be", at the end of the paragraph.

8. Where a resident of a Contracting State owns capital which, in accordance with the provisions of the Convention, may be taxed in the other Contracting State, the first-mentioned State shall allow as a deduction from the tax on the capital of that resident an amount equal to the capital tax paid in that other State. The deduction shall not, however, exceed that part of the capital tax, as computed before the deduction is given, which is attributable to the capital which may be taxed in that other State.

9. The provisions of this Article relating to the source of profits, income or gains shall not apply for the purpose of determining a credit against United States tax for any foreign taxes other than income taxes paid or accrued to Canada.

10. Where in accordance with any provision of the Convention income derived or capital owned by a resident of a Contracting State is exempt from tax in that State, such State may nevertheless, in calculating the amount of tax on other income or capital, take into account the exempted income or capital.

**Technical Explanation [1995 Protocol]**:

Paragraph 4 of Article 12 of the Protocol adds a new paragraph 10 to Article XXIV of the Convention. This paragraph provides for the application of the rule of "exemption with progression" by a Contracting State in cases where an item of income of a resident of that State is exempt from tax in that State by virtue of a provision of the Convention. For example, where under Canadian law a tax benefit, such as the goods and services tax credit, to a Canadian resident individual is reduced as the income of that individual, or the individual's spouse or other dependent, increases, and any of these persons receives U.S. social security benefits that are exempt from tax in Canada under the Convention, Canada may, nevertheless, take the U.S. social security benefits into account in determining whether, and to what extent, the benefit should be reduced.

New Article XXIX B (Taxes Imposed by Reason of Death), added by Article 19 of the Protocol, also provides relief from double taxation in certain circumstances in connection with Canadian income tax imposed by reason of death and U.S. estate taxes. However, subparagraph 7(c) of Article XXIX B generally denies relief from U.S. estate tax under that Article to the extent that a credit or deduction has been claimed for the same amount in determining any other tax imposed by the United States. This restriction would operate to deny relief, for example, to the extent that relief from U.S. income tax is claimed under Article XXIV in respect of the same amount of Canadian tax. There is, however, no requirement that relief from U.S. tax be claimed first (or exclusively) under Article XXIV. Paragraph 6 of Article XXIX B also prevents the claiming of double relief from Canadian income taxation under both that Article and Article XXIV, by providing that the credit provided by Article XXIX B applies only after the application of the credit provided by Article XXIV.

**Technical Explanation [1984]**:

Paragraph 9 provides clarification that the source rules of this Article shall not be used to determine the credit available against U.S. tax for foreign taxes other than income taxes paid or accrued to Canada (i.e., taxes of third countries). Thus, creditable third country taxes may not offset the U.S. tax on income treated as arising in Canada under the source rules of the Convention. A person claiming credit for income taxes of a third country may not rely upon the rules of paragraphs 3 and 6 for purposes of treating income that would otherwise have a U.S. source as having a foreign source. Thus, if the taxpayer elects to compute the foreign tax credit for any year using the special source rules set forth in paragraphs 3 and 6, paragraph 9 requires that a separate limitation be computed for taxes not covered by paragraph 1 without regard to the source rules of paragraphs 3 and 6, and the credit for such taxes may not exceed such limitation. The credit allowed under this separate limitation may not exceed the proportion of the Federal income taxes imposed by the Code that the taxpayer's taxable income from foreign sources (under the Code) not included in taxable income arising in Canada (and not in excess of total foreign source taxable income under the Code) bears to the taxpayer's worldwide taxable income. In any case the credit for taxes covered by paragraph 1 and the credit for other foreign taxes is limited to the amount allowed under an overall limitation computed by aggregating taxable income arising in Canada and other foreign source taxable income.

If creditable Canadian taxes exceed the proportion of U.S. tax that taxable income arising in Canada bears to the entire taxable income, such taxes may qualify to be absorbed by any excess in the separate limitation computed with respect to other taxes.

In a case where a taxpayer has different types of income subject to separate limitations under the Code (e.g., section 904(d)(1)(B) DISC dividends) the Convention rules just described apply in the context of each of the separate Code limitations.

A taxpayer may, for any year, claim a credit pursuant to the rules of the Code. In such case, the taxpayer would be subject to the limitations established in the Code, and would forego the rules of the Convention that determine where taxable income arises. In addition, any Canadian taxes covered by paragraph 1 which are not creditable under the Code would not be credited.

Thus, where a taxpayer elects to use the special source rules of this Article to compute the foreign tax credit for any year, the following computations must be made:

*Step 1(a):* Compute a hypothetical foreign tax credit limitation for Canadian income and taxes using the source rules of the Convention.

*Step 1(b):* Compute a hypothetical foreign tax credit limitation for third country income and taxes using the source rules of the Code.

*Step 1(c):* Compute an overall foreign tax credit limitation using the source rules of the Convention to the extent they resource Canadian source income as U.S. source income or U.S. source income as Canadian source income, and using the source rules of the Code with respect to any other income.

*Step 2:* Allocate the amount of creditable Canadian taxes to the amount of the limitation computed under step 1(a), and allocate the amount of creditable third country taxes to the amount of the limitation computed under step 1(b). The amount of credit to be so allocated may not exceed the amount of the respective limitation.

*Step 3:* (1) If the total credits allocated under step 2 exceed the amount of the limitation computed under step 1(c), the amount of allowable credits must be reduced to that limitation (see Rev. Rul. 82-215, 1982-2 Cum. Bull. 153 for the method of such reduction).

(2) If the total credits allocated under step 2 are less than the amount of the limitation computed under step 1(c), then (a) any amount of creditable Canadian taxes in excess of the amount of the step 1(a) limitation may be credited to the extent of the excess of the step 1(c) limitation over the total step 2 allocation, and (b) any amount of third country taxes in excess of the amount of the step 1(b) limitation may not be credited.

The following examples (in which the taxpayer's U.S. tax rate is presumed to be 46%) illustrate the application of the source rules of Article XXIV:

**Example 1.**

(a) A U.S. corporate taxpayer has for the taxable year $100 of taxable income having a U.S. source under both the Convention and the Code; $100 of taxable income having a Canadian source under both the Convention and the Code; $50 of taxable income having a Canadian source under the Convention but a U.S. source under the Code (see, for example, paragraph 1 of Article VII (Business Profits) and paragraph 3(a) of Article XXIV); and $80 of taxable income having a foreign (non-Canadian) source under the Code. The taxpayer pays $75 of Canadian income taxes and $45 of third country income taxes. All the foreign source income of the taxpayer constitutes "other" income described in Code section 904(d)(1)(C).

The source rules of the Convention are applied as follows to compute the taxpayer's foreign tax credit:

*Step 1(a):*

$\dfrac{\$150 \text{ (Canadian source taxable income under Convention)}}{\$330 \text{ (total taxable income)}} \times \$151.80$

= $69 limit for Canadian taxes.

*Step 1(b):*

$$\frac{\$80 \text{ (third country source taxable income under Code)}}{\$330 \text{ (total taxable income)}} \times \$151.80$$

= $36.80 limit for third country taxes.

*Step 1(c):*

$$\frac{\$230 \text{ (overall foreign taxable income under source rules described above)}}{\$330 \text{ (total taxable income)}} \times \$151.80$$

= $105.80 total limit.

*Step 2:* The taxpayer may tentatively credit $69 of the $75 Canadian income taxes under the step 1(a) limitation, and $36.80 of the third country income taxes under the step 1(b) limitation.

*Step 3:* Since the total amount of taxes credited under step 2 equals the taxpayer's total limitation of $105.80 under step 1(c), no additional taxes may be credited. The taxpayer has a $6 Canadian income tax carryover and an $8.20 third country income tax carryover for U.S. foreign tax credit purposes.

(b) If the taxpayer had paid only $30 of third country taxes, he would credit that $30 in step 2. Since the total amount of credits allowed under step 2 ($99) is less than the taxpayer's total limit of $105.80, and since the taxpayer has $6 of excess Canadian taxes not credited under step 2, he may also claim a credit for that $6 of Canadian income taxes, for a total credit of $105.

(c) If the taxpayer had paid $45 of third country income taxes and $65 of Canadian income taxes, the computation would be as follows:

*Step 2:* The taxpayer would credit the $65 of Canadian income taxes, and would also credit $36.80 of the $45 of third country income taxes.

*Step 3:* Although the total amount of credits computed under step 2 ($101.80) is less than the taxpayer's total limitation of $105.80, no additional credits can be claimed since the taxpayer has only excess third country income taxes. The excess third country income taxes are thus not permitted to offset U.S. tax on income that is Canadian source income under the Convention. The taxpayer would have $8.20 of third country income taxes as a carryover for U.S. foreign tax credit purposes.

**Example 2.**

A United States corporate taxpayer has for the taxable year $100 of taxable income having a Canadian source under the Convention but a U.S. source under the Code; $100 of taxable income having a U.S. source under both the Convention and the Code; $80 of taxable income having a foreign (non-Canadian) source under the Code; and $50 of loss allocated or apportioned to Canadian source income. The taxpayer pays $50 of foreign (non-Canadian) income taxes, and $20 of Canadian income taxes.

The source rules of the Convention are applied as follows to compute the taxpayer's foreign tax credit:

*Step 1(a):*

$$\frac{\$50 \text{ (Canadian source taxable income under Convention)}}{\$230 \text{ (total taxable income)}} \times \$105.80$$

= $23 limit for Canadian taxes.

*Step 1(b):*

$$\frac{\$80 \text{ (third country source taxable income under Code)}}{\$230 \text{ (total taxable income)}} \times \$105.80$$

= $36.80 limit for third country taxes.

*Step 1(c):*

$$\frac{\$130 \text{ (overall foreign taxable income under source rules described above)}}{\$230 \text{ (total taxable income)}} \times \$105.80$$

= $59.80 limit for Canadian taxes.

*Step 2:* Since the taxpayer paid $20 of Canadian income taxes, he may credit that amount in full since the step 1(a) limit is $23. Since the step 1(b) limit is $36.80, the taxpayer may credit $36.80 of the $50 foreign income taxes paid.

*Step 3:* Although the total taxes credited under step 2 ($56.80) is less than the taxpayer's total limit of $59.80, no additional credits may be claimed since the only excess taxes are third country income taxes, and those may not be used to offset any excess limitation in step 3. The $13.20 of foreign taxes not allowed as a credit is available as a foreign tax credit carryover.

**Example 3.**

The facts are the same as in Example 2, except that foreign (non-Canadian) operations result in a loss of $30 rather than taxable income of $80, and no foreign (non-Canadian) income taxes are paid. The taxpayer's credit is computed as follows:

*Step 1(a):*

$$\frac{\$50}{\$120} \times \$55.20 = \text{limit for Canadian taxes.}$$

*Step 1(b):* Since there is no third country source taxable income under the Code, the limit for third country income taxes is zero.

*Step 1(c):*

$$\frac{\$20}{\$120} \times \$55.20 = \$9.20 \text{ total limit.}$$

*Step 2:* Since the taxpayer paid $20 of Canadian income tax, he may tentatively credit that amount in full since the step 1(a) limit is $23.

*Step 3:* Since the total taxes credited under step 2 ($20) exceeds the taxpayer's total limit of $9.20, the taxpayer must reduce the total amount claimed as a credit to $9.20. The remaining $10.80 of Canadian income taxes are available as a foreign tax credit carryover.

**Example 4.**

The facts are the same as in Example 2, except that the first $100 of taxable income mentioned in Example 2 has a Canadian source under both the Convention and the Code.

*Step 1(a):*

$$\frac{\$50}{\$230} \times \$105.80 = \$23 \text{ limit for Canadian taxes.}$$

*Step 1(b):*

$$\frac{\$80}{\$230} \times \$105.80 = \$36.80 \text{ limit for third country income taxes.}$$

*Step 1(c):*

$$\frac{\$130}{\$230} \times \$105.80 = \$59.80 \text{ total limit.}$$

*Step 2:* The taxpayer credits the $20 of Canadian income tax and $36.80 of third country income tax.

*Step 3:* As explained in Example 2, the taxpayer's total credit is limited to $56.80. In this case, however, if the Canadian taxes covered by the Convention are creditable under the Code, the taxpayer could elect the Code limitation of $59.80 ($130/$230 × $105.80), which is more advantageous than the Convention limitation because that limitation does not permit third country income taxes to be credited against the U.S. tax on income arising in Canada under the Convention.

### Example 5.

The facts are the same as in Example 2, except that the corporation pays $25 of Canadian income taxes and $12 of foreign (non-Canadian) income taxes. Under step 2, the taxpayer would credit $23 of the $25 of Canadian income taxes and the full $12 of third country income taxes. Since the total amount of income taxes credited under step 2 is $35, which is less than the taxpayer's total limit of $59.80, the taxpayer may credit an amount of Canadian income taxes up to the $24.80 excess. Here, the taxpayer may claim a credit for the additional $2 of Canadian income taxes not credited under step 2, and has a total credit of $37.

### Example 6.

(a) A U.S. corporate taxpayer has for the taxable year $100 of taxable income having a Canadian source under the Convention and the Code; $50 of taxable income having a Canadian source under the Convention but a U.S. source under the Code; $80 of taxable income having a foreign (non-Canadian) source under the Code; and $50 of loss allocated or apportioned to U.S. source income. The taxpayer pays $65 of Canadian income taxes, and $45 of third country income taxes.

Step 1(a):

$$\frac{\$150}{\$230} \times \$82.80 = \$69 \text{ limit for Canadian income taxes.}$$

Step 1(b):

$$\frac{\$80}{\$180} \times \$82.80 = \$36.80 \text{ limit for third country income taxes.}$$

Step 1(c):

$$\frac{\$180}{\$180} \times \$82.80 = \$82.80 \text{ total limit.}$$

*Step 2:* The taxpayer tentatively credits the $65 of Canadian income taxes against the $69 limit of step 1(a), and $36.80 of the $45 of third country income taxes against the $36.80 limit of step 1(b).

*Step 3:* Since the total amount of credits tentatively allowed under step 2 ($101.80) exceeds the taxpayer's total limit of $82.80 under step 1(c), the taxpayer's allowable credit is reduced to $82.80 under the method provided by Rev. Rul. 82-215.

(b) If the taxpayer had paid only $40 of Canadian income taxes, the total credits tentatively allowed under step 2 is $76.80. Although that amount is less than the $82.80 total limit under step 1(c), no additional taxes may be credited since the taxpayer only has excess third country income taxes. The $8.20 of excess third country income taxes would be allowed as a foreign tax credit carryover.

The general rule for avoiding double taxation in Canada is provided in paragraph 2. Pursuant to paragraph 2(a) Canada undertakes to allow to a resident of Canada a credit against income taxes imposed under the *Income Tax Act* for the appropriate amount of income taxes paid or accrued to the United States. Paragraph 2(b) provides for the deduction by a Canadian company, in computing taxable income, of any dividend received out of the exempt surplus of a U.S. company which is an affiliate. The provisions of paragraphs 2(a) and (b) are subject to the provisions of the *Income Tax Act* as they may be amended from time to time without changing the general principle of paragraph 2. Paragraph 2(c) provides that where Canada imposes a tax on the alienation of property pursuant to the provisions of paragraph 5 of Article XIII (Gains), Canada will allow a credit for the income tax paid or accrued to the United States on such gain.

The rules of paragraph 1 are modified in certain respects by rules in paragraphs 4 and 5 for income derived by United States citizens who are residents of Canada. Paragraph 4 provides two steps for the elimination of double taxation in such a case. First, paragraph 4(a) provides that Canada shall allow a deduction from (credit against) Canadian tax in respect of income tax paid or accrued to the United States in respect of profits, income, or gains which arise in the United States (within the meaning of paragraph 3(a)); the deduction against Canadian tax need not, however, exceed the amount of income tax that would be paid or accrued to the United States if the individual were not a U.S. citizen, after taking into account any relief available under the Convention.

The second step, as provided in paragraph 4(b), is that the United States allows as a credit against United States tax, subject to the rules of paragraph 1, the income tax paid or accrued to Canada after the Canadian credit for U.S. tax provided by paragraph 4(a). The credit so allowed by the United States is not to reduce the portion of the United States tax that is creditable against Canadian tax in accordance with paragraph 4(a).

The following example illustrates the application of paragraph 4.

### Example A

- A U.S. citizen who is a resident of Canada earns $175 of income from the performance of independent personal services, of which $100 is derived from services performed in Canada and $75 from services performed in the United States. That is his total world-wide income.

- If he were not a U.S. citizen, the United States could tax $75 of that amount under Article XIV (Independent Personal Services). By reason of paragraph 3(a), the $75 that may be taxed by the United States under Article XIV is deemed to arise in the United States. Assume that the U.S. tax on the $75 would be $25 if the taxpayer were not a U.S. citizen.

- However, since the individual is a U.S. citizen, he is subject to U.S. tax on his worldwide income of $175. After excluding $75 under section 911, his taxable income is $100 and his U.S. tax is $40.

- Because he is a resident of Canada, he is also subject to Canadian tax on his worldwide income. Assume that Canada taxes the $175 at $75.

- Canada will credit against its tax of $75 the U.S. tax at source of $25, leaving a net Canadian tax of $50.

- The United States will credit against its tax of $40 the Canadian tax net of credit, but without reducing its source basis tax of $25; thus, the allowable credit is $40 - $25 = $15.

- To use a credit of $15 requires Canadian source taxable income of $37.50 ($37.50/$100 - $40 = 15). Without any special treaty rule, Canadian source taxable income would be only $25 ($100 less the section 911 exclusion of $75). Paragraph 6 provides for resourcing an additional $12.50 of income to Canada, so that the credit of $15 can be fully used.

Paragraph 5 provides special rules for the elimination of double taxation in the case of dividends, interest, and royalties earned by a U.S. citizen resident in Canada. These rules apply notwithstanding the provisions of paragraph 4, but only as long as the law in Canada allows a deduction in computing income for the portion of any foreign tax paid in respect of dividends, interest, or royalties which exceeds 15 percent of the amount of such items of income, and only with respect to those items of income. The rules of paragraph 4 apply with respect to other items of income; moreover, if the law in force in Canada regarding the deduction for foreign taxes changes, the provisions of paragraph 5 shall not apply and the U.S. foreign tax credit for Canadian taxes and the Canadian credit for U.S. taxes will be determined solely pursuant to the provisions of paragraph 4.

The calculations under paragraph 5 are as follows. First, the deduction allowed in Canada in computing income shall be made with respect to U.S. tax on the dividends, interest, and royalties before any foreign tax credit by the United States with respect to income tax paid or accrued to Canada. Second, Canada shall allow a deduction from (credit against) Canadian tax for U.S. tax paid or accrued with respect to the dividends, interest, and royalties, but such credit need not exceed 15 percent of the gross amount of such items of income that have been included in computing income for Canadian tax purposes. (The credit may, however, exceed the amount of tax

## Art. XXIV — Elimination of Double Taxation

that the United States would be entitled to levy under the Convention upon a Canadian resident who is not a U.S. citizen.) Third, for purposes of computing the U.S. tax on such dividends, interest, and royalties, the United States shall allow as a credit against the U.S. tax the income tax paid or accrued to Canada after the 15 percent credit against Canadian tax for income tax paid or accrued to the United States. The United States is in no event obliged to give a credit for Canadian income tax which will reduce the U.S. tax below 15 percent of the amount of the dividends, interest, and royalties.

The rules of paragraph 5 are illustrated by the following examples.

### Example B

- A U.S. citizen who is a resident of Canada has $100 of royalty income arising in the United States. The tentative U.S. tax before foreign tax credit is $40.
- Canada, under its law, allows a deduction for the U.S. tax in excess of 15 percent or, in this case, a deduction of $25 ($40 - $15). The Canadian taxable income is $75 and the Canadian tax on that amount is $35.
- Canada gives a credit of $15 (the maximum credit allowed is 15 percent of the gross royalty taken into Canadian income) and collects a net tax of $20.
- The United States allows a credit for the net Canadian tax against its tax in excess of 15 percent. Thus, the maximum credit is $25 ($40 - $15). But since the net Canadian tax paid was $20, the usable credit is $20.
- To be able to use a credit of $20 requires Canadian source taxable income of $50 (50% of the U.S. tentative tax of $40). Under paragraph 6, $50 of the U.S. royalty is resourced to be of Canadian source. The credit of $20 may then be offset against the U.S. tax of $40, leaving a net U.S. tax of $20.
- The combined tax paid to both countries is $40, $20 to Canada and $20 to the United States.

### Example C

A U.S. citizen who is a resident of Canada receives $200 of income with respect to personal services performed within Canada and $100 of royalty income arising within the United States. Taxable income for U.S. purposes, taking into account the rules of Code section 911, is $220. U.S. tax (before foreign tax credits) is $92. The $100 of royalty income is deemed to bear U.S. tax (before foreign tax credits) of $41.82 ($100/$220 × $92). Under Canadian law, a deduction of $26.82 (the excess of $41.82 over 15 percent of the $100 royalty income) is allowed in computing income. The Canadian tax on $273.18 of income ($300 less the $26.82 deduction) is $130. Canada then gives a credit against the $130 for $15 (the U.S. tax paid or accrued with respect to the royalty, $41.82, but limited to 15 percent of the gross amount of such income, or $15), leaving a final Canadian tax of $115. Of the $115, $30.80 is attributable to the royalty

$$\frac{\$73.18 \text{ (\$100 royalty less \$26.82 deduction)}}{\$273.18 \text{ (\$300 income less \$26.82 deduction)}} \times \$115.$$

Of this amount, $26.82 is creditable against U.S. tax pursuant to paragraph 5. (Although the U.S. allows a credit for the Canadian tax imposed on the royalty, $30.80, the credit may not reduce the U.S. tax below 15 percent of the amount of the royalty. Thus, the maximum allowable credit is the excess of $41.82, the U.S. tax imposed on the royalty income, over $15, which is 15 percent of the $100 royalty). The remaining $3.98 (the Canadian tax of $30.80 less the credit allowed of $26.82) is a foreign tax credit carryover for U.S. purposes, subject to the limitations of paragraph 5. (An additional $50.18 of Canadian tax with respect to Canadian source services income is creditable against U.S. tax pursuant to paragraphs 3 and 4(b). The $50.18 is computed as follows: tentative U.S. tax (before foreign tax credits) is $92; the U.S. tax on Canadian source services income is $50.18 ($92 less the U.S. tax on the royalty income of $41.82); the limitation on the services income is:

$$\frac{\$120 \text{ (taxable income from services)}}{\$220 \text{ (total taxable income)}} \times \$92,$$

or $50.18. The credit for Canadian tax paid on the services income is therefore $50.18; the remainder of the Canadian tax on the services income, or $34.02, is a foreign tax credit carryover for U.S. purposes, subject to the limitations of paragraph 5).

Paragraph 6 is necessary to implement the objectives of paragraphs 4(b) and 5(c). Paragraph 6 provides that where a U.S. citizen is a resident of Canada, items of income referred to in paragraph 4 or 5 are deemed for the purposes of Article XXIV to arise in Canada to the extent necessary to avoid double taxation of income by Canada and the United States consistent with the objectives of paragraphs 4(b) and 5(c). Paragraph 6 can override the source rules of paragraph 3 to permit a limited resourcing of income. The principles of paragraph 6 have effect, pursuant to paragraph 3(b) of Article XXX (Entry Into Force), for taxable years beginning on or after January 1, 1976. See the discussion of Article XXX below.

The application of paragraph 6 is illustrated by the following example.

### Example D

The facts are the same as in Example C. The United States has undertaken, pursuant to paragraph 5(c) and paragraph 6, to credit $26.82 of Canadian taxes on royalty income that has a U.S. source under both paragraph 3 and the *Internal Revenue Code*. (As illustrated in Example C, the credit, however, only reduces the U.S. tax on the royalty income which exceeds 15 percent of the amount of such income included in computing U.S. taxable income.) Pursuant to paragraph 6, for purposes of determining the U.S. foreign tax credit limitation under the Convention with respect to Canadian taxes, $64.13 (A/$220 × $92 = $26.82; A = $64.13) of taxable income with respect to the royalties is deemed to arise in Canada.

Paragraph 7 provides that any reference to "income tax paid or accrued" to Canada or the United States includes Canadian tax or United States tax, as the case may be. The terms "Canadian tax" and "United States tax" are defined in paragraphs 1(c) and 1(d) of Article III (General Definitions). References to income taxes paid or accrued also include taxes of general application paid or accrued to a political subdivision or local authority of Canada or the United States which are not imposed by such political subdivision or local authority in a manner inconsistent with the provisions of the Convention and which are substantially similar to taxes of Canada or the United States referred to in paragraphs 2 and 3(a) of Article II (Taxes Covered).

In order for a tax imposed by a political subdivision or local authority to fall within the scope of paragraph 7, such tax must apply to individuals, companies, or other persons generally, and not only to a particular class of individuals or companies or a particular type of business. The tax must also be substantially similar to the national taxes referred to in paragraphs 2 and 3(a) of Article II. Finally, the political subdivision or local authority must apply its tax in a manner not inconsistent with the provisions of the Convention. For example, the political subdivision or local authority must not impose its tax on a resident of the other Contracting State earning business profits within the political subdivision or local authority but not having a permanent establishment there. It is understood that a Canadian provincial income tax that satisfied the conditions of paragraph 7 on September 26, 1980 also satisfied the conditions of that paragraph on June 14, 1983 — i.e., no significant changes have occurred in the taxes imposed by Canadian provinces.

Paragraph 8 relates to the provisions of Article XXIII (Capital). It provides that where a resident of a Contracting State owns capital which, in accordance with the provisions of Article XXIII, may be taxed in the other Contracting State, the State of residence shall allow as a deduction from (credit against) its tax on capital an amount equal to the capital tax paid in the other Contracting State. The deduction is not, however, to exceed that part of the capital tax, computed before the deduction, which is attributable to capital which may be taxed in the other State.

**Notes**: Art. XXIV(10) added by 1995 Protocol, generally effective 1996 (see Art. 21(2) under "Application of the 1995 Protocol" above). This provision in effect confirms the interpretation of the Supreme Court of Canada in *Swantje*, [1996] 1 C.T.C. 355 for U.S. residents. The Tax Court of Canada had ruled ([1994] 1 C.T.C. 2559) that the clawback of old age security payments under ITA 180.2 was in effect a tax on exempt German pension income because it took that income into account. That decision was reversed by the higher courts.

## Article XXV — Non-Discrimination

**1.** Citizens of a Contracting State, who are residents of the other Contracting State, shall not be subjected in that other State to any taxation or any requirement connected therewith which is other or more burdensome than the taxation and connected requirements to which citizens of that other State in the same circumstances are or may be subjected.

**Technical Explanation [1984]**:

Paragraphs 1 and 2 of Article XXV protect individual citizens of a Contracting State from discrimination by the other Contracting State in taxation matters. Paragraph 1 provides that a citizen of a Contracting State who is a resident of the other Contracting State may not be subjected in that other State to any taxation or requirement connected with taxation which is other or more burdensome than the taxation and connected requirements imposed on similarly situated citizens of the other State.

**2.** Citizens of a Contracting State, who are not residents of the other Contracting State, shall not be subjected in that other State to any taxation or any requirement connected therewith which is other or more burdensome than the taxation and connected requirements to which citizens of any third State in the same circumstances (including State of residence) are or may be subjected.

**Technical Explanation [1984]**:

Paragraph 2 assures protection in a case where a citizen of a Contracting State is not a resident of the other Contracting State. Such a citizen may not be subjected in the other State to any taxation or requirement connected to taxation which is other or more burdensome than the taxation and connected requirements to which similarly situated citizens of any third State are subjected. The reference to citizens of a third State "in the same circumstances" includes consideration of the State of residence. Thus, pursuant to paragraph 2, the Canadian taxation with respect to a citizen of the United States resident in, for example, the United Kingdom may not be more burdensome than the taxation of a U.K. citizen resident in the United Kingdom. Any benefits available to the U.K. citizen by virtue of an income tax convention between the United Kingdom and Canada would be available to the U.S. citizen resident in the United Kingdom if he is otherwise in the same circumstances as the U.K. citizen.

**3.** In determining the taxable income or tax payable of an individual who is a resident of a Contracting State, there shall be allowed as a deduction in respect of any other person who is a resident of the other Contracting State and who is dependent on the individual for support the amount that would be so allowed if that other person were a resident of the first-mentioned State.

**Technical Explanation [1995 Protocol]**:

Article 13 of the Protocol amends Article XXV (Non-Discrimination) of the Convention. Paragraph 1 of Article 13 amends paragraph 3 of Article XXV to conform the treaty language to a change in Canadian law. The paragraph is intended to allow the treatment of dependents under the income tax law of a Contracting State to apply with respect to dependents who are residents of the other Contracting State. As drafted in the present Convention, the rule deals specifically only with deductions; the amendments made by the Protocol clarify that it also applies to the credits now provided by Canadian law.

**Technical Explanation [1984]**:

Paragraph 3 assures that, in computing taxable income, an individual resident of a Contracting State will be entitled to the same deduction for dependents resident in the other Contracting State that would be allowed if the dependents were residents of the individual's State of residence. The term "dependent" is defined in accordance with the rules set forth in paragraph 2 of Article III (General Definitions). For U.S. tax purposes, paragraph 3 does not expand the benefits currently available to a resident of the United States with a dependent resident in Canada. See Code section 152(b)(3).

**Notes**: Art. XXV(3) amended by 1995 Protocol, generally effective 1996 (see Art. 21(2) under "Application of the 1995 Protocol" above), to add the words "or tax payable" near the beginning. This change recognizes Canada's change in 1988 from personal exemptions (ITA 109) to personal credits (ITA 118).

**4.** Where a married individual who is a resident of Canada and not a citizen of the United States has income that is taxable in the United States pursuant to Article XV (Dependent Personal Services), the United States tax with respect to such income shall not exceed such proportion of the total United States tax that would be payable for the taxable year if both the individual and his spouse were United States citizens as the individual's taxable income determined without regard to this paragraph bears to the amount that would be the total taxable income of the individual and his spouse. For the purposes of this paragraph,

(a) the "total United States tax" shall be determined as if all the income of the individual and his spouse arose in the United States; and

(b) a deficit of the spouse shall not be taken into account in determining taxable income.

**Technical Explanation [1984]**:

Paragraph 4 allows a resident of Canada (not a citizen of the United States) to file a joint return in cases where such person earns salary, wages, or other similar remuneration as an employee and such income is taxable in the United States under the Convention. Paragraph 4 does not apply where the resident of Canada earns wages which are exempt in the United States under Article XV (Dependent Personal Services) or earns only income taxable by the United States under provisions of the Convention other than Article XV.

The benefit provided by paragraph 4 is available regardless of the residence of the taxpayer's spouse. It is limited, however, by a formula designed to ensure that the benefit is available solely with respect to persons whose U.S. source income is entirely, or almost entirely, wage income. The formula limits the United States tax with respect to wage income to that portion of the total U.S. tax that would be payable for the taxable year if both the individual and his spouse were United States citizens as the individual's taxable income (determined without any of the benefits made available by paragraph 4, such as the standard deduction) bears to the total taxable income of the individual and his spouse. The term "total United States tax" used in the formula is total United States tax without regard to any foreign tax credits, as provided in subparagraph 4(a). (Foreign income taxes may, however, be claimed as deductions in computing taxable income, to the extent allowed by the Code.) In determining total taxable income of the individual and his spouse, the benefits made available by paragraph 4 are taken into account, but a deficit of the spouse is not.

The following example illustrates the application of paragraph 4.

> A, a Canadian citizen and resident, is married to B who is also a Canadian citizen and resident. A earns $12,000 of wages taxable in the U.S. under Article XV (Dependent Personal Services) and $2,000 of wages taxable only in Canada. B earns $1,000 of U.S. source dividend income, taxed by the United States at 15 percent pursuant to Article X (Dividends). B also earns $2,000 of wages taxable only in Canada. A's taxable income for U.S. purposes, determined without regard to paragraph 4, is $11,700 ($12,000 - $2,000 (Code sections 151(b) and 873(b)(3)) + $1,700 (Code section 63)). The U.S. tax (Code section 1(d)) with respect to such income is $2,084.50. The total U.S. tax payable by A and B if both were U.S. citizens and all their income arose in the United States would be $2,013 under Code section 1(a) on taxable income of $14,800 ($17,000 - $200 (Code section 116) - $2,000 (Code section 151)). Pursuant to paragraph 4, the U.S. tax imposed on A's wages from U.S. sources is limited to $1,591.36 ($11,700/$14,800 × $2,013). B's U.S. tax liability with respect to the U.S. source dividends remains $150.

The provisions of paragraph 4 may be elected on a year-by-year basis. They are purely computational and do not make either or both spouses residents of the United States for the purpose of other U.S. income tax conventions. The rules relating to the election provided by U.S. law under Code section 6013(g) (see section 1.6013–6 of the Treasury Regulations) do not apply to the election described in this paragraph.

**5.** Any company which is a resident of a Contracting State, the capital of which is wholly or partly owned or controlled, directly or indirectly, by one or more residents of the other Contracting State, shall not be subjected in the first-mentioned State to any taxation or any requirement connected therewith which is other or more burdensome than the taxation and connected requirements to which other similar companies of the first-mentioned State, the capital of which is wholly or partly owned or controlled, directly or indirectly, by one or more residents of a third State, are or may be subjected.

**Technical Explanation [1984]:**

Paragraph 5 protects against discrimination in a case where the capital of a company which is a resident of one Contracting State is wholly or partly owned or controlled, directly or indirectly, by one or more residents of the other Contracting State. Such a company shall not be subjected in the State of which it is a resident to any taxation or requirement connected therewith which is other or more burdensome than the taxation and connected requirements to which are subjected other similar companies which are residents of that State but whose capital is wholly or partly owned or controlled, directly or indirectly, by one or more residents of a third State.

**6.** Notwithstanding the provisions of Article XXIV (Elimination of Double Taxation), the taxation on a permanent establishment which a resident of a Contracting State has in the other Contracting State shall not be less favourably levied in the other State than the taxation levied on residents of the other State carrying on the same activities. This paragraph shall not be construed as obliging a Contracting State:

(a) to grant to a resident of the other Contracting State any personal allowances, reliefs and reductions for taxation purposes on account of civil status or family responsibilities which it grants to its own residents; or

(b) to grant to a company which is a resident of the other Contracting State the same tax relief that it provides to a company which is a resident of the first-mentioned State with respect to dividends received by it from a company.

**Technical Explanation [1984]:**

Paragraph 6 protects against discrimination in the case of a permanent establishment which a resident of one Contracting State has in the other Contracting State. The taxation of such a permanent establishment by the other Contracting State shall not be less favorable than the taxation of residents of that other State carrying on the same activities. The paragraph specifically overrides the provisions of Article XXIV (Elimination of Double Taxation), thus ensuring that permanent establishments will be entitled to relief from double taxation on a basis comparable to the relief afforded to similarly situated residents. Paragraph 6 does not oblige a Contracting State to grant to a resident of the other Contracting State any personal allowances, reliefs, and reductions for taxation purposes on account of civil status or family responsibilities which it grants to its own residents. In addition, paragraph 6 does not require a Contracting State to grant to a company which is a resident of the other Contracting State the same tax relief that it grants to companies which are resident in the first-mentioned State with respect to intercorporate dividends. This provision is merely clarifying in nature, since neither the United States nor Canada would interpret paragraph 6 to provide for granting the same relief in the absence of a specific denial thereof. The principles of paragraph 6 would apply with respect to a fixed base as well as a permanent establishment. Paragraph 6 does not, however, override the provisions of Code section 906.

**7.** Except where the provisions of paragraph 1 of Article IX (Related Persons), paragraph 7 of Article XI (Interest) or paragraph 7 of Article XII (Royalties) apply, interest, royalties and other disbursements paid by a resident of a Contracting State to a resident of the other Contracting State shall, for the purposes of determining the taxable profits of the first-mentioned resident, be deductible under the same conditions as if they had been paid to a resident of the first-mentioned State. Similarly, any debts of a resident of a Contracting State to a resident of the other Contracting State shall, for the purposes of determining the taxable capital of the first-mentioned resident, be deductible under the same conditions as if they had been contracted to a resident of the first-mentioned State.

**Technical Explanation [1984]:**

Paragraph 7 concerns the right of a resident of a Contracting State to claim deductions for purposes of computing taxable profits in the case of disbursements made to a resident of the other Contracting State. Such disbursements shall be deductible under the same conditions as if they had been made to a resident of the first-mentioned State. Thus, this paragraph does not require Canada to permit a deduction to a Canadian trust for disbursements made to a non-resident beneficiary out of income derived from a business in Canada or

Canadian real property; granting such a deduction would result in complete exemption by Canada of such income and would put Canadian trusts with non-resident beneficiaries in a better position than if they had resident beneficiaries. These provisions do not apply to amounts to which paragraph 1 of Article IX (Related Persons), paragraph 7 of Article XI (Interest), or paragraph 7 of Article XII (Royalties) apply. Paragraph 7 of Article XXV also provides that, for purposes of determining the taxable capital of a resident of a Contracting State, any debts of such person to a resident of the other Contracting State shall be deductible under the same conditions as if they had been contracted to a resident of the first-mentioned State. This portion of paragraph 7 relates to Article XXIII (Capital).

**8.** The provisions of paragraph 7 shall not affect the operation of any provision of the taxation laws of a Contracting State:

(a) relating to the deductibility of interest and which is in force on the date of signature of this Convention (including any subsequent modification of such provisions that does not change the general nature thereof); or

(b) adopted after such date by a Contracting State and which is designed to ensure that a person who is not a resident of that State does not enjoy, under the laws of that State, a tax treatment that is more favorable than that enjoyed by residents of that State.

**Technical Explanation [1984]**:

Paragraph 8 provides that, notwithstanding the provisions of paragraph 7, a Contracting State may enforce the provisions of its taxation laws relating to the deductibility of interest, in force on September 26, 1980, or as modified subsequent to that date in a manner that does not change the general nature of the provisions in force on September 26, 1980; or which are adopted after September 26, 1980, and are designed to ensure that non-residents do not enjoy a more favorable tax treatment under the taxation laws of that State than that enjoyed by residents. Thus Canada may continue to limit the deductions for interest paid to certain non-residents as provided in section 18(4) of Part I of the *Income Tax Act*.

**Related Provisions**: ITA 18(4) — Thin capitalization rule.

**9.** Expenses incurred by a citizen or resident of a Contracting State with respect to any convention (including any seminar, meeting, congress or other function of a similar nature) held in the other Contracting State shall, for the purposes of taxation in the first-mentioned State, be deductible to the same extent that such expenses would be deductible if the convention were held in the first-mentioned State.

**Technical Explanation [1984]**:

Paragraph 9 provides that expenses incurred by citizens or residents of a Contracting State with respect to any convention, including any seminar, meeting, congress, or other function of similar nature, held in the other Contracting State, are deductible for purposes of taxation in the first-mentioned State to the same extent such expenses would be deductible if the convention were held in that first-mentioned State. Thus, for U.S. income tax purposes an individual who is a citizen or resident of the United States and who attends a convention held in Canada may claim deductions for expenses incurred in connection with such convention without regard to the provisions of Code section 274(h). Section 274(h) imposes special restrictions on the deductibility of expenses incurred in connection with foreign conventions. A claim for a deduction for such an expense remains subject, in all events, to the provisions of U.S. law with respect to the deductibility of convention expenses generally (e.g., Code sections 162 and 212). Similarly, in the case of a citizen or resident of Canada attending a convention in the United States, paragraph 9 requires Canada to allow a deduction for expenses relating to such convention as if the convention had taken place in Canada.

**Interpretation Bulletins**: IT-131R2: Convention expenses.

**10.** Notwithstanding the provisions of Article II (Taxes Covered), this Article shall apply to all taxes imposed by a Contracting State.

**Technical Explanation [1995 Protocol]**:

Paragraph 2 of Article 13 of the Protocol amends paragraph 10 of Article XXV of the Convention to broaden the scope of the non-discrimination protection provided by the Convention. As amended, Article XXV will apply to all taxes imposed by a Contracting State. Under the present Convention, non-discrimination protection is limited in the case of Canadian taxes to taxes imposed under the *Income Tax Act*. As amended by the Protocol, non-discrimination protection will extend, for example, to the Canadian goods and services tax and other Canadian excise taxes.

**Technical Explanation [1984]**:

Paragraph 10 provides that, notwithstanding the provisions of Article II (Taxes Covered), the provisions of Article XXV apply in the case of Canada to all taxes imposed under the *Income Tax Act*; and, in the case of the United States, to all taxes imposed under the Code. Article XXV does not apply to taxes imposed by political subdivisions or local authorities of Canada or the United States.

Article XXV substantially broadens the protection against discrimination provided by the 1942 Convention, which contains only one provision dealing specifically with this subject. That provision, paragraph 11 of the Protocol to the 1942 Convention, states that citizens of one of the Contracting States residing within the other Contracting State are not to be subjected to the payment of more burdensome taxes than the citizens of the other State.

The benefits of Article XXV may affect the tax liability of a U.S. citizen or resident with respect to the United States. See paragraphs 2 and 3 of Article XXIX (Miscellaneous Rules).

**Notes**: Art. XXV(10) amended by 1995 Protocol, generally effective 1996 (see Art. 21(2) under "Application of the 1995 Protocol" above). For 1985–1995, read:

> 10. Notwithstanding the provisions of Article II (Taxes Covered), this Article shall apply:
>
> (a) in the case of Canada, to all taxes imposed under the *Income Tax Act*; and
>
> (b) in the case of the United States, to all taxes imposed under the *Internal Revenue Code*.

## Article XXVI — Mutual Agreement Procedure

**1.** Where a person considers that the actions of one or both of the Contracting States result or will result for him in taxation not in accordance with the provisions of this Convention, he may, irrespective of the remedies provided by the domestic law of those States, present his case in writing to the competent authority of the Contracting State of which he is a resident or, if he is a resident of neither Contracting State, of which he is a national.

**Technical Explanation [1984]**:

Paragraph 1 provides that where a person considers that the actions of one or both of the Contracting States will result in taxation not in accordance with the Convention, he may present his case in writing to the competent authority of the Contracting State of which he is a resident or, if he is a resident of neither Contracting State, of which he is a national. Thus, a resident of Canada must present to the Minister of National Revenue (or his authorized representative) any claim that such resident is being subjected to taxation contrary to the Convention. A person who requests assistance from the competent authority may also avail himself of any remedies available under domestic laws.

**Notes**: See Notes to ITA 115.1 re the Canadian competent authority.

**2.** The competent authority of the Contracting State to which the case has been presented shall endeavor, if the objection appears to it to be justified and if it is not itself able to arrive at a satisfactory solution, to resolve the case by mutual agreement with the competent authority of the other Contracting State, with a view to the avoidance of taxation which is not in accordance with the Convention. Except where the provisions of Article IX (Related Persons) apply, any agreement reached shall be implemented notwithstanding any time or other procedural limitations in the domestic law of the Contracting States, provided that the competent authority of the other Contracting State has received notification that such a case exists within six years from the end of the taxable year to which the case relates.

**Technical Explanation [1984]**:

Paragraph 2 provides that the competent authority of the Contracting State to which the case is presented shall endeavor to resolve the case by mutual agreement with the competent authority of the other Contracting State, unless he believes that the objection is not justified or he is able to arrive at a satisfactory unilateral solution. Any agreement reached between the competent authorities of Canada and the United States shall be implemented notwithstanding any time or other procedural limitations in the domestic laws of the Contracting States, except where the special mutual agreement provisions of Article IX (Related Persons) apply, provided that the competent authority of the Contracting State asked to waive its domestic time or procedural limitations has received written notification that such a case exists within six years from the end of the taxable year in the first-mentioned State to which the case relates. The notification may be given by the competent authority of the first-mentioned State, the taxpayer who has requested the competent authority to take action, or a person related to the taxpayer. Unlike Article IX, Article XXVI does not require the competent authority of a Contracting State to grant unilateral relief to avoid double taxation in a case where timely notification is not given to the competent authority of the other Contracting State. Such unilateral relief may, however, be granted by the competent authority in its discretion pursuant to the provisions of Article XXVI and in order to achieve the purposes of the Convention. In a case where the provisions of Article IX apply, the provisions of paragraphs 3, 4, and 5 of that Article are controlling with respect to adjustments and corresponding adjustments of income, loss, or tax and the effect of the Convention upon time or procedural limitations of domestic law. Thus, if relief is not available under Article IX because of fraud, the provisions of paragraph 2 or Article XXVI do not independently authorize such relief.

**3.** The competent authorities of the Contracting States shall endeavor to resolve by mutual agreement any difficulties or doubts arising as to the interpretation or application of the Convention. In particular, the competent authorities of the Contracting States may agree:

(a) to the same attribution of profits to a resident of a Contracting State and its permanent establishment situated in the other Contracting State;

(b) to the same allocation of income, deductions, credits or allowances between persons;

(c) to the same determination of the source, and the same characterization, of particular items of income;

(d) to a common meaning of any term used in the Convention;

(e) to the elimination of double taxation with respect to income distributed by an estate or trust;

(f) to the elimination of double taxation with respect to a partnership;

(g) to provide relief from double taxation resulting from the application of the estate tax imposed by the United States or the Canadian tax as a result of a distribution or disposition of property by a trust that is a qualified domestic trust within the meaning of section 2056A of the *Internal Revenue Code*, or is described in subsection 70(6) of the *Income Tax Act* or is treated as such under paragraph 5 of Article XXIX B (Taxes Imposed by Reason of Death), in cases where no relief is otherwise available; or

(h) to increases in any dollar amounts referred to in the Convention to reflect monetary or economic developments.

They may also consult together for the elimination of double taxation in cases not provided for in the Convention.

**Technical Explanation [1995 Protocol]**:

Article 14 of the Protocol makes two changes to Article XXVI (Mutual Agreement Procedure) of the Convention. First, it adds a new subparagraph 3(g) specifically authorizing the competent authorities to provide relief from double taxation in certain cases involving the distribution or disposition of property by a U.S. qualified domestic trust or a Canadian spousal trust, where relief is not otherwise available.

**Technical Explanation [1984]**:

Paragraph 3 provides that the competent authorities of the Contracting States shall endeavor to resolve by mutual agreement any difficulties or doubts arising as to the interpretation or application of the Convention. In particular, the competent authorities may agree to the same attribution of profits to a resident of a Contracting State and its permanent establishment in the other Contracting State; the same allocation of income, deductions, credits, or allowances between persons; the same determination of the source of income; the same characterization of particular items of income; a common meaning of any term used in the Convention; rules, guidelines, or procedures for the elimination of double taxation with respect to income distributed by an estate or trust, or with respect to a partnership; or to increase any dollar amounts referred to in the Convention to reflect monetary or economic developments. The competent authorities may also consult and reach agreements on rules, guidelines, or procedures for the elimination of double taxation in cases not provided for in the Convention.

The list of subjects of potential mutual agreement in paragraph 3 is not exhaustive; it merely illustrates the principles set forth in the paragraph. As in the case of other U.S. tax conventions, agreement can be arrived at in the context of determining the tax liability of a specific person or in establishing rules, guidelines, and procedures that will apply generally under the Convention to resolve issues for classes of taxpayers. It is contemplated that paragraph 3 could be utilized by the competent authorities, for example, to resolve conflicts between the domestic laws of Canada and the United States with respect to the allocation and apportionment of deductions.

**Related Provisions**: Art. II:2(b)(iv) — Application to U.S. estate taxes.

**Notes**: Art. XXVI(3) amended by 1995 Protocol, generally effective 1996 (see Art. 21(2) under "Application of the 1995 Protocol" above), to renumber subpara. 3(g) as 3(h) and add new subpara. 3(g).

4. Each of the Contracting States will endeavor to collect on behalf of the other Contracting State such amounts as may be necessary to ensure that relief granted by the Convention from taxation imposed by that other State does not enure to the benefit of persons not entitled thereto. However, nothing in this paragraph shall be construed as imposing on either of the Contracting States the obligation to carry out administrative measures of a different nature from those used in the collection of its own tax or which would be contrary to its public policy (ordre public).

**Technical Explanation [1984]**:

Paragraph 4 provides that each Contracting State will endeavor to collect on behalf of the other State such amounts as may be necessary to ensure that relief granted by the Convention from taxation imposed by the other State does not enure to the benefit of persons not entitled to such relief. Paragraph 4 does not oblige either Contracting State to carry out administrative measures of a different nature from those that would be used by Canada or the United States in the collection of its own tax or which would be contrary to its public policy.

5. The competent authorities of the Contracting States may communicate with each other directly for the purpose of reaching an agreement in the sense of the preceding paragraphs.

**Technical Explanation [1984]**:

Paragraph 5 confirms that the competent authorities of Canada and the United States may communicate with each other directly for the purpose of reaching agreement in the sense of paragraphs 1 through 4.

6. If any difficulty or doubt arising as to the interpretation or application of the Convention cannot be resolved by the competent authorities pursuant to the preceding paragraphs of this Article, the case may, if both competent authorities and the taxpayer agree, be submitted for arbitration, provided that the taxpayer agrees in writing to be bound by the decision of the arbitration board. The decision of the arbitration board in a particular case shall be binding on both States with respect to that case. The procedures shall be established in an exchange of notes between the Contracting States. The provisions of this paragraph shall have effect after the Contracting States have so agreed through the exchange of notes.

**Technical Explanation [1995 Protocol]**:

Article 14 also adds a new paragraph 6 to Article XXVI (Mutual Agreement Procedure). Paragraph 6 provides for a voluntary arbitration procedure, to be implemented only upon the exchange of diplomatic notes between the United States and Canada. Similar provisions are found in the recent U.S. treaties with the Federal Republic of Germany, the Netherlands, and Mexico. Paragraph 6 provides that where the competent authorities have been unable, pursuant to the other provisions of Article XXVI, to resolve a disagreement regarding the interpretation or application of the Convention, the disagreement may, with the consent of the taxpayer and both competent authorities, be submitted for arbitration, provided the taxpayer agrees in writing to be bound by the decision of the arbitration board. Nothing in the provision requires that any case be submitted for arbitration. However, if a case is submitted to an arbitration board, the board's decision in that case will be binding on both Contracting States and on the taxpayer with respect to that case.

The United States was reluctant to implement an arbitration procedure until there has been an opportunity to evaluate the process in practice under other agreements that allow for arbitration, particularly the U.S.-Germany Convention. It was agreed, therefore, as specified in paragraph 6, that the provisions of the Convention calling for an arbitration procedure will not take effect until the two Contracting States have agreed through an exchange of diplomatic notes to do so. This is similar to the approach taken with the Netherlands and Mexico. Paragraph 6 also provides that the procedures to be followed in applying arbitration will be agreed through an exchange of notes by the Contracting States. It is expected that such procedures will ensure that arbitration will not generally be available where matters of either State's tax policy or domestic law are involved.

Paragraph 2 of Article 20 of the Protocol provides that the appropriate authorities of the Contracting State will consult after three years following entry into force of the Protocol to determine whether the diplomatic notes implementing the arbitration procedure should be exchanged.

**Related Provisions**: ITA 115.1 — Competent authority agreements.

**Notes**: Art. XXVI(6) added by 1995 Protocol, generally effective 1996 (see article 21(2) under "Application of the Provisions of the Protocol" above).

See Notes to ITA 115.1.

**Information Circulars**: 71-17R4: Requests for competent authority consideration under mutual agreement procedures in income tax conventions.

# Article XXVI A — Assistance in Collection

1. The Contracting States undertake to lend assistance to each other in the collection of taxes referred to in paragraph 9, together with interest, costs, additions to such taxes and civil penalties, referred to in this Article as a "revenue claim".

**Technical Explanation [1995 Protocol]**:

Article 15 of the Protocol adds to the Convention a new Article XXVI A (Assistance in Collection). Collection assistance provisions are included in several other U.S. income tax treaties, including the recent treaty with the Netherlands, and in many U.S. estate tax treaties. U.S. negotiators initially raised with Canada the possibility of including collection assistance provisions in the Protocol, because the Internal Revenue Service has claims pending against persons in Canada that would be subject to collection under these provisions. However, the ultimate decision of the U.S. and Canadian negotiators to add the collection assistance article was attributable to the confluence of several unusual factors.

Of critical importance was the similarity between the laws of the United States and Canada. The Internal Revenue Service, the Justice Department, and other U.S. negotiators were reassured by the close similarity of the legal and procedural protections afforded by the Contracting States to their citizens and residents and by the fact that these protections apply to the tax collection procedures used by each State. In addition, the U.S. negotiators were confident, given their extensive experience in working with their Canadian counterparts, that the agreed procedures could be administered appropriately, effectively, and efficiently. Finally, given the close cooperation already developed between the United States and Canada in the exchange of tax information, the U.S. and Canadian negotiators concluded that the potential benefits to both countries of obtaining such assistance would be immediate and substantial and would far outweigh any cost involved.

Under paragraph 1 of Article XXVI A, each Contracting State agrees, subject to the exercise of its discretion and to the conditions explicitly provided later in the Article, to lend assistance and support to the other in the collection of revenue claims. The term "revenue claim" is defined in paragraph 1 to include all taxes referred to in paragraph 9 of the Article, as well as interest, costs, additions to such taxes, and civil penalties. Paragraph 9 provides that, notwithstanding the provisions of Article II (Taxes Covered) of the Convention, Article XXVI A shall apply to all categories of taxes collected by or on behalf of the Government of a Contracting State.

**Notes**: This provision overrides the traditional rule that a court judgment based on a tax debt is not enforceable in a foreign jurisdiction (see Notes to ITA 223(3)). However, it does not let the CCRA use the IRS to collect a tax debt from a U.S. citizen or U.S.-incorporated corporation; see paragraph 8. The assistance provided under this Article can reach back to revenue claims determined since November 10, 1985; see Notes at end of Art. XXVI A.

This is the first inter-country "collection assistance" provided by any of Canada's tax treaties. The second is in Art. 26A of the Canada-Netherlands treaty, as added by a Protocol signed on August 25, 1997. The third is in Art. V(5) of the Canada-Austria treaty, under a Protocol signed on June 15, 1999 (not yet ratified).

The collection assistance provided to the U.S. under the treaty may be outside Canadian federal jurisdiction and thus constitutionally invalid, since the provinces have sole jurisdiction over property and civil rights. Case law suggests that the federal government cannot enact legislation to implement a treaty if the subject-matter of the legislation is solely within provincial jurisdiction. See Wolfe Goodman, IV(2) *Goodman on Estate Planning* (Federated Press) 187 (1995); and Bruce Lemons, Thomas Olson & L. Alan Rautenberg, "Changes in U.S.-Canadian Tax Treaty Resolve Conflicts and Present Planning Opportunities", 82(1) *Journal of Taxation* 42 (1995).

However, in *Chua*, [2000] 4 C.T.C. 159 (FCTD), the Court found that Art. XXVI-A was within federal jurisdiction, though it violated the *Charter of Rights* in its application to a tax debtor who was not a Canadian citizen when the debt arose but subsequently became a citizen. The decision has not been appealed by the Crown.

The CCRA has refused to divulge any statistics on the extent to which this provision is being used, in either direction. A complaint under the *Access to Information Act* was rejected by the Information Commissioner. An application seeking release of such statistics is underway in the Federal Court — Trial Division (*David M. Sherman v. MNR*, File T-612-00 (FCTD)).

**2.** An application for assistance in the collection of a revenue claim shall include a certification by the competent authority of the applicant State that, under the laws of that State, the revenue claim has been finally determined. For the purposes of this Article, a revenue claim is finally determined when the appli-cant State has the right under its internal law to collect the revenue claim and all administrative and judicial rights of the taxpayer to restrain collection in the applicant State have lapsed or been exhausted.

**Technical Explanation [1995 Protocol]**:

Paragraph 2 of the Article requires the Contracting State applying for collection assistance (the "applicant State") to certify that the revenue claim for which collection assistance is sought has been "finally determined." A revenue claim has been finally determined when the applicant State has the right under its internal law to collect the revenue claim and all administrative and judicial rights of the taxpayer to restrain collection in the applicant State have lapsed or been exhausted.

**Notes**: This paragraph has been carefully worded so that where there is no restriction on collection, the enforcement of collection by the other jurisdiction may begin even though the taxpayer's rights of appeal may not have expired. Thus, payroll source deductions and GST net tax remittances, the collection of which are not restricted by ITA 225.1, can be collected by the IRS on behalf of Revenue Canada (subject to para. 8) even though the taxpayer may be appealing the assessments in question.

**3.** A revenue claim of the applicant State that has been finally determined may be accepted for collection by the competent authority of the requested State and, subject to the provisions of paragraph 7, if accepted shall be collected by the requested State as though such revenue claim were the requested State's own revenue claim finally determined in accordance with the laws applicable to the collection of the requested State's own taxes.

**Technical Explanation [1995 Protocol]**:

Paragraph 3 of the Article clarifies that the Contracting State from which assistance was requested (the "requested State") has discretion as to whether to accept a particular application for collection assistance. However, if the application for assistance is accepted, paragraph 3 requires that the requested State grant assistance under its existing procedures as though the claim were the requested State's own revenue claim finally determined under the laws of that State. This obligation under paragraph 3 is limited by paragraph 7 of the Article, which provides that, although generally treated as a revenue claim of the requested State, a claim for which collection assistance is granted shall not have any priority accorded to the revenue claims of the requested State.

**4.** Where an application for collection of a revenue claim in respect of a taxpayer is accepted

(a) by the United States, the revenue claim shall be treated by the United States as an assessment under United States laws against the taxpayer as of the time the application is received; and

(b) by Canada, the revenue claim shall be treated by Canada as an amount payable under the *Income Tax Act*, the collection of which is not subject to any restriction.

**Technical Explanation [1995 Protocol]**:

Paragraph 4 of Article XXVI A provides that, when the United States accepts a request for assistance in collection, the claim will be treated by the United States as an assessment as of the time the application was received. Similarly, when Canada accepts a request, a revenue claim shall be treated as an amount payable under the *Income Tax Act*, the collection of which is not subject to any restriction.

**Notes**: See Notes to para. 1 of this Article.

**5.** Nothing in this Article shall be construed as creating or providing any rights of administrative or judicial review of the applicant State's finally determined revenue claim by the requested State, based on any such rights that may be available under the laws of either Contracting State. If, at any time pending execution of a request for assistance under this Article, the applicant State loses the right under its internal law to collect the revenue claim, the competent authority of the applicant State shall promptly withdraw the request for assistance in collection.

**Technical Explanation [1995 Protocol]**:

Paragraph 5 of the Article provides that nothing in Article XXVI A shall be construed as creating in the requested State any rights of administrative or judicial review of the applicant State's finally determined revenue claim. Thus, when an application for collection assistance has been accepted, the substantive validity of the applicant State's revenue claim cannot be challenged in an action in the requested State. Paragraph 5 furthers provides, however, that if the applicant State's revenue claim ceases to be finally determined, the applicant State is obligated to withdraw promptly any request that had been based on that claim.

**6.** Subject to this paragraph, amounts collected by the requested State pursuant to this Article shall be forwarded to the competent authority of the applicant State. Unless the competent authorities of the Contracting States otherwise agree, the ordinary costs incurred in providing collection assistance shall be borne by the requested State and any extraordinary costs so incurred shall be borne by the applicant State.

**Technical Explanation [1995 Protocol]**:

Paragraph 6 provides that, as a general rule, the requested State is to forward the entire amount collected to the competent authority of the applicant State. The ordinary costs incurred in providing collection assistance will normally be borne by the requested State and only extraordinary costs will be borne by the applicant State. The application of this paragraph, including rules specifying which collection costs are to be borne by each State and the time and manner of payment of the amounts collected, will be agreed upon by the competent authorities, as provided for in paragraph 11.

**7.** A revenue claim of an applicant State accepted for collection shall not have in the requested State any priority accorded to the revenue claims of the requested State.

**8.** No assistance shall be provided under this Article for a revenue claim in respect of a taxpayer to the extent that the taxpayer can demonstrate that

(a) where the taxpayer is an individual, the revenue claim relates to a taxable period in which the taxpayer was a citizen of the requested State, and

(b) where the taxpayer is an entity that is a company, estate or trust, the revenue claim relates to a taxable period in which the taxpayer derived its status as such an entity from the laws in force in the requested State.

**Technical Explanation [1995 Protocol]**:

Paragraph 8 provides that no assistance is to be given under this Article for a claim in respect of an individual taxpayer, to the extent that the taxpayer can demonstrate that he was a citizen of the requested State during the taxable period to which the revenue claim relates. Similarly, in the case of a company, estate, or trust, no assistance is to be given to the extent that the entity can demonstrate that it derived its status as such under the laws in force in the requested State during the taxable period to which the claim relates.

**9.** Notwithstanding the provisions of Article II (Taxes Covered), the provisions of this Article shall apply to all categories of taxes collected by or on behalf of the Government of a Contracting State.

**Notes**: The Canadian taxes covered include provincial income taxes collected by Revenue Canada, as well as goods and services tax (GST) and Harmonized Sales Tax (HST) imposed and collected under the *Excise Tax Act*. However, once the Canada Customs and Revenue Agency comes into operation it could be argued that provincial taxes are no longer being collected "by" the federal government.

**10.** Nothing in this Article shall be construed as:

(a) limiting the assistance provided for in paragraph 4 of Article XXVI (Mutual Agreement Procedure); or

(b) imposing on either Contracting State the obligation to carry out administrative measures of a different nature from those used in the collection of its own taxes or that would be contrary to its public policy (ordre public).

**Technical Explanation [1995 Protocol]**:

Subparagraph (a) of paragraph 10 clarifies that Article XXVI A supplements the provisions of paragraph 4 of Article XXVI (Mutual Agreement Procedure). The Mutual Agreement Procedure paragraph, which is more common in U.S. tax treaties, provides for collection assistance in cases in which a Contracting State seeks assistance in reclaiming treaty benefits that have been granted to a person that is not entitled to those benefits. Subparagraph (b) of paragraph 10 makes clear that nothing in Article XXVI A can require a Contracting State to carry out administrative measures of a different nature from those used in the collection of its own taxes, or that would be contrary to its public policy (ordre public).

**11.** The competent authorities of the Contracting States shall agree upon the mode of application of this Article, including agreement to ensure comparable levels of assistance to each of the Contracting States.

**Technical Explanation [1995 Protocol]**:

Paragraph 11 requires the competent authorities to agree upon the mode of application of Article XXVI A, including agreement to ensure comparable levels of assistance to each of the Contracting States.

Paragraph 3 of Article 21 of the Protocol allows collection assistance under Article XXVI A to be sought for revenue claims that have been finally determined at any time within the 10 years preceding the date on which the Protocol enters into force.

**Notes [Art. XXVI A]**: Art. XXVI-A added by 1995 Protocol, effective for revenue claims finally determined after November 9, 1985 (see Art. 21(3) under "Application of the 1995 Protocol" above).

## Article XXVII — Exchange of Information

**1.** The competent authorities of the Contracting States shall exchange such information as is relevant for carrying out the provisions of this Convention or of the domestic laws of the Contracting States concerning taxes to which the Convention applies insofar as the taxation thereunder is not contrary to the Convention. The exchange of information is not restricted by Article I (Personal Scope). Any information received by a Contracting State shall be treated as secret in the same manner as information obtained under the taxation laws of that State and shall be disclosed only to persons or authorities (including courts and administrative bodies) involved in the assessment or collection of, the administration and enforcement in respect of, or the determination of appeals in relation to the taxes to which the Convention applies or, notwithstanding paragraph 4, in relation to taxes imposed by a political subdivision or local authority of a Contracting State that are substantially similar to the taxes covered by the Convention under Article II (Taxes Covered). Such persons or authorities shall use the information only for such purposes. They may disclose the information in public court proceedings or in judicial decisions. The competent authorities may release to an arbitration board established pursuant to paragraph 6 of Article XXVI (Mutual Agreement Procedure) such information as is necessary for carrying out the arbitration procedure; the members of the arbitration board shall be subject to the limitations on disclosure described in this Article.

**Technical Explanation [1995 Protocol]:**

Article 16 of the Protocol amends Article XXVII (Exchange of Information) of the Convention. Paragraph 1 of Article 16 amends paragraph 1 of Article XXVII. The first change is a wording change to make it clear that information must be exchanged if it is "relevant" for carrying out the provisions of the Convention or of the domestic laws of the Contracting States, even if it is not "necessary." Neither the United States nor Canada views this as a substantive change. The second amendment merely conforms the language of the paragraph to the language of Article II (Taxes Covered), as amended, by referring to the taxes "to which the Convention applies" rather than to the taxes "covered by the Convention."

The Protocol further amends paragraph 1 to allow a Contracting State to provide information received from the other Contracting State to its states, provinces, or local authorities, if it relates to a tax imposed by that state, province, or local authority that is substantially similar to a national-level tax covered under Article II (Taxes Covered). However, this provision does not authorize a Contracting State to request information on behalf of a state, province, or local authority. The Protocol also amends paragraph 1 to authorize the competent authorities to release information to any arbitration panel that may be established under the provisions of new paragraph 6 of Article XXVI (Mutual Agreement Procedure). Any information provided to a state, province, or local authority or to an arbitration panel is subject to the same use and disclosure provisions as is information received by the national Governments and used for their purposes.

**Technical Explanation [1984]:**

Paragraph 1 authorizes the competent authorities to exchange the information necessary for carrying out the provisions of the Convention or the domestic laws of Canada and the United States concerning taxes covered by the Convention, insofar as the taxation under those domestic laws is not contrary to the Convention. The authority to exchange information granted by paragraph 1 is not restricted by Article I (Personal Scope), and thus need not relate solely to persons otherwise covered by the Convention. It is contemplated that Article XXVII will be utilized by the competent authorities to exchange information upon request, routinely, and spontaneously.

Any information received by a Contracting State pursuant to the Convention is to be treated as secret in the same manner as information obtained under the taxation laws of that State. Such information shall be disclosed only to persons or authorities, including courts and administrative bodies, involved in the assessment or collection of, the administration and enforcement in respect of, or the determination of appeals in relation to, the taxes covered by the Convention and the information may be used by such persons only for such purposes. (In accordance with paragraph 4, for the purposes of this Article the Convention applies to a broader range of taxes than those covered specifically by Article II (Taxes Covered).)

In specific cases a competent authority providing information may, pursuant to paragraph 3, impose such other conditions on the use of information as are necessary. Although the information received by persons described in paragraph 1 is to be treated as secret, it may be disclosed by such persons in public court proceedings or in judicial decisions.

The provisions of paragraph 1 authorize the U.S. competent authority to continue to allow the General Accounting Office to examine tax return information received from Canada when GAO is engaged in a study of the administration of U.S. tax laws pursuant to a directive of Congress. However, the secrecy requirements of paragraph 1 must be met.

**Related Provisions:** Reg. 203 — Information return where person in Canada receives income from source in the U.S. on behalf of a person outside Canada.

**Notes:** Art. XXVII(1) amended by 1995 Protocol, generally effective 1996 (see Art. 21(2) under "Application of the 1995 Protocol" above). For 1985–1995, read:

> 1. The competent authorities of the Contracting States shall exchange such information as is necessary for carrying out the provisions of this Convention or of the domestic laws of the Contracting States concerning taxes covered by the Convention insofar as the taxation thereunder is not contrary to the Convention. The exchange of information is not restricted by Article I (Personal Scope). Any information received by a Contracting State shall be treated as secret in the same manner as information obtained under the taxation laws of that State and shall be disclosed only to persons or authorities (including courts and administrative bodies) involved in the assessment or collection of, the administration and enforcement in respect of, or the determination of appeals in relation to, the taxes covered by the Convention. Such persons or authorities shall use the information only for such purposes. They may disclose the information in public court proceedings or in judicial decisions.

**2.** If information is requested by a Contracting State in accordance with this Article, the other Contracting State shall endeavor to obtain the information to which the request relates in the same way as if its own taxation was involved notwithstanding the fact that the other State does not, at that time, need such information. If specifically requested by the competent authority of a Contracting State, the competent authority of the other Contracting State shall endeavor to provide information under this Article in the form requested, such as depositions of witnesses and copies of unedited original documents (including books, papers, statements, records, accounts or writings), to the same extent such depositions and documents can be obtained under the laws and administrative practices of that other State with respect to its own taxes.

**Technical Explanation [1984]:**

If a Contracting State requests information in accordance with Article XXVII, the other Contracting State shall endeavor, pursuant to paragraph 2, to obtain the information to which the request relates in the same manner as if its own taxation were involved, notwithstanding the fact that such State does not need the information. In addition, the competent authority requested to obtain information shall endeavor to provide the information in the particular form requested, such as depositions of witnesses and copies of unedited original documents, to the same extent such depositions and documents can be obtained under the laws or administrative practices of that State with respect to its own taxes.

3. In no case shall the provisions of paragraphs 1 and 2 be construed so as to impose on a Contracting State the obligation:

(a) to carry out administrative measures at variance with the laws and administrative practice of that or of the other Contracting State;

(b) to supply information which is not obtainable under the laws or in the normal course of the administration of that or of the other Contracting State; or

(c) to supply information which would disclose any trade, business, industrial, commercial or professional secret or trade process, or information the disclosure of which would be contrary to public policy (ordre public).

**Technical Explanation [1984]:**

Paragraph 3 provides that the provisions of paragraphs 1 and 2 do not impose on Canada or the United States the obligation to carry out administrative measures at variance with the laws and administrative practice of either State; to supply information which is not obtainable under the laws or in the normal course of the administration of either State; or to supply information which would disclose any trade, business, industrial, commercial, or professional secret or trade process, or information the disclosure of which would be contrary to public policy. Thus, Article XXVII allows, but does not obligate, the United States and Canada to obtain and provide information that would not be available to the requesting State under its laws or administrative practice or that in different circumstances would not be available to the State requested to provide the information. Further, Article XXVII allows a Contracting State to obtain information for the other Contracting State even if there is no tax liability in the State requested to obtain the information. Thus, the United States will continue to be able to give Canada tax information even if there is no U.S. tax liability at issue.

4. For the purposes of this Article, the Convention shall apply, notwithstanding the provisions of Article II (Taxes Covered):

(a) to all taxes imposed by a Contracting State; and

(b) to other taxes to which any other provision of the Convention applies, but only to the extent that the information is relevant for the purposes of the application of that provision.

**Technical Explanation [1995 Protocol]:**

Paragraph 2 of Article 16 amends paragraph 4 of Article XXVII, which describes the applicable taxes for the purposes of this Article. Under the present Convention, the Article applies in Canada to taxes imposed by the Government of Canada under the *Income Tax Act* and on estates and gifts and in the United States to all taxes imposed under the *Internal Revenue Code*. The Protocol broadens the scope of the Article to apply to "all taxes imposed by a Contracting State". This change allows information to be exchanged, for example, with respect to Canadian excise taxes, as is the case with respect to U.S. excise taxes under the present Convention. Paragraph 4 is also amended to authorize the exchange of information with respect to other taxes, to the extent relevant to any other provision of the Convention.

**Technical Explanation [1984]:**

Paragraph 4 provides that, for the purposes of Article XXVII, the Convention applies, in the case of Canada, to all taxes imposed by the Government of Canada on estates and gifts and under the *Income Tax Act* and, in the case of the United States, to all taxes imposed under the *Internal Revenue Code*. Article XXVII does not apply to taxes imposed by political subdivisions or local authorities of the Contracting States. Paragraph 4 is designed to ensure that information exchange will extend to most national level taxes on both sides, and specifically to information gathered for purposes of Canada's taxes on estates and gifts (not effective for deaths or gifts after 1971). This provision is intended to mesh with paragraph 8 of Article XXX (Entry Into Force), which terminates the existing estate tax convention between the United States and Canada.

**Notes**: Art. XXVII(4) amended by 1995 Protocol, generally effective 1996 (see Art. 21(2) under "Application of the 1995 Protocol" above). For 1985–1995, read:

   4. Notwithstanding the provisions of Article II (Taxes Covered), for the purposes of this Article the Convention shall apply:

   (a) in the case of Canada, to all taxes imposed by the Government of Canada on estates and gifts and under the *Income Tax Act*; and

   (b) in the case of the United States, to all taxes imposed under the *Internal Revenue Code*.

## Article XXVIII — Diplomatic Agents and Consular Officers

Nothing in this Convention shall affect the fiscal privileges of diplomatic agents or consular officers under the general rules of international law or under the provisions of special agreements.

**Technical Explanation [1984]:**

Article XXVIII states that nothing in the Convention affects the fiscal privileges of diplomatic agents or consular officers under the general rules of international law or under the provisions of special agreements. However, various provisions of the Convention could apply to such persons, such as those concerning exchange of information, mutual agreement, and non-discrimination.

**Related Provisions**: Art. XIX — Government service.

## Article XXIX — Miscellaneous Rules

1. The provisions of this Convention shall not restrict in any manner any exclusion, exemption, deduction, credit or other allowance now or hereafter accorded by the laws of a Contracting State in the determination of the tax imposed by that State.

### Technical Explanation [1984]:

Paragraph 1 states that the provisions of the Convention do not restrict in any manner any exclusion, exemption, deduction, credit, or other allowance accorded by the laws of a Contracting State in the determination of the tax imposed by that State. Thus, if a deduction would be allowed for an item in computing the taxable income of a Canadian resident under the Code, such deduction is available to such person in computing taxable income under the Convention. Paragraph 1 does not, however, authorize a taxpayer to make inconsistent choices between rules of the Code and rules of the Convention. For example, if a resident of Canada desires to claim the benefits of the "attributable to" rule of paragraphs 1 and 7 of Article VII (Business Profits) with respect to the taxation of business profits of a permanent establishment, such person must use the "attributable to" concept consistently for all items of income and deductions and may not rely upon the "effectively connected" rules of the Code to avoid U.S. tax on other items of attributable income. In no event are the rules of the Convention to increase overall U.S. tax liability from what liability would be if there were no convention.

Notes: Art. XXIX(1) is known as the "domestic tax benefit" provision. It provides, in effect, that a taxpayer can choose between the treaty and the domestic tax law and pick the one that offers better treatment. For a discussion of the extent to which this can be done for different items by the same taxpayer, see Brian Arnold, "The Relationship Between Tax Treaties and the *Income Tax Act:* Cherry Picking", 43(4) *Canadian Tax Journal* 869-905 (1995).

**2.** Except as provided in paragraph 3, nothing in the Convention shall be construed as preventing a Contracting State from taxing its residents (as determined under Article IV (Residence)) and, in the case of the United States, its citizens (including a former citizen whose loss of citizenship had as one of its principal purposes the avoidance of tax, but only for a period of ten years following such loss) and companies electing to be treated as domestic corporations, as if there were no convention between the United States and Canada with respect to taxes on income and on capital.

### Technical Explanation [1984]:

Paragraph 2 provides a "saving clause" pursuant to which Canada and the United States may each tax its residents, as determined under Article IV (Residence), and the United States may tax its citizens (including any former citizen whose loss of citizenship had as one of its principal purposes the avoidance of tax, but only for a period of 10 years following such loss) and companies electing under Code section 1504(d) to be treated as domestic corporations, as if there were no convention between the United States and Canada with respect to taxes on income and capital.

**3.** The provisions of paragraph 2 shall not affect the obligations undertaken by a Contracting State:

(a) under paragraphs 3 and 4 of Article IX (Related Persons), paragraphs 6 and 7 of Article XIII (Gains), paragraphs 1, 3, 4, 5, 6(b) and 7 of Article XVIII (Pensions and Annuities), paragraph 5 of Article XXIX (Miscellaneous Rules), paragraphs 1, 5 and 6 of Article XXIX B (Taxes Imposed by Reason of Death), paragraphs 2, 3, 4 and 7 of Article XXIX B (Taxes Imposed by Reason of Death) as applied to the estates of persons other than former citizens referred to in paragraph 2 of this Article, paragraphs 3 and 5 of Article XXX (Entry into Force), and Articles XIX (Government Service), XXI (Exempt Organizations), XXIV (Elimination of Double Taxation), XXV (Non-Discrimination) and XXVI (Mutual Agreement Procedure);

(b) under Article XX (Students), toward individuals who are neither citizens of, nor have immigrant status in, that State.

### Technical Explanation [1995 Protocol]:

Article 17 of the Protocol amends Article XXIX (Miscellaneous Rules) of the Convention. Paragraph 1 of Article 17 modifies paragraph 3(a), the exceptions to the saving clause, to conform the cross-references in the paragraph to changes in other parts of the Convention. The paragraph also adds to the exceptions to the saving clause certain provisions of Article XXIX B (Taxes Imposed by Reason of Death). Thus, certain benefits under that Article will be granted by a Contracting State to its residents and, in the case of the United States, to its citizens, notwithstanding the saving clause of paragraph 2 of Article XXIX.

### Technical Explanation [1984]:

Paragraph 3 provides that, notwithstanding paragraph 2, the United States and Canada must respect certain specified provisions of the Convention in regard to residents, citizens, and section 1504(d) companies. Paragraph 3(a) lists certain paragraphs and Articles of the Convention that represent exceptions to the "saving clause" in all situations; paragraph 3(b) provides a limited further exception for students who have not acquired immigrant status in the State where they are temporarily present.

Notes: Art. XXIX(3)(a) amended by 1995 Protocol, generally effective 1996 (see Art. 21(2) and (4) under "Application of the 1995 Protocol" above). For 1985-1995, read:

(a) under paragraphs 3 and 4 of Article IX (Related Persons), paragraphs 6 and 7 of Article XIII (Gains), paragraphs 1, 3, 4, 5(b) and 6(b) of Article XVIII (Pensions and Annuities), paragraphs 5 and 7 of Article XXIX (Miscellaneous Rules), paragraphs 3 and 5 of Article XXX (Entry into Force), and Articles XIX (Government Service), XXI (Exempt Organizations), XXIV (Elimination of Double Taxation), XXV (Non-Discrimination) and XXVI (Mutual Agreement Procedure); and

**4.** With respect to taxable years not barred by the statute of limitations ending on or before December 31 of the year before the year in which the Social Security Agreement between Canada and the United States (signed in Ottawa on March 11, 1981) enters into force, income from personal services not subject to tax by the United States under this Convention or the 1942 Convention shall not be considered wages or net earnings from self-employment for purposes of social security taxes imposed under the *Internal Revenue Code.*

### Technical Explanation [1984]:

Paragraph 4 provides relief with respect to social security taxes imposed on employers, employees, and self-employed persons under Code sections 1401, 3101, and 3111. Income from personal services not subject to tax by the United States under the provisions of this Convention or the 1942 Convention is not to be considered wages or net earnings from self-employment for purposes of the U.S. social security taxes with respect to taxable years of the taxpayer not barred by the statute of limitations relating to refunds (under the Code) ending on or before December 31 of the year before the year in which the Social Security Agreement between Canada and the United States (signed in Ottawa on March 11, 1981) enters into force. Thus, if that agreement enters into force in 1986, a resident of Canada earning income from personal services and such person's employer may apply for refunds of the employee's and employer's shares of U.S. social security tax paid attributable to the employee's income from personal services that is exempt from U.S. tax by virtue of this Convention or the 1942 Convention. In this example, the refunds would be available for social security taxes paid with respect to taxable years not barred by the statute of limitations of the Code ending on or before December 31, 1985. For purposes of Code section 6611, the date of overpayment with respect to refunds of U.S. tax pursuant to paragraph 4 is the later of the date on which the Social Security Agreement between Canada and the United States enters into force and the date on which instruments of ratification of the Convention are exchanged.

Under certain limited circumstances, an employee may, pursuant to paragraph 5 of Article XXX (Entry Into Force), claim an exemption from U.S. tax on wages under the 1942 Convention for one year after the Convention comes into force. The provisions of paragraph 4 would not, however, provide an exemption from U.S. social security taxes for such year.

Paragraph 4 does not modify existing U.S. statutes concerning social security benefits or funding. The *Social Security Act* requires the general funds of the Treasury to reimburse the social security trust funds on the basis of the records of wages and self-employment income maintained by the Social Security Administration. The Convention does not alter those records. Thus, any refunds of tax made pursuant to paragraph 4 would not affect claims for U.S. quarters of coverage with respect to social security benefits. And such refunds would be charged to general revenue funds, not social security trust funds.

**5.** Where a person who is a resident of Canada and a shareholder of a United States S corporation requests the competent authority of Canada to do so, the competent authority may agree, subject to terms and conditions satisfactory to such competent authority, to apply the following rules for the purposes of taxation in Canada with respect to the period during which the agreement is effective:

(a) the corporation shall be deemed to be a controlled foreign affiliate of the person;

(b) all the income of the corporation shall be deemed to be foreign accrual property income;

(c) for the purposes of subsection 20(11) of the *Income Tax Act*, the amount of the corporation's income that is included in the person's income shall be deemed not to be income from a property; and

(d) each dividend paid to the person on a share of the capital stock of the corporation shall be excluded from the person's income and shall be deducted in computing the adjusted cost base to the person of the share.

**Technical Explanation [1995 Protocol]:**

Paragraph 2 of Article 17 replaces paragraphs 5 through 7 of Article XXIX of the present Convention with three new paragraphs. (Paragraph 5 in the present Convention was moved to paragraph 7 of Article XVIII (Pensions and Annuities), and paragraphs 6 and 7 were deleted as unnecessary.) New paragraph 5 provides a rule for the taxation by Canada of a Canadian resident that is a shareholder in a U.S. S corporation. The application of this rule is relatively limited, because U.S. domestic law requires that S corporation shareholders be either U.S. citizens or U.S. residents. Therefore, the rule provided by paragraph 5 would apply only to an S corporation shareholder who is a resident of both the United States and Canada (i.e., a "dual resident" who meets certain requirements, determined before application of the "tie-breaker" rules of Article IV (Residence), or a U.S. citizen resident in Canada. Since the shareholder would be subject to U.S. tax on its share of the income of the S corporation as it is earned by the S corporation and, under Canadian statutory law, would be subject to tax only when the income is distributed, there could be a timing mismatch resulting in unrelieved double taxation. Under paragraph 5, the shareholder can make a request to the Canadian competent authority for relief under the special rules of the paragraph. Under these rules, the Canadian shareholder will be subject to Canadian tax on essentially the same basis as he is subject to U.S. tax, thus eliminating the timing mismatch.

**Technical Explanation [1984]:**

Paragraph 5 provides a method to resolve conflicts between the Canadian and U.S. treatment of individual retirement accounts. Certain Canadian retirement plans which are qualified plans for Canadian tax purposes do not meet Code requirements for qualification. As a result, the earnings of such a plan are currently included in income, for U.S. tax purposes, rather than being deferred until actual distributions are made by the plan. Canada defers current taxes on the earnings of such a plan but imposes tax on actual distributions from the plan. Paragraph 5 is designed to avoid a mismatch of U.S. taxable income and foreign tax credits attributable to the Canadian tax on such distributions. Under the paragraph a beneficiary of a Canadian registered retirement savings plan may elect to defer U.S. taxation with respect to any income accrued in the plan but not distributed by the plan, until such time as a distribution is made from the plan or any substitute plan. The election is to be made under rules established by the competent authority of the United States. The election is not available with respect to income accrued in the plan which is reasonably attributable to contributions made to the plan by the beneficiary while he was not a Canadian resident.

**Notes:** Art. XXIX(5) replaced by 1995 Protocol, generally effective 1996 (see Art. 21(2) under "Application of the 1995 Protocol" above). The former Art. XXIX(5) has been broadened and moved to Art. XVIII(7). For 1985–1995, read:

5. A beneficiary of a Canadian registered retirement savings plan may elect, under rules established by the competent authority of the United States, to defer United States taxation with respect to any income accrued in the plan but not distributed by the plan, until such time as a distribution is made from such plan, or any plan substituted therefor. The provisions of the preceding sentence shall not apply to income which is reasonably attributable to contributions made to the plan by the beneficiary while he was not a resident of Canada.

**6.** For purposes of paragraph 3 of Article XXII (Consultation) of the General Agreement on Trade in Services, the Contracting States agree that:

(a) a measure falls within the scope of the Convention only if:

(i) the measure relates to a tax to which Article XXV (Non-Discrimination) of the Convention applies; or

(ii) the measure relates to a tax to which Article XXV (Non-Discrimination) of the Convention does not apply and to which any other provision of the Convention applies, but only to the extent that the measure relates to a matter dealt with in that other provision of the Convention; and

(b) notwithstanding paragraph 3 of Article XXII (Consultation) of the General Agreement on Trade in Services, any doubt as to the interpretation of subparagraph (a) will be resolved under paragraph 3 of Article XXVI (Mutual Agreement

## Art. XXIX — Miscellaneous Rules

Procedure) of the Convention or any other procedure agreed to by both Contracting States.

**Technical Explanation [1995 Protocol]:**

The Protocol adds to Article XXIX a new paragraph 6, which provides a coordination rule for the Convention and the General Agreement on Trade in Services ("GATS"). Paragraph 6(a) provides that, for purposes of paragraph 3 of Article XXII (Consultation) of the GATS, a measure falls within the scope of the Convention only if the measure relates to a tax (1) to which Article XXV (Non-Discrimination) of the Convention applies, or (2) to which Article XXV does not apply and to which any other provision of the Convention applies, but only to the extent that the measure relates to a matter dealt with in that other provision. Under paragraph 6(b), notwithstanding paragraph 3 of Article XXII of the GATS, any doubt as to the interpretation of subparagraph (a) will be resolved under paragraph 3 of Article XXVI (Mutual Agreement Procedure) of the Convention or any other procedure agreed to by both Contracting States.

GATS generally obliges its Members to provide national treatment and most-favored-nation treatment to services and service suppliers of other Members. A very broad exception from the national treatment obligation applies to direct taxes. An exception from the most-favored-nation obligation applies to a difference in treatment resulting from an international agreement on the avoidance of double taxation (a "tax agreement") or from provisions on the avoidance of double taxation in any other international agreement or arrangement by which the Member is bound.

Article XXII(3) of GATS specifically provides that there will be no access to GATS procedures to settle a national treatment dispute concerning a measure that falls within the scope of a tax agreement. This provision preserves the exclusive application of nondiscrimination obligations in the tax agreement and clarifies that the competent authority mechanism provided by the tax agreement will apply, instead of GATS procedures, to resolve nondiscrimination disputes involving the taxation of services and service suppliers.

In the event of a disagreement between Members as to whether a measure falls within the scope of a tax agreement that existed at the time of the entry into force of the Agreement establishing the World Trade Organization, Article XXII(2), footnote 11, of GATS reserves the resolution of the dispute to the Contracting States under the tax agreement. In such a case, the issue of the scope of a tax agreement may be resolved under GATS procedures (rather than tax treaty procedures) only if both parties to the existing tax agreement consent. With respect to subsequent tax agreements, GATS provides that either Member may bring the jurisdictional matter before the Council for Trade In Services, which will refer the matter to arbitration for a decision that will be final and binding on the Members.

Both Canada and the United States agree that a protocol to a convention that is grandfathered under Article XXII(2), footnote 11, of GATS is also grandfathered. Nevertheless, since the Protocol extends the application of the Convention, and particularly the nondiscrimination article, to additional taxes (e.g., some non-income taxes imposed by Canada), the negotiators sought to remove any ambiguity and agreed to a provision that clarified the scope of the Convention and the relationship between the Convention and GATS.

The purpose of new paragraph 6(a) of the Convention is to provide the agreement of the Contracting States as to the measures considered to fall within the scope of the Convention in applying Article XXII(3) of GATS between the Contracting States. The purpose of new paragraph 6(b) is to reserve the resolution of the issue of the scope of the Convention for purposes of Article XXII(3) of GATS to the competent authorities under the Convention rather than to settlement under GATS procedures.

**Technical Explanation [1984]:**

Paragraph 6 provides rules denying the benefits of the Convention in certain situations where both countries believed that granting benefits would be inappropriate. Paragraph 6(a) provides that Articles VI (Income from Real Property) through XXIV (Elimination of Double Taxation) shall not apply to profits, income or gains derived by a trust which is treated as the income of a resident of a Contracting State (see paragraph 1 of Article IV (Residence)), if a principal purpose of the establishment, acquisition or maintenance of the trust was to obtain a benefit under the Convention or the 1942 Convention for persons who are not residents of that State. For example, the provision could be applied to a case where a non-resident of the United States created a United States trust to derive dividend income from Canada and a principal purpose of the establishment or maintenance of the trust was to obtain the reduced rate of Canadian tax under Article X (Dividends) for the non-resident. Paragraph 6(b) provides that Articles VI through XXIV shall not apply to Canadian non-resident owned investment companies, as defined in section 133 of the *Income Tax Act*, or under a similar provision that is subsequently enacted. This provision operates to deny the benefits of the Convention to a Canadian non-resident owned investment company, and does not affect the grant of benefits to other persons. Thus, for example, a dividend paid by such a company to a shareholder who is a U.S. resident is subject to the reduced rates of tax provided by Article X. The denial of the benefits of Articles VI through XXIV in such cases applies notwithstanding any other provision of the Convention. A Canadian non-resident owned investment company may, however, be entitled to claim the benefits of the 1942 Convention for an additional one-year period, pursuant to paragraph 5 of Article XXX (Entry into Force). Where the provisions of this paragraph apply, the Contracting State in which the income arises may tax such income under its domestic law.

**Notes:** Art. XXIX(6) replaced by 1995 Protocol, generally effective 1996 (see Art. 21(2) under "Application of the 1995 Protocol" above). The former Art. XXIX(6) was deleted as unnecessary. For 1985–1995, read:

6. Notwithstanding any other provision of the Convention,

(a) where profits, income or gains derived by a trust is to be treated for the purposes of the Convention as income of a resident of a Contracting State, and a principal purpose for the establishment, acquisition or maintenance of the trust was to obtain a benefit under the Convention or the 1942 Convention for persons who are not residents of that State, Articles VI (Income from Real Property) through XXIV (Elimination of Double Taxation) shall not apply in relation to the profits, income or gains of the trust; and

(b) Articles VI (Income from Real Property) through XXIV (Elimination of Double Taxation) shall not apply to non-resident-owned investment corporations as defined under section 133 of the *Income Tax Act* of Canada, or under any similar provision enacted by Canada after the date of signature of the Protocol.

**7.** The appropriate authority of a Contracting State may request consultations with the appropriate authority of the other Contracting State to determine whether change to the Convention is appropriate to respond to changes in the law or policy of that other State. Where domestic legislation enacted by a Contracting State unilaterally removes or significantly limits any material benefit otherwise provided by the Convention, the appropriate authorities shall promptly consult for the purpose of considering an appropriate change to the Convention.

**Technical Explanation [1995 Protocol]:**

The Protocol also adds to Article XXIX a new paragraph 7, relating to certain changes in the law or treaty policy of either of the Contracting States. Paragraph 7 provides, first, that in response to a change in the law or policy of either State, the appropriate authority of either State may request consultations with its counterpart in the other State to determine whether a change in the Convention is appropriate. If a change in domestic legislation has unilaterally removed or significantly limited a material benefit provided by the Convention, the appropriate authorities are instructed by the paragraph to consult promptly to consider an appropriate amendment to the Convention. The "appropriate authorities" may be the Contracting States themselves or the competent authorities under the Convention. The consultations may be initiated by the authority of the Contracting State making the change in law or policy or by the authority of the other State. Any change in the Convention recommended as a result of this process can be implemented only through the negotiation, signature, ratification, and entry into force of a new protocol to the Convention.

**Technical Explanation [1984]:**

Paragraph 7 provides rules for the U.S. taxation of Canadian social security benefits paid to a resident of Canada who is a U.S. citizen. These rules are described in the discussion of paragraph 5 of Article XVIII (Pensions and Annuities).

**Notes:** Art. XXIX(7) replaced by 1995 Protocol, generally effective 1996 (see Art. 21(2) under "Application of the 1995 Protocol" above). The former Art. XXIX(7) was deleted as unnecessary. For 1985–1995, read:

> 7. One-half of the total amount of benefits under the social security legislation in Canada paid in a taxable year to a resident of Canada who is a citizen of the United States shall be exempt from taxation in the United States.

## Article XXIX A — Limitation on Benefits

**1.** For the purposes of the application of this Convention by the United States,

(a) a qualifying person shall be entitled to all of the benefits of this Convention, and

(b) except as provided in paragraphs 3, 4 and 6, a person that is not a qualifying person shall not be entitled to any benefits of the Convention.

**Proposed Amendment — Limitation on Benefits**

**Department of Finance news release, October 2, 1998:** *Canada and United States to Consult regarding Modifications to Income Tax Treaty*
[Reproduced before Article I — ed.]

**Technical Explanation [1995 Protocol]:**

*In general*

Article 18 of the Protocol adds a new Article XXIX A (Limitation on Benefits) to the Convention. Article XXIX A addresses the problem of "treaty shopping" by requiring, in most cases, that the person seeking U.S. treaty benefits not only be a Canadian resident but also satisfy other tests. In a typical case of treaty shopping, a resident of a third State might establish an entity resident in Canada for the purpose of deriving income from the United States and claiming U.S. treaty benefits with respect to that income. Article XXIX A limits the benefits granted by the United States under the Convention to those persons whose residence in Canada is not considered to have been motivated by the existence of the Convention. Absent Article XXIX A, the entity would be entitled to U.S. benefits under the Convention as a resident of Canada, unless it were denied benefits as a result of limitations (e.g., business purpose, substance-over-form, step transaction, or conduit principles or other anti-avoidance rules) applicable to a particular transaction or arrangement. General anti-abuse provisions of this sort apply in conjunction with the Convention in both the United States and Canada. In the case of the United States, such anti-abuse provisions complement the explicit anti-treaty-shopping rules of Article XXIX A. While the anti-treaty-shopping rules determine whether a person has a sufficient nexus to Canada to be entitled to treaty benefits, general anti-abuse provisions determine whether a particular transaction should be recast in accordance with the substance of the transaction.

The present Convention deals with treaty-shopping in a very limited manner, in paragraph 6 of Article XXIX, by denying benefits to Canadian residents that benefit from specified provisions of Canadian law. The Protocol removes that paragraph 6 from Article XXIX, because it is superseded by the more general provisions of Article XXIX A.

The Article is not reciprocal, except for paragraph 7. Canada prefers to rely on general anti-avoidance rules to counter arrangements involving treaty-shopping through the United States.

The structure of the Article is as follows: Paragraph 1 states that, in determining whether a resident of Canada is entitled to U.S. benefits under the Convention, a "qualifying person" is entitled to all of the benefits of the Convention, and other persons are not entitled to benefits, except where paragraphs 3, 4, or 6 provide otherwise. Paragraph 2 lists a number of characteristics, any one of which will make a Canadian resident a qualifying person. These are essentially mechanical tests. Paragraph 3 provides an alternative rule, under which a Canadian resident that is not a qualifying person under paragraph 2 may claim U.S. benefits with respect to those items of U.S. source income that are connected with the active conduct of a trade or business in Canada. Paragraph 4 provides a limited "derivative benefits" test for entitlement to benefits with respect to U.S. source dividends, interest, and royalties beneficially owned by a resident of Canada that is not a qualifying person. Paragraph 5 defines certain terms used in the Article. Paragraph 6 requires the U.S. competent authority to grant benefits to a resident of Canada that does not qualify for benefits under any other provision of the Article, where the competent authority determines, on the basis of all factors, that benefits should be granted. Paragraph 7 clarifies the application of general anti-abuse provisions.

**Notes:** Art. XXIX A is an "anti-treaty-shopping" provision that appears in most recent U.S. treaties, and denies treaty protection to taxpayers from other countries that try to set up operations in Canada in order to make use of treaty provisions. For a detailed discussion see Janice Russell, "The New Limitation-on-Benefits Article", 43(4) *Canadian Tax Journal* 964–982 (1995).

For the effective date of this rule, see Notes at end of Art. XXIX A.

**2.** For the purposes of this Article, a qualifying person is a resident of Canada that is:

(a) a natural person;

(b) the Government of Canada or a political subdivision or local authority thereof, or any agency or instrumentality of any such government, subdivision or authority;

(c) a company or trust in whose principal class of shares or units there is substantial and regular trading on a recognized stock exchange;

(d) a company more than 50 per cent of the vote and value of the shares (other than debt substitute shares) of which is owned, directly or indirectly, by five or fewer persons each of which is a company or trust referred to in subparagraph (c), provided that each company or trust in the chain of ownership is a qualifying person or a resident or citizen of the United States;

(e)

(i) a company 50 per cent or more of the vote and value of the shares (other than debt substitute shares) of which is not owned, directly or indirectly, by persons other than qualifying persons or residents or citizens of the United States, or

(ii) a trust 50 per cent or more of the beneficial interest in which is not owned, directly or indirectly, by persons other than qualifying persons or residents or citizens of the United States,

where the amount of the expenses deductible from gross income that are paid or payable by the company or trust, as the case may be, for its preceding fiscal period (or, in the case of its first fiscal period, that period) to persons that are not qualifying persons or residents or citizens of the United States is less than 50 per cent of its gross income for that period;

(f) an estate;

(g) a not-for-profit organization, provided that more than half of the beneficiaries, members or participants of the organization are qualifying persons or residents or citizens of the United States; or

(h) an organization described in paragraph 2 of Article XXI (Exempt Organizations) and established for the purpose of providing benefits primarily to individuals who are qualifying persons, persons who were qualifying persons within the five preceding years, or residents or citizens of the United States.

**Technical Explanation [1995 Protocol]:**

*Individuals and governmental entities*

Under paragraph 2, the first two categories of qualifying persons are (1) individual residents of Canada, and (2) the Government of Canada, a political subdivision or local authority thereof, or an agency or instrumentality of that Government, political subdivision, or local authority. It is considered unlikely that persons falling into these two categories can be used, as the beneficial owner of income, to derive treaty benefits on behalf of a third-country person. If a person is receiving income as a nominee on behalf of a third-country resident, benefits will be denied with respect to those items of income under the articles of the Convention that grant the benefit, because of the requirements in those articles that the beneficial owner of the income be a resident of a Contracting State.

*Publicly traded entities*

Under subparagraph (c) of paragraph 2, a Canadian resident company or trust is a qualifying person if there is substantial and regular trading in the company's principal class of shares, or in the trust's units, on a recognized stock exchange. The term "recognized stock exchange" is defined in paragraph 5(a) of the Article to mean, in the United States, the NASDAQ System and any stock exchange registered as a national securities exchange with the Securities and Exchange Commission, and, in Canada, any Canadian stock exchanges that are "prescribed stock exchanges" under the *Income Tax Act*. These are, at the time of signature of the Protocol, the Alberta, Montreal, Toronto, Vancouver, and Winnipeg Stock Exchanges. Additional exchanges may be added to the list of recognized exchanges by exchange of notes between the Contracting States or by agreement between the competent authorities.

Certain companies owned by publicly traded corporations also may be qualifying persons. Under subparagraph (d) of paragraph 2, a Canadian resident company will be a qualifying person, even if not publicly traded, if more than 50 percent of the vote and value of its shares is owned (directly or indirectly) by five or fewer persons that would be qualifying persons under subparagraph (c). In addition, each company in the chain of ownership must be a qualifying person or a U.S. citizen or resident. Thus, for example, a Canadian company that is not publicly traded but that is owned, one-third each, by three companies, two of which are Canadian resident corporations whose principal classes of shares are substantially and regularly traded on a recognized stock exchange, will qualify under subparagraph (d).

The 50-percent test under subparagraph (d) applies only to shares other than "debt substitute shares." The term "debt substitute shares" is defined in paragraph 5 to mean shares defined in paragraph (e) of the definition in the Canadian *Income Tax Act* of "term preferred shares" (see section 248(1) of the *Income Tax Act*), which relates to certain shares received in debt-restructuring arrangements undertaken by reason of financial difficulty or insolvency. Paragraph 5 also provides that the competent authorities may agree to treat other types of shares as debt substitute shares.

*Ownership/base erosion test*

Subparagraph (e) of paragraph 2 provides a two-part test under which certain other entities may be qualifying persons, based on ownership and "base erosion." Under the first of these tests, benefits will be granted to a Canadian resident company if 50 percent or more of the vote and value of its shares (other than debt substitute shares), or to a Canadian resident trust if 50 percent or more of its beneficial interest, is not owned, directly or indirectly, by persons other than qualifying persons or U.S. residents or citizens. The wording of these tests is intended to make clear that, for example, if a Canadian company is more than 50 percent owned by a U.S. resident corporation that is, itself, wholly owned by a third-country resident other than a U.S. citizen, the Canadian company would not pass the ownership test. This is because more than 50 percent of its shares is owned indirectly by a person (the third-country resident) that is not a qualifying person or a citizen or resident of the United States.

For purposes of this subparagraph (e) and other provisions of this Article, the term "shares" includes, in the case of a mutual insurance company, any certificate or contract entitling the holder to voting power in the corporation. This is consistent with the interpretation of similar limitation on benefits provisions in other U.S. treaties.

The second test of subparagraph (e) is the so-called "base erosion" test. A Canadian company or trust that passes the ownership test must also pass this test to be a qualifying person. This test requires that the amount of expenses that are paid or payable by the Canadian entity in question to persons that are not qualifying persons or U.S. citizens or residents, and that are deductible from gross income, be less than 50 percent of the gross income of the company or trust. This test is applied for the fiscal period immediately preceding the period for which the qualifying person test is being applied. If it is the first fiscal period of the person, the test is applied for the current period.

The ownership/base erosion test recognizes that the benefits of the Convention can be enjoyed indirectly not only by equity holders of an entity, but also by that entity's obligees, such as lenders, licensors, service providers, insurers and reinsurers, and others. For example, a third-country resident could license technology to a Canadian-owned Canadian corporation to be sub-licensed to a U.S. resident. The U.S. source royalty income of the Canadian corporation would be exempt from U.S. withholding tax under Article XII (Royalties) of the Convention (as amended by the Protocol). While the Canadian corporation would be subject to Canadian corporation income tax, its taxable income could be reduced to near zero as a result of the deductible royalties paid to the third-country resident. If, under a Convention between Canada and the third country, those royalties were either exempt from Canadian tax or subject to tax at a low rate, the U.S. treaty benefit with respect to the U.S. source royalty income would have flowed to the third-country resident at little or no tax cost, with no reciprocal benefit to the United States from the third country. The ownership/base erosion test therefore requires both that qualifying persons or U.S. residents or citizens substantially own the entity and that the entity's deductible payments be made in substantial part to such persons.

*Other qualifying persons*

Under subparagraph (f) of paragraph 2, a Canadian resident estate is a qualifying person, entitled to the benefits of the Convention with respect to its U.S. source income.

Subparagraphs (g) and (h) specify the circumstances under which certain types of not-for-profit organizations will be qualifying persons. Subparagraph (g) of paragraph 2 provides that a not-for-profit organization that is a resident of Canada is a qualifying person, and thus entitled to U.S. benefits, if more than half of the beneficiaries, members, or participants in the organization are qualifying persons or citizens or residents of the United States. The term "not-for-profit organization" of a Contracting State is defined in subparagraph (b) of paragraph 5 of the Article to mean an entity created or established in that State that is generally exempt from income taxation in that State by reason of its not-for-profit status. The term includes charities, private foundations, trade unions, trade associations, and similar organizations.

Subparagraph (h) of paragraph 2 specifies that certain organizations described in paragraph 2 of Article XXI (Exempt Organizations), as amended by Article 10 of the Protocol, are qualifying persons. To be a qualifying person, such an organization must be established primarily for the purpose of providing pension, retirement, or employee benefits to individual residents of Canada who are (or were, within any of the five preceding years) qualifying persons, or to citizens or residents of the United States. An organization will be considered to be established "primarily" for this purpose if more than 50 percent of its beneficiaries, members, or participants are such persons. Thus, for example, a Canadian Registered Retirement Savings Plan ("RRSP") of a former resident of Canada who is working temporarily outside of Canada would continue to be a qualifying person during the period of the individual's absence from Canada or for five years, whichever is shorter. A Canadian pension fund established to provide benefits to persons employed by a company would be a qualifying person only if most of the beneficiaries of the fund are (or were within the five preceding years) individual residents of Canada or residents or citizens of the United States.

The provisions of paragraph 2 are self-executing, unlike the provisions of paragraph 6, discussed below. The tax authorities may, of course, on review, determine that the taxpayer has improperly interpreted the paragraph and is not entitled to the benefits claimed.

**3.** Where a person that is a resident of Canada and is not a qualifying person of Canada, or a person related thereto, is engaged in the active conduct of a trade or business in Canada (other than the business of making or managing investments, unless those activities are carried on with customers in the ordinary course of business by a bank, an insurance company, a registered securities dealer or a deposit-taking financial institution), the benefits of the Convention shall apply to that resident person with respect to income derived from the United States in connection with or incidental to that trade or business, including any such income derived directly or indirectly by that resident person through one or more other persons that are residents of the United States. Income shall be deemed to be derived from the United States in connection with the active conduct of a trade or business in Canada only if that trade or business is substantial in relation to the activity carried on in the United States giving rise to the income in respect of which benefits provided under the Convention by the United States are claimed.

**Technical Explanation [1995 Protocol]:**

*Active trade or business test*

Paragraph 3 provides an eligibility test for benefits for residents of Canada that are not qualifying persons under paragraph 2. This is the so-called "active trade or business" test. Unlike the tests of paragraph 2, the active trade or business test looks not solely at the characteristics of the person deriving the income, but also at the nature of the activity engaged in by that person and the connection between the income and that activity. Under the active trade or business test, a resident of Canada deriving an item of income from the United States is entitled to benefits with respect to that income if that person (or a person related to that person under the principles of *Internal Revenue Code* section 482) is engaged in an active trade or business in Canada and the income in question is derived in connection with, or is incidental to, that trade or business.

Income that is derived in connection with, or is incidental to, the business of making or managing investments will not qualify for benefits under this provision, unless those investment activities are carried on with customers in the ordinary course of the business of a bank, insurance company, registered securities dealer, or deposit-taking financial institution.

Income is considered derived "in connection" with an active trade or business in the United States if, for example, the income-generating activity in the United States is "upstream," "downstream," or parallel to that conducted in Canada. Thus, if the U.S. activity consisted of selling the output of a Canadian manufacturer or providing inputs to the manufacturing process, or of manufacturing or selling in the United States the same sorts of products that were being sold by the Canadian trade or business in Canada, the income generated by that activity would be treated as earned in connection with the Canadian trade or business. Income is considered "incidental" to the Canadian trade or business if, for example, it arises from the short-term investment of working capital of the Canadian resident in U.S. securities.

An item of income will be considered to be earned in connection with or to be incidental to an active trade or business in Canada if the income is derived by the resident of Canada claiming the benefits directly or indirectly through one or more other persons that are residents of the United States. Thus, for example, a Canadian resident could claim benefits with respect to an item of income earned by a U.S. operating subsidiary but derived by the Canadian resident indirectly through a wholly-owned U.S. holding company interposed between it and the operating subsidiary. This language would also permit a Canadian resident to derive income from the United States through one or more U.S. residents that it does not wholly own. For example, a Canadian partnership in which three unrelated Canadian companies each hold a one-third interest could form a wholly-owned U.S. holding company with a U.S. operating subsidiary. The "directly or indirectly" language would allow otherwise available treaty benefits to be claimed with respect to income derived by the three Canadian partners through the U.S. holding company, even if the partners were not considered to be related to the U.S. holding company under the principles of *Internal Revenue Code* section 482.

Income that is derived in connection with, or is incidental to, an active trade or business in Canada, must pass an additional test to qualify for U.S. treaty benefits. The trade or business in Canada must be substantial in relation to the activity in the United States that gave rise to the income in respect of which treaty benefits are being claimed. To be considered substantial, it is not necessary that the Canadian trade or business be as large as the U.S. income-generating activity. The Canadian trade or business cannot, however, in terms of income, assets, or other similar measures, represent only a very small percentage of the size of the U.S. activity.

The substantiality requirement is intended to prevent treaty-shopping. For example, a third-country resident may want to acquire a U.S. company that manufactures television sets for worldwide markets; however, since its country of residence has no tax treaty with the United States, any dividends generated by the investment would be subject to a U.S. withholding tax of 30 percent. Absent a substantiality test, the investor could establish a Canadian corporation that would operate a small outlet in Canada to sell a few of the television sets manufactured by the U.S. company and earn a very small amount of income. That Canadian corporation could then acquire the U.S. manufacturer with capital provided by the third-country resident and produce a very large number of sets for sale in several countries, generating a much larger amount of income. It might attempt to argue that the U.S. source income is generated from business activities in the United States related to the television sales activity of the Canadian parent and that the dividend income should be subject to U.S. tax at the 5 percent rate provided by Article X of the Convention, as amended by the Protocol. However, the substantiality test would not be met in this example, so the dividends would remain subject to withholding in the United States at a rate of 30 percent.

In general, it is expected that if a person qualifies for benefits under one of the tests of paragraph 2, no inquiry will be made into qualification for benefits under paragraph 3. Upon satisfaction of any of the tests of paragraph 2, any income derived by the beneficial owner from the other Contracting State is entitled to treaty benefits. Under paragraph 3, however, the test is applied separately to each item of income.

**4.** A company that is a resident of Canada shall also be entitled to the benefits of Articles X (Dividends), XI (Interest) and XII (Royalties) if

(a) its shares that represent more than 90 per cent of the aggregate vote and value represented by all of its shares (other than debt substitute shares) are owned, directly or indirectly, by persons each of whom is a qualifying person, a resident or citizen of the United States or a person who

(i) is a resident of a country with which the United States has a comprehensive income tax convention and is entitled to all of the benefits provided by the United States under that convention;

(ii) would qualify for benefits under paragraphs 2 or 3 if that person were a resident of Canada (and, for the purposes of paragraph 3, if the business it carried on in the country of which it is a resident were carried on by it in Canada); and

(iii) would be entitled to a rate of United States tax under the convention between that person's country of residence and the United States, in respect of the particular class of income for which benefits are being claimed under this Convention, that is at least as low as the rate applicable under this Convention; and

(b) the amount of the expenses deductible from gross income that are paid or payable by the company for its preceding fiscal period (or, in the case of its first fiscal period, that period) to persons that are not qualifying persons or residents or citizens of the United States is less than 50 per cent of the gross income of the company for that period.

**Technical Explanation [1995 Protocol]:**

*Derivative benefits test*

Paragraph 4 of Article XXIX A contains a so-called "derivative benefits" rule not generally found in U.S. treaties. This rule was included in the Protocol because of the special economic relationship between the United States and Canada and the close coordination between the tax administrations of the two countries.

Under the derivative benefits rule, a Canadian resident company may receive the benefits of Articles X (Dividends), XI (Interest), and XII (Royalties), even if the company is not a qualifying person and does not satisfy the active trade or business test of paragraph 3. To qualify under this paragraph, the Canadian company must satisfy both (i) the base erosion test under subparagraph (e) of paragraph 2, and (ii) an ownership test.

The derivative benefits ownership test requires that shares (other than debt substitute shares) representing more than 90 percent of the vote and value of the Canadian company be owned directly or indirectly by either (i) qualifying persons or U.S. citizens or residents, or (ii) other persons that satisfy each of three tests. The three tests that must be satisfied by these other persons are as follows:

First, the person must be a resident of a third State with which the United States has a comprehensive income tax convention and be entitled to all of the benefits under that convention. Thus, if the person fails to satisfy the limitation on benefits tests, if any, of that convention, no benefits would be granted under this paragraph. Qualification for benefits under an active trade or business test does not suffice for these purposes, because that test grants benefits only for certain items of income, not for all purposes of the convention.

Second, the person must be a person that would qualify for benefits with respect to the item of income for which benefits are sought under one or more of the tests of paragraph 2 or 3 of this Convention, if the person were a resident of Canada and, for purposes of paragraph 3, the business were carried on in Canada. For example, a person resident in a third country would be deemed to be a person that would qualify under the publicly-traded test of paragraph 2 of this Convention if the principal class of its shares were substantially and regularly traded on a stock exchange recognized either under the treaty between the United States and Canada or under the treaty between the United States and the third country. Similarly, a company resident in a third country would be deemed to satisfy the ownership/base erosion test of paragraph 2 under this hypothetical analysis if, for example, it were wholly owned by an individual resident in that third country and most of its deductible payments were made to individual residents of that country (i.e., it satisfied base erosion).

The third requirement is that the rate of U.S. withholding tax on the item of income in respect of which benefits are sought must be at least as low under the convention between the person's country of residence and the United States as under this Convention.

**5.** For the purposes of this Article,

(a) the term **"recognized stock exchange"** means:

(i) the NASDAQ System owned by the National Association of Securities Dealers, Inc. and any stock exchange registered with the Securities and Exchange Commission as a national securities exchange for purposes of the *Securities Exchange Act of 1934*;

(ii) Canadian stock exchanges that are "prescribed stock exchanges" under the *Income Tax Act*; and

(iii) any other stock exchange agreed upon by the Contracting States in an exchange of notes or by the competent authorities of the Contracting States;

(b) the term **"not-for-profit organization"** of a Contracting State means an entity created or established in that State and that is, by reason of its not-for-profit status, generally exempt from income taxation in that State, and includes a private foundation, charity, trade union, trade association or similar organization; and

(c) the term **"debt substitute share"** means:

(i) a share described in paragraph (e) of the definition "term preferred share" in the *Income Tax Act*, as it may be amended from time to time without changing the general principle thereof; and

(ii) such other type of share as may be agreed upon by the competent authorities of the Contracting States.

**6.** Where a person that is a resident of Canada is not entitled under the preceding provisions of this Article to the benefits provided under the Convention by the United States, the competent authority of the United States shall, upon that person's request, determine on the basis of all factors including the history, structure, ownership and operations of that person whether

(a) its creation and existence did not have as a principal purpose the obtaining of benefits under the Convention that would not otherwise be available; or

(b) it would not be appropriate, having regard to the purpose of this Article, to deny the benefits of the Convention to that person.

The person shall be granted the benefits of the Convention by the United States where the competent authority determines that subparagraph (a) or (b) applies.

**Technical Explanation [1995 Protocol]:**

*Competent authority discretion*

Paragraph 6 provides that when a resident of Canada derives income from the United States and is not entitled to the benefits of the Convention under other provisions of the Article, benefits may, nevertheless be granted at the discretion of the U.S. competent authority. In making a determination under this paragraph, the competent authority will take into account all relevant facts and circumstances relating to the person requesting the benefits. In particular, the competent authority will consider the history, structure, ownership (including ultimate beneficial ownership), and operations of the person. In addition, the competent authority is to consider (1) whether the creation and existence of the person did not have as a principal purpose obtaining treaty benefits that would not otherwise be available to the person, and (2) whether it would not be appropriate, in view of the purpose of the Article, to deny benefits. The paragraph specifies that if the U.S. competent authority determines that either of these two standards is satisfied, benefits shall be granted.

For purposes of implementing paragraph 6, a taxpayer will be expected to present his case to the competent authority for an advance determination based on the facts. The taxpayer will not be required to wait until it has been determined that benefits are denied under one of the other provisions of the Article. It also is expected that, if and when the competent authority determines that benefits are to be allowed, they will be allowed retroactively to the time of entry into force of the relevant treaty provision or the establishment of the structure in question, whichever is later (assuming that the taxpayer also qualifies under the relevant facts for the earlier period).

**7.** It is understood that the fact that the preceding provisions of this Article apply only for the purposes of the application of the Convention by the United States shall not be construed as restricting in any manner the right of a Contracting State to deny benefits under the Convention where it can reasonably be concluded that to do otherwise would result in an abuse of the provisions of the Convention.

**Technical Explanation [1995 Protocol]:**

*General anti-abuse provisions*

Paragraph 7 was added at Canada's request to confirm that the specific provisions of Article XXIX A and the fact that these provisions apply only for the purposes of the application of the Convention by the United States should not be construed so as to limit the right of each Contracting State to invoke applicable anti-abuse rules. Thus, for example, Canada remains free to apply such rules to counter abusive arrangements involving "treaty-shopping" through the United States, and the United States remains free to apply its substance-over-form and anti-conduit rules, for example, in relation to Canadian residents. This principle is recognized by the Organization for Economic Cooperation and Development in the Commentaries to its Model Tax Convention on Income and on Capital, and the United States and Canada agree that it is inherent in the Convention. The agreement to state this principle explicitly in the Protocol is not intended to suggest that the principle is not also inherent in other tax conventions, including the current Convention with Canada.

**Notes [Art. XXIX A]:** Art. XXIX A added by 1995 Protocol, generally effective 1996 (see Art. 21(2) under "Application of the 1995 Protocol" above).

## Article XXIX B — Taxes Imposed by Reason of Death

**1.** Where the property of an individual who is a resident of a Contracting State passes by reason of the individual's death to an organization referred to in paragraph 1 of Article XXI (Exempt Organizations), the tax consequences in a Contracting State arising out of the passing of the property shall apply as if the organization were a resident of that State.

**Technical Explanation [1995 Protocol]:**

*In general*

Article 19 of the Protocol adds to the Convention a new Article XXIX B (Taxes Imposed by Reason of Death). The purpose of Article XXIX B is to better coordinate the operation of the death tax regimes of the two Contracting States. Such coordination is necessary because the United States imposes an estate tax, while Canada now applies an income tax on gains deemed realized at death rather than an estate tax. Article XXIX B also contains other provisions designed to alleviate death taxes in certain situations.

For purposes of new Article XXIX B, the term "resident" has the meaning provided by Article IV (Residence) of the Convention, as amended by Article 3 of the Protocol. The meaning of the term "resident" for purposes of Article XXIX B, therefore, differs in some respects from its meaning under the estate, gift, and generation-skipping transfer tax provisions of the *Internal Revenue Code*.

*Charitable bequests*

Paragraph 1 of new Article XXIX B facilitates certain charitable bequests. It provides that a Contracting State shall accord the same death tax treatment to a bequest by an individual resident in one of the Contracting States to a qualifying exempt organization resident in the other Contracting State as it would have accorded if the organization had been a resident of the first Contracting State. The organizations covered by this provision are those referred to in paragraph 1 of Article XXI (Exempt Organizations) of the Convention. A bequest by a U.S. citizen or U.S. resident (as defined for estate tax purposes under the *Internal Revenue Code*) to such an exempt organization generally is deductible for U.S. estate tax purposes under section 2055 of the *Internal Revenue Code*, without regard to whether the organization is a U.S. corporation. However, if the decedent is not a U.S. citizen or U.S. resident (as defined for estate tax purposes under the *Internal Revenue Code*), such a bequest is deductible for U.S. estate tax purposes, under section 2106(a)(2) of the *Internal Revenue Code*, only if the recipient organization is a U.S. corporation. Under paragraph 1 of Article XXIX B, a U.S. estate tax deduction also will be allowed for a bequest by a Canadian resident (as defined under Article IV (Residence)) to a qualifying exempt organization that is a Canadian corporation. However, paragraph 1 does not allow a deduction for U.S. estate tax purposes with respect to any transfer of property that is not subject to U.S. estate tax.

**Notes:** For the effective date of this rule, see Notes at end of Art. XXIX B.

**2. In determining the estate tax imposed by the United States, the estate of an individual (other than a citizen of the United States) who was a resident of Canada at the time of the individual's death shall be allowed a unified credit equal to the greater of**

(a) the amount that bears the same ratio to the credit allowed under the law of the United States to the estate of a citizen of the United States as the value of the part of the individual's gross estate that at the time of the individual's death is situated in the United States bears to the value of the individual's entire gross estate wherever situated; and

(b) the unified credit allowed to the estate of a nonresident not a citizen of the United States under the law of the United States.

The amount of any unified credit otherwise allowable under this paragraph shall be reduced by the amount of any credit previously allowed with respect to any gift made by the individual. The credit otherwise allowable under subparagraph (a) shall be allowed only if all information necessary for the verification and computation of the credit is provided.

**Technical Explanation [1995 Protocol]:**

*Unified credit*

Paragraph 2 of Article XXIX B grants a "pro rata" unified credit to the estate of a Canadian resident decedent, for purposes of computing U.S. estate tax. Although the Congress anticipated the negotiation of such pro rata unified credits in *Internal Revenue Code* section 2102(c)(3)(A), this is the first convention in which the United States has agreed to give such a credit. However, certain exemption provisions of existing estate and gift tax conventions have been interpreted as providing a pro rata unified credit.

Under the *Internal Revenue Code*, the estate of a nonresident not a citizen of the United States is subject to U.S. estate tax only on its U.S. situs assets and is entitled to a unified credit of $13,000, while the estate of a U.S. citizen or U.S. resident is subject to U.S. estate tax on its entire worldwide assets and is entitled to a unified credit of $192,800. (For purposes of these *Internal Revenue Code* provisions, the term "resident" has the meaning provided for estate tax purposes under the *Internal Revenue Code*.) A lower unified credit is provided for the former category of estates because it is assumed that the estate of a nonresident not a citizen generally will hold fewer U.S. situs assets, as a percentage of the estate's total assets, and thus will have a lower U.S. estate tax liability. The pro rata unified credit provisions of paragraph 2 increase the credit allowed to the estate of a Canadian resident decedent to an amount between $13,000 and $192,800 in appropriate cases, to take into account the extent to which the assets of the estate are situated in the United States. Paragraph 2 provides that the amount of the unified credit allowed to the estate of a Canadian resident decedent will in no event be less than the $13,000 allowed under the *Internal Revenue Code* to the estate of a nonresident not a citizen of the United States (subject to the adjustment for prior gift tax unified credits, discussed below). Paragraph 2 does not apply to the estates of U.S. citizen decedents, whether resident in Canada or elsewhere, because such estates receive a unified credit of $192,800 under the *Internal Revenue Code*.

Subject to the adjustment for gift tax unified credits, the pro rata credit allowed under paragraph 2 is determined by multiplying $192,800 by a fraction, the numerator of which is the value of the part of the gross estate situated in the United States and the denominator of which is the value of the entire gross estate wherever situated. Thus, if half of the entire gross estate (by value) of a decedent who was a resident and citizen of Canada were situated in the United States, the estate would be entitled to a pro rata unified credit of $96,400 (provided that the U.S. estate tax due is not less than that amount). For purposes of the denominator, the entire gross estate wherever situated (i.e., the worldwide estate, determined under U.S. domestic law) is to be taken into account for purposes of the computation. For purposes of the numerator, an estate's assets will be treated as situated in the United States if they are so treated under U.S. domestic law. However, if enacted, a technical correction now pending before the Congress will amend U.S. domestic law to clarify that assets will not be treated as U.S. situs assets for purposes of the pro rata unified credit computation if the United States is precluded from taxing them by reason of a treaty obligation. This technical correction will affect the interpretation of both this paragraph 2 and the analogous provisions in existing conventions. As currently proposed, it will take effect on the date of enactment.

Paragraph 2 restricts the availability of the pro rata unified credit in two respects. First, the amount of the unified credit otherwise allowable under paragraph 2 is reduced by the amount of any unified credit previously allowed against U.S. gift tax imposed on any gift by the decedent. This rule reflects the fact that, under U.S. domestic law, a U.S. citizen or U.S. resident individual is allowed a unified credit against the U.S. gift tax on lifetime transfers. However, as a result of the estate tax computation, the individual is entitled only to a total unified credit of $192,800, and the amount of the unified credit available for use against U.S. estate tax on the individual's estate is effectively reduced by the amount of any unified credit that has been allowed in respect of gifts by the individual. This rule is reflected by reducing the amount of the pro rata unified credit otherwise allowed to the estate of a decedent individual under paragraph 2 by the amount of any unified credit previously allowed with respect to lifetime gifts by that individual. This reduction will be relevant only in rare cases, where the decedent made gifts subject to the U.S. gift tax while a U.S. citizen or U.S. resident (as defined under the *Internal Revenue Code* for U.S. gift tax purposes).

Paragraph 2 also conditions allowance of the pro rata unified credit upon the provision of all information necessary to verify and compute the credit. Thus, for example, the estate's representatives will be required to demonstrate satisfactorily both the value of the worldwide estate and the value of the U.S. portion of the estate. Substantiation requirements also apply, of course, with respect to other provisions of the Protocol and the Convention. However, the negotiators believed it advisable to emphasize the substantiation requirements in connection with this provision, because the computation of the pro rata unified credit involves certain information not otherwise relevant for U.S. estate tax purposes.

In addition, the amount of the pro rata unified credit is limited to the amount of U.S. estate tax imposed on the estate. See section 2102(c)(4) of the *Internal Revenue Code*.

3. In determining the estate tax imposed by the United States on an individual's estate with respect to property that passes to the surviving spouse of the individual (within the meaning of the law of the United States) and that would qualify for the estate tax marital deduction under the law of the United States if the surviving spouse were a citizen of the United States and all applicable elections were properly made (in this paragraph and in paragraph 4 referred to as "qualifying property"), a non-refundable credit computed in accordance with the provisions of paragraph 4 shall be allowed in addition to the unified credit allowed to the estate under paragraph 2 or under the law of the United States, provided that

(a) the individual was at the time of death a citizen of the United States or a resident of either Contracting State;

(b) the surviving spouse was at the time of the individual's death a resident of either Contracting State;

(c) if both the individual and the surviving spouse were residents of the United States at the time of the individual's death, one or both was a citizen of Canada; and

(d) the executor of the decedent's estate elects the benefits of this paragraph and waives irrevocably the benefits of any estate tax marital deduction that would be allowed under the law of the United States on a United States Federal estate tax return filed for the individual's estate by the date on which a qualified domestic trust election could be made under the law of the United States.

**Technical Explanation [1995 Protocol]:**

*Marital credit*

Paragraph 3 of Article XXIX B allows a special "marital credit" against U.S. estate tax in respect of certain transfers to a surviving spouse. The purpose of this marital credit is to alleviate, in appropriate cases, the impact of the estate tax marital deduction restrictions enacted by the Congress in the *Technical and Miscellaneous Revenue Act* of 1988 ("TAMRA"). It is the firm position of the U.S. Treasury Department that the TAMRA provisions do not violate the non-discrimination provisions of this Convention or any other convention to which the United States is a party. This is because the estate — not the surviving spouse — is the taxpayer, and the TAMRA provisions treat the estates of nonresidents not citizens of the United States in the same manner as the estates of U.S. citizen and U.S. resident decedents. However, the U.S. negotiators believed that it was not inappropriate, in the context of the Protocol, to ease the impact of those TAMRA provisions upon certain estates of limited value.

Paragraph 3 allows a non-refundable marital credit in addition to the pro rata unified credit allowed under paragraph 2 (or, in the case of a U.S. citizen or U.S. resident decedent, the unified credit allowed under U.S. domestic law). However, the marital credit is allowed only in connection with transfers satisfying each of the five conditions set forth in paragraph 3. First, the property must be "qualifying property," i.e., it must pass to the surviving spouse (within the meaning of U.S. domestic law) and be property that would have qualified for the estate tax marital deduction under U.S. domestic law if the surviving spouse had been a U.S. citizen and all applicable elections specified by U.S. domestic law had been properly made. Second, the decedent must have been, at the time of death, either a resident of Canada or the United States or a citizen of the United States. Third, the surviving spouse must have been, at the time of the decedent's death, a resident of either Canada or the United States. Fourth, if both the decedent and the surviving spouse were residents of the United States at the time of the decedent's death, at least one of them must have been a citizen of Canada. Finally, to limit the benefits of paragraph 3 to relatively small estates, the executor of the decedent's estate is required to elect the benefits of paragraph 3, and to waive irrevocably the benefits of any estate tax marital deduction that would be allowed under U.S. domestic law, on a U.S. Federal estate tax return filed by the deadline for making a qualified domestic trust election under *Internal Revenue Code* section 2056A(d). In the case of the estate of a decedent for which the U.S. Federal estate tax return is filed on or before the date on which this Protocol enters into force, this election and waiver must be made on any return filed to claim a refund pursuant to the special effective date applicable to such estates (discussed below).

4. The amount of the credit allowed under paragraph 3 shall equal the lesser of

(a) the unified credit allowed under paragraph 2 or under the law of the United States (determined without regard to any credit allowed previously with respect to any gift made by the individual), and

(b) the amount of estate tax that would otherwise be imposed by the United States on the transfer of qualifying property.

The amount of estate tax that would otherwise be imposed by the United States on the transfer of qualifying property shall equal the amount by which the estate tax (before allowable credits) that would be imposed by the United States if the qualifying property were included in computing the taxable estate exceeds the estate tax (before allowable credits) that would be so imposed if the qualifying property were not so included. Solely for purposes of determining other credits allowed under the law of the United States, the credit provided under paragraph 3 shall be allowed after such other credits.

**Technical Explanation [1995 Protocol]:**

Paragraph 4 governs the computation of the marital credit allowed under paragraph 3. It provides that the amount of the marital credit shall equal the lesser of (i) the amount of the unified credit allowed to the estate under paragraph 2 or, where applicable, under U.S. domestic law (before reduction for any gift tax unified credit), or (ii) the amount of U.S. estate tax that would otherwise be imposed on the transfer of qualifying property to the surviving spouse. For this purpose, the amount of U.S. estate tax that would otherwise be imposed on the transfer of qualifying property equals the amount by which (i) the estate tax (before allowable credits) that would be imposed if that property were included in computing the taxable estate exceeds (ii) the estate tax (before allowable credits) that would be imposed if the property were not so included. Property that, by reason of the provisions of paragraph 8 of this Article, is not subject to U.S. estate tax is not taken into account for purposes of this hypothetical computation.

Finally, paragraph 4 provides taxpayers with an ordering rule. The rule states that, solely for purposes of determining any other credits (e.g., the credits for foreign and state death taxes) that may be allowed under U.S. domestic law to the estate, the marital credit shall be allowed after such other credits.

In certain cases, the provisions of paragraphs 3 and 4 may affect the U.S. estate taxation of a trust that would meet the requirements for a qualified terminable interest property ("QTIP") election, for example, a trust with a life income interest for the surviving spouse and a remainder interest for other family members. If, in lieu of making the QTIP election and the qualified domestic trust election, the decedent's executor makes the election described in paragraph 3(d) of this Article, the provisions of *Internal Revenue Code* sections 2044 (regarding inclusion in the estate of the second spouse of certain property for which the marital deduction was previously allowed), 2056A (regarding qualified domestic trusts), and 2519 (regarding dispositions of certain life estates) will not apply. To obtain this treatment, however, the executor is required, under paragraph 3, to irrevocably waive the benefit of any marital deduction allowable under the *Internal Revenue Code* with respect to the trust.

The following examples illustrate the operation of the marital credit and its interaction with other credits. Unless otherwise stated, assume for purposes of illustration that H, the decedent, and W, his surviving spouse, are Canadian citizens resident in Canada at the time of the decedent's death. Assume further that all conditions set forth in paragraphs 2 and 3 of this Article XXIX B are satisfied (including the condition that the executor waive the estate tax marital deduction), that no deductions are available under the *Internal Revenue Code* in computing the U.S. estate tax liability, and that there are no adjusted taxable gifts within the meaning of *Internal Revenue Code* section 2001(b) or 2101(c). Also assume that the applicable U.S. domestic estate and gift tax laws are those that were in effect on the date the Protocol was signed.

*Example 1.* H has a worldwide gross estate of $1,200,000. He bequeaths U.S. real property worth $600,000 to W. The remainder of H's estate consists of Canadian situs property. H's estate would be entitled to a pro rata unified credit of $96,400 (= $192,800 x (600,000/1,200,000)) and to a marital credit in the same amount (the lesser of the unified credit allowed ($96,400) and the U.S. estate tax that would otherwise be imposed on the property transferred to W ($192,800 [tax on U.S. taxable estate of $600,000])). The pro rata unified credit and the marital credit combined would eliminate all U.S. estate tax with respect to the property transferred to W.

*Example 2.* H has a worldwide gross estate of $1,200,000, all of which is situated in the United States. He bequeaths U.S. real property worth $600,000 to W and U.S. real property worth $600,000 to a child, C. H's estate would be entitled to a pro rata unified credit of $192,800 (= $192,800 x 1,200,000/1,200,000) and to a marital credit of $192,800 (the lesser of the unified credit ($192,800) and the U.S. estate tax that would otherwise be imposed on the property transferred to W ($235,000, i.e., $427,800 [tax on U.S. taxable estate of $1,200,000] less $192,800 [tax on U.S. taxable estate of $600,000])). This would reduce the estate's total U.S. estate tax liability of $427,800 by $385,600.

*Example 3.* H has a worldwide gross estate of $700,000, of which $500,000 is real property situated in the United States. H bequeaths U.S. real property valued at $100,000 to W. The remainder of H's gross estate, consisting of U.S. and Canadian situs real property, is bequeathed to H's child, C. H's estate would be entitled to a pro rata unified credit of $137,714 ($192,800 x $500,000/$700,000). In addition, H's estate would be entitled to a marital credit of $34,000, which equals the lesser of the unified credit ($137,714) and $34,000 (the U.S. estate tax that would otherwise be imposed on the property transferred to W before allowance of any credits, i.e., $155,800 [tax on U.S. taxable estate of $500,000] less $121,800 [tax on U.S. taxable estate of $400,000]).

*Example 4.* H has a worldwide gross estate of $5,000,000, $2,000,000 of which consists of U.S. real property situated in State X. State X imposes a state death tax equal to the federal credit allowed under *Internal Revenue Code* section 2011. H bequeaths U.S. situs real property worth $1,000,000 to W and U.S. situs real property worth $1,000,000 to his child, C. The remainder of H's estate ($3,000,000) consists of Canadian situs property passing to C. H's estate would be entitled to a pro rata unified credit of $77,120 ($192,800 x $2,000,000/$5,000,000). H's estate would be entitled to a state death tax credit under *Internal Revenue Code* section 2102 of $99,600 (determined under *Internal Revenue Code* section 2011(b) with respect to an adjusted taxable estate of $1,940,000). H's estate also would be entitled to a marital credit of $77,120, which equals the lesser of the unified credit ($77,120) and $435,000 (the U.S. estate tax that would otherwise be imposed on the property transferred to W before allowance of any credits, i.e., $780,000 [tax on U.S. taxable estate of $2,000,000] less $345,800 [tax on U.S. taxable estate of $1,000,000]).

*Example 5.* The facts are the same as in Example 4, except that H and W are Canadian citizens who are resident in the United States at the time of H's death. Canadian Federal and provincial income taxes totalling $500,000 are imposed by reason of H's death. H's estate would be entitled to a unified credit of $192,800 and to a state death tax credit of $300,880 under *Internal Revenue Code* sections 2010 and 2011(b), respectively. Under paragraph 6 of Article XXIX B, H's estate would be entitled to a credit for the Canadian income tax imposed by reason of death, equal to the lesser of $500,000 (the Canadian taxes paid) or $1,138,272 ($2,390,800 (tax on $5,000,000 taxable estate) less total of unified and state death tax credits ($493,680) x $3,000,000/$5,000,000). H's estate also would be entitled to a marital credit of $192,800, which equals the lesser of the unified credit ($192,800) and $550,000 (the U.S. estate tax that would otherwise be imposed on the property transferred to W before allowance of any credits, i.e., $2,390,800 [tax on U.S. taxable estate of $5,000,000] less $1,840,800 [tax on U.S. taxable estate of $4,000,000]).

**5.** Where an individual was a resident of the United States immediately before the individual's death, for the purposes of subsection 70(6) of the *Income Tax Act*, both the individual and the individual's spouse shall be deemed to have been resident in Canada immediately before the individual's death. Where a trust that would be a trust described in subsection 70(6) of that Act, if its trustees that were residents or citizens of the United States or domestic corporations under the law of the United States were residents of Canada, requests the competent authority of Canada to do so, the competent authority may agree, subject to terms and conditions satisfactory to such competent authority, to treat the trust for the purposes of that Act as being resident in Canada for such time as may be stipulated in the agreement.

**Technical Explanation [1995 Protocol]:**

*Canadian treatment of certain transfers*

The provisions of paragraph 5 relate to the operation of Canadian law. They are intended to provide deferral ("rollover") of the Canadian tax at death for certain transfers to a surviving spouse and to permit the Canadian competent authority to allow such deferral for certain transfers to a trust. For example, they would enable the competent authority to treat a trust that is a qualified domestic trust for U.S. estate tax purposes as a Canadian spousal trust as well for purposes of certain provisions of Canadian tax law and of the Convention. These provisions do not affect U.S. domestic law regarding qualified domestic trusts. Nor do they affect the status of U.S. resident individuals for any other purpose.

**Interpretation Bulletins:** IT-305R4: Testamentary spouse trusts.

**6.** In determining the amount of Canadian tax payable by an individual who immediately before death was a resident of Canada, or by a trust described in subsection 70(6) of the *Income Tax Act* (or a trust which is treated as being resident in Canada under the provisions of paragraph 5), the amount of any Federal or state estate or inheritance taxes payable in the United States (not exceeding, where the individual was a citizen of the United States or a former citizen referred to in paragraph 2 of Article XXIX (Miscellaneous Rules), the amount of estate and inheritance taxes that would have been payable if the individual were not a citizen or former citizen of the United States) in respect of property situated within the United States shall,

(a) to the extent that such estate or inheritance taxes are imposed upon the individual's death, be allowed as a deduction from the amount of any Canadian tax otherwise payable by the individual for the taxation year in which the individual died on the total of

(i) any income, profits or gains of the individual arising (within the meaning of paragraph 3 of Article XXIV (Elimination of Double Taxation)) in the United States in that year, and

(ii) where the value at the time of the individual's death of the individual's entire gross estate wherever situated (determined under the law of the United States) exceeded 1.2 million U.S. dollars or its equivalent in Canadian dollars, any income, profits or gains of the individual for that year from property situated in the United States at that time, and

(b) to the extent that such estate or inheritance taxes are imposed upon the death of the individual's surviving spouse, be allowed as a deduction from the amount of any Canadian tax otherwise payable by the trust for its taxation year in which that spouse dies on any income, profits or gains of the trust for that year arising (within the meaning of paragraph 3 of Article XXIV (Elimination of Double Taxation)) in the United States or from property situated in the United States at the time of death of the spouse.

For purposes of this paragraph, property shall be treated as situated within the United States if it is so treated for estate tax purposes under the law of the United States as in effect on March 17, 1995, subject to any subsequent changes thereof that the competent authorities of the Contracting States have agreed to apply for the purposes of this paragraph. The deduction allowed under this paragraph shall take into account the deduction for any income tax paid or accrued to the United States that is provided under paragraph 2(a), 4(a) or 5(b) of Article XXIV (Elimination of Double Taxation).

### Technical Explanation [1995 Protocol]:

*Credit for U.S. taxes*

Under paragraph 6, Canada agrees to give Canadian residents and Canadian resident spousal trusts (or trusts treated as such by virtue of paragraph 5) a deduction from tax (i.e., a credit) for U.S. Federal or state estate or inheritance taxes imposed on U.S. situs property of the decedent or the trust. This credit is allowed against the income tax imposed by Canada, in an amount computed in accordance with subparagraph 6(a) or 6(b).

Subparagraph 6(a) covers the first set of cases — where the U.S. tax is imposed upon a decedent's death. Subparagraph 6(a)(i) allows a credit for U.S. tax against the total amount of Canadian income tax payable by the decedent in the taxable year of death on any income, profits, or gains arising in the United States (within the meaning of paragraph 3 of Article XXIV (Elimination of Double Taxation)). For purposes of subparagraph 6(a)(i), income, profits, or gains arising in the United States within the meaning of paragraph 3 of Article XXIV include gains deemed realized at death on U.S. situs real property and on personal property forming part of the business property of a U.S. permanent establishment or fixed base. (As explained below, these are the only types of property on which the United States may impose its estate tax if the estate is worth $1.2 million or less.) Income, profits, or gains arising in the United States also include income and profits earned by the decedent during the taxable year of death, to the extent that the United States may tax such amounts under the Convention (e.g., dividends received from a U.S. corporation and wages from the performance of personal services in the United States).

Where the value of the decedent's entire gross estate exceeds $1.2 million, subparagraph 6(a)(ii) allows a credit against the Canadian income tax on any income, profits, or gains from any U.S. situs property, in addition to any credit allowed by subparagraph 6(a)(i). This provision is broader in scope than is the general rule under subparagraph 6(a)(i), because the United States has retained the right to impose its estate tax on all types of property in the case of larger estates.

Subparagraph 6(b) provides rules for a second category of cases — where the U.S. tax is imposed upon the death of the surviving spouse. In these cases, Canada agrees to allow a credit against the Canadian tax payable by a trust for its taxable year during which the surviving spouse dies on any income, profits, or gains (i) arising in the United States on U.S. situs real property or business property, or (ii) from property situated in the United States. These rules are intended to provide a credit for taxes imposed as a result of the death of the surviving spouse in situations involving trusts. To the extent that taxes are imposed on the estate of the surviving spouse, subparagraph 6(a) would apply as well. In addition, the competent authorities are authorized to provide relief from double taxation in certain additional circumstances involving trusts, as described above in connection with Article 14 of the Protocol.

The credit allowed under paragraph 6 is subject to certain conditions. First, where the decedent was a U.S. citizen or former citizen (described in paragraph 2 of Article XXIX (Miscellaneous Rules)), paragraph 6 does not obligate Canada to provide a credit for U.S. taxes in excess of the amount of U.S. taxes that would have been payable if the decedent had not been a U.S. citizen or former citizen. Second, the credit allowed under paragraph 6 will be computed after taking into account any deduction for U.S. income tax provided under paragraph 2(a), 4(a), or 5(b) of Article XXIV (Elimination of Double Taxation). This clarifies that no double credit will be allowed for any amount and provides an ordering rule. Finally, because Canadian domestic law does not contain a definition of U.S. situs property for death tax purposes, such a definition is provided for purposes of paragraph 6. To maximize coordination of the credit provisions, the Contracting States agreed to follow the U.S. estate tax law definition as in effect on the date of signature of the Protocol and, subject to competent authority agreement, as it may be amended in the future.

**7.** In determining the amount of estate tax imposed by the United States on the estate of an individual who was a resident or citizen of the United States at the time of death, or upon the death of a surviving spouse with respect to a qualifed domestic trust created by such an individual or the individual's executor or surviving spouse, a credit shall be allowed against such tax imposed in respect of property situated outside the United States, for the federal and provincial income taxes payable in Canada in respect of such property by reason of the death of the individual or, in the case of a qualified domestic trust, the individual's surviving spouse. Such credit shall be computed in accordance with the following rules:

(a) a credit otherwise allowable under this paragraph shall be allowed regardless of whether the identity of the taxpayer under the law of Canada corresponds to that under the law of the United States;

(b) the amount of a credit allowed under this paragraph shall be computed in accordance with the provisions and subject to the limitations of the law of the United States regarding credit for foreign death taxes (as it may be amended from time to time without changing the general principle hereof), as though the income tax imposed by Canada were a creditable tax under that law;

(c) a credit may be claimed under this paragraph for an amount of federal or provincial income tax payable in Canada only to the extent that no credit or deduction is claimed for such amount in determining any other tax imposed by the United States, other than the estate tax imposed on property in a qualified domestic trust upon the death of the surviving spouse.

**Technical Explanation [1995 Protocol]:**

*Credit for Canadian taxes*

Under paragraph 7, the United States agrees to allow a credit against U.S. Federal estate tax imposed on the estate of a U.S. resident or U.S. citizen decedent, or upon the death of a surviving spouse with respect to a qualified domestic trust created by such a decedent (or the decedent's executor or surviving spouse). The credit is allowed for Canadian Federal and provincial income taxes imposed at death with respect to property of the estate or trust that is situated outside of the United States. As in the case under paragraph 6, the competent authorities also are authorized to provide relief from double taxation in certain cases involving trusts (see discussion of Article 14, above).

The amount of the credit generally will be determined as though the income tax imposed by Canada were a creditable tax under the U.S. estate tax provisions regarding credit for foreign death taxes, in accordance with the provisions and subject to the limitations of *Internal Revenue Code* section 2014. However, subparagraph 7(a) clarifies that a credit otherwise allowable under paragraph 7 will not be denied merely because of inconsistencies between U.S. and Canadian law regarding the identity of the taxpayer in the case of a particular taxable event. For example, the fact that the taxpayer is the decedent's estate for purposes of U.S. estate taxation and the decedent for purposes of Canadian income taxation will not prevent the allowance of a credit under paragraph 7 for Canadian income taxes imposed by reason of the death of the decedent.

In addition, subparagraph 7(c) clarifies that the credit against the U.S. estate tax generally may be claimed only to the extent that no credit or deduction is claimed for the same amount of Canadian tax in determining any other U.S. tax. This makes clear, for example, that a credit may not be claimed for the same amount under both this provision and Article XXIV (Elimination of Double Taxation). To prevent double taxation, an exception to this restriction is provided for certain taxes imposed with respect to qualified domestic trusts. Subject to the limitations of subparagraph 7(c), the taxpayer may choose between relief under Article XXIV, relief under this paragraph 7, or some combination of the two.

**8.** Provided that the value, at the time of death, of the entire gross estate wherever situated of an individual who was a resident of Canada (other than a citizen of the United States) at the time of death does not exceed 1.2 million U.S dollars or its equivalent in Canadian dollars, the United States may impose its estate tax upon property forming part of the estate of the individual only if any gain derived by the individual from the alienation of such property would have been subject to income taxation by the United States in accordance with Article XIII (Gains).

**Technical Explanation [1995 Protocol]:**

*Relief for small estates*

Under paragraph 8, the United States agrees to limit the application of its estate tax in the case of certain small estates of Canadian resident decedents. This provision is intended to eliminate the "trap for the unwary" that exists for such decedents, in the absence of an estate tax convention between the United States and Canada. In the absence of sophisticated estate tax planning, such decedents may inadvertently subject their estates to U.S. estate tax liability by holding shares of U.S. corporate stock or other U.S. situs property. U.S. resident decedents are already protected in this regard by the provisions of Article XIII (Gains) of the present Convention, which prohibit Canada from imposing its income tax on gains deemed realized at death by U.S. residents on such property.

Paragraph 8 provides relief only in the case of Canadian resident decedents whose entire gross estates wherever situated (i.e., worldwide gross estates determined under U.S. law) have a value, at the time of death, not exceeding $1.2 million. Paragraph 8 provides that the United States may impose its estate tax upon property forming part of such estates only if any gain on alienation of the property would have been subject to U.S. income taxation under Article XIII (Gains). For estates with a total value not exceeding $1.2 million, this provision has the effect of permitting the United States to impose its estate tax only on real property situated in the United States, within the meaning of Article XIII, and personal property forming part of the business property of a U.S. permanent establishment or fixed base.

*Saving clause exceptions*

Certain provisions of Article XXIX B are included in the list of exceptions to the general "saving clause" of Article XXIX (Miscellaneous Rules), as amended by Article 17 of the Protocol. To the extent that an exception from the saving clause is provided for a provision, each Contracting State is required to allow the benefits of that provision to its residents (and, in the case of the United States, its citizens), notwithstanding the saving clause. General saving clause exceptions are provided for paragraphs 1, 5, and 6 of Article XXIX B. Saving clause exceptions are provided for paragraphs 2, 3, 4, and 7, except for the estates of former U.S. citizens referred to in paragraph 2 of Article XXIX.

*Effective dates*

Article 21 of the Protocol contains special retrospective effective date provisions for paragraphs 2 through 8 of Article XXIX B and certain related provisions of the Protocol. Paragraphs 2 through 8 of Article XXIX B and the specified related provisions generally will take effect with respect to deaths occurring after the date on which the Protocol enters into force (i.e., the date on which the instruments of ratification are exchanged). However, the benefits of those provisions will also be available with respect to deaths occurring after November 10, 1988, provided that a claim for refund due as a result of these provisions is filed by the later of one year from the date on which the Protocol enters into force or the date on which the applicable period for filing such a claim expires under the domestic law of the Contracting State concerned. The general effective dates set forth in Article 21 of the Protocol otherwise apply.

It is unusual for the United States to agree to retrospective effective dates. In this case, however, the negotiators believed that retrospective application was not inappropriate, given the fact that the TAMRA provisions were the impetus for negotiation of the Protocol and that the negotiations commenced soon after the enactment of TAMRA. The United States has agreed to retrospective effective dates in certain other instances (e.g., in the case of the U.S.-Germany estate tax treaty). The retrospective effective dates apply reciprocally, so that they will benefit the estates of U.S. decedents as well as Canadian decedents.

**Related Provisions [Art. XXIX B]**: ITA 60(d) — Deduction for interest accruing on estate taxes; Art. II:2(b)(iv) — Application to U.S. estate taxes; Art. XXVI:3(g) — Competent authority agreement to eliminate double taxation.

**Notes [Art. XXIX B]**: Art. XXIX B added by 1995 Protocol, generally effective for deaths after November 10, 1988, provided refund claims that would otherwise be too late are filed by November 9, 1996 (see Art. 21(4) under "Application of the 1995 Protocol" above).

## Article XXX — Entry Into Force

**1.** This Convention shall be subject to ratification in accordance with the applicable procedures of each Contracting State and instruments of ratification shall be exchanged at Ottawa as soon as possible.

**Technical Explanation [1984]:**

Paragraph 1 provides that the Convention is subject to ratification in accordance with the procedures of Canada and the United States. The exchange of instruments of ratification is to take place at Ottawa as soon as possible.

**2.** The Convention shall enter into force upon the exchange of instruments of ratification and, subject to the provisions of paragraph 3, its provisions shall have effect:

(a) for tax withheld at the source on income referred to in Articles X (Dividends), XI (Interest), XII (Royalties) and XVIII (Pensions and Annuities), with respect to amounts paid or credited on or after the first day of the second month next following the date on which the Convention enters into force;

(b) for other taxes, with respect to taxable years beginning on or after the first day of January next following the date on which the Convention enters into force; and

(c) notwithstanding the provisions of subparagraph (b), for the taxes covered by paragraph 4 of Article XXIX (Miscellaneous Rules) with respect to all taxable years referred to in that paragraph.

**Technical Explanation [1984]:**

Paragraph 2 provides, subject to paragraph 3, that the Convention shall enter into force upon the exchange of instruments of ratification. It has effect, with respect to source State taxation of dividends, interest, royalties, pensions, annuities, alimony, and child support, for amounts paid or credited on or after the first day of the second calendar month after the date on which the instruments of ratification are exchanged. For other taxes, the Convention takes effect for taxable years beginning on or after January 1 next following the date when instruments of ratification are exchanged. In the case of relief from United States social security taxes provided by paragraph 4 of Article XXIX (Miscellaneous Rules), the Convention also has effect for taxable years before the date on which instruments of ratification are exchanged.

**Notes**: Exchange of instruments of ratification took place on August 16, 1984. For the effective dates of the changes made by the 1995 Protocol, see Art. 21 of that Protocol, reproduced above (before Article I of the treaty).

**3.** For the purposes of applying the United States foreign tax credit in relation to taxes paid or accrued to Canada:

(a) notwithstanding the provisions of paragraph 2(a) of Article II (Taxes Covered), the tax on 1971 undistributed income on hand imposed by Part IX of the *Income Tax Act* of Canada shall be considered to be an income tax for distributions made on or after the first day of January 1972 and before the first day of January 1979 and shall be considered to be imposed upon the recipient of a distribution, in the proportion that the distribution out of undistributed income with respect to which the tax has been paid bears to 85 per cent of such undistributed income;

(b) the principles of paragraph 6 of Article XXIV (Elimination of Double Taxation) shall have effect for taxable years beginning on or after the first day of January 1976; and

(c) the provisions of paragraph 1 of Article XXIV shall have effect for taxable years beginning on or after the first day of January 1981.

Any claim for refund based on the provisions of this paragraph may be filed on or before June 30 of the calendar year following that in which the Convention enters into force, notwithstanding any rule of domestic law to the contrary.

**Technical Explanation [1984]:**

Paragraph 3 provides special effective date rules for foreign tax credit computations with respect to taxes paid or accrued to Canada. Paragraph 3(a) provides that the tax on 1971 undistributed income on hand imposed by Part IX of the *Income Tax Act* of Canada is considered to be an "income tax" for distributions made on or after January 1, 1972 and before January 1, 1979. Any such tax which is paid or accrued under U.S. standards is considered to be imposed at the time of distribution and on the recipient of the distribution, in the proportion that the distribution out of undistributed income with respect to which the tax has been paid bears to 85 percent of such undistributed income. A person claiming a credit for tax pursuant to paragraph 3(a) is obligated to compute the amount of the credit in accordance with that paragraph.

Paragraph 3(b) provides that the principles of paragraph 6 of Article XXIV (Elimination of Double Taxation), which provides for resourcing of certain dividend, interest, and royalty income to eliminate double taxation of U.S. citizens residing in Canada, have effect for taxable years beginning on or after January 1, 1976. The paragraph is intended to grant the competent authorities sufficient flexibility to address certain practical problems that have arisen under the 1942 Convention. It is anticipated that the competent authorities will be guided by paragraphs 4 and 5 of Article XXIV in applying paragraph 3(b) of Article XXX. Paragraph 3(c) provides that the provisions of paragraph 1 of Article XXIV (and the source rules of that Article) shall have effect for taxable years beginning on or after January 1, 1981.

Any claim for refund based on the provisions of paragraph 3 may be filed on or before June 30 of the calendar year following the year in which instruments of ratification are exchanged, notwithstanding statutes of limitations or other rules of domestic law to the contrary. For purposes of Code section 6611, the date of overpayment is the date on which instruments of ratification are exchanged, with respect to any refunds of U.S. tax pursuant to paragraph 3.

**4.** Subject to the provisions of paragraph 5, the 1942 Convention shall cease to have effect for taxes for which this Convention has effect in accordance with the provisions of paragraph 2.

**Technical Explanation [1984]:**

Paragraph 4 provides that, subject to paragraph 5, the 1942 Convention ceases to have effect for taxes for which the Convention has effect under the provisions of paragraph 2. For example, if under paragraph 2 the Convention were to have effect with respect to taxes withheld at source on dividends paid as of October 1, 1984, the 1942 Convention will not have effect with respect to such taxes.

**5.** Where any greater relief from tax would have been afforded by any provision of the 1942 Convention than under this Convention, any such provision shall continue to have effect for the first taxable year with respect to which the provisions of this Convention have effect under paragraph 2(b).

**Technical Explanation [1984]:**

Paragraph 5 modifies the rule of paragraph 4 to allow all of the provisions of the 1942 Convention to continue to have effect for the period through the first taxable year with respect to which the provisions of the Convention would otherwise have effect under paragraph 2(b), if greater relief from tax is available under the 1942 Convention than under the Convention. Paragraph 5 applies to all provisions of the 1942 Convention, not just those provisions of the Convention for which the Convention takes effect under paragraph 2(b) of this Article. Thus, for example, assume that the Convention has effect, pursuant to paragraph 2(b), for taxable years of a taxpayer beginning on or after January 1, 1985. Further assume that a U.S. resident with a taxable year beginning on April 1 and ending on March 31 receives natural resource royalties from Canada which are subject to a 25% tax under Article VI (Income from Real Property) of the Convention, as amended by the Protocol, and Canada's internal law, but which would be subject to a 15% tax under Article XI of the 1942 Convention. Pursuant to paragraph 5, the greater benefits of the 1942 Convention would continue to apply to royalties paid or credited to the U.S. resident through March 31, 1986.

**6.** The 1942 Convention shall terminate on the last date on which it has effect in accordance with the preceding provisions of this Article.

**Technical Explanation [1984]:**

Paragraph 6 provides that the 1942 Convention terminates on the last of the dates on which it has effect in accordance with the provisions of paragraphs 4 and 5.

**7.** The Exchange of Notes between the United States and Canada dated August 2 and September 17, 1928, providing for relief from double income taxation on shipping profits, is terminated. Its provisions shall cease to have effect with respect to taxable years beginning on or after the first day of January next following the date on which this Convention enters into force.

**Technical Explanation [1984]:**

Paragraph 7 terminates the Exchange of Notes between the United States and Canada of August 2 and September 17, 1928 providing for relief from double taxation of shipping profits. The provisions of the Exchange of Notes no longer have effect for taxable years beginning on or after January 1 following the exchange of instruments of ratification of the Convention. The 1942 Convention, in Article V, had suspended the effectiveness of the Exchange of Notes.

**8.** The provisions of the Convention between the Government of Canada and the Government of the United States of America for the Avoidance of Double Taxation and the Prevention of Fiscal Evasion with Respect to Taxes on the Estates of Deceased Persons signed at Washington on February 17, 1961 shall continue to have effect with respect to estates of persons deceased prior to the first day of January next following the date on which this Convention enters into force but shall cease to have effect with respect to estates of persons deceased on or after that date. Such Convention shall terminate on the last date on which it has effect in accordance with the preceding sentence.

**Technical Explanation [1984]:**

Paragraph 8 terminates the Convention between Canada and the United States for the Avoidance of Double Taxation with Respect to Taxes on the Estates of Deceased Persons signed on February 17, 1961. The provisions of that Convention cease to have effect with respect to estates of persons deceased on or after January 1 of the year following the exchange of instruments of ratification of the Convention.

**Interpretation Bulletins:** IT-173R2: Capital gains derived in Canada by residents of the United States.

## Article XXXI — Termination

**1.** This Convention shall remain in force until terminated by a Contracting State.

**Technical Explanation [1984]:**

Paragraph 1 provides that the Convention shall remain in force until terminated by Canada or the United States.

**2.** Either Contracting State may terminate the Convention at any time after 5 years from the date on which the Convention enters into force provided that at least 6 months' prior notice of termination has been given through diplomatic channels.

**Technical Explanation [1984]:**

Paragraph 2 provides that either Canada or the United States may terminate the Convention at any time after 5 years from the date on which instruments of ratification are exchanged, provided that notice of termination is given through diplomatic channels at least 6 months prior to the date on which the Convention is to terminate.

**3.** Where a Contracting State considers that a significant change introduced in the taxation laws of the other Contracting State should be accommodated by a modification of the Convention, the Contracting States shall consult together with a view to resolving the matter; if the matter cannot be satisfactorily resolved, the first-mentioned State may terminate the Convention in accordance with the procedures set forth in paragraph 2, but without regard to the 5 year limitation provided therein.

**Technical Explanation [1984]:**

Paragraph 3 provides a special termination rule in situations where Canada or the United States changes its taxation laws and the other Contracting State believes that such change is significant enough to warrant modification of the Convention. In such a circumstance, the Canadian Ministry of Finance and the United States Department of the Treasury would consult with a view to resolving the matter. If the matter cannot be satisfactorily resolved, the Contracting State requesting an accommodation because of the change in the other Contracting State's taxation laws may terminate the Convention by giving the 6 months' prior notice required by paragraph 2, without regard to whether the Convention has been in force for 5 years.

4. In the event the Convention is terminated, the Convention shall cease to have effect:

(a) for tax withheld at the source on income referred to in Articles X (Dividends), XI (Interest), XII (Royalties), XVIII (Pensions and Annuities) and paragraph 2 of Article XXII (Other Income), with respect to amounts paid or credited on or after the first day of January next following the expiration of the 6 months' period referred to in paragraph 2; and

(b) for other taxes, with respect to taxable years beginning on or after the first day of January next following the expiration of the 6 months' period referred to in paragraph 2.

**Technical Explanation [1984]:**

Paragraph 4 provides that, in the event of termination, the Convention ceases to have effect for tax withheld at source under Articles X (Dividends), XI (Interest), XII (Royalties), and XVIII (Pensions and Annuities), and under paragraph 2 of Article XXII (Other Income), with respect to amounts paid or credited on or after the first day of January following the expiration of the 6 month period referred to in paragraph 2. In the case of other taxes, the Convention shall cease to have effect in the event of termination with respect to taxable years beginning on or after January 1 following the expiration of the 6 month period referred to in paragraph 2.

## APPENDIX — EXECUTION AND COMPETENT AUTHORITIES LETTER

*September 26, 1980*

Excellency: I have the honor to refer to the Convention between the United States of America and Canada with Respect to Taxes on Income and on Capital, signed today, and to confirm certain understandings reached between the two Governments with respect to the Convention.

1. In French, the term **"société"** also means a "corporation" within the meaning of Canadian law.

2. The competent authorities of each of the Contracting States shall review the procedures and requirements for an organization of the other Contracting State to establish its status as a religious, scientific, literary, educational or charitable organization entitled to exemption under paragraph 1 of Article XXI (Exempt Organizations), or as an eligible recipient of the charitable contributions or gifts referred to in paragraphs 5 and 6 of Article XXI, with a view to avoiding duplicate application by such organizations to the administering agencies of both Contracting States. If a Contracting State determines that the other Contracting State maintains procedures to determine such status and rules for qualification that are compatible with such procedures and rules of the first-mentioned Contracting State, it is contemplated that such first-mentioned Contracting State shall accept the certification of the administering agency of the other Contracting State as to such status for the purpose of making the necessary determinations under paragraphs 1, 5 and 6 of Article XXI.

It is further agreed that the term **"family"**, as used in paragraphs 5 and 6 of Article XXI, means an individual's brothers and sisters (whether by whole or half-blood, or by adoption), spouse, ancestors, lineal descendants and adopted descendants.

3. It is the position of Canada that the so-called "unitary apportionment" method used by certain states of the United States to allocate income to United States offices or subsidiaries of Canadian companies results in inequitable taxation and imposes excessive administrative burdens on Canadian companies doing business in those states. Under that method the profit of a Canadian company on its United States business is not determined on the basis of arm's-length relations but is derived from a formula taking account of the income of the Canadian company and its worldwide subsidiaries as well as the assets, payroll and sales of all such companies. For a Canadian multinational company with many subsidiaries in different countries to have to submit its books and records for all of these companies to a state of the United States imposes a costly burden. It is understood that the Senate of the United States has not consented to any limitation on the taxing jurisdiction of the states by a treaty and that a provision which would have restricted the use of unitary apportionment in the case of United Kingdom corporations was recently rejected by the Senate. Canada continues to be concerned about this issue as it affects Canadian multinationals. If an acceptable provision on this subject can be devised, the United States agrees to reopen discussions with Canada on this subject.

# CANADA–UNITED KINGDOM TAX CONVENTION

Convention Between The Government of Canada and the Government of the United Kingdom of Great Britain and Northern Ireland for the Avoidance of Double Taxation and the Prevention of Fiscal Evasion With Respect to Taxes on Income and Capital Gains as Amended

(Enacted in Canada by S.C. 1980-81-82-83, c. 44, Part X.)

## Background

The Canada-United Kingdom Income Tax Convention, as signed on September 8, 1978 and amended by a Protocol signed on April 15, 1980 and a second Protocol signed on October 16, 1985, is reproduced below. The Convention was brought into force on December 17, 1980, the 1980 Protocol entered into force on December 18, 1980, and the 1985 Protocol entered into force on December 23, 1985. In accordance with Article 28 of the Convention and Article VI of the 1980 Protocol, the provisions thereof have effect in Canada as follows:

(a) in respect of tax withheld at the source on amounts paid or credited to non-residents on or after January 1, 1976;

(b) in respect of other Canadian taxes, for the 1976 taxation year and subsequent years;

(c) the provisions of Article 27A of the Convention, as added by Article IV of the Protocol, will have effect in Canada:

(i) in respect of tax withheld at the source on amounts paid or credited to non-residents on or after January 1, 1981;

(ii) in respect of other Canadian taxes for any taxation year beginning on or after January 1, 1981.

The provisions of the 1985 Protocol have effect in Canada as follows:

(a) for tax withheld at the source on income referred to in Articles 10, 11 and 12 of the Convention, as amended by the 1985 Protocol, with respect to amounts paid or credited on or after February 1, 1986;

(b) in relation to payments referred to in Article 17 of the Convention, as amended by the 1985 Protocol, with respect to amounts paid on or after April 6, 1986;

(c) in relation to all other provisions of the 1985 Protocol, for taxation years beginning on or after January 1, 1986.

The 1985 Protocol shall cease to be effective at such time as the Convention ceases to be effective in accordance with Article 29 of the Convention.

The Government of Canada and the Government of the United Kingdom of Great Britain and Northern Ireland, desiring to conclude a Convention for the avoidance of double taxation and the prevention of fiscal evasion with respect to taxes on income and capital gains, have agreed as follows:

## Article 1 — Personal Scope

This Convention shall apply to persons who are residents of one or both of the Contracting States.

## Article 2 — Taxes Covered

1. The taxes which are the subject of this Convention are:

(a) in Canada:

the income taxes which are imposed by the Government of Canada, (hereinafter referred to as "Canadian tax");

(b) in the United Kingdom of Great Britain and Northern Ireland:

the income tax, the corporation tax, the capital gains tax, the petroleum revenue tax and the development land tax (hereinafter referred to as "United Kingdom tax").

2. The Convention shall apply also to any identical or substantially similar taxes which are imposed after the date of signature of this Convention in addition to, or in place of, the existing taxes by either Contracting State or by the Government of any territory to which the present Convention is extended under Article 26. The Contracting States shall notify each other of changes which have been made in their respective taxation laws.

## Article 3 — General Definitions

**1.** In this Convention, unless the context otherwise requires:

(a)
  (i) the term **"Canada"** used in a geographical sense, means the territory of Canada, including any area beyond the territorial waters of Canada which is an area where Canada may, in accordance with its national legislation and international law, exercise sovereign rights with respect to the sea-bed and sub-soil and their natural resources;

  (ii) the term **"United Kingdom"** means Great Britain and Northern Ireland, including an area outside the territorial sea of the United Kingdom which in accordance with international law has been or may be hereafter designated, under the laws of the United Kingdom concerning the Continental Shelf, as an area within which the rights of the United Kingdom with respect to the sea-bed and sub-soil and their natural resources may be exercised;

(b) the terms **"a Contracting State"** and **"the other Contracting State"** means, as the context requires, Canada or the United Kingdom;

(c) the term **"person"** comprises an individual, a company, any entity treated as a unit for tax purposes or any other body of persons;

(d) the term **"company"** means any body corporate or any other entity which is treated as a body corporate for tax purposes; in French, the term **"société"** also means a "corporation" within the meaning of Canadian law;

(e) the terms **"enterprise of a Contracting State"** and **"enterprise of the other Contracting State"** mean respectively an enterprise carried on by a resident of a Contracting State and an enterprise carried on by a resident of the other Contracting State;

(f) the term **"competent authority"** means:

  (i) in the case of Canada, the Minister of National Revenue or his authorised representative;

  (ii) in the case of the United Kingdom, the Commissioners of Inland Revenue or their authorised representative;

(g) the term **"tax"** means Canadian tax or United Kingdom tax, as the context requires;

(h) the term **"national"** means:

  (i) in relation to the United Kingdom all citizens of the United Kingdom and Colonies, British Subjects under Sections 2, 13(1) or 16 of the *British Nationality Act 1948*, and British Subjects by virtue of Section 1 of the *British Nationality Act 1965*, provided they are patrial within the meaning of the *Immigration Act 1971*, so far as these provisions are in force on the date of entry into force of this Convention or have been modified only in minor respects, so as not to affect their general character; and all legal persons, partnerships, and associations deriving their status as such from the law in force in the United Kingdom;

  (ii) in relation to Canada, all citizens of Canada and all legal persons, partnerships and associations deriving their status as such from the law in force in Canada.

**Notes**: See also the provisions of the *Income Tax Conventions Interpretation Act*, reproduced before the Canada-U.S. Convention.

See Notes to ITA 115.1 re the designated Canadian "competent authority".

**2.** As regards the application of the Convention by a Contracting State any term not otherwise defined shall, unless the context otherwise requires, have the meaning which it has under the laws of that Contracting State relating to the taxes which are the subject of the Convention.

## Article 4 — Fiscal Domicile

**1.** For the purposes of this Convention, the term **"resident of a Contracting State"** means any person who, under the law of that State, is liable to taxation therein by reason of his domicile, residence, place of management or any other criterion of a similar nature. But this term does not include any person who is liable to tax in that Contracting State in respect only of income from sources therein.

**2.** Where by reason of the provisions of paragraph 1 an individual is a resident of both Contracting States, then his status shall be determined as follows:

(a) he shall be deemed to be a resident of the Contracting State in which he has a permanent home available to him. If he has a permanent home available to him in both Contracting States, he shall be deemed to be a resident of the Contracting State with which his personal and economic relations are closer (centre of vital interests);

(b) if the Contracting State in which he has his centre of vital interests cannot be determined, or if he has not a permanent home available to him in either Contracting State, he shall be deemed to be a resident of the Contracting State in which he has an habitual abode;

(c) if he has an habitual abode in both Contracting States or in neither of them, he shall be deemed to be a resident of the Contracting State of which he is a national;

(d) if he is a national of both Contracting States or of neither of them, the competent authorities of the Contracting States shall settle the question by mutual agreement.

3. Where by reason of the provisions of paragraph 1 a person other than an individual is a resident of both Contracting States, the competent authorities of the Contracting States shall by mutual agreement endeavour to settle the question and to determine the mode of application of the Convention to such person.

## Article 5 — Permanent Establishment

1. For the purposes of this Convention, the term **"permanent establishment"** means a fixed place of business in which the business of the enterprise is wholly or partly carried on.

2. The term "permanent establishment" shall include especially:

   (a) a place of management;

   (b) a branch;

   (c) an office;

   (d) a factory;

   (e) a workshop;

   (f) a mine, quarry or other place of extraction of natural resources;

   (g) a building site or construction or assembly project which exists for more than 12 months.

3. The term "permanent establishment" shall not be deemed to include:

   (a) the use of facilities solely for the purpose of storage, display or delivery of goods or merchandise belonging to the enterprise;

   (b) the maintenance of a stock of goods or merchandise belonging to the enterprise solely for the purpose of storage, display or delivery;

   (c) the maintenance of a stock of goods or merchandise belonging to the enterprise solely for the purpose of processing by another enterprise;

   (d) the maintenance of a fixed place of business solely for the purpose of purchasing goods or merchandise, or for collecting information, for the enterprise;

   (e) the maintenance of a fixed place of business solely for the purpose of advertising, for the supply of information, for scientific research, or for similar activities which have a preparatory or auxiliary character, for the enterprise.

4. A person — other than an agent of independent status to whom paragraph 5 applies — acting in a Contracting State on behalf of an enterprise of the other Contracting State shall be deemed to be a permanent establishment in the first-mentioned State if he has, and habitually exercises in that first-mentioned State, an authority to conclude contracts in the name of the enterprise, unless his activities are limited to the purchase of goods or merchandise for the enterprise.

5. An enterprise of a Contracting State shall not be deemed to have a permanent establishment in the other Contracting State merely because it carries on business in that other State through a broker, general commission agent or any other agent of an independent status, where such persons are acting in the ordinary course of their business.

6. The fact that a company which is a resident of a Contracting State controls or is controlled by a company which is a resident of the other Contracting State, or which carries on business in that other State (whether through a permanent establishment or otherwise), shall not of itself constitute either company a permanent establishment of the other.

## Article 6 — Income from Immovable Property

1. Income from immovable property, including income from agriculture or forestry, may be taxed in the Contracting State in which such property is situated.

2. For the purposes of this Convention, the term **"immovable property"** shall be defined in accordance with the law of the Contracting State in which the property in question is situated. The term shall in any case include property accessory to immovable property, livestock and equipment used in agriculture and forestry, rights to which the provisions of general law respecting landed property apply, usufruct of immovable property and rights to variable or fixed payments as consideration for the working of, or the right to work, mineral deposits, sources and other natural resources; ships, boats and aircraft shall not be regarded as immovable property.

3. The provisions of paragraph 1 shall apply to income derived from the direct use, letting, or use in any other form of immovable property and to profits from the alienation of such property.

4. The provisions of paragraphs 1 and 3 shall also apply to income from immovable property of an enterprise and to income from immovable property used for the performance of professional services.

## Article 7 — Business Profits

1. The profits of an enterprise of a Contracting State shall be taxable only in that State unless the enterprise carries on business in the other Contracting State through a permanent establishment situated therein. If the enterprise carries on or has carried on business as aforesaid, the profits of the enterprise may be taxed in the other State but only so much of

them as is attributable to that permanent establishment.

2. Subject to the provisions of paragraph 3, where an enterprise of a Contracting State carries on business in the other Contracting State through a permanent establishment situated therein, there shall be attributed to that permanent establishment profits which it might be expected to make if it were a distinct and separate enterprise engaged in the same or similar activities under the same or similar conditions and dealing wholly independently with the enterprise of which it is a permanent establishment.

**Notes**: For discussion of paras. 7(2) and (3), see David Ward, "Attribution of Income to Permanent Establishments", 48(3) *Canadian Tax Journal* 559-5576(2000).

3. In the determination of the profits of a permanent establishment situated in a Contracting State, there shall be allowed as deductions expenses of the enterprise (other than expenses which would not be deductible under the law of that State if the permanent establishment were a separate enterprise) which are incurred for the purposes of the permanent establishment including executive and general administrative expenses, whether incurred in the State in which the permanent establishment is situated or elsewhere.

4. Insofar as it has been customary in a Contracting State to determine the profits to be attributed to a permanent establishment on the basis of an apportionment of the total profits of the enterprise to its various parts, nothing in paragraph 2 shall preclude that Contracting State from determining the profits to be taxed by such an apportionment as may be customary; the method of apportionment adopted shall, however, be such that the result shall be in accordance with the principles embodied in this Article.

5. No profits shall be attributed to a permanent establishment by reason of the mere purchase by that permanent establishment of goods or merchandise for the enterprise.

6. For the purposes of the preceding paragraphs, the profits to be attributed to the permanent establishment shall be determined by the same method year by year unless there is good and sufficient reason to the contrary.

7. Where profits include items of income which are dealt with separately in other Articles of this Convention, the provisions of this Article shall not prevent the application of the provisions of those other articles with respect to the taxation of such items of income.

## Article 8 — Shipping and Air Transport

1. Profits derived by an enterprise of a Contracting State from the operation of ships or aircraft in international traffic shall be taxable only in that State.

2. Notwithstanding the provisions of paragraph 1 and Article 7, profits derived from the operation of ships used principally to transport passengers or goods exclusively between places in a Contracting State may be taxed in that State.

3. Notwithstanding the provisions of Article 7, profits of an enterprise of a Contracting State from the use, maintenance or rental of containers (including trailers and related equipment for the transport of containers) used for the transport of goods or merchandise in international traffic shall be taxable only in that State.

4. The provisions of this Article shall also apply to profits derived by an enterprise of a Contracting State from its participation in a pool, a joint business or an international operating agency.

## Article 9 — Associated Enterprises

Where

(a) an enterprise of a Contracting State participates directly or indirectly in the management, control or capital of an enterprise of the other Contracting State, or

(b) the same persons participate directly or indirectly in the management, control or capital of an enterprise of a Contracting State and an enterprise of the other Contracting State,

and in either case conditions are made or imposed between the two enterprises in their commercial or financial relations which differ from those which would be made between independent enterprises, then any income, deductions, receipts or outgoings, which would, but for those conditions, have been attributed to one of the enterprises, but, by reason of those conditions, have not been so attributed may be taken into account in computing the profits or losses of that enterprise and taxed accordingly.

## Article 10 — Dividends

1. Dividends paid by a company which is a resident of Canada to a resident of the United Kingdom may be taxed in the United Kingdom. Such dividends may also be taxed in Canada, and according to the laws of Canada, but provided that the beneficial owner of the dividends is a resident of the United Kingdom the tax so charged shall not exceed:

(a) 10 per cent of the gross amount of the dividends if the recipient is a company which controls, directly or indirectly, at least 10 per cent of the voting power in the company paying the dividends;

## Art. 10 — Dividends

> **Proposed Amendment — Withholding rate on direct dividends**
> **February 1992 budget**: [The federal government is prepared, in its tax treaty negotiations, to reduce the withholding tax rate on "direct" dividends from 10% to 5% over a five-year period beginning in 1993. See Notes to ITA 212(2).]

(b) 15 per cent of the gross amount of the dividends in all other cases.

2. Dividends paid by a company which is a resident of the United Kingdom to a resident of Canada may be taxed in Canada. Such dividends may also be taxed in the United Kingdom, and according to the laws of the United Kingdom, but provided that the beneficial owner of the dividends is a resident of Canada the tax so charged shall not exceed 15 per cent of the gross amount of the dividends.

3. However, as long as an individual resident in the United Kingdom is entitled to a tax credit in respect of dividends paid by a company resident in the United Kingdom, the following provisions of this paragraph shall apply instead of the provisions of paragraph 2 of this Article:

(a)
 (i) Dividends paid by a company which is a resident of the United Kingdom to a resident of Canada may be taxed in Canada.

 (ii) Where a resident of Canada is entitled to a tax credit in respect of such a dividend under sub-paragraph (b) of this paragraph, tax may also be charged in the United Kingdom and according to the laws of the United Kingdom, on the aggregate of the amount or value of that dividend and the amount of that tax credit at a rate not exceeding 15 per cent.

 (iii) Where a resident of Canada is entitled to a tax credit in respect of such a dividend under sub-paragraph (c) of this paragraph, tax may also be charged in the United Kingdom and according to the laws of the United Kingdom, on the aggregate of the amount or value of that dividend and the amount of that tax credit at a rate not exceeding 10 per cent.

 (iv) Except as provided in sub-paragraphs (a)(ii) and (a)(iii) of this paragraph, dividends paid by a company which is a resident of the United Kingdom to a resident of Canada who is the beneficial owner of those dividends shall be exempt from any tax which is chargeable in the United Kingdom on dividends.

(b) A resident of Canada who receives a dividend from a company which is a resident of the United Kingdom shall, subject to the provisions of sub-paragraph (c) of this paragraph and provided he is the beneficial owner of the dividend, be entitled to the tax credit in respect thereof to which an individual resident in the United Kingdom would have been entitled had he received that dividend, and to the payment of any excess of such credit over his liability to United Kingdom tax.

(c) The provisions of sub-paragraph (b) of this paragraph shall not apply where the beneficial owner of the dividend is, or is associated with, a company which, either alone or together with one or more associated companies, controls, directly or indirectly, at least 10 per cent of the voting power in the company paying the dividend. In these circumstances a company which is a resident of Canada and receives a dividend from a company which is a resident of the United Kingdom shall, provided it is the beneficial owner of the dividend, be entitled to a tax credit equal to one-half of the tax credit to which an individual resident in the United Kingdom would have been entitled had he received that dividend, and to the payment of any excess of such credit over its liability to United Kingdom tax. For the purpose of this sub-paragraph, two companies shall be deemed to be associated if one controls, directly or indirectly, more than 50 per cent of the voting power in the other company, or a third company controls more than 50 per cent of the voting power in both of them.

4. The term **"dividends"** as used in this Article means income from shares, "jouissance" shares or "jouissance" rights, mining shares, founders' shares or other rights, not being debt-claims, participating in profits, as well as income assimilated to or treated in the same way as income from shares by the taxation law of the State of which the company making the payment is a resident.

5. The provisions of paragraphs 1, 2 and 3 shall not apply if the recipient of the dividends, being a resident of a Contracting State, carries on business in the other Contracting State of which the company paying the dividends is a resident, through a permanent establishment situated therein, or performs in that other State professional services from a fixed base situated therein, and the holding in respect of which the dividends are paid is effectively connected with such permanent establishment or fixed base. In such a case, the provisions of Article 7 or Article 14, as the case may be, shall apply.

6. Where a company is a resident of only one Contracting State, the other Contracting State may not impose any tax on the dividends paid by the company, except insofar as such dividends are paid to a resident of that other State or insofar as the holding in respect of which the dividends are paid is effectively connected with a permanent establishment or a fixed base situated in that other State, nor subject the company's undistributed profits to a tax on undistributed profits, even if the dividends paid or the undistributed profits consist wholly or partly of profits or income arising in such other State.

**7.** If a resident of Canada does not bear Canadian tax on dividends derived from a company which is a resident of the United Kingdom and owns 10 per cent or more of the class of shares in respect of which the dividends are paid, then neither paragraph 2 nor 3 shall apply to the dividends to the extent that they can have been paid only out of profits which the company paying the dividends earned or other income which it received in a period ending twelve months or more before the relevant date. For the purposes of this paragraph the term **"relevant date"** means the date on which the beneficial owner of the dividends became the owner of 10 per cent or more of the class of shares referred to above.

Provided that this paragraph shall not apply if the shares were acquired for bona fide commercial reasons and not primarily for the purpose of securing the benefit of this Article.

**Information Circulars**: 76-12R4: Applicable rate of part XIII tax on amounts paid or credited to persons in treaty countries.

## Article 11 — Interest

**1.** Interest arising in a Contracting State and paid to a resident of the other Contracting State may be taxed in that other State.

**2.** However, such interest may be taxed in the Contracting State in which it arises, and according to the law of that State; but if the recipient is the beneficial owner of the interest, the tax so charged shall not exceed 10 per cent of the gross amount of the interest.

**3.** Notwithstanding the provisions of paragraph 2 of this Article,

(a) Interest arising in the United Kingdom and paid to a resident of Canada shall be taxable only in Canada if it is paid in respect of a loan made, guaranteed or insured, or a credit extended, guaranteed or insured by the Export Development Corporation; and

(b) Interest arising in Canada and paid to a resident of the United Kingdom shall be taxable only in the United Kingdom if it is paid in respect of a loan made, guaranteed or insured, or a credit extended, guaranteed or insured by the United Kingdom Export Credits Guarantee Department.

**4.** (a) Notwithstanding the provisions of paragraph 2 of this Article, interest arising in Canada and paid in respect of a bond, debenture or other similar obligation of the Government of Canada or of a political subdivision or local authority thereof shall, provided that the interest is beneficially owned by a resident of the United Kingdom, be taxable only in the United Kingdom;

(b) Notwithstanding the provisions of Article 29 Canada may, on or before the thirtieth day of June in any calendar year give to the United Kingdom notice of termination of this paragraph and in such event this paragraph shall cease to have effect in respect of interest paid on obligations issued after 31 December of the calendar year in which the notice is given.

**5.** The term **"interest"** as used in this Article means income from debt-claims of every kind, whether or not secured by mortgage, and whether or not carrying a right to participate in the debtor's profits, and in particular, income from government securities and income from bonds or debentures, including premiums and prizes attaching to bonds or debentures, as well as income assimilated to income from money lent by the taxation law of the State in which the income arises. However, the term "interest" does not include income dealt with in Article 10.

**6.** The provisions of paragraphs 1, 2 and 4 of this Article shall not apply if the recipient of the interest, being a resident of a Contracting State, carries on business in the other Contracting State in which the interest arises through a permanent establishment situated therein, or performs in that other State professional services from a fixed base, situated therein, and the debt-claim in respect of which the interest is paid is effectively connected with such permanent establishment or fixed base. In such a case, the provisions of Article 7 or Article 14, as the case may be, shall apply.

**7.** Interest shall be deemed to arise in a Contracting State when the payer is that State itself, a political subdivision, a local authority or a resident of that State. Where, however, the person paying the interest, whether he is a resident of a Contracting State or not, has in a Contracting State a permanent establishment in connection with which the indebtedness on which the interest is paid was incurred, and that interest is borne by that permanent establishment, then such interest shall be deemed to arise in the Contracting State in which the permanent establishment is situated.

**8.** Where, owing to a special relationship between the payer and the person deriving the interest or between both of them and some other person, the amount of the interest paid exceeds for whatever reason the amount which would have been paid in the absence of such relationship, the provisions of this Article shall apply only to the last-mentioned amount. In that case, the excess part of the payments shall remain taxable according to the law of each Contracting State, due regard being had to the other provisions of this Convention.

**9.** Any provision in the law of a Contracting State relating only to interest paid to a non-resident company shall not operate so as to require such interest paid to a company which is a resident of the other Contracting State to be treated as a distribution of the company paying such interest. The preceding sentence shall not apply to interest paid to a company which is a resident of a Contracting State in which more than 50 per cent of the voting power is controlled, directly or indirectly, by a person or persons resident in the other Contracting State.

**10.** The provisions of paragraph 2 of this Article shall not apply to interest where the beneficial owner of the interest
   (a) does not bear tax in respect thereof in Canada; and
   (b) sells (or makes a contract to sell) the holding from which the interest is derived within three months of the date on which such beneficial owner acquired that holding.

**Information Circulars**: 76-12R4: Applicable rate of part XIII tax on amounts paid or credited to persons in treaty countries.

## Article 12 — Royalties

**1.** Royalties arising in a Contracting State and paid to a resident of the other Contracting State may be taxed in that other State.

**2.** However, such royalties may be taxed in the Contracting State in which they arise, and according to the law of that State; but if the recipient is the beneficial owner of the royalties the tax so charged shall not exceed 10 per cent of the gross amount of the royalties.

**3.** Notwithstanding the provisions of paragraph 2 of this Article, copyright royalties and other like payments in respect of the production or reproduction of any literary, dramatic, musical or artistic work (but not including royalties in respect of motion pictures and works on film, videotape or other means of reproduction for use in connection with television broadcasting) arising in a Contracting State and beneficially owned by a resident of the other Contracting State shall be taxable only in that other State.

**4.** The term **"royalties"** as used in this Article means payments of any kind received as a consideration for the use of, or the right to use, any copyright, patent, trade mark, design or model, plan, secret formula or process, or for the use of, or the right to use, industrial, commercial or scientific equipment, or for information concerning industrial, commercial or scientific experience, and includes payments of any kind in respect of motion pictures and works on film, videotape or other means of reproduction for use in connection with television broadcasting.

**5.** The provisions of paragraphs 1, 2 and 3 shall not apply if the recipient of the royalties, being a resident of a Contracting State, carries on business in the other Contracting State in which the royalties arise through a permanent establishment situated therein, or performs in that other State professional services from a fixed base situated therein, and the right or property in respect of which the royalties are paid is effectively connected with such permanent establishment or fixed base. In such a case, the provisions of Article 7 or Article 14, as the case may be, shall apply.

**6.** Royalties shall be deemed to arise in a Contracting State when the payer is that State itself, a political subdivision, a local authority or a resident of that State. Where, however, the person paying the royalties, whether he is a resident of a Contracting State or not, has in a Contracting State a permanent establishment in connection with which the obligation to pay the royalties was incurred, and those royalties are borne as such by that permanent establishment, then such royalties shall be deemed to arise in the Contracting State in which the permanent establishment is situated.

**7.** Where, owing to a special relationship between the payer and the person deriving the royalties or between both of them and some other person, the amount of the royalties paid exceeds for whatever reason the amount which would have been paid in the absence of such relationship, the provisions of this Article shall apply only to the last-mentioned amount. In that case, the excess part of the payments shall remain taxable according to the law of each Contracting State, due regard being had to the other provisions of this Convention.

## Article 13 — Capital Gains

**1.** Gains derived by a resident of a Contracting State from the alienation of immovable property situated in the other Contracting State may be taxed in that other State.

**Related Provisions**: ITA 126(2.21), (2.22) — Foreign tax credit to emigrant for tax payable on gain accrued while resident in Canada; ITA 128.1(4)(b)(i) — Real property in Canada excluded from deemed disposition on emigration.

**2.** Gains from the alienation of movable property forming part of the business property of a permanent establishment which an enterprise of a Contracting State has in the other Contracting State or of movable property pertaining to a fixed base available to a resident of a Contracting State in the other Contracting State for the purpose of performing professional services, including such gains from the alienation of such a permanent establishment (alone or with the whole enterprise) or of such fixed base, may be taxed in that other State.

**3.** Gains derived by a resident of a Contracting State from the alienation of ships or aircraft operated in international traffic or movable property pertaining to the operation of such ships or aircraft, shall be taxable only in that Contracting State.

4. Gains from the alienation of:

(a) any right, licence or privilege to explore for, drill for, or take petroleum, natural gas or other related hydrocarbons situated in a Contracting State, or

(b) any right to assets to be produced in a Contracting State by the activities referred to in sub-paragraph (a) above or to interests in or to the benefit of such assets situated in a Contracting State,

may be taxed in that State.

5. Gains from the alienation of:

(a) shares, other than shares quoted on an approved stock exchange, deriving their value or the greater part of their value directly or indirectly from immovable property situated in a Contracting State or from any right referred to in paragraph 4 of this Article, or

(b) an interest in a partnership or trust the assets of which consist principally of immovable property situated in a Contracting State, of rights referred to in paragraph 4 of this Article, or of shares referred to in sub-paragraph (a) above,

may be taxed in that State.

6. The provisions of paragraph 5 of this Article shall not apply:

(a) in the case of shares, where immediately before the alienation of the shares, the alienator owned, or the alienator and any persons related to or connected with him owned, less than 10 per cent of each class of the share capital of the company; or

(b) in the case of an interest in a partnership or trust, where immediately before the alienation of the interest, the alienator was entitled to, or the alienator and any persons related to or connected with him were entitled to, an interest of less than 10 per cent of the income and capital of the partnership or trust.

7. For the purposes of paragraph 5 of this Article:

(a) the term **"an approved stock exchange"** means a stock exchange prescribed for the purposes of the Canadian *Income Tax Act* or a recognised stock exchange within the meaning of the United Kingdom Corporation Tax Acts; and

(b) the term **"immovable property"** does not include any property (other than rental property) in which the business of the company, partnership or trust was carried on.

8. Gains from the alienation of any property, other than that referred to in paragraphs 1, 2, 3, 4 and 5 of this Article shall be taxable only in the Contracting State of which the alienator is a resident.

9. The provisions of paragraph 8 of this Article shall not affect the right of a Contracting State to tax, according to its domestic law, gains derived by an individual who is a resident of the other Contracting State from the alienation of any property, if the alienator:

(a) is a national of the first-mentioned Contracting State or was a resident of that State for 15 years or more prior to the alienation of the property, and

(b) was a resident of the first-mentioned Contracting State at any time during the five years immediately preceding such alienation.

## Article 14 — Professional Services

1. Income derived by a resident of a Contracting State in respect of professional services or other independent activities of a similar character shall be taxable only in that State unless he has a fixed base regularly available to him in the other Contracting State for the purpose of performing his activities. If he has such a fixed base, the income may be taxed in the other Contracting State but only so much of it as is attributable to that fixed base.

**Notes:** See Notes to Art. XIV of the Canada-U.S. treaty re the meaning of "fixed base".

2. The term **"professional services"** includes independent scientific, literary, artistic, educational or teaching activities as well as the independent activities of physicians, lawyers, engineers, architects, dentists and accountants.

## Article 15 — Dependent Personal Services

1. Subject to the provisions of Articles 17 and 18, salaries, wages and other similar remuneration derived by a resident of a Contracting State in respect of an employment shall be taxable only in that State unless the employment is exercised in the other Contracting State. If the employment is so exercised, such remuneration as is derived therefrom may be taxed in that other State.

2. Notwithstanding the provisions of paragraph 1, remuneration derived by a resident of a Contracting State in respect of an employment exercised in the other Contracting State shall be taxable only in the first-mentioned State if:

(a) the recipient is present in the other State for a period or periods not exceeding in the aggregate 183 days in the calendar year concerned, and

(b) the remuneration is paid by, or on behalf of, an employer who is not a resident of the other State, and

(c) the remuneration is not borne by a permanent establishment or a fixed base which the employer has in the other State.

**3.** Notwithstanding the preceding provisions of this Article, remuneration in respect of an employment exercised aboard a ship or aircraft operated in international traffic may be taxed in the Contracting State in which the place of effective management of the enterprise is situated.

**4.** In relation to remuneration of a director of a company derived from the company the preceding provisions of this Article shall apply as if the remuneration were remuneration of an employee in respect of employment, and as if reference to employer were references to the company.

**5.** Where under the law of a Contracting State tax is required to be deducted and is so deducted from salaries, wages and other similar remuneration derived in respect of an employment exercised in that Contracting State, tax shall not be deducted therefrom on behalf of the other Contracting State.

### Article 16 — Artistes and Athletes

**1.** Notwithstanding the provisions of Articles 7, 14 and 15, income derived by entertainers, such as theatre, motion picture, radio or television artistes, and musicians, and by athletes, from their personal activities as such may be taxed in the Contracting State in which these activities are exercised.

**2.** Where income in respect of personal activities as such of an entertainer or athlete accrues not to that entertainer or athlete himself but to another person, that income may, notwithstanding the provisions of Articles 7, 14 and 15, be taxed in the Contracting State in which the activities of the entertainer or athlete are exercised.

**3.** The provisions of paragraphs 1 and 2 shall not apply:

(a) to income derived from activities performed in a Contracting State by entertainers or athletes if the visit to that Contracting State is wholly or substantially supported by public funds;

(b) to a non-profit making organization no part of the income of which is payable, or is otherwise available for the personal benefit of, any proprietor, member or shareholder thereof; or

(c) to an entertainer or athlete in respect of services provided to an organization referred to in sub-paragraph (b).

### Article 17 — Pensions and Annuities

**1.** Pensions arising in a Contracting State and paid to a resident of the other Contracting State who is the beneficial owner thereof shall be taxable only in that other State.

**2.** Annuities arising in a Contracting State and paid to a resident of the other Contracting State may be taxed in that other State. However, such annuities may also be taxed in the Contracting State in which they arise and according to the laws of that State, but if the recipient is the beneficial owner of the annuities the tax so charged shall not exceed 10 per cent of the portion thereof that is subject to tax in that State.

**3.** For the purposes of this Convention, the term **"pension"** includes any payment under a superannuation, pension or retirement plan, Armed Forces retirement pay, war veterans pensions and allowances, and any payment under a sickness, accident or disability plan, as well as any payment made under the social security legislation in a Contracting State, but does not include any payment under a superannuation, pension or retirement plan in settlement of all future entitlements under such a plan or any payment under an income-averaging annuity contract.

**4.** For the purposes of this Convention, the term **"annuity"** means a stated sum payable periodically at stated times during life or during a specified or ascertainable period of time under an obligation to make the payments in return for adequate and full consideration in money or money's worth, but does not include a pension or any payment under a superannuation, pension or retirement plan in settlement of all future entitlements under such a plan or any payment under an income-averaging annuity contract.

**Notes**: See sections 5 and 5.1 of the *Income Tax Conventions Interpretation Act*, reproduced preceding the Canada-U.S. Convention.

**5.** Notwithstanding any other provision of this Convention, alimony and similar payments arising in a Contracting State and paid to a resident of the other Contracting State who is the beneficial owner thereof shall be taxable only in that other State.

### Article 18 — Government Service

**1.** (a) Remuneration, other than a pension, paid by a Contracting State or a political subdivision or a local authority thereof to any individual in respect of services rendered to that State or subdivision or local authority thereof shall be taxable only in that State.

(b) However, such remuneration shall be taxable only in the other Contracting State if the services are rendered in that State and the recipient is a resident of that State who:

(i) is a national of that State; or

(ii) did not become a resident of that State solely for the purpose of performing the services.

2. This Article shall not apply to remuneration in respect of services rendered in connection with any trade or business carried on by one of the Contracting States or a political subdivision or a local authority thereof.

3. In this Article, the term **"political subdivision"** shall, in relation to the United Kingdom, include Northern Ireland.

## Article 19 — Students

Payments which a student, apprentice or business trainee who is or was immediately before visiting one of the Contracting States a resident of a Contracting State and who is present in the other Contracting State solely for the purpose of his education or training receives for the purpose of his maintenance, education or training shall not be taxed in that other State, provided that such payments are made to him from sources outside that other State.

## Article 20 — Estates and Trusts

1. Income received from an estate or trust resident in Canada by a resident of the United Kingdom who is the beneficial owner thereof may be taxed in Canada according to its law, but the tax so charged shall not exceed 15 per cent of the gross amount of the income.

2. The provisions of paragraph 1 of this Article shall not apply if the recipient of the income, being a resident of the United Kingdom, carries on business in Canada through a permanent establishment situated therein, or performs in Canada professional services from a fixed base situated therein, and the right or interest in the estate or trust in respect of which the income is paid is effectively connected with such permanent establishment or fixed base. In such a case, the provisions of Article 7 or Article 14, as the case may be, shall apply.

3. For the purposes of this Article, a trust does not include an arrangement whereby the contributions made to the trust are deductible for the purposes of taxation in Canada.

## Article 21 — Elimination of Double Taxation

1. In the case of Canada, double taxation shall be avoided as follows:

(a) Subject to the existing provisions of the law of Canada regarding the deduction from tax payable in Canada of tax paid in a territory outside Canada and to any subsequent modification of those provisions — which shall not affect the general principle hereof — and unless a greater deduction or relief is provided under the laws of Canada, tax payable in the United Kingdom on profits, income or gains arising in the United Kingdom shall be deducted from any Canadian tax payable in respect of such profits, income or gains.

(b) Subject to the existing provisions of the law of Canada regarding the determination of the exempt surplus of a foreign affiliate and to any subsequent modification of those provisions — which shall not affect the general principle hereof — for the purpose of computing Canadian tax, a company resident in Canada shall be allowed to deduct in computing its taxable income any dividend received by it out of the exempt surplus of a foreign affiliate resident in the United Kingdom.

The terms **"foreign affiliate"** and **"exempt surplus"** shall have the meaning which they have under the *Income Tax Act* of Canada.

2. In the case of the United Kingdom, double taxation shall be avoided as follows: subject to the provisions of the law of the United Kingdom regarding the allowance as a credit against United Kingdom tax of tax payable in a territory outside the United Kingdom (which shall not affect the general principle hereof):

(a) tax payable under the laws of Canada and in accordance with this Convention, whether directly or by deduction, on profits, income or chargeable gains from sources within Canada (excluding in the case of a dividend, tax payable in respect of the profits out of which the dividend is paid) shall be allowed as a credit against any United Kingdom tax computed by reference to the same profits, income or chargeable gains by reference to which the Canadian tax is computed; and

(b) in the case of a dividend paid by a company which is a resident of Canada to a company which is resident in the United Kingdom and which controls directly or indirectly at least 10 per cent of the voting power in the Canadian company, the credit shall take into account (in addition to any tax creditable under (a)) tax payable under the laws of Canada by the company in respect of the profits out of which such dividend is paid.

3. For the purposes of paragraphs 1 and 2 of this Article, income, profits and capital gains owned by a

resident of a Contracting State which are taxed in the other Contracting State in accordance with this Convention shall be deemed to arise from sources in that other Contracting State.

4. Where profits on which an enterprise of a Contracting State has been charged to tax in that State are also included in the profits of an enterprise of the other State and the profits so included are profits which would have accrued to that enterprise of the other State if the conditions made between the enterprises had been those which would have been made between independent enterprises dealing at arm's length, the amount included in the profits of both enterprises shall be treated for the purposes of this Article as income from a source in the other State of the enterprise of the first-mentioned State and relief shall be given accordingly under the provisions of paragraph 1 or paragraph 2 of this Article.

## Article 22 — Non-Discrimination

1. The nationals of a Contracting State shall not be subjected in the other Contracting State to any taxation or any requirement connected therewith which is other or more burdensome than the taxation and connected requirements to which nationals of that other State in the same circumstances are or may be subjected.

2. The taxation on a permanent establishment which an enterprise of a Contracting State has in the other Contracting State shall not be less favourably levied in that other State than the taxation levied on enterprises of that other State carrying on the same activities. This provision shall not be construed as obliging either Contracting State to grant to individuals not resident in its territory those personal allowances and reliefs for tax purposes which are by law available only to individuals who are so resident.

3. Nothing in this Convention shall be construed as preventing a Contracting State from imposing on the earnings attributable to permanent establishments in that State of a company which is a resident of the other Contracting State, tax in addition to the tax which would be chargeable on the earnings of a company which is a resident of the first-mentioned State, provided that the rate of any additional tax so imposed shall not exceed 10 per cent of the amount of such earnings which have not been subjected to such additional tax in previous taxation years.

4. For the purpose of paragraph 3 of this Article, the term **"earnings"** means the profits attributable to permanent establishments in a Contracting State (including gains from the alienation of property forming part of the business property of such permanent establishments) in a year and previous years after deducting therefrom:

(a) business losses attributable to such permanent establishments (including losses from the alienation of property forming part of the business property of such permanent establishments) in such year and previous years; and

(b) all taxes, other than the additional tax referred to in paragraph 3 of this Article, imposed on such profits in that State; and

(c) the profits reinvested in that State, provided that where that State is Canada, the amount of such deduction shall be determined in accordance with the existing provisions of the law of Canada regarding the computation of the allowance in respect of investment in property in Canada, and any subsequent modification of those provisions which shall not affect the general principle thereof; and

(d) five hundred thousand Canadian dollars ($500,000) or two hundred and fifty thousand pounds sterling (£250,000), whichever is the greater, less any amount deducted in that State under this subparagraph (d) by the company or a company associated therewith; for the purposes of this subparagraph (d) a company is associated with another company if one of them directly or indirectly has control of the other or both are directly or indirectly under the control of the same person, or if the two companies deal with each other not at arm's length.

5. In this Article, the term **"taxation"** means taxes which are the subject of this Convention.

## Article 23 — Mutual Agreement Procedure

1. Where a resident of a Contracting State considers that the actions of one or both of the Contracting States result or will result for him in taxation not in accordance with this Convention, he may, without prejudice to the remedies provided by the national laws of those States, address to the competent authority of the Contracting State of which he is a resident an application in writing stating the grounds for claiming the revision of such taxation.

2. The competent authority referred to in paragraph 1 shall endeavour, if the objection appears to it to be justified and if it is not itself able to arrive at an appropriate solution, to resolve the case by mutual agreement with the competent authority of the other Contracting State, with a view to the avoidance of taxation not in accordance with the Convention.

3. The competent authorities of the Contracting State shall endeavour to resolve by mutual agreement any difficulties or doubts arising as to the interpretation

or application of the Convention. In particular, the competent authorities of the Contracting States may reach agreement on:

(a) the same allocation of profits to a resident of a Contracting State and its permanent establishment situated in the other Contracting State;

(b) the same allocation of income between a resident of a Contracting State and any associated person provided for in Article 9.

**Related Provisions**: ITA 115.1 — Competent authority agreements.

**Notes**: See Notes to ITA 115.1.

**Information Circulars**: 71-17R4: Requests for competent authority consideration under mutual agreement procedures in income tax conventions.

## Article 24 — Exchange of Information

1. The competent authorities of the Contracting States shall exchange such information (being information which is at their disposal under their respective taxation laws in the normal course of administration) as is necessary for the carrying out of the provisions of this Convention or for the prevention of fraud or for the administration of statutory provisions against legal avoidance in relation to the taxes which are the subject of this Convention. Any information so exchanged shall be treated as secret and shall not be disclosed to persons other than persons (including a court or administrative tribunal) concerned with the assessment, collection or enforcement in respect of the taxes which are the subject of this Convention. No information as aforesaid shall be exchanged which would disclose any trade, business, industrial or professional secret or trade process.

## Article 25 — Diplomatic and Consular Officials

1. Nothing in this Convention shall affect the fiscal privileges of members of diplomatic or consular missions under the general rules of international law or under the provisions of special agreements.

2. This Convention shall not apply to International Organizations, to organs or officials thereof and to persons who are members of a diplomatic or permanent mission or consular post of a third State, being present in a Contracting State and not treated in either Contracting State as residents in respect of taxes on income or capital gains.

## Article 26 — Extension

1. This Convention may be extended, either in its entirety or with modifications to any territory for whose international relations either of the Contracting States is responsible, and which imposes taxes substantially similar in character to those which are the subject of this Convention and any such extension shall take effect from such date and subject to such modifications and conditions (including conditions as to termination) as may be specified and agreed between the Contracting States in notes to be exchanged for this purpose.

2. The termination of this Convention under Article 29 shall, unless otherwise expressly agreed by both Contracting States, terminate the application of this Convention to any territory to which it has been extended under this Article.

## Article 27 — Miscellaneous Rules

1. The provisions of this Convention shall not be construed to restrict in any manner any exclusion, exemption, deduction, credit or other allowance now or hereafter accorded by the law of a Contracting State in the determination of the tax imposed by that Contracting State.

2. Where under any provision of this Convention any person is relieved from tax in a Contracting State on certain income and, under the law in force in the other Contracting State, that person is subject to tax in that other State in respect of that income by reference to the amount thereof which is remitted to or received in that other State, the relief from tax to be allowed under this Convention in the first-mentioned State shall apply only to the amounts so remitted or received.

3. Nothing in this Convention shall be construed as preventing Canada from imposing a tax on amounts included in the income of a resident of Canada by virtue of the provisions of section 91 of the Canadian *Income Tax Act*, so far as they are in force on the date of entry into force of this Convention, or have been modified only in minor respects, so as not to affect their general character.

4. The aggregate of the amount or value of the dividend and the amount of the tax credit referred to in paragraph 3(b) or 3(c) of Article 10 of this Convention shall be treated as a dividend for Canadian income tax purposes.

5. Each of the Contracting States will endeavour to collect on behalf of the other Contracting State such amounts as may be necessary to ensure that relief granted by this Convention from taxation imposed by that other State does not enure to the benefit of persons not entitled thereto. However, nothing in this paragraph shall be construed as imposing on either of the Contracting States the obligation to carry out administrative measures of a different nature from those used in the collection of its own tax or which would be contrary to its public policy.

6. The competent authorities of the Contracting States may communicate with each other directly for the purpose of applying this Convention.

## Article 27A — Miscellaneous Rules Applicable to Certain Offshore Activities

1. The provisions of this Article shall apply notwithstanding any other provision of this Convention.

2. A person who is a resident of a Contracting State and carries on activities in the other Contracting State in connection with the exploration or exploitation of the sea bed and sub-soil and their natural resources situated in that other Contracting State shall, subject to paragraph 3 of this Article, be deemed to be carrying on a business in that other Contracting State through a permanent establishment situated therein.

3. The provisions of paragraph 2 of this Article shall not apply where the activities referred to therein are carried on for a period or periods not exceeding in the aggregate 30 days in any 12 month period. For the purposes of this paragraph:

(a) where a person carrying on activities referred to in paragraph 2 of this Article is associated with an enterprise carrying on substantially similar activities, that person shall be deemed to be carrying on those substantially similar activities of the enterprise with which he is associated, in addition to his own activities;

(b) two enterprises shall be deemed to be associated if one enterprise participates directly or indirectly in the management or control of the other enterprise or if the same persons participate directly or indirectly in the management or control of both enterprises.

4. Salaries, wages and similar remuneration derived by a resident of a Contracting State in respect of an employment connected with the exploration or exploitation of the sea bed and sub-soil and their natural resources situated in the other Contracting State may, to the extent that the duties are performed offshore in that other Contracting State, be taxed in that other Contracting State.

## Article 28 — Entry into Force

1. The Convention shall come into force on the date when the last of all such things shall have been done in Canada and the United Kingdom as are necessary to give the Convention the force of law in Canada and the United Kingdom respectively and shall thereupon have effect:

(a) in Canada:

(i) in respect of tax withheld at the source on amounts paid or credited to non-residents on or after 1 January 1976;

(ii) in respect of other Canadian taxes, for the 1976 taxation year and subsequent years;

(b) in the United Kingdom:

(i) in relation to any dividend to which paragraph 3 of Article 10 applied in respect of income tax and payment of tax credit, for any year of assessment beginning on or after 6 April 1973. A dividend paid on or after 1 April 1973 but before 6 April 1973 shall be treated for tax credit purposes as paid on 6 April 1973;

(ii) in relation to any other provision of this Convention, in respect of income tax and capital gains tax, for any year of assessment beginning on or after 6 April 1976;

(iii) in respect of corporation tax, for any financial year beginning on or after 1 April 1976;

(iv) in respect of petroleum revenue tax for any chargeable period beginning on or after 1 January 1976;

(v) in respect of development land tax, for any realised development value accruing on or after 1 August 1976.

2. The Governments of the Contracting States shall, as soon as possible, inform one another in writing of the date when the last of all such things have been done as are necessary to give the Convention the force of law in Canada and the United Kingdom respectively. The date specified by the last Government to fulfil this requirement, being the date on which the Convention shall come into force in accordance with paragraph 1, shall be confirmed in writing by the Government so notified.

3. Subject to the provisions of paragraph 4 of this Article the existing Agreement shall cease to have effect as respects taxes to which this Convention applies in accordance with the provisions of paragraph 1 of this Article.

4. Where, however, any greater relief from tax would have been afforded by any provision of the existing Agreement than is due under this Convention, any such provision as aforesaid shall continue to have effect

(a) in the United Kingdom for any year of assessment, chargeable period or financial year;

(b) in Canada for any taxation year;

beginning before the entry into force of this Convention.

5. The existing Agreement shall terminate on the last date on which it has effect in accordance with the foregoing provisions of this Article.

6. The termination of the existing Agreement as provided in paragraph 5 of this Article shall not revive the Agreement between the Government of Canada and the Government of the United Kingdom of Great Britain and Northern Ireland for the Avoidance of Double Taxation with respect to certain classes of Income signed at Ottawa on 6 December 1965. Upon the entry into force of this Convention that Agreement shall terminate.

7. In this Article the term **"the existing Agreement"** means the Agreement between the Government of Canada and the Government of the United Kingdom of Great Britain and Northern Ireland for the Avoidance of Double Taxation and the Prevention of Fiscal Evasion with respect to taxes on Income and Capital Gains signed at Ottawa on 12 December 1966.

8. Notwithstanding any provisions of the respective domestic laws of the Contracting States imposing time limits for applications for relief from tax, an application for relief under the provisions of this Convention shall have effect, and any consequential refunds of tax made, if the application is made to the competent authority concerned within one year of the end of the calendar year in which this Convention enters into force.

## Article 29 — Termination

This Convention shall continue in effect indefinitely but the Government of either Contracting State may, on or before 30 June in any calendar year after the year 1980 give notice of termination to the Government of the other Contracting State and, in such event, this Convention shall cease to be effective:

(a) in Canada

(i) in respect of tax withheld at the source on amounts paid or credited to non-residents on or after 1 January in the calendar year next following that in which the notice is given; and

(ii) in respect of other Canadian taxes for any taxation year ending in or after the calendar year next following that in which the notice is given;

(b) in the United Kingdom

(i) in respect of income tax and capital gains tax for any year of assessment beginning on or after 6 April in the calendar year next following that in which such notice is given;

(ii) in respect of corporation tax, for any financial year beginning on or after 1 April in the calendar year next following that in which such notice is given;

(iii) in respect of petroleum revenue tax for any chargeable period beginning on or after 1 January in the calendar year next following that in which such notice is given;

(iv) in respect of development land tax, for any realised development value accruing on or after 1 April in the calendar year next following that in which such notice is given.

IN WITNESS WHEREOF the undersigned, duly authorized thereto, have signed this Convention.

DONE in duplicate at London, this 8th day of September 1978, in the English and French languages, both texts being equally authoritative.

FOR THE GOVERNMENT OF CANADA:

Paul Martin

FOR THE GOVERNMENT OF GREAT BRITAIN AND NORTHERN IRELAND:

Frank Judd

# CURRENT STATUS OF TAX TREATIES

Reciprocal income tax treaties are currently in force between Canada and the following countries. (In some cases the treaty currently in force, signed on the date noted, replaced another treaty that had been in force from an earlier time.)

## Tax treaties in force

Algeria (February 28, 1999)
Argentina (April 29, 1993)
Australia (May 21, 1980)
Austria (December 9, 1976; and Protocol of June 15, 1999)[2]
Bangladesh (February 15, 1982)
Barbados (January 22, 1980)
Belgium (May 29, 1975)
Brazil (June 4, 1984)
Cameroon (May 26, 1982)
Chile (January 21, 1998)
China (People's Republic of) (May 12, 1986)[3]
Croatia (December 9, 1997)
Cyprus (May 2, 1984)
Czechoslovakia[4] (August 30, 1990)
Denmark (September 17, 1997)
Dominican Republic (August 6, 1976)
Egypt (May 30, 1983)
Estonia (June 2, 1995)
Finland (May 28, 1990)
France (May 2, 1975 and Protocols of January 16, 1987 and November 30, 1995)
Germany (July 17, 1981 treaty with West Germany, now considered in force for the unified Germany)
Guyana (October 15, 1985)
Hungary (April 15, 1992 and Protocol of May 3, 1994)
Iceland (June 19, 1997)
India (January 11, 1996)
Indonesia (April 1, 1998)
Ireland (November 23, 1966)
Israel (July 21, 1975)
Italy (November 17, 1977 and Protocol of March 20, 1989)
Ivory Coast (June 16, 1983)
Jamaica (March 30, 1978)
Japan (May 7, 1986; amended by Protocol of February 19, 1999)
Jordan (September 6, 1999)
Kazakhstan (September 25, 1996)
Kenya (April 27, 1983)
Korea (February 10, 1978)
Kyrgyzstan (Kyrgyz Republic) (June 4, 1998)
Latvia (Republic of) (April 26, 1995)
Lithuania (Republic of) (August 29, 1996)
Luxembourg (September 10, 1999; provisions effective January 1, 2001)
Malaysia (October 15, 1976)
Malta (July 25, 1986)
Mexico (March 16, 1990 and April 8, 1991)[5]
Morocco (December 22, 1975)
Netherlands (May 27, 1986, and Protocols of same date, March 4, 1993, and August 25, 1997)
New Zealand (May 13, 1980)
Nigeria (August 4, 1992)
Norway (November 23, 1966)
Pakistan (February 24, 1976)
Papua New Guinea (October 16, 1987)
Philippines (March 11, 1976)
Poland (May 4, 1987)
Romania (November 20, 1978)
Russia (October 5, 1995)
Singapore (March 6, 1976 and Protocol of same date)
South Africa (Republic of) (November 27, 1995)
Spain (November 23, 1976)
Sri Lanka (June 23, 1982)
Sweden (August 27, 1996)
Switzerland (May 5, 1997)
Tanzania (United Republic of) (December 15, 1995)
Thailand (April 11, 1984)
Trinidad and Tobago (Republic of) (September 11, 1995)
Tunisia (February 10, 1982)
Ukraine (March 4, 1996)
United Kingdom of Great Britain and Northern Ireland (September 8, 1978)
United States of America (September 26, 1980 and Protocols of March 17, 1995 and July 29, 1997)

---

[2] In force January 29, 2001

[3] This Convention does not apply to Hong Kong.

[4] Continues to apply to both the Czech Republic and Slovak Republic.

[5] A Convention for the exchange of information is also in force.

Uzbekistan (Republic of) (June 17, 1999)
USSR[6]
Vietnam (November 14, 1997)
Zambia (Republic of) (February 16, 1984)
Zimbabwe (April 16, 1992)

**Tax treaties or protocols signed but not yet in force**

Bulgaria (March 3, 1999)[7]
Lebanon (December 29, 1998)[7]
Portugal (June 14, 1999)[7]
Slovenia (September 15, 2000)

**Tax treaties or protocols under negotiation (re-negotiation)**

Armenia
Australia
Barbados
Belgium
Colombia
Czech Republic
Ecuador
Egypt[8]
Gabon
Germany
Greece
Ireland[8]
Italy (Republic of)
Kuwait
Mauritius (Republic of)
Mexico
Moldova
Mongolia
Norway
Romania
Saint Lucia
Senegal
Slovak Republic
Turkey
United Arab Emirates
United Kingdom
United States[9]
Venezuela

For current information regarding the status of treaty negotiations with any country, contact David Senécal at the Department of Finance, (613) 947-9860. For current information regarding CCRA administrative policy with respect to which treaties are in force, contact the International Taxation Office (613) 952-3741 or 1-800-267-5177.

---

[6]No longer applies to any former republic of the USSR.

[7]Part of Bill S-3 which received Royal Assent on June 29, 2000.

[8]Will eventually replace the existing treaty.

[9]Protocol.

# INTERPRETATION ACT

An Act respecting the Interpretation of Statutes and Regulations
REVISED STATUTES OF CANADA 1985, CHAPTER I-21, AS AMENDED.

## Short Title

Notes: For digests of cases interpreting the provisions of this Act, especially in a tax context, see McMechan & Bourgard, *Tax Court Practice* (Carswell, looseleaf).

**1. Short title** — This Act may be cited as the *Interpretation Act*.

## Interpretation

**2. (1) Definitions** — In this Act,

"**Act**" means an Act of Parliament;

"**enact**" includes to issue, make or establish;

"**enactment**" means an Act or regulation or any portion of an Act or regulation;

"**public officer**" includes any person in the public service of Canada who is authorized by or under an enactment to do or enforce the doing of an act or thing or to exercise a power, or on whom a duty is imposed by or under an enactment;

"**regulation**" includes an order, regulation, rule, rule of court, form, tariff of costs or fees, letters patent, commission, warrant, proclamation, by-law, resolution or other instrument issued, made or established

  (a) in the execution of a power conferred by or under the authority of an Act, or

  (b) by or under the authority of the Governor in Council;

"**repeal**" includes revoke or cancel.

**(2) Expired and replaced enactments** — For the purposes of this Act, an enactment that has been replaced is repealed and an enactment that has expired, lapsed or otherwise ceased to have effect is deemed to have been repealed.

Notes: 2(2) amended by *Miscellaneous Statutes Law Amendment Act* (S.C. 1999, c. 31), effective June 17, 1999. Previously read:

  (2) For the purposes of this Act, an enactment that has been replaced, has expired, lapsed or otherwise ceased to have effect is deemed to have been repealed.

## Application

**3. (1) Application** — Every provision of this Act applies, unless a contrary intention appears, to every enactment, whether enacted before or after the commencement of this Act.

**(2) Application to this Act** — The provisions of this Act apply to the interpretation of this Act.

**(3) Rules of construction not excluded** — Nothing in this Act excludes the application to an enactment of a rule of construction applicable to that enactment and not inconsistent with this Act.

## Enacting Clause of Acts

**4. (1) Enacting clause** — The enacting clause of an Act may be in the following form:

  "Her Majesty, by and with the advice and consent of the Senate and House of Commons of Canada, enacts as follows:".

**(2) Order of clauses** — The enacting clause of an Act shall follow the preamble, if any, and the various provisions within the purview or body of the Act shall follow in a concise and enunciative form.

## Operation

### Royal Assent

**5. (1) Royal Assent** — The Clerk of the Parliaments shall endorse on every Act, immediately after its title, the day, month and year when the Act was assented to in Her Majesty's name and the endorsement shall be a part of the Act.

**(2) Date of commencement** — If no date of commencement is provided for in an Act, the date of commencement of that Act is the date of assent to the Act.

**(3) Commencement provision** — Where an Act contains a provision that the Act or any portion thereof is to come into force on a day later than the date of assent to the Act, that provision is deemed to have come into force on the date of assent to the Act.

**(4) Commencement when no date fixed** — Where an Act provides that certain provisions thereof are to come or are deemed to have come into force on a day other than the date of assent to the Act, the remaining provisions of the Act are deemed to have come into force on the date of assent to the Act.

## Day Fixed for Commencement or Repeal

**6. (1) Operation when date fixed for commencement or repeal** — Where an enactment is expressed to come into force on a particular day, it shall be construed as coming into force on the expiration of the previous day; and where an enactment is expressed to expire, lapse or otherwise cease to have effect on a particular day, it shall be construed as ceasing to have effect upon the commencement of the following day.

**(2) When no date fixed** — Every enactment that is not expressed to come into force on a particular day shall be construed as coming into force

(a) in the case of an Act, on the expiration of the day immediately before the day the Act was assented to in Her Majesty's name;

(b) in the case of a regulation, on the expiration of the day immediately before the day the regulation was registered pursuant to section 6 of the *Statutory Instruments Act* or, if the regulation is of a class that is exempted from the application of subsection 5(1) of that Act, on the expiration of the day immediately before the day the regulation was made.

**(3) Judicial notice** — Judicial notice shall be taken of a day for the coming into force of an enactment that is fixed by a regulation that has been published in the *Canada Gazette*.

## Regulation Prior to Commencement

**7. Preliminary proceedings** — Where an enactment is not in force and it contains provisions conferring power to make regulations or do any other thing, that power may, for the purpose of making the enactment effective on its commencement, be exercised at any time before its commencement, but a regulation so made or a thing so done has no effect until the commencement of the enactment, except in so far as may be necessary to make the enactment effective on its commencement.

## Territorial Operation

**8. (1) Territorial operation** — Every enactment applies to the whole of Canada, unless a contrary intention is expressed in the enactment.

**(2) Amending enactment** — Where an enactment that does not apply to the whole of Canada is amended, no provision in the amending enactment applies to any part of Canada to which the amended enactment does not apply, unless it is provided in the amending enactment that it applies to that part of Canada or to the whole of Canada.

**(2.1) Exclusive economic zone of Canada** — Every enactment that applies in respect of exploring or exploiting, conserving or managing natural resources, whether living or non-living, applies, in addition to its application to Canada, to the exclusive economic zone of Canada, unless a contrary intention is expressed in the enactment.

**Notes**: See Notes to 8(2.2).

**(2.2) Continental shelf of Canada** — Every enactment that applies in respect of exploring or exploiting natural resources that are

(a) mineral or other non-living resources of the seabed or subsoil, or

(b) living organisms belonging to sedentary species, that is to say, organisms that, at the harvestable stage, either are immobile on or under the seabed or are unable to move except in constant physical contact with the seabed or subsoil

applies, in addition to its application to Canada, to the continental shelf of Canada, unless a contrary intention is expressed in the enactment.

**Notes**: 8(2.1), (2.2) added by *Oceans Act* (Bill C-26, 1996, c. 31), proclaimed in force January 31, 1997 (SI/97-21).

**(3) Extra-territorial operation** — Every Act now in force enacted prior to December 11, 1931 that expressly or by necessary or reasonable implication was intended, as to the whole or any part thereof, to have extra-territorial operation shall be construed as if, at the date of its enactment, the Parliament of Canada had full power to make laws having extra-territorial operation as provided by the *Statute of Westminster, 1931*.

## Rules of Construction

### Private Acts

**9. Provisions in Private Acts** — No provision in a private Act affects the rights of any person, except as therein mentioned or referred to.

### Law Always Speaking

**10. Law always speaking** — The law shall be considered as always speaking, and where a matter or thing is expressed in the present tense, it shall be applied to the circumstances as they arise, so that effect may be given to the enactment according to its true spirit, intent and meaning.

### Imperative and Permissive Construction

**11. "Shall" and "may"** — The expression "shall" is to be construed as imperative and the expression "may" as permissive.

## Enactments Remedial

**12. Enactments deemed remedial** — Every enactment is deemed remedial, and shall be given such fair, large and liberal construction and interpretation as best ensures the attainment of its objects.

## Preambles and Marginal Notes

**13. Preamble** — The preamble of an enactment shall be read as a part of the enactment intended to assist in explaining its purport and object.

**14. Marginal Notes and historical references** — Marginal notes and references to former enactments that appear after the end of a section or other division in an enactment form no part of the enactment, but are inserted for convenience of reference only.

Notes: The "marginal notes", which are printed as such in the official legislation as published by Parliament, are shown in this publication as titles to the provision (i.e., for this section, the bold-face words "Marginal Notes and historical references").

This provision was effectively ignored in *Corbett*, [1997] 1 C.T.C. 2 (FCA), where the Court used the marginal notes to assist in interpreting the ITA.

Similarly, in *Law Society of Upper Canada v. Skapinker*, [1984] S.C.R. 357, Estey J. stated that headings in the *Charter of Rights* "must be examined and some intent made to discern the intent of the makers of the document from the language of the heading". See also *Fleck Manufacturing Inc. v. MNR*, 98 G.T.C. 5009 (CITT).

## Application of Interpretation Provisions

**15. (1) Application of definitions and Interpretation Provisions** — Definitions or rules of interpretation in an enactment apply to all the provisions of the enactment, including the provisions that contain those definitions or rules of interpretation.

**(2) Interpretation sections subject to exceptions** — Where an enactment contains an interpretation section or provision, it shall be read and construed

(a) as being applicable only if a contrary intention does not appear, and

(b) as being applicable to all other enactments relating to the same subject-matter unless a contrary intention appears.

**16. Words in regulations** — Where an enactment confers power to make regulations, expressions used in the regulations have the same respective meanings as in the enactment conferring the power.

## Her Majesty

**17. Her Majesty not bound or affected unless stated** — No enactment is binding on Her Majesty or affects Her Majesty's rights or prerogatives in any manner, except as mentioned or referred to in the enactment.

Related Provisions: ITA 27 — Application of ITA to Crown corporations.

## Proclamations

**18. (1) Proclamation** — Where an enactment authorizes the issue of a proclamation, the proclamation shall be understood to be a proclamation of the Governor in Council.

**(2) Proclamation to be issued on advice** — Where the Governor General is authorized to issue a proclamation, the proclamation shall be understood to be a proclamation issued under an order of the Governor in Council, but it is not necessary to mention in the proclamation that it is issued under such an order.

**(3) Effective day of Proclamations** — A proclamation that is issued under an order of the Governor in Council may purport to have been issued on the day of the order or on any subsequent day and, if so, takes effect on that day.

## Oaths

**19. (1) Administration of oaths** — Where, by an enactment or by a rule of the Senate or House of Commons, evidence under oath is authorized or required to be taken, or an oath is authorized or directed to be made, taken or administered, the oath may be administered, and a certificate of its having been made, taken or administered may be given by

(a) any person authorized by the enactment or rule to take the evidence; or

(b) a judge of any court, a notary public, a justice of the peace or a commissioner for taking affidavits, having authority or jurisdiction within the place where the oath is administered.

**(2) Where justice of peace empowered** — Where power is conferred on a justice of the peace to administer an oath or solemn affirmation or to take an affidavit or declaration, the power may be exercised by a notary public or a commissioner for taking oaths.

Related Provisions: ITA 220(5) — Administration of oaths.

## Reports to Parliament

**20. Reports to Parliament** — Where an Act requires a report or other document to be laid before Parliament and, in compliance with the Act, a particular report or document has been laid before Parliament at a session thereof, nothing in the Act shall be construed as requiring the same report or document to be laid before Parliament at any subsequent session.

## Corporations

**21. (1) Powers vested in Corporations** — Words establishing a corporation shall be construed

(a) as vesting in the corporation power to sue and be sued, to contract and be contracted with by its corporate name, to have a common seal and to alter or change it at pleasure, to have perpetual succession, to acquire and hold personal property for the purposes for which the corporation is established and to alienate that property at pleasure;

(b) in the case of a corporation having a name consisting of an English and a French form or a combined English and French form, as vesting in the corporation power to use either the English or the French form of its name or both forms and to show on its seal both the English and French forms of its name or have two seals, one showing the English and the other showing the French form of its name;

(c) as vesting in a majority of the members of the corporation the power to bind the others by their acts; and

(d) as exempting from personal liability for its debts, obligations or acts individual members of the corporation who do not contravene the provisions of the enactment establishing the corporation.

**(2) Corporate name** — Where an enactment establishes a corporation and in each of the English and French versions of the enactment the name of the corporation is in the form only of the language of that version, the name of the corporation shall consist of the form of its name in each of the versions of the enactment.

**(3) Banking business** — No corporation is deemed to be authorized to carry on the business of banking unless that power is expressly conferred on it by the enactment establishing the corporation.

## Majority and Quorum

**22. (1) Majorities** — Where an enactment requires or authorizes more than two persons to do an act or thing, a majority of them may do it.

**(2) Quorum of board, court, commission, etc.** — Where an enactment establishes a board, court, commission or other body consisting of three or more members, in this section called an "association",

(a) at a meeting of the association, a number of members of the association equal to,

(i) if the number of members provided for by the enactment is a fixed number, at least one-half of the number of members, and

(ii) if the number of members provided for by the enactment is not a fixed number but is within a range having a maximum or minimum, at least one-half of the number of members in office if that number is within the range,

constitutes a quorum;

(b) an act or thing done by a majority of the members of the association present at a meeting, if the members present constitute a quorum, is deemed to have been done by the association; and

(c) a vacancy in the membership of the association does not invalidate the constitution of the association or impair the right of the members in office to act, if the number of members in office is not less than a quorum.

## Appointment, Retirement and Powers of Officers

**23. (1) Public officers hold office during pleasure** — Every public officer appointed by or under the authority of an enactment or otherwise is deemed to have been appointed to hold office during pleasure only, unless it is otherwise expressed in the enactment, commission or instrument of appointment.

**(2) Effective day of appointments** — Where an appointment is made by instrument under the Great Seal, the instrument may purport to have been issued on or after the day its issue was authorized, and the day on which it so purports to have been issued is deemed to be the day on which the appointment takes effect.

**(3) Appointment or engagement otherwise than under great seal** — Where there is authority in an enactment to appoint a person to a position or to engage the services of a person, otherwise than by instrument under the Great Seal, the instrument of appointment or engagement may be expressed to be effective on or after the day on which that person commenced the performance of the duties of the position or commenced the performance of the services, and the day on which it is so expressed to be effective, unless that day is more than sixty days before the day on which the instrument is issued, is deemed to be the day on which the appointment or engagement takes effect.

**(4) Remuneration** — Where a person is appointed to an office, the appointing authority may fix, vary or terminate that person's remuneration.

**(5) Commencement of appointments or retirements** — Where a person is appointed to an office effective on a specified day, or where the appointment of a person is terminated effective on a specified day, the appointment or termination is deemed to have been effected immediately on the expiration of the previous day.

**24. (1) Implied powers respecting public officers** — Words authorizing the appointment of a public officer to hold office during pleasure include, in the discretion of the authority in whom the power of appointment is vested, the power to

(a) terminate the appointment or remove or suspend the public officer;

(b) re-appoint or reinstate the public officer; and

(c) appoint another person in the stead of, or to act in the stead of, the public officer.

(2) **Power to act for ministers** — Words directing or empowering a minister of the Crown to do an act or thing, regardless of whether the act or thing is administrative, legislative or judicial, or otherwise applying to that minister as the holder of the office, include

(a) a minister acting for that minister or, if the office is vacant, a minister designated to act in the office by or under the authority of an order in council;

(b) the successors of that minister in the office;

(c) his or their deputy; and

(d) notwithstanding paragraph (c), a person appointed to serve, in the department or ministry of state over which the minister presides, in a capacity appropriate to the doing of the act or thing, or to the words so applying.

(3) **Restriction as to public servants** — Nothing in paragraph (2)(c) or (d) shall be construed as authorizing the exercise of any authority conferred on a minister to make a regulation as defined in the *Statutory Instruments Act*.

(4) **Successors to and deputy of public officer** — Words directing or empowering any public officer, other than a minister of the Crown, to do any act or thing, or otherwise applying to the public officer by his name of office, include his successors in the office and his or their deputy.

(5) **Powers of holder of public office** — Where a power is conferred or a duty imposed on the holder of an office, the power may be exercised and the duty shall be performed by the person for the time being charged with the execution of the powers and duties of the office.

## Evidence

**25. (1) Documentary evidence** — Where an enactment provides that a document is evidence of a fact without anything in the context to indicate that the document is conclusive evidence, then, in any judicial proceedings, the document is admissible in evidence and the fact is deemed to be established in the absence of any evidence to the contrary.

(2) **Queen's printer** — Every copy of an enactment having printed thereon what purports to be the name or title of the Queen's Printer and Controller of Stationery or the Queen's Printer is deemed to be a copy purporting to be printed by the Queen's Printer for Canada.

## Computation of Time

**26. Time limits and holidays** — Where the time limited for the doing of a thing expires or falls on a holiday, the thing may be done on the day next following that is not a holiday.

Notes: "Holiday" is defined in 35(1) to include Sundays. Where a deadline for filing a document with a government agency expires on a Saturday, the case law suggests that it may be extended to the next business day.

**27. (1) Clear days** — Where there is a reference to a number of clear days or "at least" a number of days between two events, in calculating that number of days the days on which the events happen are excluded.

(2) **Not clear days** — Where there is a reference to a number of days, not expressed to be clear days, between two events, in calculating that number of days the day on which the first event happens is excluded and the day on which the second event happens is included.

(3) **Beginning and ending of prescribed periods** — Where a time is expressed to begin or end at, on or with a specified day, or to continue to or until a specified day, the time includes that day.

(4) **After specified day** — Where a time is expressed to begin after or to be from a specified day, the time does not include that day.

Notes: In *Brunette* (TCC, 98-2080(IT)I, December 16, 1999), the Court held that 27(4) applies to exclude the day of the initial assessment from the calculation of the 3-year reassessment limit in ITA 152(3.1).

(5) **Within a time** — Where anything is to be done within a time after, from, of or before a specified day, the time does not include that day.

**28. Calculation of a period of months after or before a specified day** — Where there is a reference to a period of time consisting of a number of months after or before a specified day, the period is calculated by

(a) counting forward or backward from the specified day the number of months, without including the month in which that day falls;

(b) excluding the specified day; and

(c) including in the last month counted under paragraph (a) the day that has the same calendar number as the specified day or, if that month has no day with that number, the last day of that month.

**29. Time of the day** — Where there is a reference to time expressed as a specified time of the day, the time is taken to mean standard time.

**Notes**: This rule is somewhat counterintuitive during the summer months. See 35(1) for the definition of "standard time".

**30. Time when specified age attained** — A person is deemed not to have attained a specified number of years of age until the commencement of the anniversary, of the same number, of the day of that person's birth.

## Miscellaneous Rules

**31. (1) Reference to magistrate, etc.** — Where anything is required or authorized to be done by or before a judge, magistrate, justice of the peace, or any functionary or officer, it shall be done by or before one whose jurisdiction or powers extend to the place where the thing is to be done.

**(2) Ancillary powers** — Where power is given to a person, officer or functionary, to do or enforce the doing of any act or thing, all such powers as are necessary to enable the person, officer or functionary to do or enforce the doing of the act or thing are deemed to be also given.

**(3) Powers to be exercised as required** — Where a power is conferred or a duty imposed, the power may be exercised and the duty shall be performed from time to time as occasion requires.

**(4) Power to repeal** — Where a power is conferred to make regulations, the power shall be construed as including a power, exercisable in the same manner and subject to the same consent and conditions, if any, to repeal, amend or vary the regulations and make others.

**32. Forms** — Where a form is prescribed, deviations from that form, not affecting the substance or calculated to mislead, do not invalidate the form used.

**33. (1) Gender** — Words importing female persons include male persons and corporations and words importing male persons include female persons and corporations.

**(2) Number** — Words in the singular include the plural, and words in the plural include the singular.

**(3) Parts of speech and grammatical forms** — Where a word is defined, other parts of speech and grammatical forms of the same word have corresponding meanings.

## Offences

**34. (1) Indictable and summary conviction offences** — Where an enactment creates an offence,

(a) the offence is deemed to be an indictable offence if the enactment provides that the offender may be prosecuted for the offence by indictment;

(b) the offence is deemed to be one for which the offender is punishable on summary conviction if there is nothing in the context to indicate that the offence is an indictable offence; and

(c) if the offence is one for which the offender may be prosecuted by indictment or for which the offender is punishable on summary conviction, no person shall be considered to have been convicted of an indictable offence by reason only of having been convicted of the offence on summary conviction.

**(2) *Criminal Code* to apply** — All the provisions of the *Criminal Code* relating to indictable offences apply to indictable offences created by an enactment, and all the provisions of that Code relating to summary conviction offences apply to all other offences created by an enactment, except to the extent that the enactment otherwise provides.

**(3) Documents similarly construed** — In a commission, proclamation, warrant or other document relating to criminal law or procedure in criminal matters

(a) a reference to an offence for which the offender may be prosecuted by indictment shall be construed as a reference to an indictable offence; and

(b) a reference to any other offence shall be construed as a reference to an offence for which the offender is punishable on summary conviction.

## Powers to Enter Dwelling-houses to Carry out Arrests

**34.1 Authorization to enter dwelling house** — Any person who may issue a warrant to arrest or apprehend a person under any Act of Parliament, other than the *Criminal Code*, has the same powers, subject to the same terms and conditions, as a judge or justice has under the *Criminal Code*

(a) to authorize the entry into a dwelling-house described in the warrant for the purpose of arresting or apprehending the person, if the person issuing the warrant is satisfied by information on oath that there are reasonable grounds to believe that the person is or will be present in the dwelling-house; and

(b) to authorize the entry into the dwelling-house without prior announcement if the requirement of subsection 529.4(1) is met.

## Definitions

**35. (1) General definitions** — In every enactment,

"**Act**", as meaning an Act of a legislature, includes an ordinance of the Yukon Territory or of the Northwest Territories and a law made by the Legislature for Nunavut or continued by section 29 of the *Nunavut Act*;

Notes: Amended by 1993, c. 28, Sch. III, s. 82, to add reference to "Nunavut", in force April 1, 1999.

**"bank"** means a bank listed in Schedule I or II to the *Bank Act*;

Notes: "Bank" added by 1999, c. 28, s. 168, in force June 28, 1999.

**"British Commonwealth"** or **"British Commonwealth of Nations"** has the same meaning as "Commonwealth";

**"broadcasting"** means any radiocommunication in which the transmissions are intended for direct reception by the general public;

**"Canada"**, for greater certainty, includes the internal waters of Canada and the territorial sea of Canada;

Notes: "Canada" added by *Oceans Act* (Bill C-26, 1996, c. 31), proclaimed in force January 31, 1997 (SI/97-21).

**"Canadian waters"** includes the territorial sea of Canada and the internal waters of Canada;

Notes: "Canadian waters" added by *Oceans Act* (Bill C-26, 1996, c. 31), proclaimed in force January 31, 1997 (SI/97-21).

**"Clerk of the Privy Council"** or **"Clerk of the Queen's Privy Council"** means the Clerk of the Privy Council and Secretary to the Cabinet;

**"commencement"**, when used with reference to an enactment, means the time at which the enactment comes into force;

**"Commonwealth"** or **"Commonwealth of Nations"** means the association of countries named in the schedule;

**"Commonwealth and Dependent Territories"** means the several Commonwealth countries and their colonies, possessions, dependencies, protectorates, protected states, condominiums and trust territories;

**"contiguous zone"**,

(a) in relation to Canada, means the contiguous zone of Canada as determined under the *Oceans Act*,

(b) in relation to any other state, means the contiguous zone of the other state as determined in accordance with international law and the domestic laws of that other state;

Notes: "Contiguous zone" added by *Oceans Act* (Bill C-26, 1996, c. 31), proclaimed in force January 31, 1997 (SI/97-21).

**"continental shelf"**,

(a) in relation to Canada, means the continental shelf of Canada as determined under the *Oceans Act*, and

(b) in relation to any other state, means the continental shelf of the other state as determined in accordance with international law and the domestic laws of that other state;

Notes: "Continental shelf" added by *Oceans Act* (Bill C-26, 1996, c. 31), proclaimed in force January 31, 1997 (SI/97-21).

**"contravene"** includes fail to comply with;

**"corporation"** does not include a partnership that is considered to be a separate legal entity under provincial law;

**"county"** includes two or more counties united for purposes to which the enactment relates;

**"diplomatic or consular officer"** includes an ambassador, envoy, minister, chargé d'affaires, counsellor, secretary, attaché, consul-general, consul, vice-consul, pro-consul, consular agent, acting consul-general, acting consul, acting vice-consul, acting consular agent, high commissioner, permanent delegate, adviser, acting high commissioner, and acting permanent delegate;

**"exclusive economic zone"**,

(a) in relation to Canada, means the exclusive economic zone of Canada as determined under the *Oceans Act* and includes the seabed and subsoil below that zone, and

(b) in relation to any other state, means the exclusive economic zone of the other state as determined in accordance with international law and the domestic laws of that other state;

Notes: "Exclusive economic zone" added by *Oceans Act* (Bill C-26, 1996, c. 31), proclaimed in force January 31, 1997 (SI/97-21).

**"Federal Court"** means the Federal Court of Canada;

**Proposed Repeal — 35(1) "Federal Court"**

Application: Bill C-40 (First Reading June 15, 2000), subsec. 147(1), will repeal the definition "Federal Court" in subsec. 35(1), in force on a day to be fixed by order of the Governor in Council.

**"Federal Court–Appeal Division"** or **"Federal Court of Appeal"** means that division of the Federal Court of Canada called the Federal Court–Appeal Division or referred to as the Federal Court of Appeal by the *Federal Court Act*;

**Proposed Repeal — 35(1) "Federal Court–Appeal Division" or "Federal Court of Appeal"**

Application: Bill C-40 (First Reading June 15, 2000), subsec. 147(1), will repeal the definition "Federal Court–Appeal Division" or "Federal Court of Appeal" in subsec. 35(1), in force on a day to be fixed by order of the Governor in Council.

**"Federal Court–Trial Division"** means that division of the Federal Court of Canada so named by the *Federal Court Act*;

**Proposed Repeal — 35(1) "Federal Court–Trial Division"**

Application: Bill C-40 (First Reading June 15, 2000), subsec. 147(1), will repeal the definition "Federal Court–Trial Division" in subsec. 35(1), in force on a day to be fixed by order of the Governor in Council.

"**Governor**", "**Governor General**"; or "**Governor of Canada**" means the Governor General of Canada or other chief executive officer or administrator carrying on the Government of Canada on behalf and in the name of the Sovereign, by whatever title that officer is designated;

"**Governor General in Council**" or "**Governor in Council**" means the Governor General of Canada acting by and with the advice of, or by and with the advice and consent of, or in conjunction with the Queen's Privy Council for Canada;
Notes: This means the federal Cabinet.

"**Great Seal**" means the Great Seal of Canada;

"**Her Majesty**", "**His Majesty**", "**the Queen**", "**the King**" or "**the Crown**" means the Sovereign of the United Kingdom, Canada and Her other Realms and Territories, and Head of the Commonwealth;

"**Her Majesty's Realms and Territories**" means all realms and territories under the sovereignty of Her Majesty;

"**herein**" used in any section shall be understood to relate to the whole enactment, and not to that section only;

"**holiday**" means any of the following days, namely, Sunday; New Year's Day; Good Friday; Easter Monday; Christmas Day; the birthday or the day fixed by proclamation for the celebration of the birthday of the reigning Sovereign[1]; Victoria Day; Canada Day; the first Monday in September, designated Labour Day; Remembrance Day; any day appointed by proclamation to be observed as a day of general prayer or mourning or day of public rejoicing or thanksgiving[2]; and any of the following additional days, namely:

(a) in any province, any day appointed by proclamation of the lieutenant governor of the province to be observed as a public holiday or as a day of general prayer or mourning or day of public rejoicing or thanksgiving within the province, and any day that is a non-juridical day by virtue of an Act of the legislature of the province, and

(b) in any city, town, municipality or other organized district, any day appointed to be observed as a civic holiday by resolution of the council or other authority charged with the administration of the civic or municipal affairs of the city, town, municipality or district;

"**internal waters**",

(a) in relation to Canada, means the internal waters of Canada as determined under the *Oceans Act* and includes the airspace above and the bed and subsoil below those waters, and

(b) in relation to any other state, means the waters on the landward side of the baselines of the territorial sea of the other state;
Notes: "Internal waters" added by *Oceans Act* (Bill C-26, 1996, c. 31), proclaimed in force January 31, 1997 (SI/97-21).

"**legislative assembly**", "**legislative council**" or "**legislature**" includes the Lieutenant Governor in Council and the Legislative Assembly of the Northwest Territories, as constituted before September 1, 1905, the Commissioner in Council of the Yukon Territory, the Commissioner in Council of the Northwest Territories, and the Legislature for Nunavut;
Notes: Amended by 1993, c. 28, Sch. III, s. 82, to add reference to Nunavut, in force April 1, 1999.

"**lieutenant governor**" means the lieutenant governor or other chief executive officer or administrator carrying on the government of the province indicated by the enactment, by whatever title that officer is designated, and, in relation to the Yukon Territory, the Northwest Territories or Nunavut, means the Commissioner thereof;
Notes: Amended by 1993, c. 28, Sch. III, s. 82, to add reference to Nunavut, in force April 1, 1999.

"**lieutenant governor in council**" means the lieutenant governor acting by and with the advice of, or by and with the advice and consent of, or in conjunction with the executive council of the province indicated by the enactment and, in relation to the Yukon Territory, the Northwest Territories or Nunavut, means the Commissioner thereof;
Notes: Amended by 1993, c. 28, Sch. III, s. 82, to add reference to Nunavut, in force April 1, 1999.

"**local time**", in relation to any place, means the time observed in that place for the regulation of business hours;

"**military**" shall be construed as relating to all or any part of the Canadian Forces;

"**month**" means a calendar month;

"**oath**" includes a solemn affirmation or declaration when the context applies to any person by whom and to any case in which a solemn affirmation or declaration may be made instead of an oath, and in the same cases the expression "sworn" includes the expression "affirmed" or "declared";

"**Parliament**" means the Parliament of Canada;

"**person**" or any word or expression descriptive of a person, includes a corporation;

"**proclamation**" means a proclamation under the Great Seal;

---

[1] The Monday immediately preceding May 25 (SOR/57-55, *Canada Gazette*, Part II, February 27, 1957).

[2] The second Monday in October (SOR/57-56, *Canada Gazette*, Part II, February 27, 1957).

"**province**" means a province of Canada, and includes the Yukon Territory, the Northwest Territories and Nunavut;

**Notes**: Amended by 1993, c. 28, Sch. III, s. 82, to add reference to Nunavut, in force April 1, 1999.

"**radio**" or "**radiocommunication**" means any transmission, emission or reception of signs, signals, writing, images, sounds or intelligence of any nature by means of electromagnetic waves of frequencies lower than 3000 GHz propagated in space without artificial guide;

"**regular force**" means the component of the Canadian Forces that is referred to in the *National Defence Act* as the regular force;

"**reserve force**" means the component of the Canadian Forces that is referred to in the *National Defence Act* as the reserve force;

"**security**" means sufficient security, and "sureties" means sufficient sureties, and when those words are used one person is sufficient therefor, unless otherwise expressly required;

"**standard time**", except as otherwise provided by any proclamation of the Governor in Council that may be issued for the purposes of this definition in relation to any province or territory or any part thereof, means

(a) in relation to the Province of Newfoundland, Newfoundland standard time, being three hours and thirty minutes behind Greenwich time,

(b) in relation to the Provinces of Nova Scotia, New Brunswick and Prince Edward Island, that part of the Province of Quebec lying east of the sixty-third meridian of west longitude, and that part of Nunavut lying east of the sixty-eighth meridian of west longitude, Atlantic standard time, being four hours behind Greenwich time,

(c) in relation to that part of the Province of Quebec lying west of the sixty-third meridian of west longitude, that part of the Province of Ontario lying between the sixty-eighth and the ninetieth meridians of west longitude, Southampton Island and the islands adjacent to Southampton Island, and that part of Nunavut lying between the sixty-eighth and the eighty-fifth meridians of west longitude, eastern standard time, being five hours behind Greenwich time,

(d) in relation to that part of the Province of Ontario lying west of the ninetieth meridian of west longitude, the Province of Manitoba, and that part of Nunavut, except Southampton Island and the islands adjacent to Southampton Island, lying between the eighty-fifth and the one hundred and second meridians of west longitude, central standard time, being six hours behind Greenwich time,

(e) in relation to the Provinces of Saskatchewan and Alberta, the Northwest Territories and that part of Nunavut lying west of the one hundred and second meridian of west longitude, mountain standard time, being seven hours behind Greenwich time,

(f) in relation to the Province of British Columbia, Pacific standard time, being eight hours behind Greenwich time, and

(g) in relation to the Yukon Territory, Yukon standard time, being nine hours behind Greenwich time;

**Notes**: Despite paras. (b)–(d), all of Nunavut standard time is 6 hours behind Greenwich time, in order to keep the territory in the same time zone. This change was made by Order-in Council SOR/99-408, October 20, 1999 (*Canada Gazette* Part II, Vol. 133, November 10, 1999, No. 23).

Paragraphs (b) to (e) amended by 1993, c. 28, Sch. III, s. 82, to add references to Nunavut, in force April 1, 1999.

"**statutory declaration**" means a solemn declaration made pursuant to section 41 of the *Canada Evidence Act*;

"**superior court**" means

(a) in the Province of Prince Edward Island or Newfoundland, the Supreme Court,

(a.1) in the Province of Ontario, the Court of Appeal for Ontario and the Superior Court of Justice,

(b) in the Province of Quebec, the Court of Appeal and the Superior Court in and for the Province,

(c) in the Province of New Brunswick, Manitoba, Saskatchewan or Alberta, the Court of Appeal for the Province and the Court of Queen's Bench for the Province,

(d) in the Provinces of Nova Scotia and British Columbia, the Court of Appeal and the Supreme Court of the Province, and

(e) in the Yukon Territory or the Northwest Territories, the Supreme Court of the territory, and in Nunavut, the Nunavut Court of Justice,

and includes the Supreme Court of Canada and the Federal Court of Canada;

**Proposed Amendment — 35(1)"superior court" closing words**

and includes the Supreme Court of Canada, the Federal Court of Appeal, the Federal Court and the Tax Court of Canada;

**Application**: Bill C-40 (First Reading June 15, 2000), subsec. 147(2), will amend the closing words of the definition "superior court" in subsec. 35(1) to read as above, in force on a day to be fixed by order of the Governor in Council.

**Notes**: Amended by S.C. 1999, c. 3 to change "the Supreme Court thereof" to the existing wording (i.e., changing Nunavut reference to the Nunavut Court of Justice).

Amended by 1993, c. 28, Sch. III, s. 82, in force April 1, 1999.

"**telecommunications**" means the emission, transmission or reception of signs, signals, writing, images, sounds or intelligence of any nature by wire, cable, radio, optical or other electromagnetic system, or by any similar technical system;

**"territorial sea"**,

(a) in relation to Canada, means the territorial sea of Canada as determined under the *Oceans Act* and includes the airspace above and the seabed and subsoil below that sea, and

(b) in relation to any other state, means the territorial sea of the other state as determined in accordance with international law and the domestic laws of that other state;

Notes: "Territorial sea" added by *Oceans Act* (Bill C-26, 1996, c. 31), proclaimed in force January 31, 1997 (SI/97-21).

**"territory"** means the Yukon Territory, the Northwest Territories and, after section 3 of the *Nunavut Act* comes into force, Nunavut;

**"two justices"** means two or more justices of the peace, assembled or acting together;

**"United Kingdom"** means the United Kingdom of Great Britain and Northern Ireland;

**"United States"** means the United States of America;

**"writing"**, or any term of like import, includes words printed, typewritten, painted, engraved, lithographed, photographed or represented or reproduced by any mode of representing or reproducing words in visible form.

Notes: This definition applies to the word "written" as well. See subsec. 33(3).

(2) **Governor in Council may amend schedule** — The Governor in Council may, by order, amend the schedule by adding thereto the name of any country recognized by the order to be a member of the Commonwealth or deleting therefrom the name of any country recognized by the order to be no longer a member of the Commonwealth.

**36. Construction of "telegraph"** — The expression "telegraph" and its derivatives, in an enactment or in an Act of the legislature of any province enacted before that province became part of Canada on any subject that is within the legislative powers of Parliament, are deemed not to include the word "telephone" or its derivatives.

**37. (1) Construction of "year"** — The expression "year" means any period of twelve consecutive months, except that a reference

(a) to a "calendar year" means a period of twelve consecutive months commencing on January 1;

(b) to a "financial year" or "fiscal year" means, in relation to money provided by Parliament, or the Consolidated Revenue Fund, or the accounts, taxes or finances of Canada, the period beginning on April 1 in one calendar year and ending on March 31 in the next calendar year; and

(c) by number to a Dominical year means the period of twelve consecutive months commencing on January 1 of that Dominical year.

(2) **Governor in Council may define year** — Where in an enactment relating to the affairs of Parliament or the Government of Canada there is a reference to a period of a year without anything in the context to indicate beyond doubt whether a financial or fiscal year, any period of twelve consecutive months or a period of twelve consecutive months commencing on January 1 is intended, the Governor in Council may prescribe which of those periods of twelve consecutive months shall constitute a year for the purposes of the enactment.

**38. Common names** — The name commonly applied to any country, place, body, corporation, society, officer, functionary, person, party or thing means the country, place, body, corporation, society, officer, functionary, person, party or thing to which the name is commonly applied, although the name is not the formal or extended designation thereof.

**39. (1) Affirmative and negative resolutions** — In every Act

(a) the expression "subject to affirmative resolution of Parliament", when used in relation to any regulation, means that the regulation shall be laid before Parliament within fifteen days after it is made or, if Parliament is not then sitting, on any of the first fifteen days next thereafter that Parliament is sitting and shall not come into force unless and until it is affirmed by a resolution of both Houses of Parliament introduced and passed in accordance with the rules of those Houses;

(b) the expression "subject to affirmative resolution of the House of Commons", when used in relation to any regulation, means that the regulation shall be laid before the House of Commons within fifteen days after it is made or, if the House is not then sitting, on any of the first fifteen days next thereafter that the House is sitting and shall not come into force unless and until it is affirmed by a resolution of the House of Commons introduced and passed in accordance with the rules of that House;

(c) the expression "subject to negative resolution of Parliament", when used in relation to any regulation, means that the regulation shall be laid before Parliament within fifteen days after it is made or, if Parliament is not then sitting, on any of the first fifteen days next thereafter that Parliament is sitting and may be annulled by a resolution of both Houses of Parliament introduced and passed in accordance with the rules of those Houses; and

(d) the expression "subject to negative resolution of the House of Commons", when used in relation to any regulation, means that the regulation shall be laid before the House of Commons within fifteen days after it is made or, if the House is not then sitting, on any of the first fifteen days next thereafter that Parliament is sitting and may be annulled by a resolution of the House of Commons introduced and passed in accordance with the rules of that House.

(2) **Effect of negative resolution** — Where a regulation is annulled by a resolution of Parliament or of the House of Commons, it is deemed to have been revoked on the day the resolution is passed and any law that was revoked or amended by the making of that regulation is deemed to be revived on the day the resolution is passed, but the validity of any action taken or not taken in compliance with a regulation so deemed to have been revoked shall not be affected by the resolution.

## References and Citations

40. (1) **Citation of enactment** — In an enactment or document

(a) an Act may be cited by reference to its chapter number in the Revised Statutes, by reference to its chapter number in the volume of Acts for the year or regnal year in which it was enacted or by reference to its long title or short title, with or without reference to its chapter number; and

(b) a regulation may be cited by reference to its long title or short title, by reference to the Act under which it was made or by reference to the number or designation under which it was registered by the Clerk of the Privy Council.

(2) **Citation includes amendment** — A citation of or reference to an enactment is deemed to be a citation of or reference to the enactment as amended.

41. (1) **Reference to two or more parts, etc.** — A reference in an enactment by number or letter to two or more parts, divisions, sections, subsections, paragraphs, subparagraphs, clauses, subclauses, schedules, appendices or forms shall be read as including the number or letter first mentioned and the number or letter last mentioned.

(2) **Reference in enactments to parts, etc.** — A reference in an enactment to a part, division, section, schedule, appendix or form shall be read as a reference to a part, division, section, schedule, appendix or form of the enactment in which the reference occurs.

(3) **Reference in enactment to subsections, etc.** — A reference in an enactment to a subsection, paragraph, subparagraph, clause or subclause shall be read as a reference to a subsection, paragraph, subparagraph, clause or subclause of the section, subsection, paragraph, subparagraph or clause, as the case may be, in which the reference occurs.

(4) **Reference to regulations** — A reference in an enactment to regulations shall be read as a reference to regulations made under the enactment in which the reference occurs.

(5) **Reference to another enactment** — A reference in an enactment by number or letter to any section, subsection, paragraph, subparagraph, clause, subclause or other division or line of another enactment shall be read as a reference to the section, subsection, paragraph, subparagraph, clause, subclause or other division or line of such other enactment as printed by authority of law.

## Repeal and Amendment

42. (1) **Power of repeal or amendment reserved** — Every Act shall be so construed as to reserve to Parliament the power of repealing or amending it, and of revoking, restricting or modifying any power, privilege or advantage thereby vested in or granted to any person.

(2) **Amendment or repeal at same session** — An Act may be amended or repealed by an Act passed in the same session of Parliament.

(3) **Amendment part of enactment** — An amending enactment, as far as consistent with the tenor thereof, shall be construed as part of the enactment that it amends.

43. **Effect of repeal** — Where an enactment is repealed in whole or in part, the repeal does not

(a) revive any enactment or anything not in force or existing at the time when the repeal takes effect,

(b) affect the previous operation of the enactment so repealed or anything duly done or suffered thereunder,

(c) affect any right, privilege, obligation or liability acquired, accrued, accruing or incurred under the enactment so repealed,

(d) affect any offence committed against or contravention of the provisions of the enactment so repealed, or any punishment, penalty or forfeiture incurred under the enactment so repealed, or

(e) affect any investigation, legal proceeding or remedy in respect of any right, privilege, obligation or liability referred to in paragraph (c) or in respect of any punishment, penalty or forfeiture referred to in paragraph (d),

and an investigation, legal proceeding or remedy as described in paragraph (e) may be instituted, continued or enforced, and the punishment, penalty or forfeiture may be imposed as if the enactment had not been so repealed.

44. **Repeal and substitution** — Where an enactment, in this section called the "former enactment",

is repealed and another enactment, in this section called the "new enactment", is substituted therefor,

(a) every person acting under the former enactment shall continue to act, as if appointed under the new enactment, until another is appointed in the stead of that person;

(b) every bond and security given by a person appointed under the former enactment remains in force, and all books, papers, forms and things made or used under the former enactment shall continue to be used as before the repeal in so far as they are consistent with the new enactment;

(c) every proceeding taken under the former enactment shall be taken up and continued under and in conformity with the new enactment in so far as it may be done consistently with the new enactment;

(d) the procedure established by the new enactment shall be followed as far as it can be adapted thereto

(i) in the recovery or enforcement of fines, penalties and forfeitures imposed under the former enactment,

(ii) in the enforcement of rights, existing or accruing under the former enactment, and

(iii) in a proceeding in relation to matters that have happened before the repeal;

(e) when any punishment, penalty or forfeiture is reduced or mitigated by the new enactment, the punishment, penalty or forfeiture if imposed or adjudged after the repeal shall be reduced or mitigated accordingly;

(f) except to the extent that the provisions of the new enactment are not in substance the same as those of the former enactment, the new enactment shall not be held to operate as new law, but shall be construed and have effect as a consolidation and as declaratory of the law as contained in the former enactment;

(g) all regulations made under the repealed enactment remain in force and are deemed to have been made under the new enactment, in so far as they are not inconsistent with the new enactment, until they are repealed or others made in their stead; and

(h) any reference in an unrepealed enactment to the former enactment shall, with respect to a subsequent transaction, matter or thing, be read and construed as a reference to the provisions of the new enactment relating to the same subject-matter as the former enactment, but where there are no provisions in the new enactment relating to the same subject-matter, the former enactment shall be read as unrepealed in so far as is necessary to maintain or give effect to the unrepealed enactment.

**45. (1) Repeal does not imply enactment was in force** — The repeal of an enactment in whole or in part shall not be deemed to be or to involve a declaration that the enactment was previously in force or was considered by Parliament or other body or person by whom the enactment was enacted to have been previously in force.

**(2) Amendment does not imply change in law** — The amendment of an enactment shall not be deemed to be or to involve a declaration that the law under that enactment was or was considered by Parliament or other body or person by whom the enactment was enacted to have been different from the law as it is under the enactment as amended.

Notes: This does not mean that amendments do not change the law, but only that there is no presumption that they must change the law. See *HSC Research Development Corp.*, [1995] 1 C.T.C. 2283 (TCC) at 2293-94.

**(3) Repeal does not declare previous law** — The repeal or amendment of an enactment in whole or in part shall not be deemed to be or to involve any declaration as to the previous state of the law.

**(4) Judicial construction not adopted** — A re-enactment, revision, consolidation or amendment of an enactment shall not be deemed to be or to involve an adoption of the construction that has by judicial decision or otherwise been placed on the language used in the enactment or on similar language.

## Demise of Crown

**46. (1) Effect of demise** — Where there is a demise of the Crown,

(a) the demise does not affect the holding of any office under the Crown in right of Canada; and

(b) it is not necessary by reason of such demise that the holder of any such office again be appointed thereto or, having taken an oath of office or allegiance before the demise, again take that oath.

**(2) Continuation of proceedings** — No writ, action or other process or proceeding, civil or criminal, in or issuing out of any court established by an Act is, by reason of a demise of the Crown, determined, abated, discontinued or affected, but every such writ, action, process or proceeding remains in full force and may be enforced, carried on or otherwise proceeded with or completed as though there had been no such demise.

# SCHEDULE

(*section 35 "Commonwealth"*)

Antigua and Barbuda
Australia
The Bahamas
Bangladesh

Schedule | Schedule

| | |
|---|---|
| Barbados | Nigeria |
| Belize | Pakistan |
| Botswana | Papua New Guinea |
| Brunei Darussalam | St. Christopher and Nevis |
| Canada | St. Lucia |
| Cyprus | St. Vincent and the Grenadines |
| Dominica | Seychelles |
| Fiji | Sierra Leone |
| Gambia | Singapore |
| Ghana | Solomon Islands |
| Grenada | South Africa |
| Guyana | Sri Lanka |
| India | Swaziland |
| Jamaica | Tanzania |
| Kenya | Tonga |
| Kiribati | Trinidad and Tobago |
| Lesotho | Tuvalu |
| Malawi | Uganda |
| Malaysia | United Kingdom |
| Maldives | Vanuatu |
| Malta | Western Samoa |
| Mauritius | Zambia |
| Nauru | Zimbabwe |
| New Zealand | |

Contract - Elements
- must be offer + acceptance
- certainty of terms (ie price)
- consideration
- capacity to contract
- requirement of legality

Breach occurs when one party repudiates contract

General rule - only a party to a contract may enforce unless assigned to 3rd party

Remedies for Breach on Contract
→ Damages
→ Specific performance
→ Injunction (interim + mandatory)

Tort Law - Conditions for negligent misrepresentation:

→ must be a duty of care
→ must be a negligent misrepresentation
→ reliance on that misrepresentation
→ loss to that person arising from the misrep.

Cases to consider
↳ Hedley Byrne - would have been liable if not for express disclaimer

↳ Haig v. Bamford - concept of foreseeability

Common law remedies - deal w/ duties of directors to corp.ⁿ
   i.e act in best interest of company, not appropriate corp opp.
   etc. - while CBCA goes beyond and provides remedies for
   wronged minority SlH's

Dissent remedy (s. 190) - created entirely from statute
Oppression remedy (s. 241) - most significant adv. in
   corp. law because it so far ranging

Conflict of interest - self-dealing remedy that provides
   the parameters for a director entering into a contract w/
   a corporation in which he has an interest


Legal relationship b/w corp + S/H's is arm's length. The
S/H's owe no duty to the corp.ⁿ. Based on Dusik, the S/H's
may owe a duty to one another in respect of full disclosure
where corp.ⁿ is closely held and where the S/H's act in a
analogous manner to partners in carrying on business.

If a S/H becomes a director, 1st matter to consider is the duties
of the director

# INDEX

Note: References are to sections of the *Income Tax Act*. "Reg." references are to the *Income Tax Regulations*. "Reg. Sch. II:Cl." are references to the capital cost allowance Classes in Schedule II of the *Income Tax Regulations*, reproduced at the end of the Regulations. "ITAR" references are to the *Income Tax Application Rules*, reproduced after the text of the *Income Tax Act*.

## A

**ABIL**, *see* Allowable business investment loss
**ACB**, *see* Adjusted cost base
**ACB reduction**
- defined, for small business investment capital gain rollover, 44.1(1)

**AFB**, *see* Authorized foreign bank
**AMT (Alternative Minimum Tax)**, *see* Minimum tax
**APA**, *see* Advance Pricing Agreement
**AVC**, *see* Additional voluntary contribution (AVC) [to pension plan]
**Abatement of tax**
- corporations, 124(1)
- • manufacturing and processing credit, 125.1
- • small business deduction, 125
- individuals, re provincial schooling allowance, 120(2), Reg. 6401

**Abeyance letter**, 225.1(5)
**Aboriginal peoples**, *see* Indians
**Absconding taxpayer**, 226
**Acceleration clause exercised by creditor**, 20(1)(n)
**Access road**
- access rights to, 13(7.5)(c)
- forest, Reg. Sch. II:Cl. 10(p)

**Accident claims**, *see also* Accident insurance plan
- motor vehicle, payments exempt, 81(1)(q), Reg. 6501

**Accident insurance plan**
- death coverage is not group life insurance, Reg. 2700(2)
- employer's contribution not a taxable benefit, 6(1)(a)(i)
- payment to employee under, taxable, 6(1)(f), ITAR 19

**Accountant**, *see also* Professional practice
- penalty for misrepresentation by, 163.2

**Accounting**
- accrual method for profession, 34
- branch
- • insurer, by, 138(9)
- • 1975 election deficiency, defined, 138(12)"1975 branch accounting election deficiency"
- cash method for farmers, etc., 28(1)–(3)
- consolidation method prohibited, 61.3(1)(b)C(i), 248(24)
- equity method prohibited, 61.3(1)(b)C(i), 248(24)

**Accounting profit**
- defined, 94(1)

**Accounts**
- contingent, limitation on deductibility, 18(1)(e)
- factoring of, *see* Factoring of accounts
- penalty for failure to keep, 238(1), 239(1)(b)
- receivable, *see* Accounts receivable

- separate, for tax deductions
- • penalty for default, 238(1)
- tax, transfers of payments among, 211.2
- to be kept, 230(1)

**Accounts receivable**
- bad, *see* Bad debt
- ceasing to carry on business, on, 28(5)
- doubtful, reserve for, 12(1)(d), 20(1)(l)
- factoring of, *see* Factoring of accounts
- sale of, 22

**Accredited film or video production certificate**, 125.5(1)
**Accredited production**
- defined, for film/video production services credit, 125.5(1), Reg. 9300

**Accrual method of reporting income**
- income not previously included, ITAR 17(5)
- professional business from, 34

**Accrued interest**, *see* Interest (monetary): accrued
**Accrued return (from specified debt obligation)**
- defined, Reg. 9102(1), (3)

**Accumulated income payment**, *see* Registered education savings plan: Accumulated income payment
**Accumulated 1968 deficit**
- defined, 219(7)

**Accumulated overpayment amount**
- defined, for corporate interest offset, 161.1(1)

**Accumulated PSPA**
- defined, Reg. 8303(1)(a), 8303(2)

**Accumulated underpayment amount**
- defined, for corporate interest offset, 161.1(1)

**Accumulating fund**
- computation of, Reg. 307
- defined, Reg. 307

**Accumulating income (of trust)**
- defined, 108(1)
- election re, *see* Preferred beneficiary: election

**Accumulation of property**
- by registered charity, 149.1(8), (9)

**Acquired for consideration**
- meaning of, 108(7)

**Acquiror (re butterfly transactions)**
- defined, 55(1)"permitted exchange"(b)

**Acquisition costs**
- of insurance policy, defined, Reg. 1408(1)

**Acquisition of control**, *see* Control of corporation: change of
**Act**, *see also* Legislation
- defined, *Interpretation Act* s. 35(1)

2647

## Index

**Actions,** *see also* Offences
- none for withholding taxes, 227(1)
- recovery of tax by Crown, for, 222

**Active business,** *see also* Small business deduction
- corporation, *see* Active business corporation
- defined, 95(1), 125(7)"active business" 125(7)"income of the corporation" 248(1), Reg. 5907(1)
- income from
  - defined, 95(1), 125(7)"income of the corporation for the year from an active business"
  - foreign affiliates, 95(1), 95(2)(a)
  - investment income from associated corporation, deemed to be, 129(6)
- income incident or pertaining to, 129(4)"income"(b)(ii)

**Active business corporation**
- defined, for small business investment capital gain rollover, 44.1(1), (10)

**Active member**
- defined, Reg. 8306(4)(a), 8500(1)

**Active partner,** *see* Partner

**Actor**
- deduction from employment income, 8(1)(q)

**Actuarial liability (of insurer, re unpaid claim)**
- deduction for unpaid claim, based on, Reg. 1400(e), (e.1) [repealed]
- defined, Reg. 1404(2) [repealed]

**Actuarial report, for registered pension plan,** 147.2(3), Reg. 8410

**Actuarial surplus**
- no transfer from RPP on death, 147.3(7)(a)
- no transfer to money-purchase RPP, RRSP or RRIF, 147.3(4)(a)
- no transfer to spouse on marriage breakdown, 147.3(5)(a)
- transfer of, 60(j.01), 147.3(4.1)

**Additional tax**
- clawback of OAS, 180.2
- income not earned in a province, 120(1)
  - minimum tax and, 120(4)"tax otherwise payable under this Part"
- non-Canadian corporations carrying on business in Canada, 219
  - limitations on, 219.2
- surtax, *see* Surtax

**Additional voluntary contribution (AVC) [to pension plan]**
- defined, 248(1)
- past service, undeducted
  - refund, 60.2(1)

**Address**
- changing, deduction for costs, 62(3)(h)

**Adjusted business income**
- application in calculation of M&P credit, Reg. 5200, 5201
- defined, Reg. 5202, 5203(1)

**Adjusted cost base,** *see also* Property
- bond or debt obligation, 53(1)(g), (g.1), 53(2)(l), (l.1), (q)
- capital interest in trust, 94(5) [to be repealed], 53(1)(m.1), 53(2)(w)
- computing
  - amounts to be added, 53(1)
  - amounts to be deducted, 53(2)
  - reduction for assistance received, 53(2)(k)
  - reduction on debt forgiveness, 53(2)(g.1), 80(9)–(11)
- debts
  - owing by predecessor corporation, 87(6), (6.1), (7); ITAR 26(23)
- defined, 54
- election to increase via capital gains exemption, 110.6(19)
- excessive election for capital gains exemption, 53(2)(v)
- expropriation asset, 53(1)(k), 53(2)(n)
- farmland, 53(1)(i)
- flow-through entity, after 2004, 53(1)(p)
- identical properties, 47(1)(c), (d); ITAR 26(8)
- indexed debt obligation, 53(1)(g.1), 53(2)(l.1)
- land, 53(1)(h), (i)
- negative, deemed gain, 40(3), (3.1)
- offshore investment fund property, 53(1)(m)
- option, of, 53(2)(g.1)
  - reduction flowed through to share, partnership interest or trust interest, 49(3.01)
  - to acquire share of predecessor, reduction on amalgamation, 87(5.1)
- partnership interest, 40(3.1), 53(1)(e), 53(2)(c), (g.1); ITAR 26(9)
- partnership property, right to receive, 53(2)(o)
- property owned since before 1972, ITAR 26(3)
- shares, 53(1)(b), (c), (d), (d.3), (f.2), (j), 53(2)(a), (b), (e), (f.1), (g.1)
  - right to acquire by deceased's estate under employee stock option agreement, 53(2)(t)
- substituted property, 53(1)(f)
- surveying costs, 53(1)(n)
- trust interest, 53(1)(d.1), (d.2), (l), 53(2)(b.1), (g.1), (h), (i), (j), (q)
- valuation costs, 53(1)(n)

**Adjusted cost basis, defined,** 148(9)

**Adjusted cumulative foreign resource expense**
- defined, 66.21(1)

**Adjusted equity,** *see also* Equity
- defined, 20.2(2)
- limit on deductibility of interest relating to distributions, 20.2(1)

**Adjusted income**
- defined
  - for Child Tax Benefit, 122.6
  - for GST credit, 122.5(1)
  - for old age security clawback, 180.2(1)
  - for refundable medical expense credit, 122.51(1), 122.6

**Adjusted principal amount, defined,** 80.1(7)
- property disposed of at other than arm's length, ITAR 26(5)
- property owned on Dec. 31/71, ITAR 26(3), (4)

**Adjusted selling cost (re investment tax credits)**
- defined, 127(11.7)
- effect on qualified expenditures, 127(11.6)(d)(ii)

**Adjusted service cost (re investment tax credits)**
- defined, 127(11.7)
- effect on qualified expenditures, 127(11.6)(c)(ii)

**Adjustment**
- at-risk, *see* At-risk adjustment (for tax shelter)
- capital setoff, *see* Transfer pricing capital setoff adjustment

# Index

**Adjustment** *(cont'd)*
- income setoff, *see* Transfer pricing income setoff adjustment
- inflation, for, *see* Indexing (for inflation)
- inventory, *see* Inventory: adjustment
- unpaid claims reserve, 20(4.2)

**Adjustment time, defined**, 14(5)

**Administration fee**
- paid to non-resident, 212(1)(a)
- - defined, 212(4)

**Administration of Act**, 220–244

**Administrator**, *see also* Legal representative
- deemed to be legal representative, 248(1)"legal representative"
- defined
- - for government-sponsored retirement arrangements, Reg. 8308.4(1)
- - for scientific research tax credits, Reg. 226(1)
- - for share purchase tax credits, Reg. 227(1)
- estate, *see* Executor
- obligations of, 159
- registered pension plan, *see* Registered pension plan: administrator
- return required by, 150(3)

**Advance Pricing Agreement**
- transfer pricing, 247

**Adventure in the nature of trade**
- constitutes business, 248(1)"business"
- - deemed carries on by corporation, 10(11)
- inventory held in, no writedown until sale, 10(1.01), (9), (10)
- superficial loss not deductible, 18(14)–(16)

**Advertisement directed at the Canadian market**
- defined, 19.01(1)

**Advertising**
- expenses, limitation on deductibility
- - foreign broadcasting media, 19.1
- - foreign (other than U.S.) periodicals, 19
- materials
- - deemed to be inventory, 10(5)
- - valuation of, 10(4)
- show, ineligible for Canadian film/video credit, Reg. 1106(1)"excluded production"(b)
- show, ineligible for film/video production services credit, Reg. 9300(k)
- signs and posters, capital cost allowance, Reg. Sch. II:Cl. 11

**Advisory committee, dues paid by employee, deduction**, 8(1)(i)(vi)

**Advocate (in Quebec)**, *see* Lawyer

***Aeronautics Act*, compensation under, exemption**, 81(1)(d)

**Aeroplane**, *see* Aircraft

**Affiliate**, *see also* Affiliated person; Foreign affiliate; Subsidiary
- defined, for foreign property rules, 206(1)

**Affiliated person**
- acquisition of capital property by, 40(3.3), (3.4)
- acquisition of depreciable property by, 13(21.2)
- acquisition of eligible capital property by, 14(12)
- acquisition of inventory by
- - previously held as adventure in nature of trade, 18(14)–(16)
- - previously held by financial institution, 18(13), (15)
- defined, 251.1

**African Development Bank**
- bonds of
- - eligible for RRSP investment, Reg. 4900(1)(l)(vi)
- - excluded from foreign property, 206(1)"foreign property"(g)(iv.2)
- - trust investing in, not foreign property, Reg. 5000(7)"specified international finance trust"(c)(i)(A)

**Age**
- 7
- - under
- - - child care expenses, 63(3)"annual child care expense amount"(b)(i)
- - - Child Tax Benefit enhanced, 122.61(1)A(c)D
- 16
- - under
- - - child care expenses, 63(3)"eligible child"(c)
- - - education credit for vocational training disallowed, 118.6(2)B
- - - tuition credit disallowed, 118.5(1)(a)(ii.2)(A)
- 17
- - under, kiddie tax (split income), 120.4(1)"specified individual"
- 18
- - over
- - - RRSP overcontribution of $2,000 allowed, 204.2(1.1)(b)C
- - under, *see* Child; Minor
- 19
- - over, GST credit, 122.5(1)"eligible individual"(c)
- - under
- - - dependant for pension purposes, Reg. 8500(1)"dependant"(a)
- - - dependent child, 70(10)"child"(c), 252(1)(b)
- 21
- - over
- - - accumulated income payments from RESP, 146.1(2)(d.1)(v)(A)
- - under
- - - contributions to RESP, 146.1(2)(j)(ii)(A), (iii)(A)
- - - dependent child, ITAR 20(1.11)(c), 26(20)(c)
- - - income from personal injury award exempt, 81(1)(g.1), (g.2), 81(5)
- - - transfer of RESP beneficiary, 204.9(4)(b), 204.9(5)(c)(ii)
- - - trust for, whether amounts payable, 104(18)(b)
- 40
- - under, trust for, whether amounts payable, 104(18)(d)
- 55
- - additional lifetime retirement benefits, Reg. 8505(3)
- - early retirement pension benefits, Reg. 8503(3)(c)(i)(A)
- 60
- - early retirement pension benefits, Reg. 8503(3)(c)(ii)(A)
- - pension bridging benefits, Reg. 8503(2)(b)(ii)B(A)
- 65
- - over
- - - in-home care of, caregiver credit, 118(1)B(c.1)(iii)(A)
- - - normalized pension, lifetime retirement benefits, Reg. 8302(3)(b), (n), 8303(5)(b),

2649

Age (cont'd)
- - - 8503(2)(e)(vi)B, 8503(3)(d)(ii)B, 8504(10)(b), 8517(5)(b)
- - - pension bridging benefits, Reg. 8503(2)(b)(i), (ii)A(A), 8506(b)
- - - pension credit, 118(3)
- - - re-employment of member of pension plan, Reg. 8503(9)(b)(iv)
- - - restricted-funding member of pension plan, Reg. 8515(7)(e)(i)
- - - sale of LSVCC shares, 211.8(1)(a)B(i)(A)
- - - specified retirement arrangement, Reg. 8308.3(1)(c)
- - - trust for self, 248(1)"alter ego trust"
- - - trust for self and spouse, 248(1)"joint spouse trust"
- - under
- - - pension plan, retirement benefits, Reg. 8504(5)
- 69
- - conversion of RRSP to RRIF or annuity, 146(2)(b.4), 146(13.2), (13.3)
- - conversion of pension rights to annuity contract, 147.4(4), Reg. 8502(e)(i)(A)
- - maturation of deferred profit sharing plan, 147(2)(k), 147(10.6)
- - pre-retirement surviving spouse benefits, Reg. 8506(e)(iii)
- - pre-retirement survivor benefits, Reg. 8503(2)(f)(iii)(B)
- 75
- - exemption test life insurance policy, Reg. 307(a)
- - payments after, annuity contract issued before 1978, 20(2.2)
- 85
- - exempt life insurance policy, Reg. 306(3)(d)(ii)(B)
- 90
- - annuity to, 146(1)"qualified investment"(c.2)(v)(B), 146.3(1)"qualified investment"(b.2)(v)(B)
- 91
- - reaching, prescribed annuity contract, Reg. 304(1)(c)(iv)(C)(V), 304(2)(b)
- 94
- - RRIF payout levels out at 20%, 146.3(1)"minimum amount"
- under 18, see Minor

**Agent**
- administering property, return by, 150(3)
- insurance, reserves for, 32(1)
- liability for non-resident tax, 215(2)
- paid by commission, deductions allowed, 8(1)(f)
- - certificate of employer, 8(10)
- receiving income on behalf of non-resident, 215(1), (3)
- trustee acting as, 104(1), see also Bare trust

**Aggregate investment income**
- defined, 129(4)
- refund to private corporation of 26 ⅔%, 129(3)(a)(i)(A)

**Agreement**
- among associated/related corporations
- - to allocate base level deduction re soft costs on land, 18(2.3)
- - to allocate capital deduction among financial institutions, 190.15(2)
- - to allocate enhanced capital deduction among financial institutions, 190.17(2)
- - to allocate dividend allowance for Part VI.1 tax, 191.1(3)
- - to allocate ITC expenditure limit, 127(20)
- - to allocate reduction in ITC due to government assistance, 127(20)
- - to allocate small business deduction, 125(3)
- - to allocate UI employer premium tax credit, 126.1(9)
- - to transfer SR&ED qualified expenditure pool, 127(13)–(17)
- collection agreement with provinces, 228
- competent authority, deemed valid, 115.1
- for payment of unreasonably low rent
- - effect on proceeds of disposition of property, 69(1.2)
- for payment without withholding tax, void, 227(12)
- to issue shares to employee, 7
- to transfer forgiven amount of debt to related person, 80.04

**Agreement for sale**
- included in proceeds of disposition, 20(5), (5.1)

**Agricultural land**, see Farm land

**Agricultural organization**
- exemption, 149(1)(e), 149(2)
- information return, whether required, 149

**Air Canada, subject to tax**, 27(2), Reg. 7100

**Air conditioner**
- medical expense credit for, Reg. 5700(c.3)

**Air purifier**
- medical expense credit for, Reg. 5700(c.1)

**Air traffic control operations**, see Nav Canada

**Aircraft**
- available-for-use rule, 13(27)(h)
- broadcasting from, 19.1(4)"foreign broadcasting undertaking"
- capital cost allowance, Reg. Sch. II:Cl. 9(g)–(i), Sch. II:Cl. 16(a)–(c)
- capital tax exemption, Canada–U.S. Tax Convention Art. XXIII:3
- component manufacturer
- - exception to thin capitalization rules, 18(8)
- employment, used in
- - costs, 8(1)(j), 8(9)
- employment by U.S. resident on, Canada–U.S. Tax Convention Art. XV:3
- food consumed or entertainment enjoyed on, 67.1(4)(a)
- fuel tax rebate, see Fuel tax rebate
- GST input tax credit in respect of, 248(17)
- hangar, capital cost allowance, Reg. Sch. II:Cl. 6(h)
- international traffic, used in
- - deduction from taxable capital for large corporations tax, 181.4(d)(i)
- - income of non-resident exempt, 81(1)(c)
- lease payments, non-resident withholding tax exemption, 212(1)(d)(xi)
- manufacturer or developer of
- - exception to thin capitalization rules, 18(8)
- non-resident's income from, exempt, 81(1)(c)
- runway, capital cost allowance, Reg. Sch. II:Cl. 1(g), Sch. II:Cl. 17(c)
- - for mine, Reg. Sch. II:Cl. 10(l)(ii)
- used in international traffic, see International traffic

# Index

**Airline corporations**
- aviation fuel tax rebate, *see* Fuel tax rebate
- taxable income earned in a province, Reg. 407

**Airport, for mine, capital cost allowance**, Reg. Sch. II:Cl. 10(l)(i)

**Alarm**
- for infant prone to sudden infant death syndrome, medical expense, Reg. 5700(r)

**Alberta**, *see also* Province
- northern, *see* Northern Canada
- tax rates, *see* introductory pages

**Alimony**, *see* Support payments (spousal or child)

**All or substantially all**
- not defined (CCRA treats it as meaning "90% or more")

**Allied war veterans**
- death or disability pension exempt, 81(1)(e)

**Allocable amount (for preferred beneficiary election)**
- defined, 104(15)
- election to include in beneficiary's income, 104(14)

**Allocation**, *see also* Apportionment
- allocation in proportion to patronage, *see* Patronage
- borrowing, in proportion to, *see also* Borrowing
- by Minister, where associated corporations do not file agreement
  - base level deduction, for soft costs on land, 18(2.4)
  - dividend allowance, for Part VI.1 tax, 191.1(5)
  - expenditure limit, for investment tax credit, 127(10.4)
  - UI premium tax credit, 126.1(10)
- coal mine depletion allowance, 65(3)
- consideration, where combined transfer of property, 13(33), 68
- foreign tax credit, by trust to beneficiary, 104(22)–(22.4)
- income of trust, to beneficiaries
  - capital gains, 104(21)–(21.2)
  - dividends, 104(19), (20)
  - preferred beneficiary election, 104(13)
- liability for debt obligation, 80(2)(o)
- partnership income among partners, 103
- patronage, in proportion to, *see* Patronage
- proceeds
  - between land and building, 13(21.1), 70(5)(d)
  - between property and services, 68

**Allocation method**
- deductibility of interest relating to distributions, 20.1(3)

**Allowable business investment loss**, *see also* Business investment loss
- capital gains exemption, interaction with, 39(9), 110.6(1)"annual gains limit"B(b), 110.6(1)"cumulative gains limit"(b)
- carryforward, 111(1)(a), 111(8)"non-capital loss"
  - reduction on debt forgiveness, 80(4)(a)
- deduction, 3(d)
- defined, 38(c)
- partnership, of, 96(1.7)

**Allowable capital loss**, *see* Capital loss

**Allowable refund (of non-resident-owned investment corporation)**
- application of, to corporation's tax liability, 133(7)
- defined, 133(8)
- interest on, 133(7.01), (7.02)
- payment of, to corporation, 133(6)

**Allowable refundable tax on hand (non-resident-owned investment corporation)**
- defined, 133(9)

**Allowance**
- capital cost, *see* Capital cost allowance
- clergyman's, not taxable, 6(1)(b)(vi)
- defined
  - capital cost, 20(1)(a), Reg. 1100, *see also* Capital cost allowance
  - for alimony, maintenance, child support, 56(12)
  - for employee benefits, reasonable, 6(1)(b)(x), (xi)
  - retiring, 248(1), *see also* Retiring allowance
- depletion, *see* Depletion allowances
- depreciable property, *see* Capital cost allowance
- disabled employee: transportation and attendant, 6(16)
- employee, 6(1)(b)
  - child's schooling, 6(1)(b)(ix)
- exempt, 81(1)(d)
- family, *see* Child Tax Benefit
- inventory, repealed [was 20(1)(gg)]
- investment in property in Canada, 219(1)(j), Reg. 808
- Member of Legislative Assembly, 81(2)
- members of Canadian Forces, 6(1)(b)(ii)
- mines, Reg. Part XII
- motor vehicle, employee's, 6(1)(b)(vii.1)
  - where deemed not reasonable, 6(1)(b)(x), (xi)
- municipal officer's, 81(3)
- not income, 6(1)(b)(i)–(ix)
- oil or gas wells, Reg. Part XII
- parking, for disabled employee, not income, 6(16)
- received, as income, 6(1)(b)
- representation, not income, 6(1)(b)(iii), (iv)
- resource, 20(1)(v.1)
- resource and processing, Reg. Part XII
- retiring, *see* Retiring allowance
- support payments, defined with respect to, 56(12)
- training
  - withholding of tax, 153(1)(i)
- transportation
  - disabled employee, 6(16)
  - remote work site, 6(6)(b)
- travelling, not income, 6(1)(b)(i), (ii), (v)–(vii)
- volunteer firefighters and emergency workers
  - deduction for, 8(1)(a) [to be repealed]
  - not income, 81(4)

***Alter ego* trust**
- deduction from income, 104(6)(b)(ii.1), (iii)
- defined, 104(4)(a)(iv)(A), 248(1)
- distribution of property to person other than taxpayer, 107(4)(a)(ii)
- preferred beneficiary election by, 104(15)(a)
- transfer by, to another trust, 104(5.8)
- transfer to, rollover, 73(1.01)(c)(ii)

**Alterations to driveway**
- medical expense credit, 118.2(2)(l.6)

**Alternative basis for assessment**
- Minister allowed to raise, 152(9)

**Alternative Minimum Tax**, *see* Minimum tax

**Amalgamation**, 87, *see also* Merger
- accrual rules, 87(2)(j.4)
- affiliated corporations, 251.1(2)
- balance-due day, 87(2)(oo.1)

2651

# Index

Amalgamation *(cont'd)*
- balance of tax for year, when due, 87(2)(oo), 157(1)(b)(i)
- Canadian film/video tax credit, 87(2)(j.94)
- capital dividend account, 87(2)(z.1)
- capital dividends, 87(2)(x)(ii)
- capital property, 53(6), 87(2)(e)
- carryback of losses, 87(2.11)
- charitable gifts, 87(2)(v)
- computation of income, 87(2)(c)
- continuation of predecessors, 87(2)(g.1), (j.6)–(j.95), (qq)
  - • butterfly reorganizations, 55(3.2)(b)
- contributed surplus, 87(2)(y)
- corporation beneficiary under life insurance policy, 89(2)
- corporations deemed related, 251(3.1), (3.2)
- cross-border, 128.2
- cumulative eligible capital, 87(2)(f)
- cumulative offset account, computation, 87(2)(pp)
- debt obligation acquired, 87(2)(e.2)
- debts
  - • between two predecessor corporations, 80.01(3)
  - • owing by predecessor corporation, 87(6), (7); ITAR 26(23)
  - • owing to predecessor corporation, 87(2)(h)
- deemed proceeds of disposition, 69(13)
- defined, 87(1)
  - • pre-1972, ITAR 34(7)
- depreciable property, 87(2)(d), (d.1)
- eligible capital amount, 87(2)(f)
- eligible capital expenditure, 87(2)(f)
- eligible capital property, 87(2)(f)
- employee benefit plans, 87(2)(j.3)
- employee stock options, 7(1.4), (1.5)
- employment tax credit, 87(2)(qq)
- exchanged shares, 87(4.1), (4.2)
- farm losses, 87(2.1)
- film/video production services credit, 87(2)(j.94)
- flow-through entity, 87(2)(bb.1)
- flow-through shares, 87(4.4)
  - • renunciation of CDE as CEE, calculation of taxable capital limit, 66(12.6013)
- following debt forgiveness, deemed capital gain, 80.03(3)(a)(ii)
- foreign affiliates, 87(8), (8.1)
- foreign affiliate, shares of, 87(2)(u)
- foreign corporation with Canadian resident corporation, 128.2
- foreign investment entity, interest in, 87(2)(j.95)
- foreign tax carryover, 87(2)(z)
- insurance corporation, 87(2.2)
  - • causing demutualization, 139.1(3)(g)
- inventory, 87(2)(b)
  - • adjustment, 87(2)(j.1)
- investment tax credit, 87(2)(oo), (oo.1), (qq)
- labour-sponsored venture capital corporation, 204.85(3)
  - • permission of Minister needed, 204.85(1)
- lease, cancellation of, 87(2)(j.5)
- leasing properties, 16.1(4)
- liability for Part VI.1 tax transferred, 87(2)(ss)
- life insurance capital dividends, 87(2)(x)(ii)
- limited partnership losses, 87(2.1)
- losses

- • carryback, 87(2.11)
- • carryforward, 87(2.1)
- mark-to-market property, 87(2)(e.4)
- mutual fund corporations, 87(2)(bb)
- net capital losses, 87(2.1)
- new corporation
  - • deemed continuation of predecessors, 87(1.2), (2)(j.6)–(j.9), (l)
    - • • accrual rules, 87(2)(j.4)
    - • • bank reserves, 87(2)(g.1)
    - • • cancellation of lease, 87(2)(j.5)
    - • • charitable gifts, 87(2)(v)
    - • • deduction for Part I.3 tax, 87(2)(j.9)
    - • • deduction of Part VI tax, 87(2)(j.9)
    - • • employee benefit plans, 87(2)(j.3)
    - • • inclusion of deferred amounts for livestock, 87(2)(tt)
    - • • insurance corporations, 87(2.2)
    - • • Part III, 87(2)(z.2)
    - • • partnership interest, 87(2)(e.1)
    - • • prepaid expenses, 87(2)(j.2)
    - • • registered plans, 87(2)(q)
  - • whether Canadian corporation, 89(1)"Canadian corporation"
- new corporation deemed related to predecessors, 251(3.1), (3.2)
- non-arm's length transactions, 251(3.1)
- non-capital losses, 87(2.1)
- non-qualifying security, gift of, 87(2)(m.1)
- non-resident-owned investment corporation, 87(2)(cc)
- non-resident trust, interest in, 87(2)(j.95)
- not acquisition of control, 88(4)
- obligations, *see* debts (above)
- options
  - • expired, 87(2)(o)
  - • received on, ITAR 26(22)
  - • to acquire shares of predecessor corporation, 87(5), (5.1)
- paid-up capital, computation of, 87(3), (3.1)
- partnership interest acquired, 87(2)(e.1)
- pre-1972 capital surplus on hand, 87(2)(t)
- predecessor corporation
  - • continued, 87(2)(jj)–(ll)
  - • defined, 87(1)
- preferred shares, 87(4.1), (4.2)
- prepaid expenses, 87(2)(j.2)
- proceeds of disposition not due until later year, 87(2)(m)
- property lost, destroyed or taken, 87(2)(l.3)
- public corporation, 87(2)(ii), 87(2)(j)–(ll)
- qualifying environmental trust, interest in, 87(2)(j.93)
- refundable dividend tax on hand, 87(2)(aa)
- refundable investment tax credit, 87(2)(oo.1)
- refundable Part VII tax on hand, 87(2)(nn)
- reserves, carryover to new corporation, 87(2)(g)
- residence of predecessor corporations, deemed, 128.2
- resource and processing allowances, Reg. 1214
- resource expenses, 66.7(6)
- resource property disposition, consideration for, 87(2)(p)
- restricted farm loss, 87(2.1)
- rights, exchange of, 87(4.3)
- rules applicable, 87(2)
- scientific research expenditures, 87(2)(l)–(l.2)
- security acquired, 87(2)(e.2)

2652

# Index

**Amalgamation** *(cont'd)*
- settlement of debts between predecessors, 80.01(3)
- shares
  - deemed received, 87(1.1)
  - exchange of, 87(4.1), (4.2)
  - issued by parent, 87(9)
  - predecessor corporations, of, 87(4)
  - received on, ITAR 26(21), 65(5)
- short-form, 87(1.1), (2.11)
- special reserve, 87(2)(i), (j)
- specified debt obligation, 87(2)(e.3)
- specified property, effect on adjusted cost base, 53(6)
- subsidiary wholly-owned corporation, 87(1.4)
- tax-deferred preferred shares previously issued, 83(7)
- taxable dividends, 87(2)(x)
- taxable preferred shares, tax on, 87(2)(rr)
- taxation year, 87(2)(a)
- transitional provisions, ITAR 34
- triangular, 87(9)
- UI premium tax credit, 87(2)(mm)
- vertical
  - carryback of losses, 87(2.11)
  - deemed cost of capital properties, 87(11)(b)
  - deemed proceeds from subsidiary's shares, 87(11)(a)
- warranty outlays, 87(2)(n)

**Amateur athlete trust**, *see also* Athlete
- beneficiary, defined, 143.1(1)(e)
- death of beneficiary, 143.1(4)
- defined, 143.1(1), 248(1)
- distributions by
  - deemed
    - 8 years after last international competition, 143.1(3)
    - on death, 143.1(4)
  - included in income, 12(1)(z), 143.1(2)
  - non-resident beneficiary, to
    - tax on trust, 210.2(1.1)
    - withholding tax, 212(1)(u), 214(3)(k)
- emigration of beneficiary, no deemed disposition, 128.1(10)"excluded right or interest"(e)(ii)
- excluded from various trust rules, 108(1)"trust"(a)
- no tax payable by, 143.1(1)(f), 149(1)(v)
- rollover to new trust, 248(1)"disposition"(f)(vi)
- termination of, 143.1(3)
- trustee, defined, 143.1(1)(f)

**Amateur athletic association**
- registered Canadian, *see* Registered Canadian amateur athletic association

**Ambassador**, *see* Diplomat

**Ambulance**
- excluded from "automobile", 248(1)"automobile"(b)
- medical expense credit, 118.2(2)(f)
- technician, volunteer
  - deduction from employment income, 8(1)(a) [to be repealed]
  - exemption from employment income, 81(4)

**Amended Act**
- defined, ITAR 8

**Amendment**
- citation of, *Interpretation Act* s. 40(2)
- regulations, *Interpretation Act* s. 31(4)
- when in force
  - proclamation, *Interpretation Act* s. 18
  - Royal Assent, *Interpretation Act* s. 6(3)
- within power of Parliament, *Interpretation Act* s. 42

**Amendments to elections**, 220(3.2)

**American law**, *see* United States

**Ammonite gemstone**
- treated as mineral, 248(1)"mineral", "mineral resource"(d)(ii)

**Amortization**
- depreciable property, *see* Capital cost allowance
- expenditures, *see* Matchable expenditure

**Amortization date (for specified debt obligation)**, Reg. 9200(2)

**Amortized cost**
- defined, 248(1)
  - re loan or lending asset, 248(1)
  - re pre-1972 obligation, ITAR 26(12)
- variation in, for certain insurers, 138(13)

**Amount**
- defined, 248(1)
- list of, *see* Dollar amounts in legislation and regulations
- negative, deemed nil, 257

**Amount of remuneration**
- defined, re payment to a fisherman, Reg. 105.1(1)

**Amounts receivable**
- deceased taxpayer, by, 70(2), (3)

**Amusement parks**
- capital cost allowance, Reg. Sch. II:Cl. 37
- defined, Reg. 1104(12)

**Ancillary tuition fees, credit**, 118.5(3)

**Animal**
- breeding, defined, 80.3(1)
- inventory valuation, 28(1.2), Reg. 1802
- specified, defined, 28(1.2)
- trained to assist disabled person, medical expense credit, 118.2(2)(l)

**Anniversary day**
- investment contract, of, defined, 12(11)"anniversary day"

**Annual child care expense amount**
- defined, 63(3)

**Annual dues**
- professional membership, deduction, 8(1)(i)(i)
- trade union, etc., deductible, 8(1)(i)(iv)–(vi)

**"Annual gains limit" defined**, 110.6(1)

**Annual investment tax credit limit, defined**, 127(9)

**Annual reporting of interest**, *see* Interest (monetary): accrued

**Annuitant**
- defined
  - for Home Buyers' Plan, 146.01(1)
  - for Lifelong Learning Plan, 146.02(1)
  - for prescribed annuity contracts, Reg. 304(4)
  - for RRIF, 146.3(1), Reg. 215(1)
  - for RRSP, 146(1), Reg. 214(7)
  - for registered labour-sponsored venture capital corporations, defined, 204.8(1)

**Annuity**, Reg. Part III, *see also* Annuity contract
- accrual to date of death, 70(1)(a)
- capital element deductible, 60(a), Reg. 300

2653

# Index

Annuity (cont'd)
- contract, see Annuity contract
- deferred, out of pension plan, 254
- defined, 248(1); Canada–U.S. Tax Convention Art. XVIII:4; *Income Tax Conventions Interpretation Act* s. 5
- definitions, Reg. 310
- disposition of
  - information return, Reg. 208
  - taxable, 56(1)(d.2)
- disposition of interest in
  - information return, Reg. 217
- enlargement of, 58(7)
- government, deductible portion of, 58(1)–(3)
  - husband and wife, 58(5)
- life insurance proceeds, as, 148(6), (10)
- locked-in, held by RRIF, 146.3(1)"qualified investment"(b.2)
- money borrowed to buy
  - limitation on deductibility, 18(11)(d)
- payments
  - capital element of, Reg. 300
  - information returns, Reg. 208
  - life annuity contracts, Reg. 301
  - non-residents, to, 212(1)(o)
  - taxable, 56(1)(d)
- pension excluded from, 58(6)
- prescribed, see Prescribed annuity contract
- qualified, defined, Reg. 1408(1)
- RRSP premium refund transferred to, 60(l)
- receipt of, income, 56(1)(d), (d.2)
- valuation of, Reg. 4200
- withholding tax, 153(1)(f), 212(1)(o)

**Annuity contract**, see also Life insurance policy
- accrued interest on, taxable, 12.2
- cancellation or termination of, Reg. 303
- capital/income elements, 16(4)
- constitutes life insurance policy, 138(12)"life insurance policy"
- deduction, 20(19)
- disposition of
  - deduction, 20(20)
- emigration of beneficiary, no deemed disposition, 128.1(10)"excluded right or interest"(f)(i)
- income-averaging, see Income-averaging annuity contract
- interest on money borrowed to buy
  - amount deductible, 20(1)(c)(iv)
- prescribed, Reg. 304
- RESP investment eligibility, 146.1(1)"qualified investment"(c)
- RRIF investment eligibility, 146.3(1)"qualified investment"(b.1), (b.2)
- RRSP investment eligibility, 146(1)"qualified investment"(c)–(c.2)
- registered pension plan, 147.4
- unallocated income accrued before 1982, Reg. 305

**Anti-avoidance rules**
- abuse of the Act, 245(4)
- acquisition of option rather than shares to avoid various rules, 256(8)
- acquisition of property to defer deemed disposition by trust, 104(5.7)(c)
- arm's length rule, 246(2)
- associated corporations, 256(2.1)
- at-risk amount of limited partner, 96(2.6), (2.7)
- attribution rules, see Attribution rules
- avoidance transaction, defined, 245(3)
- back-to-back loans, see Back-to-back loans
- capital dividend, share acquired to receive, 83(2.1)
- capital gains exemption
  - allocated through partnership or trust, 110.6(11)
  - butterfly, on, 110.6(7)(a)
  - failure to declare exempt gain, 110.6(6)
  - gain of corporation converted to gain of individual, 110.6(7)(b)
  - sale of shares of corporation, 84.1(2)(a.1)(ii), 84.1(2.1)(b)
- capital gains stripping, 55(2), 110.6(7)(a)
- charity's disbursement quota, 149.1(4.1)
- corporations becoming related to transfer forgiven amount of debt, 80.04(8)
- corporations deemed associated, 256(2.1)
- cross-border purchase butterfly, 55(3.1)
- debt forgiveness reserve, 61.3(3), 160.4
- determination by Minister of tax consequences, 152(1.11), (1.12)
  - binding effect, 152(1.3)
- disbursement quota of charity, 149.1(4.1)
- disposition not at arm's length, 69(1)
- disposition of share of foreign affiliate, 93(2)–(2.3)
- dividend stripping, see Surplus stripping
- dividends deemed not to be taxable dividends, 129(1.2)
- emigration
  - deemed disposition by trust of assets transferred before emigration, 104(4)(a.3)
  - deemed disposition of assets, 128.1(4)
- exempt beneficiary, creation of interest in trust to defer deemed disposition, 104(5.5)(b)
- foreign affiliate rules, 95(6)
- foreign partnership, 96(9)(a)
  - becoming resident, 94.2(8)(a)
- foreign resource property, 85(1.11)
- foreign tax credit, 126(4.1)–(4.3)
- general rule, 245(2), see also General anti-avoidance rule
- gross revenue increases for transfer pricing rules, 247(9)
- income-splitting tax, 120.4, see also Split income
- income-splitting through spousal RRSPs, 146(8.3), 146.3(5.1)–(5.5)
- indirect loan to non-resident, 17(2)
- interest-free or low-interest loans, 56(4.1)
- investment tax credit
  - qualified expenditures, 127(24)
  - transfer of SR&ED pool, 127(16)
- kiddie tax, 120.4, see also Split income
- loan not at arm's length, 56(4.1)–(4.3)
- loan to non-resident, 17
  - through partnership, 17(4)
  - through trust, 17(5)
- loss carryover rules, on change of corporate control, 111(5.5)
- losses imported by partnership by acquiring Canadian partner, 96(8), (9)
- misuse of the Act, 245(4)
- mutual fund trust election for December 15 year-end, where beneficiaries change, 132.11(8)
- newspaper or periodical, control by non-resident, 19(8)
- offshore trusts, 94.1

2654

# Index

Anti-avoidance rules *(cont'd)*
- partnership acquiring capital properties to avoid debt forgiveness rules, 80(18)
- partnership, by, 103
- partnership capital contribution where other partner withdraws funds, 40(3.13)
- partnership with non-resident partners importing losses, 96(8), (9)
- payment of capital dividend through trust to non-resident, 212(1)(c)(i)
- penalties, *see* Penalty
- pension adjustment, artificial reduction of, Reg. 8503(14)
- pension, past service employer contributions in lieu of salary, Reg. 8503(15)
- pregnant losses, *see* Pregnant loss
- purchase butterfly, 55(1), (3.1), (3.2)
- refundable Part VII tax, 193(7)
- refundable Part VIII tax, 195(7)
- registered education savings plan, replacement of beneficiary, 204.9(4)
- registered pension plan, replacement of money purchase benefits, Reg. 8304(2)(f)
- reserve for 1995 stub period income, 34.2(7)
- residence of corporation, 250(5)
- retirement compensation arrangement
-   disposition for less than fair market value, 56(11)
- sale of shares by non-resident, 212.1
- sale of shares for dividend stripping, 84.1
- share acquired to obtain dividend refund, 129(1.2)
- small business investment rollover, 44.1(12)
- specified member of partnership, 40(3.131), 127.52(2.1)
- specified person to benefit from subsequent disposition of property, 69(11)
-   application on winding-up, 88(1)
-   incorporation during series of transactions, 69(14)
- stop-loss rules, *see* Stop-loss rules
- surplus stripping, *see* Surplus stripping
- transfer of insurance business by non-resident insurer, 138(11.7)
- transfer of property between trusts to delay deemed disposition rules, 104(5.8)
- transfer of property by tax debtor, 160
- transfer of property with pregnant loss, 13(21.2), 40(3.3), (3.4)
- transfer pricing, 247
- treaty shopping, Canada–U.S. Tax Convention Art. XXIX A
- trust distributing assets before death, 104(4)(a.2)
- trust, excessive capital interest, 104(7.1), (7.2)
- trust receiving assets before emigration, 104(4)(a.3)
- trust with accrued loss, acquisition of interest in, 107(6)
- trusts, allocation of income and capital to different beneficiaries, 104(7.1), (7.2)
- unreasonable consideration, 247

**Anti-dumping duties or countervailing duties**
- deductible, 20(1)(vv)
- included in UCC of depreciable property, 13(21)"undepreciated capital cost"D.1
- refund of
-   deducted from UCC of depreciable property, 13(21)"undepreciated capital cost"K
-   taxable, 12(1)(z.6)

*Antoine Guertin Ltée* **case overruled**, 20(1)(e.2)

**Appeal**
- books and records, 230(6)
- disposal of
-   Minister's duty after, 164(4.1)
-   reassessment, on consent, 169(3)
-   Tax Court, by, 171
- ecological property valuation, 169(1.1)
- expense of making, deduction, 60(o)
- extension of time for making, 167
- Federal Court of Appeal, to, 172(3), 180
-   documents to be transferred, 176
- frivolous, 10% penalty, 179.1
- general procedure, 175
- grounds for, whether raised in Notice of Objection, 169(2.1)
- *in camera* proceedings in Federal Court, 179
- informal procedure, 170
- large corporation by, only on grounds raised in objection, 169(2.1)
- legal costs of, 152(1.2)
- limitation on grounds for filing, 169(2), (2.1)
- Minister may change grounds for assessment, 152(9)
- notice of, Tax Court to Commissioner, 170(1)
- Part IV.1 tax, 187.6
- Part VI.1 tax, 191.4(2)
- Part XII.2 tax, 210.2(7)
- Part XII.3 tax, 211.5
- Part XII.4 tax, 211.6(5)
- repayment on, 164(1.1)
- restriction on collection action while underway, 225.1
- stay of, during action, 239(4)
- Tax Court decisions, from, 174(4.1)
- Tax Court of Canada, to, 169, 170, 174
- time not counted, 173(2), 174(5)
- transitional provisions, ITAR 62(4)–(6)
- where no reasonable grounds for, 179.1
- where right to appeal waived, 169(2.2)

**Applicable fraction (for debt forgiveness rules)**
- application of to capital losses, 80(4)
- defined, 80(2)(d)

**Apportionment**, *see also* Allocation
- bond interest to date of sale, 20(14)
- income accrued to date of death, 70(1)(a)
- proceeds of disposition, between property and services, 68
- taxable and exempt income, between, 149(6)

**Appropriate minister**
- defined, 13(21)

**Appropriate percentage**
- defined, 248(1)

*Appropriation Act*
- interest paid under
-   deduction for, 20(1)(c)(iii)

**Appropriation of amounts**
- to transfer balance between tax accounts, 221.2

**Appropriation of property**
- by shareholder, generally, 15(1), 69(4)
- legal representative, by, 159(3.1)
- on winding-up of corporation, 69(5), 84(2)

**Approved pension plan**
- included in reference to "registered" plan, ITAR 17(8)

**Approved project, defined**, 127(9)

**Approved project property**
- ascertainment of, 127(10)(c)
- defined, 127(9) [repealed]
- prescribed, Reg. 4604
- prescribed activities, Reg. 4605

**Approved share**
- clawback on disposition, 211.8(1)
- defined, 127.4(1), 211.7(1)

**Arbitration of disputes**, Canada–U.S. Tax Convention Art. XXVI:6

*Area Development Incentives Act*
- development grant under
- - capital cost allowance for property receiving, Reg. Sch. II:Cl. 20, Sch. II:Cl. 21

**Armed forces**, *see* Canadian Forces

**Arm's length**
- dividend dealings, 55(4), (5)(e)
- interest paid to non-residents in foreign currency, 212(1)(b)(iii)
- meaning of, 251(1)
- - beneficiary and trust, 251(1)(b) [draft]
- - for CCA purposes, Reg. 1102(20)
- - for currency dealings with foreign affiliate, 95(2.1)
- - for debt forgiveness rules, 80(2)(j)
- - for divisive reorganizations, 55(4), (5)(e)
- - for non-arm's length sale of shares, 84.1(2)(b), (d), 212.1(3)(c)
- - for resource expenses renounced to partnership on flow-through shares, 66(17)
- - for stock option rules, mutual fund trust, 7(1.11)
- - for tax shelter investment where information outside Canada, 143.2(14)
- - for windup of subsidiary, 88(1)(d.2)
- not deemed to confer benefit, 246(2)
- transfer, *see* Arm's length transfer
- transfer price, *see* Arm's length transfer price

**Arm's length allocation**
- defined, 247(1)

**Arm's length transfer**
- defined, 94(1)[proposed]
- price, *see* Arm's length transfer price

**Arm's length transfer price**, *see also* Transfer pricing
- defined, 247(1)
- required for transactions with related non-residents, 247(2)

**Arrears interest**
- defined, for corporate interest offset, 161.1(1)

**Arrival in Canada**, *see* Becoming resident in Canada

**Art**, *see also* Cultural property; Listed personal property
- whether CCA allowed, Reg. 1102(1)(e)

**Art flips**
- minimum $1,000 proceeds eliminated, 46(5)
- penalties for valuators and promoters, 163.2

**Art shelters**, *see* Art flips

**Artificial eye, medical expense**, 118.2(2)(i)

**Artificial kidney machine, medical expense**, 118.2(2)(i)

**Artificial limb**
- costs, as medical expenses, 118.2(2)(i)

**Artificial transactions**, *see* Anti-avoidance rules

**Artist**
- artistic endeavour, 10(6)–(8)

- expenses, deduction from employment income, 8(1)(q)
- gift of cultural property created by, 118.1(7.1)
- gift of work of art created by, 118.1(7)
- organization for, *see* Registered national arts service organization
- project grant, included in income, 56(1)(n)
- U.S. resident, Canada–U.S. Tax Convention Art. XVI
- valuation of inventory, 10(6)–(8)

**Artistic endeavour**
- defined, 10(8)
- value of inventory, 10(6), (7)

**Arts service organization**, *see* Registered national arts service organization

**"As registered" (pension plan), meaning**, 147.1(15)

**Asian Development Bank**
- bonds of
- - trust investing in, not foreign property, Reg. 5000(7)"specified international finance trust"(c)(i)(B)

**Assessable dividend (for Part IV tax)**
- defined, 186(3)
- tax on, 186(1)(a)

**Assessment**, *see also* Determination; Reassessment
- alternative basis for, permitted, 152(9)
- amounts received under RCA trust, re, 160.3(2)
- appeal from, *see* Appeal
- arbitrary, 152(7)
- consequential, of other taxation year, 152(4.3)
- date of mailing, 244(14)
- date of making, 244(15)
- derivative, 160
- determination binding, 152(1.3)–(3)
- excess refund, 160.1(3)
- failure to withhold tax, 227(10)–(10.8)
- includes reassessment, 248(1)
- incorrect or incomplete, 152(3), (8)
- irregularities in, not invalidating, 152(3), (8), 166
- issue in respect of, reference to Tax Court, 173
- jeopardy, 225.2
- losses, of, *see* Determination
- Minister, by, 152(1)
- net worth, 152(7)
- notice of, 152(2)
- - date of, 244(14), (15)
- objection to, *see* Objection
- Part IV.1 tax, 187.6
- Part VI.1 tax, 191.4(2)
- Part XII.2 tax, 210.2(7)
- Part XII.3 tax, 211.5
- Part XII.4 tax, 211.6(5)
- Part XII.5 tax, 227(10.01), 227(10.1)(c)
- Part XII.6 tax, 211.91(3)
- transitional provision, ITAR 62(1)
- valid and binding despite defects, 152(8)

**Asset**
- computation of, for debt forgiveness reserve, 61.3(1)(b)B(i)
- lending
- - defined, 248(1)
- - of insurer/moneylender
- - - limitation on deduction re, where reduced in value, 18(1)(s)

# Index

**Assignee**, *see also* Legal representative
- deemed to be legal representative, 248(1)"legal representative"
- obligations of, 159
- return required by, 150(3)
- withholding tax, liability for, 227(5), (5.1)(g)

**Assignment**
- rights to income, 56(4)
- tax refund, permitted, 220(6)

**Assistance/government assistance**
- Canadian development expense, in respect of, 66.2(5)"Canadian development expense" 66.2(5)"cumulative Canadian development expense"D, M
- Canadian exploration expense, in respect of, 66.1(6)"Canadian exploration expense" 66.1(6)"cumulative Canadian exploration expense"E, J
- Canadian film/video tax credit
  - constitutes assistance for all purposes, 125.4(5)
  - defined, 125.4(1)
- Canadian oil and gas property expense, in respect of, 66.4(5)"Canadian oil and gas property expense" 66.4(5)"cumulative Canadian oil and gas property expense"D, I
- capital cost allowance, effect on, 13(7.1)
- defined
  - for film/video production services tax credit, 125.5(1)
  - for investment tax credit, 127(9)"government assistance"
  - for resource exploration and development rules, 66(15)"assistance"
  - includes GST input tax credits, 248(16)–(18)
- eligible capital expenditure, in respect of, 14(10), (11)
- employer, provided by, for housing, 6(23)
- expired, treated as repaid, 127(10.8)
- exploration and development grant, deductible, 20(1)(kk)
- film/video production services tax credit
  - constitutes assistance for all purposes, 125.5(5)
  - defined, 125.5(1)
- flow-through mining expenditure reduced, 127(11.1)(c.2)
- GST input tax credit or rebate deemed to be, 248(16)
- GST input tax credit repaid deemed to be reduction in, 248(18)
- government, defined, 127(9)
- housing subsidy provided by employer, taxable, 6(23)
- included in income, 12(1)(x)
- increases adjusted cost base of partnership interest, 53(1)(e)(ix)
- indirect, taxable, 12(1)(x)(i)(C)
- investment tax credit reduction, 127(18)–(21)
- non-government, defined, 127(9)
- prescribed benefit under government program
  - overpayment repaid, deductible, 60(n)(ii.1)
  - taxable, 56(1)(a)(vi), Reg. 5502
- qualified expenditures, effect on, 127(18)–(21)
- reduces adjusted base of partnership interest, 53(2)(c)(ix)
- reduces adjusted cost base of property, 13(7.1), 127(11.1)(b)
- reduces claim for scientific research, 37(1)(d)
- reduces R&D expenditures, 127(11.1)(f) [repealed], 127(18)
- repayment of
  - creates capital loss, 39(13)
  - deduction for, 20(1)(hh)
  - excluded from reduction in cost base, 53(2)(k), 53(2)(s)
  - includes repaid GST input tax credit, 248(18)
  - increases investment tax credit, 127(9)"investment tax credit"(e.1), 127(10.7)
  - reduces adjusted cost base of partnership interest, 53(1)(e)(ix)(B)
- resource-related
  - allocated to member of partnership, 66.1(7), 66.2(6), (7), 66.4(6), (7)
  - increases adjusted cost base of partnership interest, 53(1)(e)(ix)

**Assistant's salary paid by employee**
- CPP contributions, UI/EI premiums deductible, 8(1)(l.1)
- deduction, 8(1)(i)(ii)
  - certificate of employer, 8(10)

**Associated charities**
- designation by Minister, 149.1(7)
- disbursement by one to another, 149.1(6)(c)

**Associated corporations**, *see also* Related persons
- anti-avoidance deeming provision, 256(2.1)
- base level deduction, 18(2.3)–(2.5)
- certain shares excluded from fair market valuations, 256(1.6)
- corporations associated with same corporation deemed associated with each other, 256(2)
- defined, 256(1)
- investment income from, 129(6)
- investment tax, allocation of expenditure limit, 127(10.2)–(10.4)
- land soft costs, allocation of base level deduction, 18(2.3)–(2.5)
- options, 256(1.4)
- parent deemed to own child's shares, 256(1.3)
- Part VI.1 tax, allocation of dividend allowance, 191.1(3)–(5)
- person deemed related to himself, 256(1.5)
- rights, 256(1.4)
- small business deduction, 125(3)–(5)
- specified class of shares, defined, 256(1.1)
- UI premium tax credit, allocation, 126.1(9)–(11)

**Associated employers (UI premium tax credit)**
- allocation of credit, 126.1(9)–(11)
- defined, 126.1(2), (3)

**Association of Universities and Colleges of Canada, exempt**, 149(1)(h.1)

**Associations**
- drilling and exploration expenses, pre-1962, ITAR 29(9), (10), (13)
- non-profit exemption, 149(1)(l)

**Assumption of debt**, 20(1)(e)(ii.2), 20(1)(e.1)(iii)
- debt forgiveness rules do not apply, 80(1)"forgiven amount"B(l)

**At-risk adjustment (for tax shelter)**
- defined, 143.2(2), (3)

**At-risk amount**, *see also* Limited partner; Tax shelter
- artificial transactions, 96(2.6), (2.7)
- as prescribed benefit for tax shelter purposes, Reg. 231(6)
- defined, 96(2.2)
- limited partner's losses restricted to, 96(2.1)

# Index

At-risk amount *(cont'd)*
- limited partnership interest acquired by subsequent person, 96(2.3)
- prescribed film production, Reg. 7500
- prescribed revenue guarantee, Reg. 7500
- resource expenditures, 66.8

**Athlete**
- association for, *see* Registered Canadian amateur athletic association
- income of, Canada–U.S. Tax Treaty, Art. XVI
- Major League Baseball Players Benefit Plan, Reg. 6800
- National Hockey League referees, Reg. 6801(c), 6802(d)
- signing bonus, taxable, 6(3), 115(2)(c.1), 115(2)(e)(v)
- trust for, *see* Amateur athlete trust
- tuition support received by, no tuition credit, 118.5(1)(a)(v)
- U.S. resident, Canada–U.S. Tax Convention Art. XVI

**Atlantic Groundfish Adjustment Program/Atlantic Groundfish Strategy**, *see* Fishing: compensation programs

**Attendant**
- for taxpayer or dependant mentally or physically impaired
  - allowance paid by employer, not income, 6(16)
  - deduction from income, 64
  - residents absent from Canada, 64.1
  - medical expense credit, 118.2(2)(b), (b.1), (c)
  - reimbursement of expenses, 118.2(3)(b)

**Attributed surplus (of financial institution)**
- defined, 181(2), 190(1.1), Reg. 8602

**Attributed surplus (non-resident insurer)**
- defined, 219(7), Reg. 2400(1)
  - Large Corporations Tax, Reg. 8600

**Attribution rules**, *see also* Income splitting
- Child Tax Benefit cheque deposited for child's benefit, 74.1(2)
- deemed receipt of dividend, 82(2)
- "designated person" defined, 74.5(5)
- gain/loss from property transferred or loaned, 74.2
  - farm property, 75.1
  - trust, to, 74.3(1)(b)
- income-splitting tax, 120.4, *see also* Split income
- indirect payments, 56(2)
- interest-free or low-interest loans, 56(4.1)
- kiddie tax, 120.4, *see also* Split income
- loan or indebtedness, 56(4.1)–(4.3)
- prescribed provincial pension plan contributions, exception for, 74.5(12)
- property transferred to child, 74.1(2), 75.1
- property transferred to spouse
  - capital gain/loss on, 74.2(1)
  - income from, 74.1(1)
- property transferred to trust
  - income, gain or loss transferor's, 75(2)
  - trusts excluded, 75(3)
- reverse attribution, excluded, 74.5(11)
- spousal RRSP premiums, exception for, 74.5(12)
- transfer or loan to child, 74.1(2)
- transfer or loan to corporation
  - income/loss from property transferred or loaned, 74.1
  - trust, to, 74.3(1)(a)

- transfer or loan to spouse, 74.1(1), 74.2(1)
- where not applicable, 74.5

**Auction of seized chattels**, 225(2)–(4)

**Audio tapes**
- talking textbooks, medical expense, Reg. 5700(w)

**Audiologist**
- certification of hearing impairment
  - for disability credit, 118.3(1)(a.2)(ii)
  - for education credit, 118.6(3)(b)(ii)
- defined, 118.4(2)

**Audit**, 231.1
- compliance required, 231.5(2), 231.7
- contemporaneous documentation for transfer pricing, 247(4)
- copies or printouts of documents, 231.5(1)
- court order for compliance, 231.7
- fishing expedition, 231.2(3)

**Aunt**, *see also* Niece/nephew
- defined, 252(2)(e)
- dependent, 118(6)(b)
- great-aunt defined, 252(2)(f)

**Australia**, *see also* Foreign government
- currency loan, *see* Weak currency debt
- stock exchange recognized, Reg. 3201(a)
- universities, gifts to, Reg. Sch. VIII s. 17

**Austria**, *see also* Foreign government
- stock exchange recognized, Reg. 3201(r)
- universities, gifts to, Reg. Sch. VIII s. 4

**Author**
- deduction from employment income, 8(1)(q)

**Authorized foreign bank**
- application of Part XIII non-resident withholding tax, 212(13.3)
- branch-establishment rollover, 142.7(3)
- branch interest tax, 218.2
- branch tax allowance, Reg. 808(8)
- capital tax rules, 181.3(3)(e), 181.3(4)(c), 190.13(d), 190.14(1)(c)
- conversion of foreign bank affiliate to branch, 142.7
- deemed resident in Canada for certain purposes, 212(13.3)
- defined, 248(1)
- foreign tax credit, 126(1.1)
- interest deduction, 18(1)(v), 20.2
- reassessment beyond 4-year deadline, 152(4)(b)(iii.1)
- taxable income earned in Canada, optional amount, 115(1)(a)(vii)
- winding up into, Reg. 9204(2.1)

**Authorized person**
- defined, re communication of taxpayer information, 241(10)

**Automobile**, *see also* Motor vehicle; Passenger vehicle
- available to shareholder, benefit, 15(5), (7)
- benefit related to operation of, includable in employee's income, 6(1)(a)(iii)
- benefit related to use of, not includable in employee's income, 6(1)(a)(iii)
- benefit to shareholder, 15(5)
- capital cost allowance
  - exclusion, Reg. 1102(1)(h), 1102(11)–(13)
  - limitation, *see* Passenger vehicle: luxury
- dealer, taxable benefit to sales employees, 6(2.1)
- defined, 248(1)

2658

Automobile *(cont'd)*
- employee's, capital cost allowance, Reg. 1100(6)
- expenses
- - employee, of, 8(1)(h.1)
- - limitations on deductibility, 13(7)(g), (h), 18(1)(r), 67.2, 67.3
- gasoline for, *see* operating costs *(below)*
- insurance, *see* operating costs *(below)*
- interest cost limit, *see* Passenger vehicle: luxury
- lease expense limit, *see* Passenger vehicle: luxury
- luxury, *see* Passenger vehicle: luxury
- maintenance, *see* operating costs *(below)*
- operating costs
- - benefit
- - - employee-owned car, 6(1)(l)
- - - employer-owned car, 6(1)(k); Reg. 7305.1
- - - shareholder, received by, 15(5)
- - deductible
- - - by employee, 8(1)(h.1)
- - - by employer, 9(1)
- parking for, taxable benefit, 6(1)(a), 6(1.1)
- provided to employee
- - amount included in income, 6(1)(e), (k), 6(2)
- - cost includes GST, 6(7)
- provided to partner
- - amount included in income, 12(1)(y)
- provided to shareholder
- - amount included in income, 15(5)
- purchase loan to employee, 15(2)(a)(iv), 15(2.4)(d)
- salesperson, standby charge for use of vehicle, 6(2.1)
- short-term rental/leasing, for
- - capital cost allowance, Reg. Sch. II:Cl. 16
- standby charge, 6(1)(e)
- - reasonable amount, 6(2)
- - salesperson, reasonable amount, 6(2.1)
- trade-in, allocation of consideration, 13(33)
- used by employee, 6(1)(e), (k), 6(2)
- used by shareholder, 15(5)
- used in employment
- - costs, 8(1)(j)

**Automotive equipment**
- capital cost allowance, Reg. Sch. II:Cl. 10(a)
- - large trucks and tractors, Reg. Sch. II:Cl. 16(g)

**Available-for-use rules**
- capital cost allowance, 13(26)–(32), Reg. 1100(2)(a)(i), (vii)
- - transfer of property to affiliated person, 13(21.2)(e)(iv)
- deduction against rental income, 20(28), (29)
- investment tax credit, 127(11.2)
- meaning of, 248(19)
- scientific research, 37(1.2)

**Average Consumer Price Index**
- defined, Reg. 8500(1)

**"Average wage" for calendar year**
- defined, 147.1(1)
- used in calculating money purchase limit, 147.1(1)"money purchase limit"

**Averaging of income**, *see also* Income-averaging annuity contract
- farmers and fishermen, 119 [obsolete]
- forward, *see* Forward averaging
- lump-sum payments, 110.2, 120.31

- RRSPs, 146(5), (8)
- - by pledging RRSP as security, 146(7), (10)
- shareholder loans, 15(2), 20(1)(j)

**Aviation fuel**, *see* Fuel tax rebate

**Aviation turbine fuel**
- failure to file fuel certificate, penalty imposed, 234.1 [repealed]
- rules respecting sales of, 69(7.1) [repealed], 69(11) [repealed]

**Avoidance of tax**, *see* Anti-avoidance rules

**Award**
- legal expenses of collecting salary, etc.
- - included in employee's income, 6(1)(j)
- personal injury
- - election re capital gains, 81(5)
- - income exempt, 81(1)(g.1), (g.2)

**Away-from-home expenses**, *see also* Special work site, employment at; Travelling expenses
- railway employees, 8(1)(e)
- transport employees, 8(1)(g)

**B**

**BAPA (Bilateral Advance Pricing Agreement)**, *see* Advance Pricing Agreement

**BIL**, *see* Business investment loss

**BN**, *see* Business number

**Baby bonus**, *see* Child Tax Benefit

**Babysitting**, *see* Child care expenses

**Back-door butterfly**, 88(1)(c)(vi), 88(1)(c.3)

**Back-to-back loans**
- attribution rules, 74.5(6)
- loan by corporation to non-resident, 17(11.2)
- thin capitalizaton rules, 18(6)

**Bad debt**
- change in control of corporation, limitation on deduction, 111(5.3)
- deductible, 20(1)(p)
- deemed disposition of, 50(1)(a)
- disposition of depreciable property, 20(4), (4.1)
- disposition of eligible capital property, 20(4.2)
- insurer/moneylender
- - inclusion in income, 12.4
- personal-use property, 50(2)
- recovered
- - capital gain, 39(11)
- - income, 12(1)(i), (i.1)
- uncollectible proceeds of disposition, 20(4)–(4.2)
- where property seized by creditor, no deduction for principal, 79.1(8)

**Balance**
- transfer of, to different CCRA account, 221.2

**Balance-due day**
- amalgamated corporation, 87(2)(oo.1)
- defined, 248(1)
- payment of tax by, 153(2), 155(1)(b), 156(1)(b), 156.1(1)"net tax owing"(b)

**Balance of annuitized voluntary contributions**
- defined, 60.2(2)

**Bank**, *see also* Financial institution
- account in foreign country, disclosure to CCRA, 233.3
- cannot make Canadian securities election, 39(5)(b)
- computation of income, 26

Bank (cont'd)
- deductions, 26(2)
- defined, *Interpretation Act* s. 35(1)
- exempt from Part IV tax, 186.1(b)
- foreign, *see* Authorized foreign bank; Foreign bank
- interference with remittance of tax, 227(5.2)–(5.4) (draft)
- liabilities of, determination for debt forgiveness reserve, 61.3(1)(b)C(ii)(B)
- mark-to-market rules, 142.2–142.6
- "Minister's rules" defined, 26(4)
- receipt of tax payments by, 229 [repealed]
- recoveries, 26(3)(b)
- remittance of source withholdings by large employers, 153(1), Reg. 110
- reserves
  - continuation of, on amalgamation, 87(2)(g.1)
  - prescribed reserve amount, Reg. 8000(a), (a.1)
- specified debt obligation that was inventory before February 1994, 142.6(4)(a)(ii)
- surtax on, 190.1(1.2)
- taxable income earned in a province, Reg. 404
- write-offs, 26(3)(a)

**Bank for International Settlements**
- no withholding tax on interest payable to, Reg. 806.1

**Banker's acceptances**
- included in capital for large corporations tax, 181.2(3)(d)
- qualified investments for deferred income plans, Reg. 4900(1)(i.2)

**Bankruptcy**
- Act, *see* Bankruptcy and Insolvency Act
- "bankrupt" defined, 248(1)
- business income, effect on, 34.1(8)(b), 34.2(6)(b)(ii), 34.2(6)(c)(ii)
- corporation
  - dividends paid to, effect on dividend refund, 129(1.1)
  - exempt from large corporations tax, 181.1(3)(b)
  - general rules, 128(1)
- debt forgiveness rules inapplicable, 80(1)"forgiven amount"B(i)
- effect on Crown's priority for taxes withheld, 227(5)
- "estate of the bankrupt" defined, 248(1)
- individual
  - Child Tax Benefit, 122.61(3.1)
  - credits allowed, 118.95
  - GST credit, 122.5(7)
  - general rules, 128(2)
  - minimum tax not applicable, 127.55
  - tuition and education credit carryforward, 128(2)(f)(iv), 128(2)(g)(ii)
- legislation, *see* Bankruptcy and Insolvency Act
- receiver
  - return to be filed by, 150(3)
  - minimum tax carryover not applicable, 120.2(4)
  - withholding tax, 153(1.3) [repealed], (1.4) [repealed], 227(5), (5.1)
- shares of corporation in, 50(1)
- trustee in, *see also* Legal representative
  - clearance certificate, 159(2)
  - deemed to be legal representative, 248(1)"legal representative"
  - obligations of, 159
  - return required by, 150(3)

- withholding tax, liability for, 227(5), (5.1)(f)

***Bankruptcy and Insolvency Act***
- charge registered under, 223(11.1)
- priority of garnishment order over, 224(1.2)

**Bare trust**, 104(1), *see also* Agent
- non-resident, transfer to, 248(25.1)
- transfer to or from, not a disposition, 248(1)"disposition"(e)(i)

**Barrister and solicitor**, *see* Lawyer

**Base level deduction**
- real property corporations, 18(2.2)–(2.5)

**Baseball players**, *see* Athlete

**Base taxation year (for OAS clawback)**
- defined, 180.2(1)

**Basic activity of daily living**
- defined, 118.4(1)(c)
- markedly restricted, disability credit, 118.3(1)

**Basic herd**
- meaning of, 29(3)
- reduction in, 29(2)
  - election re, 29(1)

**Bathtub**
- mechanical aid for getting into and out of, medical expense, Reg. 5700(g)

**Bearer bond etc.**
- coupon encashment requiring ownership certificate, 234
- withholding tax on payments to non-resident, 215(2)

**Becoming a financial institution**, 142.6(1)(a), (b)

**Becoming non-resident**, *see* Ceasing to be resident in Canada

**Becoming resident in Canada**, 128.1(1)
- corporation
  - deemed dividends, 128.1(1)(c.1),(c.2)
  - effect on non-resident shareholder's cost, 52(8)
  - foreign affiliate of Canadian resident, 128.1(1)(d)
  - paid-up capital, effect on, 128.1(2), (3)
- deemed acquisition of property, 128.1(1)(c)
- deemed disposition of property, 128.1(1)(b)
- immigration trust, five-year non-taxability, 94(1)(b)(i)(A)(III) [to be repealed], 94(1)"connected contributor"(a) [proposed]
- negative cumulative eligible capital balance, 14(8)(b)
- partner
  - cost base of properties owned by partnership, 96(8)
- taxation year-end and new taxation year, 128.1(1)(a)

**Bed**
- hospital, medical expense, Reg. 5700(h)
- reservation fee, for foster person, exempt, 81(1)(h)
- rocking, medical expense, 118.2(2)(i)

**Bees**
- keeping, constitutes farming, 248(1)"farming"

**Belgium**, *see also* Foreign government
- stock exchange recognized, Reg. 3201(b)
- universities, gifts to, Reg. Sch. VIII s. 5

**"Beneficially interested" in a trust**
- meaning of, 248(25)

**Beneficiary**
- amounts deemed not paid to, 104(13.1), (13.2)
- amounts deemed payable to, 104(24), (29)
- arm's length from personal trust, deemed not to be, 251(1)

2660

## Index

Beneficiary *(cont'd)*
- capital cost allowance, deduction for, 104(16) [repealed]
- death of
  - separate return on, 104(23)(d)
- deemed income of, 104(27), (28)
- deferred profit sharing plan, under, 147(17)
  - when plan was employees' profit sharing plan, 147(11)
- defined, 104(1.1), 104(5.5), 108(1), 248(13), Reg. 223(5), 8500(1)
- disposing of property previously held by trust
  - reduction of loss, 107(6)
- emigration of, 128.1(10)"excluded right or interest"(j), (k)
- employees profit sharing plan, under, 144(6)–(8)
  - former, refund to, 144(9)
- foreign tax credit, 104(22)–(22.4)
- immigration of, 128.1(10)"excluded right or interest"(j), (k)
- income of, 108(5)
- income payable to, 104(13)
- non-resident
  - deduction from income of trust, for dividend from non-resident-owned investment corporation, 104(10), (11)
  - distribution of property to, 107(5)
    - instalment obligation not increased, 107(5.1)
    - security to postpone payment of tax, 220(4.6)–(4.63)
  - dividends received on behalf of, 82(1)(a)(i.1)
  - estate income paid to, withholding tax, 212(1)(c)
  - limitation on deduction in computing income of trust, 104(7)
  - trust income paid to, withholding tax, 212(1)(c)
- non-resident trust, of
  - rights and obligations, 94(2) [to be repealed]
- non-taxable dividends, designation re, 104(20)
- preferred
  - defined, 108(1)
  - election re accumulating income, 104(14)
- qualifying environmental trust, credit for, 127.41
- registered education savings plan, under, 146.1(1)"beneficiary"
- rights or things transferred to, 70(3)
- share of pension etc. benefits received by testamentary trust, 104(27)–(28)
- superannuation or pension benefit, share of, 104(27)
- taxable capital gain, designation by trust, 104(21), (21.1), (21.2)
- taxable dividends received by trust, designation re, 104(19)
- trust, of
  - defined, 104(5.5), 108(1)"beneficiary"
  - depreciable property acquired with government assistance, 13(7.2)
  - inducement payments or reimbursement received by, 12(2.1)

**Benefit**
- amount, *see* Benefit amount
- automobile available to shareholder, 15(5), (7)
- automobile operation, re, 6(1)(a)(iii), 6(2.2)
- conferred on person
  - amount included in income, 56(2), 246(1)
- conferred on shareholder, 15(1), (7), (9)
  - loan forgiven, 15(1.2)
- death, *see* Death benefit
- deferred profit sharing plan, under, 147(10)–(10.2)
  - defined, 248(1)
- defined
  - Home Buyers' Plan, 146.01(1)
  - investment income tax on life insurers, Reg. 1900(1)
  - Lifelong Learning Plan, 146.02(1)
  - policy reserves in insurance business, Reg. 1408(1)
  - registered retirement savings plan, 146(1)"benefit"
- employee benefit plan, 6(1)(g)
- employment, related to, 6(1)(a)
  - automobile, 6(1)(e), (k), 6(2)
  - exclusions from income, 6(1)(a)(i)–(v)
  - GST included in benefit, 6(7)
  - group term life insurance, 6(1)(a)(i), 6(4), Reg. 2700–2704
  - housing loss, 6(19)–(22)
  - housing subsidy, 6(23)
  - loan to employee, 6(9)
  - loss in value of home on relocation, 6(19)–(22)
  - stock options, 7
- employment insurance, 6(1)(f)
- forgiveness of debt
  - owing by employee, 6(15), (15.1)
  - owing by shareholder, 15(1.2), (1.21)
- government assistance program, prescribed
  - overpayment repaid, deductible, 60(n)(ii.1)
  - taxable, 56(1)(a)(vi), Reg. 5502
- group term life insurance premium, portion taxable, 6(4)
- indirect, 56(2)
- information returns, Reg. 200
- loan to employee, officer or personal services corporation, 80.4(1)
  - deemed interest, 80.5
- loan to personal services business
  - included in income, 12(1)(w)
- loan to shareholder, 80.4(2)
  - deemed shareholder benefit, 15(9)
- northern and isolated areas
  - credit, 110.7
  - prescribed northern zone and intermediate zone, Reg. 7303.1
- paid to non-resident, 212(1)(j)
- prescribed
  - group term life insurance, Reg. 2700–2704
  - tax shelter definition, Reg. 231(6.1)
- provision, *see* Benefit provision
- registered national arts service organization, from, 56(1)(aa)
- registered retirement savings plan, under, 146(8)–(8.91)
  - defined, 146(1)"benefit"
- retirement savings, 146.3(5)
- shareholders', taxable, 15(1), (7), (9)
- stock dividend paid, 15(1.1)
- superannuation or pension, 56(1)(a)
  - defined, 248(1)
- trust, estate, contract, etc., from, 12(1)(m), 105(1)
- unemployment insurance
  - repayment of, 110(1)(i)

**Benefit on death**
- defined, Reg. 310

## Index

**Benefit provision**
- defined, Reg. 8500(1)

**Benevolent or fraternal benefit society**, *see also* Non-profit organization
- exemption, 149(1)(k)
- • limitation, 149(3), (4)

**Bequest**, *see also* Death of taxpayer
- debt forgiveness rules do not apply, 80(2)(a)

**Betting losses**, Canada–U.S. Tax Convention Art. XXII:3

**Beverages**
- expenses for, *see* Entertainment expenses (and meals)

**Bill, post-dated, sale of**, 20(1)(e), 248(1)"borrowed money"

**Bison**, 80.3(1)"breeding animals"

**Bituminous sands**
- constitutes tar sands, 248(1)"tar sands"
- defined, 248(1)
- determination of viscosity and density, Reg. 1107
- well for, is not oil or gas well, 248(1)"oil or gas well"

**Bituminous sands, included in definition of "mineral"**, 248(1)

**Bituminous sands equipment**
- defined, Reg. 1206(1)
- proceeds of disposition, 59(3.3)(c)

**Blended payment, interest and principal**, 16(1)
- paid to non-resident, 214(2)

**Blind person**, *see also* Mental or physical impairment
- computer-operating aids
- • medical expense, Reg. 5700(o)
- devices to assist, business expense, 20(1)(rr)
- guide dog, expenses, 118.2(2)(l)
- parking paid by employer, not taxable benefit, 6(16)
- print-reading aids
- • medical expense, Reg. 5700(l)
- transportation paid by employer, not taxable benefit, 6(16)

**Block of shares**
- defined, Reg. 4803(1)

**Block of units**
- defined, Reg. 4803(1)

**Blocked currency**
- income in, postponement of tax, 161(6)

**Blood relationship**
- defined, 251(6)

**Blood sugar**
- measuring device for diabetics, medical expense, Reg. 5700(s)

**Board and lodging**
- railway employees, 8(1)(e)
- special work site, 6(6)
- transport employees, 8(1)(g)
- value of, includable in income, 6(1)(a)

**Board of education**
- allowance from, exempt, 81(3)

**Board of trade**
- exemption, 149(1)(e), 149(2)
- information return, whether required, 149(12)

**Bond**, *see also* Debt obligation; Investment contract; Obligation; Specified debt obligation
- accrued interest
- • information return, Reg. 211

- • treatment of, 20(14)
- bearer, *see* Bearer bond etc.
- Canadian Government, 212(1)(b)(ii)
- certain
- • interest on, excluded from income, 81(1)(m)
- conversion of, 51.1; ITAR 26(25)
- convertible, exchanged for share, 51
- cost base, additions to, 53(1)(g)
- coupon identification, 240(2)
- credit-related gains and losses, 142.4(7)B
- discount
- • deduction for, 20(1)(j)
- • limitation on deductibility of payments on, 18(1)(f)
- • when deemed to be interest, 16(3)
- expropriation assets for sale of foreign property, 80.1
- foreign corporation, eligible for RRSP investment, Reg. 4900(1)(p)
- foreign government, eligible for RRSP investment, Reg. 4900(1)(o)
- identical properties
- • disposition of, 47(2)
- • meaning, 248(12)
- income
- • defined, 248(1)
- • foreign affiliate, issued by, 95(5)
- • interest on, deemed dividend, 15(3)
- • • non-resident corporation, 15(4)
- issued at discount, yield treated as interest, 16(3)
- predecessor corporation, of, 87(6), (7)
- provincial, taxable at reduced rate, 212(6)–(8)
- purchase of on open market, by issuer, 39(3)
- sale of, 20(21)
- small business, *see* Small business bond
- small business development, *see* Small business development bond
- stripped, cost of coupon excluded from income when sold, 12(9.1)
- transferred, interest on, 20(14)

**Bone marrow transplant**
- expenses of, tax credit for, 118.2(2)(l.1)

**Bonus**, *see also* Signing bonus
- cash, Canada Savings Bond, 12.1
- • information return, Reg. 220
- employment
- • unpaid, 78(4)
- • withholding of tax at source, 153(1)(a), Reg. 103

**Bonus interest payment**
- credit union, by
- • deduction, 137(2)
- • defined, 137(6)

**Bonus payments**
- oil or gas, ITAR 29(21), (22)

**Book**
- capital cost allowance for, Reg. Sch. II:Cl. 12(a)
- talking textbook, medical expense, Reg. 5700(w)

**Bookkeeping services**
- penalty for misrepresentation, 163.2(9)

**Books and records**, *see also* Documents
- destruction of, penalty, 239(1)
- inspections, 231.1
- outside Canada, 143.2(13), (14), 231.6
- political contributions, 230.1
- required to be kept, 230(1)

Books and records *(cont'd)*
- • electronic records, 230(4.1), (4.2)
- • failure to keep, 230(3)
- • • offence and penalty, 238(1)
- • lawyers, 230(2.1)
- • registered Canadian amateur athletic association, 230(2)
- • registered charity, 230(2)
- • retention of, 230(4)–(8), Reg. 5800
- transfer pricing, 247
- transfer pricing, for, contemporaneous, 247(4)

**Boot**, *see* Non-share consideration (boot)
**Border residents**, *see* Commuter to United States
**Borrowed money**, 20(2), (3), 20.1
- costs, capitalized, 21
- defined, 248(1)
- depreciable property, for, 21(3)
- • election to capitalize, 21(1)
- distribution, for, deductibility of interest, 20.1, 20.2
- exploration/development, for, 21(4)
- extended meaning of, 20(2), (3)
- interest paid on, 20(1)(c)
- loss of source of income, 20.1(1)
- purposes used for, deemed, 20(2), 20(3), 20.1(1), 20.2(1)
- refinanced, 20.1(6)
- used for loan to corporation, 20(3.1)
- used to acquire partnership interest, 20.1(5)
- used to invest in RRSP or RESP, no deduction for interest, 18(11)

**Borrowing**
- allocations in proportion to
- • deduction, 137(2)
- • defined, 137(6)
- expense of, 20(1)(e)

**Bovine animals**
- breeding, 80.3(1)"breeding animals"(b)
- inventory, valuation of, 28(1.2)

**Brace (limb or spinal), as medical expense**, 118.2(2)(i)
**Brady bond**
- excluded from mark-to-market rules, 142.2(1)"mark-to-market property"(e), Reg. 9002(1)(d)
- owned by bank as specified debt obligation, 142.6(4)(a)(ii)
- reserve in respect of, Reg. 8006"specified loan"

**Branch advance**
- defined, 20.2(1)

**Branch financial statements**
- defined, 20.2(1)

**Branch tax**, 219
- exemption for first $500,000 of profits, Canada-U.S. Tax Convention Art. X:6(d)
- investment allowance, Reg. 219(1)(j), 808
- non-resident investment or pension fund, exclusion, 115.2
- tax treaty dividend rate limitation to apply, 219.2

**Breakdown of marriage**, *see* Divorce and separation
**Breakwater**
- capital cost allowance for, Reg. Sch. II:Cl. 3, Sch. II:Cl. 6

**Breast prosthesis**
- medical expense, Reg. 5700(j)

**Breeding animals/herd**
- defined, 80.3(1)

**Bribes**
- no deduction for, 67.5

**Bridge**
- capital cost, 13(7.5)(b), Reg. 1102(14.3)
- capital cost allowance for, Reg. Sch. II:Cl. 1(a)

**Bridging benefits**
- defined, Reg. 8500(1)

**Britain**, *see* United Kingdom
**British Columbia**, *see also* Province
- logging tax, credit for, 127(1), (2), Reg. 700
- northern, *see* Northern Canada
- tax rates, *see* introductory pages
- Vancouver, international banking centre, 33.1(3)

**British Commonwealth**
- defined, *Interpretation Act* 35(1)

**Broadcaster**
- prescribed person for Canadian film/video tax credit, Reg. 1106(7)

**Broadcasting**
- defined, *Interpretation Act* 35(1)
- royalties paid to U.S. resident, Canada–U.S. Tax Convention Art. XII:3(d)

**Broadcasting undertaking**
- foreign, defined, 19.1(4)
- limitation re advertising expenses, 19.1(1)

**Broker**, *see also* Registered securities dealer; Securities: dealer, trader or agent
- dividend received by
- • withholding tax, 153(4), (5)
- insurance, reserve for, 32(1)

**Brother**
- deemed not related on butterfly transaction, 55(5)(e)
- dependent, 118(6)(b)
- includes brother-in-law or in common-law, 252(2)(b)

**Building**
- additions/alterations
- • capital cost allowance, Reg. Sch. II:Cl. 3, Sch. II:Cl. 6(i), Sch. II:Cl. 6(k)
- • class of property acquired, Reg. 1102(19)
- • disability-related
- • • deductible, 20(1)(qq)
- • • medical expense credit, 118.2(2)(l.2)
- capital cost allowance for, Reg. Sch. II:Cl. 1(q), Sch. II:Cl. 3, Sch. II:Cl. 5, Sch. II:Cl. 6(a), Sch. II:Cl. 8
- construction, capitalization of soft costs, 18(3.1)–(3.7)
- deduction before available for use, 20(28), (29)
- designated area, in, capital cost allowance, Reg. Sch. II:Cl. 20
- mine, capital cost allowance, Reg. Sch. II:Cl. 10(g), Sch. II:Cl. 41
- multiple-unit residential, Reg. 1101(5b), Reg. Sch. II:Cl. 31, Sch. II:Cl. 32
- • separate classes for capital cost allowance, Reg. 1101(5b)
- proceeds of disposition allocated between land and, 13(21.1), 70(5)(d)
- rent paid before acquisition, deemed CCA, 13(5.2)
- rental properties, limitation on CCA, Reg. 1100(11)–(14.2)
- scientific research expenditures, limitations, 37(8)(d)(i), (ii), Reg. 2900(11)
- scientific research expenditures on, 37(8)(d)

**Building** *(cont'd)*
- separate class, where cost over $50,000, Reg. 1101(1ac), (1ad), (5b)
- special-purpose, defined, Reg. 2903
- when available for use, 13(28)

**Bump**
- of asset costs, on windup of corporation, 88(1)(d)

**Burden of proof**
- on Minister
- • failure to report capital gain resulting in denial of exemption, 110.6(6)
- • penalty, 163(3), 15.1(5)
- on taxpayer challenging assessment, 152(7)

**Burial services**, *see* Eligible funeral arrangement; Funeral services

**Bursary**, *see* Scholarship

**Bus and truck operators**
- allocation of income among provinces
- • corporation, Reg. 409
- • individual, Reg. 2604

**Bus driver**
- expenses, 8(1)(g)

**Business**, *see also* Adventure in the nature of trade; Business or property income
- adjustment time, defined, 14(5)
- carrying on in Canada
- • extended meaning of, 253
- • non-residents, 2(3)
- cessation, *see* Ceasing to carry on business
- defined
- • for purposes of 1995 stub period reserve, 34.2(3), (7)
- • generally, 248(1)
- disposition of by proprietor, 25
- expenses, *see* Expenses
- farming or fishing, 28
- income from, *see also* Business or property income
- • defined, 9(1)
- • earned in a province, Reg. 2603
- • • limitations, Reg. 2606
- • home office expenses, conditions for deductibility, 18(12)
- • more than one business, Reg. 2605
- • reserve for 1995 stub period, 34.2(4)
- limit, *see* Business limit
- losses, *see* Non-capital loss
- more than one
- • income earned in a province, Reg. 2605
- profits, 9(1), Canada–U.S. Tax Convention Art. VII
- proprietor's income from, 11(1)
- small, *see* Small business corporation
- termination of, *see* Ceasing to carry on business
- transfer of, to corporation or spouse, 24(2)

**Business corporation, foreign**, *see* Foreign business corporation

**Business-income tax (foreign)**
- deduction for, 126(2), (2.1)
- defined, 126(7)
- • for trusts, 104(22.4)

**Business investment loss**
- allowable, *see also* Allowable business investment loss
- • carryforward, 111(1)(a), 111(8)"non-capital loss"
- • deduction for, 3(d)
- bad debt, 50(1)(a)
- change of control of corporation, rules, 111(8)"net capital loss"C(b)
- deduction from, 39(9), (10)
- meaning, 39(1)(c)
- shares of bankrupt corporation, 50(1)(b), 50(1.1)

**Business limit**
- defined, 125(2)–(5.1), 248(1)
- effect on enhanced investment tax credit, 127(10.2), 127.1(2)"qualifying corporation"
- large corporation, 125(5.1)
- limits small business deduction, 125(1)(c)

**Business number**, *see also* Social Insurance Number
- defined, 248(1)
- penalty for failure to provide, 162(6)
- provision of, to provinces and other government departments, 241(4)(l)
- regulations requiring provision of, 221(1)(d.1)
- requirement to provide, 237(1.1), (2)
- • tax shelter information return, 237.1(7)

**Business or property income**, 12
- accrued interest on debt obligation, 12(3), (4), (9)
- amounts received for services to be rendered etc., 12(1)(a), 12(2)
- automobile provided to partner, 12(1)(y)
- bad debts recovered, 12(1)(i), (i.1)
- benefits from estates, trusts, etc., 12(1)(m)
- deductions from
- • not allowed, 18
- • permitted, 20(1)
- dividends, 12(1)(j), (k)
- eligible capital amount to be included, 14(1)
- employee benefit plan
- • amounts received from, 12(1)(n.1)
- employee trust, amounts received, 12(1)(n)
- employees profit sharing plan, amounts received from, 12(1)(n)
- employment tax deduction, 12(1)(q)
- energy conversion grant, 12(1)(u)
- forfeited amounts under salary deferral arrangements, 12(1)(n.2)
- home insulation grant, 12(1)(u)
- inducement payments, 12(1)(x)
- • prescribed amount, Reg. 7300
- • received by beneficiary of trust, or partner, 12(2.1)
- insurance proceeds expended, 12(1)(f)
- interest, 12(1)(c)
- inventory adjustment, 12(1)(r)
- investment tax credit, 12(1)(t)
- life insurance policies, accumulating fund, 12.2
- partnership, 12(1)(l)
- payments based on production or use, 12(1)(g)
- personal services business
- • loan from employer, 12(1)(w)
- registered home ownership savings plan, 12(10.1)
- reimbursement, 12(1)(x)
- • prescribed amount, Reg. 7300
- • received by beneficiary of trust, or partner, 12(2.1)
- reinsurance commission, 12(1)(s)
- reserves
- • certain goods and services, for, 12(1)(e)
- • doubtful debts, for, 12(1)(d)
- • guarantees etc., for, 12(1)(d.1)

Business or property income *(cont'd)*
- • quadrennial survey, for, 12(1)(h)
- retirement compensation arrangement, amounts received under, 12(1)(n.3)
- royalties, 12(1)(o)
- scientific research deduction, 12(1)(v)
- services rendered, amounts receivable for, 12(1)(b), 12(2)
- western grain stabilization payments, 12(1)(p)

**Business property**, *see* Former business property

**Butterfly transaction**, 55(3)(b)
- back-door rule, 88(1)(c)(vi), 88(1)(c.3)
- capital gains exemption disallowed, 110.6(7)(a)
- definitions, 55(1)
- exception where gain exempted by treaty, 55(3.1)(b) [temporary]
- excluded from capital gains strip rules, 55(3)(b)
- • exception for cross-border purchase, 55(3.1) [temporary]
- • exception for purchase butterfly, 55(1), (3.1), (3.2)

## C

**CCA**, *see* Capital cost allowance

**CCDE**, *see* Cumulative Canadian development expense

**CCOGPE**, *see* Cumulative Canadian oil and gas property expense

**CCPC**, *see* Canadian-controlled private corporation

**CCPC rate reduction percentage**
- defined, 123.4(1)

**CCTB**, *see* Child Tax Benefit

**CDA**, *see* Capital dividend account

**CDE**, *see* Canadian development expense

**CEC**, *see* Cumulative eligible capital

**CEDC**, *see* Community Economic Development Corporation (Nova Scotia)

**CEDOE**, *see* Canadian exploration and development overhead expense

**CEE**, *see* Canadian exploration expense

**CESG**, *see* Canada Education Savings Grant

**CFA**, *see* Cash flow adjustment

**CIF**, *see* Canadian investment fund

**CRCE**, *see* Canadian renewable and conservation expense

**CIDA**, *see* Canadian International Development Agency

**CNIL**, *see* Cumulative net investment loss

**COGPE**, *see* Canadian oil and gas property expense

**CPI (Consumer Price Index) adjustment**, *see* Indexing (for inflation)

**CPP**, *see* Canada Pension Plan/Quebec Pension Plan

**CSOH**, *see* Pre-1972 capital surplus on hand

**CSTSP**, *see* Computer software tax shelter property

**Cable**
- fibre optic, capital cost allowance, Reg. Sch. II:Cl. 42
- included in definition of "telecommunication", *Interpretation Act* 35(1)
- systems interface equipment, Reg. Sch. II:Cl. 10(v)

**Caisse populaire**, *see* Credit union

**Calcium chloride**
- extraction of, 248(1)"mineral resource"(d)(ii)
- included in definition of "mineral", 248(1)

**Calculation period**
- defined, 20.2(1)

**Calendar year**
- defined, *Interpretation Act* 37(1)(a)

**Camp, expenses of**
- deductible as child care expenses, 63(3)"child care expense"
- not deductible, 18(1)(l)(i)

**Canada**
- defined, 255, *Income Tax Conventions Interpretation Act* 5, *Interpretation Act* 35(1), Canada–U.S. Tax Convention Art. III:1(a)
- • application to continental shelf, *Interpretation Act* s. 8(2.2)
- • application to exclusive economic zone, *Interpretation Act* s. 8(2.1)
- government of, *see* Government
- incorporated in, defined, 248(1)"corporation" "corporation incorporated in Canada"
- resident of, *see* Resident of Canada

**Canada Child Tax Benefit**, *see* Child Tax Benefit

**Canada Customs and Revenue Agency**
- account numbers, *see* Business number
- collection actions, *see* Collection of tax
- created, *Canada Customs and Revenue Agency Act* 4(1)
- delegation of powers to officials of, 220(2.01)
- employees of, 220(2), (2.01)
- fairness package, *see* "Fairness package" (1991)
- operations of, 220(1)
- procedures not followed, assessment still valid, 166
- refund payable by, *see* Refund
- staff, discipline of, communication of information for, 241(4)(h), 241(4.1)
- tax withheld, held in trust for, 227(4)–(4.2)
- transfers between tax accounts, 221.2

**Canada Deposit Insurance Corporation**, *see also* Deposit insurance corporation
- bonds, etc. issued by
- • interest deemed not from Government of Canada, 212(15)
- subject to tax, 27(2), Reg. 7100

**Canada Education Savings Grant**
- not a contribution to RESP, 146.1(1)"contribution"
- repayment of, deduction, 60(x)

**Canada Employment and Immigration Commission**
- costs of appealing decision of, deductible, 60(o)

**Canada Employment Insurance Commission**
- employment insurance benefits, *see* Employment insurance
- financial assistance from, taxable, 56(1)(r)

**Canada Gazette**
- regulations to be published in, 221(2)

*Canada Grain Act*, 76(5)
- cash purchase ticket under, 76(4)

**Canada Mortgage and Housing Corporation**
- subject to tax, 27(2), Reg. 7100

*Canada–Newfoundland Atlantic Accord Act*
- communication of information for purposes of, 241(4)(d)(vi)

**Canada–Nova Scotia Offshore Petroleum Resources Accord**
- communication of information for purposes of, 241(4)(d)(vi)

## Index

**Canada Oil Substitution Program**, *see* Energy: conversion grant

**Canada Pension Plan/Quebec Pension Plan**
- amount payable by taxpayer under, collection of, 223(1)(c)
- assignment of pension under, 56(2)
- • excluded from attribution rules, 74.1(1)
- benefits taxable
- • election to pay tax attributable to earlier years, 56(8), 120.3
- • non-resident, 212(1)(h)(ii) [repealed], 217
- • resident of Canada, 56(1)(a)(i)(B)
- constitutes earned income for RRSP, 146(1)"earned income"(b.1)
- contributions
- • by employee, as employer, deduction for, 8(1)(l.1)
- • credit for, 118.7
- • self-employed earnings
- • • credit for half, 118.7
- • • deduction for half, 60(e)
- costs of appealing decision under
- • deductible, 60(o)
- • recovery of, income, 56(1)(l)(iii)
- death benefit, taxable, 56(1)(a)(i)(F), 56(1)(a.1)
- disability pension
- • election to pay tax attributable to earlier years, 56(8), 120.3
- • included in earned income
- • • for RRSP purposes, 146(1)"earned income"(b.1)
- • • for child care expenses, 63(3)"earned income"(d)
- disclosure of confidential information for purposes of, 241(3)(b), 241(4)(a), 241(4)(e)(iii)
- emigration of taxpayer, no deemed disposition, 128.1(10)"excluded right or interest"(g)(i)
- employer's source deductions, failure to remit, 227(9.1)
- excluded from pension credit, 118(8)(b)
- non-resident withholding tax, 212(1)(h)
- • U.S. residents, Canada–U.S. Tax Convention Art. XVIII:5
- repayment of overpayment under, deduction for, 60(n)
- retirement pension under
- • assignment of, not subject to attribution, 74.1(1)
- transfer of rights to pension under, 56(4)

**Canada Savings Bond**
- cash bonus on, 12.1
- • information return, Reg. 220

**Canada security (of life insurer)**
- change in use, 138(11.3)(c), (d) [repealed]
- defined, 138(12) [repealed]
- loss on disposition of, deductible, 138(3)(b) [repealed]
- premium on acquisition of, deductible, 138(3)(d) [repealed]

**Canada Shipping Act**, *see also* Vessel
- quadrennial survey under, reserve for, 20(1)(o), Reg. 3600
- vessel, defined under, 13(21)

**Canada Student Financial Assistance Act**
- interest paid under, credit for, 118.62

**Canada Student Loans Act**
- interest paid under, credit for, 118.62

**Canada–U.K. Tax Convention**, *see* Table of Contents

**Canada–U.S. auto pact**
- payments received, income, 56(1)(a)(v)

**Canada–U.S. Tax Convention**
- prescribed provision for elections, Reg. 7400(1)
- text, *see* Table of Contents

**Canadian**
- defined, for Canadian film credit certificate, Reg. 1106(1)"Canadian"

**Canadian affiliate**
- of foreign bank, defined, 142.7(1)

**Canadian Airlines International Limited**
- rescue package, *see* Fuel tax rebate

**Canadian amateur athletic association**
- refusal to register
- • appeal from, 172(3)(a), 180
- registration
- • refusal by Minister
- • • deemed, 172(4)(a)

**Canadian art**, *see also* Cultural property
- whether CCA allowed, Reg. 1102(1)(e)

**Canadian assets (of financial institution)**
- defined, 181(2), 190(1.1), Reg. 8600, 8603

**Canadian banking business**
- defined, 248(1)

**Canadian Broadcasting Corporation**
- subject to tax, 27(2), Reg. 7100

**Canadian benefits**
- defined, 217(1)

**Canadian business property**
- defined, Reg. 2400(1)

**Canadian citizen**
- meaning of, 19(5.1)
- ownership of Canadian newspaper for advertising expenses, 19(5)"Canadian newspaper"(a)

**Canadian Commercial Corporation**
- contract payment from, investment tax credit, Reg. 4606

**Canadian-controlled private corporation**, *see also* Private corporation; Small business corporation
- corporation becoming
- • capital dividend account, 89(1.1)
- corporation ceasing to be
- • election to trigger capital gains exemption, 48.1
- defined, 125(7), 248(1)
- dividend refund, 129(1), (3)(a)
- due date for balance of tax, 157(1)(b)(i)(B)
- employee stock options in, 7(1.1)
- existing since before 1972, ITAR 50
- gain on shares of, capital gains exemption, 110.6(2.1)
- investment tax credit
- • additional credit, 127(10.1)
- • refund of credit, 127.1
- loss on share or debt of, 39(1)(c)
- reassessment deadline 3 years, 152(3.1)
- small business deduction, 125(1)
- small business development bond issued by, 15.1

**Canadian corporation**
- corporation ceasing to be, tax on, 219.1
- defined, 89(1)"Canadian corporation"
- taxable, defined, 89(1)"taxable Canadian corporation"
- winding-up of, 88(1)
- • rules, 88(2)

# Index

**Canadian Cultural Property Export Review Board**, *see also* Cultural property
- communication of information to, 241(4)(d)(xii)
- determination of cultural property, 39(1)(a)(i.1), 110.1(1)(c), 118.1(1)"total cultural gifts"
- determination of value of cultural property, 118.1(10), (11)
- • appeal of determination, *Cultural Property Export and Import Act* 33.1
- • determination applies for 2 years, 118.1(10.1)

**Canadian development expense**, *see also* Resource expenses
- borrowed money
- • capitalization of interest, 21(2), (4)
- • • reassessment, 21(5)
- conversion to Canadian exploration expense on renunciation, 66(12.601), (12.602)
- cumulative
- • adjusted, defined, 66(14.3)
- • amount to be included in income, 66.2(1)
- • deduction for, 66.2(2)
- • • short taxation year, 66(13.1)
- • • where designation not made, tax on, 196
- • deemed, 66.2(8)
- • defined, 66.2(5)
- • designation re, 66(14.2)
- • • late, 66(14.4), (14.5)
- • partner's share, 66.2(6), (7)
- • successored, deduction for, 66.7(4)
- defined, 66.2(5)
- designation re
- • late, 66(14.4), (14.5)
- • where not made, 66.5(1)
- flow-through of, to shareholder, 66(12.62)
- minimum tax, 127.52(1)(e), (e.1)
- partnership, of
- • election to exclude, 66.2(5)"Canadian development expense"(f)
- prescribed, Reg. 1218
- reclassified as Canadian exploration expense, 66.7(9)
- • expenses for preceding years, 66.1(9)
- • "restricted expense" defined, 66.1(6)
- • successor corporation, 66.7(9)
- renunciation of, 66(12.601), (12.62)
- • adjustment, statement to be filed re, 66(12.73)
- • conversion to Canadian exploration expense, 66(12.601), (12.602)
- • effect of, 66(12.63)
- • excessive, penalty for, 163(2.2)
- • form to be filed by corporation, 66(12.7)
- • • late filing, 66(12.74), (12.75)
- • Minister's powers re verification, 66(12.72)
- • partnership, return to be filed, 66(12.69)
- • • late filing, 66(12.74), (12.75)
- • restriction on, 66(12.67), (12.71)
- • successor corporation, rules, 66.7(4)
- • application, 66.6(1)

**Canadian equity property**
- defined, Reg. 2400(1)

**Canadian exploration and development expenses**, *see also* Exploration and development expenses
- borrowed money
- • interest capitalized, 21(2), (4)
- • • reassessment, 21(5)
- computation of, 66(12)
- deduction for, 66(1)–(3)
- defined, 66(15)
- limitations of, 66(12.1)
- principal-business corporation, 66(1)
- successor corporation, rules, 66.7(1)
- • application, 66.6(1)
- taxpayers other than principal-business corporations, 66(3)
- unitized oil or gas field, 66(12.2), (12.3)

**Canadian exploration and development overhead expense**, Reg. 1206(1)

**Canadian exploration expense**, *see also* Exploration and development expenses; Resource expenses
- borrowed money
- • capitalization of interest, 21(2), (4)
- • • reassessment, 21(5)
- certificate re oil/gas well ceasing to be valid, 66.1(10)
- cumulative
- • amount included in, income, 66.1(1)
- • deduction for, 66.1(3)
- • deduction from income, 66.1(2), (3)
- • defined, 66.1(6)
- • other than principal-business corporation
- • • deduction from income, 66.1(3)
- • partner's share, 66.1(7)
- • principal-business corporation
- • • deduction from income, 66.1(2)
- • trust of, reduced by investment tax credit, 127(12.3)
- defined, 66.1(6)
- designation re, 66(14.1)
- • deduction, where not made, 66.5(1)
- • • tax on, 196
- • late, 66(14.4), (14.5)
- flow-through of, to shareholder, 66(12.6)
- • expenses in first 60 days of year, 66(12.66)
- minimum tax, 127.52(1)(e), (e.1)
- prescribed, Reg. 1217
- qualified
- • prescribed expenditures for, Reg. 4608
- reclassification of Canadian development expense as, 66.7(9)
- • "restricted expense" defined, 66.1(6)
- • "specified purpose" defined, 66.1(6)
- renunciation of, 66(12.6)
- • adjustment, statement to be filed, 66(12.73)
- • effect of, 66(12.61)
- • excessive, penalty for, 163(2.2)
- • form to be filed by corporation, 66(12.7)
- • • late filing, 66(12.74), (12.75)
- • Minister's powers re verification, 66(12.72)
- • non-arm's length partnership, 66(17)
- • partnership, return to be filed, 66(12.69)
- • • late filing, 66(12.74), (12.75)
- • restriction on, 66(12.67), (12.71)
- • successor corporation, rules, 66.7(3)
- • • application, 66.6(1)

**Canadian field processing**
- defined, 248(1)
- excluded from manufacturing and processing
- • for Class 29 CCA, Reg. 1104(9)(k)
- ineligible for M&P credit, 125.1(3)"manufacturing and processsing"(k)

2667

# Index

**Canadian field processing** *(cont'd)*
- property for use in, investment tax credit, 127(9)"qualified property"(c)(ix)
- property used for, capital cost allowance, Reg. Sch. II:Cl. 29(a)(ii), Sch. II:Cl. 41(c), (d)
- sulphur processing, 12(1)(o)(v)(B), 18(1)(m)(v)(B)

**Canadian film or video production**
- capital cost allowance offsetting income from, Reg. 1100(1)(m)
- defined, 125.4(1), Reg. 1106(3)
- separate CCA class, Reg. 1101(5k.1), Reg. Sch. II:Cl. 10(x)

**Canadian film or video production certificate**
- defined, 125.4(1)
- revocation of, 125.4(6)
- tax credit where issued, 125.4(3)

**Canadian film or video tax credit**, 125.4, *see also* Canadian film or video production; Film or video production services credit
- amalgamation of corporations, 87(2)(j.94)
- prescribed person, Reg. 1106(7)
- refund of credit before assessment, 164(1)(a)(ii)

**Canadian Forces**
- allowances not income, 6(1)(b)(ii), (iii)
- members deemed resident in Canada, 250(1)(b), 250(2)
- travelling and separation allowances, not income, 6(1)(b)(ii)

**Canadian government film agency**
- defined, Reg. 1106(1)"Canadian government film agency"

**Canadian Heritage, Department of**, *see also* Minister of Canadian Heritage
- certificate issued by, for Canadian film/video credit, Reg. 1106"excluded production"
- disclosure of information re cultural property to, 241(4)(d)(xii)

**Canadian Home Insulation Program**, *see* Home insulation grant

**Canadian International Development Agency**
- prescribed international development assistance program
- - defined, Reg. 3400
- - employee under, no overseas employment tax credit, 122.3(1)(a)
- - person working on deemed resident in Canada, 250(1)(d)

**Canadian investment fund**
- defined, Reg. 2400(1)

**Canadian investment income**
- defined, 129(4) [repealed]

**Canadian investment property**
- defined, Reg. 2400(1)

**Canadian labour expenditure**
- defined, for film/video production services credit, 125.5(1)
- qualified, *see* Qualified Canadian labour expenditure

**Canadian life investment income, defined**, 211.1(3)

**Canadian manufacturing and processing profits**
- calculation of, Reg. Part LII
- defined, 125.1(3)

**Canadian National Railway**, *see also* Railway

**Canadian newspaper**
- defined, 19(5)

**Canadian newspaper or periodical**
- defined, 19(5), (8)
- subject to tax, 27(2), Reg. 7100

**Canadian oil and gas exploration expense**, Reg. 1206(1)

**Canadian oil and gas property expense**, *see also* Exploration and development expenses; Resource expenses
- borrowed money
- - interest capitalized, 21(2), (4)
- - - reassessment, 21(5)
- cumulative
- - deduction for, 66.4(2)
- - defined, 66.4(5)
- - recovery of costs, 66.4(1)
- - - short taxation year, 66(13.1)
- - successored, deduction for, 66.7(5)
- defined, 66.4(5)
- disposition, defined, 66.4(5)"disposition" and "proceeds of disposition"
- flow-through of, to shareholder, 66(12.64)
- minimum tax, 127.52(1)(e), (e.1)
- partnership, of
- - election to exclude, 66.4(5)"Canadian oil and gas property expense"(b)
- - partner's share, 66.4(6), (7)
- proceeds of disposition, defined, 66.4(5)"disposition" and "proceeds of disposition"
- renunciation of, 66(12.64)
- - adjustment, statement to be filed re, 66(12.73)
- - effect of, 66(12.65)
- - excessive, penalty for, 163(2.2)
- - form to be filed by corporation, 66(12.7)
- - - late filing, 66(12.74), (12.75)
- - Minister's powers re verification, 66(12.72)
- - partnership, return to be filed, 66(12.69)
- - - late filing, 66(12.74), (12.75)
- - restriction on, 66(12.67), (12.71)
- - successor corporation, rules, 66.7(5)
- - - application, 66.6(2)
- unitized oil or gas field, 66(12.5)

**Canadian outstanding premiums**
- defined, Reg. 2400(1)

**Canadian ownership, corporation having degree of**
- otherwise Class 8 property, capital cost allowance, Reg. Sch. II:Cl. 19

*Canadian Pacific* **case overruled**, 20.3

**Canadian partnership**
- defined, 102(1), 248(1)
- eligible, defined, 80(1)

**Canadian premiums**
- defined, Reg. 8600

**Canadian property**
- of non-resident-owned investment corporation, defined, 133(8)"Canadian property"
- taxable, *see* Taxable Canadian property

**Canadian renewable and conservation expense**
- capital cost allowance disallowed, Reg. 1102(1)(a.1)
- defined, 66.1(6), Reg. 1219
- included in CEE, 66.1(6)"Canadian exploration expense"(g.1)

**Canadian reserve liabilities**
- of financial institution, defined, 181(2), 190(1), Reg. 8602

2668

# Index

Canadian reserve liabilities *(cont'd)*
- of insurer, Reg. 2400(1)
- - Large Corporations Tax, Reg. 8600

**Canadian resource expenses**
- reduction of, on change of control, 66.7(12)

**Canadian resource profits**
- defined, Reg. 5202

**Canadian resource property**
- acquisition from exempt person, 66.6
- amount designated re
- - "outlay" or "expense" 66(15)"outlay" or "expense"
- constitutes taxable Canadian property for certain purposes, 248(1)"taxable Canadian property"(n)(i)
- defined, 66(15)
- disposition of
- - by non-resident
- - - certificate, 116(5.2)
- - - purchaser liable for tax, 116(5.2)
- - - rules, 116(5.1)
- - effect on successor rules, 66.7(14)
- - no capital gain, 39(1)(a)(ii)
- - no capital loss, 39(1)(b)(ii)
- "eligible property" for transfer to corporation by shareholder, 85(1.1)(c)
- in corporation, share is taxable Canadian property, 115(1)(b)(v)(A)(II) [to be repealed], 248(1)"taxable Canadian property"(e)(i)(B), (ii)(B)
- in partnership, constitutes taxable Canadian property, 115(1)(b)(vii)(B) [to be repealed], 248(1)"taxable Canadian property"(g)(ii)
- non-resident's income earned on, 115(4)
- non-successor acquisitions, 66.7(16)
- original owner, defined, 66(15)
- predecessor owner, defined, 66(15)
- production from, defined, 66(15)
- reserve amount, defined, 66(15)
- royalties, included in income, 12(1)(o)
- rules for trusts, 104(5.2)
- "specified stage" defined, 208(1.1)
- successor rules, 66.7(14)

**Canadian security**
- beneficiary's taxable gain from, 104(21.1), (21.2)
- defined, 39(6)
- disposition of, 39(5)
- - election re, 39(4)
- owned by partnership, 39(4.1)

**Canadian service provider**
- defined, re non-resident investment or pension fund, 115.2(1)

**Canadian surtax payable**
- defined, 125.3(4)

**Canadian tax**
- defined, Canada–U.S. Tax Convention Art. III:1(a)

***Canadian Vessel Construction Assistance Act***
- conversion cost deemed separate class, 13(17)
- deduction under, deemed depreciation, 13(13)
- disposition of deposit under, 13(19), (20)

**Canadian waters**
- defined, *Interpretation Act* 35(1)

**Canadian Wheat Board**
- participation certificates, no interest on tax due, 161(5)

***Canadian Wheat Board Act***, 76(5)

**Canals**
- capital cost allowance, Reg. Sch. II:Cl. 1(b)

**Cancellation of lease**, *see* Lease cancellation payment

**Canoes**
- capital cost allowance, Reg. Sch. II:Cl. 7

***Canterra Energy* case overruled**, 257

**Capacity test**
- for shareholder loans, 15(2.4)(e)

**Cape Breton**
- defined, 127(9)
- Development Corporation, subject to tax, 27(2), Reg. 7100

**Capital**
- allowance, *see* Capital allowance
- contribution of, addition to adjusted cost base, 53(1)(c)
- cost, *see* Capital cost; Capital cost allowance
- cost of, defined, Reg. 5204
- cumulative eligible, defined, 14(5), *see also* Cumulative eligible capital
- deemed contribution of, 53(1.1)
- defined, Reg. 5202, 5203, 5204
- - for financial institutions tax, 190.13
- - for large corporations tax, 181.2(3), 181.3(3)
- element, *see* Capital element
- "eligible capital expenditure" defined, 14(5)
- expenditure, not deductible, 18(1)(b)
- - depreciation, *see* Capital cost allowance
- - disability-related building modifications, deductible, 20(1)(qq)
- - disability-related devices or equipment, 20(1)(rr)
- - goodwill, deduction for, 20(1)(b)
- - landscaping, deduction for, 20(1)(aa)
- - scientific research and experimental development, deductible, 37
- - site investigation fees, deductible, 20(1)(dd)
- financial institutions', tax on, 190–190.211
- gains, *see* Capital gain
- income and, combined, 16(1), (4), (5)
- losses, *see* Capital loss
- outlay or loss, not deductible, 18(1)(b)
- property, *see* Capital property
- reorganization of, exchange of shares, 86(1); ITAR 26(27)
- stock, *see* Capital stock
- tax, *see* Capital tax
- thin, 18(4)–(8)

**Capital allowance**
- life insurance corporation, for Part VI capital tax
- - allowed against additional tax, 190.1(1.1)
- - defined, 190.16

**Capital cost**
- allowance, *see* Capital cost allowance
- deemed, 13(7)–(7.4)
- - depreciable property acquired with government assistance, 13(7.1), (7.2)
- - on death, 70(13)
- - reduction due to debt forgiveness, 13(7.1)(g), 80(5)
- leased property acquired, 13(5.1)
- manufacturing and processing property
- - deemed, 13(10)
- tax shelter investment, 143.2(6)
- undepreciated, *see* Undepreciated capital cost

2669

**Capital cost allowance**, *see also* Depreciable property
- access road (forest), Reg. Sch. II:Cl. 10(p)
- acquisition year rules, Reg. 1100(2)–(2.4)
  - non-arm's length exception, Reg. 1102(20)
- additional allowances
  - certified productions, Reg. 1100(1)(l)
  - Class 19, Reg. 1100(1)(n), (o)
  - Class 20, Reg. 1100(1)(p)
  - Class 21, Reg. 1100(1)(q)
  - Class 28, Reg. 1100(1)(w)
  - Class 35, Reg. 1100(1)(za.1)
  - Class 38, Reg. 1100(1)(zd)
  - Class 39, Reg. 1100(1)(ze)
  - Class 40, Reg. 1100(1)(zf)
  - Class 41, Reg. 1100(1)(y)
  - fishing vessels, Reg. 1100(1)(i)
  - grain storage facilities, Reg. 1100(1)(sb)
  - railway cars, Reg. 1100(1)(z), (z.1a)
  - railway track, Reg. 1100(1)(za), (za.1), (zb)
  - railway trestles, Reg. 1100(1)(za.2)
  - year 2000 compliant hardware/software, Reg. 1100(1)(zg), (zh)
- additions and alterations, *see also* building (*below*)
- advertising sign, Reg. Sch. II:Cl. 11
- aircraft, Reg. Sch. II:Cl. 9, Sch. II:Cl. 16
  - employee's, 8(1)(j), 13(11), Reg. 1100(6)
- airplane hangar, Reg. Sch. II:Cl. 6
- airplane runway, Reg. Sch. II:Cl. 1(g), Sch. II:Cl. 17(c)
  - for mine, Reg. Sch. II:Cl. 10(l)(ii)
- amount deductible, 20(1)(a), Reg. Parts Part XI, XVII
- amusement parks, property used in connection with, Reg. 1103(2b), 1104(12), Reg. Sch. II:Cl. 37
  - defined, Reg. 1104(12)
- apparel for rental, Reg. Sch. II:Cl. 12(k)
- automobile, Reg. 1102(1)(h)
  - definitions, Reg. 1102(11)
  - employee's, 8(1)(j)(ii), 13(11), Reg. 1100(6)
  - exclusion, Reg. 1102(1)(h)
  - general, Reg. 1102(11)–(13), Reg. Sch. II:Cl. 10(a)
  - short-term rental or leasing, for, Reg. Sch. II:Cl. 16
- automotive equipment, Reg. Sch. II:Cl. 10(a)
- available-for-use rule, 13(26)–(32), 20(28), (29), Reg. 1100(2)(a)(i), (vii)
- beneficiary of trust, deduction for, 104(16), (17.1), (17.2) [repealed]
- book (library), Reg. Sch. II:Cl. 12(a)
- breakwater, Reg. Sch. II:Cl. 3, Sch. II:Cl. 6
- bridge, Reg. Sch. II:Cl. 1(a)
- building, Reg. Sch. II:Cl. 1(q), Sch. II:Cl. 3, Sch. II:Cl. 5, Sch. II:Cl. 6(a), Sch. II:Cl. 8
  - addition/alteration, Reg. 1102(19), Reg. Sch. II:Cl. 3(g), Sch. II:Cl. 3(k), Sch. II:Cl. 6(i), Sch. II:Cl. 6(k)
  - in designated area, Reg. Sch. II:Cl. 20
  - separate class where cost over $50,000, Reg. 1101(1ac), (1ad), (5b)
- cable system interface equipment, Reg. Sch. II:Cl. 10(v)
- Canadian film or video production, Reg. 1100(1)(m), Reg. Sch. II:Cl. 10(x)
  - separate class, Reg. 1101(5k.1)
- canal, Reg. Sch. II:Cl. 1(b)
- canoe, Reg. Sch. II:Cl. 7
- catalyst, Reg. Sch. II:Cl. 26

- catch-all class, Reg. Sch. II:Cl. 8
- certified Class 34 properties, Reg. 1104(11)
- certified feature film, Reg. Sch. II:Cl. 12(n)
- certified films and video tapes, Reg. 1100(21)–(23)
- certified production, Reg. Sch. II:Cl. 10(w), Sch. II:Cl. 12(n)
  - separate classes, Reg. 1101(5k), (5l)
- chinaware, Reg. Sch. II:Cl. 12(b)
- Class 38 property
  - separate class, election, Reg. 1101(5l)
- classes of depreciable property, Reg. Sch. II
  - inclusions in, Reg. 1103
  - prescribed, Reg. 1105
  - separate, Reg. 1101
  - transfers between, Reg. 1103
- coin-operated game, Reg. Sch. II:Cl. 16(f)
- computer, *see* Computer: capital cost allowance
- computer software, Reg. Sch. II:Cl. 12(o)
  - limitation where tax shelter investment, Reg. 1100(20.1)
- concession, Reg. Sch. II:Cl. 14
- contractor's movable equipment, Reg. Sch. II:Cl. 10(h), Sch. II:Cl. 22, Sch. II:Cl. 38
- corporation having degree of Canadian ownership
  - otherwise-Class 8 property, capital cost allowance, Reg. Sch. II:Cl. 19
- culvert, Reg. Sch. II:Cl. 1(c)
- cutlery, Reg. Sch. II:Cl. 12(b)
- cutting rights, Reg. 1100(1)(e)
- cutting/shaping part in machine, Reg. Sch. II:Cl. 12(j)
- dam, Reg. Sch. II:Cl. 1(d)
  - for mine, Reg. Sch. II:Cl. 10(l)
- data communication equipment, Reg. Sch. II:Cl. 3
- deductions allowed, Reg. 1100, 1700
- deemed depreciable property, separate classes, Reg. 1101(5g), Reg. Sch. II:Cl. 36
- definitions, Reg. 1104
- dental instruments (small), Reg. Sch. II:Cl. 12(e)
- die, etc., Reg. Sch. II:Cl. 12(d)
- dock, Reg. Sch. II:Cl. 3
  - for mine, Reg. Sch. II:Cl. 10(l)
- drilling vessels, Reg. 1100(1)(va)
- drive-in theatre property, Reg. Sch. II:Cl. 10(q)
- earth-moving equipment, Reg. Sch:Cl. 22, Sch:Cl. 38
  - separate class, election, Reg. 1101(5l)
- electrical generating equipment, Reg. 1100(1)(t), (ta), Reg. Sch. II:Cl. 1(k), Sch. II:Cl. 1(m), Sch. II:Cl. 2(a), Sch. II:Cl. 8(g), Sch. II:Cl. 8(f), Sch. II:Cl. 9(e), Sch. II:Cl. 9(f), Sch. II:Cl. 29, Sch. II:Cl. 34, Sch. II:Cl. 40
  - electric energy producer/distributor, Reg. Sch. II:Cl. 2(c), Sch. II:Cl. 8(f), Sch. II:Cl. 9(a)
  - used for mining, Reg. 1102(8)–(9.2), Reg. Sch. II:Cl. 10(r)
- electronic data-processing equipment, *see* Computer: capital cost allowance, Reg. Sch. II:Cl. 10(f), Sch. II:Cl. 29, Sch. II:Cl. 40
- employee's automobile or aircraft, 8(1)(j)(ii), 13(11), Reg. 1100(6)
- excess, 1975-76, defined, 138(12)
- farming and fishing property (pre-1972), Reg. 1700–1704
- fence, Reg. Sch. II:Cl. 6
  - in amusement park, Reg. Sch. II:Cl. 37
- fibre optic cable, Reg. Sch. II:Cl. 42
- 50% rule, Reg. 1100(2)–(2.4)
  - non-arm's length exception, Reg. 1102(20)

Capital cost allowance *(cont'd)*
- film production, *see* Canadian film or video production
- films and video tapes, Reg. 1100(21)–(23), 1104(2), (10)
- first-year rule, Reg. 1100(2)–(2.4)
- fishing vessels, Reg. 1100(1)(i)
- - separate classes, Reg. 1101(2)
- franchise, Reg. 1100(1)(c), 1100(9), Reg. Sch. II:Cl. 14
- gas manufacturing/distributing equipment, Reg. Sch. II:Cl. 1(n), Sch. II:Cl. 2(d)
- generating equipment, Reg. 1100(1)(t), (ta), Reg. Sch. II:Cl. 1(k), Sch. II:Cl. 1(m), Sch. II:Cl. 2(a), Sch. II:Cl. 2(c), Sch. II:Cl. 8(f), Sch. II:Cl. 8(g), Sch. II:Cl. 9(a), Sch. II:Cl. 9(e), Sch. II:Cl. 9(f), Sch. II:Cl. 29, Sch. II:Cl. 34, Sch. II:Cl. 40
- grain storage facilities, Reg. 1100(1)(sb)
- greenhouse, Reg. Sch. II:Cl. 6
- half-year rule, Reg. 1100(2)–(2.4)
- harness, Reg. Sch. II:Cl. 10(c)
- heat production/distribution equipment, Reg. Sch. II:Cl. 1(p), Sch. II:Cl. 2(f)
- heat recovery equipment, Reg. Sch. II:Cl. 34
- heavy water, Reg. Sch. II:Cl. 26
- hydro electric installation, Reg. Sch. II:Cl. 34
- industrial mineral mines, Reg. 1100(1)(g), Reg. Sch. V
- insurer, 13(22)
- jetty, Reg. Sch. II:Cl. 1(e), Sch. II:Cl. 3
- jig, Reg. Sch. II:Cl. 12(d)
- kiln, Reg. Sch. II:Cl. 8
- kitchen utensils, Reg. Sch. II:Cl. 12(c)
- land excluded, Reg. 1102(2)
- last, Reg. Sch. II:Cl. 12(d)
- lease option agreements, separate classes, Reg. 1101(5)
- leased properties
- - buildings on, Reg. 1102(5)
- - improvements to, Reg. 1102(4)
- - leasehold interest, Reg. 1100(1)(b), 1102(4)–(6), Reg. Sch. II:Cl. 13, Reg. Sch. III
- - acquired before 1949, Reg. 1102(6)
- - Expo '67 or '86, Reg. Sch. II:Cl. 23
- - separate classes, Reg. 1101(5h)
- leasing properties, Reg. 1100(15)–(20)
- - non-arm's length exception, Reg. 1102(20)
- - separate classes, 1101(5c)
- licence, Reg. Sch. II:Cl. 14
- life insurer, 13(23)
- linen, Reg. Sch. II:Cl. 12(g)
- logging equipment, Reg. Sch. II:Cl. 10(o)
- machinery/equipment, Reg. Sch. II:Cl. 8
- manufacturing/processing business, Reg. 1102(15), (16)
- - excluded activities, Reg. 1104(9)
- - new, in designated area
- - - property used in, Reg. Sch. II:Cl. 21
- - property used in, Reg. Sch. II:Cl. 29, Sch. II:Cl. 40, Sch. II:Cl. 43
- marine railway, Reg. Sch. II:Cl. 7
- medical instruments, Reg. Sch. II:Cl. 12(e)
- mine buildings, Reg. Sch. II:Cl. 10(g), Sch. II:Cl. 41
- mine equipment etc., Reg. Sch. II:Cl. 10(k), Sch. II:Cl. 10(l), Sch. II:Cl. 10(m), Sch. II:Cl. 41
- mine property, Reg. 1100(1)(w), (x), 1100A, Reg. Sch. II:Cl. 28, Sch. II:Cl. 41

- mine shaft etc., Reg. Sch. II:Cl. 12(f)
- mining, definitions, Reg. 1104(5)–(8)
- misclassified property, 13(6)
- mold, Reg. Sch. II:Cl. 12(d)
- mole, Reg. Sch. II:Cl. 1(f), Sch. II:Cl. 3
- motion picture film, Reg. Sch. II:Cl. 10(s), Sch. II:Cl. 18
- multiple-unit residential buildings, Reg. Sch. II:Cl. 31, Sch. II:Cl. 32
- - separate classes, Reg. 1101(5b)
- non-residents, Reg. 1102(3)
- none, while election in force, ITAR 26.1(2)
- offshore drilling vessels
- - additional allowance, Reg. 1100(1)(va)
- - separate classes, Reg. 1101(2b)
- oil or gas well equipment, Reg. Sch. II:Cl. 10(j), Sch. II:Cl. 41
- oil refinery property, Reg. Sch. II:Cl. 10(u), Sch. II:Cl. 41
- oil storage tank, Reg. Sch. II:Cl. 6, Sch. II:Cl. 29, Sch. II:Cl. 40
- outdoor advertising structures, Reg. Sch. II:Cl. 8(l), Sch. II:Cl. 11
- - separate class, election, Reg. 1101(5l)
- overburden removal cost, Reg. Sch. II:Cl. 12(q)
- parking area, Reg. Sch. II:Cl. 1(g)
- - for mine, Reg. Sch. II:Cl. 10(l)
- part-year resident's otherwise-Class 8 property, Reg. Sch. II:Cl. 19
- partnership property, excluded, Reg. 1102(1a)
- patent, Reg. 1100(1)(c), 1100(9), Reg. Sch. II:Cl. 14, Sch. II:Cl. 44
- pattern, Reg. Sch. II:Cl. 12(d)
- pinball machine, Reg. Sch. II:Cl. 16(f)
- pipeline, Reg. Sch. II:Cl. 1(l), Sch. II:Cl. 2(b)
- - for mine, Reg. Sch. II:Cl. 10(l)
- - separate classes, Reg. 1101(5i), (5j)
- pollution control equipment, Reg. 1100(1)(t), Reg. Sch. II:Cl. 24, Sch. II:Cl. 27
- prescribed classes of depreciable property, Reg. 1105
- property acquired by transfer, amalgamation or winding-up, Reg. 1102(14), (14.1)
- - non-arm's length exception, Reg. 1102(20)
- property acquired in the year, Reg. 1100(2)–(2.4)
- - non-arm's length exception, Reg. 1102(20)
- property not included in classes, Reg. 1102
- pulp mill, Reg. Sch. II:Cl. 5
- radar equipment, Reg. Sch. II:Cl. 9
- radio communication equipment, Reg. Sch. II:Cl. 8, Sch. II:Cl. 9
- railway cars, Reg. 1100(1)(z), (z.1a), Reg. Sch. II:Cl. 35
- - separate classes, Reg. 1101(5d), (5d.1)
- railway locomotive, Reg. Sch. II:Cl. 6
- railway property, Reg. 1100(1)(zc)
- railway sidings, Reg. 1100(8)
- railway system, Reg. Sch. II:Cl. 4
- railway tank car, Reg. Sch. II:Cl. 6
- railway track, Reg. 1100(1)(za.1), (zb), Reg. Sch. II:Cl. 1(h)
- - for mine, Reg. Sch. II:Cl. 10(m), Sch. II:Cl. 41
- - separate classes, Reg. 1101(5e), (5e.1)
- railway traffic control equipment, Reg. Sch. II:Cl. 1(i)
- rapid transit car, Reg. Sch. II:Cl. 8
- rates for various classes of property, Reg. 1100(1)
- recapture provisions, 13(1); ITAR 20(2)

2671

# Index

Capital cost allowance *(cont'd)*
- - passenger vehicle, 13(2)
- - R&D expenditures previously deducted, 37(6)
- - rollover where property replaced, 13(4), (4.1)
- - vessels, 13(13), (15), (16)
- reclassification of property, 13(5)
- recreational property, Reg. 1102(17)
- regulations, Reg. Part XI
- rental properties, Reg. 1100(11)–(14.2)
- - non-arm's length exception, Reg. 1102(20)
- - separate class for each, Reg. 1101(1ac)–(1ae)
- revocation of certificates (Class 34 properties), Reg. 1104(11)
- river improvements, Reg. 1102(7)
- roadway, Reg. Sch. II:Cl. 1(g), Sch. II:Cl. 17
- - for mine, Reg. Sch. II:Cl. 10(l)
- roller skating rink floor, Reg. Sch. II:Cl. 10(i)
- rowboat, Reg. Sch. II:Cl. 7
- rules re property, Reg. 1102
- runway, *see* airplane runway (*above*)
- scale, metric, for retail use, Reg. Sch. II:Cl. 12(p)
- scow, Reg. Sch. II:Cl. 7
- separate classes, *see* Separate classes for capital cost allowance
- sidewalk, Reg. Sch. II:Cl. 1(g)
- sleigh, Reg. Sch. II:Cl. 10(d)
- software, *see* computer software (*above*)
- solar heating equipment, Reg. Sch. II:Cl. 34
- stable equipment, Reg. Sch. II:Cl. 10(c)
- steam generating equipment, Reg. Sch. II:Cl. 34
- storage area, Reg. Sch. II:Cl. 1(g)
- - for mine, Reg. Sch. II:Cl. 10(l)
- subway, Reg. Sch. II:Cl. 1(j)
- systems software, Reg. 1104(2), Reg. Sch. II:Cl. 10(f), Sch. II:Cl. 29, Sch. II:Cl. 40
- tableware, Reg. Sch. II:Cl. 12(b)
- tangible capital property not elsewhere specified, Reg. Sch. II:Cl. 8(i)
- tank (oil or water), Reg. Sch. II:Cl. 8
- taxation year less than 12 months, Reg. 1100(3)
- taxicab, Reg. Sch. II:Cl. 16
- telecommunication spacecraft, Reg. Sch. II:Cl. 10(f.2), Sch. II:Cl. 30
- - separate classes, Reg. 1101(5a)
- telephone/telegraph equipment, Reg. Sch. II:Cl. 3, Sch. II:Cl. 17
- telephone/telegraph system, Reg. Sch. II:Cl. 17
- television commercial, Reg. Sch. II:Cl. 12(m)
- terminal loss, 20(16)
- - limitation re passenger vehicles, 20(16.1)
- timber cutting/clearing equipment etc., Reg. Sch. II:Cl. 10(n), Sch. II:Cl. 15
- timber limits and cutting rights, Reg. 1100(1)(e)
- - separate classes, Reg. 1101(3)
- timber resource property, Reg. Sch. II:Cl. 33
- tools
- - portable, for rental, Reg. Sch. II:Cl. 10(b), Sch. II:Cl. 29, Sch. II:Cl. 40
- - small, Reg. Sch. II:Cl. 12(h)
- "total depreciation" defined, 13(21)
- townsite costs for mine, Reg. 1102(18) [repealed], Reg. Sch. II:Cl. 10(l)
- trailer, Reg. Sch. II:Cl. 10(e)
- tramways, Reg. Sch. II:Cl. 4
- transferred property, 13(5)
- trestles, Reg. 1100(1)(za.2), (zb), Reg. Sch. II:Cl. 3
- - separate classes, Reg. 1101(5e.2), (5f)
- tunnel, Reg. Sch. II:Cl. 1(j)
- undepreciated capital cost, defined, 13(21)
- underground storage cost, Reg. Sch. II:Cl. 10(f.1), Sch. II:Cl. 41
- uniforms, Reg. Sch. II:Cl. 12(k)
- vat, Reg. Sch. II:Cl. 8
- vessels, Reg. 1101(2)–(2b), Reg. Sch. II:Cl. 7
- - certified, Reg. 1100(1)(v), 1101(2a)
- - separate classes, Reg. 1101(2)–(2b)
- video game, Reg. Sch. II:Cl. 16(f)
- videotape, Reg. Sch. II:Cl. 10(s), Sch. II:Cl. 12(l), Sch. II:Cl. 12(m)
- videotape cassette for rental, Reg. Sch. II:Cl. 12(r)
- wagon, Reg. Sch. II:Cl. 10(d)
- water distributing equipment, Reg. Sch. II:Cl. 1(o), Sch. II:Cl. 10(e)
- water storage tank, Reg. Sch. II:Cl. 6, Sch. II:Cl. 29, Sch. II:Cl. 40
- wharf, Reg. Sch. II:Cl. 3, Sch. II:Cl. 6
- - for mine, Reg. Sch. II:Cl. 10(l)
- wind energy conversion system, Reg. Sch. II:Cl. 34
- windmill, Reg. Sch. II:Cl. 3
- woods assets, Reg. Sch. IV
- year 2000 compliant hardware/software, Reg. 1100(1)(zg), (zh)

**Capital deduction**
- for financial institutions tax
- - deducted in computing amount subject to tax, 190.1(1)
- - defined, 190.15
- for large corporations tax
- - deducted in computing amount subject to tax, 181.1(1)(b)
- - defined, 181.5

**Capital dividend**, 83(2)
- account, *see* Capital dividend account
- amalgamation, on, 87(2)(x)(ii)
- election to treat dividend as, 83(2), (2.2)–(2.4)
- - form and manner of making, Reg. 2101
- - where not available, 83(2.1)
- paid to non-resident, 212(2)(b)
- - through trust, 212(1)(c)(ii)
- private corporation, Reg. 2101

**Capital dividend account**
- amalgamation, on, 87(2)(z.1)
- corporation ceasing to be exempt, 89(1.2)
- defined, 89(1)
- "designated property" defined, 89(1)
- dividend payable before May 7, 1974, ITAR 32.1(4)
- gift by corporation, 89(1)"capital dividend account"(a)(i)(A)
- life insurance proceeds
- - after May 23, 1985, 89(1)"capital dividend account"(d)
- - before May 24, 1985, 89(1)"capital dividend account"(e)
- - exclusion from anti-avoidance rule, 83(2.3)
- payment out of, *see* Capital dividend
- prescribed labour-sponsored venture capital corporation, of, deemed nil, 131(11)(e)
- where control acquired, 89(1.1)

**Capital element**
- annuity, of, deductible, 60(a)

# Index

Capital element *(cont'd)*
- blended payment, 16(1), (4), (5); 20(1)(k) [repealed]
- government annuity, of, 58(4)

**Capital gain**, *see also* Capital gains and losses
- allocation of
  - - credit union, by, 137(5.1), (5.2)
- convertible property, 51
- deduction, *see* Capital gains deduction
- deemed
  - - capital gains stripping, 55(2)–(5)
  - - debt forgiveness, 80(12)
  - - negative adjusted cost base, 40(3)
  - - - of passive partnership interest, 40(3.1)
- defined, 39(1)(a), 40(1)(a)
- dividend instead of, on disposition of share of foreign affiliate, 93(1)
- donation of publicly traded shares, 38(a.1)
- exchanges of property, 44
- failure to report, 110.6(6)
- foreign affiliate, of
  - - election re, Reg. 5902
- income, 3
- life insurer's pre-1969 property, 138(11.2)
- listed personal property
  - - taxable net gain, 41
- non-resident, 115(1)(b)
  - - prorating for gains before May 1995, 40(9)
- not included in income from property, 9(3)
- principal residence
  - - exemption, 40(2)(b)
  - - farmer's, 40(2)(c)
- recovery of bad debt, 39(11)
- reserve, *see* Reserve: capital gain
- rollover, *see* Rollover
- shares, donation of, 38(a.1)
- specified, deductions for, 126(5.1)
- stripping, 55(2)–(5)
- taxable
  - - beneficiary's, designated by trust, 104(21.1), (21.2)
  - - defined, 38(a), 248(1)
  - - definitions, 54
  - - excluded from income of certain exempt organizations, 149(2)
  - - foreign affiliate, of, 95(2)(f)
  - - insurer's, 138(2)(b), 142
  - - net, of trust, 104(21.3)
  - - partnership, of, 96(1.7)
  - - trust's, designation to beneficiary, 104(21)
- taxed
  - - defined, 130(3)
- treaty rules, Canada–U.S. Tax Convention Art. XIII

**Capital gains and losses**, *see also* Capital gain; Capital loss
- adjusted cost base of property owned on Dec. 31/71, ITAR 26(3), (4)
- application of subdivision c, ITAR 26(1)
- becoming resident, on, 128.1(1)(b)
- ceasing to be resident, on, 128.1(4)(b)
- deemed, from property transferred to spouse, 74.2(2)
- deemed acquisition or disposal of property, 45
- disposition after June 18/71 where not at arm's length, ITAR 26(5)
- disposition before 1972, ITAR 26(5)
- disposition subject to warranty, 42

- disposition to corporation controlling or controlled by taxpayer, 40(2)(a)(ii)
- dividend in kind, cost of, 52(2)
- election re cost of property owned on Dec. 31/71, ITAR 26(7)
- employees profit sharing plan, allocated under, 144(4)–(4.2)
- exempt person, of, 40(2)(a)(i)
- fair market value of securities, ITAR 26(11)
- foreign affiliate, of, 95(2)(f)
- foreign exchange, 39(2)
- identical properties, 47
- "listed-personal-property loss" defined, 41(3)
- lottery prize, 40(2)(f)
- meaning of, 39(1)
- negative adjusted cost base deemed gain, 40(3), (3.1)
- non-resident taxpayer, 40(2)(a)(i)
- options, *see* Option
- partial dispositions, 43
- personal-use property, 46
  - - corporation, 46(4)
- prizes, 52(4)
- property whose value included in income, cost of, 52(1)
- purchase of bond etc. by issuer, 39(3)
- reacquired property, ITAR 26(6)
- right to receive from unit trust, cost of, 52(6)
- rollover, *see* Rollover
- stock dividends, 52(3)
- Valuation Day, ITAR 24, 25

**Capital gains deduction**, 110.6
- allowable business investment loss, interaction, with, 39(9), 110.6(1)"annual gains limit"B(b), 110.6(1)"cumulative gains limit"(b)
- anti-avoidance rules, 110.6(7)–(11)
- beneficiary of trust, 104(21.2)
- definitions, 110.6(1)
- determination of income while not resident, 110.6(13)
- double-dipping restriction, *see* Cumulative net investment loss
- election to trigger gain before corporation goes public, 48.1
- election to trigger gain on Feb. 22/94, 110.6(19)–(30); ITAR 26(29)
  - - cumulative eligible capital, 14(1)(a)(v)D, 14(9)
  - - depreciable capital property
    - - - cost, 13(7)(e.1)
    - - - no recapture, 13(21)"undepreciated capital cost"F
  - - excessive, 14(9), 110.6(19)(a)(ii)(C)(II), 110.6(22)(a)B, 110.6(28)
  - - non-qualifying real property, 110.6(21)
  - - option, 40(3.2)
  - - partnership interest, 110.6(23)
  - - penalty for late election, 110.6(29)
  - - principal residence, 40(2)(b)A, D, 40(7.1)
  - - shares from employee stock option, 110.6(19)(a)(i)(A)B
- failure to report gains, 110.6(6)
- individual deemed resident in Canada, 110.6(5)
- interest expense, effect of, *see* Cumulative net investment loss
- maximum, 110.6(4)
- non-qualifying real property, defined, 110.6(1)
- other property, 110.6(3)
- prescribed shares, Reg. 6205

Capital gains deduction *(cont'd)*
- qualified farm property, 110.6(2)
- qualified small business corporation shares, 110.6(2.1)
- real property, limitations, 110.6(1)"annual gains limit" "eligible real property gain"
- specified capital gains, 126(5.1)
- spousal trust, of, 110.6(12)
- where amount deemed proceeds of disposition rather than dividend, 183.1(7)
- where not permitted, 110.6(7), (8), (11)

**Capital gains dividend**
- investment corporation, Reg. 2104
- mortgage investment corporation, 130.1(4), Reg. 2104.1
- mutual fund corporation, 131(1)–(1.4), Reg. 2104
- non-resident-owned investment corporations, 133(7.1), Reg. 2105

**Capital gains dividend account**
- mutual fund corporation, 131(6)"capital gains dividend account"
- non-resident-owned investment corporation, of
- - defined, 133(8)

**Capital gains exemption**, *see* Capital gains deduction

**Capital gains redemptions**
- mutual fund corporation, 131(6)"capital gains redemptions"
- mutual fund trust, of, 132(1)
- - defined, 132(4)

**Capital gains refund**
- investment corporation, 130(2)
- mutual fund corporation, to, 131(2), (3)
- - interest on, 131(3.1)
- mutual fund trust, to, 132(1), (2)
- - interest on, 132(2.1)

**Capital gains stripping**
- anti-avoidance rules, 55(2), (3.1)
- exemption for butterfly transaction, 55(3)(b)
- - exclusion for cross-border purchase butterfly, 55(3.1)

**Capital interest (in a trust)**, *see* Trust (or estate): capital interest in

**Capital loss**, *see also* Capital gains and losses; Net capital loss
- allowable
- - defined, 38(b)
- - foreign affiliate, of, 95(2)(f)
- - partnership, of, 96(1.7)
- bad debt, 50(1)
- - personal-use property, 50(2)
- deduction for, 3
- defined, 39(1)(b)
- disposition of bond, etc., by corporation, 40(2)(d)
- disposition of debt, limitations on, 40(2)(e.1), (e.2), 40(2)(g)(ii)
- disposition of property to affiliated person, 40(3.3), (3.4)
- disposition of property to person controlling or controlled by corporate taxpayer, 40(3.3), (3.4)
- labour-sponsored venture capital corporation, disposition of shares of, 40(2)(i)
- net, *see* Net capital loss
- not included in loss from property, 9(3)
- personal-use property, 40(2)(g)(iii)
- pre-1986 balance, defined, 111(8)

- reassessment, 152(6)(a)
- restricted, 40(2), *see also* Stop-loss rules
- scientific research tax credit, unused, 39(8)
- shares of bankrupt corporation, 50(1)
- shares of controlled corporation, disposition of, 40(2)(h)
- shares of foreign affiliate, disposition of, 93(2)–(2.3), (4)
- stock savings plan, disposition of shares of, 40(2)(i)
- stop-loss rules, *see* Stop-loss rules
- superficial, 40(2)(g)(i), 54"superficial loss"
- unused share-purchase tax credit, 39(7)
- venture capital corporation, disposition of shares of, 40(2)(i)
- warranty, outlay or expense under, 42

**Capital property**, *see also* Disposition; Property
- adjusted cost base of, *see* Adjusted cost base
- amalgamation, on, 53(6), 87(2)(e)
- certain shares deemed to be, 54.2
- deceased taxpayer's, 70(5)
- - fair market value, 70(5.3)
- defined, 54, 248(1); ITAR 26(12)"capital property"
- depreciable, *see* Depreciable property
- eligible, *see* Eligible capital property
- "eligible property" for transfer to corporation by shareholder, 85(1.1)(a)
- gifts of, 118.1(6)
- - by corporation, 110.1(3)
- non-depreciable
- - change of control of corporation, 111(4)(c)–(e)
- share
- - loss on, 112(3)
- transfer of, to corporation, ITAR 26(5.2)

**Capital setoff adjustment**, *see* Transfer pricing capital setoff adjustment

**Capital stock**
- "class" interpretation, 248(6)
- tax-deferred preferred series, Reg. 2107

**Capital surplus**, *see* Pre-1972 capital surplus on hand

**Capital tax**
- defined, re insurance reserves, Reg. 1408(1)
- financial institutions tax, Part VI (190–190.24)
- Large Corporations Tax, Part I.3 (181–181.8)
- provincial, deductibility of, 18
- treaty restrictions, Canada–U.S. Tax Convention Art. XXIII

**Capitalization, thin**, 18(4)–(8)

**Capitalization of interest**
- election, 21

**Car**, *see* Automobile; Passenger vehicle

**Career retraining**, *see* Job retraining

**Caregiver**
- tax credit, 118(1)B(c.1)

**Caribbean Development Bank**
- bonds of
- - eligible for RRSP investment, Reg. 4900(1)(l)(iv)
- - trust investing in, not foreign property, Reg. 5000(7)"specified international finance trust"(c)(i)(C)

**Carrier**
- defined, 146.3(1)"carrier"
- - for RRIF, Reg. 215(1)

# Index

**Carryback**, *see also* Carryforward
- charitable donations, from year of death, 118.1(4)
- losses, 111(1)
  - after amalgamation, 87(2.11)
  - after emigration, against gains deemed on emigration, 128.1(8)
  - amendment to earlier return, 152(6)(c)
  - foreign accrual property, 152(6.1), Reg. 5903(1)
  - from estate, to taxpayer's year of death, 164(6)

**Carryforward**
- business losses, 111(1)(a)
- Canadian life investment losses (Part XII.3 tax), 211.1(2)
- capital losses (net capital losses)
  - against capital gains, 111(1)(b), 111(1.1)
  - against other income in year of death, 111(2)
  - defined, 111(8)"net capital loss"
  - pre-1986, against other income, 111(1.1)
- charitable donations
  - corporation, 110(1)
  - credit, 118.1(1)"total charitable gifts"
  - deduction to corporation, 110.1(1)(a)
  - individual, 118.1(1)
- deposit insurance corporation, losses of, 137.1(11)(a)
- disbursement excess of charity, 11
- education credit, 118.61
- emigration deemed gains, 128.1(8)
- expense, against reimbursement or assistance, 12(2.2)
- FAPI, foreign taxes against, 91(4)
- farm land disposed of by partnership, loss on, 101
- farm losses, 111(1)(d)
  - restricted, 111(1)(c)
- foreign accrual property losses, 95(1)"foreign accrual property income"F [to be repealed], Reg. 5903(1)
- foreign affiliate's forgiven debt, 95(1)"foreign accrual property income"A.2, G
- foreign bank's Canadian affiliate's losses, 142.7(12)
- foreign tax credits, unused, 126(2)(a), 126(2.3), 126(7)
- gifts to charity
  - credit, 118.1(1)"total charitable gifts"
  - deduction to corporation, 110.1(1)(a)
- home office expenses, undeducted, 8(13)(c), 18(12)(c)
- interest paid on purchase of shares, 20(1)(q)(ii)
- interest paid on student loan, 118.62:B
- investment tax credit, unused, 127(5), 127(9)"investment tax credit"(c)(ii)
- legal fees to obtain retiring allowance or pension benefit, 60(o.1)(i)
- limited partnership losses, 111(1)(e)
- listed personal property losses, 41(2)(b)
- minimum tax, 120.2(1)
- net capital losses, *see* Capital loss
- non-capital losses, 111(1)(a), 111(8)"non-capital loss"
- non-deductible home office expenses, 8(13)(c), 18(12)(c)
- Part I.3 tax credit, unused, 125.3(1)
- Part VI tax credit, unused, 125.2(1)
- patronage dividends, 135(2.1)
- pre-1986 capital losses, 111(1.1)
- RRSP contributions not yet deducted, 146(5)(a)
- RRSP deduction room, 146(1)"RRSP deduction limit" "unused RRSP deduction room"
- reduction of balances on debt forgiveness, 80(3), (4)
- refundable dividend tax on hand, 129(3)(c)
- repayment of support payments, 60(c.2)
- research and development expenses, 37(1)
  - partnership, disallowed, 96(1)(e.1)
- restricted farm losses, 111(1)(c)
- scientific research expenses, 37(1)
- student loan interest credit, 118.62:B
- surtax credit, unused
  - against Part I.3 tax, 181.1(4)(b)
  - against Part VI tax, 190.1(3)(b)
- tuition credit, 118.61

**Carrying charges**
- interest accrued on bond, 20(14)
- interest paid, *see* Interest (monetary): deductible
- safety deposit box rental, 9(1)

**Carrying on business in Canada**
- extended meaning of, 253
- non-Canadian corporations
  - additional tax, 219
- non-resident, 115(1)(a)
  - liability for tax on, 2(3)(b)
- part-year resident, 114

**Carrying value (of property)**
- defined
  - for draft interest deductibility rules, 20.2(3)
  - for foreign investment entities, 94.1(1), (10)
  - for small business investment capital gain rollover, 44.1(1)
- foreign property rules
  - defined, 206(1)
- interest deductibility rules [draft]
  - defined, 20.2(3)
  - limit on deductibility of interest relating to distributions, 20.2(3)

**Carryover of losses**, *see* Carryback; Carryforward

**Carve-out arrangements**
- resource properties acquired from tax-exempt person, 66.6

**Carved-out income**
- deduction under Part I, 66(14.6)
- defined, 209(1)
- partnership deemed person, 209(6)
- tax on, 209(2)
  - payment, 209(4)
  - return, 209(3)

**Carved-out property**
- defined, 209(1)
- definitions, 209(1)
- exclusions from, Reg. 7600
- prescribed property, Reg. 7600

**Cash flow adjustment**
- insurance corporation, Reg. 2412

**Cash method of computing income**
- becoming non-resident, on, 28(4), (4.1)
- changing from, 28(3)
- defined, 28(1), 248(1)
- farmers, fishermen, 28
- non-resident ceasing to carry on business in Canada, 28(4), (4.1)

**Cash purchase ticket**
- grain, for
  - when amount included in income, 76(4)

**Cash register, electronic**
- capital cost allowance, Reg. Sch. II:Cl. 12(s)(ii)

2675

## Index

**Cash surrender value**
- of insurance policy, defined, 148(9), Reg. 310, 1408(1)

**Catalyst**
- capital cost allowance for, Reg. Sch. II:Cl. 26

**Catch**
- defined, Reg. 105.1(1)

**Catheters and related products**
- medical expense credit, 118.2(2)(i.1)

**Cattle**
- basic herd maintained since 1971, deduction, 29
- breeding, 80.3(1)"breeding animals" (b)
- dairy farming, 248(1)"farming"
- exhibiting and raising, 248(1)"farming"
- inventory, valuation of, 28(1.2)

**Ceasing to be a financial institution**, 142.6(1)(a), (c)

**Ceasing to be qualifying environmental trust**, 107.3(3)

**Ceasing to be resident in Canada**, *see also* Former resident
- attribution rule, application to deemed disposition, 74.2(3)
- deemed disposition of property, 128.1(4)(b)
- - election for, 128.1(4)(d)
- - instalment obligation not increased, 128.1(5)
- - returning former resident, 128.1(6), (7)
- - stock option income excluded, 7(1.6)
- demand for payment of taxes owing, 226(1)
- departure tax, 128.1(4)
- - additional tax on corporations, 219.1, 219.3
- - security for, 220(4.5)–(4.54)
- farmer or fisherman, 28(4), (4.1)
- fiscal period end, 128.1(4)(a.1)
- foreign exploration and development expenses, deduction, 66(4)(b)(i.1)
- foreign tax credit after emigration, 126(2.21)
- - trust beneficiary, 126(2.22)
- Home Buyers' Plan income inclusion, 146.01(5)
- information return, 128.1(9)
- Lifelong Learning Plan income inclusion, 146.02(5)
- loss after emigration, 128.1(8)
- moving to United Kingdom, Canada–U.K. Tax Convention Art. 13:9
- moving to the United States, Canada–U.S. Tax Convention Art. XIII:6
- negative cumulative eligible capital balance, 14(8)(a)
- payment of tax
- - election to defer, 159(4) [to be repealed], 220(4.5)–(4.54), Reg. 1301
- post-emigration loss, 128.1(8)
- reporting of assets, 128.1(9)
- rollovers of shares after emigration ignored, 128.3
- security for departure tax, 220(4.5)–(4.54)
- seizure of goods and chattels for non-payment of tax, 226(2)
- to pursue research under grant, 115(2)(b.1)
- trust, deemed, 94(5) [proposed]
- trust deemed to dispose of property on transferor's emigration, 104(4)(a.3)

**Ceasing to carry on business**, *see also* Death of taxpayer; Sale: business, of; Winding-up
- accounts receivable, 28(5)
- business income of individual, effect on, 34.1(8)(a), 34.2(6)(c)(i)
- disposition of depreciable property after, 13(8), 20(16.3)
- eligible capital property, 24(1)
- farming business, 28(4), (4.1), (5)
- general rules, 22–25
- non-resident, 10(12), (14)
- subsequent transactions
- - repayment of assistance, deduction relating to eligible capital expenditure, 20(1)(hh.1)
- - sale of inventory, 23(1)

**Ceasing to use eligible capital property in business**
- non-resident, 14(14)

**Ceasing to use inventory in business**
- non-resident, 10(12), (14)

**Ceasing to use property in Canadian business**
- non-resident financial institution, 142.6(1.1)

**Cemetery arrangements**, *see* Eligible funeral arrangement; Funeral services

**Cemetery care trust**
- defined, 148.1(1), 248(1)
- emigration of individual, no deemed disposition, 128.1(10)"excluded right or interest"(e)(iii)
- excluded from various trust rules, 108(1)"trust"(e.1)
- rollover to new trust, 248(1)"disposition"(f)(vi)

**Cemetery services**
- defined, 248(1)
- provision of under eligible funeral arrangements, 148.1(2)(b)(i)

**Certificate**
- accredited film or video production, 125.5(1), (6)
- amount payable, re, 223(2)
- - application of, 223(1)
- - charge on land, 223(5), (6)
- - costs, 223(3)
- - registration in Court, 223(3)
- - - binding under provincial laws, 223(8)
- - - proceedings re, 223(7)
- - - sale of property, 223(9)
- - sale of property
- - - application by Minister for Federal Court order, 223(11)
- - - requirements re documentation, 223(10)
- - total amount, "prescribed rate" sufficient details, 223(12)
- before distribution of estate etc., 159(2)
- - failure to obtain, 159(3)
- Canadian film or video production, 125.4(1)
- change of ownership, Reg. 502
- clearance, 159(2), (3)
- dispositions of property by non-resident, 116(2), (4), (5.2)
- ecologically sensitive land, 110.1(1)(d), 118.1(1)"total ecological gifts"
- employer's, re employees' expenses, 8(10)
- exemption from non-resident tax, 212(1)(b)(iv), 212(14); ITAR 10(5)
- fair market value of ecological gift, 118.1(10.5)
- oil/gas well, re, 66.1(6)"Canadian exploration expense"(d)(iv)
- - ceasing to be valid, 66.1(10)
- ownership, 234, Reg. 207
- participation, Canadian Wheat Board, 161(5)

**Certification fee paid to bank**, 20(1)(i) [repealed]

2676

## Index

**Certifiable past service event**
- defined, Reg. 8300(1)

**Certified feature film**
- capital cost allowance, Reg. 1100(21)–(23), Reg. Sch. II:Cl. 12(n)
- • add-back for minimum tax purposes, 127.52(1)(c)
- defined, Reg. 1104(2)
- information returns, Reg. 225

**Certified production**
- capital cost allowance, Reg. 1100(21)–(23), Reg. Sch. II:Cl. 10(w), Sch. II:Cl. 12(n)
- • add-back for minimum tax purposes, 127.52(1)(c)
- • additional, Reg. 1100(1)(l)
- • separate class, Reg. 1101(5k), (5l)
- defined, Reg. 1104(2)
- information returns, Reg. 225

**Certified property, defined**, 127(9)

**Chamber of commerce**
- exemption, 149(1)(e), 149(2)
- information return, whether required, 149(12)

**Change in use**
- capital property, 45
- depreciable property, 13(7)(a), (b)
- property of insurer, 138(11.3), (11.31)
- research property, changed to commercial use, 127(27), (29)

**Change of address**
- cost of, deduction, 62(3)(h)

**Change of control**, *see* Control of corporation: change of

**Charging provisions**, *see* Liability for tax

**Charitable donations/gifts**, *see* Gifts and donations

**Charitable foundation**, *see also* Charity; Private foundation; Public foundation; Registered charity
- charitable purposes of, 149.1(6.1)
- corporation controlled by, 149.1(12)
- defined, 149.1(1), Reg. 3700
- disbursement quota, 149.1(1)"disbursement quota" Reg. 3701
- • deliberate reduction of, tax on, 188(3), (4)
- political activities of, 149.1(6.1)
- prescribed amount, 149.1(1)"disbursement quota"C
- • Minister's authority re determination of, 149.1(1.2)
- transfer of property
- • tax on, 188(3), (4)
- value of property, determination of, Reg. 3702

**Charitable organization**, *see also* Charity; Registered charity
- business activities of, 149.1(6)
- charitable activities of, 149.1(6.2)
- defined, 149.1(1)
- designation of registered charity as, 149.1(6.3)
- outside Canada, gifts to, 118.1(1)
- political activities of, 149.1(6.2)
- registration
- • application for, 248(1)"registered charity"
- • refusal by Minister
- • • deemed, 172(4)(a)
- • refusal or revocation, appeal, 172(3)(a)
- • revocation of, 149.1(2)
- resources of, devoted to charitable activity, 149.1(6)
- • deemed, 149.1(10)
- U.S. resident, Canada–U.S. Tax Convention Art. XXI
- universities outside Canada, Reg. 3503, Reg. Sch. VIII

- volunteers operating business, 149.1(1)"related business"

**Charity**, *see also* Registered charity
- associated
- • designation of, by Minister, 149.1(7)
- charitable purposes, defined, 149.1(1)
- defined, 149.1(1)"charity"
- designated as beneficiary of insurance policy, 118.1(5.1), (5.2)
- disclosure of information by CCRA, 149.1(15), 241(3.2)
- disposal of ecologically sensitive land, tax on, 207.31
- donations to, *see* Gifts and donations
- exemption, 149(1)(f)
- gifts received, 149.1(12)(b)
- loan to donor, 118.1(16)
- political activities, 149.1(1.1)
- specified gifts, 149.1(1.1)

**Charity trusts, employees'**
- receipts, Reg. 3502

**Chattels**
- seizure of, for unpaid tax, 225

**Cheque**
- dishonoured, 162(11) [repealed]

**Chief source of income**
- determination by Minister, 31

**Child**, *see also* Age; Dependant; Intergenerational transfers; Minor
- adopted, 252(1)
- defined, *see* extended meaning of (*below*)
- dependent, 118(6)(a)
- • credit for, 118(1)B(d), (e)
- disposition of property to, 40(1.1)
- extended meaning of, 70(10), 75.1(2), 110.6(1), 252(1); ITAR 20(1.11), 26(20)
- family farm corporation transferred to, 70(9.3)
- farm property transferred to, 44(1.1), 70(9); ITAR 26(18), (19)
- • from spouse's trust, 70(9.1)
- infirm, credit, 118(1)B(d), (e)
- maintenance payments for, *see* Support payments (spousal or child)
- property transferred to
- • gain or loss deemed to be transferor's, 75.1
- support of, deemed, 56(6), (7)

**Child Benefit**, *see* Child Tax Benefit

**Child care expenses**, 63
- cross-border commuter, 63(4)
- deduction for, 63(1), 63(2.2), 64.1
- defined, 63(3)
- "earned income" defined, 63(3)"earned income"
- eligible child, 63(3)"eligible child"
- residents absent from Canada
- • deduction, 64.1
- school or university, attendance at, 63(2.2)
- supporting person, 63(3)"supporting person"
- taxpayer's income vs. supporting person's income, 63(2), (2.1)

**Child support**, *see* Support payments (spousal or child)

**Child support amount**
- defined, 56.1(4), 60.1(4)
- whether deductible, 60(b), 60.1
- whether taxable, 56(1)(b), 56.1

## Index

**Child Tax Benefit**, 122.6–122.64
- agreement with province to vary amount, 122.63
- amount of, 122.61(1)
- attribution rules inapplicable to amounts paid, 74.1(2)
- confidentiality of information, 122.64
- definitions, 122.6
- eligible individual, 122.6, 122.62, Reg. 6300–6302
- indexing for inflation, 122.61(5)
- not to be assigned, attached, garnished, etc., 122.61(5)
- part-year residents, 122.61(3)
- Working Income Supplement, 122.61(1)A(c)C

**Child tax credit**, 122.2 (pre-1993)

**China**, *see also* Foreign government
- universities, gifts to, Reg. Sch. VIII s. 14

**Chinaware**
- capital cost allowance for, Reg. Sch. II:Cl. 12(b)

**Chiropractor**, *see* Professional practice

**Christmas party exemption**
- to meal and entertainment restriction, 67.1(2)(e)

**Chose in action, as property**, 248(1)

**Church**, *see also* Charity
- clergy employed by, deduction re residence, 8(1)(c)

**Civil law**
- application to federal, *Interpretation Act* 8.1, 8.2

**Civilian War Pensions and Allowances Act**
- pension under, exempt, 81(1)(d)

**Claim liability**
- defined, insurance policy reserves, defined, Reg. 1408(1)

**Claims, unpaid**, *see* Insurance corporation: reserve: unpaid claims; Insurance corporation: unpaid claims reserve adjustment

**Class of animal**
- defined, Reg. 1802(5)

**Class of shares**
- includes series, 248(6)

**Classes of property**, *see* Capital cost allowance

**Classification society**
- defined, Reg. 3600(2)

**Clawback**
- deduction from income for, 60(w)
- disposition of labour-sponsored funds share, 211.8(1)
- old age security, 180.2
- unemployment benefits, deduction, 60(v.1)

**Clear days**
- calculation of, *Interpretation Act* 27(1)

**Clearance certificate**, 159(2)
- failure to obtain, 159(3)

**Clearing or levelling farm land**
- cost deductible, 30

**Clergy**
- allowance received by, deduction, 6(1)(b)(vi)
- residence, expense deductible, 8(1)(c)
- employer's certificate required, 8(10)
- travelling allowance not taxable, 6(1)(b)(vi)

**Clerical services**
- no application of penalty for misrepresentation, 163.2(9)

**Closing business**, *see* Ceasing to carry on business

**Club**
- dues, no deduction, 18(1)(l)(ii)
- exemption for, 149(1)(l), 149(2)
- deemed a trust, 149(5)
- information return required, 149(12)

**Coal**, *see also* Mineral resource
- included in definition of "mineral", 248(1)
- mine, allocation of depletion allowance, 65(3)
- royalties from, taxable, 12(1)(c)(v)(C)
- royalties not deductible, 18(1)(m)(v)(C)

**Coal mine operator**
- defined, Reg. 1104(2), 1206(1)
- services rendered by, Reg. 11046.1), 1204(3)(c)

**Cod fishermen**, *see* Fishing: compensation programs

**Cogeneration**
- energy systems, Reg. Sch. II:Cl. 43.1(c)(i)

**Cohabiting spouse**
- defined, 122.6

**Collateralized preferred shares**
- restriction on dividend deductibility, 112(2.4)

**Collection agreement**
- application of payments under, 228

**Collection of tax**, 222–229
- acquisition of tax debtor's property, 224.2
- by Internal Revenue Service, Canada–U.S. Tax Convention Art. XXVI A
- debt to Her Majesty, as, 222
- deduction or set-off, by, 224.1
- garnishment, 224
- in jeopardy, 164(1.2)–(1.31)
- proceedings, 225.2
- judge's powers, 225.2(11), (12)
- judicial review of authorization, 225.2(8)–(11)
- no appeal therefrom, 225.2(13)
- interference with official, 231.5(2)
- payment of moneys seized from tax debtor, 224.3
- requirement to disclose information, 231.2(1)
- requirement to provide foreign-based document, 231.6(1)
- restricted while objection or appeal underway, 225.1
- seizure of chattels, 225
- taxpayer leaving Canada or defaulting, 226

**College**, *see* Tuition fees; University

**Colostomy pads, as medical expense**, 118.2(2)(i)

**Commencement**
- defined, *Interpretation Act* 35(1)

**Commencement day**
- defined, 56.1(4), 60.1(4)

**Commercial debt obligation**, *see also* Commercial obligation
- deemed issued where amount designated following debt forgiveness, 80.03(7)(b)(i)
- defined, 80(1), 80.01(1), 80.02(1), 80.03(1)(a), 80.04(1)
- exchanged for other commercial debt obligation, 80(2)(h)
- issued by partner, 80(2)(n)
- issued by partnership, 80(15)
- joint liability for, allocation, 80(2)(o)
- settled by deceased's estate, 80(2)(p), (q)

**Commercial obligation**, *see also* Commercial debt obligation
- debt forgiveness
  - defined, 80(1), 80.01(1), 80.02(1), 80.03(1)(a), 80.04(1)
  - disposition of in exchange for another issued by same person, 40(2)(e.2)
    - addition to adjusted cost base, 53(1)(f.12)
- foreign tax credit
  - defined, 126(7)

**Commercial traveller**, *see* Salesperson

**Commission**
- mutual fund, limited partnership financing, 18.1
- unearned, reserve for, 32
- withholding tax, 153(1)(g)

**Commission agent**
- deductions, 8(1)(f)
  - automobile or aircraft costs, 8(1)(j), 8(9), 13(11)
  - certificate of employer, 8(10)

**Commissioner of Customs and Revenue**, *see also* Deputy Minister
- appointed, *Canada Customs and Revenue Agency Act* s. 25
- authorized to exercise powers of Minister, 220(1)

**Committee, return by**, *see also* Legal representative
- deemed to be legal representative, 248(1)"legal representative"
- obligations of, 159
- return required by, 150(3)

**Common-law partner**, *see also* Spouse
- defined, 248(1)
- transfer of property to, 160(1)

**Common-law spouse**, *see* Common-law partner

**Common share**, *see also* Share
- consideration for property transferred to corporation, 85(1)(h)
- defined
  - for small business investment capital gain rollover, 44.1(1)
  - generally, 248(1)

**Commonwealth**
- defined, *Interpretation Act* 35(1)

**Communal organization**
- definitions, 143(4)
- election to allocate gifts to members, 143(3.1)
- rollover to new trust, 248(1)"disposition"(f)(vi)
- rules re, 143(1)
- specification of member of family, effect of, 143(5)
- taxable income, election re, 143(2), (3)

**Communication of information (by Revenue Canada/CCRA)**, 241
- charities, regarding, by CCRA, 149.1(15), 241(3.2)
- Child Tax Benefit, 122.64; Reg. 3003
- offence of unauthorized use or disclosure, 239(2.2)–(2.22)
- police officer, to, 241(3)(c)
- prohibition against, 241(1), (2)
- province, to, Reg. 3003
- statistical purposes, 241(1)(d)(ix), 241(4)(e)(x), 241(4)(o)

**Community Development bonds, eligible for RRSP investment**, Reg. 4900(1)(i.1)

**Community Economic Development Corporation (Nova Scotia)**
- qualified investment for deferred income plans, Reg. 4900(1)(i.11)

**Commutation of annuity, payment on**
- source withholding, 153(1)(f)

**Commutation of benefits, pension plan**, Reg. 8503(2)(m), (n), 8503(2.1)

**Commuter to United States**
- charitable gifts, 118.1(9)
- child care expenses, 63(4)
- tuition credit, 118.5(1)(c)
  - transfer of, to supporting person, 118.9(1)

***Companies' Creditors Arrangement Act***
- provisions override third-party garnishment, 224(1.2)

**Compensation**
- certain payments exempt, 81(1)(d)
- cod fisherman *see* Fishing: compensation programs
- deferred profit sharing plan
  - individual ceases to be employed by an employer, 147(5.11)
- defined for RPP purposes, 147.1(1), Reg. 8507
- depreciable property, for, 13(21)"proceeds of disposition"
- from Federal Republic of Germany, exempt, 81(1)(g)
- limits pension contribution, 147.1(8), (9)
- taxable, 5, 6, 9
- to customer or client, trust income exempt, 149(1)(w)

**Competent authority**
- agreement based on tax treaty deemed valid, 115.1
- arbitration of disputes, Canada–U.S. Tax Convention Art. XXVI:6
- defined, Canada–U.S. Tax Convention Art. III:1(g)
- exchange of information, Canada–U.S. Tax Convention Art. XXVII
- mutual agreement procedure, Canada–U.S. Tax Convention Art. XXV

**Complaint**, *see* Information or complaint

**Complete period of reduced services**
- defined, Reg. 8300(1)

**Completion date (for qualifying home under Home Buyers' Plan)**
- defined, 146.01(1)

**Compliance orders**
- after conviction of offence, 238(2)
- compliance with audit or demand, 231.7

**Compound interest**
- deduction for, 20(1)(d)
- late payments and refunds, 248(11)

**Computation of income**, 3
- amalgamation, on, 87(2)(c)
- deductions, *see* Deductions in computing income; Deductions in computing income from business or property; Deductions in computing income from office or employment
- insurance corporation, 138(1)–(6), (9)
- limitation re inclusions and deductions, 248(28)
- non-resident insurer, 138(11.91)
  - where insurance business transferred, 138(11.92)

**Computation of tax**, Reg. Part I
- corporations, 123–125.1
- deductions, *see* Deductions in computing tax
- individuals, 117–122.3

Computation of tax *(cont'd)*
- - rates, 117(2)
- Part I
- - non-resident individual, 118.94

**Computation of taxable income**, 110–114
- deductions, *see* Deductions in computing taxable income
- individual
- - order of application, 111.1
- - resident for part of year, 114, 114.1

**Computer**
- capital cost allowance
- - classification, Reg. Sch. II:Cl. 10(f), Sch. II:Cl. 29, Sch. II:Cl. 40
- - "general-purpose electronic data processing equipment" defined, Reg. 1104(2)
- - separate class for each property, Reg. 1101(5p)
- filing by, *see* Electronic filing
- software, *see* Software

**Computer-operating aids**
- medical expense, Reg. 5700(o)

**Computer software**, *see also* Software
- defined, Reg. 1104(2)

**Computer software tax shelter property**
- CCA claims limited to income from property, Reg. 1100(20.1)
- defined, Reg. 1100(20.2)
- excluded from leasing property rules, Reg. 1100(17)(b)
- separate class, Reg. 1101(5r)

**Concessions**
- capital cost allowance, Reg. 1100(1)(c), 1100(9), Reg. Sch. II:Cl. 14

**Conditional sale, repossession**, *see* Surrender: of property to creditor

**Condominium corporation**, 149(1)(l)

**Confederation Life failure**
- group disability insurance top-up payments, 6(17), (18)
- - reimbursement payment to employer, 8(1)(n.1)

**Confidentiality**, *see* Communication of information; Solicitor-client privilege

**Congregation**, *see* Communal organizations

**Connected**
- contributor, *see* Connected contributor
- defined
- - for Part IV tax, 186(4)
- - for shareholder loans, 15(2.1)
- shareholder, *see* Connected shareholder

**Connected contributor**
- defined, 94(1) [proposed]

**Connected shareholder**
- defined, Reg. 4901(2)–(2.2)

**Conservation**, *see* Energy: conservation property

**Conservation of the environment**, *see* Ecological gifts

**Consideration**, *see also* Inadequate considerations
- unreasonable
- - from non-resident, 247
- - rent, royalty, etc.
- - - non-resident, paid by, 247
- - - non-resident, paid to, 247

- whether trust interest acquired for consideration, 108(7)

**Consolidation (of shares)**
- effect on stock option rules, 110(1.5)

**Consolidation accounting method**
- prohibited for debt forgiveness reserve, 61.3(1)(b)C(i)
- prohibited for purpose of Act, 248(24)

**Construction activities**
- defined, Reg. 238(1)
- information return required, Reg. 238(2)

**Construction contracts**
- information return, Reg. 238

**Construction equipment**
- "qualified" defined, 127(9)

**Construction of building**
- home for disabled person, medical expense, 118.2(2)(l.21)
- soft costs, rules, 18(3.1)–(3.7), 20(29)

**Constructive receipts**
- indirect payments, 56(2)

**Consul**, *see* Diplomat

**Consumer goods or services**
- defined, 135(4), Reg. 4901(2)

**Consumer Price Index**
- defined, Reg. 8500(1)

**Consumer Price Index adjustment**, *see* Indexing (for inflation)

**Containers**
- deposit received for, income, 12(1)(a)(ii)
- - repayment of, deductible, 20(1)(m.2)
- reserve for, deductible, 20(1)(m)(iv)

**Contemporaneous documentation**
- required for transfer pricing audit purposes, 247(4)

**Contiguous zone**
- defined, *Interpretation Act* 35(1)

**Continental shelf**
- application of legislation to, *Interpretation Act* 8(2.2)
- defined, *Interpretation Act* 35(1)

**Contingency funds**, Reg. 3202

**Contingent liability**
- limitation on deductibility, 18(1)(e)

**Continuance outside Canada**, 219.1, 250(5.1)
- treaty rule, Canada–U.S. Tax Convention Art. IV:3 (Protocol)

**Continuity**
- previous version of Act, ITAR 75, 77

**"Contra" interest**
- on instalment payments, 161(2.2)

**Contract**
- annuity, *see* Annuity contract
- employment, consideration for entering into, 6(3)
- investment, *see* Investment contract
- life annuity, 148(10)
- payments under, combined income and capital, 16(1)
- pension plan, under, 254
- person employed to negotiate
- - expenses incurred, deduction, 8(1)(f)
- - - certificate of employer, 8(10)

**Contract payment**
- by federal government or Crown corporation, information return, Reg. 237

2680

Index

Contract payment *(cont'd)*
- defined, 127(9), (25)
- included in income, 9(1), 12(1)(x)
- paid, not counted as qualifying for ITC, 127(18)
- prescribed amount, Reg. 4606

**Contractors' movable equipment**, Reg. Sch. II:Cl. 10(h), Sch. II:Cl. 22, Sch. II:Cl. 38

**Contravene**
- defined, *Interpretation Act* s. 35(1)

**Contributed surplus**
- addition to adjusted cost base, 53(1)(c)
- calculation of, 84(10), (11)
- conversion into paid-up capital
- • amalgamations, 87(2)(y)
- • no dividend deemed, 84(1)(c.1)–(c.3)
- • restrictions, 84(10)

**Contribution**
- charitable, *see* Gifts and donations
- defined
- • for non-resident trusts and foreign investment entities, 94(1) [proposed]
- • for political contributions, Reg. 2002(1)
- political, *see* Political contribution
- to RESP, defined to exclude CESG, 146.1(1)

**Contributor**
- defined
- • for non-resident trusts and foreign investment entities, 94(1) [proposed]
- • re disposition to trust, 107.4(1)

**Control of corporation**, 112(6)(b), 256(1.2), *see also* Associated corporations
- acquired after beginning of year, investment tax credit, 127(9.2)
- acquired before end of year, investment tax credit, 127(9.1)
- acquisition of
- • because of death, effect on windup, 88(1)(d.3)
- • deemed time of, 256(9)
- • exceptions, 256(7)(a)
- • no deduction for unused Part I.3 tax credit, 125.3(3)
- amalgamation deemed not acquisition of, 88(4)
- certain shares excluded from fair market valuations, 256(1.6)
- change of
- • adjusted cost base of non-depreciable capital property, 53(2)(b.2)
- • adventure in the nature of trade, inventory writedown, 10(10)
- • application of unused surtax credit, 181.1(7), 190.1(6)
- • bad debts non-deductible, 111(5.3)
- • business investment losses, 111(8)"net capital loss"C(b)
- • Canadian resource expenses, reduction of, 66.7(12)
- • Canadian resource property acquired within 12 months, 66(11.4), (11.5)
- • capital dividend account set to zero, 89(1.1)
- • debt forgiveness rules, 80(1)"relevant loss balance"(d), (e)
- • deductions for previously disallowed pregnant losses, 13(21.2)(e)(iii)(D), 14(12)(f), 18(15)(b)(iii), 40(3.4)(b)(iii)
- • deemed year-end, 249(4)
- • depreciable property acquired in 12-month period, 13(24), (25)
- • disposal of Canadian resource properties, 66.7(14)
- • disposal of foreign resource properties, 66.7(15)
- • election re cost of capital property, 111(4)(e)
- • exploration and development expenses, 66(11), (11.3)–(11.5)
- • foreign resource expenses, reduction of, 66.7(13)
- • foreign resource property acquired within 12 months, 66(11.4), (11.5)
- • inventory writedown for adventure in the nature of trade, 10(10)
- • investment tax credit, 127(9.1), (9.2)
- • loss carryover rules
- • • anti-avoidance provision, 111(5.5)
- • losses, deductibility, 111(5)–(5.4)
- • meaning of, 256(7)(a)
- • net capital loss non-deductible, 111(4)
- • non-depreciable capital property, rules re, 111(4)(c)–(e)
- • non-successor acquisitions of resource properties, 66.7(15)
- • Part I.3 tax credit carryover, 125.3(3)
- • resource expenses, 66.7(10), (11)
- • scientific research and experimental development expenses, 37(1)(h)
- • • computation of, 37(6.1)
- • superficial loss rule inapplicable, 54"superficial loss"(f)
- • windup, 88(1)(c.3), (c.6)
- • within 12 months of incorporation, 66(11.5)
- corporation without share capital, 256(8.1)
- deemed not acquired, 256(7)
- deemed time of acquisition, 256(9)
- defined
- • directly or indirectly, 256(5.1)
- • for associated corporation rules, 256(6)
- • for Part IV tax, 186(2)
- • for stop-loss rules, 112(6)(b)
- in fact, 256(5.1)
- option, by, 251(5)(b)
- related groups, by, 251(5)(a)
- specified class of shares, defined, 256(1.1)

**Controlled corporation**, *see also* Corporation
- meaning, 256(5.1)

**"Controlled, directly or indirectly"**
- meaning, 256(5.1)

**Controlled foreign affiliate**, *see also* Foreign affiliate
- defined, 95(1), 248(1), Reg. 5907(1)
- • for loan by corporation to non-resident, 17(15)
- • foreign investment entity deemed to be, 94.1(12)
- income earned by, taxed, 91(1), *see also* Foreign accrual property income
- payment to, for services, constitutes FAPI, 95(2)(b)

**Convention**, *see* Tax treaty

**Convention expenses**
- deductible, 20(10)
- • where fee includes meals, 67.1(3)
- disallowed as R&D expense, Reg. 2902(a)(i)(F)
- held in United States, Canada–U.S. Tax Treaty, Art. XXV:9

**Convention refugee**, *see* Refugee

**Conventional lands**
- defined, 1206(1)

2681

## Conversion
- benefit, *see* Conversion benefit
- bond, deemed cost of, 51.1
- debt into debt (commercial debt obligation), 80(2)(h)
- debt into shares, 51, 80(2)(g), (g.1)
- provincial life insurance corporation to mutual, 139
- shares into other shares, 86(1)
- vessel, of
- • defined, 13(21)"appropriate minister" "conversion" and "conversion cost"

## Conversion benefit
- defined, for insurance demutualization, 139.1(1)
- flow-through by employer to employee, 139.1(16)
- taxable, *see* Taxable conversion benefit

## Conversion cost
- vessel, of
- • deemed separate class, 13(14), (17)
- • defined, 13(21)"appropriate minister" "conversion" and "conversion cost"

**Convertible debenture**, *see* Convertible property
**Convertible obligation**, 51.1
**Convertible property**, 51; ITAR 26(24)
- benefit conferred on non-arm's length person, 51(2)
- "gift portion" of, 51(2)

## Cooling-off period
- three years, labour-sponsored funds tax credit, 127.4(3)

**Cooperative corporations**, 135, 136
- investment tax credit, 127(6)
- large corporations tax, whether exempt, 181.1(3)(f)
- paid-up capital of, 89(1)"paid-up capital"(b)
- patronage dividends, 135
- • deduction, 20(1)(u)
- • non-resident, to, 212(1)(g)
- scientific research tax credit, 127.3(5)
- share of, meaning, 248(1)"share"
- share-purchase tax credit, 127.2(5)

***Coopers & Lybrand* case overruled**, 153(1.3) [repealed], 227(5)

## Copy of document
- can be used in court proceedings, 231.5(1), 244(9)

## Copyright
- royalties paid to non-resident, exempt, 212(1)(d)(vi), 212(9)(b)
- • paid to U.S. resident, Canada–U.S. Tax Convention Art. XII:3(a)

**Corporate distributions tax**, 183.1
**Corporate emigration**, 219.1
## Corporate officers
- accountability of, 242
- loans to, 80.4(1)

## Corporate partnerships
- small business deduction, 125(6)

**Corporate surplus**, *see* Surplus stripping
**Corporate surtax**, 123.2
**Corporate tax reduction**, *see* Corporation: tax rate
## Corporation
- acquiring depreciable property
- • change of control in 12-month period, 13(24), (25)
- acquisition of own shares, deemed dividend, 84(3)
- additional tax on excessive election, 184
- airline, taxable income earned in a province, Reg. 407
- allowance, re investment in property in Canada, 219(1)(j), Reg. 808
- amalgamation of, *see* Amalgamation
- annuity contract, interest in, 12.2
- appropriations of property by shareholders, 15(1), 69(4)
- • inadequate considerations, 69(5)
- appropriations to shareholders
- • on winding-up, deemed dividend, 84(2), (6)
- assets disposed of to, for shares
- • shares deemed capital property, 54.2
- associated, *see* Associated corporations
- bankrupt
- • exempt from Part I.3 tax, 181.1(3)(b)
- • exempt from Part IV tax, 186.1
- • rules applicable, 128(1)
- becoming or ceasing to be exempt, 149(10)
- • superficial loss rule inapplicable, 54"superficial loss"(g)
- becoming resident in Canada, 128.1(1)
- benefit conferred on shareholder, 15(1), (7)
- • deemed, 15(9)
- bus operators, taxable income earned in a province, Reg. 409
- buying back shares for excessive amounts
- • excess deemed dividend substitute, 183.1(3), (4)
- "Canadian"
- • defined, 89(1)
- • "taxable" defined, 89(1)"taxable Canadian corporation"
- • winding-up of, rules, 88(2)
- Canadian-controlled private, defined, 125(7)
- cancellation of shares, 84(3), (6)
- ceasing to be resident in Canada, 128.1(4)
- connected, 186(4)
- consolidation accounting method, prohibited, 248(24)
- continuance outside Canada, 219.1, 250(5.1)
- control of, *see* Control of corporation
- controlled, 186(2)
- • capital loss on property transferred to, 40(3.3), (3.4)
- • charitable foundation, by, 149.1(12)
- • disposition of shares of
- • • amalgamation, 87(2)(kk)
- • • exchanges of property, 44(7)
- • • share for share exchange, 85.1(2)(b)
- • • shares of, disposition of, 40(2)(h)
- cooperative, *see* Cooperative corporations
- Crown, *see* Crown corporation
- deduction from tax, *see* Deductions in computing tax
- deemed member of partnership, 125(6.1)
- deemed not resident, 250(5)
- deemed resident in Canada, 250(4)
- defined, 248(1), *Interpretation Act* s. 35(1)
- director of, *see* Director (of corporation)
- distributions, tax payable on, 183.1(2)
- • exceptions, 183.1(6)
- divided business, Reg. 412
- dividend received by, 112
- • dividend rental arrangements, no deduction allowed, 112(2.3)
- • short-term preferred share, on, 112(2.3)
- • where no deduction permitted, 112(2.1)–(2.9)
- drilling, prospecting, exploration and development expenses, ITAR 29(11)
- emigration of, 219.1

2682

# Index

Corporation *(cont'd)*
- execution of documents, 236
- exempt, *see* Exempt corporation; Exemptions
- family farm, *see* Family farm corporation/partnership
- farm loss
  - carryforward rules where control changed, 111(5)–(5.3)
- fiscal period of, 249.1(1)(a), 249.1(1)(b)(iii)
- foreign business corporation, *see* Foreign business corporation
- gifts made by
  - capital property, 110.1(3)
  - charitable, 110.1(1)(a)
  - deduction for, 110.1(1)
  - Her Majesty, to, 110.1(1)(b)
  - institution, to, 110.1(1)(c)
  - partnership, by, 110.1(4)
  - proof of, 110.1(2)
- grain elevator operators
  - taxable income earned in a province, Reg. 408
- housing
  - exemption, 149(1)(i), (n)
- immigration of, 128.1
- income of, defined, 125(7)"income of the corporation for the year from an active business"
- incorporated in Canada, defined, 248(1)"corporation" "corporation incorporated in Canada"
- indirect payment to person paid through intermediary as proceeds of disposition of property, 183.1(5)
- information return
  - by private corporation, under Part IV, 187(1)
  - tax under Part VII, 193(1)
- instalment payment of tax, 157(1), Reg. 5301
  - "first instalment base" defined, 161(9)(b)
  - insufficient, 161(2)
    - limitation, 161(4.1)
  - "second instalment base" defined, 161(9)(b)
- insurance, *see* Insurance corporation
- interest
  - accrued, 12(3)
  - deduction by certain corporations, 18(4)–(8)
- investment, *see* Investment corporation
- issue of stock rights, 15(1)(c)
- issuing qualifying shares, refundable tax, 192, 193
- joint exploration, *see* Joint exploration corporation
- large, tax on, *see* Large corporations tax (Part I.3)
- life insurance, *see* Life insurance corporation; Life insurer
- life insurance policy, interest in, 12.2
- loan by
  - non-resident, to, 17
  - persons connected with shareholder, to, 15(2)
  - shareholder, to, 15(2)
    - non-residents, 15(2.2), (8)
  - wholly-owned subsidiary, to, 218
- loan to, attribution rules, 74.4
- manufacturing and processing, 125.1
- member of non-resident-controlled partnership
  - specified partnership income deemed nil, 125(6.2)
- mining
  - property, etc., expenses, ITAR 29(2)–(5)
- mortgage investment, 130.1
- municipal, exempt, 149(1)(d.5)
- mutual

- provincial life insurance corporation converted into, 139
- mutual fund, *see* Mutual fund corporation
- mutual insurance, exemption, 149(1)(m)
- net capital loss non-deductible if change in control of, 111(4)
- 90% or more owned subsidiary
  - winding-up of, 88(1)
- non-arm's length non-resident, transactions with
  - extended reassessment period, 152(4)(b)(iii)
  - return required, 233.1
    - offences and penalties, 162(10)
- non-capital loss
  - carryforward rules where control changed, 111(5)–(5.4)
- non-profit
  - exemption, 149(2)
  - for scientific research and development
    - annual information return, 149(7)
    - exemption, 149(1)(j)
- non-resident, Reg. Part VIII
  - branch tax, 219
  - carrying on business in Canada, additional tax, 219
    - limitations on, 219.2
  - taxable income earned in a province, Reg. 413
- non-resident-owned investment, *see* Non-resident-owned investment corporation
- officer of, prosecution for offence of corporation, 242
- paid-up capital, *see* Paid-up capital
- patronage dividend
  - deduction, 135
- paying dividends on taxable preferred shares
  - tax payable, 191.1(1)
- payment of tax, 157
  - instalments, 157(1)
  - where instalments not required, 157(2), (2.1)
- payments to shareholders or prospective shareholders, 15(1), (7)
- pension, exempt, 149(1)(o.1), (o.2)
- personal-use property of, 46(4)
- pipeline operators, taxable income earned in a province, Reg. 411
- powers vested in, *Interpretation Act* s. 21(1)
- predecessor, *see* Predecessor corporation
- preferred-rate amount
  - credit union, 137(4.3)
- private, *see* Private corporation
- processing or fabricating, 66(15)"principal-business corporation" ITAR 29(4), (26)
- professional, *see* Professional corporation
- property appropriated to shareholder or prospective shareholder, 15(1), (7)
- provincial, exempt, 149(1)(d)–(d.4)
- provincial life insurance, converted into mutual, 139
- qualified small business, share of
  - capital gains deduction, 110.6(2.1)
  - defined, 110.6(1)
  - related person, 110.6(14)
  - rules re, 110.6(14)
- railway, *see also* Railway
- rates of tax, *see* Rates of tax
- real property rental etc.
  - base level deduction, 18(2)(f), 18(2.2)
- receiving dividends on taxable preferred shares
  - tax payable, 187.2

2683

Corporation *(cont'd)*
- redemption of shares, 40(3.6), 84(3), (6)
- reduction of paid-up capital, deemed dividend, 84(4), (4.1)
- registered investment, 204.4–204.7
- related to another, 251(3)
- - deemed, on amalgamation, 251(3.1), (3.2)
- - transfer of liability for Part VI.1 tax, 191.3
- - where deemed not, 112(2.9)
- reorganization of business, *see* Reorganization
- residence of, 250(5)
- - corporate emigration, 219.1
- - extended meaning, 250(4)
- returns
- - to be filed, 150(1)(a), (e)
- - where none filed, 150(1)(e)
- rules applicable to, 123–125.1
- scientific research and development (non-profit)
- - annual information return, 149(7)
- - exemption, 149(1)(j)
- - rules as to income, 149(9)
- scientific research tax credit, refundable tax, 195
- share-for-share exchange
- - computation of paid-up capital, 85.1(2.1)
- ship operators, taxable income earned in a province, Reg. 410
- small business deduction, 125
- small business investment, Reg. 5101(1)
- - exempt, 149(1)(o.3)
- spouse or minor, for
- - property transferred or loaned to
- - - amalgamation, corporation continued on, 87(2)(j.7)
- status of certain corporations, ITAR 50, Reg. Part XLVIII
- "stop-loss" rule, 112(3)–(7)
- subject, 186
- - deemed private corporation, 186(5)
- subsidiary, *see* Subsidiary
- successor, *see* Successor corporation
- surtax, 123.2
- tax abatement, 124
- tax on excessive capital dividend or capital gains dividend election, 184, 185
- tax on foreign property held in certain savings plans, 205–207
- tax rate, 123
- - abatements, 124
- - manufacturing or processing, 125.1
- - reductions as of 2001, 123.4
- - small business deduction, 125
- - surtax, 123.2
- taxable Canadian, defined, 89(1)"taxable Canadian corporation"
- taxable income earned in a province, Reg. Part IV
- - divided businesses, Reg. 412
- taxation year of, 249(1)(a), 249(3)
- thinly capitalized
- - interest not deductible, 18(4)–(6)
- - - exception, 18(8)
- transactions with non-resident, non-arm's length persons
- - extended reassessment period, 152(4)(b)(iii)
- - information return, 233.1
- - - offences and penalties re, 162(10)

- transfer of property to
- - attribution rules, 74.4
- - partnership, from, 85(2)
- - shareholder, from, 85(1)
- - - eligible property, 85(1.1)
- truck operators, taxable income earned in a province, Reg. 409
- trust and loan, taxable income earned in a province, Reg. 405
- when "controlled", 112(6)(b)
- wholly-owned subsidiary
- - defined, 248(1)
- without share capital, whether control acquired, 256(8.1)
- winding-up of
- - distribution deemed dividend, 84(2), (6)

**Correspondence courses**
- education credit, full-time student, 118.6(2)B

**Corruption of public officials**
- no deduction for, 67.5

**Cost**, *see also* Adjusted cost base; Capital cost; Rollover
- acquisition, of
- - capitalized interest, 21
- - land, 18(2), (3.1)
- - - included in inventory, 10(1.1)
- - non-arm's length transaction, 69(1)(a), (c)
- - property owned Dec. 31/71, ITAR 26(3), (4)
- - taxpayer becoming resident of Canada, ITAR 26(10)
- amount, *see* Cost amount
- borrowed money, of, capitalized interest, 21
- depreciable property, 13(7.1)
- farm property transferred to child
- - *inter vivos*, 73(3)(d)
- - on death, 70(9)(b)
- gift, of, 69(1)(c)
- property after immigrating to Canada, 128.1(1)(c)
- property received from partnership, 98(3), (5)
- property seized for non-payment of debt, 79.1(6)
- property whose value included in income, 52
- share of corporation that becomes resident in Canada, 52(8)
- tax shelter investment, 143.2(6)

**Cost amount**, *see also* Adjusted cost base
- defined
- - for capital interest in a trust, 108(1), 206(1)
- - generally, 248(1)
- - stock dividend, 52(3)

**Cost base of property**, *see also* Adjusted cost base
- additions to, 53(1)
- adjustments to, 53
- deductions from, 53(2)
- "relevant" to foreign affiliate, 95(4)

**Cost of capital**
- defined, Reg. 5202, 5203, 5204

**Cost of labour**
- defined, Reg. 5202, 5203, 5204

**Cost of manufacturing and processing capital**
- defined, Reg. 5202, 5204

**Cost of manufacturing and processing labour**
- defined, Reg. 5202, 5204

**Cost of the particular property**
- meaning of, for ITC recapture rules, 127(32)

## Index

**Costs**, *see* Court: costs; Legal costs

**Costumes**
- capital cost allowance for, Reg. Sch. II:Cl. 12(k)

**Counselling services**
- investment, *see* Investment counselling fees
- value of, not included in employee's income, 6(1)(a)(iv)

**Countervailing duties**, *see* Anti-dumping duties or countervailing duties

**Countries**, *see* Prescribed countries

**Country-specific foreign expenses**
- defined, for resource expenses of limited partner, 66.8(1)(a)(i)(D)

**Coupons**
- cashed for non-resident, tax and statement required, 215(2), 234
- identification of, 240(2)
- ownership certificate required, 234
- stripped bond, cost excluded from income when sold, 12(9.1)

**Court**, *see also* Judge
- appeal to, *see* Appeal; Tax Court of Canada
- compliance orders
- • after conviction of an offence, 238(2)
- • re audit or demand for information, 231.7
- costs
- • awarded against taxpayer, treated as debt owing, 222.1

**Covenant**
- ecologically sensitive land, value when donated, 110.1(5), 188.1(12)
- • valuation applies for capital gains purposes, 43(2)

**"Created by the taxpayer's will"**
- meaning of, 248(9.1)

**Credit**, *see* Tax credits

**Credit-related gains and losses, effect on securities held**, 142.4(7)B

**Credit union**, *see also* Financial institution
- "allocation in proportion to borrowing" defined, 137(6)
- allocation of taxable dividends and capital gains, 137(5.1), (5.2)
- "bonus interest payment" defined, 137(6)
- deemed not to be private corporation, 137(7)
- defined, 137(6), 248(1)
- deposit insurance corporation deemed not to be, 137.1(7)
- disposition of Canadian security, 39(5)(b)
- general provisions, 137
- insurer established to provide insurance to members, Reg. 1408(1)"acquisition costs"(a)(iv)
- member, defined, 137(6)
- member's income, 137(5)
- paid-up capital of, 89(1)"paid-up capital"(b)
- payment of tax, 157(2)
- reserves
- • maximum cumulative, defined, 137(6)
- share of, meaning, 248(1)"share"
- small business deduction, 137(3), (4)
- transitional, ITAR 58

**Creditable United States tax**
- defined, 122.7(1)

**Creditor**, *see also* Loan
- acceleration clause exercised by, 20(1)(n)
- defined, 79(1), 79.1(1), 80.01(3)
- property acquired on foreclosure by, 79
- seizure of property by, 79.1
- surrender of property to, 79

**Credits**, *see* Tax credits

**Cremation services**, *see* Eligible funeral arrangement; Funeral services

**Crew**
- defined, Reg. 105.1(1)

**Crib death monitor, medical expense**, Reg. 5700(r)

**Criminal Injuries Compensation Board**
- payments exempt, 81(1)(q), Reg. 6501

**Criminal proceedings**
- secrecy provision not applicable, 241(3)

**Croatia**, *see also* Foreign government
- universities, gifts to, Reg. Sch. VIII s. 18

**Crop insurance program**, *see* Farm Income Protection Act; Drought region

**Cross-border amalgamation**, 128.2

**Cross-border purchase butterfly**, 55(1), (3.1), (3.2)

**Cross-border worker**, *see* Commuter to United States

**Crown**, *see also* Government
- corporation, *see* Crown corporation
- death of, *Interpretation Act* s. 46
- not bound by legislation, *Interpretation Act* s. 17
- • bound by deemed trust for tax withheld, 227(4.3)
- • bound by garnishment orders, 224(1.4)
- • bound by regulations requiring information returns, 221(3)
- • bound by withholding tax requirements, 227(11)
- petroleum, natural gas etc. acquired from, for unreasonable consideration, 69(7)
- • fair market value, 69(9)
- petroleum, natural gas etc. disposed of to, for unreasonable consideration, 69(6)
- • certain persons deemed to be same person, 69(10)
- • fair market value, 69(8)

**Crown corporation**
- bonds of, no non-resident tax on interest paid, 212(1)(b)(ii)(C)(IV)
- corporation controlled by, not private corporation, 89(1)"private corporation"
- debt held by federal government, excluded from capital tax, 181(1)"long-term debt"
- debt of, as qualified investment for RRSPs etc., Reg. 4900(1)(q)
- deemed not private corporation for Part IV tax, 227(16)
- exemption for, 149(1)(d)–(d.4)
- • election to remain taxable, 149(1.11)
- • excluded where prescribed, 27(2)
- federal, prescribed, Reg. 7100
- prescribed, deemed not private corporation, 27(2)
- reporting of contract payments, Reg. 237
- subject to Part I tax, 27(2), 124(3)
- subject to Part I.3 tax, 181.71
- subject to Part IV.1 tax, 187.61
- subject to Part VI tax, 190.211
- subject to Part VI.1 tax, 191.4(3)
- transfer of unused resource expenses, 66.6(1)

**Crown foundations**
- donations after February 18/97
  - by corporation, 110.1(1)(a)(viii)
  - by individual, 118.1(1)"total charitable gifts"(g.1)
- donations before February 19/97
  - by corporation, 110.1(1)(b)(ii)
  - by individual, 118.1(1)"total Crown gifts"(c)

**Crown royalties**
- inclusion in income, 12(1)(o), 69(6), (7)
- limitation on deduction, 18(1)(m)

**Crutches**
- as medical expense, 118.2(2)(i)

**Culpable conduct**
- defined, for third-party penalty, 163.2(1)

**Cultural property**, *see also* Art; Canadian Cultural Property Export Review Board
- Canadian art, CCA claims allowed, Reg. 1102(1)(e)
- disposition of, 39(1)(a)(i.1)
  - by institution or public authority, tax on, 207.3
- excluded from capital gains rules, 39(1)(a)(i.1)
- fair market value, determination of, 118.1(10), (11)
- gift of
  - by corporation, 110.1(1)(c)
  - by individual, 118.1(1), (7.1)

**Culvert**
- capital cost allowance for, Reg. Sch. II:Cl. 1(c)

**Cumulative Canadian development expense**, *see also* Canadian development expense
- deduction for, 66.2(2)
- reduction of, on debt forgiveness, 80(8)(c)
- short taxation year, 66(13.1)

**Cumulative Canadian exploration expense**, *see also* Canadian exploration expense
- deduction for, 66.1(2), (3)
- defined, 66.1(6)
- reduction of, on debt forgiveness, 80(8)(b)
- trust, of
  - reduced by investment tax credit, 127(12.3)

**Cumulative Canadian oil and gas property expense**, *see also* Canadian oil and gas property expense
- deduction for, 66.4(2)
- defined, 66.4(5)
- reduction of, on debt forgiveness, 80(8)(d)
- short taxation year, 66(13.1)

**Cumulative deduction account**
- prescribed addition and deduction, Reg. 7200

**Cumulative eligible capital**, *see also* Eligible capital property
- amalgamation, on, 87(2)(f)
- ceasing to carry on business, on, 24
- deduction of 7% annually, 20(1)(b)
- defined, 14(5), 248(1)
- negative balance, recapture, 14(1)
  - effect of capital gains exemption election, 14(1)(a)(v)D
- partnership ceasing to exist, treatment of, 98(3)(g), 98(5)(h)
- reduction of, on debt forgiveness, 14(5)"cumulative eligible capital"F:P.1, 80(7)

**Cumulative foreign resource expense**
- defined, 66.21(1)

**"Cumulative gains limit" defined**, 110.6(1)
- computation, on amalgamation, 87(2)(pp)

**Cumulative net investment loss**
- defined, 110.6(1)
- reduced by taxable capital gains where exemption not available, 110.6(1)"investment income"(f)
- reduces capital gains exemption available, 110.6(1)"cumulative gains limit" 110.6(2)(b), 110.6(2.1)(b)

**Cumulative offset account**
- computation, on amalgamation, 87(2)(pp)
- deduction from income, 66.5(1)
  - change of control, 66.5(3)
- defined, 66.5(2)
- tax re, 196

**Cumulative reserve**
- maximum, of credit union, 137(6)

**Cumulative taxable income (of non-resident-owned investment corporation)**
- defined, 133(9)

**Curator**, *see also* Legal representative
- deemed to be legal representative, 248(1)"legal representative"
- obligations of, 159
- return required by, 150(3)

**Currency**, *see also* Foreign exchange
- blocked
  - income in, postponement of tax, 161(6)
- calculation of foreign affiliate's gain or loss in, 95(2)(f)
- fluctuation, *see* Foreign exchange: fluctuations in

**Current amount (on disposition of specified debt obligation)**, *see also* Residual portion (on disposition of specified debt obligation)
- application of, 142.4(4)
- defined, 142.4(7)

**Custodian (of eligible funeral arrangement)**
- defined, 148.1(1)
- repayment of funds by, taxable, 148.1(3), 212(1)(v)

**Custom Processing**
- treated as gross revenue from a mine, Reg. 1104(5.1)

**Customs Act**
- communication of information for enforcement of, 241(4)(d)(ii)

**Cutlery**
- capital cost allowance for, Reg. 1100(1)(e), Reg. Sch. II:Cl. 12(b)

**Cutting rights**
- capital cost allowance, separate classes, Reg. 1101(3)

**Czech Republic**, *see also* Foreign government
- universities, gifts to, Reg. Sch. VIII s. 16

## D

**DPSP**, *see* Deferred profit sharing plan

**DVD**, *see* Video laser-disk

**Daily compounding of interest**, 248(11)

**Dairy, farming**, 248(1)"farming"

**Dam**
- capital cost allowance, Reg. Sch. II:Cl. 1(d)
  - for mine, Reg. Sch. II:Cl. 10(l)

**Damages**
- wrongful dismissal, for, *see* Retiring allowance

**Dancer**
- deduction from employment income, 8(1)(q)

2686

## Index

**Data communication equipment**
- capital cost allowance, Reg. Sch. II:Cl. 3

**Data processing equipment**, *see* Computer

**Dates**, *see* Deadlines; Filing deadlines; Reassessment

**Daughter-in-law, as child of taxpayer**, 252(1)(c)

**Day camp**, *see* Child care expenses

**Day care**, *see* Child care expenses

**Day of mailing**
- constitutes date assessment or determination made, 244(15)
- presumed to be same as date appearing on notice, 244(14)

**Days**
- calculation of, *Interpretation Act* s. 27

**De facto control test**
- "controlled, directly or indirectly in any manner whatever", 256(5.1)

**Deadline**
- defined, for insurance demutualization, 139.1(1)

**Deadlines**
- extension of, by CCRA, 220(3.2)
- - labour-sponsored venture capital corporation investments, 127.4(5.1)
- - RRSP contributions, 146(22)
- payment of tax, *see* Payment of tax
- prosecution, *see* Limitation periods
- reassessments, *see* Reassessment
- returns, *see* Filing deadlines
- tax remittances, *see* Remittance of taxes withheld
- transfer pricing, *see* Documentation — due date

**Deaf person**, *see also* Hearing impairment
- devices to assist, business expense, 20(1)(rr)
- disability credit, 118.3
- guide dog, expenses, 118.2(2)(l)
- lip reading or sign language training, 118.2(2)(l.3)
- medical expenses, 118.2(2), Reg. 5700
- rehabilitative therapy, 118.2(2)(l.3)
- sign language interpretation services, 118.2(2)(l.4)

**Dealer (or trader)**
- automobile, standby charge for sales employees, 6(2.1)
- in resource rights, 66(5)
- in securities, *see* Securities: dealer, trader or agent

**Death**, *see also* Death of taxpayer
- danger of, communication of taxpayer information relating to, 241(3.1)
- funeral arrangements, *see* Eligible funeral arrangement; Funeral services
- taxpayer, of, *see* Death of taxpayer

**Death benefit**
- Canada Pension Plan, *see* Canada Pension Plan/Quebec Pension Plan: death benefit
- defined, 248(1)
- emigration of survivor, no deemed disposition, 128.1(10)"excluded right or interest"(h)
- flowed through trust or estate, 104(28)
- income, 56(1)(a)(iii)
- income averaging, ITAR 40, *see also* Averaging of income; Income-averaging annuity contract
- lump sum
- - transfer from RPP, 147.3(7)
- Saskatchewan Provincial Pension Plan, rollover to RRSP or RRIF, 60(l)(v)(B.2)
- used to purchase income-averaging annuity contract, deductible, 61(2)(c)
- withholding of tax, 153(1)(d)

**Death duties**
- deduction of, from pension benefits etc., 60(m)
- interest on, deductible, 60(d)

**Death of taxpayer**
- amounts receivable, 70(2)
- beneficiary of trust
- business income, effect on, 34.1(8)(a), 34.2(6)(c)(ii)
- business year-end income inclusion, 34.1(9)
- business year-end not calendar year, 34.1(8), (9)
- capital losses deductible against all income, 111(2)
- charitable donations carryback
- - carryback, 118.1(4)
- - claim against 100% of net income, 118.1(1)"total gifts"(a)(ii)
- - donation of non-qualifying security, 118.1(15)
- - made by will, deemed made in year of death, 118.1(5)
- - - publicly traded securities, reduced capital gain, 38(a.1)(ii)
- computation of income on, 70(1)
- consequences of, meaning, 248(8)
- debt forgiveness rules do not apply to extinguishment of debt by bequest, 80(2)(a)
- debt obligation settled by estate, 80(2)(p), (q)
- deemed proceeds of disposition of property, 70(5)–(10)
- disposition of property on, 70(5)–(10)
- - definitions, 70(10)"child"
- - legal representative, by, 164(6)
- - ordering, 70(14)
- disposition of right to share in partnership income, 96(1.5)
- elections, Reg. Part X
- eligible capital property, 70(5.1)
- entitlement to benefits on
- - deemed, spouse, 146(8.91)
- - other than spouse, by, 146(8.8), (8.9)
- forward averaging, 110.4(4) [repealed]
- funeral services provided from eligible funeral arrangement, no tax, 148.1(2)(b)(i)
- GST credit, 122.5(5)(c)
- - separate return, 104(23)(d)
- gifts, time of, 118.1(4)
- Home Buyers' Plan income inclusion or rollover, 146.01(6), (7)
- instalments not required after, 156.1(3)
- investment tax credit, income inclusion re, 70(1)(b)
- land inventories, 70(5.2)
- last annuitant under registered retirement income fund, 146.3(6)–(6.2)
- life estate in real property, termination of, 43.1(2)
- Lifelong Learning Plan income inclusion or rollover, 146.02(6), (7)
- minimum tax not applicable, 127.55
- net capital loss, 111(2)
- no inventory adjustment for farming business, 28(1)
- occurrences as a consequence of, 248(8)
- partner return, 150(4)
- partnership
- - value of rights or things, 53(1)(e)(v)
- partnership interest, transfer of, 100(3)
- payment by employer, *see* Death benefit

## Index

Death of taxpayer *(cont'd)*
- payment of tax
  - election to pay in instalments, 159(5)
- property passing to spouse or trust, 70(6)
- proprietor, return needed, 150(4)
- RPP contributions deductible, 147.2(6)
- RRIF
  - income inclusion to deceased, 146.3(6), (6.2)
  - tax-paid amounts, *see* Tax-paid amount
- RRSP
  - distribution to child or grandchild, deferral while under 18, 60(l)(v)(B.1)
  - income inclusion to deceased, 146(8.8), (8.9)
  - tax-paid amounts, *see* Tax-paid amount
- reserves not deductible, 72(1)
- resource properties, 70(5.2)
- return required, 150(1)(b), (e)
  - where none filed, 150(1)(e)
- rights or things, 70(2)
  - transferred to beneficiaries, 70(3)
- separate return, 70(2)
  - minimum tax carryover not applicable to, 120.2(4)
- single payment from deferred profit sharing plan, 147(10.1), (10.2)
- spouse or spouse trust, property transferred to, 70(6)
- stock options, effect on, 7(1)(e)
- tax on, 70(1), (5)
- termination of life estate, 43.1(2)
- transfer of partnership interest, 98.2

**Debenture**, *see* Bond; Convertible property

**Debt**, *see also* Commercial obligation; Debt obligation; Indebtedness
- amalgamation, on, 87(2)(h)
- assets acquired from foreign affiliate for settlement of, 80.1(5)
- assumption of, debt forgiveness rules do not apply, 80(1)"forgiven amount"B(l)
- bad, *see* Bad debt
- deficiency, 84.2(2), (3)
- defined, re seizure of property by creditor, 79(1), 79.1(1)
- disposition of, *see* Debt obligation: disposition of
- doubtful, reserve for, 12(1)(d), 20(1)(l)
- foreign currency, denominated in, 79(7), 80(2)(k), 80.01(11)
- forgiveness, *see* Debt forgiveness
- long-term
  - defined, 190(1)
- non-qualifying
  - owing to registered charity, 189
  - trust for benefit of spouse, 70(8)(b)
- owed by corporation, adjusted cost base, 53(2)(p)
- owing by non-resident to corporation resident in Canada, 17
- parking, *see* Debt parking
- rescheduling or restructuring, expenses deductible, 20(1)(e)(ii.2), 20(1)(e.1)(iii)
- security received in satisfaction of, 76
- seizure of property for payment of
  - effect on creditor, 79.1
  - effect on debtor, 79
- settlement of, *see* Debt forgiveness
- share issued in settlement of, 80(2)(g), (g.1)
- statute-barred, deemed settled, 80.01(9)
  - subsequent payments, 80.01(10)
- testamentary
  - trust for benefit of spouse, 70(8)(c)
- unpaid tax, etc., as, 222

**Debt forgiveness**, 80–80.04, *see also* Settlement of debt
- amalgamation, on, 80.01(3)
- application of remaining balance
  - adjusted cost base of capital property, 53(2)(g.1), 80(9)–(11)
  - allowable business investment loss carryforwards, 80(4)(a)
  - capital cost of depreciable property, 13(7.1)(g), 80(5)
  - capital gain to absorb current capital losses, 80(12)
  - capital property, 53(2)(g.1), 80(9)–(11)
  - cumulative Canadian development expense, 66.2(5)"cumulative Canadian development expense"M.1, 80(8)(c)
  - cumulative Canadian exploration expense, 66.1(6)"cumulative Canadian exploration expense"J.1, 80(8)(b)
  - cumulative Canadian oil and gas property expense, 66.4(5)"cumulative Canadian oil and gas property expense"I.1, 80(8)(d)
  - cumulative eligible capital, 14(5)"cumulative eligible capital"F:P.1, 80(2)(f), 80(7)
  - farm losses, 80(3)(b)
  - foreign exploration and development expenses, 66(4)(a)(iii), 80(8)(e)
  - income inclusion, 80(13), (14)
  - net capital losses, 80(4)(b)
  - non-capital losses, 80(3)(a), 80(4)(a)
  - ordering of rules, 80(2)(c), 248(27)
  - related corporations' shares and debt, 53(2)(g.1), 80(11)
  - resource expenditures, 80(8)
  - restricted farm losses, 31(1.1)(b), 80(3)(c)
  - successor pools, 66.7(2)(a)(ii), 66.7(3)(a)(ii), 66.7(4)(a)(iv), 66.7(5)(a)(iii), 80(8)(a)
  - undepreciated capital cost pool, 80(5)(b), 80(6)
- bequest or inheritance, rules do not apply, 80(2)(a)
- corporation to shareholder, taxable benefit, 15(1.2)
- death, rules do not apply, 80(2)(a)
- debt issued in settlement of debt, 80(2)(h)
- debt of deceased settled by estate, 80(2)(p), (q)
- employer to employee, taxable benefit, 6(15)
- foreign affiliate's gain or loss on, 95(2)(i)
- foreign currency debt, 80(2)(k), 80.01(11)
- forgiven amount, *see* Forgiven amount (re settlement of debt)
- guarantee, payment under, 80(2)(l)
- history preservation rules, 47(1), 49(3.01), 51(1), 53(4)–(6), 86(4), 87(5.1), (6.1)
  - reduction of adjusted cost base, 53(2)(g.1)
- income inclusion, 12(1)(z.3), 80(13), (14)
  - corporation in financial difficulty, 61.3
- interest deemed to be separate obligation, 80(2)(b)
- partnership, by, 80(15)
- R&D expenditures, effect on, 37(1)(f.1)
- reserve, 61.2–61.4
- residual balance
  - defined, 80(14)
  - income inclusion, 80(13)
- settlement, meaning of *see* Settlement of debt
- share issued in settlement of debt, 80(2)(g), (g.1)
- simultaneous settlement of obligations, 80(2)(i)
- subsequent disposition, capital gain, 80.03(2)

Debt forgiveness *(cont'd)*
- surrender of property
  - - by debtor to creditor, 79(3), 79.1
  - - subsequent to debt forgiveness, 80.03(2)
- transfer of forgiven amount to related person, 80.04
- winding-up, 80.01(4)

**Debt obligation**, *see also* Commercial obligation; Investment contract; Specified debt obligation
- accrued interest on, 12(3)–(10)
- adjusted cost base, 53(2)(l)
- amalgamation, acquired in, 87(2)(e.2)
- assumption of, expenses deductible, 20(1)(e)(ii.2), 20(1)(e.1)(iii)
- deduction for over-accrual, 20(21)
- defined
- discounted, *see* Bond: discount
- disposition of
  - - in exchange for other debt obligation, 40(2)(e.2)
    - - addition to adjusted cost base, 53(1)(f.12)
  - - to related person, 40(2)(e.1)
    - - addition to adjusted cost base, 53(1)(f.1), (f.11)
  - - whether capital loss allowed, 40(2)(g)(ii)
- escalating interest, accrual, Reg. 7000(2)(c.1)
- extended meaning of, 248(26)
  - - for penalties, bonuses and rate reduction payments, 18(9.1)
  - - for prepaid interest rules, 18(9.2)
  - - for purposes of scientific research tax credit, 127.3(2)"scientific research and experimental development tax credit"(d)
  - - generally, not defined
- first registered holder of
  - - election re scientific research tax credit, 127.3(9)
- increasing interest rate, accrual, Reg. 7000(2)(c.1)
- interest on, 20(14.1)
- issued by partnership, 80(13)E(a), 80(14)(b), 80(15), (18)
  - - deemed, 80(2)(n)
- owing by related person, no loss permitted on disposition, 40(2)(e.1)
- partial obligation treated the same as entire obligation, 248(27)
- prescribed
  - - accrued interest on, Reg. 7000
  - - deemed accrual of interest, 12(9)
    - - exception, 12(9.1)
  - - re donations to charities, 38(a.1)(i), Reg. 6210
- qualifying, *see* Qualifying debt obligation
- settlement of, *see* Debt forgiveness
- specified, *see* Specified debt obligation
- used or held in insurance or moneylending business
  - - "eligible property" for transfer to corporation by shareholder, 85(1.1)(g)

**Debt parking**, 80.01(6)–(8)
- deemed settlement of debt, 80.01(8)
- subsequent payment of debt, 80.01(10)

**Debt substitute share**
- defined, Canada–U.S. Tax Convention Art. XXIX A:5(c)

**Debtor**
- defined, 80(1), 80.01(1), 80.04(1)
- gain on settlement of debts, 80(1), Reg. Part LIV

**Deceased person**, *see* Death of taxpayer

**December 31, 1995 income**
- defined, 34.1(4)–(6), 34.2(1)

**Decline in value of property**
- inventory writedown, 10(1), (1.01)
- rules preventing transfer of losses, 13(21.2), 40(3.3), (3.4)

**Decoder**
- television, visually displaying vocal portion of signal
  - - medical expense, Reg. 5700(q)

**Deduction**
- or set-off, recovery of taxes by, 224.1

**Deductions in computing income**, *see also* Deductions in computing income from business or property; Deductions in computing income from office or employment; Deductions in computing taxable income
- alimony payments, 60(b)
- amounts transferred as retiring allowance, 60(j.1)
- Canadian exploration expenses, 66.1(2), (3)
- capital element of annuity, 60(a)
- "carved-out income", 66(14.6)
- child care expenses, 63
- cost of borrowed money, 21
- costs re construction of building or ownership of land, 18(3.1)–(3.7)
- cumulative Canadian development expenses, 66.2(2)
  - - short taxation year, 66(13.1)
- cumulative Canadian oil and gas property expense, 66.4(2)
  - - short taxation year, 66(13.1)
- cumulative eligible capital on ceasing business, 24
- cumulative offset account, 66.5
- deemed residents, 64.1
- deposit insurance corporation, 137.1(3)
  - - limitation, 137.1(4)
- dividend from foreign affiliate, re, 91(5)
- employee benefit plan, 32.1
- employer's contributions
  - - deferred profit sharing plan, 147(8), (9)
  - - employees profit sharing plan, 144(5)
  - - registered supplementary unemployment benefit plan, 145
- estate tax applicable to certain property, 60(m)
- foreign exploration and development expenses, 66(4)
  - - short taxation year, 66(13.1)
- foreign taxes, re, 91(4)
- income-averaging annuity contract, 61(1)
- insurance corporation
  - - amounts paid or credited to policyholders, 140(1)
- interest on death duties, 60(d)
- legal expenses of collecting or establishing right to pension benefit etc., 60(o.1)
- maintenance payments, 60(b), (c), 60.1
- mental/physical impairment
  - - attendant care expenses, 64
- mortgage on depreciable property, loss from sale of, 20(5), (5.1)
- moving expenses, 62
- Part I.2 tax payable, 60(w)
- patronage dividend, 135(1)
  - - carryover of, 135(2.1)
- provincial pension plan contributions, 60(v)
- RPP, actuarial surplus payment, 60(j.01)
- RRSP, premiums under, 60(i)
- refund of income payments, 60(q)

Index

Deductions in computing income *(cont'd)*
- refund of RRSP premium transferred to annuity, 60(l)
- refund of undeducted past service additional voluntary contributions, 60.2(1)
- repayment of overpayment of certain benefits, 60(n)
- repayment of policy loan, 60(s)
- residents absent from Canada, 64.1
- resource and processing allowances, Reg. Part XII
- resource expenses
- • successor corporation, 66.7
- retirement compensation arrangement
- • benefit from, 60(t)
- • contributions to, 20(1)(r)
- • disposition of interest in, 60(u)
- scientific research and experimental development, 37
- spousal RRSP, amounts transferred to, 60(j.2)
- succession duties applicable to certain property, 60(m.1)
- superannuation benefits transferred to another plan, 60(j)
- support payments, 60(b), (c), 60.1
- trusts of, 104(6)–(8)
- • non-resident beneficiaries, for, 104(10)
- uncollectible proceeds of disposition, 20(4)–(4.2)

**Deductions in computing income from business or property**, *see also* Deductions in computing income
- accrued interest on transferred bond, 20(14)
- amount deemed to be tax payable, 20(1)(ll)
- bad debts, 20(1)(p)
- banks, 26(2)
- CPP/QPP contributions, 8(1)(l.1), 60(e)
- cancellation of lease, 20(1)(z), (z.1)
- capital cost allowance, *see* Capital cost allowance
- cumulative eligible capital amount, 20(1)(b)
- depletion, *see* Depletion allowances
- discount on certain obligations, 20(1)(f)
- dividend from foreign affiliate, 20(13)
- employer's contributions
- • deferred profit sharing plan, 20(1)(y), 147(8), (9)
- • pension plan, 20(1)(q), 147.2(1)
- • • limitation, 20(22)
- • • special, 20(1)(r)
- • profit sharing plan, 20(1)(w)
- • supplementary unemployment benefit plan, 20(1)(x)
- expense of issuing shares or borrowing money, 20(1)(e)
- exploration and development grants, 20(1)(kk)
- foreign taxes
- • exceeding 15%, 20(11)
- guarantee fees etc., 20(1)(e.1)
- injection substances, 20(1)(ll)
- interest
- • accrued on purchased bond, 20(14)
- • compound, 20(1)(d)
- • paid on borrowed money, 20(1)(c)
- inventory adjustment, 20(1)(ii)
- investigation of site, 20(1)(dd)
- investment counsel fee, 20(1)(bb)
- landscaping, 20(1)(aa)
- life insurance corporation, 138(3)
- limitations on, 18(1), (11)
- mineral resources, 65
- mining taxes, 20(1)(v)
- oil or gas wells, 65

- patronage dividend, 20(1)(u)
- permitted, 20(1)
- prepaid expenses
- • limitation re, 18(9)
- reinsurance commission, 20(1)(jj)
- repayment of amount previously included, 20(1)(m.2)
- repayment of inducement, 20(1)(hh)
- repayment of shareholder's loan, 20(1)(j)
- representation expenses, 20(1)(cc)
- reserves, *see* Reserve
- resource allowances, 20(1)(v.1)
- salary deferral arrangements, 20(1)(oo)
- scientific research and experimental development, 37
- share transfer fees, 20(1)(g)
- terminal loss, 20(16)
- utilities service connection, 20(1)(ee)
- western grain stabilization levy, 20(1)(ff)

**Deductions in computing income from office or employment**, *see also* Deductions in computing income; Employee; Expenses
- aircraft costs, Reg. 1100(6)
- • reasonability, 8(9)
- allowed, 8(1)
- artists' expenses, 8(1)(q)
- automobile expenses, 8(1)(h.1)
- clergyman's residence, 8(1)(c)
- limitations
- • general, 8(2)
- • meals, 8(4)
- registered pension plan contributions, 8(1)(m), 147.2(4)
- retirement compensation arrangement, 8(1)(m.2)
- teachers' exchange fund, 8(1)(d)

**Deductions in computing tax**, *see also* Tax credits
- corporations
- • abatement, 124
- • income earned in province, 124(1)
- • manufacturing and processing profits, 125.1
- • small business deduction, 125
- exploration and drilling expenses, ITAR 29(32), (33)
- foreign tax, 126
- gifts, 118.1(3)
- income earned in province that provides schooling allowance, 120(2)
- *Income War Tax Act*, under, ITAR 17(1)
- international organization, levy by, 126(3)
- investment corporation, 130(1)
- investment tax credit, 127(5)–(35)
- logging tax, 127(1)
- manufacturing and processing profits, 125.1
- mortgage investment corporations, 130.1
- personal credits, 118–118.95
- political contributions, 127(3)–(4.2)
- S.C. 1947, c. 63, s. 16, under, ITAR 17(3)
- small business deduction, 125
- taxable dividends, 121

**Deductions in computing taxable income**, *see also* Tax credits; Deductions in computing income
- amounts exempt under tax agreements, 110(1)(f)(i)
- annual adjustment, 117.1
- capital gains, 110.6
- corporations
- • gifts, 110.1
- dividend

Deductions in computing taxable income *(cont'd)*
- • from foreign affiliate, 113
- • received by corporation, 112
- employee stock options, 110(1)(d), (d.1)
- home relocation loan, 110(1)(j)
- *Income War Tax Act*, under, ITAR 17(2)
- indexing, 117.1
- losses of other years, 111
- medical expenses, *see* Medical expenses
- member of religious order, 110(2)
- net capital losses, 111(1)(b), 111(1.1), (2)
- non-capital losses, 111(1)(a)
- non-resident trusts, 94(3) [to be repealed]
- order of applying provisions, 111.1
- other, permitted, 110
- Part VI.1 tax, 110(1)(k)
- part-year resident, 114
- separate returns, 114.2
- social assistance payments, 110(1)(f)(iii)
- unemployment insurance benefit repayment, 110(1)(i)
- workers' compensation payments, 110(1)(f)(ii)

**Deemed disposition**, *see* Disposition: deemed

**Deemed dividend**, *see* Dividend: deemed

**Deemed overpayment**, *see* Overpayment of tax: deemed

**Deemed realization of gains**, *see* Disposition: deemed

**Deer**, 80.3(1)"breeding animals"

**Defaulting taxpayer**, 226

**Defence forces**, *see* Canadian Forces

**Deferral**, *see also* Rollover
- amount, *see* Deferral amount
- departure tax, by posting security, 220(4.5)–(4.54)
- expenses payable but not paid, 78
- stock option benefit, 7(1.1), (1.8), (8)–(16)
- tax on distribution by trust to non-resident beneficiary, by posting security, 220(4.6)–(4.63)

**Deferral amount**
- defined, 94.2(1)(b)
- • fresh start re tax-exempt entity, 94.2(16)(c)
- • superficial disposition, 94.2(17)

**Deferred amount, defined**, 248(1)

**Deferred annuity out of pension plan**, 254

**Deferred income**
- salary deferral arrangements, 6(1)(i), 6(11)–(14)

**Deferred income plans**, 144–147.3, *see also* Deferred profit sharing plans; Registered education savings plans; Registered pension plan; Registered retirement income fund; Registered retirement savings plan; Registered supplementary unemployment benefit plan
- foreign property of, Reg. 5000
- interest on money borrowed to invest in, not deductible, 18(11)
- over-contributions to
- • tax on, 204.1–204.3
- property acquired by trusts governed by
- • tax re, 205–207
- property held by trust governed by
- • tax re, 207.1, 207.2
- qualified investments, Reg. Part XLIX
- small business investments, Reg. Part LI
- tax on non-qualified investments, 207.1

**Deferred payment**
- defined (re top-up disability payments), 8(1)(n.1)(i)

**Deferred profit sharing plan**
- age 69 maturity, 147(2)(k), 147(10.6)
- amendments to
- • anti-avoidance, 146(5.21)
- amount received from, income, 56(1)(i)
- amount taxable, 147(18), 201
- anti-avoidance rule, 147(18), (22)
- annuity purchased by, *see* purchase of annuity by (below)
- benefit under
- • estate tax on, deductible, 60(m)
- • succession duties on, deduction for, 60(m.1)
- • taxable, 147(10)–(12)
- conditions, 147(2)
- continuation of, in amalgamation, 87(2)(q)
- defined, 147(1), 248(1)
- definitions, 147(1), 204
- disposal of shares
- • deduction re amount, 110(1)(d.3)
- disposition of property to
- • capital loss nil, 40(2)(g)(iv)(A)
- distribution deemed disposition, 200
- emigration of employee, no deemed disposition, 128.1(10)"excluded right or interest"(a)(iv)
- employee contributions prohibited, 147(2)(a.1), 147(14)(c.2)
- employer's contribution
- • deductible, 20(1)(y), 147(8), (9)
- • • limitations, 18(1)(j), 147(5.1), 147(9)
- • not includable in employee's income, 6(1)(a)(i)
- • terms limiting, 147(2.1)
- • where not deductible, 147(9.1)
- "excess amount" defined, 204.2(4)
- excluded from various trust rules, 108(1)"trust"(a)
- forfeited amounts, 147(2)(i.1), 147(10.3)
- • defined, 147(1)
- • reallocation of, 147(2.2)
- forfeitures, tax on, 201
- individual ceasing to be employed by an employer
- • compensation, 147(5.11)
- initial non-qualified investment, defined, 204
- insurance corporation demutualization conversion benefit, 139.1(12), (14)
- interest on money borrowed to invest in, whether deductible, 18(11)(c)
- life insurance policies, 198(6)–(8)
- lump-sum payment
- • remuneration, Reg. 100(1)
- maturity by age 69, 147(2)(k), 147(10.6)
- money borrowed for contribution to
- • limitation on deductibility, 18(11)(c)
- non-deductible employer contributions prohibited, 147(2)(a.1), 147(14)(c.2)
- non-qualified investments of, defined, 204
- not employees profit sharing plan, 147(6)
- overcontribution to, 204.1(3)
- participating employer, meaning of, 147(1.1)
- payment out of profits, meaning of, 147(16)
- payments under
- • non-resident, to, 212(1)(m)
- • taxable, 147(10)
- • used to purchase income-averaging annuity contract, deductible, 61(2)(a)
- • withholding of tax, 153(1)(h)
- profit sharing plan, defined, 147.1(1)

2691

Deferred profit sharing plan *(cont'd)*
- property
- - appropriation of, by employer, 147(13)
- - disposition or acquisition of, for inadequate consideration, 147(18)
- purchase of annuity by, 147(2)(k)(vi)
- - before 1997, 147(10.6)
- qualified investment, defined, 204"qualified investment"
- qualified investments, Reg. Part XLIX
- - defined, 204
- registration of, 147(2)–(5), Reg. 1501
- - revocation, 147(14), (15)
- revocation of, 147(14), (22)
- revoked plan
- - defined, 204, Reg. 4901(2)
- - "excess amount" defined, 204.2(4)
- - payments under, subject to withholding of tax, 153(1)(h)
- - rules applicable, 147(15)
- shares included in single payment on retirement etc., 147(10.1), (10.2)
- - disposal of, 147(10.4), (10.5)
- single payment on withdrawal, 147(10.1), (10.2), (10.4)–(12), Reg. 1503
- tax on forfeitures, 201
- tax on initial non-qualified investments, 199
- tax on non-qualified investments, 198
- - distribution deemed disposition, 200
- - refund
- - - on disposition, 198(4)
- - - on recovery of property given as security, 198(5)
- - return required, 202(1)
- tax on overcontributions to, 204.1
- tax payable by
- - on acquisition of shares not at fair market value, 206.1
- - on foreign property, 206
- - on holding certain property, 207.1(2)
- tax re foreign property, 205–207
- tax where inadequate consideration on purchase or sale, 201
- taxation year of, 144(11)
- testamentary trust receiving benefits from, 104(27.1)
- transfer to
- - capital loss deemed nil, 40(2)(g)(iv)(A)
- - DPSP, from, 147(19)
- transfers from
- - DPSP, to, 147(19)
- - excess, 147(22)
- - registered pension plan, to, 147(19)
- - registered retirement saving plan, to, 147(19)
- - restrictions re, 147(21)
- - spousal RRSP, to, 60(j.2)
- - taxation of amount transferred, 147(20)
- - trust, through, to RPP or RRSP, 104(27.1)
- trust under, exempt, 147(7), 149(1)(s)

**Defined benefit limit**
- defined, Reg. 8500(1)

**Defined benefit provision**
- defined, 147.1(1)

**Defined contribution provision**, *see* Money purchase provision

**Definitions**, *see also* the specific defined terms
- application of, *Interpretation Act* s. 15
- capital gains exemption rules, 110.6(1)
- capital property rules, 54
- charities, 149.1(1)
- corporations, 89
- foreign affiliate rules, 95
- general, 248
- insurance rules, 138(12), 148(9), Reg. 1408
- investment tax credit rules, 127(9)
- registered pension plans, 147.1(1)
- registered retirement income funds, 146.3(1)
- registered retirement savings plans, 146(1)
- regulations, *Interpretation Act* s. 16
- relationships, 251–252
- resource taxation, 66(15), 66.1(6), 66.2(5), 66.4(5)
- small business rules, 125(7)
- terms used in regulations, *Interpretation Act* s. 16
- trusts, 108

**Delegation of powers and duties of Minister**
- administrative, 220(2.01)
- by regulation, 221(1)(f) (repealed), Reg. Part IX

**Demand**
- by Minister
- - actuarial report, for registered pension plan, Reg. 8410
- - books and records, to retain, 230(7)
- - documents, for, 231.2(1)(b)
- - information, for, 231.2(1)(a)
- - - foreign investment entity, where information not provided, 94.1(16), (17)
- - information return, for, 233
- - return, for, 150(2)
- proof of failure to comply with, 244(7), (8)
- proof of service, 244(5), (6)
- third party, *see* Garnishment for taxes unpaid

**Demutualization**, 139.1
- defined, 139.1(1)
- effect of, 139.1(4)
- holding corporation, *see* Holding corporation
- paid-up capital following, 139.1(6), (7)
- rollover of ownership rights into shares, 139.1(4)(a), (d)
- time of, 139.1(2)(i)

**Denmark**, *see also* Foreign government
- stock exchange recognized, Reg. 3201(s)

**Density**
- hydrocarbons, determination of, Reg. 1107

**Dental bills, as medical expense**, 118.2(2)(a)

**Dental instruments (small)**
- capital cost allowance for, Reg. Sch. II:Cl. 12(e)

**Dental mechanic**
- payments to, as medical expenses, 118.2(2)(p)

**Dental plan**, *see* Private health services plan

**Dentist**, *see also* Professional practice
- defined, 118.4(2)

**Department of Canadian Heritage**
- disclosure of information re cultural property to, 241(4)(d)(xii)

**Department of Energy, Mines and Resources**
- certificate re Class 34 property, Reg. 1104(11), Sch. II:Cl. 34(d), Sch. II:Cl. 34(g)

# Index

Department of Energy, Mines and Resources *(cont'd)*
- certificate re mineral deposit, 248(1)"mineral resource"(d)(i)
- certificate re oil or gas well, 66.1(6)"Canadian exploration expense"(d)(iv), 66.1(10)
- communication of information to, 241(4)(d)(v)–(vi.1)
- consultation re mine capacity, Reg. Sch. II:Cl. 1(l), Sch. II:Cl. 28(b)(ii)
- consultation re pipeline, Reg. Sch. II:Cl. 1(l), Sch. II:Cl. 2(b)
- determination of prescribed energy conservation property, 13(18.1), 241(4)(d)(vi.1)

**Department of Fisheries and Oceans Act**, *see* Northern Cod Compensation and Adjustment Program

**Department of Human Resources Development**, *see* Human Resources Development Canada

**Department of Labour Act**
- s. 5, income assistance payments under, *see* Older Worker Adjustment, Program for

**Department of National Revenue**, *see* Canada Customs and Revenue Agency

**Departure tax**, *see* Ceasing to be resident in Canada

**Dependant**
- alimony or maintenance paid to, 118(5)
- credit for, 118(1)B(b), (d)
  - apportionment of, 118(4)(e)
- deemed resident, of
  - also deemed resident, 250(1)(f)
- defined, 118(6), Reg. 8500(1)
- infirm, *see* Infirm dependant
- medical expenses of, 118.2(2)(a)
- mental or physical impairment, 118.2(2)(b), (c), 118.3(2), 118.4
- notch provision, 117(7), 118.2(1)D
- partial
  - mental or physical impairment, 118.3(3)
- spouse, 118(1)B(a)
- wholly dependent persons, credit for, 118(1)B(b)
  - limitation, 118(4)

**Dependants' relief acts, trust created by**, 70(6.1)

**Dependent personal services**, *see* Employment: income from

**Depletion allowances**, *see also* Resource allowance
- gas well, 65, Reg. Part XII
- lessee and lessor, allocation between, 65(3)
- mineral resource, 65, Reg. Part XII
  - coal mine, allocation, 65(3)
- mining exploration, Reg. 1203
- oil well, 65, Reg. Part XII
- supplementary, Reg. 1212
- timber limit, 65

**Depletion base**, *see* Earned depletion base; Mining exploration depletion base; Supplementary depletion base

**Deposit**
- eligible, *see* Eligible deposit
- insurance corporation, *see* Deposit insurance corporation
- on container
  - as income, 12(1)(a)(ii)
  - reserve for, 20(1)(m)(iv)
- specified, *see* Specified deposit

**Deposit balance**
- of insurer, defined, Reg. 2400(1)

**Deposit insurance corporation**, *see also* Canada Deposit Insurance Corporation
- amounts included in income, 137.1(1), (10)
- amounts not included in income, 137.1(2)
- capital tax, exemption from, 181.1(3)(e)
- deductions in computing income, 137.1(3)
  - limitation, 137.1(4)
  - payments to member institutions, 137.1(11)
- deemed
  - mark-to-market property, by financial institution, 142.5(2)
  - on becoming a financial institution, 142.6(1)(b)
  - on ceasing to be a financial institution, 142.6(1)(c)
  - specified debt obligation that was inventory of financial institution, 142.6(4)(a)
- deemed not credit union, 137.1(7)
- deemed not private corporation, 137.1(6)
- deeming provision re, 137.1(5.1)
- defined, 137.1(5)
- investment property, defined, 137.1(5)
- member institution
  - defined, 137.1(5)
  - payments by, deductible in computing income, 137.1(11)(a)
  - repayment deductible in computing income, 137.1(11)(b)
  - repayment excluded from income of previous year, 137.1(12)
  - security for payment of tax, 220(4.3), (4.4)
- not subject to mark-to-market rules, 142.2(1)"financial institution"(c)(iv)
- principal amount of interest payable, 137.1(10.1)
- property owned since before 1975, 137.2
- special tax rate, 137.1(9)
- wholly-owned subsidiary deemed deposit insurance corporation, 137.1(5.1)

**Depositary**
- defined, Reg. 223(5)

**Depository receipt**
- qualified investment for RRSP etc., Reg. 4900(1)(p.1)

**Deposit-taking institution**
- additional tax on, 190.1(1.1)

**Depreciable property**, *see also* Capital cost allowance
- acquired
  - amalgamation, on, 87(2)(d), (d.1)
  - by transfer, amalgamation or winding-up, Reg. 1102(14), (14.1)
  - capital cost, 13(5.2)
  - non-arm's length, 13(7)(e), Reg. 1102(20)
  - corporations controlled by one trustee, 13(7.3)
  - partner's cost, ITAR 20(4)"acquisition cost"
  - with government assistance, deemed capital cost, 13(7.1), (7.2)
- additions and alterations, Reg. 1102(19)
- amortization, *see* Capital cost allowance
- available for use, 13(26)–(32), Reg. 1100(2)(a)(i), (vii)
- borrowing money for, 21(3)
- capital, disposed of
  - capital cost, 13(5.4)
  - lease cancellation payment, 13(5.5)
  - recaptured depreciation, 13(5.3)
- capital cost, *see* Capital cost
- capital cost allowance, *see also* Capital cost allowance
  - classes, Reg. Sch. II

2693

Depreciable property *(cont'd)*
- capitalization of interest, 21(1), (3)
- - reassessment, 21(5)
- certain transactions after 1971, ITAR 20(1.2)
- change in proportions of use, 13(7)(d), 13(9)
- change in use
- - deemed acquisition/disposition, 13(7)(a), (b), 13(9)
- classes, for capital cost allowance, Reg. Sch. II
- - inclusions in, Reg. 1103
- - transfers between, Reg. 1103
- cost of money borrowed to acquire, 21(1)
- - election, 21(1)
- deductions allowed, Reg. Part XI
- - in computing income from farming or fishing, Reg. Part XVII
- deemed, Reg. 1101(5g)
- - capital cost allowance, Reg. Sch. II:Cl. 36
- - separate classes, Reg. 1101(5g)
- deemed capital cost of, 13(7.4)
- deemed disposition/reacquisition
- - capital cost, deemed, 13(7)(f)
- - on death, 70(5)
- defined, 13(21)
- - on windup of corporation, 88(1)(c.7)
- depreciation, *see* Capital cost allowance
- disposition of
- - after ceasing business, 13(8)
- - bad debt on, 20(4)
- - capital gain on, 39(1)(a)
- - on death
- - - order of disposition, 70(14)
- - - to child, 70(9)
- - - to spouse, 70(6); ITAR 20(1.1)
- - proceeds of disposition, defined, 13(21)
- - recapture, up to original cost, 13(1)
- - terminal loss, where no property left in class, 20(16)
- divided use
- - change in ratio of uses, 13(7)(d)
- - deemed cost/proceeds of income-producing part, 13(7)(c)
- dividend in kind, ITAR 20(1.4)
- election re
- - deemed, 44(4)
- exchanges of, 13(4)
- exclusions from classes, Reg. 1102
- first-year rule, Reg. 1100(2)–(2.4)
- half-year rule, Reg. 1100(2)–(2.4)
- manufacturing and processing business, acquired for
- - deemed capital cost of, 13(10)
- manufacturing and processing enterprises, Reg. 1102(15), (16)
- misclassified, 13(6)
- prescribed class, of
- - transferred to corporation by shareholder, 85(1)(e), (e.1), (e.3), (e.4)
- proceeds of disposition of, 13(21)
- receipt of government grant, 13(7.1), (7.2)
- recreational property, Reg. 1102(17)
- replacement for, 13(4), (4.1)
- rollover of
- - to corporation, 85(1)(e), 85(5)
- - to partnership, 97(2)
- - to trust, 107.4(3)(d)

- sale of, *see* disposition of (*above*)
- sale of mortgage, etc., 20(5), (5.1)
- separate classes, Reg. 1101
- transfer of
- - non-resident insurer, by, 138(11.8)
- - not at arm's length, 13(7)(e), 13(21.2)
- - on mutual fund rollover, 132.2(1)(d)
- - pre-1972, not at arm's length, ITAR 20(1.3)
- - to corporation, rules, 85(1)(e), 85(5)
- - to trust, qualifying disposition, 107.4(3)(d)
- - where UCC exceeds fair market value, 13(21.2)
- uncollectible proceeds of disposition, 20(4)–(4.2)
- undepreciated capital cost, 13(21)

**Depreciation**, *see also* Capital cost allowance
- double, in lieu of, Reg. 1100(1)(d)
- property acquired before 1972, ITAR 18

**Deputy Minister**, *see* Commissioner of Customs and Revenue

**Derivative assessment**, 160

**Designated amount**
- of trust, in respect of capital gains, 104(21.2)

**Designated area**
- defined in *Canadian Wheat Board Act*, 76(5)

**Designated beneficiary**
- defined, 210
- no deduction for income of trust paid to, 104(7)

**Designated benefit**, *see* Registered retirement income fund: designated benefit

**Designated city**
- defined, Reg. 7304(1)

**Designated Class 34 income, eg. 1100(24) [repealed]**

**Designated contributor (in respect of a trust)**, *see also* Settlor (of trust)
- application in definition of exempt beneficiary, 104(5.4)(b)(i), (ii)
- defined, 104(5.6), (5.7)(c)

**Designated corporation (re insurer)**
- loan by insurer to, 138(4.5)

**Designated cost (of offshore investment fund property)**
- application in calculation of tax, 94.1(1)(f)(i)
- defined, 94.1(2)

**Designated country**, *see also* Designated treaty country
- defined, Reg. 8006

**Designated educational institution**
- defined, 118.6(1)
- registered educational savings plan, 146.1(1)"post-secondary educational institution"(a), 146.1(1)"trust"(d)
- student enrolled at, education credit, 118.6(2)

**Designated entity**
- defined, re non-resident investment or pension fund, 115.2(3)(b)

**Designated financial institution**
- defined, 153(6)
- large remittances to be made at, 153(1)

**Designated income**, *see* Trust (or estate): designated income, tax on

**Designated insurance property**
- defined, 138(12), 248(1)

**Designated investment services**
- defined, re non-resident investment or pension fund, 115.2(1)

# Index

**Designated limited partnership**
- defined, Reg. 5000(7)
- partner's interest excluded from foreign property, Reg. 5000(1.1)(e)

**Designated overburden removal cost**, Reg. 1104(2), Reg. Sch. II:Cl. 12(q)
- defined, Reg. 1104(2)

**Designated partnership**
- defined, 212.1(3)(e)

**Designated person**
- benefit conferred on through corporation, 74.4(2)
- • exceptions, 74.4(4), 74.5(5)
- • special rules, 74.5(6)–(8)
- benefit conferred on through trust, 74.3(1)
- defined
- • for attribution rules, 74.5(5)
- • for communication of information, 241(10)

**Designated plan**
- defined, Reg. 8515(1)–(3)

**Designated property**
- capital dividend account, re
- • gain on excluded from calculation, 89(1)"capital dividend account"(a)(i)(C)(I), 89(1)"capital dividend account"(a)(ii)(C)(I)
- defined, 89(1)

**Designated rate**
- defined, Reg. 5100(1)

**Designated region, prescribed**
- credit for investment in, 127(9)"specified percentage"(a)(ii)(B), 127(9)"specified percentage"(a)(vi), 127(9)"specified percentage"(e)(i)(B)
- defined, Reg. 4607

**Designated security**
- defined, Reg. 226(1)

**Designated share**
- defined, Reg. 227(1)

**Designated shareholder**
- defined, Reg. 4901(2), (2.3)

**Designated treaty country**, Reg. 5907(11), (11.1)

**Designated underground storage cost**
- defined, Reg. 1104(2)

**Designated value**
- defined, 206(1)

**Designated withdrawal**
- defined, for Home Buyers' Plan, 146.01(1)

**Designation**
- to treat capital gain as forgiven amount, 80.03(7)

**Designation year (re capital gains of trust)**
- defined, 104(21.2)

**Determination**, *see also* Assessment
- Appropriations for Contingencies of a Bank, 26(4)
- legal fees relating to, 56(1)(l), 60(o), 152(1.2)
- Minister, by
- • general anti-avoidance rule application, 152(1.11)
- • losses, of, 152(1.1)
- • • binding on Minister and taxpayer, 152(1.3)
- • • following GAAR assessment, 152(1.11), (1.12)
- • • treated like an assessment, 152(1.2)
- • that taxpayer's chief source of income not farming, 31(2)
- notice of

- • date deemed made, 244(14), (15)
- • general anti-avoidance rule application, 152(1.11), 245(6)
- • losses, 152(1.1), 152(1.2)
- • mailing date, 244(14)
- • proof that not objected to, 244(10)
- • provisions applicable to, 152(1.2)
- partnership income or loss, 152(1.4)–(1.8)
- • objection to, 165(1.15)
- question, of, by Tax Court, 174
- redetermination, 152(1.2)
- tax consequences under general anti-avoidance rule, 245(5)
- time, defined, 110.6(1)"qualified small business corporation share"
- value of property, by Canadian Cultural Property Export Review Board, 118.1(10)

**Deuterium-enriched water**
- capital cost allowance, Reg. Sch. II:Cl. 26

**Development**, *see* Canadian development expense; Scientific research and experimental development

**Devices**
- for hearing- or sight-impaired, business expense, 20(1)(rr)
- medical, credit for, 118.2(2), Reg. 5700

**Diabetic**
- blood-sugar level measuring device, medical expense, Reg. 5700(s)

**Diagnostic procedures**
- medical expenses, 118.2(2)(o)

**Diamond**
- extraction of, 248(1)"mineral resource"(d)(ii)

**Diapers (for incontinence), medical expense**, 118.2(2)(i.1)

**Die, etc., capital cost allowance**, Reg. Sch. II:Cl. 12(d)

**Digester gas**
- defined, Reg. 1104(13)

**Digital video disc**, *see* Video laser-disk

**Diligence**, *see* Due diligence

**Diplomat**
- Canadian, abroad
- • deemed resident in Canada, 250(1)(c), 250(2)
- • reimbursement of allowance, non-taxable, 6(1)(b)(iii)
- foreign, in Canada
- • exemption from tax, 149(1)(a), Canada–U.S. Tax Convention Art. XXVIII

**Direct equity percentage, defined**, 95(4)

**Direct financing lease**
- prescribed property for specified debt obligation definition, Reg. 9004
- prescribed security for lending-asset definition, Reg. 6209(b)(iii)

**Directed person (debt forgiveness rules)**
- defined, 80(1), 80.04(1)
- eligible transferee, 80.04(2)
- obligations issued by, 80(14)

**Director, Director General**
- duties delegated to, 220(2.01), Reg. 900

**Director (of corporation)**
- fees
- • income, 6(1)(c)
- • withholding tax, 153(1)(g)

2695

## Index

Director (of corporation) *(cont'd)*
- liability of
  - - for corporation's unremitted source withholdings, 227.1
  - - for offence of corporation, 242

**Disability,** *see* Mental or physical impairment

**Disability benefit,** *see* Disability insurance; Disability pension

**Disability insurance**
- benefits under, income, 6(1)(f); ITAR 19
- employer's contribution not a taxable benefit, 6(1)(a)(i)
- top-up contributions by employer, *see* Disability policy

**Disability payments**
- military action, for
  - - exempt, 81(1)(e)

**Disability pension**
- CPP, *see* Canada Pension Plan/Quebec Pension Plan: disability pension
- RCMP, exempt, 81(1)(i)

**Disability policy**
- defined, 6(17)
- top-up payments on insolvency of insurer, 6(18)
  - - reimbursement to employer, 8(1)(n.1)

**Disability-related building modifications**
- deductible, 20(1)(qq)
- medical expense credit, 118.2(2)(l.2)

**Disability-related devices and equipment**
- deductible, 20(1)(rr)

**Disability-related employment benefits**
- when not included in income, 6(16)

**Disabled**
- defined (for pension plan), Reg. 8500(1)

**Disabled person,** *see* Mental or physical impairment

**Disbursement excess**
- registered charity, of, carryforward, 149.1(20)
  - - defined, 149.1(21)

**Disbursement quota**
- anti-avoidance rule, 149.1(4.1)
- defined
  - - for charitable foundation, 149.1(1), Reg. 3701
  - - for charitable organization, 149.1(21)(c)

**Disclaimer, defined,** 248(9)

**Disclosure of information**
- by CCRA, *see* Communication of information
- to CCRA, *see* Information return

**Discontinuance of venture capital business**
- meaning of, 204.8(2)
- penalty tax, 204.841

**Discount,** *see also* Bond: discount
- defined, pre-1972 obligation, ITAR 26(12)

**Discounted bonds,** *see* Bond: discount

**Discretion of Minister,** *see* Minister (of National Revenue)

**Discrimination,** Canada–U.S. Tax Convention Art. XXV

**Dishonoured cheque,** 162(11) [repealed]

**Disposition**
- capital gain, 39(1)(a), 40(1)
- child, to, 40(1.1)
- deceased taxpayer, of, 70(5), 164(6)
- deemed
  - - by trust, every 21 years, 104(4)
  - - mark-to-market property, by financial institution, 142.5(2)
  - - on becoming a financial institution, 142.6(1)(b)
  - - on ceasing to be a financial institution, 142.6(1)(c)
  - - on ceasing to be resident, 128.1(4)(b)
  - - on death, 70(5)–(10)
  - - on gift, 69(1)(b)(ii)
  - - specified debt obligation that was inventory of financial institution, 142.6(4)(a)
  - - where spousal trust distributes property to other person, 107(4)
- deemed contribution of capital, where, 53(1.1)
- deferral of tax on, *see* Rollover
- defined, 13(21) [to be repealed], 54 [to be repealed], 248(1) [draft]
  - - capital property, 54"disposition"
  - - depreciable property, 13(21), Reg. 1206(1)
  - - satisfaction of obligation, deemed not to be, 49.1
- depreciable, *see* Depreciable property
- income interest in trust, 106(2)
- involuntary, election re, 13(4)
  - - deemed, 44(4)
- land used in farming business of partnership, 101
- loss on, *see* Loss(es); Stop-loss rules
- non-resident, by, 116(1)–(4)
  - - certificate, 116(2)
  - - notice, 116(3)
  - - where tax deferred under tax treaty, 115.1
- of interest in life insurance policy, 148(9), Reg. 217(1)
- partnership, on ceasing to exist, 98
- personal-use
  - - capital loss nil, 40(2)(g)(iii)
- principal residence, *see* Principal residence
- proceeds of, *see* Proceeds of disposition
- purchaser corporation controlling or controlled by taxpayer, 40(2)(a)(ii)
- specified person to benefit from subsequent disposition
  - - anti-avoidance rule, 69(11)
  - - - application on winding-up, 88(1)
- subsequent to debt forgiveness, 80.03(2)
- to a trust, no change in beneficial ownership, 69(1)(b)(iii)
- together with services, allocation rule, 68
- trust, to
  - - capital loss nil, 40(2)(g)(iv)

**Disposition day (for trust)**
- defined, 104(5.3), (5.8)

**Dispute, taxes in**
- whether taxpayer required to remit, 164(1.1)(d), 225.1

**Dissolution,** *see* Winding-up

**Distance education**
- education credit, full-time student, 118.6(2)B

**Distress preferred share,** 80.02
- constitutes commercial obligation, 80(1)"commercial obligation"
- constitutes excluded security, 80(1)"excluded security"
- defined, 80(1)
- disposition of following debt forgiveness, no deemed capital gain, 80.03(2)
- settled
  - - effect of, where subsidiary wound up into parent, 80.01(5)
  - - meaning of, 80.02(2)(c), 80.02(7)(a)

# Index

**Distress preferred share** *(cont'd)*
- share ceasing to be, 80.02(7)
- substituted for debt, 80.02(3)
- substituted for other distress preferred share, 80.02(5)
- substitution of commercial debt obligation for, 80.02(4)
- substitution of other share for, 80.02(6)

**Distributing corporation**
- defined, 55(1)"distribution"

**Distribution**
- for butterfly purposes, defined, 55(1)
- of dividends or profits
  - • deduction for interest costs, 20.1, 20.2
  - • defined, 20.1(8)(b)
- of property by non-resident trust, reporting requirement, 233.5
- on winding-up, 84(2), (6)
- tax, *see* Corporate distributions tax

**Distribution equipment**
- defined (re energy conservation CCA), Reg. 1104(13)

**Distribution time**
- defined, 128.1(7)(b)

**Distribution year**
- defined
  - • for postponement of tax on distribution by trust to non-resident beneficiary, 220(4.6)(a)
  - • for foreign tax credit of trust, 126(2.22)
  - • for interest expense on money borrowed for distribution, 20.1(1)(a)

**Distributor**
- defined, 20.1(1), 20.2(1)

**District**
- defined, Reg. 1802(5)

**Dividend**
- capital, *see* Capital dividend
- capital gains dividend
  - • mutual fund corporation, election, 131(1)–(1.4)
- deemed, 84
  - • added to cost base of share, 53(1)(b)
  - • guaranteed share, on, 84(4.3)
  - • interest on income bond, 15(3)
    - • • non-resident corporation, 15(4)
  - • non-resident surplus strips, 212.1, 212.2
  - • on corporation becoming resident in Canada, 128.1(1)(c.1), (c.2)
  - • on demutualization of insurance corporation, 139.1(2)(j)
  - • on disposition of share of foreign affiliate, 93(1)
  - • on distribution by mutual holding corporation, 139.2
  - • redemption of share, 84(3)
  - • reduction of paid-up capital, on, 84(4), (4.1)
  - • term preferred share, on, 84(4.2), 258(2)
  - • windup of business, 84(2)
- deemed not received, 55(2)–(5)
- deemed paid
  - • deemed payable when, 84(7)
  - • where not deemed received, 84(8)
- deemed proceeds of disposition of share, or capital gain, 55(2)–(5)
- deemed received where attribution rules apply, 82(2)
  - • where not applicable, 84(8)
- defined, 248(1)
  - • for stop-loss rules, 112(6)(a)
  - • for treaty purposes, Canada–U.S. Tax Convention Art. X:3
- election re
  - • excessive, 184(3), (3.1)–(5)
- employees profit sharing plan, allocation by, 144(8)
- excluded from tax under Part VI.1, 191(1)
- exempt, on share of foreign affiliate, 93(3)
- foreign affiliate, from, 20(13), 95(1), 113(1), Reg. 5900
- foreign business corporation, from, received by non-resident, 213
- gross-up, 82(1)(b)
- guarantee agreement re
  - • no deduction, 112(2.2)–(2.22)
- in kind
  - • cost of, 52(2)
  - • depreciable property as, ITAR 20(1.4)
- includes stock dividend, 248(1)
- income, 12(1)(j), (k), 82(1), 90
  - • whether specified investment business, 125(7)"specified investment business"
- insurance corporation
  - • to policyholders, 140(1)
- life insurance policy, 148(2)
- money borrowed to pay, 20.1, 20.2
- mortgage investment corporation, from
  - • deemed bond interest, 130.1(2), (3)
- non-resident corporation, from, 90
- non-resident-owned investment corporation
  - • election re, 133(7.1)–(7.3)
- non-taxable
  - • portion not included in beneficiary's income
    - • • mutual fund trust, 132(3)
  - • received by trust
    - • • designation re, 104(20)
- ownership certificate required, 234
- paid
  - • in excess of elective amount, tax on, 184
  - • out of exempt surplus, 113(4)
  - • private corporation, by, 83(2)
  - • public corporation, by, 83(1)
  - • to non-resident
    - • • foreign business corporation, by, 213
    - • • tax on, 212(2)
    - • • United States resident, Canada–U.S. Tax Convention Art. X
- patronage, *see* Patronage dividends
- qualifying
  - • defined, 83(6)
  - • late-filed election, 83(3)–(5)
  - • payment of, 83(1)
- received
  - • amount included in income, 82(1), 90
  - • by broker/dealer, withholding tax, 153(4), (5)
  - • by corporation
    - • • deduction from income, 112(1), (2)
    - • • stop-loss rules, 112(2.1)–(2.9)
  - • by financial institution, 112(5)–(5.2)
  - • by prescribed venture capital corporation, deemed not taxable dividend, 186.2
  - • by spouse, transfer of, 82(3)
  - • by trust, allocation to beneficiary, 104(19), (20)
  - • gross-up, 82(1)(b)
- refund, *see* Dividend refund

Dividend *(cont'd)*
- rental arrangement, *see* Dividend rental arrangement
- short-term preferred share, 112(2.3)
- simultaneous, 89(3)
- • non-resident-owned investment corporation, 133(7.2)
- stock, *see also* 248(1)"dividend"
- • amount of, 95(7), 248(1)"amount"
- • cost of, 52(3)
- • deemed to be substituted property, 248(5)(b)
- • defined, 248(1)
- • excluded from deemed dividend, 84(1)(a)
- • paid as benefit, 15(1.1)
- "stop-loss" rule, 112(3), (3.1), (3.2), (4), (4.2), (4.3), (7)
- stripping, *see* Surplus stripping
- tax credit, 121
- taxable
- • allocation of, by credit union, 137(5.1), (5.2)
- • amalgamation, on, 87(2)(x)
- • deduction from tax otherwise payable, 121
- • defined, 89(1)"taxable dividend" 112(6)(a), 129(7), 248(1)
- • non-resident-owned investment corporation, of, 133(8)"taxable dividend"
- • received by private corporation, tax on, 186
- • received by trust, designation re, 104(19)
- taxable corporation, from
- • life insurer, received by, 138(6)
- term preferred shares, on
- • received by specified financial institution, 112(2.1)
- unclaimed at year-end
- • withholding tax, 153(4)
- • • effect of remittance, 153(5)

**Dividend payer**
- defined, for capital gains stripping rules, 55(3)(a)(iii)(A)

**Dividend recipient**
- defined, for capital gains stripping rules, 55(3)

**Dividend refund**, *see also* Refundable dividend tax on hand
- defined, 129(1)
- interest on, 129(2.1), (2.2)
- mutual fund corporation, to, 131(5)
- private corporation, to, 129
- • application to other liability, 129(2)
- • dividends deemed not to be taxable dividends, 129(1.2)

**Dividend rental arrangement**, *see also* Securities lending arrangements
- defined, 248(1)
- gross-up and credit denied, 82(1)(a)(i), 82(1)(b)
- intercorporate dividend deduction denied, 112(2.3)
- no deduction for dividends received under, 112(2.3)

**Dividend stripping**, *see* Surplus stripping

**Dividend tax**
- refundable, *see* Refundable dividend tax on hand

**Dividend tax credit**, 121

**Division of property**, *see* Partition of property

**Divisive reorganization**, 55(1), 55(3)(b)

**Divorce and separation**
- alimony, maintenance or support, *see* Support payments (spousal or child)
- attribution rules do not apply
- • generally, 74.5(3)
- • RRSP withdrawals, 146(8.3)
- registered education savings plan, rights transferred, 204.91(3)
- reimbursement of legal expenses, not taxable, 56(1)(l.1)
- separation agreement defined, 248(1)
- tracing of property transfer does not apply, 160(4)
- transfer of RPP funds to spouse's RPP, RRSP or RRIF, 147.3(5)
- transfer of RRIF funds to spouse's RRSP or RRIF, 146.3(14)
- transfer of RRSP funds to spouse's RRSP or RRIF, 146(16)(b)

**Dock**
- capital cost allowance, Reg. Sch. II:Cl. 3
- • for mine, Reg. Sch. II:Cl. 10(l)

**Documentary production**
- whether qualifies for Canadian film/video tax credit, Reg. 1106(6)

**Documentation**
- contemporaneous, for transfer pricing audit, 247(4)

**Documentation — due date**
- defined (for transfer pricing), 247(1)

**Documents**, *see also* Books and records
- demand for, 231.2(1)(b)
- examination of, where privilege claimed, 232(3.1)–(7)
- execution of, by corporations, 236
- foreign-based, 143.2(13), (14), 231.6
- proof of, 244(9), (13)
- requirement to provide, 231.2
- • compliance order, 231.5(2), 231.7
- seized
- • copies of, 231.5
- seizure of, 231.3(5)–(8)
- • where privilege claimed, 232(3), (4)–(7)
- transfer pricing, 247
- waiver of requirement to file, 220(3.1)

**Dog**, *see* Guide dog expenses; Animal

**Dollar amounts in legislation and regulations**
- $0.11/km car salesperson operating expenses benefit for 1997–99, Reg. 7305.1(1)(a)
- $0.12/km car salesperson operating expenses benefit for 2000, Reg. 7305.1(1)(a)
- $0.13/km car salesperson operating expenses benefit for 2001, Reg. 7305.1(1)(a)
- $0.14/km car operating expenses benefit for 1997–99, Reg. 7305.1(1)(b)
- $0.15/km car operating expenses benefit for 2000, Reg. 7305.1(1)(b)
- $0.16/km car operating expenses benefit for 2001, Reg. 7305.1(1)(b)
- $0.35 and $0.29 per km car allowances for 1997–99, Reg. 7306
- $0.37 and $0.31 per km car allowances for 2000, Reg. 7306
- $0.39 and $0.33 per km car allowances in territories for 1997–99, Reg. 7306
- $0.41 and $0.35 per km car allowances for 2001, Reg. 7306
- $0.41 and $0.35 per km car allowances in territories for 2000, Reg. 7306
- $0.45 and $0.39 per km car allowances in territories for 2001, Reg. 7306

Index

Dollar amounts in legislation and regulations *(cont'd)*
- $1 below which refund interest not payable, 164(3), (3.2)
- $1 per acre maximum deduction for payments on exploration and drilling rights acquired before April 11/62, ITAR 29(13)
- $2.50 per hectare of certain resource royalties not taxable, is deductible, Reg. 1211(d)(ii)
- $3.75 per day residing in prescribed intermediate zone, deduction, 110.7(1)(b)(ii)(A), 110.7(2)
- $7.50 per day maintaining household in prescribed intermediate zone, deduction, 110.7(1)(b)(ii), 110.7(2)
- $7.50 per day residing in prescribed northern zone, deduction, 110.7(1)(b)(ii)(A)
- $10 below which child tax benefit payment postponed to later month, 122.61(2)
- $10 per day penalty for trustee/receiver failing to file return, 162(3)
- $13.60 per month (federal) education credit before 1996, 118.6(2)
- $15 per day maintaining household in prescribed northern zone, deduction, 110.7(1)(b)(ii)
- $17 per month (federal) education credit for 1996, 118.6(2)
- $25 below which no instalment interest payable, 161(2.1)
- $25 per day penalty for failing to comply with obligation, 162(7), (7.1)
- $25.50 per month (federal) education credit for 1997, 118.6(2)
- $34 per month (federal) education credit after 1997, 118.6(2)
- $50 credit for U.S. social security tax changes under treaty, Canada–U.S. Tax Convention Art. XVIII:5
- $50 maximum penalty for trustee/receiver failing to file return, 162(3)
- $50 minimum interest to be reported by financial institution, Reg. 201(1) (Notes)
- $50 penalty for actions re ownership certificate, 162(4)
- $50 per day of conference expenses deemed paid for meals/entertainment, 67.1(3)
- $60 per month amount part-time education credit after 1997, 118.6(2)B(a)
- $80 per month amount for education credit before 1996, 118.6(2)
- $90 per week, certain child care expenses for child over 7 (pre-1998), 63(2)(b)(ii), 63(2.3)(c)B, 63(3)"child care expense"(c)(ii)
- $100 minimum fees for tuition credit, 118.5(1)(a), (c)
- $100 minimum penalty for failing to comply with obligation, 162(7), (7.1)
- $100 minimum penalty for false statement or omission, 163(2)
- $100 minimum penalty for issuer extending RRSP advantage, 146(13.1)(b)
- $100 minimum penalty for late renunciation, 66(12.75)
- $100 minimum penalty for non-resident corporation failing to file return, 162(2.1)(b)(i)
- $100 optional CCA deduction for timber limit or right to cut timber, Reg. Sch. VI:4
- $100 penalty for failing to provide SIN or information on a form, 162(5), (6)
- $100 per month amount for education credit for 1996, 118.6(2)
- $100 per month penalty for late designation, 66(14.5)
- $100 per month penalty for late-filed elections, 85(8), 93(6), 96(6), 220(3.5)
- $100 per partner per month penalty for failing to file partnership information return, 162(8)

- $100 per week, certain child care expenses for child over 7 (after 1997), 63(2)(b)(ii), 63(2.3)(c)B, 63(3)"child care expense"(c)(ii), 63(3)"periodic child care expense amount"
- $100 political contribution for 75% credit before 2000, 127(3)(a)
- $100 threshold for withholding on patronage dividends, 135(3)
- $100 under which GST credit paid in one lump sum, 122.5(5)(b)
- $105 annual GST credit, 122.5(3)(d), (e)
- $150 per month amount for education credit for 1997, 118.6(2)
- $150 per week, certain child care expenses per child under 7 or disabled (pre-1998), 63(2)(b)(i), 63(2.3)(c)A, 63(3)"child care expense"(c)(i)
- $170 credit to offset pension income, 118(3)
- $175 per week, certain child care expenses per child under 7 (after 1997), 63(2)(b)(i), 63(2.3)(c)A, 63(3)"child care expense"(c)(i), 63(3)"periodic child care expense amount"
- $200 below which tool, utensil or medical/dental instrument fully deductible, Reg. Sch. II:Cl. 12(c), Sch. II:Cl. 12(e), Sch. II:Cl. 12(i)
- $200 foreign currency gain or loss ignored for individual, 39(2)
- $200 maximum charitable donations for low-rate credit, 118.1(3)
- $200 per month amount for full-time education credit after 1997, 118.6(2)B(a)
- $200 political contribution for 75% credit after 1999, 127(3)(a)
- $200 work of art deemed not depreciable property, Reg. 1102(1)(e)(i)
- $215 per square metre hand-woven carpet deemed not depreciable property, Reg. 1102(1)(e)(ii)
- $250 individual surtax reduction, 180.1(1)(a)(ii)(A)
- $250 per month interest deductibility limit for automobile (purchased June 8/87–Aug/89), 67.2
- $250 per month interest deduction limit for automobile for 1997–2000, 67.2, Reg. 7307(2)
- $250 teachers' exchange fund contribution deductible, 8(1)(d)
- $300 contribution to RPP in 1944–45, income from RPP reduced, 57(4)
- $300 minimum CPP/QPP benefits, allocated to prior year, 56(8)
- $300 per month interest deduction limit for automobile before 1997 and for 2001, 67.2, Reg. 7307(2)
- $500 exemption for scholarship, bursary or prize income, 56(1)(n) [to be repealed], 56(3)(a) [draft]
- $500 maximum fine for issuing debt with interest coupons lacking "AX" or "F" marking, 240
- $500 maximum political contribution credit, 127(3)(c)
- $500 maximum refundable medical expense credit, 122.51(2)A(a)
- $500 minimum holding (each) of shares by non-insiders for corporation to be designated public or trust to be mutual fund trust, Reg. 4800(1)(b)(iv), 4800(2)(b)(iv), 4801, 4803(3), (4)
- $500 minimum penalty re tax shelter identification number, 237.1(7.4)
- $500 per month minimum penalty for late-filed R&D non-profit corporation return, 149(7.1)A(a)
- $500 per month penalty for failure to provide foreign-based information, 162(10)
- $500 per month penalty for late-filed elections, 83(4), 131(1.3), 184(5)
- $500 threshold below which no penalty for failure to remit withholdings, 227(9.1)

2699

# Index

Dollar amounts in legislation and regulations *(cont'd)*
- $525 maximum labour-sponsored funds tax credit before 1998, 127.4(5)(a)
- $550 per month leasing cost limit for automobile effective 1997, 67.3, Reg. 7307(3)
- $550 political contribution cutoff for 50% credit on excess over $200, 127(3)(b)
- $600 maximum contribution to Saskatchewan Pension Plan, Reg. 7800(2)
- $600 maximum transfer of unused tuition/education credits, 118.8, 118.9(1)
- $600 minimum RRSP contribution (pension credit offset) effective 1997, Reg. 8301(6), 8309, 8503(4)(a)(i)(B)
- $600 pension adjustment offset after 1996, Reg. 8300(1)"PA offset"(b)
- $600 per month leasing cost limit for automobile (lease entered into June 18/87–Aug. 31/89), 67.3
- $625 monthly threshold for OAS benefits withholding, 180.2(4)(a)(ii) [to be repealed]
- $650 maximum moving expenses, non-taxable reimbursement to employee, *see* Notes to 6(1)(b)
- $650 per month leasing cost limit for automobile before 1997 and for 1997–99, 67.3, Reg. 7307(3)(b)(i), (iii)
- $665 monthly threshold for OAS benefits withholding, 180.2(4)(a)(ii)
- $700 per month leasing cost limit for automobile for 2000, 67.3, Reg. 7307(3)(b)(iv)
- $750 maximum deductible health plan premium per child, 20.01(2)(c)(i)C
- $750 maximum labour-sponsored funds tax credit after 1997, 127.4(5)(a), Reg. 100(5)(a)
- $800 per month leasing cost limit for automobile for 2001, 67.3, Reg. 7307(3)(b)(iv)
- $850 maximum tuition and education credits transferred to spouse, 118.81(c)
- $1,000 antique furniture or object deemed not depreciable property, Reg. 1102(1)(e)(iv)
- $1,000 artists' employment expenses deductible, 8(1)(q)
- $1,000 instalment interest threshold below which no penalty applies, 163.1(b)
- $1,000 maximum allowable for medical expense credit air conditioner for chronic ailment, Reg. 5700(c.3)
- $1,000 maximum deduction from income of volunteer emergency worker, 8(1)(a) [to be repealed]
- $1,000 maximum exemption from income of volunteer emergency worker, 81(4)
- $1,000 maximum labour-sponsored funds tax credit 1993–1995, 127.4(2)
- $1,000 minimum ACB and proceeds of personal-use property, 46
- $1,000 minimum cost for electronic equipment to be in separate class, Reg. 1101(5p)
- $1,000 minimum fine for offence, 238(1)(a)
- $1,000 minimum penalty for false statement by third party, 163.2(3), (5)
- $1,000 minimum RRSP contribution (pension credit offset), Reg. 8301(6), 8309, 8503(4)(a)(i)(B)
- $1,000 pension adjustment offset before 1997, Reg. 8300(1)"PA offset"(a)
- $1,000 pension income, credit to offset, 118(3)
- $1,000 per month penalty for failing to provide foreign-based information, 162(10)
- $1,000 per year gain on farm that is principal residence, election to exempt, 40(2)(c)(ii)
- $1,000 threshold below which no instalments required, 156.1(1), 157(2.1)

- $1,075 maximum political contribution for credit after 1999, 127(3)(c)
- $1,150 maximum political contribution for credit before 2000, 127(3)(c)
- $1,200 deduction for income from pre-1940 annuities, 58(2), (3)
- $1,200 tax gap above which instalments due by Quebec residents, 156.1(1)
- $1,500 (indexed after 1988) threshold for medical expense credits for high-income taxpayers, 118.2(1)C
- $1,500 maximum annual RESP contributions before 1996, 146.1(1)"RESP annual limit"(a), 146.1(2)(k), 204.9(1)"excess amount"(a)
- $1,500 maximum deductible health plan premium per person, 20.01(2)(c)(i)B
- $1,500 per year of employment before 1989, additional retiring allowance transferred to RRSP, 60(j.1)(ii)(B)
- $1,722.22 defined benefit limit before 1999, Reg. 8500(1)"defined benefit limit"(a)
- $2,000 deduction from income of dining or recreational club, 149(5)(f)(i)
- $2,000 maximum annual RESP contributions effective 1996, 146.1(1)"RESP annual limit"(b), 146.1(2)(k), 204.9(1)"excess amount"(a)
- $2,000 moving expenses for person with mobility impairment, medical expense credit, 118.2(2)(l.5)
- $2,000 per year of employment before 1996, retiring allowance transferred to RRSP, 60(j.1)(ii)(A)
- $2,000 pre-1986 capital loss balance deductible against any income, 111(1.1)(b)(i)
- $2,000 RRSP overcontribution room, 204.2(1.1)(b)C
- $2,000 tax gap above which instalments due, 155(1), 156.1(1)
- $2,500 inventory adjustment for farmers in loss years (1994–95), 28(1)(c)
- $2,500 maximum penalty for failing to comply with obligation, 162(7), (7.1)
- $2,500 maximum penalty for non-resident corporation failing to file return, 162(2.1)(b)(ii)
- $2,500 minimum employment/business income for refundable medical expense credit, 122.51(1)"eligible individual"(c)
- $2,500 minimum penalty for false statement in return re distribution from foreign trust, 163(2.4)(e)(i)
- $2,500 restricted farm loss fully deductible, 31(1)
- $3,000 child care expenses per child over 7 (pre–1998), 63(1)(e)(ii)(B)
- $3,000 minimum lump-sum payment for retroactive spreading over prior years, 110.2(2)
- $3,000 scholarship exemption, 56(3)(b)(i)
- $3,500 deduction for refunds of past service AVCs, 60.2(1)(b)
- $3,500 maximum employee's RPP contribution for pre-1990 service, 147.2(4)(b), (c)
- $3,500 maximum purchase for labour-sponsored funds tax credit (1996-97), 127.4(5)(a), 127.4(6)(a)
- $3,500 per year of employment, retiring allowance transferred to RRSP, 60(j.1)(ii)
- $4,000 child care expenses per child over 7 (after 1997), 63(1)(e)(ii)(B), [to be repealed], 63(3)"annual child care expense amount"(b)(ii)
- $4,000 maximum annual RESP contributions effective 1997, 146.1(1)"RESP annual limit"(c), 204.9(1)"excess amount"(a)
- $5,000 and under non-periodic payment, withholding requirement, Reg. 103(1), (4)(a)
- $5,000 child care expenses per child under 7 or disabled (pre–1998), 63(1)(e)(ii)(A)

Index

Dollar amounts in legislation and regulations *(cont'd)*
- $5,000 deduction for income from pre-1932 annuities, 58(1)
- $5,000 income threshold to be deemed not financially dependent on annuitant, 146(1)"refund of premiums"
- $5,000 independent personal services income across U.S. border, maximum 10% withholding, Canada–U.S. Tax Convention Art. XVII.1
- $5,000 inventory adjustment for farmers in loss years (1993–94), 28(1)(c)
- $5,000 limit before 1997 to attendant care deduction or credit for disabled person, 64(c), 118.2(2)(b.1)
- $5,000 limit of cost of wheelchair-access van for medical expense credit, 118.2(2)(l.7)
- $5,000 maximum deductible cost of maintaining old residence after moving, 62(3)(g)
- $5,000 maximum education and tuition amounts transferred to spouse, parent or grandparent, 118.81(a)A(ii)
- $5,000 maximum fine for communicating confidential information or SIN, 239(2.2), (2.21), (2.3)
- $5,000 maximum gain or loss from obligation, not to be specified debt obligation, Reg. 9202(4)(c)
- $5,000 maximum purchase for labour-sponsored funds tax credit before March 6/96, 127.4(2), Reg. 6706(4)
- $5,000 maximum purchase for labour-sponsored funds tax credit effective 1998, 127.4(5)(a), 127.4(6)(a)
- $5,000 maximum RESP payments until student enrolled for 13 weeks, 146.1(2)(g.1)(ii)(B)
- $5,000 minimum FAPI for participating percentage calculation, 95(1)"participating percentage"
- $5,000 per month base for tax on excess foreign property holdings, 206(2.01)
- $6,000 (indexed after 1988) notch provision for dependant's medical expenses, 117(7), 117.1(1)(b)
- $6,000 transfer of pension/DPSP payments to spouse's RRSP (until 1994), 60(j.2)(ii)(A)
- $6,000 transitional extra RRSP overcontribution room, 204.2(1.5)(a)
- $7,000 child care expenses per child under 7 or disabled (after 1997), 63(1)(e)(ii)(A) [to be repealed], 63(3)"annual child care expense amount"(b)(i)
- $7,000 maximum federal tax at issue for Tax Court of Canada informal procedure before September 1993, *Tax Court of Canada Act* s. 18
- $7,500 inventory adjustment for farmers in loss years (1992–93), 28(1)(c)
- $8,000 limitation on RPP past service benefits, Reg. 8307(2)(b)
- $8,000 maximum penalty for late designation, 66(14.5)
- $8,000 maximum penalty for late-filed elections, 85(8), 93(6), 96(6), 220(3.5)
- $8,000 RRSP overcontribution room, 204.2(1.1)(b)M
- $8,333 basic federal tax threshold for phasing in surtax, 180.1(1)(a)(ii)(B)(II)
- $8,750 maximum restricted farm loss deduction, 31(1)
- $10,000 amount for 2/3 attendant care deduction for student, 64(b)(ii)(A)
- $10,000 attendant care deduction before 1997 for disabled person in year of death, 118.2(2)(b.1)
- $10,000 child care expenses for disabled child, 63(3)"annual child care expense amount"(a)
- $10,000 denominator for reduced small business deduction for large corporations, 125(5.1)
- $10,000 employment income of Canadian resident from U.S. or U.S. resident from Canada not taxable, Canada–U.S. Tax Convention Art. XV:2(a)
- $10,000 external income threshold for deduction of private health plan premiums, 20.01(1)(a)(ii)

- $10,000 income below which no instalments required for co-op or credit union, 157(2)(c)
- $10,000 inventory adjustment for farmers in loss years (1991–92), 28(1)(c)
- $10,000 limit for attendant care credit for disabled person, 118.2(2)(b.1)
- $10,000 limit of lump-sum payable by employer to RRSP without source withholding, Reg. 103(3.2)
- $10,000 limit to clergy residence deduction, 8(1)(c)(iv)(A)(I)
- $10,000 maximum attendant care deduction for student, 64(b)(ii)(A)
- $10,000 maximum RRSP withdrawal per year for Lifelong Learning Plan, 146.02(1)"eligible amount"(c), Reg. 104.1(1)(c)
- $10,000 minimum small business bond, 15.2(3)"qualifying debt obligation"(a)
- $10,000 minimum small business development bond, 15.1(3)"qualifying debt obligation"(a)
- $10,000 over which capital addition to building owned since 1971 by credit union deemed separate building, ITAR 58(1)(c)(i)
- $10,000 revenue over which non-profit organization must file information return, 149(12)
- $10,000 tax-free payment by employer to spouse on death, 248(1)"death benefit"
- $10,000 threshold for recoverable contribution to non-resident trust, 94(7) [proposed]
- $10,000 value of individual asset required to be reported on emigration, 128.1(10)"reportable property"(d)
- $11,500 denominator for reduced small business deduction for large corporations, 125(5.1)
- $11,500 RRSP contribution limit for 1991, 146(1)"RRSP deduction limit" 147.1(1)"money purchase limit"
- $12,000 maximum federal tax at issue for Tax Court of Canada informal procedure after August 1993, *Tax Court of Canada Act* s. 18
- $12,000 maximum penalty for failure to provide foreign-based information, 162(10)
- $12,500 basic federal tax threshold for high-income surtax before 2000, 180.1(1)
- $12,500 inventory adjustment for farmers in loss years (1990–91), 28(1)(c)
- $12,500 RRSP contribution limit for 1992–93, 146(1)"RRSP deduction limit" 147.1(1)"money purchase limit"
- $13,500 RRSP contribution limit for 1994 and 1996–2003, 146(1)"RRSP dollar limit", 147.1(1)"money purchase limit"
- $14,500 RRSP contribution limit for 1995, 146(1)"RRSP deduction limit" 147.1(1)"money purchase limit"
- $15,000 athlete/entertainer income of Canadian resident from U.S. or U.S. resident from Canada not taxable, Canada–U.S. Tax Convention Art. XVI:1
- $15,000 basis for additional CCA for grain-drying machinery, Reg. 1100(1)(sb)(iv)(B)
- $15,000 cutoff for lump sum payment, withholding requirements, Reg. 103(4)(b), (c)
- $15,000 exempt reimbursement for housing loss on relocation, 6(20)(a)
- $15,000 maximum contributions to eligible funeral arrangement for funeral services, 148.1(1)"eligible funeral arrangement"(b)(i)
- $15,000 maximum late filing penalty, 66(12.75)
- $15,000 monthly employer withholdings, remittance dates, Reg. 108(1.1)(a)

2701

Dollar amounts in legislation and regulations *(cont'd)*
- $15,500 basic federal tax threshold for high-income surtax for 2000, 180.1(1)
- $15,500 pension adjustment limitation, Reg. 8509(12)(a)(ii)
- $15,500 RRSP contribution limit for 2004, 146(1)"RRSP deduction limit" 147.1(1)"money purchase limit"
- $20,000 automobile cost cap (purchased June 18/87–Aug. 31/89), 13(2), 13(7)(g), (h), 20(4), (16.1), 67.2–67.4, 85(1)(e.4), Reg. 1101(1af), Reg. Sch. II:Cl. 10.1
- $20,000 limit in year of death for attendant care credit for disabled person, 118.2(2)(b.1)
- $20,000 maximum contributions to eligible funeral arrangement for cemetery care, 148.1(1)"eligible funeral arrangement"(b)(ii)
- $20,000 RRSP withdrawal for Home Buyers' Plan, 146.01(1)"eligible amount"(e), 46.01(1)"regular eligible amount"(e), 146.01(1)"supplemental eligible amount"(g)
- $20,000 maximum RRSP withdrawal for Lifelong Learning Plan, 146.02(1)"eligible amount"(d), Reg. 104.1(1)(d)
- $23,529 maximum base for leasing costs of automobile (leased June 18/87–Aug/89), 67.3(d)
- $24,000 automobile cost cap before 1997, 13(2), 13(7)(g), (h), 20(4), (16.1), 67.2–67.4, 85(1)(e.4), Reg. 1101(1af), 7307(1), Reg. Sch. II:Cl. 10.1
- $24,000 basic annual ITC limit for individuals, 127(9)"annual investment tax credit limit"
- $24,000 maximum penalty for failure to provide foreign-based information after demand, 162(10)
- $24,000 minimum penalty for false statement in returns re transactions with non-residents and foreign properties, 163(2.4)
- $24,000 per partner maximum penalty for failing to file partnership information return, 162(8)
- $25,000 automobile cost cap for 1997, 13(2), 13(7)(g), (h), 20(4), (16.1), 67.2–67.4, 85(1)(e.4), Reg. 1101(1af), 7307(1), Reg. Sch. II:Cl. 10.1
- $25,000 below which arm's length investment in small business permitted by RRSP, Reg. 4901(2)"connected shareholder"
- $25,000 below which leasing property rules do not apply, Reg. 1100(1.11)(c), 1100(1.13)(c), 1100(1.14), 8200(b)
- $25,000 exemption for security required for departure tax, *see* $75,000 top-bracket income
- $25,000 home relocation loan, interest deduction equivalent to, 110(1)(j)
- $25,000 maximum fine for offence, 238(1)(a)
- $25,000 maximum investment in small business by specified shareholder's RRSP, Reg. 4901(2)"designated shareholder"(a)
- $25,000 minimum depreciable property cost for pre-July 1988 approved project, 127(9)"approved project"
- $25,000 value for total assets required to be reported on emigration, 128.1(9)
- $26,000 automobile cost cap for 1998-99, 13(2), 13(7)(g), (h), 20(4), (16.1), 67.2–67.4, 85(1)(e.4), Reg. 1101(1af), 7307(1), Reg. Sch. II:Cl. 10.1
- $27,000 automobile cost cap for 2000, 13(2), 13(7)(g), (h), 20(4), (16.1), 67.2–67.4, 85(1)(e.4), Reg. 1101(1af), 7307(1), Reg. Sch. II:Cl. 10.1
- $30,000 automobile cost cap for 2001, 13(2), 13(7)(g), (h), 20(4), (16.1), 67.2–67.4, 85(1)(e.4), Reg. 1101(1af), 7307(1), Reg. Sch. II:Cl. 10.1
- $30,000 maximum UI premium tax credit for small business, 126.1

- $31,500 maximum RESP contributions for one beneficiary before 1996, 204.9(1)"excess amount"(b), 204.9(1)"RESP annual limit"(a)
- $32,000 minimum threshold for phase-out of Child Tax Benefit, 122.61(1)(B)(b)
- $35,000 maximum contributions to eligible funeral arrangement, 148.1(1)"eligible funeral arrangement"(b)(iii)
- $40,000 basic exemption from minimum tax, 127.53
- $40,000 income threshold for debt forgiveness reserve, 61.2:C
- $40,000 maximum transfer of RESP payments to RRSP (to be $50,000), 204.94(2)C(b)
- $42,000 maximum RESP contributions per beneficiary effective 1996, 146.1(2)(h), (k), 204.9(1)"excess amount"(b), 204.9(1)"RESP annual limit"(b)
- $50,000 cost of building, separate CCA class for, Reg. 1101(1ac), (1ad), (5b)
- $50,000 (indexed after 1988) income threshold for medical expense credits below 3% of income, 118.2(1)C
- $50,000 (indexed after 1988) income threshold for OAS and family allowance clawback, 180.2(2)A(b)
- $50,000 maximum accumulated income payment from RESP, no withholding, Reg. 100(1)"remuneration"(n)(iii)
- $50,000 maximum base for accelerated CCA on Year 2000 computer systems, Reg. 1100(1)(zg)(iv), 1100(1)(zh)(iv)
- $50,000 maximum transfer of RESP payments to RRSP, 204.94(2)C(b)
- $50,000 monthly employer withholdings, remittance dates, Reg. 108(1.1)(a)
- $50,000 monthly employer withholdings, requirement to remit through financial institution, Reg. 110
- $55,000 (indexed after 1988) high tax bracket cutoff, 117(2), 117.1(1)(b)
- $59,180 tax bracket threshold, 117(2)(a), (b)
- $67,000 top-bracket income exemption for security required for departure tax, 220(4.51)(a)
- $75,000 capital gains deduction, 110.6(3)
- $75,000 top-bracket income exemption for security required for departure tax before 2001, 220(4.51)(a)
- $80,000 income eligible for overseas employment tax credit, 122.3(1)(c)
- $84,000 maximum RESP contributions per beneficiary effective 1997, 146.1(2)(h), (k), 204.9(1)"excess amount"(b)
- $100,000 capital gain exempt from security required for departure tax, 220(4.51)(a)
- $100,000 capital gains exemption, 110.6(3)
- $100,000 foreign assets, reporting requirement, 233.3(1)"reporting entity"
- $100,000 maximum cost of addition to pre-1979 building, Reg. Sch. II:Cl. 6(k)
- $100,000 maximum stock option deferral for non-CCPC, 7(10)(c)(i)
- $100,000 minimum cost for accredited film/video production episode under 30 minutes, Reg. 9300(b)(i)
- $100,000 plus gross compensation, maximum civil penalty, 163.2(5)(b)(ii)
- $200,000 active business income limit for small manufacturers' M&P calculation, Reg. 5201(b)
- $200,000 active business income of CCPC taxed at low rate, 125(1)(c), 125(2)–(5), 125(7)"specified partnership income"A(b)M(i)
- $200,000 assets over which non-profit organization must file information return, 149(12)
- $200,000 income limit for enhanced R&D investment tax credit, 127(10.2)

2702

# Index

Dollar amounts in legislation and regulations *(cont'd)*
- $200,000 maximum taxable income for extra R&D credit, 127(9)"super-allowance benefit amount"(b)(ii)
- $200,000 minimum cost for accredited film/video production episode at least 30 minutes, Reg. 9300(b)(ii)
- $250,000 capital gains deduction for qualified farm property, 110.6(2)(a), 110.6(12)(c)
- $250,000 capital gains deduction for qualified small business corporation shares, 110.6(2.1)(a), 110.6(12)(c)
- $250,000 service expenses in Canada for foreign property rules, 206(1.1)(d)(iii)(C), (D)
- $375,000 capital gains deduction before 2000 for qualified farm property, 110.6(2)(a), 110.6(12)(c)
- $375,000 capital gains deduction before 2000 for qualified small business corporation shares, 110.6(2.1)(a), 110.6(12)(c)
- $400,000 additional capital gains exemption for qualified farm property and small business corporation shares, 110.6(2)(a), 110.6(2.1)(a), 110.6(3), (4)
- $400,000 phase-out limit for enhanced R&D investment tax credit, 127(10.2)A(b)
- $500,000 capital gains exemption for qualified farm property, 110.6(2)(a)
- $500,000 capital gains exemption for qualified small business corporation shares, 110.6(2.1)(a)
- $500,000 dividend allowance for Part VI.1 tax (preferred share dividends), 191.1(2)(a), 191.1(4)(a)
- $500,000 exemption from earnings subject to branch tax, Canada-U.S. tax treaty Art. X:6(d)
- $500,000 maximum cost of addition to pre-1988 building, Reg. Sch. II:Cl. 3(k)(iv)
- $500,000 maximum small business bond, 15.2(3)"qualifying debt obligation"(a)
- $500,000 maximum small business development bond, 15.1(3)"qualifying debt obligation"(a)
- $1,000,000 base level deduction for principal-business corporation, 18(2.2)–(2.4)
- $1,000,000 Canadian development expenses renounced to flow-through shareholder as Canadian exploration expenses after March 5/96, 66(12.602)(c)
- $1,000,000 minimum cost for accredited film/video production, Reg. 9300(a)
- $1,000,000 over which depreciable property is not "exempt property", Reg. 1100(1.13)(a)(i)
- $1,000,000 previous year's dividends paid on taxable preferred shares reduces dividend allowance, 191.1(2)(b), 191.1(4)(b)
- $1,000,000 threshold of transactions with related non-residents for reporting requirements, 233.1(4)
- $2,000,000 Canadian development expenses renounced to flow-through shareholder as Canadian exploration expenses before March 6, 1996, 66(12.602)(c)
- $2,000,000 expenditure limit for higher investment tax credit, 127(10.2)–(10.4)
- $2,000,000 small business investment capital gain rollover, 44.1(1)"qualifying cost"(b), 44.1(1)"qualifying portion of a capital gain"(c)
- $2,500,000 calculation for term insurance component of life insurer, for investment income tax, Reg. 1900(6)D(a)
- $5,000,000 expected drilling expenses for well, 66.1(6)"Canadian exploration expense"(d)(iv)(A)
- $5,000,000 gross revenue threshold for calculating transfer pricing penalty, 247(3)(b)(ii)
- $5,000,000 maxium cost of segregated fund, exclusion from financial institution rules, Reg. 9000(b)
- $5,000,000 threshold amount for oil and gas well, Reg. 1207(3), 4608(7), (8)
- $10,000,000 capital allowance threshold for life insurance corporation, 190.16(1)(a), 190.16(2)(a), 190.16(3)(e)
- $10,000,000 capital deduction for Large Corporations Tax, 181.1(1)(b), 181.5(1)
- $10,000,000 cost of pipeline, election for separate class, Reg. 1101(5i)
- $10,000,000 maximum investment for one corporation by LSVCC before Feb. 19/97, 204.8(1)"eligible investment"(e)
- $10,000,000 maximum investment in corporation to be "small business security" for qualified investments, Reg. 5100(2)(e)
- $10,000,000 minimum outstanding bonds for corporate bonds to be qualified investments, Reg. 4900(1)(i)(iii)
- $15,000,000 maximum investment for one corporation by LSVCC effective Feb. 19/97, 204.8(1)"eligible investment"(e)
- $15,000,000 maximum taxable capital of corporation that renounces Canadian development expense to flow-through shareholder as Canadian exploration expense, 66(12.601)(a.1)
- $25,000,000 minimum corporate capital for bonds to be qualified investments, Reg. 4900(1)(i)(iii)(A)
- $35,000,000 asset limit for corporation to be "small business security" for qualified investments, Reg. 5100(2)(f) [former version]
- $50,000,000 asset limit for corporation to be "small business security" for qualified investments, Reg. 5100(2)(f)
- $50,000,000 asset limit for eligible business entity for LSVCC, 204.8(1)"eligible investment"(f)(i)
- $50,000,000 asset limit for qualified small business corporation (share not mark-to-market property), Reg. 9001(1)(c)
- $50,000,000 maximum carrying value of small business corporation for capital gain rollover, 44.1(1)"eligible small business corporation share"(b)
- $50,000,000 of qualified property, corporation's shares deemed not foreign property, 206(1.1)(a)
- $200,000,000 basic capital deduction for financial institutions capital tax, 190.15
- $220,000,000 maximum capital deduction for financial institutions capital tax, 190.15
- $300,000,000 top capital allowance bracket for life insurance corporation, 190.16(1)(e), 190.16(2)(e), 190.16(3)(e)
- $400,000,000 enhanced capital deductions for deposit-taking financial institutions, 190.17

**Donations**, *see* Gifts and donations; Gratuities

**Double counting of deductions or credits**, 248(28)

**Double jeopardy**, 238(3), 239(3)

**Double taxation, elimination of**, Canada–U.S. Tax Convention Art. XXIV

**Doubtful debts**
- reserve for, 12(1)(d), (l)

**Downsizing**, Reg. 8505
- pension benefits, Reg. 8308(9)
- program, defined, Reg. 8505(1)
- suspension or cessation of pension, Reg. 8503(8)

**Drilling and exploration expenses**, *see also* Exploration and development expenses; Prospecting
- associations, partnerships, syndicates, ITAR 29(9), (10), (13)
- deduction by any corporation, ITAR 29(11)
- defined, ITAR 29(30)
- extended meaning of, ITAR 29(27), (28)
- general limitation, ITAR 29(31)

## Index

**Drilling and exploration expenses** *(cont'd)*
- incurred for specific considerations, ITAR 29(23), (24)
- individual, of, ITAR 29(12)
- limitation re payments for rights, ITAR 29(23), (24)
- oil or gas corporation, ITAR 29(1), (3)–(5)
- other corporations, ITAR 29(4), (5)
- potash corporations, 66(2)
- renunciation by joint exploration corporation, ITAR 29(6), (7)
- special product corporations, 66(2)

**Drilling or exploration expense**
- defined, 66(15)

**Drilling rights,** *see* Exploration and drilling rights

**Drinks,** *see* Food

**Drive-in theatre, property acquired for**
- capital cost allowance, Reg. Sch. II:Cl. 10(q)

**Driver's licence**
- change of address, deduction for, 62(3)(h)

**Driveway alterations**
- medical expense credit, 118.2(2)(l.6)

**Drought region**
- prescribed, Reg. 7305
- sales of livestock in
- • deferral of income from, 80.3(4)
- • • exceptions, 80.3(6)
- • inclusion of deferred amount, 80.3(5)
- • • amalgamation, on, 87(2)(tt)

**Drug plan,** *see* Private health services plan

**Drugs, prescription, medical expense,** 118.2(2)(n)

**Due dates,** *see* Deadlines

**Due diligence**
- defence to directors' liability, 227.1(3)
- defence to foreign reporting requirements, 233.5

**Dues**
- not deductible, 8(5)
- professional, union, etc., deduction for, 8(1)(i)
- recreational club, etc., not deductible, 18(1)(l)(ii)

**Dumping,** *see* Anti-dumping duties or countervailing duties

**Duties**
- anti-dumping or countervailing, *see* Anti-dumping or countervailing duties

**Dwelling**
- modifications to, for physically impaired person, tax credit for, 118.2(2)(l.2)

**Dwelling-house**
- entry into, 231.1

### E

**EBP,** *see* Employee benefit plan

**EBRD,** *see* European Bank for Reconstruction and Development

**ECE,** *see* Eligible capital expenditure

**ECP,** *see* Eligible capital property

**EFILE,** *see* Electronic filing

**EI (employment insurance),** *see* Unemployment insurance

**Earn-out agreement,** *see* Production or use

**Earned depletion allowances**
- computation, Reg. 1201
- deduction from income, 65

**Earned depletion base**
- capital costs of depreciable property, added to
- • proceeds of later disposition, 59(3.3)(b)
- computation, Reg. 1202, 1205
- expenses added to
- • amounts receivable, portion included in income, 59(3.3)(a)

**Earned income**
- for child care expenses, 63(3)"earned income"
- for Child Tax Benefit, 63(3)"earned income", 122.6
- for RRSP purposes, defined, 146(1)"earned income"
- for refundable medical expense credit, 122.51(1)"eligible individual"(c)

**Earnings (of foreign affiliate)**
- defined, Reg. 5907(1)

**Earnings supplement,** *see* Social assistance payment: supplementing employment income

**Earthquake reserves**
- insurers, Reg. 1400(3)L

**Easement**
- ecologically sensitive land, value when donated, 110.1(5), 118.1(12)
- • valuation applies for capital gains purposes, 43(2)

**Ecological gifts**
- by corporation, 110.1(1)(d)
- by individual, 118.1(1)"total ecological gifts"
- determination of value by Minister of Environment, 118.1(10.1)–(10.5)
- • appeal to Tax Court of Canada, 169(1.1)
- • reassessment, 118.1(11)
- easement, servitude or covenant, valuation, 110.1(5), 118.1(12)
- • valuation applies for capital gains purposes, 43(2)
- fair market value, certificate of, 118.1(10.5)
- reduced capital gain inclusion, 38(a.2)
- tax if donee disposes of the property, 207.31

**Ecologically sensitive land,** *see* Ecological gifts

**Economic profit**
- defined, for foreign tax credit, 126(7)
- none, limitation on foreign tax credit, 126(4.1)

**Economic zone,** *see* Exclusive economic zone

**Edition (of periodical)**
- meaning of, 19.01(6)

**Education credit,** 118.6(2)
- disabled student, 118.6(3)
- interest on student loan, 118.62
- loan from RRSP, *see* Lifelong Learning Plan
- part-time student, 118.6(2)B(b)
- unused
- • transfer to spouse, 118.8
- • transfer to supporting person, 118.9

**Education savings plan,** 146.1, *see also* Registered education savings plan
- appeal from refusal to register, 172(3)(e), 180
- • conditions, 146.1(2)
- defined, 146.1(1)"education savings plan"
- payment out of
- • registered plan, 56(1)(q), 146.1(7)
- registration of, 146.1(2), (4)
- • conditions, 146.1(2)
- • deemed, 146.1(3)
- • refusal by Minister
- • • deemed, 172(4)(d)

2704

# Index

Education savings plan *(cont'd)*
- trust deemed inter vivos, 146.1(11)

**Educational assistance payment**
- defined, 146.1(1)
- from registered plan, taxable, 56(1)(q), 146.1(7)
- limitations on, 146.1(2)(g), (g.1)

**Educational institution**
- certification by Human Resources Development Canada, 118.5(1)(a)(ii), 118.6(1)"designated educational institution"(a)(ii)
- designated, defined, 118.6(1)

**Educational program**
- qualifying, defined, 118.6(1)

**Educational savings plan**
- defined, 146.1(1)

**Election**, *see also* Rollover
- amounts receivable at date of death, 70(2)
- - revocation of, 70(4)
- assets acquired from foreign affiliate, 80.1(4)–(6)
- averaging provisions, ITAR 49
- basic herd, reduction of, 29(1)
- beneficiary, by, re single payment from DPSP, Reg. 1503
- beneficiary of non-resident trust, by, 107(2.002)
- branch tax, Reg. 2403
- Canadian development expenses of partnership, exclusion of, 66.2(5)"Canadian development expense"(f)
- Canadian oil and gas property expenses of partnership, exclusion of, 66.4(5)"Canadian oil and gas property expense"(b)
- capital cost allowance
- - inclusions, Reg. 1103
- - not to be deducted, ITAR 26.1(2)
- - separate class for certain office equipment, Reg. 1101(5q)
- - transfers between classes, Reg. 1103
- capital dividend, re, 83(2)–(4)
- - excessive, tax on, 184
- capital gains dividend, re
- - investment corporation, 131(1), Reg. 2104
- - mortgage investment corporation, 130.1(4), Reg. 2104.1
- - - excessive, tax on, 184
- - mutual fund corporation, 131(1), Reg. 2104
- - - excessive, tax on, 184
- capital gains exemption
- - farm property, 110.6(2)
- - gains to Feb. 22/94, 110.6(3), (19)–(30), *see also* Capital gains deduction: election to trigger gain
- - small business shares, 110.6(2.1)
- - when corporation going public, 48.1
- capital interest distribution by personal trust or prescribed trust, 107(2)
- capitalization of interest, 21
- carryforward or carryback, *see* Carryforward; Carryback
- cash method (farmers), 28(1)
- ceasing to be resident, on, 128.1(4)(b)(iv) [to be repealed], 128.1(4)(d), Reg. 1300–1302
- - on returning to Canada, 128.1(6)(a), (c), 128.1(7)(d), (g)
- - postponement of departure tax by posting security, 220(4.5)–(4.54)
- change in use of property, 45(2)

- communal organization, re taxable income, 143(2), (3)
- corporation and partners re property transferred, 85(1), (2)
- corporation and shareholder, re property transferred
- - eligible property, 85(1.1)
- cost of capital property where change in control of corporation, 111(4)(e)
- Crown corporation, to remain taxable, 149(1.11)
- death benefit, ITAR 40
- death of taxpayer, 70(6.2), Reg. Part X
- debt settled on windup of subsidiary into parent, 80.01(4)
- deemed capital loss on partnership interest, 40(3.12)
- deemed disposition of bad debt or share of insolvent corporation, 50(1)
- deemed disposition of capital property on change of control, 111(4)(e)
- deferral of "departure tax" payment, 159(4) [to be repealed], 220(4.5)–(4.54), Reg. 1301
- departure tax, *see* taxpayer ceasing to be resident (*below*)
- disposition of Canadian securities, 39(4)
- disposition of share in foreign affiliate, 93(1), (1.1)
- disposition of vessel, 13(15)(b), 13(16)
- emigration that is temporary, ignored, 128.1(6)(a), (c), 128.1(7)(d), (g)
- employees profit sharing plan, Reg. 1500
- excessive, re dividend
- - treatment of excess as loan, 184(3.1)–(5)
- - - alternative treatment of, as separate dividend, 184(3), Reg. 2106
- executor, by, to carry back losses to year of death, 164(6)
- expropriation assets, re, 80.1(1), Reg. 4500
- fiscal period, non-calendar year, 249.1(4)
- fiscal period of terminated partnership, 99(2)–(4)
- fishermen, tax deduction, Reg. 105.1
- foreign trust reporting, 233.2(5)
- forward averaging, 110.4(2) [repealed]
- - revocation, 110.4(6.1) [repealed]
- gifts by communal organizations, allocated to members, 143(3.1)
- inducement, where offset by expense, 12(2.2)
- insurer
- - non-resident, 219(5.2)
- interest on expropriation assets, 80.1(2)
- international banking centre eligible deposit, re, 33.1(6)
- - restriction on, 33.1(7)
- investment tax credit, renunciation by general partner, 127(8.4)
- involuntary dispositions, 13(4)
- joint exploration corporation, 66(10)–(10.4)
- late, 220(3.2)–(3.7); Reg. 600
- leasing properties, in respect of, 16.1(1)
- legal representative of deceased taxpayer, *see also* Legal representative of deceased taxpayer
- lump-sum payments, ITAR 40
- master trust, re proportional holdings, 206(2.1)
- mortgage investment corporation, re capital gains dividend, 130.1(4)
- - where not made, 130.1(4.1)
- mutual fund corporation, re dividend, 131(1)–(1.4)
- mutual fund reorganization, 132.2(2)"qualifying exchange"(c)

## Index

Election *(cont'd)*
- mutual fund trust status from beginning of first year, 132(6.1)
- non-resident, to file return under Part I, 216(1), 217
- • restriction on deduction, 216(8)
- non-resident-owned investment corporation, 133(7.1)–(7.3), Reg. 500
- • revocation of, Reg. 501
- non-resident parent corporation, re interest on loan, 218(3), (4)
- Part II of former Act, under, ITAR 66
- Part VI.1 tax, to pay, 191.2
- partners, by
- • re property transferred, 97(2)
- • validity of, 96(3)
- partnership ceasing to exist
- • rules applicable, 98(3), (4)
- partnership's Canadian development expenses, 66.2(5)"Canadian development expense"(f)
- partnership's Canadian oil and gas property expenses, 66.4(5)"Canadian oil and gas property expense"(b)
- pension plan payments, ITAR 40
- personal injury award, 81(5)
- personal representative, by, to carry back losses to year of death, 164(6)
- post-emigration loss, 128.1(8)
- postponement of departure tax by posting security, 220(4.5)–(4.54)
- postponement of tax on distribution of property by trust to non-resident beneficiary, by posting security, 220(4.6)–(4.63)
- preferred beneficiary, of trust, 104(12), 104(14), Reg. 2800
- principal residence, 45(3)
- • distribution by spousal trust, 107(2.01)
- • where not available, 45(4)
- property owned on Dec. 31/71, ITAR 26(7)
- proportional holdings in trust property, 259(2)
- proprietor, on disposing of business, 25
- public corporation, to be, ITAR 50(2)
- qualifying dividend
- • late-filed, 83(3)–(5)
- RPP contribution
- • additional voluntary contributions, 8(1.1)
- refund of RRSP premiums, ITAR 61(2), Reg. 5600
- replacement property, 13(4), 44(5)
- representation expense, 20(9)
- research and development, 37(8)(a)(ii)(B), 37(9)
- reserve for 1995 stub period income, 34.2
- reserves for year of death, 72(2)
- retirement compensation arrangement
- • additional voluntary contributions, 8(1)(l.1)
- • refundable tax, 207.5(2)
- rights or things on death, re, 70(2)
- • revocation of, 70(4)
- sale of accounts receivable, 22
- scientific research, 37(8)(a)(ii)(B), 37(9)
- scientific research tax credit, re first holder of share, 127.3(9)
- segregated fund trusts, Reg. 6100
- services not rendered, 20(24), (25)
- share-purchase tax credit, re first holder of share, 127.2(10)
- small business development bond, 15.1(3)
- specified leasing property not to be exempt property, Reg. 1100(1.14)

- spousal attribution rule on emigration, 74.2(3)
- subsec. 26(7) of ITAR, under, Reg. 4700
- surpluses, re, Reg. Part XXI
- tax pursuant to, deemed payable under amended Act, ITAR 49(1)
- taxpayer ceasing to be resident
- • deferral of capital gains, 128.1(4)(b)(iv) [to be repealed], Reg. 1300
- • deferral of payment of taxes, 159(4), Reg. 1301
- • realization of capital gains, 128.1(4)(d), Reg. 1302
- time of acquisition of control, re, 256(9)
- transfer of property to corporation
- • partnership, from, 85(2), (6)–(9)
- • • partnership wound up, 85(3)
- • shareholder, by, 85(1), (6)–(9)
- • • eligible property, 85(1.1)
- treat bovine animal as specified animal, 28(1.2)
- treat dividend as capital dividend, to, 83(2.2)–(2.4)
- • where not available, 83(2.1)
- trigger capital gain on small business corporation share, 48.1
- trust, by
- • accumulating income, 104(12), 104(14), Reg. 2800
- • capital distribution, no rollover, 102(2.001)
- • gains not distributed to beneficiaries, 107(2.11)
- • postponement of 21-year deemed disposition rule, 104(5.3), 108(1)"trust"(g)
- • preferred beneficiary, 104(12), 104(14), Reg. 2800
- V-day value, re, Reg. 4700
- withholding tax, 153(1)(n)
- • to increase, 153(1.2), Reg. 109
- work in progress, exclusion of, 34

**Election expenses**
- contributions deductible, 127(3)–(4.2)

**Elector**
- defined, 110.6(19)

**Electric, gas or steam corporations**
- information returns, Reg. 213

**Electrical advertising signs**
- capital cost allowance, Reg. Sch. II:Cl. 11

**Electrical energy**, *see* Energy: electrical

**Electrical furnace**
- medical expense credit for, Reg. 5700(c.2)

**Electrical generating equipment**
- capital cost allowance, Reg. Sch. II:Cl. 1(k), Sch. II:Cl. 2(a), Sch. II:Cl. 8(g), Sch. II:Cl. 8(h), Sch. II:Cl. 9(e), Sch. II:Cl. 9(f), Sch. II:Cl. 29, Sch. II:Cl. 34, Sch. II:Cl. 40, Sch. II:Cl. 41
- electrical energy producer/distributor
- • capital cost allowance, Reg. Sch. II:Cl. 1(m), Sch. II:Cl. 8(f), Sch. II:Cl. 9(a)
- for mine
- • capital cost allowance, Reg. 1102(8)–(9.2), Reg. Sch. II:Cl. 10(r), Sch. II:Cl. 41

**Electricity**, *see* Energy: electrical

**Electronic communications equipment**
- capital cost allowance, Reg. 1101(5p), Reg. Sch. II:Cl. 10(f)

**Electronic document**
- print-out as proof, 244(9)

**Electronic filing**
- E-FILE, 150.1
- information returns

## Index

**Electronic filing** *(cont'd)*
- • mandatory, Reg. 205.1
- • optional, 244(22)
- proof of return filed, 244(21)
- tax returns, 150.1

**Electronic point-of-sale equipment**
- capital cost allowance, Reg. Sch. II:Cl. 12(s)

**Electronic records**
- requirement to maintain, 230(4.1)
- • exemption, 230(4.2)

**Elevator**
- for disabled, 20(1)(qq)
- grain, 76(4), (5)

**Eligible amount**
- defined
- • for foreign retirement arrangement, 60.01
- • for Home Buyers' Plan, 146.01(1)
- • for Lifelong Learning Plan, 146.02(1)
- • for RRIF, 146.3(6.11)

**Eligible business entity**
- defined, 204.8(1)

**Eligible Canadian partnership**
- defined, 80(1), 80.04(1)
- whether a "directed person", 80(1)"directed person"

**Eligible capital amount**
- amalgamation, on, 87(2)(f)
- defined, 14(1)
- included in business income, 14(1)
- partnership ceasing to exist, on, 98(3)(g), 98(5)(h)
- treated as taxable capital gain for capital gains exemption on qualified farm property, 14(1.1)

**Eligible capital expenditure**
- amalgamation, on, 87(2)(f)
- defined, 14(5)
- partnership ceasing to exist, on, 98(3)(g)
- qualified farm property, in respect of, 14(1.1)(b)A(ii)(A)
- reduction where assistance received in respect of, 14(10), (11)
- repayment of assistance
- • deduction after ceasing to carry on business, 20(1)(hh.1)
- • while carrying on business, 14(10)(b)

**Eligible capital property**, *see also* Cumulative eligible capital
- amalgamation, on, 87(2)(f)
- deduction on ceasing to carry on business, 24
- deemed disposition of
- • on death, 70(5.1)
- defined, 54, 248(1)
- • pre-1972 obligation, ITAR 26(12)
- • disposition of
- • bad debt on, 20(4.2)
- • deemed, on death, 70(5.1)
- • income inclusion, 14(1)
- • no capital gain, 39(1)(a)(i)
- • no capital loss, 39(1)(b)(ii)
- • uncollectible portion of proceeds, 20(4.2)
- distribution by trust to beneficiary, 107(2)(f)
- "eligible property" for transfer to corporation by shareholder, 85(1.1)(e)
- excessive capital gains exemption election, 14(9)
- exchange of, 14(6)

- • replacement property, 14(7)
- incorporation expenses, IT-143R2 para. 13
- non-resident, of
- • beginning to use in Canadian business, 14(15)
- • ceasing to use in Canadian business, 14(14)
- partnership ceasing to exist, on, 98(3)(g)
- qualified farm property, relating to, 14(1.1)
- rollover
- • to corporation, 85(1)(d), (d.1), (e.1)
- • to partnership, 97(2)
- • to trust, 107.4(3)(e)
- transferred to corporation, *see* rollover (above)
- winding-up, on, 88(1)(c.1)

**Eligible corporation (for RRSP/RRIF small business investments)**
- defined, Reg. 5100(1)
- qualified investment in, Reg. 4900(6)(a)

**Eligible deposit**
- international banking centre, with, 33.1(1)
- • deductible only from IBC income, 33.1(8)

**Eligible distribution**
- defined, for foreign spin-off, 86.1(2)

**Eligible funeral arrangement**, 148.1
- defined, 148.1(1), 248(1)
- emigration of individual, no deemed disposition, 128.1(10)"excluded right or interest"(e)(iv)
- excluded from various trust rules, 108(1)"trust"(e.1)
- exemption for amount accruing in, 148.1(2)(a)
- income inclusion on return of funds, 12(1)(z.4), 148.1(3)
- information return, Reg. 202(2)(m)
- payment to non-resident, Reg. 202(2)(m)
- • information return, Reg. 202(2)(m)
- • withholding tax, 212(1)(v)
- payment to resident, Reg. 201(1)(f)
- provision of funeral services under, 148.1(2)(b)(i)
- rollover to new trust, 248(1)"disposition"(f)(vi)

**Eligible housing loss**, *see* Housing loss: eligible

**Eligible individual**
- defined
- • for Child Tax Benefit, 122.5(1), (2)
- • for GST credit, 122.6, 122.62(1); Reg. 6301, 6302
- • for refundable medical expense credit, 122.51(1)

**Eligible investment**
- defined, 204.8(1)
- of financial institution, for capital tax
- • defined, 181.3(5), 190.14(2)
- of labour-sponsored venture capital corporation
- • tax where insufficient, 204.82
- • • refund of tax, 204.83

**Eligible labour body**
- defined, 204.8(1)

**Eligible landfill site**
- defined, Reg. 1104(13)

**Eligible loan**
- made by international banking centre, 33.1(1)
- • ceasing to be eligible, rules, 33.1(11)(a)
- • where no deduction permitted, 33.1(10)

**Eligible offset**
- application on rollout of property by trust, 107(2)(c)(ii), 107(2.1)(c)(iii)
- excluded from disposition, 248(1)"disposition"(h)

2707

Eligible offset *(cont'd)*
- defined, 108(1)

**Eligible period of reduced pay**
- defined, Reg. 8500(1)

**Eligible period of temporary absence**
- defined, Reg. 8500(1)

**Eligible pooling arrangement**
- defined, for small business investment capital gain rollover, 44.1(1)

**Eligible portion (of corporation's gains or losses)**
- defined, 129(4)

**Eligible production corporation**
- defined, for film/video production services credit, 125.5(1)

**Eligible property**
- conversion of foreign bank affiliate to branch
- - defined, 142.7(1)
- shareholder/corporation rollover, for, 85(1)
- - defined, 85(1.1)
- - limitation re real property of non-resident, 85(1.2)

**Eligible real property gain**
- defined, 108(1), 110.6(1) [repealed]

**Eligible real property loss**
- defined, 108(1), 110.6(1) [repealed]

**Eligible relocation**
- defined, 248(1)
- moving expenses deductible, 62

**Eligible sewage treatment facility**
- defined, Reg. 1104(13)

**Eligible small business corporation**
- defined, for small business investment capital gain rollover, 44.1(1), (10)
- share, *see* Eligible small business corporation share

**Eligible small business corporation share**
- defined, for small business investment capital gain rollover, 44.1(1), (11)

**Eligible survivor benefit period**
- defined, Reg. 8500(1)

**Eligible taxable capital gains of trust, defined,** 108(1)"eligible taxable capital gains"

**Eligible taxation year**
- defined, for retroactive spreading of lump-sum payments, 110.2(1)

**Eligible taxpayer**
- defined, for small business investment tax credit, 127(9)

**Eligible transferee (of forgiven debt)**
- agreement to transfer forgiven amount to, 80.04(4)
- defined, 80.04(2)

**Eligible waste management facility**
- defined, Reg. 1104(13)

**Elk**, 80.3(1)"breeding animals"

**Emergency worker**
- volunteer
- - deduction from employment income, 8(1)(a) [to be repealed]
- - exemption from employment income, 81(4)

**Emigration**, *see* Ceasing to be resident in Canada

**Emigration disposition**
- defined, 74.2(3)

**Emigration year**
- defined
- - for foreign tax credit, 126(2.21)
- - for security for departure tax, 220(4.5)

**Employed**
- defined, 248(1)
- in Canada
- - deemed, 115(2)(c)
- - non-residents, tax on, 2(3), 115(1)
- - part-year residents, 114

**Employee**
- aircraft
- - capital cost allowance, 8(1)(j)(ii), 13(11)
- - deductions allowed, 8(1)(j), 8(9)
- allowances, 6(1)(b)
- - not income, 6(6)
- automobile (belonging to employee)
- - capital cost allowance, 8(1)(j)(ii), 13(11), Reg. 1100(1)(a)(x), 1100(6)
- - interest expense, 8(1)(j)(i), 67.2, 67.4
- - leasing expense, 67.3, 67.4
- automobile (belonging to employer)
- - employee of partner, 12(1)(y)
- - goods and services tax, treatment of, 6(7)
- - operating expenses, benefit, 6(1)(k), (l), Reg. 7305.1
- - rule for automobile salesperson, 6(2.1)
- - standby charge, benefit, 6(1)(e), 6(2)
- automotive products, transitional assistance benefits taxable, 56(1)(a)(v)
- benefit, *see* Benefit: employment
- benefit plan, *see* Employee benefit plan
- benefits taxable, 6(1)
- Canada Pension Plan, contribution, credit for, 118.7
- charity trust, receipts, Reg. 3502
- clergyman's residence, 8(1)(c)
- contribution to RPP deductible, 147.2(4)
- contribution to teachers' exchange fund, 8(1)(d)
- deductions, *see* Deductions in computing income from office or employment
- defined, 248(1)
- - for source deductions, Reg. 100(1)
- dues
- - deduction, 8(1)(i)
- - non-deductible, 8(5)
- dues to professional organization, deductible, 8(1)(i)(i)
- employer, as
- - deductions, 8(1)(i)(ii), 8(1)(l.1)
- - - certificate of employer, 8(10)
- employment insurance premiums
- - as employer, deductions, 8(1)(l.1)
- - credit for, 118.7
- expenses of
- - deductions, 8(1)
- - general limitation, 8(2)
- foreign country, of
- - exemption, 149(1)(a)
- - family and servants of, 149(1)(b)
- former, *see* Former employee
- group insurance premium, portion taxable, 6(4)
- housing loans to, or spouse, 15(2)(a)(ii), 15(2.4)(b)
- includes officer, 248(1)
- income maintenance plan benefits, ITAR 19
- incorporated, *see* Personal services business

2708

## Index

Employee *(cont'd)*
- international organization, of, tax deduction, 126(3)
- legal costs recovered, income, 56(1)(l)
- legal expenses of collecting or establishing right to wages, 8(1)(b)
- loan, *see* Employee loan
- meals, 8(4)
- musical instrument costs, 8(1)(p)
- negotiating contracts, expenses, 8(1)(f)
- • certificate of employer, 8(10)
- part-time
- • travelling allowance, excluded from income, 81(3.1)
- payments received from employer
- • during employment, 5(1), 6(3)
- • on death, *see* Death benefit
- • on termination or retirement, *see* Retiring allowance
- profit sharing plan, *see* Employees profit sharing plan
- railway, *see* Railway: employees, 8(1)(e)
- registered pension plan contributions, 8(1)(m), 147.2(4)
- retirement compensation arrangement, *see* Retirement compensation arrangement
- return required of, re withholding of tax, 227(2), Reg. 107
- • where not filed, 227(3)
- salary deferral arrangements, deduction for amounts forfeited under, 8(1)(o)
- salesperson's expenses, 8(1)(f)
- • certificate of employer, 8(10)
- share option benefits, 7(1)
- shares held by trustee, 7(2)
- shares purchased for, by trustee, 7(6)
- sickness and accident benefits, income, 6(1)(f)
- stock options, *see* Stock options
- transport, away-from-home expenses, 8(1)(g)
- travelling expenses of, 8(1)(h)
- • certificate of employer, 8(10)
- • limitation, 8(4)
- • • re meals, 8(4)
- trust, *see* Employee trust
- unemployment insurance premiums
- • as employer, deduction, 8(1)(l.1)
- • credit for, 118.7
- union dues, deductible, 8(1)(i)(i)

**Employee benefit plan**
- allocations, 32.1(2)
- amalgamation, on, 87(2)(j.3)
- amount received from, *see* payments out of (below)
- becoming retirement compensation arrangement
- • deemed contribution, 207.6(4)
- benefits from, 6(1)(g)
- • not includable in employee's income, 6(1)(a)(ii)
- contributions to, 6(10)
- • not deductible, 18(1)(o)
- • when deductible, 18(10)
- deduction in computing income of, 104(6)(a.1)
- deduction to employer, 32.1
- defined, 248(1)
- distribution by, 107.1
- emigration of employee, no deemed disposition, 128.1(10)"excluded right or interest"(a)(vi)
- excluded from various trust rules, 108(1)"trust"(a)
- income of, 32.1(3)
- payments out of
- • not subject to non-resident tax, 212(17)
- • to employee, taxable, 6(1)(g)
- • • source withholding, 153(1)(a)
- • to employer, taxable, 12(1)(n.1)
- prescribed arrangement, Reg. 6800

**Employee loan**, 6(9), 80.4(1)
- forgiven, amount to be included in income, 6(15)
- interest paid on money borrowed to make, 20(1)(c)(v)
- to buy motor vehicle, 15(2)(a)(iv), 15(2.4)(d)
- to buy stock, 15(2)(a)(iii), 15(2.4)(c)

**Employee trust**, 6(1)(h)
- allocations under, includable in income, 6(1)(h)
- benefits from, not includable in employee's income, 6(1)(a)(ii)
- deduction in computing income of, 104(6)(a)
- defined, 248(1)
- distribution by, 107.1
- emigration of employee, no deemed disposition, 128.1(10)"excluded right or interest"(e)(i)
- excluded from various trust rules, 108(1)"trust"(a)
- payments out of, not subject to non-resident tax, 212(17)
- receipt from, 12(1)(n)
- rollover to new trust, 248(1)"disposition"(f)(vi)
- trust not falling within definition, 108(1)"trust"(a.1)

**Employees' charity trust**
- defined, Reg. 3500

**Employees profit sharing plan**
- allocations under, income, 6(1)(d), 144(3)
- capital gains allocated, 144(4)–(4.2)
- deferred profit sharing plan not an, 147(6)
- defined, 144(1), 248(1)
- disposition of property to
- • capital loss nil, 40(2)(g)(iv)(A)
- dividend credit allocated, 144(8)
- election, Reg. 1500
- emigration of employee, no deemed disposition, 128.1(10)"excluded right or interest"(a)(v)
- employer's contribution, deduction, 20(1)(w), 144(5)
- excluded from non-resident trust rules, 94(1)"exempt foreign trust"(g) [proposed]
- excluded from various trust rules, 108(1)"trust"(a)
- flow-through entity for capital gains exemption, 39.1(1)
- foreign tax credit, 144(8.1)
- income allocated, 144(3)
- information return, Reg. 212
- interest income, allocation re, 144(8.2)
- payment under
- • portion excluded from income, 81(1)(k)
- • used to purchase income-averaging annuity contract, deductible, 61(2)(a)
- payments "out of profits" defined, 144(10)
- receipts from, 12(1)(n)
- • by employee, 144(6)–(8)
- refund to former beneficiary, 144(9)
- registration of, as DPSP, 147(3), (4)
- rollover to new trust, 248(1)"disposition"(f)(vi)
- trust not taxable, 144(2), 149(1)

**Employer**
- benefits provided by, taxable, 6(1)
- certificate re employees' expenses, 8(10)
- contributions of

# Index

Employer *(cont'd)*
- - Canada Pension Plan, to
- - - deductible, 8(1)(l.1)(i)
- - deferred profit sharing plan, to, 20(1)(y), 147(8)–(9.1)
- - - limitation on deductibility, 18(1)(j)
- - employees profit sharing plan, to, 20(1)(w), 144(5)
- - employment insurance premiums, *see* unemployment insurance premiums (below)
- - pension plan, 20(1)(q), 147.2(1)–(3), Reg. Part XXVII [Revoked]
- - - special, 20(1)(r)
- - profit sharing plan, to
- - - limitation on deductibility, 18(1)(k)
- - registered supplementary unemployment benefit plan, to, 145(5)
- - - limitation on deductibility, 18(1)(i)
- - unemployment insurance premiums
- - - deductible, 8(1)(l.1)(i), 9(1)
- - - tax credit for 1993, 126.1
- deduction re salary deferral arrangements, 20(1)(oo)
- defined, 248(1)
- - for automobile standby charge, 6(2)
- - for disability insurance top-up payments, 6(17)
- - for employee loans, 80.4(1)(b)(i)
- - for incorporated employee/RCA rules, 207.6(3)(a)
- - for municipal officer's expense allowance, 81(3)(c)
- - for source deductions, Reg. 100(1)
- - for UI premium tax credit, 126.1(1)
- - generally, 248(1)
- housing subsidy, taxable, 6(23)
- participating, defined, 147.1(1), Reg. 8308(7)
- payment to employee
- - during employment, 5(1), 6(3)
- - on death, *see* Death benefit
- - on termination or retirement, *see* Retiring allowance
- reimbursement for housing loss, 6(19)–(22)
- specified, *see* Specified employer
- union locals all deemed to be one, for pension purposes, 252.1
- withholding of tax, 153(1), Reg. 101
- - variations in deductions, Reg. 106

**Employment**
- benefits, *see* Benefit
- defined, 248(1)
- expenses, *see* Employee: expenses of
- income from, 5(1), 6(1), Canada–U.S. Tax Convention Art. XV
- - reimbursement to employer, 8(1)(n.1)
- insurance, *see* Employment insurance
- loss from, 5(2)
- office or, *see* Office or employment
- outside Canada, tax credit, 122.3
- special work site, at, 6(6)
- tax credit [repealed], 127(13)–(16), Reg. 6000
- - amalgamation, continuation of predecessor's, 87(2)(qq)
- - parent's, after subsidiary wound up, 88(1)(e.4)
- termination of, *see* Former employee; Retiring allowance

**Employment insurance**, *see also* Registered supplementary unemployment benefit plan
- benefit
- - remuneration, Reg. 100(1)
- - repayment of, 60(v.1)
- - repayment of overpayment, deduction for, 60(n)
- - right to, no disposition on emigration, 128.1(10)"excluded right or interest"(h)
- - taxable, 56(1)(a)(iv)
- - withholding tax, 153(1)(d.1), Reg. 100(1)"remuneration"(g)
- premium
- - paid by employee
- - - as employee, credit, 118.7
- - - as employer, deduction, 8(1)(l.1)
- - paid by employer, deduction, 9(1) (general accounting principles)
- - paid by employer in 1993, tax credit, 126.1
- - - deemed to be overpayment of tax, 126.1(6), (7)
- - - determination of credit by Minister, 152(3.4), (3.5)
- - - joint liability of partners for excess refund, 160.1(2.2)
- - - refund of, 164(1.6)
- - - - no interest on, 164(3)
- - short-remitting of, when credit claimed, 126.1(12)
- Program for Older Worker Adjustment, *see* Older Worker Adjustment, Program for
- tips and gratuities covered by, Reg. 100(1)"remuneration"(a.1)
- "UI premium tax credit" defined, 126.1(8)

**Employment Insurance Act**
- benefits under, *see* Employment insurance: benefit
- costs of appealing decision under, deductible, 60(o)
- - recovery of, income, 56(1)(l)(ii)
- financial assistance under, 56(1)(r)

**Enactment**, *see also* Amendments; Legislation
- defined, ITAR 12"enactment"

**End of taxation year**
- defined, Reg. 1104(1)

**Energy**
- conservation property, Reg. 8200.1, Reg. Sch. II:Cl. 43.1
- - determination of, 13(18.1)
- - disclosure of information to Energy, Mines & Resources, 241(4)(d)(vi.1)
- conversion grant
- - included in income, 12(1)(u), 56(1)(s)
- - information return re, Reg. 224
- - non-resident taxable on, 212(1)(s)
- - prescribed program, Reg. 5501
- electrical
- - corporation distributing or generating
- - - equipment for, Reg. 1102(8), (9), Sch. II:Cl. 1(m), Sch. II:Cl. 2(c)
- - - exclusion from CCA restrictions, Reg. 1100(26)(a)
- - - information return, Reg. 213(1)
- - - municipal corporation, exemption, 149(1.2)
- - equipment for processing in prescribed area, 127(9)"qualified property"(c.1)
- - generating, manufacturing & processing credit, 125.1(2)
- - producing or processing, 125.1(3)"manufacturing or processing"(h), Reg. 1104(9)(h)
- generation of, 66(15)"principal-business corporation"(h)
- property, *see* Specified energy property
- renewable, generation of, Reg. Sch. II:Cl. 43.1

# Index

Energy *(cont'd)*
- wind, conversion system, Reg. Sch. II:Cl. 34

**Energy, Mines & Resources**, *see* Department of Energy, Mines and Resources

**Enforcement of Act**, 220–244, *see also* Collection of tax

**England**, *see* United Kingdom

**Enhanced combined cycle system**
- defined, Reg. 1104(13)

**Enhanced garnishment**, 224(1.2), (1.3)

**Enhanced recovery equipment**, Reg. 1206(1)
- proceeds of disposition, 59(3.3)(d)

**Enquiry**, *see* Inquiry

**Entering Canada**, *see* Becoming resident in Canada

**Entertainer**
- U.S. resident, Canada–U.S. Tax Convention Art. XVI

**Entertainment expenses (and meals)**
- airplane, train, bus travel, 67.1(4)
- Christmas party exemption, 67.1(2)(e)
- club dues and facilities, 18(1)(l)
- "entertainment" meaning of, 67.1(4)
- general limitation on deduction for, 67.1(1)
- • exceptions, 67.1(2)
- included in convention fee
- • limitation on deductibility, 67.1(3)
- interpretation, 67.1(4)

**Entity**
- defined
- • for non-resident trusts and foreign investment entities, 94(1) [proposed]
- • for third-party civil penalty, 163.2(1)

**Entrant bank**
- defined, for conversion of foreign bank affiliate to branch, 142.7(1)

**Entry**
- Canada, into, *see* Becoming resident in Canada
- dwelling-house, into, for audit, 231.1(3), *see also* Search warrant
- • compliance required, 231.5(2)

**Environment**
- conservation of, *see* Ecological gifts

**Environmental trust**, *see* Qualifying environmental trust

**Environmentally hypersensitive person**
- equipment qualifying for medical expense credit, Reg. 5700(c)–(c.2)

**Equalization payments (family law)**
- rules on partition of property, 248(20)

**Equipment**
- administering oxygen, for, 118.2(2)(k)
- automotive, CCA, Reg. Sch. II:Cl. 10(a), *see also* Automobile
- bituminous sands
- • defined, 59(6), Reg. 1206(1)
- • proceeds of disposition, 59(3.3)(c)
- cable systems interface, CCA, Reg. Sch. II:Cl. 10(v)
- contractor's movable, CCA, Reg. Sch. II:Cl. 10(h), Sch. II:Cl. 22, Sch. II:Cl. 38
- data communication, CCA, Reg. Sch. II:Cl. 3
- disability-specific, deduction for, 20(1)(rr)
- earth-moving, separate class, Reg. 1101(5k)
- electrical energy processing, investment tax credit, 127(9)"qualified property"(c.1)

- electrical generating, Reg. 1100(1)(t), (ta), Reg. Sch. II:Cl. 1(k), Sch. II:Cl. 1(m), Sch. II:Cl. 2(a), Sch. II:Cl. 8(g), Sch. II:Cl. 9(e), Sch. II:Cl. 9(f), Sch. II:Cl. 29, Sch. II:Cl. 34, Sch. II:Cl. 40
- electronic data-processing, CCA, Reg. Sch. II:Cl. 10(f), Sch. II:Cl. 29, Sch. II:Cl. 40
- • general-purpose, defined, Reg. 1104(2)
- electronic point-of-sale, CCA, Reg. Sch. II:Cl. 12(s)
- enhanced recovery, Reg. 1206(1)
- • proceeds of disposition, 59(3.3)(d)
- for hearing- or sight-impaired, business expense, 20(1)(rr)
- gas manufacturing/distribution, CCA, Reg. Sch. II:Cl. 1(n), Sch. II:Cl. 2(d)
- gas or oil well, CCA, Reg. 1104(2), Reg. Sch. II:Cl. 10(j)
- generating, Reg. 1100(1)(t), (ta), Reg. Sch. II:Cl. 1(k), Sch. II:Cl. 1(m), Sch. II:Cl. 2(a), Sch. II:Cl. 2(c), Sch. II:Cl. 8(f), Sch. II:Cl. 8(g), Sch. II:Cl. 9(a), Sch. II:Cl. 9(e), Sch. II:Cl. 9(f), Sch. II:Cl. 29, Sch. II:Cl. 34, Sch. II:Cl. 40
- heat production/distribution, CCA, Reg. Sch. II:Cl. 1(p), Sch. II:Cl. 2(f)
- heat recovery, CCA, Reg. Sch. II:Cl. 34
- logging, CCA, Reg. Sch. II:Cl. 10(o)
- machinery and, CCA, Reg. Sch. II:Cl. 8, Sch. II:Cl. 29
- medical, 118.2(2)(m), Reg. 5700
- mining, CCA, Reg. Sch. II:Cl. 10(k), Sch. II:Cl. 10(l), Sch. II:Cl. 10(m), Sch. II:Cl. 41
- oil or gas well, CCA, Reg. Sch. II:Cl. 10(j), Sch. II:Cl. 41
- petroleum/natural gas exploration, CCA, Reg. Sch. II:Cl. 10(t), Sch. II:Cl. 41
- pollution control, Reg. 1100(1)(t), Sch. II:Cl. 24, Sch. II:Cl. 27
- prescribed
- • for sight- or hearing-impaired, business expense, 20(1)(rr)
- • medical, 118.2(2)(m), Reg. 5700
- • qualified construction equipment, Reg. 4603
- • qualified transportation equipment, Reg. 4601
- radar, CCA, Reg. Sch. II:Cl. 9
- radio communication, CCA, Reg. Sch. II:Cl. 8, Sch. II:Cl. 9
- railway traffic control, CCA, Reg. Sch. II:Cl. 1(i)
- scientific research, for, 37(8)(a)(ii)
- solar heating, CCA, Reg. Sch. II:Cl. 34
- stable, CCA, Reg. Sch. II:Cl. 10(c)
- steam generating, CCA, Reg. Sch. II:Cl. 34
- telephone/telegraph, CCA, Reg. Sch. II:Cl. 3, Sch. II:Cl. 17
- tertiary recovery, Reg. 1206(1)
- timber limit, for, CCA, Reg. Sch. II:Cl. 10(n), Sch. II:Cl. 15
- water-distributing, CCA, Reg. Sch. II:Cl. 1(o), Sch. II:Cl. 10(e)

**Equity**, *see also* Adjusted equity
- defined, 20.1(2), (7)
- limit on deductibility of interest relating to distributions, 20.1(1), (3)

**Equity accounting method**
- prohibited for debt forgiveness reserve, 61.3(1)(b)C(i)
- prohibited for purposes of Act, 248(24)

**Equity limit (of insurer)**
- defined, Reg. 2400(1)

# Index

**Equity percentage**
- defined, 95(4)
- direct, defined, 95(4)"direct equity percentage"

**Equity property**
- defined, Reg. 2400(1)

**Equity share, defined**, 204, Reg. 4803(1)

**Equivalent to married credit**, 118(1)B(b)

**Equivalent to spouse credit**, 118(1)B(b)

**Escalating interest GICs**
- income accrual, Reg. 7000(2)(c.1)

**Establishment**, *see* Permanent establishment

**Estate**, *see also* Trust (or estate)
- bankrupt, of
  - - deemed not trust or estate, 128(1)(b)
  - - defined, 248(1)
- Canada/Quebec Pension Plan death benefit taxed, 56(1)(a.1)
- carryback of losses to year of death, 164(6)
- debt of deceased settled by, 80(2)(p), (q)
- defined, 104(1), 248(1)
- flow-through of death benefits, 104(28)
- income of, paid to non-resident, 212(1)(c), 212(11)
  - - exemption for, 212(9), (10)
- information returns, Reg. 204
- life, *see* Life estate in real property
- *pur autre vie*, *see* Life estate in real property
- return required, 150(1)(c)
- transfer of rights or things to beneficiaries, 70(3)

**Estate planning**, *see also* Death of taxpayer
- attribution rule inapplicable on certain benefits through trust, 74.4(4)

**Estate tax**
- Canadian [repealed in 1972]
  - - deduction of, from pension benefits etc., 60(m)
  - - interest on, deductible, 60(d)
- U.S.
  - - credit for, Canada–U.S. Tax Convention Art. XXIX B:6, 7
  - - interest on, possibly deductible, 60(d)

**Estimate of tax, required**, 151

**Estimate of the expenses of survey**
- defined, Reg. 3600(2)

**Estimated deductions**
- defined, for source deductions, Reg. 100(1)

**European Bank for Reconstruction and Development**
- bonds of
  - - eligible for RRSP investment, Reg. 4900(1)(l)(v)
  - - excluded from foreign property, 206(1)"foreign property"(g)(iv.1)
  - - trust investing in, not foreign property, Reg. 5000(7)"specified international finance trust"(c)(i)(D)
- no withholding tax on interest payable to, Reg. 806.1

**Evasion of tax**, *see* Tax evasion, penalty for

**Evidence**, *see* Proof

**Excepted dividend**
- defined, 187.1

**Excepted gift**
- defined, 118.1(19)
- donation to charity permitted, 118.1(13)

**Excess amount (for registered education savings plan)**
- defined, 204.9(1), (2)

**Excess money purchase transfer**
- re past service event, Reg. 8303(7.1)

**Exchanges of property**
- amalgamation, effect of, 87(2)(l.3)
- capital property, 44
- corporation controlling or controlled by taxpayer, 44(7)
- depreciable property, 13(4), (4.1)
- eligible capital property, 14(6), (7)
- leasing properties, 16.1(5)–(7)
- non-qualifying security donated to charity, 118.1(15)
- non-resident, 44(7)

**Exchanges of shares**, *see* Share

**Excise Tax Act**, *see also* Goods and services tax (GST)
- communication of information for enforcement of, 241(4)(d)(ii)
- fuel tax rebate under, 12(1)(x.1)
- GST included in taxable benefit, 6(7), 15(1.3)
- input tax credit under, deemed to be government assistance, 248(16)–(18)
- rebate under, deemed not to be reimbursement, 8(11)
- tax payable under Part IX, 248(1)"goods and services tax"

**Excluded amount**
- re expenses of financing
  - - defined, 20(1)(e)(iv.1)
  - - no deduction, 20(1)(e)
- re registered education savings plan
  - - defined, 146.1(7.2)
  - - excluded from income, 146.1(7.1)(b)
- re split income
  - - defined, 120.4(1)
  - - excluded from income-splitting tax, 120.4(1)"excluded amount"

**Excluded arrangement (re tax on investment income of life insurers)**
- defined, Reg. 1900(1)

**Excluded benefits (re registered pension plan)**
- defined, Reg. 8303(5)(f)–(l), 8504(10)
- excluded from normalized pension, Reg. 8303(5)

**Excluded consideration**
- defined, re corporation attribution rules, 74.4(1)
- excluded from attribution rules, 74.4(2)(f), 74.4(3)

**Excluded contribution (to registered pension plan)**
- defined, Reg. 8300(1)
- excluded from pension credit, Reg. 8301(4)(a), 8301(5)(a), 8301(8)(e)
- excluded from provisional PSPA, Reg. 8303(8)

**Excluded corporation**
- charities, non-qualified investment rules
  - - debt excluded from non-qualified investments, 149.1(1)"non-qualified investment"(a)(ii)
  - - defined, 149.1(1)"non-qualified investment"(d)–(f)
- refundable investment tax credit
  - - defined, 127.1(2)
  - - excluded from additional credit, 127.1(2)"refundable investment tax credit"(a) pre-(f), 127.1(2.01)
  - - SRTC designation not allowed after June 15/84, 194(4.2)(c)

**Excluded dividend (for Part VI.1 tax)**
- defined, 191(1), 191(4)(d)
- excluded from dividend allowance, 191.1(2)

2712

## Index

**Excluded dividend (for Part VI.1 tax)** *(cont'd)*
- excluded from "excepted dividend" for Part IV.1 tax, 187.1(d)
- excluded from Part VI.1 tax, 191.1(1)(a)(i)–(iii)

**Excluded interest (in partnership)**
- defined, 40(3.15)–(3.18)
- grandfathered from deemed-gain rules for passive partnership interest, 40(3.1)

**Excluded investment business**
- defined, re foreign investment entities, 94.1(1)

**Excluded obligation**
- re debt forgiveness
- • defined, 80(1)
- • principal amount excluded from debt forgiveness rules, 80(1)"forgiven amount"B(j)
- • proceeds of disposition for debtor, 79(3)F(b)(iv)
- re flow-through shares
- • application to prescribed shares, Reg. 6202.1(1)(b), (c)
- • deemed not to be a guarantee, security or similar indemnity, Reg. 6202(1)(m.1)
- • defined, Reg. 6202.1(5)
- • excluded from limited partnership at-risk rules, 96(2.2)(d)(vii)
- • excluded from tax shelter at-risk adjustment, 143.2(3)(b)(iv)
- re non-resident withholding tax on interest
- • defined, 214(8)
- • sale of, by non-resident, 214(7)

**Excluded payment**
- defined, re indexed debt obligations, Reg. 7001(7)

**Excluded period**
- defined, re salary deferral arrangement, 6(13)(a)(ii)

**Excluded personal property**, *see* Excluded right or interest

**Excluded property**
- art flips, defined, 46(5)
- emigration, *see* Excluded right or interest
- personal-use property donated to charity, 46(5)

**Excluded right or interest**
- defined, 128.1(10)
- excluded from deemed disposition
- • on emigration, 128.1(4)(b)(iii)
- • on immigration, 128.1(1)(b)(iv)

**Excluded premium**
- defined
- • for Home Buyers' Plan, 146.01(1)
- • for Lifelong Learning Plan, 146.02(1)
- excluded from repayment of eligible amount
- • Home Buyers' Plan, 146.01(3)(a)
- • Lifelong Learning Plan, 146.02(3)(a)

**Excluded production (re Canadian film/video credit)**
- defined, Reg. 1106(1)
- excluded from Canadian film or video production, Reg. 1106(3)

**Excluded property**
- debt forgiveness rules
- • adjusted cost base of, not reduced, 80(9)–(11)
- • defined, 80(1)
- emigration, *see* Excluded right or interest
- foreign affiliate, of
- • accrued gains, included in FAPI, Reg. 5907(13)(b)(i)
- • defined, 95(1), Reg. 5907(1)
- • disposition of shares that are, 93(1.1)
- • • excluded from FAPI calculation, 95(1)"foreign accrual property income"B, E, 95(1)"relevant tax factor"(a)
- • • net earnings from, Reg. 5907(1)"net earnings"(d)
- • • net earnings of foreign affiliate from, Reg. 5907(1)"taxable earnings"(b)(v)
- • • net loss from, Reg. 5907(1)"net loss"(d)
- • • net loss of foreign affiliate from, Reg. 5907(1)"taxable loss"(b)(iv)
- • of second affiliate, 95(2)(a)(ii)(D)(III)
- • settlement of debt, gain or loss relating to, 95(2)(i)
- • share-for-share exchange rule inapplicable, 85.1(4)
- mark-to-market transition rules
- • defined, Reg. 8102(1), 8104(1)
- non-resident, of
- • defined, 116(6), Reg. 810
- • excluded from disposition certificate requirements, 116(1), (3), (5), (5.1)(a)
- trust, of
- • defined, 108(1)
- • excluded from 21-year deemed disposition rule, 104(4), (5.8), 104(6)(b)(iii)
- • excluded from rule re disposition to non-residents, 107(5)

**Excluded remuneration (re registered pension plan)**
- defined, Reg. 8503(14)(b)
- excluded from pension adjustment, Reg. 8503(14)(e)

**Excluded security (for debt forgiveness rules)**
- defined, 80(1)
- excluded from rule where share issued in exchange for debt, 80(2)(g)

**Excluded share**
- re foreign property rules for deferred income plans
- • defined, 206(1)
- • excluded from foreign property, 206(1)"foreign property"(d.1)
- re Part X tax on DPSPs
- • defined, 204
- • excluded from equity share, 204"equity share"(a), (b)

**Excluded trust**
- defined, 233.5(2)

**Excluded withdrawal**
- defined
- • for Home Buyers' Plan, 146.01(1)
- • for Lifelong Learning Plan, 146.02(1)
- not taxable, 146(8), (8.01)

**Exclusive economic zone**
- application of legislation to, *Interpretation Act* 8(2.1)
- defined, *Interpretation Act* 35(1)

**Executor**, *see also* Legal representative
- certificate required by, before distribution, 159(2)
- deemed to be legal representative, 248(1)"legal representative"
- obligations of, 159
- return required by, 150(3)
- withholding tax, liable for, 227(5), (5.1)(i)

**Exempt beneficiary**
- defined, 104(5.4)
- election by trust as long as there exists, 104(5.3)

**Exempt capital gains balance (re flow-through entity)**
- after 2004, added to adjusted cost base, 53(1)(p)

Exempt capital gains balance (re flow-through entity) *(cont'd)*
- defined, 39.1(1), (7)
- used to reduce capital gain, 39.1(2)–(6)

**Exempt corporation**, *see also* Exempt person
- becoming or ceasing to be exempt, 149(10)
- • capital dividend account, 89(1.2)
- • deemed disposition/acquisition of depreciable property, 13(7)(f)
- • loss carryover, restriction, 149(10)(c)
- • resource expenses, rules, 66.7(10)
- no Part I.3 tax payable, 181.1(3)(c)
- Parts IV, IV.1, VI and VI not applicable, 227(14)

**Exempt deficit (of foreign affiliate)**
- defined, Reg. 5907(1)

**Exempt earnings (of foreign affiliate)**
- defined, Reg. 5907(1)

**Exempt foreign trust**
- defined, 94(1) [proposed]

**Exempt gains balance**, *see also* Exempt capital gains balance (re flow-through entity)
- defined, 14(5)
- effect of excessive election, 14(9)

**Exempt income**
- defined, 248(1)
- under treaty, used in calculating clawback, Canada–U.S. Tax Convention Art. XXIV:10

**Exempt interest**
- defined, re foreign investment entities, 94.1(1)

**Exempt loan of transfer**
- defined, re loans to non-residents, 17(15)

**Exempt loss (of foreign affiliate)**
- defined, Reg. 5907(1)

**Exempt partnership**
- defined, for resource allowance claims, Reg. 1206(1)

**Exempt person**, *see also* Exempt corporation
- capital gains and losses, 40(2)(a)(i)
- exchanges of property, determination of gain, 44(7)
- no reserve for amount not due until later year, 20(8)
- obligation issued at discount by, 16(2), (3)
- partnership of, effect where taxable partner joins, 96(8)
- sale of Canadian resource property by, 66.6
- share-purchase tax credit, 127.2(2)
- tax on royalties paid to a government by, 208
- • exception — prescribed persons, Reg. 1216
- U.S. charitable organization, Canada–U.S. Tax Convention Art. XXI

**Exempt property**
- defined, Reg. 1100(1.13), (1.14)
- for specified leasing property CCA rules
- • defined, Reg. 1100(1.13), (1.14)
- • excluded from specified leasing property, Reg. 1100(1.11)
- for trusts
- • defined, 108(1)
- • excluded from 21-year deemed disposition rule, 104(4), (5), (5.2)

**Exempt surplus (of foreign affiliate)**
- adjustment where gain deemed due to negative adjusted cost base, 93(1)(b)(ii)
- deduction for dividend paid out of, 113(1)(a), 113(4), Reg. 5900(1)(a)
- defined, 113(1)(a), Reg. 5907(1)

**Exempt taxpayer**
- defined, re foreign investment entities, 94.1(1)

**Exempt trust (re foreign reporting)**, *see also* Exempt foreign trust
- defined, 233.2(1)

**Exemptions**, 81, 149, *see also* Grandfathering
- agricultural organizations, 149(1)(e), 149(2)
- apportionment rule, 149(6)
- Association of Universities and Colleges of Canada, 149(1)(h.1)
- basic, re minimum tax, 127.53
- benevolent or fraternal benefit society, 149(4)
- • limitation, 149(4)
- benevolent society, 149(1)(k)
- boards of trade, 149(1)(e), 149(2)
- capital gains, 110.6, *see also* Capital gains deduction
- certificate, for non-resident withholding tax, 212(1)(b)(iv), 212(14); ITAR 10(5)
- chambers of commerce, 149(1)(e), 149(2)
- charitable organization, 149(2)
- compensation by Federal Republic of Germany, 81(1)(g)
- Crown corporations, 149(1)(d)–(d.4)
- • exception, 27(1), (2)
- employee of foreign country, 149(1)(a)
- • family and servants of, 149(1)(b)
- expenses of gaining exempt income not deductible, 18(1)(c)
- fraternal benefit society/order, 149(1)(k)
- funeral arrangements, 148.1(2), 149(1)(s.1)
- general, 149
- general limitation, ITAR 31
- Governor General's stipend, 81(1)(n)
- Halifax disaster pension, 81(1)(f)
- housing corporation, 149(1)(i), 149(2)
- income from aircraft operated by non-resident, 81(1)(c)
- income from ship operated by non-resident, 81(1)(c)
- insurer of farmers and fishermen, 149(1)(t), 149(4.2)
- • limitation, 149(4.1)
- interest on certain bonds etc., 81(1)(m)
- labour organizations, 149(1)(k)
- master trust, 149(1)(o.4)
- mines, Reg. Part XIX [Revoked]
- municipal authorities, 149(1)(c)
- municipal corporations, 149(1)(d.6)
- mutual insurance corporations, 149(1)(m)
- non-profit corporation for scientific research, 149(1)(j), 149(2)
- non-profit organizations, 149(1)(l), 149(2)
- • deemed trust, 149(5)
- non-resident withholding tax, 212(1)(b)(iv), 212(14); ITAR 10(5)
- pension corporation, 149(1)(o.1), (o.2)
- pension trust, 149(1)(o)
- personal, *see* Personal credits
- personal injury award, income from, 81(1)(g.1), (g.2)
- prisoners of war, compensation paid to, 81(1)(d)
- prospecting, 81(1)(l)
- provincial corporations, 149(1)(d)–(d.4)
- provincial indemnity, 81(1)(q)
- RCA trust, 149(1)(q.1)
- RCMP pensions, 81(1)(i)

Exemptions *(cont'd)*
- registered charities, 149(1)(f)
- scientific research corporation (non-profit), 149(1)(j), 149(2)
- • control, rules re, 149(8)
- • rules as to income, 149(9)
- service and other pensions, 81(1)(d)
- service pension from other country, 81(1)(e)
- small business investment corporation, 149(1)(o.3)
- social assistance payments, 110(1)(f)(ii)
- societies, 149(1)(l), 149(2)
- • deemed a trust, 149(5)
- statutory, 81(1)(a)
- trust
- • deferred profit sharing plan, 149(1)(s)
- • employees profit sharing plan, 149(1)(p)
- • registered education savings plan, under, 149(1)(u)
- • registered retirement income fund, 149(1)(x)
- • registered retirement savings plan, 149(1)(r)
- • registered supplementary benefit plan, 149(1)(q)
- • vacation pay plan, 149(1)(y)
- war savings certificate, 81(1)(b)
- workers' compensation, 110(1)(f)(ii)

**Existing guaranteed life insurance policy**
- defined, 211, Reg. 1900(1)

**Existing plan**
- defined, Reg. 8500(1)

**Exiting Canada**, *see* Ceasing to be resident in Canada

**Expectation of profit**
- required for business deduction, 18(1)(h), 248(1)"personal or living expenses"

**Expenditure**
- defined, for tax shelter investments, 143.2(1)
- matchable, *see* Matchable expenditure

**Expenditure pool (re borrowings to make distributions)**
- defined, 20.1(8)(c), 20.1(9)

**Expenditure pool (re investment tax credit)**, *see* SR&ED qualified expenditure pool

**Expenses**, *see also* Deductions in computing income
- advertising in non-Canadian periodicals etc., not deductible, 19
- advertising on non-Canadian broadcast media, not deductible, 19.1
- allowances for
- • M.L.A.'s, 81(2)
- • municipal officer's, 81(3)
- • taxable, 6(1)(b)
- annual value of property, not deductible, 18(1)(d)
- appeal, of, 60(o)
- automobile of employee
- • deductions allowed, 8(1)(j)
- • depreciation, 13(11)
- away-from-home
- • railway employee, 8(1)(e)
- borrowing money, 18(11), 20(1)(e), 21
- cancellation of lease, payment for, 20(1)(z), (z.1)
- • limitation on deductibility, 18(1)(q)
- capital outlay, not deductible, 18(1)(b)
- clearing farm land, 30
- club dues, not deductible, 18(1)(l)(ii)
- commission agent's, 8(1)(f), 13(11)
- • automobile or aircraft, 8(1)(j), 8(9)

- • certificate of employer, 8(10)
- construction of building or ownership of land, 18(3.1)–(3.7)
- convention, 20(10)
- development, *see* Canadian development expense
- drilling and exploration, defined, 66(15)"drilling or exploration expense"
- election, tax credit for, 127(3)–(4.2)
- employee, of, 8(1), (2)
- employee's automobile or aircraft, 8(1)(j), 8(9)
- exploration, *see* Canadian exploration expense; Exploration and development expenses
- food, beverages, entertainment, *see* Entertainment expenses (and meals)
- general limitation, 67
- improving farm land, 30
- incurred to gain exempt income, not deductible, 18(1)(c)
- interest, 18(11), 20(1)(c), 20(3)
- • borrowed money, on, 20(1)(c), 20(2)
- • • used to acquire land, 18(3)
- • capitalization of, 21(1)
- • compound, 20(1)(d)
- • paid to acquire land, 18(2)
- • paid to non-resident shareholder, 18(4)–(8)
- investigation of site, 20(1)(dd)
- "investment expense" defined, 110.6(1)
- issuing units, interests or shares, 20(1)(e)
- land drainage system, 30
- landscaping, 20(1)(aa)
- limitations on deductibility, 18(1)
- listing fee, 20(1)(g)
- meals, limitation, 8(4)
- medical, *see* Medical expenses
- mining taxes, 20(1)(v)
- moving, *see* Moving expenses
- objection or appeal, of, 60(o)
- performing duties of office or employment, deduction, 8(1)(i)
- personal or living, not generally deductible, 18(1)(h)
- personal services business, limitation re, 18(1)(p)
- prepaid
- • amalgamation, on, 87(2)(j.2)
- • limitation on deductibility, 18(9)
- printing financial report, 20(1)(g)
- reasonableness criterion, 67
- recreational facilities, 18(1)(l)
- relieving telegrapher or station agent, 8(1)(e)
- representation, 20(1)(cc)
- • deemed capital cost allowance, 13(12)
- • election to defer, 20(9), Reg. 4100
- research and development, 37
- salesperson's, deduction, 8(1)(f)
- • certificate of employer, 8(10)
- scientific research and experimental development, 37
- selling units, interests or shares, 20(1)(e)
- share transfer fees, 20(1)(g)
- taxes on unproductive land, not deductible, 18(2)
- tile drainage, 30
- transport employee's, 8(1)(g)
- travelling, *see* Travelling expenses
- unpaid for more than 2 years, 78
- utilities service connection, 20(1)(ee)
- yachts, camps, clubs etc., no deduction, 18(1)(l)

**Exploration and development expenses**
- borrowing for, 21(4)
- Canadian, *see* Canadian exploration and development expenses
- foreign, *see* Foreign exploration and development expenses
- joint exploration corporation, *see* Joint exploration corporation
- limitation, 66(13)
- recovery of, 59(3.2)
- special product corporations, 66(2)
- where change in control, 66(11), (11.3)–(11.5)

**Exploration and development grants, deductions**, 20(1)(kk)

**Exploration and development shares**, *see also* Flow-through shares
- cost to taxpayer, 66.3(1)(a)(iii)
- whether inventory, 66.3(1)(a)(ii)

**Exploration and drilling rights**
- amount deductible, ITAR 29(14), (15)
- bonus payments, ITAR 29(21), (22)
- dealers in, limitation, 66(5)
- disposition of, ITAR 29(16)–(20)
- includes payments to preserve, ITAR 29(30)
- limitation, ITAR 29(13)

**Export Development Corporation**
- bonds of
- • trust investing in, not foreign property, Reg. 5000(7)"specified international finance trust"(c)(i)(E)

**Exporting resource**, Reg. 1206(1)

**Exposure to a designated country**
- defined, Reg. 8006

**Expropriation**
- amount paid constitutes proceeds of disposition, 13(21)"proceeds of disposition"(d), 54"proceeds of disposition"(d)
- foreign assets, *see* Expropriation assets
- resource properties, 59.1
- rollover where property replaced, 13(4), (4.1), 44

**Expropriation assets**
- acquired from foreign affiliate, 80.1(4)–(6)
- adjusted cost base of, 80.1(2)(b)
- adjusted principal amount, 80.1(7)
- • currency in which computed, 80.1(8)
- cost base, addition to, 53(1)(k)
- • deductions from, 53(2)(n)
- election re, 80.1(1), Reg. 4500
- income from, computation of, 80.1(2)(a)
- interest and capital amounts received at same time, 80.1(3)
- interest on
- • election re, 80.1(2)
- sale of foreign property, for, 80.1

**Extended motor vehicle warranty**
- defined (insurance policy reserves), Reg. 1408(1)

**Extension of time**
- to file appeal
- • by Tax Court, 167
- to file election or application, 220(3.2)
- to file notice of objection
- • by Minister, 166.1
- • by Tax Court, 166.2
- • deadline for requesting, 166.1(7)(a)

- to file notice of qualified dependant for Child Tax Benefit, 122.62(2)
- to file return, 220(3)
- to invest in labour–sponsored venture capital corporation, 127.4(5.1)
- to make or revoke election or designation, 220(3.2)
- to make RRSP contribution, 146(22)
- to post security for departure tax, 220(4.54)
- to transfer RRSP after death to spouse, child or grandchild, 60(1), 60(1)(iv)

**Extinct shellfish**, *see* Ammonite gemstone

**Eyeglasses, as medical expense**, 118.2(2)(j)

## F

**FAPI**, *see* Foreign accrual property income

**FEDE**, *see* Foreign exploration and development expenses

**FIE**, *see* Foreign investment entity

**FMV**, *see* Fair market value

**FRE**, *see* Foreign resource expense

**FTC**, *see* Foreign tax credit

**FTS**, *see* Flow-through share

**Facsimile machine**, *see* Fax machine

**Factoring of accounts**
- income of foreign affiliate from, 95(1)"investment business"
- • accounts arising in active business of related corporation, 95(2)(a)(iii), Reg. 5907(1)"exempt earnings"(d)(ii)(J)

**Failure to file return**, *see* Returns: failure to file, penalty

**Failure to keep records**, 230(3)

**Failure to remit withheld taxes**, 227(9)
- penalty applicable only on amounts over $500, 227(9.1)
- salary or wages, from, 227(9.5)

**Failure to withhold tax**, 227(8)
- assessment for, 227(10)
- salary or wages, from, 227(8.5)

**Fair market value**
- cultural property, donated, 118.1(10)
- deemed disposition at, *see* Disposition: deemed
- ecological gift, 118.1(10.1)–(10.5)
- • certificate, 118.1(10.5)
- inadequate considerations deemed to be, 69
- • exceptions, ITAR 32
- inventory property, of, 10(1), (4)
- property of deceased, 70(5.3)
- publicly-traded securities, ITAR 26(11)
- resource output acquired from Crown, 69(9)
- resource output disposed of to Crown, 69(8)
- share
- • disposed of on death, 70(5.3)
- • foreign affiliate, of, ITAR 26(11.1), (11.2)
- • that is not capital property, 112(4.1)
- transfer at, to spouse or minor, 74.5(1)
- trust, capital interest in, 107.4(4)
- trust for benefit of spouse, 70(8)(a)
- undivided interest in property transferred by tax debtor, 160(3.1)
- V-day election, Reg. 4700, Reg. Sch. VII

**"Fairness package" (1991)**
- late elections, 220(3.2)–(3.7)

# Index

"Fairness package" (1991) *(cont'd)*
- notice of objection
  - - filing deadline, 165(1)
  - - form of, 165(2)
- reassessments after normal reassessment period, 152(4.2), 164(1.5)
- waiver of penalty and interest, 220(3.1)

**False statement**
- defined, for third-party penalty, 163.2(1)

**False statements or omissions**
- offence, 239(1), (1.1)
- penalty, 163(2)
  - - third parties, 163.2

**Family allowances** *see* **Child Tax Benefit**

**Family farm corporation/partnership**
- farm property leased to
  - - transfer of, 70(9.8)
- interest in partnership, defined, 70(10)"interest in a family farm partnership" 110.6(1)
- share of capital stock of corporation, defined, 70(10)"share of the capital stock of a family farm corporation" 110.6(1)
- transfer of, 70(9.2), (9.3)
  - - inter vivos, 73(4)

**Family law,** *see* Province: laws of; Spouse

**Family Orders and Agreements Enforcement Assistance Act**
- Child Tax Benefit payments not garnishable under, 122.61(4)(e)
- disclosure of taxpayer information for purposes of, 122.64(3)

**Family Support Plan**
- payroll deduction reduces source withholding, Reg. 100(3)(d)

**Farm Credit Corporation, subject to tax**, 27(2), Reg. 7100

**Farm Income Protection Act,** *see also* Net income stabilization account; NISA Fund No. 2
- payment received under, taxable, 12(1)(p)
  - - information return, Reg. 234–236
- premium paid under, deductible, 20(1)(ff)

**Farm land,** *see also* Farm property
- addition to adjusted cost base, 53(1)(i)
- improving, expenses deductible, 30
- instalment on sale of, not considered payment from production, 12(1)(g)

**Farm loss**
- amalgamation, on, 87(2.1)
- defined, 111(8)"farm loss" (9), 248(1)
- determination of, by Minister, 152(1.1), (1.2), (1.3)
- drought, due to, *see* Drought region: prescribed
- limitation on deductibility, 111(3)
- partnership, from, 96(1)
- reassessment, 152(6)(c)
- reduction of, on debt forgiveness, 80(3)(b)
- restricted, 31(1), (1.1), *see also* Restricted farm loss

**Farm property**
- disposition by partnership, 101
- family farm corporation or partnership, transfer of, 70(9.2)
- investment tax credit, 127(9)"qualified property"(c)(ii)
- leased, transfer of, 70(9.8)
- qualified

- - capital gains exemption, 110.6(2)
- - defined, 110.6(1)
- transfer of
  - - from spouse's trust, to children, 70(9.1)
  - - inter vivos, to child, 73(3)
    - - - reserve, 44(1.1)
  - - to farmer's child, ITAR 26(18), (19)
    - - - on death, 70(9)
  - - to parent, 70(9.6)

**Farm quota**
- capital gains exemption, 110.6(1)"qualified farm property"(d)

**Farm risks**
- insurance of, 149(1)(t), 149(4.1)

**Farm support payments,** *see also Farm Income Protection Act*
- defined, Reg. 234(2)
- information slips for payments under, Reg. 234–236

**Farmer**
- averaging of income, 119 [obsolete]
  - - surtax, 180.1
- capital gain
  - - principal residence, exclusion of, 40(2)(c)
- cash method of computing income, 28(1)
- payment of tax, 155
- payments to, income, 12(1)(p)
- property transferred by, to child, 70(9)
- transfer of farm property by, to child
  - - inter vivos, 73(3)

**Farming**
- business
  - - cash-base method of calculation, 28
  - - ceasing to carry on, 28(4), (4.1)
  - - expenses deductible, 30
  - - inventory
    - - - acquisition of, 28(1.1)
    - - - valuation of, 28(1.2), (1.3), Reg. 1802
  - - losses, deduction for
    - - - adjustment to cost base of land, 53(1)(i), 111(6)
  - - partnership, disposition of land used in, 101, 111(7)
  - - prepaid expenses, 28(1)(e), (e.1)
- Canadian Wheat Board participation certificate, 161(5)
- capital cost allowances, Reg. Part XVII
- crop insurance, *see Farm Income Protection Act*
- defined, 248(1)
- drought, sales during, *see* Drought region: prescribed
- farm loss, defined, 111(8)
- income deferred from destruction of livestock, 80.3
- inventory
  - - acquisition of, 28(1.1)
  - - amalgamation, on, 87(2)(b)
  - - transfer to corporation, 85(1)(c.2)
  - - valuation of, 28(1.2), (1.3), Reg. 1802
  - - winding-up, on, 88(1.6)
- losses, deduction for, 31
- reduction in basic herd, 29(2)
  - - election re, 29(1)
- restricted farm loss, *see* Restricted farm loss
- stabilization payments and fees, 12(1)(p), 20(1)(ff)

**Fax machine**
- capital cost allowance, Reg. 1101(5p), Reg. Sch. II:Cl. 10(f)

2717

**Feasibility study**
- re investigation of site, deductible, 20(1)(dd)

**Federal body**
- defined, Reg. 237(1)

**Federal Court of Appeal**
- appeal to, 172(3), 180; ITAR 62
- - documents to be transferred, 176
- - refusal or revocation of registration re, 180
- defined, *Interpretation Act* s. 35(1)
- proceedings in camera, 179

**Federal Court of Canada**
- registration of certificate re amount payable, 223(3)
- - charge on land, 223(5), (6)

**Federal Crown corporation**, *see* Crown corporation

**Federal government**, *see* Government

**Federal-Provincial Fiscal Arrangements and Established Programs Financing Act**
- agreement under, 228

**Federal Republic of Germany**
- compensation paid by, exempt, 81(1)(g)

**Federal sales tax**
- refund of, taxable, 12(1)(x)(iv)

**Federal sales tax credit**, *see also* Goods and services tax (GST)

**Fees**
- directors, 6(1)(c)
- included in income, 6(1)(c)
- investment counsel, 20(1)(bb)
- share transfer, deduction for, 20(1)(g)
- withholding tax, 153(1)(g)

**Fees for an individual's tuition**
- defined, 118.5(3)

**Fellowship**, *see* Scholarship

**Fence**
- capital cost allowance for, Reg. Sch. II:Cl. 6
- in amusement park, CCA, Reg. Sch. II:Cl. 37

**Fibre optic cable**
- capital cost allowance, Reg. Sch. II:Cl. 42
- - supporting equipment, Reg. Sch. II:Cl. 3(l)

**Fiduciary**, *see* Legal representative; Trustee

**Field processing**, *see* Canadian field processing

**Fifth Supplement**, *see* Revised Statutes of Canada, 1985 (5th Supp.)

**Filing deadlines**, *see also* Deadlines
- agreement to transfer forgiven amount (debt forgiveness rules), 80.04(6)(a), 80.04(7)
- annual returns, 150(1)
- claims for SR&ED
- - deductions, 37(1), (8)
- - investment tax credits, 127(9)"investment tax credit"(m)
- designation to flow out capital gains from trust, 104(21)–(21.03)
- discontinued business, Reg. 205(2)
- election to trigger capital gains exemption, 110.6(24)
- - revocation or amendment, 110.6(25), (27)
- expiring on Sunday or holiday, *Interpretation Act* s. 26
- extension by Minister, 220(3)
- information returns (T4, etc.), Reg. 205(1)
- - distribution from foreign trusts, 233.5(1)
- - foreign affiliates, 233.4(4)

- - foreign property, 233.3(3)
- - payments to non-residents, Reg. 202(7), (8), 203(2)
- - registered pension plan, Reg. 8409
- - transfer of property to foreign trust, 233.2(4)(d), (e)
- interest offset applications, 161.1(3)(c)
- investment tax credit claims, 127(9)"investment tax credit"(m)
- preferred beneficiary election, 104(14)–(14.02)
- scientific research claims, 37(11), 127(9)"investment tax credit"(m)
- section 85 rollover, 85(6), (7)
- tax returns, 150(1)

**Filing-due date**, 150(1)
- defined, 248(1)

**Filing electronically**, *see* Electronic filing

**Film**, *see* Motion picture film

**Film agency**
- prescribed person for Canadian film/video tax credit, Reg. 1106(7)

**Film credit**, *see* Canadian film or video tax credit; Film or video production services credit

**Film or video production services credit**, 125.5, *see also* Canadian film or video tax credit
- amalgamation of corporations, 87(2)(j.94)
- refund of credit before assessment, 164(1)(a)(ii)
- refundable credit, 125.5(3)
- revocation of certificate, 125.5(6)

**Film property**
- defined, for minimum tax purposes, 127.52(3)

**Filter**
- air or water, medical expense credit, Reg. 5700(c.1)

**Financial aid**, *see* Assistance/government assistance; Reimbursement

**Financial difficulty (taxpayer in)**
- debt forgiveness reserve for insolvent corporation, 61.3
- replacement obligations, exemption from non-resident withholding tax, 212(3)
- share, 248(1)"term preferred share"(e), *see also* Distress preferred share
- small business bond, 15.2
- small business development bond, 15.1

**Financial institution**, *see also* Bank; Insurance corporation; Investment dealer; Moneylender; Restricted financial institution
- amalgamation of, 87(2)(g.2)
- bad debt deduction, 20(1)(p)(ii)
- becoming, 142.6(1)(a), (b)
- ceasing to be, 142.6(1)(a), (c)
- debt obligation owned by, *see* Specified debt obligation
- defined
- - for charitable donations, 118.1(20)
- - for financial institutions capital tax, 190(1)
- - for insurance corporations, Reg. 2400(1)
- - for Large Corporations Tax, 181(1)
- - for mark-to-market rules, 142.2(1)
- - for stop-loss rules, 112(6)(c), 142.2(1)
- - re disposition by financial institutions, Reg. 9200(1)
- dividends received by
- - mark-to-market property, 112(5)–(5.2)
- ineligible for election to treat Canadian securities as capital property, 39(5)(b)

2718

## Index

**Financial institution** *(cont'd)*
- interference with remittance of tax, 227(5.2)–(5.4) (draft)
- mark-to-market property, *see* Mark-to-market property; Specified debt obligation
- non-resident, *see* Non-resident: financial institution
- Part I.3 tax, 181.3
- Part VI tax, 190.1–190.21
- - administrative provisions, 190.2–190.211
- - calculation of, 190.1–190.15
- - credit for, 125.2
- - deductible in computing branch tax liability, 219(1)(h)(i)
- - - unused, reassessment re, 152(6)(e)
- - instalments, 157(1), (2)
- - life insurers, temporary tax on, 190.1(1.1)
- - rates, 190.1(1)
- - short taxation year, 190.1(2)
- prescribed, *see also* International banking centre
- - for financial institutions capital tax, Reg. 8604
- - for foreign affiliate rules, 95(2)(a.3), 95(2.5)"specified deposit" Reg. 7900
- - for foreign currency deposits, no withholding tax, 212(1)(b)(iii)(D), Reg. 7900
- - - return and information return by, 212(18)
- remittance of tax through, 229 [repealed]
- - by large employers, required, 153(1), Reg. 110
- reserve for doubtful debts, 20(1)(l)(ii)
- restricted, *see also* Restricted financial institution
- - election by mutual fund/investment corporation to not be, 131(10)
- - receiving dividends on taxable RFI shares
- - - information return, 187.5
- - - partnerships, 187.4
- - - tax payable, 187.3(1)
- - - time of acquisition of share, 187.3(2)
- software development by, no R&D credits, 248(1)"scientific research and experimental development"
- specified
- - defined, 248(1)
- - dividends received by, 112(2.1), (2.2)
- - guarantee agreement re shares, 112(2.2)–(2.22)
- - related corporations, 248(14)
- superficial loss of, 18(13)–(16), 142.6(7)
- windup of, *see* Winding-up: financial institution

**Financial intermediary corporation, defined**, 191(1)

**Financing fees**
- deduction for, 20(1)(e), (e.1)
- election to capitalize, 21

**Financing lease**, *see* Direct financing lease

**Financing subsidy**
- provided by employer, taxable, 6(23)

**Fine**, *see* Offences

**Finland**, *see also* Foreign government
- stock exchange recognized, Reg. 3201(t)

**Fire alarm indicator**
- visual, for the hearing impaired, medical expense credit, Reg. 5700(q.1)

**Firefighters, volunteer**
- deduction from employment income, 8(1)(a) [to be repealed]
- exemption from employment income, 81(4)

**First Nations Tax**, *see also* Indians
- federal credit for, 120(2.2)
- instalments, 156.1(1)"net tax owing"(b)B, E, F, 156.1(1.3)

**First purchaser**
- defined
- - for scientific research tax credits, Reg. 226(1)
- - for share purchase tax credits, Reg. 227(1)

**First-term shared-use-equipment, for R&D investment tax credit**
- defined, 127(9)

**First-year rule, depreciable property**, Reg. 1100(2)–(2.4)

**Fiscal period**
- business, of, 11(2)
- change of control, on, 249(4)(d)
- deemed end on emigration, 128.1(4)(a.1)
- defined, 249.1
- - of partnership, 249(2)(b)
- election for non-calendar year, 249.1(4), (5)
- - annual income inclusion where election made, 34.1
- - late filing, Reg. 600(b.1)
- election on termination of proprietorship, 25
- member of terminated partnership
- - election re, 99(2)–(4)
- qualifying, defined, 34.2(1)
- reference to, 249(2), (3)

**Fisherman**
- defined, Reg. 105.1(1)

**Fishing**
- business
- - cash method, 28(1)
- - loss from, constitutes farm loss, 111(8)"farm loss"A(a)(i)
- cod compensation, *see* compensation programs (below)
- compensation programs
- - payments received under, taxable, 56(1)(a)(vi), Reg. 5502(c)
- - - withholding of tax at source, 153(1)(m), Reg. 5502(c)
- - repayment of benefits, deductible, 60(n)(ii.1)
- defined, 248(1)
- expedition, by CCRA, 231.2(3)
- income from
- - averaging, before 1992, 119
- - election re source deductions, Reg. 105.1
- - instalments and payment of balance, 155
- - insurer exempt, 149(1)(t)
- - not eligible for manufacturing & processing credit, 125.1(3)"manufacturing or processing"(a)
- property
- - investment tax credit, 127(9)"qualified property"(c)(ii)
- - owned since before 1972, capital cost allowance, Reg. 1700–1704
- - when available for use, 13(27)(g)
- vessel
- - capital cost allowance, Reg. 1100(1)(i), 1101(2a), Reg. Sch. II:Cl. 7
- - leased to controlled corporation, investment tax credit, 127(9)"qualified property"(d)(iv)

**Fishing expedition**, 231.2(3)

2719

## Index

**Fixed-dividend share**
- interest paid on money borrowed to purchase, 20(1)(qq)

**Fixed payment obligation**
- defined, Reg. 9100

**Flared gas**, *see* Solution gas

**Flat benefit provision (of pension plan)**
- defined, Reg. 8300(1)

**Flow-through**
- adjusted cost base of option, to share, partnership interest or trust interest, 49(3.01)
- Canadian development expense, to shareholder, 66(12.62)
- Canadian exploration expense, to shareholder, 66(12.6)
- Canadian oil and gas property expense, to shareholder, 66(12.64)
- corporate income to shareholder, *see* Integration
- corporation's capital gain, untaxed portion, 83(2)
- death benefit, through trust or estate, 104(28)
- entity, *see* Flow-through entity
- intercorporate dividends, 82(1)(a)(ii)(A), 112(1)
- investment tax credits on windup, 88(1)(e.3)
- paid-up capital deficiency, on conversion of shares, 51(3), 86(2.1)
- partnership income to partner, 96(1)
  - limited to amount at risk, 96(2.1)–(2.7)
- qualifying environmental trust income to beneficiary, 107.3(1)
- shares, *see* Flow-through shares
- trust capital gains to beneficiary, 104(21)
- trust income to preferred beneficiary, 104(14)
- trust pension benefits to beneficiary, 104(27)

**Flow-through entity (re capital gains exemption)**
- adjusted cost base, addition to
  - after 2004, 53(1)(p)
  - before 2005, 53(1)(r)
- amalgamation of, 87(2)(bb.1)
- defined, 39.1(1)
- distribution of property to beneficiary, 107(2.2)
- reduction in capital gain, 39.1(2)–(6)
- sale of interest in, 39.1(7)

**Flow-through mining expenditure**
- defined, 127(9)
  - reduction for assistance received, 127(11.1)(c.2)
- investment tax credit for, 127(5)(a)(i), 127(9)"investment tax credit"(a.2)
- reduces CCEE, 66.1(1)"cumulative Canadian exploration expense"L

**Flow-through shares**, 66(12.6)–(12.75)
- amalgamation, effect of, 87(4.4)
- cost of, 66.3(3)
- defined, 66(15), 248(1)
- information return, Reg. 228
- interest on renunciation for previous year, 211.91(1)
- minimum tax, 127.52(1)(e), (e.1)
- mining exploration expenses in first 60 days of year, 66.1(8)
- not "tax shelter", 237.1(1)
- one-year look-back rule, 66(12.66)(a.1), 211.91
- paid-up capital, 66.3(4)
- prescribed, Reg. 6202.1
- renunciation, 66(12.6), (12.62), (12.64)
  - Canadian development expenses, 66(12.601), (12.62)
  - conversion to CEE, 66(12.601), (12.602)
  - Canadian exploration expenses, 66(12.6)
  - Canadian oil and gas property expenses, 66(12.64)
  - expenses in first 60 days of the year, 66(12.66)
  - member of partnership, by, 66(19)
  - mining properties excluded, 66(12.62)(b.1)
  - restrictions, 66(12.67), (12.71), (19)
- selling instrument
  - defined, 66(15)
  - filing of, 66(12.68)
  - late filing, 66(12.74), (12.75)

**Fluctuations in currency**, *see* Foreign exchange

**Food**, *see also* Entertainment expenses (and meals); Meals
- delivered after the end of the year, reserve for, 20(6)

**Football players**, *see* Athlete

**Fondaction**
- prescribed as labour-sponsored venture capital corporation, Reg. 6700(f), 6701(g)

**Foreclosure**, *see* Surrender: of property to creditor

**Foreign accrual property income**
- defined, 95(1), 95(2), 248(1)
- definitions, 95(1), (4)
- foreign affiliate purchasing goods for use in Canada, 95(2)(a.1)
- fresh start rule, 95(2)(k)
- included in income, 91(1)
- included in income of non-resident trust, 94(1)(c) [to be repealed]
- insurance of risks in Canada, 95(2)(a.2)
- loss carryback, 152(6.1), Reg. 5903(1)
- loss carryforward, 95(1)"foreign accrual property income"F [to be repealed], Reg. 5903(1)
- trusts, 94(4) [to be repealed]

**Foreign accrual tax**
- deduction from income, 91(4)
- defined, 95(1)

**Foreign affiliate**, *see also* Controlled foreign affiliate
- active business income, 95(2)(a), Reg. 5907(2)–(2.6)
- acquisition of shares of
  - from partnership, 91(7)
- assets acquired from
  - as consideration for settlement of debt, 80.1(5)
  - as dividend in kind, 80.1(4)
  - on winding-up, 80.1(6)
- becoming resident in Canada, 128.1(1)(d)
- benefit to shareholder from, 15(2)–(2.6), (7)
- capital gains
  - election re, Reg. 5902
- capital gains and losses, 95(2)(f)
  - currency fluctuation, from, 95(2)(g), (h)
- carrying on business in a country, Reg. 5906
- consolidated groups' liabilities, Reg. 5907(1.1)
- controlled, defined, 95(1)"controlled foreign affiliate"
- currency dealings of, 95(2.3), (2.5)"indebtedness"
- deductible loss, 95(1)"foreign accrual property income"F, Reg. 5903
- defined, 95(1), 248(1)
- definitions, Reg. 5907
- disposition of shares of
  - election re capital gains on, 93(1)
  - held by partnership, 93(1.2)
  - loss on, 93(2)–(2.3), (4)

2720

# Index

Foreign affiliate *(cont'd)*
- - share-for-share exchange, 85.1(3)–(6)
- disposition of shares of another foreign affiliate, 95(2)(c)
- dissolution of, 88(3), 95(2)(e), (e.1)
- dividends from, 20(13), 113(1), Reg. 5900
- - shares held by partnership, 93.1(2)
- "earnings" of, defined, Reg. 5907(1)
- "excluded property"
- - debt related to, gain or loss on settlement of, 95(2)(i)
- - defined, 95(1)
- "exempt earnings"
- - defined, Reg. 5907(1)
- - listed countries re, Reg. 5907(11)–(11.2)
- "exempt loss"
- - defined, Reg. 5907(1)
- - listed countries re, Reg. 5907(11)–(11.2)
- "exempt surplus" defined, Reg. 5907(1)
- foreign accrual property income of, defined, 95(1)
- "foreign accrual tax" defined, 95(1)
- income bonds or debentures issued by, 95(5)
- income derived from indebtedness, 95(2)(a.3), 95(2.4), (2.5)"indebtedness"
- income from services, 95(2)(b)
- - "services" defined, 95(3)
- information return re, 233.4
- insurer
- - income of, 95(1)"investment business", 95(2)(a.2)
- - subject to Canadian rules, 95(2)(k)(iv)
- investment business of, *see* Investment business
- liquidation of, 95(2)(e.1)
- loan to, 17(3), 247(7)
- merger of, 87(8), (8.1), 95(2)(d), (d.1)
- "net earnings" defined, Reg. 5907(1)
- "net loss" defined, Reg. 5907(1)
- "net surplus" defined, Reg. 5907(1)
- participating percentage, Reg. 5904
- partnership interest
- - adjusted cost base of, 95(2)(j)
- qualifying interest in, *see* Qualifying interest (in respect of foreign affiliate)
- regulations, Reg. Part LIX
- "relevant cost base" of property, 95(4)
- "relevant tax factor" defined, 95(1)
- reporting requirements, 233.4
- residence of, Reg. 5907(11.2)
- second affiliate, 95(2)(a)(ii)(D), Reg. 5907(2.8)
- settlement of debt, gain or loss from, 95(2)(i)
- share of
- - adjusted cost base, 92
- - - amalgamation, on, 87(2)(u)(i)
- - amount included in income re, 91(1)
- - - reserve where foreign exchange restriction, 91(2)
- - disposition of, 85.1(3)–(6)
- - - held by partnership, 93.1(2)
- - election re disposition, 93(1), (1.1)
- - - late-filed, 93(5)
- - - penalty, 93(6)
- - - special cases, 93(5.1)
- - - unpaid balance of penalty, 93(7)
- - exempt dividends, 93(3)
- - - on amalgamation, 87(2)(u)(ii)
- - fair market value, ITAR 26(11.1), (11.2)

- - held by partnerhip, 93.1(2)
- - issued to avoid tax, deemed not issued, 95(6)(b)
- - loss limitation on disposition of, 93(2)–(4)
- - participating percentage of, defined, 95(1)"participating percentage"
- special rules, Reg. 5905
- start-up rule, for non-active business, 95(2)(k)
- stock dividends from, 95(7)
- surplus distributions
- - order, Reg. 5901
- "surplus entitlement percentage" defined, 95(1)
- tax, *see* Foreign taxes
- "taxable earnings" defined, Reg. 5907(1)
- "taxable loss" defined, Reg. 5907(1)
- "taxable surplus" defined, Reg. 5907(1)
- taxation year, 95(1)
- taxpaying affiliates' losses, Reg. 5907(1.2)
- third affiliate, 95(2)(a)(ii)(D), Reg. 5907(2.8)
- transitional rules re 1972, ITAR 35
- "underlying foreign tax" defined, Reg. 5907(1)
- "underlying foreign tax applicable" defined, Reg. 5907(1)
- "whole dividend" paid, Reg. 5907(1)

**Foreign assets**
- reporting of, to CCRA, 233.3

**Foreign bank**, *see also* Authorized foreign bank
- defined
- - re FAPI, 95(1)
- - re foreign investment entities, 94.1(1)
- - re international banking centre, 33.1(1)
- fund deposited with, reporting requirement, 233.3

**Foreign-based information or document**
- defined, 231.6(1)
- requirement to provide, 231.6(2)
- - consequence of non-compliance or incomplete compliance, 231.6(8)
- - notice of, 231.6(3)
- - review of, 231.6(4)–(6)
- - time during review not to count, 231.6(7)
- tax shelter investment, effect on, 143.2(13), (14)

**Foreign broadcasting undertaking**
- defined, 19.1(4)
- no deduction for advertisement broadcast to Canadian market by, 19.1(1)

**Foreign business**
- defined, for FAPI rules, 95(2)(k)

**Foreign business corporation**
- deemed resident in Canada, 250(4)(b)
- defined, 213(3)
- no withholding tax on dividend from, 213(1)

**Foreign corporation**, *see* Foreign affiliate; Non-resident

**Foreign country**, *see* Foreign government; Prescribed countries

**Foreign currency**, *see also* Foreign exchange
- defined, 248(1)

**Foreign exchange**, *see also* Foreign currency
- adjustment, re specified debt obligation, Reg. 9104
- calculation of income where foreign assets expropriated, 80.1(8)
- debt obligation denominated in
- - application of debt forgiveness rules, 80(2)(k), 80.01(11)

Foreign exchange *(cont'd)*
- - assumed by non-resident in Canadian business, 76.1(2)
- - moved by non-resident from Canadian business, 76.1(1)
- - surrender of property to creditor, calculation of proceeds, 79(7)
- fluctuations in
- - capital gain or loss, 39(2)
- - debt parking and statute-barred debt rules to be ignored, 80.01(11)
- - foreign affiliate's capital gain or loss from, 95(2)(g), (h)
- - ignored in determining employee stock option deduction, 110(1)(d)(iii)
- - loan or lending asset, 248(1)"amortized cost"(c.1), (f.1)
- - specified debt obligation of financial institution, 142.4(1)"tax basis"(f), (o)
- income in blocked currency, waiver of interest on tax, 161(6)
- restriction, reserve where, 91(2), (3)

**Foreign exploration and development expenses**, *see also* Exploration and development expenses; Resource expenses
- borrowed money
- - capitalization of interest, 21(2), (4)
- - - reassessment, 21(5)
- country-by-country allocation, 66(4.1), (4.2)
- - successor rules, 66.7(2.1), (2.2)
- deduction for, 66(4)
- - on ceasing to be resident in Canada, 66(4)(b)(i.1)
- - short taxation year, 66(13.1)
- defined, 66(15)
- individual ceasing to be resident in Canada, 66(4.3)
- limitation, 66(12.4)
- reduction of, on debt forgiveness, 80(8)(e)
- short taxation year, 66(13.1)
- specified, *see* Specified foreign exploration and development expense
- successor corporation, rules, 66.7(2)
- - application, 66.6(1)
- where change in control, 66(11), (11.3)

**Foreign government**, *see also* United States
- bonds of, eligible for RRSP investment, Reg. 4900(1)(o)
- bribery of officials non-deductible, 67.5
- diplomats, exempt, 149(1)(a), Canada-U.S. Tax Convention Art. XXVIII
- employees of, exempt, 149(1)(a), Canada-U.S. Tax Convention Art. XIX, XXVIII
- expropriation by, 80.1
- social security plan of, excluded from RCA, Reg. 6802(g)
- specified debt obligation of
- - excluded from mark-to-market rules, 142.2(1)"mark-to-market property"(e)
- - owned by bank as specified debt obligation, 142.6(4)(a)(ii)
- stock exchanges recognized, Reg. 3201
- tax paid to, *see* Foreign tax credit; Foreign taxes

**Foreign immigration trust**
- five-year exemption, 94(1)(b)(i)(A)(III) [to be repealed], 94(1)"connected contributor"(a) [proposed]

**Foreign income**, *see also* Foreign accrual property income
- Canadian resident, generally taxable, 3(a)
- employment, tax credit for, 122.3
- foreign affiliate, of, *see* Foreign accrual property income
- non-resident, not taxable, 115(1)
- taxed by foreign country, *see* Foreign tax credit

**Foreign insurance subsidiary**
- defined, Reg. 8605(4)

**Foreign investment entity**, 94.1-94.2
- accrual rules, 94.1 [proposed]
- defined, 94.1(1)
- demand for information, 94.1(16), (17)
- foreign insurance policies, 94.2(10)
- fresh start year, 94.1(6)
- income allocation, 94.1(5)
- interest in
- - addition to adjusted cost base, 53(1)(m.1)
- - amalgamation of holder, 87(2)(j.95)
- - reduction in adjusted cost base, 53(2)(w)
- loss allocation, 94.1(7)
- mark to market rules, 94.2
- specified tax allocation, 94.1(8)
- tracked interests, 94.2(9)

**Foreign investment income**
- defined, 129(4)
- refund to private corporation in respect of, 129(1), (3)

**"Foreign merger" defined**, 87(8.1)

**Foreign Missions and International Organizations Act**
- employment income from international organization, tax credit, 126(3)

**Foreign mutual fund trust**
- exemption from reporting requirement, 233.2(1)"exempt trust"(c)
- reporting requirement, 233.3

**Foreign non-profit organization**
- defined, Reg. 6804(1)

**Foreign oil and gas business**
- defined, 126(7)
- foreign tax credit for, 126(5)

**Foreign plan (pension plan)**
- contributions made to, Reg. 6804(4)-(6)
- defined, Reg. 6804(1), 8308.1(1)
- electing employer with respect to, Reg. 6804(2), (3)
- PSPA of, Reg. 8308.1(5), (6)
- - information return, Reg. 8402(2)
- pension adjustment, prescribed amount, Reg. 8308.2
- pension credit of, Reg. 8308.1(2)-(4)

**Foreign policy loan**
- defined, Reg. 2400(1)

**Foreign property**, 206, Reg. Part L, *see also* Foreign reporting requirements
- acquired by certain trusts, tax re, 205-207
- acquired in non-arm's length transaction
- - consideration deemed to be fair market value, 206(4)
- - on qualifying disposition to trust, 107.4(3)(c)
- deferred income plans, Reg. 5000
- defined, 206(1), Reg. 5000(7)
- held in certain trusts, Reg. 5000
- information return, Reg. 221

2722

Foreign property *(cont'd)*
- • by corporation claiming not to be (for RRSP etc. investments), Reg. 222
- • investments in foreign property, 233.3
- limit on percentage to be held by RRSP or RRIF, 206(2)(b)
- sale of, expropriation assets for, 80.1
- security becoming, due to reorganization, 206(3.1)
- substantial Canadian presence rule, 206(1.1)(d)

**Foreign reporting requirements**, 233.1–233.7
- foreign affiliates, 233.4
- foreign property, 233.3
- foreign trusts
- • distributions from, 233.5
- • indebtedness to, 233.5
- • transfer of property to, 233.3
- transactions with related non-residents, 233.1

**Foreign resource expenses**
- defined, 66.21(1)
- reduction of, on change of control, 66.7(13)
- specified amount of, for successor rules, 66.7(13.2)
- successor of, 66.7(2.3), (13.1)

**Foreign resource income**
- defined, 66.21(1)

**Foreign resource loss**
- defined, 66.21(1)

**Foreign resource pool expense**
- deduction against taxable income earned in Canada, 115(4.1)
- defined, 248(1)

**Foreign resource property**
- acquisition of, rules, 66.7(8)
- amount designated re
- • "outlay" or "expense", 66(15)
- defined, 66(15), 248(1)
- disposal of, effect on successor rules, 66.7(15)
- disposition of, 59(1)
- • by partnership, 59(1.1)
- • no capital gain, 39(1)(a)(ii.1)
- • no capital loss, 39(1)(b)(ii)
- • successor rules, 66.7(15.1)
- "eligible property" for transfer to corporation by shareholder, 85(1.1)(d)
- eligibility for section 85 rollover, 85(1.11)
- in respect of a country, defined, 248(1)
- non-successor acquisitions, 66.7(16)
- original owner, defined, 66(15)
- predecessor owner, defined, 66(15)
- proceeds of disposition, 59(1)
- production from, defined, 66(15)"production"
- reserve amount, defined, 66(15)
- rules for trusts, 104(5.2)
- seizure of, exception to creditor rules, 79.1(2.1)
- successor rules, 66.7(15)

**Foreign retirement arrangement**
- amount credited to, exempt, 81(1)(r)
- benefit to trust, flow-through to beneficiary, 104(27)
- defined, 248(1), Reg. 6803
- eligible amount, 60.01
- emigration of retiree, no deemed disposition, 128.1(10)"excluded right or interest"(a)(x)
- excluded from non-resident trust rules, 94(1)"exempt foreign trust"(f) [proposed]
- excluded from reporting requirements, 233.2(1)"exempt trust"(a), 233.3(1)"specified foreign property"(n), 233.5(2)(a)
- excluded from various trust rules, 108(1)"trust"(a)
- exclusion from foreign accrual rules, 94(1)(b)(i)(E) [to be repealed], 94(1)"connected contributor"(a) [proposed]
- income earned in account, exempt, 81(1)(r)
- Individual Retirement Account (U.S.), Reg. 6803
- lump-sum transfer, 60(j)(ii), 60.01
- payment out of
- • eligible for transfer to RRSP, 60(j)(ii), 60.01
- • included in income, 56(1)(a)(i)(C.1)
- prescribed plan or arrangement, Reg. 6803

**Foreign service**
- for registered pension plan
- • determination of provisional PSPA, Reg. 8303(10)
- • eligibility, 8503(3)(a)(vii)

**Foreign share**
- rollover on exchange for foreign share, 85.1(5), (6)

**Foreign spin-off**, 86.1
- foreign accrual property income, 95(2)(g.2)

**Foreign stock exchanges**, Reg. 3201

**Foreign tax credit**, 126
- addition to taxable income in respect of, 110.5
- change in, reassessment within 6 years, 152(4)(b)(iii)
- deduction for specified capital gains, and, 126(5.1)
- deduction from income, 20(11), (12), (12.1), 91(4)
- deduction from Part I.1 surtax, 180.1(1.1)
- deduction from tax, 126
- • additions for, 110.5
- • calculated separately for each foreign country, 126(6)
- • definitions, 126(7)
- • emigrant, 126(2.21)
- • non-resident, re pre-Oct/96 disposition, 126(2.2)
- • trust with non-resident beneficiary, 126(2.22)
- deemed tax on income or profits, 126(5)
- definitions, 126(7)
- employees profit sharing plan, deduction, 144(8.1)
- foreign oil and gas levies, 126(5)
- former resident, 126(2.21)
- • trust beneficiary, 126(2.22)
- minimum tax, 127.54
- no economic profit, 20(12.1), 126(4.1)
- non-business income tax, 20(12)
- not deductible by life insurer, 138(5.1), (8)
- overseas employment tax credit and, choice between, 126(1)(b)(i)
- payable, adjustment, 161(6.1)
- portion of foreign tax excluded, 126(4)
- profit not material, 20(12.1), 126(4.1)
- short-term securities acquisitions, 126(4.2), (4.3)
- special, for minimum tax purposes, 127.54
- tax deemed income or profits tax, 126(5)
- trust, deduction for, 104(22)–(22.4)
- U.S. estate taxes, Canada–U.S. Tax Convention Art. XXIX B:6, (7)
- unused
- • carryover on amalgamation, 87(2)(z)
- • defined, 126(7)"unused foreign tax credit"
- • overpayment of tax as consequence of, 164(5), (5.1)
- • reassessment, 152(6)(c.1)

**Foreign tax credit** *(cont'd)*
- • rules re, 126(2.3)

**Foreign taxes**
- additional, or reimbursement of
- • reassessment within 6 years, 152(4)(b)(iv)
- credit for, *see* Foreign tax credit
- deduction for, 20(11), (12), (12.1)

**Foreign trust**, *see* Offshore trust; Trust (or estate): non-resident

**Foreign vendor**
- capital gain strip where gain exempted by treaty, 55(3.1)(b) [temporary]

**Forfeited amount**
- defined, 147(1), Reg. 8500(1)

**Forfeiture**
- under deferred profit sharing plan, 201

**Forgiven amount (re settlement of debt)**
- deemed where amount designated following debt forgiveness, 80.03(7)(b)(ii)
- defined, 6(15.1), 15(1.21), 80(1), 80.01(1), 80.03(1)(a), 80.04(1)
- transfer of, under agreement, 80.04(4)

**Forgiveness of debt**, *see* Debt forgiveness

**Form(s)**
- prescribed or authorized
- • defined, 248(1)"prescribed"
- • deviations acceptable, *Interpretation Act* s. 32
- • proof of, 244(16)
- waiver of requirement to file, 220(3.1)

**Former Act (pre-1972), references to**
- defined, ITAR 8
- para. 11(1)(a), capital cost allowance, ITAR 20(5)(b)(ii), 58(5)
- paras. 11(1)(g), (h), (i), pension plan contributions, ITAR 65(2)(b)
- subsec. 17(1), inadequate considerations, ITAR 32
- subsec. 20(6), deemed capital cost, ITAR 20(5)(a)(ii)
- subsec. 67(1), personal corporations, ITAR 57(9)(b)
- s. 68, personal corporations, ITAR 57(11)
- subsec. 79B(5), registered retirement savings plans, ITAR 65(2)(c)
- subsec. 79C(7), deferred profit sharing plans, ITAR 65(2)(d)
- s. 85I, amalgamations, ITAR 34(7), 40(6)(a)(ii)
- subsecs. 85I(1), (2), amalgamations, ITAR 34(1)
- Part II, tax on undistributed income, ITAR 66(1), (2)
- Part IID, special refundable tax, ITAR 67(1), (2), (4), (5)
- Part IV
- • continued in force, ITAR 14
- • references to, how construed, ITAR 16
- Part VIII
- • continued in force, ITAR 15
- • references to, how construed, ITAR 16

**Former business property**
- amalgamation, effect of, 87(2)(l.3)
- defined, 248(1)
- disposition of, 44(1), (6)

**Former employee**
- amount received from employer, whether taxable, 6(3)
- stock option agreement, taxable benefit, 7(4)

**Former limited-recourse indebtedness (tax shelter investment)**
- defined, 143.2(10)

**Former property**, *see also* Exchanges of property; Former business property
- defined, 13(4), 44(1)

**Former resident**, *see also* Ceasing to be resident in Canada
- credit for tax paid on emigration where stop-loss rule applies, 119
- foreign tax credit, 126(2.21), (2.22)
- returning to Canada, 128.1(6), (7)
- stop-loss credit, 119

**Former spouse, defined**, 252(3)

**Formulas**
- negative amounts in, 257

**Forward averaging**, *see also* Averaging of income; Income-averaging annuity contract
- addition to tax, 120.1(2) [repealed]
- election, 110.4(2) [repealed]

**Fossil fuel**
- defined, Reg. 1104(13)

**Fossilized shellfish**, *see* Ammonite gemstone

**Foster child**
- payment relating to, exempt, 81(1)(h)

**Foundation**, *see* Charitable foundation; Private foundation; Public foundation

**Fractional share**
- is a share, 248(1)"share"

**France**, *see also* Foreign government
- stock exchange recognized, Reg. 3201(c)
- universities, gifts to, Reg. Sch. VIII s. 3

**Franchise**
- capital cost allowance, Reg. 1100(1)(c), Reg. Sch. II:Cl. 14
- payment to U.S. resident on connection with, Canada–U.S. Tax Convention Art. XII:3(c)
- relationship not considered control, 256(5.1)
- representation expenses, 13(12), 20(1)(cc), 20(9)

**Fraternal benefit society/order**
- exemption, 149(1)(k)

**Fraud, justification for reassessment**, 152(4)(a)(i), 152(5)

**Fraudulent conveyance**
- tax equivalent to provincial legislation, 160

**Freight haulage trucks and tractors**
- capital cost allowance, Reg. Sch. II:Cl. 16(g)

**Fresh start year**
- defined, re foreign investment entity, 94.1(6)

**Freshwater Fish Marketing Corporation, subject to tax**, 27(2), Reg. 7100

*Friesen* **decision overruled**, 10(1.01)

**Frontier exploration**
- allowances, Reg. 1207
- prescribed area, Reg. 1215

**Frontier exploration base**
- defined, Reg. 1207(2)
- expenses added to
- • amounts receivable, portion included in income, 59(3.3)(e)

**Fruit growing, constitutes farming**, 248(1)"farming"

**Fuel tax rebate**
- 10 × inclusion, 12(1)(x.1)
- abatement of prior years' losses, 111(10), (11)
- amalgamation, on, 87(2)(uu)
- interest on prior year's return not to be paid, 161(7)(a)(viii)
- windup, on, 88(1)(e.2)

**Full-rate taxable income**
- defined, 123.4(1)

**Full-time student**
- defined, for Lifelong Learning Plan, 146.02(1)

**Funeral or cemetary services,** *see also* Eligible funeral arrangement
- defined, 148.1(1)
- provision of under eligible funeral arrangement, 148.1(2)(b)(i)

**Funeral services,** *see also* Eligible funeral arrangement
- defined, 148.1(1)
- provision of under eligible funeral arrangement, 148.1(2)(b)(i)

**Fur farming,** 248(1)"farming"

**Furnace**
- electric or sealed combustion, medical expense credit, Reg. 5700(c.2)

**Furniture**
- antique, whether CCA allowed, Reg. 1102(1)(e)
- capital cost allowance, Reg. Sch. II:Cl. 8(i)

**Future obligations,** *see also* Reserve
- deduction for amount paid, 20(24)

## G

**GAAP,** *see* Generally accepted accounting principles

**GAAR,** *see* General anti-avoidance rule

**GSRA,** *see* Government-sponsored retirement arrangement

**GST,** *see* Goods and services tax (GST)

***Gagnon* case overruled,** 56(12)

**Gains,** *see also* Capital gain; Capital loss; Capital gains and losses
- defined, for disposition of specified debt obligation, Reg. 9200

**Gala presentation**
- ineligible for film/video production services credit, Reg. 9300(g)

***Gallantry Awards Order Statute***
- amount received under, exempt, 81(1)(d)

**Gambling losses,** Canada–U.S. Tax Convention Art. XXII:3

**Game show**
- ineligible for Canadian film/video credit, Reg. 1106(1)"excluded production"(b)
- ineligible for film/video production services credit, Reg. 9300(e)

**Garnishment for taxes unpaid,** 224
- binding on federal and provincial governments, 224(1.4)
- enhanced, 224(1.2)
- failure to comply with order, 224(4), (4.1)
- prevented while objection or appeal underway, 225.1
- salary or wages, 224(1)
- "super" garnishment priority over secured creditors, 224(1.2)

***Garry Bowl Ltd.* case overruled,** 152(1.1)

**Gas, natural,** *see* Petroleum/natural gas

**Gas manufacturing/distributing equipment**
- capital cost allowance, Reg. Sch. II:Cl. 1(n), Sch. II:Cl. 2(d)

**Gas or oil well equipment,** Reg. 1104(2), Reg. Sch. II:Cl. 10(j)

**Gasoline expense**
- automobile, *see* Automobile: operating costs

**Gaspé Peninsula**
- defined, 127(9)
- prescribed area, for electrical energy or steam processing, 127(9)"qualified property"(c.1)
- prescribed designated region, 127(9)"specified percentage"(a)(vi), Reg. 4607
- qualified property acquired for use in, 127(9)"specified percentage"(a), (e)

**Gay couples,** *see* Common-law partner

**Gemstones,** *see also* Listed personal property
- ammonite, *see* Ammonite gemstone

**General amending provision**
- of insurance policy, defined, Reg. 1408(1)

**General anti-avoidance rule,** 245
- application of rule, 245(2), (4)
- avoidance transaction, defined, 245(3)
- determination of amounts following assessment, 152(1.11), (1.12)
- determination of tax consequences, 245(5)
- tax benefit, defined, 245(1)
- tax consequences, defined, 245(1)
- transfer pricing GAAR test, 247(2)(b)(ii)

**General procedure appeals,** 175

**General provisions**
- defined, Reg. 8006

**General-purpose electronic data-processing equipment**
- capital cost allowance, Reg. Sch. II:Cl. 10(f)
- defined, Reg. 1104(2)

**General rate reduction percentage**
- defined, 123.4(1)

**Generally accepted accounting principles**
- in computing income from business or property, 9(1)
- in determining adjusted equity, 20.2(2)

**Generating electrical energy**
- manufacturing and processing credit, 125.1(2)

**Generating equipment**
- capital cost allowance, Reg. 1100(1)(t), (ta), Reg. Sch. II:Cl. 1(k), Sch. II:Cl. 1(m), Sch. II:Cl. 2(a), Sch. II:Cl. 2(c), Sch. II:Cl. 8(f), Sch. II:Cl. 8(g), Sch. II:Cl. 9(a), Sch. II:Cl. 9(e), Sch. II:Cl. 9(f), Sch. II:Cl. 29, Sch. II:Cl. 34, Sch. II:Cl. 40

**Genstar trusts**
- anti-avoidance rule, 104(7.1)

**Germany,** *see also* Foreign government
- compensation paid by, exempt, 81(1)(g)
- stock exchange recognized, Reg. 3201(d)
- universities, gifts to, Reg. Sch. VIII s. 11

**Gifts and donations**
- art created by the donor, 118.1(7)
- art flips, 46(5)
- capital dividend account, effect on, 89(1)"capital dividend account"(a)(i)(A)
- capital property, of, 110.1(3), 118.1(6)
- carryback from year of death, 118.1(4)

## Gifts and donations *(cont'd)*
- carryforward
  - - credit, 118.1(1)"total charitable gifts"
  - - deduction to corporation, 110.1(1)(a)
- charitable
  - - commuter's, 118.1(9)
  - - corporate, deduction for, 110.1(1)(a)
  - - total, 118.1(1)
- corporation, by
  - - amalgamation, effect of, 87(2)(v)
  - - capital property, 110.1(3)
  - - deduction for, 110.1(1)
  - - partnership, made by, 110.1(4)
  - - proof of, 110.1(2)
  - - winding-up, claim by parent, 88(1)(e.6)
- Crown, to, 110.1(1)(b), 118.1(1)
  - - total, 118.1(1)
- cultural, 110.1(1)(c), 118.1(1)
- deduction from tax, 118.1(3)
- deemed disposition at fair market value, 69(1)(b)(ii)
- ecologically sensitive land, 110.1(1)(d), 118.1(1)"total ecological gifts"
  - - easement, servitude or covenant, value of, 110.1(5), 118.1(12)
    - - - valuation applies for capital gains purposes, 43(2)
- gratuities, taxable as employment income, 5(1)
- insurance proceeds, direct designation, 118.1(5.1), (5.2)
- institutions, to, 110.1(1)(c)
- member of religious order vowing perpetual poverty, 110(2)
- non-qualifying security, credit disallowed, 118.1(13)
- ordering of claims for donations
  - - credits, 118.1(2.1)
  - - deductions (corporation), 110.1(1.1)(b)
- partnership, made by, 110.1(4), 118.1(8)
- proof of, required, 118.1(2)
- property, of, 69(1)(b), (c)
- RRSP or RRIF, direct designation, 118.1(5.3)
- reassessment, 152(6)(c)
- receipts for, Reg. 3501
- shares, publicly traded, 38(a.1)
- total, 118.1(1)
- United States charities, 118.1(9); Canada–U.S. Tax Convention Art. XXI:6
- will, by, 118.1(5)
  - - publicly traded securities, reduced capital gain, 38(a.1)(ii)
- windup, on, 88(1)(e.6)

**Glasses, as medical expense**, 118.2(2)(j)

**Global foreign expenses**
- defined, for resource expenses of limited partner, 66.8(1)(a)(i)(D)

**Global foreign resource limit**
- defined, 66.21(1)

**Goats**, 80.3(1)"breeding animals"

**Golf course, expense not allowed**, 18(1)(l)

**Goods**, *see also* Property
- to be delivered
  - - amounts received for, income, 12(1)(a)(i)
    - - - repayment of, deductible, 20(1)(m.2)
- undelivered, reserve for, 20(1)(m)

**Goods and services tax (GST)**, *see also* Excise Tax Act
- change of use, timing rule for GST liability, 248(15)
- credit, *see* refundable credit *below*
- defined, 248(1)
- employee benefits
  - - GST included in taxable benefit, 6(7)
  - - rebate included in income, 6(8)
- home purchase, excluded from moving expenses, 62(3)(f)
- input tax credit
  - - deemed to be assistance, 248(16), *see also* Assistance/government assistance
  - - repaid, deemed to be reduction in assistance, 248(18)
- rebate
  - - deemed not to be reimbursement, 8(11)
  - - deemed to be assistance, 248(16), *see also* Assistance/government assistance
  - - included in income, 6(8), 12(1)(x)
  - - reduces capital cost of property, 6(8), 13(7.1)
- refundable credit, 122.5
  - - "adjusted income" defined, 122.5(1)
  - - amount of credit, 122.5(3)
  - - applied to tax liability, timing, 164(2.1)
  - - determination by Minister, 152(1)(b)
  - - "eligible individual" defined, 122.5(1)
  - - limit to one per family, 122.5(5)(a)
  - - overpayment not to require interest, 160.1(1)
  - - penalty for false statement, 163(2)(c.1)
  - - "qualified relation"
    - - - deceased eligible individual, of, 122.5(6)
    - - - defined, 122.5(1)
    - - - jointly liable for repayment of excess, 160.1(1.1)
  - - repayment where excess credit paid, 160.1(1.1)
  - - restrictions, 122.5(5)
- shareholder benefits
  - - GST included in taxable benefit, 15(1.3)

**Goodwill**, *see also* Eligible capital property
- sale of, 14(1); ITAR 21

**Governing plan**
- defined, Reg. 4901(2)

**Government**, *see also* Crown; Crown corporation
- administration of income tax, *see* Minister (of National Revenue); Canada Customs and Revenue Agency
- agreements
  - - for tax transfer payments (federal-provincial), 154
  - - with other countries, *see* Tax treaty
- annuities
  - - contracts entered into before May 26, 1932, 58(1)
  - - contracts entered into from May 25, 1932 to June 25, 1940, 58(2)
- assistance, *see* Assistance/government assistance
- bonds (and similar obligations)
  - - Canada Savings Bonds, cash bonus, 12.1
  - - "investment property" for deposit insurance corporation, 137.1(5)"qualified expenditure"
  - - issued at a discount, 16(3)
  - - no non-resident withholding tax, 212(1)(b)(ii)(C)
- bound
  - - by deemed trust for tax withheld, 227(4.3)
  - - by garnishment orders, 224(1.4)
  - - by regulations requiring information returns, 221(3)
  - - by withholding tax requirements, 227(11)

# Index

Government *(cont'd)*
- communication of confidential information to, 241(4)
- contract payments, information return, Reg. 237
- employees abroad, deemed resident, 250(1)(b)–(f)
- foreign, *see* Foreign government
- gifts to
  - by corporation, deduction, 110.1(1)(b)
  - by individual, credit, 118.1(1)
- grant, *see also* Assistance/government assistance
  - acquisition of depreciable property, towards, 13(7.1), (7.2)
  - cost base of property acquired, 53(2)(k)
  - energy conversion, 12(1)(u), 56(1)(s), *see also* Energy: conversion grant
  - home insulation, 12(1)(u), 56(1)(s), *see also* Home insulation grant
  - prescribed programs, under, 56(1)(s)
- Her Majesty, defined, *Interpretation Act* 35(1)
- international development assistance program, *see* Canadian International Development Agency
- lobbying, *see* Representation expenses
- obligation issued at discount by, 16(2), (3)
- officials, bribery of, no deduction, 67.5
- privatization of assets, debt qualifies for deferred income plans, Reg. 4900(1)(q)
- provincial, *see* Province
- public body performing function of, exempt, 149(1)(c)
- reporting of contract payments, Reg. 237
- representation, *see* Representation expenses
- rights, transitional rules, ITAR 21
- -sponsored retirement arrangement, Reg. 8308.4
  - excluded from registered pension plan eligibility, Reg. 8502(m)
  - information return, Reg. 8402.1
- support payments for farmers, information slips, Reg. 234–236
- volunteer firefighter's allowance paid by
  - deduction for, 8(1)(a) [to be repealed]
  - exemption for, 81(4)

**Government-sponsored retirement arrangement**
- defined, Reg. 8308.4(1)
- information return, Reg. 8402.1
- prescribed reduction in RRSP limit, Reg. 8308.4(2)

**Governor General in Council**
- defined, *Interpretation Act* 35(1)

**Governor General (of Canada)**
- defined, *Interpretation Act* 35(1)
- stipend exempt, 81(1)(n)

**Grain**
- delivered, amount due deemed not income debt, 76(4)

**Grain elevator operators**
- taxable income earned in a province, Reg. 408

**Grain storage facilities**
- capital cost allowance, additional, Reg. 1100(1)(sb)

**Grandchild**
- dependent, 118(6)(a)
- treated as child, *see* Child: extended meaning of

**Grandfathered plan (registered pension plan)**
- complying before March 1996 budget, Reg. 8509(13)
- defined, Reg. 8500(1)

**Grandfathered share**
- defined, 248(1)
- dividend on, where deemed to be interest, 258(3)(b)(i)
- excluded from definition of "short-term preferred share", 248(1)
- excluded from definition of "taxable preferred share", 248(1)
- excluded from restriction on dividend deductibility, 112(2.2)(d) [to be repealed], 112(2.21)(b) [draft]
- may be a taxable RFI share, 248(1)"taxable RFI share"
- Part VI.1 tax, excluded from, 191(2)(b)(iii), 191.1(2)(b), 191.1(4)(b)
- share exchanged for, excluded from Part IV.1 tax, 187.3(2)

**Grandfathering**, *see also* Grandfathered share; Transitional rules
- Canadian newspaper or periodical, 19(7)
- passive partnership interest acquired before Feb. 22/94, 40(3.1), (3.15)–(3.18)
- RESP investments, 146.1(1)"qualified investment"(d)
- taxable Canadian property only since April 26/95, prorating of gain, 40(9)
- trust established before June 18/71, low tax rates, 122(2)

**Grandparent**
- dependent, 118(6)(b)
- includes in-law or in common-law, 252(2)(d)

**Grant**, *see also* Government: grant
- Canada Oil Substitution Program, *see* Energy: conversion grant
- Canadian Home Insulation Program, *see* Home insulation grant
- exploration and development, 20(1)(kk)
- "non-government assistance" defined, 127(9)
- research
  - income from, 56(1)(o)
  - leaving Canada to pursue research under, 115(2)(b.1)

**Gratuities**, *see* Tips

**Grazing ungulates**, 80.3(1)"breeding animals"

**Great-aunt/great-uncle**
- defined, 252(2)(f)

**Green card holder**
- whether resident in U.S. for treaty purposes, Canada–U.S. Tax Convention Art. IV:1

**Greenhouse**
- capital cost allowance for, Reg. Sch. II:Cl. 6(d), Sch. II:Cl. 8(m)

**Gross Canadian life investment income**
- defined, Reg. 2400(1)

**Gross compensation**
- defined, 163.2(1), (12)(c)

**Gross cost**
- defined, Reg. 5202, 5204

**Gross entitlements**
- defined, for third-party penalty, 163.2(1)

**Gross investment revenue**
- insurer's, defined, 138(12)"gross investment revenue"

**Gross negligence**
- by issuer of small business bond, 15.2(5)
- by issuer of small business development bond, 15.1(5)
- effect on adjustment to related person's tax, Canada–U.S. tax treaty Art. IX:5
- failure to report exempt capital gain, exemption lost, 110.6(6)

Gross negligence *(cont'd)*
- penalty for failure to remit tax withheld, 227(9)(b), 227(9.1)
- penalty for failure to withhold tax, 227(8)(b)
- penalty for false statements of omissions, 163(2)
- - re flow-through share or joint exploration corporation, 163(2.2), (2.3)

Gross resource profits
- defined, Reg. 1204(1)

Gross revenue
- defined, 248(1)
- - limitation re non-profit R&D corporation, 149(9)
- - special rules re transfer pricing, 247(5), (9)
- from a mine, defined, Reg. 1104(5.1), (5.2)

Gross revenue insurance program
- payments to farmers under, income, 12(1)(p)
- premiums in respect of, deductible, 20(1)(ff)

Gross tax attributes (debt forgiveness rules)
- defined, 80(14.1)
- inclusion in residual balance, 80(14)(a)

Gross-up
- dividends, 82(1)(b)

Gross-up factor
- defined, 94.2(1)(c)

Group
- defined
- - for associated corporations, 256(1.2)(a)
- - for surplus stripping rules, 84.1(2.2), 212.1(3)(d)(i)
- related, defined, 251(4)"related group"
- unrelated, defined, 251(4)"unrelated group"

Group disability benefits
- top-up payments by employer on insolvency of insurer, 6(17), (18)
- - reimbursement to employer, 8(1)(n.1)

Group home care
- medical expense credit, 118.2(2)(b.2)

Group insurance plan
- employer's contributions to
- - top-up payments on insolvency of insurer, *see* Group disability benefits
- - whether included in employee's income, 6(1)(a)(i), 6(1)(f)

Group term insurance policy
- definition, re insurer, 138(15)
- demutualization of insurance corporation, effect on insured, 139.1(15)
- 1975–76 excess reserve, defined, 138(12)"1975–76 excess additional group term reserve"

Group term life insurance policy
- defined, 248(1)
- - for investment income tax, Reg. 1900(1)
- limitation on deduction of premiums, 18(9.01)
- taxable benefit from, 6(4), Reg. 2700–2704

Grubstaker, 35
- receipt of shares by
- - deduction from amount, 110(1)(d.2)

Guarantee
- acquired from insurer or moneylender in amalgamation, 87(2)(h)(iii)
- loan to spouse or minor, of, 74.5(7)
- payment under
- - by shareholder of corporation, 20(3.1)
- - debt forgiveness rules, 80(2)(l)
- - when treated as debt, 39(12)
- - reserve for, 12(1)(d.1), 20(1)(l.1)
- - no deduction, 20(7)
- revenue, prescribed, Reg. 7500

Guarantee agreement
- defined, 112(2.2)(a)
- no deduction for dividend, 112(2.2)–(2.22)

Guarantee fees
- deduction re, 20(1)(e.1)
- non-resident, 214(15)

Guarantee fund
- deduction for payment by insurance corporation to, Reg. 1400(3)G

Guaranteed interest
- defined, Reg. 1900(1)

Guaranteed share
- deemed dividend on reduction of paid-up capital, 84(4.3)
- restriction on dividend deductibility, 112(2.2)–(2.22), 258(3)

Guardian, return by, 150(1)(d), (e)

Guide dog expenses, 118.2(2)(l)

Guilt, *see* Offences

*Gulf Canada* case overturned re resource allowance, Reg. 1204(1)

Gypsum
- extraction of, 248(1)"mineral resource"(d)(ii)

## H

HBP, *see* Home Buyers' Plan

HBP balance
- defined, for Home Buyers' Plan, 146.01(1)

HRD, *see* Human Resources Development Canada

Habitation, right of (Quebec)
- deemed to be trust, 248(3)

Half-year rule, depreciable property, Reg. 1100(2)–(2.4)

Halifax disaster pension, exempt, 81(1)(f)

Halite
- drilling and exploration for, 66(2)
- extraction of, 248(1)"mineral resource"(d)(ii)

Handicapped persons, *see* Mental or physical impairment

Hangar, capital cost allowance, Reg. Sch. II:Cl. 6(h)

Hardship, *see* Undue hardship

Harness
- capital cost allowance, Reg. Sch. II:Cl. 10(c)

Headings in legislation
- relevance of, *Interpretation Act* s. 14

Head lease, defined, 209(1)
- "term" defined, 209(1)

Health care plan, *see* Private health services plan

Health counselling, *see* Counselling services

Health promotion surtax, 182, 183

Health services plan
- employer's contribution to
- - not includable in employee's income, 6(1)(a)(i)
- private, premiums to, 118.2(2)(q)

Hearing aid, medical expense, 118.2(2)(i)

**Hearing impairment**, *see also* Deaf person
- devices to assist person with
  - business expense, 20(1)(rr)
  - medical expense credit, Reg. 5700(q.1)
- sign language interpretation services for, 118.2(2)(l.4)

**Hearing officer**
- powers of, 231.4(3), (4)

**Hearse**
- excluded from definition of automobile, 248(1)"automobile"(c)

**Heart pacer/monitor**
- medical expense, Reg. 5700(d)

**Heat distributor**
- equipment, capital cost allowance, Reg. Sch. II:Cl. 34

**Heat production/distribution equipment**
- capital cost allowance, Reg. Sch. II:Cl. 1(p), Sch. II:Cl. 2(f)

**Heat recovery equipment**
- capital cost allowance, Reg. Sch. II:Cl. 34

**Heating expenses**
- relief from in 2000–01, 122.5[end]

**Heavy water**
- capital cost allowance for, Reg. Sch. II:Cl. 26

**Heir**, *see also* Legal representative
- deemed to be legal representative, 248.1"legal representative"
- obligations of, 159
- return required by, 150(3)

**Hepatitis C trust**
- income of, non-taxable, 81(1)(g.3)

**Her Majesty**, *see* Crown; Government

**Herd**, *see* Basic herd

**High school**, *see* Secondary school

**History preservation rules**, *see* Debt forgiveness: history preservation rules

**Hockey players or referees**, *see* Athlete

*Hoefele* **case overruled**, 6(23)

**Hogs**, *see* Swine

**Holding corporation (insurance demutualization)**
- deemed not to be taxable Canadian property, 141(4)
- deemed to be public corporation, 141(3)
- defined, 139.1(1)
- dividend received by, no tax, 112(1)

**Holiday**
- deadline expiring on, *Interpretation Act* s. 26
- defined, *Interpretation Act* s. 35(1)
- includes Sunday, *Interpretation Act* s. 35(1)"holiday"

**Holocaust survivor's compensation, exempt**, 81(1)(g)

**Home**, *see also* Principal residence
- defined, for Home Buyers' Plan withholding exemption, Reg. 104(4)
- loss in value of, reimbursement, *see* Housing loss
- maintenance of after moving away, deduction, 62(3)(g)
- sale of, *see* Principal residence

**Home Buyers' Plan**, 146.01
- death of taxpayer, 146.01(6), (7)
- definitions, 146.01(1)
- repayment of funds borrowed from RRSP, 146.01(3)
- withdrawal of funds from RRSP, 146.01(8), Reg. 104(3)
  - within 90 days of contribution, deduction disallowed, 146(5)(a)(iv.1), 146(5.1)(a)(iv)
- withholding tax exemption, Reg. 104(3)–(4)

**Home construction costs**
- medical expense, 118.2(2)(l.21)

**Home insulation grant**
- included in income, 12(1)(u), 56(1)(s)
- information return re, Reg. 224
- non-resident taxable on, 212(1)(s)
- prescribed program, Reg. 5500

**Home mortgage**, *see* Mortgage

**Home office expenses**, *see* Work space in home

**Home purchase loan**
- balance outstanding after 5 years deemed new loan, 80.4(6)
- defined, 80.4(7)
- employee or spouse, to, 15(2)(a)(ii), 15(2.4)(b)
- interest on, 80.4(4), (5)

**Home relocation loan**
- balance outstanding after 5 years deemed new loan, 80.4(6)
- deduction for, 110(1)(j)
- defined, 248(1)
- interest on, 80.4(4), (5)
- replacement of, 110(1.4)

**Home renovations (wheelchair access etc.)**
- driveway alterations, 118.2(2)(l.6)
- medical expense, 118.2(2)(l.2), Reg. 5700

**Homosexual relationships**, *see* Common-law partner

**Hong Kong**, *see also* Foreign government
- stock exchange recognized, Reg. 3201(e)
- universities, gifts to, Reg. Sch. VIII s. 19

**Horse**
- basic herd maintained since 1971, deduction, 29
- breeding, 80.3(1)"breeding animals"(a)
- inventory, valuation of, 28(1.2)
- maintaining for racing, constitutes farming, 248(1)"farming"

**Hospital bed**
- medical expense, Reg. 5700(h)

**House**
- insulation, *see* Home insulation grant
- sale of, *see* Principal residence

**House of Commons**
- election of members, contributions for, 127(3)–(4.2)

**Housing company**
- limited-dividend
  - exemption, 149(1)(n)

**Housing corporation, exemption**, 149(1)(i)

**Housing loan**, *see* Home purchase loan

**Housing loss**
- defined, 6(21)
- eligible
  - defined, 6(22)
  - taxable benefit from, 6(1)(a), 6(20)
- taxable benefit from, 6(1)(a), 6(19), (20)

**Housing subsidy**
- taxable benefit, 6(23)

**Housing unit**, *see also* Principal residence
- change in use of, ITAR 26.1(1)

## Index

**Human Resources Development Canada**
- advice re mental or physical impairment, 118.3(4)
- certification of educational institution, 118.5(1)(a)(ii), 118.6(1)"designated educational institution"(a)(ii)
- disclosure of information to, 241(4)(d)(vii.1), (x)
- eligible individuals for Child Tax Benefit, 122.62, 165(3.1), (3.2), Reg. 6301
- Social Insurance Number application, 237(1); Reg. 3800

**Husband and wife**, *see* Spouse

**Hutterite colonies, taxation**, 143, *see also* Communal organization

**Hydro electric installation**
- capital cost allowance, Reg. Sch. II:Cl. 34

**Hydrocarbons**
- determination of viscosity and density, Reg. 1107

### I

**IAAC**, *see* Income-averaging annuity contract
**IATA**, *see* International Air Transport Association
**IBC**, *see* International banking centre
**IRA**, *see* Individual Retirement Account
**IRS**, *see* Internal Revenue Service (U.S.)
**ISIP**, *see* Indexed security investment plan
**ITC**, *see* Investment tax credit

**Ice storm**
- extended deadlines
  - LSVCC investments, 127.4(5.1)
  - RRSP contributions, 146(22)
- non-taxable employee reimbursements, *Ice Storm Employment Benefits Remission Order*

**Identical properties**
- deemed, for superficial loss and pregnant loss rules
  - capital property, 40(3.5)
  - eligible capital property, 14(12)
  - inventory, 18(16)
- defined, 248(12)
  - for matchable expenditure rules, 18.1(12)
- gain or loss from, 47
- life insurance corporation, of, 138(11.1)
- non-qualifying real property, 110.6(18)
- property owned since before 1972, ITAR 26(8)–(8.5)
- whether foreign property, 206(1.4)

**Identification number**, *see* Social insurance number; Tax shelter: identification number

**Iliostomy pads, as medical expense**, 118.2(2)(i)

**Illegal payments**
- when not deductible, 67.5

**Immigration**, *see* Becoming resident in Canada

*Immigration Act*
- refugee under, *see* Refugee

**Immigration trust**
- five year non-taxability, 94(1)(b)(i)(A)(III) [to be repealed], 94(1)"connected contributor"(a) [proposed]

**Immovable property**, *see also* Real property
- defined, *Income Tax Conventions Interpretation Act* s. 5

**Immune system deficiency**
- air or water purifier for, medical expense credit, Reg. 5700(c.1), (c.2)

**Impaired loans**
- reserve for, 20(1)(l)(ii)

- no deduction when property seized by creditor, 79.1(8)
- no interest income inclusion, 12(4.1)

**Impairment**, *see* Mental or physical impairment
**Imposition of tax**, *see* Liability for tax; Rates of tax
**Imprisonment**, *see* Offences

**In camera proceedings**
- discipline etc., of authorized individual, to protect taxpayer information, 241(4.1)
- in Federal Court, 179
- review of jeopardy assessment, 225.2(10)
- review of solicitor-client privilege claim, 232(5)

**Inadequate considerations**, 69
- exceptions to fair market value deeming provision, ITAR 32
- property acquired by gift or inheritance, 69(1)(c)
- property distributed to shareholder, 69(4), (5)
- purchase price in excess of fair market value, 69(1)(a)
- sale price below fair market value, 69(1)(b)

**Income**
- accumulating in a trust, 104(14), Reg. 2800
- active business, defined, 125(7)"income of the corporation for the year from an active business"
- alimony, 56(1)(b)
- allocation, *see* Income allocation
- amount not previously included, ITAR 17(5)
- annuity, 56(1)(d), (d.2)
  - capital element, deductible, 60(a)
- assistance, *see* Older Worker Adjustment, Program for; Social assistance payment
- automobile standby charge, 6(1)(e)
  - car salesperson/lessor, 6(2.1)
  - reasonable amount, 6(2)
- automotive pact, transitional assistance, 56(1)(a)(v)
- averaging, *see* Averaging of income; Income-averaging annuity contract
- beneficiary of trust, 104(13), (14), (15)
- blocked currency, in, 161(6)
- bond, *see also* Bond
- bursary, 56(1)(n)
- business or property, from, *see* Business or property income
- Canada Pension Plan benefits, 56(1)(a)(i)
- capital and, combined, 16(1), (4), (5)
  - paid to non-resident, 214(2)
- cash method of reporting (farmers), 28
- chief source of, 31
- cod fisherman, *see* Fishing: compensation programs
- computation of, *see* Computation of income
- death benefit, 56(1)(a)(iii)
- debenture, *see* Bond
- deferred profit sharing plan, receipts from, 56(1)(i)
- destruction of livestock, from, *see also* Livestock
- determination of, by Minister, 152(1.11), (1.12)
- dividends, 82(1)
  - non-resident corporation, from, 90
- "earned" for RRSP purposes, defined, 146(1)"earned income"
- "earned in the year in a province" defined, 120(4)
- earned in the year in a province by an individual, defined, Reg. Part XXVI
- earned or realized by any corporation after 1971, 55(2), (5)(b), (c)
- employee benefits plan

2730

Index

Income *(cont'd)*
- • benefits, 6(1)(g)
- employment benefits, 6(1)
- employment insurance benefits, 6(1)(f), 56(1)(a)(iv)
- exclusions from, *see* Exemptions
- exempt, *see* Exemptions
- exploration and development expenses, recovery of, 59(3.2)
- "for the year" defined, 56(9)
- foreign resource property disposed of, 59(1)
- from active business, defined, 95(1), 125(7)
- from property, for dividend refund, 129(4)"income"
- gaining or producing, purpose, 18(1)(a), Reg. 1102(1)(c)
- grants under certain government programs, 56(1)(s)
- indirect payments, 56(2)
- international banking centre, from, 33.1(3), (4), (5), (11)(c)
- "investment income" defined, 110.6(1)
- *Labour Adjustment Benefits Act*, benefits under, 56(1)(a)(vi), Reg. 5502(a)
- legal costs recovered, 56(1)(l), (l.1)
- life insurance policy
- • proceeds of disposition of interest in, 56(1)(j)
- logging operations, from, defined, 127(2)"income for the year from logging operations in the province"
- maintenance payments, 56(1)(b), (c), (c.2)
- non-resident, of, 250.1(b)
- non-resident-owned investment corporation, 133(1)
- none, equivalent to zero income, 3(f)
- office or employment, from, 5(1), 6(1)
- old age security, 56(1)(a)(i)
- other sources of, 56–59.1
- pension, 56(1)(a)(i), 57
- place, from sources in, 4
- policyholder's, 148(1), (1.1)
- prescribed provincial pension plan benefits, 56(1)(a)(i)
- prize for achievement, 56(1)(n)
- professional business, from, 34; ITAR 23
- Program for Older Worker Adjustment, income assistance, 56(1)(a)(vi), Reg. 5502(b)
- property transferred to minor, from
- • imputed to transferor, 75(2)
- property transferred to spouse, from, 212(12)
- property transferred to spouse or minor, 74.1
- refund of payments, deductible, 60(q)
- registered education savings plan, amounts received, 56(1)(q)
- registered retirement income fund, amounts received, 56(1)(t)
- registered retirement savings plan, amounts received from, 56(1)(h)
- repeated failures to report, penalty for, 163(1)
- research grant, 56(1)(o)
- resource property disposed of
- • prior reserve for uncollected amount, 59(2)
- retirement compensation arrangement
- • benefits under, 56(1)(x), (z)
- • disposition of interest in, 56(1)(y)
- retiring allowance, 56(1)(a)(ii)
- rights to, transferred, 56(4)
- • non-resident tax not applicable, 212(12)
- salary deferral arrangement, benefit under, 56(1)(w)
- scholarship, 56(1)(n)
- • refund of, 56(1)(p)

- social assistance payments, 56(1)(u)
- source, from, 4
- splitting, *see* Attribution rules
- superannuation benefits, 56(1)(a)(i), 57
- supplementary unemployment benefits, 56(1)(g)
- support payments, 56(1)(b), (c), (c.2)
- tax on, *see also* Tax
- • non-deductible, 18(1)(t)
- taxable, *see* Taxable income
- taxation year, for, 3
- transitional assistance under auto pact, 56(1)(a)(v)
- trust, of
- • accumulating, *see* Accumulating income (of trust)
- • defined, 108(3)
- unemployment insurance benefits, 56(1)(a)(iv)
- workers' compensation benefits, 56(1)(v)

**Income allocation**
- defined, re foreign investment entity, 94.1(5)

**Income attribution**, *see* Attribution rules

**Income averaging**, *see* Averaging of income

**Income-averaging annuity contract**
- ceasing to be such, 61.1(1)
- deemed proceeds of disposition, income, 56(1)(f)
- defined, 61(4), 248(1)
- emigration of beneficiary, no deemed disposition, 128.1(10)"excluded right or interest"(f)(ii)
- information return, Reg. 208
- money borrowed to buy
- • limitation on deduction for, 18(11)(a)
- payment for, deductible, 61(1)
- payment under
- • continuing, after death, 61.1(2)
- • non-resident, to, 212(1)(n)
- • remuneration, Reg. 100(1)
- • succession duties, deduction for, 60(m.1)
- proceeds of disposition, income, 56(1)(e)
- types of payments deductible when used to purchase, 61(2)
- withholding tax, 153(1)(k)

**Income bond**
- defined, 248(1)
- interest paid on, not deductible, 18(1)(g)
- payment on deemed to be a dividend, 15(3), (4)

**Income derived from mining operations**
- defined, Reg. 3900(2)

**Income from an active business**, *see* Active business: income from

**Income from a mine**
- defined, Reg. 1104(5), (6), (6.1)

**Income from property**, *see* Property: income from

**Income interest in trust**, *see also* Trust (or estate)
- cost of, 106(1.1)
- defined, 108(1), 248(1)
- disposition of, 106(2)
- income inclusion, 106(1)
- property distributed in satisfaction of, 106(3)

**Income maintenance insurance plan**
- employer's contribution, whether a taxable benefit, 6(1)(a)(i)
- payment to employee under, taxable, 6(1)(f); ITAR 19

**Income setoff adjustment**, *see* Transfer pricing income setoff adjustment

**Income splitting**, *see also* Attribution rules
- partnership income, 103
- tax on children at high rate, 120.4, *see also* Split income: tax on
- testamentary trusts, 104(2)

**Income tax**, *see* everywhere

**Income Tax Conventions Interpretation Act**, *see* Table of Contents

**Income War Tax Act**
- para. 5(1)(a), reference to depreciation, ITAR 18(4)
- para. 5(1)(u), deduction deemed depreciation, ITAR 18(5)
- para. 6(1)(n), provisos not applicable, ITAR 18(3)
- s. 8, amounts deductible, ITAR 29(34)
- subsecs. 8(6), (7), (7a) still applicable, ITAR 17(1)

**Incontinent person**, *see also* Mental or physical impairment
- products for use by, medical expense credit, 118.2(2)(i)

**Incorporated employee**, *see also* Personal services business
- overseas employment tax credit restricted, 122.3(1.1)

**Incorporated in Canada**
- defined, 248(1)"corporation" "corporation incorporated in Canada"

**Incorporation expenses**, *see* Eligible capital property

**Increase in capital**
- defined, for non-resident owned investment corporation, 133(8)

**Indebtedness**, *see also* Debt; Loan
- defined, for deemed settlement of debt on amalgamation, 80(3)
- income of foreign affiliate from, 95(2)(a.3), 95(2.4), (2.5)"indebtedness"
- to non-resident trust, reporting requirement, 233.5(1)

**Indemnity**
- payment, provincial, excluded from income, 81(1)(q)
- reserve for, not deductible, 20(7)

**Independent personal services**, Canada–U.S. Tax Convention Art. XIV

**Indexed debt obligation**
- adjusted cost base of, 53(1)(g.1), 53(2)(l.1)
- amount deemed paid and received as interest, 16(6), Reg. 7001
- deduction from income, 20(1)(c), 16(6)
- defined, 248(1)
- excluded from annual interest accrual rules, 12(3), 12(11)"investment contract"(k)
- interest included in income, 12(1)(c), 16(6)
- prescribed amount, Reg. 7001

**Indexed payment**
- defined, re indexed debt obligation, Reg. 7001(7)

**Indexed security investment plan**
- transition for 1986, 47.1(28)

**Indexing (for inflation)**
- Child Tax Benefit, 122.61(5)
- GST Credit, 122.5(3.1)
- tax brackets and dollar thresholds, 117.1(1), (1.1)

**Indians**
- credit for First Nations Tax payable, 120(2.2)
- exemption from tax, 81(1)(a)

**Indicator re foreign trust**, *see* Non-arm's length indicator

**Indirect assistance**
- taxable, 12(1)(x)(i)(C)

**Indirect payments**
- corporation, by
- - person paid through intermediary as proceeds of disposition of property, 183.1(5)
- deemed income, 56(2)
- distribution of corporate surplus, tax on, 183.1(5)

**Individual**
- bankrupt, 128(2)
- computation of tax, 117–122.3
- computation of taxable income, order of application, 111.1
- credits, 118–118.94
- defined, 248(1)
- drilling exploration expenses, ITAR 29(12)
- fiscal period of, 249.1(1)(b)(i)
- gifts, deduction from tax, 118.1(3)
- income earned in the year in a province, Reg. Part XXVI
- "income for the year" defined, 120(3)
- instalment base, Reg. 5300
- instalment payments, 155, 156
- - "instalment base" defined, 161(9)(a)
- - insufficient instalment payments
- - interest limitation, 161(4)
- mentally or physically impaired, *see* Mental or physical impairment
- over 65, deduction, 118(2)
- - unused, transfer to spouse, 118.8
- payment of tax, 155, 156
- - instalment base, 155(2), 156(3)
- - remainder, 158
- "qualified farm property" of, defined, 108(1)
- "qualified small business corporation share" of, defined, 108(1)
- rates of tax, 117(2)
- - abatement re provincial schooling allowance, 120(2)
- - addition to tax for income not earned in province, 120(1)
- - annual adjustment, 117.1
- resident for part of year, 114, 114.1
- returns, 150(1)(d), (e)
- surtax, 180.1
- tax credits, 118
- - ordering of, 118.92
- taxation year of, 249(1)(b)

**Individual Retirement Account**, *see* Foreign retirement arrangement

**Inducement payments**
- cancellation of lease, *see* Lease cancellation payment
- election re adjusted cost base, 53(2)(s), 53(2.1)
- election to offset against outlay or expense, 12(2.2)
- included in income, 12(1)(x)
- prescribed amount, Reg. 7300
- received by beneficiary of trust, or partner, 12(2.1)
- repayment of, 20(1)(hh)

**Industrial mineral mines**
- capital cost allowance, Reg. 1100(1)(g), 1104(3), Reg. Sch. V

**Industrial minerals**
- producing, excluded from M&P credit, 125.1(3)"manufacturing or processing"(g)

# Index

**Ineligible property**
- defined, for cost base bump on windup, 88(1)(c)(iii)–(vi)

**Infant**
- prone to sudden infant death syndrome
  - alarm, medical expense, Reg. 5700(r)

**Infirm beneficiary**
- defined, 94(1)"exempt foreign trust"(a)(i)(A) [proposed]

**Infirm dependant**, *see also* Mental or physical impairment
- credit for, 118(1)B(d), (e)
- preferred beneficiary election, 108(1)"preferred beneficiary"(a)(ii)(A)
- training courses to care for, medical expense, 118.2(2)(1.8)

**Inflation adjustment period**
- defined, re indexed debt obligations, Reg. 7001(7)

**Inflation indexing**, *see* Indexing (for inflation)

**Influence over remittances**
- liability of secured creditor, 227(5.2)–(5.4) (draft)

**Informal procedure appeals**, 170

**Information**
- communication of, 241, Reg. 3003
- demand for, 231.2(1)(a)
- exchange of between tax authorities, Canada–U.S. Tax Convention Art. XXVII
- failure to provide, in return, penalty for, 162(5)
- foreign-based, 231.6
- laid, *see* Information or complaint
- outside Canada
  - foreign-based information or document, 231.6
  - tax shelter investment information, 143.2(13), (14)
- requirement to provide, 231.2(1)(a)
- return, *see* Information return

**Information or complaint**
- laid or made, 244(1)
- limitation on prosecutions, 244(4)
- territorial jurisdiction, 244(3)
- two or more offences in one, 244(2)

**Information return**, Reg. 200–237
- bond interest, accrued, Reg. 211
- Canada Savings Bonds, cash bonus, Reg. 220
- ceasing to be resident in Canada, value of assets, 128.1(9)
- certified films, Reg. 225
- charity, 149.1(14)
- construction contracts, Reg. 238
- contract payments
  - construction, Reg. 238
  - federal government, Reg. 237
- corporation
  - transactions with non-resident, non-arm's length persons, 233.1
- demand for, 233
- distribution of taxpayer's portion of, Reg. 209
- electric, gas or steam corporations, Reg. 213
- electronic filing required, Reg. 205.1
- eligible funeral arrangement, Reg. 201(1)(f)
- emigration, value of assets, 128.1(9)
- employees stock option deferral, Reg. 200(5)
- employees profit sharing plan, Reg. 212
- energy conversion program, Reg. 224
- farm support payments, Reg. 234–236
- federal government contract, Reg. 237
- foreign affiliate, 233.4
- foreign plan PSPA, Reg. 8402(2)
- foreign property, Reg. 221
  - by corporation claiming not to be (for RRSP etc. investments), Reg. 221
  - investment in, 233.3
- foreign trust
  - distributions from, 233.5
  - indebtedness to, 233.5
  - transfers to, 233.2(4)
- government contract, Reg. 237
- government-sponsored retirement arrangement, Reg. 8402.1
- home insulation program, Reg. 224
- income-averaging annuity contract, disposition of, Reg. 208
- international banking centre, 33.1(12)
- legal representative, Reg. 206
- life insurer, Reg. 217
- making of regulations re, 221(1)(d)
- NISA Fund No. 2, Reg. 201(1)(e)
- non-profit organization, 149(12), 150(1)(a)
- non-profit R&D corporation, 149(7)
- non-resident claiming treaty protection, 150(1)(a)(ii)
- non-resident transactions, 233.1–233.7
- non-residents, payments to, Reg. 202, 203
- oil substitution program, Reg. 224
- Part IV.1 tax, 187.5
- Part VI.1 tax, 191.4(1)
- partnership, Reg. 229
- past service pension adjustment, Reg. 8402
- patronage payments, Reg. 218
- penalty for failure to make, 162(7)(a)
- pension adjustment, Reg. 8401
- pension adjustment reversal, Reg. 8402.01
- political contributions, 230.1(2), Reg. 2001
- public
  - registered charity, 149.1(14)
- qualified investments, Reg. 221
- registered Canadian amateur athletic association, Reg. 216
- registered education savings plan, 146.1(13.1), (15)
- registered home ownership savings plan, Reg. 223
- registered pension plan, Reg. 8409
- registered retirement income funds, Reg. 215
- registered retirement savings plan, Reg. 214
- resource flow-through shares, Reg. 228
- SR&ED corporation, 149(7)
- scientific research tax credits, Reg. 226
- security transactions, Reg. 230
- share-purchase tax credits, Reg. 227
- social assistance payment, Reg. 233
- Social Insurance Number, use of, 237(2)
- specified retirement arrangement PSPA, Reg. 8402(3)
- stock option deferral, Reg. 200(5)
- tax shelter promoter, 237.1(7), Reg. 231
- transactions with non-residents, 233.1–233.7
- trust or corporation re Part XI tax, 207
- video tapes, Reg. 225
- withholding of tax, Reg. 210
- workers' compensation payment, Reg. 232

**Inheritance**, *see also* Death of taxpayer
- debt forgiveness rules do not apply, 80(2)(a)

**In-home care of relative**
- tax credit, 118(1)B(c.1)

**Initial deadline**
- defined, for insurance demutualization, 139.1(1)

**Initial non-qualified investment**
- defined, 204

**Initial transportation charges**
- defined (for pre-1966 cars), Reg. 1102(11)

**Injection substances**
- deduction for, 20(1)(mm)

**Injury, personal, property acquired as award for income from, exempt**, 81(1)(g.1), (g.2)

**In-laws, dependent**, 118(6)(b)

**Input tax credit**, *see* Goods and services tax (GST): input tax credit

**Inquiry**
- authorized by Minister, 231.4
- compliance required, 231.5(2)
- rights of person subjected to, 231.4(6)
- rights of witness at, 231.4(5)
- seizure of documents
- • copies of, 232(13)

**Insider of a corporation**
- defined, Reg. 4803(1)

**Insolvency**, *see also* Bankruptcy; Financial difficulty (taxpayer in)
- insurance corporation, group disability insurance top-up payments, 6(17), (18)

**Inspections**, 231.1
- compliance required, 231.5(2), 231.7
- court order for compliance, 231.7

**Inspector**
- defined, for surveys under *Canada Shipping Act*, Reg. 3600(2)

**Instalment payments**
- capital and income combined, 16(1)
- ceasing to be resident in Canada, 159(4), (4.1) [to be repealed], 128.1(5) [draft]
- dependent on use, 12(1)(g)
- sale of property, *see* Reserve
- tax, of
- • amounts deemed to be, 161(8)
- • annual, deceased taxpayer's, Reg. 1001
- • contra interest, 161(2.2)
- • corporations, 157(1), (2), (2.1), (3)
- • *de minimis* rule, 156.1(1), 157(2.1)
- • death of taxpayer, not required after, 156.1(2)
- • deduction under s. 66.5, 196(3)
- • deficient
- • • interest offset method, 161(2.2)
- • • interest payable, 161(2)
- • • limitation re corporations, 161(4.1)
- • • penalty, 163.1
- • • when certain tax credits deemed paid, 161(10)
- • • where interest not payable, 161(2.1)
- • farmers, fishermen, 155, 156.1
- • individuals, 156, 156.1
- • instalment base, defined, 161(9)(a), Reg. Part LIII
- • late, penalty for, 163.1
- • mutual fund trust, 156(2)
- • offset interest, 161(2.2)
- • Part I.3 tax, 181.7
- • Part XII.3 tax, 211.3
- • transfers between accounts, 221.2
- testamentary trust, 104(23)(e)
- trust distributing property to non-resident, 107(5.1)

**Instalment threshold**
- defined, 156.1

**Institution**
- costs of care in, as medical expense, 118.2(2)(e)
- gifts to
- • by corporation, deduction for, 110.1(1)(c)
- • by individual, credit for, 118.1(1)"total cultural gifts"

**Instrument**, *see* Musical instrument

**Insulation grant**, *see* Home insulation grant

**Insulin, medical expense**, 118.2(2)(k)

**Insurance**
- accidental death, not included in group life insurance benefit, Reg. 2700(2)
- corporation, *see* Insurance corporation
- group plans
- • employer's contributions not includable in employee's income, 6(1)(a)(i)
- • • life insurance, portion of premium taxable, 6(4)
- paid-up, deduction for, 18(9.01)
- policy, *see* Insurance policy
- premiums, *see* Premium
- proceeds
- • in respect of depreciable property, taxable, 12(1)(f)
- risks in Canada, by foreign affiliate, 95(2)(a.2)
- sickness, accident, etc., benefits taxable, 6(1)(f); ITAR 19

**Insurance agent or broker**
- reserve for unearned commissions, 32

**Insurance corporation**, *see also* Financial institution; Life insurance corporation
- amalgamation, 87(2.2)
- amortized cost, where meaning varied, 138(13)
- bad debts
- • deduction for, 20(1)(p)(ii)
- • inclusion in income, 12.4
- cash flow adjustment, Reg. 2412
- ceasing to carry on business, Reg. 8101(5)
- computation of income, 138(1), (6), 138(9), 140
- deduction for amounts paid or credited to policyholders, 140(1)
- deductions not allowed, 138(5)–(5.2), (8)
- deemed not to be private corporation, 141.1
- defined, 248(1)
- definitions, 138(12)
- demutualization, 139.1
- deposit, *see* Deposit insurance corporation
- depreciation deemed to have been allowed, 13(22)
- disposition of Canadian securities, 39(5)(e)
- earthquake reserves, Reg. 1400(3)L
- exempt under Part IV, 186.1(b)
- farmers and fishermen, of
- • exemption for, 149(1)(t), 149(4.2)
- • • limitation, 149(4.1)
- foreign affiliate, *see* Foreign affiliate: insurer
- gross investment revenue, defined, 138(12)

2734

# Index

Insurance corporation *(cont'd)*
- guarantee fund, deduction for payment to, Reg. 1400(3)G
- guarantees etc.
  - • acquired from, in amalgamation, 87(2)(h)(iii)
  - • reserve for, 20(1)(l.1)
- inclusion in computing income for 1988 taxation year, 140(2)
- income from participating life insurance business, Reg. 2402
- insolvent, group disability insurance top-up payments, 6(17), (18)
- liabilities of, determination for debt forgiveness reserve, 61.3(1)(b)C(ii)(B), (C)
- life, *see* Life insurance corporation
- loan/lending asset
  - • acquired from, in amalgamation, 87(2)(h)(ii)
  - • reduction in value of
    - • • limitation on deduction re, 18(1)(s)
- loans etc. acquired in ordinary course of business, 20(27)
- mark-to-market rules apply, 138(10)
- mutualization proposal, 139
- negative reserves, 12(1)(e.1), 20(22), Reg. 1400(2)
- 1975 branch accounting election deficiency, defined, 138(12)
- 1975–76 excess additional group term reserve, defined, 138(12)
- 1975–76 excess capital cost allowance, defined, 138(12)
- 1975–76 excess investment reserve, defined, 138(12)
- 1975–76 excess policy dividend deduction, defined, 138(12)
- 1975–76 excess policy dividend reserve, defined, 138(12)
- 1975–76 excess policy reserve, defined, 138(12)
- 1977 carryforward deduction, Reg. 2408
- 1977 excess policy dividend deduction, Reg. 2407
- non-capital loss of, 111(7.1)
- non-resident, Reg. 219(4)–(8), 800, 801, 803, 804, 2401
  - • branch tax elections, Reg. 2403
  - • change in use rules, 138(11.3)–(11.41), (11.6)
  - • computation of income, 138(11.91)
  - • domestication of branch operation, 138(11.5)
  - • eligible property for transfer to corporation by shareholder, 85(1.1)(b)
  - • excluded property, Reg. 810
  - • qualified related corporation, 138(12)
  - • registered, *see* Registered non-resident insurer
  - • transfer of insurance business
    - • • anti-avoidance provisions, 138(11.7)
    - • • computation of income, 138(11.92)
    - • • contributed surplus, computation of, 138(11.9)
    - • • depreciable property, rules re, 138(11.8)
    - • • paid-up capital, computation of, 138(11.7)
    - • • rules, 138(11.5)
  - • non-segregated property, 138(12)
  - • participating life insurance policy, defined, 138(12)
  - • policy loan, defined, 138(12), 148(9)
  - • policy reserves, Reg. 1400–1408
    - • • life insurance, 138(3)(a)(i)
      - • • • post-1995 policies, Reg. 1404
      - • • • pre-1996 policies, Reg. 1401(1)
    - • • negative, 20(1)(e.1), 20(22), Reg. 1400(2)
    - • • non-life insurance, 20(7)(c), Reg. 1400

- • • 1975-76 excess, defined, 138(12)
- • • regulations, Reg. 1400-1408
- property acquired on default in payment, 138(11.93)
- "property used by it in the year in, or held by it in the year in the course of", 138(12)
  - • • defined, Reg. 2400
- registered, *see* Registered non-resident insurer
- regulations, Reg. Part XXIV
- reserve for unpaid claims, *see also* policy reserves; unpaid claims reserve adjustment
  - • • life insurance, Reg. 138(3)(a)(ii)
    - • • • post-1995 policies, Reg. 1405
    - • • • pre-1996 policies, Reg. 1401(4)
  - • • limitation, 18(1)(e.1)
  - • • negative, 12(1)(e.1), 20(22), Reg. 1400(2)
- security used or held by
  - • • "eligible property" for transfer to corporation by shareholder, 85(1.1)(g)
- segregated funds of, 138.1, Reg. Part LXI
- subsidiary, wound up, 88(1)(g)
- surplus funds derived from operations, 138(12)
- tax payable by, under former Part IA, ITAR 60.1
- taxable capital gains, 138(2)(b), 142
- taxable income earned in a province, Reg. 403
- transfer of insurance business
  - • • by non-resident insurer, 138(11.5)
  - • • by resident insurer, 138(11.94)
- unpaid claims reserve adjustment, *see also* reserve for unpaid claims
  - • • claims incurred but not reported, Reg. 1400(3)D, E
  - • • deduction, 20(7), (26), Reg. 1400(3)D, E
  - • • inclusion of prescribed portion, 12.3
- variation in tax basis and amortized cost, 138(13)
- winding-up of, Reg. 8101(3)

**Insurance policy**
- acquisition costs, Reg. 1408(1)
- disposition of, 148
  - • no capital gain, 39(1)(a)(iii)
  - • no capital loss, 39(1)(b)(ii)
- life, *see* Life insurance policy
- loan, *see* Policy loan (life insurance)
- reserves (insurer), *see* Insurance corporation: policy reserves; Insurance corporation: reserve for unpaid claims
- rider, *see* Rider

**Insurance proceeds**
- constitute proceeds of disposition, 13(21)"proceeds of disposition"(c), 54"proceeds of disposition"(c)
- rollover where property replaced, 13(4), (4.1), 44

**Insurer**, *see also* Insurance corporation
- defined, re life annuity contracts, 148(10)(a), Reg. 217(1)

**Intangible property**, *see also* Eligible capital property
- patents, Reg. Sch. II:Cl. 14, Sch. II:Cl. 44
- relating to road, bridge, townsite, etc., capital cost, 13(7.5)(c)

**Integration**
- capital dividend flow-through, 83(2), 89(1)"capital dividend account"(b)
- corporate and personal tax, 82(1)(b), 121
- intercorporate dividend flow-through, 82(1)(a)(ii)(A), 112(1)
- Part IV tax flow-through, 186(1)(b)

**Inter vivos trust**, *see also* Trust (or estate)
- defined, 108(1)

**Inter-American Development Bank**
- bonds of
  - trust investing in, not foreign property, Reg. 5000(7)"specified international finance trust"(c)(i)(F)

**Intercorporate dividends generally tax-free**, 112, 113

**Interest (in property, etc.)**
- beneficial, in trust, meaning of, 248(25)
- capital, in trust, *see also* Trust (or estate)
- family farm partnership, in, 110.6(1)
- income, in trust, *see also* Trust (or estate)
- investment, in business, ITAR 23(5)"investment interest" "1971 receivables"
- life, in real property, *see* Life estate in real property
- partnership, *see* Partnership interest
- policy loan, re, defined, 138(12), Reg. 1408(1)
- qualifying, *see* Qualifying interest (in respect of foreign affiliate)
- real property, in, defined, 248(4)
- taxable Canadian property, in, 115(3) [to be repealed], 248(1)"taxable Canadian property"(l) [draft]
- trust, *see* Trust (or estate): interest in

**Interest (monetary)**
- accrued
  - corporations, partnerships, trusts, 12(3)
  - deduction on disposition of debt obligation, 20(21)
  - deemed, 12(9)
  - inclusion in income, 12(3), (4), (9)
  - individuals, 12(4)
  - on amalgamation, 87(2)(j.4)
  - prescribed debt obligation, on, 12(9), Reg. 7000
  - to date of death, 70(1)(a)
- allowable refund of N.R.O., on, 133(7.01), (7.02)
- annual reporting, *see* accrued (*above*)
- benefit from loan, deemed to be, 80.5
- bond
  - accrued, to date of transfer, 20(14)
    - information returns, Reg. 211
  - purchased at discount, 16(3)
- borrowed money used to acquire land, on
  - defined, 18(3)"interest on debt relating to the acquisition of land"
  - not deductible, 18(2), (2.1)
  - partner, by, 18(2.1)
- borrowed money used to acquire property no longer owned, 20.1(1)
- borrowed money used to acquire SBDB, 15.1(4)
- borrowed money used to invest in deferred income plan, 18(11)
- borrowed money used to invest in shares, 20(1)(c), 20(1)(qq)
- capital and, combined, 16(1)
  - on expropriation assets, 80.1(3)
- capital gains refund, on
  - mutual fund corporation, 131(3.1), (3.2)
  - mutual fund trust, 132(2.1), (2.2)
- capitalization into cost of property, 21
- certain bonds etc., on
  - excluded from income, 81(1)(m)
- compounded daily, 248(11)
- coupons to be identified as to taxable and non-taxable obligations, 240(2)
- debt obligation, on, 20(14.1)

  - mark-to-market property of financial institution, 142.5(3)
- debt relating to the acquisition of land, on
  - defined, 18(3)"interest on debt relating to the acquisition of land"
- deductible, *see also* borrowed money used ... (*above*)
  - authorized foreign bank, 20.2
  - distribution of dividends of profits, 20.1
  - general rule, 20(1)(c)
  - loan by partner to partnership, 20(3.1)
  - loan by shareholder to corporation, 20(3.1)
  - paid under *Income Tax Act*, not deductible, 18(1)(t)
  - payment under guarantee by shareholder, 20(3.1)
  - purchase of shares, 20(1)(qq)
- deduction by certain corporations, limitation on, 18(4)–(6)
  - exception, 18(8)
- deemed
  - amount paid by credit union re member's share, 137(4.1)
  - benefit from loan, 80.5
  - certain shares, on, 258(5)
  - non-resident tax, 214(6), (14)
  - preferred shares, on, 258(3)
- deemed received by corporation on loan to non-resident, 17
- defined, *Income Tax Conventions Interpretation Act* s. 6
- dividend refund, on, 129(2.1), (2.2)
- escalating interest GICs, Reg. 7000(2)(c.1)
- expense
  - amount deductible, 20(1)(c), (d)
  - compound, 20(1)(d)
  - election to capitalize, 21(1)
  - employee's automobile or aircraft, 8(1)(j)(i)
  - limitation on deduction by certain corporations, 18(4)–(6)
  - minimum tax, 127.52(1)(b), (c), (c.2), (e.1)
  - policy loans, on, 20(2.1), 138(12)"interest" Reg. 4001
- expropriation assets, on
  - election re, 80.1(2)
- forgiven, 80(2)(b)
- income bond, on, deemed dividend, 15(3)
  - non-resident corporation, 15(4)
- income from business or property, 12(1)(c)
  - whether specified investment business, 125(7)"specified investment business"
- increasing rates, income accrual, Reg. 7000(2)(c.1)
- instalments of tax, late or insufficient, 161(2)
  - additional 3% payable, 161(3)
  - limitation, 161(4), (4.1)
  - not deductible, 18(1)(t)
  - offset, 161(2.2)
  - scientific research tax credit, when deemed paid, 161(10)
  - share-purchase tax credit, when deemed paid, 161(10)
  - where not payable, 161(2.1)
- interest repaid, on, 164(4)
- loss carryback, effect of, 161(7)
- loss of course of income, 20.1(1)
- obligation issued at a discount, 16(3)
- offset
  - arrears interest against refund interest, 161.1

## Index

Interest (monetary) *(cont'd)*
- • early instalments against late instalments, 161(2.2)
- paid on death duties, deduction, 60(d)
- • paid or payable, deduction for, *see* deductible (*above*)
- paid to non-resident, withholding tax, 212(1)(b)
- • by wholly-owned subsidiary, 218
- • to U.S. resident, Canada–U.S. Tax Convention Art. XI
- payable
- • carryback re minimum tax, no effect, 161(7)
- penalty, on, 161(11)
- penalty or bonus, treated as interest expense, 18(9.1)
- prepaid, deduction for, 18(9), (9.2)–(9.8)
- prescribed rate, Reg. 4301
- property transferred from spouse, 74.1
- rate reduction payments, treated as interest expense, 18(9.1)
- refunds and repayments, on, 164(3)–(4)
- repayment of, deduction for, 20(1)(ll)
- spouse, property transferred to, 74.1, *see also* Attribution rules
- student loan, paid, credit for, 118.62
- tax withheld but not remitted, on, 227(9.3)
- unclaimed at year-end
- • withholding tax, 153(4)
- • • effect of remittance, 153(5)
- unpaid tax, on, 161(1), 227(9.3); ITAR 62(2)
- • adjustment of foreign tax, 161(6.1)
- • income in blocked currency, 161(6)
- • loss carryback, effect of, 164(5), (5.1)
- • none, re participation certificate, 161(5)
- • not deductible, 18(1)(t)
- • offset
- • • arrears interest against refund interest, 161.1
- • • early instalments against late instalments, 161(2.2)
- • Part III, 185(2)
- • Part IV, 187(2)
- • Part V, 189(7)
- • Part VII, 193(3), (4)
- • Part VIII, 195(3), (4)
- • Part X, 202(6)
- • Part XII.3, 211.5
- • Part XII.4 tax, 211.6(5)
- • retroactive to application date of provision, 221.1
- • waiver of, 220(3.1)
- withholding tax, 212(1)(b)

**Interest-free loan**, *see* Loan: interest-free

**Interference with remittances of tax withheld**, 227(5.2)–(5.4) (draft)

**Intergenerational transfers**
- attribution of income or loss, 74.1(2)
- farm property
- • inter vivos, 73(3)
- • on death, 70(9), (9.2)

**Interim receiver**
- withholding tax, liability for, 227(5), (5.1)(d)

**Internal Revenue Service (U.S.)**, *see also* United States
- collection of Canadian tax, Canada–U.S. Tax Convention Art. XXVI A
- competent authority procedures, Canada–U.S. Tax Convention Art. XXVI

- exchange of information with CCRA, Canada–U.S. Tax Convention Art. XXVII

**Internal waters**
- defined, *Interpretation Act* 35(1)

**International agencies, prescribed**, Reg. 806.1

**International Air Transport Association**
- employment income of non-Canadians, deduction for, 110(1)(f)(iv)

**International Bank for Reconstruction and Development**
- bonds of
- • trust investing in, not foreign property, Reg. 5000(7) "specified international finance trust"(c)(i)(G)

**International banking centre**, 33.1
- amalgamation, continuation of corporation on, 87(2)(j.8)
- definitions, 33.1(1), (2)
- designation of, 33.1(3)
- election re eligible deposit, 33.1(6)
- • restriction on, 33.1(7)
- eligible deposit, defined, 33.1(1)
- eligible loan
- • ceasing to be eligible, deemed disposition, 33.1(11)(a)
- • defined, 33.1(1)
- income/loss from
- • computation of, 33.1(4)
- • eligible deposit deductible only from, 33.1(8)
- • excluded from income, 33.1(3)
- • • exception, 33.1(9)
- • restriction, 33.1(5), (11)(c)
- information return, 33.1(12)
- loss from, not included in non-capital loss, 33.1(11)(b)

**International development assistance programs**
- employee under, no overseas employment tax credit, 122.3(1)(a)
- person working on deemed resident in Canada, 250(1)(d)
- prescribed, Reg. 3400

**International Finance Corporation**
- bonds of
- • eligible for RRSP investment, Reg. 4900(1)(l)(i.1)
- • trust investing in, not foreign property, Reg. 5000(7) "specified international finance trust"(c)(i)(H)

**International organization**
- employment income from
- • deduction, 110(1)(f)(iii)
- • tax credit, 126(3)
- interest paid to, withholding tax exemption, Reg. 806

**International shipping**
- aircraft used in
- • lease payments exempt from withholding tax, 212(1)(d)(xi)
- assets not subject to capital tax, 181.4(d)
- corporation, residence of, 250(6)
- non-resident's income from, exempt, 81(1)(c)

**International sport federation, eligibility requirements of**, *see* Amateur athlete trust

**International tax**
- conventions, *see* Tax treaty
- dividends received from foreign corporations, 90, 113
- foreign accrual property income, 91, 95

2737

International tax *(cont'd)*
- foreign tax credit, 126, *see also* Foreign tax credit
- treaties, *see* Tax treaty
- United States, rules re, *see* United States
- withholding tax, 212, *see also* Withholding tax

**International traffic**
- capital tax on ships and aircraft, Canada–U.S. Tax Convention Art. XXIII:3
- defined, 248(1), Canada–U.S. Tax Convention Art. III:1(h)
- employee employed in, Canada–U.S. Tax Convention Art. XV:3
- profits from, Canada–U.S. Tax Convention Art. VIII
- ship or aircraft operated by non-resident in
- • capital gains on, 115(1)(b)(ii)(B) [to be repealed], 248(1)"taxable Canadian property"(b)(ii) [draft]
- • deduction from taxable capital for large corporations tax, 181.4(d)(i)
- • income of non-resident exempt, 81(1)(c)
- • residence of shipping corporation, 250(6)

**Interpretation, 248–260**
- definitions, 248(1)
- *Income Tax Conventions Interpretation Act*, *see* Table of Contents
- *Interpretation Act*, *see* Table of Contents

**Interpretation services**
- sign language, medical expense credit, 118.2(2)(l.4)

**Inventory**
- adding property to, non-resident, 10(12), (14)
- adjustment
- • amalgamation, on, 87(2)(j.1)
- • deduction from income, 20(1)(ii)
- • inclusion in income, 12(1)(r)
- adventure in the nature of trade, 10(1.01)
- • superfical loss rule, 18(14)–(16)
- allowance, repealed [was 20(1)(gg)]
- amalgamation, on, 87(2)(b)
- artistic endeavour, of, 10(6)–(8)
- audit of, 231.1(1)(b)
- ceasing to use in business, non-resident, 10(12), (14)
- cost of
- • non-deductible expenses included in, 10(1.1)
- defined, 248(1)
- • specified debt obligation and mark-to-market property excluded, 142.6(3)
- "eligible property" for transfer to corporation by shareholder, 85(1.1)(f)
- examination of property in, 231.1
- exploration and development shares, 66.3(1)
- farming business, of, *see* Farming: inventory
- financial institutions, *see* Mark-to-market property
- manner of keeping, Reg. 1800
- mark-to-market rules, *see* Mark-to-market property
- non-resident, 10(12)–(14)
- removing property from, non-resident, 10(12), (14)
- reserve on sale of, 20(1)(n), 20(8)
- • where property repossessed by creditor, 79.1(4)
- sale of
- • after ceasing to carry on business, 23(1)
- • included in income, 9(1)
- • repossession by vendor in same taxation year, 79.1(5)
- share held as, stop-loss rules on disposition, 112(4)–(4.2)

- transfer to corporation, 85(1)(c.1), (e.3)
- valuation of, 10, Reg. 1801
- • adventure in the nature of trade, 10(1.01), (9)
- • • change in control of corporation, 10(10)
- • consistency required, 10(2.1)
- • farming business, 28(1.2), (1.3), Reg. 1802
- • incorrect, 10(3)
- • shares, 112(4.1)
- writedown, 10(1)
- • adventure in the nature of trade, 10(1.01), (9)
- • • change in control of corporation, 10(10)
- • of loan, denied, 18(1)(s)
- • superficial loss rule, 18(14)–(16)

**Investment**
- activity, *see* Investment activity
- allowance, *see* Investment allowance
- business, *see* Investment business
- corporation, *see* Investment corporation
- counselling, *see* Investment counselling fees
- income, *see* Investment income
- offshore, *see* Offshore investment fund
- qualified, *see* Qualified investment
- registered, tax re, 204.4–204.7
- tax credit, *see* Investment tax credit
- tax shelter, *see* Tax shelter: investment

**Investment activity (re foreign property rules)**
- defined, 206(1)

**Investment advice**, *see* Investment counselling fees

**Investment allowance**
- defined
- • for large corporations tax, 181.2(4), 181.3(4)
- • for Part XIV branch tax, 219(1)(j), Reg. 808

**Investment business**, *see also* Specified investment business
- of foreign affiliate
- • defined, 95(1)
- • excluded from active business, 95(1)"active business"(a)
- • start-up rule, 95(2)(k)(i)
- re foreign investment entity
- • defined, 94.1(1)
- re foreign property rules, *see* Investment activity

**Investment club**
- tax treatment, Information Circular 73-13 (no ITA provision)

**Investment contract**, *see also* Debt obligation
- anniversary day
- • accrued interest, 12(4)
- • defined, 12(11)
- defined, 12(11)

**Investment contract corporation, prescribed**, Reg. 6703
- exempt from Part IV tax, 186.1(b)

**Investment corporation**, 130
- deduction from tax, 130(1)
- defined, 130(3)(a), 248(1)
- election not to be restricted financial institution, 131(10)
- election re capital gains dividend, Reg. 2104
- flow-through entity for capital gains exemption, 39.1(1), (6)
- information return where share claimed to be qualified investment, Reg. 221

Investment corporation *(cont'd)*
- mortgage, *see* Mortgage investment corporation
- non-resident-owned, *see* Non-resident-owned investment corporation
- not subject to mark-to-market rules, 142.2(1)"financial institution"(c)(i)
- shares in, foreign property, 206(1)"foreign property"(e)
- special tax rate, 130
- taxed capital gains, 130(3)(a)
- that is not mutual fund corporation, 130(2)

**Investment counselling fees**
- deductible, 20(1)(bb)
- for RRSP or RRIF, non-deductible, 18(1)(u)

**Investment dealer**, *see also* Financial institution; Registered securities dealer
- defined, 142.2(1)
- subject to mark-to-market rules, 142.2(1)"financial institution"

**Investment expense, defined**, 110.6(1)

**Investment income**, *see also* Property: income from
- aggregate, *see* Aggregate investment income
- associated corporation, from, 129(6)
- Canadian, defined, 129(4)
- defined, 110.6(1)
- foreign, defined, 129(4)
- information returns, Reg. 201
- life insurer's, tax on, 211–211.6
- refundable tax on, 123.3

**Investment interest**
- in a business, ITAR 23(5)"investment interest" "1971 receivables"

**Investment loss**
- business, *see* Business investment loss

**Investment manager**
- defined, 44.1(1)"eligible pooling arrangement"

**Investment property**
- defined
  - - foreign affiliate, 95(1)
  - - foreign investment entity, 94.1(1)
  - - insurer, Reg. 2400(1)

**Investment shortfall**
- for labour-sponsored venture capital corporation, 204.82(2.1), (2.2)

**Investment tax credit**, 127(5)–(35)
- addition to, 127(10.1)
- amalgamation, on, 87(2)(oo)
- annual limit, defined, 127(9)
- assistance or government assistance, effect of, 127(18)–(21)
- - continuation of predecessors, 87(2)(qq)
- associated corporations, 127(10.3)
- - failure to file agreement, 127(10.4)
- available-for-use rule, 127(11.2), 248(19)
- certified property
- - ascertainment of, 127(10)(a), (b)
- - prescribed areas, Reg. 4602
- conversion of property to commercial use, 127(27)–(31)
- cooperative corporation, 127(6)
- deduction from Part I.1 surtax, 180.1(1.2), (1.3)
- defined, 127(9), (11.1), (12)–(12.2)
- definitions, 127(9)
- depreciable property acquired before change of control, 13(24), (25)
- expenditure limit, determination of, 127(10.2), (10.6)
- filing deadline, 37(11), 127(9)"investment tax credit"(m)
- included in income, 12(1)(t)
- - year of death, 70(1)(b)
- limited partner, of, 127(8.1)
- non-arm's length transactions, 127(11.6)–(11.8), (24)
- overpayment of tax as consequence of, 164(5), (5.1)
- parent's, after subsidiary wound up, 88(1)(e.3)
- partnership, allocation to partners, 127(8)
- - non-limited partners, 127(8.3)
- - recapture of, 127(28)
- qualified property, Reg. 4600
- - defined, 127(9), (11)
- R&D, *see* scientific research (below)
- reassessment, 152(6)(d)
- recapture of, 127(27)–(35)
- - deduction in later year, 37(1)(c.2)
- refundable, 127.1
- - defined, 127.1(2)
- - depreciable property acquired before change of control, 13(24), (25)
- renunciation of, by general partner, 127(8.4)
- repayment of assistance, 127(9)"investment tax credit"(e.1), 127(10.7)
- scientific research
- - basic 20% credit, 127(9) "investment tax credit"(a.1)
- - extra 15% credit, 127(10.1)
- small business, 127(9)"qualified small-business property" [repealed], 127(9)"specified percentage"(i)
- specified percentage, 127(9)
- super-R&D allowance by province, federal bonus, 127(9)"super-allowance benefit amount", 127(10.1)(b)
- "tax otherwise payable" defined, 127(17)
- trusts, allocation to beneficiaries, 127(7)
- - reduces cumulative Canadian exploration expense, 127(12.3)
- unpaid amounts, 127(26)
- where control of corporation acquired, 127(9.1), (9.2)
- windup of corporation, flow-through to parent, 88(1)(e.3)

**Investment trust**, *see* Mutual fund trust

**Investor (re Canadian film/video tax credit)**
- defined, 125.4(1)
- no film credit where amount can be deducted, 125.4(4)

**Involuntary dispositions**
- resource property, 59.1

**Ireland**, *see also* Foreign government
- stock exchange recognized, Reg. 3201(p)
- universities, gifts to, Reg. Sch. VIII s. 10

**Iron**
- processing ore, whether manufacturing or processing, 125.1(3)"manufacturing or processing" Reg. 5203
- production of
- - royalties not deductible, 18(1)(m)(v)(D)
- - royalties taxable, 12(1)(o)(v)(D)

**Iron lung, as medical expense**, 118.2(2)(i)

**Israel**, *see also* Foreign government
- stock exchange recognized, Reg. 3201(q)
- universities, gifts to, Reg. Sch. VIII s. 8

2739

**Israel Bonds**
- eligible for RRSPs and RRIFs, Reg. 4900(1)(o)

**Issuer**
- RRSP, defined, 146(1), Reg. 214(7)

**Italy**, *see also* Foreign government
- stock exchange recognized, Reg. 3201(f)

## J

**JEC**, *see* Joint exploration corporation

**Jail**, *see* Offences

**Jamaica**, *see also* Foreign government
- universities, gifts to, Reg. Sch. VIII s. 15

**Japan**, *see also* Foreign government
- stock exchange recognized, Reg. 3201(g)

**Jeopardy assessment or jeopardy order**
- re collection restrictions, 225.2(2)
- refund not to be paid, 164(1.2)

**Jetty, capital cost allowance for**, Reg. Sch. II:Cl. 1(e), Sch. II:Cl. 3

**Jewellery**, *see* Listed personal property

**Jig, capital cost allowance**, Reg. Sch. II:Cl. 12(d)

**Job retraining**
- reimbursed tuition fees, no credit unless included in income, 118.5(1)(a)(iii)
- unemployment insurance/employment insurance benefit, not included in income, 56(1)(a)(iv)

**Joint and several liability**, *see* Liability for tax: joint and several

**Joint election**, *see also* Election(s)
- defined, for small business development bond, 15.1(3)

**Joint exploration corporation**
- agreed portion, defined, 66(15)
- defined, 66(15), ITAR 29(8), Reg. 4608(1)
- renunciation of resource-related expenses, ITAR 29(6), (7)
  - election re, 66(10)–(10.4)
  - excessive, penalty for, 163(2.2)
  - rules, 66(10.4)
- share, adjusted cost base, 53(2)(f.1)
- shareholder corporation, defined, 66(15)

**Joint liability**, *see* Liability for tax: joint and several

**Joint partner trust**, *see also* Post-1971 partner trust; Trust (or estate): spouse, for
- deduction from income, 104(6)(b)(ii.1), (iii)
- defined, 104(4)(a)(iv)(A), 248(1)
- distribution of property to person other than taxpayer or spouse, 107(4)(a)(iii)
- preferred beneficiary election by, 104(15)(a)
- transfer by, to another trust, 104(5.8)
- transfer to, rollover, 73(1.01)(c)(iii)

**Joint spousal trust**, *see* Joint partner trust

**Judge**, *see also* Court
- application to, re seized documents, 232(4), (8)
- bribery of, non-deductible, 67.5
- defined
  - for jeopardy assessment and collection, 225.2(1)
  - for search and seizure, 231
- income from professional practice, 24.1 [repealed]
- issue of search warrant, 231.3(1)–(4)
- pension plan, Reg. 8309
- powers in jeopardy proceedings, 223(11), (12)

- review of requirement to provide foreign-based information, 231.6(5)
- RRSP contribution room, Reg. 8309(2)

**Judicial notice**
- regulations, etc., 244(12)

**Jurisdiction**
- territorial, 244(3)

**Juror's fees**
- taxable, 3 (*per* IT-377R)

**Jury duty**, *see* Juror's fees

## K

**Kaolin**
- extraction of, 248(1)"mineral resource"(d)(ii)
- included in definition of "mineral", 248(1)

**Kickbacks**, *see* Illegal payments

**Kiddie tax**, 120.4, *see also* Split income: tax on

**Kidney machine, medical expense**, 118.2(2)(i)

**Kilns**
- capital cost allowance for, Reg. Sch. II:Cl. 8

**Kilometres driven, allowance for**, Reg. 7306

**Kitchen utensils**
- capital cost allowance for, Reg. Sch. II:Cl. 12(c)

**Kiwi loans**, *see* Weak currency debt

*Krull* **case overruled**, 6(23)

## L

**LCGE (Lifetime capital gains exemption)**, *see* Capital gains deduction

**LCT**, *see* Large corporations tax (Part I.3)

**LIF**, *see* Life income fund

**LLC**, *see* Limited liability company (U.S.)

**LLP**, *see* Lifelong Learning Plan; Limited Liability Partnership

**LLP balance**
- defined, 146.02(1)

**LPP**, *see* Listed personal property

**LSVCC**, *see* Labour-sponsored venture capital corporation (LSVCC)

**Laboratory services, as medical expense**, 118.2(2)(o)

*Labour Adjustment Benefits Act*
- benefits under
  - income, 56(1)(a)(vi), Reg. 5502(a)
  - withholding of tax at source, 153(1)(m), Reg. 5502(a)
- repayment of overpayment under, deduction for, 60(n)

**Labour expenditure (re Canadian film/video tax credit)**
- defined, 125.4(1)
- qualified, *see* Qualified labour expenditure (re Canadian film/video tax credit)

**Labour organization, exemption**, 149(1)(k)

**Labour-sponsored funds tax credit**
- acquisition of share by RRSP, 127.4(1)"qualifying trust" 127.4(3), Reg. 6706(2)(c)
- computation of, 127.4(3), (4)
- cooling-off period, three years, 127.4(3)
- deduction of, 127.4(2)
- defined, 127.4(1), (6), 204.8(1), 211.7(1)
- provincial, does not reduce ACB of investment, 53(2)(k)(i)(C)
- RRSP, 127.4(1)"qualifying trust", 127.4(6)(a)

## Index

**Labour-sponsored funds tax credit** *(cont'd)*
- recovery of
  - disposition of share, 211.8
  - national LSVCC, Reg. 6706
  - provincial LSVCC, 211.7

**Labour-sponsored venture capital corporation (LSVCC)**, *see also* Labour-sponsored funds tax credit
- amalgamation or merger of, 127.4(1.1), 204.85
- deemed to be mutual fund corporation, 131(8)
- discontinuance of venture capital business, 204.8(2), 204.841
- dissolution of, 204.85
- prescribed, Reg. 6701
  - deemed not a public corporation unless listed, 89(1)"public corporation"(b), (c)
  - disposition of shares, capital loss, 40(2)(i)
  - exempt from Part IV tax, 186.1(b)
  - income eligible for dividend refund, 125(7)"specified investment business"
  - prescribed assistance, Reg. 6702
  - shares of
    - prescribed assistance, deduction from cost base, 53(2)(k)(i)(C)
- provincial, tax on, 204.82(5)
- registered, 204.8–204.87
  - deemed to be prescribed LSVCC, Reg. 6701(c)
  - defined, 248(1)
  - disposition of, clawback, 211.8
  - eligible investment, 204.8(1)
  - refund of tax where no monthly deficiency, 204.83
  - registration conditions, 204.81(1)
  - return and payment of tax, 204.86
  - revocation of registration, 204.81(6)–(9)
  - shares of
    - acquisition by RRSP, 127.4(1)"qualifying trust" 127.4(3)
    - adjusted cost base not reduced by credit, 53(2)(k)(i)(C)
    - credit for purchase, 127.4
    - redemption restrictions, 204.81(1)(c)(vii)
    - transfer restrictions, 204.81(1)(c)(vii)
  - tax where insufficient eligible investments, 204.82
- rules re, 131(11)
- voluntary de-registration, 204.81(8.1)

**Labrador**
- deduction for individuals residing in, Reg. 7303.1(1)(f)

**Land**
- adjusted cost base, additions to, 53(1)(h), (i)
- allocation of proceeds of disposition between land and buildings, 13(21.1), 70(5)(d)
- clearing, levelling, draining, 30
- costs relating to ownership of
  - limitation on deductibility, 18(3.1)–(3.7)
- defined, re restrictions on deductibility, 18(3)
- donation of, *see* Ecological gifts
- drainage system, deduction, 30
- ecological, *see* Ecological gifts
- interest on debt relating to acquisition of
  - defined, 18(3)
  - limitation on deductibility, 18(2)
- inventory
  - cost to include non-deductible expenses, 10(1.1)
  - deceased taxpayer's, 70(5.2)
- meaning of, 18(3)
- not depreciable, Reg. 1102(2)
- rent paid before acquisition, deemed depreciable property, 13(5.2)(c)
- tillage of soil, 248(1)"farming"
- unproductive
  - limitation on deductibility of expenses, 18(2)
- used in farming business, *see also* Farm land
  - disposition of
    - loss, added to cost base, 111(6)
  - transferred to child on death, 70(9)
- used in farming business of partnership
  - disposition of, 101

**Land drainage system, deduction**, 30

**Land registry**
- lien on property for various debts owing, 223(5)–(11)

**Landfill gas**
- defined, Reg. 1104(13)

**Landscaping grounds**
- deductible expense, 20(1)(aa)

**Lapse-supported policy**
- defined, Reg. 1408(1)

**Large corporation**
- appeal by, only on grounds raised in objection, 169(2.1)
- capital tax on, *see* Large corporations tax (Part I.3)
- defined, 225.1(8)
- notice of objection, requirements, 165(1.11)–(1.14)
- R&D investment tax credits limited, 127(10.2)
- required to remit ½ of taxes in dispute, 164(1.1)(d)(ii), 225.1(7)
- required to remit source withholdings through financial institution, 153(1), Reg. 110
- small business deduction limited, 125(5.1)

**Large corporations tax (Part I.3)**, 181–181.9
- capital, 181.2(3)
  - financial institutions, 181.3(3)
- capital deduction, 181.5(1)
  - related corporations, 181.5(2)–(6)
- certain corporations exempted, 181.1(3)
- deductible in computing branch tax liability, 219(1)(h)(i)
- deduction re, 125.3
- determining values and amounts, 181(3)
- financial institutions, 181.3
  - defined, 181(1)
- instalments, 157(1), (2)
- investment allowance, 181.2(4)
  - financial institutions, 181.3(4)
- limitation re inclusions and deductions, 181(4)
- long-term debt, defined, 181(1)
- mutual fund reorganization, effect on taxation year, 132.2(1)(o)(ii)
- partnership interests, value of, 181.2(5)
- payment of tax, 181.7
- reserves, defined, 181(1)
- return, 181.6
- short taxation year, 181.1(2)
- tax payable, 181.1(1)
- taxable capital, 181.2(2)
  - financial institutions, 181.3(2)
- taxable capital employed in Canada, 181.2(1)
  - financial institutions, 181.3(1)
  - non-resident corporation, 181.4

# Index

**Large employer**
- required to remit source withholdings through financial institution, 153(1), Reg. 110

**Laryngeal speaking aid, as medical expense**, 118.2(2)(i)

**Laser-disk**
- capital cost allowance, Reg. Sch. II:Cl. 12(r)

**Last, capital cost allowance**, Reg. Sch. II:Cl. 12(d)

**Late-filed elections or documents**
- detail on notice of objection, 165(1.12)
- generally, 220(3.2), Reg. 600
- resource taxation, 66(12.74)–(12.75)
- s. 85 rollover, 85(7)–(8)
- to trigger capital gain before corporation goes public, 48.1(3)

**Late-filed return**
- penalty, 162(1), 235

**Law Society**
- membership fees, deductible to employee, 8(1)(i)(i)

**Lawyer**
- appointed a judge, deferral of income, 24.1 [repealed]
- books and records required to be kept, 230(2.1)
- defined, 232(1), 248(1)
- incorporated, *see* Professional corporation
- income of, *see* Professional practice
- misrepresentation by, penalty, 163.2
- solicitor-client privilege, 232

**Lead performer (for Canadian film/video tax credit)**
- defined, Reg. 1106(5)(a)

**Lead voice (for Canadian film/video tax credit)**
- defined, Reg. 1106(5)(b)

**Learning disability**
- tutoring for, medical expense credit, 118.2(2)(l.91)

**Lease**
- financing, *see* Direct financing lease
- option to purchase, *see* Option

**Lease cancellation payment**, 13(5.5), 20(1)(z), (z.1)
- amalgamation, on, 87(2)(j.5)
- limitation on deductibility, 18(1)(q)

**Lease inducement payments**
- taxable as income, 12(1)(x)

**Lease-leaseback arrangement**
- rental payments included in cost for CCA, 13(5.4)

**Lease obligation**
- defined, for FAPI rules, 95(1)
- income of foreign affiliate from, 95(2)(a.3)

**Leasehold interest**, *see also* Interest (in property, etc.)
- capital cost allowance, Reg. 1100(1)(b), 1102(4)–(6), Reg. Sch. II:Cl. 13, Reg. Sch. III
- deemed disposition of, 13(5.1)
- Expo '67 or '86, Reg. Sch. II:Cl. 23
- property acquired, rules, 13(5.1)
- separate classes, Reg. 1101(5h)

**Leasing costs**
- non-resident withholding tax, 212(1)(d)
- passenger vehicle
- - limitation on deductibility, 67.3
- - - where more than one lessor, 67.4

**Leasing properties**
- amalgamations, 16.1(4)
- assignments, 16.1(2), (3)

- capital cost allowance, Reg. 1100(15)–(20), 1101(5c)
- defined, Reg. 1100(17)–(20)
- - non-arm's length exception, Reg. 1102(20)
- minimum tax, 127.52(1)(b), (c.2)(ii), 127.52(3)"rental or leasing property"
- replacement property, 16.1(5)–(7)
- rules re, 16.1
- rules where election filed, 16.1(1)–(4)
- subleases, 16.1(2), (3)
- windings-up, 16.1(4)

**Leaving Canada**, *see* Ceasing to be resident in Canada

**Lebanon**, *see also* Foreign government
- universities, gifts to, Reg. Sch. VIII s. 9

**Legal costs**, *see also* Court: costs
- collecting or establishing right to pension benefit
- - deduction for, 60(o.1)
- - reimbursement of, taxable, 56(1)(l.1)
- collecting or establishing right to retiring allowance or severance pay
- - deduction for, 60(o.1)
- - reimbursement of, taxable, 56(1)(l.1)
- collecting or establishing right to wages
- - deduction for, 8(1)(b)
- - reimbursement of, taxable, 6(1)(j)
- conducting appeal, of, 60(o)
- deductible, 8(1)(b), 20(1)(e), 20(1)(cc), 60(o), (o.1), 62(3)(f), 118.2(2)(l.1)(i)
- financing, 20(1)(e)
- income when awarded or reimbursed, 6(1)(j), 56(1)(l), (l.1)
- lobbying, 20(1)(cc)
- moving expenses, 62(3)(f)
- objecting to assessment, 60(o)
- objecting to determination, 152(1.2)
- purchase of new home, 62(3)(f)
- relating to organ or bone marrow transplant, 118.2(2)(l.1)(i)
- representation expenses, 20(1)(cc)
- seizure of chattels, 225(2), (4)

**Legal documents**
- cost of revising for change of address, deduction, 62(3)(f)

**Legal representative**
- appropriation of property by, 159(2.1)
- clearance certificate, 159(2)
- defined, 248(1)
- liability for taxpayer's obligations, 159(1), (3)
- obligations of, 159(1)

**Legal representative of deceased taxpayer**
- application to Minister re vesting of properties, 70(5.2), (6), (9), (9.2)
- election re amounts receivable, 70(2)
- - revocation of, 70(4)
- election re losses, 164(6)
- - reassessment, 152(6)
- election re payment of tax in instalments, 159(5)–(7)
- election re reserves, 72(2)
- information return, Reg. 206
- return of income, when due, 70(7)

**Legislation**
- amendment of, *see* Amendment
- citation of, *Interpretation Act* s. 40
- deemed remedial, *Interpretation Act* s. 12
- definitions, effect of, *Interpretation Act* s. 15

# Index

**Legislation** (cont'd)
- headings or titles, *Interpretation Act* s. 14
- in-force date, *see* Amendments: when in force
- interpretation of, *Interpretation Act*
- marginal notes, *Interpretation Act* s. 14
- repeal of, *Interpretation Act* s. 43–45
- titles of sections, *see* Marginal notes

**Legislative assembly (or Legislature)**
- defined, *Interpretation Act* s. 35(1)
- member of, expense allowance exempt, 81(2)

**Lending asset**, *see also* Specified debt obligation
- cost amount of, 248(1)"cost amount"(d.1)
- defined, 248(1)
- - for FAPI purposes, 95(1)"lending of money" closing words

**Lending of money**, *see also* Loan
- defined, for FAPI rules, 95(1)

**Lesbian couples**, *see* Common-law partner

**Level-yield method (for allocation return from specified debt obligation)**
- defined, Reg. 9102(2)

**Liabilities**
- determination of, for debt forgiveness reserve, 61.3(1)(b)C(ii)

**Liability for tax**
- alternative minimum tax, 127.7
- failure to withhold tax on payment to non-resident, 215(6)
- general, 2
- income from property transferred at non-arm's length, on, 160(1)–(3)
- income-splitting tax, 120.4(2)
- joint and several
- - assessment of, 160.1(3)
- - charitable organization and charitable foundation, 188(4)
- - charity revocation tax, 188(2)
- - debt forgiveness reserve, asset transfer, 160.4
- - debtor and transferee following transfer of forgiven amount, 80.04(11)
- - directors and corporation, source withholdings and other amount, 227.1
- - excessive election re capital dividend or capital gains dividend, 185(4)
- - GST credit overpayment, 160.1(1.1)
- - income-splitting tax, 160(1.2)
- - kiddie tax, 160(1.2)
- - legal representative and taxpayer, 159(1)
- - non-resident trust and Canadian resident beneficiary, 94(2) [to be repealed]
- - Part III tax, 185(4), (6)
- - payor and non-resident, withholding tax, 227(8.1)
- - person responsible for withholding taxes, 227(5)
- - property transferred not at arm's length, 160(1)
- - property transferred to use other taxpayer's benefit, 160(1.1)
- - RCA benefits received by another, 160.3
- - RRIF, amounts received under, 160.2(2)
- - RRSP, amounts received under, 160.2(1)
- - secured creditor, for remittances, 227(5.2)–(5.4) (draft)
- - transferred Part VI.1 tax, 191.3(1)(e)
- - trustee and person whose property is being managed, withholding, 153(1.3) [repealed], 227(5), (5.1)
- - trustee in bankruptcy and bankrupt corporation, 128(1)(e)
- - UI premium tax credit, 160.1(2.2)
- kiddie tax, 120.4(2)
- minimum tax, 127.7
- non-resident corporation
- - carrying on business in Canada, 219
- not affected by incorrect assessment, 152(3)
- Part I, 2
- Part I.1, 180.1(1)
- Part I.2, 180.2(2)
- Part I.3, 181.1(1)
- Part II, 182(1)
- Part II.1, 183.1(2)
- Part III, 184
- Part IV, 186(1)
- Part IV.1, 187.2, 187.3(1)
- Part V, 188
- Part VI, 190.1(1), (1.1), (1.2)
- Part VI.1, 191.1(1)
- Part VII, 192
- Part VIII, 194(1)
- Part IX, 196(1)
- Part X, 198(1), (3), 199(1), 201
- Part X.1, 204.1
- Part X.2, 204.6
- Part X.3, 204.82(1)–(3), (5), (6), 204.841
- Part X.4 tax, 204.91
- Part X.5 tax, 204.94(2)
- Part XI, 206(2)
- Part XI.1, 207.1
- Part XI.2, 207.3
- Part XI.3, 207.7(1)
- Part XII, 208
- Part XII.1, 209(2)
- Part XII.2, 210.2(1), (1.1)
- Part XII.3, 211.1(1)
- Part XII.4, 211.6(1)
- Part XII.5, 211.8(1)
- Part XII.6, 211.91(1)
- Part XIII, 212
- Part XIII.1, 218.2(1)
- Part XIV, 219
- transfer of property to spouse or minor, 160(3)
- trustee, etc., 159

**Library books**
- capital cost allowance, Reg. Sch. II:Cl. 12(a)

**License**
- capital cost allowance, Reg. 1100(1)(c), Reg. Sch. II:Cl. 14
- representation expense, 13(12), 20(1)(cc), 20(9)

**Licensed annuities provider**
- defined, 147(1), 248(1)
- RESP-eligible investments, 146.1(1)"qualified investment"(c)
- RRIF-eligible investments, 146.3(1)"qualified investment"(b.1), (b.2)
- RRSP-eligible investments, 146(1)"qualified investment"(c)–(c.2)

**Licensing of property**
- defined, for FAPI rules, 95(1)

**Lieutenant governor**
- defined, *Interpretation Act* 35(1)
- pension plan, Reg. 8309

# Index

Lieutenant governor *(cont'd)*
- RRSP contribution room, Reg. 8309(1)

**Life estate in real property**
- defined, 43.1(1)
- effect of retaining, 43.1(1)
- termination of, 43.1(2), 53(1)(o)

**Life income fund**, *see* Registered retirement income fund

**Life insurance**, *see also* Life insurance corporation; Life insurance policy
- business, defined, 248(1)
- definitions, 148(9)
- group plan, whether premiums an employment benefit, 6(1)(a)(i), 6(4)
- net cost of pure insurance, Reg. 308
- policy, *see* Life insurance policy
- policy loan, *see* Policy loan (life insurance)
- policyholder
  - - "adjusted cost basis" of policy, 148(9)"adjusted cost basis"
  - - "child" of, 148(9)
  - - deemed dispositions, 148(2)
  - - disposition of interest at non-arm's length, 148(7), (8)
  - - disposition of part of interest, 148(4)
  - - income from disposition of interest in policy, 148(1), (4)
- premiums, *see* Premium
- proceeds received as annuity, 148(6)
- "relevant authority" defined, 148(9)
- rules re certain policies, 148(3)

**Life insurance capital dividend**, *see also* Capital dividend account
- brought into capital dividend account, 89(1)"capital dividend account"(e)
- defined, 248(1)

**Life insurance corporation**, *see also* Insurance corporation
- accumulated 1968 deficit, defined, 138(12)
- building under construction etc., amount included in income re, 138(4.4)–(4.6), Reg. 2410
- capital gain on pre-1969 property, 138(11.2)
- capital tax, 190.1(1), 190.1(1.1)
- change in use rules, 138(11.3), (11.4), (11.41), (11.6); ITAR 26(17.1)
- computation of income, 138(1)–(6)
- deductions, 138(3), Reg. 1401
- - Part XII.3 tax, 138(3)(g)
- deemed a public corporation, 141(2)
- defined, 248(1)
- definitions, 138(12)
- demutualization, 139.1
- depreciation deemed to have been allowed to, 13(23)
- dividends from taxable corporations, 138(6)
- foreign taxes not deductible, 138(5.1), (8)
- identical properties of, 138(11.1)
- information returns, Reg. 217
- maximum tax actuarial reserve, 138(12)
- 1975–76 excess policy dividend deduction, 138(3.1)
- non-capital loss of, 111(7.2)
- non-resident, 219(4)–(8), Reg. 2401
- - branch tax elections, Reg. 2403
- provincial, conversion to mutual corporation, 139
- real property, vacant or under development, amount included in income re, 138(4.4)–(4.6) Reg. 2410

- "relevant authority" defined, 138(12)
- reserves, 138(3)(a), Reg. 1400–1408
- - policy reserves, 138(3)(a)(i)
- - - post-1995 policies, Reg. 1404
- - - pre-1996 policies, Reg. 1401(1)
- - unpaid claims, 138(3)(a)(ii)
- - - post-1995 policies, Reg. 1405
- - - pre-1996 policies, Reg. 1401(4)
- rules applicable to, 138
- segregated funds of, 138.1, Reg. 6100
- tax on investment income, 211–211.6
- - Canadian life investment income, 211.1(3)
- - interest on overdue tax, 211.5
- - payment of tax, 211.4, 211.5
- - rate of tax, 211.1(1)
- - return, 211.2
- - taxable Canadian life investment income, 211.1(2)
- taxable income of, 138(7)

**Life insurance policy**, *see also* Annuity contract
- accrued income, 12.2
- - amounts included in income on anniversary, 12.2(1)
- - anniversary day, defined, 12.2(11)
- - deduction for over-accrual, 20(20)
- acquisition costs of, Reg. 1408(1)
- "adjusted cost basis" of, to policyholder, 148(9)
- anniversary day, defined, 12.2(11)
- annuity, proceeds received as, 148(6)
- charity designated as beneficiary, 118.1(5.1), (5.2)
- corporation beneficiary under, where, 89(2)
- deemed disposition of, 148(2)
- defined, 12.2(10), 138(4.01), 138(12), 211(1), 248(1), Reg. 217(1), 310, 1900(1)
- - in Canada, 138(12), 211(1), 248(1), Reg. 310, 1408(1)
- - registered, 211, Reg. 1900(1)
- disposition by non-resident
- - certificate, 116(5.2)
- - presumption, 116(5.4)
- - purchaser liable for tax, 116(5.3)
- - rules, 116(5.1)
- disposition of
- - amount included in income, 148(1.1)
- - deduction, 20(20)
- - defined, 148(9)"disposition"
- - no capital gain, 39(1)(a)(iii)
- - no capital loss, 39(1)(b)(ii)
- - non-arm's length, 148(7), (8)
- - policyholder's income, 148(1), (4)
- - proceeds of
- - - defined, 148(9)"proceeds of the disposition"
- - - income, 56(1)(j)
- dividends, 148(2)
- enhanced capital gains deduction, effect on, 110.6(15)
- exempt policy, Reg. 306
- - defined, 12.2(11)
- group term, defined, 248(1)
- in Canada, defined, 138(12), 211(1), 248(1), Reg. 310, 1408(1)
- income from, 148
- interest in
- - amount to be included, 12.2(1)
- - owned under deferred profit sharing plan, 198(6)–(8)
- - "value" defined, 148(9)"value"

2744

**Life insurance policy** *(cont'd)*
- life annuity contract, 148(10)
- loan, *see* Policy loan (life insurance)
- mortality gains and losses, Reg. 308
- net cost of pure insurance, Reg. 308
- participating, *see* Participating life insurance
- premium, *see* Premium
- "prescribed increase" in benefit on death under, Reg. 309(2)
- prescribed premium, rules, Reg. 309
- proceeds of the disposition of, defined, 148(9)
- retirement compensation arrangement funded by, 207.6(2)
- riders, 12.2(10)
- rollover
  - to child, 148(8)
  - to spouse, 148(8.1), (8.2)
- segregated fund, 138.1, Reg. 6100
  - defined, 138(12)
- "tax anniversary date" defined, 148(9)
- third anniversary amounts, defined, 12.2(11)"anniversary day"
- transfer to child, 148(8)
- transfer to spouse
  - breakdown of marriage, on, 148(8.1)
  - death, on, 148(8.2)
- value of, for valuing shares etc. on death, emigration or immigration, 70(5.3)

**Life insurance policy in Canada**, *see* Life insurance policy: in Canada

**Life insurer**, *see also* Life insurance corporation
- defined, 248(1)

**Life interest**, *see* Life estate in real property

**Lifelong Learning Plan**, 146.02
- definitions, 146.01(1)
- income inclusions, 56(1)(h.2), 146.02(4)–(6)
- repayment of amount borrowed from RRSP, 146.02(3)
- withdrawal of funds from RRSP, 146(8), Reg. 104.1
  - within 90 days of contribution, deduction disallowed, 146(5)(a)(iv.1), 146(5.1)(a)(iv)
- withholding exemption, Reg. 104.1

**Lifetime retirement benefits**
- defined, Reg. 8500(1)

**Lift, power-operated (for wheelchair etc.)**
- medical expense, Reg. 5700(m)

**Lift truck, industrial**
- capital cost allowance, Reg. Sch. II:Cl. 29, Sch. II:Cl. 40

**Little Egypt bump**
- prevention of, 98(5)(d) (repealed)

**Limitation of benefits rule**, Canada–U.S. Tax Convention Art. XXIX A

**Limitation periods**, *see also* Filing deadlines; Reassessment; Statute-barred debt, deemed settled
- prosecution for offences, 244(4)

**Limited-dividend housing company**
- defined, Reg. 3700
- exemption, 149(1)(n)

**Limited liability company (U.S.)**
- treated as corporation, 248(1)"corporation"
- treated as foreign affiliate, Reg. 5907(11.2)(b)

**Limited liability partnership**
- at-risk rules inapplicable, 96(2.4)(a)

- capital gain not triggered by negative ACB, 40(3.14)(a)

**Limited partner**, *see also* Limited partnership; Specified member (of partnership)
- at-risk rules, 96(2.1)–(2.7)
- deemed capital gain on negative adjusted cost base, 40(3.1)(a)
- deemed not to carry on partnership's business, 253.1(b)
- defined, 96(2.4)
  - for investment tax credit, 127(8.5)
  - for minimum tax purposes, 127.52(3)
  - for partnership interest negative ACB, 40(3.14)
  - for tax shelter investments, 143.2(1)
- investment tax credit, 127(8.1)
- limit on cost of investment, 143.2(1)"tax shelter investment"(b), 143.2(6)
- minimum tax, 127.52(1)(c.1)
- research and development losses, 96(1)(g)
- resource expenses, 66.8

**Limited partnership**, *see also* Limited partner; Partnership; Tax shelter: investment
- deemed not a business of the partner, 253.1(b)
- losses, *see* Limited partnership losses
- mutual fund commissions financing, 18.1
- service of documents on, 244(20)(b)(ii)(A)
- unit
  - qualified investment for RRSP etc., Reg. 4900(1)(n)
  - small business investment, Reg. 5102

**Limited partnership losses**, *see also* Limited partnership
- adjusted cost base of partnership interest, reduction for, 53(2)(c)(i.1)
- amalgamation, on, 87(2.1)(a), (b)
- at-risk amount, 96(2.1)
  - artificial transactions to increase, 96(2.6), (2.7)
  - defined, 96(2.2)
- carryforward of, 111(1)(e)
  - non-residents, 111(10)
- deductibility, 96(2.1)
  - limitation on, 111(3)(a)
- defined, 96(2.1), 111(10), 248(1)
- determination of, by Minister, 152(1.1), (1.2), (1.3)
- minimum tax, 127.52(1)(c.1)
- order of deduction, 111(3)(b)
- partnership interest acquired by subsequent person, 96(2.3)
- winding-up, on, 88(1.1)

**Limited partnership unit**, *see* Limited partnership: unit

**Limited-recourse amount**
- defined, for tax shelter investments, 143.2(1), (7)

**Linefill**
- in pipeline, no CCA, Reg. 1102(1)(k)

**Linen**
- capital cost allowance, Reg. Sch. II:Cl. 12(g)

**Liquidator**, *see also* Legal representative
- certificate before distribution, 159(2)
- deemed to be legal representative, 248(1)"legal representative"
- obligations of, 159
- return required by, 150(3)
- withholding tax, liability for, 153(1.3) [repealed], (1.4) [repealed], 227(5), (5.1)

**List of amounts**, *see* Dollar amounts in legislation and regulations
**List of taxes and tax rates**, *see* Rates of tax
**Listed country**
- for foreign affiliate purposes, Reg. 5907(11)–(11.2)

**Listed personal property**, *see also* Art; Personal-use property
- defined, 54
- loss from
  - - defined, 41(3)
  - - reassessment, 152(6)(b)
  - - usable only against LPP gains, 3(b)(ii), 41(2)
  - - net gain from disposition, 41(2)

**Listed securities**, *see* Publicly-traded securities
**Litigation, costs of**, *see* Court: costs
**Liver extract, as medical expense**, 118.2(2)(k)
**Livestock**
- destruction of
  - - deferral of income from, 80.3(2)
  - - - exceptions, 80.3(6)
  - - inclusion of deferred amount, 80.3(3)
  - - - amalgamation, on, 87(2)(tt)
- exhibiting and raising, 248(1)"farming"
- sales of, in prescribed drought regions
  - - deferral of income, 80.3(4)
  - - - exceptions, 80.3(6)
  - - inclusion of deferred amount, 80.3(5)
  - - - amalgamation, on, 87(2)(tt)

**Living together, deemed spouses**, *see* Common-law partner
**Loan**, *see also* Borrowed money; Debt; Interest (monetary)
- acquired in ordinary course of business of insurer or moneylender, 20(27)
- back-to-back, to spouse or minor, 74.5(6)
- charity, by, 118.1(16)
- corporation to, to reduce income, 74.4(2)
  - - outstanding amount, 74.4(3)
- cost amount of, 248(1)"cost amount"(d.1)
- election to treat excess of dividend as, 184(3.1)–(5)
- eligible, by international banking centre, 33.1(1)
- employee, to, included in income, 6(9), 80.4(1)
- foreign affiliate's income from, 95(2)(a.3)
- forgiveness of, *see* Debt forgiveness
- home purchase, *see* Home purchase loan
- interest-free or low-interest
  - - to child, 74.1(2)
  - - to employee, 80.4(1)
  - - to non-arm's length person, 56(4.1)
  - - to non-resident, 17
  - - to shareholder, 15(2)–(2.6)
  - - to spouse, 74.1(1)
- inventory write-down restricted, 18(1)(s)
- minor, to, 74.1(2), 74.5(6)–(11)
  - - for value, 74.5, (2)
  - - repayment of, 74.1(3)
- non-arm's length person, to, 56(4.1)–(4.3)
  - - used to repay existing indebtedness, 56(4.3)
- non-resident, to, by corporation, 17
- partner, by, to partnership
  - - interest paid on money borrowed to make, 20(3.2)
- partnership interest, of, 96(1.8)
- personal services business, to

- - inclusion in income, 12(1)(w)
- policy, repayment of, 60(s)
- reduction in value of
  - - limitation on deduction re, 18(1)(s)
- related person, to, *see* non-arm's length person (*above*)
- shareholder, by, to corporation
  - - interest paid on money borrowed to make, 20(3.1)
- shareholder, to, by corporation, 15(2)–(2.6), 80.4(2)
  - - capacity test, 15(2.4)(e)
  - - deemed benefit, 15(9)
  - - forgiveness of, 15(1.2)
  - - interest paid on money borrowed to make, 20(1)(c)(vi)
  - - non-residents, 15(2.2), (8), 227(6.1)
  - - persons connected with, 80.4(8)
  - - repayment of, 20(1)(j)
- spouse, to, 74.1(1)
  - - for value, 74.5(2)
  - - repayment of, 74.1(3)
- value, for, to non-arm's length person, 56(4.2)
- wholly-owned subsidiary, to, 17, 218

**Loanbacks**
- property or money donated to charity, 118.1(16)

**Lobbying**, *see* Representation expenses
**Local**
- of union, deemed same employer as union, 252.1

**Locked-in annuity**
- held by RRIF, 146.3(1)"qualified investment"(b.2)

**Lodge, expense of, not deductible**, 18(1)(l)
**Lodging**, *see* Board and lodging
**Logging equipment**, Reg. Sch. II:Cl. 10(o)
**Logging operations**
- income from, in the province, defined, 127(2)"income for the year from logging operations in the province"

**Logging property**
- investment tax credit, 127(9)"qualified property"(c)(iii)

**Logging tax**
- deduction from income tax, 127(1), Reg. Part VII
- defined, 127(2)
- provincial legislation imposing, Reg. 700(3)
- rules applicable to, 127(1)

**"Long-term debt" defined**, 181(1), 190(1)
**Look-back rule (for flow-through shares)**
- interest charged as tax, 211.91(1)
- renunciation permitted, 66(12.66)(a.1)

**Loss(es)**
- allocation, *see* Loss allocation
- amalgamation, on, 87(2.1)
- business or property, from, 9(2)
- capital, *see* Capital loss
- carryback
  - - amended return, 152(6)(c)
  - - effect on interest payable, 161(7), 164(5), (5.1)
- carryforward, *see* Carryforward
- carryover of, 111
  - - corporation, by, 111(5)–(5.4)
  - - - anti-avoidance provision, 111(5.5)
  - - - change in control of corporation, 111(4)
  - - farming business, from, 111(1)(c), (d), 111(6), (7)
  - - restricted, for corporation becoming or ceasing to be exempt, 149(10)(c)

Loss(es) *(cont'd)*
- defined, for disposition of specified debt obligation, Reg. 9200
- determination of, by Minister, 152(1.1), (1.2), (1.3)
- disposition of debt in exchange for replacement obligation, 40(2)(e.2)
- disposition of debt owing by related person, deemed nil, 40(2)(e.1)
- disposition of share of, foreign affiliate, on, 93(2)–(4)
- farm, defined, 111(8)
- farming, *see also* Farm loss
  - after land disposed of, 111(6)
  - carryover of, 111(1)(d)
  - deduction limited, 31
  - effect on cost base of land, 53(1)(i)
  - limitation on deductibility, 111(3), (6), (7)
  - partnership, of, 101, 111(7)
  - reduction on debt forgiveness, 80(3)(b), (c)
  - restricted farm loss, *see* Restricted farm loss
- foreign affiliate, of
  - deductible, Reg. 5903
  - defined, Reg. 5907(1)
- foreign bank's Canadian affiliate, 142.7(12)
- housing, *see* Housing loss
- insurer's, 138(2)
- international banking centre, from, 33.1(3), 33.1(4)
- limitations on deductibility, 111(3), *see also* Stop-loss rules
- net capital, *see* Net capital loss
- non-capital, *see* Non-capital loss
- office or employment, from, 5(2)
- order of reduction, on settlement of debt, 80(2)
- place, from sources in, 4
- post-emigration, 128.1(8)
- reduction of, on property previously owned by trust, 107(6)
- resource, *see* Reource loss
- restrictions on deductibility, *see* Stop-loss rules
- share that is capital property, on, 112(3), (4)
- source, from, 4
- stop-los rules, *see* Stop-loss rules
- superficial
  - business of lending money, 18(13), (15)
  - capital property, 40(2)(g)(i), 54
  - defined, 54
  - eligible capital property, 14(12), (13)
  - inventory held as adventure in nature of trade, 18(14)–(16)
- terminal
  - deduction for, 20(16)
  - no deduction re motor vehicle, 20(16.1)
- transfer of, *see* Suspension of losses; Transfer of losses
- windup, on, 88(1.1)

**Loss allocation**
- defined, re foreign investment entities, 94.1(7)

**Loss of income source, deduction for interest expense**, 20.1

**Loss offset program**, *see* Fuel tax rebate

**Lottery**
- capital gain or loss nil, 40(2)(f)
- prize winnings, not taxed (no taxing provision)

**Lump-sum payment**
- employment income
  - averaging provisions, ITAR 40
  - defined, Reg. 103(6)
  - withholding of tax, Reg. 103(4)
- retroactive spreading over past years
  - addition to tax for earlier years, 120.31
  - deduction in current year, 110.2

**Lump-sum premium**
- defined, Reg. 2700(1)

**Luxury vehicle**, *see* Passenger vehicle: luxury

# M

**M&P**, *see* Manufacturing or processing: credit

**MIC**, *see* Mortgage investment corporation

**MLA**, *see* Member: legislative assembly

**MP**, *see* Member: Parliament

**MPP**, *see* Member: legislative assembly; Money purchase provision

**MURB**, *see* Multiple-unit residential buildings

**Machine part, cutting or shaping**
- capital cost allowance, Reg. Sch. II:Cl. 12(j)

**Machinery and equipment**
- capital cost allowance for, Reg. Sch. II:Cl. 8, Sch. II:Cl. 29

**Magazine advertising**
- limitation, 19 [to be repealed], 19.01

**Mail**
- notice of objection, 165(2)
- presumption re mailing date, 244(14)
- proof of service by, 244(5)
- receipt of things mailed, 248(7)

**Maintenance**, *see* Support payments (spousal or child)

**Maintenance costs**
- automobile, *see* Automobile: operating costs
- trust property, of, 105(2)

**Majority-interest group of partners**
- defined, 251.1(3)

**Majority interest partner**
- acquisition of control of corporation that is, 13(24), 66(11.4)
- capital loss denied on disposition to partnership, 40(3.3), (3.4), 97(3)
- defined, 248(1)

**Management fee**
- paid to non-resident, 212(1)(a)
  - defined, 212(4)

**Manitoba**, *see also* Province
- disclosure of Child Tax Benefit information to, Reg. 3003(b)
- labour-sponsored venture capital corporation of
  - recovery of LSVCC credit, 211.7
- *Mineral Exploration Incentive Program Act*, assistance under, Reg. 6202.1(5)"excluded obligation"(a)(i)
- northern, *see* Northern Canada
- Rural Development Bonds, eligible for RRSP investment, Reg. 4900(1)(i.1)
- tax rates, *see* introductory pages

**Manufacturing or processing**
- assets, capital cost allowance, Reg. Sch. II:Cl. 43
- business
  - deemed capital cost of property acquired for, 13(10)
  - new, in designated area

Manufacturing or processing *(cont'd)*
- • • capital cost allowance for property used in, Reg. Sch. II:Cl. 21
- credit, 125.1, Reg. Part LII
- defined
- • • for Class 29 CCA, Reg. 1104(9)
- • • for investment tax credit, 127(11)(a)
- • • for M&P credit, 125.1(3)"manufacturing or processing"
- • • for manufacturing and processing credit, 125.1(3)"manufacturing or processing"
- property used in, capital cost allowance, Reg. 1102(15), (16), Reg. Sch. II:Cl. 29, Sch. II:Cl. 39, Sch. II:Cl. 40
- tobacco, surtax on, 182, 183

**Marginal notes**
- effect of, *Interpretation Act* s. 14
- relevance to legislation, *Interpretation Act* s. 14

**Marine railway**
- capital cost allowance, Reg. Sch. II:Cl. 7

**Mark-to-market property**, 142.5, *see also* Specified debt obligation
- amalgamation, effect of, 87(2)(e.4), (e.5)
- annual recognition of gain or loss, 142.5(2)
- cost amount of, 248(1)"cost amount"(c.1)
- debt obligation, interest on, 142.5(3)
- deemed disposition of, 142.5(2)
- defined, 142.2(1)
- • • for stop-loss rules, 112(6)(c)
- • • for transitional rules, Reg. 8102(1), 8104(1)
- disposition of
- • • adjustment for dividends received, 112(5)–(5.2)
- • • deemed
- • • • annual, 142.5(2)
- • • • on windup, 88(1)(i)
- • • income treatment, 142.5(1)
- • • no capital gain, 39(1)(a)(ii.2)
- • • no capital loss, 39(1)(b)(ii)
- rollover not permitted, 85(1.1)(g)(iii)
- stop-loss rules restricted, 112(5.6)
- superficial loss rule not applicable, 142.6(7)
- transitional rules, 142.5(4)–(9), Reg. 8102–8105
- • • election re taxation year that includes February 22/94, 142.6(8)–(10)
- winding-up, effect of, 88(1)(a.3), (h), (i)

**Marketing board**
- patronage dividends where board used, 135(8)

**Marriage**, *see also* Spouse
- breakdown of, *see* Divorce and separation

**Married status**
- tax credit, 118(1)B(a)
- • • limitation, 118(4)

**Master trust**, *see also* Pooled fund trust
- defined, Reg. 5001
- election re proportional holdings in property of
- • • exempt from tax on foreign property holdings, 206(2.1)
- excluded from various trust rules, 108(1)"trust"(a)
- exempt from tax, 149(1)(o.4)
- foreign property holdings, tax on, 205(a)
- • • where not applicable, 206(2.1)
- information return where interest claimed to be qualified investment, Reg. 221
- minimum tax not payable, 127.55(f)(iii)

- rollover to new trust, 248(1)"disposition"(f)(vi)

**Matchable expenditure**
- deemed to be a tax shelter investment, 18.1(13)
- defined, 18.1(1)
- deduction restricted, 18.1(2)–(4)
- non-arm's length disposition, 18.1(8)–(10)
- reinsurance commissions excluded, 18.1(15)(b)

**Matrimonial regime, dissolution of**, 248(22), (23)

**Maturity**
- registered retirement savings plan, of, 146(1)"maturity"

**Maximum benefit rule**
- for registered pension plan, Reg. 8504

**Maximum tax actuarial reserve**
- defined, Reg. 1900(1)

**"May"**
- meaning of, *Interpretation Act* s. 11

**Meals**, *see also* Entertainment expenses (and meals)
- employee's, deduction limited, 8(4)

**Mean Canadian investment fund**
- defined, insurers, Reg. 2412

**Mean Canadian outstanding premiums**
- defined, insurers, Reg. 2400(1)

**Mean Canadian reserve liabilities**
- defined, insurers, Reg. 2400(1)

**Mean maximum tax actuarial reserve**
- defined, insurers, Reg. 2400(1)

**Medical devices and equipment**
- prescribed, 118.2(2)(m), Reg. 5700

**Medical doctor**, *see also* Physician
- certification for disability credit, 118.3(1)(a.2)
- defined, 118.4(2)
- fees of, medical expense credit, 118.2(2)(a)
- income of, *see* Professional practice

**Medical expenses**
- air conditioner, Reg. 5700(c.3)
- alarm for infant, Reg. 5700(r)
- ambulance, 118.2(2)(f)
- animal trained to assist impaired person, 118.2(2)(l)
- artificial eye, 118.2(2)(i)
- artificial limb, 118.2(2)(i)
- blood sugar measuring device, Reg. 5700(s)
- bone marrow transplant, 118.2(2)(l.1)
- catheters and catheter trays, 118.2(2)(i.1)
- closed-caption TV decoder, Reg. 5700(q)
- colostomy pad, 118.2(2)(i)
- credit for
- • • non-refundable, 118.2
- • • refundable, 122.51
- crutches, 118.2(2)(i)
- deemed, 118.2(3)
- deemed payment of, 118.2(4)
- defined, 118.2(2)
- denture costs, 118.2(2)(p)
- devices and equipment, Reg. 5700
- diapers for incontinence, 118.2(2)(i.1)
- driveway alterations, 118.2(2)(l.6)
- drugs, 118.2(2)(n)
- extremity pump, Reg. 5700(u)
- eyeglasses, 118.2(2)(j)
- full-time attendant for physically or mentally impaired person, 118.2(2)(b), (c)

Medical expenses *(cont'd)*
- group home care, 118.2(2)(b.2)
- guide dog, 118.2(2)(l)
- hearing aid, 118.2(2)(i)
- hearing loss, rehabilitative therapy, 118.2(2)(l.3)
- home construction for disabled person, 118.2(2)(l.21)
- home renovations, 118.2(2)(l.2)
- hospital bed, Reg. 5700(h)
- iliostomy pad, 118.2(2)(i)
- incontinence-related products, 118.2(2)(i.1)
- inductive coupling osteogenesis stimulator, Reg. 5700(v)
- infusion pump, Reg. 5700(s)
- insulin, 118.2(2)(k)
- iron lung, 118.2(2)(i)
- kidney machine, 118.2(2)(i)
- laboratory procedures, 118.2(2)(o)
- laryngeal speaking aid, 118.2(2)(i)
- learning disability, tutoring, 118.2(2)(l.91)
- limb brace, 118.2(2)(i)
- lip reading training, 118.2(2)(l.3)
- liver extract, injectible, 118.2(2)(k)
- medical equipment and devices, 118.2(2)(i), (k)
- - prescribed, 118.2(2)(m)
- medical practitioners etc., references to, 118.4(2)
- mental or physical impairment, 118.2(2)(b)–(e), 118.3
- - transfer of unused credit to spouse, 118.8
- modifications to dwelling for physically impaired person, 118.2(2)(l.2)
- moving expenses, 118.2(2)(l.5)
- notch provision, 118.2(1)D
- orthopaedic shoe, etc., Reg. 5700(e)
- oxygen, 118.2(2)(k)
- pacemaker, Reg. 5700(d)
- partial dependency, 118.3(3)
- prescribed devices and equipment, 118.2(2)(m), Reg. 5700
- private health services premiums, 118.2(2)(q)
- refundable credit, additional, 122.51
- rehabilitative therapy for hearing/speech loss, 118.2(2)(l.3)
- reimbursed, 118.2(3)
- - by employer, 118.2(3)(a)
- remuneration for attendant, 118.2(2)(b), (c)
- rocking bed, 118.2(2)(i)
- sign language interpretation services, 118.2(2)(l.4)
- sign language training, 118.2(2)(l.3)
- speech loss, rehabilitative therapy, 118.2(2)(l.3)
- speech synthesizer, Reg. 5700(p)
- spinal brace, 118.2(2)(i)
- syringe, Reg. 5700(b)
- TDD, Reg. 5700(k)
- talking textbooks, Reg. 5700(w)
- therapy, 118.2(2)(l.9)
- - for hearing or speech loss, 118.2(2)(l.3)
- training courses to care for infirm dependant, 118.2(2)(l.8)
- transportation services, 118.2(2)(g)
- - where ambulance etc. not available, 118.2(4)
- travelling expenses, 118.2(2)(h)
- truss, hernia, 118.2(2)(i)
- tutoring services, 118.2(2)(l.91)
- van for use with wheelchair, 118.2(2)(l.7)
- vitamin B12, 118.2(2)(k)
- walker, 118.2(2)(i), Reg. 5700(i)
- wheelchair, 118.2(2)(i)
- wheelchair lift, Reg. 5700(m)
- wig, Reg. 5700(a)

**Medical instruments (small)**
- capital cost allowance for, Reg. Sch. II:Cl. 12(e)

**Medical practitioner**
- defined, 118.4(2)

**Medical Research Council**
- payments to, as R&D expenditures, 37(1)(a)(ii)(B), 37(7)"approved"
- research grants, taxable, 56(1)(o)

**Member**
- credit union, defined, 137(6)"member"
- deferred profit sharing plan, defined, Reg. 8300(1)
- legislative assembly, expense allowance, 81(2)
- Parliament
- - allowance non-taxable, 61(1)(b)(i)(A)
- - election contributions
- - - credit, 127(3)
- - - records of, 230.1
- - income treated as employment income, 248(1)"office"
- - retirement compensation arrangement of, Reg. 6802.1
- - retiring allowances, 60(j.02)–(j.04)
- partnership, *see* Partner
- pension plan, defined, 147.1(1), Reg. 8300(1)

**Member of Parliament**, *see* Member: Parliament

**Member of the taxpayer's household**
- defined, Reg. 7304(1)

**Membership dues**
- employee, deduction, 8(1)(i)(i), (iv)–(vi)
- recreational club etc., not deductible, 18(1)(l)(ii)

**Mental or physical health**
- counselling related to
- - value not included in employee's income, 6(1)(a)(iv)

**Mental or physical impairment**, *see also* Blind person; Hearing impairment; Infirm dependant; Mobility impairment
- attendant care expenses, deduction from income, 64
- - residents absent from Canada, 64.1
- credit for, 118.3
- - full-time attendant, 118.2(2)(b), (c)
- - partial dependant, 118.3(3)
- - unused, transfer to spouse, 118.8
- education credit, 118.6(3)
- Minister may obtain advice from Dept. of Human Resources Development re, 118.3(4)
- modifications to dwelling, tax credit for, 118.2(2)(l.2)
- nature of, 118.4(1)
- RESP age requirements, waiver, 146.1(2.2)
- RESP enrolment requirements, part-time allowed, 146.1(2)(g.1)(i)(B)
- specified disabled person
- - defined, for Home Buyers' Plan, 146.01(1)
- - loan from RRSP to acquire home for, 146.01(1)"supplemental eligible amount"
- student, 118.6(3)
- "totally and permanently disabled"
- - meaning of, for pension plans, Reg. 8500(1)

**Merchant navy veteran pension, exempt**, 81(1)(d)

# Index

**Merger,** *see also* Amalgamation
- cross-border, 128.2
- deemed receipt of shares on, 87(1.1)
- foreign, 87(8), (8.1)
- triangular, 87(9)

**Methods of accounting prohibited,** *see* Accounting

**Metric scales, capital cost allowance,** Reg. Sch. II:Cl. 12(p)

**Mexico,** *see also* Foreign government
- certain bonds of, *see* Brady bond
- stock exchange recognized, Reg. 3201(h)

**Migration,** *see* Becoming resident in Canada; Ceasing to be resident in Canada

**Mileage allowances,** Reg. 7306

**Millennium bug,** *see* Year 2000 computer hardware and software

**Mine**
- additional allowances, Reg. 1209
- buildings, Reg. Sch. II:Cl. 10(g), Sch. II:Cl. 41
- capital cost allowance, Reg. 1100(1)(w), (x), 1100A
- - definitions, Reg. 1104(5)–(8)
- defined, Reg. 1104(6)(b), 1104(7)(a), 1206(1), 3900(2)
- depletion allowance, *see* Depletion allowances
- equipment etc., Reg. Sch. II:Cl. 10(k)–10(m), Sch. II:Cl. 41
- exempt income from, Reg. 1100A [Revoked], Part XIX [Revoked]
- exploration and development expenses, 66
- income from a, meaning of, Reg. 1104(5), (6)(a)
- industrial mineral, Reg. 1100(1)(g), Reg. Sch. V
- - separate class, Reg. 1101(4)
- new or expanded
- - separate capital cost allowance classes, Reg. 1101(4a)–(4d)
- property, Reg. Sch. II:Cl. 28, Sch. II:Cl. 41
- shafts etc., Reg. Sch. II:Cl. 12(f)
- townsite costs, *see* Townsite costs

**Mineral**
- defined, 248(1)
- - for capital cost allowances, Reg. 1104(3)
- - for mining taxes on income, Reg. 3900(1)

**Mineral ores**
- defined, Reg. 3900(2)

**Mineral resource**
- acquisition, unreasonable considerations, 69(7)
- allowance, 20(1)(v.1), 65
- defined, 248(1)
- disposition of, for unreasonable consideration, 69(6)
- regulations, 20(15)
- royalties, 12(1)(o)
- - not deductible, 18(1)(m)

**Mineral rights**
- dealers in, limitation, 66(5)

**Minimum amount**
- defined
- - for minimum tax, 127.51
- - for RRIF, 146.3(1) "minimum amount"

**Minimum tax,** 127.5–127.55
- additional tax for income not earned in a province, and, 120(4) "tax otherwise payable under this Part"
- additional tax re
- - excluded from instalment estimates for farmers and fishermen, 155(1)(a)

- adjusted taxable income, 127.52
- basic exemption, 127.53
- basic minimum tax credit, 127.531
- carryback re
- - effect on interest payable to taxpayer, 164(5), (5.1)
- - no effect on interest payable, 161(7)
- carryover, 120.2
- - additional tax, determination of, 120.2(3)
- - overseas employment tax credit not reduced by, 122.3(2) "tax otherwise payable under this Part for the year"
- - where not applicable, 120.2(4)
- excluded from "tax payable" etc. under Part I, 117(1)
- foreign tax credit, 127.54
- partnership investing in residential property or Canadian film, 127.52(2)
- Quebec abatement and, 120(4) "tax otherwise payable under this Part"
- where not applicable, 127.55

**Mining**
- defined, Reg. 1104(3)

**Mining corporation**
- prospecting, exploration and development expenses, ITAR 29(2)–(5)

**Mining expenditure**
- flow-through, *see* Flow-through mining expenditure

**Mining exploration depletion base**
- defined, Reg. 1203(2)
- expenses added to
- - amounts receivable, portion included in income, 59(3.3)(f)

**Mining exploration expenses, "grass-roots"**
- expenses in first 60 days of year, 66.1(8)
- partnership deemed not at arm's length, 66(17)

**Mining operations**
- defined, for mining taxes on income, Reg. 3900(1)

**Mining property,** *see also* Canadian resource property
- capital cost allowance, Reg. Sch. II:Cl. 28, Sch. II:Cl. 41
- defined, 35(2)
- excluded from flow-through share renunciation, 66(12.62)(b.1)
- prospector's exemption, 35

**Mining reclamation trust,** *repealed, see* Qualifying environmental trust

**Mining taxes, deduction,** 20(1)(v), Reg. 3900

**Minister of Canadian Heritage,** *see also* Canadian Heritage, Department of
- certification of accredited film/video production, 125.5(1) "accredited film or video production certificate"
- - revocation of certificate, 125.5(6)
- certification of Canadian film/video production, 125.4(1) "Canadian film or video production certificate"
- - revocation of certificate, 125.4(6)

**Minister of the Environment**
- certification of ecologically sensitive land, *see* Ecological gifts
- permission to dispose of ecologically sensitive land, 207.31

**Minister of National Revenue,** *see also* Canada Customs and Revenue Agency
- advice from Dept. of Human Resources Development re mental or physical impairment, 118.3(4)

2750

## Index

**Minister of National Revenue** *(cont'd)*
- arbitrary assessment by, 152(7)
- authority re determination of charitable foundation's "prescribed amount", 149.1(1.2)
- authorized to accept security for payment of tax etc., 220(4)–(4.4)
- burden of proof in assessing penalty, 163(3)
- certificate of exemption, 212(1)(b)(iv), (14)
- certificate re proposed disposition of property by non-resident, 116(2)
- chief source of income, determination re, 31
- consent to change of fiscal period, 249.1(7)
- consent to sale of property bound by Court-registered certificate re amount payable, 223(9), (10)
- defined, 248(1)
- delegation of powers and duties, 220(2.01), Reg. Part IX; *Interpretation Act* s. 24(2)
- designation of public corporation, ITAR 50(3)
- determination of amounts under s. 245, 152(1.11), (1.12)
- • binding effect, 152(1.3)
- determination of excessive refund, 160.1(1)
- determination of losses by, 152(1.1), (1.2)
- • binding effect, 152(1.3)
- direction re collection, 225.2
- discretion re transfer pricing adjustments, 247(10)
- duties of
- • administration and enforcement of Act, 220(1)
- • disposition of appeal, on, 164(4.1)
- • refunds, 164(4.1)
- • when objection filed, 165(3)
- inquiry authorized by, 231.4(1)
- investigatory powers re tax shelters, 237.1(8)
- not bound by return, 152(7)
- notice of, to provide information, 231.2
- permission to destroy records, 230(4), (8)
- powers
- • acquire and dispose of debtor's tax property, to, 224.2
- • extension of filing date, 220(3)
- • seize moneys restorable to tax debtor, to, 224.3
- RPP, authority to impose conditions re, 147.1(5)
- registered investments and, 204.4(2)–(5), 204.5
- required to assess tax, 152(1)
- restrictions on collection, 225.1
- • collection in jeopardy, 225.2
- revocation of registration of charity, 168
- tax shelter identification number, issuance of, 237.1(3)
- waiver of penalty or interest, 220(3.1)
- waiver of requirement to file form or document, 220(2.1)

**Minister (of religion)**, *see* Clergy

**Minor**, *see also* Age; Child
- amount payable by trust to, 104(18)
- transfers and loans to, 74.1(2)
- • corporation, through, 74.5(6)–(11)
- • deemed, 74.5(6)–(11)
- • for value, 74.5(1), (2)
- • joint liability for tax on, 160(1)–(3)
- • repayment of, 74.1(3)
- • trust, through, 74.3, 74.5(9), (10)
- trust for, 104(18)

**Misclassified property**, 13(6)

**Misrepresentation**
- justification for late reassessment, 152(4)(a)(i), 152(5)
- of other person's tax affairs, penalty, 163.2
- of own tax affairs, penalty, 163(2)

**Mobility impairment**, *see also* Disability; Impairment
- building modifications for, deductible, 20(1)(qq)
- device to permit person with, to drive vehicle
- • medical expense, Reg. 5700(m)
- driveway alterations for person with, 118.2(2)(l.6)
- moving expenses for person with, 118.2(2)(l.5)
- transportation and parking for person with, not taxable benefit, 6(16)

**Modifications (to building)**
- disability-related, deductible, 20(1)(qq)
- dwelling, for disabled person, medical expense credit, 118.2(2)(l.2)

**Modified net premium (re insurance policy)**
- defined, Reg. 1408(1), (3)

**Mold**, capital cost allowance, Reg. Sch. II:Cl. 12(d)

**Mole**, capital cost allowance, Reg. Sch. II:Cl. 1(f), Sch. II:Cl. 3

**Monetary contribution**
- for political contribution credit
- • credit for, 127(3)
- • defined, 127(4.1)

**Money**
- borrowed, *see* Borrowed money
- business of lending, *see* Moneylender
- included in definition of property, 248(1)"property"

**Money purchase limit**
- defined, 147.1(1), 248(1)
- limits pension contributions, 147.1(8), (9)
- limits RRSP contribution, 146(1)"RRSP dollar limit"

**Money purchase provision**
- defined, 147.1(1)

**Moneylender**, *see also* Financial institution
- bad debts
- • deduction for, 20(1)(p)(ii)
- • inclusion in income, 12.4
- disposition of Canadian securities, 39(5)(f)
- guarantees etc.
- • acquired from, in amalgamation, 87(2)(h)(iii)
- • reserve for, 20(1)(l.1)
- loan/lending asset
- • acquired from, in amalgamation, 87(2)(h)(ii)
- • reduction in value of
- • • limitation on deduction, 18(1)(s)
- loans etc. acquired in ordinary course of business, 20(27)
- reserve for doubtful debts, 20(1)(l)
- security used or held by
- • "eligible property" for transfer to corporation by shareholder, 85(1.1)(g)
- • superficial loss not deductible, 18(13), (15)

**Monitor**
- crib death, medical expense, Reg. 5700(r)

**Month**
- defined, *Interpretation Act* s. 35(1)

**Montreal**
- international banking centre, 33.1(3)

**Mortality experience**
- defined, Reg. 1900(1)

# Index

**Mortality gains**, Reg. 308
**Mortality loss adjustment account**
- defined, Reg. 1900(1)

**Mortality losses**, Reg. 308
**Mortgage**, *see also* Debt
- expropriation assets acquired for sale of foreign property, 80.1
- foreclosure, 79
- interest
  - - blended with principal in payments, 16(1), 214(2)
  - - deduction for, 20(1)(c), *see also* Work space in home
- investment corporation, *see* Mortgage investment corporation
- not a disposition, 248(1)"disposition"(j), (k)
- RRSP investment, Reg. 4900(1)(j)
- sale of, included in proceeds of disposition, 20(5), (5.1)
- subsidy by employer, taxable benefit, 6(23)

**Mortgage Insurance Corporation of Canada**
- payments to guarantee fund deductible, Reg. 1400(3)G

**Mortgage investment corporation**, 130.1
- allocation of gain rates during 2000, 130.1(4.3)
- deemed public corporation, 130.1(5)
- defined, 130.1(6), 248(1)
- election re capital gains dividend, 130.1(4), Reg. 2104.1
  - - where not made, 130.1(4.1)
- flow-through entity for capital gains exemption, 39.1(1), (6)
- non-qualifying taxed capital gains, 130.1(9)
- not subject to mark-to market rules, 142.2(1)"financial institution"(c)(ii)
- qualifying taxed capital gains, 130.1(9)
- reporting to shareholder of gains in 2000, 130.1(4.2)
- shareholders, how counted, 130.1(7)

**Mortgage subsidy**
- taxable benefit, 6(23)

**Motion picture film**
- Canadian film or video production credit, 125.4
- capital cost allowance, Reg. Sch. II:Cl. 10(s), Sch. II:Cl. 12(m), Sch. II:Cl. 18
- certified feature film, Reg. 1104(2), (10)
  - - capital cost allowance, Reg. 1100(21), (22), Reg. Sch. II:Cl. 12
- certified production, *see* Certified production
- film or video production services credit, 125.5
- film production, prescribed, Reg. 7500
- in-flight movies not treated as entertainment, 67.1(4)(a)
- partnership investing in
  - - capital cost allowance limitation, 127.52(2)
- payment to non-resident for use of, 212(5)
- revenue guarantee, exemption from at-risk rules, 96(2.2)(d)(ii) [repealed]

**Motor vehicle**
- accident claims, payments exempt, 81(1)(q), Reg. 6501
- capital cost allowance
  - - of employee, 8(1)(j), Reg. 1100(6)
  - - of person carrying on business, 20(1)(a), Reg. 1100(1)(a)(x)
- defined, 248(1)
- device to enable disabled person to drive, Reg. 5700(h)

- employee's allowance for use of
  - - not income, 6(1)(b)(vii.1)
  - - where deemed not reasonable, 6(1)(b)(x), (xi)
- employment by U.S. resident on, Canada–U.S. Tax Convention Art. XV:3
- expenses
  - - limitations on, *see* Passenger vehicle
  - - of employee, when deductible, 8(1)(f), (h.1)
- loan to shareholder/employee to purchase, 15(2.4)(d)
- recapture of excess CCA, 13(2)
- terminal loss rules not applicable, 20(16.1)

**Motor vehicle warranty**, *see* Extended motor vehicle warranty

**Mould**
- capital cost allowance, Reg. Sch. II:Cl. 12(d)

**Movie**, *see* Motion picture film
**Moving expenses**, *see also* Relocation
- certain students, 62(2)
- deduction for, 62(1)
  - - residents absent from Canada, 64.1
- defined, 62(3)
- medical expense credit, 118.2(2)(l.5)
- "new work location", 62(1)
- residents absent from Canada
  - - deduction, 64.1

**Multi-employer plan (RPP)**
- anti-avoidance, 147.1(14)
- defined, 147.1(1), Reg. 8500(1)
- pension adjustment limits, 147.1(9)
- registration requirements, Reg. 8510(7)
- special rules, Reg. 8510(5)
- when revocable, 147.1(9)

**Multiple counting of deductions or credits**, 248(28)

**Multiple-unit residential buildings**
- capital cost allowance, Reg. Sch. II:Cl. 31, Sch. II:Cl. 32
  - - separate classes, Reg. 1101(5b)

**Municipal waste**
- defined, Reg. 1104(13)
- used as fuel, Reg. Sch. II:Cl. 43(e)(i)(A), Sch. II:Cl. 43(d)(ix)

**Municipality**, *see also* Government
- assistance by, *see* Assistance/government assistance
- bonds of
  - - constitute qualified securities for securities lending arrangement rules, 260(1)"qualified security"(c)
  - - no non-resident withholding tax, 212(1)(b)(ii)(C)(III)
- corporation controlled by, excluded from refundable ITC, 127.1(2)"excluded corporation"(a)(ii)
- corporation owned by
  - - bonds of, no non-resident withholding tax, 212(1)(b)(ii)(C)(IV)
  - - deemed not private corporation for Part IV tax, 227(16)
  - - election to remain taxable, 149(1.11)
  - - exempt from tax, 149(1)(d.5)
- elected officer or school board trustee, expense allowance exempt, 81(3)
- exempt from tax, 149(1)(c)
- gifts to, 110.1(1)(a)(iv), 118.1(1)"total charitable gifts"(c)
  - - ecologically sensitive land
    - - - by corporation, 110.1(1)(d)(i)

## Index

Municipality (cont'd)
- • • by individual, 118.1(1)"total ecological gifts"(a)
- • • tax on disposition of without permission, 207.31
- • • generally
- • • by corporation, 110.1(1)(a)(iv)
- • • by individual, 118.1(1)"total charitable gifts"(c)
- officials, bribery of, no deduction, 67.5
- property taxes
- • • excluded from calculation of resource royalties, 12(1)(o), 18(1)(m)
- • • farmland
- • • • addition to adjusted cost base, 53(1)(i)(iii)(A)
- • • • deduction by partner where partnership disposes of land, 101(c)(i)
- • • • limitation on deduction, 18(2)(b)
- representation to, expenses deductible, 20(1)(cc)
- support payments for farmers by, information slips, Reg. 234–236
- townsite costs, see Townsite costs
- volunteer firefighter
- • • deduction for, 8(1)(a) [to be repealed]
- • • exemption for, 81(4)
- welfare, see Social assistance payment

**Musical instrument**
- capital cost allowance, Reg. Sch. II:Cl. 8(i)
- costs, to employee, 8(1)(p)

**Musician**
- deduction from employment income, 8(1)(p), (q)
- U.S. resident, Canada–U.S. Tax Convention Art. XVI

**Mute person**
- speech synthesizer, medical expense, Reg. 5700(p)

**Mutual agreement procedure**, Canada–U.S. Tax Convention Art. XXVI

**Mutual corporation**
- provincial life insurance corporation converted into, 139

**Mutual fund**, see Mutual fund corporation; Mutual fund trust

**Mutual fund corporation**, 131
- allocation of gain rates during 2000, 131(1.6)
- amalgamation, 87(2)(bb)
- capital gains dividends, election, 131(1)–(1.4), Reg. 2104
- • • interest on, 131(3.1), (3.2)
- capital gains on Canadian securities, 39(5)
- capital gains redemptions, defined, 131(6)
- deemed private corporation, 131(5)
- defined, 131(8), (8.1), 248(1)
- dividend refund to, 131(5)
- election not to be restricted financial institution, 131(10)
- first taxation year, 130.1(8)
- flow-through entity for capital gains exemption, 39.1(1), (6)
- increase in paid-up capital not deemed dividend, 131(4)
- information return where share claimed to be qualified investment, Reg. 221
- non-residents, for benefit of, 131(8.1)
- not subject to mark-to-market rules, 142.2(1)"financial institution"(c)(iii)
- payment of tax, 157(3)
- qualified investment for RRSP, RRIF, etc.
- • • bond or debenture of trust, Reg. 4900(1)(c.1)

- • • unit of trust, Reg. 4900(1)(c)
- refund to, re capital gains dividend, 131(2), (3)
- refundable capital gains tax on hand, 131(6)
- • • reduction of, 131(9)
- reporting to shareholder of gains in 2000, 131(1.5)
- rollover of property to mutual fund trust, 132.2
- shares of
- • • received on amalgamation, ITAR 65(5)
- • • transferred in exchange for units of mutual fund trust, 132.2(1)(j)
- taxed capital gains, 131(7)

**Mutual fund limited partnership**
- financing, restrictions on, 18.1

**Mutual fund trust**, 132
- amounts designated by, 132.1
- • • adjusted cost base of unit, 132.1(2)
- • • deduction for, 132.1(1)(c)
- • • • carryover, 132.1(4)
- • • • limitation, 132.1(3)
- • • inclusion in taxpayer's income, 132.1(1)(d)
- • • where designation of no effect, 132.1(5)
- capital gains on Canadian securities, 39(5)
- capital gains redemptions, defined, 132(4)
- capital gains refund to, 132(1), (2)
- • • interest on, 132(2.1), (2.2)
- defined, 132(6)–(7), 248(1)
- • • election to be from beginning of first taxation year, 132(6.1)
- • • following rollover of assets in qualifying exchange, 132.2(1)(q)
- • • retention of status to end of calendar year, 132(6.2)
- election for December 15 year-end, 132.11
- • • allocation or designation of amount to be included in income, 132.11(6)
- • • • late filing of allocation or designation, 220(3.21)(b)
- flow-through entity for capital gains exemption, 39.1(1), (6)
- information return where interest claimed to be qualified investment, Reg. 221
- instalment payments of tax, 156(2)
- interest received by, on behalf of non-residents, exemption, 212(9)(c)
- minimum tax not payable, 127.55(f)(ii)
- non-residents, for benefit of, 132(7)
- not subject to mark-to market rules, 142.2(1)"financial institution"(d)
- obligation guaranteed by, qualified investment for deferred income plan, Reg. 4900(1)(i)
- qualified investment for RRSP, RRIF, etc.
- • • bond or debenture of trust, Reg. 4900(1)(d.1)
- • • unit of trust, Reg. 4900(1)(d)
- real estate investment trust as, 132(6)(b)(ii)
- refundable capital gains tax on hand
- • • defined, 132(4)
- rollover of property to another mutual fund trust, 132.2
- taxable capital gains
- • • no surtax on, 180.1(2)(c)
- taxation year, election for December 15, 132.11
- taxed capital gains, 132(5)
- transfer of property from mutual fund corporation or trust, 132.2
- unit of
- • • adjusted cost base of, 53(1)(d.2)

2753

## Index

**Mutual fund trust** *(cont'd)*
- - "Canadian security", 39(6)
- - deemed to be a share for rollover purposes, 132.2(2)"share"
- - employee option to acquire, 7(1), 110(1)(d)
- - transferred in course of qualifying exchange, 132.2(1)(j)
- year-end, election for December 15, 132.11

**Mutual holding corporation**
- deemed dividend on distribution by, 139.2
- defined, for insurance demutualization, 139.1(1)

**Mutual insurance corporations**
- exemption for, 149(1)(m)

**Mutual life insurance corporation**
- provincial corporation converted into, 139

**Mutualization proposal (for insurer)**, 139

### N

**NISA Fund No. 2**, *see also* Net income stabilization account
- amount credited to, not taxed, 12(10.3)
- deduction by trust, limitation, 104(6)(b)(ii.1), (iii)
- deemed paid on death, 70(5.4)
- defined, 248(1)
- disposition of, 73(5)
- paid to non-resident, withholding tax, 212(1)(t), 214(3)(l)
- - information return required, Reg. 202(2.1)
- receipt from, included in income, 12(10.2)
- - constitutes active business income, 125(7)"income of the corporation for the year from an active business"
- - information return required, Reg. 201(1)(e)
- right to benefit, no tax on emigration, 128.1(10)"excluded right or interest"(i)
- rollover to corporation, 85(1)(c.1), 85(1.1)(i)
- transfer to spouse or spouse trust, 70(6.1), 73(5)(a), 104(5.1), (14.1)

**NRO**, *see* Non-resident-owned investment corporation

**NSERC**, *see* Natural Sciences and Engineering Research Council

**National arts service organization**, *see* Registered national arts service organization

**National Defence**, *see* Canadian Forces

**National Film Board**
- prescribed person for Canadian film/video tax credit, Reg. 1106(7)

**National Revenue, Department of**, *see* Minister (of National Revenue); Canada Customs and Revenue Agency

**Natural gas**, *see* Petroleum/natural gas

**Natural Sciences and Engineering Research Council**
- payments to, as R&D expenditures, 37(1)(a)(ii), 37(7)"approved"
- research grants, taxable, 56(1)(o)

**Nature Conservancy**
- prescribed donee, Reg. 3504

**Nav Canada**
- debt of, qualified investment for deferred income plans, Reg. 4900(1)(q)

**Nazi Germany**
- compensation to victims of, 81(1)(g)

**Needle/syringe**
- medical expense, Reg. 5700(b)

**Negative amounts**
- adjusted cost base, deemed gain, 40(3), (3.1)
- capital cost allowance pool, recapture, 13(1)
- cumulative eligible capital, recapture, 14(1)
- in formulas, deemed nil, 257
- investment tax credit balance, recapture, 127(27)–(35)
- taxable income cannot be less than nil, 248(1)"taxable income"
- undepreciated capital cost, recapture, 13(1)

**Negative policy reserves**
- of insurer, 12(1)(e.1), 20(22), Reg. 1400(2)

**Neglect**
- grounds for reassessment at any time, 152(4)(a)(i)

**Negligence**, *see* Gross negligence; Neglect

**Nephew**, *see* Niece/nephew

**Net capital loss**
- amalgamation, on, 87(2.1)
- carryover of, 111(1)(b)
- - limitation, 111(1.1)
- death, on, 111(2)
- defined, 111(8), (9), 248(1)
- determination of, by Minister, 152(1.1), (1.2), (1.3)
- limitation on deductibility, 111(3)
- non-deductible where control of corporation changed, 111(4)
- partnership, from, 96(1)
- reassessment, 152(6)(c)
- reduction of, on debt forgiveness, 80(4)(b)
- subsidiary's, on winding-up, 88(1.2)

**Net cost of insurance**
- defined, Reg. 1900(1)

**Net cost (of labour-sponsored funds share)**
- defined, 127.4(1), 211.7(1)

**Net cost of pure insurance**
- defined, Reg. 308
- premium deductible where used as collateral, 20(1)(e.2)

**Net earnings (of foreign affiliate)**
- defined, Reg. 5907(1)
- exempt due to tax sparing, Reg. 5907(10)
- included in exempt earnings, Reg. 5907(1)"exempt earnings"(d)(i)
- included in taxable earnings, Reg. 5907(1)"taxable earnings"(b)

**Net forgiveness amount**
- reserve for, 61.3(1)(a), 61.3(2)(a)

**Net income (on income tax return)**
- defined, 3

**Net income stabilization account**, *see also* NISA Fund No. 2
- administration fee, deductible, 20(1)(ff)
- death of taxpayer, on, 70(5.4), 70(6.1)
- defined, 248(1)
- fair market value of, for certain capital gains exemption rules, 110.6(1.1)
- money borrowed to contribute to, no deduction for interest, 18(11)(f)
- no accrual of interest income, 12(3), 12(11)"investment contract"(j)
- transfer to spouse or spouse trust, 70(6.1)

**Net interest rate**
- defined, 211(1)

2754

**Net level premium**
- defined, Reg. 1900(1)

**Net level premium reserve**
- defined, Reg. 1900(1)

**Net loss (of foreign affiliate)**
- defined, Reg. 5907(1)

**Net past service pension adjustment (net PSPA)**
- defined, 146(1), 204.2(1.3)

**Net premium for the policy**
- defined, re policy reserves, Reg. 1408(1)

**Net resource adjustment**
- defined, Reg. 5203(3.1)
- reduces adjusted business income for M&P credit, Reg. 5203(1)"adjusted business income"(b)

**Net resource income**
- defined, Reg. 5203(3)

**Net surplus (of foreign affiliate)**
- defined, Reg. 5907(1)

**Net taxable capital gains**
- defined, 104(21.3)

**Net tax owing**
- defined (for instalments), 156.1(1)

**Net worth assessment**, 152(7)

**Netherlands**, *see also* Foreign government
- stock exchange recognized, Reg. 3201(i)
- universities, gifts to, Reg. Sch. VIII s. 20

**New Brunswick**, *see also* Province
- Community Development bonds, eligible for RRSP investment, Reg. 4900(1)(i.1)
- tax rates, *see* introductory pages

**New corporation**, *see* Amalgamation; Corporation

**New law**
- defined, ITAR 12
- references to, having same number as a provision in Part IV or VIII of former Act, ITAR 16
- references to subject matter of old law, ITAR 13

**New share**
- defined, Reg. 6202.1(5)

**New Zealand**, *see also* Foreign government
- currency loan, *see* Weak currency debt
- stock exchange recognized, Reg. 3201(k)

**Newfoundland**, *see also* Province
- Canada–Newfoundland Atlantic Accord, communication of information for, 241(4)(d)(vi)
- cod fishermen compensation, *see* Northern Cod Compensation and Adjustment Program
- corporation incorporated in, before 1949
- • deemed incorporated in Canada, 248(1)"corporation incorporated in Canada"
- offshore area
- • defined, 248(1)
- • included in "province", 124(4)
- prescribed area, for electrical energy or steam processing, 127(9)"qualified property"(c.1)
- prescribed designated region, 127(9)"specified percentage"(a)(vi), Reg. 4607
- qualified property acquired for use in, 127(9)"specified percentage"(a), (e)
- tax rates, *see* introductory pages

**News show**
- ineligible for Canadian film/video credit, Reg. 1106(1)"excluded production"(b)

- ineligible for film/video production services credit, Reg. 9300(c)

**Newspaper advertising, limitation**, 19

**Niece/nephew**
- deemed related, for purposes of certain trust rules, 104(5.7)(b)
- defined, 252(2)(g)
- dependent, 118(6)(b)
- property transferred to, income attribution re, 74.1(2)

**Nil, minimum amount for formula calculations**, 257

**Nil income**
- equivalent to zero income, 3(f)

*1948 Income Tax Act*, **The, defined**, ITAR 12

**1971 receivables**, ITAR 23(5)"1971 receivables"

**1977 carryforward deduction**, Reg. 2408

**1977 excess policy dividend deduction**, Reg. 2407

**Nobel Prize, non-taxable**, Reg. 7700

**Nominee corporation**, *see* Bare trust

**Non-arm's length indicator**
- application to foreign trust, 233.2(2)

**Non-arm's length person**
- excessive payment where property surrendered to creditor, 79(3)E(a)
- interest on debt relating to acquisition of land, 18(3)"interest on debt relating to the acquisition of land"(b)
- loans to, 56(4.1)–(4.3)
- meaning of, *see* Arm's length: meaning of
- non-resident, transactions with
- • extended reassessment period, 152(4)(b)(iii)
- • information return, 233.1
- soft costs relating to construction, 18(3.1)(b), 18(3.2)(b)
- transfer of property to or from, 69(1)

**Non-arm's length transactions**
- agreement to pay low rent for property
- • effect on disposition of property, 69(1.2)
- amalgamated corporations, 251(3.1)
- corporation having, with non-resident persons
- • extended reassessment period, 152(4)(b)(iii)
- • information return, 233.1
- depreciable property acquired through, 13(7)(e)
- • corporations controlled by one trustee, 13(7.3)
- disposition at less than fair market value, 69(1)(b)
- eligible capital property acquired through, 14(3)
- foreign property acquired in
- • consideration deemed to be fair market value, 206(4)
- inadequate considerations, 69
- income or gain from property transferred
- • transferor and transferee liable for tax, 160
- lease of depreciable property, 13(32)
- life insurance policy, disposition, 148(7), (8)
- non-resident, unreasonable consideration paid to, 247
- presumption, 251(1)(a)
- property disposed of in, ITAR 26(5)
- purchases at more than fair market value, 69(1)(a)
- rights or things transferred to beneficiary
- • deemed cost, 69(1.1)
- sale of shares, 84.1
- • non-resident, by, 212.1
- share for share exchange, 85.1(2)(a)
- transfer of right to income, 56(4)

2755

**Non-arm's length transactions** *(cont'd)*
- unpaid amounts, 78(1), (2)

**Non-business income tax (foreign)**
- deduction for, 126(1)
- defined, 126(7)
- - for trust, 104(22.4)

**Non-cancellable or guaranteed renewable accident and sickness policy**
- defined, Reg. 1408(1)

**Non-capital loss**
- amalgamation, on, 87(2.1), (2.11)
- carryover of, 111(1)(a)
- - corporation, by, 111(5)–(5.4)
- - winding-up of subsidiary, on, 111(5.4)
- defined, 111(8), (9), 248(1)
- determination of, by Minister, 152(1.1), (1.2), (1.3)
- insurer's, 111(7.1)
- life insurer's, 111(7.2)
- limitation on deductibility, 111(3)
- partnership, from, 96(1)
- reassessment, 152(6)(c)
- reduction of, on debt forgiveness, 80(3)(a), 80(4)(a)
- subsidiary's, on winding-up, 88(1.1)

**Non-conventional lands, defined**, Reg. 1206(1)

**Non-discretionary trust**
- defined, 17(15), 248(1)

**Non-discrimination**, Canada–U.S. Tax Convention Art. XXV

**Non-participating life insurance policy**
- defined, 211(1), Reg. 1900(1)

**Non-periodic payments**
- tax deduction, Reg. 103

**Non-profit association**, *see* Non-profit organization

**Non-profit corporation**, *see also* Non-profit organization
- qualified investment for RRSP etc., Reg. 4900(1)(r)
- scientific research and experimental development, for
- - annual return, 149(7)
- - exemption, 149(1)(j)
- - payments to, 37(1)(a)(iii)

**Non-profit organization**, *see also* Charity, Non-profit corporation
- exemption for, 149(1)(l), 149(2)
- - deemed a trust, 149(5)
- foreign, defined, Reg. 6804(1)
- information return, whether required, 149(5), 149(12), 150(1)(a)

**Non-qualified investment**, *see also* Qualified investment
- charitable foundation
- - defined, Reg. 3700
- deferred profit sharing plan
- - acquisition of, tax on, 198(1)
- - defined, 204"qualified investment"
- - disposition of, refund of tax, 198(4)
- - excess holdings, tax on, 206(2)(a)(ii)
- - initial, 199, 204"initial non-qualified investment"
- - tax on, 207.1(2)
- private foundation
- - acquisition of, tax on, 189(1)
- - defined, 149.1(1)"non-qualified investment"
- proportional holdings election, 259(1), (3)

- registered education savings plan (RESP)
- - revocation of plan, 146.1(2.1), (12.1)
- - tax on holding, 207.1(3)
- registered retirement income fund (RRIF)
- - acquisition of, 146.3(7), (9)
- - defined, 146.3(1)"qualified investment"
- - disposition of, 146.3(8)
- - excess holdings, tax on, 206(2)(a)(ii)
- - tax on, 207.1(3)
- registered retirement savings plan (RRSP)
- - acquisition of, 146(10)
- - defined, 146(1)"non-qualified investment", "qualified investment"
- - disposition of, 146(6)
- - excess holdings, tax on, 206(2)(a)(ii)
- - tax on, 207.1(1)

**Non-qualifying corporation (for small business investment tax credit)**
- defined, 127(9)

**Non-qualifying real property**
- defined, 108(1), 110.6(1), 131(6) [all repealed]

**Non-qualifying security**
- calculation of capital gain on, 40(1.01)
- ceasing to be, 118.1(13)(b)
- defined, 118.1(18)
- donation of
- - credit disallowed to individual, 118.1(13)
- - death of donor, 118.1(15)
- - deduction disallowed to corporation, 110.1(6)
- - - amalgamation, effect on donor, 87(2)(m.1)
- - windup, effect of, 88(1)(e.2), (e.61)
- exchanged for another non-qualifying security, 118.1(14)
- reserve on donation of, 40(1.01)(c)
- - disallowed in year of death, 72(1)(c)

**Non-refundable credits**, 118–118.94

**Non-resident**, *see also* Non-resident tax; Becoming resident in Canada; Ceasing to be resident in Canada; Former resident
- agent for, liable to withhold tax, 215(3)
- alimony/maintenance paid to, 212(1)(f)
- allowance for investment in property in Canada, Reg. 808
- alternative re rents and timber royalties, 216
- amount owing to corporation resident in Canada, 17(1)
- amount paid to, re pre-1976 bond, etc.
- - prescribed countries, ITAR 10(4), Reg. 1600
- amounts received under certain contracts, 115(2)(c.1), 115(2)(e)(v)
- - withholding tax, 153(1)(o)
- annuity payments to, 212(1)(o)
- assessment under Part XIII, 227(10)
- assuming debt for Canadian business, 76.1(2)
- becoming, *see* Ceasing to be resident in Canada
- beneficiary, *see* Beneficiary: non-resident
- benefit conferred on, 246(1)(b)
- benefits paid to, 212(1)(j)
- branch tax, 219
- Canadian resource property, income earned on, 115(4)
- capital cost allowance, Reg. 1102(3)
- capital dividend paid to, 212(1)(c)(ii), 212(2)(b)
- capital gains of, taxed, 115(1)(b)
- - proration re gains before May 1995, 40(9)
- capital property, change in use, 45(1)(d)

2756

## Index

Non-resident *(cont'd)*
- carrying on business in Canada
  - - extended meaning of, 253
  - - liability for income tax, 2(3)(b)
- ceasing to be, *see* Becoming resident in Canada
- change in use (or proportions of use) of capital property, 45(1)(d)
- change in use (or proportions of use) of depreciable property
  - - "gaining or producing income" from a business, 13(9)
- corporation, *see also* Foreign affiliate
  - - bonds of, eligible for RRSP investment, Reg. 4900(1)(p)
  - - branch tax, 219(1)
  - - debt forgiveness reserve, 61.3(2)
  - - deemed, where not resident due to treaty, 250(5)
  - - dividend received by Canadian corporation from, 112(2)
  - - exempt from Part I.3 tax, 181.1(3)(d)
  - - income bond/debenture, interest on, 15(4)
  - - required to file tax return, 150(1)(a)
  - - shares of, for deferred income plans, 204"qualified investment"(h)
    - - - RESP qualified investment, 146.1(1)"qualified investment"(a)
    - - - RRSIF qualified investment, 146.3(1)"qualified investment"(a)
    - - - RRSP qualified investment, 146(1)"qualified investment"(a)
  - - taxable capital employed in Canada, 181.4
- credit for tax paid on emigration, 119
- debt owing to corporation resident in Canada, 17
- deductions allowed, in computing income from a source, 4(3)
- deferred profit sharing plan payments to, 212(1)(m)
- defined, 248(1)
- disposition of property by
  - - Canadian resource property, certificate re, 116(5.2)
  - - Canadian securities, 39(5)(g)
  - - interest in real property etc., 216(5)
  - - life insurance policy, presumption re, 116(5.4)
  - - taxable Canadian property, *see* taxable Canadian property (*below*)
  - - where tax deferred under tax treaty, 115.1
- dividend paid to, 212(2)
  - - stop-loss rule, 40(3.7)
- election to file return under Part I
  - - certain payments, 217
  - - rents and timber royalties, 216
  - - restriction on deduction, 216(8)
- eligible capital property of, 14(14), (15)
- emigration, *see* Ceasing to be resident in Canada
- employed in Canada
  - - liability for income tax, 2(3)(a)
- energy conversion grants paid to, 212(1)(s)
- entity, *see* Non-resident entity
- estate or trust income paid to, 212(11)
- exchanged for another non-qualifying security, 118.1(14)
- exchanges of property, determination of gain, 44(7)
- excluded property, defined, 116(6)
- financial institution, *see also* Authorized foreign bank
  - - beginning to use property in Canadian business, 142.6(1.2)
  - - ceasing to use property in Canadian business, 142.6(1.1)
- foreign tax credit re disposition before Oct/96, 126(2.2)
- former resident, credit for tax paid on emigration, 119
- home insulation grants paid to, 212(1)(s)
- income-averaging annuity contract payments to, 212(1)(n)
- income earned in a province, Reg. 2602
- "income for the year", 120(3)
- income from ship or aircraft, exempt, 81(1)(c)
- individual
  - - computation of Part I tax, 118.94
  - - required to file tax return, 150(1.1)(b)
  - - tax credits, 118.94
- insurance corporation, *see* Insurance corporation: non-resident
- insurer, liability for additional tax on branch profits, 219(4)–(8)
- inventory of, 10(12)–(14)
- investment fund, *see* Non-resident investment fund
- issuing obligation at discount, 16(2), (3)
- limited partnership losses, carryover of, 111(10)
- loan to, by corporation, 17
- management fees paid to, 212(1)(a)
- moving debt from Canadian business, 76.1(1)
- no reserve for amount not due until later year, 20(8)
- non-arm's length sale of shares by, 212.1
- obligation transferred or assigned to
  - - where deemed resident, 214(9)
- ownership certificate required of, 234
- partnership, withholding tax on payments to, 212(13.1)(b)
- patronage dividends paid to, 212(1)(g)
- payments from
  - - information return, Reg. 203
- payments to, 212(1)
  - - deemed, 214(3), (3.1)
  - - information returns, Reg. 202, 203
- pension benefits paid to, 212(1)(h)
- pension fund, *see* Non-resident pension fund
- pension plan for, not subject to Part XI, 205(a)
- persons, Reg. 805
  - - excluded property, Reg. 810
- plan for benefit of, re services rendered outside Canada, excluded from "retirement compensation arrangement", 248(1)
  - - exception re "resident's arrangement", 207.6(5)
- property excluded from capital cost allowances
  - - farming and fishing, Reg. 1702(4)
- real estate of, transfer to corporation, 85(1.1)(h), 85(1.2)
- refund of Part XIII tax, 227(6)
- registered education savings plan payments to, 212(1)(r)
- registered home ownership savings plan payments to, 212(1)(p)
- registered retirement income fund payments to, 212(1)(q)
- registered retirement savings plan payments to, 212(1)(l)
- remuneration for office, employment or services, 115(2)(c.1), 115(2)(e)(v)
  - - withholding tax, 153(1)(o)
- rents/royalties paid to, 212(1)(d)

2757

## Index

Non-resident *(cont'd)*
- retirement compensation arrangement, purchase price of interest in, 212(1)(j)
- retiring allowance paid to, 212(1)(j.1)
- return may be required of, 215(4)
- salary deferral arrangements, 6(13)
- shareholder
  - - loan to, from corporation, 15(2.2), (8), 227(6.1)
- spousal support payments, 212(1)(f)
- stop-loss credit, 119
- student, 115(2)
- supplementary unemployment plan benefits paid to, 212(1)(k)
- tax, *see also* Non-resident tax
  - - tax under Part I, 2(3)
- taxable Canadian property, 115(1)(b)
  - - disposition of, 2(3)(c), 116
    - - - failure to give Minister notice, offence/penalty, 238(1)
  - - prorating for gains before May 1995, 40(9)
    - - - purchaser liable for tax, 116(5)
- taxable income earned in Canada, 115
  - - deductions permitted, 115(1)(d)–(f)
- taxable income of corporation earned in a province, Reg. 413
- taxation year of, 250.1(a)
- timber royalties paid to, 212(1)(e)
- transactions not at arm's length with, 247
  - - extended reassessment period, 152(4)(b)(iii)
  - - information return re, 233.1
    - - - penalty for failure to file, 162(10)
- transfer pricing rules, *see* Transfer pricing
- trust, *see* Trust (or estate): non-resident
- unreasonable consideration from, 247
- unreasonable consideration paid to, 247
- withholding tax, 215(1), 227(10), Reg. 105, *see also* Non-resident tax
  - - joint and several liability, 227(8.1)

**Non-resident entity**
- defined, 94.1(1)

**Non-resident financial institution**, *see* Non-resident: financial institution

**Non-resident investment fund**
- deemed not carrying on business in Canada, 115.2(2)
- defined, 115.2(1)

**Non-resident-owned investment corporation**, 133, 134; ITAR 59, Reg. Part V
- allowable refund, 133(6)
  - - allowable refundable tax on hand, defined, 133(9)
  - - cumulative taxable income, defined, 133(9)
  - - defined, 133(8)"allowable refund"
- allowable refundable tax on hand, 133(9)
- amalgamation, 87(2)(cc)
- "Canadian property" defined, 133(8)
- capital gains dividend, election re, 133(7.1), Reg. 2105
  - - where not made, 133(7.3)
- capital gains dividend account, defined, 133(8)
- computation of income, 133(1)
- cumulative taxable income, 133(9)
- deemed not Canadian, taxable Canadian, or private corporation, 134
- defined, 133(8), 248(1)
- dividend paid to U.S. resident, Canada–U.S. Tax Convention Art. X:7(a)
- dividend received by trust from, for benefit of non-residents, 104(10), (11), 212(9)(a)
- exempt from corporate surtax, 123.2
- exempt from large corporations (Part I.3) tax, 181.1(3)(a)
- exempt from Part IV tax, 186.1(b)
- foreign tax not deductible, 133(4)
- interest received by trust from, for benefit of non-residents, 212(9)(a)
- no foreign affiliate of, 95(1)"foreign affiliate"
- payment of tax, 157(3)
- repealed after 2003, 133(8)"non-resident-owned investment corporation"(g)–(i)
  - - election to remain NRO for certain purposes, 134.1
- share of constitutes excluded property, 108(1)"eligible real property gain"
- simultaneous dividends, 133(7.2)
- tax rate applicable, 133(3)
- taxable dividend, 133(8)
- taxable income of, 133(2)

**Non-resident pension fund**
- deemed not carrying on business in Canada, 115.2(2)
- defined, re not carrying on business in Canada, 115.2(1)

**Non-resident person**
- defined, re international banking centre, 33.1(1)
- eligible loan to, by international banking centre, 33.1(1)

**Non-resident tax**, 212–218; ITAR 10, Reg. 800–810
- additional tax on non-resident corporation carrying on business in Canada, 219
  - - insurers, 219(4)–(8)
- alimony, 212(1)(f)
- annuity payments, 212(1)(o)
- assessment under Part XIII, 227(10)
- Canada Pension Plan benefits, 212(1)(h)(ii) [repealed]
  - - election to file return, re, 217
- certificate of exemption, 212(14)
  - - refusal by Minister
    - - - appeal from, 172(3)(d), 180
    - - - deemed, 172(4)(c)
- deemed dividends, 214(3)
- deemed income, on, 214(4)
- deemed interest, 214(6)–(14)
- deferred profit sharing payments, 212(1)(m)
  - - election to file return re, 217
- dividends, 212(2)
  - - deemed payment of, 212.1(1)
  - - from foreign business corporation, 213(1)
- eligible funeral arrangement, return of funds, 212(1)(v)
- employee benefit plan, trust payments not subject to, 212(17)
- energy conversion grant, 212(1)(s)
- estate or trust income, 212(1)(c)
  - - exemption, 212(9), (10)
- home insulation grant, 212(1)(s)
- identification of obligations, Reg. 807
- income and capital combined, 214(2)
- income imputed to transferor, not taxable, 212(12)
- insurers, Reg. 800, 801, 803, 804, 2401, 2403
- interest, 212(1)(b)
  - - government bonds, exempt, 212(1)(b)(ii)
  - - loan to wholly-owned subsidiary, 218
  - - long-term debt, exempt, 212(1)(b)(vii)
  - - on provincial bonds, 212(6)

2758

Index

Non-resident tax *(cont'd)*
- • replacement obligation where corporation in financial difficulty, 212(3)
- international organizations, prescribed, Reg. 806
- limitation on rate, ITAR 10(6)
- maintenance, 212(1)(f)
- management fee, 212(1)(a)
- • defined, 212(4)
- motion picture films, payments for use of etc., 212(5)
- no action for withholding, 227
- no deductions from income, 214(1)
- non-arm's length sale of shares by non-resident, 212.1
- obligation transferred or assigned
- • non-resident deemed resident, where, 214(9)
- Part XIV, 219
- partnership payer or payee, 212(13.1), (13.2)
- patronage dividend, 212(1)(g)
- pension benefits, 212(1)(h)
- • election to file return re, 217
- prescribed international organizations, Reg. 806
- refund of, 227(6)
- registered education savings plan, payments out of, 212(1)(r)
- registered home ownership savings plan, payments from, 212(1)(p)
- registered retirement income fund, 212(1)(q)
- registered retirement savings plan, payments out of, 212(1)(l)
- • election to file return re, 217
- regulations
- • reducing amount to be deducted or withheld, 215(5)
- • residents etc., re, 214(13)
- rent, royalties, 212(1)(d), 212(13)
- • alternative re rents and timber royalties, 216
- retiring allowances, etc., 212(1)(j.1)
- • election to file return re, 217
- securities in satisfaction of income debts, 214(4)
- spousal/child support, 212(1)(f)
- standby charges and guarantee fees, 214(15)
- supplementary unemployment benefits, 212(1)(k)
- • election to file return re, 217
- timber royalty, 212(1)(e)
- • alternative re, 216
- trust or estate income paid to, 212(1)(c)
- withholding of, 215, Reg. 105
- • reduction of, Reg. 809

**Non-resident time**
- defined, 94(1)"connected contributor" [proposed]

**Non-share-capital corporation**
- whether control acquired, 256(8.1)

**Non-share consideration (boot)**
- effect of mutual fund rollover, 132.2(1)(c)
- effect on non-arm's length sale of shares, 84.1(1)(b)
- effect on section 85 rollover, 85(1)(b)

**Non-taxable obligation, defined**, 240(1)

**Normal reassessment period**
- defined, 152(3.1)
- limitation on reassessments, 152(4), (5)

**Nortel Networks spin-off**, 55(3.02)

**Northern Canada**
- additional car allowance in Yukon and N.W.T., Reg. 7306(a)(iii)

- credit for residing in, 110.7, Reg. 7303.1
- prescribed northern zone and prescribed intermediate zone, Reg. 7303.1
- remote work site, employment at, 6(6)

**Northern Cod Compensation and Adjustment Program**, *see also* Fishing: compensation programs
- overpayments repaid, deductible, 60(n)(ii.1)
- payments received under, taxable, 56(1)(a)(vi)
- • withholding of tax at source, 153(1)(m)

**Northwest Territories**, *see also* Northern Canada
- additional $0.04 reasonable kilometrage allowance, Reg. 7306(a)(iii)
- *Risk Capital Investment Tax Credits Act*, corporation under
- • prescribed assistance under, Reg. 6702(a.2)
- • prescribed LSVCC, Reg. 6701(i)
- • prescribed venture capital corporation, Reg. 6700(a)(xiii), 6700.2
- • qualified investment, Reg. 4900(1)(i.12)
- tax rates, *see* introductory pages

**Norway**, *see also* Foreign government
- stock exchange recognized, Reg. 3201(u)

**Not-for-profit organization**, *see also* Non-profit organization
- defined, Canada–U.S. Tax Convention Art. XXIX A:5(b)

**Notary (in Quebec)**, *see* Lawyer

**Notch provision (medical expenses)**, 118.2(1)D

**Note**, *see* Promissory note

**"Nothings"**, ITAR 21, *see also* Eligible capital property

**Notice of assessment**, 152(2)
- date of, 244(14), (15)

**Notice of determination**, 152(1.2), *see also* Determination
- date of, 244(15)
- loss carryforwards, 152(1.1)
- partnership income or loss, 152(1.5)
- • objection to, 165(1.15)
- presumption re mailing date, 248(14)

**Notice of intent (to revoke RESP)**
- appeal from, 172(3)(e.1)
- defined, 146.1(12.1)

**Notice of objection**, 165, *see also* Objection
- appeal following, whether new issues can be raised, 169(2.1)
- deadline, 165(1)
- determination of partnership income or loss, 165(1.15)
- extension of time to file
- • by Minister, 166.1
- • by Tax Court, 166.2
- form, 165(1), (2)
- large corporation, issues to be specified, 165(1.11)
- limitation on grounds for objection, 165(1.1)
- service, 165(2), (6)

**Notice of revocation (of RESP)**
- defined, 146.1(12.2)
- effect of, 146.1(13)

**Nova Scotia**, *see also* Cape Breton; Province
- Community Economic Development Corporation, qualified investment for deferred income plans, Reg. 4900(1)(i.11)
- *Equity Tax Credit Act*, corporation under, qualified investment, Reg. 4900(1)(i.11)

2759

# Index

**Nova Scotia** *(cont'd)*
- offshore area
  - - amount taxable earned in, Reg. 414, 415
  - - included in "province", 124(4)"province"
  - - meaning, 248(1)
- Offshore Petroleum Resources Accord, communication of information for, 241(4)(d)(vi)
- prescribed area, for electrical energy or steam processing, 127(9)"qualified property"(c.1)
- prescribed designated region, 127(9)"specified percentage"(a)(vi), Reg. 4607
- qualified property acquired for use in, 127(9)"specified percentage"(a), (e)
- tax rates, *see* introductory pages

**Numbers**, *see* Dollar amounts in legislation and regulations

**Nurse**
- defined, 118.4(2)

**Nursery school**, *see* Child care expenses

**Nursing home**
- cost of care, as medical expense, 118.2(2)(b), (d)

## O

**OAS**, *see* Old Age Security Act benefits

**OECD**, *see* Organisation for Economic Cooperation and Development

**OSFI risk-weighting guidelines**
- defined, 248(1)

**Oaths**
- administration of, 220(5), *Interpretation Act* s. 19
- defined, *Interpretation Act* s. 35(1)

**Objection**, 165, *see also* Appeal; Notice of objection
- books and records, 230(6)
- effect of Minister's filing notice, 165(4)
- expense of making, deductible, 60(o)
- extension of time for filing, 166.1, 166.2
- Minister's duty on, 165(3)
- notice of, 165(1)
- Part IV.1 tax, 187.6
- Part VI.1 tax, 191.4(2)
- Part XII.2 tax, 210.2(7)
- Part XII.3 tax, 211.5
- Part XII.4 tax, 211.6(5)
- partnership income or loss, 165(1.15)
- repayment on, 164(1.1)
- restriction on collection action while underway, 225.1
- second notice not required after reassessment, 165(7)
- service of notice of, 165(2)
- waiver of right to object, 165(1.2), 169(2.2)

**Obligation**, *see also* Bond; Debt; Debt obligation
- assignment of
  - - non-resident tax, 214(14)
  - - where non-resident deemed resident, 214(9)
- defined, ITAR 26(12)"obligation"
- discount on, deduction for, 20(1)(f)
- identification of, Reg. 807
- issued at discount by tax-exempt person, non-resident, or government body, 16(2), (3)
- parked, 80.01(7)
- predecessor corporation, of, 87(6), (7)
- principal amount of
  - - defined, 248(1)
  - - limitation on deductibility, 18(1)(f)

- purchase of, by issuer, 39(3)
- received on amalgamation, ITAR 26(23)
- sale of
  - - non-resident tax, 214(7), (7.1)
- satisfaction of, deemed not to be disposition, 49.1
- specified, 80.01(6)
- taxable and non-taxable, defined, 240(1)

**Obsolescence**
- allowance re, limitation on deductibility, 18(1)(b)

**Occupational therapist**
- certification of impairment
  - - for disability credit, 118.3(1)(a.2)(iii)
  - - for education credit, 118.6(3)(b)(iii)
- defined, 118.4(2)
- therapy qualifying for medical expense credit, 118.2(2)(1.9)

**Offences**, 238(1), 239
- attempted evasion, 239(1)
- compliance orders, on conviction of, 238(2)
- corporation officers, 242
- court has no power to decrease punishment for, 243
- credits, false statements, 239(1.1)
- disclosure of confidential information, 239(2.2)
- failure
  - - file return, 238(1)
  - - keep records, 238(1)
  - - keep tax deductions separate, 238(1)
  - - permit investigation, 238(1)
  - - withhold tax deductions, 238(1)
- false statements, 239
- fines, no deduction for, 18(1)(t)
- minimum fines, 243
- non-resident failing to give notice under s. 116(3), 238(1)
- penalties for, *see* Penalty
- refunds, false statements, 239(1.1)
- saving provision, 238(3)
- secrecy violation, 239(2.2)
- Social Insurance Number, re, 239(2.3)
- two or more in one complaint, 244(2)

**Office, defined**, 248(1)

**Office at home**, *see* Work space in home

**Office de professions du Québec**
- dues to, deductible, 8(1)(i)(vii)

**Office of employment**
- benefits from, includable in income, 6(1)
- in home
  - - conditions for deductibility, 18(12)
- income from, 5(1)
  - - deductions, 8
  - - inclusions, 6
  - - share options, 7
- limitation on deductions, 8(2)
- loss from, 5(2)
- payment for loss of
  - - used to purchase income-averaging annuity contract, deductible, 61(2)(b)
- share option benefits, 7

**Office rent**
- paid by employee, deduction, 8(1)(i)(ii)
  - - certificate of employer, 8(10)

**Officer**
- administering and enforcing Act, 220(2)

2760

## Index

**Officer** *(cont'd)*
- bribery of, non-deductible, 67.5
- corporation, of
  - execution of documents by, 236
  - guilty of corporation's offence, 242
- defined (under "office"), 248(1)

**Official**
- defined, re communication of taxpayer information, 241(10)
- CCRA, powers and duties delegated to, 220(2.01), Reg. 900

**Official receipt**
- defined
  - for political contributions, Reg. 2002(1)
  - for donations and gifts, Reg. 3500

**Official receipt form**
- defined
  - for political contributions, Reg. 2002(1)
  - for donations and gifts, Reg. 3500

**Offset interest**
- against instalments, 161(2.2)
- arrears against refund interest, 161.1

**Offshore assets**
- disclosure of, to CCRA, 233.3

**Offshore corporation**, *see* Foreign affiliate; Non-resident

**Offshore drilling vessels**
- capital cost allowance
  - additional, Reg. 1100(1)(va)
  - separate classes, Reg. 1101(2b)

**Offshore investment fund**
- amount included in income re, 94.1
- non-resident entity, 94.1(2)

**Offshore investment fund property**
- cost base, additions to, 53(1)(m)
- designated cost, 94.1(2)
- prescribed, Reg. 6900

**Offshore region**
- prescribed, for investment tax credit, Reg. 4609

**Offshore trust**, *see also* Trust (or estate): non-resident
- distribution from, reporting requirement, 233.5
- taxation of, where Canadian beneficiary, 94–94.3
- transfer of property to, reporting requirement, 233.2

**Off-the-shelf seismic data**, *see* Seismic testing

**Oil and gas**, *see* Canadian oil and gas property expense; Flow-through shares; Petroleum/natural gas; Resource expenses

**Oil or gas field**
- unitized, *see* Unitized oil or gas field in Canada

**Oil or gas well**
- allowances, 65, Reg. 1207
  - additional, Reg. 1208
- certificate re, ceasing to be valid, 66.1(10)
- defined, 248(1)

**Oil or gas well equipment**
- capital cost allowance, Reg. Sch. II:Cl. 10(j), Sch. II:Cl. 41

**Oil refinery**
- capital cost allowance, Reg. Sch. II:Cl. 10(u), Sch. II:Cl. 41

**Oil sands, included in definition of "mineral"**, 248(1)

**Oil shale, included in definition of "mineral"**, 248(1)

**Oil Substitution Program**, *see* Energy: conversion grant

***Okalta Oils Ltd.* case overruled**, 152(1.1)

***Old Age Security Act* benefits**
- "clawback" tax on, 180.2 (Part I.2)
  - deduction from income for, 60(w)
- emigration of taxpayer, no deemed disposition, 128.1(10)"excluded right or interest"(g)(ii)
- excluded from pension income credit, 118(8)(a)
- included in income, 56(1)(a)(i)
- non-resident withholding tax, 212(1)(h)
  - U.S. residents, Canada–U.S. Tax Convention Art. XVIII:5
- reduction in RRSP annuity to reflect, 146(3)(b)(ii)
- repayment of, deduction for, 60(n)
- withholding of benefits to cover clawback tax, 180.2(3), (4)

**"Old law" defined**, ITAR 12

**Old person**, *see* Age

**Older Worker Adjustment, Program for**
- income assistance taxable, 56(1)(a)(vi), Reg. 5502(b)
- repayment of benefits, deduction, 60(n)(ii.2)
- source withholding, 153(1)(m), Reg. 5502(b)

**Ontario**, *see also* Province
- Community Economic Development bonds, eligible for RRSP investment, Reg. 4900(1)(i.1)
- northern, *see* Northern Canada
- tax rates, *see* introductory pages

**Onus**, *see* Burden of proof

**Operating costs of automobile**, *see* Automobile: operating costs

**Optic cable**, *see* Fibre optic cable

**Optical scanner, etc.**
- medical expense, Reg. 5700(l)

**Option**
- disposition of, 13(5.3)
- exchanged, rules, 7(1.4)
- exercised, 49(3), (4), (5)
  - overpayment of tax as consequence of, 164(5), (5.1)
- expiry of, 49(2)
  - amalgamation, 87(2)(o)
- granting of, disposition of property, 49(1)
- included in "taxable Canadian property", 115(3) [to be repealed], 248(1)"taxable Canadian property"(l) [draft]
- received on amalgamation, ITAR 26(22)
- stock, *see* Stock options
- to acquire, exercised, 49(3), (4)
  - effect of capital gains exemption, 49(3.2)
- to acquire interest in partnership or trust, reductions in ACB flowed through, 49(3.01)
- to acquire mutual fund trust units, *see* Stock options
- to acquire shares
  - by employee, *see* Stock options
  - deemed to be share for insurance demutualization, 139.1(1)
  - predecessor corporation, of, 87(5)
  - reductions in ACB flowed into ACB of shares, 49(3.01)
- to acquire specified property, exercise of, 49(3.01)
- to dispose, exercised, 49(3.1), (4)

**Optometrist**
- certification of sight impairment for disability credit, 118.3(1)(a.2)(i)

2761

**Optometrist** *(cont'd)*
- defined, 118.4(2)

**Ordering**
- charitable donations
  - in order of year of contributions, 110.1(1.1)(b), 118.1(2.1)
- charity loanbacks, 118.1(17)
- credits of an individual, 118.92
- debt forgiveness rules application, 80(2)(c)
- debt obligations settled simultaneously, 80(2)(i)
- deductions
  - eligible capital property, for capital gains exemption, 110.6(17)
  - in computing taxable income, 111.1
- designation of insurance properties, Reg. 2401(3)
- disposition of DPSP shares on becoming non-resident, 147(10.5)
- disposition of depreciable property on death, 70(14)
- disposition of securities acquired under employee option agreement, 7(1.3), (1.31)
- dividends, simultaneous, 89(3)
- foreign affiliate surplus distributions, Reg. 5901
- identical options, exercise of, 7(12)
- internal reorganization rules, 51(4), 86(3)
- mutual fund qualifying exchange, 132.2(1)(e)
- registered investment registration, 204.4(7)
- spousal RRIF attribution, 146.3(5.3)
- spousal RRSP attribution, 146(8.5)
- transfer of depreciable property with pregnant loss, 13(21.2)(e)(ii)

**Ordinarily resident**, 250(3)

**Ore**
- defined
  - for capital cost allowance, Reg. 1104(2)
  - for resource allowance, Reg. 1206(1)
- processing of, 125.1(3)"manufacturing or processing", Reg. 5203, Reg. Sch. II:Cl. 10(k)
- tar sands, *see* Tar sands ore

**Organ transplant**
- expenses of, tax credit for, 118.2(2)(l.1)

**Organisation for Economic Cooperation and Development**
- transfer pricing guidelines, 247

**Original acquisition**
- defined, 127.4(1), 204.8(1), 211.7(1)

**Original editorial content**
- defined, 19.01(1)

**Original owner (of resource property)**
- defined, 66(15)
  - for resource allowance, Reg. 1206(1)
- reduction of Canadian resource expenses, 66.7(12), (12.1)
- reduction of foreign resource expenses, 66.7(13)
- successor corporation rules, 66.7

**Original right**, defined, ITAR 20(3)(b)

**Orthopaedic shoes/boots**
- medical expense, Reg. 5700(e)

**Other recipient of a gift**
- defined, Reg. 3500

**Outdoor advertising structures**
- capital cost allowance, Reg. Sch. II:Cl. 8(l), Sch. II:Cl. 11(b)
  - separate class, election, Reg. 1101(5l)

**"Outstanding debts to specified non-residents"**
- defined, 18(5)
- no deduction where debt-equity ratio exceeds 3:1, 18(4)

**Outstanding premiums**
- defined, insurers, Reg. 2400(1)
- mean Canadian, *see* Mean Canadian outstanding premiums

**Overburden removal cost, designated**
- capital cost allowance, Reg. Sch. II:Cl. 12(q)

**Overcontribution to RRSP**
- tax on, 204.1(2.1), 204.2(1.1)

**Overhead expenses**
- R&D-related, 127(9)"qualified expenditure" Reg. 2900(4)–(10)

**Overpayment amount**
- defined, for corporate interest offset, 161.1(1)

**Overpayment of benefits, deductible when repaid**, 60(n)

**Overpayment of tax**
- deemed
  - Child Tax Benefit, 122.61(1)
  - GST credit, 122.5(3)
- defined, 164(7)
- refund of, 164
  - UI premium tax credit, 126.1(6), (7)

**Overseas Canadian Forces school staff**
- defined, 248(1)
- members deemed resident in Canada, 250(1)(d.1), 250(2)
- option of filing as resident, 250(1)(d.1)
- prescribed order, Reg. 6600

**Overseas employment tax credit**, 122.3
- foreign tax credit and, choice between, 126(1)(b)(i)
- incorporated employee, credit disallowed, 122.3(1.1)
- not reduced by additional minimum tax carried over, 122.3(2)"tax otherwise payable under this Part for the year"

**Owner**
- original, of resource properties, defined, 66(15)"original owner"
- predecessor, of resource property, defined, 66(15)"predecessor owner"

**Owner-occupied home**
- defined, for Home Buyers' Plan withholding exemption, Reg. 104(3.1)

**Ownership**
- certificates of, 234, Reg. 207
  - penalties for offences re, 162(4)
- change of, certificates, Reg. 502
- rights, *see* Ownership rights

**Ownership rights**
- defined, for insurance demutualization, 139.1(1)
- rollover to shares of insurance corporation, 139.1(4)(a), (d)

**Oxygen, as medical expense**, 118.2(2)(k)

# P

**PA**, *see* Pension adjustment

**PA offset**
- defined, Reg. 8300(1)

**PAR**, *see* Pension adjustment reversal

**PBC**, *see* Principal-business corporation (exploration and development); Principal-business corporation (real property)
**PSB**, *see* Personal services business
**PSPA**, *see* Past service pension adjustment
**PSPA withdrawals**
- defined, Reg. 8307(5)

**PUC**, *see* Paid-up capital
**Packaging material**
- deemed to be inventory, 10(5)
- valuation of, 10(4)

**Paid-up capital**
- amalgamation, on, 87(3), (3.1)
- computation of
- •  additions to, 84.1(3)
- •  after designation of amount re shares, 192(4.1), 194(4.2)
- •  after exchange of convertible property, 51(3)
- •  after internal reorganization, 86(2.1)
- •  after rollover of property to corporation, 85(2.1)
- •  after share-for-share exchange, 85.1(2.1)
- •  corporation becoming resident in Canada, 128.1(2), (3)
- •  insurance corporation following demutualization, 139.1(6)
- • •  holding corporation, 139.1(7)
- •  on transfer of insurance business, 138(11.7)
- contributed surplus converted into, no dividend deemed, 84(1)(c.1)–(c.3)
- cooperative corporation, of, 89(1)"paid-up capital"(b)
- credit union, of, 89(1)"paid-up capital"(b)
- deductions from, 66.3(2)
- defined, 89(1), 248(1)
- flow-through shares, 66.3(4)
- increase in, 84(1), 84(5)(d)
- •  mutual fund corporation, by, not deemed dividend, 131(4)
- non-resident shareholder, 212.1
- reduction of, deemed a dividend, 84(4), (4.1)
- stripping, 84.1, 212.1

**Paid-up insurance, deduction for premiums**, 18(9.01)
**Paid-up premium**
- defined, Reg. 2700(1)

*Panko* **case overruled**, 239(3)
**Parent (corporation)**
- continuation of wound-up subsidiary, 88(1.5)
- defined, 88(1)
- incorporated after end of subsidiary's year
- •  computation of income and tax payable, 88(1.3)

**Parent (human)**
- dependent, 118(6)(b)
- extended meaning, 252(2)

**Parity/advisory committee**
- dues paid by employee, deduction, 8(1)(i)(vi)

**Parked obligation (debt parking)**
- deemed settled, 80.01(8)(a)
- defined, 80.01(7)

**Parking**
- automobile or other vehicle
- •  excluded from benefit for operating costs and standby charge, 6(1.1)
- •  taxable benefit, 6(1)(a), 6(1.1)
- • •  exception for disabled employee, 6(16)

- debt, *see* Debt parking

**Parking area**
- capital cost allowance, Reg. Sch. II:Cl. 1(g)
- for mine, Reg. Sch. II:Cl. 10(l)

**Parliament**, *see also* Government
- defined, *Interpretation Act* 35(1)
- member of, *see* Member: Parliament

**Parson**, *see* Clergyman
**Part I.2 tax**, 180.2
- deduction for, 125.3
- •  amalgamation, on, 87(2)(j.9)
- unused credit
- •  reassessment, 152(6)(f)

**Part I.3 tax credit**
- unused, carryback of
- •  overpayment of tax as result, 164(5), (5.1)

**Part IV tax**
- imposed, 186(1)
- refund of, 129(1)

**Part VI tax**
- credit for, 125.2
- •  unused, reassessment, re, 152(6)(e)
- deduction
- •  amalgamation, on, 87(2)(j.9)

**Part VI.1 tax**
- deduction from taxable income re, 110(1)(k)
- liability for, transferred on amalgamation, 87(2)(ss)
- payment of, 157(1)

**Part VII refund, defined**, 192(2)
**Part VIII refund, defined**, 194(2)
**Part XII.2 tax**, 210.2, 210.3
- credit for, 210.2(3)
- •  included in beneficiary's income, 104(31)
- deduction for, 104(30)

**Part XII.6 tax**
- deductible, 20(1)(nn)

**Part-time attendant**
- deduction from income, 64
- medical expense credit, 118.2(2)(b.1)

**Part-year resident**, 114, 114.1
- cash method of computing income, on, 28(4)
- farmer/fisherman, 28(4)
- foreign tax credit, 126(2.2), (3)
- "income for the year", 120(3)
- otherwise-Class 8 property, capital cost allowance, Reg. Sch. II:Cl. 19
- tax credits, 118.91

**Partial debt obligation**
- treated the same as entire obligation, 248(27)

**Partial dependency**, 118.3(3)
**Partial disposition**
- cost base of property remaining, 53(2)(d)
- specified debt obligation, 142.4(9)

**Participant (re butterfly transactions)**
- defined, 55(1)"permitted exchange"(b)
- specified debt obligation, 142.4(9)

**Participate**
- defined, for third-party penalty, 163.2(1)

**Participating employer**
- deferred profit sharing plan, 147(1.1)

2763

# Index

Participating employer *(cont'd)*
- registered pension plan, 147.1(1), Reg. 8308(7)

**Participating life insurance policy**
- defined, 138(12), 211(1), Reg. 1408(1)

**Participating interest**
- defined, 94.1(1)

**Participating percentage**
- defined, 95(1)

**Participation certificate**
- no interest payable on tax due, 161(5)

**Participation period**
- defined
- - for Home Buyers' Plan, 146.01(1)
- - for Lifelong Learning Plan, 146.02(1)

**Partition of property**
- rules, 248(20)–(23)
- - disproportionate partition, 248(20)
- - proportionate partition, 248(21)

**Partner**, *see also* Partnership
- active, application of debt forgiveness rules, 80(1)"forgiven amount"B(k)
- agreement by, validity, 96(3)
- automobile provided to
- - amount included in income, 12(1)(y)
- becoming resident in Canada, 96(8)
- contribution of property to partnership, 97(1)
- debt forgiveness rules, application where partnership issued debt obligation, 80(15)
- debt owing by, where treated as partnership debt, 80(2)(n)
- deceased
- - value of rights or things to date of death, 53(1)(e)(v)
- deemed, for certain purposes, 248(13)
- depreciable property acquired with government assistance, 13(7.2)
- election by, *see* Partnership: election by members
- election re fiscal period of terminated partnership, 99(2)–(4)
- election to renounce investment tax credit, 127(8.4)
- inducement payments or reimbursement received by, 12(2.1)
- limited, *see* Limited partner
- loan by, to partnership
- - interest paid on money borrowed to make, 20(3.2)
- non-resident
- - creates non-Canadian partnership, 102(1)
- - payments to, withholding tax, 212(13.1)(b)
- notice to, 244(20)
- objection to determination of partnership's income or loss, 165(1.15)
- obligation to pay interest re land purchase, 18(2.1)
- passive, *see* Limited partner; Specified member (of partnership)
- retiring, allocation of share of income to, 96(1.1)
- - deduction, 96(1.3)
- - deemed carrying on business in Canada, 96(1.6)
- - right to share in income
- - - deemed not capital property, 96(1.4)
- return on death of, 150(4)
- rules for computing income etc., 96(1)
- share of exploration and development expense, 66.1(7), 66.2(6), (7)
- tax matters, designation by partnership, 165(1.15)

**Partnership**, *see also* Limited partnership; Partner; Partnership interest
- accrued interest income, 12(3)
- "acquisition cost", ITAR 20(4)"acquisition cost"
- acquisition of foreign affiliate from, 91(7)
- agreement by members, validity, 96(3)
- agreement to share income
- - in unreasonable proportions, 103(1.1)
- - to avoid tax, 103(1)
- allocation to retiring partner, 96(1.1)
- - deduction, 96(1.3)
- annuity contract, interest in, 12.2
- assumptions, 96(2)
- business of, continued as sole proprietorship, 98(5)
- Canadian, defined, 102(1)
- Canadian development expenses of, election to exclude, 66.2(5)"Canadian development expense"(f)
- Canadian oil and gas property expenses of, election to exclude, 66.4(5)"Canadian oil and gas property expense"(b)
- Canadian partnership, defined, 102(1)
- Canadian securities owned by, 39(4.1)
- capital cost allowance, Reg. 1102(1a)
- capital gain of, exemption for, 39.1(4)
- ceasing to exist, 98
- - continuation of, by another partnership, 98.1(2)
- - continued by new partnership, 98(6)
- - continued by proprietor, 98(5)
- - cumulative eligible capital deduction, 24(3)
- - deemed proceeds of disposition, 98(2)
- - disposition of property, 98(1)
- - property transferred to corporation, 85(3)
- - rules applicable, 98(3), (4)
- common-law, *see* Common-law partner
- continuation
- - as new partnership, 98(6)
- - by another partnership, 98.1(2)
- - by proprietor, 98(5)
- contribution of property to, 97
- - capital cost to partner exceeds proceeds, where, 97(4)
- - majority interest partner, by, 40(3.3), (3.4)
- corporate
- - gross revenue from active businesses, 125.1(4)
- - small business deduction, 125(6)
- - - "specified partnership income", 125(7)
- - - "specified partnership loss", 125(7)
- corporation deemed member, 125(6.1)
- death of partner, return, 150(4)
- debt obligation issued by, 80(13)E(a), (14)(b), (15), (18)
- deemed person for affiliated persons definition, 251.1(4)(b)
- deemed person for debt forgiveness rules, 80(1), 80.01(1)
- deemed person for flow-through share provisions, 66(16)
- deemed person for international banking centre rules, 33.1(2)(a)
- deemed person for Part IV.1 tax, 187.4(c)
- deemed person for scientific research tax credit rules, 127.3(7)
- deemed person for seizure of property by creditor, 79(1)"person" 79.1(1)"person"
- deemed person for share-purchase tax credit rules, 127.2(9)

2764

# Index

Partnership (cont'd)
- deemed person for tax on carved-out property, 209(6)
- deemed person for tax shelter identification rules, 237.1(1)
- deemed taxpayer for tax shelter investment cost rules, 143.2(1)"taxpayer"
- deemed person for withholding tax obligations, 227(5.2), (15)
- defined, nowhere (see case law)
- depreciable property, ITAR 20(3), (5)
- determination of income or loss, 152(1.4)–(1.8)
- • objection to determination, 165(1.15)
- dividend received from foreign affiliate, 93.1(2)
- • from pre-acquisition surplus, 92(4)–(6)
- drilling and exploration expenses, ITAR 29(9), (10), (13)
- election by members
- • date to be made, 96(4)
- • late-filed, 96(5)
- • • penalty, 96(6), (7)
- • • special cases, 96(5.1)
- • re property transferred, 97(2)
- • validity, 96(3)
- eligible capital property of, exemption for, 39.1(5)
- exempt, for resource allowance claims, Reg. 1206(1)
- exempt persons, anti-avoidance rule, 96(8)
- family farm, see Family farm corporation/partnership
- farming business of
- • disposition of land used in, 101
- financial institution, 142.2(1)"financial institution"(b)
- fiscal period of, 249.1(1)(b)(ii)
- flow-through entity for capital gains exemption, 39.1(1), (4), (5)
- • disposition of interest in, 39.1(2)B(c)
- foreign, partner becoming subject to Canadian tax, 96(8)
- foreign resource property disposition, 59(1.1)
- fuel tax rebate of, 111(11)
- gains and losses, determination of, 96(1.7)
- gifts made by, 118.1(8)
- • corporation's share, 110.1(4)
- includes another partnership that is a member, 102(2)
- income of, 12(1)(l), 96(1)
- • determination by CCRA, 152(1.4)–(1.8)
- • income splitting, 103
- • minimum tax applicable to partner, 127.52(2)
- information return, Reg. 229
- • failure to make, 162(7.1), (8), (8.1)
- • foreign-based information, 233.2–233.5
- • • demand for, 233(2)
- interest accrued, 12(3)
- interest in, see Partnership interest
- interest on debt relating to acquisition of land, 18(3)"interest on debt relating to the acquisition of land"(b)
- international banking centres, and, 33.1(2)
- investing in residential property or Canadian film
- • capital cost allowance limitation, 127.52(2)
- investment tax credit, allocation to partners, 127(8)
- • non-limited partners, 127(8.3)
- life insurance policy, interest in, 12.2
- limited, see Limited partnership
- limited liability, see Limited liability partnership
- loan to, by partner
- • interest paid on money borrowed to make, 20(3.2)
- loss of, minimum tax applicable to partner, 127.52(2)
- majority interest partner, 248(1)
- manufacturing etc., profits, Reg. 5204
- member, see Partner
- name, reference to on documents, 244(20)(a)
- new, continuing predecessor partnership, 98(6)
- non-Canadian
- • • withholding tax on payments to, 212(13.1)(b)
- non-existent
- • • extended deadline for assessment of non-partners, 152(1.8)
- non-resident controlled
- • • corporate member's specified income deemed nil, 125(6.2)
- • • deemed, 125(6.3)
- notice to, 244(20)
- Part IV.1 tax, 187.4
- Part XIII tax, application of, 212(13.1), (13.2)
- partner, see Partner
- payment on ceasing to be member of
- • • used to purchase income-averaging annuity contract, deductible, 61(2)(k)
- "percentage of member", ITAR 20(4)"percentage"
- personal-use property of, 46(4)
- political contributions, allocation of, 127(4.2)
- property
- • right to receive
- • • adjusted cost base, 53(2)(o)
- reference to, constitutes reference to partners, 244(20)
- renounced resource expenses, return to be filed re, 66(12.69)
- • • late filing, 66(12.74), (12.75)
- research and development expenses, no carryforward, 96(1)(e.1)
- resident of, Income Tax Conventions Interpretation Act s. 6.2
- residual interest in, 98.1(1)
- resource allowance
- • • claimed by partner, 20(1)(v.1), Reg. 1210(3)
- • • not claimed at partnership level, 96(1)(d)
- resource expenditures, by members, 66(18)
- • • allocation of assistance, 66.1(7), 66.2(6), (7), 66.4(6), (7)
- resource expenses of
- • • deemed made by partners, 66(18)
- • • election by partner to exclude, 66.2(5)"Canadian development expense"(f), 66.4(5)"Canadian oil and gas property expense"(b)
- • • not claimed at partnership level, 96(1)(d), 66.1(7), 66.2(6), (7), 66.4(6), (7)
- • • renounced, 66(12.69), (12.74), (12.75)
- resource expenses renounced to
- • • non-arm's length relationship deemed, 66(17)
- return, see information return (above)
- right to share in income
- • • disposition of, 96(1.2)
- • • • death of taxpayer, on, 96(1.5)
- • • • deduction, 96(1.3)
- • • • rules for computing income etc., 96(1)
- rollover to, 97(2)
- scientific research tax credit, 127.3(4), (7)
- service of documents on, 244(20)(b)
- share-purchase tax credit, 127.2(4), (9)
- small business bond issued by, 15.2(6)
- small business deduction, 125(6)

2765

**Partnership** *(cont'd)*
- soft costs relating to construction, 18(3.1)(b), 18(3.2)(b)(iii)
- specified member, defined, 248(1)
- taxable dividends received by, 186(6)
- taxation year of, 96(1)(b)
- terminated
  - fiscal period of, 99(1)
  - member's election re fiscal period, 99
- tiered, *see* Tiers of partnerships
- transfer of property by partner to, 97(1), (2)
- transfer of property to corporation, 85(2)
  - partnership wound up, 85(3)
- "undepreciated cost to the partnership", ITAR 20(4)"undepreciated cost to the partnership"
- unit, *see* Limited partnership unit; Partnership interest
- value of rights or things on death, 53(1)(e)(v)
- winding-up of, *see* ceasing to exist (*above*)
- withholding tax, 227(15)

**Partnership interest**, *see also* Limited partnership unit
- acquired through amalgamation, 87(2)(e.1)
- adjusted cost base
  - additions to, 53(1)(e)
  - deductions from, 53(2)(c)
  - negative, whether capital gain, 40(3)–(3.2)
  - recomputation of following debt forgiveness, 53(4)–(6)
- artificial transactions, 40(3.13)
- borrowed money used to acquire, 20.1(5)
  - deductions from, 53(2)(c)
- capital contribution where other person withdraws funds, 40(3.13)
- constitutes specified property, 54"specified property"(c)
- disposition of, 100
  - gain from, 100(2), (2.1)
  - loss from, 100(4)
  - subsequent to debt forgiveness, deemed capital gain, 80.03(2), (4)
- distributed to parent on winding-up of subsidiary, 88(1)(a.2), (c)
- expenses of selling or financing, 20(1)(e)
- foreign affiliate's, adjusted cost base of, 95(2)(j)
- limited liability partnership, *see* Limited liability partnership
- loan of, 96(1.7)
- owned on Dec. 31/71, ITAR 26(9)–(9.4)
- person having, deemed member, 248(13)
- qualified investment for RRSP etc., Reg. 4900(1)(n)
- residual, 98.1(1)
- transfer on death, 98.2
- whether taxable Canadian property, 115(1)(b)(vii) [to be repealed], 248(1)"taxable Canadian property"(g) [draft]

**Parts**
- deemed to be inventory, 10(5)
- valuation of, 10(4)

**Passenger automobile**
- defined (for pre-1966 cars only), Reg. 1102(11)

**Passenger vehicle**, *see also* Automobile
- acquired at non-arm's length
  - deemed cost of, 13(7)(h)
- capital cost limited to $24,000, 13(7)(g)
- defined, 248(1)
- interest on money borrowed to buy
  - limitation on deductibility, 67.2
- leasing costs
  - limitation on deductibility, 67.3
  - more than one lessor, limitation on deductibility, 67.4
- luxury, limitations on
  - bad debt from sales of, 20(4)
  - capital cost allowance, 13(7)(g), Reg. 1101(1af), 7307(1), Reg. Sch. II:Cl. 10.1
    - year of disposition, Reg. 1100(2.5)
  - interest deductibility, 67.2, Reg. 7307(2)
  - leasing cost, 67.3, 67.4, Reg. 7307(3), (4)
  - terminal loss disallowed, 20(16.1), Reg. 1100(2.5)
- recapture exception, 13(2)
- transferred to corporation by shareholder
  - capital cost or cost, 85(1)(e.4)

**Passive income**
- dividends, 82(1), 90
- film/video production, *see* Investor (re Canadian film/video tax credit)
- foreign affiliate, *see* Foreign accrual property income
- generally, 9(1)
- interest, 12(1)(c), 12(4)
- non-resident, of, 212

**Passive partner**, *see* Limited partner; Specified member (of partnership)

**Past service event**
- defined, 147.1(1), Reg. 8300(1), (2)
- restrictions on pension benefits, 147.1(10)

**Past service pension adjustment**
- accumulated, Reg. 8303(1)(a)
- defined, 248(1), Reg. 8303
- foreign plan, Reg. 8308.1(5), (6)
- net
  - calculation of, 204.2(1.3)
  - defined, 146(1)"net past service pension adjustment"
- occurring in 1991, Reg. 8303(2.1)
- provisional, Reg. 8303(2), (3)

**Patent**
- capital cost allowance
  - 25% rate, Reg. 1100(1)(a)(xxx), 1100(9.1), Reg. Sch. II:Cl. 44
  - allocated over life of patent, Reg. 1101(1)(c), 1100(9), Reg. Sch. II:Cl. 14
- non-resident withholding tax, 212(1)(d)
- paid to U.S. resident, Canada–U.S. Tax Convention Art. XII:3(c)

**Patient**
- defined, 118.2(2)(a)
- medical expenses for, 118.2(2)

**Patronage**
- allocation in proportion to
  - defined, 135(4), Reg. 4901(2)
  - holding forth prospect of, 135(5)
  - members/non-members, 135(2)

**Patronage dividends**, 135
- carryover of deduction, 135(2.1)
- corporation paying, tax payment, 157(2)
- deduction, 20(1)(u)
- paid to non-resident, 212(1)(g)
- payments, information return, Reg. 218
- receipt of, income, 135(7)

2766

**Patronage dividends** *(cont'd)*
- where marketing board used, 135(8)

**Pattern**
- capital cost allowance, Reg. Sch. II:Cl. 12(d)

**Pay equity**
- averaging of settlement received, 110.2, 120.31

**Pay period**
- defined, Reg. 100(1)

**Payable**
- meaning of, Reg. 104(24)

**Payee**
- defined, Reg. 237(1)

**Payoffs**
- no deduction for, 67.5

**Payment(s)**, *see also* Deductions in computing income; Expenses; Income; Payment of tax
- based on production or use, income, 12(1)(g)
- ITA, under, not deductible from business or property income, 18(1)(t)
- instalment, *see* Instalment payments
- lump sum, ITAR 40; Reg. 103
- maintenance and support, *see* Support payments (spousal or child)
- non-residents, to, Part XIII
- • information return, Reg. 202
- periodic, *see* Periodic payments
- shareholder or prospective shareholder, to, 15(7)
- • from corporation, 15(1)
- tax transfer, to provinces, 154, Reg. 3300

**Payment of tax**, 153, 156, 158
- balance due day, defined, 248(1)
- carved-out income, on, 209(4)
- certificate before distribution, 159(2)
- • failure to obtain, 159(3)
- corporations, 157
- • where instalments not required, 157(2), (2.1)
- credit union, 157(2)
- death of taxpayer, on
- • election to pay in instalments, 159(5)
- deduction at source, 153(1)
- deemed, *see also* refundable credits
- • trust, by, re non-qualified investment, 202(6)
- deferral of
- • appeal for purpose of, penalty, 179.1
- deferred income plans
- • over-contributions, 204.3
- • property acquired by, 207
- • property held by, 207.2
- departure tax
- • election to defer, 159(4) [to be repealed], 220(4.5)–(4.54), Reg. 1300
- farmers and fishermen, 155, 156.1
- individuals, 153(2), 156, 156.1
- instalment, *see also* Instalment payments
- non-residents, 215
- on behalf of others, 159
- Part I.1, 180.1(3)(b)
- Part I.2, 180.2(5)(b)
- Part I.3, 181.7
- Part II, 183(2)
- Part III, 185(2)
- Part IV, 187(2)
- Part IV.1, 187.2

- Part V, 188(1)(a), 189(6), (7)
- Part VI, 190.21
- Part VI.1, 191.1(1)
- Part VII, 192(1)
- Part VIII, 194(1)
- Part IX, 196
- Part X, 198(2)
- Part X.1, 204.3(1)
- Part X.2, 204.7(1)
- Part X.3, 204.86(c)
- Part X.4, 204.92(c)
- Part XI, 207(1)
- Part XI.1, 207.2(1)
- Part XI.2, 207.4
- Part XI.3, 207.7(3)
- Part XII, 208(2)
- Part XII.1, 209(4)
- Part XII.2, 210.2(5)(c)
- Part XII.3, 211.4
- Part XII.4, 211.6(4)
- Part XIII, 215(1)
- Part XIV, 219(1)
- patronage corporations, 157(2)
- postponement, where income in blocked currency, 161(6)
- public authorities disposing of cultural property, 207.3, 207.4
- registered investment, 204.7
- remainder payment, 158
- retirement compensation arrangement, 207.7(3)
- security for, 220(4)–(4.4), Reg. Part XXII
- tax-exempt persons, 208(2)
- tax-exempt persons paying royalties etc., 208(2)
- taxpayer leaving Canada, 226(1)
- transfer among tax accounts, 221.2
- trustee, etc., 159(1)
- • personal liability, 159(3)

**Payroll deduction**, *see also* Withholding tax
- Family Support Plan, Reg. 100(3)(d)
- income tax, 153(1), *see also* Withholding tax
- RRSP contributions, Reg. 100(3)(c)
- RPP contributions, Reg. 100(3)(a)

**Payroll taxes (provincial)**
- deductibility of, 18

**Peat**
- property for use in harvesting, 127(9) "qualified property"

**Penalty**, *see also* Offences
- appeal without reasonable grounds, 179.1
- burden of proof of offence on Minister, 163(3)
- confidential information, contraventions re, 239(2.2)
- conviction of offence, on, 238(1), 239
- • second penalty, when applicable, 239(3)
- corporation's failure to file information return, 162(10)
- court has no power to decrease punishment, 243
- deficient instalments of tax, 163.1
- destruction of records, for, 239(1)
- dishonoured cheque, for, 162(11)
- failure to file prescribed form, R&D corporation, 149(7.1)
- failure to file return, 162(1)
- • repeated penalties, 162(2)
- • trustees etc., 162(3)
- failure to remit tax withheld, 227(9)

Penalty (cont'd)
- - applicable only on amounts over $500, 227(9.1)
- - salary or wages, from, 227(9.5)
- failure to withhold tax, 227(8)
- - salary or wages, from, 227(8.5)
- false statements, 163(2), 239(1)
- - by third party or tax preparer, 163.2
- - re renunciation of resource expenses, 163(2.2)
- frivolous appeal, 179.1
- gross negligence, 163(2)
- incomplete return, 162(5)
- incorrect tax shelter identification number, for providing, 239(2.1)
- interest on, 161(11)
- large corporations, late return, 235
- late designation
- - Canadian exploration or development expense, 66(14.5)
- - refundable Part VIII tax, 194(8)
- late-filed election, 220(3.5)
- - capital gains exemption triggering, 110.6(26), (29)
- - disposition of share in foreign affiliate, 93(6)
- - partners, 96(6)
- - transfer to corporations, 85(8), (9)
- late filing of form re renunciation of resource expenses, 66(12.75)
- late filing of return, 162(1), 235
- late instalments of tax, 163.1
- misrepresentation, 163(2)
- - by third party or tax preparer, 163.2
- not deductible from income, 18(1)(t)
- ownership certificates, offences re, 162(4)
- Part IV.1 tax, 187.6
- Part VI.1 tax, 191.4(2)
- Part XII.2 tax, 210.2(7)
- Part XII.3 tax, 211.5
- Part XII.4, 211.6(5)
- partnership information return, failure to file, 162(7.1), (8.1)
- RRSP issuer extending advantage to annuitant or non-arm's length person, 146(13.1)
- regulations, failure to comply with, 162(7)
- repeated assessments of, 162(2)
- repeated failures to report an amount of income, 163(1)
- small business bond, false declaration, 15.2(5)
- small business development bond, false declaration, 15.1(5)
- Social Insurance Number
- - failure to provide, 162(6)
- - wrongful communication of, 239(2.3)
- tax advisor, 163.2
- tax shelter identification number, offences re, 237.1(7.4)
- - deduction disallowed while penalty unpaid, 237.1(6.1)
- third party, 163.2
- transfer pricing, 247(3), (11)
- waiver of, by Minister, 220(3.1)

**Pension**, *see also* Pension plan; Canada Pension Plan/Quebec Pension Plan
- adjustment, *see* Pension adjustment
- benefits
- - income, 56(1)(a)(i)
- - - exemption, 57

- - paid to non-resident, 212(1)(h)
- - - election to file return, 217
- - paid to U.S. resident, Canada–U.S. Tax Convention Art. XVIII
- - paid to widow(er), 57(5)
- - transferred to another plan, deductible, 60(j)
- - unpaid, 78(4)
- credit, *see* Pension credit
- defined, *Income Tax Conventions Interpretation Act* s. 5, Canada–U.S. Tax Convention Art. XVIII:3
- disability benefit
- - constitutes earned income for RRSP, 146(1)"earned income"(b.1)
- Halifax disaster, exempt, 81(1)(f)
- income
- - credit for, 118(3)
- - - unused, transfer to spouse, 118.8
- - defined, 118(7)
- - qualified, defined, 118(7)
- not treated as annuity, 58(6)
- paid to non-resident, 212(1)(h)
- - election to file return, 217
- paid to U.S. resident, Canada–U.S. Tax Convention Art. XVIII
- periodic payments, *see* Periodic pension payment
- plan, *see* Pension plan
- RCMP, exempt, 81(1)(i)
- service, exempt, 81(1)(d)
- - from other country, exempt, 81(1)(e)
- superannuation or pension benefits
- - defined, 248(1)
- surplus, *see* Pension surplus

***Pension Act*, pension under, exempt**, 81(1)(d)

**Pension adjustment**, *see also* Pension credit
- anti-avoidance rule (1990), 146(5.21)
- defined, 248(1), Reg. 8301(1), *see also* Pension credit
- limits, 147(5.1)(c), 147.1(8), (9), Reg. 8506(2), 8509(12)
- past service, *see* Past service pension adjustment
- reversal, *see* Pension adjustment reversal
- special rules, Reg. 8308

**Pension adjustment reversal**
- defined, 248(1)"total pension adjustment reversal", Reg. 8304.1
- effect of, 146(1)"RRSP deduction limit"R, 146(1)"unused RRSP deduction room"R, 204.2(1.1)(b)R
- regulations respecting, 147.1(18)(d), (t), Reg. 8304.1
- reporting requirements, Reg. 8402.01

**Pension benefits act, provincial**
- registration under, 147.1(2)(a)(iii)

***Pension Benefits Standards Act***
- administration of
- - communication of information obtained under ITA, 241(4)(d)(vii)
- registration under, 147.1(2)(a)(iii)

**Pension corporation**
- exemption, 149(1)(o.1), (o.2)

**Pension credit**, *see also* Pension adjustment
- artificial reduction of, Reg. 8503(14)
- calculation of, Reg. 8301
- - deferred profit sharing plan, Reg. 8301(2)
- - foreign plan, Reg. 8308.1(2)–(4)
- - registered pension plan

Pension credit *(cont'd)*
- • • defined benefit provision
- • • • multi-employer plan, Reg. 8301(7)
- • • • ordinary plan, Reg. 8301(6)
- • • • specified multi-employer plan, Reg. 8301(5)
- • • downsizing benefits, effect of, Reg. 8308(9)
- • • money purchase provision, Reg. 8301(4)
- • • non-vested termination, Reg. 8301(8), (9)
- • • remuneration for prior years, Reg. 8308(3)(b)
- • • replacement of benefits, effect of, Reg. 8304
- • • transitional rule, Reg. 8301(10)
- • rounded to nearest dollar, Reg. 8311
- • specified retirement arrangement, Reg. 8308.3(2)–(5)
- constitutes pension adjustment, Reg. 8301(1)
- DPSP contribution limits, effect on, 147(5.1)
- multi-employer plan, effect on PA limit, 147.1(9)
- non-refundable credit, for $1,000 of pension income, 118(3)
- reporting of, Reg. 8401(3)

**Pension plan**, *see also* Registered pension plan
- appeal from refusal to register, 172(3)(f), 172(5)
- benefits flowed through trust, 104(27)
- Canada, *see* Canada Pension Plan/Quebec Pension Plan
- contract under, 254
- dollar limits, *see* Pension adjustment
- foreign plan, *see* Foreign plan (pension plan)
- legal expenses of collecting or establishing right to benefit under
- • deduction for, 60(o.1)
- • income when recovered, 56(1)(l.1)
- payments, averaging provision, ITAR 40
- provincial, *see* Provincial pension plan, prescribed
- Quebec, *see* Canada Pension Plan/Quebec Pension Plan
- registered, *see* Registered pension plan
- Saskatchewan, *see* Provincial pension plan, prescribed
- surplus, *see* Pension surplus
- transfers between, 147.3

**Pension surplus**
- transfer of, 60(j.01), 147.3(4.1), (7.1)

**Pension trust**
- exempt, 149(1)(o)

**Pensionable service**
- defined, Reg. 8500(1)

**Percentage**
- rates of tax, *see* Rates of tax
- specified, *see* Specified percentage

**Period of disability**
- defined, Reg. 8500(1)

**Period of reduced services**
- defined, Reg. 8300(1)

**Periodic child care expense amount**
- defined, 63(3)

**Periodic payments**
- accrual to date of death, 70(1)(a)
- alimony/maintenance/support, 56(1)(b)–(c.2), 56.1, 60(b)–(c.2), 60.1
- pension, *see* Periodic pension payment
- tax deduction, determination of, Reg. 102

**Periodic pension payment**
- defined, *Income Tax Conventions Interpretation Act* s. 5

**Periodical**
- advertising in, limitation, 19.01(2)–(4)
- defined, 19.01(1)
- edition of, meaning, 19.01(6)

**Permanent establishment**
- defined
- • Canada–U.S. Tax Convention, Art. V
- • corporation, Reg. 400, 8600
- • for various purposes, Reg. 8201
- • individual, Reg. 2600
- dividend from non-resident corporation having, 112(2), Reg. 8201
- for allocating income among provinces
- • of corporation, Reg. 400
- • of individual, Reg. 2600
- international tax treaties
- • Canada–U.K. convention, Art. 5
- • Canada–U.S. convention, Art. V
- profits allocated to, *Income Tax Conventions Interpretation Act* s. 4
- securities lending arrangement, 260(5), Reg. 8201
- specified leasing property, 16.1(1), Reg. 8201
- tax on property forming part of, Canada–U.S. Tax Convention Art. XXIII:2

**Permitted acquisition**
- defined, for butterfly, 55(1)

**Permitted deferral**
- defined, for small business investment capital gain rollover, 44.1(1)

**Permitted exchange**
- defined, for butterfly, 55(1)

**Permitted redemption**
- defined, for butterfly, 55(1)

**Perpetual poverty, vow of**, 110(2)

**Person**, *see also* Taxpayer
- defined, 248(1), *Interpretation Act* 35(1), Canada–U.S. Tax Convention Art. III:1(e)
- • includes partnership for specific purposes, 33.1(2)(a), 66(16), 79(1), 79.1(1), 80(1), 80.01(1), 80.02(1), 80.03(1)(a), 80.04(1), 127.2(9), 127.3(7), 139.1(1), 163.2(1), 187.4(c), 209(6), 227(5.2), (15), 237.1(1), 251.1(4)(b)
- related by blood, defined, 251(6)

**Personal credits**, 118, *see also* Tax credits
- defined, for source deductions, Reg. 100(1)

**Personal injury award**
- election re capital gains, 81(5)
- income from exempt, 81(1)(g.1), (g.2)

**Personal or living expenses**
- allowance for, taxable, 6(1)(b)
- defined, 248(1)
- not deductible, 18(1)(h)

**Personal property**
- located on ship or aircraft used in international traffic, whether taxable Canadian property, 115(1)(b)(ii)(B) [to be repealed], 248(1)"taxable Canadian property"(b)(ii) [draft]

**Personal services business**
- defined, 125(7), 248(1)
- excluded from active business income, 125(7)"active business"

**Personal services business** *(cont'd)*
- expenses, limitation on deductibility of, 18(1)(p)
- incorporated employee, defined, 125(7)"personal services business"(a)
- loans, 12(1)(w), 80.4(1)
- overseas employment credit disallowed, 122.3(1.1)
- retirement compensation arrangement, 207.6(3)

**Personal trust**, *see also* Trust (or estate)
- defined, 110.6(16), 248(1)
- - effect of qualifying disposition, 107.4(3)(i)
- emigration of beneficiary, whether deemed disposition of interest, 128.1(10)"excluded right or interest"(j)
- non-arm's length with beneficiary, 251(1)(b)
- principal residence exemption, 54"principal residence"

**Personal-use property**, *see also* Listed personal property
- adjusted cost base of, 46(1), (2)
- bad debt that is, 50(2)
- defined, 54
- disposition of
- - capital loss nil, 40(2)(g)(iii)
- - in part, 46(2)
- ordinarily disposed of as a set, 46(3)

**Petro-Canada, subject to tax**, 27(2), Reg. 7100

*Petroleum and Gas Revenue Tax Act*
- amount deemed tax payable, 20(1)(ll)
- communication of information obtained under, 241(11)
- payments under not deductible, 18(1)(l.1)

**Petroleum/natural gas**
- acquisition of, for unreasonable consideration, 69(7)
- - fair market value, 69(9)
- allowances, Reg. Part XII
- corporations, *see* Drilling or exploration expense; Exploration and development expenses; Prospecting
- cost of substance injected to recover, 20(1)(mm)
- dealers in, limitation, 66(5)
- disposition of, for unreasonable considerations, 69(6)
- - certain persons deemed to be same person, 69(10)
- - fair market value, 69(8)
- exploration and development expenses, 66
- exploration equipment etc., capital cost allowance, Reg. Sch. II:Cl. 10(t), Sch. II:Cl. 41
- royalties, Reg. 1211
- - includable in income, 12(1)(o)
- - - reimbursement for, 80.2
- - not deductible, 18(1)(m)

**Phantom income**
- from provincial Crown royalties, 12(1)(o), 69(6), (7)
- - flow-through of, by trust to beneficiaries, 104(29)

**Phantom stock plan**
- emigration or immigration, no deemed disposition, 128.1(10)"excluded right or interest"(a)(vii)

**Pharmacist**
- defined, 118.4(2)

*Phénix* **case overruled**, 66.1(6)"Canadian exploration expense"(k.1), 66.2(5)"Canadian development expense"(i.1)

**Photocopier**
- capital cost allowance, Reg. 1101(5p), Reg. Sch. II:Cl. 10(f)

**Photocopy**, *see* Copy of document

**Physician**, *see* Medical doctor

**Pilot**
- away-from-home expenses, deduction, 8(1)(g)

**Pilot plants, qualify for R&D investment tax credits**, Reg. 2900(11)(c), (d)

**Pinball machine**
- capital cost allowance, Reg. Sch. II:Cl. 16(f)

**Pipeline**
- capital cost allowance, Reg. Sch. II:Cl. 1(l), Sch. II:Cl. 2(b)
- - exhausted within 15 years, Reg. Sch. II:Cl. 8(i)
- - for mine, Reg. Sch. II:Cl. 10(l)
- - gas or oil well equipment, Reg. 1104(2), Reg. Sch. II:Cl. 10(j)
- - separate classes if cost over $10 million, Reg. 1101(5i), (5j)
- defined, 1104(2)
- linefill in, no CCA, Reg. 1102(1)(k)

**Pipeline operators**
- taxable income earned in a province, Reg. 411

**Plan trust**
- defined, Reg. 4901(2)

**Planning activity**
- defined, for third-party penalty, 163.2(1)

**Plant Workers Adjustment Program**
- overpayments repaid, deductible, 60(n)(ii.1)
- payments received under, taxable, 56(1)(a)(vi), Reg. 5502
- - withholding of tax at source, 153(1)(m), Reg. 5502

**Points**
- allocated in determining whether film/video production qualifies as credit, Reg. 1106(4)

**Poland**, *see also* Foreign government
- universities, gifts to, Reg. Sch. VIII s. 12

**Police officer**
- communication of information to by CCRA, 241(3)(c)
- moneys seized from tax debtor by, 224.3
- RCMP, disability pension exempt, 81(1)(i)

**Policy**, *see* Insurance policy; Life insurance policy

**Policy anniversary**
- defined, Reg. 310

**Policy dividend**
- excess, deduction, defined, 138(12)"1975–76 excess policy dividend deduction"
- excess, reserve, defined, 138(12)"1975–76 excess policy dividend reserve"
- on demutualization, deemed not to be, 139.1(8)

**Policy liability**
- of insurer, defined, Reg. 1408(1)

**Policy loan (life insurance)**
- amount payable in respect of, 138(12), 148(9)
- defined, 138(12), 148(9), 211(1), Reg. 310, 1408(1), 1900(1)
- interest limitation, 20(2.1), Reg. 4001
- repayment of, 60(s)

**Policy reserves**, *see* see Insurance corporation; policy reserves

**Policy year**
- ending in taxation year, 6(4), (5)

**Political activities**
- of charitable foundation, 149.1(6.1)

**Political contribution**
- books and records, 230.1

2770

## Index

**Political contribution** *(cont'd)*
- information returns, Reg. 2001
- not deductible, 18(1)(n)
- receipts, Reg. 2000, 2002
- tax credit for, 127(3)–(4.2)
- "tax otherwise payable" defined, 127(17)

**Pollution control equipment**
- capital cost allowance, Reg. 1100(1)(t), Reg. Sch. II:Cl. 24, Sch. II:Cl. 27

**Pooled fund trust**, *see also* Master trust
- defined, Reg. 5000(7)
- information return where interest claimed to be qualified investment, Reg. 221

**Pornography**
- ineligible for Canadian film/video credit, Reg. 1106(1)"excluded production"(b)
- ineligible for film/video production services credit, Reg. 9300(j)

**Portfolio investments**
- dividends on, refundable Part IV tax, 186(1)
- whether foreign property, 206(1)"foreign property"(d.1)

**Post**, *see* Mail

**Post-emigration loss**, 128.1(8)

**Post-1971 partner trust**, *see also* Joint partner trust; Trust (or estate): spouse, for
- deduction from income, 104(6)(b)(ii), (iii)
- defined, 248(1)
- distribution of property to person other than spouse, 107(4)(a)(i)
- preferred beneficiary election by, 104(15)(a)
- transfer by, to another trust, 104(5.8)

**Post-1971 spousal trust**, *see* Post-1971 partner trust

**Post-1995 life insurance policy**
- defined, Reg. 1408(1)

**Post-1995 non-cancellable or guaranteed renewable accident and sickness policy**
- defined, Reg. 1408(1)

**Poultry**
- raising, constitutes farming, 248(1)"farming"

**Poverty, vow of**, 110(2)

**Pre-acquisition surplus (of foreign affiliate)**
- deduction for dividend paid out of, 113(1)(d), Reg. 5900(1)(c)
- dividend received by partnership, 92(4)–(6)

**Pre-funded group life insurance policy**
- defined, Reg. 1900(1)

**Pre-1972 capital surplus on hand**
- amalgamation, on, 87(2)(t)
- on windup of corporation, 88(2)–(2.3)

**Pre-1972 spousal trust**
- deemed disposition by, 104(4)(a.1)
- defined, 108(1)

**Pre-1986 capital loss balance**
- defined, 111(8)
- usable, $2,000 per year, 111(1.1)

**Pre-1996 life insurance policy**
- defined, Reg. 1408(1), (7)

**Pre-1996 non-cancellable or guaranteed renewable accident and sickness policy**
- defined, Reg. 1408(1), (7)

**Predecessor corporation**, *see* Amalgamation

**Predecessor employer**
- defined, Reg. 8500(1)

**Predecessor owner**
- defined, for resource allowance, Reg. 1206(1)

**Preferred beneficiary**
- defined, 108(1)
- election, 104(14), Reg. 2800
- - allocable amount, 104(15)
- - filing deadline, 104(14)–(14.02)

**Preferred-rate amount, for credit union**
- deduction based on, 137(3)
- defined, 137(4.3)

**Preferred share**, *see also* Short-term preferred share; Taxable preferred share; Term preferred share
- consideration for property transferred to corporation, 85(1)(g)
- deemed interest on, 258(3)
- defined, 248(1)
- interest paid on money borrowed to purchase, 20(1)(qq)
- issued by loss corporation
- - where dividends on not deductible, 112(2.4)–(2.9)
- tax-deferred series, Reg. 2107
- taxable, *see* Taxable preferred share

**Pregnant loss**, *see also* Superficial loss
- rules preventing transfer of,
- - capital property, 40(3.3), (3.4)
- - depreciable property, 13(21.2)
- - eligible capital property, 14(12), (13)
- - share or debt owned by financial institution, 18(13), (15)

**Premium**
- defined
- - Home Buyers' Plan, 146(1)"premium", 146.01(1)"premium"
- - investment income tax on life insurers, Reg. 1900(1)
- - life insurance as taxable benefit, Reg. 2700(2)
- - life insurance policy, 148(9)"premium"
- - Lifelong Learning Plan, 146(1)"premium", 146.02(1)"premium"
- - obligation owned since before 1972, ITAR 26(12)
- - registered retirement savings plan, 146(1)"premium"
- group term life insurance policy
- - limitation on deductibility, 18(9.01)
- - taxable benefit to employee, 6(4), Reg. 2700–2704
- health care insurance, deductible, 20.01
- home insurance, deduction after moving away, 62(3)(g)
- life insurance used as collateral, deductible, 20(1)(e.2)
- outstanding, *see* Outstanding premiums
- prescribed, Reg. 309(1)
- RRSP, under, 146(1)"premium"
- refund of, *see* Registered retirement savings plan: refund of premiums

**Premium category**
- defined, Reg. 2700(1)

**Premium paid by the policyholder**
- defined, Reg. 1408(4)

**Prepaid amounts, taxable when received**, 12(1)(a)

**Prepaid expenses**
- amalgamation, 87(2)(j.2)
- farming (cash-basis) business, 28(1)(e), (e.1)

**Prepaid expenses** *(cont'd)*
- limitation re deductibility, 18(9)

**Prepaid insurance benefit**
- defined, Reg. 2703
- included in taxable group term life insurance, 6(4), Reg. 2701(1)(b)

**Prepaid interest**
- limitations on deduction for, 18(9), 18(9.2)–(9.8)

**"Prescribed" defined**, 248(1)

**Prescribed annuity contract**, Reg. 304
- amount included in income, 56(1)(d)
- deduction, 60(a)
- excluded from accrual rule, 12(11)"investment contract" 12.2(1)(b)

**Prescribed countries**
- for intercorporate dividend from foreign affiliate, Reg. 5907(11)–(11.2)
- for lower withholding tax, debt issued before 1976, Reg. 1600
- for tax treaty elections, Reg. 7400(1)
- stock exchange recognized, Reg. 3201
- treaties with, *see* list of treaties in Table of Contents

**Prescribed debt obligation**, *see* Debt obligation: prescribed

**Prescribed film production**
- defined, Reg. 7500

**Prescribed intermediate zone**
- credit for residence in, 110.7(1)
- defined, Reg. 7303.1

**Prescribed labour-sponsored venture capital corporation**
- defined, Reg. 6701

**Prescribed northern zone**
- credit for residence in, 110.7(1)
- defined, Reg. 7303.1

**Prescribed plan or arrangement**
- retirement compensation arrangement, Reg. 6802
- • rules re, 207.6(6)

**Prescribed rate (of interest)**, Reg. Part XLIII
- "quarter" defined, Reg. 4300

**Prescribed resource loss**, *see* Resource loss

**Prescribed revenue guarantee**
- defined, Reg. 7500

**Prescribed share**
- for capital gains exemption, Reg. 6205
- for flow-through shares, Reg. 6202.1
- for lending assets, Reg. 6209
- for redemption of public corporation shares, Reg. 6206
- for resource expenditures, Reg. 6202
- for short-term preferred shares, Reg. 6201(8)
- for small business investment capital gain rollover, Reg. 6204
- for stock option rules, Reg. 6204
- for taxable preferred shares, Reg. 6201(7)
- for taxable RFI shares, Reg. 6201(4), (5.1)
- for term preferred shares, Reg. 6201(1)–(3), (5), (6)

**Prescribed stock exchange**, *see* Stock exchange

**Prescribed trust**, *see* Trust (or estate): prescribed

**Prescribed venture capital corporation**
- defined, Reg. 6700, 6700.1, 6700.2

**Prescription drugs**, as medical expense, 118.2(2)(n)

**President**, *see* Officer: corporation, of

**Priest**, *see* Clergy

**Primary currency (of specified debt obligation)**
- defined, Reg. 9100

**Primary recovery**, Reg. 1206(1)

**Prince Edward Island**, *see also* Province
- prescribed area, for electrical energy or steam processing, 127(9)"qualified property"(c.1)
- prescribed designated region, 127(9)"specified percentage"(a)(vi), Reg. 4607
- qualified property acquired for use in, 127(9)"specified percentage"(a), (e)
- tax rates, *see* introductory pages

**Principal amount (of debt obligation)**
- defined, 248(1)
- • distress preferred share, 80.02(2)(a)
- • obligation outstanding since before 1972, ITAR 26(1.1)

**Principal-business corporation (exploration and development)**
- deduction of CEE, 66.1(2)
- defined, 66(15), Reg. 4608(1)
- prescribed deductions, Reg. 1213

**Principal-business corporation (real property)**
- associated
- • base level deduction, 18(2.3)–(2.5)
- base level deduction, 18(2)(f), 18(2.2)
- excluded from limitation on CCA, Reg. 1100(12)
- specified percentage of "soft costs", 18(3.4)

**Principal residence**
- capital gains exemption election, effect on, 40(2)(b)A, D, 40(7.1)
- defined, 54
- designation, 54"principal residence"(c), (c.1), Reg. 2301
- disposed of to spouse or spousal trust, 40(4)
- disposition after 1981, 40(6)
- distribution by spouse trust, 107(2.01)
- election where change in use, 45(3), Reg. 2300
- • where not available, 45(4)
- exception to rules, 54.1
- farmer's, exclusion of, 40(2)(c)
- gain on disposition not taxed, 40(2)(b)
- property of trust, 54"principal residence"
- regulations, Reg. 2300, 2301
- relocation rule, 54.1
- satisfaction of interest in trust, 40(7)

**Principal screenwriter (for Canadian film/video tax credit)**
- defined, Reg. 1106(5)(a)

**Printout**
- as proof of electronic document, 244(9)

**Priority**, *see* Garnishment for taxes unpaid; Ordering

**Prison**, *see* Offences

**Private corporation**, *see also* Corporation
- Canadian-controlled, defined, 125(7), 248(1)
- capital dividend, election, 83(2), Reg. 2101
- cooperative deemed not to be, 136(1)
- credit union deemed not to be, 137(7)
- Crown corporation deemed not to be, 27(2)
- defined, 89(1), 248(1)
- • special cases, 27(2), 134, 136(1), 137(7), 141(2), 141.1, 186(5), 227(16)

Private corporation *(cont'd)*
- deposit insurance corporation deemed not to be, 137.1(6)
- dividend paid by, 83(2)
- dividend refund to, 129
- existing since before 1972, ITAR 50
- flow-through of income to shareholders, *see* Integration
- insurance corporation deemed not to be, 141.1
- municipal or provincial corporation deemed not to be, 227(16)
- mutual fund corporation deemed to be, 131(5)
- non-resident-owned investment corporation deemed not to be, 134
- payment of tax, 157(3)
- • deduction from tax, under provincial statute, ITAR 29(32), (33)
- • deduction of drilling and exploration expenses, ITAR 29(1), (3)–(5)
- subject corporation, 186
- tax on certain dividends received, 186

**Private foundation**
- defined, 149.1(1), 248(1)
- designation of, as public, 149.1(13)
- designation of registered charity as, 149.1(6.3)
- disbursement quota, 149.1(20)
- non-qualified investment, *see* Non-qualified investment: private foundation
- registration of
- • refusal by Minister
- • • deemed, 172(4)(a)
- • revocation of, 149.1(4)
- • revocation or refusal, appeal, 172(3)(a)

**Private health services plan**
- defined, 248(1)
- employer's contribution not a taxable benefit, 6(1)(a)(i)
- premiums
- • deductible from business income, 20.01
- • • reduction in partnership interest, 53(2)(c)(xii)
- • medical expense credit, 118.2(2)(q)

**Private holding corporation, defined,** 191(1)

**Privatization of government assets**
- debt qualifies for investment by deferred income plans, Reg. 4900(1)(q)

**Privileged documents,** *see* Solicitor-client privilege

**Prize**
- achievement, for
- • included in income, 56(1)(n)
- lottery, not taxed (no taxing provision)
- prescribed, Reg. 7700
- • not included in income, 56(1)(n)
- property acquired as, cost of, 52(4)

**Procedure and evidence,** 244

**Procedures not followed by CCRA**
- assessment still valid, 166

**Proceeds of disposition,** *see also* Proceeds of the disposition
- allocation of
- • between land and buildings, 13(21.1), 70(5)(d)
- • between property and services, 68
- deemed
- • amalgamation, on, 69(13)
- • disposition of share, on, 55(2)–(5)
- • disposition to benefit "specified person", 69(11)
- • • application on winding-up, 88(1)
- • • disposition to trust with no change in beneficial ownership, 69(1)(b)(iii)
- • former business property, 44(6)
- • property surrendered to creditor, 79(3)
- • when deemed payable, 14(2)
- defined
- • capital property, 54
- • depreciable property, 13(21)
- • for resource allowance, Reg. 1206(1)
- depreciable property, 13(21)"proceeds of disposition"
- due after year
- • amalgamation, 87(2)(m)
- income interest in trust, 106(3)
- life insurance policy, interest in, 56(1)(j), 148(9)"proceeds of the disposition"
- life insurance policy dividends deemed to be, 148(2)
- timber resource property, 20(5.1)
- unclaimed at year-end
- • withholding tax, 153(4)
- • • effect of remittance, 153(5)
- uncollectible portion, 20(4)–(4.2)
- unrealized, 40(1)(a)(iii)

**Proceeds of the disposition,** *see also* Proceeds of disposition
- defined, Reg. 310

**Processing,** *see also* Manufacturing and processing
- allowances, Reg. Part XII
- defined, for mining taxes on income, Reg. 3900(1)
- field, *see* Canadian field processing

**Processing or fabricating corporation**
- meaning, ITAR 29(26)

**Processing property**
- defined, Reg. 1206(1)

**Producer (of film or video production)**
- defined, Reg. 1106(1)"producer"

**Production**
- resource property, from, defined, 66(15)"production"
- right to receive, *see* Right to receive production

**Production or use**
- payments dependent on
- • deemed income, 12(1)(g)
- • interest paid to non-resident, 212(1)(b) (closing words)

**Production royalty**
- defined, Reg. 1206(1)

**Production tax amount**
- defined, for foreign tax credit, 126(7)

**Professional corporation,** *see also* Professional practice
- defined, 248(1)
- fiscal period of, 249.1(1)(b)(iii)

**Professional membership dues**
- employee's, deduction, 8(1)(i)(i)
- professions board, deductible, 8(1)(i)(vii)

**Professional practice**
- carried on since before 1972, ITAR 23(3)
- incorporated, *see* Professional corporation
- judge's income from, 24.1 [repealed]
- privileged information, 232(2)
- work in progress of
- • deemed to be inventory, 10(5)(a)

# Index

**Professional practice** *(cont'd)*
- - election to exclude from income, 34
- - valuation of, 10(4)(a)

**Professions board**
- dues to, deductible, 8(1)(i)(vii)

**Professor**
- exemption for travel expenses, 81(3.1)(a)(ii)

**Profit**, *see also* Income
- from business or property, income, 3(a), 9(1)
- payment based on future, 12(1)(g)
- reasonable expectation required, 18(1)(h), 248(1)"personal or living expenses"

**Profit participation payments**
- not deductible as financing expenses, 20(1)(e)(iv.1)

**Profit sharing plan**, *see also* Deferred profit sharing plan; Employees profit sharing plan
- appeal from refusal to register, 172(3)(c), 180
- defined, 147(1), 248(1)
- employer's contribution under, 20(1)(w)
- - limitation on deductibility, 18(1)(k)
- information return, Reg. 212
- registration of, as DPSP, 147(2)
- - refusal by Minister
- - - deemed, 172(4)(b)
- regulations, Reg. Part XV

**Profits**, *see* Profit

**Program for Older Worker Adjustment**, *see* Older Worker Adjustment, Program for

**Promissory note**
- conversion to other bond, debenture or note, 51.1
- issued on rollover of property to corporation, 85(1)(b)
- provided as payment, 76(1)

**Promoter**
- of education savings plan
- - defined, 146.1(1)"education savings plan"(b)
- of non-resident investment or pension fund
- - defined, 115.2(1)
- of tax shelter
- - defined, 237.1(1)
- - obligation to provide and use identification number, 237.1(5)

**Promotion expenses**, *see* Advertising

**Proof**
- burden of, *see* Burden of proof
- documents, of, 244(9), (13)
- - rebuttable, *Interpretation Act* s. 25(1)
- electronically filed return, 244(21)
- failure to comply, of, 244(7), (8)
- no appeal, of, 244(10)
- not required re signature of CCRA officer, 244(11)
- return, etc., of, 244(17)–(19)
- service, of, 244(6)
- - by mail, 244(5)
- time of compliance, of, 244(8)

**Property**, *see also* Goods
- acquired
- - as prize, 52(4)
- - by bequest etc., 70(6)
- - by gift, 69(1)(c)
- - by insurer, on default in payment, 138(11.93)
- - from spouse, deemed value of, 73
- - in the year, capital cost allowance, Reg. 1100(2)–(2.4)
- - - non-arm's length exception, Reg. 1102(20)
- - to earn income from business, expenses deductible, 20(1)(e)(ii.1), 20(1)(e.1)(ii)
- adjusted cost base
- - amounts added, 53(1)
- - amounts deducted, 53(2)
- - defined, 54
- - identical properties, 47
- - negative amount, deemed gain, 40(3), (3.1)
- amortized cost, ITAR 26(12)"capital property"
- and casualty surplus, *see* Property and casualty surplus
- annual value of, not deductible, 18(1)(d)
- appropriation of, to shareholder or prospective shareholder, 15(1), (7)
- beneficial owner of, defined re Quebec, 248(3)
- Canadian
- - non-resident-owned investment corporation, of, 133(8)"Canadian property"
- Canadian resource property, defined, 66(15)
- capital gains and losses, *see* Capital gains and losses
- "capital property" defined, 54; ITAR 26(12)"capital property"
- "certified"
- - ascertainment of, 127(10)(a), (b)
- change in use of, 45
- - before 1972, ITAR 26.1(1)
- - election, 45(2)
- - insurer, by, 138(11.3)–(11.41), (11.6)
- - principal residence, election, 45(3)
- - - where not available, 45(4)
- convertible, *see* Convertible property
- cost amount, defined, 248(1)
- cultural, *see* Cultural property
- deceased taxpayer, of, 164(6)
- deemed acquisition of
- - becoming non-resident, 128.1(4)(c)
- - becoming resident in Canada, 128.1(1)(c)
- - capital cost allowance rules, Reg. 1100(2.21)
- - change in use, on, 45
- deemed disposition of
- - becoming non-resident, 128.1(4)(b)
- - becoming resident in Canada, 128.1(1)(b)
- - capital cost allowance rules, Reg. 1100(2.21)
- - change in use, on, 45
- - death, on, 70(5)–(10)
- deemed gain from
- - added to cost base, 53(1)(a)
- - defined, 248(1)
- depreciable, *see* Depreciable property
- disposed of
- - by legal representative, Reg. 1000
- - in part, 43, 46
- - on death, definitions, 70(10)
- disposition of, *see* Disposition
- eligible capital
- - deceased, of, 70(5.1)
- - defined, 54; ITAR 26(12)"eligible capital property"
- - disposition of, 14(6)
- - exchanges of, 14(6), (7)
- exchanges of, 13(4), 44
- - replacement property, 44(5)
- "excluded" of non-resident, 116(6)

**Property** *(cont'd)*
- farm, *see* Farm property
- foreign, deferred income plans, Reg. Part L
- former, capital gain, 44(6)
- goodwill, ITAR 21
- government assistance in acquiring
  - - cost base, deductions from, 53(2)(k)
- having more than one use, 45
- identical, 47; ITAR 26(8)–(8.2)
  - - defined, 248(12)
  - - life insurance corporation, of, 138(11.1)
- income from, 9(3), 12
  - - defined, 9(1)
  - - - for dividend refund, 129(4)"income"
  - - - for FAPI purposes, 95(1)
- inter vivos gift of, 69(1)(b)
- involuntary disposition of, 13(4)
- leased
  - - buildings on, capital cost allowance, Reg. 1102(5)
  - - improvements, capital cost allowance, Reg. 1102(4)
- leasing, capital cost allowance, Reg. 1100(15)–(20)
- non-arm's length exception, Reg. 1102(20)
- separate classes, Reg. 1101(5c)
- listed personal, *see* Listed personal property
- loss from, 9(3)
  - - defined, 9(2)
- lost, destroyed or taken
  - - amalgamation, effects of, 87(2)(l.3)
- misclassified, 13(6)
- non-depreciable capital
  - - change of control, 53(2)(b.2)
- "nothings", ITAR 21
- owned on Dec. 31/71, ITAR 20(1)
- part disposition of
  - - cost base, deduction from, 53(2)(d)
- principal residence, *see* Principal residence
- proceeds of disposition of
  - - allocation of, between land and buildings, 13(21.1)
  - - defined, 54
- production from or use of, *see* Production or use
- publicly traded securities, ITAR 26(11)
- qualified (investment tax credit), Reg. 4600
  - - defined, 127(9), (11)
- reacquired, ITAR 26(6)
- real, disposition of by non-resident, 216(5)
- received as consideration for payment or loan
  - - cost base, deductions from, 53(2)(f)
- rental, capital cost allowance, Reg. 1100(11)–(14.2)
- replacement, 13(4), (4.1), 14(7), 44(5)
- repossessed, rules applicable, 79
- resource, *see* Resource property
- seizure of, by creditor, 79.1
- small business, Reg. Part LI
- substituted
  - - cost base, addition to, 53(1)(f)
  - - meaning of, 248(5)
- surrender of, to creditor, 79
- tax, *see* Municipality: property taxes
- timber resource, defined, 13(21)
- transfer of, *see* Transfer of property
- trust, proportional holdings in, 259
- upkeep by trust for beneficiary, 105(2)
- use of or production from, *see* Production or use

- value at date of death, 70(5), (6)

**Property and casualty surplus (of insurer)**
- defined, insurers, Reg. 2400(1)

**Property taxes**
- deductible after moving away from home, 62(3)(g)
- limitation on deduction as business expense, 18(2)

**Proprietor of business**
- disposing of business, 25
  - - fiscal period, 25
- income from business, 11(1)
- return on death of, 150(4)

**Proprietorship**
- continuing business of partnership, 98(5)

**Prosecution**
- indictment, upon, 239(2)
- limitation, 244(4)

**Prospecting**
- amount re share received, excluded from income, 81(1)(l)
- income from, 35
  - - exemption, 35(1)(c), 81(1)(l)

**Prospecting, exploration and development expenses**
- amalgamations, ITAR 29(11)
- deduction by any corporation, ITAR 29(11)
- extended meaning, ITAR 29(28)
- general limitation, ITAR 29(31)
- limitation, re payments for rights, ITAR 29(13)–(15)
- mining corporation, ITAR 29(2), (3), (13)
- oil and gas corporation, etc., ITAR 29(4), (5)
- renunciation by joint exploration corporation, ITAR 29(6), (7)
- successor corporation, ITAR 29(25)

**Prospector**
- defined, 35(2)
- receipt of shares by, 35
  - - deduction from amount, 110(1)(d.2)

**Protective trust**
- excluded from qualifying disposition, 107.4(1)(e)

**Province**, *see also* specific provinces by name
- bonds issued by
  - - interest paid to non-resident, 212(1)(b)(ii)(C)(II), 212(6)–(8)
- bound
  - - by garnishment orders, 224(1.4)
  - - by withholding tax requirements, 227(11)
- capital tax of, deductibility, 18
- communication of information to, 241(4)(d), Reg. 3003
- corporation incorporated in before part of Canada, 248(1)"corporation incorporated in Canada"
- corporation owned by, *see also* Crown corporation
  - - bonds issued by
  - - - interest paid to non-resident, 212(1)(b)(ii)(C)(IV)
  - - deemed not private corporation, 227(16)
  - - exemption, 149(1)(d)–(d.4)
- defined, *Interpretation Act* s. 35(1)
- exempt from federal tax, *Constitution Act 1867*, s. 125
- gift to, 118.1(1)
- government of, *see* Government
- includes Newfoundland and Nova Scotia offshore areas, 124(4)"province"
- income earned in
  - - deduction from tax, re schooling allowance, 120(2)

Index

Province *(cont'd)*
- • defined, 120(4)
- • individual, by, Reg. Part XXVI
- income not earned in
- • addition to tax for, 120(1)
- labour-sponsored venture capital corporation of
- • recovery of LSVCC credit, 211.7
- laws of
- • property transfer to spouse on death, 248(23.1)
- • support order transfers, 73(1), (1.1)
- legislature, *see* Legislative assembly (or Legislature)
- logging tax paid to, credit for, 127(1), (2), Reg. 700
- member of legislative assembly
- • expense allowance, exempt, 81(2)
- pension legislation, registration under, 147.1(2)(a)(iii)
- portion of income tax
- • refund by Minister, 164(1.4)
- refund of tax of, to be paid by CCRA, 164(1.4)
- residence of qualifying environmental trust in, 250(7)
- student loan legislation, interest paid under, credit, 118.62
- subject to withholding tax provisions, 227(11)
- super-R&D allowance, federal benefit, 127(9)"super-allowance benefit amount", 127(10.1)(b)
- tax transfer payments to, 154, Reg. 3300

**Provincial indemnities**
- excluded from income, 81(1)(q)

**Provincial laws, prescribed**, Reg. 6500–6502

**Provincial life insurance corporation**
- conversion into mutual corporation, 139

**Provincial pension plan, prescribed**
- assignment of pension under, 56(2)
- benefits taxable, 56(1)(a)(i)
- • transfer to qualifying plan, deduction for, before 1993, 60(l)(v)(B.2)
- contributions to
- • deductible from income, 60(v), Reg. 7800(2)
- • excepted from attribution rules, 74.5(12)
- • interest on money borrowed to make, no deduction, 18(11)(g)
- defined, Reg. 7800
- retirement pension under
- • assignment of, not subject to attribution, 74.1(1)
- • spousal contribution, 60(v)(i)(A)
- transfer of rights to pension under, 56(4)
- transfer to RRSP, RRIF or annuity, 146(21)

**Provision**
- defined, ITAR 74

**Provisionable assets**
- defined, Reg. 8006

**Provisional past service pension adjustment (PSPA)**
- defined, Reg. 8303(2), (3)

**Proxy amount**
- prescribed, for research and development expenses, Reg. 2900(4)–(10)
- • reduction in, 127(11.1)(f) [repealed], 127(18)

**Psychologist**
- certification of impairment
- • for disability credit, 118.3(1)(a.2)(iv)
- • for education credit, 118.6(3)(b)(iv)
- defined, 118.4(2)
- therapy qualifying for medical expense credit, 118.2(2)(l.9)

**Public authority**
- tax on disposition of cultural property, 207.3

**Public bodies, exempt**, 149(1)(c)

**Public corporation**
- amalgamation, 87(2)(ii)
- defined, 89(1), 248(1)
- election to trigger gain before corporation becomes, 48.1
- existing since before 1972, ITAR 50
- life insurance corporation deemed to be, 141(2)
- mortgage investment corporation, 130.1(5)
- qualifying dividend paid by, 83(1)
- shares of, donation to charity, 38(a.1)

**Public employees**
- annual dues deductible, 8(1)(i)(iv)

**Public foundation**
- defined, 149.1(1), 248(1)
- designation of registered charity as, 149.1(6.3)
- private foundation designated as, 149.1(13)
- registration of
- • refusal by Minister
- • • deemed, 172(4)(a)
- • revocation of, 149.1(3)
- • revocation or refusal, appeal, 172(3)(a)

**Public pension benefits**
- defined, Reg. 8500(1)

**Public safety occupation**
- defined, Reg. 8500(1)

**Public school board**
- allowance from, exempt, 81(3)

**Public utility**
- foreign
- • dividend from, paid to non-resident, 213
- • income imputed to shareholder of corporation, 213(2)
- interest on obligations, 81(1)(m)
- • amalgamation, 87(2)(jj)

**Publicly traded**
- defined, Reg. 230(1)

**Publicly-traded securities**, Reg. 4400
- donation of, to charity, reduced capital gain, 38(a.1)
- value on Valuation Day, ITAR 26(11), Reg. Sch. VII

**Puck**, *see* Paid-up capital

**Pulp mills**
- capital cost allowance, Reg. Sch. II:Cl. 5

**Punishment**, *see* Offences

**Purchase butterfly**, 55(1), (3.1), (3.2)

**Purifier**
- air or water, medical expense credit, Reg. 5700(c.1)

**Purpose**
- gaining or producing income, 18(1)(a), Reg. 1102(1)(c)

**"Put-in-use" rules**, *see* Available-for-use rules

**Q**

**QPP**, *see* Canada Pension Plan/Quebec Pension Plan

**Quadrennial survey, reserve for**
- defined, 12(1)(h), 20(1)(o), Reg. 3600(2)

**Qualified activities**
- defined, Reg. 5202

# Index

**Qualified annuity**
- defined, Reg. 1408(1)

**Qualified Canadian labour expenditure**
- defined, for film/video production services credit, 125.5(1)

**Qualified construction equipment**
- defined, 127(9) [repealed]
- prescribed, Reg. 4603

**Qualified corporation (re Canadian film/video tax credit)**
- defined, 125.4(1)

**Qualified dependant**
- Child Tax Benefit
  - credit in respect of, 122.61(1)
  - defined, 122.6, 122.62, Reg. 6300–6302
- GST credit
  - credit in respect of, 122.5(3)(c), (d)
  - defined, 122.5(1), 122.5(2)

**Qualified domestic trust**
- relief from double taxation, Canada–U.S. Tax Convention Art. XXVI:3(g)

**Qualified donee**
- defined, 149.1(1), 248(1)

**Qualified expenditure**
- pool, see SR&ED qualified expenditure pool
- reduction to reflect government assistance, 127(18)–(21)
- relating to borrowings to pay dividends or profits, 20.1(8)(d)
- scientific research, for, defined, 127(9)"qualified expenditure"

**Qualified farm property**
- capital gains deduction, 110.6(2)
- defined, 110.6(1)
  - deemed, where capital gain deemed following debt forgiveness, 80.03(8)
- eligible capital property, sale of, 14(1.1)
- individual, of, defined, 108(1)"qualified farm property"

**Qualified insurance corporation**
- defined, Reg. 810(2)
- property of, no certificate required before disposition, Reg. 810(1)(a)

**Qualified investment**, see also Non-qualified investment
- deferred profit sharing plans, 204"qualified investment"
- information returns, Reg. 221
- non-resident investment or pension fund
  - defined, 115.2(1)
- registered education savings plan, 146.1(1)"qualified investment", Reg. 4900
  - revocation of plan for failure to comply, 146.1(2.1), (12.1)
  - tax on failure to comply, 207.1(3)
- registered retirement income fund, 146.3(1)"qualified investment", Reg. 4900
  - taxes on failure to comply, 146.3(7), (9), 207.1(4)
- registered retirement savings plan, 146(1)"qualified investment", Reg. 4900
  - taxes on failure to comply, 146(10), (10.1), 207.1(1)

**Qualified labour expenditure (re Canadian film/video tax credit)**
- defined, 125.4(1)

**Qualified limited partnership**
- defined, Reg. 5000(7)

**Qualified pension income**
- defined, 118(7)
- pension credit, 118(3)B(b)

**Qualified non-resident**
- defined, 115.2(1)

**Qualified property**
- defined
  - foreign property rules, 206(1)
  - investment tax credit, 127(9), (11)

**Qualified related corporation**
- branch tax, 219(8)
- non-resident insurer, of, 138(12)"qualified related corporation"

**Qualified relation**
- GST credit
  - credit in respect of, 122.5(3)(b)
  - defined, 122.5(1), 122.5(2)

**Qualified resource**
- defined, for resource allowance claims, Reg. 1206(1)

**Qualified security**
- defined, 260(1)
- loan of, deemed dividend, 260(5)

**Qualified small business corporation**
- capital gains exemption, see Qualified small business corporation share
- share, see Qualified small business corporation share

**Qualified small business corporation share**
- capital gains deduction, 110.6(2.1)
- death of shareholder, 110.6(14)(g)
- defined, 110.6(1)
  - deemed, where capital gain deemed following debt forgiveness, 80.03(8)
- individual, of, defined, 108(1)"qualified small business corporation share"
- related person, 110.6(14)
- rules re, 110.6(14)

**Qualified small-business property**
- defined, 127(9) [repealed]
- investment tax credit for, 127(9)"specified percentage"(i)

**Qualified small business share**
- excluded from mark-to-market rules, 142.2(1)"mark-to-market property"(e)

**Qualified tertiary oil recovery project, defined**, Reg. 1206(1)

**Qualified transportation equipment**
- defined, 127(9) [repealed]
- prescribed, Reg. 4601

**Qualified trust**
- defined, 259(3)

**Qualifying acquisition**
- defined, for stock option deferral, 7(9)

**Qualifying active business**
- defined, Reg. 5100(1)

**Qualifying amount**
- defined, for retroactive spreading of lump-sum payments, 110.2(1)

**Qualifying Class A share**
- defined, for LSVCC rules, Reg. 6706(1)

Index

**Qualifying corporation**
- defined
  - for foreign investment entities, 94.1(1)
  - for refundable investment tax credit, 127.1(2)

**Qualifying cost**
- defined, for small business investment capital gain rollover, 44.1(1)

**Qualifying cost contribution arrangement**
- defined, 247(1)

**Qualifying debt obligation**
- defined
  - for small business bond, 15.2(3)
  - for small business development bond, 15.1(3)

**Qualifying disposition**
- small business investment capital gain rollover
  - defined, 44.1(1), (9)
- trusts
  - defined, 107.4(1)
  - rollover to trust, 107.4(3)
    - subsequent disposition by trust, 107.4(4)

**Qualifying dividend**
- defined, 83(6)
- paid by public corporation, 83(1)

**Qualifying educational program**
- defined
  - for education tax credit, 118.6(1)
  - for Lifelong Learning Plan withholding exemption, 104.1(2)
  - for Lifelong Learning program (loan from RRSP), 146.02(1)

**Qualifying entity**
- defined, Reg. 6804(1)

**Qualifying environmental trust** (*formerly Mining reclamation trust*)
- acquisition of, deduction, 20(1)(tt)
- amalgamation of corporation, effect of, 87(2)(j.93)
- beneficiary, credit to, 127.41
  - reduction in corporate beneficiary's instalments, 157(3)(e)
- contribution to, deduction, 20(1)(ss)
- cost amount of interest in, 248(1)"cost amount"(e.2)
- defined, 248(1)
- disposition of interest in, income, 12(1)(z.2)
- income from, 12(1)(z.1)
- residence of, 250(7)
- tax on, 211.6

**Qualifying exchange (mutual fund rollover)**
- defined, 132.2(2)
- effect of, 132.2(1)
- exemption from rules re disposition of income interest in trust, 106(2), (3)

**Qualifying fiscal period**
- defined, 34.2(1)

**Qualifying home**
- for RRSP withdrawals, 146.01(1)

**Qualifying homebuyer**
- defined, Reg. 104(3.01)

**Qualifying incomes**
- defined, for foreign tax credit, 126(7), (9)

**Qualifying individual (re approved downsizing program)**
- defined, Reg. 8505(2)(b), 8505(2.1)

**Qualifying interest (in respect of foreign affiliate)**
- defined, 95(2)(m), 95(2.2), Reg. 5907(1.02)
- income of foreign affiliate from active business, 95(2)(a)

**Qualifying losses**
- defined, for foreign tax credit, 126(7), (9)

**Qualifying obligation**
- defined, Reg. 5100(1)

**Qualifying payment**
- defined, Reg. 809(4)

**Qualifying person**
- defined
  - re eligible funeral arrangement, 148.1(1)
  - re stock option rules, 7(7)
  - re treaty shopping, Canada–U.S. Tax Convention Art. XXIX A:2

**Qualifying portion of a capital gain**
- defined, for small business investment capital gain rollover, 44.1(1)

**Qualifying portion of the proceeds of disposition**
- defined, for small business investment capital gain rollover, 44.1(1)

**Qualifying share**
- defined
  - RRSP or RRIF investment in cooperative corporation, Reg. 4901(2)
  - share-purchase tax credit, 192(6), Reg. 6203
- prescribed, Reg. 6203

**Qualifying transfers**
- re past service event, Reg. 8303(6), (6.1), Reg. 8304(2)(h)

**Qualifying trust**
- acquisition of shares for labour-sponsored funds tax credit, 127.4(3)
- defined, 127.4(1), 211.7(1)

**Qualifying withdrawals**
- defined, Reg. 8307(3)

**Quebec**, *see also* Province
- application of civil law to federal Acts, *Interpretation Act* 8.1, 8.2
- Gaspé, *see* Gaspé Peninsula
- gift of succession in, deemed to be release or surrender, 248(9)
- logging tax, credit for, 127(1), (2), Reg. 700
- matrimonial regime, 248(22), (23)
- Montreal, international banking centre, 33.1(3)
- northern, *see* Northern Canada
- Office de professions, dues deductible, 8(1)(i)(vii)
- Pension Plan, *see* Canada Pension Plan/Quebec Pension Plan
- renunciation of succession in, deemed to be disclaimed, 248(9)
- residents, federal tax abatement, 120(2)
- tax rates, *see* introductory pages
- usufructs, rights of use or habitation, and substitutions, deemed to be trusts, 248(3)

***Quebec North Shore Paper Co.* case overruled**, 20(1)(ii)

**Quebec Pension Plan**, *see* Canada Pension Plan/Quebec Pension Plan

**Queen**, *see* Crown

**Quota**
- disbursement, for charities, 149.1(1)"disbursement quota" Reg. 3700–3702

2778

# Index

**Quota** *(cont'd)*
- farm, capital gains exemption, 110.6(1)"qualified farm property"(d)

# R

**R&D**, *see* Scientific research and experimental development

**RCA**, *see* Retirement compensation arrangement

**RCA trust**
- defined, 207.5(1)
- excluded from various trust rules, 108(1)"trust"(d)

**RCGTOH**, *see* Refundable capital gains tax on hand

**RCMP pension, exemption**, 81(1)(i)

**RDTOH**, *see* Refundable dividend tax on hand

**REIT**, *see* Real estate investment trust

**REMIC**, *see* Real Estate Mortgage Investment Conduit

**REOP**, *see* Reasonable expectation of profit

**RESP**, *see* Registered education savings plan

**RESP annual limit**
- defined, 146.1(1)
- limit on RESP contributions, 146.1(2)(k)
- penalty tax on exceeding limit, 204.9"excess amount"(a)

**RESP lifetime limit**
- defined, 204.9

**RFI**, *see* Restricted financial institution

**RHOSP**, *see* Registered home ownership savings plan

**RIC**, *see* Regulated Investment Company (U.S.)

**RIF**, *see* Retirement income fund

**RLSVCC**, *see* Labour-sponsored venture capital corporation (LSVCC): registered

**RPP**, *see* Registered pension plan

**RPP annuity contract**, 147.4

**RRIF**, *see* Registered retirement income fund

**RRSP**, *see* Registered retirement savings plan

**RSP**, *see* Retirement savings plan

**R.S.C. 1985 (5th Supp.)**, *see* Revised Statutes of Canada, 1985 (5th Supp.)

**Rabbi**, *see* Clergy

**Radar equipment**
- capital cost allowance for, Reg. Sch. II:Cl. 9

**Radiocommunication equipment**
- capital cost allowance for, Reg. Sch. II:Cl. 8, Sch. II:Cl. 9
- defined, *Interpretation Act* 35(1)

**Radiological services**
- medical expense, 118.2(2)(o)

**Rail bogies or rail suspension devices**
- capital cost allowance, Reg. 1100(1)(z), Reg. Sch. II:Cl. 35(b)

*Railroad Retirement Act* **(U.S.)**
- Tier 1 benefits, Canada–U.S. Tax Convention Art. XVIII:5

**Railway**
- cars, capital cost allowance, Reg. 1100(1)(z), (z.1b), Reg. Sch. II:Cl. 35
- - separate classes, Reg. 1101(5d), (5d.1)
- companies
- - capital cost allowance, Reg. 1102(10)
- - capitalization of expenses, 36
- corporations, taxable income earned in a province, Reg. 406
- cross-border, profits exempt, Canada–U.S. Tax Convention Art. VIII:4
- employees
- - away-from-home expenses of, deduction, 8(1)(e), (g)
- - relieving telegrapher or station agent expenses, 8(1)(e)
- - U.S. retirement benefits, Canada–U.S. Tax Convention Art. XVIII:5
- expansion property, Reg. 1100(1)(zc)
- locomotive, capital cost allowance, Reg. Sch. II:Cl. 6
- modernization property, Reg. 1100(1)(zc)
- rail suspension device, capital cost allowance, Reg. 1100(1)(z), (z.1b), Reg. Sch. II:Cl. 35
- - separate classes, Reg. 1101(5d), (5d.1)
- rolling stock, exempt from non-resident tax, 212(1)(d)(vii), 212(16)
- sidings, capital cost allowance, Reg. 1100(8)
- systems, Reg. 1104(2), Reg. Sch. II:Cl. 4
- tank car, capital cost allowance, Reg. Sch. II:Cl. 6
- tier 1 pension benefits, Canada–U.S. Tax Convention Art. XVIII:5
- - U.S. resident, exempt, Canada–U.S. Tax Convention Art. XV:3
- track and related property, capital cost allowance, Reg. 1100(1)(zb), Reg. Sch. II:Cl. 1(h)
- - for mine, Reg. Sch. II:Cl. 10(m), Sch. II:Cl. 41
- - separate classes, Reg. 1101(5e), (5e.1)
- traffic control equipment, capital cost allowance, Reg. 1100(1)(za.1), Reg. Sch. II:Cl. 1(i)
- - separate classes, Reg. 1101(5e.1)
- trestles, Reg. 1100(1)(za.2), (zb), Reg. Sch. II:Cl. 3
- - separate classes, Reg. 1101(5e.2), (5f)

**Railway system**
- defined, Reg. 1104(2)

**Rapid transit car**
- capital cost allowance for, Reg. Sch. II:Cl. 8

**Rapidly depreciating electronic equipment**
- capital cost allowance, Reg. 1101(5p), Reg. Sch. II:Cl. 10(f)

**Rate reduction payment**
- treated as interest, 18(9.1)

**Rates of capital cost allowance**, Reg. 1100

**Rates of tax**, *see also* Surtax
- alternative minimum tax, 127.51
- capital tax, financial institutions, 190.1
- corporation, 123
- - abatement, 124
- - deposit insurance, 137.1(9)
- - excessive election, 184(2)
- - investment corporations, 130
- - manufacturing and processing, 125.1
- - non-resident, carrying on business in Canada, 219
- - non-resident-owned investment corporation, 133(3)
- - scientific research, 194
- - small business deduction, 125
- - surtax, 123.2
- DPSP trust
- - non-qualified investments, on, 198
- deposit insurance corporation, 137.1(9)
- income-splitting tax, 120.4(2)
- individual, 117(2)

Rates of tax *(cont'd)*
- - abatement for provincial schooling allowance, 120(2)
- - averaging, *see* Averaging of income
- - general averaging
- - - surtax, 180.1
- - income not earned in a province, 120(1)
- - indexing of, 117.1
- - over-contributions to deferred plans, 204.1
- investment corporation, 130(1)
- investment income of life insurer, 211.1(1)
- kiddie tax, 120.4(2)
- large corporations, 181.1(1)
- minimum tax, 127.51
- non-resident-owned investment corporation, 133(3)
- non-resident withholding tax, 212
- Part I (regular tax)
- - corporation, 123(1)(a), 124(1)
- - - general reduction, 123.4(2)
- - - reduction for CCPC, 123.4(3), 125
- - - surtax, 123.2
- - income not earned in a province, 120(1)
- - income splitting tax, 120.4(2)
- - individual, 117(2)
- - minimum tax, 120.4(2)
- Part I.1 (individual surtax), 180.1(1)
- Part I.2 (OAS clawback), 180.2(2)
- Part I.3 (Large Corporations Tax), 181.1(1)
- Part II (tobacco manufacturers' surtax), 182(1)
- Part II.1 (corporate distributions tax), 183.1(2)
- Part III (excessive capital dividend election), 184(2)
- Part IV (dividends received by private corporation), 186(1)
- Part IV.1 (preferred shares), 187.2
- Part V
- - charity revocation tax, 188(1)(a)
- - charitable foundation, transfer of property, 188(3)
- - private foundation, non-qualified investments, 189(1)
- Part VI (financial institutions capital tax), 190.1(1)
- Part VI.1 (preferred shares), 191.1(1)
- Part VII (share-purchase tax credit refundable tax), 192(1)
- Part VIII (scientific research tax credit refundable tax), 194(1)
- Part IX (cumulative offset account), 196(1)
- Part X
- - DPSP, inadequate consideration, 201
- - DPSP, non-qualified investments or use of assets as security, 198(1)
- Part X.1
- - DPSP with excess amount, 204.1(3)
- - RRSP overcontributions, 204.1(2.1)
- Part X.2 (registered investment holding non-prescribed investment), 204.6(1)
- Part X.3 (labour-sponsored fund insufficiently invested), 204.82(1), (3)
- Part X.4 (overcontribution to RESP), 204.91
- Part XI (deferred income plans)
- - acquisition of shares not at market value, 206.1
- - excess foreign property, 206(2)
- Part XI.1
- - DPSP holding non-qualified investment, 207.1(2)
- - RESP holding non-qualified investment, 207.1(3)
- - RRIF holding non-qualified investment, 207.1(4)
- - RRSP holding non-qualified investment, 207.1(1)
- Part XI.2 (disposition of cultural property by institution), 207.3
- Part XI.3 (retirement compensation arrangement), 207.7(1)
- Part XII (resource royalties paid by tax-exempt person), 208(1)
- Part XII.1 (carved-out income), 209(2)
- Part XII.2 (designated income of trust with non-resident beneficiary), 210.2(1)
- Part XII.3 (investment income of life insurer), 211.1(1)
- Part XII.4 (qualifying environmental trust), 211.6(1)
- Part XIII (withholding tax)
- - dividends paid to non-residents, 212(2) (as reduced by treaty)
- - film and video royalties, 212(5) (as reduced by treaty)
- - other passive income of non-residents, 212(1) (as reduced by treaty)
- Part XIII.1 (foreign bank), 218.2(1) (as reduced by treaty)
- Part XIV
- - branch tax, 219(1) (as reduced by treaty)
- - corporate emigration, 219.1
- refundable tax on corporations issuing shares, 192
- registered charities, 188
- registered investments, re, 204.4
- trust
- - governed by deferred plans, 206(2), 207.1
- - *inter vivos*, 122(1)
- - testamentary, 117(2)

**Reacquired property**, ITAR 26(6)

**Real estate**, *see* Real property

**Real estate investment trust**
- allowed as mutual fund trusts, 108(2)(b)(ii)(B), 108(2)(c), 132(6)(b)(ii)
- units provided to employees, 7(1) [1998 budget proposals]
- U.S., dividends paid by, Canada–U.S. Tax Convention Art. X:7(c)

**Real Estate Mortgage Investment Conduit**
- excess inclusion, Canada–U.S. Tax Convention Art. XI:9

**Real property**, *see also* Building; Land; Rent
- acquired
- - capital cost, 13(5.2)
- capital, taxable, Canada–U.S. Tax Convention Art. XXIII
- capital gains exemption restrictions, 110.6(1)"annual gains limit" "eligible real property gain"
- defined, *Income Tax Conventions Interpretation Act* s. 5
- disposed of
- - non-resident, by, 216(5)
- - recaptured depreciation, 13(5.3)
- income from, Canada–U.S. Tax Convention Art. VI
- interest in, defined, 248(4)
- leasehold interest in, *see* Leasehold interest
- life estate in, 43.1
- non-qualifying real property, defined, 110.6(1)
- outside Canada
- - foreign tax credit to emigrant on disposition, 126(2.21)
- - foreign tax credit to trust, 126(2.21)
- - reporting of to CCRA, 233.3

Real property *(cont'd)*
- principal-business corporations
- - associated, base level deduction, 18(2.3)–(2.5)
- - base level deduction, 18(2)(f), 18(2.2)
- - specified percentage of "soft costs", 18(3.4)
- rent paid before acquisition, deemed CCA, 13(5.2)
- trust owing, whether a unit trust, 108(2)(c)

**Reality television**
- ineligible for film/video production services credit, Reg. 9300(i)

**Reappropriations of amounts**, 221.2

**Reasonable efforts**
- to determine transfer prices
- - defined, 247(4)
- - required, 247(3)(a)(ii)(B)

**Reasonable expectation of profit**
- required for business deduction, 18(1)(h), 248(1)"personal or living expenses"
- required for loss carryforward after change in control, 111(5)(a)(i), 111(5)(b)(i)

**Reasonableness**
- criterion for expenses, 67

**Reassessment**, *see also* Assessment
- after normal reassessment period, 152(4)–(5)
- - disposition of vessel, after, 13(18)
- consequential on other change, 152(4.3)
- constitutes an assessment, 248(1)"assessment"
- deceased's estate, election re losses, 152(6)
- election to capitalize interest, on, 21(5)
- exercise of option, on, 49(4), (5)
- extended reassessment period, 152(4)(b)
- Minister, by, 152(4), (4.1), (6), 165(3)
- - after filing notice of objection, 165(5)
- - disposing of appeal, on consent, 169(3)
- normal reassessment period, defined, 152(3.1)
- second notice of objection not required, 165(7)
- unused Part I.3 tax credit, 152(6)(f)
- validity, 165(5), (6)
- within normal reassessment period, 152(4)

**Recapture**, *see also* Negative amounts
- capital cost allowance, *see* Capital cost allowance: recapture
- eligible capital property, 14(1)
- goodwill, 14(1)
- investment tax credit, 127(27)–(35)
- SR&ED expenditures, 37(6)

**Receivables**
- in later year, reserve for, 20(1)(n), 20(8)
- - where property repossessed by creditor, 79.1(4)
- 1971, ITAR 23(5)"1971 receivables"

**Receiver or receiver-manager**, *see also* Legal representative
- clearance certificate before distributing property, 159(2)
- deemed to be legal representative, 248(1)"legal representative"
- obligations of, 159
- return to be filed, 150(3)
- withholding tax, liability for, 153(1.3) [repealed], (1.4) [repealed], 227(5), 227(5.1)

**Reclamation of mines**, *see* Qualifying environmental trust

**Reclassification**
- depreciable property, change in class, 13(5)
- expenditures, R&D claims, 37(12)

**Recognized stock exchange**
- defined, Canada–U.S. Tax Convention Art. XXIX A:5(a)

**Record**, *see also* Books and records
- defined, 248(1)

**Recovery**
- labour-sponsored funds tax credit, *see* Labour-sponsored funds tax credit: recovery
- limit, *see* Recovery limit

**Recovery limit**
- defined, for non-resident trusts, 94(8)

**Recreational clubs**
- non-profit, exempt, 149(1)(l), 149(5)

**Recreational facilities**
- use of, expense not deductible, 18(1)(l)(i)

**Recreational property**
- capital cost allowance, Reg. 1102(17)

**Redemption of shares by corporation**
- capital loss denied, 40(3.6)
- deemed dividend of excess over paid-up capital, 84(3)

**Redetermination**, *see* Determination

**Reduction of tax**, *see* Abatement of tax

**Reed Stenhouse Companies Ltd.**
- Class I shares, no deemed dividend on redemption, 84(8), Reg. 6206

**Refinery**
- capital cost allowance, Reg. Sch. II:Cl. 10(u), Sch. II:Cl. 41

**Refugee**
- entitled to Child Tax Benefit, 122.6"eligible individual"(e)(iii)

**Refund**
- after normal reassessment period, 152(4.2), 164(1.5)
- "allowable refund" to non-resident-owned investment corporation, 133(6), (7), (8)"allowable refund"
- assignment of, by corporation, 220(6), (7)
- capital gains
- - mutual fund corporation, to, 131(2), (3)
- - mutual fund trust, to, 132(1), (2)
- dividend
- - mutual fund corporation, to, 131(5)
- - private corporation, to, 129(1)
- duty of Minister, 164(4.1)
- employees profit sharing plan, to former beneficiary, 144(9)
- fraudulently obtained, offence, 239(1.1)
- included in income, 12(1)(x)(iv)
- interest on, 164(3)–(4)
- labour-sponsored funds tax credit clawback, 211.9
- non-resident tax, of, 227(6)–(7)
- of payments, *see* Refund of payments
- overpayment of tax, of, 164
- - application to other taxes, 164(2)
- Part I tax, 164
- Part VIII
- - when deemed paid, 194(5)
- partial refundable investment tax credit re scientific research and development, 164(1)
- premiums, of, *see* Registered retirement savings plan: refund of premiums

2781

## Index

**Refund** *(cont'd)*
- provincial portion of income tax, 164(1.4)
- RRSP premiums, of, 146(1)"refund of premiums"
- - deemed receipt of, 146(8.1)
- reassessment to give rise to, 152(4.2)
- refundable dividend tax, 129
- - application to other liability, 129(2)
- repayment on objections and appeals, 164(1.1)
- tax, of
- - deferred profit sharing plan, to, 202(2)
- - - application to other taxes, 203
- - excessive, 160.1(1)
- tax on non-qualified investment, of
- - on disposition, 198(4), 199(2)
- - on recovery of security, 198(5)
- UI premium tax credit, 164(1.6)

**Refund benefit**
- defined, Reg. 8300(1)

**Refund interest**
- defined
- - for M&P credit on resource income, Reg. 5303(4)
- - for corporate interest offset, 161.1(1)
- payable to taxpayer, 164(3)

**Refund of payments**
- defined, for education savings plan, 146.1(1)

**Refund of premiums**, *see* Registered retirement savings plan: refund of premiums

**Refundable capital gains tax on hand**
- mutual fund corporation, of, 131(6)"refundable capital gains tax on hand"
- - carryover to mutual fund trust on qualifying exchange, 132.2(1)(l)
- - reduction of, 131(9)
- mutual fund trust of, 132(4)"refundable capital gains tax on hand"
- - addition to following reorganization, 132.2(1)(l)

**Refundable credits**
- Canadian film/video production credit, 125.4
- Child Tax Benefit, 122.61(1)
- dividend refund, 129(1)
- film or video production services credit, 125.5
- GST credit, 122.5(3)
- individual resident in Quebec, 120(2)
- investment tax credit, 127.1(1)
- medical expenses, 122.51
- qualifying environmental trust credit, 127.41(3)
- U.S. social security tax adjustment due to treaty amendment, Canada–U.S. Tax Convention Art. XVIII:5

**Refundable dividend tax on hand**, *see also* Dividend refund
- aggregate investment income, defined, 129(4)
- amalgamation, on, 87(2)(aa)
- deemed, 186(5)
- defined, 129(3)
- foreign investment income, defined, 129(4)
- "income" or "loss" defined, 129(4)
- meaning of certain expressions, 129(8)
- parent's, after subsidiary wound up, 87(2)(aa), 88(1)(e.2)
- refund of, 129(1)
- taxable dividend, defined, 129(7)

**Refundable federal sales tax credit**, 122.4 [repealed]

**Refundable goods and services tax credit**, 122.5, *see also* Goods and services tax (GST): refundable credit

**Refundable investment tax credit**
- deemed deduction from tax otherwise payable, 127.1(3)
- defined, 127.1(2)
- partial refund in respect of, 164(1)

**Refundable medical expense credit**, 122.51

**Refundable Part IV tax**, 186
- refund of, 129(1)

**Refundable Part VII tax**
- amalgamation, on hand on, 87(2)(nn)
- corporation issuing qualifying shares, 192, 193
- defined, 192(3), 248(1)
- undue deferral of, 193(6)

**Refundable Part VIII tax on hand**
- defined, 194(3), 248(1)
- undue deferral, 195(6)

**Refundable taxes**
- investment income of CCPC, 123.3, *see also* Dividend refund
- Part IV tax, 186(1)
- retirement compensation arrangement arrangement, 207.5(1)

**Registered animal**
- defined, Reg. 1802(5)

**Registered Canadian amateur athletic association**
- defined, 248(1)
- gifts to, credit for, 118.1(1), (3)
- information returns, Reg. 216
- receipts, Reg. 3500, 3501
- records to be kept, 230(2)
- refusal or revocation of registration
- - appeal from, 172(3)(a)
- revocation of registration, 168

**Registered charity**, *see also* Charity
- accumulation of property, 149.1(8), (9)
- books and records, 230(2)
- charitable activities
- - Minister may specify amount expended on, 149.1(5)
- communication of information by Minister, 149.1(15)
- corporate tax return not required, 150(1.1)(a)
- defined, 248(1)
- designation of, by Minister, as public foundation etc., 149.1(6.3)
- - appeal from, 172(3)(a.1)
- disbursement excess, 149.1(20)
- - defined, 149.1(21)
- donations to, *see* Gifts and donations
- exemption for, 149(1)(f)
- fund-raising event
- - exempted from general limitation on entertainment expense deduction, 67.1(2)(b)
- gift to another registered charity
- - revocation of registration, 149.1(4.1)
- gifts to, 118.1(1), (3)
- information returns, 149.1(14), Reg. 204(3)(c)
- loan to donor, 118.1(15)
- Minister may specify amount expended on charitable activities, 149.1(5)
- non-qualified investment, tax re, 189
- penalty taxes, 188, 189

2782

Index

Registered charity *(cont'd)*
- public information return, 149.1(14), (15)
- remainder interest in real property, disposition to, 43.1(1)
- revocation of registration, 149.1(4.1), 168
  - • tax on, 188(1), (2)
- specified gift, defined, 149.1(1)
- tax re, 188, 189
- taxation year, 149.1(1)
- transfer of property
  - • tax on, 188(3), (4)

**Registered education savings plan**, 146.1, *see also* Education savings plan
- accumulated income payment
  - • defined, 146.1(1)
  - • included in income, 146.1(7.1)
  - • restrictions on making, 146.1(2)(d.1)
- amendments to, 146.1(4.1)
- amounts received, income, 56(1)(q)
- annual limit, *see* RESP annual limit
- annuities, holding of, 146.1(1)"qualified investment"(c)
- beneficiary under
  - • amount included in income, 146.1(7)
  - • defined, 146.1(1)
  - • emigration from Canada, no deemed disposition, 128.1(10)"excluded right or interest"(a)(iii)
  - • emigration of beneficiary, no deemed disposition, 128.1(10)"excluded right or interest"(a)(iii)
- conditions for registrations, 146.1(2)
- contribution limits, *see* RESP annual limit; RESP lifetime limit
- defined, 146.1(1)
- distance education programs, 146.1(2)(g.1)
- educational assistance payment, *see* Educational assistance payment
- "excess amount" defined, 204.9(1), (2)
- excluded amount, 146.1(7.2)
- excluded from various trust rules, 108(1)"trust"(a)
- family plan, 146.1(2)(j)
- information returns
  - • by promoters, 146.1(15)
  - • by trustees, 146.1(13.1)
- interest on money borrowed to invest in, whether deductible, 18(11)(h)
- locked-in annuities, 146.1(1)"qualified investment"(c)
- money borrowed for contribution to
  - • limitation on deductibility, 18(11)(g)
- notice of intent to revoke registration, 146.1(12.1)
  - • appeal from, 172(3)(e.1)
- notice of revocation, 146.1(12.2)
- notification to beneficiaries, 146.1(2)(l)
- overcontributions to, tax on, 204.9–204.93 (Part X.4)
- payments out of
  - • non-residents, to, 212(1)(r)
  - • residents, to, 56(1)(q), 146.1(7)
- qualified investment
  - • defined, 146.1(1)
  - • holding non-qualified investment
    - • • revocation of plan, 146.1(2.1), (12.1)
    - • • tax on, 207.1(3)
- refund of payments under, 146.1(1)
- registration
  - • conditions for, 146.1(2)
  - • deemed date of, 146.1(12)
  - • • revocation of, 146.1(12.1), (12.2), (13), (14)
- revocable, 146.1(2.1)
- revocation, 146.1(13)
  - • notice of, 146.1(12.1), (12.2)
- subscriber not taxable, 146.1(6)
- tax payable by subscribers, 204.91
- transfer of property to another plan, 146.1(2)(g.2), (j)(ii)(B), 146.1(6.1), 209.4(5)
- trust
  - • rollover to new trust, 248(1)"disposition"(f)(vi)
- trust not taxable, 146.1(5), 149(1)(u)
- withholding of tax from payments, 153(1)(t), Reg. 103(6)(g), 103(8)

**Registered home ownership savings plan**, 146.2 [repealed]
- cost base of property held in, 50(3)
- defined, Reg. 223(5)
- disposal of properties, 50(3)
- income accrued before 1986, not tax, 12(10.1)
- information return, Reg. 223
- payments out of, to non-residents, 212(1)(p)

**Registered investment**
- defined, 204.4(1), 248(1)
- Minister and, 204.4(2)–(5), 204.5
- tax on
  - • on acquisition of shares not at fair market value, 206.1
  - • on foreign property, 206
  - • on holding certain property, 204.6

**Registered labour-sponsored venture capital corporation**, *see* Labour-sponsored venture capital corporation (LSVCC): registered

**Registered life insurance policy**
- defined, 211, Reg. 1900(1)

**Registered mail**
- no longer needed, for notice of objection, 165(2)

**Registered national arts service organization**
- benefits from, included in income, 56(1)(aa)
- deemed to be registered charity, 149.1(6.4)
- defined, 248(1)
- exempt from tax, 149(1)(l)
- prescribed conditions, Reg. 8700
- receipts issued by, Reg. 3500"registered organization"
- registration, 149.1(6.4)
- revocation of designation, 149.1(6.5)

**Registered non-resident insurer**
- defined, Reg. 804
- withholding requirements, Reg. 800–803

**Registered organization**
- defined, for donations and gifts, Reg. 3500

**Registered pension plan**, 147.1–147.3, Reg. Part LXXXIII–LXXXV
- actuarial report, 147.2(3), Reg. 8410
- actuarial surplus, transfer during 1988, 60(j.01)
- actuary, defined, 147.1(1)
- administrator, 147.1(6)–(7)
  - • defined, 147.1(1)
  - • obligations, 147.1(7)
  - • requirement, 147.1(6)
  - • separate liability, 147.1(16)
- amendments to, 147.1(4), (15), 172(3), (5), Reg. 8511, 8512(3)
  - • anti-avoidance, 146(5.21)

# Index

**Registered pension plan** *(cont'd)*
- annuity, rollover from RPP, 147.4
- appeal
  - - refusal to accept amendment, from, 172(3)(f.1), 172(5)
  - - refusal to register, from, 172(3)
- application for registration, 147.1(2), Reg. 8512(1)
- "as registered" meaning, 147.1(15)
- average wage, defined, 147.1(1)
- balance of annuitized voluntary contributions, 60.2(2)
- benefit provisions, transfer between, 147.3(14.1)
- benefits
  - - association of, with employers, Reg. 8305
  - - flowed through trust, 104(27)
  - - - unauthorized, 147.3(10), (12)
  - - maximum, Reg. 8504
- benefits taxable, 56(1)(a)(i)
  - - exception when contribution made before 1946, 57
- certification of past service benefit, *see* Past service event
- communication of information re, 241(4)(d)(vii)
- commutation of benefits, Reg. 8503(2)(m), (n), 8503(2.1)
- compensation, defined, 147.1(1)
- conditions, 147.1(2), (5), Reg. 8501–8506
- continuation of, in amalgamation, 87(2)
- contract under, 254
- contribution, prescribed, 147.2(2), Reg. 8516
- death of contributor, amount deductible, 147.2(6)
- defined, 248(1); ITAR 17(8)
- defined benefit provision, defined, 147.1(1)
- definitions, 147.1(1)
- designated plan, Reg. 8515
  - - special rule, Reg. 8515
- eligible contribution, defined, 147.2(2), Reg. 8515(5), 8516
- emigration of member, no deemed disposition, 128.1(10)"excluded right or interest"(a)(viii)
- employee's contribution deductible, 147.2(4), Reg. 8502(b)(i), 8503(4)(a), (b)
- employer's contribution
  - - deductible, 20(1)(q), (s), 147.2(1), Reg. Part XXVII
  - - defined benefit provision, 147.2(2)
  - - filing of actuarial report, 147.2(3)
  - - limits, 147.1(8), (9), Reg. 8506(2)
  - - not taxable benefit, 6(1)(a)(i)
- exempt from tax, 149(1)(o), (o.1)
- excluded from various trust rules, 108(1)"trust"(a)
- filing annual return, Reg. 8409
- foreign plan, *see* Foreign plan (pension plan)
- foreign property holdings, tax on, 205–207
- foreign service, *see* Foreign service
- grandfathered plan
  - - complying before March 1996 budget date, Reg. 8509(13)
  - - defined, Reg. 8500(1)
- includes references to "approved" plan, ITAR 17(8)
- income accruing in
  - - not taxed by U.S., Canada–U.S. tax treaty Art. XVIII:7
- information return, Reg. 8409
- insurance corporation demutualization conversion benefit, 139.1(12), (14)
- limits on contributions, 147.1(8), (9), 147.2(4), Reg. 8506(2)

- member of plan, defined, 147.1(1)
- Minister to obtain advice of Superintendent of Financial Institutions, 147.1(17)
- money borrowed for contribution to
  - - limitation on interest deductibility, 18(11)(c)
- money purchase limit, defined, 147.1(1)
- money purchase provision, defined, 147.1(1)
- multi-employer plan
  - - anti-avoidance, 147.1(14)
  - - becoming revocable plan, 147.1(9)
  - - defined, 147.1(1), Reg. 8500(1)
  - - pension adjustment limits, 147.1(9)
  - - registration requirements, Reg. 8510(7)
  - - specified
    - - - defined, 147.1(1), Reg. 8510(2)
    - - - rules, Reg. 8510(3), (5)–(7)
- no tax payable by, 149(1)(o), (o.1)
- non-member benefits, Reg. 8500(8)
- non-residents
  - - for, not subject to Part XI, 205(a)
  - - payment under, withholding tax, 212(1)(h)
- participating employer, defined, 147.1(1)
- past service benefits, determination of, 147.1(10)
- past service contributions
  - - additional voluntary contributions, deductible for 1986, 8(1.1)
  - - by employee
    - - - rollover where pre-March 28, 1988 commitment, 60(j.02)
  - - by employer
    - - - deductible, 147.2(2), Reg. 8516(2)
- past service event
  - - defined, 147.1(1), Reg. 8300(1), (2)
  - - restrictions on pension funding and benefits, 147.1(10), Reg. 8306, 8307(2)
- past service payments into, 57(4)
- payment under, taxable, 56(1)(a)(i), 212(1)(h), 254
- pension adjustment, *see* Pension adjustment
- pension adjustment limits, *see also* Pension adjustment
- plan as registered, 147.1(15)
- prohibited investments, Reg. 8502(h), 8514(1)
- refund of undeducted past service additional voluntary contributions, 60.2(1)
- registration of, 147.1(2), (3)
  - - additional conditions, 147.1(5)
  - - amendments, conditions for acceptance of, 147.1(4)
  - - deemed from time of application, 147.1(3)
  - - regulations, 147.1(18), Reg. Part LXXXIII–LXXXV
  - - revocation of, 147.1(13), 147.3(12)
    - - - notice, 147.1(12)
    - - - notice of intention, 147.1(11)
- reorganization of money purchase plan, 147.3(7.1)
- repayment of post-1989 benefits, 60(j.04)
- repayment of pre-1990 benefits, 60(j.03)
- reporting requirements, Reg. 8400–8410
- retiring allowances transferred to, 60(j.1)
- rollover to RPP annuity, 147.4
- salary deferral leave plan, Reg. 8508
- shared-funding arrangement, Reg. 8501(6.1)
- single amount, defined, 147.1(1)
- specified multi-employer plan
  - - defined, 147.1(1), Reg. 8510(2)
  - - rules, Reg. 8510(3), (5)–(7)

2784

Registered pension plan *(cont'd)*
- • spouse, defined, 147.1(1)
- • successor plan, Reg. 8308(8)
- tax re foreign property, 205–207
- teacher's contributions, 147.2(5)
- transfer of property between benefit provisions, 147.3(14.1)
- transfers from
- • actuarial surplus, of, 60(j.01), 147.3(4.1), (7.1)
- • another RPP, to, 147.3(1)–(8), Reg. 8517
- • death, on, 147.3(7)
- • deemed, 147.3(14)
- • division of amount transferred, 147.3(11)
- • excess, 147.3(13)
- • lump sum on death, 147.3(7)
- • marriage breakdown, on, 147.3(5)
- • money purchase plan to money purchase plan, 147.3(7.1)
- • pre-1991 contributions, 147.3(6)
- • RRIF, to, 146.3(2)(f)(v), (vi), 147.3(1), (4)–(7), (10)
- • RRSP, to, 147.3(1), (4)–(7), (10)
- • restrictions re, 147.3(12)
- • spousal RRSP, to, 60(j.2)
- • taxation of amount transferred, 147.3(9)
- transfers to
- • actuarial surplus, of, 60(j.01), 147.3(4.1), (7.1)
- • another RPP, from, 147.3, Reg. 8517
- • deferred profit sharing plan, from, 147(19)
- • • via a trust, 104(27.1)
- • marriage breakdown, on, 147.3(5)
- • money purchase plan from money purchase plan, 147.3(7.1)
- • pension benefits received through trust, of, 60(j)(ii)
- • RRSP, from, 146(16)
- • retiring allowance, 60(j.1)
- • unregistered plan, from, 60(j)(i)
- • wage measure, defined, 147.1(1)

**Registered retirement income fund**
- acceptance for registration, 146.3(2)
- administration fees, non-deductible, 18(1)(u)
- amended
- • deemed receipt, 204.2(1.4)
- amounts received, income, 56(1)(t)
- annuitant
- • defined, 146.3(1)
- • emigration from Canada, no deemed disposition, 128.1(10)"excluded right or interest"(a)(ii)
- • emigration of annuitant, no deemed disposition, 128.1(10)"excluded right or interest"(a)(ii)
- annuities, holding of, 146.3(1)"qualified investment"(b.1), (b.2)
- benefits taxable, 146.3(5)
- business carried on by, 146.3(3)(c)
- carrier, defined, 146.3(1)"annuitant"
- change in fund after registration, 146.3(11)–(13)
- common-law spouse, breakdown of relationship, 146.3(14)(b)
- death of last annuitant, 146.3(6)–(6.2)
- defined, 146.3(1)
- designated benefit
- • amount deductible, 146.3(6.2)
- • deemed received, 146.3(6.1)
- • defined, 146.3(1)"designated benefit"
- • transfer of, to spouse, child or grandchild, 146.3(6.11)
- designation of charity as beneficiary, 118.1(5.1), (5.2)
- disposition of property to
- • capital loss nil, 40(2)(g)(iv)(A)
- eligible amount, 146.3(6.11)
- excessive small business property holding, tax, 207.1(5) (repealed retroactively)
- excluded from various trust rules, 108(1)"trust"(a)
- exempt from tax, 146.3(3), 149(1)(x)
- income accruing in
- • not taxed, 146.3(3), 149(1)(x)
- • not taxed by U.S., Canada–U.S. tax treaty Art. XVIII:7
- income not subject to annual accrual, Reg. 7000(6)
- information returns, Reg. 215
- insurance corporation demutualization conversion benefit, 139.1(12), (14)
- interest income deemed not received by annuitant, 146.3(15)
- investment counselling fees, non-deductible, 18(1)(u)
- life income fund, treated as RRIF (no legislative provisions, *see* Notes to 147.3(1))
- locked-in annuities, 146.3(1)"qualified investment"(b.2)
- minimum amount
- • defined, 146.3(1)
- • requirement to pay out annually, 146.3(1)"retirement income fund"
- non-qualified investments, 146.3(7)–(9)
- non-resident, payment to, 212(1)(q)
- payments under
- • attributed to spouse, 146.3(5.1)
- • joint and several liability for tax on, 160.2(2)–(4)
- • non-resident, to, 212(1)(q)
- • • election to file return, 217
- • taxable, 146.3(5)
- • withholding of tax, 153(1)(l), Reg. 103(4), 103(6)(d.1)
- property
- • disposition or acquisition, 146.3(4)
- • transfer of, 146.3(14)
- • used as security, recovery of, 146.3(10)
- "property held" in connection with the fund, 146.3(1)
- qualified investment, defined, 146.3(1)
- registration of, 146.3(2)
- retirement income, defined, 146(1)
- retirement income fund, defined, 146.3(1)
- revocation of registration, 146.3(11)–(13)
- services in respect of, non-deductible, 18(1)(u)
- tax-paid amounts, *see* Tax-paid amount
- tax payable by
- • on acquisition of shares not at fair market value, 206.1
- • on foreign property, 206
- • on holding certain property, 207.1(4)
- transfer from
- • another RRIF, to, 146.3(2)(e), 146.3(14)(a)
- • marriage breakdown, on, 146.3(14)
- • not a disposition, 248(1)"disposition"(g)
- • RRSP, to, 146.3(14)(a)
- • spouse's RRSP, to, on marriage breakdown, 146.3(14)(b)
- transfer to
- • amount to be included in income, 146.3(5.1)

2785

## Index

Registered retirement income fund *(cont'd)*
- - another RRIF, from, 146.3(14)(a)
- - balance of annuitized voluntary contributions, pre-10/9/86, 60.2(2)
- - deceased spouse's RRSP, from, 60(l)
- - not a disposition, 248(1)"disposition"(g)
- - RPP, from, 146.3(2)(f)(v), (vi), 147.3(1), (4)–(7), (10)
- - RRSP, from 146(16), 146.3(5.1)
- - rules, 146.3(5.1)–(5.5)
- trust, not taxed, 146.3(3), 149(1)(x)
- withholding of tax, 153(1)(l), Reg. 103(4), 103(6)(d.1)

**Registered retirement savings plan**
- administration fees, non-deductible, 18(1)(u)
- age 69 maturity, 146(2)(b.4), 146(13.2)
- amended plan, 146(12)
- - deemed receipt, 204.2(1.4)
- - payments out of, subject to withholding of tax, 153(1)(j)
- amount deductible
- - excess premiums, 146(8.2)
- - - deemed not premiums, 146(8.21)
- amount included in computing income, 146(8.3)–(8.7)
- amounts received from, income, 56(1)(h), 146(8)
- annuitant
- - defined, 146(1)
- - emigration from Canada, no deemed disposition, 128.1(10)"excluded right or interest"(a)(i)
- - emigration of annuitant, no deemed disposition, 128.1(10)"excluded right or interest"(a)(i)
- annuity acquired or provided under, pre-Oct9/86
- - balance of annuitized voluntary contributions to RPP, 60.2(2)
- attribution rule re payments from spousal plan, 146(8.3)
- benefits under, 146(8)–(8.91)
- - deduction for estate tax, 60(m)
- - succession duties on, deduction for, 60(m.1)
- - where plan not registered at end of year entered into, 146(15)
- borrowing against,
- - income inclusion, 146(10)(b)
- - prohibited for depositary plan, 146(2)(c.3)(ii)
- borrowing from
- - to finance education, *see* Lifelong Learning Plan
- - to purchase a home, *see* Home Buyers' Plan
- business carried on by, 146(4)(b)
- change in, after registration, 146(12), (13)
- - advantage extended by issuer, 146(13.1)
- common-law spouse, breakdown of relationship, 146(16)
- contributions, *see* premiums (*below*)
- cumulative excess amount re, 204.1(2.1), 204.2(1.1)
- death, effect of, 146(8.8)–(8.91)
- - refund of premiums to child or grandchild, rollover to new RRSP, 60(l)(v)(B.1)
- - refund of premiums to spouse, child or grandchild, 146(1)"refund of premiums"
- deduction limit, 146(1)"RRSP deduction limit"
- - defined, 248(1)
- defined, 146(1)
- definitions, 146(1)
- designation of charity as beneficiary, 118.1(5.1), (5.2)
- disposition of property to
- - capital loss nil, 40(2)(g)(iv)(B)

- dollar limit, 146(1)"RRSP dollar limit"
- - defined, 248(1)
- election re refund of premiums, ITAR 61(2), Reg. 5600
- excess amount for a year re, 204.2(1)
- excess contributions
- - tax on, 204.1
- - withdrawal of, 146(8.2)
- excessive small business property holding, tax, 207.1(5) (repealed retroactively)
- excluded from various trust rules, 108(1)"trust"(a)
- exempt from tax, 146(4), 149(1)(r)
- foreign property of
- - defined, 206(1), Reg. 5000
- - tax re, 205–207
- Home Buyers' Plan, *see* Home Buyers' Plan
- home mortgage as investment, Reg. 4900(1)(j)
- income accruing in
- - not taxed, 146(4), 149(1)(r)
- - not taxed by U.S., Canada–U.S. Tax Convention Art. XVIII:7, Art. XXIX:5
- income not subject to annual accrual, Reg. 7000(6)
- information returns, Reg. 214
- insurance corporation demutualization conversion benefit, 139.1(12), (14)
- interest on money borrowed to invest in, not deductible, 18(11)(b)
- investment counselling fees, non-deductible, 18(1)(u)
- investment in small businesses, Reg. 4900(6), (12)
- issuer extending advantage, 146(13.1)
- "issuer" of, defined, 146(1)
- labour-sponsored venture capital corporation, 127.4(1)"qualifying trust", 127.4(6)(a)
- labour-sponsored venture capital corporation shares, acquisition of, 127.4(1)"qualifying trust" (3)
- life insurance policies, 146(11)
- Lifelong Learning Plan, *see* Lifelong Learning Plan
- maturity by age 69, 146(2)(b.4), 146(13.2)
- money borrowed to pay premium
- - limitation on interest deductibility, 18(11)(b)
- mortgage as investment, Reg. 4900(1)(j)
- net past service pension adjustment, meaning, 146(1)
- non-qualified investments, defined, 146(1)
- - disposition of, 146(6)
- non-resident withholding tax, 212(1)(l)
- overcontribution to
- - no deduction for, 146(5)
- - non-deductible, withdrawal of, 146(8.2)
- - tax on, 204.1(2.1)
- - transfer from RPP, deduction if withdrawn, 147.3(13.1)
- payments under
- - joint and several liability for tax on, 160.2(1), (3), (4)
- - non-residents, to, 212(1)(l)
- - - election to file return, 217
- - remuneration, Reg. 100(1)
- - taxable, 56(1)(h), 146(8), 212(1)(l)
- - withholding tax, 153(1)(j)
- pledging assets of, *see* borrowing against (*above*)
- premiums
- - amount deductible, 60(i), 146(5), (5.2), (6.1)
- - excess, refunded, deemed not premiums, 146(8.21)
- - minimum tax, 127.52(1)(a) [repealed]
- - paid before registration, 146(14)

2786

# Index

Registered retirement savings plan *(cont'd)*
- • refund of, on overcontribution, 146(8.2)
- • undeducted, 204.2(1.2)
- property used as security for loan, recovery of, 146(7)
- retiring allowance, transfer to, 60(j.1)
- qualified investments of, 146(1), Reg. 4900
- recontribution of certain withdrawals, deduction for, 146(6.1)
- refund of excess contributions, 146(8.2)
- refund of premiums, 146(1)
- • death before 1972, ITAR 61(2), Reg. 5600
- • deemed receipt of, 146(8.1)
- • defined, 146(1)
- • estate, to, 146(8.1)
- • transferred to annuity, RRSP or RRIF, 60(l)
- • used to purchase income-averaging annuity contract, deductible, 61(2)(d)
- registration of, 146(2), (3), (13.1)
- • change after, 146(12), (13)
- rules governing, 146
- security, not to be used as, 146(2)(c.3)(ii)
- services in respect of, non-deductible, 18(1)(u)
- spousal plan, 146(8.3)
- • attribution on withdrawals, 146(8.3)
- • defined, 146(1)
- • premiums
- • • amount deductible, 146(5.1)
- • • not subject to income attribution rules, 74.5(12)
- • transfers to, from RPP or DPSP, 60(j.2)
- spouse
- • breakdown of relationship, on, 146(16)
- • transfer to, on death, 146(1)"refund of premiums", 146(8.91)
- tax on over-contributions to, 204.1
- tax-paid amounts, *see* Tax-paid amount
- tax payable by
- • on acquisition of shares not at fair market value, 206.1
- • on foreign property, 206
- • on holding certain property, 207.1(1)
- • termination at age 69, 146(2)(b.4)
- transfer from, to other plan or RRIF, 60(l), 146(16)
- • amount to be included in income, 146.3(5.1)
- • not a disposition, 248(1)"disposition"(g)
- • rules, 146.3(5.1)–(5.5)
- • tracking of funds, 146(8.4)
- transfer to
- • another RRSP, from, 146(16)
- • capital loss deemed nil, 40(2)(g)(iv)(A)
- • capital loss denied, 40(2)(g)(iv)(B)
- • DPSP, from, 147(19)
- • deceased person's RRSP, from, 60(l)
- • not a disposition, 248(1)"disposition"(g)
- • pension benefits received through a trust, 60(j)(ii)
- • RPP, from, 147.3(1), (4)–(7), (10)
- • • division of amount transferred, 147.3(11)
- • • taxation of amount transferred, 147.3(10)
- • RRIF, from, 146.3(14)
- • retiring allowance, 60(j.1)
- • spouse, for, on marriage breakdown, 147.3(5)
- • spouse's RPP or DPSP, from, 60(j.2)
- • unregistered plan, from, 60(j)(i)
- trust
- • disposition of property by, 146(9)
- • non-qualified investments acquired by, 146(10)
- • non-qualified investments held by
- • • tax payable, 146(10.1)
- • not taxed, 146(4), 149(1)(r)
- unused deduction room, meaning, 146(1)
- United States residents, deferral, Canada-U.S. Tax Convention Art. XVIII:7
- withdrawal of funds for education, *see* Lifelong Learning Plan
- withdrawal of funds to purchase home, *see* Home Buyers' Plan
- withholding on withdrawals of funds, Reg. 103(4)

**Registered securities dealer**, *see also* Broker; Investment dealer; Securities
- defined, 248(1)
- securities lending arrangement payments to non-residents
- • exemption from withholding tax, 212(1)(b)(xii)
- • information return required, 212(18)
- • tax on excessive payments, 212(19)
- software development by, no R&D credits, 248(1)"scientific research and experimental development"(b)(ii)

**Registered segregated fund trust**
- excluded from various trust rules, 108(1)"trust"(a)

**Registered supplementary unemployment benefit plan**
- amendment of, amounts received, 145(4)
- benefits received, income, 56(1)(g)
- defined, 145(1)
- emigration of employee, no deemed disposition, 128.1(10)"excluded right or interest"(a)(xi)
- employer's contribution under, 20(1)(x), 145(5)
- excluded from various trust rules, 108(1)"trust"(a)
- rollover to new trust, 248(1)"disposition"(f)(vi)
- trust not taxable, 145(2), 149(1)(q)
- winding-up of, amounts received, 145(4)

**Registration**
- business, *see* Business number
- Canadian amateur athletic association, 248(1)"registered Canadian amateur athletic association"
- • appeal from refusal or revocation by Minister, 172(3), (4)
- certificate in Federal Court, of tax owing to Crown, 223(3)
- charity, 248(1)"registered charity"
- • appeal from refusal or revocation by Minister, 172(3), (4)
- deferred profit sharing plan, 147(2)–(5), Reg. 1501
- education savings plan, 146.1(2), (4), (12)
- employees profit sharing plan, as DPSP, 147(3), (4)
- GST, *see* Business number
- labour sponsored venture capital corporation, 204.81(1)
- multi-employer pension plan, Reg. 8510(7)
- national arts service organization, 149.1(6.4)
- • appeal from refusal or revocation by Minister, 172(3), (4)
- pension plan, 147.1(2), (3), Reg. 8512(1)
- • multi-employer plan, Reg. 8510(7)
- profit sharing plan, as DPSP, 147(2)
- registered education savings plan, *see* education savings plan (above)
- registered investment, deemed, 204.4(7)
- registered pension plan, *see* pension plan (above)

2787

# Index

Registration *(cont'd)*
- registered retirement income fund, *see* retirement income fund (below)
- registered retirement savings plan, *see* retirement savings plan (below)
- retirement income fund, 146.3(2)
- retirement savings plan, 146(2), (3), (13.1)
- revocation of, *see* Revocation of registration
- tax shelter, 237.1, *see also* Tax shelter

**Regular adjustment period**
- defined, re indexed debt obligation, Reg. 7001(7)

**Regular customers**
- defined, for FAPI rules, 95(2.4)(b)

**Regular eligible amount**
- defined, for Home Buyers' Plan, 146.01(1)

**Regulated Investment Company (U.S.)**
- dividend paid to Canadian resident, Canada–U.S. Tax Convention Art. X:7(b)

**Regulations**
- definitions in, *Interpretation Act* s. 16
- failure to comply with, penalty, 162(7)
- incorporating material amended from time to time, 221(4)
- Income Tax, reproduced after the *Income Tax Act* and *Income Tax Application Rules*
- judicial notice to be taken of, 244(12)
- meaning, 248(1)
- provision for, 147.1(18), 214(13), 215(5), 221(1)
- publication of, in *Canada Gazette*, 221(2)
- reducing amount of non-resident withholding tax, 215(5)
- residents in Canada, re, 214(13)
- retroactive effect, limitation on, 221(2)
- whether binding on Her Majesty, 221(3)

**Rehabilitative therapy**
- for hearing/speech loss, medical expense, 118.2(2)(l.3)

**Reimbursement**
- alimony or maintenance payments, 56(1)(c.2), 60(c.2)
- disability insurance top-up paid by employer, 8(1)(n.1)
- election to offset against outlay or expense, 12(2.2)
- housing loss, by employer, 6(19)–(22)
- included in income, 12(1)(x)
- - prescribed amount, Reg. 7300
- inducements, 20(1)(hh)
- legal expenses of collecting salary etc., re
- - included in employee's income, 6(1)(j)
- loss in value of home, for, 6(19)–(22)
- medical expenses, 118.2(3)(b)
- motor vehicle expenses, in respect of, 6(1)(b)(xi)
- payments as
- - election re adjusted cost base, 53(2)(s), 53(2.1)
- petroleum/natural gas etc. royalties included in income, for, 80.2
- received by beneficiary of trust, or partner, 12(2.1)
- salary or wages, of, 8(1)(n)
- support payments, 56(1)(c.2), 60(c.2)

**Reimbursement payment**
- defined (re top-up disability payments), 8(1)(n.1)(i)

**Reinsurance arrangement**
- defined, 211(1), Reg. 1900(1)

**Reinsurance commission**
- deduction, 20(1)(jj)
- defined, Reg. 1408(1)

- exclusion from matchable expenditure rules, 18.1(15)(b)
- inclusion in income, 12(1)(s)
- reserve for, 20(7)(c)

**Reinsurance recoverable**
- defined, Reg. 2400(1)

**Related**, *see* Related persons

**Related group, defined**, 251(4)

**Related persons**, *see also* Associated corporations
- deemed not to deal at arm's length, 251(1)(a)
- defined, 251(2)
- - extended meaning under debt forgiveness rules, 80(2)(j)
- - special rule for butterfly transactions, 55(5)(e)
- - special rule for deemed dispositions of trusts, 104(5.7)(b)
- - special rule for financial institutions tax, 190.15(6)
- - special rule for foreign affiliates, 95(2.2)(b), 95(6)(a)(i)
- - special rule for loans to non-residents, 17(11), (11.1)
- - special rule for transfer pricing, Canada–U.S. Tax Convention Art. IX:2

**Related segregated fund trust**, 138.1
- adjusted cost base of, 53(1)(l), 53(2)(q)
- application on qualifying disposition to trust, 107.4(3)(g)
- defined, 138.1(1)(a)
- flow-through entity for capital gains exemption, 39.1(1), (6)
- minimum tax not payable, 127.55(f)(i)
- rollover to new trust, 248(1) "disposition"(f)(vi)

**Related transactions**
- defined, for foreign tax credit, 126(7)

**Relationship, defined**, 251(6)
- for certain Part I.3 purposes, 181.3(4), 181.5(6)

**Release or surrender, defined**, 248(9)

**Relevant authority**, *see also* Competent authority
- defined
- - for policy reserves in insurance business, Reg. 1408(1)
- - for prescribed amount and recovery rate, Reg. 8006

**Relevant contribution (re eligible funeral arrangement)**
- defined, 148.1(1)

**Relevant conversion benefit**
- defined, for insurance demutualization, 139.1(16)(a)

**Relevant limit (re debt forgiveness rules, partnerships)**
- defined, 80(15)(b)
- limitation on deduction to partner, 80(15)(a)

**Relevant loss balance (for debt forgiveness rules)**
- application of, 80(3), (4)
- defined, 80(1)

**Relevant period**
- defined, 104(5.7)
- for deferred income plans, foreign property, Reg. 5000(7)
- for trust deemed disposition rules, defined, 104(5.7)

**Relevant tax factor (for FAPI)**
- defined, 95(1)

**Religious order, members' charitable gifts**, 110(2)

**Religious organization**, *see* Communal organizations; Registered charity

2788

**Relocation**, *see also* Moving expenses
- counselling, *see* Counselling services
- eligible, *see* Eligible relocation
- reimbursement for loss of value of home, *see* Housing loss

**Remainder interest, disposition of**, *see* Life estate in real property

**Remission orders**
- text of, reproduced after the *Income Tax Regulations*

**Remittance of taxes withheld**, *see also* Withholding tax
- deemed remitted on day received by Receiver General, 248(7)
- interference with, by secured creditor, 227(5.2)–(5.4) (draft)
- large employers must remit through financial institution, 153(1), Reg. 110
- small employers, quarterly remittance, Reg. 108(1.12)
- source withholdings, Reg. 108
- unclaimed dividends and interest, 153(4), Reg. 108(4)

**Remote work site, employment at**, 6(6), *see also* Northern Canada

**Remuneration**, *see also* Salary
- defined
- - for Canadian film/video tax credit, Reg. 1106(1)"remuneration"
- - for source withholdings, Reg. 100(1)
- information returns, Reg. Part II
- ranges of, Reg. Sch. I
- total
- - defined, Reg. 100(1)
- - unpaid, 78(4)
- - withholding of tax on, 153(1)(a)
- - failure to remit amounts withheld, 227(9.5)
- - failure to withhold, 227(8.5)

**Renewable energy**, *see* energy: renewable

**Renovations**
- disability-related
- - deductible, 20(1)(qq)
- - medical expense credit, 118.2(2)(l.2)

**Rent**
- accrual of, to date of death, 70(1)(a)
- deduction for, 9(1)
- future period, for
- - not "outlay" or "expense" 66(15)"outlay" or "expense"
- income
- - taxable, 9(1)
- - whether specified investment business, 125(7)"specified investment business"
- non-resident withholding tax, *see* paid to non-resident (below)
- office, paid by employee, 8(1)(i)(ii)
- - certificate of employer, 8(10)
- paid on depreciable property before acquisition, deemed CCA, 13(5.2)
- paid to non-resident, 212(1)(d), 212(13)
- - alternative tax, 216
- - re railway rolling stock, exemption, 212(1)(d)(vii)
- prepaid, non-deductible, 18(9)
- scientific research expenditures, limitations, 37(8)(d)(ii)
- treaty rules, Canada–U.S. Tax Convention Art. VI

**Rental cost**
- defined, Reg. 5202

**Rental or leasing property**
- defined, 127.52(3)
- minimum tax, 127.52(1)(b), (c)(ii)

**Rental properties**
- capital cost allowance, Reg. 1100(11)–(14.2), 1101(1ac)–(1ae)
- - non-arm's length exception, Reg. 1102(20)
- defined, Reg. 1100(14)–(14.2)
- minimum tax, 127.52(1)(b), (c.2)(ii), 127.52(3)"rental or leasing property"

**Renunciation**, *see* Flow-through shares

**Reorganization**, *see also* Amalgamation; Rollover; Winding-up
- butterfly, 55(3)(b)
- causing security of deferred income plan to become foreign property, 206(3.1)
- corporate, generally, 84–88
- divisive (butterfly), 55(3)(b)
- effect on stock options, 7(1.4), (1.5)
- mutual fund corporation or trust, 132.2
- of business, payment to shareholder deemed dividend, 84(2), (6)
- of capital, exchange of shares, 86(1); ITAR 26(27)
- property acquired in course of
- - capital cost allowance, Reg. 1100(2.2)
- treaty protection, Canada–U.S. Tax Convention Art. XIII:8

**Repaid amount (tax shelter investment)**
- defined, 143.2(10)

**Repair**
- automobile, *see* Automobile: operating costs

**Repayment**, *see also* Reimbursement
- amount previously included in income, 20(1)(m.2)
- application to other taxes, 164(2)
- employment insurance benefits, 60(n), (v.1)
- government assistance, *see* Assistance/government assistance: repayment of
- inducements, 20(1)(hh)
- overpayment of interest, by taxpayer, 164(3.1)
- - deduction for, 20(1)(ll)
- pension benefits, 60(j.03), (j.04)
- policy loan, 60(s)
- shareholder's loan, 20(1)(j)
- tax, *see* Refund
- unemployment insurance benefits, 60(n), (v.1)

**Repayment period**
- defined, for Lifelong Learning Plan, 146.02(1)

**Repeal**
- legislation, *Interpretation Act* s. 25(1)
- regulations, *Interpretation Act* s. 31(4)

**Replacement cost of property**
- value of inventory, 10(4)

**Replacement obligation**
- corporation in financial difficulty, exemption from non-resident withholding tax, 212(3)

**Replacement property**, *see also* Exchanges of property
- defined
- - for capital property, 44(5)
- - for depreciable capital property, 13(4), (4.1)
- - for eligible capital property, 14(6), (7)
- - for Home Buyers' Plan, 146.01(1)
- taxable Canadian property
- - capital property, 44(5)(c), (d)

Replacement property *(cont'd)*
- - depreciable property, 13(4.1)(c), (d)

**Replacement property**
- shares, *see* Replacement share

**Replacement share**
- defined, for small business investment capital gain rollover, 44.1(1)

**Reportable property**
- defined, 128.1(10)
- reporting of, required, 128.1(9)

**Reportable transaction**
- defined, re transactions with non-residents, 233.1(1)

**Reported reserve (of insurer)**
- defined, Reg. 1408(1)

**Reporting entity**
- foreign affiliate reporting
- - defined, 233.4(1)
- - obligation to file, 233.4(4)
- foreign property reporting
- - defined, 233.3(1)
- - obligation to file, 233.3(3)

**Reporting partnership**
- defined, re transactions with non-residents, 233.1(1)

**Reporting person**
- defined, Reg. 221(1)
- - re transactions with non-residents, 233.1(1)
- - re qualified investments and foreign property, 221(1)

**Reporting requirements**, *see* Information return

**Repossession of property**
- effect on creditor, 79.1
- - capital gains reserve, 79.1(3)
- - deemed cost of seized property, 79.1(6)
- - foreign resource property, 79.1(2.1)
- - in same taxation year as sale, 79.1(5)
- - inventory reserve, 79.1(4)
- effect on debtor, 79

**Representation allowances, not income**, 6(1)(b)(iii), (iv)

**Representation expenses**
- deductible, 20(1)(cc)
- deemed deducted as depreciation, 13(12)
- election to defer, 20(9), Reg. 4100

**Representative of deceased taxpayer**, *see* Legal representative of deceased taxpayer

**Required statement**
- defined, Reg. 809(4)

**Requirement**, *see* Demand; Garnishment for taxes unpaid

**Rescheduling of debt, expenses deductible**, 20(1)(e)(ii.2), 20(1)(e.1)(iii)

**Research and development**, *see* Scientific research and experimental development

**Research grant**
- receipt of, income, 56(1)(o)
- refund of, 56(1)(p)
- repayment of, deductible, 60(q)

**Reserve**
- allowed, 20(1)(l)–(o)
- amalgamation, on, 87(2)(g), (i), (j)
- amount not due until later year, 20(1)(n)
- - no deduction in certain circumstances, 20(8)
- business income, 1995 stub period, 34.2(4)
- capital gain, 40(1)(a)(iii), 40(2)(a)
- - donation to charity of non-qualifying security, 40(1.01)(c)
- - - disallowed in year of death, 72(1)(c)
- - on exchange of property, 44(1)(e)(iii)
- - where property repossessed by creditor, 79.1(3)
- contingent account, limitation on deductibility, 18(1)(e)
- credit unions, Reg. Part VI
- debt forgiveness, 61.2–61.4
- defined
- - for capital gains, 40(1)(a)(iii)
- - for large corporations tax, 181(1)
- - for registered labour-sponsored venture capital corporations, 204.8(1)
- disallowed, 18(1)(e), 20(7)
- donation of non-qualifying security to charity, 40(1.01)(c)
- - disallowed in year of death, 72(1)(c)
- doubtful debts, 12(1)(d), 20(1)(l)
- exchange of property, 44(1)(e)(iii)
- foreign exchange restriction, 91(2), (3)
- goods not delivered, 12(1)(e), 20(1)(m)
- guarantees etc., for, 12(1)(d.1)
- impaired debts, 20(1)(l)(ii)
- imputed to spouse on death of taxpayer, 72(2)
- insurance agent or broker, 32
- insurer, *see* Insurance corporation: policy reserves; Insurance corporation: reserve for unpaid claims
- inventory, 20(1)(n)
- - where property repossessed by creditor, 79.1(4)
- life insurer's, 138(3)
- limitation on deductibility, 18(1)(e)
- manufacturer's warranty, 20(1)(l), (m), (m.1), (n), (o)
- maximum cumulative, of credit union, 137(6)"maximum cumulative reserve"
- negative, of insurer, 20(1)(e.1), 20(22), Reg. 1400(2)
- not deductible, 18(1)(e), 20(7)
- quadrennial survey, 12(1)(h), 20(1)(o), Reg. 3600
- reported (insurer), Reg. 1408(1)
- sectoral, defined, 20(2.3)
- services not rendered, 12(1)(e), 20(1)(m)
- transportation tickets, 20(6)
- undelivered food or drink, 20(6)
- unearned commissions, 32
- unpaid claims, *see* Insurance corporation: unpaid claims reserve adjustment
- unpaid insurance policy claims
- - deduction, life insurance business, 138(3)(a)(ii)
- - deduction, non-life insurance business, 20(7)(c)
- - limitation, 18(1)(e.1)
- unrealized receivables, 20(1)(n)
- windup, on, 88(1)(e.1)
- year of death, not deductible for, 72(1)

**Reserve amount**
- re resource property, defined, 66(15)

**Reserve deficiency**
- defined, Reg. 1403(8)(d)

**Reservoir**
- substances injected into, deduction for, 20(1)(mm)

**Residence**
- cost of maintaining after move, deduction, 62(3)(g)
- loss in value of, reimbursement, *see* Housing loss

# Index

Residence *(cont'd)*
- principal, *see* Principal residence

**Resident beneficiary**
- defined, 94(1) [proposed]

**Resident compensation**
- defined, Reg. 8300(1)

**Resident contributor**
- defined, 94(1) [proposed]

**Resident of Canada**
- absent from Canada
- - child care, moving, and attendant expenses, 64.1
- becoming, *see* Becoming resident in Canada
- ceasing to be, *see* Ceasing to be resident in Canada
- corporate emigration, 219.1
- corporation, 250(4)
- corporation deemed not, 250(5)
- deemed, 250
- - for capital gains exemption, 110.6(5)
- - tuition credit, 118.5(2)
- defined, 250
- - authorized foreign bank, 212(13.3)
- - offshore trust, 94(1)(c)(i) [to be repealed], 94(3)(a) [proposed]
- entitled to U.S. treaty benefits, Canada–U.S. Tax Convention Art. XXIX A:2
- extended meaning of, 250(1), (2)
- former, *see* Former resident
- former, deemed employed in Canada, 115(2)(c)
- income earned in a province, Reg. 2601
- liability for tax, 2(1)
- ordinarily, meaning of, 250(3)
- part-year, *see* Part-year resident
- partnership, *Income Tax Conventions Interpretation Act* 6.2
- qualifying environmental trust, 250(7)
- regulations re, 214(13)
- returning, 128.1(6), (7)
- short-term, 128.1(4)(b)(iv) [draft], 128.1(4)(b)(v) [to be repealed]
- treaty purposes, Canada–U.S. Tax Convention Art. IV
- trust, 94(3)(a) [proposed]

**Residential property**
- defined, for minimum tax purposes, 127.52(3)
- partnership investing in
- - capital cost allowance limitation, 127.52(2)

**Residual balance (upon debt forgiveness)**
- defined, 80(14)
- included into income, 80(13)

**Residual portion (on disposition of specified debt obligation)**, *see also* Current amount (on disposition of specified debt obligation)
- application of, 142.4(4)
- defined, 142.4(8)
- - re disposition by financial institutions, Reg. 9200(1)

***Resman Holdings* case overruled**, 66.1(6)"Canadian exploration expense"(d)(i), 66.1(9)(a)

**Resource**
- defined, Reg. 1206(1)
- mineral, *see* Mineral resource

**Resource activity**
- defined, for resource allowance claims, Reg. 1206(1)

**Resource allowance**, 20(1)(v.1), Reg. 1210, *see also* Depletion allowances
- additional, Reg. 1210
- amalgamation, Reg. 1214
- deduction for, 20(1)(v.1), 20(15), 65, Reg. Part XII
- definitions, Reg. 1206
- earned depletion base, Reg. 1205
- not claimed at partnership level, 96(1)(d)
- partner, of, Reg. 1210(3)
- resource profits, defined, Reg. 1204

**Resource expenses**, *see also* Canadian development expense; Canadian exploration expense; Canadian oil and gas property expense
- amounts recovered included in income, 59
- Canadian development expenses, 66.2
- Canadian exploration and development expenses, 66(1)
- Canadian exploration expenses, 66.1
- Canadian oil and gas property expenses, 66.4
- change of control, rules, 66.7(10), (11)
- cumulative offset account, 66.5
- flow-through shares, 66(12.6)–(12.74), *see also* Flow-through shares
- flow-through to shareholder, 66(12.6), (12.62), (12.64)
- foreign exploration and development expenses, 66(4)
- joint exploration corporation, 66(10)–(10.4)
- limited partner, at-risk rules, 66.8
- minimum tax, 127.52(1)(e), (e.1)
- partnership, of, 96(1)(d)
- reduction of, on debt forgiveness, 80(8)
- successor rules, 66.7
- "warehousing" prohibited, 66(19)

**Resource income**
- manufacturing profits, Reg. 5203

**Resource loss**
- prescribed, Reg. 1210.1
- - income inclusion, 12(1)(z.5)

**Resource profits**
- defined, Reg. 1204(1.1), 5202

**Resource property**
- Canadian, *see* Canadian resource property
- carved-out income, *see* Carved-out income
- deceased taxpayer's, 70(5.2)
- disposition
- - consideration for, on amalgamation, 87(2)(p)
- - involuntary, 59.1
- - reserve for uncollected amount
- - - income in later year, 59(2)
- expropriation, 59.1
- foreign, *see also* Foreign resource property
- - proceeds of disposition, 59(1)
- partnership, of, 96(1)(d)
- rules for trusts, 104(5.2)
- timber, *see* Timber resource property
- trust, *see* Resource property trust

**Resource property trust**
- defined, Reg. 5000(7)
- information return where interest claimed to be qualified investment, Reg. 221

**Respiratory aids**
- medical expense, Reg. 5700(c), (c.1), (c.2)

**Respite care**, *see* Attendant

**Restricted farm loss**
- addition to adjusted cost base of land, 53(1)(i)

2791

Restricted farm loss *(cont'd)*
- amalgamation, on, 87(2.1)
- carryover of, 111(1)(c)
- deduction by partner where partnership disposes of land, 101
- defined, 31(1), (1.1), 111(9), 248(1)
- determination of, by Minister, 152(1.1), (1.2), (1.3)
- limitation on deductibility, 31(1), 111(3)
- partnership, from, 96(1)
- reassessment, 152(6)(c)
- reduction of, on debt forgiveness, 80(3)(c)

**Restricted financial institution**, *see also* Financial institution; Taxable RFI share
- defined, 248(1)
- dividends received on term preferred shares, 112(2.1)
- receiving dividends on taxable RFI shares
- • where shares acquired under securities lending arrangement, 260(9)
- software development by, no R&D credits, 248(1)"scientific research and experimental development"(b)(i)

**Restricted financial institution (RFI) shares, taxable**
- tax on dividends received by restricted financial institution, 187.3
- • information return, 187.5
- • partnership, 187.4

**Restructuring of debt, expenses deductible**, 20(1)(e)(ii.2), 20(1)(e.1)(iii)

**Retention of books and records**, 230(4), (4.1)

**Retirement benefits**
- defined, Reg. 8500(1)

**Retirement compensation arrangement**
- administration of, corporation exempt, 149(1)(o.1)(i)(B)
- amount paid in respect of
- • withholding of tax, 153(1)(p)–(r)
- amount payable under trust, not income, 12(1)(m)(ii)
- amounts received by employer under, includable in income, 12(1)(n.3)
- amounts transferred under, deduction from income, 60(j.1)
- benefits under
- • deduction from income re, 60(t)
- • includable in income, 56(1)(x), (z)
- • not includable in employee's income, 6(1)(a)(ii)
- • received by another
- • • joint and several liability for tax on, 160.3
- contribution to
- • tax on, 207.7(1)
- • withholding, Reg. 103(7)
- creation of trust, 207.6(1)
- deduction for contributions to
- • by employee, 8(1)(m.2), 60(t), (u)
- • by employer, 18(1)(o.2), 20(1)(r)
- defined, 248(1), Reg. 6802
- disposition of interest in
- • amount included in income, 56(1)(y)
- • deduction from income re, 60(u)
- disposition of property by trust, 56(11)
- distribution by trust, 107.2
- emigration of employee, no deemed disposition, 128.1(10)"excluded right or interest"(a)(ix)
- employee benefit plan becoming
- • deemed contribution, 207.6(4)

- employer contribution deductible, 20(1)(r)
- excluded from non-resident trust rules, 94(1)"exempt foreign trust"(e) [proposed]
- failure to withhold amounts in respect of, 227(8.2)
- foreign plan, *see* Foreign plan (pension plan)
- incorporated employee carrying on personal services business, 207.6(3)
- life insurance policies, 207.6(2)
- Member of Parliament, Reg. 6802.1
- money borrowed to make employee contributions
- • limitation on interest deductibility, 18(11)(e)
- non-resident compensation plan not retirement compensation arrangement
- • exception re "resident's arrangement", 207.6(5)
- payment of tax, 207.7(3)
- portion of benefits taxable, 56(1)(a)(i)
- prescribed plan or arrangement, 207.6(6), Reg. 6802
- purchase price of interest in, paid by non-resident, 212(1)(j)
- refund of tax, 207.7(2)
- refundable tax, 207.5–207.7
- • defined, 207.5(1)
- • election re, 207.5(2)
- resident's arrangement, 207.6(5)
- resident's contribution, defined, 207.6(5.1)
- severability of plan, 56(10)
- subject property
- • defined, 207.5(1)
- tax payable, 207.7(1)
- transfer to another RCA, 207.6(7)
- • no withholding, Reg. 103(7)(a)
- trust
- • corporation administering, exempt, 149(1)(o.1)(i)(B)
- • creation of, 207.6(1)
- • defined, 207.5(1)
- • exempt from tax, 149(1)(q.1)
- withholding tax, 153(1)(p)–(r), Reg. 103(7)

**Retirement counselling**, *see* Counselling services

**Retirement income, defined**, 146(1)

**Retirement income fund**, *see also* Registered retirement income fund
- registration of, 146.3(2)
- • appeal from refusal, 172(3)(g), 180
- • deemed refusal by Minister, 172(4)(f)
- • revocation of, 146.3(11)–(13)
- services relating to, non-deductible, 18(1)(u)

**Retirement payment**
- election to average, ITAR 40
- single, from deferred profit sharing plan, 147(10.1), (10.2), Reg. 1503

**Retirement savings plan**, *see also* Registered retirement savings plan
- appeal from refusal to register, 172(3)(b), 180
- deemed registered, when, 204.2(3)
- defined, 146(1)
- foreign, *see* Foreign retirement arrangement
- registration of, 146(2), (3)
- • deemed refusal by Minister, 172(4)(b)
- services relating to, non-deductible, 18(1)(u)

**Retiring allowance**
- defined, 248(1)
- emigration, no deemed disposition of right, 128.1(10)"excluded right or interest"(d)
- income, 56(1)(a)(ii)

## Index

**Retiring allowance** *(cont'd)*
- legal costs of collecting or establishing right to
  - - deduction for, 60(o.1)
  - - income when recovered, 56(1)(l.1)
- paid to non-resident, 212(1)(j.1)
  - - election to file return, 217
- repayment of, deductible, 60(n)(i.1)
- spread retroactively over prior years, 110.2, 120.31
- transferred to RRSP or RPP, 60(j.1)
- unpaid, 78(4)
- withholding tax, 153(1)(c), Reg. 103(4), (6)(e)

**Retroactive effect**, *see also* Grandfathering
- of amendments to pre-RSC 5th Supp. Act, ITAR 79
- of interest, to date of effect of amendment, 221.1
- of regulations, to date of public announcement, 221(2)

**Retroactive lump-sum payment**, *see* Lump-sum payment

**Retrospection**, ITAR 17(4)

**Return of income**
- defined, for OAS clawback, 180.2(1)

**Returning former resident**, 128.1(6), (7)

**Returns**, *see also* Information return
- alternative to withholding tax, 216(1), 217
- amended, 152(6)
- bankrupt individual, 128(2)(e), (f)
- carved-out income, tax on, 209(3)
- corporation, 150(1)(a)
- death of beneficiary, 104(23)(d)
- death of partner or proprietor, 150(4)
- deceased taxpayer, 150(1)(b), (e)
- deferred income plans
  - - over-contributions, 204.3
  - - property acquired by, 207
  - - property held by, 207.2
- demand for, by Minister, 150(2)
- designated persons, 150(1)(e)
- due date, 150(1)
- electronic filing of, 150.1
- employee's declaration, 227(2)
  - - when to be filed, Reg. 107
  - - where not filed, 227(3)
- estates, 150(1)(c)
- estimate of surtax, 180.1
- estimate of tax, 151
- extension of time for filing, 220(3)
- failure to file, penalty
  - - demand by Minister, 150(2)
  - - penalty, 162(1)
  - - - repeated, 162(2)
  - - - trustees etc., 162(3)
- false
  - - penalty for, 163(2)
  - - "understatement of income", 163(2.1)
- films, Reg. 225
- guardian, etc., 150(1)(d), (e)
- home insulation program, Reg. 224
- incomplete, penalty, 162(5)
- individual, 150(1)(d), (e)
  - - in bankruptcy, 128(2)(e)
- information, *see* Information return
- late filing, penalty, 162(1)
- Minister not bound by, 152(7)
- non-profit organization, 149(12)
- omission in, penalty, 163(2)
- Part I, 150
- Part I.1, 180.1(3)
- Part I.2, 180.2(5)(a)
- Part I.3, 181.6
- Part II, 183(1)
- Part II.1, 183.2
- Part IV, 187(1)
- Part IV.1, 187.5
- Part V, 188(1)(b), 189(6)
- Part VI, 190.2
- Part VI.1, 191.4
- Part VII, 193(1)
- Part VIII, 195(1)
- Part IX, 196(2)
- Part X, 202(1)
- Part X.1, 204.3
- Part X.2, 204.7
- Part X.3, 204.86
- Part X.4, 204.92
- Part XI, 207
- Part XI.1, 207.2
- Part XI.2, 207.4
- Part XI.3, 207.7(3)(a)
- Part XII, 208(2)
- Part XII.1, 209(3)
- Part XII.2, 210.2(5)
- Part XII.3, 211.2
- Part XII.4 (qualifying environmental trust), 211.6(1)
- Part XII.5, 211.8(2)
- Part XII.6, 211.91(2)(a)
- Part XIII.1, 218.2(5)
- Part XIV, 219(3)
- proof of, 244(17)–(19)
- public authorities (Part XI.2), 207.4
- refundable Part VII tax, 193(1)
- registered investment, 204.7
- repeated failures to report an amount of income, penalty for, 163(1)
- required of employee, 227(2)
  - - where not filed, 227(3)
- separate
  - - amounts receivable on death, 70(2)
  - - bankrupt individual, 128(2)(e), (f)
  - - death of beneficiary, 104(23)(d)
  - - death of partner or proprietor, 150(4)
  - - - 1995 stub-year reserve, 34.2(8)
  - - - off-calendar year adjustment, 34.1(9)
  - - deductions in computing taxable income, 114.2
  - - minimum tax carryover not applicable, 120.2(4)
  - - minimum tax not applicable, 127.55
- tax credits, 118.93
- tax-exempt persons (Part XII), 208(2)
- tax on foreign property of certain trusts and corporations, 207
- trustees etc., 150(3)
  - - failure to file, penalty for, 162(3)
  - - in bankruptcy, 128(2)(e)
- trusts, 150(1)(c)
- understatement of income, 163(2.1)

**Revenue Canada**, *see* Canada Customs and Revenue Agency

**Revenue guarantee**
- created tax shelter, Reg. 231(6)(b)(ii)

2793

## Index

Revenue guarantee *(cont'd)*
- prescribed, for film shelter, Reg. 7500

**Reverse attribution**, 74.5(11)

**Reverse takeover**, 256(7)(c)

**Reversionary trust**, 75(2), (3)

**Revised Statutes of Canada, 1985 (5th Supp.)**
- amendments to previous Act, ITAR 79
- continuity of previous versions of Act, ITAR 75, 77
- effective dates, ITAR 73

**Revocable living trust**
- excluded from qualifying disposition, 107.4(1)(e)

**Revocable trust**, 75(2), (3)

**Revocation of Canadian film/video production certificate**, 125.4(6)

**Revocation of elections**, 220(3.2)
- election to postpone 21-year rule by trust, 104(5.31)
- election to trigger capital gains exemption, 110.6(25)

**Revocation of film/video production services certificate**, 125.5(6)

**Revocation of registration**
- amateur athletic association, 168
- appeal from, 172(3), 180(1), 204.81(9)
- charity, 168, 188
- deferred profit sharing plan, 147(14)–(15)
- education savings plan, 146.1(12.1), (12.2), (13), (14)
- labour-sponsored venture capital corporation, 204.81(6)–(9)
- national arts service organization, 149.1(6.5)
- pension plan, 147.1(11)–(13)
- profit sharing plan, 147(14)–(15)
- retirement income fund, 146.3(11)–(13)
- retirement savings plan, 146(12)

**Revocation tax, charities**, 188

**Revoked corporation (registered labour venture capital)**
- defined (RLSVCC), 204.8(1), 211.7(1)

**Revoked plan**, *see* Deferred profit sharing plan

**Rider**
- deemed to be separate life insurance policy
  - for insurer's reserves, Reg. 1408(5), (6)
  - when added to pre-1990 policy, 12.2(10)

**Right of use or habitation (Quebec)**
- deemed to be trust, 248(3)

**Right to receive an amount**
- cost amount of, 248(1) "cost amount"(e)

**Right to receive production**
- deduction of matchable expenditure prorated, 18.1(4)
- defined, 18.1(1)
- disposition of, income inclusion, 12(1)(g.1), 18.1(6)

**Rights**
- exchange of, on amalgamation, 87(4.3)

**Rights or things**
- acquired by beneficiary
  - deemed cost, 69(1.1)
- exclusions, 70(3.1)
- transferred to beneficiaries, 70(3)
- value of, included in income at date of death, 70(2)

**Rights to drill or explore**, *see* Exploration and drilling rights

**Rights to income**
- transfer of, 56(4)

**River improvements**
- capital cost allowance, Reg. 1102(7)

**Road**, *see also* Specified temporary access road
- capital cost, 13(7.5)(b), Reg. 1102(14.3)

**Roadways**
- capital cost allowance, Reg. Sch. II:Cl. 1(g), Sch. II:Cl. 17
  - for mine, Reg. Sch. II:Cl. 10(l), Sch. II:Cl. 41

**Rocking bed, as medical expense**, 118.2(2)(i)

**Roller skating rink floor**, Reg. Sch. II:Cl. 10(i)

**"Rolling start" rule**, 13(27)(b), 13(28)(c), 13(29)

**Rollover**, *see also* Transfer of property
- accounts receivable, 22
- amalgamation, on, 87
- bare trust, to or from, 248(1) "disposition"(e)(i)
- convertible debentures, 51
- convertible property, 51
- corporation, to, 85(1)
  - by partnership, 85(2)
  - capital property, 85(1)(c.2)
  - depreciable property, 85(1)(c)
  - eligible capital property, 85(1)(d)
  - farming inventory, 85(1)(c.2)
  - from shareholder, 85(1)
    - eligible property, 85(1.1)
    - inventory, 85(1)(c.1)
    - wholly-owned corporation, 85(1)(e.2), 85(1.3)
- cumulative eligible capital
  - on transfer of business to spouse or corporation, 24(2)
- death, on
  - registered retirement savings plan, 60(l)(v)(B.1), 146(8.8)–(8.91)
  - to spouse or spouse trust, 70(6), (6.1)
- debt, in settlement of commercial debt obligation, 80(2)(h)
- demutualization of insurance corporation, 139.1(4)(a), (d)
- distress preferred share, converted to or from debt, 80.02(3)–(5)
- effect on shares held by former resident of Canada, 128.3
- exchange of property, 13(4), (4.1), 44
- exchange of shares, 51(1)
- exchange of shares on reorganization of capital, 86
- farm property, of, 70(9), (9.2), 73(3), (4)
- farming inventory, transfer to corporation, 85(1)(c.2)
- foreign share for foreign share exchange, 85.1(5), (6)
- foreign spin-off, 86.1
- insurance business, 138(11.5), (11.94)
- insurer policyholder's rights, on demutualization, 139.1(4)(a), (d)
- internal reorganization, 86
- life insurance policy
  - to child, 148(8)
  - to spouse
    - inter vivos, 148(8.1)
    - on death, 148(8.2)
- mark-to-market property prohibited, 85(1.1)(g)(iii)
- mutual fund trust or corporation, 132.2
- net income stabilization account/NISA Fund No. 2
  - to corporation, 85(1)(c.1), 85(1.1)(i)
  - to spouse or spouse trust, 70(6.1)
- non-resident insurance business, of, 138(11.5)

2794

Index

Rollover *(cont'd)*
- parent, to
  - - on death of invidudual, 70(9.6)
  - - on windup of corporation, 88(1)
- partnership, from
  - - to new partnership, 98(1)
  - - to proprietorship, 98(5)
- partnership, to, 97(2)
- qualifying disposition to a trust, 107.4
- registered pension plan to RPP annuity, 147.4
- registered retirement savings plan, on death, 60(l)(v)(B.1), 146(8.8)–(8.91)
- reorganizations, 84–88
- replacement property, 13(4), (4.1), 44
- reserves for year of death, 72(2)
- retiring allowance, to RRSP, 60(j.1)
- rights or things transferred to beneficiary, 69(1.1)
- share for share exchange, 85.1
- shareholder, from, to corporation, 85(1)
  - - eligible property, 85(1.1)
- small business investments, 44.1
- spouse or spouse trust, to
  - - death, on, 70(6), (6.1)
  - - inter vivos, 73(1)
  - - life insurance policy
    - - - inter vivos, 148(8.1)
    - - - on death, 148(8.2)
  - - registered retirement savings plan, 146(8.8)–(8.91)
- stock options, of, on corporate reorganization, 7(1.4), (1.5)
- taxable Canadian property, 85(1)(i)
- transaction, *see* Rollover transaction
- transfer of insurance business by non-resident insurer, 138(11.5)
- treaty protection, Canada–U.S. Tax Convention Art. XIII:8
- trust, from
  - - to beneficiary, 107(2)
  - - to new trust, 248(1)"disposition"(e), (f)
- trust, to, 107.4
- winding-up, on, 88(1)
- winding-up of partnership, on, 98(3)

**Rollover transaction**, *see also* Rollover
- acquisition of specified debt obligation by financial institution, 142.6(5)
- defined, 142.6(6)

**Rowboats**
- capital cost allowance, Reg. Sch. II:Cl. 7

**Royal Assent**
- amendments in force, *Interpretation Act* s. 6(3)

**Royal Canadian Mint, subject to tax**, 27(2), Reg. 7100

**Royalties**
- accrual to date of death, 70(1)(a)
- based on production or use, income, 12(1)(g)
- copyright, paid to non-resident, exempt, 212(1)(d)(vi)
- defined, Canada–U.S. Tax Convention Art. XII:4, 6
- income from
  - - whether specified investment business, 125(7)"specified investment business"
- motion picture films, paid to non-residents, 212(5)
- paid to non-resident, 212(1)(d)
  - - to U.S. resident, Canada–U.S. Tax Convention Art. XII
- paid to trust for non-resident, exemption, 212(9)(b)
- petroleum, natural gas, minerals
  - - included in income, 12(1)(o), Reg. 1211
  - - not deductible, 18(1)(m)
  - - reimbursement for, 80.2
- prepaid, non-deductible, 18(9)
- production, defined, Reg. 1206(1)
- tax re, paid to government by tax-exempt person, 208
  - - exception prescribed persons, Reg. 1216
- timber, 212(1)(e)
  - - alternative tax, 216

**Runway**, *see* Aircraft: runway

## S

**S corporation**, *see* United States: S corporation
**SBB**, *see* Small business bond
**SBDB**, *see* Small business development bond
**SBITC**, *see* Small business investment tax credit
**SDA**, *see* Salary deferral arrangement
**SDO**, *see* Specified debt obligation
**SIB**, *see* Specified investment business
**SIN**, *see* Social insurance number
**SPTC**, *see* Share-purchase tax credit
**SR&ED**, *see* Scientific research and experimental development
**SR&ED qualified expenditure pool**
- defined, 127(9)
- investment tax credit for, 127(5)(a)(i), (ii)(A), 127(9)"investment tax credit"(a.1), (f)
  - - additional, for Canadian-controlled private corporation, 127(10.1)(b)
- transfer to other taxpayer, 127(13)–(17)

**SRA**, *see* Specified retirement arrangement
**SRTC**, *see* Scientific research tax credit (expired)
**SSHRC**, *see* Social Sciences and Humanities Research Council
**Sabbatical arrangement**, Reg. 6801(a)
**Safe income**, 55(5)(b), (c)
- effect of, 55(2)

**Safe-income determination time**
- defined, 55(1)

**Salaries and Wages**, *see* Salary
**Salary**, *see also* Office or employment; Salary or wages
- accrued to date of death, 70(1)(a)
- defined, 248(1)
  - - for manufacturing and processing credit, Reg. 5202
- garnishment of, *see* Garnishment for taxes unpaid
- legal expenses of collecting or establishing right to, 8(1)(b)
- paid by employee, to assistant or substitute, 8(1)(i)(ii)
  - - certificate of employer, 8(10)
- reimbursement of, 8(1)(n)
- tax to be withheld from, 153(1)(a)
  - - failure to withhold, 227(8.5)
- unpaid, 78(4)

**Salary deferral arrangement**
- benefit from, income, 56(1)(w)
- deduction to employer, 20(1)(oo), (pp)
  - - limitation, 18(1)(o.1)
- defined, 248(1)
- emigration or immigration, no deemed disposition, 128.1(10)"excluded right or interest"(a)(vii), (b)
- forfeited amounts

2795

## Index

**Salary deferral arrangement** *(cont'd)*
- • deductible from income, 8(1)(o)
- • includable in employer's income, 12(1)(n.2)
- inclusion in income from employment, 6(1)(a)(v), 6(1)(i), 6(11), (12), (14)
- • exception for non-residents, 6(13)

**Salary deferral leave plan**, Reg. 6801(b), Reg. 8508

**Salary or wages**
- defined, 248(1)
- • re Canadian film/video tax credit, 125.4(1)
- • re film/video production services credit, 125.5(1)

**Sale**
- accounts receivable, 22
- bond, by conversion, 51.1, 77
- business, of, *see also* Ceasing to carry on business; Rollover
- • taxation year-end, 25(1)
- • to corporation for shares, 85(1)
- • to partnership, 97(2)
- • to spouse or controlled corporation, 24(2)
- defined, for informations returns on securities transactions, Reg. 230(1)
- depreciable property, *see* Capital cost allowance: recapture; Depreciable property
- mortgage included in proceeds of disposition, 20(5), (5.1)
- shares, not at arm's length, 84.1
- • by non-residents, 212.1

**Sales tax, federal**, *see* Federal sales tax credit

**Salesperson**
- automobile
- • reasonable standby charge for use of, 6(2.1)
- automobile or aircraft
- • capital cost allowance, 8(11)
- • • deemed, 13(11)
- • costs, deduction, 8(1)(j), 8(9)
- expenses, deduction, 8(1)(f)
- • certificate of employer, 8(10)
- • limitation, 8(4)

**Same-sex partner**, *see* Common-law partner

**Sand**, 248(1)"mineral"
- tar, *see* Tar sands, defined; Tar sands ore

**Saskatchewan**, *see also* Province
- northern, *see* Northern Canada
- Pension Plan, *see* Provincial pension plan, prescribed
- tax rates, *see* introductory pages

**Saskatchewan Pension Plan**
- deduction for contribution, 60(v)
- emigration of taxpayer, no deemed disposition, 128.1(10)"excluded right or interest"(g)(iii)
- prescribed as provincial pension plan, Reg. 7800(1)

**Satisfaction of obligation**
- deemed not to be disposition, 49.1

**Savings and credit unions**, 137

**Scale, metric, for retail use**
- capital cost allowance, Reg. Sch. II:Cl. 10(p)

**Scholarship**
- receipt of, income, 56(1)(n)
- • exemption, 56(3)
- refund of, 56(1)(p)
- repayment of, deductible, 60(q)

**Scholarship exemption**
- defined, 56(3)
- exempt from tax, 56(1)(n)(ii)

**School**
- attendance at, child care deduction, *see* Secondary school

**School board**
- allowance from, exempt, 81(3)

**School fees**, *see* Tuition fees

**School trustee**
- expense allowance exempt, 81(3)

**Schooling allowance, provincial tax reduction**, 120(2)

**Scientific research and experimental development**
- assistance, *see* Assistance/government assistance
- available-for-use rules, 37(1.2), 248(19)
- buildings
- • do not qualify as R&D expenditure, 37(8)(d)(i), Reg. 2900(11)
- contracted out to non-arm's length person, 127(9)"qualified expenditure"(f)
- • transfer of investment tax credit, 127(13)–(16)
- credit for, *see* investment tax credit (below)
- debt forgiveness, effect of, 37(1)(f.1)
- deduction for, 37
- • amount included in income, 12(1)(v)
- • defined, 37(8), (13), 248(1), Reg. 2900(1)
- • election to use proxy amount for overhead, 37(8)(a)(ii)(B), 37(9), Reg. 2900(4)
- expenditure pool, *see* SR&ED qualified expenditure pool
- expenditures, Reg. 2900(2)–(4)
- • change of control, 37(1)(h)
- • • computation, 37(6.1)
- • deduction for, 37(1), (2)
- • election for alternative calculation, 37(8)(a)(ii)(B), 37(9)
- • excluded, 37(8)(d)
- • on amalgamation, 87(2)(l)–(1.2)
- financial institution, by, 248(1)"scientific research and experimental development"
- investment tax credit
- • basic 20% credit, 127(9)"investment tax credit"(a.1)
- • extra 15% credit, 127(10.1)
- • refundable, 127.1
- linked work, 37(13), Reg. 2900(1)(d)
- overhead expenses, election for prescribed proxy amount
- • calculation of prescribed proxy amount, Reg. 2900(4)–(10)
- • exclusion of proxy amount from expenditure pool, 37(8)(a)(ii)(B)
- • filing of election, 37(9)
- • investment tax credit, 127(9)"qualified expenditure"
- partnership, of
- • no carryforward, 96(1)(e.1)
- • no losses for passive partners, 96(1)(g)
- pilot plants, qualify for investment tax credits, Reg. 2900(11)(c), (d)
- prescribed form required, 37(11), 127(9)"investment tax credit"(m)
- proxy amount, prescribed, Reg. 2900(4)
- • reduction in, 127(11.1)(f) [repealed], 127(18)
- qualified expenditure
- • defined, 127(9)
- • prescribed, Reg. 2901, Reg. 2902

2796

**Scientific research and experimental development** *(cont'd)*
- • subsidiary's, on winding-up, 88(1.4)
- related corporations, of, 37(1.1)
- rent for buildings, does not qualify as R&D expenditure, 37(8)(d)(ii)
- salaries, directly engaged in SR&ED, Reg. 2900(4)
- sole-purpose R&D performer, Reg. 2902(a) (closing words)
- specified employee, paid to, 37(9.1)–(9.5)
- third party payment, 37(1)(a)(i.1), (ii), (iii)
- • exclusion from prepaid expense rules, 18(9)(d)(i)

**Scientific research and experimental development financing contract**
- defined, 194(6), 248(1)

**Scientific research corporation (non-profit)**
- annual information return, 149(7)
- exemption for, 149(1)(j), 149(2)
- • rules as to control, 149(8)
- • rules as to income, 149(9)

**Scientific research tax credit (expired)**, 127.3
- information returns, Reg. 226
- refundable tax re, 194, 195
- unused
- • capital loss, 39(8)
- • defined, 127.3(2) "unused scientific research and experimental development tax credit"
- • overpayment of tax as consequence of, 164(5), (5.1)
- when deemed paid, 161(10)

*Scott* **case (1975) overruled**, 64.1

**Scow, capital cost allowance**, Reg. Sch. II:Cl. 7

**Screenwriter (for Canadian film/video tax credit)**
- principal, defined, Reg. 1106(5)(a)

**Sculptor**, *see* Artist

**Sculpture**, *see also* Cultural property; Listed personal property
- Canadian, CCA claims allowed, Reg. 1102(1)(e)

**Search and rescue volunteer**
- deduction from employment income, 8(1)(a) [to be repealed]
- exemption from employment income, 81(4)

**Search warrant**
- compliance required, 231.5(2)
- issue of, 231.3(1)–(4)

**Second affiliate**, *see* Foreign affiliate: second affiliate

**Second-term shared-use-equipment, for R&D investment tax credit**
- defined, 127(9)

**Secondary recovery method, defined**, Reg. 1206(1)

**Secondary school**
- attendance at, child care deduction, 63(2)(b)(iii), 63(2.2)(a)

**Secrecy provision**, 241

**Secretarial services**
- no application of penalty for misrepresentation, 163.2(9)

**Secretary**, *see* Officer: corporation, of

**Sectoral reserve**
- defined, 20(2.3)

**Secured creditor**
- defined, 224(1.3)
- garnishment of property of, 224(1.2)

- interference with taxpayer's remittances, 227(5.2)–(5.4) (draft)
- withholding tax, liability for, 227(5), (5.1)(h)

**Securities**
- amalgamation, acquired in, 87(2)(e.2)
- Canadian, *see* Canadian securities
- dealer, trader or agent, *see also* Broker; Registered securities dealer
- • fees of, deduction for, 20(1)(e), (bb)
- • ineligible for Canadian securities election, 39(5)(a)
- • return re securities lending arrangements and non-residents, 212(18)
- • tax re interest paid under securities lending arrangements to non-residents, 212(19)
- fair market value, ITAR 26(11)
- lending arrangements, *see* Securities lending arrangements
- prescribed, Reg. 6200
- publicly-traded, Reg. 4400
- • V-day values, Reg. Sch. VII
- received for income debt, 76
- small business, Reg. 5100(2)
- transactions
- • information returns, Reg. 230
- used or held in insurance or moneylending business
- • "eligible property" for transfer to corporation by shareholder, 85(1.1)(g)

**Securities lending arrangements**, 260, *see also* Dividend rental arrangement
- amount received deemed to be a dividend, 260(4)–(7)
- deemed dividend, 260(5)
- • dividend refund, 260(7)
- • no deduction for, 260(6)
- deemed not disposition, 260(2)
- defined, 260(1)
- disposition of right under, 260(3), (4)
- lender non-resident, effect, 260(8)
- non-resident withholding tax
- • amounts deemed to be interest, 260(8)
- • exemption, 212(1)(b)(xii)
- • special tax on securities dealers, 212(19)
- • • return required, 212(18)
- qualified security, defined, 260(1)
- restricted financial institution receiving dividend on shares acquired under, 260(9)

**Security**, *see also* Securities
- defined
- • for scientific research tax credit, Reg. 226(1)
- • for security transactions, Reg. 230(1)
- • for stock option rules, 7(7)
- • generally, *Interpretation Act* 35(1)
- granting of, not a disposition, 248(1) "disposition"(j), (k)
- non-qualifying, *see* Non-qualifying security
- qualified, *see* Qualified security

**Security for tax**, 220(4)–(4.4)
- defined, *Interpretation Act* 35(1)
- departure tax, 159(4) [to be repealed], 220(4.5)–(4.71)
- discharge, Reg. Part XXII
- taxpayer becoming non-resident, 159(4) [to be repealed], 220(4.5)–(4.71)

**Security interest**
- defined, for garnishment rules, 224(1.3)

**Seeing Eye dog**, *see* Guide dog expenses

**Segregated fund (of life insurer)**
- defined, 138.1(1), 211(1), Reg. 1408(1), 1900(1)
- related, *see* Related segregated fund trust
- rules re, 138.1
- trusts, 138.1
- • election, Reg. 6100
- • interest in, adjusted cost base, 53(1)(l), 53(2)(q)

**Segregated fund policies**
- defined, 138.1(1)(a)

**Seismic testing**
- off-the-shelf data, no renunciation of cost of, 66(12.66)(b.1)

**Seizure**
- chattels, of, 225
- documents, of, 231.3(5)–(8)
- • compliance required, 231.5(2), 232(15)
- • copies, 231.5(1)
- • where privilege claimed, 232(3), (4)–(7)
- property, for non-payment of debt
- • effect on creditor, 79.1
- • • deemed cost of property, 79.1(6)
- • • foreign resource property, 79.1(2.1)
- • • no deduction for principal portion of bad debt, 79.1(8)
- • effect on debtor, 79

**Self-contained domestic establishment, defined,** 248(1)

**Self-employed person**
- Canada Pension Plan contributions, credit, 118.7B(c)
- home office expenses, conditions for deductibility, 18(12)

**Selling cost,** *see* Adjusted selling cost (re investment tax credits)

**Senior citizen,** *see* Age

**Separate classes for capital cost allowance,** Reg. 1101
- automobile costing over $24,000, Reg. 1101(1af)
- building or MURB costing over $50,000, Reg. 1101(1ac), (1ad), (5b)
- Canadian film or video production, Reg. 1101(5k.1)
- certified productions, Reg. 1101(5k)
- computer equipment and software, Reg. 1101(5p), 1103(2g)
- computer software tax shelter property, Reg. 1101(5r)
- deemed depreciable property, 13(5.2)(c), 13(21.2)(e)(ii), Reg. 1101(5g)
- different businesses, properties for, Reg. 1101(1)
- different mines, properties for, Reg. 1101(4a)–(4d)
- excavating or moving equipment, Reg. 1101(5l)
- exempt properties, Reg. 1101(5o)
- fax machine, Reg. 1101(5p), 1103(2g)
- industrial mineral mines, Reg. 1101(4)
- leasehold interest in real property, Reg. 1101(5h)
- leasing properties, Reg. 1101(5c), (5n)
- life insurance and other insurance business, Reg. 1101(1a)
- outdoor advertising sign, Reg. 1101(5l)
- partnership and non-partnership property, Reg. 1101(1ab)
- photocopier, Reg. 1101(5p), 1103(2g)
- pipeline costing over $10,000,000, Reg. 1101(5i), (5j)
- railway assets, Reg. 1101(5d), (5e)
- rental and non-rental property, Reg. 1101(1ae)
- scientific research expenditures, 37(6)
- software, Reg. 1101(5p), 1103(2g)
- telecommunication spacecraft, Reg. 1101(5a)
- telephone equipment, Reg. 1101(5p), 1103(2g)
- timber limits and cutting rights, Reg. 1101(3)
- vessels, Reg. 1101(2), (2a), (2b)
- • conversion cost, 13(14), (17)

**Separate return,** *see* Returns: separate

**Separate school board**
- allowance from, exempt, 81(3)

**Separation agreement**
- defined, 248(1)
- payments under
- • deductible by payor, 60(b), (c)
- • taxable to recipient, 56(1)(b), (c)

**Series**
- of shares, 248(6)
- of transactions, 248(10)

**Servant**
- defined, 248(1) "employment"

**Service**
- proof of, 244(5), (6)

**Service cost,** *see* Adjusted service cost (re investment tax credits)

**Service pension**
- exemption, 81(1)(d)
- other country, from, 81(1)(e)

**Services**
- defined, for FAPI, 95(3)
- not rendered, reserve for, 20(1)(m), 20(24), (25)
- provision of, along with property disposed of
- • allocation rule, 68
- rendered, amounts receivable for, 12(1)(b), 12(2)
- to be rendered
- • amount received for, income, 12(1)(a)(i), 12(2)
- • • repayment of, deductible, 20(1)(m.2)
- • consideration for, not "outlay" or "expense", 66(15) "outlay" or "expense"

**Servitude**
- ecologically sensitive land, value when donated, 110.1(5), 118.1(12)
- • valuation applies for capital gains purposes, 43(2)

**Set-off**
- debt owing by Crown, against taxes owing, 224.1
- • communication of information to facilitate, 241(4)(d)(xiii)
- interest, on instalment payments, 161(2.2)
- refund of tax, against other debt owing to Crown or province, 164(2)
- • Part X refunds, 203
- transfer pricing adjustments, *see* Transfer pricing capital setoff adjustment; Transfer pricing income setoff adjustment

**"Settled" (debt)**
- deemed, 80.01
- defined, 80(2)(a)
- • for distress preferred shares, 80.02(2)(c), 80.02(7)(a)

**Settlement, structured,** *see* Structured settlement

**Settlement of debt,** *see also* Debt forgiveness
- deemed, 80.01
- • on amalgamation, 80.01(3)
- • on debt becoming statute-barred, 80.01(9)
- • on debt parking, 80.01(6)–(8)
- • on share ceasing to be distress preferred share, 80.02(7)

## Index

**Settlement of debt** *(cont'd)*
- • on winding-up, 80.01(4)
- distress preferred share, on winding-up, 80.01(5)
- effect of, 80(3)–(13)
- foreign affiliate's gain or loss on, 95(2)(i)
- simultaneous, 80(2)(i)
- subsequent payment following deemed settlement, 80.01(10)

**Settlement of litigation**
- property transfer, 49.1
- wrongful dismissal, 248(1)"retiring allowance"

**Settlor (of trust)**, *see also* Designated contributor (in respect of a trust)
- defined, 108(1)
- • for loan by corporation to non-resident, 17(15)

**Severance pay**, *see* Retiring allowance

**"Shall"**
- meaning of, *Interpretation Act* s. 11

**Share**
- acquired before 1976
- • cost base, deductions from, 53(2)(e)
- acquisition of
- • by corporation, deemed dividend, 84(3), (6)
- • deemed, 256(8)
- "actual cost", ITAR 26(15)–(17)
- agreement to issue, to employees, 7(1)
- average annual rate of return, capital gains deduction, 110.6(9)
- bankrupt corporation, of
- • deemed disposition of, 50(1)
- block of, defined, Reg. 4803(1)
- bought back by corporation
- • amount paid for unpaid dividends deemed dividend substitute, 183.1(4)
- calculation of consideration for
- • scientific research tax credit, 127.3(10)
- • share-purchase tax credit, 127.2(11)
- cancellation, deemed dividend, 84(3), (6)
- capital property, deemed, 39(4)
- capital stock of family farm corporation, of, 110.6(1)
- class of, series of, 248(6)
- common, defined, 248(1)
- • for mutual fund rollover rules, 132.2(2)
- controlled corporation, of
- • disposition of, 40(2)(h)
- convertible, exchanged for other shares, 51; ITAR 26(24)
- cost base of
- • additions to, 53(1)(b)–(d), (f.1)
- • deductions from, 53(2)(a)
- • deemed dividend added to, 53(1)(b)
- deductions from paid-up capital, 66.3(2)
- deemed benefit from
- • cost base, addition to, 53(1)(j)
- deemed disposition of, to corporation, 84(9)
- deemed interest on, 258(5)
- deemed receipt of, on merger, 87(1.1)
- defined, 248(1)
- • for insurance demutualization, 139.1(1)
- disposition of
- • capital gain or loss, 40(1)
- • deemed, on death, 70(5)
- • for insurance demutualization, 139.1(1)

- • order of, for employee stock option benefit, 7(1.3)
- • subsequent to debt forgiveness, deemed capital gain, 80.03(2), (4)
- • where dividend previously paid, stop-loss rules, 112(3)
- distribution of, by corporation, 84(5)
- "equity" defined, 204
- exchanged for shares, 85.1; ITAR 26(26)
- • amalgamation, on, 87(4.1), (4.2)
- • computation of paid-up capital, 85.1(2.1)
- • reorganization of capital, 86(1); ITAR 26(27)
- • rules, 7(1.5), 112(7)
- "excluded" defined, 204
- expense of issuing, 20(1)(e)
- exploration and development, 66.3(1)
- fair market value, ITAR 26(11.1), (11.2)
- first registered holder of
- • deduction from cost, 127.3(6)
- • deemed cost of acquisition, 127.2(8)
- • election re scientific research tax credit, 127.3(9)
- • election re share-purchase tax credit, 127.2(10)
- flow-through, 66(12.6)–(12.75), Reg. 6202.1
- foreign affiliate, of, *see also* Foreign affiliate
- grandfathered
- • defined, 248(1)
- guaranteed, *see* Guaranteed share
- held by trustee for employee, 7(2)
- included in single payment under DPSP, 147(10.1), (10.2)
- • deduction re amount, 110(1)(d.3)
- • disposal of, 147(10.4), (10.5)
- interest paid on money borrowed to purchase, 20(1)(c), 20(1)(qq)
- issued in exchange for property, rollover, 85(1)
- issued in settlement of debt, 80(2)(g), (g.1)
- issued to avoid tax, by foreign affiliates, 95(6)(b)
- loan to shareholder/employee to purchase, 15(2)(a)(iii), 15(2.4)(c)
- loss on, 112(3), (3.1), (3.2), (4.3)
- mark-to-market rules, *see* Mark-to-market property
- mutual fund corporation, of, received on amalgamation, ITAR 65(5)
- non-arm's length sale of, 84.1
- • by non-resident, 212.1
- non-capital property of partnership
- • loss on, 112(4.2)
- "non-participating, defined, 204"non-participating share"
- non-resident corporation, of
- • cost base, deductions from, 53(2)(b)
- not capital property
- • fair market value of, 112(4.1)
- • loss on, 112(4)
- obligation to acquire, effect of, 192(7)
- paid-up capital in respect of class of, 84.2
- paid-up capital value, defined, 204
- predecessor corporation, on amalgamation, 87(4)
- preferred, *see also* Preferred share; Term preferred share
- • deemed interest on, 258(3)
- • defined, 248(1)
- prescribed, Reg. 6201–6207
- • flow-through, Reg. 6202.1
- publicly-traded, Reg. 4400
- • V-day value, Reg. Sch. VII

**Share** *(cont'd)*
- purchase of
  - through series of transactions/events
    - tax on distribution of corporate surplus, 183.1(4)
  - trustee, by, for employees of corporation, 7(6)
- qualified small business corporation
  - capital gains deduction, 110.6(2.1)
  - defined, 110.6(1)
  - related person, 110.6(14)
  - rules re, 110.6(14)
- received on amalgamation, ITAR 26(21)
- redemption, deemed dividend, 84(3), (6)
- registered charities, held by, 189(3)–(5)
- right to acquire
  - shares deemed owned, where, 95(6)(a)
- sale of
  - non-arm's length, 84.1
- short-term preferred, defined, 248(1)
- specified shareholder's
  - adjusted cost base, 53(1)(d.3)
- subsidiary, of
  - cost of, 52(7)
- tax-deferred preferred, amalgamation where, 83(7)
- taxable preferred, *see* Taxable preferred share
- term preferred, *see* Term preferred share
- where deemed capital property, 54.2

**Share for share exchange**, 85.1

**"Share of the capital stock of a family farm corporation"**
- defined, 70(10)

**Share-funding arrangement (registered pension plan)**, Reg. 8501(6.1)

**Share options**
- employee, 7
  - where person ceases to be employee, 7(4)

**Share-purchase tax credit**, 127.2 [expired]
- deemed cost of acquisition of share, 127.2(8)
- defined, 127.2(6)
- election re
  - tax on excess, 193(7.1)
- information returns, Reg. 227
- unused
  - capital loss, 39(7)
  - defined, 127.2(6)
  - overpayment of tax as consequence of, 164(5), (5.1)

**Share transfer fees, deduction**, 20(1)(g)

**Shared-use-equipment**
- defined, 127(9)

**Shareholder**
- appropriation of property to, 15(1), 69(4), (5), 84(2)
- automobile available to, 15(5), (7)
- benefit from corporation, 15(1), (7), (9)
  - GST portion included, 15(1.3)
  - loan forgiven, 15(1.2)
- deemed disposition of share to corporation, 84(9)
- defined, 248(1)
- exchange of shares in course of reorganization, 86(1)
- guarantee by
  - interest on money borrowed for payment under, 20(3.1)
- issue of stock rights to, 15(1)(c)
- loan by, to corporation
  - interest deductible, 20(3.1)
- loan to, by corporation, *see* Loan: shareholder, to, by corporation
- non-resident
  - interest paid to, not deductible, 18(4)–(6)
    - exception, 18(8)
- persons connected with, 15(2.1), 80.4(8)
- prospective
  - benefit conferred on, by corporation, 15(1)
- share for share exchange, 85.1
- specified
  - adjusted cost base of share, 53(1)(d.3)
  - defined, 248(1)
- transfer of property by, to corporation, 85(1), (1.1)

**Shareholder corporation**
- "agreed portion" in respect of, 66(15)
- defined, 66(15), Reg. 4608(1)
- election by joint exploration corporation to renounce expenses to, 66(10)–(10.3)
- payment made to joint exploration corporation
  - reduction in adjusted cost base of property received as consideration, 53(2)(f)

**Shareholder's equity**
- determination of, for LSVCC investment shortfall, 204.82(2.2)(b), (c)

**Sheep**
- basic herd maintained since 1971, deduction, 29
- breeding, 80.3(1)"breeding animals"

**Sheitel**, *see* Wig, medical expense

**Shelf, continental**, *see* Continental shelf

**Shell Canada case overruled**, 20.3

**Shellfish**, *see* Ammonite gemstone

**Shelter**, *see* Tax shelter

**Ship**, *see also* Vessel
- non-resident's income from, exempt, 81(1)(c)
- operators, taxable income earned in a province, Reg. 410
- treaty provisions, Canada–U.S. Tax Convention Art. VIII:1–3, Art. XV:3, XXIII(3)
- used in international traffic, *see* International traffic

**Shipping**, *see* International shipping

**Shoes/boots**
- orthopaedic etc., medical expense, Reg. 5700(e)

**Shopping**, *see* Treaty shopping

**Short-form amalgamation**, 87(1.1), (2.11)

**Short-remitting of UI premiums**, 126.1(12)

**Short sale**
- dividend paid on borrowed securities not deductible, 260

**Short taxation year**
- prorating of base level deduction, 18(2.5)(b)
- prorating of capital cost allowance, Reg. 1100(3)
- prorating of cumulative eligible capital claim, 20(1)(b)
- prorating of deduction for injection substances, 20(1)(mm)(iii)
- prorating of farmer's animal valuation rules, 28(1.3)
- prorating of financial institutions capital tax, 190.1(2)
- prorating of ITC expenditure limit, 127(10.6)(b), (c)
- prorating of large corporations tax, 181.1(2)
- prorating of Part VI.1 tax dividend allowance, 191.1(6)(a)
- prorating of resource deductions, 66(13.1)

# Index

**Short taxation year** *(cont'd)*
- prorating of small business deduction, 125(5)(b)
- prorating of tax on investment income of life insurer, 211.1(4)
- - instalments, 211.3(2)A(b)

**Short-term preferred share**
- defined, 248(1)

**Shower**
- mechanical aid for getting into and out of, medical expense, Reg. 5700(g)

**Shutdown of business**, *see* Ceasing to carry on business; Winding-up

**Sickness and accident insurance**
- benefits taxable, 6(1)(f); ITAR 19
- employer's contribution not a taxable benefit, 6(1)(a)(i)

**Sidewalks, capital cost allowance**, Reg. Sch. II:Cl. 1(g)
- for mines, Reg. Sch. II:Cl. 10(l)

**Sight impairment**
- devices to assist person with, business expense, 20(1)(rr)

**Sign language**
- interpretation services, medical expense, 118.2(2)(l.4)
- training, medical expense, 118.2(2)(l.3)

**Signalling device**
- visual or vibratory, for person with hearing impairment, Reg. 5700(q.1)

**Significant interest**
- debt settlement rules
- - defined, 80.01(2)(b)
- financial institutions
- - defined, 142.2(2), (3)
- - financial institution holding, excluded from mark-to-market rules, 142.2(1)"mark-to-market property"(d)
- foreign investment entity
- - defined, 94.1(11)
- foreign property rules
- - defined, 206(1)

**Significant part of exempt capital gain attributable to unpaid dividends**, 110.6(8)

**Significant reduction in capital gain resulting from dividend**, 55(2)

**Signing bonus**
- non-resident, 115(2)(c.1), 115(2)(e)(v), 153(1)(o)
- resident, 6(3)
- withholding of tax at source, Reg. 100(1)"remuneration"(m)

**Signs, outdoor advertising**, *see* Outdoor advertising structures

*Silden* **case confirmed**, 15(2.4)(e)

**Silica, included in definition of "mineral"**, 248(1)

**Simultaneous**
- dividends, designation of order, 89(3), 133(7.2)
- settlement of debt obligations, designation of order, 80(2)(i)

**Singapore**, *see also* Foreign government
- stock exchange recognized, Reg. 3201(k)

**Singer**
- deduction from employment income, 8(1)(q)

**Single amount**
- defined, for RPPs, 147.1(1)

**Single purpose corporation**
- whether use of corporate property taxable to shareholder, 15(1)

**Single status, credit for**, 118(1)B(c)

**Sister**
- deemed not related on butterfly transaction, 55(5)(e)
- dependent, 118(6)(b)
- includes sister-in-law or in common-law, 252(2)(c)

**Site, investigation of**, 20(1)(dd)

**Skytrain trusts**
- anti-avoidance rule, 106, 108(1)"income interest"

**Sleighs**
- capital cost allowance, Reg. Sch. II:Cl. 10(d)

**Small business, investment in, by deferred income plans**, Reg. 4900(6), Part LI

**Small business bond**, 15.2
- defined, 15.2(3), 248(1)
- eligible issuer, 15.2(3)
- interest on
- - paid, no deduction for, 15.2(2)(a)
- - received, deemed to be a dividend, 15.2(1)
- maximum amount $500,000, 15.2(3)"qualifying debt obligation"(a), 15.2(7)
- minimum amount $10,000, 15.2(3)"qualifying debt obligation"(a)
- money borrowed to acquire, interest deductible, 15.2(4)
- partnership, issued by, 15.2(6), (7)
- penalty for false declaration, 15.2(5)
- qualifying debt obligation, 15.2(3)

**Small business corporation**
- attribution rules inapplicable, 74.4(2)(c)
- business investment loss on share or debt of, 39(1)(c)
- defined, 248(1)
- disposition to child, 10-year reserve, 40(1.1)(c)
- eligible for small business development bond, 15.1(3)"eligible small business corporation"(a)
- qualified, share of
- - capital gains deduction, 110.6(2.1)
- - defined, 110.6(1)

**Small business deduction**, 125
- associated corporations, 125(3)–(5)
- "business limit", 125(2)
- - special rules for, 125(5)
- corporation deemed member of partnership, 125(6.1)
- credit union, 137(3), (4)
- definitions, 125(7)
- large corporation, restricted, 125(5.1)
- multiple access, provisions preventing, 125(6)–(6.3)
- partnership, *see* Partnership
- rules for business limit, 125(5)
- two taxation years ending in year, 125(5)

**Small business development bond**, 15.1
- communal organization, issuance by, 143(1)(k)
- defined, 15.1(3)"small business development bond"(c), 248(1)
- eligible small business corporation, 15.1(3)
- interest on
- - paid, no deduction for, 15.1(2)(a)
- - received, deemed to be a dividend, 15.1(1)
- maximum amount $500,000, 15.1(3)"qualifying debt obligation"(a), 15.1(7)

2801

# Index

**Small business development bond** *(cont'd)*
- minimum amount $10,000, 15.1(3)"qualifying debt obligation"(a)
- money borrowed to acquire, interest deductible, 15.1(4)
- penalty for false declaration, 15.1(5)
- qualifying debt obligation, 15.1(3)

**Small Business Financing program**, 15.1, 15.2

**Small business investment amount, defined**, 206(1)

**Small business investment capital gain rollover**, 44.1

**Small business investment corporation**
- defined, Reg. 5101(1)
- exemption from tax, 149(1)(o.3)
- included in "small business property", 206(1)"small business property"(b)
- qualifies as RRSP or RRIF investment, Reg. 4900(6)(a)

**Small business investment limited partnership**
- defined, Reg. 4901(2), 5102
- eligible for RRSP or RRIF investment, Reg. 4900(6)(b)

**Small business investment tax credit**
- calculation of, 127(9)"qualified small-business property" [repealed], 127(9)"specified percentage"(i)
- included in investment tax credit, 127(9)"investment tax credit"(a)(i)
- not refundable, 127.1(2)"refundable investment tax credit"(d)(i)
- who can earn, 127(9)"eligible taxpayer"

**Small business investment trust**
- defined, Reg. 4901(2), 5103
- eligible for RRSP or RRIF investment, Reg. 4900(6)(c)
- information return where interest claimed to be qualified investment, Reg. 221

**Small business property**, Reg. Part LI
- defined, 206(1)

**Small business security**
- defined, Reg. 4901(2), 5100(2)
- included in "small business property", 206(1)"small business property"(a)

**Small employer**
- quarterly remittance of source deductions, Reg. 108(1.12)

**Small manufacturers' rule**, Reg. 5201

**Social assistance payment**
- deduction from taxable income, 110(1)(f)(iii)
- foster child, for, exempt, 81(1)(h)
- inclusion in income, 56(1)(r), (u)
- information return, Reg. 233
- supplementing employment income, 56(1)(r)
- • eligible for child care deduction, 63(3)"earned income"(b)

**Social benefits repayment**, 180.2

**Social club**
- dues not deductible, 18(1)(l)
- exemption for, 149(1)(l), 149(2)
- • deemed a trust, 149(5)

**Social insurance number**, *see also* Business number
- application for, 221(1)(d.1), Reg. 3800
- failure to provide, penalty, 162(5)(b), 162(6)
- information return requiring
- • reasonable effort to obtain, 237(2)(a)

- • registration of RRIF under, 146.3(1)"registered retirement income fund"
- requirement to provide, 221(1)(d.1), 237(1), (1.1)
- • attendant care receipts, 64(a)A(i), 118.2(2)(b.1)(iv), 118.2(2)(c)(iii)
- • child care receipts, 63(1)
- • farm support payment slips, for, Reg. 236
- • partnership information return, Reg. 229(1)(b)
- • penalty for failure to provide, 162(6)
- • tax shelter investor, 237.1(7)(a)
- use or communication of prohibited, 237(2)(b)
- • offence of, fine or imprisonment, 239(2.3)

**Social Sciences and Humanities Research Council**
- payments to, as R&D expenditures, 37(1)(a)(ii)(E), 37(7)"approved"
- research grants, taxable, 56(1)(o)

**Social security**
- benefits, Canada–U.S. Tax Convention Art. XVIII:5
- legislation
- • pension plan under, excluded from RCA, Reg. 6802(g)
- • social security taxes
- • • paid to U.S., Canada–U.S. Tax Convention Art. XXIV:2(a)(ii)

**Société internationale de télécommunications aéronautiques**
- employment income of non-Canadians, deduction for, 110(1)(f)(iv)

**Societies**
- exemption for, 149(1)(l), 149(2)
- • deemed a trust, 149(5)

**Soft costs**
- construction, 18(3.1)–(3.7), 20(29)

**Software**, *see also* Computer software tax shelter property
- capital cost allowance
- • applications, Reg. Sch. II:Cl. 12(o)
- • "computer software" defined, Reg. 1104(2)
- • limitation where tax shelter, Reg. 1100(20.1)
- • systems, Reg. Sch. II:Cl. 10(f), Sch. II:Cl. 29, Sch. II:Cl. 40
- • • defined, Reg. 1104(2)
- • • separate class, Reg. 1101(5p)
- development by financial institution, no R&D credits, 248(1)"scientific research and experimental development"
- non-resident withholding tax, 212(1)(d)
- royalties paid to U.S. resident, Canada–U.S. Tax Convention Art. XII:3(b)
- tax shelters
- • capital cost allowance limitation, Reg. 1100(20.1)
- • registration requirements, 237.1
- year 2000 compatible, *see* Year 2000 computer hardware and software

**Sojourning in Canada**
- 183 days, deemed resident, 250(1)(a)

**Solar heating equipment**
- capital cost allowance, Reg. Sch. II:Cl. 34

**Sole proprietorship**, *see* Proprietorship

**Sole-purpose R&D performer**
- ITCs allowed for administrative costs, Reg. 2902(a) [closing words, repealed]

**Solicitor-client privilege**
- defence, 232(2)

# Index

Solicitor-client privilege *(cont'd)*
- definitions, 232(1)
- meaning, 232(1)
- rules governing, 232
- waiver of, 232(14)

**Solution gas**
- CCA application, Reg. Sch. II:Cl. 43.1(c)(i)(B)
- defined, Reg. 1104(13)

*Solway* case overruled, 244(13.1) [repealed]

**Son-in-law, as child of the taxpayer**, 252(1)(c)

**Source(s)**
- business or property, income or loss, 9–37
- capital gains and losses, 38–55
- deductions applicable to, 4(2), (3)
- employment income, 5–8
- income from, 4(1)
- other sources of income, 56–59.1
- withholding of tax at, 153(1)
- - non-residents, 215

**Source deductions**, *see* Withholding tax

**Source withholding**, *see* Withholding tax

**South Africa**, *see also* Foreign government
- stock exchange recognized, Reg. 3201(v)
- universities, gifts to, Reg. Sch. VIII s. 19

**Spacecraft, telecommunication**, *see* Telecommunication spacecraft

**Spain**, *see also* Foreign government
- stock exchange recognized, Reg. 3201(l)
- universities, gifts to, Reg. Sch. VIII s. 13

**Speaking aid, as medical expense**, 118.2(2)(i)

**Special-purpose building, defined**, Reg. 2903

**Special refundable tax**
- under Part IID of former Act, ITAR 67

**Special work site, employment at**, 6(6)

**Specific provisions**
- defined, Reg. 8006

**Specified active business**
- defined
- - for foreign property rules, 206(1)
- - for labour-sponsored venture capital corporations, 204.8(1)

**Specified active member**
- defined, Reg. 8306(4)(b)

**Specified amount**
- defined
- - re disposition of resource properties, 66.7(12.1)
- - re flow-through share renunciations, 66(20)
- - re seizure of property by creditor, 79(1), 79.1(1)

**Specified animal**
- valuation of, 28(1.2)

**Specified beneficiary**
- re foreign reporting requirements
- - defined, 233.2(1)
- re principal residence
- - defined, 54"principal residence"(c.1)(ii)

**Specified Canadian entity**
- defined, 233.3(1)
- reporting re distribution from foreign trust, 233.5(1)
- reporting re foreign property, 233.3(3)

**Specified class**
- defined
- - associated-corporation rules, 256(1.1)
- - capital gains strips, 55(1)
- - windup of corporation, 88(1)(c.8)
- effect on corporations being associated, 256(1), (1.6)
- redemption of, 55(1)"permitted redemption"

**Specified cooperative corporation**
- defined, Reg. 4901(2)

**Specified corporation**
- defined, 55(1)

**Specified cost**
- debt forgiveness rules
- - application of, 79.1(6), (7)
- - defined, 80.01(1)
- seizure of property by creditor
- - cost of seized property includes, 79.1(6)
- - defined, 79.1(1)

**Specified debt obligation**, *see also* Lending asset; Mark-to-market property
- accrued return from, Reg. 9102(1), (3)
- amalgamation of holder, 87(2)(e.3)
- amortization date, Reg. 9200(2)
- cost amount of, 248(1)"cost amount"(d.2)
- credit-related gains and losses, 142.4(7)B
- defined, 142.2(1), Reg. 9100, 9200(1)
- disposition of, 142.4, Reg. 9200-9204
- - no capital gain, 39(1)(a)(ii.2)
- - no capital loss, 39(1)(b)(ii)
- - payment received after disposition, 142.4(11)
- early repayment of, 142.4(10)
- foreign exchange adjustment, Reg. 9104
- income inclusion and deduction prescribed, 142.3(1)
- mark-to-market property, 142.5(3)
- partial disposition of, 142.4(9)
- payment received after disposition, 142.4(11)
- prescribed obligations, Reg. 9202
- primary currency of, defined, Reg. 9100
- rollover of, 85(1.1)(g.1)
- superficial loss rule not applicable, 142.6(7)
- transfer of insurance business by non-resident holder, 138(11.5)(k.1)
- windup of holder into parent, 88(1)(a.3)

**Specified deposit**
- defined, 95(2.5)
- excluded from FAPI, 95(2)(a.3)

**Specified disabled person**
- defined, for Home Buyers' Plan, 146.01(1)
- loan from RRSP to acquire home for, 146.01(1)"supplemental eligible amount"

**Specified distribution**
- defined, Reg. 8304.1(8)

**Specified educational program**
- defined, 118.6(1)

**Specified employee**
- defined, 248(1)
- - of partnership, 15(2.7)
- remuneration of
- - calculation of prescribed proxy amount for R&D investment tax credit, Reg. 2900(7), (8)
- - excluded from R&D expenditure pool, 37(8)
- - limitation on SR&ED deduction, 37(9.1)

2803

# Index

**Specified employer**
- overseas employment tax credit
  - credit for employee, 122.3(1)(a)
  - defined, 122.3(2)
- UI premium tax credit
  - defined, 126.1(5)

**Specified energy property**
- defined, Reg. 1100(25), (27)–(29)
- limitation on capital cost allowance, Reg. 1100(24)
- separate class, Reg. 1101(5m)

**Specified event**
- defined, re stock option deduction, 110(1.6)

**Specified expense (re flow-through shares)**
- defined, 66(12.6), (12.601)

**Specified foreign exploration and development expense**
- country-by-country allocation, 66(4.1), (4.2)
  - successor corporation, 66.7(2.1), (2.2)
- defined, 66(15)

**Specified foreign property**
- defined, 233.3(1)
- over $100,000, reporting requirement, 233.3(1)"reporting entity"

**Specified foreign trust**
- defined, 233.2(1)
- reporting requirement re, 233.2(4)

**Specified fraction**
- defined, for designated limited partnership (foreign property rules), Reg. 5000(9)

**Specified future tax consequence**
- defined, 248(1)
- ignored for balance-due day of corporation, 157(1)(b)(i)(D)
- ignored for instalment threshold
  - cooperative or credit union, 157(2)(c), (d)
  - corporation, 157(2.1)(a), 161(4.1)(a)
  - farmers and fishermen, 161(4)(a)
  - individuals, 156.1(1.1), (1.2), 161(4.01)(a)
- ignored for investment tax credit of small corporation, 127(10.2)A
- ignored for penalties, 162(11)
- ignored for refundable investment tax credit, 127.1(2)"qualifying corporation"

**Specified gift**
- registered charity, of
  - defined, 149.1(1)
  - excluded from charitable expenditures and qualified gifts, 149.1(1.1)

**Specified holding corporation**
- defined, Reg. 5100(1)

**Specified individual**
- for income-splitting tax
  - defined, 120.4(1), 248(1)
  - tax on, 120.4(2)
- for LSVCCs
  - defined, 204.8(1)
  - ownership and transfer of labour-sponsored venture capital corporation shares, 204.81(1)(c)(v)–(vii)
- for pension regulations
  - defined, Reg. 8515(4)

**Specified international finance trust**
- defined, Reg. 5000(7)
- excluded from foreign property, Reg. 5000(1.1)(d)

**Specified insurance benefit**
- defined, for insurance demutualization, 139.1(1)

**Specified investment business**, *see also* Investment business
- defined, 125(7), 248(1)
- excluded from active business income, 125(7)"active business"
- included in base for dividend refund, 129(4)"income"(a)
- included in property income, 129(4)"aggregate investment income"(c)

**Specified leasing property**
- acquire in the year, Reg. 1100(2)(a)(v)
- addition or alteration to, Reg. 1100(1.19)
- amount deductible in respect of, Reg. 1100(1.1)
- defined, Reg. 1100(1.11)
- separate class, Reg. 1101(5n)

**Specified loan**
- defined, Reg. 8006

**Specified member (of partnership)**, *see also* Limited partner
- anti-avoidance rule
  - re alternative minimum tax, 127.52(2.1)
  - re negative ACB triggering gain, 40(3.131)
- CNIL of, 110.6(1)"investment expense" "investment income"
- deemed capital gain on negative adjusted cost base, 40(3.1)(a)
- defined, 248(1), (28)
- FAPI rules, 95(1)"investment business"
- investment tax credit of, 127(8)(b)
- minimum tax, 127.52(1)(c.1)
- R&D losses of, no deduction, 96(1)(g)
- real property of (capital gains exemption), 110.6(1)"non-qualifying real property"
- where interest in partnership loaned or transferred, 96(1.8)

**Specified multi-employer plan**, *see also* Registered pension plan
- defined, Reg. 8510(2), (3)

**Specified net royalty**
- defined, Reg. 1206(1)

**Specified non-resident shareholder**
- defined, 18(5)
- loans by, thin capitalization rules, 18(4)–(6)

**Specified obligation (re debt forgiveness rules)**
- defined, 80.01(6)
- parking of, deemed settled, 80.01(7), (8)

**Specified partnership income**
- defined, 125(6), (6.2), 125(7)"specified partnership income"
- small business deduction for, 125(1)(a)(ii)

**Specified partnership loss**
- defined, 125(7)
- reduces small business deduction, 125(1)(a)(iv)

**Specified percentage**
- Canadian oil and gas exploration expense, re, Reg. 1206(1)
- credit for northern residents
  - application in calculation of credit, 110.7(1)(a), (b)(ii)
  - defined, 110.7(2)
- impaired debts reserve
  - defined, 20(2.4)

Specified percentage *(cont'd)*
- interest and property taxes on vacant land
- - defined, 18(2) (application for 1988–92 only), 18(3.4)
- investment tax credit, 127(9)
- application in calculation of credit, 127(9)"investment tax credit"(a), (e.1)
- - defined, 127(9)"specified percentage"
- labour-sponsored venture capital corporation
- - defined, Reg. 6706(1)
- life insurer, inclusion in income for land/building
- - application in calculation of prescribed amount, Reg. 2410(1) (opening words)
- - defined, Reg. 2410(2)
- manufacturing and processing credit — resource income
- - application in calculation of credit, Reg. 5203(3)(d)
- - defined, Reg. 5202
- reserve for 1995 stub period
- - defined, 34.2(1)
- resource and processing allowances
- - application in calculation of earned depletion base, Reg. 1205(1)(a)(v), (vi)(A), 1205(1)(j)(iv)
- - defined, Reg. 1206(1)
- trust distribution
- - defined, 107(2)(b.1)

**Specified period**
- defined, for insurance demutualization, holding corporation, 141(4)

**Specified person**
- defined
- - for attribution rules, 74.5(8)
- - for dividend deductibility on guaranteed share, 112(2.2)(g) [to be repealed], 112(2.22)(b) [draft]
- - for flow-through shares, Reg. 6202.1(5)
- - for prescribed shares under stock option rules, Reg. 6204(3)
- - for source withholdings, 227(5.1)
- - for windup of corporation, 88(1)(c.2)
- to benefit from subsequent disposition of property
- - anti-avoidance rule, 69(11)
- - - application on winding-up, 88(1)

**Specified personal corporation, defined**, ITAR 57(11)

**Specified portion**
- defined, for retroactive spreading of lump-sum payments, 110.2(1)

**Specified predecessor, defined**, 59(3.4)

**Specified property**
- adjustment to adjusted cost base, 53(2)(g.1), 53(4)–(6)
- debt forgiveness rules
- - defined, 54
- - gain on disposition of, 80.03
- - option in respect of, when exercised, 49(3.01)
- resource allowance
- - defined, Reg. 1206(1)
- windup of corporation
- - defined, 88(1)(c.4)
- - whether subject to bump in cost based on windup, 88(1)(c.3)(i), (v)

**Specified proportion**
- defined, 206(1)

**Specified reserve adjustment**
- defined, 20(30)
- impaired debt reserve calculation, 20(1)(l)(ii)(D)(II)N

**Specified retirement arrangement**
- defined, Reg. 8308.3(1)
- PSPA of, Reg. 8308.3(4)
- - information return, Reg. 8402(3)
- pension credit under, Reg. 8308.3(2), (3)

**Specified right, defined**, ITAR 21(3)"specified right"

**Specified royalty**
- defined, Reg. 1206(1)

**Specified shareholder**
- defined, 18(5), 18(5.1), 55(3.2)(a), 88(1)(c.2)(iii), 248(1)
- interest on debt relating to the acquisition of land, 18(3)"interest on debt relating to the acquisition of land"(b)
- non-resident, loans by, thin capitalization rules, 18(4)
- soft costs relating to construction, 18(3.1)(b), 18(3.2)(b)

**Specified stage (of production from Canadian resource property)**
- defined, 208(1.1)

**Specified subsidiary corporation**
- acquisition of share by, 88(1)(c.4)(i)
- defined, 88(1)(c.5)

**Specified tax allocation**
- defined, 94.1(8)
- income inclusion, 94.1(3)(a)C

**Specified temporary access road**
- defined, Reg. 1104(2)

**Specified transaction or event**
- defined, 211(1), Reg. 1900(1)

**Specified value**
- defined, for stock option deferral rules, 7(11)

**Specified wholly-owned corporation**
- defined, 55(1)

**Speech impairment**
- certification of, for disability credit, 118.3(1)(a.2)(i.1)
- sign language interpretation services for, 188.2(2)(l.4)

**Speech-language pathologist**
- certification of speech impairment for disability credit, 118.3(1)(a.2)(i.1)
- defined, 118.4(2)

**Speech synthesizer**
- medical expense, Reg. 5700(p)

**Speech therapy**
- medical expense credit, 118.2(2)(l.3), (1.9)

**Spinal brace, as medical expense**, 118.2(2)(i)

**Split income**, 120.4
- attribution rules do not apply, 56(5), 74.4(2)(g), 74.5(13)
- deduction from regular income, 20(1)(ww)
- defined, 120.4(1), 248(1)
- tax on children, 120.4(2)
- - minimum tax carryover not allowed, 120.2(1), 120.2(1)(b)(i)
- - parent jointly liable with child, 160(1.2)

**Sporting event**, *see also* Amateur athlete trust; Athlete
- ineligible for Canadian film/video credit, Reg. 1106(1)"excluded production"(b)
- ineligible for film/video production services credit, Reg. 9300(f)

**Spousal bridging benefits**
- for registered pension plan, Reg. 8503(2)(l.1)

**Spousal equivalent credit**, 118(1)B(b)
**Spousal support**, *see* Support payments (spousal or child)
**Spousal trust**, *see also* Trust (or estate): spouse
- pre-1972
- • deemed disposition by, 104(4)(a.1)
- • defined, 108(1)

**Spouse**, *see also* Common-law partner
- alimony, *see* Support payments (spousal or child)
- common-law deemed spouse, *see* Common-law partner
- death
- • claim under provincial family law deemed to be transfer on death, 248(23.1)
- • rollover of property, 70(6)
- deemed benefits under plans, 146(8.91)
- defined, 252(3), (4)
- • re prescribed annuity contracts, Reg. 304(4)
- dividends received by, election re, 82(3)
- divorce, *see* Divorce and separation
- former
- • defined, 252(3)
- • transfer of property to, 73(1)
- government annuity, deductible portion, 58(5)
- income from property transferred to
- • joint liability for tax, 160(1)–(3)
- income splitting through RRSP transfers, 146(8.3), 146.3(5.1)–(5.5)
- joint and several liability for tax, 160
- living apart
- • commutation of RRSP, 146(8.3)
- • property transferred
- • • liability for tax on income or gain from, 160(4)
- • transfer to, 74.5(3)
- loans to, 74.1(1)
- • for value, 74.5
- • gain or loss, 74.2
- • repayment of, 74.1(3)
- maintenance, *see* Support payments (spousal or child)
- marriage breakdown, *see* Divorce and separation
- notch provision, 117(7), 118.2(1)D
- pension payments to widow(er) of contributor, 57(5)
- principal residence transferred to, 40(4)
- private health services plan premiums, medical expenses, 118.2(2)(q)
- property acquired from deceased taxpayer, 70(6)
- property in trust for, deemed disposition by trust, 104(4)(a)
- • deemed proceeds and cost, 104(5)
- property transferred between
- • valuation rules, 73
- • where transferee non-resident, Part XIII tax not exigible, 212(12)
- registered retirement savings plan for
- • amount of premiums deductible, 146(5.1)
- • meaning, 146(1)"spousal plan"
- • premiums not subject to income attribution rules, 74.5(12)
- • transfers to
- • • from RPP or DPSP, 60(j.2)
- • • income splitting via, 146(8.3), 146.3(5.1)–(5.5)
- • • marriage breakdown, on, 146(16), 146.3(5.1), 147.3(5)
- reserves allowed to, for year of taxpayer's death, 72(2)
- rollover of property

- • death, on, 70(6)
- • generally, 70(6)
- • inter vivos, 73(1)
- • reserves for year of death, 72(2)
- separation, *see* Divorce and separation
- support of
- • when living together, 118(1)B(a)
- • when separated or divorced, *see* Support payments (spousal or child)
- surviving
- • as RRIF annuitant, 146.3(1)"annuitant"(b)
- • death benefit paid to, 248(1)"death benefit"
- transfer of business to, 24(2)
- transfer of property to, 74(1) [repealed], 74.1(1)
- • for fair market value, 74.5
- • gain or loss, 74.2, 74.5
- • RRSP on marriage breakdown, 146(16)(b)
- • repayment of, 74.1(3)
- • special rules, 160(4)
- • valuation rules, 73
- trust for, *see* Trust (or estate): spouse
- unused credits transferred to, 118.8

**St. Lawrence Seaway Authority, subject to tax**, 27(2), Reg. 7100

**Stabilization account**, *see* Net income stabilization account

**Stable equipment**
- capital cost allowance for, Reg. Sch. II:Cl. 10(c)

**Stairs, power-operated climbing chair for, medical expense**, Reg. 5700(f)

**Stakeholder**
- defined, for insurance demutualization, 139.1(1)

**Standby charge**
- automobile, 6(1)(e)
- • car salesperson/lessor, reasonable amount, 6(2.1)
- • operating costs, optional one-half, 6(1)(k)(iv)
- • partner or employee of partner, 12(1)(y)
- • reasonable amount, 6(2)
- • shareholder, 15(5)
- available money, for
- • non-resident tax, 214(15)

**Start-up period**
- defined, for LSVCCs, 204.8(1)

**Stated capital**, *see* Paid-up capital

**Stated percentage**
- defined, 59(3.4)
- • for resource allowance, Reg. 1206(1)
- variation of, 59(3.5)

**Statistics**, *see* Communication of information: statistical purposes

**Statute-barred debt, deemed settled**, 80.01(9)
- subsequent payment of debt, 80.01(10)

**Statute-barred reassessments**, 152(3.1), (4)

**Statutory exemptions**, 81(1)(a)

**Stay of appeal during action to prosecute**, 239(4)

**Steam**
- deemed to be goods for M&P credit, 125.1(5)
- generating equipment, capital cost allowance, Reg. Sch. II:Cl. 34
- processing of, investment tax credit, 127(9)"qualified property"(c.1)

**Steam** *(cont'd)*
- production of, manufacturing and processing credit, 125.1(2)

**Stepchild, dependent**, 118(6)(a)

**Stock, capital**, *see* Capital stock; Share

**Stock dividend**, *see* Dividend: stock

**Stock exchange**
- prescribed
- - for charitable foundations, Reg. 3700
- - in Canada, Reg. 3200
- - outside Canada, Reg. 3201

**Stock options**
- benefit from, 7(1)
- - addition to adjusted cost base of share, 53(1)(j)
- - Canadian-controlled private corporation (CCPC), 7(1.1)
- - emigration from Canada, no income inclusion, 7(1.6)
- death of employee, 7(1)(e), 164(6.1)
- deferral, 7(8)–(16)
- - information return, Reg. 200(5)
- donation of shares to charity, 110(1)(d.01)
- emigration of employee, 7(1.6), 128.1(4)(d.1)
- employees, to, 7, 110(1)(d), (d.1)
- excluded from deemed disposition
- - on becoming non-resident, 128.1(4)(b)(vi) [to be repealed], 128.1(10)"excluded right or interest"(c)
- - on becoming resident, 128.1(1)(b)(v)
- look-through rules, 7(2)
- non-CCPC options, 7(1.8)
- prescribed shares, Reg. 6204
- return of employee shares by trustee, 8(12)
- stock split or consolidation, effect of, 110(1.5)

**Stock purchase loans**
- employee, to, 15(2)(a)(iii), 15(2.4)(c)

**Stock rights**
- issued to shareholder, 15(1)(c)

**Stock savings plan, prescribed**
- shares of
- - capital loss from disposition of, 40(2)(i)
- - prescribed assistance, deduction from cost base, 53(2)(k)(i)(C)

**Stock split**
- effect on stock option, rules, 110(1.5)

**Stone quarry**
- defined, Reg. 1104(8)

**Stop-loss rules**
- amalgamation, 87(2)(a), 87(2.1)
- ceasing to be resident in Canada, 128.1(4)(f)
- change in control of corporation, 111(4)–(5.2)
- disposition by corporation of interest in trust, 107(1)(c)
- disposition by partner of interest in trust, 107(1)(d)
- disposition by partner of share on which dividends paid, 112(3.1)
- disposition of commercial obligation in exchange for another, 40(2)(e.2)
- disposition of debt owing by related person, 40(2)(e.1)
- disposition of partnership interest, 100(4)
- disposition of property to affiliated person, 40(3.3), (3.4)
- disposition of property to controller, 40(3.3), (3.4)
- disposition of share held as inventory, 112(4)–(4.3)
- disposition of share in prescribed venture capital corporation or LSVCC, 40(2)(i)
- disposition of share of controlled corporation, 40(2)(h)
- disposition of share of corporation to itself, 40(3.6)
- disposition of share of foreign affiliate, 93(2)–(4)
- disposition of share on which dividend paid, 112(3)
- disposition of share received on reorganization, 112(7)
- dividend received by non-resident individual, 40(3.7)
- - credit where tax paid, 119
- exchanged shares, 112(7)
- losses following change of control of corporation, 111(4)–(5.2)
- mark-to-market property, 112(5.5), (5.6)
- non-resident individual, 40(3.7)
- post-emigration losses, 128.1(8)(f)
- pregnant losses, *see* Pregnant loss
- property transferred to trust, 107.4(3)(b)(ii)
- reverse takeover, 256(7)(c)
- shares held by financial institution, 112(5.2)
- windup of corporation, 88(1.1)

**Stopping business**, *see* Ceasing to carry on business; Winding-up

**Storage area, capital cost allowance**, Reg. Sch. II:Cl. 1(g)
- for mine, Reg. Sch. II:Cl. 10(l)

**Storage cost, underground**
- capital cost allowance, Reg. Sch. II:Cl. 10(f.1), Sch. II:Cl. 41

**Streamed income**
- determination of, 66.7(2.3)(b)(ii)

**Strike pay**
- not taxed (no legislative reference), *Fries* case [1990] 2 CTC 439 (SCC)

**Stripped bond**
- cost of coupon excluded from income when sold, 12(9.1)

**Stripping**, *see* Capital gains stripping; Surplus stripping

**Structured settlement**
- insurer's reserve for, Reg. 1400(3)E
- taxation of, IT-365R2 para. 5

**Stub period (1995)**
- reserve, 34.2(4)

**Student**
- commuting to U.S
- - tuition fees, credit, 118.5(1)(c)
- deemed resident, credit for tuition fees, 118.5(2)
- disabled
- - education credit, 118.6(3)
- - eligible for RESP withdrawals, 146.1(2)(g.1)(i)(B)
- - waiver of RESP age requirements, 146.1(2.2)
- education credit, *see* Education credit
- full-time, *see* Education credit
- loan payments, credit for interest on, 118.62
- moving expenses, 62(2)
- part-year resident, credit for tuition fees, 118.91
- taxpayer supporting, 118.9
- tuition fees
- - ancillary fees, 118.5(3)
- - in Canada, credit, 118.5(1)(a)
- - outside Canada, credit, 118.5(1)(b)
- U.S. resident, Canada–U.S. Tax Convention Art. XX
- unused credits, transfers of, 118.8, 118.9

***Stursberg* case confirmed**, 40(3.13)

# Index

**Subcontractors**
- construction, information return, Reg. 238

**Subdivision of property**, *see* Partition of property

**Subject corporation (for Part IV tax)**
- defined, 186(3)

**Subleases**, *see* Leasing properties

**Subordinate**
- defined, for third-party penalty, 163.2(1)

**Subscriber**
- defined, for RESPs, 146.1(1)

**Subscriber's gross cumulative excess**
- defined, for RESPs, 204.9(1)

**Subscriber's share of the excess amount**
- defined, for RESPs, 204.9(1)

**Subsidiary**, *see also* Parent (corporation)
- controlled corporation
- • defined, 248(1)"subsidiary wholly-owned corporation"
- • non-resident, *see also* Foreign affiliate
- • • loan to, 17(3), 247(7)
- cost of shares of, 52(7)
- defined, 88(1), Reg. 8605(4)
- foreign, *see* Foreign affiliate; Controlled foreign affiliate
- 90% or more owned, winding-up of
- • net capital losses, 88(1.2), (1.3)
- • non-capital losses, 88(1.1)
- • parent corporation continuation of, 88(1.5)
- • qualified expenditure, 88(1.4)
- • rules, 88(1)
- wholly-owned corporation, *see also* Control of corporation
- • amalgamation, on, 87(1.2), (1.4)
- • defined, 248(1)

**Subsidy**
- housing, provided by employer, 6(23)

**Substantial contribution of capital to partnership**
- meaning of, 40(3.16)

**Substantial increase in indebtedness**
- meaning of, re partnership interest, 40(3.16)

**Substantial interest**
- defined, for Part VI.1 tax, 191(2), (3)

**Substitute's salary paid by employee**
- deduction, 8(1)(i)(ii)
- • certificate of employer, 8(10)

**Substituted property**
- defined, 248(5)
- • for matchable expenditure rules, 18.1(8)(b)
- • for superficial loss definition, 54"superficial loss"(a)
- • for windup of corporation, 88(1)(c.3)

**Substitution (Quebec)**
- deemed to be trust, 248(3)

**Subway, capital cost allowance**, Reg. Sch. II:Cl. 1(j)

**Succession duties**
- applicable to certain property, deduction for, 60(m.1)
- interest on, deductible, 60(d)

**Successor corporation**
- Canadian resource property acquired from predecessor, 66.7(9)
- cumulative Canadian development expense, deduction for, 66.7(4)
- cumulative Canadian oil and gas property expense, deduction for, 66.7(5)
- defined, 59(3.4)
- mining exploration depletion, Reg. 1203(3)
- property acquired by, ITAR 29(25)
- resource and processing allowances, Reg. 1202(3)
- resource expenses, rules re, 66.7
- • application of, 66.6
- • exclusions from, 66.7(6)
- resource property acquired from predecessor, 66.1(10)
- resource property acquired from tax-exempt person, 66.6(1), (2)
- second
- • resource and processing allowances, Reg. 1202(3)

**Successor pool (re debt forgiveness rules)**
- defined, 80(1)
- use of to limit reductions of resource expenditures, 80(8)(a)

**Sulphur**, *see also* Canadian field processing
- resource allowance, Reg. 1204(1)(b)(i), 1206(1)"resource activity"(a)
- royalties from processing
- • not deductible, 18(1)(m)(v)(B)
- • taxable, 12(1)(o)(v)(B)
- specified stage of production, 208(1.1)(e)
- transporting, transmitting or processing, Reg. 1204(3)(a), 1206(1)"resource activity"(j)(i)(A)

**Sunday**, *see* Holiday

**Super-allowance benefit amount**
- addition to investment tax credit, 127(10.1)(b)
- • no direct ITC, 127(9)"investment tax credit"(a.1)
- defined, 127(9)

**Superannuation benefits**, *see also* Pension
- defined, 248(1)
- estate tax on, deduction for, 60(m)
- succession duties on, deduction for, 60(m.1)
- testamentary trust receiving, 104(27)
- transferred to another plan, deductible, 60(j)
- unpaid, 78(4)
- used to purchase income-averaging annuity contract, deductible, 61(2)(a)

**Superficial disposition**
- foreign investment entity, 94.2(17)

**Superficial loss**, *see also* Pregnant loss
- added to adjusted cost base of property, 53(1)(f)
- capital loss deemed nil, 40(2)(g)(i)
- capital property, 40(3.3)–(3.5), 54"superficial loss"
- defined, for capital gains purposes, 54
- eligible capital property, 14(12), (13)
- financial institution, of, 18(13)–(15)
- • no application to specified debt obligations or mark-to-market property, 142.6(7)
- inventory held as adventure in nature of trade, 18(14)–(16)

**Superior court**
- defined, *Interpretation Act* 35(1)

**Supplemental eligible amount**
- defined, for Home Buyers' Plan, 146.01(1)

**Supplementary depletion base**
- capital cost of bituminous sands equipment added to
- • proceeds of later disposition, 59(3.3)(c)
- capital cost of enhanced recovery equipment added to
- • proceeds of later disposition, 59(3.3)(d)

2808

**Supplementary depletion base** *(cont'd)*
- defined, Reg. 1212(3)

**Supplementary personal tax credit**, 118(1)B(b.1)

**Supplementary unemployment benefit plans**, 145
- amounts received under, income, 56(1)(g)
- benefits
  - withholding tax, 153(1)(e)
- defined, 145(1)
- election to file return, 217
- employer's contribution
  - limitation on deductibility, 18(1)(i)
  - not includable in employee's income, 6(1)(a)(i)
- payments to non-resident, 212(1)(k)

**Supplies**
- deemed to be inventory, 10(5)
- paid for and used by employee, 8(1)(i)(iii)
  - certificate of employer, 8(10)
- valuation of, 10(4)

**Support amount**, *see also* Child support amount
- defined, 56.1(4), 60.1(4)
- payments before agreement or court order, 56.1(3), 60.1(3)
- whether deductible, 60(b), 60.1
- whether taxable, 56(1)(b), 56.1

**Support payments (farm)**
- information slips required, Reg. 234–236

**Support payments (spousal or child)**
- "allowance" defined, 56(12)
- child support, agreement or order after April 1997
  - non-deductible, 60(b), 56.1(4)"commencement day"
  - non-taxable, 56(1)(b), 56.1(4)"commencement day"
- deductible when paid, 60(b), (c)
- enforcement of, *see* Family Orders and Agreements Enforcement Assistance Act
- income when received, 56(1)(b), (c)
- medical/educational payments, 56.1(2), 60.1(2)
- mortgage payments, 56.1(2), 60.1(2)
- no dependant credit for spouse or child when paid, 118(5)
- paid to non-resident, 212(1)(f), 217
- paid to third parties for benefit of spouse or children, 56.1, 60.1
- paid to U.S. resident, Canada–U.S. Tax Convention Art. XVIII:6
- reimbursement of, taxable, 56(1)(c.2)
- repayment of, deductible, 60(c.2)
- retroactive deductibility/taxability, 56.1(3), 60.1(3)
- taxable, 56(1)(b), (c)

**Supporting person**
- for child care expenses, defined, 63(3)
- liability for excess child tax credit refunded, 160.1(2)
- unused education credits transferred to, 118.9

**Surcharge**, *see* Surtax

**Surface construction**
- capital cost, 13(7.5)(b), Reg. 1102(14.3)

**Surplus**
- contributed
  - computation of, on transfer of insurance business, 138(11.9)
  - converted into paid-up capital, no dividend deemed, 84(1)(c.1)–(c.3)
- defined (re pension plan), Reg. 8500(1), (1.1)
- distribution of, by foreign affiliate, Reg. 5901

- exempt, *see* Exempt surplus (of foreign affiliate)
- pre-acquisition, *see* Pre-acquisition surplus (of foreign affiliate)
- stripping, *see* Surplus stripping
- taxable, *see* Taxable surplus (of foreign affiliate)

**Surplus entitlement percentage, defined**, 95(1)

**Surplus stripping**
- conversion of dividend to exempt capital gain, 110.6(8)
- non-resident former resident who will return to Canada, 128.1(6)(b), 128.1(7)(e)
- publicly-traded corporation, by, 183.1
- sale of shares by individual, 84.1
- sale of shares by non-resident, 212.1, 212.2

**Surrender**
- of property to creditor, *see also* Seizure: property
  - defined, 79(2)
  - does not constitute payment, 79(6)
  - proceeds of disposition to debtor, 79(3)
  - subsequent payment by debtor, 79(4)
- of share, partnership interest or trust interest
  - deemed capital gain, 80.03(2)
  - defined, 80.03(3)

**Surtax**, *see also* Additional tax
- corporation, 123.2
  - credit against Part I.3 tax, 181.1(4)–(7)
  - credit against Part VI tax, 190.1(3)–(6)
  - reduced by Part I.3 (before 1992), 125.3
  - reduced by Part VI tax (before 1992), 125.2
- deposit-taking financial institutions, 190.1(1.2)
- health promotion, 182, 183
- individual, 180.1
  - credit where emigration stop-loss rule applied, 180.1(1.4)
  - foreign tax credit, 180.1(1.1)
  - investment tax credit, 180.1(1.2)
- Part VI, 190.1(1.2)

**Survey, quadrennial, reserve for**, 12(1)(h), 20(1)(o), Reg. 3600

**Surveying costs**
- cost base of property, addition to, 53(1)(n)

**Surveyor**
- defined, for surveys under *Canada Shipping Act*, Reg. 3600(2)

**Surviving spouse**
- as RRIF annuitant, 146.3(1)"annuitant"(b)
- death benefit paid to, 248(1)"death benefit"
- tobacco manufacturers, 182, 183

**Suspended losses**, *see* Suspension of losses

**Suspension of losses**
- capital losses, 40(3.3)–(3.5)
- depreciable property, 13(21.2)
- eligible capital property, 14(12), (13)
- inventory held as adventure in nature of trade, 18(14)–(16)
- share or debt owned by financial institution, 18(13), (15)
- terminal losses, 13(21.2)

**Sweden**, *see also* Foreign government
- stock exchange recognized, Reg. 3201(w)

**Swine**
- basic herd maintained since 1971, deduction, 29

2809

# Index

**Switzerland**, *see also* Foreign government
- stock exchange recognized, Reg. 3201(m)
- universities, gifts to, Reg. Sch. VIII s. 6

**Sylvite**
- drilling and exploring for, 66(2)
- extraction of, 248(1)"mineral resource"(d)(ii)

**Synagogue**, *see also* Charity
- rabbi employed by, *see* Clergyman

**Syndicate**
- drilling and exploration expenses, ITAR 29(9), (10), (13)
- interest in
  - - expenses of selling, 20(1)(e)

**Synthetic speech system etc.**
- enabling blind person to use computer
  - - medical expense, Reg. 5700(o)

**Systems software**, *see also* Software
- defined, Reg. 1104(2)

## T

**T-4 information return**
- filing deadline (Feb. 28), Reg. 205(1)
- requirement for, Reg. 200(1)

**TCC**, *see* Tax Court of Canada

**TCP**, *see* Taxable Canadian property

**TPAR**, *see* Total pension adjustment reversal

**TPS**, *see* Taxable preferred share

**T-Bill**, *see* Treasury bill

**"Tainted" spouse trust**, *see also* Pre-1972 spousal trust
- relieving rule, 70(7)

**Takeover**, *see also* Control of corporation: change of
- reverse, 256(7)(c)

**Talk show**
- ineligible for Canadian film/video credit, Reg. 1106(1)"excluded production"(b)
- ineligible for film/video production services credit, Reg. 9300(d)

**Talking textbooks**
- medical expense, Reg. 5700(w)

**Tank, oil or water storage**
- capital cost allowance, Reg. Sch. II:Cl. 6, 8, 29, 40

**Tapestry**
- hand-woven, whether CCA allowed, Reg. 1102(1)(e)

**Tar sands, defined**, 248(1)

**Tar sands ore**
- defined, Reg. 1104(2), 1206(1)
- processing of, Reg. 1104(5)(a)(iii), 1104(5)(c)(iii), 1104(6)(a)(iii), 1104(9)(f)(iii), 1204(1)(b)(ii)(C), 1204(1)(b)(iii)(C), 1204(1)(b)(iv)(C), 1205(1)(a)(iv)(A)(III), 1205(1)(a)(iv)(B)(III), 1205(1)(b)(iii), 5201(c.3)
  - - excluded from M&P credit, 125.1(3)"manufacturing or processing"(f)(iii)
  - - investment tax credit, 127(9)"qualified property"(c)(vi)(C)

**Tax**
- abatement, *see* Tax abatement
- addition to, for income not earned in a province, 120(1)
- additional
  - - on non-Canadian corporations carrying on business in Canada, 219
- agreement, *see* Tax treaty
- application of payments under collection agreement, 228
- assets used as security by DPSP trust, on, 198
- attempt by partners to reduce or postpone, 103
- avoidance, *see* Anti-avoidance rules
- branch, 219
- "business-income tax" defined, 126(7)
- carved-out income, on, 209
- collection of, *see* Collection of tax
- computation of, 117(5.2), *see also* Computation of tax, Reg. Part I
- corporate distributions, on, 183.1
  - - indirect payments, 183.1(5)
  - - limitation, 183.1(6)
  - - stock dividends repurchased for excessive amount, 183.1(3)
  - - subsec. 110.6(8) not applicable, 183.1(7)
- corporations, 123–125.1
- court, *see* Tax Court of Canada
- credits, *see* Tax credits
- debt to Her Majesty, 222
- deduction at source
  - - amount of, deemed received by payee, 153(3)
  - - required of payer, 153
  - - tables, Reg. Sch. I
- deduction from
  - - employed out of Canada, 122.3
  - - re province providing schooling allowance, 120(2)
- deduction of, Reg. Part I
- deduction under s. 66.5, on, 196
- deductions in computing, *see* Deductions in computing tax
- deemed payable under amended Act, ITAR 49
- deferred income plans, on, *see also* Deferred income plans
- deferred profit sharing plans, on, 198–204
  - - tax on non-qualified investments and assets used as security, 198
- estimate to be made, 151
- evasion, *see* Tax evasion, penalty for
- excessive capital dividend or capital gains dividend elections, on, 184
- failure to remit amounts withheld, 227(9)
  - - salary or wages, from, 227(9.5)
- failure to withhold, 227(8)
  - - assessment for, 227(10)
  - - salary or wages, from, 227(8.5)
- foreign, *see* Foreign taxes
- foreign property acquired by pension and other pension and other plans, re, 205–207
- forfeiture under deferred profit sharing plan, 201
- imposed, *see* Liability for tax
- income from Canada of non-residents, on, 212–218
- income from property transferred at non-arm's length, on, 160(1)–(3)
- individuals
  - - surtax, 180.1
- interest on unpaid amount, 161(1)
- investment income of life insurers, on, 211–211.5
- large corporations, *see* Large corporations tax (Part I.3)
- liability for, *see* Liability for tax
- logging
  - - deduction for, 127(1), Reg. Part VII
  - - defined, 127(2)

2810

Index

Tax *(cont'd)*
- manufacturing and processing deduction, 125.1
- mining, deduction, 20(1)(v), Reg. 3900
- "non-business-income tax" defined, 126(7)
- non-deductible, 18(1)(t)
- non-qualified investments of deferred profit sharing plan, on, 198, 199
- non-residents, *see* Non-resident tax
- otherwise payable
  - - defined, 120(4)"tax otherwise payable under this Part" 126(7)"tax for the year otherwise payable under this Part"
- over-contributions to deferred income plans, on, 204.1–204.3
- overpayment, defined, 164(7)
- Part I.2, deduction for, 60(w)
- Part II, 182(1)
- Part II.1, 183.1
- Part IV
  - - reduction in, re Part IV.1 tax payable, 186(1.1)
- Part IV.1, 187.2, 187.3
  - - reduction in Part IV tax re, 186(1.1)
- Part VI.1, 191–191.4
- Part XII.3
  - - deductible from income of life insurer, 138(3)(g)
- payable
  - - amount deemed to be, 20(1)(ll)
  - - corporations, 123
  - - - non-resident, on branch profits, 219
  - - defined, 248(2)
  - - inter vivos trust, by, 122
- payment of, *see* Payment of tax
- property acquired by trusts, governed by deferred income plans, re, 205–207
- property disposed of by public authorities, re, 207.3, 207.4
- property held by trusts governed by deferred income plans, re, 207.1, 207.2
- rates of, *see* Rates of tax
- recovery by deduction or set-off, 224.1
- refund of overpayment, *see also* Refund
- refundable, *see* Refundable Part IV tax
- registered charities, 188, 189
- registered investments, re, 204.4–204.7
- registered securities dealers, re securities lending arrangement payments to non-residents, 212(19)
- return, *see* Returns
- revoked plans, on, 198
- royalties paid by tax-exempt person, re, 208
- security for, 220(4)–(4.4)
- shelter, *see* Tax shelter
- small business deduction, 125
- surtax
  - - corporation, 123.2
  - - individual, 180.1
- taxable dividend received by private corporation, 186
- tobacco manufacturers, 182, 183
- tobacco manufacturing income, 182
- unpaid, interest on, 227(9.3)
- withheld at source
  - - deemed to discharge debt, 227(13)
  - - failure to remit, 227(9)
  - - held in trust, 227(4), (4.1)
  - - not part of estate, 227(5)
- withholding of, *see* Withholding tax

Tax abatement
- corporations, 124
- individuals, Reg. 6401
  - - prescribed dates, Reg. 6401
  - - province providing schooling allowance, 120(2)
- manufacturing and processing, 125.1
- not available to Crown corporations, 124(3)
- small business, 125

Tax accounts
- transfer of instalments between, 221.2

Tax advisor
- penalty for misrepresentation by, 163.2

Tax agreement, *see* Tax treaty

Tax anniversary date
- defined, Reg. 310

Tax avoidance, *see* Anti-avoidance rules

Tax basis
- defined, 142.4(1), Reg. 9100, 9200(1)
  - - variation in, for certain insurers, 138(13)
- used as cost amount for specified debt obligation, 248(1)"cost amount"(d.2)

Tax benefit, 245(1)
- defined
  - - general anti-avoidance rule (GARR), 245(1)
  - - transfer pricing documentation, 247(1)

Tax consequences, defined, 245(1)

Tax convention, *see* Tax treaty

Tax Court of Canada
- appeal from, to Federal Court
  - - transfer of documents, 176
- appeal to, 169
  - - general procedure, 175
  - - informal procedure, 170
  - - only on grounds raised in objection, 169(2.1)
  - - prohibited where right waived by taxpayer, 169(2.2)
  - - time not counted, 174(5)
  - - valuation of ecological property, 169(1.1)
- application for extension of time
  - - for appeal, 167
  - - for notice of objection, 166.2
- disposal of appeal, 171
- hearing officer appointed, 231.4(2)–(4)
- reference to
  - - common questions, 174
- where no reasonable grounds for appeal, 179.1

Tax credits, *see also* Deductions in computing tax
- aged 65 and over, 118(2)
- basic minimum, 127.531
- basic personal, 118(1)B(c)
  - - additional amount for low-income taxpayer, 118(1)B(b.1)
- CPP contributions, 118.7
- caregiver, 118(1)B(c.1)
- charitable donations, 118.1
- child, 122.2
- dependants, 118(1)B(b), (d)
  - - alimony, maintenance or support payments, effect of, 118(5)
- disability, 118.3
- education credit, 118.6(2)
  - - carryforward of unused portion, 118.61

## Index

Tax credits *(cont'd)*
- • • part-time student, 118.6(2)B(b)
- • • transfer of unused portion, 118.8, 118.9
- • employment insurance premiums, 118.7
- • equivalent-to-married status, 118(1)B(b)
- • First Nations tax paid, 120(2.2)
- • foreign taxes, 126
- • fraudulently obtained, offence, 239(1.1)
- • GST, 122.5
- • gifts, 118.1
- • individual, 118
- • in-home care of relative, 118(1)B(c.1)
- • investment, 127(5)–(35), 127.1, *see also* Investment tax credit
- • labour-sponsored funds, 127.4
- • lump-sum averaging, 120.31
- • manufacturing and processing, 125.1
- • married status, 118(1)B(a)
- • medical expenses
- • • non-refundable credit, 118.2
- • • refundable credit, 122.51
- • mental or physical impairment, expenses related to, 118.2(2)(b), (c)
- • non-resident individual, 118.94
- • ordering of, 118.92
- • overseas employment, 122.3
- • part-year resident, 118.91
- • pension income, 118(3)
- • personal, 118(1)
- • • limitations, 118(4)
- • • not available to trust, 122(1.1)
- • political contributions, 127(3)–(4.2)
- • research and development, *see* Investment tax credit
- • scientific research, *see* Investment tax credit
- • separate returns, in, 118.93
- • share-purchase, 127.2
- • single status, 118(1)B(c)
- • small business, 125
- • spousal, 118(1)B(a)
- • supplementary personal, 118(1)B(b.1)
- • tuition credit, 118.5
- • • carryforward of unused portion, 118.61
- • • transfer of unused portion, 118.8, 118.9
- • unemployment insurance premium, 118.7, 126.1
- • unused
- • • carryforward, 118.61
- • • transfer to spouse, 118.8
- • • transfer to supporting person, 118.9

**Tax deferral**, *see also* Rollover
- agreement authorized by tax treaty, deemed valid, 115.1

**Tax equity**
- defined, ITAR 26(12)

**Tax evasion, penalty for**, 163, 238, 239

**Tax-exempt income**
- defined, for foreign tax credit, 126(7)

**Tax-exempt person**, *see* Exempt person

**Tax factor**
- relevant, defined, 95(1)

**Tax for year otherwise payable under Part I**
- defined, 126(7)

**Tax-free zone**
- pre-1972 capital gains, ITAR 26(3)

**Tax matters partner**
- to file objections to determination of partnership income, 165(1.15)

**Tax otherwise payable**
- defined, 120(4), 127(17)

**Tax-paid amount**
- defined, 146(1)
- excluded from RRIF income
- • generally, 146.3(5)(c)
- • on death, 146.3(6.2)A(b), (c)
- excluded from RRSP income
- • generally, 146(1)"benefit"(c.1)
- • on death, 146(8.9)A(b), (c)

**Tax payable**
- defined, 127–127.5, 248(2)
- determination of, by Minister, 152(1.11), (1.12)
- determined without reference to minimum tax, 117(1)

**"Tax payable" etc. under Part I**
- minimum tax excluded, 117(1)

**Tax return**, *see* Returns

**Tax shelter**
- art, *see* Art flips
- business does not entitle individual to June 15 filing deadline, 150(1)(d)(ii)(A)
- computer software, *see* Computer software tax shelter property
- cost of, 143.2
- deduction disallowed
- • where identification number not provided, 237.1(6)
- • where penalty unpaid, 237.1(6.1)
- defined, 237.1(1)
- film, *see* Motion picture film
- fiscal period, election for non-calendar year prohibited, 249.1(5)
- identification number
- • application for, by promoter, 237.1(2)
- • display of, required, 237.1(5)
- • issuance of, by Minister, 237.1(3)
- • penalty for false information in application, 237.1(7.4)
- • penalty for selling shelter before number issues, 237.1(7.4)
- • prerequisite for deduction, 237.1(6)
- • prerequisite of sale etc., 237.1(4)
- • provision of, to buyers, 237.1(5)
- information outside Canada, 143.2(13), (14)
- information returns, Reg. 231
- investment, 143.2
- • defined, 143.2(1)"tax shelter investment"
- • matchable expenditure, 18.1(13)
- • reassessment, no limitation period, 143.2(15)
- minimum tax on deductions, 127.52(1)(c.3)
- Minister's powers of investigation, 237.1(8)
- MURB, *see* Multiple unit residential buildings
- mutual fund limited partnership, 18.1
- prescribed benefit, Reg. 231(6), (6.1)
- promoter
- • application for identification number, 237.1(2)
- • defined, 237.1(1)
- • information return, 237.1(7)
- • provision of identification number to buyers, 237.1(5)
- sales prohibited without identification number, 237.1(4)

2812

# Index

Tax shelter *(cont'd)*
- software, *see* Computer software tax shelter property
- yacht, *see* Yacht

**Tax shelter investment**, *see* Tax shelter: investment

**Tax sparing, pre-1976 investment**, Reg. 5907(10)

**Tax transfer payments to provinces**, 154, Reg. 3300

**Tax treaty**
- amounts exempt under, deduction for, 110(1)(f)(i)
- anti-treaty shopping rule, Canada–U.S. Tax Convention Art. XXIX A
- Canada–U.K., *see* Table of Contents
- Canada–U.S., *see* Table of Contents
- competent authority agreement deemed valid, 115.1
- country with, foreign affiliate in, Reg. 5907(11)–(11.2)
- credit for departing resident to country with which Canada has, 126(2.21)
- deduction from income, 110(1)(f)(i)
- deemed resident in Canada due to family member, 250(1)(g)
- defined, 248(1)
- designated treaty country (FAPI rules), Reg. 5907(11), (11.1)
- dividend limitation in
  - applies for branch tax, 219.2
  - applies for corporate emigration tax, 219.3
- exempting Canadian corporation from tax, 250(5)
- exemption from capital gain, subsequent capital gains strip, 55(3.1) [temporary]
- gains deemed to arise in Canada, *Income Tax Conventions Interpretation Act* s. 6.3
- income exempt under, 126(7)"tax-exempt income"
- income exempt under, not earned income for RRSP, 146(1)"earned income"(c)
- interpretation of, *Income Tax Conventions Interpretation* (reproduced before the treaties)
- list of, *see* Table of Contents
- listed countries, Reg. 5907(11)–(11.2)
- non-resident under, deemed non-resident of Canada, 250(5)
- partners exempted by, new partner joining partnership, 96(8)
- property exempted under, 108(1)"exempt property"
- requirement to file return to claim exemption, 150(1)(a)(ii)
- tax on disposition of property by non-resident deferred under, 115.1
  - election, time of making, Reg. 7400(2)
  - prescribed provisions, Reg. 7400(1)

**Taxable amount**
- amount, *see* Taxable capital amount

**Taxable benefits**, *see* Benefit

**Taxable Canadian corporation**
- defined, 89(1)"taxable Canadian corporation"
- non-resident-owned investment corporation deemed not to be, 134
- prescribed, for Canadian film/video credit, Reg. 1106(2)
- property disposed of to taxpayer
  - cost base, addition to, 53(1)(f.1)

**Taxable Canadian life investment income, defined**, 211.1(2)

**Taxable Canadian property**, *see also* Property
- deemed, 128.1(4)(e)
- defined, 248(1)
  - excludes shares of demutualized life insurer or holding corporation, 141(5)
  - exclusions for branch tax purposes, 219(1.1)
- disposition of, by non-resident, 116
  - purchaser liable for tax, 116(5)
  - taxable, 2(3)(c)
- distribution to non-resident beneficiaries
  - tax on, 107(5)
    - security for tax, 220(4.6)–(4.63)
- excluded from deemed disposition
  - on becoming non-resident, 128.1(4)(b)(i) [to be repealed]
  - on becoming resident, 128.1(1)(b)(i)
- includes option, 115(3) [to be repealed], 248(1)"taxable Canadian property"(l)
- prorating for gains before May 1995, 40(9)
- replacement of
  - capital property, 44(5)(c), (d)
  - depreciable property, 13(4.1)(c), (d)
- rollover of, 85(1)(i), 85.1(1)(a)
- ship or aircraft used in international traffic, 115(1)(b)(ii)(B) [to be repealed], 248(1)"taxable Canadian property"(b)(ii)
- transitional rule re property not covered before April 26/95, ITAR 26(30)

**Taxable capital**
- for financial institutions tax
  - defined, 190.12
  - employed in Canada, defined, 190.11
- for large corporations tax
  - defined, 181.2(2), 181.3(2)
  - employed in Canada, defined, 181.2(1), 181.3(1), 181.4, Reg. 8601
    - tax on, 181.1(1)

**Taxable capital amount**
- defined, 66(12.6011)
- limit of $15 million for flow-through of CDE as CEE, 66(12.601)(a.1)

**Taxable capital employed in Canada**
- defined
  - for financial institutions tax, 190.11
  - for large corporations tax, 181.2(1), 181.3(1), 181.4
  - for renunciation of CDE as CEE on flow-through shares, 66(12.6011)

**Taxable capital gain**, *see* Capital gain

**Taxable conversion benefit**, *see also* Conversion benefit
- defined, for insurance demutualization, 139.1(1)

**Taxable deficit (of foreign affiliate)**
- defined, Reg. 5907(1)

**Taxable dividend**
- defined, 89(1), 112(6)(a), 129(1.2), 129(7), 133(8), 248(1)
  - for purposes of debt forgiveness, 80.03(1)(b)
  - for purposes of dividend refund, 129(7)
  - for purposes of non-resident-owned investment corporation, 133(8)"taxable dividend"
  - for purposes of stop-loss rules, 112(6)(a)
  - generally, 89(1), 248(1)
- partnership receiving, 186(6)

**Taxable earnings (of foreign affiliate)**
- defined, Reg. 5907(1)

**Taxable income**
- communal organization, election re, 143(2), (3)

Taxable income *(cont'd)*
- computation of, 110–114
- cumulative
  - non-resident-owned investment corporation, of, 133(9)"cumulative taxable income"
- deductions in computing, *see* Deductions in computing taxable income; Tax credits
- defined, 2(2)
- determination of, by Minister, 152(1.11), (1.12)
- earned in a province by a corporation, Reg. Part IV
- earned in Canada, *see* Taxable income earned in Canada
- earned in the year in a province, 124(4)
- life insurer, 138(7)
- non-resident, earned by in Canada, 115
- non-resident-owned investment corporation, 133(2)
- non-resident person, 115

**Taxable income earned in Canada**, 115
- defined, 115(1), 248(1)
- determination of, by Minister, 152(1.11), (1.12)
- foreign resource pool expenses, 115(4.1)

**Taxable interest expense**
- defined, 218.2(2)

**Taxable life insurance policy**
- defined, 211(1), Reg. 1900(1)

**Taxable loss (of foreign affiliate)**
- defined, Reg. 5907(1)

**Taxable net gain**
- from listed personal property, defined, 41(1), 248(1)

**Taxable obligation**
- defined, 240(1)

**Taxable preferred share**
- defined, 248(1)
- dividends excepted from tax, 187.1
- tax on corporation paying dividends on, 191–191.4
  - agreement to transfer tax liability to related corporation, 191.3
    - assessment by Minister, 191.3(3), (5)
    - payment by transferor corporation, 191.3(6)
    - where of no effect, 191.3(4)
  - amalgamation, 87(2)(rr)
  - associated corporations, 191.1(3)
    - failure to file agreement, 191.1(5)
    - total dividend allowance, 191.1(4)
  - dividend allowance, 191.1(2)
    - short years, in, 191.1(6)
    - total, for associated corporations, 191.1(4)
  - excluded dividend, defined, 191(1)
  - financial intermediary corporation, defined, 191(1)
  - information return, 191.4(1)
  - private holding corporation, defined, 191(1)
  - substantial interest, 191(2), (3)
  - tax payable, 191.1(1)
    - election, 191.2
- tax on dividends received by corporation, 187.2
  - information return, 187.5
  - partnerships, 187.4

**Taxable RFI share**
- amalgamation, effect of, 87(4.2)
- defined, 248(1)
- tax on dividend, 187.3(1)

**Taxable supplier**
- defined, 127(9)

**Taxable surplus (of foreign affiliate)**
- adjustment where gain deemed due to negative adjusted cost base, 93(1)(b)(ii)
- deduction for dividend paid out of, 113(1)(b), (c), Reg. 5900(1)(b)
- defined, 113(1)(b)(ii), Reg. 5907(1)

**Taxation year**, *see also* Fiscal period
- becoming or ceasing to be exempt, deemed year-end, 149(10)
- becoming or ceasing to be financial institution, deemed year-end, 142.6(1)
- ceasing to carry on business, 25(1)
- change of control, deemed year-end, 249(4)
- company formed by amalgamation, of, 87(2)(a)
- corporation, of
  - longer than 365 days, 249(3)
- deemed "fiscal period", 14(4)
- defined, 11(2), 104(23)(a), 132.2(1)(b), (o)(ii), 142.6(1), 149(10), 149.1(1), 249, Reg. 1104(2), 1802(5), 3700
  - of non-resident entity, 94.1(1)
- employees profit sharing plan trust, 144(11)
- first, of mortgage investment corporation, 130.1(8)
- fiscal period of business, and, 11(2)
- foreign affiliate, of, 95(1)"taxation year"
- individual, of, 11(2), Reg. 1104(2)
- less than 12 months, *see* Short taxation year
- mutual fund corporation or trust, on rollover, 132.2(1)(b), (o)(ii)
- mutual fund trust, election for December 15, 132.11
- non-resident, of, 250.1(a)
- partnership, of, 96(1)(b)
- reference to, 249(2), (3)
- registered charity, of, 149.1(1)"taxation year"
- short, *see* Short taxation year
- testamentary trust, of, 104(23)

**Taxed capital gains (of investment corporation, mutual fund corporation or mutual fund trust)**
- defined, 130(3)(b), 131(7), 132(5)

**Taxicabs**, Reg. Sch. II:Cl. 16

**Taxing country**
- defined, for foreign tax credit, 126(7)

**Taxpayer**
- absconding, 226
- bankrupt, 128
- becoming Canadian resident, ITAR 26(10)
- ceasing to be resident, *see* Non-resident: becoming
- death of, *see* Death of taxpayer
- defaulting, 226
- defined, 248(1)
  - for tax shelter investments, 143.2(1)
- investigation, under
  - rights of, at inquiry, 231.4(6)
- leaving Canada, demand for amounts owing, 226
- not limited to person liable for tax, 248(1)

**Taxpayer information**
- defined, 241(10)
- provision of
  - authorized, 241(4)
  - prohibition against, 241(1)

**Teacher**
- contribution to teachers' exchange fund, 8(1)(d)
- exemption for travel expenses, 81(3.1)(a)(ii)
- registered pension plan, contribution to, 147.2(5)

# Index

**Teacher** *(cont'd)*
- sabbatical arrangement, Reg. 6801(a)

**Telecommunication spacecraft**
- capital cost allowance, Reg. Sch. II:Cl. 10(f.2), Sch. II:Cl. 30
- - separate classes, Reg. 1101(5a)

**Telecommunications**
- defined, *Interpretation Act* s. 35(1)

**Teleglobe Canada, subject to tax**, 27(2), Reg. 7100

**Telegraph system**
- defined, Reg. 1104(2)

**Telephone and telegraph equipment**
- capital cost allowance, Reg. Sch. II:Cl. 3, Sch. II:Cl. 17

**Telephone and telegraph systems**
- capital cost allowance, Reg. Sch. II:Cl. 17
- defined, Reg. 1104(2)

**Telephone ringing indicator**
- medical expense, Reg. 5700(k)

**Teletypewriter**
- medical expense, Reg. 5700(k)

**Television commercial message**
- capital cost allowance, Reg. Sch. II:Cl. 12(m)
- defined, Reg. 1104(2)

**Television decoder (to visually display vocal portion of signal)**
- medical expense, Reg. 5700(q)

**Temporary access road**, *see* Specified temporary access road

**Temporary capital tax on life insurers**, 190.1(1.1)

**Tenant inducements**
- taxable as income, 12(1)(x)

**Term insurance**
- defined, Reg. 2700(1)

**Term preferred share**
- defined, 248(1)
- dividends on
- - deemed, 84(4.2), 258(2)
- - received by specified financial institution, 112(2.1)
- - - deemed interest on, 258(3)(a)
- reduction of paid-up capital, deemed dividend, 84(4.2)
- share-for-share exchange, 87(4.1)

**Terminal loss**
- deduction for, 20(16)
- - after ceasing to carry on business, 20(16.3)
- limitation re passenger vehicles, 20(16.1)
- limitation where property acquired by affiliated person, 13(21.2)(e)(i)

**Termination of business**, *see* Ceasing to carry on business

**Termination payment**, *see* Retiring allowance

**Territorial sea**
- defined, *Interpretation Act* 35(1)

**Territory**
- defined, *Interpretation Act* 35(1)

**Tertiary recovery equipment**, Reg. 1206(1)

**Testamentary trust**, *see* Trust (or estate): testamentary

**Textbooks, talking**
- medical expense, Reg. 5700(w)

**Therapy**
- medical expense credit
- - general, 118.2(2)(1.9)
- - rehabilitative, for speech or hearing loss, 118.2(2)(l.3)
- non-taxable employment benefit, 6(1)(a)(iv)

**Thermal waste**
- defined, Reg. 1104(13)

**Thin capitalization**
- back-to-back loans, 18(6)
- interest not deductible, 18(4)–(6)
- - exception for manufacturer of aircraft or components, 18(8)

**Things**, *see* Property; Rights or things

**Third party**
- demand, *see* Third party demand
- payment, *see* Third party payment
- penalty for misrepresentation by, 163.2

**Third party demand**
- information, for, 231.2(1)
- payment, for, *see* Garnishment for taxes unpaid

**Third party payment**, *see* Scientific research and experimental development: third party payment

**Threshold amounts**, *see* Dollar amounts in legislation and regulations

**Tiers of partnerships**
- look-through rules, 163(2.8), 233(3), 233.1(5), 233.3(2), 233.4(3), 247(6)

**Tile drainage, deduction**, 30

**Timber limits**
- capital cost allowance, Reg. 1100(1)(e), Reg. Sch. VI
- - separate classes, Reg. 1101(3)
- disposition of by non-resident, 216(5)
- equipment for use in, capital cost allowance, Reg. Sch. II:Cl. 10(n), Sch. II:Cl. 15

**Timber resource property**
- capital cost allowance, Reg. Sch. II:Cl. 33
- constitutes taxable Canadian property for certain purposes, 248(1)"taxable Canadian property"(n)(ii)
- defined, 13(21)
- disposition of
- - by non-resident, 216(5)
- - no capital gain, 39(1)(a)(v)
- - proceeds of disposition, 20(5.1)
- in corporation, share is taxable Canadian property, 115(1)(b)(v)(A)(III) [to be repealed], 248(1)"taxable Canadian property"(e)(i)(C), (ii)(C)
- in partnership, constitutes taxable Canadian property, 115(1)(b)(vii)(C) [to be repealed], 248(1)"taxable Canadian property"(g)(iii)
- non-arm's length transfer, exclusion from rule, 13(7)(e)
- undepreciated capital cost, 13(21)"undepreciated capital cost"G

**Timber royalty**
- paid to non-resident, 212(1)(e)
- - alternative re, 216

**Time**
- deadlines and time limits for taxpayers, *see* Deadlines
- expiring to recover a debt, *see* Statute-barred debt, deemed settled
- extension of, *see* Extension of time
- reassessment, for, *see* Reassessment

2815

## Index

**Tips**
- source withholding, Reg. 100(1)"remuneration"(a.1)
- taxable as employment income, 5(1)

**Titles in legislation**
- relevance of, *Interpretation Act* s. 14

**Tobacco manufacturers' surtax**, 182, 183

**Toilet**
- mechanical aid for getting on and off, medical expense, Reg. 5700(g)

**Tools**
- portable, for rental
- • capital cost allowance, Reg. Sch. II:Cl. 10(b), Sch. II:Cl. 29, Sch. II:Cl. 40
- small, capital cost allowance, Reg. Sch. II:Cl. 12(h)

**Top-up disability payment**
- defined, 6(17)
- not taxable as employee benefit, 6(18)
- reimbursement to employer, 8(1)(n.1)

**Total assets (of financial institution)**
- defined, 181(2), 190(1.1), Reg. 8600

**Total charitable gifts**
- credit for, 118.1(1)"total gifts"(a), 118.1(3)
- defined, 118.1(1)

**Total Crown gifts**
- credit for, 118.1(1)"total gifts"(b), 118.1(3)
- defined, 118.1(1)

**Total cultural gifts**
- credit for, 118.1(1)"total gifts"(c), 118.1(3)
- defined, 118.1(1)

**"Total depreciation" defined**, 13(21)

**Total ecological gifts**
- credit for, 118.1(1)"total gifts"(d), 118.1(3)
- defined, 118.1(1)

**Total pension adjustment reversal**, *see also* Pension adjustment reversal
- defined, 248(1), Reg. 8304.1

**Total premiums**
- defined, Reg. 8600

**Total remuneration**
- defined, for a taxation year, Reg. 100(1)

**Total reserve liabilities (of financial institution)**
- defined, 181(2), 190(1.1), Reg. 8600

**Total return (from fixed payment obligation)**
- defined, Reg. 9100

**Totally and permanently disabled**
- defined, Reg. 8500(1)

**Townsite costs**
- capital cost allowance, Reg. 1102(18) [repealed], Reg. Sch. II:Cl. 10(l)
- deemed capital cost, 13(7.5)(a), Reg. 1102(14.2)

**Tracked interest rules**, 94.1(9)

**Tracked property**
- defined, 94.2(9)(d)

**Tractor**
- capital cost allowance, Reg. Sch. II:Cl. 10(a), Sch. II:Cl. 16(g)

**Trade, adventure in**, *see* Adventure in the nature of trade

**Trade, board of**, *see* Board of trade

**Trade-in**
- allocation of consideration, 13(33)

**Trade mark, representation expenses**, 13(12), 20(1)(cc), 20(9)

**Trade union**, *see* Union

**Trader**, *see* Dealer (or trader)

**Trader or dealer in securities**
- defined
- • for scientific research tax credits, Reg. 226(1)
- • for security transactions, Reg. 230(1)
- • for share purchase tax credits, Reg. 227(1)

**Trailers**
- capital cost allowance, Reg. Sch. II:Cl. 10(e)
- • rail suspension device for, Reg. Sch. II:Cl. 35(b)

**Train**, *see* Railway

**Training courses**
- to care for infirm person, medical expense, 118.2(2)(1.8)

**Tramway or trolley bus system**
- capital cost allowance, Reg. Sch. II:Cl. 4
- defined, Reg. 1104(2)

**Transaction**
- defined
- • general anti-avoidance rule, 245(1)
- • information return re non-resident transactions, 233.1(1)
- • transfer pricing rules, 247(1)

**Transactions**
- series of, defined, 248(10)
- with non-resident
- • extended reassessment period, 152(4)(b)(iii)
- • reporting requirement, 233.1

**Transfer of business**, *see* Sale: business

**Transfer of forgiven amount (debt forgiveness rules)**, 80.04

**Transfer of instalment payments**, 221.2

**Transfer of losses**, *see also* Suspension of losses
- deemed proceeds of disposition, 69(11)

**Transfer of property**, *see also* Rollover
- affiliated person, to, *see* Affiliated person
- attribution rules, *see* Attribution rules
- child, to
- • gain or loss deemed to be transferor's, 75.1
- controlled corporation, to
- • capital loss denied, 40(3.3), (3.4)
- corporation, to
- • by partnership, 85(2)
- • • partnership wound up, 85(3)
- • by shareholder, 85(1)
- • • eligible property, 85(1.1)
- • • to reduce income, 74.4(2)
- • • outstanding amount, 74.4(3)
- • where benefit not granted to designated person, 74.4(4)
- deferred profit sharing plan
- • from, 147(19)
- family farm corporation or partnership, 70(9.2)
- • inter vivos, 73(4)
- • spouse trust, from, to children, 70(9.3)
- farm property, of, 73(3)
- • to child, on death, 70(9)
- • to parents, on death of child, 70(9.6)
- inter vivos, to spouse or trust, 73
- • prescribed provincial laws, Reg. Part LXV

## Index

Transfer of property *(cont'd)*
- minor, to, 74.1(2), 74.5(1), (6)–(11), 75(1) [repealed]
- • repayment of, 74.1(3)
- partnership, to, 97
- registered education savings plans, between, 146.1(2)(g.2), (i.2), 146.1(6.1)
- registered pension plan, between benefit provisions, 147.3(14.1)
- registered pension plan, from, 147.3
- registered pension plan to annuity contract, 147.4
- registered retirement income fund, from, 146.3(14)
- registered retirement savings plan, *see* Registered retirement savings plan: transfers
- retirement compensation arrangement, to second RCA, 207.6(7)
- spouse, to, 74.1(1), 74.5
- • death of taxpayer, on, 70(6)
- • deemed proceeds of disposition, 73
- • gain or loss, 74.2
- • repayment of, 74.1(3)
- transfers between, 104(5.8), 248(1)"disposition"(e), (f), 248(25.1)
- trust, by
- • to another trust, 104(5.8), 248(1)"disposition"(e), (f), 248(25.1)
- trust, to, 74.3, 74.5(9), (10), 75(3)
- • death of taxpayer, on, 70(6)
- • from another trust, 104(5.8), 248(1)"disposition"(e), (f), 248(25.1)
- • income imputed to transferor, 75(2)
- unregistered pension plan, from, 60(j), 147.1(3)(a)

**Transfer payments**
- tax, to provinces, 154

**Transfer price**
- defined, 247(1)

**Transfer pricing (re non-residents)**
- advance pricing agreements, Canada–U.S. Tax Convention Art. XXVI
- anti-avoidance rules, 247, Canada–U.S. Tax Convention Art. IX
- *bona fides* test, 247(2)(b)(ii)
- CCRA discretion to apply, 247(10)
- capital adjustment, *see* Transfer pricing capital adjustment
- capital setoff adjustment, *see* Transfer pricing capital setoff adjustment
- contemporaneous documentation, 247(4)
- income adjustment, *see* Transfer pricing income adjustment
- income setoff adjustment, *see* Transfer pricing income setoff adjustment
- loan to subsidiary excluded, 247(7)
- penalty, 247(3), (11)
- royalties, Canada–U.S. Tax Convention Art. XII:7
- rules based on OECD guidelines effective 1998, 247

**Transfer pricing capital adjustment**
- defined, 247(1)
- penalty, 247(3)(a)(i)(B)

**Transfer pricing capital setoff adjustment**
- defined, 247(1)
- reduces transfer pricing penalty, 247(3)(a)(iii)

**Transfer pricing income adjustment**
- defined, 247(1)
- penalty, 247(3)(a)(i)(B)

**Transfer pricing income setoff adjustment**
- defined, 247(1)
- reduces transfer pricing penalty, 247(3)(a)(iii)

**Transfer time**
- defined, 132.2(2)"qualifying exchange"

**Transferee corporation**
- defined, 55(1)"distribution", 55(3.2)(h)

**Transferor trust**
- defined, 107.4(2)

**Transition amount (re specified debt obligation)**
- application on disposition of specified debt obligation, 142.4(6)(c)C(i), 142.4(7)A
- defined, 142.4(1), Reg. 9201

**Transition deduction**
- insurer
- • defined, Reg. 8101(1)
- mark-to-market property
- • defined, Reg. 8103(1)

**Transition loss (mark-to-market property)**
- defined, Reg. 8105(1)

**Transitional assistance under Canada–U.S. auto pact, income,** 56(1)(a)(v)

**Transitional rules,** *see also* Grandfathering
- 1972 reform, ITAR 7–68
- mark-to-market properties, 112(5.6), 142.2(5), 142.5(4)–(9)
- R.S.C. 1985 (5th Supp.), ITAR 69–79
- specified debt obligations, 142.6(4)

**Transmission equipment**
- defined (re energy conservation CCA), Reg. 1104(13)

**Transplants, organ or bone marrow**
- medical expense, 118.2(2)(l.1)

**Transport employee**
- away-from-home expenses, deduction, 8(1)(g)

**Transportation,** *see also* International shipping
- delivered after the end of the year, reserve, 20(6)
- passengers or property, Canada–U.S. Tax Convention Art. VIII:3, 4

**Transportation equipment, qualified**
- defined, 127(9)
- prescribed, Reg. 4601

**Transportation expenses**
- allowance for, not income, 6(6)(b)
- as medical expenses, 118.2(2)(g)
- • deemed payment of, 118.2(4)

**Transportation losses,** *see* Fuel tax rebate

**Travelling expenses**
- allowance for, when not income, 6(1)(b)
- employee's, deduction for, 8(1)(h), (h.1)
- • certificate of employer, 8(10)
- • limitation, 8(4)
- food and entertainment on train, plane or bus, 67.1(4)(a)
- medical expense, as, 118.2(2)(h)
- northern Canada, residents of, 110.7(1)
- part-time employee's, excluded from income, 81(3.1)
- salesperson's, deduction for, 8(1)(f)
- • certificate of employer, 8(10)
- • limitation, 8(4)
- transport employee's, 8(1)(g)

**Treasurer,** *see* Officer: corporation, of

# Index

**Treasury bill**
- yield at maturity treated as interest, 16(3)

**Treasury Board**
- defined, 248(1)

**Treaty**, see Tax treaty

**Treaty co-production (re Canadian film/video credit)**
- defined, Reg. 1106(1)

**Treaty-protected business**
- defined, 248(1)
- losses, not usable against Canadian profits, 111(9)

**Treaty-protected property**
- cannot absorb forgiven amount, 80(1)"excluded property"
- defined, 248(1)
- losses, not usable against Canadian gains, 111(9), 115(1)(b.1)
- replacement property, 13(4.1)(d), 44(5)(d)

**Treaty shopping**, Canada–U.S. Tax Convention Art. XXIX A

**Trestle**
- capital cost allowance, Reg. 1100(1)(zb), Reg. Sch. II:Cl. 3
- separate classes, Reg. 1101(5f)

**Triangular amalgamation**, 87(9)

**Triangular foreign merger**, 87(8), (8.1)

**Trolley bus system**, Reg. Sch. II:Cl. 4

**Truck**
- capital cost allowance, Reg. Sch. II:Cl. 10(a), Sch. II:Cl. 16(g)

**Truck driver**
- away-from-home expenses, deduction, 8(1)(g)

**Truck operators**
- income from cross-border trucking, Canada–U.S. Tax Convention Art. VIII:4
- income of, earned in a province, Reg. 2604
- income of corporation in a province, Reg. 409

**Truss, as medical expense**, 118.2(2)(i)

**Trust (or estate)**, 104–108
- 21-year deemed disposition rule, 104(4), (5), (5.3)–(5.8)
- - payment of tax in instalments, 159(6.1)
- accumulating income of
- - deduction for amounts included in preferred beneficiary's income, 104(12)
- - defined, 108(1)
- - election to include in preferred beneficiary's income, 104(14), Reg. 2800
- additional units issued in payment, 107(2.11)
- agent not included, 104(1)
- allocation of capital and income to different beneficiaries, 104(7.1), (7.2)
- *alter ego, see* Alter ego trust
- amateur athlete, for, *see* Amateur athlete trust
- amount deemed not paid to beneficiary, 104(13.1), (13.2)
- amount deemed payable to beneficiaries, 104(29)
- amount payable in taxation year, 104(24)
- annuity contract, interest in, 12.2
- balance-due day of, 248(1)"balance-due day"(a)
- bare, *see* Bare trust
- "beneficially interested" in, meaning of, 248(25)
- beneficiary of, *see* Beneficiary: trust
- benefits from, income, 12(1)(m), 105
- business investment loss, deduction from, 39(10)
- capital cost allowance, determination or designation of, 104(16) [repealed]
- capital gains of
- - allocated to beneficiary, 104(21)–(21.2)
- - net taxable, 104(21.3)
- capital interest in
- - acquisition of
- - - reduction of loss on property disposed of, 107(6)
- - additions to, 53(1)(d.1)
- - adjusted cost base, 94(5) [to be repealed]
- - - computation of, 53(1)(d.1)
- - - deductions from, 53(2)(b.1), 53(2)(h)
- - cost amount of, 108(1)
- - cost of, 107(1.1)
- - defined, 108(1), 248(1)
- - disposition of, 107(1)
- - disposition of, on distribution by trust, 248(1)"disposition"(d), (h)
- - distribution in satisfaction of, 107(2)–(5), ITAR 36
- - effect of payment out of trust's income or gains, 43(3)
- - fair market value of, 107.4(4)
- - partial disposition of, 43
- - rollover to another trust, 107.4(3)(j)
- commercial, *see* personal (*below*); Unit trust
- created by will of taxpayer, meaning of, 248(9.1)
- cumulative Canadian exploration expense
- - reduced by investment tax credit, 127(12.3)
- customer/client compensation, for, exempt, 149(1)(w)
- death benefits, flow-through to beneficiary, 104(28)
- deduction in computing income, 104(6), 108(5)
- deemed disposition of property, 104(4)
- - deemed proceeds and cost, 104(5)
- deferred income plans, 207.1
- - foreign property acquisition, ITAR 65
- - tax re foreign property, 205
- - tax re property held by, 207.1
- - - return, and payment of tax, 207.2
- deferred profit sharing plan, under, 147(7)
- - exempt, 149(1)(s)
- - tax re foreign property, 205–207
- defined
- - for registered education plans, 146.1(1)
- - for specific trust rules, 108(1)
- - generally, 104(1), 248(1)
- - in Quebec, 248(3)
- definitions, 108
- designated beneficiary, defined, 210
- designated contributor, defined, 104(5.6), (5.7)(c)
- designated income, tax on, 210–210.3
- - deemed paid by beneficiary, 210.2(3)
- - designated income, defined, 210.2(2)
- - designations re partnerships, 210.2(4)
- - returns, 210.2(5)
- - tax payable, 210.2(1)
- - trustee's liability, 210.2(6)
- - trusts excepted, 210.1
- - where no designated beneficiaries, 210.3
- designation of foreign income to beneficiaries, 104(22)–(22.4)
- disposition of interest in, 106, 107
- disposition of property to, capital loss nil, 40(2)(g)(iv)

# Index

Trust (or estate) *(cont'd)*
- distribution of property by, in satisfaction of capital interest, 107(2)–(5)
  - - before death, anti-avoidance rule, 104(4)(a.2)
  - - election not to distribute gains, 107(2.11)
  - - in settlement of debt, 107(4)
  - - no capital loss on beneficiary's capital interest, 43(3)
  - - non-resident beneficiary, to, 107(5)
  - - - instalment obligation not increased, 107(5.1)
  - - - security to postpone payment of tax, 220(4.6)–(4.63)
- dividend received by, allocation to beneficiary, 104(19), (20)
- division of property among other trusts, 107.4(2)
- election by, *see* Election(s): trust
- eligible capital property, distribution to beneficiary, 107(2)(f)
- eligible taxable capital gains, defined, 108(1)
- employee, *see* Employee trust
- employees' charity
  - - receipts, Reg. 3502
- employees profit sharing plan, under, 144(2)
  - - exempt, 149(1)(p)
- environmental, *see* Qualifying environmental trust
- excluded property of, defined, 108(1)"eligible real property gain"
- exclusions for purposes of certain sections, 108(1)"trust"
- exempt beneficiary, defined, 104(5.4)
- financial institution, 142.2(1)"financial institution"(b)
- foreign, *see* non-resident (*below*)
- foreign immigration, five-year exemption, 94(1)(b)(i)(A)(III) [to be repealed], 94(1)"connected contributor"(a) [proposed]
- foreign property holdings, tax on
  - - exemption for certain master trusts, 206(2.1)
- foreign tax credit for beneficiaries, 104(22)–(22.4)
- foreign tax credit re former resident, 126(2.22)
- Hepatitis C, income of not taxable, 81(1)(g.3)
- immigration, five-year non-taxability, 94(1)(b)(i)(A)(III) [to be repealed]
- income interest in
  - - cost of, 106(1.1)
  - - - deduction for, 106(1)
  - - defined, 108(1)
  - - disposition of, 106(2)
  - - - proceeds, 106(3)
  - - personal trust, in, 108(1)"income interest"
- "income" of, 108(3)
- income of beneficiaries, 108(5)
- income paid to non-resident, 212(1)(c), 212(11)
  - - exemption, 212(9), (10)
- income payable to beneficiary, deduction for, 104(6)
  - - non-resident beneficiary, 104(7)
- information return, Reg. 204
- inter vivos
  - - deemed creation, re non-profit association, 149(5)
  - - defined, 108(1)
  - - personal tax credits not available, 122(1.1)
  - - tax payable by, 122
- interest in, *see also* "beneficially interested" in (*above*)
  - - adjusted cost base
  - - - additions to, 53(1)(d.1), (d.2), (l)

- - - deductions from, 53(2)(b.1), (h), (i), (j), (q)
- - - recomputation of, 53(4)–(6)
- interest income of, 12(3)
- investment tax credit, designation of, 127(7)
- joint partner, *see* Joint partner trust
- life insurance policy, interest in, 12.2
- loss property held by
  - - reduction of loss on disposition by person acquiring capital interest, 107(6)
- maintenance expenses, 105(2)
- master, exempt from tax, 149(1)(o.4)
- mine reclamation, *see* Qualifying environmental trust
- minor, for, 104(18)
  - - transfer of property to, 74.3, 74.5(9), (10)
- multiple
  - - basic exemption re minimum tax, 127.53(2), (3)
  - - grouped together as one trust, 104(2)
- mutual fund, *see* Mutual fund trust
- non-discretionary, defined, 17(15)
- non-resident, 94(1)"connected contributor"(a) [proposed]
  - - capital interest in cost base, deductions from, 53(2)(i)
  - - deduction from foreign accrual property income, 94(4) [to be repealed]
  - - deduction in computing taxable income, 94(3) [to be repealed]
  - - deemed resident in Canada, 94(3)(a) [proposed]
  - - deemed to be non-resident corporation, where, 94(1)(d) [to be repealed]
  - - discretionary, 94(1)(c) [to be repealed]
  - - distribution from, disclosure, 233.5
  - - financial assistance to, 94(6) [to be repealed]
  - - information return, 233.2, 233.5
  - - reporting requirements, 233.2, 233.5
  - - rights and obligations of beneficiaries, 94(2) [to be repealed]
  - - rules, 94 [to be repealed]
  - - transfer of property to
  - - - constitutes disposition, 248(1)"disposition"(e)(iii), 248(25.1)
  - - - disclosure, 233.2
- non-resident beneficiaries, 104(7)
- non-residents, for
  - - deduction for dividend from non-resident-owned investment corporation, 104(10), (11)
  - - payments to, 212(1)(c)
- non-taxable dividends received by, designation re, 104(20)
- option to acquire units in, 49(1)(c)
- payment of duties and taxes, non-disqualification, 108(4)
- pension benefits, flow-through of, 104(27)
- pension fund or plan
  - - exemption, 149(1)(o)
- personal
  - - allocation of capital and income to different beneficiaries, 104(7.1)
  - - capital interest in, defined, 108(1)"capital interest"(a)
  - - disposition of capital interest in, 107(1)(a)
  - - distribution of property to beneficiary, 107(2), (4.1)
  - - income interest in, defined, 108(1)
- personal-use property of, 46(4)
- pooled fund, *see* Pooled fund trust
- post-1971 partner, *see* Post-1971 partner trust

Trust (or estate) *(cont'd)*
- preferred beneficiary
  - defined, 108(1)
  - income of, 104(14), (15)
- prescribed, Reg. 4800.1
  - capital interest in, defined, 108(1)"capital interest"(a)
  - distribution of property to beneficiary, 107(2), (4.1)
  - flow-through entity for capital gains exemption, 39.1(1)
- principal residence
  - disposed of to taxpayer, 40(7)
  - distribution by spouse trust, 107(2.01)
- property transferred to
  - income imputed to transferor, 75(2)
  - income not imputed to transferor, 75(3)
- proportional holdings in property of, 259
- purchase of shares of corporation, for, loan to, 15(2.5)
- "qualified" defined, 259(3)
- qualified investments, *see* Qualified investment
- qualifying disposition, rollover, 107.4
- qualifying environmental, *see* Qualifying environmental trust
- reference to trustee, executor etc., 104(1)
- registered education savings plan, under, 146.1(1)"trust" 146.1(5)
  - deemed inter vivos, 146.1(11)
  - exempt, 149(1)(u)
- registered investment, 204.4–204.7
- registered pension plan, tax re foreign property, 205–207
- registered retirement income fund, exempt, 149(1)(x)
- registered retirement savings plan, under, 146(4)
  - exempt, 149(1)(r)
  - tax re foreign property, 205–207
- registered supplementary unemployment benefit plan, exempt, 149(1)(q)
- related segregated fund, Reg. 6100
- residence of, deemed, 250(6.1)
- resource property
  - rules, 104(5.2)
- retirement compensation arrangement, *see* Retirement compensation arrangement
- return to be filed, 150(1)(c)
- right of use or habitation (Quebec) deemed to be, 248(3)
- rollover of property on transfer to other trust, 107.4
- rollover to another trust, 248(1)"disposition"(e), (f)
- scientific research tax credit, 127.3(3)
- segregated fund, Reg. 6100
- self, for, *see* Alter ego trust
- settlor, defined, 108(1)
- small business investment, Reg. 5103
- spouse, for, 70(6)(a), 73(1)(c) [to be repealed], 73(1.01)(c), 104(4)(a), *see also* Joint partner trust; Post-1971 partner trust
  - deduction from taxable income of, 110.6(12)
  - deemed disposition, 104(4)
  - distribution by, in satisfaction of capital interest, 107(4)
  - double taxation relief, Canada–U.S. Tax Convention Art. XXVI:3(g)
  - family farm corporation transferred from, to children, 70(9.3)
  - farm property transferred from, to children, 70(9.1)
  - how created, 70(6.1)
  - indefeasible vesting of property in, 70(6)
  - not disqualified by certain payments, 108(4)
  - principal residence
    - disposed of to, 40(4)
    - distribution by, 107(2.01)
    - property of, 40(5)
  - property transferred to, inter vivos, 73(1)
    - capital cost, and deemed allowance, 73(2)
  - reserves allowed to, for year of taxpayer's death, 72(2)
  - special rules applicable, 70(7), (8)
  - together with self, *see* Alter ego trust
  - transfer of property to, 74.3, 74.5(9), (10)
  - transfer or distribution to, on death of taxpayer, 70(6)
  - value of property acquired, 70(6), 73
- status of, Reg. Part XLVIII
- substitution (Quebec) deemed to be, 248(3)
- supplementary unemployment benefit plan, under, 145(2)
- tax paid under Part XII.2
  - credit for, included in beneficiary's income, 104(31)
  - deduction for, 104(30)
- tax re property held by, 207.1
- taxable dividends received by
  - designation re, 104(19)
  - payable to non-resident beneficiary, 82(1)(a)(i.1)
- taxed as individual, 104(2)
- testamentary, 108(1)
  - deferred profit sharing plan benefits received by, 104(27.1)
  - instalments, 104(23)(e)
  - rules applicable, 104(23), (28)
  - superannuation or pension benefits received by, 104(27)
  - taxation year of, 104(23)(a), (b)
- transfers between, 104(5.8), 248(1)"disposition"(e), (f), 248(25.2)
- transfers to, for minor or spouse, 74.5(9), (10)
- trustee of, *see* Trustee
- unit, *see* Unit trust
- usufruct (Quebec) deemed to be, 248(3)
- vacation pay, exempt, 149(1)(y)
- voting, Reg. 4800.1(c)
- where deemed not at arm's length, 206(4)
- windup of, deemed resident, 250(6.1)

**Trust and loan corporations**
- taxable income earned in a province, Reg. 405

**Trust company**, *see also* Financial institution
- defined, for FAPI purposes, 95(1)

**Trust-purpose income**
- defined, 104(29)(c)

**Trustee**, *see also* Legal representative; Trust (or estate)
- deemed to be legal representative, 248(1)"legal representative"
- in bankruptcy, *see* Bankruptcy: trustee in
- information return, Reg. 204
- liable for Part X tax, 198(3)
- liable for Part XII.2 tax, 210.2(6)
- obligations of, 159
- public, disposition of Canadian securities, 39(5)(c)
- return required of, 150(3)
  - penalty for failure to file, 162(3)

## Index

**Trustee** *(cont'd)*
- school board, expense allowance exempt, 81(3)
- shares held by, for employee, 7(2)
- shares purchased by, for employees of corporation, 7(6)
- withholding tax, liability for, 153(1.3), (1.4), 227(5), (5.1)(a)

**Tuition fees**
- credit for, 118.5
- • ancillary fees, 118.5(3)
- • commuter's, 118.5(1)(c)
- • deemed residents, 118.5(2)
- • in Canada, 118.5(1)(a)
- • outside Canada, 118.5(1)(b)
- • unused
- • • transfer to spouse, 118.8
- • • transfer to supporting person, 118.9

**Tunnel, capital cost allowance**, Reg. Sch. II:Cl. 1(j)

**Tutoring service**
- medical expense credit, 118.2(2)(l.91)

**Twenty-one years**
- deemed realization of trust gains, 104(4), (5), (5.3)–(5.8)

**Two-year rolling start rule, when property available for use**, 13(27)(b), 13(28)(c), 13(29)

## U

**UCC**, *see* Undepreciated capital cost
**UI**, *see* Unemployment insurance
**U.S.**, *see* United States
**Uncle**, *see also* Niece/nephew
- defined, 252(2)(e)
- dependent, 118(6)(b)
- great-uncle defined, 252(2)(f)

**Undepreciated capital cost**, *see also* Capital cost; Depreciable property
- defined, 13(21)
- exceeding fair market value at time of transfer, 13(21.2), 20(16)
- reduction on debt forgiveness, 80(5)(b)
- transferred property, 13(5)

**Underlying foreign tax (of foreign affiliate)**
- defined, Reg. 5907(1)

**Underlying foreign tax applicable (of foreign affiliate)**
- defined, Reg. 5907(1)

**Underpayment amount**
- defined, for corporate interest offset, 161.1(1)

**Undertaking**
- meaning of, when investing in limited partnership, 253.1(a)

**Undertaking future obligations**
- deduction for, 20(24)

**Undivided interest**
- in property transferred by tax debtor, fair market value, 160(3.1)

**Undue hardship**
- reduction in security to be posted on emigration, 220(4.7), (4.71)
- reduction in source withholdings, 153(1.1)

**Unearned commissions, reserve for**, 32

**Unemployment insurance**, *see* Employment insurance

**Unenforceable debt**, *see* Statute-barred debt, deemed settled

**Ungulates, grazing**, 80.3(1)"breeding animals"

**Uniforms, capital cost allowance**, Reg. Sch. II:Cl. 12(i)

**Unincorporated association or organization**, *see* Non-profit organization

**Union**
- election by, re foreign pension plan, Reg. 6804(3)
- exemption, 149(1)(k)
- locals and branches deemed to be one employer for pension purposes, 252.1
- membership dues
- • deduction for, 8(1)(i)(iv), (v)
- • where not deductible, 8(5)
- strike pay taxed or exempt? no legislative reference
- venture capital, *see* Labour-sponsored venture capital corporation (LSVCC)

**Unit**
- mutual fund trust, *see* Mutual fund trust: unit of
- trust, *see* Unit trust

**Unit trust**, *see also* Mutual fund trust
- adjusted cost base of unit, 53(1)(d.1), 53(2)(h), (j)
- annuity contract, interest in, 12.2
- "block of units" defined, Reg. 4803(1)
- defined, 108(2), 248(1)
- excluded from various trust rules, 108(1)"trust"(f)
- expenses of issuing or selling, 20(1)(e)
- life insurance policy, interest in, 12.2
- non-resident
- • adjusted cost base of unit, 53(2)(j)
- right to receive from, cost of, 52(6)

**United Kingdom**, *see also* Foreign government
- defined, *Interpretation Act* 35(1)
- stock exchange recognized, Reg. 3201(n)
- Tax Convention, *see* Table of Contents
- universities, gifts to, Reg. Sch. VIII s. 2
- war pension exempt, 81(1)(e)

**United Mexican States**, *see* Mexico

**United Nations and its agencies**
- agency of, excluded from non-resident trust rules, 94(1)"exempt foreign trust"(c)(i) [proposed]
- employment income from
- • deduction, 110(1)(f)(iii)
- gifts to
- • by corporation, 110.1(1)(a)(v)
- • by individual, 118.1(1)"total charitable gifts"(e)

**United States**, *see also* Foreign government; Non-resident
- artiste or athlete, Canada–U.S. Tax Convention Art. XVI
- collection of Canadian tax by IRS, Canada–U.S. Tax Convention Art. XXVI A
- commuter to, *see* Commuter to United States
- corporate spin-off, *see* Foreign spin-off
- defined, 19(5), *Interpretation Act* s. 35(1)
- • for treaty purposes, Canada–U.S. Tax Convention Art. III:1(b)
- dividends, Canada–U.S. Tax Convention Art. X
- donations to charities in, Canada–U.S. Tax Convention Art. XXI:6; 118.1(9)
- estate taxes, Canada–U.S. Tax Convention Art. XXIX B
- franchise payment to resident of, Canada–U.S. Tax Convention Art. XII:3(c)

## Index

United States *(cont'd)*
- gambling losses in, Canada–U.S. Tax Convention Art. XXII:3
- government, employees of, Canada–U.S. Tax Convention Art. XIX, XXVIII
- green card holder, Canada–U.S. Tax Convention Art. IV:1
- income from source in, received for non-resident
  - information return, Reg. 203
- Individual Retirement Account, *see* Foreign retirement arrangement
- interest, Canada–U.S. Tax Convention Art. X
- Internal Revenue Service, *see* Internal Revenue Service (U.S.)
- limitation on treaty benefits, Canada–U.S. Tax Convention Art. XXIX A
- limited liability company, treated as foreign affiliate, Reg. 5907(11.2)(b)
- Nature Conservancy, prescribed donee, Reg. 3504
- newspaper or periodical printed in, 19(1)(b)
- pensions, Canada–U.S. Tax Convention Art. XVIII
- RRSP deferral, Canada-U.S. Tax Convention Art. XVIII:7
- *Railroad Retirement Act* Tier 1 benefits, Canada–U.S. Tax Convention Art. XVIII:5
- Real Estate Investment Trust, Canada–U.S. Tax Convention Art. X:7(c)
- Real Estate Mortgage Investment Conduit, Canada–U.S. Tax Convention Art. XI:9
- real property interest, Canada–U.S. Tax Convention Art. XVIII:3
- Regulated Investment Company, Canada–U.S. Tax Convention Art. X:7(b)
- royalties paid to resident of, Canada–U.S. Tax Convention Art. XII
- S corporation, Canada–U.S. Tax Convention Art. XXIX:5 (Protocol)
- social security benefits, Canada–U.S. Tax Convention Art. XVIII:5
- social security taxes, Canada–U.S. Tax Convention Art. XXIV:2(a)(ii)
  - credit against Canadian tax, 122.7
- state income tax, 126(5), (7)
- stock exchanges recognized, Reg. 3201(o)
- Tax Convention, *see* Table of Contents
- university, gift to, Reg. 3503; Schedule VIII, Canada–U.S. Tax Convention Art. XXI:6

**Unitized oil or gas field in Canada**
- Canadian oil and gas property expense, 66(12.5)
- exploration and development expenses, 66(12.2), (12.3)

**University**
- fees, *see* Tuition fees
- outside Canada, prescribed, Reg. 3503, Reg. Sch. VIII
  - gifts to deductible, 118.1(1)
- U.S., *see* United States: university

**Unpaid amount**
- general rules, 78
- investment tax credit limitation, 127(26)
- tax shelter investment, 143.2(1)"limited-recourse amount", 143.2(6)

**Unpaid claims reserve**, *see* Insurance corporation: reserve for unpaid claims

**Unrealized proceeds of disposition**, 40(1)(a)(iii)

**Unreasonable amount**
- expense, no deduction for, 67

- paid by non-resident, 247
- paid to non-resident, 247

**Unrecognized loss (re debt forgiveness rules)**
- defined, 80(1)
- use of to limit income inclusion, 80(13)D(a)(i)

**Unrelated group, defined**, 251(4)

**Unused foreign tax credit**, *see* Foreign tax credit: unused

**Unused Part I.3 tax credit**
- defined, 125.3(4)

**Unused Part VI tax credit**
- defined, 125.2(3)

**Unused portion of a beneficiary's exempt capital gains balance**
- defined, 144(1)

**Unused RRSP deduction room**
- defined, 146(1), 248(1)
- effect on excess RRSP contributions, 204.2(1.1)(b)A
- effect on RRSP deduction limit, 146(1)"RRSP deduction limit"A

**Unused surtax credit**
- defined, 125.3(4), 181.1(7), 190.1(6)
- reduces Part I.3 tax, 181.1(4)
- reduces Part VI tax, 190.1(6)

**Unused tuition and education tax credits**
- defined, 118.61(1)

**Use, right of (Quebec)**
- deemed to be trust, 248(3)

**Use of property**, *see* Production or use

**Usufruct (Quebec)**
- deemed to be trust, 248(3)

**Utensils**, *see* Kitchen utensils

**Utilities**
- service connection, deduction, 20(1)(ee)

## V

**V-day**, *see* Valuation day

**Vacant land**
- limitation on deductions, 18(2)–(3.7)

**Vacation pay trust**
- exemption, 149(1)(y)

**Valuation activity**
- defined, for third-party penalty, 163.2(1)

**Valuation costs**
- added to cost base of property, 53(1)(n)

**Valuation day**
- defined, ITAR 24
- fair market value on, election by individual to use, Reg. 4700
- proclamation, ITAR 25
- property held since before,
  - capital property, ITAR 26(3)
  - depreciable property, ITAR 20(1)
- publicly-traded shares and securities on, Reg. Sch. VII

**Valuation of inventory**, *see* Inventory: valuation of

**Value**, *see also* Fair market value
- defined, for insurers regulations, Reg. 2400(1)

**Value-added tax**, *see* Goods and services tax

**Van**
- wheelchair access, medical expense credit, 118.2(2)(l.7)

# Index

**Vancouver**
- international banking centre, 33.1(3)

**Variation of trust, effect of**, 108(6)

**Vatican City**, *see also* Foreign government
- universities, gifts to, Reg. Sch. VIII s. 7

**Vats, capital cost allowance**, Reg. Sch. II:Cl. 8

**Vehicle**, *see also* Automobile; Motor vehicle; Passenger vehicle
- device to permit person with mobility impairment to drive
  - medical expense, Reg. 5700(n)

**Venture capital corporation, prescribed**, *see also* Labour-sponsored venture capital corporation (LSVCC)
- assistance, Reg. Part LXVII
- defined, Reg. 6700
- disposition of shares of
  - capital loss, 40(2)(i)
- exempt from Part IV tax, 186.2
- in definition of Canadian-controlled private corporation, 125(7)
- labour-sponsored, defined, Reg. 6701
- may control private corporation, 89(1)"private corporation"
- prescribed assistance, Reg. 6702
- shares of
  - prescribed assistance, deduction from cost base, 53(2)(k)(i)(C)

**Vertical amalgamation**
- carryback of losses, 87(2.11)
- deemed cost of capital properties, 87(11)(b)
- deemed proceeds from subsidiary's shares, 87(11)(a)

**Vertical (short-form) amalgamation**, *see also* Amalgamation
- carryback of losses, 87(2.11)

**Vessel**
- capital cost allowance, Reg. 1100(1)(v), Reg. Sch. II:Cl. 7
  - separate classes, Reg. 1101(2)–(2b)
- certified
  - capital cost allowance, Reg. 1100(1)(v)
- conversion cost deemed separate class, 13(14), (17)
- defined, 13(21)
- deposit under *Canadian Vessel Construction Assistance Act*
  - disposition of, 13(19), (20)
- disposition of, 13(15)
  - election, 13(16)
- fishing, additional capital cost allowance, Reg. 1100(1)(i)
- quadrennial survey, reserve for, 20(1)(o), Reg. 3600
- reassessment in certain cases, 13(18)
- transfer of, under, *Canadian Vessel Construction Assistance Act*
  - recapture of depreciation, 13(13)

**"Vested indefeasibly"**
- meaning of, 248(9.2)

**Veterans' pensions**
- exempt, 81(1)(d), (e)

**Veterinarian**, *see* Professional practice

**VIA Rail**, *see also* Railway
- subject to tax, 27(2), Reg. 7100

**Vibratory signalling device for the hearing-impaired**
- medical expense credit, Reg. 5700(q.1)

**Victims of crime**
- compensation payments exempt, 81(1)(q), Reg. 6501

**Video games**
- capital cost allowance, Reg. Sch. II:Cl. 16(f)

**Video laser-disk** *(includes DVD)*
- rental, capital cost allowance, Reg. Sch. II:Cl. 12(r)
  - excluded from half-year rule, Reg. 1100(2)(a)(iii)

**Video tapes**
- film or video production services credit, 125.5

**Viscosity**
- hydrocarbons, determination of, Reg. 1107

**Visitor to Canada**
- 183 days, deemed resident, 250(1)(a)

**Visual signalling device for the hearing-impaired**
- medical expense credit, Reg. 5700(q.1)

**Vitamin B12, as medical expense**, 118.2(2)(k)

**Volunteer**
- emergency worker
  - deduction from employment income, 8(1)(a) [to be repealed]
  - exemption from employment income, 81(4)

**Volunteer business exemption**
- charities, 149.1(1)"related business"

**Volunteer firefighter**
- deduction from employment income, 8(1)(a) [to be repealed]
- exemption from employment income, 81(4)

**Voting trust**, Reg. 4800.1(c)
- flow-through entity for capital gains exemption, 39.1(1)

# W

**WIS**, *see* Working Income Supplement

**Wage measure**
- defined, 147.1(1)
- used in calculating "average wage", 147.1(1)

**Wagering losses**, Canada–U.S. Tax Convention Art. XXII:3

**Wages**, *see* Salary

**Wagon, capital cost allowance**, Reg. Sch. II:Cl. 10(d)

**Waiver**
- penalty or interest, of, by Minister, 220(3.1)
- pension plan conditions, by Minister, 147.1(18)(a), (k)
- RESP age requirements, where beneficiary disabled, 146.1(2.2)
- reassessment period, of, by taxpayer, 152(4)(a)(ii), 152(4.1), (5)
- requirement to file form or document, of, by Minister, 220(2.1)
- retention of document or thing seized, by Minister, 231.3(6)
- right to appeal. binding, 169(2.2)
- right to object, binding, 165(1.2), 169(2.2)
- solicitor-client privilege, of, by client, 232(14)
- tax on overcontribution to deferred income plan, by Minister, 204.1(4)
- tax on overcontribution to RESP, 204.91(2)

**Walking aids**
- medical expense, Reg. 5700(i)

**War savings certificate, income exempt**, 81(1)(b)

**War service**
- pension payments for, exempt, 81(1)(d), (e)

# Index

*War Veterans Allowance Act*
- pension under, exempt, 81(1)(d)

**Warehousing of flow-through expenses**, 66(19)

**Warrant**, *see* Option; Search warrant

**Warranty**
- disposition of property subject to, 42
- outlays, pursuant to
- - on amalgamation, 87(2)(n)
- reserve for, not allowed, 20(7)

**Water**
- distribution of, by municipal corporation, exemption, 149(1.2)

**Water distributing equipment**
- capital cost allowance, Reg. Sch. II:Cl. 1(o), Sch. II:Cl. 2(e)

**Water purifier**
- medical expense credit for, Reg. 5700(c.1)

**Water system for mine**
- capital cost allowance, Reg. Sch. II:Cl. 10(l)

**Weak currency debt**
- defined, 20.3(1)
- limit on interest deduction, 20.3(2)

**Wearing apparel for rental**
- capital cost allowance, Reg. Sch. II:Cl. 12(k)

*Webb* **case (1974) overruled**, 64.1

**Weighted Canadian liabilities**
- defined, insurers, Reg. 2400(1)

**Weighted total liabilities**
- defined, insurers, Reg. 2400(1)

*Wel Holdings* **case overruled**, 244(13.1) [repealed]

**Welfare**, *see* Social assistance payment

**Well**
- defined, for qualified CEE, Reg. 4608(1)

*Western Grain Stabilization Act*
- fees paid, deductible, 20(1)(ff)
- payment received under, income, 12(1)(p)

**Wharf, capital cost allowance**, Reg. Sch. II:Cl. 3, Sch. II:Cl. 6
- for mine, Reg. Sch. II:Cl. 10(l)

**Wheelchair**
- medical expense, 118.2(2)(i)
- power-operated lift for, Reg. 5700(m)
- ramp for
- - deduction, 20(1)(qq)
- - medical expense credit, 118.2(2)(l.2)
- van for use with, medical expense credit, 118.2(2)(l.7)

**Whole dividend (of foreign affiliate)**
- defined, Reg. 5907(1)

**Wholly-owned corporation**, *see also* Subsidiary: wholly-owned corporation
- defined, for corporate rollover rules, 85(1.3)

**Wife**, *see* Spouse

**Wig, medical expense**, Reg. 5700(a)

**Will**
- gifts by deemed made in year of death, 118.1(5)
- - publicly traded securities, reduced capital gain, 38(a.1)(ii)
- transfer, release or surrender under, 248(8)
- trust created by, 248(9.1)

**Wind energy conversion system**
- capital cost allowance, Reg. Sch. II:Cl. 34

**Winding-up**, *see also* Ceasing to carry on business
- acquisition of control because of death, 88(1)(d.3)
- appropriation of property on, 69(5), 84(2)
- assets acquired from foreign affiliate on, 80.1(6)
- Canadian corporation, rules, 88(2)
- corporation beneficiary under life insurance policy, 89(2)
- debt, settlement of, 80.01(4), (5)
- debt forgiveness reserve disallowed, 61.4(c)
- distribution on, 84(2), (6)
- farming inventory, 88(1.6)
- financial institution
- - continuing corporation for mark-to-market rules, 88(1)(h)
- - deemed disposition of mark-to-market property, 88(1)(i)
- - into parent financial institution, 88(1)(a.3)
- following debt forgiveness, deemed capital gain, 80.03(3)(a)(i)
- foreign affiliate, 88(3), 95(2)(e), (e.1)
- insurance corporation, Reg. 8101(3)
- leasing properties, 16.1(4)
- net capital losses of subsidiary, 88(1.2)
- 90% or more owned subsidiary, of, 88(1)
- - limited partnership losses, 88(1.1)
- - net capital losses, 88(1.2)
- - non-capital losses, 88(1.1)
- - parent corporation continuation of, 88(1.5)
- non-capital losses, treatment by parent, 111(5.4)
- parent incorporated after subsidiary's year-end
- - computation of income and tax payable, 88(1.3)
- partnership, *see* Partnership: ceasing to exist
- pre-1972 capital surplus on hand, 88(2.1)–(2.3)
- refundable dividend tax on hand, 87(2)(aa), 88(1)(e.2)
- resource expenses, 66.7(6)
- specified debt obligation, treatment of, 88(1)(a.3), Reg. 9204(2)
- subsidiary, of
- - non-capital losses, treatment by parent, 111(5.4)
- - where an insurance corporation, 88(1)(g)
- trust, of
- - deemed resident throughout year, 250(6.1)

**Windmill, capital cost allowance**, Reg. Sch. II:Cl. 3

**Windup**, *see* Winding-up

*Wipf* **case overruled**, 143

**Withholding tax**, 153(1), 212, 227, *see also* Remittance of taxes withheld
- agreement not to withhold, void, 227(12)
- amount of, deemed received by payee, 153(3)
- amounts deemed held in trust, 227(4), (4.1)
- amounts in trust not part of estate, 227(5)
- amounts not remitted, liability to pay, 227(9.4)
- annuity payment or commutation, 153(1)(f)
- assessment for, 227(10), (10.1)
- - definitions, 227(10.8)
- binding on federal and provincial governments, 227(11)
- commissions, 153(1)(g)
- death benefit, 153(1)(d)
- deferred profit sharing plan payment, 153(1)(h)
- directors liable for, 227.1
- dividends received by broker/dealer, 153(4), (5)

# Index

Withholding tax *(cont'd)*
- election for, 153(1)(n), 153(1.1)
  - to increase, 153(1.2), Reg. 109
- employee outside Canada, exemption, Reg. 104(2)
- employees, 153(1)(a)
- employment earnings supplement, 153(1)(s)
- employment insurance benefit, 153(1)(d.1), Reg. 100(1)"remuneration"(g)
- exemptions
  - credits on TD1 exceeding tax, Reg. 104(1)
  - employee outside Canada, Reg. 104(2)
  - Home Buyers' Plan, Reg. 104(3)–(4)
  - Lifelong Learning Plan, Reg. 104.1
- failure to remit amounts withheld, penalty, 227(9)
  - interest payable, 227(9.2)
  - salary or wages, from, 227(9.5)
- failure to withhold, 215(6), 227(8)–(10)
  - interest on amounts, 227(8.3)
  - retirement compensation arrangement, 227(8.2)
  - salary or wages, from, 227(8.5)
- fees and commissions, 153(1)(g)
- government assistance program, prescribed benefit, 153(1)(m)
- Home Buyers' Plan, exemption, Reg. 104(3)–(4)
- income-averaging annuity contract payment, 153(1)(k)
- information return, Reg. 210
- interest on amounts not deducted or withheld, 227(8.3)
- interference with remittances, 227(5.2)–(5.4) (draft)
- labour-sponsored funds share disposition, 211.8(2)
- labour-sponsored funds tax credit, 211.7(2)
- large employers, must remit through financial institution, 153(1), Reg. 110
- liability to pay amount not deducted or withheld, 227(8.4)
- Lifelong Learning Plan, exemption, Reg. 104.1
- no action against withholder, 227(1)
- non-periodic payments, Reg. 103
- non-residents, *see also* Non-resident tax
  - fees for services, Reg. 105
  - insurers, Reg. 800–804
  - interest, dividend and other passive income, 212
  - payments through an agent, 215
- not required, where, Reg. 104, 104.1
- Old Age Security benefits, 180.2(3), (4)
- partnership, 212(13.1), 227(15)
- patronage dividends, from, 135(3)
- payroll, 153(1)(a)
- penalty, 227(8)
- pension benefit, 153(1)(b)
- reduction of, Reg. 809
- refund of, 227(6), (7)
- registered education savings plan, 153(1)(t), Reg. 103(6)(g), 103(8)
- registered retirement income fund payment, 153(1)(l), Reg. 103(4), 103(6)(d.1)
- registered retirement savings plan payment, 153(1)(j)
- regulations, Reg. Part I
- remittance deadlines, source deductions, Reg. 108
- remittances to Receiver General, 153(1), Reg. 108
- retirement compensation arrangement contribution, 153(1)(p)
- retirement compensation arrangement distribution, 153(1)(q)
- retirement compensation arrangement purchase price, 153(1)(r)
- retiring allowance, 153(1)(c)
- return required of employee, 227(2)
- salary, 153(1)(a)
- severance pay, 153(1)(c)
- stock option benefit deferred, 7(15)
- superannuation benefit, 153(1)(b)
- supplementary unemployment plan benefit, 153(1)(e)
- termination pay, 153(1)(c)
- trustee etc., liability for, 153(1.3) [repealed], (1.4) [repealed], 227(5), (5.1)
- unclaimed dividends etc., 153(4), (5)
- undue hardship, 153(1.1)
- unemployment insurance benefit, 153(1)(d.1), Reg. 100(1)"remuneration"(g)
- U.S. resident, re personal services, Canada–U.S. Tax Convention Art. XVII
- wages, 153(1)(a)

**Witness**
- rights of at inquiry, 231.4(5)

**Wood waste**
- defined, Reg. 1104(13)

**Woods assets, capital cost allowance**, Reg. 1100(1)(f), Reg. Sch. IV

**Work in progress of professional business**
- deemed to be inventory, 10(5)(a)
- election to exclude from income, 34
- valuation of, 10(4)(a)

**Work space in home**
- limitation on deductibility
  - from business income, 18(12)
  - from employment income, 8(13)

**Worker Adjustment Programs**, *see* Older Worker Adjustment, Program for; Plant Workers Adjustment Program

**Workers' compensation payment**
- deduction in computing taxable income, 110(1)(f)(ii)
- disclosure of taxpayer information by CCRA, 241(4)(n)
- inclusion in income, 56(1)(v)
- information return, Reg. 232

**Working Income Supplement**, 122.61(1)A(c)C

**Working Ventures Fund**, *see* Labour-sponsored funds tax credit

**Workplace Safety and Insurance Board**, *see* Workers' compensation payment

**Writing**
- defined, *Interpretation Act* 35(1)

**Wrongful dismissal award**, *see* Retiring allowance

## X, Y, Z

**X-rays**
- cost of, as medical expense, 118.2(2)(o)

**Y2K**, *see* Year 2000 computer hardware and software

**YMPE**, *see* Year's Maximum Pensionable Earnings

**Yacht**
- expense of, not deductible, 18(1)(l)(i)
- limitation on CCA claim where rented out, Reg. 1100(15)–(20)

**Year**, *see* Calendar year; Taxation year

**Year 2000 computer hardware and software**
- accelerated CCA, Reg. 1100(1)(zg), (zh)

**Year-end**
- deemed, where control changes, 249(4)

## Index

**Year's Maximum Pensionable Earnings**
- base for SR&ED proxy amount re salaries, Reg. 2900(7)
- defined, Reg. 8500(1)

**Yukon Territory,** *see also* Northern Canada
- additional $0.04 reasonable kilometrage allowance, Reg. 7306(a)(iii)
- tax rates, *see* introductory pages

**Zero, minimum amount for formula calculations,** 257

**Zone**
- economic, *see* Exclusive economic zone
- prescribed, *see* Northern Canada
- tax-free, ITAR 26(3)

---

Protection of minority shareholders

Appraisal remedy – can elect to have shares bought at *fair* price

- limited to the following scenarios:
  1. changing any restriction on issue, transfer or ownership of shares
  2. Δ the nature of how business is carried on
  3. amalgamating or merging
  4. selling, leasing or xfring all or subst. all of the assets

Derivative action
- permits a S/H to obtain leave from court to bring an action in the name of and on behalf of the corp<u>n</u>
- must show he is acting in good faith
- must show directors refuse to bring the action themselves
- in the best interest of the corp<u>n</u> or S/H's that action is commenced

Rescuing a "locked in" shareholder
→ wind-up (may serve more as a threat)

Sec 241  ★ Oppression remedy – a statutory procedure allowing S/H's to seek a personal remedy thru the court system if they have been treated unfairly – provides greater flexibility because court can do whatever is just and appropriate under the circumstances

but must meet the meaning of oppressive → question of fact

Examples:
- restrain conduct complained of
- appoint receiver-manager
- amend articles
- order the purchase of shares
- replace directors
- set aside a contract

★ Remedy must rectify the conduct complained of and remedies must protect the interests of the complainant as security holder only

# Directors Liability checklist

1) To Corp[n]
   - damages for loss suffered by corp[n] as a result of breach
   - improper redemption of shares or pymt of dividend
   - reeission of a contract in which director has undisclosed int.
   - constructive trust of property acquired under director's mandate
   - adg for π's improperly obtained by a director
   - injunction to restrain breach of duty

2) To others
   - to employees for unpaid wages
   - liability for unpaid taxes
   - compensation to people suffering direct loss as a result of insider trading

3) Insider trading + other stat. offenses — Criminal liability

# Maintenant
## deux éditions par année

# La Loi du praticien – Loi de l'impôt sur le revenu :

## La seule édition à jour au 1$^{er}$ février 2001

*LA LOI DU PRATICIEN LOI DE L'IMPÔT SUR LE REVENU*
**David SHERMAN**
Loi annotée, incluant les notes de David Sherman
N° de commande
9267825-138
**79 $**
Couverture souple
env. 3000 pages
0-459-26782-5

Vous n'aurez plus à travailler avec une multitude de projets de loi sur votre bureau pendant la prochaine saison d'impôt. La Loi du praticien – Loi de l'impôt sur le revenu, 3$^e$ édition, intègre les dernières modifications législatives, notamment :

- les propositions législatives et notes explicatives du 21 décembre 2000;
- l'exposé énoncé économique et la mise à jour budgétaire du 18 octobre 2000;
- les projets de loi C-2 (L.C. 2000, c. 9), C-23 (L.C. 2000, c. 12), C-24 (L.C. 2000, c. 30).

Vous trouverez, sous chaque article :

- les commentaires de David Sherman;
- des articles liés, avec explication de la pertinence;
- les concordances provinciales;
- les modifications proposées, dans des zones ombrées faciles à repérer.

L'index analytique, préparé et constamment mis à jour par David Sherman, est axé sur les besoins des praticiens et vous permettra de repérer rapidement les dispositions recherchées.

*Commandez aujourd'hui pour un examen gratuit de 30 jours.*

 **CARSWELL**      **POUR COMMANDER : 1 800 387-5164**